Parts of a Dictionary Entry

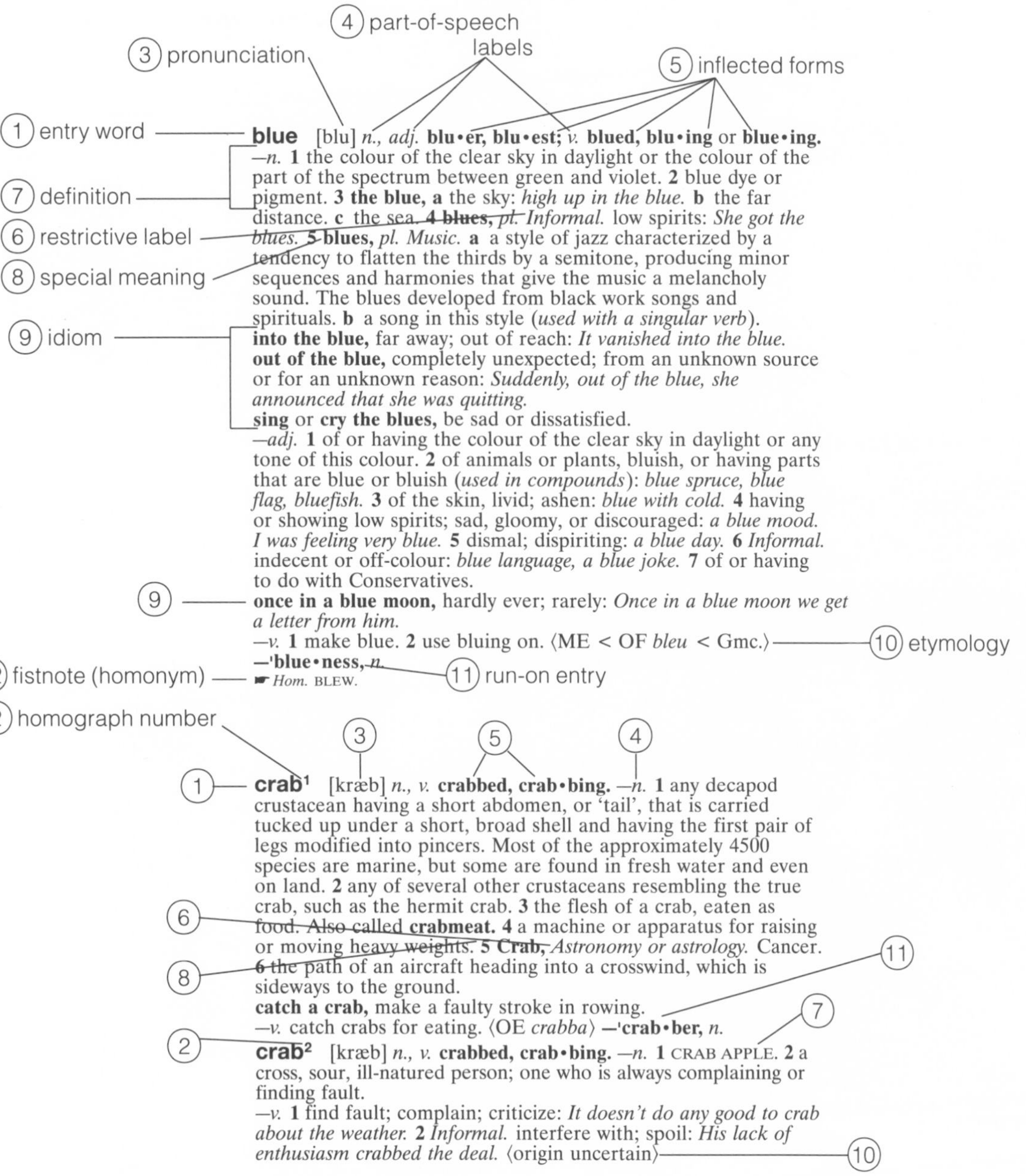

blue [blu] *n., adj.* **blu•er, blu•est;** *v.* **blued, blu•ing** or **blue•ing.**
—n. **1** the colour of the clear sky in daylight or the colour of the part of the spectrum between green and violet. **2** blue dye or pigment. **3 the blue, a** the sky: *high up in the blue.* **b** the far distance. **c** the sea. **4 blues,** *pl. Informal.* low spirits: *She got the blues.* **5 blues,** *pl. Music.* **a** a style of jazz characterized by a tendency to flatten the thirds by a semitone, producing minor sequences and harmonies that give the music a melancholy sound. The blues developed from black work songs and spirituals. **b** a song in this style (*used with a singular verb*).
into the blue, far away; out of reach: *It vanished into the blue.*
out of the blue, completely unexpected; from an unknown source or for an unknown reason: *Suddenly, out of the blue, she announced that she was quitting.*
sing or **cry the blues,** be sad or dissatisfied.
—adj. **1** of or having the colour of the clear sky in daylight or any tone of this colour. **2** of animals or plants, bluish, or having parts that are blue or bluish (*used in compounds*): *blue spruce, blue flag, bluefish.* **3** of the skin, livid; ashen: *blue with cold.* **4** having or showing low spirits; sad, gloomy, or discouraged: *a blue mood. I was feeling very blue.* **5** dismal; dispiriting: *a blue day.* **6** *Informal.* indecent or off-colour: *blue language, a blue joke.* **7** of or having to do with Conservatives.
once in a blue moon, hardly ever; rarely: *Once in a blue moon we get a letter from him.*
—v. **1** make blue. **2** use bluing on. ⟨ME < OF *bleu* < Gmc.⟩
—'blue•ness, *n.*
☛ *Hom.* BLEW.

crab[1] [kræb] *n., v.* **crabbed, crab•bing.** *—n.* **1** any decapod crustacean having a short abdomen, or 'tail', that is carried tucked up under a short, broad shell and having the first pair of legs modified into pincers. Most of the approximately 4500 species are marine, but some are found in fresh water and even on land. **2** any of several other crustaceans resembling the true crab, such as the hermit crab. **3** the flesh of a crab, eaten as food. Also called **crabmeat. 4** a machine or apparatus for raising or moving heavy weights. **5 Crab,** *Astronomy or astrology.* Cancer. **6** the path of an aircraft heading into a crosswind, which is sideways to the ground.
catch a crab, make a faulty stroke in rowing.
—v. catch crabs for eating. ⟨OE *crabba*⟩ **—'crab•ber,** *n.*

crab[2] [kræb] *n., v.* **crabbed, crab•bing.** *—n.* **1** CRAB APPLE. **2** a cross, sour, ill-natured person; one who is always complaining or finding fault.
—v. **1** find fault; complain; criticize: *It doesn't do any good to crab about the weather.* **2** *Informal.* interfere with; spoil: *His lack of enthusiasm crabbed the deal.* ⟨origin uncertain⟩

Canadian DICTIONARY

Gaelan Dodds de Wolf
Robert J. Gregg
Barbara P. Harris
Matthew H. Scargill

gage EDUCATIONAL PUBLISHING COMPANY
A DIVISION OF CANADA PUBLISHING CORPORATION
Vancouver · Calgary · Toronto · London · Halifax

This edition is a major revision of *Gage Canadian Dictionary* © 1983; *Canadian Senior Dictionary* © 1979; *The Senior Dictionary* © 1973, 1967.

Illustrations: *Lewis Parker, Lyle Glover, Lazare and Parker, Jean Galt,* and *Susan Weiss*

Cover design: Campbell Sheffield Design Inc.

Data base design, creation, and imaging: Gandalf Graphics Ltd., Toronto
Printed in the United States by Quebecor Printing Book Group

Canadian Cataloguing in Publication Data

Main entry under title:
Gage Canadian dictionary

(Dictionary of Canadian English)
ISBN 0-7715-1981-8

1. English language–Dictionaries. 2. English language–Canada–Dictionaries. 3. Canadianisms (English)–Dictionaries.* I. Avis, Walter S., 1919–1979. II. Series.

PE3237.G34 1996 423 C95-931774-0

ISBN 0-7715-**1981-8** (School)

ISBN 0-7715-**7399-5** (Trade)

1 2 3 4 5 ARC-QC 00 99 98 97 96

Gage Canadian Dictionary

Lexicographers

GAELAN DODDS DE WOLF
ROBERT J. GREGG
BARBARA P. HARRIS
MATTHEW H. SCARGILL

ROSEMARY COURTNEY
DEBBIE SAWCZAK

Gage Editorial Staff

Kathy Austin
Rebecca Carpenter
Mary Vasey Fenton
Sylvia Gilchrist
Tim Johnston
Peter Saxton
Carol Waldock

General Consulting Editor

Professor Terry Pratt
Department of English
University of Prince Edward Island
Charlottetown, Prince Edward Island

Lexicographers for previous editions

Walter S. Avis
Patrick D. Drysdale
Robert J. Gregg
Victoria E. Neufeldt
Matthew H. Scargill

Consultants

The editors wish to acknowledge all the people in various specialized fields who provided information on concepts, terms, and usage, or checked definitions. It is not possible to name them all here, but included among them are

Dr. Calvin Brown
Department of Business Computing
University of Winnipeg, Manitoba

Ruth Dyck
Department of Linguistics
University of Victoria, British Columbia

Professor Libby Garshowitz
Department of Near Eastern Studies
University of Toronto, Ontario

Professor Craig Peterkin
Department of Business Computing
University of Winnipeg, Manitoba

Dr. Margaret Thompson
Department of Genetics
Hospital for Sick Children
Toronto, Ontario

I.A. Thomson, Lieutenant Commander
Department of National Defence
North York, Ontario

Reviewers

We would like to thank the following educators for reviewing the dictionary.

Robert M. Bilan
Head of English, Oak Park H.S.
Winnipeg, Manitoba

Carol E. Chandler
Curriculum Supervisor
Halifax District School Board, Nova Scotia

Sandra Clarke
Department of Linguistics
Memorial University of Newfoundland

Jane Crosbie, Consultant
Durham Board of Education, Ontario

Pauline Johansen
Vice-Principal, McKinney Elementary School
Richmond School District #38, British Columbia

Glen Kirkland
Consultant, English/Language Arts
Edmonton Catholic School District, Alberta

We would also like to thank the many members of the public who sent in contributions, suggestions, and comments.

Photo Credits

Gage wishes to acknowledge the following for their photo contributions.

Airedale "Hold That Tiger" courtesy of Lotus Tutton; **angelfish** Bob Semple; **Aqualung** Michael Baird; **arctic fox** Ontario Ministry of Natural Resources; **asparagus** Carol Waldock; **aster** E.B. Waldock;

Bailey bridge Acrow Limited; **banjo** courtesy of B & J Music, Division of Hornberger Music Ltd.; **bassoon** Cylla von Tiedemann, courtesy of The Toronto Symphony; **beaver** Ontario Ministry of Natural Resources; **begonia** Carol Waldock; **Bennett buggy** Archives of Saskatchewan; **bird of paradise** Metropolitan Toronto Reference Library; **bison** J.D. Taylor Nature Photography; **broccoli** Carol Waldock; **Buddha** Archaeological Museum, Sarnath; **bufflehead** Ontario Ministry of Natural Resources; **bush partridge** Metropolitan Toronto Reference Library;

calèche L.P. Vallee, Québec/courtesy National Archives of Canada; **camel** Assiniboine Park Zoo, Winnipeg; **canoe** Carol Waldock; **cardinal** E.B. Waldock; **catamaran** courtesy of PDQ Yachts; **Caterpillar tractor** courtesy of Crothers Limited; **cello** Photograph courtesy of The Toronto Symphony; **château** Jeremy Ferguson; **chihuahua** Metropolitan Toronto Reference Library; **chipmunk** Ontario Ministry of Natural Resources; **chukar** Metropolitan Toronto Reference Library; **cineraria** City of Toronto, Allan Gardens/J. Mogridge; **clarinet** courtesy Boosey & Hawkes (Canada) Ltd.; **Confucius** The Bettmann Archive/Relief from the Stele in the Pei Lin de Siganfou; **corgi** Metropolitan Toronto Reference Library; **covered wagon** Glenbow Archives, Calgary, (NA-237-9); **crochet** Carol Waldock; **cromlech** Carol Waldock; **crown** Center for East Asian Studies, Western Washington University; **cupola** Robert Waldock; **curlew** Ontario Ministry of Natural Resources; **cyclamen** City of Toronto, Allan Gardens;

dahlia Royal Botanical Gardens, Hamilton; **Dalmatian** Metropolitan Toronto Reference Library; **Dandie Dinmont** Metropolitan Toronto Reference Library; **devil's club** Royal Botanical Gardens, Hamilton; **disc harrow** Agriculture Canada; **Doberman pinscher** Lia Reichman; **double bass** Photograph courtesy of The Toronto Symphony; Joel Quarrington, Principal Double Bass; **Dutchman's-breeches** Carol Waldock;

eggplant Carol Waldock; **elephant** E.B. Waldock; **Emmentaler** Carol Waldock; **Engelmann spruce** Robert Waldock; **English horn** courtesy Boosey & Hawkes (Canada) Ltd., **Eskimo dog** Kathryn Leaver; **euphonium** courtesy of Whaley, Royce & Co. Inc.;

fan Carol Waldock; **festoon** Carol Waldock; **fiddler crab** J.D. Taylor Nature Photography; **field mouse** E.B. Waldock; **fingerprint** Darleen Rotozinski; **fireweed** E.B. Waldock; **flamingo** Donald Barnes; **flügelhorn** courtesy of Whaley, Royce & Co. Inc.; **flute** Eden Robbins, courtesy of The Toronto Symphony; Nora Shulman, Principal Flute; **freesia** Carol Waldock;

gardenia Montréal Botanical Garden; **geometrid** Royal Ontario Museum, Entomology; **gerbil** Metropolitan Toronto Reference Library; **gibbon** J.D. Taylor Nature Photography; **Gioconda** Leonardo da Vinci: *Mona Lisa,* painting, Louvre, Paris/courtesy of The Bettmann Archive; **gloxinia** Montréal Botanical Garden; **goose** Ontario Ministry of Natural Resources; **Great Dane** Metropolitan Toronto Reference Library; **Great Wall of China** Consulate General of The People's Republic of China in Toronto; **grizzly bear** Industry, Science and Technology Canada Photo; **groundhog** Ontario Ministry of Natural Resources; **Guide** Girl Guides of Canada;

hare Ontario Ministry of Natural Resources; **harmonica** courtesy Boosey & Hawkes (Canada) Ltd.; **hawk** Ontario Ministry of Natural Resources; **heather** Montréal Botanical Garden; **hellebore** Niagara Parks Commission, School of Horticulture; **hollyhock** Carol Waldock; **hooded seal** Fisheries and Oceans; **houseboat** Egan Marine's Sunburst Houseboat Rentals; **hummingbird** Ontario Ministry of Natural Resources;

ichneumon wasp Royal Ontario Museum, Entomology; **impala** J.D. Taylor Nature Photography; **Indian paintbrush** Robert Waldock; **inukshuk** Dan Heringa/NWT Economic Development & Tourism;

jack pine Carol Waldock; **juke box** Wurlitzer;

kestrel no credit required; **kingfisher** Ontario Ministry of Natural Resources; **knitting** Robert Waldock; **koala** Australian Tourist Commission;

Labrador retriever Carol and Peter Brech; **lady's slipper** Robert Waldock; **larch** Carol Waldock; **Lhasa Apso** courtesy of Anne Swantee; **lion** J.D. Taylor Nature Photography;

Madonna lily Royal Botanical Gardens, Hamilton; **Maid of Orléans** *Joan of Arc*. Painting by Albert Lynch. Courtesy of The Bettmann Archive; **mandolin** courtesy of B & J Music, Division of Hornberger Music Ltd.; **maple** Carol Waldock; **meadowlark** Ontario Ministry of Natural Resources; **Ming** Royal Ontario Museum, Toronto; **mistletoe** Outdoor Oklahoma; **moccasin flower** Robert Waldock; **Mohammed** The Bettmann Archive; **mongoose** Metropolitan Toronto Reference Library; **mountain goats** Robert Waldock; **mule** J.D. Taylor Nature Photography;

narcissus City of Toronto, Allan Gardens/J. Mogridge; **Newfoundland** Metropolitan Toronto Reference Library; **nightshade** Robert Waldock;

oak Ontario Ministry of Natural Resources; **oboe** courtesy Boosey & Hawkes (Canada) Ltd.; **opossum** J.D. Taylor Nature Photography; **orangutan** J.D. Taylor Nature Photography; **orchid** E.B. Waldock; **osprey** Ontario Ministry of Natural Resources;

palomino Metropolitan Toronto Reference Library; **Parliament** Industry, Science and Technology Canada; **pasque-flower** Robert Waldock; **pelican** E.B. Waldock; **penguins** World Wildlife Fund; **percussion** Robert Waldock; **Persian cat** Metropolitan Toronto Reference Library; **platypus** Metropolitan Toronto Reference Library; **poodle** Anne Bell/Sanvar;

quail Metropolitan Toronto Reference Library;

raccoon E.B. Waldock; **red fox** Ontario Ministry of Natural Resources; **rhinoceros** Tom Rotozinski; **robin** E.B. Waldock; **rose** Carol Waldock; **Rottweiler** Janine Scheunert; **ruffed grouse** Ontario Ministry of Natural Resources;

Saint Bernard Metropolitan Toronto Reference Library; **sandpiper** Ontario Ministry of Natural Resources; **saxophone** courtesy of Whaley, Royce & Co. Inc.; **Scout** SCOUTS CANADA; **screech owl** Ontario Ministry of Natural Resources; **sea horse** Bob Semple; **seal**[2] George Calef, Government N.W.T.; **Sealyham** Metropolitan Toronto Reference Library; **secretary bird** Metropolitan Toronto Reference Library; **sequoia** Donald Barnes; **serval** Metropolitan Toronto Reference Library; **shark** Bob Semple; **skunk** Ontario Ministry of Natural Resources; **Skye terrier** Metropolitan Toronto Reference Library; **sloth** Victor Englebert; **snowy owl** Ontario Ministry of Natural Resources; **Sphinx** Royal Ontario Museum, Toronto; **stork** J.D. Taylor Nature Photography; **swallowtail** Ontario Ministry of Natural Resources;

tapir J.D. Taylor Nature Photography; **tern** Ontario Ministry of Natural Resources; **thunderhead** Robert Waldock; **tiger** Regional Municipality of Hamilton-Wentworth; **timber wolf** Ontario Ministry of Natural Resources; **toucan** Metropolitan Toronto Reference Library; **trailing arbutus** E.B. Waldock; **trillium** Robert Waldock;

ukulele courtesy of B & J Music, Division of Hornberger Music Ltd.;

violin Photograph courtesy of The Toronto Symphony; Jacques Israelievitch, Concertmaster;

walrus Lothar Dahlke/Government N.W.T.; **water lily** E.B. Waldock; **water moccasin** courtesy of Seaway Reptiles/photo by Tom Rotozinski; **weasel** Ontario Ministry of Natural Resources; **whale** Metropolitan Toronto Reference Library; **wheel** Carol Waldock; **white cedar** Carol Waldock; **white-tailed deer** Ontario Ministry of Natural Resources; **windmill** Carol Waldock; **wolverine** Ontario Ministry of Natural Resources;

xylophone courtesy Boddington Music Limited, Toronto;

yak Assiniboine Park Zoo, Winnipeg;

zebra Assiniboine Park Zoo, Winnipeg; **zither** German National Tourist Office.

Contents

Introduction

This edition of the *Gage Canadian Dictionary* represents a major revision of the edition published in 1983. It is designed not only to keep readers informed about developments in science and technology, but also to emphasize the multicultural society of Canada. Over 13 000 new entries have been added to expand the dictionary's range and bring it up to date. In addition, the entire existing text of the dictionary has been checked for accuracy, clarity, and topicality, and a large proportion of the entries have been revised or rewritten to improve them. In addition, the distinctively Canadian part of the vocabulary has been enlarged to show the richness and variety of Canadian English. This makes the new *Gage Canadian Dictionary* an authoritative, contemporary record of Canadian English that is comprehensive enough for general use by Canadians in education, business, and writing.

Among the important features of this new edition are the following:

- the use of the standard International Phonetic Alphabet (IPA) for all pronunciations, to help not only those readers whose native speech is Canadian English but those who are learning Canadian English;
- the addition of terms from various scientific and technological fields, particularly information technology;
- the inclusion of almost 200 photographs (to aid understanding);
- the organization of all charts and tables in an Appendix, enabling readers to see at once what supplementary information is available in the dictionary.

While making revisions and additions, the authors and editors have endeavoured to maintain the existing strengths of the *Gage Canadian Dictionary* and build on them. The principle of clarity and simplicity of definition has been followed for all new and revised definitions. Moreover, the liberal use of illustrative phrases and sentences, far more extensive than in comparable desk dictionaries, has been continued. Such phrases and sentences are extremely useful to distinguish, clarify, and reinforce the definitions by showing how the entry words are (or were, in the case of archaic words) actually used in the language. This feature, along with the inclusion of a great many idioms, makes the *Gage Canadian Dictionary* extremely valuable for those learning English as a second language. Also continued from the previous edition are the etymologies, the usage, homonym, spelling, and pronunciation notes, and the synonym studies.

The *Gage Canadian Dictionary* is the "senior" volume in the Dictionary of Canadian English series of graded dictionaries. The first, the *Junior*, is designed for children in grades 4, 5, and 6, who are beginning to acquire skill in the conscious use of language; the second, the *Intermediate*, is a much larger volume, tailored to the needs of students in senior elementary and junior high schools; the *Gage Canadian Dictionary* is intended for use in high schools and universities, and for general adult use. Each book in the series is based on the needs and understandings of a particular range of users, who are thus able to find the information they want in a form they can understand. Moreover, the definitions and illustrative sentences are adapted in each book to the audience for which it is intended.

The *Gage Canadian Dictionary* is a dictionary of Canadian English, written by Canadians for Canadians. Canadian English, while different from both British and American English, is in large measure a blend of both varieties; and to this blend are added many features which are typically Canadian. The explanation for this mixed character lies primarily in the settlement history of the country, for both Britain and the United States have exerted continuous influence on Canada during the past two hundred years.

Every effort has been made to ensure that all entries in the *Gage Canadian Dictionary* reflect the usage generally accepted among Canadians with respect to style, spelling, pronunciation, and vocabulary. There are hundreds of words which are native to Canada or which have meanings peculiar to Canada. As might be expected, many of these words refer to topographical features, plants, trees, fish, animals, and birds; and many others to social, political, and economic institutions and activities. Few of these words, which may be called Canadianisms, find their way into British or American dictionaries. Many entries and meanings in this dictionary, including numerous regionalisms, show vividly the richness and variety of the particularly Canadian element of our vocabulary (*conservation area, patriate, tourtière, snow apple,* (electoral) *riding, squidjigging, treaty rights, concession road, summer-fallow, loony,* and *residential school,* to name only a few).

References to Canadian places, institutions, events, and historical figures abound also in the illustrative sentences, making the dictionary one in which Canadian readers feel at home and in their own territory.

Because standard Canadian usage, especially in spelling and pronunciation, is more diverse than that of either Britain or the United States, the *Gage Canadian Dictionary* gives a greater range of alternatives than is usually available in comparable British or American dictionaries. For instance, Canadian usage is almost equally divided between *-our* and *-or* spellings in words such as *colour/color* and *honour/honor,* so both spellings are accepted by this Canadian dictionary as standard Canadian spelling. One spelling or the other must be placed first as being the more common, and in light of current trends this edition has been changed to give first place to the *-our* spelling. This is not the case for British and American dictionaries, however. The British standard spelling is *-our,* and British dictionaries reflect this by labelling *-or* spellings "U.S." Conversely, American dictionaries list *-or* as the standard spelling and label the *-our* spelling "Brit." Neither treatment covers Canadian usage.

One cannot get the most out of a dictionary unless one knows all the kinds of information it contains and how it is arranged. Moreover, a dictionary, like any other work, can be properly evaluated only if one knows what it aims to achieve. For this reason, users are urged to read the Guide to the dictionary, which begins on page viii. Particular care has been taken to make this guide to the *Gage Canadian Dictionary* explicit and easy to read; it consists, for the most part, of simple, straightforward statements followed by extensive examples from the text of the dictionary.

Attention is also drawn to the pronunciation key on the front and back endpapers. Also on the front endpaper are sample entries, in which the parts of a dictionary entry are identified by means of reference numbers keyed to the relevant sections in the Guide. Thus the number 10, identifying the etymology in the sample entry, refers also to Section 10 of the second part of the Guide, on pages xxi-xxiii, which explains in some detail how to use the etymologies. See also the Table of Contents for a list of the sections of the Guide.

In the final analysis a dictionary contains much more than information about words themselves—their spelling, pronunciation, meaning, and origin. It bears testimony to the customs and interests of the people whose language it describes; it is an inventory of the things which the people live with and talk about. For example, *muskeg, separate schools,* and the *humidex* are not just Canadian words; they are also facts of Canadian life. The *Gage Canadian Dictionary* is thus a catalogue of the things relevant to the lives of Canadians at a certain point in history. It is therefore a repository of clues to the nature of our Canadian identity.

Guide to the dictionary

Locating an entry

All main entries–single words, compound nouns and noun phrases, contractions, affixes, combining forms, abbreviations–are to be found in the same alphabetical list. However, there is a system of priorities whereby, for example, prefixes come before abbreviations having the same spelling, and abbreviations without periods come before the same forms with periods, as shown in the following sequence of entries from page 1:

ab–[1] *prefix.* from, away, away from, or off, as in *abnormal, abduct, abjure.* Also: **a-** before *m, p, v*; **abs-** before *c, t. Example*: *abstain.* ⟨< L *ab-* < *ab*, prep.⟩
ab–[2] *prefix.* to or toward; the form of AD- occurring before *b*, as in *abbreviate.*
AB[1] **1** Alberta (*used esp. in computerized address systems*). **2** ABLE SEAMAN. **3** *Baseball.* (times) at bat.
AB[2] the type of human blood containing both antigens A and B. It is one of the four blood types in the ABO system.
A.B. or **a.b.** ABLE-BODIED SEAMAN.
a•ba ['ɑbə] *or* [ə'bɑ] *n.* **1** a rough, feltlike fabric made of wool or hair fibres. **2** a loose, sleeveless outer garment worn by Arabs. ⟨< Arabic *qaba'*, woollen cloak⟩
a•ba•ca ['æbəkə] *or* [ˌæbə'kɑ] *n.* **1** a plant (*Musa textilis*) of the Philippines related to the banana, from whose leafstalks Manila hemp is obtained. **2** MANILA HEMP. ⟨< Malay⟩

For such entries one should be prepared to look a few lines above and below the place where one expects a particular item. Apart from such cases, there is only one place in the book to look for each entry.

Guide words

Guide words in a dictionary indicate the first and last entries on each page. For example, on page 8 the guide words are *Acadia* and *acceptation,* indicating that these two entries and all those that fall between them alphabetically are to be found on that page. Note that in this dictionary the guide words are placed above the outside column of each page so that they are easily seen when leafing through the book.

Homographs

Although homographs are spelled alike, they are different words because they have different meanings and origins. Homographs are entered separately and are distinguished from each other by means of small, raised numerals called superscripts:

chuck[1] [tʃʌk] *v., n. —v.* **1** pat; tap, especially under the chin. **2** *Informal.* toss: *She chucked the apple core into the garbage.* **3** *Informal.* give up or quit: *He's chucked his job.* **4** *Slang.* vomit (*used with* **up**).
—n. **1** a tap; slight blow under the chin. **2** a toss. **3** *West.* food; provisions. ⟨probably imitative⟩
chuck[2] [tʃʌk] *n.* **1** a device for holding a tool or piece of work in a machine. **2** a cut of beef between the neck and the shoulder. See BEEF for picture. ⟨var. of *chock*⟩
chuck[3] [tʃʌk] *n. Cdn. West Coast.* a large body of water, formerly especially a river, but now usually the ocean. ⟨< Chinook jargon⟩

Note that homographs may be pronounced similarly, as above, or differently, as below:

bow[1] [baʊ] *v., n. —v.* **1** bend (the head or body) in greeting, respect, worship, or submission. **2** show by bowing: *to bow one's thanks.* **3** cause to stoop: *The man was bowed by old age.* **4** submit; yield: *We must bow to necessity.*
bow and scrape, be too polite or slavish.
bow down, a weigh down: *bowed down with care.* **b** to worship.
bow out, a withdraw (*used with* **of**): *She sprained her wrist and had to bow out of the tennis tournament.* **b** usher out.
—n. a bending of the head or body in greeting, respect, worship, or submission.
make (one's) **bow, a** make an entrance. **b** make an initial appearance before the public as a performer. **c** retire from public notice.
take a bow, accept praise, applause, etc. for something done. ⟨OE *būgan*⟩
☛ *Hom.* BOUGH, BOW[3].
bow[2] [bou] *n., v. —n.* **1** a weapon for shooting arrows, usually consisting of a strip of springy wood with a string or cord stretched tight between the two ends. **2** a curve; bend. **3** a looped knot: *a bow of ribbon. I tie my shoelaces in a bow.* **4** a slender rod with horsehairs stretched on it, for playing a violin, etc. **5** something curved; a curved part: *A rainbow is a bow.* **6** bowman; archer.
—v. **1** curve; bend. **2** play (a violin, etc.) with a bow. ⟨OE *boga*⟩
—'bow•less, *adj.* **—'bow,like,** *adj.*
☛ *Hom.* BEAU.

Derivatives

Derivatives are words formed by adding prefixes or suffixes to other words or their roots. For example, the derivative *remake* is formed by adding the prefix *re-* to the verb *make*; the derivative *achievable* is formed by adding the suffix *-able* to the verb *achieve,* first dropping the final *e.*

Formed with suffixes

Derivatives formed with certain common suffixes are entered usually as "run-on" entries, that is, they are printed in boldface type at the end of the entry for their root word. Thus *churlishly* and *churlishness* are shown at the end of the entry for *churlish*:

churl•ish ['tʃɜrlɪʃ] *adj.* **1** rude; surly: *a churlish reply.* **2** niggardly; stingy; grudging; sordid. **—'churl•ish•ly,** *adv.* **—'churl•ish•ness,** *n.*

For further information on such words, see Section 11, "Run-on entries," on pages xxiii-xxiv. Derivatives formed with other suffixes are entered separately as main entries, as are all derivatives having meanings that cannot be inferred from those of their root words. Thus *absolutely* is an obvious derivative of *absolute,* but because it has a special meaning it has been entered separately:

ab•so•lute•ly ['æbsə,lutli] *or* [,æbsə'lutli] *adv.* **1** in an absolute way; especially; completely: *The water is absolutely pure. This can opener is absolutely useless.* **2** positively or definitely: *She is absolutely the finest person I know. "Can I try out your new car?" "Absolutely not!"* **3** certainly; definitely yes: *"Are you going to the game?" "Absolutely!"*

For run-on entries whose pronunciation may not be obvious, the pronunciation is indicated immediately following.

Formed with prefixes

Derivatives formed with prefixes are listed in their alphabetical place in the dictionary, except for some words that are formed with *non-, over-, re-,* and *un-* and have meanings that can be inferred from those of the prefix and the root word. These words are listed (without meanings or other information besides syllabication and stress marks) in columns at the bottom of the pages on which they would appear if listed as main entries. For example, *non-absorbent* is found in the list at the bottom of page 1005, but *nonconformist* has special meanings and therefore appears as a main entry in its proper place in the alphabetical list.

Inflected forms

Some irregular inflected forms, such as *oxen,* are entered separately. See Section 5, page xvi for more information and examples.

Subentries

Special meanings

Special uses of words, such as plural nouns, nouns or adjectives with articles, and capital-letter forms with special meanings, are treated as numbered definitions under the basic form of the word, with the special form shown in boldface type. Certain recognized phrases that do not merit separate entry are also printed in boldface type and explained within the entry for their main word (e.g., *red admiral*—a butterfly—is found under *admiral*). See Section 8, "Special meanings," on page xxi for more information and examples.

Idioms

Idiomatic expressions or phrases are defined under the entry for their most important word. For example, *have a care* will be found under *care*; *run for it, run in*, and *on the run* will be found under *run*. See Section 9, "Idioms," on page xxi, for more information and examples.

Noun phrases

Many noun phrases of two or more words function almost as if they were one-word compounds. They are found as main entries if they have a meaning that is not obvious from the meanings of their separate elements. Examples are:

affair of honour or **honor** a duel.
double agent a person who is ostensibly working as a secret agent for one side but is in fact working for the other. A double agent may even be deceiving both sides.
jolly boat *Nautical.* a small boat carried on a ship. ⟨< Danish *jolle* yawl⟩

See also Section 8, "Special meanings," page xxi for examples of noun phrases that are not entered separately but are explained within the entry for their main word.

Proper names

Except for the names of independent nations, Canadian provinces, and American states, biographical and gazetteer entries are not given in this dictionary, the space thus saved being given to enlarging the coverage of the contemporary general vocabulary and to increasing the number of illustrative phrases and sentences. However, entries are given for a number of other proper names that have passed into the general language or are frequently met with in literature.

Place names

Many mythical and legendary places are entered:

At•lan•tis [æt'læntɪs] *n.* a legendary island in the Atlantic, said to have sunk beneath the sea. ⟨< L < Gk.⟩
Cam•e•lot ['kæmə,lɒt] *n.* a legendary place in England where King Arthur had his palace and court.

In addition, some historical places and some geographical areas or features are listed, especially ones which are significant for Canadians:

A•ca•di•a [ə'keidiə] *n. Cdn.* **1** the areas of French settlement and culture in the Maritime Provinces. **2** the Maritime Provinces as a unit. **3** formerly, the French colony comprising the Maritime Provinces and adjacent parts of Québec and New England. ⟨< Latinized form of *Acadie*, a term applied in 1603 by the French to part of their territory in North America⟩
Bab•y•lon ['bæbə,lɒn] *or* ['bæbələn] *n.* **1** the capital of ancient Babylonia, on the Euphrates River and, later, of the ancient Chaldean empire. Babylon was noted for its wealth, power, magnificence, and wickedness. **2** any great, rich, or wicked city.
Canadian Shield a region of ancient rock, chiefly Precambrian granite, encircling Hudson Bay and covering nearly half the mainland of Canada. The Canadian Shield is rich in minerals, especially gold, copper, nickel, and iron ore.

Entries are also provided for some "places" of the modern world that have acquired general or figurative significance:

Bay Street *Cdn.* **1** in Toronto, a street on which there are many financial houses. **2** the financial or moneyed interests of Toronto, the largest financial centre in Canada.
Broad•way ['brɒd,wei] *n.* **1** in New York City, a street famous for its bright lights, theatres, night clubs, etc. **2** the New York commercial theatre.

Personal names

People entered are mainly: prominent figures of myth, legend, or literature, especially those whose names have acquired a general significance, representing some particular quality or ideal; central figures of great religions; people who have given their names to specific things or qualities:

Mar•y ['mɛri] *n.* in the Bible, the mother of Jesus.
Bud•dha ['bʊdə] *or* ['budə] *n.* **1** the title of Siddhartha Gautama (563?-483? B.C.), the Indian philosopher and religious teacher who founded Buddhism. Buddha means Enlightened One. **2** a statue of Buddha. ⟨< Skt.⟩
A•don•is [ə'dɒnɪs] *or* [ə'dounɪs] *n.* **1** *Roman and Greek mythology.* a handsome young man who was loved by Venus (Aphrodite). **2** any very handsome young man.
Mor•gan le Fay ['mɔrgən lə 'fei] *Arthurian legend.* a fairy and King Arthur's half sister, usually represented as trying to harm him at every opportunity.

In addition, information about many people is to be found in the etymologies or definitions of words derived from their names:

Bae•de•ker ['beidəkər] *n.* a guidebook for travellers. ⟨< Karl *Baedeker* (1801-1859), German publisher of a series of guidebooks⟩
Ba•co•ni•an [bei'kouniən] *adj., n. —adj.* **1** of or having to do with Francis Bacon (1561-1626), an English essayist, statesman, and philosopher. **2** of or suggestive of his writings or philosophy. **3** of or having to do with the theory, now no longer seriously entertained by most scholars, that Bacon wrote the plays of Shakespeare.
—n. **1** a person who supports or follows the philosophy of Francis Bacon. **2** a person who supports the theory that Bacon wrote the plays of Shakespeare.

Parts of an entry

Note: Abbreviations used in the text of the dictionary are listed and explained on the inside back endpaper.

1. Entry word—spelling and syllabication

The first item in any dictionary entry is the entry word itself, which indicates the spelling of the basic form of the word. Main entries in this dictionary are set in large boldface type:

a•rise [ə'raɪz] *v.* **a•rose, a•ris•en, a•ris•ing. 1** get up;...
ar•is•toc•ra•cy [ˌærɪ'stɒkrəsi] *or* [ˌɛrɪ'stɒkrəsi] *n., pl....*

Note that syllabication, indicating where a word may be hyphenated, is shown by the placing of a midline dot between syllables. In the case of entries made up of two or more words, syllabication is not shown for any word of the phrase for which there is a separate entry:

Legislative Assembly *Cdn.* the group of representatives elected to the legislature of any of certain provinces or the Yukon Territory.

Variant spellings

Many words in Canadian English (and some words in all dialects of English) can be spelled in two or more ways. When both spellings are equally acceptable, they are shown as alternative entry words:

col•our or **col•or** ['kʌlər]...
man•drel or **man•dril** ['mændrəl]...
judg•ment or **judge•ment** ['dʒʌdʒmənt]...

In such cases, the form given first is that which is considered to be somewhat more frequently used by educated writers across Canada. The form given first is also the one used for all occurrences of the word throughout this dictionary. It should be stressed, however, that though usage among individual writers and in particular regions may not be the same, any one writer will aim for consistency in his or her own work.

If one of two variants is considerably less common than the other, the less common variant is given toward the end of the main entry, before the etymology:

cen•tre ['sɛntər] *n., v.* **-tred, -tring.** *—n.* **1** a point within a circle or sphere equally distant from all parts of the

. . . .

story centres on her childhood experiences. **4** mark or provide with a centre: *a smooth lawn centred by a pool.* **5** *Football.* of the centre, throw (the ball) to a backfield player. Also, **center.** ⟨ME < OF *centre* < L *centrum* < Gk. *kentron* sharp point⟩
axe [æks] *n., v. —n.* **1** a tool for chopping and splitting wood, etc., consisting of a heavy metal head attached to a long wooden

. . . .

2 *Informal.* remove, restrict, end, etc.: *Several budget items were axed due to lack of funds.* Sometimes, **ax.** ⟨OE *æx*⟩ **—'axe,like,** *adj.*

For all words with two or more acceptable variants, each of the less common variants is entered in its proper alphabetical place as a cross-reference to the main entry, except in cases where it would appear adjacent to the main entry (e.g., *catalog*):

cen•ter ['sɛntər] See CENTRE.
☛ *Spelling.* Compounds and derivatives beginning with **center-** are entered under their **centre-** forms.
color ['kʌlər] *n., v.* See COLOUR.

When there is also a slight difference in pronunciation or morphology or both, the less common variant is entered separately, with the more common form given as a one-word definition (a gloss), rather than as a cross-reference:

en•quire [ɛn'kwaɪr] *v.* **-quired, -quir•ing.** inquire.

Spelling charts

It is often difficult to find the spelling of English words of which one knows only the pronunciation. The chart on the following two pages should help the reader to solve this difficulty. It gives the spellings for sounds occurring at the beginning, middle, and end of words.

Spellings of English Sounds

SOUND	BEGINNINGS OF WORDS	MIDDLES OF WORDS	ENDS OF WORDS
[i]	*e*mu, *ea*t, *ei*ther, *ae*on, *ey*rie, *ee*rie, *i*kebana	n*ee*d, t*ea*m, m*e*tre, bel*ie*ve, rec*ei*ve, k*ey*ed, mach*i*ne, C*ae*sar, ph*oe*be, p*eo*ple	b*ee*, b*e*, k*ey*, pit*y*, fl*ea*, qu*ay*, alg*ae*, origam*i*
[ju]	*u*se, *you*, *ewe*, *eu*chre	d*u*ty, f*eu*d, b*eau*ty, n*ew*t	c*ue*, f*ew*, *ewe*, *you*, q*ueue*, ad*ieu*
[ɪ]	*i*n, *e*namel, *y*ttrium	p*i*n, s*ie*ve, h*y*mn, b*ui*ld, mess*a*ge, b*u*sy, b*ee*n, w*o*men, forf*ei*t	—
[ei]	*a*ge, *ai*d, *eigh*t, *eh*, *é*lan	f*a*ce, f*ai*l, str*aigh*t, p*ay*ment, g*au*ge, br*ea*k, v*ei*n, r*ei*gn, w*eigh*t	s*ay*, sl*eigh*, bouqu*et*, th*ey*, matin*ée*, *eh*, saut*é*
[ɛ]	*e*nd, *ai*r, *ae*rial, *hei*r, *a*ny	l*e*t, d*ea*d, s*ai*d, s*ay*s, m*a*ny, h*ei*fer, l*eo*pard, fr*ie*nd, b*u*ry, phl*e*gm	—
[æ]	*a*nd, *au*nt	h*a*t, pl*ai*d, h*a*lf, l*au*gh	h*a*, b*ah*, b*aa*
[ɑ]	*ah*, *al*mond, *a*rt	c*al*m, b*a*rn, baz*aa*r, h*ea*rt, s*e*rgeant	b*aa*, hurr*ah*, f*a*
[aɪ]	*i*dol, *ei*ther, *aye*, *eye*, *ai*sle	l*i*ne, s*igh*ing, s*i*gn, sk*y*way, b*uy*ing	l*ie*, h*igh*, *aye*, *eye*, b*uy*, sk*y*, r*ye*
[aʊ]	*ow*l, *ou*r, *hou*r	b*ou*nd, h*ow*l, pl*ough*ing, T*ao*ist	n*ow*, th*ou*, b*ough*, T*ao*, pil*au*
[ʌ]	*u*p, *o*ven	c*u*p, c*o*me, fl*oo*d, tr*ou*ble, d*oe*s, w*a*s	—
[ʌu]	*ou*t	b*ou*t, dr*ough*t	—
[ə]	*a*lone, *e*ssential, *o*blige, *u*pon, *au*thority	hum*a*n, mom*e*nt, fount*ai*n, penc*i*l, butt*o*n, cauti*ou*s, circ*u*s, anal*y*sis, bott*le* [əl], pris*m* [əm], sover*ei*gn	sof*a*, wall*ah*
[əi]	*i*ce	l*i*fe, m*igh*t, b*y*te, h*eigh*t	—
[ər]	—	adv*er*tise, am*or*tize, b*ur*lesque, sug*ar*ed, arm*our*ed, adm*ir*al	wat*er*, li*ar*, az*ure*, val*our*, auth*or*, aug*ur*, zeph*yr*, fak*ir*
[ɜr]	*er*mine, *ear*ly, *ir*k, *ur*ge	t*er*m, l*ear*n, f*ir*st, t*ur*n, w*or*d, j*our*ney, m*yr*tle, c*ol*onel	det*er*, f*ir*, c*ur*, b*urr*, voyag*eur*
[ɒ]	*o*n, *aw*ful, *au*to, *augh*t, *ough*t, *e*ncore, *a*ll, *al*mond	h*o*t, b*ough*t, c*aw*ed, c*aul*k, w*al*k, w*a*tch, t*au*t, t*augh*t	p*aw*, f*augh*
[ɔ]	*o*rder, *oa*r	b*o*rn, b*oa*rd, fl*oo*ring, m*ou*rn, w*a*r, fl*uo*ride, dinos*au*r	—
[ɔɪ]	*oi*l, *oy*ster	b*oi*l, b*oy*hood, b*uoy*ant, Fr*eu*dian	b*oy*, b*uoy*, poll*oi*
[ou]	*o*pen, *oa*ts, *oh*, *ow*n	b*o*gus, s*ou*l, fl*ow*n, b*oa*t, f*ol*k, br*oo*ch, s*ew*n, y*eo*man	bl*ow*, potat*o*, t*oe*, *oh*, s*ew*, th*ough*, b*eau*
[ʊ]	—	f*u*ll, sh*oul*d, g*oo*d, w*o*lf	—

Spellings of English Sounds (continued)

SOUND	BEGINNINGS OF WORDS	MIDDLES OF WORDS	ENDS OF WORDS
[u]	*oo*ze, *u*miak, *ou*zel	r*u*le, f*oo*d, fr*ui*t, cr*ou*p, m*o*ve, n*eu*tral, man*oeu*vre, l*ew*d, S*iou*an	z*oo*, bl*ue*, thr*ew*, d*o*, carib*ou*, thr*ough*, sh*oe*, Hind*u*, Si*oux*
[p]	*p*en	ta*p*er, su*pp*er	u*p*, thor*pe*, La*pp*
[b]	*b*ad, *bu*ild, *bh*ang	ta*b*le, ra*bb*it, re*bu*ilt	ru*b*, e*bb*, tri*be*
[m]	*m*e	co*m*ing, cli*mb*ing, su*mm*er	ru*m*, co*mb*, hy*mn*, la*me*, phleg*m*
[w]	*w*ill, *wh*at, *ou*ananiche	t*w*in, q*u*ick, ch*o*ir	—
[f]	*f*at, *ph*one	hei*f*er, co*ff*ee, lau*gh*ter, go*ph*er	i*f*, bu*ff*, cou*gh*, lym*ph*, li*fe*
[v]	*v*ery	o*v*er, Ste*ph*en	re*v*, o*f*, lo*ve*
[θ]	*th*in	au*th*or	ba*th*
[ð]	*th*en	fa*th*er	smoo*th*, ba*the*
[t]	*t*ell, *Th*omas, *pt*omaine	la*t*er, la*tt*er, de*bt*or	bi*t*, mi*tt*, dou*bt*, mo*te*
[d]	*d*o, *dh*arma	do*d*o, do*dd*er, sa*dh*u	re*d*, o*dd*, hi*de*
[n]	*n*ut, *kn*ife, *gn*aw, *pn*eumonia, *mn*emonic	o*n*us, i*nn*er, anti*kn*ock, soverei*gn*ty	ma*n*, i*nn*, ma*ne*, si*gn*
[l]	*l*and, *ll*ama	on*l*y, fo*ll*ow	coa*l*, fi*ll*, fi*le*
[s]	*s*ay, *c*ent, *sc*ience, *ps*alm, *sw*ord	ma*s*on, ma*ss*ive, de*c*ent, a*sc*end, an*sw*er, e*x*tra [ks]	mi*ss*, bogu*s*, ni*ce*, ru*se*, la*x* [ks]
[z]	*z*ero, *x*ylophone, *cz*ar	si*z*ing, da*zz*le, rai*s*in, sci*ss*ors, e*x*act [gz]	bu*zz*, fe*z*, ha*s*, ho*se*
[tʃ]	*ch*ild, *c*ello, *Cz*ech, *ci*ao	ri*ch*ness, wa*tch*ing, righ*te*ous, ques*ti*on, na*t*ure, vermi*c*elli, bo*cc*ie	mu*ch*, ca*tch*
[dʒ]	*j*am, *g*em, *Dj*ibouti	en*j*oy, tra*g*ic, exa*gg*erate, ba*dg*er, sol*di*er, e*d*ucate	ra*ge*, bri*dge*, ra*j*, ve*g*
[ʃ]	*sh*e, *s*ure, *ch*auffeur, *sch*wa	a*sh*en, mi*ss*ion, ten*si*on, na*ti*on, nau*se*ous, spe*ci*al, o*ce*an, in*s*ure, con*sci*ence, i*ss*ue, ma*ch*ine, fu*chs*ia	wi*sh*, ca*che*, bor*sch*
[ʒ]	*j*alousie	divi*si*on, mea*s*ure, a*z*ure, gara*ge*d	rou*ge*
[j]	*y*oung, *J*ungian, *g*yro	can*y*on, opin*i*on, hallelu*j*ah, chamel*e*on, poi*gn*ant [nj], boui*ll*on [lj]	—
[r]	*r*un, *rh*ythm, *wr*ong	pa*r*ent, hu*rr*y, dia*rrh*ea, aw*r*y	bea*r*, bu*rr*, cata*rrh*, bo*re*
[k]	*c*oat, *ch*emist, *k*ind, *q*uick, *qu*ay, *kh*aki	ba*c*on, a*cc*ount, e*ch*o, lu*ck*y, li*qu*or, ba*cch*ant, a*cq*uire, hi*k*er, o*x*en [ks]	ba*ck*, see*k*, pi*que*, ti*c*, Ira*q*, sti*ch*, an*kh*
[g]	*g*o, *gh*ost, *gu*ess	bo*g*us, bo*gg*le, ro*gu*ish, e*x*act [gz], a*gh*ast	ba*g*, e*gg*, ro*gue*, bur*gh*
[ŋ]	—	i*n*k, si*ng*er, hara*ngu*ing	ri*ng*, to*ngue*
[h]	*h*e, *wh*o, *j*unta	a*h*ead, fa*j*ita	—

2. Homograph number

Words having identical spellings but different origins and meanings are called homographs. They are given as separate entries in this dictionary, with a superscript number following the entry word to distinguish one homograph from another. The superscript also serves to indicate to the user that there is at least one other entry word with the same spelling.

For example:

keen[1] [kin] *adj.* **1** sharp enough to cut well: *a keen blade.* **2** sharp; piercing; cutting: *a keen wind, keen hunger, keen wit, keen pain.* **3** strong; vigorous: *keen competition.* **4** able to do its work quickly and accurately: *a keen mind, a keen sense of smell.* **5** *Informal.* full of enthusiasm; eager (*often used with* **about**, **for**, *etc.*): *a keen player, keen about sailing.* ⟨ME *kene*, OE *cēne*⟩ **—'keen•ly,** *adv.* **—'keen•ness,** *n.*
☛ *Syn.* **2.** See note at SHARP. **5.** See note at EAGER.

keen[2] [kin] *n., v.* *—n.* a wailing lament for the dead. *—v.* wail; lament. ⟨< Irish *caoine*⟩ **—'keen•er,** *n.*

3. Pronunciation

Pronunciation transcriptions are given in square brackets immediately after the entry words. Pronunciation is indicated by transcriptions using symbols from the International Phonetic Alphabet shown in the key on the inside of the front and back covers:

butch•er ['bʊtʃər] *n., v.* *—n.* **1** a person whose work...
but•tress ['bʌtrɪs] *n., v.* *—n.* **1** a structure built against...
bu•ty•lene ['bjutə,lin] *n.* a gaseous hydrocarbon of the...

In the case of entries of two or more words, no pronunciation is given for words that are entered separately:

judge advocate *Military.* an officer appointed to superintend...

Whenever one word of a phrase is entered separately and the other is not, only the word that does not have its own main entry is transcribed:

bu•tyr•ic acid [bju'tirɪk] a colourless liquid...
delirium tre•mens ['trimənz] delirium characterized...

Stress

Three degrees of stress are indicated in this dictionary: primary stress [ˈ], secondary stress [ˌ], and weak stress (unmarked). The mark is placed before the syllable to which it applies. Stress is not indicated for words of one syllable unless they form part of a foreign phrase, but is shown in all transcriptions of more than one syllable, including compounds, whether hyphenated or not:

boy [bɔɪ]...
boy•ish ['bɔɪɪʃ]...
black•ber•ry ['blæk,bɛri]...
bird•bath ['bɜrd,bæθ]...
Fin•no–U•gric ['fɪnou 'jugrɪk] *or* [-'ugrɪk] *n., adj.* *—n.* a family...
non–trea•ty ['nɒn 'triti] *adj.*...

As the examples above show, some compounds may have two primary stresses. Normally, however, there is only one primary stress per word.

The stress pattern of many adjectives and adverbs whose last stress is primary varies in English with position in the sentence. For example, compare the stresses in *hard-hearted* as used in *He is very hard-hearted* and *He's a hard-hearted person.* When such a modifier occurs before the word it is modifying, the phrase acts as a single unit with regard to stress. The stress pattern of the phrase affects that of the modifier, changing its last primary stress to a secondary one and making a preceding secondary one primary. The same change can be seen for *absolutely* in *Absolute power corrupts absolutely* and *This is absolutely delicious!* and for *downtown* in *She lives downtown* and *a downtown store.* The stress indicated in the pronunciation transcriptions is for the word as it is pronounced when unaffected by phrasal stress. In some cases, both stress patterns are given:

hard–heart•ed ['hɑrd 'hɑrtɪd] *adj.* without pity; cruel; unfeeling. **—'hard-'heart•ed•ly,** *adv.* **—'hard-'heart•ed•ness,** *n.*
down•stream ['daʊn,strim] *or* [ˌdaʊn'strim] *adv., adj.*...

Variant pronunciations

The transcriptions show pronunciation variants that are common in at least some parts of Canada, for example:

fu•tile ['fjutaɪl] *or* ['fjutəl]...
khak•i ['kæki], ['kɑki], *or* ['kɑrki]...
fal•low[1] ['fælou] *or, esp. in the Prairie Provinces,* ['fɒlou]...

The first form given is the one considered to be most common in Canada as a whole, but, as with spelling, different forms are often preferred in different parts of the country or among different social groups. An individual's own usage is normally governed by that of the community to which he or she belongs, so that, unless otherwise indicated, all pronunciations given in this dictionary should be considered equally acceptable.

Labelled pronunciations

Some words are pronounced differently when they occur as different parts of speech. In such cases the transcriptions are labelled in the following manner:

ac•cent *n.* ['æksɛnt]; *v.* ['æksɛnt] *or* [æk'sɛnt]...
mod•er•ate *adj., n.* ['mɒdərɪt]; *v.* ['mɒdə,reit]...

Some words have unusual pronunciations when used by members of a profession or in other specialized contexts. In such cases the restricted pronunciation, preceded by an appropriate label, is given after the transcription for the general pronunciation:

an•gi•na [æn'dʒaɪnə]; *in medicine, often* ['ændʒənə]...
lee•ward ['liwərd] *or, in nautical use,* ['luərd]...

Pronunciation of foreign words

Where a foreign phrase is entered but has little currency in spoken English, the nearest possible approximation to the original pronunciation is given:

au jus [o'ʒy] *French.* in gravy or juice.

For words that have been Anglicized but still sometimes have their original pronunciation when used in spoken English, the Anglicized form is given first, followed by the labelled original form:

é•lan [ei'lɑn]; *French*, [e'lɑ̃] *n.* liveliness or enthusiasm combined with flair. ⟨< F *élan* < *élancer* dart⟩

4. Parts of speech

The part of speech is given for all one-word and hyphenated entries except contractions such as *can't,* which combine words having different syntactic functions. The label follows immediately after the transcription of pronunciation:

ant [ænt] *n.* any of a large family (Formicidae) of...

If a word is used as two or more parts of speech, these are listed, along with their inflected forms if required (see Section 5 below), and then the meanings are given for each part of speech in turn. The most important part of speech and its meanings are normally given first:

an•te•pe•nul•ti•mate [,æntipə'nʌltəmɪt] *adj., n.* —*adj.* third from the end; last but two.
—*n.* antepenult.

Grammatical form and function

There are certain grammatical functions of nouns and adjectives in English that require special identification. For instance, a noun such as *night* may be used adjectivally to modify another noun (as in *the night wind*), but it remains basically a noun, since it cannot be compared or modified and it cannot be used as a predicate adjective. (One can say *a very cold wind* and *the wind was cold* but one cannot say *a very night wind* or *the wind was night.*) Some nouns may also be used adverbially. Thus, the word *home* in *I am going home* is an adverbial use of what remains essentially a noun. Such uses of nouns are identified in this dictionary by abbreviations in italics, before the relevant definition. The label (*adjl.*) means adjectival; (*advl.*) means adverbial:

night [nəit] *n.* **1** the period of darkness between evening and morning; the time between sunset and sunrise. **2** the darkness of night; the dark: *She went out into the night....* **5** *(adjl.)* of or having to do with night: *cold night winds.* **6** *(adjl.)* working or for use at night: *a night light.* **7** *(advl.)* **nights,** regularly or habitually in the nighttime: *He works nights.*

home [houm] *n., v.* **homed, hom•ing.** *—n.* **1** the place where a person or family lives; one's own house. **2** the place where a person was born or brought up or now lives; one's own town or country. **3** *(advl.)* at, to, or toward one's own home: *She's not home. I want to go home.* **4** the social unit formed by a family, ... **10** *(adjl.)* of one's own country: *the home office.* **11** *Games.* the objective or goal; especially, in baseball, home plate. **12** *(adjl.) Games.* **a** having to do with or situated at or near home. **b** reaching or enabling a player to reach home. **13** *(advl.)* **a** to the thing aimed at: *to drive a nail home.* **b** to the heart or core; deep in: *Her accusing words struck home and they were ashamed.* **c** successfully or effectively: *to speak home.* **14** *(adjl.)* of, having to do with, or coming from home: *one's home country, home remedies, a home game.*

Similarly, certain adjectives are used in specific ways as nouns, without becoming true nouns; they cannot be inflected or modified by an adjective. These special nominal uses, identified by the label (*noml.*), usually require the definite article (*the*):

lat•ter ['lætər] *adj.* **1** later; more recent; nearer the end: *Friday comes in the latter part of the week.* **2** *(noml.)* **the latter,** the second of two: *Canada and the United States are in North America; the former lies north of the latter.* Compare FORMER[1]. ⟨OE *lætra* later⟩

5. Inflected forms

Certain inflected forms—the plural of nouns, the past tense and past participle of verbs, and the comparative and superlative of adjectives and adverbs—are given whenever they are not regularly formed. They are set in boldface type and come immediately after the part-of-speech listing: syllabication is indicated by midline dots, as in the entry words:

lib•er•ate ['lɪbə,reit] *v.* **-at•ed, -at•ing....**
clar•i•fy ['klærə,faɪ] *or* ['klɛrə,faɪ] *v.* **-fied, -fy•ing....**
ox [ɒks] *n., pl.* **ox•en....**
a•lum•nus [ə'lʌmnəs] *n., pl.* **-ni....**
free [fri] *adj.* **fre•er, fre•est;...**
good [gʊd] *adj.* **bet•ter, best;** *n., interj....*
cra•zy ['kreizi] *adj.* **-zi•er, -zi•est;...**

Note that the inflected forms are often abbreviated, the syllables shared with the entry word being omitted and replaced by a hyphen. Note also that the pronunciation of inflected forms is given wherever it is not obvious from that of the entry word (see *hypnosis* below), and when the inflected form is not itself an entry. Such respellings are abbreviated whenever this can be done without giving rise to confusion or ambiguity:

hyp•no•sis [hɪp'nousɪs] *n., pl.* **-ses** [-siz]....

Irregularly inflected forms are given as main entries whenever they would not come immediately before or after their root word in alphabetical order. In such cases a form is cross-referred to the entry for its root word, where the full information is to be found:

came [keim] *v.* pt. of COME.
nu•cle•i ['njukli,aɪ] *or* ['nukli,aɪ] *n.* a pl. of NUCLEUS.
ox•en ['ɒksən] *n.* pl. of OX.
hid [hɪd] *v.* pt. and a pp. of HIDE.

Variant inflected forms are given whenever appropriate:

ap•pen•dix [ə'pɛndɪks] *n., pl.* **-dix•es** or **-di•ces....**
dive [daɪv] *v.* **dived** or **dove, dived, div•ing....**
cav•il ['kævəl] *v.* **-illed** or **-iled, -il•ling** or **-il•ing;** *n....*

6. Restrictions of use

Words and meanings that are appropriate only under certain conditions are indicated in two ways: by italicized labels and by introductory phrases.

Restrictive labels
Labels are used mainly to indicate restrictions of usage in regard to level, style, currency, locality, etc. Those most commonly

used are explained below, and further information may be had by looking up the entry word for each of these terms in the body of the dictionary.

Informal The word or meaning is quite acceptable in everyday use but would in most cases be out of place in a business letter, scholarly paper, legal document, formal speech or interview, etc.:

did•dle ['dɪdəl] *v.* **-dled, -dling.** *Informal.* **1** cheat; swindle. **2** waste (time). **3** ruin. **4** fiddle with; fool around with. ⟨origin uncertain⟩

Slang The word or meaning is not established in standard use but is used mainly in speech and only by certain groups, or by others in imitation or for special effects. If a slang word survives and becomes generally known, it usually also becomes generally acceptable and therefore ceases to be slang:

clip joint *Slang.* a business establishment, especially a restaurant, nightclub, etc., that regularly overcharges its customers.

hose [houz] *n.pl.* (defs. 1 and 2), *n.sing., pl.* **hos•es** (def. 3); *v.* **hosed, hos•ing.**...

—*v.* **1** put water on with a hose (*often used with* **down**): *She hosed down the lawn furniture.* **2** *Slang.* get the better of, especially by unfair means; cheat: *He said the team was tired of being hosed by the officials in the league.* ⟨OE *hosa*⟩

Vulgar The word or meaning is considered coarse or indecent by most people, and therefore is unacceptable for use in almost any public situation:

snot [snɒt] *n.* **1** *Vulgar.* mucus from the nose. **2** *Slang.* a flippant and disrespectful person. ⟨OE *gesnot*⟩

Dialect The word or meaning is used only in the folk-speech of certain people or geographical areas:

crit•ter ['krɪtər] *n. Dialect.* **1** any living creature. **2** an animal, especially a cow, raised as livestock. ⟨alteration of *creature*⟩

Poetic The word or meaning is used only in poetry or in prose written in a poetic style:

a•wea•ry [ə'wiri] *adj. (never precedes a noun) Poetic.* weary; tired.

Archaic The word or meaning is out of place except in writings of earlier times and in modern literature that is written in the style of an earlier period:

glis•ter ['glɪstər] *v. or n. Archaic.* glisten; glitter; sparkle. ⟨< *glisten*; cf. MDu. *glisteren*⟩

breth•ren ['brɛðrən] *n.pl.* **1** *Archaic.* brothers. **2** the fellow...

Obsolete The word or meaning is no longer current, even in styles imitating that of an earlier period:

mon•gol•ism ['mɒŋgə,lɪzəm] *n. Obsolete.* DOWN SYNDROME.

Rare The word or meaning is losing currency and is now used only infrequently:

fee [fi] *n., v.* **feed, fee•ing.** —*n.* **1** a sum of money asked or paid for a service or privilege; charge: *Doctors and lawyers get fees for their services.* **2 fees,** *pl.* the money paid for instruction at a school or university. **3 a** in a feudal society, land held by a vassal on

. . . .

—*v. Rare.* give a fee to. ⟨ME < AF var. of OF *fieu* < Med.L *feudum* fief ? < Gmc.; cf. OE *feoh* money, cattle⟩

Trademark The word or form is a proprietary name, owned by a particular company and valued by it as identifying its product. Every effort has been made to label entries that are trademarks as such. The absence of such a label does not necessarily mean that a word is not a trademark:

Fre•on ['friɒn] *n. Chemistry. Trademark.* any of a class of fluorated hydrocarbons formerly used especially as refrigerants and as propellants for aerosol sprays.

Or•lon ['ɔrlɒn] *n. Trademark.* a synthetic acrylic fibre used in a number of fabrics. Orlon is used for knitted clothing, rugs, draperies, etc.

Words that are trademarks are entered only when they are considered to be established as part of the general vocabulary.

Klee•nex ['klinɛks] *n. Trademark.* a very soft, absorbent tissue, used as a handkerchief, for removing cosmetics, etc.

French, Latin, German, etc. Such language labels are used to distinguish words and phrases that, though used often in English writing and sometimes in speech, are still considered to be foreign. Such foreign words and phrases are usually italicized in print and underlined in writing or typing:

eau de vie [odəˈvi] *French.* brandy. ⟨literally, water of life⟩
Füh•rer [ˈfjʊrər]; *German,* [ˈfyRəR] *n.* **1** leader. **2 der Führer,** the title given to Adolf Hitler (1889-1945), the German dictator. Also, **Fuehrer**.
mu•ta•tis mu•tan•dis [mjuˈteitɪs mjuˈtændɪs] *or* [muˈtɑtis muˈtɑndis] *Latin.* with the necessary changes.

Cdn. Indicates that a word or meaning originated in or is now peculiar to Canada:

main•street•ing [ˈmein,stritɪŋ] *n. Cdn.* the act or practice, by a politician, etc. of walking about the main streets of a town or city in order to meet and greet potential supporters.
—ˈmain,street, *v.*
mus•pike [ˈmʌs,pəik] *n. Cdn.* a hybrid game fish crossbred from muskellunge and pike.

Brit., Scottish, U.S., etc. Other national labels are used to distinguish words, meanings, or spellings that are used chiefly or solely in some particular part of the English-speaking world:

boot[1] [but] *n., v.* —*n.* **1** a covering for the foot and lower part of the leg, made of leather, rubber, or a synthetic material such as vinyl. See SHOE for picture. **2** *Informal.* a kick. **3** the place for luggage in a horse-drawn coach. **4** *Brit.* the trunk of an automobile. **5** a bootlike protective covering or sheath for a mechanical device, etc. **6** formerly, an instrument of torture used to crush a person's leg. **7** *U.S. Slang.* a new recruit in training in the United States Navy or Marines….
lang syne [ˈlæŋ ˈzaɪn] *or* [ˈlæŋ ˈsaɪn] *Scottish.* long since; long ago.

Architecture, Hockey, Law, Music, Sports, etc. Such field labels are used to show that a word or meaning is used with reference to a specialized field of knowledge or activity:

cross–check [ˈkrɒs ,tʃɛk] *v., n.* —*v.* **1** check again, or check against another source. **2** *Hockey or lacrosse.* give (an opponent) an illegal check by holding one's stick in both hands and thrusting it in front of the opponent's face or body.
—*n.* **1** the act of cross-checking something. **2** *Hockey or lacrosse.* an illegal check made by cross-checking.
celestial globe *Astronomy.* a globe indicating the position of the heavenly bodies, similar to a globe of the earth showing the geography of continents, oceans, etc.

Restrictive phrases

Phrases (such as "in ancient Rome," "especially in Ontario") are also sometimes used at the beginning of definitions to show special reference. They may indicate that a word is used with reference to one particular region or country:

bank barn *Cdn.* especially in Ontario, a two-storey barn built into a hill so as to permit entry to the bottom level from one side and to the top level from the other side.

Position

Note in the above examples that the position of both labels and phrases varies, depending on whether the restriction applies to a particular meaning (in which case it is placed after the numeral), to the meanings for one part of speech (placed after the part-of-speech label), or to the whole entry (placed before the part-of-speech label introducing the first group of meanings).

7. Definitions

Definitions are intended to be as simple and straightforward as possible. Where there is more than one meaning for an entry, each meaning is introduced by a boldface numeral; within a single meaning, different explanations or synonyms are separated by semicolons:

for•tune [ˈfɔrtʃən] *n.* **1** a great deal of money or property; riches; wealth. **2** what is going to happen to a person; fate: *Gypsies often claim that they can tell people's fortunes.* **3** good luck; prosperity; success. **4** what happens; luck; chance: *Fortune was against us; we lost….* ⟨ME < OF < L *fortuna*⟩

Order of definitions

(*a*) Definitions are grouped by parts of speech, all the noun meanings for an entry being together, all the verb meanings being together, and so on.

(*b*) Within one part of speech, meanings are grouped in the order likely to be most useful to the reader. Normally, this is the order of frequency, the most commonly used meanings being given first. It is usual, therefore, for general meanings to be at the beginning of an entry and for specific, technical senses to come later. Sometimes, however, it is easier to understand the different meanings of a word if they are arranged in a historical or logical order. For instance, it is usually desirable for closely related senses to be kept together, as in the entry for *bar*[1]:

bar[1] [bɑr] *n., v.* **barred, bar•ring;** *prep.* —*n.* **1** an evenly shaped piece of some solid, longer than it is wide or thick: *a bar of iron, a bar of soap, a bar of chocolate.* **2** a pole or rod put across a door, gate, window, etc. to fasten or shut off something.
3 anything that blocks the way or prevents progress: *A bar of sand kept boats out of the harbour. A bad temper is a bar to*

making friends. **4** a band of colour; stripe. **5** *Music.* **a** a unit of rhythm; measure. **b** the vertical line between two such units on a staff; bar line. **6** a counter over which drinks, especially alcoholic drinks, are served. **7** a movable piece of furniture from which beverages are dispensed. **8** a room or establishment that has such a counter and in which alcoholic drinks are sold and consumed. **9** a counter, department, or other place, such as a self-serve area, where specific goods or services are sold: *a snack bar, a gas bar.* **10 the bar, a** the profession of a lawyer. A person is called to the bar after passing the prescribed law examinations. **b** lawyers as a group: *Judges are chosen from the bar.* **11** the area or railing in a court of law that separates the bench and the lawyers' seats from the rest of the court. **12** *Esp. Brit.* the place where an accused person stands in a court of law. **13** a court of law. **14** anything like a court of law: *the bar of public opinion....*

Here, definitions 6 to 9 cover one group of meanings, while definitions 10 to 13 cover another group. This is the most convenient order in which to place these entries, but it does not mean, for example, that sense 10 is necessarily less common than sense 8.

Grammatical form and function

Nouns used adjectivally or adverbially while remaining essentially nouns are grouped with noun meanings, but are specially labelled. Similarly, certain adjectives used as nouns are grouped as adjectives. See "Parts of speech" (pages xv-xvi) for more information and examples.

Parentheses in definitions

Parentheses are used to enclose words that are not strictly part of the meaning of the word being defined but are necessary in order to understand that meaning or its use. For instance, in defining a transitive verb, it is often necessary to indicate the type of word that occurs as its object:

ab•duct [æb'dʌkt] *v.* **1** carry off or take away (a person) by force or deceit. **2** of a muscle or group of muscles, serve to move (a limb, etc.) away from the median axis of the body or of one of its parts. Compare ADDUCT. ⟨< L *abductus*, pp. of *abducere* < *ab-* away + *ducere* lead⟩ **—ab'duc•tion** *n.*

The meaning of sense 1 of *abduct* is not complete unless one understands that the action is something that is done to persons; similarly, in sense 2, the words in parentheses (the supplied object) are necessary to an understanding of the meaning.

In many cases, parentheses enclose an object, or a preposition inviting one, that may be optionally included in the meaning of the verb itself, indicating that the verb can be used either transitively (with an object specified) or intransitively (with no object because the object is understood):

drink [drɪŋk] *v.* **drank, drunk, drink•ing;** *n.* *—v.* **1** swallow (liquid)....

As the parentheses in definition 1 of *drink* above indicate, the sentences *He's drinking his coffee* and *The deer come here to drink early each morning* are both proper uses of the word. In the example about the deer, it is understood that some type of liquid is being drunk (and more specifically, water). Often in such cases two illustrative sentences are given, one showing transitive use and the other intransitive, as in this case.

In addition, parentheses are used to enclose prepositions that follow verbs in specific meanings. Such required prepositions are printed in italics:

a•gree [ə'gri] *v.* **a•greed, a•gree•ing. 1** have the same opinion or opinions: *I agree with you. The two partners usually agreed on important issues.* **2** be alike or be similar to; be in harmony; correspond (*with*): *Her story agrees with theirs.* **3** get along well together. **4** consent (*to*): *We agreed to their proposal. He agreed to accompany us.* **5** come to an understanding, especially in settling a dispute. **6** concede (a fact): *We agreed that the child's behaviour had been atrocious.* **7** be suitable, healthful, etc. (*used with* **with**): *Bananas don't agree with him; they make him sick....*

In sense 1 of *agree*, *with* may be used but the verb may also occur without any preposition; in sense 2 the verb must be followed by *with*, and in sense 4, it must be followed by *to*. In such cases, the following preposition may be the only real clue as to which meaning of the verb is being used.

Expanded definitions

In many cases, especially with technical words, the normal style of gloss is not sufficient to explain a meaning, and a separate explanatory sentence is added, as in definition 4 of *aberration:*

ab•er•ra•tion [,æbə'reiʃən] *n.* **1** a wandering from the right path or usual course of action. **2** a deviation from a standard or ordinary type; abnormal structure or development. **3** a temporary mental disorder. **4** *Optics.* the failure of a lens or mirror to bring to a single focus the rays of light coming from one point. Aberration causes a blurred image or an image with a coloured rim. **5** *Astronomy.* a slight change in the apparent position of a heavenly body, caused by the combined effect of the earth's motion and of light.

Examples

Illustrative phrases and sentences, printed in italics, are widely used to support the definitions. Such examples often show the type of context in which a word may be used in a particular meaning:

ac•tion ['ækʃən] *n.* **1** the process of doing something or the state of being active or in operation: *to put a machine into action.* **2** habitual activity, especially when characterized by energy or initiative: *a man of action.* **3** something done; act. **4 actions,** *pl.* conduct; behaviour. **5** *Informal.* important or exciting activities or happenings: *to go where the action is.* **6** the effect or influence of a force or thing on something else: *the action of the wind on a ship's sails, the action of a drug....*

Examples are used also to highlight the contrast between related meanings of the same word:

beat [bit] *v.* **beat, beat•en** or **beat, beat•ing;** *n., adj....*

. . . .

—n. **1** a stroke or blow made again and again: *the beat of a drum, the beat of waves on a beach.* **2** pulsation; throb: *the beat of the heart.* **3** *Music.* **a** a unit of time; accent: *three beats to a measure.* **b** a stroke of the hand, baton, etc. showing a beat....

ob•scure [əb'skjʊr] *adj.* **-scur•er, -scur•est;** *v.* **-scured, -scur•ing.** *—adj.* **1** not clearly expressed: *an obscure passage in a book.* **2** not expressing meaning clearly: *an obscure style of writing.* **3** not well-known; attracting no notice: *an obscure little village, an obscure poet, an obscure position in the government.* **4** not easily discovered; hidden: *an obscure path, an obscure meaning.* **5** not distinct; not clear: *an obscure form, obscure sounds, an obscure view.* **6** dark; dim: *an obscure corner.* **7** indefinite: *an obscure brown, an obscure vowel.*

Pictures and diagrams

The definitions are further supported and amplified by the various types of pictorial illustration that appear throughout the book. Some of these merely provide a picture or diagram of something to complement the verbal description:

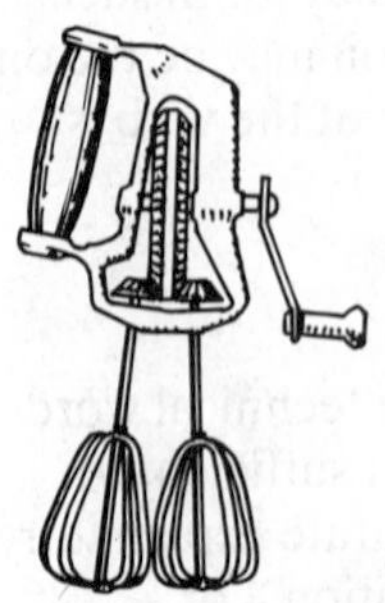

An eggbeater

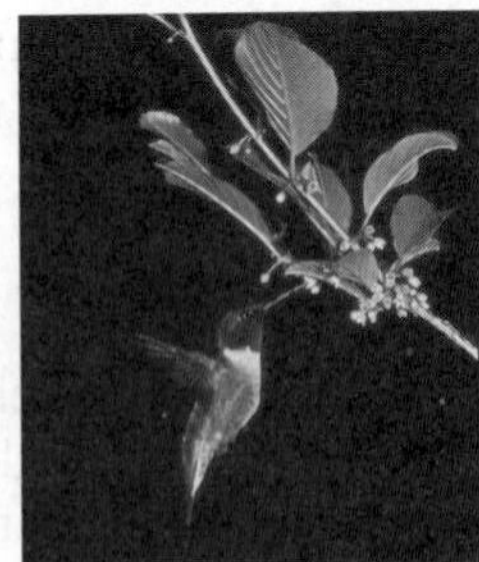

A hummingbird

Others give a considerable amount of more or less technical information, sometimes in diagram form, and these often label items that are entered elsewhere and are cross-referred to the same picture or diagram:

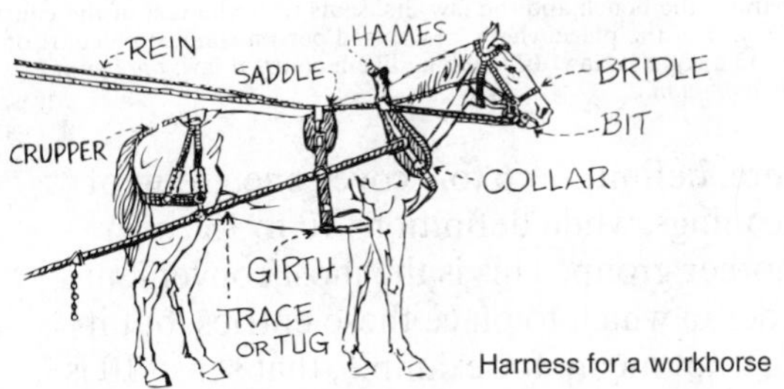

Harness for a workhorse

Still others have captions which give information that, though not strictly part of a definition, is interesting and important for a full understanding of what the entry word represents:

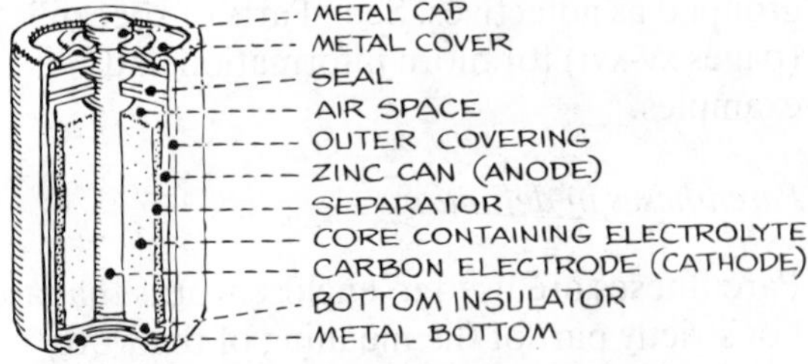

A carbon-zinc dry cell: a flashlight battery. The electrolyte, a paste of ammonium chloride, zinc chloride, manganese dioxide, and carbon, reacts with the zinc, causing it to become negatively charged. When the zinc anode and the carbon cathode are connected by a conducting wire, electrons flow from the anode to the cathode, producing an electric current.

8. Special meanings

Certain special uses of words, such as plural nouns, nouns or adjectives with articles, or capital-letter forms with special meanings, are treated as numbered definitions, but the special form is shown in regular boldface type after the definition number:

a•crop•o•lis [ə'krɒpəlɪs] *n.* **1** the fortified hill in the centre of an ancient Greek city, which served as its religious centre as well as its fortress. **2 the Acropolis,** the fortified hill of Athens, on which the Parthenon was built. ⟨< Gk. *akropolis* < *akros* topmost, outermost + *polis* city⟩

af•fair [ə'fɛr] *n.* **1** something done or to be done; matter; concern: *That's my affair.* **2 affairs,** *pl.* matters of interest or concern, especially business, commercial, or public matters: *current affairs, affairs of state.* **3** an action, event, or procedure referred to in vague terms: *The party on Saturday night was a dull affair. . . .*

Certain recognized noun phrases, etc. that do not merit separate entry are also printed in regular boldface type and explained within the entry for their basic, or main, word:

ad•mi•ral ['ædmərəl] *n.* **1** the commander-in-chief of a fleet. **2** *Canadian Forces.* in Maritime Command, the equivalent of a

. . . .

6 any of various brightly coloured butterflies (subfamily Nymphalinae), such as the **red admiral** or the **white admiral.** ⟨earlier *amiral* < OF < Arabic *amir* chief. Related to AMIR.⟩

her•pes ['hɜrpiz] *n.* any of several virus diseases of the skin or mucous membranes, characterized by clusters of blisters. **Herpes simplex** is a type of herpes marked by watery blisters especially on the mouth, lips, or genitals. ⟨< L < Gk. *herpēs* shingles < *herpein* creep⟩

9. Idioms

An idiom is a fixed phrase or expression which cannot be fully understood from the meanings of the words that form it. Idioms are defined under the entry for their most important word, and they are printed in boldface type. For example, the idiom *on the make* is explained under the noun meanings of *make*:

make [meik] *v.* **made, mak•ing;** *n. . . .*
—n. **1** the way in which a thing is made; a style, build, or

. . . .

on the make, *Informal.* trying for success, profit, etc. ⟨OE *macian*⟩

Verb phrases, such as *make out* and *make over*, and other idioms using *make* as a verb, such as *make time* and *make something of*, are entered under the meanings of the verb:

make [meik] *v.* **made, mak•ing;** *n. —v.* **1** bring into being; put together; build; form; shape: *to make a new dress, to make a poem, to make a boat, to make a medicine.* **2** have the qualities needed for: *Wood makes a good fire.* **3** cause; bring about:

. . . .

make out, a write out: *He made out his application for camp.* **b** show (to be); try to prove: *That makes me out a liar.* **c** understand: *The girl had a hard time making out the problem.* **d** see with difficulty; distinguish: *I can barely make out three ships near the horizon.* **e** *Informal.* get along; manage: *We must try to make out with what we have.* **f** *Slang.* engage in extensive kissing and caressing, and, often, sexual intercourse.
make over, a alter; make different: *to make over a dress.* **b** hand over; transfer ownership of: *Grandfather made over his farm to my mother.*
make ready, *Printing.* prepare (a form) for the press by levelling and adjusting type, plates, etc. to ensure a clear and even impression.
make something of, make an issue of.
make time, go with speed.

10. Etymologies

The etymology, or origin, of a word is given at the end of all the definitions and is enclosed in angled brackets:

a•dult [ə'dʌlt] *or* ['ædʌlt] *adj., n. —adj.* **1** fully developed and

. . . .

—n. **1** a grown-up person. **2** a person who has reached an age of legal responsibility: *In some provinces, one is an adult at 18.* **3** a full-grown animal or plant. ⟨< L *adultus*, pp. of *adolescere.* See ADOLESCENT.⟩

an•thrax ['ænθræks] *n., pl.* **an•thra•ces** ['ænθrə,siz]. **1** an infectious, often fatal, disease of cattle, sheep, etc. that may be transmitted to human beings. **2** one of the lesions caused by this disease. ⟨< LL < Gk. *anthrax* carbuncle, live coal⟩

ax•le ['æksəl] *n.* **1** a bar or shaft on which or with which a wheel turns. See DIFFERENTIAL and GYROSCOPE for pictures. **2** axletree. ⟨OE *eaxl* shoulder, crossbar; influenced by ON *öxul* axle⟩

bar•ri•cade ['bærə,keid] *or* ['bɛrə,keid], [,bærə'keid] *or* [,bɛrə'keid] *n., v.* **-cad•ed, -cad•ing.** *—n.* **1** a rough, hastily made barrier for defence. **2** any barrier or obstruction. **3** *Cdn.* large blocks of ice remaining frozen to a river or sea shore after the spring breakup.
—v. **1** block or obstruct with a barricade: *The road was barricaded with fallen trees.* **2** keep out or in with a barricade. ⟨< F *barricade*, apparently < Provençal *barricada* < *barrica* cask; originally, made of casks. Related to BARREL.⟩

duc•at ['dʌkət] *n.* **1** a gold or silver coin formerly used in some European countries. **2** *Slang.* a ticket. ⟨ME < Ital. *ducato* < Med.L < L *dux, ducis* leader⟩

ki•osk ['kiɒsk] *or* [ki'ɒsk] *for 1;* [ki'ɒsk] *for 2; n.* **1** a small building, usually with one or more sides open, used as a newsstand, bus shelter, telephone booth, etc. **2** in Turkey, Persia, etc., a light, open summerhouse. ⟨< F < Turkish *kiushk* pavilion⟩

lem•on ['lɛmən] *n., adj. —n.* **1** an acid-tasting, light yellow citrus fruit growing in warm climates. **2** a thorny tree that bears this fruit. **3** a pale yellow. **4** *Slang.* a thing (usually a car) that or person who is…
—adj. pale yellow. ⟨ME < OF *limon* < Arabic *laimun* < Persian *limun*⟩

The arrow sign (<), used to connect the earlier forms of a word given as a chain in the angled brackets, means "from," "derived from," or "taken from." Thus *adult* is from L *adultus*; *anthrax* is taken from the Late Latin word of the same form, which in its turn is taken from the Greek *anthrax* meaning "carbuncle" or "live coal." The arrow sign that stands at the opening of an angled bracket is dropped if the word is found in Old English or Middle English, as in the case of *axle*, which is a native English word found in Old English as *eaxl* meaning "shoulder."

Usually, etymological forms and their meanings are given only where they are distinctive in regard to sense, spelling, or pronunciation. Otherwise only the language symbol is given and not the form. Thus *ducat* is found in Middle English; it is derived from the Italian *ducato*, which is from the Medieval Latin word of almost identical form (*ducatus*, not given) which is derived from the Latin *dux* meaning "leader."

For Latin and Greek forms, the genitive case is also given when it sheds light on the form or spelling of the derived word, as in the case of *dux, ducis* for *ducat.*

No etymology is given for the following entries:
(*a*) abbreviations;
(*b*) words, including compounds, made up of elements separately entered in the dictionary as English forms, e.g., *humanoid* (*human* + *-oid*), *leafstalk*, *open-pit*;
(*c*) phrases of two or more words that are separately entered, e.g., *dog tag*, *officer of the day*.

However, etymologies are sometimes given for such entries when the origin would not be evident from the etymologies of the separate words:

dog days in the northern hemisphere, a period of very hot, humid, and uncomfortable weather during July and August. ⟨with reference to the rising of Sirius, the Dog Star⟩

Related words

It is often desirable to show relationships between different entries, as in the case of two words that come from an identical source but have acquired different forms as a result of different linguistic histories; such words are called doublets:

frail[1] [freil] *adj.* **1** not very strong; weak; physically delicate: *a frail child.* **2** easily broken, damaged, or destroyed; fragile: *Be careful, those branches are a very frail support.* **3** morally weak; liable to yield to temptation. ⟨ME < OF *fraile* < L *fragilis* fragile. Doublet of FRAGILE.⟩ **—'frail•ly,** *adv.* **—'frail•ness,** *n.*

frag•ile ['frædʒaɪl] *or* ['frædʒəl] *adj.* **1** easily broken, damaged, or destroyed; delicate; frail. **2** slight; ineffectual: *a fragile hope.* **3** *Informal.* nervous; hypersensitive; easily upset: *I feel fragile this morning.* ⟨< L *fragilis* (related to *frangere* break). Doublet of FRAIL.⟩ **—'frag•ile•ly,** *adv.* **—fra'gil•i•ty** [frə'dʒɪləti], *n.* **—'frag•ile•ness,** *n.*

In this case Latin *fragilis* became Old French *fraile*, resulting in the English form *frail*, while *fragile* was formed at a later date directly from the Latin.

Relationships that are slightly less close are shown by means of the phrase *related to*, or *akin to*:

fleet[2] [flit] *adj., v. —adj.* swift; rapid.
—v. pass swiftly; move rapidly. ⟨OE *flēotan*, v.; adj. < ON *fljótr.* Akin to FLOAT.⟩

beck•on ['bɛkən] *v.* **1** signal by a motion of the head or hand: *He beckoned me to follow him.* **2** entice; be attractive (*to*). ⟨OE *bēcnan*, var. of *bīecnan.* Related to BEACON.⟩

Cross references are used to direct the reader to a related entry where the etymology he or she is studying is completed:

chap•lain ['tʃæplən] *n.* a member of the clergy officially authorized to perform religious functions for a family, court, society, public institution, or unit in the armed forces. ⟨ME < OF *chapelain* < LL *capellanus* < *cappella.* See CHAPEL.⟩

chap•el ['tʃæpəl] *n.* **1** a building for worship, not so large as a church. **2** a small place for worship within a larger building such
. . . .
⟨ME < OF *chapele* < LL *cappella*; originally a shrine in which was preserved the *cappa* or cape of St. Martin⟩

Referring the reader from *chaplain* to *chapel* avoids the necessity of repeating information about the origin of Latin *cappella*, at the same time establishing the relationship between the two words. Further examples of this device are:

ben•e•fice [ˈbɛnəfɪs] *n.* **1** a permanent office or position created by ecclesiastical authority. **2** the money earned from this position or the property attached to it. ⟨ME < OF < L *beneficium* benefit < *beneficus* beneficent < *benefacere.* See BENEFACTOR.⟩

ben•e•fac•tor [ˈbɛnə,fæktər] *or* [,bɛnəˈfæktər] *n.* a person who has helped others, either by gifts of money or by some kind act. ⟨ME < LL *benefactor* < *benefacere* < *bene* well + *facere* do⟩

Occasionally no extra information is to be found at the etymology for a related word but it is worthwhile to compare the two and to note the relationship, or similarity, between the two. In such cases the direction *Cf.* is used:

as[1] [əz]; *stressed,* [æz] *adv., conj., prep., pron.* *—adv.* **1** to the

. . . .

⟨OE (unstressed) *ealswā* quite so. Cf. ALSO.⟩

al•so [ˈɒlsou] *adv.* in addition; besides; too. ⟨OE *ealswā* all so, quite so⟩

11. Run-on entries

Run-ons are derived forms listed in boldface type after the etymology position in many entries. See the first two paragraphs of the discussion of derivatives on page ix.

Further examples of run-on entries are:

ab•jure [æbˈdʒur] *v.* **-jured, -jur•ing. 1** renounce solemnly or on oath; forswear; swear to give up: *to abjure one's religion.* **2** abstain from; avoid: *to abjure alcohol.* ⟨< L *abjurāre* < *ab-* away + *jurāre* swear⟩ **—abˈjur•er,** *n.*

cool [kul] *adj., n., v.* *—adj.* **1** somewhat cold; more cold than

. . . .

stay or **keep cool,** *Slang.* keep calm. ⟨OE *cōl*⟩ **—ˈcool•ly,** *adv.* **—ˈcool•ness,** *n.*

mag•net•ize [ˈmægnə,taɪz] *v.* **-ized, -iz•ing. 1** give the properties of a magnet to. An electric current in a coil around a bar of iron will magnetize the bar. **2** attract or influence like a magnet; charm: *Her beautiful voice magnetized the audience.* **—ˈmag•net,iz•a•ble,** *adj.* **—,mag•net•iˈza•tion,** *n.* **—ˈmag•net,iz•er,** *n.*

Note that the part of speech is given for run-on entries, and that syllabication and stress marks are indicated; the rest of the pronunciation and the meaning are to be inferred from that of the root word.

Run-on entries may be given for words formed with the following suffixes:

Suffixes forming adjectives

-able "able to be —" or "capable of being —"; added to verbs:
singable = able to be sung;
adaptable = capable of being adapted or capable of adapting.

-al "of, like; having the nature of —"; added to nouns:
natural = of nature or like nature; having the nature of.
"the act or process of —"; added to verbs:
refusal = the act of refusing.

-an, -ian, -n "of or having to do with —"; added to nouns (names of places):
Albertan = of or having to do with Alberta.

-ful "full of —"; added to nouns:
cheerful = full of cheer.
"characterized by or having the qualities of —"; added to nouns:
careful = characterized by care.
"having a tendency or the ability to —"; added to verbs:
mournful = having a tendency or the ability to mourn, etc.

-ic "of or having to do with —"; added to nouns:
Icelandic = of or having to do with Iceland.
"characterized; containing; made up of —"; added to nouns:
alcoholic = containing alcohol, etc.

-ish "somewhat —"; added to adjectives:
oldish = somewhat old.
"resembling; like —"; added to nouns:
childish = like a child, etc.

-less "having no —"; added to nouns:
wingless = having no wings;
conscienceless = having no conscience.

-like "like a —" or "like a —'s"; added to nouns:
flowerlike = like a flower;
birdlike = like a bird or like a bird's.

-ous "having; having much; full of —"; added to nouns:
joyous = full of joy.
"characterized by —"; added to nouns:
zealous = characterized by zeal.
"having the nature of —"; added to nouns:
murderous = having the nature of murder, etc.

Suffixes forming nouns

-an, -ian, -n "a native or inhabitant of—"; added to nouns (names of places):
Albertan = a native or inhabitant of Alberta.

-er, -or "one that —s"; added to verbs:
deceiver = one that deceives;
extractor = one that extracts.

-ion, -ation, -tion "a —ing or being —ed"; added to verbs:
decontamination = a decontaminating or being decontaminated;
magnetization = a magnetizing or being magnetized.

-ist "one who does, makes, or has skill with"; added to nouns:
theorist = one who makes theories.
flutist = one who has skill with a flute, etc.
"one who believes in or practises –ism":
legalist = one who practises legalism.

-ity "condition or quality of –"; added to adjectives:
activity = condition of being active;
sincerity = quality of being sincere.

-ment "a –ing or being –ed"; added to verbs:
encouragement = an encouraging or being encouraged, or something that encourages;
impalement = an impaling or being impaled.

-ness "the fact or quality of being –"; added to adjectives:
exactness = the fact or quality of being exact;
timeliness = the fact or quality of being timely.

Suffixes forming adverbs

-ly "in a – way or manner"; added to adjectives:
innocently = in an innocent manner;
plainly = in a plain way.

-ally "in a – way or manner"; added to certain adjectives ending in *ic*:
schematically = in a schematic manner.

12. Fistnotes

Certain kinds of information that do not fit into the above parts of an entry are given in fistnotes, so called because they are introduced by a printer's fist: ☛ Such notes are set in smaller type than the main text. There are five kinds of fistnote, distinguished from each other by an italic label following the fist: *Hom.* (Homonym), *Syn.* (Synonym), *Usage.*, *Spelling.*, and *Pronun.* (Pronunciation).

Homonyms

Homonyms are words with identical pronunciations but different spellings. The inclusion of the homonym(s) of a given entry word can assist the user in finding a desired word when he or she is unsure of the spelling:

al•ter ['ɒltər] *v.* **1** make different; change; vary: *If this coat is too large, a tailor can alter it to fit you.* **2** become different: *Since her trip to Europe, her whole outlook has altered.* ⟨ME < OF < LL *alterāre* < L *alter* other⟩ **—'al•ter•a•ble,** *adj.* **—'al•ter•a•bly,** *adv.*
☛ *Hom.* ALTAR.

ker•nel ['kɜrnəl] *n.* **1** the softer part inside the hard shell of a nut or inside the stone of a fruit. **2** a grain or seed like wheat or corn. **3** the central or most important part: *the kernel of an argument.* ⟨OE *cyrnel* < *corn* seed, grain⟩
☛ *Hom.* COLONEL.

Synonym studies

These notes bring out differences in meaning or usage between words that have very similar definitions. Usually, the basic meaning common to the synonyms being discussed is given first, followed by the particular shades of meaning that distinguish each individual word:

flex•i•ble ['flɛksəbəl] *adj.* **1** easily bent; not stiff; bending without breaking: *Leather, rubber, and wire are flexible materials.* **2** easily adapted to fit various uses, purposes, etc.: *flexible plans. The actor's flexible voice accommodated itself to every emotion.* **3** willing and able to adapt to a variety of situations or to accommodate the needs and ideas of others. ⟨< F < L < *flexibilis* < *flexus.* See FLEX.⟩ **—,flex•i'bil•i•ty,** *n.* **—'flex•i•bly,** *adv.*
☛ *Syn.* **Flexible,** PLIANT, LIMBER[1] = easily bent. **Flexible** = capable of being bent or twisted easily and without breaking, or, used figuratively of people and their minds, etc., capable of being turned or managed with little trouble if handled skilfully: *Great thinkers have flexible minds.* **Pliant,** literally and figuratively, emphasizes having the quality of bending or adapting itself easily rather than of being easily affected by outside force: *English is a pliant language.* **Limber,** used chiefly of the body, means 'having flexible muscles and joints': *A jumper has limber legs.*

A synonym study is given under the entry for the most common of the words discussed, cross-references to the study being given under the entries for the other words:

lim•ber[1] ['lɪmbər] *adj., v.* —*adj.* bending easily; flexible: *A pianist has to have limber fingers.* … ⟨? < *limp*[2] or *limb*⟩
—'lim•ber•ness, *n.*
☛ *Syn. adj.* See note at FLEXIBLE.

Usage notes

A large number of fistnotes give information about usage. Some call attention to contrasts in meaning (see *less* and *military law*, below), some to shades of meaning or connotations (see *jargon*[1], below). Others discuss choices relating to levels of usage (see *ain't*, below) or help the reader avoid common pitfalls in usage (see *literally*, below). Additional information about etymology may also be found in some of the usage notes (see *a-*[4], below):

less [lɛs] *adj., n., adv., prep.* —*adj.* **1** smaller; not so much: *of less width, to eat less meat.* **2** fewer: *Five is less than seven.* **3** lower in age, rank, or importance: *no less a person than the Prince…*

☛ *Usage.* **Less,** LESSER. Both are used as comparative (of *little*), **less** more usually referring to size or quantity: *less time, less food*; **lesser** referring to value or importance: *a lesser writer.*

military law a system of regulations governing the armed forces and others in military service.

☛ *Usage.* **Military law** is not to be confused with MARTIAL LAW, which replaces CIVIL LAW in times of emergency and applies to civilians as well as military personnel.

jar•gon[1] ['dʒɑrgən] *n.* **1** language that fails to communicate because it is full of long or fancy words, uses more words than necessary, and contains lengthy, awkward sentences. **2** a form of speech made up of features from two or more languages, used for communication between peoples whose native languages differ: *the Chinook jargon. Pidgin English is a jargon.* **3** the language of a particular group, profession, etc.: *the jargon of sailors.*

. . . .

⟨ME < OF; probably ult. imitative⟩

☛ *Usage.* Definitions 2 and 3 carry no slur or criticism but are technical senses of **jargon** as used by linguists. They should not be confused with definition 1, which does suggest poor expression and muddled thinking.

ain't [eint] *Informal.* **1** am not, are not, or is not. **2** have not or has not.

☛ *Usage.* **Ain't** has long been used in English, though it is unacceptable to most educated speakers. It should not be used in formal English.

lit•er•al•ly ['lɪtərəli] *adv.* **1** word for word; not figuratively or imaginatively: *to translate literally.* **2** actually; without exaggeration: *I was literally penniless; I couldn't even get a cup of coffee.* **3** *Informal.* virtually.

☛ *Usage.* **Literally** is sometimes used informally as a general intensifier: *The desk was literally buried in papers.* This usage gives **literally** the exact opposite of its real meaning of 'actually; without exaggeration', and should, therefore, be avoided in formal English.

a–[4] *prefix.* not or without; the form of AN-[1] occurring before consonants except *h*, as in *atypical, atonal.*

☛ *Usage.* **A-** meaning *not* is of Greek origin and is used in words taken directly, or through Latin, from Greek, as in *apathy.* It is also used as a naturalized English prefix in new formations, as in *achromatic.* **A-,** called alpha privative, corresponds to English **un-** and Latin **in-.**

Some usage notes give grammatical information:

a[1] [ə]; *stressed,* [ei] *or* [æ] *indefinite article.* **1** a word used before singular nouns when the person or thing referred to is not specific: *There's a man at the door. I need a new coat.* **2** one: *I want a loaf of bread, a watermelon, and a dozen oranges. She took the stairs two at a time.* **3** any: *A thoughtful person would not have said that.* **4** a single: *not a one.* ⟨var. of AN[1]⟩

☛ *Usage.* **A** is used before words pronounced with an initial consonant sound whether or not that sound is shown by the spelling, as in *a woman, a year, a union, a hospital.* Most people now write *a hotel* or *a historian*, but some use *an* in these cases.

☛ *Usage.* **A** regularly comes before other modifiers but follows *many, such, what,* and any adjective preceded by *as, how, so,* or *too,* as in *many a person, such a bore, so fine a picture, too high a price.*

ad•her•ent [æd'hirənt] *n., adj.* —*n.* a faithful supporter; follower.
—*adj.* **1** sticking fast; attached. **2** *Botany.* congenitally attached.
—ad'her•ent•ly, *adv.*

☛ *Syn. n.* See note at FOLLOWER.

☛ *Usage.* **Adherent.** The preposition used with the noun **adherent** is *of*: *She was an adherent of the Liberal Party.*

Detailed grammatical information is given in the form of usage notes for such terms as *adverb* and *gerund*:

ad•verb ['ædvɜrb] *n.* a word that extends or limits the meaning of verbs but is also used to qualify adjectives or other adverbs, especially in place, time, manner, or degree: *Soon, here, very, gladly,* and *not* are adverbs. *Abbrev.*: adv. ⟨< L *adverbium* < *ad-* to + *verbum* verb⟩

☛ *Usage.* **Adverb. a forms of adverbs.** Most adverbs are formed from adjectives or participles plus the ending *-ly*: *He rowed badly. She was deservedly popular. Surely you hear that.* In informal use, certain common adverbs may occur in the same form as adjectives in some contexts. Some of these are: *cheap, close, even, loud, right, slow, tight, wrong.* For example, one can say *He sang loud* or *He sang loudly.* Their *-ly* forms are more common in formal English. There are also some other common adverbs whose two forms (with and without an *-ly* ending) are not interchangeable, each being used in a different context or with a slightly different meaning. Some of these are: *deep, first, high, near.* Thus *She can sing very high* (not *highly*) but *They praised her work very highly* (not *high*). Consult the individual entries for each form if in doubt. **b comparison of adverbs.** Degrees of the condition or manner indicated by an adverb are shown by adding *-er, -est* or by placing *more, most* before it: *hard, harder, hardest; slow, slower, slowest;* or *slowly, more slowly, most slowly. More* and *most* are used with most adverbs of more than one syllable.

ger•und ['dʒɛrənd] *n. Grammar.* a verb form used as a noun. *Abbrev.*: ger. ⟨< LL *gerundium*, ult. < L *gerere* bear⟩

☛ *Usage.* The English **gerund** ends in *-ing.* It has the same form as the present participle but differs in use. Gerund: *Running a hotel appealed to her.* Participle: *Running around the corner, he bumped into his father.* A gerund may take an object (*running a hotel*) or a complement (*being a hero*), and it may serve in any of the functions of a noun: Subject: *Kayaking always fascinated her.* Object: *He taught dancing.* Predicate noun: *Seeing is believing.* Adjectival use: *a fishing boat* (a boat for fishing, not a boat that fishes). Object of a preposition: *a great day for hiking.*

Spelling

A number of fistnotes deal with problems or variations of Canadian spelling:

ad•vis•er or **ad•vi•sor** [æd'vaɪzər] *n.* **1** a person who gives advice. **2** a person whose work is giving advice, especially a teacher or professor appointed to advise students.

☛ *Spelling.* **Adviser** has been the more common spelling, but the *-or* form, because of its similarity to *advisory,* is being increasingly used.

li•cence ['ləisəns] *n.* **1** permission given by law to do something. **2** the paper, card, plate, etc. showing such permission: *The barber hung his licence on the wall.* **3** the fact or condition of being permitted to do something. **4** freedom of action, speech, thought, etc. that is permitted or conceded. Poetic licence is the freedom from rules that is permitted in poetry and art. **5** too much liberty; disregard of what is right and proper; abuse of liberty. Also, **license.** ⟨ME < OF *licence* < L *licentia* < *licere* be allowed⟩ **—'li•cence•less,** *adj.*

☛ *Spelling.* **Licence** is one of two words that in Canadian English are usually spelled differently as nouns and verbs. The preferred spelling for the noun is **licence** and for the verb **license.** For this reason the noun and verb are entered separately in this dictionary. The spellings of the other word are **practice** and **practise.**

li•cense ['ləisəns] *v.* **-censed, -cens•ing.** *n.* —*v.* **1** give a licence to: *to license a new driver.* **2** permit or authorize, especially by law: *A doctor is licensed to practise medicine.*
—*n.* See LICENCE. **—'li•cens•er,** *n.*

☛ *Spelling.* See note at LICENCE.

Pronunciation

Variations in pronunciation are discussed in a similar way:

creek [krik] *or, often,* [krɪk] *n.* **1** a small freshwater stream. **2** a narrow bay, running inland for some distance.
up the creek, *Slang.* in difficulty. ⟨ME *creke*; cf. MDu. *creke*⟩

☛ *Hom.* CREAK [krik], CRICK [krɪk].

☛ *Pronun.* Most Canadians pronounce **creek** the same as **creak,** but in some regions, especially in parts of the West, the pronunciation (krɪk) is common.

been [bin] *or* [bɪn] *v.* pp. of BE.

☛ *Hom.* BEAN [bin], BIN [bɪn].

☛ *Pronun.* **Been.** The most common British pronunciation is [bin], and the normal American pronunciation is [bɪn]. In earlier English, [bin] was the stressed form and [bɪn] the unstressed; many Canadian speakers still employ this distinction. Otherwise, Canadian usage varies between the two forms.

A a *A a*

a or **A** [ei] *n., pl.* **a's** or **A's.** **1** the first letter of the English alphabet. **2** any speech sound represented by this letter, as in *cat, father, late,* etc. **3** a person or thing identified as *a*, especially the first in a series: *Company A in a battalion. A works twice as hard as B.* **4 A, a** a grade rating a person or thing as the best in a group: *grade A eggs.* **b** a person or thing receiving this rating: *All these exams are A's.* **5** *Music.* **a** the sixth tone in the scale of C major. **b** a symbol representing this tone. **c** a key, string, etc. that produces this tone. **d** a scale or key that has A as its keynote: *a symphony in A.* **6** *Algebra. a,* the first known quantity: $ax + by + c = 0$. **7 A, a** an antigen found in some human blood. **b** the type of human blood containing this antigen, one of the four main types in the ABO system. **8 A,** something shaped like the letter A. **9** any device, such as a printer's type, a lever, or a key on a keyboard, that produces an a or A. **10** *(adjl.)* of or being an A or a.

a[1] [ə]; *stressed,* [ei] *or* [æ] *indefinite article.* **1** a word used before singular nouns when the person or thing referred to is not specific: *There's a man at the door. I need a new coat.* **2** one: *I want a loaf of bread, a watermelon, and a dozen oranges. She took the stairs two at a time.* **3** any: *A thoughtful person would not have said that.* **4** a single: *not a one.* ⟨var. of AN[1]⟩

☛ *Usage.* A is used before words pronounced with an initial consonant sound whether or not that sound is shown by the spelling, as in *a woman, a year, a union, a hospital.* Most people now write *a hotel* or *a historian*, but some use *an* in these cases.

☛ *Usage.* A regularly comes before other modifiers but follows *many, such, what,* and any adjective preceded by *as, how, so,* or *too,* as in *many a person, such a bore, so fine a picture, too high a price.*

a[2] [ə]; *stressed,* [ei] *or* [æ] *indefinite article.* in or for each; per: *once a year, two dollars a dozen, forty dollars a day.* ⟨OE *on* on⟩

☛ *Usage.* See first note at A[1].

a–[1] *prefix.* **1** on or in: *We went aboard. They found him abed. The room was abuzz with conversation.* **2** in the act of ——ing: *a-fishing = in the act of fishing.* ⟨ME *a* < OE *ān, on* in, on, at⟩

☛ *Usage.* **a-**[1]. Adjectives originally formed with **a-** + noun (such as *alive, asleep*) are not used before a noun. We say *a man who is asleep* and *a man asleep*, but not *an asleep man.*

a–[2] *prefix.* from, away, or off; the form of AB-[1] occurring before *m, p,* and *v,* as in *avert.*

a–[3] *prefix.* to or toward; the form of AD- occurring before *sc, sp,* and *st,* as in *ascribe, aspire, astringent.*

a–[4] *prefix.* not or without; the form of AN-[1] occurring before consonants except *h,* as in *atypical, atonal.*

☛ *Usage.* **A-** meaning *not* is of Greek origin and is used in words taken directly, or through Latin, from Greek, as in *apathy.* It is also used as a naturalized English prefix in new formations, as in *achromatic.* **A-,** called alpha privative, corresponds to English **un-** and Latin **in-.**

a **1** anode. **2** alto. **3** ARE[2]. **4** before (for L *ante*). **5** atto-.

a. **1** about. **2** acre(s). **3** adjective. **4** alto. **5** in the year (for L *anno*). **6** anode. **7** anonymous. **8** answer. **9** before (for L *ante*). **10** *Heraldry.* argent. **11** *Sports.* assist; assists. **12** absent. **13** active.

A **1** ampere. **2** answer. **3** *A,* absolute temperature. **4** April. **5** August.

Å angstrom.

a•a ['ɑɑ] *n.* basaltic lava. ⟨< Hawaiian *a'a* ⟩

A1 or **A–1** *Informal.* A-one; first-class.

AA or **A.A.** **1** *Psychology.* achievement age. **2** Alcoholics Anonymous. **3** anti-aircraft.

AAA or **A.A.A.** **1** Amateur Athletic Association. **2** American Automobile Association.

aard•vark ['ɑrd,vɑrk] *n.* an African burrowing mammal (*Orycteropus afer*, of the order Tubulidentata) having large, erect ears, a long flexible snout, and a very long, flat, sticky tongue with which it catches ants and termites. An aardvark is about 1.5 m long. ⟨< Afrikaans < Du. *aarde* earth + *vark* pig⟩

aard•wolf ['ɑrd,wʊlf] *n., pl.* **-wolves** [-,wʊlvz] a carnivorous animal (*Proteles cristatus*) of the hyena family, native to South Africa. It eats grubs and termites. ⟨< Afrikaans, earth wolf⟩

ab–[1] *prefix.* from, away, away from, or off, as in *abnormal, abduct, abjure.* Also: **a-** before *m, p, v*; **abs-** before *c, t. Example: abstain.* ⟨< L *ab-* < *ab,* prep.⟩

ab–[2] *prefix.* to or toward; the form of AD- occurring before *b,* as in *abbreviate.*

AB[1] **1** Alberta (*used esp. in computerized address systems*). **2** ABLE SEAMAN. **3** *Baseball.* (times) at bat.

AB[2] the type of human blood containing both antigens A and B. It is one of the four blood types in the ABO system.

A.B. or **a.b.** ABLE-BODIED SEAMAN.

a•ba ['ɑbə] *or* [ə'bɑ] *n.* **1** a rough, feltlike fabric made of wool or hair fibres. **2** a loose, sleeveless outer garment worn by Arabs. ⟨< Arabic *qaba',* woollen cloak⟩

a•ba•ca ['æbəkə] *or* [,æbə'kɑ] *n.* **1** a plant (*Musa textilis*) of the Philippines related to the banana, from whose leafstalks Manila hemp is obtained. **2** MANILA HEMP. ⟨< Malay⟩

a•back [ə'bæk] *adv. Archaic* (*except in* **taken aback**). toward the back; backward.

taken aback, taken by surprise; startled and confused: *She was taken aback by your angry outburst.* ⟨OE *on bæc*⟩

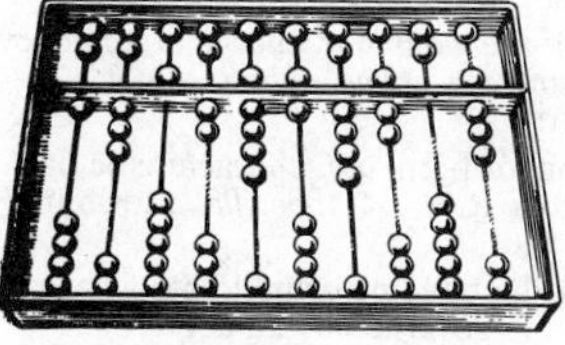

An abacus. The beads above the bar count 5 each when lowered to the bar. The beads below the bar count 1 each when raised to the bar. In the picture, the beads are set for 1 352 964 708.

ab•a•cus ['æbəkəs] *n., pl.* **-cus•es** or **-ci** [-,saɪ] *or* [-,si] **1** a calculating device consisting of a frame having rows of counters or beads that slide up and down in grooves or on wires. **2** *Architecture.* a slab forming the top of the capital of a column. ⟨< L < Gk. *abax, abacos*⟩

a•baft [ə'bæft] *adv., prep. —adv.* on a ship or boat, at or toward the stern.

—prep. behind; toward the stern from. ⟨< *a-* on + ME *baft,* OE *beæftan* < *be* by + *æftan* behind⟩

ab•a•lo•ne [,æbə'louni] *n.* any of several species of edible marine snail (genus *Haliotis*) found mainly along temperate Pacific coasts, having a single flat, ear-shaped shell with a row of small holes along one side and a mother-of-pearl lining that is used for buttons and ornaments. ⟨< Am.Sp. *abulón*⟩

a•ban•don [ə'bændən] *v., n. —v.* **1** give up entirely; relinquish: *to abandon a career, to abandon an idea.* **2** leave without intending to return; desert: *to abandon one's home.* **3** yield (oneself) completely (to a feeling, impulse, etc.): *to abandon oneself to grief.*

—n. complete freedom from restraint; spontaneous exuberance or enthusiasm: *The crowd cheered with abandon.* ⟨ME < OF *abandoner,* earlier *a ban doner* give over to another's jurisdiction < *a* to (< L *ad*) + *ban* power (< Gmc.) + *doner* give < L *donare* grant < *donum* gift⟩ **—a'ban•don•er,** *n.*

☛ *Syn. v.* **2.** See note at DESERT[2].

a•ban•doned [ə'bændənd] *adj.* **1** deserted or forsaken: *an abandoned homestead.* **2** completely unrestrained; especially, disregarding accepted standards of sexual behaviour.

a•ban•don•ment [ə'bændənmənt] *n.* **1** abandoning or being abandoned. **2** freedom from restraint; abandon.

à bas [a'ba] *French.* down with: *À bas the rebels.*

a•base [ə'beis] *v.* **a•based, a•bas•ing.** make lower in rank, esteem, or prestige; humiliate or degrade: *to abase oneself by accepting a bribe. The dictator abased his subjects by harsh treatment.* ⟨ME < OF *abaissier* bring low < LL *bassus* low⟩

a•base•ment [ə'beismənt] *n.* **1** the act of abasing. **2** the condition of being abased.

a•bash [ə'bæʃ] *v.* embarrass and confuse; make uneasy or shy and slightly ashamed: *The boys were abashed when the teacher pointed out all their mistakes.* ⟨ME < OF *esbaïss-,* a stem of *esbaïr* be astonished < VL *batare* gape⟩ **—a'bash•ment,** *n.*

a•bate [ə'beit] *v.* **a•bat•ed, a•bat•ing.** **1** become less violent, intense, etc.: *The storm has abated.* **2** make less in amount, intensity, etc.: *The medicine abated her pain.* **3** *Law.* do away with; put an end to; annul: *to abate a nuisance, to abate a writ.* **4** deduct (part of a price, etc.): *They abated ten percent from the original price for quick sale.* ⟨ME < OF *abatre* beat down < *a-* to (< L *ad-*) + *batre* beat < VL *battere* < L *battuere*⟩ **—a'bat•er,** *n.*

a•bate•ment [ə'beitmənt] *n.* **1** the act or process of abating. **2** the amount abated; reduction.

ab•a•tis or **ab•at•tis** ['æbətɪs] *or* ['æbə,ti] *n., pl.* **ab•a•tis** or **ab•at•tis.** a barricade of trees cut down and placed with their sharpened branches directed toward the enemy. ⟨< F *abatis* mass of things thrown down⟩

A battery *Electronics.* a battery for heating the filament or cathode of an electron tube to produce a stream of electrons.

ab•at•toir [,æbə'twɑr] *or* ['æbə,twɑr] *n.* slaughterhouse. ⟨< F⟩

ab•ax•i•al [æ'bæksiəl] *adj.* situated away from the axis.

ab•ba•cy ['æbəsi] *n., pl.* **-cies. 1** the position or power of an abbot. **2** the term of office of an abbot. **3** a district ruled by an abbot. ⟨< LL *abbatia* < *abbas* abbot. See ABBOT.⟩

Ab•bas•sid [ə'bæsɪd] *or* ['æbə,sɪd] *n.* any of the caliphs of Baghdad belonging to the dynasty supposed to be descended from Abbas (A.D. 566-652), uncle and helper of Mohammed. This dynasty ruled the Muslim empire from A.D. 750 to 1258.

ab•bé ['æbei] *or* [æ'bei] *n.* **1** a French abbot. **2** a title of respect given to a French priest or other cleric.

ab•bess ['æbɪs] *or* ['æbɛs] *n.* the woman in charge of an abbey of nuns. ⟨ME < OF < LL *abbatissa* < *abbas, abbatis* abbot + *-issa* Gk. fem. suffix. See ABBOT.⟩

Ab•be•vil•li•an [,æbə'vɪliən] *or* [-jən] *adj.* characteristic of a paleolithic culture that used stone axes. ⟨< *Abbeville*, a town in France⟩

ab•bey ['æbi] *n., pl.* **-beys. 1** the building or buildings where monks or nuns live a religious life governed by an abbot or abbess; a monastery or convent. **2** the monks or nuns living there. **3** a church or residence that was once an abbey or a part of an abbey: *Westminster Abbey.* ⟨ME < OF < LL *abbatia* < *abbas, -atis* abbot. See ABBOT.⟩

ab•bot ['æbət] *n.* the man in charge of an abbey of monks. ⟨OE *abbad, abbod* < LL *abbas, -atis* < LGk. < Aramaic *abbā* father⟩

abbrev. or **abbr.** abbreviation; abbreviated.

ab•bre•vi•ate [ə'brivi,eit] *v.* **-at•ed, -at•ing. 1** make (a word or phrase) shorter so that a part stands for the whole: *We can abbreviate* Alberta *to* AB. **2** make briefer; curtail: *She was asked to abbreviate her speech.* ⟨< L *abbreviare* < *ad-* to + *brevis* short. Doublet of ABRIDGE.⟩ **—ab'bre•vi,a•tor,** *n.*

☛ *Syn.* See note at SHORTEN.

ab•bre•vi•a•tion [ə,brivi'eiʃən] *n.* **1** a shortened form of a word or phrase standing for the whole, such as *Ont.* for *Ontario* or *MP* for *Member of Parliament.* **2** the act of making shorter.

☛ *Syn.* **Abbreviation,** CONTRACTION. An abbreviation is a shortened form of a word. A contraction is a combination of two words, the last of which is an abbreviation: *isn't, it's.*

ABC[1] [,ei,bi'si] *n.* Often, **ABC's: 1** the alphabet: *to learn one's ABC's.* **2** elementary principles: *This course is intended to teach you the ABC's of flying.*

ABC[2] American Broadcasting Company.

ABC soil a section of soil composed of three layers: the A horizon or topsoil, the B horizon or subsoil, and the C horizon, which is directly above the bedrock.

ab•di•cate ['æbdɪ,keit] *v.* **-cat•ed, -cat•ing. 1** give up or renounce formally (a position of authority or an office): *When King Edward VIII abdicated his throne his brother became king.* **2** give up (one's duties or responsibilities): *Do not abdicate your responsibility through cowardice.* ⟨< L *abdicare* < *ab-* away + *dicare* proclaim⟩ **—,ab•di'ca•tion,** *n.* **—'ab•di,ca•tor,** *n.*

ab•do•men ['æbdəmən] *or* [æb'doumən] *n.* **1** the part of the body containing the stomach, the intestines, and other digestive organs; belly. **2** the outer front surface of this. **3** the last of the three parts of the body of an insect or crustacean. ⟨< L⟩

ab•dom•i•nal [æb'dɒmənəl] *adj.* of, in, or for the abdomen: *the abdominal muscles.* **—ab'dom•i•nal•ly,** *adv.*

ab•dom•i•nous [æb'dɒmənəs] *adj.* potbellied.

ab•du•cent [æb'djusənt] *or* [æb'dusənt] *adj.* of a muscle, used to draw away one limb, or part of one, from another. ⟨< L *abdūcent*⟩

ab•duct [æb'dʌkt] *v.* **1** carry off or take away (a person) by force or deceit. **2** of a muscle or group of muscles, serve to move (a limb, etc.) away from the median axis of the body or of one of its parts. Compare ADDUCT. ⟨< L *abductus*, pp. of *abducere* < *ab-* away + *ducere* lead⟩ **—ab'duc•tion** *n.*

ab•duc•tor [æb'dʌktər] *n.* **1** a person who abducts another person. **2** any muscle whose function is to move a limb, etc. away from the median axis of the body or of one of its parts, as in raising an arm out to the side or spreading the fingers or toes. Compare ADDUCTOR.

a•beam [ə'bim] *adv.* **1** directly opposite to the middle part of a ship's side. **2** straight across a ship.

a•be•ce•dar•i•an [,eibisi'dɛriən] *n., adj.* *—n.* a beginner in anything that requires systematic study.
—adj. elementary. ⟨< Med.L *abecedarius* < the letters A, B, C, D⟩

a•bed [ə'bɛd] *adv.* in bed.

A•beg•weit ['æbəg,wəit] *n. Cdn.* a First Nations name for Prince Edward Island, meaning 'cradle of the waves'. ⟨< Micmac, Algonquian⟩

A•be•li•an group [ə'biliən] *or* [ə'biljən] *Mathematics.* a group of numbers or variables in an algebraic system governed by the commutative law. ⟨< N.H. *Abel*, a mathematician⟩

Ab•e•na•ki [,æbə'næki] *n., pl.* **-ki** or **-kis;** *adj.* *—n.* **1** a member of the First Nations or Native Americans living mainly in southern Québec and the State of Maine. **2** the Algonquian language spoken by the Abenaki.
—adj. of or having to do with the Abenaki or their language. Also, **Abnaki.** ⟨< Algonquin, literally, those living in the east, or easterners⟩

Ab•er•deen An•gus ['æbər,din 'æŋgəs] a breed of entirely black, hornless beef cattle having a compact body and short legs. ⟨< *Aberdeen*, a county in Scotland⟩

ab•er•rance [æ'bɛrəns] *n.* the fact or condition of being aberrant. Also, **aberrancy.**

ab•er•rant [æ'bɛrənt] *or* ['æbərənt] *adj., n.* *—adj.* deviating from what is regular, normal, or right: *aberrant behaviour.*
—n. an aberrant person or thing. ⟨< L *aberrans, -antis*, ppr. of *aberrare* < *ab-* away + *errare* wander⟩

ab•er•ra•tion [,æbə'reiʃən] *n.* **1** a wandering from the right path or usual course of action. **2** a deviation from a standard or ordinary type; abnormal structure or development. **3** a temporary mental disorder. **4** *Optics.* the failure of a lens or mirror to bring to a single focus the rays of light coming from one point. Aberration causes a blurred image or an image with a coloured rim. **5** *Astronomy.* a slight change in the apparent position of a heavenly body, caused by the combined effect of the earth's motion and of light. **—ab•er'ra•tion•al,** *adj.*

a•bet [ə'bɛt] *v.* **a•bet•ted, a•bet•ting.** encourage or help, especially in doing something wrong: *One girl did the actual stealing, but two others abetted her.* ⟨ME < OF *abeter* arouse < *a-* to + *beter* to bait⟩ **—a'bet•ment,** *n.* **—a'bet•tor** or **a'bet•ter,** *n.*

a•bey•ance [ə'beiəns] *n.* **1** temporary inactivity; a state of suspended action: *The whole question is being held in abeyance until a new committee is formed.* **2** *Law.* a lapse in succession of title until ownership or possession is established: *The inheritance was in abeyance until the rightful owner came forward.* ⟨< AF *abeiance* expectation < L *ad-* at + VL *batare* gape⟩

ab•hor [æb'hɔr] *v.* **-horred, -hor•ring.** shrink from with horror; feel disgust or hate for; detest; loathe: *to abhor liquor, to abhor snakes.* ⟨< L *abhorrere* < *ab-* from + *horrere* dread⟩ **—ab'hor•rer,** *n.*

☛ *Syn.* See note at HATE.

ab•hor•rence [æb'hɔrəns] *n.* **1** a feeling of horror or disgust. **2** something that is abhorred.

ab•hor•rent [æb'hɔrənt] *adj.* **1** causing repugnance: *abhorrent conduct.* **2** in conflict with (*used with* **to**): *abhorrent to good sense.* **—ab'hor•rent•ly,** *adv.*

a•bide [ə'baid] *v.* **a•bode** or **a•bid•ed, a•bid•ing. 1** put up with; endure; tolerate (*usually negative*): *She cannot abide stinginess.* **2** stay; remain: *"Though much is taken, much abides."* **3** dwell; continue to live (in a place). **4** stand firm. **5** *Archaic.* wait for: *He shall abide my coming.*
abide by, a accept and act upon: *We must abide by their decision.* **b** remain faithful to; fulfil: *They abided by their promise.* ⟨OE *ābīdan* stay on, and *onbīdan* wait for⟩ **—a'bid•er,** *n.*

a•bid•ing [ə'baɪdɪŋ] *adj.* unending; enduring; lasting: *an abiding interest in conservation. We hope for an abiding peace.*

ab•i•gail ['æbə,geil] *n.* a lady's maid. ⟨< *Abigail*, a character in Beaumont and Fletcher's play *The Scornful Lady*⟩

a•bil•i•ty [ə'bɪləti] *n., pl.* **-ties. 1** the power to perform or accomplish something: *He has the ability to hold an audience spellbound. This computer has the ability to solve mathematical problems.* **2** skill: *She has great ability as a hockey player.* **3** the power to do some special thing; mental gift; talent: *Musical* *ability often shows itself early in life.* ⟨< F *habileté* < L *habilitas* < *habilis* apt, fit, easily handled⟩

☛ *Syn.* **3. Ability,** TALENT = power to do or for doing something. **Ability** applies to a demonstrated physical or mental power, which may be either natural or acquired, to do a certain thing well: *She has unusual ability in science.* **Talent** applies to a capacity for doing a special thing, which is inborn in a person, never acquired, and which is or can be developed through training and use: *His Scout activities revealed a talent for leadership, which he is developing at school this year.*

☛ *Usage.* A verb following **ability** is in the infinitive and is always preceded by *to*: *She has the ability to swim like a fish.*

ab in•i•tio ['æb ɪ'nɪʃi,ou] *Latin.* from the beginning.

a•bi•o•gen•e•sis [,eibaɪou'dʒɛnəsɪs] *or* [,æbiou'dʒɛnəsɪs] *n. Biology.* the spontaneous production of life from inanimate matter.

a•bi•og•e•nist [,eibaɪ'ɒdʒənɪst] *n.* a person who believes in abiogenesis.

a•bi•ot•ic [,eibaɪ'ɒtɪk] *adj.* having to do with the absence of live organisms.

ab•ject ['æbdʒɛkt] *adj.* **1** wretched; miserable: *abject poverty.* **2** deserving contempt; degraded: *an abject flatterer.* **3** showing humiliation or complete resignation: *abject submission, an abject apology.* ⟨< L *abjectus*, pp. of *abjicere* < *ab-* down + *jacere* throw⟩ **—'ab•ject•ly,** *adv.* **—'ab•ject•ness,** *n.*

ab•jec•tion [æb'dʒɛkʃən] *n.* the state of being completely abject.

ab•ju•ra•tion [,æbdʒə'reiʃən] *n.* the act or an instance of abjuring.

ab•jure [æb'dʒur] *v.* **-jured, -jur•ing. 1** renounce solemnly or on oath; forswear; swear to give up: *to abjure one's religion.* **2** abstain from; avoid: *to abjure alcohol.* ⟨< L *abjurāre* < *ab-* away + *jurāre* swear⟩ **—ab'jur•er,** *n.*

abl. ablative.

ab•lac•ta•tion [,æblæk'teiʃən] *n.* weaning.

ab•late [æb'leit] *v.* **-lat•ed, -lat•ing. 1** remove by burning off, wearing down, cutting away, etc.; remove by ablation. **2** undergo ablation. ⟨< L *ablatus*, literally, having been carried away, pp. of *auferre* carry away⟩

ab•la•tion [æb'leiʃən] *n.* **1** the removal of an organ or body part by surgery. **2** *Geology.* the erosion of glaciers or rocks, especially by melting or the action of water. **3** *Astronautics.* the vaporizing or melting of the outer surface of the nose cone, etc. of a spacecraft, as on re-entry into the earth's atmosphere.

ab•la•tive ['æblətɪv] *adj., n. —adj.* **1** of, having to do with, or being the grammatical case, found in Latin and some other languages, that shows that a noun or pronoun refers to a source, agent, cause, etc. of an action. **2** ablating; removing by ablation. **3** undergoing ABLATION (def. 3).

—n. **1** the ablative case. **2** a word or construction in the ablative case. ⟨< L *ablativus*, literally, of removal < *ablatus*, pp. of *auferre* < *ab-* away + *ferre* carry⟩

☛ *Usage.* **Ablative case.** The work done in Latin by ablative case endings is done in English by the prepositions *at, by, from, in,* and *with* placed before the noun: *at the store, by the thief.*

ab•laut ['æblʌut]; *German,* ['ap,laʊt] *n. Linguistics.* a regular change in the quality or length of a root vowel sound, indicating a grammatical distinction. Ablaut was a feature of the early Indo-European languages and is still found in modern English in such verbs as *ring* (pt. *rang*, pp. *rung*) and *write* (pt. *wrote*, pp. *written*). ⟨< G *Ablaut* < *ab-* off + *Laut* sound⟩

a•blaze [ə'bleiz] *adv. or adj.* (*never precedes a noun*) **1** on fire; burning: *By the time we arrived, the whole building was ablaze.* **2** bright or glowing: *The great hall was ablaze with a hundred lights.* **3** in or into a state of great excitement, anger, ardour or enthusiasm: *One look from her could set his heart ablaze.*

☛ *Usage.* Used with **set.**

a•ble ['eibəl] *adj.* **a•bler, a•blest. 1** having power, means, opportunity, time, etc. (*to*): *Little children are able to walk, but they are not able to earn a living.* **2** having the necessary qualifications; competent: *an able seaman.* **3** having more competence or skill than most others; clever: *She is an able teacher.* **4** competently done: *an able speech.* ⟨ME < OF *hable*, *able* < L *habilis* fit, easily held or handled < *habere* hold⟩

☛ *Syn.* **Able,** CAPABLE, COMPETENT = having sufficient power to do or for doing something. **Able** (with *to*) emphasizes power to act or perform: *She is able to play the piano.* **Capable** emphasizes fitness for doing, capacity or ability to do something adequately, or, sometimes, general efficiency: *He has proved himself capable both as soldier and as administrator.* **Competent** emphasizes possession of sufficient skill or other requirements to do a certain kind of work satisfactorily: *A competent typist is not necessarily a competent secretary.*

☛ *Usage.* **Able** and COMPETENT may be followed by *to* plus an infinitive, but CAPABLE takes *of* plus a gerund: *able to think, competent to drive a car, capable of taking responsibility.*

–able *suffix.* **1** that can be ——ed; able to be ——ed: *obtainable = that can be obtained.* **2** likely to or suitable for: *comfortable = suitable for comfort.* **3** inclined to: *peaceable = inclined to peace.* **4** deserving to be ——ed: *lovable = deserving to be loved.* See also -IBLE. ⟨< F < L *-abilis*, a suffix forming adjectives from verbs with infinitives in *-are*, being one form of the suffix *-bilis*⟩

☛ *Usage.* Instead of **-able,** a number of words have the spelling -IBLE, which originally belonged largely to words from Latin infinitives in *-ere* or *-ire* (as in *terrible,* from Latin *terrere*). The living suffix is **-able** (*now used for passive meaning*), which should be used in coining occasional words like *jumpable.* An e which serves to make a g or c soft, as in *change*, is retained before **-able:** *changeable.*

a•ble–bod•ied ['eibəl ,bɒdid] *adj.* physically fit; strong and healthy.

able–bodied seaman an experienced sailor, especially in a merchant navy, who is qualified to perform certain routine duties at sea. *Abbrev.*: A.B. or a.b.

able seaman 1 *Canadian Forces.* in Maritime Command, a person ranking next above an ordinary seaman and below a leading seaman. *Abbrev.*: A.B. or AB. See chart of ranks in the Appendix. **2** ABLE-BODIED SEAMAN.

a•bloom [ə'blum] *adv. or adj.* (*never precedes a noun*) in bloom; blossoming.

ab•lu•ent ['æbluənt] *n.* any substance used for cleaning. ⟨< L *ablūent* < *abluere* wash⟩

ab•lu•tion [ə'bluʃən] *n.* **1** the act of washing oneself: *to perform one's ablutions.* **2** the act of washing or cleansing as a religious ceremony of purification. **3** the water or other liquid used in washing. ⟨< ME *ablucioun* < L *ablutio* a washing off⟩

a•bly ['eibli] *adv.* in an able manner; with skill.

ABM ANTIBALLISTIC MISSILE.

Ab•na•ki [æb'næki] *n., pl.* **-ki** or **-kis.** Abenaki.

ab•ne•gate ['æbnɪ,geit] *v.* **-gat•ed, -gat•ing. 1** surrender; give up (a right or privilege): *They abnegated their claim on the estate.* **2** deny; recant; renounce: *to abnegate one's God.* ⟨< L *abnegare* < *ab-* off, away + *negare* deny⟩ **—,ab•ne'ga•tion,** *n.*

ab•nor•mal [æb'nɔrməl] *adj.* **1** deviating from the normal, standard, or typical; markedly irregular: *The drug produces an abnormal dilation of the pupil of the eye.* **2** having to do with what is abnormal: *abnormal psychology.* ⟨< *ab* + *normal*⟩ **—ab'nor•mal•ly,** *adv.* **—ab'nor•mal•ness,** *n.*

☛ *Syn.* See note at IRREGULAR.

ab•nor•mal•cy [æb'nɔrməlsi] *n.* abnormality.

ab•nor•mal•i•ty [,æbnɔr'mæləti] *n., pl.* **-ties. 1** an abnormal thing or happening. **2** an abnormal condition: *He suffers from an abnormality of the blood.*

abnormal psychology the branch of psychology that deals with deviance or behaviour that is not normal.

a•board [ə'bɔrd] *adv., prep. —adv.* **1** on board; on, in, or into a ship, train, bus, aircraft, etc.: *All passengers should now be aboard.* **2** *Nautical.* alongside. **3** *Informal.* as a participant in a group: *"Welcome aboard!" We've brought two new salespeople aboard.*

all aboard, everybody on (conductor's call directing passengers to enter a train, bus, etc. about to start).

—prep. on board of: *They went aboard the ship.*

ABO blood group system a classification of human blood groups (types) based on the presence or absence of two antigens, called A and B, on the red blood cells. The four common blood groups in this system are O, A, B, and AB.

a•bode [ə'boud] *n., v. —n.* a place to live in; dwelling; residence.

—v. a pt. and a pp. of ABIDE. ⟨OE *ābād*⟩

☛ *Usage.* Often used facetiously with *humble*, as in *humble abode.*

a•boi•deau ['æbə,dou]; *French,* [abwa'do] *n., pl.* **-deaus** or **-deaux** [-,douz]; *French,* [-'do]. *Cdn.* in Nova Scotia and New Brunswick: **1** a sluice-gate in the dikes along the Bay of Fundy. **2** one of these dikes. Also, **aboiteau.** ⟨< Cdn.F⟩

a•boi•teau ['æbə,tou]; *French,* [abwa'to] *n., pl.* **-teaus** or **-teaux** [-touz]; *French,* [-to]. *Cdn.* ABOIDEAU. ⟨< Cdn.F⟩

a•bol•ish [ə'bɒlɪʃ] *v.* do away with (a law, institution, or custom) completely; put an end to: *to abolish slavery.* ⟨< F *aboliss-*, stem of *abolir*; fusion of two verbs, L *abolere* destroy, and L *abolescere* die out⟩ **—a'bol•ish•ment,** *n.*

☛ *Syn.* **Abolish,** ANNIHILATE, EXTINGUISH = put an end to something. **Abolish** applies only to things, usually long in existence, such as laws and customs: *Many countries have abolished hanging.* **Annihilate,** more general in application, suggests use of force and always retains its literal meaning of reducing to nothing, by wiping something out without a trace or by destroying its distinguishing qualities or form: *The enemy annihilated the regiment.* **Extinguish** applies to things or ideas which can be caused to die or be blotted out by overpowering force or circumstances: *You may extinguish a nation, but not the love of liberty.*

ab•o•li•tion [,æbə'lɪʃən] *n.* **1** an abolishing or being abolished. **2** the annulment of a specific law, especially: **a** in former times, the ending of slavery in Canada (1793), in the British Empire (1833) or the United States (1865). **b** the abolishing of capital punishment. ⟨< L *abolitio, -onis*⟩

ab•o•li•tion•ist [,æbə'lɪʃənɪst] *n.* a person who wishes to abolish a particular law, custom, etc., especially one in favour of abolishing capital punishment.

ab•o•ma•sum [,æbə'meisəm] *n.* the fourth stomach of cows, sheep, and other animals that chew the cud. The abomasum is the true stomach that digests the food. ⟨< NL < L *ab-* away from + *omasum* bullock's tripe⟩

A–bomb ['ei ,bɒm] *n.* atomic bomb.

a•bom•i•na•ble [ə'bɒmənəbəl] *adj.* **1** disgusting, revolting, or detestable: *abominable treatment of prisoners.* **2** *Informal.* very unpleasant, distasteful, or inferior: *abominable roads, abominable taste.* ⟨< F < L *abōminābilis* < *abōminārī.* See ABOMINATE.⟩ **—a'bom•i•na•ble•ness,** *n.* **—a'bom•i•na•bly,** *adv.*

abominable snowman a humanlike monster supposed to inhabit the higher parts of the Himalaya mountains, where huge footprints have been found in the snow. It is called 'yeti' by the Sherpa people, who inhabit this region.

a•bom•i•nate [ə'bɒmə,neit] *v.* **-nat•ed, -nat•ing. 1** feel disgust for; abhor; detest. **2** *Informal.* dislike. ⟨< L *abominari* deplore as an ill omen < *ab-* off + *ominari* prophesy < *omen, ominis* omen⟩ **—a'bom•i,na•tor,** *n.*

a•bom•i•na•tion [ə,bɒmə'neiʃən] *n.* **1** a revolting thing: *Anything that degrades people is an abomination.* **2** a shamefully wicked action or custom. **3** a feeling of disgust; hate; loathing.

ab•o•rig•i•nal [,æbə'rɪdʒənəl] *adj., n. —adj.* **1** existing in a place from the beginning; being the first or the original one or ones: *aboriginal inhabitants.* **2** of or having to do with the original or earliest known inhabitants of a region or country: *aboriginal customs, aboriginal rights.*
—n. aborigine. **—,ab•o'rig•i•nal•ly,** *adv.*
☛ *Usage.* See note at ABORIGINE.

ab•o•rig•i•ne [,æbə'rɪdʒəni] *n.* **1** one of the earliest known inhabitants of a country. **2** Usually, **Aborigine,** a member of a dark-skinned people who are the original inhabitants of Australia; a member of the Australoid race. ⟨< L *aborigines* < *ab origine* from the beginning⟩
☛ *Usage.* In the singular both **aborigine** and **aboriginal** are used, but in the plural **aborigines** is more common than **aboriginals.**

a•born•ing [ə'bɔrnɪŋ] *adv.* while just being born or produced (*used especially in* **die aborning**): *Their hopes died aborning.*

a•bort [ə'bɔrt] *v.* **1** give birth before the fetus has developed enough to survive outside the womb; have a miscarriage. **2** cause (a fetus) to be expelled before it is viable. **3** of a fetus, be expelled before it is viable. **4** cause to have an abortion. **5** *Biology.* fail to develop beyond the rudimentary stage. **6** bring to an end prematurely; cut short or cancel: *to abort a space flight.* **7** fail to develop. ⟨< L *abortus,* pp. of *aboriri* < *ab-* amiss + *oriri* be born⟩

a•bor•ti•fa•cient [ə,bɔrtɪ'feiʃənt] *n.* an agent that causes abortion. ⟨*aborti(on)* + *facient* < L *faciens,* ppr. of *facere* make⟩

a•bor•tion [ə'bɔrʃən] *n.* **1** the intentional ending of a pregnancy and destruction of the fetus by causing the fetus to be expelled, especially before it is viable. **2** MISCARRIAGE (def. 2). **3** *Biology.* **a** failure to develop beyond the rudimentary stage. **b** a creature or an organ that is incompletely or imperfectly formed. **4** the failure of anything to develop completely or properly. **5** anything incompletely or imperfectly developed: *Their revolutionary solar heating system turned out to be a sad abortion.* **6** the deliberate ending of a missile or rocket flight.

a•bor•tion•ist [ə'bɔrʃənɪst] *n.* a person who performs abortions.

a•bor•tive [ə'bɔrtɪv] *adj.* **1** unsuccessful; fruitless: *He made several abortive attempts to escape.* **2** *Biology.* not developed properly or completely; rudimentary. **3** causing abortion. **—a'bor•tive•ly,** *adv.* **—a'bor•tive•ness,** *n.*

a•bor•tus [ə'bɔrtəs] *n., pl.* **a•bor•tus•es.** the product of an abortion.

ABO system See ABO BLOOD GROUP SYSTEM.

a•bound [ə'baʊnd] *v.* **1** be plentiful: *Fish abound in the ocean.* **2** be rich (*in*): *Alberta abounds in oil.* **3** be well supplied or filled (*with*): *The ocean abounds with fish.* ⟨ME < OF *abunder* < L *abundare* < *ab-* off + *undare* flow < *unda* a wave⟩

a•bout [ə'bʌut] *prep., adv. —prep.* **1** of or having to do with: *a book about bridges.* **2** in connection with: *something peculiar about him.* **3** somewhere near; not far from: *The dog stayed about the house.* **4** on every side of; all around; around: *a fence about the garden.* **5** on (one's person); with: *She has no money about her.* **6** in many parts of; everywhere in: *to scatter papers about the room.* **7** doing; working at: *An expert worker knows what she is about.*
—adv. **1** nearly; almost: *The buckets and tubs are about full.* **2** approximately; near: *He is about my size.* **3** somewhere nearby: *A tramp has been hanging about.* **4** all around; in every direction: *The girl looked about.* **5** in many places; here and there: *A rumour went about that he was ill.* **6** in the opposite direction: *Face about! After swimming a kilometre, we turned about and swam back to the shore.* **7** one after another; by turns: *Turn about is fair play.* **8** stirring: *able to be up and about.*
about to, on the point of; going, intending, or ready to: *The plane is about to take off.*
how or **what about,** used to solicit an opinion or information: *How about a game of tennis?* ⟨OE *onbūtan, abūtan* on the outside of⟩

a•bout–face *n.* [ə'bʌut ,feis]; *v.* [ə,bʌut 'feis] *n., v.* **-faced, -fac•ing.** *—n.* a complete change or reversal of direction, point of view, opinion, etc.: *She made an about-face and hurried back to the house. At the first hint of opposition, the policy committee did an about-face.*
—v. turn or go in the opposite direction.

about turn *Military.* a command to face in the opposite direction.

a•bout–turn [ə'bʌut 'tɜrn] *n. or v.* ABOUT-FACE.

a•bove [ə'bʌv] *adv., prep., adj., n. —adv.* **1** overhead; in a higher place: *The sky is above.* **2** on the upper side or on top: *The leaves are dark above and light below.* **3** higher in rank or power: *the courts above.* **4** earlier, in a book or article: *as mentioned above.* **5** in heaven. **6** above zero on a scale of temperature: *It was 10 above that New Year's Day.*
—prep. **1** in or to a higher place than: *Birds fly above the trees.* **2** higher than; over: *He kept his head above water. A captain is above a sergeant.* **3** too high in dignity or character for; superior to: *A great person should be above mean actions.* **4** more than: *The weight is above a tonne.* **5** beyond: *Turn at the first corner above the school.*
—adj. **1** made or mentioned above: *the above remark.*
—n. **the above,** something that is written above. ⟨OE *abufan*⟩
☛ *Syn. prep.* **1, 2.** See note at OVER.

a•bove•board [ə'bʌv,bɔrd] *or* [ə'bʌv'bɔrd] *adv. or adj.* **1** in open sight: *Keep your hands aboveboard.* **2** without tricks or concealment: *The official was always aboveboard in her conduct.* **3** fairly: *to win aboveboard.*

a•bove–men•tioned [ə'bʌv ,mɛnʃənd] *adj.* previously referred to; mentioned earlier.

ab o•vo ['æb 'ouvou] *Latin.* from the beginning. ⟨literally, from the egg⟩

Abp. Archbishop.

abr. abridged.

ab•ra•ca•dab•ra [,æbrəkə'dæbrə] *n.* **1** a word supposed to have magic power, used in incantations or as a charm to ward off disease. **2** meaningless talk; jargon. ⟨< LL⟩

a•brad•ant [ə'breidənt] *n., adj.* abrasive.

a•brade [ə'breid] *v.* **a•brad•ed, a•brad•ing.** wear away by rubbing; scrape off: *The rock had been abraded over the years by blowing sand.* ⟨< L *abradere* < *ab-* off + *radere* scrape⟩ **—a'brad•er,** *n.*

a•bran•chi•ate [ei'bræŋkiɪt] *or* [ei'bræŋki,eit] *adj., n. —adj.* having no gills.
—n. a creature without gills.

a•bra•sion [ə'breiʒən] *n.* **1** a place scraped or worn by rubbing: *Abrasions of the skin are painful.* **2** a scraping off; a wearing away by rubbing. ⟨< L *abrasio, -onis* < *abradere.* See ABRADE.⟩

a•bra•sive [ə'breisɪv] *or* [ə'breizɪv] *n., adj. —n.* a substance used for grinding, smoothing, or polishing. Sandpaper, pumice, and emery are abrasives.
—adj. **1** wearing away by rubbing; causing abrasion: *the abrasive action of water on stone.* **2** causing or tending to cause irritation or annoyance: *an abrasive personality.* **—a'bra•sive•ly,** *adv.* **—a'bra•sive•ness,** *n.*

ab•re•act [ˌæbri'ækt] *v. Psychoanalysis.* release tension by talking about or acting out (some experience). ⟨< *abreaction*⟩

ab•re•ac•tion [ˌæbri'ækʃən] *n. Psychoanalysis.* the release of tension by talking about some experience. ⟨< *ab-* + *reaction*, a translation of German *Abreagierung*⟩

a•breast [ə'brɛst] *adv. or adj.* (*never precedes a noun*) side by side: *The soldiers marched three abreast.*
abreast of or **abreast with, a** up with; alongside of: *The child could barely keep abreast with his father.* **b** informed of and able to deal with: *Keep abreast of what is going on.*

a•bri [a'bʀi] *n., pl.* **a•bris** [a'bʀi] *French.* shelter.

a•bridge [ə'brɪdʒ] *v.* **a•bridged, a•bridg•ing. 1** make shorter, especially written or printed matter; condense: *The novel was abridged for publication in the magazine.* **2** make less: *The rights of citizens must not be abridged without proper cause.* **3** *Archaic.* deprive (*of*): *to abridge citizens of their rights.* ⟨ME < OF *abregier* < L *abbreviare* shorten. Doublet of ABBREVIATE.⟩
—a'bridg•a•ble [ə'brɪdʒəbəl] or **a'bridge•a•ble,** *adj.*

a•bridg•ment or **a•bridge•ment** [ə'brɪdʒmənt] *n.* **1** a shortened form, especially of a book or long article: *This book is an abridgment of a three-volume history.* **2** an abridging or being abridged.

a•broach [ə'broutʃ] *adj., adv.* **1** of a container of liquid, broached. **2** astir. ⟨< OF *abrochier*⟩

a•broad [ə'brɒd] *adv.* **1** outside one's country, especially overseas; to or in a foreign land or foreign lands: *We're going abroad this summer. She spent a year abroad, mostly in Norway.* **2** out of doors, especially away from one's home; about: *They travelled only by night because fewer enemy patrols were abroad then.* **3** going around; in circulation; current: *There is a rumour abroad that the mayor is resigning.* **4** far and wide; widely: *The news of his arrival spread abroad.*

ab•ro•ga•ble ['æbrəgəbəl] *adj.* able to be ended, usually by formal agreement; able to be repealed.

ab•ro•gate ['æbrəˌgeit] *v.* **-gat•ed, -gat•ing. 1** abolish or annul (a law or custom) by legislation; repeal. **2** do away with. ⟨< L *abrogare* < *ab-* away + *rogare* demand⟩ **—ˌab•ro'ga•tion,** [ˌæbrə'geiʃən] *n.* **—'ab•ro,ga•tor,** *n.*

a•brupt [ə'brʌpt] *adj.* **1** sudden; hasty; unexpected: *an abrupt end.* **2** very steep or sharp: *an abrupt turn, an abrupt slope.* **3** short or sudden in speech or manner; blunt. **4** disconnected: *an abrupt rhythm, an abrupt style.* **5** *Botany.* truncate: *the abrupt top of a tulip-tree leaf.* **6** *Geology.* emerging unexpectedly. ⟨< L *abruptus*, pp. of *abrumpere* < *ab-* off + *rumpere* break⟩ **—a'brupt•ly,** *adv.* **—a'brupt•ness,** *n.*
☛ *Syn.* **2.** See note at STEEP.

ab•rup•tion [ə'brʌpʃən] *n.* a sudden breaking off or termination.

abs– *prefix.* from, away, or off; the form of AB-[1] occurring before *c* and *t* as in *abscond, abstain.*

abs. **1** absent. **2** absolute. **3** abstract.

ab•scess ['æbsɛs] *or* ['æbsɪs] *n., v. —n.* a collection of pus in the tissues of some part of the body, caused by infection and often forming a red, swollen, painful lump on the skin. Pimples, boils, and carbuncles are abscesses.
—v. form an abscess: *The wound abscessed.* ⟨< L *abscessus* < *abscedere* < *ab*(*s*)- away + *cedere* go⟩

ab•scessed ['æbsɛst] *adj.* having an abscess.

ab•scind [æb'sɪnd] *v.* sever. ⟨< L *abscindere* < *ab-* off + *scindere* cut⟩

ab•scise [æb'saɪz] *v. Botany.* cut off (a leaf) from a stem. ⟨< L *abscidere*⟩

The abscissa of the point *p* is *x*; the ordinate is *y*.

ab•scis•sa [æb'sɪsə] *n., pl.* **-scis•sas** or **-scis•sae** [-'sɪsi] *or* [-'sɪsaɪ]. *Mathematics.* the first number in an ordered pair; the horizontal coordinate, or *x*-value, in a system of Cartesian coordinates. Compare ORDINATE. ⟨< L (*linea*) *abscissa* (line) cut off < pp. stem (*ab*)*sciss-* of (*ab*)*scindere* cut⟩

ab•scis•sion [æb'sɪʒən] *n.* **1** a cutting off. **2** *Botany.* the normal separation of fruits, leaves, or flowers from a plant. ⟨< L *abscissiō*⟩

ab•scond [æb'skɒnd] *v.* go away suddenly and secretly; especially, flee from the law after stealing something: *She absconded with the association's funds.* ⟨< L *abscondere* < *ab*(*s*)- away + *condere* store⟩ **—ab'scond•er,** *n.*

ab•seil ['ɑpˌzaɪl] *or* ['ɑpˌsaɪl] *n., v.* RAPPEL. ⟨< G *abseilen* descend by rope < *ab* down + *Seil* rope⟩

ab•sence ['æbsəns] *n.* **1** the state of being away: *absence from work.* **2** the time of being away: *an absence of two weeks.* **3** the fact of being without; lack: *Darkness is the absence of light.* **4** absent-mindedness.

absence of mind absent-mindedness.

ab•sent *adj.* ['æbsənt]; *v.* [æb'sɛnt] *adj., v. —adj.* **1** not present; away: *Sundar is absent from class today.* **2** lacking; not existing: *Trees are almost completely absent in some parts of the Prairies.* **3** absent-minded: *an absent reply.*
—v. take or keep (oneself) away: *to absent oneself from class.* ⟨< L *absens, -entis*, ppr. of *abesse* < *ab-* away + *esse* to be⟩

ab•sen•tee [ˌæbsən'ti] *n., adj. —n.* a person who is absent or remains absent.
—adj. of or for a voter or voters permitted to vote while absent from home.

absentee ballot *Cdn.* a system which allows a voter who is away from home to vote in an election.

ab•sen•tee•ism [ˌæbsən'tiˌɪzəm] *n.* **1** the practice or habit of being an absentee. **2** an economic system under which a landowner controls the use of land in a country or place where he or she does not live.

absentee landlord a landowner who draws an income from his or her land but lives in another part of the country, or in another country.

ab•sent•ly ['æbsəntli] *adv.* without paying attention to what is going on around one; inattentively: *He had answered her absently and later on couldn't remember what he had said.*

ab•sent–mind•ed ['æbsənt 'maɪndɪd] *adj.* **1** not aware of what is going on around one; having one's mind on other things; preoccupied. **2** chronically forgetful. **—'ab•sent-'mind•ed•ly,** *adv.* **—'ab•sent-'mind•ed•ness,** *n.*

absent without leave away without permission, as, in the army, etc. *Abbrev.*: AWOL.

ab•sinthe ['æbsɪnθ] *n.* **1** a strong, green, somewhat bitter liqueur flavoured with wormwood or a substitute and any of various other aromatics, such as aniseed or licorice. Also, **absinth. 2** the flavouring used for this liqueur, or the plant (*Artemisia absinthium*) from which it is extracted; wormwood. ⟨< F *absinthe* < L < Gk. *apsinthion* wormwood⟩

ab•sit o•men ['æbsɪt 'oumən] *Latin.* may the feared disaster, evil, etc. not take place. ⟨literally, may this (evil) omen be absent⟩

ab•so•lute ['æbsəˌlut] *or* [ˌæbsə'lut] *adj., n. —adj.* **1** complete; whole or entire; perfect: *absolute ignorance, absolute silence, absolute justice.* **2** not mixed with anything else; pure: *absolute alcohol.* **3** not limited or restricted by a constitution, parliament, etc.: *an absolute monarchy, an absolute ruler.* **4** not qualified or restricted in any way: *absolute freedom.* **5** certain; unquestionable; positive: *absolute proof, absolute certainty.* **6** not compared with or dependent on anything else; not relative: *absolute velocity, an absolute term in logic.* **7** real; actual; objective: *an absolute truth.* **8** *Grammar.* of a word, phrase, etc.: **a** forming a part of a sentence, but not connected with it grammatically. In *The train being late, we missed the boat, the train being late* is an absolute phrase. **b** used without an expressed object. In *I will not ask again, ask* is an absolute verb. **c** having its noun understood, but not expressed. In *The older pupils may help the younger, younger* is an absolute adjective. In *Your house is larger than ours, ours* is an absolute pronoun. **9** *Physics.* of or having to do with the scale of ABSOLUTE TEMPERATURE.
—n. **1** something that is absolute. **2 the absolute,** *Philosophy.* that which exists of itself and is conceivable without relation to other things. ⟨< L *absolutus*, pp. of *absolvere.* See ABSOLVE.⟩
—'ab•so,lute•ness, *n.*

absolute alcohol ethyl alcohol that contains not more than one percent by weight of water.

absolute altitude the altitude of an aircraft above the surface beneath it.

absolute ceiling *Aeronautics.* the maximum height above sea level at which an aircraft can keep flying.

absolute constant *Mathematics.* a constant that never changes in value, such as a number in arithmetic.

absolute discharge *Law.* complete freedom awarded to a person found guilty of an offence, with no record being kept of his or her conviction. Compare CONDITIONAL DISCHARGE.

absolute humidity the amount, in grams, of water vapour present in a unit volume of air: *A cubic metre of air containing ten grams of water vapour has an absolute humidity of 10.* Compare RELATIVE HUMIDITY.

ab•so•lute•ly ['æbsə,lutli] *or* [,æbsə'lutli] *adv.* **1** in an absolute way; especially; completely: *The water is absolutely pure. This can opener is absolutely useless.* **2** positively or definitely: *She is absolutely the finest person I know. "Can I try out your new car?" "Absolutely not!"* **3** certainly; definitely yes: *"Are you going to the game?" "Absolutely!"*

☛ *Usage.* In speech **absolutely** has become generalized to mean 'positively' or 'quite': *She is absolutely the finest person I know.* As an answer to a question it usually means 'yes'. It is out of place in formal writing except in its original meaning of 'completely'.

absolute magnitude *Astronomy.* the magnitude of a star if it could be seen 32 light years away.

absolute monarchy a monarchy in which the ruler has unlimited power. Compare LIMITED MONARCHY.

absolute music music, usually instrumental, which has no story or image as its basis but is supported by its structure and form alone. Compare PROGRAM MUSIC.

absolute pitch **1** the pitch of a tone determined by the frequency of its vibrations. **2** the ability to identify a note by ear; perfect pitch.

absolute temperature THERMODYNAMIC TEMPERATURE.

absolute value the value of a real number regardless of any accompanying sign: *The absolute value of* +5 *or* –5 *is* 5.

absolute zero the lowest temperature possible according to scientific theory, equal to –273.16°C, or zero kelvins; the temperature of zero thermal energy. Because the volume of a gas decreases as the temperature decreases, absolute zero is calculated as the theoretical temperature at which an ideal gas at a constant pressure would reach zero volume.

ab•so•lu•tion [,æbsə'luʃən] *n.* **1** *Christianity.* **a** release from the guilt or penalty of sins, pronounced by a priest in the name of God upon a person's confession of and sincere repentance for the sins. **b** the prescribed form of words by which such remission is granted. **2** the act of freeing or the state of being freed from guilt, blame, obligation, or promise. ⟨< L *absolutio*⟩

ab•so•lut•ism ['æbsəlu,tɪzəm] *n.* **1** a system or form of government in which the power of the ruler is not restricted; despotism. **2** the quality of being absolute; positiveness. **3** *Philosophy.* **a** belief in absolute idealism, which holds that all things are manifestations of one universal spirit, or in any proposition held to be absolute or universal rather than relative. **b** any philosophy positing some absolute principle. **4** the belief in predestination.

ab•so•lut•ist ['æbsə,lutɪst] *n., adj. —n.* a person in favour of despotism or absolutism.
—adj. having to do with, or characterized by, absolutism.

ab•solve [æb'zɒlv] *or* [æb'sɒlv] *v.* **-solved, -solv•ing. 1** declare (a person) free from sin, guilt, or blame. **2** set free (from a promise or duty). ⟨< L *absolvere* < *ab-* from + *solvere* loosen. Doublet of ASSOIL.⟩

ab•sorb [æb'zɔrb] *or* [æb'sɔrb] *v.* **1** take in or suck up (liquids): *A blotter absorbs ink.* **2** take in and make a part of itself; assimilate: *Canada has absorbed millions of immigrants.* **3** take up all the attention of; interest very much: *The puzzle has absorbed him for hours.* **4** take in and hold: *Anything black absorbs most of the light rays that fall on it; that is, few of the light rays are reflected from it.* **5** *Biology.* take (digested food, oxygen, etc.) into the bloodstream by OSMOSIS. **6** grasp with the mind; understand. **7** *Business.* **a** pay (a cost, tax, etc.) without adding it to the price of an article, etc.: *The manufacturer absorbed the new tax, and the prices remained the same.* **b** take up: *The market absorbed the whole production.* **8** take up the impact of (bumps, shocks, sound, etc.): *The ceiling insulation absorbed the noise of the children's party.* ⟨< L *absorbere* < *ab-* from + *sorbere* suck in⟩ **—ab'sorb•able,** *adj.* **—ab,sorb•a'bil•i•ty,** *n.*

☛ *Syn.* **2. Absorb,** ASSIMILATE = take something in, both literally and as used figuratively with reference to ideas. **Absorb** = swallow up a thing so that it loses its individual character or disappears: *Large companies sometimes absorb smaller ones.* **Assimilate** adds to **absorb** the idea of converting what is absorbed into an essential part of what has taken it in: *A person who reads intelligently assimilates what she reads by making it a part of her own thinking.*

ab•sorbed [æb'zɔrbd] *or* [æb'sɔrbd] *adj., v. —adj.* very much interested; completely occupied: *She was so absorbed in watching the chipmunk that she didn't hear her friend call.*
—v. pt. and pp. of ABSORB. **—ab'sorb•ed•ly,** *adv.*

ab•sorb•en•cy [æb'zɔrbənsi] *or* [æb'sɔrbənsi] *n.* **1** the quality of being absorbent. **2** the degree to which anything is absorbent. **3** the ability to be assimilated.

ab•sorb•ent [æb'zɔrbənt] *or* [æb'sɔrbənt] *adj., n. —adj.* able to take in moisture, light, or heat: *Towels are absorbent.*
—n. any thing or substance that absorbs moisture, light, or heat.

absorbent cotton raw cotton made absorbent by removing the natural wax, used for dressing wounds; COTTON BATTING.

ab•sorb•ing [æb'zɔrbɪŋ] *or* [æb'sɔrbɪŋ] *adj., v. —adj.* extremely interesting: *He has written an absorbing account of his adventure.*
—v. ppr. of ABSORB. **—ab'sorb•ing•ly,** *adv.*

ab•sorp•tion [æb'zɔrpʃən] *or* [æb'sɔrpʃən] *n.* **1** the process of absorbing or of being absorbed: *the absorption of water by a sponge. In the absorption of light rays by black objects, the light rays are changed to heat.* **2** a great interest (*in* something). **3** *Biology.* the process of taking digested food, oxygen, etc. into the bloodstream by OSMOSIS. ⟨< L *absorptio, -onis* < *absorbere.* See ABSORB.⟩

ab•sorp•tive [æb'zɔrptɪv] *or* [æb'sɔrptɪv] *adj.* able to absorb. **—ab'sorp•tive•ness** or **,ab•sorp'tiv•i•ty,** *n.*

ab•stain [æb'stein] *v.* **1** do without something voluntarily; refrain (*from*): *Athletes usually abstain from smoking.* **2** decline to vote: *Several delegates abstained because they objected to the wording of the motion.* ⟨< F *abstenir* < L *abstinere* < *ab(s)-* off + *tenere* hold⟩

☛ *Syn.* **1.** See note at REFRAIN[1].

ab•stain•er [æb'steinər] *n.* a person who abstains, especially from the use of alcoholic liquor.

ab•ste•mi•ous [æb'stimiəs] *adj.* sparing in eating and drinking; moderate; temperate. ⟨< L *abstemius* < *ab(s)-* off + *tem-,* root of *temetum* potent liquor⟩ **—ab'ste•mi•ous•ly,** *adv.* **—ab'ste•mi•ous•ness,** *n.*

ab•sten•tion [æb'stɛnʃən] *n.* the act or an instance of abstaining: *His abstention from voting was severely criticized.* ⟨< F < L *abstentio, -onis* < *abstinere.* See ABSTAIN.⟩

ab•sterge [æb'stɜrdʒ] *v.* **-sterged, -sterg•ing. 1** make clean by using a cloth. **2** empty (the bowels). ⟨< L *abstergere* < *ab* away + *tergere* wipe⟩

ab•sti•nence ['æbstənəns] *n.* **1** voluntary avoidance of indulgence in certain pleasures, foods, sex, etc. **2** the practice of avoiding certain foods, especially meat, as an act of penance. **3** the practice of refraining from drinking alcoholic liquor. ⟨< L *abstinentia* < *abstinere.* See ABSTAIN.⟩

abs•ti•nent ['æbstənənt] *adj.* abstaining. **—'ab•sti•nent•ly,** *adv.*

ab•stract *adj., n.* ['æbstrækt]; *v.* [æb'strækt] *for 1, 3, 4,* ['æbstrækt] *for 2. adj., v., n. —adj.* **1** thought of apart from any particular object or real thing; not concrete: *A lump of sugar is concrete; the idea of sweetness is abstract.* **2** expressing a quality that is thought of apart from any particular object or real thing. In *Honesty is the best policy, honesty* is an abstract noun. **3** not practical; ideal; theoretical. **4** hard to understand; difficult: *abstract theories about the nature of the soul.* **5** *Art.* representing ideas or feelings by abstracting certain qualities or elements from real things so that the result has little or no direct resemblance to these things.
—v. **1** think of (a quality, such as redness, weight, or truth) apart from any object or real thing having that quality: *How can we abstract time from the hours, minutes, and seconds by which we measure it?* **2** make an abstract of; summarize. **3** take away; remove: *We can abstract gold from ore. A thief abstracted my wallet from my pocket.* **4** withdraw (the attention).
—n. **1** a short statement giving the main ideas of an article, book, case in court, etc.; summary. **2** an abstract term or notion: *Children learn to handle abstracts at around age 10.*
in the abstract, in theory rather than in practice. ⟨< L *abstractus,* pp. of *abstrahere* < *ab(s)-* away + *trahere* draw⟩ **—ab'stract•er,** *n.* **—ab'stract•ly,** *adv.* **—ab'stract•ness,** *n.*

ab•stract•ed [æb'stræktɪd] *adj., v. —adj.* lost in thought; absent-minded.
—v. pt. and pp. of ABSTRACT. **—ab'stract•ed•ly,** *adv.* **—ab'stract•ed•ness,** *n.*

abstract expressionism a movement in painting that flourished especially in the United States in the 1950s and that emphasized the spontaneous expression of the feelings of the artist through colour and abstract forms.

ab•strac•tion [æb'strækʃən] *n.* **1** the idea of a quality thought of apart from any particular object or real thing having that quality; abstract idea or term: *Whiteness, bravery, and length are abstractions. A line that has no width is only an abstraction.* **2** the formation of such an idea. **3** a taking away; removal: *After the abstraction of the juice from an orange, only the pulp and peel are left.* **4** the state of being lost in thought; absence of mind. **5** a work of abstract art. **6** an idea that is impractical or fanciful.

ab•strac•tion•ism [æb'strækʃə,nɪzəm] *n.* the methods or principles of abstract art.

ab•strac•tion•ist [æb'strækʃə,nɪst] *n.* one who does abstract art.

abstract of title a summary of the history of ownership of a piece of real estate.

ab•struse [æb'strus] *adj.* hard to understand. ⟨< L *abstrusus*, pp. of *abstrudere* < *ab(s)*- away + *trudere* thrust⟩ **—ab'struse•ly,** *adv.* **—ab'struse•ness,** *n.*

ab•surd [æb'zɜrd] *or* [æb'sɜrd] *adj.* plainly not true or sensible; stupid; so contrary to reason that it is laughable; foolish; ridiculous. ⟨< L *absurdus* out of tune, senseless⟩ **—ab'surd•ly,** *adv.* **—ab'surd•ness,** *n.*

☛ *Syn.* See note at RIDICULOUS.

absurd•ist [æb'zɜrdɪst] *n., adj., —n.* a person who believes that life is senseless, ridiculous, etc.
—adj. having, relating to, or based on this belief: *absurdist theatre, an absurdist author.*

ab•surd•i•ty [æb'zɜrdɪti] *or* [æb'sɜrdɪti] *n., pl.* **-ties.** **1** something absurd. **2** an absurd quality or condition; folly.

a•bub•ble [ə'bʌbəl] *adj. (never used before a noun)* lively, spirited; bubbling: *The children were abubble with impatience.*

a•bu•li•a [ə'bjuliə] *or* [ə'buliə] *n.* a mental disorder which causes the loss of volition. ⟨< NL < Gk. *a-* not + *boulia* will⟩ **—a'bu•lic,** *adj.*

a•bun•dance [ə'bʌndəns] *n.* a quantity that is more than enough; great plenty; full supply. ⟨ME < OF < L *abundantia* < *abundare.* See ABOUND.⟩

a•bun•dant [ə'bʌndənt] *adj.* **1** more than enough; very plentiful. **2** filled; having in plenty; rich *(in)*: *Canada is abundant in natural resources.* **—a'bun•dant•ly,** *adv.*

a•buse *v.* [ə'bjuz]; *n.* [ə'bjus] *v.* **a•bused, a•bus•ing;** *n. —v.* **1** use wrongly; make bad use of; misuse: *to abuse a privilege.* **2** treat badly; mistreat. **3** use harsh and insulting language to.
—n. **1** a wrong or bad use. **2** harsh or severe treatment of a person: *child abuse, spouse abuse.* **3** harsh and insulting language. **4** a bad practice or custom: *Abuses multiply when citizens are indifferent.* ⟨ME < OF *abuser* < L *abusus*, pp. of *abuti* use up, misuse < *ab-* away + *uti* use⟩ **—a'bus•er,** *n.*

a•bu•sive [ə'bjusɪv] *or* [ə'bjuzɪv] *adj.* **1** using harsh and insulting language; reviling. **2** characterized by abuse: *an abusive letter, an abusive relationship.* **3** abusing; treating badly. **—a'bu•sive•ly,** *adv.* **—a'bu•sive•ness,** *n.*

a•but [ə'bʌt] *v.* **a•but•ted, a•but•ting. 1** touch at one end or edge; end *(on* or *against)*: *The sidewalk abuts on the street. The street abuts against the railway.* **2** join at a boundary; border *(on* or *upon)*: *Their land abuts on mine.* ⟨< OF *abouter* join end to end (< *a-* to + *bout* end) and OF *abuter* touch with an end (< *a-* to + *but* end)⟩

a•bu•ti•lon [ə'bjutə,lɒn] *n.* a group of related shrubs that includes the flowering maple.

a•but•ment [ə'bʌtmənt] *n.* **1** *Architecture.* a support for an arch or bridge. **2** the point or place where a support joins the thing supported. **3** the fact or state of abutting. **4** something that abuts.

a•but•tals [ə'bʌtəlz] *n. pl.* land boundaries; the lands near a border.

a•but•ter [ə'bʌtər] *n.* a person owning neighbouring land.

a•but•ting [ə'bʌtɪŋ] *adj., v. —adj.* adjacent.
—v. ppr. of ABUT.

a•buzz [ə'bʌz] *adj. (never used before a noun)* **1** filled with buzzing sounds. **2** full of excited activity, conversation, etc.: *The town was abuzz with the story of his disappearance.*

a•bysm [ə'bɪzəm] *n.* abyss. ⟨ME *abime* < OF *abisme* < L *abyssus.* See ABYSS.⟩

a•bys•mal [ə'bɪzməl] *adj.* **1** too deep to be measured; bottomless. **2** very great; profound; immeasurable: *abysmal ignorance, abysmal despair.* **3** *Informal.* immeasurably bad: *abysmal dialogue, abysmal taste.* **—a'bys•mal•ly,** *adv.*

a•byss [ə'bɪs] *n.* **1** a very deep crack in the earth; a seemingly bottomless hole; chasm. **2** the lowest depth; anything seemingly endless or measureless: *the abyss of despair.* **3** the primal chaos before Creation, according to ancient cosmogony. ⟨< L < Gk. *abyssos* < *a-* without + *byssos* bottom⟩

a•byss•al [ə'bɪsəl] *adj.* **1** of or having to do with the lowest depths of the ocean. **2** unfathomable.

abyssal zone *Ecology.* the zone along the floor of the deep part of the ocean (3600 to 6000 m); it is deeper than the BATHYAL ZONE and not as deep as the HADAL ZONE.

Ab•ys•sin•i•an [,æbə'sɪniən] *adj., n. —adj.* formerly, Ethiopian.
—n. **1** formerly, an Ethiopian. **2** a breed of medium-sized domesticated cat having short, silky, brownish hair with darker markings.

ac– *prefix.* the form of AD- occurring before *c* and *q*, as in *accede, acquaint.*

-ac *suffix.* **1** concerned with: *cardiac.* **2** having: *maniac.*

Ac **1** actinium. **2** acetate. **3** *Meteorology.* alto-cumulus.

AC, A.C., or **a.c.** **1** alternating current. Compare DC. **2** air conditioning.

A/C or **a/c** account.

A.C. **1** air commodore. **2** aircraftman or aircraftwoman.

a•ca•cia [ə'keiʃə] *n.* **1** any of a large genus *(Acacia)* of flowering trees and shrubs of the pea family found in warm regions, having fluffy clusters or spikes of yellow or white flowers, and fernlike leaves or wide, flattened, leaflike stems. Some species yield tannin or gum arabic. **2** locust tree. **3** the flower of any of these trees. **4** the gum arabic extracted from these trees. ⟨< L < Gk. *akakia*, a thorny Egyptian tree⟩

acad. academy; academic.

ac•a•deme ['ækə,dim] *n.* **1** the academic environment; university life: *She has spent all her adult life in academe.* **2** higher learning as an institution: *The government has promised more money for academe.* ⟨< F *académie* < L *academia* < Gk. *Akademeia,* a gymnasium near Athens where Plato taught.⟩

ac•a•de•mi•a [,ækə'dimiə] *n.* academe.

ac•a•dem•ic [,ækə'dɛmɪk] *adj., n. —adj.* **1** of or having to do with schools, colleges, universities, and their studies. **2** concerned with education in the arts, history, philosophy, etc. rather than with commercial, technical, or professional training. **3** scholarly. **4** theoretical; not practical: *"Which came first, the chicken or the egg?" is an academic question.* **5** following established rules and traditions, especially in art, literature, etc.; formal or conventional.
—n. **1** a person engaged in scholarly pursuits, especially at a college or university. **2 academics,** *pl.* academic courses or studies. **—,ac•a'dem•i•cal•ly,** *adv.*

ac•a•dem•i•cal [,ækə'dɛməkəl] *adj, n. —adj.* academic.
—n. **academicals,** *pl.* academic garb; gown and mortarboard.

academic freedom **1** the freedom of a teacher to investigate and discuss controversial issues and problems without fear of losing his or her position or standing. **2** the freedom of an educational institution to decide the subjects it will teach and how it will teach them. **3** the freedom of a student to explore any field, or hold any belief, without interference from the teacher.

a•cad•e•mi•cian [ə,kædə'mɪʃən] *or* [,ækədə'mɪʃən] *n.* **1** a member of a society for encouraging literature, science, or art, such as the Royal Society of Canada. **2** an artist, writer, or composer who follows traditional or conventional rules. ⟨< F *académicien*⟩

ac•a•dem•i•cism [,ækə'dɛmə,sɪzəm] *n.* the practice of following established rules and traditions, especially in art, literature, etc.; formalism or conventionalism.

academic year the part of the year during which a university or college is in regular session.

a•cad•e•mism [ə'kædə,mɪzəm] *n.* **1** Plato's school of philosophical thought. **2** academicism.

a•cad•e•my [ə'kædəmi] *n., pl.* **-mies. 1** a place for instruction. **2** a private high school. **3** a school where some special subject can be studied: *a military academy, a naval academy.* **4** a society of authors, scholars, scientists, artists, etc. for encouraging literature, science, or art. **5 Academy, a** near ancient Athens, a park where Plato taught. **b** the school for the study of philosophy started in that park. **c** Plato's disciples or their philosophy. ⟨< L *academia* < Gk. *Akadēmeia*, the grove where Plato taught⟩

A•ca•di•a [ə'keidiə] *n. Cdn.* **1** the areas of French settlement and culture in the Maritime Provinces. **2** the Maritime Provinces as a unit. **3** formerly, the French colony comprising the Maritime Provinces and adjacent parts of Québec and New England. ⟨< Latinized form of *Acadie*, a term applied in 1603 by the French to part of their territory in North America⟩

A•ca•di•an [ə'keidiən] *n., adj. —n.* **1** a native or inhabitant of Acadia. **2** a person of Acadian descent, some of whom now live in Louisiana. See CAJUN. **3** a variety of CANADIAN FRENCH spoken in the Maritimes.
—adj. of or having to do with Acadia or, sometimes, Nova Scotia.

Acadian owl *Cdn.* a small brown owl of the saw-whet family.

ac•a•jou ['ækə,ʒu] *n.* **1** the wood from any of several tropical trees, used for cabinet-making; mahogany. **2** the cashew tree (*Anarcardium occidentale*). **3** the cashew nut. ⟨< F, cashew⟩

ac•a•leph ['ækə,lɛf] *n.* any of numerous invertebrates such as jellyfishes. ⟨< NL < Gk. *akalephe* sting⟩

a•can•thus [ə'kænθəs] *n., pl.* **-thus•es, -thi** [-θaɪ] *or* [-θi]. **1** any of a genus (*Acanthus*) of herbs or shrubs native to the Mediterranean region, having large, usually spiny leaves. Some species are widely cultivated as ornamental plants. **2** *Architecture.* an ornamentation based on the leaves of *Acanthus spinosus*, used especially on classical Corinthian and Composite columns. See ORDER for picture. ⟨< L < Gk. *akanthos* < *akē* thorn⟩
—a'can•thine [ə'kænθɪn] *or* [-θin], *adj.*

a cap•pel•la [ɑ kə'pɛlə] *Music.* without instrumental accompaniment. ⟨< Ital. *a cappella* in the manner of chapel (music)⟩

a ca•pric•cio [ɑ kə'pritʃou] *Music.* with tempo and expression at the wish of the performer; freely. ⟨< Ital.⟩

ac•a•rid ['ækə,rɪd] *n.* any of an order (Acarina) of arachnids, including the mites and ticks.

a•car•pel•lous or **a•car•pel•ous** [ei'kɑrpələs] *adj. Botany.* without carpels.

a•car•pous [ei'kɑrpəs] acarpellous. ⟨< G *ákarpos*⟩

acc. **1** accusative. **2** account.

ac•cede [æk'sid] *v.* **-ced•ed, -ced•ing.** **1** give in or agree (*to*): *to accede to a proposal, to accede to popular demand.* **2** come or attain (*to* an office or dignity): *When the king died, his eldest daughter acceded to the throne.* **3** become a party (*to*): *Our government acceded to the treaty.* ⟨< L *accedere* < *ad-* to + *cedere* come⟩ **—ac'ced•ence,** *n.*

accel. accelerando.

ac•cel•er•an•do [æk,sɛlə'rændou] *or* [ə,tʃɛlə'rɑndou] *adv. or adj. Music.* gradually increasing in speed. *Abbrev.*: accel. ⟨< Ital.⟩

ac•cel•er•ant [æk'sɛlərənt] *n.* ACCELERATOR (def. 2).

ac•cel•er•ate [æk'sɛlə,reit] *v.* **-at•ed, -at•ing. 1** go or cause to go faster; increase in speed; speed up. **2** cause to happen sooner; hasten: *Sunshine, fresh air, and rest often accelerate a person's recovery from sickness.* **3** *Physics.* change the velocity of (a moving object). **4** go or put through a school program at a faster rate. ⟨< L *accelerare* < *ad-* to + *celer* swift⟩
—ac'cel•er•a•tive [ək'sɛlərətɪv] or **ac'cel•er,a•tive** [ək'sɛlə,reitɪv], *adj.*

ac•cel•er•a•tion [æk,sɛlə'reiʃən] *n.* **1** an accelerating or being accelerated. **2** *Physics.* a change in velocity. **Positive acceleration** is increase in velocity. **Negative acceleration** is decrease in velocity. **3** the rate of change in the velocity of a moving body.

acceleration of gravity *Physics.* the acceleration of a falling body in the earth's gravitational field.

ac•cel•er•a•tor [æk'sɛlə,reitər] *n.* **1 a** a device for increasing the speed of a machine, especially the pedal that controls the flow of gasoline to an automobile engine. **b** any nerve, muscle, or bodily substance that increases the speed of a movement or bodily function. **2** *Chemistry.* any substance that speeds up a chemical reaction; catalyst. **3** *Physics.* any of several kinds of apparatus used in nuclear research and in medicine and industry for accelerating electrically charged atomic particles to high velocities, thus building up extremely high amounts of energy in them. A **particle accelerator** is often called an atom smasher.

ac•cel•er•om•et•er [æk,sɛlə'rɒmətər] *n.* a device for measuring acceleration, as in an aircraft.

ac•cent *n.* ['æksɛnt]; *v.* ['æksɛnt] *or* [æk'sɛnt] *n., v. —n.* **1** a distinctive manner of pronunciation, intonation, etc. typical of a given region or group: *a Scottish accent, a Canadian accent. Klaus still speaks English with a German accent.* **2 accents,** *pl.* tone of voice or mode of speech: *speaking in tender accents.* **3** emphasis placed on a particular word or syllable; STRESS (def. 5). **4** a mark (such as ') showing such emphasis; STRESS (def. 6). **5** a mark used in writing or printing to indicate a particular sound quality, length of vowel, contraction, etc., or to indicate that a normally silent vowel is to be pronounced. Accents are used as part of the spelling system of certain languages, such as French and Greek. The accent ` in Shakespeare's phrase *despisèd tears* indicates that the final vowel in *despised* is to be pronounced. **6** an apostrophe that indicates a measurement of length, as in 5′6″ (5 feet 6 inches) or of time, as in 3′5″ (3 minutes 5 seconds); also used in mathematical notation to indicate a variable, as in a′ (a prime). **7** *Prosody.* rhythmical stress. **8** *Music.* **a** emphasis given to certain notes or chords in a piece of music, indicated by a symbol (>) above the note or chord concerned. **b** the symbol itself. **c** the regularly recurring emphasis that determines the rhythm of a piece of music. **9** intensity or emphasis: *The accent is on style.* **10** a distinguishing mark or quality: *an accent of humour.* **11** a sharply contrasting detail or an object or substance used for such contrast: *a grey and beige colour scheme with dark green accents.*
—v. **1** pronounce or write with an accent. **2** emphasize; accentuate. ⟨< L *accentus*, literally, song added to (speech) < *ad-* to + *cantus* singing < *canere* sing⟩

☛ *Syn. v.* **2. Accent,** ACCENTUATE, both mean 'emphasize', although **accent** means only to mark or say something with emphasis. **Accentuate,** the more common word, means to give emphasis to something by intensifying it or making it conspicuous: *Throughout his speech he accented the gravity of the situation. Her white dress accentuated her sunburn.*

☛ *Usage.* **Accents.** French words in English sometimes keep their accent marks: *café, outré, attaché, crêpe, tête-à-tête, à la mode.* Words that are used frequently in English usually drop the accent marks after a time unless the marks are necessary to indicate pronunciation (as in *café, attaché).*

ac•cen•tu•al [æk'sɛntʃuəl] *adj.* **1** of or formed by accent or stress. **2** of poetry, having the same accent or stress as ordinary speech.

ac•cen•tu•ate [æk'sɛntʃu,eit] *v.* **-at•ed, -at•ing. 1** emphasize: *Her black hair accentuated the whiteness of her skin.* **2** pronounce with an accent. **3** mark with an accent. **4** make greater; increase in intensity or effect: *The problems of the pioneers were accentuated by the harsh climate.* ⟨< Med.L *accentuare*⟩
—ac,cen•tu'a•tion, *n.*

☛ *Syn.* **1.** See note at ACCENT.

ac•cept [æk'sɛpt] *v.* **1** take or receive (something offered or given); consent to take: *I accept the gift.* **2** agree to; consent to; say yes to: *to accept a proposal.* **3** take as true or satisfactory; believe in: *to accept a hypothesis. She refused to accept our story of what had happened.* **4** receive with liking and approval; approve: *He was soon accepted by his new classmates.* **5** regard as normal or inevitable: *to accept one's fate. The right to an education is generally accepted today.* **6** undertake as a responsibility: *to accept a position as cashier.* **7** *Business.* agree to pay, especially by signing: *to accept a note.* **8** say yes to an invitation, offer, etc.: *They invited me to go along and I accepted.* ⟨< L *acceptare*, frequentative of *accipere* < *ad-* to + *capere* take⟩ **—ac'cept•er,** *n.*

☛ *Syn.* **1.** See note at RECEIVE.

☛ *Usage.* **Accept,** EXCEPT are often misspelled because of similarity in sound. **Accept,** always a verb, has as its basic meaning 'take to oneself' and is a synonym of *receive*: *I accepted the gift.* **Except,** sometimes a verb, sometimes a preposition, has the basic sense of 'taking out'; the verb is a synonym of *omit* and *exclude*; the preposition is a synonym of *but*: *We can call his career brilliant if we except that one serious blunder. Everyone except Lisa went home.*

ac•cept•a•bil•i•ty [æk,sɛptə'bɪləti] *n.* the quality of being acceptable or satisfactory.

ac•cept•a•ble [æk'sɛptəbəl] *adj.* **1** worth accepting: *Flowers are an acceptable gift for a sick person.* **2** good enough but not outstanding; satisfactory: *an acceptable performance.*

ac•cept•a•bly [æk'sɛptəbli] *adv.* in an acceptable way.

ac•cept•ance [æk'sɛptəns] *n.* **1** the taking of something offered or given. **2** a favourable reception; approval. **3** a believing or taking as true and satisfactory. **4** *Business.* **a** a promise or signed agreement to pay a draft or bill of exchange when it is due. **b** the draft or bill of exchange itself.

ac•cep•ta•tion [,æksɛp'teiʃən] *n.* **1** the usual meaning; generally accepted meaning; purport: *It is more important to know the acceptation of a word than its derivation.* **2** a favourable reception; approval. **3** a believing or taking as true and satisfactory.

ac•cept•ed [æk'sɛptɪd] *adj., v.* *—adj.* generally approved; conventional: *the accepted behaviour at formal dinners.*
—v. pt. and pp. of ACCEPT.

ac•cep•tor [æk'sɛptər] *n.* **1** a person who accepts. **2** a person who signs a draft or bill of exchange and agrees to pay it. **3** *Chemistry.* an atom sharing two electrons in bond with another atom but itself contributing neither electron. **4** *Electronics.* a circuit that allows reception of a certain frequency and no other. **5** *Physics.* a minute amount of a substance forming an impurity in a semiconducting crystal which attracts electrons from surrounding atoms, resulting in a hole in the crystal structure and changing its conductivity.

ac•cess ['æksɛs] *n., v.* *—n.* **1** the right to approach, enter, or use; admission: *All children have access to the library during the afternoon.* **2** the degree to which a place is reachable; approach: *Access to the mountain town was difficult because of the poor road.* **3** a way or means of approach: *A ladder was the only access to the attic. He has access to people who can help him get work.* **4** of a disease, the onset. **5** an outburst or sudden overwhelming feeling: *an access of pity and remorse.*
—v. Computer technology. get (information) out of a storage device: *The customer service department can access information on the company's product only by entering a security code.* ⟨ME < L *accessus* < *accedere.* See ACCEDE.⟩

ac•ces•sa•ry [æk'sɛsəri] See ACCESSORY.

ac•ces•si•bil•i•ty [æk,sɛsə'bɪləti] *n.* **1** the condition of being easy to reach, get at, understand, or speak with. **2** the condition of being open to influence.

ac•ces•si•ble [æk'sɛsəbəl] *adj.* **1** capable of being entered or reached; approachable: *The camp is accessible only by boat or plane.* **2** easy to get at; easy to enter: *A telephone should be put where it will be accessible.* **3** capable of being influenced; susceptible (*to*); open (*to*): *accessible to pity, accessible to reason.* **4** obtainable. **5** easy to understand or appreciate: *Her poetry is accessible to the average reader.* **—ac'ces•si•bly,** *adv.*

ac•ces•sion [æk'sɛʃən] *n., v.* *—n.* **1** the act of attaining to a right, office, etc.: *the prince's accession to the throne.* **2** the act of agreeing. **3** an increase; addition: *The accession of forty new members helped the club considerably.* **4** something added: *Each accession to the library means more expense.*
—v. enter (a new book, painting, etc.) in the record of a collection. ⟨< L *accessio, -onis* < *accedere.* See ACCEDE.⟩

ac•ces•so•rize [æk'sɛsə,raɪz] *v.* **-rized, -riz•ing.** provide or furnish with accessories: *to accessorize a basic dress.*

ac•ces•so•ry [æk'sɛsəri] *n., pl.* **-ries;** *adj.* *—n.* **1** something added that is useful in some way but not absolutely necessary: *He bought a mirror and some other accessories for his bicycle.* **2** something worn or carried, such as a hat, shoes, or a scarf, that is chosen to set off or complement a dress, suit, etc.: *The appearance of a basic dress can be changed considerably by varying the style and colour of the accessories.* **3** *Law.* a person who helps an offender against the law, without actually taking part in the commission of the offence. One who encourages, incites, or assists in the planning of a crime is called an **accessory before the fact.** One who hides the offender or fails to report the offence is called an **accessory after the fact.**
—adj. **1** additional; supplementary: *an accessory touch of colour.* **2** helping as an accessory in an offence against the law. **3** *Geology.* of or having to do with small amounts of other minerals in a particular rock.
☛ *Pronun.* This word is often mispronounced [æ'sɛsəri]. The first syllable is [æk-], as in *accident.*

access road *Cdn.* **1** a road built to permit entry to a place or an area that is otherwise sealed off, as by dense brush, muskeg, etc. **2** a road permitting entry to an expressway.

access time the time between requesting data from a computer's storage unit and receiving it.

ac•ciac•ca•tu•ra [ə,tʃɑkə'turə] *n. Music.* a short GRACE NOTE. ⟨< Ital., literally, a crushing (sound)⟩

ac•ci•dence ['æksədəns] *n.* **1** the part of grammar dealing with those changes in words that show case, number, tense, etc. **2** the basics of any subject. ⟨< L *accidens.* See ACCIDENT.⟩

ac•ci•dent ['æksədənt] *n.* **1** something harmful or unlucky that happens unexpectedly and apparently by chance: *He was killed in an automobile accident. Many accidents happen in the home.* **2** something that happens without being planned, intended, or known in advance: *Their meeting was an accident.* **3** a nonessential quality or property. **4** an irregularity in surface or structure.
by accident, by chance; not on purpose: *I dropped it by accident.* ⟨ME < OF < L *accidens, -entis,* ppr. of *accidere* < *ad-* to + *cadere* fall⟩

ac•ci•den•tal [,æksə'dɛntəl] *adj., n.* *—adj.* **1** happening unexpectedly or by chance: *They had searched for months, but the actual discovery of the treasure was accidental.* **2** of something harmful or unlucky, not intended or planned: *an accidental injury.* **3** nonessential; incidental: *Songs are essential to musical comedy, but accidental to Shakespeare's plays.* **4** *Music.* of or designating an accidental.
—n. Music. a sign showing a change in a single note in a piece of music, that is not in the key indicated by the signature. Accidentals can indicate a sharp (♯), a flat (♭), or a natural (♮).
☛ *Syn. adj.* **3. Accidental,** INCIDENTAL = not essential or of primary importance. **Accidental** emphasizes that what it describes is not an essential or necessary part, result, etc. of some larger thing or scheme of things: *Songs are essential to musical comedy, but accidental to Shakespeare's plays.* **Incidental** emphasizes that what it describes, although perhaps necessary, is subordinate to something else in importance: *My mother pays my tuition, board, and room at college, but not incidental expenses such as laundry and haircuts.*

ac•ci•den•tal•ly [,æksə'dɛntəli] *adv.* in an accidental manner; by chance.

ac•ci•dent–prone ['æksədənt ,proun] *adj.* tending to have accidents.

ac•ci•die or **ac•cid•i•a** ['æksə,di] *or* [æk'sɪdiə] *n.* spiritual apathy. ⟨< Gk. *akedia* heedlessness⟩

ac•cip•i•ter [æk'sɪpətər] *n.* any of a genus (*Accipiter*) of small and medium-sized hawks having relatively short, rounded wings and a long tail. ⟨< NL < L, hawk⟩

ac•cip•i•trine [æk'sɪpɪtrɪn] *or* [æk'sɪpɪ,trin] *adj.* belonging to the family (Accipitridae) that comprises hawks, eagles, and other birds of prey.

ac•claim [ə'kleim] *v., n.* *—v.* **1** show approval of by words or sounds; shout welcome to; applaud: *The crowd acclaimed the firefighter for rescuing two people from the burning house.* **2** announce with signs of approval; hail: *The newspapers acclaimed the firefighter a hero.* **3** *Cdn.* elect to an office without opposition: *The voters acclaimed her mayor.*
—n. a shout or show of approval; applause; welcome. ⟨< L *acclamare* < *ad-* to + *clamare* cry out⟩

ac•cla•ma•tion [,æklə'meiʃən] *n.* **1** a shout of welcome or show of approval by a crowd; applause. **2** an oral vote: *The club elected her president by acclamation.* **3** *Cdn.* the act or an instance of electing without opposition: *There were acclamations in five ridings.*
by acclamation, *Cdn.* without opposition in an election: *Since no candidate opposed him, Mr. Kress was elected by acclamation.* ⟨< L *acclamatio* a shouting. See ACCLAIM.⟩
☛ *Hom.* ACCLIMATION.

ac•cli•mate ['æklə,meit] *or* [ə'klaɪmɪt] *v.* **-mat•ed, -mat•ing.** acclimatize. ⟨< F *acclimater* < à to (< L *ad-*) + *climat* climate⟩

ac•cli•ma•tion [,æklə'meiʃən] *n.* acclimatization.
☛ *Hom.* ACCLAMATION.

ac•cli•ma•ti•za•tion [ə,klaɪmətaɪ'zeiʃən] *or* [ə,klaɪmətə'zeiʃən] *n.* an acclimatizing or being acclimatized.

ac•cli•ma•tize [ə'klaɪmə,taɪz] *v.* **-tized, -tiz•ing.** accustom or become accustomed to new climate or new surroundings or conditions: *It took him a long while to acclimatize to the high altitude. They soon became acclimatized to city life.*

ac•cliv•i•ty [ə'klɪvəti] *n., pl.* **-ties.** an upward slope (of ground). ⟨< L *acclivitas* < *acclivis, acclivus* ascending < *ad-* toward + *clivus* rising ground⟩

ac•co•lade ['ækə,leid], [,ækə'leid] *or* [,ækə'lɑd] *n.* **1** praise; recognition; award. **2** a tap on the shoulder with the flat side of a sword, given to mark the bestowal of knighthood on a person. **3** a kind of bracket { } used in music. ⟨< F < Ital. *accollata* an embrace about the neck < L *ad-* to + *collum* neck⟩

ac•com•mo•date [ə'kɒmə,deit] *v.* **-dat•ed, -dat•ing. 1** have room for; hold comfortably: *This big bedroom will accommodate two beds.* **2** help out; oblige: *She wanted change for a quarter, but I could not accommodate her.* **3** furnish with lodging, sometimes with food as well. **4** supply; furnish. **5** provide (a person) with a loan of money. **6** make or become fit or suitable; adapt: *The eye can accommodate to objects at different distances.* **7** reconcile; adjust: *to accommodate differences.* ⟨< L *accommodare* < *ad-* to + *commodare* make fit < *com-* with + *modus* measure⟩ **—ac'com•mo,dat•or,** *n.* **—ac'com•mo,dat•ive,** *adj.*
☛ *Syn.* **1.** See note at CONTAIN. **7.** See note at ADJUST.

ac•com•mo•dat•ing [ə'kɒmə,deitɪŋ] *adj.* obliging; willing to help. **—ac'com•mo,dat•ing•ly,** *adv.*

ac•com•mo•da•tion [ə,kɒmə'deiʃən] *n.* **1** lodging,

sometimes with food as well: *The hotel has accommodations for one hundred people.* **2** a help; favour; convenience: *It will be an accommodation to me if you will meet me tomorrow instead of today.* **3** a loan. **4** willingness to help out. **5** a fitting or being fitted to a purpose or situation; adjustment; adaptation: *The accommodation of our desires to a smaller income took some time.* **6** settlement of differences; reconciliation; compromise: *to arrange an accommodation with one's creditors.* **7** the adjustment of the lens of the eye for seeing objects at various distances.

accommodation paper, bill, or **note** a bank credit given to a person to allow him or her to raise money.

accommodation train *Cdn.* a train made up of passenger cars and freight cars.

ac•com•pa•ni•ment [ə'kʌmpənimənt] *or* [ə'kʌmpnimənt] *n.* **1** whatever goes along with something else: *Destruction and suffering are accompaniments of war.* **2** *Music.* a part (usually instrumental) added to help or enrich the main part (usually vocal).

ac•com•pa•nist [ə'kʌmpənɪst] *n.* a person who plays a musical accompaniment.

ac•com•pa•ny [ə'kʌmpəni] *or* [ə'kʌmpni] *v.* **-nied, -ny•ing.** **1** go along with: *to accompany a friend on a walk.* **2** be or happen in connection with: *Fire is accompanied by heat.* **3** cause to be attended by; supplement *(with)*: *to accompany a speech with gestures.* **4** play or sing a musical accompaniment for or to. ⟨ME < OF *accompagner* < *à* to + *compagnon* companion. Related to COMPANION.⟩ **—ac'com•pa•ni•er,** *n.*

☛ *Syn.* **1. Accompany,** ATTEND, ESCORT = go with someone or something. **Accompany** = go along with as a companion or (of things) as a customary addition: *She accompanied the other girls to the game. Baked or fried potatoes often accompany steak.* **Attend** = go along with to serve or assist: *The student attended the professor on a field trip.* **Escort** = go along with as a courtesy or as a protector: *He escorted a girl to the dance. Canadian destroyers escorted many Atlantic convoys during World War II.*

ac•com•plice [ə'kɒmplɪs] *n.* a person who aids another in committing a crime or other unlawful act or mischief, or one who encourages another to commit such an act: *The thief could not have got into the house so easily without an accomplice. The children were accomplices in mischief.* ⟨earlier *a complice* a confederate < F *complice* < L *complex* < *com-* together with + *plectere* twist⟩

☛ *Syn.* **Accomplice,** CONFEDERATE in technical (legal) use mean 'a partner in crime'. **Accomplice** applies to a person who deliberately gives help of any kind to another in connection with an unlawful act or crime, either before, during, or after the act itself: *Without an accomplice the thief could not have got into the house and stolen the jewels.* **Confederate** applies to a person who joins with others, or another, for the purpose of committing an unlawful act: *The head of the smuggling ring has not been found, but her confederates are in jail.*

ac•com•plish [ə'kɒmplɪʃ] *v.* **1** succeed in fulfilling; carry out (a promise, plan, etc.): *to accomplish a purpose.* **2** finish; do; complete: *to accomplish nothing.* ⟨ME < OF *accompliss-*, a stem of *acomplir* < LL *accomplere* < *ad-* + *complere* fill up⟩ **—ac'com•plish•er,** *n.*

☛ *Syn.* **1, 2.** See note at DO[1].

ac•com•plished [ə'kɒmplɪʃt] *adj., v.* *—adj.* **1** successfully carried out; achieved: *an accomplished goal.* **2** expert; skilled: *an accomplished surgeon, an accomplished host, an accomplished liar.* **3** skilled in the social arts: *Their very accomplished daughter, Tanya, entertained us.*
—v. pt. and pp. of ACCOMPLISH.

ac•com•plish•ment [ə'kɒmplɪʃmənt] *n.* **1** the act of achieving or carrying out; successful completion: *the accomplishment of a purpose.* **2** something accomplished; achievement; completed undertaking: *the major accomplishments of modern technology.* **3** skill or talent, especially in the social arts: *a man of accomplishment.*

ac•compt [ə'kaʊnt] *n. or v. Archaic.* account.

ac•cord [ə'kɔrd] *v., n.* *—v.* **1** be in harmony *(with)*; agree *(with)*: *His account of the accident accords with yours.* **2** grant (a favour, request, etc.): *We should accord Rosa praise for good work.* **3** make agree; harmonize; reconcile.
—n. **1** agreement; harmony: *Accord was finally reached. The various city groups are now in accord on the parks issue.* **2** an agreement between nations; treaty. **3** harmony of colour, pitch, or tone.
of (one's) **own accord,** without being asked; without suggestion from another; voluntarily: *He is old enough now to go to bed of his own accord.*
with one accord, all agreeing; unanimously: *They cheered with one accord when she made the jump.* ⟨ME < OF *acorder* < VL *acchordare* bring into harmony < L *ad-* to + *chorda* string⟩

ac•cord•ance [ə'kɔrdəns] *n.* **1** agreement; harmony: *What he did was in accordance with what he said.* **2** the act or fact of granting: *the accordance of certain rights.*

ac•cord•ant [ə'kɔrdənt] *adj.* agreeing; in harmony. **—ac'cord•ant•ly,** *adv.*

ac•cor•da•tu•ra [ə,kɔrdə'turə] *n. Music.* the set of tones to which a stringed instrument is tuned. ⟨< Ital.⟩

ac•cord•ing [ə'kɔrdɪŋ] *adj., v.* *—adj.* agreeing; in harmony.
according as, depending on how or whether: *Her fortunes varied according as the market fluctuated.*
according to, a on the authority of; as stated by: *According to this book, we are heading for a recession.* **b** on the basis of; in conformity with: *They try to spend according to their income. Bacteria are classified according to shape.*
—v. ppr. of ACCORD.

ac•cord•ing•ly [ə'kɔrdɪŋli] *adv.* **1** in agreement (with a given thing). **2** for this reason; therefore.

☛ *Usage.* **Accordingly** is a conjunctive adverb most appropriately used in formal writing. A co-ordinate clause introduced by **accordingly** is preceded by a semicolon: *He was told to speak briefly; accordingly he cut short his remarks.*

ac•cor•di•on [ə'kɔrdiən] *n.* **1** a portable musical wind instrument with a bellows, metallic reeds, and keys, played by pressing the keys while squeezing the bellows to force air through the reeds: *In a piano accordion, one set of keys is like a piano keyboard and the other keys are buttons.* **2** *(adjl.)* with folds like the bellows of an accordion: *a skirt with accordion pleats.* ⟨< Ital. *accordare* harmonize, tune (an instrument)⟩

ac•cor•di•on•ist [ə'kɔrdiənɪst] *n.* one who plays an accordion, especially a skilled player.

ac•cost [ə'kɒst] *v., n.* *—v.* **1** confront (someone) in a bold or hostile way; come up and speak to; address: *He was accosted by a thief.* **2** greet (a person). **3** of a prostitute, solicit.
—n. the act or an instance of greeting. ⟨< F *accoster* < Ital. < LL *accostare* < L *ad-* to + *costa* side, rib⟩

ac•couche•ment [ə'kuʃmənt]; French, [akuʃ'mɑ̃] *n.* **1** confinement for childbirth. **2** childbirth. ⟨< F *à* + *coucher*, put to bed⟩

ac•cou•cheur [,ɑku'ʃɜr] *n.* a male obstetrician or midwife.

ac•cou•cheuse [,ɑku'ʃɜz] a female obstetrician or midwife.

ac•count [ə'kaʊnt] *n., v.* *—n.* **1** a statement telling in detail about an event or thing; a report or story: *The newspaper published an account of the trial.* **2** an explanation or statement of reasons: *He could give no satisfactory account of his absence.* **3** sake: *Don't wait on my account.* **4** worth or importance: *It was an error of no account. The extra expense is of little account in comparison with the total cost.* **5** profit; advantage: *She turned the incident to her own account.* **6** Usually, **accounts,** *pl.* a statement of money received and spent: *Businesses and factories keep accounts.* **7** an arrangement for purchasing goods or services on credit; charge account: *Her firm has an account with that new advertising agency.* **8** an arrangement for depositing one's money in a bank for safekeeping, or the money deposited; bank account.
call (or **bring**) **to account, a** demand an explanation of (someone). **b** scold; rebuke; reprimand.
on account, a on the instalment plan: *She bought the coat on account.* **b** as part payment: *If you accept five dollars on account, I can pay the rest next week.*
on account of, a because of: *The game was put off on account of rain.* **b** for the sake of.
on no account, under no circumstances.
take account of, a See **take into account. b** notice.
take into account, make allowance for; consider: *When planning a holiday, you have to take travelling time into account.*
turn to account, use for one's own profit.
—v. hold to be; think of as; consider: *Solomon was accounted wise. She accounted herself lucky to have escaped with her life.*
account for, a give a reason or explanation for: *He couldn't account for the strange message.* **b** be the main or only source or reason for: *Late frosts accounted for the poor fruit crop.* **c** give a reckoning of; tell what has happened to: *The treasurer of the club has to account for all the money received. Have all the passengers been accounted for?* **d** be responsible for the defeat, destruction, or death of: *His squadron accounted for twenty enemy aircraft in the battle.* **e** make reparations: *The murderer accounted for his crime.* ⟨ME < OF *acont*, n., *aconter*, v., < VL *accomptare* < L *ad-* up + *computare* count < *com-* together + *putare* reckon⟩

ac•count•a•bil•i•ty [ə,kaʊntə'bɪləti] *n.* the state of being accountable; responsibility.

ac•count•a•ble [ə'kaʊntəbəl] *adj.* **1** responsible; liable to be called to account: *He was judged not accountable for his actions.* **2** explainable: *His bad temper is easily accountable; he has had a toothache all day.* **—ac'count•a•bly,** *adv.* **—ac'count•a•ble•ness,** *n.*

ac•count•an•cy [ə'kaʊntənsi] *n.* the profession or work of an accountant.

ac•count•ant [ə'kaʊntənt] *n.* a person trained in accounting, especially one whose work it is.

account book a book for recording business accounts.

account current a record of transactions that shows money owed.

account executive an executive in charge of the work for a particular client or clients.

ac•count•ing [ə'kaʊntɪŋ] *n.* **1** the system or procedures of recording, sorting, and analysing financial data related to business transactions, and of preparing statements of the results for individuals or businesses to use in making business decisions. **2** the activity of recording and balancing accounts and statements. **3** a statement of explanation or justification: *She was asked for an accounting of her time away from work.*

ac•cou•ple•ment [ə'kʌpəlmənt] *n.* **1** *Architecture.* the placing of columns in pairs. **2** *Carpentry.* a brace.

ac•cou•ter [ə'kutər] *v.* See ACCOUTRE.

ac•cou•ter•ment [ə'kutərmənt] See ACCOUTREMENT.

ac•cou•tre [ə'kutər] *v.* **-tred, -tring.** equip; array: *Knights were accoutred in armour.* Also, **accouter.** ⟨< F *accoutrer*⟩

ac•cou•tre•ment [ə'kutrəmənt] *or* [ə'kutərmənt] *n.* **1** the act of accoutring or the state of being accoutred. **2** Usually, **accoutrements,** *pl.* **a** clothing, equipment, accessories, etc. **b** *Military.* a soldier's outfit or equipment, other than clothing and weapons. Also, **accouterment.**

ac•cred•it [ə'krɛdɪt] *v.* **1** recognize as coming up to an official standard. **2** consider (a thing) as belonging or due (*to* a person): *We accredit the invention of the telephone to Bell.* **3** accept as true; believe; trust. **4** give authority or credibility to. **5** send or provide with credentials or a recommendation: *An ambassador is accredited as the representative of his or her own country in a foreign land.* **6** give (a person) credit for; regard (a person) as having (*usually used with* **with**): *to accredit her with kindness.* ⟨< F *accréditer* < *à* to + *crédit* credit⟩ **—ac,cred•i'ta•tion,** *n.*

☛ *Syn.* **2, 6.** See note at CREDIT.

ac•crete [ə'krit] *v.* **ac•cret•ed, ac•cret•ing. 1** grow together. **2** increase as if by growth.

ac•cre•tion [ə'kriʃən] *n.* **1** growth in size or amount: *the accretion of political power.* **2** a growing together of separate particles or parts. **3** an increase in size by gradual external addition: *the accretion of land by deposits of alluvial soil.* **4** something added to cause an increase in size. **5** a whole that results from such growths or additions. ⟨< L *accretio, -onis* < *accrescere.* See ACCRUE.⟩

ac•cru•al [ə'kruəl] *n.* **1** the process of accruing; progressive growth: *Money left in a savings account increases by the accrual of interest.* **2** the amount accrued or accruing.

ac•crue [ə'kru] *v.* **-crued, -cru•ing.** come as a growth or result: *Interest on a term deposit accrues at a higher rate than on a regular savings account. The benefits that accrue to a society through immigration are many.* ⟨< F < L *accrescere* < *ad-* to + *crescere* grow⟩ **—ac'crue•ment,** *n.*

acct. 1 account. **2** accountant.

ac•cul•tur•ate [ə'kʌltʃə,reit] *v.,* **-ated, -ating 1** of a cultural group, adapt to or adopt the culture of another group: *Inuit in some parts of the North have acculturated to the southern Canadian society.* **2** of a child, acquire the patterns of his or her own culture. **3** cause (a group, child, etc.) to do this. ⟨< *acculturation*⟩

ac•cul•tu•ra•tion [ə,kʌltʃə'reiʃən] *n.* **1** the modification of the culture of one group through the influence of the culture of another group. **2** the conditioning of a child to the ways of a particular society. ⟨< *ac-* + *culture* + *-ation*⟩

ac•cum•bent [ə'kʌmbənt] *adj.* **1** lying down. **2** *Botany.* placed against some other part. ⟨< L *accumbere* recline⟩

ac•cu•mu•late [ə'kjumjə,leit] *v.* **-lat•ed, -lat•ing. 1** collect little by little: *She accumulated a fortune by hard work.* **2** grow in amount or number; mount up: *Dust had accumulated during the three weeks that we were gone.* ⟨< L *accumulare* < *ad-* up + *cumulus* heap⟩ **—ac'cu•mu•la•ble,** *adj.*

☛ *Syn.* **1. Accumulate,** AMASS = collect a considerable or large amount. In figurative use, applied to resources, feelings, etc., **accumulate** emphasizes the idea, expressed in its literal meaning, of heaping up, little by little, pile on pile: *Through the years he accumulated sufficient money to buy a farm when he retired.* **Amass** emphasizes the idea of gathering to oneself as in a mass or in large amounts: *Before she was forty, she had amassed a fortune.*

ac•cu•mu•la•tion [ə,kjumjə'leiʃən] *n.* **1** a mass of material collected over time: *Her accumulation of old papers filled three trunks.* **2** a collecting together: *The accumulation of knowledge is one result of reading.* **3** the accruing of capital through interest.

ac•cu•mu•la•tive [ə'kjumjələtɪv] *adj.* **1** resulting from gathering into a mass. **2** anxious to ACCUMULATE (def. 1), especially to accumulate money or material things. **—ac'cu•mu•la•tive•ly,** *adv.*

ac•cu•mu•la•tor [ə'kjumjə,leitər] *n.* **1** a person or thing that accumulates matter or objects. **2** *Brit.* storage battery. **3** *Computer technology.* a type of data storage location in a calculator or the CPU of a computer.

ac•cu•ra•cy ['ækjərəsi] *n.* freedom from errors or mistakes; correctness; exactness.

ac•cu•rate ['ækjərɪt] *adj.* **1** making few or no errors: *an accurate observer.* **2** without errors or mistakes; exact; correct: *accurate measure.* ⟨< L *accuratus* prepared with care, pp. of *accurare* take care of < *ad-* to + *cura* care⟩ **—'ac•cu•rate•ly,** *adv.* **—'ac•cu•rate•ness,** *n.*

☛ *Syn.* **2.** See note at CORRECT.

ac•curs•ed [ə'kɜrsɪd] *or* [ə'kɜrst] *adj.* **1** damnable; detestable; hateful. **2** under a curse; damned. Also, **accurst.**

accus. accusative.

ac•cu•sa•tion [,ækjə'zeiʃən] *n.* **1** a charge of having done something wrong, of being something bad, or of having broken the law. **2** the offence charged. **3** an accusing or being accused.

ac•cu•sa•tive [ə'kjuzətɪv] *adj., n.* —*adj.* of, having to do with, or being the grammatical case found in some languages, that shows that a noun, pronoun, or adjective is not part of the subject of a sentence, but is a direct object of a verb or of any of certain prepositions. The English pronouns *me, her, him, us,* and *them* correspond to the accusative case in languages such as German, Latin, and Greek.
—*n.* **1** the accusative case. **2** a word or group of words in the accusative case. ⟨< L *accusativus*⟩ **—ac'cu•sa•tive•ly,** *adj.*

ac•cu•sa•to•ry [ə'kjuzə,tɔri] *adj.* of a statement, manner, etc., containing or expressing an accusation; accusing: *an accusatory glance, an accusatory tone of voice.* **—ac,cu•sa'to•ri•al,** *adj.*

ac•cuse [ə'kjuz] *v.* **-cused, -cus•ing. 1** charge with having done something wrong, with being something bad, or with having broken the law (*usually with* **of**): *He was accused of murder.* **2** find fault with; blame. ⟨ME < OF < L *accusare* < *ad-* to + *causa* cause⟩ **—ac'cus•er,** *n.* **—ac'cus•ing•ly,** *adv.*

☛ *Syn.* **1.** See note at CHARGE.

ac•cused [ə'kjuzd] *n., v.* —*n.* **the accused,** *Law.* the person or persons appearing in court on a criminal charge. Compare DEFENDANT.
—*v.* pt. and pp. of ACCUSE.

ac•cus•tom [ə'kʌstəm] *v.* make familiar with or used to something, by habit or practice (*used with* **to**): *to accustom a hunting dog to the noise of a gun.* ⟨ME < OF *acostumer* < *a-* to (< L *ad-*) + *costume* custom < L *consuescere* < *com-* + *suescere* accustom⟩

ac•cus•tomed [ə'kʌstəmd] *adj., v.* —*adj.* usual; customary: *By Monday he was back in his accustomed place.*
accustomed to, used to; in the habit of: *She was accustomed to hard work.*
—*v.* pt. and pp. of ACCUSTOM.

ace [eis] *n., v.* —*n.* **1** a playing card, domino, or side of a die having one spot. **2** a single spot or point. **3** *Sports.* **a** a point won by a single stroke. **b** *Tennis.* a serve that is impossible to return. **4** a person expert at anything. **5** a combat pilot who has shot down a large number of enemy planes. **6** (*adjl.*) of very high rank or quality; expert: *an ace football player.*
ace in the hole, a *Poker.* an ace dealt face downward and not exposed until the end. **b** *Informal.* a decisive advantage that is kept hidden until needed.
ace up one's sleeve, *Informal.* a decisive advantage that is kept hidden until needed.
within an ace of, at the brink of; on the very point of: *I came within an ace of quitting.*
—*v.* **1** *Tennis.* serve an ace against (an opponent). **2** *Golf.* make an ace on (a hole). **3** *Slang.* achieve a high mark in (an examination, etc.). **4** win (a game) or defeat (an opponent) decisively. ⟨ME < OF *as* < L *as, assis* smallest unit⟩

–acea *suffix.* of animals from a class or order: *Cetacea.*

–aceae *suffix.* of plants from a family: *Acantheaceae.*

ac•e•bu•to•lol [ˌæsəˈbjutəˌlɒl] *n.* a drug used to treat high blood pressure or angina pectoris. *Formula*: $C_{18}H_{28}N_2O_4$

ace–high [ˈeis ˈhaɪ] *adj. Cdn. Informal.* highly esteemed.

a•cen•tric [eiˈsɛntrɪk] *adj., n. —adj.* of a chromosome fragment, lacking a centromere.
—n. such a chromosome fragment.

a•ceph•a•lous [əˈsɛfələs] *or* [eiˈsɛfələs] *adj.* **1** *Biology.* without a distinct head. **2** without a leader.

a•ce•rate [ˈæsəˌreit] *or* [ˈæsərɪt] *adj. Botany.* needle-shaped. ⟨< L *aceratus* < *acus* needle⟩

a•cerb [əˈsɜrb] *adj.* **1** having or showing a bad temper. **2** sour-tasting. ⟨See ACERBITY⟩

a•cer•bate *v.* [ˈæsərˌbeit]; *adj.* [əˈsɜrbət] *v., adj. —v.* **-bat•ed, -bat•ing. 1** make sour. **2** make angry.
—adj. embittered.

a•cer•bic [əˈsɜrbɪk] *adj.* **1** sour in taste. **2** sharp, bitter, or harsh in tone, mood, or temper: *an acerbic remark, an acerbic columnist.* **—aˈcer•bi•cal•ly,** *adv.*

a•cer•bi•ty [əˈsɜrbɪti] *n., pl.* **-ties. 1** acidity combined with astringency; sharpness of taste; sourness. **2** harshness or bitterness of tone, mood, or temper. ⟨< F *acerbité* < L *acerbitas* < *acerbus* bitter⟩

ac•er•ose[1] [ˈæsəˌrous] *adj.* acerate.

ac•er•ose[2] [ˈæsəˌrous] *adj.* like chaff or containing chaff. ⟨< L *acerosus*⟩

a•cer•vate [əˈsɜrvɪt] *or* [əˈsɜrveit] *adj. Botany.* growing in clusters. ⟨< L *acervatus* < *acervare* pile up < *acervus* pile⟩

acet– *combining form.* showing the presence of acetic acid. Also, before a consonant, **aceto-.** ⟨< L *acetum* vinegar⟩

ac•e•tab•u•lum [æsəˈtæbjələm] *n., pl.* **-la** [-lə]. **1** a socket in the hipbone into which the top part of the thighbone fits. See PELVIS for picture. **2** *Biology.* one of the suctionlike cups that an octopus or a leech has as appendages. ⟨< L *acetabulum* cup-shaped holder for vinegar < *acetum* vinegar⟩

ac•e•tal [ˈæsəˌtæl] *n.* **1** a volatile liquid used as a solvent. *Formula*: $CH_3CH\ (OC_2H_5)$ **2** any one of a group of compounds of aldehyde and alcohol. ⟨< *acet-* + *al(dehyde)*⟩

ac•et•al•de•hyde [ˌæsəˈtældɪˌhaɪd] *n.* a liquid used mainly in silvering mirrors. *Formula*: CH_3CHO

ac•et•am•ide [əˈsɛtəˌmaɪd] *or* [ˌæsəˈtæmaɪd] *n.* **1** acetaldehyde. **2** a white or colourless crystalline solid, used mainly as a solvent. *Formula*: CH_3CONH_2

ac•e•ta•min•o•phen [əˌsɛtəˈmɪnəfɪn] *or* [əˌsitəˈmɪnəfɪn] *n.* acetanilide. ⟨< *acet-* + *amino* + *phenol*⟩

ac•et•an•i•lide [ˌæsəˈtænəˌlaɪd] *or* [ˌæsəˈtænəlɪd] *n.* a white crystalline compound, used in medicine to relieve pain and lessen fever. Also, **acetanilid** [-ˈtænəlɪd]. *Formula*: $C_6H_5NHCOCH_3$ ⟨< *acet-* + *aniline*⟩

ac•e•tate [ˈæsəˌteit] *n.* **1** a salt or ester of acetic acid. **2** CELLULOSE ACETATE. **3** an article or material made from this substance, such as photographic film or a kind of silklike cloth. **4** a transparency for use with an OVERHEAD PROJECTOR.

ac•e•ta•zo•la•mide [əˌsɛtəˈzɒləˌmaɪd] *or* [əˌsitəˈzɒləˌmaɪd] *n.* a drug used to treat edema and some forms of epilepsy. *Formula*: $C_4H_6N_4O_3S_2$ ⟨< *acet-* + *azole* + *amide*⟩

a•ce•tic [əˈsitɪk] *or* [əˈsɛtɪk] *adj.* of or producing vinegar. ⟨< L *acetum* vinegar⟩
☛ *Hom.* ASCETIC [əˈsɛtɪk].

acetic acid a very sour, colourless acid, the main constituent of vinegar. *Formula*: CH_3COOH

a•cet•i•fy [əˈsitəˌfaɪ] *or* [əˈsɛtəˌfaɪ] *v.* **-fied, -fy•ing.** turn into vinegar or acetic acid. **—aˌcet•i•fiˈca•tion** *n.*

a•ce•to•hex•a•mide [əˌsitouˈhɛksəˌmaɪd] *or* [əˌsɛtouˈhɛksəˌmaɪd] *n.* a drug used to control blood sugar in diabetics.

ac•e•tom•e•ter [ˌæsɪˈtɒmətər] *n.* a device to measure the amount of acetic acid in a solution. An acetometer is used in winemaking.

ac•e•tone [ˈæsəˌtoun] *n.* a colourless, volatile, flammable liquid, used as a solvent for oils, fats, resins, cellulose, etc. and in making varnishes. *Formula*: C_3H_6O **—ˌac•eˈton•ic,** *adj.*

acetous [ˈæsətəs] *adj.* vinegary; producing vinegar; tart. Also, **acetose** [ˈæsəˌtous].

a•ce•tum [əˈsitəm] *n.* a pharmaceutical preparation with weak acetic acid in it as a solvent.

a•ce•tyl [əˈsitəl], [ˈæsəˌtɪl] *or* [ˈæsətəl] *n.* the chemical group CH_3CO, found only in compounds. **—ˌac•eˈtyl•ic,** *adj.*

ac•e•tyl•cho•line [ˌæsətəlˈkoulin] *n.* a chemical secreted in body tissue. It transmits neural impulses. *Formula*: $C_7H_{17}NO_3$

acetylcholine chloride a drug used in eye surgery.

ac•e•tyl•cys•teine [əˌsitɪlˈsɔistin] *n.* a drug used as an antidote to acetaminophen poisoning. *Formula*: $C_5H_9NO_3S$

a•cet•y•lene [əˈsɛtəˌlin] *or* [əˈsɛtəlɪn] *n.* a colourless, gaseous hydrocarbon that burns with a bright light and a very hot flame. It is used mainly in preparing compounds to make synthetic fibres and vinyl plastics and, combined with oxygen, for welding and cutting metals. *Formula*: C_2H_2

ac•e•tyl•sal•i•cyl•ic acid [ˌæsətɪlˌsæləˈsɪlɪk] *or* [əˌsitəlˌsæləˈsɪlɪk] aspirin.

ace•y•deuc•y [ˈeisiˈdjusi] *or* [-ˈdusi] *n. Slang.* a variant of backgammon.

A•chae•an [əˈkiən] *adj., n. —adj.* **1** of Achaea, an ancient province in southern Greece. **2** Greek.
—n. a native or inhabitant of Achaea or Greece.

A•chai•an [əˈkeiən] *adj. or n.* Achaean.

A•cha•tes [əˈkeiˌtiz] *n.* a faithful companion. ⟨the faithful companion of Aeneas in Virgil's *Aeneid*⟩

ache [eik] *v.* **ached, ach•ing;** *n. —v.* **1** be in, or be the site of, dull, continuous pain. **2** *Informal.* be eager; wish very much: *I am just aching to hear what happened.*
—n. a dull, steady pain. ⟨OE *acan*⟩ **—ˈach•ing•ly,** *adv.*
☛ *Syn. n.* See note at PAIN.

a•chene [eiˈkin] *n. Botany.* a small, dry, hard fruit that develops from a simple ovary, having a single seed and a thin outer covering that does not burst open when ripe. The achenes of some plants, such as the sunflower, are commonly called seeds. See FRUIT for picture. ⟨< NL *achaenium* < Gk. *a-* not + *chainein* gape; because it ripens without bursting⟩

A•cher•nar [ˈeikərˌnɑr] *n.* the brightest star in the southern constellation Eridanus.

Ach•er•on [ˈækəˌrɒn] *n. Greek mythology.* **1** a river in Hades. **2** the lower world; Hades.

A•cheu•lean [əˈʃuliən] *adj.* of or relating to a Lower Paleolithic culture of the middle Pleistocene, characterized by the use of hand axes and cleavers. ⟨< *Saint Acheul* in N France, where the remains were found⟩

a•chieve [əˈtʃiv] *v.* **a•chieved, a•chiev•ing. 1** do; get done; carry out; accomplish: *to achieve one's purpose.* **2** get by effort: *He achieved distinction in mathematics.* **3** perform successfully. ⟨ME < OF *achever* < *(venir) a chief* (come) to a head < LL *ad caput (venire)*⟩ **—aˈchiev•a•ble,** *adj.* **—aˈchiev•er,** *n.*

a•chieve•ment [əˈtʃivmənt] *n.* **1** the act of achieving; completing successfully: *the achievement of one's purpose.* **2** something achieved, especially some plan or action accomplished with courage or unusual ability.
☛ *Syn.* **2.** See note at EXPLOIT.

achievement age a measure of a student's learning, determined from his or her score on a special test. It is the average age of all students having that particular score. *Abbrev.*: AA or A.A.

achievement quotient the ratio of a person's achievement age to his or her actual age, usually multiplied by 100. *Abbrev.*: AQ

ach•il•le•a [əˈkɪliə] *or* [ˌækəˈliə] *n.* yarrow. ⟨< NL < L: said to have been used medicinally by Achilles⟩

A•chil•les [əˈkɪliz] *n. Greek mythology.* the hero of Homer's *Iliad*, a Greek warrior who killed Hector at the siege of Troy, but was himself killed by Paris. Paris' arrow struck Achilles in the heel, his only vulnerable spot.

Achilles' heel a vulnerable area.

Achilles tendon the strong tendon joining the heel bone to the muscles of the calf: *The Achilles tendon helps to move the ankle joint.*

ach•kan [ˈætʃkən] *n.* a fitted Indian men's coat. ⟨< Hind. *ackan*⟩

ach•la•myd•e•ous [ˌækləˈmɪdiəs] *adj. Botany.* having no calyx or corolla. ⟨< *a-* + Gk. *chlamydes*, pl. of *chlamys* cloak⟩

a•chon•dro•pla•sia [ˌeikɒndrouˈpleiʒə] *n.* a genetic disorder of bone development causing a short-limbed type of dwarfism and other abnormalities. ⟨< Gk. *a-* without + *chondros* cartilage + *plasis* moulding⟩

ach•ro•mat•ic [ˌækrəˈmætɪk] *or* [ˌeikrəˈmætɪk] *adj.* **1** capable of refracting white light without breaking it up into the colours of the spectrum. **2** having no hue. Black, white, and neutral greys are achromatic colours. **3** *Biology.* containing or consisting of material that resists ordinary stains: *achromatic cells.* **4** *Music.* having no accidentals or changes of key; diatonic: *an achromatic scale.* ⟨< Gk. *achrōmatos* < *a-* without + *chrōma* colour⟩ **—ˌach•roˈmat•i•cal•ly,** *adv.*

ach•y [ˈeiki] *adj. Informal.* full of dull pain.

a•cic•u•la [əˈsɪkjələ] *n. Botany.* a needle-shaped point. ⟨< NL, dim. of L *acus* needle⟩

a•cic•u•late [əˈsɪkjələt] *or* [əˈsɪkjəˌleit] *adj. Botany.* having a needle-shaped point.

a•cic•u•lum [əˈsɪkjələm] *n.* acicula.

ac•id [ˈæsɪd] *n., adj.* —*n.* **1** *Chemistry.* any of various compounds that yield hydrogen ions when dissolved in water and usually react with a base to form a salt. The water solution of an acid turns blue litmus paper red. **2** a sour substance. **3** a harsh, biting, or bitter quality or character: *There was acid in his voice as he replied.* **4** *Slang.* LSD.
—*adj.* **1** of, having to do with, or containing an acid: *an acid solution.* **2** sharp or biting to the taste; sour. **3** harsh, biting, or bitter: *an acid comment, acid humour.* ⟨< L *acidus* sour⟩ **—ˈac•id•ly,** *adv.* **—ˈac•id•ness,** *n.*
☛ *Syn. adj.* See note at SOUR.

ac•i•dan•the•ra [ˌæsɪˈdænθərə] *n.* any of various plants (genus *Acidanthera*) of the iris family, found in Africa, whose flowers are pale yellow and trumpet-shaped.

acid head or **freak** *Slang.* a habitual user of LSD.

a•cid•ic [əˈsɪdɪk] *adj.* **1** acid-forming. **2** acid: *Rainfall is growing more acidic in many parts of the world.* **3** *Geology.* containing a high percentage of silica.

a•cid•i•fi•ca•tion [əˌsɪdəfəˈkeiʃən] *n.* the action or process of acidifying or the state of being acidified.

a•cid•i•fy [əˈsɪdəˌfaɪ] *v.* **-fied, -fy•ing. 1** make or become sour. **2** change into an acid. **—aˈcid•iˌfi•er,** *n.*

ac•i•dim•e•ter [ˌæsɪˈdɪmətər] *n.* an instrument for measuring acidity.

a•cid•i•ty [əˈsɪdəti] *n., pl.* **-ties. 1** an acid quality or condition; sourness: *the acidity of vinegar.* **2** excessive stomach acid.

acid number or **acid value** a number indicating the amount of free acid in a substance. The acid number is the equivalent of the amount of potassium hydroxide needed to neutralize one gram of oil.

a•cid•o•phil [əˈsɪdəˌfɪl] *n.* **1** any substance easily stained with acid dye. **2** a micro-organism that flourishes in an acidic environment. Also, **acidophile** [-ˌfail]. **—ˌa•cid•oˈphil•ic,** *adj.*

ac•i•do•sis [ˌæsəˈdousɪs] *n.* a harmful condition in which the blood and tissues are less alkaline than is normal. ⟨< *acid* + *-osis*⟩

acid precipitation ACID RAIN.

acid rain rain or snow contaminated by acids formed when industrial pollutants, especially sulphur dioxide and nitrogen oxides, undergo chemical changes in the atmosphere.

acid rock a kind of rock-and-roll dating from the late 1960s, known for its harsh and distorted electronic sounds and its association with drug culture.

acid salt a salt formed from an acid of which only part of the hydrogen has been replaced by a metal or radical.

acid test 1 a decisive test of the real worth of some person or thing. **2** a former test for gold, using nitric acid.

a•cid–tongued [ˈæsɪd ˌtʌŋd] *adj.* sarcastic; biting: *acid-tongued criticism.*

a•cid•u•late [əˈsɪdʒəˌleit] *v.* **-lat•ed, -lat•ing.** make slightly acid or sour. **—aˌcid•uˈla•tion,** *n.*

a•cid•u•lous [əˈsɪdʒələs] *adj.* slightly acid or sour. **—aˈcid•u•lous•ly,** *adv.* **—aˈcid•u•lous•ness,** *n.*

ac•i•er•ate [ˈæsiəˌreit] *v.,* **-a•ted, -a•ting.** change (iron) into steel. ⟨< F *acier* steel⟩

ac•i•form [ˈæsɪˌfɔrm] *adj. Botany.* **1** needle-shaped. **2** sharp. ⟨< L *acus* needle⟩

ac•i•nac•i•form [ˌæsɪˈnæsəˌfɔrm] *adj. Botany.* of a leaf or petal, shaped like a scimitar. ⟨< L *acinaces* sword < Gk. *akinakes*⟩

a•cin•i•form [əˈsɪnəˌfɔrm] *adj. Botany.* having the shape of a cluster of grapes. ⟨See ACINUS⟩

ac•i•nus [ˈæsənəs] *n., pl.* **-ni** [-ˌnaɪ] *or* [-ˌni] **1** a drupelet. **2** the smallest part of a gland. **3** a mass of berries growing together. ⟨< L *acinus* grape⟩ **—ˈac•i•nous,** *adj.*

ack–ack [ˈæk ˈæk] *n. Informal.* anti-aircraft fire. ⟨British radio operator's code word for A.A. (anti-aircraft)⟩

ack•ee [ˈæki] *n.* **1** a tropical African tree (*Blighia sapida*) of the soapberry family, cultivated, especially in Jamaica, for its edible fruit. **2** the fruit of this tree, eaten as a cooked vegetable, usually with salt fish. Ackee resembles scrambled eggs in appearance and taste. Also, **akee.** ⟨from an African name⟩

ac•knowl•edge [ækˈnɒlədʒ] *v.* **-edged, -edg•ing. 1** admit the existence or truth of: *I acknowledge my own faults.* **2** recognize the merit, authority, or claims of: *She was acknowledged to be the best player on the baseball team.* **3** express appreciation of (a gift, favour, etc.): *He acknowledged their help by inviting them to dinner.* **4** indicate that one has received (a service, favour, gift, message, etc.) or noticed (a person). **5** *Law.* recognize or certify as genuine: *to acknowledge a contract before a notary public.* ⟨blend of ME *aknowen* admit (< OE *oncnāwan*) and *knowleche* knowledge⟩ **—acˈknowl•edg•er,** *n.*
☛ *Syn.* **1.** See note at ADMIT.

ac•knowl•edg•ment or **ac•knowl•edge•ment** [ækˈnɒlədʒmənt] *n.* **1** a verbal, written, or other recognition of a gift, service, favour, etc.: *She waved in acknowledgment of the crowd's cheers. A receipt is an acknowledgment that a bill has been paid.* **2** the act of admitting the existence or truth of anything. **3** the recognition of authority or claims. **4** an expression of thanks. **5** an official certificate in legal form.

a•clin•ic line [eiˈklɪnɪk] MAGNETIC EQUATOR.

A.C.M. Air Chief Marshal.

ac•me [ˈækmi] *n.* the highest point; summit; culmination. ⟨< Gk. *akmé* point⟩

ac•ne [ˈækni] *n.* a skin disease in which the oil glands in the skin become clogged and inflamed, causing pimples. ⟨? < Gk. *akmē* point⟩

ac•node [ˈæknoud] *n. Mathematics.* a point on a curve that is in isolation from other points. ⟨< L *acus* needle + E *node*⟩

a•cock [əˈkɒk] *adv., adj.* askew.

ac•o•lyte [ˈækəˌləit] *n.* **1** a person who helps a priest during certain religious services; server. **2** attendant or follower. ⟨ME < Med.L *acolitus* < Gk. *akolouthos* follower⟩

ac•o•nite [ˈækəˌnəit] *n.* **1** any of a genus (*Aconitum*) of plants of the buttercup family found in cool northern regions, having blue, purple, yellow, or white hood-shaped flowers and, in some species, poisonous roots, seeds, and leaves, e.g., monkshood or wolfsbane. **2** a poisonous substance obtained from the roots of some aconites, especially a drug obtained from *Aconitum napellus*, formerly used in medicine to deaden pain, slow down the pulse, etc. ⟨< F *aconit* < L < Gk. *akoniton*⟩

a•corn [ˈeikɔrn] *n.* the nut, or fruit, of an oak tree. ⟨OE *æcern*⟩

acorn squash a type of winter squash, shaped like an acorn, about 10-15 cm in diameter, with dark green grooved skin and yellow pulp.

acorn tube a vacuum tube, the size and shape of an acorn, used to get high frequency.

a•cot•y•le•don [ˌeikɒtəˈlidən] *n.* any plant lacking a cotyledon.

a•cous•tic [əˈkustɪk] *adj.* **1** of or having to do with the sense of hearing: *acoustic nerves, an acoustic stimulus.* **2** having to do with the physical properties of sound: *acoustic phonetics, acoustic energy.* **3** designed to carry sound or to aid in hearing: *An acoustic baffle has been installed in the concert hall.* **4** designed to deaden or absorb sound: *acoustic tile.* **5** activated by sound waves: *an acoustic mine.* **6** of musical instruments, etc., not using electronic amplification: *an acoustic guitar.* ⟨< F *acoustique* < Gk. *akoustikós* having to do with hearing < *akouein* hear⟩

a•cous•ti•cal [əˈkustɪkəl] *adj.* having to do with the science of sound: *an acoustical engineer.*

a•cous•ti•cal•ly [əˈkustɪkli] *adv.* with regard to acoustics.

ac•ous•ti•cian [ˌækuˈstɪʃən] *n.* a specialist in acoustics.

a•cous•tics [əˈkustɪks] *n.* **1** the qualities of a room, hall, auditorium, etc. that determine how well sounds can be heard in it; acoustic qualities (*used with a plural verb*): *We enjoy singing in the auditorium because the acoustics are so good.* **2** the scientific study of sound (*used with a singular verb*): *Acoustics is taught in some universities.*

à cou•vert [ɑ ku'vɛr] out of danger; in or to a place of shelter or concealment. ⟨< F⟩

ac•quaint [ə'kweint] *v.* **1** inform (a person) about a thing (*used with* **with**): *Acquaint him with your intention. He acquainted me with his plan.* **2** make familiar: *He gave us a little tour to acquaint us with the neighbourhood.*
be acquainted with, have personal knowledge of: *She is acquainted with my father.* ⟨ME *acointe* < OF *acointer* < LL *adcognitare* < L *adcognitus, accognitus* < *ad-* to + *cognitus*, pp. of *cognoscere* know < *com-* with + *gnoscere* come to know⟩
☛ *Syn.* **1.** See note at INFORM.

ac•quaint•ance [ə'kweintəns] *n.* **1** a person known to one, but not a close friend. **2** a knowledge of persons or things gained from experience with them; personal knowledge.
make (someone's) **acquaintance,** get to know someone.

ac•quaint•ance•ship [ə'kweintəns,ʃɪp] *n.* **1** personal knowledge; acquaintance. **2** the relation between acquaintances: *Their acquaintanceship dates from before the war.*

ac•qui•esce [,ækwi'ɛs] *v.* **-esced, -esc•ing.** accept or agree by keeping quiet or by not making objections: *We acquiesced in their plan because we could not suggest a better one.* ⟨< F < L *acquiescere* < *ad-* to + *quiescere* to rest < *quies* rest⟩

ac•qui•es•cence [,ækwi'ɛsəns] *n.* the act of acquiescing or the state of being acquiescent.

ac•qui•es•cent [,ækwi'ɛsənt] *adj.* acquiescing; consenting or accepting. **—,ac•qui'es•cent•ly,** *adv.*

ac•quire [ə'kwaɪr] *v.* **-quired, -quir•ing. 1** receive or get as one's own: *to acquire land.* **2** get by one's own efforts or actions: *to acquire an education.* ⟨ME *acquere* < OF *acquerre* < L *acquirere* < *ad-* to + *quaerere* seek⟩ **—ac'quir•a•ble,** *adj.* **—ac'quir•er,** *n.*
☛ *Syn.* See note at GET.

acquired character *Genetics.* a character that results from environment and not heredity.

Acquired Immune Deficiency Syndrome a disease of the immune system, caused by a virus transmitted through body fluids, which makes the sufferer susceptible to other diseases from which he or she can die. *Abbrev.*: AIDS

ac•quire•ment [ə'kwaɪrmənt] *n.* **1** the act of acquiring. **2** something acquired, especially a skill; attainment: *Her musical acquirements are remarkable for a girl of her age.*

ac•qui•si•tion [,ækwə'zɪʃən] *n.* **1** the act or process of acquiring: *She spent hundreds of hours in the acquisition of skill with a yo-yo.* **2** something acquired. ⟨< L *acquisitio, -onis* < *acquirere.* See ACQUIRE.⟩

ac•quis•i•tive [ə'kwɪzətɪv] *adj.* **1** fond of acquiring; likely to get and keep (*used with* **of**): *A miser is acquisitive of money. A great scholar is acquisitive of ideas.* **2** greedy for material wealth: *She valued contentment and simplicity and found him too acquisitive.* **—ac'quis•i•tive•ly,** *adv.* **—ac'quis•i•tive•ness,** *n.*

ac•quit [ə'kwɪt] *v.* **-quit•ted, -quit•ting. 1** declare (a person) not guilty (*of* an offence): *The jury acquitted the innocent man of the crime.* **2** set free or release (from a duty, obligation, etc.). **3** pay off or settle (a debt, claim, etc.). **4** conduct (oneself); clear (oneself) (*of* a responsibility) by performing it: *She acquitted herself of her duty with good will and enthusiasm. The soldiers acquitted themselves well in battle.* ⟨ME < OF *aquiter* < *a-* to (< L *ad-*) + *quitte* free < L *quietus* quiet⟩ **—ac'quit•ter,** *n.*

ac•quit•tal [ə'kwɪtəl] *n.* **1** a setting free by declaring not guilty; release. **2** the performance (of a duty, obligation, etc.).

ac•quit•tance [ə'kwɪtəns] *n.* **1** a release from a debt or obligation. **2** a payment of a debt; settlement of a claim. **3** a written statement showing that a debt has been paid; receipt for the full amount.

a•cre ['eikər] *n.* **1** a unit for measuring land area, equal to about 4047 m^2. **2 acres,** *pl.* lands; property. **3** *Archaic.* field. **4** See GOD'S ACRE. ⟨OE *æcer* field⟩

a•cre•age ['eikərɪdʒ] *n.* **1** the number of acres: *What is the acreage of the farm?* **2** area in acres; acres collectively: *We have most of our acreage in barley this year.* **3** a piece of land of several acres: *She bought a small acreage north of town.*

a•cre–foot ['eikər 'fʊt] *n.* **1** in an artificial reservoir, 325 829 gallons. The Canadian gallon equals 4.55 dm^3. **2** the volume of water required to irrigate one acre (4047 m^2) to the depth of one foot (30.48 cm).

a•cre–inch ['eikər 'ɪntʃ] *n.* one-twelfth of an ACRE-FOOT.

ac•rid ['ækrɪd] *adj.* **1** sharp, bitter, or stinging to the nose, mouth, or skin. **2** having or showing a sharp or irritating temper: *an acrid comment.* ⟨< L *acer, acris* sharp, after *acid*⟩ **—'ac•rid•ly,** *adv.* **—'ac•rid•ness,** *n.*

ac•rid•ine ['ækrə,din] *or* ['ækrədɪn] *n.* a crystalline solid used in making some dyes and drugs. *Formula*: $C_{13}H_9N$

a•crid•i•ty [ə'krɪdəti] *n.* bitterness or sharpness.

ac•ri•fla•vine [,ækrə'fleivin] *or* [,ækrə'fleivɪn] *n.* an orange-red powder used as an antiseptic. *Formula*: $C_{14}H_{14}N_3Cl$

Ac•ri•lan ['ækrə,læn] *n. Trademark.* a synthetic acrylic fibre having a woolly texture, used for blankets, carpets, clothing, etc.

ac•ri•mo•ni•ous [,ækrə'mouniəs] *adj.* sharp and bitter in temper, language, or manner. ⟨< F *acrimonieux*⟩ **—,ac•ri'mo•ni•ous•ly,** *adv.* **—,ac•ri'mo•ni•ous•ness,** *n.*

ac•ri•mo•ny ['ækrə,mouni] *n., pl.* **-nies.** sharpness or bitterness in temper, language, or manner. ⟨< L *acrimonia* < *acer* sharp⟩

a•crit•i•cal [ei'krɪtəkəl] *adj.* **1** not showing critical judgment. **2** of an illness, not becoming critical or dangerous.

ac•ro•bat ['ækrə,bæt] *n.* a person who can perform on a trapeze, turn handsprings, walk on a tightrope, etc. ⟨< F *acrobate* < Gk. *akrobatēs* < *akros* tip (of the toes) + *-batos* going⟩

ac•ro•bat•ic [,ækrə'bætɪk] *adj.* **1** of an acrobat. **2** like an acrobat's. **—,ac•ro'bat•i•cal•ly,** *adv.*

ac•ro•bat•ics [,ækrə'bætɪks] *n.pl.* **1** the skills or performance of an acrobat. **2** feats like those of an acrobat.

ac•ro•gen ['ækrədʒən] *n.* any flowerless plant in which growth occurs only from the tip of the main stem, such as a fern or moss. ⟨< Gk. *akros* tip + E *-gen* growth < F < Gk. *-genēs* born⟩

a•cro•le•in [ə'krouliɪn] *n.* a colourless, poisonous liquid that is used as a tear gas. *Formula*: C_3H_4O ⟨< L *acer, acris* sharp + *olere* to smell + E *-in*⟩

ac•ro•lith ['ækrə,lɪθ] *n.* a wooden statue, usually early Greek, with hands, head, and feet of stone. ⟨< L *acrolithus* < Gk. *akrolithos* with stone extremities < *ákros* tip + *lithos* stone⟩

ac•ro•me•gal•ic [,ækroumə'gælɪk] *adj.* **1** having to do with acromegaly. **2** affected with acromegaly.

ac•ro•meg•a•ly [,ækrou'mɛgəli] *n.* a disease caused by abnormal activity of the pituitary gland, in which the head, hands, and feet become permanently enlarged. ⟨< F *acromégalie* < Gk. *ákros* tip + *megas, -galou* big⟩

a•cro•mi•on [ə'kroumiən] *n.* the outward end of the scapula. ⟨< Gk. *akrómion*⟩

a•cron•i•cal or **a•cron•y•cal** [ə'krɒnɪkəl] *adj. Astronomy.* taking place at sunset. ⟨< Gk. *ákros* tip + *nyx* night⟩

ac•ro•nym ['ækrə,nɪm] *n.* a word formed from the first letters or syllables of other words, such as radar (RAdio Detecting And Ranging), snafu (Situation Normal–All Fouled Up), and UNESCO (United Nations Educational, Scientific, and Cultural Organization). ⟨< Gk. *akros* tip + dial. *onoma* name⟩ **—,ac•ro'nym•ic,** *adj.*

ac•ro•pet•al [ə'krɒpətəl] *adj. Botany.* of a plant, growing from the base upwards.

ac•ro•phobe ['ækrə,foub] *n.* one who has acrophobia.

ac•ro•pho•bi•a [,ækrə'foubiə] *n. Psychiatry.* extreme, irrational fear of high places. ⟨< Gk. *akros* tip + *phobia* < *phobos* fear⟩

a•crop•o•lis [ə'krɒpəlɪs] *n.* **1** the fortified hill in the centre of an ancient Greek city, which served as its religious centre as well as its fortress. **2 the Acropolis,** the fortified hill of Athens, on which the Parthenon was built. ⟨< Gk. *akropolis* < *akros* topmost, outermost + *polis* city⟩

ac•ro•spire ['ækrou,spaɪr] *n.* the primary bud of germinating grain. ⟨< dial. *akerspire* < OE *æhher* ear' + *spir* spire'⟩

a•cross [ə'krɒs] *prep., adv.* —*prep.* **1** from one side to the other of; to the other side of; over: *a bridge laid across a river. She drew a line across the page.* **2** on the other side of; beyond: *lands across the sea.* **3** on top of and at an angle to: *She laid the board across the sawhorses. He put the coat across the back of a chair.*
across country, by way of fields, woods, etc., ignoring the roads: *We followed the winding road for 2 km and then struck out across country.*
—*adv.* **1** from one side to the other: *What is the distance across?* **2** on or to the other side: *He ran across without looking where he was going.*
come across. See COME.
get across. See GET.
put across. See PUT. ⟨< *a-* on, in + *cross*⟩

a•cross–the–board [ə'krɒs ðə 'bɔrd] *adj.* affecting all members of a group; all-embracing: *The contract called for across-the-board raises in pay.*

across the line or **lines** *Cdn.* in or to the U.S.

An acrostic of *news*

a•cros•tic [ə'krɒstɪk] *n., adj. —n.* a composition in verse or an arrangement of words in which the first, last, or certain other letters in each line, taken in order, spell a word or phrase.
—adj. in the form of an acrostic. ⟨< L < Gk. *akrostichis* < *akros* tip + *stichos* row⟩

ac•ro•tism ['ækrə,tɪzəm] *n.* weakness of the pulse. ⟨*a-*[4] + Gk. *krotos* beat + *-ism*⟩

ac•ryl•ate ['ækrə,leit] *n.* a salt or ester of acrylic acid.

acrylate resin ACRYLIC RESIN.

a•cryl•ic [ə'krɪlɪk] *adj., n. —adj.* of or having to do with ACRYLIC ACID or its derivatives.
—n. **1** an ACRYLIC RESIN. **2** a paint made with an acrylic resin base. **3** a painting done with such paints: *We bought one of her latest acrylics.* **4** an acrylic textile fibre or fabric. ⟨< *acr(olein)* + *-yl* + *-ic*⟩

acrylic acid an unsaturated organic acid in the form of a colourless liquid, from which acrylic resins are derived by polymerization. *Formula*: CH_2:COOH

acrylic fibre any of various strong, lightweight, synthetic textile fibres made by polymerizing acrylonitrile, used especially for knitwear, pile fabrics, and carpets.

acrylic resin any of a group of transparent, colourless thermoplastics made by polymerizing acrylic acid or derivatives of it, used especially in sheet form for windows, etc. and in the manufacture of paints, rubber, and adhesives.

ac•ry•lo•ni•trile [,ækrəlou'nəitrɪl] *n.* a colourless, volatile liquid used in the manufacture of acrylic textile fibres, synthetic rubber, and thermoplastics. It is poisonous and known to cause cancer. *Formula*: CH_2:CHCN

act [ækt] *n., v. —n.* **1** something done; a deed: *an act of kindness. Slapping his face was a childish act.* **2** the process of doing: *He was caught in the act of stealing.* **3** a main division of a play or opera. **4** one of several performances on a program: *the trained dog's act.* **5** a legislative decision; law. An **Act of Parliament** is a bill that has been passed by Parliament.
6 *Informal.* a display of affected or pretended behaviour: *Her bad temper was just an act and failed to convince anyone.*
clean up (one's) **act,** improve one's behaviour.
get into the act, *Informal.* to take part; join in: *Suddenly the new dance caught on and everyone was getting into the act.*
get (one's) **act together,** organize oneself in order to operate more effectively.
put on an act, put on a show of faked emotion; dissemble, especially to impress.
—v. **1** do something: *The firefighters acted promptly and saved the house.* **2** behave: *to act like a fool, to act generously.* **3** behave like; pretend to be: *Most people act the fool now and then. Just keep your mouth shut and act wise.* **4** have an effect or influence: *Yeast acts on dough and makes it rise.* **5** play (a part); perform in a play, film, or television program. **6** serve or function (*as*): *She acted as interpreter at the conference. The foam acts as insulation.* **7** serve as representative or substitute (*for*): *She is acting for the board of directors in this matter.* **8** act in accordance with; follow or obey (*used with* **on**): *He said he would act on their advice.* **9** conduct oneself as if playing a role: *She is always acting, even when she isn't on stage.* **10** of a play or role, appropriate for performance: *After years of writing, the playwright created a play that acted.*
act out, a represent in actions, as in mime: *Charades is a game in which titles or sayings are acted out.* **b** *Psychiatry.* express (subconscious feelings, attitudes, etc.) in overt actions, without awareness of the cause: *Disturbed children sometimes act out the antisocial feelings of their elders.*
act up, *Informal.* **a** behave badly: *They left when their son started acting up.* **b** be troublesome: *The knee I hurt last summer is acting up again.* ⟨ME < OF *acte,* n., < L *actus* a doing, *actum* (thing) done < *agere* do⟩ **—'act•a•ble,** *adj.*

☛ *Usage.* In the sense 'behave', **act** can be followed by an adverb or by certain adjectives: *He sometimes acts foolishly. He acts older than he is.*

ACTH a hormone obtained from the pituitary gland, used in treating arthritis, rheumatic fever, etc. ⟨*a*dreno- *c*ortico- *t*rophic *h*ormone⟩

ac•tin ['æktɪn] *n.* a globulin in the plasma of muscles which causes contraction. ⟨< L *actus* action, movement + *-in*⟩

ac•ti•nal ['æktɪnəl] *or* [æk'taɪnəl] *adj.* having rays. ⟨< Gk. *aktis, -tinos* ray⟩

act•ing ['æktɪŋ] *adj., v., n. —adj.* temporarily taking another's place and doing his or her duties: *While the principal was sick, one of the teachers was acting principal.*
—v. ppr. of ACT.
—n. the art or profession of being an actor in plays, films, etc.: *After her success in the high school play, she decided to go into acting.*

ac•tin•i•a [æk'tɪniə] *n.* a sea anemone. ⟨< Gk. *aktis, -tinos* ray⟩

ac•tin•ic [æk'tɪnɪk] *adj.* **1** of actinism. **2** producing chemical changes by radiation. Actinic rays are important in photography. ⟨< Gk. *aktis, -tinos* ray⟩

ac•tin•ide ['æktɪ,naɪd] *n.* any chemical element belonging to the series having the atomic numbers 90 through 103. All actinides are naturally radioactive.

ac•tin•ism ['æktə,nɪzəm] *n.* the property of any form of radiation of being able to produce chemical changes.

ac•tin•i•um [æk'tɪniəm] *n.* a radioactive, metallic chemical element resembling radium, found in pitchblende after uranium has been extracted. *Symbol*: Ac; *at.no.* 89; *at.mass* (227); *half-life* 21.7 years. ⟨< NL < Gk. *aktis, -tinos* ray⟩

ac•ti•nom•e•ter [,æktə'nɒmətər] *n.* an instrument for measuring the intensity of radiation, especially from the sun. ⟨< Gk. *aktis, -tinos* ray + E *-meter*⟩

ac•ti•no•my•cete [,æktɪnou'məisit] *n.* any of several soil bacteria having a radial structure. ⟨< NL < Gk. *aktis, -tinos* ray + *myketes*, pl. of *mykes* mushroom⟩

ac•ti•no•my•co•sis [,æktɪnouməɪ'kousɪs] *n.* a bone infection in people and animals in which tumours may also appear, particularly in the jaw. It is caused by actinomycetes.

ac•tin•on ['æktə,nɒn] *n.* a radioactive isotope of radon. *Symbol*: An; *at.no.* 86; *half-life* 3.92 seconds. ⟨< *actinium*⟩

ac•ti•no–u•ra•ni•um [,æktɪnou jʊ'reiniəm] *n.* a uranium isotope, the first of the actinide series.

ac•ti•no•zo•an [,æktənə'zouən] *n.* anthozoan. ⟨< NL *Actinozoa* < Gk. *aktis, -tinos* ray + *zōia*, pl. of *zōion* animal⟩

ac•tion ['ækʃən] *n.* **1** the process of doing something or the state of being active or in operation: *to put a machine into action.* **2** habitual activity, especially when characterized by energy or initiative: *a man of action.* **3** something done; act. **4 actions,** *pl.* conduct; behaviour. **5** *Slang.* important or exciting activities or happenings: *to go where the action is.* **6** the effect or influence of a force or thing on something else: *the action of the wind on a ship's sails, the action of a drug.* **7** the way in which something moves or works. **8** the working parts of a machine, instrument, etc. The keys of a piano are part of its action. **9** a minor battle. **10** combat between military forces: *I was in the armed forces but was never in action.* **11** the events forming the story or plot of a play, novel, film, etc.: *Most of the action takes place in a small town in Manitoba.* **12** lawsuit: *to bring an action against someone.* **13** an appearance of movement or activity in a painting, drawing, or sculpture.
take action, begin to act, especially in order to stop or oppose something. ⟨ME < OF < L *actio, -onis* < *agere* do⟩
—'ac•tion•less, *adj.*

☛ *Syn.* **9.** See note at BATTLE.

ac•tion•a•ble ['ækʃənəbəl] *adj.* giving cause for a lawsuit; justifying a lawsuit.

action painting a style of painting in which the random dripping of paint is used to create abstract works, developed from abstract expressionism.

ac•ti•vate ['æktə,veit] *v.* **-vat•ed, -vat•ing. 1** make active. **2** *Physics.* make radioactive. **3** *Chemistry.* make capable of reacting or of speeding up a reaction. **4** purify (sewage) by treating it with air and bacteria. **—,ac•ti'va•tion,** *n.*

activated carbon carbon treated so that molecules of other substances will adhere to its surface.

ac•ti•va•tor ['æktə,veitər] *n.* **1** something that activates. **2** *Chemistry.* catalyst.

ac•tive ['æktɪv] *adj., n. —adj.* **1** capable of acting or reacting: *an active volcano.* **2** moving much or quickly; lively or brisk: *an active child.* **3** marked by much or constant activity: *an active stock market.* **4** taking an effective part; participating: *She's an active member of the organization.* **5** real or effective: *an active interest in sports.* **6** in present use: *an active file.* **7** causing action or change: *an active ingredient.* **8** *Grammar.* of or designating a form (called the VOICE) of a verb that shows the grammatical subject of a clause as the logical subject and the agent of the action expressed in the verb. In *She broke the window, broke* is active; the subject *she* performs the action represented by the verb *broke.* Compare PASSIVE (def. 3). **9** of a verb, referring to an action rather than a state. *Throw* is an active verb, but *be* is not. **10** requiring work or activity.
—n. **1** *Grammar.* **a** the active voice. **b** a verb in the active voice. **2** a member of an organization who takes an effective part in its activities. ⟨ME < OF *actif* < L *activus* < *agere* act⟩ **—'ac•tive•ly,** *adv.* **—'ac•tive•ness,** *n.*

active immunity immunity in an organism due to the presence of antibodies produced by the organism itself.

active list a list of officers serving in the armed forces or available for service.

active service or **duty** **1** military service with full pay and regular duties. **2** service in the armed forces in time of war.

ac•tiv•ism ['æktə,vɪzəm] *n.* a doctrine or policy of direct, vigorous action or confrontation in supporting one's own point of view on a controversial social or political issue.

ac•tiv•ist ['æktəvɪst] *n., adj. —n.* a person who practises activism.
—adj. of or having to do with activism or activists.

ac•tiv•i•ty [æk'tɪvəti] *n., pl.* **-ties. 1** the state of being active; movement; use of power: *physical activity, mental activity.* **2** action; doing: *the activities of enemy spies.* **3** vigorous action; liveliness: *no activity in the market.* **4** a thing to do: *Students who have too many outside activities may find it hard to keep up with their studies.* **5** anything active; active force. **6** *Chemistry.* **a** the ability to be changed by the chemical reaction of other substances. **b** the effective concentration of a given substance in a chemical system.

activity series *Chemistry.* a list of metals in order of the degree to which they are able to take the place of other metals in solution.

ac•tiv•ize ['æktɪ,vaiz] *v.* **-ized, -iz•ing.** activate.

act of God something that could not be foreseen or prevented by human beings; a happening beyond a person's control. Floods, storms, and earthquakes are called acts of God.

Act of Union an act of the British Parliament, passed in 1840, to unite the provinces of Upper and Lower Canada.

ac•to•my•o•sin [,æktou'maiousɪn] *n.* a protein that is part of muscles and helps to cause contraction. It is a complex of actin and myasin.

ac•tor ['æktər] *n.* **1** a person who acts on the stage, in motion pictures, on radio, or on television. **2** any person who does something or takes part in something.
bad actor, *Informal.* a person, animal, or thing that is always misbehaving: *That horse is a bad actor.*

ACTRA Award ['æktrə] one of several awards presented annually by the Association of Canadian Television and Radio Artists for excellence in broadcasting.

ac•tu•al ['æktʃuəl] *adj.* **1** existing as a fact; real: *What he told us was not a dream but an actual happening.* **2** now existing; present; current: *the actual state of affairs.* ⟨ME < OF < LL *āctuālis* < L *actus* a doing. See ACT.⟩ **—'ac•tu•al•ness,** *n.*
☛ *Syn.* **1.** See note at REAL[1].

ac•tu•al•i•ty [,æktʃu'æləti] *n., pl.* **-ties. 1** actual existence; reality. **2** an actual thing; fact.

ac•tu•al•ize ['æktʃuə,laɪz] *or* ['æktʃə,laɪz] *v.* **-ized, -iz•ing. 1** make actual; realize in action or as a fact. **2** portray in a realistic manner. **—,ac•tu•al•i•'za•tion,** *n.*

ac•tu•al•ly ['æktʃuəli], ['æktʃəli], *or* ['ækʃəlɪ] *adv.* really; in fact: *Are you actually going abroad this summer?*

ac•tu•ar•i•al [,æktʃu'ɛriəl] *adj.* **1** of actuaries or their work. **2** determined by actuaries.

ac•tu•ar•y ['æktʃu,ɛri] *n., pl.* **-ar•ies.** a person whose work involves figuring risks, rates, premiums, etc. for insurance companies. ⟨< L *actuarius* account keeper < *actus* a doing. See ACT.⟩

ac•tu•ate ['æktʃu,eit] *v.* **-at•ed, -at•ing. 1** put into action: *This pump is actuated by a belt driven by an electric motor.* **2** influence to act: *He was actuated by love for his father.* ⟨< LL *actuare* < L *actus* a doing. See ACT.⟩ **—,ac•tu'a•tion,** *n.* **—'ac•tu,a•tor,** *n.*
☛ *Syn.* See note at MOVE.

ac•u•ate ['ækjuɪt] *or* ['ækju,eit] *adj. Botany.* having a sharp point. ⟨< L *acus* needle + *-ate*[1]⟩

a•cu•i•ty [ə'kjuəti] *n.* sharpness; acuteness. ⟨< Med.L *acuitas,* ult. < L *acus* needle⟩

a•cu•le•ate [ə'kjuliət] *or* [ə'kjuli,eit] *adj. Botany.* having an aculeus.

a•cu•le•us [ə'kjuliəs] *n. Biology.* **1** a sting. **2** a prickle. ⟨< L *acus* a needle⟩

a•cu•men ['ækjəmən] *or* [ə'kjumən] *n.* sharpness and quickness in seeing and understanding; keen insight, as, for example, in business. ⟨< L *acumen* < *acuere* sharpen⟩

a•cu•mi•nate [ə'kjumənɪt] *or* [ə'kjumə,neit] *adj., v.* **-nat•ed, -nat•ing.** *—adj.* pointed: *a leaf with an acuminate tip.*
—v. bring to a sharp point. ⟨< L *acuminatus,* pp. of *acuminare* point < *acumen.* See ACUMEN.⟩

ac•u•pres•sure ['ækju,prɛʃər] *n.* the application of outside pressure to pressure points on the body, instead of the needles used in acupuncture.

ac•u•punc•ture ['ækju,pʌŋktʃər] *n.* a method of relieving pain and treating disease by inserting fine needles into the body at specific points. Acupuncture has been used in the Far East for thousands of years. **—'ac•u,punc•tur•ist,** *n.*

a•cute [ə'kjut] *adj., n. —adj.* **1** having a sharp point. **2** sharp and severe: *A toothache can cause acute pain.* **3** brief and severe: *An acute disease like pneumonia reaches a crisis within a short time.* **4** keen: *Dogs have an acute sense of smell. An acute thinker is clever and shrewd.* **5** high in pitch; shrill: *Some sounds are so acute that we cannot hear them.* **6** critical; urgent: *Their situation became acute when their food supplies were exhausted.* **7** of a vowel, having an ACUTE ACCENT over it. **8** *Geometry.* less than 90°. **9** of or having to do with special care given to seriously ill patients in a hospital; intensive.
—n. an ACUTE ACCENT. ⟨< L *acutus,* pp. of *acuere* sharpen⟩ **—a'cute•ly,** *adv.* **—a'cute•ness,** *n.*
☛ *Syn.* **4.** See note at SHARP.

acute accent **1** a mark (´) written or printed to show the spoken quality of a particular letter in a word. An acute accent placed over an e in French indicates that it is pronounced something like the beginning of the English [ei] sound. **2** a mark (´) used to indicate emphasis or stress in pronunciation.

acute angle an angle less than 90°.

A.C.W. aircraftwoman.

-acy *suffix.* state: *delicacy, papacy.*

a•cy•clic [,ei'saiklɪk] *adj.* **1** not cyclic. **2** *Chemistry.* in the form of an open chain.

a•cy•clo•vir [ei'saiklə,vir] *n.* a drug used to treat certain viral infections. *Formula:* $C_{18}H_{11}N_5O_3$

ad [æd] *n.* **1** *Informal.* advertisement. **2** *Tennis.* ADVANTAGE (def. 3).
☛ *Usage.* **Ad** is the clipped form of *advertisement,* has only one *d,* and should not be followed by a period.

ad– *prefix.* to or toward, as in *admit, administer, adverb, advert.* Also: **a-** before *sc, sp, st;* **ab-** before *b;* **ac-** before *c, q;* **af-** before *f;* **ag-** before *g;* **al** before *l;* **an-** before *n;* **ap-** before *p;* **ar-** before *r;* **as-** before *s;* **at-** before *t.* ⟨< L *ad-* < *ad,* prep.⟩

–ad *suffix.* **1** a group with a certain number of members: *triad.* **2** an epic poem: *the Iliad.*

A.D. in the year of the Lord; since Christ was born (for LL *anno Domini*).

A•da ['eidə] *n. Computer technology.* a high-level computer programming language developed by the U.S. Department of Defense. ⟨after Augusta *Ada* Byron, probably the first female computer scientist, as a result of her involvement with computers in the 19th century⟩

a•dac•ty•lous [ei'dæktələs] *adj.* having no toes or fingers.

ad•age ['ædɪdʒ] *n.* a wise saying that has been much used; well-known proverb. ⟨< F < L *adagium*⟩

a•da•g•i•o [ə'dædʒiou], [ə'dɑdʒou], *or* [ə'dæʒiou] *adv., adj., n., pl.* **-gios.** *Music. —adv.* slowly.
—adj. slow.

—*n.* **1** a slow part in a piece of music. **2** a composition to be played or sung at a slow tempo. **3** *Dance.* a slow dance which emphasizes very difficult steps. **4** *Ballet.* a sequence in the PAS DE DEUX. ⟨< Ital. *ad agio* at ease⟩

Ad•am[1] [ˈædəm] *n.* in the Bible, the first man. With his wife Eve, he was driven from the Garden of Eden for eating the forbidden fruit.
the old Adam, *Christianity.* human tendency to sin.
not to know (someone) **from Adam,** *Informal.* be unable to recognize; be completely unacquainted with (someone).

Adam[2] [ˈædəm] *adj., n.* —*adj.* of, like, or having to do with a graceful, ornamented style of furniture and architecture.
—*n.* **1** this style of furniture or architecture. **2** a piece of furniture or architecture of this style. ⟨after Robert and James *Adam,* 18c. British designers and architects⟩

ad•a•mant [ˈædəmənt] *n., adj.* —*n.* **1** a legendary mineral so hard that it could not be cut or broken: *Adamant was identified at different times with the diamond and lodestone.* **2** any extremely hard substance.
—*adj.* **1** too hard to be cut or broken. **2** unyielding; firm; immovable. ⟨< OF *adamaunt* the hardest stone (= diamond) < L < Gk. *adamas, -antos* < *a-* not + *damaein* conquer, tame⟩ **—ˈad•a•mant•ly,** *adv.* **—ˈad•a•mant•ness,** *n.*

ad•a•man•tine [ˌædəˈmæntin], [ˌædəˈmæntaɪn], *or* [ˌædəˈmæntɪn] *adj.* **1** having a lustre like a diamond. **2** adamant; immovable in opinion.

Adam's ale water.

Adam's apple the lump in the front of the throat of men formed by the thyroid cartilage. See WINDPIPE for picture. ⟨translation of Hebrew *tappūach hā'ādām,* lit. meaning either 'protrusion on (the neck of) a man' or 'fruit of Adam', from the story of the forbidden fruit getting stuck in Adam's throat⟩

Adam's needle yucca.

a•dapt [əˈdæpt] *v.* **1** make or become fit or suitable; adjust: *Can you adapt yourself to a new job? She has adapted well to the new school.* **2** modify or alter for a different use: *The farmer can adapt the barn for use as a garage.* ⟨< L *adaptare* < *ad-* to + *aptare* fit⟩
☛ *Syn.* **1.** See note at ADJUST.
☛ *Usage.* **Adapt** meaning 'make suitable' is followed by the preposition *to*: *His style is not adapted to adults. Adapt* meaning 'modify' is followed by *for* or *from*: *The story was adapted for television. It was adapted from the novel.*

a•dapt•a•bil•i•ty [əˌdæptəˈbɪləti] *n.* the power to change easily to fit different conditions.

a•dapt•a•ble [əˈdæptəbəl] *adj.* easily changed or changing to fit different conditions: *an adaptable schedule, an adaptable person.* **—aˈdapt•a•ble•ness,** *n.*

ad•ap•ta•tion [ˌædæpˈteiʃən] *or* [ˌædəpˈteiʃən] *n.* **1** adapting or being adapted. **2** something made by adapting: *A movie is often an adaptation of a novel.* **3** *Biology.* a change in structure, form, or habits to fit different conditions, or the result of such a change: *Wings are adaptations of the upper limbs for flight.*

a•dapt•er [əˈdæptər] *n.* **1** a person or thing that adapts. **2** a device for fitting together parts that do not match: *An adapter can be used to fit this nozzle onto a larger hose.* **3** a device for changing the function of a machine, apparatus, etc. **4** a separate plug for attaching to the plug of an electrical appliance, etc. in order to adapt it to a different type of outlet: *North American appliances cannot be used in Europe without adapters.* **5** *Computer technology.* See CARD (def. 13). Also, **adaptor.**

a•dap•tive [əˈdæptɪv] *adj.* **1** able to adapt. **2** showing or having to do with adaptation. **—aˈdap•tive•ly,** *adv.* **—aˈdap•tive•ness,** *n.*

adaptive radiation the process through which an organism acquires many different descendants, as a result of growth of the ancestral stock and of adaptation to different environments.

a•dap•tor [əˈdæptər] See ADAPTER.

A•dar [əˈdɑr] *n.* in the Hebrew calendar, the twelfth month of the ecclesiastical year and the sixth month of the civil year, corresponding roughly to February-March in the Gregorian calendar.

A•dar She•ni [əˈdɑr ˈʃeini] a month of the Jewish year occurring every three years and falling between Adar and Nisan; Veadar.

ad•ax•i•al [æˈdæksiəl] *adj. Botany.* **1** in the side of the stem. **2** turned toward the axis, as a leaf toward the stem.

ADC, A.D.C., or **a.d.c.** aide-de-camp.

add [æd] *v.* **1** join (one thing to another); put together; put with: *Add another stone to the pile. Add 8 and 2 and you have 10.* **2** make or form an addition or increase: *The fine weather added to our pleasure.* **3** say further; go on to say or write: *She said goodbye and added that she had had a pleasant visit.* **4** perform arithmetical addition: *The little girl is learning to add and subtract.*
add in, include.
add up, a find the sum of (a column, etc. of numbers).
b *Informal.* make the correct total. **c** *Informal.* make sense; fit together: *There were many clues to the murder, but they just didn't add up.*
add up to, *Informal.* amount to: *Despite all the publicity, the highly touted politician didn't add up to much.* ⟨ME < L *addere* < *ad-* to + *dare* put⟩

add. addenda.

ad•dax [ˈædæks] *n.* a large, heavily built antelope (*Addax nasomaculatus*) of the deserts of N Africa, standing about 105 cm high at the shoulder and having very long, curving, ringed horns. ⟨< L < an African word⟩

added line *Music.* LEDGER LINE.

ad•dend [ˈædɛnd] *or* [əˈdɛnd] *n.* a number or quantity to be added to another number or quantity.

ad•den•da [əˈdɛndə] *n.* pl. of ADDENDUM.

ad•den•dum [əˈdɛndəm] *n., pl.* **-da. 1** a thing to be added. **2** the thing added; appendix. ⟨< L⟩

ad•der[1] [ˈædər] *n.* **1** the common viper (*Vipera berus*), a small poisonous snake of Europe and N Asia, from 45 to 75 cm long, usually having a black zigzag band along its back. It is the only poisonous snake native to Great Britain. **2** any of several vipers found in Africa, including the large, dangerous **puff adder** (*Bitis arietans*) and the small, less dangerous **night adder** (genus *Causus*). **3** Also, **death adder,** a very poisonous snake (*Acanthophis antarcticus*) of Australia, belonging to the same family as cobras and coral snakes, but resembling a viper. **4** Also, **blowing adder,** any of several species (genus *Heterodon*) of harmless snake found in the United States. **5** *Informal.* any snake thought to be poisonous. ⟨OE *nædre*; in ME *a nadder* was taken as *an adder*⟩

add•er[2] [ˈædər] *n.* a person or thing that adds, especially a device or machine that performs addition.

ad•der's–tongue [ˈædərz ˌtʌŋ] *n.* **1** any of various ferns (family Ophioglossaceae) of the northern hemisphere having a spore-bearing body resembling a spike or snake's tongue. **2** DOGTOOTH VIOLET.

add•i•ble [ˈædəbəl] *adj.* that can be added.

ad•dict *n.* [ˈædɪkt]; *v.* [əˈdɪkt] *n., v.* —*n.* **1** a person who is dependent on a drug, especially a narcotic drug, such as morphine or heroin. **2** a person who has given himself or herself up to a habit or obsession: *a movie addict.*
—*v.* cause (oneself or someone) to become dependent or obsessed (*usually used in the passive*): *addicted to heroin, addicted to detective novels.* ⟨< L *addictus,* pp. of *addicere* adjudge, devote < *ad-* to + *dīcere* say⟩

ad•dict•ed [əˈdɪktɪd] *adj., v.* —*adj.* slavishly following (a habit or practice); strongly inclined: *He was addicted to cigars.*
—*v.* pt. and pp. of ADDICT.

ad•dic•tion [əˈdɪkʃən] *n.* the condition of being addicted.

ad•dic•tive [əˈdɪktɪv] *adj.* that causes or tends to cause addiction.

Addison's disease a disease resulting from adrenal failure. The patient becomes extremely weak and anemic, and develops a brownish tinge to the skin. ⟨< Thomas *Addison* (1793-1860), an English physician who identified the disease⟩

ad•di•tion [əˈdɪʃən] *n.* **1** the act or process of adding. **2** the result of adding; something added. **3** a part added to a building.
in addition (to), besides; also. ⟨ME < OF < L *additio, -onis* < *addere.* See ADD.⟩

ad•di•tion•al [əˈdɪʃənəl] *adj.* added; extra; more. **—adˈdi•tion•al•ly,** *adv.*

ad•di•tive [ˈædətɪv] *n., adj.* —*n.* any substance added in small amounts to a product to add or improve certain desirable qualities or to reduce the effects of undesirable ones. Additives are put in processed foods to add a desirable colour, act as a preservative, etc. There are additives in gasoline and fuel oil to increase the efficiency of combustion.
—*adj.* of, having to do with, or involving addition.

additive inverse *Mathematics.* the number which, added to a given number, will equal zero. The additive inverse of −2 is +2.

ad•dle [ˈædəl] *v.* **-dled, -dling;** *adj.* —*v.* **1** make or become

muddled: *The wine has quite addled them.* **2** of eggs, become rotten; spoil.
–adj. **1** muddled; confused (*used only in compounds*): *They called him an addle-pated fool.* **2** of eggs, rotten. ⟨OE *adela* liquid filth⟩

add–on [ˈæd ˌɒn] *n., adj.* *–n.* anything added to a whole.
–adj. added to a whole.

ad•dress [əˈdrɛs]; *also, for n. defs. 1-4,* [ˈædrɛs] *n., v.* *–n.* **1** the place at which a person, business, etc. may be found or reached: *Send the letter to her business address.* **2** the writing on an envelope, package, etc. that shows where it is to be sent: *The letter was returned because the address was incomplete.* **3** a location or place, especially with reference to its social desirability: *It's a very good address.* **4** *Computer technology.* a code label representing the exact location of a piece of data stored in a computer memory. **5** a speech, especially a formal one: *The prime minister gave a television address.* **6** manner in conversation: *She was a person of pleasant address.* **7** skill: *The new manager shows much address in getting people to help him.* **8** a formal request to those in authority to do a particular thing: *an address from the colonists to the king, listing grievances.*
9 addresses, *pl.* attentions paid in courtship.
–v. **1** direct speech or writing to: *The Queen addressed Parliament.* **2** use titles or other forms in speaking or writing to: *How do you address a mayor?* **3** write on (a letter, package, etc.) the information that shows where it is to be sent. **4** apply (oneself) in speech (*to* a person or group): *He addressed himself to the chairperson.* **5** apply or devote (oneself) (*to*): *She addressed herself to completing the report.* **6** deal with: *to address the problem at hand.* **7** direct to the attention: *to address a warning to a friend.* **8 a** *Golf.* prepare for a stroke by placing the head of a club behind (the ball). **b** *Archery.* face (the target). **9** *Computer technology.* assign (information) to a particular computer memory location or access it afterward by using the code label. ⟨ME < OF *adresser*, v. (noun partly < F *adresse*), earlier *adrecier* < VL *addirectaire* < L *ad-* to + *directus* straight⟩ **–adˈdress•er** or **adˈdres•sor,** *n.*

☛ *Syn. n.* **5.** See note at SPEECH.

☛ *Usage.* **Addresses.** When the various parts of a person's address are written on the same line, they are separated by commas: *Send the money to Miss Louise Finney, 48 Pine St., Kingston, Ontario.*

ad•dress•ee [ˌædrɛˈsi] *or* [əˌdrɛsˈi] *n.* the person to whom a letter, package, etc. is addressed.

Ad•dres•so•graph [əˈdrɛsəˌgræf] *n. Trademark.* a machine for addressing envelopes.

ad•duce [əˈdjus] *or* [əˈdus] *v.* **-duced, -duc•ing.** give as a reason, proof, or example; cite: *The author has adduced some convincing data in support of her argument.* ⟨< L *adducere* < *ad-* to + *ducere* lead⟩ **–adˈduc•i•ble,** *adj.*

ad•du•cent [əˈdjusənt] *or* [əˈdusənt] *adj.* adducting.

ad•duct [əˈdʌkt] *v.* of a muscle or group of muscles, serve to draw (a limb, etc.) toward or beyond the median axis of the body or of one of its parts. Compare ABDUCT. ⟨< L *adductus*, pp. of *adducere.* See ADDUCE.⟩

ad•duc•tion [əˈdʌkʃən] *n.* **1** the act of adducing; the bringing forward of proof, evidence, etc. **2** the act of adducting or the state of being adducted: *the adduction of the fingers of the hand.*

ad•duc•tive [əˈdʌktɪv] *adj.* **1** adducent. **2** of or relating to ADDUCTION (def. 2).

ad•duc•tor [əˈdʌktər] *n.* any muscle whose function is to draw a limb, etc. toward the median axis of the body or one of its parts. Compare ABDUCTOR.

–ade *suffix.* **1** the act, means, or result of: *blockade, fusillade.* **2** a drink made from: *lemonade.* **3** a group involved in a joint effort: *cavalcade.*

aden– *combining form.* of a gland: *adenocarcinoma.* ⟨< Gk. *aden* gland⟩

ad•e•nine [ˈædəˌnin], [ˈædənɪn], *or* [ˈædəˌnaɪn] *n.* a purine base found in all living tissue and forming part of DNA, RNA, and ADP. *Formula*: $C_5H_5N_5$

ad•e•ni•tis [ˌædəˈnəitɪs] *n.* inflammation of any of the glands.

ad•e•noid [ˈædəˌnɔɪd] *or* [ˈædˌnɔɪd] *adj., n.* *–adj.* **1** lymphoid. **2** like a gland; glandular.
–n. See ADENOIDS.

ad•e•noi•dal [ædəˈnɔɪdəl] *or* [ædˈnɔɪdəl] *adj.* **1** adenoid. **2** having ADENOIDS (def. 2). **3** typical of a person affected with ADENOIDS (def. 2): *adenoidal breathing.*

ad•e•noid•ec•to•my [ˌædənɔɪˈdɛktəmi] *n.* surgical removal of the adenoids.

ad•e•noids [ˈædəˌnɔɪdz] *or* [ˈædnɔɪdz] *n.pl.* **1** normal lymphoid tissue in the upper part of the throat, just behind the nose, that usually shrinks and disappears in childhood, but sometimes swells and gets in the way of natural breathing and speaking. **2** swollen adenoids: *He had adenoids as a child.* ⟨< Gk. *adenoeidēs* < *adēn* gland, acorn⟩

ad•e•no•ma [ˌædəˈnoumə] *n.* **1** a tumour originating in a gland. **2** a tumour resembling a gland. ⟨< Gk. *adēn* gland + *-ōma*⟩ **–ˌad•eˈnom•a•tous** [ˌædəˈnɒmətəs], *adj.*

a•den•o•sine [əˈdɛnəˌsin] *or* [əˈdɛnəsɪn] *n.* a nucleoside whose constituents are adenine and ribose, present in all living cells in the form of a white crystalline powder. *Formula*: $C_{10}H_{13}N_5O_4$

adenosine diphosphate ADP, a nucleotide found in all living cells. When energy in the form of ADP which has been converted to ATP is later converted back to ADP, the energy is released and fuels muscular activity, photosynthesis and other vital processes. *Formula*: $C_{10}H_{12}N_5O_3H_3P_2O_7$

adenosine monophosphate AMP, a nucleotide derived from ATP, present in all living tissue and active in various cellular processes. *Formula*: $C_{10}H_{14}N_5O_7P$

adenosine triphosphate ATP, a nucleotide found in all living cells which is a source of energy for various vital processes. *Formula*: $C_{10}H_{12}N_5O_4H_4P_3O_9$

ad•en•o•sis [ˌædəˈnousɪs] *n.* any glandular disorder. ⟨< Gk. *aden* gland + *osis*⟩

ad•en•o•vi•rus [ˌædənouˈvaɪrəs] *n.* any of numerous viruses causing respiratory disease in humans.

ad•ept *n.* [ˈædɛpt] *or* [əˈdɛpt]; *adj.* [əˈdɛpt] *n., adj.* *–n.* a thoroughly skilled or expert person.
–adj. thoroughly skilled; expert. ⟨< L *adeptus*, pp. of *adipisci* attain < *ad-* to + *apisci* get⟩ **–aˈdept•ly,** *adv.* **–aˈdept•ness,** *n.*

ad•e•qua•cy [ˈædəkwəsi] *n.* the quality or state of being adequate; sufficiency.

ad•e•quate [ˈædəkwɪt] *adj.* **1** as much as is needed; sufficient: *His wages are adequate to support three people.* **2** suitable; competent: *an adequate person for the job.* ⟨< L *adaequātus*, pp. of *adaequāre* < *ad-* to + *aequus* equal⟩ **–ˈad•e•quate•ly,** *adv.* **–ˈad•e•quate•ness,** *n.*

☛ *Syn.* **1.** See note at ENOUGH.

à deux [aˈdφ] *French.* **1** for two. **2** intimate.

ad ex•tre•mum [ˌæd ɛksˈtriməm] **1** to or at the last extremity. **2** ultimately; in the end; at long last. ⟨< L⟩

ad•han [əˈdɑn] *n.* the Muslim call to prayer, uttered by a MUEZZIN, immediately before each of the five daily prayers. ⟨< Arabic⟩

ADHD attention deficit hyperactivity disorder.

ad•here [ædˈhir] *v.* **-hered, -her•ing.** **1** stick fast; remain attached *(to)*: *Mud adheres to your shoes.* **2** hold closely or firmly (*to*): *to adhere to a plan.* **3** be devoted (*to*): *Many people adhere to the religion of their parents.* ⟨< L *adhaerere* < *ad-* to + *haerere* stick⟩ **–adˈher•er,** *n.*

☛ *Syn.* **1.** See note at STICK[2].

ad•her•ence [ædˈhirəns] *n.* **1** an attachment or loyalty (to a person, group, belief, etc.); faithfulness. **2** a holding to and following closely: *rigid adherence to rules.*

ad•her•ent [ædˈhirənt] *n., adj.* *–n.* a faithful supporter; follower.
–adj. **1** sticking fast; attached. **2** *Botany.* congenitally attached. **–adˈher•ent•ly,** *adv.*

☛ *Syn. n.* See note at FOLLOWER.

☛ *Usage.* **Adherent.** The preposition used with the noun **adherent** is *of*: *She was an adherent of the Liberal Party.*

ad•he•sion [ædˈhiʒən] *n.* **1** the action of sticking fast or joining or the state of being stuck or joined together. **2** a steady or devoted attachment; faithfulness. **3** an agreement; assent. **4** *Physics.* the attraction between the molecules of different substances. Capillary attraction, which causes the surface of water to rise against the inside of a glass tube, is the result of adhesion between the liquid and the solid. Compare COHESION. **5** *Medicine.* **a** the growing together of tissues that should be separate, usually as a result of inflammation. **b** tissues abnormally joined in this way. **6** an adhering object. ⟨< L *adhaesio, -onis* < *adhaerere.* See ADHERE.⟩

ad•he•sive [ædˈhisɪv], [ædˈhizɪv] *or Informal* [əˈdizɪv] *adj., n.* *–adj.* **1** holding fast; adhering easily; sticky. **2** smeared with a sticky substance for holding something fast: *adhesive tape.*
–n. any substance, such as paste or gum, used to stick things together. **–adˈhe•sive•ly,** *adv.* **–adˈhe•sive•ness,** *n.*

ad hoc [ˈæd ˈhɒk] for or concerned with a particular purpose or case, without general application: *An ad hoc committee was appointed to discuss the problem. The decision was made ad hoc.* ⟨< L *ad hoc* for this⟩

ad hock•er•y ['æd 'hɒkəri] *n. Slang.* the act or practice of making decisions, rules, etc. on an ad hoc basis, without considering wider applications or implications. Also, **ad hocery.**

ad ho•mi•nem ['æd 'hɒmənəm] *Latin.* **1** appealing to personal prejudices, interests, etc. **2** attacking a person's character rather than replying to his or her arguments. ⟨*literally*, to the man⟩

ad•i•a•bat•ic [,ædiə'bætɪk] *adj. Physics.* of or involving expansion or contraction without gain or loss of heat: *the adiabatic expansion of air.* ⟨< Gk. *adiābatos,* not passable⟩ **—,ad•i•a'bat•i•cal•ly,** *adv.*

ad•i•aph•o•rous [,ædi'æfərəs] *or* [,ædaɪ'æfərəs] *adj.* **1** neutral. **2** *Medicine.* neither helpful nor harmful. ⟨< Gk. *adiáphoros* not different⟩

a•dieu [ə'dju] *or* [ə'du]; *French,* [a'djφ] *interj. or n., pl.* **a•dieus** or **a•dieux** [ə'djuz] *or* [ə'duz]; *French,* [a'djφ] goodbye; farewell. ⟨ME < OF *a dieu* to God⟩
☛ *Hom.* ADO [ə'du].

ad in•fi•ni•tum ['æd ,ɪnfə'naitəm] without limit; endlessly. ⟨< L⟩

ad i•ni•ti•um ['æd ɪ'nɪʃiəm] at the beginning. ⟨< L⟩

ad in•te•rim ['æd 'ɪntərɪm] for or in the meantime; temporary. ⟨< L⟩

ad•i•pose ['ædə,pous] *adj., n. —adj.* **1** of or having to do with animal fat; fatty: *adipose tissue.* **2** fat.
—n. the fat found in fatty tissue. ⟨< NL *adiposus* < L *adeps* fat⟩ **—'ad•i,pose•ness,** *n.*

ad•i•pos•i•ty [,ædə'pɒsəti] *n.* **1** an adipose condition; fatness. **2** a tendency to become fat.

ad•it ['ædɪt] *n.* **1** an approach; entrance. **2** a nearly horizontal entrance to a mine. **3** admission; access. ⟨< L *aditus* < *adire* approach < *ad-* to + *ire* go⟩

adj. **1** adjective; adjectival. **2** adjunct. **3** adjustment. **4** adjacent. **5** adjourned.

Adj. adjutant.

ad•ja•cen•cy [ə'dʒeisənsi] *n., pl.* **-cies.** nearness; a being adjacent.

ad•ja•cent [ə'dʒeisənt] *adj.* lying near or close; adjoining: *The house adjacent to ours has been sold.* ⟨ME < L *adjacens, -entis,* ppr. of *adjacere* < *ad-* near + *jacere* to lie. Doublet of EASE.⟩ **—ad'ja•cent•ly,** *adv.*

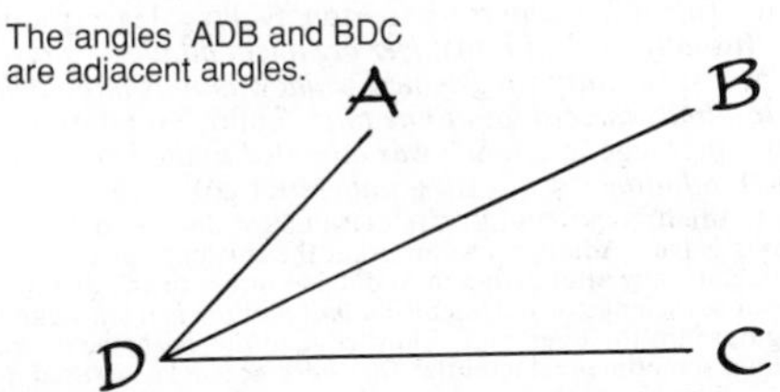

adjacent angles *Mathematics.* two angles that have the same vertex and the same line for one of their sides.

ad•jec•ti•val [,ædʒɪk'taivəl] *or* ['ædʒɪk,tɪvəl] *adj., n. —adj.* **1** of or having to do with an adjective. The ending *-like* in *childlike* is an adjectival suffix. **2** used as an adjective. The form *toy* in *toy poodle* is an adjectival use of the noun *toy.*
—n. a word or group of words used as an adjective. **—,ad•jec'ti•val•ly,** *adv.*

ad•jec•tive ['ædʒɪktɪv] *n., adj. —n.* a class of words that limit or add to the meaning of nouns. *Examples*: a *blue* shirt, a *powerful* car.
—adj. **1** of an adjective. **2** used as an adjective. *Abbrev.*: adj. or a. ⟨ME < LL *adjectivus* that which is added to < *adjicere, -jectum* put near < *ad-* to + *jacere* throw⟩ **—'ad•jec•tive•ly,** *adv.*
☛ *Usage.* **Adjectives. a forms of adjectives.** Many English adjectives are made by the addition of a suffix to a noun or verb. Some of these suffixes such as *-some* (as in *winsome*) are no longer active. Among those still in use to make new words are: *-able* (*-ible*), as in *eatable, dirigible,* and *-ed* as in *sugared, four-footed, well-lighted*; *-escent*, as in *florescent*; *-ese*, as in *Chinese*; *-ful*, as in *playful, soulful*; *-ish*, as in *babyish, cattish, womanish*; *-less*, as in *harmless, fearless*; *-like*, as in *birdlike*; *-ly*, as in *motherly, kingly*; *-y*, as in *cranky, dreamy, corny.* **b position of adjectives.** According to its use in a sentence, an adjective is attributive, appositive, or predicative. In English, **attributive adjectives** ordinarily stand immediately before the word they modify, as in *the tiny brook, horseless carriages*; but in certain phrases attributive adjectives may come after the noun: *the day following, his lady fair*, etc. **Appositive adjectives** follow the word they describe, and they are placed between commas: *The boy, weary and discouraged, went to sleep.* **Predicate adjectives** are used with some form of the verb *be* or some other linking verb (*taste, feel, turn*, etc.): *The day has turned warm. The train was crowded. That pie smells good. For a while I felt bad.* **c comparison of adjectives.** Degrees of the quality named by an adjective are shown by adding *-er* or *-est* to the adjective or by placing *more* or *most* before it: *warm, warmer, warmest; learned, more learned, most learned. More* and *most* are used with most adjectives of two syllables and all adjectives of three syllables or more.

adjl. adjectival.

ad•join [ə'dʒɔɪn] *v.* **1** be next to; be in contact with: *Canada adjoins the United States.* **2** be next to or close to each other; be in contact: *These two countries adjoin.* ⟨ME < OF *ajoindre* < L *adjungere* < *ad-* to + *jungere* join⟩

ad•join•ing [ə,dʒɔɪnɪŋ] *adj., v. —adj.* being next to or in contact with another; bordering: *adjoining rooms.*
—v. ppr. of ADJOIN.

ad•journ [ə'dʒɜrn] *v.* **1** suspend or break off for a time; especially, stop at the end of a session: *The judge adjourned the court for two hours. The meeting was adjourned at 10 o'clock.* **2** stop business or proceedings for a time: *The court adjourned for the weekend.* **3** *Informal.* go to another place to do something different: *After the meeting we adjourned to the cafeteria.* ⟨ME < OF *ajorner* < *a-* for (< L *ad-*) + *jorn* day < LL *diurnum* < L *diurnum* (neut.) daily < *dies* day⟩

ad•journ•ment [ə'dʒɜrnmənt] *n.* **1** an adjourning or being adjourned. **2** the time during which a court, legislature, etc. is adjourned.

Adjt. adjutant.

ad•judge [ə'dʒʌdʒ] *v.* **-judged, -judg•ing. 1** decree or declare by law: *The accused woman was adjudged guilty.* **2** decide or settle by law; judge: *The boy's case was adjudged in the juvenile court.* **3** award or assign by law: *The property was adjudged to the rightful owner.* ⟨ME < OF *ajugier* < L *adjudicare* < *ad-* to + *judicare* judge. Doublet of ADJUDICATE.⟩ **—ad'judg•ment** or **ad'judge•ment,** *n.*

ad•ju•di•cate [ə'dʒudə,keit] *v.* **-cat•ed, -cat•ing. 1** decide or settle by law. **2** act as judge, as in a competition or dispute; pass judgment. ⟨< L *adjudicare.* Doublet of ADJUDGE.⟩

ad•ju•di•ca•tion [ə,dʒudə'keiʃən] *n.* **1** the act or process of adjudicating. **2** a decision of a judge or court.

ad•ju•di•ca•tor [ə'dʒudə,keitər] *n.* a JUDGE (def. 3), often at a competition.

ad•junct ['ædʒʌŋkt] *n., adj. —n.* **1** something added that is less important or not necessary, but helpful. **2** an assistant or associate of a more important person. **3** *Grammar.* a word or phrase that qualifies or modifies another word or phrase. Adjectives, adjectival phrases, adverbs, and adverbial phrases are adjuncts.
—adj. non-essential though part of a whole; part-time or temporary. ⟨< L *adjunctus*, pp. of *adjungere* join to. See ADJOIN.⟩ **—ad'junct•ive,** *adj.*

ad•ju•ra•tion [,ædʒə'reiʃən] *n.* a solemn command; earnest appeal.

ad•jure [ə'dʒur] *v.* **-jured, -jur•ing. 1** command or charge (a person) on oath or under some penalty (to do something). **2** ask earnestly or solemnly: *I adjure you to speak the truth.* ⟨ME < L *adjurare* < *ad-* to + *jurare* swear⟩

ad•just [ə'dʒʌst] *v.* **1** fit or adapt (one thing to another): *to adjust a seat to the right height for a child.* **2** alter or regulate; arrange or set (machinery or controls) to work as required: *to adjust a radio dial.* **3** arrange satisfactorily; set right; settle: *to adjust a difference of opinion.* **4** accommodate oneself; get used (*to*): *We soon adjusted to army life.* **5** decide the amount to be paid in settling (a bill, insurance claim, etc.). ⟨< F *ajuster* < *a-* for (< L *ad-*) + *juste* right < L *justus*⟩ **—ad'just•a•ble,** *adj.*
☛ *Syn.* **1. Adjust,** ADAPT, ACCOMMODATE = suit one thing (or person) to another. **Adjust** emphasizes the idea of matching one thing to another: *I have to adjust my expenditure to my income.* **Adapt** emphasizes the idea of making minor changes in a thing (or person) to make it fit, suit, or fit into something: *I adapted the pattern to the material.* **Accommodate** emphasizes that the things to be fitted together are so different that one must be subordinated to the other: *We should not have to accommodate our beliefs to those of our employer.*

ad•just•er or **ad•jus•tor** [ə'dʒʌstər] *n.* **1** a thing that adjusts something else. **2** a person who adjusts claims, as in insurance.

ad•just•ment [ə'dʒʌstmənt] *n.* **1** the act or process of adjusting. **2** the state of being adjusted. **3** the orderly arrangement of parts or elements. **4** a means of adjusting, especially a mechanism or device to control machinery, etc.: *The radio has separate adjustments for volume and tone.* **5** a settlement of an insurance claim, etc.: *They accepted the adjustment.*

ad•ju•tan•cy ['ædʒətənsi] *n., pl.* **-cies.** the rank or position of an adjutant.

ad•ju•tant ['ædʒətənt] *n.* **1** *Military.* an officer who assists a commanding officer by sending out orders, writing letters, giving messages, etc. **2** helper; assistant. **3** ADJUTANT STORK. ⟨< L *adjutans, -antis,* ppr. of *adjutare* assist, frequentative of *adjuvare* < *ad-* to + *juvare* help⟩

adjutant general *pl.* **adjutants general.** the adjutant of a division or a larger military unit.

adjutant stork either of two very large, carrion-eating storks (*Leptoptilos dubius* and *L. javanicus*) of India and SE Asia closely related to and resembling the African marabou, having grey-and-white plumage, a bare head and neck, and a large pouch of skin at the front of the neck. Also called **adjutant bird.** ⟨named for their stiff-legged, military-style walk⟩

ad lib ['æd 'lɪb] *v.* **-libbed, -lib•bing;** *adv., adj.* *—v. Informal.* make (something) up as one goes along; extemporize.
—adv. freely; on the spur of the moment.
—adj. **ad-lib,** not prepared ahead of time; improvised: *an ad-lib speech.* ⟨< L, shortened form of *ad libitum*⟩

ad lib. ad libitum.

ad lib•i•tum ['æd'lɪbɪtəm] **1** to any extent; without restriction. **2** *Music.* an instruction to change, omit, or expand a passage as the performer wishes. *Abbrev.*: ad lib. ⟨< NL *ad libitum* at pleasure⟩

Adm. or **Adm** Admiral; Admiralty.

ad–man or **ad•man** ['æd ,mæn] *n.* a man whose business is advertising.

ad•min ['ædmɪn] *or* [æd'mɪn] *n. Informal.* a short form of *administration*. ⟨by clipping⟩

ad•min•is•ter [æd'mɪnɪstər] *v.* **1** manage the affairs of (a business, a city, etc.); control on behalf of others; direct: *The Minister of Defence administers a department of the government. A housekeeper administers a household.* **2** give (*to*); apply; dispense: *A doctor administers medicine to sick people. Judges administer justice and punishment.* **3** cause (an oath, a test, etc.) to be taken, done, made, etc. **4** *Law.* settle or take charge of (an estate). **5** act as administrator or executor. **6** be helpful; add something; contribute: *to administer to a person's comfort or pleasure.* ⟨ME < OF < L *administrare* < *ad-* to + *minister* servant⟩

ad•min•is•trate [æd'mɪnɪ,streit] *v.* **-strat•ed, -strat•ing.** manage or direct the affairs of (a business, school, government, etc.)

ad•min•is•tra•tion [æd,mɪnɪ'streiʃən] *n.* **1** the managing of a business, office, etc.; management. **2** a group of persons in charge: *The university administration has improved the enrolment procedure.* **3 a** the management of public affairs by government officials. **b** the officials as a group; the government. **c** the period of office of these officials or of a government. **4** a giving out or dispensing (of medicine, justice, etc.). **5** an administering (of an oath, etc.): *The Red Cross handled the administration of aid to the refugees.* **6** *Law.* the management, settling, etc. (of an estate).

ad•min•is•tra•tive [æd'mɪnɪstrətɪv] *or* [æd'mɪnɪ,streitɪv] *adj.* having to do with administration; managing; executive. **—ad'min•is•tra•tive•ly,** *adv.*

ad•min•is•tra•tor [æd'mɪnɪ,streitər] *n.* **1** a person who administers or administrates. **2** *Law.* a person appointed by a court to take charge of or settle the estate of someone who has died without making a will or appointing an executor, or at the executor's death. Compare EXECUTOR. ⟨< L⟩

ad•mi•ra•ble ['ædmərəbəl] *adj.* **1** worth admiring. **2** excellent; very good. ⟨< L *admirabilis*⟩ **—'ad•mi•ra•ble•ness,** *n.* **—'ad•mi•ra•bly,** *adv.*

ad•mi•ral ['ædmərəl] *n.* **1** the commander-in-chief of a fleet. **2** *Canadian Forces.* in Maritime Command, the equivalent of a general. *Abbrev.*: Adm. or Adm See chart of ranks in the Appendix. **3** a naval officer of similar rank in other countries. **4** any naval officer ranking above a commodore (or, in the U.S., above a captain). **5** *Cdn.* formerly, the leader of a fishing fleet in Newfoundland. **6** any of various brightly coloured butterflies (subfamily Nymphalinae), such as the **red admiral** or the **white admiral.** ⟨earlier *amiral* < OF < Arabic *amir* chief. Related to AMIR.⟩

admiral of the fleet the officer of the highest rank in the navies of certain countries, ranking above an admiral.

ad•mi•ral•ty ['ædmərəlti] *n., pl.* **-ties. 1** a law or court dealing with affairs of the sea and ships. **2 the Admiralty,** in the United Kingdom, a department of the Ministry of Defence responsible for naval affairs. **3** the office or authority of an admiral.

ad•mi•ra•tion [,ædmə'reiʃən] *n.* **1** a feeling of wonder, pleasure, and approval. **2** the act of regarding with delight and wonder (something fine or beautiful): *They paused in admiration of the beautiful view.* **3** a person or thing that is admired: *The well-dressed woman was the admiration of everyone at the party.* **4** *Archaic.* wonder.

ad•mire [æd'maɪr] *v.* **-mired, -mir•ing. 1** regard with wonder, approval, and delight: *to admire a brave deed. They stood for a while, admiring the view.* **2** think highly of; esteem: *I admire her very much.* **3** express admiration for: *He was so anxious to please that he enthusiastically admired every piece of furniture in the room.* ⟨< L *admirari* < *ad-* at + *mirari* wonder < *mirus* wonderful⟩

ad•mir•er [æd'maɪrər] *n.* **1** a person who admires. **2** a person in love with or fond of another; suitor.

ad•mir•ing [æd'maɪrɪŋ] *adj., v.* *—adj.* showing or feeling admiration: *an admiring glance. He was surrounded by a group of admiring friends.*
—v. ppr. of ADMIRE. **—ad'mir•ing•ly,** *adv.*

ad•mis•si•bil•i•ty [æd,mɪsə'bɪləti] *n.* the quality or state of being admissible.

ad•mis•si•ble [æd'mɪsəbəl] *adj.* **1** that can be permitted; allowable. **2** *Law.* that can be considered as evidence or proof. **3** having the right to enter or use (a position, occupation, group, place, etc.). **—ad'mis•si•ble•ness,** *n.* **—ad'mis•si•bly,** *adv.*

ad•mis•sion [æd'mɪʃən] *n.* **1** the act of allowing (a person, animal, etc.) to enter: *admission of aliens into a country.* **2** the power or right to enter or use an office, place, etc.; entrance. **3** the price paid for the right to enter. **4** acceptance into an office or position. **5** an acknowledging: *His admission that he was to blame kept the others from being punished.* **6** an accepting as true or valid. **7** the fact or point acknowledged; something accepted as true or valid. ⟨< L *admissio, -onis* < *admittere.* See ADMIT.⟩

ad•mit [æd'mɪt] *v.* **-mit•ted, -mit•ting. 1** say that (an undesirable or damaging fact, etc.) is true or valid; acknowledge, often unwillingly or hesitantly: *He admitted that he had lied. She admitted her mistake.* **2** accept as true or valid: *to admit a hypothesis.* **3** allow to enter a place or use something; let in: *The head waiter refused to admit him without a tie.* **4** give the right to enter to: *This ticket admits one person.* **5** allow; leave room for; permit (*usually used with* **of**): *Her argument admits of no reply.* **6** give access or entry to: *The new window admits more light. The harbour admits three ships at one time.* **7** allow to attain (*to* a position, privilege, etc.): *She was admitted to the bar last year.* ⟨ME < L *admittere* < *ad-* to + *mittere* let go⟩

☛ *Syn.* **1. Admit,** ACKNOWLEDGE, CONFESS = disclose or own that something is true. **Admit** = own or grant the existence or truth of something, usually after giving in to outside forces or the dictates of one's own conscience or judgment: *I admit that she is right.* **Acknowledge** = bring out into the open one's knowledge of the existence or truth of something, sometimes reluctantly: *They have now acknowledged defeat.* **Confess** = admit something unfavourable or embarrassing about oneself: *I confess I am a coward.*

☛ *Usage.* **Admit** is followed by *to* or *into* when it means 'give the right to enter or allow to enter': *Fifty cents will admit you to the game. The butler would not admit him into the house.* **Admit** is followed by *of* when it means 'leave room for': *Her conduct admits of no complaint.*

ad•mit•tance [æd'mɪtəns] *n.* **1** a right to enter; permission to enter. **2** the act of admitting or fact of being admitted. **3** *Electricity.* the ratio of current to voltage; the reciprocal of IMPEDANCE.

ad•mit•ted•ly [æd'mɪtədli] *adv.* without denial; by general consent.

ad•mix [æd'mɪks] *v.* add in mixing; mix in.

ad•mix•ture [æd'mɪkstʃər] *n.* **1** mixture. **2** anything added in mixing. ⟨< L *admixtus*, pp. of *admiscere* < *ad-* in addition + *miscere* mix⟩

ad•mon•ish [æd'mɒnɪʃ] *v.* **1** warn against something: *The police officer admonished her not to drive too fast.* **2** reprove gently: *The teacher admonished the student for her careless work.* **3** urge strongly; advise. **4** recall to a duty overlooked or forgotten; remind. ⟨< *admonition*⟩ **—ad'mon•ish•er,** *n.* **—ad'mon•ish•ment,** *n.*

☛ *Usage.* **Admonish.** *Of,* not *against,* is used after this rather formal synonym for *warn*: *John admonished them of the impending peril.*

ad•mo•ni•tion [,ædmə'nɪʃən] *n.* an act of admonishing; advice concerning the faults a person has shown or may show. ⟨ME < OF < L *admonitio, -onis* < *ad-* to + *monere* warn⟩

ad•mon•i•to•ry [æd'mɒnə,tɔri] *adj.* admonishing; warning.

ad nau•se•am ['æd 'nɒziəm] *or* ['æd 'nɒsiəm] to a disgusting or sickening degree or extent. ⟨< L *literally*, to (the point of) nausea⟩

a•do [ə'du] *n.* bother, fuss, or trouble: *Without more ado, he started in on the cleaning.* ⟨ME *at do* to do⟩
☛ *Hom.* ADIEU [ə'du].
☛ *Syn.* See note at STIR[1].

a•do•be [ə'doubi] *n.* **1** clay mixed with straw or grass and dried in the sun, and usually made into bricks. Adobe has been used as a building material for thousands of years. **2** a building made of adobe. **3** (*adjl.*) built or made of such bricks or material: *Adobe houses are common in Mexico and the southwestern United States.* **4** the chalky, sandy (type of) clay soil used for making adobe bricks. ⟨< Sp. *adobe* < Arabic *al-tub* the brick⟩

a•do•bo [ə'doubou] *n.* a Philippine dish of meat or chicken, marinated, simmered, and then fried.

ad•o•les•cence [,ædə'lɛsəns] *n.* **1** the period of physical and psychological growth between childhood and maturity. **2** the state of being adolescent.

ad•o•les•cent [,ædə'lɛsənt] *n., adj.* —*n.* a person in the state of growth between childhood and maturity.
—*adj.* **1** of, having to do with, or being in adolescence.
2 characteristic of an adolescent, especially with reference to immature behaviour by an adult. ⟨ME < OF < L *adolescens, -entis*, ppr. of *adolescere* < *ad-* to + *olescere* grow up. Related to ADULT.⟩

A•don•is [ə'dɒnɪs] *or* [ə'dounɪs] *n.* **1** *Roman and Greek mythology.* a handsome young man who was loved by Venus (Aphrodite). **2** any very handsome young man.

a•dopt [ə'dɒpt] *v.* **1** take or use as one's own by choice: *to adopt a new technique. I liked your idea and adopted it.* **2** accept formally: *The club adopted the motion by a vote of 20 to 5.* **3** legally take (a child of other parents) and bring up as one's own. ⟨< L *adoptare* < *ad-* to + *optare* choose⟩ **—a'dopt•a•ble,** *adj.* **—a'dopt•er,** *n.*

a•dopt•ee [ədɒp'ti] *n.* someone who has been adopted.

a•dop•tion [ə'dɒpʃən] *n.* the act of adopting or the state of being adopted: *the adoption of a new text for a course, the adoption of a child.*

a•dop•tive [ə'dɒptɪv] *adj.* **1** tending to adopt. **2** related by adoption: *adoptive parents.* **—a'dop•tive•ly,** *adv.*

a•dor•a•ble [ə'dɔrəbəl] *adj.* **1** worthy of adoration. **2** *Informal.* lovely; delightful. **—a'dor•a•bly,** *adv.*

ad•o•ra•tion [,ædə'reiʃən] *n.* **1** worship. **2** highest respect; devoted love.

a•dore [ə'dɔr] *v.* **a•dored, a•dor•ing. 1** respect very highly; love deeply. **2** worship. **3** *Informal.* like very much. ⟨ME < OF < L *adorare* < *ad-* to + *orare* pray⟩ **—a'dor•ing•ly,** *adv.*

a•dor•er [ə'dɔrər] *n.* **1** a devoted admirer; lover. **2** worshipper.

a•dorn [ə'dɔrn] *v.* **1** add beauty to; enhance the splendour or honour of; add distinction to. **2** put ornaments on; decorate. ⟨ME < OF < L *adornare* < *ad-* to + *ornare* fit out⟩ **—a'dorn•er,** *n.*
☛ *Syn.* **2.** See note at DECORATE.

a•dorn•ment [ə'dɔrnmənt] *n.* **1** something that adds beauty; ornament; decoration. **2** the act of adorning or the state of being adorned.

a•down [ə'daʊn] *adv. or prep. Poetic.* down. ⟨< OE *adūne* from the hill⟩

ADP 1 ADENOSINE DIPHOSPHATE. **2** automatic data processing.

ad rem ['æd 'rɛm] to the point at issue. ⟨< L⟩

ad•re•nal [ə'drinəl] *adj., n.* —*adj.* **1** near or on the kidney. **2** of or from the adrenal glands.
—*n.* ADRENAL GLAND. ⟨< L *ad-* near + *renes* kidneys⟩

adrenal gland either of the two ductless glands situated one on top of each kidney. The inner part of the gland, called the medulla, is controlled by the nervous system and produces adrenalin; the outer layer, called the cortex, is controlled by the pituitary gland and produces several hormones necessary to life. See KIDNEY for picture.

ad•ren•al•in [ə'drɛnəlɪn] *n.* **1** a hormone secreted by the adrenal glands. **2 Adrenalin,** *Trademark.* a white, crystalline drug prepared from this hormone, used to stimulate the heart and stop bleeding. Adrenalin is obtained from the adrenal glands of animals.
rush of adrenalin, a sudden increase in strength or endurance.

ad•ren•al•ine [ə'drɛnəlɪn] *or* [ə'drɛnə,lin] *n.* ADRENALIN (def. 1).

a•dre•no•cor•ti•co•trop•ic hormone [ə,drinou,kɔrtɪkou'trɒpɪk] See ACTH.

a•drift [ə'drɪft] *adv. or adj.* (*never used before a noun*) **1** being carried along by the current, without having control: *Having lost the paddle, we were adrift on the lake.* **2** without guidance, security, or purpose: *The team was adrift for three weeks while the coach was sick.*

a•droit [ə'drɔɪt] *adj.* **1** expert in the use of the hands; skilful. **2** clever with the mind; resourceful: *A good teacher is adroit in asking questions.* ⟨< F *adroit* < *à droit* rightly < L *ad* to, *directus* straight⟩ **—a'droit•ly,** *adv.* **—a'droit•ness,** *n.*
☛ *Syn.* See note at DEXTEROUS.

ad•sci•ti•tious [,ædsə'tɪʃəs] *adj.* additional. ⟨< L *adscīscere*, admit, adopt⟩

ad•sorb [æd'zɔrb] *or* [æd'sɔrb] *v.* **1** cause (a gas, liquid, or dissolved substance) to adhere in a very thin layer of molecules to the surface of a solid. Water can be purified by passing through a charcoal filter because molecules of substance dissolved in the water are adsorbed on the charcoal particles. **2** become adsorbed. ⟨< L *ad-* to + *sorbere* suck in⟩

ad•sorb•ate [æd'zɔrbɪt] *or* [æd'zɔrbeit], [æd'sɔr,bɪt] *or* [æd'sɔrbeit] *n.* a liquid or gas that is adsorbed.

ad•sorb•ent [æd'zɔrbənt] *or* [æd'sɔrbənt] *adj.* capable of adsorbing.

ad•sorp•tion [æd'zɔrpʃən] *or* [æd'sɔrpʃən] *n.* the adhesion of a very thin layer of molecules of a liquid, gas, or dissolved substance to the surface of a solid with which it is in contact; adsorbing or being adsorbed.

ad•sorp•tive [æd'zɔrptɪv] *or* [æd'sɔrptɪv] *adj.* having to do with adsorption.

ad•u•lar•i•a [,ædʒə'lɛriə] *n.* moonstone. ⟨< Ital. < F, ult. < *Adula*, Swiss mountain range⟩

ad•u•late ['ædʒə,leit] *v.* **-lat•ed, -lat•ing.** praise too much; flatter slavishly. ⟨< L *adulari*⟩ **—'ad•u,la•tor,** *n.*

ad•u•la•tion [,ædʒə'leiʃən] *n.* too much praise; slavish flattery.

ad•u•la•to•ry ['ædʒələ,tɔri] *adj.* praising too much; slavishly flattering.

a•dult [ə'dʌlt] *or* ['ædʌlt] *adj., n.* —*adj.* **1** fully developed and mature; full-grown; grown-up: *the adult population. An adult frog looks very different from a tadpole.* **2** of, intended for, or appealing to grown-up people: *adult education.* **3** appealing to sexual desires or interests: *adult movies, adult bookstores.* **4** Usually, **Adult,** of films, rated as recommended entertainment for adult people.
—*n.* **1** a grown-up person. **2** a person who has reached an age of legal responsibility: *In some provinces, one is an adult at 18.* **3** a full-grown animal or plant. ⟨< L *adultus*, pp. of *adolescere.* See ADOLESCENT.⟩ **—a'dult•ness,** *n.*
☛ *Pronun.* **Adult** is pronounced [ə'dʌlt] or ['ædʌlt], the choice depending generally on which best fits the rhythm of the sentence.

a•dul•ter•ant [ə'dʌltərənt] *n., adj.* —*n.* a substance used in adulterating.
—*adj.* adulterating.

a•dul•ter•ate *v.* [ə'dʌltə,reit]; *adj.* [ə'dʌltərɪt] *or* [ə'dʌltə,reit] *v.* **-at•ed, -at•ing,** *adj.* —*v.* make lower in quality by adding inferior or impure materials: *to adulterate milk with water.*
—*adj.* **1** not faithful; adulterous. **2** not real; spurious; impure. ⟨< L *adulterare* corrupt, ult. < *ad-* to + *alter (um)* other, different⟩

a•dul•ter•a•tion [ə,dʌltə'reiʃən] *n.* **1** the act of adulterating. **2** an adulterated substance; a product that has been adulterated.

a•dul•ter•er [ə'dʌltərər] *n.* a person, especially a man, guilty of adultery.

a•dul•ter•ess [ə'dʌltərɪs] *n.* a woman guilty of adultery.

a•dul•ter•ous [ə'dʌltərəs] *adj.* having to do with, characterized by, or committing adultery: *an adulterous act.* **—a'dul•ter•ous•ly,** *adv.*

a•dul•ter•y [ə'dʌltəri] *n., pl.* **-ter•ies.** sexual unfaithfulness of a husband or wife. ⟨< L *adulterium*⟩

a•dult•hood [ə'dʌlt,hʊd] *or* ['ædʌlt,hʊd] *n.* the state or condition of being an adult.

ad•um•bral [æ'dʌmbrəl] *adj.* shady.

ad•um•brate [æ'dʌmbreit] *or* ['ædəm,breit] *v.* **-brat•ed, -brat•ing. 1** indicate faintly; outline. **2** foreshadow. **3** overshadow; obscure. ⟨< L *adumbrāre* overshadow < *ad-* + *umbra* shade⟩ **—,ad•um'bra•tion,** *n.* **—ad'um•bra•tive,** *adj.*

adv. 1 adverb; adverbial. **2** advertisement. **3** advocate.

ad val. ad valorem.

ad va•lo•rem ['æd və'lɔrəm] of merchandise, in proportion to the value: *an ad valorem tax. Abbrev.*: ad val. ⟨< Med.L⟩

ad•vance [æd'væns] *v.* **-vanced, -vanc•ing;** *n.* *—v.* **1** move forward; go forward: *The troops advanced.* **2** bring forward: *The troops were advanced.* **3** make progress; improve: *We advance in knowledge.* **4** help forward; further: *to advance the cause of peace.* **5** put forward; suggest: *He advanced a new idea to help solve the city's transportation problems.* **6** raise to a higher rank; promote: *to advance her from lieutenant to captain.* **7** rise in rank; be promoted: *to advance in one's profession.* **8** raise (prices or value): *to advance the price of milk.* **9** rise in price or value: *The stock advanced three points.* **10** make earlier; hasten: *to advance the time of the meeting.* **11** move the hands of (a clock or watch) forward: *In summer, the clocks are advanced one hour.* **12** in internal-combustion engines, change (the timing) so as to cause the sparking action to take place earlier in the cycle. **13** supply beforehand: *to advance a sales rep funds for expenses.* **14** lend (money), especially on security: *to advance a loan.*
—n. **1** a movement forward: *The army's advance was very slow.* **2** the distance covered in such a movement. **3** (*adjl.*) going before: *the advance guard.* **4** a command, signal, etc. to move forward. **5** an improvement; progress. **6** a rise in price or value. **7** the furnishing of money or goods before they are due or as a loan. **8** the money or goods furnished. **9** (*adjl.*) made or provided ahead of time: *Customers were sent advance notice of the price increase.* **10 advances,** *pl.* personal approaches toward another or others to settle a difference, to make an acquaintance, etc.
in advance, a in front; ahead. **b** ahead of time. ⟨ME < OF *avancier* < VL *abantiare* < LL *abante* < *ab* from + *ante* before⟩
☛ *Syn. v.* **1. Advance,** PROCEED = move forward. **Advance** means move forward toward a definite end or destination: *In two plays the team advanced to the one-yard line.* **Proceed** means move forward toward a goal, often after a break, interruption, or delay: *If we get the money to finish the hospital, we can proceed with construction.*

ad•vanced [æd'vænst] *adj., v.* *—adj.* **1** in front of others; forward. **2** ahead of most others in progress, development, etc.: *The advanced class has studied history for three years.* **3** far along in life; very old: *She lived to the advanced age of ninety years.* **4** increased: *advanced prices.* **5** ahead of the times; progressive; unconventional: *advanced ideas on social welfare.*
—v. pt. and pp. of ADVANCE.

advanced credit or **standing** credit allowed to a student for courses to be taken at a different institution.

ad•vance•ment [æd'vænsmənt] *n.* **1** a movement forward; advance. **2** progress; improvement: *the advancement of knowledge through books.* **3** promotion to a higher rank or position: *There is good opportunity for advancement in this job.*

advance poll *Cdn.* in a general election: **1** an arrangement whereby persons expecting to be absent from their home riding on election day may cast their votes on an earlier date. **2** the number of votes cast in such a poll.

advance vote *Cdn.* a vote cast in an ADVANCE POLL (def. 1).

ad•van•tage [æd'væntɪdʒ] *n., v.* **-taged, -tag•ing.** *—n.* **1** a favourable condition, circumstance, or opportunity; benefit or profit: *Good health is always a great advantage. It would be to your advantage if you learned a second language.* **2** a better or superior position: *He had an advantage over his opponent in that he had more experience. She had the advantage of us because we had never been there before.* **3** *Tennis.* the first point scored after deuce.
have the advantage of (someone), know or recognize someone to whom one is not known: *You have the advantage of me; I'm afraid I don't know you.*
take advantage of, a make good use of for oneself: *She took advantage of the hubbub to slip out of the room.* **b** impose upon (a person or a person's good nature, innocence, ignorance, etc.); abuse.
to advantage, so as to produce a good effect or show the merits of: *a painting displayed to advantage.*
—v. give an advantage to; help; benefit. ⟨ME < OF *avantage* < *avant* before < LL *abante.* See ADVANCE.⟩
☛ *Syn. n.* **1. Advantage,** BENEFIT, PROFIT = *gain of some kind.* **Advantage** applies to a gain resulting from a position of superiority, of any kind, over others: *The girl who can think for herself has an advantage when she begins work.* **Benefit** applies to gain in personal or social improvement: *His summer in Mexico was a benefit to him.* **Profit** applies especially to material gain, but also to gain in anything valuable, such as knowledge: *There is profit even in mistakes.*

ad•van•ta•geous [,ædvən'teidʒəs] *adj.* giving advantage; favourable; helpful; profitable: *This advantageous position commands three roads.* **—,ad•van'ta•geous•ly,** *adv.* **—,ad•van'ta•geous•ness,** *n.*

ad•vec•tion [æd'vɛkʃən] *n.* the transference of heat, cold, or other property of air by the horizontal movement of a mass of air. ⟨< L *advectio, -onis* a conveying < *advehere* carry to < *ad-* to + *vehere* carry⟩ **—ad'vec•tion•al,** *adj.*

ad•vec•tive [æd'vɛktɪv] *adj.* of or having to do with advection.

ad•vent ['ædvɛnt] *n.* **1** a coming; arrival: *the advent of spring.* **2** *Christianity.* **Advent, a** the birth of Christ. **b** the season of devotion including the four Sundays before Christmas. **3** *Christianity.* **Second Advent,** the coming of Christ at the Last Judgment. ⟨< L *adventus* < *advenīre* arrive < *ad-* to + *venīre* come⟩

Advent calendar a large card with the days of December preceding Christmas, often with a pocket to open each day disclosing a scene or picture.

Ad•vent•ism ['ædvɛn,tɪzəm] *n.* the belief that Christ's second coming is near at hand.

Ad•vent•ist [æd'vɛntɪst] *or* ['ædvɛntɪst] *n., adj.* *—n.* a member of a Christian denomination that believes that the second coming of Christ is near at hand. See SEVENTH DAY ADVENTIST.
—adj. of or having to do with Adventists or Adventism.

ad•ven•ti•tious [,ædvɛn'tɪʃəs] *adj.* **1** coming from outside; additional; accidental: *The romantic life of the author gives his book an adventitious interest.* **2** *Biology.* appearing in an unusual position or place: *Adventitious roots sometimes grow from leaves.* ⟨< L *adventīcius*⟩ **—,ad•ven'ti•tious•ly,** *adv.* **—,ad•ven'ti•tious•ness,** *n.*

ad•ven•tive [æd'vɛntɪv] *adj. Biology.* introduced into a new environment; not native, though growing with cultivation.

Advent Sunday in the Christian calendar, the first of the four Sundays in Advent.

ad•ven•ture [æd'vɛntʃər] *n., v.* **-tured, -tur•ing.** *—n.* **1** a bold and difficult undertaking involving unknown risks and danger: *He had had many adventures in his career as a detective.* **2** the seeking or encountering of excitement and unknown risks or danger: *the spirit of adventure, yearning after adventure.* **3** an unusual or exciting experience: *It was an adventure to be entirely on her own in a strange city.* **4** *Archaic.* venture.
—v. **1** take part in daring or exciting undertakings: *a summer of adventuring in the wilderness.* **2** dare to do, go, etc.; venture: *to adventure upon an unknown shore.* ⟨ME < OF *aventure* < L *adventura (res)* (thing) about to happen < *advenire* arrive. See ADVENT.⟩

ad•ven•tur•er [æd'vɛntʃərər] *n.* **1** a person who seeks or has adventures. **2** a soldier ready to serve in any army that will hire him or her; a mercenary. **3** a person who lives by his or her wits; a person who schemes to get money, social position, etc. **4** speculator.

ad•ven•ture•some [æd'vɛntʃərsəm] *adj.* bold and daring; adventurous.

ad•ven•tur•ess [æd'vɛntʃərɪs] *n.* a woman who is an adventurer, especially one who schemes to get money, social position, etc.

ad•ven•tur•ism [æd'vɛntʃə,rɪzəm] *n.* the attempting of projects without sufficient forethought or preparation; imprudence.

ad•ven•tur•ist [æd'vɛntʃərɪst] *n., adj.* *—n.* a person who attempts a project or undertakes a program without sufficient forethought.
—adj. of or having to do with adventurists or adventurism.

ad•ven•tur•ous [æd'vɛntʃərəs] *adj.* **1** fond of adventures; ready to take risks; daring: *a bold, adventurous explorer.* **2** full of risk; dangerous: *An expedition to the North Pole is an adventurous undertaking.* **—ad'ven•tur•ous•ly,** *adv.* **—ad'ven•tur•ous•ness,** *n.*

ad•verb ['ædvɜrb] *n.* a word that extends or limits the meaning of verbs but is also used to qualify adjectives or other adverbs, especially in place, time, manner, or degree: *Soon, here, very, gladly,* and *not* are adverbs. *Abbrev.*: adv. ⟨< L *adverbium* < *ad-* to + *verbum* verb⟩
☛ *Usage.* **Adverb. a forms of adverbs.** Most adverbs are formed from adjectives or participles plus the ending *-ly*: *He rowed badly. She was deservedly popular. Surely you hear that.* In informal use, certain common adverbs may occur in the same form as adjectives in some contexts. Some of these are: *cheap, close, even, loud, right, slow, tight, wrong.* For example, one can say *He sang loud* or *He sang loudly.* Their *-ly* forms are more common in formal English. There are also some other common adverbs

whose two forms (with and without an *-ly* ending) are not interchangeable, each being used in a different context or with a slightly different meaning. Some of these are: *deep, first, high, near.* Thus *She can sing very high* (not *highly*) but *They praised her work very highly* (not *high*). Consult the individual entries for each form if in doubt. **b comparison of adverbs.** Degrees of the condition or manner indicated by an adverb are shown by adding *-er, -est* or by placing *more, most* before it: *hard, harder, hardest; slow, slower, slowest;* or *slowly, more slowly, most slowly. More* and *most* are used with most adverbs of more than one syllable.

ad•ver•bi•al [æd'vɜrbiəl] *adj., n. —adj.* **1** of an adverb. **2** used as an adverb. The form *home* in *I'm going home* is an adverbial use of the noun *home.*
—n. a word or group of words used as an adverb.
—ad'ver•bi•al•ly, *adv.*

ad•ver•sa•ri•al [,ædvər'sɛriəl] *adj.* **1** having to do with conflict or opposition. **2** opposed; unfriendly.

ad•ver•sar•y ['ædvər,sɛri] *n., pl.* **-sar•ies. 1** a person opposing or resisting another person; enemy. **2** a person or group on the other side in a contest. ⟨< L *adversārius*⟩
☛ *Syn.* **2.** See note at OPPONENT.

ad•ver•sa•tive [æd'vɜrsətɪv] *adj., n. Grammar. —adj.* expressing contrast or opposition. *But* and *yet* are adversative conjunctions.
—n. a word expressing contrast or opposition.

ad•verse [æd'vɜrs] *or* ['ædvɜrs] *adj.* **1** disapproving or unfriendly: *adverse criticism.* **2** unfavourable or harmful: *adverse influences. The climate had an adverse effect on his health.* **3** acting in a contrary direction; opposing: *Adverse winds hindered the ship.* **4** symmetrically opposite. **5** *Botany.* facing the stem. ⟨< L *adversus* over against, pp. of *advertere.* See ADVERT.⟩
—ad'verse•ly, *adv.* **—ad'verse•ness,** *n.*
☛ *Pronun.* The stress is on the first or last syllable when the word precedes a noun (*'adverse criticism, an ad'verse effect*) and on the last syllable when it forms part of the predicate (*The winds were ad'verse*).

ad•ver•si•ty [æd'vɜrsəti] *n., pl.* **-ties. 1** a condition of unhappiness, misfortune, or distress. **2** a stroke of misfortune; an unfavourable or harmful thing or event.
☛ *Syn.* See note at MISFORTUNE.

ad•vert[1] [æd'vɜrt] *v.* direct attention (*to*); refer (*to*): *The speaker adverted to the need for more parks.* ⟨ME *advert* < OF *avertir* < L *advertere* < *ad-* to + *vertere* turn⟩

ad•vert[2] ['ædvɜrt] *n. Brit. Informal.* advertisement.

ad•ver•tise ['ædvər,taɪz] *v.* **-tised, -tis•ing. 1** give public notice of in a newspaper, over the radio, on television, etc.: *The meeting was well advertised in the newspaper.* **2** ask by public notice (*for*): *to advertise for a job.* **3** make generally known. **4** praise the good qualities of (a product, etc.) in order to promote sales: *Manufacturers advertise things that they wish to sell.* **5** issue advertising: *It pays to advertise.* **6** call attention to (oneself). ⟨ME < OF *avertiss-,* a stem of *avertir* < L *advertere.* See ADVERT.⟩

ad•ver•tise•ment [æd'vɜrtɪsmənt], [,ædvər'taɪzmənt], *or* [æd'vɜrtɪzmənt] *n.* a public notice or announcement, as in a newspaper or magazine, over the radio, or on television.
☛ *Usage.* See note at AD.

ad•ver•tis•er ['ædvər,taɪzər] *n.* one who advertises.

ad•ver•tis•ing ['ædvər,taɪzɪŋ] *n., v. —n.* **1** the business of preparing, publishing, or circulating advertisements. **2** advertisements.
—v. ppr. of ADVERTISE.

ad•vice [æd'vəis] *n.* **1** an expressed opinion about what should be done: *Take the doctor's advice.* **2** Often, **advices,** *pl.* news or information, especially of a formal or official nature. ⟨ME < MF *advis,* var. of OF *avis* < L *ad-* + *vīsum* thing seen⟩

ad•vis•a•bil•i•ty [æd,vaɪzə'bɪləti] *n.* the quality of being advisable; propriety; expediency.

ad•vis•a•ble [æd'vaɪzəbəl] *adj.* to be recommended; wise; sensible. **—ad'vis•a•bly,** *adv.*

ad•vise [æd'vaɪz] *v.* **-vised, -vis•ing. 1** give advice to: *Advise him to be cautious.* **2** give advice: *I shall act as you advise.* **3** give notice; inform (*often used with* **of**): *We were advised of the dangers before we began our trip.* **4** recommend; suggest: *She advises caution.* ⟨ME < OF *aviser* < *avis* opinion. See ADVICE.⟩

ad•vised [æd'vaɪzd] *adj., v. —adj.* planned; considered; thought-out.
—v. pt. and pp. of ADVISE.

ad•vis•ed•ly [æd'vaɪzɪdli] *adv.* after careful consideration; deliberately.

ad•vise•ment [æd'vaɪzmənt] *n.* careful consideration: *The lawyer took our case under advisement and said she would give us an answer in two weeks.*

ad•vis•er or **ad•vi•sor** [æd'vaɪzər] *n.* **1** a person who gives advice. **2** a person whose work is giving advice, especially a teacher or professor appointed to advise students.
☛ *Spelling.* **Adviser** has been the more common spelling, but the *-or* form, because of its similarity to *advisory,* is being increasingly used.

ad•vi•so•ry [æd'vaɪzəri] *adj., n. —adj.* **1** having power to advise: *an advisory committee.* **2** containing advice.
—n. a bulletin or report containing advice or advance information: *a weather advisory.* **—ad'vi•so•ri•ly,** *adv.*

advl. adverbial.

ad•vo•ca•cy ['ædvəkəsi] *n.* a statement in favour; a public recommendation; support of a cause: *The premier's advocacy got votes for the plan.*

ad•vo•cate *v.* ['ædvə,keit]; *n.* ['ædvəkət] *or* ['ædvə,keit] *v.* **-cat•ed, -cat•ing;** *n. —v.* speak in favour of; recommend publicly: *He advocates increased spending for public transportation.*
—n. **1** a person who pleads or argues for something: *an advocate of peace.* **2** a lawyer who pleads in a law court; barrister. ⟨ME *avocat* < OF < L *advocare* < *ad-* to + *vocare* call⟩
—,ad•vo'ca•tion, *n.* **—'ad•vo,ca•tor,** *n.*

advt. advertisement.

Adzes.
A man using an adze to shape a log.

adze [ædz] *n.* a tool for shaping wood, resembling an axe, but having a curved blade with its cutting edge set across the end of the handle. Sometimes, **adz.** ⟨OE *adesa*⟩

ad•zu•ki bean [æd'zuki] **1** a bushy bean plant of China and Japan (*Phaseolus ampularis*). **2** the small bean of this plant.

ae•cid•i•um [i'sɪdiəm] *n.* aecium.

ae•ci•um ['iʃiəm] *or* ['isiəm] *n., pl.* **ae•ci•a** [-siə]. *Botany.* a cup-shaped structure containing chains of spores; it is a product of certain rust fungi.

a•e•des [ei'idiz] *n., pl.* **-des.** any of a genus (*Aedes*) of chiefly tropical and subtropical mosquitoes, including vectors of disease, such as *A. aegypti,* which transmits yellow fever and dengue. Also, **aëdes.** ⟨< NL < Gk. *aēdēs* unpleasant < *a-* not + Gk. *hēdos* pleasant. 20c. Akin to HEDONISM.⟩

ae•dile ['idaɪl] *n.* in ancient Rome, an official in charge of public buildings, games, streets, and markets. Also, **edile.** ⟨< L *aedilis* < *aedes* building⟩

ae•gis ['idʒɪs] *n.* **1** *Greek mythology.* a shield or breastplate originally used by Zeus and later by his daughter Athena. **2** protection: *under the aegis of the law. She sought the aegis of the ambassador.* **3** sponsorship; auspices: *under the aegis of the ministry of tourism.* ⟨< L < Gk. *aigis*⟩

ae•gro•tat ['aɪgrou,tæt] *n.* **1** a certificate stating that a student is unable to write an examination because of illness. **2** a pass degree awarded on the basis of such a certificate. ⟨< L *aegrotat* he is sick⟩

-ae•mi•a *combining form.* See -EMIA.

Ae•ne•as [ɪ'niəs] *n. Greek and Roman mythology.* a Trojan hero, son of Anchises (a prince of Troy) and Venus. He escaped from burning Troy, carrying his father and leading his little son. After years of wandering he reached Italy, where, it is said, his descendants founded Rome.

Ae•ne•id [ɪ'niɪd] *n.* a Latin epic poem by Virgil, describing the wanderings of Aeneas.

Ae•o•li•an[1] [i'ouliən] *adj.* **1** of Aeolus. **2 aeolian,** of, produced by, or carried by the winds. Also, **Eolian.** ⟨< Aeolus⟩

Ae•o•li•an[2] [i'ouliən] *n., adj. —n.* **1** a member of an ancient Greek people, one of the four main divisions of the early Greeks (the others being Achaean, Dorian, and Ionian), who lived in Boeotia, Thessaly, and NW Asia Minor. **2** Aeolic.
—adj. of or having to do with the Aeolians or their dialect (Aeolic). Also, **Eolian.**

aeolian harp a box with six or more tuned strings fitted across openings in the top, usually placed in a window. Air currents vibrate the strings, causing them to produce musical sounds.

Ae•o•lic [i'oulɪk] *or* [i'ɒlɪk] *n., adj. —n.* a dialect of ancient Greek, spoken mainly in Boeotia, Thessaly, and NW Asia Minor. *—adj.* Aeolian. Also, **Eolic.**

Ae•o•lus ['iələs] *n. Greek mythology.* the god of the winds.

ae•on ['iən] *or* ['iɒn] See EON.

aer•ate ['ɛreit] *or* ['eiə,reit] *v.* **-at•ed, -at•ing. 1** expose to air or increase the circulation of air in. Lawns are aerated by drilling small holes into the turf. **2** expose to and mix with air. Water in some reservoirs is aerated by being tossed high into the air in a fine spray. **3** charge with a gas. Soda water is water that has been aerated with carbon dioxide. **4** expose to chemical action with oxygen. Blood is aerated in the lungs. ⟨< L < Gk. *aēr* air⟩ **—aer'a•tion,** *n.* **—'aer•a•tor,** *n.*

aer•i•al *adj.* ['ɛriəl] *or* [ei'iriəl]; *n.* ['ɛriəl] *adj., n. —adj.* **1** of, having to do with, or existing in the air: *aerial spirits.* **2** done or performed up in the air instead of on the ground: *swallows performing an aerial ballet.* **3** like air; thin, light, and insubstantial as air. **4** ideal; imaginary. **5** of, having to do with, by, or involving an aircraft: *aerial navigation, aerial warfare, aerial bombardment.* **6** taken from or designed to be used in an aircraft: *an aerial photograph.* **7** *Botany.* growing in the air instead of in soil or water: *aerial ferns.*
—n. a radio or television antenna. ⟨< L < Gk. *aerios* < *aēr* air⟩ **—'aer•i•al•ly,** *adv.*

☛ *Pronun.* **Aerial.** For the highly literary uses of the adjective (defs. 3 and 4), it is better to retain the pronunciation with four syllables, and in verse the four syllables are often useful to the metre. For the more common uses of the adjective and for the noun, the pronunciation with three syllables is established and natural: *aerial warfare, a radio aerial.*
☛ *Hom.* AREAL.

aer•i•al•ist ['ɛriəlɪst] *n.* an acrobat who performs feats on a trapeze, a high wire, etc.

aerial ladder an extending ladder often used on fire engines.

aer•ie ['ɛri] *or* ['iri] *n., pl.* **-ies.** *Esp. U.S.* eyrie.

aer•o ['ɛrou] *adj.* of or having to do with aircraft or aviation.
☛ *Hom.* ARROW.

aero– *combining form.* **1** air, as in *aerospace, aerodynamics.* **2** gas, as in *aerosol.* **3** aircraft or aviation, as in *aeronautics.* ⟨< Gk. *aēr* air⟩

aer•o•bal•lis•tics [,ɛroubə'lɪstɪks] *n.* the science of guiding missiles in flight.

aer•o•bat•ic [,ɛrou'bætɪk] *adj.* of or having to do with aerobatics.

aer•o•bat•ics [,ɛrou'bætɪks] *n.* the performance of tricks, stunts, etc. with an aircraft in flight. ⟨< *aero-* + *(acro)batics*⟩

aer•obe ['ɛroub] *n.* a micro-organism, such as a bacterium, that can live only in air containing oxygen. Compare with ANAEROBE.

aer•o•bic [ɛ'roubɪk] *or* [,eiə'roubɪk] *adj., n. —adj.* **1** living and growing only where there is oxygen. Some bacteria are aerobic. **2** having to do with or caused by aerobic bacteria. **3** of or having to do with aerobics.
—n. **aerobics,** *pl.* exercises designed to make people breathe more efficiently. ⟨ult. < Gk. *aēr* air + *bios* life⟩

aer•o•bi•ol•o•gist [,ɛroubaɪ'ɒlədʒɪst] *n.* a person trained in aerobiology, especially one whose work it is.

aer•o•bi•ol•o•gy [,ɛroubaɪ'ɒlədʒi] *n.* the branch of biology that studies how bacteria, viruses, etc. are borne through the air. **—,aer•o,bi•o'log•i•cal,** *adj.*

aer•o•do•net•ics [,ɛroudə'nɛtɪks] *n.* the science of flying using air currents rather than engine power, usually as concerns gliders. ⟨< Gk. *aerodonetos* tossed in air < *aero-* + *donetos* pp. of *donein* toss⟩

aer•o•drome ['ɛrə,droum] *n. Brit.* an airfield or small airport. ⟨< *aero-* + *-drome* (< Gk. *dromos* racecourse)⟩

aer•o•dy•nam•ic [,ɛroudaɪ'næmɪk] *adj.* of or having to do with aerodynamics: *Airplanes are supported in the air by aerodynamic forces.* **—,aer•o•dy'nam•i•cal•ly,** *adv.*

aer•o•dy•nam•ics [,ɛroudaɪ'næmɪks] *n.* the branch of physics that deals with the motion of air and other gases, and with the forces that act on bodies moving through the air. **—,aer•o•dy'nam•i•cist,** *n.*

aer•o•em•bo•lism [,ɛrou'ɛmbə,lɪzəm] *n.* **1** an embolism produced by bubbles of air or other gases. **2** decompression sickness, especially when caused by a too sudden ascent to high altitudes, as in an unpressurized aircraft; the bends.

aer•o•gel ['ɛrou,dʒɛl] *n.* a liquid or solid in which bubbles of air or another gas are suspended. Styrofoam is an aerogel.

aer•o•gram ['ɛrou,græm] *n.* AIR LETTER. Also, **aerogramme.**

aer•o•lite ['ɛrou,ləit] *n.* meteorite. ⟨< *aero-* + *-lite* < F < Gk. *lithos* stone⟩ **—,aer•o'lit•ic,** *adj.*

aer•o•log•ic [,ɛrou'lɒdʒɪk] *adj.* of or having to do with aerology. **—,aer•o'log•i•cal,** *adj.*

aer•ol•o•gist [ɛr'ɒlədʒɪst] *n.* a person trained in aerology, especially one whose work it is.

aer•ol•o•gy [ɛr'ɒlədʒi] *n.* the branch of meteorology that deals with the study of the upper atmosphere using planes or balloons.

aer•o•me•chan•ic [,ɛroumə'kænɪk] *adj., n. —adj.* of or having to do with aeromechanics. Also, **aeromechanical.**
—n. a mechanic who works on aircraft.

aer•o•me•chan•ics [,ɛroumə'kænɪks] *n.* (*used with a singular verb*) the branch of physics that deals with air and other gases, both in motion and at rest. It includes aerodynamics and aerostatics.

aer•o•med•i•cine [,ɛrou'mɛdɪsən] *n.* the science of disorders or medical problems arising from air travel. **—,aer•o'med•i•cal,** *adj.*

aer•om•e•ter [ɛr'ɒmətər] *n.* a device for measuring the density of air and other gases.

aer•o•naut ['ɛrə,nɒt] *n.* **1** a pilot of an airship or balloon; balloonist. **2** a person who travels in an airship or balloon. ⟨< F *aéronaute* < Gk. *aēr* air + *nautēs* sailor⟩

aer•o•nau•tic [,ɛrə'nɒtɪk] *adj.* of aeronautics or aeronauts. Also, **aeronautical. —,aer•o'nau•ti•cal•ly,** *adv.*

aeronautical chart a map of the earth's surface, or one part of it, for use in flying.

aer•o•nau•tics [,ɛrə'nɒtɪks] *n.* the science or art of the design, manufacture, and operation of aircraft.

aer•o•neu•ro•sis [,ɛrounju'rousɪs] *or* [,ɛrounu'rousɪs] *n.* a nervous disorder among pilots, caused by too much stress from flying.

aer•on•o•my [ɛr'ɒnəmi] *n.* the physics and chemistry of the upper atmosphere. ⟨< *aero-* + Gk. *nomos* law, arrangement⟩

aer•o•pause ['ɛrou,pɒz] *n.* **1** the level above the earth's surface beyond which the atmosphere has no effect on flight. **2** the upper limit of manned airborne flight.

aer•o•pho•bi•a [,ɛrou'foubiə] *n.* an abnormal fear of air or other gases, especially of drafts.

aer•o•phore ['ɛrou,fɔr] *or* ['ɛrə,fɔr] *n.* a mask or other apparatus which supplies air for breathing in an oxygen shortage, or which purifies air which is otherwise unfit for breathing.

aer•o•plane ['ɛrə,plein] *n. Brit.* airplane.
☛ *Usage.* See note at AIRPLANE.

aer•o•quay ['ɛrou,ki] *n.* an airport building comprising ticket offices, shops, restaurants, etc. as well as docklike bays at which aircraft take on and let off passengers.

aer•o•sol ['ɛrə,sɒl] *n.* **1** a suspension of fine solid or liquid particles in a gas. Smoke and fog are aerosols. **2** (*adjl.*) of or designating an apparatus for dispensing a substance such as paint, insecticide, or shaving cream, under pressure as a mist or foam. The apparatus consists of a small metal can containing the paint, etc. mixed with a liquified gas that is under pressure and acts as a propellant, shooting the substance out when the valve is opened. **3** (*adjl.*) contained in such an apparatus: *aerosol shaving cream.* **4** an aerosol container together with its contents. ⟨< *aero-* + *sol*, short for *solution*⟩

aer•o•space ['ɛrou,speis] *n.* **1** the earth's atmosphere and space beyond it, considered as a continuous region or field. **2** the branch of science that deals with the earth's atmosphere and outer space, especially in relation to space travel. **3** the industry of designing, building and operating spacecraft, missiles, etc. **4** (*adjl.*) of or having to do with aerospace, space travel, or the designing, building, and operating of spacecraft, etc.: *aerospace technology.*

aer•o•stat ['ɛrou,stæt] *n.* any lighter-than-air aircraft, such as a balloon or dirigible. ⟨< *aero-* + Gk. *statos* standing⟩

aer•o•stat•ic [,ɛrou'stætɪk] *adj.* **1** of or having to do with aerostatics. **2** of or having to do with an aerostat.

aer•o•stat•ics [,ɛrou'stætɪks] *n.* (*used with a singular verb*) the branch of physics that deals with the equilibrium of air and other gases, and with the equilibrium of solid objects floating in air and other gases.

aer•o•ther•mo•dy•nam•ics [ˌɛrouˌθɜrmoudaɪ'næmɪks] *n.* the study of heat and energy in gases.

ae•ru•gi•nous [i'rudʒɪnəs] *adj.* like copper; bluish green. ⟨< L < *aerugo* verdigris < *aes* copper⟩

Aes•cu•la•pi•us [ˌɛskjə'leipiəs] *or* [ˌiskjə'leipiəs] *n. Roman mythology.* the god of medicine and healing.

Ae•sir ['eisər] *or* ['isər] *n.pl. Norse mythology.* the chief Scandinavian gods, especially Odin, Thor, Balder, Loki, and Freya. ⟨< ON, gods⟩

Ae•so•pi•an [i'soupiən] *adj.* **1** of or having to do with Aesop (620?-560? B.C.), a Greek writer of fables. **2** of or suggestive of his writings.

aes•thete ['ɛsθit] *or* ['isθit] *n.* **1** a person who is sensitive to beauty; lover of beauty. **2** a person who pretends to care a great deal about beauty; a person who gives too much attention to art and beauty. Also, **esthete.** ⟨< Gk. *aisthētēs* one who perceives⟩

aes•thet•ic [ɛs'θɛtɪk] *or* [is'θɛtɪk] *adj., n. —adj.* **1** characterized by good taste, beauty, etc.; artistic: *the aesthetic effect of a work.* **2** of or having to do with the beautiful, as distinguished from the useful, scientific, etc.: *aesthetic principles.* **3** sensitive to beauty: *an aesthetic mind.*
—n. a set of principles for the appreciation of beauty in art and nature: *following an outdated aesthetic.* Also, **esthetic.**

aes•thet•i•cal•ly [ɛs'θɛtɪkli] *or* [is'θɛtɪkli] *adv.* **1** in an aesthetic manner. **2** according to aesthetics: *an aesthetically pleasing colour combination.* Also, **esthetically.**

aes•the•ti•cian [ˌɛsθə'tɪʃən] *or* [ˌisθə'tɪʃən] *n.* a person skilled in aesthetics. Also, **esthetician.**

aes•thet•i•cism [ɛs'θɛtəˌsɪzəm] *or* [is'θɛtɪˌsɪzəm] *n.* **1** the belief in beauty as the basic standard of value in human life, underlying all moral and other considerations. **2** great love for and sensitivity to beauty and the arts. **3** an affected sensitivity to beauty and the arts. Also, **estheticism.**

aes•thet•ics [ɛs'θɛtɪks] *or* [is'θɛtɪks] *n.* the study of beauty in art and nature; philosophy of beauty; theory of the fine arts. Also, **esthetics.**

aes•ti•val ['ɛstəvəl], ['istəvəl], *or* [ɪ'staɪvəl] See ESTIVAL.

aes•ti•vate ['ɛstəˌveit] See ESTIVATE.

aet. or **aetat.** of or at the age of (for L *aetas, aetatis* age).

ae•ther ['iθər] See ETHER (defs. 2 and 3).

ae•the•re•al [ɪ'θiriəl] See ETHEREAL.

ae•ti•ol•o•gy [ˌiti'ɒlədʒi] See ETIOLOGY.

af– *prefix.* the form of AD- occurring before *f*, as in *affix.*

AF, A.F., or **a.f.** AUDIO FREQUENCY.

AF or **A.F.** Anglo-French.

a•far [ə'fɑr] *adv.* far; far away; far off.

a•feard or **a•feared** [ə'fird] *adj. Archaic or dialect.* frightened; afraid.

a•fe•brile [ei'fibraɪl] *or* [ei'fibrəl], [ei'fɛbraɪl] *or* [ei'fɛbrəl] *adj.* without a fever.

af•fa•bil•i•ty [ˌæfə'bɪləti] *n.* the state or quality of being affable; a courteous, pleasant, and friendly manner.

af•fa•ble ['æfəbəl] *adj.* easy to talk to; courteous, pleasant, and friendly. ⟨< F < L *affabilis* able to be spoken to < *affari* < *ad-* to + *fari* speak⟩ **—'af•fa•ble•ness,** *n.* **—'af•fa•bly,** *adv.*

af•fair [ə'fɛr] *n.* **1** something done or to be done; matter; concern: *That's my affair.* **2 affairs,** *pl.* matters of interest or concern, especially business, commercial, or public matters: *current affairs, affairs of state.* **3** an action, event, or procedure referred to in vague terms: *The party on Saturday night was a dull affair.* **4** an object or group of objects referred to in vague terms: *This machine is a complicated affair.* **5** a sexual relationship between two people not married to each other, especially one that lasts only a short while. ⟨ME < OF *afaire* < *à faire* to do < L *ad* to + *facere* do⟩

affair of honour or **honor** a duel.

af•fect[1] *v.* [ə'fɛkt]; *n.* ['æfɛkt] *—v.* **1** make something happen to; have an effect on; influence: *The small amount of rain last year affected the growth of crops.* **2** act on in a harmful way: *The disease so affected his mind that he lost his memory.* **3** touch the heart of; stir the emotions of; move: *The story of their plight so affected her that she immediately offered to help.*
—n. Psychology. an emotion associated with an idea or concrete object. ⟨< L *affectus*, pp. of *afficere* act upon; influence; ult. < *ad-* to + *facere* do⟩
☛ *Usage.* See note at EFFECT.

af•fect[2] [ə'fɛkt] *v.* **1** pretend (to have or feel): *He affected ignorance of the fight, but we knew that he had seen it.* **2** be fond of; like: *She affects old furniture.* **3** assume falsely or ostentatiously: *He affects a taste for abstract painting though he knows little about art.* ⟨< MF < L *affectare* strive for; ult. < *ad-* to + *facere* do⟩
☛ *Syn.* **1.** See note at PRETEND.

af•fec•ta•tion [ˌæfɛk'teiʃən] *n.* **1** an artificial or unnatural way of behaving or talking: *Her British accent is an affectation, for she has never lived outside Alberta.* **2** outward appearance; pretence: *an affectation of ignorance.*

af•fect•ed[1] [ə'fɛktɪd] *adj., v. —adj.* **1** acted on; influenced. **2** influenced injuriously. **3** touched in the heart; moved in feeling. *—v.* pt. and pp. of AFFECT[1].

af•fect•ed[2] [ə'fɛktɪd] *adj., v. —adj.* **1** put on for effect; unnatural; artificial: *His affected manner changed as soon as the guests had gone.* **2** behaving, speaking, writing, etc. unnaturally for effect: *She is very affected.*
—v. pt. and pp. of AFFECT[2]. **—af'fect•ed•ly,** *adv.*

af•fect•ing [ə'fɛktɪŋ] *adj., v. —adj.* causing emotion; touching the heart or moving the feelings.
—v. ppr. of AFFECT. **—af'fect•ing•ly,** *adv.*

af•fec•tion [ə'fɛkʃən] *n.* **1** friendly feeling; a warm liking; fondness. **2** a feeling; inclination. **3** a disease or unhealthy condition. **4** *Archaic.* a disposition; tendency.
☛ *Syn.* **1.** See note at LOVE.

af•fec•tion•al [ə'fɛkʃənəl] *adj.* having to do with the emotions.

af•fec•tion•ate [ə'fɛkʃənət] *adj.* loving; fond; tender; having or showing affection. **—af'fec•tion•ate•ly,** *adv.*

af•fec•tive [æ'fɛktɪv] *adj.* of the feelings; emotional. **—af'fect•tive•ly,** *adv.*

af•fen•pin•scher ['ɑfənˌpɪnʃər] *n.* a breed of toy dog. ⟨< G⟩

af•fer•ent ['æfərənt] *adj.* of nerves, blood vessels, etc., carrying inward to a central organ or point. Compare EFFERENT. ⟨< L *afferens, -entis*, ppr. of *afferre* < *ad-* to + *ferre* bring⟩

af•fi•ance [ə'faiəns] *v.* **-anced, -anc•ing;** *n. —v.* promise in marriage; betroth. ⟨ME < OF *afiancer* to promise < *afiance*, n., trust⟩
—n. **1** the pledging of faith; betrothal. **2** trust; confidence. ⟨ME < OF *afiance* < *afier* to trust < VL *affidare* < *ad-* to + *fidare* trust < L *fidus* faithful⟩

af•fi•anced [ə'faiənst] *or* [ˌæfi'ɑnst] *adj., v. —adj.* promised in marriage; engaged or betrothed.
—v. pt. and pp. of AFFIANCE.

af•fi•ant [ə'faiənt] *n.* one who swears an affidavit.

af•fi•da•vit [ˌæfə'deivɪt] *n.* a statement written down and sworn to be true. An affidavit is usually made before a notary public or a commissioner of oaths. ⟨< Med.L *affidavit* he has stated on oath⟩

af•fil•i•ate *v.* [ə'fɪliˌeit]; *n.* [ə'fɪliɪt] *or* [ə'fɪliˌeit] *v.* **-at•ed, -at•ing;** *n. —v.* **1** connect in close association: *The two clubs did not have the same members, but they were affiliated with each other.* **2** associate oneself (*with*): *to affiliate with a political party.* **3** bring into relationship; adopt.
—n. a person or organization that is affiliated. ⟨< LL *affiliare* adopt < L *ad-* to + *filius* son⟩

af•fil•i•a•tion [əˌfɪli'eiʃən] *n.* association; relation.

af•fine[1] [ə'faɪn] *n.* a relative by marriage. ⟨< AFFINITY⟩ **—af'fi•nal,** *adj.*

af•fine[2] ['æfaɪn] *or* [ə'faɪn] *adj. Mathematics.* relating to the reproduction of a geometric figure which remains constant despite manipulation. ⟨< L *affinis* related⟩

af•fined [ə'faɪnd] *adj.* related or connected.

af•fin•i•tive [ə'fɪnɪtɪv] *adj.* having to do with affinity.

af•fin•i•ty [ə'fɪnəti] *n., pl.* **-ties. 1** a natural attraction to a person or liking for a thing: *an affinity for dancing. They have a strong affinity for each other.* **2** *Chemistry.* an attraction or force between certain particles or substances that causes them to combine chemically. **3** a close relationship or connection, as between biological groups, languages, etc. **4** a similarity or resemblance based on relationship or connection. **5** relationship by marriage or adoption. Compare CONSANGUINITY. **6** a person to whom one is especially attracted. ⟨ME < OF *af(f)inite* < L *affinitas* < *ad-* on + *finis* boundary⟩

af•firm [ə'fɜrm] *v.* **1** declare to be true; say firmly; assert. **2** confirm; ratify: *The higher court affirmed the lower court's decision.* **3** *Law.* declare solemnly, as an alternative to taking an oath. ⟨ME < OF < L *affirmare* < *ad-* to + *firmus* strong⟩

af•firm•ance [ə'fɜrməns] *n.* affirmation.

af•fir•ma•tion [,æfər'meiʃən] *n.* **1** an assertion; positive statement. **2** an affirming; confirmation; ratification. **3** *Law.* a solemn declaration made without taking an oath. If a person's religion forbids taking oaths, he or she can make an affirmation.

af•firm•a•tive [ə'fɜrmətɪv] *adj., n. —adj.* **1** stating that a fact is so; saying yes. **2** confidently optimistic or cheerful.
—n. **1** a word or statement that gives assent or indicates agreement. **2 the affirmative,** the side arguing in favour of a resolution being debated. **3** *Radio.* another word for *yes* in radio communication.
in the affirmative, with an affirmative answer; with a word or statement meaning yes: *Asked whether she would stand for election, she replied in the affirmative.* **—af'firm•a•tive•ly,** *adv.*

affirmative action a policy, especially in employment and education, designed to increase the representation of groups that have suffered discrimination, such as women or members of racial minorities.

af•firm•er [ə'fɜrmər] *n.* one who affirms instead of swearing an oath.

af•fix *v.* [ə'fɪks]; *n.* ['æfɪks] *v., n. —v.* **1** make firm or fix (one thing to or on another). **2** add at the end. **3** make an impression of (a seal, etc.). **4** connect; assign: *to affix blame.*
—n. **1** something affixed. **2** a prefix, suffix, or infix. *Un-* and *-ly* are affixes. ⟨< Med.L *affixāre*, ult. < L *ad-* to + *figere* fix⟩
—af'fix•er, *n.*
☛ *Syn. v.* **1.** See note at ATTACH.

af•fix•a•tion [,æfɪk'seiʃən] *n.* **1** an instance of affixing. **2** *Linguistics.* the process by which an affix attaches to a stem to form a new word.

af•fla•tus [ə'fleitəs] *n.* a divine inspiration. ⟨< L *afflatus* < *afflare* < *ad-* on + *flare* blow⟩

af•flict [ə'flɪkt] *v.* cause pain to; trouble greatly; distress: *to be afflicted with troubles.* ⟨< L *afflictus*, pp. of *affligere* < *ad-* upon + *fligere* dash⟩

af•flic•tion [ə'flɪkʃən] *n.* **1** a state of pain, trouble, or distress. **2** a cause of pain, trouble, or distress.

af•flic•tive [ə'flɪktɪv] *adj.* causing misery or pain; distressing.

af•flu•ence ['æfluəns] *n.* **1** wealth; riches. **2** abundant supply; great abundance. ⟨< F < L *affluentia* < *affluere.* See AFFLUENT.⟩

af•flu•ent ['æfluənt] *adj., n. —adj.* **1** very wealthy. **2** abundant; plentiful.
—n. a stream flowing into a larger stream, lake, etc. ⟨< L *affluens, -entis*, ppr. of *affluere* < *ad-* to + *fluere* flow⟩
—'af•flu•ent•ly, *adv.*

af•flux ['æflʌks] *n.* a flow toward a place. ⟨< Med.L *affluxus* < *affluere.* See AFFLUENT.⟩

af•ford [ə'fɔrd] *v.* **1** have or spare the money for: *We can't afford a new car.* **2** manage to give, spare, have, etc.: *A busy person cannot afford delay. Can you afford the time?* **3** be able without difficulty; have the means: *I can't afford to take the chance.* **4** furnish from natural resources; yield: *Some trees afford resin.* **5** yield or give as an effect or a result; provide: *Reading affords pleasure.* ⟨OE *geforthian* further, accomplish⟩

af•ford•a•ble [ə'fɔrdəbəl] *adj.* **1** of a price, low enough to be acceptable to the consumer: *an affordable price for oil.* **2** of goods or services, having such a price: *affordable merchandise.*

af•for•est [ə'fɔrəst] *v.* plant (an area) with trees. ⟨< L *ad* + *foresta* forest⟩

af•for•est•a•tion [ə,fɔrə'steiʃən] *n.* the act or practice of afforesting.

af•fran•chise [ə'fræntʃaɪz] *v.* **-chised, -chis•ing.** enfranchise.

af•fray [ə'frei] *n.* a noisy quarrel; a fight in public; a brawl. ⟨ME < OF *affrei*, ult. < L *ex-* out of + Gmc. **fridhu* peace⟩

af•fri•cate ['æfrəkət] *n. Phonetics.* a sound that begins with a stop and ends with a fricative. The *ch* in *chin* is an affricate: it starts with [t] and ends with [ʃ]. ⟨< L *affricatus*, pp. of *affricare* < *ad-* against + *fricare* rub⟩ **—,af•fri'ca•tion** [,æfrə'keiʃən], *n.*

af•fright [ə'frəit] *Archaic. v., n. —v.* frighten; terrify.
—n. fright; terror. ⟨< ME *afrighten*, OE *āfyrhtan*⟩

af•front [ə'frʌnt] *n., v. —n.* **1** a word or act that openly expresses disrespect. **2** a slight or injury to one's dignity.
—v. **1** insult openly; offend purposely: *The boy affronted the teacher by making a face at him.* **2** meet face to face, especially in a hostile encounter; confront. ⟨ME < OF *afronter* < *a front* against the forehead < L *ad frontem*⟩
☛ *Syn. n.* **1.** See note at INSULT.

Af•ghan ['æfgæn] *or* ['æfgən] *n., adj. —n.* **1** a native or inhabitant of Afghanistan. **2** AFGHAN HOUND. **3 afghan,** a knitted or crocheted blanket or large shawl, often having a pattern of squares or zigzag stripes.
—adj. of or having to do with Afghanistan or its people.

Afghan hound a breed of tall, swift dog having a thick coat of long, silky hair, a long, narrow head, and a thin tail: *Afghan hounds came originally from the Middle East, where they were usually trained as hunting dogs.*

af•ghan•i [æf'gæni] *n.* **1** the basic unit of money in Afghanistan, divided into 100 puls. See table of money in the Appendix. **2** a coin worth one afghani.

Af•ghan•i•stan [æf'gænɪ,stæn] *n.* a country in SW Asia.

a•fi•cio•na•do [ə,fisjə'nɑdou]; *Spanish* [ɑ,fiθjo'naðo] *n., pl.* **-dos. 1** a person who is very enthusiastic about something. **2** a person who takes a very great interest in bullfighting, but who is not a bullfighter. **—a,fi•cio'na•da,** *n. fem.*

a•field [ə'fild] *adv. or adj. (never precedes a noun)* **1** away from home; away. **2** out of the way; astray.

a•fire [ə'faɪr] *adv. or adj. (never precedes a noun)* **1** on fire; ablaze: *The whole house was afire.* **2** in or into a state of great excitement or enthusiasm: *afire with patriotism.*

AFL American Football League.

a•flame [ə'fleim] *adv. or adj. (never precedes a noun)* **1** in flames; ablaze. **2** in or into a state of great excitement or enthusiasm: *aflame with curiosity.* **3** bright or glowing: *a garden aflame with colour.*

a•float [ə'flout] *adv. or adj. (never precedes a noun)* **1** floating. **2** on shipboard; at sea. **3** adrift. **4** flooded. **5** in circulation; current: *Rumours of a revolt were afloat.* **6** *Informal.* solvent; financially viable: *She had to take out a loan to keep her business afloat.*

a•flut•ter [ə'flʌtər] *adv., adj. —adv.* into a flutter or a fit of fluttering: *The excitement set his pigeons aflutter. Her voice set his heart aflutter.*
—adj. (never used before a noun) fluttering; in a flutter: *The people were aflutter with expectation. The chickens were aflutter in the yard.*

A.F.M. Air Force Medal.

a•foot [ə'fʊt] *adv. or adj. (never precedes a noun)* **1** on foot; walking. **2** going on; in progress: *Preparations for dinner were afoot in the kitchen.*

a•fore [ə'fɔr] *adv., prep., or conj. Archaic or dialect.* before. ⟨OE *onforan* (< *on foran* in front) and *ætforan* (< *æt* at + *foran* in front)⟩

a•fore•men•tioned [ə'fɔr,mɛnʃənd] *adj.* spoken of before; mentioned above.

a•fore•said [ə'fɔr,sɛd] *adj.* spoken of before.

a•fore•thought [ə'fɔr,θɒt] *adj.* thought of beforehand; deliberately planned.

a•fore•time [ə'fɔr,taɪm] *adv. Archaic.* in time past.

a for•ti•o•ri ['ei ,fɔrti'ɔri], ['ei ,fɔrti'ɔraɪ], *or* ['æ ,fɔrti'ɔri] *Latin.* for a still stronger reason; all the more.

a•foul [ə'faʊl] *adv. or adj. (never precedes a noun)* in a tangle; in a collision; entangled.
run afoul of, a get into difficulties with. **b** crash into or become entangled with: *The canoe ran afoul of the motorboat.* **c** come into conflict with: *The street gang ran afoul of the Mafia.*

Afr. Africa; African.

a•fraid [ə'freid] *adj.* **1** feeling fear; frightened: *afraid of the dark.* **2** sorry (*used to express polite regret or to soften an abrupt or possibly unwelcome statement*): *I'm afraid we won't be able to come after all. I'm afraid I'll have to ask you to leave.* ⟨originally pp. of archaic v. *affray* frighten⟩
☛ *Syn.* **Afraid,** FRIGHTENED, TERRIFIED = feeling fear. **Afraid,** which is never used before the noun, means being in a mental state ruled by fear which may have either a real or an imagined cause and may last a long or a short time: *I am afraid of snakes.* **Frightened,** commonly used instead of *afraid* before the noun, particularly means 'made afraid suddenly, often only momentarily, by a real and present cause': *The frightened child ran home.* **Terrified** means 'suddenly filled with a very great and paralysing fear': *The terrified hunter watched the approaching grizzly.*

A–frame ['ei ,freim] *n.* a building having a two-sided roof that slopes steeply almost to the ground, forming triangular, or A-shaped, front and rear walls.

af•reet ['æfrit] *or* [ə'frit] *n. Arabic mythology.* a powerful evil demon or giant. Also, **afrit.** ⟨< Arabic *ifrīt*⟩

a•fresh [ə'frɛʃ] *adv.* once more; again.

Af•ric ['æfrɪk] *adj.* African.

Af•ri•ca ['æfrəkə] *n.* a large continent south of the Mediterranean Sea, bordered by the Atlantic Ocean to the west and the Indian Ocean to the east.

Af•ri•can ['æfrəkən] *adj., n. —adj.* **1** of or having to do with Africa or its inhabitants. **2** of or designating a major race of people that includes most of the peoples traditionally inhabiting Africa south of the Sahara, distinguished by a combination of biological characteristics, including very dark skin, curly or woolly hair, and a genetic resistance to such diseases as malaria. The Blacks of North and South America and the West Indies belong to the African race.
—n. **1** a native or inhabitant of Africa. **2** a person whose recent ancestors came from Africa. **3** a member of the African race. ⟨< L *Africanus*⟩

Af•ri•can–Am•er•i•can ['æfrəkən ə'mɛrəkən] *n., adj. —n.* an American of African descent or having some African ancestors.
—adj. of or having to do with African-Americans or their history or culture.

Af•ri•can–Ca•na•di•an ['æfrəkən kə'neidiən] *n., adj. —n.* a Canadian of African descent or having some African ancestors.
—adj. of or having to do with African-Canadians or their history or culture.

Af•ri•can•ism ['æfrəkə,nɪzəm] *n.* **1** a characteristically African custom or belief. **2** *Linguistics.* a word or construction from an African language borrowed into a non-African language. **3** support of African independence and advancement.

Af•ri•can•ist ['æfrəkənɪst] *n.* **1** an expert in African art, history, culture, etc. **2** a person who supports African nationalism and African interests.

Af•ri•can•ize ['æfrəkə,naɪz] *v.* **1** make African. **2** turn over (the government, civil service, etc. of a former colony) to Africans. **—,Af•ri•can•i'za•tion,** *n.*

African violet any of several small, tropical plants (genus *Saintpaulia*) of the gloxinia family having violet, pink, or white flowers, especially *S. ionantha*, cultivated in many varieties as a house plant in temperate climates.

Af•ri•kaans [,æfrə'kɑns] *or* [,æfrə'kɑnz] *n., adj. —n.* one of the official languages of the Republic of South Africa. Afrikaans developed from 17th-century Dutch.
—adj. of or having to do with Afrikaans or Afrikaners. ⟨< Afrikaans spelling of Du. *Afrikaansch*⟩

Af•ri•kan•der [,æfrə'kɑndər] *n.* **1** Afrikaner. **2** a breed of cattle found in southern Africa. ⟨< Afrikaans *Afrikaander*, modelled after Du. *Hollander* Dutchman⟩

Af•ri•ka•ner [,æfrə'kɑnər] *n.* a native or inhabitant of the Republic of South Africa who is of European, especially Dutch, descent. ⟨< Afrikaans *Afrikaander*⟩

af•rit ['æfrit] *or* [ə'frit] *n.* afreet.

Af•ro ['æfrou] *n., pl.* **Af•ros;** *adj. —n.* a hairstyle that takes advantage of the character of very curly hair by leaving it bushy and clipping it into any of various rounded shapes.
—adj. of, for, or designating such a hairstyle: *an Afro cut.* Also, **afro.**

Afro– *combining form.* **1** African: *An Afro-American is an American of African descent.* **2** African and ——: *An Afro-Asian conference involves both African and Asian nations.*

Af•ro–A•mer•i•can [,æfrou ə'mɛrəkən] *n., adj.* AFRICAN-AMERICAN.

Af•ro–A•sian [,æfrou 'eiʒən] *or* [,æfrou 'eiʃən] *adj.* of, having to do with, or involving both Africa and Asia.

Af•ro–A•si•at•ic languages [,æfrou ,eiʒi'ætɪk] *or* [,eiʃi'ætɪk] a family of languages spoken throughout N Africa and SW Asia, made up of the Berber, Chad, Cushitic, Egyptian, and Semitic language groups. Also, **Hamito-Semitic.**

aft [æft] *adv., adj. —adv.* at, near, or toward the stern of a ship or boat or the tail of an aircraft or spacecraft; abaft.
—adj. located at or near the stern or tail: *the aft deck.* ⟨OE *æftan* from behind⟩

af•ter ['æftər] *prep., adv., adj., conj. —prep.* **1** behind (in place): *in line one after another.* **2** next to; following: *day after day.* **3** in pursuit of; in search of: *Run after him. The spy was after a special set of documents.* **4** about; concerning: *Your aunt asked after you.* **5** later in time than: *after supper.* **6** considering; in view of: *After the selfish way she acted, who could like her?* **7** in spite of: *After all her suffering, she is still cheerful.* **8** imitating; in imitation of: *He wrote a fable after the manner of Aesop.* **9** lower in rank or importance than: *A captain comes after a general.* **10** according to: *to act after one's own ideas.* **11** for: *named after his cousin.*
after all, a in spite of everything that has happened, been said, etc. to the contrary: *We decided to go after all.* **b** taking everything into consideration: *After all, what does it really matter?*
—adv. **1** behind: *to follow after.* **2** later: *three hours after.*
—adj. **1** later; subsequent: *In after years he regretted the mistakes of his boyhood.* **2** being nearer or toward the stern: *after sails.*
—conj. later than the time that: *After he goes, we shall eat.* ⟨OE *æfter* more to the rear, later⟩

af•ter•beat ['æftər,bit] *n. Music.* a note (or notes), especially in accompaniment, that follows the beat.

af•ter•birth ['æftər,bɜrθ] *n.* the placenta and membranes expelled from the uterus after childbirth.

af•ter•burn•er ['æftər,bɜrnər] *n.* in a turbojet aircraft, an extra section between the turbojet engine and the tail pipe, in which additional fuel is sprayed into the burning exhaust gases, greatly increasing the thrust of the exhaust jet and thus permitting the aircraft to attain very high speeds.

af•ter•care ['æftər,kɛr] *n.* **1** the care or treatment of convalescent patients. **2** the assistance given to people who have been discharged from prisons, psychiatric hospitals, etc.

af•ter•damp ['æftər,dæmp] *n.* a dangerous mixture of gases left in coal mines after an explosion of FIREDAMP.

af•ter•deck ['æftər,dɛk] *n.* the deck toward or at the stern of a ship.

af•ter–din•ner ['æftər 'dɪnər] *adj.* following dinner: *an after-dinner speech.*

af•ter–ef•fect ['æftər ɪ,fɛkt] *n.* a result or effect that follows something.

af•ter•glow ['æftər,glou] *n.* **1** the glow in the sky after sunset. **2** the good feeling after something exciting and pleasant has passed.

af•ter•grass ['æftər,græs] *n.* a second growth of grass in a field that has been cut.

af•ter•growth ['æftər,grouθ] *n.* a second stage of growth and development; a second growth.

af•ter–im•age ['æftər ,ɪmɪdʒ] *n.* a visual sensation that persists or recurs after the stimulus is withdrawn.

af•ter•life ['æftər,ləif] *n.* **1** life or existence after death. **2** a time later in life.

af•ter•mar•ket ['æftər,mɑrkət] *n.* the market for replacement parts and accessories for manufactured articles as distinct from the parts and accessories used in the original product: *There is a large aftermarket in the automotive industry.*

af•ter•math ['æftər,mæθ] *n.* **1** a result; consequence: *The aftermath of war is hunger and disease.* **2** a crop gathered after the first crop. ⟨< *after* + *math* a mowing < OE *mæth*⟩

af•ter•most ['æftər,moust] *adj.* **1** nearest the stern of a ship. **2** hindmost; last.

af•ter•noon [,æftər'nun] *n., adj. —n.* **1** the part of the day between noon and evening. **2** the later period of something, especially before deterioration.
—adj. of, in, or suitable for the afternoon.

af•ter•pains ['æftər,peinz] *n.* pains caused by uterine contractions after childbirth.

af•ter•shave ['æftər,ʃeiv] *n.* **1** a usually scented, astringent lotion for applying to the face after shaving. **2** (*adjl.*) of or designating a lotion, etc. for use after shaving.

af•ter•shock ['æftər,ʃɒk] *n.* a minor tremor, often one of a series, that closely follows an earthquake.

af•ter•taste ['æftər,teist] *n.* **1** a taste that remains after eating or drinking. **2** the feeling that lingers after some experience.

af•ter•thought ['æftər,θɒt] *n.* **1** a thought that comes after the time when it could have been used. **2** a later thought or explanation.

af•ter•ward ['æftərwərd] *adv.* later. ⟨OE *æfterweard*⟩

af•ter•wards ['æftər wərdz] *adv.* afterward.

af•ter•word ['æftər,wɜrd] *n.* a critical commentary at the end of a book.

af•ter•world ['æftər,wɜrld] *n.* a world believed by some to exist after this one.

ag– *prefix.* the form of **ad-** occurring before *g,* as in *agglutinate.*

Ag silver (for L *argentum).*

A.G. **1** Attorney General. **2** agent general. **3** air gunner. **4** adjutant general.

a•ga ['ɑgə] *n.* in Muslim countries, a commander or chief officer: *The Aga Khan is the leader of a Muslim sect.* Also, **agha.** ⟨< Turkish⟩

a•gain [ə'gɛn] *or* [ə'gein] *adv.* **1** once more; another time: *to try again.* **2** to the same place or person; back: *Bring us word again.* **3** moreover; besides: *Again, I must say that you are wrong.* **4** on the other hand (*often preceded by* **then**): *It might rain, and again it might not.* **5** *Archaic.* in return; in reply: *to answer again.*
again and again, often; frequently.
as much again, twice as much; twice as many. ⟨OE *ongean*⟩

a•gainst [ə'gɛnst] *or* [ə'geinst] *prep.* **1** in an opposite direction to, so as to meet; upon; toward: *to sail against the wind.* **2** in opposition to: *against reason.* **3** directly opposite to; facing: *over against the wall.* **4** in contrast to or with: *The ship appeared against the sky.* **5** in contact with: *to lean against a wall.* **6** in preparation for: *Squirrels store up nuts against the winter.* **7** from: *A fire is a protection against cold.* **8** of a charge, deducted from: *The charges were entered against the total.* ⟨ME *agenes* (< OE *ongean*) + *-t* as in *amidst.* See AGAIN.⟩

a•ga•ma [ə'geimə] *n.* any of a family (Agamidae) of lizards (genus *Agama*) of Europe, Asia, or Africa, some of which have the ability to change colour. ⟨origin uncertain⟩

ag•a•mete ['ægə,mit] *n. Biology.* a reproductive cell that develops into a new individual without being fertilized.

a•gam•ic [ə'gæmɪk] *adj. Biology.* not needing fertilization by the male. ⟨< Gk. *a-* not + *gamos* marriage⟩

ag•a•mous ['ægəməs] *adj. Biology.* asexual.

ag•a•pan•thus [,ægə'pænθəs] *n.* any of several African lilies (*Agapanthus africanus*) having blue or white flowers; African lily or lily-of-the-nile. ⟨< NL < Gk. *agape* love + *anthos* flower⟩

a•gape[1] [ə'geip] *adv. or adj.* (*never precedes a noun*) **1** gaping; with the mouth wide open in wonder or surprise. **2** wide open.

a•ga•pe[2] ['ɑgə,pei], [ə'gɑpei], *or* ['ægəpi] *n. Christianity.* **1** unselfish, brotherly love; CHARITY (def. 5). **2** a love feast, especially of the early Christians. ⟨< Gk. *agapē*⟩

a•gar ['ɑgər], ['ægər], *or* ['eigər] *n.* **1** agar-agar. **2** a preparation containing agar-agar.

a•gar–a•gar ['ɑgər 'ɑgər], ['ægər 'ægər], *or* ['eigər 'eigər] *n.* an extract, resembling gelatin, obtained from certain seaweeds and used in making cultures for bacteria, fungi, etc. and as a glue. ⟨< Malay⟩

ag•a•ric ['ægərɪk], [ə'gærɪk], *or* [ə'gɛrɪk] *n.* any of a family (Agaricaceae) of fungi that includes most edible mushrooms and many poisonous mushrooms. ⟨< L *agaricum* < Gk. *agarikon* < *Agaria,* place name⟩

ag•ate ['ægɪt] *n.* **1** a kind of quartz having different-coloured stripes, clouded colours, or mosslike formations. **2** a gem made from this stone. **3** a playing marble that resembles an agate. **4** *Printing.* a 5½ point size of type. This sentence is set in agate. ⟨< F *agathe* < L *achates* < Gk.⟩ **—'ag•ate,like,** *adj.*

ag•ate•ware ['ægɪt,wɛr] *n.* steel, iron, or ceramic household ware covered with grey enamel so as to look like agate.

a•ga•ve [ə'geivi] *n.* **1** any of a genus (*Agave*) of tropical American plants having thick, fleshy leaves and tall flower stalks. Some species are commercially important as sources of soap, sisal, and alcoholic drinks. **2** (*adjl.*) designating the family of tropical and temperate plants that includes the agaves, yuccas, and the tuberose. ⟨< NL < Gk. *Agauē,* fem. proper name, noble⟩

age [eidʒ] *n., v.* **aged, age•ing** or **ag•ing.** *—n.* **1** time of life: *He died at the age of eighty.* **2** length of life; the time anything has existed: *Her actions belie her age. The age of these elms is greater than that of any other trees in the park.* **3** a period in life: *middle age.* **4** the latter part of life: *the wisdom of age.* **5** the full or average term of life: *The age of a horse is from 25 to 30 years.* **6** a period in history: *the golden age, the space age, the Ice Age.* **7** generation: *ages yet unborn.* **8** *Informal.* a long, or apparently long, time: *We haven't been to the movies in ages.* **9** *Psychology.* the level of a person's attainment, mentally, educationally, emotionally, etc., determined by tests.
of age, old enough to have full legal rights and responsibilities.
—v. **1** grow old: *He is aging rapidly.* **2** make old: *Fear and worry aged her.* **3** improve by keeping for a time; mature: *to age wine.* ⟨ME < OF *aage* < VL *aetaticum* < L *aetas, -tatis* age⟩

–age *suffix.* **1** the act of: *breakage = the act of breaking.* **2** a collection of; group of: *baggage = a group of bags.* **3** the condition of; status of: *peerage = status of peers.* **4** the cost of: *postage = the cost of posting.* **5** a home of or for: *orphanage = a home for orphans.* ⟨< OF < L *-aticum* < Gk.⟩

a•ged ['eidʒɪd] *for adj. 1, 3, n.;* [eidʒd] *for adj. 2. adj., n. —adj.* **1** having lived a long time; old: *The aged woman was still able to look after herself.* **2** of the age of: *a child aged six.* **3** characteristic of old age. **4** made flavourful by keeping: *aged cheese.*
—n. **the aged,** *pl.* elderly people: *The aged now lead much more active lives than formerly was the custom.*
—v. pt. and pp. of AGE.

age•ism ['eidʒɪzəm] *n.* discrimination on the basis of age, especially against the elderly. **—'age•ist,** *n., adj.*

age•less ['eidʒlɪs] *adj.* never growing or seeming to grow old or older; not affected by the passage of time. **—'age•less•ly,** *adv.* **—'age•less•ness,** *n.*

age•long ['eidʒ,lɒŋ] *adj.* lasting a long time.

a•gen•cy ['eidʒənsi] *n., pl.* **-cies. 1** a means; action: *Snow is drifted by the agency of the wind.* **2** the business of a person or company that has the authority to act for another: *An agency rented my house for me.* **3** the office of such a person or company. **4** an organization, usually of the government, that provides assistance in particular areas.

agency shop in Canada, a non-union business which requires employees to give money to a union without joining a union.

a•gen•da [ə'dʒɛndə] *n.* a list or plan of things to be done or accomplished: *The agenda of the next meeting is posted on the bulletin board. What's on our agenda for this afternoon?* ⟨< L *agenda* things to be done, pl. of AGENDUM < *agere* do⟩
☛ *Usage.* **Agenda** was originally a plural noun. It is now used as a singular noun and has the regular plural **agendas.**

a•gen•e•sis [ei'dʒɛnəsɪs] *n.* **1** congenital absence of some part of the body. **2** sterility.

a•gent ['eidʒənt] *n.* **1** a person or company that has the authority to act for another. **2** a person or thing producing a particular effect: *The assassin was an agent of tragedy. Yeast is an important agent in the making of beer.* **3** a means; instrument. **4** SECRET AGENT. **5** a travelling sales representative. **6** *Chemistry.* a substance causing a reaction. ⟨< L *agens, -entis,* ppr. of *agere* do⟩

agent general *pl.* **agents general** or **agent generals.** a representative in the United Kingdom of certain Canadian provinces. *Abbrev.*: A.G.

a•gen•tive [ə'dʒɛntɪv] *adj., n. Grammar. —adj.* of or being a form that indicates agency. *-er* and *-or* are agentive suffixes in English.
—n. such a form. *Worker* is an agentive.

a•gent pro•vo•ca•teur [a'ʒɑ̃ ᴘʀɔvɔka'tœʀ] *French.* a person who incites others to do something that will make them liable to punishment.

age of consent the age at which a person is legally able to agree to marriage, sexual intercourse, medical treatment, etc. without the consent of a parent or guardian.

age–old ['eidʒ 'ould] *adj.* having existed for many ages; very old and still continuing: *the age-old question of astrology.*

ag•er•a•tum [,ædʒə'reitəm] *or* [ə'dʒɛrətəm] *n.* any of a genus (*Ageratum*) of tropical American annual plants of the composite family having compact heads of small blue, white, or pink flowers. ⟨< NL < Gk. *agēraton* < *a-* without + *gēras* old age⟩

ag•gie ['ægi] *n. Informal.* **1** AGATE (def. 3). **2** *Informal.* a student of agriculture.

ag•glom•er•ate *v.* [ə'glɒmə,reit]; *n., adj.* [ə'glɒmərɪt] *or* [ə'glɒmə,reit] *v.* **-at•ed, -at•ing;** *n., adj. —v.* gather together in a mass; cluster together.
—n. **1** a mass; collection; cluster. **2** *Geology.* a rock composed of volcanic fragments fused by heat.
—adj. packed together in a mass. ⟨< L *agglomerare* < *ad-* to + *glomus, glomeris* mass, ball⟩ **—ag'glom•er•a•tive,** *adj.*

ag•glom•er•a•tion [ə,glɒmə'reiʃən] *n.* **1** the act of agglomerating. **2** an agglomerated condition. **3** a mass of things gathered or clustered together.

ag•glu•ti•nate *v.* [ə'glutə,neit]; *adj.* [ə'glutənɪt] *or* [ə'glutə,neit] *v.* **-nat•ed, -nat•ing;** *adj. —v.* **1** stick together; join together. **2** *Linguistics.* of a language, form words by joining other words, or words and affixes, together. **3** *Bacteriology.* cause (cells, etc.) to mass together.
—adj. stuck or joined together: *'Never-to-be-forgotten' is an agglutinate word.* ⟨< L *agglutinare* < *ad-* to + *gluten, glutinis* glue⟩

ag•glu•ti•na•tion [ə,glutə'neiʃən] *n.* **1** the process of agglutinating. **2** an agglutinated condition. **3** a mass of parts sticking together. **4** *Bacteriology.* the massing together of cells, etc. **5** *Linguistics.* the forming of words by joining separate words, or words and affixes, together.

ag•glu•ti•na•tive [ə'glutənətiv] *or* [ə'glutə,neitiv] *adj.* **1** tending to stick together. **2** *Linguistics.* of a language (for example, Turkish), forming words by joining words, or words and affixes, together. Compare ANALYTIC.

ag•glu•ti•nin [ə'glutənɪn] *n.* a substance causing coagulation of the blood.

ag•glu•tin•o•gen [,æglu'tɪnədʒən] *n.* any antigen that stimulates the production of an agglutinin.

ag•grade [ə'greid] *v.* build up (a river valley, etc.) by accumulation of alluvial sediment. **—,ag•gra'da•tion** [,ægrə'deiʃən], *n.*

ag•gran•dize [ə'grændaɪz] *or* ['ægrən,daɪz] *v.* **-dized, -diz•ing.** increase in power, wealth, rank, etc.; make greater: *The dictator sought to aggrandize himself at the expense of his people.* ⟨< F *agrandiss-*, a stem of *agrandir*, ult. < L *ad-* + *grandis* large⟩ **—ag'gran,diz•er,** *n.*

ag•gran•dize•ment [ə'grændɪzmənt] *n.* an increase in power, wealth, rank, etc.; making greater.

ag•gra•vate ['ægrə,veit] *v.* **-vat•ed, -vat•ing. 1** make worse or more severe: *Her bad temper was aggravated by her headache.* **2** *Informal.* annoy; irritate; exasperate. ⟨< L *aggravare* < *ad-* on + *gravis* heavy. Doublet of AGGRIEVE.⟩ **—'ag•gra,vat•ing•ly,** *adv.* **—'ag•gra,va•tor,** *n.*

ag•gra•va•tion [,ægrə'veiʃən] *n.* **1** making or being made worse or more severe: *the aggravation of an illness.* **2** something that makes worse or more severe. **3** *Informal.* annoyance or exasperation, or a cause of this.

ag•gre•gate *adj., n.* ['ægrəgɪt] *or* ['ægrə,geit]; *v.* ['ægrə,geit] *adj., n., v.* **-gat•ed, -gat•ing.** *—adj.* **1** formed by the collection of parts or units into one body, mass, or amount; collected, whole, or total: *The aggregate value of all the gifts was $1000.* **2** *Botany.* **a** of a flower, composed of many florets forming a head. **b** of a fruit, formed from the development together of several pistils of a single flower: *The raspberry and strawberry are aggregate fruits.* **3** *Geology.* composed of mineral crystals or rock fragments: *Granite is an aggregate rock.*
—n. **1** a mass of separate things joined together or associated; collection: *The report was an aggregate of the viewpoints of the committee members.* **2** the sum total; total amount. **3** *Geology.* an aggregate rock: *volcanic aggregates.* **4** material such as broken stone, sand, or gravel, used to make concrete.
in the aggregate, together; as a whole.
—v. **1** collect together or unite. **2** amount to: *The money collected is expected to aggregate over $3000.* ⟨< L *aggregare* < *ad-* to + *grex, gregis* flock⟩ **—'ag•gre•gate•ly** *adv.*

ag•gre•ga•tion [,ægrə'geiʃən] *n.* **1** the collection of separate things into one mass or whole. **2** the resulting whole.

ag•gress [ə'grɛs] *v.* start a quarrel; be the aggressor.

ag•gres•sion [ə'grɛʃən] *n.* **1** the making by one nation of an unprovoked attack or assault on the rights or territories of another. **2** any unprovoked attack. **3** *Psychology.* an act or attitude of hostility, usually arising from feelings of inferiority or frustration. ⟨< L *aggressio, -onis* < *aggredi* < *ad-* to + *gradi* to step⟩

ag•gres•sive [ə'grɛsɪv] *adj.* **1** taking or tending to take the first step in an attack or quarrel: *aggressive behaviour, an aggressive nation.* **2** energetic and forceful: *an aggressive political campaign.* **3** unpleasantly forceful; pushy: *an aggressive salesperson.* **—ag,gres•sive•ly,** *adv.* **—,ag•gres'siv•i•ty,** *n.*

ag•gres•sor [ə'grɛsər] *n.* one that commits aggression; one that begins an attack or quarrel.

ag•grieve [ə'griv] *v.* **-grieved, -griev•ing. 1** injure unjustly; cause grief or trouble to: *He was aggrieved at the insult from his friend.* **2** infringe on the legal rights of (workers, etc.). ⟨ME *agreve* < OF *agrever* < L *aggravare.* Doublet of AGGRAVATE.⟩

ag•grieved [ə'grivd] *adj., v.* *—adj.* **1** injured or offended as to rights, position, etc.: *make amends to an aggrieved victim of injustice.* **2** feeling distressed or wronged, whether justly or not.
—v. pt. and pp. of AGGRIEVE.

a•gha ['ɑgə] *n.* aga.

a•ghast [ə'gæst] *adj.* filled with extreme surprise or horror; dumfounded; shocked (*never used before a noun*): *They were aghast at the violence of the crime.* ⟨ME pp. of obs. *agast* terrify < OE *on-* on + *gæstan* frighten. Related to GHOST.⟩

ag•ile ['ædʒaɪl] *or* ['ædʒəl] *adj.* **1** moving quickly and easily; nimble: *An acrobat has to be agile.* **2** able to think quickly;

mentally nimble. ⟨ME < OF < L *agilis* < *agere* move⟩ **—'ag•ile•ly,** *adv.* **—'ag•ile•ness,** *n.*

a•gil•i•ty [ə'dʒɪləti] *n.* the ability to move quickly and easily; activeness; liveliness; nimbleness.

ag•io ['ædʒi,ou] *n.* when converting one currency into another more valuable, the extra amount of the first paid to equal the second. ⟨< F < Ital. *aggio*⟩

ag•i•tate ['ædʒə,teit] *v.* **-tat•ed, -tat•ing. 1** move or shake violently. **2** disturb; excite (the feelings or the thoughts): *She was much agitated by the news of her brother's accident.* **3** argue about; discuss vigorously. **4** keep arguing about and discussing a matter to arouse public interest: *agitate for a shorter working week.* ⟨< L *agitare* move to and fro < *agere* drive, move⟩ **—'ag•i,tat•ed•ly,** *adv.*

ag•i•ta•tion [,ædʒə'teiʃən] *n.* **1** a violent moving or shaking. **2** a disturbed, upset, or troubled state. **3** argument or discussion to arouse public interest.

a•gi•ta•to [,ɑdʒi'tɑtou] *adj., adv.* *—adj. Music.* restless, agitated.
—adv. in a restless or agitated manner. ⟨< Ital.⟩

ag•i•ta•tor ['ædʒə,teitər] *n.* **1** a person who tries to make people discontented with things as they are. **2** a device for shaking or stirring: *the agitator in a washing machine.*

ag•it•prop ['ædʒɪt,prɒp] *n.* **1** political propaganda in the form of drama, music, or art, especially communist propaganda. **2** (*adjl.*) of or having to do with such propaganda. ⟨< Russian *agitprop*, abbrev. of *agitats'iya* agitation⟩

a•gleam [ə'glim] *adv. or adj.* (*never precedes a noun*) gleaming.

ag•let ['æglɪt] *n.* the small metal tip at the end of a shoelace.

a•glit•ter [ə'glɪtər] *adv. or adj.* (*never precedes a noun*) glittering.

a•glow [ə'glou] *adv. or adj.* (*never precedes a noun*) glowing; in a glow.

ag•lu or **ag•loo** ['æglu] *n. Cdn.* a breathing-hole in ice, made by seals. ⟨< Inuktitut⟩

ag•nos•tic [æg'nɒstɪk] *n., adj.* *—n.* a person who believes that nothing is known or can be known about the existence of God or about things outside empirical phenomena.
—adj. of agnostics or their beliefs. ⟨< Gk. *agnōstos* < *a-* not + *gnōstos* (to be) known⟩ **—ag'nos•ti•cal•ly,** *adv.*

ag•nos•ti•cism [æg'nɒstə,sɪzəm] *n.* the belief or intellectual attitude of agnostics.

Ag•nus De•i ['ægnəs 'deii] *or* ['diaɪ] *Christianity.* **1** an image of a lamb as a symbol of Christ. **2** the part of the Mass beginning "Agnus Dei." **3** the music for it. **4** a blessed cake of wax bearing the image of a lamb. ⟨< L *Agnus Dei* Lamb of God⟩

a•go [ə'gou] *adj., adv.* *—adj.* gone by; past (*always placed after the noun*): *a year ago.*
—adv. in the past: *She went long ago.* ⟨OE *āgān* gone by⟩

a•gog [ə'gɒg] *adj. or adv.* (*never precedes a noun*) in a state of great excitement, curiosity, etc. ⟨? < OF *en gogues* in happy mood⟩

a–go–go [ə 'gou ,gou] *adj.* GO-GO.

a•gon•ic [ə'gɒnɪk] *adj. Mathematics.* not making an angle. ⟨< Gk. < *a-* without + *gonia* angle⟩

agonic line an imaginary line running through the two poles, along which true north and magnetic north are the same.

a•gon•ist•ic [,ægə'nɪstɪk] *adj.* **1** overly competitive; argumentative. **2** striving to impress: *The comedian's agonistic humour disgusted the audience.*

ag•o•nize ['ægə,naɪz] *v.* **-nized, -niz•ing. 1** feel great anguish. **2** cause to suffer extreme pain; torture. **3** strive painfully; struggle. ⟨< F *agoniser* < LL *agōnizāre* < Gk. *agōnizethai* struggle < *agón* a contest⟩ **—'ag•o,niz•ing•ly,** *adv.*

ag•o•ny ['ægəni] *n., pl.* **-nies. 1** great pain or suffering. **2** the struggle often preceding death. ⟨ME < OF < LL < Gk. *agōnia* struggle⟩

☛ *Usage.* **Agony.** Often used in informal English in a light vein in such expressions as: *My shoes hurt; I'm in agony. I have to do my history assignment some time; I might as well get the agony over now.*

ag•o•ra¹ ['ægərə] *n., pl.* **-rae** [-,ri] *or* [-,raɪ]. the marketplace in an ancient Greek city. **The Agora** in Athens was used for public assemblies. ⟨< Gk. *agora*⟩

ag•o•ra² [,ɑgə'rɑ] *n., pl.* **ag•o•rot** [,ɑgə'rout]. **1** a unit of money in Israel, worth 1/100 of a shekel. **2** a coin worth one agora. ⟨< Hebrew *agora* a small coin⟩

ag•o•ra•phobe ['ægərə,foub], ['ægrə,foub] *or* [ə'gɔrə,foub] *n.* a person with agoraphobia.

ag•o•ra•pho•bi•a [,ægərə'foubiə], [,ægrə'foubiə], *or* [ə,gɔrə'foubiə] *n.* a morbid fear of open spaces or public places.

ag•o•ra•pho•bic [,ægərə'foubɪk] *adj., n. —adj.* having agoraphobia.
—n. an agoraphobe.

ag•o•rot [,ɑgə'rout] *n.* pl. of AGORA[2].

a•gou•ti [ə'guti] *n., pl.* **-tis** or **-ties.** any of a genus (*Dasyprocta*) of tropical American rodents having long legs, small ears, a very short tail, and grizzled, reddish brown to blackish fur. ⟨< F < Sp. *aguti* < native Indian name⟩

a•graffe [ə'græf] *n.* a metal ornamental clasp for clothing. Also, **agrafe.** ⟨< F⟩

a•gram•ma•tism [ei'græmə,tɪzəm] *or* [ə'græmə,tɪzəm] *n.* loss of the ability to form grammatical sentences, due to injury, stroke, or disease.

a•gran•u•lo•cy•to•sis [ei,grænjəlousəi'tousɪs] *n.* destruction of the granulocytes in the blood, causing weakness and fever.

ag•ra•pha ['ægrəfə] *n.* the sayings attributed to Christ but not found in the New Testament. ⟨< Gk.⟩

a•graph•i•a [ei'græfiə] *n.* a disorder of the brain that causes inability to write.

a•grar•i•an [ə'grɛriən] *adj., n. —adj.* **1** having to do with land, its use, or its ownership. **2** for the support and advancement of the interests of farmers. **3** agricultural.
—n. a person who favours a new division of land. ⟨< L *agrarius* < *ager* field⟩

a•grar•i•an•ism [ə'grɛriə,nɪzəm] *n.* **1** the principles, methods, or practices of agrarians. **2** an agitation for a redistribution of landed property.

a•gree [ə'gri] *v.* **a•greed, a•gree•ing. 1** have the same opinion or opinions: *I agree with you. The two partners usually agreed on important issues.* **2** be alike or be similar to; be in harmony; correspond (*with*): *Her story agrees with theirs.* **3** get along well together. **4** consent (*to*): *We agreed to their proposal. He agreed to accompany us.* **5** come to an understanding, especially in settling a dispute. **6** concede (a fact): *We agreed that the child's behaviour had been atrocious.* **7** be suitable, healthful, etc. (*used with* **with**): *Bananas don't agree with him; they make him sick.* **8** *Grammar.* have the same number, case, gender, or person: *In English, the subject and verb of a sentence have to agree in number.* ⟨ME < OF *agréer* < *à gré* to (one's) liking < L *ad* to + *gratum*, neut., pleasing⟩

☛ *Syn.* **2. Agree,** CORRESPOND, COINCIDE = be in harmony. **Agree** = not only to be consistent or harmonious in all essentials, but also to be without inconsistencies or contradictions: *The views of the two leaders agree.* **Correspond** = to agree or to equal in essentials or as a whole, in spite of differences: *Canada Day corresponds to the American Independence Day.* **Coincide** = agree so closely as to be identical: *Her tastes coincide with mine.*

☛ *Usage.* **Agree to, agree with.** One agrees *to* a plan and agrees *with* a person, but one thing agrees *with* another.

a•gree•a•bil•i•ty [ə,griə'bɪləti] *n.* the quality of being agreeable.

a•gree•a•ble [ə'griəbəl] *adj.* **1** pleasant; pleasing: *agreeable manners.* **2** ready to agree; willing: *agreeable to a suggestion.* **3** usually of a proposed arrangement, satisfactory. **4** in agreement; suitable (*to*): *music agreeable to the occasion.* ⟨< F *agréable*⟩ **—a'gree•a•ble•ness,** *n.* **—a'gree•a•bly,** *adv.*

☛ *Syn.* **1.** See note at PLEASANT.

a•greed [ə'grid] *adj., v. —adj.* fixed by common consent.
—v. pt. and pp. of AGREE.

a•gree•ment [ə'grimənt] *n.* **1** an agreeing; an understanding reached by two or more nations, persons, or groups of persons among themselves. Nations make treaties and individuals make contracts; both are agreements. **2** sameness of opinion. **3** harmony; correspondence. **4** *Grammar.* correspondence of words with respect to number, case, gender, person. In *The girls are here,* there is an agreement in number between subject and verb.

ag. rep. or **ag–rep** ['æg 'rɛp] *n. Cdn.* agricultural representative; an official appointed by a provincial government to act as adviser to farmers in a particular district.

ag•ri•busi•ness ['ægrə,bɪznəs] *n.* the whole group of businesses and industries involved in the production, processing, and marketing of agricultural products, especially as distinct from small-scale farming.

agric. agriculture.

ag•ri•cul•tur•al [,ægrə'kʌltʃərəl] *adj.* **1** having to do with farming; of agriculture. **2** promoting the interests or the study of agriculture. **—ag•ri'cul•tur•al•ly,** *adv.*

ag•ri•cul•tur•al•ist [,ægrə'kʌltʃərəlɪst] *n.* agriculturist.

ag•ri•cul•ture ['ægrə,kʌltʃər] *n.* farming; the raising of crops and livestock; the science or art of cultivating the ground. ⟨< L *agricultura* < *ager* field + *cultura* cultivation⟩

ag•ri•cul•tur•ist [,ægrə'kʌltʃərɪst] *n.* **1** a person trained in agriculture, especially one whose work it is. **2** farmer.

ag•ri•mo•ny ['ægrə,mouni] *or* ['ægrəməni] *n., pl.* **-nies.** any of a genus (*Agrimonia*) of plants of the rose family, especially *A. eupatoria*, a tall European perennial having feathery leaves that yield a yellow dye, long spikes of small yellow flowers, and fruit like small burrs. ⟨< L *agrimonia*, var. of *argemonia* < Gk. *argemōnē*⟩

ag•ri•ol•o•gy [,ægri'ɒlədʒi] *n.* the study of peoples who have little or no technology. ⟨< Gk. *ágrios* wild + *-ology*⟩

ag•ro•bi•ol•o•gist [,ægroubaɪ'ɒlədʒɪst] *n.* a person trained in agrobiology, especially one whose work it is.

ag•ro•bi•ol•o•gy [,ægroubaɪ'ɒlədʒi] *n.* the study of plant nutrition and soil management. **—,ag•ro,bi•o'log•i•cal,** *adj.*

ag•ro•chem•ic•al [,ægrou'kɛməkəl] *n.* a chemical used to increase the quantity and quality of agricultural products.

a•grol•o•gist [ə'grɒlədʒɪst] *n.* a person trained in AGROLOGY, especially one whose work it is.

a•grol•o•gy [ə'grɒlədʒi] *n.* the branch of agricultural science that deals with soils. ⟨< Gk. *agros* field + *ology*⟩

ag•ro•ma•ni•a [,ægrou'meiniə] *n.* an abnormal desire to live in the open country, away from people. ⟨< Gk. *agros* field + *mania*⟩

ag•ro•nom•ic [,ægrə'nɒmɪk] *adj.* of or having to do with agronomy. Also, **agronomical**.

a•gron•o•mist [ə'grɒnəmɪst] *n.* a person skilled in agronomy.

a•gron•o•my [ə'grɒnəmi] *n.* the science of managing farmland; the branch of agriculture dealing with crop production; husbandry. ⟨< Gk. *agronomos* < *agros* land + *nemein* manage⟩

ag•ros•tol•o•gy [,ægrə'stɒlədʒi] *n. Botany.* the study of grasses. ⟨< Gk. *agrostis* grass + *-ology*⟩

a•ground [ə'graʊnd] *adv. or adj.* (*never precedes a noun*) on or onto the shore or the bottom in shallow water: *The ship ran aground on a reef.*

agt. agent.

a•gue ['eigju] *n.* **1** a malarial fever with chills and sweating occurring at regular intervals. **2** a fit of shivering; chill. ⟨ME < OF < L *acuta (febris)* severe (fever)⟩

a•gu•ish ['eigjuɪʃ] *adj.* **1** of or like ague. **2** causing ague. **3** liable to have ague.

ah [ɑ] *interj.* an exclamation of pain, sorrow, regret, pity, admiration, surprise, joy, dislike, contempt, etc. The meaning of *ah* varies according to the context and the way it is said.

A.H. numbered in the Muslim dating system, 1A.H. corresponds to 622 A.D., the year of Mohammed's flight from Mecca to Medina. ⟨for L *anno Hegirae* year of the Hegira. See HEGIRA.⟩

a•ha [ɑ'hɑ] *interj.* an exclamation of triumph, satisfaction, surprise, etc.

a•head [ə'hɛd] *adv.* **1** in front; before: *Walk ahead of me.* **2** forward; onward: *Go ahead with this work.* **3** in advance: *Columbus was ahead of his times in his belief that the world was round.* **4** in or into the lead, as in a race or game: *The Maple Leafs shot ahead 3 to 1.*
be ahead, have gained: *When recess was over, Fatima was ahead five points.*
get ahead, *Informal.* succeed.
get ahead of, surpass; excel. ⟨< *on head*⟩

a•hem [ə'hɛm] *interj.* a word used to represent the sound made by coughing or clearing the throat, sometimes done to attract attention, express doubt, or gain time. ⟨imitative⟩

a•him•sa [ə'hɪm,sɑ] *n.* the principle of non-violence in Hinduism, Buddhism, etc. ⟨< Sanskrit *a* not + *hiṁsā* injury⟩

a•his•tor•ic•al [,eihɪ'stɔrɪkəl] *adj.* **1** not documented as history. **2** not related to history or to time.

a•hold [ə'hould] *n. Informal.* a grasp on something: *Get ahold of yourself!*
get ahold of, *Informal.* communicate with (a person).

-aholic *combining form.* one who is obsessed by something. A chocaholic is obsessed by chocolate. ⟨modified < (*alc*)*oholic*⟩

A ho•ri•zon ['ei hə,raizən] *Geology.* the topsoil in a profile of soil.

a•hoy [ə'hɔɪ] *interj.* a call used by sailors to attract the attention of persons at a distance: *When sailors call to a ship, they shout, "Ship ahoy!"* ⟨A[1] + ME *hoy* exclamation⟩

Ah•ri•man ['ɑrɪmən] *n.* ANGRA MAINYU.

A•hu•ra Maz•da [ə'hʊrə 'mæzdə] In Zoroastrianism, the supreme deity; the wise and good lord of creation; the good spirit of the cosmos.

ai ['ɑi] *n.* a large sloth of Central America (*Bradypus tridactylus*). ⟨< Portuguese⟩

AI or **A.I.** **1** *Computer technology.* artificial intelligence. **2** artificial insemination.

aid [eid] *v., n.* —*v.* give support to; help: *The Red Cross aids flood victims.*
—*n.* **1** help; support: *When my arm was broken, I could not dress without aid.* **2** a helper; assistant. **3** any assisting device: *a hearing aid.* ⟨ME < OF *aidier* < L *adjūtāre,* frequentative of *adjūvāre* < *ad-* to + *jūvāre* help⟩
☛ *Syn. v.* See note at HELP.

aide [eid] *n.* **1** AIDE-DE-CAMP. **2** an aid; helper. ⟨< F⟩

aide–de–camp ['eid də 'kæmp]; *French,* [ɛddə'kɑ̃] *n., pl.* **aides-de-camp.** a military officer who acts as an assistant and secretary to a superior officer. *Abbrev.:* ADC, A.D.C., or a.d.c. ⟨< F⟩

aide–mé•moire [ɛdme'mwaʀ] *n. French.* **1** anything that reminds, such as a calendar note. **2** a written summary or outline of a communication or proposed agreement; memorandum.

AIDS [eidz] *n.* ACQUIRED IMMUNE DEFICIENCY SYNDROME.

AIDS–related complex a condition that is often a precursor to AIDS. Its most common symptom is enlarged lymph nodes.

aid station a medical centre providing immediate medical aid to troops in the field.

ai•grette [ei'grɛt] *or* ['eigrɛt] *n.* **1** a tuft of feathers worn as an ornament on the head. **2** anything similar in shape or use. **3** egret. ⟨< F *aigrette* egret⟩

ai•guille [ei'gwil] *or* ['eigwil] *n.* **1** in mountainous regions, a thin, sharp-pointed peak of rock. **2** an instrument for boring holes, used in masonry or blasting. ⟨< F *aiguille* needle < LL *acicula, acucula,* dim. of L *acus* needle⟩

ai•guil•lette [,eigwɪ'lɛt] *n.* a tagged braid on a uniform.

ai•ki•do [aɪ'kidou] *or* [,aɪki'dou] *n.* a form of self-defence to immobilize an attacker. ⟨< Japanese *ai* co-ordinate + *ki* control of breath + *do* a way⟩

ail [eil] *v.* **1** be the matter with; trouble: *What ails the man?* **2** be ill; feel sick: *He is ailing.* **3** of a business, be in financial difficulty. ⟨OE *eglan*⟩
☛ *Hom.* ALE.

ai•lan•thus [ei'lænθəs] *n.* any of a small genus (*Ailanthus*) of trees and shrubs native to tropical Asia, having compound leaves growing along either side of the stalk. The tree of heaven is an ailanthus. ⟨< NL < Amboinan (language of Amboina in the Dutch East Indies) *aylanto* tree of heaven; form influenced by Gk. *anthos* flower⟩

ai•ler•on ['eilə,rɒn] *n.* a small, movable section on the front or back edge of the wing of an aircraft for controlling the side-to-side motion of the aircraft in flight. ⟨< F *aileron,* dim. of *aile* < L *ala* wing⟩

ail•ment ['eilmənt] *n.* a disorder of the body or mind; illness; sickness.

ailu•ro•phile [ei'lʊrə,faɪl] *or* [aɪ'lʊrə,faɪl] *n.* a cat-lover. ⟨< Gk. *aílouros* cat + *phile*⟩

ailu•ro•pho•bi•a [ei,lʊrə'foubiə] *or* [aɪ,lʊrə'foubiə] *n.* a morbid fear of cats. ⟨< Gk. *aílouros* cat + *phobia*⟩ **—ai'lu•ro,phobe,** *n.* **—ai,lu•ro'pho•bic,** *adj.*

aim [eim] *v.* **1** point or direct (a gun, blow, etc.) in order to hit a target: *to aim at something, to aim a gun.* **2** direct (words or acts): *The prime minister's speech was aimed at people in her own party.* **3** *Informal.* intend: *I aim to go.* **4** *Informal.* try; direct one's efforts: *He aims to be helpful.*
—*n.* **1** the act of aiming. **2** the direction aimed in; line of sighting. **3** purpose; intention. **4** the ability of a person or a weapon to hit a target: *This rifle has good aim.*
take aim (at), aim a weapon, words, or an act (at). ⟨ME < OF *esmer* < L *aestimare* appraise, and OF *aesmer* < VL *adæstimare*⟩

aim•less ['eimlɪs] *adj.* without aim or purpose. **—'aim•less•ly,** *adv.* **—'aim•less•ness,** *n.*

ain't [eint] *Informal.* **1** am not, are not, or is not. **2** have not or has not.
☛ *Usage.* **Ain't** has long been used in English, though it is unacceptable to most educated speakers. It should not be used in formal English.

Ai•nu ['aɪnu] *n., adj.* —*n.* **1** a member of an aboriginal, light-skinned people in N Japan, now becoming extinct. **2** the language of this people, for which no familial relationship is known.
—*adj.* of this people or their language.

air [ɛr] *n., v.* —*n.* **1** the mixture of gases that surrounds the earth; atmosphere. Air consists of nitrogen, oxygen, argon, carbon dioxide, hydrogen, and small quantities of neon, helium, and other inert gases. **2** fresh air; cool, pleasant air: *"Give me air," he cried as he left the crowded auditorium.* **3** the space overhead; sky: *Birds fly in the air.* **4** a light wind; breeze. **5** transport by aircraft: *We're going to Winnipeg by air.* **6** *Informal.* air conditioning: *Do you have air in this house?* **7** public mention: *He gave air to his opinions.* **8** the general character or appearance of anything: *an air of mystery.* **9** bearing; manner: *The famous woman had an air of importance.* **10 airs,** *pl.* unnatural or affected manners. **11** *Music.* **a** a composition to be played or sung as a solo: *Bach's Air on the G String.* **b** any tune or melody, especially a simple one. **c** the main melody in a harmonized composition, usually the soprano or treble part. **12** the medium through which radio waves travel. **13** (*adjl.*) conducting or supplying air: *an air duct.* **14** (*adjl.*) **a** compressing or confining air: *an air valve.* **b** using or worked by compressed air: *an air drill.* **15** (*adjl.*) relating to aviation; done by means of aircraft: *air photography.*
get the air, *Slang.* be dismissed or rejected.
give the air, *Slang.* dismiss, especially scornfully.
in the air, a going around: *Wild rumours were in the air.* **b** uncertain.
into thin air, without leaving a trace; completely: *He just disappeared into thin air and hasn't been seen since.*
off the air, a not broadcasting: *Our radio station is off the air from one till six a.m.* **b** not being broadcast: *That show is off the air now.*
on the air, broadcasting or being broadcast.
out of thin air, by magic or as if by magic: *She suddenly appeared out of thin air. They seem to expect us to produce a workable plan out of thin air.*
take the air, a go outdoors; take a walk or ride. **b** start broadcasting.
up in the air, a *Informal.* uncertain; unsettled. **b** *Informal.* very angry or excited.
walking on air, *Informal.* very happy or pleased.
—*v.* **1** put out in the air; let air through: *to air clothes.* **2** make known; mention publicly: *Do not air your troubles.* **3** take for a walk: *to air the dog.* **4** *Informal.* broadcast or be broadcast by radio or television: *The Olympic Games were aired to all of Canada. Her show airs every day at noon.* ⟨ME < OF < L *aer* < Gk. *aēr*⟩
☛ *Hom.* ARE[2], E'ER, ERE, ERR, EYRE, HEIR.

air alert **1** flying in anticipation of meeting enemy aircraft or receiving orders. **2** a signal to assume such flying positions.

air ambulance an aircraft used as an ambulance.

air bag a large plastic bag in a vehicle that inflates in a collision to protect the driver and passengers from possible injury.

air base headquarters and airport for military aircraft.

air bladder in most fish and in some animals and plants, a sac containing air. The air bladder in fish, usually called a swim bladder, acts as an aid in breathing and hearing or helps the fish to maintain buoyancy in the water.

air•borne ['ɛr,bɔrn] *adj.* **1** carried through the air: *airborne seeds, airborne bacteria.* **2** transported by aircraft: *airborne troops.*

3 of aircraft, in the air after taking off; flying: *After another delay, we were finally airborne.*

air brake a brake operated by a piston or pistons worked by compressed air.

air•brush ['ɛr,brʌʃ] *n., v.* *—n.* a device, operated by compressed air, used to apply a fine spray of paint, liquid colour, etc. onto a surface.
—v. apply paint or colour to (a photograph, etc.) with an airbrush, in order to remove blemishes or unwanted details or to improve finish: *to airbrush a photograph.*

air•bus ['ɛr,bʌs] *n.* a passenger aircraft, operating on a regular route and as part of a frequent service, which one may board without an advance reservation, simply by paying cash as on a bus or streetcar.

air cadet a person under military age who is undertaking basic air-command training in an organization subsidized by the armed forces.

air chamber any compartment filled with air, especially one in a hydraulic engine. See CAISSON for picture.

air chief marshal an air-force officer ranking next above an air marshall. See chart of ranks in the Appendix. *Abbrev.*: A.C.M.

air coach *Esp. U.S.* an aircraft with low passenger rates.

air cock a small opening or valve for letting air in or out.

Air Command *Cdn.* a major organizational element of the Canadian Forces, whose role is to provide combat-ready air defence forces over land and sea.

air commodore an air-force officer ranking next above a group captain and below an air vice-marshal. See chart of ranks in the Appendix. *Abbrev.*: A.C.

air–con•di•tion ['ɛr kən,dɪʃən] *v.* **1** supply with the equipment for air conditioning. **2** treat (air) by means of air conditioning.

air–con•di•tioned ['ɛr kən,dɪʃənd] *adj.* having air conditioning.

air conditioner an apparatus used to air-condition a room, building, train, etc.

air conditioning a means of treating air in buildings, rooms, trains, etc. to regulate its temperature (especially to cool it) and humidity and to free it from dust.

air–cool ['ɛr ,kul] *v.* **1** cool (an engine) by blowing air into it to remove the heat produced by combustion, friction, etc. **2** remove heat in (a room) by blowing cool air in. **—'air-,cool•er,** *n.*

air corridor an established route or passage along which aircraft are permitted to fly.

air cover the protection given to troops by aircraft.

air•craft ['ɛr,kræft] *n., pl.* **-craft.** a machine for navigation in the air, supported in the air either by aerodynamic forces acting on its surfaces (as an airplane, helicopter, or glider) or by buoyancy (as a dirigible).

aircraft carrier a warship having a large, flat deck designed as a base for aircraft.

air•craft•man ['ɛr,kræftmən] *n., pl.* **-men.** an air-force serviceman of the lowest rank. See chart of ranks in the Appendix. *Abbrev.*: A.C.

air•craft•wom•an ['ɛr,kræft,wʊmən] *n., pl.* **-wom•en.** an air-force servicewoman of the lowest rank. See chart of ranks in the Appendix. *Abbrev.*: A.W. or A.C.W.

aircrew ['ɛr,kru] *n.* the crew of an aircraft.

air curtain a mass of heated or cooled air circulated around the entrance of a building, in front of and around storage areas, etc., to hold in or keep out warm air and to serve in place of a door.

air cushion **1** an inflatable rubber or rubberized casing for use as a cushion or pad. **2** a layer of air under pressure, such as that which supports a hovercraft, lessens the shock of an impact, etc.

air–cushion vehicle ['ɛr ,kʊʃən] hovercraft.

air cylinder a cylinder in which air is compressed by a piston, for checking the recoil of a gun.

air•drop ['ɛr,drɒp] *n., v.* **-dropped, -drop•ping.** *—n.* a system for or an instance of dropping food, supplies, etc. from aircraft, especially to allies or refugees who are caught behind enemy lines, living in occupied territory, etc.
—v. deliver (supplies, etc.) in this way.

air–dry ['ɛr ,draɪ] *v.* **-dried, -dry•ing** dry by exposing to air.

Aire•dale ['ɛr,deil] *n.* a breed of large terrier, about 58 cm high at the shoulder, having a wiry tan coat with a large, dark patch on the back and sides. The Airedale is a popular family dog.
⟨< *Airedale* in Yorkshire, England⟩

An Airedale

air express a quick or direct means of sending goods by aircraft.

air–ex•press ['ɛr ɛk,sprɛs] *v.* send by air express.

air•fare ['er,fɛr] the cost of a flight in an aircraft.

air•field ['ɛr,fild] *n.* the landing field of an airport.

air•flow ['ɛr,flou] *n.* **1** the motion of air relative to the surface of a moving object, such as an aircraft or automobile. **2** a natural movement of air or wind. **3** (*adjl.*) resulting from air currents: *The airflow pattern changes when an aircraft crosses the sonic barrier.* **4** (*adjl.*) streamlined: *airflow design.*

air•foil ['ɛr,fɔɪl] *n.* any surface, such as a wing, rudder, etc. designed to help lift or control an aircraft.

air force Often, **Air Force,** the branch of the armed forces of a nation responsible for military aircraft. In Canada, the function of an air force is served by Air Command of the Canadian Forces.

air•frame ['ɛr,freim] *n.* the structure or framework, excluding engines, of an airplane, rocket, etc.

air freight **1** freight carried by aircraft. **2** the sending of freight carried by aircraft.

air–freight ['ɛr ,freit] *v.* send by air freight.

air•glow ['ɛr,glou] *n.* a glow at night that comes from the upper atmosphere in the mid and low latitudes.

air gun **1** a gun worked by compressed air. **2** an instrument to spray paint or other liquids, shaped like a gun and worked by compressed air.

air•head ['ɛr,hɛd] *n.* **1** in warfare, a place captured for the landing of aircraft by invading forces. Compare BEACHHEAD. **2** *Slang.* a giddy or silly person.

air hole **1** a hole that allows air to pass through. **2** a hole in the ice covering a body of water, often used as a breathing hole by seals, muskrats, etc. **3** AIR POCKET.

air•i•ly ['ɛrəli] *adv.* in an airy manner.

air•i•ness ['ɛrinɪs] *n.* an airy quality.

air•ing ['ɛrɪŋ] *n.* **1** exposure to air for drying, warming, etc.; putting out in the air; letting air through. **2** a walk, ride, or drive in the open air. **3** exposure to public discussion, criticism, etc.

air lane a regular route used by aircraft.

air•less ['ɛrlɪs] *adj.* **1** without fresh air; stuffy. **2** without a breeze; still.

air letter a pre-stamped letter form used for international airmail, consisting of a single sheet of paper (for writing on) which is folded, sealed, and addressed on the outside, so that no envelope is required.

air•lift ['ɛr,lɪft] *n., v.* *—n.* **1** a system or the act of using aircraft for passenger transportation and freight conveyance to a place when land approaches are closed: *the Berlin airlift.* **2** something transported by such a system.
—v. transport by such a system.

air•line ['ɛr,laɪn] *n.* **1** a company operating a system of transportation by means of aircraft. **2** the system itself. **3** (*adjl.*) of or having to do with an airline: *airline schedules.*

air line GREAT CIRCLE (def. 2).

air•lin•er ['ɛr,laɪnər] *n.* a large aircraft operated by an airline for carrying passengers.

air lock an airtight compartment in which the air pressure can be adjusted, as between the outside air and the working compartment of a caisson. See CAISSON for picture.

air•mail or **air–mail** ['ɛr,meil] *v., adj.* *—v.* send or transport by air mail.
—adj. of, having to do with, or sent by air mail.

air mail **1** mail sent by aircraft. **2** the system of sending mail by aircraft.

air•man ['ɛrmən] *n., pl.* **-men.** **1** a man connected with flying, especially as a pilot, crew member, or ground technician. **2** aircraftman. See chart of ranks in the Appendix. **3** any man serving in an air force.

air marshal an air-force officer ranking next above an air vice-marshal and below an air chief marshal. See chart of ranks in the Appendix. *Abbrev.*: A.M.

air mass a large area of the atmosphere that has nearly uniform temperature and humidity at any given level and moves horizontally over great distances without changing.

air mattress an inflatable rubber or rubberized casing designed for use as a mattress: *Air mattresses are often used by campers.*

air mile NAUTICAL MILE.

air–mind•ed ['ɛr ˌmaɪndɪd] *adj.* interested in aviation or aircraft. **—'air,mind•ed•ness,** *n.*

air•mo•bile ['ɛr,moubəl] *or* ['ɛr,moubaɪl] *adj.* able to be transported by air.

air piracy hijacking.

air pirate hijacker.

air•plane ['ɛr,plein] *n.* a mechanically driven, heavier-than-air aircraft supported in flight by the action of the air flowing past or thrusting upward on fixed wings.

☛ *Usage.* **Airplane,** AEROPLANE. **Airplane** is the usual form in North America. **Aeroplane** is more commonly used in the United Kingdom. In Canada the pronunciation ['ɛrə,plein] is used by some people who use the spelling **airplane.**

airplane cloth a lightweight cotton fabric for shirts, similar to that formerly used as a covering for the wings or fuselage of an aircraft.

air plant a plant that grows on other plants and draws nourishment from the air and the rain. Many orchids are air plants.

air•play ['ɛr,plei] *n.* the airing of songs, dialogues, etc. over radio or television: *That song got a lot of airplay during the 1970s.*

air pocket a downward air current formed by the sudden sinking of cooled air, causing a sudden, short drop in the altitude of an aircraft.

air pollution the pollution of the air by various industrial gases and chemicals.

air•port ['ɛr,pɔrt] *n.* a place where aircraft regularly come to discharge or take on passengers or freight. It usually comprises several runways, buildings for passenger and staff facilities, and facilities for sheltering, repairing, and servicing aircraft.

air power the strength of a country in military aircraft. Compare SEA POWER.

air pressure **1** the force exerted by air confined in a restricted space. **2** atmospheric pressure: *Winds are caused by the flow of air from an area of high air pressure to an area of low air pressure.*

air pump a machine for forcing air into or out of something.

air quality index a numerical value given to the air in terms of its pollution by various chemicals. See chart in the Appendix.

air raid an attack by aircraft.

air–raid shelter ['ɛr ˌreid] a place for protection during an air raid.

air rifle a rifle that is worked by compressed air and shoots a single pellet or dart.

air rights the right to use the space above a building, road, railway, etc.: *A company has bought air rights over the freight yards in order to build a huge office block above the tracks.*

air sac an air-filled space in the body of a bird, connected with the lungs.

air•scape ['ɛr,skeip] *n.* the earth viewed from a high altitude. ⟨< *air* + land*scape*⟩

air scoop ['ɛr ˌskup] *n.* a device on an aircraft for taking in air.

air shaft a passage for letting fresh air into a mine, tunnel, building, etc.

air•ship ['ɛr,ʃɪp] *n.* a dirigible.

☛ *Hom.* HEIRSHIP.

air•sick ['ɛr,sɪk] *adj.* feeling nauseated and dizzy from the motion of an aircraft. **—'air,sick•ness,** *n.*

air•space ['ɛr,speis] *n.* **1** an enclosed area containing air. **2** space in the air, especially that belonging to a particular country: *a violation of our airspace.*

air•speed ['ɛr,spid] **1** the speed of an aircraft measured in relation to the movement of the air rather than to the ground. **2** the speed of an aircraft necessary for takeoff.

air–spray ['ɛr ˌsprei] *v.* spray by means of compressed air.

air–sprayed ['ɛr ˌspreid] *adj., v.* *—adj.* dispensed by a device

that sprays liquid by using compressed air.
—v. pt. and pp. of AIR-SPRAY.

air station a headquarters and airfield for air force operations and training.

air•stream ['ɛr,strim] *n.* the stream of air created around a moving object, such as an aircraft, train, or car; airflow.

air•strike ['ɛr,strəik] *n.* an attack by missiles or aircraft.

air•strip ['ɛr,strɪp] *n.* a paved or cleared strip on which planes can land and take off; a temporary airfield.

air taxi airbus.

air•tight ['ɛr,təit] *adj.* **1** so tight that no air or gas can get in or out. **2** having no weak points open to attack: *an airtight explanation.*

air time **1** the time when a certain radio or television program begins to broadcast: *a few minutes to air time.* **2** an amount of broadcasting time: *The advertising program cost $75 000 in air time alone.*

air–to–air ['ɛr tu 'ɛr] *adj.* between two flying aircraft: *air-to-air refuelling, air-to-air missiles.*

air–to–surface ['ɛr tə 'sɜrfɪs] *adj.* of a missile, etc., directed from an aircraft toward the surface of the earth.

air–traffic controller a person who controls aircraft in an airport, giving permission to land, take off, etc.

air valve a valve for controlling the flow of air into or out of something.

air vesicle *Botany.* an air sac in various floating plants.

air vice–marshal an air-force officer ranking next above an air commodore and below an air marshal. See chart of ranks in the Appendix. *Abbrev.*: A.V.M.

air•waves ['ɛr,weivz] *n.pl.* the medium by which radio and television signals are transmitted.

air•way ['ɛr,wei] *n.* **1** a route for aircraft. **2** a passage for air, especially for breathing. **3** a specified radio frequency for broadcasting. **4 airways,** *pl.* **a** airline. **b** channels for radio or television broadcasting.

air well AIR SHAFT.

air•wo•man ['ɛr,wʊmən] *n., pl.* **-wo•men. 1** a woman who pilots an aircraft. **2** aircraftwoman. See chart of ranks in the Appendix. *Abbrev.*: AW **3** any woman serving in an air force.

air•wor•thy ['ɛr,wɜrði] *adj.* fit or safe for service in the air. **—'air,wor•thi•ness,** *n.*

air•y ['ɛri] *adj.* **air•i•er, air•i•est. 1** like air; not solid or substantial. **2** light as air; graceful; delicate. **3** light-hearted; gay. **4** open to currents of air; breezy. **5** reaching high into the air; lofty. **6** of air; in the air. **7** unnatural; affected: *His airy manner made him seem very haughty.* **8** flippant.

air•y–fair•y ['ɛri 'fɛri] *adj. Informal.* very fanciful or idealistic; unrealistic: *an airy-fairy scheme to make a million.*

aisle [aɪl] *n.* **1** a passage between rows of seats in a hall, theatre, school, church, etc. **2** the part of a church at the side of the nave, choir, or transept and set off by pillars. See BASILICA and TRANSEPT for pictures. **3** any long or narrow passageway, such as the space between shelves of goods in a supermarket. ⟨ME *ele* < OF < L *ala* wing; influenced in form by F *aile* and E *isle* and in meaning by *alley*⟩

☛ *Hom.* I'LL, ISLE.

aitch [eitʃ] *n.* the letter *h* or the sound represented by it: *She drops her aitches when she speaks fast.*

a•jar[1] [ə'dʒɑr] *adv. or adj.* (*never precedes a noun*) of a door or gate, opened a little way. ⟨ME *on char* on the turn; OE *cerr* turn⟩

☛ *Usage.* See note at A[1]-.

a•jar[2] [ə'dʒɑr] *adv. or adj.* not in harmony. ⟨< *a-* in + *jar* discord⟩

a•ji•va [ə'dʒivə] *n. Jainism:* **1** all that is not JIVA, or living soul. **2** materialism. ⟨< Sanskrit⟩

a•ju•ga ['ædʒʊgə] BUGLE[3].

a.k.a. also known as (used often in a legal sense).

ak•ee ['æki] See ACKEE.

A•ke•la [ə'keilə] *or* [ə'kilə] *n.* a pack leader of Cubs. ⟨from *Akela*, the Lone Wolf, the leader of the wolf pack in Rudyard Kipling's *The Jungle Book*⟩

a•kim•bo [ə'kɪmbou] *adj. or adv.* (*never precedes a noun*) of the arms, with the hands on the hips and the elbows bent outward. ⟨ME *in kene bowe*, apparently, in keen bow, at a sharp angle⟩

a•kin [ə'kɪn] *adj.* (*never precedes a noun*) **1** related by blood: *Your cousins are akin to you.* **2** *Linguistics.* descended from the same root: Guest *is akin to* host. **3** alike; similar: *The friends are akin in their love of sports.* ⟨for *of kin*⟩

Ak•kad ['ækæd] *or* ['ɑkɑd] *n.* the northern part of the ancient empire of Mesopotamia and now part of Iraq (formerly Babylon).

Ak•ka•di•an [ə'keidiən] *n.* **1** an inhabitant of ancient Akkad. **2** a member of the Afro-Asiatic group of languages, spoken in Akkad before the birth of Christ, and now extinct.

al– the form of AD- before *l*, as in *ally.*

–al[1] *suffix.* of; like; having the nature of: *natural = of nature or like nature; ornamental = having the nature of ornament.* ⟨< L *-alis* pertaining to⟩

–al[2] *suffix.* the act or process of ——ing: *refusal = the act of refusing.* ⟨< L *-ale*, neut. of *-alis*⟩

Al aluminum.

ala ['eilə] *n., pl.* **alae** [-li] *or* [-laɪ]. **1** a wing. **2** a winglike part.

à la or **a la** ['ælə] *or* ['ɑlə]; *French*, [ala] in the manner of; in the style of. ⟨< F⟩

☛ *Usage.* **à la, a la.** Although originally French, **a la** is now regarded as an English preposition: *a la Hollywood, a la Winston Churchill.* In formal writing and some advertising (for cosmetics and fashionable clothes), the accent mark is usually kept. It is often dropped in informal writing.

Al•a•ba•ma [,ælə'bæmə] *n.* a southern state of the United States.

al•a•bas•ter ['ælə,bæstər] *or* [,ælə'bæstər] *n., adj.* —*n.* **1** a smooth, white, translucent variety of gypsum. Alabaster is often carved into ornaments and vases. **2** a variety of calcite that is somewhat translucent and often banded like marble.
—*adj.* smooth, white, and translucent like alabaster. ⟨ME < OF < L < Gk. *alabast(r)os* alabaster⟩ **—,al•a'bas•trine** [-'bæstrɪn], *adj.*

à la carte [,æ lə 'kɑrt] *or* [,ɑ lə 'kɑrt]; *French*, [ala'kaʀt] according to the menu, on which each dish is priced separately. Compare TABLE D'HÔTE. ⟨< F *à la carte* according to the bill of fare⟩

a•lack [ə'læk] *interj. Archaic.* an exclamation of sorrow or regret; alas.

a•lack•a•day [ə'lækə,dei] *interj. Archaic.* alas! alack!

a•lac•ri•ty [ə'lækrəti] *n.* **1** cheerful willingness: *The girl took to Latin with alacrity.* **2** liveliness. ⟨< L *alacritas* < *alacer* brisk⟩ **—a'lac•ri•tous,** *adj.*

Aladdin's lamp a means of making any dream come true. ⟨< *Aladdin*, a hero of *The Arabian Nights*.⟩

à la grecque [,æ lə 'grɛk] *or* [,ɑ lə 'grɛk] cooked Greek style, in wine, olive oil, and spices.

à la king [,æ lə 'kɪŋ] *or* [,ɑ lə 'kɪŋ] creamed with mushrooms, pimento, and green pepper, often served on toast: *chicken à la king.*

à la mode or **a la mode** [,æ lə 'moud] *or* [,ɑ lə 'moud] *adv.* **1** according to the prevailing fashion; in style. **2** in a certain way. Desserts à la mode are served with ice cream. Beef à la mode is cooked with vegetables. ⟨< F⟩

a•la•mode ['ælə,moud] *or* [,ɑlə'moud] *n.* a silk fabric used in making scarves.

a•lar ['eilər] *adj.* having wings. ⟨< L *alaris* < *ala* wing⟩

a•larm [ə'lɑrm] *n., v.* —*n.* **1** sudden fear; fright; excitement caused by fear of danger. **2** a warning of approaching danger. **3** something that gives such a warning. **4** a call to arms or action. **5** a device that makes a noise to warn or awaken people.
—*v.* **1** fill with sudden fear; frighten: *He was alarmed because his friends were late in returning.* **2** warn (someone) of approaching danger. **3** call (people) to arms. ⟨ME < OF *alarme* < Ital. *allarme* < *all'arme!* to arms!⟩

☛ *Syn. n.* **1.** See note at FEAR. —*v.* **1.** See note at FRIGHTEN.

alarm clock a clock that can be set to ring a bell, etc. at any desired time, especially to waken people from sleep.

a•larm•ing [ə'lɑrmɪŋ] *adj., v.* —*adj.* of a frightening nature.
—*v.* ppr. of ALARM. **—a'larm•ing•ly,** *adv.*

a•larm•ist [ə'lɑrmɪst] *n., adj.* —*n.* one who raises alarms without good reason.
—*adj.* typical of such a person. **—a'larm•ism,** *n.*

a•lar•um [ə'lɑrəm], [ə'lɛrəm], *or* [ə'lærəm] *n. Archaic.* alarm.

a•la•ry ['eiləri] *or* ['æləri] *adj. Zoology.* **1** of or having to do with wings. **2** wing-shaped. ⟨< L *alarius* < *ala* wing⟩

a•las [ə'læs] *interj.* an exclamation of sorrow, grief, regret, pity, or dread. ⟨ME < OF *a* ah + *las* miserable < L *lassus* weary⟩

A•las•ka [ə'læskə] *n.* a northwestern state of the United States, bordering Yukon Territory.

Alaska black diamond *Cdn.* hematite.

Alaska cedar or **cypress** YELLOW CYPRESS (*Chamaecyparis nootkatensis*).

Alaska Highway a highway built in 1942 that extends from Dawson Creek, British Columbia to Fairbanks, Alaska.

A•las•kan [ə'læskən] *adj., n.* —*adj.* of or having to do with Alaska.
—*n.* a native or long-term resident of Alaska.

Alaska pine *Cdn.* a species of hemlock (*Tsuga heterophylla*).

a•late ['eileit] *adj.* having wings or winglike parts. Also, **alated.** ⟨< L *ālātus* < *āla* wing⟩

alb [ælb] *n.* a long, usually white robe with long sleeves, worn by Roman Catholic priests and by some Anglicans and Lutherans in certain church services. It is usually made of linen or linenlike fabric. ⟨< L *(vestis) alba* white (robe)⟩

al•ba•core ['ælbə,kɔr] *n., pl.* **-core** or **-cores.** a long-finned, edible fish (*Thunnus alalunga*) related to the tuna, found in the Atlantic. ⟨< Pg. *albacor* < Arabic *al-bakūra*⟩

Al•ba•ni•a [æl'beiniə] a country on the east coast of the Adriatic, between Greece and Serbia.

Al•ba•ni•an [æl'beiniən] *n., adj.* —*n.* **1** a native or inhabitant of Albania. **2** the language of the people of Albania. It is an Indo-European language.
—*adj.* of or having to do with Albania, its people, or their language.

al•ba•tross ['ælbə,trɒs] *n.* **1** any of a family (Diomedeidae) of large ocean birds found especially from about the Tropic of Capricorn south to Antarctica, having very long, narrow wings, webbed feet, a stout, hooked bill, and black, brown, or mostly white plumage. The largest species is the wandering albatross (*Diomedea exulans*), whose wingspread may reach 3.5 m, the greatest of any living bird species. **2** a burden that one is obliged to bear, especially as a consequence of one's own actions or mistakes (from Coleridge's *The Rime of the Ancient Mariner*; the Mariner shoots the albatross, which the other sailors thought a sign of good luck, and is then forced to wear the dead bird around his neck). **3** anything that continually presents problems or makes things difficult. ⟨var. of obsolete *alcatras* frigate bird < Sp. < Pg. *alcatraz* < Arabic *al-qadus* the bucket < Gk. *kados* < Phoenician⟩

al•be•do [æl'bidou] *n.* the ratio of the light reflected by a planet or satellite to that received by it. ⟨< LL *albus* whiteness + *ēdō* condition⟩

al•be•it [ɒl'biɪt] *conj.* although; even though. ⟨ME *al be it* although it be⟩

Al•ber•ta [æl'bɜrtə] *n.* a western province of Canada, east of British Columbia.

Al•ber•tan [æl'bɜrtən] *n., adj.* —*n.* a native or long-term resident of Alberta.
—*adj.* of or having to do with Alberta or Albertans.

al•bert•ite ['ælbər,təit] *n.* a bituminous mineral resembling asphalt. ⟨< *Albert* County, New Brunswick + *-ite*⟩

al•bes•cent [æl'bɛsənt] *adj.* **1** becoming white. **2** rather white. ⟨< L < *albescere* become white < *albus* white⟩

al•bi•nism ['ælbə,nɪzəm] *n.* absence of pigmentation, complete or partial, due to a heritable abnormality of pigment formation. **—,al•bi'nis•tic** or **al'bin•ic** [æl'bɪnɪk], *adj.*

al•bi•no [æl'baɪnou] *or* [æl'binou] *n., pl.* **-nos. 1** an individual who from birth lacks normal pigment in skin, hair, and eyes as a consequence of a gene defect. **2** any plant or animal with albinism. ⟨< Pg. *albino* < *albo* < L *albus* white⟩

Al•bi•on ['ælbiən] *n. Poetic.* England. ⟨< L⟩

al•bite ['ælbəit] *n.* a kind of white feldspar. ⟨< L *albus* white + *-ite*[2]⟩

al•bu•gin•e•ous [,ælbju'dʒɪniəs] *adj.* of, designating, or like the white fibrous tissue forming the white of the eye. ⟨< Med.L < L *albugo* white spot < *albus* white⟩

al•bum ['ælbəm] *n.* **1** a book with blank pages for holding pictures, stamps, autographs, etc. **2** a phonograph record or set of records, together with the cardboard slipcover or case in which it is sold and any additional material included in the package, such as lyrics of songs, posters, etc.: *In 1980 she put out a two-record album.* **3** the record or set itself. **4** the slipcover or case of a phonograph record or set of records. **5** a collection in the form of a book of pictures, musical compositions, souvenirs, etc.: *We made an album of our trip.* ⟨< L *album*, neut. of *albus* white⟩

al•bu•men [æl'bjumən] *or* ['ælbjəmən] *n.* **1** the white of an egg, consisting mostly of albumin dissolved in water. **2** *Chemistry.* albumin. **3** *Botany.* the food for a young plant stored in a seed; endosperm. ⟨< L *albumen* < *albus* white⟩
☛ *Hom.* ALBUMIN.

al•bu•men•ize [æl'bjumə,naɪz] *v.* **,-ized, -i•zing.** treat with an albuminous solution.

al•bu•min [æl'bjumən] *or* ['ælbjəmən] *n. Chemistry.* any of a class of proteins soluble in water and found in the white of egg and in many other animal and plant tissues and juices. ⟨< F *albumine* < L *albumen, -inis.* See ALBUMEN.⟩
☛ *Hom.* ALBUMEN.

al•bu•mi•nate [æl'bjumə,neit] *n.* a compound produced by the action of an acid or an alkali on albumin.

al•bu•mi•noid [æl'bjumə,nɔɪd] *n.* any protein, such as gelatin, which is difficult to dissolve in water; scleroprotein.

al•bu•mi•nose [æl'bjumə,nous] *adj.* albuminous.

al•bu•mi•nous [æl'bjumənəs] *adj.* **1** of albumin. **2** resembling albumin. **3** containing albumin.

al•bu•min•u•ria [,ælbjəmɪn'juriə] *n.* a condition characterized by albumin in the urine. It is usually a sign of kidney disease.

al•bur•num [æl'bɜrnəm] *n.* the lighter, softer part of wood between the inner bark and the harder centre of a tree; sapwood. ⟨< L *alburnum* < *albus* white⟩

Al•can Highway ['æl,kæn] ALASKA HIGHWAY. ⟨< *Al*aska + *Can*ada⟩

al•ca•zar or **al•cá•zar** ['ælkə,zɑr] *or* [æl'kæzər]; *Spanish,* [al'kaθar] *n.* **1** a palace of the Spanish Moors. **2 Alcázar,** the palace of the Moorish kings at Seville, Spain, later occupied by the Spanish royal family. ⟨< Sp. < Arabic *al-qasr* the castle < L *castrum* fort⟩

al•che•mist ['ælkəmɪst] *n.* in the Middle Ages, a student of alchemy. Alchemists tried to turn base metals into gold and find the elixir of life.

al•che•mize ['ælkə,maɪz] *v.,* **-mized, -miz•ing.** change (metals) by alchemy.

al•che•my ['ælkəmi] *n.* **1** medieval chemistry, especially the search for a process by which base metals could be turned into gold. **2** any magic power or process for changing one thing into another: *the lovely alchemy of spring.* ⟨ME < OF *alkemie* < Med.L *alchimia* < Arabic *al-kīmiyā* < LGk. *chēmeia* the extracting of medical juices < Gk. *chymeia* infusion < *chymos* juice of a plant⟩ **—al'chem•i•cal,** *adj.* **—,al•che'mis•tic** or **,al•che'mis•ti•cal,** *adj.*

al•ci•dine ['ælsə,daɪn] *or* ['ælsədɪn] *adj.* belonging to the Alcidae, a family of diving birds that includes puffins. ⟨< NL *alcidinus* < ON *alka* auk⟩

al•co•hol ['ælkə,hɒl] *n.* **1** the colourless liquid in wine, beer, whisky, gin, etc. that makes them intoxicating; GRAIN ALCOHOL; ETHYL ALCOHOL. Alcohol is used in medicine, in manufacturing, and as a fuel. *Formula*: C_2H_5OH **2** any intoxicating liquor containing this liquid. **3** *Chemistry.* any of a group of similar organic compounds. Alcohols contain a hydroxyl group and react with organic acids to form esters. Wood alcohol or methyl alcohol, CH_3OH, is very poisonous. ⟨< Med.L *alcohol* (originally, 'fine powder', then 'essence') < Arabic *al-koḥ'l* powdered antimony⟩

al•co•hol•ic [,ælkə'hɒlɪk] *adj., n.* *—adj.* **1** of or having to do with alcohol. **2** containing alcohol. **3** affected with alcoholism. *—n.* a person affected with alcoholism. **—,al•co'hol•i•cal•ly,** *adv.*

al•co•hol•ic•ity [,ælkəhɒ'lɪsɪti] *n.* alcoholic strength.

al•co•hol•ism ['ælkəhɒ,lɪzəm] *n.* **1** continual excessive and compulsive consumption of alcoholic drinks. **2** a chronic disorder resulting from this.

al•co•hol•ize ['ælkəhɒ,laɪz] *v.,* **-ized, -iz•ing. 1** make (somebody) drunk. **2** add alcohol to.

al•co•hol•o•me•ter [,ælkəhɒl'ɒmətər] *n.* a device to measure the amount of alcohol in a solution.

al•cool [æl'kul] *Cdn.* WHISKY BLANC. ⟨< F, alcohol⟩

Al•co•ran [,ælkɔ'rɑn] *or* [,ælkɔ'ræn] *n.* the Koran. ⟨< Arabic *al-qorān*⟩

al•cove ['ælkouv] *n.* **1** a recessed section of a room; nook:

Some bachelor apartments have an alcove for a bed. **2** a hollow, usually arched space in a wall, etc.; niche. **3** summerhouse. ⟨< F < Sp. *alcoba* < Arabic *al-qubbah* the vaulted chamber⟩

Al•cy•o•ne [æl'saɪə,ni] *n.* the brightest star in the constellation Pleiades.

Ald. alderman.

Al•deb•a•ran [æl'dɛbərən] *n.* the brightest star in the constellation Taurus. ⟨< Arabic *al-dabarān* the follower (i.e., of the Pleiades) < *dabar* follow⟩

al•de•hyde ['ældə,haɪd] *n.* **1** a transparent, colourless liquid with a suffocating smell, produced by the partial oxidation of ordinary alcohol. *Formula*: CH_3CHO **2** any similar organic compound. ⟨short for NL *al*(*cohol*) *dehyd*(*rogenatum*), alcohol deprived of its hydrogen⟩ **—,al•de'hy•dic,** *adj.*

al den•te [ɑl 'dɛntei] *or* [æl 'dɛnti]; *Italian,* [al 'dɛnte]. of pasta, etc., cooked so as to be still firm when eaten; not cooked to the soft stage. ⟨< Italian, to the tooth⟩

al•der ['ɒldər] *n.* any of a genus (*Alnus*) of shrubs or trees of the birch family found especially in cool, wet parts of the northern hemisphere, having toothed leaves and clusters of catkins that develop into woody cones. The bark of alders is used in tanning and dyeing. ⟨< ME *alder* < OE *alor*⟩

al•der•man ['ɒldərmən] *n., pl.* **-men.** councillor. ⟨OE (*e*)*aldormann* < *ealdor* elder, chief + *mann* man⟩

al•der•man•ic [,ɒldər'mænɪk] *adj.* of, having to do with, or characteristic of an alderman or aldermen.

Al•der•ney ['ɒldərni] *n., pl.* **-neys.** any of various breeds of cattle, such as Jersey or Guernsey, that originally came from Alderney or any of the other Channel Islands.

al•dol ['ældɒl] *n.* a liquid used in making perfumes and as a sedative. *Formula*: $CH_3CHOHCH_2CHO$ ⟨< *ald(ehyde)* + *-ol*⟩

al•dose ['ældous] *n.* a sugar containing the aldehyde group. ⟨< *ald(ehyde)* + *-ose*[2]⟩

al•dos•te•rone [æl'dɒstə,roun] *n.* a hormone produced by the cortex of the adrenal gland. It helps in the intake of sodium and potassium. ⟨< *ald(ehyde)* + *sterol* + *-one*⟩

al•drin ['ɒldrɪn] *or* ['ældrɪn] *n.* a poisonous solid used as an insecticide. *Formula*: $C_{12}H_8Cl_6$ ⟨< Kurt *Alder*, its discoverer, + *in*⟩

ale [eil] *n.* an alcoholic drink brewed from malt with a type of yeast that rises to the top, and flavoured with hops. ⟨OE *alu*⟩
☛ *Hom.* AIL.

a•le•a•to•ric [,eiliə'tɔrɪk] *adj.* **1** *Music.* selecting notes purely at random. **2** contingent upon chance; unpredictable. **3** *Law.* based on uncertainty. ⟨< L < *aleator* gambler < *alea* game of chance⟩

a•le•a•to•ry ['eiliə,tɔri] *adj.* aleatoric.

a•lee [ə'li] *adv. or adj.* on or toward the side of a ship that is away from the wind. ⟨< *a*[1]- + *lee*⟩

a•lef ['ɑlɛf] *or* ['ɑlɪf], ['eilɛf] *or* ['eilɪf], ['ælɛf] *or* ['ælɪf] *n.* the first letter of the Hebrew alphabet. See table of alphabets in the Appendix.

al•e•gar ['æləgər] *n.* soured ale; MALT VINEGAR. ⟨ME *alegre* < *ale* + *egre* sour < OF *aigre*⟩

ale•house ['eil,hʌus] *n.* formerly, a place where ale or beer was sold and drunk.

Al•e•man•ni [,ælə'mæni] *n.* a group of 3rd century Germanic tribes which settled near the Danube. ⟨< Gothic *alamannam, pl.* humankind⟩

Al•e•man•nic [,ælə'mænɪk] *adj.* the southwesterly dialects of High German, or their common ancestor, the language of the Alemanni.

a•lem•bic [ə'lɛmbɪk] *n.* **1** a glass or metal container formerly used in distilling. **2** something that transforms or refines: *Imagination is the alembic of the mind.* ⟨ME < OF < Med.L *alembicus* < Arabic *al-anbīq* the still < Gk. *ambix* cup⟩

A•len•çon [alɑ̃'sɔ̃]; *often,* [ə'lɛnsən] *n.* a kind of fine lace. ⟨< *Alençon,* a city in NW France where this lace is made⟩

a•leph–null or **a•leph–zero** ['ɑlɪf 'nʌl] *or* ['ɑlɪf 'zirou] *n.* *Mathematics.* the smallest infinite cardinal number. *Symbol:* $\aleph_0$

a•le•ri•on [ə'liriən] *n. Heraldry.* an eagle. ⟨< F *alérion*⟩

a•lert [ə'lɜrt] *adj., n., v.* *—adj.* **1** watchful; wide-awake: *A good hunting dog is alert to every sound and movement in the field.* **2** brisk; active; nimble: *A sparrow is very alert in its movements.* *—n.* **1** a signal warning of an air attack or other impending danger. **2** the period of time in which this warning is in effect: *We*

stayed at home throughout a hurricane alert. **3** a signal to troops, etc. to be ready for action.
on the alert, on the lookout; watchful; wide-awake.
—v. **1** warn. **2** draw the attention of (a person): *They alerted me to the problem.* **3** call to arms. ⟨< F *alerte* < Ital. *all' erta* on the watch, ult. < L *erigere* raise up⟩ **—a'lert•ly,** *adv.* **—a'lert•ness,** *n.*
☛ *Syn. adj.* **1.** See note at WATCHFUL.

ALERT [ə'lɜrt] *n. Trademark.* acronym for Alcohol Level Evaluation Roadside Test, a portable device for measuring the level of alcohol in a person's blood, used to test the driver of a motor vehicle for impairment.

-ales *suffix. Botany.* used to form the names of orders: *Cycadales.* ⟨< L *-alis*⟩

a•leth•i•ol•ogy [ə,liθi'ɒlədʒi] *n. Logic.* the branch of logic having to do with truth. ⟨< Gk. *aletheia* truth + *-logy*⟩

al•eu•rone ['æljʊ,roun] *or* [ə'lʊroun] *n.* a granular protein in the seed of cereal plants. ⟨< Gk.⟩

A•le•ut ['æli,ut] *n.* **1** a native or inhabitant of the Aleutian Islands, southwest of Alaska. **2** the language of the Aleuts, which is related to Inuktitut. ⟨< Russian⟩

A•leu•tian [ə'luʃən] *adj.* of or relating to the Aleutian Islands or the Aleuts, their language, etc.

al•e•vin ['æləvɪn] *n.* a very young fish, especially a very young salmon. ⟨< F < L *allevare* lift up, rear < *ad-* to + *levare* raise⟩

ale•wife[1] ['eil,wəif] *n., pl.* **-wives.** a woman who keeps an alehouse.

ale•wife[2] ['eil,wəif] *n., pl.* **-wives.** a food fish of the herring family found in sea and fresh waters of eastern North America; gaspereau. ⟨origin uncertain⟩

Al•ex•an•dri•an [,ælɪg'zændriən] *adj.* **1** of or having to do with Alexander the Great. **2** of or having to do with Alexandria, a seaport in Egypt, or the culture that flourished there in ancient times.

al•ex•an•drine or **Al•ex•an•drine** [,ælɪg'zændrɪn] *or* [,ælɪg'zændrin] *n., adj. —n.* a line of poetry having six iambic feet, with a caesura (pause) after the third foot. *Example*:
He séeks | out míght | y chárms, | to tŕou | ble sléep | y mínds.
—adj. of this metre. ⟨< F *alexandrin*; because this metre was used in OF poems on *Alexander* the Great⟩

al•ex•an•drite [,ælɪg'zændrəit] *n.* a gem which is green by daylight and violet in artificial light; a variety of chrysoberyl.

a•lex•i•a [ə'lɛksiə] *or* [ei'lɛksiə] *n.* a disorder of the brain that prevents a person from reading. ⟨< Gk. *a-*[4] + *lēxis* speech⟩

a•lex•i•phar•mic [ə,lɛksɪ'fɑrmɪk] *n., adj. —n.* antidote. *—adj.* of or being an antidote. ⟨< Gk. *alexipharmakos* < *alexein* turn away + *pharmakon* poison, drug⟩

al•fa•cal•ci•dol [,ælfə'kælsə,dɒl] *n.* a drug used to treat Vitamin D deficiency.

al•fal•fa [æl'fælfə] *n.* a European plant (*Medicago sativa*) of the pea family having clusters of small purplish flowers, compound leaves, and a deep taproot. It is widely cultivated for forage and hay. ⟨< Sp. < Arabic *al-fasfasah* the best kind of fodder⟩

al•fen•ta•nil [æl'fɛntənɪl] *n.* a drug used to control surgical pain.

al•fil•a•ri•a [æl,fɪlə'riə] *n.* a plant of the geranium family grown as food for horses and cattle. ⟨< Arabic⟩

al fi•ne [ɑl 'finei]; *Italian,* [al 'fine] *Music.* to the end.

al•fres•co or **al fres•co** [æl'frɛskou] *adv. or adj.* in the open air; outdoors. ⟨< Ital.⟩

alg. algebra.

al•ga ['ælgə] *n.* sing. of ALGAE.

al•gae ['ældʒi] *or* ['ældʒaɪ] *n.pl.* a large group of mainly aquatic, one-celled or multi-celled organisms traditionally classified as plants, having chlorophyll but lacking true stems, roots, and leaves. Seven phyla or divisions are generally recognized, but authorities differ on the placement of these phyla in a kingdom or kingdoms. ⟨< L *algae,* pl. of *alga* seaweed⟩

al•gal ['ælgəl] *adj.* of or having to do with algae.

al•gar•ro•ba or **al•ga•ro•ba** [,ælgə'roubə] *n.* **1** carob. **2** mesquite. ⟨< Sp. < Arabic *al-kharruba* the carob⟩

al•ge•bra ['ældʒəbrə] *n.* **1** a generalization of arithmetic in which letters or other symbols are used to represent any one of a set of numbers. The symbols and numbers are combined by adding, subtracting, etc. to form expressions that are used in equations and inequations for representing problem situations. Algebra is also used to illustrate properties of numbers; for example, $x \times 0 = 0$ states that the product of x (*any* number) and zero is zero. *Abbrev.*: alg. **2** *Logic.* any system with given principles that uses letters or other symbols to represent propositions. ⟨< Med.L < Arabic *al-jabr* the bone setting; hence, reduction (i.e., of parts to a whole)⟩

al•ge•bra•ic [,ældʒə'breiɪk] *adj.* of or used in algebra: *$(a + b)(a - b) = a^2 - b^2$ is an algebraic statement.* Also, **algebraical.** **—,al•ge'bra•i•cal•ly,** *adv.*

algebraic equation a polynomial equation in which a finite number of terms is equated to zero.

algebraic number **1** a number that is the root of a polynomial equation whose coefficients are rational numbers. **2** REAL NUMBER.

al•ge•bra•ist ['ældʒə,breiɪst] *n.* a person who is skilled in algebra.

Al•ge•ri•a [æl'dʒiriə] *n.* a country in N Africa.

Al•ge•ri•an [æl'dʒiriən] *n., adj. —n.* a native or inhabitant of Algeria or of Algiers, its capital.
—adj. of or having to do with Algeria or its people.

Al•ge•rine [,ældʒə'rin] *n.* **1** an Algerian. **2** *Archaic.* a pirate.

-algia *combining form.* pain: *neuralgia.* ⟨< Gk. *algo* pain⟩

al•gi•cide ['ældʒə,saɪd] *n.* a seaweed killer. ⟨< ALGAE + *-cide*[2]⟩

al•gid ['ældʒɪd] *adj. Poetic.* cold. ⟨< L *algildus* cold⟩

al•gin ['ældʒən] *n.* **1** ALGINIC ACID. **2** alginate. ⟨< *algae* + *-in*⟩

al•gi•nate ['ældʒə,neit] *n.* a soluble salt of alginic acid, used in the manufacture of textiles, as a thickening agent in foods and cosmetics, etc.

al•gin•ic acid [æl'dʒɪnɪk] an insoluble colloidal carbohydrate obtained from the cell walls of kelp, used in the manufacture of rubber tires, the preparation of emulsifiers, etc. *Formula*: $(C_6H_8O_6)_n$

al•goid ['ælgɔɪd] *adj.* like algae.

Al•gol ['ælgɒl] *n.* a bright binary star in the constellation Perseus that varies in brightness because its smaller, brighter component is periodically eclipsed by its larger, weaker one. ⟨< Arabic *al ghūl* the ghoul⟩

ALGOL or **Algol** ['æl,gɒl] *n. Computer technology.* a high-level programming language in which algorithms can be expressed in algebraic terms. It is designed for scientific and mathematical use. ⟨an acronym for *algo*rithmic *l*anguage⟩

al•go•lag•ni•a [,ælgou'lægniə] *n.* sexual pleasure derived from giving or experiencing pain. Compare SADISM, MASOCHISM. ⟨< Gk. *algos* pain + *lagneia* lust⟩ **—,al•go'lag•nic,** *adj.* **—,al•go'lag•nist,** *n.*

al•go•log•i•cal [,ælgə'lɒdʒəkəl] *adj.* of or having to do with algology. **—,al•go'log•i•cal•ly,** *adv.*

al•gol•o•gist [æl'gɒlədʒɪst] *n.* a person trained in algology, especially one whose work it is.

al•gol•o•gy [æl'gɒlədʒi] *n.* the branch of botany that deals with the study of algae.

al•gom•e•ter [æl'gɒmətər] *n.* a device for measuring pain when produced by pressure.

Al•gon•ki•an [æl'gɒŋkiən] *n. or adj.* **1** See ALGONQUIAN. **2** an earlier term for Proterozoic.

Al•gon•kin [æl'gɒŋkɪn] *n.* Algonquin.

Al•gon•qui•an [æl'gɒŋkiən] *or* [æl'gɒŋkwiən] *n., adj. —n.* **1** a stock or family of languages spoken by a large number of confederacies, peoples, and bands of the First Nations and Native Americans who traditionally occupied much of central and eastern North America, including large areas from Labrador south to Carolina and from the Atlantic west to the Rocky Mountains. Among the languages included in this family are Abenaki, Blackfoot, Cree, Malecite, Micmac, Ojibwa, and Ottawa. **2** a member of any of the First Nations or Native Americans speaking one of these languages. **3** ALGONQUIN (def. 1).
—adj. of, having to do with, or designating these peoples or their languages. ⟨< *Algonquin*⟩

Al•gon•quin [æl'gɒŋkɪn] *or* [æl'gɒŋkwɪn] *n., adj. —n.* **1** a member of the First Nations living in eastern Ontario and Québec. **2** a dialect of Ojibwa, spoken by these people.
—adj. of, having to do with, or designating these people or their language.

al•go•pho•bia [,ælgə'foubiə] *n.* an abnormal fear of pain. ⟨< Gk. *algos* pain + E *-phobia*⟩

al•go•rism ['ælgə,rɪzəm] *n.* **1** the system of Arabic numerals, using nine digits and zero; decimal system of counting. **2** the skill of computing with any system of numbers. **3** algorithm. ⟨ME < OF *algorisme* < Med.L *algorismus* < Arabic *al-khuwarizmi* < *al-Khowarizmi,* a famous Arab mathematician of the 9th century A.D.⟩

al•go•rithm ['ælgə,rɪðəm] *n.* **1** *Mathematics.* a special procedure or set of rules for solving a certain type of problem, especially one involving repetition of an operation. **2** any set of rules or step-by-step procedure for accomplishing some end. ⟨alteration of ALGORISM, influenced by Gk. *arithmos* number⟩

Al•ham•bra [æl'hæmbrə] *n.* the palace of the Moorish kings near Granada, Spain. ⟨< Sp. < Arabic *al-hamra'* the red (house)⟩

a•li•as ['eiliəs] *n., pl.* **a•li•as•es;** *adv. —n.* an assumed name; other name: *The spy's real name was Leblanc, but he sometimes went by the alias of Martinet.*
—adv. otherwise called; with the assumed name of: *Smith alias Jones.* ⟨< L *alias* at another time⟩
☛ *Usage.* In law, **alias** is still often written in italics (Harrison *alias* Johnson), in which case it stands for the Latin *alias dictus,* meaning 'otherwise called'.

al•i•bi ['ælə,baɪ] *n., pl.* **-bis;** *v.,* **-bied, -bi•ing.** *—n.* **1** *Law.* the plea that a person accused of a certain offence was somewhere else when the offence was committed. **2** *Informal.* an excuse.
—v. Informal. make an excuse. ⟨< L *alibi* elsewhere⟩

al•i•cy•clic [,ælɪ'səiklɪk] *adj. Chemistry.* having to do with cyclic compounds sharing many properties of aliphatic compounds.

al•i•dade ['ælɪ,deid] *n. Surveying.* a straightedge with a telescopic sight. ⟨< L *alhidada* < Arabic *al-'idādah,* moving radius⟩

al•ien ['eiliən] *or* ['eiljən] *n., adj. —n.* **1** a person who is not a citizen of the country in which he or she lives. **2** a foreigner; stranger. **3** a supposed being from some other planet.
—adj. **1** of or by another country; foreign: *an alien language, alien domination.* **2** unfamiliar; strange: *alien ideas.* **3** not characteristic or compatible; repugnant or opposed (*used with* **to**): *Unkindness is alien to her nature.* ⟨ME < OF < L *alienus* < *alius* other⟩

al•ien•a•ble ['eiliənəbəl] *or* ['eiljənəbəl] *adj.* capable of being transferred to another person: *alienable property.*
—,al•ien•a'bil•i•ty, *n.*

al•ien•age ['eiliənədʒ] *or* ['eiljənədʒ] *n.* the state or status of being an alien.

al•ien•ate ['eiliə,neit] *or* ['eiljə,neit] *v.* **-at•ed, -at•ing. 1** cause (a friend, etc.) to become indifferent or hostile; estrange: *His moodiness is alienating many of his friends.* **2** turn away; divert: *to alienate someone's affections.* **3** cause to become withdrawn or isolated: *She is becoming more and more alienated. Many social pressures tend to alienate our youth.* **4** *Law.* transfer the ownership of (property) to another: *Enemy property was alienated during the war.* **—'al•ien,a•tor,** *n.*

al•ien•a•tion [,eiliə'neiʃən] *or* [,eiljə'neiʃən] *n.* **1** a turning away in indifference or hostility; estrangement. **2** withdrawal or detachment from one's society or environment; isolation: *Alienation can be a serious problem in an urbanized society.*
3 *Psychiatry.* a disorder which causes one to view one's self and surroundings as unreal. **4** *Law.* a transfer of the ownership of property to another.

al•ien•ee [,eiliə'ni] *or* [,eiljə'ni] *n. Law.* a person to whom property is transferred.

al•ien•ist ['eiliənɪst] *or* ['eiljənɪst] *n.* a psychiatrist who testifies in court. ⟨< F *aliéniste* < L *alienus* insane⟩

al•ien•or ['eiliə,nɔr] *or* ['eiljə,nɔr] *n.* a person who transfers property.

a•lif ['ɑlɪf] *n.* the first letter of the Arabic alphabet. See table of alphabets in the Appendix. Also, **alef.**

al•i•form ['eilɪ,fɔrm] *or* ['ælɪ,fɔrm] *adj.* of or having to do with wings; wing-shaped. ⟨< L *ala* wing + E *-form*⟩

a•light¹ [ə'ləit] *v.* **a•light•ed** or **a•lit, a•light•ing. 1** get down; get off: *to alight from a horse.* **2** come down from the air and settle; come down from flight. **3** come by chance (*on* or *upon*). ⟨OE *ālīhtan,* ult. < *līht* light (in weight); originally, with reference to taking one's weight off a horse or vehicle⟩

a•light² [ə'ləit] *adv. or adj.* (*never precedes a noun*) **1** lighted up; illuminated: *a face alight with joy.* **2** on fire: *The candles were still alight.* ⟨OE *ālīht* illuminated⟩

a•lign [ə'laɪn] *v.* **1** bring into line or alignment: *to align the sights of a gun with the target, to align the wheels of a car.* **2** place in a line: *Lombardy poplars were aligned along the drive.* **3** bring (parties, oneself, etc.) into an alliance with or against a particular party, group, cause, etc.: *They aligned themselves in the cause of anti-racism.* Also, **aline.** ⟨< F *aligner* < *a-* to (< L *ad-*) + *ligner* < L *lineare* < *linea* line⟩

a•lign•ment [ə'laɪnmənt] *n.* **1** an arrangement in a straight line; formation in a line; bringing into line. **2** the line or lines so formed. **3** a joining together (of persons, nations, etc.) for a common purpose. **4** adjustment to a line: *The sights of the rifle were in alignment with the target.* Also, **alinement.**

a•like [ə'ləik] *adv., adj. —adv.* **1** in the same way: *Robert and his father walk alike.* **2** similarly; equally.
—adj. (*never precedes a noun*) like one another; similar: *These twins are very much alike.* ⟨OE *gelīc, onlīc*⟩

al•i•ment ['æləmənt] *n.* **1** food; nourishment. **2** a person's mental or physical support. ⟨< L *alimentum* < *alere* nourish⟩
—,al•i'ment•al, *adj.*

al•i•men•ta•ry [,ælə'mɛntəri] *adj.* **1** having to do with food and nutrition. **2** nourishing; nutritious. **3** providing support or sustenance.

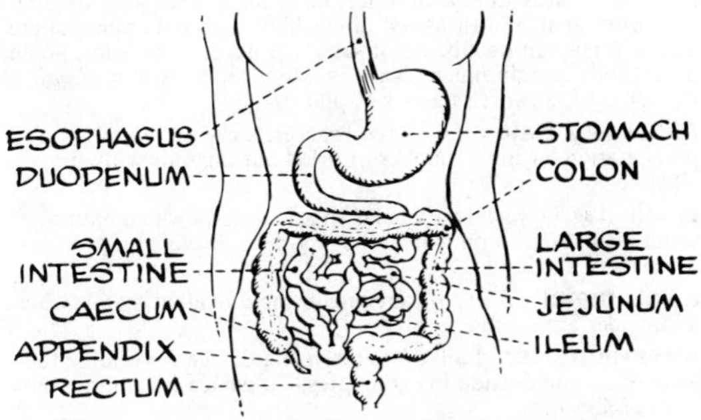

The human alimentary canal

alimentary canal the parts of the body through which food passes. The mouth, esophagus, stomach, intestines, and anus are parts of the alimentary canal.

al•i•men•ta•tion [,æləmɛn'teiʃən] *n.* **1** nourishment; nutrition. **2** maintenance; support.

al•i•mo•ny ['ælə,mouni] *n.* **1** *Law.* money paid by a person for the support of his or her spouse under a separation agreement. Compare MAINTENANCE. **2** *Informal.* money paid for the support of a former spouse after divorce. ⟨< L *alimonia* sustenance < *alere* nourish⟩

a•line [ə'laɪn] *v.* **a•lined, a•lin•ing.** See ALIGN.

A–line ['ei ,laɪn] *adj.* of a skirt, tight about the waist and widening gradually toward the bottom, but without gathers or pleats.

a•line•ment [ə'laɪnmənt] See ALIGNMENT.

Al•i•oth ['æli,ɒθ] *n.* the brightest star in the BIG DIPPER. ⟨< Arabic *alyat* sheep's tail⟩

al•i•ped ['ælɪ,pɛd] *adj., n. —adj.* web-footed.
—n. a web-footed creature.

al•i•phat•ic [,ælə'fætɪk] *adj.* of, designating or having to do with a group of organic compounds whose carbon atoms form open chains as opposed to rings. Paraffins are one type of aliphatic compound.

al•i•quant ['æləkwənt] *or* ['ælə,kwɒnt] *adj.* not able to divide a number or quantity without leaving a remainder: 5 *is an aliquant part of* 14. ⟨< L *aliquantus* somewhat < *alius* some + *quantus* how much⟩

al•i•quot ['æləkwət] *or* ['ælə,kwɒt] *adj.* able to divide a number or quantity without leaving a remainder: 3 *is an aliquot part of* 12. ⟨< L *aliquot* some < *alius* some + *quot* how many⟩

a•lit [ə'lɪt] *v. Poetic.* a pt. and a pp. of ALIGHT¹.

a•lit•er•ate [,ei'lɪtərət] *n.* someone who can read but chooses not to. **—a'lit•er•a•cy,** *n.*

a•live [ə'laɪv] *adj.* **1** living; not dead: *The man is alive.* **2** in continued activity or operation: *Keep the principles of liberty alive.* **3** of all living: *the happiest girl alive.* **4** active; lively. **5** connected with a source of electricity; charged electrically. **6** of telephones, microphones, etc. not shut off; operating or functioning.
alive to, noticing; alert to; sensitive to.

alive with, full of; swarming with: *The streets were alive with people.*
look alive! hurry up! be quick! ⟨OE *on life*⟩
☛ Usage. **Alive** is not normally used before a noun, where **live** [laɪv] and **living** may appear: *a live animal, living people.* **Alive** occurs after its noun or in the predicate: *the oldest woman alive. She is still alive.*

a•li•yah or **a•li•ya** [ˌɑli'jɑ] *or* [ɑ'lijɑ] *n.* the repatriating of Jews to the PROMISED LAND. ⟨< Mod.Hebrew⟩

a•liz•a•rin [ə'lɪzərɪn] *n.* a red dye prepared from coal tar, formerly obtained from madder. *Formula*: $C_{14}H_8O_4$ ⟨< F *alizarine* < *alizari* < Sp. < Arabic *al-'aṣara(h)* the extract⟩

al•ka•hest ['ælkəˌhɛst] *n.* **1** the mythical element sought by the alchemists which would produce gold when mixed with base metals. **2** the solution to all problems; universal panacea. ⟨< F < ML *alcahest* a coining by 15c. Swiss alchemist P.A. Paracelsus⟩

al•ka•le•mi•a [ˌælkə'limiə] *n.* abnormal alkalinity of the blood. ⟨< *alkal(i)* + *-emia*⟩

al•ka•li ['ælkəˌlaɪ] *n., pl.* **-lis** or **-lies. 1** *Chemistry.* any base or hydroxide that is soluble in water, neutralizes acids and forms salts with them, and turns red litmus blue. Lye and ammonia are alkalis. **2** any salt or mixture of salts that neutralizes acids. Some desert soils contain much alkali. ⟨< MF *alcali* < Arabic *al-qalī* the ashes of saltwort (a genus of plant)⟩

Alkali Dry Belt *Cdn.* on the Prairies, a region of low precipitation having a number of dried-out dugouts with an alkaline cover.

alkali flat in western Canada, an arid area in which natural water, as in ponds and marshes, evaporates, leaving large deposits of alkali.

alkali metal *Chemistry*. any one of the univalent metals whose hydroxides are alkalis.

al•ka•lim•e•ter [ˌælkə'lɪmətər] *n.* **1** a device for finding the level of carbon dioxide in carbonates. **2** a device for finding the level of alkalinity.

al•ka•line ['ælkəˌlaɪn] *or* ['ælkəlɪn] *adj.* **1** of or like an alkali. **2** containing an alkali: *The soil around the slough was alkaline.* **3** having a pH greater than 7.

alkaline–earth metals calcium, strontium, and barium. Some authorities include beryllium, magnesium, and radium.

alkaline earths the oxides of the alkaline-earth metals.

al•ka•lin•i•ty [ˌælkə'lɪnəti] *n.* an alkaline quality or condition.

al•ka•lin•ize ['ælkəlɪˌnaɪz] *v.* **-ized, -iz•ing.** alkalize.

al•ka•lize ['ælkəˌlaɪz] *v.* **-lized, -liz•ing.** make alkaline. **—ˌal•ka•li'za•tion,** *n.*

al•ka•loid ['ælkəˌlɔɪd] *n.* an organic substance containing nitrogen; a substance that resembles an alkali and contains nitrogen. Many alkaloids obtained from plants are drugs, such as cocaine, strychnine, morphine, and quinine. Alkaloids are often very poisonous. **—ˌal•ka'loid•al,** *adj.*

al•ka•lo•sis [ˌælkə'lousɪs] *n.* alkalemia. **—ˌal•ka'lot•ic** [-'lɒtɪk], *adj.*

al•kane ['ælkein] *n. Chemistry*. one of the **alkane series**, the series of saturated hydrocarbons having the general formula C_nH_{2n+2}. ⟨< *alk(yl)* + *(meth)ane*⟩

al•ka•net ['ælkəˌnɛt] *n.* **1** bugloss. **2 a** a Eurasian perennial plant (*Alkanna tinctoria*) of the borage family whose roots are used to make a red dye. **b** the root of this plant or the red colour it yields. **3** any of various other plants of the borage family (genus *Anchusa*) whose roots are used to make a red dye. ⟨< Sp.⟩

al•kene ['ælkin] *n.* alkane.

Al•ko•ran [ˌælkɔ'rɑn] *or* [ˌælkɔ'ræn] *n.* the Koran. ⟨< Arabic *al qor'ān*⟩

al•kyd ['ælkɪd] *n.* **1** any of several synthetic resins made by heating certain organic acids with alcohols, used especially for paints and other finishes. **2** (*adjl.*) of, containing, or designating any of these resins: *Alkyd paint is the common oil-base household paint that is thinned with turpentine or solvent.* ⟨blend of *alkyl* and *acid*⟩

alkyd resin alkyd.

al•kyl ['ælkəl] *n.* **1** any of a group of univalent hydrocarbon radicals having the general formula C_nH_{2n+1}. **2** (*adjl.*) of, designating, or containing any of these radicals. **3** an organic compound consisting of such a radical bound with one or more metal atoms. ⟨blend of *alk*ali and *-yl*⟩

al•kyl•ate ['ælkəˌleit] *v.* **-at•ed, -at•ing.** subject to the process of alkylation.

al•kyl•a•tion [ˌælkə'leiʃən] *n.* **1** a chemical reaction in which a hydrogen atom in an organic compound is replaced by an alkyl group. **2** the addition of an alkyl group to an organic compound in producing high-octane fuels.

al•kyne ['ælkaɪn] *n.* alkane. ⟨< *alky(l)* + *-(i)ne*[2]⟩

all [ɒl] *adj., pron., n., adv.* *—adj.* **1** the whole of: *all Europe.* **2** every one of: *all men.* **3** the greatest possible: *She made all haste to reach home in time.* **4** any; any whatever: *The prisoner denied all connection with the crime.*
—pron. **1** the whole number; everyone: *All of us are going.* **2** the whole quantity; everything: *All that glitters is not gold.*
above all, before everything else in importance.
after all, when everything has been considered; nevertheless.
all at once, suddenly.
all but, almost; nearly: *He was all but dead from fatigue, but he struggled on.*
all in all, a on the whole; taking everything into consideration: *All in all it was an exciting election.* **b** everything; one's all-consuming interest: *You are my all in all.*
all of, as much as; no less than: *She weighs all of 5 kg.*
at all, a under any conditions. **b** in any way.
for all (that), in spite of; notwithstanding.
in all, counting every person or thing; altogether: *There were 100 families in all.*
—n. everything one has or is: *She gave her all for the welfare of the community.*
—adv. **1** wholly; entirely: *The cake is all gone.* **2** each; apiece: *The score was even at forty all.* **3** merely; nothing but: *all words and no thought.*
all in, *Informal.* weary; worn out.
all that, *Informal.* to a particular extent or amount; very; so (*used with negatives*): *I wasn't all that keen on going.*
all the better (or **higher, farther,** etc.), even better, higher, farther, etc.: *We must work all the harder now that the holidays are over.*
go all out, use all one's resources; go the whole way, without limiting oneself: *They decided to go all out and hire a band for the dance.* ⟨OE *eall*⟩
☛ *Hom.* AWL.

al•la bre•ve ['ælə 'breivei] *Music.* **1** a measure having two or four beats in which a half note, rather than a quarter note, represents one beat. **2** the symbol indicating this. ⟨< Ital.⟩

Al•lah ['ælə] *or* ['ɑlə] *n.* the Muslim name of the one Supreme Being, or God. ⟨< Arabic *allah, al-ilāh*⟩

all–A•mer•i•can ['ɒl ə'mɛrəkən] *adj.* **1** eminently representative or typical of the United States or Americans. **2** composed entirely of Americans or American elements. **3** situated wholly within the borders of the United States. **4** of, having to do with, or involving all the nations of the western hemisphere.

al•lan•to•is [ə'læntouɪs] *n.* a membranous sac attached to embryonic birds, reptiles, and mammals to supply blood and carry away waste. ⟨< Gk.⟩ **—ˌal•lan'to•ic, al'lanˌtoid,** *adj.*

al•lar•gan•do [ˌɑlɑr'gændou] *adj. Music.* gradually becoming slower and louder. ⟨< Ital.⟩

all–a•round ['ɒl ə'raʊnd] *adj.* all-round.

al•lay [ə'leɪ] *v.* **-layed, -lay•ing. 1** put at rest; quiet: *His fears were allayed by the news of the safety of his family.* **2** relieve; check: *Her fever was allayed by the medicine.* **3** make less; weaken. ⟨OE *ālecgan*⟩

all–Ca•na•di•an ['ɒl kə'neidiən] *adj.* **1** eminently representative or typical of Canada or Canadians: *an all-Canadian menu.* **2** composed entirely of Canadians or Canadian elements: *an all-Canadian hockey team, an all-Canadian manufacturer.* **3** situated wholly within Canada's borders: *an all-Canadian route.*

all clear a signal indicating the end of an air raid or other danger.

al•le•ga•tion [ˌælə'geiʃən] *n.* **1** an assertion without proof: *He makes so many wild allegations that no one will believe him.* **2** an assertion: *The lawyer's allegation was proved.* ⟨ME < OF < L *allēgātiō, -ōnis* < *allēgāre* send a message, cite < *ad-* to + *lēgāre* commission, ult. < *lex* law⟩

al•lege [ə'lɛdʒ] *v.* **-leged, -leg•ing. 1** assert without proof. **2** state positively; assert; declare: *This person alleges that her watch has been stolen.* **3** give or bring forward as a reason, argument, or excuse. ⟨< AF *alegier* < L *ex-* out + *litigare* strive, sue; with sense of L *allegare* charge⟩ **—al'leg•er,** *n.*

al•leged [ə'lɛdʒd] *adj., v.* *—adj.* **1** asserted without proof: *The*

alleged theft never really happened. **2** asserted; declared. **3** brought forward as a reason. **4** improperly designated as such: *His alleged best friend didn't invite him to the party.*
—*v.* pt. and pp. of ALLEGE.

al•leg•ed•ly [ə'lɛdʒɪdli] *adv.* according to what is or has been alleged.

al•le•giance [ə'lidʒəns] *n.* **1** the loyalty owed by a citizen to his or her country or by a subject to his or her ruler. **2** loyalty; faithfulness to a person, cause, etc. that demands obedience or honour. ⟨ME *alegeaunce* < OF *ligeance* < *lige* liege⟩

al•le•gor•i•cal [ˌælə'gɔrəkəl] *adj.* explaining or teaching something by a story; using allegory. **—ˌal•le'gor•i•cal•ly,** *adv.*

al•le•gor•ist ['æləgərɪst] *n.* a writer of allegories.

al•le•go•rize ['æləgəˌraɪz] *v.* **-rized, -riz•ing. 1** make into an allegory. **2** treat or interpret as an allegory. **3** use allegory. **—ˌal•le•gor•iz'a•tion,** *n.*

al•le•go•ry ['æləˌgɔri] *n., pl.* **-ries. 1** a story with an underlying meaning parallel to but different from the surface meaning. An allegory may be regarded as an extended metaphor. *Pilgrim's Progress* by John Bunyan is an allegory. **2** the use of such a story to present ideas. **3** a symbol. ⟨ME < L < Gk. *allēgoria* < *allos* other + *agoreuein* speak⟩

☛ *Syn.* An **allegory,** a FABLE, or a PARABLE is a story made up to present ideas in a concrete, vivid way. The incidents of an **allegory** may stand for political, spiritual, or romantic situations; its characters may be types (*Mr. Wordly Wiseman*) or personifications (*Courtesy, Jealousy*). A **fable** has as its characters animals or inanimate objects that by acting and talking like human beings call attention to human weaknesses and teach a common-sense lesson that is usually stated at the end: *Aesop's fables.* A **parable** is a short story of everyday life used to teach a moral by comparison or by implication: *Jesus often used parables.*

al•le•gret•to [ˌælə'grɛtou] *adj., adv., n., pl.* **-tos.** *Music.* —*adj.* quick, but not as quick as allegro.
—*adv.* in allegretto tempo.
—*n.* such a part in a piece of music. ⟨< Ital. *allegretto,* dim. of allegro⟩

al•le•gro [ə'lɛgrou] *or* [ə'leigrou] *adj., adv., n., pl.* **-gros.** *Music.* —*adj.* quick; lively.
—*adv.* in allegro time.
—*n.* such a part in a piece of music. ⟨< Ital. < L *alicer,* unrecorded popular variant of *alacer* brisk⟩

al•lele [ə'lil] *n. Genetics.* **1** one of two or more genes that occupy the same position on each of a pair of chromosomes. **2** an alternative form of a given gene at a given position, or locus, on a chromosome. Most genes have numerous such forms; more than 300 alleles are known at the cystic fibrosis locus. ⟨< ALLELOMORPH⟩ **—al'lel•ic,** *adj.*

al•le•lo•morph [ə'lilouˌmɔrf] *or* [ə'lɛlouˌmɔrf] *n.* allele. ⟨< Gk. *allel-* one another + *morphe* forme, shape⟩ **—alˌle•lo'mor•phic,** *adj.*

al•le•lu•ia [ˌælə'lujə] *interj., n.* —*interj.* a liturgical form of **hallelujah,** meaning "praise the Lord."
—*n.* a hymn or shout of praise to the Lord. ⟨< L < Gk. < Hebrew *hallĕlūjāh* praise ye Jehovah⟩

al•le•mande [ˌælə'mænd] *or* [ˌælə'mɑnd]; *French* [al'mɑ̃d] *n.* **1** a German dance that became popular in France in the 1700s. **2** the music for such a dance. **3** *Music.* one of the movements of a classical suite. **4** in square dancing, a movement in which pairs of dancers interlace their right or left arms and turn in a circle. ⟨< F⟩

Allen key ALLEN WRENCH.

Allen screw a screw with a hexagonal hole for turning.

Allen wrench a wrench consisting of a small L-shaped bar with an end made to fit an ALLEN SCREW.

al•ler•gen ['ælərdʒən] *n.* any substance that causes an allergic reaction. ⟨< *aller(gy)* + *-gen*⟩

al•ler•gen•ic [ˌælər'dʒɛnɪk] *adj.* of or having to do with allergens.

al•ler•gic [ə'lɜrdʒɪk] *adj.* **1** of or caused by allergy: *Hay fever is an allergic reaction.* **2** having an allergy: *Some people are allergic to milk.* **3** *Informal.* having a strong dislike; averse (*to*): *I'm allergic to work.*

al•ler•gist ['ælərdʒɪst] *n.* a doctor who specializes in the diagnosis and treatment of allergies.

al•ler•gy ['ælərdʒi] *n., pl.* **-gies. 1** an unusual sensitiveness to a particular substance. Hay fever and asthma are often caused by allergies to certain pollens and dusts. **2** *Informal.* a strong dislike: *an allergy to work.* ⟨< NL *allergia* < Gk. *allos* different, strange + *ergon* action⟩

al•le•thrin ['æləθrɪn] *n.* a clear liquid used as an insecticide. *Formula:* $C_{19}H_{26}O_3$ ⟨< *all(ene)* (< *all(yl)* + *-ene*) + *(pyr)ethr(um)* + *-in*⟩

al•le•vi•ate [ə'liviˌeit] *v.* **-at•ed, -at•ing.** make (suffering of the body or mind) easier to endure; relieve; lessen: *Heat often alleviates pain.* ⟨< LL *alleviare* < L *ad-* up + *levis* light⟩ **—al'le•viˌa•tor,** *n.* **—al'le•vi•aˌto•ry,** *adj.*

al•le•vi•a•tion [əˌlivi'eiʃən] *n.* **1** an alleviating or being alleviated. **2** something that alleviates.

al•le•vi•a•tive [ə'liviətɪv] *or* [ə'liviˌeitɪv] *adj., n.* —*adj.* alleviating.
—*n.* anything that alleviates.

al•ley[1] ['æli] *n., pl.* **-leys. 1** a narrow back street in a city or town; alleyway. **2** a path in a park or garden, bordered by trees. **3** a long, narrow, enclosed place for bowling. **4** a building having a number of alleys for bowling. **5** *Tennis.* the narrow lane on either side of a tennis court that enlarges the court for doubles playing.
(right) up or **down one's alley,** closely related to one's work or interests. ⟨ME < OF *alee* a going < *aler* go⟩

al•ley[2] ['æli] *n., pl.* **-leys. 1** a large, white or coloured glass marble used to shoot at the other marbles in a game. **2 alleys,** any game played with such marbles. ⟨shortened form of *alabaster*⟩

alley cat a cat, usually a mongrel, that lives in back streets.

al•ley•way ['æliˌwei] *n.* **1** an alley in a city or town. **2** a narrow passageway.

All Fools' Day APRIL FOOLS' DAY.

all get out *Informal.* (to) an extreme degree (*preceded by* **as** *or* **like.**): *tired as all get out, working like all get out.*

all hail an exclamation of greeting or welcome.

All•hal•lows [ˌɒl'hælouz] *n. Christianity.* November 1, ALL SAINTS' DAY. ⟨< OE *ealra hālgena daeg*⟩

Allhallows Eve October 31, Halloween.

all•heal ['ɒlˌhil] *n.* valerian.

al•li•a•ceous [ˌæli'eiʃəs] *adj.* smelling of or flavoured with onions or garlic. ⟨< L *allium* garlic + *-aceous,* < L *-aceus* of a (certain) kind⟩

al•li•ance [ə'laɪəns] *n.* **1** a union formed by agreement; joining of interests. An alliance may be a joining of family interests by marriage, a joining of national interests by treaty, etc. **2** the nations, persons, etc. who belong to such a union. **3** an association; connection. **4** a similarity in structure or descent; relationship. ⟨ME < OF *aliance* < *alier* unite < L *alligare* < *ad-* to + *ligare* bind⟩

al•li•cin ['ælɪsɪn] *n.* an antibacterial substance extracted from garlic. ⟨ult. < L *allium* garlic⟩

al•lied [ə'laɪd]; *also, for def. 4,* ['ælaɪd] *adj.* **1** united by agreement or treaty; combined for some special purpose: *allied nations, allied armies.* **2** associated; connected: *allied industries. Reading and listening are allied activities.* **3** similar in structure or descent; related: *The dog and the wolf are allied animals.* **4 Allied,** of, involving, or designating the Allies.

Al•lies ['ælaɪz] *n.pl.* **1** the countries that fought against Germany and Austria-Hungary in World War I. **2** the countries that fought against Germany, Italy, and Japan (the Axis) in World War II.

al•li•ga•tor ['æləˌgeitər] *n.* **1** either of two species of reptile (genus *Alligator* of the family Alligatoridae) having a long, thick body and tail, four short legs, powerful jaws with sharp teeth, and eyes and nostrils set on the top of the skull. The two species are the American alligator (*A. mississipiensis*) of the southern United States and the Chinese alligator (*A. sinensis*) of the Yangtze River Valley in China. **2** leather made from the hide of an alligator. **3** (*adjl.*) made of this leather: *alligator shoes.* **4** *Cdn.* **a** formerly, a scowlike amphibious craft equipped with a winch and cable, used for towing log booms, breaking up logjams, etc. The first alligators, built about 1890, were steam-driven, sidewheel vessels. **b** a small gasoline or diesel-powered boat, usually equipped with a winch and cable, used for handling and hauling floating logs, breaking logjams, etc. ⟨< Sp. *el lagarto* the lizard < L *lacertus* lizard⟩

alligator clip a kind of toothed clip used in electrical work.

alligator pear avocado.

alligator snapper a large snapping turtle found mainly in the rivers and bayous of the Mississippi Valley.

all–im•por•tant ['ɒl ɪm'pɔrtənt] *adj.* essential; extremely important.

all–in•clu•sive ['ɒl ɪn'klusɪv] *adj.* including everything.

al•lit•er•ate [ə'lɪtə,reit] *v.* **-at•ed, at•ing. 1 a** have the same first sound. **b** loosely, have the same first letter. **2** use alliteration. **3** compose or pronounce so as to show alliteration. ⟨back formation from alliteration⟩

al•lit•er•a•tion [ə,lɪtə'reiʃən] *n.* **1** a repetition of the same first sound in a group of words or line of poetry. *Example*: "The *s*un *s*ank *s*lowly" shows alliteration of *s.* **2** less properly, repetition of the same first letter in a group of words or line of poetry. ⟨< Med.L *alliteratio, -onis* < *ad-* to + L *litera* letter⟩

al•lit•er•a•tive [ə'lɪtərətɪv] *or* [ə'lɪtə,reitɪv] *adj.* **1** having words beginning with the same sound. **2** loosely, having words beginning with the same letter. **—al'lit•er•a•tive•ly,** *adv.* **—al'lit•er•a•tive•ness,** *n.*

al•li•um ['æliəm] *n.* any plant of the genus *Allium.*

all–numeric data computer or other information consisting entirely of numbers.

allo– *combining form.* other: *allomorph.* ⟨< Gk.⟩

al•lo•bar•ic [,ælou'bɑrɪk] *adj.* of or having to do with changes in barometric pressure: *an allobaric storm.* ⟨< allo- + bar² + *-ic*⟩

al•lo•ca•ble ['æləkəbəl] *adj.* capable of being allocated.

al•lo•cat•a•ble ['ælə,keitəbəl] *adj.* allocable.

al•lo•cate ['ælə,keit] *v.* **-cat•ed, -cat•ing. 1** assign or set apart; designate; earmark: *funds allocated for capital expenditures.* **2** distribute; allot: *The money received has not yet been allocated.* **3** locate. ⟨< Med.L *allocare* < L *ad-* to, at + *locus* place⟩

al•lo•ca•tion [,ælə'keiʃən] *n.* an allotment, especially by government; distribution; assignment.

al•loch•tho•nous [ə'lɒkθənəs] *adj. Geology.* of rocks, moved by tectonic forces. ⟨< allo- + (AUTO)CHTHONOUS⟩

al•log•a•my [ə'lɒgəmi] *n. Botany.* plant cross-fertilization. **—al'log•a•mous,** *adj.*

al•lo•graft ['ælə,græft] *n.* homograft.

al•lo•graph ['ælə,græf] *n.* **1** a signature made by one person for another. **2** a legal document not made by any party to it. **3** *Linguistics.* one of two or more forms of a GRAPHEME occurring in COMPLEMENTARY DISTRIBUTION. The endings *-ie* and *-y* are allographs of each other.

al•lom•er•ism [ə'lɒmə,rɪzəm] *n.* a chemical variability without change in form. ⟨< allo- + Gk. *meros* part + *-ism*⟩ **—al'lom•er•ous,** *adj.*

al•lo•morph ['ælə,mɔrf] *n.* **1** *Chemistry.* allotrope. **2** *Linguistics.* one of the variant forms of a morpheme: *com-* in *compress, col-* in *collect, con-* in *connect,* and *cor-* in *correct* are allomorphs of the morpheme *com-.* ⟨< Gk. *allos* other + *morphē* form⟩ **—,al•lo'mor•phic,** *adj.* **—,al•lo'mor•phism,** *n.*

al•lo•nym ['ælə,nɪm] *n.* pseudonym. ⟨< allo- + Gk. dial. *onyma* name⟩

al•lo•path ['ælə,pæθ] *n.* **1** a doctor who uses allopathy. **2** a person who favours allopathy.

al•lo•path•ic [,ælə'pæθɪk] *adj.* of allopathy; using allopathy. **—,al•lo'path•i•cal•ly,** *adv.*

al•lop•a•thist [ə'lɒpəθɪst] *n.* allopath.

al•lop•a•thy [ə'lɒpəθi] *n.* a method of treating a disease by using remedies to produce effects different from the symptoms produced by the disease. Compare HOMEOPATHY. ⟨< G *Allopathie* < Gk. *állos* other + *patheia* suffering⟩

al•lo•pat•ric [,ælə'pætrɪk] *adj.* of plants or animals, found in different areas. ⟨< allo- + Gk. *patris* native land⟩ **—,al•lo'pat•ri•cal•ly,** *adv.*

al•lo•phane ['ælə,fein] *n.* a mineral appearing in blue, green, or yellow; a hydrous silicate of aluminum. ⟨< Gk. *allophanes* differently appearing < *allos* other + *phainesthai* appear⟩

al•lo•phone ['ælə,foun] *n.* **1** any one of a family of similar speech sounds that are heard as the same sound by speakers of a given language or dialect. In English, the *t* in *top* and the *t* in *stop,* although different in quality, are allophones of the phoneme *t,* and thus are not used in English to distinguish meaning. **2** especially in Québec, a speaker of a language other than French or English. ⟨< Gk. *allos* other + E *-phone* sound (< Gk. *phōnē*)⟩ **—,al•lo'phon•ic,** *adj.*

al•lo•plasm ['ælə,plæzəm] *n. Biology.* **1** that part of the cytoplasm that develops into outgrowths such as cilia, flagella, etc. **2** the nonliving material in a cell, including pigment, starch, and fat granules. **—,al•lo'plas•mic,** *adj.*

al•lo•pu•ri•nol [,ælou'pjʊrɪ,nɒl] *n.* a drug used to treat gout by lowering the level of uric acid. *Formula*: $C_5H_4N_4O$

al•lo•saur ['ælə,sɔr] *n.* any of a genus (*Allosaurus*) of large, carnivorous dinosaurs whose fossilized remains have been found in Jurassic and Cretaceous rocks of North America. ⟨< Gk. *allos* other + *sauros* lizard⟩

al•lot [ə'lɒt] *v.* **-lot•ted, -lot•ting. 1** divide and distribute in parts or shares: *The profits have all been allotted.* **2** give as a share; assign: *The teacher allotted work to each student.* ⟨< OF *aloter* < *a-* to (< L *ad-*) + *lot* lot < Gmc. Akin to LOT.⟩

☛ *Syn.* **1. Allot,** APPORTION = to give out in shares. **Allot** emphasizes giving set amounts for a definite purpose or to particular persons, and does not suggest the way in which the shares are set or distributed: *The Government is ready to allot homesteads in that area.* **Apportion** emphasizes division and distribution according to a fair plan, usually in proportions settled by some rule: *The reward money was apportioned among those who had helped in the rescue.* **2.** See note at ASSIGN.

all'ot•ta•va [,ɑlou'tɑvɑ] *adj., adv. Music.* up or down one octave, to suit the singer. ⟨< Ital.⟩

al•lot•ment [ə'lɒtmənt] *n.* **1** the act of alloting; a division or distribution in parts or shares. **2** something alloted; share or portion.

al•lo•trope ['ælə,troup] *n.* an allotropic form.

al•lo•trop•ic [,ælə'trɒpɪk] *adj. Chemistry.* occurring in two or more forms that differ in physical and chemical properties but not in the kind of atoms of which they are composed.

al•lot•ro•pism [ə'lɒtrə,pɪzəm] *n.* allotropy.

al•lot•ro•py [ə'lɒtrəpi] *n. Chemistry.* the property or fact of being allotropic. ⟨< Gk. *allotropia* < *allos* other + *tropos* manner⟩

all–out ['ɒl 'ʌut] *adj.* involving one's entire resources; total; complete: *an all-out effort to win, all-out war.*

all•o•ver ['ɒl,ouvər] *adj.* **1** covering the whole surface. **2** having a pattern that is repeated over the whole surface.

al•low [ə'laʊ] *v.* **1** let; permit: *The class was not allowed to leave until the bell rang.* **2** let have; give: *Her father allows her $10 a week as spending money.* **3** admit; acknowledge; recognize: *The judge allowed the claim of the man whose property was damaged.* **4** add or subtract to make up for something: *to allow an extra hour for travelling time.* **5** permit to happen, especially through carelessness or neglect. **6** *Informal.* say; think: *He allowed that he was going to the dance.*

allow for, take into consideration; provide for: *He purposely made the pants large to allow for shrinking.* ⟨ME < OF *alouer* < L *allaudare* (< *ad-* to + *laus* praise) and Med.L *allocare* (< L *ad-* to, at + *locus* place)⟩ **—al'low•er,** *n.*

☛ *Syn.* **1.** See note at PERMIT.

al•low•a•ble [ə'laʊəbəl] *adj.* allowed by law or by a person in authority; permitted by the rules of the game; not forbidden. **—al'low•a•ble•ness,** *n.* **—al'low•ab•ly,** *adv.*

al•low•ance [ə'laʊəns] *n., v.* *—n.* **1** a limited share set apart; definite portion or amount given out, especially, such an amount of money given regularly to a child: *Each child received a weekly allowance of $7.* **2** an amount added or subtracted to make up for something: *a car trade-in allowance of $700.* **3** an allowing; conceding: *allowance of a claim.* **4** tolerance: *allowance of slavery.* **5** the variation in dimension allowed between machine parts that fit together. **6** in coinage, the variation from the standard permitted by the mint.

—v. **1** give an allowance to. **2** provide in limited quantities.

make allowance(s) (for), a take into consideration; allow for. **b** excuse; judge leniently in view of mitigating factors.

al•loy *n.* ['ælɔɪ]; *v.* [ə'lɔɪ] *n., v.* *—n.* **1** an inferior metal mixed with a more valuable one: *This gold is not pure; there is some alloy in it.* **2** a metal made by mixing and fusing two or more metals, or a metal and a non-metal: *Brass is an alloy of copper and zinc.* **3** any injurious addition or inferior mixture.

—v. **1** make into an alloy. **2** make less valuable by mixing with a cheaper metal. **3** make worse; debase. ⟨< F *aloi,* n., *aloyer,* v., < OF *alei, aleier,* var. of *alier* unite, combine < L *alligare* < *ad-* to + *ligare* bind. Doublet of ALLY.⟩

all–pow•er•ful ['ɒl 'paʊərfəl] *adj.* having power over all people, things, etc.; almighty; omnipotent.

all–pur•pose ['ɒl 'pɜrpəs] *adj.* suitable for all purposes for which a particular product, device, etc. is generally used: *All-purpose flour is as suitable for pastry and cakes as it is for bread.*

all–red route *Cdn.* an early name for the Canadian Pacific Railway which passed through what was then British territory.

all right 1 all correct. 2 yes; agreed. 3 without doubt; certainly: *She's clever, all right.* 4 in good health; safe; uninjured: *Are you all right?* 5 satisfactory.
☛ *Usage.* See note at ALRIGHT.

all–round ['ɒl 'raʊnd] *adj.* not limited or specialized; able to do many things; useful or skilled in many ways.

All Saints' Day *Christianity.* November 1, a church festival honouring all the saints; Allhallows.

all•seed ['ɒl,sid] *n.* any plant producing many seeds, such as the goosefoot.

All Souls' Day *Roman Catholic Church.* November 2, a day when services are held and prayers said for all the souls in purgatory.

all•spice ['ɒl,spəis] *n.* 1 a spice made from the dried unripe berries of a West Indian tree (*Pimenta dioica*) of the myrtle family. Allspice has a flavour like a combination of cinnamon, nutmeg, and cloves. 2 the berry of this tree. 3 the tree itself.

all square *Informal.* 1 having paid what is due; having done what is needed. 2 having the same score; tied; even: *The teams were all square at the end of the second period.*

all–star ['ɒl ,stɑr] *adj., n.* —*adj.* made up of or involving the best players or performers.
—*n.* any player on an all-star team.

all–ter•rain vehicle ['ɒl tə'rein] *or* ['ɒl 'tɛrein] a motor vehicle designed for travel off roads, on rough land, over snow, or through water, etc. *Abbrev.*: ATV

all–time ['ɒl 'taɪm] *adj. Informal.* 1 for all time up to the present. 2 that sets a record: *an all-time high in wheat prices.*

al•lude [ə'lud] *v.* **-lud•ed, -lud•ing.** refer indirectly *(to)*; mention in passing: *Do not ask him about his failure; do not even allude to it.* ⟨< L *alludere* < *ad-* with + *ludere* play⟩
☛ *Syn.* See note at REFER.
☛ *Usage.* Do not confuse **allude** with ELUDE.

al•lure [ə'lur] *v.* **-lured, -lur•ing;** *n.* —*v.* tempt or attract very strongly; fascinate; charm.
—*n.* fascination; charm. ⟨ME < OF *alurer* < *a-* to (< L *ad-*) + *leurre* lure < Gmc. Related to LURE.⟩ **—al'lur•er,** *n.*
☛ *Syn. v.* See notes at LURE and CHARM.

al•lure•ment [ə'lurmənt] *n.* 1 an alluring or being allured. 2 something that allures.

al•lur•ing [ə'lʊrɪŋ] *adj., v.* —*adj.* 1 tempting; attracting. 2 charming; fascinating.
—*v.* ppr. of ALLURE. **—al'lur•ing•ly,** *adv.* **—al'lur•ing•ness,** *n.*

al•lu•sion [ə'luʒən] *n.* an indirect or passing reference. ⟨< L *allusio, -onis* < *alludere.* See ALLUDE.⟩
☛ *Usage.* See note at ILLUSION.

al•lu•sive [ə'lusɪv] *adj.* containing an allusion; full of allusions. **—al'lu•sive•ly,** *adv.* **—al'lu•sive•ness,** *n.*

al•lu•vi•al [ə'luviəl] *adj., n.* —*adj.* consisting of or formed by sand or mud left by flowing water. A delta is an alluvial deposit at the mouth of a river.
—*n.* alluvial soil.

alluvial fan a gently sloped, alluvial deposit in the shape of a fan, resulting from a gradual decrease in the speed of a river or stream.

al•lu•vi•on [ə'luviən] *n.* 1 alluvium. 2 the flowing of water against land. 3 a flood. 4 *Law.* an increase in land area, either by the withdrawing of sea or river water or by the deposit of sediments.

al•lu•vi•um [ə'luviəm] *n., pl.* **-vi•ums** or **-vi•a** [-viə]. the sand, mud, etc. left by flowing water. ⟨< L *alluvium,* neut. of *alluvius* alluvial < *ad-* up + *luere* wash⟩

all–weath•er ['ɒl 'wɛðər] *adj.* 1 designed to be usable or practical in all kinds of weather: *an all-weather coat, an all-weather road.* 2 done or performed in all kinds of weather.

al•ly *v.* [ə'laɪ] *or* ['ælaɪ]; *n.* ['ælaɪ] *v.* **-lied, -ly•ing;** *n., pl.* **-lies.**
—*v.* 1 combine for some special purpose; unite by formal agreement (*to* or *with*). One nation allies itself with another to protect its people and interests. 2 associate; connect: *This newspaper is allied with three others.* 3 cause to be similar in structure, descent, etc.; relate: *Dogs are allied to wolves.*
—*n.* 1 a person or nation united with another for some special purpose. See also ALLIES. 2 a related animal, plant, form, or thing. 3 a helper; supporter. ⟨ME < OF *alier* < L *alligare* < *ad-* to + *ligare* bind. Doublet of ALLOY.⟩

al•lyl ['ælɪl] *adj., n.* —*adj. Chemistry.* of or containing the monovalent group H_2C: $CHCH_2$
—*n.* this group, called the **allyl group.** ⟨< L *all(ium)* garlic + *yl*⟩ **—al'lyl•ic,** *adj.*

allyl alcohol a colourless, mustard-smelling poisonous liquid used to make herbicides, pharmaceuticals, etc.

allyl resin any of several resins that harden when heated, made from allyl alcohol and a dibasic acid and used as adhesives.

al•ma ma•ter or **Al•ma Ma•ter** ['ælmə 'mɑtər], ['ɑlmə 'mɑtər], *or* ['ælmə 'meitər] a person's school, college, or university. ⟨< L *alma mater* bounteous mother⟩

al•ma•nac ['ɒlmə,næk] *or* ['ælmə,næk] *n.* a calendar or table showing the days, weeks, and months. Many almanacs give information about the weather, sun, moon, stars, tides, church days, and other facts. ⟨ME < Med.L, probably < LGk. < Arabic *al-manākh*⟩

al•man•dine ['ælmən,din], ['ælməndɪn], *or* ['ælmən,daɪn] *n.* garnet. ⟨< F < Med.L *alabandina* < *Alabanda* ancient city where it was cut⟩

Al•mey ['ælmi] *n.* a Canadian variety of flowering crabapple having red wood, leaves, and flowers.

al•might•y [ɒl'məiti] *adj., n.* —*adj.* having supreme power; all-powerful.
—*n.* **the Almighty,** God. **—al'might•i•ly,** *adv.* **—al'might•i•ness,** *n.*

almighty dollar *Informal.* money thought of as all-powerful: *She neglects her friends and family in pursuit of the almighty dollar.*

al•mond ['ɒmənd], ['ɑmənd], ['ɒlmənd], *or* ['æmənd] *n.* 1 a small tree (*Prunus amygdalus*) of the rose family native to SW Asia but widely cultivated for its nutlike seeds. It is closely related to the peach. 2 the oval-shaped seed of this tree, eaten as a nut. 3 (*adjl.*) shaped like an almond. 4 (*adjl.*) made from or flavoured with almonds: *almond paste.* 5 the yellow-tan colour of the almond husk. ⟨ME < OF *almande* < L < Gk. *amygdalē*⟩ **—'al•mond•like,** *adj.*

al•mond–eyed ['ɒmənd ,aɪd], ['ɑmənd ,aɪd], ['ɒlmənd ,aɪd], *or* ['æmənd ,aɪd] *adj.* having eyes that appear to be oval-shaped and to have pointed ends.

al•mon•er ['ælmənər], ['ɒlmənər], *or* ['ɑmənər] *n.* a person who distributes alms for a monarch, monastery, etc. ⟨ME < OF *almosnier* < LL *elemosynarius* < L *eleēmosyna* alms. See ALMS.⟩

al•mon•ry ['ælmənri], ['ɒlmənri], *or* ['ɑmənri] *n., pl.* **-ries.** a place where alms are distributed.

al•most ['ɒlmoust] *adv.* nearly: *Nine is almost ten.* ⟨OE *eal māst* nearly⟩
☛ *Usage.* See note at MOST.

alms ['ɒmz] *or* ['ɑmz] *n. sing. or pl.* money or gifts to help the poor. ⟨OE *ælmysse* < VL **alimosina* < L *eleemosyna* < Gk. *eleēmosynē* compassion < *eleos* mercy⟩

alms•giv•er ['ɒmz,gɪvər] *or* ['ɑmz-] *n.* a person who helps the poor with money or other gifts.

alms•giv•ing ['ɒmz,gɪvɪŋ] *or* ['ɑmz-] *n. or adj.* giving help to the poor.

alms•house ['ɒmz,hʌus] *or* ['ɑmz-] *n.* a home for persons too poor to support themselves.

al•ni•co ['ælnɪ,kou] *or* [æl'nikou] *n.* an alloy containing aluminum, nickel, and cobalt, much used in making magnets. ⟨< *al*uminum + *ni*ckel + *co*balt⟩

al•oe ['ælou] *n., pl.* **-oes.** 1 any of a large genus (*Aloe*) of mainly South African succulents belonging to the lily family, having a long spike of flowers and thick, fleshy, narrow leaves. Some aloes are grown as house plants in temperate climates. 2 **aloes, a** a bitter drug made from the dried juice of the leaves of certain aloes (*used with a singular verb*). **b** the heartwood of any of the trees of the mezereum family (genus *Aquilaria*) from southeast Asia; eaglewood. ⟨OE *al(u)we* < L < Gk.⟩ **—,al•o'et•ic,** *adj.*

aloe vera ['vɛrə] *or* ['virə] 1 a kind of aloe, kept in the home for its medicinal properties. 2 the juice of the aloe vera, found in hand creams and other cosmetics.

a•loft [ə'lɒft] *adv. or adj.* (*never precedes a noun*) 1 far above the earth; high up. 2 high above the deck of a ship; up among the sails, rigging, or masts of a ship. ⟨ME < ON *á lopt* in the air⟩

a•lo•ha [ə'louə] *or* [ɑ'louhɑ] *n. or interj.* 1 greetings; hello. 2 goodbye; farewell. ⟨< Hawaiian⟩

al•o•in ['ælouɪn] *n.* a purgative obtained from aloe, in powder form.

a•lone [ə'loun] *adj., adv.* —*adj.* (*never precedes a noun*) 1 apart from other persons or things; solitary: *He was alone.* 2 without anything or anyone else; only: *He alone remained. Meat alone is*

not a good diet for humans. **3** without equal or rival: *She is alone in the field of cancer research.*
leave alone, not bother; not meddle with.
let alone, a not bother; not meddle with. **b** not to mention: *It would have been a hot day for summer, let alone early spring.*
–adv. **1** only; merely; exclusively. **2** apart from other persons or things: *One tree stood alone on the hill.* **3** without help: *I can do it alone, thank you.* ⟨ME *al one* all (completely) one⟩
–a'lone•ness, *n.*

a•long [ə'lɒŋ] *prep., adv. –prep.* **1** from one end of (something) to the other: *Flowers are planted along the path. We walked along the street.* **2** according to (often used with *lines*): *She developed her plan along the following lines.*
–adv. **1** further; onward: *Move along. Pass the word along.* **2** with one; at hand or accompanying one (*often used with* **with**): *He took his dog along.* **3** together (*with*); in association (*with*): *We had pop along with the food.* **4** *Informal.* there; present: *I'll be along in a minute.* **5** on course; ahead: *My spring cleaning is coming along nicely.*
all along, from the very beginning: *She was here all along.*
get along, a *Informal.* manage with at least some success. **b** agree. **c** go away. **d** advance. **e** succeed; prosper. ⟨OE *andlang*⟩

a•long•shore [ə,lɒŋ'ʃɔr] *adv.* near or along the shore.

a•long•side *adv.* [ə,lɒŋ'saɪd]; *prep.* [ə'lɒŋ,saɪd] *adv., prep.*
–adv. at the side; close to the side; side by side.
alongside of, *Informal.* beside; next to.
–prep. by the side of; beside.

a•loof [ə'luf] *adv., adj. –adv.* at a distance; withdrawn; apart: *One girl stood aloof from all the others.*
–adj. (*never precedes a noun*) unsympathetic; not interested; reserved. ⟨< *a-* on + *loof* windward, probably < Du. *loef*⟩
–a'loof•ly, *adv.* **–a'loof•ness,** *n.*

al•o•pe•cia [,ælə'piʃə] *n.* partial or complete loss of hair on the head; baldness. ⟨< L *alopecia* loss of hair (in foxes)⟩

a•loud [ə'laʊd] *adv.* **1** loud enough to be heard; not in a whisper. **2** in a loud voice; loudly.

alp [ælp] *n.* a high mountain. ⟨< L *Alpes* the Alps⟩

al•pac•a [æl'pækə] *n.* **1** a domesticated grazing animal (*Lama pacos*) raised in the mountains of Peru and Bolivia mainly for its long, soft, silky wool. It belongs to the same genus as the llama. **2** the wool of the alpaca. **3** a kind of warm, soft cloth made from this wool. **4** glossy, wiry cloth made of wool and cotton, usually black. ⟨< Sp. < Arabic *al* the + Peruvian *paco* alpaca⟩

al•pen•glow ['ælpən,glou] *n.* a reddish light on snowy mountain peaks at sunset or sunrise.

al•pen•horn ['ælpən,hɔrn] *n.* a long, powerful horn used in Switzerland for military signals and for calling cattle. Also, **alphorn.** ⟨< G *Alpen* Alps + *Horn* horn⟩

al•pen•stock ['ælpən,stɒk] *n.* a strong staff with an iron point, used in climbing mountains. ⟨< G *Alpen* Alps + *Stock* stick⟩

al•pes•trine [æl'pɛstrɪn] *adj. Botany.* of plants, growing on mountains below the tree line. ⟨< Med.L *alpestris* < L *Alpes* Alps⟩

al•pha ['ælfə] *n., adj. –n.* **1** the first letter of the Greek alphabet (Α, α). **2** a beginning; first in a series. **3 Alpha,** *Astronomy.* the brightest star in a constellation: *Alpha Herculis is the brightest star in the constellation Hercules.*
–adj. Chemistry. denoting the first of several positions in an organic compound that a molecule can attach to.

alpha and omega the first and the last; the beginning and the end. ⟨< Gk.⟩

al•pha•bet ['ælfə,bɛt] *n.* **1** a set of letters or characters representing sounds, used in writing a language. **2** the letters of a language, arranged in their conventional order. **3** the parts to be learned first; elementary principles. *Abbrev.:* ABC or ABC's. See table of alphabets in the Appendix. ⟨< LL *alphabetum* < LGk. *alphabetos* < *alpha* + *beta*⟩

al•pha•bet•i•cal [,ælfə'bɛtɪkəl] *adj.* **1** arranged in the order of the alphabet. **2** of the alphabet. Also, **alphabetic.**

al•pha•bet•ize ['ælfəbə,taɪz] *v.* **-ized, -iz•ing. 1** arrange in alphabetical order. **2** express by the letters of an alphabet.
–,al•pha•bet•iz'a•tion, *n.*

alpha decay *Physics.* a radioactive process that decreases the atomic number of an atom by two.

al•pha–fe•to•pro•tein [,ælfə ,fitou'proutin] *n.* a serum protein present in a normal fetus and sometimes in large amounts in adults, where it is usually a sign of disease, or, in a pregnant woman, of fetal defects.

alpha iron a soft, magnetic allotrope of iron. It is stable below 910°C.

al•pha•nu•mer•ic [,ælfənju'mɛrɪk] *or* [-nu'mɛrɪk] *adj.*
1 *Computer technology.* consisting of letters of the alphabet, digits, and possibly other characters (blanks, punctuation marks, etc.): *The Canadian postal code is an alphanumeric code.*
2 producing or using both letters and numbers: *an alphanumeric typewriter keyboard.*

alpha particle *Physics.* a positively charged particle consisting of two protons and two neutrons, released in the disintegration of radium and similar radioactive substances.

alpha ray *Physics.* a stream of alpha particles.

alpha wave a form of electrical activity in the brain, from 8 to 13 hertz, denoting relaxation. Compare BETA WAVE.

alp•horn ['ælp,hɔrn] *n.* See ALPENHORN.

al•pho•sis [æl'fousɪs] *n.* absence of skin pigment, as in albinism. ⟨< NL < Gk. *alphos* leprosy⟩

Al•pine ['ælpaɪn] *adj.* **1** of or like the Alps. **2 alpine, a** of, having to do with, or living or growing on mountains: *alpine meadows, alpine flowers.* **b** having to do with or designating downhill as opposed to cross-country skiing.

alpine fir 1 a fir tree (*Abies lasiocarpa*) found especially in the mountainous regions of western North America, having a narrow, tapering, spirelike crown and greyish green or bluish green curved needles. **2** the light, soft, relatively weak wood of this tree.

alpine forget–me–not an arctic plant (*Myosotis alpestris*), having short stems and small blue flowers.

alpine garden a rock garden.

alpine larch a small larch tree (*Larix lyallii*) found on mountain slopes at or near the timberline, from southern British Columbia south into the United States, having a short, sturdy trunk and a ragged-looking crown with gnarled branches.

al•pin•ist ['ælpənɪst] *n.* mountain climber.

alp lily an alpine and arctic wildflower (*Lloydia serotina*), having bulblike roots and small yellow and white flowers.

al•pra•zo•lam [æl'præzə,læm] *n.* a drug used to treat anxiety. *Formula:* $C_{17}H_{13}ClN_4$

al•pro•sta•dil [æl'prɒstə,dɪl] *n.* a drug used to treat heart defects in newborn babies until surgery can be performed.

Alps [ælps] *n.pl.* a range of mountains in western Europe, crossing Austria, Italy, Germany, Switzerland, and France.

al•read•y [ɒl'rɛdi] *adv.* **1** before this time; by this time; even now: *The house is already full.* **2** so soon: *Must you go already?*
3 *Informal.* an expression of impatience, used at the end of a sentence: *Enough whining already!* ⟨for *all ready*⟩
☛ *Usage.* **All ready,** as distinguished from the adverb **already,** is used as an adjective phrase meaning quite or completely ready: *He was all ready for his next job.*

al•right [ɒl'rəit] *adv. Informal.* all right.
☛ *Usage.* **All right** is the correct spelling of both the adjective phrase *(He is all right)* and the sentence adverb meaning "yes, certainly" *(All right, I'll come).* The spelling **alright** is not used in formal nor in most informal writing. Occasionally it is found in advertising and in comic strips, but it is not as yet generally accepted.

Al•sa•tian [æl'seiʃən] *n., adj. –n.* **1** a native or inhabitant of Alsace, a region in northeastern France, or the dialect of German spoken there. **2** GERMAN SHEPHERD.
–adj. of or having to do with Alsace or its people.

al•sike or **alsike clover** ['ælsɪk] *or* ['ælsəik]. *Trifolium hybridum,* a European clover grown for forage in the U.S. ⟨< *Alsike,* a town in Sweden⟩

al•so ['ɒlsou] *adv.* in addition; besides; too. ⟨OE *ealswā* all so, quite so⟩
☛ *Usage.* **Also** is an adverb; it should not be used as a connective in place of *and: The principal was strict; she was also fair. They came with tents, cooking things, and* (not *also*) *about twenty kilograms of photographic equipment.*

al•so–ran ['ɒlsou ,ræn] *n.* **1** a horse or dog that does not finish among the first three in a race. **2** a loser; a person who fails to win a contest, competition, etc., or to acquire distinction in any field.

alt. 1 alternate; alternating. **2** altitude. **3** alto.

Alta. Alberta.

Al•ta•ic [æl'teiɪk] *adj., n. –adj.* **1** of or having to do with the Altai Mountains in Central Asia. **2** of or having to do with a

family of languages that includes Turkish, Mongolian, and Manchu.
—n. this family of languages.

Al•ta•ir [æl'tɑir] *n.* a first-magnitude star in the constellation Aquila. It is about ten times as bright as the sun. ⟨< Arabic *al-ta'ir* bird, literally, flyer⟩

al•tar ['ɒltər] *n.* **1** a table or stand in the most sacred part of a church, synagogue, or temple. In Christian churches the Communion service or Mass is held at the altar. **2** a raised place built of earth or stone on which to make sacrifices or burn offerings to a god.
lead to the altar, marry. ⟨OE < LL *altare* < L *altus* high⟩
☛ *Hom.* ALTER.

altar boy *Christianity.* a boy who helps a priest during certain religious services, especially Mass; acolyte.

al•tar•piece ['ɒltər,pis] *n.* a decorated panel or wall behind and above an altar in a Christian church; reredos.

al•ta•zi•muth [ɒl'tæzɪməθ] *n.* an instrument equipped with a telescope for measuring angles vertically and horizontally, used in astronomy to determine the position of stars, planets, etc. and in surveying. A theodolite is a portable altazimuth. ⟨< *alt*(*itude*) + *azimuth*⟩

al•te•plase ['æltɪ,pleis] *n.* a drug used to treat certain heart conditions.

al•ter ['ɒltər] *v.* **1** make different; change; vary: *If this coat is too large, a tailor can alter it to fit you.* **2** become different: *Since her trip to Europe, her whole outlook has altered.* ⟨ME < OF < LL *alterāre* < L *alter* other⟩ **—'al•ter•a•ble,** *adj.* **—'al•ter•a•bly,** *adv.*
☛ *Syn.* See note at CHANGE.
☛ *Hom.* ALTAR.

al•ter•a•tion [,ɒltə'reiʃən] *n.* **1** a change in the appearance, form, or condition of anything: *to have alterations made in a dress.* **2** the act or process of making a change.

al•ter•a•tive ['ɒltərətɪv] *or* ['ɒltə,reitɪv] *adj., n.* *—adj.* **1** causing change; having the power to cause change. **2** gradually restoring healthy bodily functions.
—n. a remedy that gradually restores health.

al•ter•cate ['ɒltər,keit] *v.* **-cat•ed, -cat•ing.** dispute angrily; quarrel. ⟨< L *altercari* < *alter* other⟩

al•ter•ca•tion [,ɒltər'keiʃən] *n.* an angry dispute; quarrel: *The two teams had an altercation over the umpire's decision.*

al•ter e•go **1** another aspect of one's nature. **2** a very intimate friend. ⟨< L *alter ego*, translation of Gk. *heteros egō* other self⟩

al•ter•nate *v.* ['ɒltər,neit]; *adj., n.* ['ɒltərnɪt] *or* [ɒl'tɜrnɪt] *v.* **-nat•ed, -nat•ing;** *adj., n.* *—v.* **1** occur by turns, first one and then the other; happen or be arranged by turns: *Squares and circles alternate in this row*: □○□○□○□○. **2** arrange by turns; do by turns: *We try to alternate work and pleasure.* **3** take turns: *Lucy and her brother will alternate in setting the table.* **4** switch regularly. **5** *Electricity.* **a** of a current, reverse direction at regular intervals: *Some electric currents alternate 120 times a second.* **b** produce or be operated by such a current.
—adj. **1** placed or occurring by turns; first one and then the other: *The row has alternate squares and circles.* **2** every other: *The cleaner comes on alternate days.* **3** being an additional choice; other: *If that doesn't work, try an alternate method.* **4** *Botany.* of leaves, flowers, etc., growing singly along either side of a stem, but not directly opposite each other. Compare OPPOSITE.
—n. **1** a person appointed to take the place of another if necessary; substitute. **2** a player who relieves another during a game. ⟨< L *alternare* < *alternus* every second < *alter* other⟩

alternate angles two angles, both interior or both exterior but not adjacent, formed when two lines are crossed by a third and being on opposite sides of the third line. If the two lines are parallel, the alternate angles are equal. See ANGLE for picture.

al•ter•nate•ly ['ɒltərnɪtli] *or* [ɒl'tɛrnɪtli] *adv.* by turns, first one and then the other.

alternating current an electric current that reverses its direction at regular intervals. *Abbrev.*: A.C., a.c., or a-c. Compare DIRECT CURRENT.

al•ter•na•tion [,ɒltər'neiʃən] *n.* **1** an alternating; an occurring by turns, first one and then the other: *There is an alternation of red and white stripes on the sign outside a barber shop.* **2** *Linguistics.* the occurrence of an alternate form of a phoneme or morpheme.

alternation of generations the occurrence of different reproductive forms within the life cycle of an organism, usually a regular alternation of sexual and asexual generations. Alternation of generations occurs in many plants and some lower animals.

al•ter•na•tive [ɒl'tɜrnətɪv] *adj., n.* *—adj.* **1** giving, being, or requiring a choice between only two things. **2** giving or being a choice from among more than two things: *There are several alternative routes from Ottawa to Toronto.*
—n. **1** a choice between two things: *We have the alternative of going out or watching a TV movie.* **2** a choice from among more than two things. **3** one of the things to be chosen: *John chose the sensible alternative and stayed in school.* **—al'ter•na•tive•ly,** *adv.*
☛ *Syn. n.* See note at CHOICE.
☛ *Usage.* **Alternative** comes from Latin *alter,* meaning the second of two. Some writers, because of the word's origin, confine its meaning to one of two possibilities, but it is commonly used to mean one of several possibilities.

alternative conjunction a conjunction connecting terms that are alternative. *Examples*: either...or, neither...nor, whether...or.

alternative school a school, publicly funded, which in its curriculum, its structure, its methods of teaching, or the students it caters to, is outside the norm.

al•ter•na•tor ['ɒltər,neitər] *n.* a dynamo or generator for producing an alternating electric current.

al•the•a or **al•thae•a** [æl'θiə] *n.* **1** the rose of Sharon, a flowering garden shrub. **2** any of a genus (*Althaea*) of plants of the mallow family, such as the hollyhocks. ⟨< L *althaea* < Gk. *althaia* wild mallow, ? < *ālthainein* heal⟩

alt•horn ['ælt,hɔrn] *n.* a brass musical instrument similar to the French horn. Also, **alto horn.** ⟨< G⟩

al•though [ɒl'ðou] *conj.* even if; in spite of the fact that; though. ⟨ME *al thogh* even though⟩
☛ *Usage.* **Although,** THOUGH. There is no difference in meaning between the subordinating conjunctions **although** and **though.** Either may be used to connect an adverbial clause with the main clause of a sentence. **Although** is more likely to introduce a clause that precedes a main clause, and **though** one that follows: *Although it rained all morning, they went on the hike. They went on the hike, though it rained all morning.*

al•tim•e•ter [æl'tɪmətər] *or* ['æltɪ,mitər] *n.* any instrument for measuring altitude. Altimeters are used in aircraft to indicate height above the earth's surface. ⟨< L *altus* high + E *-meter*⟩

al•ti•tude ['æltə,tjud] *or* ['æltə,tud], ['ɒltə,tjud] *or* ['ɒltə,tud] *n.* **1** the height above the earth's surface: *The airplane was flying at an altitude of 3000 m.* **2** the height above sea level: *The altitude of Calgary, Alberta, is 1079 m.* **3** a high place: *At these altitudes snow never melts.* **4** a position of high rank or great power. **5** *Geometry.* the vertical distance from the base of a figure to its highest point. **6** *Astronomy.* the angular distance of a star, planet, etc. above the horizon. *Abbrev.*: alt. ⟨ME < L *altitudo* < *altus* high⟩ **—,al•ti'tu•di•nal,** *adj.*

altitude sickness a condition resulting from deficiency of oxygen in the body because of the thinness of the air at high altitudes. It is characterized by sleepiness, headache, muscle weakness, etc., and, in extreme cases, by unconsciousness and failure of the respiratory and circulatory systems, resulting in death.

al•to ['ɒltou] *or* ['æltou] *n., pl.* **-tos;** *adj.* *—n.* **1** the lowest female singing voice. **2** the highest adult male singing voice, above tenor; countertenor. **3** a singer whose range is alto. **4** the part sung by an alto. It is the second highest part in standard four-part harmony for men's and women's voices together. **5** an instrument having a range lower than that of the soprano, or treble, in a family of instruments.
—adj. having to do with, having the range of, or designed for an alto. *Abbrev.*: a. or alt. ⟨< Ital. < L *altus* high⟩

alto clef *Music.* a C clef which identifies middle C as being on the third line of the staff.

al•to–cu•mu•lus [,æltou 'kjumjələs] *n., pl.* **-li** [-,laɪ]. a fleecy cloud formation having rounded heaps of white or greyish clouds, often partly shaded, at heights of between 2400 and 6000 m. *Abbrev.*: Ac

al•to•geth•er *adv., n.* [,ɒltə'gɛðər] *or* ['ɒltə,gɛðər] *adv., n.* *—adv.* **1** completely; entirely: *altogether wicked.* **2** on the whole; considering everything: *Altogether, I'm sorry it happened.* **3** all included: *Altogether there were ten books.*
—n. **the altogether,** *Informal.* the condition of being nude (*used in the phrase* **in the altogether**): *They went swimming in the altogether.* ⟨ME *altogedere*⟩
☛ *Usage.* Do not confuse the adverb **altogether** with the adjective phrase **all together,** which means 'together in a group': *We found the boys all together in the kitchen.*

alto horn althorn.

al•to-re•lie•vo [,æltou rɪ'livou] *n., pl.* **-vos.** sculpture in high relief, in which the figures stand out at least half their thickness from the background. ⟨< Ital.⟩

al•to-stra•tus [,æltou 'streitəs] *or* [-'strætəs] *n., pl.* **-ti** [-taɪ] *or* [-ti]. a bluish grey, sheetlike cloud formation, ill-defined at the base, occurring at heights between 2400 and 6000 m. *Abbrev.*: As ⟨< L *altus* high + E *stratus*⟩

al•tre•ta•mine [æl'trɛtə,min] *or* [-,maɪn] *n.* a drug used to treat cancer.

al•tri•cial [æl'trɪʃəl] *adj.* of birds, helpless when hatched. ⟨< NL *altricialis* < L *altrix* nurse < *alere* feed⟩

al•tru•ism ['æltru,ɪzəm] *or* ['ɒltru,ɪzəm] *n.* **1** unselfishness; unselfish devotion to the interests and welfare of others. **2** *Philosophy.* the belief that the collective good is the responsibility of the individual. ⟨< F *altruisme* < Ital. *altrui* of or for others < L *alter* other⟩

al•tru•ist ['æltruɪst] *or* ['ɒltruɪst] *n.* an unselfish person; a person who works for the welfare of others.

al•tru•is•tic [,æltru'ɪstɪk] *or* [,ɒltru'ɪstɪk] *adj.* thoughtful of the welfare of others; unselfish. **—,al•tru'is•ti•cal•ly,** *adv.*

ALU *Computer technology.* arithmetic-logic unit; in the central processing unit of a computer, the part that carries out arithmetic and logical operations.

al•u•del ['ælju,dɛl] *n. Chemistry.* a pear-shaped vessel designed to collect sublimates and condensates. ⟨< OF < Sp. < Arabic *al uthal* the vessel⟩

al•um[1] ['æləm] *n.* **1** a white mineral salt used in medicine and in dyeing. Alum is sometimes used to stop the bleeding of a small cut. *Formula*: $KAl(SO_4)_2 \cdot 12H_2O$ **2** a colourless, crystalline salt containing ammonia, used in baking powder, in medicine, etc. *Formula*: $NH_4Al(SO_4)_2 \cdot 12H_2O$ ⟨ME < OF < L *alumen*⟩

al•um[2] [ə'lʌm] *n. Informal.* a short form for *alumnus, alumna,* etc. ⟨by clipping⟩

a•lu•mi•na [ə'lumənə] *n.* aluminum oxide, Al_2O_3. Clay is mostly alumina; emery, rubies, and sapphires are crystalline forms of alumina coloured by various impurities. ⟨< NL < L *alumen, -minis* alum⟩

a•lu•mi•nate [ə'lumə,neit] *or* [ə'lumənət] *n. Chemistry.* the salt of an acid form of aluminum hydroxide.

a•lu•mi•ni•fer•ous [ə,lumə'nɪfərəs] *adj.* containing aluminum.

al•u•min•i•um [,æljə'miniəm] *n. Brit.* aluminum.

a•lu•mi•nize [ə'lumə,naɪz] *v.,* **-nized, -niz•ing.** coat or treat with aluminum: *aluminized automobile mufflers.*

a•lu•mi•nous [ə'lumənəs] *adj.* **1** of or containing alum. **2** of or containing aluminum.

a•lu•mi•num [ə'lumənəm] *n.* a silver-white, very light, ductile, metallic chemical element that occurs in nature only in combination. It resists tarnish and is used for making utensils, instruments, etc. *Symbol*: Al; *at.no.* 13; *at.mass* 26.98. ⟨< *alumina*⟩

aluminum acetate a drug used in cream form to treat dermatitis. *Formula*: $Al(C_2H_3O_2)_3$ Its basic salt is used in the textile industry. *Formula*: $Al(C_2H_3O_2)_2OH$

aluminum foil TIN FOIL.

aluminum hydroxide a white, tasteless, odourless powder used in medicine and for dyeing, waterproofing, and ceramic glazing. *Formula*: $Al(OH_3)$

aluminum oxide alumina.

aluminum phosphate a white powder, or colourless crystals, used in making dental cements and, in ceramics, as a flux. *Formula*: $AlPO_4$

aluminum sulphate a white crystalline salt, available in powder or crystals, used in medicine and in the paper and leather industries, also in dyeing and waterproofing. *Formula*: $Al_2(SO_4)_3$

a•lum•na [ə'lʌmnə] *n., pl.* **-nae.** a female graduate or former student of a school, college, or university. ⟨< L⟩

a•lum•nae [ə'lʌmni] *n.* pl. of ALUMNA. See note at ALUMNI.

a•lum•ni [ə'lʌmnaɪ] *n.* pl. of ALUMNUS.

☛ *Pronun.* Generally, two pronunciations are given in this dictionary for Latin-derived words ending in '-ae' and '-i'. However, because of the distinction in meaning between **alumnae** and **alumni,** the two words are kept separate, one pronunciation being given for each.

a•lum•nus [ə'lʌmnəs] *n., pl.* **-ni.** a graduate or former student of a school, college, or university. ⟨< L *alumnus* foster child < *alere* nourish⟩

al•um•root ['æləm,rut] *n.* saxifrage.

al•u•nite ['æljə,nəit] *n.* a hydrous sulphate of aluminum found in volcanic igneous rock. *Formula*: $KAl_3(OH)_6(SO_4)_3$ ⟨< F *alun* (< L *alumen* alum) + E *-ite*⟩

al•ve•o•lar [æl'viələr] *or* [,ælvi'oulər] *adj., n.* *—adj.* **1** *Anatomy.* **a** of the part of the jaws where the sockets of the teeth are. **b** of, like, or having to do with an alveolus or alveoli. **2** *Phonetics.* formed by touching the tip of the tongue to or bringing it near the upper alveoli. English *t* and *d* are alveolar sounds.
—n. Phonetics. a speech sound formed in this manner.

alveolar ridge the ridge between the upper teeth and the palate.

al•ve•o•late [æl'viələt] *adj.* having alveoli.

al•ve•o•lus [æl'viələs] *or* [,ælvi'ouləs] *n., pl.* **-li** [-,laɪ] *or* [-,li]. **1** *Anatomy.* **a** a small vacuity, pit, or cell. The air cells of the lungs are alveoli. **b** the socket of a tooth. **2** Often *pl., Phonetics.* the ridge behind and above the upper teeth. ⟨< L *alveolus,* dim. of *alveus* cavity⟩

al•vine ['ælvaɪn] *or* ['ælvɪn] *adj.* intestinal or abdominal. ⟨< L *alvus* belly⟩

al•way ['ɒlwei] *adv. Archaic or poetic.* always.

al•ways ['ɒlwɪz] *or* ['ɒlweiz] *adv.* **1** every time; at all times: *Water always has some air in it.* **2** all the time; continuously: *Mother is always cheerful.* **3** forever; for all time to come: *I'll love you always.* **4** in any event: *I could always leave at four rather than five.* ⟨< *all* + *way*⟩

a•lys•sum [ə'lɪsəm] *n.* **1** any of a genus (*Alyssum*) of annual or perennial plants of the mustard family, having greyish leaves and fragrant yellow, white, pink, blue, or violet flowers. Alyssum is a popular garden flower. **2** SWEET ALYSSUM. ⟨< NL < Gk. *alysson,* name of a plant thought to cure rabies⟩

Alz•hei•mer's disease ['ɒltshaɪmərz] a degenerative disease of the brain cells, possibly hereditary, leading eventually to severe mental impairment and death. ⟨< A. *Alzheimer,* the German physician who documented it⟩

am [æm]; *unstressed,* [əm] *v.* the first pers. sing., present indicative of BE: *I am a student. I am going home tomorrow.* ⟨OE *eom*⟩

a.m. or **A.M.** before noon (*used especially to refer to a particular time after midnight and before midday*): *The appointment is for 10:00 a.m.* ⟨for L *ante meridiem*⟩

☛ *Usage.* The abbreviations **a.m.** and **p.m.** are usually written in small letters except in headlines and tables. At the beginning of a sentence the first letter only is capitalized.

Am americium.

Am. 1 America. **2** American.

AM or **A.M.** AMPLITUDE MODULATION.

A.M. air marshal.

AMA or **A.M.A.** American Medical Association.

a•ma•bi•lis fir [ə'mæbəlɪs] **1** a fir tree (*Abies amabilis*) of the western coast of North America, found especially on Vancouver Island and along the coast of the British Columbia mainland. **2** the light, soft wood of this tree, used for pulpwood and lumber.

a•mah ['ɑmə] *or* ['æmə] *n.* in India, China, etc., a European term for a nanny or maid. ⟨< Anglo-Indian < Pg. *ama*⟩

a•main [ə'mein] *adv. Archaic.* **1** at full speed. **2** in haste. **3** with full force; violently. ⟨< *a-*[1] in + *main* force⟩

a•mal•gam [ə'mælgəm] *n.* **1** an alloy of mercury with some other metal or metals. Tin amalgam is used in silvering mirrors. Silver amalgam used to be used as fillings for teeth. **2** a mixture; blend. ⟨< Med.L *amalgama* < Arabic < Gk. *malagma* emollient < *malassein* soften⟩

a•mal•gam•ate [ə'mælgə,meit] *v.* **-at•ed, -at•ing.** unite together; combine; mix; blend: *The two companies amalgamated to form one big company.* **—a'mal•gam•a•ble,** *adj.*

a•mal•gam•a•tion [ə,mælgə'meiʃən] *n.* a union; combination; mixture; blend: *Our organization is an amalgamation of three different charities.*

am•an•dine ['ɑmən,din] *adj.* cooked or served with slivered almonds.

am•a•ni•ta [,æmə'nəitə] *n.* any of various mushrooms of the genus *Amanita,* several species of which are very poisonous. ⟨< NL < Gk.⟩

am•an•ta•dine [æ'mæntə,din] *or* [-,daın] *n.* a drug used to treat flu and Parkinson's disease. *Formula*: $C_{10}H_{17}NHCl$

a•man•u•en•sis [ə,mænju'ɛnsıs] *n., pl.* **-ses** [-siz]. a person who writes down what another says, or copies what another has written. ⟨< L *amanuensis* < *(servus) a manu* literally, hand servant + *-ensis* belonging to⟩

am•a•ranth ['æmə,rænθ] *n.* **1** *Poetic.* an imaginary flower that never fades. **2** any of a genus (*Amaranthus*) of plants including some well-known garden plants, such as love-lies-bleeding, and many weeds, such as the pigweeds. **3** (*adjl.*) designating a family (Amaranthaceae) of plants native to Africa and tropical America, made up chiefly of herbs but including a few shrubs and trees. The amaranth family includes the amaranths and the cockscomb. **4** dark reddish purple. ⟨< L < Gk. *amarantos* everlasting < *a-* not + *marainein* wither; influenced by Gk. *anthos* flower⟩

am•a•ran•thine [,æmə'rænθaın], [,æmə'rænθin], *or* [,æmə'rænθın] *adj.* **1** never-fading; undying. **2** purple; purplish red. **3** of, like or having to do with the amaranth.

am•a•relle [,æmə'rɛl] *n.* SOUR CHERRY. ⟨< G < Med.L *amarellum* < L *amarus* sour, bitter⟩

am•a•ret•to [,æmə'rɛtou] *n.* an Italian liqueur flavoured with almonds.

am•a•ryl•lis [,æmə'rılıs] *n.* **1** a widely cultivated, lilylike South African plant (*Amaryllis belladonna*) having clusters of very large, fragrant, red, white, or rose flowers on a thick stalk and long narrow leaves that appear after the flowers have withered. **2** any of various other plants of the same family, having lilylike flowers. **3** (*adjl.*) designating a family (Amaryllidaceae) of mostly tropical plants that grow from bulbs, corms, or rhizomes, having long narrow leaves and large fragrant flowers with six petals, including the daffodil, jonquil, century plant, and amaryllis. ⟨< L < Gk. *Amaryllis*, typical name for a country girl⟩

a•mass [ə'mæs] *v.* heap together; pile up; accumulate: *The miser amassed a fortune for himself.* ⟨< F *amasser* < *a-* to (< L *ad-*) + *masse* mass < L *massa* kneaded dough. Related to MASS[1].⟩ **—a'mass•ment,** *n.*

☛ *Syn.* See note at ACCUMULATE.

A•mat•er•a•su [,amatɛ'rasʊ] *n.* in Shintoism, the sun goddess; the most highly revered of the many Japanese deities: *The imperial line of Japan has traditionally traced an unbroken ancestry to Amaterasu.*

am•a•teur ['æmətʃər], [,æmə'tʃʊr], ['æmə,tʃɜr], *or* [,æmə'tɜr] *n., adj.* *—n.* **1** a person who undertakes some activity for pleasure, not for money or as a profession. **2** a person who does something without showing the proper skill. **3** an athlete who is not a professional.
—adj. **1** of amateurs; made or done by amateurs. **2** being an amateur: *an amateur pianist.* ⟨< F < L *amator* lover < *amare* love⟩

am•a•teur•ish [,æmə'tʃʊrıʃ], [,æmə'tʃɜrıʃ], *or* [,æmə'tɜrıʃ] *adj.* done as an amateur might do it; not expert; not very skilful. **—,a•ma'teur•ish•ly,** *adv.* **—,a•ma'teur•ish•ness,** *n.*

am•a•teur•ism ['æmətʃə,rızəm], [,æmə'tʃʊrızəm], *or* [,æmə'tɜrızəm] *n.* **1** an amateurish way of doing things. **2** the position or rank of an amateur.

A•ma•ti [a'mati] *n.* any violin made by Nicolo Amati (1596-1684) or any member of his family.

am•a•tive ['æmətıv] *adj.* amorous. ⟨< Med.L *amativus* lovable < L *amare* love⟩

am•a•tol ['æmə,tɒl] *n.* an explosive substance composed of ammonium and trinitrotoluene. ⟨< *am(monium)* + *(trinitro)tol(uene)*⟩

am•a•to•ry ['æmə,tɔri] *adj.* of love; causing love; having to do with making love or with lovers. ⟨< L *amatorius* < *amare* love⟩

am•au•ro•sis [,æmɔ'rousıs] *n.* loss of sight. ⟨< Gk. *amauros* dark⟩ **—,am•au'rot•ic** [-'rɒtık], *adj.*

a•maut [ə'mʌut] *Cdn.* a hood in the back of a parka for an Inuit woman to carry a child. ⟨< Inuktitut⟩

a•maze [ə'meiz] *v.* **a•mazed, a•maz•ing;** *n.* *—v.* surprise greatly; strike with sudden wonder.
—n. Poetic. amazement. ⟨OE *āmasian*⟩

☛ *Syn. v.* See note at SURPRISE.

a•mazed [ə'meizd] *adj., v.* *—adj.* greatly surprised.
—v. pt. and pp. of AMAZE.

a•maz•ed•ly [ə'meizıdli] *adv.* lost in wonder or astonishment.

a•maze•ment [ə'meizmənt] *n.* great surprise; sudden wonder; astonishment.

a•maz•ing [ə'meizıŋ] *adj., v.* *—adj.* very surprising; wonderful; astonishing.
—v. ppr. of AMAZE. **—a'maz•ing•ly,** *adv.*

Am•a•zon ['æmə,zɒn] *or* ['æməzən] *n.* **1** *Greek mythology.* a member of a race of female warriors supposed to live near the Black Sea. **2** Usually, **amazon,** a tall, strong, athletic woman. ⟨ME < L *Amazon* < Gk.; origin uncertain⟩

Am•a•zo•ni•an [,æmə'zouniən] *adj.* **1** of or having to do with the Amazon River in South America or the region it drains. **2** of, having to do with, or characteristic of an Amazon.
3 Usually, **amazonian,** of a woman or girl, strong and athletic or warlike.

am•a•zon•ite ['æməzə,nəit] *n.* **1** a bright, bluish green semiprecious stone, a variety of feldspar. **2** a piece of this stone or a gem made from it. ⟨< *Amazon* (River) + *-ite[1]*⟩

am•ba•ry [æm'bari] *n.* an East Indian plant (*Hibiscus cannabinus*), yielding a jutelike fibre. ⟨< Hind.⟩

am•bas•sa•dor [æm'bæsədər] *or* [æm'bæsə,dɔr] *n.* **1** the highest-ranking diplomatic representative sent by one government or ruler to another. **2** an official representative of a government or a ruler at the meetings of an international organization, on a special mission, etc.: *The Canadian ambassador to NATO.* **3** any representative of a group who reflects its typical qualities: *Visiting Scouts can be ambassadors of good will for their country.* ⟨ME < MF *ambassadeur* < Ital. *ambasciatore*⟩

am•bas•sa•dor–at–large [æm'bæsədər ət 'lardʒ] *n.* a minister or representative appointed for a special occasion, but not accredited to any government.

am•bas•sa•do•ri•al [æm,bæsə'dɔriəl] *adj.* of an ambassador or ambassadors.

am•bas•sa•dor•ship [æm'bæsədər,ʃıp] *n.* **1** the position or rank of an ambassador. **2** the term of office of an ambassador.

am•ber ['æmbər] *n., adj.* *—n.* **1** a hard, translucent, fossilized resin, yellow or brownish yellow in colour, used for jewellery. **2** the colour of amber; brownish yellow.
—adj. **1** made of amber. **2** brownish yellow. ⟨ME < OF *ambre* < Arabic *'anbar* ambergris⟩

am•ber•gris ['æmbər,gris] *or* ['æmbərgrıs] *n.* a waxlike, greyish substance secreted by sperm whales. Ambergris is used in making perfumes. ⟨< F *ambre gris* grey amber⟩

am•ber•jack ['æmbər,dʒæk] *n.* one of several members of the genus *Seriola*, a gold-coloured fish of the Atlantic.

am•ber•oid ['æmbə,rɔıd] *n.* synthetic amber.

ambi– *combining form.* on both sides or in both ways; both, as in *ambidextrous* (dextrous with both hands). ⟨< L *ambi-* around or *ambo* both⟩

am•bi•ance ['æmbiəns], ['ambi,ãs], *or* ['æmbi,ans] See AMBIENCE.

am•bi•dex•ter•i•ty [,æmbədɛk'stɛrəti] *n.* **1** the ability to use both hands equally well. **2** unusual skilfulness. **3** deceitfulness.

am•bi•dex•trous [,æmbə'dɛkstrəs] *adj.* **1** able to use both hands equally well. **2** very skilful. **3** deceitful. ⟨< LL *ambidexter* < L *ambi-* both + *dexter* right⟩ **—,am•bi'dex•trous•ly,** *adv.* **—,am•bi'dex•trous•ness,** *n.*

am•bi•ence ['æmbiəns], ['ambi,ãs], *or* ['æmbi,ans]; *French,* [ã'bjãs] *n.* environment or atmosphere: *They felt uncomfortable in the formal ambience of the expensive restaurant.* Also, **ambiance.** ⟨< L *ambiens* from *ambire* go around < *ambi* around + *īre* go⟩

am•bi•ent ['æmbiənt] *adj.* surrounding: *the ambient temperature.* ⟨< L *ambiens, -entis*, ppr. of *ambire* < *ambi-* around + *ire* go⟩

am•bi•gu•i•ty [,æmbə'gjuəti] *n., pl.* **-ties. 1** a possibility of two or more meanings: *The ambiguity of the speaker's reply made it impossible to know which side she was on.* **2** a word or expression that can have more than one meaning. **3** lack of clarity; vagueness; uncertainty: *On his first day as a clerk in the office, the president's son was embarrassed by the ambiguity of his position.*

am•big•u•ous [æm'bıgjuəs] *adj.* **1** having more than one possible meaning: "After John hit Dick, he ran away" *is ambiguous because one cannot tell which boy ran away.* **2** doubtful; not clear; uncertain: *She was left in an ambiguous position by his friend's failure to appear and help her.* ⟨< L *ambiguus* < *ambigere* < *ambi-* in two ways + *agere* drive⟩ **—am'big•u•ous•ly,** *adv.* **—am'big•u•ous•ness,** *n.*

☛ *Syn.* **1.** See note at OBSCURE.

am•bit ['æmbɪt] *n.* **1** the bounds or limits of a district, estate, etc. **2** sphere of influence; scope.

am•bi•tion [æm'bɪʃən] *n.* **1** a strong desire for fame or honour; seeking after a high position or great power. **2** something strongly desired or sought after: *Her ambition was to be a great actor.* ⟨ME < OF < L *ambitio, -onis* a canvassing for votes < *ambire* < *ambi-* around + *ire* go⟩ **—am'bi•tion•less,** *adj.*

am•bi•tious [æm'bɪʃəs] *adj.* **1** having ambition: *an ambitious person.* **2** strongly desiring a particular thing; eager: *ambitious to succeed, ambitious of power.* **3** requiring much skill or effort: *an ambitious undertaking.* **—am'bi•tious•ly,** *adv.* **—am'bi•tious•ness,** *n.*

am•biv•a•lence [æm'bɪvələns] *n.* the state or condition of having simultaneously conflicting feelings or attitudes, such as love and hate, toward persons, places, or things. ⟨< *ambi-* + L *valentia* value < *valere* be worth⟩

am•biv•a•lent [æm'bɪvələnt] *adj.* acting in opposite ways; having conflicting feelings or attitudes, such as love and hate, at the same time: *The politician was spurred on by the ambivalent mixture of a ruthless ambition and an earnest desire to serve her country.* **—am'biv•a•lent•ly,** *adv.*

am•bi•vert ['æmbɪ,vɜrt] *n.* a person who exhibits both introversion and extroversion.

am•ble ['æmbəl] *n., v.* **-bled, -bling.** *—n.* **1** the gait of a horse when it lifts first the two legs on one side and then the two on the other. **2** an easy, slow pace in walking.
—v. **1** walk at an easy, slow pace. **2** (of a horse) move at an amble. ⟨ME < OF *ambler* < L *ambulare* walk⟩

am•bler ['æmblər] *n.* **1** a horse or mule that ambles. **2** a person who ambles.

am•blyg•o•nite [æm'blɪgə,nəit] *n.* a whitish or greyish green mineral, lithium aluminum fluorophosphate. *Formula*: $LiAl(PO_4)F_3OH$ ⟨< Gk. *amblygonios* < *amblys* blunt, obtuse + *gonia* angle⟩

am•bly•o•pi•a [,æmbli'oupiə] *n.* loss of visual acuity in the absence of any disease or damage to the eye. ⟨< Gk. *amblys* dull + *ops* eye⟩ **—,am•bly'o•pic,** *adj.*

am•bo•cep•tor ['æmbou,sɛptər] *n. Bacteriology.* an antibody that works by connecting certain proteins (called complement) to the antigen.

am•boy•na [æm'bɔɪnə] *n.* **1** a leguminous tree (*Pterocarpus indicus*) of S Asia. **2** its wood, used to make furniture. The wood is known for its curly, spotted grain.

am•bro•sia [æm'brouʒə] *or* [æm'brouziə] *n.* **1** *Greek and Roman mythology.* the food of the gods. **2** something especially pleasing to taste or smell. **3** a combination of pollen and nectar eaten by certain bees and their larvae. ⟨< L < Gk. *ambrosia* < *ambrotos* < *a-* not + *brotos* mortal⟩

am•bro•sial [æm'brouʒəl] *or* [æm'brouziəl] *adj.* **1** like ambrosia; especially pleasing to taste or smell. **2** divine; worthy of the gods.

Am•bro•sian chant [æm'brouʒən] a style of plainsong introduced by St. Ambrose in the cathedral of Milan about A.D. 384. The melody had more ornamentation than the later Gregorian chant.

am•bu•lance ['æmbjələns] *n.* a vehicle, boat, or aircraft equipped to carry sick or wounded persons. ⟨< F *ambulance* < *(hôpital) ambulant* walking hospital) < L *ambulare* walk⟩

am•bu•lant ['æmbjələnt] *adj.* walking.

am•bu•late ['æmbjə,leit] *v.* **-lat•ed, -lat•ing.** walk; move about ⟨< L *ambulare*⟩ **—,am•bu'la•tion,** *n.*

am•bu•la•to•ry ['æmbjələ,tɔri] *adj., n., pl.* **-ries.** *—adj.* **1** having to do with walking; fitted for walking. **2** capable of walking; not bedridden. **3** moving from place to place. **4** not permanent; changeable.
—n. a covered place for walking; cloister.

am•bus•cade [,æmbə'skeid] *n. or v.* **-cad•ed, -cad•ing.** ambush. ⟨< F *embuscade* < Ital. *imboscata* < *imboscare* ambush⟩ **—,am•bus'cad•er,** *n.*

am•bush ['æmbʊʃ] *n., v. —n.* **1** a surprise attack from some hiding place on an approaching enemy. **2** attackers so hidden. **3** the place where they are hidden. **4** the act of lying in wait: *They often trapped their enemies by ambush instead of meeting them in open battle.*
—v. **1** attack from an ambush. **2** wait in hiding to make a surprise attack. **3** put (soldiers, etc.) in hiding for a surprise attack: *The general ambushed his troops in the woods on either side of the road.* ⟨ME < OF *embusche*, n., *embuschier*, v. < *en* -in (< L *in-*) + *busche* wood, bush < VL *busca* < Gmc.⟩

am•ci•no•nide [æm'sɪnə,nid] *or* [-,naɪd] *n.* a drug used in a cream form to treat certain skin conditions.

a•me•ba [ə'mibə] *n., pl.* **-bas** or **-bae** [-bi] *or* [-baɪ]. See AMOEBA.

a•me•bic [ə'mibɪk] See AMOEBIC.

a•me•boid [ə'mibɔɪd] See AMOEBOID.

a•meer [ə'mir] *n.* See EMIR.

a•mel•io•ra•ble [ə'miliərəbəl] *or* [ə'miljərəbəl] *adj.* that can be improved.

a•mel•io•rant [ə'miliərənt] *or* [ə'miljərənt] *n.* anything that ameliorates.

a•mel•io•rate [ə'miliə,reit] *or* [ə'miljə,reit] *v.* **-rat•ed, -rat•ing.** **1** make better: *New housing ameliorated living conditions in the slums.* **2** become better; improve: *Living conditions ameliorated with the new housing.* ⟨< F *améliorer*, ult. < LL *meliorare* < L *a(d)* + *melior* better⟩ **—a'mel•io,rat•or,** *n.*

a•mel•io•ra•tion [ə,miliə'reiʃən] *or* [ə,miljə'reiʃən] *n.* **1** improvement. **2** *Linguistics.* the improvement in the status of what is named, as when OE *cniht* (boy) became 'a knight'.

a•mel•io•ra•tive [ə'miliərətɪv] *or* [ə'miliə,reitɪv], [ə'miljərətɪv] *or* [ə'miljə,reitɪv] *adj.* improving.

a•men [ei'mɛn] *or* [ɑ'mɛn] *interj., n. —interj.* **1** be it so; may it become true. *Amen* is said after a prayer or wish. **2** *Informal.* an expression of approval.
—n. the saying or writing of 'amen': *Several amens were heard from the crowd.* ⟨< L < Gk. < Hebrew *amen* truth, certainty < *aman* strengthen⟩

Amen ['ɑmən] *n.* one of the chief gods of ancient Egypt, who became identified with the sun god Ra and was then called **Amen-Ra.**

a•me•na•bil•i•ty [ə,minə'bɪləti] *or* [ə,mɛnə'bɪləti] *n.* the fact, quality, state, or condition of being amenable.

a•me•na•ble [ə'minəbəl] *or* [ə'mɛnəbəl] *adj.* **1** open to suggestion or advice; responsive; submissive: *A reasonable person is amenable to persuasion.* **2** accountable; answerable: *People living in a country are amenable to its laws.* **3** that can be assessed or tested according to certain principles (*used with* **to**). ⟨< AF *amener* < *a-* to (< L *ad-*) + *mener* lead < L *minare* drive (with shouts) < *minae* threats⟩ **—a'me•na•ble•ness,** *n.* **—a'me•na•bly,** *adv.*

a•mend [ə'mɛnd] *v.* **1** change the form of (a law, bill, motion, etc.) by addition, omission, etc. **2** change for the better; improve. **3** free from faults; make right; correct. ⟨ME < OF *amender* < L *emendare* < *ex-* out of + *mendum, menda* fault. Doublet of EMEND.⟩ **—a'mend•a•ble,** *adj.* **—a'mend•er,** *n.*

a•men•da•to•ry [ə'mɛndə,tɔri] *adj.* intended or tending to amend; corrective.

a•mende [ə'mɛnd]; *French* [a'mɑ̃d] *n.* **1** recompense or satisfaction for an injury done. **2** a fine or penalty. ⟨< F⟩

a•mend•ment [ə'mɛndmənt] *n.* **1** a change made in a law, bill, motion, etc. **2** a change for the better; improvement. **3** a change made to remove an error; correction.

a•mends [ə'mɛnz] *n.pl.* a payment for loss; satisfaction for an injury; compensation.

a•men•i•ty [ə'minəti] *or* [ə'mɛnəti] *n., pl.* **-ties.** **1** a pleasant way; polite act: *Saying "Thank you" and holding the door open for a person to pass through are amenities.* **2** a pleasant feature; something which makes life easier and more pleasant. **3** pleasantness; agreeableness: *the amenity of a warm climate.* ⟨ME < OF < L *amoenitas* < *amoenus* pleasant⟩

a•men•or•rhe•a [ei,mɛnə'riə] *n.* failure to menstruate; the absence of menstruation. ⟨< NL *amenorrhea* < Gk. *a-* not + *men* month + *rhoia* flux, flow⟩

A•men–Ra ['ɑmɛn 'rɑ] *n.* the principal god of ancient Egypt.

a•men•sal•ism [ei'mɛnsə,lɪzəm] *n. Biology.* a form of SYMBIOSIS in which one species is harmed but it is not clear how the other species receives benefit. Compare COMMENSALISM, MUTUALISM, and PARASITISM. ⟨< a-^{4} + *(com)mensalism*⟩

am•ent¹ ['æmənt] *or* ['eimənt] *n.* catkin. ⟨< L *amentum* thong⟩ **—,am•en'ta•ceous, ,am•en'tif•er•ous,** *adj.*

am•ent² ['eimɛnt] *n.* a person with amentia.

a•men•tia [ei'mɛnʃə] *n.* failure to develop mentally. ⟨< L, insanity < a-^{2} + *mens* mind⟩

Amer. **1** America. **2** American.

Am•er•a•sian [,æmə'reiʒən] *adj.* having an American father and an Asian mother, or vice versa.

a•merce [ə'mɜrs] *v.* **a•merced, a•merc•ing. 1** punish by a fine. **2** punish. ⟨ME < AF *amercier* < *à merci* at the mercy (of)⟩ **—a'merce•ment,** *n.* **—a'merc•er,** *n.*

A•mer•i•ca [ə'mɛrəkə] *n.* **1** the United States. **2** Often, **the Americas,** North, Central, and South America.

A•mer•i•can [ə'mɛrəkən] *n., adj. —n.* **1** an inhabitant or citizen of the United States, or of the earlier British colonies, not belonging to one of the aboriginal peoples. **2** a native or inhabitant of the western hemisphere.
—adj. **1** of or having to do with the United States or its people: *an American citizen, American technology.* **2** of, having to do with, or found in the western hemisphere: *the Amazon and other American rivers. The American robin is a different bird from the European robin.* ⟨< NL Americanus⟩

A•mer•i•ca•na [ə,mɛrə'kænə], [ə,mɛrə'kɑnə], *or sometimes* [ə,mɛrə'keinə] *n.pl.* a collection of objects, documents, books, facts, etc. about America, especially its history.

American aloe CENTURY PLANT.

American Beauty a variety of hybrid perennial rose with red blooms.

American brooklime AMERICAN SPEEDWELL.

American chameleon CHAMELEON (def. 2).

American cheese processed Cheddar.

American eagle the bald eagle, especially as the emblem or a symbol of the United States.

American Indian Amerindian.

A•mer•i•can•ism [ə'mɛrəkə,nɪzəm] *n.* **1** devotion or loyalty to the United States, its customs, traditions, etc. **2** a word, phrase, or meaning originating in the United States. **3** a custom or trait peculiar to the United States.

American ivy VIRGINIA CREEPER.

A•mer•i•can•i•za•tion [ə,mɛrəkənaɪ'zeiʃən] *or* [ə,mɛrəkənaɪ'zeiʃən] *n.* the act or process of making or becoming American in habits, customs, or character.

A•mer•i•can•ize [ə'mɛrəkə,naɪz] *v.* **-ized, -iz•ing.** make or become American in habits, customs, or character.

American organ a kind of small reed organ; melodeon.

American plan a system used in hotels where one price covers room, board, and service. See also EUROPEAN PLAN.

American Sign Language a language made up of manual and facial gestures, used by much of the North American deaf community; Ameslan. American Sign Language has its own distinct syntactic and semantic properties.

American speedwell a low-growing marsh plant (*Veronica americana*), common in Canada, having small blue flowers. Also called **American brooklime** or **veronica.**

am•er•i•ci•um [,æmə'rɪʃiəm] *n.* an artificial, radioactive, metallic chemical element. *Symbol*: Am; *at.no.* 95; *at.mass* 241.06. ⟨< NL < *America*⟩

Am•er•ind ['æmə,rɪnd] *n.* Amerindian.

Am•er•in•di•an [,æmə'rɪndiən] *adj., n. —adj.* **1** of or designating a major race of people, the original inhabitants of the western hemisphere south of the Arctic coastal regions, distinguished by a combination of biological characteristics, including straight, dark hair and light to dark-brown skin. **2** designating the aboriginal languages of the western hemisphere south of the Arctic coast, forming numerous distinct language families. **3** of or having to do with the Amerindian peoples, their cultures, or their languages.
—n. a member of the Amerindian race. ⟨< *Amer(ican)* + *Indian*⟩

Am•es•lan ['æmə,slæn] *or* ['æm,slæn] *n.* AMERICAN SIGN LANGUAGE.

am•e•thyst ['æməθɪst] *n.* **1** a purple or violet variety of quartz, a semi-precious stone, used for jewellery. **2** a piece of this stone, or a gem made from it. **3** a violet-coloured corundum, used for jewellery. **4** purple; violet. ⟨ME < OF < L < Gk. *amethystos* < *a-* not + *methy* wine; thought to prevent intoxication⟩ **—'am•e•thyst,like** or **,am•e'thys•tine** [,æmə'θɪstɪn], *adj.*

am•e•tro•pi•a [,æmɪ'troupiə] *n.* inability of the eye to focus properly. Myopia and hyperopia are types of ametropia. ⟨< NL < Gk *ametros* out of proportion (< *a-*[4] + *metron* measure) + *opia* < *ops* eye⟩

Am•har•ic [æm'hɑrɪk] *n., adj. —n.* the official and literary language of Ethiopia since the 12th century, a Semitic language of the Ethiopic group.
—adj. of or having to do with this language.

a•mi•a•bil•i•ty [,eimiə'bɪləti] *n.* good nature; friendliness; pleasantness; agreeableness.

a•mi•a•ble ['eimiəbəl] *adj.* good-natured and friendly; agreeable: *an amiable smile.* ⟨ME < OF *amiable* < LL *amicabilis* < L *amicus* friend. Doublet of AMICABLE.⟩ **—'a•mi•a•bly,** *adv.*

a•mi•an•thus [,æmi'ænθəs] *n.* any kind of asbestos having long, silky filaments. ⟨< L *amiantus* < Gk. *amiantos* not spotted < *a-*[4] + *miainein* mark, soil⟩

am•i•ca•bil•i•ty [,æməkə'bɪləti] *n.* friendliness.

am•i•ca•ble ['æməkəbəl] *adj.* peaceable; friendly: *Instead of fighting, the two nations settled their quarrel in an amicable way.* ⟨< LL *amicabilis* < L *amicus* friend. Doublet of AMIABLE.⟩ **—'am•i•ca•bly,** *adv.*

am•ice ['æmɪs] *n.* an oblong piece of white linen worn by Christian priests at Mass. It is placed around the neck and over the shoulders. ⟨ME < OF *amis* < L *amictus* cloak⟩

a•mi•cus cu•ri•ae [ə'mikəs 'kjuri,aɪ] *or* [ə'məikəs 'kjuri,i] *Law.* a person with no interest in a case who is called in to advise the judge. ⟨< NL *amicus curiae* friend of the court⟩

a•mid [ə'mɪd] *prep.* in the middle or midst of (*not used before plural nouns*). ⟨OE *amiddan* < *on middan* in the middle⟩

am•ide ['æmaɪd] *n.* **1** POTASSIUM AMIDE. **2** an inorganic compound that has the group $CONH_2$. **3** having to do with the group $CONH_2$. **4** a compound in which a metal atom replaces one of the hydrogen atoms of ammonia. *Formula*: $M(NH_2)_x$ ⟨< *am(monia)* + *-ide*⟩ **—am'i•do,** *adj.*

am•i•din ['æmɪdɪn] *n.* the part of starch that dissolves. ⟨< F *amid(on)* starch + *-in*⟩

am•i•dine ['æmɪ,din] *or* ['æmɪdɪn] *n.* **1** any monobasic compound containing the group CN_2H_3. **2** any crystalline solid with a nitrogen base and the formula $RC(:NH)NH_2$.

amido– *combining form.* showing the presence of an acid radical and the group NH_2. ⟨< *amide*⟩

am•i•dol ['æmɪ,dɒl] *n.* a developing agent in photography.

a•mid•ship [ə'mɪdʃɪp] *adv.* amidships.

a•mid•ships [ə'mɪd,ʃɪps] *adv.* in or toward the middle of a ship; halfway between the bow and stern.

a•midst [ə'mɪdst] *prep.* amid.

am•i•ka•cin [,æmɪ'keisɪn] *n.* an antibiotic drug. *Formula*: $C_{22}H_{45}N_5O_{13}$

a•mi•lo•caine [ə'mɪlə,kein] See AMYLOCAINE.

a•mi•lo•ride [ə'mɪlə,raɪd] *n.* a drug used to treat cirrhosis of the liver. *Formula*: $C_6H_8ClN_7O$

a•mine [ə'min], ['æmɪn], *or* ['æmin] *n. Chemistry.* any of a group of organic compounds formed from ammonia by replacement of one or more of its three hydrogen atoms by univalent hydrocarbon radicals. ⟨< *am(monia)* + *-ine*[2]⟩ **—a'min•ic,** *adj.*

a•mi•no•a•cid•op•a•thy [ə,minou,æsɪ'dɒpəθi] *n.* a disorder of amino acid metabolism, such as phenylketonuria.

a•mi•no acids [ə'minou] *or* ['æmə,nou] *Chemistry.* twenty complex organic acids that combine in various ways to form proteins. The amino acids are encoded in DNA as a sequence of trace of the four bases A (adenine), G (guanine), T (thymidine), and C (cytosine).

a•mi•no•ben•zo•ic acid [ə,minoubɛn'zouɪk] *or* [,æmənoubɛn'zouɪk] a substance used to make, among other things, sunscreen liquid. *Formula*: $C_7H_7NO_2$

a•mi•no•tri•a•zole [ə,minou'traɪə,zoul] *or* [,æmɪnou'traɪə,zoul] *n.* a weed killer.

a•mir [ə'mir] *n.* in Muslim countries, a commander, ruler, or prince. Also, **ameer.** ⟨< Arabic *amir* commander. Related to ADMIRAL.⟩

Am•ish ['ɑmɪʃ] *n., adj. —n.* **the Amish,** *pl.* the members of a strict Mennonite sect, founded in the 17th century in Switzerland. Today most Amish live in farming communities in southern Ontario and parts of the United States. They form part of the group often called Pennsylvania Dutch.
—adj. of, having to do with, or designating this sect or its members. ⟨after Jacob *Amen*, 17c. Mennonite preacher⟩

am•isk ['æmɪsk] *n. Cdn.* beaver. ⟨< Cree⟩

a•miss [ə'mɪs] *adv., adj. —adv.* not the way it should be; out of order; at fault.
take amiss, be offended at because of a misunderstanding: *Ravi*

had not meant to be rude to his mother but she took his answer amiss.
—adj. (*never used before the noun*) improper; wrong. ⟨ME *a mis* by (way of) fault. Related to MISS[1].⟩

am•i•to•sis [ˌæmə'tousɪs] *n. Biology.* a simple or direct method of cell division; reproduction without mitosis. In amitosis the cell separates into new cells without an exact division of the chromosomes. ⟨< *a-*[4] not + *mitosis*⟩ **—ˌa•mi'tot•ic** [-'tɒtɪk], *adj.* **—ˌa•mi'tot•i•cal•ly,** *adj.*

a•mi•trip•ty•line [ˌæmɪ'trɪptəˌlin] *n.* a drug used to treat depression.

am•i•trole ['æmɪˌtroul] aminotriazole.

am•i•ty ['æməti] *n., pl.* **-ties.** peace and friendship; friendly relations: *If there were amity between nations, there would be no wars.* ⟨ME < OF *amitié*, ult. < L *amīcus* friend⟩

am•me•ter ['æmˌmitər] *n.* an instrument for measuring in amperes the strength of an electric current. ⟨< *am*pere + *meter*⟩

am•mine ['æmin] *or* ['æmɪn] *n.* **1** one molecule of NH_3 (ammonia). **2** any compound that contains this molecule bound to a metal. ⟨< *amm(onia)* + *-ine*⟩

ammino– *combining form.* of or having to do with ammonia.

am•mo ['æmou] *n. Informal.* ammunition.

am•mo•nia [ə'mounjə] *n.* **1** a strong-smelling, colourless gas, consisting of nitrogen and hydrogen. *Formula*: NH_3 **2** this gas dissolved in water. Ammonia is very useful for cleaning. *Formula*: NH_3OH ⟨< NL; so named because obtained from sal *ammoniac*⟩

am•mo•ni•ac [ə'mouniˌæk] *n., adj. —n.* a gum resin used for medicines and as a cement for porcelain; gum ammoniac.
—adj. ammoniacal. ⟨< L *ammoniacum* < Gk. *ammōniakon*; applied to a salt obtained near the shrine of *Ammon* in Libya⟩

am•mo•ni•a•cal [ˌæmə'naɪəkəl] *adj.* of or like ammonia.

am•mo•ni•ate [ə'mouniˌeit] *v.,* **-at•ed, -at•ing.** treat with ammonia. **—amˌmo•ni'a•tion,** *n.*

ammonia water ammonia gas dissolved in water.

am•mon•ic [ə'mɒnɪk] *or* [ə'mounɪk] *adj.* of or derived from ammonia or ammonium.

am•mon•i•fy [ə'mɒnəˌfaɪ] *v.* combine or be combined with ammonia or an ammonium compound. **—amˌmon•i•fi'ca•tion,** *n.*

am•mo•nite ['æməˌnəit] *n.* the fossil shell of a mollusc extinct in the Cretaceous period, coiled in a flat spiral and up to 2 m in diameter. ⟨< NL *ammonites* < Med.L *cornu Ammonis* horn of Ammon⟩

am•mo•ni•um [ə'mouniəm] *n.* a radical NH_4 or an ion NH_4+, a group of nitrogen and hydrogen atoms present in ammonia salts. Ammonium never appears in a free state by itself, but acts as a unit in chemical reactions.

ammonium chloride colourless crystals or a white powder used in medicine, in printing on cloth, in electroplating, etc.; sal ammoniac. *Formula*: NH_4Cl

ammonium hydroxide an alkali formed when ammonia gas dissolves in water. *Formula*: NH_4OH

ammonium lactate a drug used in a liquid form to treat dry skin. *Formula*: $C_3H_9NO_3$

am•mu•ni•tion [ˌæmjə'nɪʃən] *n.* **1** bullets, shells, gunpowder, etc. for guns or other weapons; military supplies that can be used against an enemy. **2** anything that can be shot, hurled, or thrown. **3** a means of attack or defence: *Rational argument is your best ammunition.* ⟨< obsolete F *amunition*, used for *munition*⟩

am•ne•sia [æm'niʒə] *or* [æm'niziə] *n.* loss of memory caused by injury to the brain, or by disease or shock. ⟨< NL < Gk. *amnēsia* < *a-* not + *mnasthai* remember⟩

am•ne•si•ac [æm'niziˌæk] *adj., n. —adj.* of or resulting from amnesia.
—n. a person affected with amnesia.

am•ne•sic [æm'nizɪk] *or* [æm'nisɪk] *adj. or n.* amnesiac.

am•nes•ty ['æmnɪsti] *n., pl.* **-ties;** *v.* **-tied, -ty•ing.** *—n.* a general pardon for past offences against a government: *After order was restored, the queen granted amnesty to those who had plotted against her.*
—v. give amnesty to; pardon. ⟨< L < Gk. *amnēstia* < *a-* not + *mnasthai* remember⟩

am•ni•o•cen•te•sis [ˌæmniousɛn'tisɪs] *n.* a procedure for obtaining AMNIOTIC FLUID from the amniotic sac of the fetus, usually at about 16 weeks' gestation. The fluid can be used for prenatal diagnosis of a number of fetal problems, and is taken by a needle through the abdominal wall of the pregnant mother. ⟨< *amnion* + Gk. *kentesis* a pricking⟩

am•ni•on ['æmniən] *n., pl.* **-ni•ons** or **-ni•a** [-niə]. a membrane lining the sac that encloses the embryos of reptiles, birds, and mammals. ⟨< Gk. *amnion*, dim. of *amnos* lamb⟩

am•ni•ote ['æmniˌout] *n. Zoology.* any of the group of vertebrates, including reptiles, birds, and mammals, that develop amnions in their embryonic stages.

am•ni•ot•ic [ˌæmni'ɒtɪk] *adj.* **1** of or contained in the amnion: *amniotic fluid.* **2** having an amnion.

amniotic fluid the fluid filling the amniotic sac of the embryo or fetus and containing cells of fetal origin. Laboratory analysis of the fluid and cells can provide information about the health and genetic characteristics of the fetus.

am•o•bar•bi•tal [ˌæmou'bɑrbətəl] *n.* a sedative drug. *Formula*: $C_{11}H_{18}N_2O_3$

am•o•di•a•quin [ˌæmou'daɪəkwɪn] *n.* a drug used to treat malaria. *Formula*: $C_{20}H_{22}ClN_3O$

a•moe•ba [ə'mibə] *n., pl.* **-bas** or **-bae** [-bi] *or* [-baɪ]. any of a genus (*Amoeba*) of protozoans found in water or moist soil or living as parasites in humans and animals. They move by forming temporary footlike projections which are constantly changing. Sometimes, **ameba.** ⟨< Gk. *amoibē* change⟩

a•moe•bic or **a•me•bic** [ə'mibɪk] *adj.* **1** of or like an amoeba or amoebas. **2** caused by amoebas.

amoebic dysentery a type of dysentery caused by amoebae.

a•moe•bo•cyte [ə'mibouˌsəit] *n.* a cell with mobility like that of an amoeba. A corpuscle that floats about freely in the blood is an amoebocyte.

a•moe•boid or **a•me•boid** [ə'mibɔɪd] *adj.* of or like an amoeba; like that of an amoeba; related or having to do with amoebas.

a•mok [ə'mʌk] *or* [ə'mɒk] *adv., adj., n. —adv. or adj.* See AMUCK.
—n. a violent nervous disorder, occurring chiefly among the Malays; a murderous frenzy. ⟨< Malay⟩

a•mong [ə'mʌŋ] *prep.* (*used only before plural nouns*) **1** surrounded by: *a house among the trees.* **2** in with: *He fell among thieves.* **3** one of; in the number or class of: *Canada is among the largest countries in the world. That book is the best among modern novels.* **4** in comparison with: *only one among so many.* **5** to each of; by or for distribution to: *She divided the chores among the three of them. They divided the money among themselves.* **6** by the combined action of: *Among them they saved the company. We decided among ourselves to call the whole thing off.* **7** by the reciprocal actions of: *They fought among themselves.* **8** by, with, or through the whole or aggregate of: *political unrest among the people.* ⟨OE *amang* < *on gemang* in a crowd⟩
☛ *Usage.* See note at BETWEEN.

a•mongst [ə'mʌŋst] *prep.* among.

a•mon•til•la•do [əˌmɒntə'lɑdou]; *Spanish,* [aˌmɔnti'ljaðo] *n., pl.* **-dos** [-douz]; *Spanish,* [-ðos]. a pale, moderately dry sherry. ⟨< Sp. *Montilla*, a district in Spain where this wine is made⟩

a•mor•al [ei'mɔrəl] *or* [æ'mɔrəl] *adj.* **1** not involving any question of morality; non-moral. **2** having no sense of right or wrong. ⟨< *a-*[4] not + *moral*⟩ **—a'mor•al•ly,** *adv.*

a•mo•ral•i•ty [ˌeimə'rælɪti] *or* [ˌæmə'rælɪti] *n.* the quality of being amoral: *the amorality of nature.*

a•morce [ə'mɔrs] *n.* **1** an explosive to set off the main charge; priming charge. **2** a percussion cap for a toy pistol. ⟨< F < OF *amordre* bite⟩

a•mor•et•to [ˌæmə'rɛtou] *n.* a small cupid, especially in paintings of the Italian Renaissance. ⟨< Ital. dim. of *Amore* Cupid⟩

am•o•ro•so [ˌæmə'rousou] *adj., adv., n. —adj. or adv. Music.* tender(ly); loving(ly).
—n. lover. ⟨< Ital. *amoroso* loving < LL *amorosus* < L *amor* love⟩

am•o•rous ['æmərəs] *adj.* **1** inclined to love. **2** in love. **3** showing love; loving. **4** having to do with love or courtship. ⟨ME < OF *amorous* < *amour* love < L *amor*⟩ **—'am•o•rous•ly,** *adv.* **—'am•o•rous•ness,** *n.*

a•mor pa•tri•ae ['æmɔr 'pætriˌaɪ] *or* ['eimɔr 'peitriˌi] *Latin.* love of one's own country; patriotism.

a•mor•phism [ə'mɔrfɪzəm] *n.* the property of being amorphous.

a•mor•phous [ə'mɔrfəs] *adj.* **1** of no particular kind or type. **2** having no definite form; shapeless; formless; not organized. **3** *Geology.* lacking stratification or other division. **4** *Biology.*

having no definite shape or structure. **5** *Chemistry.* not consisting of crystals: *Glass is amorphous; sugar is crystalline.* ⟨< Gk. *amorphos* < *a-* without + *morphē shape*⟩ **—a'mor•phous•ly,** *adv.* **—a'mor•phous•ness,** *n.*

am•or•ti•za•tion [ˌæmərtaɪ'zeiʃən] *or* [əˌmɔrtə'zeiʃən] *n.* **1** an amortizing or being amortized. **2** the money regularly set aside for this purpose.

am•or•tize ['æmərˌtaɪz] *or* [ə'mɔrtaɪz] *v.* **-tized, -tiz•ing. 1** set money aside regularly in a special fund for future wiping out of (a debt, etc.). **2** *Accounting.* write off (expenditures, debts, etc.) proportionately over a fixed period. **3** sell or transfer (property) to a school, church, etc. for perpetual proprietorship. ⟨ME < OF *amortiss-*, a stem of *amortir* deaden < *a-* to (< L *ad-*) + *mort* death < L *mors, mortis*⟩

a•mor•tize•ment [ə'mɔrtɪzmənt] *or* [ˌæmər'taɪzmənt] *n.* amortization.

a•mount [ə'maʊnt] *n., v.* *—n.* **1** a sum; total: *What is the amount of the day's sales?* **2** the full effect, value, or extent: *the sheer amount of the evidence against him.* **3** a whole viewed as a quantity: *a great amount of intelligence.*
—v. **1** be equal (*to*); add up (*to*): *The loss from the flood amounts to ten million dollars.* **2** be equivalent in quantity, value, force, effect, etc. (*to*): *Keeping what belongs to another amounts to stealing.* ⟨ME < OF *amonter* < *a mont* up, literally, to the mountain < L *ad* to, *mons, montis* mountain⟩
☛ *Usage.* **Amount,** NUMBER. **Amount** is used of things viewed in the bulk, weight, or sum; **number** is used of persons or things that can be counted: *an amount of milk, a number of cans of milk.*

a•mour [ə'mur] *n.* **1** a love affair. **2** a secret or illicit love affair. ⟨< F *amour*, probably < Provençal < L *amor* love⟩

a•mour–pro•pre [ɑ'muʀ 'pʀɔpʀ] *n. French.* **1** self-esteem. **2** conceit.

amp¹ [æmp] *n.* ampere.

amp² [æmp] *n.* amplifier.

amp. ampere(s); amperage.

AMP ADENOSINE MONOPHOSPHATE.

am•per•age ['æmpərɪdʒ] *or* [æm'pirɪdʒ] *n.* the strength of an electric current measured in amperes. *Abbrev.*: a., a, or amp.

am•pere ['æmpir] *or* ['æmpɛr] *n.* an SI unit for measuring the rate of flow of an electric current, defined in terms of the magnetic force which a current produces. About one ampere of current is required to produce 100 watts of electric power. The ampere is one of the seven base units in the SI. *Symbol*: A ⟨after André *Ampère* (1775-1836), a French physicist⟩

am•pere–hour ['æmpir 'aʊr] *n.* a unit of electricity; the amount of current with the strength of one ampere flowing through a conductor for one hour.

am•pere–turn ['æmpir 'tɜrn] *or* ['æmpɛr] *n.* the magnetomotive force it takes for a current of one ampere to flow once through a coil. One ampere-turn equals 4π/10 or 1.257 gilberts.

am•per•sand ['æmpərˌsænd] *n.* the sign &, meaning 'and'. ⟨alteration of *and per se and,* (the symbol) & by itself (means) and⟩
☛ *Usage.* The **ampersand** is used chiefly in business correspondence and reference works.

am•phet•a•mine [æm'fɛtəˌmin] *or* [æm'fɛtəmɪn] *n.* a colourless, somewhat volatile, bitter-tasting liquid which has a strong stimulatory effect on the central nervous system, used in various preparations in medicine to treat narcolepsy, hyperkinetic behaviour in children, epilepsy, and Parkinson's disease. The drug can have dangerous side effects and can also cause addiction. *Formula*: $C_9H_{13}N$ ⟨*a*lpha-*m*ethyl-beta-*ph*enyl-*et*hyl- *amine*⟩

amphi– *combining form.* **1** around; on both sides, as in *amphitheatre.* **2** in two ways; of two kinds, as in *amphibious.* ⟨< Gk. *amphi-* < *amphi*, prep., adv.⟩

am•phi•as•ter ['æmfiˌæstər] *n.* the spindle-shaped structure that forms in a cell in the first stage of mitosis.

am•phib•i•an [æm'fɪbiən] *n., adj.* *—n.* **1** any of a class (Amphibia) of cold-blooded vertebrates, most of which have completely scaleless skin, and which produce young that at first breathe by means of gills but usually undergo a complete physical change as they mature, becoming land-living animals with lungs and legs. Frogs, toads, newts, and salamanders are amphibians. **2** an animal or plant adapted to life in the water and on land. Seals, beavers, and water snakes are sometimes called amphibians. **3** an aircraft that can take off from and come down on either land or water. **4** a vehicle that can travel across land or water.
—adj. **1** of or having to do with amphibians. **2** amphibious. ⟨< NL

Amphibia, neut. pl. of *amphibius* < Gk. *amphibios.* See AMPHIBIOUS.⟩

am•phi•bi•ot•ic [ˌæmfɪbaɪ'ɒtɪk] *adj.* living in water as a larva and on land as an adult, as the frog.

am•phib•i•ous [æm'fɪbiəs] *adj.* **1** able to live both on land and in water. **2** suited for use on land or water: *an amphibious tank.* **3** having two qualities, kinds, natures, or parts. **4** by the combined action of land, water, and air forces: *an amphibious attack.* ⟨< Gk. *amphibios* living a double life < *amphi-* both + *bios* life⟩ **—am'phib•i•ous•ly,** *adv.* **—am'phib•i•ous•ness,** *n.*

am•phi•bole ['æmfəˌboul] *n.* any of a group of rock-forming silicate minerals, including hornblende and asbestos. ⟨< F < L *amphibolus* < Gk. *amphibolos* ambiguous < *amphi-* on both sides + *-bolos* struck⟩

am•phib•o•lite [æm'fɪbəˌləit] *n.* a usually dark-green or black metamorphic rock composed mainly of amphiboles, especially hornblende.

am•phi•bol•o•gy [ˌæmfɪ'bɒlədʒi] *n.* an ambiguous expression, resulting from a peculiar construction rather than from the words that make up the expression. *Example*: *Demolish buildings and spare rooms.*

am•phi•brach ['æmfəˌbræk] *n. Prosody.* a measure or foot consisting of one strongly stressed syllable between two weakly stressed syllables, or one long syllable between two short syllables. *Example*:
Behińd shut | the póstern, | the lights sank | to reśt,
And ínto | the mídnight | we gálloped | abreást.
⟨< L *amphibrachus* < Gk. *amphibrachys* short at both ends < *amphi-* both + *brachys* short⟩

am•phi•chro•mat•ic [ˌæmfɪkrou'mætɪk] *adj.* showing two colours, as a litmus test, one in reaction to a base and the other in reaction to an acid.

am•phi•go•ry ['æmfɪˌgɔri] *n.* **1** meaningless nonsense in verse. **2** parody. ⟨< F *amphigouri*⟩

am•phi•mix•is [ˌæmfɪ'mɪksɪs] *n. Biology.* **1** sexual reproduction; union of male and female gametes from two separate organisms. **2** hybridization. ⟨< *amphi-* + Gk. *mixis* a mixing⟩

am•phi•pod ['æmfəˌpɒd] *n.* any of an order (Amphipoda) of tiny crustaceans, such as the sand flea, having two sets of feet serving different purposes. Sand fleas have one set of feet used for jumping and another for swimming. ⟨< *amphi-* + Gk. *pous, podos* foot⟩

am•phi•pro•style [ˌæmfɪ'proustaɪl] *or* [æm'fɪprouˌstaɪl] *adj. Architecture.* of a building, having columns at front and back, but not at the sides.

am•phis•bae•na [ˌæmfɪs'binə] *n.* **1** the genus of worm lizards (*Amphisbaena*). They have no legs and live in burrows. **2** a mythological serpent with a head on either end of its body. ⟨< L < Gk. *amphisbaina* < *amphis* on both sides + *bainein* go⟩ **—ˌam•phis'bae•ni•an,** *adj.*

am•phi•sty•lar [ˌæmfɪ'staɪlər] *adj. Architecture.* of a building, having columns at front and back, or at each side, but not on all sides.

am•phi•the•a•tre ['æmfəˌθiətər] *n.* **1** a circular or oval building with tiers of seats around a central open space. **2** a theatre gallery, lecture hall, etc. with ascending rows of seats, especially when forming a semicircle. **3** a place for public contests and games. **4** a level place surrounded by a steeply rising slope. Sometimes, **amphitheater.** ⟨< L < Gk. *amphitheatron* < *amphi-* on all sides + *theatron* theatre⟩

Am•phi•tri•te [ˌæmfə'trəiti] *n. Greek mythology.* the goddess of the sea. Amphitrite was the wife of Poseidon.

am•pho•ra ['æmfərə] *n., pl.* **-rae** [-ˌri] *or* [-ˌraɪ]. a tall, two-handled jar, used by the ancient Greeks and Romans. ⟨< L < Gk. *amphoreus*, short for **amphiphoreus* < *amphi-* on both sides + *phoreus* bearer; with reference to the two handles⟩

am•pho•ter•ic [ˌæmfə'tɛrɪk] *adj.* behaving both like an acid and like a base. ⟨< Gk. *amphoteros*⟩

am•pho•ter•i•cin B [ˌæmfə'tɛrəsɪn] *n.* an antifungal antibiotic drug. *Formula*: $C_{46}H_{73}NO_{20}$

am•pi•cil•lin [ˌæmpɪ'sɪlɪn] *n.* a form of penicillin effective against Gram-positive and Gram-negative bacteria. *Formula*: $C_{16}H_{19}N_3O_4S$

am•ple ['æmpəl] *adj.* **-pler, -plest. 1** large or extensive: *an ample backyard, a figure of ample proportions.* **2** enough to easily meet all requirements; plentiful; abundant: *We had ample food for the trip.* ⟨< F < L *amplus*⟩ **—'am•ple•ness,** *n.* **—'am•ply,** *adv.*

am•pli•fi•ca•tion [,æmpləfə'keiʃən] *n.* **1** the act of amplifying; expansion. **2** a detail or example that amplifies a statement, narrative, etc. **3** an expanded statement, narrative, etc. **4** an increase in the strength of electric current.

am•pli•fi•er ['æmplə,faɪər] *n.* **1** an electronic device in or attached to a radio, cassette player, etc. for strengthening electrical impulses. **2** loudspeaker. **3** any person or thing that amplifies.

am•pli•fy ['æmplə,faɪ] *v.* **-fied, -fy•ing. 1** make greater or stronger. **2** make fuller and more extensive; expand; enlarge: *to amplify a description, to amplify a point in argument.* **3** write or talk at length. **4** *Electronics.* increase the strength of (an electrical impulse) by means of an amplifier. ⟨ME < OF *amplifier* < L *amplificare* < *amplus* ample + *facere* make⟩

am•pli•tude ['æmplə,tjud] *or* ['æmplə,tud] *n.* **1** width; breadth; size. **2** abundance; fullness. **3** *Physics.* the maximum range of swing or vibration from the mean, or zero, position: *A pendulum swinging through 10° has an amplitude of 5°.* **4** *Electricity.* the maximum departure from the average cycle of an alternating current. **5** *Astronomy.* the distance between a rising star and true east or between a setting star and true west. ⟨< L *amplitudo* < *amplus* ample⟩

amplitude modulation *Radio.* **1** a method of transmitting the sound signals of a broadcast by changing the strength, or amplitude, of the carrier waves to match the audio signals. **2** a broadcasting system that uses amplitude modulation. Compare FREQUENCY MODULATION. *Abbrev.*: AM or A.M.

am•poule ['æmpul] *or* [æm'pul] *n.* a small, sealed glass container, usually holding one dose of a drug, medicine, etc. ⟨< F < L *ampulla* small bottle⟩

am•pul•la [æm'pʊlə] *n., pl.* **am•pul•lae** [-i] *or* [-aɪ]. **1** a two-handled, rounded glass or earthenware flask used in ancient Rome to hold oil, perfume, or wine. It was smaller than an amphora. **2** a vessel used in Christian churches to hold consecrated oil. **3** *Biology.* a dilated part of a canal or duct. ⟨< L⟩ **—am'pul•lar** or **,am•pul'la•ceous,** *adj.*

am•pu•tate ['æmpjə,teit] *v.* **-tat•ed, -tat•ing.** cut off, especially in a surgical operation: *to amputate a leg.* ⟨< L *amputare* < *ambi-* about + *putare* prune⟩

am•pu•ta•tion [,æmpjə'teiʃən] *n.* the act of cutting off a leg, arm, finger, etc.; a cutting off.

am•pu•tee [,æmpjə'ti] *n.* a person who has had an arm, leg, etc. amputated.

am•ri•none ['æmrɪ,noun] *n.* a drug used to treat heart failure. *Formula*: $C_{10}H_9N_3O$

am•rit ['ɑmrit] *n. Sikhism.* a sweetened water used as a sacred drink and as baptismal water. Also, **amrita** [ɑm'ritə]. Compare HOLY WATER. ⟨< Skt. *amrta* immortal⟩

am•sac•rine ['æmsə,krin] *n.* a drug used to treat leukemia.

amt. amount.

amu atomic mass unit.

a•muck [ə'mʌk] *adv. or adj.* in a murderous frenzy; with a crazy desire to attack. Also, **amok.**
run amuck, a run about in a murderous frenzy. **b** become uncontrollable. ⟨< Malay *amok* engaging furiously in battle⟩

am•u•let ['æmjəlɪt] *n.* some object worn as a magic charm against evil. ⟨< L *amuletum*⟩

a•muse [ə'mjuz] *v.* **a•mused, a•mus•ing. 1** cause to laugh or smile. **2** keep pleasantly interested; cause to feel cheerful or happy; entertain: *The new toys amused the children.* ⟨ME < OF *amuser* divert < *a-* + *muser* stare⟩ **—a'mus•er,** *n.*

☛ *Syn.* **2. Amuse,** ENTERTAIN = to keep pleasantly interested. **Amuse** emphasizes the idea of passing time by keeping one's attention occupied with something interesting and pleasing: *While waiting, she amused herself by counting the cars that passed.* **Entertain** emphasizes greater effort or more elaborate means to hold attention: *Some people entertain themselves by reading; others have to be entertained by the radio or television.*

a•mused [ə'mjuzd] *adj., v. —adj.* pleasantly entertained.
—v. pt. and pp. of AMUSE. **—a'mus•ed•ly,** *adv.*

a•muse•ment [ə'mjuzmənt] *n.* **1** the condition of being amused. **2** pleasant diversion: *They often window shop for amusement.* **3** something that amuses or entertains: *Her favourite amusement at the Exhibition is the Ferris wheel.*

amusement park an outdoor area with refreshment stands and rides, such as a roller coaster or Ferris wheel.

a•mu•si•a [ei'mjuziə], [ə'mjuʒə], *or* [ə'mjuziə] *n.* inability to identify or produce musical tones. ⟨< L < Gk. *amousos* unmusical < *a* without + *mousa* muse⟩

a•musing [ə'mjuzɪŋ] *adj., v. —adj.* **1** entertaining. **2** funny; causing laughter, smiles, etc.
—v. ppr. of AMUSE. **—a'mus•ing•ly,** *adv.*

a•myg•da•la [ə'mɪgdələ] **1** *Anatomy.* any almond-shaped structure or part, such as the tonsil. ⟨< L, almond⟩

a•myg•da•la•ceous [ə,mɪgdə'leiʃəs] *adj.* of or having to do with a group of bushes or trees bearing fruit with a single stone, such as almond, peach, and cherry trees.

am•yg•dale ['æmɪg,deil] *n.* a small pocket of some mineral, usually quartz, formed in the cavities of a volcanic rock. (See AMYGDALA)

a•myg•da•lin [ə'mɪgdəlɪn] *n.* a white, crystalline glycoside obtained from bitter almonds and used medicinally or as a flavouring. *Formula*: $C_{20}H_{27}NO_{11}$

a•myg•da•loid [ə'mɪgdə,lɔɪd] *n., adj. —n.* igneous rock that contains amygdales.
—adj. **1** of, like, or having to do with this rock. **2** almond-shaped. **—a,myg•da'loi•dal,** *adj.*

am•yl ['æməl] *n.* a group of carbon and hydrogen atoms that acts as a unit in forming compounds. *Formula*: C_5H_{11} ⟨< L < Gk. *amylon,* starch, originally, unground < *a-* not + *mylē* mill⟩ **—a'myl•ic,** *adj.*

am•y•la•ceous [,æmə'leiʃəs] *adj.* of, like, or having to do with starch.

am•yl•ase ['æmə,leis] *n.* an enzyme in saliva, the pancreatic juice, etc., or in parts of plants, that helps to change starch into sugar. ⟨< *amyl*⟩

am•yl•ene ['æmə,lin] *n.* pentene; any liquid hydrocarbon isomer having the formula C_5H_{10}.

amyl nitrite nitroglycerin.

a•my•lo•caine [æ'mɪlə,kein] *n.* a local anesthetic for babies who are teething. ⟨< L *amylum* starch + E (*co*)*caine*⟩

am•y•lol•y•sis [,æmə'lɒləsɪs] *n.* the process by which starch is changed into sugar. ⟨< *amyl* + Gk. *lyein* loose⟩

am•y•lop•sin [,æmə'lɒpsɪn] *n.* an enzyme in the pancreatic juice that changes starch into simpler compounds such as glucose. ⟨< *amyl* + (*try*)*psin*⟩

a•my•o•to•ni•a [ei,maɪou'touniə] *n.* lack of muscle tone, sometimes accompanied by spasms or extreme stiffness.

a•my•o•troph•ic lateral sclerosis [,eimaɪə'trɒfɪk] a progressive disease characterized by the deterioration of nerve cells, resulting in loss of muscle control; Lou Gehrig's disease.

an[1] [ən]; *stressed,* [æn] *indefinite article.* the form of A[1] occurring before a vowel sound.
☛ *Usage.* See note at A[1].

an[2] [ən]; *stressed,* [æn] *conj.* **1** *Dialect or informal.* and. **2** *Archaic.* if. ⟨var. of *and*⟩

An actinon.

an–[1] *prefix.* not; without, as in *anhydrous.* Also, **a-,** before consonants except *h.* ⟨< Gk.⟩

an–[2] the form of **ad-** before *n,* as in *annex.*

-an *suffix.* **1** of or having to do with ——: *Mohammedan = of or having to do with Mohammed.* **2** of or having to do with —— or its people: *Asian = of or having to do with Asia or its people.* **3** a native or inhabitant of ——: *American = native or inhabitant of America.* ⟨< L *-anus*⟩

ana– *prefix.* back; again; thoroughly; up, as in *anachronism, analysis.* ⟨< Gk. *ana-* < *ana,* prep.⟩

-ana *suffix.* sayings, writings, or articles by, belonging to or associated with ——: *Shakespeariana = things written by or associated with Shakespeare. Canadiana = things associated with Canada.* ⟨< L *-ana,* neuter pl. of *-anus,* -an⟩

an•a•bae•na [,ænə'binə] *n.* any of the algae of the genus *Anabaena.* They make drinking water taste fishy. ⟨< Gk.⟩

an•a•bap•tism [,ænə'bæptɪzəm] *n.* **1** a second baptism. **2 Anabaptism,** the doctrines, principles, and practices of the Anabaptists.

An•a•bap•tist [,ænə'bæptɪst] *n.* a member of a 16th century Protestant sect, or of any of its present-day offshoots, opposing infant baptism and requiring adult baptism.

an•a•bi•o•sis [,ænəbaɪ'ousɪs] *n.* **1** a coming to life again from a deathlike condition; resuscitation. **2** a state of suspended animation, as produced in certain organisms by drying, etc. ⟨< NL < Gk. *anabiōsis* < *anabioein* to return to life < *ana-* back, again + *bios* life⟩

an•a•bi•ot•ic [ˌænəbaɪˈɒtɪk] *adj.* of, having to do with, or showing anabiosis.

an•a•bol•ic [ˌænəˈbɒlɪk] *adj.* of or having to do with anabolism.

anabolic steroid any of various synthetic androgens used in medicine and by athletes to stimulate the growth of muscle and bone.

an•ab•o•lism [əˈnæbəˌlɪzəm] *n.* the part of the process of metabolism concerned with the synthesis of complex molecules from simple ones, by which food is changed into living tissue. ⟨< *ana-* + (*meta*)*bolism*; 19c.⟩

an•a•branch [ˈænəˌbræntʃ] *n.* a stream that leaves a river to join it again farther downstream. ⟨< *ana*(*stomotic*) *branch*⟩

a•nach•ro•nism [əˈnækrəˌnɪzəm] *n.* **1** the putting of a person, thing, or event in some time where he, she, or it does not belong: *It would be an anachronism to speak of Queen Elizabeth I riding in an automobile.* **2** something placed or occurring out of its proper time. ⟨< F < Gk. *anachronismos* < *ana-* backward + *chronos* time⟩

a•nach•ro•nis•tic [əˌnækrəˈnɪstɪk] *adj.* having or involving an anachronism. **—aˌnach•roˈnis•ti•cal•ly,** *adv.*

a•nach•ro•nous [əˈnækrənəs] *adj.* placed or occurring out of the proper time. **—aˈnach•ro•nous•ly,** *adv.*

an•a•cli•nal [ˌænəˈklaɪnəl] *adj. Geology.* of a valley, progressing in a reverse direction to that of the surrounding rock strata. ⟨< Gk. *ana-* on + *klinein* lean⟩

an•a•co•lu•thon [ˌænəkəˈluθɒn] *n., pl.* **-tha** [-θə]. a change from one grammatical construction to another in the same sentence. ⟨< LL < Gk. *anakolouthos* < *an-* not + *akolouthos* following⟩ **—ˌan•a•coˈlu•thic,** *adj.*

an•a•con•da [ˌænəˈkɒndə] *n.* **1** a very large snake (*Eunectes murinus*), a tropical American boa, having olive-green skin, often with black rings or spots, and living in trees and in and around water. Although it is not so long as the largest python, averaging about 9 m, it has a much thicker body and is considered the largest snake in the world. **2** any large snake that kills its prey by coiling around it and squeezing until it suffocates. ⟨? < Sinhalese *henakandayā*, a kind of thin, green snake⟩

an•a•cru•sis [ˌænəˈkrusɪs] *n., pl.* **-ses** [-siz]. *Music. n.* an unaccented note or notes before the first downbeat; upbeat. ⟨< NL < Gk. *anakrousis* < *anakrouein* to push back < *ana* up + *krouein* to strike⟩

a•nad•ro•mous [əˈnædrəməs] *adj.* going up rivers from the sea to spawn. Salmon are anadromous. ⟨< LGk. *anadromos* < *ana-* up + *dromos* a running⟩

a•nae•mi•a [əˈnimiə] See ANEMIA.

a•nae•mic [əˈnimɪk] See ANEMIC.

an•aer•obe [ˈænəˌroub], [æˈnɛroub], *or* [æˈneiəˌroub] *n.* **1** an organism that cannot live in the presence of free oxygen. **2** an organism that can live without free oxygen. Compare AEROBE. ⟨< NL *anaerobium* < Gk. *an-* without + *aer* air + *bios* life⟩

an•aer•o•bic [ˌænəˈroubɪk] *or* [æˌneiəˈroubɪk] *adj.* **1** living or growing where there is no free oxygen. Anaerobic bacteria get their oxygen by decomposing compounds containing oxygen. **2** of or having to do with anaerobes.

an•aes•the•sia [ˌænɪsˈθiʒə] *or* [ˌænɪsˈθiziə] *n.* See ANESTHESIA.

an•aes•thet•ic [ˌænɪsˈθɛtɪk] *adj. or n.* See ANESTHETIC.

an•aes•the•tist [əˈnisθətɪst] *or* [əˈnɛsθətɪst] *n.* See ANESTHETIST.

an•aes•the•ti•za•tion [əˌnisθətəˈzeiʃən] *or* [əˌnɛs-], [əˌnisθətaɪˈzeiʃən] *or* [əˌnɛs-] *n.* See ANESTHETIZATION.

an•aes•the•tize [əˈnisθəˌtaɪz] *or* [əˈnɛsθəˌtaɪz] *v.* **-tized, -tiz•ing.** See ANESTHETIZE.

an•a•go•ge [ˈænəˌgoudʒi], [ˈænəˌgɒdʒi], *or* [ˌænəˈgoudʒi] *n.* an abstruse method of interpreting holy writings so as to bring out a hidden spiritual or allegorical meaning, such as a reference to life after death. ⟨< LL *anagogia* < Gk. *anagoge* a lifting up < *ana-* up + *agein* lead⟩

an•a•gram [ˈænəˌgræm] *n.* **1** a word or phrase formed from another by transposing the letters. *Example*: table—bleat. **2 anagrams,** *pl.* a game in which the players make words by changing and adding letters. ⟨< NL *anagramma* < Gk. *anagrammatizein* transpose letters < *ana-* up or back + *gramma* letter⟩ **—ˌan•a•gramˈmat•ic,** *adj.*

a•nal [ˈeinəl] *adj.* **1** of the anus. **2** near the anus. **3** ANAL-RETENTIVE.

a•nal•cite [əˈnælsəit] *or* [ˈænəlˌsəit] *n.* a light-coloured crystalline zeolite consisting of hydrated aluminum silicate. *Formula*: $NaAlSi_2O_6H_2O$ ⟨< Gk. *analkes* weak + E *-ite*⟩

An•a•lects [ˈænəˌlɛkts] *n.pl. Confucianism.* the most revered and influential text containing the sayings and conversations of Confucius. ⟨< L *analecta* < Gk. *analekta* < *analegein* collect < *ana-* up + *legein* gather⟩

an•a•lem•ma [ˌænəˈlɛmə] *n.* a graduated scale in the shape of a figure eight, found on many globes, which shows the variation throughout the year between noon according to clock time and noon according to the position of the sun. The analemma also shows on which two days of the year the sun is directly overhead at midday in the low latitudes. ⟨< L, sundial < Gk. *analemma* a support < *analambanein* to recover⟩

an•a•lep•tic [ˌænəˈlɛptɪk] *adj.* **1** invigorating; stimulating. **2** of a drug or medicine, able to rouse from a drug-induced stupor. ⟨< Gk. *analeptikos* restorative < *analambanein* to recover < *ana* up + *lambanein* to take⟩

an•al•ge•si•a [ˌænəlˈdʒiziə] *or* [ˌænəlˈdʒisiə] *n.* the state of not being able to feel pain even while completely conscious. ⟨< NL < Gk. *analgēsia* < *an-* not + *algeein* feel pain⟩

an•al•ge•sic [ˌænəlˈdʒizɪk] *or* [ˌænəlˈdʒisɪk] *adj., n.* *—adj.* of, having to do with, or causing analgesia: *an analgesic drug.*
—n. a drug or other agent that causes analgesia.

an•a•log [ˈænəˌlɒg] See ANALOGUE.

an•a•log•i•cal [ˌænəˈlɒdʒɪkəl] *adj.* based on analogy; using analogy; having to do with analogy.

analogical change *Linguistics.* the alteration of a form to make it conform to a dominant pattern. *Examples*: the form *climbed* in place of earlier *clomb*, *crowed* in place of earlier *crew*, *horses* in place of earlier *hors.*

a•nal•o•gize [əˈnæləˌdʒaɪz] *v.* **-gized, -giz•ing. 1** make analogies. **2** explain by analogy.

a•nal•o•gous [əˈnæləgəs] *adj.* **1** alike in some way; similar; comparable. **2** *Biology.* corresponding in function, but not in structure and origin. **—aˈnal•o•gous•ly,** *adv.*

an•a•logue [ˈænəˌlɒg] *n., adj.* *—n.* **1** something analogous. **2** a kind of measurement in which a constantly fluctuating value, such as temperature or speed, is understood as a percentage of another value.
—adj. **1** using an analogue computer. **2** having to do with an electronic system in which the signal is linked to a visible change, as in a phonograph where sound corresponds to a groove. **3** of a dial, watch, etc., bearing hands rather than digits to indicate an amount. Compare DIGITAL.

analogue computer *Computer technology.* a computer that represents and processes data internally in a continuous form (such as voltage). Also, **analog computer**. Compare DIGITAL COMPUTER.

a•nal•o•gy [əˈnælədʒi] *n., pl.* **-gies. 1** a likeness in some ways between things that are otherwise unlike; similarity: *the analogy between words like 'man' and 'pan'.* **2** a comparison of such things: *It is easy to draw analogies between the past and the present.* **3** *Biology.* correspondence in function but not in structure and origin. **4** *Logic.* the inference that things alike in some respects will be alike in others: *It is risky to argue by analogy.* **5** *Linguistics.* ANALOGICAL CHANGE. ⟨< L < Gk. *analogia* equality of ratios, proportion⟩
☛ *Usage.* One says **analogy** *between* things, and that one thing has **analogy** *to* or *with* another.

an•al•pha•bet•ic [ænˌælfəˈbɛtɪk] *adj., n.* illiterate.

a•nal–re•ten•tive [ˈeinəl rɪˈtɛntɪv] *adj.* **1** *Psychology.* having to do with the second stage in a child's psychosexual maturation. **2** *Informal.* of a person who is obsessively neat, particular, or stingy.

a•nal•y•sand [əˈnæləˌsænd] *n.* a person who is an object of psychoanalysis.

an•a•lyse or **an•a•lyze** [ˈænəˌlaɪz] *v.* **-lysed** or **-lyzed, -lys•ing** or **-lyz•ing. 1** separate into its parts. **2** examine critically the parts or elements of with regard to form, function, interrelationships, etc.; find out the essential features of: *analyse a sentence.* **3** examine carefully and in detail. **4** *Chemistry.* subject to analysis. **5** *Mathematics.* solve a problem by means of algebra, especially by calculus. **6** examine minutely (a mind or personality); psychoanalyse. **—ˈan•aˌlys•er** or **ˈan•aˌlyz•er,** *n.*

a•nal•y•sis [əˈnæləsɪs] *n., pl.* **-ses** [-ˌsiz]. **1** the separation of a whole into its parts. Compare SYNTHESIS. **2** examination of the parts of a whole to discover their nature, relationship with each other and with the whole, etc. An analysis may be made of a book, a person's character, a medicine, soil, etc. **3** *Chemistry.* **a** the intentional separation of a substance into its ingredients or elements to determine their amount or nature. **b** the determination of the kind or amount of one or more of the constituents of a substance, whether actually obtained in separate form or not. **4** a statement giving the results of an analysis. **5** *Mathematics.* the branch of mathematics that deals with the methods and principles of algebra and calculus, as distinguished from synthetic geometry, group theory, and number theory. **6** psychoanalysis. **7** SYSTEMS ANALYSIS. **in the last** or **final analysis,** when everything has been considered. ⟨< Med.L < Gk. *analysis* a breaking up < *analyein* unloose < *ana-* up + *lyein* loose⟩

an•a•lyst [ˈænəlɪst] *n.* **1** a person who analyses, especially one who is skilled at analysis: *The analyst found traces of poison in the body.* **2** psychoanalyst. **3** SYSTEMS ANALYST.
☛ *Hom.* ANNALIST.

an•a•lyt•ic [ˌænəˈlɪtɪk] *adj.* **1** analytical. **2** *Linguistics.* of a language, using word order and function words instead of inflections or affixes to express grammatical relationships: *English is an analytic language.* Compare AGGLUTINATIVE, SYNTHETIC.

an•a•lyt•i•cal [ˌænəˈlɪtɪkəl] *adj.* **1** of analysis; using analysis. **2** inclined to or skilled in analysis: *She has an analytical mind.* **—ˌan•aˈlyt•i•cal•ly,** *adv.*

analytical psychology a school of psychology founded by Carl Jung. Universal archetypes and the collective unconscious are central concepts of analytical psychology.

analytic geometry *Mathematics.* the use of algebra and co-ordinates (or calculus) to solve problems in geometry.

an•a•lyt•ics [ˌænəˈlɪtɪks] *n.* **1** mathematical or algebraic analysis. **2** the branch of logic that deals with analysis.

an•a•lyze [ˈænəˌlaɪz] See ANALYSE.

An•a•ni•as [ˌænəˈnaɪəs] *n. Informal.* any liar. ⟨in the Bible, a member of the church at Jerusalem. He and his wife were struck dead for lying.⟩

an•a•paest or **an•a•pest** [ˈænəˌpɛst] *or* [ˈænəˌpist] *n. Prosody.* a measure or foot consisting of two weakly stressed syllables followed by a strongly stressed syllable, or two short syllables followed by one long syllable. *Example*:
From the cén | tre all róund | to the séa
I am lórd | of the fówl | and the brúte.
⟨< L *anapaestus* < Gk. *anapaistos* < *ana-* back + *paiein* strike⟩

an•a•paes•tic or **an•a•pes•tic** [ˌænəˈpɛstɪk] *or* [ˌænəˈpistɪk] *adj.* having to do with or consisting of anapests.

an•a•phase [ˈænəˌfeiz] *n.* the third stage of cell division in which the chromosomes separate and move toward either end of the cell.

an•a•pho•ra [əˈnæfərə] *n. Linguistics.* the use of a word, such as a pronoun, which replaces a noun, verb, or adverb. ⟨< Gk. *anaphorā* carrying back, repetition⟩

an•ap•tyx•is [ˌænəpˈtɪksɪs] *n. Linguistics.* vowel insertion. *Example*: *immune* + *deficiency* > *immunodeficiency*. ⟨< Gk., an opening < *anaptyssein* open < *ana-* up + *ptyssein* fold⟩

an•arch [ˈænɑrk] *n.* an anarchic leader.

an•ar•chic [æˈnɑrkɪk] *adj.* lawless; favouring anarchy.

an•ar•chi•cal [æˈnɑrkəkəl] *adj.* anarchic.

an•ar•chism [ˈænərˌkɪzəm] *n.* **1** the political theory that all systems of government and law are unnecessary and in fact harmful because they prevent individuals from reaching their greatest development. Anarchism advocates a society based on voluntary co-operation among individuals and groups. **2** the support or practice of anarchistic beliefs. **3** lawlessness or terrorism.

an•ar•chist [ˈænərkɪst] *n.* **1** a person who favours and supports anarchism as a political idea. **2** a person who uses violent means to overthrow organized government. **3** a person who promotes disorder or rebels against established laws or customs.

an•ar•chis•tic [ˌænərˈkɪstɪk] *adj.* of or having to do with anarchism or anarchists.

an•ar•chy [ˈænərki] *n.* **1** the absence of a system of government and law. **2** a state of political disorder and violence due to the absence of governmental authority. **3** disorder or confusion. ⟨< Gk. *anarkhia* < *an-* without + *arkhos* ruler⟩

an•ar•thria [æˈnɑrθriə] *n.* an inability to speak intelligibly. ⟨< NL < Gk. *anarthros* inarticulate < *an-* not + *arthron* articulation⟩

an•a•stig•mat•ic [æˌnæstɪgˈmætɪk] *adj.* of or having to do with a lens or visual device that corrects for astigmatism.

a•nas•to•mot•ic branch [əˌnæstəˈmɒtɪk] anabranch. ⟨< Gk. *anastomosis* opening < *ana-* again + *stomoein* furnish with a mouth < *stoma* mouth⟩

an•a•tase [ˈænəˌteis] *n.* a variety of native titanium oxide; octahedrite. ⟨< F *anatase* < Gk. *anatasis* extension < *ana-* up + *teinein* stretch, so named because of elongated crystals⟩

a•nath•e•ma [əˈnæθəmə] *n., pl.* **-mas. 1** a solemn curse by church authorities excommunicating a person. **2** the act of denouncing and condemning a person or thing as evil; curse. **3** a person or thing accursed. **4** a person or thing that is detested and condemned. ⟨< L < Gk. *anathema* thing devoted, esp. to evil < *ana-* up + *tithenai* set⟩

a•nath•e•ma•tize [əˈnæθəməˌtaɪz] *v.* **-tized, -tiz•ing.** pronounce an anathema against; denounce; curse. **—aˌnath•e•ma•tiˈza•tion,** *n.* **—aˈnath•e•maˌtiz•er,** *n.*

An•a•to•li•an [ˌænəˈtoulian] *adj., n. —adj.* of or having to do with Anatolia (that part of Turkey which is in Asia) or its people. *—n.* a native or inhabitant of Anatolia.

an•a•tom•i•cal [ˌænəˈtɒmɪkəl] *adj.* **1** of anatomy; having to do with anatomy. **2** structural. Also, **anatomic. —ˌan•aˈtom•i•cal•ly,** *adv.*

a•nat•o•mist [əˈnætəmɪst] *n.* **1** an expert in anatomy. **2** a person who dissects or analyses.

a•nat•o•mize [əˈnætəˌmaɪz] *v.* **-mized, -miz•ing. 1** divide (a plant or a body) into parts to study the structure; dissect. **2** examine the parts of; analyse. **—aˌnat•o•miˈza•tion,** *n.*

a•nat•o•my [əˈnætəmi] *n., pl.* **-mies. 1** the structure of an animal or plant: *The anatomy of an earthworm is much simpler than that of a human.* **2** the science of the structure of animals and plants. **3** a textbook or handbook dealing with this subject. **4** the dissecting of animals or plants to study their structure. **5** an examination of the parts or elements of a thing; analysis. ⟨< LL *anatomia* < Gk. *anatomē* dissection < *ana-* up + *temnein* cut⟩

a•na•tum peregrine falcon [əˈneitəm] a species of falcon (*Falco peregrinus anatum*) with a prominent black stripe. It is an endangered species.

-ance *noun-forming suffix.* **1** the act or fact of ——ing: *avoidance = the act or fact of avoiding.* **2** the quality or state of being ——ed: *annoyance = the quality or state of being annoyed.* **3** the quality or state of being ——ant: *importance = the quality or state of being important.* **4** something that ——s: *conveyance = something that conveys.* **5** what is ——ed: *contrivance = what is contrived.* ⟨< F < L *-antia, -entia*⟩

an•ces•tor [ˈænsɛstər] *n.* **1** a person from whom one is descended, such as one's father, mother, grandfather, or grandmother. **2** an original model or type from which others are developed: *The horseless carriage is the ancestor of the modern automobile.* **3** *Biology.* an earlier species or type from which a later or existing species is descended: *The horse and the donkey have a common ancestor.* ⟨ME < OF *ancestre* < L *antecessor* < *antecedere* < *ante* before + *cedere* go⟩

an•ces•tral [ænˈsɛstrəl] *adj.* **1** of or having to do with ancestors: *The ancestral home of the Acadians was France.* **2** inherited from ancestors: *Black hair is an ancestral trait in that family.* **—anˈces•tral•ly,** *adv.*

an•ces•try [ˈænsɛstri] *n., pl.* **-tries. 1** one's parents, grandparents, and other ancestors: *Many of the early settlers in North America had British ancestry.* **2** a line of descent from ancestors; lineage. **3** honourable descent.

Anchors. The traditional ship's anchor on the left is still often used for boats, but ships now commonly use anchors of the type shown in the centre. The grapnel, on the right, is used for dories, etc.

an•chor [ˈæŋkər] *n., v. —n.* **1** a heavy piece of shaped iron that is attached to a ship or boat by a cable and dropped to the

bottom to keep the vessel from drifting. Anchors usually have hooks of some kind that dig into the bottom. **2** something used to hold something else in place. **3** something that makes a person feel safe and secure. **4** *Sports.* **a** the last person to swim or run on a relay team. **b** the last player of a team to bowl in each frame. **c** the end player of a tug-of-war team. **5** *Radio and television.* the co-ordinator of a broadcast consisting of direct reports from several different cities or locations.
at anchor, held by an anchor.
cast anchor, a drop the anchor. **b** settle down in a place.
ride at anchor, be kept at some place by being anchored.
weigh anchor, a take up the anchor. **b** leave a place where one has settled.
—v. **1** hold in place with an anchor: *to anchor a ship.* **2** drop anchor; stop or stay in place by using an anchor. **3** hold in place; fix firmly; make secure: *to anchor a tent to the ground. A child's self-esteem is anchored in the love of a family.* **4** be an anchor for (a team, broadcast, etc.) ⟨OE *ancor* < L *ancora, anchora* < Gk. *agkyra*⟩

an•chor•age ['æŋkərɪdʒ] *n.* **1** a place to anchor. **2** money paid for the right to anchor. **3** an anchoring or being anchored. **4** something to hold on to or depend on.

an•cho•ret ['æŋkərɪt] *or* ['æŋkə,rɛt] *n.* anchorite.

anchor ice GROUND ICE (def. 1).

an•cho•rite ['æŋkə,rəit] *n.* a person who lives alone in a solitary place for religious meditation; hermit. ⟨< Med.L *anachorita* < LL < Gk. *anachōrētēs* < *anakhōrein* < *ana-* back + *chōrein* withdraw⟩ **—,an•cho'rit•ic** [-'rɪtɪk], *adj.*
☛ *Hom.* ANKERITE.

an•cho•vy ['æntʃouvi], ['æntʃəvi], *or* [æn'tʃouvi] *n., pl.* **-vies.** any of a family (*Engraulidae*) of very small fishes distantly related to the herring, used for food and also for bait. Most species are found in warm seas. ⟨< Sp., Pg. *anchova* < VL *apiuva*, probably < Gk. *aphýē*⟩

anchovy pear **1** an edible fruit with a flavour like that of a mango. **2** the tree (*Grias cauliflora*) that it grows on.

an•cienne no•blesse [ɑ̃sjɛnnɔ'blɛs] *French.* **1** in France, the nobles before the Revolution in 1789. **2** the former nobility of any society.

an•cien ré•gime [ɑ̃sjɛ̃ʀe'ʒim] *French.* **1** the social and political structure of France before the Revolution of 1789. **2** any former system; the old order of things.

an•cient ['einʃənt] *adj.* **1** of or belonging to times long past, especially the period before the fall of the Roman Empire in A.D. 476: *ancient history, ancient records. We saw the ruins of an ancient temple built six thousand years ago.* **2** of great age or early origin; very old: *the ancient hills, ancient freedoms.* **3** old-fashioned or antique: *He still wears that ancient coat.* **4** (*noml.*) a very old person. **5** (*noml.*) **the ancients, a** people who lived in ancient times, especially the Greeks, Romans, and Hebrews. **b** the writers and artists of classical Greece and Rome. ⟨ME < OF *ancien* < LL *antianus* former < L *ante* before⟩ **—'an•cient•ness,** *n.*
☛ *Syn. adj.* **1, 2.** See note at OLD.

ancient history **1** history from the earliest times to the fall of the western part of the Roman Empire in A.D. 476. **2** *Informal.* a well-known fact or event of the relatively recent past.

an•cient•ly ['einʃəntli] *adv.* in ancient times.

an•cil•lar•y [æn'sɪləri] *or* ['ænsə,lɛri] *adj., n. —adj.* **1** subordinate; dependent: *She owns a factory and several ancillary plants.* **2** supplementary; auxiliary: *ancillary information.*
—n. something subordinate or auxiliary. ⟨< L *ancillāris* < *ancilla* handmaid⟩

an•cip•i•tal [æn'sɪpɪtəl] *adj. Botany.* of stems, flat with two edges, as in some grasses. ⟨< L *anceps* (gen. *ancipitis*) having two heads < *an* for *ambi* + *caput* head⟩

an•con ['æŋkɒn] *n., pl.* **an•co•nes** [æŋ'kouniz] *Architecture.* a projection like a bracket, used to support a cornice. ⟨< L < Gk. *ankōn* bend⟩

-ancy *suffix.* a variant of *-ance,* as in *infancy.*

and [ənd] *or* [ən]; *stressed,* [ænd] *conj.* **1** as well as: *wet and cold. She sings and dances.* **2** added to; with: *4 and 2 make 6. He likes ham and eggs.* **3** as a result: *The sun came out and the grass dried.* **4** *Informal.* to: *try and do better.* **5** then; next: *She came inside and took off her boots.* **6** but; while on the other hand: *She's a traveller and he's a stay-at-home.* ⟨OE⟩
☛ *Usage.* **4.** See note at TRY.
☛ *Usage.* When joining identical words or phrases, *and* can indicate: **a** great quantity or duration: *pages and pages of fine print, waiting for hours and hours;* **b** *contrast between different types: There are movies and movies.*

and. andante.

An•da•lu•sian [,ændə'luʒən] *adj., n —adj.* of or having to do with Andalusia, a province of Spain, its people or their dialect.
—n. **1** a native or inhabitant of Andalusia. **2** the dialect of Spanish spoken in Andalusia.

an•dan•te [ɑn'dɑntei] *or* [æn'dænti] *adv., adj., n. Music.* *—adv. or adj.* moderately slow; faster than adagio, but slower than allegretto: *an andante movement.*
—n. a moderately slow movement or composition. *Abbrev.*: and. ⟨< Ital. *andante* < *andare* walk⟩

an•dan•ti•no [,ɑndɑn'tinou] *or* [,ændæn'tinou] *adv., adj., n., pl.* **-nos.** *Music. —adv. or adj.* slightly faster than andante.
—n. a composition or part of one that is played or sung andantino. ⟨< Ital. *andantino*, dim. of *andante*⟩

An•de•an [æn'diən] *or* ['ændiən] *adj.* of or having to do with the Andes, a mountain system in western South America.

An•des ['ændiz] *n.* a range of mountains running down the western side of South America.

an•des•ite ['ændə,zəit] *n.* a fine-grained igneous rock composed chiefly of plagioclase feldspar. ⟨< *Andes* + *-ite*⟩

and•i•ron ['ændaɪərn] *n.* one of a pair of metal supports for wood burned in a fireplace; a firedog. See FIREPLACE for picture. ⟨ME *aundyrne* < OF *andier*; *-iron* by association with *iron*⟩

and/or both or either.
☛ *Usage.* **And/or** is used primarily in business and legal writing. It is useful when three choices exist (both items mentioned or either one of the two), but it should not be overused. Writers can usually decide whether they mean *and* or *or.*

An•dor•ra [æn'dɔrə] a very small country between France and Spain.

an•dro•e•ci•um [,ændrou'iʃiəm] *n. Botany.* the stamen and all its constituent parts.

an•dro•gen ['ændrədʒən] *n.* a male sex hormone, such as testosterone, produced by the testes and the adrenal cortex or made synthetically. Androgens promote the development of the male sex organs and secondary masculine characteristics. ⟨< Gk. *aner, andros* man + E *-gen*⟩

an•drog•e•nous [æn'drɒdʒənəs] *adj.* producing only male offspring.
☛ *Hom.* ANDROGYNOUS.

an•dro•gyne ['ændrə,dʒaɪn] *or* ['ændrə,dʒɪn] any androgynous plant.

an•drog•y•nous [æn'drɒdʒənəs] *adj.* **1** *Botany.* having flowers with stamens and flowers with pistils in the same cluster. **2** having both male and female characteristics. ⟨< L < Gk. *androgynos* < *anēr, andros* man + *gynē* woman⟩
☛ *Hom.* ANDROGENOUS.

an•drog•y•ny [æn'drɒdʒəni] *n.* the property of being androgynous.

an•droid ['ændrɔɪd] *n.* a robot, or automaton, having the form of a human being. ⟨< Gk. *aner, andros* man + E *-oid*⟩

An•drom•e•da [æn'drɒmədə] *n.* **1** *Greek mythology.* an Ethiopian princess, who, to save her country, was to be sacrificed to a sea monster. Perseus killed the monster and married Andromeda. **2** *Astronomy.* a northern constellation. **3 andromeda,** an evergreen plant of the heath family (genera *Andromeda* and *Pieris*).

an•dro•pho•bia [,ændrə'foubiə] *n.* an abnormal fear of men. ⟨< Gk. *aner, andros* man + E *-phobia*⟩

-an•drous *combining form.* having stamens (or other male organs) as specified: *diandrous.* ⟨< Gk. *aner, andros* man⟩

-ane *combining form. Chemistry.* denoting an alkane hydrocarbon: *methane.*

an•ec•dot•age ['ænɪk,doutədʒ] *n.* **1** anecdotes collectively. **2** *Informal.* old age, with reference to the tendency of some elderly people to tell anecdotes. ⟨(def. 2) < *anecdote* + *dotage*⟩

an•ec•do•tal [,ænɪk'doutəl] *adj.* like an anecdote; of anecdotes; containing anecdotes.

an•ec•dote ['ænɪk,dout] *n.* a short account of some interesting or amusing incident or event: *Many anecdotes are told about Sir John A. Macdonald.* ⟨< Med.L *anecdota* < Gk. *anékdota* (things) unpublished < *an-* not + *ek-* out + *didónai* give⟩
☛ *Syn.* See note at STORY[1].

an•e•cho•ic [,ænɛ'kouɪk] *adj.* of a room, etc. producing or allowing no echo because constructed so as to fully absorb sound waves.

a•ne•mi•a [ə'nimiə] *n.* an insufficiency of hemoglobin or of red cells in the blood. Some forms of anemia are heritable, such as SICKLE CELL ANEMIA. Also, **anaemia.** ⟨< NL < Gk. *anaimia* lack of blood < *an-* not + *haima* blood⟩

a•ne•mic [ə'nimɪk] *adj.* of anemia; having anemia. Also, **anaemic.**

a•nem•o•graph [ə'nɛmə,græf] *n.* a machine for recording wind speed, as measured by an anemometer. ⟨< Gk. *anemos* wind + E *-graph*⟩

an•e•mom•e•ter [,ænə'mɒmətər] *n.* an instrument for measuring the speed or force of the wind. ⟨< Gk. *anemos* wind + E *-meter*⟩

a•nem•o•ne [ə'nɛməni] *n.* **1** any of a large genus (*Anemone*) of small flowers of the buttercup family having lobed or divided leaves and large, showy flowers. The prairie crocus is an anemone. **2** SEA ANEMONE. ⟨< L < Gk. *anemōnē* wind flower < *anemos* wind⟩

an•e•moph•i•lous [ænə'mɒfələs] *adj.* fertilized by pollen carried by the wind. ⟨< Gk. *anemos* wind + *-philos* loving⟩ **—,an•e'moph•i•ly,** *n.*

an•en•ceph•a•ly [,ænɛn'sɛfəli] *n.* a birth defect in which all or part of the brain is missing. ⟨< Gk. *an-* without + *enkephalos* brain⟩

a•nent [ə'nɛnt] *prep. Archaic.* concerning; about. ⟨OE *on emn, on efn* on even (ground with)⟩

an•er•gy ['ænərdʒi] *n.* **1** lack of immunity to antigens. **2** loss of energy. ⟨< NL *anergia* < Gk. *a* without + *ergon* work⟩ **—an'er•gic,** *adj.*

an•er•oid ['ænə,rɔɪd] *adj., n.* *—adj.* using no liquid.
—n. ANEROID BAROMETER. ⟨< F *anéroïde* < Gk. *a-* without + LGk. *nēros* wet⟩

aneroid barometer a barometer that records the changing pressure of air on the flexible top of an airtight metal box from which some of the air has been pumped out. The barometers commonly used in houses and offices are aneroid barometers.

an•es•the•sia [,ænəs'θiʒə] *or* [,ænəs'θiziə] *n.* an entire or partial loss of the feeling of pain, touch, cold, etc., produced by drugs, hypnotism, etc. or as the result of paralysis or disease. **General anesthesia** is the loss of feeling in the whole body, causing complete or partial unconsciousness. **Local anesthesia** is the loss of feeling in only part of the body. Also, **anaesthesia.** ⟨< NL < Gk. *anaisthēsia* insensibility < *an-* without + *aisthēsis* sensation⟩

an•es•the•si•ol•o•gist [,ænəs,θizi'ɒlədʒɪst] *n.* a medical doctor who specializes in anesthesiology. Compare ANESTHETIST.

an•es•the•si•ol•o•gy [,ænəs,θizi'ɒlədʒi] *n.* a branch of medicine dealing with anesthesia and the application of anesthetics.

an•es•thet•ic [,ænəs'θɛtɪk] *n., adj.* *—n.* a substance that produces anesthesia. Anesthetics used for surgical operations include halothane, sodium pentothal, and nitrous oxide (to produce general anesthesia) and procaine and other drugs (for local anesthesia).
—adj. of, characterized by, or causing anesthesia. Also, **anaesthetic. —,an•es'thet•i•cal•ly,** *adv.*

an•es•the•tist [ə'nisθətɪst] *or* [ə'nɛsθətɪst] *n.* a medical practitioner, not necessarily a doctor, who specializes in the application of anesthetics. Compare ANESTHESIOLOGIST. Also, **anaesthetist.**

an•es•the•ti•za•tion [ə,nisθətə'zeiʃən] *or* [ə,nɛs-], [ə,nisθətai'zeiʃən] *or* [ə,nɛs-] *n.* **1** the act or process of anesthetizing. **2** the state of being anesthetized. Also, **anaesthetization.**

an•es•the•tize [ə'nisθə,taiz] *or* [ə'nɛsθə,taiz] *v.* **-tized, -tiz•ing. 1** make unable to feel pain, touch, cold, etc.; make insensible. **2** reduce the emotional or critical responses of. Also, **anaesthetize. —an'es•the,tiz•er,** *n.*

an•eu•ploid ['ænjə,plɔɪd] *adj., n. Genetics.* *—adj.* of the number of an individual's chromosomes, not being an exact multiple of the haploid number for the species, because one or more chromosomes are missing or are present in excess. Compare EUPLOID.
—n. an individual having an aneuploid chromosome number. ⟨*an-*[1] + *eu-* + *(ha)ploid*⟩ **—'an•eu,ploid•y,** *n.*

an•eu•rin ['ænjərɪn] *n.* thiamine. ⟨< *a(nti)* + *(poly)neur(itis)* + *vitamin*⟩

an•eu•rysm or **an•eu•rism** ['ænjə,rɪzəm] *n.* a permanent swelling of an artery, caused by pressure of the blood on a part weakened by disease or injury. ⟨< Gk. *aneurysma* dilation < *ana-* up + *eurýs* wide⟩

a•new [ə'nju] *or* [ə'nu] *adv.* **1** once more; again: *At each meeting the question was raised anew.* **2** in a new form or way: *She crossed out the whole paragraph and began anew.* ⟨OE *of newe,* modelled on OF *de neuf,* L *de novo*⟩

an•ga•koq or **an•ga•kok** ['æŋgə,kɒk] *n. Cdn.* an Inuit shaman, the central religious figure in the traditional Inuit culture. ⟨< Inuktitut⟩

an•gel ['eindʒəl] *n.* **1** in certain religions, an immortal, spiritual being who is an attendant and messenger of God. **2** *Art.* a representation of such a being, shown in human form but with wings, white robes, and, often, a halo. **3** a person like an angel in goodness, innocence, or loveliness. **4** any supernatural (but not divine) spirit, either good or bad: *the angel of death.* **5** a person who provides money for a business venture such as the production of a play. **6** SNOW ANGEL. **7** an old English gold coin in use between 1465 and 1634. **8** any signal picked up by radar that is due to something besides the presence of an aircraft. ⟨OE *engel,* OF *angele* < L < Gk. *angelos* messenger⟩

angel cake ANGEL FOOD CAKE.

an•gel•fish ['eindʒəl,fɪʃ] *n., pl.* **-fish** or **-fish•es. 1** a small, tropical freshwater fish (*Pterophyllum scalare*) native to South America, usually silver and black in colour and having a deep, narrow body and long fins. Angelfish are popular for home aquariums. **2** any of various brightly coloured tropical marine fishes (family Chaetodontidae) having a deep, narrow body. **3** a shark (*Squatina squatina*) found in warm seas, having large winglike pectoral fins and reaching a length of about 120 cm.

An angelfish

angel food cake a light, springy white SPONGE CAKE containing whites of eggs but no shortening or egg yolks.

angel hair long, silky, white strings of spun glass, used to trim a Christmas tree.

angel–hair pasta very thin spaghetti.

an•gel•ic [æn'dʒɛlɪk] *adj.* **1** of angels; heavenly. **2** like an angel; pure; innocent; good and lovely. **—an'gel•i•cal•ly,** *adv.*

an•gel•i•ca [æn'dʒɛlɪkə] *n.* any of a genus (*Angelica*) of tall perennial herbs of the carrot family found in the northern hemisphere and New Zealand, having compound leaves and clusters of white or greenish flowers. Some species of angelica yield an oil used as a flavouring, in making perfume, etc. ⟨< Med.L; named from its use as an antidote⟩

angelica tree 1 a small, flowering, thorny tree (*Aralia spinosa*) of the ginseng family growing in the eastern U.S. **2** any of several trees of the same genus, having large leaves and bearing very small black fruits.

an•gel•i•cal [æn'dʒɛləkəl] *adj.* angelic.

An•ge•lus ['ændʒələs] *n. Roman Catholic Church.* **1** a prayer said in memory of Christ's assuming human form. **2** the bell, **Angelus bell,** rung at morning, noon, and night as a signal for the saying of this prayer. ⟨from the first word of the prayer in Latin⟩

an•ger ['æŋgər] *n., v.* *—n.* the feeling of wanting to retaliate that one has toward some person, animal, or thing that hurts, opposes, offends, or annoys; wrath; strong displeasure.
—v. **1** make angry: *The girl's disobedience angered her mother.* **2** become angry: *He angers easily.* ⟨ME < ON *angr* trouble⟩

☛ *Syn. n.* **Anger,** INDIGNATION, WRATH = the feeling of strong displeasure against anyone or anything that has hurt or wronged us or others. **Anger** is the general word for the emotion: *He never speaks in anger.* **Indignation** means anger mixed with contempt, caused by something mean, base, or unjust: *The atrocity caused widespread indignation.* **Wrath,** a formal word, means very great anger or indignation: *His wrath was terrible to behold.*

An•ge•vin ['ændʒəvɪn] *adj., n.* *—adj.* **1** of or from Anjou. The Plantagenet family of the kings of England was Angevin. **2** of or belonging to the Plantagenet family.
—n. **1** a member of the Plantagenet family. **2** a native or inhabitant of Anjou.

an•gi•na [æn'dʒaɪnə]; *in medicine, often* ['ændʒənə] *n.* **1** any disease of the mouth or throat, such as quinsy, croup, mumps, or diphtheria, marked by painful attacks of suffocation. **2** ANGINA PECTORIS. ⟨< L *angina* quinsy < *angere* choke⟩ **—an'gi•nal,** *adj.*

angina pec•to•ris ['pɛktərɪs] *or* [pɛk'tɔrɪs] a serious disease of the heart characterized by sharp chest pains and a feeling of suffocation, caused by a sudden decrease in the flow of blood to the heart muscles. ⟨< NL *angina pectoris* angina of the chest⟩

an•gi•o•gram ['ændʒiə,græm] *n.* an X-ray picture of blood vessels showing any abnormality in the flow of blood. ⟨< Gk. *angeion* vessel + E *-gram*⟩

an•gi•og•ra•phy [,ændʒi'ɒgrəfi] *n.* the process of making angiograms. A substance impenetrable by X rays is first injected into the bloodstream. **—,an•gi•o'graph•ic,** *adj.*

an•gi•o•ma [,ændʒi'oumə] *n.* a tumour consisting of either blood vessels or lymph vessels massed together. ⟨< Gk. *angeion* vessel + *-oma* tumour⟩

an•gi•o•plas•ty ['ændʒiə,plæsti] *n.* a procedure used to clear or repair a vein. It may involve surgery, laser, or catheters. ⟨< Gk. *angeion* vessel + *plastia* < *plastos* formed < *plassein* to form⟩

an•gi•o•sperm ['ændʒiou,spɜrm] *n.* any plant belonging to the division Magnoliophyta (also called Angiospermae); any plant producing flowers and having its seeds enclosed in an ovary which becomes the fruit after fertilization. ⟨< NL *angiospermus* < Gk. *angeion* vessel + *sperma* seed⟩ **—,an•gi•o'sperm•ous,** *adj.*

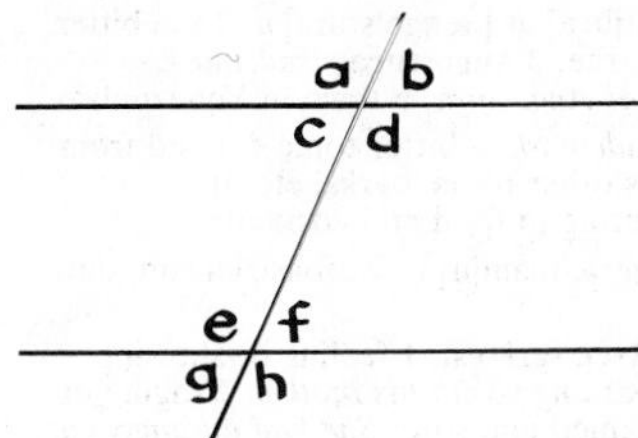

Pairs of interior angles c and e, d and f
Pairs of corresponding angles a and e, b and f, c and g, d and h
Pairs of alternate angles c and f, d and e

an•gle¹ ['æŋgəl] *n., v.* **-gled, -gling.** *—n.* **1** the space between two lines extending in different directions from the same point or two surfaces extending from the same line. **2** the figure formed by two such lines or surfaces. **3** the difference in direction between two such lines or surfaces: *The roads lie at an angle of about 45°.* **4** a corner. **5** *Informal.* point of view. **6** *Informal.* **a** a means or method of obtaining an advantage, especially an unfair one: *He always has an angle for getting the better of you.* **b** ulterior motive: *What's your angle?* **7** one aspect of something; phase.
—v. **1** move at an angle. **2** present (something) with a particular point of view or a prejudice; slant. ⟨ME < OF < L *angulus*⟩

an•gle² ['æŋgəl] *v.* **-gled, -gling. 1** fish with a hook and line. **2** try to get something by using tricks or schemes (*used with* **for**): *to angle for an invitation.* ⟨OE *angul* fish-hook⟩

An•gle ['æŋgəl] *n.* a member of a Germanic tribe that migrated from what is now Denmark to England in the 5th century A.D.

an•gled ['æŋgəld] *adj., v. —adj.* **1** placed on an angle. **2** having an angle or angles.
—v. pt. and pp. of ANGLE.

angle iron a strip of iron or steel in the shape of an angle, used for joining two other pieces at an angle.

angle of attack the acute angle between the chord of an airplane wing or other airfoil and the direction of flight.

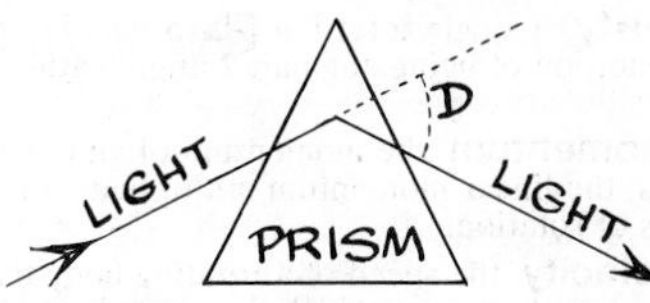

D is the angle of deviation.

angle of deviation the angle made between a ray of light as it enters a prism or other optical medium and the ray that emerges.

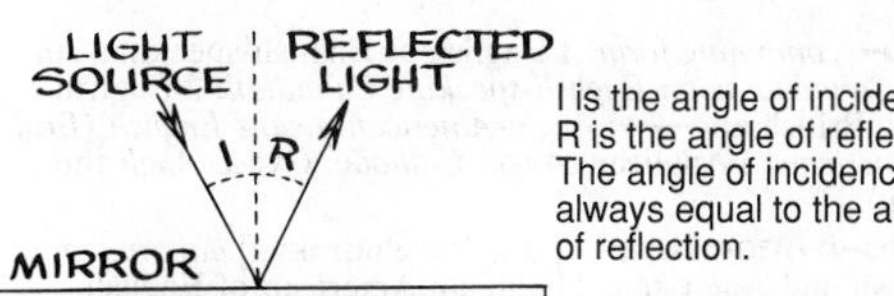

I is the angle of incidence.
R is the angle of reflection.
The angle of incidence is always equal to the angle of reflection.

angle of incidence the angle made by a ray of light falling upon a surface with a line perpendicular to that surface.

angle of reflection the angle that a ray of light makes on reflection from a surface with a line perpendicular to that surface.

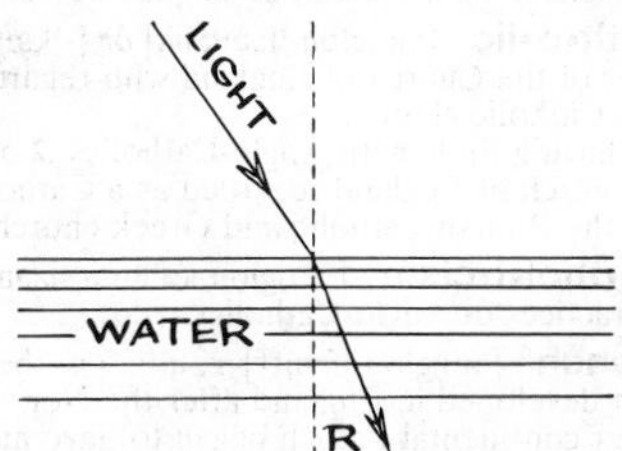

R is the angle of refraction.

angle of refraction the angle made between a ray of light refracted at a surface separating two media and a line perpendicular to the surface.

angle of repose the maximum angle at which sand, rocks, etc. will stay on a slope without sliding down.

angle of view the angle measuring the field of vision that a lens provides to the viewer.

an•gler ['æŋglər] *n.* **1** a person who fishes with a hook and line. **2** a person who tries to get something by using tricks and schemes. **3** any of an order (Pediculati, also called Lophiiformes) of bottom-living fishes that lure their prey within reach by means of a modified spine that projects from the head over the mouth, attracting other fish; especially, one species (*Lophius piscatorius*) found along the Atlantic coasts of North America and Europe. Also, **angler fish.**

an•gle•site ['æŋgəl,sɔit] *n.* a lead sulphate in colourless or grey crystalline form, found in lead ore deposits. *Formula*: $PbSO_4$ ⟨< *Anglesey*, a county in Wales, where it was discovered + *-ite*⟩

an•gle•worm ['æŋgəl,wɜrm] *n.* earthworm.

An•gli•an ['æŋgliən] *adj., n. —adj.* of or having to do with the Angles, their dialect, or customs.
—n. **1** an Angle. **2** the dialect of the Angles.

An•gli•can ['æŋgləkən] *adj., n. —adj.* of or having to do with the Anglican Church of Canada, or the Church of England or other associated churches: *The first Anglican church in Canada was built in Halifax in 1750.*
—n. a member of one of these churches.

Anglican Church of Canada a Christian church associated with the Church of England, until 1955 known as the Church of England in Canada.

An•gli•can•ism ['æŋgləkə,nɪzəm] *n.* the principles and beliefs of the Church of England or of other churches associated with it.

An•gli•cism ['æŋglə,sɪzəm] *n.* **1** a word, phrase, or meaning used in England, but not in widespread use in other English-speaking countries. **2** a custom or trait peculiar to the English.

An•gli•cize or **an•gli•cize** ['æŋglə,saiz] *v.* **-cized, -ciz•ing.** make or become English in form, pronunciation, habits, customs, or character. *Cajole, lace,* and *cousin* are French words that have been Anglicized. **—,An•gli•ci'za•tion** or **,an•gli•ci'za•tion,** *n.*

an•gling ['æŋglɪŋ] *n., v. —n.* fishing with a hook and line.
—v. ppr. of ANGLE.

An•glo ['æŋglou] *n., pl.* **Anglos. 1** *Cdn.* an English-speaking person, especially a native speaker; Anglophone. **2** a person of English or, loosely, British descent.

Anglo– *combining form.* **1** English or English-speaking: *An Anglo-Canadian is an English-speaking Canadian.* **2** English or, loosely, British and——: *Anglo-American means English (British) and American.* **3** Anglican: *Anglo-Catholic.* ⟨< LL *Angli* the English⟩

An•glo–A•mer•i•can ['æŋglou ə'mɛrəkən] *adj., n. —adj.* **1** English and American. **2** being an American of English descent.
—n. an American of English descent.

An•glo–Ca•na•di•an ['æŋglou kə'neidiən] *adj., n. —adj.* **1** English and Canadian. **2** of or having to do with English-speaking Canadians. **3** being a Canadian of English descent.
—n. **1** an English-speaking Canadian; a Canadian whose native language is English. **2** a Canadian of English descent.

An•glo–Cath•o•lic ['æŋglou 'kæθəlɪk] *or* [-'kæθlɪk] *n., adj.*
—n. a member of the Church of England who regards it as a branch of the Catholic church.
—adj. **1** of or having to do with Anglo-Catholics. **2** of or having to do with the Church of England regarded as a Catholic church, as distinct from the Roman Catholic and Greek churches.

An•glo–Ca•thol•i•cism ['æŋglou kə'θɒlə,sɪzəm] *n.* the beliefs and practices of Anglo-Catholics.

An•glo–French ['æŋglou 'frɛntʃ] *n., adj. —n.* the French language as it developed in England after the Norman Conquest, especially after continental French began to have more influence in England than the dialect of the Normans.
—adj. **1** of or referring to this language. **2** British and French: *an Anglo-French agreement.*

An•glo–In•di•an ['æŋglou 'ɪndiən] *adj., n. —adj.* **1** British and Indian. **2** of or having to do with Anglo-Indians.
—n. **1** a person of British birth living in India. **2** the dialect of English spoken by Anglo-Indians. **3** officially in India, an Indian citizen of mixed European, especially British, and Indian descent; Eurasian.

An•glo–I•rish ['æŋglou 'aɪrɪʃ] *n., adj. —n.* **1 the Anglo-Irish,** *pl.* the inhabitants of Ireland who are of English birth or descent. **2** the kind of English spoken in Ireland.
—adj. **1** of or having to do with the inhabitants of Ireland who are of English birth or descent. **2** of, having to do with, or involving Ireland and England. **3** of or having to do with the English spoken in Ireland.

An•glo–Nor•man ['æŋglou 'nɔrmən] *n., adj. —n.* **1** any of the Normans who settled in England following the Norman Conquest in 1066. **2** a descendant of an English Norman. **3** the French dialect of the Normans as used in England after 1066.
—adj. of or referring to the Anglo-Normans or their dialect.

An•glo•phile ['æŋglə,faɪl] *n.* **1** a person who greatly admires England, its people, and its culture. **2** in Canada, a French Canadian who shows particular sympathy with the policies and culture of English-speaking Canada.

An•glo•phil•i•a [,æŋglə'fɪliə] *n.* **1** a strong admiration for or devotion to England, its people, and its culture. **2** in Canada, a particular sympathy among French Canadians for the policies and culture of English-speaking Canada.

An•glo•phil•ic [,æŋglou'fɪlɪk] *adj.* **1** having to do with or characteristic of Anglophiles. **2** being an Anglophile.

An•glo•phobe ['æŋglə,foub] *n.* **1** a person who dislikes England and its people. **2** in Canada, a French Canadian who dislikes or especially fears the policies and culture of English-speaking Canadians.

An•glo•pho•bi•a [,æŋglə'foubiə] *n.* **1** a dislike of England and anything British. **2** in Canada, a strong dislike or especially fear of the policies and culture of English-speaking Canadians.

An•glo•phone ['æŋglə,foun] *n.* **1** a person whose native or principal language is English. **2** *(adjl.)* of, having to do with, or made up of people whose native or principal language is English: *an Anglophone regiment.* **—,An•glo'phon•ic** [-'fɒnɪk], *adj.*

An•glo–Sax•on ['æŋglou 'sæksən] *n., adj. —n.* **1** a member of the nation that dominated England before the Norman conquest in 1066, descended from the Germanic tribes who conquered England in the 5th century A.D. **2** the language of the Anglo-Saxons; Old English. **3** a person who is English or of English descent. **4** plain, blunt English; that part of the English vocabulary descended from Old English, as opposed to the French and Latin elements, often with reference to its inclusion of words commonly considered offensive.
—adj. **1** of or having to do with the Anglo-Saxons or their language. **2** designating that part of the vocabulary of English that is derived from Old English, including words commonly considered offensive: Food, horse, *and* hand *are Anglo-Saxon words. She cursed him in Anglo-Saxon monosyllables. Abbrev.*: AS or A.S.

Ang•mags•sa•lik [æŋ'mægsɑlɪk] *n.* a tribe of Inuit who lived on the east coast of Greenland up to the late 19th century.

An•go•la [æŋ'goulə] a country in SW Africa.

An•go•ra [æŋ'gɔrə] *n.* **1** Usually, **angora, a** the hair of the ANGORA RABBIT. **b** yarn made from this hair, used especially for knitting. **c** *(adjl.)* made from this yarn: *an angora sweater.* **d** mohair. **2** ANGORA CAT. **3** ANGORA GOAT. **4** ANGORA RABBIT. ⟨< *Angora*, the former name of the Turkish province of Ankara, the original home of the Angora cat and Angora goat⟩

Angora cat a breed of cat having long, silky hair, a bushy tail, and a ruff of hair around the neck.

Angora goat a breed of goat having spiral horns and long, silky, curly white hair that is used for making cloth. The hair of the Angora goat or cloth made from it is usually called mohair.

Angora rabbit a breed of rabbit having long, soft, usually white hair that is used for making yarns, especially for knitting. The Angora rabbit was developed from a species of European wild rabbit. ⟨named after the Angora goat since it has similar hair⟩

an•gos•tu•ra [,æŋgə'stjurə] *or* [,æŋgə'sturə] *n.* **1** the bitter bark of a South American tree. **2 Angostura,** *Trademark.* ANGOSTURA BITTERS. ⟨after *Angostura*, a town in Venezuela⟩

Angostura Bitters *Trademark.* a bitter tonic derived from angostura bark and various other roots, barks, etc. It is sometimes used as a flavouring in food and cocktails.

An•gra Main•yu ['æŋgrə 'maɪnju] in Zoroastrianism, the evil spirit of the cosmos.

an•gry ['æŋgri] *adj.* **-gri•er, -gri•est. 1** feeling or showing anger: *an angry reply. He was angry with his brother.* **2** raging or stormy: *an angry sky.* **3** inflamed and sore: *She had an angry cut on her arm.* ⟨< *anger*⟩ **—'an•gri•ly,** *adv.* **—'an•gri•ness,** *n.*

☛ *Usage.* **Angry.** In reference to a thing, **angry at** and **angry about** are used: *I was angry at his slipshod work. Do you ever get angry about the cheating you see?* In reference to a person, **angry with** is general: *She was angry with her mother.* Formal English uses **angry at** or **angry with,** making the following distinctions: when the angry feeling is being stressed, *at* is used; when the stress is on the expression of that anger upon a person, *with* is used: *We were angry at the girls for their tardiness. I was so angry with John that he drew back in fear.*

angst [ɑŋst] *or* [æŋst] *n.* a continuous, vague feeling of anxiety or dread not consciously related to any specific thing in one's environment: *adolescent angst, the angst of the rootless and the lonely.* ⟨< G⟩

ang•strom or **Ång•ström** ['æŋstrəm] *n.* a unit for measuring length, equal to one ten-millionth of a millimetre, sometimes used to measure wavelengths of light. *Symbol*: Å ⟨after Anders John *Angstrom* (1814-1874), a Swedish physicist⟩

angstrom unit angstrom. *Abbrev.*: AU

an•guish ['æŋgwɪʃ] *n., v. —n.* very great pain or grief; great suffering or distress.
—v. cause or feel anguish: *News of the flood anguished the nation. The boy anguished over the loss of his pet.* ⟨ME < OF *anguisse* < L *angustia* tightness < *angustus* narrow⟩

an•guished ['æŋgwɪʃt] *adj., v. —adj.* **1** suffering anguish. **2** full of anguish; showing anguish.
—v. pt. and pp. of ANGUISH.

an•gu•lar ['æŋgjələr] *adj.* **1** having angles; sharp-cornered: *an angular rock.* **2** measured by an angle: *angular distance.* **3** somewhat thin and bony; not plump: *She has a tall, angular body.* **4** stiff and awkward in manner or character: *angular compliments.* ⟨< L *angularis* < *angulus* angle⟩ **—'an•gu•lar•ly,** *adv.*

an•gu•lar•i•ty [,æŋgjə'lærəti] *or* [-'lɛrəti] *n., pl.* **-ties. 1** the quality or condition of being angular. **2 angularities,** *pl.* sharp corners.

angular momentum the momentum of an object rotating about an axis; the linear momentum multiplied by its distance from the axis of rotation.

angular velocity the speed of a rotating body fixed at one end, calculated as the rate at which the angle between the path of the body and the fixed point changes.

an•gu•late *adj.* ['æŋgjələt] *or* ['æŋgjə,leɪt]; *v.* ['æŋgjə,leit] *adj., v.,* **-lat•ed, -lating.** *—adj.* having angles.
—v. make or become angulate. **—'an•gu•late•ly,** *adv.*

an•gu•la•tion [,æŋgjə'leiʃən] *n.* **1** an angulating or being angulated. **2** an angular shape or position.

an•hin•ga [æn'hɪŋgə] *n.* a large bird of the tropical and sub-tropical Americas (*Anhinga anhinga*) resembling a cormorant but thinner, having a longer tail and a bill like a heron's. The adult male is mainly black; the adult female has some brown areas.

an•hy•dride [æn'haidraɪd] *or* [æn'haidrɪd] *n.* **1** any oxide that unites with water to form an acid or base. Sulphur trioxide, SO_3, is the anhydride of sulphuric acid. **2** any compound formed by the removal of water.

an•hy•drite [æn'haɪdrəit] *n.* a white to bluish grey mineral consisting of anhydrous sulphate of calcium. *Formula*: $CaSO_4$

an•hy•drous [æn'haɪdrəs] *adj.* **1** without water: *an anhydrous region.* **2** *Chemistry.* containing no water of crystallization. ⟨< Gk. *anydros* < *an-* without + *hydōr* water⟩

An•ik ['ænɪk] *Cdn. n.* one of three satellites launched by Canada to establish a domestic system of satellite communication.

an•il ['ænɪl] *n.* **1** a West Indian leguminous shrub (*Indigofera suffruticosa*) from whose leaves and stalks indigo is made. **2** indigo. ⟨< F < Pg. < Arabic *al-nil* < *al* the + *nil* indigo < Skt. *nili* indigo < *nila* dark blue⟩

an•ile ['ænaɪl] *or* ['einaɪl] *adj.* old-womanish; suitable for a weak or doting old woman. ⟨< L *anilis* < *anus* old woman⟩

a•ni•le•ri•dine [ˌænɪ'lɛrəˌdin] *n.* a drug used to relieve pain.

an•i•line ['ænəlɪn], ['ænəˌlin], *or* ['ænəˌlaɪn] *n., adj.* —*n.* a poisonous, oily liquid, obtained from coal tar and especially from nitrobenzene, used in making dyes, plastics, etc. *Formula*: $C_6H_5NH_2$
—*adj.* made from aniline. ⟨< *anil*⟩

aniline dye **1** a dye made from aniline. **2** any artificial dye.

a•nil•i•ty [ə'nɪləti] *n., pl.* **-ties. 1** an anile condition. **2** an anile act or notion.

an•i•ma ['ænəmə] *n.* **1** life; soul. **2** *Psychology.* the female part of a man's nature. ⟨< L, life, breath⟩

an•i•mad•ver•sion [ˌænəmæd'vɜrʒən] *n.* criticism; blame; unfavourable comment. ⟨< L *animadversio, -onis* < *animadvertere.* See ANIMADVERT.⟩

an•i•mad•vert [ˌænəmæd'vɜrt] *v.* make criticisms; express blame; comment unfavourably (*usually used with* **on** *or* **upon**). ⟨< L *animadvertere* < *animus* mind < *ad-* to + *vertere* turn⟩

an•i•mal [ˌænəməl] *n., adj.* —*n.* **1** any living thing that is not a plant, fungus, moneran, or protist. Most animals can move about, whereas most plants cannot; most animals are unable to make their own food from carbon dioxide, water, nitrogen, etc., but most plants can. Compare FUNGUS, MONERAN, PLANT, and PROTIST. **2** any creature other than a human being; brute; beast. **3** a person thought of as being like a brute or beast; a person seemingly without human feelings. **4** any four-footed creature: *the animals and birds of the forest.*
—*adj.* **1** of or having to do with the physical nature of human beings, as opposed to the spiritual; carnal: *animal appetites.* **2** of, having to do with, or characteristic of animals, especially the higher animals other than humans: *animal intelligence.* ⟨< L *animal* < *anima* life, breath⟩

☛ *Syn. n.* **2. Animal,** BEAST, BRUTE = a living creature of a lower order than human beings. **Animal,** the general word, suggests nothing more: *He likes animals.* **Beast** applies to four-legged animals, as distinct from birds, insects, etc.: *The horse is a noble beast.* **Brute,** used chiefly in formal or special styles, emphasizes lack of the power to reason which sets humans above animals: *With the instinct of the brute, the deer found safety.* **3.** Used figuratively, applied to humans, **animal, beast,** and **brute** express attitudes of the speaker toward the persons named. **Animal,** objective, emphasizes the body: *Those boys are healthy young animals.* **Beast,** emotional, emphasizes giving up control over physical desires: *Living only for self-indulgence, they are beasts.* **Brute,** emotional, emphasizes lack of reason as shown by mental dullness or lack of control over violent feelings and inhuman treatment of others: *That brute of a guard beat him to a pulp.*

an•i•mal•cule [ˌænə'mælkjul] *n.* a minute or microscopic animal, such as a protozoan or rotifer. ⟨< NL *animalculum,* dim. of L *animal*⟩

an•i•mal•cu•lum [ˌæni'mælkjələm] *n.* animalcule.

animal heat the body heat of an animal, produced by metabolism.

animal husbandry the science of farming with animals.

an•i•mal•ism ['ænəməˌlɪzəm] *n.* **1** the natural health and vitality typical of animals. **2** preoccupation with the satisfying of physical needs and desires. **3** the belief or doctrine that human beings are no more than animals and that they have no soul or spirit.

an•i•mal•ist ['ænəməlɪst] *n.* **1** one who believes in ANIMALISM (def. 3). **2** a sensualist. **3** an artist whose main subject is animal life. —ˌ**an•i•mal'is•tic,** *adj.*

an•i•mal•i•ty [ˌænə'mæləti] *n.* **1** animal nature or character in humans. **2** animal life.

an•i•mal•ize ['ænəməˌlaiz] *v.* **-ized, -iz•ing. 1** change into animal matter: *Food assimilated into the body is animalized.* **2** make bestial; dehumanize. **3** make sensual.
—ˌ**an•i•mal•i'za•tion,** *n.*

animal kingdom **1** the group of living creatures that can move about and do not use photosynthesis to obtain nourishment. **2** in present-day biology, one of the five basic groups into which all living things are divided: *The animal kingdom includes all living animals, birds, fish, insects, etc.*

animal magnetism the power to attract sexually.

animal spirits natural liveliness; healthy cheerfulness.

an•i•mate *v.* ['ænəˌmeit]; *adj.* ['ænəmɪt] *v.* **-mat•ed, -mat•ing;** *adj.* —*v.* **1** give life to; make alive. **2** add liveliness or zest to: *Jill's funny stories animated the whole party.* **3** move to action; stir up; incite: *A fierce desire to succeed animated her efforts.* **4** inspire; encourage: *The soldiers were animated by their captain's brave speech.* **5** put into motion; cause to act or work: *Windmills are animated by the wind.* **6** produce as an ANIMATED CARTOON: *to animate a children's story.* **7** make the drawings, etc. for (something so produced): *The television commercial was animated by a group of local artists.*
—*adj.* **1** living; having life: *Animate nature means all living plants and animals.* **2** lively; gay; vigorous. ⟨< L *animare* < *anima* life, breath⟩

an•i•mat•ed ['ænəˌmeitɪd] *adj., v.* —*adj.* **1** lively; vigorous: *an animated discussion.* **2** joyful or vivacious: *an animated smile.* **3** simulating life: *animated dolls.* **4** made as an ANIMATED CARTOON: *The movie has some animated sequences and some scenes with live actors.* **5** living; alive; animate.
—*v.* pt. and pp. of ANIMATE. —**'an•iˌmat•ed•ly,** *adv.*

animated cartoon a series of drawings arranged to be photographed and shown in rapid succession as a motion picture. Each drawing shows a slight change from the one before it so that, when the film is projected, the figures in the drawings seem to move.

an•i•ma•teur [ˌænɪmə'tɜr] *n.* one who leads a discussion, gets people involved in a meeting, etc. ⟨< F⟩

an•i•ma•tion [ˌænə'meiʃən] *n.* **1** an animating or being animated. **2** life. **3** liveliness; spirit. **4** the process or technique of making ANIMATED CARTOONS. **5** ANIMATED CARTOON: *The roster of new summer movies includes several animations.*

a•ni•ma•to [ˌɑnɪ'mɑtou] *adj. Music.* lively; gay; vigorous. ⟨< Ital.⟩

an•i•ma•tor ['ænəˌmeitər] *n.* **1** a person or thing that animates. **2** a person who makes drawings for ANIMATED CARTOONS.

a•ni•mé or **a•ni•mi** ['ænɪˌmei] *or* ['ænɪˌmi] *n.* any of several types of resin extracted from tropical American trees to make varnish. ⟨< F < Pg. or Sp. *anime* < ? Tupi word⟩

an•i•mism ['ænəˌmɪzəm] *n.* **1** a belief in the existence of soul as distinct from matter; belief in spiritual beings, such as souls, angels, and devils. **2** a belief that there are living souls in trees, stones, stars, etc. **3** *Philosophy.* the belief that the universe is animated by a spiritual force. ⟨< L *anima* life, breath⟩

an•i•mist ['ænəmɪst] *n.* a person who believes in some form of animism.

an•i•mis•tic [ˌænə'mɪstɪk] *adj.* of or associated with animism.

an•i•mos•i•ty [ˌænə'mɒsɪti] *n., pl.* **-ties.** active or violent dislike; ill will: *She felt no animosity toward the winner.* ⟨< L *animositas* < *animosus* spirited⟩

an•i•mus ['ænəməs] *n.* **1** an animating thought or spirit; intention: *Ambition was his animus.* **2** *Psychology.* the male part of a woman's nature. **3** active dislike or enmity; animosity. ⟨< L *animus* spirit, feeling⟩

an•i•on ['ænaɪən] *n.* **1** a negatively charged ion that moves toward the positive pole in electrolysis. See ELECTROLYSIS for picture. **2** an atom or group of atoms having a negative charge. ⟨< *an-*[1] + *ion*⟩ —ˌ**an•i'on•ic,** *adj.*

an•ise ['ænɪs] *n.* **1** an annual plant (*Pimpinella anisum*) of the parsley family native to the Mediterranean but widely cultivated in warm regions for its licorice-flavoured seeds. **2** aniseed. ⟨ME < OF *anis* < L < Gk. *anison*⟩

an•i•seed ['ænə,sid] *n.* the seed of anise, used as a flavouring or in medicine.

an•is•ei•ko•ni•a [,ænɪsəi'kouniə] a disorder in which the two eyes see images of different sizes. ⟨< NL *aniso* + Gk. *eikon* image + *-ia* suffix used in names of diseases⟩
—,an•is•ei'kon•ic, *adj.*

an•i•sette [,ænə'zɛt] *or* [,ænə'sɛt] *n.* a sweet, usually colourless liqueur flavoured with aniseed.

aniso– *combining form.* unequal or uneven: *anisogamy.* Also, before vowels, **anis-.** ⟨< NL *aniso* < Gk. *anisos* < *a* not + *isos* equal⟩

an•i•sog•a•my [,ænəi'sɒgəmi] *n.* sexual reproduction involving the uniting of two cells of different sizes or forms, as an ovum and a sperm.

an•i•sole ['ænɪ,soul] *n.* a sweet-smelling liquid used in perfumes and as a flavouring. *Formula:* $C_6H_5OCH_3$ ⟨< F *anisol* < OF *anis* + L *oleum* oil⟩

an•i•som•er•ous [,ænəɪ'sɒmərəs] *adj.* having floral whorls whose constituent parts, such as petals and stamens, differ in number. ⟨< NL *aniso* not equal + Gk. *meros* part⟩

an•i•so•met•ric [æ,nəisou'mɛtrɪk] *adj.* not isometric; having parts that are asymmetrical or of uneven measurements.

an•i•so•trop•ic [æ,nəisə'trɒpɪk] *adj.* **1** *Physics.* having physical properties that are not uniform throughout but depend on the direction in which they are measured. **2** *Botany.* **a** whose different parts respond differently to the same external stimulus. **b** changing position in response to an external stimulus.
—,an•i'sot•ro•py [,ænəi'sɒtrəpi], *n.*

an•is•tre•plase [æ'nɪstrə,pleis] *n.* a drug used to treat certain heart conditions.

Anjou pear a hardy winter pear, large and nearly round in shape.

an•ker•ite ['æŋkə,rəit] *n.* a grey-brown mineral similar to dolomite but containing iron and proportionately less magnesium. ⟨< M.J. *Anker,* 19c. Austrian minerologist⟩
☛ *Hom.* ANCHORITE.

ankh [ɑŋk] *or* [æŋk] *n.* an ancient Egyptian symbol of life, in the form of a cross with a loop at the top instead of a vertical arm. See CROSS for picture. ⟨< Egyptian *'nh* life; soul⟩

an•kle ['æŋkəl] *n.* **1** the part of the human leg between the foot and the calf: *slim ankles.* See LEG for picture. **2** the protruding part on the outside bottom end of each of the lower leg bones, just above the foot; anklebone: *I bumped my ankle against the chair. She has a broken ankle.* **3** the joint formed by the lower leg bones and the talus, connecting the foot and the leg: *My ankle is still stiff from when I twisted it.* **4** the part of a stocking, sock, or boot that covers the ankle. **5** in a horse, etc., the joint between the cannon bone and the pastern. ⟨ME < Scand.; cf. Danish *ankel*⟩

an•kle•bone ['æŋkəl,boun] *n.* the protruding part on the outside of the bottom of each of the lower leg bones, just above the foot. See LEG for picture.

an•klet ['æŋ,klət] *n.* **1** a short sock. **2** a chain or band worn around the ankle, especially as an ornament.

an•ky•lo•saur ['æŋkələ,sɔr] *n.* any of a suborder (Ankylosauria) of herbivorous dinosaurs that flourished in the Cretaceous period and had a heavily armoured body with short legs. ⟨< Gk. *ankylos* crooked + *sauros* lizard⟩

an•ky•lose ['æŋkə,lous] *v.* **-losed, -los•ing. 1** make or become stiff, by or as if by ankylosis. **2** of bones, grow together; unite. ⟨< Gk. *ankylosis* < *ankylos* crooked⟩

an•ky•lo•sis [,æŋkə'lousɪs] *n.* **1** a growing together of bones as a result of disease or injury. **2** stiffness of a joint caused by this. ⟨< NL < Gk. *ankylosis* < *ankyloein* stiffen < *ankylos* crooked⟩ **—,an•ky'lot•ic** [-'lɒtɪk], *adj.*

an•ky•los•to•mi•a•sis [,æŋkə,loustə'maiəsɪs] *n.* hookworm. ⟨< *Ankylostoma* hookworm genus < Gk. *ankylos* crooked + *stoma* mouth⟩

an•la•ge ['ɑn,lɑgə] *n.* **1** foundation; basis. **2** *Biology.* the earliest discernible cell grouping that will later develop into a particular part of the embryo. ⟨< G, foundation < *anlagen* lay out⟩

ann 1 annual. **2** annuity. **3** annals.

an•na ['ɑnə] *or* ['ænə] *n.* **1** a unit of money formerly used in India, Pakistan, Burma, and British East Africa, equal to one sixteenth of a rupee. **2** a coin having this value. ⟨< Hind. *ana*⟩

an•na•berg•ite ['ænə,bɜrgəit] *n.* a green monoclinic crystalline mineral, hydrated arsenide of nickel. *Formula:* $N_{13}(AsO_4)_2\ 8H_2O$

an•nal•ist ['ænəlɪst] *n.* a writer of annals. **—,an•na'lis•tic,** *adj.*
☛ *Hom.* ANALYST.

an•nals ['ænəlz] *n.pl.* **1** a written account of events year by year. **2** historical records; history. ⟨< L *annales* (*libri* books) annual record < *annus* year⟩

An•na•mese [,ænə'miz] *adj., n., pl.* **-mese.** *—adj.* of or associated with Annam or its people.
—n. **1** a native or inhabitant of Annam, a part of Vietnam. **2** the language spoken by the Annamese.

an•nat•to or **a•nat•to** [ə'nɑtou] *n.* **1** a tropical flowering tree (*Bixa orellana*) from whose seedcoats a reddish yellow dye is obtained. **2** the dye, used to colour food, fabrics, etc.

an•neal [ə'nil] *v.* **1** toughen (glass, metals, etc.) by heating and then cooling; temper. **2** toughen or strengthen (the mind, will, etc.) ⟨OE *an ælan* < *an-* on + *ælan* burn⟩

an•ne•lid ['ænəlɪd] *n.* any of more than 8000 species of segmented worms making up the phylum **Annelida.** Annelids are grouped into three classes: sea worms, earthworms, and leeches. ⟨< F *annélide* < *annel* ring < L *anellus,* double dim. of *anus* ring⟩

an•nex *v.* [ə'nɛks]; *n.* ['ænɛks] *v., n. —v.* **1** join or add to a larger thing: *England annexed Acadia in 1713.* **2** *Informal.* take as one's own; appropriate, especially without permission.
—n. **1** something added or attached; an added part: *Our hotel has an annex.* **2** *Slang.* a backhouse; outhouse. ⟨ME < Med.L *annexare* < L *annexus,* pp. of *annectere* < *ad-* to + *nectere* bind⟩
☛ *Syn. v.* **1.** See note at ATTACH.

an•nex•a•tion [,ænək'seiʃən] *n.* **1** an annexing or being annexed: *the annexation of several suburbs to the metropolitan area.* **2** something annexed.

an•nex•a•tion•ist [,ænək'seiʃənɪst] *n.* **1** a person who favours or supports annexation, as between two cities, nations, etc. **2** Sometimes, **Annexationist,** *Cdn.* a person belonging to or supporting an Annexation Movement.

Annexation Movement the name given to groups in Canada that have advocated political union with the United States.

an•ni•hi•late [ə'naɪə,leit] *v.* **-lat•ed, -lat•ing. 1** destroy completely; wipe out of existence. **2** bring to ruin or confusion. ⟨< LL *annihilāre* < L *ad-* + *nihil* nothing⟩ **—an'ni•hi,la•tor,** *n.* **—an'ni•hil•a•ble,** *adj.*
☛ *Syn.* **1.** See note at ABOLISH.

an•ni•hi•la•tion [ə,naɪə'leiʃən] *n.* **1** complete destruction. **2** *Nuclear physics.* **a** the destruction of a positron (positive electron) and an electron, the energy turning into one or more photons of radiation. **b** the uniting of an electron and a positron to produce a gamma ray.

an•ni•hi•la•tive [ə'naɪələtɪv] *or* [ə'naɪə,leitɪv] *adj.* able or likely to annihilate.

an•ni•ver•sa•ry [,ænə'vɜrsəri] *n., pl.* **-ries. 1** the yearly return of a date: *Tomorrow is the anniversary of her wedding.* **2** the celebration of the yearly return of a date. **3** (*adjl.*) of or having to do with an anniversary: *an anniversary dinner.* ⟨ME < L *anniversarius* returning annually < *annus* year + *vertere* turn⟩

an•no Dom•i•ni ['ænou 'dɒməni] *or* ['dɒmə,naɪ] *Latin.* in the year of our Lord; any year since the birth of Christ. *Abbrev.:* A.D.

an•no•tate ['ænə,teit] *v.* **-tat•ed, -tat•ing. 1** provide with explanatory notes or comments: *Shakespeare's plays are often annotated to make them easier for modern readers to understand.* **2** make explanatory notes or comments. ⟨< L *annotare* < *ad-* to + *nota* note⟩ **—'an•no,ta•tor,** *n.* **—'an•no,ta•tive,** *adj.*

an•no•ta•tion [,ænə'teiʃən] *n.* **1** the act of providing with notes; being provided with notes: *The annotation of the book required hundreds of hours.* **2** a note added to explain or criticize: *The editor's annotations were printed in small type.*

an•nounce [ə'nauns] *v.* **-nounced, -nounc•ing. 1** make known; give formal or public notice of: *to announce a wedding in the papers. She announced that she was never going to school again.* **2** make known the presence or arrival of: *The butler announced each guest in a loud voice.* **3** give or be evidence of: *Black clouds announced the coming thunderstorm.* **4** *Radio and television.* act as an announcer; be an announcer for. ⟨ME < OF *anoncier* < L *annuntiare* < *ad-* to + *nuntius* messenger. Doublet of ANNUNCIATE.⟩
☛ *Syn.* **1. Announce,** PROCLAIM, DECLARE = make known formally or publicly. **Announce** = give formal notice of something of interest to the public or a particular group: *They announced the birth of their first baby.* **Proclaim** = announce publicly and with authority something of importance to the general public: *The prime minister proclaimed an*

emergency. **Declare** = make known clearly and decisively, often formally or officially: *An armistice was declared.*

an•nounce•ment [ə'naʊnsmənt] *n.* **1** the act of announcing. **2** a public or formal notice: *Announcements of marriages appear in the newspapers.*

an•nounc•er [ə'naʊnsər] *n.* a person who announces, especially a person in radio and television who introduces programs, reads news, etc.

an•noy [ə'nɔɪ] *v.* **1** disturb or trouble, often by repetition of an act; vex; irritate: *She annoys her little brother by teasing him. The speaker was annoyed at the interruption.* **2** harass by means of repeated attacks; harry or molest: *a series of raids designed to annoy the enemy.* ⟨ME < OF *anuier* < LL *inodiare* < L* *in odio* in hatred⟩ **—an'noy•er,** *n.*
☛ *Syn.* **1.** See note at WORRY.

an•noy•ance [ə'nɔɪəns] *n.* **1** the act of annoying. **2** a feeling of being bothered or irritated; vexation: *He replied with annoyance that he had heard that story before.* **3** anything that annoys: *The heavy traffic on our street is a great annoyance.*

an•noy•ing [ə'nɔɪɪŋ] *adj.* disturbing; irritating: *an annoying background hum.* **—an'noy•ing•ly,** *adv.* **—an'noy•ing•ness,** *n.*

an•nu•al ['ænjuəl] *adj., n. —adj.* **1** coming once a year: *Your birthday is an annual event.* **2** in or for a year; covering the period of a year: *an annual salary of $36 000, annual rainfall, the earth's annual course around the sun.* **3** *Botany.* living only one year or season.
—n. **1** a book, journal, etc. published once a year. **2** a plant that lives only one year or season. Compare BIENNIAL, PERENNIAL. ⟨ME < OF *annuel* < LL *annualis* < L *annus* year⟩
—'an•nu•al•ly, *adv.*

an•nu•al•ize ['ænjʊə,laɪz] *v.* **-ized, -iz•ing.** *Finance.* calculate (rates of interest, growth, etc.) for a year based on figures from a shorter period.

annual ring in a woody plant, one of the concentric circles that can be seen in a cross section of a stem; each ring is the layer of wood produced in one growing season.

an•nu•i•tant [ə'njuətənt] *or* [ə'nuətənt] *n.* a person who receives an annuity.

an•nu•i•ty [ə'njuɪti] *or* [ə'nuɪti] *n., pl.* **-ties. 1** a sum of money paid every year. **2** the right to receive or duty to pay such a yearly sum. **3** an investment that provides a fixed yearly income during one's lifetime. ⟨ME < OF *annuité* < Med.L *annuitas* < L *annus* year⟩

an•nul [ə'nʌl] *v.* **-nulled, -nul•ling.** do away with; destroy the force of; make void: *The judge annulled the contract because one of the signers was too young.* ⟨ME < OF *anuller* < LL *annullare* < L *ad-* + *nullum* none⟩

an•nu•lar ['ænjələr] *adj.* ringlike; ring-shaped; ringed. ⟨< L *anularis* (sometimes misspelled *annularis* in late and poor MSS) < *anulus* ring. See ANNULUS.⟩

annular eclipse a solar eclipse in which the sun appears as a ring of light surrounding the dark moon.

an•nu•late ['ænjəlɪt] *or* ['ænjʊ,leit] *adj.* having rings or ringlike markings; consisting of rings.

an•nu•la•tion [,ænjə'leiʃən] *n.* **1** the act or fact of forming rings. **2** a ringlike part or structure.

an•nu•let ['ænjəlɪt] *n.* **1** a little ring. **2** *Architecture.* a narrow, ringlike moulding of wood, stone, etc. ⟨< L *anulus* ring. See ANNULUS.⟩

an•nul•ment [ə'nʌlmənt] *n.* an annulling or being annulled; cancellation.

an•nu•lus ['ænjələs] *n., pl.* **-li** [-,laɪ] *or* [-li] or **-lus•es.** a ringlike part, band, or space. ⟨< L *anulus* (sometimes misspelled *annulus* in late and poor MSS), dim. of *anus* ring⟩

an•num ['ænəm] *n. Latin.* year (acc. of *annus*).

an•nun•ci•ate [ə'nʌnsi,eit] *or* [ə'nʌnʃi,eit] *v.* **-at•ed, -at•ing.** make known; announce. ⟨< Med.L *annunciare* < L *annuntiare* < *ad-* to + *nuntius* messenger. Doublet of ANNOUNCE.⟩

an•nun•ci•a•tion [ə,nʌnsi'eiʃən] *or* [ə,nʌnʃi'eiʃən] *n.* **1** an announcement. **2 the Annunciation, a** the angel Gabriel's announcement to the Virgin Mary that she was to be the mother of Christ. **b** a painting, sculpture, etc. of this. **c** LADY DAY.

an•nun•ci•a•tor [ə'nʌnsi,eitər] *or* [ə'nʌnʃi,eitər] *n.* **1** an electrical device such as a buzzer or light, that indicates where a signal is coming from. Annunciators are used in hotel switchboards, in manually operated elevators, etc. **2** announcer.

an•nus mi•ra•bil•is ['ænəs mə'rɑbəlɪs] a year seen in retrospect as a turning-point or as full of cataclysmic events: *1867 was an annus mirabilis for Canada.* ⟨< L⟩

an•ode ['ænoud] *n.* **1** the negatively charged electrode of a primary cell or storage battery, through which the electrons leave the cell when the circuit is complete. See DRY CELL for picture. **2** the positive electrode in an electrolytic cell, that is connected to the positive terminal of a battery and carries electrons from the cell back to the battery. See ELECTROLYSIS for picture. **3** the positively charged electrode in a vacuum tube, that attracts electrons from the cathode. See CATHODE-RAY TUBE for picture. ⟨< L < Gk. *anōdos* < *ana-* up + *hodos* way⟩ **—an'od•ic,** *adj.*

an•o•dize ['ænə,daɪz] *v.,* **-dized, -diz•ing,** cover (a light metal) with a protective oxide film by electrolysis.

an•o•dyne ['ænə,daɪn] *n., adj. —n.* anything that lessens pain or provides comfort.
—adj. reducing pain; calming. ⟨< L < Gk. *anōdynos* < *an-* without + *odýnē* pain⟩

a•noint [ə'nɔɪnt] *v.* **1** put oil on; rub with ointment; smear: *Anoint sunburned skin with cold cream.* **2** put oil on in a ceremony as a sign of consecration to office; make sacred with oil: *The archbishop anointed the new king.* ⟨< OF *enoint*, pp. of *enoindre* < L *inunguere* < *in-* on + *ungere* smear⟩
—a'noint•ment, *n.* **—a'noin•ter,** *n.*

a•no•le [ə'nouli] CHAMELEON (def. 2). ⟨< F *anolis* < Carib *anoli*⟩

a•nom•a•lous [ə'nɒmələs] *adj.* departing from the common rule; irregular; abnormal: *A position as head of a department, but with no real authority, is anomalous.* ⟨< LL < Gk. *anōmalos* < *an-* not + *homalos* even⟩ **—a'nom•a•lous•ly,** *adv.*
—a'nom•a•lous•ness, *n.*

a•nom•a•ly [ə'nɒməli] *n., pl.* **-lies. 1** a departure from a general rule; irregularity. **2** something abnormal: *A dog that could not bark would be an anomaly.* **3** *Geology.* a local departure from the prevailing characteristics of an area. **4** *Astronomy.* the angle between an orbiting body, the previous point at which it was closest to the sun, and the sun. **—a,nom•a'lis•tic,** *adj.*

a•nom•ic [ə'nɒmɪk] *adj.* of, having to do with, or characterized by anomie.

an•o•mie ['ænəmi] *n.* a lack of standards for social or moral conduct in a person or society. ⟨< Med.F < Gk. *anomia* lawlessness⟩

a•non [ə'nɒn] *adv. Archaic or poetic.* **1** in a little while; soon. **2** at another time; again.
ever and anon, now and then. ⟨OE *on ān* into one, *on āne* in one, at once⟩

anon. anonymous.

an•o•nym ['ænə,nɪm] *n.* **1** pseudonym. **2** one who is anonymous.

an•o•nym•i•ty [,ænə'nɪməti] *n.* the quality or state of being anonymous: *He wrote under a pen name to preserve his anonymity.*

a•non•y•mous [ə'nɒnəməs] *adj.* **1** by or from a person whose name is not known or not given: *an anonymous letter, an anonymous poem.* **2** of unknown name; nameless: *The author of this poem is anonymous. Abbrev.*: a. or anon. **3** blending in with others due to lack of distinguishing features; nondescript: *an anonymous face in a crowd.* ⟨< Gk. *anōnymos* < *an-* without + (dialectal) *onyma* name⟩ **—a'non•y•mous•ly,** *adv.*

a•noph•e•les [ə'nɒfə,liz] *n., pl.* **-les.** any of a genus (*Anopheles*) of mosquitoes that includes all the species known to transmit malaria to humans. ⟨< NL < Gk. *anōphelēs* harmful⟩
—a'noph•e,line [-,laɪn], *adj.*

a•no•rak ['ænə,ræk] *n.* **1** a waterproof, hooded outer coat of skins, often worn by Inuit when hunting in a kayak. The lower edge of the anorak can be fastened tightly around the opening in the kayak. **2** a parka or heavy jacket, especially a waterproof one with a belt or drawstring at the waist. ⟨< Inuktitut, Greenland dial.⟩

an•o•rec•tic [,ænə'rɛktɪk] *adj. or n.* anorexic. Also, **anoretic.**

an•o•rex•i•a [,ænə'rɛksiə] *n.* **1** chronic loss of appetite. **2** ANOREXIA NERVOSA. ⟨< NL < Gk. *an-* without + *orexis* appetite⟩

anorexia ner•vo•sa [nər'vousə] an emotional disorder characterized by a refusal to eat, resulting in excessive weight loss and malnutrition which, if not corrected, can end in death.

an•o•rex•ic [,ænə'rɛksɪk] *adj., n. —adj.* of, causing, or affected with anorexia.
—n. **1** a person affected with anorexia. **2** something that causes anorexia.

an•or•thite [æn'ɔrθəit] *n.* a rare plagioclase feldspar found in volcanic rock; aluminum silicate of calcium. *Formula*: $CaAl_2(SiO_4)_2$ ⟨< Gk. *an-* not + *orthos* straight + *-ite*⟩ **–,an•or'thit•ic** [-'θɪtɪk], *adj.*

an•os•mi•a [æ'nɒzmiə] *or* [æ'nɒsmiə] *n.* partial or complete loss of the sense of smell. ⟨< NL < Gk. *an-* without + *osmē* smell⟩

an•os•mic [æ'nɒzmɪk] *or* [æ'nɒsmɪk] *adj.* of or having to do with anosmia. ⟨< NL < Gk.⟩

an•oth•er [ə'nʌðər] *adj., pron.* *–adj.* **1** one more: *Have another glass of milk.* **2** different; not the same: *That is another matter entirely.*
–pron. **1** one more: *He ate a piece of cake and then asked for another.* **2** a different one: *I don't like this book; give me another.* **3** one of the same kind: *Her mother is a scholar, and she is another.* ⟨for *an other*⟩

an•ov•u•lant [ə'nɒvjələnt] *adj., n.* *–adj.* causing the ovaries to fail to release their monthly egg.
–n. a drug that causes the ovaries to fail to release their monthly egg: *The contraceptive pill is an anovulant.*

an•ox•e•mi•a [,ænɒk'simiə] *n.* a decrease in the amount of oxygen in the blood of the arteries. ⟨< *an-¹* + *ox(ygen)* + *-emia*⟩ **–,an•ox'e•mic,** *adj.*

an•ox•i•a [æ'nɒksiə] *or* [ə'nɒksiə] *n.* **1** complete lack of oxygen. **2** inadequate supply of oxygen to body tissues by the blood. ⟨< *an-¹* + *ox(ygen)* + *-ia* disease suffix⟩ **–an'ox•ic,** *adj.*

ans. **1** answer. **2** answered.

an•sate ['ænseɪt] *adj.* having a handle. ⟨< L *ansatus* < *ansa* handle⟩

ansate cross ankh.

an•ser•ine ['ænsə,rain], ['ænsə,rin], *or* ['ænsərɪn] *adj.* **1** of or belonging to the subfamily Anserine, which includes the geese. **2** of, like, or having to do with a goose or geese. **3** stupid; foolish. ⟨< L *anserinus* < *anser* goose⟩

an•swer ['ænsər] *n., v.* *–n.* **1** words spoken or written in response to a question: *The girl gave a quick answer.* **2** a gesture or act done in return: *A nod was her only answer.* **3** a solution to a problem: *What is the correct answer to this algebra problem?* **4** a counterpart, often proposed in response (*to*): *Analytical psychology is Jung's answer to Freudian psychology.* **5** *Law.* a written defence by the defendant in response to the plaintiff's charges. **6** *Music.* the restatement of a subject in a fugue, for the second or fourth time, in another voice and key.
know all the answers, *Informal.* **a** be extremely well-informed. **b** make a boastful and annoying display of one's knowledge.
–v. **1** reply to: *She answered my question.* **2** make answer; reply: *I asked him a question, but he would not answer. She answered that she didn't need it.* **3** reply or respond by act: *He knocked on the door, but no one answered.* **4** act or move in response to (to): *She answered the doorbell. The accelerator answers to the slightest touch.* **5** serve: *This will answer your purpose. Such a poor excuse will not answer.* **6** refute; give a defence against (a charge, etc.): *to answer an accusation.* **7** bear the consequences of; be responsible (*for*): *to answer for a crime, to answer for someone's safety.* **8** correspond (*to*): *This house answers to their description.* **9** of an animal, recognize (a name) as its own (*used with* **to**): *The dog answers to Lucky.*
answer back, *Informal.* reply in a rude, saucy way. ⟨OE *andswaru* < *and-* against + *swerian* swear⟩ **–'an•swer•less,** *adj.*

an•swer•a•ble ['ænsərəbəl] *adj.* **1** responsible: *The treasurer is answerable to the club for the money that is given to her.* **2** that can be answered. **3** *Archaic.* corresponding.

answering service a business organization that takes the telephone calls of subscribers in their absence and, when they return, reports to them on the calls received.

ant [ænt] *n.* any of a large family (Formicidae) of mainly wingless insects that live in the ground or in wood in highly organized groups called colonies, which are divided into smaller groups, each with a specialized function to perform. Ants belong to the same order as bees and wasps. ⟨OE *æmete*⟩ **–'ant,like,** *adj.*

ant– the form of ANTI- before vowels and *h*, as in *antacid.*

–ant *suffix.* **1** ——ing: *buoyant = buoying, compliant = complying, triumphant = triumphing.* **2** one that ——s: *assistant = one that assists.* See also -ENT. ⟨< F < L *-ans, -antis; -ens, -entis*⟩

ant. **1** antonym. **2** antiquary.

an•ta ['æntə] *n. Architecture.* a square column added to the end of a wall or on either side of a doorway. ⟨< L⟩

ant•ac•id [ænt'æsɪd] *n., adj.* *–n.* a substance, such as baking soda or magnesia, that neutralizes acids.
–adj. tending to neutralize acids; counteracting acidity.

an•tag•o•nism [æn'tægə,nɪzəm] *n.* active opposition; conflict; hostility.

an•tag•o•nist [æn'tægənɪst] *n.* one who fights, struggles, or contends with another: *The knight defeated each antagonist.*
☛ *Syn.* See note at OPPONENT.

an•tag•o•nis•tic [æn,tægə'nɪstɪk] *adj.* having or showing conflict or hostility; opposing: *an antagonistic attitude. The two brothers have always been antagonistic.* **–an,tag•o'nis•ti•cal•ly,** *adv.*

an•tag•o•nize [æn'tægə,naɪz] *v.* **-nized, -niz•ing. 1** arouse opposition, hostility, or enmity in: *Her unkind remarks antagonized people who had been her friends.* **2** oppose or counteract. ⟨< Gk. *antagōnizesthai* < *anti-* against + *agōn* contest⟩ **–an'tag•o,niz•er,** *n.*

ant•al•ka•li [ænt'ælkə,laɪ] *n.* any substance that neutralizes alkalis. **–ant'al•ka,line** [-'ælkəlɪn] *or* [-'ælkə,laɪn], *adj.*

ant•arc•tic [æn'tɑrktɪk] *or* [æn'tɑrtɪk] *adj., n.* *–adj.* Often, **Antarctic,** of, having to do with, referring to, or living or growing in the region south of the Antarctic Circle.
–n. **the Antarctic,** the south polar region; the region south of the Antarctic Circle. ⟨ME < OF < L *antarcticus* < Gk. *antarktikos* opposite the north < *anti-* opposite + *arktikos* of the north. See ARCTIC.⟩

Antarctic Circle **1** the parallel of latitude at 66°33′ south of the equator that marks the boundary of the south polar region. **2** the polar region surrounded by this circle.

An•tar•es [æn'tɛriz] *n.* a first magnitude star in the southern constellation Scorpio. ⟨< Gk. *anti-* like *Ares* god of war⟩

ant•ar•thrit•ic [,æntɑr'θrɪtɪk] *adj., n.* *–adj.* relieving or preventing arthritis.
–n. a remedy for arthritis.

ant•asth•ma•tic [,æntæz'mætɪk] *or* [,æntæs'mætɪk] *adj., n.* *–adj.* relieving or preventing asthma.
–n. a remedy for asthma.

an•ta•zo•line [æn'tæzə,lin] *n.* a drug used to treat red, itching eyes.

ant bear the giant anteater of South America.

ant cow an aphid that yields a sweet substance on which ants feed.

an•te ['ænti] *n., v.* **-ted** or **-teed, -te•ing.** *–n.* **1** in the game of poker, a stake that every player must put up before receiving a hand or drawing new cards. **2** the amount to be paid in advance as one's share in any financial undertaking.
–v. Informal. **1** in poker, put (one's stake) into the pool. **2** pay (one's share).
ante up, a in poker, put in one's stake. **b** pay one's share. ⟨See ANTE-⟩

ante– *prefix.* **1** before; earlier: *antenatal.* **2** in front of: *anteroom.* ⟨< L *ante-* < *ante,* adv., prep.⟩
☛ *Hom.* ANTI-.

ant•eat•er ['ænt,itər] *n.* **1** any of a family (Myrmecophagidae) of toothless mammals found in the tropical forests of South America, having a long, tube-shaped head and muzzle with a small mouth opening and a long, slender, sticky, wormlike tongue with which it catches the ants and termites it eats. The giant, or great, anteater, the largest species, has a long, bushy tail and very strong front claws with which it rips open the nests of ants and termites. **2** any of several other mammals, such as the aardvark and the pangolin, that feed mainly on ants and termites but are not related to the true anteaters.

an•te–bel•lum [,ænti 'bɛləm] *adj.* **1** before the war. **2** *U.S.* before the American Civil War. ⟨< L *ante bellum* before the war⟩

an•te•cede [,æntə'sid] *v.,* **-ced•ed, -ced•ing.** precede. ⟨< L *antecēdere* precede⟩

an•te•ced•ence [,æntɪ'sidəns] *n.* **1** a going before; precedence; priority. **2** *Astronomy.* the apparent motion of a planet from east to west.

an•te•ced•ent [,æntɪ'sidənt] *n., adj.* *–n.* **1** a previous thing or event; something happening before an event and leading up to another. **2** *Grammar.* a word, phrase, or clause that is referred to by a pronoun or relative adverb. In "This is the house that Jack built," *house* is the antecedent of *that.* In "I remember the house where I was born," *house* is the antecedent of *where.* **3** *Mathematics.* the first term of a ratio; the first or third term in a proportion. **4** *Logic.* a condition upon which a theoretical conclusion depends. **5 antecedents,** *pl.* **a** past life or history: *No one knew the antecedents of the mysterious stranger.* **b** ancestors.

—*adj.* coming or happening before; preceding; previous. ⟨< L *antecedens, -entis*, ppr. of *antecedere* < *ante-* before + *cedere* go⟩ **—,an•te'ced•ent•ly,** *adv.*

an•te•ces•sor ['æntɪ,sɛsər] *n.* predecessor. ⟨< ME *antecessour* < L *antecessor* < *antecessus*, pp. of *antecedere* < *ante* before + *cedere* go⟩

an•te•cham•ber ['ænti,tʃeimbər] *n.* anteroom.

an•te•date ['ænti,deit] *n., v.* **-dat•ed, -dat•ing;** *—n.* a date, set on a document or assigned to an event, earlier than the actual date.
—v. **1** come before in time; occur earlier than: *Shakespeare's* Hamlet *antedates* Macbeth *by about six years.* **2** give too early a date to.

an•te•di•lu•vi•an [,æntidə'luviən] *adj., n. —adj.* **1** of or having to do with the period before the Flood. Compare POSTDILUVIAN. **2** very old or old-fashioned.
—n. **1** a person who lived before the Flood. **2** an old-fashioned or very old person. ⟨< *ante-* + L *diluvium* deluge⟩

an•te•fix ['æntɪ,fɪks] *n.* a small carved decoration fixed to the eaves of a tiled roof to hide the tile edges.

an•te•lope ['æntə,loup] *n., pl.* **-lope** or **-lopes. 1** any of a large group of hoofed, cud-chewing, mainly African animals belonging to the same family as cattle, goats, etc., having hollow, non-branching horns that grow upward and backward and that are not shed. **2** a very swift, hoofed, cud-chewing animal (*Antilocapra americana*) of the North American plains that is the only member of the family Antilocapridae, having horns with a permanent bony core and a black, horny outer layer that is shed every year. Also called **pronghorn antelope, pronghorn.** ⟨ME < OF *antelop* < Med.L < LGk. *antholops*⟩

an•te•me•rid•i•an [,æntimə'rɪdiən] *adj.* of or having to do with the morning, before noon.

an•te me•rid•i•em [,ænti mə'rɪdiəm] *Latin.* before noon. *Abbrev.*: a.m. or A.M.

an•te–mor•tem [,ænti 'mɔrtəm] *adj. or adv.* just before death. Compare POST-MORTEM.

an•te•na•tal [,ænti'neitəl] *adj.* occurring in, or having to do with, the time before birth.

an•ten•na [æn'tɛnə] *n., pl.* **-ten•nae** *for 1;* **-ten•nas** *for 2.* **1** one of two feelers on the head of an insect, lobster, etc. **2** *Radio and television.* a long wire or set of wires for sending out or receiving electromagnetic waves. ⟨< L *antenna*, originally, sailyard⟩

an•ten•nae [æn'tɛni] *or* [æn'tɛnai] *n.* pl. of ANTENNA (def. 1).

an•ten•nule [æn'tɛnjul] *n.* a little ANTENNA (def. 1).

an•te•nup•tial [,ænti'nʌpʃəl] *adj.* before marriage.

an•te•pen•di•um [,æntɪ'pɛndiəm] *n.* the decorative cloth hanging from the front of an altar. ⟨< Med.L *ante* before + L *pendere* hang⟩

an•te•pe•nult [,æntipə'nʌlt] *or* [,ænti'pinʌlt] *n.* the third syllable from the end of a word. In *anthropology* the syllable *pol* is the antepenult.

an•te•pe•nul•ti•mate [,æntipə'nʌltəmɪt] *adj., n. —adj.* third from the end; last but two.
—n. antepenult.

an•te•ri•or [æn'tiriər] *adj.* **1** toward the front; fore: *The anterior part of a fish's body contains the head and gills.* **2** going before; earlier; previous. Compare POSTERIOR. ⟨< L *anterior*, comparative of *ante* before⟩ **—an'te•ri•or•ly,** *adj.*

an•te•room ['ænti,rum] *or* [-,rʊm] *n.* a small room leading to a larger one; a waiting room.

an•te•type ['ænti,təip] *or* ['æntɪ,təip] *n.* prototype.

an•te•vert [,æntɪ'vɜrt] *v.* cause (an organ, such as the uterus) to lie farther forward in the body than it should. ⟨< L *antevertere* < *ante* before + *vertere* turn⟩ **—,an•te'ver•sion** [,æntɪ'vɜrʒən], *n.*

ant•he•li•on [ænt'hiliən] *or* [æn'θiliən] *n* **1** an indistinct white spot occasionally seen in the sky opposite the sun; the sun's reflection. **2** a faint glow around a shadow cast on fog or cloud. ⟨< LL < Gk. *anthelion* < *anti* against + *helios* sun⟩

an•them ['ænθəm] *n.* **1** a song of praise, devotion, or patriotism. Most countries have a **national anthem. 2** a piece of Christian sacred music, usually with words from some passage in the Bible. ⟨OE *antefne* < LL < Gk. *antiphōna* antiphon. Doublet of ANTIPHON.⟩

an•the•mi•on [æn'θimiən] *n.* an ornamental pattern of flowers or leaves, much used in ancient architecture, paintings, and carved friezes. ⟨< Gk. a flower < *anthos* flower + *-ion* diminutive suffix⟩

an•ther ['ænθər] *n.* of a flower, the part of the stamen that bears the pollen. See FLOWER for picture. ⟨< NL < Gk. *anthēra*, fem. of *anthērós* flowery < *ánthos* flower⟩

an•ther•id•i•um [,ænθə'rɪdiəm] *n., pl.* **-id•i•a** [-'rɪdiə]. the part of a fern, moss, etc. that produces male reproductive cells. ⟨< NL *antheridium.* dim of Gk. *anthēra* anther. See ANTHER.⟩ **—,an•ther'id•i•al,** *adj.*

an•ther•o•zoid [,ænθərə'zouɪd] *or* ['ænθərə,zɔid] *n.* a male reproductive cell produced in the antheridium of a fern, moss, etc. ⟨< NL *anthera* < Gk. *antheros* blooming + *zoion* animal⟩

an•the•sis [æn'θisɪs] *n.* the maturing of flower stamens. ⟨< Gk. *anthesis* < *anthein* to bloom < *anthos* flower⟩

ant•hill or **ant hill** ['ænt,hɪl] *n.* **1** a heap of dirt piled up by ants around the entrance to their underground nest. **2** a termite nest.

antho– *prefix.* flower: *anthocarpous.*

an•tho•car•pous [,ænθə'kɑrpəs] *adj.* of or being a fruit like a strawberry, formed from the enlarged ovaries of one or several blossoms. ⟨< Gk. *anthos* flower + *karpos* harvest⟩

an•tho•cy•a•nin [,ænθou'saiənɪn] *n.* any of various red or blue pigments found in plants and certain insects. ⟨< Gk. *anthos* flower + *kyanos* dark blue⟩

an•tho•di•um [æn'θoudiəm] *n.* the head of a composite plant. ⟨< NL < Gk. *anthodes* flowerlike < *anthos* flower⟩

an•thol•o•gist [æn'θɒlədʒɪst] *n.* a person who makes an anthology.

an•thol•o•gize [æn'θɒlə,dʒaɪz] *v.* **-gized, -giz•ing.** compile an anthology of or publish in an anthology: *Her poems have never been anthologized.*

an•thol•o•gy [æn'θɒlədʒi] *n., pl.* **-gies.** a collection of poems or prose selections from various authors. ⟨< L < Gk. *anthologia* < *anthos* flower + *legein* gather⟩ **—,an•tho'log•i•cal,** *adj.* **—,an•tho'log•i•cal•ly,** *adv.*

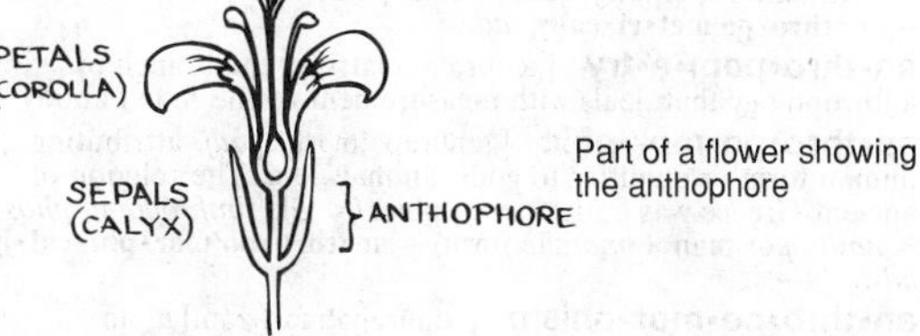

Part of a flower showing the anthophore

an•tho•phore ['ænθə,fɔr] *n.* an elongated stalk separating the calyx and corolla of a flower.

-anthous *combining form.* flowered.

an•tho•zo•an [,ænθə'zouən] *n.* any of a class (Anthozoa) of flowerlike marine animals having a body that is shaped somewhat like a cylinder, closed above and below by disks of tissue, the upper disk surrounded by a circle of hollow tentacles and having a mouth in the centre. Sea anemones and corals are anthozoans. ⟨< Gk. *anthos* flower + *zōa* animals⟩

an•thra•cene ['ænθrə,sin] *n.* a colourless, crystalline, complex compound of hydrogen and carbon. It is obtained by distilling coal tar and is used in making alizarin dyes. *Formula*: $C_{14}H_{10}$ ⟨< Gk. *anthrax* live coal⟩

an•thra•cite ['ænθrə,səit] *n.* a hard, shiny, black type of coal containing a high percentage of carbon and a low percentage of moisture, that burns with very little smoke. ⟨< L < Gk. *anthrakitēs* coal-like < *anthrax* live coal⟩ **—,an•thra'cit•ic** [-'sɪtɪk], *adj.*

an•thrac•nose [æn'θræknous] *n.* any of various fungus diseases of plants that form spores which break through the surface as blackish spots, chiefly on fruit and leaves, sometimes destroying whole crops. ⟨< Gk. *anthrax* carbuncle, live coal + *nosos* disease⟩

an•thra•coid ['ænθrə,kɔɪd] *adj.* like coal or charcoal.

an•thra•co•sis [,ænθrə'kousɪs] *n.* BLACK LUNG. ⟨< Gk. *anthrax* coal + E *-osis*⟩

an•thra•nil•ic acid [,ænθrə'nɪlɪk] a crystalline compound; an ingredient of certain dyes and medicines. *Formula*: $NH_2C_6H_4COOH$ ⟨< *anthra(cene)* + *anil(ine)* + *-ic*⟩

an•thra•qui•none [,ænθrəkwɪ'noun] *or* [,ænθrə'kwɪnoun] *n.*

a yellow, crystalline solid used to make dyes. ⟨< *anthra(cene)* + *quinone*⟩

an•thrax ['ænθræks] *n., pl.* **an•thra•ces** ['ænθrə,siz]. **1** an infectious, often fatal, disease of cattle, sheep, etc. that may be transmitted to human beings. **2** one of the lesions caused by this disease. ⟨< LL < Gk. *anthrax* carbuncle, live coal⟩

anthropo– *combining form.* of human beings, as in *anthropology, anthropometry.* ⟨< Gk. *anthrōpos* man⟩

an•thro•po•cen•tric [,ænθrəpə'sɛntrɪk] *adj.* **1** from the point of view of human beings. **2** placing human beings and their values at the centre of the universe. **—,an•thro•po'cen•trism,** *n.*

an•thro•po•gen•e•sis [,ænθrəpə'dʒɛnəsɪs] *n.* the study of the origin and development of the human species. **—,an•thro•po•ge'net•ic,** *adj.* **—,an•thro•po'gen•ic,** *adj.*

an•thro•pog•ra•phy [,ænθrə'pɒgrəfi] *n.* the science of the distribution of human populations on the basis of various anthropological characteristics such as language, cultural phenomena, physical traits, etc.

an•thro•poid ['ænθrə,pɔɪd] *adj., n.* *—adj.* humanlike; used especially with reference to members of the ape family. Also, **anthropoidal.**
—n. APE (def. 1). ⟨< Gk. *anthrōpoeidēs* < *anthrōpos* man⟩

an•thro•poi•de•a [,ænθrə'pɔɪdiə] *n. Zoology.* a suborder of mammals, including monkeys, baboons, apes, and humans.

an•thro•po•log•i•cal [,ænθrəpə'lɒdʒɪkəl] *adj.* of or having to do with anthropology. **—,an•thro•po'log•i•cal•ly,** *adv.*

an•thro•pol•o•gist [,ænθrə'pɒlədʒɪst] *n.* a person trained in anthropology, especially one whose work it is.

an•thro•pol•o•gy [,ænθrə'pɒlədʒi] *n.* the science that deals with the origin, development, and customs of people. **Physical anthropology** deals with the physiological and anatomical evolution and the racial classifications of humans; **cultural anthropology** deals with the social development, practices, and beliefs of humans.

an•thro•po•met•ric [,ænθrəpə'mɛtrɪk] *adj.* of or having to do with anthropometry. Also, **anthropometrical.** **—,an•thro•po'met•ri•cally,** *adv.*

an•thro•pom•e•try [,ænθrə'pɒmətri] *n.* the branch of anthropology that deals with measurement of the human body.

an•thro•po•mor•phic [,ænθrəpə'mɔrfɪk] *adj.* attributing human form or qualities to gods, animals, etc. The religion of ancient Greece was anthropomorphic. ⟨< Gk. *anthrōpomorphos* < *anthrōpos* man + *morphē* form⟩ **—,an•thro•po'mor•phi•cal•ly,** *adv.*

an•thro•po•mor•phism [,ænθrəpə'mɔrfɪzəm] *n.* an attributing of human form or qualities to gods or things.

an•thro•po•mor•phize [,ænθrəpə'mɔrfaɪz] *v.,* **-ized, -iz•ing.** attribute a human form or quality to (gods or things).

an•thro•po•mor•pho•sis [,ænθrəpə'mɔrfəsɪs] *n.* a metamorphosis into human shape.

an•thro•po•mor•phous [,ænθrəpə'mɔrfəs] *adj.* like a human being in form.

an•thro•pop•a•thy [,ænθrə'pɒpəθi] *n.* the attributing of human emotions and passions to gods, things, etc.

an•thro•poph•a•gy [,ænθrə'pɒfədʒi] *n.* cannibalism. ⟨< Gk. < *anthropos* man + *phagein* consume⟩

an•thro•po•pho•bia [,ænθrəpə'foubiə] *n.* an abnormal fear of people.

anti ['ænti] *n., pl.* **-tis;** *adj., prep. Informal. —n.* a person opposed to some plan, idea, political party, etc.
—adj. contrary: *He is anti by nature.*
—prep. against: *anti everything new.* (See ANTI-)
☛ *Hom.* ANTE.

anti– ['ænti] *prefix.* **1** against; opposed to ——: *anti-aircraft = against aircraft; anti-administration = opposed to the administration.* **2** not; the opposite of ——: *antisocial = the opposite of social; antiwarlike = not warlike.* **3** rival ——: *antipope = rival pope.* **4** preventing or counteracting ——: *antirust = preventing or counteracting rust.* **5** preventing, curing, or alleviating ——: *antiscorbutic = preventing, curing, or alleviating scurvy.* **6** having the appearance but not the true traits of ——: *antihero.* Also, **ant-** before vowels and *h.* ⟨< Gk. *anti-* < *anti,* prep.⟩
☛ *Usage.* **Anti-,** in this dictionary, is hyphenated only before root words beginning with a vowel and before proper nouns and proper adjectives: *anti-intellectual, anti-Confederation, anti-American.*
☛ *Pronun.* The pronunciation given here ['ænti] (or ['æntɪ]) is still the standard pronunciation in Canada. However, the variant pronunciation ['æntaɪ], which is more typical of usage in the United States, is now making headway in Canada, especially in certain words, such as **antisocial** [,æntaɪ'souʃəl]. The same trend can be seen in certain words beginning with **semi-** and **multi-.**
☛ *Hom.* ANTE-.

an•ti–air•craft ['ænti 'ɛr,kræft] *adj.* used in defence against enemy aircraft. *Abbrev.:* AA or A.A.

an•ti–at•om ['ænti ,ætəm] *n.* an atom of antimatter.

an•ti•bac•te•ri•al [,æntibæk'tiriəl] *adj.* counteracting or destroying bacteria.

an•ti•bal•lis•tic missile [,æntibə'lɪstɪk] a ballistic missile designed to intercept and destroy other ballistic missiles in flight.

an•ti•ba•ry•on [,ænti'bæriən] *or* [-'bɛriən] *n. Physics.* the antiparticle of the baryon.

an•ti•bi•o•sis [,æntibaɪ'ousɪs] *n. Biology.* an association of two organisms that is detrimental to either one. Compare SYMBIOSIS. ⟨< NL < Gk. *anti* against + Med.L *biosis* < Gk. way of life < *bios* life⟩

an•ti•bi•ot•ic [,æntibaɪ'ɒtɪk] *n. adj. —n.* a product of an organism that destroys or weakens harmful micro-organisms. Penicillin is an antibiotic.
—adj. **1** of or relating to ANTIBIOSIS. **2** of, relating to, or containing an antibiotic or antibiotics.

an•ti•bod•y ['æntɪ,bɒdi] *n., pl.* **-bod•ies.** any of various proteins produced in the blood of animals or humans in reaction to foreign substances called antigens, to provide immunity to diseases. Different antibodies are produced in reaction to different antigens.

an•tic ['æntɪk] *n.* **1** Often, **antics,** *pl.* a grotesque gesture or action; a silly trick: *The clown amused us by his antics.* **2** *Archaic.* a clown. ⟨< Ital. *antico* old (with sense of *grottesco* grotesque) < *antiquus* ancient⟩

an•ti•cho•lin•er•gic [,ænti,koulɪ'nɜrdʒɪk] *adj.* **a** of a drug, preventing the action of acetylcholine. **b** of or having to do with such a drug: *Anticholinergic effects include dry mouth, blurred vision, and constipation.* ⟨< Gk. *anti* against + *chole* bile + *ergon* work⟩

An•ti•christ ['ænti,kraɪst] *n. Christianity.* **1** the great enemy or opponent of Christ, expected by some Christians to set himself against Christ just before the Second Coming of Christ. **2** one who denies or opposes Christ. **3** one who sets himself up as Christ.

an•tic•i•pate [æn'tɪsə,peit] *v.* **-pat•ed, -pat•ing. 1** look forward to; expect: *She had anticipated a good vacation in the mountains; but when the time came, she was sick.* **2** do, make, or use in advance: *The Chinese anticipated some modern discoveries.* **3** take care of ahead of time: *The nurse anticipated all the patient's wishes.* **4** be before (another) in thinking, acting, etc. **5** consider or mention (something) before the proper time. **6** cause to happen sooner; hasten. ⟨< L *antecipare* < *ante-* before + *capere* take⟩ **—an'ti•ci,pa•tor,** *n.*

an•tic•i•pa•tion [æn,tɪsə'peiʃən] *n.* **1** the act of looking forward; expectation: *The settler cut more wood than usual in anticipation of a long winter.* **2** enjoyment in looking forward to something: *They were waiting for the holidays with great anticipation.* **3** action beforehand that provides for, takes into account, or prevents a later action or occurrence. **4** recognition, realization, or accomplishment beforehand. **5** *Genetics.* the observed tendency of many inherited diseases to appear at earlier ages in successive generations. **6** *Music.* the sounding of a note before the chord to which it belongs. Compare SUSPENSION (def. 7).

an•tic•i•pa•tive [æn'tɪsəpətɪv] *or* [æn'tɪsə,peitɪv] *adj.* involving anticipation; having a tendency to anticipate.

an•tic•i•pa•to•ry [æn'tɪsəpə,tɔri] *adj.* anticipating. **—an,ti•ci•pa'to•ri•ly,** *adv.*

an•ti•cler•i•cal [,ænti'klɛrəkəl] *adj.* opposed to the influence of the church and clergy, especially in public affairs.

an•ti•cler•i•cal•ism [,ænti'klɛrəkə,lɪzəm] *n.* opposition to the influence of the church and clergy, especially in public affairs. **—,an•ti'cler•i•cal•ist,** *n.*

an•ti•cli•mac•tic [,æntiklaɪ'mæktɪk] *adj.* of or like an anticlimax. **—,an•ti•cli'mac•ti•cal•ly,** *adv.*

an•ti•cli•max [,ænti'klaɪmæks] *n.* **1** an abrupt descent from the important to the trivial. *Example:* "Alas! Alas! what shall I do? I've lost my wife and best hat, too!" **2** a descent (in importance, interest, etc.) contrasting with a previous rise.

an•ti•cli•nal [,æntɪ'klaɪnəl] *adj.* of or like an anticline.

an•ti•cline ['æntɪ,klaɪn] *n. Geology.* an arch of stratified rock, in which the layers slope downward in opposite directions from the centre. Compare SYNCLINE. See SYNCLINE for picture. ⟨< *anti-* + Gk. *klinein* lean; modelled on *incline*⟩

an•ti•cli•no•ri•um [,æntıklaı'nɔriəm] *n. Geology*. a large formation which is anticlinal overall but is made up of a series of anticlinal and synclinal structures.

an•ti•co•ag•u•lant [,æntikou'ægjələnt] *n., adj. —n.* a substance or agent that prevents or slows up the clotting of blood, used in the treatment of certain heart diseases, etc.
—adj. preventing or delaying coagulation.

an•ti•co•lo•ni•al•ism [,æntikə'louniə,lızəm] *n.* opposition to the system whereby one country rules another as a colony.

an•ti•com•mun•ist or **an•ti–Com•mun•ist** [,ænti'kɒmjənıst] *n., adj. —n.* a person who is opposed to the principles and practices of communism.
—adj. opposed to communism.

an•ti•con•vul•sant [,æntikən'vʌlsənt] *n., adj. —n.* a substance or agent that prevents, or alleviates the effects of, convulsions.
—adj. preventing, or alleviating the effects of, convulsions. Also, **anticonvulsive**.

an•ti•cy•clone [,ænti'səikloun] *n.* **1** an area in which winds rotate around and away from a centre of high pressure, which also moves. **2** an atmospheric disturbance at the fringes of such an area.

an•ti•cy•clon•ic [,æntisəi'klɒnık] *adj.* of or having to do with an anticyclone.

an•ti•de•pres•sant [,æntidı'prɛsənt] *adj., n. —adj.* relieving depression.
—n. a drug that relieves depression.

an•ti•do•tal ['æntı,doutəl] *or* [,æntı'doutəl] *adj.* like an antidote; serving as an antidote.

an•ti•dote ['æntı,dout] *or* ['ænti,dout] *n.* **1** a medicine or remedy that counteracts a poison: *Milk is an antidote for some poisons.* **2** anything that counteracts or relieves: *The plants and paintings served as an antidote to the impersonal atmosphere of the waiting room.* ⟨< L < Gk. *antidoton* (thing) given against < *anti* against + *didonai* give⟩

an•ti•drom•ic [,æntı'drɒmık] *adj. Physiology*. that conducts neural impulses in body tissue in a direction reverse to the norm. ⟨< Gk. *anti* against + *dromos* a running⟩

an•ti•dump•ing [,ænti'dʌmpıŋ] *adj. Economy.* of or having to do with laws, agreements, tariffs, etc., that ensure that imported goods will not be sold at a lower price than in the country of origin.

an•ti–e•lec•tron [,æntiə'lɛktrɒn] *n.* positron.

an•ti–en•er•gis•tic [,ænti,ɛnər'dʒıstık] *adj.* that resists applied energy.

an•ti•fe•brile [,ænti'fibraıl], [-'fibrəl], *or* [-'fɛbrəl] *adj., n.*
—adj. counteracting fever.
—n. an antifebrile drug.

an•ti•freeze ['ænti,friz] *n.* a substance added to a liquid to lower its freezing point. Glycol is much used as an antifreeze in automobile radiators.

an•ti•fric•tion [,ænti'frıkʃən] *n.* a substance that prevents or reduces friction.

an•ti•gen ['æntədʒən] *n.* any substance that stimulates the production of antibodies or that reacts with antibodies that have already been formed. Bacteria, viruses, and other micro-organisms are sources of antigens. ⟨< *anti*(*body*) + *-gen*⟩ **—,an•ti'gen•ic,** *adj.*

antigen complex MAJOR HISTOCOMPATIBILITY COMPLEX.

An•tig•o•ne [æn'tıgəni] *n. Greek mythology.* a daughter of Oedipus. She gave her dead brother a proper burial against the orders of her uncle; when he condemned her to be buried alive, she took her own life.

an•ti•gra•vi•ty [,ænti'grævəti] *n., adj. —n. Physics.* a hypothetical force countering the force of gravity.
—adj. acting against gravity.

anti–G suit [,ænti 'dʒi] clothing for pilots and astronauts to aid circulation of the blood, which tends to pool at the extremities as an effect of rapid acceleration. Also, **G-suit.** ⟨< Gk. *anti* against + gravity + suit⟩

an•ti•he•ro ['ænti,hirou] *n.* a person in a novel, play, etc. who, though the central character, has none of the qualities normally expected of a hero.

an•ti•he•ro•ic [,æntihı'rouık] *adj., n. —adj.* opposed to the traditional or conventional idea of heroism; unlike a conventional hero or conventional heroic literature.
—n. **1** an imitation, satire, burlesque, etc. composed to ridicule conventional or traditional heroism. **2** a mock-heroic poem, verse, etc. **3 antiheroics,** writings or actions that ridicule the traditional or conventional idea of heroism.

an•ti•her•o•ine [,ænti'hɛrouın] *n.* a woman in a novel, play, etc. who, though the central character, has none of the qualities normally expected of a heroine.

an•ti•his•ta•mine [,ænti'hıstə,min] *or* [-'hıstəmın] *n.* a medicine used in the treatment of colds and allergies by neutralizing histamine. **—,an•ti,his•ta'min•ic** [,ænti,hıstə'mınık], *adj.*

an•ti–in•fla•tion [,ænti ın'fleiʃən] *adj.* counteracting INFLATION (def. 4): *an anti-inflation act*. **—,an•ti-in'fla•tion•ary,** *adj.*

an•ti•knock [,ænti'nɒk] *n., adj. —n.* a substance added to the fuel of an internal-combustion engine to reduce noise caused by too rapid combustion.
—adj. serving to reduce such noise.

an•ti•lep•ton [,ænti'lɛptɒn] *n.* an antiparticle of the LEPTON[2].

an•ti•lith•ic [,ænti'lıθık] *adj., n. Medicine*. *—adj.* counteracting the development of kidney stones, gallstones, etc.
—n. a substance that has an antilithic effect.

an•ti•log ['ænti,lɒg] *n.* antilogarithm.

an•ti•log•a•rithm [,ænti'lɒgə,rıðəm] *n.* a number corresponding to a given logarithm; the result of raising a base to the power expressed by a logarithm. The antilogarithms of the logarithms 1, 2, and 3 to the base 10 are 10, 100, and 1000.

an•til•o•gy [æn'tılədʒi] *n.* contradiction of ideas or terms.

an•ti•ma•cas•sar [,æntimə'kæsər] *n.* a small covering to protect the back or arms of a chair, chesterfield, etc. ⟨< *anti-* against + *macassar*, a hair oil from Macassar⟩

an•ti•mag•net•ic [,æntimæg'nɛtık] *adj.* resistant to magnetism by virtue of special construction or composition.

an•ti•ma•lar•i•al [,æntimə'lɛriəl] *adj., n. —adj.* counteracting malaria.
—n. an antimalarial substance.

an•ti•mask, an•ti•maske, or **an•ti•masque** ['ænti,mæsk] a performance during, and being an inverted form of, a masque, popular in Europe from the 15th to the 17th century.

an•ti•mat•ter ['ænti,mætər] *n.* a hypothetical form of matter composed of antiparticles.

an•ti•mere ['æntə,mir] *n. Zoology*. on a symmetrical animal, one of a pair of corresponding body parts. ⟨< Gk. *anti* against + *meros* part⟩ **—,an•ti'mer•ic** [-'mɛrık], *adj.*

an•ti•me•tab•o•lite [,æntimə'tæbə,ləit] *n.* a biochemical substance that is the counterpart of a metabolite, with which it competes for a given enzyme in order to slow down metabolism.

an•ti•mi•cro•bi•al [,æntiməi'kroubiəl] *adj., n. —adj.* destroying microbes or inhibiting their growth.
—n. an antimicrobial substance.

an•ti•mis•sile [,ænti'mısaıl] *or* [-'mısəl] *adj.* for use in defence against ballistic missiles, rockets, etc.

anti–missile missile a ballistic missile for destroying other missiles in flight.

an•ti•mon•ic [,æntı'mɒnık] *adj.* containing or having to do with pentavalent antimony.

an•ti•mon•ous ['æntəmənəs] *adj.* containing or having to do with trivalent antimony.

an•ti•mo•ny ['æntə,mouni] *n.* a crystalline, metallic chemical element having a bluish white lustre, that occurs chiefly in combination with other elements. It is used mainly in alloys to make them harder and in medicinal compounds. *Symbol*: Sb; *at.no.* 51; *at.mass* 121.75 ⟨< Med.L *antimonium*⟩ **—,an•ti'mo•ni•al,** *adj.*

an•ti•mo•nyl ['æntımə,nıl] *n.* anything containing the monovalent group SbO.

antimony potassium tartrate TARTAR EMETIC.

an•ti•neu•tri•no [,æntinju'trinou] *or* [,æntinu'trinou] *n.* an antiparticle of the neutrino.

an•ti•neu•tron [,ænti'njutrɒn] *or* [-'nutrɒn] *n.* the antiparticle of the neutron, having the same mass, etc. and an equal but opposite magnetic effect.

an•ti•node ['ænti,noud] *n.* the point of maximum amplitude of a STANDING WAVE between two of its adjacent nodes.

an•ti•no•mi•an [,ænti'noumiən] *adj., n.* —*adj.* of the doctrine that faith and divine grace obviate the need for any moral law. —*n.* a person who holds this belief. **—,an•ti'no•mi•an,ism,** *n.*

an•tin•o•my [æn'tɪnəmi] *n.* **1** opposition or contradiction between two laws or principles within a single one. **2** *Philosophy.* a paradox. ⟨< L *antimonia* < Gk. *anti* against + *nomos* law⟩

an•ti–nov•el ['ænti ,nɒvəl] *n.* a novel-length work of fiction that lacks most of the basic features of the traditional novel, such as character development or plot. ⟨translation of F *anti-roman.* 20c.⟩

an•ti•nu•cle•ar [,ænti'njukliər] *or* [,ænti'nukliər] *adj.* opposing the use of nuclear energy, whether for military use or as a source of domestic power: *an antinuclear demonstration.*

an•ti•nu•cle•on [,ænti'njukli,ɒn] *or* [-'nukli,ɒn] *n.* an antiproton or antineutron.

an•ti–nuke [,ænti 'njuk] *or* [-'nuk] *adj. Slang.* antinuclear. **—,an•ti-'nu•ker,** *n.*

an•ti•ox•i•dant [,ænti'ɒksədənt] *n.* any substance that inhibits oxidation, used in foods, rubber, soap, etc. to retard deterioration.

an•ti•par•al•lel [,ænti'pærə,lɛl] *or* [,ænti'pɛrə,lɛl] *adj.* **1** of vectors, parallel but pointing in opposite directions. **2** of two lines, intersecting two other lines so as to form a quadrilateral whose interior opposite angles are supplementary.

an•ti•par•ti•cle ['ænti,pɑrtəkəl] *n.* an elementary particle having the same mass as a given particle but having an electric charge or magnetic effect, etc. of equal magnitude but opposite sign. If a particle collides with an antiparticle, both are annihilated. See ANTIMATTER, ANTINEUTRON, ANTIPROTON, POSITRON.

an•ti•pas•to [,æntɪ'pæstou]; *Italian,* [,anti'pasto] *n., pl.* **-tos.** an Italian dish consisting of fish, meats, pickled vegetables, etc., served as an appetizer; hors d'oeuvres. ⟨< Ital.⟩

an•tip•a•thet•ic [æn,tɪpə'θɛtɪk] *or* [,æntɪpə'θɛtɪk] *adj.* having antipathy; contrary or opposed in nature or disposition: *Dogs and cats are antipathetic.* **—,an•ti•pa'thet•i•cal•ly,** *adj.*

an•tip•a•thet•i•cal [æn,tɪpə'θɛtəkəl] *or* [,æntɪpə'θɛtəkəl] *adj.* antipathetic.

an•tip•a•thy [æn'tɪpəθi] *n., pl.* **-thies.** a strong or fixed dislike; a feeling against. ⟨< L < Gk. *antipatheia* < *anti* against + *-patheia* < *pathos* feeling⟩

an•ti•pe•ri•od•ic [,ænti,piri'ɒdɪk] *adj., n.* —*adj.* preventing the periodic recurrence of a disease.
—*n.* an antiperiodic drug or substance.

an•ti•per•son•nel [,ænti,pɜrsə'nɛl] *adj. Military.* directed against persons rather than against mechanized equipment, supplies, etc.

an•ti•per•spi•rant [,ænti'pɜrspərənt] *n., adj.* —*n.* an astringent applied to the skin to check perspiration.
—*adj.* checking perspiration.

an•ti•phlo•gis•tic [,æntiflə'dʒɪstɪk] *adj., n.* —*adj.* preventing or relieving inflammation.
—*n.* an antiphlogistic drug or substance.

an•ti•phon ['æntə,fɒn] *n.* **1** a psalm, hymn, or prayer sung or chanted in alternate parts. **2** verses sung or chanted in response in a worship service. **3** anything sung or spoken responsively. ⟨< LL < Gk. *antiphōna* sounding in response < *anti* opposed to + *phōnē* sound. Doublet of ANTHEM.⟩

an•tiph•o•nal [æn'tɪfənəl] *adj., n.* —*adj.* like an antiphon; sung or chanted alternately.
—*n.* a book of antiphons. **—an'tiph•o•nal•ly,** *adv.*

an•ti•pho•ny [æn'tɪfəni] *n.* **1** *Music.* a clashing of sounds or the harmony resulting from this. **2** *Music.* a singing or intoning in alternation. **3** any reply or echo.

an•tip•o•dal [æn'tɪpədəl] *adj.* **1** on the opposite side of the earth. **2** directly opposite; exactly contrary.

an•ti•pode ['æntə,poud] *n.* **1** anything exactly opposite; direct opposite. **2** sing. of ANTIPODES.

an•tip•o•de•an [æn,tɪpə'diən] *adj.* antipodal.

an•tip•o•des [æn'tɪpə,diz] *n.pl.* **1** two places on directly opposite sides of the earth: *The North Pole and the South Pole are antipodes.* **2** a place on the opposite side of the earth. **3** two opposites or contraries: *Forgiveness and revenge are antipodes.* **4** the direct opposite. ⟨< L < Gk. *antipodes,* pl. of *antipous* < *anti* opposite to + *pous* foot⟩

☛ *Usage.* **Antipodes** is plural in form and plural or singular in use for defs. 2 and 4.

an•ti•pope ['ænti,poup] *n.* a pope set up by a rival group in opposition to the official pope.

an•ti•pro•ton [,ænti'proutɒn] *n.* the antiparticle of the proton, having the same mass, etc. as the proton and an equal but opposite electric charge.

an•ti•psy•cho•tic [,æntisəi'kɒtɪk] *n., adj.* —*n.* any drug used to treat psychotic states such as schizophrenia.
—*adj.* of such a drug.

an•ti•py•ret•ic [,æntipaɪ'rɛtɪk] *adj., n.* —*adj.* checking or preventing fever.
—*n.* any medicine or remedy for checking or preventing fever.

An•ti•py•rine [,æntɪ'paɪrin] *or* [-rɪn] *Trademark, n.* a sedative white crystalline powder used to counteract pain and fever, especially in treating inflammation of the middle ear. *Formula:* $C_{11}H_{12}N_2O$

an•ti•quar•i•an [,æntə'kwɛriən] *adj., n.* —*adj.* **1** having to do with antiques or antiquaries: *The antiquarian section of the museum was full of old furniture and pottery.* **2** having to do with old or rare books.
—*n.* an antiquary. **—,an•ti'quar•i•an,ism,** *n.*

an•ti•quar•y ['æntə,kwɛri] *n., pl.* **-quar•ies.** a student or collector of relics from ancient times. ⟨< L *antiquarius*⟩

an•ti•quate ['æntə,kweit] *v.* **-quat•ed, -quat•ing. 1** make old-fashioned; make out-of-date. **2** cause to look like an antique. ⟨< L *antiquare* < *antiquus* ancient⟩ **—,an•ti'qua•tion,** *n.*

an•ti•quat•ed ['æntə,kweitəd] *adj., v.* —*adj.* **1** old-fashioned; out-of-date. **2** too old for work, service, etc.
—*v.* pt. and pp. of ANTIQUATE.

an•tique [æn'tik] *adj., n., v.* **-tiqued, -tiquing.** —*adj.* **1** of a manufactured object, made in an earlier period, especially more than 100 years ago. **2** exhibiting or selling antique objects: *an antique auction.* **3** of, belonging to, or existing since times long ago; ancient. **4** in the style of former times: *antique manners. An antique gold finish is dull and slightly greenish.* **5** old-fashioned; out-of-date: *an antique hat.*
—*n.* **1** a manufactured object made in an earlier period. To antique dealers an antique is more than 100 years old. Canada Customs defines an antique as being more than 50 years old. **2** any object or relic of ancient times. **3 the antique,** an antique style in art, especially that of ancient Greece or Rome: *the proportions of the antique.* **4** *Printing.* a style of type in which the lines are of equal thickness throughout. This sentence is in antique.
—*v.* **1** make (furniture, etc.) look antique by finishing or refinishing in an antique style. **2** hunt for or collect antiques. ⟨< L *antiquus* < *ante* before⟩

an•tiq•ui•ty [æn'tɪkwəti] *n., pl.* **-ties. 1** oldness; great age. **2** times long ago; early ages of history. Antiquity usually refers to the period from 5000 B.C. to A.D. 476. **3** people of long ago. **4 antiquities,** *pl.* **a** things from times long ago. **b** the customs and life of olden times.

an•ti•ra•chit•ic [,æntirə'kɪtɪk] *adj.* preventing or curing rickets.

an•tir•rhi•num [,æntə'raɪnəm] *n.* any of a large genus (*Antirrhinum*) of plants of the figwort family, such as the snapdragon. ⟨< L < Gk. *anti* like + *rhis, rhinos* nose⟩

an•ti•scor•bu•tic [,æntiskɔr'bjutɪk] *adj., n.* —*adj.* preventing or curing scurvy.
—*n.* a remedy for scurvy.

an•ti–Sem•ite [,ænti 'sɛməit] *or* [,ænti 'siməit] *n.* a person who is anti-Semitic.

an•ti–Se•mit•ic [,ænti sə'mɪtɪk] *adj.* having or showing dislike or hatred for Jews; prejudiced against Jews. **—,an•ti-Se'mit•i•cal•ly,** *adv.*

☛ *Usage.* **Anti-Semitic.** This and the following word are based on a misunderstanding, since Jews form only one group of Semites. Other Semitic peoples include the Arabs, Syrians, etc.

an•ti–Sem•i•tism [,ænti 'sɛmə,tɪzəm] *n.* a dislike or hatred of Jews; prejudice against Jews.

☛ *Usage.* See note at ANTI-SEMITIC.

an•ti•sep•sis [,æntɪ'sɛpsɪs] *n.* **1** the prevention of infection. **2** a method or medicine that prevents infection. **3** the absence of infection-causing bacteria; the condition of being antiseptic.

an•ti•sep•tic [,æntɪ'sɛptɪk] *adj., n.* —*adj.* **1** preventing infection. **2** using antiseptics. **3** clinically free from contaminants; sterile. **4** lacking vitality; detached.
—*n.* a substance that prevents infection. Iodine, peroxide, alcohol, and boric acid are antiseptics. ⟨< NL *antisēpticus* < Gk. *anti* + *septikós* < *sepein* rot⟩

an•ti•sep•ti•cal•ly [ˌæntɪ'sɛptɪkli] *adv.* **1** by the use of antiseptics. **2** in an antiseptic way.

an•ti•se•rum ['æntɪˌsirəm] *n.* a serum containing antibodies for a given antigen, used for immunization or treatment.

an•ti•slav•er•y [ˌænti'sleivəri] *adj.* opposed to slavery; against slavery.

an•ti•so•cial [ˌænti'souʃəl] *adj.* **1** of, having to do with, or designating behaviour that violates the generally accepted rules of social interaction, personal and property rights, etc.: *acting out one's antisocial feelings. Spreading disease, stealing, and murder are antisocial acts.* **2** unsociable: *They're rather antisocial and don't like parties.* **—ˌan•ti'so•cial•ly,** *adv.*

an•ti•spas•mod•ic [ˌæntispæz'mɒdɪk] *adj., n. —adj.* preventing or curing spasms.
—n. a drug to prevent or cure spasms.

an•ti•stat•ic [ˌænti'stætɪk] *adj.* countering the effect of static electricity by preserving enough moisture to conduct the charge.

an•tis•tro•phe [æn'tɪstrəfi] *n.* **1** a part of an ancient Greek ode sung by the chorus when moving from left to right. **2** a stanza following a strophe and usually in the same metre. Compare STROPHE. ⟨< LL < Gk. *antistrophē* a turning about < *anti* against + *strephein* turn⟩ **—ˌan•ti'stroph•ic** [-'strɒfɪk], *adj.*

an•ti•tank [ˌænti'tæŋk] *adj. Military.* designed for use against armoured vehicles, especially tanks. *Abbrev.:* AT

an•tith•e•sis [æn'tɪθəsɪs] *n., pl.* **-ses** [-ˌsiz]. **1** the direct opposite: *Hate is the antithesis of love.* **2** a contrast of ideas, expressed by parallel arrangements of words, clauses, etc. *Example*: *"To err is human; to forgive, divine."* **3** the second half of such an arrangement, the first part being the thesis.
4 opposition; contrast *(of* or *between*): *antithesis of theory and fact.* ⟨< L < Gk. *antithesis* < *anti* against + *tithenai* set⟩

an•ti•thet•i•cal [ˌæntə'θɛtɪkəl] *adj.* **1** of or using antithesis. **2** contrasted; opposite. Also, **antithetic.**
—ˌan•ti'thet•i•cal•ly, *adv.*

an•ti•tox•ic [ˌænti'tɒksɪk] *adj.* **1** counteracting diseases or poisoning caused by toxins. **2** having to do with or like an antitoxin.

an•ti•tox•in [ˌænti'tɒksɪn] *n.* **1** a substance formed in the body to counteract a disease or poison. **2** a serum containing antitoxin. Diphtheria antitoxin, obtained from the blood of horses infected with diphtheria, is injected into the bloodstream to make a person immune to diphtheria, or to treat a person if already infected.

an•ti•trades [ˌænti'treidz] *n.* the winds that blow in the opposite direction to that of the trade winds, on a level above them in the tropic zone and at the earth's surface in the temperate zones.

an•ti•trust [ˌænti'trʌst] *adj.* opposed to the formation of large corporations that control the trade practices of certain kinds of business: *antitrust laws.*

an•ti•type ['æntiˌtəip] *n.* a person or symbol prefigured in an earlier type: *Noah's Ark is sometimes seen as an antitype of the Resurrection.*

an•ti•u•ni•verse [ˌænti'junəˌvɜrs] *n.* a hypothetical universe in outer space, composed of antimatter.

an•ti•ut•il•i•tar•ian [ˌæntijʊˌtɪlɪ'tɛriən] *adj., n. —adj.* not utilitarian.
—n. a person who is opposed to utilitarianism.

an•ti•ven•in [ˌænti'vɛnɪn] *n.* an antitoxin to counteract a particular venom, especially snake venom.

an•ti•vi•ral [ˌænti'vaɪrəl] *adj.* counteracting or destroying viruses.

an•ti•vi•ta•min [ˌænti'vəitəmɪn] *n.* **1** any substance that prevents or inhibits the absorption of a vitamin. **2** an enzyme that destroys vitamins.

an•ti•viv•i•sec•tion [ˌæntiˌvɪvə'sɛkʃən] *n.* opposition to the practice of vivisection, that is, cutting into or experimenting on living animals for scientific study.

an•ti•viv•i•sec•tion•ist [ˌæntiˌvɪvə'sɛkʃənɪst] *n.* a person opposed to the practice of vivisection.

ant•ler ['æntlər] *n.* **1** a branched horn of a deer or similar animal. **2** a branch of such a horn. ⟨ME *auntelere* < OF *antoillier*⟩

ant•lered ['æntlərd] *adj.* having antlers.

antlerless season *Cdn.* an open season in which young deer may be hunted legally.

ant lion **1** any of several insects of the family Myrmeleontidae found in North America and Europe, resembling a dragonfly and having short antennae and four narrow wings usually marked with brown or black. The larva of the ant lion catches small insects for food by lying in wait in a pit it has dug and seizing any insect that falls or slides in. **2** the larva of the ant lion.

an•to•nym ['æntəˌnɪm] *n.* a word that means the opposite of another word: Right *is the antonym of* wrong. *Abbrev.*: ant. Compare SYNONYM. ⟨< Gk. *antonymia* < *anti* opposite to + (dialectal) *onyma* word⟩ **—an'ton•y•mous** [æn'tɒnəməs] or **ˌan•to'nym•ic,** *adj.*

an•trorse [æn'trɔrs] *adj. Biology.* pointing to the top or front. ⟨< NL *antrarsus* < L *antr-* + *orsus* < *anterior* before + *introrsus* < **introversus* toward the inside⟩

an•trum ['æntrəm] *n., pl.* **-trums** or **-tra.** *Anatomy.* a cavity, passage or hollow, especially in a bone. ⟨< L < Gk. *antron* cave⟩

A number 1 *Informal.* A-one; first-class.

a•nu•ran [ə'njurən] *or* [ə'nurən] *n., adj. —n.* a member of the order Anura, which consists of frogs and toads.
—adj. of or relating to the anurans. ⟨< Gk. *a* without + *oura* tail + -AN⟩

an•u•re•sis [ˌænjʊ'risɪs] *n.* **1** a condition in which elimination of urine is partially or totally blocked. **2** sometimes, anuria. ⟨< NL < Gk. *a* without + *ouresis* urination < *ourein* urinate < *ouron* urine⟩ **—ˌan•u'ret•ic** [-'rɛtɪk], *adj.*

a•nu•ri•a [ə'njuriə] *n.* partial or total inability to secrete urine, due to kidney failure. ⟨< NL < Gk. *a* not + *ourein* urinate > *ouron* urine⟩ **—an'u•ric,** *adj.*

an•ur•ous [ə'njurəs] *or* [ə'nurəs] *adj.* having no tail.

a•nus ['einəs] *n.* the opening at the lower end of the alimentary canal. ⟨< L *anus*, originally, ring⟩

an•vil ['ænvəl] *n.* **1** an iron or steel block on which metals are hammered and shaped. **2** the incus of the ear. ⟨OE *anfilt*⟩

anx•i•e•ty [æŋ'zaɪəti] *or* [æŋk'saɪəti] *n., pl.* **-ties. 1** uneasy thoughts or fears about what may happen; a troubled, worried, or uneasy feeling: *We all felt anxiety when the airplane was caught in a hurricane.* **2** eager desire: *anxiety to succeed.* **3** *Psychiatry.* a state of abnormal fear or mental tension. ⟨< L *anxietas* < *anxius* troubled. See ANXIOUS.⟩

anx•i•o•lyt•ic [ˌæŋksiə'lɪtɪk] *adj., n. —adj.* relieving anxiety.
—n. an anxiolytic drug. ⟨< L *anxietas* < *anxius* anxious + Gk. *lyticos* loosing, dissolving⟩

anx•ious ['æŋkʃəs] *or* [ˌæŋʃəs] *adj.* **1** uneasy because of thoughts or fears of what may happen; troubled; worried.
2 causing or full of uneasy feelings or troubled thoughts: *an anxious moment.* **3** eagerly desiring; wishing very much: *The girl was anxious for a new bicycle.* ⟨< L *anxius* troubled < *angere* choke, cause distress⟩ **—'anx•ious•ly,** *adv.* **—'anx•ious•ness,** *n.*

☛ *Syn.* **3.** See note at EAGER.

☛ *Usage.* **Anxious.** The phrase is **anxious for** when 'eagerly desiring' is meant: *He is anxious for news of her.* When 'worried' is meant, the phrases are **anxious about,** referring to the subject of worry, and **anxious at,** referring to its cause: *Her mother was anxious about her. They became anxious at her delay.*

an•y ['ɛni] *adj., pron., adv. —adj.* **1** one (no matter which) out of many: *Any book will do. You can come any day, but you really must come some day.* **2** some (*used in questions, with negatives, and with words like* **seldom** *and* **hardly**): *Have you any fresh fruit? They seldom have any visitors. We don't have any fresh fruit.*
3 every: *Any child knows that.* **4** even one; even the smallest amount (*used with negatives and verbs of exclusion like* **forbid** *or* **refuse**): *He was forbidden to go to any movie.*
—pron. **1** some (*used in questions, with negatives, and with words like* **seldom** *and* **hardly**): *I need more paper; do you have any? I asked him for some paper, but he didn't have any.* **2** no matter which one(s): *Take any that you want.* **3** even one: *I asked three questions and didn't get an answer to any of them.*
—adv. to any extent or degree; at all (*used in questions, with negatives, and in conditional clauses.*): *Has the sick child improved any? If she leans over any farther, she'll fall.* ⟨OE *ǣnig*⟩

an•y•bod•y ['ɛniˌbʌdi] *or* ['ɛniˌbɒdi] *pron. or n., pl.* **-bod•ies.**
1 any person; anyone: *Has anybody been here?* **2** any important person: *Is she anybody?*

an•y•how ['ɛniˌhaʊ] *adv.* **1** in any way whatever: *The answer is wrong anyhow you look at it.* **2** in any case; at least: *I can see as well as you, anyhow.* **3** carelessly; in ways that are not right and proper: *He does his work anyhow.*

any more or **an•y•more** ['ɛni 'mɔr] *adv.* these days or any longer (*used with negatives, in conditional clauses, and in questions with a negative connotation*): *That book is not available any more. Who ever walks to work any more? If you want to play here any more, you'll have to learn to obey the rules.*

☛ *Usage.* **Any more** is used only in negative, interrogative, and conditional constructions in most of Canada. In certain regions, however, it is also quite commonly used informally in positive constructions with the meaning 'these days': *That's the trouble with the world any more.*

an•y•one ['ɛni,wʌn] *or* ['ɛniwən] *pron.* any person; anybody.

an•y•place ['ɛni,pleis] *adv. Informal.* anywhere.

an•y•thing ['ɛni,θɪŋ] *pron., n., adv. –pron.* any thing.
–n. a thing of any kind whatever.
anything but, not in the least; in no way: *anything but poor.*
like anything, with great enthusiasm or expense of effort: *He ran like anything to escape the tiger.*
–adv. at all: *Is he anything like his brother?*

an•y•time ['ɛni,taɪm] *adv.* at any time: *Feel free to drop in anytime.*

an•y•way ['ɛni,wei] *adv.* **1** in any way whatever. **2** in any case; at least: *I am coming anyway, no matter what you say.* **3** carelessly; in ways not right and proper.
☛ *Usage.* The form *anyways* is usually regarded as non-standard.

an•y•where ['ɛni,wɛr] *adv.* **1** in, at, or to any place. **2** at any point in some range of quantities: *The price could be anywhere from 50 to 100 dollars. I guess his age to be anywhere between 30 and 50.*
get anywhere, *Informal.* succeed to any extent: *She's not getting anywhere with that paper topic.*

an•y•wise ['ɛni,waɪz] *adv.* in any way; to any degree; at all.

An•zac ['æn,zæk] *n.* **1** a soldier in the Australian and New Zealand Army Corps of World War I. **2** any Australian or New Zealand soldier. ⟨an acronym for *A*ustralia and *N*ew *Z*ealand *A*rmy *C*orps⟩

A/O or **a/o** *Accounting.* account of.

A–O.K. or **A–OK** [,ei ou'kei] *adj. or adv. Informal.* perfectly O.K.; working, functioning, etc. very well: *Everything is A-O.K. now.* Also, **A-okay.**

A–one ['ei 'wʌn] *adj. Informal.* first-rate; first-class; excellent. Also, **A-1.**

a•o•rist ['eiərɪst] *n.* **1** one of the past tenses of Greek verbs, showing that an action took place at some time in the past without indicating whether the act was completed, repeated, or continued. **2** a tense having a similar form or purpose in other languages. **3** a verb form in the aorist. ⟨< Gk. *aoristos* < *a-* not + *horos* boundary⟩

a•or•ta [ei'ɔrtə] *n., pl.* **-tas** or **-tae** [-ti] *or* [-taɪ]. the main artery that carries the blood from the left side of the heart and, with its branches, distributes it to all parts of the body except the lungs. See HEART and KIDNEY for pictures. ⟨< NL or Med.L < Gk. *aortē* that which is hung⟩

a•or•tic [ei'ɔrtɪk] *adj.* having to do with the aorta. Also, **aortal.**

a•ou•dad ['aʊ,dæd] *n.* a large wild sheep (*Ammotragus lervia*) of N Africa having characteristics of both sheep and goats; Barbary sheep. ⟨< F < Berber *audad*⟩

ap–[1] the form of AD- before *p*, as in *apprehend.*

ap–[2] the form of APO- before vowels and *h*, as in *aphelion.*

Ap. April.

AP Associated Press.

a•pace [ə'peis] *adv.* swiftly; quickly; fast.

A•pach•e [ə'pætʃi] *n., pl.* **Apache** or **Apaches;** *adj. –n.* **1** a member of a group of American Indians of the SW U.S. **2** any of the Athapascan languages spoken by these peoples. *–adj.* of or having to do with the Apache or their languages. ⟨apparently < Am.Sp. *ápachu* enemy⟩

a•pache [ə'pɑʃ] *or* [ə'pæʃ] *n.* one of a band of gangsters of Paris, Brussels, etc. ⟨< F; special use of *Apache*⟩

ap•a•nage ['æpənɪdʒ] See APPANAGE.

a•part [ə'pɑrt] *adv., adj. –adv.* **1** to pieces; in pieces; in or into separate parts: *Take the watch apart.* **2** away from each other: *Keep the dogs apart.* **3 a** to one side; aside: *He stood apart from the others.* **b** out of consideration; excluded: *These few criticisms apart, it is a fine essay.* **4** away from others; independently: *View each idea apart.*
–adj. (never used before a noun) distinct; unique: *a people apart, a class apart.*
apart from, except for: *Apart from a little stiffness, she felt no ill effects.*
tell apart. See TELL. ⟨ME < OF *à part* aside⟩

a•part•heid [ə'pɑrt,heit] *or* [ə'pɑrt,həit] *n.* formerly, in South Africa, the policy of economic and political segregation of the native people as a principle of society upheld by law; racial segregation. Compare BAASSKAP. ⟨< Afrikaans⟩

a•part•ment [ə'pɑrtmənt] *n.* a self-contained room or rooms to live in. ⟨< F < Ital. *appartamento*, ult. < *a parte* apart⟩

apartment block **1** APARTMENT BUILDING. **2** a series of similar apartment buildings built close together by the same developer.

apartment building a building containing a number of apartments.

apartment house APARTMENT BUILDING.

ap•a•tet•ic [,æpə'tɛtɪk] *adj.* of the colouring of an animal, protecting by camouflage. ⟨< Gk. *apatetikos* deceiving < *apate* deceit⟩

ap•a•thet•ic [,æpə'θɛtɪk] *adj.* **1** with little interest in or desire for action; indifferent. **2** lacking in feeling. **–,ap•a'thet•i•cal•ly,** *adv.*

ap•a•thy ['æpəθi] *n., pl.* **-thies. 1** a lack of interest in or desire for activity; indifference: *The miser heard the old beggar's story with apathy.* **2** a lack of feeling. ⟨< L < Gk. *apatheia* < *a-* without + *pathos* feeling⟩
☛ *Syn.* **1.** See note at INDIFFERENCE.

ap•a•tite ['æpə,təit] *n.* a mineral consisting mainly of calcium phosphate, that occurs in the form of crystals or granular masses and is the main constituent of bones and teeth. *Formula:* $Ca_5(F,Cl,OH,\frac{1}{2}CO_3)\ (PO_4)_3$ ⟨< Gk. *apatē* deceit + E *-ite*, so called because its various forms were often wrongly identified⟩
☛ *Hom.* APPETITE.

ape [eip] *n., v.* **aped, ap•ing.** *–n.* **1** any of the family of tailless primates that most resemble humans, having hairless hands, feet, and faces, long front limbs and short hind limbs, and showing a tendency to stand almost erect. Chimpanzees, gibbons, gorillas, and orangutans are apes. **2** any primate other than a human being. **3** a large, clumsy or boorish person. **4** a mimic.
go ape, *Slang.* become crazy or wildly enthusiastic: *to go ape over a new style of music. He went ape for a while, but has settled down now.*
–v. imitate; mimic. ⟨OE *apa*⟩ **–'ape,like,** *adj.*

APEC or **A.P.E.C.** Atlantic Provinces Economic Council.

a•pep•si•a [ei'pɛpsiə] *n.* faulty digestion; dyspepsia. ⟨< NL < Gk. *apepsia* < *a-* not + *peptein* to digest⟩

a•per•çu [,æpər'su]; *French,* [apɛʀ'sʏ] *n.* **1** a brief glimpse or impression. **2** a short summary.

a•pe•ri•ent [ə'piriənt] *adj. or n.* laxative. ⟨< L *aperiens, -entis,* ppr. of *aperire* open⟩

a•pe•ri•od•ic [,eipiri'ɒdɪk] *adj.* **1** not periodic; irregular. **2** *Physics.* having irregular vibrations.

a•per•i•tif [ə,pɛrə'tif]; *French,* [apeʀi'tif] *n.* an alcoholic drink taken before a meal to stimulate the appetite. ⟨< F *apéritif*⟩

ap•er•ture ['æpərtʃər] *or* ['æpər,tʃʊr] *n.* **1** an opening; gap; hole. **2** in a camera, telescope, etc.: **a** the opening through which light passes. **b** the diameter of such an opening. ⟨< L *apertura* < *aperire* open. Doublet of OVERTURE.⟩

a•pet•al•ous [ei'pɛtələs] *adj.* having no petals.

a•pex ['eipɛks] *n., pl.* **a•pex•es** or **ap•i•ces** [-,siz]. **1** the highest point; peak; tip: *the apex of a triangle.* **2** climax. ⟨< L⟩

Ap•gar score ['æpgɑr] a rating given to infants immediately after birth, based on reflexes, respiration, cry, and other vital signs, with a maximum score of ten.

aph•a•nite ['æfə,nəit] *n.* rock of such fine grain that the naked eye cannot distinguish the individual crystals. ⟨< Gk. *aphanes* invisible < *a* not + *phainein* to appear⟩ **–,aph•a•'nit•ic** [-'nɪtɪk], *adj.*

a•pha•sia [ə'feiʒə] *or* [ə'feiziə] *n.* a total or partial loss of the ability to use or understand words, usually caused by injury or disease that affects the brain. ⟨< NL < Gk. *aphasia* < *a-* not + *phanai* speak⟩

a•pha•si•ac [ə'feizi,æk] *adj., n.* aphasic.

a•pha•sic [ə'feizɪk] *adj., n. –adj.* of, having to do with, or characterized by aphasia.
–n. a person affected with aphasia.

a•phe•li•on [ə'filiən] *n., pl.* **-lions** or **-li•a** [-liə]. the point in the orbit of a planet or other heavenly body where it is farthest from the sun. Compare PERIHELION. ⟨< NL *aphelium* < Gk. *apo-* away from + *hēlios* sun⟩

a•phe•li•ot•ro•pism [ə,fili'ɒtrə,pɪzəm] *n. Botany.* a tendency to grow away from sunlight. **–a,phe•li•o'trop•ic,** *adj.*

a•pher•e•sis or **a•phaer•e•sis** [ə'fɛrəsɪs] *or* [ˌæfə'risɪs] *n.* the dropping of a syllable or part of a syllable at the beginning of a word. ⟨< Gk. *aphaerein* remove⟩ **—ˌaph•e'ret•ic** [ˌæfə'rɛtɪk], *adj.*

aph•e•sis ['æfəsɪs] *n.* an instance of apheresis in which the sound dropped is a short, unstressed initial vowel. ⟨< Gk.⟩ **—a'phet•ic** [ə'fɛtɪk], *adj.* **—a'phet•i•cal•ly,** *adv.*

a•phid ['eifɪd] *or* ['æfɪd] *n.* any of a family (*Aphidae*) of tiny insects having a soft, pear-shaped body and a tube-shaped mouth adapted for piercing the stems, leaves, etc. of plants and sucking the juices. ⟨< NL *aphis, aphidis*⟩

a•phis ['eifɪs] *or* ['æfɪs] *n., pl.* **aph•i•des** ['eifəˌdiz] *or* ['æfəˌdiz]. **1** any of a genus (*Aphis*) of aphids; the plant louse. **2** any aphid.

a•pho•ni•a [ə'founiə] *or* [ei'founiə] *n.* loss of the voice. ⟨< Gk. *a-* without + *phone* sound⟩ **—a'phon•ic** [ə'fɒnɪk], *adj.*

aph•o•rism ['æfəˌrɪzəm] *n.* **1** a terse sentence expressing a general thought; maxim; proverb. *Example*: *"A bird in the hand is worth two in the bush."* **2** a concise statement of a principle. ⟨< LL < Gk. *aphorismos* definition < *apo-* off + *horos* boundary⟩
☛ *Usage.* See note at EPIGRAM.

aph•o•rist ['æfərɪst] *n.* a person who composes or uses aphorisms.

aph•o•ris•tic [ˌæfə'rɪstɪk] *adj.* of, containing, or like an aphorism or aphorisms. **—ˌaph•o'ris•ti•cal•ly,** *adv.*

aph•o•rize ['æfəˌraɪz] *v.* **-rized, -riz•ing.** compose aphorisms; write or speak in aphorisms.

a•phot•ic [ə'fɒtɪk] *or* [eɪ'foutɪk] *adj.* **1** growing without light. **2** designating that part of the ocean (below 100 m) reached by insufficient light for photosynthesis to take place. ⟨< Gk. *a* without + *phos, photos* light⟩

aph•ro•dis•i•ac [ˌæfrə'diziæk] *or* [ˌæfrə'dɪziæk] *adj., n.* *—adj.* arousing or increasing sexual desire.
—n. any drug, food, etc. that arouses or increases sexual desire. ⟨< Gk. *aphrodīsiakós* < *aphrodīsios* of Aphrodite, the goddess of love⟩

aph•ro•di•te [ˌæfrə'dəiti] *n.* a large brown northeastern North American butterfly (*Speyeria aphrodite*) with silver spots.

Aph•ro•di•te [ˌæfrə'dəiti] *n. Greek mythology.* the goddess of love and beauty, corresponding to the Roman goddess Venus.

a•phyl•lous [ə'fɪləs] *or* [ei'fɪləs] *adj.* without leaves. ⟨< Gk. *a* without + *phyllon* leaf⟩

a•pi•a•ceous [ˌeipi'eiʃəs] *adj. Botany.* bearing an umbel or umbels. ⟨< NL *apiaceae* < L *apium* celery, parsley⟩

a•pi•an ['eipiən] *adj.* of or having to do with bees.

a•pi•ar•i•an [ˌeipi'ɛriən] *adj.* of bees or the care of bees.

a•pi•a•rist ['eipiərɪst] *n.* a person who keeps bees.

a•pi•ar•y ['eipiˌɛri] *n., pl.* **-ar•ies.** a place where bees are kept; group of beehives. ⟨< L *apiarium* < *apis* bee⟩

a•pi•cal ['æpəkəl] *or* ['eipəkəl] *adj., n.* *—adj.* **1** of the apex; at the apex; forming the apex. **2** *Phonetics.* of a sound, made with the tip or apex of the tongue, such as [t].
—n. Phonetics. a sound so made.

ap•i•ces ['eipəˌsiz] *or* ['æpəˌsiz] *n.* a pl. of APEX.

a•pic•u•late [ə'pɪkjəlɪt] *or* [ə'pɪkjəˌleit] *adj.* of leaves, ending abruptly, in a short, distinct point. ⟨< NL *apiculatus* < *apiculus* tip, dim. of L *apex, apicis* apex⟩

a•pi•cul•ture ['eipəˌkʌltʃər] *n.* the raising and care of bees; beekeeping. ⟨< L *apis* bee + E *culture*⟩ **—ˌa•pi'cul•tur•al,** *adj.* **—ˌa•pi'cul•tur•ist,** *n.*

a•piece [ə'pis] *adv.* for each one; each: *These apples are forty cents apiece.*

à pied [a'pje] *French.* on foot.

ap•i•pho•bia [ˌæpɪ'foubiə] *n.* an abnormal fear of bees.

A•pis ['eipɪs] *n.* the sacred bull worshipped by the ancient Egyptians.

ap•ish ['eipɪʃ] *adj.* **1** like an ape. **2** senselessly imitative. **3** rough; clumsy. **4** foolish; silly. **—'ap•ish•ly,** *adv.*

a•pi•vo•rous [ei'pɪvərəs] *adj.* bee-eating, as certain birds.

APL *Computer technology.* a high-level, very concise computer programming language used especially in solving mathematical problems. ⟨< *A P*rogramming *L*anguage⟩

a•pla•cen•tal [ˌeiplə'sɛntəl] *adj.* having no placenta: *Marsupials are aplacental.*

ap•la•nat•ic [ˌæplə'nætɪk] *adj.* of a lens, mirror, etc. made free of spherical aberration which would cause distortion of the image. ⟨< Gk. *aplanetos* < *a* not + *planan* to wander⟩

A–plane ['ei ˌplein] *n.* an aircraft driven by atomic energy.

a•plas•tic anemia [ei'plæstɪk] anemia caused by the failure of the bone marrow to generate new blood cells. ⟨< Gk. *a* not + NL *plasia* < Gk. *plasis* moulding < *plassein* to mould⟩

a•plen•ty [ə'plɛnti] *adv. Informal.* in plenty.

a•plomb [ə'plɒm] *n.* complete self-confidence and assurance; poise. ⟨< F *aplomb* < *à plomb* according to the plummet⟩

ap•ne•a ['æpniə] *n.* a temporary failure to breathe, occasionally lasting long enough to cause unconsciousness: *Apnea is common during sleep.* ⟨< NL < Gk. *apnoia* < *a* without + *pnoie* wind⟩

apo– *prefix.* from; away; quite, as in *apostasy.* Also, **ap-**, before vowels and *h.* ⟨< Gk.⟩

ap•o•ap•sis [ˌæpou'æpsɪs] *n. Astronomy.* in the orbit of a celestial body, the point farthest from the centre of gravity.

a•poc•a•lypse [ə'pɒkəˌlɪps] *n.* **1** a revelation. **2 the Apocalypse,** the last book of the New Testament; the book of Revelation. ⟨< L *apocalypsis* < Gk. *apokalypsis* < *apo-* off, un- + *kalyptein* cover⟩

a•poc•a•lyp•tic [əˌpɒkə'lɪptɪk] *adj.* **1** of the Apocalypse. **2** like a revelation; giving a revelation. Also, **apocalyptical.** **—aˌpoc•a'lyp•ti•cal•ly,** *adv.*

ap•o•chro•mat•ic [ˌæpoukrə'mætɪk] *or* [ˌæpə-] *adj.* of a lens, mirror, etc., free from distortions of colour or shape.

a•poc•o•pate [ə'pɒkəˌpeit] *v.,* **-at•ed, -at•ing.** subject to apocope. **—aˌpoc•o'pa•tion,** *n.*

a•poc•o•pe [ə'pɒkəpi] *n.* the dropping out of the last sound, syllable, or letter in a word. *Th'* for *the* and *i'* for *in* are examples of apocope. ⟨< L < Gk. *apokopē* < *apo-* off + *koptein* cut⟩

ap•o•crine ['æpəˌkraɪn] *or* ['æpəkrɪn] *adj.* designating a glandular secretion involving loss of part of the secreting cell along with the secretion. ⟨< *apo* from + Gk. *krinein* to separate⟩

A•poc•ry•pha [ə'pɒkrəfə] *n.pl.* **1** fourteen books found in a Greek Bible of the 3rd century B.C. Eleven of them are included in the Roman Catholic Bible though none are included in the Jewish or, usually, the Protestant Bibles. **2 apocrypha,** any writings or statements of doubtful authorship or authority. ⟨ME < LL *apocrypha,* neut. pl. of *apocryphus* < Gk. *apokryphos* hidden < *apo-* from + *kryptein* hide⟩

a•poc•ry•phal [ə'pɒkrəfəl] *adj.* **1** of doubtful authorship or authority. **2** false; counterfeit. **3 Apocryphal,** of the Apocrypha.

ap•o•cyn•thi•on [ˌæpə'sɪnθiən] *n.* the point in the lunar orbit of an earth-launched spacecraft where it is farthest from the moon. Compare PERICYNTHION, APOLUNE, and PERILUNE. ⟨< *apo-* + *-cynthion* < *Cynthia* (goddess of) the moon⟩

ap•od ['æpəd] *adj., n.* *—adj.* apodal.
—n. an apodal animal. ⟨< Gk. *apous, apodos* footless < *a* without + *pous* foot⟩

ap•o•dal ['æpədəl] *adj.* having no feet, legs, or pelvic fins. Also, **apodous.**

ap•o•dic•tic [ˌæpə'dɪktɪk] *adj. Logic.* **1** demonstrably true. **2** necessarily true. ⟨< LL *apodicticus* < Gk. *apodeikticos* proving clearly < *apodeiknynai* to show by argument < *apo* from + *deiknynai* to show⟩ **—ˌap•o'dic•ti•cal•ly,** *adv.*

a•pod•o•sis [ə'pɒdəsɪs] *n.* in a conditional sentence, the clause expressing the result of the condition: *In* If the sun shines, we will go, we will go *is the apodosis.* ⟨< Med.L < Gk. giving back < *apo* from + *didonai* to give⟩

ap•o•en•zyme [ˌæpou'ɛnzaɪm] the protein constituent of an enzyme.

a•pog•a•my [ə'pɒgəmi] *n. Botany.* generation of a new individual without fusion of gametes. **—ˌap•o'gam•ic, a'pog•a•mous,** *adj.*

ap•o•gee ['æpəˌdʒi] *n.* **1** the point in orbit of a satellite of the earth or an orbiting vehicle where it is farthest from the centre of the earth. Compare PERIGEE. **2** the farthest or highest point. ⟨< F *apogée* < Gk. *apogaion* < *apo-* away from + *gē* or *gaia* earth⟩ **—ˌap•o'ge•an,** *adj.*

ap•o•ge•ot•ro•pism [ˌæpədʒi'ɒtrəˌpɪzəm] *n. Botany.* an inclination to grow away from the force of gravity or from the earth.

à point [a 'pwɛ̃] *French.* just right; just enough. A good chef cooks each dish *à point.*

a•po•lit•i•cal [ˌeipə'lɪtəkəl] *adj.* not concerned with politics or political issues: *an apolitical decision.* **—ˌa•po'lit•i•cally,** *adv.*

A•pol•lo [ə'pɒlou] *n., pl.* **-los. 1** *Greek and Roman mythology.* the god of the sun, poetry, music, prophecy, and healing. The Greeks and Romans considered Apollo the highest type of youthful, manly beauty. He was the first Greek god accepted by the Romans. **2** any extremely handsome young man.

A•poll•yon [ə'pɒljən] *n.* the Devil. ⟨< New Testament Gk., destroying < *apollyein* destroy < *apo-* from + *lyein* loose⟩

a•pol•o•get•ic [ə,pɒlə'dʒɛtɪk] *adj., n. —adj.* **1** making an apology; expressing regret or offering an excuse for a fault or failure: *an apologetic reply.* **2** suggesting uncertainty; unsure: *She answered the principal in an apologetic voice.* **3** defending by speech or writing.
—n. **1** a systematic defence of a doctrine, etc. **2 apologetics,** the branch of theology that deals with the rational defence of a religious faith (*used with a singular verb*). **—a,pol•o'get•i•cal•ly,** *adv.*

ap•o•lo•gi•a [,æpə'loudʒiə] *n.* a statement in defence or justification; apology. ⟨< L < Gk.⟩

a•pol•o•gist [ə'pɒlədʒɪst] *n.* a person who defends an idea, belief, religion, etc. in speech or writing.

a•pol•o•gize [ə'pɒlə,dʒaɪz] *v.* **-gized, -giz•ing. 1** make an apology; express regret; acknowledge a fault; offer an excuse. **2** make a defence in speech or writing. **—a'pol•o,giz•er,** *n.*

ap•o•logue ['æpə,lɒg] *n.* a fable with a moral: *Aesop's fables are apologues.* ⟨< F < L < Gk. *apologos* story, tale < *apo* off + *logos* discourse⟩

a•pol•o•gy [ə'pɒlədʒi] *n., pl.* **-gies. 1** words of regret for an offence or accident; acknowledgment of a fault or failure; the act of expressing regret and asking pardon: *to make an apology.* **2** a systematic defence of a doctrine, etc.; an explanation of the truth or justice of something: *He presented an effective apology for his course of action.* **3** a poor substitute: *It wasn't a dinner at all, but only an apology for one.* ⟨< LL < Gk. *apologia* a speech in defence, ult. < *apo-* off + *legein* speak⟩
☛ *Syn.* **1.** See note at EXCUSE.

ap•o•lune ['æpə,lun] *n.* the point in the lunar orbit of a moon-launched spacecraft where it is farthest from the moon. Compare PERILUNE, APOCYNTHION, and PERICYNTHION. ⟨< *apo-* + *-lune* < L *luna* moon⟩

ap•o•mix•is [,æpə'mɪksɪs] *n., pl.* **-mix•es** [-'mɪksiz]. asexual reproduction of plants by any of various means. ⟨< NL < Gk. *apo* from + *mixis* a mingling⟩ **—,ap•o'mic•tic** [-'mɪktɪk], *adj.*

ap•o•mor•phine [,æpə'mɔrfin] *n.* an alkaloid derivative of morphine used as an emetic and expectorant.

ap•o•neu•ro•sis [,æpounju'rousɪs] *or* [,æpounu'rousɪs] *n.* a fibrous tissue that attaches muscles to bones. ⟨< Gk.⟩

ap•o•phthegm ['æpə,θɛm] See APOTHEGM.

a•poph•y•ge [ə'pɒfədʒi] *n. Architecture.* the curve at the bottom or top of a column where it flares into the base or capital. ⟨< Gk. *apopheugein* flee away < *apo-* from + *pheugein* flee⟩

ap•o•plec•tic [,æpə'plɛktɪk] *adj.* **1** of, having to do with, or causing apoplexy. **2** suffering from or showing symptoms of apoplexy. **3** of an emotional reaction, likely to bring on apoplexy; extreme: *an apoplectic rage.* **—,ap•o'plec•ti•cal•ly,** *adv.*

ap•o•plex•y ['æpə,plɛksi] *n.* cerebrovascular accident; stroke. ⟨< LL < Gk. *apoplēxia* < *apo-* off, from + *plēssein* strike⟩

a•port [ə'pɔrt] *adv. Nautical.* to the port side; to the left.

ap•o•se•mat•ic [,æpousɪ'mætɪk] *adj.* of an animal's colouring, protecting by warning off predators. ⟨< Gk. *apo* from + *sema, sematos* sign⟩ **—,ap•o•se'mat•i•cal•ly,** *adv.*

ap•o•si•o•pe•sis [,æpə,saɪə'pisɪs] *n.* a sudden breaking off in mid-sentence as though unable to bring oneself to utter what follows; a rhetorical device. ⟨< L < Gk. *aposiopesis* < *aposiopan* to be silent < *apo* from + *siopan* to be silent⟩

ap•o•spor•y ['æpə,spɔri] *or* [ə'pɒspəri] *n. Botany.* a form of apomixis in which the sporophyte does not form spores before developing into a gametophyte.

a•pos•ta•sy [ə'pɒstəsi] *n., pl.* **-sies.** a complete forsaking of one's religion, faith, political ideology, or principles. ⟨ME < LL < Gk. *apostasia* < *apo-* away from + *stanai* stand⟩

a•pos•tate [ə'pɒsteit] *or* [ə'pɒstɪt] *n., adj. —n.* a person who completely forsakes religion, faith, political ideology, or principles.
—adj. guilty of apostasy.

a•pos•ta•tize [ə'pɒstə,taɪz] *v.* **-tized, -tiz•ing.** forsake completely one's religion, faith, party, or principles.

a pos•te•ri•o•ri ['ei pɒs,tiri'ɔraɪ] *or* ['æ pɒs,tiri'ɔri] from effect to cause; from particular cases to a general rule; based on actual observation or experience. ⟨< Med.L *a posteriori* from what comes after⟩

a•pos•til [ə'pɒstɪl] *n.* a note in the margin. ⟨< F *apostille* < *à* to + *postille* marginal note < Med.L *postilla* < L *post illa* after these⟩

a•pos•tle [ə'pɒsəl] *n.* **1 Apostle,** one of the twelve disciples, **the Apostles,** chosen by Christ to go forth and preach the gospel to all the world. **2** any early Christian leader or missionary: *Paul was frequently called the "Apostle to the Gentiles."* **3** the first Christian missionary to any country or region. **4** a leader of any reform movement or belief. **5** in the Mormon Church, one of the council of twelve administrative officials. ⟨OE < LL < Gk. *apostolos* messenger < *apo-* off + *stellein* send⟩

Apostles' Creed *Christianity.* the statement of belief that contains the fundamental doctrines of Christianity, beginning "I believe in God, the Father..." In its present form it dates back to about A.D. 600 and was formerly supposed to have been composed by the Apostles.

a•pos•to•late [ə'pɒstələt] *or* [ə'pɒstə,leit] *n.* **1** the office or work of an apostle. **2** the time during which an apostle is active.

ap•os•tol•ic [,æpə'stɒlɪk] *adj.* **1** of or having to do with any apostle. **2** of the Apostles; having to do with the Apostles. **3** according to the beliefs and teachings of the Apostles. **4** of or having to do with the Pope; papal. Also, **apostolical.**
—a,pos•to'lic•i•ty [ə,pɒstə'lɪsəti], *n.*

Apostolic Fathers 1 a group of early Christian authors who lived very soon after the Apostles. **2** the writings attributed to these authors, written probably between A.D. 95 and 150.

Apostolic See the bishopric of the Pope.

apostolic succession especially in Roman Catholic, Greek Orthodox, and Anglican churches, the unbroken line of succession from the Apostles down to the present-day bishops and priests, by which it is held that religious authority has been transmitted.

a•pos•tro•phe¹ [ə'pɒstrəfi] *n.* a sign (') used: **a** to show the omission of one or more letters in contractions and abbreviations, as in *o'er* for *over, thro'* for *through.* **b** to show the possessive forms of nouns or indefinite pronouns, as in *Julie's book, the lions' den, everybody's business.* **c** to form certain plurals, as in *2 o's, four 9's in 9999.* **d** to show that certain sounds represented in the usual spelling have not been spoken: *'lectric.* ⟨< F < LL < Gk. *apostrophos* a turning away, omission (mark) < *apostrephein* avert, get rid of. See APOSTROPHE².⟩

a•pos•tro•phe² [ə'pɒstrəfi] *n.* the addressing of words to an absent person as if he or she were present or to a thing or idea as if it could understand and appreciate the words. *Example*: *"Western wind, when wilt thou blow."* ⟨< LL < Gk. *apostrophē* < *apostrephein* < *apo-* away from + *strephein* turn⟩
—,ap•os'troph•ic [,æpə'strɒfɪk], *adj.*

a•pos•tro•phize [ə'pɒstrə,faɪz] *v.* **-phized, -phiz•ing.** in a speech, poem, etc., address (some thing or absent person), usually with emotion: *The poet apostrophizes judgment in these words: "Oh, judgment! thou art fled to brutish beasts."*

apothecaries' measure a system of units for measuring volume, traditionally used by pharmacists. One fluid ounce in apothecaries' measure is equal to about 28.4 cm³.

60 minims = 1 fluid dram
8 fluid drams = 1 fluid ounce
20 fluid ounces = 1 pint
8 pints = 1 gallon

apothecaries' weight a system of units for measuring mass, traditionally used by pharmacists. One ounce in apothecaries' weight is equal to about 31.1 g.

20 grains = 1 scruple
3 scruples = 1 dram
8 drams = 1 ounce
12 ounces = 1 pound

a•poth•e•car•y [ə'pɒθə,kɛri] *n., pl.* **-car•ies.** *Archaic.* pharmacist; druggist. ⟨ME < LL *apothecarius* warehouseman < L *apotheca* storehouse < Gk. *apothēkē* < *apo-* away + *tithenai* put⟩

ap•o•thegm ['æpə,θɛm] *n.* a short, forceful saying; maxim. *Example*: *"Beauty is only skin-deep."* Also, **apophthegm.** ⟨< Gk. *apophthegma* < *apo-* forth + *phtheggesthai* utter⟩
—,ap•o•theg'mat•ic, *adj.*
☛ *Hom.* APOTHEM.

ap•o•them ['æpə,θɛm] *n.* the line perpendicular to any side of

a regular polygon joining it with the centre. ⟨< NL < Gk. *apo* from + *thema* what is placed⟩
☛ *Hom.* APOTHEGM.

a•poth•e•o•sis [ə,pɒθi'ousɪs] *or* [,æpə'θiəsɪs] *n., pl.* **-ses.** **1** the raising of a human being to the rank of a god; deification: *The apotheosis of the emperor became a Roman custom.* **2** glorification; exaltation. **3** a glorified ideal. ⟨< L < Gk. *apotheosis,* ult. < *apo-* + *theos* god⟩

a•poth•e•o•size [ə'pɒθiə,saɪz] *or* [,æpə'θiə,saɪz] *v.* **-sized, -siz•ing. 1** raise to the rank of a god; deify. **2** glorify; exalt.

ap•o•tro•pa•ic [,æpətrou'peiɪk] *adj.* turning away evil. ⟨< Gk. *apotropaios* turning away < *apotrepein* to turn away < *apo* from + *trepein* to turn⟩ **—,ap•o•tro'pa•i•cal•ly,** *adv.*

app. 1 apparent; apparently. **2** appendix; appended. **3** apprentice. **4** appointed. **5** approved.

ap•pal or **ap•pall** [ə'pɒl] *v.* **-palled, -pall•ing.** fill with horror; dismay; terrify: *We were appalled at the thought of another war. She was appalled when she saw the river had risen to the doorstep.* ⟨ME < OF *apallir* become or make pale < *a-* to (< L *ad-*) + *pale* < L *pallidus.* Related to PALE[1].⟩

ap•pall•ing [ə'pɒlɪŋ] *adj., v. —adj.* dismaying; terrifying; horrifying.
—v. ppr. of APPAL. **—ap'pall•ing•ly,** *adv.*

ap•pa•loo•sa [,æpə'lusə] *n.* a breed of horse having mottled skin, spots or blotches of colour on the rump, and a skimpy tail. ⟨< *a Palouse* horse, named after the Palouse River country in Washington, where the breed is said to have been developed by the Nez Percé nation⟩

ap•pa•nage ['æpənɪdʒ] *n.* **1** land, property, or money set aside to support the younger children of kings, princes, etc. **2** a person's assigned portion; rightful property. **3** something that accompanies; an adjunct: *The millionaire had three houses, a yacht, and all the other appanages of wealth.* **4** a territory controlled by another country. Also, **apanage.** ⟨< F *apanage* < *apaner* give bread to, ult. < L *ad-* to + *panis* bread⟩

ap•pa•rat ['æpə,ræt] *or* [,ɑpə'rɑt] *n.* an organization, usually political, often of a communist party. ⟨< Russian < G < L. See APPARATUS.⟩

ap•pa•ra•tus [,æpə'rætəs] *or* [,æpə'reitəs] *n., pl.* **-tus** or **-tus•es. 1** the things necessary to carry out a purpose or for a particular use: *apparatus for an experiment in chemistry, gardening apparatus, our digestive apparatus.* **2** any complicated device with a particular use. **3** the system which keeps something functioning: *the apparatus of corporate affairs.* ⟨< L *apparatus* preparation < *ad-* + *parare* make ready⟩

ap•par•el [ə'pærəl] *or* [ə'pɛrəl] *n., v.* **-elled** or **-eled, -el•ling** or **-el•ing.** *—n.* clothing; dress.
—v. clothe; dress (up). ⟨ME < OF *apareil* < *apareiller* clothe, ult. < L *ad-* + *par* equal⟩
☛ *Syn.* See note at DRESS.

ap•par•ent [ə'pærənt] *or* [ə'pɛrənt] *adj.* **1** plain to see; so plain as not to be missed: *The flaw in the fabric was quite apparent.* **2** easily understood; obvious to the mind: *It was apparent that she was lying.* **3** according to appearances; seeming: *the apparent motion of the sun. An apparent truth was really a lie.* ⟨ME < OF *aparant,* ppr. of *apareir* < L *apparere.* See APPEAR.⟩ **—ap'par•ent•ness,** *n.*
☛ *Syn.* **1, 2.** See note at OBVIOUS.

ap•par•ent•ly [ə'pærəntli] *or* [ə'pɛrəntli] *adv.* **1** seemingly; as far as one can judge by appearances: *Apparently the baby had chicken pox.* **2** clearly; plainly; obviously: *He had quite apparently hurt his leg.*

ap•pa•ri•tion [,æpə'rɪʃən] *n.* **1** a ghost; phantom. **2** something strange, remarkable, or unexpected that comes into view. **3** the act of appearing; appearance. ⟨< LL *apparitio, -onis* < L *apparere.* See APPEAR.⟩ **—,ap•pa'ri•tion•al,** *adj.*
☛ *Syn.* **1.** See note at GHOST.

ap•par•i•tor [ə'pærɪtər] *or* [ə'pɛrɪtər] in ancient Rome, an officer of a civic or ecclesiastical court whose job was to carry out its orders, call witnesses, etc. ⟨< L *apparitor* public servant⟩

ap•pas•si•on•a•to [ə,pæʃə'nɑtou] *adv. or adj. Music.* with passion.

ap•peal [ə'pil] *v., n. —v.* **1** make an earnest request (*to* or *for*); apply for help, sympathy, etc.: *The children appealed to their mother for help.* **2** *Law.* ask that (a case) be taken to a higher court to be reviewed or heard again. **3** call on some person, or resort to some principle or argument, etc., to persuade someone, justify oneself, or decide some matter in one's favour. **4** be attractive, interesting, or enjoyable: *Blue and red appeal to me, but I don't like grey or yellow.*
—n. **1** an earnest request; call for help, sympathy, etc. **2** *Law.* **a** a request to have a case heard again before a higher court or judge. **b** the right to have a case heard again. **c** the case so heard: *A panel of judges presided over the appeal.* **3** a call on some person, principle, etc. for proof, decision, etc. **4** an attraction; interest: *Sports have little appeal for me.* ⟨ME < OF < L *appellare* accost, alteration of *appellere* < *ad-* up to + *pellere* drive⟩

ap•peal•ing [ə'pilɪŋ] *adj., v. —adj.* attractive; endearing; pleasant.
—v. ppr. of APPEAL. **—ap'peal•ing•ly,** *adv.*

ap•pear [ə'pir] *v.* **1** be seen; come in sight: *One by one the stars appear.* **2** seem; look: *The apple appeared sound on the outside, but it was rotten inside.* **3** be published or otherwise presented to the public: *The book appeared in the fall. The movie will appear soon.* **4** present oneself publicly or formally: *to appear on the stage.* **5** become known or apparent to the mind: *It appears that we must go.* **6** stand before an authority: *to appear in court.* ⟨ME < OF *apareir* < L *apparere* < *ad-* + *parere* come in sight⟩
☛ *Syn.* **2.** See note at SEEM.

ap•pear•ance [ə'pirəns] *n.* **1** the act of appearing: *John's appearance in the doorway, a singer's first appearance in a city.* **2** outward look; aspect: *The appearance of the house made us think that it was empty.* **3** outward show; semblance or pretence: *She found the gift ugly but gave an appearance of grateful pleasure.* **4** a thing that appears in sight; object seen. **5** *Law.* **a** in criminal law, the accused's physical attendance in court to answer the charge or charges against him or her. **b** in civil law, a document advising the court of the defendant's or respondent's intention to participate in the proceedings personally or through a lawyer.
keep up appearances, pretend to others that all is well.
make or **put in an appearance,** appear briefly.
to all appearances, as far as one can tell; supposedly.
☛ *Syn.* **2. Appearance,** ASPECT (def. 2) = the look or looks of a person or thing. **Appearance** is the general word applying to what one sees when looking at someone or something: *The appearance of the city is pleasing.* **Aspect** applies to the appearance at certain times or under certain conditions: *I love the bay in all its aspects, even its stormy, frightening aspect in winter.*

ap•pease [ə'piz] *v.* **-peased, -peas•ing. 1** satisfy (an appetite or desire): *A good dinner will appease your hunger.* **2** make calm; quiet: *to appease a crying child.* **3** give in to the demands of (especially those of a potential enemy): *Hitler was appeased at Munich.* ⟨ME < OF *apaisier* < *a-* to (< L *ad-*) + *pais* peace < L *pax*⟩ **—ap'peas•er,** *n.* **—ap'peas•ing•ly,** *adv.*
☛ *Syn.* **2. Appease,** PACIFY = make calm. **Appease** = calm or quiet a person who is excited or upset by pleasing and contenting him or her: *When he left school to go to work, he had to appease his father.* **Pacify** = quiet people or things that are quarrelling or fighting among themselves or against some condition, by making peace though not necessarily by eliminating the cause of the disturbance: *She pacified the angry mob.*

ap•pease•ment [ə'pizmənt] *n.* **1** an appeasing or being appeased; pacification; satisfaction. **2** the policy of agreeing to the demands of an unfriendly power in order to prevent an outbreak of hostilities.

ap•pel [ə'pɛl] *n. Fencing.* **1** a striking of the ball of the foot against the floor preparatory to lunging at one's opponent; a warning signal. **2** a thrust by which one tries to obtain an opening. ⟨< F, literally, a call⟩

ap•pel•lant [ə'pɛlənt] *n., adj. —n.* a person who appeals.
—adj. **1** having to do with appeals. **2** in the process of appealing.

ap•pel•late [ə'pɛlɪt] *adj.* having to do with appeals. ⟨< L *appellatus,* pp. of *appellare.* See APPEAL.⟩

appellate court a court having the power to re-examine and reverse the decisions of a lower court.

ap•pel•la•tion [,æpə'leiʃən] *n.* **1** a name or title. In *John the Baptist,* John's appellation is *the Baptist.* **2** the act of calling by a name. ⟨< L *appellatio* < pp. of *appellare.* See APPEAL.⟩

ap•pel•la•tive [ə'pɛlətɪv] *n., adj. —n.* **1** a descriptive name. **2** a common noun; one that can be applied to any member of a class.
—adj. that names; naming.

ap•pel•lee [,æpə'li] *or* [əpɛ'li] *n.* appellant.

ap•pend [ə'pɛnd] *v.* add to a larger thing; attach as a supplement: *The amendments to the association's constitution are appended to it.* ⟨< L *appendere* < *ad-* on + *pendere* hang⟩

ap•pend•age [ə'pɛndɪdʒ] *n.* **1** something attached; addition; adjunct. **2** *Biology.* any of various external or subordinate parts. Arms, tails, fins, legs, etc. are appendages.

ap•pend•ant [ə'pɛndənt] *adj., n. —adj.* added; attached in a secondary or subordinate way.
—n. something or someone that is appendant.

ap•pen•dec•to•my [ˌæpɛn'dɛktəmi] *n., pl.* **-mies.** the surgical removal of the vermiform appendix. ⟨< *append(ix)* + *-ectomy* (< Gk. *ek* out of + *-tomia* a cutting < *temnein* cut)⟩

ap•pen•di•ces [ə'pɛndəˌsiz] *n.* a pl. of APPENDIX.

ap•pen•di•ci•tis [əˌpɛndə'səitɪs] *n.* an inflammation of the vermiform appendix, the small saclike growth attached to the large intestine. ⟨< L *appendix, -icis* + E *-itis*⟩

ap•pen•dix [ə'pɛndɪks] *n., pl.* **-dix•es** or **-di•ces. 1** an addition at the end of a book or document, containing supplementary material. **2** an outgrowth of an organ, etc. The small saclike growth attached to the large intestine is the **vermiform appendix.** See ALIMENTARY CANAL for picture. ⟨< L *appendix* < *appendere.* See APPEND.⟩ **—ap•pen'dic•u•lar** [ˌæpɛn'dɪkjələr], *adj.*

☛ *Syn.* **1.** See note at SUPPLEMENT.

☛ *Usage.* The English plural **appendixes** is rapidly overtaking the Latin **appendices** and occurs more frequently except in more formal usage.

ap•per•ceive [ˌæpər'siv] *v.* **-ceived, -ceiv•ing.** *Psychology.* **1** be conscious of the act of perceiving. **2** assimilate (a perception).

ap•per•cep•tion [ˌæpər'sɛpʃən] *n. Psychology.* **1** the assimilation or interpretation of a new perception by means of ideas already in the mind. **2** a clear perception; full understanding as a result of this process. **3** sensitivity to the act of perceiving; selective perception. ⟨< F *aperception* < NL. Related to PERCEPTION.⟩

ap•per•cep•tive [ˌæpər'sɛptɪv] *adj.* of or having to do with apperception.

ap•per•tain [ˌæpər'tein] *v.* belong as a part; pertain; relate: *The control of traffic appertains to the police. Forestry appertains to geography, to botany, and to agriculture.* ⟨ME < OF *apartenir* < LL *appertinere* < L *ad-* to + *pertinere* pertain⟩

ap•pe•stat ['æpəˌstæt] *n.* the neural mechanism in the brain which controls the appetite. ⟨< *app(etite)* + Gk. *states* that stands⟩

ap•pe•tence ['æpətəns] *n.* **1** appetite; desire. **2** propensity; natural inclination. **3** chemical affinity. ⟨< L *appetentia* a craving for < ppr. of *appetere* < *ad* to + *petere* seek⟩

ap•pe•tite ['æpəˌtəit] *n.* **1** a desire for food. **2** a desire: *an appetite for amusement.* ⟨ME < OF < L *appetitus* < *ad-* + *petere* seek⟩

☛ *Hom.* APATITE.

ap•pe•tiz•er ['æpəˌtaɪzər] *n.* food or drink served, especially before a meal, to stimulate the appetite.

ap•pe•tiz•ing ['æpəˌtaɪzɪŋ] *adj.* arousing or exciting the appetite: *appetizing food.* **—'ap•peˌtiz•ing•ly,** *adv.*

ap•plaud [ə'plɒd] *v.* **1** express approval by clapping hands, shouting, etc.: *The crowd applauded lustily.* **2** express approval of (a person, speech, performance, etc.) in this way: *We applauded the speaker.* **3** approve; praise. ⟨< L *applaudere* < *ad-* to + *plaudere* clap⟩ **—ap'plaud•er,** *n.*

ap•plause [ə'plɒz] *n.* **1** approval expressed by clapping the hands, shouting, etc. **2** approval; praise. ⟨< L *applausus,* pp. of *applaudere.* See APPLAUD.⟩

ap•ple ['æpəl] *n.* **1** the firm, fleshy, roundish fruit of a tree (genus *Malus*) widely grown in temperate regions. Apples belong to the same family as the quince, pear, and hawthorn. **2** the tree. **3** any of various other fruits or fruitlike products, such as the OAK APPLE and LOVE APPLE.
apple of (someone's) **eye,** a person or thing that someone cherishes: *She is the apple of her father's eye.* ⟨OE *æppel*⟩

apple butter a smooth, jamlike spread made by boiling tart apples and apple cider together to produce a purée, and then cooking this with sugar and spices such as cinnamon and cloves.

apple cart a cart for carrying apples.
upset the apple cart, *Informal.* spoil or disrupt a plan or program: *The delegates hoped that no one would upset the apple cart before the agreement was signed.*

apple green a light green.

ap•ple•jack ['æpəlˌdʒæk] *n.* an intoxicating liquor made from apple cider.

apple of discord 1 *Greek mythology.* a golden apple inscribed "For the fairest" and claimed by Aphrodite, Athena, and Hera. Paris awarded it to Aphrodite. **2** any cause of jealousy and trouble.

apple–pie order *Informal.* perfect order or condition.

ap•ple–pol•ish ['æpəl ˌpɒlɪʃ] *v. Informal.* **1** curry favour with; flatter. **2** use flattery. **—'ap•ple-ˌpol•ish•er,** *n.*

ap•ple•sauce ['æpəlˌsɒs] *n.* **1** apples cut in pieces and cooked with sugar and water until soft. **2** *Slang.* nonsense.

apple slump BROWN BETTY.

Appleton layer the F_2 layer of the ionosphere which, together with the F_1 layer with which it overlaps, makes up the F region. The F_2 layer is from 225 to 400 km above the earth. ⟨< Sir Edward *Appleton,* 1892-1965, English scientist⟩

ap•ple•wood ['æpəlˌwʊd] *n.* the wood of the apple tree, used for cabinetmaking, firewood, etc.

ap•pli•ance [ə'plaɪəns] *n.* **1** a tool, small machine, or some other device used in doing something: *Can openers, vacuum cleaners, washing machines, refrigerators, etc. are household appliances.* **2** an applying; the act of putting into use.

ap•pli•ca•bil•i•ty [ˌæpləkə'bɪləti] *n.* the quality of being applicable.

ap•pli•ca•ble ['æpləkəbəl] *or* [ə'plɪkəbəl] *adj.* capable of being put to practical use; appropriate; suitable; fitting the situation: *The rule 'Look before you leap' is almost always applicable.*

ap•pli•cant ['æpləkənt] *n.* a person who applies (for money, position, help, office, etc.).

ap•pli•ca•tion [ˌæplə'keiʃən] *n.* **1** the act of using; the use: *The application of what you know will help you solve new problems.* **2** the act of applying; a putting on: *the application of paint to a house.* **3** range of ways of using: *'Freedom' is a word of wide application.* **4** something to be applied: *This application is made of cold cream and ointment.* **5** a request (for employment, an award, tickets, etc.): *She made an application for the position of clerk.* **6** a form or other document to be submitted in making such a request: *You must fill out the application and sign it.* **7** continued effort; close attention: *By application to his work he won promotion.* **8** applicability; relevance: *Your point has particular application to our case.* ⟨ME < MF < L *applicatio, -onis* a joining to < *applicare.* See APPLY.⟩

☛ *Syn.* **7.** See note at EFFORT.

ap•pli•ca•tor ['æpləˌkeitər] *n.* **1** any device for applying medicine, polish, paints, cosmetics, etc. **2** a person who applies something.

ap•plied [ə'plaɪd] *adj., v.* *—adj.* put to practical use; used to solve actual problems: *Engineers study applied mathematics.*
—v. pt. and pp. of APPLY.

applied science science that uses facts, laws, and theories to solve practical problems such as building a bridge, designing a radio, testing intelligence, etc.

ap•pli•qué *v.,* [ˌæplə'kei] *or* ['æpləˌkei]; *n.,* ['æpləˌkei]. *n., v.* **-quéd, -qué•ing.** *—n.* **1** the art or process of sewing or gluing pieces of fabric in various shapes and colours onto a larger piece of fabric for decoration: *Appliqué is often used to decorate clothing, table linens, etc.* **2** a cutout piece of fabric sewn or stuck onto a larger piece as a decoration: *a skirt with butterfly appliqués.* **3** (*adjl.*) trimmed with such pieces of fabric: *an appliqué skirt.*
—v. **1** trim or ornament with appliqué: *to appliqué a sweater.* **2** put on as appliqué: *to appliqué flowers on a table cloth.* **3** make by using appliqué: *an appliquéd wall hanging.* ⟨< F *appliqué* < *appliquer* apply < L *applicare*⟩

ap•ply [ə'plaɪ] *v.* **-plied, -ply•ing. 1** put on; spread: *to apply paint to a house.* **2** put to practical use; put into effect: *He knows the rule but does not know how to apply it.* **3** be useful or suitable; fit: *When does this rule apply?* **4** use for a special purpose: *to apply a sum of money to charity.* **5** make a formal request: *to apply for a job.* **6** use (a word or words) appropriately with reference to a person or thing: *to apply a nickname. Don't apply that adjective to me.* **7** set to work and stick to it (*used reflexively*): *He applied himself to learning French.* ⟨ME < OF *aplier* < L *applicare* < *ad-* on + *plicare* fold, lay⟩

ap•pog•gia•tu•ra [əˌpɒdʒiə'tʃurə] *or* [əˌpɒdʒə'turə] *n. Music.* GRACE NOTE. ⟨< Ital. *appoggiatura* < *appoggiare* lean, ult. < L *ad-* on + *podium* podium⟩

ap•point [ə'pɔɪnt] *v.* **1** name to an office or position; choose: *This man was appointed postmaster.* **2** decide on; set: *to appoint a time for the meeting.* **3** fix; prescribe. **4** furnish; equip: *a well-appointed office.* ⟨ME < OF *apointer* < LL *appunctare* < L *ad-* to + *punctum* point. Related to POINT.⟩ **—ap'point•er,** *n.*

ap•point•ee [ˌæpɔɪn'ti] *n.* a person appointed.

ap•poin•tive [ə'pɔɪntɪv] *adj.* filled by appointment: *Most positions in the Senate are appointive.*

ap•point•ment [ə'pɔɪntmənt] *n.* **1** the act of naming to an office or position; choosing: *The appointment of Ann as treasurer pleased her friends.* **2** an office or position so filled. **3** an

engagement to be somewhere or to meet someone.
4 appointments, *pl.* furniture; equipment.

ap•por•tion [ə'pɔrʃən] *v.* divide and give out in fair shares; distribute according to some rule: *The mother's property was apportioned among her children after her death.* ⟨< obsolete F *apportionner*, ult. < L *ad-* to + *portiō, -ōnis* portion⟩
☛ *Syn.* See note at ALLOT.

ap•por•tion•ment [ə'pɔrʃənmənt] *n.* the act of dividing and giving out in fair shares.

ap•pose [ə'pouz] *v.* **-posed, -pos•ing. 1** put next (*to*); place side by side; specifically, to use (an expression) in APPOSITION (def. 3). In the phrase *Louis Riel, the Métis leader*, the word *leader* is apposed to *Louis Riel.* **2** put (one thing *to* another); apply: *An official seal was apposed to the document.* ⟨< F *apposer* < *à-* to (< L *ad-*) + *poser* put (See POSE[1])⟩
☛ *Hom.* OPPOSE.

ap•po•site ['æpəzɪt] *adj.* appropriate; suitable; apt. ⟨< L *appositus*, pp. of *apponere* < *ad-* near + *ponere* place⟩
—'ap•po•site•ly, *adv.* **—'ap•po•site•ness,** *n.*

ap•po•si•tion [,æpə'zɪʃən] *n.* **1** the act of putting side by side. **2** a position side by side. **3** *Grammar.* **a** a placing together in the same relation. **b** the relation of two parts of a sentence when the one is added as an explanation to the other. In *Ms. Brown, our neighbour, has a new car, Ms. Brown* and *neighbour* are in apposition.

ap•pos•i•tive [ə'pɒzətɪv] *n., adj. Grammar. —n.* a noun added to another noun as an explanation; word, phrase, or clause in apposition.
—adj. placed beside another noun as an explanation.

ap•prais•al [ə'preizəl] *n.* **1** the act of estimating the value, amount, etc., of something; an appraising; valuation. **2** the value set on something as a result of such an act. **3** a judgment of the worth or quality of a person or thing: *He let the stranger in after a quick appraisal of his appearance and manner.*

ap•praise [ə'preiz] *v.* **-praised, -prais•ing. 1** estimate the value, amount, quality, etc. of: *An employer should be able to appraise ability and character.* **2** set a price on; fix the value of: *Property is appraised for taxation.* ⟨< *praise, apprize*[1]⟩
—ap'prais•ing•ly, *adv.*
☛ *Syn.* **1.** See note at ESTIMATE.

ap•prais•er [ə'preizər] *n.* **1** a person authorized to fix the value of property, imported goods, etc. **2** a person who appraises.

ap•pre•ci•a•ble [ə'priʃəbəl] *adj.* enough to be felt or estimated: *The difference between the two prices is appreciable.*
—ap'pre•ci•a•bly, *adv.*

ap•pre•ci•ate [ə'priʃi,eit] *v.* **-at•ed, -at•ing. 1** think highly of; recognize the worth or quality of; value; enjoy: *Almost everybody appreciates good food.* **2** have an informed opinion of the value, worth, or quality of: *to appreciate art.* **3** be sensitive to; be aware of: *A musician can appreciate small differences in sounds.* **4** be grateful for: *I really appreciate your driving me home.* **5** estimate correctly. **6** raise in value: *New buildings appreciate the value of land.* **7** rise in value: *This land will appreciate as soon as good roads are built.* ⟨< L *appretiare* appraise < *ad-* + *pretium* price. Doublet of APPRIZE[1].⟩ **—ap'pre•ci,a•tor,** *n.* **—ap'pre•ci•a,to•ry,** *adj.*
☛ *Syn.* **1.** See note at VALUE.

ap•pre•ci•a•tion [ə,priʃi'eiʃən] *n.* **1** valuing highly; sympathetic understanding: *He has no appreciation of art and music.* **2** an appreciating; valuing. **3** gratitude: *a small token of our appreciation.* **4** favourable criticism. **5** a rise in value.

ap•pre•ci•a•tive [ə'priʃətɪv] *or* [ə'priʃi,eitɪv] *adj.* having appreciation; showing appreciation or gratitude; recognizing the value: *appreciative of the smallest kindness.* **—ap'pre•ci•a•tive•ly,** *adv.* **—ap'pre•ci•a•tive•ness,** *n.*

ap•pre•hend [,æprɪ'hɛnd] *v.* **1** perceive; grasp with the mind: *They were able to apprehend his meaning from his gestures.* **2** anticipate with fear or dread: *No one had apprehended any violence.* **3** arrest: *The thief has been apprehended.* ⟨< L *apprehendere* < *ad-* upon + *prehendere* seize⟩
☛ *Usage.* See note at COMPREHEND.

ap•pre•hen•si•bil•i•ty [,æprɪ,hɛnsə'bɪləti] *n.* the quality or state of being apprehensible.

ap•pre•hen•si•ble [,æprɪ'hɛnsəbəl] *adj.* capable of being apprehended; understandable. **—,ap•pre'hen•si•bly,** *adv.*

ap•pre•hen•sion [,æprɪ'hɛnʃən] *n.* **1** expectation of something bad; fear; dread. **2** perception; grasping with the mind: *a clear apprehension of the facts.* **3** a seizing or being seized; arrest: *the apprehension of a suspect.* **4** opinion; view or interpretation: *Her apprehension of the issue is different from mine.* ⟨< L *apprehensio, -onis* < *apprehendere.* See APPREHEND.⟩

ap•pre•hen•sive [,æprɪ'hɛnsɪv] *adj.* **1** fearfully expecting danger or harm; afraid; anxious: *The captain was apprehensive for the safety of her passengers during the storm.* **2** quick to understand; able to learn. **3** having to do with mental perception: *apprehensive processes.* **—,ap•pre'hen•sive•ly,** *adv.*
—,ap•pre'hen•sive•ness, *n.*

ap•pren•tice [ə'prɛntɪs] *n., v.* **-ticed, -tic•ing.** *—n.* **1** a person learning a trade or craft by working at it under skilled supervision for a given length of time. **2** a beginner; learner.
—v. bind (oneself) or take (another) as an apprentice. ⟨ME < OF *aprentis* < *apprendre* learn < L *apprehendere.* See APPREHEND.⟩

ap•pren•tice•ship [ə'prɛntɪs,ʃɪp] *n.* **1** the condition of being an apprentice. **2** the time during which one is an apprentice.

ap•pressed [æ'prɛst] *or* [ə'prɛst] *adj.* fitted closely against something, as, a leaf to a stem.

ap•prise [ə'praɪz] *v.* **-prised, -pris•ing.** give notice to; inform (*often used with* **of**): *They were apprised by letter of a delay in the shipment.* ⟨< F *appris*, pp. of *apprendre* learn < L *apprehendere.* See APPREHEND.⟩
☛ *Hom.* APPRIZE.

ap•prize [ə'praɪz] *v.* **-prized, -priz•ing. 1** appraise. **2** esteem or appreciate. ⟨ME < OF *apriser* < L *appretiare.* Doublet of APPRECIATE.⟩
☛ *Hom.* APPRISE.

ap•proach [ə'proutʃ] *v., n. —v.* **1** come near or nearer (to) in space or time: *We're approaching the town. Winter approaches.* **2** come near or nearer to (in character, quality, amount): *The wind was approaching gale force.* **3** bring near (*to* something): *Approach the magnet to this heap of filings.* **4** make advances or overtures to: *Will you approach your father with our plan for a party?*
—n. **1** the act of coming near or nearer: *the approach of night.* **2** a way by which a place or a person can be reached; access. **3** a nearness in quality, likeness, or character; an approximation: *In mathematics there must be more than an approach to accuracy.* **4** Also, **approaches,** *pl.* an advance; overture: *Our approaches to the manager were met with disdain.* **5** a way of dealing with or accomplishing something: *a new approach to mathematics.* **6** *Golf.* a stroke by which a player tries to get his or her ball onto the putting green. ⟨ME < OF *aprochier* < LL *appropiare* < L *ad-* to + *prope* near⟩

ap•proach•a•bil•i•ty [ə,proutʃə'bɪləti] *n.* the quality or condition of being approachable.

ap•proach•a•ble [ə'proutʃəbəl] *adj.* **1** that can be approached: *The fishing camp was approachable from the south only.* **2** easy to approach: *She looks stern but is really quite approachable.*

ap•pro•ba•tion [,æprə'beiʃən] *n.* **1** approval; favourable opinion. **2** official sanction. ⟨ME < OF < L *approbatio, -onis* < *approbare* approve. See APPROVE.⟩ **—'ap•pro,ba•tive,** *adj.*

ap•pro•pri•a•ble [ə'proupriəbəl] *adj.* capable of being appropriated.

ap•pro•pri•ate *adj.* [ə'prouprit]; *v.* [ə'proupri,eit] *adj., v.* **-at•ed, -at•ing.** *—adj.* suitable; proper: *Blue jeans and a sweater are appropriate clothes for the hike.*
—v. **1** set aside for some special use: *The government appropriated money for roads.* **2** take for oneself: *You should not appropriate other people's belongings without their permission.* ⟨< LL *appropriatus*, pp. of *appropriare* < L *ad-* to + *proprius* one's own⟩
—ap'pro•pri•ate•ly, *adv.* **—ap'pro•pri•ate•ness,** *n.*
—ap'pro•pri,a•tor, *n.*
☛ *Syn. adj.* See note at FIT[1].

ap•pro•pri•a•tion [ə,proupri'eiʃən] *n.* **1** a sum of money or other thing set aside for a special use. **2** the act or an instance of appropriating: *The appropriation of the land made it possible to have a park.*

ap•prov•al [ə'pruvəl] *n.* **1** an approving; favourable opinion: *This plan has the teacher's approval.* **2** consent: sanction: *The principal gave her approval to plans for the holiday.* **3 approvals,** *pl.* items sent to a customer on approval.
on approval, so that the customer can decide whether to buy or not; on trial: *We had the car for a day on approval.*

ap•prove [ə'pruv] *v.* **-proved, -prov•ing. 1** consent to; sanction: *Everyone approved the plan. Parliament has approved the bill.* **2** give approval; think well (*often used with* **of**): *Her family did not approve of her plan to sell the farm.* **3** speak well of; express satisfaction with; commend: *His boss approved his work.* ⟨ME < OF *aprover* < L *approbare* < *ad-* to + *probus* good⟩
—ap'prov•er, *n.* **—ap'prov•ing•ly,** *adv.*

☛ *Syn.* **1.** Approve, SANCTION, RATIFY mean to give formal consent or support. **Approve,** the general word, means to consent to something one thinks favourably of: *The school board approved the budget.* **Sanction** means to give official or public consent or support: *Society does not sanction child labour.* **Ratify** expresses formal approval or confirmation in accordance with a prescribed procedure: *The club council ratified the by-laws.*

☛ *Syn.* **3.** See note at PRAISE.

approx. approximate; approximately.

ap•prox•i•mate *adj.* [ə'prɒksəmɪt]; *v.* [ə'prɒksə,meit] *adj., v.* **-mat•ed, -mat•ing.** *—adj.* **1** not accurate or precise, but nearly so; fairly close to the actual or the best: *an approximate fit. The approximate number of people expected is 500.* **2** set or located very close together. **3** very like: *The two samples are approximate in size.*
—v. **1** come near; approach in similarity or amount (*sometimes used with* **to**): *Your account of what happened approximated the truth, but there were several small errors. The crowd approximated a thousand people.* **2** bring near. *Abbrev.:* approx. ⟨< L *approximatus*, pp. of *approximare* < *ad-* to + *proximus* nearest < *prope* near⟩ **—ap'prox•i•mate•ly,** *adv.*

ap•prox•i•ma•tion [ə,prɒksə'meiʃən] *n.* **1** an approximating; approach: *an approximation to the truth.* **2** a nearly correct amount; close estimate: *Forty thousand kilometres is an approximation of the circumference of the earth.*

ap•pur•te•nance [ə'pɜrtənəns] *n.* **1** an addition to something more important; added thing; accessory. **2** a right or privilege that is subordinate to another. **3 appurtenances,** *pl.* equipment; apparatus; gear. ⟨< AF *apurtenance.* Related to APPERTAIN.⟩

ap•pur•te•nant [ə'pɜrtənənt] *adj.* pertaining; belonging; appertaining (*to*).

Apr. April.

a•prax•i•a [ə'præksiə] *or* [ei'præksiə] *n.* loss of the memory of how to perform certain muscular tasks, due to nervous disorder. ⟨< NL < Gk. *a-* not + *praxis* action⟩ **—a'prax•ic** or **a'prac•tic,** *adj.*

a•près–ski ['æprei 'ski]; *French* [apʀɛ'ski] *n.* **1** a party or other social activity held in the evening after a day of skiing. **2** (*adjl.*) of, for, or designating such an activity: *après-ski fashions.* ⟨< F *après* after + *ski*⟩

ap•ri•cot ['æprə,kɒt] *or* ['eiprə,kɒt] *n., adj. —n.* **1** a tree (*Prunus armeniaca*) of the rose family native to Africa and W Asia but cultivated throughout the warmer temperate regions of the world for its roundish, pale orange or yellow, juicy fruit. **2** the fruit of this tree. **3** a pale orange-yellow.
—adj. pale orange-yellow. ⟨earlier *apricock* (< Pg. *albricoque*), later influenced by F *abricot* < Pg. < Sp. < Arabic *al-burquq* < Gk., ult. < L *praecox* or *praecoquis* early-ripe < *prae* before + *coquere* cook, ripen⟩

A•pril ['eiprəl] *n.* the fourth month of the year. It has 30 days. *Abbrev.:* Ap. or Apr. ⟨< L *Aprilis*⟩

April fool any person who gets fooled on April Fools' Day.

April Fools' Day April 1, a day observed by fooling people with tricks and jokes.

a pri•o•ri [,ei pri'ɔri] *or* [,ei pri'ɔraɪ] **1** from cause to effect; from a general rule to a particular case. **2** based on opinion, preconception, or conjecture rather than on actual observation or experience. **3** considered to be true axiomatically; not needing experience to verify it. ⟨< Med.L *a priori* from (something) previous⟩ **—,a•pri'or•i•ty,** *n.*

a•pri•o•rism [ei'praɪə,rɪzəm] *n.* the philosophy that knowledge comes from a priori ideas and not from experience.

a•pron ['eiprən] *n., v. —n.* **1** a garment worn over the front part of the body to protect one's clothes: *a kitchen apron, a carpenter's apron.* **2** a protective shield or structure to prevent the washing away of a surface, such as a sea wall, river bank, etc. **3** a platform at the bottom of a sluice to intercept the fall of water. **4** *Logging.* a platform at the bottom of a log chute used to break the fall of the logs as they enter the water. **5** a paved area adjacent to the hangars or terminal building of an airport, especially the area immediately in front of a hangar or terminal. **6** the part of a theatre stage that extends in front of the curtain. **7** any of various other things resembling an apron in shape or in protective function. **8** *Geology.* a sheet of sand or gravel in front of a moraine.
—v. provide with an apron. ⟨ME *a napron* taken as *an apron* < OF *naperon*, dim. of *nape* < L *mappa* napkin⟩ **—'a•pron,like,** *adj.*

apron strings the ties used to fasten an apron.
tied to (one's) **mother's apron strings,** dependent on, or dominated by, one's mother.

ap•ro•pos [,æprə'pou] *adv., adj. —adv.* **1** fittingly; opportunely. **2** incidentally; by the way (to introduce some related but new point): *Apropos, what are you doing tomorrow?*
apropos of, with regard to.
—adj. fitting; suitable; to the point: *an apropos remark.* ⟨< F *à propos* to the purpose⟩

ap•ro•ti•nin [ə'prɒtənɪn] *n.* a drug used to control certain effects of surgery and certain conditions of the pancreas.

apse [æps] *n.* a semicircular or many-sided recess in a church, usually at the east end, having an arched or vaulted roof. ⟨< L *apsis* < Gk. *hapsis* loop, arch < *haptein* fasten⟩ **—,ap•si•dal,** *adj.*

ap•sis ['æpsɪs] *n., pl.* **ap•si•des** [-,diz]. **1** either extremity of an eccentric orbit. The **lower apsis** is the point closest to the centre of gravitation; the **higher apsis** is the point most distant from it. **line of apsides,** a line joining the higher and lower apsides. ⟨< L < Gk. See APSE.⟩ **—'ap•si•dal,** *adj.*

apt [æpt] *adj.* **1** fitted by nature; likely: *A careless person is apt to make mistakes.* **2** suitable; fitting: *an apt reply.* **3** quick to learn: *an apt pupil.* ⟨ME < L *aptus* joined, fitted, pp. of *apere*⟩ **—'apt•ly,** *adv.* **—'apt•ness,** *n.*

☛ *Usage.* See note at LIKELY.

apt. apartment.

ap•ter•al ['æptərəl] *adj. Architecture.* **1** built with columns at either end but not along the sides. **2** of a church, without aisles. **3** apterous. ⟨< Gk.⟩

ap•ter•ous ['æptərəs] *adj. Biology.* wingless. Lice are apterous insects. ⟨< Gk. *apteros* < *a-* without + *pteron* wing⟩

ap•ter•yg•i•al [,æptə'rɪdʒiəl] *adj.* lacking paired wings or limbs. ⟨< Gk. *apterygos* < *a-* without + *pteryx* wing⟩

ap•ter•yx ['æptə,rɪks] *n., pl.* **-yx•es** [-,ɪksɪz]. KIWI (def. 1). ⟨< NL *apteryx* < *a-* without + Gk. *pteryx* wing⟩

ap•ti•tude ['æptə,tjud] *or* ['æptə,tud] *n.* **1** a natural tendency; ability; capacity: *Edison had a great aptitude for inventing new things.* **2** readiness in learning; quickness to understand. **3** a special fitness. ⟨< LL *aptitudo* < L *aptus* joined, fitted. Doublet of ATTITUDE.⟩

aptitude test a test given to a person to find out the sort of work, studies, etc. for which he or she is specially suited.

Apus ['eipəs] *n.* a constellation in the Southern Hemisphere near the celestial south pole. ⟨< NL, a swift⟩

a•py•ret•ic [,eipaɪ'rɛtɪk] *adj.* not feverish.

aq. aqua.

AQ ACHIEVEMENT QUOTIENT.

aq•ua ['ækwə] *or* ['ɑkwə] *n., adj. —n.* **1** water. **2** *Chemistry.* a liquid solution: *aqua fortis.* **3** aquamarine.
—adj. aquamarine. *Abbrev.:* aq. ⟨< L, water⟩

aq•ua•cade ['ækwə,keid] *n.* a water entertainment consisting of swimming, diving, water skiing, group formations, etc., usually performed to the accompaniment of music. ⟨< *aqua* + *(caval)cade*⟩

aq•ua•cul•ture ['ækwə,kʌltʃər] *n.* **1** the raising of water animals and plants, especially fish, for commercial purposes. **2** (*adjl.*) of or having to do with aquaculture: *aquaculture technology.* Also, **aquiculture. —,aq•ua'cul•tur•ist,** *n.*

aq•ua for•tis ['fɔrtɪs] NITRIC ACID. ⟨< L *aqua fortis* strong water⟩

Aq•ua•lung ['ækwə,lʌŋ] *n. Trademark.* a diving apparatus consisting of cylinders of compressed air strapped to the diver's back and a watertight mask placed over the eyes and nose. The supply of air to the diver is regulated automatically by a valve.

An Aqualung

aq•ua•ma•rine [,ækwəmə'rin] *or* [,ɑkwəmə'rin] *n., adj. —n.* **1** a transparent, bluish green precious stone, a variety of beryl. **2** a gem made from this stone. **3** a colour ranging from pale to light bluish green.
—adj. having this colour. ⟨< L *aqua marina* sea water⟩

aq•ua•naut ['ækwə,nɒt] *n.* an underwater explorer. ⟨< *aqua* + *(astro)naut*⟩

aq•ua•plane ['ækwə,plein] *n., v.* **-planed, -plan•ing.** *—n.* a wide board on which a person stands as it is towed by a speeding motorboat.

—*v.* **1** ride on an aquaplane. **2** of a motor vehicle, ride on a film of water that is built up under the tires at high speed on wet roads, resulting in loss of control over braking and steering. ⟨< L *aqua* water + E *plane*[1]⟩

aq•ua re•gi•a ['ridʒiə] a mixture of nitric acid and hydrochloric acid that will dissolve gold and platinum. ⟨< NL *aqua regia* royal water, because it dissolves gold⟩

aq•ua•relle [ˌækwə'rɛl] *n.* **1** a painting done with ink and transparent water colours. **2** the method of painting in this way. ⟨< F⟩

a•quar•ist [ə'kwɛrɪst] *n.* a person who keeps an aquarium.

a•quar•i•um [ə'kwɛriəm] *n., pl.* **a•quar•i•ums** or **a•quar•i•a** [ə'kwɛriə]. **1** a pond, tank, or glass bowl in which living fish, water animals, and water plants are kept. **2** a building used for showing collections of living fish, water animals, and water plants. ⟨< L *aquarium*, neut. of *aquarius* of water < *aqua* water⟩

A•quar•i•us [ə'kwɛriəs] *n.* **1** *Astronomy.* a northern constellation thought of as representing a man standing with his left hand extended upward, and with his right pouring a stream of water out of a vase. **2** *Astrology.* **a** the 11th sign of the zodiac. The sun enters Aquarius about January 22. See ZODIAC for picture. **b** a person born under this sign. **—A'quar•i•an,** *adj.*

a•quat•ic [ə'kwɒtɪk] *or* [ə'kwætɪk] *adj., n.* —*adj.* **1** growing or living in water: *Water lilies are aquatic plants.* **2** taking place in or on water: *Swimming and sailing are aquatic sports.*
—*n.* **1** a plant or animal that lives in water. **2 aquatics,** *pl.* sports that take place in or on water. **—a'quat•i•cal•ly,** *adv.*

aq•ua•tint ['ækwəˌtɪnt] *n., v.* —*n.* **1** a process in which the spaces in a design, not the lines, are etched by acid. **2** an etching made by this process.
—*v.* etch by this process. ⟨< F *aquatinte* < Ital. *acqua tinta* < L *aqua* water, and *tincta* (fem.) dipped⟩

aq•ua•tone ['ækwəˌtoun] *n.* **1** a process of photo-engraving in which the design is transferred to a sensitized aluminum plate coated with a mixture of gelatin and celluloid. **2** a print made by this process.

aq•ua•vit ['ɑkwəˌvit] *n.* a Scandinavian spirit made from distilled potato or grain alcohol and flavoured with caraway seeds. ⟨< G < L *aqua vitae*⟩

aq•ua vi•tae ['vitaɪ] *or* ['vəiti] **1** alcohol. **2** brandy; whisky, etc. ⟨< NL *aqua vitae* water of life⟩

aq•ue•duct ['ækwəˌdʌkt] *n.* **1** an artificial channel or large pipe for bringing water from a distance. **2** a structure that supports such a channel or pipe. **3** *Anatomy.* a canal or passage. ⟨< L *aquaeductus* < *aqua* water + *ductus*, pp. of *ducere* lead, convey⟩

a•que•ous ['ækwiəs] *or* ['eikwiəs] *adj.* **1** of water; like water; watery. **2** containing water; made with water. **3** produced by the action of water: *Aqueous rocks are formed from the sediment carried and deposited by water.*

aqueous humour or **humor** the watery liquid that fills the space in the eye between the cornea and the lens. See EYE for picture.

aq•ui•cul•ture ['ækwəˌkʌltʃər] See AQUACULTURE.

aq•ui•fer ['ækwəfər] *n.* a water-bearing, underground layer of porous rock, sand, etc. which can be used as a source of water for wells. ⟨< NL *aqua* water + *-fer* < *ferre* carry⟩ **—a'quif•er•ous** [ə'kwɪfərəs], *adj.*

Aq•ui•la ['ækwələ] *n.* a northern constellation thought of as resembling the outline of an eagle. It contains the star Altair. ⟨< L *aquila* eagle⟩

aq•ui•le•gi•a [ˌækwə'lidʒiə] *n.* columbine. ⟨< NL⟩

aq•ui•line ['ækwəˌlaɪn] *or* ['ækwəlɪn] *adj.* **1** of or like an eagle. **2** curved like an eagle's beak; hooked: *an aquiline nose.* ⟨< L *aquilinus* < *aquila* eagle⟩

a•quiv•er [ə'kwɪvər] *adv. or adj. (never precedes a noun)* trembling.

ar– *prefix.* **1** to or toward; the form of AD- occurring before *r*, as in *arrive.* **2** not; without; the form of AN-[1] sometimes occurring before *r*, as in *arrhythmia*.

–ar *suffix.* **1** forming adjectives, having to do with or similar to: *circular*, *polar*. **2** forming nouns, the doer of an action: *registrar*.

Ar argon.

ar. or **ar** arrival; arrives; arriving; arrived.

Ar. **1** Arabia; Arabic. **2** Aramaic.

A•ra ['ɑrə], ['ærə] *or* ['ɛrə] *n.* a constellation in the S hemisphere, lying between Scorpio and Pavo. ⟨< L, altar⟩

Ar•ab ['ærəb] *or* ['ɛrəb] *n., adj.* —*n.* **1** a member of a Semitic people originally from the Arabian Peninsula between the Red Sea and the Persian Gulf, now widely scattered throughout the Middle East and North Africa. **2** a member of any Arabic-speaking people. **3** a breed of horse originally from the Arabian Peninsula, noted for its swiftness, gracefulness, and spirit. **4** See STREET ARAB.
—*adj.* **1** of or having to do with the Arabs: *the Arab countries.* **2** of or having to do with the Arabian Peninsula; Arabian. ⟨< F < L < Gk.⟩

☛ *Usage.* **Arab,** ARABIAN, ARABIC apply in different ways. **Arab** applies most commonly to the people or their culture: *Arab customs, the Arab world.* **Arabian** usually applies more to the territory traditionally recognized as the home of these people, specifically to the Arabian Peninsula: *Arabian sands.* **Arabic** applies to the language of the Arabs and to their literature, art, etc: *Arabic poetry.*

ar•a•besque [ˌærə'bɛsk] *or* [ˌɛrə'bɛsk] *n., adj., v.* **-besqued, -besqu•ing.** —*n.* **1** an elaborate and fanciful design of flowers, leaves, geometrical figures, etc. **2** *Ballet.* a pose in which the dancer stands on one leg with the other leg extended horizontally behind him or her. Traditionally, one arm is extended in front and the other arm behind. **3** *Music.* **a** an ornamentation, often elaborate, of a melody. **b** a short, graceful composition, often highly ornamented, resembling a rondo: *Debussy's piano arabesques.*
—*adj.* **1** carved or painted in arabesque. **2** like arabesque; elaborate; fanciful.
—*v.* **1** decorate with arabesques. **2** *Ballet.* execute an arabesque. ⟨< F < Ital. *arabesco* < *Arabo* Arab⟩

A•ra•bi•an [ə'reibiən] *adj., n.* —*adj.* **1** of or having to do with the Arabian Peninsula: *the Arabian desert, Arabian flora.* **2** of or having to do with the Arabs.
—*n.* **1** Arab. **2** a swift, graceful horse belonging to a breed of horses that originally came from Arabia.
☛ *Usage.* See note at ARAB.

Arabian camel a species of camel (*Camelus dromedarius*) found mainly in the Indian subcontinent, the Near East, and North Africa, used for riding and as a beast of burden, having long legs and one hump, and standing about 2 m high at the shoulder.

Arabian Nights *The Thousand and One Nights*, a collection of old tales from Arabia, Persia, and India, dating from the 10th century A.D.

ar•a•bic ['ærəbɪk] *or* ['ɛrəbɪk] *adj.* having to do with the acid found in gum arabic. *Formula:* $C_5H_{10}O_6$

Ar•a•bic ['ærəbɪk] *or* ['ɛrəbɪk] *n., adj.* —*n.* a Semitic language that is the main language of Saudi Arabia, Yemen, Syria, Lebanon, Jordan, Iraq, Egypt, and parts of North Africa.
—*adj.* of or having to do with the Arabs or their language.
☛ *Usage.* See note at ARAB.

Arabic numerals or **figures** the figures 1, 2, 3, 4, 5, 6, 7, 8, 9, 0. The Arabic numerals are so called because they were introduced into western Europe by Arabian scholars, but most probably they were derived from India. A more accurate name for the Arabic figures is Hindu-Arabic.

a•rab•i•nose [ə'ræbɪˌnous] *or* ['ɛrəbɪˌnous] a pentose sugar found especially in cedar or pine gum, used as a microbial culture medium. *Formula*: $C_5H_{10}O_5$ ⟨< *(gum) arab(ic)* + *-in* + *-ose*⟩

ar•a•ble ['ærəbəl] *or* ['ɛrəbəl] *adj.* fit for growing crops: *There is little arable land on the Canadian Shield.* ⟨< L *arabilis* < *arare* plough⟩ **—ˌar•a'bil•i•ty,** *n.*

Ar•ab•ist ['ærəbɪst] *or* ['ɛrəbɪst] *n.* a student of, or expert in, the Arabic language or literature or Arab culture.

Arab League an association of 13 Arab countries founded in 1945 to foster mutual social, political, and economic co-operation.

Ar•a•by ['ærəbi] *or* ['ɛrəbi] *n. Poetic.* Arabia.

A•rach•ne [ə'rækni] *n. Greek mythology.* a maiden who dared to challenge Athena to a contest in weaving, and was changed by her into a spider.

a•rach•nid [ə'ræknɪd] *n.* any of a class (Arachnida) of small, air-breathing arthropods having four pairs of walking legs, no antennae or wings, and a body usually divided into only two segments. Spiders, scorpions, mites, etc. are arachnids. ⟨< NL *Arachnida* < Gk. *arakhnē* spider, web⟩

a•rach•ni•dan [ə'ræknədən] *adj., n.* —*adj.* of or having to do with arachnids.
—*n.* arachnid.

a•rach•noid [ə'ræknɔɪd] *adj., n.* —*adj.* **1** like a cobweb. **2** of or resembling an arachnid. **3** *Physiology.* of or having to do with the thin serous membrane that envelops the brain and spinal cord. **4** *Botany.* formed of, or covered with, fine hairs or fibres resembling cobwebs.
—*n.* **1** arachnid. **2** the arachnoid membrane. ⟨< NL < Gk. *arakhnoeidés* cobweblike < *arakhnē* spider, web⟩

ar•ach•no•pho•bia [ə,ræknə'foubiə] *n.* an abnormal fear of spiders.

a•rag•o•nite [ə'rægə,nəit], ['ærəgə,nəit], *or* ['ɛrəgə,nəit] *n.* an orthorhombic crystalline mineral consisting of calcium carbonate. *Formula*: $CaCO_3$ ⟨< *Aragon*, Spain⟩

ar•ak ['ærək] *or* ['ɛrək] *n.* arrack.

Ar•a•ma•ic [,ærə'meɪɪk] *or* [,ɛrə'meɪɪk] *n., adj.* —*n.* a Semitic language or group of dialects, including Syriac and the language spoken in Palestine at the time of Christ.
—*adj.* of or in Aramaic.

a•ra•ne•id [ə'reiniɪd] *n.* spider. ⟨< L *aranea* spider⟩

ar•a•pai•ma [,ærə'paɪmə] *or* [,ɛrə'paɪmə] *n.* a long, bony Brazilian food fish. ⟨< Pg. < Tupi⟩

Ar•au•ca•ni•an [,ærɒ'keiniən] *or* [,ɛrɒ'keiniən] *n.* **1** a member of a group of aboriginal peoples of Chile and Argentina. **2** their language, which shows no relationship to any other human language. **3** of these peoples, their language or their culture. ⟨< Sp. *Araucano* < *Arauco* in Chile⟩

ar•au•car•i•a [,ærɒ'kɛriə] *or* [,ɛrɒ'kɛriə] *n.* any of the genus *Araucaria* of conifers native to the S hemisphere, including the monkey puzzle tree.
—*adj.* designating the coniferous family Araucariacea of the S hemisphere. ⟨< NL < *Arauco*, Chile⟩

A•ra•wak ['ɑrə,wɑk], ['ærəwæk], *or* ['ɛrə,wæk] *n., pl.* **Arawak** or **-waks;** *adj.* —*n.* **1** a member of a group of Indian peoples of South America and, formerly, the West Indies. **2 a** a member of one of these peoples, now living mainly along the coast of Guyana. **b** their language.
—*adj.* of or having to do with the Arawak or their language.

A•ra•wak•an [,ɑrə'wɑkən], [,ærə'wækən], *or* [,ɛrə'wækən] *n., pl.* **Arawakan** or **-kans;** *adj.* —*n.* **1** a large family of Indian languages spoken by the ARAWAK (def. 1). **2** ARAWAK (def. 1).
—*adj.* of, having to do with, or designating the Arawak peoples or their languages.

ar•ba•lest or **ar•ba•list** ['ɑrbəlɪst] *n.* a powerful crossbow having a steel bow. ⟨< OF *arbaleste* < LL *arcu-ballista* < *arcus* bow + *ballista* military engine, ult. < Gk. *ballein* throw⟩
—'ar•ba,lest•er, *n.*

ar•bi•ter ['ɑrbətər] *n.* **1** a person chosen to decide a dispute. **2** a person with full power to decide. ⟨< L *arbiter*⟩

ar•bi•tra•ble ['ɑrbətrəbəl] *adj.* capable of being decided by arbitration.

ar•bi•trage ['ɑrbətrɪdʒ] *or* ['ɑrbə,trɑʒ] *n., v.* **-traged, -trag•ing.** —*n. Business.* **1** the calculation of the prices of certain stocks, bonds, etc. in different places at the same time, allowing for exchange rates. **2** the buying and selling of stocks, bonds, etc. in several markets simultaneously, to take advantage of price differences between markets.
—*v.* practise arbitrage. ⟨< F < *arbitrer* arbitrate < L *arbitrari* < *arbiter* arbiter⟩

ar•bi•trag•eur [,ɑrbɪtrɑ'ʒɜr] *or* ['ɑrbɪ,trɑʒɜr] *n.* one who practises arbitrage.

ar•bi•tral ['ɑrbətrəl] *adj.* of arbiters or arbitration.

ar•bit•ra•ment [ɑr'bɪtrəmənt] *n.* **1** a decision by an arbitrator or arbiter. **2** the power to judge and decide.

ar•bi•trar•y ['ɑrbə,trɛri] *adj.* **1** determined by caprice or whim: *Her sudden arbitrary decision to quit the team cost us the game.* **2** done or made at random without a reason: *An arbitrary selection of a single ticket decides the winner of a lottery.* **3** determined by the decision of a judge or tribunal rather than by a specific law. **4** despotic; absolute: *arbitrary rule.*
—,ar•bi'trar•i•ly, *adv.* **—'ar•bi,trar•i•ness,** *n.*

arbitrary constant *Mathematics.* a symbol that represents an unspecified constant. For example, in the equation $ax^2 + bx + c = 0$, the symbols *a, b,* and *c* are arbitrary constants.

ar•bi•trate ['ɑrbə,treit] *v.* **-trat•ed, -trat•ing. 1** give a decision in a dispute; act as arbiter: *to arbitrate between two persons in a quarrel.* **2** settle by arbitration; submit to arbitration: *The two nations finally agreed to arbitrate their dispute.* ⟨< L *arbitrārī* < *arbiter.* See ARBITER.⟩

ar•bi•tra•tion [,ɑrbə'treiʃən] *n.* the settlement of a dispute by the decision of a judge, umpire, or arbiter. **—,ar•bi'tra•tion•al,** *adv.*

ar•bi•tra•tor ['ɑrbə,treitər] *n.* **1** a person chosen to decide a dispute. **2** a person with full power to judge and decide.

ar•bor¹ ['ɑrbər] *n.* the main shaft or axle of a machine. ⟨< F *arbre* tree⟩

ar•bor² ['ɑrbər] See ARBOUR.

ar•bo•re•al [ɑr'bɔriəl] *adj.* **1** of trees; like trees. **2** living in or among trees: *A squirrel is an arboreal animal.* ⟨< L *arbor* tree⟩

ar•bo•re•ous [ɑr'bɔriəs] *adj.* **1** wooded. **2** arboreal. **3** arborescent.

ar•bo•res•cent [,ɑrbə'rɛsənt] *adj.* like a tree in shape.
—,ar•bo'res•cence, *n.*

ar•bo•re•tum [,ɑrbə'ritəm] *n.* a place where trees and shrubs are grown for educational, scientific, and other purposes. ⟨< L *arboretum* < *arbor* tree⟩

ar•bo•ri•cul•ture ['ɑrbərə,kʌltʃər] *or* [ɑr'bɔrə,kʌltʃər] *n.* the science of growing trees or bushes.

ar•bor•ist ['ɑrbərɪst] *n.* an expert on trees.

ar•bor•vi•tae ['ɑrbər'vitaɪ] *or* ['ɑrbər'vəiti] *n., pl.* **-vi•tae** or **-vi•taes.** any of a genus (*Thuja*) of evergreen trees of the cypress family found in North America and E Asia, having small, fragrant, scalelike, overlapping leaves, small cones, and light, soft, fragrant wood that is highly resistant to decay. See also EASTERN WHITE CEDAR, WESTERN RED CEDAR. ⟨< L *arbor vitae* tree of life⟩

ar•bour or **ar•bor²** ['ɑrbər] *n.* **1** a shady place formed by trees or shrubs or, often, by vines growing on latticework. **2** the latticework itself. ⟨ME < AF *erber* < LL *herbarium* < *herba* herb. Doublet of HERBARIUM. Influenced by L *arbor* tree⟩
—'ar•boured, *adj.*

Arbour Day or **Arbor Day** a day observed in certain Canadian provinces and in some other countries by planting trees. The date varies in different places.

ar•bu•tus [ɑr'bjutəs] *n.* **1** any of a genus (*Arbutus*) of shrubs and trees of the heath family, having broad, leathery, evergreen leaves, large clusters of flowers, and red, berrylike fruit. A common arbutus of warm temperate regions is the **strawberry tree,** native to southern Europe and Ireland. Also called **madroña. 2** See TRAILING ARBUTUS. ⟨< L⟩

arc [ɑrk] *n., v.* **arced** [ɑrkt], **arc•ing** ['ɑrkɪŋ], *adj.* —*n.* **1** any continuous part of a circle or ellipse, or its angular measurement. **2** a curved line or path. **3** *Electricity.* a discharge of electricity seen as a curved stream of brilliant light or sparks, formed when a current jumps across a gap in a circuit or between electrodes. **4** *Astronomy.* the apparent path of a heavenly body above the horizon (**diurnal arc**) and below the horizon (**nocturnal arc**). **5** a cover used to protect young plants, in the form of a geodesic dome.
—*v.* **1** *Electricity.* form an arc. **2** follow a curved path or course.
—*adj. Trigonometry.* being the reverse of a trigonometric function. ⟨< L *arcus* bow⟩

ARC [ɑrk] AIDS-RELATED COMPLEX.

ar•cade [ɑr'keid] *n.* **1** a passageway with an arched roof. **2** any covered passageway: *Some buildings have arcades with small stores along either side.* **3** *Architecture.* a row of arches supported by columns. **4** a hall with video and other games, which people pay money to play. ⟨< F < Provençal *arcado*, ult. < VL *arca.* See ARCH¹.⟩

Ar•ca•di•a [ɑr'keidiə] *n.* **1** a mountain district in the southern part of ancient Greece, famous for the simple, contented life of its people. **2** any region of simple, quiet contentment, or an ideal of this. ⟨< L < Gk.⟩ **—Ar'ca•di•an,** *adj., n.*

Ar•ca•dy ['ɑrkədi] *n. Poetic.* Arcadia.

ar•cane [ɑr'kein] *adj.* mysterious; esoteric: *an arcane science, arcane knowledge.* ⟨< L. See ARCANUM.⟩

ar•ca•num [ɑr'keinəm] *n., pl.* **-nums** or **-na** [-nə]. a secret; mystery. ⟨< L *arcanum* (thing) hidden < *arca* chest⟩

arc furnace a furnace whose heat is produced by an electrical arc.

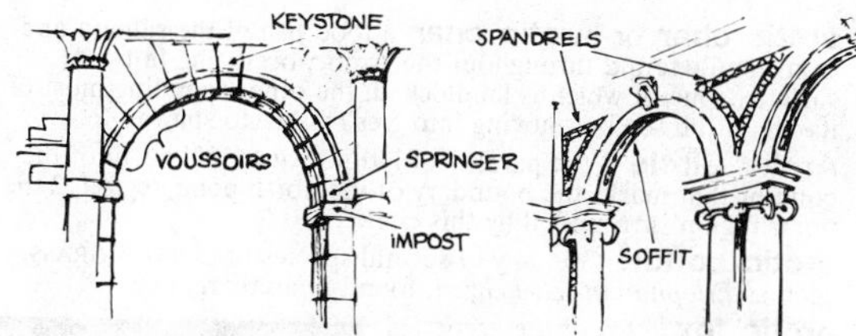

Arches: at the left, an ancient Roman arch; at the right, arches in a gallery at Osgoode Hall, Toronto

arch[1] [ɑrtʃ] *n., v.* —*n.* **1** *Architecture.* a curved structure used in bridges, gateways, etc. as a support for the weight above it. **2** a structure containing an arch or arches, built as an ornament or gateway: *a triumphal arch.* **3** any curve in the shape of an arch. **4** *Anatomy.* the curved bottom of the foot: *Fallen arches cause flat feet.* See LEG for picture. **5** something like an arch: *the great blue arch of the sky.*
—*v.* **1** bend into an arch; curve. **2** furnish with an arch. **3** form an arch over; span: *The rainbow arches the sky.* ⟨ME < OF < *arche* < VL *arca*, pl. < L *arcus* bow⟩

arch[2] [ɑrtʃ] *adj.* **1** chief; principal: *the arch villain of a story. His arch rival for the position was a younger woman.* **2** consciously playful or mischievous: *an arch look, an arch reply.* ⟨< *arch-* (prefix)⟩ —**'arch•ly,** *adv.* —**'arch•ness,** *n.*

arch– *prefix.* **1** chief; principal: *archbishop = principal bishop; archduke = principal duke.* **2** first; original: *archiblast.* Also, **archi-.** ⟨ME *arche-* < OE *arce-* < L *archi-* < Gk. *arche-*, combining form of *arkhos* chief⟩

–arch *combining form.* ruler: *matriarch, monarch.* ⟨< Gk. *-arkhes* < *-arkhein* rule⟩

arch. **1** archaic; archaism. **2** architecture; architect. **3** archipelago.

Arch. **1** Archbishop. **2** Archdeacon. **3** Archduke.

Ar•chae•an [ɑr'kiən] *n., adj.* Archaeozoic. Also **Archean.**

ar•chae•bac•te•ria [,ɑrkibæk'tiriə] *n., pl. of* ARCHAEBACTERIUM. tiny organisms much like bacteria in appearance, but with different internal structure and chemistry; thought to be ancient life forms, and sometimes classified as a separate kingdom.

archaeo– *combining form.* ancient; primitive, as in *archaeology.* ⟨< Gk. *archaios* ancient < *arkhē* beginning⟩

ar•chae•o•log•i•cal [,ɑrkiə'lɒdʒəkəl] *adj.* of or having to do with archaeology. Also, **archeological.** —**,ar•chae•o'log•i•cal•ly,** *adv.*

ar•chae•ol•o•gist [,ɑrki'ɒlədʒɪst] *n.* a person trained in archaeology, especially one whose work it is. Also, **archeologist.**

ar•chae•ol•o•gy [,ɑrki'ɒlədʒi] *n.* the study of the people, customs, and life of ancient times. Students of archaeology excavate, classify, and study the remains of ancient cities, tools, monuments, etc. Also, **archeology.** ⟨< Gk. < *archaios* ancient + E *-logy*⟩

ar•chae•op•ter•yx [,ɑrki'ɒptərɪks] *n.* the oldest-known fossil bird of the European Upper Jurassic period, about the size of a crow, having teeth, a lizardlike tail, and well-developed wings. Also, **archeopteryx.** ⟨< *archaeo-* + Gk. *pteryx* wing⟩

Ar•chae•o•zo•ic [,ɑrkiə'zouɪk] *n., adj. Geology.* —*n.* **1** the oldest era. During this era, commencing about 2 billion years ago, living things first appeared. **2** the rocks formed during this era.
—*adj.* of or having to do with this era or the rocks formed during it. Also, **Archeozoic.** ⟨< *archaeo-* + Gk. *zōē* life⟩

ar•cha•ic [ɑr'keiɪk] *adj.* **1** no longer in general use. **2** old-fashioned; out-of-date. **3** ancient. ⟨< Gk. *archaikos*, ult. < *arkhē* beginning⟩ —**ar'cha•i•cal•ly,** *adv.*

ar•cha•ism ['ɑrkei,ɪzəm] *or* ['ɑrki,ɪzəm] *n.* **1** a word or expression no longer in general use. *In sooth* and *methinks* are archaisms meaning *in truth* and *it seems to me.* **2** the use of something out of date in language or art. —**,ar•cha'ist•ic,** *adj.*

ar•cha•ize ['ɑrkei,aɪz] *or* ['ɑrki,aɪz] *v.* **-ized, -iz•ing.** put out of general use or make appear old-fashioned: *The automobile archaized the horse-drawn carriage.*

arch•an•gel ['ɑrk,eindʒəl] *n.* **1** a celestial being serving as God's chief messenger. **2** angelica. ⟨ME < LL < Gk. *archangelos* < *arch-* chief + *angelos* angel⟩

arch•bish•op ['ɑrtʃ,bɪʃəp] *n.* a bishop of the highest rank. He presides over a church district called an archbishopric or archdiocese.

arch•bish•op•ric [,ɑrtʃ'bɪʃəprɪk] *n.* **1** a church district governed by an archbishop. **2** the position, rank, or dignity of an archbishop.

arch•dea•con ['ɑrtʃ,dikən] *n.* an assistant to a bishop. In the Anglican Church, he or she superintends the work of other members of the clergy.

arch•dea•con•ate [,ɑrtʃ'dikənət] *n.* the office of an archdeacon.

arch•dea•con•ry [,ɑrtʃ'dikənri] *n., pl.* **-ries. 1** a district under the supervision of an archdeacon. **2** the position or rank of an archdeacon. **3** the residence of an archdeacon.

arch•di•o•cese [,ɑrtʃ'daɪəsɪs] *or* [,ɑrtʃ'daɪə,siz] *n.* the church district governed by an archbishop. —**,arch•di'oc•e•san** [-daɪ'ɒsəzən], *n.*

arch•du•cal [,ɑrtʃ'djukəl] *or* [,ɑrtʃ'dukəl] *adj.* of an archduke; of an archduchy.

arch•duch•ess [,ɑrtʃ'dʌtʃɪs] *n.* **1** the wife or widow of an archduke. **2** a woman with rank equal to that of an archduke. **3** a princess of the former ruling house of Austria-Hungary.

arch•duch•y [,ɑrtʃ'dʌtʃi] *n., pl.* **-duch•ies.** the territory under the rule of an archduke or archduchess.

arch•duke [,ɑrtʃ'djuk] *or* [,ɑrtʃ'duk] *n.* a prince of the former ruling house of Austria-Hungary.

Ar•che•an [ɑr'kiən] See ARCHAEAN.

arched [ɑrtʃt] *adj.* having or forming an arch or arches.

ar•che•go•ni•um [,ɑrkə'gouniəm] *n., pl.* **-ni•a** [-niə]. *Botany.* the female reproductive organ in ferns, mosses, etc. ⟨< NL *archegonium*, ult. < Gk. *arkhē* beginning + *gonos* race⟩

arch•en•e•my [,ɑrtʃ'ɛnəmi] *n., pl.* **-mies. 1** the chief enemy. **2** Satan.

ar•chen•ter•on [ɑr'kɛntə,rɒn] *n.* the primitive digestive cavity of a metazoan embryo. ⟨< *arch* chief + Gk. *enteron* intestine⟩

ar•che•o•log•i•cal [,ɑrkiə'lɒdʒəkəl] See ARCHAEOLOGICAL.

ar•che•ol•o•gist [,ɑrki'ɒlədʒɪst] See ARCHAEOLOGIST.

ar•che•ol•o•gy [,ɑrki'ɒlədʒi] See ARCHAEOLOGY.

Ar•che•o•zo•ic [,ɑrkiə'zouɪk] See ARCHAEOZOIC.

arch•er ['ɑrtʃər] *n.* **1** a person who shoots with a bow and arrows. **2 Archer,** *Astronomy or astrology.* Sagittarius. ⟨< AF < L **arcarius* < *arcus* bow⟩

arch•er•fish ['ɑrtʃər,fɪʃ] *n.* any fish of the family Toxotidae of freshwater percoids native to Australia, which shoot insects with water from the mouth to make them fall into the water.

arch•er•y ['ɑrtʃəri] *n.* **1** the practice or art of shooting with bows and arrows. **2** a troop of archers. **3** the weapons of an archer; bows, arrows, etc.

ar•che•typ•al ['ɑrkə,taɪpəl] *adj.* **1** serving as a model or pattern. **2** eminently representative or typical: *the archetypal Hollywood heroine.* —**,ar•che'typ•al•ly,** *adv.*

ar•che•type ['ɑrkə,taɪp] *n.* **1** an original model or pattern from which copies are made, or out of which later forms develop: *That little engine is the archetype of huge modern locomotives.* **2** a perfect or typical example or specimen. **3** in Jungian psychology, any of various images or patterns forming part of the collective human psyche and expressed in art and literature as specific symbols. ⟨< L < Gk. *arkhetypon*, neut. of *arkhetypos* original⟩

ar•che•typ•i•cal [,ɑrkə'tɪpəkəl] *adj.* archetypal. —**,ar•che'typ•i•cal•ly,** *adv.*

arch•fiend ['ɑrtʃ,find] *n.* **1** the chief fiend. **2** Satan.

archi– *prefix.* a variant of **arch-,** as in *archi-episcopal.*

ar•chi•blast ['ɑrkɪ,blæst] *n.* **1** the protoplasm of an egg cell. **2** the outer layer of a very immature embryo. ⟨< *arch* chief + Gk. *blastos* a sprout⟩

ar•chi•carp ['ɑrkɪ,kɑrp] *n.* the female reproductive organ in certain fungi such as mildews and yeasts. ⟨< *arch* chief + Gk. *karpos* harvest⟩

ar•chi–e•pis•co•pal [,ɑrki ə'pɪskəpəl] *adj.* of or having to do with an archbishop. —**,ar•chi•e'pis•co•pate,** *n.*

ar•chi•man•drite [,ɑrkɪ'mændrəit] *n.* in the Eastern Orthodox Church, the head of one or more monasteries.

⟨< Ecclesiastical L *archimandrita* < Ecclesiastical LGk. *archimandrites* < *arch* chief + *mandra* monastery⟩

Ar•chi•me•de•an [ˌɑrkəˈmidiən] *adj.* of, having to do with, or invented by Archimedes.

Ar•chi•me•des principle [ˌɑrkəˈmidiz] *Physics.* the principle that the apparent loss of weight of a body when partly or totally immersed in a liquid is equal to the weight of the liquid displaced. ⟨after *Archimedes* (287?-212 B.C.), a Greek mathematician, physicist, and inventor, who discovered this principle⟩

Archimedes' screw a water-raising device used by the ancients, consisting of a spiral tube around or inside a cylindrical shaft. The water was brought upward by manually turning the spiral.

ar•chi•pel•a•go [ˌɑrkəˈpɛləˌgou] *n., pl.* **-gos** or **-goes. 1** a sea having many islands in it. **2** a group of many islands: *The islands in the Arctic Ocean north of Canada are called the Canadian Archipelago. Abbrev.*: arch. ⟨< Ital. *arcipelago* < *arci-* chief (ult. < Gk. *arkhi-*) + *pelago* sea (ult. < Gk. *pelagos*); originally, the Aegean⟩ **—ˌar•chi•pe'lag•ic** [-pəˈlædʒɪk], *adj.*

ar•chi•tect [ˈɑrkəˌtɛkt] *n.* **1** a person trained in architecture, especially one whose work is designing buildings and supervising their construction. **2** a designer, planner, or maker: *the architects of modern technology.* ⟨< L *architectus* < Gk. *arkhitekton* < *arkhi-* chief + *tekton* builder⟩

ar•chi•tec•ton•ic [ˌɑrkətɛkˈtɒnɪk] *adj.* **1** having to do with architecture, construction, or design. **2** showing skill in construction or design. **—ˌar•chi•tec'ton•i•cal•ly,** *adv.*

ar•chi•tec•ton•ics [ˌɑrkətɛkˈtɒnɪks] *n.* **1** the science of architecture. **2** skill in architecture. **3** any skill in the construction or design of a work of art. **4** the product of such skill; the design or structure of a work of art.

ar•chi•tec•tur•al [ˌɑrkəˈtɛktʃərəl] *adj.* of architecture; having to do with architecture. **—ˌar•chi'tec•tur•al•ly,** *adv.*

ar•chi•tec•ture [ˈɑrkəˌtɛktʃər] *n.* **1** the science or art of building; the planning and designing of buildings. **2** a style or special manner of building: *Greek architecture made much use of columns.* **3** construction: *the flimsy architecture of some buildings.* **4** a framework or system; structure. **5** *Computer technology.* the structure of the constituent parts of a computer and how these parts affect each other.

ar•chi•trave [ˈɑrkəˌtreiv] *n. Architecture.* **1** the beam resting directly on the top, or capital, of a column; the lowest part of an entablature, below the frieze. See COLUMN for picture. **2** the moulding around a door, window, or arch. ⟨< Ital. *architrave* < *archi-* chief (ult. < Gk.) + *trave* < L *trabs, trabis* beam⟩

ar•chi•val [ɑrˈkaɪvəl] *adj.* of, having to do with, or kept in archives: *archival records.*

ar•chive [ˈɑrkaɪv] *n., v.* **ar•chived, ar•chiv•ing.** *—n.* Usually, **archives,** *pl.* **1** a place where public records or historical documents are preserved: *The National Archives of Canada are in Ottawa.* **2** the material kept in such a place.
—v. place (data) in a reserve file in a computer or other system: *We have arranged to archive all the data we have collected in the survey.* ⟨< F < L *archivum* < Gk. *archeia* < *archē* government⟩

ar•chiv•ist [ˈɑrkɪvɪst] *n.* a person in charge of archives.

ar•chi•volt [ˈɑrkɪˌvoult] *n. Architecture.* **1** decorative moulding on an arch. **2** the underside of an arch. ⟨< Ital. *archivolto* < Med.L *archivoltum* < L *arcus* arch + *volvere* to turn⟩

ar•chon [ˈɑrkɒn] *n.* **1** in ancient Athens, a chief magistrate. **2** ruler. ⟨< Gk. *arkhōn*, ppr. of *arkhein* rule⟩

arch•way [ˈɑrtʃˌwei] *n.* **1** an entrance or passageway with an arch above it. **2** an arch covering a passageway.

-ar•chy *combining form.* rule; government: *monarchy = rule by one person.* ⟨< Gk. *-arkhia* < *arkhein* rule⟩

arc lamp a lamp in which the light comes from an electric arc.

arc light 1 the brilliant light given by an ARC LAMP. **2** ARC LAMP.

arc•tic [ˈɑrktɪk] *or* [ˈɑrtɪk] *adj., n. —adj.* **1** Often, **Arctic,** of, having to do with, referring to, or living or growing in the region north of the Arctic Circle: *the arctic fox.* **2** extremely cold; frigid: *a whole week of arctic temperatures.*
—n. **1 the Arctic, a** the north polar region; the region north of the Arctic Circle. **b** the Arctic Ocean. **2 arctics,** *pl.* warm, waterproof overshoes. ⟨ME < OF < L *arcticus* < Gk. *arktikos* of the Bear (constellation) < *arktos* bear⟩

arctic char or **Arctic char** a food fish of the salmon and trout family found throughout the Arctic, occurring in two varieties, one of which is landlocked, the other spending most of its life in the sea but moving into fresh water to spawn.

Arctic Circle 1 the parallel of latitude at 66°33′ north of the equator that marks the boundary of the north polar region. **2** the polar region surrounded by this circle.

arctic cotton *Cdn.* any of several species of COTTON GRASS, such as *Eriophorum scheuchzeri*, found in arctic regions.

arctic fox a fox of the arctic regions, valued for its fur. Its coat is bluish grey or brownish grey in summer and white in winter.

An arctic fox

arctic grayling *Cdn.* a silver-grey freshwater fish (*Thymallus arcticus*) found in northern waters.

arctic ground squirrel *Cdn.* a squirrel (*Spermophilus parryii*), the largest ground squirrel of the Americas. It is greyish brown with white spots.

arctic hare *Cdn.* a large, thickset hare (*Lepus arcticus*) found in arctic Canada, from the tundra of the Northwest Territories up to the northern tip of Ellesmere Island, and also in Greenland. It is pure white in winter, except for its black-tipped ears, and varies in summer from bluish grey to almost white with a tinge of cinnamon or grey, depending on the latitude.

arctic haze a pollution problem in the far north, in which particles of pollutants suspended in the arctic air increase in concentration during the winter months.

arctic hysteria *Cdn.* CABIN FEVER

arctic loon a loon (*Gavia arctica*) similar to the common loon but smaller and grey on the head and the back of the neck. Its range is more northerly, although it winters as far south as California.

arctic poppy either of two perennial poppies having a very short stem and growing in firmly-packed soil. A subarctic variety (*Papaver nudicaule*) has yellow and white flowers; an alpine variety (*Papaver alpinum*) has white and yellow or pink and orange flowers.

arctic tern an Arctic-breeding tern (*Sterna paradisaea*) noted for the length of its migrations, from its breeding grounds in the Arctic of the Old and New Worlds south to its winter range in the oceans of the southern hemisphere.

arctic willow a low-growing willow (*Salix arctica*) of arctic tundra and northern alpine regions having trailing, freely rooting branches and pale foliage.

Arc•tu•rus [ɑrkˈtjʊrəs] *or* [ɑrkˈtʊrəs] *n.* a very bright first magnitude star in the constellation Boötes. ⟨< L < Gk.⟩

ar•cu•ate [ˈɑrkjuɪt] *or* [ˈɑrkjuˌeit] *adj.* bent like a bow. ⟨< L *arcuatus* bent like a bow < pp. of *arcuare* < *arcus* a bow⟩ **—'ar•cu•ate•ly,** *adv.*

ar•cu•a•tion [ˌɑrkjuˈeiʃən] *n.* **1** a bending or being bent into an arch. **2** the use of arches in architecture. **3** a series of arches.

arc welding a method of welding in which the heat is produced by an electric arc.

-ard or **-art** *suffix.* a person characterized by a certain quality, behaviour, actions, etc., especially excessively or conspicuously, as in *sluggard, drunkard, braggart, wizard.* ⟨< OF < Gmc.; related to G *-hard, -hart* (literally, hardy or bold)⟩

ARDA [ˈɑrdə] *Cdn.* Agriculture and Rural Development Act.

Ar•den [ˈɑrdən] *n.* **1** a land of the imagination or of romance. ⟨< the name of a wooded region of central England, the scene of Shakespeare's *As You Like It.*⟩

ar•den•cy [ˈɑrdənsi] *n.* the condition of being ardent.

ar•dent [ˈɑrdənt] *adj.* **1** full of zeal; very enthusiastic; eager. **2** burning; fiery; hot. **3** glowing. ⟨ME < OF < L *ardens, -entis,* ppr. of *ardere* burn⟩ **—'ar•dent•ly,** *adv.*

ardent spirits strong alcoholic liquor.

ar•dour or **ar•dor** [ˈɑrdər] *n.* **1** eagerness; warmth of emotion; great enthusiasm: *patriotic ardour.* **2** burning heat. ⟨ME < OF < L *ardorem* < *ardere* burn⟩

ar•du•ous [ˈɑrdjuəs] *or* [ˈɑrdʒuəs] *adj.* **1** hard to do; requiring much effort; difficult: *an arduous lesson.* **2** using up much energy; laborious; strenuous: *an arduous effort to learn the lesson.* **3** hard to climb; steep: *an arduous hill.* ⟨< L *arduus* steep⟩ **—'ar•du•ous•ly,** *adv.* **—'ar•du•ous•ness,** *n.*

are¹ [ɑr]; *unstressed*, [ər] *v.* the plural present indicative, of BE: *we are, you are, they are.* ⟨OE (Northumbrian) *aron*⟩

are² [ɛr] *or* [ɑr] *n.* a measure of area, equal to 100 m^2. *Symbol*: a ⟨< F < L *area* area⟩
☛ *Hom.* AIR, E'ER, ERE, ERR, HEIR [ɛr].

ARE Arab Republic of Egypt.

ar•e•a ['ɛriə] *n.* **1** the amount of surface; extent of surface: *The area of this floor is 60 m^2.* **2** region: *a mountainous area.* **3** range; scope: *The provincial governments often try to limit the area of federal responsibility.* **4** a field of study or activity: *He is working in the area of foreign policy.* **5** a more-or-less level surface or space: *The playing area was marked off with white lines.* **6** a yard or court of a building. ⟨< L *area* piece of level ground⟩
☛ *Hom.* ARIA ['ɛriə].

area code a three-digit number designating a particular area within the total region served by a telephone system. It is used as part of the telephone number for directly dialled long-distance calls between areas.

ar•e•al ['ɛriəl] *adj.* of or having to do with area or an area. **—'ar•e•al•ly,** *adv.*
☛ *Hom.* AERIAL ['ɛriəl].

area rug a rug covering only a small area of the floor.

ar•e•a•way ['ɛriə,wei] *n.* **1** a sunken area or court at the entrance to a cellar or basement. **2** an area serving as a passageway between buildings.

ar•e•ca ['ærɪkə], ['ɛrɪkə], *or* [ə'rikə] *n.* any of several tall, tropical Asian palms (genus *Areca*), especially the BETEL PALM. ⟨< Port. < Tamil *adaikay*⟩

a•re•na [ə'rinə] *n.* **1** a building for indoor sports, having a central space for players or competitors that is surrounded by tiers of seats for spectators: *There is a hockey game at the arena tonight.* **2** any area where contests or shows take place. **3** the central area of an ancient Roman amphitheatre, where gladiators fought. **4** any sphere of public action, especially one involving conflict: *You have to have stamina to succeed in the political arena.* **5** *Computer technology.* a smooth, round platform with a padded rest for the user's hand, on which a mouse is moved around. It reduces friction on the mouse and muscle fatigue for the user. ⟨< later var. of L *harena* sand; because the floors of Roman arenas were covered with sand⟩

ar•e•na•ceous [,ærə'neiʃəs] *or* [,ɛrə'neiʃəs] *adj.* **1** sandy; like sand. **2** arenicolous. ⟨< L *arenaceus* < *arena* sand⟩

arena theatre THEATRE-IN-THE-ROUND.

ar•e•nic•ol•ous [,ærə'nɪkələs] *or* [,ɛrə'nɪkələs] *adj.* growing in sand. ⟨< L *arena* sand + *colere* to cultivate⟩

ar•e•nite ['ærə,nəit] *or* ['ɛrə,nəit] *n.* sandstone.

aren't [ɑrnt] **1** are not. **2** am not (*used in questions*): *I'm too late, aren't I?*

a•re•o•la [ə'riələ] *n.* **-lae** [-,li] *or* [-,laɪ] or **-las. 1** a little area. **2** *Anatomy.* the small, often coloured, ring around something, as around a nipple, pimple, etc. **3** *Biology.* an interstice. The spaces between the veins of a leaf are areolae. Also, **ar•e•ole** ['ɛri,oul]. ⟨< L *āreola* dim. of *ārea* area⟩ **—a're•o•lar,** *adj.* **—a,re•o'la•tion,** *n.*

Ar•e•op•a•gus [,æri'ɒpəgəs] *or* [,ɛri'ɒpəgəs] *n.* **1** the hill of Ares in Athens. **2** the highest judicial court of ancient Athens, which met there. ⟨< Gk. *Ares* + *pagos* hill⟩ **—,Ar•e'op•a•gite** [-'ɒpə,dʒəit] *n., adj.*

Ar•es ['ɛriz] *n. Greek mythology.* the god of war, corresponding to the Roman god Mars.
☛ *Hom.* ARIES.

a•rête [ə'reit] *n.* a sharp, rocky ridge on a mountain, usually above the winter snow line. ⟨< F⟩

ar•e•thu•sa [,ærə'θuzə] *or* [,ɛrə-]; [,ærə'θusə] *or* [,ɛrə-] *n.* a rare bog orchid (*Arethusa bulbosa*) of NE North America having a single magenta flower with yellow or white hairy ridges on its pendant lip, and a single long, narrow leaf. The arethusa is rapidly becoming extinct in the more populated areas of its range. ⟨< *Arethusa*, a nymph in Greek mythology⟩

ar•ga•la ['ɑrgələ] *n.* **1** the Indian ADJUTANT STORK. **2** the African marabou. ⟨< Hind. *hargila*⟩

ar•ga•li ['ɑrgəli] *n.* a wild Asian sheep (*Ovis ammon*) having large curving horns. ⟨< Mongolian⟩

Ar•gand burner ['ɑrgənd] *n.* a type of oil or gas burner. ⟨< A. *Argand*, 18c. Swiss inventor⟩

ar•gent ['ɑrdʒənt] *n., adj. —n.* **1** *Archaic or poetic.* silver. **2** *Heraldry.* the silver or white colouring in a coat of arms. *—adj.* silvery. *Abbrev.*: a. ⟨< F < L *argentum*⟩

ar•gen•tic [ɑr'dʒɛntɪk] *adj.* of or containing divalent or trivalent silver.

ar•gen•tif•er•ous [,ɑrdʒən'tɪfərəs] *adj.* containing silver.

Ar•gen•ti•na [,ɑrdʒən'tinə] a country in SE South America.

ar•gen•tine ['ɑrdʒəntɪn], ['ɑrdʒən,tin], *or* ['ɑrdʒən,taɪn] *adj.* of or like silver. ⟨< L⟩

Ar•gen•tine ['ɑrdʒən,tin] *or* ['ɑrdʒən,taɪn] *n., adj. —n.* **1** a native or inhabitant of Argentina. **2 the Argentine,** Argentina. *—adj.* of or having to do with Argentina or its people.

Ar•gen•tin•i•an [,ɑrdʒən'tɪniən] *n. or adj.* Argentine. Sometimes, **Argentinean.**

ar•gen•tite ['ɑrdʒən,təit] *n.* a native silver sulphide, found in veins in granite and other rock strata. This dark-grey substance is an important ore of silver. *Formula*: Ag_2S ⟨< L *argentum* silver + E *-ite*[1]⟩

ar•gen•tous [ɑr'dʒɛntəs] *adj.* of or containing monovalent silver.

ar•gil ['ɑrdʒɪl] *n.* clay; especially, clay used for pottery. ⟨< F *argille* < L < Gk. *argilla* < *argos* shining⟩

ar•gil•la•ceous [,ɑrdʒə'leiʃəs] *adj.* of rock or rock deposits, containing or composed of clay or silt, etc. ⟨< L *argillaceus* < *argilla* clay < Gk. *argos* white⟩

ar•gil•lite ['ɑrdʒə,ləit] *n.* a rock composed of clay or silt that is intermediate between shale and slate. It is harder than shale but does not have the cleavage of slate. ⟨< L *argilla* white clay + E *-ite*[1]⟩

ar•gi•nase ['ɑrdʒə,neis] *n.* an enzyme in the liver that helps convert the amino acid arginine into urea and ornithine. ⟨< Gk. *arginin* < ? Gk. *arginoesis* white⟩

ar•gi•nine ['ɑrdʒə,nin] *or* ['ɑrdʒə,naɪn] *n.* a free amino acid. *Formula*: $C_6H_{14}N_4O_2$ ⟨< G *arginin* < ? Gk. *arginoesis* white⟩

Ar•give ['ɑrdʒaɪv] *or* ['ɑrgaɪv] *adj., n. —adj.* **1** of Argos, an ancient city in SE Greece. **2** Greek.
—n. **1** a native or inhabitant of Argos. **2** Greek.

Ar•go ['ɑrgou] *n. Greek mythology.* the ship in which Jason and his companions sailed in search of the Golden Fleece.

ar•gol ['ɑrgɒl] *n.* tartar; a by-product of the fermentation of grapes that collects on the inside of wine casks. It is used in dyeing and various kinds of manufacturing. ⟨< AF *argoil*⟩

ar•gon ['ɑrgɒn] *n.* a chemical element that is a colourless, odourless, inert gas forming a very small part of the air. Most ordinary light bulbs are filled with argon. *Symbol*: Ar; *at.no.* 18; *at.mass* 39.95. ⟨< NL < Gk. *argos* idle < *a-* without + *ergon* work⟩

Ar•go•naut ['ɑrgə,nɒt] *n.* **1** *Greek mythology.* one of the men who sailed with Jason in search of the Golden Fleece. **2** Often, **argonaut,** a person who participated in a gold rush in modern times, especially to California in 1849 or to the Cariboo, British Columbia, in 1862. **3** PAPER NAUTILUS. ⟨< L *Argonauta* < Gk. *Argonautēs* < *Argō*, the name of the ship used by Jason, + *nautēs* sailor⟩

ar•go•sy ['ɑrgəsi] *n., pl.* **-sies. 1** a large merchant ship. **2** a fleet of such ships. ⟨< Ital. *ragusea* ship of Ragusa, Sicilian port formerly trading extensively with England⟩

ar•got ['ɑrgou] *or* ['ɑrgət] *n.* **1** the specialized language, or jargon, of people who share a particular kind of work or way of life, especially one that is more or less secret: *underworld argot.* ⟨< F⟩

ar•gu•a•ble ['ɑrgjuəbəl] *adj.* **1** open to argument; that can be disputed or questioned. **2** supportable by argument; reasonable. **—'ar•gu•a•bly,** *adv.*

ar•gue ['ɑrgju] *v.* **-gued, -gu•ing. 1** discuss, especially with some warmth, with someone who disagrees: *to argue a question.* **2** give reasons for or against (something): *She argued against the passage of the bill.* **3** persuade by giving reasons: *He argued me into going.* **4** try to prove by reasoning; maintain: *Columbus argued that the world was round.* **5** indicate; show; prove: *Her rich clothes argue her wealth.* **6** raise objections; dispute. ⟨ME < OF *arguer* < L *argutare*, frequentative of *arguere* make clear⟩ **—'ar•gu•er,** *n.*
☛ *Syn.* **1.** See note at DISCUSS.

ar•gu•ment ['ɑrgjəmənt] *n.* **1** a discussion by persons who give reasons for and against different points of view; a debate: *He won the argument by producing figures to prove his point.* **2** an emotional disagreement; a dispute: *She had an argument with her brother about who won the card game.* **3 a** the reason or reasons given for or against something. **b** the act of giving these arguments; argumentation: *She showed by argument that his claim was false.* **4** a short statement of what is in a book, poem, etc. **5** *Mathematics.* a variable with a fixed value; an independent variable. **6** *Logic.* the term figuring in the first two statements of a syllogism but not in the conclusion. In the syllogism *All trees have roots; an oak is a tree; therefore an oak has roots, tree* is the argument. **7** *Linguistics.* a non-optional complement. *The car* is the argument of *into the car*; in *Joan ate the apple*, both *Joan* and *the apple* are arguments of *eat*.

☛ *Syn.* **1. Argument,** CONTROVERSY, DISPUTE = a discussion by persons who disagree. **Argument** applies to a discussion in which each of two persons uses facts and reasons to try to win the other over: *He won the argument by producing figures.* **Controversy** applies chiefly to a formal argument between groups, often carried on in writing or speeches: *The Canadian school controversy still continues.* **Dispute** suggests contradicting rather than reasoning, and applies to an argument marked by feeling: *The dispute over the property was settled in court.*

ar•gu•men•ta•tion [ˌɑrgjəmɛn'teiʃən] *n.* **1** the process of arguing; reasoning. **2** discussion; debate.

ar•gu•men•ta•tive [ˌɑrgjə'mɛntətɪv] *adj.* **1** fond of arguing. **2** containing argument. **—ˌar•gu'men•ta•tive•ly,** *adv.*

Ar•gus ['ɑrgəs] *n.* **1** *Greek mythology.* a giant with a hundred eyes. He was killed by Hermes, and his eyes were put in the peacock's tail. **2** any watchful guardian.

Ar•gus–eyed ['ɑrgəs ˌaɪd] *adj.* watchful; observant.

ar•gyle or **Ar•gyle** ['ɑrgaɪl] *adj., n. —adj.* of or having to do with a diamond-shaped pattern of various colours, often knitted into articles such as socks, neckties, etc.
—n. **argyles,** *pl.* socks having this pattern. ⟨< *Argyll*, a county in west Scotland⟩

ar•gyr•o•dite [ɑr'dʒɜrədəit] *n.* a shiny grey mineral composed of silver, germanium, and sulphur. *Formula*: Ag_8GeS_6

Ar•gy•rol ['ɑrdʒəˌrɒl] *or* ['ɑrdʒəˌroul] *n. Trademark.* a compound of silver and a protein, used in the treatment of inflamed mucous membranes. ⟨< Gk. *argyros* silver⟩

ar•hant ['ɑrhənt] *n. Buddhism.* a title of respect for someone who has attained enlightenment. ⟨< Skt.⟩

a•ri•a ['ɑriə], ['æriə], *or* ['ɛriə] *n.* an air or melody; a melody for a single voice with instrumental or vocal accompaniment. ⟨< Ital. < L *aer* air < Gk.⟩
☛ *Hom.* AREA ['ɛriə].

Ar•i•ad•ne [ˌæri'ædni] *or* [ˌɛri'ædni] *n. Greek mythology.* the daughter of Minos, king of Crete. She fell in love with Theseus and gave him a ball of thread to help him find his way out of the Labyrinth of the Minotaur.

Ar•i•an ['ɛriən] *adj., n. Theology. —adj.* of or having to do with the doctrine of Arius of Alexandria (4th century) who taught that Jesus Christ is not of the same substance as God the Father.
—n. a believer in this doctrine.

Ar•i•an•ism ['ɛriəˌnɪzəm] *n. Theology.* belief in or support of the Arian doctrine.

a•ri•bo•fla•vin•o•sis [eiˌraɪbouˌfleivɪ'nousɪs] *n.* a condition caused by an inadequate supply of riboflavin, resulting in distorted vision and extreme chapping of the skin around the mouth.

ar•id ['ærɪd] *or* ['ɛrɪd] *adj.* **1** dry; barren: *Desert lands are arid.* **2** dull; uninteresting: *an arid, tiresome speech.* ⟨< L *āridus* < *ārēre* be dry⟩ **—'ar•id•ly,** *adv.* **—'ar•id•ness,** *n.*
☛ *Syn.* **1.** See note at DRY.

a•rid•i•ty [ə'rɪdəti] *n.* **1** dryness; barrenness. **2** dullness; lack of interest, life, or spirit.

A•ri•el ['ɛriəl] *n.* one of the five moons of the planet Uranus.

Ar•ies ['ɛriˌiz], ['ɛrɪz], *or* ['æriz] *n.* **1** *Astronomy.* a northern constellation thought of as having the shape of a ram. **2** *Astrology.* **a** the first sign of the zodiac. The sun enters Aries about March 21. See ZODIAC for picture. **b** a person born under this sign.
☛ *Hom.* ARES ['ɛriz] *or* ['æriz].

ar•i•et•ta [ˌɑri'ɛtə] *n.* a short aria.

a•right [ə'rəit] *adv.* correctly; rightly.

A•ri•ka•ri [ˌɑrɪ'kɑri] *n.* **1** a Native American people living in western North Dakota along the Missouri River. **2** a language of the Caddoan family, spoken by these people.

ar•il ['ærɪl] *or* ['ɛrɪl] *n. Botany.* an outside covering of certain seeds. The pulpy inner pod of the bittersweet is an aril. ⟨< NL *arillus* < Med.L *arilli* raisins⟩

ar•il•late ['ærəlɪt] *or* ['ɛrəlɪt], ['ærəˌleit] *or* ['ɛrəˌleit] *adj. Botany.* having an aril.

a•ri•o•so [ˌɑri'ousou] *adj., adv., n., pl.* **-sos.** *—adj. or adv. Music.* as or like an aria or song.
—n. a passage or piece of music to be sung as an aria or song. ⟨< Ital. *arioso* songlike < *aria* aria⟩

a•rise [ə'raɪz] *v.* **a•rose, a•ris•en, a•ris•ing. 1** get up; rise: *The audience arose together.* **2** move upward; ascend: *Smoke arose from the chimney.* **3** come into being or action; appear or begin: *A great wind arose.* **4** be caused; result: *Many accidents arise through carelessness.* ⟨OE *ārīsan*⟩
☛ *Usage.* See note at RISE.

a•ris•en [ə'rɪzən] *v.* pp. of ARISE.

ar•is•toc•ra•cy [ˌærɪ'stɒkrəsi] *or* [ˌɛrɪ'stɒkrəsi] *n., pl.* **-cies. 1** people of noble rank, title, or birth; a ruling body of nobles; nobility. **2** any class that is considered superior because of birth, intelligence, culture, or wealth. **3** a government in which a privileged upper class rules. **4** a country or state having such a government; oligarchy. **5** government by the best citizens. ⟨< LL *aristocratia* < Gk. *aristokratia* < *aristos* best + *kratein* rule⟩

a•ris•to•crat [ə'rɪstəˌkræt], ['ærɪstəˌkræt], *or* ['ɛrɪstəˌkræt] *n.* **1** a person who belongs to the aristocracy; noble. **2** a person who has the tastes, opinions, manners, etc. of the upper classes. **3** a person who favours government by an aristocracy.

a•ris•to•crat•ic [əˌrɪstə'krætɪk], [ˌærɪstə'krætɪk], *or* [ˌɛrɪstə'krætɪk] *adj.* **1** having to do with, belonging to, or characteristic of aristocracy or aristocrats. **2** proud, haughty, or distinguished: *an aristocratic bearing.* **—aˌris•to'crat•i•cal•ly,** *adv.*

Ar•is•to•te•li•an [ˌærɪstə'tiljən] *or* [ˌɛrɪstə'tiljən] *adj., n. —adj.* having to do with the Greek philosopher Aristotle (384-322 B.C.) or his philosophy.
—n. a follower of Aristotle.

arith. arithmetic; arithmetical.

a•rith•me•tic *n.* [ə'rɪθməˌtɪk]; *adj.* [ˌærɪθ'mɛtɪk] *or* [ˌɛrɪθ'mɛtɪk] *n., adj. —n.* **1** the branch of mathematics dealing with computation using real numbers, especially addition, subtraction, multiplication, and division. **2** the use of arithmetic, or one's skill in it: *Their arithmetic is very weak.* **3** a textbook or handbook on this subject.
—adj. of, having to do with, or using arithmetic: *an arithmetic progression.* Also, **arithmetical.** ⟨ME < OF < L *arithmetica* < Gk. *arithmētikē* < *arithmos* number⟩ **—ˌar•ith'met•i•cal•ly,** *adv.*

a•rith•me•ti•cian [əˌriθmə'tɪʃən], [ˌærɪθmə'tɪʃən], *or* [ˌɛrɪθmə'tɪʃən] *n.* a person skilled in arithmetic.

arithmetic mean the average obtained by dividing the sum of several quantities by the number of quantities. To obtain the arithmetic mean of 3, 9, 18, and 42, add them up and divide the total by 4.

arithmetic progression a series in which there is always the same difference between a number and the one next after it. 2, 4, 6, 8, 10 are in arithmetic progression; so are 8, 5, 2, –1. Compare GEOMETRIC PROGRESSION.

arithmetic unit a component of a digital computer which carries out arithmetic tasks.

-arium a place for —— or associated with —— : *sanitarium.*

Ar•i•zo•na [ˌærɪ'zounə] *n.* a southwestern state of the United States.

Ar•ju•na ['ɑrdʒunə] *n.* a hero of the Mahabharata, a Hindu epic.

ark [ɑrk] *n.* **1** in the Bible, the large boat which God directed Noah to build in order to save himself, his family, and a pair of each kind of animal from the Flood. **2** *Informal.* any large, clumsy boat. **3** any refuge or shelter. **4** the ARK OF THE COVENANT. ⟨OE *arc* < L *arca* chest⟩

Ar•kan•sas ['ɑrkənˌsɒ] *n.* a southern state of the United States.

Ark of the Covenant 1 the wooden chest or box in which the ancient Hebrews kept the two tablets of stone containing the Ten Commandments. **2** the wooden chest or other enclosure in a synagogue that symbolizes this.

ar•kose ['ɑrkous] *n.* a sandstone made up mostly of grains of feldspar and quartz. ⟨< F⟩

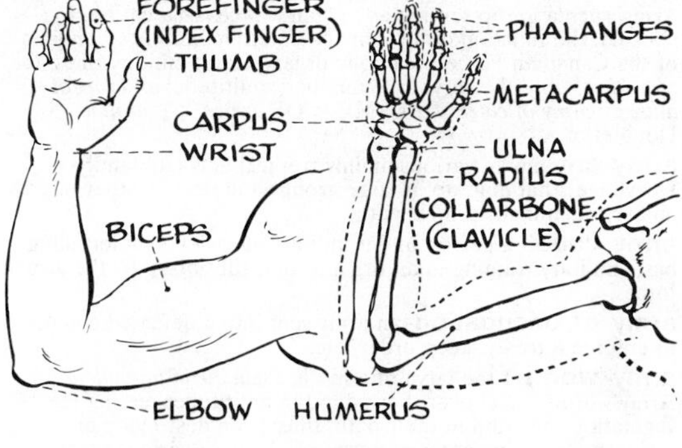

The human arm

arm[1] [ɑrm] *n.* **1** the upper limb of the human body between the shoulder and the hand. **2** a forelimb of an animal. The front legs of a bear are sometimes called arms. **3** anything resembling an arm in shape or use: *the arm of a chair, an arm of the sea.* **4** the part of a garment covering the arm. **5** power; authority: *the strong arm of the law.*
an arm and a leg, a large sum of money spent: *That platter cost an arm and a leg.*
arm in arm, with arms linked: *She walked arm in arm with her sister.*
at arm's length, a as far as the arm can reach: *He held the picture up at arm's length to look at it.* **b** far enough away to avoid familiarity: *He was never very friendly and kept everyone at arm's length.* **c** of business transactions or relationships, not involving direct influence by any of the parties over the other or others: *The new regulatory body will be at arm's length from both industry and government.*
with open arms, in a warm, friendly way; cordially. ⟨OE *earm*⟩
—'arm•less, *adj.*

arm[2] [ɑrm] *n., v.* —*n.* **1** any instrument used for fighting; weapon (*usually used in the plural*): *Arms may be used for defence or attack.* **2 arms,** *pl.* fighting; war: *Napoleon was a man of arms.* **3** a combatant branch of the armed forces. **4 arms,** *pl.* the symbols and designs used in heraldry or, as emblems of official dignity, by governments, cities, corporations, etc.; COAT OF ARMS.
bear arms, a serve as a soldier. **b** possess and display a coat of arms.
take up arms, a arm for attack or defence: *The settler took up arms against the invaders.* **b** argue militantly: *I see you've taken up arms against the new cutbacks.*
to arms! prepare for battle!
under arms, having weapons; equipped for fighting.
up in arms, a preparing for battle. **b** very angry; in rebellion.
—*v.* **1** supply with weapons; equip with armament. **2** take up weapons; prepare for war. **3** provide with a protective covering. **4** provide with a means of defence or attack: *Armed with additional statistics, she convinced the committee that more parks were necessary.* ⟨sing. of *arms*, ME *armes* < OF < L *arma*, pl.⟩

ar•ma•da [ɑr'mɑdə] *or* [ɑr'mædə] *n.* **1** a fleet of warships. **2** a fleet of military aircraft. **3 the Armada,** the Spanish fleet that was sent to attack England in 1588. ⟨< Sp. < L *armata* armed force, originally pp. neut. pl. of *armare* to arm. Doublet of ARMY.⟩

ar•ma•dil•lo [ˌɑrmə'dɪlou] *n., pl.* **-los.** any of a family (Dasypodidae) of burrowing mammals of South America and southern North America having an armourlike covering of small, jointed, bony plates, a long, narrow tongue adapted for catching insects, and strong claws. One species rolls up into a ball to protect itself when attacked. ⟨< Sp. *armadillo* dim. of *armado* armed (one) < L *armatus*, pp. of *armare* arm⟩

Ar•ma•ged•don [ˌɑrmə'gɛdən] *n.* **1** in the Bible, the scene of a great and final conflict between the forces of good and evil. **2** any great and final conflict. ⟨< LL < Gk., probably < Hebrew *har megiddon* a mountain site of great battles⟩

Ar•ma•gnac ['ɑrmən,jæk]; *French,* [aʀma'njak] *n.* a type of brandy distilled in the Gers region of France, formerly called Armagnac.

ar•ma•ment ['ɑrməmənt] *n.* **1** sometimes, **armaments,** *pl.* war equipment and supplies. **2** all the armed forces of a nation. **3** the act or process of preparing for war. **4** the weapons on a naval vessel, tank, aircraft, etc. **5** anything used for protection or defence. ⟨< L *armamentum* < *armare*⟩

ar•ma•men•tar•i•um [ˌɑrməmɛn'tɛriəm] *n.* a physician's collection of medical equipment.

ar•ma•ture ['ɑrmətʃər] *n.* **1** armour. **2** a part of an animal or plant serving for offence (teeth, claws) or defence (shells, thorns): *A turtle's shell is an armature.* **3** wire wound round and round a cable. **4** a piece of soft iron placed in contact with the poles of a magnet to preserve its magnetic power. **5** a revolving part of an electric motor or generator. See GENERATOR for picture. **6** a movable part of an electric relay or buzzer. **7** *Sculpture.* a framework which supports the clay or other substance used for modelling a figure. ⟨< L *armatura* < *armare* arm. Doublet of ARMOUR.⟩

arm•band ['ɑrm,bænd] *n.* a circlet of cloth, worn around the sleeve as a sign of rank, office, etc. Black armbands are usually a sign of mourning.

arm•chair ['ɑrm,tʃɛr] *n.* **1** a chair with side pieces to support a person's arms or elbows. **2** (*adjl.*) of or having to do with an armchair. **3** (*adjl.*) **a** of or having to do with actions, opinions, etc. based on theory rather than on practical experience or knowledge: *Armchair politicians have no idea of the real difficulties of government.* **b** sharing by reading, etc. in another's experiences: *an armchair explorer.* **c** of or having to do with work done by the intellect rather than by physical effort: *an armchair detective.*

armed[1] [ɑrmd] *adj.* **1** having an arm or arms. **2** having an arm or arms of a specified kind or number (*used in compounds*): *one-armed, long-armed.*

armed[2] [ɑrmd] *adj., v.* —*adj.* having, equipped with, or using weapons: *armed guards.*
—*v.* pt. and pp. of ARM[2].

armed forces the combined military strength of a nation, including sea, land, and air elements, or navy, army, and air force. Also called **armed services.**

Ar•me•ni•a [ɑr'minjə] *n.* a country in SW Asia.

Ar•me•ni•an [ɑr'minjən] *n., adj.* —*n.* **1** a native or inhabitant of Armenia. **2** the Indo-European language of the Armenians. —*adj.* of or having to do with Armenia, its people, or their language. ⟨< L < Gk. *Armeniā*, Old Persian *Arminà*⟩

arm•ful ['ɑrm,fʊl] *n., pl.* **-fuls.** as much as one arm or both arms can hold.

arm•hole ['ɑrm,houl] *n.* a hole for the arm in a garment.

ar•mil•lar•y ['ɑrmə,lɛri] *adj., n.* —*adj.* like a ring or circle; consisting of rings.
—*n.* **armillary sphere,** a device used by early astronomers in which the great circles of the celestial sphere were represented by rings. ⟨< L *armilla* armlet < *armus* upper arm, shoulder⟩

Ar•min•i•an [ɑr'mɪnjən] *adj., n.* —*adj.* of Jacobus Arminius, an early Dutch Protestant theologian (1560-1609), or his doctrines, e.g., that all were to be saved, not only the spiritual elect.
—*n.* a believer in Arminian doctrines.

Ar•min•i•an•ism [ɑr'mɪnjə,nɪzəm] *n.* the body of teachings of Jacobus Arminius, repudiating the doctrine of predestination and holding that divine sovereignty did not preclude the free exercise of human will.

ar•mi•stice ['ɑrməstɪs] *n.* a formal agreement between governments to cease hostilities on all fronts; especially, a permanent cessation of hostilities, as a preliminary to a peace treaty. ⟨< NL *armistitium* < L *arma* arms + *sistere* stop, stand⟩

Armistice Day **1** November 11, the date of the cessation of fighting (1918) in World War I. **2** the anniversary of this date, now called **Remembrance Day,** celebrating also the cessation of fighting in World War II.

arm•let ['ɑrmlɪt] *n.* **1** an ornamental band for the upper arm. **2** a small inlet of the sea.

arm•lock ['ɑrm,lɒk] *n. Wrestling.* a hold which uses the arm and hand to immobilize the arm of one's opponent.

ar•moire [ˌɑr'mwɑr] *n.* a large, usually ornate, wardrobe, closet, or cupboard. ⟨< F *armoire* < OF *armarie* < L *armarium* cabinet, ult. < *arma* weapons⟩

ar•mor ['ɑrmər] See ARMOUR.

ar•mo•ri•al [ɑr'mɔriəl] *adj.* having to do with coats of arms or heraldry.

armorial bearings a COAT OF ARMS.

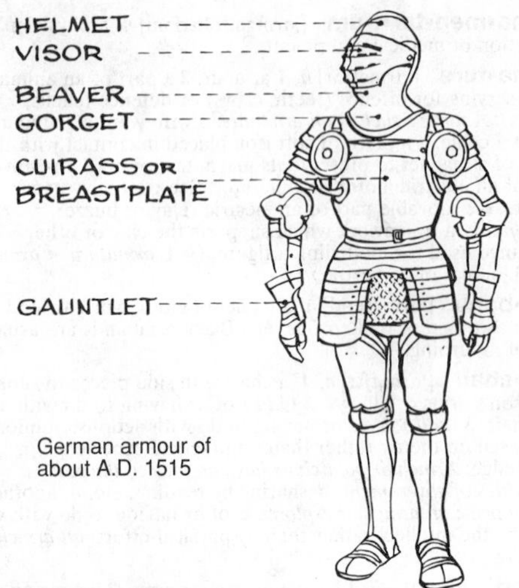

German armour of about A.D. 1515

ar•mour or **ar•mor** ['ɑrmər] *n., v.* *–n.* **1** a covering worn to protect the body in fighting. **2** any kind of protective covering. A diver's suit and the scales of a fish are armour. **3** the steel or iron plates or other protective covering of a warship, aircraft, or fortification. **4** the tanks and other armoured vehicles of an army. **5** anything that protects or defends: *An informed public opinion is the best armour against propaganda.*
–v. cover or protect with armour. ⟨ME < OF *armeüre* < L *armatura* < *armare* arm. Doublet of ARMATURE.⟩

ar•mour•bear•er or **ar•mor•bear•er** ['ɑrmər,bɛrər] *n.* formerly, an attendant who carried the armour or weapons of a warrior.

ar•moured or **ar•mored** ['ɑrmərd] *adj., v.* *–adj.* **1** covered or protected with armour: *an armoured train, car, etc.* **2** using tanks, armoured cars, etc.: *an armoured regiment.*
–v. pp. and pt. of ARMOUR.

armoured cable an electric cable with a protective covering of wire or metal binding.

armoured car **1** any vehicle with a protective covering of armour plate, used to transport large quantities of money and valuables to and from banks. **2** *Military.* a wheeled, motorized reconnaissance vehicle covered with armour plate and equipped with light arms.

ar•mour•er or **ar•mor•er** ['ɑrmərər] *n.* **1** a maker or repairer of armour. **2** a manufacturer of firearms. **3** a person in charge of firearms. The armourer of a warship takes care of the revolvers, pistols, and rifles on the ship.

ar•mour•ies or **ar•mor•ies** ['ɑrməriz] *n.pl. Cdn.* a building where reserve units of the armed forces have their headquarters and training area.

armour plate or **armor plate** steel or iron plating to protect warships, forts, etc. **–'ar•mour-,plat•ed,** *adj.*

ar•mour•y or **ar•mor•y** ['ɑrməri] *n., pl.* **-ies. 1** a place where weapons are kept; arsenal. **2** *U.S.* a place where weapons are made; arsenal. **3** armouries.

arm•pit ['ɑrm,pɪt] *n.* the hollow under the arm at the shoulder.

arm•rest ['ɑrm,rɛst] *n.* the part of a chesterfield, chair, car door, etc. that supports a person's arm.

arm–twist•ing ['ɑrm ,twɪstɪŋ] *n.* strong pressure or influence used to get what one wants; forceful persuasion: *It took some arm-twisting, but we finally got them to agree to contribute.*

ar•mure ['ɑrmjʊr] *n.* a woven silk or wool fabric with a finely pebbled surface. ⟨< F⟩

arm wrestle a round of ARM WRESTLING.

arm wrestling a kind of game with two competitors holding each other's hand, using the same hand, with their elbows on a flat surface. The object is to force the other's arm onto the flat surface: *They enrolled in an arm wrestling competition to see who was the stronger.* **–'arm-,wres•tle,** *v.*

ar•my ['ɑrmi] *n., pl.* **-mies. 1** a large, organized group of personnel trained and armed for war, especially on land. **2** Often, **Army,** such a group serving as the land forces of a nation. In Canada, the function of an army is served by Mobile Command of the Canadian Forces. **3** a body organized on military lines: *the Salvation Army.* **4** a very large number; multitude: *an army of ants, an army of caterpillars.* ⟨ME < OF *armee* < L *armata.* Doublet of ARMADA.⟩

army ant any of various mainly tropical ants (subfamily Dorylinae) that migrate in large groups and devour other insects and small animals in their path.

army cadet a person under military age who is undertaking basic military training in an organization subsidized by the armed forces.

army of occupation an army sent into a defeated country to enforce a treaty, keep order, etc.

army worm **1** the larva of a moth, *Pseudaletia unipuncta.* Army worms travel over the ground in multitudes, eating the vegetation they find in their path, thus often destroying or seriously damaging crops and grasses. **2** any of various other moth larvae that migrate in large numbers.

ar•ni•ca ['ɑrnəkə] *n.* **1** a healing liquid used on bruises, sprains, etc., prepared from the dried flowers, leaves, or roots of a plant of the genus *Arnica,* of the aster family. **2** the plant itself, which has showy yellow flowers. ⟨< NL⟩

ar•oid ['ærɔɪd] *or* ['ɛrɔɪd] *n.* any member of the arum family of plants.

a•ro•ma [ə'roumə] *n.* **1** a pleasant, sweet or savoury smell: *the aroma of a cake in the oven.* **2** a distinctive fragrance or flavour; subtle quality. ⟨ME < OF < L < Gk. *árōma* spice⟩

ar•o•mat•ic [,ærə'mætɪk] *or* [,ɛrə'mætɪk] *adj., n.* *–adj.* **1** having a sweet or spicy smell; fragrant: *The cinnamon tree has an aromatic inner bark.* **2** *Chemistry.* having to do with closed chain compounds of benzene, benzene derivatives, or compounds with at least one benzene ring. Many of these have a characteristic smell.
–n. a fragrant plant or substance. **–,ar•o'mat•i•cal•ly,** *adv.*

ar•o•ma•tize [ə'roumə,taɪz] *v.* **-tized, -tiz•ing.** *Chemistry.* make a compound aromatic.

a•rose [ə'rouz] *v.* pt. of ARISE: *She arose from her chair.*

a•round [ə'raʊnd] *prep., adv.* *–prep.* **1** in a circle about: *to travel around the world.* **2** closely surrounding: *She had a coat around her shoulders.* **3** on all sides of: *Woods lay around the house.* **4** *Informal.* here and there in: *He leaves his books around the house.* **5** *Informal.* somewhere near: *to play around the house.* **6** *Informal.* approximately; near in amount, number, etc. to: *That car cost around fifteen thousand dollars.* **7** on the far side of: *just around the corner.*
–adv. **1** in a circle. **2** in circumference: *The tree measures two metres around.* **3** on all sides: *A dense fog lay around.* **4** here and there: *We walked around to see the town.* **5** *Informal.* somewhere near: *Wait around awhile.* **6** in the opposite direction: *Turn around! You are going the wrong way.* **7** in or through a circuit or cycle: *going around to all the merchants in town. Wake me up when my turn comes around.* **8** in existence: *That kind of wallpaper just isn't around anymore.*
have been around, *Informal.* be experienced and worldly-wise.
☛ *Usage.* See note at ROUND.

a•rous•al [ə'raʊzəl] *n.* the action of arousing or the state of being aroused.

a•rouse [ə'raʊz] *v.* **a•roused, a•rous•ing. 1** awaken. **2** stir to feeling or action; excite; stimulate. **–a'rous•er,** *n.*

ar•peg•gio [ɑr'pɛdʒiou] *or* [ɑr'pɛdʒou] *n., pl.* **-gi•os.** *Music.* **1** the sounding of the notes of a chord in rapid succession instead of together. **2** a chord sounded in this way. ⟨< Ital. *arpeggio* < *arpa* harp < Gmc.⟩

ar•pent ['ɑrpənt]; *French* [aʀ'pɑ̃] *n. Cdn.* formerly: **1** an old French measure of land area, formerly used in Canada, equal to about 3400 m². An arpent contained 100 square perches. **2** a measure of length, equal to about 58 m. ⟨< F⟩

ar•que•bus ['ɑrkwəbəs] *n.* See HARQUEBUS.

arr. **1** arrange; arranged; arrangements. **2** arrival; arrive; arrived.

ar•rack ['ærək], ['ɛrək], *or* [ə'ræk] *n.* an alcoholic drink distilled from the sap of the coconut palm or from rice, sugar cane, etc. Also, **arak.** ⟨< Arabic *'araq* liquor, sweet juice⟩

ar•raign [ə'rein] *v.* **1** *Law.* bring before a court to answer a charge: *The gangster was arraigned on a charge of stealing.* **2** call into question; find fault with. ⟨ME < AF *arainer* < VL < L *ad-* to + *ratio, -onis* account⟩ **–ar'raign•er,** *n.*

ar•raign•ment [ə'reinmənt] *n.* **1** *Law.* the process of reading out the charge or charges to an accused person in court and asking the person how he or she pleads. **2** unfavourable criticism.

ar•range [ə'reindʒ] *v.* **-ranged, -rang•ing. 1** put in the proper order: *arranged by size. The army is arranged for battle.* **2** settle (a dispute). **3** plan; prepare: *Can you arrange to meet me this evening?* **4** set up (something); make the necessary agreements, reservations, etc. for: *We've arranged billeting for the entire team.* **5** *Music.* adapt (a composition) to voices or instruments for which it was not written. ⟨ME < OF *arangier* < *a-* to + *rang* rank[1] < Gmc.⟩ **—ar'rang•er,** *n.*

ar•range•ment [ə'reindʒmənt] *n.* **1** a putting or being put in proper order. **2** a way or order in which things or persons are put: *You can make six arrangements of the letters A, B, and C.* **3** an adjustment; settlement. **4** Usually, **arrangements,** *pl.* a plan; preparation: *to make arrangements for a journey.* **5** something made by arranging separate parts or things in a particular way: *an unusual flower arrangement.* **6** *Music.* **a** the adaptation of a composition to voices or instruments for which it was not written. **b** a composition so adapted.

ar•rant ['ærənt] *or* ['ɛrənt] *adj.* extreme; thoroughgoing; downright: *He was such an arrant liar that nobody ever believed him.* ⟨var. of *errant*⟩ **—'ar•rant•ly,** *adv.*

☛ *Hom.* ERRANT ['ɛrənt].

ar•ras ['ærəs] *or* ['ɛrəs] *n.* **1** a kind of tapestry. **2** a curtain or hanging of tapestry. ⟨from *Arras,* a city in France⟩

☛ *Hom.* ARRIS.

ar•ray [ə'rei] *n., v.* *—n.* **1** order: *The troops were formed in battle array.* **2** a display of persons or things: *The array of good players on the other team made our side lose confidence.* **3** military force; soldiers. **4** clothes; dress: *bridal array.* **5** *Law.* the list of jurors summoned for a trial. **6** *Mathematics.* an arrangement of data in rows and columns. **7** *Computer technology.* two or more linked items that share a common name and are kept in consecutive positions in memory.

—v. **1** arrange in order: *The general arrayed his troops for the battle.* **2** dress in fine clothes; adorn. ⟨ME < OF *a* to (< L *ad*) + *rei* order < Gmc.⟩ **—ar'ray•al,** *n.*

ar•rear•age [ə'rirɪdʒ] *n.* debts; arrears.

ar•rears [ə'rirz] *n. pl.* **1** money due but not paid; debts. **2** unfinished work; things not done on time.

in arrears, behind in payments, work, etc. ⟨ME < OF *arere* < LL *ad retro* to the rear⟩

ar•rest [ə'rɛst] *v., n.* *—v.* **1** seize a person or persons by legal authority; take to jail or court. **2** stop; check: *Filling a tooth arrests decay.* **3** catch and hold.

—n. **1** the seizing of a person or persons for the purpose of laying a criminal charge. **2** a stopping; checking.

under arrest, held by the police. ⟨ME < OF *arester* < VL *adrestare* < L *ad-* + *re-* back + *stare* stand⟩ **—ar'rest•er,** *n.*

☛ *Syn. v.* **2.** See note at STOP.

ar•rest•ing [ə'rɛstɪŋ] *adj., v.* *—adj.* catching the attention; striking: *She is not beautiful, but she has arresting eyes.*

—v. ppr. of ARREST. **—ar'rest•ing•ly,** *adv.*

ar•rhyth•mi•a [ə'rɪðmiə] *n.* irregularity in heart beat. ⟨< Gk.⟩ **—ar'rhyth•mic,** *adj.*

ar•ris ['ærəs] *or* ['ɛrəs] *n. Architecture.* **1** a sharp edge formed by two straight or curved surfaces meeting at an angle. **2** a sharp ridge. A Doric column has arrises. ⟨< OF *arest* < L *arista* ear of corn, fish bone⟩

☛ *Hom.* ARRAS.

ar•riv•al [ə'raɪvəl] *n.* **1** the act of arriving; coming. **2** a person or thing that arrives.

ar•rive [ə'raɪv] *v.* **-rived, -riv•ing. 1** reach the end of a journey; come to a place: *We arrived at noon.* **2** reach (*used with* **at**): *You must arrive at a decision soon.* **3** come; occur: *The time has arrived for you to study.* **4** be successful. ⟨ME < OF *ar(r)iver* < VL < L *ad ripam* to the shore⟩

☛ *Syn.* **2.** See note at COME.

☛ *Usage.* **Arrive** is generally followed by *at,* especially when the place reached is only a temporary stopping point: *We arrived at the bridge. The train arrived at Winnipeg. He has not yet arrived at a decision.* But *arrive in* is used before the names of countries and, sometimes, cities or towns. *We arrived in Kingston a week ago.* In informal English, **arrive** is now occasionally used without any preposition before the name of a city or town: *The flight arrived Saint John two hours late.*

ar•ri•viste [,ærɪ'vist] *or* [,ɛrɪ'vist] *n.* a person who has recently acquired money, power, prestige, etc., usually through unscrupulous behaviour; one who is overly ambitious. ⟨< F⟩

ar•ro•gance ['ærəgəns] *or* ['ɛrəgəns] *n.* too great pride; haughtiness.

ar•ro•gant ['ærəgənt] *or* ['ɛrəgənt] *adj.* too proud; haughty. ⟨ME < OF < L *arrogans, -antis,* ppr. of *arrogare* < *ad-* to + *rogāre* ask⟩ **—'ar•ro•gant•ly,** *adv.*

☛ *Syn.* See note at HAUGHTY.

ar•ro•gate ['ærə,geit] *or* ['ɛrə,geit] *v.* **-gat•ed, -gat•ing. 1** claim or take without right: *The despotic king arrogated to himself the power that belonged to the nobles.* **2** attribute to another without good reasons: *People are only too ready to arrogate dishonesty to a politician.* ⟨< L *arrogare* < *ad-* to + *rogare* ask⟩

ar•ro•ga•tion [,ærə'geiʃən] *or* [,ɛrə'geiʃən] *n.* the act of arrogating.

ar•row ['ærou] *or* ['ɛrou] *n., v.* *—n.* **1** a slender shaft or stick designed to be shot from a bow, having a pointed tip, usually barbed, and feathers at the tail end. **2** anything resembling an arrow in shape or speed. **3** a sign (→) used to show direction or position in maps, on road signs, and in writing.

—v. **1** indicate with an arrow: *The main points are arrowed in the margin.* **2** move swiftly like an arrow: *Jet planes arrowed through the sky.* ⟨OE *arwe*⟩ **—'ar•row,like** *adj.*

ar•row–back ['ærou ,bæk] *or* ['ɛrou ,bæk] *n.* a chair with balusters in the back that become broader and flatter toward the end.

ar•row•head ['ærou,hɛd] *or* ['ɛrou,hɛd] *n.* **1** the head or tip of an arrow, especially a separately made piece of stone or metal. **2** any of a genus (*Sagittaria*) of water or marsh plants found mainly in temperate and tropical regions of the western hemisphere, typically having arrowhead-shaped leaves. **3** a stylized figure of an arrowhead, often used as a symbol. In this dictionary, the sign < indicates the origin of a particular form.

arrowleaf balsamroot ['ærou,lif 'bɒlsəm,rut] *or* ['ɛrou-] a western North American plant (*Balsamorhiza sagittata*), having arrowhead-shaped leaves and smallish yellow flowers blooming in spring.

ar•row•root ['ærou,rut] *or* ['ɛrou,rut] *n.* **1** a West Indian plant (*Maranta arundinacea*) having rhizomes that yield an easily digested starch. **2** the starch obtained from this plant. **3** any of various other plants having rhizomes or roots that yield starch.

arrow sash *Cdn.* formerly, a woven belt with arrowlike markings, much traded in exchange for furs, etc.

ar•row•wood or **ar•row–wood** ['ærou,wʊd] *or* ['ɛrou,wʊd] *n.* **1** a viburnum (*Viburnum dentatum*) of E North America having coarsely toothed, rounded or oval leaves and flat clusters of white flowers followed by bluish black fruits. **2** any of various related or similar shrubs having straight, tough, pliant branches formerly much used for making arrows.

ar•row•y ['æroui] *or* ['ɛroui] *adj.* **1** of arrows. **2** like an arrow in shape or speed.

ar•roy•o [ə'rɔiou] *n., pl.* **-roy•os. 1** the dry bed of a stream; gully. **2** a small river. ⟨< Sp.⟩

ar•se•nal ['ɑrsənəl] *n.* **1** a building for storing or manufacturing weapons and ammunition for the armed forces. **2** an array or collection: *an arsenal of curious facts.* ⟨< Ital. *arsenale* < Arabic *dar accina'ah* house (of) the manufacturing⟩

ar•se•nate ['ɑrsənɪt] *or* ['ɑrsə,neit] *n.* a salt or ester of arsenic acid. **Arsenate of lead** is a poison that is used to kill insects.

ar•se•nic *n.* ['ɑrsənɪk]; *adj.* ['ɑrsənɪk] *or* [ɑr'sɛnɪk] *n., adj.* *—n.* **1** a greyish white chemical element, having a metallic lustre and volatilizing when heated. *Symbol*: As; *at.no.* 33; *at.mass* 74.92. **2** a violently poisonous, tasteless, white compound of arsenic, used in industry and in medicine. *Formula*: As_2O_3 or As_1O_6

—adj. of or containing arsenic. ⟨< L *arsenicum* < Gk. *arsenikon* < Hebrew < Old Persian **zarnika-* golden⟩

arsenic acid a colourless crystalline compound. *Formula*: H_3AsO_4

ar•sen•i•cal [ɑr'sɛnəkəl] *adj., n.* *—adj.* arsenous.

—n. a drug, pesticide, etc. containing arsenic.

ar•se•nide ['ɑrsə,naɪd] *n.* a compound of trivalent, negative arsenic and one other element or radical.

ar•se•ni•ous [ɑr'siniəs] *adj.* arsenous.

ar•se•nite ['ɑrsə,nəit] *n.* a salt or ester of arsenous acid.

ar•se•niu•ret•ted or **ar•se•niu•ret•ed** [ɑr'sɛnjə,rɛtɪd] *adj.* combined with arsenic.

ar•se•no•py•rite [,ɑrsənou'paɪrəit] *n.* a greyish white mineral composed of iron sulphide and arsenic; an ore of arsenic. *Formula*: FeAsS

ar•se•nous ['ɑrsənəs] *adj.* **1** of arsenic. **2** containing arsenic.

ar•sine ['ɑrsin], ['ɑrsɪn], *or* ['ɑrsaɪn] *n.* a colourless, poisonous gas used in various types of manufacturing and as a chemical weapon. *Formula*: AsH_3 ⟨< *ars*enic + -INE[2]⟩

ar•son [ˈɑrsən] *n.* the criminal offence of intentionally setting fire to a building or other property belonging to someone else, or to one's own insured property in order to collect insurance. ⟨< OF < LL *arsio, -onis* a burning < L *ardere* burn⟩

ar•son•ist [ˈɑrsənɪst] *n.* a person who commits arson.

art[1] [ɑrt] *n.* **1** any form of human activity that is the product of imagination and skill and that appeals mainly to the imagination; especially, drawing, painting, and sculpture, and also architecture, poetry, music, drama, dancing, etc. **2** works produced by such activity: *a museum of art.* **3** (*adjl.*) of, for, or having to do with art or artists: *an art gallery.* **4** (*adjl.*) having or showing the techniques or characteristics of art: *an art film.* **5 arts,** *pl.* in universities, a group of studies that includes literature, languages, history, philosophy, etc. and that excludes the sciences and technical or professional studies; the humanities. **6 the arts,** *pl.* fine arts: *The arts flourished in Elizabethan England.* **7** *Archaic.* learning or scholarship in general. **8** a craft or trade that requires skill and imagination: *the household arts of cooking and sewing, the weaver's art. Writing compositions is an art.* **9** a particular skill or set of working principles: *the art of making friends, the art of war. There is an art to organizing your work area.* **10** human skill or effort, as opposed to nature: *It was a well-kept, formal garden that owed more to art than to nature.* **11** artwork. **12** cunning; artfulness: *He swore he used no art to persuade them.* **13** Usually, **arts,** *pl.* cunning or skilful plans or tricks: *using arts and wiles to get one's way.* ⟨ME < OF < L *ars, artis*⟩

art[2] [ɑrt] *v. Archaic or poetic.* 2nd pers. sing., present indicative, of BE. *Thou art* means *you* (sing.) *are.* ⟨OE *eart*⟩

art. **1** article. **2** artillery. **3** artist. **4** artificial.

–art *noun-forming suffix.* See -ARD.

ARTC or **A.R.T.C.** Air Route Traffic Control.

Art Deco a decorative style of furniture, architecture, textiles, etc. having its origin in cubism and characterized by geometrical, stylized forms and utilitarian design. It flourished in the 1920s and 1930s. ⟨< F *art décoratif*⟩

ar•te•fact [ˈɑrtə,fækt] See ARTIFACT.

Ar•te•mis [ˈɑrtəmɪs] *n. Greek mythology.* the goddess of the hunt, and of the forests, wild animals, and the moon. She corresponds to the Roman goddess Diana.

ar•te•mis•i•a [,ɑrtəˈmiziə] *or* [,ɑrtəˈmiʒə] *n.* any perennial plant of the genus *Artemisia* of herbs and shrubs of the N hemisphere, such as sagebrush or mugwort. ⟨< L < Gk., ult. < *Artemis*⟩

ar•te•ri•al [ɑrˈtiriəl] *adj.* **1** *Anatomy.* having to do with or resembling the arteries. **2** *Physiology.* having to do with the bright red blood of the arteries. **3** serving as a major route of transportation, supply, etc.: *an arterial highway.* **4** being a main channel with many branches.

ar•te•ri•al•ize [ɑrˈtiriə,laɪz] *v.* **-ized, -iz•ing. 1** oxygenate (the blood of veins), converting it to arterial blood. **2** provide with a system of arteries. **3** develop blood vessels in (an organ, etc.). **—ar,te•ri•al•iˈza•tion,** *n.*

ar•te•ri•o•gram [ɑrˈtiriou,græm] *n.* an X ray produced by arteriography.

ar•te•ri•og•ra•phy [ɑr,tiriˈɒgrəfi] *n.* examination of the arteries by X ray to diagnose circulatory problems, etc.

ar•te•ri•ole [ɑrˈtiri,oul] *n.* a blood vessel, smaller than an artery and connecting it with its capillaries, which are still smaller.

ar•te•ri•o•scle•ro•sis [ɑr,tiriouskləˈrousɪs] *n.* a hardening and thickening of the walls of the arteries. It makes circulation of the blood difficult.

ar•te•ri•o•scle•rot•ic [ɑr,tiriouskləˈrɒtɪk] *adj., n.* *—adj.* of, having to do with, or affected with arteriosclerosis. *—n.* a person affected with arteriosclerosis.

ar•te•ri•o•ve•nous [ɑr,tiriouˈvinəs] *adj.* of or relating to arteries and veins.

ar•te•ri•tis [,ɑrtəˈraɪtɪs] *n.* inflammation of an artery or arteries.

ar•ter•y [ˈɑrtəri] *n., pl.* **-ter•ies. 1** *Anatomy.* any of the blood vessels or tubes that carry blood from the heart to all parts of the body. See HEART, KIDNEY, and TOURNIQUET for pictures. **2** a main road; an important channel: *Yonge Street is one of the main arteries of Toronto.* ⟨ME < L *arteria* < Gk.⟩

ar•te•sian well [ɑrˈtiʒən] a deep-drilled well, especially one from which water gushes up without pumping. ⟨< F *artésien* of Artois, an old French province where such wells were first made⟩

art•ful [ˈɑrtfəl] *adj.* **1** crafty; deceitful: *A swindler uses artful tricks to get money out of people.* **2** having or showing skill or clever art. **3** artificial. **—ˈart•ful•ly,** *adv.* **—ˈart•ful•ness,** *n.*

ar•thral•gi•a [ɑrˈθrældʒə] *n.* pain in the joints. ⟨< Gk. *arthron* joint + *algos* pain < *algein* to feel pain⟩

ar•thrit•ic [ɑrˈθrɪtɪk] *adj.* of, caused by, or affected with arthritis: *arthritic pain, arthritic joints.*

ar•thri•tis [ɑrˈθraɪtɪs] *n. Medicine.* an inflammation of a joint or joints. ⟨< L < Gk. *arthritis* < *arthron* joint⟩

ar•thro•mere [ˈɑrθrou,mir] *n.* any of the segments of an arthropod. ⟨< Gk. *arthron* joint + *meros* plant⟩

ar•thro•plas•ty [ˈɑrθrə,plæsti] *n.* **1** the making of an artificial joint to replace a natural one. **2** surgery performed on a joint. ⟨< Gk. *arthron* joint + *plastos* moulded⟩

ar•thro•pod [ˈɑrθrə,pɒd] *n.* any animal belonging to the phylum **Arthropoda,** a large group of invertebrate animals each having a segmented body and legs, including insects, spiders, mites, scorpions, and crustaceans. Arthropods range in size from tiny mites only 0.1 mm long to giant crabs having leg spans of 3.4 m; they make up about three-quarters of all the known species of animals on earth. ⟨< *arthro-* joint (< Gk. *arthron*) + Gk. *pous, podos* foot⟩ **—arˈthrop•o•dal** [ɑrˈθrɒpədəl], **arˈthrop•o•dan, arˈthrop•o•dous,** *adj.*

ar•thro•scope [ˈɒrθrə,skoup] *n.* a medical instrument which uses fibre optics to view the inside of a joint. ⟨< Gk. *arthron* joint + SCOPE⟩ **—,ar•throˈscop•ic** [-ˈskɒpɪk], *adj.*

Ar•thur [ˈɑrθər] *n. Medieval legend.* a king of ancient Britain who gathered about him a company of famous knights, who sat at a Round Table so that all would have equal rank. The real Arthur was a British chieftain or general of the 5th or 6th century A.D.

Ar•thu•ri•an [ɑrˈθjuriən] *or* [ɑrˈθuriən] *adj.* of or having to do with the legend of King Arthur and his knights.

ar•ti•choke [ˈɑrtə,tʃouk] *n.* **1** a plant (*Cynara scolymus*) of the composite family native to Europe and Asia, widely cultivated for its large flower heads having many fleshy bracts which are eaten as a vegetable. **2** the unopened flower head of this plant. **3** JERUSALEM ARTICHOKE. ⟨< Ital. *articiocco* < Provençal < Arabic *al-kharshof*⟩

ar•ti•cle [ˈɑrtəkəl] *n., v.* **-cled, -cling.** *—n.* **1** a written composition, complete in itself, but forming part of a magazine, newspaper, or book: *an article on gardening in a newspaper.* **2** a clause in a contract, treaty, statute, creed, etc.: *the third article of the club's constitution deals with fees.* **3** a particular thing; item; commodity: *Bread is a main article of food.* **4** one of the words *a, an,* or *the* or the corresponding words in certain other languages. *A(n)* is the **indefinite article;** *the* is the **definite article.**
—v. **1** bind by a contract, especially for training: *The apprentice was articled to serve the master craftsman for seven years.* **2** bring charges; accuse. ⟨ME < OF < L *articulus*, dim. of *artus* joint⟩

Articles of Confederation *U.S.* the constitution adopted by the thirteen original states of the United States in 1781. It was replaced by the present Constitution in 1789.

ar•tic•u•lar [ɑrˈtɪkjələr] *adj.* of the joints: *Arthritis is an articular disease.*

ar•tic•u•late *adj.* [ɑrˈtɪkjəlɪt]; *v.* [ɑrˈtɪkjə,leit] *adj., v.* **-lat•ed, -lat•ing.** *—adj.* **1** uttered in distinct syllables or words: *A baby cries and gurgles, but does not use articulate speech.* **2** having the power of speech: *Dogs are not articulate.* **3** having skill in putting one's thoughts into words: *Julia is the most articulate of the sisters.* **4** made up of distinct parts; distinct. **5** jointed; segmented.
—v. **1** speak distinctly: *Be careful to articulate your words so that everyone in the room can understand you.* **2** express in words: *She was overcome by a feeling she could not articulate.* **3** unite by joints. **4** fit together in a joint: *After his knee was injured, he had trouble walking because the bones did not articulate well.* **5** form or join together in a system, sequence, etc.: *An articulated English program is being introduced in all schools.* ⟨< L *articulatus*, pp. of *articulare* divide into single joints < *articulus.* See ARTICLE.⟩ **—arˈtic•u•late•ly,** *adv.* **—arˈtic•u•late•ness,** *n.* **—arˈtic•u•la,to•ry,** *adj.*

ar•tic•u•la•tion [ɑr,tɪkjəˈleiʃən] *n.* **1** a way of speaking; enunciation. **2** the act of putting ideas into words, or the result of this: *This paper is a rather poor articulation of socialist ideals.* **3** a joint. **4** *Anatomy.* the act or manner of connecting by a joint or joints: *the articulation of the bones.* **5** the act or process of forming or joining together in a system, sequence, etc.: *the* *articulation of all manufacturing processes in the plant.* **6** *Botany.* a natural separation in the stem or between a branch and a leaf.

ar•tic•u•la•tor [ɑr'tɪkjə,leitər] *n. Phonetics.* any part of the vocal apparatus whose movement results in a speech sound: *The teeth, the larynx, and the tongue are all articulators.*

ar•ti•fact or **ar•te•fact** ['ɑrtə,fækt] *n.* any thing made or any effect caused by human skill or activity, whether intentionally or not; an artificial product. ⟨< L *ars, artis* art + *factus* made⟩

ar•ti•fice ['ɑrtəfɪs] *n.* **1** a clever device; trick: *He will use any artifice to get his way.* **2** trickery; craft: *Her conduct is free from artifice.* **3** skill; cleverness. ⟨< F < L *artificium* < *ars, artis* art + *facere* make⟩

☛ *Syn.* **1.** See note at STRATAGEM.

ar•tif•i•cer [ɑr'tɪfəsər] *n.* **1** a skilled worker; craftsperson. **2** a maker; inventor.

ar•ti•fi•cial [,ɑrtə'fɪʃəl] *adj.* **1** made by human skill or labour; not natural: *When you read at night, you read by artificial light.* **2** made as a substitute for or in imitation of; not real: *artificial flowers, artificial silk.* **3** assumed; false; affected: *an artificial tone of voice, an artificial manner.* **4** *Botany.* of plants, not native or growing naturally in a place; cultivated. ⟨< L *artificiālis*⟩ **—,arti'fi•cial•ly,** *adv.* **—,arti'fi•cial•ness,** *n.*

☛ *Syn.* **1, 2. Artificial,** SYNTHETIC = not natural. **Artificial** describes things which are made by human skill and labour, in contrast to those produced in nature, but which often correspond to natural things: *You can get burned by the artificial light of a sun lamp.* **Synthetic** describes things which are put together in a laboratory by chemical combination or treatment of natural substances, and which often serve as substitutes for natural products: *Nylon is a synthetic fabric.*

artificial horizon **1** a gyroscopic flight instrument giving the aircraft's position relative to the horizontal. **2** a level reflective surface, such as that of mercury, used by astronomers to calculate the distance to a celestial body whose image it reflects.

artificial insemination insemination by artificial techniques, using donor sperm.

artificial intelligence the ability of some computers to recognize and solve problems in ways that simulate human learning and reasoning.

ar•ti•fi•ci•al•i•ty [,ɑrtə,fɪʃi'æləti] *n., pl.* **-ties. 1** an artificial quality or condition. **2** something unnatural or unreal.

artificial respiration the process of restoring the breathing of a person by rhythmically forcing air into and out of his or her lungs, as by breathing directly into the mouth or alternately applying and releasing pressure on the diaphragm.

artificial turf any of various matlike synthetics imitating natural sod and used to cover playing fields for baseball, football, etc.

ar•ti•gi or **ar•tig•gi** ['ɑrtəgi] *or* [ɑr'tigi] *n. Cdn.* atigi.

ar•til•ler•y [ɑr'tɪləri] *n.* **1** mounted guns; cannon. **2** the part of an army that uses and manages big guns. **3** the science of firing, and co-ordinating the firing of, guns of larger calibre than machine guns. ⟨ME < OF *artillerie* < *artiller* equip⟩

ar•til•ler•y•man [ɑr'tɪlərimən] *n., pl.* **-men.** a soldier who belongs to the artillery; gunner.

ar•ti•o•dac•tyl [,ɑrtiou'dæktəl] *n.* any placental member of the order Artiodactyla of ungulates whose hooves have an even number of toes, such as pigs, cattle, and deer. ⟨< NL < Gk. *artios* even + *daktylos* finger⟩ **—,ar•ti•o'dac•ty•lous,** *adj.*

ar•ti•san ['ɑrtəzən] *or* ['ɑrtə,zæn] *n.* a person skilled in some industry or trade; craftsperson. ⟨< F < Ital. *artigiano* < L *ars, artis* art⟩

☛ *Syn.* See note at ARTIST.

art•ist ['ɑrtɪst] *n.* **1** a person who draws or paints pictures, especially one who does so as a profession. **2** a person skilled in any of the fine arts, such as sculpture, music, dance, or literature. **3** a person who does work with skill and good taste. **4** a professional in the performing arts; an actor, singer, musician, etc; artiste. ⟨< F < Ital. *artista* < VL < L *ars, artis* art⟩

☛ *Syn.* **3. Artist,** ARTISAN = a person who does work with skill. **Artist** emphasizes use of taste, imagination, and creative ability in addition to skill, and usually applies to a person working in the fine arts: *Her creative interpretation makes that dancer an artist.* **Artisan** emphasizes skill, and usually applies to a person working in the manual or industrial arts: *Factories want artisans in all departments.*

ar•tiste [ɑr'tist] *n.* a very skilful performer or worker. An artiste may be a singer, a dancer, or a cook. ⟨< F⟩

ar•tis•tic [ɑr'tɪstɪk] *adj.* **1** of, having to do with, or characteristic of art or artists: *The artistic imagination.* **2** done or made with skill, imagination, and good taste: *an artistic design, an artistic presentation.* **3** having skill in art or an appreciation of art: *You are very artistic.*

ar•tis•ti•cal•ly [ɑr'tɪstɪkli] *adv.* **1** with skill and good taste. **2** from an artistic point of view.

art•ist•ry ['ɑrtɪstri] *n., pl.* **-ries.** artistic work; expertise of an artist.

art•less ['ɑrtlɪs] *adj.* **1** not artificial or studied; natural and uncontrived: *She walked with artless grace. Small children ask many artless questions.* **2** without guile or deceit; sincere; innocent: *artless flattery, an artless youth.* **3** lacking knowledge or skill; crude, uncultured, or clumsy. **—'art•less•ly,** *adv.* **—'art•less•ness,** *n.*

Art Nou•veau [aʀnu'vo] *French.* a movement in the arts at the end of the 19th century in which very rounded stylizations of natural forms predominated.

art•sy ['ɑrtsi] *adj.* **art•si•er, art•si•est.** *Informal.* making a pretence or show of being artistic.

art•sy–craft•sy [,ɑrtsi 'kræftsi] *adj. Informal.* of or having to do with an art or craft, especially when made, done, or working in a fussy, trendy, or superficial way.

art•work ['ɑrt,wɜrk] *n.* **1** pictures and other decorative or illustrative material in a magazine, book, etc.: *That magazine always has excellent artwork.* **2** one or more works of art.

art•y ['ɑrti] *adj.* **art•i•er, art•i•est.** *Informal.* artsy. **—'ar•ti•ness,** *n.*

Arty. artillery.

A•ru•ban [ɑ'rubən] *n., adj. —n.* a native or inhabitant of Aruba, an island in the Caribbean.
—adj. of Aruba or its people.

a•ru•gu•la [ə'rugələ] *n.* MUSTARD (def. 4).

ar•um ['ɛrəm] *n.* **1** any of a genus (*Arum*) of Old World plants having small flowers densely clustered on an upright fleshy part called a spadix which is more or less enclosed by a leafy part called a spathe. See SPADIX for picture. **2** any of various other plants of the same family, such as the **water arum** or **wild calla** (*Calla palustris*), a common Canadian marsh plant having a greenish white spathe surrounding a yellow spadix. **3** (*adjl.*) designating the family (Araceae) of plants that includes the arums and other plants, such as the jack-in-the-pulpit, sweet flag, and skunk cabbage. ⟨< L < Gk. *aron*⟩

a•run•di•na•ceous [ə,rʌndɪ'neiʃəs] *adj.* reedlike; of or having to do with reeds.

–ary *suffix.* **1** a place for ——: *infirmary, library.* **2** a collection of ——: *dictionary, statuary.* **3** a person or thing that is, does, belongs to, etc. ——: *adversary, boundary, commentary.* **4** of or having to do with ——: *legendary, missionary.* **5** being; having the nature of ——: *secondary, supplementary.* **6** characterized by ——: *customary, honorary.* ⟨< L *-arius* or (neut.) *-arium*⟩

Ar•y•an ['æriən] *or* ['ɛriən], ['ærjən] *or* ['ɛrjən] *adj., n. —adj.* **1** of, having to do with, or designating the Indo-European family of languages or the hypothetical language from which they developed. **2** of or having to do with a hypothetical prehistoric people who spoke this original language, or any of their supposed descendants. **3** of or having to do with the Indo-Iranian languages or the peoples who speak them.
—n. **1** a member of the hypothetical prehistoric people who spoke the Aryan language, or any of their supposed descendants. **2** a member of any of the peoples speaking Indo-European languages. **3** in Nazi use, a non-Jewish person of European descent, especially the so-called Nordic type. **4** the hypothetical parent language of the Indo-European languages. ⟨< Skt. *aryas* noble⟩

ar•yl ['ærɪl] *or* ['ɛrɪl] *adj.* having to do with or being a member of the ARYL GROUP.

aryl group any of the organic groups derived from an aromatic hydrocarbon by removing one hydrogen atom.

ar•y•ten•oid [ə'rɪtə,nɔɪd], [,ærə'tinɔɪd], *or* [,ɛrə-] *adj.* **1** of or having to do with the two small triangular cartilages linked to the vocal cords. **2** of or having to do with the three muscles serving to close the opening between the vocal cords.

as[1] [əz]; *stressed,* [æz] *adv., conj., prep., pron. —adv.* **1** to the same degree or extent; equally: *as black as coal.* **2** for example: *Some animals, as dogs and cats, eat meat.*
as for, in the case of; with regard to: *We're leaving now; as for Sonia, she'll have to come on her own.*
as good as, practically; almost: *He looks as good as dead.*
as if, as it would be if: *The car looked as if it had been driven on rough roads.*

as is, *Informal.* in the present condition: *If you buy the car as is, you will have to put it in running order yourself.*
as though, as it would be if.
as well, also; besides.
as well as, in addition to; besides.
as yet, up to this time; so far: *Nothing has been done as yet.*
—conj. **1** to the same degree or extent that: *She worked just so much as she was told to.* **2** in the same way that: *Run as I do.* **3** during the time that; when; while: *He sang as he worked.* **4** because: *As he was a skilled worker, he received good wages.* **5** though: *Brave as they were, the danger made them afraid.* **6** that the result was: *The child so marked the picture as to spoil it.* **7** *Informal.* that; if; whether: *I don't know as that's such a good idea.*
as it were, so to speak.
—prep. **1** in the character or status of; doing the work of: *She is regarded as a model citizen. Who will act as teacher?* **2** like: *They treat me as their own child.*
as for, in the case of; with regard to: *We're leaving now; as for Sonia, she'll have to come on her own.*
as from, as of.
as of, beginning on; dating from: *As of April 7, we will be on daylight-saving time.*
as to, a about; concerning; referring to: *We have no information as to the cause of the riot.* **b** according to: *The scarves were grouped as to colour.*
—pron. **1** a condition or fact that: *She is very careful, as her work shows.* **2** that: *Do the same thing as I do.* ⟨OE (unstressed) *ealswā* quite so. Cf. ALSO.⟩
☛ *Syn. conj.* **4.** See note at BECAUSE.
☛ *Usage.* **As to** is often a clumsy substitute for a single preposition, usually *about* or *of*: *Practice usually proves the best teacher as to (in, for, of) the use of organ stops.*
☛ *Usage.* See note at LIKE[1].

as[2] [æs] *n., pl.* **as•ses** ['æsɪz] **1** an ancient Roman unit for measuring mass, equal to about 328 g. **2** the standard unit of money in ancient Rome. **3** a bronze or copper coin worth one as. ⟨< L⟩
☛ *Hom.* ASS.

as– *prefix.* a form of AD- before *s*, as in *assist.*

As **1** arsenic. **2** alto-stratus.

AS or **A.S.** Anglo-Saxon.

as•a•fet•i•da or **as•a•foet•i•da** [,æsə'fɛtədə] *or* [,æsə'fɪtɪdə] *n.* a gum resin with a garliclike odour, used in medicine and cooking. Also, **assafetida, assafoetida.** ⟨< Med.L *asafetida* < *asa* mastic (< Persian *azā*) + L *fœtidus* stinking⟩

ASAP as soon as possible.

as•bes•tos [æs'bɛstəs] *or* [æz'bɛstəs] *n.* **1** a mineral, a silicate of calcium and magnesium, that does not burn or conduct heat, usually occurring in fibres. **2** formerly, a fireproof fabric made of these fibres. **3** (*adjl.*) made of asbestos. ⟨ME < OF < L < Gk. *asbestos* unquenchable (originally, of quicklime) < *a-* not + *sbennunai* quench⟩ **—as'bes•tine** [-tin], *adj.*

as•bes•to•sis [,æsbɛs'tousɪs] *n.* a disease of the lungs caused by the inhalation of asbestos dust and fibres over a period of time.

as•car•id ['æskə,rɪd] *n.* any parasitic roundworm or other nematode of the family Ascaridae (genus *Ascaris*), often found in the intestines of humans and pigs.

as•cend [ə'sɛnd] *v.* **1** go up; rise; move upward: *She watched the airplane ascend higher and higher.* **2** climb; go to or toward the top of: *Another expedition is planning to ascend Mt. Everest.* **3** *Music.* rise in pitch. **4** incline upward. **5** go upstream along: *ascend a river.*
ascend the throne, become king, queen, etc. ⟨ME < L *ascendere* < *ad-* up + *scandere* climb⟩
☛ *Syn.* **2.** See note at CLIMB.

as•cend•ance [ə'sɛndəns] *n.* ascendancy. Also, **ascendence.**

as•cend•an•cy [ə'sɛndənsi] *n.* a controlling influence; domination; rule. Also, **ascendency.**

as•cend•ant [ə'sɛndənt] *adj., n. —adj.* **1** ascending; rising. **2** superior; dominant; ruling; controlling. **2** *Astrology.* of or being an ascendant.
—n. **1** a position of power; controlling influence. **2** *Astrology.* **a** the point of the apparent path of the sun rising above the horizon at a certain time. **b** HOROSCOPE (def. 1). Also, **ascendent.**
in the ascendant, a supreme; dominant. **b** increasing in influence.

as•cend•ence [ə'sɛndəns] See ASCENDANCE.

as•cend•ency [ə'sɛndənsi] See ASCENDANCY.

as•cend•ent [ə'sɛndənt] See ASCENDANT.

as•cend•er [ə'sɛndər] *n.* **1** a person or thing that ascends. **2** *Printing.* **a** the upper part of a lower-case letter such as b, d, h, or k. **b** any such letter. Compare DESCENDER.

ascend•ing [ə'sɛndɪŋ] *adj., v. —adj.* **1** rising or sloping upwards; mounting. **2** *Botany.* rising or gradually curving upward to a vertical position.
—v. ppr. of ASCEND.

as•cen•sion [ə'sɛnʃən] *n.* **1** the act of ascending; ascent. **2** *Christianity.* **Ascension, a** the bodily passing of Christ from earth to heaven. **b** Also, **Ascension Day,** a Christian church festival in honour of this on the fortieth day after Easter. ⟨< L *ascensio, -onis* < *ascendere.* See ASCEND.⟩

as•cent [ə'sɛnt] *n.* **1** the act of going up; rising. **2** the act of climbing. **3 a** a place or way that slopes up. **b** the amount or degree of slope. ⟨< *ascend*; modelled after *descent*⟩
☛ *Hom.* ASSENT.

as•cer•tain [,æsər'tein] *v.* find out; determine. ⟨ME < OF *acertener* < *a-* to + *certain* certain < L *certus* sure⟩ **—,as•cer'tain•a•ble,** *adj.* **—,as•cer'tain•a•bly,** *adv.*

as•cer•tain•ment [,æsər'teinmənt] *n.* an ascertaining.

as•cet•ic [ə'sɛtɪk] *n., adj. —n.* **1** a person who practises unusual self-denial or severe discipline of self for religious reasons. **2** a person who refrains from pleasures and comforts.
—adj. refraining from pleasures and comforts; self-denying. ⟨< Gk. *askētikos* < *askein* exercise; hence, discipline⟩
—as'cet•i•cal•ly, *adv.*
☛ *Hom.* ACETIC.

as•cet•i•cism [ə'sɛtə,sɪzəm] *n.* **1** the life or habits of an ascetic. **2** the doctrine that by abstinence and self-denial a person can train himself or herself to be in conformity with God's will.

as•cid•i•an [ə'sɪdiən] *n.* SEA SQUIRT.

as•cid•i•um [ə'sɪdiəm] *n., pl.* **-cid•i•a** [-'sɪdiə]. *Botany.* a baglike or pitcherlike part of a plant. ⟨< NL < Gk. *askidion,* dim of *askos* bag⟩

ASCII ['æski] *n., adj. Computer technology. —n.* American Standard Code for Information Interchange: *a common code used to represent characters of data in a computer.*
—adj. represented or stored using ASCII: *an ASCII file.*

as•ci•tes [ə'saitiz] *n.* dropsy of the peritoneum. ⟨< LL < Gk. *askites* dropsy < *askos* wineskin, bladder⟩

a•scle•pi•a•da•ceous [æs,klipiə'deiʃəs] *adj.* of or belonging to a family (Asclepiadaceae) of flowering plants such as milkweed, whose pollen is waxy. ⟨< NL *Asclepias* genus name < L < Gk. *asklepias* after Asclepius⟩

as•co•carp ['æskə,karp] *n. Botany.* a round structure which holds the spore sacs in an ascomycete. ⟨< NL *asco* < Gk. *askos* wineskin, bladder + *karpos* harvest⟩ **—,as•co'car•pous,** *adj.*

as•co•go•ni•um [,æskə'gouniəm] *n.* the female reproductive body in certain ascomycetes. ⟨< NL < Gk. *askos* wineskin, bladder + *gonos* seed, offspring⟩

as•co•my•cete [,æskə'maisit] *or* [,æskoumai'sit] *n.* any of a class (Ascomycetes) of fungi that includes yeasts, moulds, truffles, and mildews. ⟨< Gk. *askos* bag + *mykēs, mykētos* fungus⟩ **—,as•co•my'cet•ous,** *adj.*

as•cor•bate [ə'skɔrbeit] *n.* a salt of ascorbic acid.

a•scor•bic acid [ə'skɔrbɪk] *or* [ei'skɔrbɪk] vitamin C. *Formula*: $C_6H_8O_6$ ⟨< *a-*[4] + *scorb(ut)ic*⟩

as•co•spore ['æskə,spɔr] *n.* any of the spores developed in the spore sac of an ascomycete.

as•cot ['æskət] *or* ['æskɒt] *n.* a neck scarf with broad ends that is worn turned over in a loose single knot at the throat, with the ends laid one over the other. It is usually worn inside the collar. ⟨from *Ascot,* famous English race-track⟩

as•cribe [ə'skraɪb] *v.* **-cribed, -crib•ing. 1** assign; attribute (*to*): *The police ascribed the automobile accident to fast driving.* **2** consider as belonging (*to*): *People have ascribed their own characteristics to their gods.* ⟨ME < OF < L *ascribere* < *ad-* to + *scribere* write⟩ **—as'crip•tive,** *adj.*
☛ *Syn.* **1.** See note at ATTRIBUTE.

as•crip•tion [ə'skrɪpʃən] *n.* **1** the act of ascribing: *the ascription of selfishness to a miser.* **2** a statement or words ascribing something. ⟨< L *ascriptio, -onis* < *ascribere.* See ASCRIBE.⟩ **—as'crip•tive,** *adj.*

-ase *suffix.* enzyme: *amylase.* ⟨< *diastase* F < Gk. *diastasis,* a separation⟩

a•sep•sis [ei'sɛpsɪs] *or* [ə'sɛpsɪs] *n.* **1** an aseptic condition. **2** aseptic methods or treatment.

a•sep•tic [ei'sɛptɪk] *or* [ə'sɛptɪk] *adj.* free from germs causing infection. **—a'sep•ti•cal•ly,** *adv.*

a•sex•u•al [ei'sɛkʃuəl] *adj. Biology.* **1** having no sex. **2** independent of sexual processes. In the liverworts and mosses, and in some of the lower animals, sexual and asexual reproduction alternate. **—a'sex•u•al•ly,** *adv.*

As•gard ['æsgɑrd] *or* ['æzgɑrd] *n. Norse mythology.* the home of the Norse gods and heroes. ⟨< ON *Asgarthr* < *ass* god + *garthr* garden⟩

ash¹ [æʃ] *n.* **1** what remains of a thing after it has been thoroughly burned or oxidized by chemical means: *There was a cigarette ash on the carpet. We cleaned the ashes out of the fireplace.* **2 ashes,** *pl.* **a** ruins: *a whole city laid in ashes.* **b** the remains of a dead person: *He was buried beside the ashes of his forefathers.* **3** the light-grey colour of ashes from wood. **4** fine particles of lava from an erupting volcano. **5** (*adjl.*) like ash in colour, etc. ⟨OE *æsce*⟩

ash² [æʃ] *n.* **1** any of a genus (*Fraxinus*) of trees of the olive family found in the northern hemisphere, having compound leaves and greyish twigs. **2** the tough, straight-grained wood of an ash, valued especially for making tool handles, etc. **3** See MOUNTAIN ASH. ⟨OE *æsc*⟩

ash³ [æʃ] *n.* the name of an Old English letter, written æ, Æ.

a•shamed [ə'ʃeimd] *adj.* **1** feeling shame; disturbed or uncomfortable because one, or someone close to one, has done something wrong, improper, or silly: *I was ashamed when I sobbed at the movies. She was ashamed of her dishonesty. Don't be ashamed of your less affluent friends.* **2** unwilling because of shame: *I was ashamed to tell my parents that I had failed.*

☛ *Syn.* **1. Ashamed,** HUMILIATED, MORTIFIED = feeling embarrassed and disgraced. **Ashamed** emphasizes a feeling of having disgraced oneself by doing something wrong, improper, or foolish: *I was ashamed when I sobbed aloud at the movies.* **Humiliated** emphasizes a painful feeling of being lowered and shamed in the eyes of others: *Parents are humiliated if their children behave badly when guests are present.* **Mortified** = feeling greatly embarrassed and humiliated, sometimes ashamed: *He was mortified when he forgot his speech.*

A•shan•ti [ə'ʃænti] *or* [ə'ʃɑnti] *n., pl.* **-ti** or **-tis;** *adj. —n.* **1** the native people of the Ashanti region of Ghana. **2** a native of this region. **3** the language of its people.
—adj. of or having to do with the Ashanti region or its people.

ash•can ['æʃ,kæn] *n.* any receptacle, such as a barrel, drum, or large can, for holding garbage, ashes, etc.

ash•en¹ ['æʃən] *adj.* **1** like ashes; pale as ashes. **2** of ashes.

ash•en² ['æʃən] *adj.* **1** of the ash tree. **2** made from the wood of the ash tree.

ash•e•ry ['æʃəri] *n., pl.* **-ries.** *Cdn.* formerly, a place for making potash.

Ash•ke•naz•ic [,æʃkə'næzɪk] *or* [,ɑʃkə'nɑzɪk] *adj.* of, having to do with, or descended from the Ashkenazim.

Ash•ke•naz•im [,æʃkə'næzɪm] *or* [,ɑʃkə'nɑzɪm] *n.pl.* the Jews of central and eastern Europe, distinguished from the Spanish and Portuguese Jews, who are called the Sephardim. The Yiddish language developed among the Ashkenazim. ⟨< Hebrew, a German from the ancient kingdom of *Ashkenaz*⟩

ash•lar or **ash•ler** ['æʃlər] *n.* **1** a square stone used in building. **2** masonry composed of ashlars. ⟨ME < OF *aisselier* < VL *axillarium* < *axis* plank⟩

ash–leaf maple ['æʃ ,lif] *Cdn.* the MANITOBA MAPLE.

a•shore [ə'ʃɔr] *adv. or adj.* **1** to or toward the shore; to land. **2** on the shore; on land.

ash•ram ['æʃrəm] *or* ['ɑʃrəm] *n.* a place for Hindu religious instruction and retreat. ⟨< Hind. < Skt. *āsrama*⟩

Ash•to•reth ['æʃtə,rɛθ] *n.* Astarte. Also, **Ashtaroth.**

ash•tray ['æʃ,trei] *n.* a small receptacle to put tobacco ashes in.

Ash Wednesday the first day of Lent; the seventh Wednesday before Easter. Often, ashes are put on the foreheads of Christians observing this day, as a sign of repentance.

ash•y ['æʃi] *adj.* **ash•i•er, ash•i•est. 1** of or covered with ashes. **2** very pale; ashen.

A•sia ['eiʒə] *or* ['eiʃə] *n.* large continent including the Far East and parts of the Middle East.

A•sian ['eiʒən] *or* ['eiʃən] *adj., n. —adj.* **1** of, having to do with, or characteristic of Asia or its people. **2** Asiatic.
—n. **1** a native or inhabitant of Asia. **2** a person whose recent ancestors come from Asia. **3** a member of the Asiatic race. ⟨< LL *Asianus* < Gk.⟩

Asian flu a kind of influenza, first identified in Hong Kong in 1957.

A•si•at•ic [,eiʒi'ætɪk], [,eiʃi'ætɪk], [,eizi'ætɪk], *or* [,eisi'ætɪk] *adj., n. —adj.* **1** of or designating a major race of people that includes the traditional inhabitants of most of eastern Asia, Japan, Taiwan, the Philippines, and Indonesia, and, usually, the Inuit of North America, Greenland, and Siberia. They are distinguished by a combination of biological characteristics, including straight, dark hair, light brown skin, and an inner fold in the upper eyelid. **2** Asian.
—n. **1** a member of the Asiatic race. **2** Asian.

Asiatic cholera cholera.

a•side [ə'saɪd] *adv., n. —adv.* **1** on or to one side: *Move the table aside. John spoke aside to Tom without our hearing him.* **2** out of one's thoughts, consideration, etc.: *Put your troubles aside.* **3** kept back for future use: *The salesperson put the coat aside for me.* **4** notwithstanding; in spite of: *Kidding aside, I must tell you what I think of the matter.*
aside from, a apart from. **b** *Informal.* except for.
—n. words meant not to be heard by someone; especially, in the theatre, an actor's remark that is meant to be heard by the audience but not by the other characters in the play.

as•i•nine ['æsə,naɪn] *adj.* **1** of asses. **2** like an ass. **3** stupid; silly. ⟨< L *asininus* < *asinus* ass⟩ **—'as•i,nine•ly,** *adv.*

as•i•nin•ity [,æsə'nɪnəti] *n., pl.* **-ties.** silliness.

-asis *suffix.* a disorder characterized by —— : *elephantiasis.* ⟨< Gk. *asis* state of⟩

ask [æsk] *v.* **1** try to find out by words; inquire: *If you don't know, why don't you ask? She asked about our health. Ask the way.* **2** seek the answer to: *Ask any questions you wish.* **3** put a question to; inquire of: *Ask him how old he is.* **4** try to get by words; request (*often with* **for**): *Ask Kate to sing. I asked for a bike for my birthday.* **5** claim; demand: *to ask too high a price for a house.* **6** invite: *She asked ten guests to the party.* **7** need; require (*often with* **for**): *This job asks for hard work.*
ask for, *Informal.* invite (trouble); act so as to cause a fight, argument, etc.: *He's really asking for a fight by interrupting the meeting in that way.* ⟨OE *āscian*⟩

☛ *Syn.* **1. Ask,** INQUIRE = try to find out by a question. **Ask** is the general word meaning to seek information from someone: *Joe asked about you. Ask someone where that street is.* **Inquire** is more formal, but also suggests going into a subject more deeply, asking in an effort to get definite information: *He inquired about you, wanted to know where you are going and when you are leaving. You had better inquire how to get there.*

☛ *Syn.* **4. Ask,** REQUEST (def. 1), SOLICIT (def. 1). **Ask** is the general word: *I asked permission to do it. She asked me to give this to you.* **Request,** a more formal word, means to ask in a polite and more formal way: *We request contributions to the library. We request that you smoke outside.* **Solicit,** also more formal, means to request respectfully or earnestly: *They are soliciting funds for a new hospital.* **Solicit** can take only a noun phrase as its object.

a•skance [ə'skæns] *adv.*
look askance, a look with suspicion or disapproval: *The students looked askance at the suggestion of classes on Saturday.* **b** look sideways or to one side. Also, **askant.** ⟨origin uncertain⟩

a•skew [ə'skju] *adv. or adj.* to one side; out of the proper position; turned or twisted the wrong way: *Her hat is on askew. The bottom line of printing is askew.*

asking price the price asked in a sale of property, especially real estate. The actual selling price may be lower.

ASL AMERICAN SIGN LANGUAGE.

a•slant [ə'slænt] *adv., prep., adj. —adv.* in a slanting direction.
—prep. slantingly across.
—adj. (*never precedes a noun*) slanting.

a•sleep [ə'slip] *adj., adv. —adj.* (*never used before a noun or pronoun*) **1** in a condition of sleep; sleeping: *The cat is asleep.* **2** temporarily without feeling; numb, especially as a result of poor circulation: *My foot is asleep.* **3** sluggish; not alert; inactive: *asleep on the job.* **4** dead.
—adv. **1** into a condition of sleep: *The tired girl fell asleep.* **2** into a condition of numbness or inactivity.

a•slope [ə'sloup] *adv. or adj.* (*never precedes a noun*) at a slant.

a•so•cial [ei'souʃəl] *adj.* **1** paying no attention to social customs or laws; not interested in the welfare of society. **2** avoiding association with others; not sociable.

asp[1] [æsp] *n.* **1** the Egyptian cobra (*Naja haje*), a very poisonous snake, about 180 cm long. It was sacred to the Egyptians and became a symbol of royalty. **2** a small, poisonous snake (*Vipera aspis*) of Europe, a species of viper also called **asp viper.** ⟨< L *aspis* < Gk.⟩

asp[2] [æsp] *n. Archaic.* aspen. ⟨OE *æspe*⟩

a•spa•ra•gi•nase [ə'spærədʒə,neis] *or* [ə'spɛrədʒə,neis] *n.* a drug used to treat leukemia.

a•spar•a•gine [ə'spærə,dʒin] *or* [-,dʒɪn], [ə'spɛrə,dʒin] *or* [-,dʒɪn] *n.* a nonessential amino acid found especially in asparagus, beets, and potatoes. *Formula*: $NH_2COCH_2CH(NH_2)COOH$

as•par•a•gus [ə'spærəgəs] *or* [ə'spɛrəgəs] *n.* **1** any of a genus (*Asparagus*) of perennial plants of the lily family having many-branched stems with tiny, scalelike leaves; especially, one species (*A. officinalis*) widely cultivated for its edible young shoots. Several other species (such as *A. plumosa*), usually called **asparagus ferns,** are grown as ornamental plants. **2** the young shoots of *A. officinalis*, which are cooked and eaten as a vegetable. ⟨< L < Gk. *asparagos*⟩

Asparagus

a•spar•kle [ə'sparkəl] *adj. (never precedes a noun)* sparkling.

a•spar•tame [ə'spɑr,teim] *n.* an artificial sweetener many times sweeter than ordinary sugar and virtually noncaloric. *Formula*: $C_{14}H_{18}N_2O_5$ ⟨< *aspart(ic acid)* + *(phenyl)a(lanine) m(ethyl) e(ster)*⟩

as•pect ['æspɛkt] *n.* **1** one side, part, or view (of a subject): *various aspects of a plan.* **2** look; appearance: *the wintry aspect of the countryside.* **3** countenance; expression: *the solemn aspect of a judge.* **4** direction in which anything faces; EXPOSURE (def. 4): *This house has a western aspect.* **5** a side fronting in a given direction; *the southern aspect of a house.* **6** *Astrology.* the relative position of planets as determining their supposed influence upon human affairs. **7** *Grammar.* **a** the nature of the action of a verb, regarded as beginning, continuing, ending, being repeated, etc. **b** a verb form that expresses action as beginning, continuing, ending, being repeated, etc.: *Aspects indicate a quality of the action; tenses indicate time.* **c** in English, a verbal construction performing a similar function. The phrase *is walking* is, properly speaking, an aspect of the verb *walk.* **d** set of such forms or phrases for the various persons: *The Russian verb has many aspects.* **8** *Physics.* the position of a plane surface relative to a fluid or gas through which it moves. ⟨< L *aspectus* < *aspicere* < *ad-* at + *specere* look⟩

☛ *Syn.* **2.** See note at APPEARANCE.

as•pec•tu•al [æ'spɛktʃuəl] *adj., n.* —*adj. Grammar.* of or having to do with ASPECT (def. 7).
—*n. Grammar.* a verb form indicating aspect.

as•pen ['æspən] *n., adj.* —*n.* any of several trees (genus *Populus*) of the willow family having flattened leaf stalks that cause the leaves to flutter in the slightest breeze, such as the trembling aspen of North America and the common aspen (*P. tremula*) of Europe. See also TREMBLING ASPEN.
—*adj. Archaic.* trembling or quaking. ⟨earlier meaning 'of the asp[2]'⟩

as•per ['æspər] *n.* a Turkish money of account, equal to $\frac{1}{120}$ of a piaster, formerly a silver coin.

as•per•gil•lum [,æspər'dʒɪləm] *n. Roman Catholic Church.* an instrument for sprinkling holy water, either a brush or a perforated spherical container. ⟨< L *aspergillum* < *aspergere.* See ASPERSE.⟩

as•per•gil•lus [,æspər'dʒɪləs] *n.* any ascomycetous fungus of the genus *Aspergillus* whose chains of spores attached by stalks to a club-shaped branch resemble bristles on the end of a brush.

as•per•i•ty [ə'spɛrəti] *n., pl.* **-ties.** roughness; harshness; severity. ⟨ME *asprete* < OF < L *asperitas* < *asper* rough⟩

as•perse [ə'spɜrs] *v.* **-persed, -pers•ing. 1** spread damaging or false reports about; slander. **2** sprinkle. ⟨< L *aspersus*, pp. of *aspergere* < *ad-* on + *spargere* sprinkle⟩ **—as'per•ser,** *n.*

as•per•sion [ə'spɜrʒən] *or* [ə'spɜrʃən] *n.* **1** a damaging or false report; slander. **2** a sprinkling with water.
cast aspersions on, make slanderous comments about.

as•per•so•ri•um [,æspər'sɔriəm] *n.* **1** a basin or font containing holy water. **2** aspergillum.

as•phalt ['æsfɒlt] *or, sometimes,* ['æʃfɒlt] *n., v.* —*n.* **1** a dark-coloured, almost solid, tarry substance found in natural deposits in many parts of the world and also obtained by evaporating petroleum; bitumen. **2** a mixture of this substance with sand or crushed rock, used for pavements, roofs, etc. **3** (*adjl.*) consisting of or covered with asphalt.
—*v.* surface or seal with asphalt. ⟨< LL < Gk. *asphaltos*⟩ **—as'phal•tic,** *adj.*

asphalt jungle *Informal.* a densely populated city area in which crime and violence are common.

as•phal•tite [æs'fɒltəit], [æs'fæltəit], *or* ['æsfəl,təit] *n.* a naturally occurring, asphaltlike hydrocarbon. It is purer and has a higher melting point than asphalt.

as•phal•tum [æs'fæltəm] *n.* asphalt.

as•pho•del ['æsfə,dɛl] *n.* **1** any of various European plants (genera *Asphodelus* and *Asphodeline*) of the lily family, having spikes of white or yellow flowers. **2** an immortal flower of Greek legend, said to cover the fields of Elysium. ⟨< L < Gk. *asphodelos*⟩

as•phyx•i•a [æs'fɪksiə] *n.* suffocation or an unconscious condition caused by lack of oxygen and excess of carbon dioxide in the blood. ⟨< NL < Gk. *asphyxia* < *a-* without + *sphyxis* pulse < *sphyzein* throb⟩

as•phyx•i•ant [æs'fɪksiənt] *n., adj.* —*n.* a cause of asphyxiation.
—*adj.* causing or producing asphyxiation.

as•phyx•i•ate [æs'fɪksi,eit] *v.* **-at•ed, -at•ing.** suffocate through lack of oxygen and excess of carbon dioxide in the blood. **—as,phyx•i'a•tion,** *n.* **—as'phyx•i,a•tor,** *n.*

as•pic[1] ['æspɪk] *n.* a kind of jelly made of meat or fish stock, tomato juice, etc., often set in a mould with seafood, meat, etc. ⟨< F⟩

as•pic[2] ['æspɪk] *n. Poetic.* ASP[1]. ⟨< F *aspic*, var. (by influence of *piquer* to sting) of L *aspis.* See ASP[1].⟩

as•pi•dis•tra [,æspə'dɪstrə] *n.* any of a genus (*Aspidistra*) of plants of the lily family native to E Asia, especially a cultivated species (*A. lurida*) commonly called the cast-iron plant, popular as a house plant. ⟨< NL < Gk. *aspis*, *aspidos* shield + *astra* stars⟩

as•pir•ant [ə'spaɪrənt] *or* ['æspərənt] *n., adj.* —*n.* a person who aspires; a person who seeks a position of honour, advancement, etc.
—*adj.* aspiring.

as•pi•rate *v.* ['æspə,reit]; *adj., n.* ['æspərɪt] *v.* **-rat•ed, -rat•ing;** *adj., n.* —*v.* **1** *Phonetics.* **a** begin (a word or syllable) with an *h*-sound, as in *hoot* [hut]. **b** pronounce (a stop) with a following or accompanying puff of air. *P* is aspirated in *pin* but not in *spin* or *nip.* **2** draw (air) into the lungs; breathe. **3** *Medicine.* suction out (liquid or gas) from a body cavity.
—*adj.* pronounced with a breathing or *h*-sound. The *h* in *here* is aspirate; so is the *t* in *turn.*
—*n.* an aspirated sound. English *p* is an aspirate in *pat*, but not in *tap.* ⟨< L *aspirare.* See ASPIRE.⟩

as•pi•ra•tion [,æspə'reiʃən] *n.* **1** an earnest desire or ambition; longing to achieve or attain. **2** an object of desire or ambition; goal. **3** the act of breathing, especially drawing air into the lungs. **4** *Phonetics.* **a** an aspirating (of sounds). In English, the [t] sounds in *table* and *stable* are distinguished by aspiration: the former is followed by a puff of air while the latter is not. **b** an aspirated sound. **5** *Medicine.* the suctioning of liquid or gas from a body cavity.

as•pi•ra•tor ['æspə,reitər] *n.* an apparatus or device employing suction: *A vacuum cleaner is an aspirator.*

as•pi•ra•to•ry [ə'spaɪrə,tɔri] *adj.* **1** of or for breathing or suction. **2** of or for aspiration, the removal of fluid by suction.

as•pire [ə'spaɪr] *v.* **-pired, -pir•ing.** have an ambition for something; desire earnestly: *Scholars aspire after knowledge. Ruth aspired to be captain of the team.* ⟨< L *aspirare* < *ad-* toward + *spirare* breathe⟩ **—as'pir•ing•ly,** *adv.* **—as'pir•er,** *n.*

as•pi•rin ['æspərɪn] *n.* acetylsalicylic acid, used to relieve pain or fever. *Formula*: $C_9H_8O_4$ ⟨< a former trademark⟩

As•pi•rin ['æspərɪn] *n. Trademark.* a brand of tablets of acetylsalicylic acid. ⟨< A(cetyl) + spir(ea) + *-in*⟩

a•squint [ə'skwɪnt] *adv. or adj.* with a squint; sideways. ⟨origin uncertain, perhaps Du.⟩

ass [æs] *n.* **1** donkey. **2** any of several wild animals (genus *Equus*) of Asia and Africa, smaller than the horse but very fast

and having long, erect ears, a very short mane, and a long tail with a tuft of long hair at the end. The wild ass of Africa is the ancestor of the common domestic donkey. **3** a silly or stupid person; fool. ⟨OE *assa* < Celtic < L *asinus*⟩
☛ *Hom.* AS.

as•sa•fet•i•da or **as•sa•foet•i•da** [ˌæsəˈfɛtədə] *or* [ˌæsəˈfitədə] See ASAFETIDA.

as•sa•gai [ˈæsəˌgaɪ] See ASSEGAI.

as•sa•i [əˈsaɪ]; *Italian,* [asˈsaɪ] *adv. Music.* very: *allegro assai,* very fast.

as•sail [əˈseil] *v.* **1** set upon with violence; attack: *to assail a fortress.* **2** set upon vigorously with arguments, abuse, etc. **3** come over (a person); trouble: *He was assailed with feelings of panic.* **4** embark energetically upon (a task or problem): *She assailed the problem head on.* **5** overwhelm or have an impact on (usually the senses): *The smell of garlic assailed her nostrils.* ⟨ME < OF *asalir* < VL *adsalire* < L *ad-* at + *salire* leap⟩ **—as'sail•a•ble,** *adj.*
☛ *Syn.* **1.** See note at ATTACK.

as•sail•ant [əˈseilənt] *n.* a person who attacks: *The injured man did not know his assailant.*

As•sa•mese [ˌæsəˈmiz] *adj., n. —adj.* of Assam, its people, or their language or culture.
—n. **1** a native or inhabitant of Assam. **2** the state language of Assam, an Indo-European language related to Bengali.

as•sas•sin [əˈsæsɪn] *n.* **1** a murderer, especially of a politically important person. An assassin may be a hired murderer or a political fanatic. **2** any person who destroys or does serious damage: *a character assassin.* ⟨< F < Ital. < Arabic *hashshāshīn* hashish eaters; with reference to murderers under the influence of hashish⟩

as•sas•si•nate [əˈsæsəˌneit] *v.* **-nat•ed, -nat•ing. 1** murder (someone, especially a politically important person) by a sudden or secret attack. **2** destroy or do serious damage to, especially by slander, treachery, etc. **—as'sas•si,na•tor,** *n.*

as•sas•si•na•tion [əˌsæsəˈneiʃən] *n.* the act of assassinating.

as•sault [əˈsɒlt] *n., v. —n.* **1** an attack, especially a sudden, vigorous attack. **2** the final phase of a military attack; closing with the enemy in hand-to-hand fighting. **3** *Law.* a threat or an attempt to do physical harm to another person.
—v. make an assault on. ⟨ME < OF *asauter* < L *ad-* at + *saltare* leap⟩ **—as'sault•er,** *n.*
☛ *Syn. v.* See note at ATTACK.

assault and battery *Law.* the striking of a person; intentionally doing physical harm to a person.

as•say *v.* [əˈsei]; *n.* [ˈæsei] *or* [əˈsei] *v., n. —v.* **1** analyse (an ore, alloy, etc.) to find out the quantity of gold, silver, or other metal in it. **2** try; test; examine. **3** of ore, contain, as shown by analysis, a certain proportion of metal. **4** *Archaic.* attempt.
—n. **1** an analysis of an ore, alloy, etc. to find out the amount of metal in it. **2** a trial; test; examination. **3** the substance analysed or tested. **4** a list of the results of assaying an ore, drug, etc. ⟨ME < OF *a(s)sayer,* variant of *essayer,* ult. < LL < VL *exagere* weigh⟩ **—as'say•er,** *n.*

as•se•gai [ˈæsəˌgaɪ] *n., pl.* **-gais. 1** a slender spear or javelin of hard wood, often tipped with iron, used in South Africa. **2** a South African tree (*Curtisea faginea*) of the dogwood family whose wood is used for making such spears. Also, **assagai.** ⟨< Sp. *azagaya* < Arabic *az zaghayah* < Berber⟩

as•sem•blage [əˈsɛmblɪdʒ] *n.* **1** a group of persons gathered together; assembly. **2** a collection; group. **3** a bringing together; coming together; meeting. **4** a putting together: *the assemblage of the parts of a machine.* **5** a type of art form in which all manner of diverse objects are glued together as a collage.

as•sem•ble [əˈsɛmbəl] *v.* **-bled, -bling. 1** gather or bring together: *All the writer's papers have been assembled into one collection. They were finding it hard to assemble a crew for the yacht.* **2** come together; meet: *After lunch, the delegates assembled in the auditorium.* **3** put together the parts of; fit together: *The chair should be easy to assemble.* **4** *Computer technology.* convert (anything written in ASSEMBLY LANGUAGE) into machine language. ⟨ME < OF *as(s)embler* < VL *assimulare* bring together < L *assimulare* compare, ult. < *ad-* to + *similis* like, or *simul* together⟩
☛ *Syn.* **1.** See note at GATHER.

as•sem•bler [əˈsɛmblər] *n.* **1** a person or device that assembles. **2** *Computer technology.* a computer program designed specifically to convert ASSEMBLY LANGUAGE into machine language.

as•sem•bly [əˈsɛmbli] *n., pl.* **-blies. 1** a group of people gathered together for some purpose; meeting. A reception, a worship service, or a political rally may be called an assembly. **2** Often, **Assembly,** *Cdn.* in Québec, the National Assembly. **3** any lawmaking body; especially, in some countries, the lower house or branch of a legislature. **4** the act of fitting together: *the assembly of the parts of an automobile.* **5** the set of parts fitted or required to be fitted together: *the wing assembly of a model plane.* **6** *Military.* a signal on a bugle or drum for troops to form in ranks. **7** the act of gathering or coming together: *unlawful assembly.* **8** *Computer technology.* the conversion of a program in ASSEMBLY LANGUAGE into machine language.
☛ *Syn.* **1.** See note at MEETING.

assembly language *Computer technology.* a low-level computer language using words and abbreviations which will be converted into the digital instructions of machine language.

assembly line a row of workers and machines along which work is passed until the final product is made: *Automobiles are produced on an assembly line.*

as•sem•bly member *n.* **1** in Prince Edward Island, one of fifteen members of the Legislative Assembly elected by both property-holders and non-property-holders; a member of the Legislative Assembly who is not a councillor. **2** in the United States, a member of a state legislature, especially of a lower house.

as•sent [əˈsɛnt] *v., n. —v.* express agreement; agree.
—n. an acceptance of a proposal, statement, etc.; agreement. ⟨ME < OF < L *assentari* < *ad-* along with + *sentire* feel, think⟩ **—as'sent•er,** *n.* **—as'sent•ing•ly,** *adv.* **—,as•sen'ta•tion,** *n.*
☛ *Syn. v.* See note at CONSENT.
☛ *Hom.* ASCENT.

as•sert [əˈsɜrt] *v.* **1** state positively; declare. **2** insist on (a right, a claim, etc.); defend: *to assert one's independence.*
assert oneself, put oneself forward; make oneself noticed, especially in insisting on one's rights: *You'll never get waited on in that place if you don't assert yourself.* ⟨< L *assertus,* pp. of *asserere* < *ad-* to + *serere* join⟩ **—as'sert•er** or **as'ser•tor,** *n.*
☛ *Syn.* **1.** See note at DECLARE.

as•ser•tion [əˈsɜrʃən] *n.* **1** a positive statement; declaration. **2** an insisting on one's right, a claim, etc.

as•ser•tive [əˈsɜrtɪv] *adj.* **1** confident and certain; positive: *Katie is an assertive woman, standing up for her rights and opinions.* **2** declarative: *an assertive sentence.* **—as'ser•tive•ly,** *adv.* **—as'ser•tive•ness,** *n.*

as•sess [əˈsɛs] *v.* **1** estimate the value of (property or income) for taxation. **2** fix the amount of (a tax, fine, damages, etc.). **3** put a tax on or call for a contribution from (a person, property, etc.): *Each member of the club will be assessed one dollar to pay for the trip.* **4** portion out as a tax; apportion. **5** examine critically and estimate the merit, significance, value, etc. of: *The committee met to assess the idea of establishing a new university.* ⟨ME < OF < VL *assessare* fix a tax < L *assidere* < *ad-* by + *sedere* sit⟩ **—as'sess•a•ble,** *adj.*

as•sess•ment [əˈsɛsmənt] *n.* **1** the act of assessing. **2** the amount assessed. **3** an evaluation; critical appraisal.

as•ses•sor [əˈsɛsər] *n.* a person who estimates the value of property or income for taxation.

as•set [ˈæsɛt] *n.* **1** something having value; resource or advantage: *Her main asset as a politician is her ability to sway a crowd.* **2 assets,** *pl.* **a** the entire property of a person, company, etc. **b** property that can be used to pay debts. **c** *Accounting.* the entries on a balance sheet showing total resources. ⟨< OF *asez* enough < L *ad-* + *satis* enough⟩

as•sev•er•ate [əˈsɛvəˌreit] *v.* **-at•ed, -at•ing.** declare solemnly; state positively. ⟨< L *asseverare* < *ad-* + *severus* serious⟩ **—as'sev•er•a•tive,** *adj.*

as•sev•er•a•tion [əˌsɛvəˈreiʃən] *n.* a solemn declaration; emphatic assertion.

as•si•du•i•ty [ˌæsəˈdjuəti] *or* [ˌæsəˈduəti] *n., pl.* **-ties.**
1 careful and steady attention; diligence; perseverence.
2 solicitous behaviour.

as•sid•u•ous [əˈsɪdʒuəs] *or* [əˈsɪdjuəs] *adj.* careful and attentive; diligent. ⟨< L *assiduus* < *assidere* sit at. See ASSESS.⟩ **—as'sid•u•ous•ly,** *adv.* **—as'sid•u•ous•ness,** *n.*

as•sign [əˈsaɪn] *v., n. —v.* **1** give as a share, task, duty, etc.: *The teacher has assigned ten problems for tonight's homework.*
2 appoint (to a post or duty): *The captain assigned two soldiers to guard the gate.* **3** name definitely; fix; set: *The judge assigned a day for the trial.* **4** ascribe; attribute: *His breakdown was assigned to overwork.* **5** *Law.* transfer or hand over (property, rights, etc.): *He was finally obliged to assign his farm to his creditors.*

—*n. Law.* a person to whom property or a right is assigned; assignee. ⟨ME < OF *assigner* < L *assignare* < *ad-* to, for + *signare* to mark < *signum* mark⟩ **—as'sign•a•ble,** *adj.* **—as'sign•er,** *n.*

☛ *Syn. v.* **1. Assign,** ALLOT = give something to a particular person or purpose as a share or responsibility. **Assign** emphasizes giving something that has been established as due by some plan or principle: *The teacher assigned me a seat near the window.* **Allot** suggests giving an amount or part that is set more or less by chance: *Each student was allotted two tickets.*

as•sig•nat ['æsɪg,næt]; *French,* [asi'nja] *n.* a piece of paper money issued from 1789 to 1796 in France by a revolutionary government. Assignats were based on the value of confiscated lands. ⟨< F < L *assignatum* < *assignare.* See ASSIGN.⟩

as•sig•na•tion [,æsɪg'neiʃən] *n.* **1** an appointment for a meeting, especially a secret meeting between lovers; tryst. **2** the meeting or meeting place. **3** the act of assigning or alloting. **4** the thing, portion, etc. assigned.

as•sign•ee [əsaɪ'ni] *or* [,æsə'ni] *n.* **1** *Law.* a person to whom some property, right, etc. is transferred. **2** a person assigned to be someone's agent.

as•sign•ment [ə'saɪnmənt] *n.* **1** something assigned, especially a piece of work to be done. **2** the act of assigning. **3** *Law.* a transfer of some property, right, etc., or the document by which it is effected.

as•sign•or [əsaɪ'nɔr] *or* [,æsə'nɔr] *n. Law.* a person who transfers to another some property, right, etc.

as•sim•i•la•ble [ə'sɪmələbəl] *adj.* that can be assimilated. **—as,sim•i•la'bil•i•ty,** *n.*

as•sim•i•late [ə'sɪmə,leit] *v.* **-lat•ed, -lat•ing. 1** absorb; digest, either physically or mentally: *Mike reads too fast to assimilate everything. The human body will not assimilate sawdust.* **2** make or become like (people of a nation, etc.) in customs and viewpoint: *Canada has assimilated people from many lands. People of many nations have assimilated readily in this country.* **3** *Phonetics.* make or become like. A consonant is frequently assimilated to the consonant it precedes; *ads-* becomes *ass-*; *comr-, corr-*; *disf-, diff-*; etc. **4** become similar or alike. ⟨< L *assimilare* < *ad-* to + *similis* like⟩ **—as'sim•i,la•tor,** *n.*

☛ *Syn.* **1.** See note at ABSORB.

as•sim•i•la•tion [ə,sɪmə'leiʃən] *n.* assimilating or being assimilated: *Nutrition depends on the assimilation of food.*

as•sim•i•la•tion•ism [ə,sɪmə'leiʃə,nɪzəm] *n.* a policy that seeks to blend minority groups into the general population by intermarriage or education; the belief that such a policy is necessary and desirable: *Canada subscribes to a cultural mosaic policy rather than assimilationism.* **—as,sim•i'la•tion•ist,** *adj., n.*

as•sim•i•la•tive [ə'sɪmələtɪv] *or* [ə'sɪmə,leitɪv] *adj.* assimilating.

As•sin•i•boine [ə'sɪnə,bɔɪn] *n., adj.* —*n.* **1** a member of the First Nations living mainly in Alberta, Saskatchewan, and Montana: *The Assiniboines are a Siouan people.* **2** the Siouan language of the Assiniboines.
—*adj.* of or having to do with the Assiniboines or their language.

as•sist [ə'sɪst] *v., n.* —*v.* **1** help; give aid to. **2** take part or have a hand (*in*): *He assisted in the scoring of the goal.*
—*n.* **1** an instance of giving help: *With an assist from me, he soon climbed the fence.* **2** *Sports.* **a** the act of a player who helps a teammate score a goal, put an opposing player out, etc. **b** the credit given to a player for such an act. ⟨< F < L *assistere* < *ad-* by + *sistere* take a stand⟩

☛ *Syn. v.* **1.** See note at HELP.

as•sist•ance [ə'sɪstəns] *n.* help; aid.

as•sist•ant [ə'sɪstənt] *n., adj.* —*n.* **1** a helper; aid. **2** ASSISTANT PROFESSOR.
—*adj.* helping; assisting.

assistant professor a college or university teacher ranking below an associate professor but above a lecturer.

as•size [ə'saɪz] *n.* **1 assizes,** *pl.* **a** periodical sessions of a court of law. **b** the time or the place of these sessions. **2** an inquest or the verdict of the inquest. ⟨ME < OF *as(s)ise* < *asseeir* < VL *assedere* sit at < L *assidere.* See ASSESS.⟩

assn. or **Assn.** association.

assoc. or **Assoc.** associate; association.

as•so•ci•a•ble [ə'souʃəbəl] *adj.* able to be associated in thought: *ideas so opposed as to be hardly associable.*

as•so•ci•ate *v.* [ə'souʃi,eit] *or* [ə'sousi,eit] *n., adj.* [ə'souʃiɪt] *or* [ə'sousiɪt] *v.* **-at•ed, -at•ing;** *n., adj.* —*v.* **1** connect in thought: *We associate camping with summer.* **2** mix socially (*with*); keep company (*with*): *She associates only with people interested in sports.* **3** make (oneself or another person or persons) a partner or companion in some matter, organization, etc.: *He was associated with a law firm for several years. She has associated herself with the reform movement in the party.* **4** join or combine (two or more persons or parties) for a common purpose: *They have been associated in a number of business enterprises.*
—*n.* **1** a partner or colleague. **2** a companion or friend. **3** something that is connected with or usually accompanies something else. **4** a member of an institution, association, etc., who does not have full rights and privileges.
—*adj.* (*only before a noun*) **1** joined in companionship, interest, action, etc. **2** having partial rights and privileges in an institution, association, etc.: *an associate member.* **3** connected; related. ⟨< L *associare* < *ad-* to + *socius* companion⟩ **—as'so•ci,a•tor,** *n.*

associate professor a university or college teacher ranking below a professor but above an assistant professor.

as•so•ci•a•tion [ə,sousi'eiʃən] *or* [ə,souʃi'eiʃən] *n.* **1** an associating or being associated. **2** a group of people joined together for some purpose; society. **3** companionship; partnership; friendship. **4** the connection of ideas in thought. **5** *Chemistry.* the linking of identical or distinct molecules by weak bonds. **6** *Ecology.* a group of related organisms sharing an environment and forming part of a larger ecological community. *Abbrev.:* assn. or Assn., assoc. or Assoc.

association football soccer.

as•so•ci•a•tive [ə'souʃətɪv] *or* [ə'sousi,eitɪv] *adj.* **1** of, having to do with, or dependent on association, as of ideas or images. **2** *Mathematics.* of or referring to a rule that any change in the grouping of elements in an operation will not affect the result: *Addition and multiplication are associative. Example*: (7 + 3) + 8 = 7 + (3 + 8).

as•soil [ə'sɔɪl] *v. Archaic.* **1** absolve. **2** atone for. ⟨ME < OF *assoil,* pres. indicative of *as(s)oldre* < L *absolvere.* Doublet of ABSOLVE.⟩

as•so•nance ['æsənəns] *n.* **1** a partial rhyme in which the vowels are alike but the consonants are different. *Examples: brave—vain, lone—show.* **2** The repetition of similar vowel sounds for effect, as the sounds [i], [u], and [ɜr] in the following example: "She moved near me to soothe my gloomy fear/And murmured fervent verses in my ear." ⟨< F < L *assonans,* ppr. of *assonare* < *ad-* to + *sonāre* sound⟩

as•sort [ə'sɔrt] *v.* **1** sort out; classify; arrange by sorts. **2** furnish with an assortment of goods. **3** group (*with*). **4** agree in sort or kind; fall into a class. **5** associate (*with*). ⟨< F *assortir* < *a-* to (< L *ad-*) + *sorte* sort < L *sors, sortis,* originally, lot⟩ **—as'sort•er,** *n.* **—as'sort•a•tive,** *adj.*

assortative mating *Genetics.* nonrandom selection of mates in a population of organisms. In **positive assortative mating,** the partners resemble each other more closely than if they had been randomly selected; in **negative assortative mating,** the partners are less alike.

as•sort•ed [ə'sɔrtɪd] *adj., v.* —*adj.* **1** selected so as to be of different kinds; various: *assorted cakes.* **2** arranged by kinds; classified: *The socks are assorted by size.* **3** matched; suited to one another: *They are a poorly assorted couple, always quarrelling.*
—*v.* pt. and pp. of ASSORT.

as•sort•ment [ə'sɔrtmənt] *n.* **1** a collection made up of various kinds of things, persons, etc.; miscellaneous collection: *an assortment of candy.* **2** the act of assorting; separation into classes.

asst. or **Asst.** assistant.

as•suage [ə'sweidʒ] *v.* **-suaged, -suag•ing. 1** make easier or milder: *to assuage pain.* **2** satisfy; appease; quench: *to assuage thirst.* ⟨ME < OF *assouagier,* ult. < L *ad-* + *suavis* sweet⟩ **—as'suag•er,** *n.*

as•suage•ment [ə'sweidʒmənt] *n.* **1** an assuaging or being assuaged. **2** something that assuages.

as•sume [ə'sum] *or* [ə'sjum] *v.* **-sumed, -sum•ing. 1** take for granted; suppose: *He assumed that the train would be on time.* **2** take upon oneself; undertake: *to assume the leadership of a group, to assume control.* **3** take or put (an attitude, etc.) on oneself: *to assume an air of superiority.* **4** pretend: *to assume ignorance.* ⟨ME < L *assumere* < *ad-* to + *sumere* take⟩

☛ *Syn.* **4.** See note at PRETEND.

as•sumed [ə'sumd] *or* [ə'sjumd] *adj., v.* —*adj.* **1** pretended; not real. **2** supposed; taken for granted.
—*v.* pt. and pp. of ASSUME.

as•sum•ing [ə'sumɪŋ] *or* [ə'sjumɪŋ] *adj., v.* —*adj.* taking too

much on oneself; presumptuous: *She is too assuming.*
—*v.* ppr. of ASSUME.

as•sump•tion [ə'sʌmpʃən] *or* [ə'sʌmʃən] *n.* **1** the act of assuming: *She bustled about with an assumption of authority.* **2** the thing assumed: *John's assumption that he would win the prize proved incorrect.* **3** presumption; arrogance; unpleasant boldness. **4 the Assumption,** *Roman Catholic Church.* **a** the bodily taking of the Virgin Mary from earth to heaven after her death. **b** a church festival in honour of this, held on August 15. ⟨ME < L *assumptio, -onis* < *assumere.* See ASSUME.⟩ **—as'sump•tive,** *adj.*

as•sur•ance [ə'ʃʊrəns] *n.* **1** the act of making sure or certain. **2** a positive declaration inspiring confidence. **3** a security; certainty; confidence. **4** self-confidence. **5** impudence; too much boldness. **6** *Brit.* insurance.
☛ *Syn.* **3, 4.** See note at CONFIDENCE.

as•sure [ə'ʃʊr] *v.* **-sured, -sur•ing. 1** make sure or certain: *The man assured himself that the bridge was safe before crossing it.* **2** tell confidently or positively: *The captain of the ship assured the passengers that there was no danger.* **3** make safe; secure. **4** *Brit.* make safe against loss; insure. **5** give or restore confidence to; reassure. ⟨ME < OF *aseürer* < VL < L *ad-* + *securus* safe⟩ **—as'sur•er,** *n.*

as•sured [ə'ʃʊrd] *or* [ə'ʃɜrd] *adj., n., v.* —*adj.* **1** sure; certain. **2** confident; bold. **3** insured against loss.
—*n.* **1** a person whose life or property is insured. **2** a person who is the beneficiary of an insurance policy.
—*v.* pt. and pp. of ASSURE. **—as'sur•ed•ly** [ə'ʃʊrɪdli], *adv.* **—as'sur•ed•ness** [ə'ʃʊrɪdnəs] *or* [ə'ʃʊrdnəs], *n.*

as•sur•gent [ə'sɜrdʒənt] *adj.* ascending.

As•syr•i•an [ə'siriən] *n., adj.* —*n.* **1** a native or inhabitant of Assyria, an ancient country and empire in SW Asia. **2** the Semitic language of the Assyrians.
—*adj.* of or having to do with the Assyrians or their language. ⟨< L < Gk.⟩

As•tar•te [ə'stɑrti] *n. Phoenician mythology.* the goddess of love and fertility, known to the Hebrews as Ashtoreth.

a•stat•ic [ei'stætɪk] *adj.* **1** *Physics.* not tending to take a fixed or definite position: *A magnetic needle may be made astatic by neutralizing it.* **2** not stationary; unstable. **—a'stat•ic•al•ly,** *adv.*

astatic galvanometer a galvanometer whose needle is not influenced by the magnetic field of the earth.

as•ta•tine ['æstə,tin] *or* ['æstətɪn] *n.* a radioactive chemical element of the halogen group, produced artificially by bombarding bismuth with alpha particles and also formed naturally by radioactive decay. *Symbol*: At; *at.no.* 85; *at.mass* (210). ⟨< Gk. *astatos* unstable (*a-* not + *statos* stable) + E *-ine*[2]⟩

as•te•mi•zole [ə'stɛmɪ,zoul] *n.* an antihistamine drug.

as•ter ['æstər] *n.* **1** any of a genus (*Aster*) of perennial and annual plants of the composite family having daisylike, usually lavender, blue, pink, or white flowers. Many species are common North American wildflowers. **2** any of several other composite plants having similar flowers, such as the **China aster** (*Callistephus chinensis*), cultivated in several varieties as a garden flower, or the **golden asters** (genus *Chrysopsis*) of North America, having yellow flowers. **3** *Biology.* a star-shaped structure arising around the centrosome during cell division. ⟨< L < Gk. *aster* star⟩

Asters

-aster[1] *combining form.* starlike.

-aster[2] *suffix.* inferior; worthless; *poetaster.* ⟨< L, dim. suffix⟩

as•te•ri•at•ed [ə'stiri,eitɪd] *adj.* **1** star-shaped. **2** exhibiting asterism.

as•ter•isk ['æstə,rɪsk] *n., v.* —*n.* a star-shaped mark (*) used in printed or written material to call attention to a footnote, indicate an omission, show a hypothetical form, etc.
—*v.* mark with an asterisk. ⟨< LL < Gk. *asteriskos*, dim. of *aster* star⟩

as•ter•ism ['æstə,rɪzəm] *n.* **1** *Astronomy.* **a** a group of stars. **b** a constellation. **2** *Geology.* a starlike figure produced in some crystallized minerals by reflected or transmitted light.

a•stern [ə'stɜrn] *adv.* **1** at or toward the rear of a ship or aircraft. **2** backward. **3** behind.

a•ster•nal [ei'stɜrnəl] *adj.* **1** not attached to the sternum. **2** lacking a sternum.

as•ter•oid ['æstə,rɔɪd] *n., adj.* —*n.* **1** *Astronomy.* any of the many very small planets revolving around the sun between the orbit of Mars and the orbit of Jupiter. **2** any starfish.
—*adj.* **1** starlike. **2** resembling a starfish. ⟨< Gk. *asteroeidēs* starlike < *aster* star⟩

as•the•ni•a [æs'θiniə] *n.* lack or loss of strength; debility. ⟨< NL *asthenia* < Gk. *astheneia* < *asthenēs* weak < *a-* without + *sthenos* strength⟩

as•then•ic [æs'θɛnɪk] *adj.* **1** of or having to do with asthenia; weak. **2** characterized by a tall, lean physique.

as•then•o•sphere [æs'θɛnə,sfir] *n.* a region within the mantle of the earth that seems to be partly melted.

asth•ma ['æzmə] *or* ['æsmə] *n.* a chronic disease that causes coughing, difficulty in breathing, and a feeling of suffocation. ⟨ME *asma* < Med.L < Gk. *asthma* panting < *azein* breathe hard⟩

asth•mat•ic [æz'mætɪk] *or* [æs'mætɪk] *adj., n.* —*adj.* **1** of or having to do with asthma. **2** affected with asthma.
—*n.* a person affected with asthma.

as•tig•mat•ic [,æstɪg'mætɪk] *adj.* **1** having astigmatism. **2** having to do with astigmatism. **3** correcting astigmatism.

a•stig•ma•tism [ə'stɪgmə,tɪzəm] *n.* **1** a defect of an eye or of a lens that makes objects look indistinct or gives imperfect images. With perfect focus, all the rays of light from any one point of an object converge at one point on the retina of the eye or other receiving surface; with astigmatism they do not. **2** imperfect or distorted understanding or judgment. ⟨< *a-*[4] without + Gk. *stigma* point⟩

a•stir [ə'stɜr] *adv. or adj.* (*never precedes a noun*) **1** out of bed; up and around: *It was only six o'clock, but already the girls were astir.* **2** in motion.

a•stom•a•tous [ei'stɒmətəs], [ei'stoumətəs], *or* [æ'stɒmətəs] *adj. Biology.* not having a stoma.

as•ton•ish [ə'stɒnɪʃ] *v.* surprise greatly; amaze: *The gift of fifty dollars astonished the child.* ⟨var. of *astoun* < OF *estoner* < VL **extonare*; cf. L *tonare* thunder⟩
☛ *Syn.* See note at SURPRISE.

as•ton•ish•ing [ə'stɒnɪʃɪŋ] *adj., v.* —*adj.* very surprising; amazing: *an astonishing sight.*
—*v.* ppr. of ASTONISH. **—as'ton•ish•ing•ly,** *adv.*

as•ton•ish•ment [ə'stɒnɪʃmənt] *n.* **1** great surprise; amazement; sudden wonder. **2** anything that causes great surprise.

as•tound [ə'staʊnd] *v.* shock with alarm or surprise; surprise very greatly; amaze. ⟨earlier *astoun.* See ASTONISH.⟩

as•tound•ing [ə'staʊn,dɪŋ] *adj., v.* —*adj.* very shocking or surprising.
—*v.* ppr. of ASTOUND. **—as'tound•ing•ly,** *adv.*

astr. astronomer; astronomy.

a•strad•dle [ə'strædəl] *adv. or adj.* (*never precedes a noun*) astride.

as•tra•gal ['æstrəgəl] *n. Architecture.* **1** a small, convex moulding cut into the form of a string of beads. **2** plain, convex moulding. ⟨< L *astragalus* < Gk. See ASTRAGALUS.⟩

as•trag•a•lus [ə'strægələs] *n., pl.* **-li** [-,lai] *or* [-,li]. the uppermost bone of the tarsus; talus. ⟨< L < Gk. *astragalos* anklebone, small round moulding⟩

as•tra•khan or **as•tra•chan** ['æstrəkən] *n.* **1** the curly, furlike wool of young lambs from Astrakhan, a district in SW Asia. **2** a woollen cloth that looks like this. **3** a variety of apple having a reddish skin and crisp, white flesh.

as•tral ['æstrəl] *adj.* **1** of or having to do with the stars. **2** consisting of stars; starry. **3** *Biology.* having to do with the aster of a dividing cell. ⟨< LL *astralis* < L *astrum* star < Gk. *astron*⟩

astral body a spiritual counterpart, or double, of the human body, believed to be able to leave it at will.

astral lamp an oil lamp so made that it casts no shadow on the table below.

a•stray [ə'strei] *adj. or adv.* (*never precedes a noun*) off the right path or out of the right way.

a•stride [ə'straɪd] *adj., adv., prep.* —*adj. or adv.* (*never precedes a noun*) **1** with one leg on each side. **2** with legs far apart.
—*prep.* with one leg or end part on each side of (something).

as•trin•gen•cy [ə'strɪndʒənsi] *n.* the property of being astringent.

as•trin•gent [ə'strɪndʒənt] *adj., n.* —*adj.* **1** causing the

contraction of soft body tissues; styptic: *an astringent lotion, such as witch hazel.* **2** severe or austere: *astringent criticism.*
—n. a substance or agent that has an astringent effect. Alum is an astringent. ⟨< L *astringens, -entis*, ppr. of *astringere* < *ad-* to + *stringere* bind⟩ **—as'trin•gent•ly,** *adv.*

astro– *combining form.* **1** a star, planet, or other heavenly body: *astrophysics.* **2** space; outer space: *astronaut.* **3** having to do with the aster of a dividing cell: *astrosphere.*

as•tro•bi•ol•o•gist [ˌæstroubaɪ'ɒlədʒɪst] *n.* a person trained in astrobiology, especially one whose work it is.

as•tro•bi•ol•o•gy [ˌæstroubaɪ'ɒlədʒi] *n.* the branch of biology that deals with the discovery and study of life on other planets, etc.

as•tro•bot•a•ny [ˌæstrou'bɒtəni] *n.* the branch of botany that deals with the discovery and study of plant life on other planets, etc.

as•tro•chem•is•try [ˌæstrou'kɛmɪstri] *n.* the branch of chemistry that deals with the chemical properties of heavenly bodies.

as•tro•com•pass ['æstrou,kʌmpəs] *n.* an instrument used to determine direction by sighting on a heavenly body.

as•tro•cyte ['æstrə,səit] *n.* a star-shaped cell in the brain and the spinal cord. **—ˌas•tro'cyt•ic** [-'sɪtɪk], *adj.*

as•tro•dy•nam•ics [ˌæstroudaɪ'næmɪks] *n.* the branch of dynamics that deals with the motion of bodies in outer space and the forces acting upon them.

as•tro•ge•o•lo•gist *n.* [ˌæstroudʒi'ɒlədʒɪst] a person trained in astrogeology, especially one whose work it is.

as•tro•ge•o•lo•gy *n.* [ˌæstroudʒi'ɒlədʒi] the science that deals with the nature of rocks on other planets and the moon.

as•tro•labe ['æstrə,leib] *or* ['æstrə,læb] *n.* an astronomical instrument formerly used for measuring the altitude of the sun or stars. ⟨ME < OF *astrelabe* < Med.L < Gk. *astrolabon*, orginally, star-taking < *astron* star + *lambanein* take⟩

as•trol•o•ger [ə'strɒlədʒər] *n.* a person who claims to interpret the influence of the stars and planets on persons, events, etc.

as•tro•log•i•cal [ˌæstrə'lɒdʒəkəl] *adj.* having to do with astrology. **—ˌas•tro'log•i•cal•ly,** *adv.*

as•trol•o•gy [ə'strɒlədʒi] *n.* **1** a pseudo-science that interprets the supposed influence of the stars and planets on persons, events, etc.; the study of the stars to foretell what will happen. **2** *Archaic.* practical astronomy. ⟨ME < L < Gk. *astrologia* < *astron* star + *-logos* treating of⟩

as•trom•e•try [ə'strɒmətri] *n.* the branch of astronomy having to do with the measurement of the positions and movements of heavenly bodies. **—ˌas•tro'met•ric** [ˌæstrə'mɛtrɪk], *adj.*

astron. astronomer; astronomical; astronomy.

as•tro•naut ['æstrə,nɒt] *n.* a pilot or member of the crew of a spacecraft; a person who travels in outer space. ⟨< *astro* + (*Argo*)*naut*⟩ **—ˌas•tro'nau•tic,** *adj.*

as•tro•nau•ti•cal [ˌæstrə'nɒtɪkəl] *adj.* having to do with space travel and spacecraft. **—ˌas•tro'nau•ti•cal•ly,** *adv.*

as•tro•nau•tics [ˌæstrə'nɒtɪks] *n.* **1** the designing, manufacturing, and operating of space vehicles. **2** space travel.

as•tron•o•mer [ə'strɒnəmər] *n.* a person trained in astronomy, especially one whose work it is. *Abbrev.*: astr.

as•tro•nom•i•cal [ˌæstrə'nɒməkəl] *adj.* **1** of or having to do with astronomy. **2** enormous; like the numbers reported in astronomy. Also, **astronomic. —ˌas•tro'nom•i•cal•ly,** *adv.*

astronomical latitude the angle between the plane of the celestial equator and the plumbline at a particular point on the earth's surface.

astronomical unit a unit used in astronomy for measuring length or distance, equal to 149 600 gigametres, which is the mean distance of the earth from the sun. The astronomical unit is used with the SI. *Abbrev.*: AU

astronomical year the period of the earth's revolution around the sun; solar year. It lasts 365 days, 5 hours, 48 minutes, and 45.51 seconds.

as•tron•o•my [ə'strɒnəmi] *n.* **1** the science that deals with the sun, moon, and other heavenly bodies. It includes the study of their composition, motions, positions, distances, sizes, etc. **2** a textbook or handbook dealing with this science. *Abbrev.*: astr. ⟨ME < L < Gk. *astronomia* < *astron* star + *nomos* distribution⟩

as•tro•phys•i•cal [ˌæstrou'fɪzəkəl] *adj.* of or having to do with astrophysics.

as•tro•phys•ics [ˌæstrou'fɪzɪks] *n. (used with a singular verb)* the branch of astronomy that deals with the physical and chemical characteristics of heavenly bodies.

as•tro•sphere ['æstrə,sfir] *n. Biology.* **1** centrosphere. **2** the aster of a cell, not including the centrosome.

As•tro•turf ['æstrou,tɜrf] *or* ['æstrə,tɜrf] *n. Trademark.* artificial turf made to look like grass, used on playing fields, tennis courts, etc.

as•tute [ə'stjut] *or* [ə'stut] *adj.* **1** having or showing a keen, discovering mind; clever; sagacious: *an astute remark.* **2** having or showing hard-headed shrewdness; crafty: *an astute business deal.* ⟨< L *astutus* < *astus* sagacity, cunning⟩ **—as'tute•ly,** *adv.* **—as'tute•ness,** *n.*

☛ *Syn.* **2.** See note at SHREWD.

a•sty•lar [ei'staɪlər] *adj. Architecture.* having no columns. ⟨< Gk. *a* without + *stylos* pillar⟩

a•sun•der [ə'sʌndər] *adv., adj. —adv.* in pieces; into separate parts: *torn asunder.*
—adj. apart; separate (*never precedes a noun*). ⟨OE *on sundran*⟩

a•swarm [ə'swɔrm] *adv. or adj. (never precedes a noun)* in a crowded, swarming state: *The bleachers were aswarm with baseball fans.*

a•sy•lum [ə'saɪləm] *n.* **1** formerly, an institution for the support and care of the mentally ill, the poor, the aged, etc. **2** refuge; shelter: *The author who had been accused of a political crime was given asylum in another country.* ⟨ME < L < Gk. *asylon* refuge < *a-* without + *sylē* right of seizure⟩

a•sym•met•ric [ˌeisə'mɛtrɪk] *or* [ˌæsə'mɛtrɪk] *adj.* asymmetrical.

a•sym•met•ri•cal [ˌeisə'mɛtrəkəl] *or* [ˌæsə'mɛtrəkəl] *adj.* not symmetrical; lacking symmetry.

The outline of the tree on the left is asymmetric; the one on the right is symmetric.

a•sym•me•try [ei'sɪmətri] *or* [æ'sɪmətri] *n.* lack of symmetry.

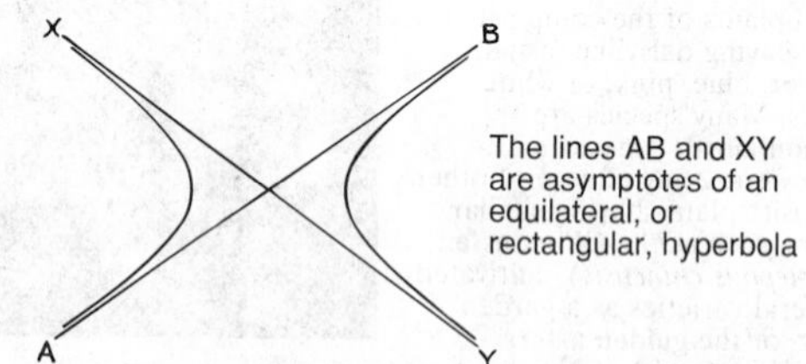

The lines AB and XY are asymptotes of an equilateral, or rectangular, hyperbola

as•ymp•tote ['æsɪm,tout] *n. Mathematics.* a straight line that continually approaches a curve, but does not meet it within a finite distance. ⟨< Gk. *asymptōtos* < *a-* not + *syn-* together + *ptōtos* apt to fall⟩

as•ymp•tot•ic [ˌæsɪmp'tɒtɪk] *adj.* having to do with an asymptote. **—ˌas•ymp'tot•i•cal,** *adj.* **—ˌas•ymp'tot•i•cal•ly,** *adv.*

a•syn•chro•nism [ei'sɪŋkrə,nɪzəm] *n.* lack of correspondence in time.

a•syn•chron•ous [ei'sɪŋkrənəs] *adj.* not synchronous.

a•syn•de•ton [ə'sɪndətən] *n.* the leaving out of a conjunction. ⟨< LL < Gk. *a* not + *syndetos* joined with < *syndein* to join < *syn-* together + *dein* to find⟩

at¹ [ət]; *stressed,* [æt] *prep.* **1** in; on; near: *at school, at the front door.* **2** toward; in the direction of: *to aim at the mark. Look at me.* **3** in the place, manner, or condition of: *at right angles, at war, at a crawl.* **4** on or near the time of: *at midnight.* **5** through; by way of: *Smoke came out at the chimney.* **6** engaged in; trying to do: *at work.* **7** because of; as a result of: *The shipwrecked sailors were happy at the arrival of the rescue ship.* **8** for: *two books at a* *dollar each.* **9** according to: *at will.* **10** from: *The sick woman got good treatment at the hands of the doctor.* **11** with respect to: *poor at math.* ⟨OE *æt*⟩

☛ *Usage.* **At,** IN are used to bring into a sentence a word stating a place or a time. **At** is used when the place or time is thought of as a point, as on a map or a clock. **In** is used when the place or time is thought of as having boundaries and the idea to be expressed is that of being *inside* or *within* the boundaries: *On our trip we stopped at Toronto and stayed two days in Montréal. We left Montréal at noon and in the afternoon drove to Québec.*

at² [ɑt] *n.* **1** a unit of money in Laos, equal to 1/100 of a kip. See money table in the Appendix. **2** a coin worth one at. Also, **att.** ⟨< Thai⟩

at– *prefix.* to or toward; the form of AD- occurring before *t,* as in *attain.*

at. **1** atmosphere(s). **2** atomic. **3** airtight.

At astatine.

AT antitank.

At•a•lan•ta [,ætə'læntə] *n. Greek mythology.* a maiden famous for her beauty and for her speed in running. She required each of her suitors to run a race with her; those who lost the race were killed.

at•a•rac•tic [,ætə'ræktɪk] *adj., n.* —*adj.* **1** able to soothe. **2** of a drug, inducing calmness.
—*n.* an ataractic drug.

at•a•rax•ia [,ætə'ræksiə] *n.* emotional serenity. Also, **ataraxy** ['ætə,ræksi]. ⟨< Gk. *a-* not + *tarassein* disturb⟩

at•a•vism ['ætə,vɪzəm] *n.* **1** in a plant or animal, the reappearance of a characteristic that has been absent for several generations. **2 a** this characteristic. **b** an individual showing such a characteristic; throwback. ⟨< L *atavus* ancestor⟩

at•a•vis•tic [,ætə'vɪstɪk] *adj.* **1** having to do with atavism. **2** having a tendency to atavism.

a•tax•i•a [ə'tæksiə] *n.* an inability to co-ordinate voluntary muscular movements, as in some nervous disorders. ⟨< NL < Gk. *ataxia* < *a-* without + *taxis* order⟩ **—a'tax•ic,** *adj.*

ATC or **A.T.C.** **1** air traffic control. **2** Air Transport Command.

ate [eit] *v.* pt. of EAT.

A•te ['eiti] *n. Greek mythology.* the goddess of recklessness and mischief, later regarded as the goddess of revenge. ⟨< Gk⟩.

-ate¹ *suffix.* **1** of or having to do with: *novitiate = having to do with novices.* **2** having; containing: *compassionate = having compassion.* **3** having the form of; like: *stellate = having the form of a star.* **4** ——ed or able to be ——ed: *duplicate = duplicated; determinate = able to be determined.* **5** become: *maturate = become mature.* **6** cause to be: *alienate = cause to be alien.* **7** produce: *ulcerate = produce ulcers.* **8** supply or treat with: *aerate = treat with air.* **9** combine with: *oxygenate = combine with oxygen.* **10** a person or thing that is a participant in, or product of, some process: *graduate = a person who is graduating; condensate = the product of condensation.* ⟨< L *-atus, atum,* pp. endings⟩

-ate² *suffix.* a salt made from ——ic acid: *nitrate = salt made from nitric acid.* ⟨special use of *-ate¹*⟩

-ate³ *suffix.* the office, rule, domain, or condition of: *caliphate = rule of a caliph.* ⟨< L *-atus,* from 4th declension nouns⟩

at•el•ier [,ætə'ljei] *n.* a workshop, especially an artist's studio. ⟨< F *atelier* originally, pile of chips < OF *astele* chip < L *astula*⟩

a tem•po [ɑ 'tɛmpou] *Music.* in time; returning to the former speed. ⟨< Ital.⟩

a•te•no•lol [ə'tɛnə,lɒl] *n.* a drug used to treat high blood pressure. *Formula:* $C_{14}H_{22}N_2O_3$

Ath•a•na•sian Creed [,æθə'neiʒən] *or* [,æθə'neiʃən] *Christianity.* one of the three main Christian creeds or professions of faith, the other two being the Apostles' Creed and the Nicene Creed. Its authorship is unknown, but it was probably composed around A.D. 430. ⟨< St. *Athanasius* (296 ?-373), bishop of Alexandria, formerly supposed to be the author of the creed⟩

Ath•a•pas•can [,æθə'pæskən] *n., adj.* —*n.* **1** a major group of languages of the First Nations and Native Americans spoken in northwestern Canada, Alaska, and the SW United States, including Chippewayan, Dogrib, Sarcee, Slave, and Navaho. **2** a member of a nation speaking any of these languages.
—*adj.* of, having to do with, or referring to this group of languages or any of the peoples speaking them.

a•the•ism ['eiθi,ɪzəm] *n.* the belief that there is no God. ⟨< F *athéisme* < Gk. *atheos* denying the gods < *a-* without + *theos* a god⟩

a•the•ist ['eiθiɪst] *n.* a person who believes that there is no God.

a•the•is•tic [,eiθi'ɪstɪk] *adj.* of atheism or atheists. Also, **atheistical. —,a•the'is•ti•cal•ly,** *adv.*

ath•el•ing ['æθəlɪŋ] *n.* an Anglo-Saxon prince or noble, especially a crown prince. ⟨OE *ætheling* < *æthelu* noble family + *-ling* belonging to⟩

A•the•na [ə'θinə] *n. Greek mythology.* the goddess of wisdom, arts, industries, and prudent warfare, corresponding to the Roman goddess Minerva. Also called **Pallas, Pallas Athena, Athene.**

ath•e•nae•um or **ath•e•ne•um** [,æθə'niəm] *n.* **1** a scientific or literary club. **2** a reading room; library. ⟨< L < Gk. *Athēnaion* temple of Athena, where men of learning gathered⟩

Ath•e•nae•um [,æθə'niəm] *n.* in Athens, the temple of Athena. Poets and learned men gathered there.

A•the•ne [ə'θini] *n.* Athena.

A•the•ni•an [ə'θiniən] *or* [ə'θinjən] *adj., n.* —*adj.* of Athens, the capital of Greece, or its people.
—*n.* **1** a person having the right of citizenship in ancient Athens. **2** a native or inhabitant of Athens.

Ath•ens *n.* ['æθənz] **1** the capital city of Greece. **2** any city thought of as being a centre of art and literature like the ancient Greek city of Athens.

a•ther•man•cy [ei'θɜrmənsi] *n.* the inability to transmit heat or infrared radiation. ⟨< Gk. *a* without + *thermansis* heating < *thermanein* to heat < *therme* heat⟩ **—a'ther•ma•nous,** *adj.*

ath•er•o•ma [,æθə'roumə] *n.* a fatty deposit on or in the inner lining of an artery. ⟨< L < Gk. *athērē* mush + *-ōma* tumour⟩ **—,ath•er'om•a•tous** [,æθə'rɒmətəs] *or* [,æθə'roumətəs], *adj.*

ath•er•o•scle•ro•sis [,æθərousklə'rousɪs] *n.* a form of arteriosclerosis characterized by a narrowing and hardening of the arteries due to deposits of cholesterol and fatty acids along the artery walls. ⟨< NL < Gk. *ather* chaff + SCLEROSIS⟩ **—,ath•er•o•scle'rot•ic** [-sklə'rɒtɪk], *adj.*

a•thirst [ə'θɜrst] *adj. (never precedes a noun)* **1** thirsty. **2** eager.

ath•lete ['æθlit] *n.* a person trained in exercises of physical strength, speed, and skill. Ballplayers, runners, boxers, and swimmers are athletes. ⟨< L *athleta* < Gk. *athlētēs* < *athlēo* contend for a prize *(athlon)*⟩

athlete's foot a contagious skin disease of the feet, caused by a fungus; ringworm of the feet.

athlete's heart an enlargement of the heart due to overexercise.

ath•let•ic [æθ'lɛtɪk] *adj.* **1** active and strong; generally enjoying active games and sports and showing natural skill in them: *I'm not very athletic but I do enjoy swimming and horseback riding.* **2** of, like, or suited to an athlete. **3** having to do with active games and sports. **—ath'let•i•cal•ly,** *adv.* **—ath'let•i,cism,** *n.*

ath•let•ics [æθ'lɛtɪks] *n.* **1** *(usually pl. in use)* exercises of strength, speed, and skill; active games and sports: *Athletics include baseball and basketball.* **2** *(usually sing. in use)* the study or science of the practice and principles of athletic training: *Athletics is recommended for every student.*

athletic support an elasticized belt and pouch for supporting the genitals, worn by men for athletics and other physical activity.

ath•o•dyd ['æθə,dɪd] *or* ['æθə,daɪd] *n.* ramjet. ⟨< *a(ero)th(erm)ody(namic) d(uct)*⟩

at–home [ət 'houm] *n.* an informal reception, usually in the afternoon.

a•thwart [ə'θwɔrt] *adv., prep.* —*adv.* **1** crosswise; across from side to side. **2** so as to prevent passage.
—*prep.* **1** across. **2** across the line or course of. **3** in opposition to; against. ⟨< *a-* on + *thwart,* adv.⟩

—atic *suffix.* of; having the nature of ——: *problematic.*

at•i•gi ['ætəgi] *or* [ə'tigi] *n. Cdn.* **1** a hooded, knee-length inner shirt made of summer skins with the hair inside against the body, used in winter especially by Inuit, often for indoor wear. **2** a hooded outer garment of fur or other material; parka. Also, **artigi, artiggi.** ⟨< Inuktitut⟩

a•tilt [ə'tɪlt] *adj. (never precedes a noun) or adv.* **1** at a tilt; tilted. **2** in a jousting encounter or TILT (def. 3).

a•tin•gle [ə'tɪŋgəl] *adj. (never precedes a noun) or adv.* tingling; in or into a tingling or excited condition.

–ation *suffix.* **1** the act or state of ——ing: *admiration = act or state of admiring.* **2** the condition or state of being ——ed: *cancellation = condition or state of being cancelled.* **3** the result of ——ing: *civilization = result of civilizing.* ⟨< L *-atio, -onis* < *-at-* of pp. stem (cf. *-ate*[1]) + *-io* (cf. *-ion*)⟩

–ative *suffix.* **1** tending to ——: *talkative = tending to talk.* **2** having to do with ——: *qualitative = having to do with quality.* ⟨< F *-ative* (fem. of *-atif* < L *-ativus*) or directly < L *-ativus* < *-at-* of pp. stem (cf. *-ate*[1]) + *-ivus* (cf. *-ive*)⟩

At•ka mackerel ['ætkə] an important food fish of the greenling family found in the waters off the Aleutian Islands. ⟨< *Atka* Island⟩

At•lan•te•an [,ætlæn'tiən] *adj.* **1** resembling Atlas; strong. **2** having to do with the legendary island of Atlantis. ⟨< L *Atlanteus* < Gk.⟩

At•lan•tic [æt'læntɪk] *n., adj. —n.* the Atlantic Ocean. *—adj.* **1** of the Atlantic Ocean: *Atlantic currents.* **2** on, in, over, or near the Atlantic Ocean: *Atlantic air routes.* **3** of or designating NATO: *the Atlantic alliance.* ⟨< L < Gk. *Atlantikos* pertaining to Atlas⟩

Atlantic Charter the joint declaration of U.S. President Roosevelt and British Prime Minister Churchill on August 14, 1941, asserting the need for guaranteed freedom of all nations.

Atlantic hump–backed dolphin a dolphin (*Sousa teuszii*) of the coastal waters off W Africa. It is an endangered species.

Atlantic Provinces Newfoundland, Prince Edward Island, Nova Scotia, and New Brunswick.

☛ *Usage.* See note at MARITIME PROVINCES.

Atlantic salmon a salmon (*Salmo salar*) found along the Atlantic coasts of North America and Europe, very highly valued as a game and food fish. The ouananiche, or landlocked salmon, is a variety of Atlantic salmon that spends all its life in fresh water.

At•lan•tis [æt'læntɪs] *n.* a legendary island in the Atlantic, said to have sunk beneath the sea. ⟨< L < Gk.⟩

at•las ['ætləs] *n., pl.* **at•las•es. 1 Atlas, a** *Greek mythology.* one of the Titans who rebelled against Zeus. He was punished by being made to support the heavens with his head and hands. **b** a person who bears a great burden. **c** a man who is exceptionally strong. **2** a book of maps. The first such books always had at the front a picture of Atlas supporting the world. **3** a book of plates, tables, or charts illustrating a particular subject. ⟨< L < Gk.⟩

atm 1 STANDARD ATMOSPHERE(s). **2** atmospheric.

ATM *Computer technology.* automated teller machine.

at•man *n.* ['ɑtmən] *Hinduism.* **1** the soul which is capable of reincarnation; the individual's spiritual self. **2** Also, **Atman**, the universal soul; the spiritual principle animating all of creation.

at.mass ATOMIC MASS.

at•mom•e•ter [æt'mɒmətər] *n.* an instrument for measuring rate of evaporation. ⟨< Gk. *atmos* vapour + E *-meter*⟩

at•mos•phere ['ætməs,fir] *n.* **1** air that surrounds the earth, consisting mainly of nitrogen and oxygen. More than 99 percent of the total mass of the earth's atmosphere lies in the region up to about 80 km above the earth's surface. See also TROPOSPHERE, STRATOSPHERE, MESOSPHERE, THERMOSPHERE, EXOSPHERE. **2** the mass of gases that surrounds any heavenly body. **3** air in any given place: *a damp atmosphere.* **4** STANDARD ATMOSPHERE. **5** mental and moral environment; surrounding influence: *an atmosphere of poverty, the atmosphere of old Vienna.* **6** the colouring or feeling that pervades a work of art: *the sombre atmosphere of* The Scarlet Letter. **7** *Informal.* a pleasant, usually creative, effect brought about by the décor, lighting, etc. of a place: *This pub has a lot of atmosphere.* ⟨< NL *atmosphaera* < Gk. *atmos* vapour + *sphaira* sphere⟩

at•mos•pher•ic [,ætməs'fɛrɪk] *adj., n. —adj.* **1** of or having to do with the atmosphere: *Atmospheric conditions prevented observation of the stars.* **2** occurring in or produced by the atmosphere: *atmospheric moisture, atmospheric disturbances.* *—n.* **atmospherics,** *pl.* **1** interference in the form of crackling or hissing sounds in a radio receiver, caused by electrical disturbance in the atmosphere. **2** electrical disturbance in the atmosphere produced by a natural cause such as lightning. Also, **atmospherical. —,at•mos'pher•i•cal•ly,** *adv.*

atmospheric pressure the pressure exerted by the air on the surface of the earth and everything existing on it, caused by the force of gravity. The standard atmospheric pressure is about 101 kilopascals; the highest atmospheric pressure ever recorded was about 108 kilopascals, in Siberia.

at.no. ATOMIC NUMBER.

at•oll ['ætɒl] *or* [ə'tɒl] *n.* a ring of coral that has built up on a sunken land bank or volcano top in the open sea, parts of the ring showing above water as solid coral islands that support vegetation. The pool in the centre of an atoll is called a lagoon. ⟨< Maldive (lang. of the Maldive Islands in the Indian Ocean), ? < Malayalam *adal* uniting⟩

at•om ['ætəm] *n.* **1** the smallest part of an element that has all the properties of the element and can take part in a chemical reaction without being permanently changed. The basic particles making up an atom are protons and neutrons (themselves made up of quarks) constituting its central portion, or nucleus, and electrons orbiting the nucleus. **2** the atom considered as a source of potential energy: *the power of the atom.* **3** a very small particle, thing, or quantity; bit: *not an atom of strength left. The plate was smashed to atoms.* ⟨< L < Gk. *atomos* indivisible < *a-* not + *tomos* a cutting⟩

atom bomb ATOMIC BOMB.

a•tom•ic [ə'tɒmɪk] *adj.* **1** of or having to do with atoms: *atomic research.* **2** of, having to do with, or using ATOMIC ENERGY or ATOMIC POWER: *an atomic submarine.* **3** of or involving weapons that use ATOMIC ENERGY: *atomic warfare.* **4** extremely small; minute. **—a'tom•i•cal•ly,** *adv.*

atomic age the era that began in 1945 with the first use of ATOMIC ENERGY.

atomic bomb a bomb that uses the energy released by the very rapid splitting of atoms to cause an explosion of tremendous force.

atomic clock a highly accurate clock that is run by controlled radio waves.

atomic disintegration a process by which a radioactive nucleus is changed, resulting in a different mass, energy, or ATOMIC NUMBER.

atomic energy the energy that exists in atoms. Some atoms can be made to release this atomic energy, either slowly (in a reactor) or very suddenly (in a bomb); it is generated through alteration of an atomic nucleus, by fission or fusion.

at•o•mic•i•ty [,ætə'mɪsəti] *n.* **1** *Chemistry.* **a** the number of atoms in one molecule of an element. **b** valence. **c** the number of atoms or groups that can be replaced in the molecule of a compound. **2** the state or condition of being composed of atoms.

atomic mass the mass of an atom, equal to its ATOMIC WEIGHT times the ATOMIC MASS UNIT, and expressed in atomic mass units. *Abbrev.*: at.mass

atomic mass unit a unit of mass equalling $\frac{1}{12}$ of the mass of a neutral atom of carbon-12, i.e., 1.6605×10^{-24} g. *Abbrev.*: amu

atomic number *Chemistry and physics.* a number used in describing a chemical element, giving its relation to other elements and determining its place in the periodic table. The atomic number of an element represents the number of protons (positive charges) in the nucleus of one of its atoms. *Abbrev.*: at.no.

atomic pile NUCLEAR REACTOR.

atomic power NUCLEAR POWER.

a•tom•ics [ə'tɒmɪks] *n. (used with a singular verb)* the science that deals with the structure and behaviour of atoms, especially as they relate to the generation of nuclear energy.

atomic theory 1 any theory proposing that matter is made up of atoms and that all happenings can be explained by the interaction of these atoms. **2** *Physics.* the view that the atom has a particular atomic structure, consisting of a nucleus bearing a positive charge and containing protons and neutrons, surrounded by electrons which bear a negative charge. **3** *Philosophy.* ATOMISM (def. 2).

atomic volume the ATOMIC WEIGHT of an element divided by its density.

atomic weight the ratio of the average mass per atom of an element to one-twelfth of the mass of an atom of carbon-12.

at•om•ism ['ætə,mɪzəm] *n.* **1** *Psychology.* the theory that all psychological states are composed of basic units. **2** *Philosophy.* the theory that the universe is made up of distinct particles. **—,at•om'ist•ic,** *adj.*

at•om•ize ['ætə,maɪz] *v.* **-ized, -iz•ing. 1** reduce to separate atoms. **2** change (a liquid) into a fine spray. **—,at•om•i'za•tion,** *n.*

at•om•iz•er ['ætə,maɪzər] *n.* a device used to convert a liquid to a spray of very small drops.

atom smasher cyclotron.

at•o•my[1] ['ætəmi] *n., pl.* **-mies.** *Archaic.* **1** a very small thing; atom. **2** a tiny being; pygmy. ⟨< L *atomi,* pl. of *atomus.* See ATOM.⟩

at•o•my[2] ['ætəmi] *n., pl.* **-mies.** *Archaic.* skeleton. ⟨for *anatomy* taken as *an atomy*⟩

a•ton•al [ei'tounəl] *adj. Music.* not having a central or dominant tone, or key; having all tones in equal relation to each other. Atonal music is often based on the chromatic scale of twelve tones. **—a'ton•al•ly,** *adv.*

a•to•nal•i•ty [,eitə'næləti] *n. Music.* the state or condition of being atonal; absence of tonality.

a•tone [ə'toun] *v.* **a•toned, a•ton•ing. 1** make amends or reparation (*for*): *to atone for a sin or crime. He tried to atone for his thoughtlessness by sending flowers to his hosts.* **2** expiate (a fault, etc.): *to atone guilt, to atone a loss.* ⟨back formation < *atonement*⟩

a•tone•ment [ə'tounmənt] *n.* **1** a making up for something; giving satisfaction for a wrong, loss, or injury; amends. **2 the Atonement,** *Christianity.* the reconciliation of God with sinners through the sufferings and death of Christ in their place. **3** See DAY OF ATONEMENT. ⟨< *at onement* being at one, i.e., in accord; *onement* < ME *onen* unite, ult. < OE *ān* one⟩

a•top [ə'tɒp] *adv., prep. —adv.* on or at the top.
—prep. on the top of.

ATP ADENOSINE TRIPHOSPHATE.

at•ra•bil•ious [,ætrə'bɪljəs] *adj.* **1** melancholy. **2** hypochondriac. **3** bad-tempered. ⟨< L *atra bilis* black bile⟩

a•tra•cu•ri•um [,ætrə'kjuriəm] *n.* a muscle relaxant.

a•tre•sia [ə'triʒə] *n.* the absence or closure of a normal body opening or tubular structure. ⟨< NL < Gk. *a-* not + *tresis* opening, hole⟩

a•tri•o•ven•tric•u•lar [,eitriouvɛn'trɪkjulər] *adj. Anatomy.* of or relating to the atria and the ventricles.

a•tri•um ['eitriəm] *or* ['ætriəm] *n., pl.* **a•tri•a** ['eitriə] *or* ['ætriə]. **1** the main room of an ancient Roman house. **2** a hall or court, often open to the sky. **3** either of the upper chambers of the heart that receive the blood from the veins. See HEART for picture. **4** any of various other cavities in the body. ⟨< L *atrium* (def. 1) < Etruscan⟩

a•tro•cious [ə'trouʃəs] *adj.* **1** very wicked or cruel; very savage or brutal: *The crime was so atrocious that many details were never made public.* **2** *Informal.* very bad; abominable: *atrocious weather, an atrocious pun.* ⟨< L⟩ **—a'tro•cious•ly,** *adv.* **—a'tro•cious•ness,** *n.*

a•troc•i•ty [ə'trɒsəti] *n., pl.* **-ties. 1** very great wickedness or cruelty. **2** a very cruel or brutal act. **3** *Informal.* a very bad blunder. ⟨< L *atrocitas* < *atrox, -ocis* fierce < *ater* dark⟩

at•ro•phy ['ætrəfi] *n., v.* **-phied, -phy•ing.** *—n.* **1** the wasting away of tissue or an organ, etc. in the body: *muscular atrophy.* **2** the failure of a part or organ to develop properly. **3** any decline; degeneration, especially due to lack of use or cultivation: *the atrophy of a skill.*
—v. **1** waste away or cause to waste away, especially through disuse. **2** fail to develop. ⟨< LL < Gk. *atrophia* < *a-* without + *trophē* nourishment⟩ **—a'troph•ic** [ə'trɒfɪk], *adj.*

at•ro•pine ['ætrə,pin] *or* ['ætrəpɪn] *n.* a poisonous drug obtained from belladonna and similar plants, used in medicine to relax muscles and dilate the pupil of the eye. Also, **atropin.** *Formula*: $C_{17}H_{23}NO_3$ ⟨< NL *Atropa* belladonna < Gk. *Atropos* one of the Fates⟩

At•ro•pos ['ætrə,pɒs] *n. Greek mythology.* one of the three Fates. Atropos cuts the thread of life.

att [at] See AT[2].

att. **1** attention. **2** attorney. **3** attached.

at•tach [ə'tætʃ] *v.* **1** fasten (*to*): *She attached the boat to the pier by means of a rope.* **2** connect with for duty, etc: *He was attached as mate to the ship* Clio. **3** add at the end; affix: *We attached our names to the petition.* **4** attribute: *The world at first attached little importance to the policies of Hitler.* **5** fasten itself; belong: *The blame attaches to you.* **6** bind by affection: *May is much attached to her cousin.* **7** *Law.* take (person or property) by legal authority: *Her property was attached by the court because she had not paid her debts.* ⟨ME < OF *atachier* < L *ad-* to + Gmc. source of OF *tache* a fastening, a nail. Related to TACK.⟩ **—at'tach•a•ble,** *adj.*

☛ *Syn.* **4. Attach,** AFFIX, ANNEX = to add one thing to another. **Attach,** the general word, used literally and figuratively, suggests only joining or fastening one thing to another by some means: *He attached a trailer to his car.* **Affix** suggests putting one thing, usually something smaller or less important, on another firmly and permanently: *She affixed her seal to the document.* **Annex** = add to and make a part of (usually something larger): *The Board annexed the suburb to the school district.*

at•ta•ché [ə'tæʃei] *or* [,ætə'ʃei] *n.* a specialist on the official staff of an ambassador or minister to a foreign country: *a cultural attaché, a press attaché.* ⟨< F⟩

attaché case a briefcase shaped like a small, thin suitcase with a rigid frame and sides.

at•tach•ment [ə'tætʃmənt] *n.* **1** an attaching or being attached. **2** something that is or can be attached: *A vacuum cleaner has various attachments.* **3** a means of attaching; fastening. **4** affection. **5** *Law.* **a** the legal seizure of property. **b** the arrest of a person. **c** the writ authorizing either of these.

at•tack [ə'tæk] *v., n. —v.* **1** use force or weapons on to hurt; go against as an enemy; begin fighting against: *The dog attacked the cat.* **2** talk or write against. **3** begin to work vigorously on: *The hungry girls attacked their dinner as soon as it was served.* **4** act harmfully on: *Certain bacteria attack tooth enamel.* **5** make an attack: *The enemy attacked at dawn.*
—n. **1** the act of attacking; especially, a hostile manoeuvre or onslaught, sharp criticism, etc.: *The attack of the enemy took the town by surprise. The chairperson's speech consisted mainly of an attack on wasteful government spending.* **2** the sudden onset of illness, discomfort, etc.: *an attack of malaria, an attack of remorse.* **3** any start to an undertaking or chore. **4** the manner of this start. **5** *Music.* the exactness and timing with which one begins a musical phrase. ⟨< F < Ital. *attaccare* (from the same source as OF *atachier*). See ATTACH.⟩ **—at'tack•er,** *n.*

☛ *Syn. v.* **1. Attack,** ASSAIL, ASSAULT = set upon with force. **Attack,** the general word, emphasizes the idea of falling upon a person or enemy without warning, sometimes without cause, or of starting the fighting: *Germany attacked Belgium in 1914.* **Assail** = attack with violence and repeated blows: *The enemy assailed our defence positions.* **Assault** = attack suddenly with furious or brutal force, and always suggests actual contact as in hand-to-hand fighting: *In a rage he assaulted his neighbour with a knife.*

at•tain [ə'tein] *v.* **1** arrive at; reach: *to attain years of discretion.* **2** gain; accomplish.
attain to, succeed in coming to or getting: *to attain to a position of great influence.* ⟨ME < OF *ataindre* < VL *attingere* < L *ad-* to + *tangere* touch⟩

at•tain•a•bil•i•ty [ə,teinə'bɪləti] *n.* the quality of being attainable.

at•tain•a•ble [ə'teinəbəl] *adj.* that can be attained: *The office of prime minister is one of the highest attainable in Canada.*

at•tain•der [ə'teindər] *n.* formerly, the loss of property and civil rights as the result of being sentenced to death or being outlawed. ⟨ME < OF *ataindre* attain; influenced by E *taindre* taint⟩

at•tain•ment [ə'teinmənt] *n.* **1** the act of attaining. **2** something attained; an accomplishment: *Leonardo da Vinci was a man of varied attainments; he was a painter, engineer, and inventor.*

at•taint [ə'teint] *v., n. —v.* **1** formerly, punish or condemn by attainder. **2** *Archaic.* disgrace; sully.
—n. Archaic. a disgrace. ⟨< OF *ataint,* pp. of *ataindre.* See ATTAIN.⟩ **—at'taint•ment,** *n.*

at•tar ['ætər] *n.* a perfume made from the petals of roses or other flowers. Also, **ottar.** ⟨< Persian *'aṭar* < Arabic *'uṭur* aroma⟩

attar of roses a fragrant oil made from rose petals.

at•tempt [ə'tɛmpt] *v., n. —v.* **1** make an effort at; try. **2** try to take or destroy (life, etc.).
—n. **1** a putting forth of effort to accomplish something, especially something difficult. **2** an attack: *The rebels made an unsuccessful attempt on the queen's life.* ⟨< OF < L *attemptare* < *ad-* to + *temptare* try⟩

☛ *Syn. v.* **1.** See note at TRY.

at•tend [ə'tɛnd] *v.* **1** be present at: *Children must attend school.* **2** give care and thought; pay attention: *Attend to the laboratory instructions.* **3** apply oneself: *Attend to your music if you want to play well.* **4** go with; accompany: *Noble ladies attend the queen.* **5** go with as a result: *Danger attends delay. Success often attends hard work.* **6** wait on; care for; serve (*sometimes with* **on**): *Nurses attend the sick.* **7** do something about; deal with or dispose of by action (*used with* **to**): *Someone should attend to this matter immediately.* ⟨ME < OF < *atendre* < L *attendere* < *ad-* toward + *tendere* stretch⟩

☛ *Syn.* **4.** See note at ACCOMPANY.

at•tend•ance [əˈtɛndəns] *n.* **1** being present; attending: *Attendance at all classes is compulsory.* **2** the people present; the number attending: *The attendance at the meeting was over 200 last Friday.* **3** the degree of constancy in showing up at an event: *This event always has high attendance.*
dance attendance on, wait on with excessive attentions: *The ambitious courtier danced attendance on any noble he thought might help him.*
in attendance, waiting (*on*); attending; on duty.

at•tend•ant [əˈtɛndənt] *n., adj.* —*n.* **1** a person who waits on another, or provides a service: *An attendant will look after your coat. The princess had five attendants.* **2** an accompanying thing or event: *Hatred had developed as an attendant on fear.* **3** a person who is present; attendee.
—*adj.* **1** waiting on another to help or serve: *an attendant nurse.* **2** going with as a result; accompanying: *weakness attendant on illness, attendant circumstances.* **3** present: *attendant hearers.*

at•tend•ee [ˌətɛnˈdi] *n.* a person who is present at a meeting, function, etc.: *attendees at a conference.*

at•ten•tat [atɑ̃ˈta] *French. n.* an unsuccessful terrorist attempt, especially on the life of a political figure.

at•ten•tion [əˈtɛnʃən] *n., interj.* —*n.* **1** the application of the mind to something; concentration: *He gave the speaker his undivided attention.* **2** notice or observation: *She called my attention to the cat stalking the squirrel.* **3** care and thought; consideration: *The matter requires our immediate attention.* **4** thoughtfulness and courtesy; attentiveness: *He showed his mother much attention.* **5 attentions,** *pl.* acts of courtesy or devotion, especially of a suitor. **6** *Military.* a standing position taken by a soldier, etc., in which the body is straight, with the heels together, arms straight down at the sides, and eyes looking forward. The position is taken to prepare for another command: *soldiers at attention.*
—*interj.* **1** an order to take notice. **2** *Military.* an order to assume the position of attention. ⟨ME < L *attentio, -onis* < *attendere.* See ATTEND.⟩

attention deficit (hyperactivity) disorder the most common psychiatric disorder of childhood, in which children are restless and cannot concentrate. In some cases it persists into adulthood.

at•ten•tive [əˈtɛntɪv] *adj.* **1** paying attention; observant. **2** considerate; thoughtful; solicitous: *an attentive host. The nurse was attentive to the patient's needs.* **—atˈten•tive•ly,** *adv.* **—atˈten•tive•ness,** *n.*

at•ten•u•ate *v.* [əˈtɛnju,eit]; *adj.* [əˈtɛnjuɪt] *or* [əˈtɛnju,eit]; *v.* **-at•ed, -at•ing.** —*v.* **1** make or become thin or slender. **2** weaken; reduce. **3** make less dense; dilute. **4** *Bacteriology.* make (micro-organisms, etc.) less harmful. **5** *Electronics.* decrease the amplitude of (an electrical signal). ⟨< L *attenuare* < *ad-* + *tenuis* thin⟩

at•ten•u•a•tion [ə,tɛnjuˈeiʃən] *n.* an attenuating or being attenuated.

at•ten•u•a•tor [əˈtɛnju,eitər] *n.* a person or thing that attenuates, especially a device for reducing the amplitude of an electrical signal without distorting it.

at•test [əˈtɛst] *v.* **1** give proof or evidence of: *The child's good health attests her parents' care.* **2** declare to be true or genuine; certify. **3** bear witness; testify: *The handwriting expert attested to the genuineness of the signature.* **4** put (a witness, etc.) on oath. ⟨< L *attestari* < *ad-* to + *testis* witness⟩ **—atˈtest•er** or **atˈtest•or,** *n.*

at•tes•ta•tion [ˌætɛˈsteiʃən] *n.* **1** the act of attesting. **2** proof; evidence. **3** testimony.

at•tic [ˈætɪk] *n.* a room or space in a house just below the roof and above the other rooms. ⟨< F *attique* < L *Atticus* Attic < Gk.⟩

At•tic [ætɪk] *adj., n.* —*adj.* **1** of Attica or Athens; Athenian. **2** of a style of writing, etc., simple and elegant.
—*n.* the speech of Attica, the dialect of ancient Greek used by Plato, Sophocles, Euripides, and Pericles. ⟨< L *Atticus* < Gk. *Attikos*⟩

At•ti•cism [ˈætɪ,sɪzəm] **1** simple elegance of expression in speech or writing. **2** an instance of this.

Attic salt or **wit** incisive wit.

at•tire [əˈtaɪr] *v.* **-tired, -tir•ing;** *n.* —*v.* clothe, especially in rich or formal clothes; array: *She was attired in full military uniform.* —*n.* clothes. ⟨ME < OF *atirer* arrange < *a-* to (< L *ad-*) + *tire* row < Gmc.⟩
☛ *Syn. n.* See note at DRESS.

at•ti•tude [ˈætə,tjud] *or* [ˈætə,tud] *n.* **1** a way of thinking, acting, or feeling: *His attitude toward school changed from dislike to great enthusiasm.* **2** a position of the body suggesting an action, purpose, emotion, etc: *She stood there in an attitude of defiance.* **3** the position of an aircraft or spacecraft in relation to some line or plane, such as the horizon or the horizontal.
strike an attitude, pose for effect. ⟨< F < Ital. *attitudine* < LL *aptitudo.* Doublet of APTITUDE.⟩

at•ti•tu•di•nal [ˌætəˈtjudənəl] *or* [ˌætəˈtudənəl] of, having to do with, or expressing an attitude or attitudes.

attn. attention.

atto– *SI prefix.* one quintillionth; 10^{-18}. *Symbol:* a

at•tor•ney [əˈtɜrni] *n., pl.* **-neys. 1** a person who has legal power to act for another. **2** *Esp. U.S.* lawyer. *Abbrev.:* atty. ⟨ME < OF *atourne,* pp. of *atourner* assign, appoint < *a-* to (< L *ad-*) + *tourner* turn < L *tornare* turn on a lathe < *tornus* lathe < Gk.⟩

attorney at law *Esp. U.S.* lawyer.

attorney general or **Attorney General** *pl.* **attorneys general** or **attorney generals. 1** a chief law officer. **2 Attorney General,** *Cdn.* **a** the chief law officer of Canada: *The Attorney General is the head of the Department of Justice and is a member of the Cabinet.* **b** the chief law officer of a province. Compare SOLICITOR GENERAL. Also, **attorney-general.**

at•tract [əˈtrækt] *v.* **1** draw to oneself: *A magnet attracts iron.* **2** be pleasing to; win the attention and liking of: *Bright colours attract children.* ⟨< L *attractus,* pp. of *attrahere* < *ad-* to + *trahere* draw⟩
☛ *Syn.* See note at CHARM.

at•trac•tant [əˈtræktənt] *n.* a substance that attracts, especially a pheromone or something imitating it.

at•trac•tion [əˈtrækʃən] *n.* **1** the act or power of attracting. **2** anything that delights or attracts people: *The elephants were the chief attraction at the circus.* **3** charm; fascination. **4** *Physics.* the force exerted by molecules on one another, tending to draw or hold them together.

attraction sphere CENTROSPHERE (def. 1).

at•trac•tive [əˈtræktɪv] *adj.* **1** capable of winning attention and liking; pleasing: *an attractive hat, an attractive personality, an attractive job offer.* **2** having to do with or having the power to attract: *the attractive force of a magnet.* **—atˈtrac•tive•ly,** *adv.* **—atˈtrac•tive•ness,** *n.*

attrib. attribute; attributive.

at•trib•ut•a•ble [əˈtrɪbjətəbəl] *adj.* able to be attributed: *Some diseases are attributable to lack of cleanliness.*

at•trib•ute *v.* [əˈtrɪbjut]; *n.* [ˈætrə,bjut] *v.* **-ut•ed, -ut•ing;** *n.* —*v.* **1** consider as belonging or appropriate: *They attribute a great deal of intelligence to their dog.* **2** regard as an effect of; think of as caused by: *They attributed her success to intelligence and hard work.* **3** state as having been said or written by: *The newly discovered poem has been attributed to Emily Dickinson.*
—*n.* **1** a quality considered as belonging to a person or thing; a characteristic: *Prudence is an attribute of a judge.* **2** an object considered appropriate to a person, rank, or office; symbol: *The eagle was the attribute of Jupiter.* **3** an adjective; a word or phrase used as an adjective. ⟨ME < L *attributus,* pp. of *attribuere* < *ad-* to + *tribuere* assign, originally, divide among the tribes < *tribus* tribe⟩
☛ *Syn. v.* **Attribute,** ASCRIBE = consider something as belonging or due to someone or something, and are often interchangeable. But **attribute** suggests believing something appropriate to a person or thing or belonging to it by nature or right: *We attribute importance to the words of great leaders.* **Ascribe** suggests guessing or basing a conclusion on evidence and reasoning: *I ascribe his failure to his careless habits.*

at•tri•bu•tion [ˌætrəˈbjuʃən] *n.* **1** the act of attributing. **2** the thing attributed; attribute.

at•trib•u•tive [əˈtrɪbjətɪv] *adj., n.* —*adj.* **1** *Grammar.* of an adjective or other modifier, expressing a quality or attribute, especially when coming before or immediately after the noun it modifies. An attributive adjective is in the same part of the sentence as the noun it modifies; a predicate adjective is separated from its noun by a linking verb. **2** that attributes. **3** of or like an attribute.
—*n. Grammar.* an attributive noun or adjective. *General* is an attributive in *general store* and in *governor general.* **—atˈtrib•u•tive•ly,** *adv.*
☛ *Usage.* **Attributive.** An adjective that stands before or immediately after its noun is **attributive** (a *blue* shirt), as contrasted with a **predicate** adjective that is related to its noun by a linking verb (The shirt is *blue*). An attributive adjective that comes immediately after its noun is **postpositive** (the man *asleep*).

at•tri•tion [əˈtrɪʃən] *n.* **1** a wearing away by rubbing: *Pebbles become smooth by attrition.* **2** any gradual process of wearing down: *a war of attrition.* **3** a gradual reduction in the number of employees, due to natural events such as retirement and resignation. **4** sorrow for one's sins, less perfect than contrition because arising from fear rather than love of God. ⟨ME < LL *attritio, -onis* < *atterere* < *ad-* against + *terere* rub⟩

at•tune [ə'tjun] *or* [ə'tun] *v.* **-tuned, -tun•ing. 1** bring into harmony; adjust: *He could not attune his ears to the sounds of the big city.* **2** make sensitive (*to*); make responsive (*to*): *Her years in politics had attuned the minister to the shifts in public opinion.*
—at'tune•ment, *n.*

atty. attorney.

ATV ALL-TERRAIN VEHICLE.

at.vol. ATOMIC VOLUME.

a•twit•ter [ə'twɪtər] *adj., adv. Informal.* (*never comes before a noun*) in or into a state of twittering, especially from excitement.

at.wt. ATOMIC WEIGHT.

a•typ•i•cal [ei'tɪpəkəl] *or* [æ'tɪpəkəl] *adj.* not typical; irregular; abnormal. **—a'typ•i•cal•ly,** *adv.*

Au gold (for L *aurum).*

AU 1 angstrom unit. **2** astronomical unit.

au•bade [ou'bɒd] *or* [ou'bæd] *n.* a musical composition, lyric poem, etc. about or appropriate to the morning. ⟨< F ⟩

au•berge [ou'bɛrʒ] *n.* inn. ⟨< F⟩

au•ber•gine ['oubər,ʒin] *or* ['oubərdʒin] *n.* **1** EGGPLANT. **2** the deep purple colour of an eggplant. ⟨< F < Catalan *albergínia* < Arabic *al badhinjan* < Persian *badindjan*⟩

au•bre•tia [ɒ'briʃə] *n.* any of a genus (*Aubrieta*; family Cruciferae) of flowering, trailing plants native to Europe and the Middle East. Also, **au•brie•ta** [ɒ'britə]. ⟨< NL after Claude *Aubriet*, French painter⟩

au•burn ['ɒbərn] *n. or adj.* reddish brown. ⟨ME < OF *auborne* < L *alburnus* whitish < *albus* white; apparently confused with ME *brun* brown⟩

Au•bus•son [oby'sɔ̃] *n. French.* **1** a rich tapestry of scenes or figures used for wall hangings, upholstery, etc. **2** a rug woven like an Aubusson tapestry. ⟨< *Aubusson*, France, where these tapestries were first made in the 16c.⟩

A.U.C. from the founding of the city (of Rome) (for L *ab urbe condita).*

au cou•rant [oku'ʀɑ̃] *French.* in the current (of events); well informed; up-to-date on the topics of the day.

auc•tion ['ɒkʃən] *n., v. —n.* **1** a public sale in which each thing is sold to the person who offers the most money for it. **2** AUCTION BRIDGE. **3** the competitive calling or bidding in bridge prior to play.
—v. sell at an auction (*often used with* **off**). ⟨< L *auctio, -onis* < *augere* increase⟩

auction bridge a card game for four people playing in two opposing pairs. Tricks made by the highest-bidding team in excess of their bid may be counted toward a game. Compare CONTRACT BRIDGE.

auc•tion•eer [,ɒkʃə'nir] *n., v. —n.* a person who conducts an auction or auctions.
—v. **1** sell at an auction. **2** conduct an auction.

auc•to•ri•al [ɒk'tɔriəl] *adj.* of an author. ⟨< L *auctor* author⟩

au•cu•ba ['ɒkjəbə] *n.* an evergreen shrub of the genus *Aucuba*, having bright red berries. It is often grown as an ornamental plant. ⟨< NL < Japanese < *ao* green + *ki* tree + *ha* leaf⟩

aud [ɒd] *v. Education.* listen attentively; understand by listening. ⟨< *audition*⟩
☛ *Hom.* ODD.

aud. auditor.

au•da•cious [ɒ'deiʃəs] *adj.* **1** bold; daring. **2** too bold; impudent. ⟨< L⟩ **—au'da•cious•ly,** *adv.* **—au'da•cious•ness,** *n.*

au•dac•i•ty [ɒ'dæsəti] *n., pl.* **-ties. 1** boldness; reckless daring. **2** rudeness; impudence. **3** an instance of audacious speech or behaviour: *This and other audacities shocked the dignified hearers.* ⟨< L *audacia* < *audax* bold < *audere* dare⟩

au•di•bil•i•ty [,ɒdə'bɪləti] *n.* **1** the fact of being audible. **2** the relative loudness of a sound, usually measured in decibels.

au•di•ble ['ɒdəbəl] *adj.* capable of being heard; loud enough to be heard. ⟨< LL *audibilis* < L *audire* hear⟩ **—'au•di•bly,** *adv.*

au•di•ence ['ɒdiəns] *n.* **1** the people gathered to hear or see a performance or presentation: *The audience cheered the mayor's speech.* **2** the people reached by radio or television broadcasts, by books, etc.: *The book is intended for a juvenile audience.* **3** a chance to be heard; hearing: *The committee will give you an audience to hear your plan.* **4** a formal interview with a person of high rank: *The king granted an audience to the famous singer.* **5** the act or fact of hearing. ⟨ME < OF < L *audientia* hearing < *audire* hear⟩

au•dile ['ɒdaɪl] *adj.* having to do with hearing; auditory.

au•di•o ['ɒdiou] *adj., n. —adj.* **1** of or having to do with sound. **2** *Television.* having to do with the broadcasting or receiving of sound as opposed to images: *An audio problem is a sound problem; a video problem involves the image that appears on the screen.*
—n. sound reproduction. ⟨< L *audio* < *audire* hear⟩

audio– *combining form.* sound: *audiovisual*.

audio frequency a frequency corresponding to audible sound vibrations, from about 20 hertz to about 20 000 hertz for the normal human ear. *Abbrev.*: AF, A.F., or a.f.

au•di•ol•o•gy [,ɒdi'ɒlədʒi] *n.* the science dealing with the sense and organs of hearing, including diagnosis and treatment of hearing disorders. **—,au•di'ol•o•gist,** *n.*
—,au•di•o'log•i•cal, *adj.*

au•di•om•e•ter [,ɒdi'ɒmətər] *n.* an instrument for measuring the power of hearing.

au•di•o•phile ['ɒdiə,faɪl] *n.* a person who is greatly interested in the high-fidelity reproduction of sound.

au•di•o•phone ['ɒdiə,foun] *n.* an aid for the hearing-impaired, which, when placed against some part of the skull (such as the teeth or the bone behind the ear) allows the bones of the head to pick up sound vibrations and carry them to the auditory nerve.

au•di•o–vid•e•o ['ɒdiou 'vɪdiou] *adj.* of or having to do with the transmission or reception of both sounds and pictures.

au•di•o•vis•u•al [,ɒdiou 'vɪʒuəl] *adj.* of, having to do with, or involving the use of both hearing and sight: *Language courses often use audiovisual aids, such as films. Abbrev.*: AV or A.V.

au•dit ['ɒdɪt] *v., n. —v.* **1** examine and check (business accounts) officially. **2** at a college or university, attend (a class) as a listener without being allowed to take the examinations or get credit for the course.
—n. **1** an official examination and check of business accounts. **2** a statement of an account that has been examined and checked authoritatively. ⟨< L *auditus* a hearing < *audire* hear⟩

au•di•tion [ɒ'dɪʃən] *n., v. —n.* **1** a trial performance in which an actor, singer, dancer, or other performer demonstrates his or her skills. **2** the act of hearing. **3** the power or sense of hearing.
—v. **1** hear (a singer) at an audition: *The producer auditioned six singers for the lead in the musical.* **2** hold an audition or auditions: *They are auditioning now for the production and have shortlisted six performers.* **3** give an audition; perform at an audition: *She auditioned for the role of the maid.* ⟨< L *auditio, -onis* a hearing < *audire* hear⟩

au•di•tor ['ɒdətər] *n.* **1** a hearer; listener. **2** a person who audits business accounts. **3** at a college or university, a person permitted to attend a class as a listener without being allowed to take the examinations or get credit for the course.

auditor general or **Auditor General** *pl.* **auditors general** or **auditor generals.** in Canada, an officer, appointed by the Governor General, who is responsible for auditing the accounts of the federal government and making an annual report of the findings to Parliament.

au•di•to•ri•um [,ɒdə'tɔriəm] *n.* **-to•ri-ums** or **-to•ri•a** [-'tɔriə]. **1** a large room for an audience in a church, theatre, school, etc.; a large hall. **2** a building specially designed for lectures, concerts, etc. ⟨< L⟩

au•di•to•ry ['ɒdə,tɔri] *adj., n., pl.* **-ries.** *—adj.* of or having to do with hearing, the sense of hearing, or the organs of hearing: *the auditory nerve.*
—n. Archaic. **1** audience. **2** auditorium. **—,au•di'to•ri•ly,** *adv.*

au fait [ou'fei] *or* [ou'fɛ] *French.* **1** well-informed; familiar *(with).* **2** expert; very skilled.

Aug. August.

Au•ge•an stables [ɒ'dʒiən] *Greek mythology.* the stables, sheltering 3000 oxen, that remained uncleaned for 30 years, until Hercules turned two rivers through them.

au•gend ['ɒdʒɛnd] *n. Mathematics.* a number or quantity to which another, the addend, is to be added. ⟨< L *augendum*, gerund of *augere* to increase⟩

au•ger ['ɒgər] *n.* **1** a tool for boring holes in wood. **2** a tool for boring holes in the earth or ice: *a post-hole auger.* **3** a similar

device having a continuous spiral channel inside a tube, used for moving bulk substances such as grain or snow: *An auger is used to move grain from an elevator to a boxcar.* ⟨OE *nafugār*, originally, a nave borer < *nafu* nave of a wheel + *gār* spear; ME *a nauger* taken as *an auger*⟩
☛ *Hom.* AUGUR.

Au•ger effect [ou'ʒei] the absorption of energy into an inner electron shell, resulting in the emission, by an excited atom, of an electron rather than a proton. ⟨< Pierre *Auger* (1899-), French physicist⟩

Au•ger shower a shower of electrons, protons, etc. occasioned by primary cosmic rays striking atomic nuclei on entering the earth's atmosphere.

aught[1] [ɒt] *n., adv.* —*n.* anything: *You may resign your job for aught I care.*
—*adv. Archaic.* in any way; to any degree; at all: *Help came too late to avail aught.* ⟨OE *āwiht* < *ā* ever + *wiht* a thing⟩
☛ *Hom.* OUGHT.

aught[2] [ɒt] *n.* zero; cipher; nothing. ⟨< *naught*; *a naught* taken as *an aught; naught,* OE *nāwiht* < *nā* no + *wiht* a thing⟩
☛ *Hom.* OUGHT.

au•gite ['ɒdʒəit] *n.* a pure black, bluish, or greenish mineral, found mostly in volcanic rocks. ⟨< L *augites* < Gk. *augitēs*, ult. < *augē* lustre⟩

aug•ment [ɒg'mɛnt] *v.* increase; enlarge: *He had to augment his income by working in the evenings. The orchestra was augmented to play the large-scale work.* ⟨ME < LL *augmentare* < *augmentum* < *augere* increase⟩ **—aug'men•ta•ble,** *adj.*
☛ *Syn.* See note at INCREASE.

aug•men•ta•tion [,ɒgmɛn'teiʃən] *n.* **1** enlargement; increase. **2** *Music.* the transformation of a melody by increasing the time values of the notes.

aug•men•ta•tive [ɒg'mɛntətɪv] *adj. Grammar.* of or having to do with a word or affix that when added indicates an increase in size, duration, intensity, etc. *Example*: Spanish *-isimo; grande* big > *grandisimo* very big.

aug•ment•ed [ɒg'mɛntɪd] *adj., v.* —*adj. Music.* **1** of or having to do with an interval that is one half step higher than the corresponding normal interval. **2** of an orchestra or choir, enlarged to perform a specific piece.
—*v.* pt. and pp. of AUGMENT.

au grat•in [ou'grætən] *or* [ou'grɑtən]; *French,* [ogʀa'tɛ̃] with crumbs; cooked with crumbs and cheese on top; cooked with cheese. ⟨lit., with grated (cheese)⟩

au•gur ['ɒgər] *n., v.* —*n.* **1** in ancient Rome, a priest who made predictions and gave advice. **2** a prophet; fortuneteller.
—*v.* **1** predict; foretell. **2** be a sign or promise (of).
augur ill, be a bad sign.
augur well, be a good sign. ⟨< L *augur,* apparently, increase, growth (of crops), personified in ritual service < *augere* increase⟩
☛ *Hom.* AUGER.

au•gu•ry ['ɒgjəri] *n., pl.* **-ries. 1** the art or practice of foretelling the future by the flight of birds, the appearance of the internal organs of sacrificed animals, thunder and lightning, etc. **2** a prediction; indication; sign; omen. **3** a rite or ceremony performed by an augur. ⟨ME < L⟩

Au•gust ['ɒgəst] *n.* the eighth month of the year. It has 31 days. *Abbrev.*: Aug. ⟨after *Augustus* Cæsar (63 B.C.-A.D. 14), first emperor of Rome⟩

au•gust [ɒ'gʌst] *or* ['ɒgʌst] *adj.* inspiring reverence and admiration; majestic; venerable. ⟨< L *augustus* < unrecorded *augus* increase, power < *augere* to increase⟩ **—au'gust•ly,** *adv.* **—au'gust•ness,** *n.*

Au•gus•tan [ɒ'gʌstən] *adj., n.* —*adj.* of the Roman emperor Augustus or his reign.
—*n.* any writer during the AUGUSTAN AGE of Latin or English literature.

Augustan age 1 the period of Latin literature covering the reign of Emperor Augustus, from 27 B.C. to A.D. 14. **2** the period of English literature from about 1700 to 1750, noted for classicism and elegance of style.

Au•gus•tin•i•an [,ɒgə'stɪniən] *adj., n.* —*adj.* of or having to do with Saint Augustine (A.D. 354-430), his teachings, or the religious orders named for him.
—*n.* **1** a person who follows the teachings of Saint Augustine. **2** a member of any of the religious orders named for Saint Augustine.

au jus [o'ʒy] *French.* in gravy or juice.

auk [ɒk] *n.* **1** any of various swimming and diving sea birds (family Alcidae) found along northern coasts. The **great auk,** (*Pinguinus impennis*), a flightless bird about the size of a goose, has been extinct for over a century. See also AUKLET and RAZORBILL. **2** (*adjl.*) designating the family (Alcidae) of heavy-bodied, short-winged sea birds that includes the auks. Murres, guillemots, and puffins also belong to the auk family and are sometimes called auks. ⟨< ON *álka*⟩

auk•let ['ɒklɪt] *n.* any of about six species of small sea birds (family Alcidae) of the N Pacific, having black-and-white plumage and, in breeding season, head plumes and brightly coloured bill plates similar to those of the related puffins.

au lait [o'le]; *French,* [o'lɛ] with milk.

auld lang syne ['ɒld 'læŋ 'saɪn] *or* ['ɒld 'læŋ 'zaɪn] *Scottish.* old times; long ago in one's life.

au na•tu•rel [onaty'ʀɛl] *French.* **1** in the plainest or simplest manner. **2** natural; lifelike. **3** nude.

aunt [ænt] *n.* **1** a sister of one's father or mother. **2** one's uncle's wife. ⟨ME < OF *ante* < L *amita* father's sister⟩
☛ *Pronun.* The pronunciation [ænt] is usual in Canada, but [ɑnt] is common in New Brunswick and parts of Nova Scotia.

au pair [ou 'pɛr] **1** a person, especially a girl or young woman, who works in another country as a housekeeper, mother's helper, etc., usually temporarily in order to learn the language of the country. Au pairs usually receive a small wage in addition to room and board. **2** (*adjl.*) of or designating such a person: *an au pair girl.* ⟨< F *au pair* on equal terms; originally used to refer to an exchange student living with a family in a foreign country to learn the language, etc.⟩

au poivre [o'pwavʀ] *French.* with peppercorns and, usually, a peppery sauce.

au•ra ['ɔrə] *n., pl.* **au•ras** or **au•rae** ['ɔri] *or* ['ɔraɪ] **1** something supposed to come from a person or thing and surround him, her, or it as an atmosphere: *An aura of holiness surrounded the saint.* **2** a delicate or slight fragrance arising, as from flowers. **3** *Medicine.* a peculiar sensation that usually announces the onset of a seizure. ⟨< L < Gk. *aura*⟩

au•ral[1] ['ɔrəl] *adj.* of or having to do with the ear or the sense of hearing. ⟨< L *auris* ear⟩ **—'au•ral•ly,** *adv.*
☛ *Hom.* ORAL.

au•ral[2] ['ɔrəl] *adj.* of or like an aura.
☛ *Hom.* ORAL.

au•ra•no•fin [ɔ'rænəfɪn] *n.* a drug prepared from gold and used to treat rheumatoid arthritis. *Formula*: $C_{20}H_{34}Au_9PS_1$

au•rar ['ɔrɑr] *or* ['aʊrɑr] *n.* pl. of EYRIR.

au•re•ate ['ɔriɪt] *adj.* **1** golden; gilded. **2** shining or splendid. **3** of a writing style, etc., ornate; overly fancy. ⟨< LL *aureatus* < *aurum* gold⟩

au•re•o•la [ɔ'riələ] *n.* aureole.

au•re•ole ['ɔri,oul] *n.* **1** an encircling radiance; halo. **2** *Astronomy.* a ring of light surrounding the sun. ⟨< L *aureola* (*corona*) golden (crown) < *aurum* gold⟩

au•re•o•my•cin [,ɔriou'məisɪn] *n.* an antibiotic, similar to penicillin. ⟨< L *aureus* golden + Gk. *mykēs* fungus⟩

au re•voir [ɔʀ'vwaʀ] *French.* goodbye; till we see each other again.

au•ric ['ɔrɪk] *adj.* **1** of or having to do with gold. **2** containing gold, especially gold with a valence of 3. ⟨< L *aurum* gold + -IC⟩

au•ri•cle ['ɔrəkəl] *n.* **1** the outer part of the ear. **2** an earlike part. ⟨< L *auricula,* dim. of *auris* ear⟩
☛ *Hom.* ORACLE.

au•ric•u•lar [ɔ'rɪkjələr] *adj.* **1** of, having to do with, or near the ear. **2** heard by or addressed to the ear. **3** shaped like an ear. **4** of or having to do with an auricle.

au•ric•u•late [ɔ'rɪkjəlɪt] *or* [ə'rɪkjə,leit] *adj. Biology.* having ears or ear-shaped parts.

au•rif•er•ous [ɔ'rɪfərəs] *adj.* yielding gold. ⟨< L *aurifer* < *aurum* gold + *ferre* bear⟩

au•ri•form ['ɔrɪ,fɔrm] *adj.* shaped like an ear. ⟨< L *auris* ear + *-formis* < *forma* form⟩

Au•ri•ga [ɔ'rigə] *n.* a large northern constellation supposed to represent a charioteer kneeling in his chariot. ⟨< L *Auriga* charioteer⟩

Au•rig•na•cian [,ɔrɪg'neiʃən] *adj.* of or relating to an Upper Paleolithic culture which saw the extensive use of tools made out of flint, bone, and antler, and the introduction of cave painting and early religion. ⟨< F *Aurignacien,* after F village of *Aurignac*⟩

au•rist ['ɔrɪst] *n.* a doctor who specializes in diseases of the ear. ⟨< L *auris* ear⟩

au•rochs ['ɔrɒks] *n., pl.* **-rochs. 1** a wild ox (*Bos primigenius*) extinct since the 17th century, thought to be one of the ancestors of the modern cattle breeds of Europe and America. It was a huge, black animal, about 185 cm high at the shoulder. **2** WISENT. ⟨< G *Auerochs* < OHG *ūr-ohso* < *ūr* wild bull + *ohso* ox⟩

au•ro•ra [ɔ'rɔrə] *or* [ə'rɔrə] *n.* **1** dawn. **2** streams or bands of light appearing in the sky at night. **3 Aurora,** *Roman mythology.* the goddess of the dawn, corresponding to the Greek goddess Eos. ⟨< L⟩

aurora aus•tra•lis [ɒ'stræləs] streamers or bands of light appearing in the southern sky at night. ⟨< NL⟩

aurora bo•re•al•is [,bɔri'ælɪs] *or* [,bɔri'eilɪs] streamers or bands of light appearing in the northern sky at night; northern lights. ⟨< NL⟩

au•ro•ral [ɔ'rɔrəl] *adj.* **1** of or like the dawn; first; rosy. **2** of the AURORA BOREALIS or the AURORA AUSTRALIS. **3** shining; bright.

aurora trout a very rare, nonspotted subspecies of the brook trout (*Salvelinus timigamiensis*) found only in certain lakes of northern Ontario. It was originally described as a distinct species. It is an endangered species.

au•ro•thi•o•glu•cose [,ɔrə,θaɪə'glukous] *n.* a drug prepared from gold and used to treat rheumatoid arthritis.

au•rous ['ɔrəs] *adj.* **1** of or having to do with gold. **2** containing gold, especially gold with a valence of 1. ⟨< L *aurum* gold + -OUS⟩

aus•cul•tate ['ɒskəl,teit] *v.* **-tat•ed, -tat•ing.** *Medicine.* listen to; examine by auscultation.

aus•cul•ta•tion [,ɒskəl'teiʃən] *n.* **1** the act of listening. **2** *Medicine.* the act of listening, usually with a stethoscope, to sounds within the human body to determine the condition of the heart or lungs. ⟨< L *auscultatio, -onis* < *auscultare* listen⟩

aus•pice ['ɒspɪs] *n., pl.* **aus•pic•es** ['ɒspəsɪz] **1** a favourable circumstance; indication of success. **2** an omen; sign. **3** a divination or prophecy, especially one made from the flight of birds.
under the auspices of, under the patronage of: *The school fair was held under the auspices of the Home and School Association.*
⟨< F < L *auspicium* < *avis* bird + *specere* look at. See def. 3.⟩

aus•pi•cious [ɒ'spɪʃəs] *adj.* **1** showing signs of success; favourable. **2** fortunate. **—aus'pi•cious•ly,** *adv.*
☛ *Syn.* **1.** See note at FAVOURABLE.

Aus•sie ['ɒzi] *adj. or n. Slang.* Australian.

Aust. 1 Austria; Austrian. **2** Australia; Australian.

aus•ten•ite ['ɒstə,nəit] *n.* a solid solution of carbon in iron produced at temperatures above 723°C in steel containing a high proportion of carbon. ⟨< F after British metallurgist Sir Roberts-*Austen* + -ITE[2]⟩

aus•tere [ɒ'stir] *adj.* **1** harsh; stern: *Frank's father was a silent, austere man, very strict with his children.* **2** strict in moral discipline: *The Puritans were austere.* **3** severely simple: *The tall, plain columns stood against the sky in austere beauty.* **4** sour-tasting. ⟨ME < OF < L < Gk. *austēros* < *auein* dry⟩ **—aus'tere•ness,** *n.* **—aus'tere•ly,** *adv.*

aus•ter•i•ty [ɒ'stɛrəti] *n., pl.* **-ties. 1** sternness; strictness; severity. **2** severe simplicity. **3** economic stringency or restriction. **4 austerities,** *pl.* severe practices, such as going without food or sitting up all night to pray.

Austl. 1 Australia. **2** Australasia.

aus•tral ['ɒstrəl] *adj.* **1** southern. **2 Austral,** having to do with or from Australia. ⟨< L *australis* < *auster* the south wind⟩

Austral. 1 Australian; Australia. **2** Australasian.

Aus•tral•a•sian [,ɒstrə'leiʒən] *or* [,ɒstrə'leiʃən] *adj., n. —adj.* of or having to do with Australasia, the islands of the SW Pacific Ocean, or the people of these islands.
—n. a native or inhabitant of Australasia.

Aus•tral•ia [ɒ'streiljə] *or* [ə'streiljə] *n.* a country and island continent in the SW Pacific Ocean.

Aus•tral•ian [ɒ'streiljən] *or* [ə'streiljən] *n., adj. —n.* a native or inhabitant of Australia.
—adj. **1** of or having to do with the country of Australia or its people. **2** of, having to do with, or living or growing in the geographical region that includes the continent of Australia and nearby islands. **3** Australoid.

Australian crawl a form of the crawl in which each stroke of the swimmer's arm is accompanied by a double kick.

Aus•tra•loid ['ɒstrə,lɔɪd] *adj., n. —adj.* of or designating a major race of people that consists of the original inhabitants of the continent of Australia, distinguished by a combination of biological characteristics including medium brown to very dark skin and almost complete absence of blood type B. The Australoid race was separated from other humans for thousands of years before modern times.
—n. a member of the Australoid race.

Aus•tra•lo•pith•e•cine [,ɒstrəlou'pɪθə,sin] *n., adj. —n.* any of the primates of the genus *Australopithecus*, now extinct, but believed to have lived in southern Africa during the Pleistocene epoch.
—adj. having to do with that genus.

Aus•tri•a ['ɒstriə] *n.* a country in central Europe.

Aus•tri•an ['ɒstriən] *n., adj. —n.* **1** a native or inhabitant of Austria. **2** a person of Austrian descent.
—adj. of or having to do with Austria or its people.

Austrian pine a pine (*Pinus nigra*) native to N Europe but now commonly cultivated in Canada, having very long, stiff, dark green needles.

Aus•tro–[1] *combining form.* Austrian; Austrian and ——: *Austro-Hungarian.*

Aus•tro–[2] *combining form.* southern: *Austro-Asiatic.* ⟨< L *auster* south wind⟩

Aus•tro–A•si•at•ic [,ɒstrou ,eiʒi'ætɪk] *n.* a hypothetical language family uniting Austronesian, Mon-Khmer and certain other language families of SE Asia.

Aus•tro•ne•sian [,ɒstrə'niʒən] *or* [-ʃən] *adj., n. —adj.* of or having to do with Austronesia, the islands of the central and S Pacific, or the peoples of these islands.
—n. Malayo-Polynesian.

au•su•bo [aʊ'subou] *n.* balata. ⟨origin uncertain⟩

aut– the form of AUTO- before vowels and *h*, as in *authentic.*

au•ta•coid ['ɒtə,kɔɪd] *n.* **1** a hormone. **2** any of a group of natural secretions, such as histamine, whose effects on the blood, etc., resemble those of drugs. ⟨< *auto-* + Gk. *akos* cure + E *-oid*⟩

au•tar•chic [ɒ'tɑrkɪk] *adj.* of, having to do with, or resembling autarchy.

au•tar•chy ['ɒtɑrki] *n., pl.* **-chies. 1** absolute or autocratic rule; despotism. **2** the domain ruled by a despot or autocrat. ⟨< Gk. *autarchos* absolute ruler < *autos* self + *archein* rule⟩
☛ *Hom.* AUTARKY.

au•tar•ky ['ɒtɑrki] *n., pl.* **-kies.** the state of being self-sufficient, especially of being independent of imports from other nations. ⟨< Gk. *autarkeia* < *auto-* self + *arkein* suffice⟩ **—au'tar•kic,** *adj.*
☛ *Hom.* AUTARCHY.

au•te•col•o•gy [,ɒtɪ'kɒlədʒi] *n.* the ecological study of a single plant, animal, etc.

au•teur [ou'tɜr] *n.* a film director, especially when considered as having the main creative role in a motion picture. ⟨< F *auteur* author⟩

au•then•tic [ɒ'θɛntɪk] *adj.* **1** genuine: *A comparison of signatures showed that the letter was authentic.* **2** reliable: *an authentic account.* **3** of a document, properly executed and so legally valid. **4** *Music.* PERFECT (def. 10b). Compare PLAGAL. ⟨ME < OF *autentique* < LL < Gk. *authentikos* < *autos-* by oneself + *hentēs* one who acts⟩
☛ *Syn.* **2.** See note at GENUINE.

au•then•ti•cal•ly [ɒ'θɛntɪkli] *adv.* **1** genuinely. **2** reliably.

au•then•ti•cate [ɒ'θɛntə,keit] *v.* **-cat•ed, -cat•ing. 1** establish the authenticity of; show to be valid or genuine. **2** establish the authorship of. **—au'then•ti,ca•tor,** *n.*
☛ *Syn.* **1.** See note at CONFIRM.

au•then•ti•ca•tion [ɒ,θɛntə'keiʃən] *n.* authenticating or being authenticated.

au•then•tic•i•ty [,ɒθɛn'tɪsəti] *n.* **1** genuineness; validity: *to question the authenticity of a signature.* **2** reliability.

au•thor ['ɒθər] *n., v. —n.* **1** a person who writes books, stories, plays, or articles. **2** an author's publications: *Do read this author.* **3** a person who creates or begins anything.
—v. be the author of; write: *She has authored a number of plays as*

well as two novels. ⟨ME < OF *autor* < L *auctor* < *augēre* increase⟩ **—au'tho•ri•al** [ɒ'θɔriəl], *adj.*

au•thor•i•tar•i•an [ə,θɔrə'tɛriən] *adj., n.* *—adj.* favouring obedience to authority instead of individual freedom.
—n. a person who favours obedience to authority instead of individual freedom.

au•thor•i•tar•i•an•ism [ə,θɔrə'tɛriə,nɪzəm] *n.* the principle of requiring obedience to the authority of one person or of a small group of persons.

au•thor•i•ta•tive [ə'θɔrə,teitɪv] *adj.* **1** having authority; officially ordered: *Authoritative orders came from the general.* **2** commanding: *In authoritative tones the policeman shouted, "Keep back!"* **3** that ought to be believed or obeyed; having the authority of expert knowledge. **—au'thor•i,ta•tive•ly,** *adv.* **—au'thor•i,ta•tive•ness,** *n.*

au•thor•i•ty [ə'θɔrəti] *n., pl.* **-ties. 1** the power to enforce obedience; right to command or act: *Parents have authority over their children.* **2** a person who has such power or right. **3 the authorities, a** officials of the government. **b** persons in control. **4** a government body that runs some activity or business on behalf of the public: *the St. Lawrence Seaway Authority.* **5** an influence that creates respect and confidence. **6** a source of correct information or wise advice: *A good dictionary is an authority on the meanings of words.* **7** an expert on some subject. ⟨ME < OF *autorite* < L *auctoritas*⟩

☛ *Syn.* **1. Authority,** CONTROL, INFLUENCE = power to direct or act on others. **Authority** applies to rightful power, given by a person's position or office, to give commands and enforce obedience: *Teachers have authority over pupils.* **Control** applies to power, regardless of its source, to direct people and things: *Lords had control over their serfs.* **Influence** applies to personal power, coming from a person's character, personality, or position, to have some effect on the actions of others: *Some teachers have great influence over young people.*

au•thor•i•za•tion [,ɒθərə'zeiʃən] *or* [,ɒθəraɪ'zeiʃən] *n.* **1** the act of authorizing: *the general's authorization of the attack.* **2** a legal right; sanction; warrant.

au•thor•ize ['ɒθə,raɪz] *v.* **-ized, -iz•ing. 1** give authority to; empower: *The prime minister authorized her to set up a committee.* **2** give authoritative consent or approval to; sanction: *The expenditure was never authorized by Parliament. This dictionary authorizes the two spellings* honour *and* honor.

au•thor•ized ['ɒθə,raɪzd] *adj., v.* *—adj.* **1** having authority; accepted as authoritative. **2** sanctioned by formal or legal authority.
—v. pt. and pp. of AUTHORIZE.

Authorized Version the English translation of the Bible first published in 1611; the King James Version. *Abbrev.*: A.V.

au•thor•ship ['ɒθər,ʃɪp] *n.* **1** the occupation of an author; writing. **2** the origin as to author: *What is the authorship of that novel?* **3** the origin or source of anything.

au•tism ['ɒtɪzəm] *n.* a cognitive, emotional, and behavioural disorder characterized by difficulty in understanding, or making sense of, what one sees and hears, and in responding to it. Some people with autism have normal or even high intelligence, and many can be helped through special educational programs to cope with their condition.

au•tis•tic [ɒ'tɪstɪk] *adj.* affected with autism.

au•to ['ɒtou] *n., pl.* **au•tos.** automobile.

auto– *combining form.* **1** coming from or having to do with the self: *An autobiography is the story of one's own life.* **2** independent(ly): *An automobile is self-propelled.* ⟨< Gk.⟩

au•to•an•a•lys•er [,ɒtou'ænə,laɪzər] *n.* a machine that performs tests and analyses of blood and urine samples, chemicals, etc.

au•to•an•ti•bod•y [,ɒtou'æntɪ,bɒdi] *n.* an antibody that reacts with substances in the body in which it is produced, so that it fights against the system it is supposed to protect.

au•to•bi•og•ra•pher [,ɒtəbaɪ'ɒgrəfər] *n.* a person who writes the story of his or her own life.

au•to•bi•o•graph•ic [,ɒtə,baɪə'græfɪk] *adj.* **1** having to do with the story of one's own life. **2** telling or writing the story of one's own life: *Her writings are all autobiographic.* Also, **autobiographical. —,au•to,bi•o'graph•i•cal•ly** *adv.*

au•to•bi•og•ra•phy [,ɒtəbaɪ'ɒgrəfi] *n., pl.* **-phies.** the story of a person's life written by himself or herself.

au•to•bog•gan ['ɒtə,bɒgən] *n. Cdn.* a sled that is powered by a gasoline motor. ⟨< *auto-* + (*to*)*boggan*⟩

au•to•bus ['ɒtou,bʌs] *n.* BUS (def. 1).

au•to•ca•tal•y•sis [,ɒtoukə'tæləsɪs] *n.* the catalysis of a chemical reaction, one of whose products is itself also a catalyst.

au•to•ceph•a•lous [,ɒtou'sɛfələs] *adj.* autonomous; applied to certain member churches of the Eastern Orthodox communion. ⟨< *auto-* + L *cephalicus* of the head < Gk. *kephalikos* < *kephale* head⟩

au•toch•thon [ɒ'tɒkθən] *n.* **1** an aboriginal inhabitant. **2** an indigenous plant or animal. ⟨< Gk. *autochthon* sprung from the land itself < *auto-* self + *chthōn* earth, soil⟩

au•toch•tho•nous [ɒ'tɒkθənəs] *adj.* originating where found; aboriginal; indigenous. **—au'toch•tho•nous•ly,** *adv.*

au•to•clave ['ɒtə,kleiv] *n., v.* *—n.* **1** a strong, closed vessel that develops superheated steam under pressure, used for sterilizing, cooking, etc. **2** a strong vessel for effecting chemical reactions under high pressure.
—v. cook or sterilize in an autoclave. ⟨< F *autoclave* < *auto-* self + L *clavis* key⟩

au•toc•ra•cy [ɒ'tɒkrəsi] *n., pl.* **-cies. 1** a government having absolute power over its citizens. **2** a country having such a government. **3** absolute authority; unlimited power over a group. ⟨< Gk. *autokrateia* absolute power < *autos* self + *kratia* rule < *kratos* strength⟩

au•to•crat ['ɒtə,kræt] *n.* **1** a ruler having absolute power over his or her subjects. **2** a person who uses power in a harsh or unrestricted way: *She thinks her parents are autocrats.* ⟨< Gk. *autokratēs* < *auto-* self + *kratos* power, strength⟩

au•to•crat•ic [,ɒtə'krætɪk] *adj.* of or like an autocrat; absolute in authority; ruling without checks or limitations. **—,au•to'crat•i•cal•ly,** *adv.*

au•to–da–fé [,ɒtou də 'fei] *or* [,ʌutou-] *n., pl.* **au•tos-da-fé. 1** a public ceremony accompanying the passing of sentence by the Spanish Inquisition. **2** the carrying out of such a sentence. **3** the burning of a heretic. ⟨< Pg. *auto-da-fé* act of the faith < L *actus* act and *fides* faith⟩

au•to•di•dact [,ɒtou'daɪdækt] a self-educated person. **—,au•to•di'dac•tic,** *adj.*

au•to•dyne ['ɒtə,daɪn] *adj.* designating a type of heterodyne reception of radio signals in which the oscillator also functions as amplifier.

au•toe•cism [ɒ'tisɪzəm] *n.* the property of some parasites of spending the whole life cycle on a single host. ⟨< *auto-* + Gk. *oikos* house + -ISM⟩ **—au'toe•cious,** *adj.* **—au'toe•cious•ly,** *adv.*

au•to•e•rot•i•cism [,ɒtoui'rɒtə,sɪzəm] *n.* sexual self-stimulation, as through masturbation. Also, **autoerotism** [,ɒtou'ɛrə,tɪzəm].

au•tog•a•my [ɒ'tɒgəmi] *n.* self-fertilization, such as that of a flower pollinated by its own stamens or of a fungus, etc., by the union of gametes in a single individual.

au•to•gen•e•sis [,ɒtou'dʒɛnəsɪs] *n.* the independent generation of living organisms from nonliving matter, now believed to be impossible.

Au•to•gi•ro or **au•to•gy•ro** [,ɒtə'dʒaɪrou] *n., pl.* **-ros.** *Trademark.* an aircraft powered by a single ordinary propeller but deriving its lift mainly from a set of free-wheeling rotors that turn as the aircraft moves forward. ⟨< Sp. *autogiro* < Gk. *auto-* self + *gyros* circle⟩

au•to•graft ['ɒtə,græft] *n.* a graft, such as a skin graft, taken from the same person to whom it is given.

au•to•graph ['ɒtə,græf] *n., v.* *—n.* **1** a person's signature. **2** something written in a person's own handwriting.
—v. **1** write one's signature in or on. **2** write with one's own hand. ⟨< L *autographum, autographus* written with one's hand < Gk. *autographos*⟩

au•to•graph•ic [,ɒtə'græfɪk] *adj.* **1** of or for an autograph. **2** in one's own handwriting. Also, **autographical. —,au•to'graph•i•cal•ly,** *adv.*

Au•to•harp ['ɒtou,hɑrp] *n. Trademark.* a kind of zither with dampers that allow only certain pre-selected strings to be heard.

au•to•hyp•no•sis [,ɒtouhɪp'nousɪs] *n.* the act or state of self-induced hypnosis. **—,au•to•hyp'not•ic** [-hɪp'nɒtɪk], *adj.*

au•to•im•mune [,ɒtouɪ'mjun] *adj.* having to do with the development of antibodies hostile to the body's own molecules. **—,au•to•im'mu•ni•ty,** *n.*

autoimmune disease a disorder caused by autoantibodies.

au•to•in•fec•tion [,ɒtouɪn'fɛkʃən] *n.* infection due to agents already present in the organism.

au•to•in•tox•i•ca•tion [,ɒtouɪn,tɒksə'keiʃən] *n.* poisoning by toxic substances produced within the body.

au•to•load•ing ['ɒtou,loudɪŋ] *adj.* self-loading; of a firearm, semi-automatic.

au•tol•o•gous [ɒ'tɒləgəs] *adj.* having the same organism as its origin.

au•tol•y•sate [ɒ'tɒlə,seit] *n.* a product of autolysis.

au•to•lyse ['ɒtə,laɪz] *v.* **-lysed, -lysing.** subject to, or undergo, autolysis. ⟨< *auto-* + Gk. *lysis* a loosening⟩

au•tol•y•sin [ɒ'tɒləsɪn] *n.* an agent of autolysis.

au•tol•y•sis [ɒ'tɒləsɪs] *n.* a process by which enzymes destroy the very cells and tissues of which they are a part, as in the decay of a dead organism. **—,au•to'lyt•ic** [,ɒtə'lɪtɪk], *adj.*

au•to•mat ['ɒtə,mæt] *n.* a restaurant in which food is obtained from compartments that open when coins are inserted in slots. ⟨short for *automatic*⟩

au•to•mate ['ɒtə,meit] *v.* **-mat•ed, -mat•ing. 1** convert to automatic operation or automation: *Fewer people are employed in a plant when it is automated.* **2** make use of automation: *Many industries now face the problem of whether to automate or not.* ⟨back formation from *automation*⟩

automated teller machine *Computer technology.* a machine that allows the user to carry out various banking functions (deposits, cash withdrawals, transfers, etc.) without the aid of a human teller.

au•to•mat•ic [,ɒtə'mætɪk] *adj., n. —adj.* **1** made or done without thought or attention, as from force of habit, etc.; spontaneous or mechanical: *His automatic reply to questions from reporters was, "No comment."* **2** mainly or entirely involuntary; reflex: *Breathing is automatic.* **3 a** of a mechanism, machine, etc., made or set to move or act by itself; self-regulating or self-acting: *an automatic lock. His car has an automatic transmission.* **b** performed with the aid of such a machine or mechanism: *an automatic urinalysis.* **4** of a firearm, having a mechanism for repeatedly firing, throwing out the used shell, and reloading until the pressure on the trigger is released or the ammunition is used up. **5** as a necessary consequence; without exception or restriction: *automatic promotion after a year of service. Any violation of the rules means automatic disqualification.* *—n.* **1** an automobile equipped with an automatic transmission: *Is your car an automatic?* **2** an automatic firearm. **3** any other automatic machine. ⟨< Gk. *automatos* self-acting⟩ **—,au•to•ma'tic•i•ty** [-'tɪsəti], *n.*

au•to•mat•i•cal•ly [,ɒtə'mætɪkli] *adv.* in an automatic manner.

automatic pilot a gyroscopic mechanism designed to keep an aircraft, missile, etc. on a given course and at a given altitude without human assistance.

au•to•ma•tion [,ɒtə'meiʃən] *n.* **1** a method of making a manufacturing process, a production line, etc. operate more efficiently by the use of built-in or supplementary controls in a machine or number of machines. **2** the state of functioning by automated means. ⟨< *autom(atic)* + *(oper)ation*⟩

au•tom•a•tism [ɒ'tɒmə,tɪzəm] *n.* **1** the quality or state of being automatic. **2** an automatic action. **3** *Psychology.* **a** action not controlled by the conscious mind. **b** the power of acting in such a way. **c** action not subject to outside stimuli. **4** the suspension of conscious control of the mind, as sought or practised by some artists and writers, to permit free expression of the subconscious. **5** *Philosophy.* the belief that the living body is a machine controlled by the laws of physics rather than by the conscious mind. **—au'tom•a•tist,** *n.*

au•tom•a•ton [ɒ'tɒmə,tɒn] *n., pl.* **-ta** [-tə]. **1** an apparatus that is made to resemble a human being or an animal and operates by a concealed mechanism, by preprogrammed instructions, or by remote control; robot. **2** a person or animal that acts or appears to act in an automatic or mechanical way. ⟨< Gk. *automaton,* neut., self-acting⟩

au•to•mo•bile ['ɒtəmə,bil] *n.* **1** a passenger vehicle that carries its own engine and is driven on roads and streets; car. **2** (*adjl.*) of, having to do with, or for an automobile: *an automobile engine.* ⟨< F⟩

au•to•mo•bil•ist ['ɒtəmə,bilɪst] *n.* a person who uses an automobile.

au•to•mo•tive [,ɒtə'moutɪv] *adj.* **1** of or having to do with cars, trucks, and other self-propelled vehicles. Automotive engineering deals with the design and construction of automobiles. **2** self-propelling.

au•to•nom•ic [,ɒtə'nɒmɪk] *adj.* **1** autonomous. **2** not controlled by the conscious mind. **3** having to do with the AUTONOMIC NERVOUS SYSTEM. **4** *Biology.* arising from inside causes. Mutation is an autonomic process. **—,au•to'nom•ic•al•ly,** *adv.*

autonomic nervous system *Physiology.* the ganglia and nerves of the nervous system of vertebrates, which control digestive, reproductive, respiratory, and other involuntary functions of the body.

au•ton•o•mist [ɒ'tɒnəmɪst] *n.* a person who advocates autonomy.

au•ton•o•mous [ɒ'tɒnəməs] *adj.* **1** self-governing; independent. **2** *Biology.* **a** independent from other parts in function and development. **b** producing its own food; autotrophic. **c** AUTONOMIC (def. 4). **—au'ton•o•mous•ly,** *adv.*

au•ton•o•my [ɒ'tɒnəmi] *n., pl.* **-mies. 1** self-government; independence. **2** a self-governing community. ⟨< Gk. *autonomia* < *auto-* of oneself + *nomos* law⟩

au•to•pho•bia [,ɒtə'foubiə] *n.* an abnormal fear of being alone.

au•to•phyte ['ɒtə,fəit] *n.* a plant that produces its food from non-living matter. **—,au•to'phyt•ic** [-'fɪtɪk], *adj.*

au•to•pi•lot ['ɒtou,paɪlət] *n.* AUTOMATIC PILOT.

au•to•plas•ty ['ɒtə,plæsti] *n.* autograft. ⟨< *auto-* + Gk. *plastia* < *plastos* formed < *plassein* to form⟩

au•top•sy ['ɒtɒpsi] *or* ['ɒtəpsi] *n., pl.* **-sies. 1** an examination and dissection of a dead body to find the cause of death or the nature or extent of the damage done to the body by disease, injury, etc. Compare BIOPSY. **2** a critical examination of a finished product or event, as a book, performance, relationship, treaty, etc.: *an autopsy of the Meech Lake Accord.* ⟨< NL < Gk. *autopsia* < *auto-* for oneself + *opsis* a seeing⟩

au•to•ra•di•o•graph [,ɒtou'reidiə,græf] *n.* an X-ray photograph revealing the existence and location of radioactive material in an object, whose own radiation in turn exposes the photographic plate or film. **—,au•to,ra•di•o'graph•ic,** *adj.*

au•to•ra•di•o•graph•y [,ɒtou,reidi'ɒgrəfi] *n.* a laboratory technique in which a radiograph is made by photographic recording of the radiation emitted by an object which has been labelled by a radioactive marker.

au•to•route ['ɒtou,rut] *n.* expressway. ⟨< F⟩

au•to•some ['ɒtə,soum] *n.* a chromosome that is not sex-determining. In the human there are 22 pairs of autosomes and one pair of sex chromosomes. **—,au•to'som•al,** *adj.*

au•to•sug•ges•tion [,ɒtousə'dʒestʃən] *or* [,ɒtousəg'dʒɛstʃən] *n. Psychology.* the suggestion to oneself of ideas that produce subconscious changes in attitudes, behaviour, or physical condition.

au•to•tel•ic [,ɒtə'tɛlɪk] *adj.* being its own end; done for its own sake. ⟨< Gk. *autoteles* complete in itself < *autos* self + *telos* an end⟩

au•to•ther•a•py [,ɒtou'θɛrəpi] *n.* **1** self-treatment. **2** a spontaneous cure.

au•tot•o•mize [ɒ'tɒtə,maɪz] *v.,* **-mized, -miz•ing.** cast off or be cast off by autotomy.

au•tot•o•my [ɒ'tɒtəmi] *n.* the reflex-activated severing of a body part of an animal, such as the tail of a lizard, in response to an injury or as an escape mechanism, after which the lost part is regenerated. ⟨< *auto-* + Gk. *tome* a cutting⟩ **—,au•to'tom•ic** [,ɒtə'tɒmɪk], *adj.*

au•to•tox•e•mi•a [,ɒtoutɒk'simiə] *n.* autointoxication.

au•to•tox•in ['ɒtou,tɒksɪn] *n.* a toxic substance generated within the organism that is poisoned by it.

au•to•trans•form•er [,ɒtoutræns'fɔrmər] *n. Electricity.* a transformer in which the primary and secondary circuits share all or part of the windings.

au•to•troph ['ɒtə,trɒf] *n.* an organism that manufactures its own food from inorganic substances, such as a plant by photosynthesis or a bacterium by chemosynthesis. ⟨< *auto-* + Gk. *trophe* food < *trephein* to feed⟩

au•to•troph•ic [,ɒtə'trɒfɪk] *adj.* of or having to do with an autotroph. **—,au•to'troph•i•cal•ly,** *adv.*

au•tox•i•da•tion [ɒ,tɒksɪ'deiʃən] *n.* **1** oxidation by exposure to air. **2** oxidation that is a concomitant of another oxidizing reaction. **—au'tox•i,da•tive,** *adj.*

au•tumn ['ɒtəm] *n.* **1** the season of the year between summer and winter; fall. **2** a time of maturity and the beginning of decay. **3** (*adjl.*) of, in, like, or characteristic of autumn: *autumn flowers, autumn rains.* ⟨ME < OF < L *autumnus*⟩

au•tum•nal [ɒ'tʌmnəl] *adj.* of or coming in autumn.

autumnal equinox the equinox occurring about September 22.

autumn crocus a plant (*Colchicum autumnale*) of the family Liliaceae, native to Europe and N Africa. Its flowers, which bloom in autumn, are usually pink or purple.

aux. auxiliary.

aux•il•ia•ry [ɒg'zɪləri] *or* [ɒg'zɪljəri] *adj., n., pl.* **-ries.** *—adj.* 1 supplementary or additional: *auxiliary troops. The building has an auxiliary power supply in case of a blackout.* 2 assisting or supporting: *Intellect and imagination should be auxiliary to each other.* 3 of a sailing vessel, equipped with an engine to supplement the power of the sails. 4 having to do with the non-fighting ships of a navy, as tankers.
—n. 1 a supplementary or supporting person, group, organization, or thing. 2 a sailing vessel equipped with an engine. 3 a naval vessel, such as a hospital ship, designed for duties other than fighting. 4 **auxiliaries,** *pl.* foreign or allied troops that help the army of a nation at war. 5 AUXILIARY VERB. ⟨< L *auxiliarius* < *auxilium* aid⟩

auxiliary verb a verb used to form the tenses, moods, aspects, or voices of other verbs, such as *be, do, have, shall,* and *will. Examples:* I *am* going; he *will* go; they *are* lost; they *have* lost.

aux•in ['ɒksən] *n.* a plant hormone, natural or synthetic, which controls the growth of various parts of a plant. ⟨< Gk. *auxein* to increase⟩

aux•o•chrome ['ɒksə,kroum] *n.* an atom group that is added to a potentially pigment-producing or colouring substance, turning it into a dye and making it adhere to the fabric. ⟨< Gk. *auxein* to increase + *chroma* colour⟩

aux•o•troph•ic [,ɒksə'trɒfɪk] *adj.* of or relating to an organism which, having failed to inherit from its parent the capacity to produce a certain enzyme necessary to synthesize its own growth factors, needs an abnormal quantity of nutrients. ⟨< Gk. *auxein* to increase + *trophe* food < *trephein* to feed⟩ **—'aux•o,troph,** *n.*

Av [æv] *n.* in the Hebrew calendar, the fifth month of the ecclesiastical year, and the eleventh month of the civil year.

av. 1 average. 2 avoirdupois.

av. or **Av.** Avenue.

AV audiovisual.

A.V. 1 Authorized Version. 2 audiovisual.

a•vail [ə'veil] *v., n. —v.* be of use or value (to): *Money will not avail you after you are dead. Talk will not avail without work.*
avail oneself of, take advantage of; profit by; make use of: *While she was in Québec she availed herself of the opportunity to improve her French.*
—n. use; advantage or help for a purpose (*used especially with a negative meaning*): *Crying is of little avail now. He tried again and again, but to no avail.* ⟨apparently < *a-* to (< L *ad-*) + *vail* < F < L *valere* be worth⟩

a•vail•a•bil•i•ty [ə,veilə'bɪləti] *n.* the quality or state of being available: *The availability of water power helped make southern Ontario an industrial region.*

a•vail•a•ble [ə'veiləbəl] *adj.* 1 ready or handy to be used; that can be used: *The available water supply had dried up.* 2 that can be obtained: *All available tickets were sold.* 3 willing or free to do something: *He said he was available for the job now.* **—a'vail•a•bly,** *adv.*

av•a•lanche ['ævə,lænt∫] *n., v.* **-lanched, -lanch•ing.** *—n.* 1 a large mass of snow and ice, or of dirt and rocks, sliding or falling down a mountainside. 2 anything like an avalanche: *an avalanche of questions.*
—v. move like an avalanche. ⟨< F < Swiss F *lavenche* (< a pre-Latin Alpine language), influenced by F *avaler* go down < *à val* < L *ad vallem* to the valley⟩

avalanche lily any of several species (genus *Erythronium*) of wildflowers of the lily family found in the mountains of W North America, especially *E. grandiflorum,* the glacier lily.

Av•a•lon ['ævə,lɒn] *n. Celtic legend.* an earthly paradise in the western seas, to which King Arthur and other heroes were carried at death.

a•vant–garde [,ævɑ̃ 'gɑrd]; French, [avɑ̃'gaʀd] *n., adj. —n.* the people who develop new and experimental ideas, especially in the arts.
—adj. of or having to do with such people or the movements started by them: *an avant-garde artist, avant-garde ideas.* ⟨< F *avant-garde* literally, advance guard⟩

a•vant–gard•ism [,ævɑ̃ 'gɑrdɪzəm] *n.* 1 a movement or trend in the arts characterized by emphasis on what is new or startling. 2 the quality of being avant-garde.

a•vant–gard•ist [,ævɑ̃ 'gɑrdɪst] *n.* a person who supports or belongs to the avant-garde in art, etc.

av•a•rice ['ævərɪs] *n.* an extreme desire for money or property; greed: *It was avarice, not a desire for security, that made them scrimp and save all those years.* ⟨ME < OF < L *avaritia* < *avarus* greedy⟩

av•a•ri•cious [,ævə'rɪ∫əs] *adj.* greedy for wealth. **—,av•a'ri•cious•ly,** *adv.* **—,av•a'ri•cious•ness,** *n.*

a•vast [ə'væst] *interj. Nautical.* a command to stop: *"Avast there!" shouted the sailor.* ⟨probably < Du. *houd vast* hold fast⟩

av•a•tar ['ævə,tɑr] *n.* 1 *Hinduism.* the descent of a god to earth in bodily form; incarnation. 2 a manifestation in bodily form. ⟨< Skt. *avatāra* descent < *ava* down + *tar-* pass over⟩

a•vaunt [ə'vɒnt] *or* [ə'vɑnt] *interj. Archaic.* a command to get out, go away, etc. ⟨ME < OF *avant* < L *ab ante* forward, in front⟩

avdp. avoirdupois.

a•ve ['ɑvei] *interj., n. —interj. Latin.* hail! farewell!
—n. **Ave,** the prayer Ave Maria.

ave. or **Ave.** Avenue.

A•ve Ma•ri•a ['ɑvei mə'riə] *Roman Catholic Church.* 1 "Hail, Mary!", the first words of the Latin form of a prayer. 2 the prayer.

a•venge [ə'vɛndʒ] *v.* **a•venged, a•veng•ing.** 1 inflict punishment in return for; take vengeance for: *to avenge an insult.* 2 take vengeance on behalf of (oneself or another): *The clan avenged their slain chief. He had the power to avenge himself on his betrayers.* 3 get revenge (*used in the passive*): *She swore to be avenged.* ⟨ME < OF *avengier* < *a-* to (< L *ad-*) + *vengier* < L *vindicare* punish < *vindex* champion⟩ **—a'veng•er,** *n.*
☛ *Syn.* See note at REVENGE.

av•ens ['ævɪnz] *n.* 1 any of several perennial plants (genus *Geum*) of the rose family found in temperate and arctic regions, including several common Canadian wildflowers, such as the three-flowered avens (*Geum triflorum*) of the Prairies. 2 See MOUNTAIN AVENS. ⟨ME < OF *avence*; origin unknown⟩

a•ven•tu•rine [ə'vɛnt∫ə,rin] *or* [ə'vɛnt∫ərɪn] *n.* 1 a kind of quartz containing bright specks of mica or some other mineral. 2 a type of glass shot with glittery pieces of metal. ⟨< F < Ital. *avventurino* < *avventura* chance < L *adventura*; because discovered accidentally. See ADVENTURE.⟩

av•e•nue ['ævə,nju] *n.* 1 a wide or main street. 2 a road or walk bordered by trees. 3 a way of approach or departure; passage: *avenues to fame.* 4 in some cities, a thoroughfare running at right angles to others usually called 'streets'. ⟨< F *avenue,* fem. pp. of *avenir* < L *advenire* < *ad-* to + *venire* come⟩

a•ver [ə'vɜr] *v.* **a•verred, a•ver•ring.** state to be true; assert. ⟨ME < OF *averer,* ult < L *ad-* + *verus* true⟩ **—a'ver•ment,** *n.*

av•er•age ['ævrɪdʒ] *or* ['ævərɪdʒ] *n., adj., v.* **-aged, -ag•ing.** *—n.* 1 an arithmetic mean; the quantity found by dividing the sum of several quantities by the number of those quantities: *The average of 3, 5, and 10 is 6.* 2 a usual kind or quality; ordinary amount or rate: *His achievement at school was definitely above the average.* 3 *Business.* **a** a small charge payable by the master of a ship, covering the cost of pilotage, towing, etc. **b** a loss or expense arising as a result of damage at sea to ship or cargo. **c** the fair, proportionate distribution of such loss or expense among all the parties involved.
on (the) average, calculated as an average; generally speaking: *She worked 35 hours a week on the average.*
—adj. 1 obtained by averaging; being an average: *an average price, the average temperature.* 2 usual; ordinary: *average intelligence.*
—v. 1 find the average of. 2 amount to on an average; come close to: *The cost for lunch at the cafeteria averages about seven dollars a day.* 3 do, get, yield, etc. on an average: *He averages six hours work a day. We averaged eight litres per 100 kilometres.* 4 divide among several proportionately: *We averaged our gains according to what each had put in.* 5 *Finance.* buy or sell set amounts of stock at varying prices in order to get a better average cost (*used with* **up** *or* **down**).
average out, come to an average over time: *The expenses averaged out over several months. Abbrev.:* av. ⟨ME < F *avarie* damage to ship or cargo < Arabic *'awārīya* damage from sea water. In English, extended to 'equal distribution' (at first, 'of loss')⟩

A•ver•nus [ə'vɜrnəs] *n.* 1 *Roman mythology.* the lake on the shores of which lay the entrance to Hades. Avernus is the Latin name for Averno, a lake in the crater of an extinct volcano near Naples, Italy. 2 the lower world itself; Hades.

a•verse [ə'vɜrs] *adj.* **1** opposed; having an active distaste; reluctant (*used with* **to**): *He was averse to fighting.* **2** *Botany.* not facing the principal stem. ⟨< L *aversus,* pp. of *avertere.* See AVERT.⟩ **—a'verse•ness,** *n.* **—a'verse•ly,** *adv.*

a•ver•sion [ə'vɜrʒən] *or* [ə'vɜrʃən] *n.* **1** a strong or fixed dislike; antipathy. **2** a thing or person disliked. **3** unwillingness.
☛ *Usage.* Either *to* or *for* follows **aversion:** *She has an aversion to moving fast and working hard. We'll eat alone; they have an aversion for fried shrimp.*

a•ver•sive [ə'vɜrsɪv] *adj.* causing avoidance of an unpleasant stimulus; tending to repel: *Aversive conditioning is sometimes used by therapists to help a patient overcome a serious bad habit, etc.*

a•vert [ə'vɜrt] *v.* **1** prevent; avoid: *He averted the accident by a quick turn of the steering wheel.* **2** turn away; turn aside: *She averted her eyes from the wreck.* ⟨ME < OF < L *avertere* < *ab-* from + *vertere* turn⟩

A•ves•ta [ə'vɛstə] *n.* the sacred writings of the ancient Zoroastrian religion, still in use by the Parsi.

A•ves•tan [ə'vɛstən] *n., adj.* *—n.* the language, closely related to Old Persian and being the oldest attested Indo-European language, in which the Avesta was written.
—adj. of or relating to the Avesta or its language.

avg. average.

av•gas ['æv,gæs] *n.* aviation gasoline.

av•go•le•mo•no [,ɑvgou'lɛmə,nou] *n.* a Greek soup whose main ingredients are lemon juice, beaten eggs, rice, and meat stock. ⟨< Gk. *augon* egg + *lemonion* lemon⟩

a•vi•an ['eiviən] *adj.* of or having to do with birds. ⟨< L *avis* bird⟩

a•vi•ar•y ['eivi,ɛri] *n., pl.* **-ar•ies.** an enclosure or large cage in which to keep birds. ⟨< L *aviarium* < *avis* bird⟩

a•vi•a•tion [,eivi'eiʃən] *or* [,ævi'eiʃən] *n.* **1** the designing, manufacturing, and operating of aircraft, especially airplanes. **2** airplanes, their personnel, and their equipment. ⟨< F *aviation* < L *avis* bird⟩

a•vi•a•tor ['eivi,eitər] *or* ['ævi,eitər] *n.* a person who flies an aircraft; pilot.

a•vi•cul•ture ['eivi,kʌltʃər] *n.* the rearing or keeping of birds. ⟨< L *avis* bird + *cultura* culture⟩

a•vi•cul•tur•ist [,eivə'kʌltʃərɪst] *n.* a bird expert or fancier.

av•id ['ævɪd] *adj.* **1** enthusiastic: *She is an avid reader.* **2** eager; greedy: *The miser was avid for gold.* ⟨< L *avidus* < *avere* crave⟩ **—'av•id•ly,** *adv.*

av•i•din ['ævədɪn] *n.* a protein found in raw egg white that binds biotin so that it cannot be absorbed and used by the body of the person or animal eating the egg. ⟨< L *avidus* + E -INE[2]⟩

a•vid•i•ty [ə'vɪdəti] *n.* **1** eagerness; greediness. **2** *Chemistry.* the relative strength of an acid or base.

a•vi•fau•na [,eivə'fɒnə] *n., pl.* the birds of a particular region, environment, or time. ⟨< NL < L *avis* bird + LL *fauna* sister of⟩

a•vi•on•ics [,eivi'ɒnɪks] *n.* the division of electronics which concerns electronic apparatus as it is used in aircraft and rockets. **—,a•vi'on•ic,** *adj.*

a•vir•u•lent [,ei'virjələnt] *adj.* not virulent; no longer virulent.

a•vi•ta•min•o•sis [,ei,vəitəmɪ'nousɪs] *n.* any disorder which is a result of vitamin deficiency.

A.V.M. Air Vice-Marshal.

av•o ['ɑvou] *n.* a unit of money in Macao, equal to 1/100 of a pataca. See table of money in the Appendix.

The fruit and seed of an avocado plant

av•o•ca•do [,ævə'kɑdou] *or* [-'kɒdou] *n., pl.* **-dos,** *adj.* *—n.* **1** the pear-shaped or egg-shaped fruit of a tropical American tree (*Persea americana*) of the laurel family, having a dark green or blackish skin, soft, greenish yellow, edible pulp, and a very large stone. Also called **alligator pear. 2** the tree producing this fruit. **3** yellowish green.
—adj. yellowish green. ⟨< Sp. *avocado,* var. of *aguacate* < Aztec *ahuacatl*⟩

av•o•ca•tion [,ævə'keiʃən] *n.* **1** something that a person does besides his or her regular business; a minor occupation; hobby: *Mrs. Gomez is a lawyer, but writing stories is her avocation.* **2** *Informal.* one's regular business; occupation. ⟨< L *avocatio, -onis* < *avocare* < *ab-* away + *vocare* to call⟩

av•o•cet ['ævə,sɛt] *n.* any of several long-legged, web-footed wading birds (genus *Recurvirostra*) of temperate and tropical regions, having a long, slender bill that curves upward. Also, **avoset.** ⟨< F *avocette* < Ital. *avosetta*⟩

A•vo•gad•ro's law [,ɑvə'gɑdrouz] *Physics.* the law stating that equal volumes of different gases, under like conditions of pressure and temperature, contain the same number of molecules. ⟨after Count Amedeo *Avogadro* (1776-1856), an Italian physicist, who stated it⟩

Avogadro's number the number of molecules in one MOLE[4] of any substance, equalling 6.022137×10^{23} per mole. Also, **Avogadro's constant.**

a•void [ə'vɔɪd] *v.* **1** keep (away) from; keep out of the way of: *We avoided driving through large cities on our trip.* **2** prevent the need for or the occurrence of: *You can avoid costly repairs by regular cleaning. Avoid spills in the lab.* **3** *Law.* make void; annul. ⟨< AF var. of OF *esvuidier* empty, quit < *es-* out (< L *ex-*) + *vuidier* < VL *vocitare* empty⟩

a•void•a•ble [ə'vɔɪdəbəl] *adj.* **1** that can be escaped or avoided. **2** *Law.* voidable.

a•void•ance [ə'vɔɪdəns] *n.* **1** avoiding; a keeping away from. **2** the fact of being or becoming vacant: *the avoidance of the office of vice-president.* **3** *Law.* the act of making void; an invalidating; annulment.

av•oir•du•pois [ə'vwɑrdjʊ,pwɑ] *or* ['ævərdə,pɔɪz] *n.* **1** avoirdupois weight: *The package weighs three pounds avoirdupois.* **2** *Informal.* a person's mass or weight. ⟨ME < OF *aveir de peis* goods of weight < L *habere* have, *de* of, and *pensum* weight < *pendere* weight⟩

avoirdupois weight the ordinary system of weighing in Canada before the change to the SI, or metric system. One pound in avoirdupois weight is equal to about 0.454 kilograms. Compare APOTHECARIES' WEIGHT and TROY WEIGHT. See table of measures in the Appendix.

av•o•set ['ævə,sɛt] See AVOCET.

a•vouch [ə'vʌutʃ] *v.* **1** declare to be true. **2** guarantee. **3** acknowledge; affirm. ⟨ME < OF *avochier* < *a-* to (< L *ad-*) + *vochier* call < L *vocare*⟩ **—a'vouch•ment** *n.*

a•vow [ə'vaʊ] *v.* declare frankly or openly; confess; admit; acknowledge: *He avowed that he could not sing.* ⟨ME < OF *avouer* < *a-* to (< L *ad-*) + *vouer* vow < VL *votare* < L *advocare*⟩

a•vow•al [ə'vaʊəl] *n.* a frank or open declaration; confession; admission; acknowledgment.

a•vowed [ə'vaʊd] *adj., v.* *—adj.* openly declared; admitted: *Her avowed intention was to try for the party leadership.*
—v. pt. and pp. of AVOW.

a•vow•ed•ly [ə'vaʊɪdli] *adv.* admittedly; openly.

a•vul•sion [ə'vʌlʃən] *n.* **1** the tearing away or separation of a part or structure; often, a surgical procedure accomplishing this. **2** the sudden removal of soil from a person's land by flooding, etc. **3** anything so removed, torn away, etc. ⟨< L *avulsio* < *a-* from + pp. of *vellere* pull⟩

a•vun•cu•lar [ə'vʌŋkjələr] *adj.* **1** of an uncle. **2** like an uncle. ⟨< L *avunculus* mother's brother, dim. of *avus* grandfather⟩

aw [ɒ] *interj.* an exclamation expressing mild disagreement, resignation, pleading, pity, etc.
☛ *Hom.* AWE.

A.W. aircraftwoman.

a•wait [ə'weit] *v.* **1** wait for; look forward to: *to await someone's arrival.* **2** be ready for; be in store for: *They had no idea what awaited them at the end of the trip.* ⟨ME < OF *awaitier* < *a-* for (< L *ad-*) + *waitier* wait < Gmc.⟩
☛ *Usage.* See note at WAIT.

a•wake [ə'weik] *v.* **a•woke** or **a•waked, a•wok•en** or **a•waked, a•wak•ing;** *adj.* *—v.* **1** cease or cause to cease sleeping; wake up: *We awoke from a sound sleep. The alarm clock awoke me.* **2** make or become active or alert: *The song awoke old memories.*

—adj. (never used before a noun) **1** not asleep; roused from sleep or inactivity: *Jerry is always awake early.* **2** on the alert; watchful: *awake to danger.* ⟨OE *āwacian* + OE *onwæcnan*⟩

a•wak•en [ə'weikən] *v.* awake.

a•wak•en•ing [ə'weikənɪŋ] *n., adj., v. —n.* a waking up or arousing: *an awakening to new possibilities.*
—adj. waking or reviving: *the awakening birds.*
—v. ppr. of AWAKEN.

a•ward [ə'wɔrd] *v., n. —v.* **1** give after careful consideration of merit; grant: *A medal was awarded to the woman who saved the child.* **2** decide or settle by law; adjudge: *The court awarded damages of $5000.*
—n. **1** something given after careful consideration; a prize: *Frank's dog won the highest award.* **2** *Law.* a decision by a judge. ⟨< AF var. of OF *esguarder* observe, decide < VL *ex-* from + **wardare* guard < Gmc.⟩ **—a•ward'ee, a'ward•er,** *n.*

a•ware [ə'wɛr] *adj.* knowing; realizing; conscious (*of*): *I was too sleepy to be aware how cold it was. She was not aware of his presence.* ⟨OE *gewær*⟩ **—a'ware•ness,** *n.*
☛ *Syn.* See note at CONSCIOUS.

a•wash [ə'wɒʃ] *adv. or adj. (never precedes a noun)* **1** level with the surface of the water; just covered with water. **2** carried about by water; floating. **3** flooded.

a•way [ə'wei] *adv., adj. —adv.* **1** from a place; to or at a distance: *Get away from the fire. The sailor was far away from home.* **2** gone; absent: *How many students are away today?* **3** in another direction; aside: *turn away.* **4** out of one's possession, notice, or use: *He gave his boat away.* **5** out of existence: *The sounds died away.* **6** without stopping; continuously: *She worked away at her job.* **7** without waiting; at once: *I'll do it right away.* **8** somewhere else; aside, often in its appropriate place: *Put your book away until supper is over.* **9** off; used to launch an action or undertaking: *Away we went, our schoolbags in hand.*
away back, *Informal.* far back in space or time.
away with, take someone or something away: Away with you *means* go away.
do away with, a put an end to; get rid of. **b** kill.
—adj. **1** at a distance; far. **2** absent; gone. **3** not at home: *an away game.* **4** *Golf.* of a golf ball, to be played first because it is at the greatest distance from the hole. **5** *Baseball.* out: *Two away in the top of the fifth.* ⟨OE *onweg*⟩
☛ *Hom.* AWEIGH.

awe [ɒ] *n., v.* **awed, aw•ing.** *—n.* **1** wonder and reverence inspired by something sacred, mysterious, or magnificent: *They gazed in awe at the mountains towering above them.* **2** great respect and admiration mixed with fear, inspired by power and authority: *They stood in awe of the old woman's disapproval.*
—v. **1** cause to feel awe; fill with awe: *The majesty of the mountains awed us.* **2** influence or restrain by awe. ⟨ME *age* < ON *agi*⟩
☛ *Hom.* AW.

a•wea•ry [ə'wiri] *adj. (never precedes a noun) Poetic.* weary; tired.

a•weath•er [ə'wɛðər] *adj. (never precedes a noun) or adv.* on or toward the windward, or weather, side.

a•weigh [ə'wei] *adj. (never precedes a noun)* raised off the bottom: *The ship sailed off as soon as its anchor was aweigh.*
☛ *Hom.* AWAY.

awe–in•spir•ing ['ɒ ɪn,spaɪrɪŋ] *adj.* awesome.

awe•less ['ɒlɪs] *adj.* not awed; not feeling awe. **—'awe•less•ness,** *n.*

awe•some ['ɒsəm] *adj.* **1** causing awe: *A great fire is an awesome sight.* **2** showing awe; awed: *awesome admiration.* **—'awe•some•ly,** *adv.* **—'awe•some•ness,** *n.*

awe–struck ['ɒ ,strʌk] *adj.* filled with awe. Also **awe-stricken** ['ɒ ,strɪkən].

aw•ful ['ɒfəl] *adj.* **1** dreadful; terrible: *an awful storm.* **2** *Informal.* very bad, great, ugly, etc.: *The room was in an awful mess.* **3** deserving great respect and reverence; sublime: *the awful power of God.* **4** filling with awe; impressive. **5** (*advl.*) *Informal.* very: *She was awful mad.* ⟨< *awe* + *-ful*⟩ **—'aw•ful•ness,** *n.*
☛ *Usage.* In formal English **awful** = filling with awe. In familiar and informal English it is a general word of disapproval: *awful manners, an awful cold, an awful mistake.* As a result, the word is seldom used in careful writing; **awe-inspiring** and **awesome** have taken its place.
☛ *Hom.* OFFAL.

aw•ful•ly ['ɒfli] *or* ['ɒfəli] *adv.* **1** dreadfully; terribly. **2** *Informal.* very: *I'm awfully sorry that I hurt your feelings.*

a•while [ə'waɪl] *adv.* for a short time.

awk•ward ['ɒkwərd] *adj.* **1** clumsy; not graceful or skilful: *The seal is very awkward on land, but quite at home in the water.* **2** not well suited to use: *The handle of this pitcher has an awkward shape.* **3** not easily managed: *This is an awkward corner to turn.* **4** embarrassing: *He asked me an awkward question.* ⟨< obs. *awk* perversely, in the wrong way (ME < ON *afugr* turned the wrong way) + *-ward*⟩ **—'awk•ward•ly,** *adv.* **—'awk•ward•ness,** *n.*
☛ *Syn.* **1. Awkward,** CLUMSY, UNGAINLY = not graceful. **Awkward** = lacking grace, ease, quickness, and skill: *An awkward person is no help in the kitchen.* **Clumsy** suggests moving heavily and stiffly: *The clumsy girl bumped into the furniture.* **Ungainly** = awkward in moving one's body: *He is as ungainly as a newborn calf.*

awl [ɒl] *n.* a pointed tool used for making small holes in leather or wood. ⟨OE *al*⟩
☛ *Hom.* ALL.

A.W.L. *Military.* absent without leave. Also, **A.W.O.L.**

awn [ɒn] *n.* one of the bristly hairs extending from the spikelets of some cereal grains and other grasses. ⟨ME < ON *ögn* chaff⟩ **—'awn•less,** *adj.*
☛ *Hom.* ON.

awned [ɒnd] *adj.* of cereal grains, etc., having awns; bearded.

awn•ing ['ɒnɪŋ] *n.* a rooflike structure consisting of metal, canvas, wood, or plastic spread over a frame and attached over a door, window, etc. as a protection from the sun or rain. ⟨origin uncertain⟩

a•woke [ə'wouk] *v.* pt. and pp. of AWAKE.

A.W.O.L., a.w.o.l., or **AWOL** ['ei,wɒl] *when used as acronym.* A.W.L.

a•wry [ə'raɪ] *adv. or adj. (never precedes a noun)* **1** with a twist or a turn to one side: *His hat was blown awry by the wind.* **2** wrong: *Our plans have gone awry.* ⟨< *a-* in + *wry*⟩

axe [æks] *n., v. —n.* **1** a tool for chopping and splitting wood, etc., consisting of a heavy metal head attached to a long wooden handle, the head having a blade, or cutting edge, parallel to the handle. **2** a tool or weapon similar to this.
get the axe, *Informal.* **a** be dismissed from a job; get fired. **b** be axed; be removed, restricted, ended, etc.
have an axe to grind, a have a special, usually selfish, purpose or reason for being involved. **b** have a personal grievance to settle.
—v. **1** split, shape, or trim with an axe. **2** *Informal.* remove, restrict, end, etc.: *Several budget items were axed due to lack of funds.* Sometimes, **ax.** ⟨OE *æx*⟩ **—'axe,like,** *adj.*

ax•el ['æksəl] *n. Figure skating.* a jump in which the skater takes off from one foot, makes one and a half turns in the air, and lands on the other foot. ⟨< *Axel* Paulson, a Norwegian skater⟩
☛ *Hom.* AXLE.

axe•man ['æksmən] *n., pl.* **-men. 1** a man who uses an axe in chopping or fighting. **2** hatchetman. Sometimes, **axman.**

a•xe•nic [ei'zinɪk] *or* [ei'zɛnɪk] *adj.* uncontaminated by unwanted micro-organisms, as a culture medium. ⟨< Gk. *a* without + *xenos* foreign⟩

ax•es[1] ['æksiz] *n.* pl. of AXIS.

ax•es[2] ['æksəz] *n.* pl. of AXE.

ax•i•al ['æksiəl] *adj.* **1** of or forming an axis. **2** on or around an axis. **—'ax•i•al•ly,** *adv.*

axial flow the flow of air along the longitudinal axis of a jet engine.

ax•il ['æksɪl] *n. Botany.* the angle between the upper side of a leaf or stem and the supporting stem or branch. ⟨< L *axilla* armpit⟩

ax•ile ['æksaɪl] *adj.* of or having to do with an axis.

ax•il•la [æk'sɪlə] *n., pl.* **ax•il•lae** [-i] *or* [-aɪ] **1** armpit. **2** axil. ⟨< L⟩

ax•il•lar ['æksələr] *adj., n. —adj.* axillary.
—n. any of the feathers on the underside of a bird's wing where it joins the body.

ax•il•lar•y ['æksə,lɛri] *adj., n., pl.* **-aries.** *—adj.* **1** of or near the armpit. **2** in or growing from an axil.
—n. axillar.

ax•i•o•log•i•cal [,æksiə'lɒdʒəkəl] *adj.* of or having to do with axiology. **—,ax•i•o'log•i•cal•ly,** *adv.*

ax•i•ol•o•gist [,æksi'ɒlədʒɪst] *n.* a person who studies or specializes in axiology, especially one whose work it is.

ax•i•ol•o•gy [,æksi'ɒlədʒi] *n.* the branch of philosophy dealing with the nature and criteria of moral and aesthetic values and value judgments. ⟨< Gk. *axios* worthy + *logis* word⟩

ax•i•om ['æksiəm] *n.* **1** a statement seen to be true without proof; a self-evident truth: *It is an axiom that if equals are added to equals the results will be equal.* **2** an established principle. ⟨< L < Gk. *axiōma* < *axios* worthy⟩

ax•i•o•mat•ic [,æksiə'mætɪk] *adj.* **1** self-evident: *That a whole is greater than any of its parts is axiomatic.* **2** full of axioms or maxims.

ax•is ['æksɪs] *n., pl.* **ax•es** [-siz]. **1** an imaginary or real straight line that passes through an object and about which an object turns or seems to turn. The earth's axis is an imaginary line through the North and South Poles. **2** a central or principal line around which parts are arranged regularly. The axis of a cone is the straight line joining its apex and the centre of its base. **3** a central or principal structure extending lengthwise. The axis of a plant is the stem. The axis of the skeleton is the spinal column. **4** *Aeronautics.* any of three straight lines representing the length, height, and width of the aircraft, and intersecting at the centre of gravity of the aircraft. **5** *Optics.* **a** the line going through the middle of a lens from its inner to its outer surface. **b** the line between the object seen and the point at which vision is sharpest. **6** an important line of relation: *the Berlin-Rome axis.* **7 the Axis,** in World War II, Germany, Italy, Japan, and their allies. ⟨< L⟩

ax•le ['æksəl] *n.* **1** a bar or shaft on which or with which a wheel turns. See DIFFERENTIAL and GYROSCOPE for pictures. **2** axletree. ⟨OE *eaxl* shoulder, crossbar; influenced by ON *öxul* axle⟩
☛ *Hom.* AXEL.

ax•le•tree ['æksəl,tri] *n.* a crossbar that connects two opposite wheels.

Ax•min•ster ['æks,mɪnstər] *n.* a kind of carpet with a finely tufted velvetlike pile. ⟨< *Axminster*, a town in England where such carpets were first made⟩

ax•o•lotl ['æksə,lɒtəl] *n.* any of several species (genus *Ambystoma*) of salamander found in certain lakes of Mexico and the W United States, that ordinarily never lose their gills and larval form but otherwise live and breed like other salamanders. ⟨< Sp. < a Nahuatl word meaning 'water doll'; literally, servant of water⟩

ax•on ['æksɒn] *n.* the part of a nerve cell that carries impulses away from the body of the cell. See NEURON for picture. Also, **axone** ['æksoun]. ⟨< NL < Gk. *axōn* axis⟩ **—'ax•on•al** ['æksənəl], *adj.*

ax•seed ['æks,sid] *n.* CROWN VETCH.

ay[1] [ei] See AYE[1].

ay[2] [aɪ] See AYE[2].

a•yah ['ɑjə] *n.* a maid or nurse in India and related cultures. ⟨< Hind. *āya* < Pg. *aia* governess⟩

a•ya•tol•lah [,ɑjə'toulə] *n.* **1** a title of respect given to the most eminent scholars in Shiite Islamic theology and law. **2** *Informal.* a person having or aspiring to great authority: *the ayatollahs of the media.* ⟨< Persian < *ayat* religious mark or sign + *ollah* Allah, God⟩

aye[1] or **ay** [ei] *adv.* always; ever. ⟨ME < ON *ei*⟩

aye[2] or **ay** [aɪ] *adv., n.* —*adv.* yes: *Aye, aye, sir.*
—*n.* an affirmative answer, vote, or voter: *The ayes were in the majority when the vote was taken.* ⟨origin uncertain⟩
☛ *Hom.* EYE, I.

aye–aye ['aɪ ,aɪ] *n.* a squirrel-like lemur of Malagasy. ⟨< F < Malagasy *aiay*⟩

a•yin ['ɑjɪn] *n.* the seventeenth letter in the Hebrew alphabet, silent and represented by a midline dot in transliteration. See table of alphabets in the Appendix.

Ayr•shire ['ɛr,ʃir] *or* ['ɛrʃər] *n.* a breed of hardy dairy cattle that are red and white or brown and white. ⟨< *Ayrshire*, a county in SW Scotland⟩

ay•ur•ve•da [,ɑjʊr'veidə] *n.* traditional Hindu herbal medicine dating from the 1st century A.D.

az. **1** azimuth. **2** azure.

a•zal•ea [ə'zeiljə] *n.* **1** any of various species and cultivated varieties of rhododendron (genus *Rhododendron*), especially those having funnel-shaped flowers and deciduous leaves. **2** the flower or cluster of flowers of any of these plants. ⟨< NL < Gk. *azaleos* dry < *azein* parch⟩

a•zan [ɑ'zɑn] *or* [ə'zæn] *n.* the Muslim call to public prayer, proclaimed five times a day by the muezzin, or crier, from the minaret of a mosque. ⟨< Arabic *adhān* invitation⟩

az•a•ta•dine ma•le•ate [ə'zætə,din 'mæli,eit] an antihistamine drug.

az•a•thi•o•prine [,æzə'θaɪə,prin] *n.* a drug used to suppress rejection of transplanted organs, and to treat rheumatoid arthritis. *Formula*: $C_9H_7N_7O_2S$

a•zed•a•rach [ə'zɛdə,ræk] *n.* **1** the astringent bark of a tropical Asian tree (*Melia azederach*), used medicinally. **2** the tree itself, also called **chinaberry.** ⟨< F *azédarac* < Sp. *acedaraque* < Arabic *azadirakht* < Persian *azad diraht*⟩

a•ze•o•trope [ə'ziə,troup] *n.* a mixture of liquids whose boiling point remains constant at a given pressure. ⟨< Gk. *a* not + *zein* to boil + *tropos* a turn⟩ **—,az•e•o'trop•ic** [,eiziə'trɒpɪk], *adj.*

A•zer•bai•jan [,æzərbaɪ'dʒɑn] *n.* a country in SW Asia. **—,A•zer•bai'jan•i** [-'dʒɑni], *n., adj.*

az•ide ['æzaɪd] *n.* any compound that contains the radical N_3.

A•zil•i•an [ə'zɪljən] *adj.* of or relating to a Paleolithic culture of the Pyrenees (c. 9500 B.C.) characterized by bone and antler harpoon heads.

az•i•muth ['æzəməθ] *n. Astronomy.* the angular distance east or west from the north point: *The azimuth of the North Star is 0°. A star due northeast from the observer has an azimuth of 45°E. Abbrev.*: az. ⟨ME < OF *azimut* < Arabic *as-sumūt* the ways < *samt* way⟩ **—,az•i'muth•al** [,æzɪ'muθəl], *adj.*

az•ine ['æzin], ['eizin], *or* ['æzɪn] *n.* any organic chemical compound, such as diazine or triazine, having a six-membered ring with at least one nitrogen atom. ⟨< azo- + -INE[2]⟩

az•lon ['æzlɒn] *n.* any synthetic fibre made from a chemically produced protein. ⟨< azo- + (*ny*)*lon*⟩

az•o– ['æzou] *or* ['eizou] containing nitrogen. ⟨< F *azote* nitrogen < Gk. *a-* not + *zōē* life, because nitrogen does not support life⟩

az•o•ben•zene [,æzou'bɛnzin] *or* [,æzoubɛn'zin], [,eizou'bɛnzin] *or* [,eizoubɛn'zin] *n.* an orange crystalline solid compound used in making dyes. *Formula*: $C_6H_5N{:}NC_6H_5$

a•zo•ic [ei'zouɪk] *or* [ə'zouɪk] *adj.* lifeless; showing no evidence of life.

az•ole ['æzoul] *n.* any organic chemical compound having a five-membered ring. ⟨< azo- + L *oleum* oil⟩

a•zon•al [ei'zounəl] *adj.* **1** of soil, not having distinct zones or layers. **2** of soil, having a profile largely determined by factors not related to local climate or vegetation.

a•zo•o•sper•mi•a [,eizouə'spɜrmiə] *n.* failure to form sperm; absence of sperm in the semen.

az•o•te•mi•a [,æzou'timiə] *n.* uremia. ⟨< F *azote* nitrogen + Gk. *haima* blood⟩ **—,az•o'te•mic,** *adj.*

az•o•tize ['æzə,taɪz] *or* ['eizə,taɪz] *v.,* **-tized, -tiz•ing.** nitrogenize.

Az•ra•el ['æzriəl] *n. Islamic and Jewish mythology.* the celestial being that takes the soul from the body. ⟨< Hebrew *Azrael* the Lord helped⟩

Az•tec ['æztɛk] *n., adj.* —*n.* **1** a member of the Indians who ruled Mexico before its conquest by the Spaniards in 1519. **2** the language of the Aztecs.
—*adj.* of or having to do with the Aztecs or their language.

az•ure ['æʒʊr], ['æʒər], *or* ['eiʒər] *n., adj.* —*n.* **1** blue; sky blue. **2** *Poetic.* the clear sky.
—*adj.* blue; sky blue. ⟨ME < OF *l'azur* the azure < Arabic < Persian *lajward* lapis lazuli⟩

az•u•rite ['æʒə,rəit] *n.* **1** a blue copper ore; a basic carbonate of copper. *Formula*: $2CuCO_3{\cdot}Cu(OH)_2$ **2** a gem made from it.

az•y•gous ['æzɪgəs] *adj.* occurring singly rather than in a pair. ⟨< Gk. *azygos* unmatched < *a* not + *zygon* yoke⟩

B b *B b*

b or **B** [bi] *n., pl.* **b's** or **B's. 1** the second letter of the English alphabet. **2** any speech sound represented by this letter. **3** a person or thing identified as **b,** especially the second in a series: *Company B in a battalion.* **4 B, a** a grade rating a person or thing as good but not excellent, the second level from the top, or best: *grade B beef.* **b** a person or thing receiving this rating. **5** *Music.* **a** the seventh tone in the scale of C major. **b** a symbol standing for this tone. **c** a key or string that produces this tone. **d** a scale or key that has B as its tonic. **6** *Algebra.* Usually, *b*, the second known quantity: $ax + by + c = 0$. **7 B, a** an antigen found in some human blood. **b** the type of human blood containing this antigen, one of the four types in the ABO system. **8 B,** a symbol used on pencils to indicate the degree of softness of the lead: *A 2B pencil is quite soft; 6B is very soft.* Compare **H** and **HB.** **9 b, a** bit. **b** binary. **10** something shaped like the letter B. **11** (*adjl.*) of or being a B or b. **12** any device, such as a printer's type, a lever, or a key on a keyboard, that produces a b or B. **13 b,** boliviano.
☛ *Hom.* BE, BEE.

B 1 boron. **2** *Chess.* bishop. **3** byte. **4** brightness. **5** magnetic induction.

B. 1 Bay. **2** Bible. **3** British. **4** bacillus.

B. or **b. 1** born. **2** book. **3** base. **4** baseman. **5** bat. **6** bass. **7** basso. **8** bachelor. **9** bolivar.

ba [bɑ] *Egyptian mythology.* the soul in the form of a bird.

Ba barium.

BA or **B.A. 1** British Airways. **2** batting average.

baa [bæ] *or* [bɑ] *n., v.* **baaed, baa•ing.** bleat. ⟨imitative⟩

Ba•al [beiəl] *or* [beil] *n., pl.* **Ba•al•im** ['beiəlɪm] **1** any of a number of local deities among the ancient Semitic peoples. **2** the chief god of the Canaanites and Phoenicians. In some places he was the god of fertility; in others, he was the sun god. **3** a false god. ⟨< Hebrew *bá'al* lord, master⟩ **—'Ba•al,ism,** *n.* **—'Ba•al,ite,** *n.*

baas•skap ['bɑskɑp] *n.* the total subordination of indigenous South Africans to European settlers. Compare APARTHEID. ⟨< Afrikaans *baas* master + *-skap* -ship⟩

ba•ba ['bɑbə]; *French* [ba'ba] *n.* a small, light cake, made with yeast and flavoured with rum, kirsch, etc. ⟨< F < Polish *baba,* originally, old woman⟩

ba•ba gha•nouj [gə'nuʒ] *or* [gɑ'nuʒ] a Middle Eastern appetizer consisting of eggplant flavoured with tahini, garlic, and lemon.

ba•bas•su [,bɑbə'su] *n.* any of a genus (*Orbignya*) of Brazilian palm trees. Its edible nuts are a source of oil. ⟨< Pg. *babaçú*⟩

bab•bitt ['bæbɪt] *n., v.* *—n.* a whitish alloy of tin, antimony, and copper, or a similar alloy, used in bearings, etc. to lessen friction. *—v.* furnish (a bearing) with babbitt. ⟨after Isaac *Babbitt* (1799-1862), an American inventor⟩

Babbitt metal babbitt.

bab•ble ['bæbəl] *v.* **-bled, -bling;** *n.* *—v.* **1** make indistinct sounds like a baby. **2** talk or speak foolishly. **3** talk too much; tell secrets. **4** reveal foolishly: *to babble a secret.* **5** murmur, as a brook does.
—n. **1** talk that cannot be understood: *A confused babble filled the room.* **2** foolish talk. **3** a murmur: *the babble of the brook.* ⟨ME *babel*; imitative⟩ **—'bab•bler,** *n.*

babe [beib] *n.* **1** a baby. **2** an innocent or inexperienced person; a person who is like a child. ⟨ME⟩

babe in arms 1 a very young baby. **2** an innocent or gullible person.

babe in the wood or **woods** a naïve, gullible, or childlike person; one who is so innocent or inexperienced as to be a likely victim of an unscrupulous person or plan.

Ba•bel ['bæbəl] *or* ['beibəl] *n.* **1** Babylon. **2 Tower of Babel,** in the Bible, a high tower built to reach heaven. God punished the builders by changing their language into several new languages. When they could not understand one another, they had to leave the tower unfinished. **3** Also, **babel, a** a confusion of many different sounds; noise. **b** a place of noise and confusion. **4** a plan that is impossible to fulfil. ⟨< Hebrew⟩

bab•e•si•o•sis [,bæbə'zaɪəsɪs], [,bæbə'saɪəsɪs], *or* [bə,bizi'ousɪs] *n.* an infectious cattle disease, carried by ticks, which affects the red blood cells; Texas fever.

ba•biche [bæ'biʃ] *or* ['bæbɪʃ] *n. Cdn.* rawhide thongs or lacings: *Babiche is often used in making snowshoes.* ⟨< Cdn.F < Algonquian⟩

Ba•bin•ski reflex [bə'bɪnski] a curling of the toes in response to a stroking of the sole of the foot: *The Babinsky reflex is normal in babies, but otherwise is a sign of nerve damage.* ⟨after J.F.F. *Babinski* (d. 1932), French neurologist⟩

bab•i•ru•sa, bab•i•rous•sa, or **bab•i•rus•sa** [,bæbə'rusə] *or* [,bɑbə'rusə] *n.* a wild pig (*Babyrousa babyrussa*) of the East Indies. The boar has long, curved tusks. It is an endangered species. ⟨< Malay *bābi* hog + *rūsa* deer⟩

Bab•ism ['bɑbɪzəm] *n.* a minority religion of Persia, founded in 1844, prohibiting polygamy, dealing in slaves, the consumption of alcohol, and begging. Also, **Babi.** **—'Bab•ist,** *n., adj.*

bab•ka ['bɑbkə] *or* ['bʌbkə] *n.* a light, sometimes rum-flavoured raisin bread often covered with a sweet glaze. ⟨< Polish⟩

ba•boo ['bɑbu] See BABU.

ba•boon [bə'bun] *n.* **1** any of various large, fierce monkeys of Africa and the Arabian peninsula having a doglike face and a short tail. **2** a clumsy, uncouth person; lout. ⟨ME < OF *babouin* stupid person⟩ **—ba'boon•er•y,** *n.* **—ba'boon•ish,** *adj.*

ba•bu ['bɑbu] *n., pl.* **-bus.** in India: **1** a form of address more or less corresponding to *Mr.*, used before the full name or following the first name of a man. **2** formerly, an Indian clerk who could write English. Also, **baboo.** ⟨< Hind. *bābū* father⟩

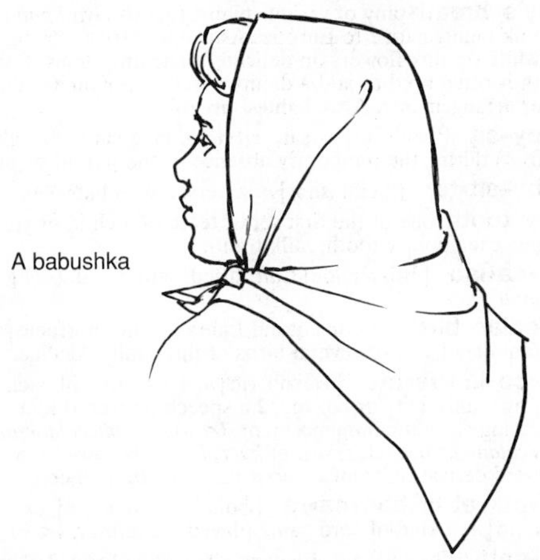
A babushka

ba•bush•ka or **ba•boush•ka** [bə'bʊʃkə]; *Russian,* [bɑ'buʃkə] *n.* **1** a woman's scarf or kerchief worn on the head and knotted under the chin. **2** a polite form of address when speaking to an elderly woman, not necessarily a relative. ⟨< Russian *babushka* grandmother, dim. of *baba* old woman⟩

ba•by ['beibi] *n., pl.* **-bies;** *v.* **-bied, -by•ing.** *—n.* **1** a very young child or animal. **2** the youngest of a family or group. **3** a person who acts like a baby; childish person. **4** *Slang.* a plan, idea, project, etc. that a person, group, etc. creates or is responsible for, especially one that is held dear or is a source of pride: *The society's baby for next year is the building of a new theatre.* **5** *Slang.* any person or thing: *That guy is a tough baby. This baby here is our best sedan.* **6** (*adjl.*) **a** of or for a baby: *baby shoes.* **b** very young: *a baby bird.* **c** small of its kind: *my baby finger, a baby grand piano.* **d** like that of a baby or child: *a baby face.*
—v. **1** treat as a baby; pamper or indulge: *to baby a sick child.* **2** operate or handle very carefully: *to baby a new computer.* ⟨ME *babe*⟩ **—'ba•by,like,** *adj.*

baby beef 1 the prime beef of a calf that has been fattened for one to two years before slaughtering. **2** a calf thus fattened.

baby blue pale blue.

baby bonus *Cdn. Informal.* the FAMILY ALLOWANCE.

baby boom the marked increase in the birth rate that characterized the period following the end of World War II during the years 1946–1965, peaking in 1961: *The baby boom caused a shortage of schools in the fifties and sixties.* **–baby boomer,** *n.*

baby buggy *Informal.* BABY CARRIAGE.

baby carriage a light, four-wheeled carriage used for wheeling a baby about.

baby doll a woman's short, sheer nightgown, worn with bikini panties. **–'ba•by-,doll,** *adj.*

ba•by–faced ['beibi ,feist] *adj.* **1** appearing to have extreme youth and innocence. **2** having a rather round, chubby, smooth face.

baby grand a small GRAND PIANO.

ba•by•hood ['beibi,hʊd] *n.* **1** the condition or time of being a baby. **2** babies as a group.

ba•by•ish ['beibiɪʃ] *adj.* like a baby; childish; silly. **–'ba•by•ish•ly,** *adv.* **–'ba•by•ish•ness,** *n.*

Bab•y•lon ['bæbə,lɒn] *or* ['bæbələn] *n.* **1** the capital of ancient Babylonia, on the Euphrates River and, later, of the ancient Chaldean empire. Babylon was noted for its wealth, power, magnificence, and wickedness. **2** any great, rich, or wicked city.

Bab•y•lo•ni•an [,bæbə'louniən] *adj., n. –adj.* **1** of or having to do with Babylonia, an ancient empire in SW Asia, or Babylon. **2** sinful, decadent, wealthy, etc.
–n. **1** a native or inhabitant of ancient Babylonia or Babylon. **2** the language of the ancient Babylonians.

Babylonian Captivity **1** the period spent by the Jews in exile in Babylonia from 597 to 538 B.C. under Nebuchadnezzar. **2** the period (A.D. 1309–1377) during which the popes were confined to Avignon in France.

baby's breath any of various plants (genus *Gypsophila*) of the pink family native to Europe, Asia, and Africa, having many tiny white or pink flowers on delicate branching stems. Baby's breath is often used to add a dainty touch to bouquets and to flower arrangements. Also, **babies'-breath**.

ba•by–sit ['beibi ,sɪt] *v.* **-sat, -sit•ting.** take care of (a child or children) during the temporary absence of the parent or parents.

ba•by–sit•ter ['beibi ,sɪtər] *n.* a person who baby-sits.

baby tooth one of the first set of teeth of a child or young animal; a temporary tooth; milk tooth.

bac•ca•lao [,bækə'leiou] *Cdn.* dried, salted cod. ⟨< Pg. *bacalhau*⟩

baccalao bird *Cdn.* in coastal Labrador and northeast Newfoundland, any of several birds of the family Alcidae.

bac•ca•lau•re•ate [,bækə'lɔriɪt] *n.* **1** a degree of bachelor given by a university or college. **2** a speech delivered to a graduating class at commencement. ⟨< Med.L *baccalaureatus* < *baccalaureus* bachelor, var. of *baccalarius*, because of a supposed derivation from L *bacca* berry + *laurus* laurel⟩

bac•ca•rat or **bac•ca•ra** [,bɑkə'rɑ], ['bɑkə,rɑ], *or* ['bækə,rɑ] *n.* a kind of card game played for money. ⟨< F⟩

bac•cate ['bækeit] *adj.* **1** having a berrylike form. **2** producing berries. ⟨< L *baccatus* < *bacca* berry⟩

Bac•chae ['bæki] *or* ['bækaɪ] *n.pl.* **1** female companions or worshippers of Bacchus. **2** priestesses of Bacchus. **3** women taking part in the Bacchanalia. ⟨< Gk.⟩

bac•cha•nal ['bækənəl], ['bɑkənəl], *or* [,bækə'næl] *adj., n.*
–adj. **1** having to do with Bacchus or his worship. **2** wild and noisy; orgiastic.
–n. **1** a worshipper of Bacchus. **2** a drunken reveller. **3** a wild, noisy party; bacchanalia. **4 Bacchanals,** *pl.* Bacchanalia. **5** a song, dance, poem, etc., for or about Bacchus. ⟨< L *bacchanalis* < *Bacchus* god of wine < Gk. *Bakchos*⟩

Bac•cha•na•li•a [,bækə'neiliə] *or* [,bækə'neiljə] *n.pl.* **1** in ancient Rome, a wild, noisy festival in honour of Bacchus. **2 bacchanalia,** a wild, noisy party; drunken revelry; orgy.

bac•cha•na•li•an [,bækə'neiliən] *or* [,bækə'neiljən] *adj., n.*
–adj. **1** having to do with the Bacchanalia. **2** drunken and riotous.
–n. a drunken reveller.

bac•chant ['bækənt] *n., pl.* **bac•chants** or **bac•chan•tes** [bə'kæntiz]; *adj. –n.* **1** a priest or worshipper of Bacchus. **2** a drunken reveller.
–adj. **1** devoted to Bacchus. **2** engaging in wild, drunken parties. ⟨< L *bacchans, -antis*, ppr. of *bacchari* celebrate the festival of Bacchus⟩ **–bac'chan•tic,** *adj.*

bac•chan•te [bə'kænti], [bə'kænt], [bə'kɑnt], *or* ['bækənt] *n.* **1** a priestess or female worshipper of Bacchus. **2** a woman who takes part in wild, drunken parties. ⟨< F⟩

Bac•chic ['bækɪk] *adj.* **1** of Bacchus or his worship. **2** Also, **bacchic,** drunken; riotous.

Bac•chus ['bækəs] *n. Greek and Roman mythology.* the god of wine. The Greeks also called him Dionysus.

bac•cif•er•ous [bæk'sɪfərəs] *adj.* bearing berries. ⟨< L *baccifer* < *bacca* berry + *ferre* carry⟩

bac•ci•form ['bæksə,fɔrm] *adj.* having the form of a berry. ⟨< L *bacca* berry + *forma* shape⟩

bac•civ•or•ous [bæk'sɪvərəs] *adj.* berry-eating. ⟨< L *bacca* berry + *vorare* devour⟩

bach [bætʃ] *v. Informal.* live independently as a single person; keep house for oneself (*often used with* **it**): *She's baching while her parents are away. He's been baching it for two years now.* ⟨< *bachelor*⟩
☛ *Hom.* BATCH.

bach•e•lor ['bætʃələr] *n.* **1** an unmarried man. **2** (*adjl.*) of, for, or designating a person who is not married or who lives alone: *a bachelor apartment.* **3** a bachelor apartment or flat: *The apartments on this floor are all bachelors.* **4** a person who holds the first degree offered by a university or college. **5** in the Middle Ages, a young knight serving under the banner of another. **6** a young male animal, not yet mated. ⟨ME < OF *bacheler* squire < Med.L *baccalarius* the holder of a small farm, a young man⟩

bachelor apartment a small apartment with a kitchen and bathroom but no separate bedroom.

bach•e•lor–at–arms ['bætʃələr ət 'ɑrmz] *n., pl.* **bachelors-at-arms.** BACHELOR (def. 5).

bachelor chest a chest of drawers to hold a man's clothing.

bach•e•lor•ette [,bætʃələ'rɛt] *n. Cdn.* a very small apartment consisting of one room with kitchen facilities and a bathroom; often, an illegal dwelling unit with less than the minimum floor space required by law.

bach•e•lor•hood ['bætʃələr,hʊd] *n.* the condition of being a bachelor.

bach•e•lor's–but•ton ['bætʃələrz 'bʌtən] *n.* **1** an annual plant (*Centaurea cyanus*) of the composite family, native to Europe but often grown in North America for its bright blue, mauve, pink, or white flowers; cornflower. **2** Often, **bachelor's buttons,** a perennial garden plant (*Ranunculus acris*) of the buttercup family native to Europe, having bright yellow double flowers.

bachelor suite BACHELOR APARTMENT.

Bach•i•an ['bɑxiən] *or* ['bɑkiən] *adj., n. –adj.* **1** of or having to do with Johann Sebastian Bach (1685-1750), a German composer of music. **2** in the style of his music.
–n. an interpreter or admirer of Bach's music.

ba•cil•lar [bə'sɪlər] *or* ['bæsələr] *adj.* **1** of or like a bacillus. **2** characterized by bacilli. **3** rod-shaped. Also, **bacillary** ['bæsɪ,lɛri].

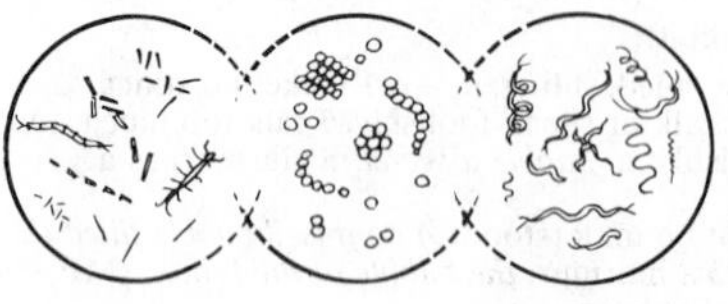

Three main types of bacteria, classified according to shape

ba•cil•li [bə'sɪlaɪ] *or* [bə'sɪli] *n.* pl. of BACILLUS.

ba•cil•li•form [bə'sɪlə,fɔrm] *adj.* rod-shaped.

ba•cil•lus [bə'sɪləs] *n.* **-cil•li. 1** any of a genus (*Bacillus*) of rod-shaped aerobic bacteria. **2** any rod-shaped bacterium. **3** loosely, any bacterium. ⟨< LL *bacillus*, dim. of *baculus* rod⟩

ba•ci•tra•cin [,bæsɪ'treisɪn] *n.* an antibiotic derived from a certain bacillus (*Bacillus subtilis*) used to treat skin infections. ⟨20c., < *bacillus* + *Tracy*, the name of the American girl whose infected wounds were found to contain the bacillus⟩

back [bæk] *n., adj., v., adv. –n.* **1** the part of a person's body opposite to the face and to the front part of the body: *a broad back. She turned her back to the wind.* **2** the upper part of an animal's body from the neck to the end of the backbone. **3** SPINAL COLUMN. **4** that part of a piece of clothing that fits over the back. **5** the side opposite or behind the front: *the back of the head, the back of the room.* **6** the upper, outer, or farther side or part: *the back of the hand, the back of the garden.* **7** the reverse or wrong side; the undecorated, unfinished, etc. side that is not meant to be displayed: *the back of a rug.* **8** the part of a chair, chesterfield, etc. that supports the back of a person sitting down. **9 a** the part of a book where pages are sewn or glued together. **b** the spine of the binding of a book. **10** *Sports.* **a** a player whose position is behind the front line, as a halfback in football. **b** the position of such a player.

behind (someone's) **back,** secretly and with a mean or scheming purpose: *He seemed to be a good friend but then I found out he was talking about me behind my back.*

get (one's or someone's) **back up,** *Informal.* make or become angry and stubbornly opposed: *She didn't mean to be critical, so don't get your back up.*

get off (someone's) **back,** *Informal.* stop nagging or criticizing someone: *I finally told him if he didn't get off my back I wouldn't do it at all.*

on (one's) **back,** helpless or incapacitated; especially, sick in bed: *He's flat on his back with the flu.*

on (someone's) **back,** *Informal.* continually nagging or criticizing a person.

put (one's) **back into, a** work hard at. **b** expend great effort on.

put (someone's) **back up,** *Informal.* make angry and stubbornly opposed: *It wasn't what she said, but the way she said it that put my back up.*

turn (one's) **back on, a** reject or ignore in contempt, anger, or indifference: *How can you turn your back on those people when they so obviously need help?* **b** forsake; renounce: *He turned his back on success and returned to his home town.*

with (one's) **back to the wall,** in a desperate situation; no longer able to run away: *Now, with their backs to the wall, they finally had to admit that they needed help.*

—adj. **1** opposite or behind the front: *the back seat of a car, the back fence.* **2** directed backward; performed facing backward: *a back step, a back flip.* **3** belonging to the past; not current: *the back numbers of a newspaper.* **4** due but not yet paid; overdue: *He still has some back debts to clear up.* **5** *Phonetics.* pronounced at the back of the mouth. The *o* in *go* is a back vowel. **6** in distant or frontier regions: *back country.*

—v. **1** support or help (*often used with* **up**): *Most of her friends backed her plan. If you make the request, we'll back you up.* **2** take financial responsibility for: *The show is backed by a group of local business people.* **3** move backward: *She backed away from the gun. She started the car and backed out into the street.* **4** cause to move backward: *to back a car.* **5** countersign: *to back a cheque.* **6** bet on: *to back a horse.* **7** be a background for: *A forest backed the little farm.* **8** have the back facing toward (*used with* **on** *or* **onto**): *Our house backs on a park.* **9** provide with a back or backing: *to back satin with crepe. The picture was backed with cardboard.* **10** *Meteorology.* of the wind, switch direction so as to blow counterclockwise.

back and fill, a trim sails so as to keep a boat in a channel and floating with the current. **b** of cars and trucks, go forward and backward alternately in order to get out of mud or snow, or to make a difficult turn. **c** *Informal.* be undecided; keep changing one's mind.

back down, give up a challenge or claim; withdraw.

back into, *Informal.* gain (something) mainly by accident: *He backed into a place on the hockey team when our star defenceman fell ill.*

back off, a move a short distance to the rear. **b** retreat from a previously-held claim or stance; stop insisting on something: *The salesperson backed off when the customer threatened to leave the store.*

back out (of), *Informal.* **a** withdraw from (an undertaking). **b** break (a promise).

back up, a move backward. **b** support or help. **c** make or become clogged or jammed: *Traffic was backed up because of the accident. The drain has backed up.* **d** *Computer technology.* make a backup (of): *All files on the hard disk are backed up onto tape every night.*

back water, a make a boat go backward. **b** reverse one's course; withdraw from a position, claim, etc.

—adv. **1** to or toward the rear; backward; behind: *Please step back.* **2** in or into the place or condition from which something or somebody came: *Put the books back. Let's go back to square one.* **3** in or toward the past: *some years back.* **4** in return: *Pay back what you borrow.* **5** in reserve: *Keep back enough sugar to do the icing.* **6** in check: *Hold back your temper.*

back and forth, first one way and then the other: *She paced back and forth impatiently.*

back of or **in back of,** *Informal.* behind: *The garden is back of the house.*

go back on, *Informal.* **a** fail to live up to: *to go back on one's word.* **b** not be faithful or loyal to: *He went back on his friends.* ⟨OE *bæc*⟩

☛ *Usage.* **Back of, in back of.** The form **in back of,** still not accepted by some speakers, has become much more common throughout Canada. It is now widely accepted, along with the form **back of.**

back•ache ['bæk,eik] *n.* a continuous pain in the back.

back bacon *Cdn.* bacon cut from the loin, having little fat and a hamlike flavour.

back•beat ['bæk,bit] *n. Music.* in 4/4 time, an accent on the second and fourth beats.

back bench Usually **back benches,** *pl.* **1** the seats in a parliament or legislative assembly occupied by backbenchers. **2** the position or rank of a backbencher: *He spent his entire political career on the back benches.*

back–bench or **back•bench** ['bæk ,bɛntʃ] *adj.* of or designating a backbencher or backbenchers: *back-bench MPs, a back-bench revolt.*

back•bench•er ['bæk,bɛntʃər] *n.* member of parliament or a legislative assembly who is not a member of the cabinet or one of the leading members of an opposition party.

back•bend ['bæk,bɛnd] *n.* an exercise in which the gymnast bends the body backward until the hands can touch the floor.

back•bit ['bæk,bɪt] *v.* pt. and a pp. of BACKBITE.

back•bite ['bæk,bəit] *v.* **-bit, -bit•ten** or **-bit, -bit•ing.** say spiteful or malicious things about (an absent person). **—'back,bit•er,** *n.*

back•bit•ten ['bæk,bɪtən] *v.* a pp. of BACKBITE.

back•board ['bæk,bɔrd] *n.* **1** a board that forms the back of something or acts as a support. **2** a board above and behind the basket on a basketball court. **3** a pediment.

back•bone ['bæk,boun] *n.* **1** in human beings and other vertebrates, the series of small bones along the middle of the back; spinal column. See SPINAL COLUMN for picture. **2** anything like a backbone, such as the keel of a ship, the spine of a book, or a range of mountains. **3** the most important part; the chief strength or support: *She is the backbone of the organization.* **4** strength of character: *A coward lacks the backbone to stand up for her beliefs.*

back•break•ing ['bæk,breikɪŋ] *adj.* physically very exhausting or tiring. **—'back,break•ing•ly,** *adv.*

back burner a heating element at the back of a stove.
on the back burner, *Informal.* in abeyance.

back•chat ['bæk,tʃæt] *n. Informal.* impudent or insolent retorts; talking back.

back•check[1] ['bæk,tʃɛk] *n., v. —n.* the examination of completed work to verify its accuracy.
—v. examine (completed work) to verify its accuracy.

back•check[2] ['bæk,tʃɛk] *v. Hockey.* skate back toward one's own goal to cover an opponent's rush, used especially of forwards who have themselves been attacking.

back–comb ['bæk ,koum] *v.* give (hair) a fuller appearance by lifting it in strands and combing the underlayers back toward the scalp.

back concessions *Cdn.* mainly in Ontario and Québec, rural or bush districts, as opposed to urban centres: *They have a small farm on the back concessions.*

back country a region away from any centre of population; rural or undeveloped areas; backwoods. **—'back-,coun•try,** *adj.*

back court **1** *Basketball.* **a** the part of the court containing one's team's own basket. **b** the defensive players in this area. **2** *Tennis.* the part of the court between the base line and the service line.

back•cross ['bæk,krɒs] *v., n. —v. Horticulture.* cross (a hybrid) with its parent or with a specimen genetically similar to its parent.
—n. the act or result of crossing two such specimens.

back•date ['bæk,deit] *v.* **-dat•ed, -dat•ing. 1** put a date on (something) earlier than the actual date. **2** count as being from a date earlier than the actual one.

back•door ['bæk'dɔr] *adj.* **1** secret; underhand; sly. **2** of or near the entrance at the back of a building: *Leave it by the backdoor stairway.*

back•drop ['bæk,drɒp] *n.* **1** the curtain at the back of a stage. **2** a background.

back East *Cdn.* in or to eastern Canada: *Many people in western Canada speak of Ontario as being back East.*

back•er ['bækər] *n.* a person who backs or supports another person, a contestant in a horse race, some plan or idea, a theatrical production, etc.

back•field ['bæk,fild] *n.* **1** *Football.* the players behind the front line: the quarterback, two halfbacks, flying wing, and fullback. In American football there is no flying wing. **2** *Baseball.* the outfield.

back•fill ['bæk,fɪl] *v., n.* —*v.* refill (an excavation) with soil or other material.
—*n.* the soil or other material used. **—'back,fill•er,** *n.*

back•fire ['bæk,faɪr] *n., v.* **-fired, -fir•ing.** —*n.* **1** in an automobile engine, an explosion, either of fuel igniting too soon in a cylinder or of unburned exhaust gases in the muffler. **2** a fire set to check a forest fire or prairie fire by burning off the area in front of it. **3** an explosion going the wrong way in a gun.
—*v.* **1** explode too soon or the wrong way. **2** use a backfire. **3** *Informal.* of a plan or scheme designed to gain something, have an unexpected result that is to the detriment or misfortune of the planner.

back formation a word formed from another word of which it appears to be the root. *Examples*: *burgle* from *burglar*; *edit* from *editor*; *pea* from *pease* taken as plural.

back forty *Cdn.* the back forty acres (almost half a hectare), that part of a farm most remote from the house and barn.

back•gam•mon ['bæk,gæmən] *or* [,bæk'gæmən] *n.* a game for two played on a special board with pieces moved according to the throw of dice. ⟨< *back*[1] + *gammon* game; because the pieces are sometimes set back⟩

back•ground ['bæk,graʊnd] *n., v.* —*n.* **1** the part of a picture or scene farthest from the viewer: *In this photograph, the cottage stands in the foreground with the mountains in the background.* **2** a surface against which things are seen; a surface upon which things are made or placed: *a cotton print with pink flowers on a white background.* **3** earlier or contemporaneous conditions or events, or any other facts, that help to explain some other condition or event: *the background of the two-party system.* **4** circumstances which provide contrast to an event: *MPs enjoying excessive perks against the background of a severe recession.* **5** one's past experience, knowledge, and training. **6** the accompanying music or sound effects in a play, film, etc. **7** static or other natural interference in radio or television signal.
in the background, out of sight; not in clear view; not prominent: *Though she remained in the background, her work was very important.*
—*v.* supply with a background. **—'back,ground•er,** *n.* **—'back,ground•ing,** *n.*

back•hand ['bæk,hænd] *n., adj., adv., v.* —*n.* **1** a stroke made with the back of the hand turned forward, especially in games like tennis, table tennis, or badminton. **2** handwriting in which the letters slope to the left.
—*adj. or adv.* backhanded.
—*v.* hit or catch backhanded.

back•hand•ed ['bæk,hændɪd] *adj., adv.*—*adj.* **1** done or made with the arm across the body and the back of the hand turned forward, as, in a tennis stroke. **2** of handwriting, slanting to the left. **3** awkward; clumsy. **4** ambiguous or sarcastic: *An example of a backhanded compliment is "I knew right away that you had made it yourself."*
—*adv.* using a backhand: *She did it backhanded.*
—'back,hand•ed•ly, *adv.* **—'back,hand•ed•ness,** *n.*

back•haul ['bæk,hɒl] *n., v.*—*n.* a return trip made empty by a truck or cargo ship after delivering a load.
—*v.* make such a return trip.

back•hoe ['bæk,hou] *n., v.* **-hoed, -hoe•ing.** —*n.* a machine for digging trenches for water mains, etc.
—*v.* use such a machine.

back•house ['bæk,hʌus] *n., pl.* **-hous•es** [-,haʊziz]. **1** a small outside toilet; privy. **2** a small building at the back of a main one.

back•ing ['bækɪŋ] *n., v.* —*n.* **1** support; help. **2** financial support. **3** supporters; helpers. **4** something placed at the back of anything to support or strengthen it. **5** *Informal.* musical accompaniment.
—*v.* ppr. of BACK.

back lake *Cdn.* formerly, in Upper Canada, one of the many lakes inland from the north shore of Lake Ontario, such as Lake Simcoe, Rice Lake, etc.

back•lash ['bæk,læʃ] *n.* **1** a sudden hostile reaction to an earlier action or series of actions that were not originally seen as a serious threat: *a backlash of anger. The fear of rebellion resulted in a pro-government backlash.* **2** a jarring reaction between worn or badly fitting parts of a machine or mechanism. **3** the movement or play of such parts. **4** a tangle in the part of a fishing line still on the reel after a cast.

back•less ['bæklɪs] *adj.* **1** having no back. **2** of women's dresses, swimsuits, etc., having the back of the bodice cut very low.

back•light ['bæk,ləit] *v.* **-lit, -light•ing.** light from behind.

back•list ['bæk,lɪst] *n., v.* —*n.* **1** the books of a publisher that have been previously advertised and are still in print. **2** a list or catalogue of such books.
—*v.* place on a backlist.

back•log ['bæk,lɒg] *n., v.,* **back•logged, back•log•ging.** —*n.* **1** an accumulation of orders, commitments, etc. that have not yet been filled: *The company hired extra staff to help clear the backlog of orders.* **2** a reserve supply; something saved or stored. **3** a large log at the back of a fire in a fireplace.
—*v.* of orders, commitments, etc., accumulate in this manner.

back nine *Golf.* the last nine holes (10 through 18).

back number **1** an old issue of a magazine or newspaper. **2** *Informal.* a person or thing that is old-fashioned or out-of-date.

back order an order for goods not currently in stock, received and acknowledged for filling at a later date.

back–or•der ['bæk ,ɔrdər] *v.* hold an order for (out-of-stock goods) for filling at a later date.

A backpack

back•pack ['bæk,pæk] *n., v.* —*n.* **1** a lightweight bag of nylon, canvas, etc., usually attached to a tubular metal frame that is strapped onto a person's back, used for carrying food, clothing, equipment, etc. **2** something, such as equipment, carried on the back, as by a radio operator, astronaut, etc. **3** a device attached to people or animals to provide information as to their condition, location, etc. **4** (*adj.*) of or designating a way of travelling, especially on foot, while carrying all one's belongings in a backpack: *We're going on a backpack holiday.*
—*v.* **1** travel in this way: *They backpacked 200 km last summer.* **2** carry (something or someone such as a baby) in a backpack. **—'back,pack•er,** *n.*

back•pack•ing ['bæk,pækɪŋ] *n., v.* —*n.* the action or sport of travelling, especially on foot, with all one's belongings carried in a backpack: *I had had no experience in wilderness backpacking.*
—*v.* ppr. of BACKPACK.

back•ped•al ['bæk,pedəl] *v.* **-alled** or **-aled, -al•ling** or **-al•ing. 1** move the pedals of a bicycle backward, especially to give a braking action. **2** *Boxing.* move backward to keep away from an advancing opponent. **3** modify or retreat from an opinion, promise, policy, etc.

back•rest ['bæk,rɛst] *n.* **1** anything that supports the back. **2** a support at the back, as on a lathe.

back road any little-used road, especially one in the country; side road.

back•room ['bæk,rum] *or* ['bæk,rʊm] *adj.* **1** working behind the scenes or away from public view: *the backroom movers of politics.* **2** done, performed, or decided without public knowledge: *He played a backroom role in the election.*

back•scat•ter ['bæk,skætər] *n., v.* —*n. Nuclear physics.* the deflecting of rays or particles at more than 90° from their source.
—*v.* deflect rays or particles at more than 90° from their source.

back•scratch•er ['bæk,skrætʃər] *n.* **1** any device for scratching the back. **2** *Informal.* a person who tries to gain advancement or maintain a position by flattering a superior; toady.

back•scratch•ing ['bæk,skrætʃɪŋ] *n. Informal.* the giving and taking of favours for reciprocal advantage.

back seat **1** a seat at or in the back. **2** *Informal.* a place of inferiority or insignificance.

back–seat driver **1** a passenger in an automobile who criticizes and advises the driver. **2** a person who offers criticism and advice without himself or herself assuming any responsibility.

back•set ['bæk,sɛt] *n.* a check to progress; setback.

back•sheesh or **back•shish** ['bʌkʃiʃ], ['bɑkʃiʃ], *or* ['bækʃiʃ] See BAKSHEESH.

back•side ['bæk,saɪd] *n.* **1** the back. **2** the rump; buttocks.

back•sight ['bæk,səit] *n. Surveying.* **1** a sighting taken in reverse. **2** something that marks such a sighting.

back•slap ['bæk,slæp] *v.,* **back•slapped, back•slap•ping.** slap (someone) on the back in a friendly or effusive manner: *He backslaps constantly, always looking for votes.*

back•slap•per ['bæk,slæpər] *n. Informal.* **1** a person who habitually slaps others on the back. **2** any person whose friendly manner is so hearty and effusive as to seem insincere.

back•slid ['bæk,slɪd] *v.* pt. and a pp. of BACKSLIDE.

back•slid•den ['bæk,slɪdən] *v.* a pp. of BACKSLIDE.

back•slide ['bæk,slaɪd] *v.* **-slid, -slid** or **-slid•den, -slid•ing.** slide back into wrongdoing; lose one's enthusiasm, especially for religion. **—'back,slid•er,** *n.*

back•space ['bæk,speis] *v.,* **-spaced, -spac•ing;** *n.* *—v.* move the carriage or element carrier of a typewriter or the cursor on a computer screen backward one space or a set number of spaces.
—n. **1** the key that controls this operation. **2** (*adjl.*) of or having to do with this key: *the backspace key.*

back•spin ['bæk,spɪn] a reverse spin given to a ball, hoop, etc., causing it to rebound from a surface at a different angle from the angle at which it hit.

back–stab•ber ['bæk ,stæbər] *n. Informal.* a person who secretly tries to harm another, usually by slander or betrayal.

back•stage ['bæk'steidʒ] *adv., adj.* *—adv.* **1** in the dressing rooms of a theatre. **2** toward the rear of a stage.
—adj. **1** located backstage. **2** of or having to do with people and activities backstage. **3** not known to the general public; confidential: *backstage negotiations.*

back•stairs ['bæk'stɛrz] *adj.* secret or underhand: *backstairs political bargaining, a backstairs romance.* Also, **backstair.**

back stairs **1** formerly, stairs in the back part of a house, used mainly by servants. **2** a secret or underhanded method or course: *Some people never do anything in the open but approach every deal by the back stairs.*

back•stamp ['bæk,stæmp] *n.* a stamp put on the back of an envelope to show the date of arrival.

back•stay ['bæk,stei] *n.* **1** a rope extending from the top of the mast to a ship's side and helping to support the mast. **2** a spring, rod, strap, or other support at the back of something.

back•stitch ['bæk,stɪtʃ] *n., v.* *—n.* **1** a stitching method in which the thread doubles back each time on the preceding stitch. **2** a stitch made in this way.
—v. sew with such stitches.

back•stop ['bæk,stop] *n., v.* **-stopped, -stop•ping.** *—n.* **1** *Sports.* a fence or screen used to keep the ball from going too far away. **2** *Sports.* a player who stops balls that get past another player. **3** any person or thing that acts as a support.
—v. Informal. **1** serve as a backstop (for). **2** support; reinforce.

back•stretch ['bæk,strɛtʃ] **1** the part of a horseracing track farthest from the winning post. **2** the stables, bunkhouses, etc., near a racetrack.

back•stroke ['bæk,strouk] *n., v.* **-stroked, -strok•ing.** *—n.* **1** a swimming stroke made with the swimmer lying on his or her back. **2** a competition in which each swimmer uses this stroke: *She won the backstroke.* **3** a backhanded stroke.
—v. **1** cover (a distance) by swimming the backstroke. **2** perform any backhanded stroke. **3** hit with such a stroke.

back•swim•mer ['bæk,swɪmər] an insect of the family Notonectidae, which uses its long legs to swim on its back.

back•swing ['bæk,swɪŋ] *n. Golf, Tennis, etc.* a raising of the club or racket up and behind the player's hands to give momentum to a following forward stroke.

back talk *Informal.* a talking back; impudent answers.

back–to–back ['bæk tə 'bæk] *adj.* **1** with the backs against each other or close together and the fronts or faces turned in opposite directions: *back-to-back seats in a train.* **2** *Informal.* consecutive: *They had four back-to-back wins.*

back•track ['bæk,træk] *v.* **1** go back over a course or path. **2** withdraw from an undertaking, position, etc.: *Luc backtracked on the claim he made last week.*

back•up ['bæk,ʌp] *n.* **1** a person, group, or thing that serves as a support, substitute, or reinforcement: *We need some sort of backup if we're going to convince them. I appointed Luc as backup in case Alice can't make it.* **2** (*adjl.*) serving as a support, substitute, or reinforcement: *backup advice.* **3** an accumulation or buildup because of delay, obstruction, etc.: *a backup of traffic.* **4** *Computer technology.* in computer systems, a copy of important programs or data stored on a disk or in a separate file in case the originals are destroyed or lost. **5** (*adjl.*) *Computer technology.* of or for such copying: *a backup disk, an automatic backup function.*

back•ward ['bækwərd] *adv., adj.* *—adv.* **1** toward the back: *She glanced backward.* **2** with the back foremost: *The little girl was trying to walk backward. He tumbled backward.* **3** toward the starting point: *The rolling ball came to a stop and began to roll backward.* **4** opposite to the usual way; in the reverse way: *to read backward.* **5** from better to worse: *Educational conditions in the town went backward.* **6** toward the past: *She looked backward forty years and talked about her childhood.* Also, **backwards.**
—adj. **1** directed toward the back: *a backward look.* **2** with the back first. **3** directed to or toward the starting point; returning: *a backward movement.* **4** done in the reverse way or order: *a backward process.* **5** reaching back into the past. **6** slow in development: *Backward children need special help in school.* **7** shy; bashful. **8** late; behind time: *This is a backward season; spring is two weeks late.* ⟨ME *bakward* < *bak* back + *-ward*⟩ **—'back•ward•ness,** *n.* **—'back•ward•ly,** *adv.*

☛ *Usage.* **Backward** and BACKWARDS are used interchangeably as adverbs: *Try doing the work backward. Try doing the work backwards.* Only *backward* is used as an adjective: *He hurried off without a backward glance.*

back•wards ['bækwərdz] *adv.* backward.
fall, lean, or **bend over backwards,** try extremely hard; be especially accommodating.

☛ *Usage.* See note at BACKWARD.

back•wash ['bæk,wɒʃ] *n.* **1** the water thrown back by oars, paddle wheels, the passing of a ship, etc. **2** a backward current. **3** a furor caused by some action.

back•wa•ter ['bæk,wɒtər] *n.* **1** a stretch of still, often stagnant water close to the bank of a river or stream. **2** a stretch of water that is held or pushed back, as by a dam. **3** a condition or place that is thought of as backward, stagnant, etc.: *The small, provincial town was often referred to as a cultural backwater.* **4** a backward current; backwash. **5** (*adjl.*) of or like a backwater: *backwater conditions.*

back•woods ['bæk,wʊdz] *n.pl., adj.* *—n.* uncleared forests or wild regions far away from towns.
—adj. **1** of the backwoods. **2** crude; rough.

back•woods•man ['bæk,wʊdzmən] *n., pl.* **-men.** a person who lives or works in the backwoods.

back•yard ['bæk'jɑrd] *n.* a yard behind a house: *They have a vegetable garden in their backyard.*
in (one's) **own backyard,** within one's own domain or area: *We have a lot of talented people right here in our own backyard.*
not in my backyard, an expression of protest indicating refusal to tolerate something viewed as unpleasant in one's vicinity.

ba•con ['beikən] *n.* salted and smoked meat from the back and sides of a pig. See PORK for picture.
bring home the bacon, *Informal.* **a** be successful; win the prize. **b** be the breadwinner. ⟨ME < OF < Gmc.⟩

Ba•co•ni•an [bei'kouniən] *adj., n.* *—adj.* **1** of or having to do with Francis Bacon (1561-1626), an English essayist, statesman, and philosopher. **2** of or suggestive of his writings or philosophy. **3** of or having to do with the theory, now no longer seriously entertained by most scholars, that Bacon wrote the plays of Shakespeare.
—n. **1** a person who supports or follows the philosophy of Francis Bacon. **2** a person who supports the theory that Bacon wrote the plays of Shakespeare.

bac•te•re•mia [,bæktə'rimiə] *n.* the existence of bacteria in the blood. ⟨< NL *bacter(ium)* + *-emia* < Gk. *bacterion* little staff + *haima* blood⟩

bac•te•ri•a [bæk'tiriə] *n.* pl. of BACTERIUM. a large, diverse group of one-celled micro-organisms found wherever there is life, in soil, water, and air, and within the bodies of other organisms. Many soil bacteria produce nitrogens that are useful for other organisms; some bacteria produce decay; some of the bacteria that live in other organisms cause disease. Bacteria have traditionally been classified as plants, but most authorities today place them in a separate kingdom. Bacteria are different from viruses. Compare VIRUS.

bac•te•ri•al [bæk'tiriəl] *adj.* of or caused by bacteria: *bacterial life, bacterial diseases.* **—bac'te•ri•al•ly,** *adv.*

bac•te•ri•cid•al [bæk,tirə'saɪdəl] *adj.* destructive to bacteria.

bac•te•ri•cide [bæk'tirə,saɪd] *n.* a substance that destroys bacteria. ⟨< *bacterium* + *-cide²*⟩

bac•te•ri•o•log•i•cal [bæk,tiriə'lɒdʒəkəl] *adj.* having to do with bacteriology. **—bac,te•ri•o'log•i•cal•ly,** *adv.*

bac•te•ri•ol•o•gist [bæk,tiri'ɒlədʒɪst] *n.* a person trained in bacteriology, especially one whose work it is.

bac•te•ri•ol•o•gy [bæk,tiri'ɒlədʒi] *n.* the science that deals with bacteria.

bac•te•ri•ol•y•sis [bæk,tiri'ɒləsɪs] *n.* the destruction or elimination of bacteria. ⟨< NL < Gk. *bacterion* little staff + *lysis* a breaking up⟩ **—bac,te•ri•o'lyt•ic** [bæk,tiriə'lɪtɪk], *adj.*

bac•te•ri•o•phage [bæk'tiriou,feidʒ] *or* [bæk'tiriə-] *n.* a virus that causes infection in a bacterium.

bac•te•ri•o•sta•sis [bæk,tiriə'steisɪs] *n.* the cessation of growth or spreading of bacteria. **—bac,te•ri•o'stat•ic** [-'stætɪk], *adj.*

bac•te•ri•um [bæk'tiriəm] *n.* sing. of BACTERIA. ⟨< NL < Gk. *bactērion*, dim. of *baktron* stick, staff⟩

bac•te•roid ['bæktə,rɔɪd] *adj., n.—adj.* having a form like that of bacteria.
—n. a bacterium whose structure has been altered.

Bac•tri•an camel ['bæktriən] a camel (*Camelus bactrianus*) of the highlands of central Asia, having two humps and somewhat shorter legs and a heavier build than the Arabian camel. It cannot travel as fast as the latter, but it can keep its pace longer in a caravan. ⟨< *Bactria*, an ancient country in Asia⟩

bac•u•lum ['bækjələm] *n.* a thin, rigid bone in the penis of many animals including carnivores, rodents, and some primates, to support erection. ⟨< L, a stick⟩

bad [bæd] *adj.* **worse, worst;** *adv. —adj.* **1** not good; not acceptable; poor or inferior in quality or skill: *bad poetry, a bad shipment, a bad singer. The light was bad. That desk shows bad construction.* **2** unfavourable, unpleasant, or distressing: *bad news. He came at a bad time.* **3** severe: *a bad cold, a bad storm.* **4** evil; wicked: *a bad influence. He said they were bad through and through.* **5** naughty: *Don't be a bad girl!* **6** disagreeable or sullen: *a bad mood. She's in a bad temper.* **7** harmful: *It is bad for your eyes to read in dim light.* **8** sick; suffering: *He's feeling very bad with his cold.* **9** sorry; regretful: *I feel bad about losing your baseball.* **10** worthless; not valid: *a bad cheque, a bad debt.* **11** incorrect; faulty: *a bad guess, bad grammar.* **12** rotten; spoiled: *The fish is bad; we'll have to throw it out.* **13** run-down; partly ruined, especially because of neglect: *bad teeth. The car was in bad condition.* **14** (*noml.*) **the bad,** that which is bad; a bad condition, quality, etc.: *She realized she'd have to take the bad with the good.*
go bad, a become spoiled or rotten: *We forgot about the leftovers and they went bad.* **b** develop a bad moral character.
in bad, *Informal.* in disfavour (with someone): *I'm in bad with my sister because I accidentally sat on her banjo.*
not bad, *Informal.* average; acceptable: *The movie's not bad, but I've seen better.*
not half bad, *Informal.* better than average; rather good: *I wasn't expecting much of the movie, but it's really not half bad.*
not so bad, *Informal.* better than expected: *I was dreading the test, but it wasn't so bad.*
to the bad, a toward a degenerative or ruined state: *a promising youth who went to the bad.* **b** in debt: *That last foolish deal put her several hundred dollars to the bad.*
—adv. Slang. badly: *It hurts bad.* ⟨ME *badde*; ? < OE *bæddel* hermaphrodite⟩ **—'bad•ness,** *n.*
☛ *Hom.* BADE.
☛ *Usage.* **Bad,** BADLY. In standard English a linking verb is followed by the adjective **bad**, not the adverb **badly:** *She feels bad about the loss.* However, **badly** is common and generally accepted in informal speech: *She feels badly about the loss.*

bad actor someone or an animal that misbehaves: *That horse is a bad actor.*

Ba•da•ri•an [bə'dæriən] *or* [bə'dɛriən] *adj.* of or designating an Egyptian Neolithic culture characterized by the manufacture of pottery and ornaments, and the raising of cattle. ⟨< *Badari*, a village in Egypt where remains were found⟩

bad blood an unfriendly feeling; hate: *The bad blood between the two men grew to a full-scale feud.*

bad cheque a cheque for which there is insufficient money in the account.

bad•die or **bad•dy** ['bædi] *n., pl.* **-dies.** *Informal.* a bad person; an enemy or opponent in public opinion, in a story or film, etc.: *The heroine easily routs the baddies.*

bade [bæd] *or* [beid] *v.* a pt. of BID (defs. 1, 2, 5, 7).
☛ *Hom.* BAD [bæd].
☛ *Usage.* **Bade** is used chiefly in formal and literary English: *The king bade her remain.*

bad egg *Informal.* a bad person.

badge [bædʒ] *n.* **1** something worn to show that a person belongs to a certain occupation, school, class, club, society, etc.: *The Red Cross badge is a red cross on a white background.* **2** a symbol; sign: *The traditional badge of office of a mayor is a chain.* ⟨ME *bage*; origin unknown⟩

badg•er ['bædʒər] *n., v. —n.* **1** any of various nocturnal burrowing animals of the weasel family having a wide, heavy body with long, grizzled fur, a long snout, and long, sharp claws on the forefeet. The American badger (*Taxidea taxus*), the only New World species, is found from the Canadian prairies south to Mexico. **2** the fur of a badger.
—v. **1** keep after (someone); try again and again to convince: *A car salesman has been badgering my father for weeks.* **2** harass by persistent questioning: *The judge objected to the way the lawyer was badgering the witness.* ⟨? < *badge*; with reference to the white spot on its head⟩

badge reader *Computer technology.* an electronic scanner capable of reading information coded magnetically or optically on a badge.

bad•i•nage [,bædə'nɑʒ] *or* ['bædə,nɑʒ] *n.* good-natured joking; banter. ⟨< F *badinage* < *badiner* banter < *badin* silly < VL *batare* gape⟩

bad•lands ['bæd,lændz] *n.* a barren region marked by ridges, gullies, and weird rock formations caused by erosion, as found in parts of southern Saskatchewan and Alberta.

bad•ly ['bædli] *adv.* **1** in a bad manner. **2** greatly; very much: *Rain is badly needed.*
☛ *Usage.* See note at BAD.

bad•man ['bæd,mæn] *n.* a villain of the Old West.

bad•min•ton ['bædmɪntən] *n.* a game in which either two or four players use light rackets to volley a shuttlecock over a high net. ⟨< *Badminton*, the Duke of Beaufort's estate in Gloucestershire, England⟩

bad–mouth ['bæd ,mʌuθ] *v. Slang.* speak badly of; disparage or criticize: *to bad-mouth a political opponent.*

bad–tem•pered ['bæd 'tɛmpərd] *adj.* **1** having a bad temper or disposition; angry or cross: *a bad-tempered horse.* **2** displaying irritation: *a bad-tempered remark.*

Bae•de•ker ['beidəkər] *n.* a guidebook for travellers. ⟨< Karl *Baedeker* (1801-1859), German publisher of a series of guidebooks⟩

baff [bæf] *v., n. —v.* **1** *Golf.* strike the ground with the sole of the club in making a stroke. **2** *Scottish.* strike a blow.
—n. **1** *Golf.* the act of baffing. **2** *Scottish.* a blow. ⟨probably < OF *baffe* a blow⟩

baf•fle ['bæfəl] *v.* **-fled, -fling;** *n. —v.* **1** be too hard for (a person) to understand or solve; confuse: *This puzzle baffles me.* **2** hinder or thwart. **3** struggle without success: *The ship baffled bravely with the storm.* **4** control (radio interference) with a baffle.
—n. **1** a wall, screen, or similar device controlling the flow of air, water, etc. by hindering its movement or changing its course. **2** a device that stops sound wave interference between the front and back of the loudspeaker in a radio or other audio equipment. ⟨? < Scots *bauchle* ridicule⟩ **—'baf•fler,** *n.*
☛ *Syn. v.* **2.** See note at FRUSTRATE.

baf•fle•gab ['bæfəl,gæb] *n. Slang.* meaningless or incomprehensible talk designed to impress or confuse a listener, avoid making a direct statement, etc.: *political bafflegab.*

baf•fle•ment ['bæfəlmənt] *n.* the act of baffling or the state of being baffled.

baf•fling ['bæflɪŋ] *adj., v.—adj.* **1** puzzling. **2** hindering; thwarting.
—v. ppr. of BAFFLE.

bag [bæg] *n., v.* **bagged, bag•ging.** *—n.* **1** a container made of paper, cloth, plastic, leather, etc. that can be pulled together or folded over to close at the top. **2** the amount that a bag can hold: *She ate a whole bag of cookies.* **3** a bag and its contents: *Could you please buy a bag of milk?* **4** a baglike membrane or sac in an animal's or human's body. **5** anything suggesting a bag by its use or shape, such as a suitcase. **6 a** the game killed or caught at one time by a hunter. **b** the container which the game is put in. **7** *Baseball.* a base. **8** a person's particular interest, activity, skill, etc.: *Math was never his bag.* **9** a woman's purse; handbag.
bag and baggage, with all one's belongings; entirely.
in the bag, *Informal.* certain to succeed or be achieved; sure: *Don't worry; the contract's in the bag.*
leave (someone) **holding the bag,** *Informal.* leave (someone) to take all the responsibility or blame alone instead of sharing it: *We had agreed to do the dishes, but after dinner he suddenly remembered a phone call he had to make and left me holding the bag.*
—v. **1** put into a bag or bags: *to bag vegetables.* **2** swell or bulge, or cause to do so: *His trousers bag at the knees.* **3** hang loosely. **4** *Hunting.* kill or catch. **5** *Slang.* catch; take; steal; collect. ⟨ME < ON *baggi* pack⟩
☛ *Syn. n.* **1. Bag,** SACK = a container made of paper, cloth, etc. that can be closed at the top. **Bag** is the general word, applying to any such container of suitable size and material: *Fresh vegetables are sometimes sold in cellophane bags.* **Sack,** in Canada and the United Kingdom, applies particularly to a large bag made of coarse cloth: *a sack of grain or potatoes.* In parts of the United States, **sack** is the general word.

ba•gasse [bə'gæs] *n.* the pulp of sugar cane after the juice has been extracted. ⟨< F < Provençal *bagasso* husks⟩

bag•a•telle [,bægə'tɛl] *or* ['bægə,tɛl] *n.* **1** a mere trifle; thing of no importance. **2** a game resembling billiards. **3** *Music.* a short, light composition. ⟨< F < Ital. *bagatella,* dim. of *baga* berry⟩

bag boom *Cdn.* a type of boom used in towing logs, loosely packed and enclosed by linked boom logs.

ba•gel ['beigəl] *n.* a doughnut-shaped roll of yeast dough that is simmered in water and then baked. ⟨< Yiddish *beigel* < *beigen* twist; related to OE *bēag* ring⟩

ba•gel•ry ['beigəlri] *n., pl.* **-ries.** a store that makes and sells bagels.

bag•ful ['bæg,fʊl] *n.,* **1** the contents of a full bag. **2** *Informal.* a lot.

bag•gage ['bægɪdʒ] *n.* **1** suitcases, bags, etc. packed with belongings, that a person takes with him or her on a trip; luggage. **2** the equipment that an army takes with it, such as tents, blankets, ammunition, etc. **3** anything superfluous or useless or which acts as an impediment. ⟨ME < OF *bagage* < *bagues* bundles⟩
☛ *Syn.* **Baggage** (def. 1) and LUGGAGE are synonymous; however, the former term is usual in the United States, the latter in the United Kingdom. In Canada, both terms are used, but **luggage** often has special reference to suitcases, overnight bags, and other bags carried by hand; **baggage** is the usual term for heavier and more bulky items such as trunks, boxes, and crates, or for items that are checked or sent separately. Only **luggage** is used for suitcases, etc. when they are empty: *She bought a new set of luggage.*

baggage car a railway car used to carry passengers' baggage, mail bags, etc.

bag•gage•mas•ter ['bægɪdʒ,mæstər] *n.* a person in charge of receiving and dispatching baggage, especially at a railway station.

bag•gat•a•way [bə'gætə,wei] *n. Cdn.* formerly, a game of the First Nations of eastern Canada, from which lacrosse developed. It was sometimes played between nations, with as many as 200 men to a team. Also, **baggatiway.** ⟨< Algonquian⟩

bagged [bægd] *adj. Slang.* **1** drunk. **2** exhausted.

bag•ger ['bægər] *n.* a person whose work is putting goods, especially merchandise purchased in a store, into bags.

Bag•gie ['bægi] *n. Trademark.* a small plastic bag designed for storing food.
☛ *Hom.* BAGGY.

bag•ging ['bægɪŋ] *n., v. —n.* cloth for making bags.
—v. ppr. of BAG.

bag•gy ['bægi] *adj.* **-gi•er, -gi•est. 1** swelling; bulging. **2** hanging loosely: *baggy trousers.* **—'bag•gi•ly,** *adv.* **—'bag•gi•ness,** *n.*
☛ *Hom.* BAGGIE.

bag lady a poor, homeless woman who lives on the street and carries her possessions in shopping bags.

bagn•io ['bænjou] *or* ['bɑnjou] *n., pl.* **bagn•ios.** brothel. ⟨< Ital. *bagno* bath or bathhouse < L < Gk. *balaneion* bath⟩

bag•pipe ['bæg,pəip] *n.* Usually, **bagpipes,** *pl.* a musical wind instrument in which the sound is produced by a reed melody pipe and several drone pipes. The latter are supplied with air from a bag that is inflated by blowing through a mouthpiece or operating a bellows with the arm.

bag•pip•er ['bæg,pəipər] *n.* a person who plays the bagpipes.

ba•guette [bæ'gɛt] *n.* **1** a gem cut in a narrow oblong shape. **2** such a shape. **3** a narrow, long loaf of bread. **4** *Architecture.* a small, half-round moulding. ⟨< F < Ital. *bachetta* small stick⟩

bag•worm ['bæg,wɜrm] *n.* a moth (family Psychidae) whose larvae spin bag-shaped cocoons. The female has no wings or legs even when fully developed, and remains in the cocoon.

bah [bɑ] *interj.* an exclamation of scorn or contempt.

Ba•hai [bə'haɪ] *or* ['bɑhaɪ] *n., adj. —n.* **1** a person who believes in Bahaism. **2** Bahaism.
—adj. of or having to do with Bahaism. ⟨< Persian⟩

Ba•ha•ism [bə'haɪɪzəm] *or* ['bɑhaɪ,ɪzəm] *n.* a religious system founded in 1863 by Mirza Hussein Ali Nuri, a Persian religious leader who taught the basic unity of all religions. **—Ba'ha•ist,** *n.*

Ba•ha•mas [bə'hɑməz] *n.* **The Bahamas,** a country of 700 islands off the E Florida coast. See HAÏTI for map.

Ba•ha•mi•an [bə'heimiən] *or* [bə'hɑmiən] *n., adj. —n.* a native or inhabitant of the Bahamas.
—adj. of or having to do with the Bahamas.

Ba•ha•sa In•do•ne•sia [bɑ'hɑsə ,ɪndou'niʒə] the official language of Indonesia, based on a form of Malay that was widely used in SE Asia as a lingua franca.

Ba•ha Ul•lah [bɑ,hɑ ʊ'lɑ] *n.* the prophet and founder of Bahaism, who was born Mirza Hussein Ali in Persia, A.D. 1817.

Bah•rain [bɑ'rein] *n.* a country consisting of several islands in the Persian Gulf off the E coast of Saudi Arabia.

Bah•rai•ni [bɑ'reini] *n., adj.—n.* a native or inhabitant of Bahrain.
—adj. of or having to do with Bahrain.

baht [bɑt] *n.* **1** the basic unit of money in Thailand, divided into 100 satang. See table of money in the Appendix. **2** a coin worth one baht. ⟨< Thai *bāt*⟩

bai•dar•ka ['baɪdɑrkə] *or* [baɪ'dɑrkə] *n. Cdn.* a kayaklike skin boat with two or three cockpits. ⟨< Russian⟩

bai•ji ['baɪdʒi] *n.* a dolphin (*Lipotes vexillifer*) of the Yangtze River in China. It is an endangered species.

bail¹ [beil] *n., v. —n.* **1** a security necessary to set a person free from arrest until he or she is due to appear for trial. **2** the amount guaranteed. **3** the temporary freedom which this security grants: *She was allowed bail.*
go (or **stand**) **bail for, a** supply bail for. **b** vouch for; guarantee: *I'll go bail for their good behaviour on the trip.*
jump bail, disobey the orders of the court by not appearing at one's trial.
out on bail, released from jail temporarily while awaiting trial, on the strength of someone's having paid bail.
—v. **1** obtain the freedom of (a person under arrest) by guaranteeing to pay bail. **2** deliver (goods) in trust without change of ownership.
bail out, a supply bail for. **b** help (someone) out of a difficulty. ⟨ME < OF *bail* custody < *baillier* deliver < L *bajulare* carry⟩
☛ *Hom.* BALE.

bail² [beil] *n.* **1** the arched handle of a kettle or pail. **2** a hooplike support. The bails of a covered wagon hold up the canvas. **3** the part of a typewriter that holds the paper against the roller. ⟨ME < ON *beygla* sword guard⟩
☛ *Hom.* BALE.

bail³ [beil] *n., v.* *—n.* a scoop or pail used to throw water out of a boat.
—v. throw (water) out of (a boat) with a pail, a dipper, or any other container.
bail out, a make an emergency jump with a parachute from an aircraft. **b** throw accumulated water out of (something) with a pail, a dipper, or any other container. ⟨< F *baille* < L *bajulus* carrier⟩
☛ *Hom.* BALE.

bail⁴ [beil] *n.* **1** *Cricket.* either of two small bars that form the top of a wicket. **2** a partition separating horses in a stable. ⟨ME < OF *bail* barrier⟩
☛ *Hom.* BALE.

bail•a•ble ['beiləbəl] *adj.* **1** capable of being bailed. **2** permitting bail to be paid: *a bailable offence.*

bail•ee [bei'li] *n.* one to whom goods are committed in bailment.

bail•ey ['beili] *n., pl.* **-eys.** the outer wall or court of a medieval castle. ⟨var. of *bail⁴*⟩
☛ *Hom.* BAILIE.

Bail•ey bridge ['beili] a portable bridge made from prefabricated steel sections in a lattice design. ⟨after Sir Donald C. *Bailey*, an English engineer⟩

A Bailey bridge

bail•ie ['beili] *n.* in Scotland, an official of a town or city corresponding to an alderman. ⟨ME < OF *baillis*, variant of *baillif.* See BAILIFF.⟩
☛ *Hom.* BAILEY.

bail•iff ['beilɪf] *n.* **1** an official in charge of writs, processes, arrests, etc.; an assistant to a sheriff. **2** the officer of a court who has charge of prisoners while they are in the courtroom. **3** the overseer or steward of an estate. The bailiff collects rents, directs the work of employees, etc., for the owner. **4** formerly, in the United Kingdom, the chief magistrate in certain towns. **5** a person who is brought in by a landlord or other creditor to seize goods in lieu of rent or payment: *The bailiff repossessed our car when we couldn't make the payments.* ⟨ME < OF *baillif* < *baillir* govern < *bail* guardian, manager < L *bajulus* carrier⟩

bail•i•wick ['beilə,wɪk] *n.* **1** the district over which a sheriff or bailiff has authority. **2** the place or locality that a person is identified with: *She is a big name in her own bailiwick.* **3** a person's field of knowledge, work, or authority. ⟨< *bailie* + *wick* office < OE *wīce*⟩

bail•ment ['beilmənt] *n.* **1** *Law.* the delivery of goods by one person to another in trust. **2** the act of bailing an accused person.

bail•or ['beilər] *or* ['beilɔr] *n. Law.* one who commits goods in bailment to the bailee.

bail•out ['beil,ʌut] *n.* **1** the act of one who bails out. (See BAIL¹ and BAIL³.) **2** financial assistance of an enterprise by a government to keep it from going bankrupt.

bails•man ['beilzmən] *n., pl.* **-men.** a person who gives bail.

Bai•ly's beads ['beiliz] spots of light seen around the edge of the moon immediately before or after a total eclipse of the sun, as the sunlight shines through depressions on the moon's surface.

Bain wagon [bein] *Cdn.* formerly, a large freight wagon that was widely used in the West in the late 19th and early 20th centuries.

Bai•ram [baɪ'ram] *n.* either of two Muslim festivals, the **lesser Bairam**, following immediately after Ramadan, or the **greater Bairam**, occurring 70 days later. ⟨< Turkish⟩

bairn [bɛrn] *n. Scottish.* child. ⟨OE *bearn* < pp. of *beran* to bear, influenced by ON *barn* child⟩

bai•sa ['baɪsɑ] *n., pl.* **baisa.** a unit of money in Oman, $\frac{1}{1000}$ of a rial. See money table in the Appendix.

Bai•sak•hi Day [,bəi'sɑki] in Sikhism, the festival commemorating the day, April 13th or 14th, on which Guru Gobind Singh, the tenth and last of the founding gurus, created the Khalsa, or community of baptized Sikhs.

bait [beit] *n., v.* *—n.* **1** anything, especially food, used to attract fish, birds, or animals to catch them. **2** anything used to lure or attract.
—v. **1** put bait on (a hook) or in (a trap, etc.). **2** lure or attract. **3** set dogs to attack (a chained animal, etc.): *Bears and bulls were formerly baited as sport.* **4** torment or worry by unkind or annoying remarks, etc. **5** *Archaic.* stop and feed: *The coachman baited his horses.* ⟨ME < ON *beita* hunt with dogs, cause to bite and ON *beita* food, bait for fish, influenced also by ON *beit* pasture⟩ **—'bait•er,** *n.*
☛ *Hom.* BATE.

bait–and–switch ['beit ən 'swɪtʃ] *n.* a fraudulent method of selling something in which the customer is first lured by the promise of something cheaper which may or may not actually exist.

bait–cast•ing ['beit ,kæstɪŋ] *adj.* of or having to do with fishing equipment that uses the weight of the bait to unroll the line from the reel.

bait•fish ['beit,fɪʃ] *n.* fish caught for use as bait.

bait station a site at which poisoned bait is put out to destroy wolves and other marauding animals.

baize [beiz] *n.* a thick woollen or cotton cloth with a nap, used especially for pool table covers: *Baize is usually dyed green.* ⟨< F *baies*, pl. of *bai* chestnut-coloured < L *badius*⟩

bake [beik] *v.* **baked, bak•ing;** *n.* *—v.* **1** cook (food) by dry heat without exposing it directly to the fire. Breads and cakes are cooked by baking. **2** dry or harden by heat: *to bake bricks or china.* **3** become baked: *Cookies bake quickly.* **4** make or become very warm: *It is no longer safe to lie in the sun and bake.*
—n. an act of baking. ⟨OE *bacan*⟩

bake•ap•ple ['beik,æpəl] *n. Cdn., esp. Atlantic Provinces.* **1** a creeping plant (*Rubus chamaemorus*) of the rose family that grows in swampy areas, having single white flowers and amber-coloured, edible berries like small raspberries; cloudberry. **2** the berry of this plant.

baked Alaska a dessert consisting of ice cream in a meringue coating, sometimes with a base of cake. It is put in a hot oven for a few minutes to brown the meringue.

baked–ap•ple ['beikt ,æpəl] *n.* bakeapple.

baked beans haricot beans baked for a long time in a closed container with tomato sauce and spices.

Ba•ke•lite ['beikə,ləit] *or* ['beik,ləit] *n. Trademark.* a hard, heat-resistant plastic used to make beads, stems of pipes, umbrella handles, fountain pens, electric insulators, etc. ⟨after L.H. *Baekeland* (1863-1944), who invented it⟩

bake–off ['beik ,ɒf] *n.* a competition in baking.

bak•er ['beikər] *n.* **1** a person who makes or sells bread, pies, cakes, etc. **2** a dish or utensil in which to bake something. **3** a small portable oven.

baker's dozen thirteen.

bak•er•y ['beikəri] *n., pl.* **-er•ies.** a baker's shop; a place where bread, pies, cakes, etc. are made or sold.

bake sale a sale of homemade baked goods, especially one held by a charitable organization, etc. to raise money.

bake shop bakery.

bak•ing ['beikɪŋ] *n., v.* *—n.* **1** the process of cooking in dry heat. **2** the process of drying or hardening by heat. **3** the amount baked at one time; a batch.
—v. ppr. of BAKE.

baking powder a mixture of BICARBONATE OF SODA, starch, and an acid compound such as cream of tartar, used as a leavening agent in making biscuits, cakes, etc.

baking soda BICARBONATE OF SODA.

bak•la•va or **bac•la•va** ['bɑklə,vɑ] *or* [,bɑklə'vɑ] a Greek pastry made with nuts and honey. ⟨< Turkish⟩

bak•sheesh or **bak•shish** ['bʌkʃiʃ], ['bɑkʃiʃ], *or* ['bækʃiʃ] *n.* in Egypt, Turkey, India, etc., money given as a tip. Also, **backsheesh, backshish.** ⟨< Persian < *bakhshidan* give⟩

bal. balance.

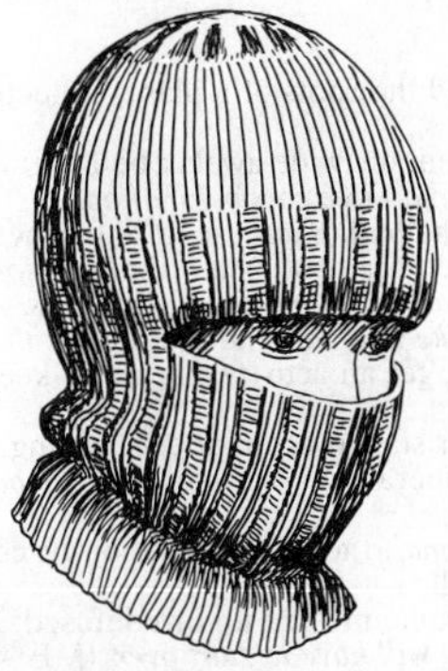
A balaclava

bal•a•clav•a [ˌbæləˈklɑvə] *or* [ˌbæləˈklævə] *n.* a type of knitted woollen headgear that covers all of the head and neck except the eyes. Also, **balaclava helmet.** ⟨< *Balaklava,* site of a battle in the Crimean War⟩

bal•a•lai•ka [ˌbæləˈləikə] *or* [ˌbɑləˈləikə] *n.* a Russian musical instrument resembling a guitar, but having only three strings and a triangular body. ⟨< Russian⟩

bal•ance [ˈbæləns] *n., v.* **-anced, -anc•ing.** *—n.* **1** an instrument for weighing, especially a device consisting of a horizontal bar freely suspended by its centre and having a matched platform or shallow pan at either end; something to be weighed is placed on one platform and objects of known mass are added to the other until the bar is exactly horizontal. It is often used as a symbol of justice. **2** equality in mass, amount, force, effect, etc. **3** a comparison of mass, value, importance, etc.; estimate. **4** the power to make decisions. **5** good proportion in design, etc.; harmony: *a balance of colours.* **6** a steady condition or position; steadiness: *He lost his balance and fell off the ladder.* **7** mental steadiness; poise. **8** anything that counteracts the effect, mass, etc. of something else. **9** *Accounting.* **a** the difference between the credit and debit sides of an account. **b** equality of debit and credit in an account. **10** the part that is left over; remainder: *They were dismissed from school for the balance of the term.* **11** a wheel that regulates the rate of movement of a clock or watch. **12** the greatest mass, amount, or power. **13** the rhetorical placing of two sentences or figures of speech in equivalent constructions. **14** *Dancing.* a balancing movement. **15 Balance,** *Astrology.* Libra.
in the balance, a undecided. **b** at stake.
on balance, overall; all things considered.
—v. **1** weigh in a balance or in one's hands to see which of two things is heavier. **2** make or be equal (to) in mass, amount, force, effect, etc. **3** compare the value, importance, etc., of. **4** make or be proportionate (to). **5** bring into or keep in a steady condition or position: *Can you balance a coin on its edge?* **6** counteract the effect, influence, etc. of; make up for. **7** *Accounting.* **a** make the credit and debit sides of (an account) equal: *to balance a budget.* **b** be equal in credit and debit: *The account doesn't balance.* **c** find a difference between the credit and debit sides of (an account). **8** manage (an account) by settling one's debts. **9** hesitate; waver. ⟨ME < OF < LL *bilanx, bilancis* two-scaled < *bi-* two + *lanx* scale[2]⟩ **—ˈbal•anc•er,** *n.*

balance beam a long, narrow piece of wood set up at some distance from the floor, on which gymnasts perform exercises.

balance billing *Cdn.* a system by which a doctor charges more than the rates allowed under the provincial health program, billing the difference (or balance) to the patient. This is illegal in some provinces.

bal•anced [ˈbælənst] *adj., v.—adj.* **1** of two or more things, in equilibrium. **2** consisting of different elements in good proportion: *a balanced curriculum.* **3** mentally and emotionally stable.
—v. pt. and pp. of BALANCE.

balanced diet a diet having the correct amounts of all the kinds of food from the four food groups necessary for health.

balance of nature *Ecology.* equilibrium among interacting communities of animals or plants and their habitat, maintained by natural processes such as adaptation and competition.

balance of payments a calculation of the credit and debit of an organization or country in respect to debtors and creditors in the same or another country.

balance of power **1** an even distribution of military and economic power among nations or groups of nations. **2** any even distribution of power. **3** the power of a small group to give control to a large group by joining forces with it.

balance of trade the difference between the value of all the imports and that of all the exports of a country.

balance point the place along the length of an object at which the mass of each side is equal.

balance sheet a written statement showing the profits and losses, the assets and liabilities, and the net worth of a business.

balance wheel a wheel for regulating motion. A clock or watch has a balance wheel that controls the movement of the hands. See ESCAPEMENT for picture.

bal•as [ˈbæləs] *or* [ˈbeiləs] *n.* a semiprecious stone, a type of orange or pink ruby. ⟨ME *baleis* < OF *balais* < Med.L *balascius* < Arabic *balakhsh,* after Persian *Badahšān,* a province in Afghanistan where the stone is found⟩

bal•a•ta [ˈbælətə] *n.* **1** a hard, non-elastic, rubberlike substance made by drying the milky juice of a tropical American tree (*Manilkara bidentata*) of the sapodilla family, used in making golf balls, belting, etc. **2** the tree itself. ⟨< Sp.⟩

bal•bo•a [bælˈbouə] *n.* **1** a unit of money in Panama, equal to 100 centésimos. See table of money in the Appendix. **2** a coin worth one balboa. ⟨< Vasco de *Balboa* (1475-1517), a Spanish explorer⟩

bal•brig•gan [bælˈbrɪgən] *n.* **1** a type of knitted cotton cloth, used for stockings, underwear, etc. **2** a similar type of knitted woollen cloth. **3 balbriggans,** *pl.* knitted cotton stockings or pyjamas. ⟨originally made at *Balbriggan,* Ireland⟩

bal•co•nied [ˈbælkənid] having a balcony. ⟨< balcony⟩

bal•co•ny [ˈbælkəni] *n., pl.* **-nies. 1** an outside projecting platform with an entrance from an upper floor of a building. **2** in a theatre or hall, a projecting upper floor with seats for an audience. ⟨< Ital. *balcone* < *balco* scaffold < OHG *balcho* beam⟩

bald [bɒld] *adj.* **1** wholly or partly without hair on the head. **2** without its natural covering: *A mountaintop with no trees or grass on it is bald.* **3** bare; plain; unadorned. **4** undisguised: *The bald truth is that she is a thief.* **5** of tires, having little or no tread remaining. **6** *Zoology.* having white on the head: *the bald eagle.* ⟨ME *balled,* apparently < obsolete *ball* white spot⟩ **—ˈbald•ly,** *adv.* **—ˈbald•ness,** *n.*

bal•da•chin or **bal•da•quin** [ˈbɒldəkɪn] *or* [ˈbældəkɪn] *n.* **1** a canopy of stone, metal, or other material over an altar, throne, etc. **2** a canopy of silk brocade or other fabric carried in solemn procession. **3** a similar canopy above a dais, etc. **4** a heavy brocade, formerly made of silk and gold. ⟨< F *baldaquin* < Ital. *baldac(c)hino* < *Baldacco,* Italian name of Baghdad, where the silk was made⟩

bal•da•chi•no [ˌbɒldəˈkinou] *or* [ˌbældəˈkinou] *n.* baldachin.

bald cypress a large coniferous tree (*Taxodium distichum*) of the same family as the redwood, native to swampy parts of the SE United States and Mexico, having feathery leaves, a thick trunk, and 'knees', produced by the root system, that project above the surface of the water. It is named for the fact that, unlike most conifers, it loses its leaves each fall.

bald eagle a large North American eagle (*Haliacetus leucocephalus*) having plumage that is mainly dark brown on the body and wings and pure white on the head, neck, and tail. Bald eagles feed mainly on fish. They are an endangered species.

Bal•der [ˈbɒldər] *n. Norse mythology.* the god of light, beauty, goodness, wisdom, and peace. Also, **Baldor, Baldur.**

bal•der•dash [ˈbɒldərˌdæʃ] *n., interj.* nonsense. ⟨< 16c. slang, meaning a senseless mixture of drinks such as milk and beer⟩

bald–faced [ˈbɒld ˌfeist] *adj.* **1** of animals, having a white face or white markings on the face. **2** open and without shame or embarrassment: *a bald-faced lie.*

bald•head [ˈbɒldˌhɛd] *n.* **1** a person who has a bald head. **2** a breed of pigeon. **3** any of various birds with a whitish spot on the head.

bald•head•ed [ˈbɒldˌhɛdɪd] *adj.* **1** having little or no hair on the head. **2** *Cdn.* devoid of trees or brush: *baldheaded prairie.*

bald•ing [ˈbɒldɪŋ] *adj.* going bald; becoming bald.

Bal•dor [ˈbɒldər] *n.* See BALDER.

bald•pate [ˈbɒldˌpeit] *n.* **1** a person who has a bald head. **2** a wild duck (*Anas americana,* also classified as *Mareca americana*) found throughout W North America, the male having a noticeable white patch on the forehead and crown; widgeon.

bald prairie that part of the western prairie which is almost without trees.

bal•dric ['bɒldrɪk] *n.* a belt hung from one shoulder and across the chest to the opposite side of the body, used to support a sword, horn, etc. ⟨ME *baudry* < OF *baudrei*, of obscure origin; akin to MHG *balderich* girdle⟩

Bal•dur ['bɒldər] See BALDER.

Bald•win ['bɒldwɪn] *n.* a type of apple with red skin and piquant flesh.

bal•dy ['bɒldi] *n. Informal.* someone who is bald.

bale[1] [beil] *n., v.* **baled, bal•ing.** *—n.* **1** a large bundle of merchandise or material securely wrapped or bound for shipping or storage: *bales of hay, a bale of paper.* **2** a group of turtles.
—v. make into bales; tie in large bundles. ⟨ME, probably < Flemish < OF < OHG *balla* ball[1]⟩
☛ *Hom.* BAIL.

bale[2] [beil] *n. Archaic or poetic.* **1** evil; harm. **2** sorrow; pain. ⟨OE *bealu*⟩
☛ *Hom.* BAIL.

ba•leen [bə'lin] *or* [bei'lin] *n.* **1** an elastic horny substance that grows in large, fringed, parallel plates or sheets from the roof of the mouth of baleen whales. It traps the plankton taken into the whale's mouth with water. **2** BALEEN WHALE. ⟨ME < OF *baleine* < L *balena*, var. of *balaena* < Gk. *phalaina* whale⟩

baleen whale any of a suborder (Mysticeti) of mostly large whales that includes the right whales, rorquals, and the blue whale, all lacking teeth but having baleen for trapping the plankton and small crustaceans on which they feed, and having paired blowholes.

bale•fire ['beil,faɪr] *n. Archaic.* **1** an outdoor bonfire. **2** a signal fire. **3** a pyre.

bale•ful ['beilfəl] *adj.* **1** evil; harmful. **2** *Archaic.* sorrowful; miserable. **—'bale•ful•ly,** *adv.* **—'bale•ful•ness,** *n.*

bal•er ['beilər] *n.* **1** a person who bales. **2** a machine that compresses and ties up into bundles such things as hay, straw, paper, and scrap metal.

Ba•li•nese [,bɑlə'niz] *n., pl.* **-nese;** *adj. —n.* **1** a native or inhabitant of Bali, an island in Indonesia. **2** the language of the Balinese. **3** a breed of domestic cat related to the Siamese, having blue eyes and long, pale hair with darker patches on the face, ears, feet, and tail.
—adj. of or having to do with Bali, its people, or their language.

bal•ise [bə'liz] *Cdn.* one of a series of evergreen shrubs set up as markers at intervals of about 10 m to outline the edges of winter roads, ice-roads, etc. ⟨< F⟩

balk [bɒk] or [bɒlk] *v., n. —v.* **1** stop short and stubbornly; refuse to go on. **2** thwart; hinder; check: *The police balked the robber's plans.* **3** fail to use; let slip; miss. **4** *Sports.* make an incomplete or misleading move. **5** *Baseball.* cause (a runner on third base) to score by illegally faking a pitch. **6** draw back in fear or distaste: *The child balked at the rice pudding.*
—n. **1** an act of balking. **2** a hindrance; check; defeat. **3** a blunder or mistake. **4** *Sports.* an incomplete or misleading motion, especially an illegal false move to throw the ball, made by a baseball pitcher when there are runners on base. **5** *Billiards.* a space between the cushions and the BALKLINE. **6** a ridge between furrows; a strip left unploughed. **7** a large beam or timber. ⟨OE *balca* ridge⟩
☛ *Hom.* BOCK [bɒk].

Bal•kan ['bɒlkən] *adj.* **1** of or having to do with the Balkan Peninsula in SE Europe. **2** of or having to do with the countries of the Balkan Peninsula or their inhabitants. **3** of or having to do with the Balkan Mountains in Bulgaria.

bal•kan•ize ['bɒlkə,naɪz] *v.* **-ized, -iz•ing.** divide (a country or territory) into small independent units, as the countries of the Balkan Peninsula were divided after World War I.
—,bal•kan•i'za•tion *n.* ⟨< *Balkan* countries + *-ize*⟩

balk•line ['bɒk,laɪn] *or* ['bɒlk,laɪn] *n. Billiards.* a line on the table from behind which the player first shoots with the cue ball.

balk•y ['bɒki] *or* ['bɒlki] *adj.* **balk•i•er, balk•i•est.** balking or likely to balk: *a balky horse.* **—'balk•i•ly,** *adv.* **—'balk•i•ness,** *n.*

ball[1] [bɒl] *n., v. —n.* **1** a round or oval object that is thrown, kicked, knocked, bounced, or batted about in various games. **2** a game in which some kind of ball is thrown, hit, or kicked. **3** a ball in motion: *a fast ball.* **4** the game of baseball. **5** *Baseball.* a delivery of a ball pitched too high, too low, or not over the plate and not struck at by the batter. **6** bullet, cannonball, or such projectiles collectively. **7** anything round or roundish; something that resembles a ball: *a ball of string, the ball of the thumb.* **8** a globe or sphere; the earth. **9** the roots of a plant, collected in a bundle for transshipment.
be on the ball, *Slang.* be mentally wide awake; be alert: *He's really on the ball today; he sold three cars before noon.*
get or **have something on the ball,** *Slang.* acquire or have quickness of mind and good judgment: *She must have something on the ball, because she's already figured out the answers. Anybody who would do a silly thing like that can't have much on the ball.*
get or **keep the ball rolling,** get an activity started or keep it going.
play ball, a begin a game or start it again after stopping. **b** get busy. **c** work together; co-operate: *If everyone will play ball, we can get the job done quickly.*
the whole ball of wax, *Informal.* the entire situation or collection.
—v. make or form into a ball.
ball up, *Slang.* make or become messed up or confused: *They have balled it up so badly we will have to start over.* ⟨ME < ON *böllr*⟩
☛ *Hom.* BAWL.

ball[2] [bɒl] *n.* **1** a large, formal party with dancing. **2** *Informal.* a very good time; a lot of fun: *We had a ball at the party.* ⟨< F *bal* < *baler* to dance < LL *ballare*⟩
☛ *Hom.* BAWL.

bal•lad ['bæləd] *n.* **1** a simple song. **2** a poem that tells a story in a simple verse form, especially one that tells a popular legend and is passed orally from one generation to another: *Troubadours used to sing ballads.* **3** the music for such a poem. **4** a popular love song, usually slow. ⟨ME < OF *balade* < Provençal *balada* dancing song⟩

bal•lade [bə'lɑd] *n. French.* **1** a poem having three stanzas of eight or ten lines each, followed by an envoy of four or five lines. The last line of each stanza and of the envoy are the same, and the same rhyming sounds recur throughout. **2** *Music.* an instrumental composition, usually rather simple and romantic: *Chopin's ballades.* ⟨< F < OF *balade.* See BALLAD.⟩

bal•lad•eer [,bælə'dir] *n.* **1** a writer or singer of ballads. **2** *Informal.* a writer or singer of popular songs.

bal•lad•ry ['bælədri] *n.* **1** ballads collectively. **2** the composition of ballads.

ballad stanza the common four-line verse form of ballads, with the rhyme scheme *a b c b.*

ball and chain **1** a heavy metal ball attached by a short chain to the leg of a prisoner to prevent his or her escaping. **2** *Informal.* anything that restricts one's freedom of action.

ball–and–sock•et joint a flexible joint formed by a ball or knob fitting in a socket, such as the shoulder or hip joint, and permitting some motion in every direction. See SOCKET for picture.

bal•last ['bæləst] *n., v. —n.* **1** something heavy carried in a ship to steady it. **2** the weight carried in a balloon or dirigible to control it. **3** anything that steadies a person or thing. **4** the gravel or crushed rock used in making the bed for a road or railway track.
—v. **1** put ballast in (ships, balloons, etc.). **2** put gravel or crushed rock on. ⟨apparently < Scand.; cf. ODanish *barlast* < *bar* bare + *last* load⟩ **—'bal•last•er,** *n.*

ballast tube in fluorescent lighting, etc., a device to keep the electric current constant, usually consisting of an iron wire in a vacuum tube filled with hydrogen. Its varying resistance counteracts changes of voltage.

ball bearing **1** a bearing in which the shaft turns upon a number of freely moving metal balls contained in a grooved ring around the shaft. Ball bearings are used to lessen friction. **2** any of the metal balls so used.

ball boy *Sports.* a boy who collects loose balls during a game, keeping them out of play, or has charge of extra balls used for practice, drills, etc.

ball cock a valve for regulating the supply of water in a tank, cistern, etc., opened or closed by the fall or rise of a hollow, floating ball.

bal•le•ri•na [,bælə'rinə] *n., pl.* **-nas.** a female ballet dancer. ⟨< Ital.⟩

bal•let [bæ'lei] *or* ['bælei] *n.* **1** an artistic dance that usually tells a story or expresses a mood, performed by either a soloist or a group of dancers in a theatre, concert hall, etc. **2** the art of creating or performing ballets. **3** a performance of a ballet. **4** the music for a ballet. **5** a company of dancers that performs ballets. ⟨< F *ballet*, dim. of *bal* dance. See BALL[2].⟩

bal•let•ic [bæ'lɛtɪk] *adj.* of or having to do with ballet. **—bal'let•i•cal•ly,** *adv.*

bal•let•o•mane [bæ'lɛtə,mein] *n.* a person who is enthusiastic about ballet. ⟨< F *balletomane* < *ballet* + *-mane* < *manie* < Gk. *mania* enthusiasm⟩ **—,bal•let•o'ma•nia,** *n.*

ball•game ['bɒl,geim] *n.* any game in which a ball is thrown, kicked, or dribbled, especially a baseball game.
a whole new ballgame, *Informal.* a matter needing new handling because it has changed unexpectedly.

ball girl *Sports.* a girl who collects loose balls during a game, keeping them out of play, or has charge of extra balls used for practice, drills, etc.

ball•hand•ler ['bɒl,hændlər] *n. Sports.* **1** the player who has the ball at any point in a game. **2** a player with reference to his or her skill in controlling the ball.

ball hockey a hockeylike game played with hockey sticks and a tennis ball, usually on pavement.

bal•lis•ta [bə'lɪstə] *n., pl.* **-tae** [-ti] *or* [-taɪ]. a machine used in wars in ancient times to throw stones and other heavy missiles. ⟨< L *ballista*, ult. < Gk. *ballein* throw⟩

bal•lis•tic [bə'lɪstɪk] *adj.* **1** having to do with the motion or throwing of projectiles. **2** having to do with the science of ballistics. **3** designating exercises composed of jerky stop/start motions.
go ballistic, *Slang.* become suddenly angry or excited.
—bal'lis•ti•cal•ly, *adv.*

ballistic missile a projectile powered by a rocket engine or engines but reaching its target as a result of aim at the time of launching, used especially as a long-range weapon of offence.

bal•lis•tics [bə'lɪstɪks] *n.* **1** the properties of a bullet, etc., that affect its trajectory. **2** the science that deals with the motion of projectiles.

bal•lis•to•car•di•o•gram [bə,lɪstou'kɑrdiə,græm] *n.* a record made by a ballistocardiograph.

bal•lis•to•car•di•o•graph [bə,lɪstou'kɑrdiə,græf] *n.* a machine that records the barely perceptible movement of the body in reaction to each contraction of the heart, as an indicator of the strength of the heartbeat.

ball joint a BALL-AND-SOCKET JOINT transferring motion from the tie rods to the wheels as part of the steering mechanism of a motor vehicle.

ball lightning lightning occurring very infrequently in the form of a red-orange ball that moves quickly through the air or along the ground for a very short time before disintegrating.

bal•lon [bæ'loun]; *French,* [ba'lɔ̃] *n.* a dancer's way of moving that creates the impression of floating. ⟨< F⟩

bal•lo•net [,bælə'nɛt] *n.* a small bag inside a balloon or airship that holds air or gas to regulate ascent or descent. ⟨< F *ballonnet*, dim. of *ballon* balloon⟩

bal•loon [bə'lun] *n., v.* —*n.* **1** an airtight bag filled with air or a gas lighter than air, so that it will rise and float. Small balloons are used as toys and decorations; larger balloons can be used as signals, advertisements, etc. **2** a large such airtight bag from which is suspended either a gondola to carry two or more persons or a container to carry instruments. **Observation balloons** are used to observe and record data on weather, atmospheric radiation, etc. **3** (*adjl.*) puffed out like a balloon: *balloon sleeves.* **4** in cartoons, an outlined space in which the words of a speaker are written.
—*v.* **1** swell out like a balloon. **2** ride in a balloon. ⟨< Ital. *ballone* < *balla* ball⟩ **—bal'loon,like,** *adj.*

balloon barrage an anti-aircraft screen of BARRAGE BALLOONS.

bal•loon•ist [bə'lunɪst] *n.* **1** a person who goes up in balloons. **2** a pilot of a dirigible balloon.

balloon sail a large, lightweight sail used on a yacht instead of or with conventional sails, for speed downwind.

balloon tire a large tire containing air under low pressure.

bal•lot ['bælət] *n., v.* **-lot•ed, -lot•ing.** —*n.* **1** a piece of paper or other object used in voting. **2** the total number of votes cast. **3** vote; voting: *The ballot went in favour of the new party.* **4** a method of secret voting that uses paper slips, voting machines, etc. **5** the list of candidates for an election: *He was too late to get on the ballot.* **6** permission to vote: *Only registered union members have the ballot.*
—*v.* vote or decide by using ballots. ⟨< Ital. *ballotta*, dim. of *balla* ball⟩

ballot box the box into which voters put their ballots.

bal•lotte•ment [bə'lɒtmənt] *n. Medicine.* a method of palpating internal organs to check for pregnancy or injury, or to diagnose the size of a tumour. ⟨< F *ballotter* to toss < *ballotte* < Ital. *ballotta* dim. of *palla* ball⟩

ball•park ['bɒl,pɑrk] *n.* a stadium for playing baseball or football.
a ballpark figure, *Informal.* a rough estimate.
in the ballpark, *Informal.* **a** of an estimate, fairly close or accurate. **b** meeting minimum requirements or criteria.

ball–peen hammer ['bɒl ,pin] a hammer having one end of the head rounded like a ball, for shaping metal, etc. The other end has the usual cylindrical shape.

ball•play•er ['bɒl,pleiər] *n.* **1** a baseball player. **2** a person who plays ball.

ball•point or **ball–point** ['bɒl,pɔɪnt] *n.* a pen having a small metal ball in place of a nib. The movement and pressure of writing make the ball turn against a cartridge of semisolid ink, transferring some of the ink to the paper.

ball•room ['bɒl,rum] *or* ['bɒl,rʊm] *n.* a large room for dancing.

ballroom dancing a type of formal dancing in couples, including waltzes, foxtrots, etc.

bal•lute [bə'lut] *n.* a combination balloon and parachute, to keep ejecting fighter pilots out of range of enemy ground fire until rescue planes can retrieve them in midair. ⟨< *ball(oon)* + *parach(ute)*⟩

ball valve part of a plumbing fixture in which a ball acts as a valve, controlled by the pressure of water.

bal•ly•hoo *n.* ['bæli,hu]; *v.* ['bæli,hu] *or* [,bæli'hu] *n., pl.* **-hoos;** *v.,* **-hooed, -hoo•ing.** *Slang.* —*n.* **1** noisy advertising; a sensational way of attracting attention. **2** an uproar or outcry.
—*v.* advertise noisily; make exaggerated or false statements about. ⟨origin uncertain⟩ **—'bal•ly,hoo•er,** *n.*

balm [bɒm] *or* [bɑm] *n.* **1** any of various fragrant, oily, resinous substances obtained from certain tropical trees, used for relieving pain or healing. **2** any fragrant ointment or oil used for soothing or healing. **3** anything that soothes or comforts: *Kind words are a balm for wounded feelings.* **4** any of various plants of the mint family, especially a Eurasian herb (*Melissa officinalis*) cultivated for its fragrant leaves which are used as flavouring in foods and drinks and also for making perfume. **5** fragrance; sweet smell. ⟨ME < OF *basme* < L < Gk. *balsamon* balsam. Doublet of BALSAM.⟩
☛ *Hom.* BOMB [bɒm].

bal•ma•caan [,bælmə'kɑn] *n.* a type of overcoat having a generous cut and raglan sleeves. ⟨< *Balmacaan* in Scotland⟩

balm of Gil•e•ad **1** a fragrant ointment prepared from the resin of a small evergreen tree (*Commiphora opobalsumum*) of Asia and Africa. **2** the tree itself. **3** a North American hybrid poplar (*Populus gileadensis*) closely resembling the balsam poplar but having a broader crown and leaves that are almost heart-shaped. **4** *Cdn.* BALSAM FIR. **5** anything having a soothing or healing effect.

bal•mor•al [bæl'mɔrəl] *n.* **1** a brimless Scottish cap having a round, soft, more or less flat crown that projects all around. See CAP for picture. **2** a walking shoe fastened with laces. **3** a woollen petticoat made to show under a looped skirt. ⟨< *Balmoral* in Scotland⟩

Bal•mung ['balmʊŋ] *n.* Siegfried's sword in the Nibelungenlied.

balm•y[1] ['bɒmi] *or* ['bɑmi] *adj.* **balm•i•er, balm•i•est. 1** mild; gentle; soothing: *a balmy breeze.* **2** fragrant. ⟨< *balm*⟩ **—'balm•i•ly,** *adv.* **—'balm•i•ness,** *n.*

balm•y[2] ['bɒmi] *or* ['bɑmi] *adj.* **balm•i•er, balm•i•est.** *Slang.* silly; crazy. ⟨var. of *barmy*⟩

bal•ne•al ['bælniəl] *adj.* having to do with baths or bathing. ⟨< LL *balneum* bath⟩

bal•ne•ol•ogy [,bælni'ɒlədʒi] *n.* the study of medicinal waters, baths, etc. ⟨< L *balneum* bath < Gk. *balaneion* + L *-logia* word < Gk. *logos*⟩

ba•lo•ney [bə'louni] *n.* **1** *Slang.* nonsense. **2** *Informal.* bologna. Also, **boloney.** ⟨< *bologna*⟩

bal•sa ['bɒlsə] *n.* **1** a tropical American tree (*Ochroma lagopus*) with very light, strong wood. **2** its wood. **3** a raft, especially one consisting of two or more floats fastened to a framework. ⟨< Sp. *balsa* raft⟩

bal•sam ['bɒlsəm] *n.* **1** any of various fragrant, resinous substances containing benzoic acid, used in medicine and perfume. **2** any of various other fragrant and usually resinous substances used especially for healing or soothing. **3** any of various turpentines. **4** a tree that yields balsam, especially the balsam fir. **5** a garden plant (*Impatiens balsamina*) having large leaves and double, usually red or pink, flowers. **6** BALM (def. 3). ⟨< L < Gk. *balsamon.* Doublet of BALM.⟩ **—bal'sam•ic** [bɒl'sæmɪk], *adj.*

balsam fir **1** a fir tree (*Abies balsamea*) found throughout E Canada and parts of the Prairie Provinces and the N United States, having a narrow, symmetrical crown tapering to a spirelike top and shiny, dark green needles. It is often used as a Christmas tree and its resin is used in making varnish. The species found in British Columbia is *Abies amabilis*. **2** the soft, light, weak wood of this tree, used especially for pulp.

balsam of Peru a resin extracted from a Central American tree (*Myroxylon pereirae*), used in medicines, fragrances, and other preparations.

balsam of Tolu tolu.

balsam poplar **1** a poplar (*Populus balsamifera*) found throughout Canada and along the northern border of the United States, having oval leaves that are shiny dark green above and whitish green below and having resin-coated buds that give the tree a strong balsam odour; tacamahac. **2** the wood of this tree, used for lumber, veneer, etc.

bal•sam•root ['bɒlsəm,rut] *n.* a wildflower (*Balsamorhiza sagittata*), having large leaves shaped like arrowheads and yellow, daisylike flowers.

Bal•tic ['bɒltɪk] *adj., n.* *—adj.* **1** having to do with the Baltic Sea in N Europe. **2** having to do with the Baltic States, Estonia, Latvia, and Lithuania. See LATVIA for map. **3** of or having to do with the languages of this region, a branch of Indo-European.
—n. a group of Indo-European languages of this region.

Bal•ti•more oriole ['bɒltə,mɔr] a North American oriole (*Icterus galbula*) common throughout central and eastern North America, having a loud, piping whistle. The adult male has a black head and back and mostly black wings, with bright orange-yellow underside, rump, and upper tail feathers. The adult female has an olive upper body with black spots, dull orange underparts, and wings with two white bars and white edging. ⟨from its colours, which are those of the coat of arms of Lord *Baltimore*, English statesman and founder of the state of Maryland⟩

Ba•lu•chi [bə'lutʃi] *n., pl.* **-chi.** **1** a native or inhabitant of Baluchistan, a province of Pakistan. **2** the Iranian language of Baluchistan.

bal•us•ter ['bæləstər] *n.* one of a set of often ornamental posts supporting a railing or coping, as along the edge of a staircase, balcony, or terrace. ⟨< F *balustre* < Ital. < L < Gk. *balaustion* pomegranate blossom; from the shape⟩

bal•us•trade ['bælə,streid] *or* [,bælə'streid] *n.* an ornamental railing along a staircase, balcony, etc. together with its supporting balusters. ⟨< F *balustrade* < *balustre.* See BALUSTER.⟩

bam•bi•no [bæm'binou] *n., pl.* **-nos** or **-ni** [-ni]. *Italian.* **1** a baby; little child. **2** an image or picture of the baby Jesus. ⟨< Ital. *bambino*, dim. of *bambo* silly⟩

Bamboo

bam•boo [bæm'bu] *n., pl.* **-boos.** **1** any of a family (Bambuseae) of treelike tropical or semitropical grasses having hollow or solid, stiff, jointed stems and evergreen or deciduous leaves. **2** the stems of certain bamboos, used for building, furniture, poles, etc. **3** (*adjl.*) made of bamboo: *a bamboo fishing pole, a bamboo chair.* ⟨< Du. *bamboes*, probably < Malay⟩

Bamboo Curtain an imaginary wall or dividing line between China and non-communist nations.

bam•boo•zle [bæm'buzəl] *v.* **-zled, -zling.** *Informal.* **1** impose upon; cheat; trick. **2** puzzle; perplex. ⟨origin uncertain⟩ **—bam'boo•zler, bam'booz•le•ment,** *n.*

ban¹ [bæn] *v.* **banned, ban•ning;** *n.* *—v.* **1** prohibit; forbid by law or authority: *Swimming is banned in this lake.* **2** pronounce a curse on.
—n. **1** the forbidding of an act or speech by authority of the law, the church, or, unofficially, by public opinion; prohibition. **2** a solemn curse by the church; excommunication or condemnation. **3** a sentence of outlawry or banishment. ⟨OE *bannan* summon⟩

ban² [bæn] *n.* **1** a public proclamation or edict. **2** in medieval times: **a** the summoning of the king's vassals for war. **b** the whole body of these vassals. ⟨fusion of OE *gebann* summons and Old North French *ban* proclamation, jurisdiction < Gmc.⟩

ban³ [bɑn] *n., pl.* **ba•ni** ['bɑni] a unit of money in Moldova and Romania, equal to $^1/_{100}$ of a leu. See table of money in the Appendix. ⟨< Romanian⟩

ba•nal [bə'næl] *or* [bə'nɑl] *for def. 1,* ['beinəl] *for def. 2. adj.* **1** commonplace; trite or trivial: *He made some banal remarks about the weather before coming to the point of his visit.* **2** formerly, available to the whole community: *banal mills.* ⟨< F *banal* < *ban* proclamation < Gmc.; original sense 'of feudal service'; later, 'open to the community'⟩ **—ba'nal•ly** or **'ba•nal•ly,** *adv.*

ba•nal•i•ty [bə'næləti] *n., pl.* **-ties.** **1** commonplaceness; triteness; triviality. **2** a trite or trivial remark.

ba•na•na [bə'nænə] *n.* **1** the elongated, curved fruit of any of various tropical plants (genus *Musa*), having sweet, whitish pulp and a thick, yellow skin. **2** any of the treelike, herbaceous plants producing such fruit, especially *Musa sapientum*, widely cultivated in the tropics. **3** (*adjl.*) designating a family (Musaceae) of plants that includes bananas, plantains, and the bird-of-paradise flower.
go bananas, *Slang.* become crazy or wildly enthusiastic, distressed, etc.: *The whole audience went bananas when she stepped onto the stage.* ⟨< Pg. or Sp.⟩

banana belt *Cdn. Informal, often facetious.* a region having a relatively mild climate: *the banana belt of southwestern B.C.*

banana oil **1** a colourless liquid having a smell resembling that of bananas, used in flavourings and as a solvent. **2** *Slang.* pretentious but insincere talk; excessive flattery.

banana republic a small country such as some of those in Central and South America, dependent on a single crop.

banana spider a spider (*Heteropoda venatoria*) found among bananas. It is big and yellow.

ba•nau•sic [bə'nɒsɪk] *or* [bə'nɒzɪk] *adj.* **1** mechanical. **2** concerned with mundane or worldly matters; materialistic. ⟨< Gk. *banausikos*, for mechanics⟩

band¹ [bænd] *n., v.* *—n.* **1** a group of persons or animals moving or acting together: *a band of robbers, a band of wild dogs.* **2** a group of musicians organized to play together, especially on brass, woodwind, and percussion instruments: *We hired a five-piece band for our dance.* Compare ORCHESTRA. **3** *Cdn.* a group of Canadian First Nations people of a particular region or reserve, recognized by the Federal Government as an administrative unit.
—v. unite or cause to unite in a group. ⟨< MF *bande* < Med.L *banda*, prob. < Gmc. Related to BANNER.⟩

band² [bænd] *n., v.* *—n.* **1** a thin, flat strip of material for binding, trimming, etc.: *a narrow band of lace. The oak box was strengthened with bands of iron.* **2** a loop or ring of material used for holding something together: *I put a rubber band around the bundle of letters.* **3** a stripe: *a white cup with a gold band near the rim.* **4** **bands,** *pl.* two strips hanging from the front of a collar in certain academic, clerical, or legal costumes. **5** a particular range of wavelengths or frequencies of sound or light. **6** any of the separate sections on a phonograph record. **7** anything that binds or restrains. **8** a narrow strip of anything. **9** a ring worn on the finger: *a wedding band.*
—v. **1** put a band on. **2** mark with stripes. ⟨ME < MF *bande, bende* < Gmc. Related to BAND¹, BEND².⟩

band³ [bænd] *n.* anything that ties, binds, or unites. Compare BOND. ⟨ME < ON *band.* Related in Gmc. to BAND².⟩

band•age ['bændɪdʒ] *n., v.* **-aged, -ag•ing.** *—n.* **1** a strip of cloth or other material used in binding up and dressing a wound, injured leg or arm, etc. **2** something like this used to support or

protect when there is no injury: *Racehorses often have bandages on their legs.*
—*v.* bind, tie up, or dress with a bandage. ⟨< F *bandage* < *bande.* See BAND[1].⟩ —**'band•ag•er,** *n.*

Band–Aid ['bæn,deid] *n. Trademark.* a small bandage for minor wounds, consisting of a thin gauze pad attached to the middle of a strip of adhesive tape.
☛ *Usage.* **Band-Aid** is sometimes used metaphorically to mean a temporary solution or stopgap.

ban•dan•a or **ban•dan•na** [bæn'dænə] *n.* a large, coloured handkerchief. ⟨probably < Hind. *bandhnu* tying cloth to produce a design when dyed⟩

band•box ['bænd,bɒks] *n.* a light cardboard box for holding hats, collars, etc.
bandbox neat, very neat.

band council *Cdn.* a group of Canadian First Nations people elected to govern a BAND[1] (def. 3).

ban•deau [bæn'dou] *or* ['bændou] *n., pl.* **-deaux** [-'douz] *or* [-douz]. **1** a band worn around the head. **2** a narrow band. **3** a narrow brassiere. ⟨< F *bandeau,* dim. of *bande* band[1], ult. < Gmc.⟩

ban•de•ril•la [,bændə'riljə] *or* [,bɑn-] *n.* any of several decorated darts which are stuck into the bull in a bullfight. ⟨< Sp.⟩

ban•de•ril•le•ro [,bændəri'ɛrou] *or* [,bændəril'jɛrou]; *Spanish,* [,bandəri'ljero] *n.* the man in a bullfight whose job it is to stick banderillas into the bull.

ban•de•role or **ban•de•rol** ['bændə,roul] *n.* **1** a small flag or streamer on a lance, mast, etc. **2** a scroll in the form of a ribbon, bearing some saying or dedication, or the representation of such a scroll, found on tombstones, buildings, etc. ⟨< F < Ital. *banderuola* < *bandiera* banner < LL *bandum* < Gmc.⟩

ban•di•coot ['bændə,kut] *n.* **1** any of about 20 species of small grey or tan marsupial (family Peramelidae) found in Australia and neighbouring islands, resembling kangaroos but belonging to a different family. Bandicoots are active at night and sleep during the day. **2** BANDICOOT RAT. ⟨< Telugu *pandikokku* pig-rat⟩

bandicoot rat any of several large, burrowing, ratlike rodents (genera *Bandicota* and *Nesokia*) found in India and Sri Lanka, having a body about 30 to 38 cm long and a very long tail, and having a short head and a broad muzzle. They live in forests, cultivated land, and towns, and destroy crops, stored grains, and poultry.

ban•dit ['bændɪt] *n., pl.* **ban•dits** or **ban•dit•ti** [bæn'dɪti]. **1** a highwayman; robber. **2** anyone who steals, cheats, or defrauds. ⟨< Ital. *bandito,* pp. of *bandire* banish, proscribe, ult. < Gmc. Akin to BAN.⟩

ban•dit•ry ['bændɪtri] *n.* **1** the work of bandits. **2** bandits.

ban•dit•ti [bæn'dɪti] *n.* a pl. of BANDIT.

band•lead•er ['bænd,lidər] *n.* the chief player in a BAND[2].

band leader an important person in a Canadian BAND[1] (def. 3).

band•mas•ter ['bænd,mæstər] *n.* the conductor of a BAND[1] (def. 2).

ban•do•lier or **ban•do•leer** [,bændə'lir] *n.* **1** a broad belt worn over one shoulder and across the breast. Some bandoliers have loops for carrying cartridges; others have small cases for bullets, gunpowder, etc. **2** one of these cases. ⟨< F *bandoulière* < Sp. *bandolera* < *banda* band[1], ult < Gmc.⟩

ban•dore [bæn'dɔr] *or* ['bændɔr] *n.* a musical instrument resembling a guitar, used in ancient times. ⟨< Sp. *banduria* < LL *pandura* < Gk. *pandoura* three-stringed instrument⟩

band–pass filter ['bænd ,pæs] *Radio.* a filter which will let through only certain selected frequencies.

band saw a saw in the form of an endless steel belt.

band shell an outdoor platform for musical concerts that has a shell-shaped, rear wall extending up over the platform and serving as a sounding board.

bands•man ['bændzmən] *n., pl.* **-men.** a member of a band of musicians.

band•stand ['bænd,stænd] *n.* **1** an outdoor platform, usually roofed, for band concerts. **2** a similar platform indoors.

band•wag•on ['bænd,wægən] *n.* a wagon that carries a musical band in a parade.
climb or **get on the bandwagon,** *Informal.* join what appears to be the winning side in a political campaign, contest, public issue, etc.

band width *Radio and telecommunications.* the range of frequencies necessary to send a certain signal.

ban•dy[1] ['bændi] *v.* **-died, -dy•ing 1** throw back and forth; toss about. **2** give and take; exchange: *To bandy words with a foolish person is a waste of time.* ⟨Cf. F *bander* bandy, *se bander* band together < Gmc.⟩

ban•dy[2] ['bændi] *adj.* bent or curved outward: *bandy legs.* ⟨< F *bandé* bent⟩

ban•dy–leg•ged ['bændi ,lɛgɪd] *or* [,lɛgd] *adj.* having legs that curve outward; bowlegged.

bane [bein] *n.* **1** a cause of death, ruin, or harm: *Wild animals were the bane of the mountain village.* **2** destruction of any kind. **3** poison (*only used in compounds*): *ratsbane.* ⟨OE *bana* murderer⟩

bane•ber•ry ['bein,bɛri] *n., pl.* **-ries. 1** any of several plants (genus *Actaea*) of the buttercup family having spikes of small white flowers and clusters of white or red poisonous berries. **2** a berry of any of these plants.

bane•ful ['beinfəl] *adj.* deadly; harmful. —**'bane•ful•ly,** *adv.*

bang[1] [bæŋ] *n., v., interj.* —*n.* **1** sudden, loud noise: *the bang of a gun.* **2** a violent or noisy blow. **3** (*advl.*) violently and noisily: *The girl on the bicycle went bang into a tree.* **4** (*advl.*) precisely; squarely: *The concert ended bang at ten.* **5** vigour, impetus: *They wanted to start the campaign off with a bang.* **6** *Slang.* thrill: *They really got a bang out of the incident.*
bang on, *Informal.* exactly correct or on target: *Your answer is bang on.*
—*v.* **1** make a sudden loud noise: *We heard the door bang.* **2** hit violently or sharply: *I banged my head when I fell. The snowball banged against the window.* **3** shut with a noise; slam: *He banged the door as he went out.* **4** handle roughly (usually used with **around**): *They really banged our suitcases around.*
bang up, *Informal.* physically harm: *The thugs banged up all the cars on the street.*
—*interj.* an imitation of gunfire: *"Bang! Bang!" shouted the children.* ⟨? < ON *banga* to hammer⟩
☛ *Hom.* BHANG.

bang[2] [bæŋ] *n., v.* —*n.* **1** Usually, **bangs,** *pl.* a fringe of hair cut short and worn over the forehead: *She has long hair with bangs.*
—*v.* cut hair in this way: *She wears her hair banged.* ⟨< short for *bangtail* docked tail (of a horse)⟩
☛ *Hom.* BHANG.

Ban•gla•desh [,bʌŋglə'dɛʃ] *or* [,bæŋglə'dɛʃ] *n.* a country in S Asia, part of the Indian subcontinent. It was formerly the province of East Pakistan.

Ban•gla•desh•i [,bʌŋglə'dɛʃi] *or* [,bæŋglə'dɛʃi] *adj., n.* —*adj.* of or having to do with Bangladesh or its people.
—*n.* a native or inhabitant of Bangladesh.

ban•gle ['bæŋgəl] *n.* **1** a ring worn around the wrist, arm, or ankle. **2** a small ornament suspended from a bracelet. ⟨< Hind. *bangri, bangli* glass bracelet⟩

Bang's disease [bæŋz] an infectious disease in cattle that often results in abortion. ⟨< Bernhard *Bang* (1848-1932), the Danish physician who described it⟩

bang•tail ['bæŋ,teil] *n. Informal.* a racehorse with its tail cut below the tail bone, straight through the hair.

bang–up ['bæŋ 'ʌp] *adj. Slang.* good; excellent: *You've done a bang-up job.*

ba•ni ['bɑni] *n.* pl. of BAN[3].

ban•ian ['bænjən] *or* ['bænjæn] *n.* **1** a Hindu merchant of a caste that eats no meat. **2** See BANYAN. ⟨< Pg. *banian,* probably < Arabic *banyan* < Gujarati (a lang. of W India), ult. < Skt.⟩

ban•ish ['bænɪʃ] *v.* **1** condemn to leave a country; exile. **2** force to go away; send away; drive away. ⟨ME < OF *baniss-,* a stem of *banir* < LL *bannire* ban < Gmc.⟩ —**'ban•ish•er,** *n.*
☛ *Syn.* **1. Banish,** EXILE, DEPORT = force to leave a country. **Banish** = to force a person, by order of authority, to leave his or her own or a foreign country, permanently or for a stated time: *Napoleon was banished to Elba.* **Exile** also means to compel a person to leave his or her own country or home, but the authority may be the force of circumstances or his or her own will: *The Kaiser was exiled from Germany after World War I.* **Deport** = to banish a person from a country of which he or she is not a citizen: *We deport immigrants who enter Canada illegally.*

ban•ish•ment ['bænɪʃmənt] *n.* **1** the act of banishing. **2** the state of being banished; exile.

ban•is•ter ['bænɪstər] *n.* **1** Usually, **banisters,** *pl.* the railing of a staircase together with the supporting balusters. **2** the railing alone. **3** baluster. Also, **bannister.** ⟨var. of *baluster*⟩

ban•jo ['bændʒou] *n., pl.* **-jos** or **-joes.** a stringed musical instrument played with the fingers or a plectrum. ⟨< alteration of *bandore* < Sp. < LL < Gk. *pandoura,* a three-stringed instrument⟩

A banjo

ban•jo•ist ['bændʒouɪst] *n.* a person who plays a banjo, especially a skilled player.

bank[1] [bæŋk] *n., v.* —*n.* **1** a long pile or heap: *a bank of snow.* **2** the ground bordering a river, lake, etc. **3** a shallow place in an ocean, sea, etc.; shoal: *the fishing banks of Newfoundland.* **4** a slope: *the bank of a corner on a race track.* **5** the tilting of an airplane to one side when making a turn. **6** *Mining.* **a** the top of a shaft. **b** the face being worked in a coal mine. **7** *Billiards.* the cushion around the edge of the table.
—*v.* **1** raise a ridge or mound about; border with a bank or ridge. **2** form into a bank; pile up; heap up: *The wind had banked snow against the wall. Clouds are banking along the horizon.* **3** slope: *The pavement of a curve on an expressway should be well banked, upward and outward from the centre.* **4** make (an airplane) tilt when making a turn. **5** of an airplane, tilt when turning. **6** lessen the draft and cover (a fire) with ashes or fresh fuel so that it will burn slowly. **7** *Basketball.* score by bouncing (the ball) off the backboard into the basket. **8** *Billiards.* hit (a ball) so as to make it bounce back off the cushion. ⟨ME < ON; cf. Old Icelandic *bakki*⟩

bank[2] [bæŋk] *n., v.* —*n.* **1 a** an institution for keeping, lending, exchanging, and paying out money. **b** the building housing such an institution. **2** a container used for saving small sums at home: *a plastic piggy bank.* **3** *Gambling.* the funds kept by the dealer or manager for use in a game. **4** *Games.* a stock of pieces from which players draw. **5** a place where something is stored for future use: *a blood bank, a data bank.* **6** *Computer technology.* a section of memory.
—*v.* **1** operate or manage a bank. **2** keep money in a bank: *He banks at the branch near his office.* **3** put (money) in a bank: *She banked half her pay cheque.* **4** act as banker in a gambling game.
bank on, *Informal.* depend on; be sure of. ⟨< F *banque* < Ital. *banca,* originally, bench, later applied to the table used by money changers < Gmc.⟩

bank[3] [bæŋk] *n., v.* —*n.* **1** a row or close arrangement of things: *a bank of switches, a bank of machines.* **2** a row of keys on an organ, typewriter, etc. **3 a** a tier or row of oars in a galley. **b** a bench for the rowers in a galley. **c** the rowers in a galley. **4** a subheading in a newspaper.
—*v.* arrange in rows. ⟨ME < OF *banc* < LL *bancus* < Gmc. Akin to BENCH.⟩

bank•a•ble ['bæŋkəbəl] *adj.* **1** capable of being accepted by a bank. **2** likely to be profitable.

bank account **1** an arrangement for depositing one's money in a bank for safekeeping until it is needed, involving a record of deposits and withdrawals: *to open a bank account.* **2** the sum of money kept by a bank for a person or company: *My bank account is very low right now.*

bank barn *Cdn.* especially in Ontario, a two-storey barn built into a hill so as to permit entry to the bottom level from one side and to the top level from the other side.

bank bill BANK NOTE.

bank•book ['bæŋk,bʊk] *n.* a book in which a record of a person's account at a bank is kept.

bank discount an amount of money deducted from a loan by a bank at the time the loan is made, equal to the interest chargeable from the date the loan is made until the date when the final payment is due.

bank draft a kind of cheque drawn by a bank on another bank.

bank•er[1] ['bæŋkər] *n.* **1** a person or company that manages a bank. **2** a dealer or manager in a gambling game. **3** *Informal.* any person who lends or advances money in order to make a profit: *a banker in a loan shark operation.*

bank•er[2] ['bæŋkər] *n. Cdn.* **1** a fisher who fishes off the GRAND BANKS. **2** a fishing vessel that operates off the GRAND BANKS.

bank holiday any day on which banks are legally closed; a statutory holiday.

bank•ing ['bæŋkɪŋ] *n., v.*—*n.* **1** the business of operating a bank. **2** any business with a bank: *I have to do my banking today.*
—*v.* ppr. of BANK.

bank note **1** a piece of paper currency. In Canada, all bank notes are issued by the Bank of Canada and serve as the currency of this country. **2** formerly, a note issued by a bank, that could be redeemed at any time for a specific amount of money, gold, etc.

Bank of Canada the agent of the Government of Canada that issues all Canadian bank notes and carries out monetary policy on behalf of the government.

bank paper **1** bank notes as a group. **2** any note or bill that is acceptable by a bank.

bank rate the standard rate of discount for a specified type of note, security, etc., set by a central bank, such as the Bank of Canada, or by a chartered bank.

bank•roll ['bæŋk,roul] *n., v.* —*n. Informal.* the amount of money a person has in his or her possession or easily available.
—*v. Slang.* provide or put up the money for: *A group of businesses bankrolled the opera company's tour.*

bank•rupt ['bæŋk,rʌpt] *adj., n., v.* —*adj.* **1** unable to pay one's debts; declared legally unable to pay debts. **2** at the end of one's resources; destitute. **3** completely lacking in something or failing: *The story was entirely bankrupt of any new ideas.*
—*n.* **1** a person declared by a law court to be unable to pay his or her debts and whose property is distributed among or administered on behalf of his or her creditors. **2** a person who is unable to pay his or her debts. **3** a person who is completely lacking in something: *a moral bankrupt.*
—*v.* make bankrupt. ⟨< F *banqueroute* < Ital. *bancarotta* bankruptcy < *banca* bank + *rotta,* fem. pp. of *rompere* break < L *rumpere*⟩

bank•rupt•cy ['bæŋkrəpsi] *or* ['bæŋkrʌptsi] *n., pl.* **-cies.** the condition of being bankrupt.

bank•sia ['bæŋksiə] *n.* an Australian evergreen bush of the genus *Banksia,* having prickly leaves and clusters of small flowers. ⟨after Sir Joseph *Banks* (1743-1820), English botanist⟩

ban•ner ['bænər] *n.* **1** a flag. **2** a piece of cloth with some design or words on it, often an advertisement, slogan, greeting, etc., attached by its upper edge to a pole or staff, strung across a room, or pulled through the air by an airplane. **3** a newspaper headline in large type, usually extending across the entire width of the page. **4** (*adjl.*) leading or outstanding; foremost: *a banner year in sports.* ⟨ME < OF *baniere* < LL *bandum* < Gmc.⟩

ban•ner•et ['bænə,rɛt] *n.* **1** formerly, a knight entitled to lead his vassals into battle under his own banner. **2** a rank of knighthood, senior to that of knight bachelor. ⟨ME < OF *baneret* < *banere* banner + *-et* -ate[1]⟩

ban•ner•ette or **ban•ner•et** [,bænə'rɛt] *n.* a small banner.

ban•nis•ter ['bænɪstər] See BANISTER.

ban•nock ['bænək] *n.* **1** a flat cake, usually unleavened, made of oatmeal or barley flour. **2** *Cdn.* a flat, round cake, made of unleavened flour, salt, and water. Baking powder is sometimes added. ⟨OE *bannuc* bit, piece⟩

banns [bænz] *n.pl.* a public notice, given three times in church, that a man and a woman are to be married. ⟨pl. of *bann,* var. of *ban* proclamation, OE *gebann*⟩

ban•quet ['bæŋkwɪt] *n., v.* **-quet•ed, -quet•ing.** —*n.* **1** a feast. **2** a formal dinner with speeches.
—*v.* **1** entertain with a banquet: *The visiting celebrity was banqueted by the city.* **2** take part in a banquet. ⟨< F < Ital. *banchetto,* dim. of *banco* bench < Gmc.⟩
☛ *Syn. n.* See note at FEAST.

ban•quette [bæŋ'kɛt] *n.* **1** a platform along the inside of a parapet or trench for soldiers to stand on when firing. **2** an upholstered bench, especially one along a wall in restaurants, etc. ⟨< F⟩

ban•shee ['bænʃi] *or* [,bæn'ʃi] *n.* a spirit whose wails are supposed to mean that there will soon be a death in the family. ⟨< Irish *bean sidhe* woman of the fairies⟩

ban•tam ['bæntəm] *n.* **1** Often, **Bantam,** any of a number of breeds of dwarf ornamental fowl, raised mainly as a hobby because of the striking colours and arrangement of their feathers. Bantams usually weigh only about 680 g. **2** a very small person, especially one fond of fighting. **3** (*adjl.*) small and light.

4 *Sports.* **a** a class for players under 15 years. **b** a player in such a class. **c** bantamweight. **5** (*adjl.*) *Sports.* of or designating a class of players under 15 years: *a bantam hockey league.* ⟨probably from *Bantam*, a city in Java, where the small fowl originated⟩

ban•tam•weight [ˈbæntəm,weit] *n.* a boxer who weighs at least 51 kg and not more than 54 kg.

ban•ter [ˈbæntər] *n., v.* —*n.* playful teasing; joking: *She didn't mind her friends' banter about her freckles.*
—*v.* **1** tease or make fun of playfully. **2** talk in a joking way. ⟨origin unknown⟩ **—ˈban•ter•er,** *n.* **—ˈban•ter•ing•ly,** *adv.*

Ban•tu [ˈbæntu] *n., pl.* **-tu** or **tus;** *adj.* —*n.* **1** a member of a large group of peoples who occupy central and southern Africa. The Bantu are not a uniform group, but include peoples of very different cultures. **2** a group of African languages widely spoken throughout central and southern Africa, including Swahili, Zulu, and Kikuyu.
—*adj.* of or having to do with these peoples or their languages.

ban•ty [ˈbænti] *n. Informal.* **1** BANTAM (def. 1), also called **banty hen.** **2** a small, feisty person.

ban•yan [ˈbænjən] *or* [ˈbænjæn] *n.* **1** an east Indian tree (*Ficus bengalensis*) of the mulberry family, closely related to the fig but having inedible fruit. The branches of a banyan have hanging roots that grow down to the ground and start new trunks, so that one tree may cover half a hectare of ground. **2** a loose shirt or undershirt worn in India. **3** a member of a Hindu caste of merchants. Also, **banian.** ⟨var. of *banian*; originally a specific tree under which stood a banian pagoda⟩

ban•zai [ˈbɑn,zaɪ] *or* [,bɑnˈzaɪ] *interj.* **1** a Japanese greeting or patriotic cheer meaning: "May you live ten thousand years!" **2** the battle cry of Japanese soldiers in a BANZAI ATTACK. ⟨< Japanese *ban* ten thousand + *sai* year⟩

banzai attack a suicidal assault by Japanese soldiers, usually on an entrenched position.

ba•o•bab [ˈbeiou,bæb] *or* [ˈbɑou,bæb] *n.* a tall, tropical African tree (*Adansonia digitata*) having a very thick trunk, sometimes up to 15 m in diameter. The fibres of baobab bark are used for making rope, cloth, etc. ⟨origin uncertain⟩

bap•tism [ˈbæptɪzəm] *n.* **1** a baptizing or being baptized. **2** the rite or sacrament of baptizing or being baptized. **3** an experience that cleanses a person or introduces him or her into a new kind of life. ⟨ME *bapteme*⟩

bap•tis•mal [bæpˈtɪzməl] *adj.* having to do with baptism; used in baptism: *baptismal vows.* **—bapˈtis•mal•ly,** *adv.*

baptism of fire **1** the first time that a soldier is under fire. **2** a severe trial or test; ordeal.

Bap•tist [ˈbæptɪst] *n., adj.* —*n.* **1** a member of a Christian church that believes that baptism should be given to adults only, usually immersing the whole person under water. **2 baptist,** a person who baptizes.
—*adj.* of or having to do with the Baptists.

bap•tis•ter•y [bæpˈtɪstəri] *n., pl.* **-ter•ies.** a place where baptism is performed. A baptistery may be a section of a church or a separate building. Also, **baptistry** [ˈbæptɪstri].

bap•tize [ˈbæptaɪz] *or* [bæpˈtaɪz] *v.* **-tized, -tiz•ing.** **1** dip (a person) into water or wash with water as a sign of purification from sin and of admission into a Christian church. **2** purify; cleanse. **3** give a first name to (a person) at baptism; christen. **4** give a name to. ⟨ME < OF *baptiser* < LL < Gk. *baptizein* < *baptein* dip⟩ **—bapˈtiz•er,** *n.*

bar¹ [bɑr] *n., v.* **barred, bar•ring;** *prep.* —*n.* **1** an evenly shaped piece of some solid, longer than it is wide or thick: *a bar of iron, a bar of soap, a bar of chocolate.* **2** a pole or rod put across a door, gate, window, etc. to fasten or shut off something. **3** anything that blocks the way or prevents progress: *A bar of sand kept boats out of the harbour. A bad temper is a bar to making friends.* **4** a band of colour; stripe. **5** *Music.* **a** a unit of rhythm; measure. **b** the vertical line between two such units on a staff; bar line. **6** a counter over which drinks, especially alcoholic drinks, are served. **7** a movable piece of furniture from which beverages are dispensed. **8** a room or establishment that has such a counter and in which alcoholic drinks are sold and consumed. **9** a counter, department, or other place, such as a self-serve area, where specific goods or services are sold: *a snack bar, a gas bar.* **10 the bar, a** the profession of a lawyer. A person is called to the bar after passing the prescribed law examinations. **b** lawyers as a group: *Judges are chosen from the bar.* **11** the area or railing in a court of law that separates the bench and the lawyers' seats from the rest of the court. **12** *Esp. Brit.* the place where an accused person stands in a court of law. **13** a court of law. **14** anything like a court of law: *the bar of public opinion.* **15** formerly, the mouth of a harbour. **16** *Heraldry.* a horizontal or diagonal stripe: *a bar sinister.*
cross the bar, die.
—*v.* **1** put bars across; fasten or shut off with a bar: *They bar the doors every night.* **2** block; obstruct: *The exits were barred by chairs.* **3** exclude; forbid: *All talking is barred during a study period.* **4** mark with stripes or bands of colour.
—*prep.* except; excluding: *Dale is the best student, bar none.* ⟨ME *barre* < OF < VL *barra* thick ends of bushes (collectively) < Celtic⟩
☛ *Hom.* BARRE.

bar² [bɑr] *n.* a unit for measuring pressure, equivalent to 100 kilopascals. *Symbol*: bar. ⟨< Gk. *baros* weight⟩
☛ *Hom.* BARRE.

bar. **1** barometer; barometric. **2** barrel.

ba•ra•chois [,bærəˈʃwɑ] *or* [,bɛrəˈʃwɑ], [ˈbærə,ʃwɑ] *or* [ˈbɛrə,ʃwɑ]; *French,* [baʀaˈʃwa] *n. Cdn.* a narrow strip of sand or gravel rising above the surface of the adjacent water; causeway. ⟨< Cdn.F, sandbar at the mouth of a river⟩

barb¹ [bɑrb] *n., v.* —*n.* **1** a point projecting backward from the main point. **2** *Zoology.* one of the hairlike branches on the shaft of a bird's feather. **3** a long, thin growth hanging from the mouth; barbel: *the barbs of a catfish.* **4** *Botany.* a plant growth resembling a hook. **5** something sharp and wounding: *the stinging barbs of unfair criticism.* **6** *Zoology,* the central part of a feather; a quill. **7** a strip of white linen covering the neck and chin of certain nuns.
—*v.* equip with a barb; furnish with barbs. ⟨ME < OF *barbe* < L *barba* beard⟩

barb² [bɑrb] *n.* **1** a kind of horse that has great speed, endurance, and gentleness. **2** a kind of domestic pigeon, related to the carrier pigeon, having a short, stout beak. ⟨< F *barbe* < *Barbarie* Barbary⟩

Bar•ba•di•an [bɑrˈbeidiən] *or* [bɑrˈbeidʒən] *n., adj.* —*n.* a native or inhabitant of Barbados.
—*adj.* of or having to do with Barbados or its people.

Bar•ba•dos [bɑrˈbeidous] *n.* an island country in the West Indies.

bar•bar•i•an [bɑrˈbæriən] *or* [bɑrˈbɛriən] *n., adj.* —*n.* **1** a member of a people thought to be uncivilized. **2** a foreigner differing from the speaker or writer in language and customs. In ancient times a barbarian was successively a person who was not a Greek, a person outside of the Roman Empire, or a person who was not a Christian. **3** a person without sympathy for literary culture or art; boor. **4** a brutal, vicious person.
—*adj.* **1** of or like a barbarian; not civilized; cruel and coarse. **2** differing from the speaker or writer in language and customs. ⟨< F *barbarien* ult. < Gk. *barbaros* foreign. See BARBAROUS.⟩
☛ *Syn. adj.* **1. Barbarian,** BARBARIC, BARBAROUS = not considered civilized. **Barbarian** suggests nothing more: *The Roman Empire was conquered by barbarian peoples.* **Barbaric** emphasizes lack of refinement, taste, or moderation: *barbaric colour schemes, a barbaric noise.* **Barbarous** emphasizes harshness and cruelty: *Torturing prisoners is a barbarous custom.*

bar•bar•i•an•ism [bɑrˈbæriə,nɪzəm] *or* [bɑrˈbɛriə,nɪzəm] *n.* the state or condition of being a barbarian.

bar•bar•ic [bɑrˈbærɪk] *or* [bɑrˈbɛrɪk] *adj.* **1** resembling barbarians; rough and rude. **2** crudely rich or splendid. ⟨ME < L < Gk. *barbarikos* < *barbaros* foreign. See BARBAROUS.⟩ **—barˈbar•i•cal•ly,** *adv.*
☛ *Syn.* See note at BARBARIAN.

bar•ba•rism [ˈbɑrbə,rɪzəm] *n.* **1** an act, custom, etc. that is brutal or harsh. **2** the condition of being barbarous or a barbarian. **3** an act, expression, or object that offends against accepted standards of decency or good taste. **4** a word or construction, or the use of one, that is considered substandard or wrong.

bar•bar•i•ty [bɑr'bærəti] *or* [bɑr'bɛrəti] *n., pl.* **-ties. 1** brutal cruelty. **2** an act of cruelty. **3** a barbaric manner, taste, or style.

bar•ba•rize ['bɑrbə,raɪz] *v.* **-rized, -riz•ing.** make or become barbarous. **—,bar•ba•ri'za•tion,** *n.*

bar•ba•rous ['bɑrbərəs] *adj.* **1** not civilized; primitive in culture and customs. **2** rough and rude; coarse; unrefined. **3** cruelly harsh; brutal: *the barbarous treatment of prisoners.* **4** unpleasant in sound. ⟨< L *barbarus* < Gk. *barbaros* foreign, apparently originally, stammering < the reduplication of the syllable *bar* suggesting unintelligible speech⟩ **—'bar•ba•rous•ly,** *adv.* **—'bar•ba•rous•ness,** *n.*

☛ *Syn.* See note at BARBARIAN.

Bar•ba•ry ['bɑrbəri] *n.* the Muslim countries west of Egypt on the northern coast of Africa.

Barbary ape a tailless monkey that lives in N Africa and on the Rock of Gibraltar.

Barbary sheep aoudad.

Barbary States a former name for Morocco, Algeria, Tunisia, and Tripoli, once noted as pirate strongholds.

bar•bas•co [bɑr'bæskou] *n.* a Mexican plant of the genus *Dioscoria*, having a large root whose extract is used in making steroid hormones. ⟨< Am.Sp. < L⟩

bar•bate ['bɑrbeit] *adj.* **1** having a beard. **2** of plants, having awns, typical of barley, oats, etc. ⟨< L *barbatus* < *barba* beard⟩

bar•be•cue ['bɑrbɪ,kju] *n., v.* **-cued, -cu•ing;** *adj. —n.* **1** an outdoor grill or open fireplace for cooking meat, etc., usually over charcoal. **2** an outdoor meal prepared on a barbecue. **3** food prepared on a barbecue or in a highly seasoned tomato sauce. **4** a feast at which animals are roasted whole. **5** an animal roasted whole. **6** a restaurant which serves barbecued food.
—v. **1** roast (meat, etc.) over an open fire. **2** cook (meat or fish) in a highly seasoned tomato sauce. **3** roast (an animal) whole.
—adj. **1** for use at a barbecue. **2** cooked on a barbecue: *barbecue chicken*. ⟨< Sp. *barbacoa* < Haitian *barboka* framework of sticks⟩

barbed [bɑrbd] *adj., v. —adj.* **1** having a barb or barbs. **2** sharp and wounding: *barbed sarcasm.*
—v. pt. and pp. of BARB.

barbed wire twisted wire with sharp points fixed to it at short intervals, used for fences, etc.

bar•bel ['bɑrbəl] *n.* **1** a long, thin growth hanging from the mouth of some fishes. **2** any of several large freshwater fishes (genus *Barbus*) of Europe having such growths. ⟨ME < OF < LL *barbellus*, dim. of *barbus* a kind of fish < L *barba* beard⟩

bar•bell ['bɑr,bɛl] *n.* a device for performing lifting exercises, similar to a dumb-bell but having a longer bar and provision for weights at each end. ⟨< BAR[1] + *(dumb)bell*⟩

bar•bel•late ['bɑrbə,leit] *or* [bɑr'bɛlɪt] *adj. Botany*. covered with hairy growths resembling bristles or hooks. ⟨< L⟩

bar•ber ['bɑrbər] *n., v. —n.* a person whose business is cutting hair and shaving or trimming beards.
—v. **1** cut the hair or shave or trim the beard of. **2** work as a barber. ⟨ME < AF *barbour* < L *barba* beard⟩

barber pole a pole placed outside a barber's shop to signify the trade, having spiral stripes of red and white dating back to the barber's ancient sideline as a surgeon.

bar•ber•ry ['bɑr,bɛri] *n., pl.* **-ries. 1** any of a genus (*Berberis*) of spiny shrubs having yellow flowers and sour, oblong, red berries. **2** the berry of a barberry. **3** (*adjl.*) designating a family of mostly spiny shrubs or herbs found mainly in north temperate regions. The May apple and the barberries belong to the barberry family. ⟨ME *barbere* < OF *berberis* < Med.L *barbaris*, *berberis*⟩

bar•ber•shop ['bɑrbər,ʃɒp] *n., adj. —n.* a barber's place of business.
—adj. of, having to do with, or suggesting a barbershop quartet: *barbershop harmony.*

barbershop quartet or **quartette** a quartet that sings and improvises on popular sentimental ballads, usually in close harmony.

barber's itch a fungoid infection of the hair follicles of the neck and face.

bar•bet ['bɑrbət] *n.* a bird of the family Capitonidae, having brightly coloured plumage, two fore and two hind toes on each foot, and a large beak with beardlike bristles at its base. ⟨< F, dim. of *barbe* beard⟩

bar•bette [bɑr'bɛt] *n.* **1** a platform in a fort from which guns may be fired over the side. **2** an armoured cylinder protecting a gun turret on a warship. ⟨< F, dim. of *barbe* beard < L *barba*⟩

bar•bi•can ['bɑrbə,kæn] *or* ['bɑrbəkən] *n.* a tower for defence built over a gate or bridge leading into a city or castle. See CASTLE for picture. ⟨ME < OF *barbacane* < Med.L *barbacana*⟩

bar•bi•cel ['bɑrbə,sɛl] *n.* part of a feather; one of the small hooks that fasten the barbules together. ⟨< L *barba*, beard⟩

bar•bi•tal ['bɑrbə,tɒl] *or* ['bɑrbə,tæl] *n.* a drug containing barbituric acid, used as a sedative or hypnotic. *Formula*: $C_7O_3N_2H_{12}$

bar•bi•tu•rate [bɑr'bɪtʃə,rɪt] *or* [bɑr'bɪtʃəreit], [,bɑrbə'tʃʊrɪt] *or* [,bɑrbə'tʃureit] *n.* **1** a salt or ester of barbituric acid. **2** any of several drugs derived from barbituric acid, used as sedatives or hypnotics.

bar•bi•tu•ric acid [,bɑrbə'tʃʊrɪk] an acid much used as the basis of sedatives and hypnotics. *Formula*: $C_4H_4N_2O_3$ ⟨*barbituric* < NL *(Usnea) barbata*, a kind of lichen (< L *barba* beard) + E *-uric*⟩

bar•bule ['bɑrbjul] *n.* part of a feather; one of the hairlike parts on each side of the barb. ⟨< L *barbula* dim. of *barba* beard⟩

barb•wire ['bɑrb,waɪr] *n.* BARBED WIRE.

bar•ca•role or **bar•ca•rolle** ['bɑrkə,roul] *n.* **1** a traditional Venetian boat song. **2** any music in the style of a barcarole. ⟨< F *barcarolle* < Ital. *barcarola* boatman's song < *barca* bark[3]⟩

Bar•ce•lo•na chair [,bɑrsə'lounə] *Trademark.* a soft, armless leather chair having a frame of steel tubing in the shape of an X.

bar•chan [bɑr'kɒn] *or* ['bɑrkɒn] *n.* a sand dune of inland deserts, formed into a crescent shape by the wind. ⟨< Russian⟩

bar chart BAR GRAPH.

bar code a set of lines printed on a package, so that a computer can read the price. Bar codes can also be used on mail.

bar–code reader *Computer technology.* an electronic device capable of reading information printed as a bar code: *The cashier used a bar-code reader to scan the price.*

bard [bɑrd] *n.* **1** a poet and singer of long ago. Bards sang their own poems to the music of their harps. **2** a poet. ⟨< Irish and Scots Gaelic *bàrd* poet⟩

bar•dic ['bɑrdɪk] *adj.* of or having to do with bards or their poetry.

Bard of Avon Shakespeare. ⟨< *Avon*, the river on which Stratford (his birthplace) stands⟩

Bar•do•li•no [,bɑrdə'linou] *or* [,bɑrdou-] *n.* a light Italian wine, usually red, with a fruity taste.

bare[1] [bɛr] *adj.* **bar•er, bar•est;** *v.* **bared, bar•ing.** *—adj.* **1** without covering; not clothed; naked: *bare hands. Trees grew part way up the hill, but the top was bare.* **2** not concealed or not disguised; open: *the bare truth.* **3** not furnished; empty: *The room was bare.* **4** plain; unadorned: *He told us just the bare facts.* **5** much worn; threadbare. **6** only that and no more; mere: *She won by a bare five percent plurality. He earns a bare living by his work.* **7** *Archaic.* without a hat or other headdress.
lay bare, uncover; expose; reveal: *The plot was laid bare.*
—v. make bare; uncover; reveal: *to bare one's feelings. The dog bared its teeth.* ⟨OE bær⟩

☛ *Hom.* BEAR.

☛ *Syn.* **1. Bare,** NAKED, NUDE = without covering. **Bare** emphasizes the idea of being without the usual covering and therefore lying open to view: *The sun burned her bare shoulders.* **Naked** emphasizes the idea of being stripped of all covering, especially customary protective covering, and laid open to view: *The little boy wandered naked through the streets.* **Nude** = unclothed, but expresses an objective attitude toward the body: *Many famous artists have painted nude models.*

bare[2] [bɛr] *v. Archaic.* a pt. of BEAR[1].

☛ *Hom.* BEAR.

bare•back ['bɛr,bæk] *adv. or adj.* without a saddle; on the bare back of a horse, etc.: *to ride bareback, a bareback rider.*

bare•bones ['bɛr,bounz] *n., adj. —n.* a very skinny person.
—adj. **1** meagre: *Her barebones generosity will not make us rich.* **2** basic; simple; without embellishment.

bare•faced ['bɛr,feist] *adj.* **1** with the face bare. **2** not disguised. **3** shameless; impudent: *a barefaced lie.* **—'bare,fac•ed•ly,** *adv.* **—'bare,fac•ed•ness,** *n.*

bare•fist•ed ['bɛr,fɪstəd] *adj.* **1** without boxing gloves. **2** ruthless; unprincipled: *The industrialist was notorious for his barefisted treatment of competitors.*

bare•foot ['bɛr,fʊt] *adj. or adv.* without shoes or stockings on: *a barefoot child. If you go barefoot, watch out for broken glass.*

barefoot doctor *Informal.* a doctor who works in primitive conditions, and without much pay, in a developing country.

bare•foot•ed ['bɛr,fʊtɪd] *adj. or adv.* barefoot.

ba•rège or **ba•rege** [bə'rɛʒ] *n.* a light, flimsy cloth of cotton and wool or silk and wool, used for dresses, veils, etc. ⟨< *Barèges,* a town in France⟩

bare•hand•ed ['bɛr,hændɪd] *adj. or adv.* **1** without any covering on the hands. **2** without weapons or tools in the hands: *He fought the dog barehanded.*

bare•head•ed ['bɛr,hɛdɪd] *adj. or adv.* wearing nothing on the head.

bare•knuck•le ['bɛr,nʌkəl] *adj.* **1** without boxing gloves. **2** in which quarter is neither asked nor given: *a bare-knuckle argument.*

bare•leg•ged ['bɛr,lɛgɪd] *or* ['bɛr,lɛgd] *adj. or adv.* without stockings.

bare•ly ['bɛrli] *adv.* **1** only just; scarcely: *barely old enough to vote. They have barely enough money to live on.* **2** poorly or scantily: *a barely furnished room.* **3** openly or plainly: *She put the question to them barely, and they were obliged to answer.*
☛ *Syn.* **1.** See note at HARDLY.

bare•ness ['bɛrnɪs] *n.* the state or condition of being bare; a lack of covering; lack of furnishings and contents.

barf [bɑrf] *v. Slang.* vomit. ⟨? imitative⟩

bar•fly ['bɑr,flaɪ] *n., pl.* **-flies.** a person who spends much time in bars or taverns.

bar•gain ['bɑrgən] *n., v.* —*n.* **1** an agreement to trade or exchange goods, money, services, concessions, etc.: *If you will take $5 for your book, it's a bargain.* **2** something offered for sale cheap, or bought cheap. **3** a good trade or exchange; price below the real value.
into the bargain, besides; also: *It's late and I'm tired into the bargain.*
strike a bargain, make a bargain; reach an agreement.
—*v.* **1** try to get good terms. **2** make a bargain; come to terms. **3** trade.
bargain for or **on,** be ready for; expect: *The rain wasn't so bad, but the hail was more than we bargained for.* ⟨ME < OF *bargaigne*⟩
—'bar•gain•er, *n.*

bargain basement part of a store, often below ground, where goods are sold cheaply.

bargain counter a small area of a store where goods are sold cheaply.

bargaining chip a helpful factor in negotiation.

barge [bɑrdʒ] *n., v.* **barged, barg•ing.** —*n.* **1** a large, flat-bottomed boat for carrying freight. **2** a large boat furnished and decorated for use in excursions, pageants, and other special occasions. **3** a large motorboat or rowboat used by the commanding officer of a flagship. **4** any old or ill-constructed boat.
—*v.* **1** carry by barge. **2** move heavily or clumsily like a barge. **3** push oneself rudely or abruptly: *Everyone turned as she barged into the room.* **4** intrude (*used with* **in**): *He's forever barging in where he's not wanted.* ⟨ME < OF < L < Gk. *baris* boat used on the Nile⟩

barge•board ['bɑrdʒ,bɔrd] *n.* a carved piece of wood used to embellish gabled façades.

barge couple *Architecture.* one of the two exterior beams projecting beyond the wall in a gabled roof.

bar•gee [bɑr'dʒi] *n. Esp. Brit.* bargeman.

barge•man ['bɑrdʒmən] *n., pl.* **-men.** a man who works on a barge.

barge•pole ['bɑrdʒ,poul] *n.* the long stick used to steer a barge.
would not touch (something) **with a bargepole,** avoid touching or being involved with in any way: *I wouldn't touch that topic with a bargepole.*

barge•wom•an ['bɑrdʒ,wʊmən] *n., pl.* **barge•wom•en** [-,wɪmən] a woman who works on a barge: *The bargewoman threw Toad into the river.*

bar graph a chart or diagram showing different quantities by means of vertical or horizontal bars of proportional lengths.

bar•hop ['bɑr,hɒp] *v.,* **bar•hopped, bar•hop•ping.** *Informal.* go from bar to bar, drinking at each one, usually as a group party event.

bar•i•a•tri•cian [,bæriə'trɪʃən] *or* [,bɛriə'trɪʃən] *n.* a physician trained in bariatrics.

bar•i•at•rics [,bæri'ætrɪks] *or* [,bɛri'ætrɪks] *n.* the scientific study of obesity and its management.

bar•ic[1] ['bærɪk] *or* ['bɛrɪk] *adj. Physics.* having to do with weight, usually that of the atmosphere. ⟨< *bar*[2]⟩

bar•ic[2] ['bærɪk] *or* ['bɛrɪk] *adj. Chemistry.* having to do with barium.

bar•ite ['bærəit] *or* ['bɛrəit] *n.* a rock that consists mostly of barium sulphate. ⟨< Gk. *barys* weighty + -ITE[1]⟩

bar•i•tone ['bærə,toun] *or* ['bɛrə,toun] *n., adj.* —*n.* **1** a male voice between tenor and bass. **2** *Music.* **a** a singer with such a voice. **b** a part for such a voice or for a corresponding instrument. **c** an instrument playing such a part. **3** *Music.* a brass B-flat musical instrument used in bands.
—*adj.* **1** of or for a baritone. **2** that can sing or play a baritone part. ⟨< Gk. *barytonos* < *barys* deep + *tonos* pitch⟩

bar•i•um ['bæriəm] *or* ['bɛriəm] *n.* a soft, silvery white metallic element. *Symbol*: Ba; *at.no.* 56; *at.mass* 137.33. ⟨< NL < Gk. *barytēs* weight⟩

barium sulphate a medium used for diagnosis of diseases of the gastrointestinal tract. *Formula*: $BaSO_4$

bark[1] [bɑrk] *n., v.* —*n. Botany.* **1** the tough outer covering of the stems and roots of woody plants, including an outside layer of dead cells, a cortex, which in twigs and small branches contains chlorophyll, and an inner layer, the phloem, containing the tubes which carry food along the stem or root. **2** any of several particular kinds of bark, such as tanbark, used in tanning, or circhona, used in medicine.
—*v.* **1** strip bark from; especially, cut out a ring of bark around (a tree) to kill it by interrupting the flow of food. **2** treat or tan with bark. **3** scrape the skin from (shins, knuckles, etc.): *I fell down the steps and barked my shins.* ⟨ME < ON *börkr*⟩
☛ *Hom.* BARQUE.

bark[2] [bɑrk] *n., v.* —*n.* **1** the short, sharp sound that a dog makes. **2** a sound like this: *the bark of a fox, a squirrel, a gun, or a cough.*
—*v.* **1** make this sound or one like it. **2** speak or utter sharply or gruffly: *The officer barked out the order.* **3** *Informal.* cough. **4** *Informal.* call or shout to attract people into a circus tent, sideshow at a fair, store, etc. **5** advertise (goods) loudly.
bark at the moon, make a noise or fuss to no effect.
bark up the wrong tree, go after something by mistake or use wrong means to get at something. ⟨OE *beorcan*⟩
☛ *Hom.* BARQUE.

bark[3] [bɑrk] *n.* See BARQUE.

bark beetle any of a family (Scolytidae) of small beetles that bore through the bark and wood of trees. Bark beetles are carriers of the fungus that causes Dutch elm disease.

bar•keep ['bɑr,kip] *n. Esp. U.S.* barkeeper.

bar•keep•er ['bɑr,kipər] *n.* **1** a person who tends a bar where alcoholic drinks are sold. **2** the owner of such a bar.

bar•ken•tine ['bɑrkən,tin] *n.* a three-masted ship with the foremast square-rigged and the other masts fore-and-aft-rigged. Also, **barquentine.** ⟨< *bark*[3]; modelled on *brigantine*⟩

bark•er ['bɑrkər] *n.* **1** one that barks. **2** a person who stands in front of a circus tent, sideshow at a fair, store, etc. urging people to go in. ⟨< *bark*[2]⟩

bar•ley ['bɑrli] *n.* **1** any of various cereal grasses (genus *Horedum*) of temperate regions, especially *H. vulgare,* widely cultivated for forage and for its grain. **2** the grain or seed of barley, used in soups, etc. and also for making malt for beer and whisky. ⟨OE *bærlic*⟩

bar•ley•corn ['bɑrli,kɔrn] *n.* **1** a grain of barley. **2** an old measure of length, equal to 0.85 cm.

Bar•ley•corn ['bɑrli,kɔrn] *n.* **John Barleycorn,** a name for intoxicating liquor, especially whisky.

barley sugar a clear, brittle candy, originally made by boiling sugar with an extract of barley.

barley water water in which barley has been boiled, formerly much used as a drink for invalids and babies.

bar line *Music.* the vertical line between two measures, or bars, on a staff.

barm [bɑrm] *n.* a foamy yeast that forms on malt liquors while they are fermenting. ⟨OE *beorma*⟩

bar magnet a permanent magnet shaped like a bar or rod: *A bar magnet suspended horizontally from a string can serve as a compass.*

bar•maid ['bɑr,meid] *n.* a woman who works in a bar, serving alcoholic drinks to customers.

bar•man ['bɑrmən] *n., pl.* **-men.** a male barkeeper.

Bar•me•cide feast ['bɑrmə,saɪd] **1** a pretended feast with empty dishes. **2** the empty pretence of hospitality, generosity, etc. ⟨from *Barmecide*, a wealthy man in the *Arabian Nights* who gave a beggar a pretended feast on empty dishes⟩ **—,bar•me'cid•al,** *adj.*

bar mitz•vah ['bɑr 'mɪtsvə] **1** a ceremony marking the formal admission of a boy into the Jewish religious community, usually held when the boy is thirteen years old. Compare BAS MITZVAH. **2** a boy who has reached the age of thirteen, the age of religious responsibility. Also, **Bar Mitzvah.** ⟨< Hebrew *bar mitzvāh* son of the commandment⟩

barm•y ['bɑrmi] *adj.* **barm•i•er, barm•i•est. 1** full of barm; fermenting. **2** *Informal.* silly; crazy; flighty.

barn [bɑrn] *n.* **1** a building for storing hay, grain, farm machinery, etc. and often for sheltering livestock. **2** any place that resembles a barn in use or appearance. **3** *Nuclear physics.* a measurement of area, equal to 10^{-24} m². ⟨OE *bern* < *bere* barley + *ærn* storing place⟩ **—'barn,like,** *adj.*

bar•na•cle ['bɑrnəkəl] *n.* **1** any of a large group of marine crustaceans (subclass Cirripedia) that spend their entire adult life attached to some underwater object like a rock, ship bottom, or wharf pile, or a sea creature like a turtle or whale. In the first two of the three stages of a barnacle's life, it has no shell and can swim about freely. **2** BARNACLE GOOSE. **3** *Informal.* any person or thing that will not go away. ⟨ME *bernacle* < OF (cf. F *barnacle, bernicle*); earlier ME *bernake* < OF *bernaque*⟩

bar•na•cled ['bɑrnəkəld] *adj.* covered with barnacles.

barnacle goose a northern European wild goose (*Branta leucopsis*).

bar•na•cles ['bɑrnəkəls] *n.pl.* **1** an instrument for controlling a disobedient horse by pinching the nose. **2** an instrument of torture resembling this.

barn burner *Informal.* something or someone spectacular.

barn dance 1 a dance held in a barn. **2** a lively dance resembling a polka.

barn owl a common brown and white owl (*Tyto alba*) which lives in barns and eats mice.

barn raising a gathering of neighbours to build a barn. In pioneer days, such gatherings were usually social affairs, the day's work being followed by dancing, eating, and drinking.

barn•storm ['bɑrn,stɔrm] *v. Informal.* **1** act plays, make speeches, etc. in (small towns and country districts). **2** tour (country districts) giving short airplane rides, exhibitions of stunt flying, etc. **—'barn,storm•er,** *n.*

barn swallow a swallow (*Hirundo rustica*) found throughout the world, having a dark steel-blue back and reddish brown throat and breast, and a deeply forked tail. Barn swallows often nest in crevices of buildings. See SWALLOW for picture.

barn•yard ['bɑrn,jɑrd] *n.* **1** the yard around a barn for livestock, etc. **2** (*adjl.*) of or having to do with a barnyard: *barnyard animals.* **3** (*adjl.*) fit for a barnyard; dirty; lewd: *barnyard morals*.

baro– *combining form.* weight; atmospheric pressure: *Barometer = something that measures (i.e., a meter of) atmospheric pressure.* ⟨< Gk. *baros* weight⟩

bar•o•gram ['bærə,græm] *or* ['bɛrə,græm] *n.* a record made by a barograph or similar instrument.

bar•o•graph ['bærə,græf] *or* ['bɛrə,græf] *n.* a barometer that automatically records pressure changes on a revolving drum. **—,bar•o'graph•ic,** *adj.*

Ba•ro•lo [bə'roulou] *or* [bɑ-] a dry red Italian wine which is full in flavour.

ba•rom•e•ter [bə'rɒmətər] *n.* **1** an instrument for measuring atmospheric pressure. Barometers are used to indicate probable changes in the weather and for determining the height above sea level. **2** something that indicates changes: *Newspapers are often barometers of public opinion.* ⟨< Gk. *báros* + *métron* measure⟩

bar•o•met•ric [,bærə'mɛtrɪk] *or* [,bɛrə'mɛtrɪk] *adj.* **1** of a barometer. **2** indicated by a barometer. **—,bar•o'met•ric•al•ly,** *adv.*

bar•o•met•ri•cal [,bærə'mɛtrəkəl] *or* [,bɛrə'mɛtrəkəl] *adj.* barometric.

barometric gradient the rate at which barometric pressure falls in a given place during a given period.

barometric pressure pressure exerted by the atmosphere as measured by a barometer. It is measured in kilopascals.

bar•on ['bærən] *or* ['bɛrən] *n.* **1** a British nobleman of the lowest hereditary rank. **2** a Japanese or European nobleman with a similar rank. **3** during the Middle Ages, a British nobleman who held his lands directly from the king. **4** a powerful merchant or financier: *a railway baron.* **5** a large cut of meat: *a baron of beef.* ⟨ME < OF < OHG *baro* man, fighter⟩

☛ *Hom.* BARREN.

☛ *Usage.* In the United Kingdom, a **baron** is referred to as *Lord M—*, rather than as *Baron M—* as is the case in other European countries.

bar•on•age ['bærənɪdʒ] *or* ['bɛrənɪdʒ] *n.* **1** barons collectively. **2** the nobility. **3** the rank or title of a baron. **4** the domain of a baron.

bar•on•ess ['bærənɪs] *or* ['bɛrənɪs] *n.* **1** a noblewoman holding a rank equal to that of a baron. A British baroness has the title *Lady* before her surname. **2** the wife or widow of a baron.

bar•on•et [,bærə'nɛt] *or* [,bɛrə'nɛt], ['bærənɪt] *or* ['bɛrənɪt] *n.* **1** in the United Kingdom, a man below a baron in rank and next above a knight. A baronet has *Sir* before his name and *Bart.* after it, as in *Sir John Brown, Bart.* **2** the hereditary rank or title of a baronet. *Abbrev.*: Bart. or Bt.

bar•on•et•age ['bærə,nɛtədʒ] *or* ['bɛrə,nɛtədʒ], ['bærənətədʒ] *or* ['bɛrənətədʒ] *n.* **1** barons collectively. **2** baronetcy.

bar•on•et•cy ['bærənɪtsi] *or* ['bɛrənɪtsi] *n., pl.* **-cies. 1** the rank or position of a baronet. **2** a document that makes a person a baronet.

ba•rong [bə'rɒŋ] *n.* a large ornamental knife, used by the Moros of the Philippines. ⟨< Malay⟩

ba•ro•ni•al [bə'rouniəl] *adj.* **1** of a baron; of barons. **2** suitable for a baron; splendid; stately; magnificent.

bar•o•ny ['bærəni] *or* ['bɛrəni] *n., pl.* **-nies. 1** the lands of a baron. **2** the rank or title of a baron. **3** a vast region or undertaking under private ownership or control. ⟨< OF⟩

ba•roque [bə'rouk] *or* [bə'rɒk] *adj., n.* *—adj.* **1** Often, **Baroque**, of or having to do with a style of art, architecture, poetry, or music that flourished in Europe, especially in the 17th and early 18th centuries, and was characterized by rich and elaborate ornamentation. **2** Often, **Baroque**, of or having to do with this period. **3** ornate or fantastic in style. **4** of pearls, irregular in shape.
—n. the baroque style. ⟨< F < Pg. *barroco* irregular⟩

bar•o•re•cep•tor [,bærourɪ'sɛptər] *or* [,bɛrou-] *n.* a nerve ending which responds to pressure.

bar•o•scope ['bærə,skoup] *or* ['bɛrə,skoup] *n.* an instrument for showing changes in the pressure or density of the air. ⟨< Gk. *baros* weight + E *-scope* instrument for viewing < Gk. *skopein* look at⟩

ba•rouche [bə'ruʃ] *n.* a four-wheeled carriage with two seats facing each other, and a folding top. ⟨< dial. G *Barutsche* < Ital. < L *birotus* two-wheeled < *bi-* two + *rota* wheel⟩

A barque of the late 19th century

barque [bɑrk] *n.* **1** *Poetic.* any boat or ship. **2** a sailing ship with three masts, square-rigged on the first two masts and fore-and-aft rigged on the other. Also, **bark.** ⟨< F *barque* < Ital. *barca* < LL⟩

☛ *Hom.* BARK.

bar•quen•tine ['bɑrkən,tin] See BARKENTINE.

bar•quette [bɑr'kɛt] *n.* a pastry shell in the shape of a boat, filled with fruit or custard, etc.

bar•rack[1] ['bærək] *or* ['bɛrək] *n., v.* —*n.* Usually, **barracks** (*used with a sing. or pl. verb*), **1** a building or group of buildings for members of the armed forces to live in. **2** *Cdn.* a building housing local detachments of the Royal Canadian Mounted Police. **3** *Cdn. Informal.* a training centre of the Royal Canadian Mounted Police: *Her brother is training at the RCMP barracks in Regina.* **4** a large, plain building housing many people.
—*v.* house (soldiers, etc.) in barracks. ⟨< F *baraque* < Ital. *baracca*⟩

bar•rack[2] ['bærək] *or* ['bɛrək] *v. Brit. and Australian. Informal.* express opinions noisily, especially to jeer at (a player, team, speaker, etc.). ⟨< Australian slang *barracking* banter⟩

bar•ra•cu•da [,bærə'kudə] *or* [,bɛrə'kudə] *n., pl.* **-da** or **-das.** any of several pikelike fishes (genus *Sphyraena*) found in warm seas, having long, pointed jaws with razor-sharp teeth, and ranging in length from about 90 cm to about 120 cm. Because a barracuda will pursue anything that moves in the water, it is considered by some to be more dangerous than a shark. ⟨< Sp. < West Indian name⟩

bar•rage [bə'rɑʒ] *for n. 1,3 and v.,* ['bɑrɪdʒ] *for n. 2*; *n., v.* **-raged, -rag•ing.** —*n.* **1** a barrier of artillery fire to check the enemy or to protect one's own soldiers in advancing or retreating. **2** an artificial barrier in a river; dam. **3** any heavy onslaught or attack: *a barrage of words.*
—*v.* fire with artillery at; subject to a barrage. ⟨< F *barrage* < *barrer* to bar⟩

barrage balloon a large balloon intended to force enemy aircraft out of bombing range. It floats from a cable and is equipped with a self-sealing, bulletproof fabric.

bar•ra•mun•di [,bærə'mʌndi] *or* [,bɛrə-] *n.* **1** a fish (*Neoceratodus forsteri*) having one lung and fins like paddles, common in Australia. **2** a similar Australian fish of the genus *Scleropages*, living in fresh water. Also, **barramunda** [-mʌndə]. ⟨< aboriginal language of Australia⟩

bar•ran•ca [bə'ræŋkə] *n.* a steep canyon in the southwestern U.S. ⟨< Sp. < VL < Gk. *pharanx* chasm⟩

bar•ra•tor ['bærətər] *or* ['bɛrətər] *n.* someone guilty of BARRATRY (def. 1).

bar•ra•try ['bærətri] *or* ['bɛrətri] *n.* **1** *Law.* fraud or gross negligence by a ship's officer or seaman against owners, insurers, etc. **2** the act of stirring up lawsuits or quarrels. **3** trade in church or civil positions. ⟨ME < OF *baraterie* < *barater* to exchange, cheat. Related to BARTER.⟩ —**'bar•ra•trous,** *adj.*

Barr body *Genetics.* the SEX CHROMATIN, a chromatin mass seen in somatic cells of human females, representing an inactive X chromosome. ⟨after Murray *Barr* (1908-), Canadian anatomist⟩

barre [bɑr] *n.* the supporting rail that ballet dancers use when practising. ⟨< F⟩
☛ *Hom.* BAR.

barred [bɑrd] *adj., v.* —*adj.* **1** having bars: *a barred window.* **2** marked with stripes: *a chicken with barred feathers.* **3** not permitted; forbidden: *Smoking is barred in the library.*
—*v.* pt. and pp. of BAR.

barred owl a fairly large owl with a round head, no ear tufts, and coloured brown and white. Its breast is striped or barred.

bar•rel ['bærəl] *or* ['bɛrəl] *n., v.* **-relled** or **-reled, -rel•ling** or **-rel•ing.** —*n.* **1** a large container shaped somewhat like a cylinder, having a flat, round top and bottom and slightly bulging sides, usually made of boards held together by hoops. **2** the amount that a barrel can hold. **3** a unit for measuring volume of oil, equal to about 0.159 m^3 (159 L). **4** any container, case, or part shaped like a barrel: *the barrel of a drum.* **5** the metal tube of a firearm, through which the bullet travels. See FIREARM for picture. **6** any similar tube, such as that in a microscope. **7** *Informal.* a large quantity or number: *a barrel of fun.*
have (someone) **over a barrel,** *Informal.* have (someone) entirely in one's power.
—*v.* **1** put in a barrel or barrels. **2** *Informal.* move in a rush: *She was barrelling along the highway at 130 km/h.* ⟨ME < OF *baril,* probably < VL *barra* bar, stave⟩
☛ *Hom.* BERYL ['bɛrəl].

barrel chair *Esp. U.S.* TUB CHAIR.

bar•rel–chest•ed ['bærəl ,tʃɛstɪd] *or* ['bɛrəl] *adj.* having a large, rounded rib cage.

bar•rel•ful ['bærəl,fʊl] *or* ['bɛrəl,fʊl] *n.* the amount that a barrel can hold.

bar•rel•house ['bærəl,hʌus] *or* ['bɛrəl-] *n., v.* **-housed, -hous•ing.** *Music.* a kind of jazz, known for its roughness and hard rhythms. ⟨so called from its origins in saloons with barrels stacked along the walls.⟩
—*v.* play such jazz.

barrel organ a HAND ORGAN.

barrel racing a sport in which riders perform a kind of slalom around barrels. **—barrel racer.**

barrel roll an airplane stunt in which the plane describes a spiral while turning over completely.

barrel vault *Architecture.* a vault built in the shape of a half-barrel.

bar•ren ['bærən] *or* ['bɛrən] *adj., n.* —*adj.* **1** not producing anything: *A sandy desert is barren.* **2** not able to bear offspring; sterile. **3** without interest; not attractive; dull. **4** fruitless; unprofitable. **5** completely lacking; without (*used with* **of**): *barren of imagination.*
—*n. Cdn.* **1** Usually, **barrens,** *pl.* a barren stretch of land; a wasteland. **2 the Barrens,** *pl.* the BARREN GROUND. **3** a group of mules. ⟨ME < OF *baraine*⟩ **—'bar•ren•ly,** *adv.*
—'bar•ren•ness, *n.*
☛ *Hom.* BARON.

Barren Ground or **Grounds** *Cdn.* the treeless, thinly populated region in northern Canada, lying between Hudson Bay on the east and Great Slave Lake and Great Bear Lake on the west: *Much of the Barren Ground is covered, in season, with short grass, moss, and small flowering plants.* Also, **Barren Lands.**

bar•rette [bə'rɛt] *n.* a pin with a clasp used for holding the hair in place. ⟨< F *barrette,* dim. of *barre* bar⟩

bar•ri•cade ['bærə,keid] *or* ['bɛrə,keid], [,bærə'keid] *or* [,bɛrə'keid] *n., v.* **-cad•ed, -cad•ing.** —*n.* **1** a rough, hastily made barrier for defence. **2** any barrier or obstruction. **3** *Cdn.* large blocks of ice remaining frozen to a river or sea shore after the spring breakup.
—*v.* **1** block or obstruct with a barricade: *The road was barricaded with fallen trees.* **2** keep out or in with a barricade. ⟨< F *barricade,* apparently < Provençal *barricada* < *barrica* cask; originally, made of casks. Related to BARREL.⟩

bar•ri•ca•do [,bærə'keidou] *or* [,bɛrə'keidou] *n., pl.* **-does.** barricade.

bar•ri•er ['bæriər] *or* ['bɛriər] *n.* **1** something that stands in the way; something stopping progress or preventing approach. **2** something that separates things or people or keeps them apart. **3** *Horse racing.* a movable starting gate. ⟨ME < AF *barrere* < LL *barraria* < *barra* bar < Celtic⟩

barrier cream a skin cream used to prevent infection or irritation by forming a barrier against bacteria and irritants.

barrier reef a long line of rocks or coral reef not far from the mainland.

bar•ring ['bɑrɪŋ] *prep., v.* —*prep.* except; not including: *Barring accidents, we shall reach Vancouver at twelve o'clock.*
—*v.* ppr. of BAR.

bar•rio ['bɑriou], ['bæriou], *or* ['bɛriou] *n.* **1** a city district or neighbourhood in Spain or its former colonies. **2** a rural settlement in Central or South America or the Philippines. **3** any district in an American city whose inhabitants are Spanish-speaking, especially those from Latin America. ⟨< Sp.⟩

bar•ris•ter ['bærɪstər] *or* ['bɛrɪstər] *n.* **1** a lawyer who pleads in court. **2** in the United Kingdom, a lawyer entitled to plead in any court, as opposed to a solicitor. ⟨< *bar* + *-ster*⟩

bar•room ['bɑr,rum] *or* [-,rʊm] *n.* a room with a bar for the sale of alcoholic drinks.

bar•row[1] ['bærou] *or* ['bɛrou] *n.* **1** a frame with two short handles at each end, used for carrying a load. **2** wheelbarrow. **3** handcart. ⟨OE *bearwe.* Related to BEAR[1].⟩

bar•row[2] ['bærou] *or* ['bɛrou] *n.* a mound of earth or stones over an ancient or prehistoric grave. ⟨OE *beorg*⟩

bar•row[3] ['bærou] *or* ['bɛrou] *n.* a young gelded pig. ⟨ME *barow* < OE *beorg*⟩

barrow pit especially in the West, a BORROW PIT.

bar sinister **1** BEND SINISTER. **2** the fact or the stigma of being of illegitimate birth.

Bart. Baronet.

bar•tend•er ['bɑr,tɛndər] *n.* a person who mixes or serves alcoholic drinks.

bar•ter ['bɑrtər] *v., n.* —*v.* **1** trade by exchanging one kind of goods or services for other goods or services without using money. **2** exchange (*used with* **for**): *He bartered his boat for a car.* **3** give or trade without an equal return (*used with* **away**): *In his eagerness to make a fortune, he bartered away his freedom.*
—*n.* **1** the act of bartering. **2** something bartered. ⟨< OF *barater* to exchange. Related to BARRATRY.⟩ —**'bar•ter•er,** *n.*
☛ *Usage.* **Barter** and BARGAIN are not the same. **Barter** means to trade goods without money changing hands, but **bargain** means to negotiate for a better price.

Barth•i•an ['bɑrθiən] *adj. Theology.* having to do with the neo-Orthodox doctrine of Karl Barth, Swiss theologian (1886-1968). Barthian philosophy promotes tolerance and ecumenicalism and emphasizes people's need for God's grace.

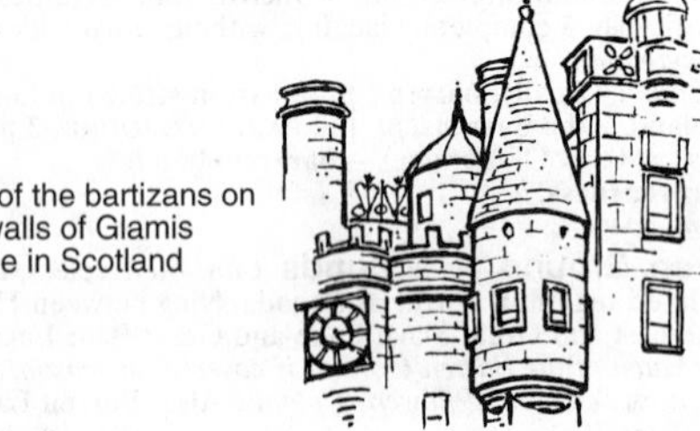

One of the bartizans on the walls of Glamis Castle in Scotland

bar•ti•zan ['bɑrtəzən] *or* ['bɑrtə,zæn] *n. Architecture.* a small overhanging turret on a wall or tower. ⟨alteration of *bratticing* < *brattice* parapet < OF *bretesche*, probably < OE *brittisc* British (type of fortification)⟩

Bart•lett pear ['bɑrtlɪt] a large, juicy kind of pear. ⟨after E. *Bartlett*, who introduced it into America⟩

bar•y•on ['bæri,ɒn] *or* ['bɛri,ɒn] *n. Physics.* any of a class of elementary particles, including the proton and neutron and the hyperons, having a spin of ½ and generally having a mass greater than that of the mesons. ⟨< Gk. *barys* heavy + *on*⟩

bar•y•sphere ['bærəs,fir] *or* ['bɛrəs,fir] *n.* the heavy inside part of the earth within the outer crust. ⟨< Gk. *barys* heavy + E *sphere*⟩

ba•ry•ton ['bærɪtən] *n.* an obsolete stringed instrument of the 18th century. ⟨< F < Ital. *baritono* low voice < Gk. *barytonos* deep-sounding⟩

bas•al ['beisəl] *adj.* **1** of the base; at the base; forming the base. **2** fundamental; basic. **3** *Botany.* growing from the bottom of a stem. —**'bas•al•ly,** *adv.*

basal metabolism the minimum amount of energy used for the vital life processes of an individual at rest. It is measured as oxygen consumption in kilojoules per minute per kilogram of body mass. The basal metabolism of an average 30-year-old male is about 5.5 kJ/min to 6 kJ/min.

ba•salt ['beisɒlt], ['bæsɒlt], *or* [bə'sɒlt] *n.* **1** a hard, dark-coloured rock of volcanic origin. **2** BASALT WARE. ⟨< LL *basaltes*, a manuscript corruption of L *basanites* < Gk. *basanos* touchstone⟩

ba•sal•tic [bə'sɒltɪk] *adj.* **1** of or having to do with basalt. **2** like basalt.

basalt ware a black, unglazed pottery having a dull gloss, developed by Josiah Wedgwood (1730-1795).

bas•cule ['bæskjul] *n.* a device in which one end is counterbalanced by the other, as in a teeter-totter. ⟨< F *bascule* seesaw, ult. < *battre* beat (influenced by *bas* low) + *cul* posterior⟩

bascule bridge a type of drawbridge that is raised and lowered by means of a bascule. See BRIDGE[1] for picture.

base[1] [beis] *n., v.* **based, bas•ing;** *adj.* —*n.* **1** an underlying support: *The machine rests on a wide base of steel.* **2** a fundamental principle; basis; foundation. **3** the most important element of anything; essential part. **4** *Architecture.* **a** the part of a column on which the shaft rests. See COLUMN for picture. **b** the part at the bottom of a wall or monument. **5** *Biology.* **a** the part of an organ nearest its point of attachment. **b** the point of attachment. **6** *Chemistry.* a compound that reacts with an acid to form a salt. Calcium hydroxide is a base. **7 a** an undercoat of paint. **b** a foundation layer of make-up. **8** *Baseball.* any of the four corners of the diamond, which runners have to touch in order to score. **9** a starting place or goal in any of various sports and games. **10 a** the place from which a military force operates and from which supplies are obtained; headquarters. **b** the starting point for a mountaineering or exploring expedition. **11** a permanent camp or other place where units of the armed forces are stationed: *There is a large base at Gagetown, New Brunswick.* **12** the number that is a starting point for a system of numeration or logarithms. In arithmetic, 10 is the base of the decimal system, 2 the base of the binary system used in computers. **13** *Geometry.* a line or surface forming that part of a geometrical figure on which it is supposed to stand: *Any side of a triangle can be its base.* **14** *Surveying.* a line used as the starting point. **15** *Linguistics.* the form of a word to which affixes are attached; root; stem. **16** in business, a starting point for certain calculations.
cover all the bases, examine all angles of something.
get to first base, make the first step successfully: *I worked on the problem for an hour, but couldn't even get to first base.*
off base, *Informal.* incorrect; absurdly mistaken: *I think your answer was off base.*
touch base (or **bases**), make contact (*with* someone).
—*v.* **1** make or form a base or foundation for. **2** establish; found (*on* or *upon*): *Her large business was based on good service.* **3** station or locate at a base: *The company is based in Ottawa. The research team is based at York University but does fieldwork all over the province.*
—*adj.* serving as a beginning point: *base line, base pay.* ⟨ME < MF < L < Gk. *basis* base; literally, a step. Doublet of BASIS.⟩
☛ *Hom.* BASS[1].
☛ *Syn. n.* **1, 2. Base,** BASIS, FOUNDATION = the part of anything on which the rest stands for support. **Base,** chiefly used literally, applies to the bottom and supporting part of objects: *The Christmas tree must have a base.* **Basis,** chiefly used figuratively, applies to the part that supports beliefs, arguments, etc.: *The basis of his opinion is something he read in the paper.* **Foundation,** used literally and figuratively, emphasizes the firmness and solidness of the base or basis: *Her honesty and willingness to work are the foundation of her success.*
☛ *Usage.* **Base,** BASIS. The plural of this word is regular: **bases** ['beisɪz]. The plural of **basis** is spelled **bases** but pronounced ['beisiz].

base[2] [beis] *adj.* **bas•er, bas•est. 1** morally low; mean; selfish; cowardly: *To betray a friend is a base action.* **2** fit for an inferior person or thing; menial; unworthy: *No needful service is to be looked on as base.* **3** *Archaic.* of humble birth or origin. **4** having little comparative value; inferior: *Iron and lead are base metals; gold and silver are precious metals.* **5** debased; counterfeit: *base coin.* **6** deep or grave in sound. ⟨ME < MF *bas* < LL *bassus* low. Doublet of BASSO.⟩ —**'base•ly,** *adv.* —**'base•ness,** *n.*
☛ *Hom.* BASS[1].
☛ *Syn. adj.* **1. Base,** VILE, LOW = morally inferior and contemptible. **Base** = reduced to a low moral state, without honour or without moral standards, usually by selfishness or cowardliness: *To betray a friend for a reward is base.* **Vile** = without moral standards or sense of decency; evil; disgustingly dirty: *In the slums of some cities even small children learn vile habits.* **Low** = without a sense of decency or of what is honourable: *To steal from the collection plate in church is low.*

base•ball ['beis,bɒl] *n.* **1** a game played with bat and ball by two teams of nine players each, on a field with four bases. **2** the ball used in this game.

base•board ['beis,bɔrd] *n.* **1** a line of boards around the walls of a room, next to the floor. **2** a board forming the base of anything.

baseboard heating a method of heating a room or building with small radiators near the floor.

base•born ['beis,bɔrn] *adj. Archaic.* **1** born of slaves, peasants, or other humble parents. **2** born of a mother who was not married; illegitimate. **3** dishonourable; contemptible.

base•burn•er ['beis,bɜrnər] *n.* a stove or furnace fed automatically as the fuel below is burned.

base hit *Baseball.* a successful hitting of the ball by a batter so that he or she gets at least to first base without the help of an error.

base•less ['beislɪs] *adj.* groundless; without foundation: *A rumour is baseless if it is not supported by facts.*
—**'base•less•ness,** *n.*

base level *Geology.* **1** the limit of erosion of a river. **2** SEA LEVEL.

base line **1** a line used as a base for measuring or calculating, especially in land surveys, etc. **2** Often, **baseline,** a basic standard of value against which things are measured or compared: *the artistic baseline of the cinema.* **3** *Baseball.* a lane inside which a runner must keep when running between bases. **4** *Tennis and basketball.* the line marking the limit of play at either end of a court.

base•man ['beismən] *n., pl.* **-men.** *Baseball.* a player guarding one of the bases.

base map a map empty of details which can then be entered.

base•ment ['beismənt] *n.* **1** the lowest storey of a building, partly or wholly below the ground; cellar. **2** (*adjl.*) of, having to do with, or in a basement: *a basement rec room.*

base metal **1** any of the non-precious metals, such as lead, zinc, iron, etc. **2** the chief metallic element in an alloy.

ba•sen•ji [bə'sɛndʒi] *n.* a breed of small dog originally from Africa, having a smooth, brown coat and a curled tail. Basenjis cannot bark. ⟨< Bantu⟩

base pair *Genetics.* a pair of complementary nucleotide bases, AT or GC, located in the DNA double helix like a step on a ladder.

base pairing *Genetics.* the complementary pairing of bases in DNA, A with T and G with C.

base pay basic remuneration for any job, not counting bonuses, overtime, etc.

base runner *Baseball.* a member of the team at bat who is on a base or trying to reach a base.

ba•ses[1] ['beisiz] *n.* pl. of BASIS.

bas•es[2] ['beisɪz] *n.* pl. of BASE[1].

bash [bæʃ] *v., n.* *—v. Informal.* strike violently: *She bashed the intruder on the head. They bashed down the door.*
—n. **1** *Informal.* a smashing blow: *a bash on the head.* **2** *Slang.* an entertaining or exciting social event; a party or spree: *The mayor's fete was one of the most successful bashes of the year.* **3** *Slang.* an attempt: *Let me have a bash at it.* ⟨? imitative⟩ **—'bash•er,** *n.*

ba•shaw [bə'ʃɒ] *n.* **1** a pasha, a Turkish official. **2** an important person. ⟨< Turkish *basha*⟩

bash•ful ['bæʃfəl] *adj.* uneasy and awkward in the presence of strangers; shy. ⟨< *bash*, v. (var. of *abash*) + *-ful*⟩ **—'bash•ful•ly,** *adv.* **—'bash•ful•ness,** *n.*
☛ *Syn.* See note at SHY[1].

Bash•kir [bæʃ'kir] *n.* **1** any of a people of SW Asia, formerly in the Soviet Union. **2** their Turkic language.

ba•sic ['beisɪk] *adj., n.* *—adj.* **1** of, at, or forming the base; fundamental: *a basic principle. Addition, subtraction, multiplication, and division are the basic processes of arithmetic.* **2** being a basis or introduction; elementary: *a basic course in drawing.* **3** standard minimum, excluding extras: *a basic salary of $38 000.* **4** *Chemistry.* of, having the character of, or containing a base. **5** *Geology.* of or having to do with igneous rocks having a small proportion of silica.
—n. Usually, **basics,** *pl.* a fundamental fact, principle, etc.: *the basics of flying. Many parents felt that the schools were paying too little attention to basics.*

BASIC ['beisɪk] a computer language that uses ordinary words. ⟨*B*eginner's *A*ll-purpose *S*ymbolic *I*nstruction *C*ode⟩

ba•si•cal•ly ['beisɪkli] *adv.* **1** as a basic principle; fundamentally. **2** *Informal.* essentially; in simple terms.

basic defect *Genetics.* a defect that underlies and leads to others. Compare CONGENITAL DEFECT.

Basic English a simplified system of English, consisting of 700 essential words and a further 150 scientific words. It was invented by C.K. Ogden (1889-1957). ⟨*Basic*, considered as an acronym for *B*ritish, *A*merican, *S*cientific, *I*nternational, *C*ommercial⟩

ba•sic•i•ty [bei'sɪsəti] *n. Chemistry.* **1** the state or quality of being a base. **2** the ability of an acid to combine with bases, dependent on the number of replaceable hydrogen atoms contained in a molecule of the acid.

ba•sid•io•my•cete [bə,sɪdiou'maisit] *n. Botany.* a type of fungus, including mushrooms and puffballs. ⟨< NL < L *basidium* + Gk. *myketes* pl. of *mykes* mushroom⟩

ba•sid•i•um [bə'sɪdiəm] *n. Botany.* any of several long cells found in certain fungi, having spores at the ends of small stems.

bas•i•fy ['beisə,fai] *v.,* **bas•i•fied, bas•i•fy•ing.** *Chemistry.* reduce to a base; make alkaline.

bas•il ['bæzəl] *n.* **1** an annual herb (*Ocimum basilicum*) of the mint family having strongly aromatic leaves used as a seasoning in cookery; sweet basil: *Basil is especially good with tomatoes and tomato dishes.* **2** any of several other herbs (genus *Ocimum*) of the mint family, not used for cooking. ⟨ME < OF *basile* < L < Gk. *basilikon* royal < *basileus* king⟩

bas•i•lar ['bæsələr] *adj. Anatomy.* of the base; at the base.

ba•sil•ic [bə'sɪlək] *adj.* **1** of or having to do with a basilica. **2** of or having to do with a large vein of the upper arm.

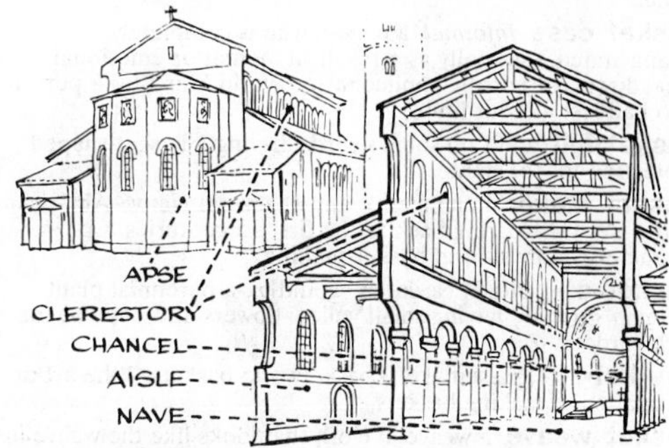

Basilica (def. 2). The 6th-century basilica of Sant'Apollinaire in Classe, Ravenna, Italy

ba•sil•i•ca [bə'sɪləkə] *n.* **1** an oblong hall with an aisle or gallery at each side, separated from the main area by a row of columns, and usually having an apse with a raised platform at one end. **2** an early Christian church built in this form. **3** a Roman Catholic church having certain rights and privileges. ⟨< L < Gk. *basilikē (oikia)* royal (house) < *basileus* king⟩ **—ba'sil•ic•an,** *adj.*

bas•i•lisk ['bæzə,lɪsk] *or* ['bæsə,lɪsk] *n.* **1** any of various tropical American lizards (genus *Basiliscus*) of the same family as the iguanas, noted for their ability to run on their hind legs in an almost upright position. Male basilisks have a crest on the head. **2** a lizardlike reptile of classical legend whose breath and look were fatal. It had a black-and-yellow skin and fiery red eyes. ⟨< L *basiliscus* < Gk. *basiliskos*, dim. of *basileus* king⟩

ba•sin ['beisən] *n.* **1** a wide, shallow bowl, usually with sloping sides, used especially for holding liquids. **2** the amount that a basin can hold. **3** a sink, especially in a bathroom. **4** a relatively shallow depression in land, usually containing water. **5** a sheltered area where boats may be moored. **6** all the land drained by a river and the streams that flow into it: *the St. Lawrence basin.* **7** *Geology.* a large, hollowed area in which the rock strata lean inward to a centre. ⟨ME < OF *bacin* < LL *baccinum* < *bacca* water vessel < Celtic⟩

bas•i•net ['bæsə,nɛt] *n.* a round steel helmet. ⟨ME < OF *bacinet*, dim. of *bacin.* See BASIN.⟩
☛ *Hom.* BASSINET.

ba•sip•e•tal [bei'sɪpətəl] *adj. Botany.* of plant tissues or hormones, moving from the top to the bottom of the stem.

ba•sis ['beisɪs] *n., pl.* **ba•ses** [-siz]. **1** the base or main part; foundation. **2** a fundamental principle or set of principles; criterion. **3** the principal ingredient: *The basis of this medicine is an oil.* **4** the timing of any regularly scheduled event: *I am paid on a monthly basis. Reviews are conducted on a quarterly basis.* **5** the foundation of a feeling or relationship: *Agreement was reached on an amicable basis.* ⟨< L < Gk. *basis.* Doublet of BASE[1].⟩
☛ *Syn.* **1, 2.** See note at BASE[1].
☛ *Usage.* See note at BASE[1].

basis point one one-hundredth of one percent, used in calculating interest, exchange rates, etc.

bask [bæsk] *v.* **1** warm oneself pleasantly: *The cat was basking before the fire.* **2** take great pleasure: *He basked in the praise of his friends.* ⟨ME < ON *bathask* bathe oneself⟩

Bas•ker•ville ['bæskər,vɪl] *n.* a type font of an elegant design. ⟨after John *Baskerville* (1706-1775), English printer⟩

bas•ket ['bæskɪt] *n.* **1** a container made of twigs, grasses, fibres, strips of wood, etc. woven together. **2** the amount that a basket holds: *She bought a basket of peaches.* **3** anything that looks like or is shaped like a basket. **4** the structure beneath a balloon for carrying passengers or ballast. **5** *Basketball.* **a** a net shaped like a basket but open at the bottom, used as a goal. **b** a score made by tossing the ball through the basket. ⟨ME; origin unknown⟩ **—'bas•ket,like,** *adj.*

bas•ket•ball ['bæskɪt,bɒl] *n.* **1** a game between two teams, usually of five players each, who try to score by sinking a large round ball in the opposing team's basket. **2** the ball used in this game.

basket case *Informal.* a person who is completely incapacitated, especially as a result of mental or emotional breakdown. ⟨originally applied, after World War I, to a person who had lost all four limbs⟩

basket hilt a hilt on some swords, having a basket-shaped protection for the hand.

Basket Maker a member of any of several Native Americans of the SW U.S., dating back to the first six centuries A.D., characterized by skill in basket-making.

basket–of–gold ['bæskɪt əv 'gould] *n.* a perennial plant (*Aurinia saxatilis*) having small yellow flowers and popular for rock gardens.

bas•ket•ry ['bæskɪtri] *n.* **1** basketwork; baskets. **2** the art or occupation of making baskets.

basket weave a weave in cloth that looks like the weave in a basket.

bas•ket•work ['bæskɪt,wɜrk] *n.* **1** work woven as a basket is; wickerwork. **2** the art or occupation of making baskets.

basking shark a very large shark (*Cetorhinus maximus*) found chiefly in temperate seas, having two dorsal fins and very long gill clefts, and, unlike most sharks, not carnivorous but feeding on plankton. It is named for its habit of floating at the surface of the water.

bas mitz•vah ['bɑs 'mɪtsvə] **1** a ceremony marking the formal admission of a girl into the Jewish religious community, usually held when the girl is twelve years old. Compare BAR MITZVAH. **2** a girl who is assuming religious responsibility. Also, **bat mitzvah, bath mitzvah.** ⟨< Hebrew *bat mitzwāh* daughter of the commandment⟩

ba•so•phil or **ba•so•phile** ['beisəfɪl] *or* ['beisə,faɪl] *n.* part of the body, such as some leucocytes, that readily takes a basic dye. **—,ba•so'phil•ic,** *adj.*

Basque [bæsk] *n., adj.* —*n.* **1** a member of a people living in the Pyrenees in S France and in N Spain. **2** the language of the Basques, having no known relationship with any other language. **3 basque,** a woman's garment consisting of a close-fitting bodice extending over the hips.
—*adj.* of or having to do with the Basques or their language.

bas–re•lief [,bɑ rɪ'lif] *or* [,bæs rɪ'lif], ['bɑ rɪ,lif] *or* ['bæs rɪ,lif] *n.* relief sculpture in which the modelled forms stand out only slightly from the background and no part of the forms is undercut. See RELIEF for picture. ⟨< F < Ital. *basso-rilievo* low relief⟩

bass¹ [beis] *n., pl.* **bass•es;** *adj.* —*n.* **1** the lowest adult male singing voice: *He sings bass.* **2** a singer who has such a voice. **3** the part sung by a bass. Bass is the lowest part in standard four-part harmony for men's and women's voices together. **4** an instrument having the lowest range in a family of musical instruments, especially a DOUBLE BASS. **5** the lower half of the whole musical range for voice or instrument, or for sound reproduction. Compare TREBLE. **6** a deep, low-pitched voice or musical sound.
—*adj.* **1** having to do with, having the range of, or designed for a bass. **2** having to do with or referring to the lower half of the musical range: *the bass clef.* ⟨var. of *base²*; after Ital. *basso*⟩
☛ *Hom.* BASE.

bass² [bæs] *n., pl.* **bass** or **bass•es. 1** any of various perchlike, spiny-finned marine fishes (family *Serranidae*) found in temperate and warm seas throughout the world, highly valued as food and game fishes. **2** any of several large, important freshwater game fishes (genus *Micropterus*) of the sunfish family native to eastern and central North America, especially the **largemouth bass** (*M. salmoides*) and **smallmouth bass** (*M. dolomieui*). See OTTER for picture. ⟨var. of *barse* perch, OE *bears*⟩

bass³ [bæs] *n.* **1** basswood. **2** bast. ⟨alteration of *bast*⟩

bass clef [beis] *Music.* **1** a symbol (𝄢) showing that the pitch of the notes on a staff is below middle C. **2** the range of notes that appear on such a staff. In the bass clef, the F below middle C is on the fourth line from the bottom of the staff. See CLEF for picture.

bass drum [beis] a large double-headed drum that produces a deep sound of indefinite pitch. See DRUM for picture.

bas•set¹ ['bæsɪt] *n.* a breed of hunting dog having short legs and a long body, similar to a dachshund, but bigger. ⟨< F *basset,* dim. of *bas* low⟩

bas•set² ['bæsɪt] *n., v.* —*n. Geology.* the edge of a rock stratum, etc. appearing at ground surface; outcropping.
—*v.* appear or crop out at the surface.

basset horn a woodwind instrument, similar to the clarinet but having a wider range, set in the key of F.

basset hound BASSET¹.

bass horn [beis] tuba.

bas•si•net [,bæsə'nɛt] *or* ['bæsə,nɛt] *n.* **1** a baby's basketlike cradle, usually with a hood and set on a stand. **2** a baby carriage of similar shape. ⟨< F *bassinet,* dim. of *bassin* basin⟩
☛ *Hom.* BASINET.

bass•ist ['beisɪst] *n.* a person who plays a double bass, especially a skilled player.

bas•so ['bæsou]; *Italian,* ['basso] *n., pl.* **bas•sos;** *Italian,* **bas•si** ['bassi]. a singer with a bass voice. ⟨< Ital. < LL *bassus* low. Doublet of BASE².⟩

Bassoons

bas•soon [bə'sun] *n.* a deep-toned wind instrument with a double reed, having a long wooden body with a second tube attached at the side, leading to a curved metal mouthpiece. ⟨< F < Ital. *bassone* < *basso* basso⟩

bas•soon•ist [bə'sunɪst] *n.* one who plays a bassoon, especially a skilled player.

basso pro•fun•do [prə'fʌndou]; *Italian,* [pro'fondo] **1** the lowest bass voice. **2** a singer with such a voice. **3** a part for such a voice. ⟨< Ital. *profondo* < L *profundus* deep⟩

bass viol [beis] **1** VIOLA DA GAMBA. **2** DOUBLE BASS.

bass•wood ['bæs,wʊd] *n.* **1** a tall North American shade tree (*Tilia americana*), a kind of linden, having heart-shaped leaves. **2** the light, fine-grained, white wood of this tree.

bast [bæst] *n.* **1** tough fibres obtained from the phloem of plants such as flax and hemp, used in making rope, matting, etc. **2** phloem. ⟨OE *bæst*⟩

bas•ta ['bʌstə]; *Italian,* ['basta] *interj.* enough!

bas•tard ['bæstərd] *n., adj.* —*n.* **1** a child born of parents not legally married. **2** anything inferior or not genuine. **3** *Slang.* a cruel, treacherous or unpleasant person.
—*adj.* **1** born of parents not legally married. **2** inferior; not genuine. **3** irregular or unusual in shape, size, style, etc. ⟨ME < OF *bastard,* originally, mule < *bast* packsaddle + *-ard* (< Gmc.)⟩ **—'bas•tard•ly,** *adj.*

bas•tard•ize ['bæstər,daɪz] *v.* **-ized, -iz•ing. 1** show or prove to be a bastard. **2** decrease the value or worth of; make inferior or corrupt; debase. **—,bas•tar•di'za•tion,** *n.*

bas•tard•y ['bæstərdi] *n.* illegitimacy.

baste¹ [beist] *v.* **bast•ed, bast•ing.** drip or pour melted fat or butter on (meat, etc.) while it is roasting: *Meat is basted to keep it from drying out and to improve its flavour.* ⟨originally pp. of a verb < OF *basser* moisten. Related to BASIN.⟩ **—'bast•er,** *n.*

baste² [beist] *v.* **bast•ed, bast•ing.** sew with long, loose stitches to hold the cloth until the final sewing. ⟨ME < OF *bastir* < Gmc.; cf. OHG *besten* tie up, sew with bast⟩ **—'bast•er,** *n.*

baste³ [beist] *v.* **bast•ed, bast•ing. 1** beat; thrash. **2** abuse verbally. ⟨< ON *beysta*⟩

Bas•tille [bæs'til]; *French,* [bas'tij] *n.* **1** in Paris, an old fort used as a prison, especially for political offenders. It was captured and destroyed by a mob on July 14, 1789. **2 bastille** or **bastile,** a prison, especially one considered oppressive. ⟨< F < LL *bastilia* < *bastire* build⟩

bas•ti•na•do [,bæstə'nɑdou] *or* [,bæstə'neidou] *n., pl.* **-does;** *v.,* **-doed, -do•ing.** —*n.* **1** a beating with a stick, especially on the soles of the feet. **2** a stick; cudgel.
—*v.* beat or flog with a stick, especially on the soles of the feet. ⟨< Sp. *bastonada* < *baston* cudgel, ult. < L⟩

bast•ing ['beistɪŋ] *n., v.* —*n.* long, loose stitches to hold cloth in place until the final sewing.
—*v.* ppr. of BASTE.

bas•tion ['bæstʃən] *or* ['bæstiən] *n.* **1** a projecting part of a fortification made so that the defenders can fire at attackers from as many angles as possible. See FORT for picture. **2** any fortification or fortified area. **3** something that provides or acts as a stronghold: *a bastion of freedom.* ⟨< F < Ital. *bastione* < *bastire* build < LL⟩

bas•tioned ['bæstʃənd] *or* ['bæstiənd] *adj.* provided with or defended by bastions.

bat[1] [bæt] *n., v.* **bat•ted, bat•ting.** *—n.* **1** *Sports.* **a** a specially shaped stick or club, used for hitting the ball as in baseball or cricket. **b** the act of hitting the ball with such a stick or club. **c** a turn at hitting the ball: *It's her bat next.* **2** *Informal.* a squash racket, table tennis paddle, etc. **3** *Informal.* a stroke or blow. **4** *Slang.* a drinking spree or binge. **5** BATTING (def. 1). **6** a jockey's whip.
at bat, in position to bat; having a turn at batting.
go to bat for, *Informal.* support the cause of: *I'm sure she'll go to bat for you if you explain exactly what happened.*
right off the bat, *Informal.* immediately; without hesitation: *He accepted the offer right off the bat.*
—v. **1** hit with or as if with a bat. **2** use a bat: *She's batting well this season.* **3** have a turn at batting: *Who'll bat first?* **4** *Baseball.* have a given batting average: *Any player who bats over 400 is valuable.*
bat around, a *Baseball.* go right through the batting order in one inning. **b** *Slang.* go here and there with no definite purpose: *He is always batting around town in his new car.* **c** *Slang.* discuss (a topic) freely and informally. ⟨ME < OF *batte* club < *battre* strike⟩ **—'bat•ter,** *n.*

bat[2] [bæt] *n.* any of several hundred species making up an order (Chiroptera) of flying mammals, resembling other small mammals like mice and shrews in their general body form, but having membranes between the very long bones of the forelimbs, which enable them to fly, hind feet adapted for clinging, and a special radarlike sense organ that enables them to fly in the dark. Bats sleep during the day by clinging upside down to the ceilings in caves, dark corners of buildings, etc.
blind as a bat, completely blind.
have bats in the belfry, *Informal.* be or appear odd, peculiar, or insane. ⟨alteration of ME *bakkee* < Scand.⟩ **—'bat,like,** *adj.*

bat[3] [bæt] *v.* **bat•ted, bat•ting.** *Informal.* flutter; wink; blink (an eye). ⟨variant of obsolete *bate* flutter⟩
not bat an eye at, not be the least bit surprised at.

bat. **1** battalion. **2** battery.

bat•boy ['bæt,bɔɪ] *n.* a boy who looks after the bats in a baseball game, and helps the players generally.

batch[1] [bætʃ] *n.* **1** a quantity of bread, cookies, etc., made at one baking. **2** the quantity of dough needed for such a baking. **3** a quantity of anything made as one lot or set: *a batch of candy.* **4** a number of persons or things taken together: *a batch of essays.* **5** *Computer technology.* a set of instructions, etc. for a computer to perform in one run. ⟨ME *bacche* < OE *bacan* bake⟩
☛ *Hom.* BACH.

batch[2] [bætʃ] *n. or v. Informal.* BACH ⟨shortened form of *bachelor*⟩

batch file *Computer technology.* in some computers, a file containing commands to the operating system.

batch processing *Computer technology.* a method of processing in which records are collected into batches before being processed.

batch program *Computer technology.* **a** a computer program which has little or no interactive communication with users while it is executing. **b** a program that does batch processing. **c** a program that, when submitted, is placed in a queue and later selected for execution by the operating system.

bate [beit] *v.* **bat•ed, bat•ing.** abate; lessen; hold back.
with bated breath, holding the breath in great fear, awe, interest, etc.: *The children listened with bated breath to the sailor's stories of his adventures.* ⟨var. of *abate*⟩
☛ *Hom.* BAIT.

ba•teau or **bat•teau** [bæ'tou] *n., pl.* **-teaux** [-'touz]; *adj. —n. Cdn.* **1** a light, flat-bottomed river boat about 9 m long, having a tapered bow and stern, and propelled by oars, poles, or sails. Bateaux were used especially in the late 18th and early 19th centuries to carry freight or passengers, especially on the upper St. Lawrence River. **2** any of several similar, usually smaller, light river boats.
—adj. of or having to do with a wide neckline, as on a woman's dress, extending to the shoulders; boat neck. ⟨< Cdn.F < F *bâteau* boat, ult. < OE *bāt* boat⟩

bat•fish ['bæt,fɪʃ] *n.* **1** any of a family (Ogcocephalidae) of angler fishes. **2** a ray (*Myliobatis californica*) of the eastern Pacific, shaped like a bat.

bath [bæθ] *n., pl.* **baths** [bæðz]; *v. —n.* **1** a washing of the body. **2** the water, etc. for a bath: *Your bath is ready.* **3** a tub, room, or other place for bathing: *In ancient Rome, baths were often elaborate public buildings which were used also as clubs.* **4** a resort having baths for medical treatment. **5** a liquid for washing or dipping something, such as a solution for fixing photographic prints or film or a liquid for controlling the temperature of something placed in it. **6** the container holding the liquid.
take a bath, *Informal.* lose a lot of money.
—v. **1** give a bath to. **2** take a bath. ⟨OE *bæth*⟩

Bath chair an early form of wheelchair having a covering for the head, often made of wickerwork. ⟨< *Bath* in England, where these chairs originated⟩

bathe [beið] *v.* **bathed, bath•ing. 1** take a bath. **2** give a bath to. **3** apply water to; wash or moisten with, or immerse in, any liquid: *The doctor told me to bathe my eyes with the lotion.* **4** go swimming; go into a pool, river, lake, etc. for pleasure. **5** cover; surround: *The valley was bathed in sunlight.* ⟨OE *bathian*⟩ **—'bath•er,** *n.*

ba•thet•ic [bə'θɛtɪk] *adj.* showing bathos; characterized by bathos. **—ba'thet•ic•al•ly,** *adv.*

bath•house ['bæθ,hʌus] *n., pl.* **-hous•es** [-,haʊziz] **1** a house or building fitted up for bathing. **2** a building containing one or more dressing rooms for swimmers.

bathing cap a tight-fitting rubber cap worn to protect the hair while swimming.

bathing suit ['beiðɪŋ] a garment worn for swimming.

bath•mat ['bæθ,mæt] *n.* a small mat of towelling or other washable material, to stand on when getting out of the bath or shower.

bath mitzvah ['bɑθ 'mɪtsvə] BAS MITZVAH.

bath•o•lith ['bæθə,lɪθ] *n. Geology.* a great mass of intruded igneous rock, often forming the base of a mountain range and uncovered only by erosion. There is a batholith in British Columbia that is about 2400 by 160 km. ⟨< Gk. *bathos* depth + *lithos* stone⟩ **—,bath•o'lith•ic,** *adj.*

ba•thom•et•er [bə'θɒmətər] *n.* a gauge for measuring the depth of water. ⟨< Gk. *báthos* depth⟩

ba•thos ['beiθɒs] *or* ['beiθous] *n.* **1** dullness or triteness in speech or writing, especially when immediately following more elevated expression. *Example: The exile came back to his home, crippled, unfriended, and hatless.* **2** strained or insincere pathos. ⟨< Gk. *bathos* depth⟩

bath•robe ['bæθ,roub] *n.* a loose garment worn when going to and from a bath or when resting or lounging.

bath•room ['bæθ,rum] *or* [-,rʊm] *n.* **1** a room fitted up for taking baths, usually equipped with a washbasin, a toilet, and a bathtub. **2** toilet.
go to the bathroom, *Informal.* urinate or defecate.

bath•tub ['bæθ,tʌb] *n.* a tub to bathe in.

bath•y•al zone ['bæθiəl] the area of the continental shelf between 100 and 2000 fathoms (about 183 to 3658 m).

bath•y•met•ric [,bæθə'mɛtrɪk] *adj.* of or having to do with bathymetry. **—,bath•y'met•ri•cal•ly,** *adv.*

ba•thym•e•try [bə'θɪmətri] *n.* **1** the measurement of the depth of oceans, seas, and lakes. **2** the data resulting from this measurement, most often expressed in a topographical map. ⟨< Gk. *bathys* deep + *metron* measure⟩

bath•y•scaph ['bæθə,skæf] *n.* a self-contained diving vessel for deep-sea observation, designed to reach great depths in the ocean, consisting of a heavy steel cabin for the observers attached to the underside of a large light hull called a float. The bathyscaph descends by allowing sea water into the float and ascends again by releasing iron ballast from the float. The record dive for a bathyscaph is 10 916 m, made in 1960. Also, **bathyscaphe** [-,skeif]. ⟨< Gk. *bathys* deep + *skaphos* ship⟩

bath•y•sphere ['bæθə,sfir] *n.* a ball-shaped, steel, watertight vessel having portholes, formerly used for observing plant and animal life in the ocean depths. The bathysphere was suspended from a boat by a cable and was able to descend to a depth of about 900 m. ⟨< Gk. *bathys* deep + E *sphere*⟩

bath•y•therm•o•graph [,bæθə'θɜrmə,græf] *n.* an instrument for measuring the temperature of the ocean waters at depths down to 1800 m. ⟨< Gk. *bathys* deep + *therme* heat + *graphe* a drawing, writing⟩

ba•tik [bə'tik] *or* ['bɑtik] *n., v. —n.* **1** the art and method of making designs on cloth by dyeing only part at a time, the rest being protected by a removable coating of melted wax. **2** cloth dyed in this way. **3** a design formed in this way. **4** (*adjl.*) of or like

batik: *a batik wall hanging.*
—*v.* dye by batik. ⟨< Malay⟩

ba•tiste [bə'tist] *n.* **1** a fine, thin cotton cloth in a plain weave. **2** any of various similar fabrics made of polyester, rayon, etc. ⟨< F *Baptiste,* probably the name of the maker⟩

bat•man ['bætmən] *n., pl.* **-men.** a private soldier assigned to act as an officer's servant. ⟨< OF *bast* packsaddle + *man*⟩

bat mitz•vah ['bɑt 'mɪtsvə] BAS MITZVAH.

ba•ton [bə'tɒn] *n.* **1** a staff or stick used as a symbol of office or authority. **2** a stick used by the leader of an orchestra, chorus, etc. to indicate the beat and direct the performance. **3** a stick passed from runner to runner in a relay race. **4** a light, hollow metal rod twirled by a drum major or majorette as a showy display. **5** *Heraldry.* a short, narrow, diagonal stripe on a shield, especially one running from upper left to lower right (from the bearer's point of view), indicating bastardy. ⟨< F *baton* stick⟩

ba•ton•nier [bɑtɒn'jei]; *French,* [batɔn'je] *n. Cdn.* an official of the Québec Bar Association. ⟨< F⟩

bat•ra•chi•an [bə'treikiən] *n., adj.* —*n.* an amphibian, especially a frog or toad.
—*adj.* froglike; of or having to do with amphibians, especially frogs and toads. ⟨< Gk. *batrakhos* frog⟩

bat•ra•cho•tox•in ['bætrəkou,tɒksɪn] *or* [bə'trækou,tɒksɪn] a naturally poisonous substance found in the skin of frogs of the genus *Phyllobates* and used for poisoned arrows. *Formula*: $C_{31}H_{42}N_2O_6$ ⟨< Gk. *batracheios* having to do with frogs + *toxikon* poison⟩

bats•man ['bætsmən] *n., pl.* **-men.** *Cricket.* a player who is batting. ⟨< *bat*[1]⟩

batt [bæt] *n.* COTTON BATTING.

batt. **1** battalion. **2** battery.

bat•tal•ion [bə'tæljən] *n.* **1** a formation of four companies within a regiment of infantry, usually commanded by a lieutenant-colonel. **2** any large number of soldiers organized to act together. **3** any large group organized to act together: *A battalion of volunteers helped to rescue the flood victims. Abbrev.*: Bn. ⟨< F *bataillon* < Ital. *battaglione,* dim. of *battaglia* battle < LL *battalia.* See BATTLE.⟩

bat•teau [bæ'tou] *n., pl.* **-teaux** [-'touz] bateau.

bat•ten[1] ['bætən] *v.* **1** grow fat. **2** fatten. **3** feed greedily. ⟨< ON *batna* < *bati* improvement⟩

bat•ten[2] ['bætən] *n., v.* —*n.* **1** a long, thick, board used for flooring. **2** a thin strip of wood used to reinforce or support lathing, etc., seal a joint, hold a tarpaulin in place over a ship's hatch, etc. **3** *Theatre.* **a** a wooden or metal bar from which to hang lights, scenery, etc. **b** the lights hung from such a bar.
—*v.* fasten down or strengthen with strips of wood.
batten down the hatches, a prepare for a storm at sea by covering all entranceways to the lower decks with boards. **b** prepare for any onslaught or other emergency. ⟨var. of *baton*⟩

bat•ter[1] ['bætər] *v.* **1** beat with repeated blows; beat so as to bruise, break, or knock out of shape; pound: *Violent storms battered the coast for days. Stop battering on my door, I'm coming!* **2** damage by hard use. **3** abuse physically: *He was charged with battering his wife.* ⟨< ME *bateren* < OF *batre*⟩

bat•ter[2] ['bætər] *n.* a mixture of flour, milk, eggs, etc. that becomes solid when cooked. Cakes, pancakes, etc. are made from batter. ⟨ME *batour,* probably < OF *bature* beating < *batre*⟩

bat•ter[3] ['bætər] *n. Baseball.* a player who is batting. ⟨< *bat*[1]⟩

bat•tered ['bætərd] *adj., v.* —*adj.* **1** beaten, bruised or broken: *a battered ship.* **2** physically abused: *a shelter for battered wives.*
—*v.* pt. and pp. of BATTER[1].

battering ram **1** a heavy beam of wood with metal at the striking end, used in ancient and medieval warfare for battering down walls, gates, etc. **2** any heavy object used to break down a door, wall, etc.

bat•ter•y ['bætəri] *n., pl.* **-ter•ies. 1** a container holding materials that produce electricity by chemical action; a single electric cell. See DRY CELL for picture. **2** a set of two or more electric cells that produce electric current: *a car battery.* **3** any set of similar or connected things or people: *a battery of loudspeakers, a battery of tests, a battery of lawyers.* **4** a set of guns or other weapons such as mortars, machine guns, and artillery pieces for combined action in attack or defence. **5** a formation of several troops in an artillery regiment. **6** a platform or fortification equipped with big guns. **7** the armament, or one part of it, of a warship. **8** *Baseball.* the pitcher and catcher together. **9** *Law.* assault causing actual bodily harm. ⟨< F *batterie* < *battre* beat < L *battuere.* Related to BAT[1], BATTLE.⟩

bat•ting ['bætɪŋ] *n., v.* —*n.* **1** sheets or layers of pressed cotton, wool, or a synthetic fibre, used for lining quilts, stuffing mattresses, packing, etc. **2** the act or manner of hitting a ball with a bat: *Her batting has improved.*
—*v.* ppr. of BAT.

batting average **1** *Baseball.* a player's ratio of base hits to the number of times at bat. **2** any record or indicator of performance or accomplishments: *Two promotions in two years is a pretty good batting average.*

batting cage *Baseball.* an enclosure of screens or net leaving only one side open, for batting practice and to trap loose balls.

batting helmet *Baseball.* a helmet of strong plastic with an earpiece or earpieces, to protect the head when batting.

bat•tle ['bætəl] *n., v.* **-tled, -tling.** —*n.* **1** a fight between opposing armed forces. **2** fighting or war: *wounds received in battle.* **3** any fight or contest: *a battle of words.*
do (or **give**) **battle,** begin fighting; fight.
half the battle, half the task: *Admitting you have a problem is half the battle.*
—*v.* **1** take part in a battle. **2** fight; struggle or contend (with): *The brave little ship battled the storm for hours.* ⟨ME *batayle* < OF *bataille* < LL *battalia* < L *battuere* beat. Related to BAT[1], BATTERY.⟩ —**'bat•tler,** *n.*

☛ *Syn.* **1. Battle,** ACTION, ENGAGEMENT = a fight between armed forces. **Battle** applies to a fight between large forces, such as armies, navies or air forces, lasting some time: *The battle for Caen lasted many weeks.* **Action** applies to a lively offensive or defensive part of a battle or campaign: *The Normandy landing during World War II was a decisive action.* **Engagement** emphasizes the meeting of forces, large or small, in combat: *The engagement at Dieppe cost the attacking Canadians many casualties.*

battle array **1** the order of troops, ships, etc. ready for battle. **2** armour and equipment for battle.

bat•tle–axe ['bætəl ,æks] *n.* a kind of axe used as a weapon of war. Sometimes, **battle-ax.**

battle cruiser a large, fast warship, not as heavily armoured as a battleship.

battle cry **1** the shout of soldiers in battle. **2** a motto or slogan in any contest.

bat•tle•dore ['bætəl,dɔr] *n.* **1** a small, light racket used in the game battledore and shuttlecock. **2** the game itself; battledore and shuttlecock. ⟨ME *batyldore,* apparently < Pg. *batedor* beater < *bater* beat < L *battuere*⟩

battledore and shuttlecock an old-fashioned game resembling badminton, played by two persons.

battle dress a two-piece uniform consisting of pants and a short, loose jacket, usually called a blouse, that ends in a fitted waistband. Battle dress is worn by the armed forces for field training and combat.

battle fatigue a neurosis caused by prolonged anxiety and emotional tension during combat.

bat•tle•field ['bætəl,fild] *n.* **1** the place where a battle is fought or has been fought. **2** any sphere of contention.

bat•tle•front ['bætəl,frʌnt] *n.* **1** the place where actual fighting between two armies is taking place. **2** the position of direct confrontation in any struggle.

bat•tle•ground ['bætəl,graʊnd] *n.* battlefield.

bat•tle•ment ['bætəlmənt] *n.* **1** a wall for defence at the top of a tower or wall, with indentations through which soldiers could shoot. See CASTLE and FORT for pictures. **2** a wall built like this for ornament. ⟨ME *batelment* < OF *bateillier* fortify + E *-ment*⟩ —**'bat•tle,ment•ed,** *adj.*

battle royal **1** a fight in which several people take part; riot. **2** a long, hard fight. **3** a prolonged and intense argument.

bat•tle–scarred ['bætəl ,skɑrd] *adj.* scarred from involvement in battles or fights: *a battle-scarred old coyote.*

bat•tle•ship ['bætəl,ʃɪp] *n.* the largest, most powerful, and most heavily armoured type of warship. Battleships are seldom used now because they are very vulnerable to attacks from the air.

battle stations **1** the positions taken by parts of an army, navy, etc. ready for battle. **2** a state of readiness for any conflict.

bat•tue [bæ'tju] *or* [bæ'tu] *n.* **1** the driving of game from cover toward the hunters. **2** a hunt where this is done. **3** a general slaughter. ⟨< F *battue,* fem. pp. of *battre* beat < L *battuere*⟩

bat•wing sleeve ['bæt,wɪŋ] a sleeve shaped like the wing of a bat, tapering from a broad end (at the body) to a narrow end (at the wrist).

bau•ble ['bɒbəl] *n.* **1** a showy trifle having no real value. Useless toys and trinkets are baubles. **2** a jester's staff. **3** an elastic band wound with thread and decorated with one or two small coloured balls, used especially by small girls to hold braids or ponytails together. ⟨ME *babel, babulle* < OF *babel, baubel* toy, of uncertain origin⟩
☛ *Hom.* BOBBLE.

baud [bɒd] *n.pl.* **1** a unit of speed in sending a message by telegraph. **2** *Computer technology.* a unit of speed in a computer system, calculated in bits per second. ⟨< F *baud* < J.M.E. *Baudot* (1845-1903), a French engineer⟩
☛ *Hom.* BAWD, BOD.

baud rate *Computer technology.* data transmission speed measured in baud: *Changing to a higher baud rate improved the response time at the bank teller's terminal.*

Bau•haus ['baʊ,hʌus] *n.* a school and style of architecture, founded in Germany in 1919 by Walter Gropius and emphasizing the merging of technology with architecture.

bau•hin•ia [bɒ'hɪniə] *n.* a small tropical tree of the genus *Bauhinia*, having large showy flowers in purple or white, and double-lobed leaves.

baulk [bɒk] *or* [bɒlk] See BALK.

Bau•mé [bou'mei] *adj. Physics.* having to do with either of two scales used to measure the specific gravity of liquids. *Abbrev.*: Bé. ⟨after A. *Baumé* (1728–1804), French chemist⟩

baum marten [baʊm] **1** a European marten (*Martes martes*). **2** its dark brown fur. ⟨< G *Baummarder* < *Baum* tree + *Marder* marten⟩

baux•ite ['bɒksəit] *n.* a claylike mineral from which aluminum is obtained. It is also used in making alum and firebricks. *Formula*: $Al_2O_3.2H_2O$ ⟨from Les *Baux*, France⟩

Ba•var•i•an [bə'vɛriən] *n., adj.* —*n.* **1** a native or inhabitant of Bavaria, a state in SW Germany, formerly a duchy and a kingdom. **2** the German dialect spoken in Bavaria and in Austria.
—*adj.* of or having to do with Bavaria, its people, or their dialect.

Bavarian cream a dessert made of fruit, whipped cream, and eggs and thickened with gelatin.

bawd [bɒd] *n.* **1** a woman who keeps a brothel. **2** a prostitute. ⟨ME < OF *bald* bold < Gmc.⟩
☛ *Hom.* BAUD, BOD.

bawd•ry ['bɒdri] *n. Archaic.* lewd or obscene talk or writing.

bawd•y ['bɒdi] *adj.* **bawd•i•er, bawd•i•est;** *n.* —*adj.* humorously and exuberantly lewd or indecent: *bawdy songs.*
—*n.* humorously lewd or obscene talk or writing. —**'bawd•i•ly,** *adv.* —**'bawd•i•ness,** *n.*
☛ *Hom.* BODY .

bawd•y–house ['bɒdi,hʌus] *n.* brothel.

bawl [bɒl] *v., n.* —*v.* **1** shout or call out noisily: *The peddler bawled her wares in the street. The sergeant bawled out a command.* **2** weep loudly: *The small boy bawled whenever he hurt himself.*
bawl out, *Informal.* scold severely or loudly: *They got bawled out for leaving their bicycles in the driveway.*
—*n.* a loud shouting or weeping. ⟨probably < Med.L *baulare* bark⟩ —**'bawl•er,** *n.*
☛ *Hom.* BALL.

bay[1] [bei] *n.* **1** a part of a sea or lake extending into the land; a wide indentation that is usually larger than a cove and smaller than a gulf. **2 the Bay,** *Cdn. Informal.* **a** formerly, Hudson Bay. **b** the Hudson's Bay Company. ⟨ME < OF *baie* < LL *baia*⟩
☛ *Hom.* BEY.

bay[2] [bei] *n.* **1** a space or division of a wall or building between columns, pillars, buttresses, etc. **2** a space with a window or set of windows in it, projecting out from a wall; BAY WINDOW. **3** a projecting wing of a building. **4** a place in a barn for storing hay or grain; mow. **5** a compartment in an aircraft, especially one for carrying bombs. **6** a recess, platform, or other area for a specified purpose: *an unloading bay, a sick bay.* ⟨ME < OF *baie* opening < VL *batare* gape⟩
☛ *Hom.* BEY.

bay[3] [bei] *n., v.* —*n.* **1** a long, deep howl or bark, especially as made by hounds, etc. when pursuing or closing in on prey. **2** the situation or position of a hunted animal when escape is impossible and it is forced to face its pursuers: *The quarry was brought to bay. The stag stood at bay on the edge of the cliff.* **3** the position or situation of a person forced to face an enemy, a serious difficulty, persecution, etc. **4** the position of the pursuers or enemies who are being kept off: *The stag held the hounds at bay.*
bring to bay, put in a position from which escape is impossible.
—*v.* **1** utter a howl or prolonged barks: *The dogs sat and bayed at the moon.* **2** call out; shout. **3** bark at or pursue with barking. **4** bring to or hold at bay. ⟨ME *bay, abay,* n. < OF *abai* a barking; ME *bayen,* v. (< OF *bayer* bark) and ME *abayen* (< OF *abayer* bark)⟩
☛ *Hom.* BEY.

bay[4] [bei] *n.* **1** LAUREL (def. 1) (*Laurus nobilis*), a shrub or tree of the Mediterranean region. Bay leaves are used for flavouring food. **2** any of several other trees resembling the laurel, such as the magnolia. **3 bays,** *pl.* **a** a laurel wreath worn by poets and victors. **b** honour; renown; fame. ⟨< OF *baie* < L *baca* berry⟩
☛ *Hom.* BEY.

bay[5] [bei] *n., adj.* —*n.* **1** reddish brown. **2** a reddish brown horse.
—*adj.* reddish brown: *a bay mare.* ⟨< OF *bai* < L *badius*⟩
☛ *Hom.* BEY.

ba•ya•dere or **ba•ya•deer** [bɑjə'dir]; *French,* [baja'diʀ] *n.* a type of cloth with brightly coloured horizontal stripes. ⟨< F *bayadère* dancing girl < Pg. *bailadeira* < *bailar* dance < L *ballare*⟩

bay•ard ['beiərd] *n., adj. Archaic.* —*n.* **1** a bay horse. **2** a mock-heroic name for any horse.
—*adj.* bay-coloured. ⟨< OF *baiard* a red-brown horse < *bai* bay[5]⟩

Bay•ard ['beiɑrd] *or* ['beiərd]; *French,* [ba'jaʀ] *n.* a man of heroic nature. ⟨< Pierre du Terrail, Chevalier de *Bayard* (1473?-1524), a heroic French knight⟩

bay•ber•ry ['bei,bɛri] *n., pl.* **-ries;** *adj.* —*n.* **1** a North American shrub (*Myrica pensylvanica*) of the wax-myrtle family, having clusters of round nuts covered with greyish white wax. The leaves of the bayberry are aromatic, and candles made from the wax of the berries burn with a pleasant fragrance. **2** the fruit of this shrub. **3** a West Indian tree (*Pimenta racemosa*) of the myrtle family having leaves that yield an aromatic oil used in making BAY RUM.
—*adj.* designating a family of fragrant dicotyledons (*Myricales Myricaceae*).

Ba•yeux Tapestry [bei'ju]; *French,* [ba'jœ] a famous tapestry of the 11th century that pictures events leading to the Norman Conquest of England. ⟨from *Bayeux,* a town in N France, where it is preserved⟩

bay ice *Cdn.* ice of recent formation in bays and sheltered places.

bay laurel LAUREL (def. 1).

bay leaf the dried, aromatic leaf of the LAUREL (def. 1), used as a flavouring in making soups, stews, meat sauces, etc.

bay lynx bobcat.

bay•o•net [,beiə'nɛt] *or* ['beiənɪt] *n., v.* **-net•ed, -net•ing.** —*n.* **1** a heavy, daggerlike blade for piercing or stabbing, made to be attached to the end of the barrel of a rifle. **2** any object similar to a bayonet, either in the way it attaches or its form.
—*v.* pierce or stab with a bayonet. ⟨< F *baïonnette*; from *Bayonne,* France⟩

bay•ou ['baɪju] *or* [baɪ'ju] *n., pl.* **-ous.** *Esp. U.S.* a marshy inlet or outlet of a lake, river, or gulf. ⟨< Louisiana F < Choctaw *bayuk* small stream⟩

bay rum a fragrant liquid originally made from the leaves of the West Indian bayberry, used in medicine and cosmetics.

Bay Street *Cdn.* **1** in Toronto, a street on which there are many financial houses. **2** the financial or moneyed interests of Toronto, the largest financial centre in Canada.

bay window **1** a window or set of windows projecting out from a wall, providing extra space in a room. **2** *Informal.* a large abdomen: *He was a short, fat man, whose expensive watch chain called attention to his bay window.*

bay•wood ['bei,wʊd] *n.* **1** a tropical tree (*Swietenia macrophylla*) growing from SE Mexico to South America. **2** the light, soft wood of this tree, resembling mahogany.

ba•zaar [bə'zɑr] *n.* **1** especially in Middle Eastern countries and the Indian subcontinent, a street or streets full of shops and stalls. **2** a place for the sale of many kinds of goods. **3** a sale of things donated by various people, held for some special purpose, often to raise money for charity. ⟨< F < Arabic < Persian *bazar*⟩
☛ *Hom.* BIZARRE.

ba•zoo•ka [bə'zukə] *n.* a rocket gun used against tanks. ⟨from its resemblance to a trombonelike instrument created and named by Bob Burns (1896-1956), American humorist⟩

BB ['bibi] *n., pl.* **BB's.** **1** a standard size of shot, approximately

0.45 cm in diameter. 2 a shot of this size, especially for use in an air rifle.

BBC or **B.B.C.** British Broadcasting Corporation.

BB gun AIR RIFLE. Also, **bee-bee gun.**

bbl. barrel.

bbls. barrels.

BBS *Computer technology.* BULLETIN-BOARD SYSTEM.

BC British Columbia (*used esp. in computerized address systems*).

B.C. 1 before Christ (*used to indicate years, numbering back from the birth of Christ*): *The year 350 B.C. is 100 years earlier than 250 B.C.* 2 British Columbia.

B.C.E. Before the Christian (or Common) Era (*used to indicate years* B.C.).

B complex the set of all of the types of vitamin B.

bd. 1 board. 2 bond. 3 bound.

bd. ft. board foot; board feet.

Bdr or **Bdr.** Bombardier.

be [bi] *v. pres. indic. sing.* **am, are, is,** *pl.* **are;** *pt. indic.* **was, were, was,** *pl.* **were;** *pp.* **been;** *ppr.* **be•ing. 1** have reality; live; exist: *The days of the pioneers are no more.* **2** take place; happen: *The circus was last month.* **3** have a particular place or position; remain; continue: *They will be here all year. The food is on the table.* **4** equal; represent: *Let "x" be the unknown quantity.* **5** belong to a particular group or class: *The new baby is a boy. My mother is a doctor. Elephants and mice are mammals.* **6** have or show a particular quality or condition: *I am sad. You are wrong. The book is red.* **7 Be** is also used as an auxiliary verb with: **a** the present participle of another verb to form the progressive tense: *I am asking. They were asking. You will be asking.* **b** the past participle of another verb to form the passive voice: *I am asked. She was asked. You will be asked.* **8 Be** is also used to express future time, duty, intention, and possibility: *He is to arrive here at nine. No shelter was to be seen. You are to keep this strictly confidential.* **9 Be** is also used as an auxiliary with the past participle of some intransitive verbs to form an archaic or poetic perfect tense: *The sun is risen.*
be off, (*usually imperative*) leave. ⟨OE *bēon*⟩
☛ *Hom.* B, BEE.

be– *prefix.* **1** thoroughly; all around, as in *bespatter.* **2** at; on; to; for; about: *bewail* = *wail about*; makes an intransitive verb transitive. **3** make; cause to seem, as in *belittle.* **4** provide with, as in *bespangle.* ⟨OE *be-*, unstressed form of *bī* by⟩

Be beryllium.

Bé. Baumé.

beach [bitʃ] *n., v. —n.* the almost flat shore of sand or small stones beside a lake or the sea over which the water washes when high or at high tide.
—v. run or drive up on shore: *We beached the boat in a little inlet. The newspaper reported that a whale was beached on the island.* ⟨origin uncertain⟩ **—'beach•less,** *adj.*
☛ *Hom.* BEECH.

beach ball a large, inflated rubber or plastic ball for use on the beach or in water.

beach buggy a small open vehicle for use on the beach; DUNE BUGGY.

beach•comb ['bitʃ,koum] *v.* live or work as a beachcomber.

beach•comb•er ['bitʃ,koumər] *n.* **1** a vagrant or loafer on beaches or in wharf areas, especially in islands of the south Pacific. **2** a long wave rolling in from the ocean. **3** *Cdn.* in British Columbia, a person who salvages logs broken loose from log booms and returns them to the logging companies for a fee.

beach flea a small saltwater crustacean that jumps like a flea.

beach•head ['bitʃ,hɛd] *n.* **1** the first position established by an invading army on an enemy shore. **2** a position from which to launch any aggressive effort.

beach•side ['bitʃ,saɪd] *n.* **1** the area beside a beach. **2** (*adjl.*) for or in such an area: *a beachside pool.*

beach umbrella a large, usually coloured umbrella stuck on its pointed handle into the sand to provide shade.

beach•wear ['bitʃ,wɛr] *n.* articles of clothing, such as bathing suits, shorts, or robes, for wearing at a beach.

bea•con ['bikən] *n., v. —n.* **1** a fire or light used as a signal to guide or warn. **2** a marker, signal light, or radio station that guides aircraft through fogs, storms, etc. **3** a tall tower for a signal; lighthouse. **4** anything that guides or inspires.
—v. **1** provide with a beacon or beacons. **2** serve as a beacon. **3** provide light for. ⟨OE *bēacn*⟩

bead [bid] *n., v. —n.* **1** a small ball or bit of glass, metal, etc. with a hole through it, so that it can be strung on a thread with others like it. **2 beads,** *pl.,* **a** a string of beads. **b** a rosary; string of beads for keeping count in saying prayers. **3** any small, round object like a drop or bubble: *beads of sweat.* **4** a small metal knob or ball at the front of a rifle or pistol barrel, used for taking aim. **5** a narrow, semicircular moulding. **6** the froth on a carbonated drink, beer, etc., when newly poured. **7** the part of a tire that attaches to the rim of the wheel. **8** *Architecture.* a moulding shaped like a row of beads.
draw a bead on, aim at.
tell, count, or **say** (one's) **beads,** say prayers using a rosary.
—v. **1** supply, trim, or cover with beads or beading: *Her forehead was beaded with sweat.* **2** form into beads or drops: *Water will bead on an oily surface.* **3** string together like beads. ⟨OE *bedu* prayer. See def. 2b.⟩ **—'bead,like,** *adj.*

bead•ed ['bidɪd] *adj., v. —adj.* **1** trimmed or covered with beads; having beads: *beaded fabric, a beaded moulding.* **2** formed into beads; like beads: *beaded bubbles winking at the brim.*
—v. pt. and pp. of BEAD.

bead•ing ['bidɪŋ] *n., v. —n.* **1** a trimming made of beads threaded into patterns. **2** a narrow lace or openwork trimming through which ribbon may be run. **3** on woodwork, silver, etc., a pattern or edge made of small beads. **4** BEAD (def. 5). **5** BEAD (def. 8).
—v. ppr. of BEAD.

bea•dle ['bidəl] *n.* **1** in the Church of England, a minor officer. Formerly, if a person slept in church during a service, the beadle would wake him or her up. **2** a minor officer in a synagogue, who helps with the organization. ⟨OE *bydel*⟩

bea•dle•dom ['bidəldəm] *n.* stupid officiousness.

beads•man ['bidzmən] *n., pl.* **-men.** formerly, a person who said prayers for others, especially one hired to do so.

beads•wom•an ['bidz,wʊmən] *n., pl.* **-wom•en.** formerly, a woman who said prayers for others, especially one hired to do so.

bead•work ['bid,wɜrk] *n.* beading.

bead•y ['bidi] *adj.* **bead•i•er, bead•i•est. 1** small, round, and shiny: *beady eyes.* **2** trimmed with beads. **3** covered with drops or bubbles.

bea•gle ['bigəl] *n.* a breed of small hunting dog having smooth hair, short legs, and drooping ears. ⟨ME *begle* < ? OF *begueule* wide throat⟩

beak [bik] *n.* **1** a bird's bill, especially one that is strong and hooked and useful in striking or tearing. Eagles, hawks, and parrots have beaks. **2** a similar part in other animals, such as some turtles or fish. **3** the projecting bow of an ancient warship. **4** *Slang.* a person's nose, especially a large or hooked nose. **5** a spout. ⟨ME < OF *bec* < L *beccus* < Celtic⟩ **—'beak,like,** *adj.*

beaked [bikt] *adj.* **1** having a beak. **2** shaped like a beak; hooked.

beak•er ['bikər] *n.* **1** a large cup or drinking glass. **2** the contents of a beaker. **3** a thin glass or metal cup with a small lip for pouring and no handle, used in laboratories. ⟨ME < ON *bikarr* < LL *becarium,* var. of *bacarium.* Related to BASIN.⟩

beak•y ['biki] *adj.* **1** having a beaklike nose; beaklike. **2** prying; meddlesome.

be–all and end–all **1** the main purpose or reason of anything. **2** *Informal.* the most important person or thing: *He thinks he is the be-all and end-all.* ⟨coined by Shakespeare in *Macbeth*⟩

beam [bim] *n., v. —n.* **1** a large, long piece of timber, ready for use in building. **2** a similar piece of metal, stone, reinforced concrete, etc. **3** any of the main horizontal supports of a building or ship. See FRAME for picture. **4** the part of a plough by which it is pulled. **5** the crossbar of a balance, from the ends of which the scales or pans are suspended. **6** the balance itself. **7** a ray or shaft of light: *the beam of a flashlight, a moonbeam.* **8** a bright look or smile. **9** a straight, narrow stream of electromagnetic radiation, nuclear particles, etc.: *a laser beam.* **10** a radio signal directed in a straight line, used to guide aircraft, ships, etc. **11** the side of a ship, or the direction at right angles to the keel, with reference to wind, sea, etc. **12** the greatest width of a ship. **13** the measurement of the hips: *a broad beam.* **14** *Gymnastics.* BALANCE BEAM. **15** either of the two large cylindrical devices on a loom. One holds the threads to be woven, the other the completed material. **16** the principal branch of a deer's antler.
off the beam, a of an aircraft, off the course indicated by directing signals. **b** *Informal.* on the wrong track; mistaken.

on the beam, a at right angles to the keel of a ship. **b** of an aircraft, in the right path as indicated by directing signals. **c** *Informal.* just right; on the right track. **d** performing well; sharp and alert.
—*v.* **1** send out rays of light; shine. **2** smile radiantly. **3** direct (a broadcast, a light source, etc.): *to beam programs at the Yukon. Beam your flashlight over here.* ⟨OE *bēam* tree, piece of wood, ray of light⟩

☛ *Syn.* **7. Beam,** RAY = a line of light. **Beam** applies to a shaft, long and with some width, coming from something that gives out light: *The beam from the flashlight showed a kneeling man.* **Ray** applies to a thin line of light, usually thought of as radiating, or coming out like the spokes of a wheel, from something bright: *There was not a ray of moonlight in the forest.*

beamed [bimd] *adj., v.* —*adj.* built so as to expose the beams: *a beamed ceiling.*
—*v.* pt. and pp. of BEAM.

beam–ends ['bim ˌɛndz] *n.pl.* the ends of a ship's beams.
on her beam-ends, of a ship, almost capsizing.
on (one's) **beam-ends,** seriously short of money; impoverished.

beam•er ['bimər] *n.* a bone implement for scraping hides, made from the cannon bone of a moose or caribou. It is used by holding it in both hands and pushing it along the skin away from the user.

beam•ing ['bimɪŋ] *adj., v.* —*adj.* **1** shining; bright. **2** smiling brightly; cheerful.
—*v.* ppr. of BEAM. —**'beam•ing•ly,** *adv.*

beam–on ['bim 'ɒn] *adv.* of a ship, with the beam ahead; against the beam.

beam trawler a fishing vessel that drags its net along the ocean floor.

bean [bin] *n., v.* —*n.* **1** any of a number of climbing or bushy plants (genus *Phaseolus*) of the pea family, including many cultivated varieties, that produce edible, usually kidney-shaped seeds in long pods. The pods themselves of some of these plants are also edible when immature. **2** the dried mature seed of a bean plant: *Baked beans are often eaten as the main part of a meal.* **3** the immature green or yellow pod of a bean plant with its seeds, used as a vegetable, usually cooked. **4** any of various other seeds or fruits related to or resembling a bean: *Coffee beans are the seeds of the coffee plant.* **5** *Slang.* the head.
full of beans, *Slang.* lively; in high spirits: *She's really full of beans today.*
not know beans about, *Informal.* have no knowledge of; be uninformed about.
old bean, *Esp. Brit. Slang.* chap; friend (*used as a form of address*): *How are you, old bean?*
spill the beans, tell a secret.
—*v. Slang.* hit (someone) on the head, especially with a baseball or other thrown object: *The pitcher beaned one batter twice.* ⟨OE *bēan*⟩ —**'bean,like,** *adj.*
☛ *Hom.* BEEN [bin].

bean•bag ['bin,bæg] *n.* a small cloth bag loosely filled with dry beans, used to toss in play: *Beanbags are often made in the shape of animals.*

beanbag chair a soft chair, usually made of vinyl and stuffed with polystyrene beads, that can change shape to suit the sitter.

bean•ball ['bin,bɒl] *n. Baseball.* a pitch sent on purpose near the batter's head.

bean curd tofu.

bean•er•y ['binəri] *n.* a low-class restaurant.

bean•ie ['bini] *n.* a small cap, often having no peak, formerly worn especially by schoolboys as part of their uniform, but now often by youth of both sexes.

bean•pole ['bin,poul] *n.* **1** a pole stuck in the ground for bean vines to climb on as they grow. **2** *Slang.* a tall, thin person.

bean sprout *n.* the sprout of any of various bean seeds used as a vegetable, either raw, as for salads, or cooked.

bean•stalk ['bin,stɒk] *n.* the stem of a bean plant.

bear¹ [bɛr] *v.* **bore, borne** or (for 6 or 7 when used in the passive voice) **born, bear•ing. 1** carry; transport: *A voice was borne upon the wind.* **2** support: *The ice is too thin to bear your weight.* **3** put up with; abide; tolerate: *I can't bear that song.* **4** undergo or experience without giving way; endure: *She cannot bear any more pain.* **5** produce; yield: *This tree bears fine apples. Our apple tree bears well.* **6** give birth to; have (offspring): *That woman has borne four boys. He was born on June 4.* **7** produce; create; cause to come into existence: *On the opening night of the play a star was born. The idea of the plot was born at a secret meeting.* **8** have a connection or effect; relate: *Her answer did not bear on the question.* **9** behave; conduct: *He bore himself with great dignity.* **10** bring forward; give: *to bear company, to bear a hand. A person who has seen an accident can bear witness to what happened.* **11** hold in mind; harbour or cherish: *to bear a grudge, to bear affection for someone.* **12** have as an identification or characteristic: *He bears the name of John, the title of earl, and a reputation for learning.* **13** have as a duty, right, privilege, etc.: *The queen bears sway over the empire.* **14** take on oneself as a duty: *to bear the cost, responsibility, etc.* **15** press; push: *Don't bear so hard on the lever.* **16** move; go in a certain direction: *The ship bore north.* **17** lie; be situated: *The land bore due north of the ship.* **18** allow; permit: *The accident bears two explanations.* **19** carry and give (a message). **20** bring it upon oneself: *She couldn't bear to tell him.* **21** be directed toward (*used with* **on** *or* **upon**): *The cannons are set to bear on the barricade.*
bear a hand, assist; lend a hand.
bear down, of a woman in childbirth, use effort to expel the baby.
bear down (on), a put pressure on; press or push: *Don't bear down so hard on him.* **b** move toward; approach. **c** try hard; work seriously: *You'll have to bear down if you expect to pass the examination.*
bear out, support; prove.
bear up, keep one's courage; not lose hope or faith; cope: *How is she bearing up?*
bear with, put up with; be patient with.
bring to bear (on), cause to have an influence (on). ⟨OE *beran*⟩
☛ *Hom.* BARE.
☛ *Syn.* **4. Bear,** ENDURE, STAND = to undergo something hard to take. **Bear,** the general word, suggests only being able to hold up: *He is bearing his grief very well.* **Endure** = to bear hardship or misfortune for a long time without giving in: *The pioneers endured many hardships in settling the West.* **Stand** is the informal word used interchangeably with **bear**, but it suggests bearing stubbornly and bravely: *She can stand more pain than anyone else I know.*

bear² [bɛr] *n.* **1** any of a family (Ursidae) of large, heavily built mammals found mainly in the temperate regions of the northern hemisphere, having thick, coarse, shaggy hair, a very short tail, short, rounded ears, and large, flat, five-toed paws with powerful claws. Bears are carnivorous animals but they also feed on berries, young shoots and buds, etc. **2** a gruff, surly person. **3** a person who sells shares or stocks in anticipation of a price decline, in order to make a profit by buying later at the lower price. Compare BULL¹ (def. 5). **4** (*adjl.*) of, having to do with, or designating a stock market in which prices are declining. Compare BULL¹ (def. 6). **5 Bear.** See GREAT BEAR and LITTLE BEAR.
be a bear for punishment, be capable of enduring harsh circumstances; enjoy challenge. ⟨OE *bera*⟩ —**'bear,like,** *adj.*
☛ *Hom.* BARE.

bear•a•ble ['bɛrəbəl] *adj.* that can be borne; endurable: *The pain was severe but bearable.* —**'bear•a•ble•ness,** *n.* —**'bear•a•bly,** *adv.*

bear•bait•ing ['bɛr,beitɪŋ] *n.* **1** a sport that was popular for several hundred years, in which dogs were set to torment a chained bear. Bearbaiting declined in popularity from the 17th century on and was finally outlawed by Parliament in 1835. **2** the unfair attacking of someone by a group.

bear•ber•ry ['bɛr,bɛri] *n., pl.* **-ries.** *Cdn.* **1** a trailing evergreen shrub (*Arctostaphylos uva-ursi*) of the heath family having small, pale pink flowers, red berries, and astringent leaves. It is found especially in rocky or sandy regions of Canada and the United States and in the British Isles. **2** a closely related arctic and alpine shrub (*A. alpina*) having black berries.

bear•cat ['bɛr,kæt] *n.* **1** PANDA (def. 2). **2** a person who is strong, aggressive, etc.

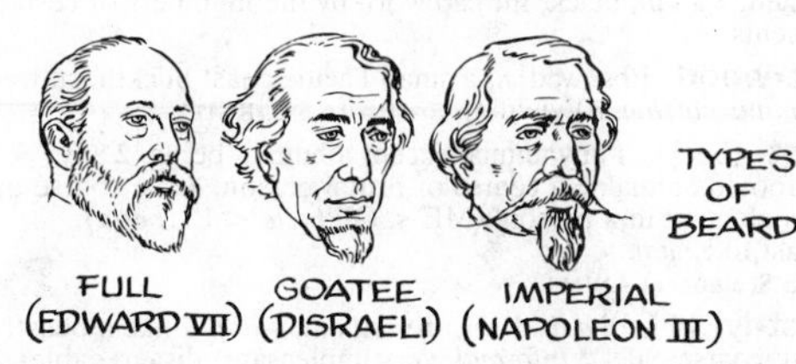

beard [bird] *n., v.* —*n.* **1** the hair that grows on the chin, cheeks, and upper throat of a man: *a three days' growth of beard.* **2** the growth formed by this hair, allowed to grow freely or cut or trimmed in any of various styles: *a full beard, an imperial beard.*

3 a tuft or growth of hair or bristles on the face or under the chin of any of certain animals or birds. **4** a tuft or crest of hairs or bristles on a plant, such as the awns of some grasses.
—v. **1** face boldly; defy. **2** grasp by the beard. ⟨OE⟩ **—'beard,like,** *adj.*

beard•ed ['birdɪd] *adj., v. —adj.* having a beard.
—v. pt. and pp. of BEARD.

bearded seal *Cdn.* a very large seal (*Erignathus barbatus*) found along the arctic coasts of the world, distinguished especially by its square foreflippers and long, whiskerlike bristles about the mouth.

bearded vulture a large vulture (*Gypaetus barbatus*) of the eastern hemisphere, having dark grey plumage with white streaks, and bristles below the beak.

beard•less ['birdlɪs] *adj.* **1** having no beard. **2** too young to have a beard: *a beardless youth.* **3** young and inexperienced.

beard•tongue ['bird,tʌŋ] *n.* a plant of the genus *Penstemon,* having showy flowers of various colours, and five stamens, one of which is sterile and bears bristles.

bear•er ['bɛrər] *n.* **1** a person or thing that carries. **2** a person who holds or presents a cheque, draft, or note for payment. **3** a tree or plant that produces fruit or flowers: *This apple tree is a good bearer.* **4** the holder of a rank or office. **5** pallbearer.
6 (*adjl.*) payable to the bearer: *bearer bonds.*

bear garden **1** formerly, a place for bearbaiting. **2** any place which is noisy or unruly.

bear•grass ['bɛr,græs] *n.* a plant (*Xerophyllum tenax*) of the lily family, native to W North America.

bear•hug ['bɛr,hʌg] *n.* an embrace, often by a bigger person hugging tightly.

bear•ing ['bɛrɪŋ] *n., v. —n.* **1** a way of standing, sitting, walking, etc.; manner: *a military bearing.* **2** connection in thought or meaning; reference or relation: *His foolish question has no bearing on the problem.* **3** a part of a machine on which another part turns or slides. See GYROSCOPE for picture. **4** the act, time, or power of producing fruit, young, etc. **5** a crop. **6** a supporting part. **7** *Heraldry.* a device or figure on a shield; charge.
8 bearings, *pl.* **a** direction; position in relation to other things: *The pilot radioed her bearings.* **b** comprehension of one's position in relation to other things: *Without a guide in the bush, he would soon have lost his bearings.*
—v. ppr. of BEAR[1].

☛ *Syn.* **1. Bearing,** CARRIAGE = manner of carrying oneself. **Bearing** applies to a person's manner of managing his or her whole body, including his or her gestures, mannerisms, posture, the way he or she holds his or her head, and the way he or she walks and sits: *His manly bearing won the confidence of his young charges.* **Carriage** applies only to a person's way of holding his or her head and body when he or she stands and walks: *Her awkward carriage prevented the pretty girl from becoming a model.*

bear•ish ['bɛrɪʃ] *adj.* **1** like a bear; rough; surly. **2** marked by, tending toward, or expecting lower prices in the stock market. Compare BULLISH. **3** expecting the worst. **—'bear•ish•ly,** *adv.*
—'bear•ish•ness, *n.*

bé•ar•naise sauce ['beiərneiz] a French sauce made with egg yolks and butter, flavoured with wine or herbs and served with meat or fish.

bear•pit session ['bɛr,pɪt] *Cdn.* a frank gathering of political party members at a convention, when members of Parliament or a legislature must defend their policies or positions.

bear•skin ['bɛr,skɪn] *n.* **1** the skin of a bear with the fur attached. **2** a tall, black, fur cap worn by the members of certain regiments.

bear•wood ['bɛr,wʊd] *n.* a small Pacific coast buckthorn tree (*Rhamnus purshiana*) yielding CASCARA SAGRADA.

beast [bist] *n.* **1** any animal except a human being. **2** any four-footed animal. **3** a coarse or brutal person. **4** the coarse or brutal element in a person. ⟨ME < OF *beste* < LL *besta*⟩
—'beast,like, *adj.*

☛ *Syn.* See note at ANIMAL.

beast•ly ['bistli] *adj.* **-li•er, -li•est;** *adv. —adj.* **1** like a beast; brutal; coarse; vile. **2** *Informal.* very unpleasant; disagreeable: *a beastly headache.*
—adv. Informal. very; unpleasantly: *It was beastly cold.*
—'beast•li•ness, *n.*

beast of burden an animal used for carrying loads.

beast of prey any animal that hunts and kills other animals for its food.

beat [bit] *v.* **beat, beat•en** or **beat, beat•ing;** *n., adj. —v.* **1** strike again and again; strike; whip; thrash: *The cruel man beat his horse.* **2** throb: *Her heart beat fast with joy.* **3** drive by blows; force by blows: *He beat the savage dog away from him.* **4** defeat or overcome: *Their team beat ours by a huge score.* **5** *Informal.* baffle: *This problem beats me.* **6** *Informal.* cheat; swindle. **7** make flat; shape with a hammer: *to beat gold into thin strips.* **8** make flat by much walking; tread (a path). **9** mix by stirring; mix by striking with a fork, spoon, or other utensil: *to beat eggs.* **10** move up and down; flap: *The bird beat its wings.* **11** make a sound by being struck: *The drums beat loudly.* **12** mark (time) with drumsticks or by tapping with hands or feet: *to beat a tattoo.*
13 *Music.* show (a unit of time or accent) by a stroke of the hand, baton, etc. **14** go through (woods or underbrush) in a hunt: *The men beat the woods in search of the lost child.* **15** move against the wind by a zigzag course: *The sailboat beat along the coast.* **16** outdo; surpass: *Nothing can beat yachting as a sport.*
17 come to the end or to an end before (someone else); be first in doing something: *They beat us to the theatre.*
beat about, search around; try to discover: *She beat about in vain for a fitting answer.*
beat a retreat, a run away; retreat. **b** sound a retreat on a drum.
beat around (or **about**) **the bush,** approach a matter indirectly; avoid coming to the point: *Stop beating around the bush and tell me what you want.*
beat back, force to retreat; push back: *The enemy advance was successfully beaten back.*
beat down, *Informal.* **a** force to set a lower price. **b** of the sun, shine intensely. **c** subdue; suppress.
beat it, *Slang.* go away; scram: *I got tired of his teasing and told him to beat it.*
beat off, a drive off or away by blows: *He beat off the two men who attacked him.* **b** drive away; repel: *We beat off our fear by singing to each other.*
beat (someone) **to it,** be the first to do something.
beat the rap, *Slang.* be freed from an accusation or charge without any penalty: *She was charged with dangerous driving, but managed to beat the rap.*
beat up, *Slang.* thrash severely.
—n. **1** a stroke or blow made again and again: *the beat of a drum, the beat of waves on a beach.* **2** pulsation; throb: *the beat of the heart.* **3** *Music.* **a** a unit of time; accent: *three beats to a measure.* **b** a stroke of the hand, baton, etc. showing a beat. **c** rhythm; pattern of timed accents: *She likes music with a fast beat.* **4** a regular round or route, especially one taken by a police officer or a sentry. **5** *Informal.* something that excels: *I've never seen the beat of that.* **6** *Slang.* beatnik. **7** a person's regular work or environment, sphere of knowledge, etc.: *That sort of thing is off my beat.* **8** *Radio.* one cycle of a frequency.
—adj. **1** *Informal.* worn out; exhausted: *She was beat after a hard day at the factory.* **2** *Slang.* of or characteristic of beatniks: *the beat generation of the 50s.* ⟨OE *bēatan*⟩

☛ *Hom.* BEET.

☛ *Syn. v.* **1. Beat,** HIT, POUND = to strike. **Beat** = to strike again and again, but does not suggest how hard nor with what: *The cruel driver beat his horse.* **Hit** = to strike a single blow with force and aim: *The batter hit the ball.* **Pound** = to hit hard again and again with the fist or something heavy: *The child pounded the floor with a hammer.*

beat•en ['bitən] *v., adj. —v.* a pp. of BEAT.
—adj. **1** whipped; struck: *a beaten dog.* **2** shaped by blows of a hammer: *beaten silver.* **3** much walked on or travelled: *a beaten path.* **4** discouraged by defeat; overcome: *They were a beaten lot.*
5 exhausted.
off the beaten path or **track, a** in an out-of-the-way or remote place. **b** unconventional; different.

beat•er ['bitər] *n.* **1** a person who beats, especially a person hired to rouse game during a hunt. **2** a device or utensil for beating eggs, cream, etc.: *an electric beater.* **3** *Cdn.* a young harp seal, about three or four weeks old, that is learning to swim and has developed its first spotted coat.

be•a•tif•ic [,biə'tɪfɪk] *adj.* showing or producing blessedness; blissful: *The woman in the painting had a beatific smile.*
—,be•a'tif•ic•al•ly, *adv.*

be•at•i•fi•ca•tion [bi,ætəfə'keiʃən] *n.* **1** a making blessed or being made blessed. **2** *Roman Catholic Church.* **a** an official declaration by the Pope that a dead person is among the blessed in heaven. **b** the inquiry investigating the dead person prior to this pronouncement.

be•at•i•fy [bi'ætə,faɪ] *v.* **-fied, -fy•ing. 1** make supremely happy; bless. **2** *Roman Catholic Church.* declare (a dead person) by a papal decree to be among the blessed in heaven. ⟨< L *beatificare* < *beatus* happy + *facere* make⟩

beat•ing ['bitıŋ] *n., v.* —*n.* **1** the act of beating. **2** punishment by repeated blows; whipping. **3** defeat: *They took a beating in the game.* **4** throbbing; pulsation: *He could hear the beating of his own heart as he waited.*
—*v.* ppr. of BEAT.

be•at•i•tude [bi'ætə,tjud] *or* [bi'ætə,tud] *n.* **1** supreme happiness; bliss. **2** a blessing. **3 the Beatitudes,** *pl.* the declarations of blessedness made by Jesus in the Sermon on the Mount. ⟨< L *beatitudo* < *beatus* blessed⟩

beat•nik ['bitnık] *n.* a person who adopts a mode of life calculated to show indifference to or contempt for conventions and accepted standards in dress, speech, art expression, etc. ⟨< *beat* + Yiddish *-nik*⟩

beat–up ['bit 'ʌp] *adj. Slang.* **1** in very bad condition; worn out. **2** completely exhausted.

beau [bou] *n., pl.* **beaus** or **beaux** [bouz]. **1** a young man courting a young woman; suitor; lover. **2** a man who pays much attention to the way he dresses and to the fashionableness or stylishness of his clothes. ⟨< F *beau* handsome < L *bellus* fine⟩
☛ *Hom.* BOW[2].
☛ *Usage.* **Beaux** is the more formal plural form; ordinarily, use **beaus.**

Beau Brum•mell ['bou 'brʌməl] **1** the nickname of George Bryan Brummell (1778-1840), an English leader in men's fashions. **2** any dandy.

Beau•fort scale ['boufərt] an internationally used scale of wind velocities, using code numbers from 0 to 17. See chart in the Appendix. ⟨after Admiral Sir Francis *Beaufort*, who devised the scale in 1805⟩

beau geste ['bou 'ʒɛst] *pl.* **beaux gestes** ['bou 'ʒɛst]. *French.* **1** a graceful or kindly act. **2** a pretence of kindness or unselfishness merely for effect.

beau i•dé•al ['bou, idei'æl]; *French,* [boide'al] a perfect type of excellence or beauty; the highest ideal or model. ⟨< F, ideal beauty⟩

Beau•jo•lais [,bouʒə'lei] *or* ['bouʒə,lei] *n.* a light red or white table wine, especially that from the Beaujolais region in France.

beau monde ['bou 'mɒnd]; *French,* [bo'mɔ̃d] fashionable society. ⟨< F⟩

beaut [bjut] *n. Slang.* a person or thing that is exceptionally fine, splendid or beautiful. ⟨< *beauty*⟩
☛ *Usage.* Sometimes used ironically of something bad.
☛ *Hom.* BUTTE.

beau•te•ous ['bjutiəs] *adj. Esp. Poetic.* beautiful. —**'beau•te•ous•ly,** *adv.* —**'beau•te•ous•ness,** *n.*

beau•ti•cian [bju'tıʃən] *n.* a specialist in the use of cosmetics, especially a person who works in a beauty salon.

beau•ti•fi•ca•tion [,bjutəfə'keiʃən] *n.* the act or process of making something, especially a place, more beautiful: *plans for the beautification of the city.*

beau•ti•ful ['bjutəfəl] *adj., interj.* —*adj.* very pleasing to see or hear; delighting the mind, spirit, or senses: *a beautiful picture, beautiful music.*
—*interj.* an exclamation of pleasure or delight. —**'beau•ti•ful•ly,** *adv.* —**'beau•ti•ful•ness,** *n.*
☛ *Syn.* **Beautiful,** LOVELY, HANDSOME = pleasing the senses or mind. **Beautiful** suggests delighting the senses by excellence and harmony, and often also giving great pleasure to the mind by an inner goodness: *Looking at a beautiful painting always gives one satisfaction.* **Lovely** suggests appealing to the emotions and giving delight to the heart as well as to the senses and mind: *Her lovely smile shows a sweet disposition.* **Handsome** = pleasing to look at because well formed, well proportioned, etc.: *That is a handsome chest of drawers.*

beau•ti•fy ['bjutə,faı] *v.* **-fied, -fy•ing. 1** make beautiful or more beautiful; embellish: *Flowers beautify a yard.* **2** become beautiful. ⟨< *beauty* + *-fy*⟩ —**'beau•ti,fi•er,** *n.*

beau•ty ['bjuti] *n., pl.* **-ties. 1** a quality or combination of qualities that gives great pleasure to the senses or to the mind and spirit: *The richness and beauty of the great hall were almost beyond description. "A thing of beauty is a joy forever." There is great beauty in your poetry.* **2** a person or thing that has beauty, especially a beautiful woman: *She is a renowned beauty.* **3** a feature or trait that gives special pleasure to the mind or senses: *the beauties of the countryside in spring. The beauty of her writing style is its simplicity.* **4** *Informal.* a notable or exceptional example of its kind: *That catch was a beauty! You should see her black eye; it's a beauty!* ⟨ME < OF *beaute* < *beau* beautiful < L *bellus* fine⟩

beauty mark BEAUTY SPOT (def. 2).

beauty parlour or **parlor** BEAUTY SALON.

beauty salon or **shop** a place that provides women with such services as hairdressing, manicuring, and facial skin treatments.

beauty sleep *Informal.* **1** any short nap. **2** the hours of sleep taken before midnight, supposed to be those that are most beneficial.

beauty spot 1 a small, black patch formerly worn on the face to show off by contrast the whiteness of the skin. **2** a mole or small spot or mark on the skin. **3** any place or natural feature of especial beauty.

beaux [bouz] *n.* a pl. of BEAU.

beaux–arts ['bo'zaʀ] *n.pl. French.* fine arts; painting, sculpture, music, etc.

A beaver

bea•ver[1] ['bivər] *n., pl.* **-vers** or (def. 1) **-ver;** *v.* —*n.* **1** either of two species comprising a family (Castoridae) of large rodents that live in and around water, having a thickset body, a broad, flat, scaly tail which is used as a rudder in swimming, large webbed hind feet, and long, chisel-like front teeth. The North American beaver (*Castor canadensis*) has been an emblem of Canada for over two hundred years. Some authorities consider the North American beaver to be of the same species as the Old World beaver (*Castor fiber*). **2** the thick, soft, glossy, brown fur of a beaver, highly valued for coats, etc. **3** a man's high silk hat, formerly made of beaver fur. **4** a heavy woollen cloth. **5** *Informal.* an especially hard-working person; an EAGER BEAVER. **6 Beaver,** a member, aged five to seven, of the Scouts.
—*v. Informal.* work hard or energetically (*often used with* **away**): *He has been beavering away all day.* ⟨OE *beofor*⟩

bea•ver[2] ['bivər] *n.* **1** a movable piece of armour that protects the chin and mouth. See ARMOUR for picture. **2** the movable front part of a helmet; a visor. ⟨ME < OF *bavière*, originally, bib < *bave* saliva⟩

Beaver ['bivər] *n., pl.* **-ver** or **-vers. 1** a member of a group of Athapaskan First Nations of the Peace River valley in Alberta. **2** the language of this group. ⟨translation of Beaver name meaning 'dwellers among beavers'⟩

Bea•ver•board ['bivər,bɔrd] *n. Trademark.* a lightweight material resembling very thick, strong cardboard, used for making ceilings, partitions, etc.

be•bee•rine [bı'birin] *or* [-rın] *n.* a drug obtained from the bark of the bebeeru tree and similar to quinine, prescribed for malaria. *Formula*: $C_{36}H_{38}N_2O_6$

be•bee•ru [bı'biru] *n.* a tropical tree (*Nectandra rodioei*) growing in South America. It is evergreen and related to the laurels. Its bark yields bebeerine. ⟨< a Guianan name⟩

be•bop ['bi,bɒp] *n. Music.* a style of jazz that evolved in the 1940s, characterized by more complex harmony and more syncopation than in swing; bop. ⟨imitative⟩

be•calm [bı'kɒm] *or* [bı'kɑm] *v.* **1** keep (a ship, boat, etc.) from moving because of lack of wind (*usually used in the passive*): *We were becalmed for several hours.* **2** make calm; soothe.

be•came [bı'keim] *v.* pt. of BECOME.

be•cause [bı'kʌz] *or* [bı'kɒz] *conj.* for the reason that; since: *We play ball because we enjoy the game.*
because of, by reason of; on account of: *Mark did not go because of the rain.* ⟨ME *bi cause* by cause⟩
☛ *Syn.* **Because,** AS, SINCE, FOR. **Because** introduces a subordinate clause that gives the reason for the main clause: *Because we were late, we hurried.* **As** can be used in such clauses, but is less definite and more characteristic of informal speech than of writing. **Since** has a similar function but may be ambiguous since it can refer to time as well as cause: *Since she went away, he has taken to drink.* **For,** used only to introduce a clause following the main clause, is a more formal word.

bec•ca•fi•co [,bɛkə'fikou] *n.* a small European bird of the genus *Sylvia,* noted for its song and, especially in Italy, for its delicate flavour when eaten. ⟨< Ital. < *beccare* peck + *fico* fig⟩

bé•cha•mel [,beiʃɑ'mɛl] a creamy white sauce seasoned with onion and other spices. ⟨< F; named after King Louis XIV's steward⟩

be•chance [bı'tʃæns] *v.* **-chanced, -chanc•ing.** *Archaic.* happen; happen to; befall.

bêche-de-mer ['bɛʃ də 'mɛr] *n., pl.* **bêches-de-mer. 1** a sea cucumber used in Malaysia to make soup. **2** a hybrid languag containing much pidgin English, used for trade among South Pacific islanders. ⟨< F < Pg. *bicho do mar* sea slug⟩

Bech•u•a•na [ˌbɛtʃu'ɒnə] *or* [bɛtʃ'wɒnə] *n.* **1** a member of a people living in Botswana. **2** their language, a form of Bantu.

beck [bɛk] *n.* a motion of the head or hand meant as a call or command.
at (someone's) **beck and call,** ready to do whatever someone orders or wants: *He had three servants at his beck and call.*
⟨< *beck*, v., short for *beckon*⟩

beck•on ['bɛkən] *v.* **1** signal by a motion of the head or hand: *He beckoned me to follow him.* **2** entice; be attractive (*to*). ⟨OE *bēcnan*, var. of *bīecnan.* Related to BEACON.⟩

be•clo•meth•a•sone di•pro•pi•on•ate [ˌbɛklə'mɛθəˌsoun daɪ'proupiəˌneit] a drug used as an inhalant to treat asthma. *Formula*: $C_{28}H_{37}ClO_7$

be•cloud [bɪ'klaʊd] *v.* **1** hide by a cloud or clouds. **2** make obscure: *Too many big words becloud the meaning.*

be•come [bɪ'kʌm] *v.* **be•came, be•come, be•com•ing. 1** come to be; grow to be: *He became wiser as he grew older.* **2** be suitable for; suit: *The rude comment did not become his position as chair.* **3** look good on: *That dress becomes her.*
become of, happen to: *What will become of her? What has become of the box of candy?* ⟨OE *becuman*⟩
☛ *Usage.* **Become** is one of the common linking verbs: *At his words she became more angry. Become* differs from the linking verb *be* in that it adds a meaning of its own to its linking function, suggesting change or development rather than identity.

be•com•ing [bɪ'kʌmɪŋ] *adj., v.* —*adj.* **1** suitable; appropriate: *becoming conduct for a formal occasion.* **2** that looks good on the person wearing it: *a becoming dress.*
—*v.* ppr. of BECOME. **—be'com•ing•ly,** *adv.*
☛ *Syn.* See note at FITTING.

bec•que•rel [ˌbɛkə'rɛl] an SI unit for measuring radioactivity, or the rate at which the atoms of radioactive elements disintegrate. One becquerel is equal to one disintegration per second. *Symbol*: Bq ⟨after A.H. *Becquerel* (1852-1908), a French physicist⟩

Becquerel rays the original name of GAMMA RAYS.

bed [bɛd] *n., v.* **bed•ded, bed•ding.** —*n.* **1 a** a piece of furniture to sleep or rest on. A bed usually consists of a mattress raised upon a support and covered with sheets and blankets.
b sometimes, only the support or frame, or only the sheets and blankets: *an unmade bed. Don't forget, you have to add the cost of a mattress to the price of a bed.* **2** any place where people or animals rest or sleep. **3** a flat base on which anything rests; foundation: *They set the lathe in a bed of concrete.* **4** the ground under a body of water: *the bed of a river.* **5** the piece of ground in a garden in which plants are grown. **6** *Geology.* a layer or stratum: *a bed of coal.* **7** the time at which one goes to bed: *You must have finished your homework before bed.*
bed and board, sleeping accommodation and meals.
get up on the wrong side of the bed, be irritable or bad-tempered.
go to bed with, *Informal.* have sexual intercourse with.
put to bed, a make (a child or invalid) go to bed. **b** prepare (an edition of a newspaper) for printing.
take to (one's) **bed,** stay in bed because of sickness or weakness.
—*v.* **1** provide with a bed or sleeping place; put to bed (*usually used with* **down**): *Wendy bedded her horse down with straw.* **2** go to bed; lie down to sleep (*used with* **down**): *He bedded down on a couch in the basement.* **3** fix or set in a permanent position; embed. **4** plant in a garden bed: *These roses should be bedded in rich soil.* **5** form a compact layer. **6** lay flat or in order so as to form a bed. **7** *Informal.* have sexual intercourse with. ⟨OE *bedd*⟩

bed and breakfast an establishment offering overnight accommodation and breakfast the next morning.
—bed-and-breakfast, *adj.*

be•daub [bɪ'dɒb] *v.* **1** smear with something dirty or sticky. **2** ornament in a gaudy or showy way.

be•daz•zle [bɪ'dæzəl] *v.* **-zled, -zling.** dazzle completely; confuse by dazzling: *She was bedazzled by the brilliant lights.*

bed•board ['bɛdˌbɔrd] *n.* a rigid piece of wood placed under a mattress to provide firm support.

bed•bug ['bɛdˌbʌg] *n.* a small, reddish brown bug (*Cimex lectularius*) about 5 mm long, having a broad, flat body covered with short hairs and bristles, small useless wings, and scent glands that give off a disagreeable odour. Bedbugs are bloodsucking parasites on human beings; they hide during the day in folds of mattresses, cracks in bedsteads, behind baseboards, etc. and come out at night to feed.

bed•cham•ber ['bɛdˌtʃeimbər] *n.* bedroom.

bed chesterfield a chesterfield that opens out into a bed.

bed•clothes ['bɛdˌklouðz] *or* ['bɛdˌklouz] *n.pl.* sheets, blankets, quilts, etc.

bed•cov•er ['bɛdˌkʌvər] *n.* a bedspread; coverlet.

bed•ding ['bɛdɪŋ] *n., v.* —*n.* **1** sheets, blankets, quilts, etc.; bedclothes. **2** material for beds: *Straw is used as bedding for cows and horses.* **3** a foundation; bottom layer. **4** *Geology.* rocks in a layered structure.
—*v.* ppr. of BED.

bedding plant a small plant such as that of a flower, ready for transplanting into a flower bed.

be•deck [bɪ'dɛk] *v.* adorn; decorate.

be•dev•il [bɪ'dɛvəl] *v.* **-illed** or **-iled, -il•ling** or **-il•ing.** **1** trouble greatly; torment. **2** confuse completely; muddle. **3** put under a spell; bewitch.

be•dev•il•ment [bɪ'dɛvəlmənt] *n.* **1** great trouble; torment. **2** complete confusion; muddle. **3** the state of being under a spell; a being bewitched.

be•dew [bɪ'dju] *or* [bɪ'du] *v.* make wet with dew or as if with dew: *Tears bedewed her cheeks.*

bed•fast ['bɛdˌfæst] *adj.* confined to bed; bedridden.

bed•fel•low ['bɛdˌfɛlou] *n.* **1** the person with whom one shares a bed. **2** a close associate: *The anti-war movement has produced some strange bedfellows.*

Bed•ford cord ['bɛdfərd] a heavy cloth ribbed like corduroy. ⟨< *Bedford*, a town in S England⟩

be•dight [bɪ'dəit] *adj. Archaic.* adorned; arrayed. ⟨< *be-* + *dight*⟩

be•dim [bɪ'dɪm] *v.* **-dimmed, -dim•ming.** make dim; darken; obscure.

be•di•zen [bɪ'daɪzən] *or* [bɪ'dɪzən] *v.* dress in gaudy clothes; ornament with showy finery. ⟨< *be-* + *dizen*⟩
—be'diz•en•ment, *n.*

bed jacket a short sweater or coat worn over night clothes by women, often when sick and sitting up in bed.

bed•lam ['bɛdləm] *n.* **1** uproar; confusion: *When the home team won, there was bedlam in the arena. The whole house was bedlam for the first few days.* **2 Bedlam,** the traditional popular name for a hospital for the mentally ill in London, England, originally the Hospital of St. Mary of Bethlehem, but now officially named Bethlehem Royal Hospital. ⟨ME *Bedlem*, a variant form of *Bethlehem*⟩

bed•lam•er ['bɛdləmər] *n. Cdn.* a young seal, especially a harp seal, about one to five years old, having a creamy brown coat with large, dark blotches on the flanks. ⟨prob. a corruption of F *bête de la mer* sea beast⟩

bed linen sheets and pillowcases for a bed.

Bed•ling•ton terrier ['bɛdlɪŋtən] a breed of medium-sized terrier having rough, woolly fur, usually greyish brown, noted for its speed and pluck. It is usually clipped to resemble a lamb. ⟨< *Bedlington*, a town in England⟩

bed of roses *Informal.* a situation of ease and comfort (*usually in negative sentences*): *Life isn't a bed of roses.*

Bed•ou•in ['bɛduɪn] *n., adj.* —*n.* **1** a nomad of the deserts and steppes of the Middle East and N Africa: *Most of the Bedouins of northern Africa are Berbers; those of the Middle East are Arabs.* **2** a wanderer; nomad.
—*adj.* of or having to do with the Bedouins. ⟨ME < OF < Arabic *badawin*, pl. of *badawiy* desert dweller⟩

bed•pan ['bɛdˌpæn] *n.* **1** a pan used as a toilet by sick people in bed. **2** a pan filled with hot coals for warming a bed, especially formerly.

bed•post ['bɛdˌpoust] *n.* an upright support at a corner of a bed.

be•drag•gle [bɪ'drægəl] *v.* **-gled, -gling.** make wet or soiled with or as if with rain, mud, etc.

be•drag•gled [bɪ'drægəld] *adj., v.* —*adj.* **1** thoroughly wet and straggly or ragged-looking: *bedraggled hair. He arrived home two hours later, tired and bedraggled.* **2** soiled by or as if by being dragged in dirt or mud: *a bedraggled hem.*
—*v.* pt. and pp. of BEDRAGGLE.

bed•rail ['bɛdˌreil] *n.* either of the two planks running the length of the bed, between the head of the bed and the foot.

bed rest a period of resting in bed, as, after illness, surgery, etc.: *The doctor has prescribed bed rest.*

bed•rid ['bɛd,rɪd] *adj.* bedridden. ⟨OE *bedreda, bedrida,* literally, bed rider⟩

bed•rid•den ['bɛd,rɪdən] *adj.* confined to bed for a long time because of sickness or weakness. ⟨var. (by confusion with *ridden*) of *bedrid*⟩

bed•rock ['bɛd,rɒk] *n.* **1** the solid rock beneath the soil and looser rocks. **2** a firm foundation. **3** the lowest level; bottom. **4** basic truths.

bed•roll ['bɛd,roul] *n.* bedding that can be rolled up and tied to a saddle, etc.

bed•room ['bɛd,rum] *or* ['bɛd,rʊm] *n.* **1** a room to sleep in. **2** (*adjl.*) *Informal.* having to do with or suggestive of sex: *bedroom eyes.*

bedroom suburb or **community** a suburb or community inhabited by people who work outside that area and only return there in the evening.

bed•sheet any sheet used on a bed.

bedsheet ballot a paper ballot that is very long and complicated.

bed•side ['bɛd,saɪd] *n.* **1** the side of a bed. **2** (*adjl.*) with or attending the sick: *Young doctors need bedside practice. She has a good bedside manner.*

bed–sit•ting room a bachelor apartment lacking separate sleeping accommodation, with a sofa that can open up into a bed.

bed sofa a sofa that can open up into a bed.

bed•sore ['bɛd,sɔr] *n.* a sore caused by lying too long in the same position.

bed•spread ['bɛd,sprɛd] *n.* a cover that is spread over other bedclothes to keep them clean and neat and lend a decorative effect.

bed•spring ['bɛd,sprɪŋ] *n.* **1** a set of springs forming the part of the bed that supports the mattress. **2** one of these springs.

bed•stead ['bɛd,stɛd] *n.* the wooden or metal framework of a bed.

bed•straw ['bɛd,strɒ] *n.* any of a genus (*Galium*) of low-growing, perennial plants of the madder family having small white or yellow flowers. The plants were formerly dried and used as straw for beds.

bed throw a coverlet or bedspread, usually of patterned cloth.

bed•tick ['bɛd,tɪk] *n.* the cloth covering of a mattress or a box spring.

bed•tick•ing ['bɛd,tɪkɪŋ] *n.* the strong cotton cloth from which bedticks are made.

bed•time ['bɛd,taɪm] *n.* the usual time for going to bed.

bed–wet•ting ['bɛd 'wɛtɪŋ] *n.* a lack of bladder control at night, so that urine is passed in the bed during sleep; enuresis. **—'bed-,wet•ter,** *n.*

bee[1] [bi] *n.* any of about 20 000 species making up a superfamily (Apoidea) of insects that feed their young with a mixture of pollen and honey stored in their nests. Some species of bees are social, living in large, highly organized colonies, but most species are solitary. The best-known social bees are the honeybee and the bumblebee.
have a bee in (one's) **bonnet,** *Informal.* **a** be preoccupied or overenthusiastic about one thing. **b** be slightly crazy. ⟨OE *bēo*⟩
the bee's knees, *Slang.* a person extremely well-matched to some activity or thing.
☛ *Hom.* B, BE.

bee[2] [bi] *n.* a gathering for work, competition, or amusement: *a husking bee, a spelling bee, a quilting bee.* ⟨? < E dialect *bean* or *been* help from neighbours < OE *bēn* prayer, related to ON *bón* petition. Compare BOON.⟩
☛ *Hom.* B, BE.

bee[3] [bi] BEE BLOCK.
☛ *Hom.* B, BE.

bee•balm ['bi,bɒm] *or* ['bi,bɑm] **1** a plant of the mint family (*Monarda didyma*) with clusters of bright red flowers. **2** a tea made from the leaves of this plant. **3** another plant of the mint family (*Melissa officinalis*) having white flowers, and scented leaves used in medicine, liqueurs, and in flavouring food.

bee–bee gun AIR RIFLE; BB gun.

bee block on a sailing ship, a spar on either side of the bowsprit, to which ropes from the mast can be fastened.

bee•bread ['bi,brɛd] *n.* a brownish, bitter substance consisting of pollen, or pollen mixed with honey, used by bees as food.

beech [bitʃ] *n.* **1** any of a genus (*Fagus*) of trees found in North America and Europe, having smooth, grey bark, dark green, glossy leaves, and small, sweet, edible nuts. **2** the hard, heavy, strong wood of a beech. **3** (*adjl.*) made of this wood: *a beech table.* **4** (*adjl.*) designating a family (Fagaceae) of trees that includes some species highly valued for their timber. Beeches, oaks, and chestnuts belong to the beech family. ⟨OE *bēce*⟩
☛ *Hom.* BEACH.

beech•drops ['bitʃ,drɒps] *n.* a plant of the broom family (*Epifagus virginiana*) common in North America, and having clusters of pale purple flowers. It lives as a parasite on the roots of beech trees.

beech•en ['bitʃən] *adj.* made of beechwood.

beech•mast ['bitʃ,mæst] *n.* a pile of beechnuts on the ground.

beech•nut ['bitʃ,nʌt] *n.* the small, triangular, edible nut of the beech tree.

beech•wood ['bitʃ,wʊd] *n.* the wood of a beech tree.

bee eater a small tropical bird of the family Meropidae, having brightly coloured plumage, a strong, sharp bill, and fused front toes. It feeds on bees and other insects.

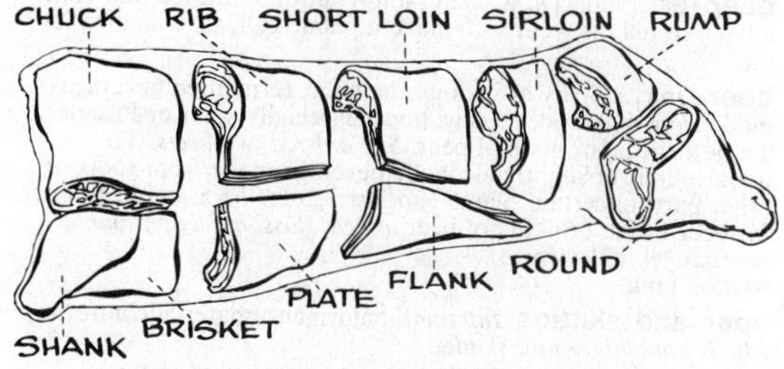

The main cuts of beef

beef [bif] *n., pl.* **beeves** (def. 2), **beefs** (def. 4); *v.* —*n.* **1** the meat from a steer, cow, or bull. **2** a steer, cow, or bull when full-grown and fattened for food, or such animals collectively. **3** *Informal.* strength or muscle; brawn. **4** *Slang.* complaint or grievance: *We answered all his beefs.*
—*v.* **1** *Informal.* strengthen (*used with* **up**): *You could beef up your argument by adding more examples.* **2** *Slang.* complain: *They're always beefing about something.* ⟨ME < OF *boef* < L *bos, bovis* ox⟩ **—'beef•er,** *n.* **—'beef•less,** *adj.*

beef•a•lo ['bifə,lou] *n.* a cross between bison and cattle, raised for its meat. ⟨< *beef* + (*buff*)*alo*⟩

beef bouillon a clear, thin soup or broth made with beef or bouillon cubes.

beef•cake ['bif,keik] *n. Slang.* photographs or photography displaying men with muscular physiques. Compare CHEESECAKE.

beef cattle cattle bred and raised primarily for meat.

beef•eat•er ['bif,itər] *n.* **1** one who eats beef, especially as an example of good living. **2** the common nickname for a yeoman of the guard who acts as a warder and official guide of the Tower of London.

beef extract an extract of beef or beef juices, for use in making broth, gravy, sauce, etc.

beef•steak ['bif,steik] *n.* a slice of beef for broiling or frying.

beefsteak tomato a very large tomato.

beef tea a strong beef broth.

beef Wellington a dish of best roast beef covered in liver pâté and pastry and then baked.

beef•y ['bifi] *adj.* **beef•i•er, beef•i•est. 1** like beef: *a beefy taste.* **2** strong; muscular. **3** heavy; solid. **—'beef•i•ness,** *n.*

bee•hive ['bi,haɪv] *n.* **1** a hive or house for bees. **2** a busy, swarming place. **3** a raised hairstyle using backcombing, popular in the 1950s.

bee•keep•er ['bi,kipər] *n.* a person who keeps bees for their honey and wax.

bee•keep•ing ['bi,kipɪŋ] *n.* the art of caring for and managing colonies of honeybees so that they will produce more honey than they need for themselves. The extra honey stored by the bees is collected for human use.

bee•line ['bi,laɪn] *n.* the straightest way or line between two places.
make a beeline for, *Informal.* go as quickly and directly as possible to: *The startled calf made a beeline for its mother.*

Be•el•ze•bub [bi'ɛlzə,bʌb] *n.* **1** the Devil. **2** in Milton's poem *Paradise Lost,* the fallen angel next to Satan in power. ⟨OE *Belzebub,* ultimately from Hebrew *ba'alzebūb,* the name of a Philistine god, lit., 'lord of the flies'. See BAAL.⟩

bee moth a moth (*Galleria melonella*) whose larvae are raised in beehives, where they eat the beeswax.

been [bin] *or* [bɪn] *v.* pp. of BE.
☛ *Hom.* BEAN [bin], BIN [bɪn].
☛ *Pronun.* **Been.** The most common British pronunciation is [bin], and the normal American pronunciation is [bɪn]. In earlier English, [bin] was the stressed form and [bɪn] the unstressed; many Canadian speakers still employ this distinction. Otherwise, Canadian usage varies between the two forms.

beep [bip] *n., v.* —*n.* **1** *Radio.* a short, sharp sound occurring as a signal. **2** any short, sharp sound: *the beep of a car horn.*
—*v.* **1** cause (something) to emit short, sharp sounds. **2** emit such sounds. ⟨imitative⟩

beep•er ['bipər] *n.* a small radio-controlled device that emits a beep to tell the wearer to make a phone call, take medication, etc.

beer [bir] *n.* **1** any of various alcoholic, fermented beverages made from malt and, usually, hops, especially lager or Pilsener. **2** a bottle, can, or glass of beer: *She ordered two beers.* **3** a nonalcoholic or slightly alcoholic beverage made from roots or other parts of certain plants: *root beer, ginger beer.* **4** (*adjl.*) of or for beer or the drinking of beer: *a beer glass, a beer parlour, a beer garden.* ⟨OE *bēor*⟩
☛ *Hom.* BIER.

beer and skittles *Informal.* enjoyment; material comforts: *Life is not all beer and skittles.*

beer–bel•ly ['bir ,bɛli] *n.* a paunch or protruding abdomen caused by excessive drinking of beer.

beer•fest ['bir,fɛst] *n. Informal.* a celebration at which much beer is drunk.

beer garden a pub or outdoor café where beer is sold and drunk.

beer hall a large building where beer is sold and drunk.

beer mat a small coaster, often of cardboard, used in a bar or pub to protect furniture from spilled beer.

beer parlour or **parlor** *Cdn.* a room in a hotel or tavern where beer is sold and drunk; beverage room.

Beer•she•ba [bir'ʃibə] *or* ['birʃibə] *n.* a city in central Israel, near the southern boundary of the former Palestine.
from Dan to Beersheba, from one end of a place to the other.

beer•y ['biri] *adj.* **beer•i•er, beer•i•est. 1** of beer. **2** like beer. **3** caused by beer. **4** slightly drunk on beer. **—'beer•i•ly,** *adv.* **—'beer•i•ness,** *n.*

beest•ings ['bistɪŋz] *n.pl.* the first milk from a cow after it has given birth to a calf; colostrum. ⟨OE *bȳsting* < *bēost* beestings⟩

bees•wax ['biz,wæks] *n., v.* —*n.* a yellowish, pleasant-smelling wax secreted by worker bees for constructing the cell walls of their honeycombs. Beeswax is processed for making candles, furniture polish, modelling wax, etc.
none of (someone's) **beeswax,** *Slang.* none of that person's concern: *What I do with my money is none of your beeswax.*
—*v.* rub, polish, or treat with beeswax.

bees•wing ['biz,wɪŋ] *n.* **1** a thin film that forms in some old wines. **2** an old wine that has such a film.

beet [bit] *n.* **1** a biennial plant (*Beta vulgaris*) of the goosefoot family widely cultivated in many varieties, especially in temperate regions, for its thick, fleshy, red, yellowish, or white root or its edible leaves. The red roots of some varieties are eaten as a vegetable; the white roots of other varieties yield sugar. See also MANGEL and SWISS CHARD. **2** the root of a beet. ⟨< L *beta*⟩ **—'beet,like,** *adj.*
☛ *Hom.* BEAT.

bee•tle[1] ['bitəl] *n., v.* —*n.* **1** any of an order (Coleoptera) of insects having four wings, the front pair of which are modified into horny coverings that are folded along the back when at rest, hiding the rear pair of wings. Beetles include some of the largest insects, such as an Asian beetle that is about 18 cm long, and others so small they are almost invisible to the naked eye. **2** any similar insect.
—*v. Informal.* move quickly; scurry (*used with* **off, along,** *etc.*): *beetling along the road. She grabbed her jacket and beetled off.* ⟨OE *bitela* < *bītan* bite⟩
☛ *Hom.* BETEL.

bee•tle[2] ['bitəl] *n., v.* **-tled, -tling.** —*n.* **1** a heavy wooden mallet for ramming, crushing, or smoothing. **2** a wooden household utensil for beating or mashing. **3** an apparatus that puts a shine on material by crushing its fibres between rollers.
—*v.* **1** pound with a beetle. **2** put a shine on (material) with a beetle. ⟨OE *bīetel* < *bēatan* beat⟩
☛ *Hom.* BETEL.

bee•tle[3] ['bitəl] *v.* **-tled, -tling;** *adj.* —*v.* project; overhang: *Great cliffs beetled above the narrow path.*
—*adj.* of eyebrows, shaggy and projecting: *His eyes were fierce beneath his beetle brows.* ⟨< *beetle-browed*⟩
☛ *Hom.* BETEL.

beetle–browed ['bitəl ,braʊd] *adj.* **1** having projecting or overhanging eyebrows. **2** scowling; sullen. ⟨ME *bitel* biting + *brow.* Related to BEETLE[1].⟩

bee•tling ['bitəlɪŋ] *adj., v.* —*adj.* projecting; overhanging.
—*v.* ppr. of BEETLE.

bee tree **1** any hollow tree used by bees to house a hive. **2** a tall North American shade tree (*Tilia americana*), a kind of linden, having heart-shaped leaves.

beet•root ['bit,rut] *Brit.* red beet.

beet sugar the sugar obtained from white beets.

beeves [bivz] *n.* pl. of BEEF[1] (def. 2).

be•fall [bɪ'fɒl] *v.* **-fell, -fall•en, -fall•ing. 1** happen to: *Be careful that no harm befalls you.* **2** happen. ⟨OE *befeallan*⟩

be•fall•en [bɪ'fɒlən] *v.* pp. of BEFALL.

be•fell [bɪ'fɛl] *v.* pt. of BEFALL.

be•fit [bɪ'fɪt] *v.* **-fit•ted, -fit•ting.** be suitable or proper for: *clothes that befit the occasion.*

be•fit•ting [bɪ'fɪtɪŋ] *adj., v.* —*adj.* suitable; proper.
—*v.* ppr. of BEFIT. **—be'fit•ting•ly,** *adv.*

be•fog [bɪ'fɒg] *v.* **-fogged, -fog•ging. 1** surround with fog; make foggy. **2** obscure; confuse.

be•fool [bɪ'ful] *v. Archaic.* fool; deceive; dupe.

be•fore [bɪ'fɔr] *prep., adv., conj.* —*prep.* **1** earlier than: *Come before five o'clock.* **2** rather than; sooner than: *We would choose death before dishonour.* **3** in the presence of or in the sight of: *to stand before the king.* **4** in front or ahead of: *She walked before them.* **5** under consideration by: *The bill has been put before the House.* **6** not yet reached by: *The hardest exams are still before us.*
—*adv.* **1** earlier: *Come at five o'clock, not before.* **2** until now; in the past: *I didn't know that before.* **3** in front or ahead: *He went before to see if the road was safe.*
—*conj.* **1** previously to the time when: *Before she goes, I would like to talk to her.* **2** rather than; sooner than: *I'll give up the trip before I'll go with them.* ⟨OE *beforan*⟩

be•fore•hand [bɪ'fɔr,hænd] *adv. or adj.* (*never precedes a noun*). ahead of time; in advance: *I am going to get everything ready beforehand.*

be•fore•time [bɪ'fɔr,taɪm] *adv. Archaic.* formerly.

be•foul [bɪ'faʊl] *v.* **1** make dirty; cover with filth. **2** entangle: *The rope was befouled by weeds and sticks.* **3** speak ill of (someone); besmirch. **—be'foul•ment,** *n.*

be•friend [bɪ'frɛnd] *v.* act as a friend to; help: *They were eager to befriend their new neighbours.*

be•fud•dle [bɪ'fʌdəl] *v.* **-dled, -dling. 1** stupefy; confuse. **2** make stupid with alcoholic drink. **—be'fud•dle•ment,** *n.*

beg [bɛg] *v.* **begged, beg•ging. 1** ask for help or charity: *He was finally reduced to begging for a living.* **2** ask for (food, money, clothes, etc.) as a charity: *The homeless man begged his meals.* **3** ask as a favour; ask earnestly or humbly: *He begged his mother to forgive him.* **4** ask for formally and courteously: *I beg your pardon.*
beg off, ask to be excused or released from (an engagement or obligation): *She asked me to go along, but I begged off. I'll have to beg off dinner tonight.*
beg the question, a take for granted the very thing argued about. **b** avoid the matter being argued about.
go begging, find no acceptance: *The architect's suggestion went begging.* ⟨ME *beggen* < AF *begger* < MF *begard,* of uncertain origin⟩
☛ *Syn.* **3. Beg,** IMPLORE, BESEECH = to ask earnestly. **Beg** = to ask earnestly or humbly: *He begged me to think about his offer.* **Implore,** more formal, adds to **beg** the idea of pleading with warm feeling or great

humility: *We implored him not to ruin his life by doing anything so foolish.* **Beseech,** formal, suggests greater earnestness and humility than **beg:** *The mother besought the queen to pardon her son.*

be•gan [bɪˈgæn] *v.* pt. of BEGIN.

be•gat [bɪˈgæt] *v. Archaic.* a pt. of BEGET.

be•get [bɪˈgɛt] *v.* **be•got** or (*archaic*) **be•gat, be•got•ten** or **be•got, be•get•ting. 1** become the father of. **2** cause to be; produce: *Hate begets hate.* ⟨ME *begete(n), begite(n)*, alteration of earlier unrecorded *beyiten* (OE *begitan*) under the influence of *gete(n)* get (< ON *geta*)⟩ **—be'get•ter,** *n.*

beg•gar [ˈbɛgər] *n., v.* —*n.* **1** a person who makes his or her living by begging. **2** a very poor person. **3** a fellow: *That dog's a friendly little beggar.*
—*v.* **1** bring to poverty: *Your reckless spending will beggar your parents.* **2** make to seem inadequate or useless: *The grandeur of Niagara Falls beggars description.*

beg•gar–lice [ˈbɛgər ˌləis] *n., pl.* **beg•gar-lice.** BEGGAR'S-LICE.

beg•gar•ly [ˈbɛgərli] *adj.* fit for a beggar; poor. **—'beg•gar•li•ness,** *n.*

beg•gar's–lice [ˈbɛgərz ˌləis] *n., pl.* **beg•gar's-lice. 1** any of various plants of the borage family having prickly fruits that adhere to clothing, fur, etc. **2** beggarticks. **3** the prickly fruit of any of these plants. Also, **beggar-lice.**

beg•gar's–ticks [ˈbɛgərz ˌtɪks] *n., pl.* **beg•gar's-ticks.** beggarticks.

beg•gar•ticks [ˈbɛgərˌtɪks] *n., pl.* **beg•gar•ticks. 1** any of a genus (*Bidens*) of weedy plants of the composite family having yellow flowers and small, pointed fruits with barbed awns that catch in clothing, fur, etc. **2** the fruits of any of these plants. **3** any of a genus (*Desmodium*) of plants of the pea family, having small purple flowers in clusters, and pods with prickly spines. Also, **beggar's-ticks.**

beg•gar•weed [ˈbɛgərˌwid] *n.* a plant (*Desmodium purpureum*) found in Caribbean countries, having seeds in pods.

beg•gar•y [ˈbɛgəri] *n.* **1** a condition of great poverty; the state of being a beggar. **2** beggars collectively.

be•gin [bɪˈgɪn] *v.* **be•gan, be•gun, be•gin•ning. 1** do the first part; start: *Let's begin. She began to speak.* **2** do the first part of: *I began reading the book yesterday.* **3** come into being: *The club began two years ago.* **4** bring into being: *Two sisters began the club ten years ago.* **5** be near; come near: *That suit doesn't even begin to fit you.* **6** be first in a series; form the first part of: The Fellowship of the Ring *begins Tolkien's trilogy.* ⟨OE *beginnan*⟩

☛ *Syn.* **1, 2. Begin,** COMMENCE, START = to get something going. **Begin** is the general word, more formal than **start** but less formal than **commence:** *We will begin work soon.* **Commence** is formal and applies particularly to beginning a formal action or event: *The dedication ceremonies will commence at two o'clock.* **Start** emphasizes taking the first step in doing something, or setting about doing it: *At last they have started building that hotel.* **Start** also means to set (a machine) in motion.

☛ *Usage.* **Begin** is followed by *at* when the meaning is 'start from': *Let us begin at the third chapter.* It is followed by *on* or *upon* when the meaning is 'set to work at': *We must begin on the government survey tomorrow.* When the meaning is 'take first in an order of succession', the idiom is *begin with*: *We always begin with the hardest problems.*

be•gin•ner [bɪˈgɪnər] *n.* **1** a person who is doing something for the first time; a person who lacks skill and experience. **2** a person who begins anything.

be•gin•ning [bɪˈgɪnɪŋ] *n., adj., v.* —*n.* **1** a start: *make a good beginning.* **2** the time when anything begins: *"In the beginning God created the heaven and the earth."* **3** the first part: *The beginning of the book is good, but then it gets boring.* **4** a first cause; source; origin. **5 beginnings,** *pl.* an early period or type of: *the beginnings of Gothic architecture.*
—*adj.* **1** that forms a beginning; first in order: *a beginning course.* **2** for beginners: *a beginning dictionary.* **3** that is just starting: *a beginning student.*
—*v.* ppr. of BEGIN.

be•gird [bɪˈgɜrd] *v.* **-girt** or **-gird•ed, -gird•ed.** *Poetic.* encircle; gird around.

be•gone [bɪˈgɒn] *interj.* be gone; go away; depart: *"Begone!" the old lady cried out to the intruder in her garden.*

be•go•ni•a [bɪˈgounjə] *or* [bɪˈgouniə] *n.* **1** any of a large genus (*Begonia*) of flowering plants, including many varieties and hybrids grown for their showy, waxy flowers and often coloured leaves. **2** (*adj.*) designating the family (Begoniaceae) of tropical and subtropical plants that includes the begonias and a few other species. Most of the plants belonging to the begonia family are herbs native to South America. ⟨after Michel *Bégon* (1638-1710), a French colonial governor⟩

A begonia

be•got [bɪˈgɒt] *v.* a pt. and a pp. of BEGET.

be•got•ten [bɪˈgɒtən] *v.* a pp. of BEGET.

be•grime [bɪˈgraɪm] *v.,* **-grimed, -griming.** make grimy, soiled and dirty.

be•grudge [bɪˈgrʌdʒ] *v.* **-grudged, -grudg•ing. 1** be reluctant to give (something); grudge: *She is so stingy that she begrudges food to her dog.* **2** resent (someone) because of (something they have or enjoy): *They begrudge us our new house.* **3** disapprove of. **—be'grudg•ing•ly,** *adv.*

be•guile [bɪˈgaɪl] *v.* **-guiled, -guil•ing. 1** deceive; cheat: *His pleasant ways beguiled me into thinking that he was my friend.* **2** take something from deceitfully or cunningly (*used with* **of**): *They beguiled him of his money.* **3** entertain; amuse; charm. **4** pass or while away (time) pleasantly. **—be'guil•er,** *n.* **—be'guile•ment,** *n.*

be•guil•ing [bɪˈgaɪlɪŋ] *adj., v.* —*adj.* **1** deceiving. **2** entertaining; amusing; charming.
—*v.* ppr. of BEGUILE. **—be'guil•ing•ly,** *adv.*

be•guine [bɪˈgin] *n.* **1** a dance originating in Martinique. **2** the music for this dance. ⟨< F *béguin* flirtation⟩

be•gum [ˈbeigəm] *n.* a Muslim title of honour for a woman, used especially in India and Pakistan. The title is equivalent to princess. ⟨< Hind. *begam*⟩

be•gun [bɪˈgʌn] *v.* pp. of BEGIN.

be•half [bɪˈhæf] *n.* interest; favour; support: *My friends will act in my behalf.*
in behalf of, in the interest of; for: *We worked for weeks in behalf of the Community Chest.*
on behalf of, a as a representative of: *The lawyer spoke convincingly on behalf of her client.* **b** in behalf of. ⟨ME *behalve* beside, on the side of⟩

be•have [bɪˈheiv] *v.* **-haved, -hav•ing. 1** conduct (oneself): *The little girl behaves herself badly in school. The ship behaves well.* **2** act well; do what is right: *Did you behave today?* **3** act: *Water behaves in different ways when it is heated and when it is frozen.* ⟨< *be-* + *have*⟩

☛ *Usage.* **Behave.** In speaking to or of children, **behave** (def. 2) = behave properly or use good manners: *Did you behave at the party, Mary?* Otherwise, **behave,** meaning 'act or conduct oneself in a certain way', is ordinarily modified by a qualifying word: *They behaved well in spite of their boredom.*

be•hav•iour or **be•hav•ior** [bɪˈheivjər] *n.* **1** a way of acting; actions; acts: *His sullen behaviour showed that he was angry.* **2** manners; deportment. **3** the observable reaction of an animal or plant to stimulation. **4** the way of functioning of a machine.

☛ *Syn.* **1.** See note at CONDUCT.

be•hav•iour•al or **be•hav•ior•al** [bɪˈheivjərəl] *adj.* of or having to do with behaviour: *Sociology and psychology are behavioural sciences.*

be•hav•iour•ism or **be•hav•ior•ism** [bɪˈheivjəˌrɪzəm] *n.* the theory that the objectively observable behaviour of persons and animals is the chief or only subject matter of psychology.

be•hav•iour•ist or **be•hav•ior•ist** [bɪˈheivjərɪst] *n.* an adherent of behaviourism.

be•hav•iour•is•tic or **be•hav•ior•is•tic** [bɪˌheivjəˈrɪstɪk] *adj.* of or having to do with behaviourists or behaviourism.

behaviour or **behavior modification** *Psychology.* a method for conditioning a subject's behaviour in which rewards are given for desirable behaviour and punishments for undesirable behaviour.

behaviour or **behavior therapy** any treatment using the methods of behaviour modification.

be•head [bɪˈhɛd] *v.* cut off the head of.

be•held [bɪˈhɛld] *v.* pt. and pp. of BEHOLD.

be•he•moth [bɪˈhiməθ] *or* [ˈbiəməθ] *n.* **1** in the Bible, a huge and powerful animal of unknown identity. **2** any large and powerful person or animal. **3** something that is especially large and powerful. ⟨< Hebrew *b'hēmōth*, pl. of *b'hēmah* beast⟩

be•hest [bɪˈhɛst] *n.* a command or order. ⟨OE *behæs* promise⟩

be•hind [bɪ'haɪnd] *prep., adv., n. —prep.* **1** at the back of; in the rear of: *The child hid behind the sofa.* **2** at or on the far side of: *A beautiful valley lies behind the hill.* **3** concealed by: *Treachery lurked behind the spy's smooth manner.* **4** less advanced than: *She is behind the other children in her class.* **5** later than; after: *The milkman is behind his usual time today.* **6** remaining after: *The dead man left a family behind him.* **7** in support of; supporting: *His friends are behind him.* **8** in (someone's) past; over for: *Her difficulties were behind her.* **9** in the happenings preceding or related to: *A scandal lies behind his accession to power.*
—adv. **1** at or toward the back; in the rear: *The dog's tail hung down behind.* **2** farther back in place or time: *The rest of the hikers are still far behind.* **3** in reserve: *More supplies are behind.* **4** not on time; slow; late: *The train is behind today.* **5** of bills or accounts, in an unpaid or unsettled state: *His payments are behind.*
—n. Informal. buttocks; seat. ⟨OE *behindan* < *be-* by + *hindan* from behind⟩

be•hind•hand [bɪ'haɪnd,hænd] *adj. (never used before a noun) or adv.* **1** behind time; late. **2** behind others in progress; backward; slow. **3** in debt; in arrears.

be•hold [bɪ'hould] *v.* **be•held, be•hold•ing;** *interj. —v.* **1** see; perceive: *He beheld a strange figure approaching him.* **2** look at; observe: *He beheld the figure with apprehension.*
—interj. look! see! ⟨OE *behealdan*⟩ **—be'hold•er,** *n.*

be•hold•en [bɪ'houldən] *adj.* under an obligation or in debt to somebody: *I am much beholden to you for your help.*

be•hoof [bɪ'huf] *n. Archaic.* use; advantage; benefit: *The father toiled for his children's behoof.* ⟨OE *behōf* need⟩

be•hoove [bɪ'huv] *v.* **-hooved, -hoov•ing.** be necessary or proper for: *It behooves us to answer the challenge.* ⟨OE *behōfian* to need⟩

be•hove [bɪ'houv] *v.* **-hoved, -hov•ing.** behoove.

beige [beiʒ] *n. or adj.* very light, greyish brown; a neutral colour. ⟨< F⟩

beig•net [bɛ'njei] *n.* **1** a small fritter with a filling of cheese, meat, fruit, etc. **2** a deep-fried confection sprinkled with icing sugar. ⟨< F⟩

be•ing ['biɪŋ] *n., adj., v. —n.* **1** a person or other living creature: *human beings.* **2** life; existence: *A new era came into being.* **3** nature; constitution: *Her whole being thrilled to the beauty of the music.*
—adj.
for the time being, for the present time; for now: *Let's leave that problem for the time being and come back to it later.*
—v. ppr. of BE.
being as or **that,** since the situation is such that.

be•jew•el [bɪ'dʒuəl] *v.* **-elled** or **-eled, -el•ling** or **-el•ing.** adorn with jewels, or as if with jewels: *The sky is bejewelled with stars.*

bel [bɛl] *n.* a unit for comparing levels of power, equal to ten decibels. ⟨after Alexander Graham *Bell* (1847-1922), Scottish inventor⟩

be•la•bour or **be•la•bor** [bɪ'leibər] *v.* **1** beat vigorously: *The man belaboured his poor donkey.* **2** abuse or ridicule: *The politician was belaboured by the press.* **3** work at or on longer than necessary; harp on: *to belabour a point in an argument.*

Be•la•rus [,bɛlə'rus] *n.* a country in E Europe.

be•lat•ed [bɪ'leitɪd] *adj.* **1** delayed; happening or coming late or too late: *a belated birthday card. Her belated attempt to make amends was rejected.* **2** overtaken by darkness: *The belated travellers lost their way.* **—be'lat•ed•ly,** *adv.* **—be'lat•ed•ness,** *n.*

be•lay [bɪ'lei] *v.* **be•layed, be•lay•ing;** *n. —v.* **1** fasten (a line or rope) by winding it around a pin, cleat, piton, etc.
2 *Mountaineering.* secure (a climber) at the end of a rope.
3 *Nautical. Informal.* stop (*usually used in the imperative*): *Belay there!*
—n. Mountaineering. **1** the action or method of obtaining a hold by securing a rope around an object. **2** an object, such as a projecting piece of rock, to which a rope is secured. ⟨OE *belecgan*⟩

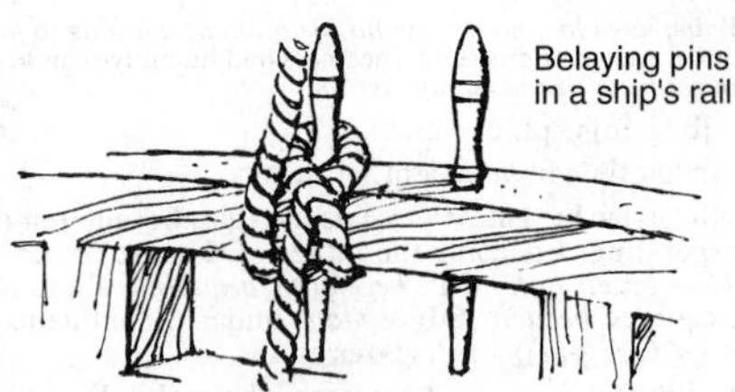
Belaying pins in a ship's rail

belaying pin a removable pin on the rail of a ship or boat, used for fastening rigging lines. Removing the pin unties the knot.

bel canto [bɛl 'kɑntou] *Music.* a style of singing marked by fullness and breadth of tone and the display of great technical skill. It originated in Italy in the 17th century. ⟨< Ital. *bel canto,* literally, fine singing⟩

belch [bɛltʃ] *v., n. —v.* **1** expel gas from the stomach through the mouth. **2** throw out with force: *The volcano belched fire and smoke.* **3** utter or express (blasphemous or obscene words) vigorously.
—n. the act of belching. ⟨Cf. OE *bealcian*⟩ **—'belch•er,** *n.*

bel•dam or **bel•dame** ['bɛldəm] *n. Archaic.* **1** an old woman. **2** an ugly old woman; hag. ⟨< *bel-* grand- (< OF *bel, belle* fair) + *dam* dame < OF *dame*⟩

be•lea•guer [bɪ'ligər] *v.* **1** besiege: *The people of the beleaguered city refused to give in.* **2** torment; beset: *Beleaguered by debts, she was finally forced into bankruptcy.* ⟨< Du. *belegeren* < *leger* camp⟩

bel•em•nite ['bɛləm,nəit] *n.* the fossil of an extinct sea mollusc of the order Belemnoidea of the Mesozoic era. ⟨< Gk. *belemnon* a dart, arrow + -E *ite*[1]⟩

bel–es•prit ['bɛl ɛ'spri] *n., pl.* **beaux-es•prits** [bouz]. a refined, cultivated person. ⟨< F⟩

bel•fry ['bɛlfri] *n., pl.* **-fries. 1** a tower or steeple containing a bell or bells. **2** a room in a tower, or a cupola or turret, in which a bell or bells are hung. ⟨ME *berfrey* < OF *berfrei* < Gmc.⟩

Bel•gae ['bɛldʒi] *n.* an ancient people who lived in Belgium and northern France. ⟨< L ⟩

Bel•gian ['bɛldʒən] *n., adj. —n.* **1** a native or inhabitant of Belgium. **2** a person of Belgian descent. **3** a breed of large, strong draft horse.
—adj. of or having to do with Belgium or its people.

Belgian endive the whitish forced shoots of chicory, used raw in salads and also as a cooked vegetable.

Belgian hare a breed of large European rabbit having reddish brown hair, raised in many countries for its fur and its meat: *The Belgian hare is the typical domestic rabbit.*

Belgian sheepdog a breed of large black dog used as a shepherd or guide dog.

Belgium ['bɛldʒəm] *n.* a small country in NW Europe. See NETHERLANDS for map.

Bel•gra•vi•an [bɛl'greiviən] *adj.* of or having to do with Belgravia, a wealthy district in London, England.

Be•li•al ['biliəl] *or* ['biljəl] *n.* **1** the Devil. **2** in Milton's poem *Paradise Lost,* a fallen angel. ⟨< Hebrew⟩

be•lie [bɪ'laɪ] *v.* **-lied, -ly•ing. 1** give a false idea of; misrepresent: *Her frown belied her usual good nature.* **2** show to be false; contradict: *Your actions belie your words.* **3** fail to come up to; disappoint: *He stole again, and so belied our hopes.* ⟨OE *belēogan*⟩ **—be'li•er,** *n.*

be•lief [bɪ'lif] *n.* **1** confidence in any person or thing; faith; trust: *a belief in God, belief in a person's honesty.* **2** mental acceptance as true or real; acceptance of a statement or fact: *a belief in the existence of ghosts. That statement is unworthy of belief.* **3** the thing believed; a statement or condition accepted as true: *Your beliefs are different from mine.* **4** opinion: *It's my belief that we're in for a cold winter.* ⟨ME *bileafe* < OE⟩
☛ *Syn.* **1. Belief,** FAITH (def. 1), CONVICTION (def. 5) = what is held true. **Belief** is the general word: *His belief in superstition gets him into trouble.* **Faith** applies to a belief without proof, based on one's trust in a person or thing: *I have faith in her ability to succeed.* **Conviction** applies to a firm belief based on one's own certainty after one has been convinced by someone or something: *It is my conviction that she will succeed.*

be•liev•a•ble [bɪ'livəbəl] *adj.* that can or is likely to be believed: *a believable story.* **—be'liev•a•bly,** *adv.* **—be,liev•a'bil•i•ty,** *n.*

be•lieve [bɪ'liv] *v.* **-lieved, -liev•ing. 1** have faith; trust (*used* *with* **in**): *to believe in God. I believe in their sincerity.* **2** accept (a statement, fact, etc.) as true or real: *We believe that the earth revolves around the sun. I don't believe her story. Do you believe in ghosts?* **3** think that (another person) tells the truth: *I don't believe him.* **4** have religious faith: *All who believe are asked to pray for peace.* **5** think or suppose: *I believe they're planning a big reception for the wedding.* ⟨ME *bileve(n)* < OE *belefan*⟩

be•liev•er [bɪ'livər] *n.* a person who believes, especially a follower of some religion.

be•like [bɪ'ləik] *adv. Archaic.* very likely; probably; perhaps.

be•lit•tle [bɪ'lɪtəl] *v.* **-tled, -tling.** cause to seem little, unimportant, or less important; speak slightingly of; disparage: *Jealous people belittled the explorer's great discoveries.* **—be'lit•tler, be'lit•tle•ment,** *n.* **—be'lit•tling•ly,** *adv.*

Be•lize [bə'liz] *n.* a country in Central America.

Be•li•ze•an [bə'liziən] *n., adj. —n.* a native or inhabitant of Belize.
—adj. of or having to do with Belize.

bell[1] [bɛl] *n., v. —n.* **1** a hollow device of metal or sometimes glass, etc., usually shaped like a cup with a flared opening, that makes a musical sound when struck by a clapper or a hammer. **2** the sound of a bell. **3 a** on shipboard, the stroke of a bell to indicate a half hour of time. 1 bell = 12:30, 4:30, or 8:30; 2 bells =1:00, 5:00, or 9:00; and so on up to 8 bells = 4:00, 8:00, or 12:00. **b** any one of these half-hour periods. **4** Usually, **bells,** *pl.* a percussion instrument having metal tubes or bars that produce bell-like tones when struck. **5** anything shaped like a bell, such as the flared opening of a trumpet, etc., or the corolla of some flowers.
ring a bell, produce a response in one's mind; seem familiar: *I didn't recognize her at first, but the name rang a bell.*
—v. **1** put a bell on. **2** swell out like a bell.
bell the cat, take on oneself a dangerous role for the common good. ⟨OE *belle*⟩ **—'bell-,like,** *adj.*
☛ *Hom.* BELLE.

bell[2] [bɛl] *v. or n.* bellow; roar; cry. ⟨OE *bellan*⟩
☛ *Hom.* BELLE.

Bel•la Bel•la ['bɛlə 'bɛlə] *n., pl.* **Bella Bella** or **Bella Bellas. 1** a member of a people of the First Nations, of the southern part of the British Columbian coast. **2** the Wakashan language of the Bella Bella.

Bel•la Coo•la ['bɛlə 'kulə] *n., pl.* **Bella Coola** or **Bella Coolas. 1** a member of a people of the First Nations, living near Queen Charlotte Sound, B.C. **2** the Salishan language of the Bella Coola.

bel•la•don•na [,bɛlə'dɒnə] *n.* **1** a very poisonous perennial plant (*Atropa belladonna*) of the nightshade family native to Europe, having reddish, bell-shaped flowers and small, shiny black berries; deadly nightshade. **2** the dried leaves or roots of this plant, or any of the alkaloid drugs, such as atropine, prepared from them. ⟨< Ital. *belladonna*, literally, fair lady⟩

belladonna lily an amaryllis (*Amaryllis belladonna*) of S Africa cultivated for its large, fragrant, white or pink flowers.

bell–bot•toms ['bɛl ,bɒtəmz] *n.pl.* pants having legs that flare out downward from the knee into wide bottoms. **—'bell-,bot•tom** or **'bell-,bot•tomed,** *adj.*

bell•boy ['bɛl,bɔɪ] *n.* a man or boy whose work is carrying hand baggage and doing errands for the guests of a hotel or club.

bell buoy a buoy with a bell that is rung by the movement of the waves.

bell captain a person who supervises the work of the bellboys in a hotel or club.

bell curve the standard variation on a statistical graph, with low numbers at each end and the highest in the middle, thus forming a bell-like shape.

belle [bɛl] *n.* **1** a beautiful woman or girl. **2** the prettiest or most admired woman or girl: *the belle of the ball.* ⟨< F *belle*, fem. of *beau.* See BEAU.⟩
☛ *Hom.* BELL.

Bel•leek [bə'lik] *n.* a kind of thin, delicate porcelain having a multicoloured glaze. ⟨< *Belleek*, a town in Northern Ireland, where this porcelain is made⟩

belle é•poque [bɛl ei'pɒk]; *French,* [bɛle'pɔk] *n.* life in Paris from 1890 to 1914, emphasizing luxury and merriment. ⟨< F, beautiful period⟩

Bel•ler•o•phon [bə'lɛrə,fɒn] *n. Greek mythology.* a hero who killed a dreadful monster, the chimera, with the help of the winged horse Pegasus.

belles–let•tres ['bɛl 'lɛtrə] *n.pl.* literature, such as poetry, drama, fiction and personal essays, considered for its artistic appeal rather than for any practical value such as giving information. ⟨< F⟩ **—bel'let•rist,** *n.* **—,bel•le'tris•tic,** *adj.*

bell•flow•er ['bɛl,flaʊər] *n.* **1** any of various plants (genus *Campanula*) found in temperate regions of the northern hemisphere having bell-shaped flowers, usually blue, purple, or white. Some bellflowers are grown as garden flowers. **2** (*adjl.*) designating the family (Campanulaceae) of temperate and subtropical plants that includes the bluebell and the bellflowers.

bell glass a bell-shaped container or cover made of glass.

bell•hop ['bɛl,hɒp] *n. Informal.* bellboy.

bel•li•cose ['bɛlə,kous] *adj.* warlike; fond of fighting. ⟨< L *bellicosus* < *bellum* war⟩ **—'bel•li,cose•ly,** *adv.*

bel•li•cos•i•ty [,bɛlə'kɒsəti] *n.* a bellicose quality or attitude.

bel•lig•er•ence [bə'lɪdʒərəns] *n.* **1** a warlike attitude; fondness for fighting. **2** fighting; war.

bel•lig•er•en•cy [bə'lɪdʒərənsi] *n.* **1** the state of being a belligerent. **2** belligerence.

bel•lig•er•ent [bə'lɪdʒərənt] *adj., n. —adj.* **1** having or showing an aggressive or quarrelsome attitude; warlike: *She gets very belligerent if you don't agree with her.* **2** at war; engaged in war; fighting. **3** having to do with nations or states at war.
—n. **1** a person engaged in fighting with another person. **2** a nation or state at war: *The belligerents agreed on a truce.* ⟨< L *belligerans, -antis*, ppr. of *belligerare* < *bellum* war + *gerere* wage⟩ **—bel'lig•er•ent•ly,** *adv.*

bell jar a bell-shaped container or cover made of glass, used especially in scientific experiments requiring reduced air pressure.

bell•man ['bɛlmən] *n., pl.* **-men. 1** TOWN CRIER. **2** bellboy.

bell metal a metal from which bells are made, usually an alloy of copper and tin.

Bel•lo•na [bə'lounə] *n. Roman mythology.* the goddess of war; the sister, wife, or, in some cases, daughter of Mars.

bel•low ['bɛlou] *v., n. —v.* **1** roar as a bull does. **2** shout loudly: *The lifeguard bellowed at the boys to stay near the shore.* **3** roar with pain or anger: *The pain of the burn made him bellow.*
—n. **1** a roar like a bull's. **2** a deep, loud shout, roar of pain or anger, etc. ⟨ME *belwe*, akin to OE *bellan* roar and *bylgan* bellow⟩ **—'bel•low•er,** *n.*

bel•lows ['bɛlouz] *n.pl. or sing.* **1** an instrument for producing a strong current of air, used for blowing a fire to make it burn or for sounding an organ, accordion, etc. **2** in certain cameras, the folding part behind the lens. ⟨ME *belwes, pl.* of *belu* < *OE belgas*, pl. of *belg* bag, belly⟩

bell pepper a sweet pepper (*Capsicum frutescens*) which grows in Central and South America. It is used raw in salads or cooked as a vegetable. Its immature state is green; when mature it is red.

Bell's palsy a disease causing sudden paralysis on one side of the face. ⟨after C. *Bell* (1774-1842), the Scottish anatomist who identified it⟩

bell tower a tower built to house a bell or bells, often as part of a larger building, such as a church.

bell•weth•er ['bɛl,wɛðər] *n.* **1** a male sheep that wears a bell and leads the flock. **2** any leader, especially of a group thought to resemble sheep in lack of foresight, intelligence, etc.: *a bellwether of the mob.* **3** *Cdn.* any person, group, or thing thought of as setting a standard or pattern: *Our riding is considered the political bellwether for the rest of the province.*

bell•wort ['bɛl,wɜrt] *n.* a spring lily (*Uvularia grandiflora*), having yellow flowers up to 5 cm long. It grows in woodlands and has some medicinal uses.

bel•ly ['bɛli] *n., pl.* **-lies;** *v.* **-lied, -ly•ing.** *—n.* **1** the lower part of the human body that contains the stomach and intestines, or the front of this; abdomen. **2** the under part of an animal's body. **3** the stomach. **4** the bulging part of anything. **5** the space deep inside anything: *the belly of the cargo plane.* **6** *Archaic.* the womb.
—v. swell out; bulge: *The ship's sails bellied in the wind.* ⟨ME *bely* < OE *belg, belig* bag⟩

bel•ly•ache ['bɛli,eik] *n., v.* **-ached, -ach•ing.** *Informal. —n.* **1** a pain in the abdomen. **2** an excuse for complaining; grievance.
—v. complain or grumble, especially over trifles.
—'bel•ly,ach•er, *n.*

bel•ly•band ['bɛli,bænd] *n.* **1** a strap around the middle of an animal's body to keep a saddle, harness, etc. in place. **2** formerly, clothes that were tied around the middle of a newborn infant, to prevent an umbilical hernia.

belly button *Informal.* navel.

belly dance a Middle Eastern dance performed by a woman with a naked navel, consisting of gyrations of the hips. **—'bel•ly-,dance,** *v.* **—'bel•ly-,danc•er,** *n.*

bel•ly•flop ['bɛli,flɒp] *v.* **-flopped, -flop•ping;** *n. Slang. —v.* **1** ride prone on a sled, with the stomach downward. **2** *Diving.* strike the water with the chest, or with the chest and abdomen.
—n. a dive or sled ride executed in this manner.

bel•ly•ful ['bɛli,fʊl] *n. Informal.* an amount that is more than one wants or can stand: *After listening to complaints for two hours, the store clerk had had a bellyful.*

belly laugh a deep, resounding laugh.

bel•ly–up [,bɛli 'ʌp] *adv.* on the back: *The dead fish floated belly-up.*
go belly-up, *Informal.* of an organization, business, etc., fail: *The firm went belly-up after only a year.*

be•long [bɪ'lɒŋ] *v.* **1** have a proper place: *That book belongs on this shelf.* **2** have the required traits or background to be accepted into the group: *She doesn't belong in this club.*
belong to, a be the property of. **b** be a part of; be connected with. **c** be a member of. **d** be the duty or concern of: *This responsibility belongs to the club secretary.* ⟨ME *bilonge(n)* < *bi-* by + *longen* belong, ult. < OE *gelang* belonging to⟩

be•long•ing [bɪ'lɒŋɪŋ] *n., v. —n.* **1** inclusion; a being accepted; companionship: *a sense of belonging.* **2 belongings,** *pl.* the things that belong to a person; possessions.
—v. ppr. of BELONG.

be•lov•ed [bɪ'lʌvɪd] *or* [bɪ'lʌvd] *adj., n. —adj.* dearly loved; dear.
—n. a person who is loved; darling.

be•low [bɪ'lou] *adv., prep. —adv.* **1** in or to a lower place, position, or degree: *She stopped at the top of the hill and looked down on the road below.* **2** on or to a lower floor or deck; downstairs: *The sailor went below.* **3** on earth. **4** in hell. **5** at the bottom of the page or farther on in an article, essay, book, etc.: *The problem is dealt with below.* **6** below zero on a scale of temperature: *It was four below last night.*
—prep. **1** lower than; under: *below the third floor.* **2** lower in rank, amount, or degree than: *an income below $10 000. The temperature rarely goes below freezing.* **3** unworthy of; beneath: *He said it would be below him to argue the point.* ⟨ME *biloghe* by low⟩
☛ *Syn. prep.* **1.** See note at UNDER.

belt [bɛlt] *n., v. —n.* **1** a strip of leather, cloth, etc. worn around the body to hold in or support clothing, to hold tools or weapons, or as a decoration. **2** any broad strip or band: *a belt of trees.* **3** a region having distinctive characteristics; zone: *The wheat belt is the region where wheat is grown.* **4** an endless band that transfers motion from one wheel or pulley to another: *a fan belt.* **5** *Slang.* a sharp blow: *a belt on the chin.* **6** *Slang.* a drink, as of liquor, especially when gulped hurriedly or greedily: *He took a belt of whisky before leaving.* **7** a jolt of excitement.
below the belt, unfair or unfairly: *He's hitting below the belt with his personal remarks.*
tighten (one's) **belt,** become more thrifty; cut down on expenditures.
under (one's) **belt,** *Informal.* **a** in one's stomach: *With a good dinner under his belt, he felt more relaxed.* **b** in one's possession or experience; to one's credit: *With five years' training under her belt, she could easily find another job.*
—v. **1** put a belt around. **2** fasten on with a belt. **3** beat with a belt. **4** hit suddenly and hard: *The boxer belted his opponent across the ring.* **5** *Slang.* drink hurriedly or greedily (*usually used with* **down**): *They belted down a couple of drinks and took off.* **6** *Slang.* sing forcefully or raucously (*used with* **out**): *They stood around the piano, belting out one song after another.* ⟨OE *belt,* apparently ult. < L *balteus* girdle⟩

Bel•tane ['bɛltein] *n.* **1** in Scotland, May 1 (Old Style Calendar). **2** an ancient Celtic May Day celebration when fires were lit. **3** May 1, a festival in Wicca. ⟨< Scots Gaelic *bealltainn* May Day, the May festival⟩

belt•ed ['bɛltɪd] *adj., v. —adj.* **1** having a belt: *a belted jacket.* **2** wearing a special belt as a sign of honour: *a belted earl.* **3** marked by a belt or band of colour: *a belted kingfisher.*
—v. pt. and pp. of BELT.

belt•er ['bɛltər] *n. Informal.* one who sings loudly.

belt•ing ['bɛltɪŋ] *n., v. —n.* **1** material for making belts or lining waistbands. **2** belts. **3** a beating.
—v. ppr. of BELT.

belt line a railway, bus line, etc. that takes a more or less circular route around a city or other special area.

belt•way ['bɛlt,wei] *n.* a road encircling an urban centre.

be•lu•ga [bə'lugə] *n.* **1** a white toothed whale (*Delphinapterus leucas*) of the same family as the narwhal, found in the Arctic and as far south as the Gulf of St. Lawrence, usually about 4 m long, having broad, rounded flippers and lacking a dorsal fin. It was formerly called the 'sea canary' by Arctic whalers because of its musical trilling voice. It is an endangered species. Also called **white whale. 2** a very large white sturgeon (*Acipenser huso*) of the Black and Caspian Seas and the Sea of Azov. It is the largest inland fish, sometimes reaching a length of 7 m, and is the source of most European caviar. ⟨def. 1 < Russian *beluga,* def. 2 < Russian *belukha;* both from *bielo-* white⟩

bel•ve•dere ['bɛlvə,dir] *or* [,bɛlvə'dir] *n.* a structure, sometimes set high on a building, designed to be open on several sides to afford a wide view. ⟨< Ital. *belvedere* fine view⟩

be•ma ['bimə] *n., pl.* **be•ma•ta** ['bimətə] or **be•mas** ['biməs]. **1** in ancient Greece, a platform for a speaker to speak or read from. **2** in a synagogue, a platform from which the Scripture is read. **3** in the Eastern Orthodox Church, the enclosed area around the altar. ⟨< Gk. *bema* platform⟩

Bem•ba ['bɛmbə] *n.* **1** a member of a people living in northern Zambia. **2** the Bantu language of this people.

be•mire [bɪ'maɪr] *v.* **-mired, -mir•ing. 1** make dirty with mud. **2** cause to sink in mud.

be•moan [bɪ'moun] *v.* **1** moan about; bewail. **2** mourn.

be•mock [bɪ'mɒk] *v. Archaic.* mock; mock at.

be•muse [bɪ'mjuz] *v.* **-mused, -mus•ing. 1** bewilder; confuse; stupefy. **2** absorb in thought (*usually passive*). **—be'mused,** *adj.* **—be'mus•ed•ly,** *adv.* **—be'muse•ment,** *n.*

ben•act•y•zine [bɛn'æktə,zin] *or* [-zɪn] *n.* a drug used in the manufacture of tranquillizers. *Formula*: $C_{20}H_{25}NO_3$

bench [bɛntʃ] *n., v. —n.* **1** a long seat, often backless, usually of wood or stone. **2** a backless seat running athwart a boat. **3** the worktable of a carpenter, or of any worker with tools and materials. **4** the seat where judges sit in a court of law. **5 the bench, a** a judge or group of judges presiding in a court of law. **b** the position or office of a judge: *The lawyer was appointed to the bench.* **c** a court of law. **6** *Sports.* **a** the place where team members sit while waiting their turn or opportunity to play. **b** these players collectively. **7** a long, narrow, open plateau between a river or lake bed and nearby hills: *Apples are grown on the benches of the Okanagan Valley in British Columbia.* **8** a ledge in a rockface or in a mine. **9** a platform on which dogs or cats are placed for judging at a show. **10** a pet show.
on the bench, a sitting in a court of law as a judge. **b** sitting among the substitute players.
—v. **1** furnish with benches. **2** assign a seat on a bench. **3** take (a player) out of a game. **4** show (a dog or cat) at a pet show. ⟨OE *benc*⟩

bench•er ['bɛntʃər] *n.* **1** a person who sits on a bench, especially a judge, magistrate, etc. **2** in Canada, one of the elected officials of a provincial law society, who, through committees, govern the affairs of the society. **3** in the United Kingdom, one of the senior members governing a society of lawyers and law students called an Inn of Court.

bench•land ['bɛntʃ,lænd] *n.* level stretches of land forming terraces lying between a river or lake and the nearby hills or plateau.

bench•mark or **bench mark** ['bɛntʃ,mark] *n.* **1** *Surveying.* a mark made on a rock or other permanent landmark of known position and elevation for use as a starting point or reference for topographical surveys. **2** a standard or point of reference for measuring or evaluating other things: *The court's ruling will serve as a benchmark for future cases.* **3** *Computer technology.* a test used to measure the performance of computer hardware or software.

bench penalty or **bench minor** *Cdn. Hockey.* a minor (two-minute) penalty imposed against a team and served by a player designated by the team's coach or manager.

bench press a manner of lifting weights with the arms while lying flat on one's back on a bench, with one's feet on the floor. **—'bench-,press,** *v.*

bench warrant a written order from a court of law or a judge for the arrest of an accused person or a witness who has not appeared in court as required.

bend¹ [bɛnd] *v.* **bent, bend•ing;** *n.* *—v.* **1** make, be, or become curved or crooked: *The branch began to bend as I climbed along it.* **2** stoop; bow: *She bent to the ground and picked up a stone.* **3** force to submit: *"I will bend you or break you!" cried the villain.* **4** submit: *But the hero would not bend.* **5** move or turn in a certain direction; direct or apply (one's mind or effort): *He bent his mind to the task. She bent her steps toward home.* **6** fasten (a sail, rope, etc.).
—n. **1** a part that is not straight; curve or turn: *There is a sharp bend in the road here.* **2** the act of bending: *a bend of the knee.* **3** *Nautical.* a knot for tying two ropes together or tying a rope to something else. **4 the bends,** *Informal.* DECOMPRESSION SICKNESS.
around or **round the bend,** *Slang.* crazy: *That incessant noise is driving me around the bend.* ⟨OE *bendan* bind, band⟩

bend² [bɛnd] *n. Heraldry.* a broad stripe extending across a shield from the upper right to the lower left, from the wearer's point of view. ⟨OE *bend* strap, influenced by OF *bende* band⟩

Ben•day process ['bɛn'dei] a method of printing which adds tone or shading to a drawing by means of an overlay of dots. ⟨< after *Ben(jamin) Day* (1838-1916), a New York printer⟩

bend•ed ['bɛndɪd] *v. Archaic.* pt. and a pp. of BEND: *On bended knee, he asked her forgiveness.*

bend•er ['bɛndər] *n.* **1** a person or thing that bends. **2** *Slang.* a drinking spree.

ben•dro•flu•me•thia•zide [ˌbɛndrouˌfluməˈθaɪəˌzaɪd] *n.* a diuretic drug used to treat edema and high blood pressure.

A shield showing a bend sinister

bend sinister *Heraldry.* a broad stripe drawn from the upper left to the lower right of a shield (from the bearer's point of view), indicating bastardy.

be•neath [bɪ'niθ] *adv., prep.* *—adv.* below, underneath: *The man climbed into the hammock and his dog settled itself beneath.*
—prep. **1** below; under; lower than: *The dog sat beneath the tree.* **2** unworthy of; worthy not even of: *A traitor is so as to be beneath contempt.* ⟨OE *beneothan* < *be-* by + *neothan* below⟩
☛ *Syn. prep.* **1.** See note at UNDER.

ben•e•dic•i•te [ˌbɛnəˈdɪsəti] *n., interj.* *—n.* **1** a blessing. **2 Benedicite, a** a hymn of praise to God of which "Benedicite" is the first word in Latin. **b** a musical setting for this hymn.
—interj. bless (you, them, etc.). ⟨< L *benedicite,* 2nd person pl. imperative of *benedicere* bless < *bene* well + *dicere* say⟩

ben•e•dict ['bɛnəˌdɪkt] *n.* **1** a recently married man, especially one who was a bachelor for a long time. **2** a married man. Also, **Benedick.** ⟨< *Benedick,* character in Shakespeare's *Much Ado About Nothing*⟩

Ben•e•dic•tine [ˌbɛnəˈdɪktin] *or* [ˌbɛnəˈdɪktɪn] *adj., n.* *—adj.* of Saint Benedict (480?-543?), the founder of the first order of monks, or of a religious order following his rule.
—n. **1** *Roman Catholic Church.* a monk or nun following the rule of Saint Benedict or of the order founded by him. **2** a kind of liqueur. ⟨< F *bénédictin*⟩

Benedictine rule the set of rules for a plan of life, used in monasteries and convents established by Saint Benedict.

ben•e•dic•tion [ˌbɛnəˈdɪkʃən] *n.* **1** the asking of God's blessing at the end of a religious service. **2** a blessing or being blessed. **3** mercy. **4** in the Roman Catholic Church, a special service held in the presence of, and with the blessing of, the Host. ⟨< L *benedictio, -onis* < *benedicere* bless. See BENEDICITE. Doublet of BENISON.⟩ **—ˌbe•neˈdic•to•ry,** *adj.*

Ben•e•dic•tus [ˌbɛnəˈdɪktəs] *n.* **1** a short hymn or canticle beginning in English "Blessed is He that cometh in the name of the Lord." **2** a canticle or hymn beginning in English "Blessed be the Lord God of Israel." **3** a musical setting of either of these canticles. ⟨< L *benedictus*, pp. of *benedicere.* See BENEDICITE.⟩

ben•e•fac•tion [ˌbɛnəˈfækʃən] *n.* **1** a doing good; kind act. **2** a benefit conferred; gift for charity; help given for any good purpose.

ben•e•fac•tor ['bɛnəˌfæktər] *or* [ˌbɛnəˈfæktər] *n.* a person who has helped others, either by gifts of money or by some kind act. ⟨ME < LL *benefactor* < *benefacere* < *bene* well + *facere* do⟩

ben•e•fac•tress ['bɛnəˌfæktrɪs] *or* [ˌbɛnəˈfæktrɪs] *n.* a woman who has helped others, either by gifts of money or by some kind act.

ben•e•fice ['bɛnəfɪs] *n.* **1** a permanent office or position created by ecclesiastical authority. **2** the money earned from this position or the property attached to it. ⟨ME< OF < L *beneficium* benefit < *beneficus* beneficent < *benefacere.* See BENEFACTOR.⟩

be•nef•i•cence [bəˈnɛfəsəns] *n.* **1** the quality of being kind. **2** a charitable act or donation. ⟨< L *beneficentia* < *beneficus.* See BENEFICE.⟩

be•nef•i•cent [bəˈnɛfəsənt] *adj.* **1** kindly; doing good. **2** having good results: *beneficent acts.* **—beˈnef•i•cent•ly,** *adv.*

ben•e•fi•cial [ˌbɛnəˈfɪʃəl] *adj.* favourable; helpful; good; productive of good: *Sunshine and moisture are beneficial to plants.* **—ˌben•eˈfi•cial•ly,** *adv.*

ben•e•fi•ci•ar•y [ˌbɛnəˈfɪʃəri] *or* [ˌbɛnəˈfɪʃiˌɛri] *n., pl.* **-ar•ies.** **1** a person who receives benefit: *All the children are beneficiaries of the new playground.* **2** a person who receives or is to receive money or property from an insurance policy, a trust fund, a will, etc. **3** one who holds a BENEFICE (def. 1).

ben•e•fit ['bɛnəfɪt] *n., v.* **-fit•ed, -fit•ing.** *—n.* **1** anything for the good of a person or thing; an advantage: *Universal peace would be of great benefit to the world.* **2** *Archaic.* an act of kindness; a favour. **3** money paid to the sick, disabled, etc. **4** a performance at the theatre, a game, etc. to raise money that goes to a special person or persons or to a worthy cause.
—v. **1** give benefit to; be good for: *Rest will benefit a sick person.* **2** receive good; profit: *She benefited by the medicine. They will benefit from the new way of doing business.* ⟨ME < AF *benfet* < L *benefactum* < *bene-* well + *factum*, pp. of *facere* do⟩
☛ *Syn. n.* **1.** See note at ADVANTAGE.

benefit of clergy **1** formerly, the privilege of being tried in church courts instead of regular courts. **2** the services and rites or approval of the church.

benefit society or **association** a group which, through membership fees, provides its members with certain benefits, such as insurance.

Ben•e•lux ['bɛnəˌlʌks] *n.* the economic association of Belgium, the Netherlands, and Luxembourg, first organized in 1948 and now part of the European Common Market. ⟨< *Be*lgium, *Ne*therlands, *Lux*embourg⟩

be•nev•o•lence [bəˈnɛvələns] *n.* **1** good will; kindly feeling. **2** an act of kindness; something good that is done; a generous gift. **3** formerly, a forced loan levied by certain medieval English kings. ⟨ME < OF < L *benevolentia* < *bene* well + *velle* wish⟩

be•nev•o•lent [bəˈnɛvələnt] *adj.* kindly; charitable. **—beˈnev•o•lent•ly,** *adv.*

Ben•gal [bɛŋˈgɒl], [ˈbɛŋgɒl], *or* [bɛnˈgɒl] *n.* a region to the NE of India, comprising West Bengal and Bangladesh.

Ben•ga•lese [ˌbɛŋgəˈliz] *or* [ˌbɛngəˈliz] *n., pl.* **-lese;** *adj.* *—n.* a native of Bengal.
—adj. of Bengal, its people, or their language.

Ben•ga•li [bɛŋˈgɒli] *or* [bɛnˈgɒli] *adj., n.* *—adj.* of Bengal, its people, or their language.
—n. **1** a native of Bengal. **2** the language of Bengal.

Bengal light a signal flare that burns with a steady blue flame.

ben•ga•line [ˌbɛŋgəˈlin] *or* [ˈbɛŋgəˌlin] *n.* a corded silk or rayon cloth with wool or cotton in it. ⟨< F⟩

be•night•ed [bɪˈnəitɪd] *adj.* **1** not knowing right from wrong; ignorant. **2** overtaken by night; being in darkness. ⟨< obsolete verb *benight* < *be-* + *night*⟩

be•nign [bɪˈnaɪn] *adj.* **1** gentle; kindly: *a benign old lady.* **2** favourable; mild: *a benign climate.* **3** *Medicine.* **a** mild; doing no permanent harm: *benign leukemia.* **b** of tumours, not likely to recur after removal or to spread; not malignant. ⟨ME *benigne* < OF < L *benignus* < *bene* well + *-gnus* born⟩ **—beˈnign•ly,** *adv.*

be•nig•nan•cy [bɪˈnɪgnənsi] *n.* a benignant quality.

be•nig•nant [bɪˈnɪgnənt] *adj.* **1** kindly; gracious: *a benignant ruler.* **2** favourable; beneficial. **3** BENIGN (def. 3). **—beˈnig•nant•ly,** *adv.*

be•nig•ni•ty [bɪˈnɪgnəti] *n., pl.* **-ties.** **1** the quality of kindliness or graciousness. **2** a kind act; favour.

Be•nin [bɛ'nin] *n.* a country in W Africa on the Gulf of Guinea.

Be•nin•ese [bɛ'niniz] *or* [ˌbɛnɪ'niz] *n., adj.* —*n.* a native or inhabitant of Benin.
—*adj.* of or having to do with Benin.

ben•i•son ['bɛnəzən] *or* ['bɛnəsən] *n.* a blessing. Compare MALISON. ⟨ME < OF *beneison* < L *benedictio, -onis.* Doublet of BENEDICTION.⟩

Ben•nett buggy ['bɛnət] *Cdn.* in the Depression of the 1930s, an automobile drawn by horses because the owner could not afford gas, oil, or a licence for it. Bennett buggies usually had the engine removed, and the horses were hitched to poles attached to the front bumper. ⟨after R.B. *Bennett*, prime minister of Canada from 1930 to 1935, because his government had not succeeded in solving Canada's economic problems as promised⟩

A Bennett buggy

ben•ny ['bɛni] *n., pl.* **-nies.** *Slang.* an amphetamine tablet taken as a stimulant, especially Benzedrine. ⟨shortened from *Benzedrine.* 20c.⟩

ben•se•ra•zide [bɛn'sɛrəˌzaid] *n.* a drug used to treat Parkinson's disease.

bent[1] [bɛnt] *v., adj., n.* —*v.* pt. and pp. of BEND.
—*adj.* **1** not straight; curved; crooked. **2** strongly inclined; determined: *He was bent on going home.* **3** bound (for): *toward Jerusalem bent.* **4** *Slang.* unscrupulous; cheating.
bent out of shape, *Slang.* in a state of agitation or anger.
—*n.* an inclination; a tendency: *a bent for drawing.*

bent[2] [bɛnt] *n.* **1** any of a genus (*Agrostis*) of annual and perennial grasses found especially in temperate and cool parts of the world, including several species, such as red top, valued for use as forage or in lawn mixtures. **2** any stiff or reedy grass. **3** *Archaic.* heath or moor. ⟨OE *beonet-*⟩

bent grass BENT[2] (def. 1).

Ben•tham•ism ['bɛnθəˌmɪzəm] *n.* the philosophical doctrine held by Jeremy Bentham and his followers, that the aim of life should be the greatest happiness of the greatest number; utilitarianism. ⟨after Jeremy *Bentham* (1748-1832), English philosopher⟩ —**'Ben•tham,ite,** *n.*

ben•thos ['bɛnθɒs] *n.* **1** the region at the bottom of the sea. **2** all the organisms that live at the bottom of the sea. ⟨< NL < Gk. depth of the sea⟩ —**'benth•ic,** *adj.*

ben•ton•ite ['bɛntəˌnəit] *n.* a highly absorbent clay formed from the decomposition of volcanic ash, used extensively in industry as a binding, filling, and filtering agent. ⟨after Fort *Benton*, Montana, where the clay is found⟩

bent•wood ['bɛntˌwʊd] *n.* **1** wood bent into various shapes by steam and pressure. **2** (*adjl.*) denoting furniture made of such wood: *a bentwood chair.*

be•numb [bɪ'nʌm] *v.* **1** make numb; deaden. **2** stupefy; make inactive: *A benumbing boredom had set in.* ⟨OE *benumen*, pp. of *beniman* deprive < *be-* + *niman* take⟩ —**be'numb•ing•ly,** *adv.*

ben•zal•de•hyde [bɛn'zɒldəˌhaɪd] *or* [bɛn'zældəˌhaɪd] *n.* a clear liquid with a pleasant smell, found in bitter almond oil and used in the manufacture of perfumes, dyes, etc. *Formula*: C_6H_5CHO ⟨< *benz(ene)* + aldehyde⟩

ben•zal•ko•ni•um [ˌbɛnzæl'kouniəm] *n.* an antiseptic and disinfectant. *Formula*: $C_8H_{10}NRCl$

ben•zene ['bɛnzin] *or* [bɛn'zin] *n.* a colourless, volatile, flammable liquid hydrocarbon that has a pleasant odour. It is obtained chiefly from coal tar and is used in the manufacture of many chemical products, including detergent, insecticides, and motor fuels. *Formula*: C_6H_6 ⟨< *benzoin*⟩
☛ *Hom.* BENZINE.

benzene ring the hexagonal molecular structure of benzene and benzene compounds, in which six carbon atoms are bonded to each other and to six hydrogen atoms.

ben•ze•tho•ni•um chloride [ˌbɛnzə'θouniəm] a drug used as an antiseptic cleanser and to treat itching. *Formula*: $(C_{27}H_{42}O_2N)Cl\text{-}H_2O$

ben•zine ['bɛnzin] *or* [bɛn'zin] *n.* a clear, colourless, flammable liquid consisting of a mixture of hydrocarbons obtained by the fractional distillation of petroleum, used especially as a solvent and cleaning fluid. ⟨< *benzoin*⟩
☛ *Hom.* BENZENE.

ben•zo•ate ['bɛnzouɪt] *or* ['bɛnzouˌeit] *n.* a salt or ester of benzoic acid. **Benzoate of soda** is used as a food preservative.

ben•zo•caine ['bɛnzəˌkein] *n.* a white powder without odour, which is used as a local anesthetic. *Formula*: $C_6H_4NH_2COOC_2H_5$

ben•zo•dia•ze•pine [ˌbɛnzoudaɪ'æzəˌpin] *n.* a class of drugs used as minor tranquillizers.

ben•zo•ic acid [bɛn'zouɪk] an acid occurring in benzoin, cranberries, etc. that is used as an antiseptic or as a food preservative. *Formula*: C_6H_5COOH

ben•zo•in ['bɛnzouɪn], [bɛn'zouɪn], *or* ['bɛnzɔɪn] *n.* **1** a fragrant resin obtained from certain species of trees (genus *Styrax*) of Java, Sumatra, etc. and used in perfume and medicine. **2** a substance resembling camphor made from this resin. **3** any of various fragrant trees or bushes of the laurel family (genus *Lindera*) native to eastern North America; spicebush. ⟨< F *benjoin* < Sp. or Pg. < Arabic *luban jawi* incense of Java⟩

ben•zol ['bɛnzɒl] *or* ['bɛnzoul] *n.* **1** benzene. **2** a liquid, about 70 percent benzene and 20 to 30 percent toluene. It is obtained from coal tar and is used in making dyes.

ben•zon•a•tate [bɛn'zɒnəˌteit] *n.* a drug used to treat coughs. *Formula*: $C_{30}H_{53}NO_{11}$

ben•zo•py•rene [ˌbɛnzou'paɪrin] *n.* a yellow, crystalline hydrocarbon found in coal tar and tobacco smoke. It is known to be carcinogenic. *Formula*: $C_{20}H_{12}$

ben•zo•yl ['bɛnzouˌɪl] *n.* the group C_6H_5CO-, occurring in benzoic acid and derived substances.

benz•py•rene [bɛnz'paɪrin] *n.* benzopyrene.

Be•o•thic [bi'ɒθɪk] *or* [bi'ɒtɪk] *n., pl.* **-thic** or **-thics.** beothuk.

Be•o•thuk [bi'ɒθək] *or* [bi'ɒtək] *n., pl.* **-thuk** or **-thuks. 1** an extinct nation, the aboriginal inhabitants of Newfoundland. **2** a member of this people. The last Beothuk died in 1829. **3** the language of this people. Also, **Beothic.**

Be•o•wulf ['beiəˌwʊlf] *n.* **1** an Old English epic poem in alliterative verse, composed in England probably about A.D. 700. **2** the hero of this poem.

be•praise [bi'preiz] *v.* **-praised, -prais•ing.** praise greatly; praise too much.

be•queath [bɪ'kwiθ] *or* [bɪ'kwið] *v.* **1** give or leave (property, etc.) by a will: *The father bequeathed the farm to his daughter.* **2** hand down to posterity: *One age bequeaths its civilization to the next.* ⟨OE *becwethan* < *be-* to, for + *cwethan* say⟩
—**be'queath•er,** *n.*

be•queath•al [bɪ'kwiðəl] *n.* the act of bequeathing.

be•quest [bɪ'kwɛst] *n.* **1** something bequeathed; legacy: *Mrs. Quail died and left a bequest of ten thousand dollars to the university.* **2** the act of bequeathing. ⟨ME *biqueste*⟩

be•rate [bɪ'reit] *v.* **-rat•ed, -rat•ing.** scold sharply; upbraid.

Ber•ber ['bɜrbər] *n., adj.* —*n.* **1** a member of a group of peoples who are the original European or Caucasoid inhabitants of N Africa. The Berbers, most of whom are now farmers, make up a considerable portion of the populations of Libya, Algeria, and Morocco. **2** a branch of the Afro-Asiatic language family, spoken by more than ten million people scattered through N Africa. **3** any one of these languages.
—*adj.* of or having to do with the Berbers or their languages.

ber•ber•ine ['bɜrbəˌrin] *n.* a bitter-tasting, yellow substance obtained from the barberry plant and used in medicine. *Formula*: $C_{20}H_{17}NO_4\text{-}6H_2O$ ⟨< NL *berberina* < Med.L *barberis* barberry⟩

ber•ceuse [bɛʀ'søz] *n. French.* **1** lullaby. **2** *Music.* a vocal or instrumental composition that has a soothing rhythm.

be•reave [bɪ'riv] *v.* **be•reaved** or **be•reft, be•reav•ing.** **1** deprive *(of)* ruthlessly; rob: *bereave of hope.* **2** leave desolate. ⟨OE *berēafian* < *be-* away + *rēafian* rob⟩

be•reaved [bɪ'rivd] *adj., v.* —*adj.* deprived *(of)* by death: *Bereaved of their mother at an early age, the children learned to take care of themselves.*
—*v.* a pt. and a pp. of BEREAVE.

be•reave•ment [bɪ'rivmənt] *n.* the fact or state of being bereaved, especially the loss of a relative or friend by death.

be•reft [bɪ'rɛft] *adj., v.* —*adj.* deprived; dispossessed: *Bereft of hope and friends, the old man led a wretched life.*
—*v.* a pt. and a pp. of BEREAVE.

be•ret [bə'rei] *n.* a soft, round cap of wool, felt, etc. See CAP for picture. ⟨< F *béret* < Provençal *birret* < LL *birretum.* See BIRETTA.⟩

be•ret•ta [bəˈrɛtə] biretta.

berg [bɜrg] *n.* iceberg.
☛ *Hom.* BURG.

ber•ga•mot¹ [ˈbɜrgə,mɒt] *n.* **1** a small citrus tree (*Citrus bergamia*) cultivated especially in S Italy for its pear-shaped fruit, whose rind yields a fragrant essential oil used in perfumes. **2** this fruit, which is inedible. **3** any of several plants of the mint family, such as a Mediterranean mint (*Mentha citrata*) that yields an oil with a similar fragrance. **4** the oil thus derived. ⟨from *Bergamo*, a town in Italy⟩

ber•ga•mot² [ˈbɜrgə,mɒt] *n.* a kind of pear with a fine flavour. ⟨< F *bergamote* < Ital. *bergamotta* < Turkish *beg-armudi* prince's pear < *beg* prince + *armudi* pear⟩

ber•gère or **ber•gere** [bɛrˈʒɛr] *n.* a kind of chair in 18th century style, either upholstered, or made of cane and used with cushions. ⟨< F, literally, shepherdess⟩

berg•schrund [ˈbɛrkʃrʊnt] *or* [ˈbɜrgʃrʊnd] *n.* a deep crack in the top of a glacier. ⟨< G *Berg* mountain + *Schrund* crack⟩

Berg•so•ni•an [bɜrgˈsouniən] *adj., n. —adj.* of or having to do with Henri Bergson (1859-1941), a French philosopher who thought of the universe as being in a continual process of creative evolution.
—n. a person who supports or believes in the philosophy of Bergson.

Berg•son•ism [ˈbɜrgsə,nɪzəm] *n.* the philosophy of Bergson.

be•rib•boned [bɪˈrɪbənd] *adj.* **1** trimmed with many ribbons. **2** decorated with ribbons: *a beribboned general.*

ber•i•ber•i [ˈbɛri,bɛri] *n.* a disease caused by a lack of thiamine, affecting the heart or nervous system and in extreme cases resulting in heart failure or paralysis. ⟨< Sinhala (language of Sri Lanka), a reduplication of *beri* weakness. 19c.⟩

Berke•le•ian [ˈbɑrkliən] *or* [ˈbɜrkliən] *adj., n. —adj.* of or having to do with George Berkeley (1685-1753), an Irish philosopher who held that things exist only in the mind.
—n. an adherent of Berkeley's philosophy.

Berke•le•ian•ism [ˈbɑrkliə,nɪzəm] *or* [ˈbɜrkliə,nɪzəm] *n.* the philosophy of Berkeley.

ber•ke•li•um [bərˈkiliəm] *n.* an artificial, radioactive, metallic element produced by bombarding americium with alpha particles. *Symbol*: Bk; *at.no.* 97; *at.mass* 249.08. ⟨< *Berkeley*, California (site of the University of California campus where berkelium was first produced in 1949)⟩

Berk•shire [ˈbɜrkʃər], *Brit.* [ˈbɑrkʃər] *n.* a breed of black-and-white pig. ⟨< *Berkshire*, a county in S England⟩

ber•lin [bərˈlɪn] *or* [ˈbɜrlɪn] *n.* **1** a four-wheeled carriage with two hooded seats and a platform in the rear for footmen. **2** a soft woollen yarn. ⟨from *Berlin*, Germany⟩

berm [bɜrm] *n.* **1** a high embankment or ridge of earth, etc. functioning as a protective barrier or as a base or covering for a pipeline, etc. Berms are sometimes built along expressways to protect neighbouring residential districts from traffic noise. **2** a narrow strip of grass beside a street or road. **3** a narrow ledge, path, or shelf between a moat and a rampart in a fortification. ⟨< F *berme* < Du. *berm*, prob. cognate with ON *barmr* brim. 18c.⟩

berm house a modern house which is built into the earth on one side.

Ber•mu•da [bərˈmjudə] *n.* a British colony consisting of a group of islands off the SE coast of the United States.

Ber•mu•dan or **Ber•mu•di•an** [bərˈmjudən] *or* [bərˈmjudiən] *n., adj. —n.* a native or inhabitant of Bermuda.
—adj. of or having to do with Bermuda.

Bermuda onion a large variety of onion with a mild flavour similar to that of the Spanish onion.

Bermuda shorts short tailored pants that reach to just above the knee, for men or women.

Bermuda Triangle a region of the Atlantic, bounded by Florida, Bermuda, and Puerto Rico, in which ships and planes are said to have mysteriously disappeared.

Ber•noul•li's principle [bərˈnuli] *Physics.* the finding by Bernoulli that the pressure exerted by a liquid against the walls of a passage varies inversely with the speed at which the liquid is coursing through that passage. ⟨after Daniel *Bernoulli* (1700-1782), Swiss scientist⟩

ber•ried [ˈbɛrid] *adj.* **1** of a lobster, crayfish, etc., bearing eggs. **2** having berries.
☛ *Hom.* BURIED.

ber•ry [ˈbɛri] *n., pl.* **-ries;** *v.* **-ried, -ry•ing.** *—n.* **1** any small, juicy, edible fruit having many seeds instead of a single stone or pit: *Strawberries and currants are berries.* **2** *Botany.* a simple fruit having two or more seeds in the pulp and having a skin or rind, such as grapes, tomatoes, currants, and bananas. See FRUIT for picture. **3** the dry seed or kernel of certain kinds of grain or other plants: *a wheat berry.* **4** the fruit of the coffee tree. Coffee is made from the beans (seeds) found inside ripe coffee berries. **5** an egg of a lobster or fish.
—v. **1** gather or pick berries. **2** bear or produce berries: *a berrying shrub.* **—ˈber•ry,like,** *adj.* ⟨OE *berie*⟩
☛ *Hom.* BURY.

ber•serk [bərˈzɜrk] *or* [bərˈsɜrk] *adj. or adv., n. —adj. or adv.* in a frenzy.
—n. berserker. ⟨< Icelandic *berserkr* (accus. sing. *berserk)* wild warrior < *ber-* bear + *serkr* shirt⟩

ber•serk•er [bərˈzɜrkər] *or* [bərˈsɜrkər] *n.* **1** a fierce Norse warrior. **2** one who behaves violently or wildly. ⟨< Icelandic *berserkr*⟩

berth [bɜrθ] *n., v. —n.* **1** a place to sleep on a ship, train, or aircraft. **2** enough clear space around a ship for it to manoeuvre safely in the water; sea room. **3** the place where a ship stays when at anchor or at a wharf. **4** a place for a truck or other motor vehicle to load or unload, etc. **5** an appointment or position; job. **6** *Cdn.* a stand of timber in which an individual or company has the right to fell trees; TIMBER LIMIT (def. 2). **7** *Sports.* a place or standing: *to win a berth in the final.*
give (a person or thing) **a wide berth,** keep well away from (a person or thing); pass well clear of: *I gave the dog a wide berth.*
—v. **1** put in a berth; provide with a berth. **2** have or occupy a berth. ⟨? < *bear¹*⟩
☛ *Hom.* BIRTH.

ber•tha [ˈbɜrθə] *n.* a woman's wide collar that often extends over the shoulders. ⟨after *Berthe*, mother of Charlemagne⟩

berth•ing [ˈbɜrθɪŋ] *n., v. —n.* space to berth a ship, motorboat, etc. in a harbour or beside a pier.
—v. ppr. of BERTH.

Ber•til•lon system [ˈbɜrtə,lɒn] a system, once widely used, for identifying persons, especially criminals, by their physical measurements, such as length of arms and legs and width and length of the skull. The Bertillon system has been replaced by fingerprinting. ⟨after A. *Bertillon* (1853-1914), the French police officer who introduced the system⟩

ber•yl [ˈbɛrəl] *n.* **1** a very hard, clear or cloudy mineral, usually green or greenish blue, a silicate of beryllium and aluminum. **2** a piece of this stone, or a gem made from it. Emeralds and aquamarines are beryls. ⟨ME < OF < L < Gk. *bēryllos*, cognate with Skt. *vaidurya* cat's-eye⟩
☛ *Hom.* BARREL [ˈbɛrəl].

be•ryl•li•o•sis [bə,rɪliˈousɪs] *n.* a lung disease caused by inhalation of poisonous beryllium fumes.

be•ryl•li•um [bəˈrɪliəm] *n.* a hard, strong, steel-grey metallic element, used mainly in alloys as a hardening agent. *Symbol*: Be; *at.no.* 4; *at.mass* 9.01. ⟨< *beryl*⟩

be•seech [bɪˈsitʃ] *v.* **-sought** or **-seeched, -seech•ing.** ask earnestly; beg. ⟨ME *biseche(n)* < *be-* thoroughly + *seche(n)* seek⟩ **—beˈseech•er,** *n.*
☛ *Syn.* See note at BEG.

be•seech•ing [bɪˈsitʃɪŋ] *adj., v. —adj.* that beseeches.
—v. ppr. of BESEECH. **—beˈseech•ing•ly,** *adv.*

be•seem [bɪˈsim] *v.* be proper for; be fitting to: *It does not beseem you to leave your friend without help.*

be•set [bɪˈsɛt] *v.* **-set, -set•ting. 1** attack on all sides; surround: *In the swamp we were beset by mosquitoes.* **2** continue to trouble; afflict: *a task beset with many difficulties.* **3** set; stud: *Her bracelet was beset with gems.* ⟨OE *besettan* < *be-* around + *settan* set⟩ **—beˈset•ment,** *n.*

be•set•ting [bɪˈsɛtɪŋ] *adj., v. —adj.* habitually attacking or troubling: *Laziness is a loafer's besetting sin.*
—v. ppr. of BESET.

be•shrew [bɪˈʃru] *v. Archaic.* call down evil upon; curse mildly. ⟨ME *beshrewe(n)*⟩

be•side [bɪˈsaɪd] *prep., adv. —prep.* **1** by the side of; near; close to: *Grass grows beside the brook.* **2** compared with: *Andy seems dull beside his sister.* **3** *Archaic.* in addition to; besides: *Other men beside ourselves were helping.* **4** away or aside from; not related to: *That question is beside the point.*
beside oneself, extremely excited or upset; wild or crazy: *beside oneself with fear. He was beside himself with joy.*
—adv. Archaic. in addition; besides. ⟨OE *be sīdan* by side⟩

☛ *Usage.* Do not confuse the preposition **beside** with the adverb and preposition BESIDES. Although both can mean 'in addition (to)', only **beside** can mean 'close to'.

be•sides [bɪ'saɪdz] *adv., prep.* —*adv.* **1** also; moreover; further: *He didn't want to quarrel; besides, he wasn't completely sure he was right.* **2** in addition: *We tried two other ways besides.* **3** otherwise; else: *She is ignorant of politics, whatever she may know besides.*
—*prep.* **1** in addition to; over and above: *The picnic was attended by others besides our own club members.* **2** except; other than: *We spoke of no one besides you.*

☛ *Usage.* See note at BESIDE.

be•siege [bɪ'sidʒ] *v.* **-sieged, -sieg•ing. 1** make a prolonged attempt to get possession of (a place) by armed force; surround and try to capture: *For ten years the Greeks besieged the city of Troy.* **2** crowd around: *Hundreds of admirers besieged the astronaut.* **3** overwhelm with requests, questions, etc.: *During the flood the Red Cross was besieged with calls for help.* **—be'sieg•er,** *n.*

be•smear [bɪ'smir] *v.* **1** smear over. **2** sully; dishonour: *The lies and half-truths in the newspaper article besmeared the diplomat's reputation.*

be•smirch [bɪ'smɜrtʃ] *v.* **1** make dirty; soil. **2** sully; dishonour: *to besmirch a good reputation.* **—be'smirch•er,** *n.*

be•som ['bizəm] *n.* a broom made of twigs. ⟨OE *besma*⟩

be•sot [bɪ'sɒt] *v.* **-sot•ted, -sot•ting.** stupefy or make foolish, as with liquor, infatuation, etc.

be•sought [bɪsɒt] *v.* a pt. and a pp. of BESEECH.

be•spake [bɪ'speik] *v. Archaic.* a pt. of BESPEAK.

be•span•gle [bɪ'spæŋgəl] *v.* **-gled, -gling.** adorn with spangles or anything like them.

be•spat•ter [bɪ'spætər] *v.* **1** spatter all over; soil by spattering. **2** slander. **—be'spat•ter•er,** *n.*

be•speak [bɪ'spik] *v.* **-spoke** or (*archaic*) **-spake, -spo•ken** or **-spoke, -speak•ing. 1** engage in advance; order; reserve: *to bespeak tickets to a play.* **2** show; indicate: *A neat appearance bespeaks care.* **3** point to; foreshadow: *Their early successes bespeak a great future.*

be•spec•ta•cled [bɪ'spɛktəkəld] *adj.* wearing glasses.

be•spoke [bɪ'spouk] *v., adj.* —*v.* a pt. and a pp. of BESPEAK.
—*adj. Brit.* made-to-order: *bespoke tailoring, a bespoke overcoat.*

be•spo•ken [bɪ'spoukən] *v.* a pp. of BESPEAK.

be•spread [bɪ'sprɛd] *v.* **-spread, -spread•ing.** spread something over.

be•sprent [bɪ'sprɛnt] *adj. Archaic or poetic.* sprinkled or strewn. ⟨OE *besprenged*, pp. of *besprengan*⟩

be•sprin•kle [bɪ'sprɪŋkəl] *v.* **-kled, -kling.** sprinkle all over.

Bes•se•mer converter ['bɛsəmər] a large container for making molten iron into steel by the BESSEMER PROCESS.

Bessemer process a method of making steel by burning out carbon and impurities in molten iron with a blast of compressed air. ⟨after Sir Henry *Bessemer* (1813-1898), the English engineer who invented the process⟩

Bessemer steel steel made by the BESSEMER PROCESS.

best [bɛst] *adj.* (superlative of GOOD), *adv.* (superlative of WELL), *n., v.* —*adj.* **1** the most desirable, valuable, superior, etc.: *the best food, the best students, the best quality of crystal.* **2** of the greatest advantage, usefulness, etc.: *the best thing to do.* **3** largest; greatest: *We spent the best part of the day just getting organized.*
—*adv.* **1** in the most excellent way; most thoroughly: *Who reads best?* **2** in the highest degree: *I like this book best.*
as best one can, *Informal.* as well as possible; to the best of one's abilities.
had best, should; ought to; will be wise to: *We had best postpone the party.*
—*n.* **1** the person, thing, part, quality, or state that is best: *She is the best in the class. We want the best. The story represents journalism at its best.* **2** utmost: *I did my best to finish the work on time.* **3** one's most elegant outfit: *He came to the meeting dressed in his best.*
(all) for the best, favourable in the end: *at first we were unhappy about the plan, but it turned out to be all for the best.*
at best, a even under the most favourable circumstances: *Summer is at best very short.* **b** even when interpreted most favourably: *It was a sad effort at best.*
get the best of, defeat or outwit.
make the best of, do as well as possible with: *We'll just have to make the best of a bad job.*
with the best, as well as anyone: *She can swim with the best.*
—*v. Informal.* outdo; defeat: *Our team was bested in the final game.* ⟨OE *betst*⟩

best–ball ['bɛst ,bɒl] *n. Golf.* a team game for two partners who share a ball, following on from the better drive of the two.

be•stead [bɪ'stɛd] *v.* **-stead•ed, -stead•ed** or **-stead, -stead•ing;** *adj. Archaic.* —*v.* help; assist; serve.
—*adj.* placed; situated. ⟨< *be-* + *stead*, v., help⟩

bes•tial ['bistʃiəl], ['bɛstʃəl], *or* ['bɛstiəl] *adj.* **1** beastly; brutal; vile. **2** of or having to do with beasts. ⟨ME < OF < L *bestialis* < *bestia* beast⟩ **—'bes•tial•ly,** *adv.* **—'bes•ti•al,ize,** *v.*

bes•ti•al•i•ty [,bistʃi'æləti], [,bɛstʃi'æləti], *or* [,bɛsti'æləti] *n.* **1** bestial character or conduct. **2** sexual activity between a person and an animal.

bes•ti•ar•y ['bɛstʃi,ɛri] *or* ['bistʃi,ɛri] *n.* a medieval collection of allegorical descriptions of real or mythical animals. ⟨< Med.L *bestiarum* < L *bestiarius* having to do with beasts < *bestia* beast⟩

be•stir [bɪ'stɜr] *v.* **-stirred, -stir•ring.** stir up; rouse; exert: *to bestir oneself to action.*

best man the chief attendant of the bridegroom at a wedding.

be•stow [bɪ'stou] *v.* **1** give (something) as a gift; give; confer (*used with* **on** *or* **upon**). **2** make use of; apply: *We bestowed a great deal of thought on the plan.* **3** *Archaic.* put safely; put; place. **4** *Archaic.* find quarters for; lodge. ⟨ME *bistowe(n)*⟩

be•stow•al [bɪ'stouəl] *n.* the act of bestowing.

be•strad•dle [bɪ'strædəl] *v.* **-dled, -dling.** bestride; straddle.

be•strew [bɪ'stru] *v.* **-strewed, -strewn** or **-strewed, -strew•ing. 1** strew; scatter; sprinkle: *The children bestrewed the path with flowers.* **2** strew (things) around; scatter about. **3** lie scattered over: *Flowers bestrewed the path.* ⟨OE *bestrēowian*⟩

be•strewn [bɪ'strun] *adj., v.* —*adj.* scattered all over.
—*v.* a pp. of BESTREW.

be•strid [bɪ'strɪd] *v.* a pt. and a pp. of BESTRIDE.

be•strid•den [bɪ'strɪdən] *v.* a pp. of BESTRIDE.

be•stride [bɪ'straɪd] *v.* **-strode** or **-strid, -strid•den** or **-strid, -strid•ing. 1** get on or sit on (something) with one leg on either side: *One can bestride a horse, a chair, or a fence.* **2** stand over (something) with one leg on each side. **3** stride across; step over. ⟨OE *bestrīdan*⟩

be•strode [bɪ'stroud] *v.* a pt. of BESTRIDE.

best•sell•er or **best seller** ['bɛst'sɛlər] *n.* **1** anything, especially a book, that has a very large sale. **2** the author of a book with a very large sale.

bet[1] [bɛt] *n., v.* **bet** or **bet•ted, bet•ting.** —*n.* **1** an agreement between two persons or groups that the one who is proved wrong about the outcome of an event will give a particular thing or sum of money to the one who is proved right: *I made a two-cent bet that I wouldn't pass.* **2** the thing or sum of money risked in a bet; the stake: *I did pass; so I lost my bet (that is, my two cents).* **3** a thing to bet on: *That horse is a good bet.*
—*v.* **1** promise (money or something else) to (a person) if that person is proved right about the outcome of an event: *I bet you two cents I won't pass this test.* **2** make a bet: *Did you bet on the race?* **3** *Informal.* be very sure: *I bet you're wrong about that.*
you bet, *Informal.* certainly; of course: *You bet I'm going to object. "Are you going to the game?" "You bet!"* ⟨origin uncertain⟩

bet[2] [bɛt]; *Hebrew,* [beit] *or* [beis] *n.* the second letter of the Hebrew alphabet. See Appendix for table.

be•ta ['beitə] *or* ['bitə] *n., adj.* —*n.* **1** the second letter of the Greek alphabet (Β, β). **2** the second of a series. **3 Beta** or **Betamax,** *Trademark.* a type of videocassette recorder and player, and the format of the videocassette itself. **4 Beta,** *Astronomy.* in a constellation, the name of the second brightest star. This name is followed by the name of the constellation in the genetive: *Beta Cygni.*
—*adj. Chemistry.* denoting the second of several positions in an organic compound that a molecule can attach to.

beta blocker a type of drug used to control high blood pressure.

beta decay radioactive decay of a substance, resulting in a new substance and the emission of a BETA PARTICLE.

beta emitter a radioactive chemical element that emits a BETA PARTICLE in the course of changing into another element.

beta en•dor•phin [ɛn'dɔrfən] a chemical substance in the brain which acts as a pain reliever.

be•ta•his•tine [,beitə'hɪstin] *or* [,bitə-] *n.* a drug used to treat the vertigo and ringing in the ears associated with Ménière's Syndrome.

be•take [bɪ'teik] *v.* **-took, -tak•en, -tak•ing.** (*used reflexively*)

1 go: *to betake oneself to the mountains.* 2 devote or apply (oneself) (*to*): *to betake oneself to hard work.*

be•tak•en [bɪ'teikən] *v.* pp. of BETAKE.

be•ta•meth•a•sone [ˌbeitə'mɛθəˌsoun] *or* [ˌbitə-] *n.* a drug used in various compounds to treat a wide variety of medical conditions. *Formula*: $C_{22}H_{29}FO_5$

beta particle an electron or positron emitted by a nucleus in the process of radioactive decay.

beta ray a stream of BETA PARTICLES.

be•ta•tron ['beitəˌtrɒn] *or* ['bitəˌtrɒn] *n.* an accelerator that uses magnetic induction produced by rapid changes in a magnetic field to increase the velocity of electrons. ⟨< *beta* ray + (*elec*)*tron*⟩

beta wave a form of electrical activity in the brain, with frequencies from 13 to 30 hertz, denoting mental alertness. Compare ALPHA WAVE.

be•tel ['bitəl] *n.* a climbing pepper plant (*Piper betle*) of tropical Asia, the dried leaves of which are commonly chewed, together with pieces of betel nut and lime, throughout S Asia. See also BETEL NUT, BETEL PALM. ⟨< Port. < Malayalam *vettila*⟩
☛ *Hom.* BEETLE.

Be•tel•geuse ['bitəlˌdʒuz] *n.* a very large reddish star in the constellation Orion. ⟨< F ? < Arabic *bīt-al-jāuza* house of the twins⟩

betel nut the mildly narcotic seed of the betel palm, boiled and dried for chewing with betel leaves. See also BETEL, BETEL PALM.

betel palm a palm tree (*Areca catechu*) of tropical Asia having pinnate leaves and producing large seeds called betel nuts.

betel pepper a plant (*Piper betle*) of the pepper family, growing in hot regions of Asia.

bête noire ['bɛt 'nwɑr] a thing or person especially dreaded or detested. ⟨< F *bête noire* black beast⟩

be•than•e•chol [bə'θænəˌkɒl] *n.* a drug used to treat certain bladder conditions. *Formula*: $C_7H_{17}ClN_2O_2$

beth•el ['bɛθəl] *n.* 1 a holy place; a place of worship. 2 a church or chapel for seamen. ⟨< Hebrew *beth-el* house of God⟩

be•think [bɪ'θɪŋk] *v.* **-thought, -think•ing. 1** cause (oneself) to consider or reflect. 2 remind (oneself). 3 think about; call to mind. ⟨OE *bethencan*⟩

be•thought [bɪ'θɒt] *v.* pt. and pp. of BETHINK.

be•tide [bɪ'taɪd] *v.* **-tid•ed, -tid•ing.** happen or happen to; befall: *Woe betide anyone who touches Lisa's stamp collection.* ⟨ME *betiden* < *be-* + *tiden* happen⟩

be•times [bɪ'taɪmz] *adv. Archaic.* 1 early: *He rose betimes in the morning.* 2 soon; before it is too late. ⟨ME *bitime* by time⟩

bê•tise [bɛ'tiz] *n., pl.* **bê•tises** [-'tiz]. 1 a stupid remark. 2 stupidity. ⟨< F *bête* animal⟩

be•to•ken [bɪ'toukən] *v.* 1 be a sign or token of; indicate; show: *His smile betokens satisfaction.* 2 foreshadow; anticipate.

bet•o•ny ['bɛtəni] *n.* 1 a plant of the genus *Stachys* of the mint family, having white, yellow, or purple flower spikes, and formerly used in medicine. 2 a plant of the genus *Pedicularis* of the figwort family, having yellow, pink, or purple flower spikes and divided leaves. ⟨< ME *betonike* < OE *betonice* < LL *betonica*, altered < L *vettonica* after the *Vettones*, an ancient Iberian people⟩

be•took [bɪ'tʊk] *v.* pt. of BETAKE.

be•tray [bɪ'trei] *v.* 1 deliver into the enemy's hands by treachery: *The traitor betrayed her country.* 2 be unfaithful to: *He betrayed his friends.* 3 mislead; deceive. 4 give away (a secret); disclose unintentionally. 5 reveal; show: *His mistakes betrayed his lack of education.* ⟨ME *bitraie(n)* < *be-* (intensive) + *traie(n)* betray < OF < L *tradere* hand over⟩ **—be'tray•er,** *n.*

be•tray•al [bɪ'treiəl] *n.* betraying or being betrayed.

be•troth [bɪ'trouð] *or* [bɪ'trɒθ] *v.* promise in marriage; engage: *His daughter was betrothed to a rich man.* ⟨ME *betrouthe(n)*, var. of *betreuthien* < *be-* + *treuthe* < OE *trēowth* pledge⟩

be•troth•al [bɪ'trouðəl] *or* [bɪ'trɒθəl] *n.* a promise of marriage; engagement.

be•trothed [bɪ'trouðd] *or* [bɪ'trɒθt] *adj., n., v. —adj.* engaged to be married.
—n. the person to whom one is engaged to be married.
—v. pt. and pp. of BETROTH.

bet•ta ['bɛtə] *n.* a fish of the genus *Betta*, found in fresh water in hot regions of Asia, and including the Siamese fighting fish. ⟨< NL⟩

bet•ter[1] ['bɛtər] *adj.* (comparative of GOOD), *adv.* (comparative of WELL), *n., v. —adj.* 1 more desirable, valuable, etc.; of higher quality: *a better brand, better facilities.* 2 of greater advantage, usefulness, etc.: *a better thing to do.* 3 less sick: *The child is better today.* 4 larger or greater: *Four days is the better part of a week.*
—adv. 1 in a more excellent way; more thoroughly, desirably, etc.: *He'll do better next time.* 2 in a higher degree; more: *I know her better than I know her brother.* 3 more: *It took better than three hours to remove the stump.* 4 *Informal.* had better; should: *We better go; it's late.*
better off, a in a better condition: *The theatre was full, and we would have been better off if we had stayed at home watching television.* **b** having more money: *That family is better off than we are.*
had better, should; ought to; would be wise to: *You had better be there on time.*
think better of, think over and change one's mind: *I was going to go out, but thought better of it and decided to stay home.*
—n. 1 a person, thing, part, quality, or state that is better: *That is the better of the two routes.* 2 Usually, **betters,** *pl.* one's superiors, especially in rank or merit: *They were told to listen to the advice of their betters.*
for the better, to more desirable circumstances; to improvement: *Her illness took a turn for the better.*
get or **have the better of,** be superior to; defeat or outwit.
—v. 1 make or become better: *to better one's work, to better the lot of the poor.* 2 do better than; surpass: *They were unable to better the other school academically.* ⟨OE *betera*⟩

bet•ter[2] or **bet•tor** ['bɛtər] *n.* a person who bets.

better half *Informal.* spouse.

bet•ter•ment ['bɛtərmənt] *n.* 1 improvement: *Doctors work for the betterment of their patients' health.* 2 Usually, **betterments,** *pl. Law.* an improvement of real estate property.

bet•ty ['bɛti] *n.* a pudding made of diced bread or toast, fruit, and sweetening: *apple brown betty.*

be•tween [bɪ'twin] *prep., adv. —prep.* 1 in or into the space, position, or time separating; in the middle in relation to (two persons, things, etc.): *Many cities lie between Halifax and Toronto. There are no more holidays between now and the end of school. A sergeant ranks between a corporal and a warrant officer.* 2 in or into a position thought of as being in the middle in relation to two or more persons, things, or ideas: *Between dying in captivity and getting killed in escaping, he had little to choose from. Choose between me and my sister.* 3 within the range separating two or more quantities, qualities, or times: *a shade between pink and red. The temperature is probably between 20°C and 25°C. She made between $400 and $500 on the deal.* 4 connecting in space: *There is a paved highway between Flin Flon and The Pas.* 5 connecting in a state or condition; involving: *war between two nations. There was a strong bond of affection between them.* 6 in the joint ownership of: *They own the property between them.* 7 by the combined action or effort of: *The girls caught 12 fish between them. Settle the matter between you.* 8 in or into portions for: *The estate was divided between the grandchildren.* 9 restricted to: *We kept the matter between us.* 10 in or into a position separating: *They were fast friends and would let no quarrel come between them.* 11 throughout the range separating two or more conditions, qualities, or quantities: *all numbers between 1 and 50.*
between the devil and the deep blue sea. See DEVIL.
between you and me, as a secret; confidentially: *Between you and me, I don't think he has a chance of winning.*
no love lost between (persons), strong dislike involving two people; mutual enmity: *There's no love lost between them.*
—adv. in or into an intermediate space or time: *We could no longer see the moon, for a cloud had come between. The speeches seemed very long because there was no break between.*
in between, a in the middle: *We folded the blanket and put the mirror in between.* **b** in the middle of. ⟨OE *betwēonum* < *be-* by + *twā* two⟩
☛ *Usage.* **Between,** AMONG. **Between** is used when the reference is to two persons or things only: *My brother and I had less than a dollar between us.* **Among** is usually preferred when the reference is to more than two persons or things: *The money was divided among the four of us. However,* **between** is used also when the reference is to a number of persons or things that are thought of in pairs: *Leave a line space between paragraphs.*
☛ *Usage.* **Between you and me.** Since prepositions are followed by the objective form of a pronoun, standard English requires *me* in this expression, not *I.* Similarly, standard English requires: *between you and him* (not *he*), *between you and us* (not *we*), etc.

be•tween•times [bɪ'twinˌtaɪmz] *adv.* at intervals. Also, **betweenwhiles.**

be•twixt [bɪ'twɪkst] *prep. or adv.* between.
betwixt and between, in the middle; neither one nor the other. ⟨OE *betweox*⟩

BeV [bɛv] *U.S.* gigaelectronvolt (GeV). ⟨abbrev. of *b*illion *e*lectron*v*olts⟩

bev•a•tron ['bɛvə,trɒn] *n.* the synchrotron at the University of California, Berkeley, that accelerates electrified particles to 6BeV. ⟨< *BeV* + (*cyclo*)*tron*⟩

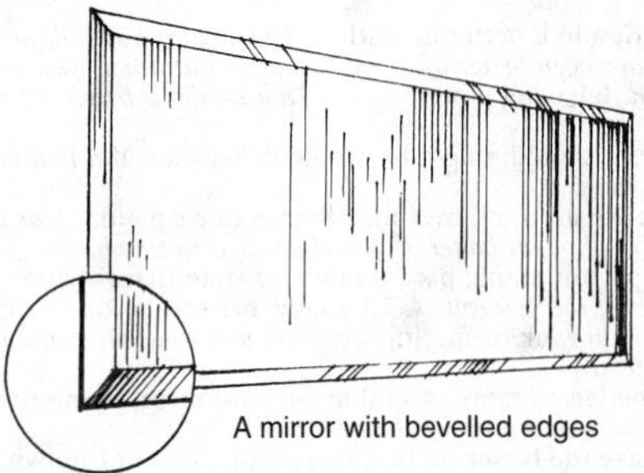

A mirror with bevelled edges

bev•el ['bɛvəl] *n., v.* **-elled** or **-eled, -el•ling** or **-el•ing.** *—n.* **1** a sloping edge, as on plate glass, moulding, etc. **2** also, **bevel square,** an instrument for measuring or drawing angles or adjusting a surface or edge that is to be given a bevel. **3** (*adjl.*) slanting; oblique.
—v. **1** cut at an angle other than a right angle; make slope: *This mirror has bevelled edges.* **2** be inclined; slope. ⟨? < OF⟩

bevel gear a gear which connects to another gear at an angle.

bev•er•age ['bɛvərɪdʒ] *n.* a liquid used or prepared for drinking. *Examples: milk, tea, coffee, beer, and wine.* ⟨ME < OF *bevrage* < *bevre* drink < L *bibere*⟩

beverage room *Cdn.* BEER PARLOUR.

bev•y ['bɛvi] *n., pl.* **bev•ies. 1** a group: *a bevy of quail, a bevy of girls.* **2** a group of roebucks. ⟨ME *bevey* ? < AF *bevée* a drinking group⟩

be•wail [bɪ'weil] *v.* mourn or lament: *to bewail one's fate.*

be•ware [bɪ'wɛr] *v.* be on one's guard; be cautious or wary (*used only in the imperative or infinitive*): *Beware of pickpockets.* ⟨< *be* + *ware*⟩

☛ *Usage.* **Beware** is a more formal word for 'be careful'. It is followed by *of* preceding a noun or pronoun or by *lest, how,* or *that...not* introducing a subordinate clause: *Beware of the sharpers at the fair. They were told to beware lest they wake him. We must beware how we approach them. Beware that you do not anger her.* **Beware** is sometimes followed directly by its object: *Beware the dog.*

be•wigged [bɪ'wɪgd] *adj.* wearing a wig.

be•wil•der [bɪ'wɪldər] *v.* confuse completely; cause doubt and uncertainty: *The little girl was bewildered by the crowds. Difficult problems in arithmetic bewilder me.* ⟨< *be-* + OE *wilder* lead astray⟩ **—be'wil•der•ment,** *n.*

☛ *Syn.* See note at PUZZLE.

be•wil•der•ing [bɪ'wɪldərɪŋ] *adj., v. —adj.* perplexing; confusing: *a bewildering assortment of sizes and colours.*
—v. ppr. of BEWILDER. **—be'wil•der•ing•ly,** *adv.*

be•witch [bɪ'wɪtʃ] *v.* **1** put under a spell; use magic on. **2** charm; delight; fascinate: *a smile that bewitches.*
—be'witch•er, *n.* **—be'witch•ment,** *n.*

be•witched [bɪ'wɪtʃt] *adj., v. —adj.* **1** under the influence of magic. **2** charmed; delighted; fascinated.
—v. pt. and pp. of BEWITCH.

be•witch•ing [bɪ'wɪtʃɪŋ] *adj., v. —adj.* fascinating; delightful; charming.
—v. ppr. of BEWITCH. **—be'witch•ing•ly,** *adv.*

be•wray [bɪ'rei] *v. Archaic.* reveal; make known. ⟨ME *bewreie(n)* < *be-* + *wreie(n)* < OE *wrēgan* accuse⟩

bey [bei] *n., pl.* **beys. 1** in the Ottoman Empire, the governor of a province. **2** a Turkish title of respect for a person of rank. **3** formerly, a native ruler of Tunis or Tunisia. ⟨< Turkish *beg*⟩

☛ *Hom.* BAY.

bey•gel ['beigəl] bagel.

be•yond [bɪ'jɒnd] *prep., adv., n. —prep.* **1** on or to the farther side of: *He lives beyond the sea.* **2** farther on than: *The school is beyond the last house on this street.* **3** later than; past: *They stayed beyond the set time.* **4** out of the reach, range, or understanding of: *The dying man was beyond help.* **5** more than; exceeding: *The price of the suit was beyond what she could pay.* **6** in addition to; besides: *I will do nothing beyond the job given me.*
—adv. **1** farther away: *Beyond were the hills.* **2** in addition: *The farmer had ten cows, and a flock of sheep beyond.*
—n.
the beyond or **the great beyond,** life after death. ⟨OE *begeondan* < *be-* at, near + *geondan* beyond⟩

bez•el ['bɛzəl] *n.* **1** a slope, or bevel, especially on the edge of a cutting tool. **2** the sloping sides or faces of a cut jewel. **3** a grooved rim or ring holding a jewel, watch crystal, etc. in place. ⟨< OF form of F *biseau*⟩

be•zique [bə'zik] *n.* a card game resembling pinochle. ⟨< F *bésigue*, origin uncertain⟩

bf. boldface (type).

B/F or **b/f.** *Bookkeeping.* brought forward (from a previous column).

B.Gen. or **BGen** BRIGADIER-GENERAL.

Bha•ga•vad Gi•ta ['bʌgəvəd 'gitə] *Hinduism.* a philosophical dialogue embodied in the *Mahabharata*, an ancient Sanskrit epic. ⟨< Skt. *Song of the Blessed One*⟩

bhak•ti ['bʌkti] *or* ['bɑkti] *n. Hinduism.* worship of only one of the gods. ⟨< Skt. *bhakti-* a share < *bhajati* (he) distributes⟩

bhang [bæŋ] *n.* **1** hemp. **2** cannabis (def. 2). ⟨< Hind. < Skt. *bhanga* hemp⟩

☛ *Hom.* BANG.

bhik•ku ['bɪku] *n. Buddhism.* a fully ordained monk. ⟨< Skt. *bhiksu*⟩

bhik•ku•ni [bɪ'kuni] *n. Buddhism.* a fully ordained nun.

bhp BRAKE HORSEPOWER.

Bhu•tan [bu'tɑn] *n.* a country between China and India in the Himalayas.

Bhu•tan•ese [,butə'niz] *n., adj. —n.* a native or inhabitant of Bhutan.
—adj. of or having to do with Bhutan or its people.

bi– *prefix.* **1** twice, as in *biannual, bimonthly.* **2** doubly, as in *bipolar, biconcave.* **3** joining or involving two, as in *bilateral, bilabial.* **4** appearance or occurrence in intervals of two; every two, as in *bimonthly, biennial.* **5** *Chemistry.* **a** in a compound, the solution that has twice as much of a chemical as the other part of the compound: *sodium bicarbonate.* **b** in an organic compound, containing two radicals of similar type: *biphenyl.* ⟨ME, < L⟩

☛ *Usage.* See note at BIMONTHLY.

Bi bismuth.

bia•ly ['bjɑli] *or* [bi'ɑli] *n.* a flat roll covered with onions, etc. ⟨< Yiddish, after *Bialy*(*stok*) in NE Poland, where it was first made⟩

bi•an•nu•al [baɪ'ænjuəl] *adj.* occurring twice a year: *Our doctor recommends a biannual visit to the dentist.*
—bi'an•nu•al•ly, *adv.*

☛ *Usage.* See note at BIMONTHLY.

bi•an•nu•late [baɪ'ænjə,lɪt] *or* [-leit] *adj. Zoology.* having two rings or bands of colour.

bi•as ['baɪəs] *n., adv., v.* **bi•assed** or **bi•ased, bi•as•sing** or **bi•as•ing.** *—n.* **1** a slanting or oblique line. Cloth is cut on the bias when it is cut diagonally across the weave. **2** (*adjl.*) slanting across the threads of cloth; oblique; diagonal: *a bias cut, cloth with a bias print.* **3** an inclination or preference that makes it difficult or impossible to judge fairly in a particular situation; a general opinion that has an unfair influence on a specific decision: *The newspaper account of the trial showed a bias in favour of the defendant.* **4** *Lawn bowling.* **a** the lopsided shape of a bowl that makes it swerve when rolled on the green. **b** the tendency of a bowl to swerve or the force that makes it do so. **5** *Statistics.* **a** the deviation of the true value of a statistic obtained in random sampling from its estimated value. **b** distortion of a statistic due to neglect of a factor or factors. **6** *Radio.* the set voltage attached to an electrode, used to control the flow of the current.
—adv. diagonally across the weave: *cloth cut bias.*
—v. **1** cause to have an inclination or preference that interferes with fair judgment; prejudice: *Several bad experiences biassed her against teenage drivers.* **2** *Radio.* attach a bias to (an electrode). ⟨< F *biais* slant < VL *biaxius* having a double axis⟩

bias ply tire a car tire with rubber ribs in a pattern of crossed diagonal lines. Compare RADIAL TIRE.

bi•assed or **bi•ased** ['baɪəst] *adj., v. —adj.* having or showing BIAS (def. 3): *a biassed judge. He was biassed where his children were concerned.*
—v. pt. and pp. of BIAS.

bi•ath•lon [baɪ'æθlɒn] *or* [baɪ'æθlən] *n.* an Olympic event or contest in which skiers with rifles race along a 20 km cross-country course, shooting at four targets spaced along the way. ⟨< *bi-* + Gk. *athlon* contest, as in *pentathlon*⟩

bi•aur•ic•u•late [ˌbaɪɔ'rɪkjəlɪt] *—adj. Zoology.* having two ears. ⟨< *bi-* + L *auricula*, dim. of *auris* ear⟩

bi•ax•i•al [baɪ'æksiəl] *adj.* having two axes: *a biaxial crystal.* **—bi'ax•i•al•ly,** *adv.*

bib [bɪb] *n., v.* **bibbed, bib•bing.** *—n.* **1** a cloth worn under the chin, especially by babies and small children to protect their clothing. **2** the part of an apron or overalls extending above the waist in front.
—v. Archaic. drink; tipple. ⟨ME < *bib* drink, ? < L *bibere*⟩
☛ *Hom.* BIBB.

bib and tucker *Informal.* clothes: *Put on your best bib and tucker, we're going out to dinner.*

bibb [bɪb] *n.* **1** bibcock. **2** a piece of wood fixed to a ship's mast to hold up the beams that support the crosstrees, etc. of the mast. ⟨< *bib* from its resemblance to a child's bib⟩
☛ *Hom.* BIB.

bib•ber ['bɪbər] *n.* a drinker: *a wine bibber.*

bibb lettuce a type of lettuce with dark green, crisp leaves. ⟨after Jack *Bibb* (1789-1884), American horticulturist⟩

bib•cock ['bɪbˌkɒk] *n.* a tap having a nozzle bent downward.

bi•be•lot ['bɪblou] *or* ['bɪbəlou]; *French,* [bi'blo] *n.* **1** a small object valued for its beauty, rarity, or interest. **2** an unusually small book. ⟨< F⟩

Bi•ble ['baɪbəl] *n.* **1** the collection of sacred writings belonging to the Christian religion and comprising the Old and New Testaments. **2** the sacred writings of Judaism, identical with the Old Testament of the Christian Bible. **3** the sacred writings of any religion. **4** a copy or version of any of these: *We have three different Bibles at home.* **5 bible,** any book accepted as an indisputable authority in a particular field: *The* Canada Year Book *is the Canadian geographer's bible.* ⟨ME < OF < Med.L < Gk. *biblia*, pl. dim. of *biblos* book⟩
☛ *Usage.* **Bible,** referring to the Christian scriptures, is capitalized: *You will find it in the Bible.* **Bible** in the sense of an authoritative book is not capitalized: *'Smith's Manual', the botanist's bible, was most useful to the medical students.*

Bible Belt an area where fundamentalist Christianity is predominant, and the clergy are influential, such as parts of Alberta and British Columbia.

bib•li•cal or **Bib•li•cal** ['bɪbləkəl] *adj.* **1** of or having to do with the Bible: *biblical literature.* **2** according to the Bible: *biblical history.* **3** in the Bible: *a biblical reference to Esther.* **4** conforming to the Bible's teachings. **—'bib•li•cal•ly** or **'Bib•li•cal•ly,** *adv.*

bib•li•cist ['bɪbləsɪst] *n.* **1** a person who believes that everything in the Bible is literally true. **2** a biblical scholar. **—'bib•li,cism,** *n.*

biblio– *combining form.* book or books: *bibliophile = a lover of books.* ⟨< Gk. *biblion* book⟩

bib•li•og•ra•pher [ˌbɪbli'ɒgrəfər] *n.* **1** a person who investigates the authorship, edition, dates, etc. of books or other publications or manuscripts. **2** someone who assembles a bibliography for a certain work or on a certain topic.

bib•li•o•graph•i•cal [ˌbɪbliə'græfəkəl] *adj.* of bibliography. Also, **bibliographic. —,bib•li•o'graph•i•cal•ly,** *adv.*

bib•li•og•ra•phy [ˌbɪbli'ɒgrəfi] *n., pl.* **-phies. 1** a list of references used by an author in a certain work. **2** a list of books, articles, etc. about a subject or person. **3** a list of books, articles, etc. by a certain author. **4** a study of the authorship, editions, dates, etc. of books, articles, etc.

bib•li•o•ma•ni•a [ˌbɪbliə'meiniə] *n.* an excessive preoccupation with collecting books.

bib•li•o•ma•ni•ac [ˌbɪbliə'meiniˌæk] *n.* a person who is excessively preoccupied with collecting books.

bib•li•op•e•gy [ˌbɪbli'ɒpədʒi] *n.* the art and craft of bookbinding. ⟨< Gk. *biblion* book + *pegia* < *pegnynai* bind, fasten⟩

bib•li•o•phage ['bɪbliəˌfeidʒ] *n.* a person who loves reading; bookworm.

bib•li•o•phile ['bɪbliəˌfaɪl] *n.* a lover of books, especially one who likes to collect books. Also, **bibliophil** [-ˌfɪl].
—,bib•li•o'phil•ic [-'fɪlɪk], *adj.*

bib•li•o•phobe ['bɪbliəˌfoub] *n.* a person who hates and fears books. **—,bib•li•o'pho•bic,** *adj.*

bib•li•o•ther•a•py [ˌbɪbliou'θɛrəpi] *n.* a form of psychological treatment involving reading books dealing with problems similar to one's own. **—,bib•li•o'ther•a•pist,** *n.*

bib•u•lous ['bɪbjələs] *adj.* **1** fond of drinking alcoholic liquor. **2** absorbent. ⟨< L *bibulus* < *bibere* drink⟩ **—'bib•u•lous•ly,** *adv.* **—'bib•u•lous•ness,** *n.*

bi•cam•er•al [bəi'kæmərəl] *adj.* **1** having or consisting of two legislative assemblies: *The Canadian Parliament is bicameral; it has both a Senate and a House of Commons.* **2** having two parts that work together: *the bicameral mind.* ⟨< *bi-* two + L *camera* chamber < Gk. *kamara*⟩

bi•cap•su•lar [bəi'kæpsjələr] *adj. Botany.* comprising two seedcases.

bi•car•bo•nate [bəi'kɑrbənɪt] *or* [bəi'kɑrbəˌneit] *n.* SODIUM BICARBONATE, especially when used in cooking as a leavening agent or in medicine as an antacid.

bicarbonate of soda SODIUM BICARBONATE.

bice [bəɪs] *n.* **1** a kind of green paint. **2** a kind of blue paint. ⟨< F *bis* dark grey < ?⟩

bi•cen•ten•ar•y [ˌbaɪsɛn'tɛnəri] *or* [ˌbaɪsɛn'tinəri] *adj., n., pl.* **-nar•ies.** *—adj.* having to do with a period of 200 years.
—n. **1** a period of 200 years. **2** a 200th anniversary. **3** its celebration.

bi•cen•ten•ni•al [ˌbaɪsɛn'tɛnjəl] *or* [ˌbaɪsɛn'tɛniəl] *adj., n.* *—adj.* **1** having to do with a period of 200 years. **2** recurring every 200 years.
—n. **1** a 200th anniversary. **2** its celebration.

bi•ceph•a•lous [bəi'sɛfələs] *adj.* having two heads. ⟨< *bi-* two + L *cephalicus* < Gk. *kephalikos* < *kephale* head⟩

bi•ceps ['baɪsɛps] *n. sing. or pl. —n., pl.* **-ceps** or **-ceps•es. 1** any muscle having two heads, or points of origin, especially the large muscle at the front of the upper arm or the large muscle at the back of the upper leg. See ARM for picture. **2** *Informal.* muscular strength, especially in the upper arm. ⟨< L *biceps* two-headed < *bi-* two + *caput* head⟩

bi•ce•to•ni•um [ˌbaɪsɪ'touniəm] *n.* a drug used to treat oral infections.

bi•chlo•ride [ˌbaɪ'klɔraɪd] *or* [bəi'klɔrɪd] *n.* **1** dichloride. **2** MERCURIC CHLORIDE; bichloride of mercury.

bi•chro•mate [bəi'kroumeit] *n.* a salt containing two atoms of chromium combined with another element or radical.

bi•cip•i•tal [bəi'sɪpətəl] *adj. Anatomy.* **1** having two heads or ends. **2** of or having to do with the biceps. ⟨< NL < L *biceps, bicipitis* < *bis* two + *caput* head⟩

bick•er ['bɪkər] *v., n. —v.* **1** express annoyance to each other over trifles; squabble; engage in a petty quarrel: *The children bickered all afternoon.* **2** move quickly with a babbling or pattering noise: *a bickering stream.* **3** of light, a flame, etc., flash or flicker.
—n. **1** a mild quarrel over a trifle or trifles: *After a short bicker, they decided on a movie they both wanted to see.* **2** a bickering sound. ⟨ME *biker(en)*⟩ **—'bick•er•er,** *n.*

bi•coast•al [bəi'koustəl] *adj.* having to do with the Atlantic and Pacific coasts of North America: *This bicoastal movie star has homes in New York and Los Angeles.*

bi•col•oured or **bi•col•ored** ['baɪˌkʌlərd] *adj.* having two colours: *bicoloured roses.*

bi•con•cave [bəi'kɒnkeiv] *or* [ˌbaɪkɒn'keiv] *adj.* concave on both sides. See CONCAVE for picture.

bi•con•cav•i•ty [ˌbaɪkɒn'kævəti] *n.* the quality or state of being biconcave.

bi•con•ic•al [bəi'kɒnəkəl] *adj.* having two points: *a biconical tent.*

bi•con•vex [bəi'kɒnvɛks] *or* [ˌbaɪkɒn'vɛks] *adj.* convex on both sides. See CONVEX for picture.

bi•con•vex•i•ty [ˌbaɪkɒn'vɛksəti] *n.* the quality or state of being biconvex.

bi•corn ['baɪkɔrn] *adj.* **1** having two horns. **2** shaped like a crescent moon. ⟨< L *bicornis* < *bi-* two + *cornu* horn⟩

bi•cron ['bəikrɒn] *n.* a unit for measuring length, equal to one billionth of a metre.

bi•cul•tur•al [bəi'kʌltʃərəl] *adj.* **1** having two distinct cultures existing side by side in the same country, province, etc. 2 *Cdn.* having to do with the coexistence of English and French cultures.

bi•cul•tur•al•ism [bəi'kʌltʃərə,lɪzəm] *n.* **1** the fact or condition of being bicultural. **2** a policy that favours a country, province, etc. being bicultural. **3** the practice or support of such a policy.

bi•cus•pid [bəi'kʌspɪd] *n., adj. —n.* a double-pointed tooth. A human adult has eight bicuspids. See TEETH for picture.
—adj. having two points. ⟨< *bi-* two + L *cuspis, -pidis* point⟩ **—bi'cus•pid•ate,** *adj.*

bicuspid valve *Anatomy.* in the heart, the valve between the left ventricle and the left atrium; mitral valve. The bicuspid valve stops blood from passing back into the atrium.

bi•cy•cle ['bəisəkəl] *n., v.* **-cled, -cling.** *—n.* a vehicle consisting of a metal frame with two wheels, set one behind the other, handles for steering, and a seat for the rider. An ordinary bicycle has pedals; a motor bicycle has an engine.
—v. **1** go by bicycle. **2** take or move on a bicycle. ⟨< F *bicycle* < *bi-* two (< L *bis*) + Gk. *kyklos* circle, wheel⟩ **—'bi•cy•cler,** *n.*

bi•cyc•lic [bəi'sɪklɪk] *adj.* **1** having two circles or cycles. **2** *Chemistry.* having molecules in two circles.

bi•cy•clist ['bəisəklɪst] *n.* a bicycle rider; cyclist.

b.i.d. of medicine, (take) twice a day. ⟨for L *bis in die*⟩

bid [bɪd] *v.* **bade** or **bid, bid•den** or **bid, bid•ding** *for defs. 1, 2, 4, 6,* **bid, bid•ding** *for defs. 3, 5; n. —v.* **1** command: *Do as I bid you.* **2** say or tell: *His friends came to bid him goodbye.* **3** offer or state (a price): *She bid $50 for the table. Several companies will bid for the contract.* **4** proclaim; declare: *He bade defiance to them all.* **5** *Card games.* state what one proposes to make or win. **6** *Archaic or dialect.* invite: *They bade us come again.*
bid fair, seem likely; have a good chance: *The plan bids fair to succeed.*
bid in, at an auction, overbid on behalf of the owner with the intention of keeping the article unsold.
bid up, at an auction, etc. raise the price of something by bidding more.
—n. **1** an offer of a specified amount, or price, as at an auction or for a contract: *Are you going to make a bid on that table?* **2** the amount of such an offer: *His bid was $140. The lowest bid for building the bridge was $800 000.* **3** an attempt to secure, achieve, etc.: *She made a bid for our sympathy.* **4** *Card games.* **a** the statement of what a player proposes to make or win. **b** the amount of the bid. **c** a player's turn to bid. **5** *Archaic.* an invitation. ⟨OE *biddan* ask; meaning influenced by OE *bēodan* offer⟩
☛ *Usage.* In the sense 'command', now somewhat archaic, **bid** in the active voice is usually followed by an infinitive without *to: You bade me forget what is unforgettable.* With the passive, *to* is used: *They were bidden to assemble.*

bid•da•ble ['bɪdəbəl] *adj.* **1** obedient; docile. **2** that is suitable to bid on in card games.

bid•den ['bɪdən] *v.* a pp. of BID.

bid•der ['bɪdər] *n.* a person who bids, especially at an auction or in a card game.

bid•ding ['bɪdɪŋ] *n., v. —n.* **1** a request or command, or an invitation. **2** the making of offers, or bids, at an auction: *The bidding was slow at first but soon became lively.* **3** *Card games.* the bids collectively.
do (someone's) **bidding,** obey: *They did his bidding without question.*
—v. ppr. of BID.

bid•dy[1] ['bɪdi] *n.* hen. ⟨< a call to poultry, *chickabiddee*⟩

bid•dy[2] ['bɪdi] *n.* a talkative old woman. ⟨Anglo-Irish *Biddy,* dim. of *Bridget*⟩

bide [baɪd] *v.* **bode** or **bid•ed, bid•ed, bid•ing.** *Archaic* (*except in* **bide one's time**). **1** dwell; abide. **2** stay or wait; tarry. **3** wait for. **4** bear; endure; suffer.
bide (one's) **time,** wait for a good chance: *If you bide your time, you will probably get a good bargain.* ⟨OE *bīdan*⟩

bi•den•tate [baɪ'dɛnteit] *adj.* having two teeth.

bi•det [bɪ'dei] *or* ['bidei] *n.* a bathroom fixture similar to a toilet but shallower and having taps, a fountain, and a drain like a sink, used for bathing the genital areas of the body. ⟨< F *bidet* a small horse⟩

bi•di•rec•tion•al [,baɪdə'rɛkʃənəl] *adj.* **1** capable of working in two directions at once, as, to send or receive signals: *a bidirectional antenna.* **2** *Computer technology.* of a computer printer, printing, or capable of printing, first from left to right and then from right to left.

Bie•der•mei•er ['bidər,maɪər] *adj.* **1** of or having to do with a kind of German furniture style of the 19th century, known for its heavy design, and similar to the Empire style. **2** bourgeois in taste and style; unimaginative and conformist, especially in intellectual and artistic matters. ⟨after Gottlieb *Biedermeier,* a fictitious German author⟩

bi•en•na•le [,biən'ɑli] *n.* an art exhibition held every other year. ⟨< Ital.⟩

bi•en•ni•al [baɪ'ɛniəl] *adj., n. —adj.* **1** of plants, lasting two years. **2** occurring every two years.
—n. **1** any plant that lives two years, usually producing flowers and seeds the second year. Carrots and onions are biennials. Compare ANNUAL, PERENNIAL. **2** an event that occurs every two years. ⟨< L *biennium* < *bi-* two + *annus* year⟩ **—bi'en•ni•al•ly,** *adv.*
☛ *Usage.* See note at BIMONTHLY.

bi•en•ni•um [baɪ'ɛniəm] *n.* a period of time lasting two years.

bier [bir] *n.* a movable stand on which a coffin or dead body is placed. ⟨OE *bēr* < *beran* bear[1]⟩
☛ *Hom.* BEER.

biff [bɪf] *n. or v. Slang.* hit; slap. ⟨probably imitative⟩

bif•fy ['bɪfi] *n. Slang. Esp. Cdn.* **1** toilet. **2** bathroom. **3** outhouse. ⟨origin uncertain⟩

bi•fid ['baɪfɪd] *adj.* divided into two parts by a cleft. ⟨< L *bifidus* < *bi-* two + *fid-* base of *findere* cleave⟩ **—'bi•fid•ly,** *adv.* **—bi'fid•i•ty,** *n.*

bi•fo•cal [bəi'foukəl] *or* ['baɪ,foukəl] *adj., n. —adj.* having two focuses. Bifocal eyeglasses have two parts: the upper part for far vison, the lower for near vision.
—n. **1 bifocals,** *pl.* eyeglasses having bifocal lenses. **2** a bifocal lens.

bi•fo•li•ate [bəi'fouli,eit] *or* [bəi'fouliət] *adj. Botany.* bearing two leaves.

bi•fo•li•o•late [bəi'fouliələt] *or* [bəi'fouliə,leit] *adj. Botany.* bearing two leaflets.

Bif•rost ['bifrɒst] *n. Norse mythology.* the rainbow bridge between Asgard and earth.

bi•fur•cate *v.* ['baɪfər,keit] *or* [,baɪ'fɜrkeit]; *adj.* ['baɪfər,keit] *or* [,baɪ'fɜrkɪt] *v.* **-cat•ed, -cat•ing;** *adj. —v.* divide into two parts or branches.
—adj. divided into two branches; forked. ⟨< Med.L *bifurcatus* < L *bifurcus* < *bi-* two + *furca* fork⟩

bi•fur•ca•tion [,baɪfər'keiʃən] *n.* **1** a splitting into two parts. **2** the place where the split occurs.

big [bɪg] *adj., adv.* **big•ger, big•gest.** *—adj.* **1** great in extent, amount, size, etc.; large: *a big room, a big book, big business.* **2** grown up: *He said he wants to be a firefighter when he's big.* **3** *Informal.* important; great: *This is big news.* **4** full or loud: *a big voice.* **5** generous: *She has a big heart and will always help you out.* **6** boastful: *big talk.* **7** *Informal.* popular: *Fax machines are very big these days.* **8** of a sibling, older: *My big sister graduated last week.* **9** overflowing with; full of (*used with* **with**): *He pranced in, big with self-importance.*
be big on, have a strong interest in or liking for: *She's big on Kantian philosophy at the moment.*
big with child, pregnant, especially in the later months.
in a big way, very much; to a great extent.
—adv. Informal. boastfully: *He talks big.*
think big, aspire to great things; think on a grandiose scale. ⟨ME⟩ **—'big•ness,** *n.*
☛ *Syn.* **1.** See note at GREAT.

big•a•mist ['bɪgəmɪst] *n.* a person who commits bigamy.

big•a•mous ['bigəməs] *adj.* **1** guilty of bigamy. **2** involving bigamy. **—'big•a•mous•ly,** *adv.*

big•a•my ['bɪgəmi] *n.* the criminal offence of marrying someone while still legally married to someone else. ⟨ME < OF *bigamie* < *bigame* < Med.L *bigamus* < *bi-* twice + Gk. *gamos* married⟩

big•ar•reau ['bɪgə,rou] *n.* a kind of sweet cherry, having firm flesh. ⟨< F < *bigarré* flecked, mottled⟩

big band a group of 15 to 20 musicians that plays jazz selections and music to dance to. **—'big-,band,** *adj.*

big bang theory the scientific theory, now generally accepted, that the universe as we know it began with an enormous explosion. Compare STEADY-STATE THEORY.

Big Ben [bɛn] **1** in London, England, a huge bell in the clock tower of the Houses of Parliament. **2** *Informal.* the clock. **3** *Informal.* the tower.

Big Ber•tha ['bɜrθə] *Informal.* **1** in World War I, a long-range gun used by the Germans to fire on Paris. **2** any powerful artillery gun. **3** anything large or of great range for its kind.

Big Brother a tyrannical dictator or government whose subjects are kept constantly under secret observation. ⟨after the dictator, who is frequently mentioned, but never appears, in George Orwell's novel *1984*, pub. 1949⟩

big cheese an important person.

big deal *Slang.* something or someone important (*often used ironically*).

Big Dipper the seven principal stars in the constellation Ursa Major, arranged in a form that suggests a dipper. The two end stars of the Big Dipper are in a line with the North Star. Compare LITTLE DIPPER.

bi•gem•i•nal [baɪ'dʒɛmənəl] *adj.* happening in pairs. **—bi'gem•i•ny,** *n.*

bi•ge•ne•ric [,baɪdʒə'nɛrɪk] *adj.* of or having to do with a cross between one genus and a different genus.

Big•foot ['bɪg,fʊt] *n.* the Sasquatch of the Coast Range.

big game **1** large animals sought by hunters. Elephants, tigers, lions, moose, and elk are big game. **2** a very important thing that is sought.

big•gie ['bɪgi] *n. Slang.* a person or thing that is very big, important, influential, etc.: *Her next film promises to be a biggie.*

big•gish ['bɪgɪʃ] *adj.* quite big.

big gun *Slang.* an important or high-ranking person: *They brought in a couple of big guns from Toronto to negotiate the deal.*

big–head ['bɪg ,hɛd] *n.* **1** any of several diseases of animals, especially sheep, characterized by swelling about the head. **2** infectious sinusitis in turkeys. **3** Also, **big head,** *Informal.* **a** a conceited attitude. **b** a conceited or arrogant person. **—'big-,head•ed,** *adj.*

big–heart•ed ['bɪg 'hɑrtɪd] *adj.* kindly; generous. **—'big-,heart•ed•ly,** *adv.*

big•horn ['bɪg,hɔrn] *n., pl.* **big•horn** or **big•horns.** a large, heavy-bodied wild mountain sheep (*Ovis canadensis*) found mainly in the Rocky Mountains, brown with a white muzzle and rump patch, having long, slender legs and huge brown horns that curl back and down from the forehead.

big house, the *Slang.* prison.

bight [bəit] *n., v.* *—n.* **1** a long curve in a coastline, mountain range, etc. **2** BAY[1]. **3** a bend; angle; corner. **4** a loop of rope; the slack of rope between the fastened ends. **5** the width of sewing-machine stitch selected for making a buttonhole.
—v. tie with a bight of cord. ⟨OE *byht*⟩
☛ *Hom.* BITE, BYTE.

big league **1** MAJOR LEAGUE. **2** Often, **big leagues,** *pl.* the group, place, etc. that is recognized as the best and has the most power and influence within its sphere: *The star of the new musical is definitely from the big leagues.* **—'big-'leagu•er,** *n.* **—'big-'league,** *adj.*

big•mouth ['bɪg,mʌuθ] *n.* someone who talks a lot, especially to spread gossip, reveal secrets, or influence opinion.

big name *Informal.* a well-known person, often in a particular community or field: *She became a big name in politics.*

big noise *Slang.* an important person; bigwig.

big•no•ni•a [bɪg'nouniə] *n.* any of a genus (*Bignonia*) of mainly tropical American woody vines of the trumpet-creeper family, having compound leaves and trumpet-shaped flowers. ⟨< NL, named after Abbé *Bignon*, librarian to Louis XIV⟩

bi•gos ['bɪgɒs] *n.* a Polish dish, a hunter's stew consisting of meat from the hunt (originally wild boar) and sweet and sour cabbage, recooked several times before serving.

big•ot ['bɪgət] *n.* a bigoted person; an intolerant, prejudiced person. ⟨< F⟩

big•ot•ed ['bɪgətɪd] *adj.* sticking to an opinion, belief, party, etc. unreasonably and without tolerating other views; intolerant. **—'big•ot•ed•ly,** *adv.*

big•ot•ry ['bɪgətri] *n., pl.* **-ries.** bigoted conduct or attitude; intolerance.

big shot *Slang. n.* an important person; BIG WHEEL. **—'big,shot,** *adj.*

big stick negotiation backed by a show of force, usually in the political arena.

big–tick•et ['bɪg 'tikət] *adj. Informal.* costing a lot: *big-ticket items such as a car.*

big time *Slang.* **1** in public affairs, the arts, sports, etc., the top level of advancement or achievement. **2** in an extreme way or to an extreme degree: *He was taken to court and lost big time.* **—'big,time,** *adj.* **—'big-'tim•er,** *n.*

big top **1** the main tent for a circus performance. **2** *Informal.* the circus as a way of life.

big tree a giant coniferous tree (*Sequoiadendron giganteum*) found in California, not generally quite so tall as the redwood, but having a thicker trunk (the trunk of one specimen has a diameter of 10 m at the base).

big wheel *Informal.* an important and influential person, as in a particular organization, etc.: *He's a big wheel in publishing.*

big•wig ['bɪg,wɪg] *n. Informal.* an important person.

bi•jou ['biʒu] *or* [bi'ʒu] *n., pl.* **-joux** [-ʒuz]. **1** a jewel. **2** something small and fine. ⟨< F⟩

bi•jou•te•rie [bɪ'ʒutəri] *or* [bi,ʒutə'ri] *n.* jewellery or jewels as a group. ⟨< F⟩

bi•ju•gate ['baɪdʒə,geit], [baɪ'dʒugɪt], *or* [baɪ'dʒugeit] *adj. Botany.* having two pairs of leaflets. Also, **bijugous** ['baɪdʒəgəs]. ⟨< *bi-* two + L *jugatus* yoked⟩

bike [bəik] *n., v.* **biked, bik•ing.** *—n.* **1** bicycle. **2** motorcycle. *—v.* go by bike. ⟨< *bicycle*⟩

bik•er ['bəikər] *n.* a motorcyclist, especially one who wears leather and belongs to a motorcycle club.

bike•way ['bəik,wei] *n.* a special path for bicycles.

bi•ki•ni [bɪ'kini] *n.* **1** a very brief, two-piece swimsuit for women and girls. **2** a pair of brief, close-fitting underpants or men's swimming trunks. ⟨< *Bikini*, an atoll in the Marshall Islands in the W Pacific Ocean, site of a series of U.S. atomic bomb tests⟩

bi•la•bi•al [baɪ'leibiəl] *adj., n.* *—adj.* **1** having two lips. **2** *Phonetics.* produced by closing or nearly closing the lips: *Bilabial consonants are* m, p, *and* b.
—n. Phonetics. a bilabial speech sound.

bi•la•bi•ate [,baɪ'leibiɪt] *or* [baɪ'leibi,eit] *adj. Botany.* having an upper and lower lip.

bi•lat•er•al [baɪ'lætərəl] *adj.* **1** having two sides. **2** on two sides: *bilateral symmetry.* **3** affecting or influencing two sides equally: *a bilateral treaty.* **—bi'lat•er•al•ly,** *adv.* **—bi'lat•er•al,ism,** *n.*

bil•ber•ry ['bɪl,bɛri] *n., pl.* **-ries. 1** any of several shrubs (genus *Vaccinium*) of the heath family, closely related to the blueberries, but having flowers that grow singly or in very small clusters. **2** the sweet, edible, bluish or blackish berry of any of these shrubs. ⟨apparently Scand.; cf. Danish *böllebær*⟩

bil•bo ['bɪlbou] *n., pl.* **-boes.** *Archaic.* **1** Usually, **bilboes,** *pl.* a long iron bar with sliding shackles and a lock, formerly used to confine the feet of prisoners. **2** a type of sword having a very fine-tempered and resilient blade. ⟨apparently short for *Bilboa*, English name for Bilbao, a Spanish town, famous for its ironworks and steel⟩

Bil•dungs•ro•man ['bɪldʊŋzrou'mɑn]; *German,* ['bɪldʊŋksʀo'man] *n.* a novel that deals with the mental and moral development of its hero or heroine. ⟨< G⟩

bile [baɪl] *n.* **1** a bitter, yellow or greenish liquid secreted by the liver and stored in the gall bladder. It is discharged into the small intestine, where it aids digestion by neutralizing acids and emulsifying fats. **2** ill humour; anger. ⟨< F < L *bilis*⟩

bile duct the tube leading between the liver and the gall bladder.

bilge [bɪldʒ] *n., v.* **bilged, bilg•ing.** *—n.* **1** the lowest part of a ship's hold; bottom of a ship's hull. **2** BILGE WATER. **3** the bulging part of a barrel. **4** *Informal.* nonsense.
—v. **1** break in the bottom of (a ship). **2** spring a leak in the bilge. **3** come to rest or settle on the bilge. **4** bulge; swell out. ⟨origin uncertain⟩

bilge water the dirty water that collects by seeping or leaking in the bottom of a ship or boat.

bil•gy ['bɪldʒi] *adj.* having the look or smell of bilge water.

bil•har•zi•a [bɪl'hɑrziə] *or* [-'hɑrtsiə] *n.* **1** a serious, debilitating disease of humans in tropical and subtropical regions caused by a parasitic flatworm, a blood fluke, which is picked up in water as a tiny larva that burrows through the skin and enters the bloodstream; schistosomiasis. **2** any of a genus (*Schistosoma*) of flatworms causing this disease; schistosome. ⟨after the 19c. parasitologist T. *Bilharz*⟩

bil•har•zi•a•sis [,bɪlhɑr'zaɪəsɪs] *or* [-hɑrt'saɪəsɪs] *n.* BILHARZIA (def. 1).

bil•i•ar•y ['bɪli,ɛri] *adj.* **1** of bile. **2** carrying bile. **3** caused by trouble with the bile; bilious.

bi•lin•e•ar [baɪ'lɪniər] *adj.* of, having to do with, or involving two lines.

bi•lin•gual [baɪ'lɪŋgwəl] *or* [baɪ'lɪŋgjuəl] *adj., n.* —*adj.* **1** able to speak two languages, especially with the fluency of a native speaker. **2** of, containing, or conducted or expressed in two languages: *a bilingual dictionary, a bilingual meeting.* **3** *Cdn.* **a** able to speak both English and French. **b** having to do with or catering to speakers of both English and French: *bilingual courts, a bilingual school.*
—*n.* a bilingual person. ⟨< L *bilinguis* speaking two languages < *bi-* two + *lingua* language⟩ **—bi'lin•gual•ly,** *adv.*

bilingual district *Cdn.* a region established under the federal Official Languages Act, in which all federal services must be provided in both English and French.

bi•lin•gual•ism [baɪ'lɪŋgwə,lɪzəm] *n.* **1** the ability to speak two languages, especially with the fluency of a native speaker. **2** *Cdn.* the ability to speak both English and French. **3** the principle that two languages should enjoy equal status in a country, province, etc. **4** *Cdn.* the policy of according equal status to English and French throughout Canada.

bi•lin•gual•ize [baɪ'lɪŋgwə,laɪz] *v.* **-ized, -iz•ing.** *Cdn.* make bilingual: *to bilingualize the public service.*
—bi,lin•gual•i'za•tion, *n.*

bil•ious ['bɪljəs] *adj.* **1** having to do with bile. **2** having or caused by some trouble with the bile or the liver: *a bilious person, a bilious attack.* **3** peevish; cross; bad-tempered. **4** as though having or connected to some ailment of the bile or liver; disgusting: *He lay on the couch, a bilious look on his face. The dress was a bilious ochre colour.* ⟨< L *biliosus* < *bilis* bile⟩
—'bil•ious•ly, *adv.* **—'bil•ious•ness,** *n.*

bi•li•ru•bin [,bɪlə'rubən] *n.* a reddish yellow pigment in bile, found also in blood and urine. An excessive amount in the blood causes jaundice. ⟨< NL⟩

bi•li•ver•din [,bɪlə'vɜrdən] *or* [,baɪlə-] *n.* a dark green pigment in bile, that changes to bilirubin in humans.

bilk [bɪlk] *v., n.* —*v.* **1** avoid payment of. **2** defraud; cheat; deceive. **3** succeed in avoiding or escaping from: *The robber bilked the constable.*
—*n.* **1** a fraud; deception. **2** a person who avoids paying his or her bills; petty swindler. ⟨origin uncertain⟩ **—'bilk•er,** *n.*

bill[1] [bɪl] *n., v.* —*n.* **1** a list or statement showing an amount of money owed or paid for work done or things supplied; an invoice or cash register receipt: *We got the bill yesterday.* **2** the amount of money shown on such a statement: *Our phone bill was high last month.* **3** a piece of paper money: *a five-dollar bill.* **4** a written or printed public notice; advertisement; poster; handbill. **5** a written or printed statement; list of items: *a bill of fare.* **6** a theatre program. **7** the entertainment in a theatre. **8** a proposed law presented to a lawmaking body for its approval. In Canada, a bill becomes an act if it receives a majority vote in Parliament. **9** BILL OF EXCHANGE. **10** a written request or complaint presented to a court.
fill the bill, *Informal.* satisfy requirements fully or exactly.
foot the bill, *Informal.* pay; accept the responsibility to settle the bill.
—*v.* **1** send a statement of charges to: *The store will bill us on the first of the month.* **2** enter or charge in a bill: *The cost of the books was billed to the school.* **3** advertise or announce through public notices or posters: *It was billed as the greatest show on earth.* **4** list on a theatrical program, poster, etc.: *She was billed as the star.* **5** book for shipping. ⟨ME *bille*, Anglo-L *billa*, alteration of Med.L *bulla* document, seal, bull[2]. See BULL[2].⟩ **—'bill•er,** *n.*

bill[2] [bɪl] *n., v.* —*n.* **1** the horny part of the jaws of a bird; beak. **2** a mouth part shaped like a bird's bill: *the bill of a turtle.*
—*v.* **1** of doves, etc., touch or rub bills.
bill and coo, kiss, caress, and talk as lovers do. ⟨OE *bile*⟩

bill[3] [bɪl] *n.* **1** a spear with a hook-shaped blade. **2** a billhook; tool for pruning or cutting. ⟨OE *bil*⟩

bil•la•bong ['bɪlə,bɒŋ] *n. Australian.* **1** a branch of a river flowing away from the main stream. **2** a backwater; stagnant pool which exists only after rain. ⟨native Australian name < *billa* river + *bung* dual⟩

bill•board ['bɪl,bɔrd] *n.* a large board, usually outdoors, on which advertisements or notices are displayed.

bill•bug ['bɪl,bʌg] *n.* a weevil of the family Curculionidae, the larvae of which eat crops such as grain.

billed [bɪld] *adj., v.* —*adj.* having a bill or beak.
—*v.* pt. and pp. of BILL.

bil•let[1] ['bɪlɪt] *n., v.* **-let•ed, -let•ing.** —*n.* **1** a written order to provide board and lodging for troops, especially in a private home. **2** a place where a person is assigned to be lodged, especially as a guest in a private home: *We will require twenty billets for the visiting team.* **3** the place where a sailor is told he or she can sleep. **4** a job; position.
—*v.* **1** provide lodging for by billet or as a guest in a private home. **2** write a billet order for. **3** have a billet; be quartered. ⟨ME *billette*, dim. of *bille* bill[1]⟩

bil•let[2] ['bɪlɪt] *n.* **1** a thick stick of wood, such as firewood. **2** a bar of iron or steel or, sometimes, other metal. ⟨< F *billette*, dim. of *bille* log, tree trunk⟩

bil•let–doux [,bɪli 'du]; *French,* [bije'du] *n., pl.* **bil•lets-doux** [,bɪli 'duz]; *French,* [bije'du]. a love letter. ⟨< F⟩

bill•fish ['bɪl,fɪʃ] *n.* any fish which has a long, narrow mouth like a beak, such as the marlin.

bill•fold ['bɪl,fould] *n.* a folding case for carrying money, papers, etc.; wallet.

bill•head ['bɪl,hɛd] *n.* **1** a sheet of paper with the name and the address of a business firm printed at the top, used in making out bills. **2** the name and address of a business firm printed at the top of such a sheet of paper.

bill•hook ['bɪl,hʊk] *n.* a tool with a hooked blade, used for pruning or cutting.

bil•liard ['bɪljərd] *adj., n.* —*adj.* of or for billiards.
—*n. Billiards.* a score made by striking one ball so that it hits the other two; carom.

Billiards

bil•liards ['bɪljərdz] *n.* a game played with two white balls and a red one on a special table. A long stick called a cue is used to hit the balls. ⟨< F *billard(s)*, dim. of *bille* log, tree trunk⟩

bill•ing ['bɪlɪŋ] *n., v.* —*n.* **1** on a playbill or similar advertisement: **a** the order in which the names of the performers, acts, etc. are listed. **b** the position in such a listing: *She received star billing.* **2** a listing of the total amount of money owed by a client or customer: *They thought the company's billings were too high.*
—*v.* ppr. of BILL.

bil•lings•gate ['bɪlɪŋz,geit] *n.* vulgar, abusive language. ⟨< *Billingsgate*, a fish market in London, England, once notorious for the abusive language used by the fish sellers⟩

bil•lion ['bɪljən] *n. or adj.* **1** in Canada and the United States, a thousand million; 1 000 000 000. **2** in the United Kingdom and Germany, a million million; 1 000 000 000 000. ⟨< F *billion* < *bi-* two (i.e., to the second power) + *(mi)llion* million⟩

bil•lion•aire ['bɪljə,nɛr] *or* [,bɪljə'nɛr] *n.* a person whose wealth adds up to at least a billion dollars, pounds, marks, francs, etc.

bil•lionth ['bɪljənθ] *adj., n.* **1** last in a series of a billion. **2** one, or being one, of a billion equal parts.

bill of attainder formerly, an act of a lawmaking body that deprived a person of property and civil rights because of a sentence of death or outlawry.

bill of exchange a written instruction to pay a certain sum of money to a specified person.

bill of fare a list of the articles of food served at a meal or of those that can be ordered; menu.

bill of goods a shipment of merchandise.
sell (someone) **a bill of goods,** *Slang.* mislead or seek to mislead.

bill of health a certificate stating whether or not there are infectious diseases on a ship or in the port which the ship is leaving. A ship is not allowed to dock unless it has a clean bill of health from the port it left last.
clean bill of health, a a bill of health showing absence of infectious diseases. **b** *Informal.* a clean record; a favourable report.

bill of lading a receipt given by a shipping or express company, etc. showing a list of goods delivered to it for transportation. *Abbrev.*: b.l. or B/L

bill of rights **1** a statement of the fundamental rights of the people of a nation. **2 Bill of Rights, a** in Canada, a statement of human rights and fundamental freedoms enacted by Parliament in 1960; since 1982 it has been largely superseded by the Canadian Charter of Rights and Freedoms. **b** in the United Kingdom, a declaration of rights and liberties, which also established the succession to the throne, enacted under William III in 1689. **c** in the United States, the first ten amendments to the Constitution.

bill of sale a written statement transferring ownership of something from the seller to the buyer.

bil•lon ['bɪlən] *n.* an alloy of gold or silver with copper or other metal, used for coins. ⟨< OF, ingot < *bille* log⟩

bil•low ['bɪlou] *n., v.* —*n.* **1** a great wave or surge of the sea. **2** any great wave: *billows of smoke.*
—*v.* **1** rise or roll, as big waves. **2** swell or bulge out, especially from the action of the wind: *skirts billowing in the wind.* **3** cause to swell or bulge out. ⟨< ON *bylgja*⟩

bil•low•y ['bɪloui] *adj.* **-low•i•er, -low•i•est. 1** rising or rolling in big waves. **2** swelling out; bulging. —**'bil•low•i•ness,** *n.*

bill•post•er ['bɪl,poustər] *n.* a person whose work is putting up advertisements or notices in public places. —**'bill,post•ing,** *n.*

bil•ly[1] ['bɪli] *n., pl.* **-lies.** a small club or stick, especially one carried by a police officer; truncheon. ⟨< *billet*[2]⟩

bil•ly[2] ['bɪli] *n., pl.* **-lies.** billycan.

bil•ly•can ['bɪli,kæn] *n.* a can or metal pot used for boiling water, especially over a campfire, or for holding hot liquids, etc. ⟨< native Australian *billa-* water + E *can*⟩

billy goat a male goat.

bi•lob•ate [baɪ'loubeit] *adj. Biology.* having two lobes; divided into two lobes. Also, **bilobed.**

bi•loc•u•lar [baɪ'lɒkjələr] *adj. Biology.* having two cells or chambers; divided into two cells or chambers. ⟨< *bi-* two + NL *loculus* < L, dim of *locus* a place⟩

bil•tong ['bɪltɒŋ] *n.* in South Africa, strips of dried lean meat of antelope, buffalo, etc. ⟨< Afrikaans *biltong* < Du. *bil* buttock + *tong* tongue⟩

bi•ma•nous [baɪ'meinəs] *adj. Zoology.* having two hands. ⟨< NL *bimanus* < L *bi-* two + *manus* hand⟩

bi•man•u•al [baɪ'mænjuəl] *adj.* using or needing two hands. —**bi'man•u•al•ly,** *adv.*

bi•mes•tri•al [baɪ'mɛstriəl] *adj.* **1** bimonthly. **2** having a duration of two months. ⟨< L *bimestris* < *bi-* two + *mensis* month⟩

bi•met•al ['baɪmɛtəl] *n.* an alloy of two different metals.

bi•me•tal•lic [,baɪmə'tælɪk] *adj.* **1** using or consisting of two metals. **2** of or based on bimetallism.

bi•met•al•lism [,baɪ'mɛtə,lɪzəm] *n.* the use of gold and silver together, at a fixed ratio, as the standard of value for the currency of a country.

bi•mo•lec•u•lar [,baɪmə'lɛkjələr] *adj.* having to do with, or formed from, two molecules.

bi•month•ly [baɪ'mʌnθli] *adj., adv., n., pl.* **-lies.** —*adj.* **1** happening once every two months: *bimonthly meetings.* **2** happening twice a month.
—*adv.* **1** once every two months: *The magazine is published bimonthly.* **2** twice a month.
—*n.* a periodical published bimonthly.
☛ *Usage.* **Bimonthly,** BIWEEKLY, and BIYEARLY originally meant 'every two months', etc. but are now often used to mean 'twice a month', etc. To avoid confusion, use *semi-monthly* or *twice a month* for one meaning and *every two months* for the other. However, BIANNUAL has only the one meaning: 'twice a year'. The word for 'every two years' is BIENNIAL.

bi•morph ['baɪmɔrf] *n.* two fused crystals used to increase voltage. ⟨< *bi-* two + Gk. *morphe* form⟩

bi•morph•em•ic [,baɪmɔr'fimɪk] *adj. Linguistics.* comprising two morphemes.

bin [bɪn] *n., v.* **binned, bin•ning.** —*n.* a box or enclosed place for holding grain, coal, etc.
—*v.* put or store in a bin. ⟨OE *binn*⟩
☛ *Hom.* BEEN [bɪn].

bi•na•ry ['baɪnəri] *adj., n., pl.* **-ries.** —*adj.* **1** having to do with, consisting of, or involving two; dual. **2** *Mathematics, Computer technology.* of, having to do with, using, or expressed in BINARY DIGITS: *Binary notation is a number system used in computers.*
—*n.* **1** something composed of two parts or things. **2** *Mathematics, Computer technology.* a number expressed in BINARY NOTATION. **3** BINARY STAR. ⟨< L *binarius* < *bini* two at a time⟩

binary compound *Chemistry.* a compound comprising two units, such as two elements or groups.

binary digit either of the digits 0 or 1, serving as the basic unit of information in a digital computing system. The two digits can be represented as the *off* and *on* states, respectively, of an electric circuit. Also called **bit.**

binary fission *Biology.* in protists, asexual reproduction by splitting into two parts.

binary notation a number system used in computers, using the BINARY DIGITS 0 and 1.

binary (number) system BINARY SCALE.

binary scale *Mathematics.* a numerical system having a base of 2 rather than 10, so that 1 in the base-10 (decimal) system is expressed as 1 in the binary system, 2 as 10, 3 as 11, 4 as 100, and so on. It is used especially in digital computers.

binary star a pair of stars that revolve around a common centre of gravity, often appearing as a single object.

bi•nate ['baɪneit] *adj. Botany.* growing in pairs; double. ⟨< NL *binatus* < L *bini* two at a time⟩ —**'bi•nate•ly,** *adv.*

bi•na•tion•al [baɪ'næʃənəl] *adv.* of or having to do with two nations.

bin•aur•al [baɪ'nɔrəl] *or* [bɪ'nɔrəl] *adj.* **1** of, for, or having to do with both ears: *a binaural stethoscope.* **2** of or having to do with two speakers, etc.; stereophonic: *binaural broadcasting.* **3** having two ears. —**bin'aur•al•ly,** *adv.*

bind [baɪnd] *v.* **bound, bind•ing;** *n.* —*v.* **1** tie together; hold together; fasten: *She bound the package with a bright ribbon.* **2** stick together. **3** hold by some force; restrain. **4** hold by a promise, love, duty, law, etc.; obligate: *in duty bound to help.* **5** put under legal obligation to serve as an apprentice: *bound out to be a carpenter.* **6** put a bandage on: *bind up a wound.* **7** put a band or wreath around. **8** put a border or edge on (a seam, etc.) to strengthen or ornament. **9** fasten (sheets of paper) into a cover; put a cover on (a book): *The pages were bound into a small book.* **10** constipate. **11** stiffen or harden: *Wait until the glue binds before using that plate again.* **12** be confining or restraining.
bind hand and foot, a tie up thoroughly. **b** restrict or constrain without choice or freedom: *The strict contract bound us hand and foot.*
bind over, *Law.* force (to appear in court or keep the peace, etc.)
—*n.* **1** anything that binds or ties. **2** *Music.* a TIE (def. 7). **3** *Informal.* a situation that is very inconvenient or restrictive: *It'll put me in a real bind if he doesn't pay me back today.* ⟨OE *bindan*⟩

bind•er ['baɪndər] *n.* **1** a person who binds, especially a bookbinder. **2** anything that ties, sticks, or holds things together. **3** a cover for holding loose sheets of paper together. **4** a machine that cuts stalks of grain and ties them in bundles.

binder twine *Cdn.* a strong, coarse string used especially for binding up grain into sheaves.

bind•er•y ['baɪndəri] *n., pl.* **-er•ies.** a place where books are bound.

bin•di ['bɪndi] *n.* a small red dot worn on the forehead by women of high caste in India. ⟨< Hind.⟩

bind•ing ['baɪndɪŋ] *n., adj., v.* —*n.* **1** the covering of a book. **2** a strip protecting or ornamenting an edge. Binding is sometimes used on the seams of garments. **3** the foot fastening on a ski. **4** a substance in a mixture that causes its elements to cohere. **5** bandage; dressing.
—*adj.* **1** that binds, fastens, or connects. **2** having force or power to hold to some agreement, pledge, etc.; obligatory: *a binding contract.*
—*v.* ppr. of BIND. —**'bind•ing•ly,** *adv.*

binding energy *Physics.* **1** the energy necessary to break a particular atomic nucleus into its smaller component particles. **2** the energy necessary to remove an electron from an atom.

bin•dle ['bındəl] *n. Slang.* a bundle of clothing, toilet articles, etc., usually tied to a stick carried by a hobo over his shoulder. ⟨? < *bundle*⟩

bin•dle•stiff ['bındəl,stıf] *n. Slang.* hobo.

bind•weed ['baınd,wid] *n.* any of various plants that twine around other plants or a support, especially any of several species (genus *Convolvulus*) in the morning-glory family, such as the **hedge bindweed** (*C. sepium*), or any of several species (genus *Polygonum*) of the buckwheat family, such as **black bindweed** (*P. convolvulus*).

bine [baın] *n.* the twisting stem of any climbing plant, such as the hop. ⟨dialect form of BIND⟩

Bing cherry a dark red, sweet and juicy cherry.

binge [bındʒ] *n., v.* **binged, binge•ing.** *—n. Slang.* **1** a heavy drinking session. **2** a bout or spree of indulgence in anything.
—v. have a binge (*used with* **on**): *to binge on doughnuts.* ⟨< dial. E *binge* to soak⟩

binge eating an eating disorder characterized by alternate bouts of eating a lot and vomiting; bulimia.

bin•go ['bıŋgou] *n., interj. —n.* **1** a game of chance in which each player has a card with randomly numbered squares, which he or she covers with markers as the numbers are drawn and called out by a caller. **2** an event at which people play bingo for prizes: *They held a bingo to raise money.*
—interj. the word called out by the winner of a game of bingo, sometimes used metaphorically. ⟨origin uncertain⟩

bin•na•cle ['bınəkəl] *n.* a box or stand that contains a ship's compass, placed near the person who is steering. ⟨alteration of *bittacle* < Sp. *bitácula* or Pg. *bitácola* < L *habitaculum* dwelling place < *habitare* dwell⟩
☛ *Hom.* BINOCLE.

bin•o•cle ['bınəkəl] *n.* a telescope or field glass for both eyes. ⟨< F < L *bini* two each + *oculus* eye⟩
☛ *Hom.* BINNACLE.

bin•ocs [bə'nɒks] *n. Slang.* binoculars.

bin•oc•u•lar [bə'nɒkjələr] *or* [baı'nɒkjələr] *adj., n. —adj.* of, having to do with, using, or for both eyes.
—n. Usually, **binoculars,** *pl.* a double telescope joined as a unit for use with both eyes: *Field glasses and opera glasses are binoculars.* ⟨< L *bini* two at a time + *oculi* eyes⟩

bi•no•mi•al [baı'noumiəl] *adj., n. —adj.* consisting of two terms.
—n. **1** *Algebra.* an expression consisting of two terms connected by a plus or minus sign. **2** *Biology.* a two-part name (genus and species) by which a plant or animal is identified according to an international system of classification. The binomial of the North American beaver is *Castor canadensis.* Also, **binominal.** ⟨< LL *binomius* having two names < *bi-* two + *nomen* name⟩
—bi'no•mi•al•ly, *adv.*

binomial coefficients *Mathematics.* the coefficients in the expansion of $(x + y)^n$. For example, $(x + y)^3 = x^3 + 3x^2y + 3xy^2 + y^3$, so the binomial coefficients are 1, 3, 3, and 1.

binomial distribution *Genetics and Mathematics.* the distribution obtained by expansion of the binomial $(p + q)^n$, where p and q are two alternative probabilities and n the number of occurrences. Family size, for example, is distributed binomially, with p and q the probability of a male or female at any birth respectively, and n the number of children in the family.

binomial nomenclature *Biology.* the system of classification in which plants or animals are given two names, the first being that of the genus and the second that of the species. *Example*: *Alkanna tinctoria.*

binomial theorem *Mathematics.* an algebraic system, invented by Sir Isaac Newton, for raising a binomial to any power. *Example*: $(a + b)^2 = a^2 + 2ab + b^2$

bi•nom•i•nal [baı'nɒmənəl] *adj., n. Biology.* See BINOMIAL.

bin•tu•rong ['bıntjʊ,rɒŋ] *or* ['bıntʊ,rɒŋ] *n.* a type of Asian civet (*Arctitis binturong*), having tufted ears and a long prehensile tail. ⟨< Malay⟩

bi•nu•cle•ate [baı'njukliıt] *or* [baı'njukli,eit], [baı'nukliıt] *or* [baı'nukli,eit] *adj.* having two nuclei.

bio ['baıou] *n. Informal.* biography, especially one in capsule form.

bio– *combining form.* **1** life; living things: *biology = the science of life.* **2** biological: *biochemistry = biological chemistry.* ⟨< Gk. *bios* life⟩

bi•o•ac•cu•mu•la•tion [,baıouə,kjumjə'leiʃən] *n. Ecology.* the process by which poisonous substances collect in living matter. Also, **biological accumulation.**

bi•o•a•cous•tics [,baıouə'kustıks] *n.* the science of sound with reference to sounds produced and received by animals.

bi•o•act•ive [,baıou'æktıv] *adj. Biology.* responsive to living matter. **—,bi•o•ac'tiv•i•ty,** *n.*

bi•o•as•say [,baıou'æsei] *n., v. Pharmacology. —n.* the technique of assessing the strength of a drug by comparing its effects on a test animal with those of a standard dosage.
—v. test (a drug) by this method.

bi•o•as•tro•nau•tics [,baıou,æstrə'nɒtıks] *n.* the science of assessing the effects of travel in outer space on animals and humans.

bi•o•ce•no•sis [,baıousə'nousıs] *n. Ecology.* an ecological system in which the needs of plants and animals are balanced. ⟨< NL < *bio-* life + Gk. *koinosis* a mingling < *koinoun* to share < *koinos* common⟩

bi•o•chem•i•cal [,baıou'kɛməkəl] *adj.* of or having to do with biochemistry. **—,bi•o'chem•i•cal•ly,** *adv.*

biochemical oxygen demand the quantity of oxygen required to break up organic material in water. Also, **biological oxygen demand.**

bi•o•chem•ist [,baıou'kɛmıst] *n.* a person trained in biochemistry, especially one whose work it is.

bi•o•chem•is•try [,baıou'kɛmıstri] *n.* the chemistry of living animals and plants; biological chemistry.

bi•o•cide ['baıə,saıd] *n.* a poison that kills living matter, especially micro-organisms.

bi•o•clean ['baıou,klin] *adj.* free from all micro-organisms; aseptic.

bi•o•cli•ma•tol•o•gy [,baıou,klaımə'tɒlədʒi] *n.* the science that studies the effects of climate on living organisms.

bi•o•de•grad•a•ble [,baıoudı'greidəbəl] *adj.* capable of being broken down, or decomposed, by a natural process such as the action of bacteria: *Plastic containers are not biodegradable.*
—,bi•o•de,grad•a'bil•i•ty, *n.*

bi•o•dyne ['baıə,daın] *n.* a substance, produced by an injured cell, that aids recovery by promoting growth, reproduction, etc. It is similar in effect to a hormone. ⟨< *bio-* + *-dyne* < Gk. *dynamis* power⟩

bi•o•en•gi•neer•ing [,baıou,ɛndʒə'nirıŋ] *n.* the science dealing with the relationship of engineering with living matter, such as in the development of prostheses, pacemakers, etc.

bi•o•eth•ics [,baıou'ɛθıks] *n.* the study of the ethical problems arising from research projects or medical procedures involving human beings or live animals, or from the application of new scientific and medical advances. **—,bi•o'eth•i•cal,** *adj.*

bi•o•feed•back [,baıou'fid,bæk] *n.* the technique of controlling normally involuntary or unconscious body processes, such as heartbeat, body temperature, or blood pressure, by making them perceptible to the senses, often with the aid of electronic devices, and then using mental concentration to manipulate them.

bi•o•fla•vo•noid [,baıou'fleivə,nɔıd] *or* [,baıou'flævə,nɔıd] *n.* a substance found in citrus and other fruits, that reduces the chance of hemorrhaging by strengthening the blood vessels' capillary walls. ⟨< *bio-* + G *flavon* < L *flavus* yellow⟩

biog. biographical; biography.

bi•o•gas ['baıou,gæs] *n.* a gas, such as methane, produced from the fermentation of animal dung and vegetable waste, especially for use as fuel.

bi•o•gen•e•sis [,baıou'dʒɛnəsıs] *n.* **1** the theory that living things can be produced only by other living things. **2** the production of living things from other living things.

bi•o•ge•net•ic [,baıoudʒə'nɛtık] *adj.* of or having to do with biogenesis. **—,bi•o•ge'net•ic•al•ly,** *adv.*

bi•o•ge•og•ra•phy [,baıoudʒi'ɒgrəfi] *n.* the branch of biology that deals with the geographical distribution of plants and animals. **—,bi•o,ge•o'graph•ic,** *adj.*

bi•og•ra•pher [baı'ɒgrəfər] *n.* a person who writes a biography.

bi•o•graph•i•cal [,baıə'græfəkəl] *adj.* **1** of a person's life: *biographical information.* **2** having to do with biography. Also, **biographic. —,bi•o'graph•i•cal•ly,** *adv.*

bi•og•ra•phy [baɪ'ɒgrəfi] *n., pl.* **-phies. 1** the written story of a person's life. **2** the part of literature that consists of biographies.

bi•o•herm ['baɪou,hɜrm] *n.* a large reeflike area under the sea. ⟨< *bio-* + Gk. *herma* a reef⟩

biol. biology; biological.

bi•o•log•i•cal [,baɪə'lɒdʒəkəl] *adj., n.* —*adj.* **1** of plant and animal life. **2** having to do with biology. Also, **biologic**.
—*n.* a drug prepared from animal tissue or some other living source. **—,bi•o'log•i•cal•ly,** *adv.*

biological accumulation bioaccumulation.

biological clock a hypothetical mechanism inherent in living things that is responsible for various periodic physiological processes or responses, especially those synchronized to the cycle of day and night. It is the human biological clock that is responsible for the feeling known as JET LAG.

biological control control of pests, such as insects, by natural means, such as predators, rather than by chemical substances.

biological magnification the accumulation of chemicals in animals high up in the food chain, through feeding on creatures lower in the food chain that each contained small amounts of the chemical.

biological oxygen demand BIOCHEMICAL OXYGEN DEMAND.

biological warfare the waging of war by using disease-producing bacteria or other micro-organisms to destroy crops, livestock, or human life.

bi•ol•o•gist [baɪ'ɒlədʒɪst] *n.* a person trained in biology, especially one whose work it is.

bi•ol•o•gy [baɪ'ɒlədʒi] *n.* **1** the science of life or living matter in all its forms and phenomena; the study of the origin, reproduction, structure, etc. of plant and animal life. **2** the plant and animal life of a particular area or region. **3** the biological facts about a particular kind of plant or animal. **4** a textbook or handbook dealing with biology.

bi•o•lu•min•es•cence [,baɪou,lumɪ'nɛsəns] *n.* the ability of certain living organisms, such as fireflies, to change chemical energy in the body into light. **—,bi•o,lu•min'es•cent,** *adj.*

bi•o•mag•net•ics [,baɪoumæg'nɛtɪks] *or* [,baɪoumәg'nɛtɪks] *n.* the science that studies the effects of magnetism on living matter.

bi•o•mass ['baɪou,mæs] *n.* **1** the total amount or mass of living organisms in a given area: *the biomass of plankton.* **2** organic waste.

bi•o•math•e•mat•ics [,baɪou,mæθə'mætɪks] *n. Biology.* the use of mathematical techniques to study living material.

bi•ome ['baɪoum] *n.* an extensive ecological community, especially one having one dominant type of vegetation: *the tundra biome.* ⟨< *bio-* + Gk. *-oma* group, mass⟩

bi•o•me•chan•ics [,baɪoumə'kænɪks] *n.* the science that deals with the effects of forces on a living organism, especially the effects of gravity.

bi•o•med•i•cal [,baɪou'mɛdəkəl] *adj.* concerning the relationship of biology with medicine: *biomedical engineering.*

bi•o•med•i•cine [,baɪou'mɛdəsɪn] *n.* the science dealing with aspects of the relationship of biology to medicine, such as the adaptation of humans to travel in outer space.

bi•o•me•te•or•ol•o•gy [,baɪou,mitiə'rɒlədʒi] *n.* the science concerning the effects of weather on people and animals.

bi•o•met•rics [,baɪə'mɛtrɪks] *n.* BIOMETRY (def. 2).

bi•om•e•try [baɪ'ɒmətri] *n.* **1** the calculation of the probable duration of human life. **2** the branch of biology that deals with living things by measurement and statistical analysis. ⟨< Gk. *bios* life + E *-metry*⟩

bi•on•ic [baɪ'ɒnɪk] *adj.* **1** of or having to do with bionics. **2** referring to an artificial body part or a device that strengthens or replaces a natural body function, especially one that operates electronically: *a bionic arm.* **3** in science fiction, designating a person, etc. having certain physiological parts or functions replaced or strengthened by electronic equipment.
—bi'on•i•cal•ly, *adv.*

bi•on•ics [baɪ'ɒnɪks] *n.* (*used with a singular verb*) the study of human and animal biological functions, especially functions of the brain, that might be applied to the development of electronic equipment, such as computers and robots. ⟨< *bio-* + (*electr*)*onics*⟩

bi•o•phys•i•cal [,baɪou'fɪzəkəl] *adj.* of or having to do with biophysics.

bi•o•phys•i•cist [,baɪou'fɪzəsɪst] *n.* a person trained in biophysics, especially one whose work it is.

bi•o•phys•ics [,baɪou'fɪzɪks] *n.* (*used with a singular verb*) the science dealing with the application of the principles of physics to biology and biological problems.

bi•o•pic ['baɪou,pɪk] *n. Informal.* a biographical film. ⟨< *bio*(*graphy*) + *pic*(*ture*)⟩

bi•op•sy ['baɪɒpsi] *n., pl.* **-sies.** the removal and examination of tissue taken from a living person or animal as an aid to medical diagnosis. A biopsy is often done to find out if cancer cells are present in a particular part of the body. Compare AUTOPSY. ⟨< *bio-* + Gk. *opsis* a viewing⟩

bi•o•rhythm ['baɪə,rɪðəm] *n.* a theoretical bodily or mental cycle of functions, from several of which it is said one can predict one's performance in various areas of life at any given time.

bi•o•so•cial [,baɪou'souʃəl] *adj.* concerning the connections between social conditions and biology.

bi•o•sphere ['baɪə,sfir] *n.* the parts of the earth and its atmosphere in which living things are found.

bi•o•strome ['baɪə,stroum] *n. Geology.* a thin stratum of limestone, containing mainly the remains of living material, such as fossils. ⟨< *bio-* + Gk. *stroma* bed⟩

bi•o•syn•the•sis [,baɪou'sɪnθəsɪs] *n.* the formation of chemical compounds in living matter. **—,bi•o•syn'thet•ic** [-sɪn'θɛtɪk], *adj.*

bi•o•ta [baɪ'outə] *n.* all the living organisms of a particular place or time. ⟨< Gk. *biote* way of life < *bios* life⟩

bi•o•tech•nol•o•gy [,baɪoutɛk'nɒlədʒi] *n.* **1** a science that relates biology with technology. **2** the use of living organisms to make industrial products, such as the use of recombinant DNA research by the pharmaceutical industry for the development of new drugs. **—,bi•o,tech•no'log•ic•al,** *adj.*
—,bi•o•tech'nol•o•gist, *n.*

bi•o•ther•a•py [,baɪou'θɛrəpi] *n.* the use of substances derived from living matter, such as vaccines, to treat or prevent disease.

bi•ot•ic [baɪ'ɒtɪk] *adj.* of or having to do with life or living things. ⟨< Gk. *biōtikos* < *bios* life⟩

biotic potential the ability of a living organism to survive and reproduce in an optimal environment.

bi•o•tin ['baɪətɪn] *n.* a colourless crystalline vitamin of the B complex that promotes growth and is found especially in yeast, liver, and egg yolk. *Formula*: $C_{10}H_{16}N_2O_3S$ ⟨< (*biot*)*ic* + *-in*⟩

bi•o•tite ['baɪə,tait] *n.* black or dark-coloured mica. ⟨after J. B. *Biot*, French mineralogist⟩

bi•o•tope ['baɪə,toup] *n. Ecology.* a part of a larger ecosystem, such as a tidal pool, with its own particular community. ⟨< *bio-* + Gk. *topos* place⟩

bi•o•type ['baɪə,taip] *n.* a set of living organisms which share genetic factors. **—,bi•o'typ•ic** [-'tɪpɪk], *adj.*

bip•a•rous ['bɪpərəs] *adj.* **1** *Zoology.* of animals, bringing forth two at a birth. **2** *Botany.* of flower clusters, having two axes or branches. ⟨< *bi-* two + L *parere* to produce + E *-ous*⟩

bi•par•ti•san [bəi'partəzən] *or* [bəi'partə,zæn] *adj.* of or representing two political parties: *Bipartisan foreign policy has the support of the two main political parties of a nation.*
—bi'par•ti•san•ship, *n.*

bi•par•tite [bəi'partəit] *adj.* **1** having or consisting of two parts. An oyster has a bipartite shell. **2** *Botany.* divided into two parts nearly to the base: *a bipartite leaf.* **3** involving two parties: *a bipartite contract.* ⟨< L *bipartitus*, pp. of *bipartire* < *bi-* two + *partire* divide⟩

bi•par•ti•tion [,baɪpar'tɪʃən] *n.* division into two parts.

bi•par•ty [bəi'parti] *adj.* combining two different political groups, religious groups, etc.

bi•ped ['baɪpɛd] *n., adj.* —*n.* an animal having two feet. Birds are bipeds.
—*adj.* having two feet. ⟨< L *bipes* < *bi-* two + *pes, pedis* foot⟩
—bi'ped•al, *adj.*

bi•ped•al•ism [bəi'pɛdə,lɪzəm] *n.* **1** two-footedness. **2** movement on two feet.

bi•per•i•den [bəi'pɛrədən] *n.* a drug used to treat Parkinson's disease.

bi•pet•al•ous [bəi'pɛtələs] *adj. Botany.* having two petals.

bi•phen•yl [baɪˈfɛnəl] *or* [-ˈfinəl] *n.* a colourless, crystalline hydrocarbon used especially as a heat-transfer agent and fungicide and in the manufacture of dyes. *Formula*: $C_6H_5C_6H_5$

bi•pin•nate [baɪˈpɪnɪt] *or* [baɪˈpɪneit] *adj. Botany.* doubly pinnate. A leaf with leaflets on each side of a stalk is pinnate; a pinnate leaf with pinnate leaflets is bipinnate. **—bi'pin•nate•ly,** *adv.*

bi•plane [ˈbaɪplein] *n.* an airplane having two sets of wings, one above the other.

bi•pod [ˈbaɪpɒd] *n.* a stand with two legs. Compare TRIPOD.

bi•po•lar [baɪˈpoulər] *adj.* **1** having two poles, or extremes. **2** of, having to do with, or occurring in both polar regions. **3** characterized by two opposing opinions. **—ˌbi•po'lar•i•ty** [ˌbaɪpəˈlærəti] *or* [-ˈlɛrəti], *n.*

bipolar affective disorder *Psychiatry.* a condition in which periods of depression and manic behaviour succeed each other, often including periods of normalcy; manic-depressive psychosis.

bi•quad•rat•ic equation [ˌbaɪkwɒˈdrætɪk] an algebraic equation of the fourth degree. Also called a **quartic**.

bi•ra•cial [baɪˈreiʃəl] *adj.* of or having to do with two races: *a biracial community.*

bi•rad•ial [baɪˈreidiəl] *adj.* having both a bilateral and a radial arrangement of parts: *biradial symmetry.*

birch [bɜrtʃ] *n., v.* *—n.* **1** any of a genus (*Betula*) of trees and shrubs found in the northern hemisphere, having light green oval or triangular leaves and usually light-coloured, smooth outer bark that in many species peels off easily in thin layers. **2** the hard, close-grained wood of a birch, often used in making furniture. **3** (*adjl.*) made of this wood: *a birch chair.* **4** a bundle of birch twigs or a birch stick, used for flogging. **5** (*adjl.*) designating a family (Betulaceae) of deciduous trees and shrubs found mainly in the northern hemisphere, having simple, serrate leaves that grow alternately along the stems, and flowers in drooping catkins. Alders, hazelnuts, and birches belong to the birch family.
—v. whip with a birch; flog. ⟨OE *bierce*⟩

birch•bark [ˈbɜrtʃˌbɑrk] *n.* **1** the bark of a birch, especially the white, or paper, birch. Birchbark was traditionally used by First Nations peoples of the eastern woodlands to make canoes. **2** (*adjl.*) made of or covered with birchbark: *a birchbark torch, a birchbark canoe.* **3** a canoe made of birchbark.

birch partridge *Cdn.* See RUFFED GROUSE.

birch•rind [ˈbɜrtʃˌraɪnd] *n. Cdn.* part of the bark of a birch tree, used to make canoes.

bird [bɜrd] *n., v.* *—n.* **1** any of a class (Aves) of warm-blooded, egg-laying vertebrates having a body covered with feathers, and forelimbs modified into wings by means of which most species can fly. All birds have keen vision. **2** a bird hunted for sport; game bird. **3** shuttlecock. **4** *Informal.* person: *He's a strange bird.* **5** *Slang.* a rude noise made by vibrating the lips. **6** *Slang.* BALLISTIC MISSILE. **7** CLAY PIGEON.
bird in the hand, something certain because one already has it.
birds of a feather, people with the same kind of ideas or interests.
eat like a bird, have a very small appetite.
for the birds, *Informal.* not worth considering; ridiculous, boring, etc.: *The movie was for the birds. I think housecleaning is for the birds.*
give (someone) **the bird,** jeer or ridicule someone, especially a performer.
have a bird, *Slang.* be in a state of frenzy; have a fit.
kill two birds with one stone, get two things done by one action.
the birds and the bees, *Informal.* the basic facts of sexual reproduction and development.
—v. engage in bird-watching. ⟨OE *bridd,* bird⟩ **—'bird,like,** *adj.* **—'bird•er,** *n.*

bird•bath [ˈbɜrdˌbæθ] *n.* a shallow basin raised off the ground and filled with water for birds to bathe in or drink from.

bird•box [ˈbɜrdˌbɒks] *n.* a kind of birdhouse.

bird•brain [ˈbɜrdˌbrein] *n. Slang.* a stupid or scatterbrained person. **—'bird,brained,** *adj.*

bird call **1** the sound that a bird makes. **2** an imitation of it. **3** an instrument for imitating the sound that a bird makes.

bird dog *n.* **1** any of several breeds of dog trained to locate game birds and to bring them back to the hunter after they have been shot. The various breeds of setter and retriever are usually trained as bird dogs. **2** *Informal.* a person whose work is seeking something for someone else, such as a talent scout or canvasser.

bird–dog [ˈbɜrd ˌdɒg] *v.,* **-dogged, -dog•ging.** *Informal.* **1** pursue or follow closely. **2** look for new talent, prospective candidates, etc.

bird•house [ˈbɜrdˌhʌus] *n.* **1** a small roofed box with one or more openings, placed on a pole, in a tree, etc., for wild birds to nest in. **2** an aviary.

bird•ie [ˈbɜrdi] *n., v.,* **bird•ied, bird•ie•ing.** *—n.* **1** *Informal.* a little bird. **2** *Golf.* a score of one stroke less than par for any hole on a golf course. **3** shuttlecock.
—v. score one less than par on (any hole).

bird•ing [ˈbɜrdɪŋ] *n.* BIRD-WATCHING. **—'bird•er,** *n.*

bird•lime [ˈbɜrdˌlaɪm] *n., v.* **-limed, -lim•ing.** *—n.* **1** a sticky substance smeared on trees to catch small birds. It is often made from the inner bark of holly or mistletoe. **2** anything that ensnares.
—v. **1** smear with birdlime; lime. **2** catch (birds) with birdlime.

bird louse a parasitic insect of the order Mallophaga, using birds as hosts.

bird•man [ˈbɜrdmən] *n., pl.* **-men.** *Informal.* **1** an aviator. **2** a person who catches or sells birds; fowler. **3** one who studies birds; ornithologist.

bird of ill omen **1** a person who is always bringing bad luck. **2** an unlucky person.

bird of paradise **1** any of about 40 species of songbird (family Paradiseidae) of New Guinea and nearby islands, the male of many species having vividly-coloured plumes which it displays in elaborate rituals during the mating season. The largest of these birds is the cinnamon-coloured **great bird of paradise** (*Paradisaea apoda*), having a yellow and emerald green head and long, pale yellow plumes rising over the back. **2** an African plant (genus *Strelitzia*) of the banana family, whose bright blue and orange flowers form a crest like that of the bird of paradise.

A bird of paradise

bird–of–par•a•dise flower any of a genus (*Strelitzia*) of tropical African plants of the banana family, especially *S. reginae*, having large, showy, orange and purple blossoms resembling an exotic bird in flight.

bird of passage **1** a bird that flies from one region to another as the seasons change. **2** *Informal.* a person who roams from place to place.

bird of peace a dove.

bird of prey any of many species of bird that kill animals and other birds for food. Eagles, hawks, and owls are birds of prey.

bird pepper a red pepper (*Capsicum frutescens*) that grows in Central and South America and bears small, hot-tasting fruits.

bird•seed [ˈbɜrdˌsid] *n.* a mixture of small seeds used to feed birds.

bird's–eye [ˈbɜrdˌzaɪ] *n.* **1** an allover woven pattern for cloth, consisting of small diamonds, each having a dot in the centre. **2** cloth of cotton, linen, or synthetic fibres woven with such a pattern. **3** any of various plants (especially of genera *Primula* and *Veronica*) having small, round, bright-coloured flowers. **4** in wood, a small spot resembling a bird's eye. **5** (*adjl.*) having markings resembling birds' eyes: *bird's-eye maple.*

bird's–eye primrose CANADIAN PRIMROSE.

bird's–eye view **1** a view from above or from a distance: *You get a bird's-eye view of the town from that hill.* **2** a general or overall view: *This summary will give you a bird's-eye view of the project.*

bird's–foot [ˈbɜrdzˌfʊt] *n., pl.* **-foots.** any of several plants whose leaves or flowers look like a bird's foot.

bird's–foot trefoil a plant (*Lotus corniculatus*) of the pea family, having bright yellow flower clusters. It is used to feed livestock.

bird's–foot violet a plant (*Viola pedata*) of the violet family, found in North America, having divided leaves and large purple flowers. It grows in E North America from Ontario south.

bird shot a small size of lead shot, used in shooting birds.

bird–watch ['bɜrd ˌwɒtʃ] *v.* observe and study wild birds in their natural surroundings. ⟨back formation < *bird watcher*⟩

bird–watch•er ['bɜrd ˌwɒtʃər] *n.* a person for whom bird-watching is a pastime.

bird–watch•ing ['bɜrd ˌwɒtʃɪŋ] *n.* the observation and study of wild birds in their natural surroundings.

bi•re•fring•ence [ˌbaɪrɪ'frɪndʒəns] *n. Physics.* the bisection of a ray of light into two rays travelling at different speeds and in different directions; double refraction. **—ˌbi•re'fring•ent,** *adj.*

bi•reme ['baɪrim] *n.* in ancient times, a ship with two rows of oars on each side, one above the other. ⟨< L *biremis* < *bi-* two + *remus* oar⟩

bi•ret•ta [bə'rɛtə] *n.* a stiff, square cap having at the top three or four thin, upright pieces radiating out from the centre to the edge. Birettas are worn by Roman Catholic priests on certain occasions. Also, **beretta.** ⟨< Ital. *berretta* < LL *birretum* cap, dim. of L *birrus* cloak⟩

birl [bɜrl] *v.* **1** rotate (a log) in the water by moving the feet while standing on it. **2** spin rapidly. **—'birl•er,** *n.* ⟨< *birr*[1], influenced by *whirl*⟩
☛ *Hom.* BURL.

birl•ing ['bɜrlɪŋ] *n., v.* —*n.* a competition for two loggers, to see who can stay longest on a log which both are birling.
—*v.* ppr. of BIRL.

birr[1] [bɜr] *n., v.* —*n. Esp. Scottish.* **1** the force of the wind or of something moving; momentum. **2** vigour. **3** a whirring sound.
—*v.* make or move with a whirring sound. ⟨< ON *byrr* favouring wind⟩
☛ *Hom.* BURR.

birr[2] [bɜr] *n., pl.* **bir•rotch** ['bɜrɒtʃ]. **1** the basic unit of money in Eritrea and Ethiopia, divided into 100 cents. See table of money in the Appendix. **2** a note worth one birr. ⟨< Amharic, silver⟩
☛ *Hom.* BURR.

birth [bɜrθ] *n., v.* —*n.* **1** a coming into life; a being born: *the birth of a child.* **2** a beginning or origin: *the birth of a nation.* **3** a bringing forth: *the birth of a plan.* **4** natural inheritance: *a musician by birth.* **5** descent; parentage: *She is of Spanish birth. He was a man of humble birth.* **6** noble family or descent: *He is a man of birth and breeding.* **7** *Archaic.* a person that is born or a thing that is produced.
give birth (to), a bear or bring forth (young, a child, etc.). **b** be the author, origin, or cause of.
—*v.* give birth (to). ⟨ME *birthe*, probably < ON *burthr*⟩
☛ *Hom.* BERTH.

birth control **1** the control of the birth rate by artificial means. **2** the use of contraceptive methods or devices. **—'birth-conˌtrol,** *adj.*

birth•day ['bɜrθˌdei] *n.* **1** the day on which a person is born. **2** the day on which something began: *July 1, 1867, was the birthday of Canada.* **3** the anniversary of the day on which a person was born, or on which something began.

birthday honours or **honors** in the United Kingdom, the titles and decorations awarded annually by the sovereign on his or her official birthday.

birthday suit a state of nakedness; one's bare skin.

birth defect an abnormality present at birth.

birthing room a room, often part of a hospital, which is set up to provide a homelike atmosphere for the act of birth.

birth•mark ['bɜrθˌmɑrk] *n.* a congenital mark on the skin.

birth mother the natural or biological mother.

birth name the surname that a woman used before her marriage; maiden name: *Mrs. Petrovich's birth name was Drury.*

birth•place ['bɜrθˌpleis] *n.* **1** the place where a person was born. **2** the place of origin.

birth rate the proportion of the number of births per year to the total population or to some other stated number.

birth•right ['bɜrθˌrɔit] *n.* **1** the rights belonging to a person by virtue of being the eldest in the family. **2** a right enjoyed by a person because he or she was born in a certain country, because of any other circumstance about his or her birth, or simply by virtue of being a human being: *"Freedom is our birthright!" she shouted.*

birth•stone ['bɜrθˌstoun] *n.* a jewel associated with a certain month of the year. It is supposed to bring good luck when worn by a person born in that month.

birth•wort ['bɜrθˌwɜrt] *n.* a vine (genus *Aristolochia*) having brown or purple flowers in the shape of an S. It was formerly supposed to be helpful in childbirth.

bis [bis] *or* [bɪs] *adv.* **1** twice; again; encore. **2** *Music.* a direction to repeat a passage. ⟨< L *bis*⟩

bis•cuit ['bɪskɪt] *n., pl.* **-cuits** or (rarely) **-cuit;** *adj.* —*n.* **1 a** a kind of bread baked in small, soft cakes, made with baking powder, soda, or yeast. **b** one of these cakes; tea biscuit or scone. **2** a cracker. **3** pottery or china that has been fired (baked) once but not yet glazed. **4** a pale brown. **5** *Brit.* a cookie.
—*adj.* pale brown. ⟨< OF *bescuit* < *bes* twice (< L *bis*) + *cuit*, pp. of *cuire* cook < L *coquere*⟩

bise [biz] *n.* a cold wind blowing from the north or northeast, common in the Swiss Alps. ⟨ME⟩

bi•sect [bɔi'sɛkt] *v.* **1** divide into two parts; halve. **2** *Mathematics.* divide (a geometric figure) into two equal parts. ⟨< *bi-* two + L *sectus*, pp. of *secare* cut⟩

bi•sec•tion [bɔi'sɛkʃən] *n.* **1** the act of bisecting. **2** the place of bisecting. **3** one of two equal parts. **—bi'sec•tion•al,** *adj.*

bi•sec•tor [bɔi'sɛktər] *n. Mathematics.* a line that bisects something.

bi•ser•rate [bɔi'sɛrɪt] *or* [bɔi'sɛreit] *adj.* **1** *Botany.* of a leaf, with serrated serrations; having two sets of serrations. **2** *Zoology.* of antennae, with indentations on either side.

bi•sex•u•al [bɔi'sɛkʃuəl] *adj., n.* —*adj.* **1** of, having to do with, or involving both sexes. **2** having male and female reproductive organs in one individual. Earthworms are bisexual. **3** sexually attracted to members of both sexes.
—*n.* a plant, animal, or person that is bisexual. **—bi'sex•u•al•ly,** *adv.*

bi•sex•u•al•ism [bɔi'sɛkʃuəˌlɪzəm] *n.* a bisexual condition or quality.

bi•sex•u•al•i•ty [bɔiˌsɛkʃu'ælətі] *n.* the quality or state of being bisexual.

bish•op ['bɪʃəp] *n.* **1** in some Christian churches, a high ranking member of the clergy who has certain spiritual duties and who administers the religious affairs of a district called a diocese or see. **2** *Chess.* one of two pieces held by a player that may be moved diagonally across any number of unoccupied spaces of one colour. **3** a hot, sweet drink of port wine flavoured with an orange stuck with cloves. ⟨OE *bisc(e)op* < VL *(e)biscopus*, var. of L *episcopus* < Gk. *episkopos* overseer < *epi-* on, over + *skopos* watcher⟩

bish•op•ric ['bɪʃəprɪk] *n.* **1** the position, office, or rank of bishop. **2** a church district under the charge of a bishop; diocese or see. ⟨OE *bisceoprīce* < *bisceop* bishop + *rīce* dominion. See BISHOP.⟩

bishop's–cap a small plant (*Mitella nuda*) growing in bogs, whose divided seedcase resembles a bishop's cap.

bis•muth ['bɪzməθ] *n.* a brittle, reddish white, metallic chemical element. Some compounds are used in medicine and in alloys. *Symbol*: Bi; *at.no.* 83; *at.mass* 208.98. ⟨< G⟩

bis•muth•ic [bɪz'mʌθɪk], [bɪz'mjuθɪk], *or* ['bɪzməθɪk] *adj.* of or containing bismuth with a valence of five.

bis•muth•ous ['bɪzməθəs] *adj.* of or containing bismuth with a valence of three.

bi•son ['baɪzən] *or* ['bɔisən] *n., pl.* **-son.** either of two species making up a genus (*Bison*) of bovine animals found in Europe and North America. The North American bison (*Bison bison*) is commonly called a buffalo; the European bison (*Bison bonasus*) is the wisent. ⟨< L < Gmc.⟩

A bison

bisque[1] [bisk] *or* [bɪsk] *n.* **1** a thick soup made from shellfish such as crayfish or lobsters, or from the meat of birds or rabbits. **2** a smooth, creamy soup made of strained tomatoes, asparagus, etc. **3** ice cream containing powdered macaroons or crushed nuts. ⟨< F⟩

bisque[2] [bɪsk] *or* [bisk] *n.* **1** biscuit (def. 3) that is purposely left unglazed, used especially in figurines, dolls, etc. **2** the bricklike colour of unglazed biscuit. ⟨shortened from *biscuit*⟩

bis•sex•tile [bɔi'sɛkstaɪl] *or* [bɔi'sɛkstəl] *adj.* containing the extra day of leap year. February is the bissextile month. ⟨< L *bissextilis (annus)* leap (year) < *bis* twice + *sextus* sixth. The Julian calendar added an extra day every fourth year after the *sixth* day before the calends of March.⟩

bis•tort ['bɪstɔrt] *n.* a plant (genus *Polygonum*) of the buckwheat family, growing in cool or upland regions, having a twisted root that yields an astringent. ⟨< MF *bistorte* < ML *bistorta* twice twisted⟩

bis•tre ['bɪstər] *n.* **1** a dark brown colouring matter made from soot. **2** a dark brown. Also, **bister.** ⟨< F *bistre*⟩

bis•tro ['bistrou] *n.* a small restaurant, wine bar, or café. ⟨< F⟩

bi•sul•cate [bəi'sʌlkeit] *adj.* **1** having two grooves. **2** *Zoology.* having cloven hoofs. ⟨< *bi-* + L *sulcatus,* pp. of *sulcare* to furrow < *sulcus* a furrow⟩

bi•sul•phate or **bi•sul•fate** [bəi'sʌlfeit] *n.* a salt of sulphuric acid in which half of the hydrogen is replaced by a metal; acid sulphate.

bi•sul•phide or **bi•sul•fide** [bəi'sʌlfaɪd] *or* [bəi'sʌlfɪd] *n.* disulphide.

bi•sym•met•ric•al [,baɪsɪ'mɛtrəkəl] *adj.* having both sides symmetrical.

bit[1] [bɪt] *n., v.* **bit•ted, bit•ting.** *—n.* **1** the part of a bridle that goes in a horse's mouth. See HARNESS for picture. **2** anything that curbs or restrains. **3** the biting or cutting part of a tool. **4** the part of a drill or similar tool that does the actual drilling or boring. A drill or BRACE AND BIT usually has several interchangeable bits. **5** the part of a key that goes into a lock and makes it turn.

take the bit in (one's) **teeth, a** of a horse, bite on the bit so that it cannot be pulled against the soft part of the mouth. **b** take control and act on one's own, especially in an irresponsible or willful manner: *The young soldier took the bit in his teeth and charged the enemy, despite the order to wait for the lieutenant's signal.*

—v. **1** put a bit in the mouth of; bridle. **2** curb; restrain. **3** make the bit on (a key). ⟨OE *bite* a bite < **bītan* bite⟩

☛ *Hom.* BITT.

bit[2] [bɪt] *n.* **1** a small piece or amount. **2** a small degree or extent: *She wasn't a bit sorry. I'm a bit tired.* **3** BIT PART. **4** *Informal.* a short time: *Stay a bit.* **5** *Informal.* a group of actions, situations, or attitudes associated with a particular role, lifestyle, etc.: *the whole do-it-yourself bit.* **6** a former Spanish coin worth 12½ cents.

bit by bit, gradually; piecemeal.

do (one's) **bit,** do (one's) share.

every bit, completely.

two bits, a quarter; 25 cents. ⟨OE *bita* < **bītan* bite⟩

☛ *Hom.* BITT.

bit[3] [bɪt] *v.* pt. and pp. of BITE.

☛ *Hom.* BITT.

bit[4] [bɪt] *n. Computer technology.* the basic unit of information in an electronic computer; BINARY DIGIT. ⟨< *b(inary) dig(it)*⟩

☛ *Hom.* BITT.

bi•tar•trate [bəi'tartreit] *n.* an acid salt of tartaric acid, containing the radical $C_4H_5O_6$.

bitch [bɪtʃ] *n., v. —n.* **1** a female dog, wolf, fox, etc. **2** *Slang.* anything that is very unpleasant or difficult. **3** *Slang.* a complaint; gripe: *He had a bitch about every single thing I did.*

—v. Slang. **1** complain; grumble: *He's always bitching about something.* **2** botch; bungle (*usually with* **up**). ⟨OE *bicce*⟩

bitch•y ['bɪtʃi] *adj. Slang.* ill-tempered or malicious. **—'bitch•i•ness,** *n.* **—'bitch•i•ly,** *adv.*

bite [bəit] *v.* **bit, bit•ten** or **bit, bit•ing;** *n. —v.* **1** seize, cut into, or cut off with the teeth: *to bite into an apple, to bite one's fingernails.* **2** wound with teeth, fangs, or a sting: *That dog won't bite. A mosquito bit me.* **3** cut or pierce, as with a sword or other sharp weapon. **4** nip; snap: *a dog biting at fleas.* **5** cause a sharp, smarting pain (to): *Her fingers were bitten by frost.* **6** take a tight hold on; grip: *The wheels bite the rails.* **7** take a bait; be caught: *The fish are biting well today.* **8** eat into: *Acid bites metal.* **9** intrigue or control, as a passion, interest, etc. (*used in the passive*): *He was bitten by the excitement of politics.*

bite back, hold back (words, temper, etc.) by biting the lips.

bite off more than (one) **can chew,** attempt more than (one) is able to accomplish.

bite the bullet, brace oneself to confront or accept something stoically (from a former practice, in battlefield surgery without anesthetic, of giving the patient a bullet to bite on).

bite the dust, *Informal.* **a** fall dead. **b** be defeated.

bite the hand that feeds one, show ingratitude.

bitten by, a addicted to. **b** cheated by.

—n. **1** a piece bitten off; bit of food; mouthful: *Have the whole apple, not just a bite.* **2** a light meal; a snack: *We usually have a bite before going to bed.* **3** the act of biting: *The dog gave a bite or two at the bone.* **4** the result of a bite, wound, sting, etc.: *Mosquito bites itch.* **5** a sharp, smarting pain: *the bite of a cold wind.* **6** a cutting or wounding quality: *the bite of his sarcasm. There was a sharp bite to her humour.* **7** a tight hold or grip: *the bite of train wheels on the rails.* **8** the action of acid in eating into a metal, etc. **9** *Informal.* an amount or part taken away: *Hotels took a big bite out of our travel budget.* **10** *Dentistry.* the way in which the upper and lower teeth meet when the mouth is closed naturally; occlusion. Braces are sometimes needed to correct a person's bite.

put the bite on, *Slang.* ask for or demand money from, as a loan or bribe. ⟨OE *bītan*⟩ **—'bit•er,** *n.*

☛ *Hom.* BIGHT, BYTE.

bite–size or **bite–sized** ['bəit ,saɪz] *or* ['bəit ,saɪzd] small enough to be taken in one mouthful: *bite-size pieces of fruit.*

bite•wing ['bəit,wɪŋ] *n.* a dental X-ray film having a projection which is held by the teeth during exposure, so as to show the crowns of the upper and lower teeth in one picture.

bit•ing ['bəitɪŋ] *adj., v. —adj.* **1** sharp; cutting: *a biting wind.* **2** sarcastic; sneering: *a biting remark.*

—v. ppr. of BITE. **—'bit•ing•ly,** *adv.*

bit part a small role in a play or film, including some spoken lines.

bits per second *Computer technology.* a measure of the speed at which data is transmitted in a computer system: *This modem operates at 9600 bits per second.*

bitt [bɪt] *n., v. —n.* a strong post on a ship's deck to which ropes, cables, etc. are fastened.

—v. put (ropes, cables, etc.) around the bitts. ⟨var. of BIT[1]⟩

☛ *Hom.* BIT.

bit•ten ['bɪtən] *v.* a pp. of BITE.

bit•ter ['bɪtər] *adj., n., adv. —adj.* **1** having a sharp, harsh, unpleasant taste: *bitter medicine. Orange rind is bitter.* **2** unpleasant to the mind or feeling; hard to admit or bear: *a bitter defeat. Failure is bitter.* **3** (*noml.*) **the bitter,** that which is bitter: *You must take the bitter with the sweet.* **4** harsh or cutting: *bitter words.* **5** causing pain; sharp; severe: *a bitter wound, a bitter fight.* **6** of weather, very cold: *a bitter wind.* **7** expressing grief, pain, misery, etc.: *a bitter cry.* **8** feeling wretched, resentful, cynical, etc.: *She is bitter about her loss.*

to the bitter end, a until the very last. **b** to death.

—n. Brit. a somewhat bitter-tasting draft beer strongly flavoured with hops.

—adv. to an extreme degree: *It was bitter cold.* ⟨OE *biter.* Related to BITE.⟩ **—'bit•ter•ly,** *adv.* **—'bit•ter•ness,** *n.*

bitter almond an almond with bitter seeds that are a source of hydrocyanic acid.

bitter apple 1 a vine (*Citrullus colocynthis*) growing in Asia and Africa, having small fruits which yield a cathartic. **2** one of these fruits. **3** the cathartic which it yields; colocynth.

bitter cassava a species of cassava (*Manihot esculenta*), having a poisonous root from which tapioca is obtained.

bitter end[1] *Informal.* the very end or last extremity, such as defeat or death.

bitter end[2] the inboard end of a ship's anchoring rope or cable.

bit•ter–end•er ['bɪtər 'ɛndər] *n.* one who refuses to give in even when all is lost; a die-hard.

bit•tern[1] ['bɪtərn] *n.* any of a small subfamily (Botaurinae) of wading birds of the same family as herons, resembling the herons, but having somewhat shorter legs and neck. Bitterns are solitary, secretive birds, seldom seen, but noted for their booming call. ⟨ME < OF *butor*⟩

bit•tern[2] ['bɪtərn] *n.* the acrid fluid remaining after salt has crystallized in brine.

bit•ter•nut ['bɪtər,nʌt] *n.* **1** an eastern American hickory tree (*Carya cordiformis*), whose nuts are bitter. **2** its nut.

bit•ter•root ['bɪtər,rut] *n.* a low-growing herb (*Lewisia rediviva*) of the purslane family found in the Rocky Mountains, having small, fleshy leaves, large, showy pink flowers, and starchy, edible roots.

bit•ters ['bɪtərz] *n.pl.* a liquid, usually alcoholic, flavoured with some bitter plant. It is sometimes used as medicine.

bit•ter•sweet ['bɪtər,swit] *n., adj. —n.* **1** a woody climbing vine (*Solanum dulcamara*) of the nightshade family, native to Europe but now common in North America, having clusters of purple flowers and poisonous leaves and poisonous scarlet berries. The bittersweet is so named because its taste is at first bitter and then sweet. **2** a North American climbing shrub (*Celastrus scandens*) having greenish white flowers, short, pointed

leaves, and orange berrylike fruits that open when ripe, showing red seeds. **3** sweetness and bitterness mixed.
—adj. being bitter and sweet at the same time; especially, being pleasant but including also suffering or regret: *bittersweet memories.*

bit•ter•weed ['bɪtər,wid] *n.* any herb which tastes bitter, such as ragweed or horseweed.

bi•tu•men [bə'tjumən], [bə'tumən], *or* ['bɪtʃəmən] *n.* **1** a heavy, almost solid form of petroleum occurring in natural deposits, as in the Athabasca tar sands. Bitumen is also often called pitch or asphalt. **2** any of various tarry substances obtained as a residue from the distillation of petroleum, coal tar, etc. ⟨< L⟩ **—bi'tum•i,noid,** *adj.*

bi•tu•mi•nize [bɪ'tjumə,naɪz] *or* [bɪ'tumə,naɪz] *v.* **-nized, -niz•ing. 1** turn into bitumen. **2** soak with bitumen.
—bi,tu•mi•ni'za•tion, *n.*

bi•tu•mi•nous [bə'tjumənəs] *or* [bə'tumənəs] *adj.* **1** containing or made with bitumen. **2** like bitumen.

bituminous coal a type of soft, black coal containing less carbon and more moisture than anthracite and burning with a smoky flame. It is the most important and most plentiful type of coal.

bi•va•lence [baɪ'veiləns] *or* ['bɪvələns] *n.* the quality or condition of being bivalent.

bi•va•lent [baɪ'veilənt] *or* ['bɪvələnt] *adj., n. —adj.* **1** *Chemistry.* having a valence of two. **2** *Chemistry.* having two valences. **3** *Biology.* of a chromosome, double; formed from two equal chromosomes fused during meiosis.
—n. Biology. such a chromosome. ⟨< *bi-* + L *valens, -entis,* ppr. of *valere* be worth⟩

bi•valve ['baɪvælv] *n., adj. —n.* any of a class (Bivalvia) of molluscs having gills for respiration and a shell consisting of two hinged sections, called valves. Clams, oysters, and mussels are bivalves.
—adj. **1** having to do with, belonging to, or designating the class Bivalvia. **2** of a seed, etc., having or consisting of two similar parts: *a bivalve seed capsule.*

biv•ou•ac ['bɪvu,æk] *n., v.* **-acked, -ack•ing.** *—n.* a temporary camp outdoors without tents or with very small tents, as made by soldiers, etc.
—v. camp outdoors in this way. ⟨< F, probably < G *Beiwacht* additional night guards⟩

bi•week•ly [baɪ'wikli] *adj., n., pl.* **-lies;** *adv. —adj.* **1** happening once every two weeks. **2** happening twice a week; semiweekly.
—n. a newspaper or magazine published biweekly.
—adv. **1** once every two weeks. **2** twice a week; semiweekly.
☛ *Usage.* See note at BIMONTHLY.

bi•year•ly [baɪ'jirli] *adj., adv. —adj.* **1** once every two years: *a biyearly magazine.* **2** *Informal.* biannual: *You can get a biyearly crop if the weather is right.*
—adv. **1** *Informal.* twice a year: *You can harvest it biyearly.* **2** appearing every two years: *The magazine comes out biyearly.*
☛ *Usage.* See note at BIMONTHLY.

biz [bɪz] *n. Slang.* business: *the magazine biz.*

bi•zarre [bə'zɑr] *adj.* odd; queer; fantastic; grotesque. ⟨< F < Sp. *bizarro* handsome, brave < Basque *bezar* beard⟩
—bi'zarre•ly, *adv.* **—bi'zarre•ness,** *n.*
☛ *Hom.* BAZAAR.

bk. **1** bank. **2** book. **3** block.

Bk berkelium.

bkg. banking.

bks. **1** books. **2** barracks.

bkt. **1** basket. **2** bracket.

bl. **1** bale. **2** barrel. **3** blue.

b.l. or **B/L** bill of lading.

blab [blæb] *v.* **blabbed, blab•bing;** *n. —v.* tell (secrets); talk too much.
—n. **1** blabbing talk; chatter. **2** a person who blabs. ⟨ME *blabbe*⟩

blab•ber ['blæbər] *v., n. —v.* chatter.
—n. one who chatters.

blab•ber•mouth ['blæbər,mʌuθ] *n. Informal.* a person who talks too much, especially one who reveals secrets.

black [blæk] *adj., n., v. —adj.* **1** of the colour of coal or soot; opposite to white: *This print is black.* **2** without any light; very dark: *The room was black as night.* **3** Also, **Black, a** of, having to do with, or being a Black: *a black Trinidadian.* **b** by, for, or about Blacks as a group: *black theatre, black studies.* **4** *Archaic.* having dark hair and eyes and, usually, dark skin. **5** covered with dirt, soot, grease, etc.: *The windows facing the highway were black.* **6** of

coffee, without cream or milk. **7** calamitous: *It was a black day for us when the stocks fell.* **8** hopeless: *a black outlook.* **9** being funny about unpleasant matters: *black humour.*
—n. **1** the colour of coal or soot; the opposite of white: *Black is the darkest colour; pure black reflects no light.* **2** black colouring matter. **3** black clothes; mourning. **4** Usually, **Black,** a member of the African race or a person having some African ancestors. **5** *Archaic.* any person with dark hair, eyes, and skin. **6** *Chess, checkers, or backgammon.* **a** the black or dark-coloured pieces. **b** the player holding these pieces. **c** the black or dark-coloured squares or other shapes on the board. **7** utter darkness: *the black of night.*
in the black, showing a profit, or at least no loss.
—v. **1** make or become black. **2** put blacking on boots, shoes, etc.
black out, a lose consciousness temporarily: *I don't know what happened after that, because I blacked out.* **b** darken completely. **c** hold back; suppress: *The government blacked out all news of the invasion. The boxing match will be blacked out in Vancouver.* **d** cause a BLACKOUT (def. 2) in: *The storm has blacked out some parts of the city.* ⟨OE *blæc*⟩ **—'black•er,** *n.* **—'black•ly,** *adv.* **—'black•ness,** *n.*

black alder an eastern American tree (*Ilex verticillata*) of the holly family, having red berries, and leaves that turn black before falling.

black–and–blue ['blæk ənd 'blu] *adj.* severely bruised.

Black and Tan a member of the constabulary force sent to Ireland in 1919-1921 by the British government to put down the rebellion there, so called because members of the force wore a black and tan uniform.

black and white *n., adj. —n.* **1** print or writing: *I asked him to put his promise down in black and white.* **2** a drawing, photograph, film, etc. in black, white, and shades of grey rather than in colour.
—adj. **black-and-white 1** designating such a drawing, photograph, etc.: *a black-and-white studio portrait.* **2** *before a noun.* recorded in print: *a black-and-white statement.* **3** with black parts and white parts: *a black-and-white sweater. The lost cat is black and white.* **4** having or showing a tendency to think, respond, etc. in terms of extremes, especially to view things as either all good or all evil: *Her whole world view is black and white. The book advocates a black-and-white morality.*

Black Angus a breed of cattle; ABERDEEN ANGUS.

black art BLACK MAGIC.

black•ball ['blæk,bɒl] *v., n. —v.* **1** vote against. **2** ostracize.
—n. a vote against a person or thing. ⟨from the practice of voting against a candidate by placing a black ball in the ballot box⟩
—'black,ball•er, *n.*

black bass BASS[2] (def. 2).

black bear **1** a North American bear (*Ursus americanus;* formerly *Euarctos americanus*) found in forest regions and swamp areas from Mexico north to the edge of the tundra, about 170 cm long, able to swim and climb well, often climbing trees to eat young buds and fruit and to protect itself against attack. Most black bears are black except for a tan muzzle and a white V on the chest, but much lighter colours occur; cinnamon-coloured black bears are common in western Canada. **2** a bear (*Selenarctos thibetanus*) found in the tropical forests of central and E Asia, having a black coat with a white V on the chest.

black belt **1** the highest major level of skill recognized in judo or karate, symbolized by a black belt or sash. **2** the belt awarded for achieving this level. **3** a person who has achieved this level of skill.

black•ber•ry ['blæk,bɛri] *n., pl.* **-ries;** *v.* **-ried, -ry•ing.** *—n.* **1** the small, black or dark purple, edible fruit of various bushes and vines (genus *Rubus*) of the rose family. **2** a bush or vine that produces blackberries.
—v. gather blackberries.

blackberry lily a plant (*Belamcanda chinensis*) of the iris family, having orange flowers and black seeds that grow in clusters like blackberries. It is grown for ornament.

black bindweed BUCKWHEAT (def. 4).

black•bird ['blæk,bɜrd] *n.* **1** any of several mainly black species of songbird (family Icteridae) ranging in size from about 18 to 33 cm long. Among the species of blackbird found in Canada are the red-winged blackbird, the rusty blackbird, and the common grackle. **2** a European bird (*Turdus merula*) of the thrush family, the male having black feathers and an orange bill, and the female having dusky brown feathers and a dark bill. The blackbird is one of the commonest birds of the British Isles. Its song is beautiful.

black blizzard *Cdn.* on the Prairies, a dust storm.

black•board ['blæk,bɔrd] *n.* a black chalkboard.

black body a theoretical surface or body that can absorb all the radiation that falls on it.

black book **1** a book containing the names of people to be criticized or punished. **2** *Informal.* a man's book of women's names for dates.
be in someone's black book(s), be regarded with disfavour by someone.

black box **1** any self-contained electronic or automatic device for recording data, controlling a mechanical process, etc. One type is used to record all events in the flight of a plane. **2** anything capable of sophisticated behaviour but whose internal mechanisms cannot be observed or understood, as certain processes of the human mind.

black bread heavy, coarse, dark rye bread.

black•buck ['blæk,bʌk] *n.* an antelope (*Antilope cervicapra*) of India, having long horns, a dark back, and a white belly.

black•cap ['blæk,kæp] *n.* **1** a BLACK RASPBERRY. **2** a bird whose head has a black top, such as the chickadee.

black•cock ['blæk,kɒk] *n.* the male of the BLACK GROUSE.

black•cod ['blæk,kɒd] *n. Cdn.* a large, dark grey or black fish (*Anoplopoma fimbria*) of the N Pacific coasts, having a slender, streamlined body with two dorsal fins, one behind the other. The blackcod is an important commercial food fish. Also called **sablefish.**

black comedy humorous material satirizing morbid themes.

black•damp ['blæk,dæmp] *n.* suffocating air containing large amounts of carbon dioxide and nitrogen, as found in some mines.

Black Death a violent outbreak of the bubonic plague that spread through Asia and Europe in the 14th century, peaking in 1348.

black diamond **1** an opaque, dark type of diamond found chiefly in Brazil. **2 black diamonds,** *pl.* coal.

black•en ['blækən] *v.* **-ened, -en•ing. 1** make or become black or very dark. **2** damage the reputation or good name of; defame. **—'black•en•er,** *n.*

Black English a variety of English spoken by black people, especially in the U.S., varying from the standard form in its sound system, vocabulary, and syntax.

black eye **1** a bruise around an eye. **2** *Informal.* **a** a severe blow: *The insult gave his pride a black eye.* **b** a cause of disgrace, discredit, or disfigurement: *The substandard housing in that section is a black eye to the whole community.*

black–eyed Su•san ['blæk ,aɪd 'suzən] either of two North American wildflowers (*Rudbeckia hirta* and *R. serotina*) of the composite family having flower heads with bright golden yellow ray flowers and a round-topped cluster of dark brown or purplish disk flowers.

black•face ['blæk,feis] *n.* **1** an actor made up as a caricature of a Black, especially for a minstrel show. **2** the make-up for such a role. **3** *Printing.* a heavy style of type; boldface.

Black•feet ['blæk,fit] *n.pl.* BLACKFOOT CONFEDERACY.

black•fin ['blæk,fɪn] *n.* **1** a West Indian fish (*Lutjanus buccanella*) related to the snappers. **2** a North American fish (*Coregonus nigripinnis*) related to the ciscos.

black•fish ['blæk,fɪʃ] *n.* **1** any of various dark-coloured fishes, such as the sea bass, tautog, etc. **2** a small freshwater fish (*Dallia pectoralis*) of Alaska and Siberia having broad, fanlike pectoral fins and a slightly projecting lower jaw. **3** PILOT WHALE.

black flag JOLLY ROGER.

black fly ['blæk ,flaɪ] *n., pl.* **-flies.** any of many species of small, mostly black or grey fly (family Simuliidae), found throughout the world and having mouth parts adapted for sucking blood. The bite of a black fly can be very painful.

Black•foot ['blæk,fʊt] *n., pl.* **-foot. 1** a member of a people of the First Nations of the Plains, one of the three Algonquian peoples forming the Blackfoot confederacy. **2** a member of this confederacy. **3** the Algonquian language spoken by the peoples of the Blackfoot confederacy. ⟨a translation of the name *Siksika*, believed to refer to their moccasins⟩

Blackfoot confederacy a confederacy of three Algonquian peoples of the Plains, the Blackfoot, Blood, and Piegan.

black–foot•ed ferret ['blæk ,fʊtəd] a mink-sized mammal (*Mustela nigripes*) of the weasel family formerly found throughout the North American grasslands from Texas to the southern Canadian Prairies, having a creamy-white coat with black feet, tail, and face mask. This animal is now extinct in Canada and very rare in the remainder of its range.

Black Forest cake a rich chocolate cake, layered with cherries and whipped cream.

Black Forest ham a fine, lean type of ham which is cured by a special method.

Black Friar a Dominican friar.

Black Friday any Friday on which some calamity happens. ⟨< Friday, September 24th, 1869, when the U.S. began a financial depression⟩

black frost weather cold enough to turn vegetation black, without hoarfrost.

black gold *Informal.* oil.

black grouse **1** a large N European grouse (*Lyrurus tetrix*), the male of which has bluish black plumage and a lyre-shaped tail; the female has mottled brown and black plumage. **2** a similar, related W Asian species (*Lyrurus mlokosiewiczi*).

black•guard ['blægɑrd] *or* ['blægərd] *n., v.* *—n.* scoundrel.
—v. **1** abuse with vile language. **2** behave like a blackguard. ⟨< *black* + *guard*⟩ **—'black•guard•ly,** *adj., adv.*

Black Hand any of various secret societies dedicated to violence and terrorism, such as a Sicilian organization, formed in the late 19th century, that operated in the United States in the early 20th century.

black haw a shrub of the honeysuckle family, with blue berries.

black•head ['blæk,hɛd] *n.* **1** a small, black-tipped lump of dead cells and oil plugging a pore of the skin. **2** any of various birds that have a black head. **3** an infectious, often fatal intestinal disease that attacks turkeys and chickens, turning their combs black.

black•heart ['blæk,hɑrt] *n.* **1** a variety of dark-skinned cherry. **2** a plant disease, especially of potatoes, in which the internal tissues turn black.

black hole[1] a hypothetical entity, a region in space, produced by the collapse of a star, resulting in such a strong gravitational field that anything caught in this field, including light, can never escape.

black hole[2] a cell or dungeon; a place of punishment. ⟨< the *Black Hole of Calcutta*, a small cell in which many British prisoners were supposedly confined in 1756⟩

black humour BLACK COMEDY.

black ice *Cdn.* **1** thin ice on water, appearing black because of its transparency. **2** similar thin ice on the surface of a road, which makes driving conditions dangerous.

black•ing ['blækɪŋ] *n., v.* *—n.* a black polish used on shoes, stoves, etc.
—v. ppr. of BLACK.

black•ish ['blækɪʃ] *adj.* somewhat black.

black•jack ['blæk,dʒæk] *n., v.* *—n.* **1** a club with a flexible handle, used as a weapon. **2** a large drinking cup or jug, formerly made of leather. **3** the black flag of a pirate. **4** a small oak tree (*Quercus marilandica*) of the S and SE United States having black bark. **5 a** a card game in which the players try to get a count of twenty-one. **b** a count of twenty-one with only two cards, namely an ace and a ten or any face card. **6** a dark kind of zinc ore in the form of zinc sulphide. *Formula*: ZnS
—v. **1** hit (a person) with a blackjack. **2** coerce.

black lead graphite.

black•leg ['blæk,lɛg] *n.* **1** *Informal.* swindler. **2** *Brit.* a worker who refuses to strike with his or her fellows. Compare SCAB. **3** an infectious, usually fatal disease of cattle and sheep. **4** a disease of various root vegetables.

black letter *Printing.* Gothic (a typeface).

black light invisible ultraviolet or infrared radiation.

black list a list of names of persons who are believed to deserve punishment, blame, suspicion, etc. Also, **blacklist.**

black•list ['blæk,lɪst] *v.* put on a BLACK LIST.

black lung a disease common among coal miners, caused by long-term breathing of coal dust which settles in the lungs and hardens them; anthracosis.

black magic evil magic. Compare WHITE MAGIC.

black•mail ['blæk,meil] *n., v.* —*n.* **1** the extortion of money, etc. by threats, especially threats of disgracing a person by revealing his or her unsavoury secrets. **2** manipulation or coercion of a person by unfair pressure, moral intimidation, etc: *It is emotional blackmail to say, "If you love me, let me move in with you."* **3** the money or other advantage obtained in this way. —*v.* get or try to get blackmail from. ⟨< *black* + *mail* rent, tribute, coin < OF *maille* < *mail, medaille* coin, medal⟩
—'black,mail•er, *n.*

Black Ma•ri•a [mə'raiə] **1** *Slang.* a police patrol wagon or prison van. **2** hearse.

black mark a mark of criticism or punishment.

black market **1** the selling of goods at illegal prices or in illegal quantities or the selling of smuggled goods. **2** a place where such trade is carried on. **—'black-,mark•et,** *v.*

black mar•ke•teer [,markə'tir] one who deals on the black market.

Black Mass **1** a Mass for the dead at which black vestments are worn by the priest. **2** a ceremony in which the Mass of Christian worship is caricatured by followers of the devil or Satan.

black measles a severe form of measles.

black medic NONESUCH (def. 2).

Black Muslim a member of a branch of Islam among black people in the U.S.

black nightshade a poisonous nightshade (*Solanum nigrum*) native to Europe, but now a common weed throughout eastern North America, having dark green leaves, white flowers, and black berries.

black oak an oak tree (*Quercus velutina*) of eastern North America having dark grey or black bark rich in tannin.

black•out ['blæk,ʌut] *n.* **1** a turning out or concealing of all the lights of a city, district, etc. as a protection against an air raid. **2** a power failure. **3** a temporary loss of vision, memory, or consciousness due to lack of circulation of blood in the brain. It may occur as a result of extreme exertion, rapid changes of velocity or direction, as in an aircraft, etc. **4** a temporary failure of memory. **5** a turning off of all the lights on the stage of a theatre to suggest the passing of time, or to mark the end of a scene. **6** a failure in radio reception. **7** the holding back of news or other information by censorship: *News blackouts are common in wartime.* **8** suppression of television coverage of a sports event in the area where it is taking place, in order to avoid a reduction in attendance.

black pepper a hot-tasting seasoning made from the ground dried berries of the pepper vine (*Piper nigrum*). Compare WHITE PEPPER.

black•poll ['blæk,poul] *n.* a bird (*Dendroica striata*), native to North America, of the warbler family. The top of the head is black in the male in the spring but olive green in the fall; the female is greenish grey in the spring and olive green in the fall.

Black Power a movement among Blacks, especially in the United States, to obtain social equality by consolidating their political and economic resources, in order to bargain from a position of power, rather than by seeking integration into white society. Also, **black power.**

black raspberry **1** a species of raspberry bush (*Rubus occidentalis*) of the rose family, bearing aggregate purple-black fruit. **2** the fruit of this bush.

Black Rod **1** in Canada, the chief usher of the Senate. **2** the chief usher in the British House of Lords, whose symbol of authority is a black rod. **3** the chief usher in various other legislatures of the British Commonwealth.

black rot any of several diseases of cultivated plants caused by various bacteria or fungi and producing dark brown discoloration and decay.

black sheep a person who has not lived up to the expectations of his or her family or group and is considered a disgrace to it.

Black•shirt ['blæk,ʃɜrt] **1** formerly, a member of the Italian Fascists, who wore a black shirt as part of their uniform. **2** a member of any similar fascist organization. Compare BROWN SHIRT.

black•smith ['blæk,smiθ] *n.* a person who makes and repairs things of iron, such as tools or horseshoes, using a forge. ⟨with ref. to black metals, e.g., iron⟩

black•snake ['blæk,sneik] *n.* **1** a harmless, swift-moving snake (*Coluber constrictor*) of southeastern Canada and the eastern United States, belonging to the same family as the garter snake, having a glossy black back and bluish grey belly, and usually about 120 cm long. Blacksnakes eat insects, frogs, mice, and other snakes and will climb trees to get birds' eggs and young birds. **2** any of various other black or nearly black snakes, such as the poisonous Australian blacksnake (*Pseudechis porphyriacus*). **3** a heavy whip made of braided leather.

black spruce **1** a spruce (*Picea mariana*) found in moist climates throughout northern Canada up to the edge of the tundra, having small, egg-shaped cones and short, dark, bluish green needles. The black spruce is the commonest tree of the northern forest. **2** its soft, moderately light wood.

black•strap molasses ['blæk,stræp] a thick, dark molasses from the final process of making cane sugar, having less sugar than other molasses.

black•tailed deer ['blæk,teild] *Cdn.* a deer (*Odocoileus hemionus columbianus*) related to the mule deer and found in NW North America. Its tail is black on top. Also called **blacktail.**

black tea tea leaves that have been allowed to wither and ferment in the air for some time before being dried in ovens.

black•thorn ['blæk,θɔrn] *n.* **1** a thorny European shrub (*Prunus spinosa*), a species of plum having white flowers that appear before the leaves and bearing very small, bluish black fruits usually called sloes. **2** a walking stick or club made from the stem of this shrub.

black tie **1** a black tie, especially a black bow tie, for wear with a dinner jacket or tuxedo. **2** a dinner jacket or tuxedo, as opposed to full evening dress, or tails: *The men will wear black tie for the dinner.* Compare WHITE TIE.

black•top ['blæk,tɒp] *n., v.* **-topped, -top•ping.** —*n.* **1** asphalt mixed with crushed rock, used as a pavement for highways, roads, runways, etc. **2** any surface so paved, such as a highway, driveway, etc.
—*v.* pave or surface with blacktop.

black walnut **1** a medium-sized North American walnut tree (*Juglans nigra*). **2** the heavy, hard, strong brown wood of this tree, highly valued for making furniture, interior panelling, etc. **3** the oily, round, edible nut of this tree.

black•wa•ter fever ['blæk,wɒtər] a fever accompanying malaria, in which the patient's heart beats rapidly and his or her urine is dark.

black widow any of a genus (*Latrodectus*) of poisonous black spiders found in many warm regions of the world, especially *L. mactans*, which is found in the S United States, as well as many other regions, having a red hourglass-shaped spot on the underside of its abdomen. ⟨named for its colour and the fact that the female often eats the male after mating⟩

black•work ['blæk,wɜrk] *n.* iron wrought or forged by blacksmiths, not brightened by burnishing, filing, etc.

blad•der ['blædər] *n.* **1** a soft, thin bag of membrane in the body of an animal, which holds urine received from the kidneys until it is discharged. **2** any similar bag that stores or holds liquid or air in an animal body: *the swim bladder of a fish.* **3** a strong bag, often made of rubber, that will hold liquids or air: *The rubber bag inside a football is a bladder.* **4** a hollow, air-filled bag in plants, as in certain seaweeds, or surrounding some fruits. ⟨OE *blædre*⟩

bladder campion a plant (*Silene cucubalus*) related to the pinks, whose sepals are filled with air.

blad•der•wort ['blædər,wɜrt] *n.* **1** any of a genus (*Utricularia*) of mainly small, rootless plants found throughout the world, but especially in tropical regions, having many small bladders or bags on their leaves in which they trap insect larvae, small crustaceans, etc. Most bladderworts are water or bog plants. **2** (*adjl.*) designating a family (Lentibulariaceae) of carnivorous plants including the bladderworts, butterworts, etc.

blade [bleid] *n.* **1** the cutting part of anything like a knife or sword. See SWORD for picture. **2** sword. **3** swordsman. **4** a smart or dashing fellow. **5** a leaf of grass. **6** *Botany.* the flat, wide part of a leaf as distinguished from the stalk. **7** a flat, wide part of anything: *the blade of an oar or paddle, the shoulder blade.* **8** the metal part underneath a skate, which makes contact with the ice. **9** a cut of meat. See VEAL for picture. **10** *Phonetics.* the upper part of the tongue, just behind the tip. ⟨OE *blæd*⟩
—'blade,like, *adj.*

blad•ed ['bleidid] *adj.* having a blade or blades.

blah [blɑ] *n., adj. —n. Slang.* **1** silly or boring talk or chatter. **2 the blahs,** *pl.* a feeling of apathy, boredom, and vague but general dissatisfaction: *the February blahs.*
—adj. uninteresting and mediocre; insipid: *a blah speech.* ⟨imitative⟩

blain [blein] *n.* an inflamed swelling or sore; blister; pustule. ⟨OE *blegen*⟩

blam•a•ble ['bleiməbəl] *adj.* deserving blame. Also, **blameable. —'blam•a•bly,** *adv.*

blame [bleim] *v.* **blamed, blam•ing;** *n. —v.* **1** hold responsible (*for* something bad or wrong): *We blamed the fog for our accident.* **2** find fault with: *The teacher will not blame us if we do our best.*
be to blame, deserve blame: *Who is to blame for this?*
blame on, attribute (some unfortunate fact or event) to: *The accident was blamed on the icy road.*
—n. **1** the responsibility for something bad or wrong: *Lack of care deserves the blame for many mistakes.* **2** finding fault; reproof. ⟨ME < OF *blasmer* < L *blasphemare* < Gk. *blasphēmeein,* ult. < *blas-* false, slanderous + *phēmē* word. Doublet of BLASPHEME.⟩ **—'blam•er,** *n.*

☛ *Syn.* **2. Blame,** CENSURE, REPROACH = find fault with. **Blame,** the least formal word, means find fault with a person for doing something that is wrong or that the person passing judgment thinks is wrong: *We blame people for doing what they know is wrong.* **Censure** adds to *blame* the idea of expressing disapproval, often publicly: *People often censure the government.* **Reproach** adds to *censure* the idea of expressing one's personal feelings of displeasure or resentment, sometimes unjustly: *She reproached him for being late.*

blamed [bleimd] *adj., v. —adj. Informal.* darned; confounded: *Now where did I put the blamed thing?*
—v. pt. and pp. of BLAME.

blame•less ['bleimlɪs] *adj.* not deserving blame: *a blameless act.* **—'blame•less•ly,** *adv.* **—'blame•less•ness,** *n.*
☛ *Syn.* See note at INNOCENT.

blame•wor•thy ['bleim,wɜrði] *adj.* deserving blame. **—'blame,worth•i•ly,** *adv.* **—'blame,worth•i•ness,** *n.*

blanch [blæntʃ] *v.* **1** turn white; become pale: *to blanch with fear.* **2** loosen the skins of (raw vegetables, nuts, etc.) by plunging them first in boiling water and then in cold water. **3** keep (growing celery, etc.) from becoming green by covering with earth, etc. so as to exclude sunlight. **4** boil (vegetables, meat, etc.) briefly to prepare for freezing, remove a bitter taste, etc. **5** make white; bleach. ⟨ME < OF *blanchir* < *blanc* white⟩

blanc•mange [blə'mɑ̃ʒ] *n. French.* a jellylike dessert made with milk, sugar, etc. thickened with cornstarch or gelatin. ⟨ME < OF *blancmanger* white food⟩

bland [blænd] *adj.* **1** smooth; mild; gentle; soothing: *a bland spring breeze, a bland diet.* **2** agreeable; polite, especially in an ingratiating manner. **3** lacking a distinctive character; uninteresting; dull: *a bland election campaign. His poems are very bland.* ⟨< L *blandus* soft⟩ **—'bland•ly,** *adv.* **—'bland•ness,** *n.*

blan•dish ['blændɪʃ] *v.* coax by flattering. ⟨ME < OF *blandiss-,* a stem of *blandir* < L *blandiri* flatter⟩ **—'blan•dish•er,** *n.*

blan•dish•ment ['blændɪʃmənt] *n.* **1** the act of blandishing. **2** Usually, **blandishments,** *pl.* flattering remarks, etc. meant to persuade.

blank [blæŋk] *adj., n., v. —adj.* **1** not written or printed on: *blank paper.* **2** with spaces to be filled in: *a blank form.* **3** having or showing no idea or understanding: *Her only answer was a blank stare. Her mind suddenly went blank in the middle of the exam.* **4** utter; absolute: *a blank refusal. He looked at her in blank dismay.* **5** incomplete or lacking some usual feature. A blank cartridge contains powder but no bullet. **6** unmarked; having no ornamentation.
—n. **1** a space left empty or to be filled in: *Leave a blank after each word.* **2** a paper with spaces to be filled in: *an application blank.* **3** an empty or vacant place or space: *Her mind was a complete blank for several hours after the accident.* **4** a lottery ticket that does not win anything. **5** a partly formed piece ready to be stamped, filed, forged, etc. into a finished object: *a key blank.* **6** a mark, usually a long dash, indicating an omitted word, especially an oath or vulgarism. **7** BLANK CARTRIDGE. **8** the white spot in the centre of a target.
draw a blank, end an attempt without success; be unsuccessful: *He tried to get support for his nomination, but he drew a blank with us.*
—v. **1** become confused or distracted (*used with* **out**): *Just when I wanted to introduce them, I blanked out and couldn't remember their names.* **2** keep (an opponent) from scoring in a game. **3** cancel; erase (*used with* **out**). **4** imprint with a die. ⟨< F *blanc* white, shining < Gmc.⟩ **—'blank•ly,** *adv.* **—'blank•ness,** *n.*

blank cartridge a cartridge with no bullet or shot.

blank cheque 1 a cheque form that has not been filled out. **2** a signed cheque that allows the bearer to fill in the amount. **3** *Informal.* freedom or permission to do as one pleases; carte blanche.

blan•ket ['blæŋkɪt] *n., v. —n.* **1** a soft, heavy covering woven from wool, cotton, or other material, used to keep people or animals warm. **2** anything like a blanket: *A blanket of snow covered the ground.* **3** (*adjl.*) covering all instances, members of a group or class, etc.: *a blanket insurance policy, a blanket wage increase.*
—v. **1** cover with a blanket: *Snow blanketed the ground.* **2** cover; hinder; obscure: *Fog blanketed the city.* **3** stifle or suppress: *They have blanketed all debate on the issue.* **4** intercept the wind from the sails of (another boat), as in a race, by passing on the side from which the wind is blowing. ⟨ME < OF *blankete* < *blanc* white < Gmc. Related to BLANK.⟩

blanket endorsement wholesale approval of a SLATE (def. 4), etc.

blan•ket•flow•er ['blæŋkɪt,flaʊər] *n.* a perennial plant (*Gaillardia aristata*), having yellow flowers.

blanket stitch a needlework stitch resembling BUTTONHOLE STITCH, but with the stitches spaced about half a centimetre. This stitch is used for edging thick fabric such as blankets.

blank verse unrhymed poetry having a metre based on five iambic feet in each line: *Shakespeare's plays are written mainly in blank verse.*

blan•quette [blɑŋ'kɛt]; *French,* [blɑ̃'kɛt] *n.* a dish of chicken or veal in a creamy sauce with onions and mushrooms.

blare [blɛr] *v.* **blared, blar•ing;** *n. —v.* **1** make a loud, harsh sound: *The trumpets blared, announcing the queen's arrival.* **2** utter harshly or loudly.
—n. **1** a loud, harsh sound: *The blare of the horn was startling.* **2** brilliance of colour; glare. ⟨ME < MDu. *blaren*⟩

blar•ney ['blɑrni] *n., v.* **-neyed, -ney•ing.** *—n.* flattering, coaxing talk.
—v. flatter; coax.
kiss the Blarney Stone, get skill in flattering and coaxing people. ⟨< the *Blarney Stone,* a stone in a wall of Blarney Castle near Cork, Ireland, said to give skill in flattery to anyone who kisses it⟩

bla•sé [blɑ'zei] *or* ['blɑzei] *adj.* **1** tired of pleasures; bored; world-weary. **2** unconcerned about something due to being over-exposed to it; jaded: *We're all excited about our daughter starting school this fall, but she's very blasé about it.* ⟨< F *blasé,* pp. of *blaser* exhaust with pleasure⟩

blas•pheme [blæs'fim] *or* ['blæsfim] *v.* **-phemed, -phem•ing. 1** speak about (God or sacred things) with abuse or contempt; utter blasphemy. **2** utter profanities or curses. ⟨ME *blasfemen* < OF *blasfemer* < L *blasphemare* < Gk. *blasphēmeein.* Doublet of BLAME.⟩ **—blas'phem•er,** *n.*

blas•phe•mous ['blæsfəməs] *adj.* showing contempt for God or sacred things; profane: *a blasphemous utterance.* **—'blas•phe•mous•ly,** *adv.* **—'blas•phe•mous•ness,** *n.*

blas•phe•my ['blæsfəmi] *n., pl.* **-mies. 1** abuse of or contempt for God or sacred things. **2** irreverence or disrespect toward something considered immune from criticism. **3** profanity; curses.

blast [blæst] *n., v., interj. —n.* **1** a strong, sudden rush of wind or air: *the icy blasts of winter.* **2 a** the blowing of a trumpet, horn, etc. **b** the sound so made. **3** a current of air used in smelting, etc. A furnace is **in blast** when in operation; it is **out of blast** when stopped. **4** a charge of dynamite or some other explosive that blows up rocks, earth, etc. **5** a blasting; explosion. **6** a rush of air following an explosion: *The windows were all blown out by the blast.* **7** a cause of withering, blight, or ruin. **8** *Slang.* an outburst of anger, severe criticism, etc. **9** *Slang.* **a** a large, wild party. **b** a lot of fun: *That new game is a blast!*
(in or **at) full blast,** in full operation; at full volume or speed: *to play the stereo full blast.*
—v. **1** blow up (rocks, earth, etc.) with dynamite, or some other explosive. **2** wither; blight; ruin: *The intense heat blasted the vines. His conviction for fraud blasted his reputation.* **3** blow (a trumpet, horn, whistle, etc.). **4** criticize angrily and severely. **5** make by blasting: *They blasted a hole in the rock face.*
—interj. an exclamation of frustration, anger, etc.
blast off, of rockets, missiles, etc., fire; take off: *Make ready to blast off.* ⟨OE *blǣst*⟩ **—'blast•er,** *n.*

blast•ed ['blæstɪd] *adj., v. —adj.* **1** withered; blighted; ruined.

2 *Informal.* a word used as an intensive, to express impatience or anger: *This blasted pen won't write.*
—*v.* pt. and pp. of BLAST.

blas•te•ma [blæ'stimə] *n.* the undifferentiated tissue of an embryo, which develops into cells, organs, etc. ⟨< NL < Gk. *blastema* a bud < *blastanein* to bud < *blastos* a sprout⟩
—blas'te•mic, *adj.*

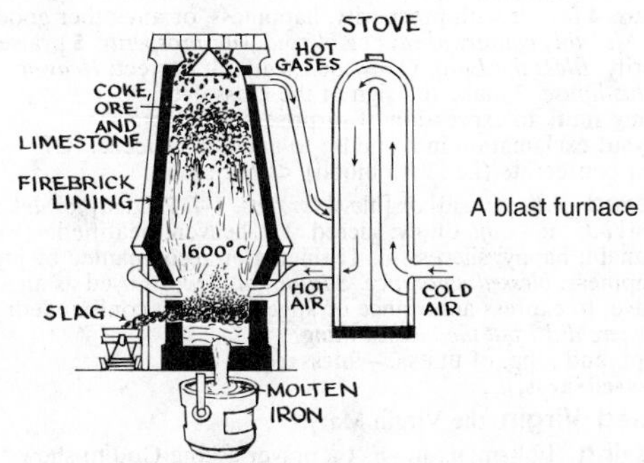

A blast furnace

blast furnace a furnace in which ores are smelted by blowing a strong current of air from the bottom to produce intense heat.

blas•to•coele or **blas•to•cele** ['blæstou,sil] *n.* the space in the centre of a blastula or ovum. ⟨< Gk. *blastos* a sprout + *koilia* body cavity < *koilos* hollow⟩

blas•to•cyst ['blæstou,sɪst] *n.* the embryo of a human being or other mammal, in an early stage before it has reached the uterus; blastula. ⟨< Gk. *blastos* a sprout + *kystis* sac, bladder⟩

blas•to•derm ['blæstə,dɜrm] *n. Biology.* a layer of cells formed by the growth of a fertilized egg. It later divides into three layers, from which all parts of the animal are formed. ⟨< Gk. *blastos* germ + E *-derm* (< Gk. *derma* skin)⟩
—,blas•to'derm•ic, *adj.*

blas•to•disk ['blæstə,dɪsk] *n.* the small disk of protoplasm, containing the egg nucleus, in the yolk of a fertilized egg.

blast•off or **blast–off** ['blæst,ɒf] *n.* the process or moment of launching a rocket, spacecraft, etc.

blas•to•mere ['blæstou,mir] *n.* any of the cells into which a fertilized ovum first divides. ⟨< Gk. *blastos* a sprout + *meros* a part⟩ **—,blas•to'mer•ic** [-'mɛrɪk], *adj.*

blas•to•my•cete [,blæstou'maisit] *or* [,blæstoumai'sit] *n.* a fungus of the genus *Blastomyces,* which can cause disease in people and animals. ⟨< Gk. *blastos* a sprout + *myketes,* pl. of *mykes* mushroom⟩

blas•to•pore ['blæstou,pɔr] *n.* the opening of the cavity of a gastrula. ⟨< Gk. *blastos* a sprout + *poros* a passage⟩

blas•tu•la ['blæstʃələ] *n., pl.* **-lae** [-li] *or* [-,laɪ]. *Zoology.* the embryo of an animal. It usually consists of a sac or hollow sphere formed by a single layer of cells. ⟨< NL *blastula,* dim. of Gk. *blastos* sprout, germ⟩

blas•tu•lar ['blæstʃələr] *adj.* having to do with, or resembling, a blastula.

blat [blæt] *v.* **blat•ted, blat•ting,** *n.* —*v.* **1** cry like a calf or sheep; bleat. **2** *Informal.* say loudly and foolishly; blurt out.
—*n.* the sound of a bleat, or of something being squashed. ⟨imitative⟩

bla•tan•cy ['bleitənsi] *n.* a blatant quality.

bla•tant ['bleitənt] *adj.* **1** offensively obvious; forced on one's attention: *blatant lies, blatant stupidity.* **2** disagreeably noisy; clamorous. ⟨coined by Spenser < L *blatire* babble⟩ **—'bla•tant•ly,** *adv.*

blath•er ['blæðər] *n., v.* —*n.* foolish talk.
—*v.* talk foolishly. Also, **blether.** ⟨ME < ON *blathr*⟩
—'blath•er•er, *n.*

blath•er•skite ['blæðər,skait] *n. Informal.* a person who talks much but says little worth saying; a windbag. ⟨< ON *blathr* foolish talk + Scottish *skate* a term of contempt⟩

blau•bok ['blaʊ,bɒk] *n.* an extinct antelope (*Hippotragus leucophaeus*) which lived in South Africa and had bluish grey fur. ⟨< Afrikaans *blauwbok* blue buck⟩

blaze¹ [bleiz] *n., v.* **blazed, blaz•ing.** —*n.* **1** a bright flame or fire. **2** a glow of brightness; intense light; brilliance or glare: *the blaze of the noon sun.* **3** a bright display. **4** a violent outburst: *a blaze of temper.*
go to blazes, *Slang.* go to hell.
—*v.* **1** burn with a bright flame; be on fire: *A fire was blazing in the fireplace.* **2** show bright colours or lights: *On Christmas Eve the big house blazed with lights.* **3** make a bright display. **4** burst out in anger or excitement: *She blazed at the insult.*
blaze away, a fire a gun, etc. **b** talk rapidly and excitedly. ⟨OE *blæse*⟩
☛ *Syn. n.* **1.** See note at FLAME.

blaze² [bleiz] *n., v.* **blazed, blaz•ing.** —*n.* **1** a mark made on a tree by chipping off a piece of bark. **2** a white mark on an animal's forehead.
—*v.* **1** mark (a tree) by chipping off a piece of the bark. **2** mark by blazing trees: *The hunters blazed a trail through the bush.* ⟨< LG *bläse*⟩

blaze³ [bleiz] *v.* **blazed, blaz•ing.** make known; proclaim. ⟨< MDu. *blasen* blow⟩

blaz•er ['bleizər] *n.* **1** a jacket cut like a suit coat, and usually worn by men with tailored trousers as dressy but informal wear. **2** a similar loose or slightly fitted, unbelted jacket worn by women or men, usually having a notched collar and patch pockets.

blazing star a wildflower (*Liatris cylindraceae*) of the composite family, having purple or white flowers and stiff, narrow, pointed leaves. It blooms from July to September in dry, open places from southern Ontario south.

bla•zon ['bleizən] *v., n.* —*v.* **1** make known; proclaim: *Big posters blazoned the wonders of the coming circus.* **2** decorate; adorn. **3** describe or paint (a coat of arms). **4** display; show, especially colourfully or brightly.
—*n.* **1** coat of arms. **2** a description or painting of a coat of arms. **3** a bright or colourful display; a show. ⟨ME < OF *blason* shield⟩
—'bla•zon•ment, *n.*

bla•zon•ry ['bleizənri] *n.* **1** a bright decoration or display. **2** a coat of arms. **3** a description or painting of a coat of arms.

bldg. building.

bleach [blitʃ] *v., n.* —*v.* **1** whiten by exposing to sunlight: *Bleached bones lay on the deserts.* **2** whiten or lighten by using chemicals: *We bleached the stains out of the shirt.* **3** turn white or pale; lose colour.
—*n.* **1** a chemical used in bleaching. **2** the act of bleaching. **3** the amount of whiteness after bleaching. ⟨OE *blǣcean* < *blac, blǣce* pale. Related to BLEAK.⟩
☛ *Syn. v.* **1, 2.** See note at WHITEN.

bleach•er ['blitʃər] *n.* **1** a person or thing that bleaches or an agent used in bleaching. **2 bleachers,** *pl.* **a** the roofless rows or tiers of seats for spectators at outdoor games such as football or baseball. **b** the similar rows of seats at indoor games such as basketball.

bleaching powder **1** any powder used in bleaching. **2** CHLORIDE OF LIME.

bleak [blik] *adj.* **1** swept by winds; bare: *bleak and rocky mountain peaks.* **2** chilly; cold: *a bleak wind.* **3** dreary; dismal: *All their savings were gone, and the future looked bleak.* ⟨ME *bleke* pale < Scand., related to OE *blac, blǣce.* See BLEACH.⟩
—'bleak•ly, *adv.* **—'bleak•ness,** *n.*

blear [blir] *adj., v.* —*adj.* bleary.
—*v.* make dim or blurred. ⟨ME *blere(n)*⟩

blear–eyed ['blir ,aɪd] *adj.* having inflamed or watery eyes. Also, **bleary-eyed.**

blear•y ['bliri] *adj.* **blear•i•er, blear•i•est.** of the eyes or vision, dim or blurred, especially from tiredness or tears.
—'blear•i•ly, *adv.* **—'blear•i•ness,** *n.*

bleat [blit] *n., v.* —*n.* **1** the cry made by a sheep, goat, or calf. **2** a sound like a bleat.
—*v.* **1** make the cry of a sheep, goat, or calf, or a sound like it. **2** complain, especially feebly or with a whine. **3** blather; babble. ⟨OE *blǣtan*⟩ **—'bleat•er,** *n.*

bleb [blɛb] *n.* **1** a blister. **2** a bubble. ⟨variant of *blob*⟩

bled [blɛd] *v.* pt. and pp. of BLEED.

bleed [blid] *v.* **bled, bleed•ing;** *n.* —*v.* **1** lose blood: *This cut is bleeding.* **2** shed one's blood; suffer wounds or death: *He bled to death. He fought and bled for his country.* **3** take blood from: *Doctors used to bleed sick people.* **4** lose sap, juice, etc.: *The injured elm is bleeding.* **5** take sap, juice, etc. from. **6** feel pity, sorrow, or grief. **7** *Informal.* get money from by extortion.

8 *Printing.* **a** extend to the edge of (a page), leaving no margin: *This photograph will look best on the page if it bleeds both sides.* **b** print (an illustration) or trim (a page) so that there is no margin. **9** show through one coat of paint, as a dark colour under a lighter one. **10** spread, as colours in wet cloth. **11** empty (a container) of liquid or gas.
bleed white, take all the power, strength, money, etc. of: *Blackmailers and gamblers have bled him white.*
one's heart bleeds, one has sympathy (sometimes meant ironically).
—n. **1** *Printing.* **a** an illustration or page that bleeds. **b** the paper trimmed off such a page. **2** a valve or tap. **3** (*adjl.*) of a page on which trimming the outer edge will eliminate print or part of a picture. ⟨OE *bledan* < *blod* blood⟩

bleed•er ['blidər] *n.* a person having a condition in which the blood fails to clot, so that bleeding is hard to stop; hemophiliac.

bleeding heart **1** a spring-flowering Japanese perennial herb (*Dicentra spectabilis* of the family Fumariaceae) widely cultivated for its drooping, heart-shaped, pink flowers. **2** any of several other cultivated plants of the same genus. **3** *Informal.* a person who is excessively sentimental and allows feelings of pity and sympathy to override his or her judgment.

bleeding station a laboratory which takes blood samples for analysis elsewhere.

bleep [blip] *n., v.* *—n.* a short, high-pitched sound, especially a signal from electronic equipment, used as a warning, to indicate direction, etc.; beep.
—v. **1** emit such a sound. **2** *Radio and television.* censor (a word, etc.) in a broadcast by substituting a bleep (*often used with* **out**).

blem•ish ['blɛmɪʃ] *n., v.* *—n.* **1** a stain; spot; scar: *A mole is a blemish on a person's skin.* **2** an imperfection; fault: *A quick temper was the only blemish in his character.*
—v. **1** make stained or scarred. **2** injure; mar: *One bad deed can blemish a good reputation.* ⟨ME < OF *blemiss-*, a stem of *ble(s)mir* make livid⟩ **—'blem•ish•er,** *n.*

blench[1] [blɛntʃ] *v.* draw back; shrink away. ⟨apparently < OE *blencan* deceive⟩

blench[2] [blɛntʃ] *v.* **1** turn pale. **2** make white. ⟨var. of *blanch*⟩

blend [blɛnd] *v.* **blend•ed** or (*Poetic*) **blent, blend•ing;** *n.* *—v.* **1** mix together; mix or become mixed so thoroughly that the things mixed cannot be distinguished or separated: *Oil and water will not blend. Blend the first three ingredients in a saucepan.* **2** make by mixing several kinds together: *to blend tea.* **3** shade into each other, little by little; merge: *The colours of the rainbow blend into one another.* **4** go well together; harmonize: *The colours in that print do not blend. Your voices blend well.*
—n. **1** the act of blending. **2** something produced by blending: *a blend of several coffees. This fabric is a blend.* **3** a word made by fusing two words, often with a syllable in common. *Blotch* is a blend of *blot* and *botch.* **4** a consonant cluster in which the second consonant is a liquid: *Blends are often hard for young children to pronounce.* ⟨ME < ON *blanda* mix⟩
☛ *Hom.* BLENDE.
☛ *Syn. v.* **1.** See note at MIX.

blende [blɛnd] *n.* **1** the chief ore of zinc; zinc sulphide. **2** any of certain other sulphides. ⟨< G *Blende* < *blenden* blind, deceive; because the yield from the ore is disappointing⟩
☛ *Hom.* BLEND.

blend•er ['blɛndər] *n.* **1** a person or thing that blends. **2** a mechanical device for mixing things uniformly. **3** a small household appliance for mixing ingredients, usually into a liquid.

blending inheritance a mixture of characteristics from two disparate parents. A white dog crossed with a black bitch can produce a grey dog.

Blen•heim spaniel ['blɛnəm] a dog first bred at Blenheim Palace in England, a kind of small spaniel having reddish brown spots on a white body.

blen•ny ['blɛni] *n., pl.* **-ny** or **-nies. 1** any of a family (Blenniidae) of small, scaleless, bottom-living fishes found in the coastal waters of most oceans, having a large head and a tapering body. **2** any of numerous other, mostly small, fishes belonging to the same suborder (Blennioidei), typically having a slender, elongated body with a long dorsal fin. ⟨< L *blennius*, var. of *blendius* < Gk. *blennos* < *blenna* slime⟩

blent [blɛnt] *v. Poetic.* a pt. and a pp. of BLEND.

ble•o•my•cin [ˌbliou'mɔisɪn] *n.* a drug used to treat some forms of cancer. *Formula:* $C_{55}H_{84}N_{17}O_{21}S_3$

bleph•a•ri•tis [ˌblɛfə'rɔitɪs] *n.* inflammation of the eyelids, especially round the edges. ⟨< Gk. *blepharon* eyelid + E *-itis*⟩

bleph•a•ro•plas•ty ['blɛfərouˌplæsti] *n.* cosmetic surgery involving lifting of the eyelids. ⟨< Gk. *blepharon* eyelid + *plastos* formed⟩

bless [blɛs] *v.* **blessed** or **blest, bless•ing. 1** make holy or sacred: *to bless a church.* **2** ask God's favour for: *Bless these little children.* **3** wish good to; feel grateful to: *They blessed her for her kindness.* **4** favour with prosperity, happiness, or any other good thing: *May this country always be blessed with prosperity.* **5** praise or glorify: *Bless the Lord, O my soul.* **6** guard; protect: *Heaven bless this house.* **7** make the sign of the cross over.
bless my soul! an expression of surprise or pleasure.
bless you! exclamation in response to another's sneeze. ⟨OE *blētsian* consecrate (i.e., with blood) < *blōd* blood⟩

bless•ed *adj.* ['blɛsɪd] *or* [blɛst] *for defs. 1-4,* ['blɛsɪd] *for def. 5; v.* [blɛst] *adj., v.* *—adj.* **1** holy; sacred. **2** in heaven; beatified. **3** fortunate; happy; successful. **4** bringing or accompanied by joy or happiness: *blessed ignorance.* **5** *Informal.* a word used as an intensive, to express annoyance or anger; darned; confounded: *Now where did I put the blessed thing?*
—v. a pt. and a pp. of BLESS. **—'bless•ed•ly,** *adv.* **—'bless•ed•ness,** *n.*

Blessed Virgin the Virgin Mary.

bless•ing ['blɛsɪŋ] *n., v.* *—n.* **1** a prayer asking God to show His favour; benediction: *At the end of the church service, the bishop gave the blessing.* **2** a giving of God's favour. **3** grace said before meals. **4** a wish for happiness or success: *When she left home, she received her parents' blessing.* **5** approval or consent: *The marriage had the blessing of all four parents.* **6** anything that makes one happy or contented; boon or benefit: *A good temper is a great blessing.*
—v. ppr. of BLESS.

blest [blɛst] *v., adj.* *—v.* a pt. and a pp. of BLESS.
—adj. blessed.

bleth•er ['blɛðər] *n. or v.* blather.

blew [blu] *v.* pt. of BLOW[2] and BLOW[3].
☛ *Hom.* BLUE.

blight [blɔit] *n., v.* *—n.* **1** any of several plant diseases that cause leaves, stems, or other parts to wither and die: *The apple crop was wiped out by blight.* **2** a fungus, insect, etc. that causes such a disease: *Rust, smut, and mildew are blights.* **3** anything that destroys, impairs or prevents growth, etc.: *a region suffering from the blight of high unemployment.* **4** a person or thing that frustrates or disappoints hopes or ambitions. **5** the condition of being spoiled, ruined, etc.: *the causes of urban blight.*
—v. **1** cause to wither and die: *Mildew blighted the June roses.* **2** destroy; ruin. **3** disappoint or frustrate: *All their hopes were blighted.* **4** suffer from blight. ⟨origin uncertain⟩ **—'blight•er,** *n.*

blimp [blɪmp] *n. Informal.* **1** a small, non-rigid dirigible airship. **2** any dirigible. ⟨apparently from Type *B limp*, the most common type of limp dirigible in World War I⟩ **—'blimp•ish,** *adj.*

Blimp or **blimp** [blɪmp] *n.* an ultra-conservative, stupidly short-sighted person. ⟨< Colonel *Blimp*, a British newspaper cartoon character created by David Low⟩ **—'blimp•ish,** *adj.*

blin [blɪn] *n., pl.* **bli•ni** ['blɪni]. a Russian dish, a thin crepe covered with sour cream and caviar.

blind [blaɪnd] *adj., adv., v., n.* *—adj.* **1** not able to see; not having the sense of sight: *The woman with the white cane is blind.* **2** of or for blind persons. **3** not based on evidence, judgment, or reason: *blind faith, a blind fury. Love is blind.* **4** unable or unwilling to understand or perceive (*used with* **to**): *blind to the beauty of one's environment.* **5** hard to see; hidden: *a blind seam, a blind curve on a highway.* **6** without an opening: *a blind wall.* **7** with only one opening: *a blind canyon.* **8** made or done without preparation, knowledge of certain facts, etc.: *a blind purchase.* **9** done without the help of sight, using only instruments: *The pilot made a blind landing.* **10** not producing buds, etc.: *a blind shoot.* **11** of a boil, etc., not having come to a head. **12** *Slang.* drunk. **13** secret; unlisted: *A blind copy of the letter was sent to the director.*
turn a blind eye (to), refuse to see or take notice of.
—adv. **1** without being able to see properly: *driving blind in the fog.* **2** using only instruments: *to fly blind.* **3** without complete knowledge, etc. **4** extremely (drunk).
—v. **1** make unable to see: *The bright lights blinded me for a moment. She was blinded in an accident in childhood.* **2** make hard to see; conceal: *Clouds blind the stars from view.* **3** rob of power to understand or judge: *His prejudices blinded him.*
—n. **1** a screen on a spring roller that can be rolled down in front of a window in order to shut out light or heat: *We have blinds on our bedroom windows.* **2** a similar device using vertical or

horizontal slats: *We have vertical blinds in the office, and a Venetian blind in the kitchen.* **3** any thing or person that conceals an action or purpose; decoy or screen. **4** a hiding place for a hunter or photographer. ⟨OE⟩ **—'blind•ly,** *adv.* **—'blind•ness,** *n.*

blind alley **1** a passageway closed at one end. **2** anything that gives no chance for progress or improvement.

blind date **1** a social date arranged by a third person for a couple who have not met. **2** either of the two persons thus dated.

blind•er ['blaɪndər] *n.* a leather flap designed to keep a horse from seeing to the side; blinker.

blind•fish ['blaɪnd,fɪʃ] *n.* any small fish that cannot see and lives in deep water or underground caves, etc.

blind flying the act of piloting an airplane by instruments only.

blind•fold ['blaɪnd,fould] *v., adj., adv., n.* *—v.* **1** cover the eyes to prevent seeing: *The robbers blindfolded, gagged, and bound their victim.* **2** prevent (someone) from understanding.
—adj. or adv. **1** with the eyes covered: *He said he could walk the line blindfold.* **2** reckless(ly).
—n. **1** something covering the eyes to prevent seeing: *Putting a blindfold on the horse, the woman led it from the burning barn.* **2** anything that prevents understanding. ⟨OE *blindfellian,* ult. < *blind* blind + *fell,* var. of *fiell* a fall; influenced by *fold*⟩

blind•man's buff ['blaɪnd,mænz 'bʌf] a game in which a blindfolded person tries to catch and identify one of the other players. Also, **blindman's bluff.**

blind pig *Slang.* a place where one can buy liquor illegally. Blind pigs usually operate outside the normal hours for taverns or bars.

blind•side ['blaɪnd,saɪd] *v.* **-sid•ed, -sid•ing. 1** attack (someone) while unseen. **2** criticize (someone who has poor or no defence). **3** *Football.* tackle (a player on the opposing team) from the side on which he or she is not looking.

blind side the side on which a person is not looking.

blind spot **1** a round spot on the retina of the eye that is not sensitive to light. The optic nerve enters the eye at the blind spot. See EYE for picture: *The motorist did not see the cyclist as the cyclist was riding in her blind spot.* **2** a matter on which a person does not know that he or she is prejudiced or poorly informed. **3** an area of poor radio reception. **4** an area of poor visibility: *There is a blind spot where the road dips on that steep curve.*

blind staggers STAGGER (n. 3).

blind•stitch ['blaɪnd,stɪtʃ] *v., n.* *—v.* sew with stitches not visible on the right side of the work.
—n. Also, **blind stitch,** a stitch or stitching of this kind.

blind•sto•rey ['blaɪnd,stɔri] *n. Architecture.* **1** a storey without windows. **2** a storey without windows above the main arches of a Gothic church; windowless clerestory.

blind trust an arrangement whereby the stocks, bonds, etc. held by a person, such as an MP or other public servant, are administered and traded on his or her behalf so that he or she does not know about the transactions and so cannot be caught in a conflict of interest.

blind•worm ['blaɪnd,wɜrm] *n.* a small, legless, burrowing lizard (*Anguis fragilis*) of Eurasia having a snakelike body and small eyes. Also called **slowworm.**

bli•ni ['blɪni] *n.* pl. of BLIN.

blink [blɪŋk] *v., n.* *—v.* **1** look with the eyes opening and shutting: *Nico blinked at the sudden light.* **2** close the eyes and open them again quickly; wink: *We blink every few seconds.* **3** shine with an unsteady or flashing light: *A little lantern blinked in the night.* **4** make, send, cause to be, etc. by blinking: *He blinked away his tears. The light blinked a message to the boat.* **4** look with indifference (at); ignore: *Don't blink the fact that there is a risk of war. She blinks at all his faults.*
—n. **1** a blinking. **2** a flash or flicker of light. **3** a glimpse. **4** especially in the Far North, a reflection of sunlight on cloud caused by ice or snow in the distance.
on the blink, *Informal.* not working properly; out of order: *Our TV set is on the blink again.* ⟨ME *blenken*⟩

blink•er ['blɪŋkər] *n., v.* *—n.* **1** blinder. **2** a warning or message signal with flashing lights.
—v. **1** put blinders on. **2** constrict the vision, thinking, etc. of: *blinkered by prejudice.*

blintz or **blintze** [blɪnts] *n.* a thin, rolled pancake filled with cheese, fruit, jam, etc. ⟨< Yiddish *blintz* < Ukrainian *blynci*⟩

blip [blɪp] *n., v.* **blipped, blip•ping.** *—n.* **1** an image on a radar screen, in the form of a small dot of light, showing that radar waves are being reflected from an object. The blip shows the location of the object and the direction in which it is moving. **2** a short, high-pitched, light or crisp sound.
—v. make or show a blip.

bliss [blɪs] *n., v.* *—n.* **1** great happiness; perfect joy. **2** the joy of heaven; blessedness.
—v. Slang. induce or undergo intense gratification from or as from drugs (*used with* **out**): *He blissed out when she kissed him.* ⟨OE *blīths* < *blīthe* blithe⟩
☛ *Syn.* **1.** See note at HAPPINESS.

bliss•ful ['blɪsfəl] *adj.* very happy; joyful. **—'bliss•ful•ly,** *adv.* **—'bliss•ful•ness,** *n.*

Blis•sym•bol•ics ['blɪssɪm'bɒlɪks] *n. Trademark.* a method for a person with a disability to communicate by pointing to language symbols on a board. ⟨after Charles *Bliss,* its inventor⟩

blis•ter ['blɪstər] *n., v.* *—n.* **1** a little baglike swelling in the skin filled with watery matter, often caused by a burn or by abrasion. **2** a swelling on the surface of a plant, on metal, or on painted wood, etc. **3** a bulge below the waterline in the hull of a ship, for protection against torpedoes. **4** a bulgelike, often transparent, projection on the fuselage of an aircraft, for an observer, navigator, or air gunner. **5** a bubblelike shell of transparent plastic used to protect and display a piece of merchandise.
—v. **1** raise a blister or blisters on. **2** become covered with blisters; have blisters. **3** attack with sharp words. ⟨ME < OF *blestre* tumour, lump < ON *blastr* swelling⟩ **—'blis•ter•y,** *adj.*

blister beetle any of various soft-bodied beetles (family Meloidae) having body fluids containing a substance that causes skin to blister.

blis•ter•ing ['blɪstərɪŋ] *adj., v.*—*adj.* scathing; *a blistering remark.*
—v. ppr. of BLISTER. **—'blis•ter•ing•ly,** *adv.*

blister rust a fungous disease of white pine trees.

blithe [blaɪð] *or* [blaɪθ] *adj.* **1** happy; cheerful; light-hearted: *She had a blithe and carefree spirit.* **2** airy; casual; unheeding: *blithe indifference.* ⟨OE *blīthe*⟩ **—'blithe•ly,** *adv.* **—'blithe•ness,** *n.*

blith•er•ing ['blɪðərɪŋ] *adv.* talking nonsense; jabbering; blathering: *a blithering idiot.* ⟨var. of *blathering*⟩

blithe•some ['blaɪðsəm] *or* ['blaɪθsəm] *adj.* cheerful and light-hearted. **—'blithe•some•ly,** *adv.* **—'blithe•some•ness,** *n.*

blitz [blɪts] *n., v.* *—n.* **1** blitzkrieg. **2** a sudden, violent attack using many airplanes and tanks. **3** any concentrated effort: *The United Way launched a house-to-house blitz in a last attempt to meet their goal.*
—v. to subject to a blitz. ⟨< G *Blitz* lightning⟩

blitz•krieg ['blɪts,krig] *n.* **1** a type of offensive action designed by its speed and violence to crush the enemy quickly. **2** any violent onslaught. ⟨< G *Blitzkrieg* lightning war⟩

bliz•zard ['blɪzərd] *n., v.*—*n.* **1** a violent, long-lasting, blinding snowstorm usually accompanied by temperatures of -10°C or colder: *Blizzards sometimes last for more than a day.* **2** any violent winter windstorm with much blowing snow. **3** *Informal.* an overwhelming number or amount: *a blizzard of angry letters.*
—v. blow a blizzard: *It's blizzarding out there.* ⟨origin uncertain⟩ **—'bliz•zard•y,** *adj.*

blk. **1** black. **2** block. **3** bulk.

bloat [blout] *v., n.* *—v.* **1** swell up; puff up: *His face was bruised and bloated after the fight.* **2** preserve (herring) by salting and smoking.
—n. **1** a swelling of the stomach of cattle, sheep, etc. caused by an accumulation of gases brought on by eating moist feed that ferments. **2** *Informal.* needless or wasteful expansion of staff, budget, etc. ⟨ME *blout* soft with moisture < ON *blautr* soft, pulpy⟩

bloat•ed ['bloutɪd] *adj., v.* *—adj.* **1** puffy and swollen. **2** pampered; glutted. **3** inflated. **4** cured as a BLOATER: *a bloated herring.*
—v. pt. and pp. of BLOAT.

bloat•er ['bloutər] *n.* **1** a herring preserved by salting and smoking. **2** a small Great Lakes cisco trout (*Coregonus hoyi*).

blob [blɒb] *n., v.* **blobbed, blob•bing.** *—n.* **1** a small, soft drop or lump: *Blobs of wax covered the candlestick.* **2** a splash or daub of colour. **3** something seen indistinctly.
—v. mark or put on with blobs. ⟨ME *blobe* a bubble⟩

bloc [blɒk] *n.* a group of persons, companies, or nations, etc. united for a purpose. ⟨< F < OF *bloc.* See BLOCK.⟩

block [blɒk] *n., v.* *—n.* **1** a usually solid piece of wood, stone, metal, concrete, etc., with rectangular sides. **2** a child's building

toy in the shape of a brick. **3** a space in a city or town bounded by four streets: *one city block.* **4** the length of one side of a block, in a city or town: *Walk one block east.* **5** a number of townships, usually surrounded by land that has not been surveyed: *the Peace River Block.* **6** a group of things of the same kind, or a continuous stretch of something: *a block of seats in a theatre, a block of time, blocks of colour.* **7** a building containing a number of units: *an apartment block, an office block.* **8** a number of buildings close together: *an industrial block.* **9** a short section of railway track with signals for spacing trains. **10** formerly, a piece of wood placed under the neck of a person being beheaded. **11** a platform where things are put up for sale at an auction. **12** a pulley on a hook. **13** a mould on which things are shaped. **14** *Printing.* a piece of engraved metal, wood, or other substance; cut. **15** *Slang.* a person's head. **16** *Sports.* the hindering of an opponent's play. **17** *Computer technology.* a portion of data already entered, which is identified as a unit and can then be moved. **18** something that prevents progress; an obstruction or hindrance: *writer's block.* **19** an emotional repression of speech or thought on some subject: *a psychological block.* **20** one of two small pieces of wood placed on a track to assist a runner in starting: *starting blocks.* **21** (*adjl*). arranged on a page without indentations, and with a space between paragraphs: *block style.* **22** the metal shell containing the cylinders of an internal-combustion engine; cylinder block. **23** *Philately.* a group of four or more attached stamps in the shape of a rectangle. **24** (*adjl.*) in the shape of a block or blocks: *block lava.*
go to the block, a have one's head cut off. **b** be for sale at an auction.
on the block, for sale, especially at an auction.
—*v.* **1** fill so as to prevent passage or progress (*often used with* **up**): *The country roads were blocked with snow.* **2** put things in the way of; obstruct; hinder: *Her sickness blocks my plans for the party.* **3** mount on a block. **4** shape on a block: *Felt hats are blocked.* **5** *Printing.* stamp with a block. **6** *Sports.* hinder the play of (an opponent). **7** prevent (a nerve) from transmitting impulses. **8** plan roughly; outline (*usually used with* **in** *or* **out**): *to block in a sketch.* **9** introduce an obstruction into, so as to make unfit for passage, etc. (*often used with* **off**): *to block off a street.* **10** support with or on a block. **11** stop the normal transaction of (money, assets, etc.). **12** *Theatre.* plan the moves of actors in (a scene, play, etc.). **13** *Computer technology.* designate (a portion of text) as a block. ⟨ME < OF *bloc* < Gmc.⟩

block•ade [blɒ'keid] *n., v.* **-ad•ed, -ad•ing.** —*n.* **1** in war, the closing off of a harbour, city, etc. by enemy ships or other forces to keep people or supplies from getting through. **2** the forces used to set up a blockade. **3** anything that blocks up or obstructs.
run the blockade, try to get into or out of a port that is being blockaded.
—*v.* **1** put under blockade. **2** block up; obstruct. **—block'ad•er,** *n.*
☛ *Syn. n.* **1.** See note at SIEGE.

blockade runner a ship that tries to get into or out of a port that is being blockaded.

block•age ['blɒkɪdʒ] *n.* **1** a blocking or being blocked. **2** something that blocks: *We cleared the blockage from the pipe.*

block and tackle an arrangement of pulleys and ropes used in lifting heavy weights.

block•bust•er ['blɒk,bʌstər] *n. Informal.* **1** an aerial bomb that weighs two or more tonnes, capable of destroying a large area. **2** any person or thing that has a very strong impact or effect: *The new musical is a blockbuster.* **3** a person, corporation, etc. that engages in blockbusting.

block•bust•ing ['blɒk,bʌstɪŋ] *n.* the process or practice of developers buying up one or two houses in a city block or area and either razing them or letting them fall to ruin to induce other residents to sell their property quickly, often at a loss, for fear of depreciating property values. Purchases for prospective group homes, halfway houses, etc., often have a similar effect.

block diagram **1** *Geology.* a diagram in perspective, showing the topography or geology of the terrain, generally including vertical cross sections. **2** *Computer technology.* a diagram illustrating the sequence of operations and the relationship between different elements in a computer system; flowchart.

block•er ['blɒkər] *n.* **1** *Football.* a player who hinders an opponent's play. **2** a drug which hinders a chemical process in the body: *a beta blocker.*

block•head ['blɒk,hɛd] *n.* a stupid person; fool.

block heater an electrical device for keeping the engine block of a motor vehicle slightly warm, making it possible to start the engine even in extremely cold weather.

block•house ['blɒk,hʌus] *n.* **1** a military fortification built of heavy timbers or concrete, and having loopholes to shoot from. **2** a heavily reinforced building used as a control centre and place of observation for operations involving danger from intense heat, radiation, etc.: *The launching of space vehicles is controlled from a blockhouse.*

block•ish ['blɒkɪʃ] *adj.* stupid. **—'block•ish•ly,** *adv.* **—'block•ish•ness,** *n.*

block letter a capital letter, usually hand printed: *Print your name in block letters.*

Block Parent a designated adult to whose home, identified by a special logo in the window, neighbourhood children may go when in need of help. The Block Parent program is administered by a community-level municipal organization.

block party a party by or for all the residents of a given street block, during which the street is closed to traffic.

block plane a small plane used to smooth the ends of boards across the grain.

block printing printing from engraved blocks of wood, etc.

block signal a signal to show whether a short section of railway track ahead has a train on it or not.

block system the system of dividing a railway track into short sections with signals to warn a train when the section ahead is not clear.

block•y ['blɒki] *adj.* **block•i•er, block•i•est. 1** like a block; chunky. **2** having patches of light and shade. **—'block•i•ly,** *adv.* **—'block•i•ness,** *n.*

Bloc Québécois ['blʌk ,keibɛ'kwɑ] a Canadian federal political party, comprising MPs from Québec and championing Québec's interests, especially in seeking to separate from Canada.

bloke [blouk] *n. Informal.* fellow; chap.

blond [blɒnd] *adj., n.* —*adj.* **1** light-coloured: *blond hair, blond furniture.* **2** having yellow or light brown hair, usually blue or grey eyes, and light skin; fair: *blond people.*
—*n.* a blond man or boy. ⟨< F < Gmc.⟩ **—'blond•ness,** *n.*
☛ *Usage.* **Blond,** BLONDE. As a noun, **blond** is used for men and boys, while **blonde** is used for women and girls; in ambiguous or doubtful cases, **blond** is used: *Mary and her brother are both blonds.* The normal form of the adjective is **blond** for all cases, but some people prefer to use **blonde** as an adjective when referring to women or girls: *a blond young man, a blond woman* or *a blonde woman.* All of these distinctions are based on a French grammatical pattern.

blonde [blɒnd] *n., adj.* —*n.* a woman or girl having fair hair. —*adj.* of a woman or girl, blond. ⟨< F *blonde,* feminine form of *blond*⟩
☛ *Usage.* See note at BLOND.

blood [blʌd] *n., pl.* (def. 9) **Bloods** or **Blood;** *v.* —*n.* **1** in vertebrates, the red liquid in the veins and arteries. Blood is circulated by the heart, carrying oxygen and digested food to all parts of the body and taking away waste materials. **2** the corresponding liquid in other animals: *The blood of most insects looks yellowish.* **3** bloodshed; slaughter. **4** family; birth; relationship; parentage; descent: *Love of the sea runs in his blood.* **5** high lineage, especially royal lineage: *a prince of the blood.* **6** temper; state of mind: *There was bad blood between them.* **7** a fashionable man; dandy. **8** of animals, pure breeding; thoroughbred stock. **9 Blood,** a member of a First Nations people of the Plains, one of the three Algonquian nations making up the Blackfoot confederacy. **10** people seen as an influx of energy into a group or organization: *What this corporation needs is new blood.*
blood is thicker than water, the ties that bind families are stronger than those that link friends.
draw first blood, hit or score first.
have someone's blood on one's hands or **head,** be guilty of murder.
in cold blood, on purpose and without emotion: *He lay in wait for the spy and then shot him down in cold blood.*
in one's blood, natural; original: *Love of country is in my blood.*
make (one's) **blood boil,** make one very angry: *Unfair comments like that make my blood boil.*
make (one's) **blood run cold,** fill one with terror: *"The Arctic trails have their secret tales/That would make your blood run cold."*
—*v.* give the first taste or experience of blood to: *to blood a hunting dog, to blood raw troops in a battle.* ⟨OE *blōd*⟩

blood–and–thun•der ['blʌd ən 'θʌndər] *adj.* characterized by highly dramatic, sensational adventures: *a blood-and-thunder movie.*

blood bank **1** a place for storing blood to be used in transfusions. **2** the blood kept in storage.

blood bath savage or widespread killing; massacre.

blood–brain barrier a layer of cells in the capillaries of the brain which prevent certain substances from passing from the blood into brain tissue.

blood brother **1** a brother by birth. **2** a person who goes through a ceremony of mixing some of his blood with another person's. **—blood brotherhood.**

blood count a count of the number of red and white corpuscles or platelets in a sample of a person's blood.

blood•cur•dling ['blʌd,kɜrdlɪŋ] *adj.* terrifying; horrible: *a bloodcurdling story.*

blood donor a person who donates blood to a hospital or for storage in a blood bank.

blood•ed ['blʌdɪd] *adj.* **1** coming from good stock; of good breed: *blooded horses.* **2** having blood or a temperament of a certain kind (*used only in compounds*): *Snakes are called cold-blooded; lions are warm-blooded. She is very hot-blooded and gets angry quickly.*

blood fluke any of various parasitic flatworms (class Digenea) that live in the blood of humans and other vertebrates.

blood group any of four main groups into which human blood is classified according to the presence or absence of genetically determined antigens: A, B, AB, and O.

blood•guil•ty ['blʌd,gɪlti] *adj.* guilty of murder or bloodshed. **—'blood,guilt•i•ness,** *n.*

blood heat the normal temperature of human blood, about 37°C.

blood•hound ['blʌd,haʊnd] *n.* **1** a breed of large dog with a very keen sense of smell, long, drooping ears, and a wrinkled face. A trained bloodhound can follow a trail several hours old. **2** a keen and relentless pursuer. **3** *Slang.* detective.

blood•less ['blʌdlɪs] *adj.* **1** without blood; pale. **2** without bloodshed: *a bloodless revolution.* **3** without energy or emotion; spiritless. **4** cold-hearted or cruel. **—'blood•less•ly,** *adv.* **—'blood•less•ness,** *n.*

blood•let•ting ['blʌd,lɛtɪŋ] *n.* **1** taking blood from a vein as a treatment for disease. Bloodletting was formerly common, but few diseases are treated in this way today. **2** bloodshed.

blood•line ['blʌd,laɪn] *n.* a line of direct descent; family or pedigree.

blood•mo•bile ['blʌdmə,bil] *n.* a van equipped for taking blood from blood donors.

blood money **1** money paid to have somebody murdered. **2** money paid as compensation to the next of kin of a person who has been murdered. In Anglo-Saxon England, blood money was paid to the family of a murdered person by the family of the murderer. **3** money gained at the cost of another person's life, freedom, welfare, etc.

blood plasma the colourless, liquid part of blood, as distinct from the corpuscles.

blood platelet any of the numerous colourless cells in the blood that promote clotting.

blood poisoning a diseased condition that occurs when the bloodstream is invaded by poisonous substances or disease-causing bacteria from a local source of infection.

blood pressure the pressure of the blood against the inner walls of the blood vessels, varying with exertion, excitement, health, age, etc.

blood–red ['blʌd 'rɛd] *adj.* **1** having the colour of blood, a deep, full red. **2** made red with blood: *a blood-red sword.*

blood relation or **relative** a person related by birth.

blood•root ['blʌd,rut] *n.* a North American plant (*Sanguinaria canadensis*) of the poppy family having a red root, red sap, and a white flower that blooms in early spring.

blood royal the royal family.

blood•shed ['blʌd,ʃɛd] *n.* the shedding of blood; slaughter.

blood•shot ['blʌd,ʃɒt] *adj.* of the eyes, red and sore; having the whites tinged with blood from swollen or burst blood vessels: *Your eyes become bloodshot if you get dirt in them.*

blood sport any sport, such as fox hunting, that involves the killing of animals.

blood•stain ['blʌd,stein] *n.* a mark or stain left by blood.

blood•stained ['blʌd,steind] *adj.* **1** stained with blood. **2** guilty of murder or bloodshed.

blood•stone ['blʌd,stoun] *n.* **1** a dark green semiprecious stone having flecks of bright red jasper or impure quartz through it. Bloodstone is a kind of translucent quartz. **2** a gem made from this stone.

blood•stream ['blʌd,strim] *n.* **1** the blood flowing in the circulatory system of a living body. **2** the necessary part or support of something: *the bloodstream of our economy.*

blood•suck•er ['blʌd,sʌkər] *n.* **1** leech. **2** a person who gets all he or she can from others. **—'blood,suck•ing,** *adj.*

blood sugar the level of glucose in the blood, which can be tested to diagnose such diseases as diabetes.

blood test an examination of a sample of a person's or animal's blood to determine the type of blood, to diagnose illness, etc.

blood•thirst•y ['blʌd,θɜrsti] *adj.* eager for bloodshed; cruel; murderous. **—'blood,thirst•i•ly,** *adv.* **—'blood,thirst•i•ness,** *n.*

blood transfusion an injection of blood from one person or animal into another.

blood type BLOOD GROUP.

blood vessel any tube in the body through which the blood circulates. Arteries, veins, and capillaries are blood vessels.

blood•y ['blʌdi] *adj.* **blood•i•er, blood•i•est;** *adv., v.* **blood•ied, blood•y•ing.** *—adj.* **1** bleeding: *a bloody nose.* **2** covered or stained with blood: *a bloody bandage, a bloody sword.* **3** with much bloodshed: *a bloody battle.* **4** eager for bloodshed; cruel. **5** like blood; blood-red. **6** *Slang.* a word used as an intensive, especially to express irritation or anger; cursed; confounded: *He's a bloody fool.*
—adv. Slang. a word used as an intensive to express irritation or anger: *I worked bloody hard.*
—v. **1** cause to bleed: *My nose was bloodied in the fight.* **2** stain with blood. **—'blood•i•ly,** *adv.* **—'blood•i•ness,** *n.*
☛ *Usage.* **Bloody,** in its slang use as an intensive, is sometimes considered vulgar.

blood•y–mind•ed ['blʌdi 'maɪndɪd] *adj.* **1** obstinate; contrary. **2** cruel; murderous. **—'blood•y-'mind•ed•ly,** *adv.* **—'blood•y-'mind•ed•ness,** *n.*

bloom[1] [blum] *n., v. —n.* **1** a flower; blossom. **2** the condition or time of flowering. **3** the condition or time of greatest health, vigour, or beauty: *in the bloom of youth.* **4** a glow of health and beauty. **5** the powdery or downy coating on some fruits and leaves. There is a bloom on grapes and plums and on the needles of some species of spruce. **6** a cloudy patch that appears on a bright surface, as of a coin. **7** *Ecology.* the sudden appearance of large clumps of algae on the surface of lake water, sea water, etc.
—v. **1** have flowers; open into flowers; blossom: *Many plants bloom in the spring.* **2** be in the condition or time of greatest health, vigour, or beauty. **3** glow with health and beauty. ⟨ME < ON *blōm*⟩

bloom[2] [blum] *n.* **1** an unmelted, spongy mass of wrought iron. **2** a bar of iron or steel. ⟨OE *blōma* lump⟩

bloom•er[1] ['blumər] *n.* **1** something that blooms. **2** a person with regard to how or when he or she develops: *She's a late bloomer.*

bloom•er[2] ['blumər] *n. Brit. Slang.* a blunder or mistake.

bloom•ers ['blumərz] *n.pl.* **1** loose shorts, gathered above the knee, formerly worn by women and girls for athletics. **2** underwear, pajama, or swimsuit bottoms, etc. made like these, but shorter. ⟨first referred to in a magazine published by Amelia J. *Bloomer* in 1851⟩

bloom•ing ['blumɪŋ] *adj., v.* **1** having flowers; blossoming. **2** flourishing. **3** *Esp. Brit. Informal.* a word used as an intensive: *a blooming genius. It's a blooming shame.*
—v. ppr. of BLOOM. **—'bloom•ing•ly,** *adv.*
☛ *Usage.* **Blooming** (def. 3), in its informal usage, is a euphemism for BLOODY (def. 6).

Blooms•bu•ry ['blumzbəri] *adj.* having to do with the **Bloomsbury set,** a loose association of writers and artists in the early 20th century, centered originally around Bloomsbury in London, and including such artists and intellectuals as Leonard and Virginia Woolf, Vanessa Bell, Duncan Grant, and John Maynard Keynes.

bloom•y ['blumi] *adj.* **1** covered in blossoms. **2** having a BLOOM (defs. 5 or 6).

bloop•er ['blupər] *n. Slang.* a silly or stupid, embarrassing mistake made in public, often in the media; boner.

blos•som ['blɒsəm] *n., v. —n.* **1** a flower, especially of a tree or other plant that produces fruit: *apple blossoms.* **2** the condition or time of flowering: *a cherry tree in blossom.*
—v. **1** have flowers; open into flowers. **2** open out; develop: *Her talent blossomed under the teacher's expert guidance.* ⟨OE *blōstma*⟩

blos•som•y ['blɒsəmi] *adj.* full of blossoms.

blot[1] [blɒt] *v.* **blot•ted, blot•ting;** *n.* —*v.* **1** make blots (on); stain or spot. **2** dry (ink, etc.) with paper or other material that absorbs: *She blotted her signature before folding the letter.* **3** blemish; disgrace. **4** erase (the memory of) (*often used with* **out**): *I've blotted that whole incident from my mind.*
blot (one's) **copybook,** spoil one's record or reputation: *He failed to get his promotion after blotting his copybook at the staff party.*
blot out, a hide; cover up. **b** wipe out; destroy. **c** erase; expunge.
—*n.* **1** a spot or stain: *an ink blot.* **2** a blemish; disgrace. ⟨ME; origin uncertain⟩

blot[2] [blɒt] *n.* a piece in backgammon which is next to no other and can therefore be taken. ⟨origin uncertain⟩

blotch [blɒtʃ] *n., v.* —*n.* **1** a large, irregular spot or stain. **2** a place where the skin is discoloured or broken out.
—*v.* cover or mark with blotches. ⟨blend of *blot* and *botch*⟩

blotch•y ['blɒtʃi] *adj.* **blotch•i•er, blotch•i•est.** having or consisting of a blotch or blotches. —**'blotch•i•ness,** *n.*

blot•ter ['blɒtər] *n.* **1** a piece of blotting paper. **2** a book for writing down happenings or transactions: *A police station blotter is a record of arrests.* **3** anything that soaks up or absorbs: *She has a blotter of a mind; she remembers everything.* **4** *Slang.* drunkard.

blotting paper a soft paper used to dry writing by soaking up excess ink.

blot•to ['blɒtou] *adj. Slang.* inebriated to the point of unconsciousness. ⟨< *blot*[1]⟩

blouse ['blaʊz] *or* [blʌus] *n., v.* **bloused, blous•ing.** —*n.* **1** a loose or partly fitted, light garment for the upper part of the body, worn by women and girls. **2** any loosely fitted garment for the upper part of the body. Sailors wear blouses. **3** the upper part of a battle dress. **4** a kind of smock reaching to the knees, worn by European peasants and workmen to protect their clothes.
—*v.* of a shirt or blouse, be tucked in so as to flow over the waist in loose folds; tuck in (one's shirt) so that it flows over the waist in such a manner. ⟨< F < Provençal *(lano) blouso* short (wool)⟩
—**'blouse,like,** *adj.*

blous•on [blu'zɒn] *or* ['bluzɒn]; *French,* [blu'zɔ̃] *adj., n.*—*adj.* of a garment, having the top styled like a blouse.
—*n.* a garment in this style. ⟨< F⟩

blow[1] [blou] *n.* **1** a hard hit; knock; stroke. **2** a sudden happening that causes misfortune or loss; severe shock; misfortune: *His mother's death was a great blow to him.* **3** a sudden attack or assault: *The army struck a swift blow at the enemy.*
at one blow, by one act or effort.
come to blows, start fighting.
without striking a blow, with no effort; without even trying. ⟨ME *blaw*⟩
☛ *Syn.* **1. Blow,** STROKE[1] = a sudden, hard hit. **Blow,** both figuratively and literally, emphasizes the force, roughness, and heaviness of a hard knock against something or a hit with the fist or something heavy: *He got a blow on the head.* **Stroke** emphasizes the sharpness and precision of a hit with the hand or something long and narrow, but is most often used in specific senses, as in tennis or art, and figuratively: *His scar was made by a sword stroke across the face.*

blow[2] [blou] *v.* **blew, blown, blow•ing;** *n.* —*v.* **1** send forth (a strong current of air): *The fan blew fresh air into the room. She blew on the soup to cool it.* **2** move in a current, especially rapidly or with power: *The wind was blowing from the east.* **3** drive or carry, or be driven or carried, by a current of air: *The wind blew the curtains. His hat blew away.* **4** force a current of air into, through, or against: *She blew the embers into flame.* **5** clear or empty by forcing air through: *We blew the eggs before colouring them for Easter.* **6** produce or shape by means of blown or injected air: *to blow bubbles, to blow glass.* **7** be windy: *It's blowing like rain.* **8** cause (a wind instrument) to make a sound: *to blow a trumpet.* **9** make (a sound) by means of a current of air or steam: *The whistle blew at noon. The bugle blew taps.* **10** break by an explosion; blow up, open, etc.: *The thieves blew the safe.* **11** be out of breath: *The horse was blowing at the end of the race.* **12** make out of breath; cause to pant. **13** *Informal.* boast; brag. **14** of whales, spout water and air. **15** of insects, lay eggs (in). Some flies blow fruit. **16** *Slang.* **a** spend recklessly: *She blew her whole allowance in the bookstore.* **b** treat; entertain. **17** melt or burn out (a fuse, etc.): *A short circuit will blow a fuse. That bulb in the hall light just blew.* **18** publish or spread (news). **19** *Slang.* handle badly; bungle: *The last time we asked him to help, he blew the job.* **20** *Slang.* leave; get out of: *She blew town.* **21** of an engine, cause or undergo a breakdown, usually by overwork or misuse: *The engine blew from overwork. The mechanic blew the engine.*
blow hot and cold, change from a favourable opinion to an unfavourable one; view something with fluctuating enthusiasm.
blow in, a *Informal.* appear unexpectedly; drop in. **b** of an oil well, start production; come into production.
blow off, get rid of noisily or explosively.
blow (one's) **cool,** *Slang.* lose one's composure.
blow (one's or someone's) **cover,** reveal (one's or someone's) real self, intention, etc.
blow (one's) **own horn,** speak braggingly about one's accomplishments.
blow (one's) **top** (or **stack** or **cork,** etc.), *Slang.* become very angry.
blow out, a extinguish or be extinguished by a puff of breath or other current of air: *Please blow out the candle. The candle has blown out.* **b** have or cause to have a blowout. **c** disperse (itself), usually said of bad weather; fade away: *The storm blew itself out.*
blow over, a pass by or over: *The storm has blown over.* **b** of some scandal, etc., be forgotten.
blow (someone) **away,** *Informal.* **a** kill, usually with a firearm. **b** overwhelm with admiration, surprise, etc.; shock.
blow (someone's) **mind,** surprise greatly; astonish.
blow the whistle (on), reveal someone's guilty secret; tattle-tale (on).
blow up, a explode. **b** fill with air. **c** *Informal.* become very angry. **d** *Informal.* scold; abuse. **e** arise; begin: *A storm suddenly blew up.* **f** enlarge (a photograph). **g** exaggerate.
—*n.* **1** the act or fact of forcing air into, through, or against something; blast: *a blow of the whistle. One blow cleared the pipe.* **2** a gale of wind: *Last night's big blow brought down several trees.* ⟨OE *blāwan*⟩

blow[3] [blou] *v.* **blew, blown, blow•ing;** *n.* —*v.* burst into flower; bloom (*now used mostly as a past participle*): *a full-blown rose.*
—*n.* the state of blooming: *The garden was in full blow.* ⟨OE *blōwan*⟩

blow–by–blow ['blou baɪ 'blou] *adj.* of a report, account, etc., very detailed: *He gave us a blow-by-blow account of the game.*

blow–dry ['blou ,draɪ] *v.* **blow-dried, blow-dry•ing.** dry and style (the hair) using a blow dryer.

blow dry•er or **blow–dry•er** ['blou ,draɪər] *n.* a hand-held electrical apparatus for drying the hair by means of a strong current of hot air. It has a nozzle for directing the air to a particular part of the hair so that the hair can be styled as it is being dried.

blow•er ['blouər] *n.* **1** a person or thing that blows: *a glass blower.* **2** a fan or other machine for forcing air into a building, furnace, mine, etc. **3** whale. **4** *Informal.* telephone.

blow•fish ['blou,fɪʃ] PUFFER (def. 2).

blow•fly ['blou,flaɪ] *n., pl.* **-flies.** any of several species of large fly (family Calliphoridae), including bluebottles, having metallic blue, green, or bronze bodies and making a loud buzzing sound in flight. Blowflies are similar to the common housefly, except that they breed mainly in dead flesh, and their larvae will sometimes infest open wounds, causing serious disease.

blow•gun ['blou,gʌn] *n.* **1** a tube through which a person blows arrows or darts. **2** peashooter.

blow•hard ['blou,hɑrd] *n. Slang.* braggart.

blow•hole ['blou,houl] *n.* **1** a hole where air or gas can escape. **2** a hole for breathing, in the top of the head of whales and some other animals. **3** a hole in the ice where whales, seals, etc. come to breathe. **4** a defect in a piece of metal due to a bubble of air or gas. **5** a defect; flaw.

blown [bloun] *adj., v.* —*adj.* **1** out of breath; exhausted: *He was blown after climbing the steep hill.* **2** tainted by flies; flyblown; tainted. **3** shaped by blowing: *blown glass.* **4** of cattle, having the stomach distended by eating too much green food; bloated.
—*v.* pp. of BLOW[2] and BLOW[3].

blow•off ['blou,ɒf] *n.* **1** an explosive output of steam or water. **2** a blowing away of topsoil by the wind. **3** the topsoil lost through wind erosion. **4** *Slang.* a self-important person.

blow•out ['blou,ʌut] *n.* **1** the bursting of a container or casing, such as an automobile tire, by the pressure of the enclosed air, etc. on a weak spot. **2** the sudden, uncontrolled eruption of an oil or gas well. **3** the melting of an electric fuse caused by an overload in a circuit or line. **4** *Slang.* a big party or meal or other celebration.

blow•pipe ['blou,pəip] *n.* **1** a tube for blowing air or gas into a flame to increase the heat. **2** blowgun. **3** a long metal tube used for blowing molten glass into the required shape. **4** *Medicine.* an instrument for blowing air into a body cavity for cleaning or examination.

blows•y or **blowz•y** ['blaʊzi] *adj.* **blows•i•er, blows•i•est** or **blowz•i•er, blowz•i•est. 1** untidy; frowzy. **2** red-faced and coarse-looking. ⟨< obs. *blouze* wench⟩ **—'blows•i•ly** or **'blowz•i•ly,** *adv.* **—'blows•i•ness** or **'blowz•i•ness,** *n.*

blow•torch ['blou,tɔrtʃ] *n.* a small torch that shoots out a hot flame. It is used to melt metal and burn off paint.

blow•up ['blou,ʌp] *n.* **1** explosion. **2** *Informal.* **a** an outburst of anger. **b** a quarrel. **3** *Informal.* an enlargement (of a photograph).

blow•y ['bloui] *adj.* **blow•i•er, blow•i•est.** windy.

bls. 1 barrels. **2** bales.

BLT a bacon, lettuce, and tomato sandwich.

blub•ber ['blʌbər] *n., v.* —*n.* **1** the fat of whales and some other sea animals. **2** unwanted fat on a human being. **3** a noisy weeping.
—*v.* **1** weep noisily. **2** utter while crying and sobbing: *The child blubbered an apology.* **3** disfigure or swell with crying: *a face all blubbered.* ⟨probably imitative⟩ **—'blub•ber•y,** *adj.*

blub•ber•bag or **blub•ber–bag** ['blʌbər,bæg] *Informal.* a sausage-shaped rubber container for carrying oil on an aircraft.

blu•cher ['blutʃər] *or* ['blukər] *n.* formerly, a shoe or half-boot whose tongue and front part were made from one piece of leather. ⟨after Field Marshal von *Blücher* (1742-1819), a Prussian general⟩

bludg•eon ['blʌdʒən] *n., v.* —*n.* a short, heavy club, used as a weapon.
—*v.* **1** strike with a club. **2** bully; threaten. ⟨origin unknown⟩ **—'bludg•eon•er,** *n.*

blue [blu] *n., adj.* **blu•er, blu•est;** *v.* **blued, blu•ing** or **blue•ing.**
—*n.* **1** the colour of the clear sky in daylight or the colour of the part of the spectrum between green and violet. **2** blue dye or pigment. **3 the blue, a** the sky: *high up in the blue.* **b** the far distance. **c** the sea. **4 blues,** *pl. Informal.* low spirits: *She got the blues.* **5 blues,** *pl. Music.* **a** a style of jazz characterized by a tendency to flatten the thirds by a semitone, producing minor sequences and harmonies that give the music a melancholy sound. The blues developed from black work songs and spirituals. **b** a song in this style (*used with a singular verb*).
into the blue, far away; out of reach: *It vanished into the blue.*
out of the blue, completely unexpected; from an unknown source or for an unknown reason: *Suddenly, out of the blue, she announced that she was quitting.*
sing or **cry the blues,** be sad or dissatisfied.
—*adj.* **1** of or having the colour of the clear sky in daylight or any tone of this colour. **2** of animals or plants, bluish, or having parts that are blue or bluish (*used in compounds*): *blue spruce, blue flag, bluefish.* **3** of the skin, livid; ashen: *blue with cold.* **4** having or showing low spirits; sad, gloomy, or discouraged: *a blue mood. I was feeling very blue.* **5** dismal; dispiriting: *a blue day.* **6** *Informal.* indecent or off-colour: *blue language, a blue joke.* **7** of or having to do with Conservatives.
once in a blue moon, hardly ever; rarely: *Once in a blue moon we get a letter from him.*
—*v.* **1** make blue. **2** use bluing on. ⟨ME < OF *bleu* < Gmc.⟩
—'blue•ness, *n.*
☛ *Hom.* BLEW.

blue baby a baby born with cyanosis as a result of malfunctioning of the lungs or heart. Blood transfusion is necessary.

blue•back ['blu,bæk] *n.* **1** a young HOODED SEAL. **2** BLUEBACK SALMON.

blueback salmon a three-year-old coho.

Blue•beard ['blu,bird] *n.* **1** *Legend.* a man who murdered six of his wives and hid their bodies in a room which he forbade anyone to enter. **2** any man who marries women with the intention of killing them.

Bluebeard's chamber any place where mysteries or terrible secrets are hidden.

blue•bell ['blu,bɛl] *n.* **1** a common wildflower (*Campanula rotundifolia*) of north temperate regions having long, slender stems and blue, bell-shaped flowers. Bluebells are found throughout most of Canada. **2** any of various other plants having bell-shaped blue flowers, such as a European woodland plant (*Endymion nonscriptus*, also classified as *Scilla nonscriptus*) of the lily family.

blue•ber•ry ['blu,bɛri] *n., pl.* **-ries. 1** the small, sweet, blue berry of any of several shrubs (genus *Vaccinium*) of the heath family. **2** a shrub bearing these berries.

blue•bill ['blu,bɪl] *n.* the scaup or any other American duck with a bluish beak.

blue•bird ['blu,bɜrd] *n.* any of a small genus (*Sialia*) of North American songbirds, all three species about 18 cm long including the tail, and the males all having mainly bright blue plumage. Bluebirds belong to the subfamily Turdinae, the thrushes.

blue•black ['blu,blæk] *adj. or n.* bluish black; very dark blue.

blue blood 1 aristocratic descent. **2** aristocrat.

blue–blood•ed ['blu ,blʌdɪd] *adj.* aristocratic.

blue•bon•net ['blu,bɒnɪt] *n.* **1** a round, brimless cap made of blue woollen cloth, formerly worn in Scotland. **2** a person wearing such a cap. **3** a Scot. **4** an annual lupin (*Lupinus subcarnosus*) of the SW United States, especially Texas, having clusters of small, bonnet-shaped, blue flowers. **5** a blue cornflower.

blue book 1 a book that lists socially prominent people. **2** a booklet with a blue paper cover, used for writing answers to examinations. **3 Blue Book,** an official statement of public accounts, published annually by the Government of Canada. **4 Blue Book,** a parliamentary or other official publication.

blue•bot•tle ['blu,bɒtəl] *n.* **1** any of several species of blowfly having a bright, metallic-blue body. **2** any similar fly. **3** cornflower.

blue camas a wildflower (*Camassia quamash*) growing from a bulb, and having bright blue flowers. It blooms in spring in high wet areas from British Columbia south.

blue cheese any cheese that is veined with mould, such as Gorgonzola or Danish Blue.

blue–chip ['blu ,tʃɪp] *adj.* **1** of or having to do with any relatively low-yield, high-security stock. **2** *Informal.* of good quality.

blue cohosh a tall, early spring flower (*Caulophyllum thalictroides*) having smooth, purplish grey stems, small greenish yellow flowers, and bright blue berries. It blooms from eastern Canada south, and also in eastern Asia.

blue–col•lar ['blu ,kɒlər] *adj.* of or having to do with industrial or manual workers as a group, or their jobs, attitudes, etc.: *He said he would prefer any blue-collar job to working in an office.* ⟨referring to a common colour for workshirts; coined in contrast to *white-collar*⟩

blue crab 1 an edible crab (*Callinectes sapidus*) of the Atlantic seaboard of the U.S., having blue legs and edible flesh. **2** any other crab of this genus.

Blue Cross *Trademark.* a system of medical insurance, either to obtain benefits beyond what provincial medicare provides, or when travelling abroad.

blue–curls ['blu ,kɜrlz] a plant of the genus *Trichostema* of the mint family, having blue flowers and narrow leaves with fuzz on them.

blue devils 1 the blues; low spirits. **2 a** DELIRIUM TREMENS. **b** horrible things seen during delirium tremens.

blue–eyed grass ['blue ,aɪd] a plant *(Sisyrinchium angustifolium)* of the iris family, having short, narrow leaves like grass, and small blue or white flowers. It blooms in spring in meadows across North America.

blue•fin ['blu,fɪn] *n.* a type of tuna.

blue•fish ['blu,fɪʃ] *n., pl.* **-fish** or **-fish•es. 1** a large, blue-and-silver game and food fish (*Pomatomus saltatrix*) of tropical and temperate parts of the Atlantic and Indian Oceans, distantly related to the sea basses. **2** any of various other bluish fishes.

blue flag any of several blue-flowered wild irises, especially a common North American wildflower (*Iris versicolor*) found in marshy places.

blue fox 1 a rare colour phase of the ARCTIC FOX. **2** its bluish grey fur.

blue•gill ['blu,gɪl] *n.* a bluish-coloured sunfish (*Lepomis macrochirus*), found in fresh water.

blue goose *Cdn.* the SNOW GOOSE in its "blue" colour phase, with mainly bluish grey upper parts and wings, greyish brown or whitish under parts, and white head and neck.

blue•grass ['blu,græs] *n.* **1** any of several grasses (genus *Poa*) having bluish green stems, especially **Kentucky bluegrass** (*P. pratensis*), widely cultivated as a pasture, forage, and lawn grass. **2** a type of country music with fast rhythms and bluesy harmony.

blue gum any of several Australian eucalyptus trees, especially a tall species (*Eucalyptus globulus*) widely cultivated for its aromatic leaves, which yield a medicinal oil, and for its hard wood. The young leaves of the blue gum have a bluish tinge.

blue heart or **Blue Heart** a plant (*Buchnera americana*) of the figwort family, found in the southern U.S. and having purple flowers with hairy stems.

blue•ing ['bluɪŋ] *n.* See BLUING.

blue•ish ['bluɪʃ] See BLUISH.

blue•jack ['blu,dʒæk] *n.* a small oak tree (*Quercus incana*) of the southern U.S.

blue•jack•et ['blu,dʒækɪt] *n.* a sailor in the navy.

Bluejays—about 30 cm long including the tail

blue•jay or **blue jay** ['blu,dʒei] *n.* **1** a jay (*Cyanocitta cristata*) found in southern Canada and the United States, having a crest on the head, a very long tail, and a blue upper body and head, with a broad black band around the neck. **2** in British Columbia, the Steller's Jay (*Cyanocitta stelleri*), having a blue forehead.

blue•jeans or **blue jeans** ['blu,dʒinz] *n.pl.* men's or women's casual pants usually made of blue denim, often having the pockets and fell seams sewn in thread of a contrasting colour.

blue laws any very strict and puritanical laws.

blue•line ['blu,laɪn] *n.* either of the two blue lines drawn midway between the centre of a hockey rink and each goal: *The blueline plays an important part in the rules of hockey.*

blue lobelia a wildflower (*Lobelia siphiliticata*) having bright blue flowers, and growing tall at the edge of wet ground or low in bogs. It was once used as a cure for syphilis.

blue mould a fungus of the genus *Penicillium*, having bluish spores, and found on bread and some cheeses.

Blue•nose ['blu,nouz] *n. Informal.* **1** a Nova Scotian; less often, a New Brunswicker. **2** (*adjl.*) of or associated with Nova Scotia. **3** a ship built in Nova Scotia and manned by Nova Scotians. **4** a famous schooner built in Nova Scotia and launched in 1921. The *Bluenose* was never defeated as the holder of the International Fisherman's Trophy, given to the fastest sailing vessel in the North Atlantic fishing fleets. It was wrecked and lost off Haïti in 1946. The name is generally supposed to come from a nickname given to Nova Scotians. See SCHOONER for picture. **5 bluenose,** a prudish or puritanical person.

blue note *Music.* a minor third or seventh, as used in some jazz.

blue–pen•cil ['blu 'pɛnsəl] *v.* **-cilled** or **-ciled, -cil•ling** or **-cil•ing.** change or cross out, especially by using a pencil with a blue lead, such as editors sometimes use.

blue phlox a wildflower (*Phlox divaricata*), having broad pink or purple flowers and sharp-pointed leaves. It blooms in spring in open ground from Québec and Ontario south.

blue•point ['blu,pɔɪnt] *n.* a type of small, edible oyster harvested at Blue Point on Long Island, New York.

blue•print ['blu,prɪnt] *n., v.* —*n.* **1** an exact photographic copy of an original drawing of a building plan, map, etc., usually showing white lines on a blue background. **2** a detailed plan for any enterprise.
—*v.* **1** make a blueprint of. **2** make or explain (a plan) in detail.

blue racer a dark blue or greenish blue subspecies of the blacksnake (*Coluber constrictor*) found in central and western North America. It is an endangered species.

blue ribbon first prize; highest honour. —**'blue-'rib•bon,** *adj.*

blues [bluz] *n.* See BLUE (defs. 4, 5).

blue spruce a spruce tree (*Picea pungens*) having bluish green needles, native to the W United States but commonly used as an ornamental tree throughout North America.

blue•stem ['blu,stɛm] *n.* a grass of the genus *Andropogon*, native to the U.S. and used to feed livestock.

blue•stock•ing ['blu,stɒkɪŋ] *n. Informal.* a woman who displays great interest in intellectual or literary subjects, especially if pedantic or affected. ⟨< nickname "*Blue Stocking* Society" given to a group of women in London, England, who met (about 1750) to discuss literature⟩

blue•stone ['blu,stoun] *n.* **1** bluish sandstone. **2** BLUE VITRIOL.

blue streak *Informal.* anything as fast or vivid as lightning. **talk a blue streak,** *Informal.* speak rapidly and excitedly and at length.

blue•sy ['bluzi] *adj. Music.* related to or reminiscent of blues.

blu•et ['bluɪt] *n.* a small plant of North America having pale bluish flowers. ⟨< F *bluet*, dim of *bleu* blue < Gmc.⟩

blue–throat•ed macaw ['blu ,θroutɪd] a type of parrot (*Ara glaucogularis*) native to flooded savannahs in Bolivia, having a blue head and throat patch, green wings, and a long tail. It is an endangered species.

blue violet a small wildflower (*Viola papilionacea*) having pale purple flowers. It is the provincial flower of New Brunswick.

blue vitriol hydrous COPPER SULPHATE. *Formula*: $CuSO_4.5H_2O$

blue•weed ['blu,wid] a tall plant (*Echium vulgare*) having pale to deep blue flowers. It was naturalized in North America from European plants. Also known as **viper's bugloss**.

blue whale a dark greyish blue baleen whale (*Balaenoptera musculus*) found in all the oceans of the world. It is the largest animal that has ever existed on earth, reaching a maximum length of about 30 metres and mass of about 130 tonnes.

blue–winged teal ['blu ,wɪŋd] a small duck (*Anas discors*) found on ponds and rivers across the U.S. and Canada, and having blue and green wings and a bluish bill.

bluff[1] [blʌf] *n., adj.* —*n.* **1** a high, steep bank or cliff. **2** *Cdn.* a clump of trees standing on the flat prairie; copse: *The farmhouse was screened from the wind and the sun by a poplar bluff.*
—*adj.* **1** of a cliff, the bow of a ship, etc., rising steeply with a straight, broad front. **2** frank and rough in a good-natured way. ⟨probably < Du. *blaf* broad flat face⟩ —**'bluff•ly,** *adv.* —**'bluff•ness,** *n.*

☛ *Syn. adj.* **2.** See note at BLUNT.

bluff[2] [blʌf] *n., v.* —*n.* **1** a show of pretended confidence, used to deceive or mislead. **2** a threat that cannot be carried out. **3** a person who bluffs.
call (someone's) **bluff,** challenge or expose a bluff: *He backed down when I called his bluff.*
—*v.* **1** deceive (someone) by a show of pretended confidence. **2** frighten (someone) with a threat that cannot be carried out.
bluff (one's) **way,** get something one wants by bluffing: *She bluffed her way through this test but she'll never make the final exam.* ⟨? < Du. *bluffen*, baffle; mislead; brag⟩ —**'bluff•er,** *n.*

blu•ing or **blue•ing** ['bluɪŋ] *n., v.*—*n.* a blue liquid or powder put in water when rinsing white fabrics, in order to prevent them from turning yellow.
—*v.* ppr. of BLUE.

blu•ish ['bluɪʃ] *adj.* somewhat blue. Also, **blueish.**

blun•der ['blʌndər] *n., v.* —*n.* a stupid mistake.
—*v.* **1** make a stupid mistake. **2** do (something) clumsily or wrongly; bungle. **3** move clumsily or blindly; stumble. **4** blurt out; say clumsily or foolishly. ⟨ME *blondre(n)*; origin uncertain⟩
blunder on, discover by chance —**'blun•der•er,** *n.*

blun•der•buss ['blʌndər,bʌs] *n.* **1** a short gun with a wide muzzle, formerly used to fire a quantity of shot a short distance. **2** a person who blunders. ⟨alteration of Du. *donderbus* thunder gun⟩

blunge [blʌndʒ] *v.* **blunged, blunging.** *Ceramics.* blend (clay) with water. ⟨? < *bl*(*end*) + (*pl*)*unge*⟩

blunt [blʌnt] *adj., v.* —*adj.* **1** without a sharp edge or point. **2** plain-spoken; outspoken; frank. **3** slow in perceiving or understanding.
—*v.* **1** make less sharp or keen: *to blunt a knife, to blunt someone's enthusiasm.* **2** become less sharp or keen. ⟨ME; origin uncertain⟩ —**'blunt•ly,** *adv.* —**'blunt•ness,** *n.*

☛ *Syn. adj.* **1.** See note at DULL. **2. Blunt,** BLUFF, CURT = abrupt in speaking or manner. **Blunt** emphasizes speaking plainly and frankly and sometimes tactlessly: *He thinks that blunt speech proves he is honest.* **Bluff** suggests a frank and rough manner of speaking and acting combined with heartiness and genuineness: *Everyone likes the bluff police officer on the beat.* **Curt** = rudely abrupt and brief: *A curt nod was the only notice he gave that he knew she was there.*

blur [blɜr] *v.* **blurred, blur•ring;** *n.* —*v.* **1** make or become confused in form or outline: *Mist blurred the hills.* **2** make or become unable to see clearly: *Tears blurred my eyes. Her eyes blurred with tears.* **3** smear; blot; smudge: *She blurred the writing by touching the ink before it was dry.*
—*n.* **1** a blurred condition; dimness or indistinctness. **2** something seen dimly or indistinctly. **3** a smear; blot; smudge. ⟨? var. of *blear*⟩

blurb [blɜrb] *n. Informal.* an advertisement or announcement, especially of a book, and especially one that is full of extremely high praise. ⟨supposedly coined in 1907 by Gelett Burgess (1866-1951), an American humorist⟩

blur•ry ['blɜri] *adj.* **blur•ri•er, blur•ri•est. 1** dim; indistinct. **2** smeary; full of blots and smudges. **—'blur•ri•ness,** *n.*

blurt [blɜrt] *v.* say suddenly or without thinking (often used with **out**): *In his anger he blurted out the secret.* ⟨imitative⟩

blush [blʌʃ] *n., v.* —*n.* **1** a reddening of the skin caused by shame, confusion, or excitement. **2** a rosy colour. **3** BLUSHER (def. 2).
at first blush, at first appearance or consideration.
—*v.* **1** make or become red because of shame, confusion, or excitement: *She was so shy that she blushed every time she was spoken to.* **2** be ashamed: *I blush to observe the errors in my manuscript.* **3** be or become rosy. ⟨ME *blusche* < OE *blyscan* redden⟩

blush•er ['blʌʃər] *n.* **1** one who blushes. **2** a red or pink cosmetic applied to the face to heighten its colour.

blush wine any wine of a pink colour, made in the manner of rosé from red and white grapes, but technically a dry white wine.

blus•ter ['blʌstər] *v., n.* —*v.* **1** storm or blow noisily and violently: *The wind blustered around the house.* **2** talk noisily and boastfully or threateningly: *He blusters a lot but he's really a coward.* **3** do or say noisily and violently: *She blustered an oath and slammed the door.* **4** make or get by blustering.
—*n.* **1** stormy noise and violence. **2** noisy and boastful or threatening talk. ⟨apparently < LG *blüstern* blow violently⟩
—'blus•ter•er, *n.*

blus•ter•y ['blʌstəri] *adj.* blustering.

blvd. boulevard.

BM *Informal.* bowel movement.

bm BOARD MEASURE.

BMR basal metabolism rate.

Bn. battalion.

BNA Act or **B.N.A. Act** BRITISH NORTH AMERICA ACT.

B'nai B'rith [bə'nei 'brɪθ] *or* [bə'rɪθ] an international Jewish fraternal society. ⟨< Hebrew *bene berith*, sons of the covenant⟩

BO or **B.O.** *Informal.* **1** body odour. **2** box office. **3** branch office.

bo•a ['bouə] *n., pl.* **bo•as. 1** any of various non-poisonous tropical snakes (family Boidae) that give birth to live young, unlike most snakes, and that kill their prey by coiling around it and squeezing until it suffocates. Boas range in length from about 45 cm to 9 m. One of the smallest boas, called the **rubber boa**, is found in the valleys in the extreme south of British Columbia. **2** a long scarf made of fur or feathers, worn around a woman's neck. ⟨< L *boa*, a type of serpent⟩

boa constrictor 1 a large tropical American boa (*Boa constrictor*) having tan skin with brown markings and averaging about 340 cm in length. **2** any large snake that kills its prey by squeezing it until it suffocates.

boar [bɔr] *n.* **1** an uncastrated male of the domestic pig. **2** WILD BOAR. ⟨OE *bār*⟩
☛ *Hom.* BORE.

board [bɔrd] *n., v.* —*n.* **1** a long, flat piece of sawed lumber for use in building, etc. **2** a flat piece of wood or other material used for some special purpose: *an ironing board.* **3 the boards,** *pl.* **a** the stage of a theatre. **b** *Hockey.* the wooden guard fence surrounding the ice of a hockey rink. **c** *Basketball.* backboard. **4** pasteboard: *a book with covers of board.* **5** a flat, specially marked piece of wood, cardboard, etc. on which to play a game: *a chessboard.* **6** a table to serve food on; table. **7** the food served on a table. **8** meals provided for pay. **9** a group of people managing something; council: *a board of health.* **10** the side of a ship. **11** chalkboard; blackboard. **12** *Computer technology.* CIRCUIT BOARD. **13** *Computer technology.* CARD (def. 13). **14** a printed catalogue of the stocks for sale on a specific stock exchange, with their prices.
across the board, affecting everybody or everything of a group equally: *Prices have increased across the board again.*
go by the board, a of a ship mast, etc., fall over the side. **b** be given up, neglected, or ignored.
on board, on a ship, train, etc.
tread the boards, act in a play.
—*v.* **1** cover with boards (*usually used with* **up**): *to board up a broken window.* **2** provide with regular meals, or room and meals, at one's own home or another's, for pay: *They boarded John at his uncle's house for a while.* **3** get meals, or room and meals, for pay: *Mrs. Cohen boards at our house.* **4** get on (a ship, train, etc.). **5** come alongside of or against (a ship). **6** *Hockey.* bodycheck (an opposing player) into the boards. ⟨OE *bord*⟩

board check *Hockey.* a check made by bodychecking an opposing player into the boards of a rink, the checker being subject to a penalty if the referee judges the act to have been violent; boarding.

board–check ['bɔrd ˌtʃɛk] *v.* give a BOARD CHECK to (an opposing player).

board•er ['bɔrdər] *n.* **1** a person who pays for regular meals, or for room and meals, at another's house. **2** a person assigned to go on board an enemy ship. **3** a resident pupil at a BOARDING SCHOOL.
☛ *Hom.* BORDER.

board foot a unit of measure equal to the volume of a board one foot square and one inch thick (about 30 cm^2 × 2.54 cm), used for measuring logs and lumber; 144 cubic inches (about 2360 cm^3). *Abbrev.*: bd.ft.

board game any game played by moving pieces on a marked board, often according to the throw of dice.

board•ing ['bɔrdɪŋ] *n., v.*—*n.* **1** *Hockey.* the act of checking an opposing player into the boards of the rink in a rough and illegal manner. **2** wood cut into boards: *We have to order the boarding for our new fence.* **3** a structure made of boards. **4** the act of going on board a ship or plane. **5** (*adjl.*) having to do with boarding: *a boarding pass.*
—*v.* ppr. of BOARD.

boarding house a house where meals, or room and meals, are provided for pay.

boarding school a school that provides lodging and food during the school term for some or all of its students or pupils.

board measure a system for measuring logs and lumber. The unit is the BOARD FOOT.

board of control the executive branch of the governing council of certain large cities, consisting of the mayor and two or more controllers.

board of education a group of people, usually elected, who manage the schools in a certain area; school board.

board of health the department of a local government in charge of public health.

board of trade 1 an association of business people to protect and advance their interests. **2 Board of Trade,** in the United Kingdom, the governmental department in charge of commerce and industry.

board•room ['bɔrd,rum] *or* [-ˌrʊm] *n.* **1** a room that is regularly used to hold meetings of a board of directors, etc. **2** (*adjl.*) of or having to do with business executives: *boardroom politics.*

board rule a measuring instrument for determining the number of board feet in an amount of lumber.

board•sail•ing ['bɔrd,seilɪŋ] *n.* a water sport in which one rides a sailboard; sailboarding; windsurfing.

board•walk ['bɔrd,wɒk] *n.* a sidewalk or promenade made of boards, usually along a waterfront.

boar•fish ['bɔr,fɪʃ] *n.* a fish of the Caproidae family. It is small and red, has a snout like a pig's, and lives in deep water.

boar•hound ['bɔr,haʊnd] *n.* any of several breeds of large dog, especially the Great Dane, formerly used in hunting wild boars.

boast [boust] *v., n.* —*v.* **1** speak highly of oneself or one's accomplishments or possessions; brag. **2** brag about: *He boasts his skill at soccer. She boasted that she was the best player on the team.* **3** have and be proud of: *Our town boasts many fine parks.*
—*n.* **1** a praising of oneself; bragging. **2** something to be proud of. ⟨ME *boste(n)*; origin uncertain⟩ **—'boast•er,** *n.* **—'boast•ing•ly,** *adv.*
☛ *Syn. v.* **1. Boast,** BRAG = to praise oneself. **Boast** = talk too much

about something one has done or about one's possessions, family, etc., even though there may be some reason to be proud: *She boasts about her new convertible.* **Brag** is informal, and always suggests showing off and exaggerating: *He is always bragging about what he can do with a car.*

boast•ful ['boustfəl] *adj.* **1** boasting; speaking too well about oneself. **2** fond of boasting. **—'boast•ful•ly,** *adv.* **—'boast•ful•ness,** *n.*

boat [bout] *n., v.* *—n.* **1** a small, open vessel for travelling on water. **2** ship. **3** a boat-shaped dish for gravy, sauce, etc.
burn (one's) **boats,** cut off all chances of retreat.
in the same boat, in the same position or condition; taking the same chances: *We're all in the same boat, so stop complaining.*
miss the boat, *Informal.* miss an opportunity; lose one's chances.
rock the boat, *Informal.* disturb the status quo.
—v. **1** use a boat; go in a boat. **2** put or carry in a boat. ⟨OE *bāt*⟩

boat–billed heron ['bout ,bɪld] a wading bird (*Cochlearius cochlearius*) of Central and South America, having a large, wide beak. It is nocturnal.

boat•el [bou'tɛl] *n.* a motel for people arriving by boat; a hotel on the waterfront or near a dock. ⟨< *boat* + (*hot*)*el*⟩

boat•er ['boutər] *n.* **1** one who sails a boat. **2** a straw hat with a brim and a flat top.

boat•hook ['bout,hʊk] a pole having a metal hook at one end, used for pulling or pushing a boat, raft, etc.

boat•house ['bout,hʌus] *n., pl.* **-hous•es** [,haʊzɪz]. a house or shed for sheltering a boat or boats.

boat•ing ['boutɪŋ] *n., v.—n.* rowing; sailing.
—v. ppr. of BOAT.

boat livery a boathouse where boats are hired out.

boat•load ['bout,loud] *n.* **1** as much or as many as a boat can hold or carry. **2** the load that a boat is carrying.

boat•man ['boutmən] *n., pl.* **-men. 1** a man who rents out boats or takes care of them. **2** a man whose work is rowing or sailing small boats or who is skilled in their use.

boat neck a wide, shallow, scooped neckline.

boat people refugees who have escaped from their native country by boat and are seeking asylum in another country, especially South Asians who fled the Communist takeover of Vietnam in 1975.

boat song *Cdn.* a song used by the VOYAGEURS to help them maintain a steady rhythm with their paddles. Also, **paddling song.**

boat•swain ['bousən]; *less often,* ['bout,swein] *n.* a ship's officer in charge of the deck crew, the anchors, ropes, rigging, etc. Also, **bo's'n, bosun.**

boat train a train that waits at a port for passengers transferring from a ship. The train is scheduled to meet the boat, but will wait if the boat is delayed.

bob[1] [bɒb] *v.* **bobbed, bob•bing;** *n. —v.* **1** move up and down, or to and fro, with short, quick motions: *The bird bobbed its head up and down. The little boat bobbed on the waves.* **2** curtsy quickly. **3** try to catch with the teeth something floating or hanging: *One game at the party was to bob for apples in a bowl of water.*
bob up, appear suddenly or unexpectedly.
—n. **1** a short, quick motion up and down, or to and fro. **2** a quick curtsy. ⟨ME; origin uncertain⟩

bob[2] [bɒb] *n., v.* **bobbed, bob•bing.** *—n.* **1** a short haircut. **2** a small ringlet or curl of hair. **3** a horse's docked tail. **4** a weight on the end of a pendulum or plumb line. **5** a float for a fishing line. **6** a bobsled.
—v. **1** cut (hair) short. **2** fish with a bob. ⟨ME *bobbe* bunch; origin uncertain⟩

bob[3] [bɒb] *n., v.* **bobbed, bob•bing.**
—n. a light rap; tap.
—v. rap lightly; tap. ⟨ME; origin uncertain⟩

bob•ber ['bɒbər] *n.* **1** BOB[2] (def. 4). **2** any person or thing that bobs.

bob•bin ['bɒbən] *n.* a reel or spool for holding thread, yarn, etc. Bobbins are used in spinning, weaving, machine sewing, and lacemaking. Wire is also wound on bobbins. ⟨< F *bobine*⟩

bob•bi•net [,bɒbə'nɛt] *or* ['bɒbə,nɛt] *n.* a cotton netting or lace made by machines. ⟨< *bobbin* + *net*[1]⟩

bobbing shack ICE HUT.

bob•ble ['bɒbəl] *n., v.* **bob•bled, bob•bling.** *—n.* **1** a small, round, fluffy ball used for decoration on hangings. **2** a quick movement up and down, or to and fro. **3** a fumbling of the ball in football, basketball, etc.
—v. fumble (the ball). ⟨< *bob*[1]⟩
☛ *Hom.* BAUBLE.

bob•by ['bɒbi] *n., pl.* **-bies.** *Brit. Informal.* police constable. ⟨after Sir *Robert* Peel (1788-1850), who improved the London police system⟩

bobby pin a flat wire clip for the hair, having prongs that press close together.

bob•cat ['bɒb,kæt] *n.* a lynx (*Lynx rufus*) found mostly in the United States, closely related to the Canada lynx but generally smaller and having much smaller ear tufts or none at all, and smaller paws. The bobcat has silky brownish fur with dark spots.

bob•o•link ['bɒbə,lɪŋk] *n.* a New World songbird (*Dolichonyx oryzivorus*) of the same family as the orioles and meadowlarks, that breeds in N North America and winters in central South America. The male in breeding season has a white back and rump and black under parts. ⟨imitative⟩

bob•skate ['bɒb,skeit] *n.* a child's skate that consists of two sections of double runners and is adjustable for size.

bob•sled ['bɒb,slɛd] *n., v.* **-sled•ded, -sled•ding.** *—n.* a long sled with two sets of runners, a continuous seat, a steering wheel, and brakes.
—v. ride or coast on a bobsled.

bob•sleigh ['bɒb,slei] *n. or v.* **-sleighed, -sleigh•ing.** BOBSLED.

bob•stay ['bɒb,stei] *n.* on a ship, a rope or chain to hold a bowsprit down.

bob•tail ['bɒb,teil] *n., v.—n.* **1** a short tail; tail cut short. **2** a horse or dog having a bobtail. **3** (*adjl.*) having a bobtail.
—v. cut short the tail of (an animal).

bob•white ['bɒb,wɔit] *n.* a quail (*Colinus virginianus*) of southern Ontario and the eastern United States, a small, plump game bird having a reddish brown back and striped sides.

bob•wire ['bɒb,waɪr] *n.* barbed wire.

boc•cie, boc•ce, or **boc•ci** ['bɒtʃi] an Italian bowling game played on a boarded court of sand with wooden balls. ⟨< Ital. *bocce* wooden balls⟩

bock [bɒk] *n.* BOCK BEER.

bock beer a strong, sweet, dark beer brewed in the winter and stored until the spring. ⟨< G *Bockbier* for *Eimbocker Bier* beer of *Eimbock,* variant of Einbeck, a city in Germany⟩

BOD BIOCHEMICAL OXYGEN DEMAND.

bod [bɒd] *n. Informal.* **1** the body. **2** a person.
☛ *Hom.* BAUD, BAWD.

bode[1] [boud] *v.* **bod•ed, bod•ing.** be a sign of; indicate beforehand: *Dark clouds boded rain.*
bode ill, be a bad sign.
bode well, be a good sign. ⟨OE *bodian* < *boda* messenger⟩

bode[2] [boud] *v.* a pt. of BIDE.

bo•de•ga [bou'deigə] *n.* a small Spanish grocery store or wine store. ⟨< Sp.⟩

bod•hi ['boudi] *n. Buddhism.* **1** the state of enlightenment attained by one who has achieved salvation. **2** the awakening into nirvana. ⟨< Skt.⟩

Bod•hi•satt•va [,boudi'sʌtvə] *n. Buddhism.* one who has attained enlightenment yet remains in the world to save others. ⟨< Skt.⟩

bod•ice ['bɒdɪs] *n.* **1** the part of a dress from the shoulders to the waist. **2** an outer garment for women and girls, worn over a blouse and laced up the front. The bodice is part of the traditional dress of peasant women in some European countries. ⟨var. of pl. of *body,* part of a dress⟩

–bodied *combining form.* having a body of a certain kind: *a full-bodied wine, able-bodied helpers.*

bod•i•less ['bɒdilɪs] *adj.* **1** without a body; lacking the trunk. **2** having no material form: *bodiless spirits.*

bod•i•ly ['bɒdəli] *adj., adv. —adj.* of or in the body: *bodily pain, assault causing bodily harm.*
—adv. **1** in person: *The man we thought dead walked bodily into the room.* **2** all together; as one body: *The audience rose bodily.* **3** by taking hold of the body: *She carried the kicking child bodily from the room.*

bod•ing ['boudɪŋ] *n., adj., v.—n.* a feeling that something bad is about to happen; presentiment.
—adj. ominous.
—v. ppr. of BODE. ⟨ME *bodynge* < OE *bodung* < *bodian* bode⟩

bod•kin ['bɒdkɪn] *n.* **1** a large, blunt needle with a large eye, used for pulling tape or ribbon through a casing, etc. **2** a long ornamental hairpin. **3** a small, pointed tool for making holes in fabric or leather. **4** *Archaic.* dagger; stiletto. ⟨ME *boydekyn* dagger; origin unknown⟩

Bod•lei•an ['bɒdliən] *or* [bɒd'liən] *n.* a great library in Oxford, England, housing a copy of the Magna Carta among other important books and papers. ⟨after Sir T. *Bodley* (1545-1613)⟩

Bo•do•ni [bə'douni] *n.* an elegant 18th century type font. ⟨after Giombattista *Bodoni* (1740-1813), the Italian printer who designed it⟩

bod•y ['bɒdi] *n., pl.* **bod•ies;** *v.* **bod•ied, bod•y•ing.** *—n.* **1** the whole material part of a human being, animal, or plant: *This girl has a strong, healthy body.* **2** the main part, or trunk, of a human being or animal, excluding the head and limbs. **3** the main part of anything, such as the nave of a church, the hull of a ship, etc. **4** the material part of a person, as distinct from the spiritual part. **5** the part of a vehicle that holds the passengers or the load. **6** the fuselage of an airplane. **7** the main part of a speech or document, excluding the introduction, etc. **8** a group of persons considered together; collection of persons or things: *A large body of children sang at the concert.* **9** *Informal.* a person: *She is a good-natured body.* **10** a dead person; corpse. **11** a mass; portion of matter: *A lake is a body of water.* **12** matter; substance; density; substantial quality: *Thick soup has more body than thin soup.* **13** that part of a garment that covers the trunk of the body. **14** the largest percentage of a group of people or objects: *The body of the antiques is kept in the basement.* **15** any object with a substantive form or physical reality. Planets and stars are celestial bodies. **16** of sounds and flavours, mellowness or richness: *a red wine with body; a baritone with body.*
keep body and soul together, keep alive.
over my dead body, not with my consent; not if I can hinder it.
—v. provide with a body; give substance to; embody.
body forth, a be a sign of; represent. **b** lend shape or substance to; make concrete. ⟨OE *bodig*⟩
☛ *Hom.* BAWDY.

body bag a large rubber bag fastened with a zipper, used for carrying a dead body, especially in war.

body blow **1** *Boxing.* a blow received between the bust and the navel. **2** a setback resulting in great loss.

bod•y•build•ing ['bɒdi,bɪldɪŋ] *n.* the practice of developing the muscles of the body through weightlifting and other strenuous exercises.

bod•y•check ['bɒdi,tʃɛk] *n., v. —n. Hockey, lacrosse, etc.* a defensive play by which a player impedes an opponent's progress by body contact. Also, **body check.**
—v. employ a bodycheck (against). **—'bod•y,check•er,** *n.*

body clock BIOLOGICAL CLOCK.

body count a count of the dead in a war.

bod•y•guard ['bɒdi,gɑrd] *n.* **1** a person or persons who guard someone. **2** a retinue; escort.

body language gesture, attitude, and position of the body, used as silent communication.

body pack a portable set of microphone and transmitter, worn by police.

body politic the people forming a political group with an organized government.

body rub a form of massage.

body–rub parlour a massage parlour.

body shirt or **bod•y•shirt** ['bɒdi,ʃɜrt] *n.* a fitted shirt or blouse for women or girls that ends in a kind of brief pantie with a fastening at the crotch.

body shop a garage which specializes in repairing the body of a vehicle.

body snatcher a person who steals bodies from graves.

body stocking a lightweight, close-fitting, stretchable garment consisting of a top, briefs, and, often, stockings, in one piece. Body stockings may be worn for exercising, by dancers, or, when made of very elastic fabric, as a light support for the body.

body suit a BODY SHIRT OR BODY STOCKING. Also, **bodysuit.**

bod•y•surf ['bɒdi,sɜrf] *v.* ride waves without a surfboard.

Boe•o•tian [bi'ouʃən] *n., adj. —n.* **1** a native or inhabitant of Boeotia, a district in ancient Greece. The Boeotians were considered stupid. **2** a stupid person.
—adj. **1** of or having to do with Boeotia or its people. **2** stupid.

Boer [bur] *or* [bɔr] *n.* a Dutch colonist or a person of Dutch descent living in South Africa. ⟨< Du. *boer* farmer⟩
☛ *Hom.* BOOR [bur].

Boer War the war between Great Britain and the Boers of South Africa, which lasted from 1899 to 1902.

boeuf bour•gig•non ['bʊf ,burgin'jɔ̃] beef cut up and cooked for a long time in red wine, with mushrooms and onions.

bof•fin ['bɒfɪn] *n. Slang.* an expert, especially in science. ⟨< origin uncertain⟩

bof•fo ['bɒfou] *adj. Informal.* **1** outstandingly successful or popular: *He gave a boffo recital.* **2** sensational; great. ⟨< Ital. *buffa* jest or *buffo* a puff of wind⟩

bog [bɒg] *n., v.* **bogged, bog•ging.** *—n.* soft, wet, spongy ground; a marsh or swamp.
—v. sink or get stuck in a bog.
bog down, get stuck or cause to get stuck as if in mud: *Let's not get bogged down in the details.* ⟨< Irish or Scots Gaelic *bog* soft⟩

bo•gan ['bougən] *n. Esp. Cdn.* in the Maritimes, a backwater or quiet tributary stream of a river. ⟨< Algonquian *pokelogan.* Doublet of LOGAN.⟩

bog asphodel **1** a wildflower (*Narthecium americanum*) of New Jersey, having yellow flowers. **2** any other plant of the genus *Narthecium*, growing in bogs.

bog•bean ['bɒg,bin] buckbean.

bo•gey[1] ['bougi] *n., pl.* **-geys;** *v. —n. Golf.* **1** one stroke over par: *He shot a bogey on the seventh hole.* **2** the standard score that players try to equal; par.
—v. play (a hole) in one stroke over par. ⟨< Colonel *Bogey*, imaginary partner⟩

bo•gey[2] or **bo•gy** ['bʊgi] *or* ['bougi] *n., pl.* **-geys. 1** an evil spirit or goblin. **2** a person or thing that causes annoyance or fear; bugaboo: *His bogey was mathematics.* **3** *Slang.* an unidentified aircraft. Also, **bogie, bogle.** ⟨< obs. *bog* bugbear⟩

bo•gey•man ['bʊgi,mæn] *or* ['bougi,mæn] *n.* an imaginary fearful being mentioned, especially formerly, to frighten children into obedience.

bog•gle ['bɒgəl] *v.* **-gled, -gling;** *n. —v.* **1** be or become overwhelmed, as by the unexpectedness, difficulty, etc. of something: *Her mind boggled at the thought of so much responsibility.* **2** overwhelm: *The sheer number of stars boggles the mind.* **3** hesitate or shy away. **4** bungle; botch.
—n. the act or an instance of boggling. ⟨? < Scottish *bogle*⟩
—'bog•gler, *n.* **—'bog•gling•ly,** *adv.*

bog•gy ['bɒgi] *adj.* **-gi•er, -gi•est.** soft and wet like a bog; marshy; swampy.

bo•gie ['bʊgi] *or* ['bougi] See BOGEY[2].

bo•gle ['bougəl] *n.* BOGEY[2].

bog rosemary an evergreen shrub (*Andromeda glaucophylla*), having pink flowers and needlelike bluish leaves, and growing in European and North American bogs.

bo•gus ['bougəs] *adj.* not genuine; counterfeit; sham: *a bogus twenty-dollar bill.* ⟨origin unknown; U.S.⟩

bo•gy ['bougi] *n., pl.* **-gies.** See BOGEY[2].

Bo•he•mi•a [bou'himiə] *or* [bou'himjə] *n.* **1** a former country in central Europe, now a region of Slovakia. **2** Often, **bohemia,** a free and easy, unconventional sort of life, or a place where artists, writers, etc., live such a life.

Bo•he•mi•an [bou'himiən] *or* [bou'himjən] *n., adj. —n.* **1** a native or inhabitant of Bohemia. **2** the language of Bohemia; Czech. **3** Often, **bohemian,** an artist, writer, etc., who lives in a free and easy, unconventional way. **4** gypsy.
—adj. **1** of Bohemia, its people, or their language. **2** Often, **bohemian,** free and easy; unconventional.

Bo•he•mi•an•ism [bou'himiə,nɪzəm] *or* [bou'himjə,nɪzəm] *n.* Often, **bohemianism,** a free and easy way of living; unconventional habits.

bohemian waxwing a brownish grey waxwing (*Bombycilla garrulus*) found throughout N Eurasia and NW North America.

boil[1] [bɔɪl] *v., n. —v.* **1 a** of liquids, bubble up and give off steam or vapour: *Water boils when heated to about* 100°C. **b** reach BOILING POINT: *Water boils faster at high altitudes.* **2** cause to boil. **3** cook in boiling water or other liquid: *to boil eggs.* **4** of a container, have its contents boil: *The kettle is boiling.* **5** clean or sterilize by putting in boiling water. **6** be very excited; be stirred up, especially by anger: *She is still boiling over the incident.* **7** move violently.
boil down, a reduce the bulk of by boiling: *to boil a sauce down.* **b** reduce by getting rid of unimportant parts: *He boiled down his*

notes to a list of important facts. **c** be essentially equivalent (*to*): *Jealousy, that's what it boils down to.*
boil over, a come to the boiling point and overflow. **b** show excitement or anger.
—n. **1** an act of boiling. **2** a boiling condition. ⟨ME *boille* < OF *boillir* < L *bullire* form bubbles⟩
☛ *Syn. v.* **6. Boil,** SIMMER, SEETHE, figuratively used, mean 'to be emotionally excited'. **Boil** suggests being so stirred up by emotion, usually anger, that one's feelings and, often, blood are thought of as heated to boiling point: *My blood boils at the suggestion.* **Simmer** suggests less intense emotion or greater control, so that one's feelings are just below the boiling point: *I was simmering with laughter.* **Seethe** suggests being violently stirred up, so that a person's mind or feelings or a group of people are thought of as churning and foaming: *The people seethed with discontent.*

boil² [bɔɪl] *n.* a hard, round abscess in the skin and the tissues just beneath it, consisting of pus around a hard core. Most boils are caused by bacteria entering an oil or sweat gland, a hair follicle, or a small wound.
blind boil, a boil that has no visible pus sac. ⟨OE *bȳl(e)*⟩

boiled [bɔɪld] *adj., v.—adj. Slang.* extremely drunk.
—v. pt. and pp. of BOIL.

boil•er ['bɔɪlər] *n.* **1** a container for heating liquids. **2** a tank for making steam to heat buildings or drive engines. **3** a tank for holding hot water.

boil•er•mak•er ['bɔɪlər,meikər] *n.* **1** a person who makes or repairs boilers. **2** *Informal.* a drink of whisky followed by beer.

boiling point 1 the temperature at which a liquid boils. The boiling point of water at sea level is 100 degrees Celsius. **2** the point at which matters come to a head or one loses one's temper.

bois–brû•lé ['bwɑ bru'lei]; *French* [bwabʀy'le] *Cdn.* formerly, Métis. ⟨< Cdn.F *bois brûlé* charred wood, referring to the dark complexion of most Métis⟩

bois•ter•ous ['bɔɪstərəs] *adj.* **1** noisily cheerful: *a boisterous game.* **2** violent; rough: *a boisterous wind, a boisterous child.* ⟨ME *boistrous,* earlier *boistous*; origin unknown⟩ **—'bois•ter•ous•ly,** *adv.* **—'bois•ter•ous•ness,** *n.*

bok choy ['bɒk 'tʃɔɪ] CHINESE CABBAGE.

bo•la ['boulə] *n.* a weapon consisting of stone or metal balls tied to cords. South American cowboys throw the bola so that it winds around the animal at which it is aimed. Also, **bolas** ['bouləs]. ⟨< Sp. and Pg. *bola* ball < L *bulla* bubble⟩

bold [bould] *adj.* **1** without fear; daring: *a bold knight, a bold explorer.* **2** showing or requiring courage: *a bold act.* **3** too free in manner; impudent: *The bold little boy made faces at us as we passed.* **4** striking; vigorous; free; clear: *The mountains stood in bold outline against the sky.* **5** steep; abrupt: *Bold cliffs overlooked the sea.* **6** printed in heavy, black type.
make bold, take the liberty; dare. ⟨OE *bald*⟩ **—'bold•ly,** *adv.* **—'bold•ness,** *n.*
☛ *Syn.* **3. Bold,** BRAZEN, FORWARD = too free in manner. **Bold** suggests lacking proper shame and modesty and pushing oneself forward too rudely: *He swaggered into school late with a bold look on his face.* **Brazen** = defiantly and insolently shameless: *She is brazen about being expelled.* **Forward** suggests being too sure of oneself, too disrespectful of others, too pert in pushing oneself forward: *With her forward ways, that girl will make no friends.*

bold•face ['bould,feis] *n., adj. Printing.* a heavy type that stands out clearly. **This sentence is in boldface.** *Abbrev.*: bf.
—adj. printed in this style.

bold•faced ['bould,feist] *adj.* cheeky; presumptuous.

bole¹ [boul] *n.* the trunk of a tree. ⟨ME < ON *bolr*⟩
☛ *Hom.* BOLL, BOWL.

bole² [boul] *n.* red clay which is easily ground to powder. ⟨< ME *bol* clay⟩
☛ *Hom.* BOLL, BOWL.

bo•le•ro [bə'lɛrou] *n., pl.* **-ros. 1** a lively Spanish dance in 3/4 time. **2** the music for it. **3** a short, loose jacket worn open at the front. ⟨< Sp.⟩

bo•lide ['boulaɪd] *or* ['boulɪd] *n.* a large, bright meteor, that explodes into meteorites that fall to earth. ⟨< F < L *bolis, bolidis* fiery meteor < Gk. *bolis* missile⟩

bol•i•var ['bɒləvər]; *Spanish* [bo'livar] *n.* **1** a unit of money in Venezuela, divided into 100 centimos. See table of money in the Appendix. **2** a coin worth one bolivar. ⟨< Simon *Bolivar* (1783-1830), Venezuelan general and statesman⟩

bo•liv•i•a [bə'lɪviə] *n.* a soft, woollen cloth resembling plush. ⟨< *Bolivia,* a country in South America⟩

Bo•liv•i•a [bə'lɪviə] *n.* a country in central South America.

Bo•liv•i•an [bə'lɪviən] *n., adj. —n.* a native or inhabitant of Bolivia.
—adj. of or having to do with Bolivia or its people.

bo•liv•i•a•no [bə,lɪvi'ɑnou] *n.* the major unit of currency in Bolivia, divided into 100 centavos. See table of money in the Appendix.

boll [boul] *n.* a rounded seed pod or capsule of a plant, especially that of cotton or flax. ⟨var. of *bowl*⟩
☛ *Hom.* BOLE, BOWL.

bol•lard ['bɒlərd] *n.* a strong post, usually concrete, on a wharf, round which a ship's mooring ropes are fastened. ⟨probably < ME *bol* stem, trunk < ON *bolr*⟩

boll weevil a weevil (*Anthonomus grandis*) of the S United States, Mexico, and Central America, that is a serious pest of cotton plants, both as larva and adult, feeding on the buds and bolls.

boll•worm ['boul,wɜrm] *n.* any of various moth caterpillars, such as the **pink bollworm** (*Pectinophora gossypiella*), that feed on cotton bolls.

bo•lo ['boulou] *n., pl.* **-los.** a long, heavy knife, used in the Philippine Islands. ⟨< Sp. < Philippine dial.⟩

bo•lo•gna [bə'louni] *or* [bə'lounə] *n.* a large sausage made of beef, veal, and pork. ⟨< *Bologna,* a city in Italy⟩

Bo•lo•gnese [,boulə'niz] *or* [,boulən'jiz] *adj., n.—adj.* of or having to do with the city of Bologna in northern Italy.
—n. **1** a native or inhabitant of Bologna. **2** the dialect of Italian spoken there.

bo•lo•graph ['boulə,græf] *n.* a record of the measurements taken by a bolometer. ⟨< Gk. *bole* ray + E *-graph*⟩

bo•lom•e•ter [bou'lɒmətər] *n.* an instrument used to measure the intensity of radiant energy, especially in small amounts. ⟨< Gk. *bolē* ray + E *-meter*⟩

bo•lo•ney [bə'louni] *n. Esp. Brit.* baloney.

bolo tie a tie made of thin cord, its ends kept together with an ornament which slides along them.

Bol•she•vik ['boulʃə,vɪk] *or* ['bɒlʃə,vɪk] *n., pl.* **Bol•she•viks** or **Bol•she•vi•ki** [,boulʃə'viki] *or* [,bɒlʃə'viki]. *adj. —n.* **1** a member of the radical wing of the Russian Social Democratic Party, which seized power in November, 1917. The Bolsheviks formed the Communist party in 1918. **2** a Communist. **3** Often, **bolshevik,** any extreme radical, especially a political revolutionary.
—adj. **1** of or having to do with the Bolsheviks or Bolshevism. **2** Often, **bolshevik,** extremely radical. ⟨< Russian *bolshevik* < *bolshe* greater; because it was at one time the majority wing. Opposed to MENSHEVIK.⟩

Bol•she•vism or **bol•she•vism** ['boulʃə,vɪzəm] *or* ['bɒlʃə,vɪzəm] *n.* **1** the doctrines and methods of the Bolsheviks. **2** extreme radicalism.

Bol•she•vist ['boulʃəvɪst] *or* ['bɒlʃəvɪst] *n. or adj.* Bolshevik. **—,Bol•she'vis•tic,** *adj.*

Bol•she•vize or **bol•she•vize** ['boulʃə,vaɪz] *or* ['bɒlʃə,vaɪz] *v.* **-vized, -viz•ing.** make Bolshevistic. **—,Bol•she•vi'za•tion** or **,bol•she•vi'za•tion,** *n.*

bol•ster ['boulstər] *n., v. —n.* **1** a long pillow for a bed. **2** a pad or cushion, often ornamental.
—v. **1** support with or as if with a bolster (*often used with* **up**): *The baby was bolstered with pillows.* **2** give support or a boost to; prop (*often used with* **up**): *to bolster a theory with additional evidence.* ⟨OE⟩

bolt¹ [boult] *n., v., adv. —n.* **1** a rod made to hold parts together, having a head at one end and a thread on the other. A bolt is placed through holes that have been drilled for it, and is held in place by a nut screwed onto the threaded end. **2** a sliding fastener for a door, gate, etc. **3** the part of a lock moved by a key. **4** a sliding bar that opens and closes the breech of a rifle, etc. The opening and closing of the bolt after firing ejects the used cartridge case and places a new one in position for firing. **5** a short arrow with a thick head. Bolts were shot from crossbows. **6** a discharge of lightning. **7** a dash; a running away. **8** a roll of cloth or wallpaper. **9** refusal to support one's political party or its candidates.
bolt from the blue, a sudden, unexpected happening; surprise.
shoot (one's) **bolt,** do as much or as well as one can; do all one can so that further effort is either useless or impossible: *He would like to have tried again for the championship, but he was over age and had shot his bolt.*
—v. **1** fasten with a bolt. **2** dash away; run away: *The horse bolted.* **3** break away from or refuse to support one's political party or its

candidates. **4** move suddenly; rush. **5** swallow (food) without chewing. **6** of cultivated plants, go to seed too quickly. Some kinds of lettuce often bolt in hot weather. **7** roll (fabric, wallpaper, etc.) into a bolt.
—adv.
bolt upright, stiff and straight: *Awakened by a noise, she sat bolt upright in bed.* ⟨OE *bolt* arrow⟩

bolt[2] [boult] *v.* **1** sift through a cloth or sieve: *Flour is bolted to remove the bran.* **2** examine carefully; separate. ⟨ME *bulte* < OF *bulter*⟩

bolt•er[1] ['boultər] *n.* **1** a horse that runs away. **2** a person who breaks away from or refuses to support his or her political party or its candidates. ⟨< *bolt[1]*⟩

bolt•er[2] ['boultər] *n.* a cloth or sieve used for sifting flour, meal, etc. ⟨< *bolt[2]*⟩

bolt–hole ['boult ˌhoul] *n.* **1** a place that one can escape to and hide in. **2** a way out; a way to escape some situation.

bol•to•nia [boul'touniə] *n.* any perennial plant of the genus *Boltonia,* having white or purple flowers arranged like those of a daisy, and native to the Americas. ⟨< NL after J. *Bolton,* 18c. English naturalist⟩

bo•lus ['bouləs] *n.* **1** a small, rounded mass, especially of medicine. **2** a lump of masticated food, ready to swallow. **3** any small, rounded mass. ⟨< L < Gk. *bōlos* lump⟩

bomb [bɒm] *n., v. —n.* **1** a container filled with an explosive charge or a chemical substance and exploded by a fuse or a timing mechanism, or by contact when something hits or touches it. **2** a container filled with liquid under pressure, such as paint, insect poison, etc.: *We used a bomb to rid the house of moths.* **3** a sudden, unexpected happening; disturbing surprise. **4** *Slang.* a miserable failure. **5 the bomb,** nuclear weapons: *Many nations already have the bomb.* **6** *Medicine.* a machine containing radioactive material, used for X-ray treatment: *cobalt bomb.*
drop a bomb, make a very unexpected announcement.
—v. **1** attack, damage, or destroy with a bomb or bombs, especially by dropping bombs from aircraft. **2** *Slang.* fail completely and miserably: *All the jokes he made in his speech bombed because he was so nervous.* **3** *Computer technology.* fail suddenly; crash. **4** *Slang.* move quickly: *bombing along the highway.* ⟨< MF *bombe* < Ital. < L *bombus* < Gk. *bombos* boom[1]⟩
☛ *Hom.* BALM [bɒm].

bom•bard [bɒm'bɑrd] *v.* **1** attack with heavy fire of shot and shell from big guns: *The artillery bombarded the enemy all day.* **2** drop bombs on: *Aircraft bombarded the hydro-electric plant and destroyed it.* **3** keep attacking vigorously: *The lawyer bombarded the witness with question after question.* **4** *Physics.* subject (atomic nuclei) to a stream of fast-moving particles, thus changing the structure of the nuclei. ⟨< F *bombarder* < *bombarde* cannon < Med.L *bombarda* < L *bombus.* See BOMB.⟩
—bom'bard•ment, *n.*

bom•bar•dier[1] [ˌbɒmbə'dir] *or* ['bɒmbəˌdir] *n.* **1** the member of the crew of a bomber who aims and releases the bombs. **2** a corporal in the artillery. *Abbrev.:* Bdr or Bdr. ⟨< MF *bombardier* < *bombarde* cannon. See BOMBARD.⟩

Bom•bar•dier[2] [ˌbɒmbə'dir] or [bɒm'bɑrdjei] *n. Cdn. Trademark.* a large covered vehicle used for travelling over snow and ice, usually equipped with tracked wheels at the rear and a set of skis at the front. ⟨after Armand *Bombardier* (1908-1964), inventor and manufacturer of the machine⟩

bom•bar•don ['bɒmbərdən] *or* [bɒm'bɑrdən] *n.* **1** a bass reed stop on a pipe organ. **2** a bass musical instrument resembling a shawm. **3** a deep-toned brass valved musical instrument like a bass tuba. ⟨< Ital. *bombardone*⟩

bom•ba•sine [ˌbɒmbə'zin] *or* ['bɒmbəˌzin] See BOMBAZINE.

bom•bast ['bɒmbæst] *n.* high-sounding, pompous language. ⟨earlier *bombace* < OF *bombace, bambace* < Med.L < Med.Gk. *bambax* cotton < Gk. *bombyx* silkworm, silk⟩

bom•bas•tic [bɒm'bæstɪk] *adj.* using bombast.
—bom'bas•ti•cal•ly, *adv.*

bom•bax ['bɒmbæks] *n.* **1** a large genus of tropical deciduous trees of the family Bombacaceae, having palmate leaves, large, showy, white or pink flower clusters, and dry, woolly fruit. **2** any tree of this family, such as the baobab or silk-cotton tree. ⟨< NL < Med.L cotton⟩

bom•ba•zine [ˌbɒmbə'zin] *or* ['bɒmbəˌzin] *n.* a twilled cloth made of silk and wool or cotton and wool. Also, **bombasine.** ⟨< early modern F *bombasin* < Ital. *bambagino* made of cotton, ult. < Med.Gk. *bambax* cotton. See BOMBAST.⟩

bomb bay the space or compartment in the underside of a combat aircraft in which bombs are carried and from which they are dropped.

bombe [bɒm], [bɒmb], *or* [bɔ̃b] *n.* a dessert made with eggs and sugar encased in ice cream, usually of a round shape. ⟨< F⟩

bombed [bɒmd] *adj., v.—adj. Slang.* completely under the influence of alcohol or drugs.
—v. pt. and pp. of BOMB.

bomb•er ['bɒmər] *n.* **1** a combat aircraft used to drop bombs on enemy troops, factories, cities, etc. **2** a person who throws or drops bombs.

bom•bi•nate ['bɒmbəˌneit] *v.* **-nat•ed, -nat•ing.** buzz like a fly or bee. ⟨< NL *bombinatus,* pp. of *bombinare* < L *bombitare* to buzz < *bombus* a buzzing⟩ **—ˌbom•bi'na•tion,** *n.*

bomb•proof ['bɒmˌpruf] *adj., n. —adj.* strong or deep enough to be safe from bombs and shells.
—n. a bombproof shelter.

bomb•shell ['bɒmˌʃɛl] *n.* **1** a bomb. **2** a sudden, unexpected happening; disturbing surprise.

bomb•sight ['bɒmˌsəit] *n.* an instrument used to find that point in the flight of an airplane where dropping a bomb will cause the bomb to fall exactly on the target.
☛ *Hom.* BOMBSITE.

bomb•site ['bɒmˌsəit] *n.* a district or area that has suffered damage from bombs.
☛ *Hom.* BOMBSIGHT.

bo•na•ci [ˌbounɑ'si] *n.* any of various large basses (genus *Myctero perca*) native to the Gulf of Mexico. ⟨< Am.Sp.⟩

bo•na fi•de ['bounə 'faɪd], ['bounə 'faɪdi], *or* ['bounə 'fidei] in good faith; genuine; without make-believe or fraud. ⟨< L⟩

bo•na fi•des ['bounə 'faɪdiz] *or* ['bounə 'fideis] assurance of honest intent.

bo•nan•za [bə'nænzə] *n.* **1** a rich mass of ore in a mine. **2** *Informal.* any rich source of profit. ⟨< Sp. *bonanza* fair weather, prosperity < L *bonus* good⟩

Bo•na•parte's gull ['bounəˌpɑrts] a small gull with grey on the back and folded wings, mainly white wing tips marked with black, and the rest of the plumage white. It breeds in western Alaska and the forests of British Columbia, and winters in Ontario, Massachusetts south to northern Mexico, Bermuda, and Cuba.

Bo•na•part•ist ['bounəˌpɑrtɪst] *n.* a follower or supporter of Napoleon Bonaparte (1769-1821) and his family.

bon ap•pé•tit *French,* [bɔ̃nape'ti] good appetite, a wish for someone about to eat.

bon•bon ['bɒnˌbɒn] *n.* a piece of candy. Bonbons often have fancy shapes. ⟨< F, reduplication of *bon* good⟩

bond[1] [bɒnd] *n., v. —n.* **1** anything that ties, binds, or unites: *a bond of affection between sisters.* **2** a certificate of debt issued by a government or company that is borrowing money, promising to pay back, by a certain date, the money borrowed plus interest. **3 a** *Law.* a written agreement by which a person says he or she will pay a certain sum of money if he or she does not perform certain duties properly. **b** the sum of money. **4** any agreement or binding engagement. **5** a person who acts as surety for another. **6** BOND PAPER. **7** the condition of goods placed in a warehouse until taxes are paid: *Imported jewellery is held in bond until customs duty has been paid.* **8** the condition of passengers on an international flight: *Passengers to Toronto may not leave the aircraft at Montréal as they are in bond.* **9** a way of arranging bricks, stones, or boards to bind them together. **10** a substance that binds together the other ingredients of a mixture: *Cement is the bond in concrete.* **11** the sticking together of substances; adhesion: *You get much better bond with this glue.* **12** *Chemistry.* the attraction that joins two or more atoms to form a unit, such as a molecule. **13 bonds,** *pl.* **a** chains; shackles. **b** imprisonment.
—v. **1** issue bonds on; mortgage. **2** take out an insurance policy to pay for any losses caused by (an employee): *The company bonds all its cashiers to protect itself in case any of them proves to be dishonest.* **3** put (goods) under bond. **4** bind or join (things) firmly together: *This glue bonds instantly.* **5** place (boards, bricks, etc.) in a particular arrangement so as to guarantee strength. **6** develop emotional ties: *The two orphans bonded.* ⟨var. of *band[2]*⟩
—'bond•a•ble, *adj.* **—'bond•er,** *n.*
☛ *Syn. n.* **1. Bond,** TIE, used figuratively, mean something that joins people. **Bond** applies particularly to a connection that brings two people or a group so closely together that they may be considered as one: *The members of the club are joined by bonds of fellowship.* **Tie** may be used interchangeably with **bond,** but applies particularly to connections of a

more involved and less voluntary nature: *When they went away, they severed all ties with their old life.*

bond² [bɒnd] *adj.* in slavery; captive; not free. ⟨ME < ON *bóndi* peasant, originally, dweller⟩

bond•age ['bɒndɪdʒ] *n.* **1** the lack of freedom; slavery. **2** the condition of being under some power or influence. **3** the status of a feudal serf.

bond•ed ['bɒndɪd] *adj., v.—adj.* **1** guaranteed by a bond or bonds: *The company's drivers are bonded.* **2** put in a warehouse until taxes are paid.
—v. pt. and pp. of BOND.

bond•hold•er ['bɒnd,houldər] *n.* a person who owns bonds issued by a government or company.

bond•ing ['bɒndɪŋ] *n., v.—n.* the close relationship that occurs between people in a family or social group: *Bonding between mother and child begins in the first few minutes after birth.*
—v. ppr. of BOND.

bond•maid ['bɒnd,meid] *n.* a girl or woman slave.

bond•man ['bɒndmən] *n., pl.* **-men. 1** a male slave; one who is not free. **2** in the Middle Ages, a serf.

bond paper a good quality of strong paper, made at least partly from rag pulp. Bond paper was originally used for documents.

bond•ser•vant ['bɒnd,sɜrvənt] *n.* **1** a servant bound to work without pay, sometimes for a specified time only. **2** a slave.

bonds•man ['bɒndzmən] *n., pl.* **-men. 1** a person who becomes responsible for another by giving a bond. **2** a slave. **3** in the Middle Ages, a serf.

bond•wom•an ['bɒnd,wʊmən] *n., pl.* **-wom•en.** a female slave; a woman held in involuntary servitude.

bone [boun] *n., v.* **boned, bon•ing.** *—n.* **1** one of the parts of the skeleton of a vertebrate. **2** the hard substance of which bones are made. **3** anything like bone. Ivory is sometimes called bone. **4 bones,** *pl.* **a** *Slang.* dice. **b** wooden clappers used in keeping time to music. **c** an end man in a minstrel show. **d** a skeleton; a dead person's remains. **5** a small thing given to soothe or make quiet, especially in order to avoid trouble: *throwing a bone to angry workers in the form of a small pay increase.* **6** BONE WHITE.
bone of contention, the subject of an argument.
feel in (one's) **bones,** be sure without knowing why.
have a bone to pick, have cause for argument or complaint.
make no bones, *Informal.* have no scruples; show no hesitation.
near the bone, a very exacting; mean: *A harsh employer comes near the bone.* **b** nearly indecent or obscene: *The speaker's jokes were very near the bone.*
—v. **1** take bones out of: *to bone fish.* **2** stiffen by putting whalebone or steel strips in. **3** *Informal.* study intensively, as for an examination (*usually used with* **up**): *You'd better bone up on your facts before you go for the interview.* ⟨OE *bān*⟩ **—'bone•less,** *adj.* **—'bone,like,** *adj.*

bone ash white ash resulting from burning bones in the open air, and used in the manufacture of bone china and fertilizers.

bone•black ['boun,blæk] *n.* a black powder made by roasting bones in closed containers, used to remove colour from liquids and as a colouring matter.

bone china a particularly white and translucent type of china made by mixing bone ash or calcium phosphate with clay.

boned ['bound] *adj., v.—adj.* **1** having a particular kind of bone: *long-boned.* **2** having the bones removed: *Is this fish boned?*
—v. pt. and pp. of BONE.

bone–dry ['boun 'draɪ] *adj.* very dry.

bone•fish ['boun,fɪʃ] *n.* any of a family (Albulidae) of silvery, small-boned marine game fishes found in warm, shallow waters.

bone•head ['boun,hɛd] *n. Informal.* a stupid person.
—'bone-,head•ed•ness, *n.*

bone meal crushed or ground bones, used as fertilizer and as food for animals.

bon•er ['bounər] *n. Slang.* a foolish mistake; stupid error; blunder.

bone•set ['boun,sɛt] *n.* a North American plant (*Eupatorium perfoliatum*) of the composite family having flat clusters of small white flowers formerly used in folk medicine.

bone–weary ['boun 'wiri] *adj.* very tired; exhausted.

bone white a colour, as of paint, that is off-white or nearly white.

bone•yard ['boun,jɑrd] *n.* **1** a graveyard. **2** *Informal.* a place where ideas are abandoned or things are lost forever.

bon•fire ['bɒn,faɪr] *n.* a large fire built on the ground outdoors. ⟨ME *bonefire* bone fire⟩

bon•go¹ ['bɒŋgou] *n., pl.* **-gos** or **-goes.** one of a pair of small connected drums, one slightly larger than the other, that are played with the hands, usually while being held between the knees. They are used for Latin American music. Also, **bongo drum.** ⟨< Am.Sp.⟩

bon•go² ['bɒŋgou] *n.* an antelope native to Africa (*Tragelaphus eurycerus*), with brown-red colouring and white stripes. It is an endangered species. ⟨< an African language⟩

bon•ho•mie [,bɒnə'mi] *or* ['bɒnəmi] *n.* good nature; courteous and pleasant ways. ⟨< F *bonhomie* < *bonhomme* good fellow⟩ **—'bon•hom•ous,** adj.

Bon•homme [bɒ'nɒm] *or* [bʌn'ʌm]; *French,* [bɔ'nɔm] *n. Cdn.* a traditional character of the winter carnival in Québec City. The Bonhomme is a giant snowman. ⟨< Cdn.F. See BONHOMIE.⟩

bon•i•face ['bɒnəfɪs] *or* ['bɒnɪ,feis] *n.* **1** an innkeeper. **2** the owner of a hotel, restaurant, etc. ⟨< *Boniface,* innkeeper in the play *The Beaux' Stratagem* by George Farquhar (1678-1707)⟩

bo•ni•to [bə'nitou] *n., pl.* **-tos** or **-toes.** any of several food and game fishes (especially genus *Sarda*) of the mackerel family, steel blue and silvery in colour, with dark, narrow stripes, found mainly in tropical seas. Bonitos are similar in form to tuna, but smaller. ⟨< Sp. *bonito* pretty < L *bonus* good⟩

bon•jour [bɔ̃'ʒuʀ] *French.* good morning; good day.

bonk [bɒŋk] *v.,n.* *—v. Slang.* hit, especially on the head.
—n. **1** a hit on the head. **2** the sound of such a hit. ⟨imitative⟩

bon•kers ['bɒŋkərz] *adj. Slang.* crazy.

bon mot [bɒn 'mou] *pl.* **bons mots** [bɒn 'mouz]; *French,* [bɔ̃'mo] *French.* a clever saying; witty remark.

bonne [bʌn] *n.* a maid. ⟨< F *bonne* maid⟩
☛ *Hom.* BUN.

bon•net ['bɒnɪt] *n., v.* *—n.* **1** a head covering usually tied under the chin with strings or ribbons, worn by babies and little girls. **2** a similar head covering formerly worn by girls and women. **3** a round, brimless cap worn by men and boys in Scotland. **4** WAR BONNET. **5** a metal covering or hood over a machine, chimney, etc. **6** *Brit.* the hood covering the engine of a car, truck, etc.
—v. put a bonnet on. ⟨ME < OF *bonet, bonnet,* originally, fabric for hats⟩

bon•nie or **bon•ny** ['bɒni] *adj.* **-ni•er, -ni•est. 1** pretty; handsome. **2** fine; excellent. **3** healthy-looking. ⟨ME *bonie,* apparently < OF *bon, bonne* good < L *bonus*⟩ **—'bon•ni•ly,** *adv.* **—'bon•ni•ness,** *n.*

bon•ny•clab•ber ['bɒnɪ,klæbər] *n.* thick sour milk or cream. ⟨< Irish *bainne* milk + *claba* thick⟩

bon•sai ['bɒnsaɪ] *or* ['bounsaɪ] *n.* **1** a small potted tree or shrub that has been dwarfed by a special process that includes the pruning of branches and roots, placement in a shallow dish, etc. **2** the art of dwarfing trees and shrubs in this way.
⟨< Japanese *bon* basin + *sai* plant⟩

bon•soir [bɔ̃'swaʀ] *French.* good evening.

bon•spiel ['bɒn,spil] *n. Curling.* a tournament among different clubs or among teams of the same club. ⟨< Scots < Du. *bond* contract, league + *spel* game⟩

bon•te•bok ['bɒntə,bɒk] *n.* a large South African antelope (*Damaliscus dorcas*) with dark brown fur. ⟨< Afrikaans < Du. *bont* variegated + *bok* buck⟩

bon ton [bɔ̃'tɔ̃] *French.* **1** good style; fashion. **2** fashionable society. **3** good breeding.

bo•nus ['bounəs] *n., v.* *—n.* something extra; something given in addition to what is due: *The company gave all its employees a Christmas bonus.*
—v. Cdn. offer a bonus for (work to be done, as for the construction of a railway line); subsidize. ⟨< L *bonus* good⟩

bon vi•vant [bɔ̃vi'vɑ̃] *pl.* **bons vi•vants** [bɔ̃vi'vɑ̃] *French.* a person who is fond of good food and luxury.

bon vo•yage [bɔ̃vwa'jaʒ] *French.* goodbye; a farewell for someone going on a trip.

bon•y ['bouni] *adj.* **bon•i•er, bon•i•est. 1** of bone. **2** like bone. **3** full of bones. **4** having big bones that stick out. **5** thin. **6** of a fish, having bone instead of cartilage. **—'bon•i•ness,** *n.*

bonze [bɑnz] *n.* a Buddhist monk. ⟨< F< Pg. *bonzo* < Japanese *bonso*⟩

boo [bu] *n., pl.* **boos;** *interj., v.* **booed, boo•ing.** *—n. or interj.* a

sound made to show dislike or contempt or to frighten.
—*v.* **1** make such a sound. **2** cry "boo" at.
☛ *Hom.* BOUT².

boob [bub] *n., v.* —*n. Slang.* **1** a stupid person; fool; dunce. **2** a silly mistake; booboo: *I made a real boob on the exam.*
—*v. Slang.* make a silly mistake. ⟨< *booby.* See BOOBY.⟩

boo•boo ['bu,bu] *n. Slang.* a silly mistake. ⟨< *booby*⟩
☛ *Hom.* BOUBOU.

boob tube *Slang.* television.

boo•by ['bubi] *n., pl.* **-bies. 1** a stupid person; fool; dunce. **2** a kind of large sea bird of the tropics. **3** the person who does worst in a game or contest. ⟨probably < Sp. *bobo* (defs. 1, 3) < L *balbus* stammering⟩

booby prize a prize given to the person who does worst in a game or contest.

booby trap 1 a trick arranged to annoy some unsuspecting person. **2** a bomb arranged to explode when an object is grasped, pushed, etc. by an unsuspecting person.

boo•by–trap ['bubi,træp] *v.* **boo•by-trapped, boo•by-trap•ping.** fit with a booby trap: *Look out! That doorway may be booby-trapped!*

boo•dle ['budəl] *n. Slang.* **1** graft; money from bribes. **2** caboodle. **3** stolen goods; haul; loot. ⟨< Du. *boedel* goods⟩

boo•gie ['bugi] *n., v.* **boo•gied, boo•gy•ing.** —*n.* rock and roll.
—*v.* **1** *Slang.* go; move: *I'm going to boogie down to the drugstore.* **2** dance to rock and roll music. ⟨origin uncertain⟩

boo•gie–woo•gie ['bʊgi 'wʊgi] *or* ['bugi 'wugi] *n. Music.* a style of jazz characterized by a repeating rhythmic pattern of dotted eighth notes in the bass, accompanying a melody that is often improvised. Boogie-woogie is usually played on the piano.

boo•hoo ['bu'hu] *v.* **-hooed, -hoo•ing;** *n., pl.* **-hoos.** —*v.* cry loudly.
—*n.* loud crying. ⟨imitative⟩

book [bʊk] *n., v.* —*n.* **1** a set of written or printed sheets of paper stitched or glued together along one edge and usually having attached covers at the front and back: *a book of poetry.* **2** a long work, or composition, that is written or printed: *She writes books about camping.* **3** a set of blank sheets bound together along one edge, used for taking notes, drawing, keeping records, etc. **4** a main division of a literary work: *the books of the Bible.* **5** something fastened together like a book: *a book of tickets, a book of matches.* **6** the words of an opera, operetta, etc.; libretto. **7** the script of a play. **8 the Book,** the Bible. **9** something thought of as providing knowledge if it is studied or 'read' like a book: *the book of nature, the book of life.* **10** a record of bets. **11** in certain card games, a trick or a specified number of tricks forming a set. **12 books,** *pl.* **a** the complete records of a business: *She keeps the books for their business.* **b** academic study: *After the holiday she returned to her books.* **13 the book, a** the telephone directory of a particular town or city: *Are you in the book?* **b** any authoritative volume.
a closed book, secretive; obscure; full of unknowns.
an open book, not secret; easy to know and understand: *His life is an open book.*
bring to book, a demand an explanation from. **b** rebuke.
by the book, according to the proper or accepted way; strictly according to the rules: *When she was chairperson, our meetings were always run by the book.*
close the books, a stop entering items in an account book. **b** bring (an affair) to a close or stop keeping track of it (*used with* **on**): *Let's just close the books on the whole sorry business.*
every trick in the book, *Informal.* all possible ways to deceive, gain one's own ends, etc.
in (one's) **book,** *Informal.* in one's opinion or judgment: *In my book, swearing is always unnecessary.*
in (one's) **good** (or **bad**) **books,** in favour (or disfavour) with one: *He may be wild, but he is still in my good books.*
know (someone) **like a book,** understand very well; know everything about: *My mother knows me like a book, and can always tell when I have a problem.*
one for the book, an item or case worthy of mention.
on the books, a on the official list (of members of a club, university, etc.). **b** on the record.
read (someone) **like a book,** guess accurately what a person is thinking, feeling, or planning: *He tried to hide it, but I can always read him like a book and I knew he was afraid.*
throw the book at, a *Slang.* punish as severely as the law allows: *This is his third offence, so the judge will probably throw the book at him.* **b** *Informal.* marshal every possible argument against (a defendant).
—*v.* **1** enter in a book or list. **2** *Informal.* record a charge against (a person) at a police station: *She was booked on a charge of*

theft. **3** engage (a place, passage, etc.); make a reservation (for): *to book a room in a hotel, to book theatre tickets.* **4** hire; make engagements for: *The lecturer is booked for every night this week.* ⟨OE *bōc*⟩ —**'book•er,** *n.* —**'book•less,** *adj.*

book•bind•er ['bʊk,baɪndər] *n.* a person whose work or business is binding books.

book•bind•er•y ['bʊk,baɪndəri] *n., pl.* **-er•ies.** an establishment for binding books.

book•bind•ing ['bʊk,baɪndɪŋ] *n.* **1** the binding of a book. **2** the art or business of binding books.

book•case ['bʊk,keis] *n.* a piece of furniture with shelves for holding books.

book club a business organization that regularly supplies selected books to subscribers.

book•end ['bʊk,ɛnd] *n.* a support placed at the end of a row of books to hold them upright.

book•ie ['bʊki] *n. Informal.* BOOKMAKER (def. 1).

book•ing ['bʊkɪŋ] *n., v.* —*n.* **1** an engagement to perform, lecture, etc.: *The pianist has bookings for a six-week tour.* **2** a reservation: *He made a booking for his flight to Yellowknife. We have a booking at the hotel.*
—*v.* ppr. of BOOK.

book•ish ['bʊkɪʃ] *adj.* **1** fond of reading or studying. **2** knowing books better than real life. **3** having to do with books. **4** learned; pedantic. —**'book•ish•ly,** *adv.* —**'book•ish•ness,** *n.*

book•keep•er ['bʊk,kipər] *n.* a person whose work is bookkeeping.

book•keep•ing ['bʊk,kipɪŋ] *n.* the process or practice of recording, classifying, and summarizing data about the business transactions of a company, according to a particular system.

book–learn•ed ['bʊk ,lɜrnɪd] *adj.* knowing a lot of things from books, not from real life.

book learning knowledge learned from books, not from real life.

book•let ['bʊklɪt] *n.* a little book; a thin book or pamphlet. It usually has paper covers.

book•lore ['bʊk,lɔr] *n.* BOOK LEARNING.

book•mak•er ['bʊk,meikər] *n.* **1** a person who makes a business of accepting bets on horse races. **2** a maker of books.

book•mak•ing ['bʊk,meikɪŋ] *n.* **1** the business of taking bets on horse races, etc. at odds fixed by the takers. **2** the compiling and manufacture of books.

book•man ['bʊkmən] *n.* **1** a scholar or literary man. **2** a publisher, editor, or other person engaged in the book business.

book•mark ['bʊk,mark] *n.* **1** something put between the pages of a book to mark the place. **2** a bookplate.

book matches a strip of paper matches enclosed in a cardboard folder.

book•mo•bile ['bʊkmə,bil] *n.* a large van or trailer that serves as a travelling branch of a public library.

book of account 1 ACCOUNT BOOK. **2** financial records needed to audit business accounts.

Book of Changes the I CHING.

Book of Common Prayer the book containing the prayers and services of the Church of England or the Anglican Church of Canada.

Book of Mormon the sacred book of the Mormon Church.

Book of the Dead a collection of ancient Egyptian religious maxims that were intended to guide the soul on its way out of this world.

book•plate ['bʊk,pleit] *n.* a label for pasting in books, having the owner's name or emblem printed on it.

book•rack ['bʊk,ræk] *n.* **1** a rack for holding an open book. **2** a rack for holding a row of books.

book•rest ['bʊk,rɛst] *n.* a stand for holding a book open to read.

book review an article written about a book, discussing its merits, faults, etc.

book•sell•er ['bʊk,sɛlər] *n.* a person whose business is selling books.

book•shelf ['bʊk,ʃɛlf] *n.* a shelf for holding books.

book•shop ['bʊk,ʃɒp] *n.* bookstore.

book•stall ['bʊk,stɒl] *n.* a place where books, usually second-hand, are sold, often outdoors.

book•stand ['bʊk,stænd] *n.* **1** a stand for holding an open book. **2** a stand or counter for showing books for sale. **3** a place where books are sold; bookstall.

book•store ['bʊk,stɔr] *n.* a store where books are sold.

book•trail•er ['bʊk,treilər] *n.* bookmobile.

book value **1** the value of anything as it appears on the account books of the owner. It may be higher or lower than the real or present value. **2** the actual capital worth of a business, as measured by the greater ratio of assets to liabilities.

book•work ['bʊk,wɜrk] *n.* **1** the keeping of records, ledgers, etc. for a business. **2** the study or use of books: *He always did far better in the laboratory than in his bookwork.*

book•worm ['bʊk,wɜrm] *n.* **1** any of various insects whose adult forms or larvae gnaw the bindings or pages of books. The silverfish is one of the most widely known kinds of bookworm. **2** a person who is extremely fond of reading and studying.

Boo•le•an algebra ['buliən] a mathematical system dealing with the relationship between sets, used to solve problems in logic, engineering, etc., and to program computers. ⟨after George *Boole* (1815-1864), English mathematician⟩

boom[1] [bum] *n., v.* —*n.* **1** a deep, hollow sound like the roar of cannon or of big waves: *a sonic boom.* **2** the deep, hollow call of some animals, as the bittern or bullfrog. **3** a sudden activity and increase as in business, prices, or values of property; rapid growth: *Our town is having such a boom that it is likely to double its size in two years.* **4** (*adjl.*) produced by a boom: *boom prices.*
—*v.* **1** make a deep, hollow sound: *The man's voice boomed out above the rest. You could hear the bullfrogs booming.* **2** utter with such a sound: *The big guns boomed their message.* **3** increase suddenly in activity; grow rapidly: *Business is booming.* **4** cause to increase suddenly or grow rapidly. ⟨imitative ? < Du. *bommen*⟩ **—'boom•er,** *n.*

boom[2] [bum] *n.* **1** a long pole or beam, used to extend the bottom of a sail. See SLOOP for picture. **2** the lifting or guiding pole of a derrick. **3** *Lumbering.* **a** a chain, cable, or line of timbers used to keep logs from floating away. **b** the enclosure formed by such a chain, etc.: *The logs were held in booms upstream from the mill.* **c** a collection of logs held together by a chain, etc. for towing by water. **4** a chain line of timbers, etc. used to block the passage of boats or ships. **5** an overhead pole in a recording studio bearing microphones, lights, etc. ⟨< Du. *boom* tree, pole⟩

boom•box ['bum,bɒks] *n. Slang.* a large, powerful, portable radio combined with a cassette-player, and, often, a CD player.

boom carpet the area affected by SONIC BOOMS from aircraft.

boom•er ['bumər] *n.* **1** an itinerant construction worker. **2** *Informal.* a person born during the BABY BOOM; baby boomer. **3** (*adjl.*). of or for baby boomers: *Her radio was tuned to her favourite boomer station.*

boom•er•ang ['bumə,ræŋ] *n., v.* —*n.* **1** a narrow, flat, curved or angular piece of wood used as a throwing weapon by aboriginal peoples of Australia. One type can be thrown so that it will return to the thrower if it misses its target. **2** anything that recoils or reacts to harm the doer or user.
—*v.* act as a boomerang. ⟨< native dial. of New South Wales⟩

booming ground *Cdn.* the part of a river, lake, or ocean where logs are dumped to be gathered into booms, or where booms of logs are held.

boom•let ['bumlɪt] *n.* a small BOOM[1] (def. 3).

boom town a town that has grown up suddenly, usually as a result of an increase in economic activity. Boom towns are often found near newly discovered oil fields, gold strikes, etc.

boon[1] [bun] *n.* **1** a blessing; great benefit. **2** *Archaic.* something asked or granted as a favour. ⟨ME < ON *bón* petition⟩

boon[2] [bun] *adj.* **1** jolly; merry: *a boon companion.* **2** *Poetic.* kindly; pleasant. ⟨ME < OF *bon* good < L *bonus*⟩

boon•docks ['bundɒks] *n.pl. Slang.* rough backwoods; bush country. ⟨< Tagalog *bundók* mountain⟩

boon•dog•gle ['bun,dɒgəl] *v.* **-gled, -gling;** *n.* —*v. Informal.* do trivial, unnecessary, or pointless work.
—*n.* **1** *Informal.* trivial, unnecessary, or pointless work or its product, often at public expense. **2** *Cdn.* a device used to take up the slack in a chin strap, such as a large wooden bead. ⟨origin uncertain⟩ **—'boon•dog•gler,** *n.*

boon•ies ['buniz] *n.pl. Slang.* boondocks.

boor [bur] *n.* **1** a rude, bad-mannered, insensitive person. **2** a person who is clumsy and awkward in unfamiliar social situations; yokel. ⟨< LG *bur* or Du. *boer* farmer⟩
☛ *Hom.* BOER.

boor•ish ['burɪʃ] *adj.* rude; having bad manners; clumsy. **—'boor•ish•ly,** *adv.* **—'boor•ish•ness,** *n.*

boost [bust] *n., v. Informal.* —*n.* **1** a push or shove that helps a person in rising or advancing: *a boost over the fence.* **2** an increase: *a boost in salary.* **3** a promotion of some activity, idea, product, etc. **4** a start given to a motor vehicle by connecting it with booster cables to the battery of another vehicle: *Can you please give me a boost?*
—*v.* **1** lift or push from below or behind. **2** raise; increase: *to boost prices, to boost sales.* **3** help by speaking well of or promoting actively: *to boost a new product.* **4** increase the voltage in (an electric current or battery). ⟨blend of *boom* and *hoist*⟩

boost•er ['bustər] *n.* **1** a person or thing that boosts or promotes an idea, product, or organization. **2** the first stage of a multistage rocket. **3** the device used to orbit an artificial satellite. **4** any auxiliary device for increasing force, power, voltage, etc. **5** *Informal.* BOOSTER SHOT.

booster cables a pair of heavy, insulated cables each fitted with a spring clip at each end for connecting the terminals of two batteries, used to start a motor vehicle with a weak or discharged battery by means of power from another battery. Also called **jumper cables.**

boost•er•ism ['bustə,rɪzəm] *n.* the practice of promoting an event, region, city, etc. aggressively or extravagantly.

booster shot a supplementary injection of vaccine or serum, given to reinforce an earlier inoculation.

booster station a television or radio installation that picks up, amplifies, and relays signals from the main transmitting station.

boot[1] [but] *n., v.* —*n.* **1** a covering for the foot and lower part of the leg, made of leather, rubber, or a synthetic material such as vinyl. See SHOE for picture. **2** *Informal.* a kick. **3** the place for luggage in a horse-drawn coach. **4** *Brit.* the trunk of an automobile. **5** a bootlike protective covering or sheath for a mechanical device, etc. **6** formerly, an instrument of torture used to crush a person's leg. **7** *U.S. Slang.* a new recruit in training in the United States Navy or Marines. **8** *Computer technology.* the start-up of a computer program. **9 the boot,** *Slang.* rude or abrupt dismissal, as from a job.
bet your boots, *Informal.* depend on it; be sure: *You can bet your boots that our team will win.*
die with (one's) **boots on, a** die in battle; die fighting. **b** die working, especially for a cause.
have (one's) **heart in** (one's) **boots,** be dejected or discouraged.
lick (a person's) **boots,** flatter (a person); follow or obey slavishly.
the boot is on the other leg, the situation is reversed; the responsibility is on the other party.
too big for (one's) **boots,** *Informal.* having an excessively high opinion of (oneself); conceited: *When he won the athlete-of-the-year award, he got to be much too big for his boots.*
wipe (one's) **boots on,** treat in an insulting way.
—*v.* **1** put boots on. **2** give a kick to; drive or move by kicking: *She booted the stone off the sidewalk.* **3** *Slang.* dismiss or get rid of rudely or abruptly (*usually used with* **out**). **4** *Computer technology.* **a** make (a computer, especially a microcomputer) ready for use by causing the operating system to load itself into memory (if necessary) and initialize itself. A system is often booted automatically when the computer is turned on. **b** of a computer system, undergo this process (*often used with* **up**). ⟨ME < OF *bote* < Gmc.⟩ **—'boot•less,** *adj.*

boot[2] [but] *n., v.* —*n. Archaic.* profit; benefit.

to boot, in addition; besides: *She gave me her knife for my book and fifty cents to boot.*
—*v. Archaic.* benefit; avail. ⟨OE *bōt* advantage⟩ **—'boot•less,** *adj.*

boot•black ['but,blæk] *n.* a person whose work is shining shoes and boots.

boot camp an initial training camp for military recruits.

boot•ed ['butəd] *adj., v.—adj.* wearing boots: *He was booted and spurred.*
—*v.* pt. and pp. of BOOT.

boot•ee ['buti] *or* [bu'ti] *n.* **1** a baby's soft shoe. **2** a woman's short boot. Also, **bootie** ['buti].
☛ *Hom.* BOOTY ['buti].

Bo•ö•tes [bou'outiz] *n. Astronomy.* a northern constellation that includes the star Arcturus. ⟨< L < Gk. *boōtēs* ox-driver < *bous* ox⟩

booth [buθ] *n., pl.* **booths** [buðz] *or* [buθs]. **1** a place where goods are displayed for sale at a fair, market, etc. **2** a small, closed place for a telephone, movie projector, etc. **3** a small, closed place for voting at elections. **4** a partly enclosed space in a restaurant, café, etc., containing a table and seats for a few persons. ⟨ME < Scand.; cf. ODanish **bóth*⟩

boot•ie ['buti] *n.* bootee.

boot•jack ['but,dʒæk] *n.* a device to help in pulling off boots.

boot•leg ['but,lɛg] *v.* **-legged, -leg•ging;** *adj., n.* —*v.* sell, transport, or make unlawfully.
—*adj.* made, transported, or sold unlawfully.
—*n.* **1** the leg of a boot. **2** *Informal.* alcoholic liquor made, sold, or transported unlawfully. ⟨modern use from the practice of smuggling liquor in boot legs⟩

boot•leg•ger ['but,lɛgər] *n. Informal.* a person who bootlegs.

boot•lick ['but,lɪk] *v. Informal.* fawn on (a person) to try to gain favour; toady: *She was determined to make it on her own, without bootlicking. They would bootlick anyone with influence.*

boot•lick•er ['but,lɪkər] *n. Informal.* a person who fawns on another in order to gain favour; flatterer; toady.

boots [buts] *n. Brit.* a servant who shines shoes and boots and does other menial tasks.

boots and saddles formerly, a bugle call to mount horses.

boot•strap ['but,stræp] *n.* **1** a strap or loop at the top of a boot, used for pulling it on. **2** (*adjl.*) done or undertaken without outside help: *a bootstrap campaign.* **3** *Computer technology.* a short routine which instructs the computer to take in other routines or information.
by (one's) **own bootstraps,** by (one's) own efforts; without help from others: *He raised himself to his present position by his own bootstraps.*

boot tree a wooden or metal device shaped like a foot and put into a boot to keep it in shape.

boo•ty ['buti] *n., pl.* **-ties. 1** things taken from the enemy in war. **2** things seized by violence and robbery; plunder: *The pirates fought over the booty from the raided town.* **3** any valuable thing or things obtained; prize. ⟨Related to BOOT[2]⟩
☛ *Syn.* **1, 2.** See note at PLUNDER.
☛ *Hom.* BOOTEE ['buti].

booze [buz] *n., v.* **boozed, booz•ing.** *Informal.* —*n.* **1** any intoxicating liquor. **2** a spree.
—*v.* drink heavily. ⟨probably < MDu. *busen* drink to excess⟩
—'booz•er, *n.*

booz•y ['buzi] *adj.* **booz•i•er, booz•i•est. 1** rather drunk, especially as a habitual state. **2** involving the drinking of too much intoxicating liquor: *a long, boozy lunch.* **—'booz•i•ly,** *adv.* **—'booz•i•ness,** *n.*

bop[1] [bɒp] *n., v.* **bopped, bop•ping.** *Slang.* —*n.* a blow with the hand, a club, etc.
—*v.* hit; strike. ⟨imitative⟩

bop[2] [bɒp] *n., v.,* **bopped, bopping.** —*n.* bebop.
—*v.* go about or carry oneself in a cheerful, casual way: *She's been bopping around town all morning.*

bor. borough.

bo•ra ['bɔrə] *n.* a strong, cold, northerly wind common on the Adriatic coast of Italy. ⟨< Ital. dialect for *borea* < L *boreas* < Gk. *boreas* north wind⟩

bo•rac•ic [bə'ræsɪk] *adj.* boric.

bo•ra•cite ['bɔrə,sait] *n.* a mineral found in two forms: hard crystals or a soft white mass. *Formula:* $Mg_6Cl_2B_{14}O_{26}$ When its temperature rises it can create electric dipoles. ⟨< *borax* + *-ite*⟩

bor•age ['bɔrɪdʒ] *or* ['bɜrɪdʒ] *n.* **1** a plant (*Borago officinalis*) having hairy leaves and blue or purplish flowers, native to S Europe. It is used in salads, in flavouring beverages, and in medicine. **2** (*adjl.*) designating the family (Boraginaceae) of flowering plants of temperate and tropical regions that includes borage, heliotrope, and forget-me-not. ⟨< OF *bourrache* < Med.L *borrago* < *burra* rough hair⟩

bo•ral ['bɔrəl] *n.* a compound of aluminum tartrate and borate, used as an astringent and in reactors. ⟨< *bor*(*on*) + *al*(*uminum*)⟩

bo•rate *n.* ['bɔreit]; *v.* ['bɔreit], *n., v.* **-rat•ed, -rat•ing.** —*n.* a salt or ester of boric acid.
—*v.* mix or treat with boric acid or borax.

bo•rax ['bɔræks] *n.* white, crystalline powder, used as an antiseptic, in washing clothes, in fusing metals, and in preserving foods; sodium borate. *Formula*: $Na_2B_4O_7$ ⟨ME *boras* < Med.L < Arabic *buwraq* < Persian *bōrah*⟩

Bor•a•zon ['bɔrə,zɒn] *n. Trademark. Chemistry.* a crystalline compound of boron and nitrogen, as hard as diamond and having a higher melting point. ⟨< *bor*(*on*) + *azo* + *n*(*itrogen*)⟩

bor•bo•ryg•mus [,bɔrbə'rɪgməs] *n., pl.* **-mi** [-mi] *or* [-maɪ]. stomach rumbling. Also, **borborygm** ['bɔrbə,rɪgəm]. ⟨< Gk. *borborygmos* < *borboryzein* rumble⟩

Bor•deaux [bɔr'dou] *n.* **1** a red or white wine made in the Bordeaux region of SW France. **2** any similar wine.

Bordeaux mixture a liquid mixture of copper sulphate, lime, and water, used as a fungicide.

bor•de•laise sauce [,bɔrdə'leiz] a dark sauce for meat, made with meat juices thickened with flour, and flavoured with onions and seasonings. ⟨< F fem. of *Bordelais* of Bordeaux⟩

bor•del•lo [bɔr'dɛlou] *n.* brothel. ⟨< Ital. < Med.L *bordellus,* dim. of *borda* cottage⟩

bor•der ['bɔrdər] *n., v.* —*n.* **1** an edge, rim, or outer part of something: *a plate with a fluted border.* **2** the line separating two countries, provinces, etc., or two geographical regions; boundary; frontier. **3** a strip on or near the edge of anything for strength or ornament: *a handkerchief with a lace border. Our lawn has a border of flowers.* **4 the border,** the border between Canada and the U.S.: *We reached Detroit by crossing the border at Windsor. The government discourages shopping over the border.*
—*v.* **1** form a boundary to; bound. **2** put a border on; edge. **3** touch at the border; be adjacent (*used with* **on** *or* **upon**). **4** approach in character; verge (*used with* **on**): *The accusations in the newspaper article border on libel.* ⟨ME < OF *bordure* < *border* to border < *bord* side < Gmc.⟩
☛ *Hom.* BOARDER.

bor•der•er ['bɔrdərər] *n.* a person who lives on the border of a country or region.

bor•der•land ['bɔrdər,lænd] *n.* **1** the land forming, or next to, a border. **2** an uncertain district, space, or condition: *the borderland between sleeping and waking.*

bor•der•line ['bɔrdər,laɪn] *n., adj.* —*n.* a boundary; dividing line.
—*adj.* **1** on a border or boundary. **2** of uncertain status; doubtful; in between; especially, verging on something unacceptable or abnormal.

bor•dure ['bɔrdʒər] *n. Heraldry.* a border around a shield, covering one fifth of its surface. ⟨earlier form of *border*⟩

bore[1] [bɔr] *v.* **bored, bor•ing;** *n.* —*v.* **1** make (a hole) by means of a tool that keeps turning, or by penetrating as a worm does in fruit. **2** make (a hole, passage, entrance, etc.) by or as if by pushing through or digging out: *A mole has bored its way under the hedge.* **3** make a round hole in; hollow out evenly. **4** be capable of being bored by a tool: *Soft wood bores easily.*
—*n.* **1** a hole made by a revolving tool. **2** the hollow space inside a pipe, tube, or gun barrel: *He cleaned the bore of his gun.* **3** the distance across the inside of a hole or tube. ⟨OE *borian*⟩
☛ *Hom.* BOAR.

bore[2] [bɔr] *v.* **bored, bor•ing;** *n.* —*v.* make weary by dull or tiresome behaviour or conversation.
—*n.* a dull, tiresome person or thing. ⟨origin unknown⟩
☛ *Hom.* BOAR.

bore[3] [bɔr] *v.* pt. of BEAR[1].
☛ *Hom.* BOAR.

bore[4] [bɔr] *n.* a sudden, high tidal wave that rushes up a channel with great force. ⟨< ON *bára* wave⟩
☛ *Hom.* BOAR.

bo•re•al ['bɔriəl] *adj.* **1** northern. **2** of or having to do with Boreas.

boreal chickadee a bird, a chickadee native to the northeastern coast of Canada and the U.S., with a brown head and a black throat.

boreal forest a vast primeval forest almost completely encircling the northern part of the globe, consisting mainly of spruce, fir, pine, and larch, with some birch, aspen, and elder. In Canada, the boreal forest stretches from the tundra down to the mountains and prairies, the Great Lakes, and the Gaspé. ⟨< *Boreas*, the north wind⟩

Bo•re•as ['bɔriəs] *n.* the north wind. ⟨< Gk.⟩

bore•dom ['bɔrdəm] *n.* a bored condition; weariness caused by dull, tiresome people or events.

bor•er ['bɔrər] *n.* **1** a tool for boring holes. **2** an insect or worm that bores into wood, fruit, etc. **3** a person whose work is boring holes.

bore•some ['bɔrsəm] *adj.* boring; dull; tiresome.

bo•ric ['bɔrɪk] *adj.* of or containing boron. Also, **boracic.**

boric acid a white, crystalline substance used as a mild antiseptic, as a food preservative, etc. *Formula*: $B(OH)_3$

bo•ride ['bɔraɪd] *n.* a compound of boron and another element.

bor•ing ['bɔrɪŋ] *n., adj.* —*n.* **1** a hole produced by something that bores. **2 borings,** *pl.* the bits cast up from a hole that is bored.
—*adj.* tiresome; dull; tedious. —**'bor•ing•ly,** *adv.*
—**'bor•ing•ness,** *n.*

born [bɔrn] *adj., v.* —*adj.* **1** brought into life; brought forth. **2** thought up; conceived. **3** by birth; by nature: *a born athlete.*
in all my born days, in my whole life.
—*v.* a pp. of BEAR[1].
was not born yesterday, is not gullible or naive: *You can't fool me with that trick—I wasn't born yesterday.* ⟨pp. of *bear[1]*⟩
☛ *Hom.* BOURN.

born–again ['bɔrn ə'gɛn] *adj.* with one's spiritual life renewed: *a born-again Christian.*

borne [bɔrn] *v.* a pp. of BEAR[1].
☛ *Hom.* BOURN.

born•ite ['bɔrnəit] *n.* a copper ore that is brownish red in its natural state but tarnishes to purple when broken up. *Formula*: Cu_5FeS_4 ⟨after Ignaz von *Born* (1742-91), Austrian metallurgist⟩

bo•ron ['bɔrɒn] *n.* a non-metallic, chemical element found in borax. *Symbol*: B; *at.no.* 5; *at.mass* 10.81. ⟨blend of *bor(ax)* and *(carb)on*⟩

boron carbide a hard mineral made up of carbon and boron, used primarily in nuclear reactors. *Formula*: B_4C

bo•ro•sil•i•cate [,bɔrou'sɪləkɪt] *n.* a kind of glass that can support temperatures of up to 500°C. Pyrex is a brand of borosilicate.

bor•ough ['bɜrou] *n.* **1** a town or township having its own local government: *East York is Canada's only remaining borough.* **2** in England: **a** a town with a municipal corporation and a charter that guarantees the right of local self-government. **b** a town that sends representatives to Parliament. ⟨OE *burg* < *burh*, a town of a certain political importance⟩
☛ *Hom.* BURRO, BURROW.

bor•row ['bɔrou] *v.* **1** get (something) from another person with the understanding that it is to be returned. **2** take and use as one's own; take: *Rome borrowed many ideas from Greece.* **3** take (a word or expression) from another language to use like a native word. The word *mukluk* was borrowed from Inuktitut. Many words we think of as English were borrowed from French hundreds of years ago. **4** *Arithmetic.* in subtraction, decrease the digit in one column of the minuend by 1 in order to increase the value in the column on its right by 10; regroup.
borrow trouble, worry about something before there is reason to. ⟨OE *borgian* < *borg* pledge, surety⟩ —**'bor•row•er,** *n.*

bor•row•ing ['bɔrouɪŋ] *n., v.* —*n.* **1** something borrowed. **2** a word taken directly from one language into another; loanword. The English word *voyageur* is a borrowing from Canadian French.
—*v.* ppr. of BORROW.

borrow pit *Cdn.* a pit or ditch from which earth has been dug for use as fill, especially in road or railway construction.

borsch [bɔrʃ] *n.* a Russian soup containing meat stock, beets, etc. Also, **borscht** [bɔrʃt]. ⟨< Russian *borshch*⟩

bort or **bortz** [bɔrt] *or* [bɔrts] *n.* a dark, unevenly crystallized kind of diamond, used mainly in industry as an abrasive.

bor•zoi ['bɔrzɔɪ] *n.* a breed of tall, slender, swift dog having long, silky hair. The borzoi was developed in Russia and was originally used to hunt wolves. ⟨< Russian *borzoy* swift⟩

bos•cage ['bɒskɪdʒ] *n.* a small woods; thicket. ⟨ME < OF *boscage* < *bosc* < Gmc.; cf. Frankish *busk* woods. Related to BUSH.⟩

bosh[1] [bɒʃ] *n. or interj. Informal.* nonsense; foolish talk or ideas. ⟨< Turkish *boş* empty, worthless⟩

bosh[2] [bɒʃ] *n.* **1** the lower, tapered part of a blast furnace. **2** a trough for cooling hot metal, such as ingots. ⟨< G *Böschung* slope⟩

bosk [bɒsk] *n.* a grove; small woods; thicket. ⟨var. of *busk*, dial. for *bush*⟩

bosk•y ['bɒski] *adj.* **bosk•i•er, bosk•i•est. 1** wooded. **2** shady.

bo's'n ['bousən] *n.* boatswain.

Bos•ni•a–Her•ce•go•vi•na ['bɒzniə ,hɛrtsə'gouvinə] a country in E Europe, part of the former Yugoslavia.

bos•om ['bʊzəm] *or* ['buzəm] *n., v.* —*n.* **1** the upper, front part of the human body, especially the female breasts. **2** the part of a garment covering the bosom. **3** the centre or inmost part: *She did not mention it even in the bosom of her family.* **4** the heart; the seat of one's thoughts, affections, desires, etc.: *He kept the secret in his bosom.* **5** the surface or depths (of a sea, lake, river, the ground, etc.). **6** (*adjl.*) close; trusted: *a bosom friend.*
—*v.* **1** cherish; embrace. **2** hide in the bosom. ⟨OE *bōsm*⟩

bos•om•y ['bʊzəmi] *or* ['buzəmi] *adj.* having large breasts.

bo•son ['bousɒn] *n.* any of a class of elementary particles that includes mesons and the photon, having a spin that is zero or an integral number. ⟨after S.N. *Bose* (1858-1937), Indian physicist⟩

boss[1] [bɒs] *Informal. n., v., adj.* —*n.* **1** a person who hires workers or watches over or directs them; foreman or manager. **2** a person who controls a political organization.
—*v.* **1** give orders to: *He likes to boss people. Don't boss me around!* **2** direct; control: *Who is bossing this job?*
—*adj.* **1** that is in charge. **2** *Slang.* excellent: *a boss piece of writing.* ⟨< Du. *baas*⟩

boss[2] [bɒs] *n., v.* —*n.* **1** an ornamentation of silver, ivory, or other material rising above a flat surface or projecting from the centre of a vaulted ceiling: *The boss in this church is made of stone.* **2** in machinery, the enlarged part of a shaft. **3** *Geology.* a domelike body of igneous rock protruding above the surface or into a stratum of other rock.
—*v.* decorate with bosses. ⟨ME *boce* < OF⟩

bos•sa no•va ['bɒsə 'nouvə] **1** a dance originating in Brazil, resembling the samba. **2** the music for this dance. ⟨< Pg., literally, new trend⟩

boss•ism ['bɒsɪzəm] *n.* control by political bosses.

boss•y[1] ['bɒsɪ] *adj.* **boss•i•er, boss•i•est.** *Informal.* fond of telling others what to do and how to do it; domineering. ⟨< *boss[1]*⟩

boss•y[2] ['bɒsi] *adj.* decorated with bosses. ⟨< *boss[2]*⟩

bos•sy[3] or **bos•sie** ['bɒsi] *n.* a familiar name for a calf or cow. ⟨< dial. E *borse, boss* young calf⟩

Boston baked beans haricot or other beans cooked for a long time over low heat, and flavoured with salt pork and molasses.

Boston bull ['bɒstən] BOSTON TERRIER.

Boston cream the creamy whipped filling of **Boston cream pie** (actually a layer cake) and **Boston cream doughnuts.**

Boston fern a variety of sword fern having long, drooping fronds, popular as a house plant.

Boston ivy a woody Asian vine (*Parthenocissus tricuspidata*) of the grape family having broad, glossy, three-lobed leaves, widely cultivated as an ornamental covering for walls.

Boston lettuce a variety of butterhead lettuce.

Boston Tea Party a raid on some British ships in Boston harbour in 1773. Disguised as Native Americans, colonists threw chests of tea overboard as a protest against taxation by the British Parliament.

Boston terrier a breed of small dog having smooth, short, dark hair with white feet, chest, and face. Also called **Boston bull.**

bo•sun ['bousən] *n.* boatswain.

Bos•well ['bɒzwɛl] *or* ['bɒzwəl] *n.* an author of a biography of a close friend. ⟨< James *Boswell* (1740-1795), the Scottish author of a famous biography of Samuel Johnson⟩

bot [bɒt] *n.* the larva of a botfly. It is a parasite of horses, cattle, and sheep. Also, **bott.** ⟨ME; origin uncertain⟩
☛ *Hom.* BOUGHT.

bo•tan•ic [bəˈtænɪk] *adj.* botanical. ⟨< Med.L *botanicus* < Gk. *botanikos* < *botanē* plant⟩

bo•tan•i•ca [bəˈtænɪkə] *n.* a small store selling herbs, magic charms, etc.

bo•tan•i•cal [bəˈtænɪkəl] *adj., n.* —*adj.* **1** of or having to do with plants and plant life. **2** of or having to do with botany.
—*n.* a drug made from parts of a plant. **—boˈtan•i•cal•ly,** *adv.*

botanical garden a place where native or rare plants are grown and studied, open to the public for viewing.

bot•a•nist [ˈbɒtənɪst] *n.* a person trained in botany, especially one whose work it is.

bot•a•nize [ˈbɒtəˌnaɪz] *v.* **-nized, -niz•ing. 1** study plants in their natural environment. **2** collect plants for study. **3** explore the plant life of. **—ˈbot•aˌniz•er,** *n.*

bot•a•ny [ˈbɒtəni] *n., pl.* **-nies. 1** the science of plants; the branch of biology that deals with the structure, growth, classification, diseases, etc. of plants. **2** the plant life of a particular area: *the botany of the Canadian Shield.* **3** the botanical facts and characteristics concerning a particular type or group of plants: *the botany of roses.* ⟨< *botanic*⟩

Botany wool a fine merino wool used in high quality yarns and fabrics. ⟨< *Botany* Bay, Australia, near which it was originally grown⟩

botch [bɒtʃ] *v., n.* —*v.* **1** spoil by poor workmanship; bungle. **2** patch or mend clumsily.
—*n.* **1** a poor piece of workmanship. **2** a clumsy patch. ⟨ME *bocchen*; origin uncertain⟩ **—ˈbotch•er,** *n.*

botch•y [ˈbɒtʃi] *adj.* **botch•i•er, botch•i•est.** botched; poorly made or done.

bot•fly [ˈbɒtˌflaɪ] *n., pl.* **-flies.** any of various two-winged flies (families Gasterophilidae and Oestridae) whose larvae are parasites in mammals. Several species of botfly attack livestock.

both [bouθ] *adj., pron., adv., conj.* —*adj.* two, when only two are considered; the one and the other: *Both houses are white.*
—*pron.* the two together: *Both belong to him. Both of us like it. They are both too small.*
—*adv., conj.* together; alike; equally: *She can both sing and dance. She is both strong and healthy.* ⟨ME, apparently < ON *báthir*⟩
☛ *Usage.* **Both** is used in informal English to emphasize the fact that two persons or places or things are involved in a situation: *The twins were both there.* Strictly speaking, the word *both* is redundant in this sentence, but it gives emphasis.

both•er [ˈbɒðər] *v., n., interj.* —*v.* **1** take trouble; concern oneself: *Don't bother about my breakfast; I'll eat what is here.* **2** make uneasy, worried, or annoyed; irritate: *Hot weather bothers me.* **3** interrupt; disturb: *Don't bother me just now.*
—*n.* **1** worry; fuss; trouble. **2** a person or thing that causes worry, fuss, or trouble.
—*interj.* a word used to express mild annoyance: *Oh, bother! I've forgotten the sugar.* ⟨apparently an Anglo-Irish modification of *pother*⟩

both•er•a•tion [ˌbɒðəˈreiʃən] *n. or interj. Informal.* bother.

both•er•some [ˈbɒðərsəm] *adj.* causing worry or fuss; troublesome.

bo tree [bou] *Buddhism.* the sacred tree under which Buddha was sitting when he achieved enlightenment. ⟨< Sinhalese *bo* < Pali *bodhi* < *bodhi-taru* < *bodhi* wisdom < Skt. *budh* to know + *taru* tree⟩

bots [bɒts] *n.* a disease of cattle caused by botfly larvae infesting the stomach and intestines. Also, **botts.**

Bot•swa•na [bɒtˈswɑnə] *n.* a republic in S Africa, a member of the Commonwealth.

bott [bɒt] See BOT.
☛ *Hom.* BOUGHT.

bot•tle [ˈbɒtəl] *n., v.* **-tled, -tling.** —*n.* **1 a** a container for holding liquids, made of glass, plastic, etc., usually without handles and with a narrow neck and mouth that can be closed with a cap or stopper. **b** such a container whose cap includes a nipple, used for feeding a baby. **2** the amount that a bottle can hold. **3** the contents of a bottle. **4** a bottle and its contents. **5 the bottle,** alcoholic liquor.
hit the bottle, *Slang.* drink alcoholic liquor to excess.
—*v.* **1** put into bottles: *to bottle milk.* **2** hold in; keep back; control (*often used with* **up**): *to bottle one's feelings, to bottle up one's anger.* ⟨ME *botel* < OF *botele, botaille* < VL *butticula*, dim. of LL *buttis* butt[4]⟩ **—ˈbot•tleˌlike,** *adj.* **—ˈbot•tler,** *n.* **—ˈbot•tleˌful,** *n.*

bot•tle•brush [ˈbɒtəlˌbrʌʃ] *n.* **1** a long narrow brush for washing the inside of bottles. **2** a semitropical bush of the genus *Callistemon* of the myrtle family, having tall red or yellow flower clusters resembling a narrow brush.

bottled gas gas, usually propane, made liquid and stored under pressure in portable containers.

bottle gentian a wildflower (*Gentiana andrewsii*) having purple blooms 3 cm long. It grows in meadows or bogs from Québec to Saskatchewan and south to Georgia, Arkansas, and Nebraska.

bottle green a very dark green.

bot•tle•neck [ˈbɒtəlˌnɛk] *n., v.* —*n.* **1** the neck of a bottle. **2** a narrow passageway or street. **3** a person or thing that hinders progress. **4** a situation in which progress is hindered: *They have hit a bottleneck that could delay the decision for weeks.*
—*v.* act as a bottleneck in.

bot•tle•nose [ˈbɒtəlˌnouz] *n.* **1** BOTTLENOSED DOLPHIN. **2** a whale of the genus *Hyperoodon*, having a snout like a dolphin, and teeth.

bot•tle•nosed dolphin [ˈbɒtəlˌnouzd] a dolphin (*Tursiops truncatus*) widely distributed in temperate and warm seas, having a short, somewhat upturned beak. Also called **bottlenose dolphin, bottlenose.**

bot•tom [ˈbɒtəm] *n., v., adj.* —*n.* **1** the lowest part: *The berries at the bottom of the basket were small.* **2** underside: *The bottom of the shelf was left unpainted. Don't set the glass on the table if the bottom is wet.* **3** the base on which something rests: *There is an inscription around the bottom of the statue.* **4** the lowest position: *She was at the bottom of the class.* **5** the ground under a body of water: *the bottom of the sea.* **6** Often, **bottoms,** *pl.* the low land along a river. **7** the seat of a chair: *This chair needs a new bottom.* **8 bottoms,** *pl.* pyjama pants. **9** the buttocks. **10** the part of a ship's hull below the water line. **11** a ship, especially a cargo ship. **12** *Baseball.* the second half of an inning: *the bottom of the ninth.* **13** the area farthest from the entrance or beginning: *the bottom of the garden.* **14** ability to withstand; endurance.
at bottom, basically; actually: *At bottom, she's a kind person.*
be at the bottom of, be the cause or source of: *He is at the bottom of this mischief.*
bottoms up! *Informal.* drain your glass! drink up!
get to the bottom of, discover the underlying source, cause, or meaning of.
—*v.* **1** put a seat on. **2** get to the bottom of; understand fully. **3** touch or rest on the bottom: *The submarine bottomed on the ocean floor.*
bottom out, reach a low point and level off: *It seems the stock market has bottomed out.*
—*adj.* **1** lowest; last: *bottom prices.* **2** underlying; fundamental.
bet one's bottom dollar, *Slang.* bet all that one has; be absolutely certain. ⟨OE *botm*; for def. 11, see BOTTOMRY⟩

bottom land the low land along a river.

bot•tom•less [ˈbɒtəmlɪs] *adj.* **1** without a bottom. **2** so deep that the bottom cannot be reached; extremely deep. **3** endless or inexhaustible.

bottom line 1 the final line of a financial statement, showing profit and loss. **2** the most fundamental point or principle: *What's the bottom line in your negotiations?*

bot•tom•most [ˈbɒtəmˌmoust] *adj.* deepest; lowest.

bot•tom•ry [ˈbɒtəmri] *n., pl.* **-ries.** *Law.* a contract by which a shipowner mortgages his or her ship in order to get money to make a voyage. If the ship is lost, the lender loses the money. ⟨< *bottom* ship, after Du. *bodemerij*⟩

botts [bɒts] See BOTS.

bo•tu•lin [ˈbɒtʃəlɪn] *n.* the poison that causes botulism.

bo•tu•lin•us [ˌbɒtʃəˈlaɪnəs] *n.* a bacterium that produces the poison causing botulism.

bot•u•lism [ˈbɒtʃəˌlɪzəm] *n.* acute FOOD POISONING caused by a potent toxin produced in imperfectly preserved food, etc. by a bacterium (*Clostridium botulinum*). ⟨< L *botulus* sausage; because originally thought to be produced especially by eating sausages⟩

bou•bou [ˈbuˌbu] *n.* a long flowing garment worn in some parts of Africa.
☛ *Hom.* BOOBOO.

bou•clé [buˈklei] *n.* **1** a crimped, looped yarn. **2** fabric made with this yarn, having a spongy feel and tiny loops and curls on its surface. ⟨< F *bouclé* curled⟩

bou•din [ˈbudɪn]; *French,* [buˈdɛ̃] *n.* a boiled sausage. It exists in two forms: **boudin blanc** made with white meat, and **boudin noir** made with pork, blood, and spices.

bou•doir ['budwɑr] *or* [bu'dwɑr] *n.* a lady's private dressing room or sitting room. ⟨< F *boudoir* < *bouder* sulk⟩

bouf•fant [bu'fɑnt]; *French,* [bu'fɑ̃] *adj.* puffed out: *bouffant sleeves, a bouffant hairdo.* ⟨< F⟩

bou•gain•vil•le•a [ˌbugən'vɪliə] *n.* any of several tropical climbing shrubs having large, brilliant, deep-red leaves surrounding tiny flowers. ⟨after L.A. de *Bougainville* (1729-1811), French navigator and explorer⟩

bough [baʊ] *n.* **1** one of the main branches of a tree. **2** a branch cut from a tree. ⟨OE *bōg* bough, shoulder⟩
☛ *Hom.* BOW[1], BOW[3].
☛ *Syn.* See note at BRANCH.

bought [bɒt] *v.* pt. and pp. of BUY.
☛ *Hom.* BOT, BOTT.

bought•en ['bɒtən] *adj. Dialect.* bought; not homemade.
☛ *Usage.* **Boughten** is a nonstandard expression used only in certain North American dialects: *Is that a boughten dress?*

bou•gie ['buʒi] *or* [bu'ʒi] *n.* **1** a candle made of wax. **2** *Medicine.* a narrow tool inserted into a body passage, such as the rectum or urethra. ⟨< F, candle⟩

bouil•la•baisse [ˌbuljə'beis]; *French,* [buja'bɛs] *n.* a fish chowder highly seasoned with wine, herbs, etc. ⟨< F *bouillabaisse* < Provençal *bouiabaisso* < *boui* boil + *abaisso* go down (from its being brought quickly to boil and then simmered down)⟩

bouil•lon ['bʊljən] *or* ['bʊljɒn]; *French,* [bu'jɔ̃] *n.* **1** a clear, thin soup or broth. **2** a liquid, nutritive medium used for growing cultures of bacteria. ⟨< F *bouillon* < *bouillir* boil < L *bullire*⟩
☛ *Hom.* BULLION ['bʊljən].

bouillon cube a small cube of concentrated stock from which one can make bouillon by adding water.

boul•der ['bouldər] *n.* a large rock rounded or worn by the action of water or weather. ⟨for *boulderstone,* ME < Scand.; cf. Swedish *bullersten* < *bullra* roar + *sten* stone⟩

bou•le ['buli] *n.* in ancient Greece: **1** a group of older men who advised the ruler. **2** later, an elected parliament who made laws and ran the country. ⟨< Gk. *ballein* throw⟩

boul•e•vard ['bʊlə,vɑrd] *n.* **1** a broad street. **2** the strip of grass between a sidewalk and a curb. **3** the centre strip dividing a road into two lanes for traffic going in opposite directions. **4** such a road. *Abbrev.:* blvd. ⟨< F, originally, the passageway along a rampart < MLG < MDu. *bolwerc.* Akin to BULWARK.⟩

boulle [bul] *n.* **1** wood inlaid with tortoise-shell, ivory, or bright metals in elaborate patterns, used for furniture. **2** this method of decorating wood, or the furniture made with such wood. Also, **buhl.** ⟨< G *Buhl* < F *boulle* < André C. *Boulle* (1642-1732), French cabinetmaker⟩

bounce [baʊns] *v.* **bounced, bounc•ing;** *n.* —*v.* **1** spring, often repeatedly, into the air after striking something, as a rubber ball does: *The baby likes to bounce on the bed. The ball bounced off the porch railing.* **2** cause to bounce: *She bounced the basketball off the backboard.* **3** come or go energetically, noisily, angrily, etc.: *He bounced out of the room.* **4** *Slang.* throw out (a person who is disorderly). **5** *Slang.* discharge from work or employment. **6** *Informal.* of a cheque, be returned by a bank as a result of the person who signed the cheque having insufficient funds in his or her account to meet it.
bounce back, recover health or good spirits quickly.
—*n.* **1** a bound; a spring; a bouncing. **2** impudence or bluster. **3** springiness; ability to bounce: *This ball has lots of bounce.* **4** *Informal.* energy; spirit: *She was in hospital for a week, but she is as full of bounce as ever.* **5 the bounce,** *Slang.* rude or abrupt dismissal or ejection: *The club owner gave him the bounce.* ⟨ME *bunse(n)*; cf. Du. *bonzen* thump⟩

bounc•er ['baʊnsər] *n.* **1** *Slang.* a person employed by a cabaret, restaurant, etc. to restrain or remove people who are drunk or disorderly. **2** any person or thing that bounces.

bounc•ing ['baʊnsɪŋ] *adj., v.* —*adj.* strong, healthy, and vigorous: *a bouncing baby girl.*
—*v.* ppr. of BOUNCE.

bouncing Bet soapwort.

boun•cy ['baʊnsi] *adj.* **boun•ci•er, boun•ci•est. 1** elastic; resilient: *a bouncy surface.* **2** cheerful and spirited; exuberant: *A week after the accident, he was as bouncy as always.* —**'boun•ci•ly,** *adv.* —**'boun•ci•ness,** *n.*

bound[1] [baʊnd] *adj., v.* —*adj.* **1** under some obligation; obliged: *bound by law to keep the peace. He felt himself duty-bound to volunteer.* **2** certain; sure: *It's bound to rain before morning.* **3** confined (*used especially in compounds*): *housebound. We were snowbound for three days.* **4** *Informal.* determined; resolved: *She was bound to go, whether or not we were going.* **5** of a book or a set of pages, having covers; having a binding: *Our workbook consisted of 40 bound tests from previous years.* **6** *Linguistics.* of a morpheme, unable to stand alone as a word. The *-ing* in *going* is a bound morpheme. **7** constrained as by being tied. **8** linked or associated.
bound up in or **with, a** closely connected with. **b** very devoted to.
—*v.* pt. and pp. of BIND. ⟨pp. of *bind;* ME *bounden*⟩

bound[2] [baʊnd] *v., n.* —*v.* **1** spring lightly along; move by leaping: *The deer bounded into the woods and was gone.* **2** of a ball, etc., spring back after striking a surface; rebound; bounce: *The ball bounded from the wall and hit the car.*
—*n.* **1** a leap or spring upward or onward. **2** the act of rebounding; bounce: *I caught the ball on the bound.* ⟨< F *bondir* leap, originally, resound, ? < L *bombus.* See BOMB.⟩

bound[3] [baʊnd] *n., v.* —*n.* **1** Usually **bounds,** *pl.* a limit or limiting line: *the farthest bounds of the estate. Keep your hopes within bounds.* **2 bounds,** *pl.* land on or near a boundary.
out of bounds, outside the area allowed by rules, custom, or law: *He kicked the ball out of bounds. The town is out of bounds to the soldiers.*
—*v.* **1** be or form the boundary of: *A poplar bluff bounds the property to the north. The garden is bounded by a flagstone walk.* **2** be next to; adjoin (*used with* **on**): *Canada bounds on the United States.* ⟨ME *bunne* < AF *bounde* < OF *bodne* < LL *butina*⟩

bound[4] [baʊnd] *adj.* going; on the way (*often used in compounds*): *westbound. I am bound for home.* ⟨ME *boun* < ON *búinn,* pp. of *búa* get ready⟩

bound•a•ry ['baʊndəri] *n., pl.* **-ries. 1** a limiting line; something that functions as a dividing line, especially between properties, provinces, countries, etc.: *The Ottawa River forms part of the boundary between Ontario and Québec.* **2** *Cricket.* **a** a limit of the field. **b** a hit to or beyond this limit. ⟨< *bound*[3] + *-ary*⟩

boundary layer *Physics.* in a coursing liquid containing solid objects, the layer of fluid surrounding the solid. The liquid in the boundary layer flows more slowly than the rest of the liquid.

bound•en ['baʊndən] *adj.* **1** required; obligatory: *They considered it their bounden duty.* **2** *Archaic.* under obligation; obliged. ⟨*Archaic* pp. of *bind*⟩

bound•er ['baʊndər] *n. Esp. Brit. Informal.* a rude, vulgar person; upstart; cad.

bound form *Linguistics.* a form which cannot stand alone as a word, but can only be part of another word. The *-ly* in *slowly* is a bound form.

bound•less ['baʊndlɪs] *adj.* **1** not limited; infinite; vast: *boundless space.* **2** seemingly without bounds; vast: *the boundless ocean.* —**'bound•less•ly,** *adv.* —**'bound•less•ness,** *n.*

boun•te•ous ['baʊntiəs] *adj. Poetic.* **1** generous; given freely. **2** plentiful; abundant. —**'boun•te•ous•ly,** *adv.* —**'boun•te•ous•ness,** *n.*

boun•ti•ful ['baʊntəfəl] *adj.* **1** plentiful; abundant. **2** generous; giving freely. —**'boun•ti•ful•ly,** *adv.* —**'boun•ti•ful•ness,** *n.*

boun•ty ['baʊnti] *n., pl.* **-ties. 1** something given with generosity. **2** generosity. **3** a reward or premium, especially one given by a government. Governments have sometimes offered bounties to hunters for killing animals considered a nuisance. ⟨ME < OF *bonte* < L *bonitas* < *bonus* good⟩

bounty hunter a person who makes a living by hunting animals (or, formerly, outlaws) for their bounty. —**bounty hunting.**

bou•quet [bu'kei] *or* [bou'kei] *for 1;* [bu'kei] *for 2 and 3. n.* **1** a bunch of flowers. **2** a fragrance; aroma. **3** a group of pheasants. ⟨< F *bouquet* little wood, dim. of OF *bosc* wood < Gmc. **busk.* See BOSCAGE.⟩

bouquet gar•ni [bu'kei gɑr'ni] a collection of herbs and seasonings fastened in a little cloth bag which is added to a stew while cooking, and then removed. ⟨< F⟩

bour•bon ['bɜrbən] *n.* a kind of whisky, distilled from a grain mash containing at least 51 percent corn. ⟨< *Bourbon* County, Kentucky, where this whisky was originally made⟩

Bour•bon ['burbən], *occasionally* ['bɜrbən] *n.* a person who clings to old ideas and opposes any change; an extreme conservative. ⟨< *Bourbon,* the name of a former royal family of France, Spain, Naples, and Sicily⟩

Bour•bon•ism ['burbə,nɪzəm]; *occasionally,* ['bɜrbə,nɪzəm] *n.*

1 support of the Bourbons. **2** extreme conservatism in politics, etc.

bour•don ['bʊrdən] *n.* **1** the drone of a bagpipe. **2** an organ stop that sounds like the drone of a bagpipe. ⟨< F < ML *burdo* drone⟩

bour•geois [bur'ʒwɑ] *or* ['burʒwɑ]; *French,* [buʀ'ʒwa] *n., pl.* **-geois,** *fem.* **-geoise** [-ʒwɑz]. *adj.* *—n.* **1** a person of the middle class. **2** a property owner or business person, as contrasted with a member of the working class. **3** *Cdn.* formerly, a partner in a fur-trading company, in charge of a trading post or expedition; wintering partner. **4** *Cdn.* formerly, employer; boss. **5** formerly, a free townsman. **6** one whose outlook and customs are typically middle-class.
—adj. **1** of the middle class. **2** like the middle class; ordinary; conventional. **3** influenced chiefly by the interests of property ownership and business. ⟨< F *bourgeois* < LL *burgensis* < *burgus* fort < Gmc. Doublet of BURGESS.⟩

bour•geoi•sie [ˌburʒwɑ'zi] *n.* **1** the middle class. **2** property owners and business people as a class, as contrasted with the proletariat. ⟨< F⟩

bourn[1] or **bourne**[1] [bɔrn] *n.* a small stream; brook. ⟨OE *burna*⟩
☛ *Hom.* BORN, BORNE.

bourn[2] or **bourne**[2] [bɔrn] *n.* **1** *Archaic.* a boundary; limit. **2** a goal. ⟨< OF *borne.* Akin to BOUND[3].⟩
☛ *Hom.* BORN, BORNE.

bour•rée [bu'rei] *n.* **1** a spirited French dance in 2/4 time. **2** the music for this dance, popular in the 17th century. ⟨< F *bourrir,* a reference to the wing-beating and posturing of birds⟩

bourse [burs] *n.* **1** an exchange, especially the stock exchange in Paris or in any of certain other European cities. **2** a sale of stamps or coins at a conference for collectors. ⟨< F *bourse,* originally, purse < LL *bursa* < Gk. *byrsa* hide, wineskin. Doublet of BURSA, PURSE.⟩

bouse [bʌus] *or* [baʊz] *v.* **boused, bous•ing.** *Nautical.* hoist with a block and tackle.

bou•stro•phe•don [ˌbustrə'fidən] *n.* formerly, an arrangement of writing in which the lines read alternately one way and then the other, following on from the end of the previous line. ⟨< Gk. *boustrophēdon* turning like oxen in ploughing⟩

bout[1] [bʌut] *n.* **1** a trial of strength; contest. **2** a spell; a period, especially one involving illness, effort, or endurance: *I have just had a long bout of the flu. Are you ready for a bout of house-cleaning? They went on a drinking bout.* ⟨var. of *bought* a bending, turn. Related to BOW[1].⟩

bout[2] [bu] *n.* *Cdn.* formerly, one of the paddlers or rowers at either end of a canoe, bateau, etc. ⟨< Cdn.F < F *bout* end⟩
☛ *Hom.* BOO.

bou•tique [bu'tik] *n.* a small shop or a department in a large store that specializes in fashionable clothes or accessories, or in gifts, etc. ⟨< F⟩

bou•ton•niere or **bou•ton•nière** [ˌbutə'njɛr] *or* [ˌbutə'nir]; *French,* [butɔ'njɛʀ] *n.* a flower or flowers worn in a buttonhole. ⟨< F *boutonnière* buttonhole⟩

bou•var•dia [bu'vɑrdiə] *n.* a plant of the genus *Bouvardia,* of the madder family, having showy red, yellow, or white tubular flowers prized as ornamental. ⟨< C. *Bouvard,* 17c. French physician⟩

bou•vi•er ['buvi,ei] *n.* BOUVIER DES FLANDRES. ⟨< C. *Bouvard,* 17c. French physician⟩

bouvier des Flan•dres ['flændərz] *or* ['flɑndrə] a breed of large, heavily built dog having a rough, somewhat tousled coat, originally from Belgium where it was used especially for herding cattle. ⟨< F, lit., cowherd of Flanders⟩

bou•zou•ki [bu'zuki] *n.* a Greek stringed musical instrument resembling a mandolin. ⟨< Mod.Gk. *mpouzouki,* possibly < Turkish *büjük* large⟩

bo•vid ['bouvɪd] *adj., n.* *—adj.* belonging to or characteristic of the family Bovidae, a group of cud-chewing, hoofed mammals with permanent, non-branching, hollow horns.
—n. an animal of the family Bovidae, including domestic cattle, true antelope, buffalo, bison, the yak, sheep, goats, and the musk-ox.

bo•vine ['bouvaɪn] *adj., n.* *—adj.* **1** belonging to or characteristic of a tribe (Bovini) of bovid mammals that includes buffalo, bison, the yak, and domestic cattle. **2** slow and somewhat stupid. **3** without emotion; stolid.
—n. a bovine animal; ox (def. 2). ⟨< LL *bovinus* < L *bos, bovis* ox, cow⟩

bow[1] [baʊ] *v., n.* *—v.* **1** bend (the head or body) in greeting, respect, worship, or submission. **2** show by bowing: *to bow one's thanks.* **3** cause to stoop: *The man was bowed by old age.* **4** submit; yield: *We must bow to necessity.*
bow and scrape, be too polite or slavish.
bow down, a weigh down: *bowed down with care.* **b** to worship.
bow out, a withdraw (*used with* **of**): *She sprained her wrist and had to bow out of the tennis tournament.* **b** usher out.
—n. a bending of the head or body in greeting, respect, worship, or submission.
make (one's) **bow, a** make an entrance. **b** make an initial appearance before the public as a performer. **c** retire from public notice.
take a bow, accept praise, applause, etc. for something done. ⟨OE *būgan*⟩
☛ *Hom.* BOUGH, BOW[3].

bow[2] [bou] *n., v.* *—n.* **1** a weapon for shooting arrows, usually consisting of a strip of springy wood with a string or cord stretched tight between the two ends. **2** a curve; bend. **3** a looped knot: *a bow of ribbon. I tie my shoelaces in a bow.* **4** a slender rod with horsehairs stretched on it, for playing a violin, etc. **5** something curved; a curved part: *A rainbow is a bow.* **6** bowman; archer.
—v. **1** curve; bend. **2** play (a violin, etc.) with a bow. ⟨OE *boga*⟩ **—'bow•less,** *adj.* **—'bow,like,** *adj.*
☛ *Hom.* BEAU.

bow[3] [baʊ] *n.* **1** the forward part of a ship, boat, or airship. **2** the person who rows with the oar nearest the bow of a boat.
on the port (or starboard) bow, contained in the right angle to the left (or right) of the point immediately ahead. ⟨probably of LG or Scand. origin. Akin to BOUGH.⟩
☛ *Hom.* BOUGH, BOW[1].

bowd•ler•ize ['baʊdlə,raɪz] *or* ['boudlə,raɪz] *v.* **-ized, -iz•ing.** purge of words and passages thought to be improper. ⟨< Dr. T. *Bowdler* (1754-1825), who published an expurgated edition of Shakespeare in 1818⟩ **—'bowd•ler,ism,** *n.* **—,bowd•ler•i'za•tion,** *n.*

bow•el ['baʊəl] *n.* **1** a part of the bowels; intestine. **2** Usually, **bowels,** *pl.* a tube in the body into which digested food passes from the stomach; intestines. **3 bowels,** *pl.* **a** the inner part; depths: *Miners dig for coal in the bowels of the earth.* **b** *Archaic.* pity; tender feelings.
move (one's) **bowels,** defecate. ⟨ME < OF *boel* < L *botellus,* dim. of *botulus* pudding, sausage⟩

bowel movement 1 discharge of waste matter from the large intestine. **2** the waste matter discharged; feces.

bow•er[1] ['baʊər] *n.* **1** a shelter of leafy branches. **2** a summerhouse or arbour. **3** *Archaic.* bedroom. **4** an erection of twigs built by the male bowerbird for courting purposes. ⟨OE *būr* dwelling⟩ **—'bow•er,like,** *adj.*

bow•er[2] ['baʊər] *n.* an anchor carried at the bow of a ship. ⟨< *bow*[3]⟩

bow•er[3] ['baʊər] *n.* the high card in certain games. The **right bower** is a jack of the suit that is trump; the **left bower,** the jack of the suit of the same colour as trump; the **best bower,** the joker. ⟨< G *Bauer* jack (in cards), peasant⟩

bow•er[4] ['baʊər] *n.* one who bows or stoops.

bow•er[5] ['bouər] *n.* one who uses a bow (in a specified way) as on a violin, etc. *The first violinist is a very expressive bower.*

bow•er•bird ['baʊər,bɜrd] *n.* an Australian songbird of the Ptilorhynchidae family, the male of which builds an elaborate bower of twigs, lavishly decorated with shells, etc., to attract the female.

bow•er•y ['baʊəri] *adj.* like a bower; leafy; shady.

bow•fin ['bou,fɪn] *n.* a voracious freshwater fish (*Amia calva*) found in shallow, weedy waters in E North America, having a dull green, roundish body with a very long dorsal fin. The bowfin is the only living representative of the order Amiiformes. Also called **dogfish, mudfish.**

bow–front ['bou ,frʌnt] designating a style or piece of furniture, especially a chest of drawers, whose front is convex.

bow hand the hand that holds the bow in playing stringed instruments, or in archery.

bow•head ['bou,hɛd] *n.* a right whale (*Balaena mysticetus*) having a very large head that is almost one third of its total length of about 18 m and a great mouth, with the lower lip curving upward in a high bow on each side. It is an endangered species.

bow•hunt•er ['bou,hʌntər] *n.* one who hunts animals with a bow and arrow. **—'bow,hunt•ing,** *n.*

bow•ie knife ['boui] *or* ['bui] a long, single-edged hunting knife carried in a sheath. ⟨after Col. James *Bowie* (1796-1836), American pioneer⟩

bow•ing ['bouɪŋ] the manner of moving the bow back and forth when playing a stringed instrument: *It looks better if the whole violin section of the orchestra uses the same bowing. Mark the bowing on your score.*

bow•knot ['bou,nɒt] *n.* a slipknot such as is made in tying shoelaces. It may be tied as a single bow or as a double bow.

bowl¹ [boul] *n.* **1** a hollow, rounded dish. **2** the amount that a bowl can hold. **3** a bowl-shaped or concave part: *the bowl of a spoon or a pipe.* **4** a large drinking cup. **5** a drink. **6** a bowl-shaped structure such as an amphitheatre or a stadium. ⟨ME *bolle* < OE *bolla*⟩ **—'bowl,like,** *adj.*
☛ *Hom.* BOLE, BOLL.

bowl² [boul] *n., v.* —*n.* **1** a fairly large, heavy ball used in certain games, especially the weighted or slightly flattened ball used in lawn bowling. **2** in lawn bowling or bowling, a throw.
3 bowls, *pl.* (*usually used with a singular verb*) **a** lawn bowling.
b skittles or tenpins.
—*v.* **1** *Bowling.* **a** take part in a game of bowling. **b** roll (a ball) in bowling. **c** make a score of. **2** roll or move along rapidly and smoothly: *Our car bowled along on the good road.* **3** *Cricket.* **a** send (the ball) to the batsman by an overarm throw. **b** dismiss (a batsman), especially by knocking off the bails or knocking down a wicket.
bowl down, knock down.
bowl over, a knock over. **b** *Informal.* make helpless and confused; stun: *I was bowled over by the bad news.* ⟨ME *boule* < L *bulla* ball, bubble⟩
☛ *Hom.* BOLE, BOLL.

bowl•der ['bouldər] See BOULDER.

bow•leg ['bou,lɛg] *n.* **1** a leg that curves outward at or below the knee. **2** an outward curve of the legs.

bow•leg•ged ['bou,lɛgɪd] *or* [-,lɛgd] *adj.* having the legs curved outward at or below the knee.

bowl•er¹ ['boulər] *n.* **1** a person who bowls, as in the games of bowling or lawn bowling. **2** *Cricket.* the player who sends the ball to the wicket by an overarm throw. ⟨< *bowl²*, v.⟩

bowl•er² ['boulər] *n.* DERBY (def. 3). ⟨after J. *Bowler*, a 19c. London hatter⟩

bowl•ful ['boul,fʊl] as much as a bowl can hold.

bow•line ['boulən] *or* ['bou,laɪn] *n.* **1** a knot used in making a fixed loop. See KNOT for picture. **2** the rope tied to the edge of a square sail nearest the wind. It holds the sail steady when sailing into the wind. ⟨ME; *bow³* + *line¹*⟩

bowline knot BOWLINE (def. 1).

bowl•ing ['boulɪŋ] *n., v.* —*n.* **1** a game played indoors, in which balls are rolled down an alley at bottle-shaped wooden pins. Fivepins, ninepins, and tenpins are forms of bowling. **2** LAWN BOWLING. **3** *Cricket.* the act of a bowler in delivering the ball to the batsman: *He was practising his bowling.*
—*v.* ppr. of BOWL.

bowling alley **1** the lane or alley down which balls are rolled. **2** an establishment having a number of lanes for bowling: *There is a snack bar at the bowling alley.*

bowling green a smooth, flat stretch of grass for lawn bowling.

bowls [boulz] *n.* LAWN BOWLING.

bow•man¹ ['boumən] *n., pl.* **-men.** a soldier armed with bow and arrows; archer.

bow•man² ['baʊmən] *n. Rowing.* the oarsman nearest the bow of the boat.

Bowman's capsule ['boumənz] a cup-shaped structure in the nephron for removing waste from the kidney. ⟨after William *Bowman* (1816-1892), English anatomist⟩

bow net [bou] a wickerwork trap for catching lobsters and other shellfish. ⟨< *bow²* + *net*⟩

bow•shot ['bou,ʃɒt] *n.* **1** a shot from a bow. **2** the distance that a bow will shoot an arrow.

bow•sprit ['baʊ,sprɪt] *or* ['bou,sprɪt] *n.* a pole or spar projecting forward from the bow of a ship. Ropes from the bowsprit help to steady sails and masts. See SCHOONER for picture. ⟨probably < LG or Du.⟩

bow•string ['bou,strɪŋ] *n., v.* **-stringed** or **-strung, -string•ing.** —*n.* **1** a strong cord stretched between the two ends of a bow and pulled back by the archer to send the arrow forward. **2** a cord like this.
—*v.* strangle with a bowstring; garrote.

bow tie [bou] a necktie worn in a small bowknot.

bow window [bou] a curved BAY WINDOW.

bow–wow ['baʊ 'waʊ] *n., v.* —*n.* **1** the bark of a dog, or an imitation of this sound. **2** a child's word for a dog.
—*v.* bark like a dog. ⟨imitative⟩

bow•yer ['boujər] *n.* a maker or seller of archery bows.

box¹ [bɒks] *n., v.* —*n.* **1** a rectangular container, usually with a lid, made of wood, metal, cardboard, paper, etc. to pack or put things in. **2** the amount that a box can hold: *We ate a whole box of cereal.* **3** a separate, partly enclosed area in a theatre, etc., for a small group of people. **4** an enclosed space in a courtroom, as for a jury, witness, or prisoner. **5** a small shelter: *a sentry box.* **6** a small country house used by hunters. **7** anything shaped or used like a box. **8** a hollow part that encloses or protects some piece of machinery. **9** the driver's seat on a coach, carriage, etc.
10 *Baseball.* **a** the place where a pitcher stands to throw the ball. **b** the place where the batter stands to hit the ball. **11** *Cdn.* an enclosed area for playing lacrosse. **12** a compartment for a horse in a stable or a vehicle. **13** in newspapers, magazines, etc., a space set off by enclosing lines. **14** a receptacle in a post office from which a subscriber collects mail. **15 the box,** *Informal.* television: *What's on the box tonight?*
in a box, in a problematic situation from which there is no escape.
—*v.* **1** pack in a box; put into a box. **2** confine as if in a box; surround or hem in (*usually used with* **in** *or* **up**): *We couldn't get out of our parking space because another car had boxed us in.*
box in, put (someone) in a problematic situation from which they have no way out.
box the compass, a name the points of a compass in order. **b** go all the way around and end up where one started.
box up, surround; confine. ⟨specialization of meaning of *box³*⟩
—'box,like, *adj.*

box² [bɒks] *n., v.* —*n.* a blow with the open hand or the fist, especially on the side of the head: *She gave him a box on the ear.*
—*v.* **1** strike such a blow. **2** fight as a sport with the fists, which are usually covered with padded gloves: *He had not boxed since he left school.* ⟨origin uncertain⟩

box³ [bɒks] *n.* **1** any of a genus (*Buxus*) of evergreen shrubs and small trees, especially the **common box** (*B. sempervirens*), often used for hedges, borders, etc. **2** the hard, durable wood of a box; boxwood. ⟨< L *buxus* < Gk. *pyxos* a box made of boxwood⟩

box•ber•ry ['bɒks,bɛri] *n.* **1** a creeping shrub (*Gaultheria procumbens*) having evergreen leaves, bell-shaped white flowers, and edible berries. **2** an evergreen climbing plant (*Mitchella repens*) of the madder family, having round leaves, pink flowers, and red berries; partridgeberry.

box•board ['bɒks,bɔrd] *n.* a stiff, non-corrugated cardboard used to make small boxes, as cereal boxes, shoeboxes, etc.

box camera a simple camera in the form of a box which does not fold up and which has a fixed focus.

box•car ['bɒks,kɑr] *n.* a railway freight car enclosed on all sides.

box coat **1** a heavy overcoat such as that formerly worn by coachmen. **2** a loose overcoat without darts or belt.

box elder MANITOBA MAPLE.

box•er¹ [bɒksər] *n.* a person or machine whose work is to pack things in boxes. ⟨< *box¹* + *-er*⟩

box•er² ['bɒksər] *n.* **1** a person who fights with his fists, usually in padded gloves and according to special rules. **2** a breed of medium-sized dog having a stocky, strong body with a deep chest, short brownish hair, and a short, square muzzle. **3 Boxer,** in China, a member of a society opposed to foreigners and Christianity. The Boxers rose in armed rebellion in 1900, but were defeated by foreign soldiers. ⟨< *box²*⟩

boxer shorts loose-fitting shorts with an elastic waistband, worn as underwear.

box•ing¹ ['bɒksɪŋ] *n., v.* —*n.* the sport of fighting with the fists.
—*v.* ppr. of BOX². ⟨< *box²*⟩

box•ing² ['bɒksɪŋ] *n., v.* —*n.* **1** the material used for boxes. **2** the sides of a window; casing. **3** the act of packing things in boxes.
—*v.* ppr. of BOX¹. ⟨< *box¹*⟩

Boxing Day December 26, a legal holiday in all provinces except Québec. Formerly, 'boxes' or presents were given on this day to employees, letter carriers, etc.

boxing gloves the padded gloves worn when boxing.

box kite a kite consisting of two rectangular boxes with open ends, joined together one above the other.

box lacrosse *Cdn.* a form of lacrosse played by teams of seven players on an enclosed playing area about the size of a hockey rink.

box lunch a portable lunch of sandwiches, etc., packed by a catering firm in a box for one person, or carried to work, school, etc., in a lunchbox.

box office **1** the place where tickets are sold in a theatre, hall, etc. **2** the money taken in at the box office. **3** the power to attract ticket buyers, or a show or performer having this power: *Adventure movies are good box office.*

box pleat a double pleat with the cloth folded under at each side.

box score *Baseball.* a complete record of the plays of a game arranged in a table by the names of the players.

box seat a chair or seat in a box of a theatre, hall, auditorium, stadium, etc.

box set *Theatre.* a stage set with back and side walls.

box social *Cdn.* especially formerly, a social gathering where boxes of sandwiches or other food are auctioned to male bidders, the successful bidder having the privilege of eating and dancing with the woman who prepared the box.

box spring a base for a bed, consisting of coil springs set in a cloth-covered frame: *A box spring is designed to be used under a mattress.*

box stall a stall for a horse, cow, etc. being a rectangular enclosure too small for the animal to move about in.

box•thorn ['bɒks,θɔrn] *n.* a shrub of the genus *Lycium* of the nightshade family, having small pink flowers and red berries.

box turtle or **tortoise** any of a genus (*Terrapene*) of small North American turtles whose shells have a hinged lower half and can be entirely closed. They live mostly on land.

box•wood ['bɒks,wʊd] *n.* **1** the hard, fine-grained, durable wood of a BOX[3], especially the common box (*Buxus sempervirens*), used for making tool handles, musical instruments, inlays, etc. **2** a box tree or shrub.

box•y ['bɒksi] *adj.* like a box in shape or function.

boy [bɔɪ] *n., interj. —n.* **1** a male child. **2** son: *Is that your boy?* **3** a male servant. **4** a boy or man employed to run errands, carry things, etc. **5** *Informal.* any man; fellow: *the boys at the office. He's a local boy.*
—interj. Informal. an exclamation of surprise, admiration, pleasure, contempt, etc.: *Boy, is it hot! Boy, is he a liar!* ⟨ME *boy, boi*; origin uncertain⟩
☛ *Hom.* BUOY.

boy•ar [bou'jɑr] *or* ['bɔɪər] *n.* a former Russian aristocrat of high rank. ⟨< Russian *bojarin*⟩

boy•cott ['bɔɪ,kɒt] *v., n. —v.* **1** combine against and have nothing to do with (a person, business, nation, etc.). If people are boycotting someone, they do not associate with him or her, or buy from or sell to him or her, and they try to keep others from doing so. **2** refuse to buy or use (a product, etc.).
—n. the act of boycotting. ⟨after Captain *Boycott* (1832-1897), an English land agent in Ireland who was so treated⟩
—'boy,cot•ter, *n.*

boy•friend ['bɔɪ,frɛnd] *n.* **1** a male companion of a girl or woman; escort, sweetheart, or lover: *She has a new boyfriend.* **2** a boy who is one's friend.

boy•hood ['bɔɪ,hʊd] *n.* **1** the time or condition of being a boy. **2** boys as a group: *the boyhood of the nation.*

boy•ish ['bɔɪɪʃ] *adj.* **1** of a boy. **2** like a boy: *The warm spring weather made him feel almost boyish again.* **3** like a boy's: *a boyish grin.* **4** fit for a boy: *boyish games.* **—'boy•ish•ly,** *adv.* **—'boy•ish•ness,** *n.*

Boyle's law [bɔɪlz] *Physics.* the principle that at a constant temperature the volume of a gas varies inversely with the pressure to which it is subjected. ⟨< Robert *Boyle* (1627-1691), the Irish scientist and philosopher who formulated this law⟩

boy•o ['bɔɪou] *n. Irish.* fellow; man.

boy•sen•ber•ry ['bɔɪzən,bɛri] *n., pl.* **-ries. 1** a purple berry like a blackberry in size and shape, and like a raspberry in flavour, probably a cross of loganberry, raspberry, and blackberry. **2** the plant it grows on. ⟨after R. *Boysen* of California, the botanist who developed it⟩

bp. birthplace.

Bp. Bishop.

BP **1** *Geology.* before the present. **2** See B/P.

B/P or **b/p** **1** bills payable. **2** blood pressure.

bpi *Computer technology.* bits per inch.

bpl birthplace.

bps *Computer technology.* bits per second.

Bq becquerel.

br. **1** branch. **2** brand. **3** brother. **4** bronze. **5** bills receivable. **6** bedroom.

Br bromine.

Br. **1** Britain; British. **2** branch. **3** Brother.

BR or **B/R** **1** bills receivable. **2** bedroom.

bra [brɑ] *n.* brassiere.

brace [breis] *n., v.* **braced, brac•ing.** *—n.* **1** something that holds parts together or in place; a support: *An iron rod or a piece of timber used to support a roof or a wall is called a brace.* **2** a pair; couple: *a brace of ducks.* **3** a handle for a tool or drill used for boring. See DRILL[1] for picture. **4** either of these signs { } used to enclose words, figures, lines, or staves of music, indicating that they are to be considered together. **5 braces,** *pl.* a pair of straps, usually elasticized, for supporting pants, worn over the shoulders and fastened to the pants at the back and front; suspenders. **6** Often, **braces,** *pl.* an arrangement of wires attached to crooked teeth in order to correct their position. **7** a device to strengthen a weak or deformed part of the body: *She had braces on her legs for many years.* **8** a leather thong that slides up and down the cord of a drum, used to regulate the tension of the skins and thus the pitch.
—v. **1** give strength, tension, or firmness to; support with or as if with a brace or braces. **2** enliven; invigorate. **3** tighten the muscles of (one's hands or feet) so as to get a good grip. **4** make ready for something demanding: *The walk braced us for the next job.*
brace (oneself) or **brace up,** *Informal.* summon one's strength or courage to face a shock or trouble. ⟨ME < OF *bracier* embrace < *brace* the two arms < L *bracchia,* pl. of *bracchium* < Gk. *brakhion* upper arm⟩

brace and bit a tool for boring, consisting of a bit fitted into a crank-shaped handle.

brace•let ['breislɪt] *n.* **1** a band or chain worn for ornament around the wrist or arm. **2** the band of a wristwatch, especially a metal band: *My watch has an expansion bracelet.* **3** *Informal.* handcuff. ⟨ME < OF *bracelet,* dim. of *bracel,* ult. < L *bracchium* arm < Gk. *brakhion*⟩ **—'brace•let•ed,** *adj.*

brac•er ['breisər] *n.* **1** a person or thing that braces; a support. **2** *Slang.* a stimulating drink.

brachi•a ['brækiə] *or* ['breikiə] *n.* pl. of BRACHIUM.

bra•chi•al ['brækiəl] *or* ['breikiəl] *adj.* **1** of or having to do with the arm or forelimb: *the brachial artery.* **2** armlike: *the brachial appendages of a starfish.* ⟨< L *bracchialis* of the arm < *bracchium* arm < Gk. *brakhion* upper arm⟩

bra•chi•ate ['bræki,eit] *or* ['breiki,eit] *v.* **bra•chi•at•ed, bra•chi•at•ing;** *adj. —v.* move by swinging from branch to branch, arm over arm, as monkeys and some apes do.
—adj. Botany. bearing branches that grow in diverging directions. ⟨< L *brachialis* < *brachium* arm + -ATE[1]⟩. **—,bra•chi'a•tion,** *n.*

brach•i•o•pod ['brækiə,pɒd] *or* ['breikiə,pɒd] *n.* any of a phylum (Brachiopoda) of small, invertebrate animals of the sea bottom, all having a shell consisting of an upper and a lower valve, and, inside the shell, two coiled arms called brachia on either side of the mouth, used to draw in food-bearing water. Some brachiopods look very much like clams, but the two groups are not related. ⟨< NL *brachiopoda,* pl. < Gk. *brakhion* arm + *pous* foot⟩

bra•chi•o•saur•us [,brækiə'sɔrəs] *n.* the largest herbivorous dinosaur (genus *Brachiosaurus*) of the Jurassic and Cretaceous eras.

bra•chis•to•chrone [brə'kɪstə,kroun] *n. Physics.* the curving path of an object falling from a higher point to a lower point, subject to no force other than gravity.

bra•chi•um ['brækiəm] *or* ['breikiəm] *n., pl.* **-chi•a. 1** the part of the arm from the elbow to the shoulder; upper arm. **2** a corresponding part in an animal. **3** *Zoology.* any armlike appendage. ⟨< L *bracchium* arm < Gk. *brakhion* upper arm⟩

brach•y•ce•phal•ic [ˌbrækəsəˈfælɪk] *adj.* having a short, broad skull; having a skull whose breadth is 80 percent or more of its length; broad-headed. Compare DOLICHOCEPHALIC. Also, **brachycephalous** [ˌbrækəˈsɛfələs]. ⟨< Gk. *brachys* short + *kephalē* head⟩

brach•y•dac•tyl•ic [ˌbrækɪdækˈtɪlɪk] *adj.* having short fingers or toes. ⟨< Gk. *brachys* short + *dactylos* finger⟩

bra•chyp•ter•ous [brəˈkɪptərəs] *adj. Ornithology.* having short wings. ⟨< Gk. *brachys* short + *pteron* wing⟩

brac•ing [ˈbreisɪŋ] *adj., n., v.* —*adj.* giving strength and energy; refreshing.
—*n.* a brace or system of braces.
—*v.* ppr. of BRACE. —**ˈbrac•ing•ly,** *adv.*

bra•cio•la [bræˈtʃoulə] *n.* an Italian dish consisting of a thin slice of meat, rolled and stuffed with other meat, chopped vegetables, etc.

brack•en [ˈbrækən] *n.* **1** a large, coarse fern (*Pteridium aquilinum*) found almost throughout the world, having large, triangular fronds and creeping underground stems. **2** any of various other large ferns, especially of genus *Pteridium.* **3** a growth or clump of such ferns. Also called **brake.** ⟨ME *braken*, apparently < Scand.⟩

brack•et [ˈbrækɪt] *n., v.* —*n.* **1** a flat-topped piece of stone, wood, etc., projecting from a wall or column to support a cornice, statue, etc. **2** a usually L-shaped support fixed to a wall to hold a shelf, light fixture, etc. **3** a small shelf supported by brackets. **4** a light fixture projecting from a wall. **5** either of the signs [ ], used to enclose words, symbols, or figures. **6** either of the signs ( ); parenthesis. **7** either of the signs { }; brace. **8** a classification or grouping according to age, income, etc.: *a middle-income bracket, the junior age bracket.* **9** the distance between two shots, one fired beyond and one short of a target, in finding the correct range for artillery. **10** a pair of shots like this.
—*v.* **1** support with brackets. **2** enclose within brackets. **3** consider or think of together; group: *She is usually bracketed with the avant-garde in music.* **4** fire beyond and short of (a target) in order to find the correct range for artillery. ⟨< F *braguette* < Sp. *bragueta*, dim. of *braga* swaddling clothes < L *bracae* breeches; by confusion with *brachia* arms⟩

bracket fungus a variety of shelflike fungus (genus *Basidiomycotina*) found on tree trunks.

brack•ish [ˈbrækɪʃ] *adj.* **1** of water, slightly salty. **2** distasteful; unpleasant. ⟨< E dial. *brack* salty < MLG *brac*; cf. Du. *brak.* 16c.⟩ —**ˈbrack•ish•ness,** *n.*

bract [brækt] *n.* a small leaf at the base of a flower or flower stalk. See FLOWER for picture. ⟨< L *bractea* thin metal plate⟩ —**ˈbrac•te•al,** *adj.*

brac•te•ate [ˈbræktiɪt] *or* [ˈbrækti,eit] *adj.* having bracts.

bract•let [ˈbræktlət] *n.* a small or secondary bract at the base of a flower.

brad [bræd] *n, v.* **brad•ded, brad•ding.** —*n.* a small, thin nail with a small head.
—*v.* fasten with brads. ⟨var. of *brod* < ON *broddr* spike⟩

brad•awl [ˈbræd,ɒl] *n.* an awl with a cutting edge for making small holes for brads, etc.

brad•y•car•dia [ˌbrædɪˈkɑrdiə] *n.* a heartbeat slower than 60 beats a minute. ⟨< Gk. *bradys* slow + *kardia* heart⟩

brae [brei] *n. Scottish.* a slope; hillside. ⟨ME *bra* < ON *brá-* (first member of a compound) brow; intermediate sense being 'brow of a hill'⟩
☛ *Hom.* BRAY.

brag [bræg] *v.* **bragged, brag•ging.** *n.;*
—*v.* boast.
—*n.* **1** a boast. **2** boastful talk. **3** a person who boasts. ⟨ME; origin uncertain⟩ —**ˈbrag•ger,** *n.*
☛ *Syn. v.* See note at BOAST.

brag•ga•do•ci•o [ˌbrægəˈdouʃiou] *or* [ˌbrægəˈdoutʃiou] *n., pl.* **-ci•os. 1** a boasting or bragging. **2** a boaster; braggart. ⟨coined by Spenser as the name of a character in his *Faerie Queene*⟩

brag•gart [ˈbrægərt] *n.* **1** boaster. **2** (*adjl.*) boastful. ⟨< F *bragard* < *braguer* brag⟩

brah•ma [ˈbrɑmə] *or* [ˈbreimə] *n.* a breed of large chicken with feathered legs and small wings and tail. ⟨< *Brahmaputra*, a river in E India⟩

Brah•ma [ˈbrɑmə] *n.* **1** *Hinduism.* a divinity widely worshipped as the highest god, the creator of all things. **2** BRAHMAN (defs. 1, 3). ⟨< Skt.⟩

Brah•man [ˈbrɑmən] *n., pl.* **-mans. 1** *Classical Hinduism.* the eternal, supreme reality that is the basis of the universe. **2** a member of the priestly caste, the highest caste in India. **3** any of several breeds of humpbacked cattle developed in the S United States by crossing breeds of Indian zebu cattle with American beef breeds. Also, **Brahmin.** —**Brahˈman•ic** [brɑˈmænɪk], *adj.*

Brah•man•ism [ˈbrɑmə,nɪzəm] *n.* **1** the orthodox form of Hinduism wherein the priestly caste, the Brahmans, have great power and prestige and sacrificial rituals are very important. **2** the principles and practices of the Brahmans themselves.

Brah•min [ˈbrɑmɪn] *n., pl.* **-min. 1** See BRAHMAN. **2** highbrow intellectual, especially one belonging to an upper-class family. —**Brahˈmin•ic,** *adj.*

Brah•min•ism [ˈbrɑmɪ,nɪzəm] *n.* **1** Brahmanism. **2** the beliefs, attitudes, etc., of Brahmins; intellectual snobbery.

braid [breid] *n., v.* —*n.* **1** a narrow length of hair, ribbon, straw, etc., formed by weaving together three or more strands or bunches. **2** ribbon or cord, usually consisting of interwoven strands, used to trim or bind clothing, etc. **3** a band, etc., for binding the hair. **4** (*adjl.*) formed of braiding: *a braid rug.*
—*v.* **1** weave together three or more strands or bunches of: *Her mother always braids her hair.* **2** form or make in this way: *to braid a rug.* **3** trim or bind with braid. **4** *Poetic.* bind or ornament (the hair) with ribbons, flowers, etc. ⟨OE *bregdan*⟩ —**ˈbraid•er,** *n.*

braid•ed [ˈbreidɪd] *adj., v.* —*adj.* **1** formed by weaving together three or more strands of hair, ribbon, straw, etc. **2** trimmed or bound with braid.
—*v.* pt. and pp. of BRAID.

braid•ing [ˈbreidɪŋ] *n., v.* —*n.* **1** braid used as trimming. **2** anything braided.
—*v.* ppr. of BRAID.

brail [breil] *n., v.* —*n.* **1** a rope fastened to a sail, used in drawing the sail up or in. **2** brailer.
—*v.* **1** draw in, or furl, (a sail) using the brails. **2** unload (fish) from a seine or trap onto a boat. ⟨ME < OF < VL *bracale* belt < *bracae* breeches. See BRACKET.⟩
☛ *Hom.* BRAILLE.

brail•er [ˈbreilər] *n.* a scoop or basket used to brail fish.

braille or **Braille** [breil] *n., v.* **brailled, brail•ling.** —*n.* **1** a system of writing and printing for blind people. The letters in braille are made of specially arranged groups of up to six raised dots that are read by touch. **2** the letters themselves.
—*v.* encode in braille characters. ⟨named after Louis *Braille* (1809-1852), a French teacher of the blind⟩
☛ *Hom.* BRAIL.

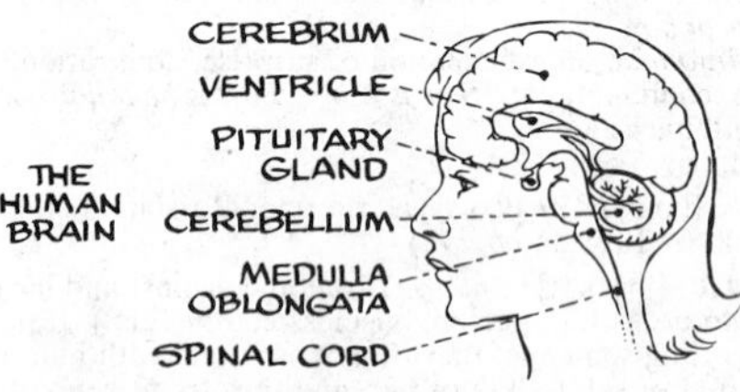

brain [brein] *n., v.* —*n.* **1** the mass of nerve tissue enclosed in the skull of vertebrates. The brain interprets impulses received by the senses of sight, touch, hearing, etc., controls and co-ordinates bodily activities, and is the centre of thought and feeling. **2** in invertebrates, the part of the nervous system corresponding to the brain of vertebrates. **3** mind; intellect: *He has a good brain.* **4** *Slang.* a very intelligent person. **5** Usually, **brains,** *pl.* **a** intelligence: *She has more brains than anyone else in the family.* **b** the main planner of an organization or project: *She is the brains of the firm.* **6** an electronic device thought of as comparable to a brain.
beat or **rack** or **cudgel** (one's) **brain(s),** try hard to think of something.
have on the brain, *Informal.* to be extremely interested in or fanatical about: *He has ballet on the brain.*
pick (someone's) **brains,** to extract useful information or material from (someone).
—*v.* **1** kill by smashing the skull of: *The trapper brained the injured wolf with a large stone.* **2** hit hard on the head. ⟨OE *brægen*⟩

brain cell a nerve cell in the brain.

brain•child [ˈbrein,tʃaild] *n., pl.* **-chil•dren** [ˌtʃɪldrən]. an original product of a person's thought or imagination, such as an invention, idea, or plan, especially one that the person is particularly pleased with or proud of.

brain coral a large coral of the genera *Diploria* or *Meandrina*, whose stony surface looks like a brain.

brain dead having no functioning in the brain; according to some, legally dead. **—brain death.**

brain drain *Informal.* a departure of the most highly trained or educated people from a country or region because of better opportunities elsewhere.

brain•less ['breinlɪs] *adj.* **1** without a brain. **2** stupid; foolish. **—'brain•less•ly,** *adv.* **—'brain•less•ness,** *n.*

brain•pan ['brein,pæn] *n.* the part of the skull enclosing the brain; cranium.

brain–pow•er ['brein ,paʊər] *n.* **1** the power of the mind; brains. **2** intellect thought of as a force or as an instrument to be used.

brain•sick ['brein,sɪk] *adj.* crazy; insane. **—'brain,sick•ness,** *n.*

brain stem the base of the human brain lying beneath the cerebrum and the cerebellum, which connects the spinal cord with the forebrain.

brain•storm ['brein,stɔrm] *n., v.* *—n.* **1** *Informal.* a sudden inspired idea. **2** a sudden and violent, but temporary, mental disturbance.
—v. attempt to solve a problem in a group, committee, etc., by having the members suggest every possible solution they can think of. Discussion is postponed until suggestions are exhausted. **—'brain,storm•er,** *n.*

brain trust or **brains trust** **1** a group of experts acting as advisers to an administrator, a political leader, or an executive. **2** a group of experts in various fields who discuss on the radio or television problems sent in for their attention.

brain•wash ['brein,wɒʃ] *v.* change the ideas or beliefs of by brainwashing.

brain•wash•ing ['brein,wɒʃɪŋ] *n., v.* *—n.* **1** a process of systematic and intensive forced indoctrination designed to purge a person's mind of existing political, religious, or social beliefs and to replace them with a completely different set of beliefs. **2** *Informal.* persuasion through long or intensive exposure to advertising or propaganda.
—v. ppr. of BRAINWASH.

brain wave **1** a rhythmic increase and decrease of voltage between parts of the brain that produces an electric current. Brain waves can be recorded by means of an electroencephalograph. **2** *Informal.* a sudden inspiration or bright idea.

brain•work ['brein,wɜrk] *n.* work requiring the use of the mind primarily, as distinguished from manual or mechanical work.

brain•y ['breini] *adj.* **brain•i•er, brain•i•est.** *Informal.* intelligent; clever. **—'brain•i•ness,** *n.*

braise [breiz] *v.* **braised, brais•ing.** brown (meat) quickly and then cook it long and slowly in a covered pan with very little water. ⟨< F *braiser* < *braise* hot charcoal < Gmc.⟩
☛ *Hom.* BRAZE.

brake¹ [breik] *n., v.* **braked, brak•ing.** *—n.* **1** a device used to decrease or stop the motion of a wheel or vehicle by pressing or scraping. **2** a tool or machine for breaking up flax or hemp into fibres. **3** a machine for kneading or rolling. **4** a BREAK (def. 7). **5** anything that retards or holds back: *a brake on progress.* **6** a heavy harrow used to separate clumps of earth.
—v. **1** slow down or stop by using a brake or brakes: *She had to brake fast to avoid hitting the car ahead. She braked the truck.* **2** break up (flax or hemp) into fibres. ⟨< MLG or MDu. *braeke.* Akin to BREAK.⟩ **—'brake•less,** *adj.*
☛ *Hom.* BREAK.

brake² [breik] *n.* thicket. ⟨Cf. MLG *brake*⟩
☛ *Hom.* BREAK.

brake³ [breik] *n.* bracken. ⟨probably var. of *bracken*⟩
☛ *Hom.* BREAK.

brake⁴ [breik] *v. Archaic.* a pt. of BREAK.

brake•age ['breikɪdʒ] *n.* **1** the use of brakes. **2** the capacity of a machine, such as a vehicle, to brake.
☛ *Hom.* BREAKAGE.

brake band on a winch, hoist, etc., a flexible band encircling the brake drum, that is tightened to slow down or stop a turning wheel or shaft.

brake drum on the wheel, axle, or transmission shaft of a vehicle, a metal cylinder against which a shoe or brake band is pressed in braking.

brake horsepower *Physics.* the horsepower of an engine calculated as the resistance of a brake connected at the drive shaft.

brake lining a pad of mineral or metal (formerly asbestos) attached to a brake band to provide the friction needed to stop.

brake•man ['breikmən] *n., pl.* **-men. 1** a person who works as assistant to the conductor or engineer of a railway train. Brakemen used to work the brakes on steam locomotives. **2** the rear person on a bobsled team, who applies the brake.

brake shoe part of a brake mechanism on railway cars, automobiles, and other vehicles; a shaped block which rubs against a wheel, drum, or other surface in motion to provide friction when the brakes are applied.

bra•less ['brɒləs] *or* ['brɑlɪs] *adj.* not wearing a bra.

bram•ble ['bræmbəl] *n.* **1** any of a genus (*Rubus*) of shrubs of the rose family, most of which have prickly stems. Blackberry and raspberry bushes are brambles. **2** any rough, prickly shrub. ⟨OE *bræmbel,* var. of *brēmel* < *brōm* broom⟩

bram•bling ['bræmblɪŋ] *n.* a European finch (*Fringilla montifringilla*) with brightly coloured plumage. ⟨< earlier *bramline,* perhaps < ME *brembel* < OE *bræmel* < *brom* broom⟩

bram•bly ['bræmbli] *adj.* **-bli•er, -bli•est. 1** full of brambles. **2** like brambles; prickly.

bran [bræn] *n.* the broken coat of the grains of wheat, rye, etc., separated from the flour or meal. Bran is used as fodder and in cereal, bread, and other foods. ⟨ME < OF⟩ **—'bran•ny,** *adj.*

branch [bræntʃ] *n., v.* *—n.* **1** a subdivision of the stem of a large woody plant, especially a stem growing from the trunk or another stem of a tree or from the main or a secondary stem of a shrub. **2** any division or part of a main body or source, like a branch of a tree: *the branches of a deer's antlers, a branch of a river.* **3** a division or part of a system, subject, etc.: *a branch of a family. Botany is a branch of biology.* **4** a local office: *The company's head office is in Moncton, but it has branches in several other cities.* **5** *Computer technology*. an instruction to choose the next task from a set of alternatives.
—v. **1** put out branches; spread in branches (*often used with* **out**). **2** divide into branches: *The trunk branches near the ground. The road branches at the bottom of the hill.* **3** go off in another direction; diverge from the main route, topic, etc. (*often used with* **off**): *With this remark he branched off into a long discourse about his rich relatives. They live on a small street that branches off Highway 5.* **4** extend or expand business, activities, interests, etc. (*often used with* **out**): *His brokerage firm is considering branching out into investment counselling.* **5** *Computer technology.* proceed by means of a branch to a command in another section of a program. ⟨ME < OF *branche* < LL *branca* paw⟩ **—'branch•less,** *adj.* **—'branch,like,** *adj.*
☛ *Syn.* **1. Branch,** BOUGH, LIMB = a part of a tree growing out from the trunk or from another similar part. **Branch** is the general word, and applies to any of the woody outgrowths, large or small, of a tree or shrub: *The branches waved in the breeze.* **Bough** applies particularly to a main branch, but often is used to suggest any branch covered with blossoms, fruit, etc., especially when it has been cut from the tree: *Those boughs of flowering plum are beautiful on the table.* **Limb** applies to a main or large branch: *The wind broke a whole limb from the tree.*

branched chain *Chemistry*. a molecular structure in which atoms, usually carbon, form a straight line, with other atoms branching from it at intervals.

bran•chi•a ['bræŋkiə] *n., pl.* **bran•chi•ae** ['bræŋki,i]. either of the gills of an animal, such as a fish, that lives in water. ⟨< L < Gk. pl. of *brankhion* a gill⟩ **—'bran•chi•al,** *adj.*

bran•chi•o•pod ['bræŋkiə,pɒd] *n.* any of a subclass (Branchiopoda) of small, mainly freshwater crustaceans, including the water fleas, having many pairs of flattened appendages used for swimming, respiration, etc. ⟨< NL < Gk. *brankhia* gills + *pous, podos* foot⟩

branch•let ['bræntʃlɪt] *n.* a small branch.

branch plant a business that is owned and controlled by a company having its headquarters elsewhere. A corporation may have branch plants in several countries, or in several parts of the same country.

branch–plant ['bræntʃ ,plænt] *adj.* characterized by or arising from the existence of branch plants and the resulting dependence on decisions made elsewhere: *a branch-plant economy.*

brand ['brænd] *n., v.* *—n.* **1** a certain kind, grade, or make: *a popular brand of shampoo, a good brand of coffee.* **2** BRAND NAME or trademark. **3** a mark made by burning the skin with a hot iron: *Cattle and horses on big ranches are marked with brands to show*

who owns them. 4 BRANDING IRON. 5 a mark of disgrace. 6 a piece of wood that is burning or partly burned. 7 a disease of garden plants caused by a fungus (*Puccinia arenariae*), in which the leaves develop brown spots that look like burns. 8 *Archaic or poetic.* sword.
—*v.* 1 mark by burning the skin with a hot iron: *In former times criminals were often branded.* 2 expose or mark as deserving disgrace: *He has been branded as a traitor.* ⟨OE⟩ —**'brand•er,** *n.*

brand–building or **brand building** ['brænd ˌbɪldɪŋ] *n.* the widespread advertising of a product with a brand name, to familiarize customers with the brand name.

bran•died ['brændid] *adj.* prepared, mixed, or flavoured with brandy.

branding iron an iron stamp for burning an identification mark on hide, wood, etc.

bran•dish ['brændɪʃ] *v., n.* —*v.* wave or shake threateningly; flourish: *The knight drew his sword and brandished it at his enemy.*
—*n.* a threatening shake; flourish. ⟨< OF *brandiss-*, stem of *brandir* < *brand* sword < Gmc.⟩

brand•ling ['brændlɪŋ] *n.* 1 a small red or yellowish worm used as bait in fishing. 2 a young salmon.

brand name 1 a name given to a product, process, or service by its manufacturer or seller to distinguish from similar ones produced or sold by someone else; trade name. A brand name may be registered and protected as a trademark. 2 a product with a well-known trade name. —**'brand-'name,** *adj.*

brand–new ['brænd 'nju] *or* ['nu] *adj.* very new; as new as if just made.

bran•dy ['brændi] *n., pl.* **-dies;** *v.* **-died, -dy•ing.** —*n.* 1 a strong alcoholic liquor distilled from wine. 2 an alcoholic liquor distilled from fermented fruit juice.
—*v.* mix, flavour, or preserve with brandy. ⟨< Du. *brandewijn* burnt (i.e., distilled) wine⟩

bran•ni•gan ['brænəgən] *n.* a rowdy fight or brawl. ⟨< an Irish surname⟩

brant [brænt] *n., pl.* **brants** or (*esp. collectively*) **brant.** a small wild goose (*Branta bernicla*) that breeds in the Arctic tundra and winters in the temperate regions of the Atlantic and Pacific Oceans, having a black head, neck, and breast, dark grey upper parts, and a narrow white crescent on either side of the neck. ⟨origin uncertain⟩

brash[1] [bræʃ] *adj.* 1 hasty; rash. 2 impudent; saucy. ⟨origin uncertain⟩ —**'brash•ly,** *adv.* —**'brash•ness,** *n.*

brash[2] [bræʃ] *n.* small fragments of ice broken off from an ice pack or floe. ⟨? < MF *breche* breach⟩

bra•sier ['breiʒər] *or* ['breiziər] See BRAZIER.

brass [bræs] *n.* 1 a yellow metal, an alloy of copper and zinc. 2 something made of brass, such as door fittings or ornaments. 3 (*adjl.*) made of brass. 4 a musical wind instrument, usually made of brass, such as the trumpet, trombone, tuba, or French horn. 5 (*adjl.*) of or for such instruments. 6 often, **brasses,** *pl.* the section of an orchestra or band composed of brass instruments. 7 *Informal.* shamelessness; impudence; nerve. 8 high-ranking officials, especially military officers. 9 a memorial plate of brass marked with an effigy, coat of arms, inscription, etc. 10 *Esp. Brit. dialect.* money. ⟨OE *bræs*⟩

bras•sard ['bræsərd] *or* [brə'sɑrd] *n.* 1 a band worn above the elbow as a badge. 2 armour for the upper part of the arm. ⟨< F *brassard* < *bras* arm⟩

bras•sart ['bræsərt] *n.* BRASSARD (def. 2).

brass band a group of musicians playing brass wind instruments.

brass•bound ['bræs,baʊnd] *adj.* 1 *Informal.* keeping strictly to rule. 2 bound with brass: *a brassbound box.*

bras•se•rie ['bræsəri] *or* [ˌbræsə'ri] *n.* a bar or small restaurant serving food and alcoholic drinks, especially beer. ⟨< F *brasser* brew, stir; 19c.⟩

brass hat *Slang.* a high-ranking military officer, such as a general or staff officer.

bras•sie ['bræsi] *n. Golf.* the number 2 wood golf club.

bras•siere or **bras•sière** [brə'zir] *n.* a woman's undergarment worn to support the breasts; bra. ⟨< F *brassière* bodice < *bras* arm⟩

brass instrument a musical instrument made of brass or other metal and played by blowing, such as a trumpet, horn, trombone, or tuba.

brass knuckles a metal bar that fits across the knuckles, used in street fighting.

brass ring the highest prize, distinction, or position of honour, power, prominence, etc.: *As a politician she was not ambitious enough to reach for the brass ring.* ⟨from a brass ring that used to hang above the riders on a merry-go-round; anyone catching hold of the ring got a free ride⟩

brass tacks *Informal.* the actual facts or details: *Let's get down to brass tacks.* ⟨< Cockney rhyming slang for *facts*⟩

brass•ware ['bræs,wɛr] *n.* things made of brass.

brass•y ['bræsi] *adj.* **brass•i•er, brass•i•est.** 1 of brass. 2 like brass: *a brassy hair colour.* 3 loud and harsh. 4 *Informal.* shameless; impudent. —**'brass•i•ly,** *adv.* —**'brass•i•ness,** *n.*

brat [bræt] *n.* a spoiled or irritating child. ⟨? special use of ME *brat* coarse garment, OE *bratt* cloak, covering, probably < Celtic; with reference to a bib⟩ —**'brat•tish,** *adj.*

brat•tice ['brætɪs] *n.* 1 formerly, a rampart put up during a siege. 2 *Mining.* a dividing wall of wood or other material, used to make a passage for air. ⟨ME *bretice, bretasce* < OF *bretesche* wooden tower < Med. L *brittisca* < OHG *brittissa* lattice, balcony < *bret* board⟩

brat•ty ['bræti] *adj.* **brat•ti•er, brat•ti•est.** *Informal.* like a brat; cheeky; disobedient. —**'brat•ti•ness,** *n.*

brat•wurst ['bræt,wɜrst]; *German,* ['bʀat,vʊʀst] *n.* a veal and pork sausage, highly seasoned. ⟨< G < OHG *brato* lean meat + *wurst* sausage⟩

bra•va•do [brə'vɑdou] *n.* a great show of boldness without much real courage; boastful defiance without much real desire to fight. ⟨< Sp. *bravada* < *bravo.* See BRAVE.⟩

brave [breiv] *adj.* **brav•er, brav•est;** *n., v.* **braved, brav•ing.**
—*adj.* 1 having the strength of mind to control fear and act firmly in the face of danger or difficulties; courageous: *He showed he was brave when he stood up to the bully.* 2 showing bravery: *a brave act.* 3 making a fine appearance; showy: *The fair had brave displays.* 4 *Archaic.* fine; excellent.
—*n.* 1 a courageous person. 2 a First Nations warrior.
—*v.* 1 meet bravely: *Soldiers brave much danger.* 2 dare; defy: *She braved the odds.* ⟨< F < Ital. *bravo* brave, bold < Sp. *bravo* vicious, courageous < L *barbarus* barbarous⟩ —**'brave•ly,** *adj.* —**'brave•ness,** *n.*

brav•er•y ['breivəri] *n., pl.* **-er•ies.** 1 strength of mind in the face of danger or difficulties; courage. 2 fine appearance; showy dress; finery.

bra•vo[1] ['brɑvou] *or* [brɑ'vou] *interj., n., pl.* **-vos.** —*interj.* well done! fine! excellent!
—*n.* the cry of "Bravo!" ⟨< Ital. See BRAVE.⟩

bra•vo[2] ['brɑvou] *n., pl.* **-voes** or **-vos.** a hired fighter or murderer. ⟨< Ital. See BRAVE.⟩

bra•vu•ra [brə'vjurə] *n.* 1 a piece of music requiring skill and spirit in the performer. 2 a display of daring; attempt at brilliant performance; dash; spirit. 3 (adjl.) requiring or showing skill, spirit, or daring. ⟨< Ital. *bravura* bravery⟩

braw [brɒ] *adj. Scottish.* 1 making a fine appearance. 2 excellent; fine. ⟨var. of *brave*⟩

brawl[1] [brɒl] *n., v.* —*n.* 1 a noisy and disorderly quarrel: *The hockey game turned into a brawl.* 2 a babble.
—*v.* 1 quarrel in a noisy and disorderly way. 2 babble. ⟨ME *brallen*⟩ —**'brawl•er,** *n.*

brawl[2] [brɒl] *n.* 1 an old French folk dance similar to the cotillion. 2 the music for this dance. 3 *Slang.* a dance or party. ⟨< *brawl*[1] influenced by MF *branle* dance⟩

brawn [brɒn] *n.* 1 firm, strong muscles. 2 muscular strength: *Football requires brains as well as brawn.* 3 boiled and pickled meat from a boar or pig. 4 headcheese. ⟨ME < OF *braon* < Gmc.⟩

brawn•y ['brɒni] *adj.* **brawn•i•er, brawn•i•est.** strong; muscular. —**'brawn•i•ness,** *n.*

brax•y ['bræksi] *n.* an acute inflammatory disease of the fourth stomach of sheep, caused by a bacterium (*Clostridium septicum*), and followed by convulsions and death. ⟨< OE *brǣc* rheum⟩

bray[1] [brei] *n., v.* —*n.* 1 the loud, harsh sound made by a donkey. 2 any noise like it.
—*v.* 1 make this sound: *The man brayed with laughter.* 2 utter in a loud, harsh voice. ⟨ME < OF *braire*⟩
☛ *Hom.* BRAE.

bray[2] [brei] *v.* pound or crush into fine bits; grind into a powder. ⟨ME < OF *breier*⟩ —**'bray•er,** *n.*
☛ *Hom.* BRAE.

braze[1] [breiz] *v.* **brazed, braz•ing. 1** cover or decorate with brass. **2** make like brass. ⟨OE *brasian* < *bræs* brass⟩ **—'braz•er,** *n.*
☛ *Hom.* BRAISE.

braze[2] [breiz] *v.* **brazed, braz•ing.** solder with any of various solders having a high melting point. ⟨? < F *braser* < OF *braise* embers⟩ **—'braz•er,** *n.*
☛ *Hom.* BRAISE.

bra•zen ['breizən] *adj., v. —adj.* **1** shameless; impudent. **2** made of brass. **3** like brass in colour or strength. **4** loud and harsh.
—v. make shameless or impudent.
brazen (a thing) **out** or **through,** act as if one did not feel ashamed of it. ⟨OE *bræsen* < *bræs* brass⟩ **—'bra•zen•ly,** *adv.* **—'bra•zen•ness,** *n.*
☛ *Syn. adj.* **1.** See note at BOLD.

bra•zen•faced ['breizən,feist] *adj.* shameless; cheeky.

bra•zier[1] ['breiʒər] *or* ['breiziər] *n.* a metal container to hold burning charcoal or coal: *Braziers are used in some countries for heating rooms.* Also, **brasier.** ⟨< F *brasier* < *braise* hot coals⟩

bra•zier[2] ['breiʒər] *or* ['breiziər] *n.* a person who works with brass. Also, **brasier.** ⟨< *braze[1]*⟩

Bra•zil [brə'zɪl] *n.* a large republic in South America.

Bra•zil•ian [brə'zɪljən] *n., adj. —n.* a native or inhabitant of Brazil.
—adj. of or having to do with Brazil or its people.

Brazil nut 1 a large, triangular, edible nut of a tropical South American tree (*Bertholletia excelsa*). **2** the tree bearing these nuts.

bra•zil•wood [brə'zɪl,wʊd] *n.* the red wood of any of several tropical trees (genus *Caesalpina*) used in cabinetwork and, especially formerly, as a source of red or purple dye.

breach [britʃ] *n., v. —n.* **1** an opening made by breaking down something solid; gap. **2** the breaking or neglect of a law, promise, duty, etc.: *For you to go away today would be a breach of duty.* **3** a breaking of friendly relations; quarrel. **4** a whale's leap clear of the sea.
—v. **1** break through; make an opening in: *The enemy's fierce attack finally breached the wall.* **2** of whales, rise or leap clear of the sea. ⟨ME *breche* < OF < Gmc.⟩
☛ *Hom.* BREECH.

breach of faith a breaking of a promise.

breach of promise a breaking of a promise to marry.

breach of the peace a public disturbance; riot.

breach of trust improper behaviour by a trustee of property.

bread [brɛd] *n., v. —n.* **1** a food made of flour or meal mixed with milk or water and, usually, yeast, that is kneaded, shaped into loaves, and baked. **2** food; livelihood. **3** *Slang.* money.
break bread, a share a meal. **b** administer or take Communion.
cast (one's) **bread upon the waters,** do good with little or no prospect of reward.
know which side (one's) **bread is buttered on,** know what is to one's advantage.
take the bread out of (someone's) **mouth, a** to take away a person's livelihood. **b** to take from a person what he or she is on the point of enjoying.
—v. cover with bread crumbs before cooking. ⟨OE *brēad*⟩
—'bread•less, *adj.*

bread and butter 1 bread spread with butter. **2** *Informal.* necessities; a living.

bread–and–butter ['brɛd ən 'bʌtər] *adj.* **1** *Informal.* prosaic; commonplace. **2** expressing thanks for hospitality: *a bread-and-butter letter.* **3** having to do with the work, etc. relied on for living.

bread•bas•ket ['brɛd,bæskɪt] *n.* **1** a basket or tray for bread. **2** a region that is a chief source of grain: *The Prairies are the breadbasket of Canada.* **3** *Slang.* the stomach.

bread•board ['brɛd,bɔrd] *n.* **1** a board on which to slice bread, knead dough, roll pastry, etc. **2** a board on which electrical circuits are laid out experimentally.

bread•box ['brɛd,bɒks] *n.* a container for bread to keep it fresh.

bread•crumb or **bread–crumb** ['brɛd,krʌm] *n., v. —n.* **1** a crumb of bread. **2** the soft part of bread as distinguished from the crust.
—v. cover with breadcrumbs.

bread•fruit ['brɛd,frut] *n.* **1** a large, round, starchy, tropical fruit of the Pacific islands, much used for food. When baked, it tastes somewhat like bread. **2** the tree (*Artocarpus altilis*) that it grows on.

bread line a line of people waiting to get food issued as charity or relief.

bread•root ['brɛd,rut] *n.* **1** a North American prairie plant (*Psoralea esculenta*) of the pea family, having blue flowers and an edible starchy root. **2** the root of this plant.

bread stick dough baked into the form of a stick about 20 cm long, served with soup and other dishes.

bread•stuff ['brɛd,stʌf] *n.* **1** grain, flour, or meal for making bread. **2** bread.

breadth [brɛdθ] *or* [brɛtθ] *n.* **1** how broad a thing is; the distance across; width: *The breadth of his shoulders suggested great strength.* **2** a piece of a certain width: *a breadth of cloth.* **3** freedom from narrowness in views or taste: *She is known for her breadth of mind.* **4** great extent or scope. **5** in art, a broad, sweeping quality in which details are made subservient to the whole. ⟨ME *bredethe* < *brede* breadth, OE *brædu* < *brād* broad⟩

breadthways ['brɛdθ,weiz] *or* ['brɛtθ-] *adv. or adj.* in the direction of the breadth.

breadth•wise ['brɛdθ,waɪz] *or* ['brɛtθ-] *adv. or adj.* breadthways.

bread•win•ner ['brɛd,wɪnər] *n.* the member of a family who earns the family's living.

break [breik] *v.* **broke** or (*archaic*) **brake, bro•ken** or (*archaic*) **broke, break•ing;** *n. —v.* **1** cause to come to pieces by a blow or pull: *How did you break my glasses?* **2** come apart; crack; burst: *The plate broke into pieces when it fell on the floor.* **3** destroy the evenness, wholeness, etc. of: *to break a five-dollar bill.* **4** damage, ruin, or destroy; make inoperative: *She broke her watch by winding it too tightly.* **5** fracture the bone of: *to break one's arm.* **6** fail to keep; act against: *to break a law, to break a promise.* **7** escape or become free from: *to break jail. The boat broke its moorings in the storm.* **8** force open: *to break the enemy's ranks, to break a safe.* **9** force one's way: *to break loose from prison, to break into a house.* **10** come suddenly: *The storm broke within ten minutes.* **11** become less or stop suddenly: *The spell of rainy weather has broken.* **12** decrease the force of; lessen: *Because the bushes broke his fall, he was not hurt.* **13** be crushed by sorrow, stress, or disappointment; give way: *The dog's heart broke when its master died. Eventually their nerve broke.* **14** dawn; appear: *The day is breaking.* **15** of plants: **a** to bud. **b** to flower too soon. **16** stop; put an end to: *to break one's fast.* **17** reduce in rank: *The captain was broken for neglect of duty.* **18** train to obey; tame: *to break a colt.* **19** ruin the health, morale, etc. of. **20** ruin financially; make bankrupt. **21** go beyond; exceed: *The speed of the new train has broken all records.* **22** dig or plough (land), especially for the first time: *In the forests of Upper Canada the pioneers had to work hard to break the ground.* **23** of boxers, come out of a clinch. **24** make known; reveal: *to break the bad news gently.* **25** train away from a habit: *He's trying to break himself of nail biting.* **26** open (an electric circuit). **27** interrupt: *to break a journey. The government spokeswoman broke her long silence and issued a statement.* **28** decipher; solve: *to break a code.* **29** *Tennis:* win a game against (an opponent who is serving). **30** stop doing something temporarily, as, work: *Let's break for lunch.* **31** fall apart; disintegrate: *The waves broke against the headland.* **32** *Computer technology.* interrupt a program. **33** cut into (fog, etc.); pierce through: *The light of the flashlight broke the darkness.* **34** of a crowd, separate in various directions (*used with* **for**): *When the rain came they broke for shelter in all directions.* **35** cease functioning: *Our washing machine broke.* **36** of prices or markets, drop suddenly. **37** emerge abruptly from the water's surface, as a fin or a submarine part. **38** start a game of pool with a break.
break a leg! an ironic good luck send-off, especially to an actor.
break away, a leave or escape, especially suddenly: *He broke away from his captors. She finally broke away from her parents and got an apartment of her own.* **b** start before the signal: *The horse was disqualified for breaking away.*
break down, a go out of order; cease to work. **b** collapse; become weak: *Her health broke down.* **c** begin to cry. **d** analyse; separate into components: *Water can be broken down into its component elements by passing an electric current through it. We broke our total holiday budget down into expenses for food, hotels, transportation, and extras.* **e** vanquish; put down.
break even, *Informal.* finish with the same amount one started with; not win or lose: *She had hoped to sell her bicycle at a profit, but she could only break even.*
break in, a enter illegally or by force: *The thieves broke in through the cellar.* **b** interrupt. **c** train (a beginner). **d** use (an engine) gently for a time. **e** accustom (anything new) to use.
break in on, disturb; interrupt.

break into, a enter suddenly, by force, or illegally: *Our house was broken into while we were away. She broke into the room, yelling, "Who took my sweater?"* **b** begin suddenly: *I almost fell off when my horse broke into a gallop. She broke into song.* **c** interrupt: *He didn't want to break into the conversation, so he kept quiet.* **d** enter (a profession or activity), especially with some difficulty: *He's been trying for months to break into the advertising business.*
break off, a stop suddenly. **b** stop being friends or dating.
break out, a begin or arise suddenly or unexpectedly: *War broke out. Fire broke out in the basement.* **b** have an eruption of pimples, rashes, etc. on the skin: *The child broke out in measles.* **c** escape from prison: *Ten convicts have broken out in the last year.*
break trail, *Cdn.* move ahead of a dog team, vehicle, or person, making a way through deep snow: *The leader went ahead on snowshoes, breaking trail for the dogs.*
break up, a scatter: *The fog is breaking up.* **b** stop; put an end to: *We broke up our meeting early today.* **c** *Informal.* upset; disturb greatly. **d** break into pieces: *to break up lumps of earth.* **e** *Informal.* stop being a team, married, friends, etc.: *They've broken up.* **f** *Informal.* begin or cause to begin to laugh uncontrollably. **g** stop (a fight) (*usually* **break it up**).
break with, a stop being friends with. **b** depart from; dissociate oneself from: *She decided to break with her bourgeois upbringing and pursue a radical lifestyle.*
—n. **1** a broken place; gap; crack: *There's a break in the dam.* **2** a breaking or shattering; fracture; rupture. **3** a forcing of one's way out. **4** an abrupt or marked change. **5** a short interruption in work, athletic practice, etc. **6 a** the act or fact of making an electric circuit incomplete. **b** *Computer technology.* a special signal used to interrupt a computer program. **7** a large, four-wheeled, horse-drawn carriage or wagon. **8** *Slang.* an awkward remark; mistake in manners. **9** *Slang.* a chance or opportunity. **10 a** in billiards, an uninterrupted series of points. **b** the first shot in pool, meant to scatter the balls across the table. **11** *Music.* a short, often improvised, section in which one member of a jazz band keeps playing after the others have stopped. **12** *Printing.* a division in a word, paragraph, etc., as at the end of a line, column, or page.
get all the breaks, *Informal.* have things come easily; have lots of luck.
give (someone) **a break,** *Informal.* stop criticizing or nagging.
make a break for it, attempt a run for shelter or in order to escape: *The rain has almost stopped; let's make a break for it.* ⟨OE *brecan*⟩
☛ *Hom.* BRAKE.
☛ *Syn. v.* **1. Break,** SHATTER, SMASH = to make something come or go to pieces. **Break,** the general word = to divide something into two or more pieces by pulling, hitting, or striking it: *I broke the handle off a cup.* **Shatter** = to break suddenly into a number of pieces that fly in all directions. *I shattered the cup when I dropped it on the floor.* **Smash** = to break to pieces with sudden violence and noise: *He smashed the headlights when he hit the wall.*

break•a•ble ['breikəbəl] *adj., n.—adj.* that can be cracked or shattered, especially objects of glass, china, etc., or delicate mechanisms: *Is there anything breakable in this box?*
—n. something fragile: *Be careful with the breakables.*

break•age ['breikɪdʒ] *n.* **1** the act or fact of breaking; break. **2** damage or loss caused by breaking. **3** an allowance made for such damage or loss.
☛ *Hom.* BRAKEAGE.

break and enter the act or an instance of BREAKING AND ENTERING. Also called **break and entry.**

break•a•way ['breikə,wei] *n.* **1** the act or fact of separating sharply from a group or pattern. **2** the separation of the shock wave from the fireball of an atomic explosion as it moves ahead. **3** *Slang.* in the theatre, a stage property made so that it breaks easily and harmlessly when struck by or against something. **4** a start: *Three of the horses in the race got well ahead of the others at the breakaway.* **5** *Hockey or lacrosse.* a situation in which a player of one team launches an attack on goal, the defensive players being caught out of position in their opponents' zone. **6** (*adjl.*) of or being or resulting from a breakaway.

break dancing a modern style of dancing in which dancers jerk, wriggle, and bend the arms and legs and often spin on their backs on the floor. It is performed by individuals or groups to music with a strong beat. **—'break-,dance,** *v.* **—break dancer,** *n.*

break•down ['breik,daʊn] *n.* **1** a failure to work. **2** a loss of health; weakness; collapse: *a mental breakdown.* **3** a noisy, lively dance. **4** the division of anything into parts; an analysis. **5** chemical decomposition or analysis.

break•er¹ ['breikər] *n.* **1** a wave that breaks into foam on the shore, rocks, etc. **2** a machine for breaking things into smaller pieces. **3** a person or thing that breaks. ⟨< *break*⟩
☛ *Syn.* **1.** See note at WAVE.

break•er² ['breikər] *n.* a small water cask for use in a boat. ⟨alteration of Sp. *barrica*⟩

break–even ['breik 'ivən] *adj.* of a point or situation where profits and losses are equal.

break•fast ['brɛkfəst] *n., v. —n.* the first meal of the day. *—v.* eat breakfast. ⟨< *break* + *fast²*⟩

breakfast food cereal eaten at breakfast.

break–in ['breik ,ɪn] *n., adj. —n.* a burglary.
—adj. of or being a time or process of breaking something or someone in: *a break-in period of six weeks.*

breaking and entering *Law.* the entry by force or guile into private or business premises with the object of committing a crime.

breaking point **1** the point at which a person's mental or physical endurance or resistance gives way under stress. **2** the point at which anything breaks under strain.

break•neck ['breik,nɛk] *adj.* likely to cause a broken neck; very dangerous: *breakneck speed, a breakneck slope.*

break of day the dawn.

break•out ['breik,ʌut] *n.* **1** the act or condition of escaping from a prison, etc. **2** BREAKTHROUGH (def. 2).

break•point ['breik,pɔɪnt] *n.* BREAKING POINT.

break•through ['breik,θru] *n.* **1** the solution of a problem, especially in science or technology, that has an important effect on all future research and development. The development of the transistor was a major breakthrough in electronics. **2** an offensive military operation that gets all the way through a defensive system into the unorganized area in the rear. **3** a solving of the major problem or problems hindering any undertaking or advance: *a moral breakthrough.*

break–up or **break•up** ['breik ,ʌp] *n.* **1** *Cdn.* the breaking of the ice on a river or lake in spring: *We stood on the bridge and watched the break-up.* **2** *Cdn.* especially in the North, the time when this happens; spring: *They planned to start work on the new road after break-up.* **3** a scattering; separation. **4** a stopping; end, especially of a relationship or of a joint activity: *the break-up of a marriage or of a friendship.* **5** a collapse; decay.

break•wa•ter ['breik,wɒtər] *n.* a wall or barrier built near the shore to break the force of waves and make an area of calm water for a harbour or beach.

bream¹ [brim] *n., pl.* **bream** or **breams. 1** any of several European freshwater fishes (genus *Abramis*) of the minnow family, especially a common food and game fish (*A. brama*), having a deep, compressed body and silvery scales. **2** any of various other cyprinid fishes. **3** any of various freshwater sunfishes. **4** SEA BREAM. ⟨ME *breme* < OF *bre(s)me* < Gmc.⟩

bream² [brim] *v.* formerly, clean (a ship's bottom) by heating and scraping. ⟨Cf. MDu. *brem* broom⟩

breast [brɛst] *n., v. —n.* **1** either of the two milk-producing glands on the chest of the human female. **2** a similar gland in certain female primates. **3** the similar non-developed gland in the human male. **4** the upper, front part of the human body; chest. **5** the corresponding part in animals. See LAMB and VEAL for pictures. **6** the upper, front part of a coat, dress, etc. **7** anything suggesting the human breast in shape, position, or function. **8** the heart or feelings.
beat one's breast, express grief, guilt, remorse, etc., publicly and emotionally.
make a clean breast of (it), confess fully; tell everything.
—v. oppose; face; struggle with; advance against: *The experienced swimmer was able to breast the waves. She breasted every trouble as it came.* ⟨OE *brēost*⟩

breast•beat•ing ['brɛst,bitɪŋ] *n.* the public, emotional expression of grief, guilt, remorse, etc.

breast•bone ['brɛst,boun] *n.* the thin, flat bone in the front of the chest to which the ribs are attached; sternum. See COLLARBONE for picture.

breast–feed ['brɛst ,fid] *v.* **-fed, -feed•ing.** feed (a baby) at the mother's breast rather than from a bottle; nurse; suckle.

breast•pin ['brɛst,pɪn] *n.* an ornamented pin worn on the breast, especially to close a garment.

breast•plate ['brɛst,pleit] *n.* **1** a piece of armour for the chest. See ARMOUR for picture. **2** in ancient times, a vestment set with jewels, worn by Jewish high priests.

breast stroke or **breast•stroke** ['brɛst,strouk] *n.* *Swimming.* a stroke performed while face down in the water, the swimmer bringing both arms forward from the breast and then sweeping them out to the sides and back down, while moving the legs in a frog kick.

breast•work ['brɛst,wɜrk] *n.* a low, hastily built wall for defence.

breath [brɛθ] *n.* **1** air drawn into and forced out of the lungs. **2** the act of breathing. **3** moisture from breathing: *You can see your breath on a very cold day.* **4** the ability to breathe easily: *Running makes you lose your breath. Take a moment to get your breath back.* **5 a** a single drawing in and forcing out of air from the body. **b** the air drawn in. **c** the time required for one breath; a moment. **6** a slight movement of the air. **7** a whisper. **8** a short pause or rest; breather: *Let's take a breath here.* **9** life. **10** *Phonetics.* an expulsion of air without vibration of the vocal cords, as in pronouncing *s, f, p, t, k.* **11** the fragrance given off by flowers, etc. **12** a trace or suggestion: *a breath of suspicion.*
below (one's) **breath,** in a whisper.
catch (one's) **breath, a** gasp; pant. **b** stop for breath; rest: *They sat down on a rock to catch their breath.*
hold (one's) **breath,** check exhalation.
in the same breath, at the same time or almost the same time.
out of breath, breathing very hard as a result of exertion: *She was so out of breath from the run that she could hardly speak.*
save (one's) **breath,** *Informal.* avoid useless effort in trying to convince: *I know he won't help, so you might as well save your breath.*
take (one's) **breath away,** leave one breathless because of awe, surprise, etc.
under (one's) **breath,** in a whisper: *She was talking under her breath so we couldn't hear her.* ⟨OE *bræth* odour, steam⟩
waste one's breath, waste energy discussing or advising.

breath•a•ble ['briðəbəl] *adj.* **1** suitable for being breathed: *The air in this place is hardly breathable.* **2** of a fabric, etc., allowing air to pass through. **—,breath•a'bil•i•ty,** *n.*

Breath•a•lys•er ['brɛθə,laɪzər] *n. Trademark.* a device for measuring the alcoholic content in a person's blood by a test of the breath. Also, *U.S.,* **Breathalyzer.** ⟨< *breath* + (*an*)*alyser*⟩

breathe [brið] *v.* **breathed, breath•ing. 1** draw (air) into the lungs and force it out. **2** stop for breath; rest: *I need a moment to breathe.* **3** say softly; whisper; utter: *"Don't move until I give the signal," he breathed.* **4** be alive; live. **5** *Phonetics.* utter with breath and not with voice. **6** draw into the lungs; inhale. **7** send out from the lungs; exhale: *The dragon breathed fire and smoke.* **8** inspire; impart; give: *Her enthusiasm breathed new life into the team.* **9** blow lightly. **10** make apparent; exude: *His whole appearance breathes confidence.* **11** of a fabric, leather, etc., allow air to pass through: *Some synthetic fabrics are uncomfortable because they don't breathe.* **12** allow to rest after exertion: *to breathe a horse.* **13** of wine, be exposed to air after being opened, to improve the flavour. **14** carry the odour of on one's breath: *He leaned over me, breathing garlic and onions.*
breathe again or **breathe freely** or **easily,** feel relieved: *The guard passed and she could breathe again.*
breathe down (someone's) **neck,** pursue or watch a person closely: *His supervisor was always breathing down his neck.*
breathe one's last, die.
not breathe a word of, not mention to anyone; keep (information) completely hidden. ⟨ME *brethen* < *breth* breath⟩

breath•er ['briðər] *n.* **1** a short stop for breath; rest. **2** a small vent in an enclosure, container, etc. **3** a person or animal that breathes in a certain way: *a noisy breather.*

breath•ing ['briðɪŋ] *n., v.—n.* **1** respiration. **2** a single breath. **3** the time needed for a single breath.
—v. ppr. of BREATHE.

breathing space room or time enough to breathe easily; an opportunity to rest.

breathing spell a pause to catch one's breath.

breath•less ['brɛθlɪs] *adj.* **1** out of breath: *Running very fast makes you breathless.* **2** holding one's breath because of fear, interest, excitement, etc.: *The beauty of the scenery left Theo breathless.* **3** without breath; lifeless. **4** without a breeze. **5** of writing, exciting and fast-paced. **—'breath•less•ly,** *adv.* **—'breath•less•ness,** *n.*

breath•tak•ing ['brɛθ,teikɪŋ] *adj.* thrilling; exciting: *a breathtaking roller-coaster ride, a breathtaking view.* **—'breath,tak•ing•ly,** *adv.*

breath•y ['brɛθi] *adj.* characterized by audible sounds of breathing. **—'breath•i•ly,** *adv.* **—'breath•i•ness,** *n.*

brec•ci•a ['brɛtʃiə] *or* ['brɛʃiə] *n. Geology.* a kind of sedimentary rock consisting of angular fragments of older rocks naturally cemented together in a matrix. ⟨< Ital. < Gmc. Akin to BREAK.⟩

bred [brɛd] *v.* pt. and pp. of BREED.

breech [britʃ] *n., v. —n.* **1** the lower part; back part. **2** in a firearm, the opening, directly behind the barrel, where the shells are inserted. **3** the rump or buttocks.
—v. **1** clothe with breeches. **2** provide (a gun) with a breech. ⟨back formation from *breeches*⟩ **—breech•less,** *adj.*
☛ *Hom.* BREACH.

breech birth a birth in which the baby's feet are presented first instead of the head.

breech•block ['britʃ,blɒk] *n.* in an old type of gun, a block which receives the force of the charge.

breech•cloth ['britʃ,klɒθ] *n.* a covering for the loins consisting of a length of cloth or leather passed between the legs and fastened around the waist; loincloth. Breechcloths were formerly worn by some First Nations.

breech•clout ['britʃ,klʌut] *n.* breechcloth.

breech delivery BREECH BIRTH.

breech•es ['brɪtʃɪz] *or* ['britʃɪz] *n.pl.* **1** short pants covering the hips and thighs and fastened snugly at or just below the knees. **2** *Informal.* pants.
too big for one's breeches, having too high an opinion of oneself, and expressing this; forward. ⟨OE *brēc,* pl. of *brōc* breech⟩

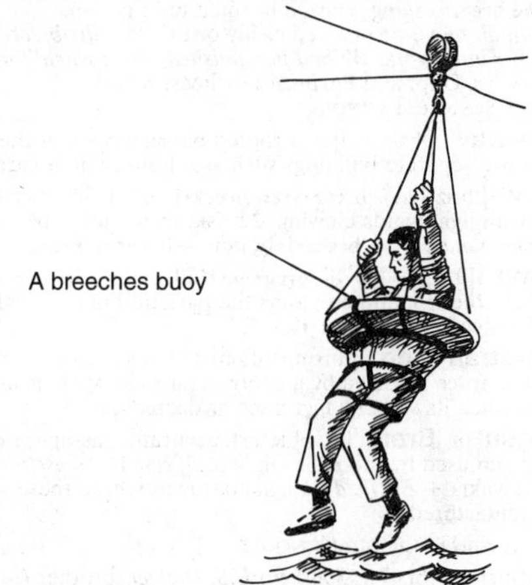

A breeches buoy

breeches buoy a pair of short canvas pants fastened to a belt or life preserver. A breeches buoy slides along a rope on a pulley and is used to move people from one ship to another or from ship to shore, especially in rescue operations.

breech•ing ['brɪtʃɪŋ] *or* ['britʃɪŋ] *n., v.—n.* the part of a harness that passes around a horse's rump to help hold the vehicle when going downhill.
—v. ppr. of BREECH.

breech•load•er ['britʃ,loudər] *n.* a gun that is loaded from behind the barrel, instead of at the mouth.

breech•load•ing ['britʃ,loudɪŋ] *adj.* of guns, loading from behind the barrel instead of at the mouth.

breed [brid] *v.* **bred, breed•ing;** *n. —v.* **1** produce young; reproduce: *Rabbits breed rapidly.* **2** of animals, pair for reproduction; mate: *Polar bears breed only every other year.* **3** cause to mate. **4** develop (different or superior types of an animal or plant) by selective mating of outstanding individuals of one type or of two closely related types: *She breeds horses for harness racing.* **5** bring about; be the cause of: *Despair often breeds violence. Careless driving breeds accidents.* **6** be produced or caused; come into being. **7** bring up; nurture and train: *born and bred in the city.* **8** *Nuclear physics.* produce (fissionable material) by nuclear reaction.
—n. **1** a distinctive type of a particular species of animal or, sometimes, plant, having recognizable inherited characteristics that are the result of a long period of selective mating. By mating only animals showing tendencies toward desired characteristics, people have produced many breeds of dog, horse, pigeon, etc., that suit specific purposes of usefulness or beauty. **2** kind; sort: *It takes a strong, tough breed of person to survive in the wilderness.* ⟨OE *brēdan*⟩

breed•er ['bridər] *n.* **1** a person who breeds animals or plants: *a cattle breeder, a dog breeder.* **2** an animal that produces offspring. **3** a source; cause: *Great inequalities are breeders of revolutions.* **4** BREEDER REACTOR.

breeder reactor a nuclear reactor that produces more fissionable material than it uses up in the chain reaction.

breed•ing ['bridɪŋ] *n., v.*—*n.* **1** the producing of offspring. **2** the propagation of animals or plants, especially to produce different or superior varieties. **3** upbringing or training in social behaviour: *Politeness is a sign of good breeding.* **4** good upbringing: *She is a woman of breeding.* **5** *Nuclear physics.* the process in a reactor by which more fissionable material is produced than is consumed.
—*v.* ppr. of BREED.

breeding ground **1** a place where animals, insects, etc. breed, or to which they return to breed. **2** a place where anything easily grows or flourishes: *Colonialism made Africa a breeding ground of nationalism.*

breeks [briks] *n. Informal.* breeches.

breeze ['briz] *n., v.* **breezed, breez•ing.** —*n.* **1** a light wind. **2** *Meteorology.* any air current blowing at a rate of 6 to 49 km/h. See Beaufort scale in the Appendix. **3** *Informal.* a disturbance; quarrel. **4** *Informal.* an easy task: *That math problem was a breeze.*
in a breeze, *Informal.* easily; with little effort.
shoot the breeze, *Slang.* engage in small talk; gossip.
—*v. Informal.* move or proceed easily or briskly: *She breezed through her homework. We had just finished lunch when Tom breezed in.* ⟨< OSp. and Pg. *briza* northeast wind⟩
☛ *Syn. n.* **1.** See note at WIND[1].

breeze•way ['briz,wei] *n.* a roofed passage open at the sides between two separate buildings such as a house and a garage.

breez•y ['brizi] *adj.* **breez•i•er, breez•i•est. 1** that has a breeze; with light winds blowing. **2** brisk; lively; jolly: *We like his breezy joking manner.* —**'breez•i•ly,** *adv.* —**'breez•i•ness,** *n.*

breg•ma ['brɛgmə] *n., pl.* **breg•ma•ta** [-mətə]. the part of the skull where the frontal bone joins the parietal bone. ⟨< NL < Gk. forehead⟩ —**breg'mat•ic,** *adj.*

brems•strah•lung ['brɛm,ʃtrɑlʊŋ] *n. Nuclear physics.* the radioactive force released by a charged particle, such as an electron, when its velocity increases or decreases.

Bren gun or **Bren** [brɛn] a fast, accurate, gas-operated machine gun used by the Allies in World War II. ⟨< *Br(no),* Czechoslovakia + *En(field),* England, towns where these guns were manufactured⟩

brent [brɛnt] *n.* the BRANT GOOSE.

br'er [brɛr] *or* [brər] *n. Southern U.S. Dialect.* brother (*used before a name*): *Tales of Br'er Rabbit.*

breth•ren ['brɛðrən] *n.pl.* **1** *Archaic.* brothers. **2** the fellow members of a church, society, or religious order.
☛ *Usage.* See note at BROTHER.

bret•on ['brɛtən] *n.* a hat having a shallow crown and a slightly rolled brim. ⟨< *Breton*⟩

Bret•on ['brɛtən] *n., adj.* —*n.* **1** a native or inhabitant of Brittany, a region in NW France. **2** the Celtic language of the people of Brittany.
—*adj.* of or having to do with Brittany, its people, or their language. ⟨< F < L *Bretto, -onis*⟩

bre•ty•li•um [brɛ'tiliəm] *n.* a drug used to treat irregular heartbeat.

breve [briv] *or* [brɛv] *n.* **1** the curved mark ˘ put over a vowel or syllable to show that it is short. **2** *Music.* a note equal to two whole notes. ⟨< Ital. < L *brevis* short⟩

bre•vet [brə'vɛt] *n., adj., v.* **-vet•ted** or **-vet•ed, -vet•ting** or **-vet•ing.** —*n.* a commission promoting an army officer to a higher rank without an increase in pay.
—*adj.* having or giving rank by a brevet.
—*v.* give rank by a brevet. ⟨ME < OF *brevet,* diminutive of *bref* letter < OF *bref* short. See BRIEF.⟩

bre•vi•ar•y ['brivi,ɛri] *or* ['brɛvi,ɛri] *n., pl.* **-ar•ies.** in the Roman Catholic Church, a book of prescribed prayers to be said daily by certain clergy and religious. ⟨< L *breviarium* summary < *brevis* short⟩

bre•vier [brə'vir] *n.* a size of type; 8 point. This sentence is in brevier. ⟨< G or OF < L *breviarium,* from its use in printing breviaries. See BREVIARY.⟩

brev•i•rost•rate [,brɛvə'rɒstreit] *adj.* of a bird, having a short beak. ⟨< L *brevis* brief + *rostratus* having a rostrum (beaklike part)⟩

brev•i•ty ['brɛvəti] *n., pl.* **-ties.** the quality of shortness, conciseness, or briefness. ⟨< L *brevitas* < *brevis* short⟩

brew [bru] *v., n.* —*v.* **1** make (beer, ale, etc.) from malt, etc., by steeping, boiling, and fermenting. **2** make (a drink) by steeping, boiling, or mixing: *Tea is brewed in boiling water.* **3** of such a drink, undergo this process: *Your tea has been brewing for 20 minutes now.* **4** bring about; plan; plot: *Those boys are brewing some mischief.* **5** begin to form; gather: *Dark clouds show that a storm is brewing.*
—*n.* **1** a drink made by brewing. **2** the quantity brewed at one time. **3** *Slang.* (a glass or bottle of) beer. ⟨OE *brēowan*⟩

brew•age ['bruɪdʒ] *n.* **1** anything brewed, especially whisky. **2** the process of brewing.

brew•er ['bruər] *n.* a person who brews beer, ale, etc.

brewer's yeast a selected strain of yeast used in brewing beer and available in tablet form.

brew•er•y ['bruəri] *n., pl.* **-er•ies.** a place where beer, ale, etc., are brewed.

brew•ing ['bruɪŋ] *n., v.*—*n.* **1** the preparing of a brew. **2** the amount brewed at one time.
—*v.* ppr. of BREW.

brewis [bruz] *or* ['bruɪs] *n.* in Newfoundland, a kind of stew prepared by boiling hardtack with codfish, pork fat, and vegetables. Also, **brose.** ⟨variant of *brose*⟩
☛ *Hom.* BRUISE [bruz].

bri•ar ['braɪər] See BRIER.

bri•ard [bri'ɑrd] *n.* a large dog with a long, bushy coat and ears that are held erect. ⟨< F, one from Brie⟩

bri•ar-root ['braɪər ,rut] See BRIER-ROOT.

bri•ar•wood ['braɪər,wʊd] See BRIERWOOD.

bri•ar•y ['braɪəri] See BRIERY.

bribe [braɪb] *n., v.* **bribed, brib•ing.** —*n.* **1** an inducement offered to a person to act dishonestly or against the law for the benefit of the giver. **2** a reward for doing something that one does not want to do: *He should not need a bribe to do well in school.*
—*v.* influence by giving a bribe; give or offer a bribe (to). ⟨ME < OF *bribe* bit of bread given to a beggar⟩ —**'brib•a•ble,** *adj.* —**'brib•er,** *n.*

brib•er•y ['braɪbəri] *n., pl.* **-er•ies. 1** the giving or offering of a bribe. **2** the taking of a bribe.

bric or **BRIC** [brɪk] *v. Cdn.* sell shares in a public corporation. ⟨< BCRIC, British Columbia Resources Investment Corporation⟩

bric-a-brac or **bric-à-brac** ['brɪk ə ,bræk] *n.* a collection of interesting or curious knick-knacks used as decorations; small ornaments, such as vases, old china, or small statues. ⟨< F⟩
☛ *Usage.* **Bric-a-brac** is a collective noun; it never adds *s* to form the plural, nor is it ever modified by *a*: *The bric-a-brac showed her good taste.*

brick [brɪk] *n., pl.* **bricks** or (*esp. collectively*) **brick;** *v.* —*n.* **1** a block of clay baked by sun or fire, used in building and paving. **2** such blocks considered together as building material: *Our fireplace is built of brick.* **3** (*adjl.*) made or built of bricks. **4** anything shaped like a brick: *a brick of ice cream.* **5** a light-coloured, semisoft cheese made from whole milk, having numerous small holes and resembling mild Cheddar in flavour. A whole cheese is shaped like a brick. **6** *Informal.* a good fellow; a person who is generous and dependable.
hit the bricks, *Slang.* go on strike.
make bricks without straw, do anything without the wherewithal.
—*v.* **1** build or pave with bricks. **2** cover or line with bricks: *Harry's mother bricked the walk in front of her house.* **3** close or fill with bricks (*used with* **in** *or* **up**): *The old doorway was bricked up.* ⟨< F *brique* < MDu. *bricke*⟩ —**'brick,like,** *adj.*

brick•bat ['brɪk,bæt] *n.* **1** a piece of broken brick, especially one used as a missile. **2** *Informal.* an insult.

brick•lay•er ['brɪk,leiər] *n.* a person whose work is building with bricks.

brick•lay•ing ['brɪk,leiɪŋ] *n.* the act or work of building with bricks.

brick–red ['brɪk 'rɛd] *adj.* yellowish red or brownish red.

brick wall **1** a wall made of bricks. **2** anything that is impossible to pierce, circumvent, etc., or a person who is stubborn or unresponsive.

brick•work ['brɪk,wɜrk] *n.* **1** anything made of bricks. **2** the act or process of building with bricks; bricklaying.

brick•yard ['brɪk,jɑrd] *n.* a place where bricks are made or sold.

bri•co•lage [,brikou'lɑʒ] *n.* **1** the act of making something from found materials. **2** anything made in this way. ⟨< F⟩

brid•al ['braɪdəl] *adj., n. —adj.* of a bride or a wedding. *—n.* wedding. ⟨OE *brȳdealo* bride ale⟩
☛ *Hom.* BRIDLE.

bridal attendant a woman who attends a bride at her wedding.

bridal register a list kept at a store of the bride's choice of patterns in china, silverware, etc., so that wedding guests can give the desired pattern and not duplicate gifts.

bridal wreath a commonly cultivated shrub (*Spiraea prunifolia*) having long sprays of small, white flowers that bloom in the spring.

bride [braɪd] *n.* a woman just married or about to be married. ⟨OE *brȳd*⟩

bride•groom ['braɪd,grum] *n.* a man just married or about to be married. ⟨OE *brȳdguma* < *brȳd* bride + *guma* man; influenced by *groom*⟩

brides•maid ['braɪdz,meid] *n.* a woman, usually unmarried, who attends the bride at a wedding; bridal attendant.

bride•well ['braɪd,wɛl] *n.* a house of correction for vagrants and disorderly persons; jail. ⟨from a former prison at St. Bride's Well in London⟩

A bascule bridge on the Welland Canal in Ontario

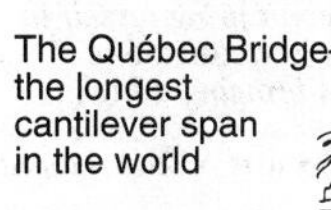

The Québec Bridge—the longest cantilever span in the world

The suspension bridge at Dunvegan, Alberta

bridge[1] [brɪdʒ] *n., v.* **bridged, bridg•ing.** *—n.* **1** a structure built over a river, road, etc., to carry a road, walkway, or railway. **2** the platform above the deck of a ship for the officer in command. **3** the upper, bony part of the nose. **4** a mounting for a false tooth or teeth fastened to the real teeth nearby. **5** a piece of wood on the box of a violin, guitar, etc., over which the strings are stretched. **6** *Music.* a passage in a composition connecting one theme, movement, etc., to another. **7** the curved central part of a pair of eyeglasses that rests on the nose. **8** *Electricity.* an apparatus for measuring the electrical resistance of a conductor. **9** *Billiards.* a player's hand arched to steady the cue in long shots, or a notched wooden or metal piece at the end of a long rod used for the same purpose. **10** any other thing like a bridge in form or use.
burn (one's) **bridges,** cut off all chances of retreat.
—v. **1** build a bridge over: *The engineers bridged the river.* **2** form a bridge over; extend over; span: *A log bridged the brook.* **3** make a way over: *Politeness will bridge many difficulties.* ⟨OE *brycg*⟩

bridge[2] [brɪdʒ] *n.* a card game based on whist, for two teams of two players each, played with 52 cards. Auction bridge and contract bridge are two varieties of this game. ⟨origin uncertain⟩

bridge•a•ble ['brɪdʒəbəl] *adj.* that can be bridged: *bridgeable differences.*

bridge•board ['brɪdʒ,bɔrd] *n.* a piece of notched wood forming the structure of a staircase, to support wooden treads and risers.

bridge•head ['brɪdʒ,hɛd] *n.* **1** a position obtained and held by advance troops within enemy territory, used as a starting point for further attack. **2** any position taken as a foothold from which to make further advances: *She was able to make her first television job a bridgehead to a spectacular career in broadcasting.* **3** a fortification protecting the end of a bridge nearer to the enemy.

bridge line a line of inexpensive clothing produced by a major designer who normally sells expensive clothes.

Bridge of Sighs **1** in Venice, the bridge through which prisoners were led for trial. **2** in New York City, the bridge leading to the Tombs prison.

bridge table a small, square or round table, about 75 cm^2 or 90 cm in diameter, having legs that fold under the table top, used for playing cards, etc.

bridge•work ['brɪdʒ,wɜrk] *n.* a number of false teeth in a mounting fastened to the adjacent natural teeth.

bridg•ing ['brɪdʒɪŋ] *n., v. —n.* the braces placed between two beams to strengthen them and to keep them apart.
—v. ppr. of BRIDGE.

bri•dle ['braɪdəl] *n., v.* **-dled, -dling.** *—n.* **1** a harness fitted about a horse's head, consisting of a headstall, bit, and reins, used to guide or control the horse. See HARNESS for picture. **2** anything that holds back or controls. **3** *Cdn.* the loop of a snowshoe in which the toe of the boot or moccasin is placed.
—v. **1** put a bridle on. **2** hold back; check; control: *Bridle your temper.* **3** hold the head up high with the chin drawn back to express pride, vanity, scorn, or anger. **4** take umbrage (*at*). ⟨OE *brīdel, brigdels* < *bregdan* to braid⟩ **—'bri•dler,** *n.*
☛ *Hom.* BRIDAL.

bridle path a path for people riding horses.

Brie [bri] *n.* a variety of soft, white cheese originating in Brie in France. ⟨< F⟩

brief [brif] *adj., n., v. —adj.* **1** lasting only a short time: *a brief meeting.* **2** using few words: *a brief announcement.* **3** of clothes, very short; barely covering. **4** brusque to the point of being rude.
—n. **1** a short statement or a summary. **2** a formal statement of opinion for submission to an authority: *She submitted a brief to the Royal Commission on Taxation.* **3** a statement of the facts and the points of law concerning a case to be pleaded in court. **4** *Informal.* a client; a case at law to plead. **5** a briefing. **6** *Roman Catholic Church.* a papal letter, less formal than a bull. **7 briefs,** *pl.* short, close-fitting underpants.
hold a brief for, argue for; support; defend.
hold no brief for, have no commitment or desire to argue for or support: *He is my friend, but I hold no brief for his political opinions.*
in brief, in a few words.
—v. **1** make a brief of; summarize. **2** furnish with a brief. **3** retain as a lawyer or counsel. **4** give a briefing to. ⟨ME *bref* < OF < L *brevis* short⟩ **—'brief•ly,** *adv.* **—'brief•ness,** *n.*
☛ *Syn. adj.* **1.** See note at SHORT.

brief•case ['brif,keis] *n.* a flat container with or without a handle, for carrying loose papers, books, drawings, etc.

brief•ing ['brifɪŋ] *n., v. —n.* **1** the act or an instance of giving necessary information or exact instructions for a specific job, assignment, etc.: *The briefing for the combat mission was given by the commanding officer.* **2** the information or instruction given. **3** a summary of a current situation to inform or provide background.
—v. ppr. of BRIEF.

brief•less ['briflɪs] *adj.* of a lawyer, having no work.

bri•er[1] ['braɪər] *n.* **1** any of various kinds of thorny or prickly bush, especially the wild rose. **2** a thorn or thorny twig. **3** a tangled growth of briers. Also, **briar.** ⟨OE *brēr*⟩

bri•er[2] ['braɪər] *n.* **1** an evergreen shrub (*Erica arborea*) of the heath family native to S Europe, having a hard, woody root used for making tobacco pipes. **2** a tobacco pipe made of brier-root. Also (esp. def. 2), **briar.** ⟨< F *bruyère* heath < Celtic⟩

Bri•er ['braɪər] *n. Cdn.* the competition or bonspiel that determines the curling champions of Canada. ⟨< name of the trophy, formerly the Macdonald *Brier* Tankard, now the Labatt Tankard *Brier*⟩

bri•er–root ['braɪər ,rut] *n.* **1** the root of the brier (*Erica arborea*) used for tobacco pipes. **2** a pipe made of this root. Also, **briar-root.**

bri•er•wood ['braɪər,wʊd] *n.* brier-root. Also, **briarwood.**

bri•er•y ['braɪəri] *adj.* full of thorns or briers: *briery undergrowth.* Also, **briary.**

brig [brɪg] *n.* **1** a square-rigged ship with two masts. **2** the prison on a warship. **3** any military prison. ⟨short for *brigantine*⟩

Brig. **1** Brigadier. **2** Brigade.

bri•gade [brɪ'geid] *n., v.* **bri•gad•ed, bri•gad•ing.** *—n.* **1** a part of an army, usually made up of two or more regiments. **2** any group of people organized for a particular purpose: *A fire brigade puts out fires.* **3** *Cdn.* a fleet of canoes, bateaux, Red River carts, dog sleds, etc., carrying trade goods, supplies, etc., to and from inland posts; caravan.
—v. form into a brigade. ⟨< F *brigade* < Ital. *brigata* < *brigare* strive, fight < *briga* strife < Celtic⟩

brig•a•dier [,brɪgə'dir] *n.* BRIGADIER-GENERAL. ⟨< F *brigadier* < *brigade.* See BRIGADE.⟩

brig•a•dier–gen•er•al ['brɪgə,dir 'dʒɛnərəl] *or* ['dʒɛnrəl] *n., pl.* **brig•a•dier-gen•er•als.** an officer in the armed forces, ranking next above a colonel and below a major-general. See chart of ranks in the Appendix. *Abbrev.*: B.Gen. or BGen

brig•and ['brɪgənd] *n.* a person who robs travellers on the road; a robber; bandit. ⟨ME < OF < Ital. *brigante* fighter < *brigare* to brawl. See BRIGADE.⟩

brig•and•age ['brɪgəndɪdʒ] *n.* robbery; plundering.

brig•an•dine ['brɪgən,din] *or* ['brɪgən,daɪn] *n.* a coat of armour made of linen, leather, etc. strengthened with metal rings or thin metal pieces. ⟨< MF *brigandine* armour for a brigand < *brigant* < Ital. *brigante* fighter. See BRIGAND.⟩

brig•an•tine ['brɪgən,tin] *n.* **1** a two-masted ship having the foremast square-rigged and the mainmast fore-and-aft-rigged. **2** a similar ship but with a square-rigged topsail on the mainmast. ⟨< F < Ital. *brigantino* < *brigare.* See BRIGAND, BRIGADE.⟩

bright [brəit] *adj.* **1** giving or reflecting much light; shining: *The sun is too bright to look at directly. Chrome is very bright.* **2** very light or clear: *a bright day.* **3** quick-witted; clever: *She's a bright girl and learns quickly.* **4** vivid; glowing: *bright colours.* **5** lively; cheerful: *a bright smile.* **6** hopeful; happy: *a bright attitude toward life.* **7** likely to turn out well; favourable: *a bright outlook for the future.* **8** splendid; glorious: *The knight was a bright example of courage in battle.* **9** (*advl.*) in a bright manner: *The fire shines bright.* **10** (*noml.*) **brights,** *pl.*, high-beam headlights on a motor vehicle. ⟨OE *briht, beorht*⟩ **—'bright•ly,** *adv.*

☛ *Syn. adj.* **1. Bright,** RADIANT, BRILLIANT = shining. **Bright** is the general word, and applies to anything thought of as giving out or reflecting light: *Her silver earrings are bright.* **Radiant** suggests giving out light in rays as the sun does, shining with a light that comes from deep within the thing or person described: *Her radiant face told us of her happiness.* **Brilliant** = very bright or excessively bright and often suggests sparkling or flashing: *The surface of the water is brilliant in the sunlight.*

bright•en ['brəitən] *v.* **1** make or become bright or brighter: *The sky brightened. He brightened the room with flowers.* **2** make or become happy or cheerful: *Their faces brightened.*

bright–line spectrum ['brəit ,laɪn] an emission spectrum consisting of separate bright lines against a dark background.

bright•ness ['brəitnɪs] *n.* **1** the quality or state of anything that is bright. **2** *Physics.* the degree of light in a colour. The colour white has the maximum amount of light, while black has no light whatsoever.

Bright's disease inflammation of the parts of the kidney that produce urine. ⟨after R. *Bright* (1789-1858), an English physician⟩

bright•work ['brəit,wɜrk] *n.* polished metal fittings or trim on ships, motor vehicles, etc.

brill [brɪl] *n., pl.* **brill** or **brills.** a European flatfish (*Scophthalmus rhombus*) closely related to the turbot, valued for food. ⟨origin uncertain⟩

bril•liance ['brɪljəns] *n.* **1** great brightness; radiance; sparkle. **2** splendour; magnificence. **3** great ability: *brilliance as a pianist.* **4** *Music.* clarity and vividness of sound: *the brilliance of modern high-frequency recordings.* Also, **brilliancy.**

bril•liant ['brɪljənt] *adj., n. —adj.* **1** shining brightly; sparkling: *brilliant jewels, brilliant sunshine.* **2** strikingly bright and strong: *a brilliant red.* **3** splendid; magnificent; distinguished: *They say she has a brilliant future in politics.* **4** having or showing great ability: *a brilliant performance, a brilliant scholar.*
—n. **1** a diamond or other gem cut to sparkle brightly. **2** a small size of type; 3½ point. ⟨< F *brilliant*, ppr. of *briller* shine, ? < L *beryllus* beryl⟩ **—'bril•liant•ly,** *adv.*

☛ *Syn. adj.* **1.** See note at BRIGHT.

bril•lian•tine ['brɪljən,tin] *n.* **1** an oily preparation used to make the hair glossy. **2** a glossy cloth of cotton and wool. ⟨< F *brillantine*⟩

Brill's disease [brɪlz] a form of typhus in which symptoms recur up to years after the disease was first caught. ⟨after N.E. *Brill* (1860-1925), American physician⟩

brim [brɪm] *n., v.* **brimmed, brim•ming.** *—n.* **1** the edge of a cup, bowl, etc.; rim. **2** the projecting edge of something: *The hat has a wide brim.* **3** *Archaic.* the edge of a body of water.
—v. fill or be full to the brim: *The pond is brimming with water as a result of the hard rains.* ⟨ME *brimme*⟩ **—'brim•less,** *adj.*

brim•ful ['brɪm,fʊl] *adj.* full to the brim; full to the very top.

brim•mer ['brɪmər] *n.* a cup, bowl, etc., full to the brim.

brim•stone ['brɪm,stoun] *n.* sulphur. ⟨ME *brinston* < *brinnen* burn + *ston* stone⟩

brin•dle ['brɪndəl] *adj., n. —adj.* brindled.
—n. **1** a brindled colouring. **2** a brindled animal. ⟨< *brindled*⟩

brin•dled ['brɪndəld] *adj.* grey, tan, or tawny with darker streaks and spots. ⟨earlier *brinded*, ME *brended.* Probably related to BRAND.⟩

brine [braɪn] *n., v.* **brined, brin•ing.** *—n.* **1** very salty water: *Pickles are often kept in brine.* **2** a salt lake or sea; ocean.
—v. soak in brine. ⟨OE *brȳne*⟩

Bri•nell number [brɪ'nɛl] a number indicating the hardness of a metal, calculated with the **Brinell test.** The Brinell test assesses the hardness of a metal by applying a steel ball to it and measuring the diameter of the imprint made by that ball. ⟨after J.A. *Brinell* (1849-1925), Swedish engineer⟩

brine shrimp a small FAIRY SHRIMP of the genus *Artemia*, found in salt water and used as tropical fish food.

bring [brɪŋ] *v.* **brought, bring•ing. 1** carry or take with oneself to a place; come to a place with: *I didn't bring enough money. He brought his cousin to the party. Bring me a clean plate, please. The bus brought us home from school.* **2** cause to come: *What brings you into town today?* **3** cause to do something; persuade; induce: *Our arguments finally brought him to agree. I can't bring myself to finish another page tonight.* **4** present before a law court: *She brought a charge against me.* **5** sell for: *Meat is bringing a high price this week.*
bring about, cause; cause to happen: *The flood was brought about by heavy rain.*
bring around or **bring round, a** restore to consciousness. **b** convince; persuade. **c** influence (someone) to be in a better mood.
bring forth, a give birth to; bear; produce; generate. **b** reveal; show.
bring forward, a reveal; show. **b** *Accounting.* carry over from one page to another.
bring home to, a prove beyond doubt to. **b** make realize.
bring in, a introduce or try out. **b** report or announce officially; return: *to bring in a verdict.* **c** cause to flow by drilling: *to bring in an oil well.* **d** yield or produce (money).
bring off, cause to happen; carry to a successful conclusion.
bring on, cause; cause to happen: *I think my cold was brought on by lack of sleep.*
bring out, a reveal; show: *His paintings bring out the loneliness of the North.* **b** offer to the public: *She brought out a new book of poems.* **c** introduce (a young woman) to society.
bring over, convince; persuade.
bring to, a restore to consciousness: *We tried to bring him to by loosening his clothing.* **b** stop; check.
bring up, a care for in childhood. **b** educate or train, especially in social behaviour: *His good manners showed that he had been well brought up.* **c** suggest for action or discussion. **d** stop suddenly: *The rider brought her horse up at the high fence.* **e** vomit. ⟨OE *bringan*⟩ **—'bring•er,** *n.*

bring•ing–up ['brɪŋɪŋ 'ʌp] *n.* **1** care in childhood. **2** education; training.

brink [brɪŋk] *n.* **1** the edge at the top of a steep place. **2** any edge, such as the shore of a river, etc.
on the brink of, very near. ⟨ME; probably < Scand.⟩

brink•man•ship ['brɪŋkmən,ʃɪp] *n.* **1** the maintaining or urging of a foreign policy to the brink of war before giving ground. **2** the fact or process of manoeuvering any dangerous situation to the very limits of safety before giving ground. Also, **brinksmanship.**

brin•y ['braɪni] *adj.* **brin•i•er, brin•i•est;** *n. —adj.* of or like brine; salty.
—n. **the briny,** *Slang.* sea. **—'brin•i•ness,** *n.*

brio ['briou] *n. Music.* liveliness and vigour of style. ⟨< Italian⟩

bri•oche [bri'ɒʃ] *or* ['briɒʃ] *n.* a roll or bun rich in butter and eggs. ⟨< F⟩

bri•o•ny ['braɪəni] *n.* bryony.

bri•quette or **bri•quet** [brɪ'kɛt] *n.* **1** a block of compressed charcoal, coal dust, etc. used for fuel in furnaces or barbecues. **2** a small brick or similar block of anything else. ⟨< F *briquette,* dim. of *brique* brick⟩

bris [brɪs] *n. Judaism.* a ceremony held when a boy is eight days old, during which he is circumcised. ⟨< Yiddish < Hebrew *berit*⟩

brisk [brɪsk] *adj.* **1** acting, moving, or happening quickly; energetic: *The storekeeper told us that business was brisk. He went for a brisk walk.* **2** keen; sharp: *brisk weather.* ⟨? akin to *brusque*⟩ **—'brisk•ly,** *adv.* **—'brisk•ness,** *n.*

bris•ket ['brɪskɪt] *n.* **1** the meat from the breast of an animal. See BEEF for picture. **2** the breast of an animal. ⟨ME < OF *bruschet* < Gmc.⟩

bris•ling ['brɪslɪŋ] *n.* a sardinelike Norwegian food fish, packed in oil. ⟨< Norwegian dialect < older Danish *bretling*⟩

bris•tle [brɪsəl] *n., v.* **-tled, -tling.** *—n.* **1** one of the short, stiff hairs of a hog or wild boar, used to make brushes. **2** any short, stiff hair of an animal or plant. **3** a synthetic substitute for a hog's bristles: *My toothbrush has nylon bristles.*
—v. **1** provide with bristles. **2** of hair, stand up straight: *The angry dog's hair bristled.* **3** cause (hair) to stand up straight. **4** have one's hair stand up straight: *The dog bristled.* **5** show that one is aroused and ready to fight: *The whole country bristled with indignation.* **6** be thick (with); be thickly set: *Our path bristled with difficulties.* ⟨ME *bristel* < OE *byrst* bristle⟩

bris•tle•cone pine ['brɪsəl,koun] a bushy or shrublike pine (*Pinus aristata*) with cones that bear long prickles or bristles. Bristlecone pines are found in the western U.S., and are among the oldest trees in existence.

bris•tle•tail ['brɪsəl,teil] *n.* any of about 400 species making up two orders (Thysanura and Diplura) of mostly tiny, wingless insects found throughout the world, having compound eyes, long, segmented feelers, and three or two long, movable appendages at the end of the abdomen. Silverfish are bristletails.

bris•tly ['brɪsli] *adj.* **-tli•er, -tli•est. 1** rough with bristles or hair that is like bristles. **2** resembling bristles; short and stiff; prickly.

Bris•tol board ['brɪstəl] a fine, smooth pasteboard. ⟨after the city of *Bristol,* England⟩

brit [brɪt] *n., pl.* **brit. 1** a young herring. **2** a small sea creature such as some crustaceans, providing food for fish and whales. ⟨< Cornish < Old Celtic *brith* varicoloured⟩

Brit. Britain; British; Briticism.

Brit•ain GREAT BRITAIN.

Bri•tan•ni•a [brɪ'tænjə] *n.* **1** *Poetic.* GREAT BRITAIN. **2** *Poetic.* the British Empire. **3** a woman symbolizing Britain, shown (as on coins) with helmet, shield, and trident.

Britannia metal a white alloy of tin, copper, and antimony, used in making tableware.

Bri•tan•nic [brɪ'tænɪk] *adj.* of Britain; British.

brit•ches ['brɪtʃɪz] *n.pl. Informal.* breeches.

Brit•i•cism ['brɪtə,sɪzəm] *n.* a word or phrase used especially by the British. *Wings* meaning *fenders* (of a car) is a Briticism.

Brit•ish ['brɪtɪʃ] *adj., n. —adj.* of or having to do with Great Britain or the United Kingdom, or its people.
—n. **the British,** the people of Great Britain or the United Kingdom. ⟨OE *brittisc* < *Brittas* Britons < Celtic⟩

British Co•lum•bi•a [kə'lʌmbiə] *n.* the westernmost province of Canada.

British Co•lum•bi•an [kə'lʌmbiən] *n., adj. —n.* a native or long-term resident of British Columbia.
—adj. of or having to do with British Columbia or its people.

British Commonwealth of Nations an association of a large number of countries, many of them now completely independent, that were once under British law and government, and are now united under the British monarchy. All the independent members of the British Commonwealth of Nations, including Canada and the United Kingdom, have equal status.

British English English as spoken and written in the United Kingdom.

Brit•ish•er ['brɪtɪʃər] *n.* a native or inhabitant of Great Britain.

British Isles Great Britain, Ireland, and the Isle of Man.

British North America Act the Act of Parliament that in 1867 created the Government of Canada for the union of Ontario, Québec, Nova Scotia, and New Brunswick. The other six provinces joined the federation as follows: Manitoba, 1870; British Columbia, 1871; Prince Edward Island, 1873; Alberta, 1905; Saskatchewan, 1905; and Newfoundland, 1949. *Abbrev.:* BNA Act or B.N.A. Act. Since 1981 it has been called the **Constitution Act,** 1867.

British subject 1 a citizen of the United Kingdom. **2** a citizen of any country, such as Canada, of which the British monarch is the official head of state.

British thermal unit a unit for measuring heat; the amount of heat necessary to raise the temperature of one pound of water one degree Fahrenheit (about 1.06 kJ). *Abbrev.:* B.T.U.

Brit•on ['brɪtən] *n.* **1** a native or inhabitant of Great Britain. **2** a member of a Celtic people who lived in Great Britain before the Roman conquest. ⟨< Med.L *Brito, -onis* < Celtic⟩

Brit•ta•ny spaniel ['brɪtəni] a breed of orange and white or liver and white spaniel, having long legs and no tail, or a very short tail. ⟨after *Brittany* in France, region where the dog is bred⟩

brit•tle ['brɪtəl] *adj., n. —adj.* **1** rigid but very easily broken; apt to break with a snap rather than bend: *Thin glass and dead twigs are brittle.* **2** harsh and clipped: *a brittle voice.* **3** of a person, not flexible or adaptable and therefore likely to be defeated by adversity.
—n. a sweet made with caramelized sugar and nuts: *peanut brittle.* ⟨ME *britel* < OE *brēotan* break⟩ **—'brit•tle•ness,** *n.*

brittle star an invertebrate sea animal having a round central part and five long, narrow limbs that break easily but regenerate.

Brix scale [brɪks] a scale for measuring the proportion of sugar in a solution. ⟨after A.F. *Brix* (1798-1890), German chemist⟩

bro. or **Bro.** brother.

broach [broutʃ] *n., v. —n.* **1** a pointed tool for making and shaping holes. **2** a sharp-pointed, slender rod on which meat is roasted.
—v. **1** open by making a hole: *to broach a barrel of cider.* **2** begin to talk about: *to broach a subject.* **3** make or shape (a hole) with a broach. ⟨ME < OF < L *broccus* projecting⟩ **—'broach•er,** *n.*
☛ *Hom.* BROOCH.

broad [brɒd] *adj.* **1** large across; wide: *Many cars can go on that broad road.* **2** extensive: *broad experience.* **3** not limited; liberal; tolerant: *broad ideas.* **4** not detailed; general: *Give a broad outline of the speech.* **5** clear; full: *broad daylight.* **6** plain; obvious; unmistakable: *a broad hint, a broad accent.* **7** coarse; not refined: *broad jokes.* **8** *Phonetics.* **a** pronounced with the vocal passage open wide. The *a* in *father* is broad. **b** indicating pronunciation in general terms: *a broad phonetic transcription.* ⟨OE *brād*⟩ **—'broad•ly,** *adv.* **—'broad•ness,** *n.*
☛ *Syn.* **1.** See note at WIDE.

broad•axe ['brɒd,æks] *n., pl.* **-ax•es.** an axe with a broad blade. Sometimes, **broadax.**

broad•band ['brɒd,bænd] *adj. Radio.* operating over a wide range of frequencies: *broadband radio transmission.*

broad–based ['brɒd ,beist] *adj.* built on a broad base; having a wide range; not narrow or limited: *A broad-based economy relies on many products.*

broad bean a smooth, kidney-shaped edible seed borne in long pods by a European vetch.

broad•bill ['brɒd,bɪl] *n.* any bird with a wide beak, such as the spoonbill.

broad•brim ['brɒd,brɪm] *n.* formerly, **a** a hat with a very wide brim, such as the kind once worn by the Quakers. **b** Quaker.

broad•cast ['brɒd,kæst] *v.* **-cast** or (*sometimes for def. 1*) **-cast•ed, -cast•ing;** *n., adj., adv. —v.* **1** send out (messages, programs, etc.) by radio or television: *Her speech will be broadcast tonight. The new channel will begin broadcasting next month.* **2** scatter or spread widely: *to broadcast seed.* **3** make widely known: *He broadcast that story all over town.*
—n. **1** a radio or television program. **2** the act of broadcasting.
—adj. **1** sent out by radio or television: *a broadcast message.* **2** scattered or spread widely: *broadcast sowing.*
—adv. over a wide surface: *She scattered the seed broadcast.* **—'broad,cast•er,** *n.*

broad•cloth ['brɒd,klɒθ] *n.* **1** a fine, closely woven cloth with a smooth finish, made of cotton, silk, rayon, synthetics, or blends of these fibres and used for shirts, dresses, pyjamas, etc. **2** a smooth, closely woven woollen cloth having a glossy surface and a short nap, used in making suits, coats, etc. ⟨originally wider, or broader, than about 74 cm⟩

broad•en ['brɒdən] *v.* make or become broad or broader: *to broaden one's outlook. The river broadens at its mouth.*

broad gauge a width of railway track greater than the standard gauge of about 144 cm, especially, a width of track of about 168 cm. Compare NARROW GAUGE. **—'broad-,gauge,** *adj.*

broad•gauged ['brɒd,geidʒd] *adj.* BROAD-GAUGE.

broad jump LONG JUMP.
standing broad jump, a long jump from a standing start.

broad•leaf ['brɒd,lif] *n.* a kind of tobacco with wide leaves, used for making cigars.

broad–leaved cattail ['brɒd ,livd] a marsh plant (*Typha latifolia*) having swordlike leaves and spikes of tiny flowers which fall off, leaving the spike. It blooms in spring throughout North America, Europe, and Asia.

broad–leaved spring beauty a small plant (*Claytonia caroliniana*) having tiny bulbs and fragrant pink flowers. It blooms in spring in woodlands across North America.

broad–leaved stonecrop a rock plant (*Sedum spathulifolium*) having yellow flowers and thick leaves. It blooms on the Pacific coast of North America.

broad–leaved willow herb an Arctic plant (*Epilobium latifolium*) having low-growing pink flowers. Also called **mountain fireweed** and **river beauty.**

broad•loom ['brɒd,lum] *adj., n., v. —adj.* woven on a loom or machine at least 1.8 m wide: *a broadloom carpet.*
—n. carpeting made on a broad loom, sold by the metre and cut to fit the exact dimensions of a room: *We have broadloom in the living room.*
—v. cover (a floor, walls, etc.) with such material: *We broadloomed the office.*

broad–mind•ed ['brɒd 'maɪndɪd] *adj.* respecting opinions, customs, or beliefs, that are different from one's own; liberal; not prejudiced or bigoted. **—'broad-'mind•ed•ly,** *adv.* **—'broad-'mind•ed•ness,** *n.*

broad•sheet ['brɒd,ʃit] *n.* a large sheet of paper printed on one side as a newsletter, advertisement, etc.

broad•side ['brɒd,saɪd] *n.* **1** the whole side of a ship above the waterline. **2** all the guns that can be fired from one side of a ship. **3** the firing of all these guns at the same time. **4** a violent attack in words; a storm of abuse: *She was met with a broadside from her sister the minute she got home.* **5** a broad surface or side, as of a house. **6** (*advl.*) with the side turned toward an object or point: *The ship drifted broadside to the pier. His car hit the other vehicle broadside.* **7** a large sheet of paper printed on one or both sides: *Kids were distributing broadsides announcing a big sale.*

broad–spec•trum ['brɒd 'spɛktrəm] *adj.* having a wide range of use or application: *a broad-spectrum drug.*

broad•sword ['brɒd,sɔrd] *n.* a sword with a broad, flat blade.

broad•tail ['brɒd,teil] *n.* **1** Also, **broadtail sheep,** a kind of Asiatic sheep having a broad tail. **2** the skin of a prematurely born broadtail lamb, having dark, flat, wide curls. **3** a coat or other garment made from such skins.

Broad•way ['brɒd,wei] *n.* **1** in New York City, a street famous for its bright lights, theatres, night clubs, etc. **2** the New York commercial theatre.

Brob•ding•nag•i•an [,brɒbdɪŋ'næɡiən] *adj., n. —adj.* **1** of or like Brobdingnag, the land of giants in Jonathan Swift's *Gulliver's Travels*. **2** gigantic; huge; enormous.
—n. giant.

bro•cade [brou'keid] *n., v.* **-cad•ed, -cad•ing.** *—n.* a heavy cloth woven with a raised design on it: *silk brocade, velvet brocade.*
—v. weave or decorate with raised designs. ⟨< Sp., Pg. *brocado,* pp. of *brocar* embroider⟩

bro•cad•ed [brou'keidɪd] *adj., v. —adj.* woven or wrought into a brocade.
—v. pt. and pp. of BROCADE.

bro•ca•telle [,brɒkə'tɛl] *n.* a heavy brocaded cloth, usually made of linen and silk. ⟨< F *brocatelle* < Ital. *broccatello,* dim. of *broccato,* pp. of *brocare* to embroider⟩

broc•co•flow•er ['brɒkou,flaʊər] *n.* a cross between broccoli and cauliflower, looking like light green cauliflower. ⟨*brocco(li)* + *(cauli)flower*⟩

broc•co•li ['brɒkəli] *n.* **1** a variety of cabbage (*Brassica oleracea italica*) having dense clusters of green flower heads at the ends of the branches. **2** the flower heads and upper stems of this plant, cut for use as a cooked or raw vegetable when the flower buds are still closed. **3** a particular variety of cauliflower with green flowers. ⟨< Ital. *broccoli,* pl., sprouts < L *broccus* projecting⟩

Broccoli

bro•chette [brou'ʃɛt] *n.* **1** meat and vegetables broiled on a skewer. **2** the skewer itself. ⟨< F *broche* pin, spit⟩

bro•chure [brou'ʃʊr] *n.* a printed booklet or folder, usually having colourful pictures, that advertises or gives information about a place, a product, etc.: *The provincial government puts out a brochure on its parks.* ⟨< F *brochure* < *brocher* stitch⟩

brock [brɒk] *n.* a badger. ⟨< ME *brok*⟩

brock•et ['brɒkət] *n.* **1** a small South American red deer of the genus *Mazama,* having unbranched horns. **2** a male European red deer in the second year, having the first year's growth of horns. ⟨< ME *broket*⟩

bro•gan ['brougən] *n.* a heavy, strong work shoe reaching to the ankle. ⟨< Irish, Scots Gaelic *brógan,* dim. of *bróg* shoe⟩

brogue[1] [broug] *n.* **1** any heavy, strong shoe. **2** an oxford shoe made for comfort and long wear. ⟨< Irish, Scots Gaelic *bróg* shoe⟩

brogue[2] [broug] *n.* **1** an Irish accent in the speaking of English. **2** the accent or pronunciation peculiar to any dialect. ⟨probably < Irish *barróg* defect of speech⟩

broi•der ['brɔɪdər] *v. Archaic.* embroider. ⟨ME < OF *broder;* influenced by archaic E *broid* braid⟩ **— 'broi•der•y,** *n.*

broil[1] [brɔɪl] *v., n. —v.* **1** cook by placing on a rack directly over a fire or in a pan directly under an electric coil or gas flame; grill. **2** make or be very hot: *You will broil in this hot sun.*
—n. broiled meat, etc. ⟨ME *brule; bruyle* < OF *bruler; bruillir* burn⟩

broil[2] [brɔɪl] *n., v. —n.* an angry quarrel or struggle; brawl.
—v. quarrel; fight. ⟨< OF *brouiller* to disorder⟩

broil•er ['brɔɪlər] *n.* **1** a person or thing that broils. **2** a pan or rack for broiling food. **3** a young chicken suitable for broiling. **4** a heating element in the top of an oven under which food is placed for broiling.

broke [brouk] *v., adj. —v.* **1** a pt. of BREAK. **2** *Archaic.* a pp. of BREAK; broken.
—adj. Informal. without money.
go for broke, *Informal.* stake everything on a risky venture.

bro•ken ['broukən] *v., adj. —v.* a pp. of BREAK.
—adj. **1** not whole; in pieces: *a broken cup.* **2** not in working order: *a broken toaster.* **3** weakened in strength, spirit, etc.; tamed; crushed: *He was a broken man after his loss.* **4** divided, as by divorce: *She comes from a broken home.* **5** rough; uneven: *broken ground, a broken voice.* **6** violated; not kept: *a broken promise.* **7** imperfectly spoken: *He speaks broken French.* **8** interrupted: *broken sleep.* **9** bankrupt; ruined. **10** incomplete: *broken sizes.* **—'bro•ken•ly,** *adv.* **—'bro•ken•ness,** *n.*

bro•ken–down ['broukən 'daʊn] *adj.* **1** shattered; ruined: *broken-down health.* **2** no longer fit for use.

bro•ken–heart•ed ['broukən 'hɑrtɪd] *adj.* crushed by sorrow or grief; heartbroken.

broken home a family with only one parent, usually because of divorce.

broken wind heaves.

bro•ken–wind•ed ['broukən 'wɪndɪd] *adj.* of a horse, breathing with sudden, short efforts; suffering from heaves.

bro•ker ['broukər] *n., v. —n.* a person who acts as an agent for other people in arranging contracts, purchases, or sales in return for a fee or commission.
—v. be a broker of or for. ⟨ME < AF *brocour* tapster, retailer of wine. Akin to BROACH.⟩

bro•ker•age ['broukərɪdʒ] *n.* **1** the business of a broker. **2** the money charged by a broker for his or her services.

brol•ly ['brɒli] *n. Brit. Informal.* umbrella.

bro•maz•e•pam [brə'mæzə,pæm] *n.* a drug used to treat anxiety.

brome [broum] *n.* any of a genus (*Bromus*) of grasses of temperate regions, typically having loose, drooping clusters of flowers, especially any of several species, such as *B. inermis*, that are important for hay and as pasture grasses. Also called **brome grass.** ⟨< NL < L *bromos* < Gk. *bromos* oats, rustling < *bremein* to rustle⟩

bro•me•li•ad [brou'mili,æd] *n.* any member of the pineapple family, having tough leaves and bright flower spikes, such as Spanish moss. ⟨< NL *Bromelia*, after O. *Bromel* (1639-1705), Swedish botanist⟩

bro•mic ['broumɪk] of or containing bromine with a valence of five.

bromic acid *Chemistry.* an acid that produces bromate salts. Bromic acid is used to make dyes and pharmaceuticals. *Formula*: $HBrO_3$

bro•mide ['broumaɪd] *or* ['broumɪd] *n.* **1** a compound of bromine with another element or radical. **2** potassium bromide, a drug used to induce sleep, as a tranquillizer, sedative, etc. *Formula*: KBr **3** a commonplace idea; trite remark.

bro•mid•ic [brou'mɪdɪk] *adj. Informal.* like a bromide; commonplace; trite.

bro•mi•nate ['broumi,neit] *v.* **-nat•ed, -nat•ing.** *Chemistry.* mix with bromine. Also, **bromate** ['broumeit].

bro•mine ['broumin] *n.* a heavy, non-metallic element that evaporates quickly, resembling chlorine and iodine. Bromine is a dark brown liquid that gives off an irritating vapour. It is used in drugs and dyes and in developing photographs. *Symbol*: Br; *at.no.* 35; *at.mass* 79.90. ⟨< Gk. *bromos* stench⟩

bro•mism ['broumɪzəm] *n.* a toxic condition caused by abuse of bromides. Also, **brominism** ['broumə,nɪzəm].

bro•mo•cryp•tine or **bro•mo•crip•tine** [,broumə'krɪptin] *or* [-taɪn] *n.* a drug used to alleviate Parkinson's disease or promote fertility. *Formula*: $C_{32}H_{40}BrN_5O_5$

brom•phe•ni•ra•mine [,brɒmfə'nirə,min] *n.* an antihistamine drug. *Formula*: $C_{16}H_{19}BrN_2$

Bromp•ton mixture ['brɒmptən] a mix of several drugs given to relieve severe pain, often with terminally ill patients. ⟨< *Brompton* in England⟩

bronc [brɒŋk] *n. Informal.* bronco.

bron•chi ['brɒŋkaɪ] *or* ['brɒŋki] *n.* pl. of BRONCHUS. **1** the two main branches of the windpipe, one going to each lung. **2** the smaller, branching tubes in the lungs.

bron•chi•a ['brɒŋkiə] *n.pl.* the bronchial tubes, especially the smaller tubes.

bron•chi•al ['brɒŋkiəl] *adj.* of or having to do with the bronchi or their branches.

bronchial pneumonia inflammation and congestion of the smaller bronchial tubes and adjacent air cells in the lungs.

bronchial tube either of the bronchi or any of their branching tubes. See LUNG for picture.

bron•chi•ole ['brɒŋki,oul] *n. Anatomy* the smallest tube leading from the bronchi and ending in the alveoli.

bron•chit•ic [brɒŋ'kɪtɪk] *adj.* **1** of or having to do with bronchitis. **2** having bronchitis.

bron•chi•tis [brɒŋ'kəitɪs] *n.* inflammation of the lining of the bronchial tubes. ⟨< NL < *bronchus* + *-itis*⟩

bron•cho ['brɒŋkou] See BRONCO.

bron•cho•pneu•mo•ni•a BRONCHIAL PNEUMONIA.

bron•cho•scope ['brɒŋkə,skoup] *n. Medicine.* an instrument consisting of a narrow tube equipped with an electric light, for examining and treating the bronchi. **—,bron•cho'scop•ic** [-'skɒpɪk], *adj.* **—bron'cho•scop•y** [brɒŋ'kɒskəpi], *n.*

bron•chus ['brɒŋkəs] *n., pl.* **-chi** [-kaɪ] *or* [-ki]. one of the bronchi. ⟨< NL < Gk. *bronchos* windpipe⟩

bron•co ['brɒŋkou] *n., pl.* **-cos.** a western pony, often wild or only half tamed. Also, **broncho.** ⟨< Sp. *bronco* rough, rude; 19c.⟩

bron•co•bust•er ['brɒŋkou,bʌstər] *n. Slang.* in the West, one who breaks wild horses to the saddle. **—'bron•co,bust•ing,** *n.*

bron•to•sau•rus [,brɒntə'sɔrəs] *n.* any of a genus (*Apatosaurus*, also called *Brontosaurus*) of giant, plant-eating dinosaurs having a long neck, small head, and long tail, and walking on four legs. Also, **brontosaur** ['brɒntə,sɔr]. ⟨< NL < Gk. *brontē* thunder + *sauros* lizard⟩

Bronx cheer [brɒŋks] *Slang.* a scornful noise made with the tongue and lips; RASPBERRY (def. 4). ⟨< *the Bronx*, a borough of New York City⟩

bronze [brɒnz] *n., adj., v.* **bronzed, bronz•ing.** *—n.* **1** a brown metal, an alloy of copper and tin. **2** a similar alloy of copper with zinc or other metals. **3** a statue, medal, etc., made of bronze: *She won a bronze in the swimming competition.* **4** a moderate yellowish brown colour.
—adj. **1** made of bronze. **2** having the colour bronze.
—v. **1** tan: *The sailor was bronzed from the sun.* **2** cover with bronze: *They had his baby shoes bronzed.* ⟨< F < Ital. *bronzo* bell metal⟩

Bronze Age the period in human culture following the Stone Age, characterized by the use of bronze tools, weapons, etc. The European Bronze Age began about 3000 B.C.; that of the Middle East somewhat earlier.

bronze medal a medal made of bronze or similar metal, awarded to a contestant taking third place.

bronze•smith ['brɒnz,smɪθ] *n.* a person who works with bronze.

bronz•y ['brɒnzi] *adj.* **bronz•i•er, bronz•i•est. 1** tinged with bronze colour. **2** resembling bronze.

brooch [broutʃ] *n.* an ornamental pin having the point secured by a clasp or catch. ⟨var. of *broach*, n.⟩
☛ *Hom.* BROACH.

brood [brud] *n., v. —n.* **1** the young birds hatched at one time in the nest or cared for together. **2** young animals or humans who are cared for by the same mother. **3** a group of hens. **4** a breed; kind. **5** (*adjl.*) kept for breeding: *a brood mare.*
—v. **1** sit on (eggs) in order to hatch them. **2** think or worry a long time about some one thing: *She broods a lot these days.* **3** dwell on in thought: *For years he brooded vengeance.* **4** float above in an ominous manner: *The brooding clouds bode ill for our day at the beach.*
brood on or **over, a** keep thinking about. **b** hover over; hang close over. ⟨OE *brōd*⟩

brood•er ['brudər] *n.* **1** a closed place that can be heated, used in raising chicks, etc. **2** somebody or something that broods. **3** a hen brooding or ready to brood eggs.

brood•mare ['brud,mɛr] *n.* a mare kept for breeding.

brood•y ['brudi] *adj.* **brood•i•er, brood•i•est. 1** inclined to ponder or think moodily on a subject. **2** of hens, ready to brood eggs. When hens become broody, they stop laying. **—'brood•i•ly,** *adv.* **—'brood•i•ness,** *n.*

brook[1] [brʊk] *n.* a small, natural freshwater stream; creek. ⟨OE *brōc*⟩

brook[2] [brʊk] *v.* put up with; endure; tolerate: *Her pride would not brook such insults.* ⟨OE *brūcan* use⟩

brook•let ['brʊklət] *n.* a little stream.

brook•lime ['brʊk,laɪm] *n.* a small plant (*Veronica americana*) having purple flowers and growing near streams. Also called **American speedwell** or **veronica.**

brook trout a freshwater food and game fish (*Salvelinus fontinalis*) of North America having a long, quite narrow, deep body, a large head, and a square tail; speckled char; mud trout. The colouring of brook trout varies from olive green to dark brown.

broom [brum] *or* [brʊm] *n.* **1** a long-handled brush for sweeping, originally of broom twigs. **2** a shrub of the same family as the pea, having slender branches, small leaves, and yellow flowers.
a new broom, a new person or management that starts actively and tries to put everything right at once, from the saying "A new broom sweeps clean." ⟨OE *brōm*⟩
☛ *Hom.* BRUME.

broom•ball ['brum,bɒl] *or* ['brʊm,bɒl] *n. Cdn.* a game similar to hockey but using cornbrooms and a volleyball, usually played on a hockey rink.

broom•corn ['brum,kɔrn] *or* ['brʊm,kɔrn] *n.* a tall plant resembling corn, having flower clusters with long, stiff stems used for making brooms.

broom•rape ['brum,reip] *or* ['brʊm,reip] *n.* a plant of the genus *Orobanche*, having no leaves and growing as a parasite on the roots of other plants.

broom•stick ['brum,stɪk] *or* ['brʊm,stɪk] *n.* the long handle of a broom.

bros. or **Bros.** brothers.

brose [brouz] *n.* **1** brewis. **2** oatmeal with boiling water or milk added to it.

broth [brɒθ] *n.* **1** a thin soup made from water in which meat or fish and, often, vegetables have been boiled. **2** a thick soup, such as Scotch broth. **3** a medium in which cultures of bacteria are grown. ⟨OE⟩

broth•el ['brɒθəl] *n.* an establishment where prostitutes are available to be hired for sexual acts. ⟨ME < OE *brēothan* go to ruin⟩

broth•er ['brʌðər] *n., pl.* **broth•ers** or (*archaic except for defs. 4, 5*) **breth•ren;** *interj.* **1** a son of the same parents; sometimes, a son only of the same mother or father (a half brother). **2** a male who is a very close friend or companion; one who fills the role of a brother: *My cousin is a brother to me.* **3** a male who shares a duty, purpose, ideal, or allegiance: *The two soldiers were brothers in arms. All men are brothers.* **4** a male fellow member of a church who is not a priest. **5** a male member of a religious order who is not a priest; monk. **6** (*adjl.*) being in or of the same profession or calling: *brother officers.* **7** an informal term of address for a man: *Watch your step, brother, it's pretty slippery out there.*
–interj. Slang, an emphatic exclamation, often of annoyance: *Oh, brother!* ⟨OE *brōther*⟩ **–'broth•er•less,** *adj.* **–'broth•er,like,** *adj.*

☛ *Usage.* **Brothers** is the normal plural. **Brethren** is now used only of fellow members of a church or society, the names of certain religious groups, such as the *Plymouth Brethren.*

broth•er•hood ['brʌðər,hʊd] *n.* **1** the relationship between brothers: *He claimed brotherhood with the heir.* **2** a spiritual bond between brothers or as if between brothers: *The two inventors had worked closely together for so long that they had a strong feeling of brotherhood.* **3** an association of men with some common aim, characteristic, belief, profession, etc.: *the brotherhood of locomotive engineers.*

broth•er–in–law ['brʌðər ɪn ,lɒ] *n., pl.* **broth•ers-in-law. 1** the brother of one's spouse. **2** the husband of one's sister. **3** the husband of the sister of one's spouse.

Brother Jonathan *Archaic.* **1** the United States or its people. **2** an inhabitant of the United States.

broth•er•ly ['brʌðərli] *adj.* **1** of or having to do with a brother or brothers. **2** showing the affection of a brother; friendly; kindly: *He gave her a brotherly hug and wished her luck in the exam.*
–'broth•er•li•ness, *n.*

brougham ['brouəm] *or* ['bruəm] *n.* **1** a closed four-wheeled carriage or automobile having an outside seat for the driver. **2** an early type of car, especially one powered by electricity. ⟨after Lord *Brougham* (1778-1868), a British statesman⟩

brought [brɒt] *v.* pt. and pp. of BRING.

brou•ha•ha ['bruhɑ,hɑ] *or* [bru'hɑhɑ] *n.* an uproar or commotion: *The proposed government spending cuts caused a nationwide brouhaha.* ⟨< F, of imitative origin⟩

brow [braʊ] *n.* **1** the forehead. **2** the arch of hair over the eye; eyebrow. **3** the ridge or prominence above the eye, on which the eyebrow grows. **4** the edge of a steep place; top of a slope: *the brow of a hill.* ⟨OE *brū*⟩

bro•wal•lia [brou'weiliə] *or* [brou'weiljə] *n.* a plant of the genus *Browallia* of the nightshade family, having blue and white flowers.

brow•band ['braʊ,bænd] *n.* the part of a horse's bridle that goes across its forehead in front of the ears.

brow•beat ['braʊ,bit] *v.* **-beat, -beat•en, -beat•ing.** frighten into doing something by overbearing looks or words; bully; intimidate. **–'brow,beat•er,** *n.*

-browed *combining form.* having brows of a particular kind: *beetle-browed.*

brown [braʊn] *n., adj., v.* *–n.* **1** a colour like that of toast, cinnamon, or coffee. **2** a paint or dye having this colour. **3** clothing having this colour: *He was dressed in brown.*
–adj. **1** of or having a colour like that of toast, cinnamon, or coffee. **2** dark-skinned; tanned: *She was very brown from a summer in the sun.*
do up brown, *Slang,* do (something) perfectly well.
–v. make or become brown: *Brown the onions in butter.*
browned off, *Slang.* fed up; exasperated. ⟨OE *brūn*⟩
–'brown•ness, *n.*

brown algae a phylum of multicellular marine algae, generally dark brown to olive green due to the presence of a brown pigment as well as chlorophyll. The kelps are brown algae.

brown–bag ['braʊn ,bæg] *v.* **-bagged, -bag•ging.** *Informal.* carry lunch to work or school, usually in a brown paper bag. Often, **brown-bag it.** **–'brown-,bag•ger,** *n.*

brown bear the largest and most widespread species of bear (*Ursus arctos*), found throughout the northern parts of the world, having a short neck and large, doglike head and a thick coat of fur varying in colour from cream to blueblack. The grizzly is a subspecies of the brown bear.

brown belt 1 a degree just below the highest in judo, karate, or other martial art. **2** the belt awarded to a practitioner who has achieved this level. **3** the practitioner who has been awarded the brown belt. Compare BLACK BELT.

brown betty a baked pudding made of apples, bread crumbs, sugar, and spices.

brown bread bread made at least partly from whole wheat flour, sometimes containing extra bran and often flavoured and coloured with molasses or caramel.

brown coal lignite.

brown fat a special tissue, brown in colour, in parts of the body of a hibernating animal, which keeps it warm.

Brown•i•an movement or **motion** ['braʊniən] *Physics.* a rapid oscillatory motion often observed in very minute particles suspended in water or other liquids. ⟨after Dr. Robert *Brown* (1773-1858), a Scottish botanist⟩

brown•ie ['braʊni] *n.* **1** a good-natured, helpful elf or fairy. **2 Brownie,** a member, aged six to nine, of the Girl Guides. **3** a small square or bar of a kind of rich, dense chocolate cake usually containing nuts.

brownie points *Informal.* credit earned for good behaviour, performing some special service, etc., especially to curry favour with a superior. ⟨from the points awarded to Brownies for merit⟩

brown•ish ['braʊnɪʃ] *adj.* rather brown.

brown lung a fibrous hardening of lung tissue in textile workers, caused by long-term breathing of cotton dust; byssinosis. Also called **brown lung disease.**

brown•out ['braʊn,ʌut] *n.* a partial BLACKOUT (def. 2).

Brown Owl the leader of a Brownie pack.

brown race the Malay people living mainly in Malaya and Polynesia.

brown recluse spider a very poisonous spider (*Loxosceles reclusa*) of medium size, having six eyes and a violin-shaped mark on its thorax.

brown rice rice grains that have not had the outer layer containing the bran removed; unpolished rice.

brown rot a disease of some fruits, caused by a fungus (*Monilinia fructicola*) and resulting in rotting.

Brown Shirt 1 a member of the group of German storm troopers that was organized by Adolf Hitler in 1923 and discontinued in 1934. **2** any Nazi. Also, **Brownshirt.** Compare BLACKSHIRT.

brown•stone ['braʊn,stoun] *n.* **1** a reddish brown sandstone used as a building material. **2** a building, especially a house, built of this sandstone.

brown study the condition of being absorbed in thought; a serious reverie.

brown sugar 1 refined sugar in which the crystals are coated with dark molasses-flavoured syrup. **2** sugar that is only partly refined and so retains the original brown colour of the molasses that is naturally in sugar.

Brown Swiss a breed of large dairy cattle originating in Switzerland, having a brown hide.

brown–tail moth ['braʊn ,teil] a brown and white moth (*Euproctis pharaeorrhoea*), whose larvae feed on the foliage of fruit trees.

brown thrasher a thrasher (*Toxostoma rufum*) found in North America east of the Rockies, having bright reddish brown upper parts and whitish under parts streaked with brown.

brown trout a game fish stocked in North America but originating in Europe, having golden-brown scales (*Salmo trutto*).

browse [braʊz] *v.* **browsed, brows•ing;** *n.* *–v.* **1** feed on growing plants, especially the tender parts of trees and bushes: *The deer moved through the woods, browsing on young shoots and leaves.* **2** read here and there in a book or in books; especially, pass the time looking at books in a library or bookstore. **3** look casually at articles for sale in a store. **4** *Computer technology.* **a** look through a series of records by having sets of them displayed successively on a computer monitor. **b** search casually for material of interest on the WORLD WIDE WEB.
–n. **1** tender shoots, leaves, and twigs of trees and shrubs considered as food for animals. **2** the act of browsing. ⟨apparently < early Mod.F *broust* a bud, shoot, *brouster* feed on buds and shoots < Gmc. 16c.⟩ **–'brows•er,** *n.*

brows•er ['braʊzər] *n.* **1** a person or thing that browses.

2 *Computer technology.* a piece of software which enables the user to access and browse on the WORLD WIDE WEB.

bru•cel•lo•sis [ˌbrusə'lousɪs] *n.* a disease of cattle which causes abortion, and which can be passed to people, caused by a bacterium of the genus *Brucella.* ⟨after Sir David *Bruce* (1855-1931), Scottish physician⟩

bru•in ['bruən] *n.* a bear, especially a brown bear as featured in fables and children's stories. ⟨< MDu. *bruin* brown⟩

bruise [bruz] *n., v.* **bruised, bruis•ing.** *—n.* **1 a** an injury to the body, caused by a fall or a blow, that breaks blood vessels without breaking the skin: *The bruise on my arm was quite painful.* **b** the resulting discoloured area: *She had a bruise as big as the palm of my hand.* **2** an injury to the outside of a fruit, vegetable, plant, etc. **3** an emotional hurt or injury: *His insult was a bruise to her pride.*
—v. **1** make or cause a bruise on: *I bruised my leg. Handle the tomatoes carefully so you don't bruise them.* **2** cause to be hurt: *The harsh words bruised his feelings.* **3** become bruised: *I bruise easily.* **4** pound or crush (drugs or food). ⟨fusion of ME *bruse* < OE *brȳsan* crush and AF *bruser*, OF *bruisier* break, shatter⟩
☛ *Hom.* BREWIS [bruz].

bruis•er ['bruzər] *n. Informal.* **1** PRIZE FIGHTER. **2** a bully. **3** a very muscular person.

bruit [brut] *v., n. —v.* spread (a report or rumour): *Rumours of the princess's engagement were bruited about.*
—n. Archaic. a report or rumour. ⟨< OF *bruit* noise, rumour < *bruire* roar⟩
☛ *Hom.* BRUT, BRUTE.

bru•lé or **bru•le** [bru'lei] *or* ['brulei] *n. Cdn.* **1** a forest area that has been destroyed by fire. **2** rocky, untillable land. ⟨< F *brûlé* burnt⟩

brume [brum] *n.* fog; mist.
☛ *Hom.* BROOM.

brunch [brʌntʃ] *n.* a meal, taken in the late morning, that combines breakfast and lunch. ⟨< *br(eakfast)* + *(l)unch*⟩

Bru•nei [bru'naɪ] *n.* **Brunei Darussalam,** a country in NW Borneo, consisting of two separate areas.

bru•net [bru'nɛt] *adj., n. —adj.* **1** dark-coloured; having an olive colour. **2** having dark brown or black hair, usually brown or black eyes, and, sometimes, a dark skin.
—n. a man or boy having dark hair. ⟨< F *brunette*, fem., dim. of *brun* brown < Gmc.⟩

bru•nette [bru'nɛt] *n.* a woman or girl having dark hair. ⟨< F⟩

Bruns•wick stew ['brʌnzwɪk] a dish formerly made with rabbit or squirrel and now with chicken, stewed with corn, beans, and other vegetables.

brunt [brʌnt] *n.* the main force or violence; hardest part: *to bear the brunt.* ⟨ME *brunt* a blow; origin uncertain⟩

brush¹ [brʌʃ] *n., v. —n.* **1** a tool for cleaning, sweeping, scrubbing, painting, etc. A brush is made of bristles, hair, or wires set in a stiff back or fastened to a handle. **2** a brushing; a rub with a brush. **3** a light touch in passing. **4** an encounter or confrontation: *a brush with the law, a brush with death.* **5** the bushy tail of an animal, especially of a fox. **6** a piece of carbon, copper, etc. used to conduct the electricity from the revolving part of a motor or generator to the outside circuit. **7** BRUSH DISCHARGE. **8** *Slang.* brushoff: *to give someone the brush.* **9** the style of an artist: *He paints with a bold brush.*
—v. **1** clean, sweep, paint, etc. with a brush; use a brush on. **2** wipe away; remove with a light sweeping motion: *The child brushed the tears from his eyes.* **3** touch lightly in passing. **4** move quickly.
brush aside or **away,** cast aside; refuse to consider.
brush off, *Informal.* refuse or dismiss (a request, person, etc.) in a curt or disdainful way: *He brushed us off when we asked for his autograph.*
brush up (on), refresh the memory by study; review: *I have to brush up on some theorems for the geometry test tomorrow.* ⟨ME *brusshe* < OF *broisse* < Gmc.⟩ **—'brush•er,** *n.* **—'brush,like,** *adj.*

brush² [brʌʃ] *n.* **1** branches broken or cut off. **2** shrubs, bushes, and small trees growing thickly together. **3** thinly settled country; backwoods. ⟨ME *brusche* < OF *broche*⟩

brush•cut ['brʌʃˌkʌt] *n.* a very short haircut in which the hair on top of the head stands straight out from the scalp.

brush discharge a luminescent electrical discharge, as around a high voltage wire, like a brush in appearance.

brushed [brʌʃt] *adj., v. —adj.* of cloth or leather, rubbed with a brush so as to raise the nap.
—v. pt. and pp. of BRUSH.

brushfire war a small conflict.

brush•off ['brʌʃˌɒf] *n. Informal.* a curt or offhand dismissal of a request, person, etc.: *When I asked for a date, I got a brushoff.*

brush•stroke ['brʌʃˌstrouk] *n.* **1** a movement of the brush in painting. **2** the method of using brushstrokes in painting, or its effect: *This reproduction is so authentic that you can see the brushstrokes. She uses a very heavy brushstroke to give texture.*

brush•up ['brʌʃˌʌp] *n.* **1** a refreshing of memory or a reviewing of knowledge, skill, etc. **2** a smartening or freshening of one's appearance.

brush wolf *Cdn.* coyote.

brush•wood ['brʌʃˌwʊd] *n.* BRUSH² (defs. 1 and 2).

brush•work ['brʌʃˌwɜrk] *n.* **1** the application of paint with a brush. **2** an artist's characteristic technique in applying paint with a brush.

brush•y¹ ['brʌʃi] *adj.* **brush•i•er, brush•i•est.** like a brush; rough and shaggy. ⟨< *brush¹*⟩ **—'brush•i•ness,** *n.*

brush•y² ['brʌʃi] *adj.* **brush•i•er, brush•i•est.** covered with bushes, shrubs, etc. ⟨< *brush²*⟩ **—'brush•i•ness,** *n.*

brusque [brʌsk] *or* [brusk] *adj.* abrupt in manner or speech; blunt. ⟨< F < Ital. *brusco* coarse < LL *bruscus*, blend of *ruscum* broom and Gaulish *brucus* broom⟩ **—'brusque•ly,** *adv.* **—'brusque•ness,** *n.*

brus•que•rie ['brʌskəri] *or* ['bruskəri]; *French,* [bʀyskə'ʀi] *n.* brusqueness.

Brus•sels carpet ['brʌsəlz] a carpet with a pattern made of small loops of yarn having various colours. ⟨< *Brussels*, Belgium⟩

Brussels lace a heavy lace with a very elaborate design.

Brussels sprouts **1** a variety of cabbage (*Brassica oleracea gemmifera*) that bears many small green heads, like tiny cabbages, along its tall, thick stem. **2** the heads of this plant, eaten as a vegetable.

brut [brut] *adj.* of champagne, very dry, with only a little sugar added. ⟨< F < ME and OF *brut* < L *brutus* heavy, dull⟩
☛ *Hom.* BRUIT, BRUTE.

bru•tal ['brutəl] *adj.* **1** coarse and savage. **2** harsh; unrelenting: *brutal weather, the brutal facts.* **—'brut•al•ly,** *adv.*
☛ *Syn.* **1.** See note at CRUEL.

bru•tal•i•ty [bru'tæləti] *n., pl.* **-ties. 1** brutal conduct; cruelty; savageness. **2** a cruel or savage act.

bru•tal•ize ['brutəˌlaɪz] *v.* **-ized, -iz•ing. 1** make brutal: *War brutalizes many people.* **2** become brutal. **3** treat brutally: *The judge had harsh criticism for police officers who brutalized people they were questioning.* **—ˌbru•tal•i'za•tion,** *n.*

brute [brut] *n., adj. —n.* **1** an animal without power to reason. **2** a cruel, coarse, or sensual person. **3** animal nature.
—adj. **1** not having power to reason: *brute creatures.* **2** cruel; coarse; sensual. **3** without feeling: *Humans have struggled long with the brute forces of nature.* ⟨< F *brut* < L *brutus* heavy, dull⟩
☛ *Syn. n.* See note at ANIMAL.
☛ *Hom.* BRUIT, BRUT.

brut•ish ['brutɪʃ] *adj.* coarse; savage. **—'brut•ish•ly,** *adv.* **—'brut•ish•ness,** *n.*

brux•ism ['brʌksɪzəm] *n.* the act or habit of grinding one's teeth while asleep. ⟨< Gk. *ebryxa* < *brykein* to gnash the teeth⟩

bry•ol•o•gy [braɪ'ɒlədʒi] *n.* a branch of botany that deals with mosses and liverworts. ⟨< Gk. *bryon* moss + E *-logy*⟩ **—ˌbry•o'log•i•cal,** *adj.* **—bry'ol•o•gist,** *n.*

bry•o•ny ['braɪəni] *n., pl.* **-nies.** any of a genus (*Bryonia*) of herbaceous climbing plants of the gourd family native to Europe and N Africa, having greenish flowers and red or black berries. Also, **briony.** ⟨< L < Gk. *bryonia* < *bryein* swell⟩

bry•o•phyte ['braɪəˌfəit] *n.* any of a division (Bryophyta) of perennial plants having stems and leaves but no true roots, and reproducing by spores. The division includes the mosses and liverworts. ⟨< NL *bryophia* < Gk. *bryon* tree moss + *phyton* plant < *phyein* grow⟩ **—ˌbry•o'phy•tic** [ˌbraɪə'fɪtɪk], *adj.*

bry•o•zo•an [ˌbraɪə'zouən] *n.* a tiny water creature of the phylum Bryozoa, that reproduces by budding and forms colonies. Fossils of bryozoans have been found on Baffin Island. ⟨< NL < Gk. *bryon* moss + *zoion* animal⟩

Bryth•on ['brɪθən] *n.* any member of a large Celtic group once living in South Britain but later driven into Wales, Cornwall, and ancient Cumbria, who spoke Brythonic languages. ⟨< Welsh *Brython* < Old Celtic *Britton* a Briton⟩

Bry•thon•ic [brɪ'θɒnɪk] *adj., n. —adj.* **1** of or having to do with the Brythons. **2** of, having to do with, or denoting the Celtic language group to which Breton, Cornish, and Welsh belong. *—n.* one of the two main divisions of the Celtic language (the other being Goidelic), including Breton, Cornish, and Welsh; Cymric.

b.s. **1** bill of sale. **2** balance sheet.

bskt. basket.

B.S.M. battery sergeant-major.

bsmt. basement.

Bt. baronet.

btl. bottle.

Btn. or **btn.** battalion.

btry. battery.

Btu, BTU, or **B.T.U.** BRITISH THERMAL UNIT or units.

bu. **1** bushel(s). **2** bureau.

bu•bal or **bu•bale** ['bjubəl] *n.* a rare subspecies of the hartebeest (*Alcelaphus bucelaphus*), found in North Africa. ⟨< NL *Bubalis* < Gk. *boubalis* buffalo, antelope⟩

bub•ble ['bʌbəl] *n., v.* **-bled, -bling.** *—n.* **1** a thin round film of liquid enclosing air or gas: *soap bubbles. The surface of boiling water is covered with bubbles.* **2** a pocket of air or gas in a liquid or solid, as in ice or glass. **3** the act or process of bubbling; a sound of bubbling: *the bubble of boiling water.* **4** something shaped like a bubble. A round, domed skylight is often called a bubble. **5** a plan or idea that looks good, but soon goes to pieces. **6** anything that does not last or has little substance. **7** *Archaic.* a swindle: *the South Sea Bubble.*
—v. **1** have or form bubbles. **2** flow with bubbles: *Water bubbled up between the stones.* **3** make sounds like water boiling; gurgle.
bubble over, a be very full; overflow. **b** be very enthusiastic: *The girls were bubbling over with ideas for the canoe trip.* ⟨ME *bobel, probably imitative*⟩ **—'bub•bling•ly,** *adv.*

bubble and squeak a British dish consisting of previously cooked cabbage and potato, mashed together and fried, sometimes with meat.

bubble bath **1** a bath with a mass of bubbles on the surface, formed by adding a special liquid or gel. **2** the liquid or gel.

bubble chamber a small vessel filled with a superheated liquid, especially pentane or hydrogen under pressure, through which sub-atomic particles make a bubbly track by means of which they may be isolated and identified.

bubble gum chewing gum that is very elastic and can be blown up into bubbles from the mouth.

bub•ble–gum•mer ['bʌbəl ˌgʌmər] *n. Slang.* a young person.

bub•ble•head ['bʌbəl,hɛd] *n. Slang.* a stupid person.

bubble pack **1** a method of packaging in which the objects are sealed between a clear, rigid plastic covering and a cardboard back. Also, **blister pack.** **2** any object so packaged. **3** a packing material consisting of two layers of plastic, the space between them being entirely filled with small bubbles.

bub•ble–top ['bʌbəl ˌtɒp] *n.* a transparent plastic top or canopy, often retractable, on a vehicle or airplane.

bubble tower a device for separating petroleum into various components by distillation.

bub•bly ['bʌbli] *adj., n. —adj.* **1** full of bubbles; like bubbles. **2** showing enthusiasm or high spirits: *She has a bubbly personality.*
—n. Informal. champagne.

bu•bo ['bjubou] *n., pl.* **bu•boes.** an inflammatory swelling of a lymphatic gland, especially in the groin or armpits. ⟨< LL *bubo* < Gk. *boubon* groin⟩

bu•bon•ic [bju'bɒnɪk] *adj.* of or having to do with inflamed swelling of the lymphatic glands, especially in the armpit and groin.

bubonic plague a dangerous infectious disease, accompanied by fever, chills, and swelling of the lymphatic glands, carried to human beings by fleas from rats or squirrels.

bu•bon•o•cele [bju'bɒnə,sil] *n.* a swelling in the groin caused by a partial hernia.

buc•cal ['bʌkəl] *adj. Anatomy.* **1** of the cheek. **2** of the mouth or of the sides of the mouth. ⟨< L *bucca* cheek, mouth⟩
☛ *Hom.* BUCKLE.

buc•ca•neer [ˌbʌkə'nir] *n.* a pirate or freebooter. ⟨< F *boucanier* < *boucaner* cure flesh on a boucan or barbecue < Tupi *boucan* frame for curing meat, as done by the French in Haïti⟩

buc•ci•na•tor ['bʌksə,neitər] *n. Anatomy.* the muscle in the cheek responsible for contraction and for pulling the inner cheek against the teeth, as in chewing.

Buch•man•ism ['bʌkmə,nɪzəm] *n.* a 20th century religious movement; Moral Rearmament. ⟨< Frank *Buchman* (1878-1961), U.S. evangelist and founder of the movement⟩

buck[1] [bʌk] *n.* **1** an adult male deer, goat, hare, rabbit, antelope, or sheep. **2** *Informal.* a man, especially a young man who is lively, bold, and dashing. **3** *Archaic.* a dandy. **4** (*adjl.*) male. ⟨a fusion of OE *buc* male deer, and OE *bucca* male goat⟩

buck[2] [bʌk] *v., n. —v.* **1** fight against; resist stubbornly: *The swimmer bucked the current with strong strokes. You can't buck progress.* **2** *Informal.* push or hit with the head; butt. **3** *Football.* charge into (the opposing line) with the ball. **4** of horses, jump into the air with back curved and come down with the front legs stiff. **5** throw or attempt to throw (a rider) in this way. **6** *Informal.* of an automobile, motor, etc., run unevenly; jerk, as when the fuel supply is low or the motor cold.
buck up, cheer up; be brave or energetic: *Buck up; everything will be all right.*
—n. a throw or an attempt to throw by bucking. ⟨special use of *buck[1]*⟩ **—'buck•er,** *n.*

buck[3] [bʌk] *n., v. —n.* **1** a sawhorse; sawbuck. **2** *Gymnastics.* a padded, adjustable frame used for vaulting, etc.
—v. cut (wood, especially felled trees) into lengths, as with a bucksaw. ⟨short for *sawbuck*⟩

buck[4] [bʌk] *n.* formerly, a marker placed before a designated player in poker to show that he or she had the responsibility for dealing the cards.
pass the buck, *Informal.* shift the responsibility or blame to someone else: *Whenever his plans don't work out, he passes the buck and someone else gets blamed.* ⟨origin uncertain⟩

buck[5] [bʌk] *n. Slang.* dollar. ⟨origin uncertain⟩

buck•a•roo [ˌbʌkə'ru] *or* ['bʌkə,ru] *n., pl.* **-roos.** cowboy. ⟨< alteration of Sp. *vaquero* < *vaca* cow < L *vacca*⟩

buck•bean ['bʌk,bin] *n.* a plant (*Menyanthes trifoliata*) of the gentian family, having shiny trifoliate leaves and white flowers. It grows in bogs. ⟨< Du. *boksboon*, literally, goat's bean⟩

buck•board ['bʌk,bɔrd] *n.* an open four-wheeled carriage having a seat fastened to a platform of long, springy boards instead of having a body and springs. ⟨< *buck[2]* + *board*⟩

buck•er ['bʌkər] *n.* a logger who trims the trees. ⟨< *buck[3]*⟩

buck•et ['bʌkɪt] *n., v.* **-et•ed, -et•ing.** *—n.* **1** a pail, especially a wooden one used for carrying water, milk, etc. **2** the amount that a bucket can hold. **3** the scoop of a backhoe, one of the cups on a water wheel, or any other bucketlike thing. **4** *Slang.* a ship, car, etc., especially one that is old and slow.
kick the bucket, *Slang.* die.
—v. **1** lift or carry in a bucket or buckets. **2** ride (a horse) hard. **3** *Informal.* **a** move fast. **b** move jerkily and irregularly. **4** swing forward too hurriedly before taking the stroke in rowing. **5** conduct a BUCKET SHOP. ⟨ME < AF *buket* washtub, milk pail, perhaps < OE *būc* belly, vessel, pitcher⟩

bucket brigade a line of people passing buckets of water from hand to hand from the source, to put out a fire.

buck•et•ful ['bʌkɪt,fʊl] *n., pl.* **-fuls.** the amount that a bucket can hold.

bucket seat a single, stooped or contoured, low-slung seat with a curved back, used especially in sports cars, small airplanes, etc.

bucket shop a fraudulent establishment conducted ostensibly for buying and selling stocks or commodities, but really for making bets on the rise and fall of their prices, with no actual buying and selling.

buck•eye ['bʌk,aɪ] *n.* **1** *Esp. U.S.* any of various North American trees (genus *Aesculus*) of the horse chestnut family. The **Ohio buckeye** (*A. glabra*) gave Ohio the nickname 'Buckeye State'. **2** the shiny brown seed of this tree, encased in a spiky covering. ⟨< *buck[1]* + *eye*; with reference to mark on the seed⟩

Buck•ing•ham Palace ['bʌkɪŋhəm] *or* ['bʌkɪŋəm] the official London residence of all British sovereigns since 1837.

buck•le[1] ['bʌkəl] *n., v.* **-led, -ling.** *—n.* **1** a device used to fasten the loose end or both ends of a belt or strap, usually consisting of a metal or plastic frame through which the end of the belt or strap is pulled. **2** a metal ornament, especially one for a shoe.
—v. fasten together with a buckle.
buckle down (to), begin to work hard (at): *She promised to buckle down to her homework right after supper.* ⟨ME *bocle* < OF *boucle* < L *buccula* cheek strap on helmet, dim. of *bucca* cheek⟩
☛ *Hom.* BUCCAL.

buck•le² ['bʌkəl] *v.* **-led, -ling;** *n.* —*v.* bend; bulge; give way under a heavy weight or strain: *The heavy snowfall caused the roof of the arena to buckle.*
buckle under, give in; yield.
—*n.* a bend; bulge; kink or wrinkle. ⟨< F *boucler* bulge⟩
☛ *Hom.* BUCCAL.

buck•ler ['bʌklər] *n.* **1** a small, round shield. **2** a protection; defence. ⟨ME < OF *boucler* shield, originally, one with a boss < *boucle* boss < L *buccula.* See BUCKLE¹.⟩

buck•o ['bʌkou] *n. Slang.* fellow; man.

buck•pas•sing ['bʌk,pæsɪŋ] *n. Slang.* avoidance of responsibility, blame, work, etc. by shifting it to someone else. **—'buck,pas•ser,** *n.*

buck private *U.S. Slang.* a common soldier below the rank of lance corporal.

buck•ram ['bʌkrəm] *n., v.* —*n.* **1** a coarse cotton or linen cloth made stiff with glue, used in bookbinding and to stiffen hats and other clothing. **2** (*adjl.*) made of or resembling buckram.
—*v.* pad or stiffen with buckram. ⟨ME < AF ? ult. < *Bukhara,* var. of *Bokhara,* a city in Uzbekistan⟩

buck•saw ['bʌk,sɒ] *n.* a saw set in a light H-shaped frame and held with both hands. Bucksaws are used for sawing wood.

buck•shee ['bʌkʃi] *adj. Slang.* free: *We were given two buckshee tickets for the dance.* ⟨< *baksheesh*⟩

buck•shot ['bʌk,ʃɒt] *n.* a coarse lead shot for shotgun shells, used for hunting large game such as deer.

buck•skin ['bʌk,skɪn] *n.* **1** the skin of a male deer. **2** a soft, strong, yellowish or greyish leather made from this skin, usually having a suede finish. Buckskin is tougher and coarser than deerskin. **3** a similar leather made from sheepskin. **4 buckskins,** *pl.* clothing, especially breeches, made from BUCKSKIN (def. 2). **5** a yellowish or greyish horse. **6** (*adjl.*) made of buckskin: *my buckskin boots.*

buck•thorn ['bʌk,θɔrn] *n.* **1** any of several thorny trees or shrubs (genus *Rhamnus*) having small green flowers followed by bluish black berries. **2** (*adjl.*) designating the family (Rhamnaceae) of trees, shrubs, and climbing vines that includes the buckthorns.

buck•tooth ['bʌk,tuθ] *n., pl.* **-teeth.** a tooth that sticks out.

buck•toothed ['bʌk,tuθt] *or* [-,tuðd] *adj.* having protruding upper front teeth.

buck•wheat ['bʌk,wit] *n.* **1** any of a genus (*Fagopyrum*) of annual plants native to Europe and Asia. Two species of buckwheat have been extensively grown in North America for their edible seeds, which are used as cereal grains; the plants have escaped from cultivation, becoming common weeds in many parts of Canada. **2** the seed of a buckwheat, used as food. **3** a dark flour made from this seed. **4 wild buckwheat,** a twining annual plant (*Polygonum convolvulus*) native to Europe, but now growing as a weed throughout Canada. Also called **black bindweed. 5** (*adjl.*) designating a family (Polygonaceae) of annual or perennial herbs or shrubs found mainly in the northern hemisphere. Rhubarb, sorrel, dock, and smartweed belong to the buckwheat family. ⟨< *buck* (< OE *bōc* beech) + *wheat*; from its beechnut-shaped seeds⟩

buckwheat cake a pancake made of buckwheat flour.

bu•col•ic [bju'kɒlɪk] *adj., n.* —*adj.* **1** of shepherds or their lifestyle; pastoral: *Bucolic poetry is seldom written by shepherds themselves.* **2** rustic; rural.
—*n.* **1** a poem about shepherds. **2** a rustic person. ⟨< L *bucolicus* < Gk. *boukolikos* rustic < *boukolos* shepherd⟩ **—bu'col•i•cal•ly,** *adv.*

bud [bʌd] *n., v.* **bud•ded, bud•ding.** —*n.* **1** on a plant, a small swelling that will develop into a flower, leaf, or branch. **2** a partly opened flower or leaf. **3** a person or thing not yet developed or mature. **4** anything in its beginning stage. **5** a minute, bud-shaped part or organ: *a taste bud.* **6** *Informal.* buddy. **7** *Biology.* a growth on the body of certain lower life forms which will eventually form a new member of the species.
in bud, budding: *The pear tree is in bud.*
nip in the bud, stop at the very beginning.
—*v.* **1** put forth buds: *The rosebush has budded.* **2** graft (a bud) from one kind of plant into the stem of a different kind. See GRAFT for picture. **3** begin to grow or develop. **4** sprout: *That calf is budding horns.* ⟨ME *budde*⟩ **—'bud•der,** *n.* **—'bud,like,** *adj.*

Bud•dha ['bʊdə] *or* ['budə] *n.* **1** the title of Siddhartha Gautama (563?-483? B.C.), the Indian philosopher and religious teacher who founded Buddhism. Buddha means Enlightened One. **2** a statue of Buddha. ⟨< Skt.⟩

A statue of Buddha

Bud•dhism ['bʊdɪzəm,] *or* ['budɪzəm] *n.* a religion based on the doctrine of Buddha that pain and suffering cannot be avoided so long as one is subject to worldly desires, but that through meditating and leading a strictly moral life one can eventually reach nirvana, a state of liberation and spiritual illumination that is beyond pleasure or pain. Buddhism is widely practised today in many parts of eastern and central Asia, especially in Myanmar, Thailand, Sri Lanka, Japan, Cambodia, Laos, and Tibet.

Bud•dhist ['bʊdɪst] *or* ['budɪst] *n., adj.* —*n.* a believer in Buddhism.
—*adj.* of or having to do with Buddha or Buddhism.
—Bud,dhist•ic, *adj.*

bud•ding ['bʌdɪŋ] *adj., v., n.* —*adj.* potential: *a budding physicist.*
—*v.* ppr. of BUD.
—*n.* a type of asexual reproduction in lower animals and some plants, in which the new individual forms as an outgrowth on the parent.

bud•dle•ia [bəd'liə] *or* ['bʌdliə] *n.* a tropical bush or tree (genus *Buddleia*) of the logonia family, having yellow or purple flowers. ⟨< NL after A. *Buddle,* 17c. English botanist⟩

bud•dy ['bʌdi] *n., pl.* **-dies.** *Informal.* **1** a good friend; pal. **2** fellow (*used as a form of address*): *Say, buddy, can you change a quarter?*

bud•dy–bud•dy ['bʌdi ,bʌdi] *or* ['bʌdi 'bʌdi] *adj. Slang.* effusively friendly, often in an insincere way.

buddy system an arrangement in dangerous kinds of work or sport, by which two people operate together as a safety precaution in case of accident.

bu•des•o•nide [bju'dɛsə,naɪd] *n.* a drug used as an inhalant to treat bronchial asthma.

budge [bʌdʒ] *v.* **budged, budg•ing.** move or cause to move: *He wouldn't budge from his chair.* ⟨< F *bouger* stir < VL * *bullicare* boil furiously < L *bullire* boil⟩

budg•er•i•gar ['bʌdʒərɪ,gar] *n.* a small, long-tailed parrot (*Melopsittacus undulatus*) native to Australia, but very popular in many countries as a cage bird. The plumage of wild budgerigars is green below and yellow above, with blue and black stripes, but the cage birds have been bred to produce individuals of many different colours. ⟨< native Australian *budgereegah* < *budgeri* good + *gar* cockatoo⟩

budg•et ['bʌdʒɪt] *n., v.* **-et•ed, -et•ing.** —*n.* **1** an estimate of the amount of money that will be spent for various purposes in a given time by a government, school, business, family, etc.: *We made a budget for our holiday trip so that we wouldn't run out of money before the end.* **2** the amount of money allotted for a particular use or period of time: *I've already spent my budget for movies this month.* **3** a stock or collection: *a budget of news.*
—*v.* **1** make a plan for spending or using: *to budget one's time. He budgets his earnings carefully.* **2** allot (money) for a particular purpose: *I forgot to budget for extras so I couldn't buy the tape.* **3** draw up or prepare a budget. ⟨ME < OF *bougette,* dim. of *bouge* leather bag < L *bulga* < Celtic⟩

budg•et•ar•y ['bʌdʒə,tɛri] *adj.* of a budget.

bud•get•eer [,bʌdʒə'tir] *n.* **1** a person who prepares a budget. **2** a person who sticks closely to a budget.

budg•ie ['bʌdʒi] *n. Informal.* budgerigar.

bud run *Cdn.* the third run of sugar maple sap, which makes syrup or sugar of a poor quality. Compare with FROG RUN and ROBIN RUN.

bud scale any of the scales covering some plant buds in winter.

bud vase a tall, narrow vase used for holding a single rosebud or other flower.

bud•worm ['bʌd,wɜrm] *n.* SPRUCE BUDWORM.

bu•fex•a•mac [bju'fɛksə,mæk] *n.* an anti-inflammatory drug used in a cream or ointment form.

buff[1] [bʌf] *n., adj., v.* —*n.* **1** a strong, soft, dull yellow leather having a fuzzy surface, made from buffalo skin or oxhide. **2** a soldier's coat made of this leather. **3** a dull yellow. **4** a polishing wheel or stick covered with leather. **5** *Informal.* bare skin: *swimming in the buff.*
—*adj.* **1** made of buff leather. **2** having the colour buff.
—*v.* **1** polish with a buff. **2** stain or dye a dull yellow. **3** make smooth or soft like buff. ⟨earlier *buffle* < F *buffle* < Ital. *bufalo.* See BUFFALO.⟩

buff[2] [bʌf] *n. Informal.* fan; enthusiast: *a hockey buff, a theatre buff.* ⟨origin uncertain⟩

buff[3] [bʌf] *n. Cdn. Informal.* buffalo.

buf•fa•lo ['bʌfə,lou] *n., pl.* **-loes, -los,** or (*esp. collectively*) **-lo;** *v.* **-loed, -lo•ing.** —*n.* **1** a large mammal (*Bison bison*) of the North American plains having a prominent shoulder hump and a large head that is carried below the level of the shoulders, short, curved horns, and coarse, dark brown hair that is long and shaggy on the forequarters. The buffalo is Canada's largest land mammal; a large bull may weigh up to one tonne. **2** any of several large hoofed mammals (family Bovidae) of Africa and India generally having long horns that curve upward and backward. Some species, such as the water buffalo of India, have been domesticated. **3** BUFFALO FISH. **4** a loose garment or a blanket or rug made of buffalo hide.
—*v.* **1** *Slang.* make unable to answer, proceed, etc.; baffle: *We were all buffaloed by the last question on the exam.* **2** *Slang.* intimidate or overawe. ⟨< Ital. *bufalo* < L *bubalus* < Gk. *boubalos* wild ox⟩

buffalo berry **1** a shrub (*Shepherdia argentea*) of the oleaster family native to W North America, having silvery foliage and edible red berries. **2** the berry of this shrub. **3** SOAPBERRY (def. 4).

buffalo fish any of several North American suckers (genus *Ictiobus*) having a deep body with a humped back.

buffalo grass a short grass (*Buchloë dactyloides*) of the plains east of the Rocky Mountains, valued especially for winter pasture.

buffalo jump *Cdn.* a place where the First Nations people of the Plains slaughtered buffalo by stampeding them over a precipice.

buffalo robe a kind of wrap made of tanned and cured buffalo hide.

buff•er[1] ['bʌfər] *n., v.* —*n.* **1** an apparatus that softens the shock of a blow. **2** anything helping to soften or sustain a shock or to neutralize opposing forces: *Mother was a buffer between my brother's anger and me.* **3** any substance in a solution that neutralizes acid or alkali. **4** *Computer technology.* a repository for data being held temporarily prior to transfer to a storage device or another place in the memory.
—*v.* act as a buffer for or against. ⟨< *buff* deaden force, (earlier meaning) strike; cf. OF *buffe* a blow⟩

buff•er[2] ['bʌfər] *n.* a person or thing that polishes, especially a leather or cloth-covered device for polishing or buffing. ⟨< *buff*[1]⟩

buffer state a small country between two larger countries that are enemies or competitors, thought of as lessening the danger of open conflict between them.

buffer zone a neutral area established as a barrier between two adjoining enemy or rival areas. NO-MAN'S-LAND (def. 1) is a buffer zone.

buf•fet[1] ['bʌfɪt] *n., v.* **-fet•ed, -fet•ing.** —*n.* **1** a blow of the hand or fist. **2** a knock; stroke; hurt.
—*v.* **1** strike with the hand or fist. **2** knock about; strike; hurt: *The waves buffeted her.* **3** fight or struggle (against): *He was exhausted from buffeting the storm.* ⟨ME < OF *buffet,* dim. of *buffe* blow⟩

buf•fet[2] [bə'fei] *or* [bʊ'fei] *n.* **1** a low cabinet with a flat top, for holding dishes, silver, and table linen. **2** a counter where food and drinks are served. **3** a restaurant with such a counter. **4** a meal at which guests serve themselves from food laid out on a separate table. ⟨< F⟩

buffet car a railway car having a small area where light meals may be obtained.

buffet lunch a BUFFET[2] (def. 4).

buffet supper a BUFFET[2] (def. 4), served at night.

A bufflehead

buf•fle•head ['bʌfəl,hɛd] *n.* a small, black-and-white, North American diving duck (*Bucephala albeola*), the male of which has long, fluffy feathers forming puffs on the sides of the head. ⟨< obs. *buffle* buffalo + *head*⟩

buf•fo ['bufou]; *Ital;* ['buffo] *n., adj.* —*n.* a male singer of comic operatic roles, usually a basso.
—*adj.* comic. ⟨< Ital. *buffo*⟩

buf•foon [bə'fun] *n., v.* —*n.* **1** a person who amuses people with tricks, pranks, and jokes; clown. **2** a person given to coarse or undignified jesting.
—*v.* behave like a buffoon. ⟨< F *bouffon* < Ital. *buffone* < *buffa* jest⟩ **—buf'foon•ish,** *adj.*

buf•foon•er•y [bə'funəri] *n., pl.* **-er•ies. 1** the tricks, pranks, and jokes of a clown. **2** undignified or rude joking. **3** the behaviour of a buffoon.

A buffy-tufted-ear marmoset

buffy–tufted–ear marmoset a marmoset (*Callithrix aurita*) of S Brazil, having tufts of hair around the ears and large incisors. It eats fruit, flowers, and sap.

bu•fo•ten•ine [,bjufə'tɛnin] *or* [-ɪn] *n.* a poison obtained from toadstools and the skin glands of toads. It causes hallucinations, and can also be made synthetically. *Formula:* $C_{12}H_{16}N_2O$ ⟨< L *bufo* toad⟩

bug [bʌg] *n., v.* **bugged, bug•ging.** —*n.* **1** any of an order (Heteroptera) of sucking insects made up of about 20 000 species, including the bedbug, having generally horizontal wings that overlap on the body when at rest. Most families of bugs have scent glands that produce a characteristic odour. **2** any insect or insectlike animal. The ladybug and June bug are really beetles. Ants, spiders, cockroaches, etc. are sometimes called bugs, especially when thought of as pests. **3** *Informal.* a disease bacterium or virus: *the flu bug.* **4** *Informal.* a mechanical defect; any structural fault or difficulty: *a bug in the fire alarm system.* **5** *Informal.* a person who is very enthusiastic about something: *a camera bug.* **6** *Informal.* a very small hidden microphone, installed for the purpose of secretly listening in on or recording conversation. **7** *Computer technology.* an error in the hardware or software of a computer: *The incorrect invoices were the result of bugs in the billing system.* **8** a strong interest or passion: *stung by the motorcycle bug.*
—*v.* **1** *Slang.* annoy; irritate: *His constant grumbling bugs me.* **2** *Informal.* fit (a room, telephone, etc.) with a very small concealed microphone. **3** *Informal.* secretly listen in on or record by means of a hidden microphone: *to bug a meeting.* **4** of eyes, be so wide open from astonishment, fear, etc., as to seem to protrude like a bug's: *Their eyes bugged at the unbelievable sight.*
bug off, *Slang.* go away and stop being a nuisance.
bug out, a *Informal.* of an army camp, move to another location. **b** *Slang.* (*imperative*) go away; mind your own business.
⟨? < obsolete Welsh *bwg* ghost⟩

bug•a•boo [ˈbʌgə,bu] *n., pl.* **-boos.** a cause of fear; something, usually imaginary, that frightens: *The child was frightened by tales of witches, ghosts, and other bugaboos.* ⟨< *bug* bogy + *boo*⟩

bug•bane [ˈbʌg,bein] *n.* a perennial plant (genus *Cimicifuga*) of the buttercup family, having spikes of small white flowers whose unpleasant smell is supposed to drive insects away.

bug•bear [ˈbʌg,bɛr] *n.* **1** bugaboo. **2** something that causes difficulties; a snag. ⟨< *bug* bogy + *bear*[2]⟩

bug–eyed [ˈbʌg ˌaɪd] *adj. Slang.* having eyes wide open and bulging, especially from wonder or excitement.

bug•ger [ˈbʌgər] *n., v.* —*n.* **1** a person who commits buggery; a sodomite. **2** *Slang.* a humorous term for a person or thing.
bugger all, *Slang.* nothing.
—*v.* commit buggery (with).
bugger around, *Slang.* trifle; meddle; fool around.
bugger up, *Slang.* foul up; make a mess of. ⟨< OF *bougre* < Med.L *Bulgarus* Bulgarian, the Eastern Orthodox Bulgarians being considered heretics⟩

bug•ger•y [ˈbʌgəri] *n.* sexual relations involving anal intercourse between a man and another person or an animal; sodomy.

bug•gy[1] [ˈbʌgi] *n., pl.* **-gies. 1** a light, four-wheeled carriage having a single large seat, and drawn by one horse. **2** a wheeled cart used for shopping in a grocery store, etc. **3** BABY CARRIAGE. **4** *Slang.* an old car. ⟨origin uncertain⟩

bug•gy[2] [ˈbʌgi] *adj.* **-gi•er, -gi•est. 1** swarming with bugs. **2** *Slang.* crazy. ⟨< *bug*⟩

bug•house [ˈbʌg,hʌus] *n., adj. Slang.* —*n.* a psychiatric hospital.
—*adj.* crazy.

bu•gle[1] [ˈbjugəl] *n., v.* **-gled, -gling.** —*n.* a wind instrument like a small trumpet, made of brass or copper, and sometimes having keys, or valves. Bugles are sometimes used in the armed services for sounding calls and orders.
—*v.* **1** blow a bugle. **2** direct or summon by or as if by blowing on a bugle. ⟨ME < OF < L *buculus*, dim. of *bos* ox; with reference to early hunting horns⟩

bu•gle[2] [ˈbjugəl] *n.* a small, tubular glass or plastic bead used for trimming on dresses, blouses, etc. Also called **bugle bead.** ⟨origin uncertain⟩

bu•gle[3] [ˈbjugəl] *n.* a low-growing plant (genus *Ajuga*) of the mint family, having blue, pink, or white flowers; ajuga.

bu•gler [ˈbjuglər] *n.* a person who plays a bugle, especially a skilled player.

bu•gle•weed [ˈbjugəl,wid] *n.* a plant (genus *Lycopus*) of the mint family, having small white or light blue flowers.

bu•gloss [ˈbjuglɒs] *n.* any of various weedy Eurasian plants of the borage family having bristly leaves and stems and small, bright blue flowers. Some species, such as *Lycopsis arvensis*, have become naturalized in North America. ⟨< F < L *buglossa* < Gk. *bouglōssos* ox tongue < *bous* ox + *glōssa* tongue⟩

bug–out [ˈbʌg ˌʌut] *n. Informal.* a move of an army camp to another location.

buhl [bul] *n.* See BOULLE.

buhr•stone [ˈbɜr,stoun] *n.* **1** a hard kind of rock containing a high proportion of silica, used for making grinding stones. **2** a grinding stone made of this rock. Also, **burrstone.** ⟨< *buhr*, var. of *burr*, probably of Scand. origin⟩

build [bɪld] *v.* **built** or (*archaic*) **build•ed, build•ing;** *n.* —*v.* **1** make by putting materials together; construct: *People build houses, dams, bridges, and roads.* **2** form gradually; develop: *to build a business, to build an empire.* **3** establish; base: *to build a case on facts.* **4** rely; depend: *We can build on that woman's honesty.* **5** make a structure: *We've bought the land, but we won't start to build until next year.* **6** order, supervise, or pay for the construction of (a building). **7** grow larger, heavier, etc., by increments: *The tension between the factions has been building.*
build in, build so as to include in the whole structure.
build up, a form gradually; develop: *The firm has built up a wide reputation for fair dealing.* **b** gather; come together: *Clouds were building up on the horizon.* **c** fill with houses, etc. **d** accumulate, causing congestion: *The traffic always builds up at the toll bridge at rush hours.* **e** promote: *They're using TV ads to build up their new product.* **f** encourage; foster the self-esteem of.
—*n.* a form, style, or manner of construction; structure or physique: *An elephant has a heavy build.* ⟨OE *byldan* < *bold* dwelling⟩

build–down [ˈbɪld ˌdaʊn] *n. Informal.* a slow reduction in the number of nuclear weapons and soldiers.

build•ed [ˈbɪldɪd] *v. Archaic.* a pt. and a pp. of BUILD.

build•er [ˈbɪldər] *n.* **1** a person or animal that builds. **2** a person in the construction business. **3** a component, usually an abrasive, added to a cleaning agent to improve its efficacy.

build•ing [ˈbɪldɪŋ] *n., v.* —*n.* **1** something built, such as a house, factory, barn, store, etc. **2** the business, art, or process of making houses, stores, bridges, ships, etc. **3** a group of rocks.
—*v.* ppr. of BUILD.

☛ *Syn.* **1. Building,** EDIFICE, STRUCTURE = something constructed. **Building** is the general word and has a wide range of uses because it does not suggest purpose, size, materials, etc.: *From the hill we could see the buildings in the city.* **Edifice** is a formal word, applying to a large and imposing building: *The cathedral is a handsome edifice.* **Structure** emphasizes the type of construction: *The new library is a fireproof structure.*

build•up or **build–up** [ˈbɪld ˌʌp] *n.* **1** the act or process of building up: *a buildup of military strength.* **2** favourable publicity in advance; promotion: *The actor received a tremendous buildup in the local papers before the play opened.* **3** congestion: *a traffic buildup.*

built [bɪlt] *v.* a pt. and a pp. of BUILD.

built–in [ˈbɪlt ˈɪn] *adj.* **1** built as part of a larger structure, especially a building; not detachable: *a built-in closet. We can't move the bookcase, because it's built-in.* **2** having as a part of one's nature, or as an integral part: *a built-in sense of humour.*

Bulb (def. 1): onion

bulb [bʌlb] *n.* **1** a kind of bud produced underground by certain plants, such as onions, lilies, and tulips, that permits the plants to survive cold or dry periods. It is in effect a compressed plant in a dormant state, consisting of a stem base, one or more growing buds, and root cells, surrounded by layers of fleshy leaves serving as a source of food. **2** any plant that produces bulbs. **3** a thick underground stem resembling a bulb, such as a corm or tuber. **4** LIGHT BULB. **5** the rounded end of any object: *the bulb of a thermometer.* ⟨< L *bulbus* < Gk. *bolbos* onion⟩ —**ˈbulb•less,** *adj.* —**ˈbulb,like,** *adj.*

bulb•ar [ˈbʌlbər] *adj.* of or having to do with a bulb-shaped organ, especially the medulla oblongata, which is the lowest part of the brain.

bul•bif•er•ous [bʌlˈbɪfərəs] *adj.* of a plant, having many small bulbs including those on the stem.

bul•bil [ˈbʌlbɪl] *n.* an aerial bud with fleshy scales, growing in the leaf axils or taking the place of flowers. ⟨< NL *bulbillus* < L *bulbus* bulb⟩

bulb•let [ˈbʌlblɪt] *n.* a small flower or vegetable bulb.

bulb•ous [ˈbʌlbəs] *adj.* **1** shaped like a bulb; rounded and swollen: *a bulbous nose.* **2** producing or growing from bulbs: *Daffodils are bulbous plants.*

bul•bul [ˈbʊl,bʊl] *n.* **1** any of a family (Pycnonotidae) of mainly brownish songbirds of tropical Asia and Africa. **2** a songbird often mentioned in Persian poetry, thought to be a nightingale. ⟨< Arabic or Persian⟩

Bul•gar [ˈbʌlgɑr] *or* [ˈbʊlgɑr] *adj. or n.* Bulgarian.

Bul•ga•ria [bʌlˈgɛriə] *n.* a republic in SE Europe.

Bul•gar•i•an [bʌlˈgɛriən] *n., adj.* —*n.* **1** a native or inhabitant of Bulgaria. **2** the Slavic language of the Bulgarians.
—*adj.* of or having to do with Bulgaria, its people, or their language.

bulge [bʌldʒ] *v.* **bulged, bulg•ing;** *n.* —*v.* **1** swell outward: *His pockets bulged with apples and candy.* **2** cause to swell outward: *The apples bulged her pockets.*
—*n.* **1** an outward swelling. **2** of a ship: **a** the bottom of the hull; bilge. **b** a structure attached outside the hull to protect it from mines, torpedoes, etc.; a blister. **3** a temporary increase: *The graph shows a bulge in the birth rate.* ⟨ME < OF *boulge* < L *bulga* bag⟩

bul•gur [ˈbʌlgər] *or* [ˈbʌlgʊr] *n.* a Middle Eastern cereal food made from cracked wheat. Also, **bulghur.** ⟨< Turkish⟩

bulg•y ['bʌldʒi] *adj.* **bulg•i•er, bulg•i•est.** having a bulge or bulges.
—'bul•gi•ness, *n.*

bu•lim•i•a [bə'limiə] *n.* an eating disorder characterized by alternate bouts of bingeing and purging or self-induced vomiting. Also, **bulimia nervosa.** **—bu'lim•ic,** *adj.*

bulk [bʌlk] *n., v., adj.* *—n.* **1** size, especially large or unwieldy size: *an elephant of great bulk.* **2** the largest part; main mass: *The ocean forms the bulk of the earth's surface.* **3** a ship's cargo or hold. **4** soft, undigested food which helps the body to eliminate solid waste.
in bulk, a loose, not in packages. **b** in large quantities.
—v. **1** have size or importance. **2** grow or cause to grow large; swell.
—adj. of or having to do with merchandise in bulk: *bulk buying, a bulk food store.* ⟨< Scand.; cf. O Icelandic *bulki* heap⟩
☛ *Syn. n.* **1.** See note at SIZE[1].

bulk carrier a lake freighter designed to carry bulk commodities such as ore and grain.

bulk•er ['bʌlkər] *n.* BULK CARRIER.

bulk•head ['bʌlk,hɛd] *n.* **1** one of the upright partitions dividing a ship into watertight compartments. **2** a similar partition in an aircraft, etc. **3** a wall or partition built to hold back water, earth, rocks, air, etc. **4** a boxlike structure covering the top of a staircase or other opening.

bulk•y ['bʌlki] *adj.* **bulk•i•er, bulk•i•est. 1** taking up much space; large: *Bulky shipments are often sent by freight.* **2** hard to handle; clumsy: *He dropped the bulky package of curtain rods twice.* **—'bulk•i•ly,** *adv.* **—'bulk•i•ness,** *n.*

bull[1] [bʊl] *n., v.* *—n.* **1** the adult male of cattle, buffalo, etc. **2** the adult male of the moose, whale, elephant, seal, and other large animals. **3** (*adjl.*) like a bull; large and strong. **4** a person whose size or loudness resembles that of a bull. **5** a person who tries to raise prices in the stock market, etc. Compare BEAR. **6** (*adjl.*) marked by or having to do with rising prices in the stock market, etc. Compare BEAR. **7** *Slang.* foolish or boastful, insincere talk. **8** bulldog. **9** *Esp. Brit.* bull's-eye. **10 Bull,** *Astronomy or astrology.* Taurus.
shoot the bull, *Slang.* talk idly; speculate or boast.
take the bull by the horns, deal bravely and directly with a dangerous or difficult situation.
—v. **1** push or force one's way. **2** try to raise prices of (stocks). **3** try to raise prices in (a stock market). **4** *Slang.* engage in glib, empty talk or foolish boasting; bluff: *She can bull her way through any oral exam.* ⟨ME *bole* < ON *boli.* Related to BULLOCK.⟩

bull[2] [bʊl] *n.* **1** *Roman Catholic Church.* a formal announcement, edict, or official order from the Pope. **2** the round lead seal attached to this document; bulla. ⟨< Med.L *bulla* document, seal < L *bulla* amulet, bubble⟩

bull[3] [bʊl] *n.* an absurd and amusing mistake in language, especially one that is self-contradictory. *Example*: *If you don't receive this letter, write and let me know.* ⟨origin uncertain⟩

bull. bulletin.

bul•la ['bʊlə] *n.* **1** BULL[2] (def. 2). **2** *Medicine.* blister.

bul•late ['bʊlɪt] *or* ['bʊleit] *adj.* **1** having blisters. **2** blistered or puckered in appearance, as some leaves. **3** swollen like a blister. ⟨< L *bullatus* < *bulla* a bubble⟩
☛ *Hom.* BULLET ['bʊlɪt].

bull•bait•ing ['bʊl,beitɪŋ] *n.* formerly, a sport like bearbaiting, with the dogs tormenting a chained bull. See also BEARBAITING.

bull•bat ['bʊl,bæt] *n.* a bird (*Chordeiles minor*) of the goatsucker family, common in Canada and having long wings and a slightly forked tail, a very small bill, and dark, mottled plumage; nighthawk. It is active during the day or night.

bull•cook ['bʊl,kʊk] *n.* a janitor or handyman in a lumber camp. In some camps it used to be his duty to prepare mash for the oxen used in hauling logs.

bull•dog ['bʊl,dɒg] *n., v.* **-dogged, -dog•ging.** *—n.* **1** a breed of heavily built dog with a large head and short hair. Bulldogs are not large, but they are very muscular and courageous. **2** (*adjl.*) like that of a bulldog: *bulldog courage.* **3** a large-calibre revolver with a short barrel. **4** *Cdn.* a kind of horsefly about the size of a bumblebee, having a vicious bite and a great appetite for blood. Also, **bulldog fly** or **bull fly.**
—v. in the western parts of Canada and the United States, throw (a steer, etc.) to the ground by grasping its horns and twisting its neck.

bulldog edition the first edition of a morning newspaper, which is sent to other places.

bull•doze ['bʊl,douz] *v.* **-dozed, -doz•ing. 1** move, clear, dig, or level with a bulldozer. **2** *Informal.* coerce (into doing something) by manipulation or threats; bully. ⟨back formation < *bulldozer*⟩

bull•doz•er ['bʊl,douzər] *n.* **1** a powerful tractor that moves dirt, etc., for grading, road building, etc., by means of a wide steel blade attached to the front. **2** *Informal.* one who bulldozes.

bul•let ['bʊlɪt] *n.* **1** a round or pointed piece of lead, steel, or other metal designed to be shot from a rifle, pistol, or other relatively small firearm. **2** *Printing.* a small dot used to draw attention to an item in a list. ⟨< F *boulette,* dim. of *boule* ball⟩
☛ *Hom.* BULLATE ['bʊlɪt].

bul•let•head ['bʊlɪt,hɛd] *n.* **1** a short, round head. **2** a person with such a head. **3** *Informal.* a stubborn, pig-headed person.

bul•let–head•ed ['bʊlɪt 'hɛdɪd] *adj.* having a round head.

bul•le•tin ['bʊlətɪn] *n., v.* *—n.* **1** a short statement of news: *In times of crisis newspapers publish bulletins about the latest happenings. Doctors issue bulletins about the condition of a sick person.* **2** a magazine or newspaper appearing regularly, especially one published by a club or society for its members. **3** a leaflet handed out in some churches, containing the order of service, announcements, etc.
—v. make known by a bulletin. ⟨< F < Ital. *bullettino,* double dim. of *bulla* bull[2]⟩

bulletin board a board or a sheet of cork, etc., used for posting notices.

bul•le•tin–board system ['bʊlətɪn ,bɔrd] *Computer technology.* a computer system that allows users to exchange information by providing facilities to post general announcements, leave messages for other users, download and upload programs and data, etc.

bul•let•proof ['bʊlɪt,pruf] *adj., v.* *—adj.* made so that a bullet cannot pass through: *a bulletproof jacket.*
—v. make bulletproof.

bullet train 1 any high-speed train such as the one in Japan. **2** the rail system for such a train.

bull fiddle *Informal.* DOUBLE BASS.

bull•fight ['bʊl,fəit] *n.* a traditional public performance or ritual in which a man, called a matador, confronts a fierce bull in an arena and performs a series of skilful manoeuvres in avoiding the horns of the charging bull, usually killing the bull with a sword. Bullfights are common in Spain, Mexico, Colombia, Peru, and Venezuela, but illegal in Canada.

bull•fight•er ['bʊl,fəitər] *n.* matador.

bull•fight•ing ['bʊl,fəitɪŋ] *n.* the act or ritual of fighting a bull in a public arena.

bull•finch ['bʊl,fɪntʃ] *n.* **1** a small, plump-bodied finch (*Pyrrhula pyrrhula*) found in the forests of the British Isles, Europe, and Asia, having a short bill and black head, wings, and tail. The male bullfinch has a pinkish breast and a bluish back, the female a brownish grey breast and back. **2** any of various other finches.

bull fly ['bʊl,flaɪ] *n.* BULLDOG (def. 4).

bull•frog ['bʊl,frɒg] *n.* any of a genus (*Rana*) of very large frogs found in North America, Africa, and India, the male having a loud call that has been compared to the bellow of a bull. The American bullfrog is olive green or reddish brown.

bull•head ['bʊl,hɛd] *n.* **1** any of several North American freshwater catfishes (genus *Ictalurus,* also called *Ameiurus*), such as the **brown bullhead** (*I. nebulosus*) of E and central North America. **2** any of various other large-headed fishes, such as the sculpin. **3** a stupid or stubborn fellow; a blockhead.

bull•head•ed ['bʊl,hɛdɪd] *adj.* stupidly stubborn; obstinate. **—'bull,head•ed•ness,** *n.* **—'bull,head•ed•ly,** *adv.*

bull•horn ['bʊl,hɔrn] *n.* a megaphone with an electric amplifier.

bul•lion ['bʊljən] *n.* **1** gold or silver in their untouched state. **2** bricks or bars of gold or silver. ⟨< AF *bullion* < *bouillir* boil; influenced by OF *billon* debased metal⟩
☛ *Hom.* BOUILLON ['bʊljən].

bull•ish ['bʊlɪʃ] *adj.* **1** like a bull. **2** marked by, tending toward, or expecting higher prices in the stock market. Compare BEARISH. **3** optimistic. **—'bull•ish•ly,** *adv.* **—'bull•ish•ness,** *n.*

bull mastiff a breed of large, powerful, thickset dog with a short brown or brindled coat, developed in the late 19th century in England from a cross between a bulldog and a mastiff.

bull•necked ['bʊl,nɛkt] *adj.* having a thick neck.

bull nose a contagious disease of pigs, characterized by swellings of the snout and mouth which are later sloughed off. It is caused by a bacillus (*Fusobacterium necrophorum*).

bull•ock ['bʊlək] *n.* **1** a castrated bull; an ox or steer. **2** a young bull. ⟨OE *bulluc* bull calf⟩

bull pen **1** *Baseball.* **a** a place outside the playing limits in which pitchers warm up during a game. **b** the pitchers in this area. **2** any place in which people are gathered together for a specific purpose. Also, **bullpen**.

bull ring **1** an enclosed arena for bullfights. **2** the floor of this arena. Also, **bullring**.

bull•roar•er ['bʊl,rɔrər] *n.* **1** a flat piece of wood tied to a string so as to produce a roaring sound when whirled in the air, used in religious rites by certain North American First Nations, Australian aborigines, etc. **2** a similar device used as a toy.

bull session an informal, rambling group discussion.

bull's–eye ['bʊl ,zaɪ] *n.* **1** the centre of a target. **2** a shot that hits the centre. **3** any answer, effort, etc., that is exactly right or meets an objective. **4** a thick disc of glass set in a roof, pavement, the deck or side of a ship, etc., to let in light. **5** a convex lens with a short focal distance, used to concentrate light. **6** a lantern with such a lens. **7** any small, round opening or window. **8** a small, hard, round candy.

bull•snake ['bʊl,sneik] *n.* a large North American snake (genus *Pituophis*) which eats mice and rabbits. It is not poisonous.

bull terrier a breed of strong, active dog, having a long head and stiff, usually white, hair, originally bred as a cross between a bulldog and a terrier.

bull thistle the common thistle (*Cirsium vulgare*), having purple brushlike flowers and spiny leaves. Although a native of Eurasia, it grows as an aggressive weed across southern Canada and the United States.

bull trout **1** SALMON TROUT. **2** DOLLY VARDEN TROUT.

bull•whip ['bʊl,wɪp] *n., v.* **-whipped, -whip•ping.** *—n.* a long, heavy leather whip.
—v. strike with a bullwhip.

bull work rough chores; manual labour: *He did the bull work around the camp.*

bul•ly ['bʊli] *n., pl.* **-lies;** *v.* **-lied, -ly•ing;** *adj., interj.* *—n.* a person who teases, frightens, or hurts smaller or weaker people.
—v. **1** be a bully. **2** frighten into doing something by noisy talk or threats.
—adj. **1** *Informal.* first-rate; excellent. **2** jovial; gallant; spirited.
—interj. Informal. bravo! well done! ⟨origin uncertain, probably < M.Du. *boele* an affectionate or reproachful term⟩

bully beef canned or pickled beef. ⟨? < F *bouilli* boiled beef < *bouillir* boil⟩

bully boy *Informal.* a man who is hired to carry out certain plans by force. **—'bul•ly-,boy,** *adj.*

bul•ly•rag ['bʊli,ræg] *v.* **-ragged, -rag•ging.** *Informal.* bully; tease; abuse.

bully tree balata.

bul•rush ['bʊl,rʌʃ] *n.* **1** any of a genus (*Typha*) of tall marsh plants found in North America, Europe, and Asia, having very long, stiff, flat leaves and long, thick, fuzzy, brown flower spikes; cat-tail: *Bulrushes are often used as decoration and also, sometimes, as torches outdoors.* **2** any of a genus (*Scirpus*) of grasslike marsh plants of the sedge family found in North America, Europe, and Asia, having long, spongy, usually leafless stems and small flowers growing in a cluster of spikelets: *The stems of the common bulrush of Europe and Asia are used for making mats, baskets, chair seats, thatch, etc.* **3** the papyrus of Egypt, also belonging to the sedge family. ⟨ME *bulrysche* < *bule* (see BULL[1], n. def. 2) + *rysche*, OE *rysc* rush⟩

bul•wark ['bʊlwərk] *n., v.* *—n.* **1** a support or safeguard; any thing, person, or idea that serves as a defence: *They believe that free speech is a bulwark of democracy. Her common sense was our bulwark during the crisis.* **2** an earthwork or other wall for defence against an enemy. **3** a breakwater for protection against the force of the waves. **4** Usually, **bulwarks,** *pl.* the part of a ship's side that extends above the deck level. See SCHOONER for picture.
—v. **1** defend; protect. **2** provide with a bulwark or bulwarks. ⟨ME *bulwerk*, apparently < *bole* + *work*, a work made of tree trunks. Akin to BOULEVARD.⟩

bum[1] [bʌm] *n., v.* **bummed, bum•ming;** *adj.* **bum•mer, bum•mest.** *Informal.* *—n.* **1** an idle or good-for-nothing person; loafer. **2** a tramp or vagrant. **3** a drunken spree. **4** a person who devotes himself or herself to a sport or recreation, to the exclusion of other activities or responsibilities: *a ski bum.*
on the bum, a living as a bum: *He spent two years on the bum.* **b** *Informal.* not functioning; in disrepair: *Our toaster is on the bum.*
the bum's rush, *Slang.* a forcible ejection (of a person from a place).
—v. Informal. **1** loaf around; idle about. **2** live by taking advantage of the kindness of other people. **3** get (something) by taking advantage of the kindness of other people: *She tried to bum a ride.*
bum (someone) **out,** *Slang.* disappoint; irritate; upset, etc.
—adj. **1** of poor quality. **2** injured or lame: *a bum knee.* **3** false or unfair: *a bum rap.* ⟨partly Scottish dial. *bum* a lazy, dirty person (a special use of *bum*[2]); partly a shortening of earlier American *bummer* loafer < G *Bummler*⟩ **—'bum•mer,** *n.*

bum[2] [bʌm] *n. Informal.* the fleshy part of a person's body, where the legs join the back; seat; buttocks; bottom. ⟨ME *bom*, probably < *botem* bottom⟩

bum•bail•iff [,bʌm'beilɪf] *n. Brit.* a bailiff or sheriff's officer, especially one employed in serving attachments and making arrests. ⟨< *bum*[2] + *bailiff*⟩

bum•ble ['bʌmbəl] *n., v.* **-bled, -bling.** *—n.* an awkward mistake.
—v. act in a bungling or awkward way; blunder; botch. ⟨origin uncertain, perhaps < *b(ung)* + *(st)umble*⟩

bum•ble•bee ['bʌmbəl,bi] *n.* any of a family (Bombini) of large bees, especially any of a genus (*Bombus*) of social bees having a thick, hairy body usually banded with yellow. ⟨< *bumble* < ME *bumme, bumbe* buzz + *bee*⟩

bum•ble•dom ['bʌmbəldəm] *n.* incompetent, officious people collectively. ⟨< *Bumble*, the pompous beadle in Dickens' *Oliver Twist*, + *-dom*⟩

bum•bling ['bʌmblɪŋ] *n., adj., v.* *—n.* an awkward blundering.
—adj. blundering; inefficient.
—v. ppr. of BUMBLE.

bum•boat ['bʌm,bout] *n.* a boat used for peddling small wares and provisions to ships in port or offshore. ⟨? < LG *Bumboot*, a broad-beamed boat⟩

bumf or **bumph** [bʌmf] *n. Slang.* useless and unwelcome paper material, especially when official. ⟨< *bumfodder* toilet paper⟩

bum•mer ['bʌmər] *n. Slang.* **1** a bad or depressing experience or time: *The whole day was a bummer.* **2** a person who lives at other people's expense.

bump [bʌmp] *v., n.* *—v.* **1** push or strike (against something fairly large or solid: *to bump one's head*). **2** move or proceed with bumps: *Our car bumped along the rough road.* **3** hit or come (against) with heavy blows: *That truck bumped our car.* **4** *Slang.* remove (someone) from an airplane seat or other reserved position; displace: *The local performer was bumped from the program in favour of a bigger name from abroad.* **5** *Slang.* (*used with* **up**) increase (a price, a bet, etc.).
bump into, a bump against. **b** *Informal.* meet by chance.
bump off, *Slang.* kill.
—n. **1** a blow, knock, or jolt. **2** a swelling caused by a blow or knock. **3** a projection or bulge: *a bump on a road.* **4** a rising air current that gives an aircraft a jolt. **5** an earthquakelike shock or concussion caused by rock subsidence in and around mines. ⟨? < Scandinavian, imitative⟩

bump•er ['bʌmpər] *n.* **1** the bar or bars of metal or hard rubber across the front and back of a car, bus, or truck that protect it from being damaged if bumped. **2** a person or thing that bumps. **3** a fender used to protect a boat or dock. **4** a cup or glass filled to the brim. **5** *Informal.* something unusually large of its kind. **6** (*adj.*) unusually large: *We had a bumper crop of wheat last year.*

bumper–to–bumper ['bʌmpər tə 'bʌmpər] *adj.* of a long line of vehicles, travelling very closely together and slowly.

bumper sticker a piece of gummed paper having a slogan, catchword, or witty saying printed on it, for sticking on the bumper of a motor vehicle.

bump•kin ['bʌmpkɪn] *n.* **1** a person from the country who is socially awkward in unfamiliar surroundings, especially in cities. **2** *Nautical.* a short spar which sticks out and is used for tying ropes. ⟨< MDu. *bommekyn* little barrel⟩

bump•tious ['bʌmpʃəs] *adj.* unpleasantly assertive or

conceited. ⟨< *bump*⟩ —**'bump•tious•ly,** *adv.* —**'bump•tious•ness,** *n.*

bump•y ['bʌmpi] *adj.* **bump•i•er, bump•i•est. 1** having bumps on the surface; uneven: *a bumpy road.* **2** causing bumps or jolts; rough: *a bumpy ride.* —**'bump•i•ly,** *adv.* —**'bump•i•ness,** *n.*

bun [bʌn] *n.* **1** a small piece of yeast dough that has been separately baked. Buns are often slightly sweetened and may contain spice, raisins, or fruit. **2** hair coiled at the back of the head in a knot suggesting a bun. ⟨ME *bunne*; origin uncertain⟩
☛ *Hom.* BONNE.

bu•na ['bjunə] *or* ['bunə] *n.* an artificial rubber made from butadiene. ⟨< *bu*(*tadiene*) + *Na*, symbol for sodium⟩

bunch [bʌntʃ] *n., v.* —*n.* **1** a group of things of the same kind growing, fastened, placed, or thought of together: *a bunch of grapes, a bunch of flowers.* **2** *Informal.* a group of people, animals, etc.: *They're a friendly bunch.* **3** *Informal.* a large quantity: *There is a whole bunch of paint in the basement.*
—*v.* **1** come together in one place: *The sheep bunched in the shed to keep warm.* **2** bring together and make into a bunch: *We have bunched the flowers for you to carry home.* —**'bunch•er,** *n.* ⟨ME *bunche*; origin uncertain⟩
☛ *Syn. n.* **1.** See note at BUNDLE.
☛ *Usage.* **Bunch.** Formal English limits the use of **bunch** to objects that grow together or can be fastened together: *a bunch of radishes, a bunch of flowers, a bunch of keys.* Informal English, however, clings to the older usage of **bunch,** applying it to a collection or group of any kind—including people: *A bunch of us meet at the Grill every night.*

bunch•ber•ry ['bʌntʃ,bɛri] *n., pl.* **-ries.** a small dogwood (*Cornus canadensis*) growing about 15-20 cm high, having showy blossoms consisting of four petal-like bracts surrounding a cluster of tiny flowers which mature into clusters of bright red berrylike fruits. The bunchberry is common throughout Canada.

bunch•flow•er ['bʌntʃ,flaʊər] *n.* a tall North American plant (*Melanthium virginicum*) of the lily family, having white flowers growing in clusters.

bunch grass any of various grasses that grow in clumps or tufts, such as brome.

bunch•y ['bʌntʃi] *adj.* **bunch•i•er, bunch•i•est. 1** having bunches. **2** growing in bunches. —**'bunch•i•ness,** *n.*

bun•co ['bʌŋkou] *n., pl.* **-cos;** *v.* **-coed, -co•ing.** *Informal.* —*n.* a scheme in which swindlers join to cheat an unsuspecting person. —*v.* swindle in this way. Also, **bunko.** ⟨short for *buncombe*⟩

bun•combe or **bun•cum** ['bʌŋkəm] *n. Informal.* bunkum.

Bund [bʊnd]; *German,* [bʊnt] *n., pl.* **Bün•de** ['bʏndə]. *German.* an association; society; league.

Bun•des•rat ['bʊndəs,rɑt]; *German,* ['bʊndəs,ʀat] *n.* **1** in Germany, the upper house of the federal legislature. **2** in Switzerland or the former German Empire, the federal council or chief executive authority. ⟨< G *Bund* league, federation + *Rat* council⟩

Bun•des•tag ['bʊndəs,tɑg]; *German,* ['bʊndəs,tak] *n.* in Germany, the lower house of the federal legislature.

Bun•des•wehr ['bʊndəs,vɛr] *n.* the federal defence forces of Germany.

bun•dle ['bʌndəl] *n., v.* **-dled, -dling.** —*n.* **1** a number of things tied or wrapped together. **2** a parcel or package. **3** *Informal.* a large number or amount; a bunch; a lot: *a bundle of money. The book gave us a bundle of new ideas.* **4** *Botany.* a collection of fibres that strengthens a plant or conducts water. **5** *Anatomy.* a collection of nerve or muscle fibres.
—*v.* **1** wrap or tie together; make into a bundle. **2** send or go away in a hurry; hustle (*usually used with* **off**): *They bundled him off to the hospital in spite of his protests.* **3** collect; gather together in a mass. **4** share a bed with one's sweetheart while fully dressed (a courting custom formerly practised especially in New England).
bundle up, dress warmly: *Make sure you bundle up when you go out.* ⟨< ME *bundel* cf. MDu. *bondel.* Akin to BIND.⟩
—**'bun•dler,** *n.*
☛ *Syn. n.* **1, 2. Bundle,** BUNCH, PARCEL = something fastened or wrapped together. **Bundle** suggests a number of things of the same or different sizes and shapes bound or wrapped together, often clumsily: *We gave away several bundles of old newspapers and magazines.* **Bunch** suggests a number of things of the same kind bound or fastened together, usually closely and neatly: *I bought a bunch of flowers.* **Parcel** suggests one or more things wrapped and tied neatly for mailing or carrying: *I had too many parcels to carry on the bus.*

bundle of nerves a person in a state of extreme nervousness and tension: *By the time we got there, he was a bundle of nerves.*

Bundt pan or **mould** [bʊnt] *Trademark.* a cake pan with a hollow centre tube and fluted sides.

bung [bʌŋ] *n., v.* —*n.* **1** a stopper for closing the hole in the side or end of a barrel, keg, or cask. **2** bunghole.
—*v. Brit. Slang.* hurl; throw.
bung up, a close (a bunghole) with a stopper. **b** stop up; choke up. **c** *Slang.* bruise. ⟨probably < MDu. *bonghe*⟩

bun•ga•low ['bʌŋgə,lou] *n.* a one-storey house, often small; a house having no living space above the main floor. ⟨< Hind. *bangla* of Bengal⟩

Bun•gay or **Bun•gi** ['bʌŋgɪ] *n.* a member of a First Nations people of the Assiniboine valley.

Bun•gee ['bʌŋgi] *n.* **1** a lingua franca spoken in the 19th century in the Red River area in Manitoba. **2** an Ojibwa or Salteaux.

bun•gee ['bʌndʒi] *n.* a tension device, such as a set of springs, an elastic cable, or a rubber cord, used in an aircraft to assist in moving the controls, on other vehicles to secure loads, etc. ⟨origin unknown⟩

bungee jumping the sport of leaping off a bridge or other high place, with an elasticized cable tied to one's ankles for safety.

bung•hole ['bʌŋ,houl] *n.* a hole in the side or end of a barrel, keg, or cask through which it is filled and emptied.

bun•gle ['bʌŋgəl] *v.* **-gled, -gling;** *n.* —*v.* spoil (something) by doing or making in a clumsy, unskilful way.
—*n.* a clumsy, unskilful performance or piece of work. ⟨origin uncertain⟩ —**'bun•gler,** *n.* —**'bun•gling•ly,** *adv.*

bun•ion ['bʌnjən] *n.* an enlargement of the first joint of the big toe, caused by the toe having been permanently bent inwards, due to ill-fitting shoes. ⟨? < obsolete *bunny* a swelling⟩

bunk¹ [bʌŋk] *n., v.* —*n.* **1** a narrow bed attached to a wall like a shelf. **2** a narrow bed, usually one of two or occasionally three built one above the other. **3** *Informal.* any place to sleep.
—*v.* **1** *Informal.* spend the night (*at*): *It was too late to go home so Brigitta bunked at our house.* **2** sleep in or occupy a makeshift bed: *We bunked in an old barn.* **3** provide with a bunk or bed: *This cabin bunks three people.* ⟨? < *bunker*⟩

bunk² [bʌŋk] *n. Slang.* insincere talk; humbug; bunkum. ⟨short for *buncombe*⟩

bunk bed 1 one of two or occasionally three beds, usually built one above the other. **2** the entire structure.

bunk•er ['bʌŋkər] *n., v.* —*n.* **1** a bin or other place for storing fuel on a ship. **2** fuel oil in bulk; BUNKER FUEL. **3** a sandy hollow or mound of earth on a golf course, constituting an obstacle. **4** a steel-and-concrete fortification, usually part of a defence system and built partly or entirely below ground.
—*v.* **1** hit (a golf ball) into a bunker. **2** supply (a ship) with coal or other fuel. ⟨origin uncertain⟩

bunker fuel or **oil** a thick, heavy oil transported in bulk for use as fuel, especially for ships.

bunk•house ['bʌŋk,hʌus] *n.* a building equipped with bunks for sleeping.

bun•ko ['bʌŋkou] See BUNCO.

bun•kum ['bʌŋkəm] *n. Informal.* insincere talk; humbug. Also, **buncum, buncombe.** ⟨after *Buncombe* Co., N.C., whose congressman kept making pointless speeches "for Buncombe"⟩

bun•ny ['bʌni] *n., pl.* **-nies.** a pet name for a rabbit. ⟨origin uncertain⟩

bun•ra•ku [bʊn'rɑku] *n.* a form of Japanese theatre in which life-size manikins are manipulated by two or three men dressed in black, while the voices are those of off-stage actors.

Bun•sen burner ['bʌnsən] a gas burner with a very hot, blue flame, used in laboratories. Air is let in at the base of the burner and mixed with gas. ⟨after Robert *Bunsen* (1811-1899), the German chemist who invented it⟩

bunt¹ [bʌnt] *v., n.* —*v.* **1** strike with the head or horns, as a goat does. **2** push; shove. **3** *Baseball.* hit (a ball) lightly so that it goes to the ground and rolls only a short distance.
—*n.* **1** push; shove. **2** *Baseball.* **a** a hit made by hitting the ball lightly so that it goes to the ground and rolls only a short distance. **b** a baseball that is bunted. ⟨Cf. *butt³*⟩ —**'bunt•er,** *n.*

bunt² [bʌnt] *n., v.* —*n.* **1** the central, bellying part of a square sail. **2** the bagging part of a fishing net.
—*v.* swell out; belly: *sails bunting before the wind.*
bunt up, haul (a sail) up to a yard. ⟨origin uncertain⟩

bunt³ [bʌnt] *n.* **1** a disease of wheat in which a parasitic fungus turns the centre kernels into a foul-smelling black powder. **2** the fungus itself. ⟨origin uncertain⟩

bun•ting[1] ['bʌntɪŋ] *n., v.* *—n.* **1** a thin cloth used for flags. **2** long pieces of cloth having the colours and designs of a flag, used to decorate buildings and streets on holidays and special occasions; flags. **3** sometimes, **bunting bag,** a baby's winter garment like a bag with a hood and no armholes or legholes, fastened up the front.
—v. ppr. of BUNT. ⟨? < ME *bonten* sift, since the cloth was used for sifting⟩

bun•ting[2] ['bʌntɪŋ] *n.* any of numerous finches, especially of the New World genus *Passerina* and the Old World genus *Emberiza.* See also INDIGO BUNTING, LARK BUNTING, SNOW BUNTING. ⟨origin uncertain⟩

bunt•line ['bʌntlɪn] *or* ['bʌnt,laɪn] *n.* a rope fastened to a sail, used to haul it up to the yard for furling. ⟨< *bunt,* middle part of a sail (origin uncertain), + *line[1]*⟩

Bun•yan ['bʌnjən] See PAUL BUNYAN.

buoy [bɔɪ] *or* ['bui] *n., v.* *—n.* **1** a floating object anchored on the water to warn or guide. Buoys mark hidden rocks or shallows, show the safe part of the channel, can be used to moor a boat, etc. **2** a cork or plastic belt, ring, or jacket used to keep a person from sinking; a life buoy or life preserver.
—v. **1** furnish or mark with a buoy or buoys. **2** keep from sinking (*often used with* **up**). **3** support or encourage (*often used with* **up**): *Hope buoyed him up when things began to go wrong.* ⟨< OF *boie* (< Gmc.; akin to E *beacon*) and MDu. *boeie* (< OF *boie*)⟩
☛ *Hom.* BOY [bɔɪ].

buoy•an•cy ['bɔɪənsi] *n.* **1** the power to float: *Wood has more buoyancy than iron.* **2** the power to keep things afloat: *Salt water has greater buoyancy than fresh water.* **3** a tendency to rise. **4** the ability to rise above or recover quickly from low spirits; light-heartedness; cheerfulness; hopefulness. **5** a body's loss in mass when immersed in a liquid.

buoy•ant ['bɔɪənt] *adj.* **1** able to float: *Wood and cork are buoyant in water; iron and lead are not.* **2** able to keep things afloat: *Air is buoyant; balloons float in it.* **3** tending to rise. **4** light-hearted; cheerful; hopeful: *Even in the hospital, her spirits were buoyant.* **—'buoy•ant•ly,** *adv.*

BUP British United Press.

bu•piv•a•caine [bju'pɪvə,kein] *n.* an anesthetic. *Formula:* $C_{18}H_{28}N_2O$

bu•pres•tid [bju'prɛstɪd] *n.* a beetle of the family Buprestidae, whose larvae feed on shrubs and trees. ⟨< NL < L *buprestis* < Gk. *bouprestis* a kind of poisonous beetle⟩

bur [bɜr] *n., v.* **burred, bur•ring.** See BURR.

bur. bureau.

bu•ran [bu'rɑn] *n.* a strong NE wind which blows across the Russian steppes, bringing snowstorms in the winter and duststorms in the summer. ⟨< Russian < Turkish⟩

Bur•ber•ry ['bɜrbəri] *n. Trademark.* a light coat of waterproof material.

bur•ble ['bɜrbəl] *v.* **-bled, -bling. 1** make a bubbling noise. **2** speak in a confused, excited manner. **3** *Aeronautics.* of an airflow, cease to blow smoothly, as over an aircraft wing presented at too sharp an angle. ⟨probably imitative⟩
—'bur•bler, *n.*

bur•bot ['bɜrbət] *n., pl.* **-bot** or **-bots.** a freshwater food fish (*Lota lota*) having a slender body, related to the cod. ⟨< F *bourbotte* < L *barba* beard; influenced by F *bourbe* mud⟩

burbs [bɜrbz] *n.pl. Informal.* the suburbs.

bur•den[1] ['bɜrdən] *n., v.* *—n.* **1** something carried; a load of things, duty, work, etc. **2** anything difficult to carry or bear; a heavy load. **3** the quantity of freight that a ship can carry; the mass of a ship's cargo.
—v. **1** put a burden on; load. **2** load too heavily; oppress. ⟨OE *byrthen.* Related to BEAR[1].⟩
☛ *Syn. n.* **1, 2.** See note at LOAD.

bur•den[2] ['bɜrdən] *n.* **1** the main idea or message: *The burden of his speech was the conservation of our natural resources.* **2** a repeated verse in a song; chorus; refrain. ⟨< MF *bourdon* humming, drone of bagpipe < LL *burda* pipe⟩

burden of proof the obligation of proving a statement or accusation that has been made. In any court case, the burden of proof lies with the accuser.

bur•den•some ['bɜrdənsəm] *adj.* hard to bear; very heavy or oppressive: *a burdensome tax, burdensome duties.*
—'bur•den•some•ly, *adv.* **—'bur•den•some•ness,** *n.*
☛ *Syn.* See note at HEAVY.

bur•dock ['bɜrdɒk] *n.* any of a genus (*Arctium*) of weedy herbs of the composite family, having broad, heart-shaped leaves and prickly fruits. ⟨< *bur* + *dock[4]*⟩

bu•reau ['bjʊrou] *n., pl.* **bu•reaus** or **bu•reaux** ['bjʊrouz]. **1** dresser; chest of drawers. **2** a desk or writing table with drawers. **3** a certain kind of office or business: *a travel bureau.* **4** *Esp. U.S.* a branch of a government department. ⟨< F *bureau* desk (originally cloth-covered) < OF *burel,* dim. of *bure* coarse woollen cloth < LL *burra*⟩

bu•reauc•ra•cy [bjʊ'rɒkrəsi] *n., pl.* **-cies. 1** government by groups of officials. **2** the officials administering the government. **3** an excessive concentration of power in administrative offices. **4** excessive insistence on rigid routine; red tape. ⟨< F *bureaucratic* < *bureau* + *-cratie* < Med.L *cratia* < Gk. *kratia* rule⟩

bu•reau•crat ['bjʊrə,kræt] *n.* **1** an official in a bureaucracy. **2** a formal, pretentious government official.

bu•reau•crat•ese [bjʊ,rɒkrə'tiz] *n. Informal.* the language of bureaucrats, when it is long-winded, full of jargon, and often incomprehensible.

bu•reau•crat•ic [,bjʊrə'krætɪk] *adj.* **1** having to do with a bureaucracy or a bureaucrat. **2** arbitrary. **—,bu•reau'crat•i•cal•ly,** *adv.*

bu•reau•crat•ize [bjʊ'rɒkrə,taɪz] *v.* **-ized, -iz•ing.** make into a bureaucracy; cause to become bureaucratic.
—bu,reau•crat•i'za•tion, *n.*

bu•rette or **bu•ret** [bjʊ'rɛt] *n.* a graduated glass tube with a valve at the bottom, used for accurately measuring out small amounts of a liquid or gas. ⟨< F *burette,* dim. *buire* vase⟩

burg or **burgh** [bɜrg] *n. Informal.* a town or city. ⟨var. of *borough*⟩
☛ *Hom.* BERG.

bur•gee ['bɜrdʒi] *n.* a small, swallow-tailed flag or pennant, used on merchant ships and yachts. ⟨origin uncertain⟩

bur•geon ['bɜrdʒən] *v., n.* *—v.* **1** bud; sprout: *burgeoning leaves.* **2** grow; flourish: *the burgeoning talent of the young painter.*
—n. a bud or sprout. ⟨ME < OF *burjon,* apparently < Gmc.⟩

bur•ger ['bɜrgər] *n. Informal.* HAMBURGER (def. 2).
☛ *Hom.* BURGHER.

-burger *combining form.* **1** a fried or grilled patty of —— in a split bun: *fishburger.* **2** a HAMBURGER (def. 2) with ——: *cheeseburger.*

bur•gess ['bɜrdʒɪs] *n.* **1** the citizen of a borough. **2** *Cdn.* in Saskatchewan, a property owner who has the right to vote on money by-laws in a municipality. ⟨ME < OF *burgeis* < LL *burgensis* citizen. Doublet of BOURGEOIS.⟩

burgh [bɜrg] *n.* **1** burg. **2** in some countries, a chartered town. ⟨var. of *borough*⟩
☛ *Hom.* BERG.

burgh•er ['bɜrgər] *n.* a citizen of a burgh or town; citizen.
☛ *Hom.* BURGER.

bur•glar ['bɜrglər] *n.* a person who breaks into a dwelling to steal or commit some other crime. ⟨< Anglo-L *burglator,* ? partly < OE *burgbryce*⟩

bur•glar•i•ous [bər'glɛriəs] *adj.* having to do with burglary.
—bur'glar•i•ous•ly, *adv.*

bur•glar•ize ['bɜrglə,raɪz] *v.* **-ized, -iz•ing.** *Informal.* break into (a dwelling) to steal.

bur•glar•proof ['bɜrglər,pruf] *adj.* so strong or safe that burglars cannot break in.

bur•glar•y ['bɜrgləri] *n., pl.* **-glar•ies.** the act or criminal offence of breaking into a dwelling to steal or commit some other crime.

bur•gle ['bɜrgəl] *v.* **-gled, -gling.** *Informal.* burglarize. ⟨back formation < *burglar*⟩

bur•go•mas•ter ['bɜrgə,mæstər] *n.* in the Netherlands, Flanders, Austria, and Germany, the mayor of a town. ⟨< Du. *burgemeester* < *burg* borough + *meester* master⟩

bur•goo ['bɜrgu] *or* [bər'gu] *n.* formerly, a thick stew made from whatever meat and vegetable might be available. ⟨< Brit. dialect *burgoo* porridge⟩

Bur•gun•di•an [bər'gʌndiən] *n., adj.,* *—n.* a native or inhabitant of Burgundy, a region in E France.
—adj. of or having to do with Burgundy or its people.

bur•gun•dy ['bɜrgəndi] *n., adj.* *—n.* a dark purplish red.
—adj. having this colour.

Bur•gun•dy ['bɜrgəndi] *n., pl.* **-dies. 1** a red or white wine made in Burgundy, a region in E France. 2 a similar wine made elsewhere.

bur•i•al ['bɛriəl] *n.* **1** the act or process of putting a dead body in a grave, in a tomb, or in the sea; burying. **2** (*adjl.*) of or having to do with burying: *a burial service.*

burial ground a graveyard or cemetery.

bu•ried ['bɛrid] *or* ['bɜrɪd] *v.* pt. and pp. of BURY.
☛ *Hom.* BERRIED ['bɛrɪd].

bu•rin ['bjʊrɪn] *n.* **1** an engraver's pointed steel tool for cutting. **2** a similar instrument used to shape bone tools. ⟨< F < OF < Old Ital. *burino, borino* < Langobardic *boro* borer⟩

bur•ka ['bʊrkə] *n.* a veil worn by Muslim women that covers the body from head to toe. ⟨< Urdu *burqa* < Arabic⟩

burke [bɜrk] *v.* **burked, burk•ing. 1** murder by suffocation so as to leave no marks on the body. **2** suppress; hush up. ⟨< William *Burke* (1792-1829), hanged for murder; he suffocated his victims so that he could sell their unmarked bodies for dissection⟩

Bur•ki•na Fa•so [bʊr'kinə 'fɑsou] *n.* a country in W Africa. See SENEGAL for map.

Bur•kitt's lym•pho•ma ['bɜrkɪts lɪm'foumə] *n.* a cancerous tumour in lymphoid tissue, found in the lymph nodes and bone marrow of children in temperate countries, and in the jaws of children in Africa.

burl [bɜrl] *n., v.* —*n.* a knot in wool, cloth, or wood.
—*v.* remove knots from. ⟨< MF *bourle* < LL *burra* flock of wool⟩
☛ *Hom.* BIRL.

bur•lap ['bɜrlæp] *n.* coarse and heavy plain-weave fabric made of jute, hemp, or cotton, used mainly for making sacks, wall coverings, draperies, and sometimes clothing. ⟨ME *borel* coarse cloth + *lappa* garment flap⟩

bur•lesque [bər'lɛsk] *n., adj., v.* **-lesqued, -les•quing;** —*n.* **1** a literary or dramatic composition in which a serious subject is treated ridiculously, or with mock seriousness: *The movie is a burlesque of the classical detective story.* **2** a cheap or debasing imitation or representation; mockery: *making a burlesque of parliamentary democracy.* **3** theatre entertainment featuring broadly humorous or bawdy skits or jokes, striptease, etc.
—*adj.* of, having to do with, or characteristic of burlesque.
—*v.* imitate or represent in a humorous or mocking way. ⟨< F < Ital. *burlesco* < *burla* jest⟩ **—bur'les•quer,** *n.*

bur•ley or **Bur•ley** ['bɜrli] *n., pl.* **-leys.** a kind of thin-leaved tobacco. ⟨origin uncertain⟩
☛ *Hom.* BURLY.

bur•ly ['bɜrli] *adj.* **-li•er, -li•est. 1** big, strong, and sturdy; husky. **2** bluff; rough. ⟨OE *borlīce* excellently⟩ **—'bur•li•ly,** *adv.* **—'bur•li•ness,** *n.*
☛ *Hom.* BURLEY.

Bur•ma ['bɜrmə] *n.* Myanmar.

Bur•man ['bɜrmən] *n. or adj.* Burmese.

bur marigold a plant (genus *Bidens*) of the composite family, having yellow flowers like daisies, and fruit with spines.

Bur•mese [bər'miz] *n., pl.* **-mese;** *adj.* —*n.* **1** a native or inhabitant of Burma. **2** the Sino-Tibetan language of the Burmese. **3** BURMESE CAT.
—*adj.* of or having to do with Burma, its people, or their language.

Burmese cat a breed of cat resembling the Siamese but having a dark brown or grey coat.

burn[1] [bɜrn] *v.* **burned** or **burnt, burn•ing;** *n.* —*v.* **1** be on fire; use up fuel while giving off heat and light and gases; blaze: *The campfire burned all night.* **2** set on fire; cause to burn, especially in order to destroy: *They raked up all the leaves and burned them.* **3** be destroyed, damaged, or ruined by fire or heat: *Many important documents burned in the fire. I forgot the roast and it burned to a crisp.* **4** ruin, damage, or injure by fire, heat, acid, electricity, or radiation: *I burned the roast. She burned her finger when she touched the hot pan.* **5** make or produce by burning: *The cigar ashes burned a hole in the tablecloth.* **6** become sunburned: *Do you burn easily?* **7** be dissipated by warm sunshine (*used with* **off**): *The fog burned off before noon.* **8** use as fuel: *The stove burns wood or coal. Our car burns too much gas.* **9** fire (a rocket engine): *The commander gave the order to burn the engines.* **10** give light; shine, as if from fire: *Lamps were burning in every room.* **11** feel hot: *the burning sands of the desert. Her forehead burned with fever.* **12** produce or feel pain as if from fire or heat: *My hands were burning from the cold. That ointment burns.* **13** be or become very excited, eager, angry, etc.: *burning with enthusiasm, burning with resentment. It made me burn to see the way he got the better of them.* **14** *Informal.* make angry or annoyed (*usually used with* **up**): *Her smug attitude really burns me up.* **15** harden, glaze, etc., by fire or heat: *to burn bricks.* **16** transform into energy by metabolism (*usually used with* **off** *or* **up**): *He's trying to burn off some weight by jogging.* **17** cauterize. **18** disappoint; deceive; defraud: *I got burned in that deal.*

burn down, a burn to the ground: *Their house burned down but most of their possessions were saved.* **b** burn less strongly as fuel gets low: *Get more wood—the fire's beginning to burn down.*

burn (one's) **boats** or **bridges,** cut off all means of retreat for oneself; commit oneself to a particular course: *She burned her boats when she resigned from her old job before she had found a new one.*

burn out, a destroy the inside or contents of by burning: *The store was completely burned out, leaving just a shell.* **b** cease to burn; become extinguished: *The campfire had burned out and we were in darkness.* **c** make or become unserviceable; make or become worn out, especially through long or improper use: *to burn out a motor. One of the light bulbs is burned out.* **d** deprive of a home through fire: *The family was burned out last year and had to live with relatives for two months. The marauders burned the villagers out of their homes.* **e** bring to a state of physical, mental, or emotional exhaustion: *He burned himself out with worry and overwork.*

burn up, burn completely: *By the time the police got there, the papers were burned up.*

have (something) **to burn,** have enough of something, usually money or time, to waste.

—*n.* **1** an injury caused by fire, heat, acid, electricity, or radiation: *How do you treat a burn?* **2** a burned place or spot: *Those are cigarette burns on the floor.* **3** a sunburn. **4** the firing of a rocket engine, especially to change the course of a spacecraft in flight: *The burn lasted 43 seconds.* ⟨coalescence of OE *beornan* be on fire and OE *bærnan* consume with fire⟩ **—'burn•a•ble,** *adj.*

☛ *Syn. v.* **3, 4. Burn,** SCORCH, SEAR = to injure or be injured by fire, heat, or acid. **Burn,** the general word, suggests any degree of damage from slight injury to destruction by fire, heat, or acid: *The toast burned.* **Scorch** = to burn the surface enough to discolour it, sometimes to damage the texture, by heat or fire: *The cigarette scorched the paper.* **Sear** = to burn or scorch the surface enough to dry or harden it, by heat, fire, or acid, and applies particularly to burning the tissues of people or animals: *Wounds are cauterized by searing.*

☛ *Usage.* **Burn.** The past tense and past participle of **burn** are either **burned** or **burnt.** Many people keep **burned** for the verb and use **burnt** when the participle is adjectival: *They hastily burned all the old letters before they left. The partially burnt papers gave us little help in solving the mystery.*

burn[2] [bɜrn] *n. Scottish.* a small stream; creek; brook. ⟨OE *burna*⟩

burn•er ['bɜrnər] *n.* **1** the part of a stove, furnace, etc., where the flame or heat is produced. **2** an apparatus or part that works by burning: *an oil burner. A combustion chamber in a jet engine is sometimes called a burner.* **3** any person or thing that burns.

on the back burner, *Informal.* in or into a state of temporary inactivity; in or into abeyance: *The issue was put on the back burner until after the election.*

bur•net ['bɜrnɪt] *n.* **1** a plant (genus *Sanguisorba*) of the rose family, having red, white, purple, or green flowers. **2** a herb (*Poterium sanguisorba*) having edible leaves also used to make a herbal tea. ⟨ME < OF *burnet, brunet*⟩

burn•ing ['bɜrnɪŋ] *adj., v.* —*adj.* **1** glowing hot; hot. **2** vital; urgent: *a burning issue.*
—*v.* ppr. of BURN. **—'burn•ing•ly,** *adv.*

burning bush any of a number of American bushes (genus *Euonymus*) bearing scarlet fruit or leaves.

burning glass a convex lens used to produce heat or set fire to a substance by focussing the sun's rays on it.

bur•nish ['bɜrnɪʃ] *v. or n.* polish; shine. ⟨ME < OF *burniss-*, a stem of *burnir* make brown, polish < *burn* brown < Gmc.⟩ **—'bur•nish•er,** *n.*

bur•noose or **bur•nous** [bər'nus] *or* ['bɜrnus] *n.* **1** a long, loose cloak with a hood, traditionally worn by Arabs. **2** a similar garment worn by women or men for casual wear. ⟨< F *burnous* < Arabic *burnus*⟩

burn•out ['bɜrn,ʌut] *n.* **1** a failure due to burning or extreme heat. **2** the termination of operation of a jet or rocket engine, because the fuel has been either used up or shut off. **3** the point at which burnout occurs. **4** mental and physical exhaustion through overwork.

burn•sides or **Burn•sides** ['bɜrn,saɪdz] *n.pl.* a growth of hair on the cheeks but not on the chin. Also, **sideburns.** ⟨after Gen. A.E. *Burnside*⟩

burnt [bɜrnt] *v.* a pt. and a pp. of BURN[1].
☛ *Usage.* See note at BURN[1].

burnt offering 1 the burning of an animal, harvest fruits, etc. on an altar as a religious sacrifice. **2** the thing so burned. **3** anything offered as a sacrifice.

burnt sienna 1 a dark brown colour. **2** a pigment of this colour, especially when made by burning raw sienna to powder.

burnt umber 1 a reddish brown colour. **2** a pigment of this colour.

bur oak a white oak (*Quercus macrocarpa*) of central and E North America having acorns partly enclosed in a deep cup covered with large, knobby scales.

burp [bɜrp] *Informal. n., v. —n.* a belch.
—v. **1** belch. **2** cause to belch: *to burp a baby.* ⟨imitative⟩

burr[1] or **bur** [bɜr] *n., v. —n.* **1** the prickly, clinging seedcase, fruit husk, or flowers of various plants. **2** a plant bearing burrs. **3** a person or thing that clings like a burr. **4** a rough ridge or edge left by a tool on metal, wood, etc., after cutting or drilling it. **5** any of several small cutting tools with a rough head, such as a dentist's drill.
—v. **1** remove burrs from. **2** leave a rough edge or ridge on. ⟨ME, probably < Scand.; cf. Danish *borre* burdock⟩ **—'bur•ry,** *adj.*
☛ *Hom.* BIRR.

burr[2] [bɜr] *n., v. —n.* **1** a prominent trilling of *r*, as in Scottish pronunciation. **2** a pronunciation in which *r* sounds are trilled: *a Scottish burr.* **3** a whirring sound.
—v. **1** pronounce (*r*) with a trill: *He burrs his r's.* **2** speak with a burr. **3** make a whirring sound. ⟨probably imitative⟩ **—'bur•ry,** *adj.*
☛ *Hom.* BIRR.

burr[3] [bɜr] *n.* **1** a washer placed on the end of a rivet before swaging it. **2** a disk or blank punched out of a sheet of metal. ⟨ME *burwe* circle < Scand.; Cf. Icelandic *borg* wall⟩
☛ *Hom.* BIRR.

bur•ri•to [bʊ'ritou] *n.* a Mexican dish consisting of a wheat tortilla rolled around a filling of ground beef, beans, etc., and often topped with melted cheese.

bur•ro ['bɜrou] *n., pl.* **-ros.** a small donkey, especially one used as a beast of burden in Latin America and the SW United States. ⟨< Sp. *burro* < *burrico* small horse < LL *burricus*⟩
☛ *Hom.* BOROUGH, BURROW.

bur•row ['bɜrou] *n., v. —n.* **1** a hole dug in the ground by an animal for refuge or shelter: *Rabbits live in burrows.* **2** a similar passage for dwelling, shelter, or refuge.
—v. **1** dig (a hole, etc.) in the ground: *The mole soon burrowed out of sight.* **2** live in burrows. **3** hide. **4** dig; make burrows in: *Rabbits have burrowed the ground near the river.* **5** make a thorough search. ⟨Cf. OE *beorg* burial place, *byrgen* grave⟩
☛ *Hom.* BOROUGH, BURRO.

bur•row•er ['bɜrouər] *n.* one who burrows.

burrowing owl a small round-headed owl (*Speotyto cunicularia*) of the interior of British Columbia and the prairies, having no ear tufts, long, slim, unfeathered legs, and a short tail. Its plumage is basically sandy, with brown and white markings. It is active by day and by night, especially on the ground, and nests in abandoned mammalian burrows.

burr•stone ['bɜr,stoun] *n.* See BUHRSTONE.

bur•sa ['bɜrsə] *n., pl.* **-sae** [-si] *or* [-saɪ] or **-sas.** a sac or pouch in the body, especially one located between joints and containing a lubricating fluid. ⟨< LL *bursa* < Gk. *byrsa* hide, wineskin. Doublet of BOURSE, PURSE.⟩

bur•sar ['bɜrsər] *or* ['bɜrsɑr] *n.* a treasurer, especially of a university or college. ⟨< Med.L *bursarius* < LL *bursa* purse⟩

bur•sa•ry ['bɜrsəri] *n., pl.* **-ries. 1** a grant of money to a student at a college or university. **2** a treasury, especially of a college or university.

burse [bɜrs] *n.* **1** a purse. **2** a BURSARY (def. 1) **3** in the Roman Catholic church, a silk case for carrying the altar cloth used in Communion. ⟨< F *bourse* a purse, exchange⟩

bur•se•ra ['bɜrsərə] *adj.* of or having to do with the family Burseraceae of bushes and trees, including the balm of Gilead and myrrh. ⟨< NL genus name, after J. *Burser* (1593-1649), German botanist⟩

bur•si•tis [bər'saitɪs] *n.* inflammation of a bursa, usually in the shoulder or the hip. ⟨*bursa* + *-itis*⟩

burst [bɜrst] *v.* **burst, burst•ing;** *n. —v.* **1** fly apart suddenly and with force; explode; break open: *The balloon burst when it touched the light bulb.* **2** be full to the breaking point: *The granaries were bursting with grain. She is bursting with enthusiasm.* **3** go, come, do, etc., by force or suddenly: *He burst into the room. The door burst open. The sun burst through the clouds.* **4** open suddenly or violently: *The buds burst into bloom after the rain. She burst the lock with a screwdriver.* **5** begin an action suddenly in a way suggesting a break or explosion: *She burst into loud laughter. He burst into tears.* **6** cause to break open or into pieces; shatter: *to burst a blood vessel. The prisoner burst his chains.*
—n. **1** a sudden and violent issuing forth; sudden opening to view or sight. **2** a bursting; split; explosion. **3** an outbreak: *a burst of laughter.* **4** a sudden display of activity or energy: *a burst of speed.* **5** a series of shots fired by one pressure of the trigger of an automatic weapon. ⟨OE *berstan*⟩

bur•then ['bɜrðən] *n. or v. Archaic.* BURDEN[1].

Bu•run•di [bə'rʊndi] *n.* a country in central Africa.

Bu•run•di•an [bə'rʊndiən] *n., adj. —n.* a native or inhabitant of Burundi.
—adj. of or having to do with Burundi or its people.

bur•weed ['bɜr,wid] *n.* any of various plants having burrs, such as a cocklebur or burdock.

bur•y ['bɛri] *or* ['bɜri] *v.* **bur•ied, bur•y•ing. 1** put (a dead body) in the earth, a tomb, the sea, etc., usually with a ceremony of some kind. **2** cover up with earth or some other material: *The treasure was buried under the old oak tree. We found the essay buried under a lot of papers.* **3** hide from view: *He buried his face in his hands. The story of her exploits was buried in the back pages of the newspaper.* **4** occupy (oneself) with great concentration: *She buried herself in her work.* **5** put out of mind; put an end to: *They buried their differences and became friends again.* ⟨OE *byrgan*⟩ **—'bur•i•er,** *n.*
☛ *Hom.* BERRY ['bɛri].

bus [bʌs] *n., pl.* **bus•es** or **bus•ses;** *v.* **bused, bus•ing** *—n.* **1** a large motor vehicle with seats inside and sometimes also upstairs, used to carry passengers along a certain route. **2** *Informal.* an automobile or airplane. **3** (*adjl.*) of, having to do with, or for buses: *a bus driver, a bus depot.* **4** *Computer technology.* a hardware pathway in a computer, along which data is transferred. **5** busbar.
miss the bus, *Slang.* lose an opportunity.
—v. **1** transport or travel by bus: *She buses to work. We were bused to another airport.* **2** serve as BUS BOY. ⟨short for *omnibus*⟩
☛ *Hom.* BUSS.

bus. business.

bus•bar ['bʌs,bɑr] *n.* an electrical conductor or set of conductors to which several circuits are connected.

bus boy a waiter's assistant. He brings bread and butter, fills glasses, carries off dishes, etc.

bus•by ['bʌzbi] *n., pl.* **-bies. 1** a tall fur hat with a cloth bag hanging from the top over the right side, worn by hussar regiments. **2** BEARSKIN (def. 2). ⟨origin uncertain⟩

bu•ser•e•lin [bju'sɛrəlɪn] *n.* a drug used to treat prostate cancer.

bush [bʊʃ] *n., v., adj. —n.* **1** any woody plant having many separate branches starting from or near the ground; shrub: *A bush is usually smaller than a tree.* **2** forested wilderness, especially the vast forests beyond settled areas. **3** *Cdn.* a tree-covered area on a farm; a bush lot or woodlot: *The bush was right behind the houses.* **4** *Cdn.* on the Prairies, wooded land on the edge of the plains: *There's more bush west of here.* **5** anything bushlike, as a beard or tail.
beat around (or **about**) **the bush,** approach a matter in a roundabout way; not come straight to the point: *Tell me the truth right away and don't beat around the bush.*
—v. **1** spread out like a bush; grow thickly (*often used with* **out**). **2** set (ground) with bushes; cover with bushes. **3** *Cdn.* set out bushes or small trees to mark (a route) across a frozen river, lake, etc. (*often used with* **out**).
—adj. Slang. unpolished; rough-and-ready; suited to a BUSH LEAGUE: *The course, the play, and the golfers were all bush.* ⟨ME *busch*, var. of *busk* < ON *buskr* < Gmc. **busk-*⟩

bush. bushel.

bush baby any of several species (family Galagidae) of small, furry, nocturnal primates of the African forests. They move very nimbly on trees and have a childlike cry and large eyes.

bush bean a plant (*Phaseolus vulgaris*) bearing common beans, which grows like a bush. Compare POLE BEAN.

bush bread *Cdn.* bannock.

bush•buck ['bʊʃ,bʌk] *n.* a small antelope of the African forests (*Tragelaphus scriptus*), having spirally twisted horns.

bush•craft [ˈbʊʃ,kræft] *n.* knowledge of how to keep alive and find one's way in the bush.

bushed [bʊʃt] *adj., v. —adj.* **1** lost in the bush. **2** *Informal. Cdn.* acting strangely as a result of having been isolated from people. **3** *Informal.* exhausted.
—v. pt. and pp. of BUSH.

bush•el¹ [ˈbʊʃəl] *n.* **1** a unit for measuring the volume of grain, fruit, vegetables, and other dry things, equal to about 0.036 m³. One bushel is equal to 4 pecks or 32 quarts. **2** a container holding a bushel. ⟨ME < OF *boissiel*, dim. of *boisse* a measure⟩

bush•el² [ˈbʊʃəl] *v.* **-elled** or **-eled, -el•ling** or **-el•ing.** repair or alter (clothing). ⟨origin uncertain⟩ **—ˈbush•el•ler** or **ˈbush•el•er,** *n.*

bushel basket a round basket holding one bushel.

bush flying flying over and in remote areas.

Bu•shi•do or **bu•shi•do** [ˈbuʃi,dou] *or* [,buʃiˈdou] *n.* in Japan, the moral code of the Samurai, the feudal knights and warriors; chivalry. In its fully developed form, Bushido lasted from the 12th to the 19th centuries. ⟨< Japanese *bushi* warrior + *do* way⟩

bush•ing [ˈbʊʃɪŋ] *n.* **1** a removable metal lining used to protect parts of machinery from wear. **2** a metal lining inserted in a hole, pipe, etc., to reduce its size. **3** a lining for a hole, to insulate one or more wires or other electrical conductors passing through. ⟨< *bush* bushing < MDu. *busse* box⟩

bush jacket a jacket that comes down to the hips, usually made of cotton and in a sandy or olive colour, having a belt and patch pockets that fasten with buttons; worn in tropical climates, especially when on safari.

bush league *Slang.* **1** *Baseball.* a minor league. **2** any second-rate or unimportant group or organization: *Her brilliant performance in court shows that this lawyer is no longer in the bush league.* **—ˈbush-,league,** *adj.* **—ˈbush ,leag•uer,** *n.*

bush line *Cdn.* an airline that transports freight and passengers over the northern bush country.

bush lot *Cdn.* that part of a farm where the trees have been left standing to provide firewood, fence posts, etc.; woodlot.

bush•man [ˈbʊʃmən] *n., pl.* **-men. 1** *Australian.* a settler in the bush. **2** a person who knows much about living in the woods; woodsman. **3 Bushman, a** a member of a nomadic people of SW Africa. The Bushmen were traditionally hunters. **b** any of the Khoisan languages spoken by the Bushmen.

bush•master [ˈbʊʃ,mæstər] *n.* the largest poisonous snake (*Lachesis muta*) of Central and South America.

bush partridge *Cdn.* a bird found in Canada and the N United States; spruce grouse.

A bush partridge

bush pig a wild pig (genus *Potamochoerus*) that lives in African forests.

bush pilot *Cdn.* an aviator who does most of his or her flying in the bush country of the far north.

bush•rang•er [ˈbʊʃ,reindʒər] *n.* **1** a person who lives in the bush. **2** *Australian.* a criminal who hides in the bush and lives by robbery.

bush telegraph 1 any of various means of communication between people in wild country: *The call to arms seemed to have spread instantly over the whole area by the amazing bush telegraph.* **2** GRAPEVINE (def. 2): *I heard on the bush telegraph that you were being nominated for president of our club.*

bush•tit [ˈbʊʃ,tɪt] *n.* a small brownish grey bird (*Psaltriparus minimus*) of southwestern British Columbia, having a short bill and a long tail. It lives in woodland and makes a large, complicated nest.

bush•wa or **bush•wah** [ˈbʊʃwɑ] *or* [ˈbʊʒwɑ] *n. Slang.* nonsense; rubbish.

bush•whack [ˈbʊʃ,wæk] *v.* **1** live or work in the bush or backwoods. **2** beat, cut, or make one's way through the bush. **3** ambush or raid, as in guerrilla warfare.

bush•whack•er [ˈbʊʃ,wækər] *n.* **1** a person who lives or works in the bush or backwoods. **2** a scythe for cutting bushes. **3** a guerrilla fighter.

bush•work•er [ˈbʊʃ,wɜrkər] *n. Cdn.* a person who works in the bush, especially a logger.

bush•y [ˈbʊʃi] *adj.* **bush•i•er, bush•i•est. 1** spreading out like a bush; growing thickly: *a bushy beard.* **2** overgrown with bushes: *a bushy hill.* **—ˈbush•i•ness,** *n.*

bus•ied [ˈbɪzid] *v.* pt. and pp. of BUSY.

bus•i•ly [ˈbɪzəli] *adv.* in a busy manner; actively.

busi•ness [ˈbɪznɪs] *n.* **1** activities of buying and selling; trade; commercial dealings: *This store does a big business.* **2** a commercial enterprise; an industrial establishment: *a bakery business. They sold their business for ten million dollars.* **3** whatever one is busy at; one's work or occupation: *Business comes before pleasure.* **4** a matter or affair: *His dismissal was a sad business.* **5** the right to act; responsibility: *It's not your business to decide what I should do.* **6** a special job or concern: *My business is to find out who was involved in the cover-up.* **7** (*adjl.*) used for or having to do with business: *a business suit, business envelopes.* **8** a group of ferrets. **9** *Theatre.* a movement or action in a play to add realism, reveal character, etc.
in business, all set for operation: *Once our new computers arrive, we'll be in business.*
like nobody's business, as fast or as hard as one can.
mean business, *Informal.* be in earnest; be serious.
mind (one's) **own business,** avoid interfering in the affairs of others. ⟨< *busy* + *-ness*⟩
☛ *Syn.* **3.** See note at OCCUPATION.

business card a calling card for use in business, printed with the owner's name, position, business address and telephone number, etc.

business college an institution that gives training in business-related subjects, especially secretarial skills such as shorthand, typewriting, and office procedures.

business end *Informal.* the area or part of something that does the important or essential work: *The nib is the business end of a pen.*

busi•ness•like [ˈbɪznɪs,ləik] *adj.* having system and method; well-managed; practical: *He ran his store in a businesslike manner.*

busi•ness•man [ˈbɪznəs,mæn] *or* [ˈbɪznɪsmən] *n., pl.* **-men. 1** a man in business. **2** a man who is good at business: *He's no businessman.*

busi•ness•per•son [ˈbɪznəs,pɜrsən] *n.* a businessman or businesswoman.

business school BUSINESS COLLEGE.

busi•ness•wom•an [ˈbɪznəs,wʊmən] *n., pl.* **-wom•en.** [-,wɪmɪn] **1** a woman in business. **2** a woman who is good at business: *She's more of a businesswoman than her mother.*

busk•er [ˈbʌskər] *n. Esp. Brit.* a strolling entertainer of passers-by, theatre line-ups, subway patrons, etc. ⟨< dial. *busk* peddle, provide entertainment, etc.⟩

bus•kin [ˈbʌskɪn] *n.* **1** a boot reaching to the calf or knee, especially an open laced boot worn in ancient times. **2** a similar boot having a very thick sole, worn by actors in Greek and Roman tragedies. **3** tragedy; tragic drama. Compare SOCK¹. ⟨probably < OF *brousequin* < MDu. *brosekin*⟩

bus•king [ˈbʌskɪŋ] *n.* the activity of buskers; street entertainment.

bus•man [ˈbʌsmən] *n.* a conductor or driver of a bus.

busman's holiday a holiday spent in doing something similar to what one does at one's daily work: *A letter carrier who goes for a walk on her day off is taking a busman's holiday.*

bu•spi•rone [bjuˈspaɪroun] *n.* a drug used to treat anxiety.

buss [bʌs] *v. or n. Archaic or dialect.* kiss. ⟨probably < G dialect *bus*, Welsh and Gaelic *bus* kiss, lip⟩
☛ *Hom.* BUS.

bus•ses [ˈbʌsɪz] *n.* a pl. of BUS.

bust¹ [bʌst] *n.* **1** a piece of sculpture representing a person's head, shoulders, and chest. **2** the breasts of a woman. **3** the measurement around a woman's body at the level of the breasts: *a 92 cm bust.* ⟨< F < Ital. < L *bustum* funeral monument⟩

bust² [bʌst] *v.* **1** *Slang or dialect.* burst. **2** *Slang.* make or become bankrupt. **3** *Informal.* punch; hit: *He busted me on the nose.* **4** *Slang.* **a** arrest: *She was busted for possessing stolen goods.* **b** raid. **5** *Slang.* reduce to a lower rank; demote: *He was busted to private.* **6** *Slang.* break or break down: *Don't bust my watch.* **7** tame: *bronco busting.* **8** break up (a monopoly, etc.).
—n. **1** *Slang.* a failure; flop. **2** *Informal.* a punch: *I gave him a bust*

on the head. 3 *Informal.* spree. 4 *Slang.* a raid or arrest. ⟨var. of *burst*⟩

bus•tard ['bʌstərd] *n.* any of a family (Otididae) of large game birds having long legs and heavy bodies, found on the deserts and plains of Africa, Europe, and Asia. ⟨blend of OF *bistarde* and *oustarde*, both < L *avis tarda* slow bird⟩

–busted *combining form.* having a certain kind of bust: *small-busted = having a small bust.*

bust•er ['bʌstər] *n. Slang.* 1 boy, fellow, etc. (*used as a form of address*): *Look, buster, don't talk to me like that.* 2 something remarkable or outstanding. 3 a dashing fellow. 4 a wild frolic; spree. 5 *Australian.* a terrific gale.

bus•tic ['bʌstɪk] *n.* a tropical tree (*Dipholis salicifolia*) of the sapodilla family, yielding a dark, hard wood used in cabinetmaking.

bus•tier ['bustjei] *n.* a tight-fitting, sleeveless and strapless bodice, usually worn under the clothes.

bus•tle[1] ['bʌsəl] *v.* **-tled, -tling;** *n.* —*v.* 1 be noisily busy and in a hurry. 2 make (others) hurry or work hard.
—*n.* noisy or excited activity: *There was a great bustle as the party broke up.* ⟨? imitative⟩ —**'bus•tler,** *n.*
☛ *Syn. n.* See note at STIR[1].

bus•tle[2] ['bʌsəl] *n.* a pad or framework used in the late 19th century to puff out the upper back part of a woman's skirts. ⟨? special use of *bustle*[1]⟩

bust–up ['bʌst ˌʌp] *n. Slang.* 1 a quarrel. 2 a fight.

bu•sul•phan [bju'sʌlfən] *n.* a drug used to treat leukemia. *Formula*: $C_6H_{14}O_6S_2$

bus•y ['bɪzi] *adj.* **bus•i•er, bus•i•est;** *v.* **bus•ied, bus•y•ing.**
—*adj.* 1 working; active: *a busy person.* 2 in use: *I tried to phone her but her line was busy.* 3 indicating that something is in use: *I got a busy signal the first time I dialled.* 4 full of work or activity: *a busy day, a busy street.* 5 *Informal.* having too much design, ornament, etc.: *a busy drawing, busy decoration.* 6 meddlesome.
—*v.* make or keep busy: *The stagehands busied themselves in setting up the stage.* ⟨OE *bisig*⟩ —**bus•i•ly,** *adv.* —**'bus•y•ness,** *n.*
☛ *Syn. adj.* **1. Busy,** INDUSTRIOUS, DILIGENT = actively or attentively occupied. **Busy** = habitually active or working steadily or at the moment: *She is a busy woman, and it is hard to get an appointment with her.* **Industrious** = hard-working by nature or habit: *He is an industrious worker.* **Diligent** = hard-working at a particular thing, usually something one likes or especially wants to do: *She is a diligent mother, but a poor housekeeper.*

bus•y•bod•y ['bɪzi,bɒdi] *or* ['bɪzi,bʌdi] *n., pl.* **-bod•ies.** a person who pries into other people's affairs; meddler.

bus•y•work ['bɪzi,wɜrk] *n.* work done or assigned, especially to students, merely to fill time or to appear to be busy.

but[1] [bʌt]; *unstressed,* [bət] *conj., prep., adv., n.* —*conj.* 1 yet; still; however: *It rained, but I went anyway.* 2 rather; on the contrary: *He is not snobbish but merely shy.* 3 without the result that; unless: *It never rains but it pours.* 4 that: *I don't doubt but she will come.* 5 that not: *He is not so sick but he can eat.*
—*prep.* 1 except; save: *She works every day but Sunday.* 2 other than: *We can do nothing but accept their conditions.*
—*adv.* no more than; only; merely: *He is but a boy.*
all but, nearly; almost: *The book was all but finished when the author died.*
but for, were it not for; excepting; save: *She was right but for one thing.*
but that, were it not that: *I would have come but that I felt too ill.*
—*n.* objection: *Not so many buts, please.* ⟨OE *būtan* without, unless < *be-* + *ūtan* outside < *ūt* out⟩
☛ *Hom.* BUTT.
☛ *Syn. conj.* **1. But,** HOWEVER express a relationship in which two things or ideas are thought of as standing in opposition or contrast to each other. **But** expresses the contrast or contradiction clearly and sharply by placing the two things or ideas side by side in perfect balance: *He is sick, but he can eat.* **However** is more formal, and suggests that the second idea should be compared and contrasted with the first: *We have not yet reached a decision; however, our opinion of your plan is favourable.* —*prep.* **1.** See note at EXCEPT.

but[2] [bʌt] *n.* BUTT[5].

bu•ta•bar•bi•tal [ˌbjutə'bɑrbətəl] *n.* a barbiturate drug used as a sedative. *Formula*: $C_{10}H_{15}N_2NaO_3$

bu•ta•di•ene [ˌbjutə'daiin] *n.* a colourless, flammable gas obtained from petroleum, used especially in making synthetic rubber. *Formula*: C_4H_6 ⟨< *buta(ne)* + *di-* + *-ene,* chemical suffix (< L *-enus*)⟩

bu•tane ['bjutein] *or* [bju'tein] *n.* a colourless, flammable gas obtained from natural gas or petroleum, used as a fuel. *Formula*: C_4H_{10} ⟨< L *butyrum* butter < Gk. *boutyron*⟩

bu•ta•none ['bjutə,noun] *n.* a clear, extremely flammable liquid used as a solvent; methyl ethyl ketone. *Formula*: CH_3COC_2

butch [bʊtʃ] *n., adj. Slang.* —*n.* 1 a woman, sometimes specifically a lesbian, who is masculine in dress, manner, etc. 2 a tough or rugged man.
—*adj.* of a woman, masculine in appearance, manner, etc. ⟨probably from *Butch,* a boy's nickname⟩

butch•er ['bʊtʃər] *n., v.* —*n.* 1 a person whose work is killing animals and cutting up meat to be sold for food. 2 a person who only cuts up and sells the meat. 3 a brutal killer or murderer. 4 *Informal.* a person who botches or bungles something.
—*v.* 1 kill and cut up (animals) for food. 2 kill cruelly or needlessly: *Many village inhabitants were butchered in the invasion.* 3 spoil by poor work; botch: *She butchered the song by singing it much too loudly.* ⟨ME < OF *bocher* < *boc* he-goat, buck[1] < Gmc.⟩ —**'butch•er•er,** *n.*

butch•er•bird ['bʊtʃər,bɜrd] *n.* 1 any of various shrikes that impale their prey on thorns or wedge it into cracks in order to feed upon it or store it. 2 any of a genus (*Cracticus*) of Australian songbirds that treat their prey in a similar way.

butcher block a hardwood block made of narrow strips of wood, similar to that used by a butcher for chopping meat, used as a tabletop or counter top.

butcher's broom a plant (*Ruscus aculeatus*) of the lily family, having flat branches and small white flowers followed by red berries.

butcher shop a butcher's place of business.

butch•er•y ['bʊtʃəri] *n., pl.* **-er•ies.** 1 brutal or wholesale killing or murder. 2 a slaughterhouse; butcher shop. 3 a butcher's work; the act or business of killing animals for food. 4 something botched or spoiled, or the act of botching or spoiling.

bu•te•o ['bjuti,ou] *n.* any of a genus (*Buteo*) of hawks found in many parts of the world, having a thick-set body, broad wings, and a short, broad tail. Buteos will soar high in the air for hours while hunting. ⟨< NL < L type of hawk⟩

but•ler ['bʌtlər] *n.* 1 the chief male servant of a household, whose duties include supervising other servants, directing the serving of meals, and personal services for his employers. 2 a male servant in charge of wines and liquors; wine steward. ⟨ME < AF var. of OF *bouteillier* < *bouteille* bottle. See BOTTLE.⟩

butler's pantry a small room between the kitchen and dining room, for use by a butler, serving maid, etc.

but•su•dan [ˌbutsu'dɑn] *n.* in Japanese tradition: 1 the altar in a temple upon which Buddhist statues are enshrined. 2 the shrine in a Buddhist household, containing statues, pictures, and memorial tablets of family ancestors.

butt[1] [bʌt] *n., v.* —*n.* 1 the thicker end of anything: *The butt of a gun.* See FIREARM for picture. 2 the end that is left over; a stub or stump: *a cigar butt.* 3 *Slang.* buttocks; rump. See LAMB and PORK for pictures. 4 a ridge between furrows; strip of land. 5 *Slang.* an (unsmoked) cigarette: *Can you lend me a butt?*
—*v.* extinguish (a cigarette or cigar) by pressing and rubbing the lit end against something (*often used with* **out**). ⟨fusion of ME *but, bott* (related to *buttocks*) and OF *bout* end < Gmc.⟩
☛ *Hom.* BUT.

butt[2] [bʌt] *n., v.* —*n.* 1 target. 2 an object of ridicule or scorn: *He was the butt of their jokes.* 3 **a** on a rifle, archery, or artillery range, a mound of earth or sawdust behind the target to stop shots. **b** a mound on which an archery target is set. 4 also, **butt joint,** a joint where two boards or timbers meet end to end. 5 a hinge that fits behind two surfaces, as between the door and the jamb. 6 a small, open shelter for grouse shooting. 7 **the butts,** a place to practise shooting in.
—*v.* 1 join end to end. 2 attach with a butt hinge. ⟨< F *bout* end < Gmc.⟩
☛ *Hom.* BUT.

butt[3] [bʌt] *v., n.* —*v.* 1 strike or push by knocking hard with the head. 2 place (a timber, etc.) with its end against something; put (planks, etc.) end to end. 3 cut off the rough ends of (boards, logs, etc.). 4 project; run out; jut (out or into): *One wing of the house butted out as far as the roadway.*
butt in, *Slang.* meddle; interfere.
butt out! *Slang.* mind your own business!
—*n.* a push or blow with the head. ⟨ME < OF *bouter* thrust < Gmc.⟩
☛ *Hom.* BUT.

butt[4] [bʌt] *n.* 1 a large barrel for wine or beer. 2 a former unit for measuring liquids, equal to two hogsheads, about 476 L. ⟨ME < OF *botte* < LL *butta*⟩
☛ *Hom.* BUT.

butt⁵ [bʌt] *n.* any of a number of flatfishes, like the halibut or the flounder. Also, **but.**

butte [bjut] *n. Cdn.* a steep, often flat-topped hill standing alone. Buttes are common in southern Alberta. ⟨< F⟩
☛ *Hom.* BEAUT.

butt–end•ing ['bʌt ˌɛndɪŋ] *n. Hockey.* the illegal jabbing or thrusting of the handle end of the stick into an opponent's body.

but•ter ['bʌtər] *n., v.* —*n.* **1** the solid, yellowish fat obtained by churning cream or whole milk. **2** something like butter in consistency or use: *peanut butter, apple butter, cocoa butter.* **3** *Informal.* flattery.
—*v.* **1** put butter on. **2** *Informal.* flatter in order to get something (*used with* **up**): *We tried buttering him up, but he still wouldn't lend us his car.* ⟨OE *butere* < L *butyrum* < Gk. *boutyron*⟩
—**'but•ter•less,** *adj.*

butter–and–eggs ['bʌtər ən 'ɛgz] *n.* a wildflower, the common toadflax (*Linaria vulgaris*), having showy yellow and orange flowers and growing across North America and Eurasia.

but•ter•ball ['bʌtər,bɒl] *n.* **1** bufflehead. **2** *Informal.* a plump person.

butter bean any light-coloured bean, as the wax bean or lima bean.

but•ter•bur ['bʌtər,bɜr] *n.* **1** a plant (*Petasites hybridus*) of the composite family, having large kidney-shaped leaves. **2** any other plant of the genus *Petasites.*

butter clam a large clam (genus *Saxidomus*) native to the North American Pacific coast. Butter clams are edible.

but•ter•cup ['bʌtər,kʌp] *n.* **1** any of a number of wildflowers (genus *Ranunculus*) found especially in meadows and damp places, having yellow flowers and leaves that are usually deeply lobed. **2** (*adjl.*) designating a large family (Ranunculaceae) of annual or perennial plants found in temperate and cold regions, especially in the northern hemisphere, including many herbs, such as the buttercups, columbines, and anemones, and a few woody vines, such as the clematis. The buttercup family is also called the **crowfoot** family.

but•ter•fat ['bʌtər,fæt] *n.* the fatty content of milk from which butter is made. Whole milk from cows usually contains about 3.8 percent butterfat.

but•ter•fin•gered ['bʌtər,fɪŋgərd] *adj.* awkward; clumsy; always letting things drop or slip through one's fingers.

but•ter•fin•gers ['bʌtər,fɪŋgərz] *n. Informal.* a clumsy or awkward person who drops things: *Don't let her handle the china; she's a real butterfingers.*

but•ter•fish ['bʌtər,fɪʃ] *n., pl.* **-fish** or **-fish•es.** a gunnel (*Pholis gunnellus*) of coastal regions of the North Atlantic, having a slippery body covered with fine scales.

but•ter•fly ['bʌtər,flaɪ] *n., pl.* **-flies. 1** any of a large group of about six families of diurnal insects (order Lepidoptera) having a slender body, long, slender antennae with thick, knoblike tips, and four large, often brightly coloured wings. Compare MOTH. **2** a person who suggests a butterfly by his or her delicate beauty, bright clothes, fickleness, etc. **3** a swimming stroke performed face down, in which the outstretched arms move in a circular motion together while the legs are kicking up and down together. **4 butterflies,** *pl.* an uneasy or queasy feeling caused by nervous anxiety about something that is to happen: *I get butterflies in my stomach just thinking about being in front of all those people.* **5** the butterfly-shaped metal clasp which secures the post of an earring in a pierced ear. **6** WING NUT. ⟨OE *buterflēoge*⟩

butterfly fish a small tropical fish of the family Chaetodontidea, having brightly coloured, usually yellow scales.

butterfly orchid a South American orchid (*Oncidium papilio*), having red flowers.

butterfly stroke BUTTERFLY (def. 3).

butterfly valve a valve consisting of a disk turning on an axis. A damper on a furnace and a throttle valve in a carburetor are examples.

butterfly weed a milkweed (*Asclepias tuberosa*) with orange-coloured flowers.

but•ter•head lettuce ['bʌtər,hɛd] a variety of lettuce having soft leaves forming a loose head. The bibb and Boston lettuces are butterheads.

but•ter•milk ['bʌtər,mɪlk] *n.* **1** the sour, fat-free liquid left after butter has been churned from cream. **2** milk that has been soured by adding certain bacteria.

but•ter•nut ['bʌtər,nʌt] *n.* **1** a North American tree (*Juglans cinerea*) of the walnut family. **2** the oily, edible nut of this tree. **3** a brown dye made from butternut bark. **4** the wood of this tree.

butternut squash a type of smooth winter squash with ochre skin and pulp.

but•ter•scotch ['bʌtər,skɒtʃ] *n., adj.* —*n.* a candy or syrup made from brown sugar and butter.
—*adj.* flavoured with brown sugar and butter.

butter tart *Cdn.* a rich, sweet tart having a filling made from butter, brown sugar, corn syrup, raisins, spices, etc. Recipes for butter tarts vary somewhat and the filling may be runny or firm.

but•ter•wort ['bʌtər,wɜrt] *n.* any of a genus (*Pinguicula*) of herbs of the bladderwort family having fleshy leaves that secrete a sticky substance that traps insect prey and digests it.

but•ter•y¹ ['bʌtəri] *adj.* **1** like butter. **2** containing butter; spread with butter. **3** flattering. ⟨< *butter*⟩

but•ter•y² ['bʌtəri] *n., pl.* **-ter•ies.** pantry. ⟨ME < OF *boterie* < *botte* butt⁴ < LL *butta*⟩

but•tocks ['bʌtəks] *n.pl.* the fleshy hind part of the body where the legs join the back; rump. ⟨OE *buttuc* end, small piece of land⟩

but•ton ['bʌtən] *n., v.* —*n.* **1** a knob or disk of plastic, metal, wood, etc. fixed on clothing or other things, serving to hold parts together when passed through a buttonhole or loop, or used simply to decorate. **2** a knob or small disk or plate that is pushed or turned to open or close an electric circuit: *an elevator button. You push that button to start the machine.* **3** a usually round badge of metal or plastic having a catchword, slogan, logo, etc., printed on it, and a pin at the back, for attaching to clothing: *The publisher was giving away buttons to promote the new book.* **4** anything that resembles or suggests a button. **5** a young or undeveloped mushroom. **6** the small knob on the end of a fencing foil. **7** *Slang.* the centre of the chin, especially as a target for a blow. **8 buttons,** *pl., Brit. Informal.* a bellboy or page in a hotel, etc. **9** a small piece of wood on a nail to hold the door of a farm building.
on the button, *Informal.* exactly; precisely: *She was there at five o'clock on the button.*
—*v.* **1** close or fasten with buttons. **2** have buttons for fastening: *The dress buttons down the front.*
button up, *Informal.* **a** complete satisfactorily: *button up the details of a contract.* **b** keep quiet; keep a secret. ⟨ME < OF *boton* < *bouter* thrust. See BUTT³.⟩ —**'but•ton•less,** *adj.* —**'but•ton,like,** *adj.*

but•ton•ball ['bʌtən,bɒl] *n.* the common North American sycamore tree (*Platanus occidentalis*).

button blanket *Cdn.* among West Coast First Nations, a highly ornamental blanket with contrasting colour designs and totems outlined with numerous mother-of-pearl buttons.

but•ton•bush ['bʌtən,bʊʃ] *n.* a North American wildflower (*Cephalanthus occidentalis*), having tiny, fragrant flowers clustered on a spiky sphere, and growing in wooded swamps.

but•ton–down ['bʌtən 'daʊn] *adj.* **1** of a shirt collar, fastening, at the tips, with small buttons to the body of the shirt. **2** staid; conventional or tense: *a button-down smile.*

but•ton•hole ['bʌtən,houl] *n., v.* **-holed, -hol•ing.** —*n.* **1** the slit through which a button is passed. **2** a flower or flowers worn in a buttonhole.
—*v.* **1** make buttonholes in. **2** sew with the stitch used in making buttonholes. **3** force (someone) to listen, as if by holding him or her by the buttonhole of the coat: *He buttonholed me as I tried to sneak out of the room.* —**'but•ton,hol•er,** *n.*

buttonhole stitch a series of parallel and interlooping stitches placed close together, to strengthen an edge such as that of a buttonhole.

but•ton•hook ['bʌtən,hʊk] *n.* a hook for pulling the buttons of shoes, gloves, etc., through the buttonholes.

button tree any of various small West Indian trees (genus *Conocarpus*) bearing button-shaped fruit.

but•ton•wood ['bʌtən,wʊd] *n.* buttonball; sycamore.

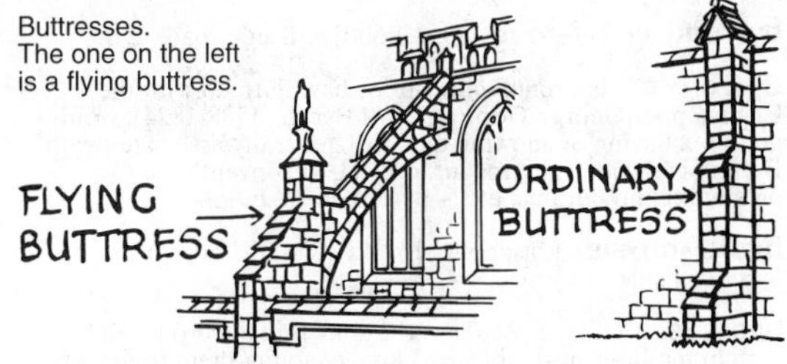

Buttresses.
The one on the left is a flying buttress.

but•tress ['bʌtrɪs] *n., v.* *–n.* **1** a structure built against a wall or building to strengthen or support it. **2** something resembling a buttress, such as a projecting rock. **3** any support; prop: *The experience was a buttress to his faith.*
–v. **1** strengthen with a buttress. **2** support and strengthen; bolster: *The pilot's report of the flight was buttressed with photographs.* ⟨ME < OF *bouterez* (pl.) < *bouter* thrust against. See BUTT[3].⟩

butt weld a butt joint that has been welded.

bu•tut [bʊ'tut] *n.* the lesser currency of Gambia, equal to $\frac{1}{100}$ of a dalasi. See money table in the Appendix.

bu•tyl ['bjutəl] *n.* any of the four univalent radicals obtained from butane. Butyl is used in making inner tubes, insulation for electrical appliances, etc. *Formula:* C_4H_9

butyl alcohol any of four liquid, isomeric alcohols derived from oil products and used as solvents; butanol. *Formula:* C_4H_9OH

bu•tyl•at•ed hy•drox•y•an•i•sole ['bjutə,leitɪd haɪ,drɒksi'ænə,soul] *n.* a food preservative. *Formula:* $C_{11}H_{16}O_2$

bu•ty•lene ['bjutə,lin] *n.* a gaseous hydrocarbon of the ethylene series, often used in making synthetic rubber. *Formula:* C_4H_8 ⟨< L *butyrum* butter⟩

bu•ty•ra•ceous [,bjutə'reiʃəs] *adj.* of butter; like butter; containing butter. ⟨< L *butyrum* butter + *-aceous*⟩

bu•ty•rate ['bjutə,reit] *n.* any salt or ester of butyric acid.

bu•tyr•ic acid [bju'tirɪk] a colourless liquid that has an unpleasant odour and is formed by fermentation in rancid butter, cheese, etc. *Formula:* $C_4H_8O_2$ ⟨*butyric* < L *butyrum* butter < Gk. *boutyron*⟩

bux•om ['bʌksəm] *adj.* vigorously healthy and plump; used especially of a full-bosomed woman. ⟨ME *buhsum* < OE *būgan* bend⟩ **–'bux•om•ly,** *adv.* **–'bux•om•ness,** *n.*

buy [baɪ] *v.* **bought, buy•ing;** *n.* *–v.* **1** get by paying a price: *You can buy a pencil for 20 cents.* **2** buy things; shop: *I won't buy there again.* **3** bribe: *It was charged that two members of the jury had been bought.* **4** *Informal.* accept as valid, feasible, etc.: *If you say it's true, I'll buy it.* **5** enable one to acquire or purchase: *Fifty dollars buys you a seat on the train.* **6** work as a buyer.
buy into, a obtain an interest or footing in by purchase: *She bought into the new aluminum company, obtaining 500 shares.* **b** commit oneself to (a principle, philosophy, etc.)
buy off, get rid of by paying money to; bribe.
buy out, a buy all the shares, rights, etc., of. **b** buy up.
buy time, extend a situation, often by making excuses, in order to bring something to a favourable close.
buy up, buy all that one can of; buy.
–n. **1** *Informal.* something bought; a purchase. **2** *Informal.* a bargain: *a good buy.* ⟨OE *bycgan*⟩ **–'buy•a•ble,** *adj.*
☛ *Hom.* BY, BYE.
☛ *Syn. v.* **1. Buy,** PURCHASE = to get something by paying a price. **Buy** is the general word: *You can buy anything in that store if you have the money.* **Purchase** is used in more formal style and suggests buying after careful planning or by business dealings or on a large scale: *The bank has purchased some property on which to construct a new building.*
☛ *Usage.* **Buy** is used with *from* but, informally, also with *off*: *He bought it from a stranger on the street.* (Informal.) *She bought it off a kid at work.*

buy•back ['baɪ,bæk] *n.* **1** the repurchase of something one has sold. **2** a purchase made as a condition of sale, as when a supplier agrees to buy its customer's product. **3** purchase by a company of its own shares, to reduce the number of shares available.

buy•er ['baɪər] *n.* **1** a person who buys. **2** a person whose work is buying goods, especially for a retail store.

buyer's market an economic situation in which the buyer has the advantage because goods are plentiful and prices tend to be low. Compare SELLER'S MARKET.

buy•out ['baɪ,ʌut] *n.* the purchase of a whole company, as by its employees.

buzz [bʌz] *n., v.* *–n.* **1** a humming sound made by flies, mosquitoes, or bees, and also by machines. **2** a low, indistinct, murmuring sound of many people talking quietly: *The buzz of conversation stopped when the teacher entered the room.* **3** *Informal.* a telephone call: *Give me a buzz tonight.* **4 a** busy movement; stir; state of activity or excitement. **b** the sound of such activity. **5** *Slang.* a haircut, especially a short one. **6** *Slang.* a state of happiness produced as by drugs or alcohol. **7** *Slang.* news: *What's the buzz about Tilda?*
–v. **1** make a loud, steady humming sound on one pitch: *The radio needs to be fixed; it buzzes when you turn it on.* **2** make a low, indistinct murmuring sound: *The whole room buzzed with the news of the class excursion.* **3** murmur; whisper: *"Here they come," she buzzed in my ear.* **4** approach quickly and pass by closely with an aircraft or a small boat: *A pilot buzzed our school yesterday.* **5** signal by pressing a buzzer: *She buzzed her secretary.* **6** *Informal.* to telephone: *I'll buzz you when I find out.* **7** *Slang.* give a haircut to, especially a short one.
buzz about, move about busily.
buzz off, *Slang.* go away. ⟨imitative⟩

buz•zard ['bʌzərd] *n.* **1** any of several species of vulture of the western hemisphere, especially the turkey vulture, or turkey buzzard. **2** *Esp. Brit.* buteo. **3** a mean, greedy person. ⟨ME < OF *busart*, ult. < L *buteo* hawk⟩

buzz bomb a type of unguided missile heavily loaded with explosives and propelled by a pulsejet, that was invented in Germany and used against England in World War II, especially in the bomb attacks on London. ⟨with reference to the buzzing sound it made⟩

buzz•er ['bʌzər] *n.* **1** something that buzzes, especially an electric device that makes a buzzing sound as a signal. **2** the sound of a buzzer: *At the buzzer, they all rushed from the room.*

buzz saw a circular saw.

buzz•word ['bʌz,wɜrd] *Slang.* the newest piece of jargon.

B.V.M. Blessed Virgin Mary (for L *Beata Virgo Maria*).

B/W or **BW** black and white, as distinct from coloured; said of a film or television program.

B.W.I. British West Indies.

bx. box.

by [baɪ] *prep., adv., adj., n.* *–prep.* **1** near; beside: *The garden is by the house.* **2** along; over; through: *to go by the bridge.* **3** through the action of: *the thief was captured by the police. The house was destroyed by fire.* **4** through the means or use of: *They keep in touch by letter. He never travels by plane.* **5** combined with in multiplication or relative dimensions: *a room five by ten metres.* **6** in the measure of: *Eggs are sold by the dozen.* **7** to the extent of: *larger by half.* **8** according to: *They all work by the rules.* **9** in relation to: *He did well by his children.* **10** taken separately as units or groups in a series: *two by two. Algebra must be mastered step by step.* **11** during: *by day.* **12** not later than: *by six o'clock.* **13** toward: *The island lies south by east from here.*
by (oneself), **a** having no company; alone. **b** single-handedly; unaided.
by the way, aside from the main point; incidentally: *By the way, what time is it?*
–adv. **1** at hand: *close by.* **2** past: *days gone by. A car dashed by.* **3** aside or away: *to put something by.* **4** *Informal.* in or into (another's house) when passing: *Please come by and see me when you can.*
by and by, after a while; soon: *You will feel stronger by and by.*
by and large, on the whole; in general: *It has some faults, but by and large it is a good book.*
–adj. **1** situated at the side; out of the way; private. **2** away from the main purpose; secondary.
–n. See BYE[1].
by the by, incidentally. ⟨OE *bī*⟩
☛ *Hom.* BUY, BYE.
☛ *Syn. prep.* **3. By,** THROUGH (def. 4), WITH (def. 4) = by means of. **By** in this sense is used before words for things: *She travelled by snowmobile.* **Through** is used before words for feelings or conditions or for people considered as intermediaries: *They lost the match through sheer carelessness. We found out through a friend in Vancouver.* **With** is used before things named as instruments: *We cut the meat with a knife.*

by– *combining form.* **1** secondary; minor; less important: *by-product = less important product.* **2** nearby: *bystander = person standing nearby.*

by–and–by ['baɪ ən 'baɪ] *n.* the future.

by–blow ['baɪ ,blou] *n.* **1** a glancing blow. **2** *Archaic.* an illegitimate child.

bye[1] [baɪ] *n.* **1** *Sports.* **a** the condition of being the odd player or team not required to play one round of a contest in which players or teams are grouped in pairs: *Our team had a bye to the semifinal.* **b** the player or team not required to play a round. **2** *Cricket.* a run made on a missed ball. **3** *Golf.* the holes not played after one player has won.
by the bye, incidentally. ⟨var. of *by*, prep.⟩
☛ *Hom.* BUY, BY.

bye[2] or **'bye** [baɪ] *interj. Informal.* goodbye.
☛ *Hom.* BUY, BY.

bye–bye ['baɪ 'baɪ] *interj. Informal.* goodbye.

by–e•lec•tion ['baɪ ɪ,lɛkʃən] *n.* an election held in one riding because of the death or resignation of its Member of Parliament or Legislative Assembly.

by•gone ['baɪ,gɒn] *adj., n. —adj.* gone by; past; former: *The Romans lived in bygone days.*
—n. **1** something in the past. **2** the past.
let bygones be bygones, let past offences be forgotten.

by–law ['baɪ ,lɒ] *n.* **1** a local law; a law made by a city, company, club, etc., for the control of its own affairs: *Our city has by-laws to control parking, traffic, and building practices.* **2** a secondary law or rule; not one of the main rules. ⟨ME, probably < earlier *byrlaw* < ON *býr* town + *lög* law; meaning influenced by *by-*⟩

by–line ['baɪ ,laɪn] *n.* a line at the beginning of a newspaper or magazine article giving the name of the writer. **—'by,lin•er,** *n.*

by•name ['baɪ,neim] *n.* a secondary name or nickname.

BYOB bring your own bottle (or beer).

by•pass ['baɪ,pæs] *n., v. —n.* **1** a road or passage around or to one side, especially a highway around a city or town. **2** a channel, pipe, etc., for a liquid or gas, providing a secondary or alternative passage for a distance and connecting again with the main channel. **3** *Electricity.* a shunt. **4** in medicine, the grafting of a section of blood vessel onto a blocked or narrow blood vessel, usually a coronary artery, to carry blood around the obstruction.
—v. **1** provide a secondary passage for. **2** make a detour around: *bypass a city.* **3** ignore (an intermediate person or level) in order to deal directly with a higher authority. **4** set aside or ignore (regulations, etc.) in order to reach a desired objective. **5** get away from; avoid; escape: *bypass a question.* **6** *Military.* flank.

by–path ['baɪ ,pæθ] *n.* a side path; byway.

by–play ['baɪ ,plei] *n.* especially in a dramatic production, a secondary action that is carried on on the side while the main action proceeds.

by–prod•uct ['baɪ ,prɒdəkt] *n.* **1** something of value produced in making or doing something else: *Kerosene is a by-product of petroleum refining.* **2** a side effect; a secondary and sometimes unexpected result: *Her new self-confidence is a by-product of her experience as club president.*

byre [baɪr] *n.* a cowhouse or cow shed. ⟨OE *byre*⟩

by•road or **by–road** ['baɪ ,roud] *n.* a side road.

By•ron•ic [baɪ'rɒnɪk] *adj.* **1** of or having to do with the English poet George Gordon, Lord Byron (1788-1824), or his poetry. **2** having or showing qualities generally associated with Byron or his poetry; arrogant, cynical, unconventional, passionate, mysterious, etc. **—By'ron•ic•al•ly,** *adv.*

bys•si•no•sis [,bɪsɪ'nousɪs] *n.* BROWN LUNG. ⟨< NL < L *byssinus* made of byssus⟩

bys•sus ['bɪsəs] *n. Zoology.* the silky threads produced by certain molluscs of the bivalve class, enabling them to attach themselves to rocks, walls, etc.

by•stand•er ['baɪ,stændər] *n.* a person who stands near or looks on but does not take part.

bystreet or **by–street** ['baɪ ,strit] *n.* a side street.

byte [bəit] *n. Computer technology.* a sequence of usually eight binary digits (bits) processed as a single unit of information by a computer. ⟨probably a blend of *bite* and *bit*[4]. 20c.⟩
☛ *Hom.* BIGHT, BITE.

By•town ['baɪ,taʊn] a former name for Ottawa. ⟨< Colonel *By* (1779-1836), builder of the Rideau Canal⟩

by•way or **by–way** ['baɪ,wei] *n.* **1** a side path or road; a way that is little used. **2** a less important activity.

by•word ['baɪ,wɜrd] *n.* **1** a common saying; proverb. **2** a word which one uses habitually. **3** a person or thing commonly or proverbially taken as typifying a certain characteristic, especially an unfavourable one: *They had become a byword for hospitality throughout the region.* **4** an object of contempt; something scorned: *His cowardice made him a byword to all who knew him.* ⟨OE *bīword*⟩

Byz•an•tine ['bɪzən,tin], [bɪ'zæntɪn], *or* ['bɪzən,taɪn] *adj., n.* *—adj.* **1** of or having to do with Byzantium, an ancient city on the Bosporus. **2** of or having to do with the art or architecture of Byzantium. **3** Sometimes, **byzantine,** complex; intricate and devious: *byzantine plots.* **4** of or having to do with the Eastern Orthodox Church.
—n. **1** a native or inhabitant of Byzantium. **2** *Architecture.* a style developed in Byzantium in the 5th and 6th centuries, characterized by rounded arches, domes, and a lavish use of mosaics and murals. **3** *Art.* a style developed in Byzantium in the 6th century, characterized by brilliant colours, formal designs, and distorted proportions. ⟨< L *Byzantinus*⟩

Byzantine Empire the eastern part of the Roman Empire after the division in A.D. 395. It ceased to exist after the fall of its capital Constantinople in 1453.

Bz. benzene.

C c C c

c or **C** [si] *n., pl.* **c's** or **C's. 1** the third letter of the English alphabet. **2** any speech sound represented by this letter. **3** a person or thing identified as *c*, especially the third in a series. **4** a person or thing considered as belonging to the third best group: *grade C eggs, C grade in Latin.* **5** *Music.* **a** the first tone in the scale of C major; the third tone of A minor. **b** a symbol representing this tone. **c** a key, string, etc., that produces this tone. **d** the scale or key that has C as its keynote. **6** **C,** the Roman numeral for 100. **7** *Algebra.* Usually **c,** the third known quantity: $ax + by + c = 0$. **8** something shaped like the letter C. **9** (*adjl.*) of or being a C or c. **10** *Computer technology.* a computer programming language. **11** any device, such as a printer's type, a lever, or a key on a keyboard, that produces a c or C.
☛ *Hom.* SEA, SEE, SI.

c centi- (an **SI** prefix).

c. 1 cent(s). **2** approximately (for L *circa*). **3** *Sports.* catcher. **4** century. **5** centre. **6** copyright. **7** cubic. **8** *Physics.* capacity. **9** cathode. **10** chapter. **11** current. **12** hundredweight. **13** city.

C 1 Celsius. **2** carbon. **3** central. **4** *Mathematics.* constant. **5** coulomb.

C. 1 Cape. **2** Catholic. **3** Conservative. **4** Celtic. **5** Church.

C1 CHIEF PETTY OFFICER 1st class.

C2 CHIEF PETTY OFFICER 2nd class.

C14 CARBON-14.

ca about; approximately (for L *circa*). Also, **c.**

Ca calcium.

CA 1 *Psychology.* chronological age. **2** controlled atmosphere.

C.A. 1 Chartered Accountant. **2** Central America. **3** Consular Agent. **4** Court of Appeal.

C/A or **c/a 1** capital account. **2** credit account. **3** current account.

CAA or **C.A.A. 1** Canadian Automobile Association. **2** Canadian Authors' Association.

Caa•ba ['kɑbə] See KAABA.

CAAT or **C.A.A.T.** College of Applied Arts and Technology.

cab [kæb] *n.* **1** an automobile that can be hired with a driver; taxi. **2** a horse-drawn carriage that can be hired with a driver. **3** the enclosed part of a locomotive, truck, etc., where the operator or driver stands or sits. ⟨a shortened form of *cabriolet*⟩

CAB or **C.A.B. 1** Canadian Association of Broadcasters. **2** *U.S.* Civil Aeronautics Board.

ca•bal [kə'bæl] *n., v.* **-balled, -bal•ling.** *—n.* **1** a small group of people working or plotting in secret. **2** a secret scheme of such a group; plot.
—v. form such a group; conspire. ⟨< F < Med.L *cabbala.* See CABALA.⟩

cab•a•la ['kæbələ], ['kɑbələ], *or* [kə'bɑlə] *n.* **1** a secret religious philosophy of the Jewish rabbis, based on a mystical interpretation of the Scriptures. **2** a mystical belief; secret doctrine. ⟨< Med.L *cabbala* < Hebrew *qabbalah* tradition⟩

cab•a•lism ['kæbə,lɪzəm] *n.* **1** the secret belief of the cabala. **2** any secret belief.

cab•a•lis•tic [,kæbə'lɪstɪk] *adj.* **1** of or having to do with the Jewish cabala. **2** having a mystical meaning; secret.

cab•al•le•ro [,kæbə'lɛrou] *or* [,kæbəl'jɛrou]; *Spanish,* [,kaba'ljero] *n., pl.* **-ros. 1** gentleman. **2** knight. **3** horseman. ⟨< Sp. < LL *caballarius* horseman < L *caballus* horse⟩

ca•ba•ña [kə'bɑnə], [kə'bɑnjə], *or* [kə'bænə] *n.* **1** a shelter on the beach for changing or shade. **2** bathhouse. **3** CABIN (def. 1). ⟨< Sp. < LL *capanna.* Doublet of CABIN.⟩

cab•a•ret [,kæbə'rei] *or* ['kæbə,rei] *n.* **1** a restaurant where singing and dancing are provided as entertainment. **2** the entertainment provided there. ⟨< F *cabaret* tavern⟩

cab•bage ['kæbɪdʒ] *n.* **1** a cultivated plant (*Brassica oleracea capitata*) having large, round leaves that are closely folded into a compact head growing from a short stem. **2** the head of a cabbage, used as a vegetable. **3** the Mediterranean plant (*Brassica oleracea*) of the mustard family from which the garden cabbage, cauliflower, Brussels sprouts, and broccoli have been developed. ⟨< F *caboche* < Provençal, ult. < L *caput* head⟩

cabbage butterfly a small white butterfly (*Pieris rapae*) whose caterpillars feed on the green leaves of cabbage and other plants.

cabbage rose a Caucasian rose (*Rosa centifolia*) having large, double, very fragrant pink flowers. It has been a popular garden rose for centuries.

cab•bage•town ['kæbɪdʒ,taʊn] *n. Cdn.* a run-down urban area; slum. ⟨< *Cabbagetown,* formerly, a depressed area on the east side of the older part of downtown Toronto, so-called from the supposed diet of the area's English population⟩

cab•bage•worm ['kæbɪdʒ,wɜrm] *n.* the larva of any insect, such as the cabbage butterfly, that feeds on the green leaves of cabbage and other plants.

cab•by ['kæbi] *n., pl.* **-bies.** *Informal.* cabdriver.

cab•dri•ver ['kæb,draɪvər] *n.* one who drives a taxi.

ca•ber ['keibər] *n.* a long, heavy pole or beam tossed as a trial of strength in Scottish Highland games. ⟨< Scots Gaelic *cabar*⟩

ca•ber•net [,kæbər'nei] *n.* **1** a kind of grape. **2** a red wine made from these grapes.

cabernet sau•vig•non [,souvi'njɒn]; *French,* [sovi'njɔ̃] **1** the finest kind of cabernet grape. **2** a red wine made from these grapes, especially in Bordeaux.

ca•be•zon ['kæbə,zɒn] *n.* a fish (*Scorpaenichthys marmoratus*) related to the sculpins and inhabiting waters off the west coast of North America. ⟨< Sp. *cabeza* head⟩

cab•in ['kæbən] *n., v. —n.* **1** a small, often roughly built house; hut: *a hunting cabin in the woods.* **2** COTTAGE (def. 1). **3** a room for passengers or crew in a ship or boat. **4** a place for passengers in an aircraft.
—v. **1** live in a cabin. **2** *Archaic.* confine; cramp. ⟨< F *cabane* < LL *capanna.* Doublet of CABAÑA.⟩

cabin boy a boy whose work is to wait on the officers and passengers on a ship.

cabin class a class of accommodation on a passenger ship, above tourist and below first class.

cabin cruiser a motorboat having a cabin and equipped with facilities for living on board.

cab•i•net ['kæbənɪt] *n.* **1** an upright piece of furniture having shelves or drawers to store or display things: *a china cabinet, a medicine cabinet.* **2** (*adjl.*) suitable in value, beauty, etc., for display in a cabinet. **3** an upright case holding a radio or televison receiver, record turntable, etc. **4** a body of advisers to a head of state, a prime minister, etc. **5** Usually, **Cabinet,** in Canada: **a** an executive committee of the federal government chosen by the prime minister, from members of the majority party in the House of Commons. Members of the Cabinet have the title of Minister of the Crown. **b** a similar committee of a provincial government. **6** (*adjl.*) of or having to do with a political cabinet. **7** *Archaic.* a small, private room. **8** (*adjl.*) of a size suitable for a small room. ⟨dim. of *cabin*⟩

cab•i•net•mak•er ['kæbənɪt,meikər] *n.* a person skilled in constructing and finishing fine wooden furniture, especially one whose work it is. **—'cab•i•net,mak•ing,** *n.*

cabinet minister the head of a department of the government of certain countries, including Canada, or of a province; a member of the Cabinet.

ca•bi•ne•try ['kæbənətri] *n.* cabinetwork.

cab•i•net•work ['kæbənɪt,wɜrk] *n.* **1** any beautifully made furniture or woodwork. **2** the making of such furniture and woodwork.

cabin fever *Cdn.* **1** a state of mental depression or hysteria resulting from a long period of isolation and confinement, especially as occurs in isolated parts of the North toward the end of the long, dark winter. **2** *Informal.* restlessness due to long confinement indoors.

cabin ship a ship carrying only one class of passengers.

ca•ble ['keibəl] *n., v.* **-bled, -bling.** *—n.* **1** a strong, thick rope, usually made of wires twisted together. **2** the rope or chain by which an anchor is raised and lowered. **3** CABLE'S LENGTH. **4** an insulated bundle of wires made to carry an electric current. Telegraph messages are sent under the ground or under the ocean by cable. **5** a message sent by cable; cablegram. **6** an

ornament with a design like that of a cable. 7 CABLE TELEVISION. 8 (*adjl.*) of or having to do with cable television.
—v. 1 tie or fasten with a cable. 2 send (a message) by cable. 3 send a cable to (someone): *Cable me when you arrive.* ⟨ME < OF < Provençal < L *capulum* halter⟩

cable car a car pulled, often up a steep hill, by a moving cable that is operated by an engine.

ca•ble•cast ['keibəl,kæst] *v.* **-cast, -cast•ing;** *n.* *—v.* send (a television picture or program) directly by cable.
—n. the television picture or program thus sent.

ca•ble•gram ['keibəl,græm] *n.* a message sent across the ocean by underwater cable.

cable's length a unit of length traditionally used at sea, defined as approximately 184 m (607.56 feet) by the Canadian and British navies and approximately 220 m (720 feet) by the United States navy.

Cable stitch

cable stitch *Knitting.* a combination of stitches that produces a pattern resembling a twisted cable.

cable television a system by which signals from various television stations are picked up by a very tall or elevated central antenna and sent by cable to the sets of individual subscribers. A television set that is hooked up to cable television does not need an antenna. Also, **cable TV**.

ca•ble•vi•sion ['keibəl,vɪʒən] *n.* CABLE TELEVISION.

cab•o•chon ['kæbə,ʃɒn]; *French,* [kabɔ'ʃɔ̃] *n.* 1 a rounded, unfacetted, highly polished gem. 2 the manner of cutting such gems. ⟨< MF *cabochon* < *caboche* head. See CABBAGE.⟩

ca•bom•ba [kə'bɒmbə] *n.* 1 a water lily (*Cabomba caroliniana*) with wide, flat leaves on the surface of the water, and narrow leaves below the surface. 2 any other member of this genus. ⟨< Sp.⟩

ca•boo•dle [kə'budəl] *n. Informal.* lot; pack; crowd (*used especially in the phrases* **the whole caboodle, the whole kit and caboodle**): *We put the whole caboodle into one box.* ⟨< *ca-* informal intensifying prefix (< G *ge-*) + Du. *boedel* property, estate⟩

ca•boose [kə'bus] *n.* 1 a small car on a freight train in which the train crew can work, eat, and sleep. It is usually the last car. 2 a kitchen on the deck of a ship. 3 *Cdn.* a mobile bunkhouse used by loggers, threshing crews, etc. 4 *Cdn.* a horse-drawn vehicle consisting of a small cabin mounted on runners and equipped with benches and a stove: *My aunt remembers driving to school in a caboose in winter.* 5 *Cdn.* in the North, a bunkhouse or cookhouse on runners for the crew of a cat-train, etc. 6 *Cdn.* in the North, a portable house. ⟨< Du. *kabuis* wretched hut, cabin < MLG *kabūse*; cf. CAMBOOSE⟩

cab•o•tage ['kæbə,tɑʒ] *or* ['kæbətɪdʒ]; *French,* [kabɔ'taʒ] *n.* 1 navigation or trade between ports along a coast. 2 transportation or trade between points within one country. 3 the right to ply such trade, especially as given to traders from another country. ⟨< F *cabotage* coastal trade < *caboter* sail along a coast⟩

cab•o•teur [,kæbə'tɜr]; *French,* [kabɔ'tœʀ] *n. Cdn.* 1 a ship engaged in coastal trade, especially along the St. Lawrence River and in the Gulf of St. Lawrence. 2 a captain or a member of the crew of such a ship. ⟨< Cdn.F < F. See CABOTAGE.⟩

Ca•bo•tia [kə'bouʃiə] *n. Cdn.* formerly, a name proposed for a British province incorporating the general area of the Atlantic Provinces. ⟨< John *Cabot* (Italian name Giovanni Caboto), 1450?-1498, explorer of the E North American coast for England⟩

ca•brilla [kə'brɪlə] a Caribbean food fish of the family Serranidae. ⟨< Sp. *cabrilla* prawn, dim. of < *cabra* goat⟩

cab•ri•ole ['kæbri,oul] *n., adj.* *—n.* 1 a curved, tapering furniture leg with a decorated foot, characteristic of Queen Anne and Chippendale furniture. The foot was usually carved as a claw grasping a ball. 2 a ballet step in which one leg is raised and then the other beaten against it.
—adj. 1 done or made in this style. 2 having such legs. ⟨< F *cabriole*, var. of *capriole* a leap, because it resembled the foreleg of an animal making a capriole⟩

cab•ri•o•let [,kæbriə'lei] *n.* 1 an automobile resembling a coupe but having a folding top. 2 a light, one-horse carriage with one or two seats, two wheels, and, often, a folding top. ⟨< F *cabriolet* < *cabrioler* caper < Ital. < L *caper* goat; from bouncing motion⟩

cab•stand ['kæb,stænd] *n.* TAXI STAND.

ca•ca•o [kə'keiou] *or* [kə'kɑou] *n., pl.* **-ca•os. 1** a tropical American evergreen tree (*Theobroma cacao*) that produces seeds from which chocolate, cocoa, and cocoa butter are obtained. 2 the seed of this tree, also called **cacao bean.** ⟨< Sp. < Mexican *caca-uatl*⟩

cac•cia•to•re [,kɑtʃə'tɔri]; *Italian,* [,katʃa'tɔre] *adj.* cooked in a casserole with tomatoes, onions, and spices: *chicken cacciatore.* ⟨< Ital., hunter < pp. of *cacciare* to hunt, chase⟩

cach•a•lot ['kæʃə,lɒt] *or* ['kæʃə,lou] *n.* SPERM WHALE. ⟨< F < Pg. *cachalote*⟩

cache [kæʃ] *n., v.* **cached, cach•ing.** *—n.* 1 a hiding place. 2 *Cdn.* a place for storing supplies, furs, equipment, etc., away from foraging animals and the weather. 3 *Cdn.* a supply of goods stockpiled for future use. 4 *Cdn.* a hut, tent, lean-to, or other structure used as a storehouse. 5 the things hidden or stored in a cache. 6 a blind used in hunting game. 7 *Computer technology.* a dedicated data storage area, either a section of the main memory or supplied by a special chip, that can be accessed many times more quickly than regular memory.
—v. 1 hide or conceal. 2 *Cdn.* deposit in a cache. ⟨< F *cache* < *cacher* conceal⟩
☛ *Hom.* CASH.

ca•chet [kæ'ʃei] *or* ['kæʃei] *n.* 1 a private seal or stamp: *The letter was sealed with the king's cachet.* 2 a distinguishing mark of quality or genuineness. 3 stylish distinction; prestige. 4 a capsule for enclosing a medicine with an unpleasant taste. 5 a slogan, design, etc., stamped or printed on mail, especially to show off commemorative stamps. 6 *Philately.* an insignia on an envelope commemorating some event in history, particularly stamp history. ⟨< F *cachet* < *cacher* hide⟩

ca•chex•ia [kə'kɛksiə] *n. Medicine.* a general wasting of the body through long-term illness or malnutrition. ⟨< NL < Gk. *kachexia* bad (bodily) habit < *kakos* bad + *hexis* habit⟩

cach•in•nate ['kækə,neit] *v.* **-nat•ed, -nat•ing.** laugh loudly. ⟨< L *cachinnare*⟩ **—,cach•in'na•tion,** *n.*

ca•chou [kæ'ʃu] *or* [kə'ʃu] *n.* 1 a pill or lozenge, composed of cashew nuts and other ingredients and used to perfume the breath, thus cloaking the odour of tobacco smoke, alcohol, etc. 2 catechu. ⟨< F *cachou*⟩
☛ *Hom.* CASHEW [kə'ʃu].

ca•chu•cha [kə'tʃutʃə] *n.* 1 an Andalusian dance in 3/4 time. 2 the music for this dance. ⟨< Sp.⟩

ca•cique [kə'sik] *n.* 1 formerly, a native Indian chief in Spanish America. 2 a local political boss in Latin America or Spain. 3 any of various tropical American orioles (especially of genus *Cacicus*). ⟨< Sp. < Haitian⟩

cack•le ['kækəl] *v.* **-led, -ling;** *n.* *—v.* 1 of a hen, make a shrill, intermittent cry, especially after laying an egg. 2 laugh with shrill, harsh, or intermittent sounds: *The old man cackled after each joke.* 3 chatter.
—n. the act or sound of cackling. ⟨ME *cakelen*; imitative⟩

caco– *prefix.* bad; poor; unpleasant. Also, before vowels, **cac-**. ⟨< Gk. *kakos* bad⟩

ca•cog•ra•phy [kə'kɒgrəfi] *n.* 1 poor handwriting. 2 wrong spelling.

cac•o•mis•tle ['kækə,mɪsəl] *n.* a carnivorous mammal (*Bassariscus astutus*) rather like a cat, but having a long, ringed tail and related to the raccoon; native to SW U.S. and Mexico. ⟨< Mexican Spanish < Nahuatl *tlacomiztli* < *tlaco* half + *miztli* lion⟩

ca•coph•o•nous [kə'kɒfənəs] *adj.* harsh and clashing; dissonant; discordant. **—ca'coph•o•nous•ly,** *adv.*

ca•coph•o•ny [kə'kɒfəni] *n., pl.* **-nies.** a harsh, clashing sound; dissonance; discord. ⟨< NL *cacophonia* < Gk. *kakophōnia* < *kakos* bad + *phōnē* sound⟩

cac•tus ['kæktəs] *n., pl.* **-tus•es** or **-ti** [-taɪ] *or* [-ti]. any of a family (Cactaceae) of plants found especially in deserts, having thick, fleshy stems with spines or scales instead of leaves and often having large, showy flowers. ⟨< L < Gk. *kaktos*⟩

ca•cu•mi•nal [kə'kjumənəl] *adj., n. Phonetics. —adj.* uttered with the tongue-tip curled backward against or near the hard palate.
—n. a sound uttered in this way. ⟨< L *cacumen* top⟩

cad [kæd] *n.* a man who does not act like a gentleman; an ill-bred man. ⟨< *caddie*⟩

CAD *Computer technology.* COMPUTER-AIDED (or ASSISTED) DESIGN.

ca•das•tre [kə'dæstər] *n.* a public register of the ownership, value, and extent of land as a basis of taxation. Also, **cadaster.** ⟨< LL *capitastrum* register of poll tax < L *caput*, *-itis* head⟩ **—ca'das•tral,** *adj.*

ca•dav•er [kə'dævər] *n.* a dead body, especially a human body intended for dissection; corpse. ⟨< L⟩

ca•dav•er•ous [kə'dævərəs] *adj.* **1** of or like a cadaver. **2** pale and ghastly. **3** thin and worn. **—ca'dav•er•ous•ly,** *adv.* **—ca'dav•er•ous•ness,** *n.*

Cad•bo•ro•sau•rus [ˌkædbərə'sɔrəs] *n. Cdn.* a monster sea serpent supposed to frequent the waters off Victoria, B.C. ⟨< *Cadboro* Bay⟩

cad•die or **cad•dy** ['kædi] *n., v.* **-died, -dy•ing.** *—n.* **1** *Golf.* a person who helps a golfer by carrying his or her clubs, finding the ball, etc. **2** a small trolley with two wheels, used for carrying golf clubs.
—v. help a golfer in this way. ⟨< F *cadet* younger brother. See CADET.⟩

cad•dis fly ['kædɪs] any of an order (Trichoptera) of aquatic insects found throughout the world, having two pairs of membranous wings and slender, jointed antennae. Many caddis flies resemble moths. See also CADDIS WORM. ⟨origin uncertain⟩

cad•dish ['kædɪʃ] *adj.* like a cad; ungentlemanly. **—'cad•dish•ly,** *adv.* **—'cad•dish•ness,** *n.*

caddis worm the omnivorous larva of the CADDIS FLY. It is found in fresh water, carrying around its own protective case that it has constructed of silk and bits of sand and debris.

Cad•do ['kædou] *n.* **1** a member of a group of American Indians now living in Oklahoma but formerly of Louisiana, Arkansas, and E Texas. **2** the language of these people.

cad•dy¹ ['kædi] *n., pl.* **-dies. 1** a small box, can, or chest, often used to hold tea. **2** any container or storage device. ⟨< Malay *kati* a small weight⟩

cad•dy² ['kædi] *n., pl.* **-dies;** *v.* **-died, -dy•ing.** See CADDIE.

cade¹ [keid] *adj.* of a young animal, neglected by its mother and reared by people: *a cade lamb.* ⟨< Late ME, a pet⟩

cade² [keid] *n.* a juniper bush (*Juniperus oxycedrus*) native to Mediterranean regions, yielding a medicinal oil used to treat skin conditions. ⟨< F⟩

ca•dence ['keidəns] *n.* **1** rhythm; the measure or beat of any rhythmical movement: *the steady cadence of a march.* **2** a fall of the voice, as at the end of a sentence. **3** a rising and falling sound; modulation: *She speaks with a pleasant cadence.* **4** *Music.* a series of chords, a trill, etc., that brings part of a composition to an end. ⟨< F < Ital. *cadenza* < L *cadentia.* Doublet of CADENZA and CHANCE.⟩

ca•den•za [kə'dɛnzə] *n. Music.* an elaborate flourish or showy passage for a solo voice or instrument in an aria, concerto, etc. ⟨< Ital. < L *cadentia* < *cadere* fall. Doublet of CADENCE and CHANCE.⟩

ca•det [kə'dɛt] *n., adj.—n.* **1** a young man or woman in training to be an officer in the armed forces. **2** a young man or woman undergoing training for a police force. **3** a person under military age who is undertaking basic military training in an organization subsidized by the armed forces. **4 Cadet,** a member of the GIRL GUIDES, aged 15 to 17, who is training for leadership. **5** *Archaic.* a younger son or brother.
—adj. descended from a younger son or daughter: *the cadet branch of the family.* ⟨< F < Gascon *capdel* < L *capitellum*, dim. of *caput* head⟩

ca•det•ship [kə'dɛtʃɪp] *n.* the rank or position of a cadet.

cadge [kædʒ] *v.* **cadged, cadg•ing. 1** *Dialect.* peddle. **2** *Informal.* beg. ⟨origin uncertain⟩ **—'cadg•er,** *n.*

cadge crib *Cdn. Logging.* formerly, a raft equipped with a windlass driven by horsepower and having the function of drawing, by means of a cable, booms of logs to a desired anchoring spot.

ca•di ['kɑdi] *or* ['keidi] *n., pl.* **-dis.** a Muslim judge responsible for making judgments in religious cases, such as those involving inheritance, marriage, or divorce. ⟨< Arabic *qadi* judge⟩

Cad•me•an ['kædmiən] *or* [kæd'miən] *adj.* having to do with Cadmus. The Cadmean alphabet was the earliest form of writing used by the ancient Greeks. ⟨< L *Cadme(us)* < Gk. *Kadmeios* of Cadmus⟩

cad•mi•um ['kædmiəm] *n.* a soft, bluish white, ductile metallic chemical element resembling tin, used in plating to prevent rust and in making certain alloys. *Symbol*: Cd; *at.no.* 48; *at.mass* 112.41. ⟨< NL < L *cadmia* zinc ore < Gk. *kadmeia*⟩ **—'cad•mic,** *adj.*

Cad•mus ['kædməs] *n. Greek mythology.* a Phoenician prince who killed a dragon and sowed its teeth. Armed men sprang up from the teeth and fought each other until only five survived. With these five men, Cadmus founded the Greek city of Thebes.

ca•dre ['kædri] *or* ['kædrei], ['kɑdri] *or* ['kɑdrei] *n.* **1** framework. **2** the staff of trained military personnel necessary to establish and train a new military unit. **3** a similar group of people working closely together or as the nucleus of an organization. ⟨< F < Ital. < L *quadrum* square⟩

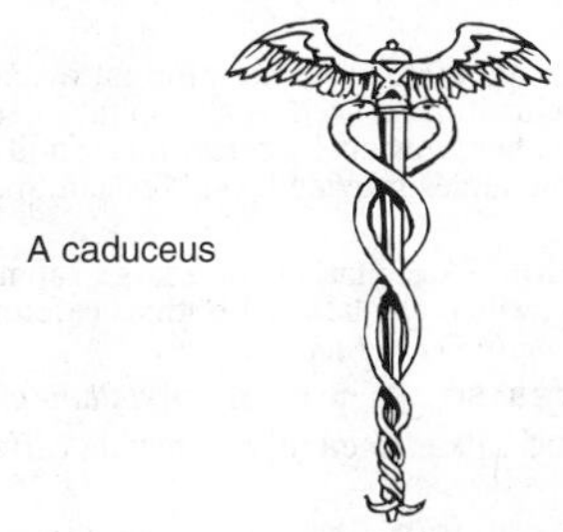
A caduceus

ca•du•ce•us [kə'djusiəs] *or* [kə'dusiəs] *n., pl.* **-ce•i** [-si,aɪ] *or* [-si,i]. a staff with two snakes twined around it and a pair of wings on top. Mercury, or Hermes, the messenger of the gods, is usually shown carrying a caduceus. The caduceus is often used as an emblem of the medical profession. ⟨< L < dial. Gk. *karykeion* herald's staff⟩

ca•du•ci•ty [kə'djusəti] *or* [kə'dusəti] *n.* **1** the condition of spoiling or decaying. **2** the condition of growing feeble in old age. ⟨< F *caducité* < LL *caducitas* < L *caducus* falling < *cadere* fall⟩

cae•cum ['sikəm] *n., pl.* **-ca** [-kə]. the large pouch, closed at one end, that forms the beginning of the large intestine. See ALIMENTARY CANAL for picture. Also, **cecum.** ⟨< L *caecum* blind (thing)⟩

Cae•lum ['siləm] a small constellation in the southern sky.

Caer•phil•ly [kɛr'fɪli] *n.* a soft cheese. ⟨< *Caerphilly* in Wales⟩

Cae•sar ['sizər] *n.* **1** a title of the Roman emperors from Augustus to Hadrian, and later of the heir to the throne. **2** emperor. **3** dictator; tyrant. ⟨< Gaius Julius *Caesar* (100?-44 B.C.), a Roman general, statesman, and historian, conqueror of Gaul⟩

Cae•sar•e•an [sɪ'zɛriən] *adj., n. —adj.* **1** of Julius Caesar or the Caesars. **2** by CAESAREAN SECTION: *a Caesarean birth.*
—n. CAESAREAN SECTION. Also, **Caesarian** or (sometimes for *n.* and *adj.*, def. 2) **Cesarean** or **Cesarian.**

Caesarean section a method of delivering a child by cutting through the wall of the abdomen and uterus of the mother. Also called **C-section.** ⟨from the belief that Julius Caesar was born in this way⟩

Cae•sar•i•an [sɪ'zɛriən] See CAESAREAN.

cae•sar•ism ['sizə,rɪzəm] *n.* dictatorship; autocracy. **—'cae•sar•ist,** *adj., n.*

Caesar salad a salad of greens, cheese, and croutons, dressed in beaten raw egg and oil, seasoned with garlic.

cae•si•um ['siziəm] See CESIUM.

cae•su•ra [sɪ'zjʊrə] *or* [sɪ'ʒʊrə] *n., pl.* **-sur•as. 1** a pause in a line of verse, generally agreeing with a pause required by the sense. The caesura is the chief pause if there is more than one. In Greek and Latin poetry the caesura falls within a foot, not far from the middle of a line. Whenever it occurs in English poetry, it usually comes near the middle of a line, either within or after a metrical foot. *Example*: *"To err is human, | to forgive, divine."* Also, **cesura. 2** a similar pause in music. ⟨< L *caesura* cutting < *caedere* cut⟩

CAF or **C.A.F.** Canadian Armed Forces.

C.A.F. or **c.a.f. 1** cost and freight. **2** cost, assurance, and freight.

CAFE corporate average fuel economy.

ca•fé [kæ'fei] *or* [kə'fei] *n.* **1** a small, informal restaurant, especially one that serves light meals, often specializing in different coffees and teas, pastries, etc. **2** *French.* coffee. ⟨< F⟩

☛ *Syn.* **Café** usually refers only to a small, informal place to eat. RESTAURANT may refer to any public eating place, from a very formal dining room to a small place with a counter and perhaps two or three tables.

ca•fé au lait [kɑ'fei ou 'lei] *or* ['kæfi-]; *French,* [kafeo'lɛ] *French.* **1** coffee made with milk or cream. **2** brownish yellow.

café curtains short, usually sheer curtains hung by rings on a rod to cover the lower half of a window.

café filtre [kafe'filtʀ] *French.* coffee made by pouring boiling water over coffee grounds in a filtering device.

ca•fé noir [kafe'nwaʀ] *French.* coffee without milk or cream; black coffee.

caf•e•te•ri•a [,kæfə'tiriə] *n.* an informal restaurant, especially in an institution, such as a hospital or school, or in an office building, where customers select their food at a counter and take it to the tables provided. ⟨< Mexican Sp. *cafeteria* coffee shop⟩

caf•e•to•ri•um [,kæfə'tɔriəm] *n.* a large room in a school or similar building, which can be used both as cafeteria and as auditorium. ⟨*cafet*(*eria*) + (*audit*)*orium*⟩

caf•fé es•pres•so [,kafe ɛs'prɛsso] *Italian.* espresso coffee.

caf•fein•at•ed ['kæfə,neitəd] *adj.* having caffeine as an ingredient.

caf•feine or **caf•fein** [kæ'fin] *or* ['kæfin] *n.* a stimulating drug found in coffee and tea. *Formula*: $C_8H_{10}N_4O_2$ ⟨< F *caféine* < *café* coffee⟩

caf•fein•ism ['kæfi,nɪzəm] *n.* excessive dependence on caffeine; addiction to caffeine.

caf•tan ['kæftæn], ['kæftən], *or* ['kɑftɑn] *n.* **1** a loose, ankle-length, long-sleeved garment worn with a kind of sash. Caftans are traditionally worn in eastern Mediterranean countries. **2** a similar garment worn in western countries for lounging or recreation. Also, **kaftan.** ⟨< Turkish *qaftan*⟩

cage [keidʒ] *n., v.* **caged, cag•ing.** *—n.* **1** a frame or box closed in with wires, bars, etc. for confining an animal. Birds are kept in cages. **2** anything shaped or used like a cage: *The car or closed platform of a mine elevator is a cage.* **3** a prison or anything that confines like a prison. **4** *Hockey.* the network structure forming the goal. **5** *Baseball.* a screen used to stop balls during batting practice. **6** *Basketball.* the basket.
—v. put or keep in a cage. ⟨ME < OF < L *cavea* cell < *cavus* hollow⟩

cage•ling ['keidʒlɪŋ] *n.* a bird kept in a cage.

cag•er ['keidʒər] *n. Slang.* a basketball player.

ca•gey or **ca•gy** ['keidʒi] *adj.* **ca•gi•er, ca•gi•est.** **1** *Informal.* shrewd: *a cagey lawyer.* **2** cautious; wary: *He was too cagey to commit himself completely.* **—'ca•gi•ly,** *adv.* **—'ca•gi•ness,** *n.*

CAHA or **C.A.H.A.** Canadian Amateur Hockey Association.

ca•hoots [kə'huts] *n. Slang.*
in cahoots, in partnership, especially for a wrongful purpose; in league: *She was found to be in cahoots with the thief. The two of them are probably in cahoots.* ⟨origin uncertain⟩

ca•hot [kə'hou] *n. Cdn.* **1** a ridge of snow on a road: *The cahots made the ride a very bumpy one.* **2** a ridge or bump in an unpaved road. ⟨< F⟩

CAI computer-assisted instruction.

cai•man ['keimən] *n., pl.* **-mans.** See CAYMAN.

Cain [kein] *n.* **1** in the Bible, the oldest son of Adam and Eve and the murderer of his brother Abel. **2** any murderer.
raise Cain, *Slang.* make a great disturbance.

ca•ïque [kɑ'ik] *n.* **1** a long, narrow Turkish rowboat, much used on the Bosporus. **2** a Mediterranean sailing ship. ⟨< F < Ital. *caicco* < Turkish *qāyik*⟩

cairn [kɛrn] *n.* **1** a pile of stones heaped up as a memorial, tomb, or landmark. **2** CAIRN TERRIER. ⟨< Scots Gaelic *carn* heap of stones⟩

cairn•gorm ['kɛrn,gɔrm] *n.* **1** a yellow or smoky-brown variety of quartz. **2** a gem made of this stone. Cairngorms are often used for brooches and other ornaments, especially by the Scots. ⟨< *Cairngorm*, a peak in the Grampians, Scotland⟩

cairn terrier a breed of small, long-haired, working terrier originally bred in Scotland, having a soft undercoat and a hard, wiry topcoat.

caisse pop•u•laire ['kɛs pɒpjə'lɛr]; *French,* [,kɛspɔpy'lɛʀ] *Cdn.* especially in Québec, credit union. Often, **caisse.** ⟨< Cdn.F⟩

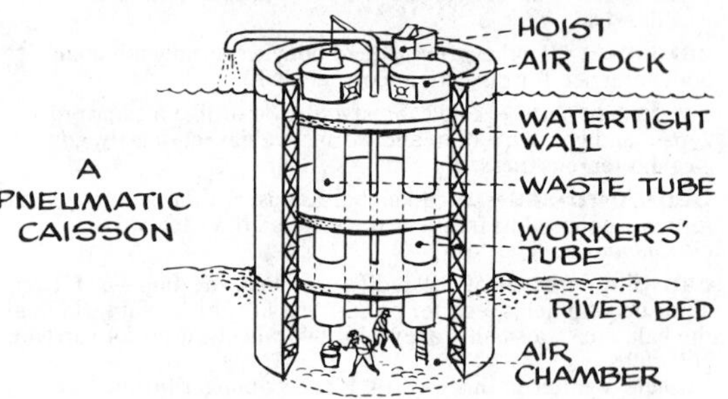

A PNEUMATIC CAISSON

cais•son ['keisɒn] *or* ['keisən] *n.* **1** a watertight box or chamber within which work can be carried on under water. Caissons are used in the construction of bridge piers. **2** a watertight float used in raising sunken ships. **3** a box for ammunition. **4** a wagon to carry ammunition. ⟨< F *caisson* < *caisse* chest < L *capsa* box⟩

caisson disease DECOMPRESSION SICKNESS.

cai•tiff ['keitɪf] *n., adj. —n. Archaic.* a mean, contemptible person; coward.
—adj. vile; cowardly; contemptible. ⟨ME < OF *catif* < L *captivus* captive. Doublet of CAPTIVE.⟩

ca•jole [kə'dʒoul] *v.* **-joled, -jol•ing.** persuade by flattery or false promises, especially to overcome reluctance; coax: *His older sister cajoled him into cutting the lawn.* ⟨< F *cajoler*⟩ **—ca'jol•er,** *n.* **—ca'jol•ing•ly,** *adv.*

ca•jol•er•y [kə'dʒouləri] *n., pl.* **-er•ies.** persuasion by flattering or deceitful words; flattery; coaxing.

Ca•jun ['keidʒən] *n., adj.—n.* **1** a native or inhabitant of a French-speaking area of Louisiana. **2** the French dialect of these people.
—adj. of or having to do with Cajuns: *Cajun cooking.* ⟨< *Acadian*⟩

cake [keik] *n., v.* **caked, cak•ing.** *—n.* **1** a baked mixture of flour, sugar, eggs, flavouring, and other things: *a sponge cake, a fruit cake.* **2** batter that has been fried or baked in a small, flat, usually round shape: *buckwheat cakes.* **3** any small, flat mass of food fried on both sides: *a fish cake.* **4** a hard, shaped mass: *a cake of soap, a cake of maple sugar.*
take the cake, *Slang.* **a** win first prize. **b** excel. **c** used ironically, be the last or worst in a series of disappointments, troubles, etc.
—v. form into a solid mass; harden: *Mud cakes as it dries.* ⟨ME, probably < ON *kaka*⟩

cake flour a fine wheat flour having a low gluten content, used for baking cakes, cookies, etc.

cakes and ale good things; the pleasures of life.

cake•walk ['keik,wɒk] *n., v. —n.* **1** formerly, among Blacks of the United States, an entertainment in which people performed a kind of promenade or walk to music, with a prize of a cake for the best or most original steps. **2** a popular high-stepping dance based on this walk. **3** music for this dance. **4** *Informal.* something easy to do: *The election campaign was a cakewalk.*
—v. do a cakewalk. **—'cake,walk•er,** *n.*

cal. 1 calendar. **2** calibre. **3** calorie(s).

cal•a•bash ['kælə,bæʃ] *n.* **1** a tropical American tree (*Crescentia cujete*) of the trumpet creeper family, having funnel-shaped flowers and very large, hard-shelled fruits. **2** the fruit of this tree. **3** a utensil, such as a bowl or dipper, made from the shell of this fruit. **4** GOURD (def. 1). ⟨< F *calebasse* < Sp. *calabaza*, probably < Persian *kharbuz* melon⟩

cal•a•boose ['kælə,bus] *or* [,kælə'bus] *n. Informal.* a jail or prison. ⟨< Sp. *calabozo* dungeon⟩

ca•la•di•um [kə'leidiəm] *n.* any of several tropical American plants (genus *Caladium*) of the arum family, grown in many varieties for their colourful foliage. Caladiums are popular as house plants in cooler regions. ⟨< Malay *kelady*⟩

cal•a•man•co [,kælə'mæŋkou] *n.* a glossy woollen cloth, checked or brocaded in the warp so that the pattern shows on one side only. ⟨origin uncertain⟩

ca•la•ma•ri or **ca•la•ma•ry** [,kɑlə'mɑri] *or* ['kælə,mɛri] *n.* a giant squid served as food. ⟨< L *calamarius* < *calamus* a reed⟩

cal•a•mine ['kælə,maɪn] *or* ['kæləmɪn] *n.* a pink, odourless, tasteless powder consisting of zinc oxide and a small amount of ferric oxide, used in skin lotions and ointments. ⟨< F < Med.L *calamina* < L *cadmia.* See CADMIUM.⟩

cal•a•mint ['kælə,mɪnt] *n.* a plant (*Calamintha nepeta*) of the mint family, related to savory. ⟨< ME *calaminte* < OF *calamente* < Med.L *calamentum* < L *calaminthe* < Gk. *kalaminthe*⟩

ca•lam•i•tous [kə'læmətəs] *adj.* causing a calamity; accompanied by a calamity; disastrous. **—ca'lam•i•tous•ly,** *adv.* **—ca'lam•i•tous•ness,** *n.*

ca•lam•i•ty [kə'læməti] *n., pl.* **-ties. 1** an event causing great misery or destruction: *The fire was the worst calamity of the decade for the town.* **2** serious trouble; misery: *Calamity may come to anyone.* ⟨< F *calamité* < L *calamitas*⟩

☛ *Syn.* **1.** See note at DISASTER.

cal•a•mon•din [,kælə'mɒndɪn] *n.* **1** a small citrus tree (*Citrofortunella mitis*) native to the Philippines. **2** the fruit of this tree, a tart orange with a flavour like that of a tangerine. ⟨< Tagalog *kalamunding*⟩

cal•a•mus ['kæləməs] *n., pl.* **-mi** [-,maɪ] *or* [-,mi]. **1** the aromatic rootstock of the sweet flag, used as a flavouring and in the manufacture of perfume and insecticide. **2** the plant itself; sweet flag. **3** any of various tropical Asian palms (genus *Calamus*) from which rattan is obtained. **4** the shaft of a feather; quill. ⟨< L < Gk. *kalamos* reed⟩

ca•lan•do [kə'lændou] *adv. Music.* fading away; with a gradual decrease in volume and speed. ⟨< Ital. gerund of *calare* to decrease < L < Gk. *chalan* to slacken⟩

ca•lash [kə'læʃ] *n.* **1** a light, four-passenger carriage with small wheels and a folding top. **2** *Archaic.* calèche. **3** a folding carriage top. **4** a woman's folding hood or bonnet, worn in the 18th and 19th centuries. ⟨< F *calèche*⟩

cal•a•ver•ite [,kælə'vɛrəit] *n.* a naturally occurring compound of gold and tellurium. Symbol: $AuTe_2$ ⟨< *Calaveras* County, California, where it was first discovered⟩

cal•ca•ne•us [kæl'keiniəs] *n., pl.* **-ne•i** [-ni,aɪ]. **1** the human heel bone. **2** a similar bone in four-footed animals. ⟨< L *calcaneum* heel⟩

cal•car•e•ous [kæl'kɛriəs] *adj.* **1** of or containing lime or limestone. **2** of or containing calcium. ⟨< L < *calx* lime⟩

cal•ces ['kælsiz] *n.* a pl. of CALX.

calci– *combining form.* lime or calcium; of or containing lime or calcium. Also (before vowels), **calc-.**

cal•cif•er•ous [kæl'sɪfərəs] *adj.* containing calcite.

cal•ci•fi•ca•tion [,kælsəfə'keiʃən] *n.* **1** the process of calcifying. **2** a calcified part. **3** the accumulation of calcium in certain soils.

cal•ci•fuge ['kælsə,fjudʒ] *n.* a plant that thrives in calcium-poor soil. **—cal'sif•u•gous** [kæl'sɪfjəgəs], *adj.*

cal•ci•fy ['kælsə,faɪ] *v.* **-fied, -fy•ing.** make or become hard by the deposit of lime. An injured cartilage sometimes calcifies.

cal•ci•mine ['kælsə,maɪn] *or* ['kælsəmɪn] *n., v.* **-mined, -min•ing.** *—n.* a white or coloured liquid consisting of a mixture of water, colouring matter, glue, etc., used especially on plastered ceilings and walls.
—v. cover with calcimine.

cal•ci•na•tion [,kælsə'neiʃən] *n.* **1** the act or operation of calcining. **2** anything formed by calcining.

cal•ci•na•tor ['kælsə,neitər] *n.* a furnace or incinerator that reduces radioactive waste to ashes, so that it can be transported and dumped with greater care and safety.

cal•cine ['kælsaɪn] *or* ['kælsɪn] *v.* **-cined, -cin•ing. 1** heat (an inorganic substance) to a high temperature, but not high enough to melt or fuse it, in order to bring about evaporation of certain

matter in it or cause chemical changes such as oxidation: *Limestone is calcined to produce lime.* **2** undergo this process. **3** burn (something) to a powder or fine ash. ⟨ME < OF *calciner* < L *calx* lime⟩

cal•cite ['kælsəit] *n.* a mineral composed of CALCIUM CARBONATE. It occurs as limestone, chalk, marble, etc. *Formula*: $CaCO_3$

cal•ci•to•nin [,kælsə'tounɪn] *n.* a hormone used to treat certain bone diseases.

cal•cit•ri•ol [kæl'sɪtri,ɒl] *n.* a hormone which is an active form of vitamin D_3. *Formula*: $C_{27}H_{44}O_3$

cal•ci•um ['kælsiəm] *n.* a soft, silver-white, metallic element that is a part of limestone, chalk, milk, bone, etc. Calcium is used in alloys or as a medicine, and its compounds are used in making plaster, in cooking, and as bleaching agents. *Symbol*: Ca; *at.no.* 20; *at.mass* 40.08. ⟨< L *calx, calcis* lime⟩

calcium car•bide ['kɑrbaɪd] a heavy, grey, crystalline compound that reacts with water to form acetylene gas. *Formula*: CaC_2

calcium car•bi•mide ['kɑrbə,maɪd] a drug used to treat alcoholism.

calcium car•bo•nate ['kɑrbə,neit] a mineral occurring in rocks as marble and limestone, in animals as bones, shells, teeth, etc., and to some extent in plants; calcite. *Formula*: $CaCO_3$

calcium chlo•ride ['klɔraɪd] a very absorbent compound of calcium and chlorine, used mainly as a drying agent, preservative, and refrigerant, and also in medicine. *Formula*: $CaCl_2$

calcium di•so•di•um ed•e•tate [dəi'soudiəm 'ɛdə,teit] a drug used to treat lead poisoning.

calcium glu•co•hep•to•nate [,glukou'hɛptə,neit] a calcium dietary supplement used to treat osteoporosis.

calcium glu•co•nate ['glukə,neit] a first aid treatment for certain acid burns. *Formula*: $CaC_{12}H_{22}O_{14}$

calcium hy•drox•ide [haɪ'drɒksaɪd] slaked lime. *Formula*: $Ca(OH)_2$

calcium light a strong, white light produced by making lime incandescent with a very hot flame; limelight.

calcium ox•ide ['ɒksaɪd] quicklime. *Formula*: CaO

calcium phos•phate ['fɒsfeit] a compound of calcium and phosphoric acid, used in medicine, in making enamels, etc. It is found in bones and as rock. *Formula*: $Ca_3(PO_4)_2$

cal•cu•la•ble ['kælkjələbəl] *adj.* **1** that can be calculated. **2** reliable; dependable. **—'cal•cu•la•bly,** *adv.*

cal•cu•late ['kælkjə,leit] *v.* **-lat•ed, -lat•ing. 1** find out by adding, subtracting, multiplying, or dividing; figure: *to calculate the cost of furnishing a house.* **2** find out beforehand by any process of reasoning; estimate: *Calculate the day of the week on which Christmas will fall.* **3** rely; depend; count (*on*): *A waitress working evenings here can calculate on making $60 a week in tips.* **4** *Informal.* plan; intend: *That remark was calculated to hurt my feelings.* **5** *Informal.* think; believe; suppose.
calculate on, *Informal.* estimate or anticipate: *We calculated on ten guests, but only two arrived.* ⟨< L *calculare* < *calculus* pebble used in counting, dim. of *calx* stone⟩

cal•cu•lat•ing ['kælkjə,leitɪŋ] *adj., v.* *—adj.* **1** that calculates: *calculating machines.* **2** shrewd; careful. **3** scheming; selfish.
—v. ppr. of CALCULATE. **—'cal•cu,lat•ing•ly,** *adv.*

cal•cu•la•tion [,kælkjə'leiʃən] *n.* **1** the act of calculating: *The calculation of the total cost will take some time.* **2** a plan or result found by calculating: *All my calculations are correct.* **3** careful thinking; deliberate planning or scheming.

cal•cu•la•tive ['kælkjələtɪv] *or* ['kælkjə,leitɪv] *adj.* **1** having to do with calculation. **2** tending to be calculating.

cal•cu•la•tor ['kælkjə,leitər] *n.* **1** a machine that performs mathematical calculations mechanically or electronically, especially one that solves difficult mathematical problems. **2** a person who operates such a machine. **3** a person who calculates by hand. **4** a table or chart facilitating routine calculations.

cal•cu•lous ['kælkjələs] *adj.* caused by or containing a CALCULUS (def. 2).

☛ *Hom.* CALCULUS.

cal•cu•lus ['kælkjələs] *n., pl.* **-lus•es** or **-li** [-,laɪ] *or* [-,li]. **1** *Mathematics.* a method of reasoning using a highly specialized system of notation. See also DIFFERENTIAL CALCULUS and INTEGRAL CALCULUS. **2** a stone or hard mass formed in the

body. **3** a hard substance that has collected on the teeth, formed by the action of bacteria on saliva and food particles; tartar. ⟨< L *calculus.* See CALCULATE.⟩
☛ *Hom.* CALCULOUS.

cal•dar•i•um [kæl'dɛriəm] *n.* in ancient Rome, a special room for taking a hot bath. ⟨< L < *caldarius* having to do with warming < *calidus* warm, hot; akin to *calor* heat⟩

cal•de•ra ['kɒldərə] *or* ['kældərə] *n.* a depression at the top of a volcano, larger than a crater, formed by an explosion or the collapse of part of the cone. ⟨< Sp. < L *caldarium*⟩

cal•dron ['kɒldrən] *n.* See CAULDRON.

ca•lèche [kə'lɛʃ] *n. Cdn.* a light, two-wheeled, one-horse carriage for two passengers, having a seat in front for the driver and, usually, a folding top. Also, **calash.** ⟨< F⟩
☛ *Usage.* The alternative form **calash** was once more common than it is today. Since the vehicle is now little used except as a conveyance for sightseers in Québec City and Montréal, **calèche,** the French form of the word, is generally used.

A calèche

Cal•e•do•ni•a [,kælə'dounjə] *or* [,kælə'douniə] *n. Poetic.* Scotland. **—,Cal•e'do•ni•an,** *adj., n.*

cal•en•dar ['kæləndər] *n., v. —n.* **1** a table showing the months and weeks of the year and the day of the week on which each day of the month comes. **2** a system by which the beginning, length, and divisions of the year are fixed. **3** a list or schedule; record of planned events; register: *We have three winter carnivals on our calendar. The trial had to be delayed because the court calendar was filled.* **4** a volume or booklet issued annually by a university or college listing regulations, courses to be given, etc.
—v. enter in a calendar or list; register. ⟨ME < AF *calender* < L *calendarium* account book < *calendae* calends (day bills were due)⟩
☛ *Hom.* CALENDER.

calendar day the 24 hours from one midnight to the next midnight.

calendar month one of the 12 named parts into which a year is divided; month.

calendar stick *Cdn.* a stick notched each day to keep track of the date, used by trappers and others isolated in the wilderness.

calendar year a period of 365 days (or in leap year, 366 days) that begins on January 1 and ends on December 31.

cal•en•der ['kæləndər] *n., v. —n.* a machine in which cloth, paper, etc., is smoothed and glazed by pressing between rollers.
—v. make smooth and glossy by pressing in a calender. ⟨< F *calandre* < L < Gk. *kylindros* cylinder⟩
☛ *Hom.* CALENDAR.

ca•len•dri•cal [kə'lɛndrəkəl] *adj.* of or having to do with a calendar.

cal•ends ['kæləndz] *n.pl.* in the ancient Roman calendar, the first day of the month. Also, **kalends.** ⟨ME < L *calendae*⟩

ca•len•du•la [kə'lɛndʒələ] *or* [kə'lɛndjələ] *n.* **1** any of a genus (*Calendula*) of small, closely related herbs of the composite family having yellow or orange flowers. The best-known calendula is the pot marigold. **2** the flower of any of these herbs, often used in medicine. ⟨< NL *calendula,* dim. of *calendae* the calends⟩

cal•en•ture ['kæləntʃər] *or* ['kælən,tʃʊr] *n.* a tropical fever accompanied by delirium. ⟨< F < Sp. *calentura* < L *calere* be hot⟩

calf[1] [kæf] *n., pl.* **calves. 1** the young of the domestic cow or of a related animal such as the buffalo. **2** a young elephant, whale, seal, etc. **3** leather made from the skin of a calf. **4** *Informal.* a clumsy, silly child or youth. **5** a small mass of ice that has become detached from a glacier, iceberg, etc.
kill the fatted calf, prepare a feast to celebrate something or to welcome someone. ⟨OE⟩

calf[2] [kæf] *n., pl.* **calves.** the thick, fleshy part of the back of the human leg below the knee. See LEG for picture. ⟨< ON *kálfi*⟩

calf love PUPPY LOVE.

calf's–foot jelly gelatin made by boiling the feet of calves. Also, **calves's-foot jelly.**

calf•skin ['kæf,skɪn] *n.* **1** the skin of a calf. **2** leather made from it.

Cal•i•ban ['kælə,bæn] *n.* a bestial or degraded man. ⟨in Shakespeare's play *The Tempest,* a beastlike slave⟩

cal•i•ber ['kæləbər] See CALIBRE.

cal•i•brate ['kælə,breit] *v.* **-brat•ed, -brat•ing. 1** determine, check, or adjust the scale of (a thermometer, gauge, or other measuring instrument). This is usually done by comparison with a standard instrument. **2** find the calibre of. **3** *Informal.* measure. **—'cal•i,bra•tor,** *n.* **—,cal•i'bra•tion,** *n.*

cal•i•bre ['kæləbər] *n.* **1** diameter, especially inside diameter: *A .45 calibre revolver has a barrel with an inside diameter of 45/100 of an inch* (*about* 114 mm). **2** degree of quality or worth: *a person of high calibre. How can we improve the calibre of our schools?* Also, **caliber.** ⟨< F *calibre* < Arabic *qalib* mould⟩

ca•li•che [kə'litʃi] *or* [kə'litʃə] *n.* **1** naturally occurring sodium nitrate, found in South America. *Formula*: $NaNO_3$ **2** calcium carbonate formed on dry soil by evaporation. *Formula*: $CaCO_3$ ⟨< Am.Sp. < Sp. *cal* lime < L *calx*⟩

cal•i•co ['kælə,kou] *n., pl.* **-coes** or **-cos;** *adj. —n.* a cotton cloth that usually has coloured patterns printed on one side.
—adj. **1** made of calico. **2** spotted in colours: *a calico cat.* ⟨< *Calicut,* India⟩

calico salmon *Cdn.* CHUM[3].

ca•lif ['keilɪf] *or* ['kælɪf] See CALIPH.

ca•lif•ate ['keilə,feit] *or* ['kælə,feit] See CALIPHATE.

Cal•i•for•nia [,kælə'fɔrnjə] *or* [,kælə'fɔrniə] *n.* a large west coast state of the United States.

California laurel a shrub or tree (*Umbellaria californica*) of the laurel family, growing on the west coast of the United States and bearing bay leaves.

California poppy 1 a plant (*Eschscholtzia californica*) of the poppy family having finely divided bluish green leaves and cream-coloured, yellow, orange, or red flowers. It is native to the Pacific coast of North America. **2** the flower of this plant.

California rosebay a shrub or tree (*Rhododendron californicum*) growing on the west coast of North America and bearing large red flowers.

cal•i•for•ni•um [,kælə'fɔrniəm] *n.* a highly radioactive artificial element, produced by bombarding curium with helium isotopes. *Symbol*: Cf; *at.no.* 98; *at.mass* 251.08. ⟨after the University of *California,* where it was first produced in 1950⟩

cal•i•per ['kæləpər] See CALLIPER.

ca•liph ['keilɪf] *or* ['kælɪf] *n.* a traditional title, since the time of Mohammed, of the religious and political leader of the Muslim community. The office of the caliph was suspended in 1926 until such time as the Muslim peoples can again form one community. Also, **calif, khalif.** ⟨< OF *calife* < Med.L < Arabic *khalifah* successor, vicar⟩

ca•liph•ate ['keilə,feit] *or* ['kælə,feit] *n.* the rank, reign, government, or territory of a caliph. Also, **califate.**

cal•i•sa•ya bark [,kælə'seijə] the bark of the cinchona tree, which yields quinine. ⟨< Am.Sp. < ? Quechua⟩

cal•is•then•ic [,kælɪs'θɛnɪk] See CALLISTHENIC.

cal•is•then•ics [,kælɪs'θɛnɪks] See CALLISTHENICS.

calk[1] [kɒk] See CAULK[1].

calk[2] [kɒk] See CAULK[2].

call [kɒl] *v., n. —v.* **1** speak or say loudly; cry; shout (*often used with* **out**): *She called from downstairs. I called out all the names.* **2** of a bird or animal, utter its characteristic sound. **3** give a signal (*to*): *The bugle called the men to assemble.* **4** issue commands for (some event): *call a ceasefire.* **5** rouse; waken: *Call me at seven o'clock.* **6** summon or command: *Obey when duty calls.* **7** convene; assemble: *They have called a meeting for Thursday.* **8** bring to action; begin to consider: *Her case will be called in court tomorrow.* **9** give a name or label to: *They called the baby Luke. I hit him because he called me a coward.* **10** consider; think of as being: *Everyone called the party a success. I call that a rude remark.* **11** make a short visit or stop (*used with* **on**): *They called on us last night. We must call on our new neighbour.* **12** read over aloud: *The teacher called the roll of the class.* **13** end; stop: *The ball game was called on account of rain.* **14** contact on the telephone; telephone: *Call me tomorrow morning.* **15** demand payment of: *The bank called my loan.* **16** shout the steps and instructions for (a square dance). **17** in a game of pool, announce the shot one is aiming for. **18** *Poker.* **a** demand a show of (hands). **b** match (the preceding bet). **c** challenge (another player). **19** *Sports.* make a ruling on, as an umpire: *The umpire called the player out.*

call attention to, bring to people's notice.
call away, cause someone to leave: *I'm sorry, she's not here; she's been called away.*
call back, a ask a person to return; recall: *Call the letter carrier back.* **b** take back; retract. **c** telephone (someone who has called earlier).
call down, *Informal.* scold.
call for, a go and get; stop and get: *You can call for the pictures any time after three o'clock.* **b** need; require: *This recipe calls for two eggs. Your remark was uncalled for.* **c** predict: *The forecast calls for showers today.* **d** ask for: *to call for the waiter. People are calling for a new law.*
call forth, bring into action or being; get in response: *a play that calls forth strong emotions.*
call in, a summon for advice or consultation: *to call in a lawyer, doctor, etc.* **b** withdraw from free action, circulation, or publicity: *to call in a book.* **c** collect as debts: *to call in a mortgage.*
call into existence, create; cause to be: *Computers have called many new words into existence.*
call into question, raise doubts about.
call it a day, *Informal* See DAY.
call off, a order back; order away: *Call off your dog.* **b** cancel: *We called off our trip.* **c** read aloud from a list: *The names were called off alphabetically.*
call on or **upon, a** visit. **b** appeal to: *We call on all people everywhere to fight against racism.*
call out, a summon into service or action: *to call out troops.* **b** order (workers) to strike. **c** elicit; bring into play. **d** shout loudly.
call (someone's) **bluff,** challenge or confront someone with the fact that he or she is bluffing.
call to order, make (an assembly) ready for the business of the meeting.
call up, a bring to mind; bring back. **b** telephone. **c** summon to the service of the country.
—n. **1** a shout; a cry. **2** the characteristic sound of a bird or other animal. **3** a signal given by sound: *Army calls are played on the bugle.* **4** a calling by telephone: *I want to make a call to Montréal.* **5** an invitation; request; command; summons. **6** a claim or demand: *A busy person has many calls on her time.* **7** a need; occasion: *You have no call to meddle in other people's business.* **8** a short visit or stop. **9** a demand for payment. **10** a notice requiring actors and stagehands to attend a rehearsal. **11** the attraction of something: *the call of the big city.* **12** *Poker.* the demand that all hands still active be shown after their players have matched the current bet. **13** *Bridge.* a bid or a pass. **14** *Square dancing.* an instruction that is chanted or shouted. **15** a calling or vocation. **16** the act of calling.
call of nature, *Informal.* the need to relieve oneself.
on call, a subject to payment on demand. **b** available at any time: *There are three doctors on call tonight.*
within call, near enough to hear a call. ⟨OE *callian, dial. var. of ceallian⟩
☛ *Hom.* CAUL, COL.
☛ *Syn. v.* **5. Call,** SUMMON, INVITE = ask or order someone to come. **Call** is the general and informal word: *The principal called the student leaders together for a talk.* **Summon** = call with authority, and is used especially of a formal calling to duty or to some formal meeting: *The principal summoned the student leaders to her office.* **Invite** = ask politely, and suggests giving a person a chance to do something he or she would like to do, but allowing him or her to refuse: *The principal invited the student leaders to come in and talk things over.*

cal•la ['kælə] *n.* **1** a bog plant (*Calla palustris*) comprising a separate genus of the arum family found in northern temperate and subarctic regions, having heart-shaped leaves and a white spathe surrounding a yellow spadix whose flowers develop into brilliant red berries. Also called **water arum. 2** CALLA LILY. ⟨< NL⟩

call•a•ble ['kɒləbəl] *adj.* payable on demand, as, a loan.

calla lily 1 any of several plants (genus *Zantedeschia*) of the arum family cultivated as house or greenhouse plants, especially *Z. aethiopica,* native to southern Africa, having a large, white, flaring spathe surrounding a yellow spadix. **2** the flower of any of these plants.

call•back ['kɒl,bæk] *n. Informal.* **1** a recalling of workers who were previously laid off, of successful auditioners, etc. **2** an additional visit or call to a client or customer: *The sales representative made no new calls, but spent the whole day on callbacks.*

call•board ['kɒl,bɔrd] *n.* a notice board in a theatre, used for posting rehearsal times, casting, notice of closure, etc.

call•box ['kɒl,bɒks] *n.* the booth containing a public telephone.

call•boy ['kɒl,bɔɪ] *n.* **1** a bellboy in a hotel, ship, etc. **2** a boy who calls actors from their dressing rooms when they are due to appear on the stage.

call•er ['kɒlər] *n.* **1** a person who makes a short visit. **2** a person who calls, especially a person who calls out the dance steps at a square dance.
☛ *Hom.* CHOLER, COLLAR .

call girl a prostitute with whom appointments may be made by telephone.

cal•li•bo•gus [,kælə'bougəs] *or* ['kælə,bougəs] *n.* a drink popular in the Atlantic Provinces, made of rum, molasses, and spruce beer. ⟨origin unknown⟩

cal•lig•ra•pher [kə'lɪgrəfər] *n.* **1** a person having good handwriting, especially one practising the art of elegant penmanship. **2** a professional transcriber of manuscripts; penman.

cal•lig•ra•phy [kə'lɪgrəfi] *n.* **1** handwriting. **2** the art of beautiful handwriting. ⟨< Gk. *kalligraphia* < *kallos* beauty + *graphein* write⟩ **—,cal•li'graph•ic** [,kælə'græfɪk], *adj.*

call•ing ['kɒlɪŋ] *n., v. —n.* **1** a business; occupation; profession; trade. **2** an invitation; command; summons. **3** a spiritual or divine summons to a special service or office; call.
—v. ppr. of CALL.

calling card 1 a small card with a person's name on it. It is used when visiting someone formally, in acknowledging gifts, etc. **2** an identifying or characteristic sign or trace.

cal•li•o•pe [kə'laɪəpi] *n.* **1** a musical instrument having a series of steam whistles played by a keyboard similar to that of an organ. **2 Calliope,** *Greek mythology.* the Muse of eloquence and heroic poetry. ⟨< L < Gk. *Kalliopē* beautiful-voiced < *kallos* beauty + *ops* voice⟩

cal•li•op•sis [,kæli'ɒpsɪs] *n.* coreopsis.

cal•li•per or **cal•i•per** ['kæləpər] *n., v. —n.* **1** Usually, **callipers,** *pl.* an instrument consisting of a pair of hinged legs, used to measure the diameter or thickness of something. **2** the part of a bicycle or vehicle brake that provides friction.
—v. measure with callipers. ⟨var. of *calibre*⟩

calliper rule SLIDE RULE.

cal•lis•then•ic or **cal•is•then•ic** [,kælɪs'θɛnɪk] *adj.* of callisthenics; developing a strong and graceful body.

cal•lis•then•ics or **cal•is•then•ics** [,kælɪs'θɛnɪks] *n.* **1** exercises without the use of special equipment, designed to develop a strong and graceful body. **2** the practice or art of callisthenics. ⟨< Gk. *kallos* beauty + *sthenos* strength⟩

Cal•lis•to [kə'lɪstou] *n.* **1** in Greek and Roman mythology, a nymph loved by Zeus and changed into a bear. **2** a satellite of the planet Jupiter.

call letters the identification letters of a radio or television station, or of a ham radio operator.

call loan a loan that must be paid back on demand.

call money a sum of money borrowed that must be paid back on demand.

call number a combination of letters and numbers that is part of a system by which a book is classified and assigned to a place on a library shelf.

cal•los•i•ty [kə'lɒsəti] *n., pl.* **-ties. 1** CALLUS (def. 1). **2** lack of feeling; hardness of heart.

cal•lous ['kæləs] *adj., v.* **1** hard; hardened. Parts of the skin that are subjected to friction often become callous. **2** unfeeling; insensitive: *Only a callous person can see suffering without trying to relieve it.*
—v. make or become callous. ⟨< L *callosus* < *callus* hard skin⟩ **—'cal•lous•ly,** *adv.* **—'cal•lous•ness,** *n.*
☛ *Hom.* CALLUS.

call–out ['kɒl ,ʌut] *n. Military.* an officer temporarily commissioned for a special assignment or duty.

cal•low ['kælou] *adj.* **1** young and inexperienced. **2** not fully developed. **3** of birds, without feathers sufficiently developed for flight. ⟨OE *calu* bald⟩ **—'cal•low•ness,** *n.*

call sign the combination of letters or letters and numbers used to identify a radio station, operator, office, etc.

call–up ['kɒl ,ʌp] *n.* a summoning to training or duty, especially military training or duty.

cal•lus ['kæləs] *n., pl.* **-lus•es,** *v. —n.* **1** a hard, thickened place on the skin. **2** a new growth that unites the ends of a broken

bone. **3** a substance that grows over the wounds of plants. —*v.* form or develop a callus. ⟨< L. Related to CALLOUS.⟩
☛ *Hom.* CALLOUS.

calm [kɒm] *or* [kɑm] *adj., n., v.* —*adj.* **1** not stormy or windy; quiet; still; not moving: *a calm sea.* **2** peaceful; not excited: *Although she was frightened, she answered in a calm voice.*
—*n.* **1** the absence of motion or wind; quietness; stillness. **2** the absence of excitement; peacefulness. **3** *Meteorology.* a condition in which the wind has a velocity of less than two kilometres per hour (on the Beaufort scale, force 0). See chart in the Appendix.
—*v.* **1** become calm (*usually with* **down**): *The crying baby soon calmed down.* **2** make calm: *She soon calmed the baby.* ⟨ME < OF *calme* < Ital. < VL < Gk. *kauma* heat of the day; hence, time for rest, stillness⟩ —**'calm•ly,** *adv.* —**'calm•ness,** *n.*
☛ *Syn. adj.* **2. Calm,** COMPOSED, COLLECTED = not disturbed or excited. **Calm** = being or seeming to be completely undisturbed, showing no sign of being confused or excited: *Mother's calm behaviour quieted the frightened boy.* **Composed** = calm as the result of having or having got command over one's thoughts and feelings and, sometimes, an inner peace: *She looked composed at the funeral.* **Collected** emphasizes having control over one's actions, thoughts, and feelings, especially at times of danger or disturbance: *He looked collected as he led the rescuers.*

cal•o•mel ['kælə,mɛl] *n.* mercurous chloride, a white, tasteless, crystalline powder, used in medicine as a cathartic. *Formula*: Hg_2Cl_2 ⟨< Gk. *kalos* beautiful + *melas* black⟩

ca•lop•o•gon [kə'lɒpə,gɒn] *n.* a wild orchid (*Calopogon pulchellus*) having vivid pinkish purple flowers but no scent. It grows in cool, acid bogs from Newfoundland south to Florida.

ca•lor•ic [kə'lɔrɪk] *n., adj.* —*n. Archaic.* heat.
—*adj.* **1** having to do with heat. **2** of or having to do with calories.

cal•o•rie ['kæləri] *n., pl.* **-ries. 1** either of two units for measuring heat. A **calorie,** or **small calorie,** represents the quantity of heat necessary to raise the temperature of a gram of water one degree Celsius. A **Calorie,** or **large calorie,** represents the amount of heat necessary to raise the temperature of one kilogram of water one degree Celsius. A calorie is equal to about 4.18 joules; a Calorie is equal to about 4.18 kilojoules. **2** a unit corresponding to a calorie, used to measure the heat or energy produced by food as it is burned in the body: *Thirty grams of brown sugar produce about 100 calories.* **3** an amount of food capable of producing energy equal to one calorie: *You are not consuming enough calories.* ⟨< F < L *calor* heat⟩

cal•o•rif•ic [,kælə'rɪfɪk] *adj.* **1** producing heat. **2** caloric.

cal•o•rim•e•ter [,kælə'rɪmətər] *n.* an apparatus for measuring the quantity of heat, the specific heat of different substances, the heat of chemical combination, etc.

cal•o•rim•et•ry [kælə'rɪmətri] *n.* measurement of heat.

cal•o•yer ['kæləjər] *or* [kə'lɔɪər] *n.* a monk of the Eastern Orthodox Church. ⟨< F < Med.Gk. *kalogeros* < *kalos* beautiful + *geras* old age⟩

calque [kælk] *n. Linguistics.* a borrowing from another language by translating each part of a compound word. ⟨< F copy, tracing < *calquer* trace⟩

cal•trop ['kæl,trɒp] *n.* **1** a spiked implement designed to be stuck in the ground to impede enemy cavalry. **2** a bar with spikes to puncture the tires of vehicles going the wrong way. **3** *Botany.* any plant with spikes on the flower or fruit, such as the chestnut. ⟨< ME *calketrappe* < OE *calcatrippe* star thistle and OF *chaucetrape* both < Med.L *calcatrippa* < L *calcare* to tread upon⟩

cal•u•met ['kælјə,mɛt] *n. Cdn.* a long, ornamented tobacco pipe formerly used by peoples of the First Nations of the plains and eastern woodlands, especially in formal peacemaking ceremonies. ⟨< F < L *calamus* < Gk. *kalamos* reed⟩

ca•lum•ni•ate [kə'lʌmni,eit] *v.* **-at•ed, -at•ing.** say false and injurious things about; slander. ⟨< L *calumniari* < *calumnia* false accusation. Doublet of CHALLENGE, v.⟩ —**ca'lum•ni,a•tor,** *n.*

ca•lum•ni•a•tion [kə,lʌmni'eiʃən] *n.* a slandering; calumny.
☛ *Hom.* COLUMNIATION.

ca•lum•ni•ous [kə'lʌmniəs] *adj.* slanderous.
—**ca'lum•ni•ous•ly,** *adv.*

cal•um•ny ['kæləmni] *n., pl.* **-nies.** a false statement made to injure someone's reputation; slander. ⟨< L *calumnia.* Doublet of CHALLENGE, n.⟩

cal•u•tron ['kæljətrɒn] *n.* a mass spectrometer used to separate isotopes. ⟨< *Cal(ifornia) U(niversity),* where it was developed, + Gk. *-tron,* suffix denoting an instrument⟩

Cal•va•dos or **cal•va•dos** ['kælvə,dous] *n.* a kind of brandy distilled from hard cider and originating in Normandy, France. ⟨after *Calvados,* a department of NW France⟩

Cal•va•ry ['kælvəri] *n.* **1** the place where Jesus died on the cross. **2 calvary,** any agonizing experience.

calve [kæv] *v.* **calved, calv•ing. 1** give birth to a calf. **2** of a glacier, produce or set loose (an iceberg or icebergs): *When an advancing arctic glacier reaches the sea, the heavy weight of the ice in the water causes the glacier to calve huge chunks of ice that float away as icebergs.* ⟨OE *calfian* < *calf* calf[1]⟩

calves [kævz] *n.* pl. of CALF[1] AND CALF[2].

Cal•vin•ism ['kælvə,nɪzəm] *n.* the religious teachings of John Calvin (1509-1564), a French leader of the Protestant Reformation at Geneva, and his followers. Calvinism teaches that certain persons, the elect, were chosen by God to be saved and these are saved only by God's grace. —**'Cal•vin•ist,** *n., adj.* —**,Cal•vin'is•tic,** *adj.*

calx [kælks] *n., pl.* **calx•es** or **cal•ces** ['kælsiz]. **1** an ashy substance left after a metal or a mineral has been calcined or burned. **2** lime or chalk. **3** the heel. ⟨< L *calx* lime⟩

cal•y•ces ['kælə,siz] *or* ['keilə,siz] *n.* a pl. of CALYX.

cal•y•cine ['kæləsɪn] *or* ['keiləsɪn], ['kælə,saɪn] *or* ['keilə,saɪn] *adj.* of or having to do with a calyx.

ca•lyp•so [kə'lɪpsou] *n.* **1** a kind of ballad that originated in Trinidad, characterized by syncopated rhythms and improvisation and usually having satirical or humorous lyrics. **2** the music characteristic of such ballads. **3** (*adj.*) of or designating these ballads or this music. **4 Calypso,** in Homer's *Odyssey,* a sea nymph who kept Ulysses on her island for seven years. **5** a Canadian wild orchid (*Calypso bulbosa*) growing in the depths of forests from Newfoundland to Alaska. It has two forms: one east of the Rockies with a yellow beard, and one on the west coast with a white beard. Also called **fairy slipper.** ⟨? < *Calypso*⟩

ca•lyx ['keilɪks] *or* ['kælɪks] *n., pl.* **ca•lyx•es** or **cal•y•ces** ['kæləsiz] *or* ['keiləsiz]. **1** *Botany.* the outer leaves that surround the unopened bud of a flower. The calyx is made up of sepals. See FLOWER for picture. **2** *Zoology.* any cuplike structure or organ. ⟨< L < Gk. *kalyx* covering⟩

cal•zo•ne [kæl'zouni] *n.* an Italian dish consisting of a pastry casing filled with meat, cheese, and vegetables. ⟨< Ital.⟩

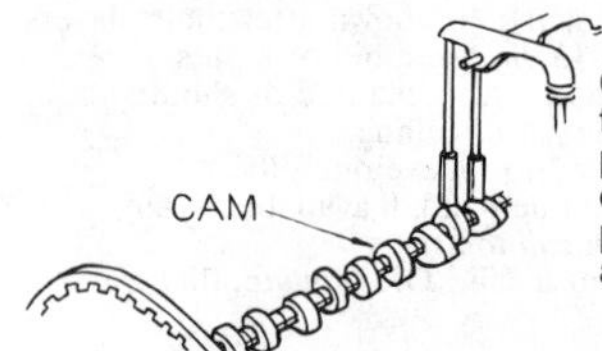

Cams. The cam turns with the shaft. The wheel of the plunger follows the irregular curve of the cam, causing the plunger to move up and down.

cam [kæm] *n.* a projection on a wheel or shaft that changes a regular circular motion into an irregular circular motion or into a back-and-forth motion. ⟨< Du. *kam* cog, comb⟩

CAM *Computer technology.* computer-aided (or assisted) manufacturing.

ca•ma•ra•de•rie [,kɑmə'rɑdəri] *or* [,kæmə'rædəri] *n.* comradeship; friendliness and loyalty among comrades. ⟨< F⟩

cam•a•ril•la [,kæmə'rɪlə]; *Spanish,* [,kama'rilja] *n.* **1** a group of private advisers; cabal; clique. **2** the small room where they meet. ⟨< Sp. *camarilla,* dim. of *cámara* chamber⟩

cam•as or **cam•ass** ['kæməs] *n.* any of a genus (*Camassia*) of plants of the lily family native to W North America, especially *C. quamash,* which has clusters of blue or white flowers and an edible bulb. The bulb was formerly a staple food of the northwestern Native peoples. ⟨< Chinook *quamash* bulb⟩

cam•ber ['kæmbər] *v., n.* —*v.* arch slightly; bend or curve upward in the middle.
—*n.* a slight arch; an upward bend or curve in the middle, such as the curve of an airfoil, a ship's deck, a road, or a piece of timber. ⟨< F *cambre* bent < L *camur* crooked⟩

Cam•ber•well beauty ['kæmbər,wɛl] a butterfly (*Nymphalis antiopa*) of North America and Europe, having dark-brown wings bordered with yellow, and purple spots. Also called **mourning cloak.** ⟨after *Camberwell,* a former borough of London, England, where it was first noted⟩

cam•bi•um ['kæmbiəm] *n.* the layer of soft, growing tissue between the phloem (inner bark) and xylem (wood) of trees and shrubs, from which new bark and new wood grow. ⟨< LL *cambium* exchange⟩ —**'cam•bi•al,** *adj.*

Cam•bo•dia [kæm'boudiə] *n.* the former name of Kampuchea.

cam•boose [kæm'bus] *n. Cdn.* formerly: **1** the living quarters of a gang of loggers or shantymen; SHANTY[1] (def. 2). **2** an open fireplace in such a building. ⟨< Cdn.F < F *cambuse* store, hut < Du. *kambuis* < MLG; cf. CABOOSE⟩

Cam•bri•a ['kæmbriə] *n.* an old name for Wales. ⟨Variant of *Cumbria*, Med.L name for Wales < Welsh *Cymru* (pronun. ['kɪmri]) Wales or *Cymry* Welshman⟩

Cam•bri•an ['kæmbriən] *or* ['keimbriən] *adj., n.* —*adj.* **1** *Geology.* of, having to do with, or designating the first period of the Paleozoic era of geological time, or the rock formed during this time. The Cambrian period began about 600 million years ago. See geological time chart in the Appendix. **2** Welsh. —*n.* **1 the Cambrian,** the Cambrian period or its rock system. **2** a Welsh person.

cam•bric ['keimbrɪk] *n.* a fine, thin linen or cotton cloth. ⟨< *Cambrai*, France⟩

cambric tea a drink made of hot water, milk, and sugar, often flavoured with a little tea.

cam•cord•er ['kæm,kɔrdər] *n.* a hand-held combination of a TV camera and a video recorder. ⟨< *cam(era)* + *(re)corder*⟩

came [keim] *v.* pt. of COME.

A camel

cam•el ['kæməl] *n.* **1** either of two species comprising a genus (*Camelus*) of large, cud-chewing desert mammals of Africa and Asia having one or two humps on the back in which fat is stored for use as food and as a source of water. See also ARABIAN CAMEL and BACTRIAN CAMEL. **2** a light yellowish brown colour. **3** (*adjl.*) camel-hair: *a camel coat.* **4** a waterproof box used in the retrieval of shipwrecks. **5** a log raft moored by a quay to cushion docking ships. ⟨< L *camelus* < Gk. *kamēlos;* of Semitic origin⟩

camel hair or **camel's hair** **1** the hair of the camel, used especially for weaving into cloth. **2** a soft cloth, usually a light yellowish brown in colour, made from this hair or a blend of this hair and wool, etc. **3** (*adjl.*) **camel-hair** or **camel's-hair,** made of this cloth: *a camel-hair coat.*

ca•mel•lia [kə'miljə] *or* [kə'miliə] *n.* **1** any of several E Asian evergreen shrubs and trees (genus *Camellia*), especially *C. japonica*, cultivated in several varieties as a greenhouse plant, having large, waxy, roselike flowers that may be white, pink, or red. **2** the flower of any of these plants. ⟨after G. J. *Kamel* or *Camellus* (1661-1706), missionary in the Philippines⟩

ca•mel•o•pard [kə'mɛlə,pɑrd] *n. Archaic.* giraffe. ⟨< LL < L < Gk. *kamēlopardalis* < *kamēlos* camel + *pardalis* leopard; so called from its camel-like neck and leopardlike spots⟩

Ca•mel•o•par•dus [kə,mɛlə'pɑrdəs] *n.* a northern constellation thought to look somewhat like a giraffe.

Cam•e•lot ['kæmə,lɒt] *n.* a legendary place in England where King Arthur had his palace and court.

Cam•em•bert ['kæməm,bɛr] *or* [,kæməm'bɛr] *n.* a rich, soft cheese. ⟨after *Camembert*, France⟩

cam•e•o ['kæmi,ou] *n., pl.* **-e•os. 1** a precious or semiprecious stone, especially one made up of layers of different colours, carved so that there is a raised part of one colour on a background of another colour. Agates are commonly used for cameos. **2** the technique of carving cameos. **3** a short literary sketch of a certain character or event. **4** an appearance by a famous actor or actress in a minor film role, usually in a single brief scene, that presents a distinctive character or is especially suited to the star's talents: *In this movie, he has a cameo as an eccentric landlord.* **5** a brooch showing a single object in relief. ⟨< Ital. *cammeo*⟩

cam•er•a ['kæmərə] *n., pl.* **-er•as** *for 1 and 2,* **-er•ae** [-ə,ri] *or* [-ə,raɪ] *for 3.* **1** a lightproof box or chamber for taking photographs, videotapes, or movies, in which film or plates are exposed and the image is formed by means of a lens. **2** *Television.* the part of the transmitter that converts images into electronic impulses for transmitting. **3** a judge's private office.
in camera, a in a judge's private office. **b** of a trial, parliamentary session, or other meeting, with the press and public excluded. **c** privately.
on or **off camera,** *Film.* placed so as to fall in or outside of the field of vision of the camera. ⟨< L *camera* arched chamber, arch < Gk. *kamara.* Doublet of CHAMBER.⟩

camera lu•ci•da ['lusədə] an instrument by which the image of an object is made to appear on a sheet of paper, etc., on which it may be traced.

cam•er•a•man ['kæmərəmən] *n., pl.* **-men.** a man who operates a camera, especially a movie or television camera.

camera ob•scu•ra [ɒb'skjʊrə] a camera in which images of external objects, received through an aperture, are exhibited in their natural colours on a surface arranged to receive them. The camera obscura is used for sketching, exhibition purposes, etc. ⟨< NL⟩

cam•er•a–read•y ['kæmərə ,rɛdi] *adj.* ready to be photographed for printing: *camera-ready copy.*

camera–shy ['kæmərə, ʃaɪ] *adj.* reluctant to have one's picture taken.

Ca•me•roun [,kæmə'run] *n.* a country in west central Africa.

cam•i•on ['kæmiən] *n.* **1** a low, heavy cart; dray. **2** a truck for carrying cannons. ⟨< F⟩

ca•mise [kə'miz] *or* [kə'mis] *n.* a loose doublet or tunic. ⟨< Arabic *qamis* < LL *camisia* shirt, tunic⟩

cam•i•sole ['kæmə,soul] *n.* a waist-length, sleeveless undergarment worn by women and girls, especially one trimmed with lace or embroidery and worn under a sheer blouse or shirt. ⟨< F < Sp. *camisola*, dim. of *camisa* shirt. Akin to CHEMISE.⟩

cam•let ['kæmlɪt] *n.* **1** a cloth of silk and wool made in the Orient. **2** a strong, waterproof cloth. ⟨< F *camelot* < Arabic *khamlat* wool plush < *khaml* nap[2]⟩

cam•o•mile ['kæmə,maɪl] *or* ['kæmə,mɪl] *n.* **1** any of a genus (*Anthemis*) of aromatic herbs of the composite family, especially *A. nobilis*, a European plant having finely divided leaves and daisylike flowers often used as medicine. **2** any plant of the related genus *Matricaria.* Also, **chamomile.** ⟨ME < OF < LL *camomilla*, var. of L *chamaemelon* < Gk. *chamaimēlon* earth apple⟩

Ca•mor•ra [kə'mɔrə] *n.* **1** a secret society formed in Naples, Italy, about 1820, which developed into a powerful political organization. Later it was associated with blackmail, robbery, etc. **2 camorra,** a secret society like the Camorra.

cam•ou•flage ['kæmə,flɑʒ] *n., v.* **-flaged, -flag•ing.** —*n.* **1** an outward appearance that makes a person, animal, or thing seem to be part of its natural surroundings. The white fur of a polar bear is a natural camouflage, for it prevents the bear from being easily seen against the snow. **2** the practice of giving soldiers, weapons, etc., a false appearance to conceal them from the enemy. **3** materials or other means by which something or someone is disguised or concealed: *A camouflage of earth and branches effectively hid the guns.*
—*v.* give a false appearance to in order to conceal; disguise: *The hunters were camouflaged with shrubbery so that they blended with the green landscape. The boy camouflaged his embarrassment by laughing.* ⟨< F *camouflage* < *camoufler* disguise⟩
—'cam•ou,flag•er, *n.*

camp [kæmp] *n., adj., v.* —*n.* **1** a temporary shelter such as a tent, trailer, or cabin, or the ground on which it is set up: *Her camp was right in the bush. It took us three hours to get back to camp.* **2** a temporary community of people living in tents, trailers, cabins, etc., in the country or forest, especially for holidays or outings, and often with a structured program of activities in sports, woodcraft, or some other skill: *a wilderness camp, a music camp. They always go to camp for two weeks in summer.* **3** the people in a camp: *The camp was up by seven o'clock.* **4** a group of people who promote a particular theory, political doctrine, etc.: *the liberal camp.* **5** a way of thinking; an ideological outlook or position: *They're in the same camp, politically.* **6** military life. **7** a place where athletes or army recruits train together. **8** *Slang.* a fashionably sophisticated kind of humour, based on the affectation or exaggeration of styles, decoration, etc., normally considered trite, corny, or vulgar.
—*adj. Slang.* characterized by this kind of humour.
break camp, pack up tents and equipment and leave.
make camp, set up a camp; set up tents, etc.: *We hiked until sunset and then made camp beside a creek.*
—*v.* **1** make a camp; put up tents, huts, etc.: *We decided to camp by the river the first night.* **2** live in a camp (*often used with* **out**):

We camped out all summer. **3** live simply without comforts for a time: *We had to camp in the house until our furniture arrived.*
camp it up, *Slang.* act in a camp way. ⟨< F < Ital. < L *campus* field. Doublet of CAMPUS.⟩

cam•paign [kæm'pein] *n., v.* —*n.* **1** a series of related military operations that have some special purpose in view: *The general's staff planned a campaign to capture the enemy's most important city.* **2** a series of connected activities planned to achieve some goal or to acquire something; a planned course of action for some special purpose: *a campaign to raise money for a college, a campaign to advertise some article, a campaign to elect someone to political office.*
—*v.* take part in or serve in a campaign; go on a campaign. ⟨< F *campagne* open country < Ital. *campagna* < LL *campanea, campania* level country < L *campus* field. Doublet of CHAMPAIGN.⟩ **—cam'paign•er,** *n.*

cam•pa•ni•le [,kæmpə'nili] *n., pl.* **-ni•les** or **-ni•li** [-'nili]. a bell tower, especially one that is near, but not attached to, a church. ⟨< Ital. < LL *campana* bell⟩

cam•pa•nol•o•gist [,kæmpə'nɒlədʒɪst] *n.* **1** a bell-ringer. **2** one versed in the art of campanology.

cam•pa•no•lo•gy [,kæmpə'nɒlədʒi] *n.* **1** bell-ringing. **2** the study of bells. ⟨< LL *campana* bell + *-logia* -logy⟩

cam•pan•u•la [kæm'pænjələ] *n.* any of a genus (*Campanula*) of plants having bell-shaped flowers, including the bluebell and the bellflowers. ⟨< LL *campanula*, dim. of *campana* bell⟩

cam•pan•u•late [kæm'pænjəlɪt] *or* [kæm'pænjə,leit] *adj. Botany.* of a flower, bell-shaped.

camp bed a lightweight folding cot or bed.

camp boss the person in charge of a logging camp or other camp.

camp chair a lightweight folding chair.

camp•craft ['kæmp,kræft] *n.* the skills needed to be a successful outdoor camper.

cam•per ['kæmpər] *n.* **1** a person who camps. **2** a member of a summer camp for children or adolescents. **3** a vehicle equipped for camping, such as a small covered trailer or a pickup truck with a roomlike unit fitted onto the back. Campers often have built-in beds, cupboards, etc.

cam•pe•si•no [,kæmpə'sinou] *n., pl.* **-nos.** *Spanish.* farmer or peasant.

camp•fire ['kæmp,faɪr] *n.* **1** a fire in a camp, for warmth or cooking. **2** a social gathering for soldiers, scouts, etc.

camp follower **1** a civilian hanger-on in an army camp, especially a prostitute or a seller of small wares. **2** *Informal.* any person who attaches himself or herself for his or her own profit to a more important person, a group, a cause, etc.

camp•ground ['kæmp,graʊnd] *n.* **1** a place where a camp is. **2** a place where one is permitted to park a camper, trailer, or motor home for the night. **3** the place where a camp meeting is held.

cam•phene ['kæmfin] *or* [kæm'fin] *n.* a poisonous, colourless hydrocarbon prepared from turpentine oil. *Formula*: $C_{10}H_{16}O$ ⟨< *camphor* + *-ene* < L *-enus* < Gk. *-enos* adjective suffix⟩

cam•phor ['kæmfər] *n.* a white, crystalline compound with a strong odour and a bitter taste. It is used in the manufacture of film, lacquers, etc., and in medicine. *Formula*: $C_{10}H_{16}O$ ⟨< Med.L *camphora* < Arabic, ult. < Malay *kāpūr*⟩

cam•phor•at•ed ['kæmfə,reitɪd] *adj.* containing camphor: *camphorated oil.*

camphor ball mothball.

camphor tree an evergreen tree (*Cinnamomum camphora*) of the laurel family, found in SE Asia and yielding camphor.

camp•ing ['kæmpɪŋ] *n., v.* —*n.* the practice or recreation of living outdoors in a temporary shelter or in a vehicle.
—*v.* ppr. of CAMP.

cam•pi•on ['kæmpiən] *n.* any of various plants (genera *Lychnis* and *Silene*) of the pink family having pink, red, or white flowers. ⟨< L *campus* field⟩

camp meeting a religious gathering held outdoors or in a large tent, usually lasting several days.

cam•po•ree [,kæmpə'ri] *n.* **1** a gathering of Scouts or Guides for competitions in campcraft, etc. **2** a kind of bivouac outing for a troop. ⟨*camp* + (*jamb*)*oree*⟩

camp robber *Cdn.* CANADA JAY.

camp•site ['kæmp,səit] *n.* **1** a place where people may camp. Many provincial parks contain well-managed campsites. **2** any place where someone camps or has camped: *We made our campsite in the bush.* **3** the site of an ancient or prehistoric camp: *The archaeologists found a Stone Age campsite.*

camp•stool ['kæmp,stul] *n.* a lightweight folding seat.

cam•pus ['kæmpəs] *n., adj.* —*n.* **1** the grounds and buildings of a university, college, or school. **2** the grounds and buildings of a factory, hospital, etc.
—*adj.* of or having to do with a university, college, or school: *a campus newspaper.* ⟨< L *campus* field, plain. Doublet of CAMP.⟩

cam•py ['kæmpi] *adj. Slang.* of, having to do with, or characterized by CAMP (def. 8).

cam•shaft ['kæm,ʃæft] *n.* a rod or shaft on which a cam is fastened, or of which a cam forms an essential part. See CAM for picture.

can[1] [kæn]; *unstressed*, [kən] *v. pres. sing. and pl.* (*all persons*) **can,** *pt.* **could.** (*used as an auxiliary followed by an infinitive without* **to**) **1** have the knowledge or power to; be able to: *Can you come tomorrow? I can swim quite well. I can't see because you're standing in my way.* **2** *Informal.* have the right to, by permission, agreement, custom, or law: *You can cross the street here. You can go at 4 o'clock.* **3** be designed to: *This calculator can do much more than the other one.* **4** be likely to: *It can't be that bad. Can he be serious?* ⟨OE *can(n)* know, know how, can (infinitive, *cunnan*)⟩

☛ *Usage.* **Can,** MAY. In formal English we usually distinguish between **may,** meaning 'be allowed to' or 'have permission to', and **can,** meaning 'know how to' or 'be able to': *You may go now. You may if you can. She can walk with crutches.* In informal English **can** is widely used to mean both 'be allowed to' and 'be able to': *Can I go now? You can if you want to. I can run faster than any of my friends.*

can[2] [kæn] *n., v.* **canned, can•ning.** —*n.* **1** a metal container, usually having a separate lid: *a garbage can, an oil can, a milk can.* **2** a small metal container in which foods are sealed to preserve them for later use; tin can. **3** the contents of a can. **4** a can and its contents. **5** the amount that a can holds: *I ate a whole can of beans.* **6** *Slang.* jail. **7** *Slang.* toilet. **8** *Slang.* **a** a depth charge. **b** destroyer.
can of worms, *Informal.* **a** a mess: an awkward or muddled state of affairs. **b** a complicated and unsavoury problem or situation.
in the can, *Slang.* of movie film, ready to show; completed.
—*v.* **1** preserve by putting in airtight cans or jars: *to can fruit.* **2** *Slang.* dismiss from a job: *He says he's been canned.* **3** *Slang.* put an end to; stop: *Can that racket!* **4** *Slang.* make a recording of: *to can applause for a later broadcast. She sings to canned accompaniment.* ⟨OE *canne* vessel⟩ **—'can•ner,** *n.*

can. **1** canon. **2** canto.

Can. **1** Canada. **2** Canadian.

Ca•naan ['keinən] *n.* **1** an ancient region in Palestine between the Jordan River and the Mediterranean. In the Bible, God promised Canaan to Abraham and his descendants. **2** a land of promise.

Ca•naan•ite ['keinə,nəit] *n.* **1** an inhabitant of Canaan before its conquest by the Hebrews. **2** the Semitic language of the Canaanites.

Can•a•da ['kænədə] *n.* a large country occupying the northern part of North America except Alaska. ⟨< a word for 'village' in an extinct Iroquoian language⟩

Canada Act the Act of 1791 that divided the province of Québec into Upper and Lower Canada.

Canada anemone a white-flowered anemone (*Anemone canadensis*) found in moist places across Canada.

Canada balsam a sticky, transparent, yellow resin obtained from the balsam fir. Because it is transparent when it solidifies, it is used as a cement and mounting medium for preparing specimens for examination through a microscope.

Canada bird *Cdn.* the white-throated sparrow, *Zonotrichia albicollis.*

Canada Council a body founded by Parliament in 1957 to administer funds for the encouragement of writing, music, painting, and other cultural activities. *Abbrev.*: C.C.

Canada Day July 1st, Canada's national holiday, formerly called Dominion Day. The Dominion of Canada was established on July 1, 1867. The name was officially changed to Canada Day in October, 1982.

Canada goldenrod a wild autumn flower (*Solidago canadensis*) having clusters of small golden flowers once used to make a yellow dye or as a medicine.

Canada goose a large, wild goose (*Branta canadensis*) of

North America, having a black head and neck, a white throat, and a brownish grey body.

Canada holly a bog plant (*Ilex verticillata*) having bright red berries, and common from Newfoundland to Ontario. Also called **winterberry.**

Canada jays - about 28 cm long

Canada jay a jay (*Perisoreus canadensis*) that is common throughout Canada and the N United States, having loose, fluffy grey feathers on the body and a white-and-black head without a crest; grey jay. The Canada jay has a number of nicknames, including lumberjack, moosebird, and whisky-jack.

Canada lynx a North American subspecies of the LYNX (def. 1) sometimes classified as a separate species (*Felis canadensis*), found mainly in northern Canada and Alaska, having very large paws, pointed ears with long tufts, and a thick coat of long, silky, greyish fur mixed with black and dark brown. Its large, well-furred paws enable it to run fast over snow in winter.

Canada Medal an award for conspicuous bravery to civilians or military personnel, established in 1943. See MEDAL for picture.

Ca•na•darm ['kænə,dɑrm] *or* [,kænə'dɑrm] *n.* an extension, built in Canada, of a spacecraft, which allows astronauts to manipulate objects in space.

Canada thistle a kind of thistle that is a very common and troublesome weed throughout Canada. Canada thistles have small rose-purple, pink, or, sometimes, white flowers.

Ca•na•di•an [kə'neidiən] *n., adj.* *—n.* a native, inhabitant, or citizen of Canada.
—adj. of or having to do with Canada or its people.

Ca•na•di•a•na [kə,neidi'ænə] *or* [kə,neidi'ɑnə] *n.* things relating to Canada and its history, especially early Canadian furniture, textiles, books, etc.

Canadian Armed Forces CANADIAN FORCES.

Canadian bacon *Esp. U.S.* BACK BACON.

Canadian Brick *Cdn.* a fairly mild, straw-coloured cheese.

Canadian Charter of Rights and Freedoms See CHARTER OF RIGHTS AND FREEDOMS.

Canadian English the kind of English spoken by English-speaking Canadians.

Canadian Forces the armed forces of Canada, grouped into several main organizations called commands, each responsible for a particular military function. *Abbrev.*: CF or C.F.

Canadian French the kind of French spoken by French-speaking Canadians.

Canadian Girls in Training an organization for girls similar in focus to the Girl Guides.

Ca•na•di•an•ism [kə'neidiə,nɪzəm] *n.* **1** a word or expression originating in or peculiar to Canada. The words *muskeg* and *caribou* are Canadianisms. **2** a custom peculiar to Canada. **3** loyalty to Canada as an independent nation and devotion to its customs, traditions, and laws. **4** the state of being Canadian; Canadian quality.

Ca•na•di•an•ize [kə'neidiə,naɪz] *v.* **-ized, -iz•ing. 1** make Canadian in character or custom: *Our new neighbours have become so Canadianized they've already taken up curling.* **2** change the content or subject matter of (a book, television program, scientific report, etc.) to reflect Canadian situations or points of view. **3** bring under Canadian ownership or control: *to Canadianize a foreign-owned industry.* **—Ca,na•di•an•i'za•tion,** *n.*

Canadian Labour Congress the confederation of trade unions in Canada.

Canadian Legion ROYAL CANADIAN LEGION.

Canadian parrot *Cdn.* the crossbill (*Loxia curvirostra* or *Loxia leucoptera*).

Canadian primrose a spring and summer wildflower (*Primula mistassinica*), having pink flowers with yellow centres. Also called **bird's-eye primrose.**

Canadian Radio-television and Telecommunications Commission a Federal Government body established in 1968 to regulate radio and television broadcasting in Canada. It has the power to enforce broadcasting policy and regulate public and private radio and television and cable systems. *Abbrev.*: CRTC

Canadian Shield a region of ancient rock, chiefly Precambrian granite, encircling Hudson Bay and covering nearly half the mainland of Canada. The Canadian Shield is rich in minerals, especially gold, copper, nickel, and iron ore.

Canadian Space Agency the body which controls space flights from Canada, oversees astronauts, etc. Compare NASA.

Canadian whisky a blended whisky containing a high proportion of rye whisky; RYE (def. 6).

Ca•na•di•an•ness [kə'neidiənnɪs] *n.* the quality or state of being Canadian.

Ca•na•di•en [kə,neidi'ɛn]; *French,* [kana'djɛ̃] *n.* a French Canadian.

Ca•na•di•enne [kə,neidi'ɛn]; *French,* [kana'djɛn] *n.* **1** a French-Canadian girl or woman. **2** a breed of cow bred in Québec since the 17th century.

ca•naille [kə'naɪ] *or* [kə'neil]; *French,* [ka'naj] *n.* the lowest class of people; rabble; riffraff. ⟨< F < Ital. *canaglia* < *cane* dog < L *canis*⟩

ca•nal [kə'næl] *n., v.* **-nalled** or **-naled, -nal•ling** or **nal•ing.** *—n.* **1** a waterway dug across land. Some canals are for boats and ships; others are for carrying water to places that need it. **2** a river altered to allow ships to pass, as by straightening, locks, etc. **3** a passage or series of passages in the body or in a plant for carrying food, liquid, air, etc.: *the alimentary canal.* **4** a long arm of a large body of water. **5** any of the long, narrow markings sometimes visible on the surface of the planet Mars.
—v. **1** dig or cut a canal through or across. **2** furnish with canals. ⟨< L *canalis* trench, pipe. Doublet of CHANNEL.⟩

canal boat a long, narrow boat used on canals. Canal boats are sometimes pulled along by horses. Also, **canalboat.**

can•a•lic•u•lus [,kænə'lɪkjələs] *n., pl.* **-li** [-,laɪ] *or* [,li]. a small canal or duct in the body. Canaliculi connect the small cavities in the bones. ⟨< L dim. of *canalis* trench, pipe⟩

ca•nal•i•za•ton [kə,nælə'zeiʃən], [,kænələ'zeiʃən], *or* [,kænəlaɪ'zeiʃən] *n.* **1** the act of canalizing. **2** a system of canals. **3** the draining of wounds by surgical means rather than by the use of tubes.

ca•nal•ize [kə'nælaɪz] *or* ['kænə,laɪz] *v.* **-ized, -iz•ing. 1** make a canal or canals through. **2** make into or like a canal. **3** lead in a desired direction so as to control or regulate; channel: *an attempt to canalize the energies of children into worthwhile activities.*

can•a•pé [,kænə'pei] *or* ['kænəpi] *n.* a cracker, a thin piece of toasted or fried bread, etc., spread with a seasoned mixture of fish, cheese, etc. ⟨< F *canapé,* originally, a couch with curtains of mosquito netting. See CANOPY.⟩

ca•nard [kə'nɑrd] *n.* a false rumour; an exaggerated report; hoax. ⟨< F *canard,* literally, duck⟩

ca•nar•y [kə'nɛri] *n., pl.* **-nar•ies;** *adj.* *—n.* **1** a small yellow or greenish yellow finch (*Serinus canaria*) native to the Canary Islands. Canaries are often kept as cage birds for their bright plumage and also for their singing. **2** CANARY YELLOW. **3** a usually sweet wine from the Canary Islands. **4** *Slang.* a tattletale; informer.
—adj. CANARY YELLOW. ⟨after the *Canary Islands*⟩

canary grass 1 an annual Old World grass (*Phalaris canariensis*) which yields seeds used for bird food. **2** a perennial grass (*Phalaris arundinacea*) grown for cattle food.

canary seed seed of canary grass, used as food for caged birds.

canary yellow light yellow.

ca•nas•ta [kə'næstə] *n.* **1** a card game similar to rummy, played by two to six players using two decks of cards. In canasta the players try to earn as many points as possible by getting sets of seven or more cards. **2** a seven-card set in this game. ⟨< Sp. basket < *canasto* contraction < *canastro* < Gk. *kanastron* wicker basket < *kanna* a reed⟩

canc. 1 cancelled. **2** cancellation.

can•can ['kæn,kæn] *n.* a kind of dance marked by extravagant high kicking, performed by women (often in a chorus line) and originating in 19th-century Paris. ⟨< F⟩

can•cel ['kænsəl] *v.* **-celled** or **-celed, -cel•ling** or **-cel•ing;** *n.* —*v.* **1** cross out; mark, stamp, or punch something so that it cannot be used or used again: *to cancel a stamp.* **2** annul; make without value: *The debt was cancelled.* **3** *Mathematics.* **a** reduce a fraction by dividing both the numerator and the denominator by (a given quantity). **b** reduce an equation by dividing both members by (a common factor). **4** put an end to or withdraw; call off; stop: *He cancelled his order for the books. The meeting has been cancelled.* **5** balance or match; neutralize (*often used with* **out**): *crossness cancelled out by a smile.* **6** *Music.* nullify the power of a sharp or a flat by inserting the sign ♮.
—*n.* cancellation. ⟨< L *cancellare* cross out with latticed lines < *cancelli* crossbars, dim. of *cancri,* altered from *carcer,* originally, network, grating⟩ **—'can•cel•ler** or **'can•cel•er,** *n.*

can•cel•la•tion [,kænsə'leiʃən] *n.* **1** a cancelling or being cancelled. **2** the marks made when something is cancelled or crossed out: *You can hardly see the cancellation on this stamp.* **3** something cancelled.

can•cer ['kænsər] *n.* **1 Cancer, a** *Astronomy.* a northern constellation thought of as having the shape of a crab. **b** *Astrology.* the fourth sign of the zodiac. The sun enters Cancer about June 21. See ZODIAC for picture. **c** a person born under this sign. **d** See TROPIC OF CANCER. **2** a harmful, uncontrolled growth of new tissue or cells in the body that tends to spread and destroy healthy tissue; a malignant tumour. **3** a condition marked by such harmful growths. **4** any evil or harmful thing that tends to spread: *the cancer of jealousy.* ⟨< L *cancer* crab, tumour. Doublet of CANKER, CHANCRE.⟩

can•cer•ous ['kænsərəs] *adj.* **1** of cancer: *a cancerous growth.* **2** having cancer: *a cancerous rat.*

can•cer•pho•bia [,kænsər'foubiə] *n.* extreme fear of contracting cancer.

Can•con ['kæn,kɒn] *n. Cdn. Informal.* Canadian content as determined by regulations for radio and television stations.

Can•cult ['kæn,kʌlt] *n. Cdn. Informal.* Canadian culture.

can•de•la [kæn'dɛlə] *or* [kæn'dilə] *n.* an SI unit for measuring luminous intensity, or candlepower, which is the amount of light shining in one direction from a glowing object. One candela is the amount of light produced by the inside of a ceramic box that has been heated until it glows; the light is measured as it shines out through a hole in the box. The candela is one of the seven base units in the SI. *Symbol:* cd ⟨< L *candela* candle⟩

can•de•la•bra [,kændə'læbrə] *or* [,kændə'lɑbrə] *n., pl.* **-bras** [-brəz]. candelabrum.

☛ *Usage.* Though **candelabrum** is the original form, its plural, **candelabra,** is now often treated as singular, with its own plural **candelabras.**

can•de•la•brum [,kændə'læbrəm] *or* [,kændə'lɑbrəm] *n., pl.* **-bra** [-brə] or **-brums.** an ornamental candlestick with several branches for holding candles, or an electric light in imitation of this. ⟨< L *candelabrum* < *candela* candle⟩

can•de•lil•la [,kændə'lijə] *or* [,kændə'lɪlə] *n.* **1** a shrub (*Euphorbia antisiphylitica*) of the spurge family, found in SW U.S. and Mexico, yielding a commercially valuable wax. **2** a similar shrub (*Pedilanthus pavonis*) which yields a similar wax. ⟨< Am.Sp. < Sp. dim. of *candela* candle⟩

can•des•cent [kæn'dɛsənt] *adj.* glowing with heat; incandescent. ⟨< L *candescens, -entis,* ppr. of *candescere* begin to glow⟩ **—can'des•cent•ly,** *adv.* **—can'des•cence,** *n.*

can•did ['kændɪd] *adj.* **1** frank; sincere: *a candid reply.* **2** fair; impartial: *a candid decision.* **3** of a photograph, not posed; often, taken without the subject's knowledge: *The magazine story included several candid shots of the premier's family.* ⟨< L *candidus* white⟩ **—'can•did•ly,** *adv.*

☛ *Syn.* **1.** See note at FRANK.

can•di•da•cy ['kændədəsi] *n.* the state of being a candidate: *Please support my candidacy for treasurer.*

can•di•date ['kændə,deit] *or* ['kændədɪt] *n.* **1** a person who seeks or is proposed for an honour, prize, position, office, etc.: *There were three possible candidates for the award. All the job candidates have been interviewed.* **2** a person who is sitting or about to sit an examination. **3** a person who seems to have a particular fate in store: *a candidate for fame and fortune, a likely candidate for prison.* ⟨< L *candidatus* clothed in a white toga⟩

can•di•da•ture ['kændədətʃər], ['kændə,deitʃər], *or* ['kændədə,tʃʊr] *n.* candidacy.

candid camera 1 a small camera with a fast lens for photographing persons unposed and, often, unaware that their picture is being taken. **2** any very small camera.

can•di•di•a•sis [,kændɪ'daɪəsɪs] *n., pl.* **-ses** [-,siz]. a skin infection caused by a yeast (*Candida albicans*), occurring in warm, moist areas of the body such as under the arms.

can•died ['kændid] *adj.* **1** glazed, soaked, or cooked with sugar: *candied cherries, a candied apple.* **2** of honey, etc., crystallized. **3** made deceptively sweet or agreeable: *Her candied words of congratulations hid a great bitterness.*

can•dle ['kændəl] *n., v.* **-dled, -dling.** —*n.* **1** a stick of wax or tallow with a wick in it, burned to give light. **2** anything shaped or used like a candle: *Sulphur candles are burned to disinfect rooms.* **3** candela.

burn the candle at both ends, try to do more than one's energy or resources allow; make unreasonable demands on one's physical and mental resources.

not hold a candle to, not compare with: *The cake from the bakery could not hold a candle to the one John made.*

not worth the candle, not worth doing.

—*v.* **1** test eggs for freshness and quality by holding them in front of a light in order to see the size of the air pocket and the position and size of the yolk. **2** *Cdn.* of ice, form into CANDLE ICE. ⟨OE *candel* < L *candela* < *candere* shine⟩

can•dle•fish ['kændəl,fɪʃ] *n.* oolichan.

can•dle•hold•er ['kændəl,houldər] *n.* candlestick.

candle hour a unit of light equivalent to the energy derived in one hour from a source of light equal to one CANDLE (def. 3).

candle ice or **candled ice** *Cdn.* ice on a river, lake, etc., that has deteriorated into candlelike shapes, usually occurring shortly before break-up.

can•dle•light ['kændəl,ləit] *n.* **1** the light from a candle or candles. **2** the time when candles are lighted; dusk; twilight; nightfall.

can•dle•lit ['kændəl,lɪt] *adj.* lit by candlelight.

Can•dle•mas ['kændəlməs] *n.* February 2, a Christian church festival in honour of the purification of the Virgin Mary and the presentation of the infant Jesus in the Temple. It is celebrated with lighted candles. ⟨OE *candelmæsse*⟩

can•dle•nut ['kændəl,nʌt] *n.* **1** a tree (*Aleurites moluccana*) of the spurge family, growing in the islands of the South Pacific. **2** the fruit of this tree, yielding an oil, and often burned by the indigenous peoples as a candle.

can•dle•pin ['kændəl,pɪn] *n.* **1** one of a set of thin, cylindrical bowling pins. **2 candlepins,** *pl.* a game of tenpins played with these bowling pins.

can•dle•pow•er ['kændəl,paʊər] the intensity of light given by a standard candle, measured in candelas.

can•dle•stick ['kændəl,stɪk] *n.* a holder for a candle, to make it stand upright.

can•dle•wick ['kændəl,wɪk] *n., adj.* —*n.* **1** the wick of a candle. **2** a soft, loosely twisted cotton thread similar to that used for candlewicks.
—*adj.* having a pattern made with tufts of such threads: *a candlewick bedspread.*

can•dour or **can•dor** ['kændər] *n.* **1** frankness; open-heartedness in giving one's view or opinion. **2** fairness; impartiality. ⟨< L *candour* whiteness, purity < *candere* shine⟩

CANDU or **Candu** ['kæn'du] a nuclear reactor made in Canada. ⟨< *Can(ada)* + *d*euterium + *u*ranium⟩

C and W country and western music.

can•dy ['kændi] *n., pl.* **-dies;** *v.* **-died, -dy•ing.** —*n.* **1** a confection made with sugar or syrup, flavouring, and other ingredients: *He doesn't eat much candy.* **2** a piece of this: *She took a candy from the box.*
—*v.* **1** cook or soak in sugar, or glaze with sugar. **2** of honey, etc., become crystallized into sugar. **3** make deceptively sweet or agreeable. ⟨< F *(sucre) candi* (sugar) candy < Persian *quand* sugar⟩

candy bar U.S. CHOCOLATE BAR.

candy cane a stick of brittle, white peppermint candy having spiralling red and green stripes and shaped like a walking stick with a curved handle.

candy floss spun sugar candy; COTTON CANDY.

can•dy–pull ['kændi ,pʊl] *n.* **1** a social gathering where candy, while it is still soft enough to handle, is pulled and twisted to the colour and consistency of taffy. **2** a turn at doing this.

candy stripe a narrow stripe of two alternating colours, generally red and white. **—'can•dy-,striped,** *adj.*

can•dy•strip•er ['kændi,strəipər] *n.* a teenage girl who does volunteer work in a hospital. ⟨from the uniform of a jumper with vertical red and white stripes, worn over a white blouse⟩

can•dy•tuft ['kændi,tʌft] *n.* any of various plants (genus *Iberis*) of the mustard family, widely cultivated for their clusters of white, pink, purple, or red flowers. ⟨< *Candia,* former name of Crete + *tuft*⟩

cane [kein] *n., v.* **caned, can•ing.** *—n.* **1** a rod or stick, usually of wood and having a curved end, or head, for holding with the hand, used to help a person in walking. **2** a long, hollow or pithy, jointed stem, such as that of various woody grasses or reeds. **3** a plant having such stems, as sugar cane, bamboo, or rattan. **4** strips of such stems used for wickerwork, chair backs and seats, etc. **5** (*adjl.*) made of cane: *a cane chair bottom.* **6** a long, slender stem of woody plants such as roses and raspberries, usually growing directly from the ground. **7** any of a genus (*Arundinaria*) of coarse grasses of the S United States having long, stiff stems. **8** formerly, a flexible stick used for inflicting punishment.
—v. **1** make or repair with strips of rattan, bamboo, etc.: *to cane a chair seat.* **2** beat with or as if with a flexible stick or rod. ⟨< F < L *canna* < Gk. *kanna* reed. Doublet of CANNA.⟩ **—'can•er,** *n.*

cane•brake ['kein,breik] *n.* a thicket of cane plants.

ca•nel•la [kə'nɛlə] *n.* a spice similar to cinnamon, obtained from the inner bark of a tropical American tree (*Canella winterana*). ⟨< Med.L cinnamon < L *canna* reed⟩

ca•nes•cent [kə'nɛsənt] *adj.* **1** becoming white or greyish. **2** of leaves, etc., covered with a white or greyish bloom. ⟨< L *canescens* ppr. of *canescere* grow white < *canere* be white < *canus* white, hoary⟩

cane sugar sugar made from SUGAR CANE.

Ca•nes Ve•na•ti•ci ['keiniz və'nætə,si] *n.* a northern constellation between Boötes and Ursa Major.

Can•ex ['kænɛks] *n. Cdn.* a supply place for Canadian Forces personnel; a military supermarket.

Ca•nic•u•la [kə'nɪkjələ] *n.* Sirius, the dog star. ⟨< L dim. of *canis* dog⟩

ca•nine ['keinaɪn] *adj., n. —adj.* **1** of or having to do with dogs. **2** like that of a dog: *His little brother followed him around with canine devotion.* **3** of or having to do with the dog family (Canidae), a group of meat-eating, four-footed animals that includes the domestic dog, wolf, coyote, Australian dingo, and jackal.
—n. **1** dog. **2** any member of the dog family. **3** CANINE TOOTH. ⟨< L *caninus* < *canis* dog⟩

canine tooth one of the four pointed teeth next to the incisors; cuspid. See TEETH for picture.

Ca•nis Ma•jor ['keinɪs] *Astronomy.* a group of stars southeast of Orion that contains Sirius, the brightest of the stars. ⟨< L *canis major* greater dog⟩

Ca•nis Mi•nor ['keinɪs] *Astronomy.* a group of stars east of Orion, separated from Canis Major by the Milky Way. ⟨< L *canis minor* lesser dog⟩

can•is•ter ['kænɪstər] *n.* **1** a small covered box or can, especially one used for keeping tea, flour, sugar, coffee, or other dry products. **2** formerly, a bullet-filled case shot from a cannon. **3** the boxlike part of a vacuum cleaner, containing the motor and dirt bag. **4** the part of a gas mask that contains the air filters. ⟨< L *canistrum* < Gk. *kanastron* basket⟩

can•ker ['kæŋkər] *n., v. —n.* **1** a spreading sore, especially one in the mouth. **2** a disease of plants that causes slow decay. **3** the decayed part of a woody plant. **4** anything that causes rot or decay or that destroys by a gradual eating away.
—v. infect or be infected with canker; decay; rot. ⟨OE *cancer* < L *cancer* crab, tumour, gangrene. Doublet of CANCER, CHANCRE.⟩

can•ker•ous ['kæŋkərəs] *adj.* **1** affected with, caused by, or like canker. **2** causing canker.

can•ker•worm ['kæŋkər,wɜrm] *n.* the larva of any of various geometrid moths, which injures or destroys fruit or shade trees by feeding on the buds and foliage; especially, either of two North American tree pests, *Paleacrita vernata* or *Alsophila pometaria.*

Can•Lit ['kæn'lɪt] *n. Cdn. Informal.* Canadian Literature.

can•na ['kænə] *n.* **1** any of a genus (*Canna,* constituting the family Cannaceae) of tropical herbs widely cultivated for their showy clusters of red, pink, or yellow flowers. **2** the flower of any of these plants. ⟨< L *canna* reed. Doublet of CANE.⟩

can•na•bis ['kænəbɪs] *n.* **1** the dried flowering tops of the female hemp plant. Compare MARIJUANA, HASHISH. **2** hemp. ⟨< L *cannabis* hemp < Gk. *kánnabis*⟩

canned [kænd] *adj., v. —adj.* **1** preserved by being put in an airtight can or jar. **2** preserved on a phonograph record or tape; recorded: *canned music.* **3** *Informal.* drunk; intoxicated. **4** *Slang.* fired; terminated; out of work. **5** *Slang.* cancelled, scrapped.
—v. pt. and pp. of CAN[2].

can•nel coal ['kænəl] a kind of bituminous coal in large lumps that burns with a bright flame and a lot of smoke. Also called **cannel.** ⟨apparently var. of *candle*⟩

can•nel•lo•ni [,kænə'louni] *n.pl.* an Italian dish consisting of large noodles stuffed with meat or cheese and baked in a tomato sauce. ⟨< Italian < *cannello* tube⟩

can•ner•y ['kænəri] *n., pl.* **-ner•ies.** a factory where food is canned.

can•ni•bal ['kænəbəl] *n.* **1** any person who eats human flesh. **2** an animal or fish that eats others of its own kind. **3** (*adjl.*) of or like cannibals. ⟨< Sp. *Canibal* < *Caribe* Carib⟩

can•ni•bal•ism ['kænəbə,lɪzəm] *n.* **1** the practice of eating the flesh of one's own kind. **2** barbarity; extreme cruelty.

can•ni•bal•is•tic [,kænəbə'lɪstɪk] *adj.* of cannibals; characteristic of cannibals.

can•ni•bal•ize ['kænəbə,laɪz] *v.* **-ized, -iz•ing.** use the parts of (an old or unserviceable piece of equipment) to assemble or repair another: *My sister built this radio set by cannibalizing two old ones that would not work.*

can•ni•kin ['kænəkɪn] *n.* a small can; cup. ⟨< *can*[2] + *-kin*⟩

can•ning ['kænɪŋ] *n., v. —n.* the process or business of preserving food by putting it in airtight cans or jars.
—v. ppr. of CAN[2].

can•no•li [kə'nouli] *n.* a dish consisting of a rolled pastry tube or shell, fried and filled with a sweetened mixture of ricotta cheese, bitter chocolate, and orange peel. ⟨< Italian, plural of *cannolo,* diminutive of *canna* pipe, tube⟩

can•non ['kænən] *n., pl.* **-non** or **-nons;** *v. —n.* **1** a big gun that is fixed to the ground or mounted on a carriage, especially the old-fashioned type of gun that fired cannon balls. **2** the CANNON BONE. **3** *Mechanics.* a hollow, cylindrical piece that revolves or is capable of revolving on and independently of a shaft. **4** the metal loop by which a bell is suspended; ear. **5** *Billiards.* a carom.
—v. **1** fire a cannon. **2** attack with a cannon. **3** *Billiards.* carom. **4** come into collision: *to cannon against a tree.* ⟨< F *canon* < Ital. < L *canna* reed, tube < Gk. *kanna*⟩
☛ *Hom.* CANON.

can•non•ade [,kænə'neid] *n., v.* **-ad•ed, -ad•ing.** *—n.* **1** a continued firing of cannon. **2** *Informal.* a verbal assault: *a furious political cannonade.*
—v. attack with cannon. ⟨< F *canonnade*⟩

cannon ball **1** a large iron or steel ball, formerly fired from cannons. **2** a rapid express train. **3** in tennis, a driving serve. **4** a jump into water with the body in a curled-up position. Also, **cannonball.**

cannon bone in hoofed animals, the long bone between the hock and the fetlock. See HORSE for picture.

cannon cracker a large firecracker.

can•non•eer [,kænə'nir] *n.* an artilleryman; gunner.

cannon fodder military personnel considered as being expendable in war.

can•non•ry ['kænənri] *n., pl.* **-ries. 1** a continuous firing of cannons. **2** artillery.
☛ *Hom.* CANONRY.

cannon shot **1** cannon balls or other shot for a cannon. **2** the range of a cannon.

can•not [kə'nɒt] *or* ['kænɒt]; *stressed,* ['kæn'nɒt] *v.* can not.

can•ny ['kæni] *adj.* **-ni•er, -ni•est. 1** shrewd and cautious, especially in business. **2** thrifty. **3** *Esp. Scottish.* fortunate or lucky. **4** *Esp. Scottish.* nice, good, pleasant, etc. ⟨< *can*[1]⟩ **—'can•ni•ly,** *adv.* **—'can•ni•ness,** *n.*

A canoe

ca•noe [kə'nu] *n., v.* **ca•noed, ca•noe•ing.** *—n.* a light, narrow boat having low, curving sides that come together in a point at each end, and that is moved by one or more paddles.
—v. **1** paddle a canoe; go in a canoe. **2** take or carry in a canoe. ⟨< Sp. < Haitian *canoa* < Arawakan⟩

Canoe Country *Cdn.* formerly, an area of land in central British Columbia.

ca•noe•ist [kə'nuɪst] *n.* a person who paddles a canoe, especially one who is skilled at doing this.

ca•noe•man [kə'numən] *n., pl.* **-men.** *Cdn.* **1** voyageur. **2** a man skilled in handling a canoe.

Ca•no•la [kə'noulə] *n. Cdn. Trademark.* **1** any of several varieties of the rape plant having seeds that contain no more than 5 percent erucic acid and no more than 3 mg per gram of glucosinolate (an anti-nutritional substance containing sulphur). **2** the seed or an edible oil or livestock meal prepared from the seed. ⟨< *Can*ada + *colza.* 20c.⟩

can•on¹ ['kænən] *n.* **1** a law of a church; a body of church law. **2** a rule by which a thing is judged; standard: *the canons of good taste.* **3** the official list of the books contained in the Bible; the books of the Bible accepted by the Christian church as being inspired by God. **4** a list of the accepted works of an author: *the Shakespearian canon.* **5** the list of saints. **6** any official list. **7** *Roman Catholic Church.* the part of the Mass coming after the offertory. **8** *Music.* a kind of composition in the style of a fugue, the different voice parts repeating the same subject one after another either at the same or at a different pitch; round. **9** a large size of type; 48 point. ⟨OE < L < Gk. *kanōn*⟩
☛ *Hom.* CANNON.

can•on² ['kænən] *n.* **1** a member of the clergy belonging to a cathedral or to certain churches. **2** *Roman Catholic Church.* a member of a group of clergy living according to a certain rule. ⟨ME < OF < L *canonicus* canonical < *canon* canon¹⟩
☛ *Hom.* CANNON.

ca•ñon ['kænjən] See CANYON.

ca•non•i•cal [kə'nɒnəkəl] *adj., n. —adj.* **1** according to or prescribed by the laws of a church. **2** in the canon of the Bible. **3** authorized; accepted. **4** *Music.* having to do with or in the form of a canon.
—n., pl. **canonicals.** the vestments worn by clergy for a church service. **—ca'non•i•cal•ly,** *adv.*

canonical hours in certain churches, the periods of the day fixed by canon law for prayer and worship.

can•on•ize ['kænə,naɪz] *v.* **-ized, -iz•ing. 1** declare (a dead person) to be a saint; place in the official list of saints: *Joan of Arc was canonized by the Roman Catholic Church in 1920.* **2** treat as a saint; glorify. **3** make or recognize as canonical. **4** authorize. **—,can•on•i'za•tion,** *n.*

canon law the laws of a church that govern ecclesiastical affairs.

ca•non•ry ['kænənri] *n.* **1** the position of a canon. **2** canons as a group.
☛ *Hom.* CANNONRY.

ca•noo•dle [kə'nudəl] *v.* **ca•noo•dled, ca•noo•dling.** *Slang.* kiss; pet; fondle. ⟨< G *knudeln* to cuddle, akin to LG *knuddel* a knot, clump, dim. of dial. *knude*; akin to OHG *knodo*, OE *cnotta* knot⟩

Ca•no•pus [kə'noupəs] *n.* a very bright, first magnitude star in the southern constellation Argo or Carina. It is the second brightest star in the sky; only Sirius is brighter.

can•o•py ['kænəpi] *n., pl.* **-pies;** *v.* **-pied, -py•ing.** *—n.* **1** a covering fixed over a bed, throne, entrance, etc., or carried on poles over a person: *There is a striped canopy over the entrance to the hotel.* **2** a rooflike covering; a shelter or shade: *The trees formed a canopy over the old road. Many species of birds live in the canopy of the tropical forest.* **3** the sky. **4** the umbrellalike supporting surface of a parachute. **5** the clear shell over the cockpit of an aircraft.
—v. cover with a canopy. ⟨< F *canapé* < Med.L < L *conopeum* < Gk. *kōnōpeion* a couch with curtains of mosquito netting < *kōnōps* gnat⟩

ca•not du maître [kanody'mɛtʀ] *Cdn. French.* MONTRÉAL CANOE. ⟨literally, master's canoe⟩

ca•not du nord [kanody'nɔʀ] *Cdn. French.* NORTH CANOE.

canst [kænst] *v. Archaic.* 2nd pers. sing., present tense, of CAN¹. *Thou canst* means *You* (sing.) *can.*

cant¹ [kænt] *n., v. —n.* **1** insincere talk; moral and religious statements that many people make, but few really believe or follow. **2** the peculiar language of a special group, including many words incomprehensible to outsiders: *thieves' cant.* **3** a whining manner of speaking, especially as adopted by beggars. **4** (*adj.*) of, marked by, or being cant: *the cant language of thieves.*
—v. use cant; talk in cant. ⟨< L *cantus* song⟩ **—'cant•er,** *n.* **—'cant•ing•ly,** *adv.*

cant² [kænt] *n., v. —n.* **1** a slope or bevel. **2** a sloping surface or edge. **3** an outside corner or angle, especially of a building. **4** a sudden movement producing a tilt. **5** the tilt or angle produced in this way.
—v. **1** give a cant, or slope, to; bevel. **2** tip or tilt. **3** overturn, especially with a sudden movement. **4** slant. ⟨probably < MDu., MLG < OF < *cant* < L *cant(h)us* corner, side < Celtic⟩

can't [kænt] cannot or can not.

Cantab. of Cambridge, England (for L *Cantabrigiensis*).

can•ta•bi•le [kɑn'tɑbi,lei] *adj. or adv. Music.* in a smooth and flowing style; songlike. ⟨< Ital. < L *cantare* < *canere* sing⟩

Can•ta•brig•i•an [,kæntə'brɪdʒiən] *adj., n. —adj.* of Cambridge, England or Cambridge, Massachusetts, or of Cambridge or Harvard University.
—n. **1** a native or inhabitant of Cambridge, England or Cambridge, Massachusetts. **2** a student or graduate of Cambridge or Harvard University. ⟨< *Cantabrigia*, Latin form of *Cambridge*⟩

can•ta•loupe or **can•ta•loup** ['kæntə,loup] *n.* **1** a cultivated variety of muskmelon (*Cucumis melo cantalupensis*) with a hard, rough rind and sweet, juicy, orange flesh. **2** any other variety of muskmelon. ⟨< F *cantaloup* < Ital. *Cantalupo*, place where first cultivated⟩

can•tan•ker•ous [kæn'tæŋkərəs] *adj.* showing a disagreeable and ill-natured disposition; quarrelsome and perverse: *a cantankerous way of speaking. She's very cantankerous these days, arguing about everything.* ⟨alteration, influenced by *rancorous*, of earlier **conteckerous* < ME *contecker* contentious person < *conteck* strife, quarrelling⟩ **—can'tan•ker•ous•ly,** *adv.* **—can'tan•ker•ous•ness,** *n.*

can•ta•ta [kən'tɑtə] *or* [kən'tætə] *n.* a musical composition consisting of a story or play to be sung, but not acted, by a chorus and soloists, usually with orchestral accompaniment. ⟨< Ital. < L *cantare* < *canere* sing⟩

can•teen [kæn'tin] *n.* **1** a small, often compressed and cloth-covered container for carrying water or other drinks. **2** a place in a school, camp, factory, etc. where food and drink and, sometimes, other articles are sold or given out. **3** a store, recreation hall, or club for members of the armed forces. **4** a place in a disaster area where cooked food is given out to victims; SOUP KITCHEN. **5** a box of cooking utensils for use in camp. **6** a set of cutlery in a box or case. ⟨< F < Ital. *cantina* cellar < LL *cant(h)us* side⟩

can•ter ['kæntər] *n., v. —n.* a horse's gait faster than a trot but slower than a gallop.
—v. move with this gait. ⟨for *Canterbury gallop*, the supposed easy pace of pilgrims riding to Canterbury⟩
☛ *Hom.* CANTOR ['kæntər].

Can•ter•bur•y bell ['kæntər,bɜri] *or* ['kæntər,bɛri] a biennial bellflower (*Campanula medium*) with tall stalks of bell-shaped flowers, usually purplish blue, pink, or white.

can•thar•i•din [kæn'θærədɪn] *or* [kæn'θɛrədɪn] *n.* a drug used to treat warts.

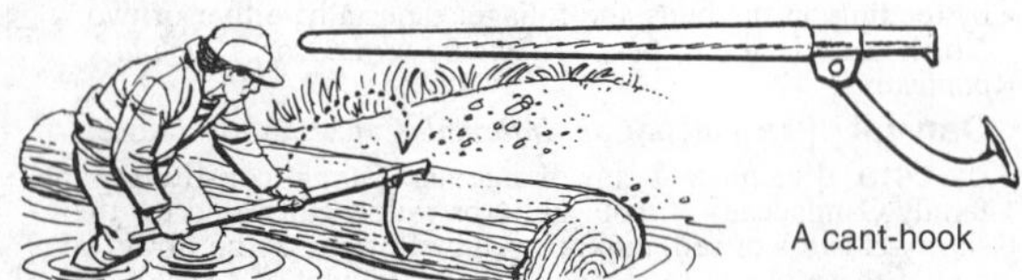
A cant-hook

cant–hook ['kænt ,hʊk] *n. Cdn.* a lever used for handling logs, consisting of a wooden handle with a blunt steel tip and a movable steel hook at its lower end. Compare PEAVEY. ⟨< *cant* a slabbed log < *cant*[2] + *hook*⟩

can•thus ['kænθəs] *n.* either corner of the eye. ⟨< NL < Gk. *kanthos*⟩

can•ti•cle ['kæntəkəl] *n.* **1** a song, hymn, or chant, especially a hymn with words taken from the Bible, used in certain church services. **2 Canticles,** Song of Solomon (*used with a singular verb*). Also called (in the Douay Bible) **Canticle of Canticles.** ⟨< L *canticulum* little song < *cantus* song⟩

can•ti•le•na [,kæntə'linə] *n. Music.* a smoothly flowing, lyrical passage of music for voice or, sometimes, instrument. ⟨< Ital. < L, song < *cantare* sing⟩

can•ti•lev•er ['kæntə,livər] *or* [-,lɛvər] *n., v.* —*n.* a large, projecting bracket or beam that is fastened at one end only.
—*v.* **1** build with cantilevers or a cantilever: *Our balcony is cantilevered; theirs is supported by pillars.* **2** extend outward on or as a cantilever: *The artist's studio cantilevers out over a sheer cliff.* ⟨origin uncertain⟩

cantilever bridge a bridge made of two cantilevers whose projecting ends meet but do not support each other. See BRIDGE[1] for picture.

can•til•late ['kæntə,leit] *v.,* **-lat•ed, -lat•ing.** sing or recite (Jewish liturgy) with given phrasing. ⟨< L *cantillare* sing low, hum⟩ **—,can•til'la•tion,** *n.*

can•tle ['kæntəl] *n.* the part of a saddle that sticks up at the back. ⟨< OF < Med.L *cantellus* little corner⟩

can•to ['kæntou] *n., pl.* **-tos. 1** one of the main divisions of a long poem. A canto of a poem corresponds to a chapter of a novel. **2** *Music.* the soprano part; melody. ⟨< Ital. < L *cantus* song⟩

can•ton *n.* ['kæntən], ['kæntɒn], *or* [kæn'tɒn]; *French,* [kɑ̃'tɔ̃]; *v.* [kæn'tɒn] *n., v.* —*n.* **1** a small part or political division of a country: *Switzerland is made up of 22 cantons.* **2** township. **3** in Québec, a municipal unit roughly equal to a township.
4 *Heraldry.* a small, rectangular portion of a shield or flag, in the upper corner.
—*v.* **1** divide into parts; subdivide. **2** allot quarters to or provide quarters for (soldiers, etc.). ⟨< F *canton* corner, portion < OF *cant.* See CANT[2].⟩

can•ton•al ['kæntənəl] *adj.* of a canton.

Can•ton crepe ['kæntən] a soft silk cloth with a crinkled surface. ⟨after Canton, China. See CANTONESE.⟩

Can•ton•ese [,kæntə'niz] *n., pl.* **-ese;** *adj.* —*n.* **1** a native or inhabitant of Canton, a city in S China. **2** the Chinese language spoken in Canton and the surrounding area, in Hong Kong, etc.
—*adj.* of or having to do with Canton, its people or their language.

Can•ton flannel ['kæntən] a strong cotton cloth that is soft and fleecy on one side.

can•ton•ment [kæn'tɒnmənt] *or* [kæn'tounmənt] *n.* **1** a place where soldiers live; quarters. **2** the act of cantoning troops. ⟨< F⟩

can•tor ['kæntər] *or* ['kæntɔr] *n.* **1** a singer who leads the singing of a choir or congregation. **2** a soloist in a synagogue. ⟨< L *cantor* singer < *canere* sing⟩
☛ *Hom.* CANTER ['kæntər].

can•tus fir•mus ['kæntəs 'fɜrməs] *Music.* a principal melody to which polyphonic parts are added. ⟨< Med.L, fixed song⟩

Ca•nuck [kə'nʌk] *n. or adj. Cdn. Informal.* **1** Canadian. **2** French Canadian. ⟨origin uncertain⟩

Ca•nuck•o•phile [kə'nʌkə,faɪl] *n., adj.* —*n. Informal.* a lover of Canada and Canadians.
—*adj. Informal.* showing a love of Canada and Canadians.

can•vas ['kænvəs] *n., v.* —*n.* **1** a strong cloth made of cotton, flax, or hemp, used to make tents and sails, certain articles of clothing, etc. **2** (*adjl.*) made of canvas. **3** something made of canvas. **4** a sail or sails. **5** a piece of canvas on which to paint a picture, especially in oils. **6** a picture painted on canvas: *She's got seven canvases ready for the show.* **7** a tent or tents, as, for a circus. **8 the canvas,** the floor of a boxing ring. **9** any coarse, stiffened fabric of wide weave used for working tapestry, as a basis for embroidery, etc. **10** *Rowing.* **a** either of the tapering covered ends of a racing boat. **b** the length of this: *They won the race by a canvas.*
under canvas, a in tents. **b** with sails spread: *The boat left the harbour under canvas.*
—*v.* cover, line, or furnish with canvas. ⟨ME < OF *canevas* < L *cannabis* hemp⟩
☛ *Hom.* CANVASS.

can•vas•back ['kænvəs,bæk] *n.* a North American diving duck (*Aythya valisineria*) having a long, blackish bill and distinctive sloping forehead, the male having a rusty-brown head, black upper back, breast, and tail, and whitish back, wings, and abdomen.

can•vass ['kænvəs] *v., n.* —*v.* **1** go about (a street or community) asking for subscriptions, votes, orders, etc.: *Each student canvassed his or her own block for contributions to the Red Cross.* **2** ask for votes, orders, donations, etc.: *She's out canvassing.* **3** examine carefully; examine: *Dale canvassed the papers, hunting for job ads.* **4** discuss: *The city council canvassed the mayor's plan thoroughly.* **5** examine and count (the votes cast in an election).
—*n.* **1** the act or process of canvassing, especially a personal visiting of homes or stores in a district to sell something, ask for votes, etc. **2** a discussion. ⟨< *canvas,* originally, toss (someone) in a sheet, later, shake out, discuss⟩ **—'can•vass•er,** *n.*
☛ *Hom.* CANVAS.

can•yon ['kænjən] *n.* a narrow valley with high, steep sides, usually with a stream at the bottom. Also, **cañon.** ⟨< Sp. *cañón* tube < L *canna* cane⟩

can•zo•net [,kænzə'nɛt] *n.* a short, light song. ⟨< Ital. *canzonetta,* ult. < L *cantare* sing⟩

caou•tchouc [kʌu'tʃuk], [kʌutʃuk], *or* ['kʌutʃʊk] *n.* the gummy, coagulated juice of various tropical plants; rubber. ⟨< F < Sp. < South Am.Ind.⟩

Caps: several different types

cap[1] [kæp] *n., v.* **capped, cap•ping.** —*n.* **1** a close-fitting covering for the head usually having little or no brim. **2** a special head covering worn to show rank, occupation, etc.: *a nurse's cap.* **3** something that serves as a cover, especially to protect an end, tip, etc., or to close off the end of a pipe, tube, bottleneck, etc.: *a lens cap, a bottle cap.* **4** CERVICAL CAP. **5** a top part like a cap: *The top of a mushroom is called a cap.* **6** the highest part; top. **7** a small quantity of explosive in a wrapper or covering. **8** a limit; imposed maximum: *They've put a cap on departmental budgets.*
cap in hand, in humble fashion.
set (one's) **cap for,** *Informal.* try to get as one's spouse or lover.
—*v.* **1** put a cap on. **2** put a top on; cover the top of: *pudding capped with whipped cream.* **3** match (one thing) with something good or better: *The two clowns kept on capping each other's jokes.* **4** form or serve as a cap, covering, or crown to; lie on top of. **5** *Scottish.* confer an academic degree on. **6** place the white cap of a nurse upon (a nursing school graduate). **7** be the finishing touch to. **8** limit; set a maximum to.
cap the climax, go to the extreme limit; go beyond expectation or belief. ⟨OE *cæppe* < LL *cappa.* Doublet of CAPE[1]. Cf. L *caput* head.⟩ **—'cap•per,** *n.* **—'cap•less,** *adj.* **—'cap,like,** *adj.*

cap[2] [kæp] *n., v.* **capped, cap•ping.** —*n.* **1** a capital letter. **2** (*adjl.*) capital; uppercase.
—*v.* capitalize; put in upper case. ⟨< capital⟩

cap. 1 capital letter. **2** capitalize. **3** capacity. **4** capital. **5** chapter (for L *caput*).

ca•pa•bil•i•ty [,keipə'bɪləti] *n., pl.* **-ties. 1** ability to learn or do; power or fitness; capacity. **2** legal or moral qualifications: *A contract has the capability of binding people to a common purpose.* **3** potential not yet realized.

ca•pa•ble ['keipəbəl] *adj.* having fitness, power, or ability; able; efficient; competent: *a capable teacher.*
capable of, a having ability, power, or fitness for: *Some airplanes are capable of going 1500 km/h.* **b** open to; ready for: *a statement capable of many interpretations.* ⟨< LL *capabilis* < L *capere* take⟩ **—'ca•pa•ble•ness,** *n.* **—'ca•pa•bly,** *adv.*
☛ *Usage.* See note at ABLE.

ca•pa•cious [kə'peiʃəs] *adj.* able to hold much; roomy; large: *a capacious closet.* **—ca'pa•cious•ly,** *adv.* **—ca'pa•cious•ness,** *n.*

ca•pa•ci•tance [kə'pæsətəns] *n.* the ability of a capacitor to collect and store a charge of electricity.

ca•pa•ci•tate [kə'pæsɪ,teit] *v.,* **-tat•ed, -tat•ing.** make capable or fit; qualify.

ca•pac•i•tor [kə'pæsətər] *n.* CONDENSER (def. 2).

ca•pac•i•ty [kə'pæsəti] *n., pl.* **-ties. 1** the amount of room or space inside; the largest volume that can be held by a container: *This can has a capacity of 4 L.* **2** the maximum number or amount that can be accommodated: *The theatre has a capacity of 500. The arena was filled to capacity.* **3** (*adjl.*) being a maximum number or amount: *a capacity crowd.* **4** the power or ability to receive and hold: *the heat capacity of a metal.* **5** ability to learn or do; power or aptitude: *a great capacity for learning.* **6** a position or relation: *A person may act in the capacity of guardian, trustee, voter, friend, etc.* **7** capacitance. ⟨< L *capacitas* < *capere* take⟩

cap and bells a cap trimmed with bells, worn by a jester.

cap and gown a flat cap, or mortarboard, and loose gown, worn by university professors and students on certain occasions.

cap–a–pie or **cap–à–pie** [,kæpə'pi] *adv.* from head to foot; completely. ⟨< OF⟩

ca•par•i•son [kə'pærəsən] *or* [kə'pɛrəsən], [kə'pærəzən] *or* [kə'pɛrəzən] *n., v.* *—n.* **1** an ornamental covering for a horse. **2** any rich clothing or equipment.
—v. dress richly; fit out. ⟨< F *caparasson* < Provençal *capa* cape⟩

cape[1] [keip] *n.* an outer garment, or part of one, without sleeves, that falls loosely from the shoulders. ⟨< F < *cape* < Sp. < LL *cappa.* Doublet of CAP.⟩

cape[2] [keip] *n.* **1** a point of land extending into the water. **2 the Cape,** the Cape of Good Hope, in SW South Africa. ⟨< F *cap* < Provençal < L *caput* head⟩

Cape Breton Island a large island to the northeast of Nova Scotia, noted for rugged beauty and for mining.

Cape buffalo a large, wild buffalo (*Syncerus caffer*) of southern Africa, having large horns that curve downward and then upward.

Cape Cod 1 a peninsula in Massachusetts. **2** a style of house architecture of 1½ storeys, with gables and dormer windows.

cap•e•lin ['kæpəlɪn], ['keiplɪn], *or* ['kæplɪn] See CAPLIN. ⟨< F < Provençal *capelan* chaplain⟩

Ca•pel•la [kə'pɛlə] *n.* the brightest star in the constellation Auriga, one of the six brightest stars in the sky. ⟨< L *capella,* dim. of *caper* goat⟩

ca•per[1] ['keipər] *v., n.* *—v.* leap or jump about playfully.
—n. **1** a playful leap or jump. **2** a playful trick, scheme, or pursuit: *Her newest caper is to tell everyone she's an orphan.* **3** a dishonest scheme or enterprise; racket: *He did five years for that caper.*
cut a caper or **cut capers,** behave in a frolicsome, playful way: *We really cut a caper at the party last night.* ⟨A shortened form of E *capriole,* first used in 16c. See CAPRIOLE.⟩

ca•per[2] ['keipər] *n., adj.* *—n.* **1** a low, prickly Mediterranean shrub (*Capparis spinosa*) cultivated for its edible flower buds. **2** one of the flower buds of this plant, pickled for use as a condiment.
—adj. of or having to do with various plants of the Capparaceae family. The bee plant and cleome are caper plants. ⟨ME *capres* < F < L *capparis* < Gk. *kapparis*⟩

cap•er•cail•lie [,kæpər'keilji] *n.* a large, black grouse (*Tetrao urogallus*) of the woodlands of N Europe. ⟨< Scots Gaelic *capullcoille,* lit. forest horse⟩

cape•skin ['keip,skɪn] *n.* a soft, durable leather made of lambskin or sheepskin, used for gloves, jackets, etc. ⟨after *Cape* of Good Hope, where the strong leather from its goats was first made⟩

Ca•pe•tian [kə'piʃən] *adj., n.* *—adj.* of or having to do with Hugh Capet (A.D. 938?-996), King of France from 987 to 996, or the kings named Capet who reigned over France till 1328.
—n. one of these rulers.

Cape Ver•de ['vɛrdi] *n.* a country of islands in the Atlantic off the west coast of Africa.

cap•ful ['kæp,fʊl] *n.* a quantity equal to the contents of the cap of a bottle or jar.

cap gun a toy gun having a hammer action for setting off a small explosive charge, or cap; cap pistol.

ca•pi•as ['keipiəs] *or* ['kæpiəs] *n. Law.* a writ ordering an officer to arrest a certain person. ⟨< L *capias* you may take⟩

cap•il•la•ceous [,kæpə'leiʃəs] *adj.* **1** having threads like hairs. **2** like a hair. ⟨< L *capillaceus* hairlike < *capillus* hair⟩

cap•il•lar•i•ty [,kæpə'lærəti] *or* [,kæpə'lɛrəti] *n.* **1** CAPILLARY ATTRACTION OR REPULSION. **2** the quality of having or causing capillary attraction or repulsion.

cap•il•lar•y [kə'pɪləri] *or* ['kæpə,lɛri] *n., pl.* **-lar•ies;** *adj.* *—n.* **1** one of the very tiny blood vessels connecting the smallest arteries with the smallest veins. **2** any tube having a very slender opening, or bore.
—adj. **1** of, in, or having to do with capillaries. **2** hairlike; very slender. ⟨< L *capillaris* of hair, hairlike < *capillus* hair⟩

capillary attraction *Physics.* the force that causes a liquid to rise against a vertical surface, resulting when the attraction between the molecules of the liquid is less than the attraction between them and a solid surface. Capillary attraction causes the surface of water in a glass tube to be slightly higher at the sides where it touches the glass than in the middle. See MENISCUS for picture.

capillary repulsion *Physics.* the force that causes a liquid to move away from a vertical surface, resulting when the attraction between the molecules of the liquid is greater than the attraction between them and a solid surface. Capillary repulsion causes the surface of mercury in a glass tube to be slightly higher in the middle than at the sides where it touches the glass. See MENISCUS for picture.

capillary tube a tube with a very slender, hairlike opening or bore.

cap•i•ta ['kæpətə] *n. Latin.* pl. of CAPUT.

cap•i•tal[1] ['kæpətəl] *n., adj.* *—n.* **1** the city where the government of a country, province, or state is located. **2** a chief centre for an industry, etc.: *the sugar capital of the Caribbean.* **3** a capital letter, as distinct from a, b, c, etc. **4** the amount of money or property that a company or a person uses in carrying on a business: *The Dahn Company has a capital of $60 000.* **5** a source of power or advantage; resources. **6** national or individual wealth as produced by industry and available for reinvestment in the production of goods. **7** *Accounting.* **a** the net worth of a business after the deduction of taxes and other liabilities. **b** the total investment of owners in a business, often expressed as capital stock. **8** capitalists as a group.
make capital of, take advantage of; use to one's own advantage: *He made capital of his mother's fame to get the job.*
—adj. **1** of or having to do with capital. **2** important; leading: *The invention of the telephone was a capital advance in communications.* **3** main; chief. **4** *Informal, esp. Brit.* of the best kind; excellent: *A maple tree gives capital shade.* **5** involving death; punishable by death: *Murder is a capital crime in many countries.* **6** in which the seat of government is located: *the capital city.* ⟨ME < OF < L *capitalis* chief, pertaining to the head < *caput* head. Doublet of CATTLE and CHATTEL.⟩
☛ *Hom.* CAPITOL.

cap•i•tal[2] ['kæpətəl] *n.* the top part of a column or pillar. See COLUMN for picture. ⟨ME < OF *capitel* < L *capitellum,* dim. of *caput* head⟩
☛ *Hom.* CAPITOL.

capital expenditure in a business, the money spent on renovations and rebuilding, as opposed to that spent on operating expenses.

capital gain profit realized from the sale of assets, such as real estate: *capital gains tax.*

capital goods *Economics.* goods such as machinery or equipment that can be used to produce other goods. Compare CONSUMER GOODS.

cap•i•tal–in•ten•sive ['kæpətəl ɪn'tɛnsɪv] *adj.* requiring much money or capital goods rather than labour. Compare LABOUR-INTENSIVE.

cap•i•tal•ism ['kæpətə,lɪzəm] *n.* an economic system in which the means of production, such as land or factories, are for the most part privately owned by individuals or corporations which compete with one another to produce goods and services that are offered on a free market for whatever profit may be made. Compare COMMUNISM and SOCIALISM.

cap•i•tal•ist ['kæpətəlɪst] *n.* **1** a person whose money and property are used in carrying on business. **2** *Informal.* a wealthy person. **3** a person who supports capitalism. **4** (*adjl.*) capitalistic.

cap•i•tal•is•tic [,kæpətə'lɪstɪk] *adj.* **1** of or having to do with capitalism. **2** favouring or supporting capitalism.
—,cap•i•tal'is•ti•cal•ly, *adv.*

cap•i•tal•i•za•tion [,kæpətələ'zeiʃən] *or* [,kæpətəlaɪ'zeiʃən] *n.* **1** a capitalizing or being capitalized. **2** the amount at which a company is capitalized; the capital stock of a business.

cap•i•tal•ize ['kæpətə,laɪz] *v.* **-ized, -iz•ing. 1** write or print with a capital initial letter. **2** set the capital of (a company) at a certain amount. **3** turn into capital; use as capital. **4** supply (an operation) with the necessary starting capital. **5** take advantage; use to one's own advantage (*used with* **on**): *The children capitalized on the hot weather by setting up lemonade stands at the bus stops.*

capital letter the large form of a letter; A, B, C, D, etc., as distinguished from a, b, c, d, etc.

capital levy a tax on the capital of a company or, sometimes, an individual.

cap•i•tal•ly ['kæpətəli] *adv.* very well; excellently.

capital murder murder punishable by death.

capital punishment the death penalty for a crime.

capital ship a large warship; battleship.

capital stock capital used in carrying on a business. It is divided into shares.

cap•i•tate ['kæpə,teit] *adj.* **1** larger at the head end. **2** *Botany.* of a flower, shaped like a head.

cap•i•ta•tion [,kæpə'teiʃən] *n.* **1** a tax or fee of a fixed amount per person. **2** the act or process of assessing by counting individuals. ⟨< LL *capitatio, -onis* < L *caput* head⟩

Cap•i•tol ['kæpətəl] *n.* **1** in Washington, D.C., the building in which the United States Congress meets. **2** *U.S.* Often, **capitol,** the building in which a state legislature meets. **3** in Rome: **a** the ancient temple of Jupiter on the Capitoline hill. **b** the Capitoline hill. ⟨ME < ONF *capitolie* < L *Capitolium* chief temple (of Jupiter) < *caput* head⟩
☛ *Hom.* CAPITAL.

Cap•i•to•line ['kæpətə,laɪn] *or* [kə'pɪtə,laɪn], ['kæpətə,lin] *or* [kə'pɪtə,lin] *n., adj.* —*n.* in Rome, one of the seven hills on which ancient Rome was built. —*adj.* having to do with the hill or the Capitol.

ca•pit•u•late [kə'pɪtʃə,leit] *v.* **-lat•ed, -lat•ing. 1** surrender under certain terms or conditions: *The men in the fort capitulated on the condition that they be allowed to go free.* **2** give up completely; stop resisting: *He capitulated when he realized that arguing was useless.* ⟨< Med.L *capitulare* draw up under separate heads, arrange in chapters < L *caput* head⟩ **—ca'pit•u,la•tor,** *n.*

ca•pit•u•la•tion [kə,pɪtʃə'leiʃən] *n.* **1** the act of capitulating. **2** the terms or conditions of surrender. **3** statement of the main facts of a subject; summary.

cap•let ['kæplɪt] *n.* a type of pharmaceutic pill coated like a capsule.

cap•lin or **cape•lin** ['kæplɪn] *or* ['keiplɪn] *n.* a small fish (*Mallotus villosus*) of the smelt family found in N Atlantic and Pacific coastal waters, used for food and as bait for cod.

Cap'n [kæpn] *or* [kæpm] Captain.

ca•po¹ ['keipou] *n.* a device fastened over the strings of a guitar to change key. ⟨< Ital. *capo* chief, head⟩

ca•po² ['kɑpou] *or* ['kæpou] *n.* the head of a criminal organization. ⟨< Ital. *capo* head < L *caput*⟩

ca•pon ['keipɒn] *or* ['keipən] *n.* a rooster that has been castrated to improve the flesh for eating. ⟨OE *capūn* < OF < L *capo, caponis*⟩

ca•pon•ize ['keipə,naɪz] *v.* **-ized, -iz•ing.** make (a young male chicken) into a capon.

ca•pot [kæ'pou] *n.* a hooded frock-coat, worn in former times. ⟨< F dim. of *cape* cape⟩

ca•pote [kə'pout] *n.* **1** a long, cloaklike outer garment, usually having a hood. **2** a bonnet formerly worn by women and girls. ⟨< F *capot*⟩

cap•puc•ci•no [,kæpə'tʃinou] *n.* coffee, especially espresso, served with hot milk or cream, and sometimes flavoured with cinnamon or chocolate powder. ⟨< Ital., literally Capuchin; because its light-brown colour is like that of a Capuchin's habit⟩

cap•ric acid ['kæprɪk] a component of natural oils, used in making perfumes and artificial flavours. *Formula*: $CH_3(CH_2)_8COOH$

ca•pric•ci•o [kə'pritʃiou]; *Italian* [ka'pritʃo] *n., pl.* **-ci•os. 1** a caper; prank; caprice. **2** *Music.* a lively composition in a free, irregular style. ⟨< Ital. *capriccio* < *capro* he-goat < L *caper.* Doublet of CAPRICE.⟩

ca•pric•ci•o•so [kə,pritʃi'ousou]; *Italian,* [,kapri'tʃoso] *adj. Music.* to be played in a light, fanciful style.

ca•price [kə'pris] *n.* **1** a sudden change of mind without any reason; unreasonable notion or desire: *Her decision to wear only blue clothes was pure caprice.* **2** a tendency to change suddenly and without reason. **3** CAPRICCIO (def. 2). ⟨< F < Ital. *capriccio.* Doublet of CAPRICCIO.⟩

ca•pri•cious [kə'prɪʃəs] *or* [kə'priʃəs] *adj.* likely to change suddenly and without reason; changeable; fickle: *a spoiled and capricious child, capricious weather.* **—ca'pri•cious•ly,** *adv.* **—ca'pri•cious•ness,** *n.*

Cap•ri•corn ['kæprə,kɔrn] *n.* **1** *Astronomy.* a southern constellation thought of as having the shape of a goat. **2** *Astrology.* **a** the tenth sign of the zodiac. The sun enters Capricorn about December 22 and leaves about January 21. See ZODIAC for picture. **b** a person born under this sign. **3** See TROPIC OF CAPRICORN. ⟨< L *capricornus* < *caper* goat + *cornu* horn⟩

cap•ri•fig ['kæprə,fɪg] *n.* the wild fig tree (*Ficus carica*) of southern Europe and the Middle East, used to fertilize cultivated figs. ⟨< L *caprificus* wild fig < *caper* he-goat + *ficus* fig⟩

cap•ri•ole ['kæpri,oul] *n., v.* **-oled, -ol•ing.** —*n.* **1** a high leap made by a horse without moving forward. **2** a leap; caper. —*v.* **1** of a horse, make a high leap without moving forward. **2** leap; caper. ⟨< F < Ital. *capriola* leap < *capriolo* roebuck, dim. of *caper* goat. See CAPRICCIO.⟩

ca•pro•ic acid [kə'prouɪk] a natural fatty acid that occurs in animal fats such as butter or lard, used to make esters. *Formula*: $CH_3(CH_2)_4COOH$

caps or **caps. 1** capital letters. **2** capsule.

cap•sa•i•cin [kæp'seiəsɪn] *n.* a drug used to treat neuralgia, extracted from capsicum. *Formula*: $C_{18}H_{27}NO_3$

cap screw a bolt that screws into an opening, used to secure a cover, etc.

cap•si•cum ['kæpsəkəm] *n.* **1** any of a genus (*Capsicum*) of small, tropical shrubs of the nightshade family, some of which are widely grown for their edible fruit. Green peppers, chilis, and pimentos are the fruits of cultivated varieties of capsicum. **2** the fruit of any of these shrubs. **3** the pods of these shrubs, used in medicine as a gastric stimulant. ⟨< NL < L *capsa* box⟩

cap•size ['kæpsaɪz] *or* [kæp'saɪz] *v.* **-sized, -siz•ing.** of a ship, boat, etc., turn bottom side up; upset; overturn. ⟨origin unknown⟩

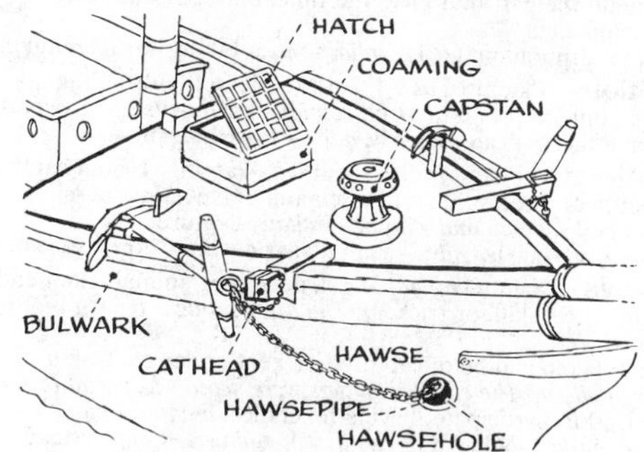

The forward part of a sailing ship

cap•stan ['kæpstən] *n.* **1** a machine for lifting or pulling that revolves on an upright shaft or spindle. Sailors on early sailing ships hoisted the anchor by turning the capstan by means of spokes inserted into the shaft; on later ships the capstan was operated by an engine. **2** a device in a tape recorder to keep the tape driven past the head at a constant speed. ⟨< Provençal *cabestan* < L *capistrum* halter < *capere* take⟩

capstan bar a pole used to turn a capstan.

cap•stone ['kæp,stoun] *n.* **1** the top stone of a wall or other structure. **2** a finishing touch; climax.

cap•su•lar ['kæpsələr] *or* ['kæpsjələr] *adj.* **1** of or having to do with a capsule. **2** in a capsule. **3** shaped like a capsule.

cap•su•late *adj.* ['kæpsəlɪt] *or* ['kæpsjəlɪt]; *v.* ['kæpsə,leit] *or* ['kæpsjə,leit] *adj., v.* **-lat•ed, -lat•ing.** —*adj.* enclosed in a capsule.
—*v.* **1** enclose in a capsule. **2** make a brief summary of.

cap•sule ['kæpsəl] *or* ['kæpsjul] *n., v.* **cap•suled, cap•sul•ing.** *—n.* **1** a small container made of gelatin or other soluble substance for enclosing a dose of medicine. **2** the enclosed front section of a rocket, made to carry instruments, astronauts, etc., into space. In flight, the capsule can separate from the rest of the rocket and go into orbit or be directed back to earth. **3** any of various compact containers or coverings. **4** *Botany.* a dry seedcase that opens when ripe. See FRUIT for picture. **5** *Anatomy.* **a** a membrane enclosing an organ; a membranous bag or sac. **b** either of two folds of white matter in the brain. **6** a concise summary. **7** *(adjl.)* condensed; concise: *She gave a capsule description of the entire plan.* **8** *(adjl.)* very small; miniature: *a capsule radio transmitter.*
—v. **1** furnish with or enclose within a capsule: *It will be capsuled in a cylinder.* **2** condense. ⟨< L *capsula,* dim. of *capsa* box⟩

cap•sul•ize ['kæpsə,laɪz] *or* ['kæpsjə,laɪz] *v.* **-ized, -iz•ing.** **1** condense into or express in a compact form. **2** enclose in a capsule.

Capt. or **Capt** captain.

cap•tain ['kæptən] *n., v. —n.* **1** a leader; chief. **2** *Canadian Forces.* **a** an officer ranking next above a lieutenant and below a major. *Abbrev.*: Capt. or Capt **b** in Maritime Command, the equivalent of a colonel. *Abbrev.*: Capt.(N) or Capt(N) See chart of ranks in the Appendix. **3** an officer of similar rank in the armed forces of other countries. **4** the commander of a ship. **5** *Sports.* the leader of a team. *Abbrev.*: Capt. **6** a police or fire department officer ranking next above a lieutenant. **7** the leader of a troop of Girl Guides.
—v. lead or command as captain: *Pearl will captain the team.* ⟨ME < OF *capitain(e)* < LL *capitaneus* chief < L *caput* head. Doublet of CHIEFTAIN.⟩
☛ *Hom.* CAPTAN.

cap•tain•cy ['kæptənsi] *n., pl.* **-cies.** the rank, commission, term of office, or authority of a captain.

cap•tain•ship ['kæptən,ʃɪp] *n.* **1** captaincy. **2** ability as a captain; leadership.

cap•tan ['kæptæn] *or* ['kæptən] *n.* a fungicidal powder used on flowers, fruits, etc. *Formula*: $C_9H_8Cl_3NO_2S$
☛ *Hom.* CAPTAIN ['kæptən].

cap•tion ['kæpʃən] *n., v. —n.* **1** a title or heading at the beginning of a page, article, chapter, etc. **2** an explanation or title accompanying a picture. **3** in films, subtitle. **4** of a legal document, the part that gives the time, place, or authority for the document.
—v. put a caption on. ⟨< L *captio, -onis* a taking < *capere* take⟩

cap•tious ['kæpʃəs] *adj.* **1** hard to please; faultfinding. **2** made only to pick a quarrel: *captious arguments.* ⟨< L *captiosus* < *capere* take⟩ **—'cap•tious•ly,** *adv.* **—'cap•tious•ness,** *n.*

cap•ti•vate ['kæptə,veit] *v.* **-vat•ed, -vat•ing.** **1** hold captive by beauty or interest; charm; fascinate: *The children were captivated by the animal story.* **2** *Archaic.* capture. **—'cap•ti,vat•ing•ly,** *adv.* **—,cap•ti'va•tion,** *n.* **—'cap•ti,va•tor,** *n.*

cap•tive ['kæptɪv] *n., adj. —n.* a person or animal taken and held by force, skill, or trickery: *The army brought back a thousand captives.*
—adj. **1** taken and held; captured or kept under control: *a captive balloon. The captive soldiers were kept in a special prison.* **2** obliged to participate; having no choice: *a captive audience, a captive market.* ⟨ME < OF *captif* < L *captivus* < *capere* take. Doublet of CAITIFF.⟩

cap•tiv•i•ty [kæp'tɪvəti] *n., pl.* **-ties.** the state of being held captive: *Some animals cannot bear captivity and die after a few weeks in a cage.*

cap•to•pril ['kæptə,prɪl] *n.* a drug used to treat high blood pressure. *Formula*: $C_9H_{15}NO_3S$

cap•tor ['kæptər] *n.* a person who takes or holds a prisoner.

cap•ture ['kæptʃər] *v.* **-tured, -turing;** *n. —v.* **1** take by force, skill, or trickery; seize: *They were captured during the raid.* **2** attract and hold: *The brightly coloured toy immediately captured the baby's attention.* **3** succeed in preserving: *The artist was able to capture the mood of a rainy fall day.*
—n. **1** taking or being taken by force, skill, or trickery. **2** a person or thing taken in this way. ⟨< F < L *captura* taking < *capere* take⟩ **—'cap•tur•er,** *n.*

ca•puche [kə'puʃ] *or* [kə'putʃ] *n.* a long, pointed hood such as that worn by the Capuchins. ⟨< F < Ital. *cappucio* hood⟩

cap•u•chin ['kæpju,ʃɪn] *or* ['kæpju,tʃɪn] *n.* **1** any of a genus (*Cebus*) of South American monkeys typically having a thick, cowl-like crown of hair. **2** a woman's cloak with a hood. **3 Capuchin,** a friar belonging to a branch of the Franciscan order. Capuchins are distinguished by their long, pointed hood or cowl. ⟨< F < Ital. *cappuccio* hood⟩

ca•put ['kæpət] *or* ['keipət] *n., pl.* **cap•i•ta** ['kæpətə]. *Latin.* head.

cap•y•ba•ra [,kæpə'bɑrə] *n.* either of two species of semiaquatic rodent constituting the genus *Hydrochoerus,* found in Central and South America. The best-known is *H. hydrochaeris* of South America, the largest living rodent, reaching a length of 1.2 m. ⟨< Pg. *capybara* < the Brazilian native name⟩

car [kɑr] *n.* **1** a passenger vehicle that carries its own engine and is used on roads and streets. **2** any vehicle that moves on wheels. **3** a vehicle that runs on rails and is used to carry passengers or freight, such as a railway car or a streetcar. **4** the closed platform of an elevator, balloon, etc., for carrying passengers or cargo. **5** a crate measuring 6.5 m × 10 m, designed to hold live lobsters until they are sold. **6** *Poetic or archaic.* chariot. ⟨ME < ONF *carre* < Med.L *carra* < L *carrus* two-wheeled cart⟩
☛ *Usage.* **Car** now commonly replaces *automobile, auto, motorcar,* and other terms for four-wheeled vehicles powered by a gasoline engine. But it is not used in referring to trucks, vans, or buses.

car. carat.

ca•ra•ba•o [,kɑrə'bɑou] *or* ['kɛrə,baʊ] *n., pl.* **-ba•os.** WATER BUFFALO. ⟨< Sp. < Malay *karbau*⟩

car•a•bi•neer or **car•a•bi•nier** [,kærəbə'nir] *or* [,kɛrəbə'nir] *n.* formerly, a cavalry soldier armed with a carbine. Also, **carbineer.** ⟨< F⟩

car•a•bi•ner [,kærə'binər] *or* [,kɛrə'binər] *n.* in mountaineering, a D-shaped ring with a spring latch, used to fasten a rope to the piton. Also, **karabiner.** ⟨< Austrian G *Karabiner* shortening of G *Karabinerhaken* carbine hook⟩

car•a•bi•ni•ere [,kɑrəbi'njɛrei]; *Italian,* [karabi'njere] *n., pl.* **carabinieri** [-'njɛri]; *Italian,* [-'njeri]. an Italian police officer.

car•a•cal ['kærə,kæl] *or* ['kɛrə,kæl] *n.* **1** a small, slender, long-legged wildcat (*Lynx caracal,* also classified as *Felis caracal*) of African and Asian desert regions, having reddish brown fur with black-tipped ears. Also called **Persian lynx, desert lynx.** **2** its fur.

ca•ra•ca•ra [,kɑrə'kɑrə], [,kærə'kærə], *or* [,kɛrə'kɛrə] *n.* any of several vulturelike hawks of South and Central America and the southern U.S. ⟨< Sp. *caracara* < Tupi⟩

car•a•cole ['kærə,koul] *or* ['kɛrə,koul] *n., v.* **-coled, col•ing.** *—n.* a half turn to the right or left, made by a horse and rider. *—v.* make such half turns; prance from side to side. ⟨< F < Ital. < Sp. *caracol* spiral shell⟩

car•a•cul ['kærəkəl] *or* ['kærə,kʌl], ['kɛrəkəl] *or* ['kɛrə,kʌl] *n.* **1** a type of flat, loose, curly fur made from the skin of newborn karakul lambs. **2** KARAKUL (def. 1). ⟨< *Kara Kul,* a lake in Turkestan⟩

ca•rafe [kə'ræf] *n.* a glass bottle for holding water, wine, etc., at table. ⟨< F < Ital. *caraffa* < Sp. < Arabic *gharrâf* drinking vessel⟩

car•a•ga•na [,kærə'gænə] *or* [,kɛrə'gænə] *n.* any of a genus (*Caragana*) of shrubs or small trees of the legume family, having feathery, pale green foliage and yellow flowers that appear in early spring. Caraganas are widely grown on the Prairies as hedges and windbreaks because they can survive in a dry climate. ⟨< NL < Tatar⟩

caragana break a hedge of caragana serving as a windbreak.

ca•ra•geen ['kærə,gin] *or* ['kɛrə,gin] *n.* See CARRAGEEN.

ca•ra•geen•an [,kærə'ginən] *or* [,kɛrə'ginən] *n.* See CARRAGEENAN.

car•a•mel ['kærəməl], ['kɛrəməl], *or* ['kɑrməl] *n.* **1** sugar browned or burned over heat, used for colouring and flavouring food. **2** a small block of chewy candy flavoured with this sugar. **3** the colour of browned sugar. ⟨< F < Sp. *caramelo*⟩

car•a•mel•ize ['kærəmə,laɪz], ['kɛrəmə,laɪz], *or* ['kɑrmə,laɪz] *v.,* **-ized, -iz•ing.** change into caramel. **—,car•a•me•li'za•tion,** *n.*

car•a•pace ['kærə,peis] *or* ['kɛrə,peis] *n.* the shell on the back of a turtle, lobster, etc. ⟨< F < Sp. *carapacho*⟩

car•at ['kærət] *or* ['kɛrət] *n.* **1** a unit of mass for precious stones, equal to 200 mg. **2** See KARAT. ⟨< F < Ital. < Arabic < Gk. *keration,* a small horn-shaped bean used as a weight, dim. of *keras* horn⟩
☛ *Hom.* CARET, CARROT, KARAT.

car•a•van ['kærə,væn] *or* ['kɛrə,væn] *n., v.* **-vanned, -van•ning.** *—n.* **1** a group of people travelling together,

especially for safety. **2** the vehicles or beasts of burden used by such a group. **3** *Brit.* a mobile home, especially one pulled by a car; trailer. **4** a large covered vehicle such as those used by a circus or by Gypsies. **5** *Military.* a mobile headquarters for a senior officer.
—v. travel in a caravan. ⟨< F *caravane* < Persian *karwan*⟩

car•a•van•sa•ry [ˌkærəˈvænsəri] *or* [ˌkɛrəˈvænsəri] *n., pl.* **-ries. 1** an inn or hotel where caravans stop to rest in the Orient: *There used to be many caravansaries on the trade routes from China to Arabia.* **2** any large inn or hotel. Also, **caravanserai** [-səˌraɪ] *or* [-səˌrei]. ⟨< Persian *karwansarai* < *karwan* caravan + *sarai* inn⟩

A 15th-century caravel, lateen-rigged

car•a•vel [ˈkærəˌvɛl] *or* [ˈkɛrəˌvɛl] *n.* any of various small sailing ships of former times. One type, with a broad bow and a high stern, was used by Columbus and other navigators of the same period. Also, **carvel.** ⟨< OF *caravelle* < Ital. < LL *carabus* < Gk. *karabos* kind of light ship < ancient Macedonian⟩

car•a•way [ˈkærəˌwei] *or* [ˈkɛrəˌwei] *n.* **1** a biennial herb (*Carum carvi*) of the parsley family having finely divided leaves and a fragrant fruit used in cooking and medicine. **2** the dried fruit, usually called **caraway seed,** of this plant, used especially in flavouring cheeses and breads. ⟨< Med.L *carui* < Arabic *karawya*⟩

car•ba•chol [ˈkɑrbəˌkɒl] *n.* a drug used to contract the pupil of the eye. *Formula:* $C_6H_{15}ClN_2O_2$

car•ba•maz•e•pine [ˌkɑrbəˈmæzəˌpin] *n.* a drug used to treat neuralgia and some forms of epilepsy. *Formula:* $C_{15}H_{12}N_2O$

car•bam•ic acid [kɑrˈbæmɪk] a presumed acid known only in the form of its salts, including ammonium carbamate, or its esters, including urethane. *Formula:* NH_3CO_2 ⟨< *carb*on + *am*ido + *-ic*⟩

car•ban•i•on [kɑrˈbænaɪən] *or* [kɑrˈbænaɪˌɒn] *n.* an organic ion containing a negatively charged ion of carbon. Compare CARBONIUM. ⟨< L *carbo, carbonis* coal + ANION⟩

car•ben•i•cil•lin [ˌkɑrbɛnəˈsɪlɪn] *n.* an antibiotic drug, a form of penicillin. *Formula:* $C_{17}H_{16}N_2Na_2O_6S$

car•bide [ˈkɑrbaɪd] *n.* a compound of carbon with a metal, especially calcium carbide.

car•bi•do•pa [ˌkɑrbəˈdoupə] *n.* a drug used along with levodopa to treat Parkinson's disease.

car•bine [ˈkɑrbaɪn] *or* [ˈkɑrbin] *n.* **1** a short, light rifle, originally designed for cavalry use. **2** a light automatic or semi-automatic rifle. ⟨< F *carabine*⟩

car•bi•neer [ˌkɑrbəˈnir] *n.* See CARABINEER.

carbo– *combining form.* containing carbon. Also, **carb-** before vowels.

car•bo•hy•drate [ˌkɑrbəˈhaɪdreit] *n.* any of a group of compounds composed of carbon, hydrogen, and oxygen that take part in the chemical processes in living plants and animals. Sugar and starch are carbohydrates. In sunlight, green plants make carbohydrates from carbon dioxide and water. ⟨< *carbo(n)*+ *hydrate*⟩

car•bo•lat•ed [ˈkɑrbəˌleitɪd] *adj.* containing carbolic acid.

car•bol•ic [kɑrˈbɒlɪk] *adj.* made from carbon or coal tar. ⟨< L *carbo* coal + *oleum* oil⟩

carbolic acid a poisonous, corrosive, white crystalline compound present in coal tar and wood tar, used in solution as a disinfectant and antiseptic; phenol. *Formula:* C_6H_5OH

car•bo•lize [ˈkɑrbəˌlaɪz] *v.* **-lized, -liz•ing.** add carbolic acid to; treat with carbolic acid.

car•bon [ˈkɑrbən] *n., adj. —n.* **1** a very common non-metallic element found in combination with other elements in all plants and animals. Carbon forms organic compounds in combination with hydrogen, oxygen, etc. Diamonds and graphite are pure carbon; coal and charcoal are impure carbon. *Symbol:* C; *at.no.* 6; *at.mass* 12.01. **2** a piece of carbon used in batteries, arc lamps, etc. **3** a piece of CARBON PAPER. **4** a copy made with carbon paper.
—adj. of carbon; like carbon; treated with carbon: *a carbon copy.* ⟨< F *carbone* < L *carbo, -onis* coal⟩

carbon-12 the most common isotope of carbon, now adopted instead of oxygen as the standard for determining the atomic mass of chemical elements.

carbon-13 a heavy, stable isotope of carbon having an atomic number of 13, used as a tracer in physiological studies, especially in cancer research.

carbon-14 a heavy, radioactive isotope of carbon, produced by the bombardment of nitrogen atoms. It is used as a tracer in biological research and in CARBON DATING. *Abbrev.:* C14

car•bo•na•ceous [ˌkɑrbəˈneiʃəs] *adj.* **1** of or containing carbon. **2** like or containing coal.

car•bo•na•do¹ [ˌkɑrbəˈneidou] *n., v. —n.* a piece of meat, fish, etc., scored and then broiled.
—v. **1** score and broil. **2** *Archaic.* slash; hack. ⟨< Sp. *carbonada* something cooked in coals < *carbon* charcoal < L *carbo, -onis*⟩

car•bo•na•do² [ˌkɑrbəˈneidou] *n.* a bulky, dark-coloured type of diamond, used for drills and found mostly in Brazil; black diamond. ⟨< Pg. *carbonado* carbonized (from its colour)⟩

car•bo•na•ra [ˌkɑrbəˈnɑrə] *n., adj.—n.* a sauce for pasta, made with bacon, onions, egg yolks, and grated Parmesan cheese.
—adj. of pasta, served with this sauce. ⟨< LL *carbonaria* brazier⟩

carbon arc 1 a curved stream of light or sparks formed when a strong electric current jumps from one carbon electrode or conductor to another. **2** an ARC LAMP having carbon electrodes emitting such a stream of light or sparks.

car•bon•ate *n.* [ˈkɑrbənɪt] *or* [ˈkɑrbəˌneit]; *v.* [ˈkɑrbəˌneit] *n., v.* **-at•ed, -at•ing.** *—n.* a salt or ester of carbonic acid.
—v. **1** change into a carbonate. **2** charge with carbon dioxide. Soda water is carbonated to make it bubble and fizz. **3** burn to carbon; char; carbonize. **—car•bon'a•tion,** *n.*

carbon black a smooth, black pigment of pure carbon formed by deposits from burning gas, oil, etc.; a black soot, finer than lampblack.

carbon copy 1 a copy made by using CARBON PAPER. **2** anything that appears to be a duplicate of something else: *His ideas are a carbon copy of his mother's.*

carbon cycle 1 *Physics.* the process whereby nuclear changes in the interior of stars bring about the liberation of atomic energy that gradually transforms hydrogen to helium. **2** *Biology.* the circulation of carbon in nature.

car•bon–date [ˈkɑrbən ˌdeit] *v.* **-dat•ed, -dat•ing.** measure the age of (any carbonaceous material, especially a once-organic archaeological or geological specimen by examining the extent to which the carbon-14 in it has disintegrated. **—carbon dating.**

carbon dioxide a heavy, colourless, odourless gas, present in the atmosphere. Plants absorb it from the air to make plant tissue. The air that comes from an animal's lungs contains carbon dioxide. *Formula:* CO_2

carbon disulphide or **disulfide** a colourless, poisonous, highly flammable liquid used in the manufacture of plastics, insecticides, etc. *Formula:* CS_2

car•bon•ic [kɑrˈbɒnɪk] *adj.* of or containing carbon.

carbonic acid the acid made when carbon dioxide is dissolved in water. *Formula:* H_2CO_3

Car•bon•if•er•ous [ˌkɑrbəˈnɪfərəs] *n., adj. —n.* **1** *Geology.* the period, beginning approximately 360 million years ago, when the warm, moist climate produced a rank growth of tree ferns, horsetail rushes, and conifers, whose remains form the great coal beds. See geological time chart in the Appendix. **2** the rocks and coal beds formed during this period.
—adj. **1** of this period. **2** denoting the period of the Paleozoic era which gave rise to these coal beds. **3 carboniferous,** containing coal. ⟨< *carbon* + *-ferous* containing (< L *ferre* to bear)⟩

car•bo•ni•um [kɑrˈbouniəm] *n.* an organic ion containing a positively charged ion of carbon. Compare CARBANION. ⟨< *carb(on)* + *(amm)onium*⟩

car•bon•i•za•tion [ˌkɑrbənəˈzeiʃən] *or* [ˌkɑrbənaɪˈzeiʃən] *n.* a carbonizing or being carbonized.

car•bon•ize ['kɑrbə,naɪz] *v.* **-ized, -iz•ing. 1** change into carbon by burning. **2** cover or combine with carbon.

carbon monoxide a colourless, odourless, poisonous gas, formed when carbon burns with an insufficient supply of air. It is part of the exhaust gases of automobile engines. *Formula*: CO

carbon paper a thin paper having a preparation of carbon or other inky substance on one surface, used for making copies of written or typed material. Carbon paper is placed between sheets of ordinary paper to make a copy of whatever is written or typed on the top sheet.

carbon process a method of printing photographs by using paper specially coated with a gelatin that hardens on exposure to light.

carbon tetrachloride a poisonous, colourless, nonflammable liquid, often used in fire extinguishers and in cleaning fluids. *Formula*: CCl_4

car•bon•yl ['kɑrbə,nɪl] *n.* a bivalent radical occurring in aldehydes, ketones, acids, etc. *Formula*: -CO
—car•bon'yl•ic, *adj.*

car•bo•pla•tin [,kɑrbə'pleitɪn] *n.* a drug used to treat certain forms of cancer.

Car•bo•run•dum [,kɑrbə'rʌndəm] *n. Trademark.* an extremely hard compound of carbon and silicon, used for grinding, polishing, etc. *Formula*: SiC ⟨< *carbo(n)* + *(co)rundum*⟩

car•box•y•he•mo•glo•bin [kɑr,bɒksə'himə,gloubɪn] *n.* a compound in which carbon monoxide replaces oxygen on the hemoglobin molecule. The formation of carboxyhemoglobin often results in cell death. ⟨< *carbon* + oxy-[2] + hemoglobin⟩

car•box•yl [kɑr'bɒksɪl] *n.* a univalent radical existing in many organic acids. *Formula*: -COOH

carboxylic acid [,kɑrbɒk'sɪlɪk] any organic acid, all of which typically contain the carboxyl group.

car•boy ['kɑrbɔɪ] *n.* a very large bottle of glass or plastic, usually enclosed in a protective basket, box, or crate, used for keeping liquids safely. ⟨< Persian *qarabah* large flagon⟩

car•bro•mal ['kɑrbrə,mæl] *n.* a sedative barbiturate drug.

car•bun•cle ['kɑrbʌŋkəl] *n.* **1** a severe abscess of the skin and tissues just beneath the skin, forming a hard, painful, dark red swelling that looks like a group of boils. A carbuncle discharges pus through several openings. **2** *Archaic.* a round garnet or other deep red jewel not cut in facets. ⟨ME < OF < L *carbunculus* < *carbo* coal⟩ **—car'bun•cu•lar** [kɑr'bʌŋkjələr], *adj.*

car•bu•ret ['kɑrbə,reit] *or* ['kɑrbjə,reit] *v.* **-ret•ted** or **-ret•ed, -ret•ting** or **-ret•ing. 1** mix (air or gas) with carbon compounds, such as gasoline, benzine, etc. **2** combine with carbon. ⟨< *carbon*⟩

car•bu•re•tion [,kɑrbə'reiʃən] *or* [,kɑrbjə'reiʃən] *n.* a carburetting or being carburetted.

car•bu•re•tor ['kɑrbə,reitər] *n.* a device for sending air through or over a liquid fuel, so as to produce an explosive mixture. Also, **carburettor.**

car•bur•ize ['kɑrbə,raɪz] *v.* **-ized, -iz•ing. 1** carburet. **2** heat (iron) with carbon to make steel. **—,car•bu•ri'za•tion,** *n.*

car•ca•jou ['kɑrkə,ʒu] *n. Cdn.* wolverine. ⟨< Cdn.F < Algonquian⟩

car•ca•net ['kɑrkə,nɛt] *n. Archaic.* an ornamental, usually jewelled necklace, collar, or headband. ⟨< F *carcan* + E *-et*⟩

car•cass ['kɑrkəs] *n.* **1** the body of a dead animal. A human body or corpse is sometimes contemptuously called a carcass. **2** the whole trunk of a butchered animal, after removal of the head, limbs, and offal. **3** the lifeless shell or husk of anything: *the carcass of his disappointed hopes.* **4** the shell or framework of a structure, as of a building, ship, or piece of furniture. **5** the foundation structure of a tire, consisting of layers of corded fabric. Also (Brit.), **carcase.** ⟨< F < Ital. *carcassa*⟩

car•ci•no–em•bry•on•ic antigen ['kɑrsənou ,ɛmbri'ɒnɪk] a protein which, in urine, serum, etc., often indicates the presence of a tumour. Regulating this protein is helpful in the treatment of cancer patients.

car•cin•o•gen [kɑr'sɪnədʒən] *n.* any substance or agent that causes cancer. **—,car•cin•o'gen•e•sis,** *n.*

car•cin•o•gen•ic [,kɑrsɪnə'dʒɛnɪk] *adj.* **1** tending to cause cancer: *The drug was taken off the market because it was found to be carcinogenic.* **2** caused by cancer. **—,car•ci•no•ge'nic•i•ty** [,kɑrsənoudʒə'nɪsəti], *n.*

car•ci•no•ma [,kɑrsə'noumə] *n., pl.* **-mas, -ma•ta** [-mətə]. a cancerous growth, especially in the skin or the lining of a tube or cavity in the body. ⟨< L < Gk. *karkinōma* ulcer⟩
—,car•ci'no•ma•tous, *adj.*

car•ci•no•ma•to•sis [,kɑrsə,noumə'tousɪs] *n.* a spreading of a carcinoma throughout the body.

car coat a short topcoat for casual wear, cut for ease and comfort when driving.

card[1] [kɑrd] *n., v. —n.* **1** a piece of stiff paper, thin cardboard, or plastic, usually small and oblong: *a business card, a credit card.* **2** PLAYING CARD. **3 cards,** *pl.* **a** any of various games played with a set of playing cards: *She enjoys cards.* **b** the playing of such a game: *Many of the guests were busy at cards.* **4** a piece of paper, usually folded, printed with a message or greeting and an illustration and sent in an envelope to mark a special occasion such as Christmas, a birthday, etc.: *Did you send him a card?* **5** a printed program of sporting or other events, especially a horse race. **6** a card on which spectators record the progress of a game; score card. **7** the round of contests that make up a boxing match. **8** formerly, a dance program at a ball, in which a lady wrote the names of her partners. **9** a piece of cardboard to which are attached small items for sale. **10** a postcard. **11** a small card for writing and filing information: *index cards.* **12** COMPASS CARD. **13** *Informal.* an amusing person. **14** *Brit.* cardboard. **15** *Computer technology.* **a** a circuit board that is inserted into an expansion slot of a computer to give the computer additional capabilities: *graphics card, communications card.* Also called **expansion card, adapter, board. b** PUNCHED CARD.
a card up (one's) **sleeve,** a plan in reserve; extra help kept back until needed.
hold all the cards, have complete control.
in or **on the cards,** sure to happen: *It was in the cards that it would rain; nothing has gone right all day.*
play (one's) **cards well** (or **right,** etc.), deal or act cleverly.
put (one's) **cards on the table,** be perfectly frank about one's plans, resources, etc.
show (one's) **cards,** reveal one's plans.
—v. **1** provide with a card. **2** put on a card. ⟨< F *carte* < L *charta* < Gk. *chartēs* a leaf of papyrus. Doublet of CHART.⟩

card[2] [kɑrd] *n., v. —n.* **1** a toothed tool or wire brush for raising the nap on cloth or for cleaning or combing fibres to be spun. **2** a machine, or part of one, that performs the same function.
—v. clean or comb (fibres to be spun) with such a tool or machine. ⟨ME < OF *carde* < Provençal < L *carere* to card; influenced by L *carduus* thistle⟩

Card. Cardinal.

car•da•mom or **car•da•mum** ['kɑrdəməm] *n.* **1** a spice consisting of the dried fruit, whole or ground, of a perennial East Indian herb (*Elettaria cardamomum*) of the ginger family. Cardamom is used in curry dishes and in Scandinavian pastries. **2** the plant producing this fruit, cultivated especially in S Asia and Central America. **3** any of a number of related plants bearing fruit whose aroma is similar to that of the spice. Also, **cardamon** [-mən]. ⟨< L < Gk. *kardamōmon*⟩

card•board ['kɑrd,bɔrd] *n., adj. —n.* a fairly thick kind of stiff paper, used to make cards, boxes, cartons, etc.
—adj. **1** made of cardboard. **2** weak or infirm: *a cardboard government.* **3** unrealistic or poorly developed: *cardboard characters in a novel.*

card–car•ry•ing ['kɑrd ,kæriŋ] *or* [-,kɛriŋ] *adj.* being a member of a political party or other organization, or a firm adherent of some ideology: *a card-carrying anarchist.*

card catalogue a reference catalogue of cards individually listing books and other items in a library or collection; card index.

card•er ['kɑrdər] *n.* a person who or machine that cards wool, cotton, flax, etc.

card file a set of cards arranged systematically and containing data or information.

card game a game played with playing cards: *Would you like to learn a new card game?*

car•di•ac ['kɑrdi,æk] *adj., n. —adj.* **1** of or having to do with the heart: *cardiac symptoms.* **2** having to do with the upper part of the stomach.
—n. **1** a medicine that stimulates the heart. **2** a heart patient: *the cardiac in room 43.* ⟨< L *cardiacus* < Gk. *kardiakos* < *kardia* heart⟩

cardiac arrest heart failure: *A patient with cardiac arrest can be revived if the right treatment is given in time.*

car•di•al•gia [ˌkardiˈældʒə] *n.* **1** heartburn. **2** any uncomfortable feeling in the area of the heart.

car•di•gan [ˈkardəgən] *n.* a sweater or knitted jacket that opens down the front and, usually, is collarless. ⟨after the Earl of *Cardigan* (1797-1868)⟩

Car•di•gan [ˈkardɪgən] *n.* a kind of Welsh corgi dog.

car•di•nal [ˈkardənəl] *adj., n.*
—adj. **1** of first importance; main; chief; principal: *Her idea was of cardinal importance to the plan.*
2 bright red.
—n. **1** a bright red. **2** *Roman Catholic Church.* one of the high officials appointed by the Pope to the College of Cardinals, and second to him in rank. **3** a North American songbird (*Richmondena cardinalis*) related to the finches, having a pointed crest on the head and a heavy, reddish bill, the male having bright red plumage marked with grey and black, and the female being mainly brownish, with reddish wings, tail, and crest.
4 CARDINAL NUMBER. ⟨ME < OF < L *cardinalis* chief, having to do with a hinge < *cardo* hinge⟩ **—ˈcar•di•nalˌship,** *n.*

A cardinal (def. 3)

car•di•nal•ate [ˈkardənəlɪt] *or* [ˈkardənəˌleit] *n.* **1** the position or rank of cardinal. **2** the Sacred College of cardinals.

cardinal flower **1** a perennial plant (*Lobelia cardinalis*) that is a common wildflower of E North America and Central America and is also cultivated for its spikes of brilliant red flowers. **2** the flower of this plant.

cardinal grosbeak a CARDINAL (def. *n.* 3).

cardinal number any of the numbers such as one, two, three, fifteen, eight hundred, etc., that show quantity and are used in simple counting. Compare ORDINAL NUMBER.

cardinal points the four main directions of the compass; north, south, east, and west.

cardinal virtues prudence, fortitude, temperance, and justice. They were considered by the ancient philosophers to be the basic qualities of a good character.

card index a file of cards each referring to a separate item in a collection, list, research study, etc., so arranged as to aid in finding items desired; card catalogue.

card•ing [ˈkardɪŋ] *n., v.* *—n.* the preparation of the fibres of wool, cotton, flax, etc. for spinning by combing them.
—v. ppr. of CARD[2].

cardio– *combining form.* **1** the heart: *Cardiology = the science of the heart.* **2** the heart and——: *Cardiovascular = relating to the heart and blood vessels.* ⟨< Gk. *kardia* heart⟩

car•di•o•gram [ˈkardiəˌgræm] *n.* a graphic record of the action of the heart, made by a cardiograph.

car•di•o•graph [ˈkardiəˌgræf] *n.* an instrument that records the strength and nature of movements of the heart.

car•di•og•ra•phy [ˌkardiˈɒgrəfi] *n., pl.* **-phies.** the examination of the action of the heart by means of a cardiograph.

car•di•oid [ˈkardiˌɔɪd] *n. Mathematics.* the heart-shaped path traced by a point on a circle which is rolling around an equal-sized fixed circle.

car•di•ol•o•gist [ˌkardiˈɒlədʒɪst] *n.* one who studies the heart and its functions, or who specializes in the treatment of heart diseases.

car•di•ol•o•gy [ˌkardiˈɒlədʒi] *n.* the study of the heart and its functions, and the diagnosis and treatment of heart diseases.

car•di•o•my•o•pa•thy [ˌkardioumaɪˈɒpəθi] *n.* any of several diseases affecting the muscle of the heart. ⟨< Gk. *kardia* heart + *mys, myos* muscle + *pathos* suffering, disease⟩

car•di•o•pul•mo•na•ry [ˌkardiouˈpʌlmənɛri] *adj.* having to do with the heart and lungs and their interaction.

cardiopulmonary resuscitation a method of saving life by combining mouth-to-mouth respiration with rhythmic pressure on the heart. *Abbrev.*: CPR

car•di•o•ta•chom•e•ter [ˌkardioutəˈkɒmətər] *n.* an instrument for measuring the heartbeat.

car•di•o•vas•cu•lar [ˌkardiouˈvæskjələr] *adj.* of or having to do with both the heart and the blood vessels: *Hardening of the arteries is a cardiovascular disease.*

car•di•tis [karˈdəitɪs] *n.* inflammation of the heart. ⟨< NL < Gk. *kardia* heart + *-tis*⟩

car•doon [karˈdun] *n.* a composite plant (*Cynara cardunculus*) of the Mediterranean area, having edible roots and leaves. ⟨< F *cardon* ult. < L⟩

card•sharp [ˈkardˌʃarp] *n.* a person who cheats at cards, especially one who does so for a livelihood. Also, **cardsharper.**

card table a small, square, folding table used for playing card games.

care [kɛr] *n., v.* **cared, car•ing.** *—n.* **1** watchful keeping; charge: *The child was left in her sister's care.* **2** food, shelter, and protection: *Your child will have the best of care.* **3** kind or tender attention to another's emotional needs. **4** serious attention; caution: *A good cook works with care.* **5** a troubled state of mind because of fear of what may happen; worry: *Few people are completely free from care.* **6** an object of worry, concern, or attention: *Keeping records is the care of the secretary of the club.*
care of or **in care of,** at the address or in the charge of: *Send it care of his father. Symbol*: c/o
have a care, be careful.
take care, a be careful. **b** *Informal.* a generalized expression of farewell.
take care of, a attend to; take charge of: *The waiter will take care of your order.* **b** look after; provide for: *She has a pension to take care of her basic needs. His brother took care of him while he was sick.* **c** be careful with; watch over: *Take care of your money.*
—v. **1** be concerned; feel an interest: *She cares about conservation. I don't care what they said.* **2** conduct oneself with care (n. 3); pay kind attention to others' emotional needs: *teachers who care.* **3** want; wish: *They said they didn't care to come.* **4** to object; mind (*usually used with negatives or in questions*): *Will he care if I borrow his sweater? They don't care if we come home late once in a while.*
care for, a have a liking or fondness for: *She doesn't care for him.* **b** want; wish: *I don't care for any dessert tonight.* **c** look after: *The nurse will care for him during the night.* **d** minister to the emotional needs of.
couldn't care less, be completely unconcerned. Sometimes, ironically or in error, **could care less.** ⟨OE *caru*⟩ **—ˈcar•er,** *n.*

☛ *Syn. n.* **5. Care,** CONCERN, SOLICITUDE = a troubled, worried, or anxious state of mind. **Care** emphasizes the idea of a burden which weighs a person down with responsibilities of worries and fears: *It is care that has made her sick.* **Concern** suggests uneasiness over someone or something one likes or is interested in: *He expressed concern over her health.* **Solicitude** suggests great concern, often together with loving care: *Her friends wait on her with solicitude.*

ca•reen [kəˈrin] *v.* **1** lean to one side; tilt; tip: *The ship careened in the strong wind.* **2** cause to lean to one side: *The strong wind careened the ship.* **3** lay (a ship) over on one side for cleaning, painting, repairing, etc. **4** clean, paint, or repair (a ship laid on its side). **5** rush along with a bobbing, leaning movement: *The waitress careened among the tables, balancing a heavy tray on one hand.* ⟨< F < L *carina* keel⟩

ca•reer [kəˈrir] *n., v., adj.* *—n.* **1** a way of making a living; occupation; profession: *Lisa planned to make law her career.* **2** a general course of action or progress through life: *It is interesting to read of the careers of great men and women.* **3** speed; full speed: *We were in full career when we struck the post.*
—v. rush along wildly; dash: *The runaway horse careered through the streets.*
—adj. having to do with someone who seriously follows a profession: *a career diplomat.* ⟨< F *carrière* race course < L *carrus* wagon⟩

ca•reer•ist [kəˈrirɪst] *n.* a person interested only in advancing in his or her profession, often at the expense of other people. **—caˈreer•ism,** *n.*

care•free [ˈkɛrˌfri] *adj.* without worry; light-hearted; happy.

care•ful [ˈkɛrfəl] *adj.* **1** thinking before one speaks; watching what one does; taking pains; watchful; cautious. **2** done with thought or effort; exact; thorough: *a careful investigation, a careful reading of a text.* **3** full of care or concern; attentive or protective: *She was always careful of the feelings of others.*
4 *Archaic.* anxious; worried. **—ˈcare•ful•ly,** *adv.*
—ˈcare•ful•ness, *n.*

☛ *Syn.* **1. Careful,** CAUTIOUS, WARY = watchful in speaking and acting. **Careful** = being observant and giving serious attention and thought to what one is doing, especially to details: *He is careful to tell the truth at all times.* **Cautious** = very careful, looking ahead for possible risks or dangers, and guarding against them by taking no chances: *He is cautious about making promises.* **Wary** emphasizes the idea of being suspicious and on the alert for danger or trouble: *She is wary of people who suddenly become very friendly.*

care•giv•er [ˈkɛrˌgɪvər] *n.* a person who looks after someone else, whether paid or not.

care•less ['kɛrlɪs] *adj.* **1** not thinking what one says; not watching what one does; not taking enough pains; not watchful or cautious: *One careless step here could cost a life.* **2** done without enough thought or effort; not exact or thorough: *careless work, a careless worker.* **3** not troubling oneself; indifferent; unconcerned: *Careless of danger, he walked boldly into the enemy camp.* **4** carefree; untroubled. **5** without art or study; natural; *careless charm.* **—'care•less•ly,** *adv.* **—'care•less•ness,** *n.*

ca•ress [kə'rɛs] *n., v.* *—n.* **1** a gentle, loving touch, stroke, or kiss. **2** any light or gentle touch: *the caress of a summer breeze.* *—v.* touch or stroke gently, lightly, or lovingly: *He talked to the kitten softly as he caressed it. The wind caressed the treetops.* ⟨< F *caresse* < Ital. *carezza* < L *carus* dear⟩

car•et ['kærət] *or* ['kɛrət] *n.* a mark (‸) to show where something should be put in, used in writing and in proofreading. ⟨< L *caret* is lacking, from *carere* be without; 17c.⟩
☛ *Hom.* CARAT, CARROT, KARAT.

care•tak•er ['kɛr,teikər] *n.* **1** a person, especially a janitor, who takes care of a building, estate, etc. **2** (*adjl.*) of a government or management, carrying on the functions of an office on a temporary basis pending an election or the accession of a new administration.

care•worn ['kɛr,wɔrn] *adj.* showing the effects of continuous worry and care.

car•fare ['kɑr,fɛr] *n.* the money that has to be paid for riding on a streetcar, bus, etc.: *He had just enough money for the carfare home.*

car•ful ['kɑr,fʊl] *n., pl.* **-fuls.** as much as a car will hold; enough to fill a car: *a carful of children.*

car•go ['kɑrgou] *n., pl.* **-goes** or **-gos.** the load of goods carried on a truck, ship, or aircraft; freight: *a cargo of wheat.* ⟨< Sp. *cargo* < *cargar* load, ult. < L *carrus* wagon⟩

car•hop ['kɑr,hɒp] *n. Informal.* a person who serves customers at a drive-in restaurant.

Car•ib ['kærɪb] *or* ['kɛrɪb] *n.* **1** a member of an Indian people who formerly inhabited NE South America and some islands in the Caribbean. **2** the language of the Caribs. ⟨< Sp. *caribe* cannibal⟩

Car•ib•be•an [,kærə'biən], [,kɛrə'biən], *or* [kə'rɪbiən] *adj.* **1** of or having to do with the Caribbean Sea or the islands in it. **2** of or having to do with the Caribs or their language.

ca•ri•be [kə'ribei] *or* [kə'ribi] *n.* piranha. ⟨< Sp., cannibal⟩

Car•i•boo ['kærə,bu] *or* ['kɛrə,bu] *n.* **the Cariboo,** a region in the western foothills of the Cariboo Mountains in east central British Columbia, the site of a famous gold rush that began in 1860. ⟨See CARIBOU⟩

car•i•bou ['kærə,bu] *or* ['kɛrə,bu] *n., pl.* **-bou** or **-bous. 1** any of several subspecies of reindeer found in northern North America, of which the most widely spread are the **barren-ground caribou** (*Rangifer tarandus groenlandicus*) and the **woodland caribou** (*Rangifer tarandus caribou*). **2** the hide of a caribou: *a parka of caribou.* **3** (*adjl.*) made of this hide: *caribou moccasins.* ⟨< Cdn.F < Algonquian *xalibu* pawer, from its habit of pawing snow in search of grass⟩

caribou bird *Cdn.* CANADA JAY.

Caribou Eskimo a member of a group of Inuit living in the Barren Ground west of Hudson Bay. ⟨with reference to their living on caribou⟩

car•i•ca•ture ['kærəkətʃər] *or* ['kɛr-], ['kærəkə,tʃʊr] *or* ['kɛr-] *n., v.* **-tured, -tur•ing.** *—n.* **1** a picture, cartoon, description, etc. that deliberately exaggerates the peculiarities or defects of a subject. **2** the art of making such pictures or descriptions. **3** a very poor imitation. **4** a character in a book, movie, etc. that is very stereotyped or oversimplified.
—v. make or be a caricature of. ⟨< F < Ital. *caricatura* < *caricare* overload, exaggerate⟩

car•i•ca•tur•ist ['kærəkətʃərɪst] *or* ['kɛr-], ['kærəkə,tʃʊrɪst] *or* ['kɛr-] *n.* a person skilled in drawing caricatures, especially one whose work it is.

car•ies ['kɛriz] *or* ['kɛri,iz] *n.* **1** the decay of teeth, bones, or tissues: *Caries of the teeth is caused by bacteria.* **2** a cavity in a tooth, caused by caries: *You have a caries in your lower left canine.* ⟨< L⟩

car•il•lon ['kærə,lɒn], ['kɛrə,lɒn], *or* [kə'rɪljən] *n.* **1** a set of bells arranged for playing melodies: *There is a carillon in the Peace Tower in Ottawa.* **2** a melody played on such bells. **3** a part of an organ that imitates the sound of bells. **4** an electronic instrument simulating the sound of these bells by striking metal bars and tubes. ⟨< F, ult. < L *quattuor* four; originally consisted of four bells⟩

car•il•lon•neur [,kærələ'nɜr], [,kɛr-], *or* [kə,rɪljə'nɜr] *n.* a person who plays a carillon.

Ca•ri•na [kə'rinə] *or* [kə'raɪnə] *n.* a southern constellation which includes the bright star Canopus. It is also called **Argo.**

car•ing ['kɛrɪŋ] *adj., v.* *—adj.* attentive to the needs, especially emotional needs, of others: *We have found a very caring nanny for our kids.*
—v. ppr. of CARE.

car•i•o•ca [,kæri'oukə] *or* [,kɛr-] *n.* **1** a dance of South America. **2** the music for this dance. **3 Carioca,** a native or inhabitant of Rio de Janeiro. ⟨< Brazilian Portuguese *carioca*⟩

car•i•ole[1] or **car•ri•ole[1]** ['kæri,oul] *or* ['kɛr-] *n.* **1** a small, one-horse carriage. **2** a covered cart. ⟨< F < Ital. *carriuola* < L *carrus* wagon⟩

car•i•ole[2] or **car•ri•ole[2]** ['kæri,oul] *or* ['kɛr-] *n., v.* **-oled, -ol•ing.** *Cdn.* *—n.* **1** a light, open sleigh having a single seat for the driver, drawn by one or two horses or, sometimes, by dogs. **2** a light sleigh usually drawn by two horses and having seats for a driver and two passengers. **3** a dogsled, often ornately decorated, for carrying freight or equipped to carry one person lying down: *The sick trapper was brought to the post on a cariole.*
—v. ride in a cariole. ⟨< Cdn.F⟩

car•i•ous ['kɛriəs] *adj.* having caries; decayed. ⟨< L *cariosus* < *caries* decay⟩

ca•ri•tas ['kɑrɪ,tɑs], ['kærɪ,tɑs], *or* ['kɛrɪ,tɑs] *n.* love for humanity. ⟨< L⟩

car•jack ['kɑr,dʒæk] *v. Informal.* **1** steal (a car) by using force or threats against the driver. **2** force or threaten (a driver) into yielding possession of a car. ⟨< *car* + hi*jack*⟩ **—'car,jack•ing,** *n.*

car jockey *Informal.* **1** a person employed by a hotel, restaurant, etc. to park customers' cars and return them to the customers when needed. **2** a person employed by a car rental agency to deliver cars to customers and to collect cars returned by customers.

cark•ing ['kɑrkɪŋ] *adj. Archaic.* troublesome; worrying. ⟨< obs. *cark* burden, worry < AF *karke,* ult. < LL *carricare* load⟩

car•ling ['kɑrlɪŋ] *n.* a short beam running fore and aft under a ship's deck to support a mast or brace an opening such as a hatch. ⟨< F *carlingue* < ON *kerling* old woman⟩

car•load ['kɑr,loud] *n.* **1** the number or amount that an automobile can carry: *We passed a carload of people bound for the party.* **2** the amount that a freight car can hold or carry: *a carload of grain.* **3** a specification of the exact amount of any substance designated as a carload for the purpose of determining shipping charges.

carload rate the special low price for shipping by freight carload.

Car•lo•vin•gi•an [,kɑrlə'vɪndʒiən] *adj. or n.* Carolingian.

Car•ma•gnole [,kɑrmən'joul] *or* ['kɑrmən,joul]; *French,* [kaʀma'ɲɔl] *n.* **1** a dance and song popular during the French Revolution. **2** the street uniform of the French revolutionaries, comprising a short jacket, black pants, a red cap, and a tricolour sash. ⟨< F *Carmagnola,* a town in Piedmont taken by the revolutionaries⟩

Car•mel•ite ['kɑrmə,ləit] *n., adj.* *—n.* a mendicant friar or nun of a religious order founded in the 12th century or earlier.
—adj. of or having to do with this order.

car•min•a•tive ['kɑrmənətɪv], [kɑr'mɪnətɪv], *or* ['kɑrmə,neitɪv] *adj., n.* *—adj.* expelling gas from the stomach and intestines.
—n. a medicine that does this. ⟨< L *carminatus* carded; cleansed⟩

car•mine ['kɑrmaɪn] *or* ['kɑrmən] *n., adj.* *—n.* **1** a deep red with a tinge of purple. **2** a light crimson. **3** a crimson colouring matter found in cochineal, used to stain microscopic slides and formerly as a dye.
—adj. **1** deep red with a tinge of purple. **2** light crimson. ⟨< Med.L *carminium* < Arabic *qirmiz* the kermes insect, and L *minium* red lead. See CRIMSON.⟩

car•nage ['kɑrnɪdʒ] *n.* the slaughter of a great number of people, as in war. ⟨< F < Ital. *carnaggio* < L *caro, carnis* flesh⟩

car•nal ['kɑrnəl] *adj.* **1** having to do with the desires and pleasures of the body; sensual: *Gluttony and drunkenness have been called carnal vices.* **2** sexual: *carnal knowledge.* **3** worldly; not spiritual. ⟨< L *carnalis* < *caro, carnis* flesh. Doublet of CHARNEL.⟩ **—'car•nal•ly,** *adv.*

car•nal•i•ty [kɑr'nælәti] *n., pl.* **-ties. 1** worldliness. **2** sensuality.

car•nal•lite ['kɑrnә,lәit] *n.* a form of potash yielding potassium. *Formula*: $MgCl_2 \cdot KCl \cdot 6H_2O$ ⟨< Rudolf von *Carnall* (1804-1874), German mineralogist⟩

car•nas•sial [kɑr'næsiәl] *adj., n. —adj.* of or having to do with the teeth of a carnivorous animal, adapted for slicing rather than tearing.
—n. a carnassial tooth, especially one of the last upper premolars or the first lower molars. ⟨< F *carnassier* meat-eating⟩

car•na•tion [kɑr'neiʃәn] *n., adj. —n.* **1** any of numerous cultivated varieties of pink derived from the clove pink, widely grown in gardens and greenhouses for their large, many-petalled flowers which usually have a spicy fragrance. **2** the flower of a carnation: *He wore a carnation in his lapel.* **3** a pink to light red colour. **4** a crimson colour.
—adj. having either of these colours. ⟨< F < Ital. *carnagione* flesh colour < *carnaggio.* See CARNAGE.⟩

car•na•u•ba [,kɑr'naʊbә] *or* [kɑr'nubә] *n.* **1** a Brazilian palm tree (*Copernicia cerifera*) whose leaves yield wax used to make polishes, phonograph records, electric insulation, etc. **2** Usually, **carnauba wax**, the wax from this tree. ⟨< Brazilian Portuguese⟩

car•nel•ian [kɑr'niliәn] *or* [kɑr'niljәn] *n.* **1** a red or reddish brown variety of chalcedony used in jewellery. The colour is caused by traces of iron oxide. **2** a gem made from this stone. Also called **cornelian.** ⟨alteration of *cornelian;* influenced by L *caro* flesh⟩

car•net [kɑr'nei]; *French*, [kaʀ'nɛ] **1** a document such as a customs certificate needed to cross a border. **2** a book of tickets for a subway, bus, etc.

car•nie ['kɑrni] *n., pl.* **-nies.** *Slang.* **1** carnival. **2** a person who works or performs in a carnival. Also, **carny.**

car•ni•val ['kɑrnәvәl] *n.* **1** a place of amusement, especially a travelling show having merry-go-rounds, sideshows, etc. **2** feasting and merrymaking; celebration. **3** an organized program of events involving a particular sport, institution, etc.: *a water carnival.* **4** in some traditionally Roman Catholic cultures, a time of feasting and merrymaking just before Lent. ⟨< Ital. *carnevale* < Med.L *carnevalarium* < L *carnem levare* the putting away of meat (before Lent)⟩

car•ni•vore ['kɑrnә,vɔr] *n.* **1** any of an order (Carnivora) of mammals that feed chiefly on flesh or other animal matter rather than plants. Cats, dogs, weasels, raccoons, bears, seals, etc., are carnivores. **2** an insect-eating plant. ⟨< F⟩

car•niv•o•rous [kɑr'nɪvәrәs] *adj.* **1** feeding or subsisting on flesh or other animal matter. **2** of a plant, able to use animal substance as food. Carnivorous plants such as the pitcher plant trap and digest insects and other small animals. **3** of or having to do with carnivores or the order Carnivora. ⟨< L *carnivorus* < *caro, carnis* flesh + *vorare* devour⟩ **—car'niv•or•ous•ly,** *adv.* **—car'niv•or•ous•ness,** *n.*

car•no•tite ['kɑrnә,tәit] *n.* a yellowish, radioactive mineral found in the W and SW United States. It is a source of radium and uranium. ⟨after Adolphe *Carnot* (1839-1920), a French inspector-general of mines⟩

car•ny ['kɑrni] See CARNIE.

car•ob ['kærәb] *or* ['kɛrәb] *n.* **1** a Mediterranean evergreen tree (*Ceratonia siliqua*) of the pea family having compound leaves, red flowers, and long, blackish pods. **2** the edible pod of this tree, having a sweet pulp. ⟨< F *caroube* < Med.L *carrubia* < Arabic *kharrub* bean pod⟩

car•ol ['kærәl] *or* ['kɛrәl] *n., v.* **-olled** or **-oled, -ol•ling** or **-ol•ing.** *—n.* **1** a song of joy. **2** a hymn of joy: *Christmas carols.*
—v. **1** sing; sing joyously: *The birds were carolling in the trees.* **2** praise or celebrate with carols: *carolling the arrival of spring.* ⟨ME < OF *carole*, probably < L < Gk. *choraulēs* flute player accompanying a choral dance < *choros* dance + *aulos* flute⟩ **—'car•ol•ler** or **'car•ol•er,** *n.*
☛ *Hom.* CARREL.

Car•o•li•na allspice [,kærә'laɪnә] *or* [,kɛrә'laɪnә] any of a genus (*Calycanthus*) of plants having reddish brown, fragrant flowers.

Car•o•line ['kærә,laɪn] *or* ['kɛr-], ['kærәlɪn] *or* ['kɛr-] *adj.* of or having to do with Charles, especially Charles I or Charles II of England, Scotland, and Ireland.

Car•o•lin•gi•an [,kærә'lɪndʒiәn] *or* [,kɛr-] *adj., n. —adj.* of or having to do with the second Frankish dynasty. It ruled in France from A.D. 751 to 987, in Germany from A.D. 751 to 911, and in Italy from A.D. 751 to 887.
—n. a ruler during this dynasty. Also, **Carlovingian**.

Car•o•lin•i•an [,kærә'lɪniәn] *or* [,kɛr-] *adj., n. —adj.* **1** Carolingian. **2** of North or South Carolina or both.
—n. a native or inhabitant of North Carolina or South Carolina.

car•om ['kærәm] *or* ['kɛrәm] *n., v. —n.* **1** *Billiards.* a kind of shot in which the ball struck with the cue hits two balls, one after the other. **2** a similar shot in other games. **3** a hitting and bouncing off.
—v. **1** make a carom. **2** hit something and bounce off. ⟨< F < Sp. *carambola*, ? < Malay *carambil*, name of fruit⟩

car•o•tene ['kærә,tin] *or* ['kɛrә,tin] *n.* a red or yellow crystalline pigment found in the carrot and other plants, and in animal tissues, and converted by the body into vitamin A. *Formula*: $C_{40}H_{56}$ Also, **carotin.** ⟨< L *carota* carrot⟩

ca•rot•en•oid [kә'rɒtә,nɔɪd] *n.* any of a group of yellow to dark red pigments found in various plant and animal tissues. The group includes carotene.

ca•rot•id [kә'rɒtɪd] *n., adj., —n.* either of two large arteries, one on each side of the neck, that carry blood to the head.
—adj. having to do with these arteries. ⟨< F < Gk. *karōtides* < *karos* stupor (state produced by compression of carotids); 17c.⟩

ca•rouse [kә'raʊz] *n., v.* **-roused, -rous•ing.** *—n.* a noisy feast; drinking party.
—v. drink heavily; take part in noisy feasts or revels. ⟨< obs. adv. < G *gar aus(trinken)* (drink) all up⟩ **—ca'rous•al,** *n.* **—ca'rous•er,** *n.*

car•ou•sel or **car•rou•sel** ['kærә,sɛl] *or* ['kɛr-], [,kærә'sɛl] *or* [,kɛr-] **1** a merry-go-round. **2** at an airport, a revolving circular platform onto which the baggage of arriving passengers is delivered from a central chute. **3** a rotating object such as a slide holder, from which slides are projected one by one. ⟨< F < Ital. *carosello* < L *carrus* cart⟩

carp[1] [kɑrp] *v.* find fault; complain. ⟨< ON *karpa* wrangle⟩ **—'carp•er,** *n.* **—'carp•ing•ly,** *adv.*

carp[2] [kɑrp] *n., pl.* **carp** or **carps. 1** a freshwater food fish (*Cyprinus carpio*) of the minnow family having large scales, a long dorsal fin, and two barbels on each side of the upper jaw. It is native to Asia, but has been introduced into Europe and North America. **2** any of various other comparatively large fishes of the same family. **3** any of various suckers. ⟨ME < OF *carpe* < Provençal < LL *carpa* < Gmc.⟩

car•pac•cio [kɑr'pɑtʃou] *or* [kɑr'pɑtʃi,ou] *n.* a dish of thinly sliced raw beef, served as an appetizer with a strong vinaigrette or mustard sauce.

car•pal ['kɑrpәl] *adj., n. —adj.* of or having to do with the carpus.
—n. a bone of the carpus. ⟨< NL *carpalis* < Gk. *karpos* wrist⟩
☛ *Hom.* CARPEL.

carpal tunnel syndrome pain or numbness in the hand and wrist due to highly repetitive movements as in keyboarding, crocheting, etc. Tissues surrounding a nerve in the wrist swell and pinch the nerve.

car park 1 a parking lot where one must pay to park. **2** *Esp. Brit.* any parking lot.

car•pe di•em ['kɑrpei 'diәm] *or* ['kɑrpi 'daɪәm] *Latin.* enjoy today; make the most of the present. ⟨lit. 'seize the day'⟩

car•pel ['kɑrpәl] *n.* the central part of a flower, containing the ovules, which develop into seeds. Some flowers, such as the pea and bean, have a simple pistil composed of only one carpel; other flowers, such as the iris and mock orange, have a compound pistil composed of several carpels fused together. See FLOWER for picture. ⟨< Gk. *karpos* fruit⟩ **—'car•pel,la•ry** or **'car•pel•late** [-lɪt] *or* [-,leit], *adj.*
☛ *Hom.* CARPAL.

car•pen•ter ['kɑrpәntәr] *n., v. —n.* a person skilled in carpentry, especially one whose work it is.
—v. do carpentry. ⟨ME < ONF *carpentier* < L *carpentarius* < *carpentum* wagon⟩

carpenter ant any of several large ants (genus *Camponatus*) who make their home by eating out complex passages in wood.

carpenter bee *n.* any of several bees (family Anthophoridae) who tunnel through wood to lay their eggs.

car•pen•try ['kɑrpәntri] *n.* the trade or art of building, finishing, and repairing wooden objects or structures.

car•pet ['kɑrpɪt] *n., v. —n.* **1** a thick, heavy, woven covering for floors and stairs. **2** the fabric used for such a covering; carpeting. **3** anything like a carpet: *a carpet of grass.*

on the carpet, a being considered or discussed. b *Informal.* being scolded or rebuked.
—*v.* cover with a carpet: *In the spring, the ground was carpeted with violets.* ⟨ME < OF < Med.L *carpeta* thick cloth < L *carpere* card (wool)⟩

car•pet•bag ['kɑrpɪt,bæg] *n.* a travelling bag made of carpeting: *Carpetbags were common in the 19th century.*

car•pet•bag•ger ['kɑrpɪt,bægər] *n.* **1** any of the politicians, merchants, etc. from the north of the United States who travelled south to benefit from the chaotic aftermath of the American Civil War. **2** any opportunistic foreign politician, promoter, etc., disliked by the native population. ⟨so called from the type of bag carried by 19c. carpetbaggers⟩

carpet beetle any of various small beetles (family Dermestidae, especially genus *Anthrenus*) whose larvae destroy carpets and other fabrics and furs. Also, **carpet bug.**

car•pet–bomb ['kɑrpɪt,bɒm] *v.* bomb (a place) over a wide area with many bombs, as a softening-up process preparatory to advance by ground troops. **—'car•pet-,bomb•ing,** *n.*

car•pet•ing ['kɑrpətɪŋ] *n., v.* *—n.* **1** a fabric for carpets. **2** carpets in general.
—*v.* ppr. of CARPET.

carpet sweeper a device for cleaning carpets and rugs with a rotating brush, operated by hand or electricity.

car•pet•weed ['kɑrpɪt,wid] an annual plant (*Mollugo verticillata*) growing as a ground cover weed in North America.

carp•ing ['kɑrpɪŋ] *adj., v.* *—adj.* faultfinding; naggingly critical: *a carping tongue, carping critics.*
—*v.* ppr. of CARP[1]. **—'carp•ing•ly,** *adv.*

car•pol•o•gy [kɑr'pɒlədʒi] *n.* the study of the structure of fruits and seeds. ⟨< Gk. *karpos* fruit + *-logy*⟩

car pool **1** an arrangement by which members of a group take turns at providing transportation in their own cars, especially to and from work. **2** such a group of people.

car•port ['kɑr,pɔrt] *n.* a roofed shelter for one or more automobiles. It is usually attached to a house and open on at least one side.

carp•suck•er ['kɑrp,sʌkər] *n.* quillback.

car•pus ['kɑrpəs] *n., pl.* **-pi** [-paɪ] *or* [-pi]. *Anatomy.* **1** the group of short bones forming the joint between the forearm and the hand; the bones of the wrist. See ARM[1] for picture. **2** the corresponding part of the foreleg of an animal; the knee joint. ⟨< NL < Gk. *karpos* wrist⟩

car•rack ['kærək] *or* ['kɛrək] *n.* a large, regularly heavily armed, European merchant ship used from the 14th to the 17th centuries, similar to a caravel but larger and broader. The carrack was the forerunner of the three-masted ships. ⟨ME < OF *carraque* < Sp. < Arabic *qaraqir*, pl.⟩

car•ra•geen or **car•ra•gheen** ['kærə,gin] *or* ['kɛrə,gin] *n.* a small, purplish, edible seaweed (*Chondrus crispus*) found along rocky coasts of the North Atlantic, yielding an emulsifying agent used in medicines, certain foods, cosmetics, etc. Also, **carageen.** ⟨< *Carragheen*, near Waterford, Ireland, where it is abundant⟩

car•ra•geen•an [,kærə'ginən] *or* [,kɛrə'ginən] *n.* a derivative of carrageen used as an emulsifier. Also, **carageenan.**

Car•ra•ra marble [kə'rɑrə] the finest kind of white marble quarried in Italy. ⟨< *Carrara*, a commune near Florence⟩

car•re•four ['kærə,fʊr] *or* ['kɛrə-], [,kærə'fʊr] *or* [,kɛrə-] *n.* **1** a four-way intersection. **2** a public square. ⟨< F < LME *quarefour* < MF *quarrefour* < VL **quadrifurcum* < L *quadri-* four + *furca* fork⟩

car•rel ['kærəl] *or* ['kɛrəl] *n.* an enclosed space for individual study in a library, usually containing a desk and bookshelves. Sometimes, **carrell.** ⟨alteration of ME *carole* ring. See CAROL.⟩
☛ *Hom.* CAROL.

car•riage ['kærɪdʒ] *or* ['kɛrɪdʒ]; *for 6 & 7, also* ['kæriɪdʒ] *or* ['kɛriɪdʒ] *n.* **1** a vehicle that moves on wheels. Carriages are usually pulled by horses and are used to carry people. **2** a baby carriage; perambulator. **3** a wheeled frame which supports a gun and by which it is moved from place to place. **4** a moving part of a machine that supports some other part: *the carriage of a typewriter.* **5** the manner of holding the head and body; bearing: *She has a queenly carriage.* **6** the act of taking persons or goods from one place to another; carrying; transporting: *carriage charges.* **7** the cost or price of carrying. **8** *Archaic.* management. ⟨ME < ONF *cariage* < *carier.* See CARRY.⟩
☛ *Syn.* **5.** See note at BEARING.

carriage bolt a bolt having a round shaft with a square part just under the head, formerly used chiefly to fasten together parts of a carriage.

carriage dog Dalmatian.

carriage return **1** the realignment of a typewriter carriage so that the next character typed will be at the beginning of a line. **2** *Computer technology.* RETURN (n. 8).

carriage trade the wealthy patrons, or customers, of a theatre, restaurant, hotel, store, etc., so called because such persons formerly drove in private carriages.

carrick bend ['kærɪk] *or* ['kɛrɪk] a type of knot used to tie two ropes together. ⟨var. of *carrack*⟩

car•ri•er ['kæriər] *or* ['kɛriər] *n.* **1** a person or thing that carries something: *Letter carriers deliver mail. Trains, buses, and ships are carriers.* **2** one who delivers messages or parcels. **3** anything designed to carry something or someone in or on. **4** a person or thing that carries or transmits a disease. Healthy persons who are immune to a particular disease may be carriers. **5** *Telecommunications.* a radio-frequency wave used to transmit, or carry, the audio-frequency waves representing the sounds being broadcast. Also called **carrier wave. 6** a company that transports goods, people, etc., usually over certain routes and according to fixed schedules: *Bus systems, railways, airlines, and truck companies are carriers.* **7** AIRCRAFT CARRIER. **8** CARRIER PIGEON. **9** a company that provides insurance for a corporation, an individual, etc. **10** *Genetics.* an individual carrying a particular mutant allele paired with a normal allele.

Car•ri•er ['kæriər] *or* ['kɛriər] *n.* **1** a member of a people of the First Nations living in the interior of British Columbia. **2** the Athapascan language of the Carriers. ⟨from the custom of a Carrier widow carrying the charred bones of her dead husband in a net bag⟩

carrier pigeon **1** a HOMING PIGEON, especially one trained to fly home from great distances carrying written messages. **2** a breed of large show pigeon.

carrier wave CARRIER (def. 5).

car•ri•ole ['kæri,oul] *or* ['kɛri,oul] See CARIOLE.

car•ri•on ['kæriən] *or* ['kɛriən] *n., adj.* *—n.* **1** dead and decaying flesh. **2** rottenness; filth.
—adj. **1** dead and decaying. **2** feeding on dead and decaying flesh. **3** rotten; filthy. ⟨ME < OF *carogne*, ult. < L *caro* flesh. Doublet of CRONE.⟩

carrion crow a common European crow (*Corvus corone*).

carrion flower **1** a vine (Smilax herbacea) of the lily family, bearing green, pungent flowers. **2** the stinking flower of this plant.

car•ro•nade [,kærə'neid] *or* [,kɛrə'neid] *n.* formerly, a short cannon with a large bore. ⟨after *Carron*, Scotland⟩

car•rot ['kærət] *or* [kɛrət] *n.* **1** a cultivated biennial herb (*Daucus carota sativa*) of the parsley family having feathery, finely divided leaves, flat clusters of tiny white flowers, and a long, thick, tapering orange root. See also WILD CARROT. **2** the root of this plant, eaten raw or cooked as a vegetable. **3** a promise of reward, used as an incentive or lure. ⟨< F *carotte* < L < Gk. *karōton*⟩
☛ *Hom.* CARAT, CARET, KARAT.

car•rot•y ['kærəti] *or* ['kɛrəti] *adj.* **1** like a carrot in colour; orange-red. **2** red-haired. **3** containing carrots; tasting like carrots: *The carrot cake at that café is really carroty.*

car•rou•sel ['kærə,sɛl] *or* ['kɛr-], [,kærə'sɛl] *or* [,kɛr-] See CAROUSEL.

car•ry ['kæri] *or* ['kɛri] *v.* **-ried, -ry•ing;** *n., pl.* **-ries.** *—v.* **1** a hold and take from one place to another: *Buses carry passengers. He carried the sleepy child up to bed.* **b** have on one's person: *Everyone should carry proper identification.* **2** bear the weight of; hold up; support; sustain: *Those columns carry the roof.* **3** hold (one's body and head) in a certain way; have a certain kind of posture: *This boy carries himself well.* **4** comport oneself in a particular way: *She carries herself like a queen.* **5** capture; win: *Our troops carried the enemy's fort.* **6** get (a motion or bill) passed or adopted: *The motion to adjourn was carried.* **7** garner majority approval (in or by): *The amendment carried. The liberals carried nine ridings.* **8** continue; extend: *to carry a road into the mountains.* **9** cover the distance; have the power of throwing or driving: *Her voice carried easily to the back of the room. This gun will carry one kilometre.* **10** keep in stock: *This store carries men's clothing.* **11** of a newspaper, magazine, etc., print (an article, etc.) in its pages: *The evening papers carried a review of the new play.* **12** sing with correct or nearly correct pitch: *She can carry a tune.* **13** sing or play (a melody, part, etc.): *The first violins carry* *the melody.* **14** act as a medium for the conveying of, especially in the context of sound transmission. **15** influence greatly; lead: *His acting carried the audience.* **16** cause to go: *His business carried him overseas.* **17** have as a result; have as an attribute, property, etc.; involve: *Her judgment carries great weight.* **18** keep on the account books of a business. **19** bear the financial burden of. **20** *Mathematics.* transfer a number from one place or column in the sum to the next one on the left: *A 10 in the 1's column must be carried to the 10's column.* **21** be pregnant with: *I'm carrying twins.* **22** drink (alcohol) without showing the effect: *He never could carry his liquor.*

carry away, arouse strong feeling in; influence beyond reason.

carry everything before (one), meet with uninterrupted success; be very successful in spite of opposition.

carry forward, a go ahead with; make progress with. **b** in bookkeeping, re-enter (an item or items already entered) on the next or a later page or column of an accounting record.

carry off, a win (a prize, honour, etc.). **b** succeed with: *It was her first speech, but she carried it off all right.* **c** take away by force.

carry on, a do; manage or conduct: *He carried on a successful business for many years.* **b** go ahead with; go on with after being stopped. **c** keep going; continue: *We must carry on in our effort to establish world peace.* **d** *Informal.* behave wildly or foolishly: *The small boys really carried on at the party.* **e** have a love affair.

carry out, do; get done; accomplish; complete.

carry over, a have left over; be left over. **b** keep until later; continue; extend. **c** transfer.

carry the ball, *Informal.* take the chief part in promoting or completing a plan or activity.

carry the day, a be victorious in battle. **b** be successful against opposition.

carry through, a get done; accomplish; complete. **b** bring through trouble; keep from being discouraged.

—n. **1** the distance covered or the distance that something goes. **2** the act of carrying boats and supplies from one body of water to another; portage. **3** a place where this is done. **4** *Golf.* the distance a ball travels in the air before hitting the ground. ⟨< ONF *carier* < LL *carricare* < L *carrus* wagon, cart. Doublet of CHARGE.⟩

☛ *Syn. v.* **1. Carry,** CONVEY, TRANSPORT = to take or bring from one place to another. **Carry,** the general word, emphasizes the idea of holding and moving a person or thing in or with something, such as a vehicle, container, hands, or paws: *Sandra was carrying a heavy box.* **Convey** emphasizes getting a person or thing to a place by some means or through some channel, and therefore is used figuratively in the sense of communicate: *Language conveys ideas.* **Transport** = to carry or convey people or goods in a ship, plane, or vehicle: *Trucks transport freight.*

car•ry•all[1] ['kæri,ɒl] *or* ['kɛri-] *n.* **1** *Cdn.* a covered one-horse carriage. **2** cariole. ⟨alteration of *cariole*⟩

car•ry•all[2] ['kæri,ɒl] *or* ['kɛri-] *n.* **1** any of several vehicles so named because of their large capacity. **2** a large bag or basket.

carry cot a collapsible, boxlike cradle equipped with handles and used for carrying a baby.

carrying capacity the number of individuals belonging to a particular species that an environment can support.

carrying charge the interest charged on money owing for goods or services bought on credit. Also, **carry charge.**

car•ry•ing–on ['kæriŋ 'ɒn] *or* ['kɛri-] *n., pl.* **carry•ings-on.** *Informal.* **1** a loud disturbance; fuss. **2** conspicuous, uninhibited, indiscreet behaviour.

carrying place *Cdn.* a portage.

carry–on ['kæri ,ɒn] *or* ['kɛri ,ɒn] *adj.* describing a piece of luggage small enough to go under an airplane seat or in an overhead rack, and so not having to be checked: *my carry-on bag.*

car•ry–out ['kæri ,ʌut] *or* ['kɛri ,ʌut] *n., adj. U.S.* TAKEOUT (adj. 1, n. 4).

car•ry–o•ver ['kæri ,ouvər] *or* ['kɛri-] *n.* **1** something left over. **2** an item carried forward in an accounting record.

car seat 1 the seat of an automobile. **2** a small safety seat for a child, designed to be put on top of a standard automobile seat and held in place by the car's seat belt passed through its frame. The child is comfortably restrained by any of various arrangements of straps, buckles, snaps, etc.

car–sick ['kɑr ,sɪk] *adj.* nauseated as a result of the motion of a car, train, etc. **—'car-,sick•ness,** *n.*

cart [kɑrt] *n., v. —n.* **1** a vehicle with two wheels, used to carry heavy loads: *Horses, donkeys, and oxen are often used to pull carts.* **2** a light wagon, used to deliver goods, etc. **3** any of various small, wheeled vehicles for carrying loads, moved by hand.

put the cart before the horse, reverse the proper or natural order of things.

—v. **1** carry in or as if in a cart. **2** move (someone) by force: *The demonstrators were carted off to the police station.* **3** *Informal.* carry (something) awkwardly. **4** *Informal.* traipse. ⟨ME < ON *kartr*⟩

☛ *Hom.* CARTE, KART.

cart•age ['kɑrtɪdʒ] *n.* **1** the act of carting. **2** the cost of carting.

carte[1] [kɑrt] *n.* **1** card. **2** BILL OF FARE. **3** map; chart. ⟨< F. See CARD[1].⟩

☛ *Hom.* CART, KART.

carte[2] [kɑrt] *n. Fencing.* a thrust or parry. ⟨< F *quarte* < Ital. *quarta* fourth⟩

☛ *Hom.* CART, KART.

carte blanche [kaʀt'blɑ̃ʃ] *French.* **1** full authority; freedom to use one's discretion. **2** freedom to do whatever one pleases. ⟨< F, literally, white card⟩

carte du jour [,kɑrt du 'ʒʌr]; *French,* [kaʀtdy'ʒuʀ] a menu, especially one for a particular day.

car•tel [kɑr'tɛl] *n.* **1** a combination of independent businesses formed to regulate prices, production, and marketing of goods. **2** a written agreement between countries at war for the exchange of prisoners or for some other purpose. **3** an alliance of political groups for a common cause. **4** formerly, a written challenge to a duel. ⟨< F < Ital. *cartello* little card[1], specifically one used for a written challenge to a duel⟩

car•tel•ize [kɑr'tɛlaɪz] *or* ['kɑrtə,laɪz] *v.* **-ized, -iz•ing. 1** combine in a cartel. **2** join with other businesses to form a cartel.

cart•er ['kɑrtər] *n.* **1** a person whose work is driving a cart or truck. **2** a person who runs a trucking business.

Car•te•sian [kɑr'tiʒən] *adj., n. —adj.* **1** of or having to do with René Descartes (1596-1650), a French philosopher and mathematician. **2** of or suggestive of his doctrines or methods. *—n.* a follower of Descartes or of his doctrines or methods. ⟨< NL *Cartesianus* < *Cartesius,* Latinized form of *Descartes*⟩ **—Car'te•sian,ism,** *n.*

Cartesian coordinates *Geometry.* an ordered pair (or triple) of numbers which can plot the location of any point in space, from a given starting point.

Cartesian set *Mathematics and logic.* the set of all ordered pairs that can be formed by matching each member of one set in turn with each member of a second set.

Car•tha•gin•i•an [,kɑrθə'dʒɪniən] *n., adj. —n.* a native or inhabitant of Carthage, an ancient city and seaport in N Africa. *—adj.* of or having to do with Carthage.

cart horse DRAFT HORSE.

Car•thu•sian [kɑr'θuʒən] *n., adj. —n. Roman Catholic Church.* a monk or nun of an order founded by St. Bruno in 1086. *—adj.* of this order. ⟨< *Cartusia,* now *Chartreuse,* the village in the French Alps where the first monastery of the order was founded⟩

car•ti•lage ['kɑrtəlɪdʒ] *n.* **1** a tough, elastic tissue that forms most of the skeleton of very young vertebrates and, in higher vertebrates, is for the most part changed into bone as the animal matures; gristle. Cartilage is found in adults at the ends of the long bones, between the bones of the spine, in the nose, etc. **2** a part formed of cartilage. ⟨< F < L *cartilago*⟩

car•ti•lag•i•nous [,kɑrtə'lædʒənəs] *adj.* **1** of or like cartilage; gristly. **2** having the skeleton formed mostly of cartilage: *Sharks are cartilaginous fish.*

cart•load ['kɑrt,loud] *n.* as much as a cart can hold or carry.

car•to•gram ['kɑrtə,græm] *n.* a map that gives information by means of dots, lines, etc.

car•tog•ra•pher [kɑr'tɒgrəfər] *n.* a person skilled in making maps or charts, especially one whose work it is.

car•to•graph•ic [,kɑrtə'græfɪk] *adj.* having to do with cartography or cartographers.

car•tog•ra•phy [kɑr'tɒgrəfi] *n.* the making of maps or charts. ⟨< Med.L *carta* chart, map + E *-graphy*⟩

car•ton ['kɑrtən] *n., v.* **1** a box or other container made of cardboard: *The books were packed in cartons. Milk can be bought in cartons.* **2** the amount that a carton can hold. **3** a carton and its contents.

—*v.* pack in a carton for transport or storage. ⟨< F *carton* cardboard < Ital. *cartone* < *carta* < L *charta.* Related to CARD[1].⟩

car•toon [kɑr'tun] *n., v.* —*n.* **1** a humorous drawing, often having a caption, that shows ridiculous or exaggerated situations; a pictorial joke: *Many magazines and newspapers have cartoons.* **2** an exaggerated drawing or caricature, often accompanied by words, meant to make fun of a political figure or current happenings: *The editorial page of our paper has a cartoon every day.* **3** COMIC STRIP. **4** a movie made up of a series of drawings; animated film: *Cartoons often show animals engaging in human activities.* **5** a full-size sketch to be traced or copied as the design for a fresco, mosaic, tapestry, etc.
—*v.* **1** make a cartoon of. **2** make cartoons. ⟨var. of *carton;* because drawn on paper⟩

car•toon•ist [kɑr'tunɪst] *n.* a person skilled in drawing cartoons, especially one whose work it is.

car•top•per ['kɑr,tɒpər] *n. Informal.* something that goes on top of a car, such as a canoe.

car•touche [kɑr'tuʃ] *n.* **1** an oblong or oval figure found on ancient Egyptian monuments, framing the hieroglyphics representing the name of a ruler. **2** an elaborate frame for a painted or bas-relief inscription on a building. **3** a paper or cardboard container for gun cartridges or for the explosive in a firework. ⟨< F⟩

car•tridge ['kɑrtrɪdʒ] *n.* **1** a cylindrical metal tube containing a charge of explosive and, usually, a bullet, for use in a rifle or pistol. **2** a shell for a shotgun. **3** a usually long, more or less cylindrical case containing a refill of material, such as ink for a fountain pen or toner for a printer. **4** a sealed plastic case containing a spool of film together with a take-up spool, designed for use with certain types of camera: *The cartridge is simply dropped into the back of the camera.* **5** a sealed plastic case containing film or magnetic tape in an endless loop wound on a single reel. The film or tape unwinds from the centre of the reel and rewinds around the outside. **6** (*adjl.*) of a film projector or tape recorder, designed for use with cartridges. **7** a removable unit in the tone arm of a record player, containing the needle, or stylus, and a crystal or magnet that changes the movements of the needle into electric waves. ⟨alteration of F *cartouche* roll of paper⟩

cartridge paper a heavy, uncoated type of paper used for drawing and also, especially formerly, for making cartridges or shells.

cart•wheel ['kɑrt,wil] *n., v.* —*n.* **1** the wheel of a cart. **2** a sideways handspring or somersault, made with the arms and legs stretched out stiffly like the spokes of a wheel. **3** *Archaic. Slang.* a large coin, such as a silver dollar.
—*v.* **1** make a sideways handspring or somersault. **2** move like a rotating wheel.

car•un•cle ['kɑrʌŋkəl] *or* [kə'rʌŋkəl] *n.* a fleshy protuberance. ⟨< L *caruncula* < *caro* flesh⟩

car•va•crol ['kɑrvə,krɒl] *or* ['kɑrvə,kroul] *n.* a thick extract of various oils, smelling like mint, and used as a disinfectant or insecticide, or to make perfume. *Formula:* $C_{10}H_{14}O$ ⟨< F *carvi* caraway + L *acer* sharp + E- *ol*⟩

carve [kɑrv] *v.* **carved, carv•ing. 1** cut (meat) into slices or pieces: *to carve the roast at the table.* **2** cut; make by cutting: *Statues are often carved from marble, stone, or wood.* **3** decorate with figures or designs cut on the surface: *to carve a wooden tray.* **4** cut (a design, etc.) on or into a surface: *They carved their initials on the tree.* **5** make as if by cutting: *He ruthlessly carved himself a financial empire.*
carve out, *Informal.* form or make by planned effort: *She is carving out quite a reputation for herself.* ⟨OE *ceorfan*⟩

car•vel ['kɑrvəl] *n.* caravel.

car•vel–built ['kɑrvəl ,bɪlt] *adj.* of the hull of a boat, made of boards or metal plates that lie edge to edge, forming a smooth surface. Compare CLINKER-BUILT. ⟨< carvel < LME *carvile* < Du. *karveel* caravel + BUILT⟩

carv•en ['kɑrvən] *adj. Archaic or poetic.* carved; decorated by carving.

carv•er ['kɑrvər] *n.* **1** a person who carves. **2** a large knife for carving meat.

carv•ing ['kɑrvɪŋ] *n., v.* —*n.* **1** the act or art of a person who carves. **2** a piece of carved work; a carved decoration: *a wood carving.*
—*v.* ppr. of CARVE.

carving fork a large, usually two-pronged fork with a long handle used to hold roast meat steady while carving it.

carving knife a large, sharp knife for carving roast meat.

carving set a carving knife, carving fork, and a long steel for sharpening the knife.

car•wash ['kɑr,wɒʃ] *n.* a place where cars, vans, and light trucks are washed, usually by machine. Some carwashes offer interior cleaning as well.

car•y•at•id [,kæri'ætɪd] *or* [,kɛri'ætɪd] *n., pl.* **-ids, -i•des** [-ə,diz]. *Architecture.* a supporting column carved in the form of a woman. Compare TELAMON. ⟨< L *Caryatides* < Gk. *Karyatides* women of Caryae⟩

car•y•op•sis [,kæri'ɒpsɪs] *or* [,kɛri'ɒpsɪs] *n.* a small, dry seed fruit, especially of grasses: *A grain of wheat is a caryopsis.* ⟨< NL < Gk. *karyon* nut, kernel + *opsis* sight < *ops* eye⟩

ca•sa•ba or **cas•sa•ba** [kə'sɑbə] *or* [kə'sɒbə] *n.* a variety of winter muskmelon with a yellow rind and sweet green or white flesh. ⟨< *Kasaba,* a town near Izmir (formerly Smyrna), Turkey⟩

Cas•a•no•va [,kæsə'nouvə] *or* [,kæzə'nouvə] *n.* a man who has many affairs with women, especially an immoral adventurer with women. ⟨< Giovanni Jacopo *Casanova* (1725-1798), an Italian adventurer, known for his *Memoirs*⟩

Cas•bah ['kɑzbɑ], ['kɑzbə], *or* ['kæzbə] *n.* **1** the Arab section of Algiers. **2 casbah,** the Arab section of any city with a large Arab population. **Also, kasbah, Kasbah.** ⟨< Arabic *qasaba* fortress, citadel⟩

cas•cade [kæ'skeid] *or* ['kæskeid] *n., v.* **-cad•ed, -cad•ing.**
—*n.* **1** a small waterfall. **2** anything like a waterfall: *a cascade of ruffles.* **3** a series of pieces of apparatus serving to continue or develop a process. **4** a series of reactions in which one causes or produces another. **5** a series of connected electrical parts.
—*v.* fall, occur, or cause to fall or occur, in a cascade. ⟨< F < Ital. *cascata* < L *cadere* fall⟩

cas•car•a [kæ'skɛrə] *or* [kæ'skɑrə] *n.* **1** a buckthorn (*Rhamnus purshiana*) found along the Pacific coast of North America, yielding cascara sagrada. **2** CASCARA SAGRADA. ⟨< Sp. *cáscara* bark⟩

cascara sa•gra•da [sə'grɑdə], [sə'grædə], *or* [sə'greidə] the dried bark of cascara, used as a laxative. ⟨< Sp. *cáscara sagrada* sacred bark⟩

cas•ca•ril•la [,kæskə'rɪlə] *n.* **1** Also, **cascarilla bark,** the bitter, aromatic bark of a West Indian shrub (*Croton eluteria*) of the spurge family used as flavouring for tobacco or as a tonic. **2** the shrub itself. ⟨< Sp. *cascarilla,* dim. of *cáscara.* See CASCARA.⟩

case[1] [keis] *n.* **1** an instance; example: *a case of poor work.* **2** a set of circumstances; situation; state: *You are in a worse case than I.* **3** the actual condition; real situation; true state: *He said he had done the work, but that was not the case.* **4** an instance of a disease or injury: *a case of measles.* **5** a person who has a disease or injury; patient. **6** a matter for a court of law to decide. **7** a statement of facts raising a point of view for a court to consider. **8** the set of arguments or supporting facts to justify an action, situation, etc.: *the case for a guaranteed annual income.* **9** *Informal.* a peculiar or unusual person. **10** *Grammar.* **a** a distinct form of a noun, pronoun, or adjective that shows its relation to other words in a sentence. **b** the relation shown by such a distinct form. English does not have a case system like German or Latin. English nouns and most pronouns have only two forms indicating grammatical relation: a common, or simple, form (e.g. *boy, woman, somebody*) and a possessive form (*boy's, woman's, somebody's*). Six English pronouns have three case forms: the subjective form (*I, we, he, she, they, who*), objective form (*me, us, him, her, them, whom*), and possessive form (*mine, ours, his, hers, theirs, whose*). English adjectives do not indicate grammatical relation at all.
get on (off) someone's case begin (or leave off) nagging someone or interfering in his or her concerns.
in any case, under any circumstances; no matter what happens; in any event; anyhow: *In any case, you should prepare for the worst.*
in case, if it should happen that; if; supposing.
in case of, if there should be; in the event of: *In case of fire, walk to the nearest door.*
in no case, under no circumstances. ⟨ME < OF *cas* < L *casus* a falling, chance < *cadere* fall⟩

☛ *Syn.* **1. Case,** INSTANCE = example. **Case** applies to a fact, actual happening, situation, etc., that is typical of a general kind or class: *His accident is a case of reckless driving.* **Instance** applies to an individual case used to illustrate a general idea or conclusion: *Going through a stop signal is an instance of his recklessness.*

☛ *Usage.* **Case.** Writers often make unnecessary and ineffective use of expressions containing the word **case:** *Although I read many stories, in not* *one case was I satisfied with the ending. She used the same plot before in the case of a short story about pioneer days.* In the first sentence, *case* is entirely unnecessary. The second can be improved by dropping *the case of.*

case² [keis] *n., v.* **cased, cas•ing.** *—n.* **1** a strong, heavy box: *a packing case. There is a big case full of books in the hall.* **2** the quantity in a box, etc.: *a case of ginger ale.* **3** a covering; sheath; a container designed for a specific object: *a guitar case. Put the knife back in the case.* **4** an outer protective part: *My watch has a steel case.* **5** a frame; casing. **6** *Printing.* a tray for type, with a space for each letter. **7** the covers and spine for a hardbound book, especially before being attached to the book.
—v. **1** put in a case; cover with a case. **2** *Informal.* look over surreptitiously; inspect; examine, with a view to crime: *The thieves cased the bank.* ⟨ME < ONF *casse* < L *capsa* box < *capere* hold. Doublet of CASH¹, CHASE³.⟩

ca•se•ate ['keisi,eit] *v.* **-at•ed, -at•ing.** undergo caseation.

ca•se•a•tion [,keisi'eiʃən] *n.* **1** the formation of cheese by precipitation of casein. **2** *Medicine.* the degeneration of tissue into a cheeselike substance, as in tuberculosis.

case•book ['keis,bʊk] *n.* a book in which details of a case are recorded, to be used as the basis of a lecture, thesis, etc.

case–bound ['keis ,baʊnd] *adj.* of a book, hardbound.

ca•se•fy ['keisə,faɪ] *v.* **-fied, -fy•ing.** make or become like cheese. ⟨< L *caseus* cheese + E *-fy*⟩

case•hard•en ['keis,hɑrdən] *v.* **1** harden (iron or steel) on the surface. **2** render callous; make unfeeling.

case history all the facts about a person or group that may be useful in deciding what medical or psychiatric treatment, social services, etc. are needed.

ca•sein ['keisin] *or* ['keisiɪn] *n.* the protein found especially in milk and which is the main ingredient of cheese. Casein is used in making plastics, paints, and adhesives. ⟨< L *caseus* cheese⟩

case knife **1** a knife carried in a case. **2** a table knife.

case law law based on previous judicial decisions rather than on statutes.

case•load ['keis,loud] *n.* the number of cases handled by a court, a social worker, etc. in a given time.

case•mate ['keismeit] *n.* **1** a bombproof chamber in a fort or rampart, with openings through which cannon may be fired. **2** an armoured enclosure protecting guns on a warship. ⟨< F < Ital. *casamatta* (influenced by *casa* house), earlier *camata*, apparently < Gk. *chasmata* openings⟩

case•ment ['keismənt] *n.* **1** a window opening on vertical hinges. **2** *Poetic.* any window. **3** a casing; covering; frame.

ca•se•ous ['keisiəs] *adj.* of or like cheese. ⟨< L *caseus* cheese⟩

ca•sern or **ca•serne** [kə'zɜrn] *n.pl.* formerly, barracks or a billet for soldiers in a fortified town. ⟨< F < Sp. *caserna* < L *casa* house⟩

case study **1** a method of research in which a single representative case, such as a person or community, is studied intensively. **2** a study of one such case, or a report of it. **3** an apt or pertinent example: *a failing business that was a case study in poor management.*

case system **1** a method of legal training in which individual cases are studied in detail. **2** *Linguistics.* the set of grammatical cases of a particular language.

case•work ['keis,wɜrk] *n.* a thorough study of the character and present and past circumstances of a maladjusted person, family, or group, carried out by a social worker to serve as a basis for guidance or treatment. **—'case,work•er,** *n.*

case•worm ['keis,wɜrm] *n.* any larva that builds a shell around itself.

cash¹ [kæʃ] *n., v., adj. —n.* **1** money in the form of coins and bills; ready money. **2** money, or something recognized as the equivalent of money, such as a cheque, paid at the time of buying something: *I don't like charge accounts; I prefer to pay cash.* **3** *Informal.* the place in a store, restaurant, etc., where purchases are paid for: *You pay at the cash.*
—v. **1** get ready money for: *I'll have to cash a cheque to pay for it.* **2** give ready money for: *That teller will cash your cheque.*
cash in (one's) **chips, a** *Informal.* change poker chips, etc., into cash. **b** *Slang.* die. **c** *Slang.* close or sell a business; retire.
cash in on, *Informal.* **a** make a profit from. **b** take advantage of; use to advantage.
—adj. of, for, using, or requiring cash: *a cash sale.* ⟨< F *caisse* < Provençal < L *capsa* box, coffer. Doublet of CASE², CHASE³.⟩ **—'cash•less,** *adj.* **—'cash•a•ble,** *adj.*
☛ *Hom.* CACHE.

cash² [kæʃ] *n., pl.* **cash. 1** in China, India, etc., a coin of small

value. **2** in China, a copper coin with a square hole in it. ⟨< Tamil *kasu*⟩
☛ *Hom.* CACHE.

cash–and–car•ry ['kæʃ ən 'kæri] *or* ['kæʃ ən 'kɛri] *adj.* **1** with immediate payment for goods and without delivery service. **2** operated on this basis: *a cash-and-carry store.*

cash bar a bar at a party, reception, etc., at which one pays for one's own drinks.

cash•book ['kæʃ,bʊk] *n.* a book in which a record is kept of money received and paid out.

cash cow *Slang.* a ready source of income: *We taxpayers are cash cows for the government.*

cash crop a crop grown for sale, rather than for consumption on the farm.

cash discount a price reduction which applies only to a purchase paid for within a certain period of time.

cash•ew ['kæʃu] *or* [kə'ʃu] *n.* **1** an evergreen tree (*Anacardium occidentale*) native to tropical and subtropical America, cultivated for its kidney-shaped nuts. **2** the nut of this tree, edible when roasted. **3** (*adj.*) designating the family (Anacardiaceae) of trees and shrubs that includes the cashew as well as pistachio, mango, and the sumacs. ⟨< F *acajou* < Brazilian Pg. *acajú* < Tupi-Guarani⟩
☛ *Hom.* CACHOU [kə'ʃu].

cash flow **1** the regular movement of funds into and out of a business, household, etc. **2** the balance between income and expenditure of a company or individual: *plenty of assets, but a negative cash flow.*

cash•ier¹ [kæ'ʃir] *n.* **1** a person who has charge of money in a bank or business. **2** the person who takes money for goods at a checkout in a supermarket, hardware store, etc. ⟨< F *caissier* treasurer < *caisse.* See CASH¹.⟩

cash•ier² [kæ'ʃir] *v.* dismiss from the armed forces for some dishonourable act; discharge in disgrace. ⟨< Du. *casseren* < F < L *quassare* shatter and LL *cassare* annul⟩

cashier's cheque a cheque drawn by a bank on its own funds and signed by its cashier.

cash•mere ['kæʃmir] *n.* **1** the soft, downy fibre forming the undercoat of a breed of goats raised especially in Kashmir and Tibet. **2** a fine, soft cloth made from this fibre. **3** any fine, soft woollen cloth. **4** a garment, shawl, etc. made of cashmere: *Did you borrow my cashmere?* ⟨< *Kashmir*, in N India⟩

cash on delivery payment when goods are delivered. *Abbrev.*: C.O.D. or c.o.d.

cash register a machine that records and shows the amount of a sale. It usually has a drawer to hold money.

cas•ing ['keisɪŋ] *n., v. —n.* **1** something to put around something else to cover or contain it; case: *The air in a rubber tire is contained inside a casing made of layers of rubberized cord fabric.* **2** a lining or liner, especially metal tube or pipe used to line a water, oil, or gas well. **3** a frame: *A window fits in a casing.* **4** a long, narrow space between two layers of fabric, formed by two parallel lines of stitching, used to insert a rod, as for curtains, or a drawstring or elastic, as for clothing. **5** a membrane used to encase sausage meat. It may be the cleaned intestine of cattle, pigs, etc., or a synthetic substitute.
—v. ppr. of CASE².

ca•si•no [kə'sinou] *n., pl.* **-nos. 1** a building or room for gambling, public shows, dancing, etc. **2** cassino. **3** a small Italian country house. ⟨< Ital. *casino*, dim. of *casa* house < L *casa*⟩

cask [kæsk] *n.* **1** a cylindrical container with outward-curving sides usually made of wooden staves bound by iron hoops, and having a flat top and bottom; barrel. Casks are used especially for holding beer, wine, etc. **2** the amount that a cask holds. **3** a cask and its contents. ⟨< Sp. *casco* skull, cask of wine, ult. < L *quassare* break⟩
☛ *Hom.* CASQUE.

cas•ket ['kæskɪt] *n., v.* **1** a small box or chest used to hold jewels, letters, etc. **2** coffin.
—v. put into a casket; enclose in a casket. ⟨origin uncertain⟩

casque [kæsk] *n.* **1** armour for the head; helmet. **2** *Zoology.* any part looking like or functioning as a helmet. ⟨< F < Sp. *casco.* See CASK.⟩
☛ *Hom.* CASK.

cas•sa•ba [kə'sɑbə] *or* [kə'sɒbə] See CASABA.

Cas•san•dra [kə'sændrə] *n.* **1** *Greek mythology.* a daughter of King Priam of Troy. Apollo gave her the gift of prophecy, but later in anger decreed that no one should believe her. **2** any person who prophesies misfortune but is not believed.

cas•sa•ta [kə'sɑtə] *or* [kə'sɒtə] *n.* an Italian ice cream containing chopped fruits and nuts.

cas•sa•tion [kæ'seiʃən] *n.* an annulment; reversal. ⟨< LL *cassatio, -onis* < *cassare* annul⟩

cas•sa•va [kə'sɑvə] *or* [kə'sævə] *n.* **1** any of several tropical American plants (genus *Manihot*) of the spurge family grown for their large, starchy rootstocks. **2** a starch from its roots, used as a staple food in the tropics. Tapioca is made from cassava. ⟨< F *cassave* < Sp. < Haitian *cacábi* < Arawakan⟩

cas•seau [kæ'sou] *n. Cdn.* formerly, a birchbark box for collecting the sap of the sugar maple, and also for storing maple syrup and maple sugar. ⟨< Cdn.F⟩

Cas•se•grain ['kæsə,grein] *n., adj.* *—n.* a type of telescope in which light is reflected from a large concave mirror onto a small convex mirror near the top of the tube, which then reflects converging beams back through an opening in the large mirror. The observer looks in the direction of the star.
—adj. of or having to do with such a telescope. ⟨< after N. *Cassegrain,* 17c. French scientist⟩ **—,Cas•se'grain•i•an,** *adj.*

cas•se•role ['kæsə,roul] *n.* **1** a baking dish in which food can be both cooked and served. **2** the food cooked and served in a casserole: *a chicken-and-rice casserole.* **3** a small, deep dish with a handle, used in chemical laboratories. ⟨< F *casserole* < *casse* pan < VL *cattia* < Gk. *kyathion*, dim. of *kyathos* cup⟩

cas•sette [kə'sɛt] *n.* **1** a sealed plastic case containing magnetic tape on a reel together with a take-up reel, designed for use with certain types of tape recorder or player. **2** (*adjl.*) of a tape recorder or player, designed for use with cassettes. Cassette recorders are very simple to operate. **3** a lightproof plastic case for holding film, as for a 35 mm camera. **4** a sealed plastic case containing a spool of film together with a take-up spool; CARTRIDGE (def. 4). **5** *Cdn.* formerly, a specially made box or trunk used by the fur traders for transporting personal effects on journeys inland. **6** a sealed case containing instructions for a computer. ⟨< F *cassette* small case < OF *casse* CASE²⟩

cas•sia ['kæʃə] *or* ['kæsiə] *n.* **1** a spice similar to cinnamon, but coarser, obtained from the bark of a tropical Asian tree (*cinnamomum cassia*). **2** the tree itself. **3** any of a genus (*Cassia*) of mainly tropical herbs, shrubs, and trees of the pea family, especially any of several species whose leaves or pods yield a mild laxative called senna. **4** the pods or pulp of a cassia. ⟨OE < L < Gk. < Hebrew *q'tsi'ah*⟩

cas•si•mere ['kæsə,mir] *n.* a soft, lightweight, woollen cloth sometimes used for men's suits. ⟨variant of *cashmere*⟩

cas•si•no or **ca•si•no** [kə'sinou] *n.* a card game in which the ten of diamonds and the two of spades have special counting value. ⟨var. of *casino*⟩

Cas•si•o•pe•ia [,kæsiə'piə], [,kæʃiə'piə], *or* [,kæʃə'piə] *n.* **1** *Greek mythology.* the wife of an Ethiopian king and mother of Andromeda. **2** *Astronomy.* a northern constellation thought to resemble Cassiopeia sitting in a chair.

cas•sis [kə'sis] *n.* a liqueur made from black currants and often served with vermouth. ⟨< F *cassis* black currant⟩

cas•sit•e•rite [kə'sɪtə,rəit] *n.* dioxide of tin, found pure in nature, which is the chief source of tin; tinstone. *Formula*: SnO_2 ⟨< Gk. *kassiteros* tin⟩

cas•sock ['kæsək] *n.* a long outer garment, usually black, worn by a member of the clergy. ⟨< F *casaque* < Ital. *casacca*⟩ **—'cas•socked,** *adj.*

cas•sou•let [,kæsʊ'lei] *n.* a dish of beans baked in a casserole with several kinds of meat. ⟨< F originally dial. dim. of *cassolo* stoneware bowl, dim. of *casso* < Provençal *cassa*⟩

cas•so•war•y ['kæsə,wɛri] *n., pl.* **-war•ies.** any of three species making up a genus (*Casuarius*) of large, flightless birds found in the forests of New Guinea, northern Australia, and nearby islands, having glossy black, hairlike plumage and a blue, featherless head and neck with a high, bony, helmetlike growth on the head. The cassowaries are the sole members of the family Casuariidae. ⟨< Malay *kasuari*⟩

cast [kæst] *v.* **cast, cast•ing;** *n., adj.* *—v.* **1** throw, fling, or hurl. **2** toss the dice. **3** throw one end of a fishing line out into the water. **4** throw off; shed; let fall: *The snake cast its skin.* **5** direct or turn: *He cast a glance of surprise at me.* **6** shape by pouring or squeezing into a mould to harden. Metal is first melted and then cast. **7** arrange: *He cast his plans into final form.* **8** *Theatre.* **a** assign the various parts of (a play). **b** appoint (actors) for the parts. **c** fill (a part) by assigning an actor to it. **9** add; calculate. **10** *Nautical.* in launching, steer the bow of (a ship) to port or starboard. **11** of a ship, turn its stern to the wind: *The ship cast starboard.* **12** drop or let down (an anchor or fishing net) into the water.
cast a ballot, vote.
cast about, search or seek; look around.
cast aside, reject.
cast aspersions on, reflect badly on; criticize (someone).
cast away, a abandon. **b** shipwreck.
cast back, a return in memory or speech: *Cast your mind back to our wedding.* **b** make reference to something in the past. **c** resemble an ancestor.
cast down, a turn downward; lower. **b** make sad or discouraged: *She was cast down by the bad news.*
cast lots, use lots to decide something: *We cast lots for first chance to try out the raft.*
cast off, a let loose; set free: *to cast off a boat from its moorings.* **b** *Knitting.* make the last row of stitches. **c** *Printing.* estimate the printed space needed for (a given quantity of manuscript).
cast on, *Knitting.* make the first row of stitches.
cast out, drive away; banish or expel.
cast up, a turn upward; raise: *He cast up his eyes and groaned in exasperation.* **b** add up; find the sum of.
the die is cast, the future is decided.
—n. **1** the distance a thing is thrown: *She made a long cast with her line.* **2** the act of throwing a fishing line: *She made a skilful cast from the river bank.* **3** something made by casting; something that is moulded. **4** a mould used in casting. **5** *Pathology.* a substance accumulated and moulded in the hollows of certain diseased organs. **6** a plaster support used to keep a broken bone in place while it is mending: *He had his arm in a cast for more than a month.* **7** the actors in a play, movie, etc. **8** the outward form or appearance: *Her face had a gloomy cast.* **9** a kind or sort. **10** a slight amount of colour; tinge: *a white dress with a pink cast.* **11** a slight squint. **12** a group of hawks.
—adj. made by casting: *cast iron.* ⟨ME < ON *kasta* throw⟩
☛ *Hom.* CASTE.
☛ *Syn. v.* **1.** See note at THROW.

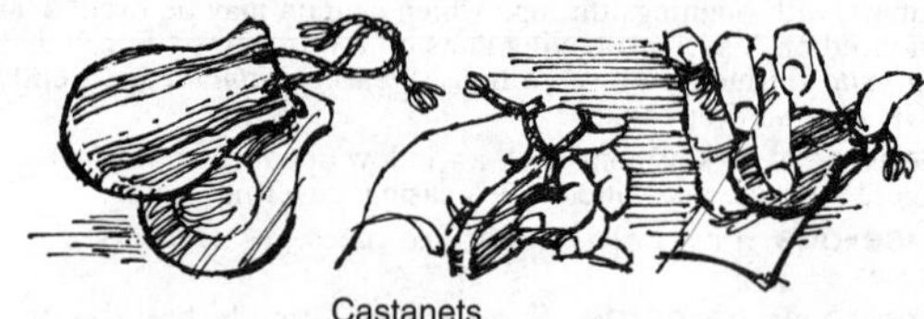

Castanets

cas•ta•net [,kæstə'nɛt] *n.* a small rhythm instrument made of ivory, hardwood, or plastic, usually used in pairs, consisting of two parts which are held in the hand and clicked together rhythmically, especially to accompany dancing, particularly Spanish dancing. ⟨< Sp. *castaneta* < L *castanea.* See CHESTNUT.⟩

cast•a•way ['kæstə,wei] *adj., n.* *—adj.* **1** thrown away; cast adrift. **2** outcast.
—n. **1** a shipwrecked person. **2** an outcast.

caste [kæst] *n.* **1** one of the four main social classes of India, formerly officially supported by the state and still part of the Hindu religion. Castes have traditionally been hereditary; one could never change one's caste or marry somebody from another caste. **2** the system or basis of this division. **3** an exclusive social group; distinct class. **4** a social system having distinct classes separated by differences of birth, rank, wealth, or position. **5** *Zoology.* any of the forms of a social insect differentiated by function.
lose caste, lose social rank or position. ⟨< Sp., Pg. *casta* race < L *castus* pure. Doublet of CHASTE.⟩
☛ *Hom.* CAST.

cas•tel•lan ['kæstələn] *n.* the governor of a castle. ⟨< L *castellanus* occupant of a stronghold < *castellum.* See CASTLE.⟩

cas•tel•lat•ed ['kæstə,leitɪd] *adj.* **1** like a castle; having turrets and battlements. **2** having many castles.
—,cas•tel'la•tion, *n.*

cast•er¹ ['kæstər] *n.* a person who or thing that casts.

cast•er² or **cast•or** ['kæstər] *n.* **1** a small wheel on a swivel, set into the base of a piece of furniture or other heavy object to make it easier to move. **2** a bottle containing salt, mustard, vinegar, or other seasoning for table use. **3** a stand or rack for such bottles.

cas•ti•gate ['kæstə,geit] *v.* **-gat•ed, -gat•ing.** criticize, rebuke, or punish severely. ⟨< L *castigare,* ult. < *castus* pure⟩ **—,cas•ti'ga•tion,** *n.* **—'cas•ti,ga•tor,** *n.*

Cas•tile soap or **cas•tile soap** [kæ'stil] *or* ['kæstil] **1** a pure, hard soap made from olive oil and sodium hydroxide. **2** any fine, mild soap made from another oil, such as coconut oil. ⟨< *Castile,* a region in north and central Spain⟩

Cas•til•ian [kæ'stɪljən] *or* [kə'stɪljən] *n., adj.* *—n.* **1** a native or inhabitant of Castile, a region and former kingdom of Spain. **2** the standard form of Spanish used in Spain, originally the dialect of Castile.
—adj. of or having to do with Castile, its people, or their dialect, or modern standard Spanish.

cast•ing ['kæstɪŋ] *n., v.* *—n.* **1** something shaped by being poured into a mould to harden. **2** the process of making casts in a mould. **3** the assignment of the parts in a play, film, etc. **4** earth excreted by a worm at the end of digestion.
—v. ppr. of CAST.

casting vote a vote by the presiding officer to decide a question when the votes of an assembly, council, board, or committee are evenly divided.

cast iron an alloy of iron, carbon, and silicon, poured into moulds to harden.

cast–i•ron ['kæst 'aɪərn] *adj.* **1** made of cast iron. **2** hard; not yielding: *He has a cast-iron will.* **3** hardy; strong or impregnable: *a cast-iron stomach, a cast-iron alibi.*

cast–iron plant an aspidistra (*Aspidistra lurida*) often grown as a house plant, having long, tough, glossy leaves which grow from the base of the plant.

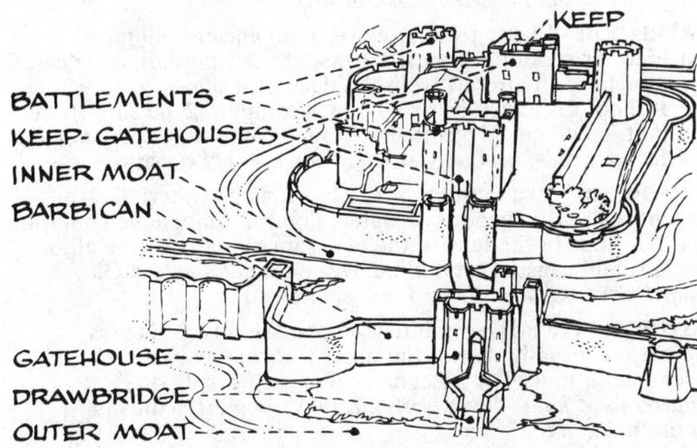

Caerphilly Castle in Glamorgan, Wales, built in the 13th century

cas•tle ['kæsəl] *n., v.* **-tled, -tling.** *—n.* **1** a building or group of buildings with thick walls, towers, and other defences against attack. **2** a palace that once had defences against attack. **3** a large and imposing residence. **4** *Chess.* rook.
—v. **1** place in or as if in a castle. **2** *Chess.* **a** move the castle, or rook, next to the king and then the king to the other side of the rook in the same turn, a move allowed only under certain conditions. **b** (of the king) be moved in this way. ⟨< L *castellum,* dim. of *castrum* fort. Doublet of CHÂTEAU.⟩

castle in the air or **in Spain** something imagined but not likely to come true; a daydream.

cast•off ['kæst,ɒf] *adj., n.* *—adj.* thrown away; abandoned.
—n. **1** something that has been thrown away or put aside as no longer useful. **2** a person who has been abandoned or cast aside. **3** an estimate of the number of printed pages resulting from a given quantity of manuscript.

cas•tor[1] ['kæstər] See CASTER[2].

cas•tor[2] ['kæstər] *n.* **1** a hat made of beaver fur. **2** a pungent, oily substance secreted by beavers, used in making perfume and in medicines. **3** beaver. ⟨< L < Gk. *kastōr* beaver⟩

Cas•tor ['kæstər] *n.* **1** *Greek and Roman mythology.* the mortal twin brother of Pollux. **2** *Astronomy.* the second brightest star in the constellation Gemini. Pollux, the brightest star in the constellation, lies near it.

castor bean **1** the poisonous seed of the castor-oil plant. **2** CASTOR-OIL PLANT.

castor oil a yellow oil obtained from castor beans, used as a cathartic, a lubricant, etc.

cas•tor–oil plant ['kæstər ,ɔɪl] a tall, tropical herb (*Ricinus communis*) of the spurge family, native to India, having very large, fanlike leaves. It is cultivated as an ornamental plant and also for its seeds, which yield an oil used as an industrial lubricant and also as a laxative.

cas•trate ['kæstreit] *v.* **-trat•ed, -trat•ing;** *n.* *—v.* **1** remove the testicles of; geld. **2** take away the basic strength or vitality of. *—n.* a castrated animal or person. ⟨< L *castrare*⟩ **—cas'tra•tion,** *n.*

cas•tra•to [kæ'strɑtou]; *Italian,* [ka'strɑto] *n., pl.* **cas•tra•ti** [-ti]. a man who was castrated in youth to preserve his high voice; a practice common in Italy from the 16th-18th century.

cast steel steel that has undergone fusion. **—'cast-'steel,** *adj.*

cas•u•al ['kæʒuəl] *adj., n.* *—adj.* **1** happening by chance; not planned or expected; accidental: *a casual meeting.* **2** having or showing lack of concern or interest; careless, nonchalant, or indifferent: *He gave the painting only a casual glance. She takes a very casual approach to her work.* **3** informal; relaxed; easygoing: *casual manners, casual living.* **4** designed for informal use: *casual clothes, casual furniture.* **5** not given or done with any serious purpose or commitment; superficial: *a casual interest in the arts. She's just a casual acquaintance.* **6** happening, active, or employed on an irregular basis; occasional: *casual employment, a casual labourer.*
—n. **1** a casual labourer or worker. **2** a member of the armed forces temporarily attached to a post or station while awaiting transportation to his or her unit, to a permanent assignment, etc. **3 casuals,** casual clothes, shoes, etc. ⟨< L *casualis* < *casus* chance⟩ **—'cas•u•al•ly,** *adv.* **—'cas•u•al•ness,** *n.*

casual labour a worker or workers hired by the day.

cas•u•al•ty ['kæʒuəlti] *or* ['kæʒəlti] *n., pl.* **-ties. 1** an accident. **2** an unfortunate accident; mishap. **3** a member of the armed forces who has been wounded, killed, or captured as a result of enemy action. **4** a person injured or killed in an accident or disaster, or as a result of enemy action: *The earthquake caused many casualties.* **5** anything lost, destroyed, etc. by accident.

cas•u•a•ri•na [,kæʒuə'rinə] *n.* a tree of the genus *Casuarina,* found in Australia and having jointed branches bearing leaves in a whorl pattern. ⟨< NL < Malay *kasuari* cassowary (because its twigs resemble the feathers)⟩

cas•u•ist ['kæʒuɪst] *n.* **1** a person who decides questions of right and wrong in conduct, duty, etc. **2** a person who reasons cleverly but falsely, especially in regard to right and wrong. ⟨< F *casuiste* < L *casus* case⟩

cas•u•is•tic [,kæʒu'ɪstɪk] *adj.* **1** of or like casuistry. **2** too subtle; sophistic. Also, **casuistical. —,cas•u'is•ti•cal•ly,** *adv.*

cas•u•ist•ry ['kæʒuɪstri] *n., pl.* **-ries. 1** the act or process of deciding questions of right and wrong in regard to conduct, duty, etc. **2** clever but false reasoning.

ca•sus bel•li ['kɑsʊs 'bɛli] *or* ['keisəs 'bɛlaɪ] *Latin.* a cause for war.

cat [kæt] *n., v.* **cat•ted, cat•ting.** *—n.* **1** a small domestic mammal (*Felis catus*) of the cat family having furry paws with soft pads and retractable claws, a rounded face with a short muzzle, short, pointed ears, and soft fur. Cats are kept as pets and for catching mice. **2** any of a family (Felidae) of mostly wild, flesh-eating, tree-climbing mammals characterized by lithe, muscular bodies, spiny tongues, teeth adapted for stabbing, holding, and cutting, but not for chewing, and claws that are retractable in all species but the cheetah. The cat family is divided into two main groups: the big roaring cats, including the lion, tiger, leopard, snow leopard, and jaguar; and the purring cats, including the lynx, wildcat, cougar, and domestic cat. **3** an animal resembling a cat. **4** *Slang.* a mean, spiteful woman. **5** catfish. **6** cat-o'-nine-tails. **7** the tackle for hoisting an anchor. **8** *Slang.* fellow; guy.
let the cat out of the bag, tell a secret: *It was supposed to be a surprise party, but he let the cat out of the bag.*
rain cats and dogs, rain very hard.
—v. hoist (an anchor) and fasten it to a beam on the ship's side. ⟨OE *catt(e),* probably < LL *catta*⟩

cat. **1** catalogue. **2** catechism.

CAT **1** CLEAR-AIR TURBULENCE. **2** COMPUTERIZED AXIAL TOMOGRAPHY.

cata– *prefix.* down; against; entirely, as in *cataract.* Also, **cat-** before vowels and *h,* as in *category, cathode.* ⟨< Gk. *kata-* < *kata,* prep.⟩

ca•tab•o•lism [kə'tæbə,lɪzəm] *n. Biology.* the process of breaking down living tissues into simpler substances or waste matter, thereby producing energy. Also, **katabolism.** ⟨probably

< *metabolism*, by substitution of *cata-* down⟩ —,**ca•ta'bol•ic,** *adj.* —,**ca•ta'bol•i•cal•ly,** *adv.*

ca•tab•o•lite [kə'tæbə,ləit] *n.* a waste product of catabolism.

ca•tab•o•lize [kə'tæbə,laɪz] *v.* **-lized, -liz•ing.** undergo catabolism; make (something) undergo catabolism.

cat•a•chre•sis [,kætə'krisɪs] *n., pl.* **-ses** [-siz]. the misuse of words, especially the use of a word in an inappropriate or meaningless context. ⟨< L < Gk. *katachrēsis* misuse < *kata-* amiss + *chrēsthai* use⟩ —,**cat•a'chres•tic** [-'krɛstɪk], *adj.* —,**cat•a'chres•ti•cal•ly,** *adv.*

cat•a•clysm ['kætə,klɪzəm] *n.* **1** a flood, earthquake, or any sudden, violent change in the earth. **2** any violent change: *World War II was a cataclysm for all of Europe.* ⟨< L *cataclysmos* < Gk. *kataklysmos* flood < *kata-* down + *klyzein* wash⟩

cat•a•clys•mic [,kætə'klɪzmɪk] *adj.* of or like a cataclysm; extremely sudden and violent. Also, **cataclysmal.**

cat•a•comb ['kætə,koum] *n.* Usually, **catacombs,** *pl.* an underground gallery forming a burial place. ⟨< LL *catacumbae*, pl. < *cata* (< Gk. *kata*) *tumbas* (< Gk. *tymbos*) among the tombs⟩

ca•ta•di•op•tric [,kætədaɪ'ɒptrɪk] *adj.* of or having to do with a telescope or other optical instrument that is both reflecting and refracting. ⟨< *cato(ptric)* + *dioptric* < Gk. *katoptrikos* relating to a mirror + *dioptrikos* relating to the diopter⟩

ca•tad•ro•mous [kə'tædrəməs] *adj.* of freshwater fishes, returning to the sea to spawn. ⟨< Gk. *kata-* down + *-dromos* < *dramein* run⟩

cat•a•falque ['kætə,fælk] *n.* a stand or frame to support the coffin in which a dead person lies. ⟨< F < Ital. *catafalco*, of uncertain origin⟩

Cat•a•lan ['kætə,læn] *or* ['kætələn] *n., adj.* —*n.* **1** a native or inhabitant of Catalonia, a region in NE Spain. **2** the Romance language of the Catalans, also spoken especially in Valencia, Andorra, and the Balearic Islands.
—*adj.* of or having to do with Catalonia, its people, or their language.

cat•a•lec•tic [,kætə'lɛktɪk] *adj. Prosody.* of a line of verse, missing part of the last metrical foot. ⟨< *cata-* + Gk. *legein* to end⟩

cat•a•lep•sy ['kætə,lɛpsi] *n.* a kind of fit during which a person loses consciousness and the power to feel, and his or her muscles become rigid. Also, **catalepsis.** ⟨< LL *catalepsis* < Gk. *katalēpsis* seizure < *kata-* down + *lambanein* seize⟩

cat•a•lep•tic [,kætə'lɛptɪk] *adj., n.* —*adj.* **1** of catalepsy. **2** having catalepsy.
—*n.* a person who has catalepsy.

ca•ta•lo ['kætə,lou] *n.* See CATTALO.

cat•a•logue ['kætə,lɒg] *n., v.* **-logued, -logu•ing.** —*n.* **1** a list of items in a collection, identifying each item very briefly and sometimes describing it. A library has a catalogue of its books, arranged in alphabetical order. A company sometimes prints a catalogue with pictures and prices of the things that it sells. **2** a volume or booklet issued by a university or college listing rules, courses to be given, etc.; calendar. **3** a list; series: *a catalogue of lies, tricks, and deceits.*
—*v.* make a catalogue of; put in a catalogue: *He catalogued all the insects in his collection.* Also, *esp. U.S.*, **catalog.** ⟨< F < LL < Gk. *katalogos* list < *kata-* down + *legein* count⟩ —'**cat•a,logu•er,** *n.* —'**cat•a,logu•ist,** *n.*
☛ *Syn. n.* See note at LIST[1].

ca•tal•pa [kə'tælpə] *n.* any of a small genus (*Catalpa*) of North American and Asian trees having large, heart-shaped leaves, clusters of bell-shaped flowers, and long pods. ⟨< NL < Creek Indian *kutuhlpa*⟩

ca•tal•y•sis [kə'tæləsɪs] *n., pl.* **-ses** [-,siz]. *Chemistry.* the changing, especially the speeding up, of a chemical reaction by the presence of a substance that is not itself permanently changed.

cat•a•lyst ['kætəlɪst] *n.* **1** *Chemistry.* a substance that causes catalysis. **2** an agent that causes or speeds up the occurrence of an event, especially one that is not directly involved or affected by the results.

cat•a•lyt•ic [,kætə'lɪtɪk] *adj.* **1** of catalysis. **2** causing catalysis. —,**cat•a'ly•ti•cal•ly,** *adv.*

catalytic converter a device in the exhaust system of a vehicle, designed to control, by a chemical reaction, the emission of pollution.

cat•a•lyse ['kætə,laɪz] *n.* be the catalyst of. —'**cat•a,lys•er,** *n.*

cat•a•ma•ran [,kætəmə'ræn] *n.* **1** a boat having two hulls or floats joined side by side by a frame. Compare TRIMARAN. **2** *Cdn.* a type of platform on two runners, used for hauling lumber, etc. **3** a raft made of two or more logs fastened beside each other but some distance apart, used in parts of India, South America, etc. ⟨< Tamil *kattamaram* tied tree⟩

A catamaran

cat•a•mite ['kætə,məit] *n.* a boy who has a sexual relationship with a man. ⟨< L *Catamitus* < Gk. *Ganymedes* Ganymede⟩

cat•a•mount ['kætə,maʊnt] *n.* any of various wildcats, such as the cougar or lynx. ⟨short for *catamountain* cat of (the) mountain⟩

ca•ta•phyll ['kætə,fɪl] *n. Botany.* an undeveloped leaf, prior to leafing out. ⟨< NL < Gk. *kata-* down + *phyllon* a leaf⟩

ca•ta•pla•sia [,kætə'pleiʒə] *n., pl.* **-si•ae** [-ʒi,i]. degeneration of a cell or tissue, characterized by regression to an earlier form. ⟨< NL < Gk. *kata-* down + *plasis* moulding < *plassein* mould⟩ —,**ca•ta'plas•tic** [-'plæstɪk], *adj.*

cat•a•plex•y ['kætə,plɛksi] *n.* a momentary loss of muscular power and control, without loss of consciousness. ⟨< Gk. *kataplexis* < *kataplessein*, strike down⟩

cat•a•pult ['kætə,pʌlt] *n., v.* —*n.* **1** an ancient military machine for shooting stones, arrows, etc. **2** slingshot. **3** a device for launching an aircraft from the deck of a ship.
—*v.* **1** shoot or launch by or as if by a catapult. **2** be shot from a catapult; move quickly as if shot from a catapult. ⟨< L *catapulta* < Gk. *katapeltēs*, probably < *kata-* down + *pallein* hurl⟩

cat•a•ract ['kætə,rækt] *n.* **1** a large, steep waterfall. **2** a violent rush or downpour of water; flood. **3** an opaque condition that develops in the lens of the eye, sometimes covering all of the lens and causing total blindness. ⟨< L *cataracta* < Gk. *katarrhaktēs* < *kata-* down + *arassein* dash⟩

ca•tarrh [kə'tɑr] *n.* an inflamed condition of a mucous membrane, usually that of the nose or throat, causing a discharge of mucus or phlegm. ⟨< F *catarrhe* < L < Gk. *katarrhous* < *kata-* down + *rheein* flow⟩ —**ca'tarrh•ous** or **ca'tarrh•al,** *adj.*

ca•tas•ta•sis [kə'tæstəsɪs] *n.* in ancient Greek drama, the build-up to the catastrophe. ⟨< Gk. *katastasis* arrangement⟩

ca•tas•tro•phe [kə'tæstrəfi] *n.* **1** a sudden, widespread, or extraordinary disaster; great calamity or misfortune: *A big fire or flood is a catastrophe.* **2** *Geology.* an unexpected, cataclysmic change, such as an earthquake. **3** the outcome; unhappy ending: *The catastrophe of a tragedy usually brings death or ruin to the leading character.* **4** a disastrous end; ruin. ⟨< Gk. *katastrophē* overturning < *kata-* down + *strephein* turn⟩
☛ *Syn.* **1.** See note at DISASTER.

cat•a•stroph•ic [,kætə'strɒfɪk] *adj.* **1** of or caused by disaster; calamitous. **2** being a catastrophe; sudden, violent, and having a very profound effect. —,**cat•a'stroph•i•cal•ly,** *adv.*

ca•tas•tro•phism [kə'tæstrə,fɪzəm] *n.* **1** the doctrine that vast geological changes in the earth were caused by sudden catastrophes rather than by slow evolutionary change. **2** an attitude of expecting catastrophe. —**ca'ta•stroph•ist,** *n.*

cat•a•to•nia [,kætə'touniə] *n.* a symptom, especially of schizophrenia, characterized by rigid muscles and stupor, often alternating with psychotic excitement. ⟨< Gk. *kata-* down + *tonos* tension < *teinein* to tend⟩ —,**cat•a'ton•ic** [-'tɒnɪk], *adj.*

Ca•taw•ba [kə'tɒbə] *n., pl.* **-bas. 1** an American Indian group of South Carolina. **2** their Siouan language. **3** a light red grape of North America. **4** a light wine made from it. ⟨< Shawnee *kataapa*⟩

cat•bird ['kæt,bɜrd] *n.* **1** a mainly slate grey North American songbird (*Dumetella carolinensis*) belonging to the same family as the mockingbird and the thrashers. The catbird has a call like the mewing of a cat. **2** any of several Australian songbirds (family Ptilonorhynchidae) having a mewing call.

catbird seat a position of advantage or power; an enviable position: *He wasn't at all worried, since he was sitting in the catbird seat.*

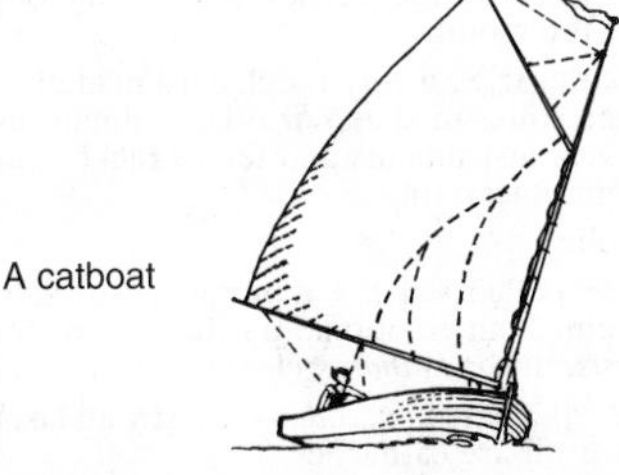
A catboat

cat•boat ['kæt,bout] *n.* a sailboat having a broad beam and one mast set far forward. It has no bowsprit or jib.

cat brier any of various vines (genus *Smilax*) bearing small thorns and, commonly, black berries; greenbrier.

cat burglar a burglar who enters by skilful feats of climbing.

cat•call ['kæt,kɒl] *n., v.* —*n.* a shrill cry or whistle to express disapproval: *Poor actors are sometimes greeted by catcalls from the audience.*
—*v.* **1** make catcalls. **2** attack with catcalls: *The audience catcalled the actor.*

catch [kætʃ] *v.* **caught, catch•ing;** *n.* —*v.* **1** seize and hold, especially after chasing or going after: *She caught the child just as he reached the street. The thief was caught five days after the robbery.* **2** seize; take hold of by a device: *The fox's paw was caught in the trap.* **3** stop the motion of and hold on to: *I caught the ball with one hand. She caught the glass just before it fell.* **4** become affected by; take or get: *to catch the spirit of the celebration. Paper catches fire easily. I think I've caught a cold.* **5** touch; strike: *The ball caught her on the head.* **6** become or cause to become accidentally hooked, pinched, or entangled: *My dress caught in the door.* **7** start burning; take fire: *Tinder catches easily.* **8** come on (someone) suddenly; surprise in the act of doing something: *He was caught stealing. My mother caught me hiding her present.* **9** take or get suddenly or briefly: *to catch a quick nap. They caught a glimpse of him before he disappeared into the crowd.* **10** attract: *Bright colours catch the eye. I tried to catch his attention but he didn't look my way.* **11** reach or get to in time: *If we hurry, we can just catch the next bus.* **12** take notice of; discover: *He thought I wouldn't catch his error.* **13** represent in a picture, statue, description, etc.: *You've caught her likeness.* **14** apprehend by the senses or intellect; hear, see, understand, etc., by an effort: *I couldn't catch what she was saying.* **15** *Baseball.* act as catcher: *Who's catching?* **16** check suddenly: *She caught her breath.*
catch alight, a begin to burn. **b** become enthusiastic.
catch as catch can, a grab or wrestle in any way. **b** take whatever chances one gets.
catch at, try to take hold of; grab at: *He caught at the rope as it swung by him.*
catch in the act or **catch red-handed,** find someone in the process of doing something wrong.
catch it, *Informal.* be scolded or punished: *We'll catch it if we're late again.*
catch on, *Informal.* **a** understand; get the idea: *to catch on to a joke. They were kidding me but I didn't catch on.* **b** become popular or widely used and accepted: *The song never caught on.*
catch out, discover doing wrong: *to catch him out cheating.*
catch sight of, notice; become aware of: see: *The dog suddenly caught sight of the cat.*
catch up, a come up even (with) or overtake a person or thing going the same way: *He ran hard, trying to catch up with his sister.* **b** pick up suddenly; seize; grab: *He caught the laughing child up in his arms.* **c** become too much for (*used with* **with**): *His late nights were beginning to catch up with him.* **d** bring or become up to date; make up for lost time: *to catch up on the news. She's missed a lot of school, but it shouldn't take her too long to catch up.* **e** involve, especially unwillingly; ensnare (*used in the passive*): *They were both caught up in the scandal.* **f** absorb completely; engross (*used in the passive*): *He is all caught up in his new boat.* **g** take or hold up in loops or folds.
catch up on, make up for (something lost): *I need to catch up on my sleep.*
—*n.* **1** the act of catching: *Maria made a fine catch with one hand.* **2** a game of throwing and catching a ball: *They're outside playing catch.* **3** something caught, especially the total quantity caught: *They made a good catch today. Her catch was six trout.* **4** something that holds something else in place: *We can't fasten the windows because the catch is broken.* **5** *Informal.* a person worth catching as a spouse, especially because of wealth, position, etc. **6** a hidden or tricky condition or meaning; some difficulty that does not appear on the surface: *There's a catch to that question, so think carefully before you answer.* **7** (*adjl.*) tricky or deceptive: *a catch question.* **8** a short stopping or blocking of the voice or breath: *There was a catch in his voice as he described the accident.* **9** *Music.* a ROUND (def. 12). **10** a scrap or fragment of anything: *She sang catches of songs.* ⟨ME < OF *cachier* < LL *captiare* < L *capere* take. Doublet of CHASE[1].⟩

catch–all ['kætʃ ,ɒl] *n.* **1** a container for odds and ends. **2** a term, question, etc., used to cover a number of possible examples: *The word 'etc.' in this definition is a catch-all.*

catch–as–catch–can [,kætʃ əz ,kætʃ 'kæn] *n., adj., adv.* —*n.* **1** a situation in which one must take whatever chances one gets. **2** a style of wrestling in which one may use the legs and feet, or hold one's opponent's legs and feet, to gain advantage.
—*adj.* **1** unrestrained; free-for-all. **2** haphazard; random.
—*adv.* in a catch-as-catch-can way.

catch basin **1** a sievelike receptacle at the entrance of a sewer to retain matter that might block the flow of sewage. **2** a reservoir for catching and holding surface drainage over large areas.

catch crop an additional crop planted when the ground is normally unused, as between the cultivation of two major crops.

catch•er ['kætʃər] *n.* a person who or thing that catches; especially, in baseball, the player who stands behind the batter to catch balls thrown by the pitcher that are not hit by the batter.

catch•fly ['kætʃ,flaɪ] *n., pl.* **-flies.** a carnivorous plant of the genus *Silene,* which catches insects on its sticky stems.

catch•ing ['kætʃɪŋ] *adj., v.* —*adj.* **1** liable to spread from one to another; contagious; infectious: *Colds are catching.* **2** attractive; fascinating.
—*v.* ppr. of CATCH.

catch•ment ['kætʃmənt] *n.* **1** the act or fact of catching drainage. **2** a reservoir for catching drainage. **3** the water collected in such a reservoir.

catchment area **1** a land area where the rainfall is drained by one river system. Also called **catchment basin.** **2** the area whose residents are served by a given social institution.

catch•pen•ny ['kætʃ,pɛni] *adj., n., pl.* **-nies.** —*adj.* showy but worthless or useless; made to sell quickly.
—*n.* a showy but worthless article.

catch phrase a phrase designed to attract attention and be memorable; slogan: *Sheila is trying to think of a good catch phrase to advertise the contest.*

catch•pole or **catch•poll** ['kætʃ,poul] *n.* formerly, a deputy sheriff or bailiff whose duties included arresting debtors for non-payment. ⟨ME *cacchepol* tax collector < AF *cache-pol* chicken chaser⟩

catch stitch a stitch that makes parallel rows of lines as in a herringbone design.

catch–22 ['kætʃ ,twɛntɪ 'tu] *n.* a condition whereby one loses or fails no matter what action is taken. ⟨< *Catch-22,* title of a novel (1961) by Joseph Heller, b. 1923⟩

catch•weight ['kætʃ,weit] *adj., adv. Horseracing.* with none of the usual restrictions on weight: *The jockeys will ride catchweight.*

catch•word ['kætʃ,wɜrd] *n.* **1** a word or phrase used again and again until it becomes accepted as representative of a party, point of view, etc.; slogan: *"Canada first" was a catchword of a late 19th-century movement for cultural independence.* **2** a word placed so as to catch attention, such as a guide word in a dictionary. **3** a verbal cue for an actor, usually the last word of the previous speech.

catch•y ['kætʃi] *adj.* **catch•i•er, catch•i•est.** **1** easy to remember; attractive: *The new musical play has several catchy tunes.* **2** tricky; misleading; deceptive: *The third question on the test was catchy; nearly everyone in the class gave the wrong answer.*
—'catch•i•ly, *adv.* **—'catch•i•ness,** *n.*

cate [keit] *n. Archaic.* Usually, **cates,** *pl.* a delicacy; choice food. ⟨var. of ME *acate* < ONF *acat* a purchase < *acater* buy < VL *accaptare* acquire < L *ad-* to + *capere* take⟩

cat•e•che•sis [,kætə'kisɪs] *n., pl.* **-ses** [-siz]. teaching by catechism.

cat•e•chet•i•cal [,kætə'kɛtəkəl] *adj.* **1** teaching by questions and answers. **2** like or according to a catechism. Also, **catechetic.**

cat•e•chin ['kætə,tʃɪn] *or* ['kætə,kɪn] *n.* a yellow acid used in tanning, dyeing, etc. *Formula*: $C_{15}H_{14}O_6$ ⟨< *catech(u)* + *-in*⟩

cat•e•chism ['kætə,kɪzəm] *n.* **1** a book of questions and answers, especially one used for teaching religious doctrine. **2** any set of questions. **—,cat•e'chis•mal,** *adj.*

cat•e•chist ['kætəkɪst] *n.* a person who catechizes.

cat•e•chize ['kætə,kaɪz] *v.* **-chized, -chiz•ing. 1** teach by questions and answers. **2** question closely. ⟨< L *catechizare* < Gk. *katēchizein* teach orally < *katēchein* < *kata-* thoroughly + *ēchein* sound⟩ **—'cat•e,chiz•er,** *n.* **—,cat•e•chi'za•tion,** *n.*

cat•e•chol•a•mine [,kætə'koulə,min] *or* [,kætə'tʃoulə,min] *n.* any of a group of chemically related hormones and neurotransmitters, including adrenalin, noradrenalin, and dopamine. ⟨< NL *catechu* an astringent substance obtained from plants⟩

cat•e•chu ['kætə,tʃu] *or* ['kætə,kju] *n.* any of several hard, brittle, astringent substances used in dyeing and tanning and in medicine, obtained from tropical plants, especially an acacia tree (*Acacia catechu*) of S Asia. ⟨< NL < Malay *kachu*⟩

cat•e•chu•men [,kætə'kjumən] *n.* **1** a person who is being taught the elementary doctrines of Christianity. **2** a person who is being taught the fundamentals of any field of study. ⟨< LL *catechumenus* < Gk. *katēchoumenos* one being instructed, ppr. passive of *katēchein.* See CATECHIZE.⟩

cat•e•gor•i•cal [,kætə'gɔrəkəl] *adj.* **1** without conditions or qualifications; positive. **2** of or in a category. **—,cat•e'gor•i•cal•ly,** *adv.*

categorical imperative 1 the doctrine of Immanuel Kant (1724-1804) that one should do the same as one would prescribe for all others in similar circumstances. **2** the dictate of conscience.

cat•e•gor•i•za•tion [,kætəgərə'zeiʃən] *or* ['kætəgəraɪ'zeiʃən] *n.* the act or fact or process of categorizing.

cat•e•gor•ize ['kætəgə,raɪz] *v.* **-ized, -iz•ing.** place in a category; classify. **—'cat•e•gor,iz•er,** *n.*

cat•e•go•ry ['kætə,gɔri] *n., pl.* **-ries. 1** a group or division in a general system of classification; class: *She groups all people into two categories: those she likes and those she dislikes.* **2** in various systems of philosophy, any of certain basic concepts underlying knowledge or into which all existing things can be resolved. ⟨< L *categoria* < Gk. *katēgoria* assertion < *kata-* down + *agoreuein* speak⟩

ca•te•na [kə'tinə] *n., pl.* **-nas** or **nae** [-ni] *or* [-naɪ]. a linked series of writings, especially those of the early Christian fathers. ⟨< L *catena* chain⟩

cat•e•nar•y ['kætə,nɛri] *or* [kə'tinəri] *n., pl.* **-nar•ies.** *adj. Mathematics.* *—n.* the curve formed by a heavy flexible cord hanging freely from two points not in a vertical line.
—adj. of or having to do with a catenary. ⟨< L *catenarius* relating to a chain < *catena* chain⟩ **—,cat•e'na•ri•an,** *adj.*

cat•e•nate ['kætə,neit] *v.* **-nat•ed, -nat•ing.** link together like a chain; connect in a series. ⟨< L *catenare* < *catena* chain⟩ **—,cat•e'na•tion,** *n.*

ca•ter ['keitər] *v.* **1** provide food or supplies (*for*): *He has a small hotel and also caters for weddings and parties.* **2** provide what is needed or wanted (*used with* **to**): *There is a new magazine catering to people interested in crafts.* ⟨verbal use of *cater*, n., ME *acatour* buyer of provisions < OF *acateor* < *acater* buy. See CATE.⟩

cat•er–cor•nered ['kætə ,kɔrnərd] *adj. or adv.* kitty-corner. Also, **cater-corner.** ⟨< E dial. *cater* diagonally (< F *quatre* four) + *cornered*⟩

ca•ter•er ['keitərər] *n.* a person or company whose business is to provide food or supplies for entertainments, parties, etc.

cat•er•pil•lar ['kætər,pɪlər] *or* ['kætə,pɪlər] *n.* the wormlike larva of certain insects, especially butterflies and moths, often brightly coloured and covered with long hairs or spines. ⟨Cf. OF *chatepelose* hairy cat⟩

Cat•er•pil•lar ['kætər,pɪlər] *n. Trademark.* a brand of tractor with cogged wheels in a moving belt for use on rough ground.

A Caterpillar tractor

cat•er•waul ['kætər,wɒl] *v., n.* *—v.* **1** howl like a cat; screech. **2** quarrel noisily.
—n. such a howl or screech. ⟨ME *caterwrawe* < *cater*, apparently, cat + *wrawe* wail, howl⟩

cat•fish ['kæt,fɪʃ] *n., pl.* **-fish** or **-fish•es.** any of an order (Siluriformes) of mostly freshwater fishes of almost worldwide distribution, having long, whiskerlike barbels about the mouth.

cat•gut ['kæt,gʌt] *n.* a very tough cord made from the dried and twisted intestines of sheep or other animals, used for stringing musical instruments and tennis rackets, and for surgical stitches. ⟨origin uncertain⟩

Cath. Catholic.

ca•thar•sis [kə'θɑrsɪs] *n.* **1** a purging, especially of the digestive system. **2** an emotional purification or relief. ⟨< NL < Gk. *katharsis*, ult. < *katharos* clean⟩

ca•thar•tic [kə'θɑrtɪk] *n., adj.* *—n.* a strong laxative. Epsom salts and castor oil are cathartics.
—adj. of or bringing about catharsis; purifying.

Ca•thay [kæ'θei] *n. Poetic or archaic.* China. ⟨< Med.L *Cataya* < Vighur *khitay*, a Mongol people who ruled in Beijing from 936-1122⟩

cat•head ['kæt,hɛd] *n.* **1** a projecting beam on a ship's side near the bow, to which the hoisted anchor is fastened. See CAPSTAN for picture. **2** in oil drilling, a spinning drum used to control a chain.

ca•the•dra [kə'θidrə] *or* ['kæθədrə] *n.* **1** a bishop's throne in a cathedral. **2** a seat of authority. See also EX CATHEDRA. ⟨< L < Gk. *kathedra* seat < *kata-* down + *hedra* seat. Doublet of CHAIR.⟩

ca•the•dral [kə'θidrəl] *n., adj.* *—n.* **1** the official church of a bishop. **2** a large or important church.
—adj. **1** containing a bishop's throne. **2** of, like, or having to do with a cathedral. **3** authoritative; official. ⟨< Med.L *cathedralis* of the (bishop's) seat < L < Gk. *kathedra* seat. See CATHEDRA.⟩

ca•thep•sin [kə'θɛpsɪn] *n.* any of a class of intracellular enzymes found in the liver, spleen, kidney, and intestines, that act as a catalyst to break down protein in some diseases and after death. ⟨< Gk. *kathepsein* boil down < *kata-* down + *hepsein* boil⟩

Cath•e•rine wheel ['kæθrɪn] *or* ['kæθərɪn] **1** *Heraldry.* a figure of a wheel with projecting spikes. **2** a firework that revolves while burning; pinwheel. ⟨< St. *Catherine* of Alexandria, condemned to torture on the wheel⟩

cath•e•ter ['kæθətər] *n.* a slender tube to be inserted into a passage or cavity of the body. A catheter is used to distend an anatomical passage, remove urine from the bladder, etc. ⟨< LL < Gk. *kathetēr* < *kata-* down + *hienai* send⟩

cath•e•ter•ize ['kæθətə,raɪz] *v.* **-ized, -iz•ing.** insert a catheter into. **—,cath•e•ter•i'za•tion,** *n.*

cath•ode ['kæθoud] *n.* **1** the positively charged electrode of a primary cell or storage battery. The cathode of a carbon-zinc dry cell is a mixture of manganese dioxide and carbon powder packed around a central carbon rod. See DRY CELL for picture. **2** the negative electrode of an electrolytic cell, through which electrons enter the cell. See ELECTROLYSIS for picture. **3** *Electronics.* the electrode that is the main source of electrons in a vacuum tube. See CATHODE-RAY TUBE for picture. ⟨< Gk. *kathodos* a way down < *kata-* down + *hodos* way⟩ **—ca'thod•ic** [kə'θɒdɪk], *adj.*

cathode ray a high-speed, invisible stream of electrons from the heated cathode of a vacuum tube.

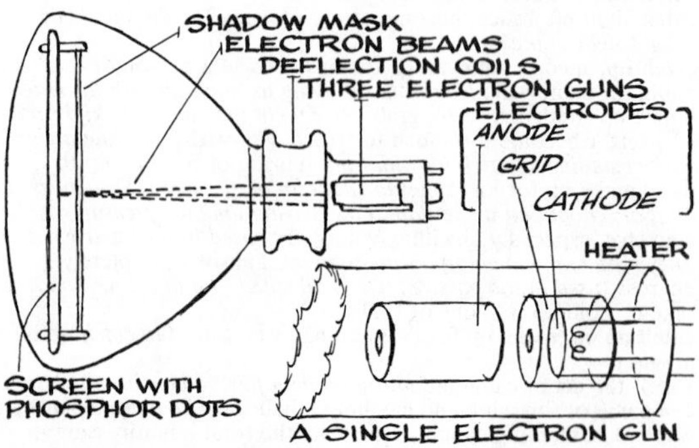

Cathode-ray tube: a colour television picture tube

cathode–ray tube a kind of tapered vacuum tube used in electronic equipment to display information. A cathode at the narrow end is heated to give off electrons, which are accelerated as a beam through a collector and strike a fluorescent screen at the other end, causing it to glow.

cath•o•lic ['kæθəlɪk] *or* ['kæθlɪk] *adj.* **1** very broad; general; all-inclusive; universal: *Music has a catholic appeal.* **2** having sympathies with all; broad-minded; liberal. **3** of the whole Christian church. ⟨< L *catholicus* < Gk. *katholikos* < *kata-* in respect to + *holos* whole⟩ **—'cath•o•li•cal•ly,** *adv.*

Cath•o•lic ['kæθəlɪk] *or* ['kæθlɪk] *n., adj. —n.* **1** a member of the Christian church that recognizes the Pope as its supreme temporal leader and whose tenets include belief in the factual truth of the gospel of Christ as recorded in the Bible and interpreted by the council of bishops together with the Pope, acceptance of seven sacraments (baptism, penance, Eucharist, confirmation, holy orders, matrimony, and extreme unction), and the doctrine of apostolic succession. **2** a member of any church that has its origins in or claims continuity with the ancient undivided Christian church. **3** a member of the ancient undivided Christian church.
—adj. of or having to do with any of these churches or with Catholicism.

Ca•thol•i•cism [kə'θɒlə,sɪzəm] *n.* **1** the faith, doctrine, organization, and practice of the Catholic Church. **2 catholicism,** catholicity.

cath•o•lic•i•ty [,kæθə'lɪsəti] *n.* **1** universality; wide appeal or application. **2** broad-mindedness; liberalness. **3 Catholicity,** the fact or quality of being Catholic.

ca•thol•i•cize [kə'θɒlə,saɪz] *v.* **-cized, -ciz•ing. 1** make or become catholic or universal. **2 Catholicize,** convert to the Roman Catholic Church.

cat•house ['kæt,hʌus] *n. Slang.* brothel.

cat•i•on ['kætaɪən] *n.* an ion having a positive charge. During electrolysis, cations move toward the cathode. See ELECTROLYSIS for picture. ⟨< Gk. *kation* going down < *kata-* down + *ienai* go⟩ **—,cat•i'on•ic** [-aɪ'ɒnɪk], *adj.*

cat•kin ['kætkɪn] *n.* the downy or scaly spike of the flowers of willows, poplars, birches, etc.; ament. ⟨< Du. *katteken* little cat⟩

cat•like ['kæt,ləik] *adj.* **1** like a cat. **2** noiseless; stealthy. **3** active; nimble.

cat•lin•ite ['kætlə,nəit] *n.* a smooth, hard, bright red clay, used by American Indian Prairie peoples for tobacco pipes. ⟨< George *Catlin* (1796-1872), an American artist + *ite*⟩

cat•mint ['kæt,mɪnt] *n. Esp. Brit.* catnip.

cat•nap ['kæt,næp] *n., v.* **-,napped, -nap•ping.** *—n.* a short nap or doze.
—v. take a catnap.

cat•nip ['kæt,nɪp] *n.* a plant (*Nepeta cataria*) of the mint family having scented leaves that cats like. ⟨< *cat* + *nip*, var. of *nep* catnip < L *nepeta*⟩

cat–o'–nine–tails [,kæt ə 'naɪn ,teilz] *n., pl.* **-tails.** a whip consisting of usually nine pieces of knotted cord fastened to a handle.

ca•top•trics [kə'tɒptrɪks] *n.* the branch of optics that deals with the reflection of light from mirrors. ⟨< Gk. *katoptrikos* < *katoptron* mirror < *kata-* down + *ops* eye, face⟩ **—ca'top•tric,** *adj.*

cat power *Cdn. Slang.* tracked work vehicles, such as bulldozers, Caterpillar tractors, etc.

cat rig a sailboat with one large sail on a mast close to the bow. **—'cat-,rigged,** *adj.*

CAT scan [kæt] **1** *Medicine.* an examination of the body, especially the brain, for diagnosis using COMPUTERIZED AXIAL TOMOGRAPHY. **2** the X-ray picture obtained from this process. **—CAT scanner.**

cat's cradle 1 a game in which a loop of string, stretched over the fingers in an intricate pattern, is passed from one player to another with the object of forming a new pattern each time. **2** something mixed up.

cat's–eye ['kæts,aɪ] *n.* **1** a gem showing beautiful changes of colour suggesting a cat's eye. **2** one of a row of small reflectors set on a road or curb to act as guides by catching the headlights of approaching vehicles. **3** a type of playing marble containing a green or blue swirl in the middle.

cat•skin•ner ['kæt,skɪnər] *n. Cdn.* a person who operates a Caterpillar tractor. ⟨< *Cat*erpillar + *skinner*, after *mule-skinner*⟩

cat's–paw or **cats•paw** ['kæts ,pɒ] *n.* **1** a person used by another to do something unpleasant or dangerous. **2** a light breeze that ruffles a small stretch of water. **3** a type of hitch or knot, used for attaching a tackle to a hook.

cat•sup ['kætsəp] *or* ['kɛtʃəp] *n.* ketchup.

cat–swing ['kæt ,swɪŋ] *n. Cdn.* CAT-TRAIN.

cat–tail or **cat•tail** ['kæt ,teil] *n.* any of a genus (*Typha*) of tall marsh plants having long, flat leaves, and flowers that form long, thick brown spikes; BULRUSH (def. 1). Cat-tails are often used as decoration.

cat•tal•lo ['kætə,lou] *n. Cdn.* an experimental cross between beef cattle and North American buffalo. Cattalo are usually sterile. Also, **catalo.** ⟨< *catt(le)* + *(buff)alo*⟩

cat•tish ['kætɪʃ] *adj.* **1** catlike. **2** catty. **—'cat•tish•ly,** *adv.* **—'cat•tish•ness,** *n.*

cat•tle ['kætəl] *n.* **1** domesticated bovine animals; cows, bulls, steers, or oxen. **2** *Archaic.* any farm animals; livestock. ⟨ME < OF *catel* < L *capitale* property, neut. of *capitalis.* Doublet of CAPITAL[1] and CHATTEL.⟩

cat•tle•man ['kætəlmən] *n., pl.* **-men.** a man who raises or takes care of cattle.

catt•le•ya ['kætliə] *n.* a tropical American orchid of the genus *Cattleya*, with large flowers. ⟨< NL, after Wm. *Cattley*, 19c. English horticulturist⟩

cat–train ['kæt ,trein] *n. Cdn.* a series of large sleds pulled by a Caterpillar tractor. Cat-trains are used in the North for hauling goods over the frozen muskeg in wintertime.

cat•ty ['kæti] *adj.* **-ti•er, -ti•est. 1** mean; spiteful. **2** of or like cats. **—'cat•ti•ly,** *adv.* **—'cat•ti•ness,** *n.*

cat•ty–cor•nered ['kæti ,kɔrnərd] *adj. or adv.* KITTY-CORNER. Also, **catty-corner.** ⟨alteration of *cater-cornered*⟩

cat•walk ['kæt,wɒk] *n.* a high, narrow place to walk, as on a bridge.

Cau•ca•sian [kɒ'keiʒən] *or* [kə'keiʒən] *n., adj. —n.* **1** a native or inhabitant of the Caucasus, a mountainous region in SE Europe between the Black and Caspian Seas. **2** Caucasoid. **3** either of two separate families of languages spoken in the Caucasus, including Circassian and Georgian.
—adj. **1** of or having to do with the Caucasus or its inhabitants. **2** Caucasoid. **3** of or in any of the Caucasian languages.

Cau•ca•soid ['kɒkə,sɔɪd] *adj., n. —adj.* describing one of the major groups of human beings that includes peoples of Europe, most of the Indian subcontinent, the Middle East, and N Africa.
—n. a member of this group.

cau•cus ['kɒkəs] *n., v. —n.* **1 a** in Canada, a meeting of the members of Parliament of one party to discuss policy, plan strategy, etc. **b** these members as a group, whether meeting or not. **2** in the United States, **a** a meeting of members or leaders of a political party to make plans, choose candidates, decide how to vote, etc. **b** the members attending such a meeting. **3** a committee within a political party, whose function is to determine party policy. **4** *Esp. Brit.* a faction within a political party, especially a powerful or semi-secret faction.
—v. hold a caucus. ⟨prob. from Algonquian; cf. Virginian *caucauasu* counsellor. Formerly thought to be from Med.L *caucus, caucum* drinking vessel < Med.Gk. *kaukos.* 18c.⟩
☛ *Hom.* COCCUS.

cau•dad ['kɒdæd] *adv. Anatomy, zoology.* toward the tail or rear. Compare CEPHALAD. ⟨< L *cauda* tail + *-ad* toward⟩

cau•dal ['kɒdəl] *adj.* **1** of, at, or near the tail. See SPINAL COLUMN for picture. **2** tail-like. ⟨< NL *caudalis* < L *cauda* tail⟩ **—'cau•dal•ly,** *adv.*
☛ *Hom.* CAUDLE, CODDLE.

cau•date ['kɒdeit] *adj.* having a tail. ⟨< NL *caudatus* < L *cauda* tail⟩

cau•dex ['kɒdɛks] *n.* **1** the stem of a perennial plant which survives until the next year. **2** the trunk of a tree or shrub. ⟨< L, tree trunk, log⟩

cau•dil•lo [kɒ'diljou]; *Spanish,* [kaʊ'ðiljo] *n.* a leader or head of state, especially a military one. ⟨< Sp. < L *capitellum* little head⟩

cau•dle ['kɒdəl] *n.* formerly, a warm drink for sick people; gruel sweetened and flavoured with wine, ale, spices, etc. ⟨< ONF *caudel* < L *calidus* warm⟩
☛ *Hom.* CAUDAL, CODDLE.

Caugh•na•waugh•a [,kɒknə'wɒgə] *n., pl.* **-waugh•a** or **-waugh•as.** a member of the Mohawk nation living on the Caughnawaugha Reserve on the south shore of the St. Lawrence opposite Montréal. Also, **Kahnawake.**

caught [kɒt] *v.* pt. and pp. of CATCH.
☛ *Hom.* COT .

caul [kɒl] *n.* **1** a portion of the membrane enclosing a child in the womb that is sometimes found clinging to the head at birth. It was supposed to be a good omen, especially against drowning. **2** the fold of the peritoneum stretching from the stomach to the large intestine; great omentum. ⟨ME *calle,* perhaps < OF *cale* a little cap⟩
☛ *Hom.* CALL, COL.

caul•dron or **cal•dron** ['kɒldrən] *n.* **1** a large kettle or boiler. **2** anything thought to resemble a boiling cauldron or its bubbling contents: *a cauldron of political intrigue and unrest.* ⟨ME *caudron* < ONF < LL *caldaria* pot for boiling (L *calidus* warm)⟩

cau•li•flow•er ['kɒli,flaʊər] *n.* **1** a garden plant (*Brassica oleracea botrytis*) that is a variety of cabbage, having a tightly set flower cluster that forms a solid, white head with a few leaves around it. **2** the head itself, eaten raw as in salads, or cooked as a vegetable. ⟨half-translation of NL *cauliflora* < *caulis* cabbage + *flos, floris* flower⟩

cauliflower ear an ear that has been misshapen by injuries received in boxing, etc.

cau•lis ['kɒlɪs] *n.* the main stem of a plant. ⟨< L < Gk *kaulos* stalk⟩

caulk[1] [kɒk] *v.* **1** fill up (a seam, crack, or joint) to make it watertight or airtight: *to caulk the seams of a boat, to caulk the cracks in a window frame.* **2** fill up the seams, cracks, or joints of (something) to make leakproof: *to caulk a boat, to caulk a window.* Sometimes, **calk.** ⟨< OF *cauquer* < L *calcare* tread, press in⟩ **—'caulk•er,** *n.*
☛ *Hom.* COCK.

caulk[2] [kɒk] *n., v.* *—n.* **1** a projecting piece on a horseshoe that catches in the ground or ice and prevents slipping. **2** one of a number of sharp spikes set into the sole of a boot or shoe or into a metal plate fitted over the sole to prevent slipping. **3** a metal plate studded with caulks and fastened to a boot or shoe. **4** a boot or shoe with caulks, worn especially by loggers, etc.
—v. **1** provide or fit with caulks: *caulked boots.* **2** wound with a caulk. Also, **calk.** ⟨< L *calx* heel or *calcar* spur⟩
☛ *Hom.* COCK.

caulk•ing ['kɒkɪŋ] *n., v.* *—n.* a soft, puttylike compound used to CAULK[1] things.
—v. ppr. of CAULK.

caus•a•ble ['kɒzəbəl] *adj.* capable of being caused.

caus•al ['kɒzəl] *adj.* **1** of, having to do with, or being a cause. **2** involving or having to do with cause and effect. **3** *Grammar.* showing a cause or reason. **Because** is a causal conjunction. **—'caus•al•ly,** *adv.*

cau•sal•gia [kɒ'zældʒiə] *or* [kɒ'zældʒə] *n.* a neuralgia characterized by severe burning pain in certain nerves, often of the hands and arms. ⟨< NL < Gk. *kausos* fever + *algos* pain⟩

cau•sal•i•ty [kɒ'zæləti] *n., pl.* **-ties. 1** the relation between cause and effect. **2** the principle that nothing happens or exists without a cause. **3** the fact or condition of being a cause.

cau•sa•tion [kɒ'zeiʃən] *n.* **1** a causing or being caused. **2** whatever produces an effect; cause or causes. **3** causality.

caus•a•tive ['kɒzətɪv] *adj., n.* *—adj.* **1** being a cause; productive. **2** *Grammar.* expressing causation. In *enrich, en-* is a causative prefix.
—n. Grammar. a causative form. **—'caus•a•tive•ly,** *adv.* **—'caus•a•tive•ness,** *n.*

cause [kɒz] *n., v.* **caused, caus•ing.** *—n.* **1** whatever produces an effect; a person or thing that makes something happen: *The flood was the cause of much damage.* **2** an occasion for action; reason; ground; motive: *cause for celebration.* **3** a good reason; reason enough: *He was angry without cause.* **4** a goal or movement in which people are interested and to which they give their support: *World peace is the cause she works for.* **5** *Law.* a matter for a court to decide; lawsuit.
make common cause with, join efforts with; side with; help and support.
—v. produce as an effect; make happen or do; bring about: *What caused the fire?* ⟨< L *causa*⟩ **—'caus•er,** *n.*
☛ *Syn. n.* **2, 3.** See note at REASON.

cause cé•lè•bre ['kouz sei'lɛbrə] *or* ['kɒz sə'lɛb]; *French,* [kozse'lɛbʀ] *French.* **1** *Law.* a famous case. **2** a notorious case or incident.

cause•less ['kɒzlɪs] *adj.* **1** without any known cause; happening by chance. **2** without good reason; not having reason enough. **—'cause•less•ly,** *adv.*

cau•se•rie [,kouzə'ri] *n.* **1** an informal talk or discussion; chat. **2** a short written article. ⟨< F *causerie* < *causer* chat⟩

cause•way ['kɒz,wei] *n., v.* *—n.* a long, raised road or path, usually built across wet ground or shallow water.
—v. **1** provide with a causeway. **2** pave with cobbles or pebbles. ⟨var. of dialect or archaic *causey* (influenced by *way*) < ME *cauci* < ONF *caucie* < LL *calciata* paved way < L *calx* limestone⟩

caus•tic ['kɒstɪk] *n., adj.* *—n.* a substance that burns or eats away by chemical action; corrosive substance.
—adj. **1** able to burn or eat away by chemical action; corrosive. Lye is caustic soda or caustic potash. **2** sarcastic; stinging; biting: *The director's caustic remarks made the actors very angry.* ⟨< L *causticus* < Gk. *kaustikos*⟩ **—'caus•ti•cal•ly,** *adv.*

caustic potash POTASSIUM HYDROXIDE.

caustic soda a brittle, white alkaline compound used in bleaching and in making soap, rayon, paper, etc.; sodium hydroxide. *Formula:* NaOH

cau•ter•i•za•tion [,kɒtərə'zeiʃən] *or* [,kɒtəraɪ'zeiʃən] *n.* **1** the act of cauterizing or the state of being cauterized. **2** a cauterized place.

cau•ter•ize ['kɒtə,raɪz] *v.* **-ized, -iz•ing.** destroy (defective tissue) or seal (a wound) by burning with heat or a chemical agent: *Doctors often remove warts by cauterizing them.*

cau•ter•y ['kɒtəri] *n., pl.* **-ter•ies. 1** cauterization. **2** an instrument or substance used in cauterizing. ⟨< L *cauterium* < Gk. *kautērion,* dim. of *kautēr* branding iron⟩

cau•tion ['kɒʃən] *n., v.* *—n.* **1** the practice of taking care to be safe, or of never taking chances; a being very careful: *Use caution in crossing streets.* **2** a warning: *A sign with 'Danger' on it is a caution.* **3** *Law.* a formal warning to an accused person that anything he or she says may be used as evidence against him or her. **4** *Informal.* a person or thing that is amusing, unusual, startling, etc.
—v. **1** warn; urge to be careful. **2** *Law.* warn (an accused person) that anything he or she says may be used as evidence against him or her. ⟨ME < OF < L *cautio, -onis* < *cavere* beware⟩ **—'cau•tion•er,** *n.*
☛ *Syn. v.* See note at WARN.

cau•tion•ar•y ['kɒʃə,nɛri] *adj.* warning; urging care.

cau•tious ['kɒʃəs] *adj.* very careful; taking care to be safe; never taking chances: *a cautious driver.* **—'cau•tious•ly,** *adv.* **—'cau•tious•ness,** *n.*
☛ *Syn.* See note at CAREFUL.

cav•al•cade ['kævəl,keid] *or* [,kævəl'keid] *n.* **1** a procession of persons riding on horses, in carriages, or in automobiles. **2** a series of scenes or events: *a cavalcade of sports.* ⟨< F < Ital. *cavalcata* < *cavalcare* ride horseback < LL *caballicare* < L *caballus* horse⟩

cav•a•lier [,kævə'lir] *or* ['kævə,lir] *n., adj.* *—n.* **1** a courteous gentleman, especially a lady's escort. **2** *Archaic.* a horseman, especially a mounted soldier or knight. **3 Cavalier,** a supporter of Charles I in his struggle with Parliament (1641-1649).
—adj. **1** too free and easy; careless in manner; offhand: *a cavalier disregard for danger.* **2** haughty and arrogant; supercilious. **3 Cavalier, a** of or having to do with the supporters of Charles I in his struggle with Parliament. **b** of, having to do with, or designating a group of English lyric poets of the 17th century, most of whom were associated with the court of Charles I. ⟨< F < Ital. *cavalliere* < *cavallo* horse < L *caballus* horse⟩ **—,cav•a'lier•ly,** *adv.* **—,cav•a'lier•ness,** *n.*

cav•al•ry ['kævəlri] *n., pl.* **-ries. 1** the branch of an army made up of troops trained to fight on horseback or, in recent times, in armoured vehicles. **2** (*adjl.*) of, having to do with, or belonging to the cavalry. ⟨< F *cavalerie* < Ital. *cavalleria* knighthood < *cavalliere.* See CAVALIER.⟩

cav•al•ry•man ['kævəlrimən] *n., pl.* **-men.** a cavalry soldier.

cav•a•ti•na [,kævə'tinə] *n.* **1** *Music.* a short, simple song; melody; air. **2** a lyrical, non-vocal composition. ⟨< Ital.⟩

cave [keiv] *n., v.* **caved, cav•ing.** *—n.* a hollow space underground, often having an opening in the side of a hill or cliff.
—v. **1** form a cave in or under; hollow out. **2** take part in the sport or pastime of exploring caves.
cave in, a fall in or down; collapse: *The weight of the snow caused the roof of the arena to cave in.* **b** cause to fall in or down; smash. **c** *Informal.* yield completely; give in to an argument, strain, or hardship. ⟨ME < OF < L *cava* hollow (places)⟩ **—'cave,like,** *adj.*

ca•ve•at ['kævi,æt] *or* ['keivi,æt] *n.* **1** a warning. **2** *Law.* a notice given to a law officer or some legal authority not to do something until the person giving notice can be heard. ⟨< L *caveat* let (him) beware⟩

caveat emp•tor ['ɛmptɔr] *Latin.* let the buyer beware; you buy at your own risk.

cave dweller 1 a person who lived in a cave in prehistoric times. 2 any person who lives in a cave.

cave•in ['keiv,ɪn] *n.* 1 a falling-in, or collapse, of a mine, tunnel, etc. 2 the site of such a collapse.

cave man 1 CAVE DWELLER. 2 *Informal.* a rough, crude man who treats women without respect.

cav•en•dish ['kævəndɪʃ] *n.* leaf tobacco that has been softened, sweetened with molasses, and pressed into cakes. ⟨origin uncertain⟩

cav•er ['keivər] *n.* one who explores caves as a hobby or scientific activity; spelunker.

cav•ern ['kævərn] *n.* a large cave. ⟨ME < MF *caverne* < L *caverna* < *cavus* hollow⟩

cav•ern•ous ['kævərnəs] *adj.* 1 like or characteristic of a cavern; large, dark, hollow, etc.: *a cavernous doorway, cavernous eyes.* 2 full of caverns: *cavernous mountains.* 3 full of small holes; porous. **—'cav•ern•ous•ly,** *adv.*

ca•vet•to [kə'vɛtou] *n. Architecture.* a concave moulding whose side view is a quarter circle. ⟨< Ital. dim. of *cavo* hollow < L *cavus*⟩

cav•i•ar or **cav•i•are** ['kævi,ɑr] *or* [,kævi'ɑr] *n.* a salty relish made from the eggs of sturgeon or other large fish.
caviar to the general, too good a thing to be appreciated by ordinary people. ⟨< F < Ital. < Turkish *khaviar*⟩

ca•vi•corn ['kævə,kɔrn] *adj.* having hollow as distinct from bony horns: *Cattle and sheep are cavicorn.* ⟨< L *cavus* hollow + *cornu* horn⟩

cav•il ['kævəl] *v.* **-illed** or **-iled, -il•ling** or **-il•ing;** *n.* *—v.* find fault unnecessarily; raise trivial objections.
—n. a petty objection; trivial criticism. ⟨< F < L *cavillari* jeer⟩ **—'cav•il•ler** or **'cav•il•er,** *n.*

cav•ing ['keivɪŋ] *n.* the sport or pastime of exploring caves; spelunking.

ca•vi•ta•tion [,kævɪ'teiʃən] *n.* the formation and collapse of vapour pockets in flowing liquid, caused by a vacuum created by mechanical force. It causes damage to propellers, etc.: *Cavitation occurs when the speed of a propeller blade, or a hydrofoil, reaches a point where it leaves a cavity in the water.*

cav•i•ty ['kævəti] *n., pl.* **-ties.** 1 a hole; hollow place: *a cavity in a wall.* 2 an enclosed space inside the body: *the abdominal cavity, the four cavities of the heart.* 3 a hole in a tooth, caused by decay: *Too much sugar can cause cavities.* ⟨< F *cavité* < LL *cavitas* < L *cavus* hollow⟩
☛ *Syn.* See note at HOLE.

ca•vort [kə'vɔrt] *v. Informal.* prance about; jump around in a frisky way: *The colt cavorted in the pasture.* ⟨origin uncertain⟩

CAVU *Aeronautics.* ceiling and visibility unlimited.

ca•vy ['keivi] *n., pl.* **-vies.** any of a small family (Caviidae) of mostly rat-sized South American rodents having a very short tail and rough grey or brown hair; especially, any of the genus *Cavia,* which includes the guinea pig. ⟨< NL *Cavia* < Galibi (a Carib language) *cabiai*⟩

caw [kɒ] *or* [kɑ] *n., v. —n.* the harsh cry made by a crow or raven.
—v. make this cry. ⟨imitative⟩

cay [kei] *or* [ki] *n.* a low island; reef; KEY². ⟨< Sp. *cayo* shoal, rock⟩
☛ *Hom.* KEY [ki], QUAY [ki].

cay•enne [kaɪ'ɛn] *or* [kei'ɛn] *n.* RED PEPPER (def. 1). ⟨< *Cayenne,* French Guiana⟩

cay•man ['keimən] *n., pl.* **-mans.** a large alligator of tropical America. Also, **caiman.** ⟨< Sp. *caiman* < Carib⟩

Cay•man Islands ['keimən] a country of several islands in the Caribbean Sea.

Ca•yu•ga [kei'jugə] *or* [kaɪ'jugə] *n., adj. —n.* 1 a member of an American Indian people living mainly in New York state and, later, in Ontario. The Cayuga belonged to the Iroquois Confederacy. 2 the Iroquoian language of the Cayuga.
—adj. of or having to do with the Cayuga or their language.

cay•use [kaɪ'jus] *n.* **1 Cayuse,** a member of an American Indian people living in Oregon. **2 Cayuse,** their Senecan language. 3 in western Canada and the United States, an Indian pony. 4 in NW U.S., a cold easterly wind.

Cb columbium.

CB CITIZENS' BAND. See also GENERAL RADIO SERVICE.

C.B. 1 Cape Breton. 2 Companion of (the Order of) the Bath. 3 Confined to Barracks.

CBC the Canadian Broadcasting Corporation.

C.B.E. Commander of (the Order of) the British Empire.

CBT *Computer technology.* computer-based training.

cc or **c.c.** 1 cubic centimetre(s). Now written cm³. 2 CARBON COPY.

CC *Cdn.* Companion of (the Order of) Canada.

C.C. or **CC** CANADA COUNCIL.

C.C.A. 1 Canadian Conference of the Arts. 2 Canadian Council for Architecture.

CCF or **C.C.F.** a Canadian political party established in 1932. It joined with the Canadian Labour Congress to form the New Democratic Party in 1961. The name CCF is an abbreviation for Co-operative Commonwealth Federation.

CCG Canadian Coast Guard.

C clef *Music.* a symbol that means that the line on which it is placed represents middle C.

cd candela.

cd. cord(s).

Cd cadmium.

C.D. or **CD** 1 Civil Defence. 2 Canadian (Forces) Decoration. 3 COMPACT DISC. 4 CERTIFICATE OF DEPOSIT.

CDC Canada Development Corporation.

cd.ft. CORD FOOT; cord feet.

Cdn. Canadian.

cDNA COMPLEMENTARY DNA.

Cdn. Fr. CANADIAN FRENCH.

Cdr. or **Cdr** commander.

CD–ROM ['si di 'rɒm] *Computer technology.* compact disc–read-only memory.

CDS *Cdn.* Chief of the Defence Staff.

Ce cerium.

C.E. 1 CIVIL ENGINEER. Also, **CE.** 2 CHURCH OF ENGLAND. 3 chief engineer. 4 chemical engineer. 5 COMMON ERA or CHRISTIAN ERA (*used to indicate years* A.D.).

CE 1 CANADIAN ENGLISH. 2 CIVIL ENGINEER.

cease [sis] *v., n. —v.* **ceased, ceas•ing.** 1 come to an end: *The music ceased suddenly.* 2 put an end to: *They have ceased their endeavours. Cease your complaining. The plant in Burlington will cease production on Tuesday.*
—n. Archaic. ceasing; cessation.
without cease, without ceasing; continuously: *It rained for hours without cease.* ⟨ME < OF < L *cessare*⟩
☛ *Syn.* See note at STOP.

cease–fire ['sis ,faɪr] *n.* the formal cessation of combat between opposing armed forces, especially for a specified period of time in order to remove the dead and wounded, discuss peace, etc.

cease•less ['sislɪs] *adj.* never stopping; going on all the time; continual: *the ceaseless noise of distant traffic.* **—'cease•less•ly,** *adv.* **—'cease•less•ness,** *n.*

ce•cro•pi•a moth [sə'kroupiə] a large, colourful silkworm moth (*Samia cecropia*) of E North America having a wingspan of over 15 cm. ⟨< NL *Cecropia,* a type of mulberry⟩

ce•cum ['sikəm] See CAECUM.

ce•dar ['sidər] *n.* 1 any of a genus (*Cedrus*) of North African and Asian evergreen trees of the pine family having long cones and short, sharp needles growing in flat spirals. The best known of these trees is the **cedar of Lebanon,** which often appears in art and literature as a symbol of power and long life. 2 any of various other trees, especially of the cypress family, such as arborvitae and junipers. 3 the durable, fragrant, usually reddish wood of any of these trees. Most kinds of cedar are insect repellent and resistant to decay. 4 (*adjl.*) made of cedar: *a cedar chest.* ⟨ME < OF *cedre* < L < Gk. *kedros*⟩
☛ *Hom.* SEEDER.

cedar canoe *Cdn.* a light, seaworthy canoe made of cedar and capable of carrying a sail.

cedar chest a chest made of cedar wood, in which one stores woollens and furs to protect them against moths.

cedar waxwing a North American waxwing (*Bombycilla cedrorum*) found throughout most of the continent, smaller than the bohemian waxwing and having mainly cinnamon brown upper parts and yellowish under parts.

cede [sid] *v.* **ced•ed, ced•ing. 1** surrender; hand over to another: *In 1763, France ceded Canada to Britain.* **2** concede; admit the validity of: *His argument was so convincing that I ceded the point.* ⟨< L *cedere* yield⟩
☛ *Hom.* SEED.

ce•di ['seidi] *n.* **1** the basic unit of money in Ghana, divided into 100 pesewas. See table of money in the Appendix. **2** a note worth one cedi.

ce•dil•la [sə'dɪlə] *n.* a mark resembling a comma put under *c* (ç) before *a*, *o*, or *u* in certain words borrowed from French to show that it has the sound of *s*. *Example*: *façade.* ⟨< Sp. *cedilla*, dim. of *ceda* < L *zeta*, the letter *z* < Gk.⟩

C.E.F. Canadian Expeditionary Force (World War I).

cef- or **ceph-** *combining form.* used to form names of compounds belonging to the cephalosporin group of antibiotics.

CEGEP [sei'ʒɛp] *French.* Collège d'Enseignement Général et Professionel (General and Vocational College).

ceiba ['seibə] *or* ['sibə] *n.* any of several silk-cotton trees (genus *Ceiba*) found in tropical climates. ⟨< NL < Sp.⟩

ceil [sil] *v.* **1** put a ceiling in. **2** cover the ceiling of. ⟨? < F *ciel* canopy, sky < L *caelum* heaven⟩
☛ *Hom.* SEAL.

cei•lidh ['keili] *n.* an informal social gathering featuring traditional Scottish or Irish stories, songs, and dances. ⟨< Gaelic⟩

ceil•ing ['silɪŋ] *n.*, *v.* —*n.* **1** the inside, top covering of a room; the surface opposite the floor. **2** the greatest height to which an aircraft can go under certain conditions. **3** the distance between the earth and the lowest clouds. **4** an upper limit: *A ceiling was placed on the amount of rent landlords could charge.*
hit the ceiling, *Slang.* react with a strong burst of anger: *When she saw the repair bill she hit the ceiling.*
—*v.* ppr. of CEIL. ⟨< *ceil*⟩

ceil•om•e•ter [si'lɒmətər] *or* [sɪ'lɒmətər] *n.* a device for reckoning the height of clouds, using a beam of light.

cel•a•don ['sɛlə,dɒn] *or* ['sɛlədən] *n.* **1** a delicate greyish green colour. **2 a** a glaze of this colour. **b** pottery with this glaze. ⟨< F *céladon* pale green, after Céladon, principal character in *Astree* by H. D'urfe (1610) < L after character in Ovid's *Metamorphoses*⟩

cel•an•dine ['sɛlən,daɪn] *or* ['sɛlən,din] *n.* **1** a biennial herb (*Chelidonium majus*) of the poppy family having yellow flowers. **2** the **lesser celandine,** a perennial herb (*Ranunculus ficaria*) of the buttercup family native to Europe but now naturalized in North America. ⟨ME < OF *celidoine* < L < Gk. *chelidonion* < *chelidōn* swallow[2]⟩

cel•e•brant ['sɛləbrənt] *n.* **1** a person who performs a ceremony or rite. **2** a priest who performs Mass. **3** anyone who celebrates; celebrator.

cel•e•brate ['sɛlə,breit] *v.* **-brat•ed, -brat•ing. 1** observe (a special time or day) with the proper ceremonies or festivities: *to celebrate Christmas. On her birthday she was too sick to celebrate.* **2** perform publicly with the proper ceremonies and rites: *The priest celebrates Mass in church.* **3** make known publicly; proclaim. **4** praise; honour: *to celebrate the glory of nature.* **5** have a joyful time; make merry: *The people celebrated when the war ended.* ⟨< L *celebrare*⟩ **—'cel•e•bra•tive,** *adj.* **—'cel•e,bra•tor,** *n.* **—'cel•e•bra,to•ry,** *adj.*

cel•e•brat•ed ['sɛlə,breitɪd] *adj.*, *v.* —*adj.* famous; well-known; much talked about: *a celebrated author.*
—*v.* pt. and pp. of CELEBRATE.

cel•e•bra•tion [,sɛlə'breiʃən] *n.* **1** the act of celebrating. **2** whatever is done to celebrate something: *A Canada Day celebration often includes a display of fireworks.* **3** a performance of a solemn ceremony: *the celebration of the Mass.*

ce•leb•ri•ty [sə'lɛbrəti] *n.*, *pl.* **-ties. 1** a famous person; a person who is well-known or much talked about. **2** fame; being well-known or much talked about.

ce•ler•i•ac [sə'lɛri,æk] *n.* **1** a variety of celery (*Apium graveolens rapaceum*) cultivated for its edible, bulblike root. **2** the root itself, eaten raw or cooked as a vegetable.

ce•ler•i•ty [sə'lɛrəti] *n.* swiftness; speed. ⟨ME < OF < L *celeritas* < *celer* swift⟩

cel•er•y ['sɛləri] *or* ['sɛlri] *n.* **1** a biennial herb (*Apium graveolens*) of the carrot family having long, crisp, pale green stalks with leaves at the top; especially, a cultivated variety (*A. graveolens dulce*). **2** the stalks of this plant, eaten raw or cooked as a vegetable. ⟨< F *céleri* < dial. Ital. < L < Gk. *selinon* parsley⟩

celery salt a seasoning made of salt mixed with ground celery seed.

ce•les•ta [sə'lɛstə] *n.* a musical instrument with a keyboard, the bell-like tones being made by hammers hitting steel plates. Also, **celeste** [-'lɛst]. ⟨< F < L *caelestis* heavenly < *caelum* heaven⟩

ce•les•tial [sə'lɛstʃəl] *adj.*, *n.* —*adj.* **1** of or having to do with the sky or the heavens. The sun, moon, planets, and stars are celestial bodies. **2** heavenly; divine; very good or beautiful: *celestial music.* **3 Celestial,** of the Chinese people or the former Chinese Empire. **Celestial Empire** is a translation of a Chinese name for the empire.
—*n.* a heavenly being. ⟨ME < OF *celestiel* < L *caelestis* heavenly < *caelum* heaven⟩ **—ce'les•tial•ly,** *adv.*

celestial equator *Astronomy.* the imaginary great circle that represents the intersection of the plane of the earth's equator with the celestial sphere. See ECLIPTIC for picture.

celestial globe *Astronomy.* a globe indicating the position of the heavenly bodies, similar to a globe of the earth showing the geography of continents, oceans, etc.

celestial latitude *Astronomy.* the angular distance of a heavenly body from the nearest point on the ecliptic.

celestial longitude *Astronomy.* the angular distance of a point on the celestial sphere from a point where the star, the ecliptic, and the great circle intersect.

celestial navigation *Astronomy.* a method of navigation in which the position of a ship or an aircraft is calculated from the position of heavenly bodies.

celestial pole *Astronomy.* each of the two points on the celestial sphere at which the earth's axis, if extended, would intersect, and about which the stars seem to rotate.

celestial sphere *Astronomy.* the imaginary sphere that apparently encloses the universe, of a size approaching infinity. See ECLIPTIC and NADIR for pictures.

cel•es•tite ['sɛlə,staɪt] *n.* a mineral, strontium sulphate, occurring in white or sometimes blue crystals, the chief ore of strontium. *Formula*: $SrSO_4$ ⟨< L *caelestis* celestial (because of its blueness) + E *-ite*⟩

ce•li•ac ['sili,æk] *adj.* **1** of or having to do with the abdominal cavity. **2** of or suffering from CELIAC DISEASE. Also, **coeliac.** ⟨< L *coeliacus* < Gk. *koiliakos* < *koilia* bowels, belly < *koilos* hollow⟩

celiac disease a chronic intestinal disorder usually of childhood, resulting in diarrhea, swelling of the abdomen, etc.

cel•i•ba•cy ['sɛləbəsi] *n.*, *pl.* **-cies. 1** the state of being unmarried, especially because of religious vows. **2** habitual abstinence from sexual intercourse.

cel•i•bate ['sɛləbɪt] *or* ['sɛlə,beit] *n.* **1** an unmarried person, especially one who takes a vow to remain single. **2** one who habitually abstains from sexual intercourse.
—*adj.* being a celibate. ⟨< L *caelibatus* < *caelebs* unmarried⟩

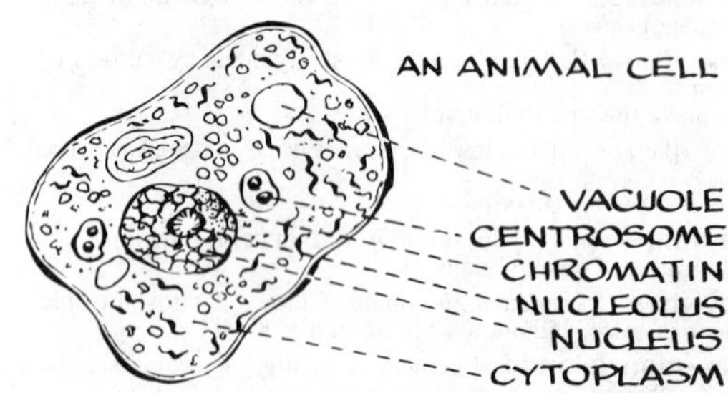

cell [sɛl] *n.* **1** a small room in a prison, convent, or monastery. **2** a convent or monastery annexed to a larger one. **3** the small dwelling of a hermit. **4** a small, hollow place: *Bees store honey in the cells of a honeycomb.* **5** *Biology.* the smallest structural unit of living matter that can function independently. Most cells consist of protoplasm, have a nucleus near the centre, and are enclosed by a cell wall or membrane. Plants and animals are made of cells. **6 a** a device for producing electricity by chemical means, consisting of one positive and one negative electrode immersed in an electrolyte. **b** a division of a storage battery. **7** Often, **cell group,** a small group that acts as the basic unit of an organization, especially a revolutionary political movement or a

large religious congregation. **8** a group of people who are the subjects of research, as in sociology, sociolinguistics, etc. Samples of subjects are divided into cells on the basis of specific characteristics, e.g., age, sex, etc. **9** a small enclosed receptacle or cavity in an organism or tissue. **10** *Computer technology.* **a** in a spreadsheet, the intersection of a row and column, where a single entry (number, label, formula, etc.) is stored. **b** a unit of computer memory in which a single data item can be stored. ⟨< L *cella* small room⟩
☛ *Hom.* SELL.

cel•la ['sɛlə] *n.* in an ancient Greek or Roman temple, an inner room housing a statue of the god or goddess. ⟨See CELL.⟩

cel•lar ['sɛlər] *n., v. —n.* **1** an underground room or space, usually under a building, used for storing food, fuel, etc. **2** such a room for wines. **3** a supply of wines.
—v. put into a cellar; store as if in a cellar. ⟨ME *celer* < OF *celier* < L *cellarium* < *cella* small room⟩
☛ *Hom.* SELLER.

cel•lar•age ['sɛlərɪdʒ] *n.* **1** the space in a cellar. **2** cellars. **3** a charge for storage in a cellar.

cel•lar•er ['sɛlərər] *n.* a person who takes care of a cellar and the food or wines in it.

cel•lar•et [,sɛlə'rɛt] *n.* a cabinet for wine bottles, glasses, etc.

cel•lar•man ['sɛlərmən] *n., pl.* **-men. 1** a man in charge of or employed in a cellar, especially a wine cellar. **2** a wine merchant.

cel•lar•way ['sɛlər,wei] *n.* an outside entrance to a cellar, consisting of steps leading to a cellar door.

cell block an individual building of cells in a prison.

cell body the nucleus of a neuron. See NEURON for picture.

cell culture the process of growing living cells in the laboratory under controlled conditions, for use in research. See also TISSUE CULTURE.

cell cycle the sequence of events from one cell division to the next.

cell division the division of a living cell to form two daughter cells. See MEIOSIS, MITOSIS.

cel•list or **'cel•list** ['tʃɛlɪst] *n.* a person who plays the cello, especially a skilled player.

cell lineage cells derived from a progenitor cell by repeated cell division and differentiation.

cell•mate ['sɛl,meit] *n.* one who shares a prison cell.

cell membrane the thin membrane that forms the outer wall of the protoplasm of a cell; plasma membrane.

cel•lo or **'cel•lo** ['tʃɛlou] *n., pl.* **-los.** the second largest instrument of the modern violin family, much larger than the violin and having a lower, mellow tone. When a cello is played it rests upright on the floor and is held between the knees of the player, who is seated. ⟨shortened form of *violoncello*⟩

A cello

cel•loi•din [sə'lɔɪdɪn] *n.* a concentrated, soft form of pyroxylin used to embed specimens to be looked at under a microscope.

cel•lo•phane ['sɛlə,fein] *n.* a shiny, transparent substance made from cellulose in the form of thin sheets. It is used especially for packaging foods, candy, tobacco, etc. ⟨< *cell(ul)o(se)* + Gk. *phanein* appear⟩

cellophane noodle a long, clear noodle used in Oriental cooking.

cell plate a sheet of cellulose that forms in a plant cell near the end of cellular division, separating the two new cells.

cell theory a theory in biology which states that all living organisms consist of cells, that the cell is the basic unit of structure, and that all cells come from other cells.

cel•lu•lar ['sɛljələr] *adj.* **1** having to do with cells. **2** consisting of cells: *All animal and plant tissue is cellular.* **3** of or involving CELLULAR RADIO.

cellular radio a telecommunication system that allows moving vehicles to send and receive messages.

cellular telephone a telephone using radio frequencies to send messages in small areas called cells. The frequency needed

in moving from one cell to another is obtained with no interruption: *She has a cellular telephone in her car.*

cel•lule ['sɛljul] *n.* a tiny cell. ⟨< L *cellula*, dim. of *cella* small room⟩

cel•lu•lite ['sɛljə,lait] *n.* adipose deposits on the hips and buttocks. ⟨< F *cellulitis*⟩

cel•lu•loid ['sɛljə,lɔɪd] *n.* **1** a hard, transparent, combustible substance made from cellulose nitrate and camphor, used now for eyeglass frames, photographic film, etc. Celluloid was the first plastic to be widely used commercially; it has now been largely replaced by less flammable plastics. **2 Celluloid.** *Trademark.* a brand of this substance. **3** (*adjl.*) made of celluloid. **4** movie film or movies collectively. **5** (*adjl.*) of or having to do with films. ⟨< *cellul(ose)* + *-oid*⟩

cel•lu•lose ['sɛljə,lous] *n.* a polymeric carbohydrate that is the chief constituent of the walls of plant cells and of plant fibres. It is used extensively in the manufacture of paper, plastics, textiles, explosives, etc. *Formula*: $(C_6H_{10}O_5)_n$ ⟨< L *cellula* small cell⟩
—,cel•lu'lo•sic, *adj.*

cellulose acetate any of several compounds produced by the action of acetic acid and sulphuric acid on cellulose, used in making textile fibres, lacquers, photographic film, etc.

cellulose nitrate a nitric acid ester of cellulose; a group of compounds made by treating cellulose (wood, linen, cotton, etc.) with a mixture of nitric acid and sulphuric acid. It is used for manufacturing plastics, lacquers or varnishes, explosives, etc.

cel•lu•lous ['sɛljələs] *adj.* **1** full of cells. **2** made of cells.

cell wall the hard, transparent outer covering of a plant cell, made up mostly of cellulose and surrounding the cell membrane.

ce•lom ['siləm] See COELOM.

ce•lo•sia [sə'louʃə] *or* [sə'lousiə] *n.* a plant of the genus *Celosia*, having small red or yellow flowers in spikes; cockscomb. ⟨< NL apparently derived irregularly from Gk. *keleos* burning⟩

Celsius ['sɛlsiəs] *or* ['sɛlʃəs] *adj.* of, based on, or according to a scale for measuring temperature, in which 0 degrees is the temperature at which water freezes and 100 degrees is the temperature at which water boils under normal atmospheric pressure. A **Celsius thermometer** is a thermometer marked off according to this scale. *Symbol*: C See THERMOMETER for picture. ⟨after Anders *Celsius* (1701-1744), a Swedish astronomer, who invented it⟩

celt [sɛlt] *n.* a prehistoric stone or metal tool shaped like an axe head with a bevelled edge. ⟨< NL *celtes* chisel⟩

Celt [kɛlt] *or* [sɛlt] *n.* **1** a member of an ancient people of W Europe and the British Isles, including the Britons and Gauls. **2** a descendant of one of these peoples. The Irish, most Highland Scots, Welsh, and Bretons are Celts. Also, **Kelt.** ⟨< L *Celtae*, pl. < Gk. *Keltoi*⟩

Celt•ic ['kɛltɪk] *or* ['sɛltɪk] *adj., n. —adj.* of the Celts or their language.
—n. a group of Indo-European languages, including Irish and Scots Gaelic, Manx, Welsh, Breton, and Cornish. Also, **Keltic.**

Celtic cross a cross having a circle or circles intersecting the four arms. The design is of Celtic origin. See CROSS for picture.

cel•tuce ['sɛltəs] *n.* a crisp, leafy type of lettuce (*Lactuca sativa asparagina*) that tastes like both lettuce and celery.

cem•ba•lo ['tʃɛmbə,lou] *n.* harpsichord. ⟨< Ital., harpsichord, cymbal < L *cymbalum*⟩

ce•ment [sə'mɛnt] *n., v. —n.* **1** a fine, grey powder made by burning clay and limestone. **2** this substance mixed with water and sand, gravel, or crushed stone to form concrete, used to make sidewalks, basement walls and floors, etc.: *Cement becomes hard like stone.* **3** any soft substance that hardens to make things stick together: *rubber cement.* **4** a substance used to fill cavities in teeth or to fasten fillings into them. **5** cementum. **6** anything that joins together or unites. **7** *Metallurgy.* sand, metal dust, or charcoal powder used in cementation.
—v. **1** fasten together with cement. **2** pour or spread concrete for: *to cement a sidewalk.* **3** join firmly; make firm: *The shared dangers cemented their friendship.* ⟨ME < OF *ciment* < L *caementum* chippings of stone < *caedere* cut⟩ **—ce'ment•er,** *n.*

ce•men•ta•tion [,simɛn'teiʃən] *n.* **1** a cementing or being cemented. **2** *Metallurgy.* the process of surrounding a solid with another material in powder form (the cement) and heating both together until they chemically combine into a new material. Steel is made by cementation of iron with charcoal powder.

ce•ment•ite [sə'mɛntəit] *n.* the iron carbide that strengthens steel and cast iron. *Formula*: Fe_3C

ce•ment•um [sə'mɛntəm] *n.* the bony tissue forming the outer crust of the root of a tooth.

cem•e•ter•y ['sɛmə,tɛri] *n., pl.* **-ter•ies.** a place for burying the dead; graveyard. ⟨< LL *coemeterium* < Gk. *koimētērion* < *koimaein* lull to sleep⟩

cen. central.

cen•a•cle ['sɛnəkəl] *n.* **1 Cenacle,** *Christianity.* the room in which the Last Supper was held. **2** any group of people meeting for a special purpose, as, writers, nuns, etc. ⟨< F *cénacle* < L *cenaculum* dining room < *cena* dinner < OL *cesnas*⟩

ce•no•bite ['sinə,bəit] *or* ['sɛnə,bəit] *n.* a member of a religious group living in a monastery or convent. Also, **coenobite.** ⟨< LL *coenobita* < *coenobium* < Gk. *koinobion* convent < *koinos* common + *bios* life⟩ **—'ce•no,bit•ism,** *n.*

ce•no•bit•ic [,sinə'bɪtɪk] *or* [,sɛnə'bɪtɪk] *adj.* **1** of or having to do with a cenobite. **2** living in community: *Monks in a monastery are cenobitic.*

ce•no•spe•cies ['sinou,spisiz] *or* [-,spiʃiz], ['sɛnou,spisiz] *or* [-,spiʃiz] *n. Genetics.* different species of animals or plants whose hybrids are fertile. ⟨< Gk. *koinos* common + E *species*⟩

cen•o•taph ['sɛnə,tæf] *n.* **1** a monument in memory of a dead person whose body is elsewhere. **2** a monument in memory of many dead persons, such as all those from one country, city, etc. killed in a war. ⟨< L *cenotaphium* < Gk. *kenotaphion* < *kenos* empty + *taphos* tomb⟩

Ce•no•zo•ic [,sinə'zouɪk] *or* [,sɛnə'zouɪk] *adj., n.* *—adj. Geology.* **1** of, having to do with, or designating the era extending from the end of the Mesozoic, about 63 million years ago, to the present time. The Cenozoic era is the age of mammals. See geological time chart in the Appendix. **2** of, having to do with, or designating the rock formed during this era.
—n. **the Cenozoic,** the Cenozoic era or its rock system. ⟨< Gk. *kainos* recent + *zoē* life⟩

cense [sɛns] *v.;* **censed, cens•ing.** burn incense in, on, or to.
☛ *Hom.* SENSE.

cen•ser ['sɛnsər] *n.* a container in which incense is burned. ⟨ME < OF *(en)censier,* ult. < L *incensum* incense⟩
☛ *Hom.* CENSOR, SENSOR.

cens et rentes [sɑ̃ze'ʀɑ̃t] *Cdn. French.* formerly, in New France and Lower Canada, a payment in cash (*cens*) and kind (*rentes*) to a seigneur in recognition of his rights. ⟨< Cdn.F⟩

cens•i•taire [sɑ̃zi'tɛʀ] *n. Cdn. French.* formerly, in French Canada, a habitant qualified to vote. ⟨< Cdn.F, payer of the *cens*⟩

cen•sor ['sɛnsər] *n., v.* *—n.* **1** a person authorized by a government or other organization to examine and, if necessary, change books, letters, motion pictures, etc., to ensure they contain nothing obscene, libellous, politically incorrect, or dangerous, etc. **2** in ancient Rome, a magistrate who took the census and supervised the conduct of citizens. **3** a person who exercises supervision over the morals or behaviour of others. **4** a person who likes to find fault. **5** in earlier psychoanalytic parlance, the part of the unconscious responsible for censorship.
—v. **1** examine as a censor, often making changes or cutting out parts: *All letters from the battlefront were censored.* **2** take out (a part or parts of news reports, letters, books, films, etc.): *Two scenes in the movie had been censored.* ⟨< L *censor* < *censere* appraise⟩
☛ *Hom.* CENSER, SENSOR.

cen•so•ri•al [sɛn'sɔriəl] *adj.* of or suitable for a censor.

cen•so•ri•ous [sɛn'sɔriəs] *adj.* too ready to find fault; severely critical. **—cen'so•ri•ous•ly,** *adv.* **—cen'so•ri•ous•ness,** *n.*

cen•sor•ship ['sɛnsər,ʃɪp] *n.* **1** the act, practice, or system of censoring: *Censorship of news is common in time of war.* **2** the position or work of a censor. **3** *Psychoanalysis.* the process by which disturbing thoughts and images are prevented from entering consciousness, except in dream form.

cen•sure ['sɛnʃər] *n., v.* **-sured, -sur•ing.** *—n.* **1** strong disapproval, especially official criticism or condemnation: *a vote of censure.* **2** an expression of such disapproval: *The minister's speech included a censure of the press for biassed reporting.*
—v. express disapproval of; criticize officially or publicly. ⟨ME < OF < L *censura* < *censere* appraise⟩ **—'cen•sur•a•ble,** *adj.* **—,cen•sur•a'bil•i•ty,** *n.* **—'cen•sur•a•bly,** *adv.* **—'cen•sur•er,** *n.*
☛ *Syn. v.* See note at BLAME.

cen•sus ['sɛnsəs] *n.* an official count of the people of a country or district. A census is taken to find out the number of people living there and the numbers in different age groups, occupations, etc. ⟨< L < *censere* appraise⟩

cent [sɛnt] *n.* **1** a unit of money in Australia, Bahamas, Barbados, Bermuda, Canada, Cayman Islands, Fiji, Grenada, Guyana, Hong Kong, Jamaica, Liberia, Marshall Islands, Namibia, New Zealand, Singapore, Solomon Islands, Taiwan, Trinidad and Tobago, United States, West Indies (Leeward Islands, Windward Islands), and Zimbabwe, equal to 1/100 of a dollar; in Ethiopia, 1/100 of a birr; in Surinam and the Netherlands, 1/100 of a gulden; in Sierra Leone, 1/100 of a leone; in Cyprus and Malta, 1/100 of a pound; in South Africa, 1/100 of a rand; in Brunei, 1/100 of a ringgit; in Mauritius and Sri Lanka, 1/100 of a rupee; in Kenya and Uganda, 1/100 of a shilling; in Kazakhstan, 1/100 of a tenge; in Taiwan, 1/100 of a yuan and 1/10 of a chiao; in Swaziland, 1/100 of a lilangeni. See table of money in the Appendix. *Symbol*: ¢ **2** a coin worth one cent. ⟨< F < L *centum* hundred⟩
☛ *Hom.* SCENT.

cent. 1 central. **2** century. **3** centigrade.

cen•ta ['sɛntə] *n.* a unit of money in Lithuania, equal to 1/100 of a lita. See table of money in the Appendix.

cen•tal ['sɛntəl] *n.* **1** a unit of weight used for grain, equivalent to a hundredweight (45.3 kg). **2** a British hundredweight of 112 pounds (50.9 kg).

cen•taur ['sɛntɔr] *n.* **1** *Greek mythology.* one of a race of creatures that had the head, arms, and chest of a man, and the body and legs of a horse. **2 Centaur,** the constellation Centaurus. ⟨< L *centaurus* < Gk. *kentauros*⟩

Cen•taur•us [sɛn'tɔrəs] *n.* a southern constellation thought to resemble a centaur, having Alpha Centauri as its brightest star.

cen•ta•vo [sɛn'tɑvou] *or* [sɛn'tɒvou] *n.* **1** a unit of money equal to 1/100 of the basic unit of money in certain countries: 1/100 of a peso in Argentina, Bolivia, Chile, Colombia, Cuba, the Dominican Republic, Guinea-Bissau, and Mexico; 1/100 of a metical in Mozambique; 1/100 of an escudo in Portugal; 1/100 of a colon in El Salvador; 1/100 of a cordoba in Nicaragua; 1/100 of a real in Brazil; 1/100 of a lempira in Honduras; 1/100 of a quetzal in Guatemala; 1/100 of a sucre in Ecuador. See table of money in the Appendix. **2** a coin worth one centavo. ⟨< Sp. < L *centum* hundred⟩

cen•te•nar•i•an [,sɛntə'nɛriən] *n., adj.* *—n.* a person who is 100 years old or more.
—adj. **1** 100 years old or more. **2** of 100 years.

cen•ten•ar•y [sɛn'tɛnəri,], [sɛn'tinəri], *or* ['sɛntə,nɛri] *n., pl.* **-ar•ies;** *adj.* *—n.* **1** a period of 100 years. **2** a 100th anniversary. **3** the celebration of the 100th anniversary.
—adj. having to do with a period of 100 years. ⟨< L *centenarius* relating to a hundred < *centum* hundred⟩

cen•ten•ni•al [sɛn'tɛnjəl] *or* [sɛn'tɛniəl] *adj., n.* *—adj.* **1** of or having to do with 100 years or a 100th anniversary: *a centennial exhibition.* **2** happening every 100 years or being of 100 years' duration. **3** 100 years old.
—n. **1** a 100th anniversary. Canada celebrated its centennial in 1967. **2** the celebration of the 100th anniversary. ⟨< L *cent(um)* hundred + E *(bi)ennial*⟩ **—cen'ten•ni•al•ly,** *adv.*

cen•ter ['sɛntər] See CENTRE.
☛ *Spelling.* Compounds and derivatives beginning with **center-** are entered under their **centre-** forms.

cen•tes•i•mal [sɛn'tɛsəməl] *adj.* **1** 100th. **2** divided into 100ths. ⟨< L *centesimus* hundredth⟩ **—cen'tes•i•mal•ly,** *adv.*

cen•tes•i•mo [sɛn'tɛsə,mou]; *Italian,* [tʃɛn'tesi,mo]; *Spanish,* [sɛn'tesi,mo] *n., pl.* **cen•tes•i•mi** [-mi] or **cen•tes•i•mos.** a unit of money in Uruguay, equal to 1/100 of a peso; in Panama, equal to 1/100 of a balboa; and in Italy, equal to 1/100 of a lira. ⟨< Sp. < L *centesimus* hundredth⟩

centi– *combining form.* **1** an SI prefix meaning hundredth. A centimetre is one hundredth of a metre. *Symbol*: c **2** one hundred, as in *centigrade, centipede.* ⟨< L *centum* hundred⟩

cen•ti•are ['sɛnti,ɛr] *n.* 1/100 of an are; one square metre. ⟨< F⟩

cen•ti•grade ['sɛntə,greid] *adj.* **1** divided into or consisting of 100 degrees. **2** Celsius. ⟨< F < L *centum* hundred + *gradus* degree⟩

cen•time [sɒn'tim]; *French,* [sɑ̃'tim] *n.* **1** a unit of money equal to 1/100 of the basic unit in certain countries: 1/100 of a franc in Belgium, Benin, Burkina Faso, Burundi, Cameroon, Central African Republic, Chad, Congo Republic, Djibouti, Equatorial Guinea, France, Gabon, Guinea, Ivory Coast, Liechtenstein, Luxembourg, Madagascar, Mali, Monaco, Niger, Rwanda,

Senegal, Switzerland, Togo, and Upper Volta; 1/100 of a dinar in Algeria; 1/100 of a gourde in Haïti; 1/100 of a dirham in Morocco; 1/100 of a rupee in Seychelles. See table of money in the Appendix. **2** a coin worth one centime. ⟨< F < L *centum* hundred⟩

cen•ti•me•tre ['sɛntə,mitər] *n.* an SI unit for measuring length, equal to one hundredth of a metre, or ten millimetres: *A nickel has a diameter of just over two centimetres. Symbol*: cm Also, **centimeter.** ⟨< F⟩

cen•ti•me•tre–gram–sec•ond ['sɛntə,mitər 'græm 'sɛkənd] *adj.* having to do with a system of measurement in which the centimetre is the unit of length, the gram is the unit of mass, and the second is the unit of time. *Abbrev.*: cgs

cen•ti•mo ['sɛntə,mou] *n.* a unit of money equal to 1/100 of the basic unit in certain countries: 1/100 of a colon in Costa Rica; 1/100 of a dobra in São Tome e Principe; 1/100 of a guarani in Paraguay; 1/100 of a peseta in Spain; 1/100 of a bolivar in Venezuela; 1/100 of a sol in Peru. See table of money in the Appendix. ⟨< Sp. < F *centime*⟩

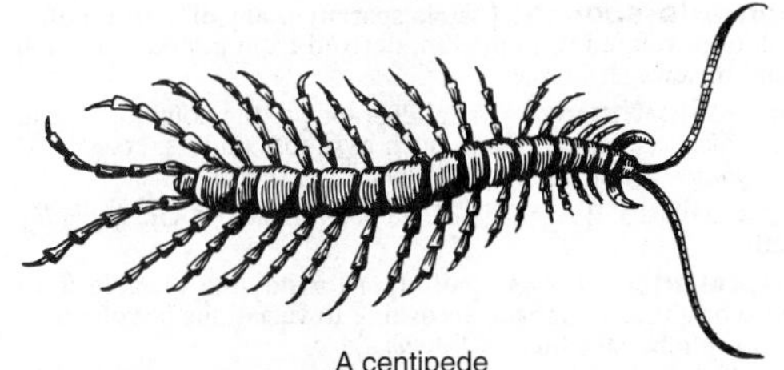

A centipede

cen•ti•pede ['sɛntə,pid] *n.* any of a class (Chilopoda) of small, wormlike arthropods having a long, flat body with a great many segments and one pair of legs to each segment. The front pair of legs is modified into poison fangs. ⟨< L *centipeda* < *centum* hundred + *pes, pedis* foot⟩

cen•ti•stere ['sɛntə,stir] *n.* one hundredth of a stere (a cubic metre).

cen•tral ['sɛntrəl] *adj., n. —adj.* **1** of the centre; being or forming the centre. **2** at, in, or near the centre: *the central part of the city.* **3** from the centre. **4** equally distant from all points; easy to get to or from: *They are looking for a good central location to set up their shop.* **5** main; chief: *What is the central idea in the story?* **6** *Anatomy.* **a** of or designating the brain and spinal cord as a major division of the nervous system of vertebrates. **b** arising from or affecting these parts of the nervous system: *central anesthesia.* **7** *Phonetics,* of a vowel, pronounced halfway between front and back in the mouth: *The* [ʌ] *in 'come' is a central vowel.*
—n. **1** a telephone exchange. **2** a telephone operator. ⟨< L *centralis* < *centrum.* See CENTRE.⟩ **—'cen•tral•ly,** *adv.* **—'cen•tral•ness,** *n.*

Central African Republic a country in central Africa. See SUDAN for map.

Central American *adj., n. —adj.* of or having to do with Central America or its people.
—n. a native or inhabitant of Central America, the isthmus joining North and South America.

central dogma *Genetics.* the theory that DNA is the pattern for its own reproduction and the formation of RNA, and that RNA governs the formation of proteins.

cen•tral•ism ['sɛntrə,lɪzəm] *n.* a theory or system of concentrating control in a central agency, especially a government. **—,cen•tral'ist•ic,** *adj.*

cen•tral•ist ['sɛntrəlɪst] *n.* a person who promotes or favours centralism.

cen•tral•i•ty [sɛn'træləti] *n.* a central position or character.

cen•tral•i•za•tion [,sɛntrələ'zeiʃən] *or* [,sɛntrəlaɪ'zeiʃən] *n.* **1** a coming or bringing to a centre. **2** concentration at a centre: *Centralization of relief agencies may prevent waste of effort.* **3** the concentration of administrative power in a central government.

cen•tral•ize ['sɛntrə,laɪz] *v.* **-ized, -iz•ing. 1** collect at a centre; gather together. **2** bring or come under one control. **—'cen•tra,liz•er,** *n.*

central nervous system the brain and spinal cord. Compare PERIPHERAL NERVOUS SYSTEM.

Central Powers during World War I, Germany and Austria-Hungary, sometimes also their allies Turkey and Bulgaria.

central processing unit *Computer technology.* the part of a computer that controls the computer's operations by interpreting and executing program instructions.

cen•tre ['sɛntər] *n., v.* **-tred, -tring.** *—n.* **1** a point within a circle or sphere equally distant from all parts of the circumference or surface. **2** the middle part or place: *the centre of a room, the centre of the forehead, the centre of the stage.* **3** a person, thing, or group in a middle position. **4** a person or thing that is most important; the chief object of attention, interest, etc.: *He was the centre of attention. The new city hall was the centre of a huge controversy.* **5** a place of influence or activity; a main area or point: *a shopping centre, a community centre. Toronto is a centre for trade.* **6** *Sports.* the player who has the middle position of a forward line. **7** *Football.* in beginning play, the player of the offence who throws the ball between the legs to a backfield player. **8** a political attitude or policy characterized by moderate views that are neither right (conservative) nor left (reformist or radical). **9** all the people and parties having moderate views. **10** a mass of nerve cells closely connected and acting together; nerve centre: *the respiratory centre, the centre of balance.* **11** the main body of an army, as distinct from the flanks.
—v. **1** place in or at the centre. **2** gather together; concentrate: *She centred her hopes on obtaining the premiership. The troops were centred at a temporary camp.* **3** be concentrated; focus: *The story centres on her childhood experiences.* **4** mark or provide with a centre: *a smooth lawn centred by a pool.* **5** *Football.* of the centre, throw (the ball) to a backfield player. Also, **center.** ⟨ME < OF *centre* < L *centrum* < Gk. *kentron* sharp point⟩
☛ *Syn. n.* **1, 2.** See note at MIDDLE.
☛ *Usage.* **Centre around** is an informal idiom: *The story centres around a robbery.* The idiom in written and formal English is *centre on* or *upon.*

centre bit a drill bit with a long, sharp centre and cutting sides.

cen•tre•board ['sɛntər,bɔrd] *n.* a movable keel of a sailboat. It is lowered through a slot in the bottom of a boat to prevent drifting to leeward. Also, **centerboard.**

cen•tred ['sɛntərd] *adj., v. —adj.* **1** located in the centre. **2** having a given thing as its defining factor or interest, focus, etc., (*used to form compounds*): *a student-centred curriculum.*
—v. pt. and pp. of CENTRE. Also, **centered.**

centre field *Baseball.* the section of the outfield behind second base. **—centre fielder.**

cen•tre•fold ['sɛntər,fould] *n.* **1** a large illustration, such as a photograph, that extends across the two facing pages forming the centre of a magazine. **2** the subject of such a photograph.

centre ice *Hockey.* **1** the centre of the ice surface from which play begins at the start of each period. **2** the area of ice surface between the bluelines.

centre line *Hockey.* a red line passing through CENTRE ICE at an equal distance from each of the bluelines.

centre of gravity the point in something around which its mass is evenly balanced.

centre of mass a point in a body or system of bodies which moves as though it bore the entire mass of the body or system, usually identical with the centre of gravity.

cen•tre•piece ['sɛntər,pis] *n.* **1** an ornamental piece of glass, lace, etc. for the centre of a table. **2** the main item in a display or collection: *A simple navy skirt is the centrepiece of our elegant new fall wardrobe.* Also, **centerpiece.**

cen•tric ['sɛntrɪk] *adj.* **1** central. **2** having a centre. **—'cen•tri•cal•ly,** *adv.*

-centric *combining form.* **1** having (something) as a centre: *heliocentric.* **2** having a centre or centres of a particular kind or number.

cen•trif•u•gal [sɛn'trɪfjəgəl] *or* [,sɛntrə'fjugəl] *adj.* **1** moving away from the centre. **2** making use of or acted upon by centrifugal force. **3** *Physiology.* drawing blood, nerve impulses, etc. away from a centre; efferent. **4** *Botany.* of a flower cluster, growing outward from the centre. ⟨< NL *centrifugus* < L *centrum* centre + *fugere* flee⟩ **—cen'trif•u•gal•ly,** *adv.*

centrifugal force the inertia of a body that tends to move it away from the centre around which it revolves.

cen•trif•u•ga•tion [sɛn,trɪfjə'geiʃən] *n.* the separation of materials of different densities by centrifugal force.

cen•tri•fuge ['sɛntrə,fjudʒ] *n., v.* **-fuged, -fug•ing.** *—n.* a machine for separating cream from milk, bacteria from a fluid, etc. by means of centrifugal force.

—*v.* **1** separate with a centrifuge. **2** rotate in a centrifuge; subject to centrifugal force. ⟨< F⟩

cen•tri•ole ['sɛntri,oul] *n.* either of two bundles of rodlike bodies, within the centrosome of most animal cells, that form the spindle fibres along which chromatids move during mitosis.

cen•trip•e•tal [sɛn'trɪpətəl] *adj.* **1** moving toward the centre. **2** making use of or acted upon by centripetal force. **3** *Physiology.* drawing blood, nerve impulses, etc. toward a centre; afferent. **4** *Botany.* of a flower cluster, growing inward toward the centre. ⟨< NL *centripetus* < L *centrum* centre + *petere* seek⟩ **—cen'trip•e•tal•ly,** *adv.*

centripetal force a force that tends to move things toward the centre around which they are turning. Gravitation is a centripetal force.

cen•trist ['sɛntrɪst] *n., adj.* —*n.* a person who holds moderate views, especially in politics.
—*adj.* of such people or their views. **—'cen•trism,** *n.*

cen•troid ['sɛntrɔɪd] *n.* **1** the CENTRE OF MASS. **2** in geometry, the point of intersection of the medians of a triangle.

cen•tro•mere ['sɛntrə,mir] *n. Genetics.* the primary constriction on a chromosome, at which the paired sister chromatids are held together until the end of cell division, and at which the kinetochore, the attachment of the spindle fibres, is formed. ⟨< Gk. *kentron* centre + *meros* part⟩
—,cen•tro'mer•ic [-'mɛrɪk] *or* [-'mirɪk], *adj.*

cen•tro•some ['sɛntrə,soum] *n.* a tiny spherical region in the cytoplasm of many animal cells, close to the nucleus, which contains the centrioles. See CELL for picture. ⟨< Gk. *kentron* centre + *soma* body⟩ **—,cen•tro'som•ic** [-'soumɪk] *or* [-'sɒmɪk], *adj.*

cen•tro•sphere ['sɛntrə,sfir] *n.* **1** centrosome. **2** *Geology.* the extremely dense central part of the earth. ⟨< *centro* centre (< L *centrum* and Gk. *kentron*) + *sphere*⟩

cen•tum ['kɛntəm] *or* ['kɛntʊm] *adj. Linguistics.* of or having to do with the language groups in which Indo-European palato-velars became velar, as opposed to the satem language groups where they became palatal. The centum language group includes Germanic, Italic, Anatolian, and Celtic. Compare SATEM. ⟨< L hundred, because the initial [k] of this word is an example of the velarization of the Indo-European palato-velar stop⟩

cen•tu•ple [sɛn'tjupəl] *or* [sɛn'tupəl], ['sɛntjəpəl] *or* ['sɛntəpəl] *adj. or n., v.* **-pled, -pling.** —*adj. or n.* 100 times as much or as many; a hundredfold.
—*v.* make 100 times as much or as many; increase a hundredfold. ⟨< F < LL *centuplus* hundredfold⟩

cen•tup•li•cate *adj., n.* [sɛn'tjupləkɪt] *or* [sɛn'tupləkɪt]; *v.* [sɛn'tjuplɪ,keit] *or* [sɛn'tuplɪ,keit] *adj. or n., v.* **-cat•ed, -cat•ing.**
—*adj. or n.* a hundredfold.
—*v.* increase by a hundred times.

cen•tu•ri•on [sɛn'tʃʊriən] *or* [sɛn'tjʊriən] *n.* in the ancient Roman army, a commander of a group of about 100 soldiers. ⟨< L *centurio, -onis* < *centuria.* See CENTURY.⟩

cen•tu•ry ['sɛntʃəri] *n., pl.* **-ries. 1** each 100 years, counting from some special time, such as the birth of Christ. **2** any period of 100 years: *From 1824 to 1924 is a century.* **3** a group of 100 people or things. **4** in the ancient Roman army, a body of soldiers, originally probably consisting of 100 soldiers. **5** in ancient Rome, a division of the people for voting. Each century had one vote. **6** *Cricket.* an individual score of 100 runs. ⟨< L *centuria* a division of a hundred units < *centum* hundred⟩
☛ *Usage.* **Centuries.** The 5th century A.D. runs from the beginning of the year 401 to the end of the year 500, the 19th century from January 1, 1801, through December 31, 1900, and so on. That is, to name the century correctly, add one to the number of its hundred. Similarly, the 1st century B.C. runs back from the birth of Christ through 100, the 2nd century from 101 through 200, the 5th century from 401 through 500, and so on.

century plant a large, tropical American agave (*Agave americana*) that flowers only once, usually when it is more than 10 years old, and then dies.

CEO CHIEF EXECUTIVE OFFICER.

ceorl [tʃɜrl] *n.* in medieval times, a freeman of low rank; CHURL (def. 4). ⟨OE⟩

cep or **cèpe** [sɛp] *n.* an edible mushroom (*Boletus edulis*) growing wild under evergreens, and having a brown cap and a white stem. ⟨< F < Gascon dial. *cep* mushroom < L *cippus* a stake, post⟩

ceph•a•lad ['sɛfə,læd] *adv.* toward the head. Compare CAUDAD. ⟨< Gk. *kephalē* head + L *-ad* toward⟩

ce•phal•ic [sə'fælɪk] *adj.* **1** of or having to do with the head. **2** near, on, or in the head. **3** toward the head. ⟨< L *cephalicus* < Gk. *kephalikos* < *kephalē* head⟩

cephalic index the ratio of the breadth of the human skull to its length, multiplied by 100. Also called **cranial index.**

ceph•a•li•za•tion [,sɛfələ'zeiʃən] *or* [,sɛfəlaɪ'zeiʃən] *n.* a specialization of the forward part of the body into a distinct head in which nerve tissue and sensory organs are concentrated.

ceph•a•lom•e•ter [,sɛfə'lɒmətər] *n.* a device for measuring the circumference of the skull; craniometer. ⟨< L *cephalius* < Gk. *kephalikos* < *kephale* head + -METER[2]⟩

ceph•a•lo•pod ['sɛfələ,pɒd] *n.* any of a class (Cephalopoda) of molluscs including squids, octopuses, and cuttlefishes, having long, armlike tentacles around the mouth, a pair of large, highly developed eyes, and a sharp, birdlike beak. ⟨< NL *cephalopoda,* pl. < Gk. *kephalē* head + *pous, podos* foot⟩

ceph•a•lo•spo•rin [,sɛfələ'spɔrən] *n.* any of a group of antibiotics related to penicillin, derived from a mould originally found in sewage.

ceph•a•lo•tho•rax [,sɛfələ'θɔræks] *n.* the combined head and thorax of some animals, such as crabs, spiders, etc. ⟨< *cephalo-* the head (< Gk. *kephalē*) + *thorax*⟩

ceph•a•lous ['sɛfələs] *adj.* having a head. ⟨< Gk. *kephalē* head⟩

Ce•phe•id variable ['sifiɪd] *or* ['sɛfiɪd] *n.* a variable star whose brightness changes according to variations in volume. Also, **cepheid variable.** ⟨< *Cepheus*⟩

Ce•phe•us ['sifiəs] *or* ['sifjus] *n.* **1** *Greek mythology.* the father of Andromeda. **2** *Astronomy.* a northern constellation near Cassiopeia.

ce•ra•ceous [sə'reiʃəs] *adj.* waxy. ⟨< L *cera* wax⟩

ce•ram•ic [sə'ræmɪk] *adj., n.* —*adj.* of or having to do with earthenware, porcelain, brick, etc. or with their manufacture.
—*n.* **1 ceramics,** the art or process of making articles from baked clay (*used with a singular verb*): *Ceramics is taught in art class.* **2** an article of earthenware, porcelain, etc.: *They had some beautiful ceramics at the craft show.* ⟨< Gk. *keramikos* < *keramos* potter's clay⟩

cer•a•mist ['sɛrəmɪst] *or* [sə'ræmɪst] *n.* **1** an expert in ceramics. **2** a manufacturer of ceramics; potter. Also, **ceramicist** [sə'ræməsɪst].

ce•ras•tes [sə'ræstiz] *n.* a poisonous snake (*Cerastes cornultus*) found in Africa and Asia, having a horny spike above each eye; horned viper. It moves sideways like a sidewinder. ⟨< NL < L < Gk. *kerastes* horned < *keras* horn⟩

ce•rate ['sirɪt] *or* ['sireit] *n.* a firm ointment made of lard or oil mixed with wax, resin, etc. ⟨< L *ceratum,* pp. neut. of *cerare* to wax < *cera* wax⟩

cer•a•toid ['sɛrə,tɔɪd] *adj.* horny; hard like a horn; shaped like a horn. ⟨< Gk. *keratoeides* < *keras* horn⟩

cer•a•top•si•an [,sɛrə'tɒpsiən] *n.* a horned, plant-eating dinosaur.

Cer•ber•us ['sɜrbərəs] *n.* **1** *Greek and Roman mythology.* a three-headed dog that guarded the entrance to Hades. **2** a surly, watchful guard. **—Cer'be•re•an** [sər'biriən], *adj.*

cer•cis ['sɜrsɪs] *n.* any shrub of the genus *Cercis,* found in North America and Eurasia, and including the Judas tree. ⟨< NL < Gk. *kerkis*⟩

cer•cus ['sɜrkəs] *n., pl.* **cer•ci** ['sɜrsaɪ]. one of a pair of antennalike appendages at the back of the abdomen in many insects, serving as sensory organs. ⟨< NL < Gk. *kerkos* tail⟩
☛ *Hom.* CIRCUS.

cere [sir] *n.* a waxy-looking membrane near the beak of certain birds, especially birds of prey and parrots, in which the nostrils open. ⟨< L *cera* wax < Gk. *kēros*⟩
☛ *Hom.* SEAR, SEER, SERE.

ce•re•al ['siriəl] *n., adj.* —*n.* **1** any grass that produces a grain used as food. Wheat, rice, corn, oats, and barley are cereals. **2** the grain. **3** food, especially breakfast food, made from grain. Oatmeal and corn flakes are cereals.
—*adj.* of or having to do with grain or the grasses producing it. ⟨< L *Cerealis* of or having to do with Ceres⟩
☛ *Hom.* SERIAL.

cer•e•bel•lum [,sɛrə'bɛləm] *n.* **-bel•lums, -bel•la** [-'bɛlə]. a major division of the brain situated below the cerebrum. It controls the co-ordination of the muscles and the maintenance of bodily equilibrium. See BRAIN for picture. ⟨< L *cerebellum* dim. of *cerebrum* brain⟩ —ˌcer•eˈbel•lar, *adj.*

ce•re•bral [səˈribrəl] *or* [ˈsɛrəbrəl] *adj.* **1** of the brain: *Paralysis may be caused by a cerebral hemorrhage.* **2** of the cerebrum: *The cerebral cortex is the outer layer of the cerebrum.* **3** involving or appealing to thought and reason; intellectual: *She enjoys cerebral games like chess.* ⟨< L *cerebrum* brain⟩

cerebral accident a STROKE[1] (def. 11).

cerebral hemisphere either of the two halves of the cortex.

cerebral palsy a disorder resulting from brain damage, especially before or during birth, and characterized by impaired muscular function, lack of co-ordination, spastic movement, etc.

cer•e•brate [ˈsɛrəˌbreit] *v.* **-brat•ed, -brat•ing.** use the brain; think.

cer•e•bra•tion [ˌsɛrəˈbreiʃən] *n.* **1** the action of the brain. **2** the act of thinking.

ce•re•bro•spi•nal [səˌribroˈspaɪnəl] *or* [ˌsɛrəbrouˈspaɪnəl] *adj.* of or affecting both the brain and spinal cord.

cerebrospinal fluid the liquid which occupies spaces in the brain, and around the brain and spinal cord.

cerebrospinal meningitis the full name for meningitis.

ce•re•bro•vas•cu•lar [səˌribrouˈvæskjələr] *or* [ˌsɛrəbrouˈvæskjələr] *adj.* of or having to do with the blood vessels of the brain.

cerebrovascular accident sudden partial or complete loss of consciousness with paralysis and loss of sensation, caused by the rupture or the obstruction by a clot, etc., of an artery in the brain; stroke.

ce•re•brum [səˈribrəm] *or* [ˈsɛrəbrəm] *n., pl.* **-brums, -bra** [-brə]. **1** the part of the human brain that is responsible for mental activities such as memory, understanding, and the ability to reason, and also controls fine movements of the smaller muscles of the face, hands, and toes, and the senses of sight, hearing, etc. See BRAIN for picture. **2** the part of the brain in all other vertebrates that corresponds structurally to the human cerebrum but has fewer functions. ⟨< L⟩

cere•cloth [ˈsirˌklɒθ] *n.* **1** waxed cloth. **2** the waxed cloth in which a dead person is wrapped for burial. ⟨originally *cered cloth*; *cere* wax < L *cerare* < *cera* wax. See CERE.⟩

cere•ment [ˈsirmənt] *n.* Usually, **cerements,** *pl.* the cloth or garment in which a dead person is wrapped for burial; shroud. ⟨< obs. *cere* wrap for burial, wax < L *cerare.* See CERECLOTH.⟩

cer•e•mo•ni•al [ˌsɛrəˈmouniəl] *adj., n.* —*adj.* **1** of or having to do with ceremony or ceremonials: *a ceremonial occasion. The ceremonial costumes were grand.* **2** very formal; ceremonious. —*n.* **1** a formal action suitable for an occasion. Kneeling is a ceremonial of religion. **2** a rite or ceremony. **3** a formality of courtesy or manners. —ˌ**cer•eˈmo•ni•al•ly,** *adv.* —ˌ**cer•eˈmo•ni•al•ism,** *n.*

☛ *Usage.* **Ceremonial,** CEREMONIOUS differ in meaning and use. **Ceremonial** = having to do with ceremony, and applies to things involving or belonging to the ceremonies and formalities of the church, law, polite conduct, fraternities, etc.: *Shriners wear ceremonial costumes.* **Ceremonious** = full of ceremony, and applies to things done with ceremony or showy formality or to people who pay very strict attention to the details of polite conduct: *The banquet was a ceremonious affair.*

cer•e•mo•ni•ous [ˌsɛrəˈmouniəs] *adj.* **1** full of ceremony. **2** very formal; extremely polite. —ˌ**cer•eˈmo•ni•ous•ly,** *adv.* —ˌ**cer•eˈmo•ni•ous•ness,** *n.*

☛ *Usage.* See note at CEREMONIAL.

cer•e•mo•ny [ˈsɛrəˌmouni] *n., pl.* **-nies. 1** a special form or set of acts to be done on special occasions such as weddings, funerals, graduations, religious holidays, etc. **2** the occasion or observance of such acts. **3** very polite conduct; a way of conducting oneself that follows all the rules of polite social behaviour: *The old gentleman showed us to the door with a great deal of ceremony.* **4** an empty form; meaningless formality. **5** formality; formalities: *The democratic prince disliked the traditional ceremony of court life.* **6** complicated affair; fuss or bother: *I had no idea getting this permit would be such a ceremony. He makes a ceremony of every little thing.*

stand on ceremony, be very formal; insist on formal behaviour: *The Premier does not stand on ceremony but always makes the people she meets feel comfortable and relaxed.* ⟨< L *caerimonia* rite⟩

☛ *Syn.* **1. Ceremony,** RITE = a form followed on special occasions. **Ceremony** applies to a special form or procedure used on religious, public, or other solemn occasions: *The graduation ceremony was inspiring.* **Rite** applies to a ceremonial procedure that is laid down to be followed in a religious service or other solemn ceremony and in which both the acts to be done and the words to be said are prescribed: *A priest went to administer the last rites to the dying victims of the explosion.*

Ce•res [ˈsiriz] *n. Roman mythology.* the goddess of agriculture, corresponding to the Greek goddess Demeter.

ce•re•us [ˈsiriəs] *n.* **1** any of a genus (*Cereus*) of tropical American cactuses. **2** the **night-blooming cereus,** any of several cactuses with fragrant flowers that open at night, such as *Selenicereus grandiflorus.* ⟨< L *cereus* wax candle < *cera* wax⟩

☛ *Hom.* SERIOUS.

ce•ria [ˈsiriə] *n.* a white powder, cerium dioxide, used in ceramics and glass polishing. *Formula*: CeO_2

ce•ric [ˈsirɪk] *or* [ˈsɛrɪk] *adj.* of or containing cerium with a valency of four. Compare CEROUS.

ce•rif•er•ous [səˈrɪfərəs] *adj.* yielding wax.

ce•rise [səˈriz] *or* [səˈris] *n. or adj.* bright pinkish red. ⟨< F *cerise* cherry < VL < LGk. *kerasia* cherry tree < Gk. *kerasos* cherry. Doublet of CHERRY.⟩

ce•ri•um [ˈsiriəm] *n.* a greyish metallic chemical element. *Symbol*: Ce; *at.no.* 58; *at.mass* 140.12. ⟨< NL *cerium,* from the asteroid *Ceres*⟩

cer•met [ˈsɜrmɛt] *n.* an alloy of heat-resistant compound and a metal, used in combustion chambers, turbojet engines, etc. Cermets combine the properties of ceramic and metallic materials. ⟨< *cer(amic)* + *met(al)*⟩

ce•ro [ˈsirou] *or* [ˈsɛrou] *n.* an edible fish of the family Scombridae, having spiny fins and native to the warmer areas of the N Atlantic Ocean. ⟨< Sp. *sierra* < L *serra* a saw⟩

ce•rous [ˈsirəs] *adj.* of or containing cerium with a valency of three. Compare CERIC.

cer•tain [ˈsɜrtən] *adj., pron.* —*adj.* **1** settled; fixed; definite: *a certain hour. Each investor will receive a certain percentage of the profit.* **2** that cannot be disputed; established beyond any doubt: *It is certain that 2 and 3 do not make 6.* **3** sure to happen; inevitable: *Death is certain.* **4** bound (*to*); sure (*to*): *She is certain to do well in her profession.* **5** reliable; dependable: *The police have certain evidence of his guilt.* **6** definite but not named: *A certain person donated $2000 to the project.* **7** having or showing no doubt; confident; positive: *She was certain of her facts. His reply was quick and certain.* **8** of a particular but unspecified character, amount, or degree: *There was a certain reluctance in his voice, but he agreed to go. The room had a certain charm that made it very inviting. To a certain extent we are all at fault.* —*pron. Formal.* a definite but unspecified number; some particular ones: *Certain of the students will be asked to give a detailed report.*

for certain, surely, without a doubt: *It will rain for certain.* ⟨ME < OF < L *certus* sure⟩ —ˈ**cer•tain•ness,** *n.*

☛ *Syn. adj.* **7.** See note at SURE.

cer•tain•ly [ˈsɜrtənli] *adv.* **1** surely; without doubt; with certainty. **2** *Informal.* yes; of course: *May I borrow your music? Certainly, you may.* **3** *Informal.* very: *I'm certainly pleased that you came.*

cer•tain•ty [ˈsɜrtənti] *n., pl.* **-ties. 1** a being certain; freedom from doubt: *The man's certainty was amusing, for we could all see that he was wrong.* **2** something certain; a fact: *The annual recurrence of the seasons is a certainty.*

of a certainty, *Archaic or formal.* beyond doubt; surely.

cer•tes [ˈsɜrtiz] *adv. Archaic.* certainly; in truth. ⟨ME < OF < VL *certas* surely⟩

cer•ti•fi•a•ble [ˈsɜrtəˌfaɪəbəl] *adj.* **1** that can be certified. **2** mentally ill enough to be legally committed to a psychiatric hospital. —ˈ**cer•tiˌfi•a•bly,** *adv.*

cer•tif•i•cate *n.* [sərˈtɪfəkɪt]; *v.* [sərˈtɪfəˌkeit] *n., v.* **-cat•ed, -cat•ing.** —*n.* a written or printed statement that declares something to be a fact: *Your birth certificate gives your full name and the date and place of your birth.* —*v.* **1** give a certificate to. **2** authorize or declare by a certificate. ⟨< Med.L *certificatum,* neut. pp. of *certificare.* See CERTIFY.⟩

certificate of deposit a document given by a bank, showing that it has received a certain sum of money from an individual, which is to be held for a certain length of time as an interest-gaining deposit. *Abbrev.*: C.D. or CD

certificate of fran•ci•sa•tion or **fran•ci•ci•sa•tion** [ˌfrænsəˈzeiʃən] *or* [ˌfrænsəsəˈzeiʃən] *Cdn.* a document certifying that the dominant language used in a company is French. It is required to operate a company in Québec.

cer•ti•fi•ca•tion [ˌsɜrtəfəˈkeiʃən] *n.* **1** a certifying or being certified. **2** a certified statement.

cer•ti•fied [ˈsɜrtəˌfaɪd] *adj., v.* —*adj.* **1** guaranteed: *The water*

is certified to be pure. **2** having a certificate. **3** committed to a psychiatric hospital.
—v. pt. and pp. of CERTIFY.

certified cheque a cheque that has been guaranteed as good by the bank on which it is drawn. When a bank certifies a cheque, money to cover it is immediately withdrawn from the account on which the cheque is written.

certified mail a postal service for businesses that provides proof of delivery of a letter or parcel by means of a card that is signed by the receiver of the mail and is then returned to the sender. Certified mail is similar to registered mail, but cheaper.

certified milk raw or pasteurized milk guaranteed to meet certain official standards.

cer•ti•fi•er ['sɜrtə,faɪər] *n.* one that certifies.

cer•ti•fy ['sɜrtə,faɪ] *v.* **-fied, -fy•ing. 1** declare to be true or correct by spoken, written, or printed statement: *The doctor certified that the cause of death was a heart attack.* **2** legally commit (a person) to a psychiatric hospital; declare to be legally insane. **3** guarantee the quality or value of. **4** assure; make certain. **5** *Banking.* guarantee in writing on the face of (a cheque) that sufficient funds have been set aside from the drawer's account to cover the cheque. ⟨ME < OF < Med.L *certificare* < L *certus* sure + *facere* make⟩

cer•ti•o•rar•i [,sɜrʃiə'rɛri] *or* [-'rɛraɪ] *n. Law.* an order from a higher court to a lower one, calling for the record of a case for review. ⟨< LL *certiorari* be informed⟩

cer•ti•tude ['sɜrtə,tjud] *or* ['sɜrtə,tud] *n.* certainty; sureness. ⟨< LL *certitudo* < *certus* sure⟩

ce•ru•le•an [sə'ruliən] *adj. or n.* sky blue. ⟨< L *caeruleus* dark blue⟩

ce•ru•men [sə'rumən] *n.* a waxlike substance in the ears; earwax. ⟨< NL < L *cera* wax⟩ **—ce'ru•men•ous,** *adj.*

ce•rus•site ['sirə,sɔit] *or* [sə'rusɔit] *n.* natural lead carbonate, an ore of lead. *Formula*: $PbCO_3$ ⟨< L *cerussa*⟩

cer•ve•lat [,sɛrvə'lɑ] *or* [,sɛrvə'lɑt] *n.* a smoked beef and pork sausage. ⟨< F⟩

cer•vi•cal ['sɜrvəkəl] *adj.* of or having to do with a cervix. See SPINAL COLUMN for picture.

cervical cap a contraceptive device shaped like a flexible cap and fitted over the cervix. Although it is not permanently inserted like the IUD, it may be left in for relatively long periods of time.

cervical smear a few cells scraped from the cervix (the neck of the uterus) to be tested for malignancy. Also called **Pap test.**

cer•vi•ces ['sɜrvɪ,siz] *or* [sər'vɔisiz] *n.* a pl. of CERVIX.

cer•vi•ci•tis [,sɜrvə'sɔitɪs] *n.* inflammation of the cervix.

cer•vid ['sɜrvɪd] *adj.* of or having to do with the deer family of animals. ⟨< L *cervus* stag⟩

cer•vine ['sɜrvaɪn] *or* ['sɜrvɪn] *adj.* of or like a deer. ⟨< L *cervinus* < *cervus* deer⟩

cer•vix ['sɜrvɪks] *n., pl.* **cer•vix•es** or **cer•vi•ces. 1** the neck, especially the back of the neck. **2** a necklike part, especially the narrow opening of the uterus. ⟨< L⟩

Ce•sar•e•an or **Ce•sar•i•an** [sɪ'zɛriən] See CAESAREAN.

ce•si•um or **cae•si•um** ['siziəm] *n.* a silvery metallic chemical element. *Symbol*: Cs; *at.no.* 55; *at.mass* 132.91. ⟨< NL *caesium* < L *caesius* bluish grey⟩

ces•sa•tion [sɛ'seiʃən] *n.* a ceasing; pause; stop: *There is still hope for a cessation of fighting.* ⟨< L *cessatio, -onis* < *cessare* cease⟩

ces•sion ['sɛʃən] *n.* a handing over to another; the act of ceding, giving up, or surrendering. ⟨< L *cessio, -onis* < *cedere* yield⟩
☛ *Hom.* SESSION.

cess•pit ['sɛs,pɪt] *n.* a large hole in the ground for garbage, human waste, etc. ⟨< *cess(pool)* + *pit*⟩

cess•pool ['sɛs,pul] *n.* **1** a pool or pit for house drains to empty into. **2** any filthy place. ⟨origin uncertain⟩

ces•ta ['sɛstə] *n.* in jai alai, the narrow, curved basket fitted to a handle with a glove on the end, used for throwing and receiving the ball. ⟨< Sp. *cesta* basket⟩

ces•tode ['sɛstoud] *n.* any of a class (Cestoda) of flatworms that live as parasites in the intestines of various animals. Tapeworms are cestodes. ⟨< Gk. *kestos* girdle⟩

ces•toid ['sɛstɔɪd] *adj.* of an animal, shaped like a ribbon: *A tapeworm is cestoid.*

ces•tus¹ ['sɛstəs] *n.* **1** in ancient Greece, a woman's girdle or belt. **2** the girdle of Venus, adorned with love-arousing objects. ⟨< Gk. *kestos* girdle < *kentein* stitch⟩

ces•tus² ['sɛstəs] *n.* a boxer's hand covering made of strips of leather, often loaded with metal, used in ancient Rome. ⟨< L *caestus*, ? var. of *cestus* girdle < Gk. *kestos*⟩

ce•su•ra [sə'ʒʊrə] *or* [sɪ'zjʊrə] *n., pl.* **-su•ras, -su•rae** [-'ʒʊri], ['ʒʊraɪ], [-'zjʊri], *or* [-'zjʊraɪ] See CAESURA.

ce•ta•cean [sə'teiʃən] *n., adj. —n.* any of an order (Cetacea) of fishlike mammals that live in the water, especially in the ocean. Whales, dolphins, and porpoises are cetaceans.
—adj. of, having to do with, or designating an animal of this order. ⟨< NL < L *cetus* whale < Gk. *kētos*⟩ **—ce'ta•ceous,** *adj.*

ce•tane ['sitein] *n.* a colourless, liquid hydrocarbon of the alkane group, found in petroleum and some plants, and used as a solvent and to test fuel oils. *Formula*: $C_{16}H_{34}$ ⟨< L *cetus* whale + *-ane*⟩

cete [sit] *n.* a group of badgers. ⟨origin uncertain⟩
☛ *Hom.* SEAT.

ceteris paribus ['kɛtərɪs 'pɑrɪbʊs], ['sɛtərɪs 'pærəbəs], *or* ['sɛtərɪs 'pɛrəbəs] *Latin.* all other things being equal.

ce•to•log•i•cal [,sitə'lɒdʒɪkəl] *adj.* of or having to do with cetology.

ce•tol•o•gist [si'tɒlədʒɪst] *n.* a person trained in cetology, especially one whose work it is.

ce•tol•o•gy [si'tɒləji] *n.* the branch of zoology that deals with whales. ⟨< L *cetus* whale + Gk. *logos* word⟩

Ce•tus ['sitəs] *n.* a constellation near the celestial equator. ⟨< L *Cetus* < Gk. *Kētos* the Whale⟩

ce•vi•che [sə'vitʃei] *n.* a Spanish dish popular in South America, consisting of chopped fish soaked in lime juice with chilies and vegetables, served cold. Also, **seviche.** ⟨< Sp.⟩

Cey•lon moss [sɪ'lɒn] any of various East Indian red algae (genus *Gracilaria*), used to produce agar.

cf. compare (for L *confer*).

c/f *Bookkeeping.* carried forward.

Cf californium.

CF or **C.F.** CANADIAN FORCES.

CFA *Cdn., Nfld. & P.E.I.* come from away (a visitor or outsider).

CFB Canadian Forces Base.

CFC chlorofluorocarbon.

CFDC Canadian Film Development Corporation.

C.F.I. or **c.f.i.** cost, freight, and insurance.

CFL or **C.F.L.** Canadian Football League.

cfm cubic feet per minute.

cfs cubic feet per second.

C.G.I.T. or **CGIT** CANADIAN GIRLS IN TRAINING.

C.G.M. Conspicuous Gallantry Medal.

cgs centimetre-gram-second.

ch. or **Ch. 1** chapter. **2** church. **3** chaplain. **4** child; children. **5** CHAIN (def. 4). **6** champion. **7** chief.

C.H. Companion of Honour.

Cha•blis [ʃə'bli] *or* ['ʃæbli] *n.* **1** a dry white Burgundy wine from the area around Chablis, France. **2** any similar white wine.

cha•bouk or **cha•buk** ['tʃɑbʊk] *n.* in the Orient, a long whip used to punish people. ⟨< Persian or Hind. *chabuk*⟩

cha–cha ['tʃɑ ,tʃɑ] *n.* CHA-CHA-CHA.

cha–cha–cha ['tʃɑ 'tʃɑ 'tʃɑ] *n., v. —n.* **1** a ballroom dance with a fast, strongly-marked rhythm, originally Latin American. **2** the music for such a dance.
—v. dance the cha-cha-cha. Also, **cha-cha.** ⟨imitative⟩

cha•conne [ʃə'kɒn] *n. Music.* **1** a stately Spanish dance in 3/4 time. **2** the music for this dance. **3** a musical form consisting of variations based on a chordal sequence. ⟨< F < Sp. *chacona*⟩

Chad [tʃæd] *n.* a country in north central Africa. See SUDAN for map.

Chad•i•an ['tʃædiən] *n., adj. —n.* a native or inhabitant of Chad.
—adj. of or having to do with Chad.

cha•dor ['tʃʌdər] *n.* a large piece of cloth used as a long cloak and veil by some Muslim women, especially in Iran. ⟨< Hind. < Persian *chaddar, chadur* veil, sheet⟩

chae•to•pod ['kitə,pɒd] *n.* any member of the Chaetopoda family of annelids, having equal body segments. Earthworms and leeches are chaetopods.

chafe [tʃeif] *v.* **chafed, chaf•ing;** *n.* —*v.* **1** rub to make warm: *She chafed her cold hands.* **2** wear or be worn away by rubbing. **3** make or become sore by rubbing: *The rough collar chafed my neck.* **4** annoy or make angry: *Their teasing chafed him.* **5** become annoyed or angry: *He chafed under their teasing.*
chafe at, become impatient at: *They chafed at the long delay.*
chafe under, become annoyed about (something done to one): *He chafed under their teasing.*
—*n.* **1** a sore or injury caused by chafing. **2** a state of irritation or anger. ⟨ME < OF *chaufer* < L *calefacere* < *calere* be warm + *facere* make⟩

chaf•er ['tʃeifər] *n.* any of various large beetles (subfamily Melolonthinae) of the family Scarabaeidae, such as the cockchafer. ⟨OE *ceafor*⟩

chaff[1] [tʃæf] *n.* **1** husks of wheat, oats, rye, etc., especially when separated from grain by threshing. **2** hay or straw cut fine for feeding cattle. **3** worthless stuff. **4** strips of aluminum foil dropped by aircraft to confuse enemy radar systems. ⟨OE *ceaf*⟩

chaff[2] [tʃæf] *v., n.* —*v.* make fun of (someone) in a good-natured way: *The girls chaffed the English boy about his French.*
—*n.* good-natured joking about a person to his or her face. ⟨origin uncertain⟩

chaf•fer ['tʃæfər] *v., n.* —*v.* **1** dispute about a price; bargain. **2** make conversation.
—*n.* a disputing about price; bargaining. ⟨ME *chaffare* < OE *cēap* bargain + *faru* journey⟩ —**'chaf•fer•er,** *n.*

chaf•finch ['tʃæfɪntʃ] *n.* a European finch (*Fringilla coelebs*) having black and white wings, the male having a reddish breast and bluish grey head. The chaffinch has a pleasant, short song, and is often kept as a cage bird. ⟨OE *ceaffinc* < *ceaf* chaff[1] + *finc* finch⟩

chaff•y ['tʃæfi] *adj.* **-i•er, -i•est. 1** full of chaff. **2** worthless.

chafing dish a dish with a heating apparatus under it, used to cook food at the table or to keep it warm.

Cha•gas' disease ['ʃɑgəs] an infectious disease caused by the parasite *Trypanosoma*, which is carried by insects, and characterized by fever, leading to damage to the heart, intestines and nerves. ⟨after Carlos *Chagas,* a Brazilian doctor who identified it in 1909⟩

cha•grin [ʃə'grɪn] *n., v.* —*n.* a feeling of embarrassment or vexation caused by disappointment, failure, or humiliation.
—*v.* cause to feel chagrin. ⟨< F < MF *chagrin* sad, gloomy⟩

chain [tʃein] *n., v.* —*n.* **1** a flexible, connected series of links or rings used to bind, connect, or hold, or to decorate: *a gold chain, a steel chain, a paper chain.* **2** a series of things joined or linked together: *a mountain chain, a chain of events, a chain of thoughts.* **3** anything that binds or restrains. **4** a measuring instrument consisting of 100 links of iron or steel: *A surveyor's chain is about 20 m long. An engineer's chain is about 30 m long.* **5** a number of restaurants, stores, theatres, etc., owned and operated by one person or company. **6 chains,** *pl.* **a** bonds; fetters. **b** imprisonment; bondage. **7** *Chemistry.* a number of atoms of the same element bonded together like a chain. **8** *Biology.* a group of organisms, as bacteria, connected end to end.
—*v.* **1** join together or fasten with a chain. **2** restrain with chains; fetter. **3** bind; restrain. **4** keep in prison; make a slave of.
chained to, entirely responsible for; unable to leave: *chained to the house. She is simply chained to her job and never has a vacation.* ⟨ME < OF *chaeine* < L *catena*⟩

chain gang in S United States, a gang of convicts, etc. chained together while at work outdoors or on their way to work.

chain letter 1 a letter that each receiver is asked to copy and send to several other people in order to get some supposed benefit. **2** a letter that circulates from one person to the next within a closed group, each person adding his or her news or other communication.

chain lightning lightning that moves quickly across the sky.

chain–link ['tʃein ,lɪŋk] *adj.* of or having to do with a fence made of interwoven steel links.

chain mail a kind of flexible armour made of metal rings linked together.

chain•man ['tʃeinmən] *n., pl.* **-men.** *Surveying.* a man who carries the measuring chain.

chain measure a system of measurement used in surveying:
100 links = 1 chain (about 20 m)
10 chains = 1 furlong (about 200 m)
8 furlongs = 1 mile (about 1.61 km)

chain–react ['tʃein ri,ækt] *v.* play a part in or undergo a chain reaction.

chain reaction 1 *Chemistry or physics.* a process that goes on automatically when it has once been started because it yields energy or products that cause further reactions of the same kind. A reactor is designed to produce a controlled chain reaction; the explosion of an atomic bomb is an uncontrolled chain reaction. **2** any series of events or happenings, each caused by the one that precedes it.

chain reference 1 one of a system of cross-references in which each reference leads to a new or different related place in the text. **2** such a system of cross-references.

chain–ref•er•ence ['tʃein ,rɛfrəns] *adj., v.* **-enced, -enc•ing.**
—*adj.* provided with a CHAIN REFERENCE: *a chain-reference Bible.*
—*v.* provide (a text) with a CHAIN REFERENCE.

chain saw a portable power saw having teeth linked together in an endless chain.

chain–smoke ['tʃein ,smouk] *v.* **-smoked, -smok•ing.** smoke cigarettes one after another, lighting one from a previous one. —**'chain-,smok•er,** *n.*

chain stitch a kind of crochet or embroidery stitch in which each stitch makes a loop through which the next stitch is taken. —**'chain-,stitch,** *v.*

chain store one of a group of retail stores owned and operated by a single company.

chair [tʃɛr] *n., v.* —*n.* **1** a separate seat for one person, having legs and a back and, often, arms. **2** a seat of rank, dignity, or authority. **3** the position or authority of a person who has such a seat: *Professor Eagle occupies the chair of Philosophy at this university.* **4** the chairman of a meeting or committee. **5** the position of the leader of an instrumental section of an orchestra. **6** a covered chair carried on poles by two people; a sedan chair. **7** ELECTRIC CHAIR.
get the chair, *Informal.* die or be sentenced to die in the electric chair.
take the chair, a begin a meeting. **b** be in charge of or preside at a meeting: *Ms. James will take the chair.*
—*v.* **1** put or carry in a chair. **2** carry high up, as if in a chair: *The winning team chaired their captain.* **3** put in a position of authority. **4** act as chairman of: *My sister chaired the meeting.* ⟨ME < OF *chaiere* < L < Gk. *kathedra* seat. Doublet of CATHEDRA.⟩

chair lift an apparatus for conveying people, especially skiers, up a slope or between two points, consisting of a number of chairs suspended from an endless cable. Also, **chairlift.**

chair•man ['tʃɛrmən] *n., pl.* **-men. 1** a person who presides at or is in charge of a meeting. **2** the head of a committee. **3** in New Brunswick, the elected head of a village council. **4** a man whose work is carrying or wheeling people in a chair.

☛ *Usage.* **Chairman,** CHAIRPERSON, CHAIRWOMAN. The word **chairman** may be used for either a man or a woman in charge of a meeting or committee. The word **chairperson** is now widely used, so that the term **chairwoman** is less frequently needed. Of the three terms, only **chairman** is used as a form of address: *Mr. Chairman, Madam Chairman.*

chair•man•ship ['tʃɛrmən,ʃɪp] *n.* **1** the position of chairman. **2** the period of time one is a chairman.

chair•per•son ['tʃɛr,pɜrsən] *n.* **1** a person who presides at or is in charge of a meeting. **2** the head of a committee.
☛ *Usage.* See note at CHAIRMAN.

chair•wom•an ['tʃɛr,wʊmən] *n., pl.* **-wom•en. 1** a woman who presides at or is in charge of a meeting. **2** a woman at the head of a committee.
☛ *Usage.* See note at CHAIRMAN.

chaise [ʃeiz] *or* [ʃɛz] *n.* **1** any of several kinds of light carriage, often with a folding top, having two or four wheels and drawn by one or two horses. **2** CHAISE LONGUE. ⟨< F *chaise* chair, var. of *chaire*, OF *chaiere.* See CHAIR.⟩

chaise longue ['ʃeiz 'lɒŋ]; *French,* [ʃɛz'lɔ̃g] a couchlike chair with a long seat, in which a person can sit with outstretched legs. ⟨< F *chaise longue* long chair⟩

chaise lounge ['ʃeiz 'laʊndʒ] CHAISE LONGUE. ⟨misreading of *longue*, influenced by *lounge*⟩

chak•ra ['tʃɑkrə], ['tʃʌkrə], *or* ['tʃækrə] *n.* in yoga, any of the points of psychic power that are located in six or seven areas of the body. They are personified by gods, and their energy is released through exercises. ⟨origin uncertain⟩

cha•la•zi•on [kə'leiziən] *n.* a sty that will not heal. ⟨< NL < Gk. dim. of *chalaza* hail, lump⟩

chal•can•thite [kæl'kænθəit] *n.* copper sulphate crystals found in nature; blue vitriol. *Formula*: $CuSO_4 \cdot 5H_2O$ ⟨< L *chalcanthum* < Gk. *kalkanthon* vitriol⟩

chal•ced•o•ny [kæl'sɛdəni] *or* ['kælsə,douni] *n., pl.* **-nies. 1** a variety of quartz having a waxy lustre that occurs in various colours and forms. Agate, onyx, carnelian, jasper, etc., are chalcedony. **2** a gem made from this stone. ⟨< L *chalcedonius* < Gk. *chalkēdōn*⟩

chal•cid ['kælsɪd] *n.* any of a large superfamily (Chalcidoidea) of mostly very small insects whose larvae live as parasites on other insects. ⟨< Gk. *chalkos* copper; in reference to their colour⟩

chal•co•cite ['kælkə,səit] *n.* a shiny grey sulphide of copper, an important copper ore. *Formula*: Cu_2S ⟨< Gk. *chalkos* copper⟩

chal•cog•ra•phy [kæl'kɒgrəfi] *n.* the art of engraving on brass or copper. ⟨< NL *chalcographia* printing < Gk. *chalkos* copper, brass + *-graphy*⟩

chal•co•py•rite [,kælkə'paɪrəit] *or* [-'pirəit] *n.* a rich copper ore consisting of a sulphide of copper and iron; copper pyrites. *Formula*: $CuFeS_2$ ⟨< Gk. *chalkos* copper + E *pyrite*⟩

Chal•da•ic [kæl'deiɪk] *adj. or n.* Chaldean.

Chal•de•a [kæl'diə] *n.* a region of ancient Babylonia lying on either side of the lower part of the Euphrates River, near the Persian Gulf.

Chal•de•an [kæl'diən] *n., adj.* *—n.* **1** a member of an ancient Semitic people who dominated Babylonia from the late 700s to the late 600s B.C. **2** the Semitic language of the Chaldeans. **3** an astrologer or magician.
—adj. of or having to do with ancient Chaldea, its people, or their language. ⟨< L *Chaldaeus* < Gk. *Chaldaios*⟩

Chal•dee [kæl'di] *or* ['kældi] *adj. or n.* Chaldean.

cha•let [ʃæ'lei] *or* ['ʃælei] *n.* **1** a herder's hut or cabin in the Alps. **2** a Swiss house with wide, overhanging eaves and a steeply pitched roof. **3** any house of similar design. ⟨< Swiss F⟩

chal•ice ['tʃælɪs] *n.* **1** a cup; goblet, especially one used in the Communion service. **2** a flower shaped like a cup. ⟨ME < OF < L *calix* cup⟩

chalice flower a spring flower of western North America (*Anemone occidentalis*) having cream, cup-shaped flowers with yellow centres, which develop into wind-blown seeds. Also called **western anemone** and **wind flower.**

chal•iced ['tʃælɪst] *adj.* **1** having a flower shaped like a cup. **2** contained in a chalice.

chalk [tʃɒk] *n., v.* *—n.* **1** a soft, white or grey limestone, made up mostly of tiny fossil sea shells. Chalk is used for making lime. **2** a substance like chalk, especially in the form of a crayon used for writing or drawing on a hard, smooth surface such as a chalkboard. **3** a crayon of chalk. **4** a record of credit given; tally.
by a long chalk, *Esp. Brit. Informal.* by far.
not by a long chalk, *Esp. Brit. Informal.* not at all; by no means.
—v. **1** mark, write, or draw with chalk. **2** mix or rub with chalk; whiten with chalk. **3** score; record. **4** of paint, become chalky or powdery when dry.
chalk up, a write down; record. **b** score. **c** attribute: *Chalk it up to simple human error.* ⟨OE *cealc* < L *calx, calcis* lime⟩
—'chalk,like, *adj.*
☛ *Hom.* CHOCK.

chalk•board ['tʃɒk,bɔrd] *n.* a board having a smooth, hard surface for writing or drawing on with chalk.

chalk talk a lecture illustrated by drawings and diagrams in chalk on a chalkboard.

chalk•y ['tʃɒki] *adj.* **chalk•i•er, chalk•i•est. 1** of chalk; containing chalk. **2** like chalk; white as chalk: *The clown's face was chalky.* **—'chalk•i•ness,** *n.*

chal•lah ['xʌlə] *or* ['xɑlə] *n.* the loaf of rich white bread, made with yeast and eggs, and braided, traditionally eaten on the Jewish Sabbath. ⟨< Yiddish *Khale* < Hebrew *chala* loaf of bread⟩

chal•lenge ['tʃæləndʒ] *v.* **-lenged, -leng•ing;** *n.* *—v.* **1** call to engage in a fight or contest: *to challenge someone to a duel. The new school has challenged us to a basketball tournament.* **2** stop (a person) and question his or her right to do what he or she is doing or to be where he or she is: *When she tried to enter the building, the guard challenged her.* **3** demand proof of; question or dispute (something): *My friends challenged my statement that Fredericton was the oldest city in Canada.* **4** *Law.* object formally to, especially to a juror or jury. **5** demand action or effort from; stimulate: *The possibility of space travel has challenged the human imagination for centuries.* **6** call upon the inner resources of (someone): *He is challenged by his disability.*
—n. **1** a call to a fight or contest: *We have accepted the challenge.* **2** a call to justify or account for oneself or one's actions: *The sentry called out a challenge as they approached.* **3** a demand for proof; a questioning of the truth of something: *Their challenge led me to read up on the history of our country.* **4** any activity which presents interesting problems: *I enjoy a challenge.* **5** *Law.* a formal objection, especially to a juror or jury. ⟨ME < OF *chalenge*, n., earlier *chalonge* (also OF *chalenger*, v., < L *calumniari* to slander) < L *calumnia* false accusation. Doublet of CALUMNIATE, CALUMNY.⟩ **—'chal•lenge•a•ble,** *adj.*
—'chal•leng•er, *n.*

chal•lis ['ʃæli] *n.* a lightweight, usually printed, fabric of wool, wool and cotton, or a synthetic fibre, used for dresses, blouses, etc. ⟨origin uncertain⟩

chal•one ['kæloun] *n.* an endocrine substance secreted within body tissue to suppress activity in the tissue, such as cell division. ⟨< Gk. *chalon.* ppr. of *chalan* slacken⟩

chal•u•meau ['ʃælə,mou] *n. Music.* **1** the low register of the clarinet. **2** a woodwind instrument with a single reed, popular in the 17th and 18th centuries. ⟨< F < OF *chalemel* < L *calemellus*, dim. of *calamus* reed⟩

cha•lyb•e•ate [kə'lɪbiɪt] *or* [kə'lɪbi,eit] *adj., n.* *—adj.* **1** containing salts of iron. **2** tasting like iron.
—n. water, medicine, etc., containing salts of iron. ⟨< NL **chalybeatus* < L < Gk. *chalyps* steel⟩

cham [kæm] *n. Archaic.* KHAN[1]. ⟨< ME (c(h)aan (spelled *khan* since 19c.) < OF *chan* or Med.L *canus* < Turkic *khan* lord, prince < Mongolian *qan, qajan*⟩

Cha•mae•leon [kə'miliən] *n.* a southern constellation near the south celestial pole.
☛ *Hom.* CHAMELEON.

cham•ber ['tʃeimbər] *n., v.* *—n.* **1** *Archaic or poetic.* a room in a house, especially a bedroom. **2** a room in an official residence in which visitors are received. **3** a hall where a legislature or a governing body meets. **4** a group of lawmakers; a legislative or judicial body: *The Canadian Parliament has two chambers, the Senate and the House of Commons.* **5** a group of people organized for some business purpose: *Chamber of Commerce.* **6 chambers,** *pl.* **a** a set of rooms in a building to live in or use as offices. **b** the office of a lawyer or judge. **7** an enclosed space, or cavity, in the body of an animal or plant: *The human heart has four chambers.* **8** an enclosed space in machinery, especially the part of the bore of a gun that holds the charge or any of the spaces for cartridges in a revolver. **9** (*adjl.*) of, having to do with, or performing CHAMBER MUSIC: *a chamber group.* **10** CHAMBER POT.
—v. provide with or put into a chamber. ⟨ME < OF *chambre* < L *camera* < Gk. *kamaru* vaulted place. Doublet of CAMERA.⟩

chamber concert a concert of CHAMBER MUSIC.

cham•bered ['tʃeimbərd] *adj.* having a chamber or chambers; divided into compartments.

cham•ber•lain ['tʃeimbərlɪn] *n.* **1** the person who manages the household of a sovereign or a lord; steward. **2** a high official of a royal court. **3** treasurer: *the city chamberlain.* ⟨ME < OF *chamberlenc* < L *camera* vault + Gmc. *-ling*⟩

cham•ber•maid ['tʃeimbər,meid] *n.* a maid who makes the beds, cleans the bedrooms, etc., now especially in hotels.

chamber music music suited to a room or small hall; music for a trio, quartet, small orchestra, etc.

Chamber of Commerce an organization of business people whose aim is to increase business opportunities in the community in which they live.

chamber orchestra a smaller orchestra than a symphony orchestra, suitable for playing chamber music.

chamber pot a receptacle for urine, etc., used in the bedroom in the absence of indoor plumbing.

cham•bray ['ʃæmbrei] *n.* a fine cloth, especially of cotton, in a plain weave, combining coloured warp threads with white filling threads in various designs. ⟨var. of *cambric*⟩

cha•me•le•on [kə'miljən] *or* [kə'miliən] *n.* **1** any of a family (Chamaeleontidae) of mainly tree-dwelling Old World lizards having a prehensile tail, independently swivelling eyes, a very long, slender tongue, and the ability to change the colour of their skin according to changes in their environment. **2** any of various New World lizards (family Iguanidae, especially of genus *Anolis*). **3** *Informal.* a changeable or fickle person. ⟨< L *chamaeleon*

< Gk. *chamaileōn*, literally, ground lion < *chamai* on the ground, dwarf + *leōn* lion⟩
☛ *Hom.* CHAMAELEON [kə'miliən].

cham•fer ['tʃæmfər] *n., v.* *—n.* **1** a flat, slanting surface made by cutting off an edge or corner; bevel. **2** a groove or furrow. *—v.* **1** cut off at an edge or corner to make a slanting surface. **2** make a groove or furrow in; flute. ⟨< F *chamfrain*, apparently < *chant fraindre* (< L *cantum frangere*) break the side⟩

cham•ois ['ʃæmi] *or, for def. 1,* [ʃæm'wɑ] *or* ['ʃæmwɑ] *n., pl.* **-ois,** *adj., v.* **cham•oised** ['ʃæmid], **cham•ois•ing** ['ʃæmiɪŋ]. *—n.* **1** an animal (*Rupicapra rupicapra*) native to the mountains of Europe and SW Asia, belonging to the same family (Bovidae) as goats and antelope and having characteristics of both. **2** a very soft suede leather originally made from the hide of this animal, now made from the hide of sheep or goats. **3** a piece of this leather, used for polishing glass and metal. **4** a yellowish brown. *—adj.* **1** made of chamois. **2** yellowish brown. *—v.* polish with a chamois. ⟨< F < LL *camox*⟩

cham•o•mile ['kæmə,maɪl] *or* ['kæmə,mɪl] See CAMOMILE.

champ[1] [tʃæmp] *v.* **1** bite and chew noisily. **2** bite on impatiently: *The racehorse champed its bit.*
champ (at) the bit, be restless or impatient: *After months with his leg in plaster, the boy was champing at the bit to go skiing again.* ⟨? related to CHAP[3]⟩

champ[2] [tʃæmp] *n. Informal.* champion.

champac or **cham•pak** ['tʃæmpæk] *or* ['tʃʌmpʌk] *n.* a tree (*Michelia champaca*) of the magnolia family, native to Asia, having fragrant yellow or orange flowers and yielding an oil used in making perfume. ⟨< Hind. *champak*⟩

cham•pagne [ʃæm'pein] *n., adj.* *—n.* **1** a sparkling, bubbling wine, first made in Champagne, France. **2** a very pale, yellowish brown or orange yellow.
—adj. having the colour champagne.
☛ *Hom.* CHAMPAIGN.

cham•paign [ʃæm'pein] *n., adj.* *—n.* a wide plain; level, open country.
—adj. level and open. ⟨ME < OF *champaigne* < LL *campania* < L *campus* field. Doublet of CAMPAIGN.⟩
☛ *Hom.* CHAMPAGNE.

cham•pi•gnon [ʃæm'pɪnjən] *or* ['ʃæmpɪn,jɔ̃]; *French,* [ʃɑ̃pi'njɔ̃] *n.* an edible mushroom, especially the common meadow mushroom (*Agaricus campestris*) having a white cap with brown or pinkish gills underneath. ⟨< MF⟩

cham•pi•on ['tʃæmpiən] *n., v.* *—n.* **1** a person, animal, or thing that wins first place in a game or contest: *the swimming champion of the world.* **2** (*adjl.*) having won first place; ahead of all others: *a champion boxer, a champion rose.* **3** a person who fights or speaks for another or for a cause; defender; supporter: *a great champion of peace.* **4** a brave fighter.
—v. fight or speak in behalf of; defend; support: *Jean-Luc championed his friends.* ⟨ME < OF < LL *campio, -onis* < L *campus* field (i.e., of battle)⟩ **—'cham•pi•on•less,** *adj.*

cham•pi•on•ship ['tʃæmpiən,ʃɪp] *n.* **1** the position of a champion; first place. **2** defence; support. **3** a competition or series of competitions to decide a winner. **4** (*adjl.*) of or being such a competition or series: *the championship game.*

chance [tʃæns] *n., v.* **chanced, chanc•ing.** *—n.* **1** an opportunity: *a chance to make some money.* **2** the likelihood of something happening; probability: *There's a good chance that she'll show up in time for dinner.* **3** fate; luck; destiny. **4** an unplanned happening; fortuity: *Chance led to the finding of the diamond mine.* **5** a risk: *He took a chance when he swam the Channel.* **6** (*adjl.*) not expected or planned; happening by accident: *a chance meeting.* **7** *Baseball.* any handling of the ball which results in a putout, an assist, or an error by a defensive player. **8** *Cricket.* a possible catch. **9** a lottery or raffle ticket.
by chance, a accidentally: *The meeting came about by chance.* **b** by some turn of events: *If by chance the weather clears, we can go for a swim.*
on the chance, depending on the possibility.
on the off chance, depending on luck: *She went to the theatre on the off chance of getting a returned ticket.*
stand a chance, have favourable prospects: *Our team still stands a chance of winning the cup.*
(the) chances are (that), it is likely (that).
—v. **1** happen. **2** accept the danger of; risk: *I wouldn't chance a canoe ride without a life jacket.*
chance it, *Informal.* take a risk.
chance on or **upon,** happen to find or meet: *There they chanced on a real treasure—a first edition.* ⟨ME < OF *cheance* < L *cadentia* a falling < *cadere* fall. Doublet of CADENCE, CADENZA.⟩

chan•cel ['tʃænsəl] *n.* the space around the altar of a church, used by the clergy and the choir. It is often separated from the rest of the church by a railing, lattice, or screen. See BASILICA for picture. ⟨ME < OF < L *cancelli* a grating⟩

chan•cel•ler•y ['tʃænsələri] *n., pl.* **-ler•ies. 1** the position of a chancellor. **2** the office of a chancellor. **3** the office of an ambassador in a foreign country. Also, **chancellory.**

chan•cel•lor ['tʃænsələr] *n.* **1** a high official who is the secretary of a monarch or noble, or the chief secretary of an embassy. **2** the chief judge of a court of chancery or equity. **3** the prime minister or other very high official of some European countries. **4** any of various high British government officials, especially: **a** the CHANCELLOR OF THE EXCHEQUER. **b** the LORD CHANCELLOR. **5** the honorary head of a university, who presides over convocation and is usually a member of the university senate and the board of governors. ⟨ME < AF *canceler, chanceler* < LL *cancellarius* officer stationed at a tribunal < *cancelli* a grating, bars (which enclosed the chancel)⟩

Chancellor of the Exchequer in the United Kingdom, the highest official of the treasury.

chan•cel•lor•ship ['tʃænsələr,ʃɪp] *n.* **1** the position of a chancellor. **2** the term of office of a chancellor.

chan•cel•lor•y ['tʃænsələri] *n.* chancellery.

chan•cer•y ['tʃænsəri] *n., pl.* **-cer•ies. 1** *Brit.* the court of the Lord Chancellor; a division of the High Court of Justice. **2** a court that deals with cases involving fairness and justice outside the scope of common law or statute law. **3** an office where public records are kept. **4** the office of a chancellor. **5** the principle of equity; the spirit rather than the letter of the law. **6** *Wrestling.* a grip on the head.
in chancery, a in a court of equity. **b** in a helpless position. ⟨var. of CHANCELLERY⟩

chan•cre ['ʃæŋkər] *n.* a hard, reddish ulcer or sore that is the first symptom of syphilis. ⟨< F < L *cancer.* Doublet of CANCER, CANKER.⟩ **—'chanc•rous,** *adj.*

chanc•y ['tʃænsi] *adj.* **chanc•i•er, chanc•i•est.** *Informal.* **1** subject to chance; risky; uncertain. **2** *Scottish.* lucky; favourable.

chan•de•lier [,ʃændə'lir] *n.* a fixture with branches for lights, usually hanging from the ceiling. ⟨ME < OF < VL *candelarius* < L *candela* candle < *candere* shine. Doublet of CHANDLER.⟩

chan•delle [ʃæn'dɛl] *n., v.* **-delled, -del•ling.** *—n. Aeronautics.* a fast climbing turn in which the aircraft's momentum increases the rate of climb.
—v. make a chandelle. ⟨< F *chandelle* candle⟩

chan•dler ['tʃændlər] *n.* **1** a maker or seller of candles. **2** a dealer in groceries and supplies: *a ship chandler.* ⟨ME < AF *chandeler* < VL *candelarius.* Doublet of CHANDELIER.⟩

Chan•dler wobble a small, uneven oscillation of the earth's axis, occurring every 416 to 433 days. ⟨< after Seth *Chandler* (1846-1913), American astronomer⟩

chan•dler•y ['tʃændləri] *n., pl.* **-dler•ies. 1** a storeroom for candles. **2** the warehouse, goods, or business of a chandler.

change [tʃeindʒ] *v.* **changed, chang•ing;** *n.* *—v.* **1** become different: *He had changed since they had seen him last. The bus schedule has changed again.* **2** of the male voice during adolescence, lower in pitch. **3** make different: *She changed the room by painting the walls green.* **4** get rid of, stop, or remove (something or someone) in favour of something else: *We are changing to a new format. I am thinking of changing my lawyer.* **5** pass from one position or state to another: *The wind changed from east to west.* **6** exchange: *I changed seats with my sister.* **7** get or give small units of money that equal (a larger unit): *to change a five-dollar bill for two twos and a loony.* **8** put fresh clothes or coverings on: *to change the baby, to change the bed.* **9** put on other clothing: *I want to change first.* **10** transfer from one bus, plane, etc., to another: *It's not a direct flight; you have to change at Winnipeg.*
change around, exchange places or directions.
change for the better, improve.
change hands. See HAND.
change off, alternate with another in doing something; take turns: *We changed off hoeing and raking to make the job easier.*
change over, a exchange places or tasks. **b** adopt a new system, method, etc.: *Canada changed over to the metric system more than 20 years ago.*
change places with, have someone else's lifestyle or job.
—n. **1** a changing; a passing from one position or state to another. **2** a changed condition. **3** the lack of sameness; variety:

Let me drive for a change. **4** a thing to be used in place of another of the same kind: *a change of clothes.* **5** the money returned to a person when he or she has given an amount larger than the price of what he or she buys. **6** smaller units of money given in place of a large unit of money: *Please give me change for this five-dollar bill.* **7** coins: *I have five dollars and some change.* **8 changes,** *pl.* the different ways in which a set of bells can be rung.
ring the changes, a ring a set of bells in all its different ways. **b** do or express something in many different ways. ⟨ME < OF *changer* < LL *cambiare*⟩ **—'chang•er,** *n.*

☛ *Syn. v.* **1, 2. Change,** ALTER = make or become different. **Change** is the general word, but emphasizes the idea of a fundamental difference in the make-up of the person or thing, of making or becoming completely different: *She used to be shy, but has changed since she went to college.* **Alter** = change in one particular way, without changing the person or thing as a whole: *We can alter the kitchen enough to put in a freezer if we rehang the door.*

'change [tʃeindʒ] *n. Archaic.* an exchange; a place where people trade. Also, **Change.**

change•a•ble ['tʃeindʒəbəl] *adj.* **1** that can change; likely to change. **2** that can be changed; likely to be changed. **3** having a colour or appearance that changes: *Silk is called changeable when it looks different in different lights.* **—,change•a'bil•i•ty** or **'change•a•ble•ness,** *n.* **—'change•a•bly,** *adv.*

change•ful ['tʃeindʒfəl] *adj.* full of changes; likely to change; changing. **—'change•ful•ly,** *adv.* **—'change•ful•ness,** *n.*

change•less ['tʃeindʒlɪs] *adj.* not changing; not likely to change; constant; steadfast. **—'change•less•ly,** *adv.* **—'change•less•ness,** *n.*

change•ling ['tʃeindʒlɪŋ] *n.* **1** a child secretly substituted for another. **2** a strange, stupid, or ugly child, supposed to have been left by fairies in place of a child carried off by them.

change of heart a profound change of attitude; conversion.

change of life menopause.

change of venue 1 a change of the place of a trial. **2** a change in place for any activity.

change–o•ver ['tʃeindʒ ,ouvər] *n.* **1** conversion from one method, model, system, etc., to a completely different one. **2** a transfer of ownership or control.

change ringing the art of ringing a peal of bells in regularly varying order. There are many styles of change ringing, each with its own name.

chan•nel ['tʃænəl] *n., v.* **-nelled** or **-neled, -nel•ling** or **-nel•ing.** *—n.* **1** the bed of a stream, river, etc. **2** a body of water joining two larger bodies of water: *the English Channel.* **3** the deeper part of a waterway: *There is shallow water on both sides of the channel in this river.* **4** a passage for liquids; groove. **5** a means of communication or expression: *The information came through secret channels.* **6** a course of action; field of activity: *He sought to find a suitable channel for his enthusiasm.* **7** a narrow band of radio or television frequencies, sufficient for one-way transmission.
—v. **1** convey through or as if through a channel. **2** form a channel in; cut out as a channel: *The river had channelled its way through the rocks.* **3** to direct into a particular course; concentrate. **4** be a channel for. **5** *New Age.* receive spiritual energy, awareness, etc. from some supernatural source through meditation, etc. **6** put grooves or fluting in (a column, etc.) ⟨ME < OF *chanel* < L *canalis.* Doublet of CANAL.⟩

chan•son [ʃɑ̃'sɔ̃] *n. French.* song.

chan•son•nier [ʃɑ̃sɔ'nje] *n. French.* a songwriter or singer, especially one who sings his own compositions in cabarets, etc.

chan•son•nière [ʃɑ̃sɔ'njɛʀ] *n. French.* a female chansonnier.

chant [tʃænt] *n., v. —n.* **1** song. **2** a song in which several syllables or words are sung on one tone. Chants are used in some Christian church services. **3** a psalm, prayer, mantra, or other words for chanting. **4** a rhythmic, monotonous way of talking. **5** the melody played on a bagpipe.
—v. **1** sing. **2** sing to a chant, or utter in the manner of a chant. A choir chants psalms or prayers. **3** repeat rhythmically and monotonously: *We chanted, "Go, team, go!"* ⟨ME < OF *chanter* < L *cantare* < *canere* sing⟩

chan•te•cler ['tʃæntə,klir] *n.* See CHANTICLEER.

chan•ter ['tʃæntər] *n.* **1** a person who sings or chants. **2 a** one who sings in a choir; chorister. **b** the chief singer in a choir; cantor. **3** *Roman Catholic Church.* a priest who sings Mass in a chantry. **4** in a bagpipe, the pipe on which the melody, or chant, is played.

chan•te•relle [,ʃæntə'rɛl] *or* [,tʃæntə'rɛl] *n.* any of a genus (*Cantharellus*) of orange or yellow mushrooms with a funnel-shaped cap, especially *C. cibarius,* an edible species, yellow in colour and having an apricotlike odour when fresh. ⟨< F < L *cantharus* cup < Gk. *kantharos*⟩

chan•teuse [ʃɑ̃'tøz] *n. French.* a female singer.

chant•ey ['ʃænti] *or* ['tʃænti] *n., pl.* **chant•eys.** See SHANTY[2].

chan•ti•cleer ['tʃæntə,klir] *n.* rooster. Also, **chantecler.** ⟨ME < OF *chantecler* < *chanter* sing + *cler* clear; from the name of the cock in the medieval tale of *Reynard the Fox*⟩

Chan•til•ly [ʃæn'tɪli]; *French,* [ʃɑ̃ti'ji] *n.* a type of fine lace, having a netlike pattern of six-pointed stars. ⟨< *Chantilly,* a town in N France, formerly famous for lace manufacturing⟩

chan•try ['tʃæntri] *n., pl.* **-tries.** *Roman Catholic Church.* **1** a chapel attached to a church, used for the less important services. **2** an endowment to pay for the singing or saying of Masses for a person's soul. **3** a chapel, altar, or part of a church similarly endowed. **4** the priests thus endowed. ⟨ME < OF *chanterie* singing < *chanter* sing⟩

chant•y ['ʃænti] *or* ['tʃænti] *n., pl.* **chant•ies.** See SHANTY[2].

Cha•nu•kah or **Cha•nuk•kah** ['xanəkə] *or* ['xanʊ,ka]; *Hebrew,* ['xanʊ,ka] See HANUKKAH.

cha•os ['keiɒs] *n.* **1** great confusion; complete disorder: *The whirlwind left chaos behind it.* **2** the infinite space or formless matter thought to have existed before the universe came into being. ⟨< L < Gk.⟩

cha•ot•ic [kei'ɒtɪk] *adj.* in great confusion; very confused; completely disordered. **—cha'ot•i•cal•ly,** *adv.*

chap[1] [tʃæp] *v.* **chapped, chap•ping;** *n. —v.* of skin, crack open; make or become rough: *A person's lips often chap in cold weather. Cold weather chapped his hands.*
—n. a place where the skin is chapped. ⟨ME *chappe(n)* cut⟩

chap[2] [tʃæp] *n. Informal.* a fellow; man; boy. ⟨a shortened form of *chapman*⟩

chap[3] [tʃæp] *n.* CHOP[2]. ⟨? < *chap*[1]⟩

chap. 1 chapter. **2** chaplain. **3** chapel.

cha•pa•re•jos [,ʃæpə'reious]; *Spanish,* [,tʃapa'rehos] *n.pl.* in the SW United States, strong leather trousers worn by cowboys; chaps. Also, **chaparajos,** *Spanish,* [-'rahos]. ⟨< Mexican Sp.⟩

chap•ar•ral [,ʃæpə'ræl] *or* [,tʃæpə'ræl] *n.* in the SW United States, a thicket of low shrubs, etc., especially dwarf evergreen oaks. ⟨< Sp. *chaparral* < *chaparro* evergreen oak⟩

chaparral pea a spiky evergreen bush (*Pickeringia montana*) of the legume family, growing in chaparrals and having large purple flowers.

cha•pa•ti [tʃə'pɑti] *n.* a flat bread like a pancake, made of whole-wheat flour and cooked on a griddle, common in India. Also, **chapatti.** ⟨< Hind. *capati* flat⟩

chap•book ['tʃæp,bʊk] *n.* a small book or pamphlet of poems, ballads, etc. ⟨because formerly sold by *chapmen*⟩

cha•peau [ʃæ'pou]; *French,* [ʃa'po] *n., pl.* **-peaux** [-'pou] *or* **-peaus** [-'pouz]; *French,* [-'po]. ⟨< F < OF *chapel* hat < VL *cappellum* < LL *cappa* cape. Related to CAP, CAPE.⟩

chap•el ['tʃæpəl] *n.* **1** a building for worship, not so large as a church. **2** a small place for worship within a larger building such as a church or synagogue. **3** a room or building for worship in a palace, school, etc. **4** a religious service in a chapel: *We were late for chapel.* **5** *Brit.* **a** a place of worship of Nonconformist groups. **b** Nonconformist doctrine or practices. **6** an association of journeymen printers for regulating conditions of work among themselves. ⟨ME < OF *chapele* < LL *cappella;* originally a shrine in which was preserved the *cappa* or cape of St. Martin⟩

chap•er•on•age ['ʃæpərənɪdʒ] *n.* the activities of a chaperone; protection of a chaperone.

chap•er•one or **chap•er•on** ['ʃæpə,roun] *or* [ʃæpə'roun] *n., v.* **-oned, -on•ing.** *—n.* **1** especially formerly, a married woman or an older woman who accompanies a young, unmarried woman in public for the sake of convention and protection. **2** an older person who attends young people's parties, student dances, etc., to ensure proper behaviour.
—v. act as a chaperone to. ⟨< F *chaperon* hood, protector < *chape* cape < LL *cappa.* Related to CAP, CAPE.⟩

chap•fall•en ['tʃæp,fɒlən] *or* ['tʃɒp,fɒlən] *adj.* **1** having the lower jaw hanging loose from being tired. **2** dejected; discouraged; humiliated. Also, **chopfallen.** ⟨< *chap*[3]⟩

chap•i•ter ['tʃæpətər] *n. Architecture.* the capital of a column. ⟨< OF *chapitre.* Doublet of CHAPTER.⟩

chap•lain ['tʃæplən] *n.* a member of the clergy officially authorized to perform religious functions for a family, court, society, public institution, or unit in the armed forces. ⟨ME < OF *chapelain* < LL *capellanus* < *cappella.* See CHAPEL.⟩

chap•lain•cy ['tʃæplənsi] *n.* the position of a chaplain.

chap•lain•ship ['tʃæplən,ʃɪp] *n.* chaplaincy.

chap•let ['tʃæplɪt] *n.* **1** a wreath worn on the head. **2** a string of beads. **3** *Roman Catholic Church.* **a** a string of beads, one third as long as a rosary, used for keeping count in saying prayers. **b** the prayers said with such beads. **4** *Architecture.* a rounded moulding looking like a string of beads. ⟨ME *chapelet* < OF, dim. of *chapel* headdress. See CHAPEAU.⟩
—'chap•let•ed, *adj.*

Chap•lin•esque [,tʃæplɪn'ɛsk] *adj.* of or having to do with Sir Charles Chaplin (1889-1977) or his style of films.

chap•man ['tʃæpmən] *n., pl.* **-men.** *Archaic.* **1** peddler. **2** a man whose business is buying and selling; merchant; trader; dealer. ⟨OE *cēapman* < *cēap* trade + *man* man⟩

chaps [ʃæps] *or* [tʃæps] *n.pl.* backless leggings of tough leather, worn by cowboys to protect their legs when riding. ⟨short for *chaparajos*⟩

chap•ter ['tʃæptər] *n., v.* *—n.* **1** a main division of a book or other writing, dealing with a certain part of the story or subject. **2** anything like a chapter; part or section of something thought of as a story: *The development of television is an interesting chapter in modern science.* **3** a local division of an organization; branch of a club, society, etc. **4** a group of clergy, usually attached to a cathedral, or of monastics. **5** a meeting of such a group.
—v. divide into chapters; arrange in chapters. ⟨ME < OF *chapitre* < L *capitulum*, dim. of *caput* head⟩

chapter and verse **1** the exact reference for a passage of Scripture. **2** precise authority (*for*): *He cited chapter and verse for his opinions.* **3** exact information and complete detail.

chapter house **1** the building where a CHAPTER (def. 4) meets. **2** the house of a college fraternity or sorority.

char¹ [tʃɑr] *v.* **charred, char•ring;** *n.* **1** burn to charcoal. **2** burn slightly; scorch.
—n. anything burned, such as charcoal.
⟨? < *charcoal*⟩

char² [tʃɑr] *n., v.* **charred, char•ring.** *Esp. Brit.* *—n.* **1** charwoman. **2** an odd job; chore.
—v. **1** do housework by the day or hour. **2** do odd jobs. ⟨OE *cerr* turn, occasion. Doublet of CHORE.⟩

char³ [tʃɑr] *n., pl.* **char.** any of a genus (*Salvelinus*) of mostly freshwater fish belonging to the salmon and trout family. The arctic char, brook trout, and lake trout are common Canadian char. ⟨origin uncertain⟩

char•a•banc ['ʃærə,bæŋ] *or* ['ʃɛrə-], ['ʃærə,bæŋk] *or* ['ʃɛrə-] *Brit.* a large motorbus, used for excursions. Also, **char-à-banc.** ⟨< F *char-à-bancs* car with benches⟩

char•a•cin ['kærəsɪn] *or* ['kɛrəsɪn] *n.* any small freshwater fish of the family Characidae, native to tropical areas and having powerful jaws. ⟨< NL < Gk. *charax*⟩

char•ac•ter ['kærɪktər] *or* ['kɛrɪktər] *n.* **1** the combination of qualities or features that distinguishes one person, group, or thing from another; kind; sort; nature: *The two organizations have similar goals but differ greatly in character. The character of the soil in the southern part of the province is different from that in the central part.* **2** a famous figure, usually in history. **3** the combined moral, emotional, and mental qualities that a person or group has: *a person of shallow, changeable character.* **4** moral firmness; integrity: *It takes character to endure hardship for very long.* **5** the estimate formed of a person's qualities; reputation: *His meanness was a stain on his character.* **6** position; status; role: *In his character as club secretary, he is responsible for all correspondence.* **7** a person or animal portrayed in a play, novel, or story: *The main character is a miner.* **8** (*adjl.*) *Theatre or film.* of, for, or acting in roles that emphasize strong characteristics of personality that may be very different from those of the actor himself or herself: *a character actor, a character part.* **9** *Informal.* a person who attracts attention for being different or eccentric: *I'd like to meet him; I hear he's really a character.* **10** *Genetics.* a distinctive structure, function, or quality that is determined by heredity: *Marquis wheat is valued for its character of rust resistance.* **11** in writing or printing, a letter, symbol, or other mark, including a space. *A, a,* %, +, –, *1, 2,* and *3* are characters. **12** a style in printing or calligraphy. **13** *Computer technology.* a letter, digit, or other symbol that can be stored and processed (though not necessarily displayed) by a computer. **14** CHARACTER SKETCH. **15** a written testimonial, especially from a former employer, describing the qualities and capacities of an employee.
in character, a *Theatre.* true to character: *The actor remained in character throughout the play.* **b** consistent with a person's known character; as expected: *Her stinging letter to the editor was entirely in character.*
out of character, a *Theatre.* not true to character. **b** not consistent with a person's known character; not as expected: *It was out of character for her to go off without letting anyone know.*
⟨ME < OF *caractere* < L < Gk. *charaktēr* stamped mark < *charassein* engrave⟩
☛ *Syn.* **1, 3. Character,** PERSONALITY, INDIVIDUALITY = the qualities that make a person what he or she is. **Character** applies to the moral qualities that determine the way a person thinks, feels, and acts in the important matters of life, especially in relation to the principles of right and wrong. **Personality** applies to the personal qualities that make one person different from another and determine the way he or she acts in his or her social and personal relations. **Individuality** applies to the particular qualities that make a person himself or herself, an individual: *He has a weak character, but a winning personality and great individuality.*

character actor an actor who can play a variety of roles, especially those with unusual characteristics.

char•ac•ter•is•tic [,kærɪktə'rɪstɪk] *or* [,kɛrɪktə'rɪstɪk] *adj., n.* *—adj.* distinguishing (a person or thing) from others; special; typical: *Such outbursts are characteristic of insecure people. Bananas have a characteristic smell.*
—n. **1** a special quality or feature; whatever distinguishes one person or thing from others: *Cheerfulness is a characteristic that we admire in people. An elephant's trunk is its most noticeable characteristic.* **2** *Mathematics.* the integral part of a logarithm. In the logarithm 2.954 24, the characteristic is 2 and the mantissa is .954 24.
☛ *Syn. n.* **1.** See note at FEATURE.

char•ac•ter•is•ti•cal•ly [,kærɪktə'rɪstɪkli] *or* [,kɛrɪktə'rɪstɪkli] *adv.* in a way that shows characteristics; specially; typically.

char•ac•ter•i•za•tion [,kærɪktərə'zeiʃən] *or* [,kɛr-], [,kærɪktəraɪ'zeiʃən] *or* [,kɛr-] *n.* **1** the act of characterizing; description of characteristics. **2** the creation of characters in a play, book, etc.

char•ac•ter•ize ['kærɪktə,raɪz] *or* ['kɛrɪktə,raɪz] *v.* **-ized, -iz•ing. 1** describe the special qualities or features of (a person or thing); describe. **2** be a characteristic of; distinguish: *A camel is characterized by the humps on its back and the ability to do without water for several days.* **3** give character to: *The author characterized his heroine in a few short paragraphs.*

char•ac•ter•less ['kærɪktərlɪs] *or* ['kɛrɪktərlɪs] *adj.* **1** without character. **2** without distinction; uninteresting.

char•ac•ter•o•log•i•cal [,kærəktərə'lɒdʒəkəl] *or* [,kɛrəktərə'lɒdʒəkəl] *adj.* of or having to do with character: *a characterological study.*

character sketch a brief description of a person's qualities.

char•ac•ter•y ['kærɪktəri] *or* ['kɛrɪktəri] *n., pl.* **-ter•ies.** the set of signs or symbols used to express ideas.

cha•rade [ʃə'reid] *n.* **1** a word represented by a pantomime, picture, or tableau. **2 charades,** *pl.* a parlour game in which a word, title, proverb, etc. is acted out by a group of people while others try to guess what it is. **3** a very obvious pretence. ⟨< F < Provençal *charrada* < *charra* chatter⟩

char•broil or **char–broil** ['tʃɑr,brɔɪl] *v.* cook on a rack over burning charcoal.

char•coal ['tʃɑr,koul] *n., v.* *—n.* **1** the black substance, a form of carbon, made by partly burning wood or bones in a place from which the air is shut out. Charcoal is used as a fuel, filter, and absorbent. **2** a stick, pencil, or crayon of charcoal for drawing. **3** a drawing made with such a stick, pencil, or crayon. **4** a very dark grey.
—v. mark, write, or blacken with charcoal. ⟨ME *charcole*⟩

charcoal burner **1** anything in which charcoal is burned, such as a stove. **2** a person whose work is making charcoal.

chard [tʃɑrd] *n.* a variety of white beet; Swiss chard. ⟨< F *charde* < L *carduus* thistle, artichoke⟩

Char•don•nay [,ʃɑrdə'nei] *n.* **1** a white grape used to make wine. **2** a dry, white wine made from these grapes.

charge [tʃɑrdʒ] *v.* **charged, charg•ing;** *n.* *—v.* **1** ask for as a price; ask (someone) for a price of: *He charged us $45 for*

repairing the radio. **2** record as an obligation or debt: *This store will charge things that you buy.* **3** put down a debt or obligation against: *Please charge my account.* **4** require monetary payment (*for*): *They charge for hot water in the cafeteria.* **5** load; fill. A gun is charged with powder and shot. A battery is charged with electricity. **6** restore the active materials of (a storage battery): *The battery of a car is charged automatically when the motor is running.* **7** give a task, duty, or responsibility to: *The law charges the police with keeping order.* **8** give an order or command to; direct: *She charged us to keep the plan secret. The judge charged the jury.* **9** accuse, especially in a court of law: *The driver was charged with speeding.* **10** attack; rush with force: *The soldiers charged the enemy.* **11** attribute (a fault, etc.) to a person. **12** *Heraldry.* **a** place (a bearing or charge) on an escutcheon, shield, etc.: *to charge crosses on a field.* **b** place a bearing or charge upon (an escutcheon, shield, etc.): *to charge a field with crosses.* **13** *Cdn. Hockey.* try to stop (an opposing player) illegally by taking more than two steps toward him or her in a direct attack.
charge off, **a** subtract as a loss. **b** charge up.
charge out, **a** check (books) out of a library. **b** check out of a hotel, etc.
charge up, ascribe: *A bad mistake must be charged up to experience.*
—n. **1** a price asked for or put on something. *Taxes are a charge on property.* **2** a debt to be paid: *Will that be cash or charge?* **3** the quantity needed to load or fill something. A gun is fired by exploding the charge of powder and shot. **4** an amount of electricity. **5** a task; duty; responsibility: *Arresting criminals is the charge of the police.* **6** care; management: *Doctors and nurses have charge of sick people.* **7** a person, persons, or thing under the care or management of someone: *Sick people are the charges of doctors and nurses.* **8** an order; command; direction: *a judge's charge to the jury.* **9** an accusation, especially in a court of law: *She admitted the charge and paid the fine.* **10** an attack; forceful rush: *The charge drove the enemy back.* **11** *Heraldry.* a device borne on an escutcheon; bearing. **12** *Informal.* a thrill; pleasant stimulation: *I get a charge out of watching my daughter play tennis.*
in charge, in command; having control or management: *Who's in charge here?*
in charge of, having control, management, or supervision of: *Dr. Lois Hsing is in charge of the case.*
in the charge of, under the control or management of; in the custody of: *The suspect was placed in the charge of a police constable.* ⟨ME < OF *charger* < LL *carricare* load < L *carrus* wagon. Doublet of CARRY.⟩
☛ *Syn. v.* **9. Charge,** ACCUSE = put the blame on (a person). **Charge** (followed by **with**) may suggest the blame for some minor wrongdoing, such as breaking a rule, but it commonly suggests a serious offence, such as breaking a law, and making a formal statement before the proper authority: *He was charged with leaving the grounds without permission.* **Accuse** (followed by **of**) suggests making the charge directly to the person blamed and expressing disapproval, but not necessarily taking him or her before authority: *He accused me of lying.*
—n. **1.** See note at PRICE.

charge•a•ble [ˈtʃɑrdʒəbəl] *adj.* **1** that can be charged; likely to be charged: *If you take anything that belongs to someone else, you are chargeable with theft. Taxes are chargeable against the owners of property.* **2** liable to become a public charge.

charge account an arrangement with a business firm for purchasing goods or services on credit: *We have charge accounts at two department stores.*

charge card CREDIT CARD.

charge–coupled device a small electronic device based on a semiconductor silicon chip, used as a light sensor in video systems and astronomy, and used instead of a transistor to control electric currents in computers.

charged [tʃɑrdʒd] *adj.* that has been loaded; filled.

char•gé d'af•faires [ʃɑrˌʒei dəˈfɛr]; *French,* [ʃaʀʒedaˈfɛʀ] *pl.* **char•gés d'af•faires** [ʃɑrˌʒeiz dəˈfɛr]; *French,* [ʃaʀʒedaˈfɛʀ] an official who takes the place of an ambassador, minister, or other diplomat. ⟨< F, (*one*) entrusted with affairs⟩

charged particle a particle, as a proton, electron, or helium ion, which bears a positive or negative charge.

charge plate a CREDIT CARD embossed with the holder's name and account number so that these may be printed on a bill, receipt, etc.

charg•er[1] [ˈtʃɑrdʒər] *n.* **1** a horse ridden in war. **2** a person or thing that charges. **3** a device that gives an electrical charge to storage batteries. ⟨< *charge*⟩

charg•er[2] [ˈtʃɑrdʒər] *n. Archaic.* a large, flat dish; platter. ⟨< OF **chargeour* or *chargeoir* < *charger* load. See CHARGE.⟩

charg•ing [ˈtʃɑrdʒɪŋ] *n., v.* *—n.* **1** the act of loading; filling. **2** *Hockey.* an illegal action involving a direct forward attack of more than two steps against an opponent in an attempt to take him or her out of the play.
—v. ppr. of CHARGE.

Chari–Nile [ˈʃɑri ˈnaɪl] *n.* a subgroup of the Nilo-Saharan language family. Sudanic belongs to the Chari-Nile language family. ⟨after the *Chari* and *Nile* Rivers in Africa⟩

char•i•ot [ˈtʃæriət] *or* [ˈtʃɛriət] *n.* **1** a two-wheeled vehicle pulled by horses, used in ancient times for fighting, for racing, and in processions. **2** a four-wheeled carriage or coach. ⟨ME < OF *chariot* < *char* < L *carrus* four-wheeled cart⟩

char•i•ot•eer [ˌtʃæriəˈtir] *or* [ˌtʃɛriəˈtir] *n.* **1** a person who drives a chariot. **2 Charioteer,** the northern constellation Auriga.

char•ism [ˈkærɪzəm] *or* [ˈkɛrɪzəm] *n.* charisma.

cha•ris•ma [kəˈrɪzmə] *n., pl.* **-ma•ta** [-mətə]. **1** *Theology.* a spiritual gift or grace giving a person the gift of prophesying, healing, etc. **2** magnetic and compelling personal power, especially as attributed to leaders who gain the enthusiastic support of large numbers of people. ⟨< Gk. *charisma, -atos*⟩

char•is•mat•ic [ˌkærɪzˈmætɪk] *or* [ˌkɛrɪzˈmætɪk] *adj., n.* *—adj.* **1** of or having to do with a charisma. **2** having charisma; capable of inspiring popular allegiance. **3** of or having to do with a Christian religious group emphasizing the charismata and spontaneity in worship. *—n.* **1** an adherent of such a religious group. **2** a person having charisma.

char•i•ta•ble [ˈtʃærətəbəl] *or* [ˈtʃɛrətəbəl] *adj.* **1** of or for charity. **2** generous in giving help to poor or suffering people. **3** kindly in judging people and their actions.
—ˈchar•i•ta•ble•ness, *n.* **—ˈchar•i•ta•bly,** *adv.*

char•i•ty [ˈtʃærəti] *or* [ˈtʃɛrəti] *n., pl.* **-ties.** **1** the giving of help to the poor or suffering. **2** the help, money, etc. given. **3** a fund, institution, or organization for helping the poor or suffering. **4** kindness in judging the faults of other people. **5** love for one's fellow human beings. **6** kindliness. ⟨ME < OF *charite* < L *caritas* dearness < *carus* dear⟩

cha•riv•a•ri [ˌʃɪvəˈri] *or* [ʃəˌrɪvəˈri] *n., pl.* **-ris.** shivaree. ⟨< F⟩

char•la•tan [ˈʃɑrlətən] *n.* a person who pretends to have more knowledge or skill than he or she really has; quack. ⟨< F < Ital. *ciarlatano,* ult. < Mongolian *dzar* proclaim, tell lies⟩

char•la•tan•ism [ˈʃɑrlətəˌnɪzəm] *n.* the practices or methods of a charlatan; quackery. Also, **charlatanry.**

Charles's Law [ˈtʃɑrlzɪz] the principle that the volume of a gas varies directly with its temperature. ⟨after J. *Charles* (1746-1823), French physicist⟩

Charles's Wain [ˈtʃɑrlzɪz ˈwein] *Brit.* BIG DIPPER. ⟨OE *Carles Wœgn* Carl's (Charlemagne's) wagon⟩

Charles•ton [ˈtʃɑrlstən] *n., v.* *—n.* a lively dance especially popular in the 1920s, in which the heels are kicked out to the side at each step.
—v. dance the Charleston. ⟨< *Charleston,* the early capital of South Carolina⟩

char•ley horse [ˈtʃɑrli] *Informal.* a very painful cramp or stiffness in a muscle, especially of the leg or arm, caused by strain. ⟨ballplayers' slang, circa 1888, most likely referring to a lame racehorse⟩

char•lock [ˈtʃɑrlək] *n.* WILD MUSTARD. ⟨OE *cerlic*⟩

char•lotte russe [ˈʃɑrlət ˈrus] a dessert made of a mould of sponge cake filled with whipped cream or custard. ⟨< F *charlotte russe* Russian charlotte (a type of dessert)⟩

charm [tʃɑrm] *n., v.* *—n.* **1** the power of delighting or fascinating; attractiveness: *the charm of novelty. We were much impressed with the grace and charm of our hostess.* **2** a very pleasing or fascinating quality or feature: *One of her many charms.* **3** a small ornament or trinket worn on a watch chain, bracelet, etc. **4** a word, verse, act, or thing supposed to have magic power to help or harm people. **5** *Physics.* a theoretical property by which one class of quarks may be distinguished from the several others thought to exist. **6** a group of finches.
—v. **1** please greatly; delight; fascinate; attract: *The old sailor's stories of his adventures charmed the children.* **2** engage in the practice of magic. **3** act on as if by magic: *Laughter charmed away his troubles.* **4** give magic power to; protect as by a charm: *Sir Galahad seemed to bear a charmed life.* ⟨ME < OF *charme* < L *carmen* song, enchantment (? earlier **canmen*) < *canere* sing⟩ **—ˈcharm•less,** *adj.*
☛ *Syn. v.* **1. Charm,** ATTRACT, ALLURE = win a person by pleasing. **Charm** emphasizes winning and holding a person's attention and admiration by giving delight: *Her beautiful voice charms everyone.* **Attract**

emphasizes drawing attention and good will by being pleasing: *She attracts everyone she meets.* **Allure** emphasizes attracting a person by appealing to the senses and feelings: *Mountain scenery allures many tourists to the Rockies.*

charmed [tʃɑrmd] *adj., v.* —*adj.* **1** delighted; fascinated. **2** enchanted. **3** protected as by a charm: *She bears a charmed life.* **4** *Physics.* having CHARM (def. 5): *charmed quarks.*
—*v.* pt. and pp. of CHARM.

charm•er ['tʃɑrmər] *n.* one who charms, delights, or fascinates.

char•meuse [ʃɑr'muz]; *French,* [ʃaʀ'møz] *n.* a soft, lightweight fabric with a satiny finish. ⟨< F, fem. of *charmeur,* literally, charmer⟩

charm•ing ['tʃɑrmɪŋ] *adj., v.* —*adj.* very pleasing; delightful; fascinating; attractive.
—*v.* ppr. of CHARM. —**'charm•ing•ly,** *adv.*

char•nel ['tʃɑrnəl] *n., adj.* —*n.* CHARNEL HOUSE.
—*adj.* **1** of or used for a charnel. **2** like a charnel; deathlike; ghastly. ⟨ME < OF < LL *carnale,* originally neut. of L *carnalis.* Doublet of CARNAL.⟩

charnel house *Archaic.* a place where dead bodies or bones are laid.

Char•o•lais [ˌʃɑrə'lei] *n.* a breed of large white beef cattle. ⟨< F < *Charolles,* a province in France where the breed originated⟩

Char•on ['kɛrən] *n.* **1** *Greek mythology.* the boatman who ferried the spirits of the dead across the river Styx to Hades. **2** a satellite of Pluto.

char•poy ['tʃɑrpɔɪ] *n.* a light bed used in India. ⟨< Hind. *carpal*⟩

char•ry ['tʃɑri] *adj.* **-ri•er, -ri•est.** like charcoal.

chart [tʃɑrt] *n., v.* —*n.* **1** a map, especially one for the use of navigators. A sailor's chart shows the coasts, rocks, and shallow places of a sea. The course of a ship is marked on a chart. **2** an outline map for showing special conditions or facts other than just geographical information: *a weather chart.* **3** a sheet giving information in lists, pictures, tables, or diagrams. **4** such a list, table, picture, or diagram. **5** usually, **charts,** *Informal.* a listing of the best-selling recordings: *no. 3 in the charts.*
—*v.* **1** make a chart of; show on a chart: *chart a course.* **2** plan in detail. ⟨< F *charte* < L *charta* < Gk. *chartēs* leaf of paper. Doublet of CARD[1].⟩ —**'chart•less,** *adj.*
☛ *Syn.* **1.** See note at MAP.

char•ter ['tʃɑrtər] *n., v.* —*n.* **1** a written grant by a government to a colony, a group of citizens, a commercial company, etc., bestowing the right of organization, with other privileges, and specifying the form of organization. All Canadian banks must have charters from the federal government. **2** a written order from the authorities of a society, giving to a group of persons the right to organize a new chapter, branch, or lodge. **3** a document setting forth the fundamental principles or the aims and purposes of a group of nations, organizations, or individuals in a common undertaking: *the Charter of the United Nations, the Canadian Charter of Rights and Freedoms.* **4** the hiring or leasing of a bus, ship, aircraft, etc., together with a driver or pilot, for temporary private use. **5** the contract or arrangement covering this. **6** (*adjl.*) arranged by charter: *a charter flight.* **7** a special right, privilege, or immunity.
—*v.* **1** give a charter to. **2** hire or lease (a bus, ship, aircraft, etc.) for temporary private use: *We chartered a bus for the trip to the film festival.* ⟨ME < OF *chartre* < L *chartula,* dim. of *charta.* See CHART.⟩ —**'char•ter•er,** *n.* —**'char•ter•less,** *adj.*

chartered accountant a member of an accountants' institute that is chartered by the Crown. *Abbrev.*: C.A.

chartered bank in Canada, any of the privately owned banks chartered by Parliament and working under the provisions of the Bank Act with an extensive network of branches.

charter member one of the original members of a club, society, or company.

Charter of Rights and Freedoms *Cdn.* principles enshrined in the Constitution Act, 1982, guaranteeing to everyone certain fundamental freedoms, democratic rights, mobility rights, legal rights, equality rights, and minority language educational rights.

charter school *Cdn.* a school which holds a charter directly from the government, by-passing the regular local school board. It has customized curriculum and different teaching methods from the board schools.

Chart•ism ['tʃɑrtɪzəm] *n.* **1** in England, a reform movement making the political system more democratic. The movement was active between 1838 and 1848. **2** the principles of this movement, embodied in the People's Charter of 1838.

Chart•ist ['tʃɑrtɪst] *n., adj.* —*n.* an adherent of Chartism.
—*adj.* of or having to do with Chartism.

chart•ist ['tʃɑrtɪst] *n.* a stock market specialist who predicts market trends on the basis of the analysis of charts recording the price and volume of shares traded on the world's stock exchanges.

char•treuse [ʃɑr'trʊz] *or* [ʃɑr'truz]; *French,* [ʃaʀ'tʀøz] *n., adj.* —*n.* **1** a green, yellow, or white liqueur first made by Carthusian monks. **2** a light, yellowish green.
—*adj.* having the colour chartreuse. ⟨< F *chartreuse* Carthusian⟩

char•wom•an ['tʃɑrˌwʊmən] *n., pl.* **-wom•en.** *Esp. Brit.* a woman whose work is cleaning homes, offices, or public buildings; cleaning woman. ⟨OE *cerr* turn, occasion + *woman*⟩

char•y ['tʃɛri] *adj.* **char•i•er, char•i•est. 1** careful: *A cat is chary of wetting its paws.* **2** shy: *A bashful person is chary of strangers.* **3** sparing; stingy: *A jealous person is chary of praising others.* ⟨OE *cearig* < *caru* care⟩ —**'char•i•ly,** *adv.*
—**'char•i•ness,** *n.*
☛ *Hom.* CHERRY.

Cha•ryb•dis [kə'rɪbdɪs] *n.* a dangerous whirlpool off the northeastern coast of Sicily. See SCYLLA.
between Scylla and Charybdis, between two dangers, one of which must be met.

chase[1] [tʃeis] *v.* **chased, chas•ing;** *n.* —*v.* **1** run or follow after to catch or kill. **2** drive; drive (something or someone) away. **3** hunt. **4** follow; pursue: *The catcher chased the ball.*
chase after, pursue.
chase around or **about,** *Informal.* rush; hurry: *She is always chasing around.*
chase up, search for.
—*n.* **1** a going after to catch or kill: *The thieves were caught after a short chase.* **2** hunting as a sport: *He was very fond of the chase.* **3** a hunted animal: *The chase escaped the hunter.* **4** *Brit.* an open piece of privately owned ground or other place reserved for hunting animals.
give chase, run after; chase. ⟨ME < OF *chacier* < LL *captiare.* Doublet of CATCH.⟩

chase[2] [tʃeis] *v.* **chased, chas•ing.** engrave. ⟨var. of *enchase*⟩

chase[3] [tʃeis] *n., v.* **chased, chas•ing.** —*n.* **1** a groove; furrow; trench. **2** *Printing.* an iron frame to hold type that is ready to print or make plates from.
—*v.* cut a groove or recess in. ⟨< F *châsse* < L *capsa* box. Doublet of CASE[2], CASH[1].⟩

chas•er[1] ['tʃeisər] *n.* **1** a person or thing that chases or pursues, such as a hunter or small, speedy aircraft or ship for pursuing the enemy. **2** a gun on the bow or stern of a ship, used when chasing, or being chased by, another ship. **3** *Informal.* a drink of water or something mild after a drink of strong liquor. ⟨< *chase[1]*⟩

chas•er[2] ['tʃeisər] *n.* **1** engraver. **2** a tool for engraving. ⟨< *chase[2]*⟩

Chasid ['hæsɪd] *or* [xɑ'sid] *n., pl.* **Chasidim** ['hæsɪdɪm] *or* [xɑsi'dim]. See HASID.

chasm ['kæzəm] *n.* **1** a deep opening or crack in the earth; a narrow gorge or abyss. **2** a wide difference of feelings or interests between people or groups: *The chasm between Britain and the American colonies grew wider and wider until it finally resulted in the American Revolution.* **3** a break in continuity. ⟨< L *chasma* < Gk.⟩ —**'chas•mic,** *adj.*

chas•sé [ʃæ'sei] *n., v.* **-séd, -sé•ing.** —*n.* a gliding dance step in which one foot is in front of the other.
—*v.* perform this step.

chas•seur [ʃæ'sɜr]; *French,* [ʃa'sœʀ] *n.* **1** a soldier of a group of cavalry or infantry equipped and trained to move rapidly. **2** hunter. **3** an attendant or servant in uniform. ⟨< F⟩

chas•sis ['ʃæsi] *or* ['tʃæsi] *n., pl.* **chas•sis** ['ʃæsiz] *or* ['tʃæsiz]. **1** the frame that supports the body of an automobile, aircraft, etc. **2** the parts of an aircraft used specifically on land or in the water, as wheels, shock absorbers, etc. **3** the frame that encloses and supports the working parts of a radio, television set, etc. **4** the frame on which a gun carriage moves backward and forward. **5** *Slang.* a person's body, especially a woman's. ⟨< F < OF *châsse* frame or sash⟩

chaste [tʃeist] *adj.* **1** virginal. **2** abstaining from sexual activity outside of marriage. **3** decent or modest in speech or behaviour. **4** simple in taste or style; not ornamented. ⟨ME < OF < L *castus* pure. Doublet of CASTE.⟩ **—'chaste•ly,** *adv.* **—'chaste•ness,** *n.*

chas•ten ['tʃeisən] *v.* **1** discipline with the intention of improving: *The teacher chastened the children.* **2** make more restrained, humble, etc.; subdue: *The experience chastened them.* ⟨< obs. v. *chaste* < F < L *castigare* make pure < *castus* pure⟩ **—'chas•ten•er,** *n.*

chas•tise [tʃæs'taɪz] *v.* **-tised, -tis•ing. 1** inflict punishment on, especially by beating or whipping. **2** rebuke or scold severely; castigate: *The coach chastised the players for being late.* ⟨< obs. *chaste.* See CHASTEN.⟩ **—chas'tise•ment,** *n.* **—chas'tis•er,** *n.*

chas•ti•ty ['tʃæstəti] *n.* **1** sexual purity; virtue. **2** decency; modesty. **3** simplicity of style or taste; absence of excessive decoration.

chas•u•ble ['tʃæzəbəl] *or* ['tʃæzjəbəl] *n.* a sleeveless, capelike outer vestment worn over other vestments by a Christian priest when celebrating Mass, or Eucharist. ⟨ME *chesible* < OF < LL *casubula* < L *casa* cottage. Akin to CASSOCK.⟩

chat[1] [tʃæt] *n., v.* **chat•ted, chat•ting.** *—n.* **1** an easy, familiar talk. **2** any of several birds having a chattering cry.
—v. talk in an easy, familiar way.
chat up, *Informal.* talk with, usually in a flirtatious or flattering manner. ⟨short for *chatter*⟩

chat[2] [tʃæt] *n.* any of various tree seeds or flowers, as, a catkin or samara. ⟨< F, cat⟩

châ•teau or **cha•teau** [ʃæ'tou] *or* [ʃə'tou]; *French,* [ʃa'to] *n., pl.* **-teaux** [-'touz]; *French,* [-'to] **1** in France, a castle. **2** a large country house in France. **3** a building resembling such a house. **4** formerly, in French Canada: **a** the residence of a governor or a seigneur.

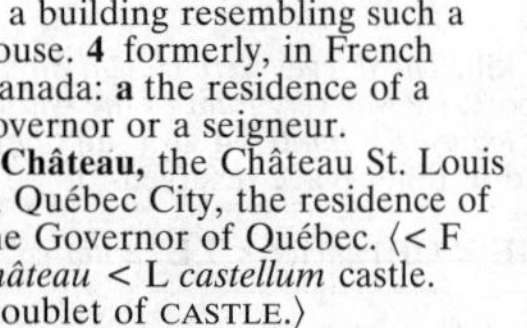

b Château, the Château St. Louis in Québec City, the residence of the Governor of Québec. ⟨< F *château* < L *castellum* castle. Doublet of CASTLE.⟩

A chateau

cha•teau•bri•and [ʃæ,toubri'ɑ̃]; *French,* [ʃatobʀi'ɑ̃] *n.* a thick tenderloin steak, usually grilled or broiled and served with a sauce. ⟨after François René *Chateaubriand* (1768-1848), French statesman and writer⟩

chat•e•laine [,ʃætə'lein] *or* ['ʃætə,lein] *n.* **1** the mistress, or lady, of a castle, château, or any large, fashionable household. **2** a chain or clasp formerly worn at a woman's waist for carrying keys, a watch, purse, etc. ⟨< F *châtelaine,* fem. of *châtelain* keeper of a castle < L *castellanus.* See CASTELLAN.⟩

cha•toy•ant [ʃə'tɔɪənt] *adj., n.* *—adj.* usually of a cloth or gem, having a changing colour or sheen.
—n. a precious stone that has such a sheen. Cat's-eye is a chatoyant. ⟨< F, ppr. of *chatoyer* change lustre⟩
—cha'toy•ance, *n.*

chat•tel ['tʃætəl] *n.* a movable possession; a piece of property that is not real estate. Furniture, automobiles, and domestic animals are chattels. ⟨ME < OF *chatel* < L *capitale,* neut. of *capitalis.* Doublet of CAPITAL[1] and CATTLE.⟩

chat•ter ['tʃætər] *v., n.* *—v.* **1** talk constantly, rapidly, and foolishly. **2** make rapid, indistinct sounds: *Monkeys chatter.* **3** rattle together: *Fear or cold sometimes makes a person's teeth chatter.*
—n. **1** rapid, foolish talk. **2** rapid, indistinct sounds: *The chatter of sparrows annoyed her.* ⟨imitative⟩ **—'chat•ter•er,** *n.*

chat•ter•box ['tʃætər,bɒks] *n.* a person who is given to chattering.

chat•ty ['tʃæti] *adj.* **-ti•er, -ti•est. 1** fond of friendly, familiar talk. **2** having the style and manner of friendly, familiar talk: *He wrote us a nice, chatty letter about his trip.* **—'chat•ti•ly,** *adv.* **—'chat•ti•ness,** *n.*

Chau•ce•ri•an [tʃɒ'siriən] *adj., n.* *—adj.* **1** of or having to do with Geoffrey Chaucer (1340?-1400), an English poet and author of *The Canterbury Tales.* **2** of or suggestive of his writings.
—n. a student of Chaucer or a specialist in his writings.

chauf•feur [ʃou'fɜr] *or* ['ʃoufər] *n., v.* *—n.* a person whose work is driving an automobile, usually as the employee of a private person or company: *The president of our bank has a chauffeur.*
—v. act as a chauffeur to; drive around. ⟨< F *chauffeur* stoker < *chauffer* heat; from the days of steam automobiles⟩

chaul•moo•gra [tʃɒl'mugrə] *n.* any of several trees native to SE Asia, of the genera *Hydnocarpus* or *Taraktogenos,* whose seeds yield **chaulmoogra oil,** formerly used to treat leprosy and skin diseases. ⟨< Bengali *calmugra*⟩

chaunt [tʃɒnt] *n. or v. Archaic.* chant.

chausses [ʃous] *n. pl.* **1** medieval chain mail for the legs and feet. **2** medieval tights for men, covering the legs and feet. ⟨< OF *chauces,* pl. < Med.L *calcea* < L *calceus* shoe < *calx* heel⟩

chau•tau•qua or **Chau•tau•qua** [ʃə'tɒkwə] *n.* an assembly for education and entertainment of adults by lectures, concerts, etc., held for several days. ⟨with reference to meetings of a religious and educational nature, the first of which were held at *Chautauqua,* New York⟩

chau•vin•ism ['ʃouvə,nɪzəm] *n.* **1** unreasoning enthusiasm for the military glory of one's country; boastful, warlike patriotism. **2** a strong, unreasoning conviction of the natural superiority of one's own group, beliefs, etc. ⟨< F *chauvinisme;* after Nicolas *Chauvin,* an over-enthusiastic French patriot and supporter of Napoleon I⟩

chau•vin•ist ['ʃouvənɪst] *n., adj.* *—n.* a person given to chauvinism.
—adj. chauvinistic.

chau•vin•is•tic [,ʃouvə'nɪstɪk] *adj.* **1** of or having to do with chauvinism or chauvinists. **2** showing chauvinism: *a chauvinistic remark.* **—,chau•vin'is•ti•cal•ly,** *adv.*

chaw [tʃɒ] *interj. Cdn.* a call directing a team of dogs to swing to the left.

cha•yo•te [tʃɑ'joutei] *or* [tʃɑ'jouti] *n.* **1** a tropical, perennial American vine (*Sechium edule*) of the gourd family, having triangular leaves and small, white flowers. **2** the edible fruit of this plant, which is green or white and shaped like a pear. ⟨< Sp. < Nahuatl⟩

cheap [tʃip] *adj., n.* *—adj.* **1** low in price or cost; not expensive: *Eggs are cheap now.* **2** costing less than it is worth; obtained at a bargain price. **3** charging low prices: *a cheap market.* **4** easily obtained; costing little effort: *a cheap victory.* **5** of little merit or value; common: *cheap entertainment, cheap jewellery.* **6** of little account; not esteemed: *Life was cheap in those days.* **7** of money, obtainable at a low rate of interest. **8** reduced in value or purchasing power, as money depreciated by inflation: *cheap silver.* **9** reduced in price for a special occasion or in prescribed circumstances: *the cheap rate.* **10** (*advl.*) cheaply: *After the accident he sold his car cheap.* **11** stingy; mean: *Don't be so cheap!* **12** of a person, spending little money.
feel cheap, feel inferior and ashamed.
hold cheap, value little: *The lord held the lives of his servants cheap.*
—n.
on the cheap, with little expense; at low cost: *travelling on the cheap, with a backpack.* ⟨short for *good cheap* a good bargain; OE *cēap* price, bargain < Gmc. (cf. OHG *kouf*) < L *caupō* small tradesman⟩ **—'cheap•ly,** *adv.* **—'cheap•ness,** *n.*
☛ *Hom.* CHEEP.
☛ *Syn. adj.* **1. Cheap,** INEXPENSIVE = costing little. **Cheap** = low in price, but often is used to express an attitude toward the thing, suggesting low quality that is worth no more or even less than the price: *Eggs are cheap now. I won't wear cheap shoes.* **Inexpensive** = not expensive, worth the price or even more, and usually expresses a more impersonal attitude: *An inexpensive car gives good mileage.*

cheap•en ['tʃipən] *v.* **1** make or become cheap; lower the price of. **2** lower the reputation of; reduce the dignity of: *He cheapened himself by his slovenly appearance.* **—'cheap•en•er,** *n.*

cheap•ie ['tʃipi] *n. Informal.* something bought at a low price, therefore either of inferior quality or a good bargain.

cheap•jack ['tʃip,dʒæk] *n., adj.* *—n.* a person who deals in cheap or worthless goods.
—adj. worthless; inferior.

cheap•skate ['tʃip,skeit] *n. Slang.* a stingy, miserly person.

cheat [tʃit] *v., n.* *—v.* **1** deceive or trick; play or do business (with) in a way that is not honest. **2** deprive or dispossess by such trickery: *The peddler cheated the woman of ten cents in change.* **3** act in a dishonest way, by practising fraud or violating rules secretly: *to cheat at cards, to cheat in an exam.* **4** escape; foil: *to cheat death.*
cheat on, be sexually unfaithful to (one's spouse or lover).
cheat (out) of, deprive of, as by cheating: *She claimed that her mother's will cheated her out of her due inheritance.*
—n. **1** a person who is not honest and does things to deceive and

trick others. **2** a fraud or trick. ⟨var. of *escheat*⟩ **—'cheat•a•ble,** *adj.* **—'cheat•er,** *n.*

☛ *Syn. v.* **Cheat,** DECEIVE, TRICK = use underhanded means for a purpose. **Cheat** = do something dishonest in an underhanded way to get something one wants: *He cheated to pass the test.* **Deceive** means to lead others to believe what is not true in order to hide the truth or to get what one wants: *He deceived the teacher by lying.* **Trick** emphasizes using a sly scheme or device to deceive and indirectly to get what one wants: *Mission Centre used fake plans to trick the spy.*

cheat•ers ['tʃitərz] *n. pl. Slang.* sunglasses.

check [tʃɛk] *v., n., interj.* *—v.* **1** stop suddenly: *They checked their steps.* **2** hold back; control; restrain: *to check one's anger.* **3** rebuff; repulse; reverse: *to check an enemy attack.* **4** *Hockey.* **a** impede the progress of (the puck-carrier), using either the stick or the body. **b** force or drive in this way: *to check a person into the boards.* **5** correspond accurately when compared, usually with a duplicate or the original (*often with* **out**): *The two copies check.* **6** **a** examine or compare to prove true or right: *Check your answers against mine.* **b** verify the status, progress, welfare, etc., of: *Could you check the cake in the oven? Excuse me while I check the kids.* **7** find out; investigate: *When he checked, he found the money was gone.* **8** mark (something dealt with, examined, or compared) with a check (✓): *How many answers did the teacher check as right?* **9** leave or take for safekeeping: *to check one's coat. The hotel checked our baggage.* **10** send (baggage) to a particular place: *I will check my bag through to Halifax.* **11** mark in a pattern of squares. **12** of wood, steel, paintwork, etc., crack or split. **13** cause to crack. **14** *Chess.* have (an opponent's king) in a position of danger so that it must be moved or the danger avoided in some other way. **15** *Nautical.* lessen the tension on (a line) by releasing it little by little. **16** *Poker.* refuse to start off a round of betting.

check in, arrive and register at a hotel, etc.

check off, mark as checked and found true or right or finished.

check on or **check up on,** find out about; seek more information on: *The police were checking up on her.*

check out, **a** leave and pay for a hotel or motel room, or leave a hospital: *We checked out of the hotel at noon.* **b** in a supermarket or other self-service store, have one's purchases totalled at the cash desk and pay for them: *It took a long time to check out.* **c** *Slang.* die. **d** verify: *to check out a statement.* **e** inspect; examine: *to check out a plane before takeoff.* **f** borrow from a library: *She checked out two books on pets.* **g** *Slang.* look at (especially something remarkable): *Hey, check out Jeff's new bike!* **h** accord; JIBE[3]: *Her testimony checks out with what we heard earlier.*

check over, inspect.

check up, **a** examine or compare to prove true, correct, or in order (*often with* **on**). **b** examine the health of: *Let your doctor check you up.*

—n. **1** a sudden stop: *The message gave a check to our plans.* **2** a holding back; control; restraint. **3** any person, thing, or event that controls or holds back action: *Her calm, practical attitude acted as a check on her partner's impulsiveness.* **4** *Hockey.* **a** an impeding of the progress of the puck-carrier, by means of either the body or the stick. **b** a forward who is covered by an opposing forward: *The coach told him to keep better watch on his check.* **5** a rebuff; repulse; reverse. **6** a test for correctness made by comparing: *My work will be a check on yours.* **7** a mark (✓) to show that something has been counted, examined, verified, etc.: *She put a check beside the right answers.* **8** (*adjl.*) used in checking. **9** a ticket or metal piece given in return for a coat, hat, baggage, package, etc., to show ownership. **10** a bill for a meal, etc. **11** *Esp. U.S.* See CHEQUE. **12** a pattern of squares: *Do you want a check or a stripe for your new dress?* **13** one of these squares: *The checks are small in this pattern.* **14** (*adjl.*) marked in a pattern of squares. **15** a crack; split. **16** *Chess.* **a** a call warning that an opponent's king is in danger. **b** the position of an opponent's king when it is in danger and must be moved or the threatening piece blocked off or removed.

in check, held back; controlled.

—interj. **1** *Chess.* a call warning that an opponent's king is in danger and must be moved or protected. **2** *Informal.* OK. ⟨ME < OF *eschec* a check at chess (v., *eschequier*), ult. < Persian *shāh* king, king at chess⟩ **—'check•a•ble,** *adj.*

☛ *Syn. v.* **1.** See note at STOP. **2. Check,** RESTRAIN, CURB = hold someone or something back. **Check** suggests use of some means that slows up or stands in the way of action or progress: *The awning checked his fall.* **Restrain** suggests use of some force to keep down or within limits or to prevent completely: *A bystander restrained him from jumping off the bridge.* **Curb** suggests use of a control that pulls back suddenly or keeps from acting freely: *Her good sense curbed her impulse to hit the man.*

☛ *Hom.* CHEQUE.

check•book ['tʃɛk,bʊk] *Esp. U.S.* See CHEQUEBOOK.

checked [tʃɛkt] *adj., v.* *—adj.* **1** marked in a pattern of

squares. **2** *Phonetics.* **a** of a syllable, ending in a consonant. **b** of a vowel, spoken in such a syllable.

—v. pt. and pp. of CHECK.

check•er[1] ['tʃɛkər] *v., n.* *—v.* **1** mark in a pattern of squares of alternate different colours, like a chessboard: *The bathroom wall was checkered with blue and white tiles.* **2** mark off in patches contrasting: *The ground under the trees was checkered with sunlight and shade.* **3** cause to have ups and downs; change.

—n. **1** a pattern of squares of different colours. **2** one of these squares. **3** one of the flat, round pieces used in the game of checkers. Also, **chequer.** ⟨ME < AF *escheker* < Med.L *scaccarium* chessboard⟩

check•er[2] ['tʃɛkər] *n.* a person who or thing that checks, especially a cashier in a self-service store or supermarket.

check•er•ber•ry ['tʃɛkər,bɛri] *n., pl.* **-ries. 1** the red berry of any of various plants, especially the spicy, edible fruit of a North American wintergreen (*Gaultheria procumbens*). **2** a plant bearing such fruit. **3** partridgeberry.

check•er•bloom ['tʃɛkər,blum] *n.* a western North American perennial plant (*Sidalcea malviflora*) of the mallow family, having pink or purple flowers.

check•er•board ['tʃɛkər,bɔrd] *n.* a square board marked in a pattern of 64 squares of two alternating colours and used in playing checkers or chess. Also, **chequerboard.**

check•ered ['tʃɛkərd] *adj., v.* *—adj.* **1** marked in a pattern of squares of different colours. **2** marked in patches. **3** often changing; varied; irregular: *a checkered career.*

—v. pt. and pp. of CHECKER. Also, **chequered.**

check•ers ['tʃɛkərz] *n.* a game played by two people, each having twelve round, flat pieces to move on a checkerboard (*used with a singular verb*). Also, **chequers.**

check•list ['tʃɛk,lɪst] *n.* a complete list of things, such as names, articles on inventory, steps in a procedure, etc., used for checking or comparing.

check mark a mark (✓) to show that something has been counted, examined, verified, etc.; a CHECK (*n.* def. 7).

check•mate ['tʃɛk,meit] *v.* **-mat•ed, -mat•ing;** *n., interj.* *—v.* **1** *Chess.* put (an opponent's king) in indefensible check and so win the game. **2** defeat completely. **3** foil; thwart; outmanoeuvre: *The spy checkmated his pursuers at every turn.*

—n. **1** *Chess.* **a** a move that ends the game by putting the opponent's king in check where it cannot be protected. **b** such a position of the king. **2** a complete defeat.

—interj. Chess. a declaration that the opposing king is in check and cannot be defended. ⟨ME < OF *eschec et mat* < Persian *shāh māt* king is dead⟩

check•off ['tʃɛk,ɒf] *n.* **1** a system of collecting union dues through wage deductions made by the employer on the union's behalf. **2** the amount deducted under such a system.

check•out ['tʃɛk,ʌut] *n.* **1** in a supermarket or other self-service store: **a** the process by which purchases are checked and paid for: *The checkout took only about a minute.* **b** the counter where this is done: *I went to the express checkout.* **2** Often, **checkout time,** in a hotel or motel, the time by which one must leave and pay for a room: *We missed the checkout and had to pay for an extra day.* **3** an inspection of a machine.

checkout counter CHECKOUT (def. 1b).

check•point ['tʃɛk,pɔint] *n.* a point or place where a check is made, especially a place on a road or highway where vehicles or persons are inspected by authorities.

check•rein ['tʃɛk,rein] *n.* **1** a short rein to keep a horse from lowering its head. **2** a short rein connecting the bit of one of a team of horses to the driving rein of the other.

check•room ['tʃɛk,rum] *or* [-,rʊm] *n.* a place where coats, hats, baggage, packages, etc., can be left until required again.

check•up ['tʃɛk,ʌp] *n.* **1** a thorough physical examination. **2** a careful examination.

Ched•dar ['tʃɛdər] *n.* a hard, smooth, white or yellow cheese made in three main degrees of sharpness. Also, **cheddar.** ⟨after *Cheddar*, in Somerset, England⟩

che•der ['xeidər] *n., pl.* **-da•rim** [xeidə'rim] See HEDER.

chee•cha•ko [tʃi'tʃɑkou] *or* [tʃi'tʃækou] *n. Cdn. West Coast.* a newcomer; tenderfoot; greenhorn: *It took the cheechako many months to learn the ways of the Yukon.* ⟨< Chinook jargon < Chinook *t'shi* new + *chakho* come⟩

cheek [tʃik] *n.* **1** the side of the face below either eye. **2** something suggesting the human cheek in form or position.

3 *Slang.* buttock. 4 *Informal.* saucy talk or behaviour; impudence: *The girl's cheek annoyed the neighbours.*
cheek by jowl, a side by side; close together. b close; intimate; familiar.
turn the other cheek, not retaliate when wronged. ⟨OE *cēce*⟩

cheek•bone ['tʃik,boun] *n.* a bone just below either eye.

–cheeked *combining form.* having cheeks of a particular kind: *rosy-cheeked.*

cheek•piece ['tʃik,pis] *n.* one of the two side straps of a bridle. They connect the band around the head with the bit. Also, **cheek strap**.

cheek pouch a pouch in the cheek for holding food. Squirrels have cheek pouches.

cheek•y ['tʃiki] *adj.* **cheek•i•er, cheek•i•est.** *Informal.* saucy; impudent. **—'cheek•i•ly,** *adv.* **—'cheek•i•ness,** *n.*

cheep [tʃip] *v., n. —v.* make a short, sharp sound like a young bird; chirp; peep.
—n. a short, sharp sound like that of a young bird; chirp; peep. ⟨imitative⟩ **—'cheep•er,** *n.*
☛ *Hom.* CHEAP.

cheer [tʃir] *n., v. —n.* 1 joy; gladness; comfort; encouragement: *The warmth of the fire and a good meal brought cheer to our hearts again.* 2 a shout of encouragement, approval, praise, etc. 3 food and/or drink: *We were invited for Christmas cheer.* 4 a state of mind; condition of feeling: *My friends encouraged me to be of good cheer.*
what cheer? *Archaic, poetic, or facetious.* how are you?
—v. 1 fill with cheer; give joy to; gladden; comfort; encourage: *Our visit cheered the old lady.* 2 shout encouragement, approval, praise, etc. 3 urge on with cheers: *Everyone cheered our team.* 4 greet or welcome with cheers.
cheer up, make or become happier; be glad. ⟨ME *chere* < OF < LL *cara* face < Gk. *kara* head, face⟩ **—'cheer•er,** *n.*
☛ *Syn. v.* **1. Cheer,** GLADDEN = raise a person's spirits. **Cheer** suggests either making a person feel less downhearted by giving comfort and encouragement (often *cheer up)* or putting him or her in high spirits by giving pleasure or joy: *The news cheered everyone.* **Gladden** suggests putting a person in good spirits by giving delight and making him or her feel happy: *The sight of the countryside gladdened the city children.*

cheer•ful ['tʃirfəl] *adj.* 1 full of cheer; joyful; optimistic: *a smiling, cheerful person.* 2 filling with cheer; pleasant; bright: *a cheerful, sunny room.* 3 willing: *a cheerful giver.* **—'cheer•ful•ly,** *adv.* **—'cheer•ful•ness,** *n.*

cheer•i•o ['tʃiri,ou] *interj. n., pl.* **-i•os.** *Esp. Brit. Informal.* 1 goodbye. 2 hello. 3 hurrah.

cheer•lead•er ['tʃir,lidər] *n.* a person who leads the organized cheering of a crowd, especially at high-school or university sports events.

cheer•lead•ing ['tʃir,lidɪŋ] *n.* 1 the act or practice of leading a crowd in cheers; the activity of a cheerleader. 2 the act of leading in business, politics, etc.

cheer•less ['tʃirlɪs] *adj.* without joy or comfort; gloomy; dreary. **—'cheer•less•ness,** *n.* **—'cheer•less•ly,** *adv.*

cheers [tʃirz] *interj.* a toast before drinking.

cheer•y ['tʃiri] *adj.* **cheer•i•er, cheer•i•est.** cheerful; pleasant; bright. **—'cheer•i•ly,** *adv.* **—'cheer•i•ness,** *n.*

cheese[1] [tʃiz] *n., v. —n.* 1 a solid food made from the curds of milk. 2 a mass of this substance pressed into a shape.
say cheese, *Informal.* smile for a photograph.
—v. Slang. upset or annoy (*used with* **off**): *His attitude cheeses me off. She's cheesed off about something.* ⟨OE *cēse* < L *caseus*⟩ **—'cheese,like,** *adj.*

cheese[2] [tʃiz] *n. Slang.* 1 something that becomes a fad precisely because it is so out-of-date or conservative. 2 See BIG CHEESE. ⟨< Hind. *chiz* a thing⟩ **—'chees•y,** *adj.*

cheese•burg•er ['tʃiz,bɜrgər] *n.* a hamburger with a slice of cheese melted on top of the meat.

cheese•cake ['tʃiz,keik] *n.* 1 a rich dessert made of cream cheese or cottage cheese, eggs, sugar, etc., baked or mixed together. 2 *Slang.* photographs or photography emphasizing the figure and legs of an attractive young woman. Compare BEEFCAKE.

cheese•cloth ['tʃiz,klɒθ] *n.* a thin, loosely woven cotton cloth, originally used for wrapping cheese.

cheese•par•ing ['tʃiz,pɛrɪŋ] *n., adj. —n.* 1 something as insignificant or worthless as the parings of rind from cheese. 2 stinginess.
—adj. stingy; miserly.

chees•y ['tʃizi] *adj.* **chees•i•er, chees•i•est.** 1 of or like cheese. 2 *Slang.* not well made; inferior; tacky or cheap. ⟨< *cheese*[1]⟩ **—'chees•i•ness,** *n.*

chee•tah ['tʃitə] *n.* a tall, rangy, long-legged African and Asian animal (*Acinonyx jubatus*) of the cat family, thought to be the fastest mammal on earth, having doglike feet with hard pads and claws that cannot be retracted, a small head, and a reddish yellow coat with black spots. Cheetahs that have been captured and trained to hunt are often called hunting leopards. ⟨< Hind. *chita*⟩

chef [ʃɛf] *n.* 1 a head cook. 2 a cook. ⟨< F *chef (de cuisine)* < L *caput* head. Doublet of CHIEF.⟩

chef–d'oeu•vre [ʃei'dœvrə]; *French,* [ʃɛ'dœvʀ] *n., pl.* **chefs-d,oeuvre** [ʃei'dœvrə]. masterpiece. ⟨< F⟩

che•la ['kilə] *n., pl.* **-lae** [-li] *or* [-laɪ]. a pincerlike claw, such as that of a lobster, crab, or scorpion. ⟨< L < Gk. *chēlē* claw⟩

che•late ['kileit] *adj., n., v.* **-lat•ed, -lat•ing.** *—adj.* having a chela.
—n. Chemistry. a co-ordination compound in which a central metal ion is bonded to other atoms in such a way that a ring is formed.
—v. combine or react so as to form a chelate. **—che'la•tion,** *n.*

che•lif•er•ous [kə'lɪfərəs] *adj.* having chelae.

che•li•form ['kilə,fɔrm] *adj.* having the form of a chela.

che•li•ped ['kilə,pɛd] *n.* either of the limbs of a crustacean bearing a chela. ⟨< Gk. *chele* claw + L *pes pedis* foot⟩

che•lo•ni•an [kɪ'louniən] *n., adj. —n.* any of an order (Chelonia) of reptiles, including tortoises and turtles, having the body enclosed in a protective, bony shell.
—adj. of, having to do with, or belonging to the order Chelonia. ⟨< NL *Chelonia* < Gk. *chelōnē* tortoise⟩

chem. chemistry; chemical; chemist.

chem•ic ['kɛmɪk] *adj. Archaic.* 1 chemical. 2 of alchemy.

chem•i•cal ['kɛməkəl] *adj., n. —adj.* 1 of, having to do with, used in, or produced by chemistry: *chemical knowledge, a chemical process, a chemical compound.* 2 producing or using chemicals: *the chemical industry.* 3 made of or working by chemicals: *a chemical fertilizer, a chemical toilet.* 4 of or having to do with a psychotropic drug or alcohol: *chemical addiction.*
—n. 1 a substance that has been produced by chemical processes in a laboratory, using raw materials such as crude petroleum, rocks, or plant parts, or using basic substances already made in this way, to produce more complex substances and finished products. Phosphates, coal tar, plastics, drugs, paints, and insecticides are chemicals. 2 a psychotropic drug or alcohol.

chemical abuse the habitual overuse of a psychotropic drug or alcohol.

chemical change *Chemistry.* a change in which one substance is converted into one or more substances with different properties.

chemical engineering the science or profession of using chemistry for industrial purposes. **—chemical engineer.**

chem•i•cal•ly ['kɛmɪkli] *adv.* 1 according to chemistry. 2 by chemical processes.

chemical warfare the technique or use of gases, flames, smoke, or any chemicals other than explosives as weapons.

chem•i•lu•mi•nes•cence [,kɛmə,lumə'nɛsəns] *n.* luminescence resulting from chemical action and not involving heat. Bioluminescence is a kind of chemiluminescence. ⟨< *chemi(cal)* + *luminescence*⟩

chemin de fer [ʃə'mɛ̃ də 'fɛr] *or* [ʃə'mæn də 'fɛr] *n.* a gambling game like baccarat, using cards. ⟨< F⟩

che•mise [ʃə'miz] *n.* 1 a loose, shirtlike undergarment worn by women or girls. 2 a loose, straight-cut dress. ⟨< F < LL *camisia* shirt < Celtic⟩

chem•i•sette [,ʃɛmɪ'zɛt] *n.* a garment worn by women and girls, consisting of a false blouse front to fill in a neckline.

chem•ist ['kɛmɪst] *n.* 1 a person trained in chemistry, especially one whose work it is. 2 *Brit.* druggist. ⟨var. of *alchemist*⟩

chem•is•try ['kɛmɪstri] *n., pl.* **-tries.** 1 the science that deals with elements or simple substances, the changes that take place when they combine to form compounds, and the laws of their combination and behaviour under various conditions. 2 the application of this to a certain subject: *the chemistry of foods.* 3 chemical processes, properties, phenomena, etc.: *Some people have acne because of their body chemistry.* 4 qualities of personality in interaction: *The addition of new members altered* *the chemistry of the group.* **5** the significance of this in some sphere of human activity: *the chemistry of love.*

chemo– *combining form.* of or involving chemical reactions: *chemotherapy.* Also, before vowels, **chem-**.

che•mo•pro•phy•lax•is [ˌkimouˌproufəˈlæksɪs] *or* [ˌkɛmou-], [ˌkimouˌprɒfəˈlæksɪs] *or* [ˌkɛmou-] *n.* the prevention of disease by the use of drugs or food nutrients.

chem•o•re•cep•tor [ˌkimourɪˈsɛptər] *or* [ˌkɛmourɪˈsɛptər] *n.* a nerve ending or sense organ that reacts to chemical stimulation.

chem•os•mo•sis [ˌkimɒzˈmousɪs] *or* [ˌkɛmɒzˈmousɪs] *n.* chemical action between components separated by a semi-permeable covering.

chem•o•sphere [ˈkɛməˌsfir] *or* [ˈkiməˌsfir] *n. Meteorology.* a region of the atmosphere beginning about 35 km above the earth, where the sun's radiation produces predominant photochemical activity.

che•mo•stat [ˈkiməˌstæt] *or* [ˈkɛməˌstæt] *n.* a set-up for growing a bacterial colony indefinitely while maintaining the population and environment constant.

che•mo•ster•i•lant [ˌkimouˈstɛrələnt] *or* [ˌkɛmouˈstɛrələnt] *n.* a chemical substance that destroys the ability of an organism, such as an insect, to reproduce.

chem•o•sur•ge•ry [ˌkimouˈsɜrdʒəri] *or* [ˌkɛmouˈsɜrdʒəri] *n.* the excising of tumours or affected tissue by chemical methods.

che•mo•syn•thes•is [ˌkimouˈsɪnθəsɪs] *or* [ˌkɛmouˈsɪnθəsɪs] *n.* the use by an organism of chemical reaction as an energy source, instead of the sun, to synthesize its organic compounds. Compare with PHOTOSYNTHESIS.
—ˌche•mo•synˈthet•ic [-sɪnˈθɛtɪk], *adj.*
—ˌche•mo•synˈthet•ic•al•ly, *adv.*

che•mo•ther•a•py [ˌkimouˈθɛrəpi] *or* [ˌkɛmouˈθɛrəpi] *n.* the treatment or control of disease, especially cancer, by means of chemical agents.

chem•ur•gist [ˈkɛmərdʒɪst] *n.* a person trained in chemurgy, especially one whose work it is.

chem•ur•gy [ˈkɛmərdʒi] *n.* the branch of chemistry that deals with the use of farm products, such as casein and cornstalks, for purposes other than food and clothing. ⟨< *chem(istry)* + *-urgy* (< Gk. *ergon* work + *ia*)⟩ **—chemˈur•gic** [kɛˈmɜrdʒɪk], *adj.*

che•nille [ʃəˈnil] *n.* **1** a fabric, usually cotton, made with a filling of rows of tufted cord arranged in various designs and forming a soft, piled surface. Chenille is used for bedspreads, robes, rugs, etc. **2** a tufted cord of silk, cotton, or worsted, used in embroidery, fringe, etc. ⟨< F *chenille* caterpillar < L *canicula* little dog; from its furry look⟩

chenin blanc [ʃənɛ̃ˈblɑ̃] *n. French.* **1** a white wine, varying from dry to semisweet. **2** the grape used to make this wine. ⟨< F < OF *(reisin) chenin* (grape) of the dog + *blanc* white⟩

che•no•de•ox•y•cho•lic acid [ˌkinoudiˌɒksɪˈkoulɪk] *or* [ˌkɛnoudiˌɒksɪˈkoulɪk] a naturally occurring bile salt which can dissolve gallstones.

che•no•pod [ˈkinəˌpɒd] *or* [ˈkɛnəˌpɒd] *n.* any plant of the goosefoot family, such as spinach. ⟨< NL *Chenopodium* < Gk. *chen* goose + *pous, podas* foot⟩

cheong•sam or **cheong sam** [ˌtʃɒŋˈsæm] *n.* a Chinese woman's dress with a mandarin collar and slits up the sides of the skirt. ⟨< Chinese⟩

cheque [tʃɛk] *n.* **1** a written order directing a bank to take money from the account of the signer and pay it to the person or company named on it: *He pays his bills by cheque.* **2** a blank form on which to write such an order. Sometimes, *esp. U.S.,* **check.**
☛ *Hom.* CHECK.

cheque•book [ˈtʃɛkˌbʊk] *n.* a book of blank cheques. Sometimes, *esp. U.S.,* **checkbook.**

cheq•uer [ˈtʃɛkər] See CHECKER[1].

cheq•uer•board [ˈtʃɛkərˌbɔrd] See CHECKERBOARD.

cheq•uered [ˈtʃɛkərd] See CHECKERED.

cheq•uers [ˈtʃɛkərz] See CHECKERS.

Cheq•uers [ˈtʃɛkərz] *n.* the official country residence of the British prime minister, in Buckinghamshire, northwest of London.

chequing account a bank account against which cheques may be drawn.

cher•i•moy•a [ˌtʃɛrəˈmɔɪə] *n.* **1** a fruit tree (*Annona cherimola*) found in tropical America, having velvety leaves and fragrant yellow flowers. **2** the large, edible, heart-shaped fruit of this tree. ⟨< Sp. *chirimoya*⟩

cher•ish [ˈtʃɛrɪʃ] *v.* **1** hold dear; treat with affection; care for tenderly: *He cherished his little daughter.* **2** keep in mind; cling to: *For many years the old woman cherished the hope that her wandering son would come home.* ⟨ME < OF *cheriss-*, a stem of *cherir* < *cher* dear < L *carus*⟩
☛ *Syn.* **2. Cherish,** FOSTER, HARBOUR, used figuratively, mean 'keep and care for in the mind'. **Cherish,** which literally means 'hold dear', emphasizes treasuring an idea or feeling and watching over it with loving care: *She cherishes friendship.* **Foster** suggests nourishing an idea or feeling, and helping it to grow: *He tries to foster tolerance.* **Harbour,** which literally means 'give shelter to', suggests letting in a bad idea or feeling and brooding over it: *She harbours a grudge.*

cher•no•zem [ˈtʃɜrnəˌzɛm] *or* [ˈtʃɛrnəˌzɛm] *n.* a fertile soil typical of wet grasslands, consisting of a rich, black layer with a high organic content, overlying a layer of accumulated lime. ⟨< Russian *chernozem* < *chernyi* black + *zemlja* land, soil⟩

Cher•o•kee [ˈtʃɛrəˌki] *or* [ˌtʃɛrəˈki] *n., pl.* **-kee** or **-kees. 1** a member of an American Indian people now living mostly in Oklahoma. **2** the Iroquoian language of the Cherokee. ⟨alteration of native *Tsalagi* or *Tsaragi*⟩

Cherokee rose a white climbing rose (*Rosa laevigata*), native to China but now naturalized in the southern U.S. It is the state flower of Georgia.

che•root [ʃəˈrut] *n.* a cigar cut off square at both ends. ⟨< F *chéroute* < Tamil *shuruttu* roll⟩

cherries jubilee a dessert dish of dark cherries flambéd in brandy and often served with vanilla ice cream.

cher•ry [ˈtʃɛri] *n., pl.* **-ries;** *adj.* *—n.* **1** a small, round, edible, juicy fruit having a pit, or stone, in the centre, produced by any of various trees and shrubs (genus *Prunus*) of the rose family. **2** a tree or shrub that produces this fruit. **3** the wood of any of these trees or shrubs. **4** *(adjl.)* made of this wood. **5** a bright red. *—adj.* **1** bright red. **2** made with cherries: *cherry brandy.* **3** tasting like cherries. ⟨ME *chery*, back formation from *cherys* < ONF *cherise* < VL < LGk. *kerasia* cherry tree < Gk. *kerasos* cherry. Doublet of CERISE.⟩
☛ *Hom.* CHARY.

cherry bomb a kind of firecracker, the colour and shape of a cherry.

cherry laurel any of various evergreen bushes (genus *Prunus*) of the rose family, bearing thick, shiny leaves.

cherry picker *Informal.* a type of crane consisting of a jointed or telescoping arm with a large bucket at the end, in which a person can stand to carry out operations high above the ground, such as repairs to power lines, or to pick something up off ice.

cherry plum 1 a tree (*Prunus cerasifera*) of the rose family, bearing edible yellow or red fruit, and often used in grafting other kinds of plums. **2** the fruit of this tree. Also called **myrobalan.**

cher•ry•stone [ˈtʃɛriˌstoun] *n.* the quahog, a clam with a round, hard shell. Also called **cherrystone clam.**

cherry tomato a miniature tomato a little bigger than a cherry, used in salads.

chert [tʃɜrt] *n.* a dark, impure mineral resembling flint and containing quartz and hydrated silica. ⟨origin unknown⟩
—ˈchert•y, *adj.*

cher•ub [ˈtʃɛrəb] *n., pl.* **cher•u•bim** *for 1 and 2,* **cher•ubs** *for 3 and 4.* **1** a celestial being representing divine justice. **2** a picture or statue of a child with wings, or of a child's head with wings but no body. **3** a beautiful or good child. **4** a person with a chubby, innocent face. ⟨< Hebrew *kerūb*⟩

che•ru•bic [tʃəˈrubɪk] *adj.* **1** of or like a cherub; angelic. **2** innocent; good. **3** chubby. **—cheˈru•bi•cal•ly,** *adv.*

cher•u•bim [ˈtʃɛrəˌbɪm] *or* [ˈtʃɛrjəˌbɪm] *n.* **1** a pl. of CHERUB. **2** *(pl., formerly used as sing.)* CHERUB (def. 1).

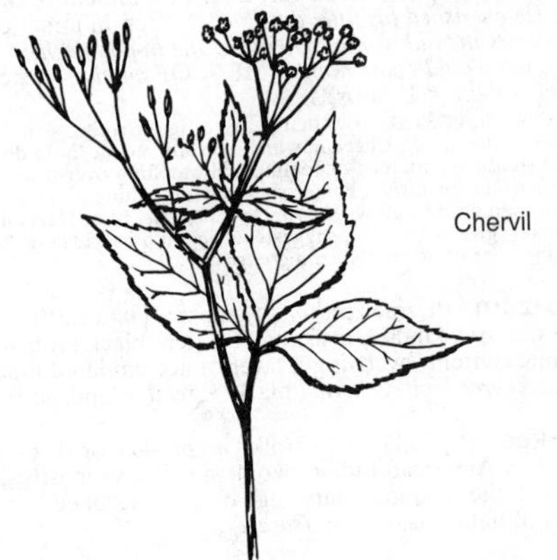
Chervil

cher•vil ['tʃɜrvəl] *n.* **1** an aromatic Eurasian herb (*Anthriscus cerefolium*) of the parsley family having finely divided leaves that are used to flavour soups, salads, fish, etc. **2** a similar plant (*Chaerophyllum bulbosum*) having an edible root like a carrot. ⟨OE *cerfille* < L < Gk. *chairephyllon* < *chairein* rejoice + *phyllon* leaf⟩

cher•vo•nets [tʃər'vounɛts] *n., pl.* **-von•tsi** [-'vountsi]. **1** a former monetary unit of the Soviet Union. **2** a gold coin worth one chervonets. ⟨< Russian⟩

Chesh•ire ['tʃɛʃər] *n.* a crumbly cheese, similar to Cheddar, either white or coloured red. Some red Cheshire develops a blue veining as it ripens. ⟨< *Cheshire*, a county in NW England⟩

Cheshire cat anybody with a fixed grin. ⟨the grinning cat in *Alice in Wonderland* by Lewis Carroll⟩

chess¹ [tʃɛs] *n.* a game played on a chessboard by two people. Each has 16 pieces that have to be moved in various ways, with the object of capturing those of the other player. ⟨ME < OF *esches*, pl. of *eschec.* See CHECK¹.⟩

chess² *n.* a kind of brome grass (*Bromus secalinus*) growing as a weed among cultivated grains. ⟨origin unknown⟩

chess•board ['tʃɛs,bɔrd] *n.* a board marked in a pattern of 64 squares of two alternating colours, used in playing chess.

chess•man ['tʃɛs,mæn] *or* [-mən] *n., pl.* **-men.** one of the pieces used in playing chess. Each player has 16 chessmen at the start of the game: 1 king, 1 queen, 2 rooks (or castles), 2 knights, 2 bishops, and 8 pawns.

chest [tʃɛst] *n.* **1** the part of the body of a person or animal enclosed by the ribs. **2** the front outside part of this. **3** the measurement around a person's body at the widest part of the chest: *He has a 100 cm chest.* **4** (*adjl.*) of or involving the chest: *a chest cold.* **5** a large, sturdy box with a lid, used for storing or shipping things: *a linen chest, a tool chest.* **6** a piece of furniture with drawers. **7** a small cabinet for keeping first-aid supplies and drugs: *the medicine chest.* **8** a sealed container for gas, steam, etc. **9** *Rare.* **a** a place where money of a public or charitable institution is kept; treasury. **b** the money itself.
get something off one's chest, relieve one's mind by talking about some problem. ⟨OE *cest, cist* < L *cista* < Gk. *kistē* box⟩

-chested *combining form.* having a ——chest: *broadchested* = *having a broad chest.*

ches•ter•bed ['tʃɛstər,bɛd] *n. Cdn.* a chesterfield that can be opened out to form a bed.

ches•ter•field ['tʃɛstər,fild] *n.* **1** *Cdn.* a long, upholstered seat for several people, having a back and, usually, arms; sofa; couch. **2** a single-breasted, knee-length, man's overcoat usually having the buttons concealed by an overlapping flap. ⟨after a 19c. Earl of *Chesterfield*⟩

Ches•ter White ['tʃɛstər] a breed of large, white pig. ⟨after *Chester* County, Pennsylvania⟩

chest•nut ['tʃɛsnʌt] *or* [-nət] *n., adj.* —*n.* **1** any of a genus (*Castanea*) of trees of the beech family native to north temperate regions having flowers in long catkins and producing burrlike fruits containing two or three edible nuts. **2** the nut of any of these trees. **3** the wood of any of these trees. **4** a reddish brown. **5** a brown or reddish brown horse. **6** *Informal.* a stale joke or story. **7** See HORSE CHESTNUT, WATER CHESTNUT. **8** the hard knob in the skin of a horse at the inner side of the foreleg.
—*adj.* having the colour chestnut. ⟨< obs. *chesten* chestnut (< OF *chastaigne* < L *castanea* < Gk. *kastanea* or *kastaneia* < *kastanon*) + *nut*⟩

chestnut blight a disease of chestnut trees, especially the American chestnut, in which the bark gradually falls off, killing the tree. It is caused by a fungus (*Endothia parasitica*).

chest of drawers a piece of furniture consisting of a wooden casing in which are housed several drawers, for keeping clothes, etc.

chest register the lowest register of any singing voice.

chest wader a waterproof garment like overalls, used by hunters for wading through swamps.

chest•y ['tʃɛsti] *adj. Informal.* **1** having a large chest or thorax. **2** bosomy. **3** conceited. **4** *Brit.* having, inclined to, or due to weak lungs, bronchitis, pneumonia, etc.

che•tah ['tʃitə] *n. Archaic.* See CHEETAH.

chet•nik ['tʃɛtnɪk] *n., pl.* **-niks** or **chet•ni•ci** [tʃɛt'nitsi]. in the former Yugoslavia, one of a guerrilla force that was active against the Nazis during World War II. ⟨< Serbian *chetnik* < *cheta* band⟩

chet•rum ['tʃɛtrʊm] *n.* the smaller monetary unit of Bhutan, equal to 1/100 of a ngultrum.

che•val–de–frise [ʃə'væl də 'friz]. *n., pl.* **che•vaux-de-frise** [ʃə'vou də 'friz]. **1** a piece of wood with spikes sticking out, formerly used to hinder the advance of enemy cavalry. **2** a row of spikes or broken glass along the top of a wall. ⟨< F, literally horse of Friesland; first used by Frisians to make up for their lack of cavalry⟩

che•val glass [ʃə'væl] a tall mirror mounted in a frame so that it swings between its supports. ⟨*cheval* < F *cheval* horse, support < L *caballus* horse⟩

chev•a•lier [ʃɛvə'lir] *or* [ʃəvæl'jei]; *French,* [ʃval'je] *or* [ʃfal'je] *n.* **1** *Archaic.* a knight. **2** in France, a member of the lowest rank in the Legion of Honour. ⟨< F *chevalier* < *cheval* horse < L *caballus*⟩

Chev•i•ot ['tʃɛviət] *or* ['tʃiviət] *for def. 1;* ['ʃɛviət] *for def. 2. n.* **1** a breed of sheep that originated in the Cheviot Hills on the boundary between England and Scotland. **2 cheviot, a** a rough woollen cloth with a nap, used for coats and suits. **b** a heavy, coarse cotton cloth used for shirts.

chev•re ['ʃɛvrə]; *French,* [ʃɛvʀ] *n.* goat's-milk cheese. ⟨< F *chèvre* goat⟩

chev•ron ['ʃɛvrɒn] *or* ['ʃɛvrən] *n.* **1** a V-shaped bar, usually of cloth, often worn on the sleeve of a uniform by members of the armed forces, a police force, etc., to show rank or years of service: *A sergeant wears three chevrons.* **2** any V-shaped design. ⟨ME < OF *chevron* rafter < *chevre* goat < L *caper*⟩

chev•ro•tain ['ʃɛvrə,tein] *or* ['ʃɛvrətən] *n.* any very small, deerlike ruminant of the family Tragulidae, found in W Africa, S Asia, the Malay peninsula, and other tropical regions; mouse deer. ⟨< F *chevrotin* a fawn under 6 months old < OF *chevrot* kid⟩

chev•y [tʃɛvi] *n., pl.* **chev•ies;** *v.* **chev•ied, chev•y•ing.** *Brit.* —*n.* **1** a hunting cry. **2** a hunt; chase.
—*v.* **1** hunt; chase. **2** scamper; race. **3** worry; harass. ⟨shortened form of *Chevy Chase*, from the ballad of that name⟩

chew [tʃu] *v., n.* —*v.* **1** crush, grind, or gnaw with the teeth. **2** mark, crush, etc., as if by chewing (*usually used with* **up**): *The wheels of the truck had chewed up the lawn.* **3** *Informal.* consider or discuss at length (*used with* **over**): *She chewed it over for several days before making her decision.* **4** chew tobacco: *Does he chew?*
chew out, *Slang.* reprimand.
chew the fat or **rag,** *Slang.* converse casually or idly: *We sat around for an hour or so, chewing the fat.*
—*n.* **1** an act of chewing. **2** something chewed or to be chewed: *a chew of tobacco.* ⟨OE *cēowan*⟩ **—'chew•a•ble,** *adj.* **—'chew•er,** *n.*

chewing gum a gummy preparation for chewing, usually made of chicle that has been sweetened and flavoured.

che•wink [tʃɪ'wɪŋk] *n.* TOWHEE (def. 1). ⟨imitative⟩

chew•y ['tʃui] *adj.* requiring chewing; becoming sticky and pliable when chewed.

Chey•enne [ʃaɪ'ɛn] *or* [ʃaɪ'æn] *n., pl.* **-enne** or **-ennes. 1** a member of American Indian people now living in Montana and Oklahoma. **2** the Algonquian language of the Cheyenne. ⟨< the Sioux name *Shahi'yena, Shai-ena* people of alien speech⟩

Cheyne–Stokes respiration ['tʃein 'stouks] respiration

typical of coma and heart failure patients, in which deep breathing alternates with shallow breathing. ⟨< after John *Cheyne* (1777-1836), Scottish physician, and William *Stokes* (1804-1878), Irish physician⟩

chez [ʃei] *French.* at the home of.

chg. charge(s).

chgd. charged.

chi [xaɪ] *or* [kaɪ] *n.* the twenty-second letter of the Greek alphabet (Χ, χ), appearing as *ch*, but usually sounded as *k*, in English words of Greek origin.

Chi•an•ti [ki'ɑnti] *or* [ki'æntі] *n.* **1** a dry, red Italian wine. **2** any similar wine. ⟨< the *Chianti* Mountains in Italy⟩

chi•a•o ['tjaʊ] *or* [dʒjaʊ] *n., pl.* **chiao. 1** a unit of money in the People's Republic of China and Taiwan, equal to 1/10 of a yuan. **2** a coin worth one chiao.

chi•a•ro•scu•ro [ki,ɑrə'skjurou]; *Italian,* [,kjarɔ'skuro] *n., pl.* **-ros. 1** the treatment of light and shade in a picture. **2** the effect of light and shade in a picture. **3** a style of painting, drawing, etc. that uses only light and shade. **4** a picture, especially a painting, in which chiaroscuro is used. **5** stylistic effects of variation, relief, contrast, etc., used in any of the arts. ⟨< Ital. < *chiaro* clear (< L *clarus)* + *oscuro* dim (< L *obscurus*)⟩

chi•as•ma [kaɪ'æzmə] *n. Genetics.* the crossing of chromosome strands seen at a stage of the first meiotic division in the formation of reproductive cells, thought to be cytological evidence of exchange of chromosomal material (recombination) between homologous chromosomes. ⟨< Med.L < Gk. *chiasma* a crosspiece < *chiasmos* placing crosswise < *chiazein* to mark with a chi⟩

Chib•cha ['tʃıbtʃə] *n.* **1** any member of an extinct Indian people who lived where Bogota, Colombia, now stands. **2** the language of this people.

Chib•chan ['tʃıbtʃən] *adj.* of or having to do with a family of languages of Central America, Colombia, and Ecuador.

chic [ʃik] *n., adj. —n.* style.
—adj. stylish. ⟨< F⟩ **—'chic•ly,** *adv.*
☛ *Hom.* SHEIK.

chi•ca•lo•te [,tʃıkə'louti] *or* [,tʃıkə'loutei] *n.* a poppy plant (*gemone platyceras*) of Mexico and SW U.S., having large, white flowers. Also called **prickly poppy.** ⟨< Am.Sp. < Nahuatl *chicalotl* < *chicaloyo* thorny⟩

chi•cane [ʃı'kein] *n., v.* **-caned, -can•ing.** *—n.* chicanery.
—v. **1** use chicanery (on); trick. **2** get by chicanery. ⟨< F *chicane* < *chicaner* quibble⟩

chi•can•er•y [ʃı'keinəri] *n., pl.* **-er•ies.** low trickery; unfair practice; quibbling: *Only a dishonest lawyer would use chicanery to win a lawsuit.*

Chi•ca•no [tʃı'kɑnou] *n., pl.* **-nos,** *feminine,* **Chicana** [tʃı'kɑnə]; *adj. —n.* a citizen or inhabitant of the United States who is a native of Mexico or is of Mexican descent.
—adj. of or having to do with Chicanos. ⟨< dial. pronun. of Am. Sp. *Mexicano* Mexican⟩

chi–chi ['ʃi ,ʃi] *adj. Informal.* very smart and stylish, especially in an affected, arty way: *a chi-chi little boutique.*

chick [tʃık] *n.* **1** a young chicken. **2** a young bird. **3** child. ⟨ME *chicke*, var. of *chicken*⟩

chick•a•dee ['tʃıkə,di] *n.* any of several North American songbirds (genus *Parus*) of the titmouse family, having a plump body, long tail, short bill, and a large black or brown caplike patch on the top of the head. The **black-capped chickadee** (*P. atricapillus*) is the commonest species, found across North America. ⟨imitative of its cry⟩

chick•a•ree ['tʃıkə,ri] *n.* a North American red squirrel. See RED SQUIRREL. ⟨imitative of its cry⟩

Chick•a•saw ['tʃıkə,sɒ] *n.* **1** any member of an American Indian people who formerly lived in northern Mississippi and now live in Oklahoma. **2** the Muskogean language of this people.

chic•kee [tʃı'ki] *or* ['tʃıki] *n.* a house of the Seminole people, with open sides and thatched with palm leaves. ⟨< Mikasuki *ciki* dwelling⟩

chick•en ['tʃıkən] *n., v. —n.* **1** the common domestic fowl, bred in many varieties for its flesh or eggs. All breeds of chicken are descended from a wild fowl (*Gallus gallus*) of the jungles of SE Asia. **2** a young hen or rooster. **3** the flesh of a chicken used for food. **4** any of various other birds when young. **5** *Cdn. Informal.* PRAIRIE CHICKEN. **6** (*adjl.*) young or small: *a chicken lobster.* **7** *Slang.* coward: *Don't be such a chicken.* **8** (*adjl.*) *Slang.* cowardly.
count one's chickens before they are hatched, reckon on success or good fortune which may not become fact.
play chicken, take part in any of various games in which each person risks his or her own safety on the assumption that the other person will give up or back down first.
—v. Slang. back out, or withdraw, because of a loss of courage (*used with* **out**): *She chickened out at the last minute and refused to go on stage.* ⟨OE *cicen*⟩

chick•en•burg•er ['tʃıkən,bɜrgər] *n.* a burger made with cooked chicken instead of ground beef.

chicken divan a dish of boneless chicken breast cooked in a casserole with vegetables and a cheese sauce.

chicken feed *Slang.* a small or insignificant amount of money: *He said he left the job because it paid chicken feed.*

chicken hawk any of various hawks that raid poultry yards.

chick•en–heart•ed ['tʃıkən ,hɑrtıd] *adj.* cowardly; timid.

chicken Ki•ev [ki'ɛv] *or* ['kiɛf] a dish of boneless chicken breast pounded flat, rolled around chunks of herbed butter, breaded, and deep fried. ⟨after *Kiev*, Ukraine⟩

chick•en–liv•ered ['tʃıkən ,lıvərd] *adj. Informal.* cowardly.

chicken pox a contagious disease, usually of childhood, marked by pus-filled skin eruptions similar to those of smallpox but milder, and usually accompanied by a fever.

chicken snake any of various large, benign snakes (genus *Elaphe*), native to eastern and southwestern North America, which feed on rodents; rat snake.

chicken wire a light wire netting of six-sided mesh, used for fencing, on cages for pets, to protect young trees, etc.

chick pea 1 an annual plant (*Cicer arietinum*) of the pea family, native to Asia but now widely grown in the western hemisphere for its edible seeds, which grow in short pods. **2** the seed of this plant, resembling the garden pea in shape and flavour.

chick•weed ['tʃık,wid] *n.* any of several plants (especially of genera *Stellaria* and *Cerastium*) of the pink family, some of which have leaves and seeds that are attractive to birds. The common chickweed (*Stellaria media*) is well-known as a weed in gardens.

chic•le ['tʃıkəl] *n.* a tasteless, gumlike substance, the main ingredient of chewing gum, that is prepared from the milky juice of the sapodilla tree. ⟨< Am.Sp. < Mexican *jiktli* < Nahuatl *chietli*⟩

chic•o•ry ['tʃıkəri] *n., pl.* **-ries. 1** a European perennial herb (*Cichorium intybus*) of the composite family having small blue flowers. It is widely cultivated for its leaves, which are used in salads, and also for its roots, which are dried and ground for use as a coffee substitute. It is a common Canadian weed. **2** the dried, ground roots of this plant, used as a substitute for coffee. ⟨< F *chicorée* < L < Gk. *kichōrion*⟩

chid [tʃıd] *v.* a pt. and a pp. of CHIDE.

chid•den ['tʃıdən] *v.* a pp. of CHIDE.

chide [tʃaɪd] *v.* **chid•ed** or **chid, chid•ed, chid,** or **chid•den, chid•ing.** reproach; blame; scold: *She chided her son for getting his sweater dirty.* ⟨OE *cīdan*⟩ **—'chid•er,** *n.* **—'chid•ing•ly,** *adv.*
☛ *Syn.* See note at SCOLD.

chief [tʃif] *n., adj. —n.* **1** the head of a group; leader; the person highest in rank or authority. **2 Chief,** engineer or petty officer highest in rank. **3** the head of a tribe or clan. **4** *Heraldry.* the upper third of a shield.
in chief, a at the head or in the highest position. **b** chiefly.
—adj. **1** leading; at the head; in authority: *the chief engineer of a building project.* **2** main; most important: *The chief attraction of the midway was the ferris wheel.* ⟨ME < OF < L *caput* head. Doublet of CHEF.⟩ **—'chief•less,** *adj.*

chief•dom ['tʃifdəm] *n.* the position or authority of a chief, or the territory ruled by him or her.

chief executive officer the head of the executive branch of a government or large corporation. *Abbrev.*: CEO

chief justice 1 in Canada and some other Commonwealth countries, a judge who is appointed as the senior judge of a supreme court. The Supreme Court of Canada is made up of the chief justice of Canada and eight puisne judges. **2** in the United States: **a** a similar official. **b** a judge who presides over a court made up of a group of judges.

chief•ly ['tʃifli] *adv., adj. —adv.* **1** mainly; mostly: *This juice is made up chiefly of tomatoes.* **2** first of all; above all.
—adj. of or proper to a chief: *his chiefly bearing.*

chief of staff the senior staff officer serving as principal adviser to the commander of a military organization or formation.

Chief of the Defence Staff *Cdn.* the highest-ranking military officer.

chief petty officer **1** *Canadian Forces.* in Maritime Command, either of two ranks: chief petty officer 2nd class (*abbrev.*: C2), equivalent to a master warrant officer; chief petty officer 1st class (*abbrev.*: C1), equivalent to a chief warrant officer. See chart of ranks in the Appendix. **2** a naval, non-commissioned officer of similar rank in other countries. *Abbrev.*: CPO or C.P.O.

chief•tain ['tʃiftən] *n.* **1** the chief of a tribe or clan. **2** a leader; the head of a group. ⟨ME *chevetaine* < OF < LL *capitaneus.* Doublet of CAPTAIN.⟩

chief•tain•cy ['tʃiftənsi] *n.* the position or rank of a chieftain.

chief•tain•ship ['tʃiftən,ʃɪp] *n.* chieftaincy.

chief warrant officer the highest ranking non-commissioned officer in the armed forces. *Abbrev.*: C.W.O. or CWO See chart of ranks in the Appendix.

chiff•chaff ['tʃɪf,tʃæf] *n.* a small bird (*Phylloscopus collybita*) of the warbler family, native to Europe, having green and brown plumage and feeding mostly on insects. ⟨imitative of the bird's call⟩

chif•fe•robe ['ʃɪfə,roub] *n.* a piece of furniture having both hanging space and drawers or shelves. Also, **chifforobe.** ⟨< *chiff(onier)* + *(ward)robe*⟩

chif•fon [ʃə'fɒn] *or* ['ʃɪfɒn] *n.* **1** a delicate, very thin, usually soft fabric, made of silk, rayon, etc., and used for dresses, scarves, veils, etc. **2 chiffons,** *pl. Rare.* ribbons, laces, etc., used to ornament a woman's dress. **3** (*adjl.*) made of chiffon. **4** (*adjl.*) of fabric, soft and lightweight: *chiffon velvet.* **5** (*adjl.*) of cakes, etc., having a light texture, as from the addition of beaten egg whites. ⟨< F *chiffon* < *chiffe* rag⟩

chif•fo•nier [,ʃɪfə'nir] *n.* a high chest of drawers, often having a mirror. ⟨< F *chiffonnier* < *chiffon.* See CHIFFON.⟩

chig•ger ['tʃɪgər] *n.* **1** the larva of any of various mites (family Trombiculidae) that sucks the blood of people and animals, causing intense irritation of the skin. **2** chigoe. ⟨alteration of *chigoe*⟩

chi•gnon ['ʃinjɒn]; *French,* [ʃi'njɔ̃] *n.* a knot or roll of hair worn at the back of the head by women. ⟨< F *chignon* nape of the neck < VL *catenio* < L *catena* chain; referring to the vertebrae⟩

chig•oe ['tʃɪgou] *n.* **1** a tropical flea (*Tunga penetrans*), the female of which burrows under the skin of people and animals, causing intense irritation; sand flea. **2** chigger. ⟨< W Indian⟩

chi•hua•hua [tʃə'wɑwɑ] *n.* an ancient breed of tiny dog originally developed in Mexico, having large, protruding eyes, short hair, and large, erect ears. ⟨< *Chihuahua,* a state and city in N Mexico⟩

A chihuahua

chil•blain ['tʃɪl,blein] *n.* Usually, **chilblains,** *pl.* an itching sore or redness on the hands or feet, caused by cold. ⟨< *chill* + *blain*⟩ **—'chil,blained,** *adj.*

Chil•cot•in [tʃɪl'koutɪn] *n.* **1** a tribe of Athapascan people of the First Nations living in the valley of the Chilcotin River, British Columbia. **2** a member of this people. **3** the Athapascan language of the people.

child [tʃaɪld] *n., pl.* **chil•dren.** **1** baby. **2** an unborn baby; fetus. **3** a boy or girl, especially one up to the early or mid teens. **4** a son or daughter: *All their children are already married.* **5** descendant. **6** an adult who behaves in a childish way, as if he or she has not grown up: *My father is such a child when he is sick.* **7** an adult who is more innocent, naive, and unsophisticated than most other adults: *When it comes to politics or business dealings, Uncle Joe is a child.* **8** a product or result: *The new system is entirely the child of her ingenuity.* **9** a person regarded as belonging to or produced by a particular time, place, or environment: *a child of the sea, a child of the nuclear age.*
with child, pregnant. ⟨OE *cild*⟩

child•bear•ing ['tʃaɪld,bɛrɪŋ] *n., adj.* *—n.* the act or process of conceiving and giving birth to children.
—adj. of or having to do with this act or process.

child•bed ['tʃaɪld,bɛd] *n.* the condition of a woman giving birth to a child.

childbed fever infection of the genital tract occurring after childbirth.

child•birth ['tʃaɪld,bɜrθ] *n.* the act or process of giving birth to a child.

child care the care of a child or children, especially by a paid caregiver while the parents are at work: *funds for child care.* **—'child-,care,** *adj.*

Chil•der•mas ['tʃɪldərməs] *n.* a Christian holy day (December 28) in memory of the infant boys killed on Herod's orders; Holy Innocents' Day. ⟨ME *childermasse* < OE *cildramæsse* < *cildra* of infants + *mæsse* mass⟩

child•hood ['tʃaɪld,hʊd] *n.* **1** the condition of being a child: *the carefree days of childhood.* **2** the time during which one is a child: *Her childhood was very happy.* **3** an early stage of anything.

child•ish ['tʃaɪldɪʃ] *adj.* **1** of a child. **2** like a child: *a childish person.* **3** not suitable for a grown person; weak; silly; foolish: *It was childish of her to make such a fuss.* **—'child•ish•ly,** *adv.*
☛ *Usage.* **Childish,** CHILDLIKE differ widely. **Childish** emphasizes the physical helplessness, lack of control over feelings, and undeveloped mind of a child, and therefore expresses an unfavourable opinion when used of an adult: *Such irresponsible behaviour is childish.* **Childlike** emphasizes the innocence, simplicity, and frankness of children, and suggests a favourable opinion: *She has a childlike belief in her son's innocence.*

child•ish•ness ['tʃaɪldɪʃnɪs] *n.* **1** the fact or condition of being like a child. **2** immaturity; silliness.

child labour or **labor** work done by children in factories, business, etc.

child•less ['tʃaɪldlɪs] *adj.* having no child.
—'child•less•ness, *n.*

child•like ['tʃaɪld,ləik] *adj.* **1** like a child; innocent; frank; simple: *The charming old woman had an open, childlike manner.* **2** suitable for a child. **—'child,like•ness,** *n.*
☛ *Usage.* See note at CHILDISH.

child•proof ['tʃaɪld,pruf] *adj., v., —adj.* so arranged as to prevent damage by or to a young child: *Is your home childproof?* *—v.* make (usually, a home) free of danger to or from a child: *How to childproof your home.*

chil•dren ['tʃɪldrən] *n.* pl. of CHILD.

children of Israel *Archaic.* Israelites; Hebrews; Jews.

Children's Crusade an unsuccessful expedition to recover the Holy Sepulchre, undertaken by thousands of French and German children in 1212.

child's play something very easy to do.

chil•e ['tʃɪli] *n.* See CHILI.

Chi•le ['tʃilei] *n.* a country in SW South America.

Chil•e•an [tʃə'leiən] *n., adj.* *—n.* a native or inhabitant of Chile. *—adj.* of or having to do with Chile or its people.

Chile saltpetre ['tʃɪli] SODIUM NITRATE.

chi•les rel•le•nos ['tʃileis rə'jeinous] a Mexican dish consisting of green chilies stuffed with cheese or, sometimes, ground beef, then breaded and fried or baked.

chil•i ['tʃɪli] *n., pl.* **chil•ies.** **1** the small, hot-tasting pod, or fruit, of any of several varieties of PEPPER (def. 5), used for seasoning. Chilies are also dried and ground up to make red pepper. **2** the plant that it grows on, a tropical American shrub (*Capsicum frutescens*) grown in southern U.S. **3** CHILI CON CARNE: *We had chili for supper last night.* Also, **chilli.** ⟨< Sp. *chile* < Mexican *chilli*⟩
☛ *Hom.* CHILLY.

chil•i•ad ['kɪli,æd] *n.* **1** a thousand. **2** a thousand years. ⟨< L *chilias* < Gk. *chilias* < *chilioi* a thousand⟩

chil•i con car•ne ['tʃɪli kən 'kɑrni] ground or cubed beef cooked with chilies or chili powder and, usually, with red or kidney beans and tomatoes. ⟨< Sp., chili with meat⟩

chili dog a dish consisting of a hot dog served with chili con carne.

chili powder dried ground chili pods with cumin, oregano, etc., used as a seasoning.

chili sauce a sauce made of red peppers, tomatoes, and spices. Also, **chilli sauce.**

Chil•kat ['tʃɪlkæt] *n.* **1** an American Indian people of the Tlingits, formerly living mainly in SE Alaska, noted for their making of brightly coloured blankets of mountain-goat wool and cedar bark. **2** a member of this people.

Chilkat blanket or **robe** *Cdn.* a D-shaped blanket woven of mountain-goat wool with a warp of yellow cedar bark, into which are worked symbolic designs, originally made by the Chilkat people and later adopted by other peoples of the west coast.

chill [tʃɪl] *n., adj., v.* *—n.* **1** a moderate but unpleasant coldness: *a chill in the air.* **2** a sudden coldness of the body, often accompanied by shivering. **3** a mild cold or other illness due to cold or damp conditions: *I seem to have caught a chill.* **4** unfriendliness; lack of warmth of feeling: *I felt the chill of his greeting.* **5** a check on enthusiasm; depressing influence: *The announcement of renewed fighting cast a chill over the assembled group.* **6** a sudden feeling of fear or dread: *A chill went through her at the thought of the coming night.* **7** *Metallurgy.* a metal mould, or a piece of iron in a sand mould, for making chilled castings.
—adj. **1** unpleasantly cold. **2** cold in manner; unfriendly. **3** depressing; discouraging.
—v. **1** make cold: *We chilled the pop in the refrigerator.* **2** become cold; feel cold. **3** depress; dispirit; fill with dread. **4** *Metallurgy.* **a** harden (cast iron, etc.) on the surface by cooling it suddenly. **b** of cast iron, etc., become hard on the surface through sudden cooling.
chill out, *Slang.* calm down. ⟨OE *ciele*⟩ **—'chill•ness,** *n.*

chill•er ['tʃɪlər] *n.* **1** a person who or thing that chills. **2** *Informal.* a horror story or film.

chill factor WIND CHILL. See table in the Appendix.

chil•li ['tʃɪli] See CHILI.

chill•ing ['tʃɪlɪŋ] *adj.* that chills: *a chilling wind, a chilling glance.* **—'chill•ing•ly,** *adv.*

chilli sauce See CHILI SAUCE.

chill•y ['tʃɪli] *adj.* **chill•i•er, chill•i•est. 1** unpleasantly cool; rather cold: *a chilly day.* **2** cold in manner; unfriendly: *a chilly greeting.* **—'chill•i•ness,** *n.*
☛ *Hom.* CHILI.
☛ *Syn.* **1.** See note at COLD.

Chil•tern Hundreds ['tʃɪltərn] *Brit.* an office under the Crown that members of the House of Commons are said to apply for when they wish to resign; a legal fiction.

chi•mae•ra [kə'mirə] *or* [kaɪ'mirə] **1** a fish of the family Chimaeridae, having a smooth skin and a narrowing body, the male having a spiky, grasping organ over the mouth. **2** See CHIMERA.

chime [tʃaɪm] *n., v.* **chimed, chim•ing.** *—n.* **1** usually, **chimes,** *pl.* **a** a set of bells tuned to the musical scale, usually played by hammers or simple machinery. **b** a set of metal tubes hung vertically from a frame, played by striking with a hammer held in the hand, used in orchestras; tubular bells. **2** the musical sound made by a bell or set of tuned bells: *The old clock has a pleasant chime.* **3** a pleasantly harmonious sound, suggesting bells: *the chime of children's laughter.* **4** agreement; harmony. **5** carillon. **6** an apparatus or arrangement for striking a bell or set of bells so as to produce a musical sound.
—v. **1** make musical sounds on (a set of tuned bells). **2** ring out musically: *The bells chimed at midnight. The clock chimed the hours.* **3** produce (a musical sound) from a bell (or the like) by striking it or using means other than ringing. **4** agree; be in harmony. **5** say or utter in cadence, unison, or singsong.
chime in, a be in harmony; agree: *Her ideas chimed in with mine.* **b** *Informal.* break into or join in a conversation. ⟨ME *chymbe,* ult. < L < Gk. *kymbalon.* See CYMBAL.⟩ **—'chim•er,** *n.*

chi•me•ra or **chi•mae•ra** [kə'mirə] *or* [kaɪ'mirə] *n., pl.* **-ras. 1 Chimera.** *Greek mythology.* a female monster with a lion's head, a goat's body, and a serpent's tail, supposed to breathe out fire. **2** a horrible creature of the imagination. **3** an absurd or impossible idea; wild fancy: *The idea of changing lead to gold was a chimera.* **4** *Biology.* an individual composed of cells from two zygotes, as a result of an unusual event of early development. Chimeric mice are generated by injection of embryonic stem cells into a genetically different mouse embryo at the blastocyst stage. ⟨ME < OF < L < Gk. *chimaira* she-goat⟩

chi•mer•ic [kə'mɛrɪk] *or* [kaɪ'mɛrɪk] *adj.* **1** unreal; imaginary. **2** absurd; impossible: *chimeric schemes for getting rich.* **3** wildly fanciful; visionary. **4** of a chimera. Also, **chimerical.** **—chi'mer•i•cal•ly,** *adv.*

chim•ney ['tʃɪmni] *n., pl.* **-neys. 1** an upright structure used to make a draft for a fire and carry away smoke. **2** the part of this structure that rises above a roof. **3** a glass tube put around the flame of a lamp. **4** a crack or opening in a rock, mountain, volcano, etc. **5** an upright block of ore. ⟨ME *chimenee* < OF *cheminee* < LL *caminata* < L *caminus* oven < Gk. *kaminos*⟩ **—'chim•ney•less,** *adj.*

chimney corner **1** a recess by a fire, equipped with seats. **2** the corner or side of a fireplace; a place near the fire.

chimney piece mantlepiece.

chimney pot a pipe of earthenware or metal fitted on top of a chimney to increase the draft.

chimney swallow **1** the chimney swift of North America. **2** the European barn swallow.

chimney sweep a person whose work is cleaning out chimneys.

chimney swift a short-tailed, dark grey swift (*Chaetura pelagica*) that often nests inside chimneys. The chimney swift ranges from southern Saskatchewan east to Nova Scotia and south to the upper Amazon region of South America.

chi•mo ['tʃimou] *or* ['tʃaɪmou] *interj. Cdn.* especially in the North, a call or exclamation of greeting. ⟨< Inuktitut⟩

chimp [tʃɪmp] *n. Informal.* chimpanzee.

chim•pan•zee [ˌtʃɪmpæn'zi], ['tʃɪmpænˌzi], *or* [tʃɪm'pænzi] *n.* an anthropoid ape (*Pan troglodytes*) of Africa, smaller than a gorilla. The chimpanzee is probably the most intelligent ape. ⟨< a Bantu name⟩

chin [tʃɪn] *n., v.* **chinned, chin•ning.** *—n.* **1** the front of the lower jaw below the mouth. **2** the whole lower surface of the face, below the mouth. **3** *Informal.* a chat; gossip.
keep (one's) **chin up,** bear adversity without flinching or complaining.
take it on the chin, *Informal.* **a** suffer severed hardship. **b** endure stoically.
—v. **1** *Informal.* chat; gossip. **2** *Informal.* place (a violin) under the chin in order to play it.
chin (oneself), do a chin-up or chin-ups. ⟨OE *cinn*⟩ **—'chin•less,** *adj.*

chi•na ['tʃaɪnə] *n., adj.* *—n.* **1** a fine, white, translucent ceramic ware made of pure clay that has been baked at high temperatures; porcelain. Coloured designs can be baked into china. **2** dishes, vases, ornaments, etc. made of china. **3** ceramic dishes of any kind.
—adj. made of china: *a china teapot.* ⟨short for earlier *china-ware* ware from China⟩

Chi•na ['tʃaɪnə] *n.* a large country in E Asia, properly called the People's Republic of China.

China aster an annual plant (*Callistephus chinensis*) of the composite family, similar to an aster, and native to the Far East, bearing large white, yellow, red, blue, or purple flowers, cultivated as a garden flower.

chi•na•ber•ry ['tʃaɪnəˌbɛri] *n., pl.* **-ber•ries. 1** a tree (*Melia azedarach*) of the same family as the mahogany, native to Asia and widely cultivated in warm regions for its purplish flowers and yellow, berrylike fruits, and for shade. **2** its fruit. **3** the soapberry of the southern U.S., northern Mexico, and the West Indies.

China rose **1** a rose (*Rosa chinensis*) of China, having fragrant red, pink, or white flowers. From it many modern roses have been bred. **2** a large, tropical Asian shrub (*Hibiscus rosa-sinensis*) of the mallow family, having showy red flowers.

Chi•na•town ['tʃaɪnəˌtaʊn] *n.* a section of a city inhabited mainly by Chinese people and having a large number of Chinese stores, restaurants, etc.

chi•na•ware ['tʃaɪnəˌwɛr] *n.* **1** dishes, vases, ornaments, etc., made of china. **2** earthen dishes of any kind.

chinch [tʃɪntʃ] *n. U.S.* **1** bedbug. **2** Usually, **chinch bug,** a small black-and-white hemipterous insect (*Blissus leucopterus*) that sucks the juice of grain plants. ⟨< Sp. *chinche* < L *cimex* bug⟩

chin–che•rin•chee [ˌtʃɪn tʃə'rɪntʃi] *n.* a poisonous plant (*Ornithogalum thyrsoides*) with spiky white or yellow flowers, native to South Africa. ⟨origin unknown⟩

chin•chil•la [tʃɪn'tʃɪlə] *n.* **1** a small, stocky rodent (*Chinchilla laniger*) native to the mountains of South America, widely bred in captivity for its soft, fine silver-grey fur. **2** the highly valued fur of a chinchilla. **3** (*adjl.*) made of this fur: *a chinchilla coat.* **4** a thick woollen fabric woven in small, closely set tufts, used for overcoats. **5** a kind of Persian cat, usually white. ⟨< Sp. *chinchilla,* dim. of *chinche*⟩

chine [tʃaɪn] *n., v.* **chined, chin•ing.** *—n.* **1** the backbone; spine. **2** a piece of an animal's backbone with the meat on it, suitable for cooking. **3** a ridge; crest. **4** the join between the bottom and either side of a boat.

–*v.* cut (a carcass) along or across the backbone. ⟨ME < OF *eschine* < Gmc.⟩

Chi•nese [tʃaɪ'niz] *n., pl.* **-nese;** *adj.* –*n.* **1** a native or inhabitant of China. **2** a person of Chinese descent. **3** any of the Sino-Tibetan languages of China, especially Mandarin.
–*adj.* of or having to do with China, its people, or their languages.

Chinese boxes a set of progressively larger boxes, each of which nests into the one bigger.

Chinese cabbage any of several edible plants (*Brassica pekinensis* or *Brassica chinensis*) native to Asia, related to and tasting like cabbage but having a looser and more cylindrical head.

Chinese calendar the ancient lunar calendar formerly used in China, having cycles of 60 years, 12 months in a year, 29 or 30 days in a month, with an extra month added after each half cycle. The Chinese adopted the Georgian calendar in 1912, the first year of the Republic, and years are now counted from that date.

Chinese checkers a game played by two to six persons using small marbles on a board patterned as a six-pointed star. The object of the game is to be the first player to move all one's marbles into the corresponding positions on the opposite side of the board. Also, **Chinese chequers.**

Chinese chestnut a chestnut (*Castanea mollissima*) having large, sweet nuts. It is often hybridized with other chestnuts as it resists chestnut blight.

Chinese Empire China before it became a republic in 1912, including Manchuria, Mongolia, Tibet, and Sinkiang.

Chinese lantern 1 a lantern of thin, coloured paper that can be folded up accordion-style. **2** Often, **Chinese lantern plant,** a perennial plant (*Physalis alkekengi*) cultivated for its hollow, red fruit casing.

Chinese puzzle something that is very complicated and hard to solve. ⟨from the wood and metal puzzles invented by the Chinese⟩

Chinese red a specific shade of red for paint, usually a bright orange red.

Chinese white a white colour base for watercolours and inks, made of zinc oxide.

chink[1] [tʃɪŋk] *n., v.* –*n.* a narrow opening; crack; slit: *The chinks between the logs of the cabin let in the wind and snow.*
–*v.* **1** fill up the chinks in: *The cracks in the walls of the cabin were chinked with mud.* **2** make chinks in. ⟨? < ME *chine* fissure < OE *cinu*⟩

chink[2] [tʃɪŋk] *n., v.* –*n.* a short, sharp, ringing sound like coins or glasses hitting together.
–*v.* **1** make a short, sharp, ringing sound. **2** cause to make such a sound: *He chinked the coins in his pocket.* ⟨imitative⟩

chi•no ['tʃinou] *or* ['ʃinou] *n.* **1** a twilled cotton or cotton-blend fabric of medium weight with a smooth, lustrous finish, used especially for sportswear. **2 chinos,** *pl.* pants made of chino. **3** (*adjl.*) made of chino: *chino pants.* ⟨origin unknown⟩

chi•noi•se•rie [ʃin,wɑzə'ri], [,ʃinwɑzə'ri], *or* [ʃin'wɑzə,ri] *n.* **1** a style of design and decoration for furniture, ceramics, etc., based on traditional Chinese designs and motifs. **2** an article or articles made in this style: *She collects chinoiserie.* ⟨< F < *chinois* Chinese + *-erie* -ery⟩

chi•nook [ʃə'nʊk] *n., v. Cdn.* –*n.* a warm, usually dry, winter wind that blows from the west or southwest across the Rocky Mountains from the Peace River to Colorado, sometimes extending across Alberta and into Saskatchewan. A chinook usually causes a dramatic rise in temperature.
–*v.* blow a chinook: *It didn't chinook again until March.*

Chi•nook [ʃə'nʊk] *or* [tʃə'nuk] *n., pl.* **-nook** or **-nooks. 1** a member of an American Indian people who lived along the Columbia River in the NW United States. **2** the Chinookan language of the Chinook and other peoples of the region. **3** CHINOOK JARGON. **4** (*adjl.*) of or having to do with the Chinook, their language, or Chinook jargon. ⟨< Salishan⟩

Chi•nook•an [ʃə'nʊkən] *n., adj.* –*n.* a family of languages spoken by American Indians and First Nations peoples of the N Pacific coast of North America.
–*adj.* of this family of languages.

chinook arch *Cdn.* an arch of blue sky above the western horizon, often seen just before or during a chinook.

chinook belt *Cdn.* that part of southern Alberta and Saskatchewan most influenced by chinooks.

Chinook jargon *Cdn.* a relatively simple trade language of the Pacific coast of North America based on Chinook, with words from Nootka, Salishan, English, and French. Chinook jargon was formerly used by American Indians or First Nations peoples and Europeans in their dealings with each other.

chinook salmon a spring salmon, especially a large one.

chin•qua•pin ['tʃɪŋkə,pɪn] *n.* **1** a shrubby tree (*Castanea pumila*) of the beech family, native to SE U.S. and having rectangular leaves and small, edible nuts; especially, the dwarf chestnut. **2** an evergreen tree (*Castanopsis chrysophylla*) of the beech family, native to the Pacific coasts of North America and Asia, having dark green needles and inedible nuts. **3** the nut of either of these trees. ⟨< Algonquian⟩

chintz [tʃɪnts] *n.* a firm, plain-woven, cotton fabric, usually printed with colourful designs and having a glazed surface. Chintz is used mostly for draperies and slipcovers. ⟨originally pl., < Hind. *chint* < Skt. *citra* variegated⟩

chintz•y ['tʃɪntsi] *adj.* **1** like chintz. **2** *Informal.* showy or gaudy and cheap. **3** *Informal.* trivial or petty: *a chintzy motel room, a chintzy thing to do.*

chin–up ['tʃɪn ,ʌp] *n.* the exercise of hanging by the hands from a bar and pulling oneself up until one's chin is level with the bar.

chip [tʃɪp] *n., v.* **chipped, chip•ping.** –*n.* **1** a small piece cut or broken off. **2** a place in china or stone from which a small piece has been broken: *One of the new plates has a chip.* **3** a small or thin piece of food or candy: *chocolate chips, dried banana chips.* **4** POTATO CHIP (def. 1): *We ate a whole bag of chips.* **5** FRENCH FRY: *fish and chips.* **6** *Games.* a round, flat piece of plastic, etc. used as a counter, to represent money, etc. **7** *Electronics.* **a** a tiny wafer of semiconductor material, such as silicon, used as the basis for an integrated circuit or an electronic component or device such as a transistor. **b** INTEGRATED CIRCUIT. **8** a strip of wood, palm leaf, or straw used in making baskets or hats. **9** a piece of dried dung, used for fuel in some regions: *buffalo chips.* **10** *Golf.* CHIP SHOT.
cash in (one's) **chips, a** change poker chips into cash. **b** *Slang.* close or sell a business; retire. **c** *Slang.* die.
chip off the old block, *Informal.* a person who is like his or her parent.
chip on (one's) **shoulder,** *Informal.* **a** a permanent sense of grievance. **b** a readiness to quarrel or fight.
in the chips, *Slang.* wealthy; affluent.
when the chips are down, when the moment of decision or definite action arrives; in a crisis.
–*v.* **1** cut or break off in small pieces from wood, stones, dishes, etc.: *He chipped off the old paint.* **2** become chipped: *This china chips easily.* **3** shape by cutting at the surface or edge with an axe or chisel. **4** *Golf.* make a chip shot.
chip in, *Informal.* **a** join with others in giving (money or help). **b** put in (a remark) when others are talking. ⟨OE *(for)cippian*⟩
–'chip•per, *n.*

chip•board ['tʃɪp,bɔrd] *n.* a building material made in large, rigid sheets, consisting of wood chips and fibres pressed together, using a synthetic resin as a binding agent.

Chip•e•wy•an [,tʃɪpə'waɪən] *n., pl.* **-an** or **-ans. 1** a member of a people of the First Nations living in northern Manitoba and Saskatchewan and the Northwest Territories. The Chipewyans were traditionally a nomadic people who hunted the caribou. **2** the Athapascan language of the Chipewyan. **3** (*adjl.*) of or having to do with the Chipewyans or their language. Also, **Chipewayan.**

chip•munk ['tʃɪpmʌŋk] *n.* any of several small North American animals (genera *Eutamias* and *Tamias*) of the squirrel family that live mainly on the ground, having mostly brown fur with black stripes along the back that are separated by pale grey or creamy stripes. Chipmunks are smaller than squirrels and have a less bushy tail. ⟨< obs. Cdn. dial. *chitmunk* < Algonquian; cf. Ojibwa *atchitamon* one who descends trees head first⟩

A chipmunk

chi•pot•le [tʃɪ'poutlei]; *Spanish,* [tʃi'pɔtle] *n.* a Mexican red pepper, eaten either as a pickle or as an ingredient of meat dishes. ⟨< Mexican Sp. < Nahuatl *xipotli*⟩

chipped beef dried, smoked beef sliced very thin and usually served hot, with a cream sauce.

Chip•pen•dale ['tʃɪpən,deil] *adj., n.* –*adj.* of, like, or having to do with a graceful, often richly ornamented style of furniture. —*n.* **1** this style of furniture. **Chinese Chippendale** reflects an Oriental influence. **2** a piece of furniture in this style. ⟨after Thomas *Chippendale* (1718-1779), an English cabinetmaker⟩

chip•per ['tʃɪpər] *adj. Informal.* lively; cheerful. ⟨origin uncertain; cf. Northern E dial. *kipper* frisky⟩

Chip•pe•wa ['tʃɪpə,wɑ], ['tʃɪpə,wɒ], *or* ['tʃɪpə,wei] *n., pl.* **-wa** or **-was.** Ojibwa.

chipping sparrow a small sparrow (*Spizella passerina*) found throughout North America except for the far North, having a reddish cap and black and white streaks on the side of the head. ⟨< *chip*, imitative of its cry⟩

chip•py ['tʃɪpi] *n., pl.* **-pies;** *adj.* —*n.* **1** CHIPPING SPARROW. **2** chipmunk.
—*adj. Cdn. Slang.* **1** short-tempered; quarrelsome; aggressive: *He was known as a chippy player.* **2** having much rough and short-tempered play: *a chippy hockey game.*

chip shot *Golf.* a short, lofted shot used to get the ball onto the green.

chi•ral•i•ty [kaɪ'ræləti] *n.* the tendency of a compound toward a molecular structure that spirals in a clockwise or counterclockwise direction. ⟨< Gk. *cheir* hand + *-al*[1] + *-ity*⟩ **—'chi•ral,** *adj.*

chirk [tʃɜrk] *v.* cheer (*up*). ⟨ME *chirken* twitter⟩

chi•rog•ra•pher [kaɪ'rɒgrəfər] *n.* **1** a person who writes by hand, especially a calligraphist. **2** a person who studies handwriting.

chi•rog•ra•phy [kaɪ'rɒgrəfi] *n.* handwriting, especially a particular form of handwriting, or calligraphy. ⟨< Gk. *cheir* hand + E *-graphy* writing < Gk. *graphein* write⟩ **—,chi•ro'graph•ic,** *adj.*

chi•ro•man•cy ['kaɪrə,mænsi] *n.* the art of predicting a person's future from the lines on the palm of the hand; palmistry. ⟨< Gk. *cheir* hand + ME *mancy* < OF *-mancie* < LL *-mantia* < Gk. *manteia* divination < *mantis* prophet⟩

Chi•ron ['kaɪrɒn] *n. Greek mythology.* a wise and kindly centaur, teacher of many Greek heroes. Chiron was famous for his medical skill.

chi•rop•o•dist [kə'rɒpədɪst] *n.* a person trained and licensed to practise chiropody.

chi•rop•o•dy [kə'rɒpədi] *n.* the health specialty concerned with the diagnosis and treatment of disorders, injuries, and diseases of the human foot. Increasingly called **podiatry.** ⟨< Gk. *cheir* hand + *pous, podos,* foot; originally, treatment of hands and feet⟩

chi•ro•prac•tic [,kaɪrə'præktɪk] *n., adj.* —*n.* the treatment of disorders of the bones, muscles, and nerves by manipulation of the bony segments of the body, especially the spine.
—*adj.* having to do with the treatment of diseases by manipulating the spine. ⟨< Gk. *cheir* hand + *praktikos* referring to practice (< *prassein* do)⟩

chi•ro•prac•tor ['kaɪrə,præktər] *n.* a person who is qualified to practise chiropractic and whose work it is.

chi•rop•te•ran [kaɪ'rɒptərən] *n., adj.* —*n.* any mammal of the order Chiroptera, the bats. Also, **chiropter.**
—*adj.* of, having to do with, or designating the order Chiroptera. Also, **chiropterous.** ⟨< NL < Gk. *cheir* hand + *pteron* wing⟩

chirp [tʃɜrp] *v., n.* —*v.* **1** make a short, sharp sound such as certain small birds and insects make: *The sparrows and crickets chirped outside the house.* **2** utter with a chirp. **3** greet or urge on by chirping: *He chirped his horses on.* **4** make any similar sound.
—*n.* a short, sharp sound such as certain small birds and insects make. ⟨? var. of *chirk* be cheerful, OE *circian* roar⟩
—'chirp•er, *n.*

chirp•y ['tʃɜrpi] *adj.* **-i•er, -i•est.** *Informal.* **1** disposed to chirp. **2** lively and cheerful; enthusiastic. **—'chirp•i•ly,** *adv.* **—'chirp•i•ness,** *n.*

chirr [tʃɜr] *v., n.* —*v.* make a shrill, trilling sound: *The grasshoppers chirred in the fields.*
—*n.* a shrill, trilling sound. Also, **churr.** ⟨imitative⟩

chir•rup ['tʃirəp] *or* ['tʃɜrəp] *v.* **-rupped** or **-ruped, -rup•ping** or **-rup•ing;** *n.* —*v.* **1** chirp again and again: *He chirrupped to his horse to make it go faster.* **2** utter with chirps or sounds like this.
—*n.* the sound of chirruping. ⟨< *chirp*⟩ **—'chir•rup•y,** *adj.*

chi•rur•geon [kaɪ'rɜrdʒən] *n. Archaic.* surgeon. ⟨ME < OF *cirurgien* < *cirurgie* surgery. See SURGERY.⟩

chi•rur•ger•y [kaɪ'rɜrdʒəri] *n. Archaic.* surgery. **—chi'rur•gi•cal,** *adj.*

Chis•an•bop ['tʃɪzən,bɒp] *n.* a system of counting using the fingers and thumbs, to which values have been assigned. Numbers are added and subtracted by lifting or pressing down fingers and thumbs. ⟨< Korean *chisanbop* < *chi* finger + *san* calculation + *bop* method⟩

chis•el ['tʃɪzəl] *n., v.* **-elled** or **-eled, -el•ling** or **-el•ing.** —*n.* a cutting tool with a sharp edge at the end of a strong blade, used to cut or shape wood, stone, or metal.
—*v.* **1** cut or shape with a chisel. **2** *Slang.* use unfair practices (on); cheat; swindle. **3** get (something) by swindling. ⟨ME < OF < VL *cisellum*, var. of *caesellum* < L *caedere* cut⟩

chis•elled or **chis•eled** ['tʃɪzəld] *adj., v.* —*adj.* **1** cut, shaped, or wrought with a chisel. **2** having clear and sharp outlines, as if cut with a chisel: *his chiselled features.*
—*v.* pt. and pp. of CHISEL.

chis•el•ler or **chis•el•er** ['tʃɪzələr] *or* ['tʃɪzlər] *n. Slang.* a cheat; swindler.

chi–square test ['kaɪ ,skwɛr] *n. Statistics.* a test of the validity of a specific frequency distribution, made by matching the results obtained from the actual data with the results expected in theory.

chit[1] [tʃɪt] *n.* **1** child. **2** a saucy, forward girl. ⟨related to KITTEN. Cf. dial. *chit* kitten.⟩

chit[2] [tʃɪt] *n.* **1** a note; memorandum. **2** a signed note or something like it, given for a purchase, a meal, etc., that is to be paid for later. **3** a receipt for which expenses will be claimed: *a chit for cab fare.* ⟨short for *chitty* < Hind. *chitthi* letter < Sanskrit *chitra* a spot, mark⟩

chit–chat ['tʃɪt ,tʃæt] *n., v.* **-chat•ted, -chat•ting.** —*n.* **1** friendly, informal or superficial talk; chat. **2** gossip.
—*v.* talk in a friendly, informal or superficial way. ⟨< *chat*⟩

chi•tin ['kəitən] *n.* a semitransparent, horny substance forming the hard outer covering of beetles, lobsters, crabs, etc. ⟨< F *chitine* < Gk. *chiton* tunic⟩
☛ *Hom.* CHITON.

chi•tin•ous ['kəitənəs] *adj.* of or like chitin.

chi•ton ['kəitɒn] *or* ['kəitən] *n.* **1** in ancient Greece, a long, loose garment worn next to the skin by both men and women. **2** a mollusc of the class Amphineura, which clings to rocks. ⟨< Gk.⟩
☛ *Hom.* CHITIN ['kəitən].

chit•ter ['tʃɪtər] *v.* twitter: *The birds chittered.* ⟨imitative⟩

chit•ter•lings ['tʃɪtərlɪŋz] *n.pl.* the small intestines of pigs, cooked as food. ⟨ME; origin uncertain⟩

chiv•al•ric ['ʃɪvəlrɪk] *or* [ʃə'vælrɪk] *adj.* **1** having to do with chivalry: *the chivalric code.* **2** chivalrous.

chiv•al•rous ['ʃɪvəlrəs] *adj.* **1** having or showing the qualities of an ideal knight; brave, courteous, helpful, generous, and honourable: *a chivalrous action. He was a chivalrous escort.* **2** of or having to do with chivalry in the Middle Ages.
—'chiv•al•rous•ly, *adv.* **—'chiv•al•rous•ness,** *n.*

chiv•al•ry ['ʃɪvəlri] *n.* **1** the qualities of an ideal knight. Chivalry includes bravery, honour, courtesy, respect for women, protection of the weak, generosity, and fairness to enemies. **2** in the Middle Ages, the rules and customs of knights; system of knighthood. **3** knights as a group. **4** gallant warriors or gentlemen. **5** courteous behaviour, especially a manifestation of the traditional courtesies expected of a gentleman. ⟨ME *chivalrie* < OF *chevalerie* horsemanship, knighthood < Med.L *caballerius* horseman < L *caballus* horse⟩

chiv•a•ree [,ʃɪvə'ri] See SHIVAREE.

chive [tʃaɪv] *n.* Usually, **chives,** *pl.* a plant (*Allium schoenoprasum*) closely related to and resembling the onion, but milder in flavour and having a very small bulb. The long, slender, hollow leaves of chives are used to flavour soups, stews, salads, etc. ⟨ME < OF < L *caepa* onion⟩

chiv•vy or **chiv•y** ['tʃɪvi] *v.* **chiv•vied** or **chiv•ied, chiv•vy•ing** or **chiv•y•ing. 1** pursue or nag; harass: *She was chivvied into taking up the challenge.* **2** get by chivvying: *She chivvied a dollar out of me.* ⟨origin uncertain⟩

Ch.J. Chief Justice.

chla•myd•i•a [klə'mɪdiə] *n., pl.* **-diae** [-di,i]. **1** any parasite of the genus *Chlamydia*, which causes various infections. **2** a venereal disease of the genito-urinary tract, caused by the bacterium *Chlamydia trachomatis.* It can lead to sterility.

chla•mys ['kleimɪs] *or* ['klæmɪs] *n., pl.* **chla•my•des** [-mɪ,diz]. a short cloak worn by men in ancient Greece. ⟨< L < Gk.⟩

chlo•as•ma [klou'æzmə] *n.* a condition in which light brown patches appear on the skin, especially on the face and chest, caused by pregnancy, exposure to sunlight, malnutrition, or various diseases. ⟨< NL < LGk. greenness < Gk. *chloazein* to be green < *chloos* green⟩

chlor•ac•ne [klɔr'ækni] *n.* a skin condition, similar to acne, resulting from overexposure to chlorine.

chlo•ral ['klɔrəl] *n.* **1** a colourless, oily, liquid compound that is very irritating to the lungs, used in making DDT and chloral hydrate. *Formula*: CCl_3CHO **2** CHLORAL HYDRATE. ⟨< *chlo(rine)* + *al(cohol)*⟩

chloral hy•drate ['haɪdreit] a white, crystalline drug used to quiet nervousness and induce sleep. *Formula*: $CCl_3CH(OH)_2$

chlo•ram•bu•cil [klɔ'ræmbjə,sɪl] *n.* a drug used to treat leukemia. *Formula*: $C_{14}H_{19}Cl_2NO_2$

chlo•ram•phe•ni•col [,klɔræm'fɛnə,kɒl] *n.* an antibiotic drug. *Formula*: $C_{11}H_{12}Cl_2N_2O_5$

chlo•rate ['klɔreit] *or* ['klɔrɪt] *n.* a salt of chloric acid.

chlor•cy•cli•zine [klɔr'səiklə,zin] *n.* an antihistamine used in the treatment of allergies. *Formula*: $C_{18}H_{21}ClN_2$

chlor•di•az•e•pox•ide [,klɔrdaɪ,æzə'pɒksaɪd] *n.* a drug used to relieve anxiety. *Formula*: $C_{16}H_{14}ClN_3O$

chlo•rel•la [klɔ'rɛlə] *n.* any of a genus (*Chlorella*) of single-celled green algae regarded as a potential source of low-cost nutrients.

chlor•hex•i•dine [klɔr'hɛksə,din] *n.* an antibacterial ointment used to dress wounds and burns.

chlo•ric ['klɔrɪk] *adj.* of or containing chlorine. **Chloric acid,** $HClO_3$, occurs as a colourless solution or in the form of chlorates.

chlo•ride ['klɔraɪd] *n.* any of a group of chemical compounds consisting of chlorine and another element or radical, especially a salt of hydrochloric acid.

chloride of lime a white powder used for bleaching and disinfecting, made by treating slaked lime with chlorine. *Formula*: $CaOCl_2$ Also called **chlorinated lime.**

chlo•rin•ate ['klɔrə,neit] *v.* **-at•ed, -at•ing. 1** combine or treat with chlorine: *Paper pulp is chlorinated to bleach it.* **2** disinfect with chlorine: *The water in the city reservoirs is chlorinated.*

chlo•rin•a•tion [,klɔrə'neiʃən] *n.* a chlorinating or being chlorinated.

chlo•rine [klɔ'rin] *or* ['klɔrin] *n.* a poisonous, greenish yellow chemical element that is a gas at normal temperatures, used in making drugs, dyes, explosives, and plastics, and in bleaching and disinfecting. Chlorine has a sharp, unpleasant smell and is very irritating to the nose, throat, and lungs. *Symbol*: Cl; *at.no.* 17; *at. mass* 35.45. ⟨< Gk. *chlōros* green⟩

chlo•rite ['klɔrəit] *n.* a salt of chlorous acid.

chlor•mez•a•none [klɔr'mɛzə,noun] *n.* a drug used to relieve anxiety.

chloro– *combining form.* **1** green: *chlorophyl.* **2** chlorine. Also, before a vowel, **chlor-**.

chlo•ro•ben•zene [,klɔrou'bɛnzin] *n.* a colourless, flammable liquid used as a solvent. *Formula*: C_6H_5Cl

chlo•ro•fluo•ro•car•bon [,klɔrou,flɔrou'kɑrbən] *or* [-,fluərou'kɑrbən] *n.* any of several compounds of carbon used in refrigerators and aerosol cans, etc., and thought to be responsible for damaging the ozone layer of the earth's atmosphere. *Abbrev.*: CFC, *pl.* CFCs.

chlo•ro•form ['klɔrə,fɔrm] *n., v. —n.* a colourless liquid with a sweetish smell, used as an anesthetic and to dissolve rubber, resin, wax, and many other substances. *Formula*: $CHCl_3$
—v. **1** make (a person or animal) unconscious or unable to feel pain by giving chloroform. **2** kill with chloroform. ⟨< *chloro-* + *form(yl)*⟩

chlo•ro•hy•drin [,klɔrou'haɪdrɪn] *n.* **1** any of several organic compounds in which a chlorine atom replaces a hydroxyl group. **2** a clear liquid used mainly as a solvent and in the making of dyes. *Formula*: $CH_2OHCHOHCH_2Cl$ ⟨< *chloro-* + *hydro-* + *-in*⟩

chlo•ro•phyl or **chlo•ro•phyll** ['klɔrə,fɪl] *n.* **1** *Botany.* the green colouring matter of plants, produced only in the presence of sunlight and where iron is available in the plant cell. It converts carbon dioxide and water into carbohydrates, such as starch and sugar. **2** a dark green, waxy plant extract, containing chlorophyl, that is used as a dye and for its supposed deodorizing qualities. ⟨< F *chlorophylle* < Gk. *chlōros* pale green + *phyllon* leaf⟩

chlo•ro•pic•rin [,klɔrou'pɪkrɪn] *n.* a clear, poisonous, tear-inducing liquid used as a pesticide, fungicide, etc. and as tear gas. *Formula*: CCl_3NO_2 ⟨< *chloro-* + *picr(ic acid)* + *-in*⟩

chlo•ro•plast ['klɔrə,plæst] *n. Botany.* the part of a plant cell that contains chlorophyl. Also, **chloroplastid.** ⟨< Gk. *chlōros* pale green + *plastos* formed⟩

chlo•ro•prene ['klɔrə,prin] *n.* a colourless liquid used in making synthetic rubber. *Formula*: C_4H_5Cl ⟨< *chloro-* + *(iso)prene*⟩

chlo•ro•pro•caine [,klɔrou'proukein] *n.* a drug used as a local anesthetic.

chlo•ro•quine ['klɔrə,kwaɪn] *n.* a drug used to treat malaria.

chlo•ro•sis [klə'rousɪs] *n.* **1** *Botany.* a blanching or yellowing of plants, usually resulting from a lack of iron and other minerals in the soil. **2** an iron-deficiency anemia affecting young girls, especially formerly, and characterized by a greenish pallor, hysteria, etc. ⟨< NL *chlorosis* < Gk. *chlōros* pale green + *-osis*⟩ **—chlo'rot•ic** [-'rɒtɪk], *adj.*

chlo•ro•thi•a•zide [,klɔrou'θaɪə,zaɪd] *n.* a diuretic drug used to treat high blood pressure. *Formula*: $C_7H_6ClN_3O_4S_2$

chlo•rous ['klɔrəs] *adj.* of or containing trivalent chlorine.

chlor•phe•nir•a•mine [,klɔrfə'nirə,min] *n.* an antihistamine drug. *Formula*: $C_{20}H_{23}ClN_2O_4$

chlor•prom•a•zine [klɔr'prɒmə,zin] *n.* an antipsychotic drug. *Formula*: $C_{17}H_{19}ClN_2S$

chlor•prop•a•mide [klɔr'prɒpə,maɪd] *n.* a drug used to treat diabetes. *Formula*: $C_{10}H_{13}ClN_2O_3S$

chlor•pro•thix•ene [,klɔrprou'θɪksin] *n.* a drug used to treat schizophrenia and nausea.

chlor•tet•ra•cy•cline [,klɔr,tɛtrə'səiklin] *n.* an antibiotic drug used as an ointment. *Formula*: $C_{22}H_{23}ClN_2O_8$

chlor•thal•i•done [klɔr'θælə,doun] *n.* a drug used to treat high blood pressure and as a diuretic. *Formula*: $C_{14}H_{11}ClN_2O_4S$

chm. or **chmn.** chairman.

chock [tʃɒk] *n., v., adv. —n.* **1** a block; wedge. A chock can be put under a barrel or wheel to keep it from rolling. A boat on a ship's deck is put on chocks. **2** on a ship or boat, a heavy piece of metal or wood with two arms curving inward for a rope to pass through.
—v. **1** provide or fasten with chocks. **2** put (a boat) on chocks.
—adv. as close or as tight as can be: *chock up against the wall.* ⟨apparently < ONF *choque* log⟩
☛ *Hom.* CHALK.

chock–a–block ['tʃɒk ə ,blɒk] *adj.* **1** *Nautical.* with the blocks drawn close together. **2** jammed together; crowded; packed.

chock–full ['tʃɒk 'fʊl] *adj.* as full as can be; completely full. Also, **chuck-full.**

choc•o•late ['tʃɒklɪt] *or* ['tʃɒkəlɪt] *n., adj. —n.* **1** a dark brown, bitter-tasting substance, the finely ground, roasted seeds of the cacao tree, used as a food or flavouring. The basic form of chocolate is a liquid, called **chocolate liquor,** that is produced when the seeds are ground. **2** a hot or cold drink made of chocolate or cocoa, milk or water, and sugar. **3** candy made of chocolate and sugar. **4** dark brown.
—adj. **1** made of or flavoured with chocolate: *chocolate cake.* **2** dark brown. ⟨< Sp. < Aztec *chocolatl*⟩ **—'choc•o•lat•y** or **'choc•o•lat•ey,** *adj.*

chocolate bar a confection consisting of an oblong piece or bar of chocolate or a mixture of things such as nuts, sugar, syrup, marshmallow, raisin, flavouring, etc., coated with chocolate.

choc•o•la•tier [,tʃɒklə'tir] *n.* a maker or seller of fine chocolates. ⟨< F⟩

Choc•taw ['tʃɒktɒ] *n.* **1** a member of an American Indian people now living mostly in Oklahoma. **2** their Muskogean language.

choice [tʃɔɪs] *n., adj.* **choic•er, choic•est.** *—n.* **1** the act of choosing; selection: *Leave the choice of background music to her.* **2** the power or chance to choose: *Her parents have given her a choice between tennis and golf lessons. He had no choice but to accept their statement.* **3** the person or thing chosen or to be chosen: *My choice was cabbage rolls.* **4** an alternative. **5** a quantity and variety to choose from: *There is a wide choice of vegetables in the market.* **6** best; cream: *a team made up of the choice of the league.*
of choice, preferred: *the treatment of choice.*
—adj. **1** of fine quality; excellent; superior: *a choice steak.*

2 carefully chosen: *choice arguments.* ⟨ME *chois* < OF *choisir* < Gmc.⟩ —**'choice•ly,** *adv.* —**'choice•ness,** *n.*

☛ *Syn. n.* **3. Choice,** ALTERNATIVE, PREFERENCE = the thing chosen or to be chosen. **Choice,** the general and most informal word, emphasizes freedom in choosing, both in the way one chooses and in the number of possibilities from which to choose: *Take your choice of the puppies.* **Alternative** emphasizes limitation of the possibilities, usually to two but sometimes several, between which one must choose: *You have the alternative of sheltering from the rain or getting drenched.* **Preference** emphasizes choosing according to one's own liking: *Which is your preference? —adj.* **1.** See note at FINE[1].

choir [kwaɪr] *n., v. —n.* **1** an organized group of singers who sing in Christian church services. **2** the part of a church set aside for such a group. **3** any organized group of singers: *the university choir.* **4** instruments of the same class in an orchestra: *the string choir, a brass choir.* **5** in medieval Christian theology, any of the nine orders of angels.
—v. Poetic. sing together. ⟨ME *quer* < OF *cuer* < L *chorus.* Doublet of CHORUS.⟩
☛ *Hom.* QUIRE.

choir•boy ['kwaɪr,bɔi] a boy who sings in a choir.

choir loft a high place such as a balcony or gallery, where a Christian church choir sings.

choir•mas•ter ['kwaɪr,mæstər] *n.* the director or conductor of a choir.

choke [tʃouk] *v.* **choked, chok•ing;** *n. —v.* **1** keep from breathing by squeezing or blocking up the windpipe: *The smoke almost choked the firefighters.* **2** be unable to breathe: *He choked when some food stuck in his throat.* **3** check or extinguish by cutting off the supply of air: *to choke a fire.* **4** control; hold back; suppress (*used with* **down** *or* **back**): *He choked back his anger and said nothing.* **5** fill up or block; clog (*often used with* **up**): *a street choked with traffic. Sand is choking the river.* **6** reduce or close the air intake in (an internal-combustion engine) in order to make a richer fuel mixture, especially in starting. **7** retard or stop the development or growth of: *The flowers had become choked by weeds.* **8** put an end to; stop (*often used with* **off**): *to choke off rebellion. The rock slide choked off our water supply.*
choke down, swallow with difficulty: *She managed to choke down the dry bread.*
choke up, fill with emotion; be or cause to be on the verge of tears: *She choked up from stage fright. We were all choked up when the heroine in the movie died.*
—n. **1** the act of choking: *He gave a slight choke but then got his breath.* **2** the sound of choking: *We heard a choke behind us.* **3** something that chokes, such as a valve that cuts off the supply of air to an internal-combustion engine. **4** a narrow or constricted part of a tube, etc., as in a chokebore. ⟨OE **cēocian*, var. of *ācēocian*⟩

choke•ber•ry ['tʃouk,bɛri] *n.* **1** the berry of a shrub of the rose family (genus *Aronia*), having a bitter taste. **2** the shrub that the berry grows on.

choke•bore ['tʃouk,bɔr] *n.* **1** a shotgun bore that narrows toward the muzzle in order to keep the shot from scattering too widely. **2** a shotgun with such a bore.

choke•cher•ry ['tʃouk,tʃɛri] *n., pl.* **-ries. 1** a North American shrub or small tree (*Prunus virginiana*) of the rose family having small black or dark red edible astringent fruit. **2** the fruit of this tree.

choke coil *Electricity.* a coil of wire around a core of iron or air, used to control alternating currents in an electric circuit.

choke collar a collar for training a dog, which tightens round its neck when the dog pulls on it instead of keeping to heel. Also, **choke chain.**

choke•damp ['tʃouk,dæmp] *n.* a heavy, suffocating gas, mainly carbon dioxide and nitrogen, that gathers in mines, old wells, etc.

chok•er ['tʃoukər] *n.* **1** a necklace that fits closely around the neck: *a pearl choker.* **2** a high, stiff, close-fitting collar, neckband, etc. **3** *Cdn. Logging.* a cable and hook used in hauling and loading logs. **4** any person or thing that chokes.

cho•ky ['tʃouki] *adj.* **cho•ki•er, cho•ki•est.** *Informal.* **1** inclined to choke, especially with emotion. **2** tending to choke one; suffocating: *a choky collar.*

cho•late ['kouleit] *n.* a salt or ester of cholic acid.

chol•e•cal•cif•e•rol [,kɒləkæl'sɪfə,rɒl] *n.* the commonest form of vitamin D, found in fish-liver oils or produced in the skin by the action of sunlight. *Formula*: $C_{27}H_{43}OH$ ⟨< Gk. *chole* bite + E *calcif*(*erous ergost*)*erol*⟩

chol•e•cyst ['kɒlə,sɪst] *n.* the gall bladder. ⟨< NL *cholecystis* < Gk. *chole* bile + *kystis* bladder⟩

chol•e•cyst•ec•to•my [,kɒləsɪ'stɛktəmi] *n.* surgical removal of the gall bladder.

chol•e•cys•ti•tis [,kɒləsɪ'stəitɪs] *n.* inflammation of the gall bladder.

cho•lent ['tʃoulənt] *or* ['tʃʌlənt] *n.* a Jewish dish consisting of beef, potatoes, beans, etc., stewed for a long time and prepared overnight for the Sabbath. ⟨< Yiddish⟩

chol•er ['kɒlər] *n.* **1** an irritable disposition; anger. **2** in ancient physiology, yellow bile, the one of the four humours believed to cause irritability. **3** bilious disorder. ⟨ME *colre* < OF < L < Gk. *cholera* cholera, apparently < *cholē* bile⟩
☛ *Hom.* CALLER, COLLAR.

chol•er•a ['kɒlərə] *n.* **1** an acute, infectious disease of the stomach and intestines caused by a bacterium (*Vibrio comma*), characterized by vomiting, cramps, and diarrhea. Cholera is often fatal if untreated. **2** any of several diseases occurring chiefly in hot weather and causing acute diarrhea. ⟨< L < Gk. See CHOLER.⟩

cholera mor•bus ['mɔrbəs] an old term applied to any inflammation of the intestines accompanied by diarrhea, fever, and pain; gastroenteritis. ⟨< L, cholera disease⟩

chol•er•ic ['kɒlərɪk] *adj.* **1** easily made angry; irritable. **2** enraged; angry: *a choleric outburst of temper.*

cho•les•ter•ol [kə'lɛstə,rɒl] *or* [kə'lɛstərəl] *n.* a crystalline fatty alcohol produced by all vertebrates and found in the highest concentration in the brain, nerves, and spinal cord. It is used by the body to make acids which aid digestion and also to make some hormones. The human body produces most of its own cholesterol, but some enters the body in food and is not always properly absorbed. *Formula*: $C_{27}H_{45}OH$ ⟨< Gk. *cholē* bile + *stereos* solid⟩

cho•lic acid ['koulɪk] **1** an acid found in bile, related to cholesterol. *Formula*: $C_{24}H_{40}O_5$ **2** an extract of beef bile, used to make drugs.

cho•line ['koulin] *or* ['koulɪn] *n.* a constituent of the vitamin B complex, present in many animal and plant tissues, which prevents the accumulation of fat in the liver. *Formula*: $C_5H_{15}NO_2$ ⟨< Gk. *chole* bile⟩

cho•li•ner•gic [,koulɪ'nɜrdʒɪk] *adj.* producing or activated by acetylcholine or a similar chemical substance: *a cholinergic nerve fibre.* ⟨< *choline* + Gk. *ergon* work + E *-ic*⟩

cho•li•nes•te•rase [,koulɪ'nɛstə,reis] *n.* an enzyme which prevents the accumulation of acetylcholine at the nerve endings by stimulating its hydrolysis. ⟨< *choline* + *esterase*⟩

chol•la ['tʃoulјə] *or* ['tʃoujə] *n.* a spiny, treelike cactus (genus *Opuntia*) of the SW U.S. and Mexico. ⟨< Sp., skull, head⟩

chomp [tʃɒmp] *v.* **1** chew noisily: *to chomp one's food.* **2** bite down: *He chomped on his cigar.* ⟨variation of CHAMP[1]⟩

Chom•sky•an ['tʃɒmskiən] *adj., n. —adj.* of Noam Chomsky (1928–), an American linguist who formulated the non-behaviourist transformational generative grammar, or his ideas.
—n. a supporter or proponent of Chomsky's ideas.

chon•drich•thi•an [kɒn'drɪkθiən] *n.* any of a class of fishes whose skeletons are formed of cartilage and whose gills are thin and platelike; elasmobranch. Sharks and rays belong to this class. ⟨< Gk. *chondros* cartilage + *ichthys* fish⟩

chon•drite ['kɒndrəit] *n.* a type of stony meteorite containing small masses of silicate minerals. ⟨< Gk. *chondros* cartilage + E *-ite*⟩ —**chon'drit•ic** [kɒn'drɪtɪk], *adj.*

chon•dro•ma [kɒn'droumə] *n., pl.* **-mas** or **-mata** [-mətə]. a benign cartilaginous tumour. ⟨< Gk. *chondros* cartilage + E *-oma*⟩

choose [tʃuz] *v.* **chose, cho•sen, choos•ing. 1** pick out; select from a number: *She chose a book from the library.* **2** prefer and decide on: *I would always choose comfort over style.* **3** think fit; want and decide (*with an infinitive*): *She did not choose to go. He chose to run for election.* **4** make a choice; decide: *You must choose.*
cannot choose but, cannot take an alternative; must: *Since he had received both first prizes, he could not choose but be satisfied.* ⟨OE *cēosan*⟩ —**'choos•er,** *n.*

choos•y ['tʃuzi] *adj.* **choos•i•er, choos•i•est.** *Informal.* particular or fussy in one's preferences; fastidious; selective. —**'choos•i•ness,** *n.*

chop[1] [tʃɒp] *v.* **chopped, chop•ping;** *n. —v.* **1** cut by hitting with something sharp: *to chop wood with an axe.* **2** cut into small

pieces: *to chop up cabbage.* **3** make quick, sharp movements; jerk. **4** make by cutting: *The explorer chopped her way through the bushes.* **5** *Tennis, cricket, etc.* slice or cut at (a ball); hit with a chop stroke. **6** cut off or reduce: *The government has chopped welfare payments.*
chop back, *Informal.* severely reduce.
chop down, cause to fall by chopping: *to chop down a tree.*
–n. **1** a cutting stroke or blow. **2** a slice of lamb, pork, veal, etc., on a piece of rib, loin, or shoulder. **3** a short, irregular, broken motion of waves. **4** an area of rough or choppy water. **5** a special short, sharp downward movement in boxing, judo, karate, etc. ⟨ME *choppe(n)*⟩
☛ *Syn. v.* **1.** See note at CUT.

chop² [tʃɒp] *n.* **1** the jaw. **2 chops,** *pl.* the cheeks or jaws, especially the fleshy covering of an animal's jaws: *The cat is licking the milk off its chops.*
lick (one's) **chops,** *Informal.* relish the prospect of something good to come: *licking their chops over the prospect of a fat fee.* ⟨< *chop¹*⟩

chop³ [tʃɒp] *v.* **chopped, chop•ping.** change suddenly; shift quickly: *The wind chopped around from west to north.*
chop and change, change one's tactics or ways; make frequent changes; change about. ⟨var. of obs. *chap* buy and sell, exchange. Related to CHEAP.⟩

chop•fall•en ['tʃɒp,fɒlən] *adj.* chapfallen.

chop•house ['tʃɒp,hʌus] *n.* a restaurant that makes a specialty of serving chops, steaks, etc.

cho•pine [tʃou'pin] *or* ['tʃɒpɪn] *n.* a woman's shoe with a very thick sole, worn especially in the 17th century. ⟨< Sp. *chapin* < *chapa* piece of leather⟩

chop•per ['tʃɒpər] *n., v. –n.* **1** a person who chops. **2** a tool or machine for chopping, such as a short-handled axe or a heavy knife. **3** *Informal.* helicopter. **4** *Slang.* a motorcycle, especially one with high handlebars. **5 choppers,** *pl. Slang.* teeth. **6** a device for changing direct electric current into alternating current. **7** a device for stopping an electric current or beam of light, and then starting it again, on a regular basis.
–v. Informal. fly or transport by helicopter: *Workers were choppered out to the rig.*

chopping block a large wooden block on which meat and vegetables are cut.

chop•py¹ ['tʃɒpi] *adj.* **-pi•er, -pi•est. 1** making quick, sharp movements; jerky: *a choppy ride.* **2** moving in short, irregular, broken waves: *The lake is choppy today.* ⟨< *chop¹*⟩
–'chop•pi•ness, *n.*

chop•py² ['tʃɒpi] *adj.* **-pi•er, -pi•est.** changing suddenly; shifting quickly. ⟨< *chop³*⟩

chop•stick ['tʃɒp,stɪk] *n.* one of a pair of small, shaped sticks used especially by the Chinese, Japanese, Vietnamese, and Koreans to raise food to the mouth. ⟨< Chinese Pidgin English *chop* quick + E *stick¹*⟩

chop su•ey ['tʃɒp 'sui] a Chinese-American dish consisting of small pieces of meat with vegetables such as bean sprouts, mushrooms, and greens all cooked together in their own juices. Chop suey is usually served with rice. ⟨alteration of Chinese *tsa-sui* odds and ends⟩

cho•ra•gus [kə'reigəs] *n.* **1** in an ancient Greek play, the leader of the chorus. **2** in ancient Greece, someone who paid for the chorus. **3** any conductor of a choir or orchestra. ⟨< L < Gk. *choregos* < *choros* chorus + *agein* lead⟩ **–cho'rag•ic** [-'rædʒɪk], *adj.*

cho•ral *adj.* ['kɔrəl]; *n.* [kə'ræl] *or* [kə'rɑl] *adj., n. –adj.* **1** of or having to do with a choir or chorus: *She belongs to a choral group.* **2** sung or designed to be sung by a choir or chorus: *a choral arrangement of a song.*
–n. See CHORALE.
☛ *Hom.* CORAL.

cho•rale [kə'ræl] *or* [kə'rɑl] *n.* **1** a slow, stately hymn tune, originally sung in unison, especially in the Lutheran church. **2 a** a composition for voices or orchestra based on such a tune. **b** a composition like a cantata, but shorter, simpler, and less dramatic. **3** a group of singers, especially for singing Christian church music; choir. Sometimes, **choral.** ⟨< G *Choral(gesang)*⟩

choral speaking the recitation of poetry, etc. by a group of people together.

chord¹ [kɔrd] *n., v. –n. Music.* a combination of two or more notes sounded together in harmony.
–v. **1** harmonize with chords. **2** play the piano or guitar in chords only, without a melody line. ⟨var. of *cord*, var. of *accord*, n.⟩
☛ *Hom.* CORD.

chord² [kɔrd] *n.* **1** *Geometry.* a straight line or segment between two points on a curve. See CIRCLE for picture. **2** *Anatomy. Archaic.* See CORD (def. *n.* 4). **3** *Archaic or Poetic.* a string of a harp, etc. **4** a feeling, especially an emotional response: *to touch a sympathetic chord.* **5** *Engineering.* a main horizontal part of a truss. **6** *Aeronautics.* an imaginary straight line between the leading and trailing edges of an airfoil. ⟨< L < Gk. *chordē* string made of gut; string of a lyre. Doublet of CORD.⟩
☛ *Hom.* CORD.

chord•al ['kɔrdəl] *adj. Music.* **1** of or having to do with the strings of an instrument. **2** of or having to do with chords.

chor•date ['kɔrdeit] *n., adj. –n.* any of a phylum (Chordata) of animals that includes vertebrates and all other animals that have an internal skeleton (a notochord in primitive forms) and a central nervous system located along the back.
–adj. of or having to do with this group. ⟨< NL *chordata* < L *chorda* chord. See CHORD².⟩

chore [tʃɔr] *n.* **1** an odd job; minor task, especially one that must be done daily: *Feeding the chickens was Maria's chore on the farm.* **2** a task that is disagreeable or irritating: *She found the work quite a chore.* ⟨OE *cyrr*, var. of *cierr*, *cerr* turn, business. Cf. CHAR².⟩

cho•re•a [kɔ'riə] *n.* a nervous disorder characterized by involuntary twitching of the muscles; St. Vitus's dance. ⟨< NL < Gk. *choreia* dance⟩

chore–boy ['tʃɔr ,bɔɪ] *n.* a boy who does odd jobs or routine tasks around a farm, ranch, tourist resort, logging camp, etc.

cho•re•o•graph ['kɔriə,græf] *v.* **1** arrange or compose choreography for (a ballet, etc.). **2** arrange or plan the details of (anything complicated). ⟨< Gk. *choreia* dance + *graphein* write⟩

cho•re•og•ra•pher [,kɔri'ɒgrəfər] *n.* a creator or designer of ballets and other stage dances.

cho•re•o•graph•ic [,kɔriə'græfɪk] *adj.* **1** of or having to do with the art of dancing. **2** of or having to do with choreography.

cho•re•o•graph•i•cal•ly [,kɔriə'græfɪkli] *adv.* **1** in a choreographic manner. **2** in terms of choreography.

cho•re•og•ra•phy [,kɔri'ɒgrəfi] *n.* **1** the art of creating, designing, and arranging dances, such as ballet, for performance on stage. **2** the steps and sequences of such a dance. **3** notation used for representing dance movements. **4** the art of stage dancing.

cho•ri•amb ['kɔri,æmb] *or* ['kɔri,æm] *n. Prosody.* a metrical foot consisting of two short syllables between two long ones, or two unaccented syllables between two accented ones. *Example: Give to a child.* ⟨< L *choriambus* < Gk. *choriambos* < *choreios* trochee + *iambos* iamb⟩

cho•ric ['kɔrɪk] *adj.* of, having to do with, or for a chorus, especially one in an ancient Greek play.

cho•rine ['kɔrin] *n. Informal.* CHORUS GIRL.

cho•ri•on ['kɔri,ɒn] *n.* **1** the outermost membrane, enclosing the amnion, of the sac which envelops the embryo or fetus of the higher vertebrates and eventually forms the placenta, persisting until birth. **2** the eggshell of insects and other invertebrates. ⟨< Gk.⟩

cho•ri•on•ic villus sampling [,kɔri'ɒnɪk] a procedure in which a sample of embryonic or fetal tissue containing chorionic villi is obtained from a pregnant woman. The tissue sample can be tested directly for certain abnormalities, or cultured for subsequent testing. *Abbrev.*: CVS

cho•ri•zo [tʃou'rizou] *or* [tʃou'risou] *n.* a Spanish or Mexican dish consisting of a highly spiced pork sausage which is then smoked and dried. ⟨< Sp.⟩

cho•rog•ra•phy [kə'rɒgrəfi] *n.* **1** the art and science of mapping or describing a region. **2** the resulting map or description. ⟨< L < Gk. *chorographia* < *choros* open area + *graphein* write⟩ **–,cho•ro'graph•ic,** *adj.*

chor•is•ter ['kɔrəstər] *n.* **1** a singer in a choir, especially a choirboy. **2** the leader of a choir. ⟨< Med.L *chorista* chorister < L *chorus.* See CHORUS.⟩

cho•roid ['kɔrɔɪd] *n., adj. –n.* the vascular membrane of the eyeball between the retina and the sclera. See EYE for picture.
–adj. of or designating this membrane. ⟨< Gk. *choroeidēs* < *chorion* membrane + *eidos* resemblance⟩

chor•tle ['tʃɔrtəl] *v.* **-tled, -tling;** *n. –v.* chuckle and snort at the same time: *He chortled in his joy.*

—*n.* a combined chuckle and snort. ⟨blend of *chuckle* and *snort*; coined by Lewis Carroll⟩ —**'chor•tler,** *n.*

cho•rus ['kɔrəs] *n., pl.* **-rus•es;** *v.* **-rused, -rus•ing.** —*n.* **1** a group of singers who sing together, such as a choir. **2** a musical composition to be sung by a large number of singers in several harmonizing voice parts: *The opera ends in a splendid chorus.* **3** the part of a song that is repeated after each stanza; refrain. **4** a refrain sung by all present after a solo verse. **5** the principal melody of a jazz piece, succeeding the introduction. **6** a jazz solo, commonly an improvisation of the main melody of the piece. **7** a short song of praise or worship, sung in informal Christian services, based on a passage of Scripture and set to contemporary music, not in stanza form. Compare HYMN. **8** a similar or identical utterance by many at the same time: *My question was answered by a chorus of no's.* **9** a group of singers and dancers: *She was in the chorus of our school musical.* **10** *Classical Drama.* **a** an actor or group of actors who comment on the action of a play. **b** the part of a play performed by the chorus.
in chorus, all together at the same time.
—*v.* sing or speak all at the same time: *The birds were chorusing around me.* ⟨< L < Gk. *choros* dance, band of dancers. Doublet of CHOIR.⟩

chorus boy a young man who sings and dances in a chorus of a musical comedy or revue.

chorus girl a young woman who sings and dances in a chorus of a musical comedy or revue.

chose [tʃouz] *v.* pt. and an archaic pp. of CHOOSE: *Selma chose a red dress for the Christmas party.*

cho•sen ['tʃouzən] *v., adj.* —*v.* a pp. of CHOOSE.
—*adj.* picked out; selected from a group: *the chosen book.*

chou•croute [ʃu'krut]; *French,* [ʃu'kRut] *n.* **1** sauerkraut. **2** a dish consisting of sauerkraut cooked with sausages, ham, or pork. ⟨< F⟩

chough [tʃʌf] *n.* **1** either of two Old World birds (genus *Pyrrhocorax*) related to and resembling the crows, having glossy, blue-black plumage, a down-curved bill, and red legs. The common chough (*P. pyrrhocorax*) has a red bill; the alpine chough (*P. graculus*) has a yellow bill. **2** a similar but unrelated bird (*Corcorax melanorhamphus*) of Australia, having white wing patches and a black bill. ⟨ME *choughe*⟩
☛ *Hom.* CHUFF.

chow [tʃaʊ] *n.* **1** CHOW CHOW. **2** *Slang.* **a** food. **b** the time when food is served. ⟨short for *chow-chow*⟩
☛ *Hom.* CIAO.

chow chow or **Chow Chow** a breed of medium-sized dog having a curled tail, large head, compact body, and a thick, usually brown or black coat. ⟨< Chinese dial.⟩

chow–chow ['tʃaʊ ˌtʃaʊ] *n.* **1** a Chinese mixed preserve. **2** any mixed pickles chopped up. ⟨< Chinese Pidgin English⟩

chow•der ['tʃaʊdər] *n.* a thick soup or stew, often made of clams or fish with potatoes, onions, etc. in a milk base. ⟨apparently < F *chaudière* pot, ult. < L *calidus* hot⟩

chow mein ['tʃaʊ 'mein] a Chinese-American dish consisting of a thickened stew of onions, celery, meat, etc. served over fried noodles. ⟨< Chinese *ch'ao mien* fried flour⟩

chres•tom•a•thy [krɛs'tɒməθi] *n., pl.* **-thies. 1** a collection of literary passages chosen to help in the learning of a language. **2** a selection of passages from the works of one author. ⟨< Gk. *chrēstomatheia* < *chrēstos* useful + *-matheia* learning⟩

chrism ['krɪzəm] *n.* **1** the consecrated oil used by some Christian churches in baptism and other sacred rites. **2** a sacramental anointing; the ceremony of confirmation, especially as practised in the Greek Orthodox church. ⟨OE *crisma* < L *chrisma* < Gk. *chrisma* < *chriein* anoint⟩ —**'chris•mal,** *adj.*

chris•ma•to•ry ['krɪzməˌtɔri] *n.* a vessel used to house the chrism.

Christ [krəist] *n.* **1** the Messiah; the deliverer foretold by the ancient Jewish prophets. **2** Jesus of Nazareth, regarded by Christians as the incarnate Son of God and the true Messiah. ⟨OE *Crīst* < L *Christus* < Gk. *Christos* one who is anointed, a translation of Hebrew *māshīach*⟩

Chris•ta•del•phi•an [ˌkrɪstə'dɛlfiən] *n.* a member of a Christian religious sect founded in the United States about 1850 by Dr. John Thomas. This sect rejects the doctrine of the Trinity and holds that only the righteous attain immortality. ⟨< L < Gk. *Christadelphos* brother of Christ < Gk. *Christos* Christ + *adelphos* brother + E *-ian*⟩

chris•ten ['krɪsən] *v.* **1** admit to a Christian church by baptism; baptize. **2** give a name to (someone) at baptism. **3** give a name to: *The new ship was christened before it was launched.* **4** *Informal.* make the first use of. ⟨OE *cristnian* make Christian < *cristen* Christian < LL < LGk. *christianos* Christian; belonging to Christ⟩

Chris•ten•dom ['krɪsəndəm] *n.* **1** countries whose people are traditionally or predominantly Christian; the so-called Christian part of the world. **2** all Christians. ⟨OE *cristendōm* < *cristen* Christian + *-dōm* state < *dōm* statute⟩

chris•ten•ing ['krɪsənɪŋ] *n., v.* —*n.* the act or ceremony of baptizing and naming; baptism.
—*v.* ppr. of CHRISTEN.

Chris•tian ['krɪstʃən] *n., adj.* —*n.* one who believes in Jesus as the Christ and follows his teachings; a believer in Christianity.
—*adj.* **1** of or having to do with Jesus Christ, his teachings, or Christianity: *the Christian religion, Christian ethics.* **2** being a Christian or made up of Christians: *Christian organizations, a Christian businessman.* **3** showing kindness, goodness, or humility: *a Christian act.* —**'Chris•tian,like,** *adj.* —**'Chris•tian•ly,** *adj., adv.*

Christian Era the time since the birth of Christ. The label A.D. is used for dates in this era; B.C. for dates before it.

Chris•ti•an•ia [ˌkrɪstʃi'æniə] *or* [ˌkrɪsti'ɑniə] *n.* Christie.

Chris•ti•an•i•ty [ˌkrɪstʃi'ænəti] *or* [ˌkrɪsti'ænəti] *n.* **1** a religion that grew out of Judaism and that separated itself from Judaism through its acceptance of Jesus of Nazareth as the Son of God and as the Messiah of Hebrew prophecy. The sacred Scriptures of Christianity, the Bible, comprise the Hebrew Bible (Old Testament) and the New Testament. **2** the Christian beliefs, spirit, or character. **3** all Christians; Christendom. **4** the state of being Christian.

Chris•tian•ize ['krɪstʃəˌnaɪz] *or* ['krɪstjəˌnaɪz] *v.* **-ized, -iz•ing.** make Christian; convert to Christianity.
—**ˌChris•tian•i'za•tion,** *n.* —**'Chris•tian,iz•er,** *n.*

Christian name given name. It is so called from the traditional practice, in many Christian churches, of formally giving the name to an infant at christening.

Christian Science a Christian religion based on the belief that physical healing is possible through spiritual healing. Evil, pain, and disease are believed to be caused by a sinful mind, and they can be overcome through prayer and by following the teachings of Jesus. Christian Science was founded by Mary Baker Eddy in the United States in 1806.

Christian Scientist a believer in Christian Science.

Chris•tie ['krɪsti] *n.* in skiing, a skidding turn in which the skis are kept parallel, the weight of the skier is shifted forward in the direction of the turn, and the skier springs just enough to remove weight from the skis. Also, **Christiania.** ⟨< *Christiana* old name of Oslo, where the technique originated⟩

Christ•like ['krəistˌləik] *adj.* like Jesus Christ; showing the spirit of Jesus Christ. —**'Christ,like•ness,** *n.*

Christ•ly ['krəistli] *adj.* of Christ; Christlike.
—**'Christ•li•ness,** *n.*

Christ•mas ['krɪsməs] *n., pl.* **Christ•mas•es. 1** the yearly Christian celebration commemorating the birth of Christ; in most Christian churches, December 25. **2** the season of Christmas. **3** (*adjl.*) for Christmas: *Christmas music.* ⟨OE *Cristes mæsse* Christ's Mass⟩

Christmas cactus a cactus plant (*Schlumbergera bridgesii*), native to Brazil, having red flowers that bloom at Christmas time.

Christmas Day December 25.

Christmas Eve December 24.

Christ•mas•tide ['krɪsməsˌtaɪd] *n. Archaic or Poetic.* Christmastime. ⟨< *Christmas* + *tide* time⟩

Christ•mas•time ['krɪsməsˌtaɪm] *n.* the Christmas season, especially from Christmas Eve to New Year's Day, or, more traditionally, to Epiphany (January 6).

Christmas tree 1 an evergreen tree, such as a spruce or pine, or an imitation of one, hung with decorations indoors at Christmastime. **2** *Cdn.* a party held at Christmastime for entertaining children and presenting gifts to them, usually sponsored by a church, school, or other organization. **3** in oil drilling, a complex arrangement of pipes, valves, etc. to control the flow of oil.

Chris•tol•o•gy [krɪ'stɒlədʒi] *n.* the study of the teachings and life of Christ. —**ˌChris•to'log•i•cal,** *adj.*

Christ's–thorn ['krəists ˌθɔrn] *n.* any of certain Old World shrubs reputed to have been the source of Christ's crown of thorns; especially the Jerusalem thorn (*Paliurus spina-christi*) or the jujube (*Ziziphus jujuba*).

chro•mate ['kroumeit] *n.* a salt of chromic acid.

chro•mat•ic [krou'mætɪk] *adj.* **1** of or having to do with colour or colours. **2** *Music.* **a** of or involving the use of sharpened or flattened notes that are foreign to the diatonic key in which they occur: *chromatic chords, chromatic harmony.* **b** of, having to do with, or based on the CHROMATIC SCALE.
c designating an instrument capable of producing all the tones of the chromatic scale. ⟨< L *chromaticus* < Gk. *chrōmatikos* < *chrōma, -atos* colour⟩ **—chro'mat•i•cal•ly,** *adv.*

chromatic aberration failure of the different colours of light to meet in one focus when refracted through a convex lens. Also called **chromatism.**

chromatics [krou'mætɪks] *n.* (*used with a singular verb*). the scientific study of colours with reference to hue and intensity or brightness.

chromatic scale *Music.* a scale in which the octave is divided into 12 semitones.

chro•ma•tid ['kroumətɪd] *n.* either of the two portions of a chromosome that has doubled in preparation for cell division, held together at the middle by a centromere. During cell division, the centromere of each doubled chromosome divides and the chromatids separate into two complete chromosomes that are identical to the parent chromosome.

chro•ma•tin ['kroumətɪn] *n.* the substance, consisting of DNA and proteins, in the nucleus of a plant or animal cell in a resting stage, forming a spongy network of chromosomes. See CELL for picture.

chro•ma•tism ['kroumə,tɪzəm] *n.* CHROMATIC ABERRATION.

chromato– *combining form.* **1** colour; coloured. **2** chromatin. Also, before a vowel, **chromat-.** ⟨< Gk. *chroma, chromatos* colour⟩

chro•mat•o•gram [krou'mætə,græm] *n.* the pattern formed on an adsorbent by the components of a mixture separated by chromatography.

chro•mat•o•graph [krou'mætə,græf] *v., n.* *—v.* separate (the components of a mixture) by chromatography.
—n. **1** a system for separating the components of a mixture by chromatography. **2** a record of the results of chromatography.

chro•mat•o•graph•ic [krou,mætə'græfɪk] *adj.* of or having to do with chromatography. **—chro,mat•o'graph•i•cal•ly,** *adv.*

chro•ma•tog•ra•phy [,kroumə'tɒgrəfi] *n.* the separation of a mixture of liquids or gases for the purpose of analysis by passing it through an adsorbent, such as a column of clay. The different components of the mixture are adsorbed at different rates into different sections of the adsorbent.

chro•mat•o•phore [krou'mætə,fɔr] *or* ['kroumətə,fɔr] *n.* **1** one of the specialized pigment-bearing bodies in the cells of plants, such as a chloroplast or chromoplast. **2** a pigment-bearing skin cell which can expand or contract so as to change the colour of certain animals such as the chameleon.

chrome [kroum] *n., v.* **chromed, chrom•ing.** *—n.* **1** chromium. **2** any of various pigments or dyes containing chromium. **3** CHROME STEEL.
—v. cover or plate with chrome. ⟨< F < Gk. *chrōma* colour⟩

chrome alum an alum containing chromium, especially potassium chromium sulphate, used in dyeing. *Formula:* $KCr(SO_4)_2 \cdot 12H_2O$

chrome green **1** a green colouring matter made from chromic oxide. *Formula:* Cr_2O_3 **2** a green colouring matter consisting of chrome yellow and Prussian blue.

chrome red lead chromate, a red powder. *Formula:* $PbCrO_4 \cdot PbO$

chrome steel an extremely hard, strong steel containing chromium.

chrome yellow a yellow colouring matter made from lead chromate. *Formula:* $PbCrO_4$

chro•mic ['kroumɪk] *adj.* of or containing chromium.

chromic acid an acid found in nature only in its salts. *Formula:* H_2CrO_4

chro•mite ['kroumait] *n.* **1** a mineral containing iron and chromium. *Formula:* $FeCr_2O_4$ **2** a salt of chromium.

chro•mi•um ['kroumiəm] *n.* a shiny, hard, brittle metallic element that does not rust or become dull easily; chrome. Chromium is used in alloys and in plating. *Symbol:* Cr; *at.no.* 24; *at.mass* 52.00. ⟨< Gk. *chrōma* colour⟩

chromium steel CHROME STEEL.

chro•mo ['kroumou] *n., pl.* **-mos.** chromolithograph.

chromo– *combining form.* colour. Before vowels, **chrom-.** ⟨See CHROME⟩

chro•mo•dy•nam•ics [,kroumoudaɪ'næmɪks] *n.* the branch of physics that deals with the forces of gluons, especially in interactions between quarks. ⟨with reference to 'colour' as the name for one of the hypothetical properties distinguishing quarks⟩

chro•mo•gen ['krouməd3ən] *n.* **1** any pigment, such as a substance in organic fluids, that forms coloured compounds when oxidized. **2** a compound that can become a dye. **3** a bacterium that can produce a colour.

chro•mo•lith•o•graph [,kroumou'lɪθə,græf] *n.* a coloured picture produced by the lithographic process, using a series of plates each of a different colour. Often shortened to **chromo.**

chro•mo•phore ['kroumə,fɔr] *n.* a group of atoms which produce the colour in the molecules of a coloured organic compound.

chro•mo•plast ['kroumə,plæst] *n.* a body in the cytoplasm of a plant cell containing colouring matter other than chlorophyl.

chromosomal aberration *Genetics.* any abnormality of chromosome number or structure.

chro•mo•some ['kroumə,soum] *n. Genetics.* any of the long, thin strands, or fibres, found in the nucleus of every plant and animal cell, composed of protein and DNA, which carry the coded information for heredity in units called genes. A chromosome has two arms, short (p) and long (q), joined at a centromere and each ending in a telomere. During cell division, the chromosomes form into pairs of short, fat rods, of a characteristic number for each species. **—,chro•mo'so•mal,** *adj.*

chromosome banding *Genetics.* a technique for staining chromosomes in unique patterns of crosswise bands, used to identify individual chromosomes and chromosomal abnormalities.

chromosome set *Genetics.* the set of chromosomes characteristic of an individual or a species. See also KARYOTYPE.

chromosome walking *Genetics.* a standard technique used in molecular genetics to find a specific gene within a region of a chromosome. It involves the sequential isolation of clones carrying overlapping DNA sequences, so that eventually long stretches of the chromosome are cloned.

chro•mo•sphere ['kroumə,sfir] *n.* **1** a scarlet layer of gas around the sun, forming the lower part of the sun's atmosphere, below the corona. The chromosphere consists mainly of hydrogen. **2** a similar layer around a star. **—,chro•mo'spher•ic** [-'sfɛrɪk], *adj.*

chrom•ous ['krouməs] *adj.* containing chromium with a valence of two.

chrom•yl ['kroumɪl] *adj.* containing chromium with a valence of six, in the form of chromyl chloride. *Formula:* CrO_2Cl_2

chron. **1** chronological. **2** chronology.

chron•ic ['krɒnɪk] *adj., n.* *—adj.* **1** of a disease, lasting a long time: *The doctor told him rheumatism was a chronic disease.* **2** constant; habitual: *a chronic liar, a chronic smoker.* **3** of, for, or having had an illness for a long time: *a chronic patient, chronic care.*
—n. a chronic patient. ⟨< L *chronicus* < Gk. *chronikos* < *chronos* time⟩ **—chro'nic•i•ty** [krə'nɪsəti], *n.* **—'chron•i•cal•ly,** *adv.*

chronic fatigue syndrome a medical disorder, thought to be caused by a virus, in which the patient feels very tired all the time.

chron•i•cle ['krɒnəkəl] *n., v.* **-cled, -cling.** *—n.* **1** a record of happenings in the order in which they happened. **2** a narrative; account.
—v. record in a chronicle; write the history of; tell the story of. ⟨ME < AF var. of OF *cronique* < L < Gk. *chronika* annals, neut. pl. of *chronikos.* See CHRONIC.⟩

chron•i•cler ['krɒnəklər] *n.* the writer of a chronicle; a recorder of events; historian.

chrono– *combining form.* time: *chronometer = an instrument that measures time.* Also, before vowels, **chron-.** ⟨< Gk. *chronos* time⟩

chron•o•bi•ol•ogy [,krɒnoubaɪ'ɒləd3i] *n.* the study of the rhythms of natural life. **—,chron•o,bi•o'log•ic•al,** *adj.*

chron•o•gram ['krɒnə,græm] *n.* **1** a chronograph recording. **2** an inscription in which Roman letters add up to a date.

chron•o•graph ['krɒnə,græf] *n.* **1** an instrument that measures very short intervals of time accurately; stopwatch. **2** an instrument for recording the exact instant of an astronomical or other occurrence. ⟨< Gk. *chronos* time + E *-graph*⟩

chro•nol•o•ger [krə'nɒlədʒər] *n.* chronologist.

chron•o•log•i•cal [,krɒnə'lɒdʒəkəl] *adj.* arranged in the order in which the events happened: *In telling a story, a person usually arranges the events in chronological order.* Also, **chronologic.** **—,chron•o'log•i•cal•ly,** *adv.*

chro•nol•o•gist [krə'nɒlədʒɪst] *n.* a person who investigates the exact dates of events and the order in which the events happened. Also, **chronologer.**

chro•nol•o•gy [krə'nɒlədʒi] *n., pl.* **-gies. 1** an arrangement in the form of a table, chart, or list giving the exact dates of events arranged in the order in which they happened. **2** the science of measuring time or periods of time and of determining the proper order and dates of events.

chro•nom•e•ter [krə'nɒmətər] *n.* a clock or watch that measures time very accurately, especially a **marine chronometer,** used to provide the exact time for observation of celestial bodies to determine the position of a ship at sea. **—,chron•o'met•ric,** *adj.*

chron•o•scope ['krɒnə,skoup] *n.* an instrument for measuring very small intervals of time, especially by visual means, such as a pendulum or a falling rod.

chrys•a•lid ['krɪsəlɪd] *n., adj. —n.* chrysalis.
—adj. of a chrysalis.

chrys•a•lis ['krɪsəlɪs] *n., pl.* **chrys•a•lis•es** or **chry•sal•i•des** [krə'sælə,diz]. **1** the resting stage, or pupa, of a butterfly, during which it develops into a winged adult. **2** the hard outer covering of the butterfly during this stage. When the transformation has been completed, the chrysalis splits and the adult butterfly emerges. **3** a stage of development or change. ⟨< L < Gk. *chrysallis* golden sheath < *chrysos* gold⟩

chry•san•the•mum [krə'sænθəməm] *n.* **1** any of various plants (genus *Chrysanthemum*) of the composite family, some of which are widely cultivated for their large, showy, usually double flowers that bloom in late summer or autumn. **2** the flower of any of these plants: *Chrysanthemums are usually yellow, white, bronze, red, or rose.* ⟨< L < Gk. *chrysanthemon* < *chrysos* gold + *anthemon* flower⟩

chrys•a•ro•bin [,krɪsə'roubɪn] *n.* a mixture of yellow compounds obtained from Goa powder, used to treat psoriasis and other skin disorders. *Formula*: $C_{15}H_{12}O_3$ ⟨< Gk. *chrysos* gold + Pg. *araroba* < Tupi name for the tree which is the source of the powder⟩

chrys•o•ber•yl ['krɪsə,bɛrəl] *n.* **1** a yellow or pale gren semiprecious stone; beryllium aluminate. *Formula*: $BeAl_2O_4$ **2** a piece of this stone, or a gem made from it. ⟨< L < Gk. *chrysoberyllos* < *chrysos* gold + *beryllos* beryl⟩

chrys•o•lite ['krɪsə,ləit] *n.* **1** a green or yellow silicate of magnesium and iron, a semiprecious stone; olivine. **2** a piece of this stone, or a gem made from it. ⟨< L < Gk. *chrysolithos* < *chrysos* gold + *lithos* stone⟩

chrys•o•prase ['krɪsə,preiz] *n.* **1** a light green kind of chalcedony, a semiprecious stone. **2** a piece of this stone, or a gem made from it. ⟨< L < Gk. *chrysoprasos* < *chrysos* gold + *prason* leek⟩

chrys•o•tile ['krɪsə,taɪl] *n.* a green, grey, or white mineral occurring in the form of silky fibres; a variety of serpentine that constitutes commercial asbestos. ⟨< Gk. *chrysos* gold + *tilos* fine hair⟩

chtho•ni•an ['θouniən] *adj. Greek mythology.* of or having to do with the world of the dead, and with its gods and spirits. Also, **chthonic** ['θɒnɪk]. ⟨< Gk. *chthonios* in the earth < *chthon* earth⟩

chub [tʃʌb] *n., pl.* **chub** or **chubs. 1** any of various freshwater game fishes of the cyprinid, or minnow, family. The lake chub (*Couesius plumbeus*) is found throughout Canada and in parts of the N United States. *Leuciscus cephalus* is a common European chub. **2** any of several North American whitefishes. ⟨ME *chubbe*; origin unknown⟩

chub•by ['tʃʌbi] *adj.* **-bi•er, -bi•est.** round and plump: *chubby cheeks.* **—'chub•bi•ness,** *n.*

chuck[1] [tʃʌk] *v., n. —v.* **1** pat; tap, especially under the chin.
2 *Informal.* toss: *She chucked the apple core into the garbage.*
3 *Informal.* give up or quit: *He's chucked his job.* **4** *Slang.* vomit (*used with* **up**).
—n. **1** a tap; slight blow under the chin. **2** a toss. **3** *West.* food; provisions. ⟨probably imitative⟩

chuck[2] [tʃʌk] *n.* **1** a device for holding a tool or piece of work in a machine. **2** a cut of beef between the neck and the shoulder. See BEEF for picture. ⟨var. of *chock*⟩

chuck[3] [tʃʌk] *n. Cdn. West Coast.* a large body of water, formerly especially a river, but now usually the ocean.
⟨< Chinook jargon⟩

chuck–full ['tʃʌk 'fʊl] *adj.* chock-full.

chuck•hole ['tʃʌk,houl] *n.* a deep depression or hole in a street or road; pothole.

chuck•le ['tʃʌkəl] *v.* **chuck•led, chuck•ling;** *n. —v.* laugh quietly, as when mildly amused: *He chuckled as he watched the antics of the puppy.*
—n. a soft, quiet laugh. ⟨< obs. *chuck* cluck, laugh; imitative⟩
—'chuck•ler, *n.*

chuck•le•head ['tʃʌkəl,hɛd] *n. Informal.* **1** a thick or large head. **2** a stupid person. **—'chuck•le,head•ed,** *adj.*
—'chuck•le,head•ed•ness, *n.*

chuck race CHUCKWAGON RACE.

chuck•wag•on ['tʃʌk,wægən] *n.* in the western parts of Canada and the United States, a wagon that carries food and cooking equipment for cowboys, harvest hands, etc.

chuckwagon race *Cdn.* a race between chuckwagons drawn by horses, a thrilling and highly popular event at rodeos and stampedes in western Canada.

chuck–will's–widow ['tʃʌk ,wɪlz 'wɪdou] *n.* a large goatsucker (*Caprimulgus carolinensis*) with bristles on the sides of the beak, and mostly brown plumage. It breeds from southern Ontario south. ⟨imitative of its song⟩

chuff [tʃʌf] *n. or v.* chug. ⟨imitative⟩
☛ *Hom.* CHOUGH.

chug [tʃʌg] *n., v.* **chugged, chug•ging.** *—n.* a short, loud, explosive sound: *the chug of an engine.*
—v. **1** make short, loud, explosive sounds. **2** *Informal.* go or move with short, loud, explosive sounds: *The engine chugged along.* **3** *Informal.* of work, etc., proceed at a steady, moderate pace: *"How are you doing with that research paper?" "Oh, it's chugging along."* ⟨imitative⟩

chug–a–lug ['tʃʌg ə ,lʌg] *v.,* **-lugged, -lug•ging,** *Slang.* drink (liquor) all in one gulp, or steadily until it is consumed. ⟨imitative⟩

chu•kar [tʃə'kɑr] *or* ['tʃʌkər] *n.* a partridge (*Alectoris graeca*) native to SE Europe and Asia but introduced to many other countries as a game bird, having red legs and bill and mainly brown plumage barred with black. ⟨< Hind. *chakor* < Skt. *chakora*⟩

A chukar

Chuk•chi ['tʃʊktʃi] *n.* **1** any member of an aboriginal people now living in NE Siberia. **2** their language.

chuk•ka boot ['tʃʌkə] an ankle-high leather boot with pairs of eyelets or a strap and buckle. ⟨alteration of *chukker*, from its similarity to a polo player's boot⟩

chuk•ker or **chuk•kar** ['tʃʌkər] *n.* in polo, one of the periods of play, lasting about eight minutes. ⟨< Hind. *chakkar*⟩

chum[1] [tʃʌm] *n., v.* **chummed, chum•ming.** *Informal. —n.* **1** a close friend. **2** a roommate.
—v. **1** be close friends: *Chaim and Ravi have chummed for years.* **2** room together. ⟨? shortened form of *chamber mate, chamber fellow*⟩

chum[2] [tʃʌm] *n., v.* **chummed, chum•ming.** *—n.* bait for fish, especially chopped fish scattered on the water to attract fish.
—v. scatter chum to attract fish. ⟨origin unknown⟩

chum[3] [tʃʌm] *n. Cdn.* a Pacific salmon (*Oncorhynchus keta*) found especially along the coasts of British Columbia and Alaska, metallic blue and silver in colour and having pale pink flesh. ⟨< Chinook jargon *tzum* spotted⟩

chum•my ['tʃʌmi] *adj.* **-mi•er, -mi•est.** *Informal.* like a chum; very friendly; intimate. **—'chum•mi•ly,** *adv.* **—'chum•mi•ness,** *n.*

chump [tʃʌmp] *n.* **1** *Informal.* a foolish or stupid person; blockhead. **2** a short, thick block of wood. **3** a thick, blunt end. **4** *Esp. Brit. Slang.* the head.
off one's chump, *Esp. Brit. Slang.* off one's head; out of one's senses. ⟨origin uncertain⟩

chunk [tʃʌŋk] *n. Informal.* **1** a thick piece or lump: *a chunk of* *earth.* **2** a considerable amount or part: *The preparation took quite a chunk out of the day.* **3** a thick-bodied, short-legged horse. ⟨var. of *chuck*²⟩

chunk•y ['tʃʌŋki] *adj.* **chunk•i•er, chunk•i•est.** *Informal.* **1** like a chunk; short and thick. **2** stocky. **3** containing chunks, as of meat or potatoes: *chunky soup.* **—'chunk•i•ly,** *adv.* **—'chunk•i•ness,** *n.*

chun•nel ['tʃʌnəl] *n.* the Channel tunnel between Great Britain and France.

church [tʃɜrtʃ] *n., v.* —*n.* **1** a building for public, especially Christian, worship or religious services: *There is a big church at the end of our street.* **2** public worship or religious service in a church: *They go to church regularly.* **3 the church,** all Christians. **4** Usually, **Church,** a body or organization of persons having the same religious beliefs and usually under one authority; denomination: *the Presbyterian Church, the Roman Catholic Church.* **5** a group of people who worship together; congregation: *The whole church spent the weekend at the lake.* **6** the organization of a church; ecclesiastical authority or power: *The church forced Galileo to deny his discoveries.* **7** the profession of the clergy: *He has a sister in the church.* **8** (*adjl.*) of or having to do with church or a church.
—*v.* **1** bring to church. **2** in certain churches, conduct a special ceremony of thanksgiving for (especially a woman after childbirth). ⟨OE *circe* < Gk. *kyriakon (doma)* (house) of the Lord < *kyrios* lord⟩ **—'church•less,** *adj.* **—'church,like,** *adj.*

church day a day on which a festival of the Christian church is celebrated: *Ascension Day is a church day.*

churched [tʃɜrtʃt] *adj., v.* —*adj.* associated with or belonging to a church.
—*v.* pt. and pp. of CHURCH.

church•go•er ['tʃɜrtʃ,gouər] *n.* a person who goes to church, especially one who goes regularly. **—'church,go•ing,** *n., adj.*

Church•ill•i•an [tʃər'tʃiliən] *adj.* **1** of, having to do with, or resembling Sir Winston Churchill (1874-1965). **2** of or suggestive of his writings, speeches, etc: *Churchillian rhetoric.*

church•ly ['tʃɜrtʃli] *adj.* **1** of a church. **2** suitable for a church. **—'church•li•ness,** *n.*

church•man ['tʃɜrtʃmən] *n., pl.* **-men. 1** a male member of the clergy. **2** a male member of a church.

Church of Christ, Scientist the official name of the Christian Science Church.

Church of England the Christian church that is recognized as the national church of England. The Anglican Church of Canada is affiliated with the Church of England.

Church of Jesus Christ of Latter–day Saints the official name of the Mormon Church.

Church of Rome ROMAN CATHOLIC CHURCH.

church•ward•en ['tʃɜrtʃ,wɔrdən] *n.* **1** *Anglican Church*: a lay official who manages the business matters of a church. **2** a clay tobacco pipe with a very long stem.

church•wom•an ['tʃɜrtʃ,wʊmən] *n., pl.* **-wom•en. 1** a woman who is a member of the clergy. **2** a woman who is a member of a church.

church•yard ['tʃɜrtʃ,jɑrd] *n.* the ground immediately surrounding and belonging to a church, especially a part used as a burial ground.

churl [tʃɜrl] *n.* **1** a rude, surly person. **2** a person of low birth; peasant. **3** a person who is stingy in money matters; niggard; miser. **4** in Anglo-Saxon and medieval England, a freeman of the lowest rank; ceorl. ⟨OE *ceorl* freeman (of low rank)⟩

churl•ish ['tʃɜrlɪʃ] *adj.* **1** rude; surly: *a churlish reply.* **2** niggardly; stingy; grudging; sordid. **—'churl•ish•ly,** *adv.* **—'churl•ish•ness,** *n.*

churn [tʃɜrn] *n., v.* —*n.* **1** a container or machine in which butter is made from cream or milk by beating and shaking. **2** a violent stirring.
—*v.* **1** stir or shake (cream or milk) in a churn. **2** make (butter) by using a churn. **3** stir violently; make or become foamy: *The propeller of the steamboat churned the waves. The water churns in the rapids.* **4** move as if beaten and shaken: *The excited crowd churned about the speaker's platform.*
churn out, *Informal.* produce as if mechanically. ⟨OE *cyrn*⟩ **—'churn•er,** *n.*

churr [tʃɜr] *v. or n.* See CHIRR.

chute¹ [ʃut] *n., v.* **chut•ed, chut•ing.** —*n.* **1** an inclined trough, tube, etc., used for dropping or sliding things such as mail, laundry, or coal to a lower level. **2** a narrow waterfall or rapids in a river. **3** a steep slope. **4** a narrow passageway or stall for controlling an animal while branding or disinfecting it. **5** a similar stall in which a rodeo animal is held before being released into the ring.
—*v.* send or go down a chute. ⟨apparently blend of F *chute* fall (of water) and E *shoot*⟩
☛ *Hom.* SHOOT.

chute² [ʃut] *n. or v.* **chut•ed, chut•ing.** *Informal.* parachute.
☛ *Hom.* SHOOT.

chut•ney ['tʃʌtni] *n., pl.* **-neys.** a spicy sauce or relish made of fruits, herbs, pepper, etc. ⟨< Hind. *chatni*⟩

chutz•pah ['xʊtspə] *or* ['hʊtspɑ] *n. Slang.* bold self-confidence; nerve; gall. Also, **hutzpah.** ⟨< Yiddish *khutspe*⟩

chyle [kaɪl] *n.* the milky fluid in the lymphatic vessels of the body, consisting of lymph and the digested fats that have been absorbed from the intestines. Chyle is carried by the lymphatic vessels, called lacteals, into the bloodstream. ⟨< Med.L < Gk. *chylos* < *cheein* pour⟩ **—chy'la•ceous** [kaɪ'leiʃəs] or **'chy•lous,** *adj.*

chy•lo•mi•cron [,kaɪlou'maikrɒn] *n.* a tiny particle, composed mostly of triglycerides, whose function is to convey digested fats through the lymph.

chyme [kaɪm] *n.* the thick semiliquid mass that is the product of the first stage of digestion in the stomach. The chyme passes from the stomach into the duodenum and small intestine, where digestion is completed. ⟨< Med.L < Gk. *chymos* < *cheein* pour⟩ **—'chy•mous,** *adj.*

chy•mo•pa•pa•in [,kaɪmoupə'peɪn] *or* [,kaɪmoupə'paɪɪn] *n.* an enzyme, a form of papain, used in medicine to soften a slipped disc. ⟨< Gk. *chymos* juice + E *papain*⟩

chy•mo•tryp•sin [,kaɪmou'trɪpsɪn] *n.* an enzyme used in cataract surgery. It is secreted by the pancreas and, in its natural state, aids the digestion of protein.

Ci curie.

CIA or **C.I.A.** *U.S.* Central Intelligence Agency.

ciao [tʃaʊ] *interj. Informal.* hello or goodbye. ⟨< Ital.⟩
☛ *Hom.* CHOW.

ci•bo•ri•um [sə'bɔriəm] *n., pl.* **-ri•a** [-riə]. **1** a covered container used to hold the sacred bread of the Eucharist. **2** a dome-shaped canopy over an altar. ⟨< Med.L *ciborium* canopy over an altar < L *ciborium* drinking cup < Gk. *kiborion* cuplike seed vessel⟩

ci•ca•da [sə'keidə] *or* [sə'kɑdə] *n., pl.* **-das, -dae** [-di] *or* [-daɪ]. any of a family (Cicadidae) of medium- to large-sized insects, found mostly in tropical and subtropical regions, having two pairs of transparent wings and noted especially for the loud buzzing sound that the male makes by vibrating membranes on its abdomen. Several species of cicada have very long cycles of development; one species found in eastern North America lives underground as a larva for 17 years before becoming an adult. ⟨< L⟩

cic•a•trice ['sɪkətrɪs] *n.* cicatrix.

cic•a•trix ['sɪkətrɪks] *or* [sɪ'keitrɪks] *n., pl.* **cic•a•tri•ces** [,sɪkə'traɪsiz]. **1** *Medicine.* the scar left by a healed wound. **2** *Botany.* **a** the scar left on a tree or plant by a fallen leaf, branch, etc. **b** the scar on a seed where it was attached to the pod or seed container. **c** on a tree or plant, the traces of an old wound. Also, **cicatrice.** ⟨< L⟩ **—,cic•a'tri•cial** [-'trɪʃəl], *adj.*

cic•a•trize ['sɪkə,traɪz] *v.* **-trized, -triz•ing.** heal by forming a scar. **—,cic•a•tri'za•tion,** *n.*

cic•e•ro•ne [,sɪsə'rouni]; *Italian,* [tʃitʃe'rone] *n., pl.* **-nes** or **-ni** [-ni]. a guide for sightseers that explains curiosities, antiquities, etc. ⟨< Ital. < L *Cicero, -onis* Cicero⟩

Cic•e•ro•ni•an [,sɪsə'rouniən] *adj.* **1** resembling the literary style of M.T. Cicero (106-43 B.C.), a Roman orator, writer, and statesman. **2** eloquent.

cich•lid ['sɪklɪd] *n.* a freshwater fish of the family Cichlidae, of South America, Africa, and southern Asia, resembling the American sunfishes. ⟨< Gk. *kichle* sea fish⟩

CIDA Canadian International Development Agency.

–cide¹ *combining form.* killing of: *regicide* (def. 1) = *killing of a king.* ⟨< L *-cidium* the act of killing < *caedere* kill⟩

–cide² *combining form.* killer of: *regicide* (def. 2) = *killer of a king.* ⟨< L *-cida* killer < *caedere* kill⟩

ci•der ['saɪdər] *n.* **1** the juice pressed out of apples, for use as a drink and in making vinegar. **Sweet cider** is the unfermented juice; **hard cider,** the fermented juice. **2** the juice pressed from other fruits. ⟨ME *sidre* < OF < LL *sicera* < Gk. < Hebrew *shēkār* liquor⟩

cider press a machine for pressing the juice out of apples.

ci–de•vant [sid'vɑ̃] *adj. French.* former: *The ci-devant general led the revolt against his government.*

CIE. or **cie.** company (for F *compagnie*).

C.I.F. or **c.i.f.** cost, insurance, and freight.

ci•gar [sə'gɑr] *n.* a tight roll of dried tobacco leaves for smoking. ⟨< Sp. *cigarro*⟩

cig•a•rette [ˌsɪgə'rɛt] *or* ['sɪgəˌrɛt] *n.* a small roll of finely cut tobacco enclosed in a thin sheet of generally white paper for smoking. Sometimes (*esp. U.S.*), **cigaret.** ⟨< F *cigarette*, dim. of *cigare* cigar⟩

cig•a•ril•lo [ˌsɪgə'rɪlou] *or* [ˌsɪgə'rijou] *n., pl.* **-los.** a small, thin cigar. ⟨< Sp. *cigarillo* cigarette, dim. of *cigarro* cigar⟩

cig•ua•te•ra [ˌsɪgwə'tɛrə] *or* [ˌsɪgwə'tirə] *n.* a serious kind of food poisoning, often having neurological consequences, resulting from eating contaminated fish. ⟨< Am.Sp. < *cigua* a marine snail⟩

cil•i•a ['sɪliə] *n.pl., sing.* **cil•i•um** ['sɪliəm]. **1** eyelashes. **2** *Biology.* tiny hairlike projections found on the surface of many different types of cell, including those lining the human windpipe. In some one-celled animals cilia cover the entire surface of the organism and function like oars, allowing the animal to move through the liquid surrounding it. ⟨< L⟩

cil•i•ar•y ['sɪliˌɛri] *adj.* **1** of or having to do with cilia. **2** of or having to do with the CILIARY BODY in the eye.

ciliary body the part of the choroid layer of tissue in the front of the eyeball that contains the muscles used to focus the eye by changing the shape of the lens. See EYE for picture.

cil•i•ate ['sɪliɪt] *or* ['sɪliˌeit] *adj., n.* —*adj.* having cilia.
—*n.* any of a large class (Cileatea) constituting a subphylum of protozoans having cilia on all or part of the body.

Ci•li•cian [sə'lɪʃən] *adj., n.* —*adj.* of or having to do with Cilicia, an ancient country in SE Asia Minor.
—*n.* a native or inhabitant of Cilicia.

cil•i•um ['sɪliəm] *n.* singular of CILIA.

cim•ba•lom or **cym•ba•lom** ['sɪmbələm] *n.* a type of zither used for Hungarian folk music. ⟨< Hungarian *czimbalom* < L *cymbalum* cymbal⟩

ci•mex ['saɪmɛks] *n., pl.* **cim•i•ces** ['sɪməˌsiz]. a bug of the genus *Cimex*, including the bedbug. ⟨< NL < L a bug⟩

Cim•me•ri•an [sə'miriən] *n., adj.* —*n. Greek mythology.* one of a mythical people said to live in perpetual mists and darkness.
—*adj.* very dark and gloomy. ⟨< L < Gk.⟩

C. in C. commander-in-chief.

cinch [sɪntʃ] *n., v.* —*n.* **1** a strong band or belt, usually of leather, for fastening a saddle or pack on a horse. **2** *Informal.* a firm hold or grip. **3** *Informal.* something sure or easy: *It was a cinch we would win. This puzzle is a cinch.*
—*v.* **1** fasten on with a cinch; bind firmly. **2** *Informal.* get a firm hold on. **3** *Informal.* make sure of: *We've got to cinch that win.* ⟨< Sp. *cincha* < L *cincta* girdle < *cingere* bind⟩

cin•cho•na [sɪŋ'kounə] *or* [sɪn'kounə] *n.* **1** any of a genus (*Cinchona*) of tropical evergreen trees and shrubs of the madder family, native to South America. A few species of cinchona are cultivated in other parts of the world, especially Indonesia, because their bark is a source of quinine, quinidine, and other similar drugs. **2** the bitter bark of any species of cinchona tree, from which these drugs are obtained. ⟨< NL; after Francesca de Ribera, Countess *Chinchón* (?-1641?), the wife of a Spanish viceroy of Peru⟩

cin•chon•i•dine [sɪŋ'kɒnəˌdin] *or* [sɪŋ'kɒnədɪn], [sɪn'kɒnəˌdin] *or* [sɪn'kɒnədɪ] *n.* a white substance obtained from cinchona bark and used to treat malaria and fevers. *Formula*: $C_{19}H_{22}N_2O$

cin•chon•ism ['sɪŋkəˌnɪzəm] *or* ['sɪnkəˌnɪzəm] *n.* poisoning by excessive use of cinchona products such as quinine, characterized by headache, deafness, and ringing in the ears.

cinch•y ['sɪntʃi] *adj.* **-i•er, -i•est.** *Informal.* very easy.

cinc•ture ['sɪŋktʃər] *n., v.* **-tured, -tur•ing.** —*n.* **1** a belt; girdle. **2** a border; enclosure.
—*v.* encircle; surround. ⟨< L *cinctura* < *cingere* bind, gird⟩

cin•der ['sɪndər] *n.* **1** a piece of burned-up wood or coal. **2 cinders,** *pl.* **a** wood or coal partly burned but no longer flaming. **b** ashes. **3** slag, especially slag produced in making pig iron in a blast furnace. **4** a fragment of lava ejected from a volcano. ⟨OE *sinder*⟩

Cin•der•el•la [ˌsɪndə'rɛlə] *n.* **1** a girl who suddenly achieves success or fame after being neglected or ridiculed, etc. **2** any person whose real worth or beauty is not recognized. **3** (*adjl.*) of or having to do with sudden or dramatic success: *a Cinderella story.* ⟨< *Cinderella*, the beautiful young heroine of a fairy tale, who is cruelly treated by her stepmother and stepsisters but is then helped by her fairy godmother⟩

cinder track a race track surfaced with fine cinders.

cin•é•aste or **cin•e•aste** ['sɪniˌæst]; *French* [sine'ast] *n.* **1** a film enthusiast. **2** someone who makes films. ⟨< F < *ciné* cinema + *-aste* as in *enthousiaste* enthusiast. 20c.⟩

cin•e•ma ['sɪnəmə] *n.* **1** a movie theatre. **2 the cinema,** movies as an art form: *She is more interested in the cinema than in live theatre.* ⟨short for *cinematograph*⟩

Cin•e•ma•scope ['sɪnəməˌskoup] *n. Trademark.* a filming process developed in the 1950s, in which the image is projected on a wide, curved screen to give some illusion of depth and of natural field of vision. The process involves the use of a special camera lens that photographs an area twice as large as an ordinary lens, but compresses it so that it can be recorded on regular film. This distorted film image is corrected before it reaches the screen by a special lens in the projector, which expands it to its normal width.

cin•e•ma•theque [ˌsɪnəmə'tɛk] *n.* a building in which films are shown and stored; film library or museum. ⟨< F *cinémathèque* < *cinéma* + (*biblio*)*thèque* library⟩

cin•e•mat•ic [ˌsɪnə'mætɪk] *adj.* of or having to do with cinema: *cinematic style, a cinematic presentation.*
—ˌ**cin•e'mat•i•cal•ly,** *adv.*

cin•e•mat•o•graph [ˌsɪnə'mætəˌgræf] *n.* **1** *Brit.* a machine for projecting movies on a screen. **2** a camera for taking movies.

cin•e•ma•tog•ra•pher [ˌsɪnəmə'tɒgrəfər] *n.* a person who makes movies, especially the head camera operator.

cin•e•ma•tog•ra•phy [ˌsɪnəmə'tɒgrəfi] *n.* the art and science of making movies, especially from a photographic point of view.

ci•né•ma vé•ri•té [sinema veʀi'te] *French.* a filming style that aims to reflect reality by filming spontaneous action.

ci•ne•phile ['sɪnəˌfaɪl] *n.* a lover of the cinema.

Cin•er•am•a [ˌsɪnə'ræmə] *or* [ˌsɪnə'rɑmə] *n. Trademark.* a wide-screen presentation of film using 70 mm film and a special lens to produce an image on a large, deeply curved screen, giving the illusion of three dimensions. ⟨< *cine*(*ma*) + (*pano*)*rama*⟩

cin•e•rar•i•a [ˌsɪnə'rɛriə] *n.* any of several varieties of house and greenhouse plant derived from a perennial herb (*Senecio cruentus*) of the composite family, native to the Canary Islands. Cinerarias have heart-shaped leaves and clusters of daisylike flowers in several colours. ⟨< NL < L *cinerarius* of ashes; with reference to down on leaves⟩

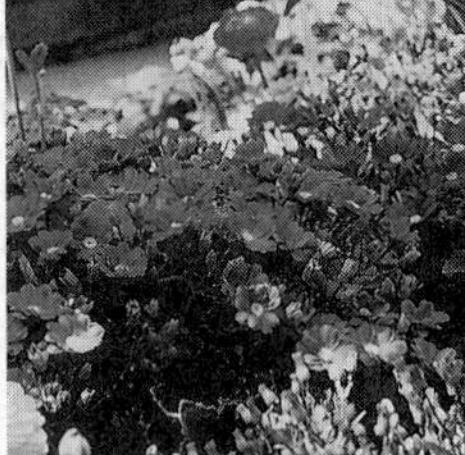
Cinerarias

cin•e•rar•i•um [ˌsɪnə'rɛriəm] *n.* **-rar•i•a.** a place for keeping the ashes of cremated bodies. ⟨< L⟩

cin•e•rar•y ['sɪnəˌrɛri] *adj.* **1** used to hold the ashes of a cremated body. **2** of or for ashes.

ci•ne•re•ous [sɪ'niriəs] *adj.* **1** of or having to do with ashes. **2** ash grey.

cin•gu•lum ['sɪŋgjələm] *n. Zoology.* a belt or band of colour. ⟨< L, girdle, belt < *cingere* to encircle⟩

cin•na•bar ['sɪnəˌbɑr] *n., adj.* —*n.* **1** a reddish or brownish mineral that is the chief source of mercury; native mercuric sulphide. *Formula*: HgS **2** artificial mercuric sulphide, used as a red pigment in making paints, dyes, etc. **3** a bright red; vermilion.
—*adj.* bright red; vermilion. ⟨< L < Gk. *kinnabari*; ult. < Persian *šängärf*⟩

cin•nam•ic [sə'næmɪk] *adj.* **1** of or having to do with cinnamon. **2** relating to an organic acid obtained from benzaldehyde, derived from cinnamon. *Formula*: $C_6H_5 \cdot CH = CH \cdot COOH$

cin•na•mon ['sɪnəmən] *n., adj.* —*n.* **1** a fragrant spice, used especially as a flavouring in baked goods, desserts, and candy, that is the dried inner bark of a tropical evergreen tree (*Cinnamomum zeylanicum*) of the laurel family. Most cinnamon comes from Sri Lanka and India. **2** this bark. **3** the tree or shrub yielding this bark. **4** the colour of cinnamon, a light reddish brown.
—*adj.* **1** flavoured with cinnamon: *cinnamon rolls.* **2** having the colour cinnamon. ⟨ME < OF *cinnamome* < LL < Gk. *kinnamon*; of Semitic origin⟩

cinnamon bear a reddish brown variety of the black bear of North America.

cinnamon stone essonite.

cin•quain ['sɪŋkein] *n.* **1** a stanza of five lines. **2** a five-line poem, usually unrhymed, the lines having 2, 4, 6, 8, 2 syllables or 1, 2, 3, 4, 1 words, respectively. **3** any group of five. ⟨< F *cinq* five, on the analogy of *quatrain*⟩

cin•que•cen•tist [,tʃɪŋkwə'tʃɛntɪst] *n.* an Italian writer or artist of the 16th century.

cin•que•cen•to [,tʃɪŋkwə'tʃɛntou] *n., adj.* —*n.* the 16th century, especially with regard to the art and architecture of Italy at that time.
—*adj.* of or having to do with the 16th century. ⟨< Ital. *cinquecento* short for *mil cinque cento* one thousand five hundred⟩

☛ *Usage.* Note that *cinquecento* refers to the 1500s, and so to the 16th rather than the 15th century.

cinque•foil ['sɪŋk,fɔɪl] *n.* **1** any of a genus (*Potentilla*) of plants of the rose family found mainly in the northern hemisphere, having compound leaves with three to seven leaflets and usually yellow or white flowers with five roundish petals. Several species of cinquefoil are common Canadian weeds. **2** *Architecture.* an ornament made up of five arcs or part circles joined in a circle. ⟨ME *synkefoile* < OF (unrecorded) < L *quinquefolium* < *quinque* five + *folium* leaf⟩

ci•on ['saɪən] *n.* See SCION (def. 2).

ciop•pi•no [tʃə'pinou] *n.* a hearty Italian fish and shellfish stew, with tomatoes, onions, and spices. ⟨< dial. Ital.⟩

ci•paille [sɪ'paɪ]; *French,* [sɪ'paj] *n. Cdn.* a pie with any number of meats (pork, veal, chicken, or wild game) baked in alternate layers with pastry. ⟨< F⟩

ci•pher ['səifər] *n., v.* —*n.* **1** a method of secret writing based on a key or set pattern; code: *She sent me a telegram in cipher.* **2** something in secret writing or code. **3** the key to a method of secret writing or code. **4** a zero; 0. **5** a person or thing of no importance. **6** any Arabic numeral. **7** a pattern of interlaced initials; monogram.
—*v.* **1** express (a message or information) in cipher. **2** *Rare.* do arithmetic or work out (a problem) by arithmetic. Also, **cypher.** ⟨ME < Med.L *ciphra* < Arabic *sifr* empty. Doublet of ZERO.⟩

cip•o•lin ['sɪpəlɪn] *n.* a type of Italian marble with green and white streaks. ⟨< F < Ital. *cipollino* little onion < L *cepa* onion (because it is layered)⟩

cir•ca ['sɜrkə] *prep. or adv.* about: *Mohammed was born circa A.D. 570. Abbrev.*: c. or ca. ⟨< L⟩

cir•ca•di•an [sər'keidiən] *adj.* of, having to do with, or designating biological processes that have a cycle or periodicity of approximately 24 hours. ⟨< L *circa* about + *dies* day + E *-an*; 20c.⟩

Cir•cas•sian [sər'kæʃən] *or* [sər'kæʃiən] *n., adj.* —*n.* **1** a native or inhabitant of Circassia, a region in southern Russia on the Black Sea. **2** a language of the northern Caucasus.
—*adj.* of or having to do with Circassia, its people, or their language.

Circassian walnut the hard wood of the English walnut tree. It can be dark brown or even purplish, and has a distinctive grain.

Cir•ce ['sɜrsi] *n.* **1** *Greek mythology.* an enchantress who changed men to beasts. **2** any enchantress.

cir•ci•nate ['sɜrsə,neit] *adj.* **1** rolled up into a coil. **2** *Botany.* coiled from tip toward the base: *The new leaves of a fern are circinate.* ⟨< L *circinatus* made round, pp. of *circinare* < *circinus* pair of compasses < Gk. *kirkinos*⟩ —**'cir•ci,nate•ly,** *adv.*

Cir•ci•nus ['sɜrsənəs] *n.* a southern constellation near Centaurus, known as the Compasses.

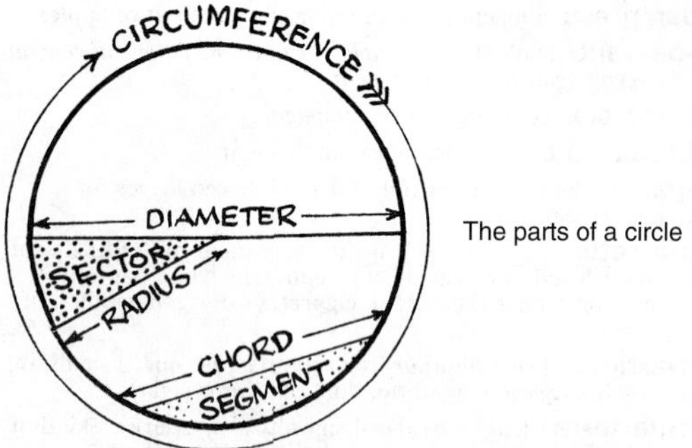

The parts of a circle

cir•cle ['sɜrkəl] *n., v.* **-cled, -cling.** —*n.* **1** a continuously curving line, every point of which is equally distant from a fixed point called the centre. **2** a plane figure bounded by such a line. **3** a halo, crown, or anything shaped like a circle or part of one. **4** a ring: *The girls danced in a circle.* **5** a set of seats in the balcony of a theatre. **6** a complete series or course of something that is repeated; cycle: *A year is a circle of 12 months.* **7** *Astronomy.* **a** the orbit of a heavenly body. **b** the period of revolution of a heavenly body. **8** a group of people held together by the same interests: *the family circle, a circle of friends.* **9** a sphere of influence, action, etc. **10** a set of parts that form a connected whole: *the circle of the sciences.* **11** *Logic.* flawed reasoning in which two propositions are used, each to prove the other: *reasoning in a circle.*
—*v.* **1** go around in a circle; revolve around: *The moon circles the earth. The airplane circled before it landed.* **2** identify by drawing a circle around: *Circle the number of the answer you think is correct.*
come full circle, return to the starting point of a circular route or of a cyclical series of stages. ⟨ME < OF *cercle* < L *circulus*, dim. of *circus* ring⟩ —**cir'cler,** *n.*

☛ *Syn. n.* **8. Circle,** CLIQUE = a group of people held together by a common tie. **Circle** applies to a group held together around a person or a common interest, cause, occupation, etc.: *The book is praised in literary circles.* **Clique** applies to a small, exclusive, sometimes snobbish, group, and often expresses an attitude of disapproval on the part of the speaker: *Every school has its cliques.*

cir•clet ['sɜrklɪt] *n.* **1** a small circle. **2** a round ornament worn on the head, neck, arm, or finger.

circs ['sɜrks] *n.pl. Esp. Brit. Informal.* circumstances: *We can't very well ask him again, under the circs.*

cir•cuit ['sɜrkɪt] *n., v.* —*n.* **1** a complete course, journey, or route, especially one that is more or less circular or that goes around something: *It takes a year for the earth to make its circuit of the sun.* **2** the complete path followed by an electric current. **3** an arrangement of connected electronic components or elements forming such a path. **4** the plan of such an arrangement. **5** a route followed repeatedly at regular intervals, having a number of stopovers and returning to the starting point: *the circuit of a travelling theatre company.* **6** a periodic journey along such a route. **7** the district or region covered by such a route. **8** a group or association of theatres, cinemas, resorts, etc., at which the same plays, films, or other entertainments are presented in turn. **9** an association of athletic teams or clubs or a series of sporting events involving the same players. **10** the distance around any space. **11** a line enclosing any space; boundary line. **12** the space enclosed.
—*v.* go around in, or make, a circuit. ⟨ME < L *circuitus* a going around < *circum* around + *ire* go⟩ —**'cir•cuit•al,** *adj.*

circuit board **1** a panel of circuit breakers. **2** a flat board made of insulating material on which electronic components are mounted and interconnected. Also called **board.**

circuit breaker a switch that automatically opens or interrupts an electric circuit when the current gets too strong.

cir•cu•i•tous [sər'kjuətəs] *adj.* roundabout; not direct: *To avoid unpaved roads, we took a circuitous route home.* —**cir'cu•i•tous•ly,** *adv.* —**cir'cu•i•tous•ness,** *n.*

circuit rider formerly, a Methodist minister who rode from place to place over a circuit to preach.

cir•cuit•ry ['sɜrkətri] *n., pl.* **-ries. 1** the science of electrical or electronic circuits. **2** the component parts of a circuit. **3** a system of circuits.

cir•cu•i•ty [sər'kjuəti] *n.* **1** a circuitous quality. **2** a roundabout, indirect manner of speaking, moving, etc.

cir•cu•lar ['sɜrkjələr] *adj., n.* —*adj.* **1** having the form of a circle: *The full moon is circular.* **2** moving in a circle; going around a circle: *a circular movement of the arms.* **3** having to do with a circle: *circular measure.* **4** sent to each of a number of people: *a circular letter.* **5** roundabout; indirect: *a circular explanation.* **6** in an argument, etc., using as one's proof an assertion that assumes what one is trying to prove: *Circular reasoning is futile because it inevitably comes back to the starting point.* **7** moving or occurring in a round or cycle of repetition: *a circular sequence of events.*
—*n.* a letter, notice, or advertisement sent to each of a number of people. ⟨ME < AF < LL *circularis* < *circulus.* See CIRCLE.⟩
—'cir•cu•lar•ly, *adv.*

cir•cu•lar•i•ty [ˌsɜrkjə'lærəti] *or* [ˌsɜrkjə'lɛrəti] *n., pl.* **-ties.** circular quality or form.

cir•cu•lar•ize ['sɜrkjələˌraɪz] *v.* **-ized, -iz•ing. 1** send circulars to. **2** make circular. **3** canvass. **—ˌcir•cu•lar•i'za•tion,** *n.* **—'cir•cu•larˌiz•er,** *n.*

circular measure 1 a system for measuring angles. There are two main circular measures: **degree measure,** based on the division of a circle into 360°, and **radian measure,** based on a standard angle in which the length of the arc subtending the angle is equal to the radius of the circle. **2** the measurement of the radius, circumference, area, etc., of a circle.

circular mil a measure of the thickness of wire, based on the area of a cross-section. It equals the area of a circle with a diameter of one mil.

circular saw a thin steel disk with saw teeth round its edge, turned at high speed by machinery.

cir•cu•late ['sɜrkjəˌleit] *v.* **-lat•ed, -lat•ing. 1** move around in a circuit; follow a course, especially one that returns to the starting point: *The blood circulates through the body. The house is heated by hot water circulating through a system of pipes.* **2** pass from place to place or person to person freely and continuously: *The gossip circulated rapidly. Money circulates as it goes from person to person.* **3** send around from person to person or place to place: *She circulated the news of the holiday. The book has been widely circulated among our friends.* **4** move about in a social circle. **5** move around at a gathering, talking to different people. ⟨< L *circulare* < *circulus.* See CIRCLE.⟩ **—'cir•cuˌla•tor,** *n.*

circulating library lending library.

circulating medium the coins, notes, bills, etc. that are in use as money; currency.

cir•cu•la•tion [ˌsɜrkjə'leiʃən] *n.* **1** the movement of anything in a circuit, especially a closed circuit: *Open windows increase the circulation of air in a room.* **2** specifically, the circular movement of the blood in the human body: *Cold feet are often the result of poor circulation.* **3** the passage of anything from person to person or place to place: *the circulation of money, the circulation of information or news, the circulation of magazines.* **4** the number of copies of a book, newspaper, magazine, etc. that are sent out at a certain time: *The magazine has a circulation of 50 000.*

cir•cu•la•to•ry ['sɜrkjələˌtɔri] *adj.* having to do with circulation: *Arteries and veins are parts of the human body's circulatory system.*

circum– *prefix.* in a circle; around: *circumnavigate = navigate around*; *circumpolar = around the North or South Pole.* ⟨< L⟩

cir•cum•am•bi•ent [ˌsɜrkəm'æmbiənt] *adj.* surrounding; encircling. **—ˌcir•cum'am•bi•ence,** *n.*

cir•cum•am•bu•late [ˌsɜrkəm'æmbjəˌleit] *v.* **-lat•ed, -lat•ing. 1** walk around, especially ceremoniously. **2** talk evasively or circuitously. **—ˌcir•cumˌam•bu'la•tion,** *n.* **—ˌcir•cum'am•bu•laˌto•ry,** *adj.* **—ˌcir•cum'am•buˌla•tor,** *n.*

cir•cum•bo•re•al [ˌsɜrkəm'bɔriəl] *adj.* having to do with animals and plants of the northern regions of North America and Eurasia.

cir•cum•cen•tre ['sɜrkəmˌsɛntər] *n.* the centre of a circle that is circumscribed around another figure: *The circumcentre of a triangle is the centre of the circle circumscribed about it.*

cir•cum•cise ['sɜrkəmˌsaɪz] *v.* **-cised, -cis•ing. 1** cut off the foreskin of. **2** ceremonially cut the genitals of (a female). ⟨ME < L *circumcisus,* pp. of *circumcidere* < *circum* around + *caedere* cut⟩ **—'cir•cumˌcis•er,** *n.*

cir•cum•ci•sion [ˌsɜrkəm'sɪʒən] *or* ['sɜrkəmˌsɪʒən] *n.* the act or practice of circumcising.

cir•cum•fer•ence [sər'kʌmfərəns] *n.* **1** the boundary line of a circle. Every point on the circumference of a circle is at the same distance from the centre. See CIRCLE for picture. **2** the boundary line of any figure enclosed by a curve. **3** the distance around a circle or an object bounded by a curved surface: *The big tree had a circumference of 3 m.* ⟨< L *circumferentia* < *circum* around + *ferre* bear⟩

cir•cum•fer•en•tial [sərˌkʌmfə'rɛnʃəl] *adj.* of a circumference; located at or near the circumference.
—cirˌcum•fer'en•tial•ly, *adv.*

cir•cum•flex ['sɜrkəmˌflɛks] *n., adj.* —*n.* a mark (ˆ, ⌒, or ˜) used especially over a vowel in certain languages and phonetic spelling systems to show length, contraction, or quality. The circumflex was used originally in ancient Greek over long vowels to show a rising-falling tone. The circumflex in the French word *fête* (Old French *feste*) marks the loss of the letter *s.*
—*adj.* **1** written with a circumflex. **2** of or characterized by the quality, length, etc. shown by a circumflex. **3** *Anatomy.* bending or curving around: *a circumflex nerve.* ⟨< L *circumflexus* bent around < *circum* around + *flectere* bend⟩

circumflex accent a circumflex.

cir•cum•flu•ent [sər'kʌmfluənt] *adj.* flowing around; surrounding. Also, **circumfluous.** ⟨< L *circumfluens, -entis,* ppr. of *circumfluere* < *circum* around + *fluere* flow⟩

cir•cum•fuse [ˌsɜrkəm'fjuz] *v.* **-fused, -fus•ing. 1** pour or spread around. **2** surround; suffuse. ⟨< L *circumfusus,* pp. of *circumfundere* < *circum* around + *fundere* pour⟩
—ˌcir•cum'fu•sion, *n.*

cir•cum•lo•cu•tion [ˌsɜrkəmlə'kjuʃən] *n.* a roundabout way of speaking. *The wife of your father's brother* is a circumlocution for *Your aunt.* ⟨< L *circumlocutio, -onis* < *circum* around + *loqui* speak⟩ **—ˌcir•cum'loc•uˌto•ry** [-'lɒkjətɔri], *adj.*

cir•cum•nav•i•gate [ˌsɜrkəm'nævəˌgeit] *v.* **-gat•ed, -gat•ing.** sail completely around: *Magellan's ship circumnavigated the earth.* **—ˌcir•cum'nav•iˌga•tor,** *n.* **—ˌcir•cumˌnav•i'ga•tion,** *n.*

cir•cum•po•lar [ˌsɜrkəm'poulər] *adj.* **1** around the North or South Pole. **2** around either celestial pole.

cir•cum•ra•di•us [ˌsɜrkəm'reidiəs] *n.* the radius of a circle circumscribed around a triangle.

cir•cum•scribe [ˌsɜrkəm'skraɪb] *or* ['sɜrkəmˌskraɪb] *v.* **-scribed, -scrib•ing. 1** draw a line around; mark the boundaries of. **2** surround. **3** limit; restrict: *A prisoner's activities are circumscribed.* **4** *Geometry.* **a** draw (a figure) around another figure so as to touch as many points as possible: *A circle that is circumscribed around a square touches it at four points.* **b** be so drawn around: *A circle can circumscribe a hexagon.* **c** enclose (a solid figure) within another solid figure, as, a cube within a cylinder. ⟨< L *circumscribere* < *circum* around + *scribere* write, draw⟩ **—ˌcir•cum'scrib•er,** *n.*

cir•cum•scrip•tion [ˌsɜrkəm'skrɪpʃən] *n.* **1** a circumscribing or being circumscribed. **2** the thing that circumscribes, such as an outline or boundary or a restriction. **3** an inscription around the edge of a coin, medal, etc. **4** a space circumscribed. ⟨< L *circumscriptio, -onis* < *circumscribere.* See CIRCUMSCRIBE.⟩

cir•cum•spect ['sɜrkəmˌspɛkt] *adj.* careful; cautious; prudent. ⟨< L *circumspectus,* pp. of *circumspicere* < *circum* around + *specere* look⟩ **—'cir•cumˌspect•ly,** *adv.*
—'cir•cumˌspect•ness, *n.*

cir•cum•spec•tion [ˌsɜrkəm'spɛkʃən] *n.* care; caution; prudence.

cir•cum•stance ['sɜrkəmˌstæns] *n.* **1** a condition that contributes to or modifies an act or event: *You ought to consider all the circumstances before you judge her action.* **2** a happening; occurrence: *Her arrival on the scene was a fortunate circumstance.* **3 circumstances,** *pl.* financial condition: *in good or easy circumstances, in bad or reduced circumstances.* **4** something that is not essential; additional information; detail: *It was his success, not the circumstances of the achievement, that interested his family.* **5** all the unavoidable factors contributing to an event or situation; the sum of the direct and indirect controlling influences (*used only as a singular noun and without* **the** *or* **a**): *a victim of circumstance.* **6** ceremony; display (*used only as a singular noun and without* **a**): *The royal procession advanced with pomp and circumstance.* **7** luck; chance.
under no circumstances, never; no matter what the conditions.
under the circumstances, because of conditions; things being as they are or were. ⟨< L *circumstantia* surrounding condition < *circumstans, -antis,* ppr. of *circumstare* < *circum* around + *stare* stand⟩

cir•cum•stan•tial [,sɜrkəm'stænʃəl] *adj.* **1** depending on or based on circumstances: *circumstantial evidence.* **2** incidental; not essential; not important: *Minor details are circumstantial compared with the main facts.* **3** giving full and exact details; complete: *a circumstantial report of an accident.* **4** ceremonial. **—,cir•cum'stan•tial•ly,** *adv.*

circumstantial evidence events or facts that make certain conclusions apparent. If stolen jewels are found in a person's possession, it is circumstantial evidence that he or she stole them; if somebody saw him or her steal them, that would be direct evidence.

cir•cum•stan•ti•al•ity [,sɜrkəm,stænʃi'æləti] *n., pl.* **-ties. 1** the quality of being circumstantial. **2** detail. **3** *Psychiatry.* an excessively roundabout way of talking in details that eventually leads to the point: a symptom of some disorders.

cir•cum•stan•ti•ate [,sɜrkəm'stænʃi,eit] *v.* **-at•ed, -at•ing.** give the circumstances of; support or prove with details. **—,cir•cum,stan•ti'a•tion,** *n.*

cir•cum•vent [,sɜrkəm'vɛnt] *v.* **1** defeat or get the better of by skilful planning; outwit; frustrate: *to circumvent the law. The rebels' plans to take over the radio station were circumvented by the police.* **2** avoid by going around: *We can circumvent the heavy traffic by taking this route.* **3** *Archaic.* surround, especially with evil, hatred, malice, etc., so as to trap or ensnare. ⟨< L *circumventus*, pp. of *circumvenire* < *circum* around + *venire* come⟩ **—,cir•cum'ven•tion,** *n.* **—,cir•cum'ven•tor,** *n.* **—,cir•cum'ven•tive,** *adj.*

cir•cus ['sɜrkəs] *n.* **1** a travelling show of acrobats, clowns, horses, riders, and wild animals. **2** the performers who give the show or the performances they give. **3** the circular area where circus performances are given; ring. **4** *Informal.* an amusing person or thing. **5** *Informal.* a lively but disorderly time or place: *Our place was a circus that last night, as we were trying to get organized for the trip.* **6** in ancient Rome, a round or oval open-air stadium with tiers of seats around it, used for chariot races, etc. **7** *Brit.* a more or less circular open area at an intersection of several streets (*used especially in place names*): *Piccadilly Circus.* ⟨< L *circus* ring. Doublet of CIRQUE.⟩
☛ *Hom.* CERCUS.

Circus Max•i•mus ['mæksəməs] in ancient Rome, a huge amphitheatre.

ci•ré [si'rei] *adj.* having a smooth, glossy surface as if waxed. ⟨< F waxed, pp. of *cirer* to wax < *cire* wax⟩

cirque [sɜrk] *n.* **1** a circular space. **2** *Poetic.* a circlet; ring. **3** *Geology.* a steep-sided mountain rock basin, or hollow, formed by glacial erosion and often containing a small lake or glacier. ⟨< F *cirque* < L *circus.* Doublet of CIRCUS.⟩

cir•rho•sis [sə'rousɪs] *n.* a chronic progressive disease of the liver characterized by the death of liver cells and excessive formation of connective tissue followed by contraction of the organ. ⟨< NL < Gk. *kirrhos* orange yellow⟩ **—cir'rhot•ic** [-'rɒtɪk], *adj.*

cir•ri•ped ['sirə,pɛd] *n.* any of a subclass (Cirripedia) of marine crustaceans, such as barnacles, that have threadlike appendages instead of legs. As adults, cirripeds are parasitic or permanently attached to a surface. ⟨< NL *Cirripeda* < L *cirrus* curl + *pes, pedis* foot⟩

cir•ro•cu•mu•lus [,sirou'kjumjələs] *n.* a cloud made up of rows or groups of small, fleecy clouds. ⟨< *cirrus* + *cumulus*⟩

cir•ro•stra•tus [,sirou'streitəs] *or* [-'strætəs] *n.* a thin, veil-like cloud high in the air. ⟨< *cirrus* + *stratus*⟩

cir•rus ['sirəs] *n., pl.* **cir•ri** ['siraɪ] *or* ['siri]. **1** a thin, curling, wispy cloud very high in the air. **2** the tendril of a plant. **3** the antenna or other thin appendage of an insect. ⟨< L *cirrus* curl⟩

cis– prefix. **1** on this side of; on the near side of. **2** *Chemistry.* of an isomer, having two atoms or groups on one side of a given plane in the molecule. ⟨< L⟩

CIS COMMONWEALTH OF INDEPENDENT STATES.

cis•al•pine [sɪs'ælpaɪn] *or* [sɪs'ælpɪn] *adj.* on the southern side of the Alps.

cis•at•lan•tic [,sɪsæt'læntɪk] *adj.* on this (the speaker's or writer's) side of the Atlantic Ocean.

cis•co ['sɪskou] *n., pl.* **-coes** *or* **-cos.** any of various whitefishes (genus *Coregonus*) found throughout the lakes of Canada and the NE United States. Some ciscoes are valuable food fish. ⟨< Cdn.F *ciscoette* < ? Algonquian⟩

cis•lu•nar [sɪs'lunər] *adj.* in the moon's vicinity.

cis•mon•tane [,sɪsmɒn'tein] *or* [sɪs'mɒntein] *adj.* on this (the speaker's or writer's) side of the mountains, especially the Alps.

cis•plat•in [sɪs'plætɪn] *n.* a drug used to treat certain forms of cancer. *Formula*: $PtCl_2H_6N_2$ ⟨< *cis-* + *platin(um)*⟩

cis•soid ['sɪsɔɪd] *n., adj. Geometry.* —*n.* a curve with two branches forming a cusp at the point of origin.
—*adj.* of an angle, formed by the concave sides of two intersecting curves. ⟨< Gk. *kissoeides* ivy-shaped < *kissos* ivy⟩

Cis•ter•cian [sɪ'stɜrʃən] *n., adj.* —*n. Roman Catholic Church.* a monk or nun of a very strict order founded in France in 1098 as an offshoot of the Benedictines.
—*adj.* of or having to do with this order. ⟨< Med.L *Cistercium* Citeaux, where the order was founded⟩

cis•tern ['sɪstərn] *n.* **1** a large artificial reservoir, especially a tank, usually underground, for storing rainwater. **2** the tank holding water at the back of, or above, a toilet. **3** *Anatomy.* a cavity or space holding a bodily fluid. ⟨< L *cisterna* < *cista* box⟩

cis•tron ['sɪstrɒn] *n. Genetics.* the smallest unit of DNA capable of forming a polypeptide chain; gene. ⟨< *cis-tr*(ans), after a test defining the unit as either cis or trans⟩

cis•tus ['sɪstəs] *n.* a plant of the genus *Cistus* of the rockrose family, having roselike white or purple flowers. ⟨< NL < Gk. *kistos* rockrose⟩

cit. **1** citation; cited. **2** citizen.

cit•a•del ['sɪtədəl] *or* ['sɪtə,dɛl] *n.* **1** a fortress commanding a city. **2** a strongly fortified place; stronghold. **3** a strong, safe place; refuge. ⟨< F *citadelle* < Ital. *cittadella*, dim. of *città* city⟩

ci•ta•tion [səi'teiʃən] *n.* **1** a quotation or reference given as an authority for facts, opinions, etc. **2** the act of citing. **3** a specific mention in an official dispatch. **4** an honourable mention for bravery in war. **5** the official commendation of a civilian for public service. **6** a summons to appear before a court of law: *a traffic citation for a speeding violation.*

cite [səit] *v.* **cit•ed, cit•ing. 1** refer to (a passage, book, or author), especially as an authority: *He cited the Bible and Shakespeare to prove his statement.* **2** refer to; mention as an example: *The lawyer cited another case similar to the one being tried.* **3** mention for bravery in war. **4** mention publicly in recognition of and praise for outstanding service to humanity, one's country, etc. **5** summon to appear before a court of law. **6** *Archaic.* arouse to action; summon. ⟨< F *citer* < L *citare* summon < *ciere* set in motion⟩ **—'cite•a•ble** or **'cit•a•ble,** *adj.*
☛ *Hom.* SIGHT, SITE.
☛ *Syn.* **1.** See note at QUOTE.

cith•a•ra ['sɪθərə] *n.* an ancient musical instrument resembling a lyre. Also, **cither.** ⟨< L < Gk. *kithara.* Doublet of GUITAR and ZITHER.⟩

cith•ern ['sɪθərn] *n.* cittern.

cit•i•fied ['sɪtɪ,faɪd] *adj. Informal.* having city ways or fashions.

cit•i•fy ['sɪtə,faɪ] *v.* **-fied, -fy•ing.** cause to conform to an urban way of life. **—,cit•i•fi'ca•tion,** *n.*

cit•i•zen ['sɪtəzən] *or* ['sɪtəsən] *n.* **1** a person who by birth or by choice (i.e., naturalization) is a member of a nation or state, thereby owing allegiance to it and in turn being entitled to protection and the enjoyment of certain rights. **2** a civilian, as distinguished from a member of the armed forces, police, etc. **3** an inhabitant of a city or town; resident. ⟨ME < AF *citisein* < OF *cite.* See CITY.⟩

citizen of the world a person who is interested in the affairs of the whole world; cosmopolitan.

cit•i•zen•ry ['sɪtəzənri] *or* ['sɪtəsənri] *n., pl.* **-ries.** citizens as a group.

citizen's arrest an arrest of a criminal made by an ordinary member of the public, not a police officer.

citizens' band a range of radio frequencies reserved for use by the public. See also GENERAL RADIO SERVICE. *Abbrev.*: CB

cit•i•zen•ship ['sɪtəzən,ʃɪp] *or* ['sɪtəsən,ʃɪp] *n.* **1** the condition of being a citizen: *She has Canadian citizenship but her husband doesn't.* **2** the duties, rights, and privileges of a citizen.

cit•ral ['sɪtrəl] *n.* a yellow liquid aldehyde which smells like lemons, obtained from lemons or oranges, or made synthetically, and used to make perfumes and artificial flavourings. *Formula*: $C_{10}H_{16}O$. ⟨< *citric* + *al(dehyde)*⟩

cit•rate ['sɪtreit] *n.* a salt or ester of citric acid.

cit•re•ous ['sɪtriəs] *adj.* yellow like a lemon.

cit•ric ['sɪtrɪk] *adj.* of or from citrus fruits.

citric acid a white, odourless, sour-tasting acid that occurs in such fruits as lemons, limes, etc. It is used as a flavouring, as a medicine, and in making dyes. *Formula*: $C_6H_8O_7$

cit•ri•cul•ture ['sɪtrə,kʌltʃər] *n.* the growing of citrus fruits as a crop.

cit•rine ['sɪtrɪn] *or* ['sɪtrin] *n., adj. —n.* **1** pale yellow like a lemon. **2** a yellow kind of quartz like a topaz.
—adj. pale yellow. ⟨< F *citrin* < L *citrus* citrus tree⟩

cit•ron ['sɪtrən] *n.* **1** a pale yellow citrus fruit resembling a lemon but larger, less acid, and with a thicker rind. **2** the tree (*Citrus medica*) that this fruit grows on. **3** a small, round variety of watermelon (*Citrullus vulgaris citroides*) generally considered inedible except for its rind, which is used in preserves. Also called **citron melon**. **4** the preserved or candied rind of either of these fruits. ⟨< F < Ital. *citrone* < L *citrus* citrus tree⟩

cit•ron•el•la [,sɪtrə'nɛlə] *n.* **1** an oil used in making perfume, soap, liniment, etc., and for keeping mosquitoes away. **2** the fragrant tropical grass (*Cymbopogon nardus*) that yields this oil. ⟨< NL; from its citronlike smell⟩

cit•ron•el•lal [,sɪtrə'nɛlæl] *n.* a colourless liquid smelling of lemons, obtained from citrus fruits and used to make perfumes and artificial flavourings. *Formula*: $C_{10}H_{18}O$

citron melon CITRON (def. 3).

cit•rous ['sɪtrəs] *adj.* having to do with fruits such as lemons, limes, oranges, etc.
☛ *Hom.* CITRUS.

cit•rus ['sɪtrəs] *n.* **1** any of a genus (*Citrus*) of trees or shrubs of the rue family grown in warm regions, bearing sweet or tart, edible fruit. **2** (*adjl.*) of or designating this genus or the fruits borne by these trees or shrubs: *Oranges, lemons, limes, grapefruit, and citrons are citrus fruits.* ⟨< L⟩
☛ *Hom.* CITROUS.

citrus fruit the fruit of a citrus tree: *Oranges, lemons, limes, grapefruit, and citrons are citrus fruits.*

cit•tern ['sɪtərn] *n.* a musical instrument resembling a guitar, popular in the 16th and 17th centuries. Also, **cithern.** ⟨blend of L *cithara* cithara and E *gittern*⟩

cit•y ['sɪti] *n., pl.* **cit•ies. 1** a large and important town. **2** in Canada, an incorporated community with fixed boundaries that has been granted status as a city by its provincial government, usually having more financial and social responsibilities and more sources of revenue than a town. A city is the largest urban municipal unit and in most provinces must have a minimum population of several thousand. **3** in the United Kingdom, a town or district that has a royal charter for the title of city and is usually a cathedral town. **4** in the United States, a municipality, usually with a large population, having a charter granted by the state. **5** the people living in a city. **6** the government of a city: *The city has decided to make more land available for parks.* **7** a city-state. **8 the City,** in London, England, the business and financial district. **9** (*adjl.*) of, having to do with, or in a city: *city politics. I hate city driving.* ⟨ME < OF < L *civitas* citizenship, state, city < *civis* citizen⟩

city chicken breaded cubes of veal or pork, skewered and then baked or pan-fried.

City Council the administrative body of a city.

city councillor a municipal politician at the city level.

city editor 1 the newspaper editor in charge of collecting and editing local news. **2** *Brit.* business or financial editor.

city fathers or **mothers** the councillors, magistrates, or other leading citizens of a city.

city hall 1 the headquarters of the local government in a city: *The mayor's office is in the city hall.* **2** a building housing a local government. **3** the officials of a municipal government, considered collectively. **4** petty bureaucracy: *fight city hall.*

city manager a person appointed by a city council or commission to manage the government of a city.

city of David 1 Jerusalem. **2** Bethlehem.

City of God heaven.

City of Seven Hills Rome.

cit•y•scape ['sɪti,skeip] *n.* **1** the visual aspects of a city; the buildings, streets, parks, etc. of a city viewed as scenery. **2** a photograph, painting, etc. of a city or part of a city. **3** a view of a city from the air, the water, or a high building, showing buildings seen against the horizon.

city slicker *Slang.* a city dweller who is looked on with scorn or suspicion by rural people because of the way he or she dresses and behaves.

city–state ['sɪti ,steit] *n.* an independent state consisting of a city and the territories depending on it, as in ancient Greece and Renaissance Italy.

ci•ty•wide ['sɪti'waɪd] *adj. or adv.* throughout the city.

civ•et ['sɪvɪt] *n.* **1** a fatty, yellowish, musky-smelling fluid secreted by civet cats, used as a fixative in perfumes. It can be removed from captive animals every two or three weeks. **2** CIVET CAT. **3** the fur of a civet cat. ⟨< F *civette* < Ital. < Arabic *zabad*⟩

civet cat any of various catlike, carnivorous mammals (family Viverridae) of the Old World having anal glands that secrete civet, a fatty fluid with a powerful, musky smell.

civ•ic ['sɪvɪk] *adj.* **1** of a city. **2** of or having to do with citizenship: *Every person has some civic duties, such as obeying the law, voting, or paying taxes.* **3** of citizens. ⟨< L *civicus* < *civis* citizen⟩ **—'civ•i•cal•ly,** *adv.*

civic centre 1 the headquarters of a municipal government. **2** a building serving as a centre for community activities, concerts, games, etc.

civ•ics ['sɪvɪks] *n.* the study of the duties, rights, and privileges of citizens.

civ•ies ['sɪviz] See CIVVIES.

civ•il ['sɪvəl] *adj.* **1** of or having to do with a citizen or citizens. **2** of or having to do with the government, state, or nation: *civil servants.* **3** not connected with the armed forces or the church: *a civil court, a civil marriage.* **4** polite; courteous: *The girl answered our questions in a very civil way.* **5** having to do with the private rights of individuals or with legal proceedings connected with these rights: *a civil lawsuit.* **6** such as occurs among citizens of one community, state, or nation: *civil war, civil strife.* **7** of, belonging to, or based on Roman civil law, or civil law derived from it. ⟨< L *civilis* < *civis* citizen⟩ **—'civ•il•ly,** *adv.*
☛ *Syn.* **4.** See note at POLITE.

civil defence a program of procedures and planned action for civilian volunteers to cope with a general emergency, such as enemy attack or a major natural disaster.

civil disobedience refusal because of one's principles to obey the law, especially by not paying taxes.

civil engineer a person trained in civil engineering, especially one whose work it is.

civil engineering the planning and directing of the construction of bridges, roads, harbours, etc.

ci•vil•ian [sə'vɪljən] *n., adj. —n.* a person who is not in the armed forces or the police.
—adj. of civilians; not of the armed forces or the police: *Soldiers often wear civilian clothes when on leave.*

ci•vil•i•ty [sə'vɪləti] *n., pl.* **-ties. 1** politeness; courtesy. **2** an act or remark of politeness or courtesy.

civ•i•li•za•tion [,sɪvələ'zeiʃən] *or* [,sɪvəlaɪ'zeiʃən] *n.* **1** a civilized condition; an advanced stage of social and political organization. **2** the nations and peoples thought of as having reached an advanced stage of social and political organization. **3** a civilizing or being civilized. **4** the total culture of a nation or people at a given time: *Inuit civilization, 19th-century Canadian civilization.* **5** modern comforts, as found in a town or city: *After the ten-day canoe trip in Algonquin Park, it was nice to get back to civilization.* **6** populated area: *to reach the edge of civilization.*

civ•i•lize ['sɪvə,laɪz] *v.* **-lized, -liz•ing. 1** change (a so-called primitive social and political system) to a much more complex one that includes knowledge of the arts and sciences: *The Romans civilized a great part of their world.* **2** improve (someone) in culture and good manners; refine: *They were given the job of trying to civilize their niece.* ⟨< Med.L *civilizare* < L *civilis.* See CIVIL.⟩ **—'civ•i,liz•er,** *n.*

civ•i•lized ['sɪvə,laɪzd] *adj., v. —adj.* **1** having a complex social and political system. **2** of nations or persons so advanced: *civilized entertainments.* **3** showing culture and good manners; refined.
—v. pt. and pp. of CIVILIZE.

civ•i•liz•ing ['sɪvə,laɪzɪŋ] *adj., v. —adj.* that civilizes; promoting civilization.
—v. ppr. of CIVILIZE.

civil law 1 the body of law that regulates and protects private rights and is controlled and used by civil (not military) courts: opposed to CRIMINAL LAW and MILITARY LAW. **2** the legal system of a particular country. **3** Roman law or a system of law based on Roman law.
☛ *Usage.* See note at MILITARY LAW.

civil liberty the right of a person to do, think, and say what he or she pleases as long as he or she does not harm anyone else or break established laws.

civil list 1 a list of sums appropriated to pay the members of the civil government and civil servants (obsolete in Canada). 2 in the United Kingdom, a list of sums appropriated by Parliament as allowances for the sovereign and members of the royal family.

civil marriage a marriage performed by a government official, rather than by a member of the clergy.

civil rights the constitutional rights of every citizen to vote, to be a free worker, and to have equal treatment and the protection of the law.

civil servant a member of the civil service. A cabinet minister has a staff of civil servants. A deputy minister is a civil servant.

civil service 1 the service responsible for the day-to-day administrative work of the various departments of the government of a country, province, etc., such as the collection of taxes and issuing of pensions. 2 the body of officials, clerks, etc., who do this work. The civil service is not usually affected by changes of government.

civil war 1 a war between two groups of citizens of one nation. 2 **Civil War, a** in England, the war between the king and Parliament, 1642-1646 and 1648-1652. **b** in the United States, the war between the northern and southern states, 1861-1865.

civil year CALENDAR YEAR.

civ•vies ['sɪviz] *n.pl. Informal.* civilian clothes, as distinguished from military (or, sometimes, other) uniform. Also, **civies.**

ck. cask.

cl. 1 class. 2 clause. 3 clerk. 4 a member of the clergy.

Cl chlorine.

clab•ber ['klæbər] *n., v. —n.* thick, sour milk.
—v. become thick in souring; curdle. ⟨< Irish *clabar* curds, short for *bainne clabair* bonnyclabber (curdled milk)⟩

clack [klæk] *v., n. —v.* 1 make or cause to make a short, sharp, rather loud sound: *typewriter keys clacking against the paper.* 2 chatter.
—n. 1 a short, sharp, rather loud sound: *We heard the clack of her heels on the sidewalk.* 2 something that makes a short, sharp sound. 3 chatter. ⟨imitative⟩ **—'clack•er,** *n.*

Clac•to•ni•an [klæk'touniən] *adj.* of or having to do with a Lower Paleolithic culture, characterized by making tools by flaking. ⟨after *Clacton*-on-Sea, England, where flaked tools were found⟩

clad[1] [klæd] *v.* a pt. and a pp. of CLOTHE.

clad[2] [klæd] *v.* **clad, clad•ding.** sheathe or face (a surface, metal, etc.) with a protective coating, etc.: *Aluminum pots are sometimes clad with copper for better heat distribution.* ⟨OE *clæthan* clothe, now obsolete in that sense⟩

clad•ding ['klædɪŋ] *n., v. —n.* 1 material used for facing the outside walls of a building, etc.: *aluminum cladding for a house.* 2 a layer or coating of metal bonded to another metal, as for protection of the metal underneath. 3 the process of applying cladding.
—v. ppr. of CLAD[2]. ⟨See CLAD[2]⟩

cla•dis•tics [klə'dɪstɪks] *n.* the theory that classifies biological organisms into **clades** according to shared characteristics believed to indicate descent from a common ancestor. ⟨< NL < Gk. *klados* a branch, shoot⟩ **—cla'dis•tic,** *adj.* **—'cla•dism** ['kleidɪzəm], *n.*

clad•o•phyll ['klædə,fɪl] *n.* a branch or stem resembling and functioning as a leaf. Also called **cladode.** ⟨< Gk. *klados* branch + *phyllon* leaf⟩

claim [kleim] *v., n. —v.* 1 say that one has and demand that others recognize (a right, title, possession, etc.); assert one's right to: *to claim a tract of land.* 2 demand as one's own or one's right: *Does anyone claim this pencil?* 3 declare as a fact; say strongly; maintain: *She claimed that her answer was correct.* 4 require; call for; deserve: *Business claims his attention.*
—n. 1 a demand for something due; assertion of a right. 2 a right or title to something. 3 something that is claimed. 4 a piece of public land that a settler or prospector marks out for himself or herself. When the government offers the land for sale, the settler must buy his or her claim or forfeit it. 5 the assertion of something as a fact.
jump a claim, illegally seize a piece of land that has been staked for mining by another but not yet formally recorded.
lay claim to, declare (one's) right to; assert (one's) ownership of; claim: *Since nobody laid claim to the video, we took it home.*
put in a or (one's) **claim for,** ask for as a right; claim: *I'm putting in my claim right now for my share of the saskatoons we picked.*
stake (out) a claim, a claim an area of land for mining rights by setting out stakes to mark its boundaries: *After staking out a claim, a person must record it at the proper government office within a certain length of time to make it permanent.* **b** claim anything, especially space, for one's own: *The new house has four bedrooms; the kids have already staked their claims.* ⟨ME < OF *claim(e)* < *clamer*, v. < L *clamare* call, proclaim⟩ **—'claim•a•ble,** *adj.* **—'claim•er,** *n.*
☛ *Syn. v.* 2. See note at DEMAND.

claim•ant ['kleimənt] *n.* one who makes a claim.

claiming race a horserace in which the horses are for sale at a price fixed before the race.

clair•au•di•ence [klɛr'ɒdiəns] *n.* the ability to perceive sounds that are out of hearing. Compare CLAIRVOYANCE.

cláirsach ['klɑrsæx] *n., pl.* **cláirseach** ['klɑrsæx] the ancient festival harp of Ireland and Scotland, having from 29 to 58 strings. ⟨< Gaelic⟩

clair•voy•ance [klɛr'vɔiəns] *n.* 1 the power of knowing about things that are out of sight. Compare CLAIRAUDIENCE. 2 exceptional insight. ⟨< F⟩

clair•voy•ant [klɛr'vɔiənt] *adj., v. —adj.* 1 having the power of seeing things that are out of sight. 2 having exceptionally keen insight.
—n. a person who has, or claims to have, the power of seeing things that are out of sight: *The clairvoyant claimed to be able to locate lost articles, and to give news of faraway people.* ⟨< F *clairvoyant* clear-sighted < *clair* clear + *voyant*, ppr. of *voir* see⟩ **—clair'voy•ant•ly,** *adv.*

clam [klæm] *n., v.* **clammed, clam•ming.** *—n.* 1 any of various bivalve molluscs having a shell closed by two muscles at opposite ends, and a powerful, muscular foot with which they burrow into sand or mud. Some clams, such as the quahog and soft-shell clam, are edible. 2 the fleshy part of such a mollusc, eaten raw or cooked. 3 *Informal.* a person who speaks very little.
—v. go out after clams; dig for clams.
clam up, *Slang.* refuse to speak or give information. ⟨apparently special use of *clam* pair of pincers; OE *clamm* fetter⟩ **—'clam,like,** *adj.*

clam•bake ['klæm,beik] *n.* 1 a picnic where clams are baked or steamed. A clambake may be an elaborate meal, with much to eat besides clams. 2 the food served at a clambake. 3 *Informal.* a large, noisy entertainment or social gathering.

clam•ber ['klæmbər] *v., n. —v.* 1 climb, using both hands and feet; climb awkwardly or with difficulty; scramble. 2 of plants, climb by means of tendrils, etc.
—n. an awkward or difficult climb. ⟨ME *clambre(n)*. Related to CLIMB.⟩ **—'clam•ber•er,** *n.*

clam•my ['klæmi] *adj.* **-mi•er, -mi•est.** unpleasantly cold and damp. ⟨ME; probably < *clammen* smear < OE *clæman*; cf. OE *clām* clay⟩ **—'clam•mi•ness,** *n.* **—'clam•mi•ly,** *adv.*

clamor ['klæmər] See CLAMOUR.

clam•or•ous ['klæmərəs] *adj.* 1 noisy; shouting. 2 making noisy demands or complaints. **—'clam•or•ous•ly,** *adv.* **—'clam•or•ous•ness,** *n.*

clam•our or **clam•or** ['klæmər] *n., v. —n.* 1 a loud, continual uproar; shouting. 2 a noisy demand or complaint. 3 any loud, sustained noise.
—v. 1 make a loud noise or continual uproar; shout. 2 demand or complain noisily.
clamour or **clamor for,** demand noisily: *The children were clamouring for candy.* ⟨ME < OF < L *clamour* < *clamare* cry out⟩ **—'clam•our•er** or **'clam•or•er,** *n.*

clamp [klæmp] *n., v. —n.* any of various mechanical devices for binding or pressing two or more things firmly together.
—v. 1 put in a clamp or fasten together or strengthen with a clamp. 2 impose: *to clamp a tax on imports.*
clamp down on, *Informal.* put pressure on; take strict measures against: *The police clamped down on speeding.* ⟨< MDu. *klampe*⟩

clamp•down ['klæmp,daʊn] *n.* crackdown; repression; censorship.

clams casino clams broiled in their bottom shell with a topping of bread crumbs, bacon, garlic, and butter.

clam•shell ['klæm,ʃɛl] *n.* 1 the shell of a clam. 2 a bucket, box, or the like, hinged like a clamshell, used in dredging and loading.

clan [klæn] *n.* **1** especially in Scotland, a group of related families that claim to be descended from a common ancestor. **2** a group of people closely joined together by some common interest. **3** any extended family: *We're having the clan over for Thanksgiving.* ⟨< Scots Gaelic *clann* family⟩ **—'clan,like,** *adj.*

clan•des•tine [klæn'dɛstən] *adj.* secret; concealed; underhand: *a clandestine plan.* ⟨< L *clandestinus* < *clam* secretly⟩ **—clan'des•tine•ly,** *adv.* **—clan'des•tine•ness,** *n.*
☛ *Syn.* See note at SECRET.

clang [klæŋ] *n., v.* *—n.* a loud, harsh, resonant sound such as that caused by metal striking metal: *The clang of the fire alarm aroused the town.*
—v. **1** make or cause to make such a sound. **2** strike together with a clang. **3** move with a clang: *The firetruck clanged along the road.* ⟨imitative⟩

clang•er ['klæŋər] *n. Informal.* a bad or blatant mistake.
☛ *Hom.* CLANGOUR.

clangor ['klæŋər] *or* ['klæŋgər] *n.* See CLANGOUR.

clan•gor•ous ['klæŋərəs] *or* ['klæŋgərəs] *adj.* clanging.

clan•gour or **clang•or** ['klæŋər] *or* ['klæŋgər] *n.* a loud clang or continued clanging: *the clangour of many bells.* ⟨< L *clangor* < *clangere* clang⟩
☛ *Hom.* CLANGER ['klæŋər].

clank [klæŋk] *n., v.* *—n.* a sharp, harsh sound like the rattle of a heavy chain.
—v. **1** make a sharp, harsh sound: *The swords clashed and clanked as the men fought one another.* **2** cause to clank. **3** move with a clanking sound. ⟨imitative; probably < Du. *klank*⟩

clan•nish ['klænɪʃ] *adj.* **1** of or having to do with a clan. **2** closely united and not liking outsiders. **—'clan•nish•ly,** *adv.* **—'clan•nish•ness,** *n.*

clans•man ['klænzmən] *n., pl.* **-men.** a member of a clan.

clans•wom•an ['klænz,wʊmən] *n., pl.* **-wom•en.** a female member of a clan.

clap [klæp] *n., v.* **clapped, clap•ping.** *—n.* **1** a sudden, loud noise, such as a single burst of thunder, the sound of the hands struck together, or the sound of a loud slap. **2** the act of clapping the hands: *They gave the speaker a polite clap.* **3** a hit or blow; slap: *a clap on the shoulder.*
—v. **1** strike together loudly: *to clap one's hands.* **2** applaud by striking the hands together. **3** strike lightly with a quick blow: *to clap someone on the back.* **4** put or place quickly and effectively: *The police clapped the thief into jail.* **5** of a bird, flap (the wings).
clap eyes on, *Informal.* look at; see: *I liked her from the first time I clapped eyes on her.* ⟨OE *clæppan*⟩

clap•board ['klæp,bɔrd] *or* ['klæbərd] *n., v.* *—n.* **1** one of a series of thin boards, thicker along one edge than along the other, used overlappingly to cover the outer walls of wooden buildings. **2** these boards collectively: *I like clapboard for siding.* **3** (*adjl.*) covered with clapboard: *Maritime towns are full of clapboard houses.*
—v. cover with clapboards.

clap•per ['klæpər] *n.* **1** a person who or thing that claps. **2** the movable part inside a bell that strikes and rings the outer part. **3** a device for making a striking noise: *We had horns and clappers at the party.*

clap•trap ['klæp,træp] *n., adj.* *—n.* empty talk aimed merely at getting attention or applause.
—adj. cheap and showy.

claque [klæk] *n.* **1** a group of persons hired to applaud in a theatre. **2** a group that applauds or follows another person for selfish reasons. ⟨< F *claque* < *claquer* clap⟩

clar•et ['klærət], ['klɛrət], *or* [klɑ'rei] *n., adj.* *—n.* **1** a kind of dry, red table wine, originally one made in Bordeaux, France. **2** a dark, purplish red.
—adj. dark purplish red. ⟨ME < OF *claret* light-coloured, dim. of *cler.* See CLEAR.⟩

claret cup an iced drink composed of claret, soda water, lemon juice, and brandy.

clar•i•fi•ca•tion [,klærəfə'keiʃən] *or* [,klɛrəfə'keiʃən] *n.* **1** the act, means, or process of clarifying. **2** the state of being clarified.

clar•i•fi•er ['klærə,faɪər] *or* ['klɛrə,faɪər] *n.* **1** a substance used to clarify liquids. **2** a large metal pan used in clarifying sugar.

clar•i•fy ['klærə,faɪ] *or* ['klɛrə,faɪ] *v.* **-fied, -fy•ing. 1** make or become free of impurities; purify: *We clarified the cloudy liquid by using a filter.* **2** make clear to the understanding; explain: *The news reporter asked her to clarify her statement for the public.* ⟨ME < OF *clarifier* < LL *clarificare* < L *clarus* clear + *facere* make⟩

clar•i•net [,klærə'nɛt] *or* [,klɛrə'nɛt] *n.* a wind instrument consisting of a straight metal or wooden tube ending in a slightly flared bell, having a single reed and played by means of holes and keys. ⟨< F *clarinette* < Ital. *clarinetto* < *clarino* trumpet, ult. < L *clarus* clear⟩

A clarinet

clar•i•net•tist or **clar•i•net•ist** [,klærə'nɛtɪst] *or* [,klɛrə'nɛtɪst] *n.* a person who plays a clarinet, especially a skilled player.

clar•i•on ['klæriən] *or* ['klɛriən] *adj., n.* *—adj.* clear and sharp.
—n. **1** an ancient trumpet with clear, sharp tones. **2** *Poetic.* the sound made by this trumpet. **3** *Poetic.* a clear, sharp sound like it. ⟨< Med.L *clario, -onis* < L *clarus* clear⟩

clar•i•o•net [,klæriə'nɛt] *or* [,klɛriə'nɛt] *n. Archaic.* clarinet.

clar•i•ty ['klærəti] *or* ['klɛrəti] *n.* clearness. ⟨< L *claritas*⟩

clar•kia ['klɑrkiə] *n.* an annual wildflower of the evening-primrose family, popular in flower gardens for its bright colours. ⟨< NL after W. *Clark* (1770-1838), American soldier and explorer⟩

cla•ry ['klæri] *or* ['klɛri] *n.* **1** any plant of the genus *Salvia* of the mint family. **2** a plant (*Salvia sclarea*) grown as a herb.

clash [klæʃ] *v., n.* *—v.* **1** make or cause to make a loud, harsh, discordant sound like that of two hard things running into each other, or of metal striking metal, or of bells rung together but not in harmony. **2** throw, shut, etc., with such a sound. **3** come into or be in conflict: *The two armies clashed. Your feeling and your judgment sometimes clash.* **4** of colours, fail to harmonize.
—n. **1** a loud, harsh, discordant sound. **2** strong disagreement or conflict: *a clash of opinions.* ⟨imitative⟩ **—'clash•er,** *n.* **—'clash•ing•ly,** *adv.*

clasp [klæsp] *n., v.* *—n.* **1** a device, usually having a hook of some kind, to fasten two parts or pieces together: *This suede belt has a gold clasp.* **2** a close hold with the arms or hands. **3** a firm grip with the hand: *She gave my hand a warm clasp.* **4** a small bar of metal placed across the ribbon of a military medal, indicating the battle area, etc. in which the medal was won.
—v. **1** fasten together with a clasp. **2** hold closely with the arms or hands: *The mother clasped her baby to her breast.* **3** grip firmly with the hand. ⟨ME *claspe(n)*⟩ **—'clasp•er,** *n.*

clasp knife a knife with a blade or blades folding into the handle, especially one with a clasp to hold each blade open.

class [klæs] *n., adj., v.* *—n.* **1** a group of persons or things alike in some way; kind; sort. **2** a group of students taught together. **3** the meeting of such a group: *The class was at nine o'clock.* **4** a group of students starting school together and graduating in the same year: *The class of 1996 graduated in 1996.* **5** a rank or division of society: *the middle class.* **6** a system of ranks or divisions in society. **7** *U.S.* a group of military draftees of the same age. **8** high rank in society. **9** grade; quality: *First class is the best and most costly way to travel.* **10** *Informal.* elegance or style. **11** *Biology.* a major category in the classification of plants and animals, more specific than the phylum (or division) and more general than the order. See classification chart in the Appendix.
in a class by itself/oneself, superior to all others; unique.
—adj. Informal. of excellent quality; showing elegance and style: *a class act.*
—v. put or be in a class or group. ⟨< L *classis* class, fleet < dial. Gk. *klasis* a calling, summoning⟩

class. **1** classical. **2** classified.

class action a legal action brought on behalf of all the people in a group directly affected by a case.

class•book ['klæs,bʊk] *n.* **1** a book in which a teacher records the absences and keeps the grades of students. **2** an annual book usually published by the graduating class of a high school or college. It contains pictures of the students, teachers, school buildings, etc.

class–con•scious ['klæs 'kɒnʃəs] *adj.* very aware of one's status as a member of a particular social or economic class. **—'class-'con•scious•ness,** *n.*

clas•sic ['klæsɪk] *adj., n. —adj.* **1** of the highest rank or quality; serving as an example of excellence for its kind: *a classic example of clear, attractive handwriting, the classic 1937 Ford. The golf champion has a classic swing.* **2** having to do with the literature and art of ancient Greece and Rome; classical. **3** of or according to established principles of quality in the arts and sciences; elegantly simple, regular, and restrained: *the classic style of Bach's music. We admired the classic lines of the new bridge.* **4** established in literature, art, or history as a model or outstanding example: *the classic smile of the Mona Lisa, Coco Chanel's classic suit.*
—n. **1** a work of literature or art long considered to be of the highest quality: The Tin Flute *is a classic.* **2** an author or artist of acknowledged excellence whose works serve as a standard, model, or guide: *Shakespeare is a classic.* **3** a famous traditional event: *The Kentucky Derby is a classic.* **4** something considered as a typical or outstanding example of its type. **5** something simple in style and likely to remain in fashion for a long time. **6** a car made between 1925 and 1942. **7 the classics,** the literature of ancient Greece and Rome. ⟨< L *classicus* < *classis.* See CLASS.⟩

clas•si•cal ['klæsəkəl] *adj.* **1** of, having to do with, or designating ancient Greece and Rome, especially with respect to their art and literature: *classical studies.* **2** knowledgeable about ancient Greece and Rome, especially their languages, art and literature: *a classical scholar.* **3** modelled on or resembling this literature and art: Ulysses *is a classical poem by Tennyson.* **4** orthodox and sound, but not new or up to date: *classical physics.* **5** of or designating any music composed in the European tradition of written music as developed from early Christian church music, especially works composed during the last 300 years or so: *She prefers classical music to popular or folk music.* **6 Classical,** *Music.* of, having to do with, or designating the music of 18th century European composers such as Mozart and Haydn, as distinct from the Romantic music of composers like Beethoven and Tchaikovsky. **—'clas•si•cal•ly,** *adv.*

classical college *Cdn.* in French Canada, an educational establishment at the secondary-school and college levels that offers an eight-year course, mainly in the classics and liberal arts, leading to the B.A. degree which is conferred by the university with which the college is affiliated.

clas•si•cism ['klæsə,sɪzəm] *n.* **1** the principles of the literature and art of ancient Greece and Rome. They include simplicity, regularity, and restraint. **2** the following of these principles. **3** knowledge of the languages and literature of ancient Greece and Rome; classical scholarship. **4** an idiom or form from Greek or Latin introduced into another language. **5** a style of music, art, literature, etc. developed in Europe during the latter half of the 18th century, characterized by simplicity, dignity, proportion, and elegance.

clas•si•cist ['klæsəsɪst] *n.* **1** a follower of the principles of classicism in literature, music, and art. **2** an expert in the languages and literature of ancient Greece and Rome. **3** a person who urges the study of Greek and Latin.

clas•si•co ['klæsɪ,kou] *adj.* made of grapes from a particular Italian region known for its high-quality wine: *Orvieto classico.*

clas•si•fi•ca•tion [,klæsəfə'keiʃən] *n.* **1** an arranging in classes or groups on the basis of similar qualities or features; act of grouping according to some system. **2** the arrangement or grouping so made: *This library has worked out a simple classification for its books.* **3** *Biology.* the arranging of plants and animals in groups according to shared characteristics such as body structure. See biological classification chart in the Appendix. **—'class•i•fi•ca,to•ry,** *adj.*

clas•si•fied ['klæsə,faɪd] *adj., n., v. —adj.* **1** of government documents, having a classification as secret, confidential, or restricted. **2** *Informal.* secret.
—n. **classifieds,** *pl.* CLASSIFIED ADVERTISEMENTS.
—v. pt. and pp. of CLASSIFY.

classified advertisement an advertisement inserted in a designated part of a newspaper, magazine, etc., under one of a set of special headings.

clas•si•fy ['klæsə,faɪ] *v.* **-fied, -fy•ing.** arrange in classes or groups; group according to some system: *In the post office, mail is classified according to the places where it is to go.* ⟨< L *classis* class + E *-fy*⟩ **—'clas•si,fi•a•ble,** *adj.* **—'clas•si,fi•er,** *n.*

class•ism ['klæsɪzəm] *n.* discrimination against people of a different social class or level. **—'class•ist,** *n., adj.*

class•less ['klæslɪs] *adj.* not divided into classes, especially social and economic classes: *a classless society.*
—'class•less•ness, *n.*

classmate ['klæs,meit] *n.* a member of the same class in school.

class•room ['klæs,rum] *or* [-,rʊm] *n.* a room where classes meet in school or college; schoolroom.

class struggle any conflict between divisions of society, especially between capital and labour.

class•y ['klæsi] *adj.* **-i•er, -i•est.** *Informal.* of high class or quality; stylish; elegant; refined; noble. **—'class•i•ly,** *adv.* **—'class•i•ness,** *n.*

clas•tic ['klæstɪk] *adj.* **1** of or having to do with a model for the study of anatomy whose parts can be removed to show the inner structure. **2** *Geology.* composed of bits of older rocks. ⟨< Gk. *klastos* broken < *klan* to break⟩

clat•ter ['klætər] *n., v. —n.* **1** a rattling noise: *the clatter of dishes.* **2** noisy talk.
—v. **1** move or fall with a rattling noise; make a commotion: *The horses clattered over the stones.* **2** talk fast and noisily. **3** cause to clatter. ⟨OE *clatrian*⟩ **—'clat•ter•er,** *n.*

clau•di•ca•tion [,klɒdə'keiʃən] *n.* **1** lameness; a limp. **2** lack of proper blood circulation in the leg. ⟨< L *claudicatio* < *claudicatus,* pp. of *claudicare* to limp⟩

clause [klɒz] *n.* **1** *Grammar.* that part of a sentence having a subject and predicate. In *He came before we left, He came* is a **main clause,** and *before we left* is a **subordinate clause.** A subordinate clause functions as a noun, adjective, or adverb. **2** a single provision of a law, treaty, or any other written agreement: *There is a clause in our contract that says we may not keep a dog in this building.* ⟨< Med.L *clausa* for L *clausula* close of a period < *claudere* close⟩ **—'claus•al,** *adj.*

claus•tro•pho•bi•a [,klɒstrə'foubiə] *n.* **1** a morbid fear of enclosed spaces. **2** a feeling of being confined or stifled. ⟨< NL < L *claustrum* closed place + E *-phobia* fear⟩

claus•tro•pho•bic [,klɒstrə'foubɪk] *adj., n. —adj.* **1** of or having to do with claustrophobia. **2** causing a feeling of confinement; stifling.
—n. a person with claustrophobia. **—,claus•tro'pho•bi•cal•ly,** *adv.*

cla•vate ['kleiveit] *adj.* club-shaped. Also, **claviform.** ⟨< L *clavatus* < *clava* club⟩

clave[1] [kleiv] *v. Archaic.* a pt. of CLEAVE[2].

cla•ve[2] ['klɑvei] *n.* one of a pair of wooden sticks that are beaten together to provide a percussive rhythm base for music, especially in the Latin style. ⟨< Am.Sp. < L *clavis* key⟩

clav•i•chord ['klævə,kɔrd] *n.* an early stringed musical instrument with a keyboard. The piano evolved from it. It is still being made for use in early music. ⟨< Med.L *clavichordium* < L *clavis* key + *chorda* string⟩

clav•i•cle ['klævəkəl] *n.* the collarbone. See ARM for picture. ⟨< L *clavicula* bolt, dim. of *clavis* key⟩ **—cla'vic•u•lar** [klə'vɪkjələr], *adj.*

clav•i•corn ['klævɪ,kɔrn] *adj.* of or having to do with a group of beetles having club-shaped antennae. ⟨< NL *clavicornia* < L *clava* club + *cornu* horn⟩ **—,clav•i'cor•nate,** *adj.*

clav•i•er ['klæviər] *or* [klə'vir] *n.* **1** the keyboard of a piano, organ, etc. **2** a soundless keyboard used for practice. **3** any musical instrument having a keyboard, such as the harpsichord and the clavichord. ⟨< G *Klavier* < F *clavier,* orig. key bearer < *clef* key < L *clavis*⟩

clav•i•form ['klævə,fɔrm] *adj.* clavate.

claw [klɒ] *n., v. —n.* **1** a sharp, hooked nail on each toe of a bird. **2** a similar nail on each toe of certain animals: *The cat's claws were dangerous.* **3** a foot with such sharp, hooked nails: *The gopher was held tightly in the hawk's claws.* **4** one of the pincers of a lobster, crab, etc. **5** anything like a claw. The part of a hammer used for pulling nails is the claw.
—v. scratch, tear, seize, or pull with claws or fingernails. ⟨OE *clawu*⟩ **—'claw,like,** *adj.*

A claw hammer

claw hammer **1** a hammer with one end of the head curved like a claw and forked for pulling nails. **2** *Informal.* a dress coat; swallowtail coat.

clay [klei] *n.* **1** a stiff, sticky kind of earth with little or no animal or vegetable matter in it, that can be easily shaped when wet and hardens after drying or baking. Bricks and dishes may be made from clay. **2** earth. **3** *Poetic.* the human body.
feet of clay. See FEET. ⟨OE *clæg*⟩

clay•bank ['klei,bæŋk] *n., adj.* —*n.* **1** a dull brownish yellow, as of a bank of clay. **2** a claybank-coloured horse.
—*adj.* dull brownish yellow.

clay•ey ['kleii] *adj.* **clay•i•er, clay•i•est. 1** of, like, or containing clay. **2** covered or smeared with clay.

clay•ish ['kleiɪʃ] *adj.* clayey.

clay•more ['klei,mɔr] *n.* **1** a heavy, two-edged sword, formerly used by Scottish Highlanders. **2** a sword with a basket hilt, worn as part of ceremonial dress by Scottish regiments. ⟨< Scots Gaelic *claidheamh mor* great sword⟩

clay•pan ['klei,pæn] *n.* **1** a layer of clay in the soil that holds water. **2** *Australian.* a depression in the earth that fills with water in a heavy rain; billabong.

clay pigeon a saucerlike clay disk thrown in the air as a flying target for skeet shooting.

clay•to•nia [klei'touniə] *n.* any plant of the genus *Claytonia,* of the purslane family, having pink or white flowers that bloom in the spring. ⟨< NL, after John *Clayton,* American botanist (1693–1773)⟩

CLC CANADIAN LABOUR CONGRESS.

–cle *suffix.* **1** little: *corpuscle, particle.* **2** other meanings: *receptacle, vehicle.* ⟨< L *-culus, -cula, -culum* (dim.) or < F *-cle* (< L)⟩

clean [klin] *adj., adv., v.* —*adj.* **1** free from dirt or filth; not soiled or stained; washed: *clean clothes.* **2** pure; innocent: *a clean heart.* **3** decent; not obscene: *a clean joke.* **4** having the habit of keeping oneself and one's quarters clean: *Cats are clean animals.* **5** of atomic weapons, causing little or no radioactive fall-out. **6** fit for food: *Muslims and Jews do not consider pork a clean meat.* **7** ceremonially pure. **8** clear; even; regular: *a clean cut.* **9** smooth; skilful; free from any clumsiness: *a clean jump.* **10** complete; entire; total: *a clean escape.* **11** honest; fair, as in sports: *a clean player, a clean fighter.* **12** having few or no corrections or alterations: *I have to make a clean copy to hand in.* **13** blank; new: *I need a clean page.* **14** of printer's proofs, relatively free from corrections or alterations. **15** not using drugs: *The athlete was found to be clean.*
—*adv.* **1** completely; entirely; totally: *The horse jumped clean over the brook.* **2** in a clean manner.
come clean, a *Informal,* confess the truth. **b** be clean as a result of washing.
—*v.* **1** make clean: *to clean a room.* **2** prepare (fish, game, chicken, etc.) for cooking by removing entrails, scales, or feathers, etc. **3** undergo cleaning: *This room cleans easily because it doesn't have much furniture in it.* **4** do cleaning: *I'm going to clean this morning.* **5** take away, remove (dirt, mess, etc.) so as to make something clean: *Clean the paint marks off this chair. I cleaned the junk out of my drawer.*
clean out, a make clean by emptying: *Clean out your desk.* **b** empty; use up: *The girls cleaned out a whole box of cookies.* **c** *Slang.* leave without money; take all the money of.
clean up, a make clean by removing dirt, rubbish, etc. **b** groom oneself. **c** put (things, a place, etc.) in order. **d** *Informal.* finish; complete. **e** *Slang.* make money; profit. *She sure cleaned up on that deal.* ⟨OE *clæne*⟩ —**'clean•ness,** *n.*
☛ *Syn. v.* **1. Clean,** CLEANSE = make free from dirt or filth. **Clean** is the general word meaning 'to remove dirt, impurities, or stains', especially from objects: *The men cleaned the streets.* **Cleanse,** formal or archaic in the sense of 'make clean', is used commonly in the sense of 'make pure', applying particularly to removing impurities by chemical or other technical processes: *Health experts are trying to cleanse the air in cities. We cleanse wounds.* It is also often used with an abstract meaning: *to cleanse one's mind of unwholesome thoughts, to be cleansed from sin.*

clean and jerk in weightlifting, a lift in which the barbell is raised to the shoulders in one movement, and then lifted above the head with the arms straight.

clean–cut ['klin 'kʌt] *adj.* **1** having clear, sharp outlines. **2** well-shaped. **3** clear; definite; distinct. **4** having a neat and wholesome appearance: *a clean-cut young man.*

clean•er ['klinər] *n.* **1** a person whose work is keeping buildings, windows, etc., clean. **2** a tool or machine for cleaning. **3** anything that removes dirt, grease, or stains; cleanser. **4** DRY CLEANER: *I must take my coat to the cleaner's.*
take (someone) **to the cleaners,** *Slang.* take all (a person's) money, as in gambling.

cleaning woman or **lady** a woman whose work is cleaning homes, offices, or public buildings.

clean–limbed ['klin 'lɪmd] *adj.* having well-shaped limbs.

clean•li•ness ['klɛnlinɪs] *n.* cleanness; habitual cleanness.

clean•ly *adv.* [klinli]; *adj.* [klɛnli] *adv., adj.* **-li•er, -li•est.** —*adv.* in a clean manner: *The butcher's knife cut cleanly through the meat.*
—*adj.* always keeping oneself or one's surroundings clean: *The cat is a cleanly animal.* ⟨OE *clænlīce*⟩

clean room a sterilized and pressurized room for laboratory work.

cleanse [klɛnz] *v.* **cleansed, cleans•ing. 1** make clean. **2** make pure. ⟨OE *clænsian* < *clæne* clean⟩ —**'cleans•a•ble,** *adj.*
☛ *Syn.* See note at CLEAN.

cleans•er ['klɛnzər] *n.* a substance that cleans, especially a soap, detergent, disinfectant, or bleaching agent used in household cleaning.

clean–shav•en ['klin 'ʃeivən] *or* ['klin ,ʃeivən] *adj.* with the face shaved.

clean–up ['klin ,ʌp] *n.* **1** a cleaning up. **2** *(adjl.)* having to do with cleaning up: *a clean-up process.* **3** *Slang.* an exceptional amount of money made on a transaction; large profit.

clear [klir] *adj., v., adv., n.* —*adj.* **1** not cloudy, misty, or hazy; bright; light: *a clear day.* **2** easy to see through; transparent: *clear glass.* **3** having a pure, even colour: *a clear blue.* **4** easily seen, heard, or understood; plain; distinct: *a clear idea, a clear voice.* **5** free from blemishes: *clear skin.* **6** perceiving distinctly; keen: *a clear eye, a clear mind.* **7** sure; certain; obvious: *It is clear that it is going to rain.* **8** not blocked or obstructed; open: *a clear view.* **9** without touching; without being caught: *The ship was clear of the iceberg.* **10** free from blame or guilt; innocent: *A careful investigation showed that the suspect was clear.* **11** free from debts or charges: *clear profit.* **12** without limitation; complete: *the clear contrary.* **13** of lumber, free from knots or other imperfections.
make clear, state definitely: *She made clear that she would not take part in such an arrangement.*
—*v.* **1** make clear or free of obstruction: *She cleared the land of trees. He cleared his throat before he began to speak. She cleared her desk.* **2** become clear: *It rained and then it cleared.* **3** remove to leave a space clear: *She cleared the dishes from the table.* **4** get by or over without touching or being caught: *The horse cleared the fence.* **5** make free from blame or guilt; prove to be innocent: *The jury's verdict cleared the accused man.* **6** make as profit free from debts or charges: *We cleared $90 on the used book sale.* **7** get (a ship or cargo) free by meeting requirements on entering or leaving a port. **8** leave (a port) after doing this. **9** get permission from (an authority) to proceed: *It took us half an hour to clear customs.* **10** get permission or approval for (a proposed action, etc.): *Have you cleared this idea with the principal?* **11** exchange (cheques and bills) and so settle accounts between different banks. **12** settle (a business account) or certify (a cheque) as valid. **13** settle (a debt, misunderstanding, etc.)
clear away or **off, a** remove to leave a space clear: *to clear away underbrush. Clear those papers off, please, I need the desk.* **b** leave; go away: *She cleared off as soon as she heard there was work involved.*
clear out, a make clear by throwing out or emptying. **b** *Informal.* go away; leave: *You'll have to clear out of the gym by four o'clock because they need it for basketball practice.*
clear up, a make or become clear. **b** put in order by clearing. **c** explain: *John cleared up the question of why he had not been there by saying that he had been ill.* **d** become clear after a storm. **e** cure or be cured; heal: *This cream should clear up his acne. Her cold cleared up.*
—*adv.* **1** in a clear manner. **2** completely; entirely: *The bullet went clear through the door.*
—*n.*
in the clear, a between the outside parts; in interior measurement: *The house was 15 m wide, in the clear.* **b** *Informal.* free of guilt or blame; innocent: *Her report shows that the suspect is in the clear.* **c** free from limitations or encumbrances: *Having paid all his debts, he was finally in the clear again.* **d** in plain text; not in cipher or code. ⟨ME *cler* < OF < L *clarus*⟩ —**'clear•ly,** *adv.* —**'clear•ness,** *n.*

clear air turbulence moving air that shakes an aircraft but is not the result of a storm. *Abbrev.:* CAT

clear•ance ['klirəns] *n.* **1** the act of clearing. **2** a clear space, especially the distance between objects or parts that allows free movement: *We had to wait for the other car to move, because there wasn't enough clearance to get our car out. The underpass has a clearance of 4 m.* **3** the meeting of requirements to get a ship or cargo free on entering or leaving a port. **4** a certificate showing this. **5** official permission to go ahead; authorization to do a certain thing or have access to a certain place: *The pilot had to wait for clearance from the control tower.* **6** the exchanging of cheques and bills and settling of accounts between different banks. **7** CLEARANCE SALE.

clearance sale a sale held by a store, etc., to clear out old stock in order to make room for new.

clear–cut ['klir 'kʌt] *adj., v.* **-cut, -cut•ting.** *—adj.* **1** having clear, sharp outlines. **2** clear; definite; distinct: *He had clear-cut ideas about his work.*
—v. cut down all the trees in (a wooded area).

clear•cut•ting ['klir,kʌtɪŋ] *n.* **1** the clearing from a forest area of all standing timber. **2** the area so cleared.

clear–eyed ['klir ,aɪd] *adj.* **1** having bright, clear eyes. **2** having acute and undistorted perception.

clear–head•ed ['klir ,hɛdɪd] *adj.* having or showing a clear understanding. **—'clear-'head•ed•ly,** *adv.* **—'clear-'head•ed•ness,** *n.*

clear•ing ['klirɪŋ] *n., v. —n.* **1** an open space of cleared land in a forest. **2** the exchanging of cheques and bills and settling of accounts between different banks.
—v. ppr. of CLEAR.

clearing house a place where banks exchange cheques and bills and settle their accounts.

clearing pass *Cdn. Hockey.* a forward pass of the puck intended to get it out of the defending team's end of the rink.

clear–sight•ed ['klir ,səitɪd] *adj.* **1** able to see clearly. **2** able to understand or think clearly. **—'clear-'sight•ed•ly,** *adv.* **—'clear-'sight•ed•ness,** *n.*

clear•sto•rey ['klir,stɔri] *n., pl.* **-ries.** See CLERESTOREY.

clear•wing ['klir,wɪŋ] *n.* a moth of the family Aegeriidae, having translucent wings without scales, and often harmful to plants.

cleat [klit] *n., v. —n.* **1** one of several studs or bars of leather, plastic, etc. attached to the sole of a football boot, soccer boot, etc. to prevent slipping. **2** a strip of wood, metal, leather, etc. fastened across anything for support or for sure footing. A gangway has cleats to keep people from slipping. **3** one of the raised bars placed at intervals across the track of a vehicle that travels over snow. The cleats on a snowmobile track permit a firmer grip on snow. **4** a small, wedge-shaped block fastened to a mast, spar, etc. as a support, check, etc. **5** a piece of wood, metal, or plastic having projecting arms or ends, fixed to a boat, wharf, flagpole, stage scenery, etc. and used for securing ropes or lines.
—v. **1** fasten to or with a cleat. **2** furnish with cleats. ⟨ME *cleete*⟩

cleav•age ['klivɪdʒ] *n.* **1** the site of a split or division. **2** the action of cleaving, or splitting. **3** *Biology.* cell division, especially any of the series of divisions by which a fertilized egg forms smaller cells called blastomeres, and thus develops into an embryo. **4** *Chemistry.* the breaking up of a molecule into simpler molecules. **5** *Mineralogy.* the tendency of a crystallized substance or rock to split along definite planes. **6** *Informal.* the division between a woman's breasts, especially as revealed by a low neckline.

cleave[1] [kliv] *v.* **cleft** or **clove** or **cleaved, cleft** or **cleaved** or **clo•ven, cleav•ing. 1** cut, divide, or split open: *With one blow of the axe he cleft the log in two.* **2** pass through; pierce; penetrate: *The airplane clove the clouds.* **3** make by cutting: *to cleave a path through the wilderness.* ⟨OE *clēofan*⟩ **—'cleav•a•ble,** *adj.*

cleave[2] [kliv] *v.* **cleaved,** *or archaic,* **clave, cleav•ing.** hold fast (*to*); cling; be faithful *(to)*: *to cleave to an idea.* ⟨OE *cleofian*⟩

cleav•er ['klivər] *n.* **1** one who cleaves. **2** a cutting tool with a heavy blade and a short handle: *A butcher uses a cleaver to chop through meat or bone.*

cleav•ers ['klivərz] *n.* **1** a North American plant (*Galium aparine*) of the madder family, having spiny stems and small white or yellow flowers. **2** any other species of this genus.

clef [klɛf] *n. Music.* **1** a symbol indicating the pitch of the notes on a staff. **2** the range of pitch indicated by the symbol. See BASS CLEF, TREBLE CLEF. ⟨< F < L *clavis* key⟩

cleft [klɛft] *v., adj., n. —v.* a pt. and a pp. of CLEAVE[1].
—adj. split; divided.
—n. a space or opening made by splitting; crack. ⟨OE *(ge)clyft*⟩

cleft palate a narrow opening running lengthwise in the roof of the mouth, caused by failure of the two parts of the palate to join.

cleis•tog•a•mous [kləi'stɒgəməs] *adj. Botany.* having small, closed, self-pollinating flowers in addition to regular flowers.

cleis•tog•a•my [kləi'stɒgəmi] *n. Botany.* self-fertilization taking place in flowers that do not open. ⟨< Gk. *kleistos* closed + *-gamia* < *gamos* marriage⟩ **—,cleis•to'gam•ic** [,kləistə'gæmɪk], *adj.*

clem•a•tis [klə'mætəs], ['klɛmətɪs], *or* [klə'meitɪs] *n.* any of a genus (*Clematis*) of mainly climbing shrubs of the buttercup family, some having evergreen leaves, cultivated in many species and varieties for their showy flowers. ⟨< L < Gk. *klēmatis* < *klēma* vine branch⟩

clem•en•cy ['klɛmənsi] *n., pl.* **-cies. 1** mercy; mildness in exercising authority or power: *The Crown recommended clemency for the defendant.* **2** mildness of climate or weather.
☛ *Syn.* **1.** See note at MERCY.

clem•ent ['klɛmənt] *adj.* **1** merciful. **2** mild and clear: *clement weather.* ⟨< L *clemens, -entis*⟩ **—'clem•ent•ly,** *adv.*

clem•ent•ine ['klɛmən,taɪn] *or* ['klɛmən,tin] *n.* a small, tangerinelike type of orange.

clench [klɛntʃ] *v., n. —v.* **1** close tightly together: *to clench one's fists, to clench one's teeth.* **2** grasp firmly; grip tightly: *The policeman clenched his prisoner's arm.* **3** clinch (a nail, etc.).
—n. **1** a firm grasp; tight grip: *I felt the clench of her hand on my arm.* **2** the clinch of a nail, staple, etc. ⟨OE *(be)clencan* hold fast⟩ **—'clench•er,** *n.*
☛ *Syn. v.* **Clench,** CLINCH agree in their basic meaning of holding fast or making hold fast, but differ in emphasis and application. **Clench** emphasizes the idea of holding fast by clamping together and is used in the senses of 'close tightly' (fist, teeth, lips, etc.) and 'grasp firmly' (a hammer, etc.). **Clinch** emphasizes the idea of fastening firmly and securely, and applies chiefly to fastening nails and bolts, etc. or fastening things together.

cle•o•me [kli'oumi] *n.* any tropical, strong-smelling plant of the genus *Cleome*, of the caper family, having showy white, pink, green, yellow, or purple flowers; spider plant. ⟨origin uncertain⟩

clep•sy•dra ['klɛpsədrə] *n., pl.* **-dras, -drae** [-,dri] *or* [-,draɪ]. a device used in ancient times for measuring time by the flow of water, mercury, etc. through a small opening. ⟨< L < Gk. *klepsydra* < *kleptein* steal + *hydōr* water⟩

clere•sto•rey ['klir,stɔri] *n., pl.* **-ries. 1** *Architecture.* the upper part of the wall of a church, having windows in it above the roofs of the aisles. **2** any similar structure. Also, **clearstorey.** ⟨apparently < *clere* clear + *storey*⟩

cler•gy ['klərdʒi] *n., pl.* **-gies. 1** a body or order of persons specially trained and ordained to perform religious services. Ministers, pastors, priests, and rabbis are members of the clergy. Compare LAITY. **2** all the persons commissioned or otherwise designated for religious duties, including deacons, religious, lay ministers, etc. ⟨ME < OF *clergie*, ult. < L *clericus.* See CLERIC.⟩

cler•gy•man ['klərdʒimən] *n., pl.* **-men.** a man who is a member of the clergy.

Clergy Reserves *Cdn.* the lands set aside in Lower and Upper Canada in 1791 for the support of a Protestant clergy. In practice, this was interpreted to mean the Church of England clergy.

cler•ic ['klɛrɪk] *n., adj. —n.* a member of the clergy.
—adj. of the clergy; clerical. ⟨< L *clericus* < Gk. *klērikos* < *klēros* clergy; originally, lot, allotment; first applied (in the Septuagint) to the Levites, the service of God being the priest's lot. Doublet of CLERK.⟩

cler•i•cal ['klɛrəkəl] *adj., n. —adj.* **1** of or for a clerk or clerks: *Keeping records or accounts and copying letters are clerical jobs in an office.* **2** of, having to do with, or characteristic of the clergy

or a member of the clergy: *clerical robes.* **3** supporting the power or influence of the clergy in politics.
—n. **1** a member of the clergy. **2** a supporter of the power or influence of the clergy in politics. **3 clericals,** *pl.* the clothes worn by members of the clergy. ⟨< LL *clericalis* < L *clericus.* See CLERIC.⟩ **—'cler•i•cal•ly,** *adv.*

clerical collar a stiff, white collar which is fastened at the back, worn by some members of the clergy.

cler•i•cal•ism ['klɛrəkə,lɪzəm] *n.* **1** the power or influence of the clergy in politics. **2** the support of such power or influence. **—'cler•i•cal•ist,** *n., adj.*

cler•i•hew ['klɛrə,hju] *n.* a short, rhyming, humorous poem about a person, with couplets and lines of uneven length. ⟨after E. *Clerihew* Bentley (1875-1956), English writer⟩

cler•i•sy ['klɛrəsi] *n.* educated people as a class; intelligentsia. ⟨< ME *clericia* < LL *clericus.* See CLERIC.⟩

clerk [klɜrk] *n., v. —n.* **1** a person whose work is waiting on customers and selling goods in a store; a salesperson in a store. **2** a person whose work is keeping records or accounts, copying letters, etc., in an office. **3** an official who keeps records and takes care of regular business in a court of law, legislature, etc. **4** a layman who has minor church duties. **5** in a hotel, one who registers guests, assigns rooms, etc. **6** a worker in a post office or mail room. **7** *Archaic.* clergyman. **8** *Archaic.* a person who can read and write; scholar.
—v. work as a clerk in a store: *He clerks in a drugstore.* ⟨partly OE *clerc, cleric,* partly < OF *clerc* < L *clericus.* Doublet of CLERIC.⟩

clerk•ly ['klɜrkli] *adj.* **1** of or like a clerk. **2** of the clergy. **3** *Archaic.* scholarly.

clerk•ship ['klɜrkʃɪp] *n.* the position or work of a clerk.

clev•er ['klɛvər] *adj.* **1** having a quick mind; bright; intelligent. **2** skilful or expert in doing some particular thing: *a clever carpenter.* **3** showing skill or intelligence: *a clever trick, a clever answer.* **4** showing a glib, facile, or superficial intelligence: *You can never have a really good talk with them because they are always being clever. Enough of your clever remarks.* **5** *Informal.* good-natured; obliging. ⟨ME *cliver;* origin uncertain⟩
—'clev•er•ly, *adv.* **—'clev•er•ness,** *n.*
☛ *Syn.* **1. Clever,** INGENIOUS = having a quick mind. **Clever** is the general word, and suggests a natural quickness in learning things and skill in using the mind: *He had no training, but was clever enough to become a good salesman.* **Ingenious** = quick to see ways of doing things, skilful in inventing and making things: *Some ingenious person designed the first electric can opener.*

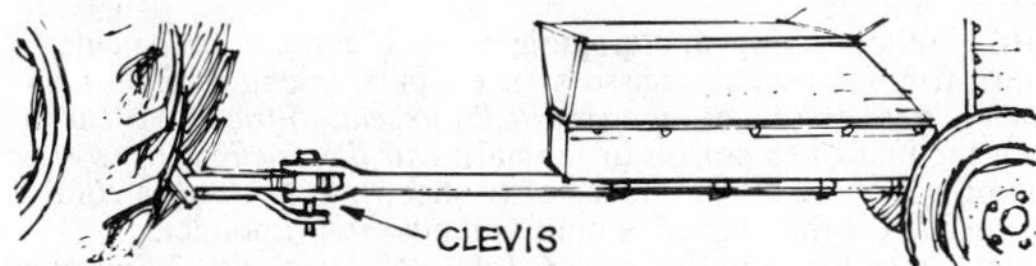

clev•is ['klɛvɪs] *n.* a U-shaped piece of metal with a bolt or pin through the ends. A clevis may be used to fasten a wagon, plough, etc., to a tractor. ⟨related to CLEAVE[1]⟩

clew [klu] *n., v. —n.* **1** a ball of thread or yarn. **2** a lower corner of a sail. **3** a metal ring fastened there.
—v. **1** raise or lower a sail by the clews (*used with* **up** *or* **down**). **2** wind into a ball or coil. ⟨OE *cleowen*⟩
☛ *Hom.* CLUE.

cli•ché [kli'ʃei] *n., adj. —n.* **1** a timeworn expression or idea. **2** a printing plate made of cast metal.
—adj. clichéd. ⟨< F *cliché,* pp. of *clicher* stereotype⟩

cli•chéd [kli'ʃeid] *adj.* **1** trite or overused: *the clichéd setting of a novel, clichéd expressions.* **2** full of clichés: *a clichéd speech.* Also, **cliché.**

click [klɪk] *n., v. —n.* **1** a light, sharp sound: *We heard the click as he turned his key in the lock.* **2** a locking device in a ratchet mechanism, such as a pawl, that operates with such a sound. **3** *Phonetics.* any of a group of voiceless speech sounds characteristic especially of some African languages, made by sucking air into the mouth and rapidly drawing the tongue down from the teeth or the roof of the mouth.
—v. **1** make a light, sharp sound. **2** cause to make such a sound: *The soldier clicked his heels together and saluted.* **3** *Slang.* get along well together; be congenial; hit it off: *We clicked from the start.* **4** *Informal.* succeed; go or do well: *This movie should click; it has well-known actors and a popular theme.* **5** *Informal.* suddenly make sense or become clear: *Then something clicked and she realized that she had seen the man before.* **6** *Computer technology.* depress and release a button on a mouse to make a selection or cause an operation (save, delete, etc.) to take place: *Having finished editing her document, she clicked on the print option in order to get a hard copy.* ⟨imitative⟩
☛ *Hom.* CLIQUE.

click beetle any of a family (Elateridae) of beetles that are able to right themselves with a clicking or snapping sound when put on their backs.

cli•ent ['klaɪənt] *n.* **1** a person for whom a lawyer or other professional person acts. **2** customer. **3** in ancient Rome, a poor or humble person depending on a noble or wealthy man for assistance. **4** a personal follower; dependant. **5** someone who receives help from a social agency. **6** a country which depends on another country economically or politically. ⟨< L *cliens, -entis* (related to *clinare* lean)⟩ **—'cli•ent•less,** *adj.*

cli•en•tele [,klaɪən'tɛl] *or* [,kliɑn'tɛl] *n.* **1** clients; customers. **2** personal followers. **3** the number of clients: *She has a large clientele.* ⟨< F < L *clientela*⟩

cliff [klɪf] *n.* a steep, high face of rock or earth; precipice: *Great cliffs overhung the canyon.* ⟨OE *clif*⟩ **—'cliff,like,** *adj.*

cliff dweller **1** a person living in a cave or house built in a cliff. **2** *Slang.* a person living in a high-rise apartment building.

cliff dwelling a cave or house built in a cliff.

cliff–hang•er ['klɪf ,hæŋər] *n. Slang.* **1** a story, television show, etc. that is full of suspense, especially a serial in which each episode ends with the hero or heroine in an extremely dangerous situation. **2** a race, election, or other contest in which the result is in doubt until the very end. Also, **cliffhanger.**

cliff swallow a swallow (*Petrochelidon pyrrhonota*) of North and South America having a relatively short, squarish tail. It builds a bottle-shaped nest of mud, straw, and feathers, usually attached to a cliff or wall.

cli•mac•ter•ic [klaɪ'mæktərɪk] *or* [,klaɪmæk'tɛrɪk] *n., adj. —n.* **1** the time when some important event occurs, changing the course of things; crucial period. **2** the period of life around middle age when important physical and emotional changes usually take place in both male and female. The climacteric in women is usually called the menopause.
—adj. of, having to do with, or designating a climacteric. ⟨< L < Gk. *klimaktērikos* of a critical period < *klimaktēr* rung of a ladder < *klimax* ladder⟩

cli•mac•tic [klaɪ'mæktɪk] *adj.* of or forming a climax. **—cli'mac•ti•cal•ly,** *adv.*

cli•ma•graph ['klaɪmə,græf] *n.* a graph showing the typical climate of a selected location in terms of its average monthly temperature and precipitation. Also, **climograph.**

cli•mate ['klaɪmɪt] *n.* **1** the kind of weather patterns a place has over a period of years. Climate includes conditions of heat and cold, moisture and dryness, clearness and cloudiness, wind and calm. **2** any geographical region, with reference to its usual conditions of heat and cold, rainfall, wind, sunlight, etc: *The doctor ordered her to go to a drier climate.* **3** the prevailing state or trend: *the climate of public opinion.* ⟨< L *clima, -atis* < Gk. *klima* slope (of the earth) < *klinein* incline⟩

cli•mat•ic [klaɪ'mætɪk] *adj.* of or having to do with climate. **—cli'mat•i•cal•ly,** *adv.*

cli•ma•tol•o•gist [,klaɪmə'tɒlədʒɪst] *n.* a person trained in climatology, especially one whose work it is.

cli•ma•tol•o•gy [,klaɪmə'tɒlədʒi] *n.* the science that deals with climate. **—,cli•ma•to'log•i•cal,** *adj.*

cli•max ['klaɪmæks] *n., v. —n.* **1** the highest point; point of greatest interest; most exciting part. **2** *Rhetoric.* the arrangement of ideas in a rising scale of force and interest. **3** orgasm. **4** *Ecology.* CLIMAX COMMUNITY.
—v. bring or come to a climax. ⟨< LL < Gk. *klimax* ladder⟩

climax community *Ecology.* the last community of plants or animals to develop in a particular area: *The climax community will continue provided there is no change in soil conditions or climate in the area.*

climb [klaɪm] *v., n. —v.* **1** go up, especially by using the hands or feet, or both; ascend: *The painter climbed the ladder. We had been climbing for hours but we had not reached the top of the mountain.* **2** rise slowly or with steady effort in rank or fortune: *It took her twelve years to climb to the position of executive director.* **3** grow upward by holding on or twining around. Some vines climb. **4** slope upward: *The road climbed for more than a kilometre before it began its descent toward the coast.* **5** increase: *The price of coffee has climbed during the past year.* **6** get (into or

out of something) with effort: *The heavy woman climbed out of the car.*
climb down, a go down by using the hands and feet. **b** *Informal.* give in; back down; withdraw from an impossible position or unreasonable attitude.
—n. **1** a climbing; ascent: *Our climb took two hours.* **2** a place to be climbed. **3** increase: *a climb in price.* **4** upward slope. ⟨OE *climban*⟩
☛ *Hom.* CLIME.
☛ *Syn. v.* **1. Climb,** ASCEND, MOUNT = go to or toward the top. **Climb** is the general word but suggests greater effort than do *ascend* and *mount*: *This car will never climb that hill.* **Ascend** is more formal, but suggests going straight up: *She ascended the steps like a princess.* **Mount** is close to **ascend**, but in contrast to it can also mean 'to get on top of': *He mounted the stepladder. She mounted the stage.*

climb•er ['klaɪmər] *n.* **1** a person who or thing that climbs. **2** *Informal.* a person who is always trying to get ahead socially. **3** a spike attached to a shoe to help in climbing. **4** any climbing plant.

climbing fern a tropical plant of the genus *Lygodium*, having vines and tendrils.

climbing iron one of a pair of frames having metal spikes, attached to boots to help in climbing.

climbing perch a fish (*Anabas testudineus*) of SE Asia, that can leave the water briefly and travel over land.

climbing rose any rose plant that has tendrils and can climb around supports.

clime [klaɪm] *n. Poetic.* **1** a country; region. **2** climate. ⟨< L *clima.* See CLIMATE.⟩
☛ *Hom.* CLIMB.

clim•o•graph ['klaɪmə,græf] *n.* See CLIMAGRAPH.

clinch [klɪntʃ] *v., n.* *—v.* **1** fasten (a driven nail, a bolt, etc.) firmly by bending over or flattening the end that has been driven through something and projects from the other side. **2** fasten (things) together in this way. **3** fix firmly; settle decisively: *A deposit of five dollars clinched the bargain.* **4** confirm (a victory). **5** *Boxing and wrestling.* grasp one another tightly; grapple: *When the boxers clinched, the crowd hissed.* **6** *Slang.* embrace. **7** clench.
—n. **1** *Boxing and wrestling.* a tight grasp; close grip: *The referee broke the boxers' clinch.* **2** *Slang.* embrace. **3** a kind of sailor's knot in which the end of the rope is lashed back. **4** a fastening made by bending back a nail, bolt, etc. ⟨var. of *clench*⟩
☛ *Syn. v.* See note at CLENCH.

clinch•er ['klɪntʃər] *n.* **1** a tool for clinching nails, bolts, etc. **2** *Informal.* an argument, statement, act, etc. that is decisive.

cline [klaɪn] *n.* **1** any gradual progression. **2** a gradual change in an organism. **3** *Biology.* within a species, a gradual variation in a characteristic in populations geographically or environmentally separated, so that the most widely separated populations may differ considerably. **4** a continuum. ⟨< Gk. *klinein* lean⟩
—'cli•nal, *adj.*

cling [klɪŋ] *v.* **clung, cling•ing;** *n.* *—v.* **1** attach oneself firmly; grasp; hold tightly: *The child clung to his mother.* **2** stick; be attached: *A vine clings to its support.* **3** remain attached to a belief, idea, etc.: *They clung to the beliefs of their parents.* **4** keep or remain near: *clouds clinging to the mountains.*
—n. **1** the act of clinging. **2** STATIC CLING. ⟨OE *clingan*⟩

cling•fish ['klɪŋ,fɪʃ] *n.* a fish of the family Gobiesocidae, having suckers that enable it to cling to rocks, boats, etc.

cling•ing ['klɪŋɪŋ] *adj., v.* *—adj.* that clings or holds fast.
—v. ppr. of CLING.

cling•stone ['klɪŋ,stoun] *n., adj.* *—n.* a peach whose flesh clings to the stone.
—adj. having such a stone.

clin•ic ['klɪnɪk] *n.* **1** a part of a hospital where people are treated for certain kinds of illness without having to stay overnight: *They have the latest equipment in the eye clinic.* **2** a place, separate from a hospital, where a group of doctors work together: *My aunt is a heart specialist in the new clinic.* **3** a session held to treat or prevent certain illnesses or injuries, or to provide a special service: *a blood donor clinic, a rabies clinic for pets.* **4** the practical instruction of medical students by examining or treating patients in the presence of the students. **5** a class of students receiving such instruction. **6** a brief course of practical instruction in some non-medical field: *a football clinic, a writing clinic.* ⟨< L < Gk. *klinikos* of a bed < *klinē* bed⟩

clin•i•cal ['klɪnəkəl] *adj., n.* *—adj.* **1** of or having to do with a clinic. **2** having to do with the diagnosis and treatment of disease by observation of the patient, as opposed to laboratory testing, research, etc.: *clinical medicine, clinical psychology.* **3** detached, unemotional, and thorough, suggesting a medical examination or report: *The interviewer looked the applicant over with a clinical eye and then said, "You'll do."* **4** bare, neat, and functional, suggesting a hospital: *The kitchen looked clinical, very different from the large, friendly kitchen in the old house.* **5** *Psychiatry.* of depression, so severe as to constitute a disease or disorder; pathological.
—n. CLINIC (defs. 4,5): *I just finished the most gruelling part of my nurse's training—we had clinicals the last two months.*
—'clin•i•cal•ly, *adv.*

clinical ecology a branch of medicine which treats many diseases as allergies to synthetic pollutants.

clinical thermometer a thermometer for measuring the temperature of the body.

cli•ni•cian [klɪ'nɪʃən] *n.* a person, such as a physician or psychiatrist, trained and specializing in the treatment of patients, as distinct from one specializing in medical research or laboratory work.

clink[1] [klɪŋk] *n., v.* *—n.* a light, sharp, ringing sound like that of glasses hitting together.
—v. **1** make a clink. **2** cause to clink. ⟨ME, ? < Du. *klinken*⟩

clink[2] [klɪŋk] *n. Informal.* a prison. ⟨< *Clink* Street in London, the site of a former prison⟩

clink•er ['klɪŋkər] *n.* **1** a piece of the rough, hard mass left in a furnace or stove after coal has been burned; large, rough cinder. **2** a very hard brick. **3** a mass of bricks fused together. **4** slag. **5** *Informal.* a bad or stupid mistake, or its result. **6** *Informal.* a failure; flop: *The movie was a clinker.* ⟨< Du. *klinker* brick < *klinken* ring⟩

clink•er–built ['klɪŋkər ,bɪlt] *adj.* made of boards or metal plates that overlap one another: *The lifeboat was clinker-built.* Compare CARVEL-BUILT. ⟨*clinker*, dial. var. of *clincher*⟩

cli•nom•e•ter [klaɪ'nɒmətər] *or* [klə'nɒmətər] *n.* an instrument for measuring deviation from the horizontal. ⟨< L *clinare* incline + E *-meter*⟩

clin•to•nia [klɪn'touniə] *n.* a plant of the genus *Clintonia*, of the lily family, having broad leaves and white, yellow, or pink flowers, and blue berries. ⟨< NL, after De Witt *Clinton* (1769–1828), American statesman⟩

Clio ['klaɪou] *n. Greek mythology.* the Muse of history.

cli•o•met•rics [,klaɪə'mɛtrɪks] *n. pl.* (*used with a singular verb*) the analysis of historical data using mathematics, statistics, and computers.

clip[1] [klɪp] *v.* **clipped, clip•ping;** *n.* *—v.* **1** cut; cut out or cut short; trim with shears, scissors, or clippers: *to clip the hair. I often clip interesting newspaper articles to send to friends.* **2** cut or trim the hair of (a person or animal): *Our dog is clipped every summer.* **3** shear off the fleece of (a sheep). **4** damage (a coin) by cutting off the edge. **5 a** omit (sounds) in pronouncing. **b** shorten (a form) in this way. **6** *Informal.* move fast. **7** *Informal.* hit or punch sharply. **8** *Slang.* cheat, especially by overcharging: *We got clipped in that restaurant.*
—n. **1** the act of clipping. **2** the amount of wool clipped from sheep at one shearing or during one season. **3** anything that has been clipped off, such as a section of filmed material. **4** *Informal.* a fast pace: *Our bus passed through the village at quite a clip.* **5** *Informal.* a sharp blow or punch. **6** *Informal.* one time; single occasion: *at one clip.* **7** a CLIPPED FORM: *Mob, bus, and flu are clips.* ⟨ME *clippe(n)* < ON *klippa*⟩

clip[2] [klɪp] *v.* **clipped, clip•ping;** *n.* *—v.* **1** hold tight; fasten: *to clip papers together.* **2** *Football.* tackle from behind (a player who does not have the ball). Clipping is an illegal move.
—n. **1** something used for clipping things together: *a paper clip.* **2** of certain firearms: **a** a metal holder for cartridges. **b** the rounds it holds. ⟨ OE *clyppan* embrace⟩

clip•board ['klɪp,bɔrd] *n.* **1** a small board with a tight spring clip at one end for holding papers while writing. **2** *Computer technology.* in an interactive computing environment, a storage area where data is stored temporarily during some operation (move, copy, etc.).

clip–fed ['klɪp ,fɛd] *adj.* of a firearm, automatically reloaded from a CLIP[2] (def. *n.* 2).

clip joint *Slang.* a business establishment, especially a restaurant, nightclub, etc., that regularly overcharges its customers.

clip–on ['klɪp ,ɒn] *adj., n.* *—adj.* designed to be attached by means of a clip: *clip-on earrings.*
—n. a clip-on earring.

clipped form *Linguistics.* a word formed by the shortening of another. *Admin* is the clipped form of *administration.*

clip•per ['klıpər] *n.* **1** a person who clips or cuts. **2** Often, **clippers,** *pl.* a tool for cutting. **3** a sailing ship of the mid-19th century, built and rigged for great speed. **4** a large, fast aircraft.

clip•ping ['klıpıŋ] *n., v.* —*n.* **1** a piece cut from or out of something, especially a piece cut out of a newspaper or magazine. **2** something cut from anything else: *hair clippings.* **3** a shortened word.
—*v.* ppr. of CLIP.

clipping service a company which monitors newspapers and magazines for mention of its clients, and sends each client such clippings.

clique [klik] *or* [klık] *n., v.,* **cliqued, cliqu•ing.** —*n.* a small, exclusive group of people within a larger group: *Members complained that the club was being run by a clique.*
—*v. Informal.* form or associate in a clique. ⟨< F *clique* < *cliquer* click⟩
☛ *Hom.* CLICK [klık].
☛ *Syn.* See note at CIRCLE.

cliqu•ey or **cliqu•y** ['kliki] *or* ['klıki] *adj.* cliquish.

cliqu•ish ['klikıʃ] *or* ['klıkıʃ] *adj.* **1** like a clique. **2** tending to form a clique. —**'cliqu•ish•ly,** *adv.* —**'cliqu•ish•ness,** *n.*

cli•tel•lum [klı'tɛləm] *or* [kləi'tɛləm] *n.* a grandular swelling around certain sections of an annelid from which a viscous fluid, which forms a cocoon for the eggs, is secreted. ⟨< NL < L *clitellae* packsaddle⟩

clit•or•i•dec•to•my [,klıtərə'dɛktəmi] *or* [,kləitərə'dɛktəmi] *n.* surgical removal of the clitoris, often practised as a ritual in certain societies; female circumcision.

clit•o•ris ['klıtərıs] *or* ['kləitərıs] *n.* a small, erectile organ that is part of the female genitals, situated at the front of the vulva. ⟨< NL < Gk. *kleitoris*⟩ —**'clit•o•ral,** *adj.*

cli•via ['klıviə] *or* ['klaıviə] *n.* a plant of the genus *Clivia*, of the lily family, native to South Africa and having evergreen leaves and red spring flowers.

clo•a•ca [klou'eikə] *n., pl.* **-cae** [-si] *or* [-saı], [-ki] *or* [-kaı]. **1** sewer. **2** privy. **3** a cavity in the body of birds, reptiles, amphibians, etc. into which the intestinal, urinary, and generative canals open. **4** a similar cavity in mammals which lay eggs, such as the platypus, and in certain invertebrates. ⟨< L *cloaca*, probably < *cluere* purge⟩

cloak [klouk] *n., v.* —*n.* **1** an outer garment, usually loose, with or without sleeves. **2** anything that hides or conceals.
—*v.* **1** cover with a cloak. **2** hide; conceal: *to cloak evil purposes under friendly words.* ⟨ME < OF *cloque* < LL *clocca*, originally, bell < OIrish *cloc.* Doublet of CLOCHE, CLOCK[1].⟩

cloak–and–dag•ger ['klouk ən 'dægər] *adj., adv.* —*adj.* of or having to do with spies and espionage, secret intrigue, and adventure.
—*adv.* in a manner suggestive of spies, secrecy, intrigue, and adventure.

cloak•room ['klouk,rum] *or* [-,rʊm] *n.* a room, especially in a school or other public building, where coats, hats, etc. can be left for a time.

clob•ber ['klɒbər] *v. Slang.* **1** beat or strike violently. **2** defeat severely. **3** attack verbally; criticize vehemently: *They were clobbered by the press.* ⟨origin unknown⟩

clo•be•ta•sol [klou'bitə,sɒl] *n.* a drug used to treat certain skin conditions.

cloche [klouʃ] *n.* **1** a bell-shaped glass cover to protect tender plants. **2** a woman's close-fitting hat popular in the 1920s and 1930s. ⟨< F *cloche* bell, ult. < LL *clocca.* Doublet of CLOAK, CLOCK[1].⟩

clock[1] [klɒk] *n., v.* —*n.* **1** an instrument for measuring and showing time, specifically one that is not carried around like a watch. **2** anything resembling a clock in appearance or function, such as a time clock or taximeter, etc. **3** *Computer technology.* an electronic circuit that generates a signal used to synchronize the internal operations of computer system components.
against the clock, under strong pressure from a deadline: *working against the clock to get the newsletter out on time.*
around the clock, all day and all night.
put or **turn the clock back,** return to an earlier time or to an out-of-date fashion or way of doing things.
—*v.* **1** measure or record the time of; time: *The coach clocked the three girls to see who was the fastest runner.* **2** attain (a time, distance, number, etc.) recorded mechanically: *The racing car clocked 240 km/h.*
clock in or **out,** register on a time card the beginning or end of a day's work. ⟨ME < MDu. *clocke* < OF *cloque* or LL *clocca.* Doublet of CLOAK, CLOCHE.⟩ —**'clock•er,** *n.* —**'clock,like,** *adj.*

clock[2] [klɒk] *n.* an ornamental pattern sewn or woven on the side of a stocking, extending up from the ankle. ⟨origin uncertain⟩

clock•mak•er ['klɒk,meikər] *n.* a person whose business is making or repairing clocks.

clock radio a radio with a built-in clock that can be set to turn the radio on or off at any desired time, used as or instead of an alarm clock.

clock speed *Computer technology.* the rate at which a clock in a computer system component produces its signals: *This microprocessor has a clock speed of 33 megahertz.*

clock•wise ['klɒk,waız] *adv. or adj.* in the direction in which the hands of a clock rotate.

clock•work ['klɒk,wɜrk] *n.* **1** machinery used to run a clock, consisting of gears, wheels, and springs. **2** any mechanism like this. Many mechanical toys are run by clockwork.
like clockwork, with great regularity and smoothness.

clod [klɒd] *n.* **1** a lump of earth; lump. **2** earth; soil. **3** a stupid person; blockhead. ⟨OE *clod*⟩

clod•hop•per ['klɒd,hɒpər] *n.* **1** a clumsy boor. **2** a large, heavy shoe.

clo•fi•brate [klou'faıbreit] *or* [klou'fıbreit] *n.* a drug used to treat certain forms of high cholesterol. *Formula*: $C_{12}H_{15}ClO_3$

clog [klɒg] *v.* **clogged, clog•ging;** *n.* —*v.* **1** block by filling up; stop up: *Greasy water clogged the drain.* **2** become blocked or filled up: *The drain has clogged with leaves.* **3** hinder the operation or movement of; interfere with; hold back: *Heavy clothes clogged the swimmer. Sand clogged the reel of the fishing rod.* **4** perform a CLOG DANCE.
clog up, block; hinder: *Traffic is often clogged up on holiday weekends.*
—*n.* **1** something that hinders or interferes. **2** any weight, such as a block of wood, fastened to the leg of an animal to hinder motion. **3** a heavy shoe or sandal with a wooden sole. **4** a lighter shoe with a wooden sole, used in clog dancing. **5** CLOG DANCE. ⟨ME *clogge* block; origin uncertain⟩

clog dance a dance performed while wearing CLOGS (def. *n.* 4) which produce a rhythmic clattering sound on the floor. —**clog dancer.** —**clog dancing.**

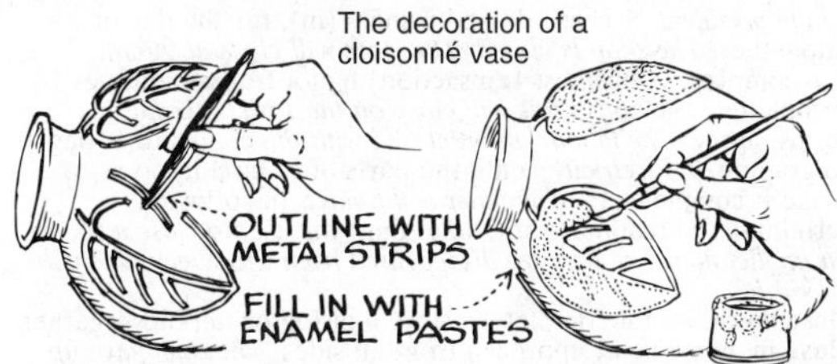

The decoration of a cloisonné vase

cloi•son•né [,klɔızə'nei]; *French,* [klwazɔ'ne] *n., adj.* —*n.* **1** enamelware in which the different colours of enamel are separated by thin metal strips set on edge on the surface. **2** the method for producing such enamelware.
—*adj.* of, having to do with, or made by cloisonné. ⟨< F *cloisonné* partitioned < *cloison* partition, ult. < L *clausus*, pp. of *claudere* close⟩

clois•ter ['klɔıstər] *n., v.* —*n.* **1** a covered walk along the wall of a building, with a row of pillars on the open side. A cloister is often built around the courtyard of a monastery, church, or university building. **2** a place of religious retirement; convent or monastery. **3** a quiet place shut away from the world.
—*v.* shut away in a cloister or other quiet place. ⟨ME < OF < L *claustrum* closed place, lock < *claudere* close⟩

clois•tered ['klɔıstərd] *adj., v.* —*adj.* **1** secluded. **2** having a cloister. **3** in a cloister.
—*v.* pt. and pp. of CLOISTER.

clois•tral ['klɔıstrəl] *adj.* **1** like a cloister. **2** of or suitable for a convent, monastery, etc.

clomb [kloum] *v. Archaic.* a pt. and a pp. of CLIMB.

clo•mip•ra•mine [klə'mıprə,min] *n.* a drug used to treat depression.

clo•naz•e•pam [klə'næzə,pæm] *n.* a drug used to treat certain forms of epilepsy. *Formula*: $C_{15}H_{10}ClN_3O_3$

clone [kloun] *n., v.* **cloned, clon•ing.** *–n.* **1** all the cells or organisms derived from a single individual by means such as cuttings or bulbs, by fission, or by the development of an unfertilized ovum. **2** a single organism produced in this way. **3** a person or thing that appears to be identical to another; copy. **4** *Computer technology.* computer hardware or software designed to imitate closely hardware or software produced by another company. **5** *Biology.* one or a group of genetically identical individuals or cells, derived by mitosis from a single parent cell. **6** *Genetics.* a copy of a particular DNA sequence, made by recombinant DNA technology. **7** the process of making a clone; cloning.
–v. **1** produce (a new, genetically identical individual) by means of cuttings or bulbs (for plants), fission, or the development of an unfertilized ovum. **2** *Informal.* reproduce; duplicate: *They cloned the computer of a rival company.* ⟨< Gk. *klon* a twig; 20c.⟩

clon•ing ['klounıŋ] *n., v. –n.* **1** the technique of producing a duplicate of an organism by replacing the nucleus of an unfertilized ovum, or egg, with the nucleus of a body cell of the parent organism, causing the ovum to develop into a new organism that is genetically identical to the parent organism. **2** an individual produced by or as if by cloning; a CLONE (defs. 2 and 3).
–v. ppr. of CLONE.

clonk [klɒŋk] *n., v. Informal. –n.* a sound like that of something striking a hard surface; clunk: *The golf ball fell to the floor with a clonk.*
–v. make such a sound; move or strike with such a sound: *The car door clonked when I closed it. The golf club clonked me on the head.* ⟨imitative⟩

clo•nus ['klounəs] *n.* a series of muscular spasms. ⟨< NL < Gk. *klonus* turmoil⟩ **–'clon•ic** ['klɒnık], *adj.*

clop [klɒp] *n., v.* **clopped, clop•ping.** *–n.* a sharp, hard sound such as is made by a horse's hoof on a paved road.
–v. make such a sound. ⟨imitative⟩

clo•qué [klou'kei] *n.* a cloth with an embossed or quilted design. ⟨< F blistered, pp. of *cloquer* to blister < *cloque* a blister⟩

close¹ [klouz] *v.* **closed, clos•ing;** *n. –v.* **1** shut: *Close the door. The sleepy child's eyes are closing.* **2** stop up; fill; block: *to close a gap.* **3** bring together; come together: *to close the ranks of troops.* **4** end; finish: *to close a debate. The meeting closed with a speech by the president.* **5** cease doing business (in), for the day or altogether: *The shop is closed. The store will close at 9 p.m.* **6 a** complete (a business transaction) **b** of a transaction, be completed: *The house sale will close on the 15th.* **7** come to terms; agree: *The labour union closed with the company.* **8** begin to grapple. **9** *Electricity.* unite the parts of (a circuit) so as to make it complete. **10** *Computer technology.* in software, terminate the readiness of (something) for use: *to close a file or an application. The window disappeared from the screen when she closed it.*
close down, a shut completely; stop. **b** of fog or darkness, gather.
close in, come near; approach from all sides: *The thief gave up when the police closed in. Night closed in swiftly.*
close in on, come near and surround or shut in on all sides: *The wolves closed in on the moose. I felt that the walls were closing in on me.*
close on, get nearer to, in a race: *Lucky Lady is closing on the winning horse.*
close out, a sell to get rid of: *to close out old stock.* **b** go out of business: *They are closing out next month.*
close up, a shut completely; stop up; block. **b** bring or come nearer together. **c** of a wound, heal.
–n. **1** the act of closing. **2** the end; finish. ⟨ME < OF *clos-*, stem of *clore* < L *claudere* close⟩ **–'clos•a•ble,** *adj.* **–'clos•er,** *n.*
☛ *Hom.* CLOTHES [klouz].

close² [klous] *adj.* **clos•er, clos•est;** *adv., n. –adj.* **1** not far off; near: *close to home, close to death.* **2** with very little in between; near together; near: *close teeth.* **3** fitting tightly; tight; narrow: *close quarters.* **4** having its parts near together; dense or compact: *a close texture.* **5** intimate; dear: *a close friend.* **6** careful; exact: *a close translation.* **7** thorough; strict: *close attention.* **8** stifling; stuffy: *With the windows shut, the room soon became hot and close.* **9** not fond of talking; keeping quiet about oneself. **10** secret; hidden. **11** strictly guarded; confined: *to keep a man close at home.* **12** restricted; limited. **13** stingy. **14** hard to get; scarce. **15** with the outcome in doubt till the end: *a close contest.* **16** closed; shut; not open. **17** *Phonetics.* of a vowel, pronounced with some part of the tongue raised to a point near the palate, as the vowels in *leap* and *loop.*
–adv. **1** *Informal.* in a close manner: *to listen close.* **2** nearby: *They live close.*
close to the wind, a with the ship pointed as nearly as possible in the direction from which the wind is blowing. **b** *Informal.* just barely following rules or laws.
come close to, a almost do: *I came close to drowning.* **b** almost amount to: *That comes pretty close to fraud.*
close up, from a close vantage point; at close quarters.
–n. **1** an enclosed place. **2** the grounds around a cathedral or abbey. **3** a cul-de-sac. ⟨ME < OF < L *clausum* closed place < *claudere* close⟩ **–'close•ly,** *adv.* **–'close•ness,** *n.*

close call [klous] *Informal.* a narrow escape from disaster: *I had a close call this morning when a car went through a red light and almost hit me.*

closed [klouzd] *adj., v. –adj.* **1** restricted to certain people; limited by certain conditions, etc.: *a closed meeting.* **2** not open to new ideas: *a closed mind.* **3** of a syllable, ending in a consonant. **4** not open to further discussion: *a closed question.* **5** *Mathematics.* **a** of a curve, endless. **b** of a set, yielding another member of the same set whenever an operation is performed on any of its members.
–v. pt. and pp. of CLOSE¹.

closed–captioned ['klouzd 'kæpʃənd] *adj.* of a television program, showing words for the deaf which can only be seen by using a special device. **–closed captioning.**

closed chain an arrangement of atoms in a closed figure, as a circle.

closed–cir•cuit ['klouzd 'sɜrkıt] *adj.* denoting or having to do with television broadcasting that is limited to a certain audience, as in a chain of theatres, a school, etc.

closed–door ['klouzd 'dɔr] *adj.* of a meeting, secret.

closed–end ['klouzd 'ɛnd] *adj.* of or having to do with investment trusts or companies that have a fixed capitalization of shares which are traded on the free market and do not have to be redeemed on demand of the holder.

closed gentian BOTTLE GENTIAN.

closed season any part of the year when hunting or fishing is restricted.

closed shop a factory or business that employs only members of labour unions. Compare OPEN SHOP, PREFERENTIAL SHOP.

closed syllable a syllable that ends in a consonant sound. *Example*: *can-* [kæn-] in *candy* ['kændi]. Compare OPEN SYLLABLE.

close–fist•ed ['klous 'fıstıd] *adj.* stingy. **–'close-'fist•ed•ness,** *n.*

close–fit•ting ['klous 'fıtıŋ] *adj.* fitting tightly; tight.

close–grained ['klous 'greind] *adj.* having a fine, close grain. Mahogany is a close-grained wood.

close–hauled ['klous 'hɒld] *adj.* having sails set for sailing as nearly as possible in the direction from which the wind is blowing.

close–knit ['klous 'nıt] *adj.* firmly united by affection or common interests: *a close-knit family.*

close–lipped ['klous 'lıpt] *adj.* close-mouthed.

close–mouthed ['klous 'maʊðd] *or* ['mʌuθt] *adj.* tending to be silent; taciturn; secretive.

close quarters [klous] **1** a place or position with little space: *They were living in very close quarters.* **2** the condition of fighting or struggling close together.
at close quarters, very close; at close range: *I had never seen a bear at close quarters before.*

close shave [klous] *Informal.* a narrow escape; CLOSE CALL.

clos•et ['klɒzıt] *n., v. –n.* **1** a small room or cupboard used for storing clothes or household supplies: *Most houses and apartments these days have built-in closets.* **2** a small, private room for prayer or study. **3** water closet; toilet. **4** (*adjl.*) private or secret; unadmitted: *a closet drinker.* **5** (*adjl.*) speculative; inclined to the theoretical, as opposed to actual: *closet strategies, a closet politician.*
out of the closet, in or into the open; in or to public knowledge or view: *More separatists were coming out of the closet.*
–v. **1** shut up in a private room for a secret talk: *The president was closeted with her personal advisers for several hours.* **2** shut up in or as if in a closet: *to closet oneself in the house.* ⟨ME < OF, dim. of *clos.* See CLOSE².⟩

close–up ['klous ˌʌp] *n., adj. –n.* **1** a picture taken at close range. **2** a close view.
–adj. being or using a close-up: *a close-up photo of the prime minister.*

close–wo•ven ['klous 'wouvən] *adj.* woven so that the threads are close together.

clos•ing ['klouzɪŋ] *n., adj., v.* —*n.* **1** a meeting for settling matters between buyer and seller at the time real property is sold and title of ownership is transferred. **2** the settlement made at such a meeting. **3** any other act of one that closes.
—*adj.* final; that constitutes a close: *closing price, closing remarks.*
—*v.* ppr. of CLOSE[1].

clos•trid•i•um [klɒ'strɪdiəm] *n., pl.* **-trid•i•a** [-'trɪdiə]. any of a genus (*Clostridium*) of anaerobic bacteria, some species of which produce potent toxins causing botulism, tetanus, and other serious diseases. ⟨< NL *Clostridium*, genus name < Gk. *kloster* spindle, rod; from their shape⟩

clo•sure ['klouʒər] *n.* **1** the act of closing or the condition of being closed. **2** a thing that closes. **3** the end; finish; conclusion. **4** in a legislative body, a means of ending a debate and getting an immediate vote on the question being discussed. In Canada, a closure may be moved after due notice by a cabinet minister. **5** *Geology.* the distance between the apex of an anticline and the lowest contour enclosing it. ⟨ME < OF < LL *clausura* < L *clausus*, pp. of *claudere* close⟩

clot [klɒt] *n., v.* **clot•ted, clot•ting.** —*n.* **1** a half-solid lump; thickened mass: *A clot of blood formed in the cut and stopped the bleeding.* **2** a clod.
—*v.* **1** form into clots: *Milk clots when it turns sour.* **2** cause to clot; cover with clots. ⟨OE *clott*⟩

cloth [klɒθ] *n., pl.* **cloths** [klɒðz] *or* [klɒθs]. **1** material made from wool, cotton, silk, linen, hair, synthetic fibres, etc. by weaving, knitting, or rolling and pressing. **2** a piece of such material used for a special purpose: *a cloth for the table.* **3** (*adjl.*) made of cloth. **4 the cloth, a** the customary clothing worn by the clergy. **b** the clergy. ⟨OE *clāth*⟩

cloth•bound ['klɒθ,baʊnd] *adj.* of a book, having hard covers faced with cloth.

clothe [klouð] *v.* **clothed** or **clad, cloth•ing. 1** put clothes on; cover with clothes; dress. **2** provide with clothes. **3** cover or wrap as if with clothes: *The sun clothes the earth with light.* **4** provide; endue; invest: *A judge is clothed with the authority of the state.* **5** express: *The moral of a fable is usually clothed in simple words.* **6** disguise: *murderous intentions clothed in friendship.* ⟨OE *clāthian* < *clāth* cloth⟩

☛ *Syn.* **1. Clothe,** DRESS = put clothes on. **Clothe** always requires an object and usually a modifying word or phrase telling how or with what: *He clothed himself in an old tweed suit.* **Dress** can be followed by an object and/or modifier but does not have to be. Without them it emphasizes the idea of getting ready, putting on whatever clothes are needed or appropriate: *She dressed in a hurry. It's time to dress for the party.*

clothes [klouðz] *or* [klouz] *n.pl.* **1** coverings for a person's body; garments; apparel; clothing: *summer clothes.* **2** the coverings for a bed.
☛ *Hom.* CLOSE[1] [klouz].

clothes•horse [klouðz,hɔrs] *or* ['klouz,hɔrs] *n.* **1** a frame to hang clothes on in order to dry or air them. **2** *Informal.* a person who places great value on being well and fashionably dressed.

clothes•line ['klouðz,laɪn] *or* ['klouz,laɪn] *n.* a rope, wire, etc. to hang clothes on in order to dry or air them.

clothes moth any of various moths (family Tineidae, especially of genera *Tineda* and *Tinea*) whose larvae feed on wool, fur, or feathers.

clothes•peg ['klouðz,pɛg] *or* ['klouz,pɛg] *n.* **1** a peg for hanging clothes on. **2** clothespin.

clothes•pin ['klouðz,pɪn] *or* ['klouz,pɪn] *n.* a clip, usually of plastic or wood, to hold clothes on a clothesline.

clothes•pole ['klouðz,poul] *or* ['klouz,poul] the pole that a clothesline is fastened to.

clothes•press ['klouðz,prɛs] *or* ['klouz,prɛs] *n.* a chest, cupboard, or closet in which to keep clothes.

clothes tree **1** an upright pole with branches on which to hang coats and hats. **2** a similar device but with larger branches and lines strung between them, for hanging clothes to dry.

cloth•ier ['klouðjər] *or* ['klouðiər] *n.* **1** a seller or maker of clothing. **2** a seller of cloth.

cloth•ing ['klouðɪŋ] *n., v.* —*n.* **1** clothes. **2** covering.
—*v.* ppr. of CLOTHE.

Clo•tho ['klouθou] *n. Greek mythology.* one of the three Fates. Clotho spins the thread of life.

cloth of gold cloth made of gold threads woven with silk or wool threads.

cloth yard formerly, a unit of length for measuring cloth, set by Edward VI at 37 inches (about 94 cm). It was also used as a length for arrows.

clo•ture ['kloutʃər] *n. Esp. U.S.* CLOSURE (def. 4).

cloud [klaʊd] *n., v.* —*n.* **1** a white, grey, or almost black mass in the sky, made up of tiny drops of water or ice particles. **2** a mass of smoke or dust. **3** a great number of things moving close together through the air: *a cloud of birds, a cloud of arrows.* **4** a mass of gas or dust in outer space; nebula. **5** a blemish or spot on a polished stone or gem. **6** anything that darkens, obscures, or dims. **7** a cause of gloom, trouble, suspicion, or disgrace.
in the clouds, a far above the earth. **b** fanciful; theoretical; not practical. **c** daydreaming; absent-minded.
under a cloud, a under suspicion; in disgrace. **b** in gloom or trouble.
—*v.* **1** cover with a cloud or clouds. **2** become cloudy: *The sky clouded.* **3** streak; spot, especially of a clear or shiny surface. **4** make or become gloomy or troubled; darken; dim: *His face clouded as he thought of the quarrel.* **5** make or become suspected or disgraced. ⟨OE *clūd* a mass of rock, hence, a mass of vapour⟩
—**'cloud•less,** *adj.* —**'cloud,like,** *adj.*

cloud•ber•ry ['klaʊd,bɛri] *n., pl.* **-ries.** *Cdn.* **1** a creeping herbaceous plant (*Rubus chamaemorus*) of the rose family found in northern latitudes, having white flowers and edible, amber-coloured berries. **2** a berry produced by this plant, resembling a raspberry. **3** *Cdn.* bakeapple.

cloud•burst ['klaʊd,bɜrst] *n.* a short, sudden, very heavy rainfall.

cloud–capped ['klaʊd ,kæpt] *adj.* tall enough to be covered by clouds: *cloud-capped towers.* ⟨coined by Shakespeare in *The Tempest*⟩

cloud chamber a large vessel filled with a vapour, especially a vapour of hydrogen and methyl alcohol, through which subatomic particles may be caused to move, leaving a trail by which they may be identified.

cloud•land ['klaʊd,lænd] *n.* the realm of the imagination, fancy, etc.

cloud•let ['klaʊdlɪt] *n.* a little cloud.

cloud nine or **Cloud Nine** *Informal.* a state or place of great happiness or bliss: *I still haven't come down from cloud nine!*
on cloud nine, in a very happy state.

cloud rack a group of broken clouds.

cloud seeding a scattering, usually from aircraft, of particles of carbon dioxide or certain other chemicals in clouds to produce rain.

cloud•y ['klaʊdi] *adj.* **cloud•i•er, cloud•i•est. 1** having clouds; covered with clouds: *a cloudy sky.* **2** characterized by a sky covered with clouds: *The morning was cloudy and cold.* **3** of or like clouds: *A cloudy veil hid the mountaintop.* **4** of a liquid, not clear; murky: *The pond water was cloudy.* **5** streaked; spotted: *cloudy marble.* **6** of ideas, etc., dim or unclear; hazy; clouded by ignorance, etc.: *He had some cloudy, half-formed notions, but no real plan of action.* **7** full of gloom or trouble; made dark or dim by grief, anger, fear, etc.: *a cloudy future.* —**'cloud•i•ly,** *adv.* —**'cloud•i•ness,** *n.*

clough [klʌf] *or* [klaʊ] *n.* a narrow valley; glen. ⟨OE *clōh*⟩

clout [klʌut] *n., v.* —*n.* **1** *Informal.* a hit, especially with the hand; cuff: *a clout on the head.* **2** *Baseball. Informal.* a long hit. **3** *Informal.* power and influence: *That newspaper doesn't carry any real clout. She has a lot of political clout.* **4** *Archery.* **a** a white cloth on a frame, used as a target. **b** a shot that hits this. **5** *Archaic or dialect.* a cloth or leather patch.
—*v. Informal.* hit hard: *She finally got exasperated with his teasing and clouted him.* ⟨OE *clūt* small piece of cloth or metal⟩

clove[1] [klouv] *n.* **1** the strongly fragrant, dried flower bud of a tropical tree (*Eugenia aromatica*) of the myrtle family, used as a spice. **2** the tree itself. ⟨ME *cloue* (apparently misread as *clove*) < OF *clou* < L *clavus* nail⟩

clove[2] [klouv] *n.* a small, separable section of a bulb: *a clove of garlic.* ⟨OE *clufu*⟩

clove[3] [klouv] *v.* a pt. of CLEAVE[1].

clove hitch a knot used in tying a rope around a pole, spar, etc. See KNOT for picture.

clo•ven ['klouvən] *v., adj.* —*v.* a pp. of CLEAVE[1].
—*adj.* split; divided.

cloven foot CLOVEN HOOF.

clo•ven–foot•ed ['klouvən ˌfʊtɪd] *adj.* **1** having cloven feet. **2** devilish.

cloven hoof a hoof divided into two parts. Cows have cloven hoofs. The Devil is traditionally pictured with cloven hoofs.

clo•ven–hoofed ['klouvən ˌhuft] *or* [-ˌhʊft] *adj.* **1** having cloven hoofs. **2** devilish.

clove pink an Old World pink (*Dianthus caryophyllus*) having single, flesh-coloured, clove-scented flowers. The many cultivated varieties of carnation are all derived from the clove pink.

clo•ver ['klouvər] *n.* **1** any of a genus (*Trifolium*) of low herbs of the pea family, having leaves consisting of three leaflets and rounded heads of small red, white, or yellow flowers. Several species of clover are grown as food for horses and cattle. **2** any of various related plants, such as sweet clover.
in clover, *Informal.* enjoying a life of pleasure and luxury without work or worry. ⟨OE *clāfre*⟩

clo•ver•leaf ['klouvər,lif] *n.* a series of ramps or turning lanes at the intersection of two main roads or highways, so arranged that traffic may move from one highway to the other without having to cross in front of other traffic.

clown [klaʊn] *n., v.* —*n.* **1** a person whose work is to amuse and entertain by tricks, jokes, and antics: *Circuses always have clowns.* **2** a person who is always acting silly or trying to be funny: *Arnie is the class clown.* **3** an ill-mannered, awkward, or uneducated person.
—*v.* act like a clown; play tricks and jokes; act silly: *We were clowning around on the lawn.* ⟨origin uncertain; cf. Icelandic *klumni* clumsy person, boor⟩

clown•er•y ['klaʊnəri] *n., pl.* **-er•ies.** the tricks and jokes of a clown; clownish act.

clown•ish ['klaʊnɪʃ] *adj.* like a clown; like a clown's. **—'clown•ish•ly,** *adv.* **—'clown•ish•ness,** *n.*

clox•a•cil•lin [ˌklɒksə'sɪlɪn] *n.* an antibiotic drug, a form of penicillin. *Formula*: $C_{19}H_{17}ClN_3NaO_5S$

cloy [klɔɪ] *v.* **1** overload with something originally pleasurable, such as rich or sweet food, so as to cause dislike: *She was cloyed with sweets before the holidays ended.* **2** of something originally pleasant, disgust or make weary through excess: *Her constant helpfulness soon begins to cloy.* ⟨ME *acloy, ancloy* drive a nail into, stop up, fill full < OF *encloyer* < *en-* in (< L *in-*) + *clou* nail (< L *clavus*)⟩ **—'cloy•ing•ly,** *adv.* **—'cloy•ing•ness,** *n.*

cloze test [klouz] a test of comprehension of reading, in which certain words are replaced by blanks for the reader to supply a suitable word. ⟨alteration of *close*[1]⟩

club [klʌb] *n., v.* **clubbed, club•bing.** —*n.* **1** a heavy stick of wood, thicker at one end, used as a weapon. **2** *Sports.* a stick or bat used in some games to hit a ball: *golf clubs.* **3** a group of people joined together for some special purpose: *a tennis club.* **4** an athletic team associated with some organization that sponsors it. **5** a building or rooms used by a club. **6** a nightclub. **7** a playing card with one or more black designs on it shaped like this: ♣ **8 clubs,** *pl.* a suit of cards marked with this design. **9** CLUB SANDWICH.
—*v.* **1** beat or hit with or as if with a club. **2** gather, unite, or combine for a common purpose (*usually used with* **together**). ⟨ME < ON *klubba*⟩

club•ba•ble ['klʌbəbəl] *adj.* sociable; suitable to be a member of a club. ⟨coined by Samuel Johnson, an 18c. English writer⟩

club•by ['klʌbi] *adj. Informal.* **1** very sociable or friendly. **2** of a place, having an atmosphere like a social club.

club car a railway passenger coach for day travel, more luxurious than ordinary coaches.

club chair a deep upholstered chair such as found in clubs, having upholstered arms and a low back.

club•foot ['klʌb,fʊt] *n., pl.* **-feet. 1** a deformity of the foot present at birth, in which the foot is twisted and misshapen, often resembling a club. **2** a foot having this deformity.

club•foot•ed ['klʌb,fʊtɪd] *adj.* having a clubfoot.

club fungus a large class of fungi including smuts, rusts, mushrooms, and puffballs, characterized by the formation of spores on a club-shaped structure.

club•hand ['klʌb,hænd] *n.* **1** a deformity of the hand present at birth, resembling a clubfoot. **2** a hand with this deformity.

club•house ['klʌb,hʌus] *n.* **1** a building used by a club. **2** an enclosed, often air-conditioned part of a race-track grandstand containing a restaurant.

club•man ['klʌbmən] *n., pl.* **-men. 1** a man who is a member of a fashionable club or clubs, especially one who makes frequent use of them. **2** a male member of a service club.

club moss any of an order (Lycopodiales) of mosslike plants having creeping or erect stems covered with tiny, overlapping leaves that resemble pine needles.

club•room ['klʌb,rum] *or* [-ˌrʊm] *n.* a room used for club meetings and activities.

club•root ['klʌb,rut] *n.* a disease of cabbages and similar plants, in which the roots become enlarged. It is caused by a mould (*Plasmodiaphora brassicae*).

club sandwich a thick sandwich consisting of toast and at least two layers of meats (especially chicken), lettuce, tomato, etc.

club soda SODA WATER.

club steak a small piece of beef cut from the loin.

club•wom•an ['klʌb,wʊmən] *n., pl.* **-wom•en. 1** a woman who belongs to a fashionable club or clubs, especially one who makes frequent use of them. **2** a female member of a service club.

cluck [klʌk] *n., v.* —*n.* **1** the sound made by a hen calling her chickens. **2** a sound like this. **3** *Slang.* a stupid person; blockhead; fool.
—*v.* **1** of a hen, make a cluck when calling the chickens. **2** make a sound like this; express with such a sound: *She clucked her disapproval.* ⟨imitative⟩

clue [klu] *n., v.* —*n.* a guide to the solving of a mystery or problem: *The police could find no clues to help them in solving the crime. This crossword puzzle has some very hard clues.*
—*v.* **1** indicate something by or as if by means of a clue. **2** *Informal.* tell; give information to (*usually used with* **in**): *"So what's happening? Clue me!" She promised to clue him in on their doings.*
clue up, *Esp. Brit. Informal.* provide (someone) with the essential details or information: *The new minister is not yet clued up about the working of her department.* ⟨var. of *clew*⟩
☛ *Hom.* CLEW.

clue•less ['klulɪs] *adj. Informal.* **1** not having any idea; not knowing; in the dark: *I always feel clueless about politics.* **2** generally ignorant or incompetent: *Boy, is he clueless—he just asked me where the cow's nest was!*

clum•ber ['klʌmbər] *n.* a breed of spaniel with short legs, a long, heavy body, and a silky, mainly white coat. ⟨< *Clumber*, an estate of the Duke of Newcastle, England⟩

clump [klʌmp] *n., v.* —*n.* **1** a cluster: *a clump of trees.* **2** a lump: *a clump of earth.* **3** the sound of heavy, clumsy walking.
—*v.* **1** form or cause to form a clump or clumps. **2** walk heavily and clumsily. ⟨earlier *clumper*, OE *clympre* lump of metal⟩

clump•y ['klʌmpi] *adj.* **1** full of clumps. **2** like a clump or clumps. **3** heavy and clumsy.

clumsy ['klʌmzi] *adj.* **-si•er, -si•est. 1** not graceful or skilful; awkward. **2** awkwardly done; poorly contrived: *a clumsy apology.* **3** not well-shaped or well-made. ⟨< *clumse* be numb with cold, probably < Scand.⟩ **—'clum•si•ly,** *adv.* **—'clum•si•ness,** *n.*
☛ *Syn.* **1.** See note at AWKWARD.

clung [klʌŋ] *v.* pt. and pp. of CLING.

clunk [klʌŋk] *n., v.* —*n.* **1** a dull sound like that of something hard striking the ground; thump. **2** a dull or stupid person.
—*v.* make such a sound; move or strike with such a sound: *clunk a person on the head.* ⟨imitative⟩

clunk•er ['klʌŋkər] *n. Slang.* **1** an old, run-down machine, especially a car or truck. **2** something worthless, unsuccessful, etc. **3** a mistake: *She really pulled a clunker on that one!* **4** something that clunks.

clunk•y ['klʌŋki] *adj.* **clunk•i•er, clunk•i•est.** *Informal.* **1** making a dull or thumping sound: *clunky footsteps.* **2** bulky and heavy; not elegant or graceful in appearance: *clunky shoes, clunky furniture.* **3** dull, clumsy, or poor: *a clunky film.* **—clunk•i•ly,** *adv.*

Cluny lace ['kluni] a kind of lace made of heavy linen or cotton thread. ⟨< *Cluny*, town in E France⟩

clu•peid ['klupiɪd] *n., adj.* —*n.* a fish of the family Clupeidae, including herrings and sardines.
—*adj.* of or having to do with this family of fishes. ⟨< NL⟩

clus•ter ['klʌstər] *n., v.* —*n* **1** a number of things of the same kind growing or fastened together; bunch: *a cluster of curls.* **2** a group of persons or things. **3** *Phonetics.* a sequence of two or more vowels or, especially, consonant sounds. *Str-* in *string* is a consonant cluster. **4** *Astronomy.* a group of stars relatively close to each other and often found to have a common motion in space. **5** *U.S.* a small metal device placed on the ribbon standing

for a military medal, to show that the same medal has been awarded again. **6** a bunch of grapes.
—*v.* form into a cluster; gather in clusters; group together closely: *The girls clustered around their teacher.* ⟨OE⟩

clutch[1] [klʌtʃ] *n., v.* —*n.* **1** a tight grasp; a firm hold by claw, paw, or hand: *The eagle loosened its clutch and the rabbit escaped.* **2** a grasping claw, paw, hand, etc.: *He just managed to stay out of reach of the bear's clutches.* **3** Usually, **clutches,** *pl.* control; power: *in the clutches of the police.* **4** any of several devices for connecting and disconnecting two working parts of a machine: *The clutch in a car connects the engine with the drive shaft, which turns the wheels.* **5** the lever or pedal that operates such a device. **6** CLUTCH PURSE.
—*v.* **1** grasp tightly: *The girl clutched her puppy to her breast.* **2** depress the clutch pedal of a car, van, or truck.
clutch at, grasp eagerly for; try to seize or take hold of: *She clutched at the branch, but missed it and fell.* ⟨OE *clyccan* bend, clench⟩
☛ *Syn. v.* **1.** See note at SEIZE.

clutch[2] [klʌtʃ] *n.* **1** a nest of eggs. **2** a brood of chickens. **3** a group of people or things: *There was a clutch of journalists covering the story.* ⟨var. of *cletch* < *cleck* hatch < ON *klekja*⟩

clutch purse a woman's handbag that is carried under the arm; a purse without handles or strap. Also, **clutch bag.**

clut•ter ['klʌtər] *n., v.* —*n.* **1** a litter; confusion; disorder. **2** confused noise; loud clatter.
—*v.* **1** litter with things: *Her desk was all cluttered with books and papers.* **2** make a confused noise; clatter loudly. ⟨< *clot*⟩

Clydes•dale ['klaɪdz,deil] *n.* a breed of large, strong draft horse. ⟨< *Clydesdale,* Scotland, where they were raised originally⟩

cm centimetre(s). The symbol for cubic centimetre is cm^3.

Cm curium.

CM *Cdn.* Member of the Order of Canada.

CMA Canadian Medical Association.

Cmdr. or **Cmdr** commander.

Cmdre. or **Cmdre** commodore.

C.M.G. Companion of (the Order of) St. Michael and St. George.

CMHC or **C.M.H.C.** Canada Mortgage and Housing Corporation.

CMM *Cdn.* Commander of the Order of Military Merit.

C.M.R. Collège Militaire Royale.

CN Canadian National Railways. Formerly, **CNR.**

CNE Canadian National Exhibition.

CNIB Canadian National Institute for the Blind.

cni•dar•ian [nɪ'dɛriən] *n.* coelenterate. ⟨< NL *Cnidaria* phylum name < Gk. *knidē* nettle; because they sting⟩

C–note ['si,nout] *n.* a 100-dollar bill.

CNS CENTRAL NERVOUS SYSTEM.

co– *prefix.* **1** with; together: *co-operate = act with or together.* **2** joint; fellow: *co-author = joint or fellow author.* **3** equally: *co-extensive = equally extensive.* **4** *Mathematics.* complement of: *cosine = complement of a sine.* ⟨< L *co-,* var. of *com-*⟩

c.o. or **c/o** **1** in care of. **2** carried over.

Co cobalt.

Co. or **co.** **1** company. **2** county.

C.O. **1** Commanding Officer. **2** *Informal.* CONSCIENTIOUS OBJECTOR.

coach [koutʃ] *n., v.* —*n.* **1** formerly, a large, closed carriage with seats inside and a high seat in front for the driver, especially a stagecoach. **2** a passenger car of a railway train, containing adjustable seats but no sleeping accommodation. **3** a closed automobile, especially a large, luxurious one. **4** bus. **5** a person who teaches or trains athletic teams, etc.: *a football coach.* **6** *Baseball.* a person stationed near first or third base to direct base runners and the batter. **7** a private teacher who helps a student prepare for a special test. **8** an instructor who supervises the training of actors, singers, etc.: *a drama coach, a music coach.* **9** a class of accommodation on a commercial airline, cheaper than first class.
—*v.* **1** carry or ride in a coach. **2** be a coach for or in: *She coached a winning team that fall. He coaches baseball. She coached the young singer for the exam.* **3** work as a coach: *He is coaching this winter.* ⟨ME < MF *coche* prob. < Magyar *kocsi,* after *Kocs,* a Hungarian village where coaches were supposedly made first⟩
☛ *Usage.* **Coach** (defs. 5-8). The senses of *instructor, teacher, trainer,* and the related verb meanings appear to derive from the idea of a university tutor being a means for carrying, or driving, the student through his or her examinations.

coach–and–four ['koutʃ ən 'fɔr] *n.* formerly, a coach pulled by four horses.

coach dog Dalmatian.

coach•man ['koutʃmən] *n., pl.* **-men.** a person whose work is driving a coach or carriage.

co•ac•tion [kou'ækʃən] *n. Ecology.* the interdependent interaction of two organisms, as in symbiosis.

co•ad•ju•tor [kou'ædʒətər] *or* [,kouə'dʒutər] *n.* **1** an assistant; helper. **2** a bishop appointed to assist another bishop. ⟨ME < LL < L *co-* with + *adjutor* helper < *adjuvare* < *ad-* + *juvare* help⟩

co•ag•u•lant [kou'ægjələnt] *n.* a substance that produces coagulation.

co•ag•u•late [kou'ægjə,leit] *v.* **-lat•ed, -lat•ing.** change from liquid form into a thickened mass; thicken; clot: *Cooking coagulates the white of an egg. Blood coagulates in air.* ⟨< L *coagulare* < *coagulum* means of curdling < *co-* together + *agere* drive⟩ **—co'ag•u•,la•tor,** *n.* **—co'ag•u•la•ble,** *adj.*

co•ag•u•lase [kou'ægjə,leis] *n.* an enzyme produced by certain bacteria, which causes clotting of blood.

co•ag•u•la•tion [kou,ægjə'leiʃən] *n.* **1** the act of coagulating. **2** a coagulated mass.

co•ag•u•la•tive [kou'ægjələtɪv] *or* [kou'ægjə,leitɪv] *adj.* tending to coagulate or cause coagulation.

coal [koul] *n., v.* —*n.* **1** a black or brownish black combustible substance containing varying amounts of carbon, used as a natural fuel and for the manufacture of coal gas, coal tar, etc. Coal is a kind of sedimentary rock formed over millions of years from the partial decomposition of vegetable matter away from air and under varying degrees of pressure. **2** a piece of coal. **3** a piece of burning or charred coal, wood, etc.; ember. **4** charcoal.
carry coals to Newcastle. See NEWCASTLE.
haul, rake, drag, or **call over the coals,** scold; blame.
heap coals of fire on (someone's) **head,** make (a person) sorry by returning good for evil.
—*v.* **1** supply with or take in coal: *The ship stopped to coal.* **2** burn (something) until it becomes charcoal. ⟨OE *col*⟩
☛ *Hom.* COLE, KOHL.

coal car a railway car used for freighting coal from the mine.

coal•er ['koulər] *n.* **1** a ship, railway, freight car, etc. used for carrying or supplying coal. **2** a worker or merchant who supplies coal.

co•a•lesce [,kouə'lɛs] *v.* **-lesced, -lesc•ing.** **1** grow together. **2** unite into one body, mass, party, etc.; combine: *Two political groups coalesced to form a new party.* ⟨< L *coalescere* < *co-* together + *alescere* grow⟩

co•a•les•cence [,kouə'lɛsəns] *n.* **1** a growing together. **2** union; combination. **—,co•a'les•cent,** *adj.*

coal field a region where beds of coal are found.

coal•fish ['koul,fɪʃ] *n.* POLLOCK (def. 1).

coal gas **1** a gas made by distilling bituminous coal, used for heating and lighting. **2** the toxic gas given off by burning coal.

coal hod COAL SCUTTLE.

coal•i•fi•ca•tion [,kouləfə'keiʃən] *n.* the natural process by which plant material is changed into coal.

coaling station a place where ships, trains, etc. are supplied with coal.

co•a•li•tion [,kouə'lɪʃən] *n.* **1** a union; combination. **2** a formal arrangement by which politicians, political parties, etc., agree to work together for a certain period of time or for a special purpose. ⟨< Med.L *coalitio, -onis* < L *coalescere.* See COALESCE.⟩ **—,co•a'li•tion•ist,** *n.*

coal measures **1** beds of coal; strata containing coal. **2** carboniferous rocks including coal deposits.

coal oil **1** kerosene: *coal oil lamps.* **2** petroleum.

coal pit **1** a coal mine. **2** a place where charcoal is made.

Coal•sack ['koul,sæk] *n. Astronomy.* a dark nebula in the southern constellation Crux, which blacks out that part of the Milky Way behind it.

coal scuttle a bucket or large scoop for holding or carrying coal.

coal tar a dark brown or black, heavy, sticky liquid obtained as a residue after the distillation of bituminous coal, used especially in making dyes, perfumes, medicines, and explosives.

coal•y ['kouli] *adj.* **-i•er, -i•est. 1** filled with coal. **2** black like coal.

coam•ing ['koumɪŋ] *n.* **1** a raised edge around a hatch or opening in the deck of a ship to prevent water from running down below. See CAPSTAN for picture. **2** any similar raised edge around an opening. ⟨origin uncertain⟩

coarse [kɔrs] *adj.* **coars•er, coars•est. 1** made up of fairly large parts; not fine: *coarse sand.* **2** heavy and rough in appearance or texture; not smooth and fine: *Burlap is coarse fabric.* **3** intended for rough work: *a coarse file.* **4** common; of ordinary or inferior quality: *coarse food. The peasants wore the same coarse clothing, summer and winter.* **5** rude; rough; vulgar: *coarse manners, a coarse laugh.* ⟨adjectival use of *course*, n., meaning 'ordinary'⟩ **—'coarse•ly,** *adv.* **—'coarse•ness,** *n.*

☛ *Hom.* COURSE, CORSE.

☛ *Syn.* **4, 5. Coarse,** VULGAR = not refined in feelings, manners, language, taste. **Coarse** emphasizes roughness and crudeness: *The soldier's coarse language was fit only for the barracks.* **Vulgar** suggests being deliberately and offensively rude, indelicate, or unrefined: *He is so vulgar that no one at school likes him.*

coarse–grained ['kɔrs 'greind] *adj.* **1** having a coarse texture; made up of large, coarse fibres or grains. **2** not delicate or refined; crude.

coars•en ['kɔrsən] *v.* make or become coarse.

coast [koust] *n., v.* *—n.* **1** the land along the edge of the sea; seashore. **2** a region near a coast. **3 the Coast,** in Canada and the United States, the region along the Pacific Ocean. **4** a ride or slide down a hill or along a flat road by momentum, without the use of power. **5** a slope for sliding downhill on a sled, etc.
the coast is clear, no one is in the way; the danger or hindrance is gone.
—v. **1** go along or near the coast of. **2** sail from port to port of a coast. **3** ride or slide down a hill without using power. **4** allow (a vehicle or vessel) to continue to move by its own momentum. **5** move or advance with little effort or exertion: *to coast along through school.* ⟨ME < OF < L *costa* side⟩ **—'coast•al,** *adj.*

coast•er ['koustər] *n.* **1** a person who or thing that coasts. **2** a ship trading along a coast. **3** a sled to coast on. **4** an amusement railway whose track dips and curves abruptly; ROLLER COASTER. **5** a little tray or mat on which a glass or bottle may be placed to protect the surface underneath.

coaster brake a brake on the rear wheel of a bicycle, worked by pushing back on the pedals.

coast guard 1 in Canada, a government service responsible mainly for search-and-rescue operations at sea, establishing and maintaining lighthouses, buoys, and other navigation aids, and icebreaking and moving cargo in the North. **2** a coastal patrol whose work is preventing smuggling and protecting lives and property along the coast: *The coast guard is often part of the armed forces of a country.* **3** a member of such a patrol.

coasting trade 1 the trade carried on by ships between the ports of one country. **2** the trade carried on by ships along the coasts of several countries.

coast•land ['koust,lænd] *n.* the land along a coast.

coast•line ['koust,laɪn] *n.* the outline or contour of a coast: *the rugged coastline of Newfoundland.*

Coast Salish 1 a people of the First Nations living in southern British Columbia, including the southeastern part of Vancouver Island, famous for their skill in basketry and weaving. **2** a member of this people. **3** their language.

coast–to–coast ['koust tə 'koust] *adj., adv.* in Canada, nationwide; transcontinental.

coast•ward ['koustwərd] *adv. or adj.* toward the coast. Also (*adv.*), **coastwards.**

coast•wise ['koust,waɪz] *adv. or adj.* along the coast. Also, **coastways.**

coat [kout] *n., v.* *—n.* **1** an outer garment of cloth, fur, etc. with sleeves. **2** an outer covering: *a dog's coat of hair, a coat of bark on a tree.* **3** a layer covering a surface: *a coat of paint.*
—v. **1** provide with a coat. **2** cover with a layer: *The old books were coated with dust.* ⟨ME < OF *cote* < Gmc.⟩ **—'coat•er,** *n.* **—'coat•less,** *adj.*

☛ *Hom.* COTE.

coated paper paper that has been coated with clay or sizing to give a glossy, smooth surface especially suitable for reproducing half-tone illustrations.

coat hanger a specially shaped piece of strong wire, plastic, or wood on which to hang clothes, with a hook in the top by which to hang it on a bar.

co•a•ti [kou'ɑti] *n., pl.* **-ties.** any of a genus (*Nasua*) of tropical American mammals related to and somewhat resembling raccoons, but larger and having a long, flexible snout and coarse grey, reddish, or brown fur. ⟨< Tupi⟩

co•a•ti–mun•di [kou'ɑti 'mʌndi] *n.* coati.

coat•ing ['koutɪŋ] *n., v.* *—n.* **1** a layer covering a surface: *a coating of paint.* **2** cloth for making coats.
—v. ppr. of COAT.

coat of arms 1 a group of symbols or designs which show the marks of distinction of a noble family, a government, a city, etc.: *In the Middle Ages, each knight or lord had his own coat of arms.* **2** a shield, or drawing of a shield, marked with such symbols or designs. ⟨translation of F *cotte d'armes*, a light coat decorated with heraldic designs worn over armour by knights in the Middle Ages⟩

coat of mail a garment made of metal rings or plates, worn as armour.

coat•tail ['kout,teil] *n.* **1** the back part of a coat below the waist; one of a pair of tails or flaps on such a part of a coat. **2 coattails,** *pl.* the skirts of a formal coat.
ride on (someone's) **coattails,** advance in career or popularity by associating with a more successful or more popular person.

co–au•thor [kou 'ɒθər] *n., v.* *—n.* a joint author.
—v. write with the help of another.

coax [kouks] *v.* **1** persuade by soft words; influence by pleasant ways: *She coaxed her father to let her go to the dance.* **2** get by coaxing: *The nurse coaxed a smile from the baby.* **3** urge gently. ⟨< obs. *cokes* a fool⟩ **—'coax•er,** *n.*

co•ax•i•al [ko'æksiəl] *adj.* **1** having a common axis. **2** of or having to do with a COAXIAL CABLE.

coaxial cable 1 a cable enclosing two or more concentric, insulated conductors capable of operating singly or in combination to carry radio, television, telegraph, and telephone signals. **2** a large cable containing a system of many coaxial cables to carry several video circuits and a large number of telephone circuits.

cob [kɒb] *n.* **1** the centre part of an ear of corn, on which the kernels grow. **2** a strong horse with short legs, often used for riding. **3** a male swan. ⟨ME *cob, cobbe* < Scand. and LG, a word suggesting something round or plump⟩

co•bal•a•min [kou'bæləmɪn] *n.* VITAMIN B_{12}.

co•balt ['koubɒlt] *n.* **1** a silvery-white, metallic element with a pinkish tint that occurs with and is similar to nickel and iron, used especially in alloys and for making pigments. *Symbol*: Co; *at.no.* 27; *at.mass* 58.93. **2** COBALT BLUE. ⟨< G *kobalt*, var. of *kobold* goblin⟩

cobalt blue 1 a bright blue pigment made from a mixture of cobalt and aluminum oxides. **2** bright medium blue.

cobalt bomb *Cdn.* a device for the use of cobalt-60 in the treatment of cancer.

co•bal•tic [kou'bɒltɪk] *adj.* **1** of cobalt. **2** of or containing cobalt with a valency of three.

co•balt•ite ['koubɒl,təit] *or* [kou'bɒltəit] *n.* a silvery-white mineral containing cobalt, arsenic, and sulphur. It is an important ore of cobalt. *Formula*: CoA_5S

co•bal•tous [kou'bɒltəs] of or containing cobalt with a valency of two.

cobalt–60 a heavy, radioactive form of cobalt used as a source of gamma rays for radiotherapy, in industry for detecting flaws in the internal structure of materials, etc.

cob•ble[1] ['kɒbəl] *v.* **-bled, -bling. 1** mend (shoes, etc.); repair; patch. **2** put together clumsily: *The proposal was quickly cobbled together by the constitutional experts.* ⟨probably akin to COB⟩

☛ *Hom.* COBLE.

cob•ble[2] ['kɒbəl] *n., v.* **-bled, -bling.** *—n.* **1** cobblestone. **2** a round lump of coal about the size of a cobblestone.
—v. pave with cobblestones. ⟨apparently dim. of ME *cob, cobbe.* See COB.⟩

☛ *Hom.* COBLE.

cob•bler ['kɒblər] *n.* **1** a person whose work is mending or making shoes; shoemaker. **2** a clumsy worker. **3** a fruit pie baked in a deep dish, usually with a crust only on top. **4** an iced drink made of wine, fruit juice, etc.

cob•ble•stone ['kɒbəl,stoun] *n.* a rounded stone formerly much used in paving streets, sidewalks, etc. ⟨ME *cobel ston*⟩

co–bel•lig•er•ent [ˌkou bəˈlɪdʒərənt] *n.* a nation that helps another nation carry on a war.

co•bia [ˈkoubiə] *n.* a large fish (*Rachycentron canadum*) found in warm oceans and having a black stripe along each side. ⟨origin unknown⟩

co•ble [ˈkoubəl] *or* [ˈkɒbəl] *n.* a small fishing boat used off the northerly coasts of Great Britain. ⟨ME *cobel* < OE *cuopel*⟩
☛ *Hom.* COBBLE.

cob•nut [ˈkɒbˌnʌt] *n.* hazelnut; filbert.

CO•BOL [ˈkoubɒl] *n. Computer technology.* an abbreviation of Common Business Oriented Language, the first computer language designed to handle business transactions.

co•bra [ˈkoubrə] *n.* **1** any of several very poisonous snakes (genus *Naja*) of Asia and Africa that, when excited, will spread out their upper ribs, causing the skin just below the head to expand into a hoodlike shape. **2** any of various related snakes. **3** leather made from the skin of any cobra. ⟨short for *cobra de capello*⟩

cobra de cap•el•lo [ˈkoubrə di kəˈpɛlou] *pl.* **cobras de capello.** a type of colourful Indian cobra (*Naja naja*) with an eye-shaped marking on its head. ⟨< Pg. serpent of the hood < L *colubra* a snake⟩

cob•web [ˈkɒbˌwɛb] *n.* **1** a spider's web or the stuff it is made of. **2** anything fine-spun or entangling like a spider's web. ⟨OE *(ātor)coppe* spider + *web*⟩

cob•web•by [ˈkɒbˌwɛbi] *adj.* **1** of or like a cobweb. **2** covered with or full of cobwebs.

co•ca [ˈkoukə] *n.* **1** any of several South American shrubs (genus *Erythroxylon*), especially *E. coca* from whose leaves cocaine and other alkaloids are obtained. **2** the dried leaves of a coca. **3** (*adjl.*) of or having to do with a family (Erythroxylaceae) of trees and shrubs. ⟨< Peruvian *cuca*⟩

co•caine [kouˈkein] *or* [ˈkoukein] *n.* a white, bitter, crystalline drug obtained from coca leaves, used to deaden pain and illegally as a stimulant. *Formula*: $C_{17}H_{21}NO_4$ Also, **cocain.** ⟨< *coca*⟩

co•cain•ism [kouˈkeinɪzəm] *n.* addiction to cocaine, causing a diseased condition.

co•cain•ize [kouˈkeinəɪz] *v.* **-ized, -iz•ing.** use cocaine therapeutically on (a person) as an anesthetic.

coc•cid [ˈkɒksɪd] *n.* a scale insect of the family Coccidae, having an outer covering of soft wax.

coc•cid•i•oi•do•my•co•sis [kɒkˌsɪdiˌɔɪdoumaɪˈkousɪs] *n.* a disease of people and animals, caused by inhaling spores of a fungus (*Coccidioides immitis*) and characterized by fever, respiratory infection, and red bumps on the skin. It is common in dry areas of the SW U.S. and Mexico, where it is often called **desert fever.**

coc•ci•di•o•sis [ˌkɒksɪdiˈousɪs] *n.* an infectious animal disease caused by an intestinal parasite (order Coccidia). ⟨< NL < L *coccidium* little berry + E *-osis*⟩

coc•cus [ˈkɒkəs] *n., pl.* **coc•ci** [ˈkɒksi] *or* [ˈkɒksaɪ]. **1** a bacterium shaped like a sphere. See BACILLI for picture. **2** *Botany.* one of the carpels making up the compound pistil of such plants as the carrot and celery. Each coccus contains one seed and breaks away when the fruit is mature. **—ˈcoc•coid,** *adj.* ⟨< NL < Gk. *kokkos* seed, berry⟩
☛ *Hom.* CAUCUS.

coc•cyx [ˈkɒksɪks] *n., pl.* **coc•cy•ges** [kɒkˈsaɪdʒiz] in humans and tailless apes, a small triangular bone at the base of the spinal column. It consists of several fused vertebrae. See SPINAL COLUMN and PELVIS for pictures. ⟨< L < Gk. *kokkyx*, originally, cuckoo; because shaped like cuckoo's bill⟩

Co•chin or **co•chin** [ˈkoutʃɪn] *or* [ˈkɒtʃɪn] *n.* a breed of large domestic fowl developed in Asia, having thickly feathered legs. ⟨after *Cochin China*, a former French colony in S Indo-China, now part of South Vietnam⟩

coch•i•neal [ˌkɒtʃəˈnil] *or* [ˈkɒtʃəˌnil] *n.* a bright red dye formerly made from the dried bodies of the females of a scale insect that lives on cactus plants of tropical America. ⟨< F < Sp. *cocinilla*, ult. < L *coccinus* scarlet < Gk. *kokkos* berry (gall) of a kind of oak⟩

cochineal insect any of various scale insects (family Dactylopiidae) with scarlet body fluid, native mainly to Mexico, and once used in the making of cochineal.

coch•le•a [ˈkɒkliə] *n., pl.* **-le•ae** [-liˌi] *or* [-liˌai]. *Anatomy.* a spiral-shaped cavity of the inner ear, containing the sensory ends of the auditory nerve. See EAR[1] for picture. ⟨< L < Gk. *kochlias* snail⟩ **—ˈcoch•le•ar,** *adj.*

coch•le•ate [ˈkɒkliɪt] *or* [ˈkɒkliˌeit] *adj.* spiral-shaped, like the shell of a snail.

cock[1] [kɒk] *n., v.* *—n.* **1** an adult male chicken; rooster. **2** the adult male of other birds. **3** a tap used to turn the flow of a liquid or gas on or off. **4** the hammer of a gun. **5** the position of the hammer of a gun when it is pulled back ready to fire. **6** weathercock. **7** woodcock. **8** *Informal.* leader; head; main person. **9** *Curling.* the mark aimed at.
cock of the walk, a person who thinks he or she has supreme power over a group or situation: *swaggering around like the cock of the walk.*
—v. pull back the hammer of (a gun), ready to fire. ⟨OE *cocc*⟩
☛ *Hom.* CAULK.

cock[2] [kɒk] *v., n.* *—v.* **1** turn or tilt upward and to one side: *The little bird cocked its eye at me. The dog cocked its ears.* **2** set (one's hat) at a jaunty angle on the head. **3** turn up the brim of (one's hat).
—n. **1** an upward turn or tilt of the nose, eye, or ear. **2** the turn of a hat brim. ⟨apparently < *cock*[1]⟩
☛ *Hom.* CAULK.

cock[3] [kɒk] *n., v.* *—n.* a small pile of hay, rounded on top.
—v. make into such piles. ⟨ME⟩
☛ *Hom.* CAULK.

A cockade on a hat

cock•ade [kɒˈkeid] *n.* a knot of ribbon or a rosette worn on the hat as a badge. ⟨alteration of *cockard* < F *cocarde* < *coq* cock⟩

cock–a–hoop [ˈkɒk ə ˈhup] *adj. Esp. Brit.* elated; triumphant and boastful.

Cock•aigne [kɒˈkein] *n.* an imaginary land of luxury and idleness. ⟨ME < OF *cokaigne* < MLG *kokenje* little sugar cake, ult. < L *coquere* cook⟩

cock•a•leek•ie [ˌkɒkəˈliki] *n.* a Scottish soup made of chicken broth with leeks and sometimes oatmeal. ⟨< *cocky-leekie*, < *cocky*, dim. of cock + *leeky*, dim. of leek⟩

cock•a•lo•rum [ˌkɒkəˈlɔrəm] *n.* **1** a little man with an exaggerated sense of his own importance. **2** boastful talk. ⟨< *cock*[1] + fanciful ending *-alorum*, based on L gen. pl. *-orum*; 18c.⟩

cock•a•ma•mie [ˈkɒkəˌmeimi] *adj.* **1** of inferior quality; cheap. **2** foolish; laughable. ⟨alteration of *decalcomania*, probably influenced by *cock-a-nee-nee*, 19c. New York name for a cheap molasses candy⟩

cock–and–bull story [ˈkɒk ən ˈbʊl] an absurd, incredible story.

cock•a•poo [ˈkɒkəˌpu] *n.* a dog that is a cross between a cocker spaniel and a poodle.

cock•a•tiel [ˈkɒkəˌtil] *or* [ˌkɒkəˈtil] *n.* a small Australian parrot with a crest and a long tail (*Nymphicus hollandicus*) that is sometimes kept as a pet. ⟨< Du. *kaketielje*⟩

cock•a•too [ˈkɒkəˌtu] *or* [ˌkɒkəˈtu] *n., pl.* **-toos.** any of various large parrots (especially genus *Kakatoe*) of Australia and the East Indies, having mainly white plumage and a crest on the head. ⟨< Du. *kaketoe* < Malay *kakatua*⟩

cock•a•trice [ˈkɒkətrɪs] *n.* a fabled serpent hatched from a cock's egg, whose look was supposed to cause death. ⟨ME < OF *cocatris* (influenced by *coq* cock) < L *calcatrix* trampler < *calcare* tread⟩

cock•boat [ˈkɒkˌbout] *n.* a small rowboat; cockleboat.

cock•chaf•er [ˈkɒkˌtʃeifər] *n.* a large European beetle (*Melolontha melolontha*) that destroys plants. The larva of the cockchafer feeds on roots and the adult feeds on the green parts of plants.

cock•crow ['kɒk,krou] *n.* **1** the crowing of a rooster. **2** the time when roosters begin to crow; dawn.

cocked hat **1** a hat with the brim turned up. **2** a hat pointed in front and at the back.
knock into a cocked hat, *Slang.* defeat; destroy completely; ruin.

cocker ['kɒkər] *n.* COCKER SPANIEL.

cock•er•el ['kɒkərəl] *n.* a young rooster, not more than one year old.

cocker spaniel a breed of small spaniel having long, silky hair and drooping ears.

cock•eye ['kɒk,aɪ] *n.* an eye that squints.

cock–eyed ['kɒk ,aɪd] *adj.* **1** cross-eyed. **2** *Slang.* tilted or twisted to one side. **3** *Slang.* foolish; silly; way off the mark.

cock•fight ['kɒk,fəit] *n.* a fight between roosters or between gamecocks armed with steel spurs.

cock•fight•ing ['kɒk,fəitɪŋ] *n.* fighting by roosters or gamecocks for the entertainment of spectators. Cockfighting is illegal in Canada.

cock•horse ['kɒk,hɔrs] *n.* a child's hobbyhorse; rocking horse.

cock•le[1] ['kɒkəl] *n., v.* **-led, -ling.** *—n.* **1** any of various saltwater clams (family Cardiidae) having a shell consisting of two round, convex valves with ridges radiating out from the hinge; especially a common, edible, European species (*Cardium edule*). **2** cockleshell. **3** a wrinkle or pucker, as in paper or cloth. **4** cockleboat.
cockles of (one's) **heart,** the inmost part of one's heart or feelings: *a welcome that warms the cockles of one's heart.*
—v. wrinkle; pucker: *Paper sometimes cockles when you paste it.* ⟨ME < MF *cokille* < VL < L *conchylia*, pl. of *conchylium* < Gk. *konchylion*, ult. < *konchē* conch⟩

cock•le[2] ['kɒkəl] *n.* any of several weeds often found in grainfields, especially several plants (such as *Saponaria vaccaria* and *Lychnis alba*) of the pink family. ⟨OE *coccel*, ? < L < Gk. *kokkos* berry⟩

cock•le•boat ['kɒkəl,bout] *n.* a small, light, shallow boat.

cock•le•bur ['kɒkəl,bɜr] *n.* any of a genus (*Xanthium*) of plants of the composite family found especially along roadsides and in pastures and fields, having spiny burrs.

cock•le•shell ['kɒkəl,ʃɛl] *n.* **1** the shell of a cockle or one of the valves of the shell. **2** the shell of any similar mollusc. **3** a small, light, shallow boat.

cock•loft ['kɒk,lɒft] *n.* a small attic; garret.

Cock•ney or **cock•ney** ['kɒkni] *n., pl.* **-neys;** *adj. —n.* **1** a native or inhabitant of London, England, especially a native of its East End or the City of London proper who speaks a particular dialect of English. **2** this dialect.
—adj. **1** of or like this dialect. **2** of or like Cockneys. ⟨ME *cokeney* cock's egg, pampered child, city fellow < *cocken* of cocks (OE *cocc*) + *ey* egg (OE *æg*)⟩

cock•ney•ism ['kɒkni,ɪzəm] *n.* any peculiarity of Cockney speech, such as a pronunciation, idiom, etc.

cock•pit ['kɒk,pɪt] *n.* **1** a place where the pilot sits in an aircraft. **2** the open place in a boat where the pilot or passengers sit. **3** an enclosed place for cockfights. **4** a scene of many fights or battles: *Belgium is often called the cockpit of Europe.* **5** formerly, an apartment or rooms below deck in a warship, used as quarters for junior officers, or as a hospital during battle. **6** the driver's seat in a racing car.

cock•roach ['kɒk,routʃ] *n.* any of an order (Blattaria) of insects, most of which are active at night, having long feelers and a long, flat, shiny body. Some species of cockroach are household pests. ⟨alteration of Sp. *cucaracha*⟩

cocks•comb ['kɒks,koum] *n.* **1** the fleshy, red crest on the head of a rooster. **2** a pointed cap somewhat like this, worn by a jester or clown. **3** any of several garden plants (genus *Celosia*) of the amaranth family having large, feathery red, orange, or yellow flower heads. **4** COXCOMB (def. 1).

cocks•foot ['kɒks,fʊt] *n.* ORCHARD GRASS.

cock•spur ['kɒk,spɜr] *n.* **1** the spur on the leg of a rooster. **2** a North American hawthorn (*Crataegus crusgalli*) having wide-spreading branches and long, slender thorns.

cock•sure ['kɒk'ʃʊr] *adj.* **1** too sure; cocky: *Her cocksure attitude is very irritating.* **2** perfectly sure; absolutely certain: *He hesitated, not being cocksure of his position.* **—'cock'sure•ly,** *adv.* **—'cock'sure•ness,** *n.*

cock•swain ['kɒksən] *or* [-,swein] See COXSWAIN.

cock•tail ['kɒk,teil] *n.* **1** an iced drink, often composed of gin or whisky mixed with bitters, vermouth, fruit juices, etc. **2** an appetizer: *a tomato juice cocktail.* **3** shellfish served in a small glass with a highly seasoned sauce: *a seafood cocktail.* **4** mixed fruits, diced and usually served in a glass. **5** (*adjl.*) of, for, or involving the serving and drinking of cocktails: *a cocktail party.* **6** (*adjl.*) of clothing, semiformal: *a cocktail dress.* **7** any mixture.

cocktail lounge a room in a hotel, restaurant, etc. where alcohol is served.

cocktail party a party at which cocktails are served.

cocktail table COFFEE TABLE.

cock•y ['kɒki] *adj.* **cock•i•er, cock•i•est.** *Informal.* conceited; swaggering. **—'cock•i•ly,** *adv.* **—'cock•i•ness,** *n.*

co•co ['koukou] *n., pl.* **co•cos. 1** COCONUT PALM. **2** its fruit; coconut. **3** (*adjl.*) made of the fibres of coconut husks: *coco mats.* ⟨< Pg. *coco* grinning face⟩
☛ *Hom.* COCOA.

co•coa ['koukou] *n.* **1** a reddish brown powder made from chocolate liquor by pressing out most of the fat. **2** a hot drink made from cocoa, milk or water, and sugar. **3** medium reddish brown.
—adj. having the colour cocoa. ⟨var. of *cacao*⟩
☛ *Hom.* COCO.

cocoa bean the seed of the cacao.

cocoa butter a yellowish white fat obtained from chocolate liquor, used in making soap, cosmetics, candy, etc.

co•co•nut ['koukə,nʌt] *or* ['koukənət] *n.* **1** the large, roundish fruit of the coconut palm, having edible white meat in a hard, brown shell. The shell of a coconut is enclosed in a thick, fibrous husk which is itself covered by a smooth rind. **2** the meat of the coconut, often shredded, used as a food or flavouring.

coconut milk a sweet, whitish liquid found in the hollow centre of an unripe coconut: *Coconut milk is good to drink.*

coconut oil the oil obtained from the dried meat of coconuts, used for making soap, candles, etc.

coconut palm a tall, tropical palm (*Cocos nucifera*) which produces coconuts. It has a crown of giant leaves with many leaflets growing along the centre rib of each.

co•coon [kə'kun] *n., v. —n.* **1** a covering prepared by the larva of many kinds of insect, including the ant and the moth, to protect itself while it is changing into an adult. Cocoons are usually of silk fibres produced by the insect, but some kinds include bits of leaves, twigs, etc. **2** any similar protective covering.
—v. **1** wrap or enclose in or as if in a cocoon; encase. **2** surround with protection. **3** engage in COCOONING. ⟨< F *cocon* < *coque* shell⟩

co•coon•ing [kə'kunɪŋ] *n., v. —n.* the practice of staying at home instead of going out, relying on home entertainment, take-out or delivery food instead of restaurant dining, and, increasingly, an office or workstation in one's own home instead of a job to which one commutes.
—v. ppr. of COCOON.

coco palm COCONUT PALM.

co•cotte [kou'kɒt] *n.* **1** a promiscuous woman. **2** an individual casserole. ⟨< F, originally hen < *coq* cock < OF⟩

co•co•zel•le [,koukə'zɛli] *n.* a kind of summer squash, having dark green skin striped with light green, and shaped like a club. ⟨< dialect form of Italian *cocuzza* gourd⟩

cod [kɒd] *n., pl.* **cod** or **cods. 1** a very important food fish (*Gadus morhua*) of the colder parts of the N Atlantic Ocean, having soft fins, a barbel on the chin, and a small, square tail. The cod is the source of cod-liver oil. **2** any of several related fishes, especially a closely related Pacific fish (*Gadus macrocephalus*). **3** (*adjl.*) designating a family (Gadidae) of fish found in cold and temperate waters, including the cods, haddock, hakes, and pollocks. Some of the world's most valuable food fishes are in the cod family. ⟨ME; origin uncertain⟩

C.O.D. or **c.o.d.** CASH ON DELIVERY; COLLECT ON DELIVERY.

co•da ['koudə] *n.* **1** *Music.* a separate and distinct passage at the end of a movement or composition, designed to bring it to a satisfactory close. **2** *Ballet.* the concluding section of a *pas de deux.* **3** *Linguistics.* the consonant or consonants closing a syllable. The coda of *spilt* is [lt] and the coda of *spin* is [n]. *Snow* has no coda. ⟨< Ital. < L *cauda* tail⟩

cod•der ['kɒdər] *n. Cdn. Maritimes.* **1** a boat used for cod fishing. **2** a cod fisher.

cod•dle ['kɒdəl] *v.* **-dled, -dling. 1** treat tenderly; pamper: *coddle sick children.* **2** cook in hot water without boiling: *coddle an egg.* ⟨var. of n. *caudle* gruel < OF < L *calidus* hot⟩
—'cod•dler, *n.*
☛ *Hom.* CAUDAL, CAUDLE.

code [koud] *n., v.* **cod•ed, cod•ing.** *—n.* **1** a collection of the laws of a country. **2** any set of rules: *A moral code is made up of the notions of right and wrong conduct held by a person, a group of persons, or a society.* **3** a system of signals for sending messages by telegraph, flags, etc. The Morse code is used in telegraphy. **4** *Computer technology.* **a** a system of symbols for representing information in a computer system. **b** a set of instructions written in a computer programming language: *The code for the payroll system still contains bugs.* **5** a system of secret writing; arrangement of words, figures, etc. to keep a message short or secret. **6** GENETIC CODE. **7** *Linguistics.* a language or dialect, especially regarded functionally as a vehicle of thought and expression.
reveal codes, display computer codes on the screen.
—v. **1** change or translate into a code; encode. **2** mark, provide, or program with a code. **3** *Computer technology.* write instructions for a computer; program: *She will begin to code the seat-selection module next week.* ⟨< F < L *codex* codex. Doublet of CODEX.⟩ **—'co•der,** *n.*

co•de•fen•dant [,koudi'fɛndənt] *n.* a joint defendant.

co•deine ['koudin] *or* ['koudiɪn] *n.* a white crystalline drug obtained from opium, used to relieve pain and cause sleep. Also, **codein.** *Formula:* $C_{18}H_{21}NO_3$ ⟨< Gk. *kōdeia* poppy head⟩

code word a euphemism for a socially or politically unacceptable term or idea.

co•dex ['koudɛks] *n., pl.* **co•di•ces.** ['koudə,siz] *or* ['kɒdə,siz]. a manuscript; a volume of manuscripts. ⟨< L *codex,* var. of *caudex* tree trunk, block, book. Doublet of CODE.⟩

cod•fish ['kɒd,fɪʃ] *n., pl.* **-fish** or **-fish•es.** cod.

codg•er ['kɒdʒər] *n. Informal.* a peculiar person, especially an older one. ⟨origin uncertain⟩

cod–haul•er ['kɒd ,hɒlər] *n. Cdn. Slang.* Newfoundlander.

co•di•ces ['koudə,siz] *or* ['kɒdə,siz] *n.* pl. of CODEX.

cod•i•cil ['kɒdəsɪl] *or* ['kɒdəsəl] *n.* **1** *Law.* something added to a will to change it, add to it, or explain it. **2** something added. ⟨< L *codicullus,* dim. of *codex.* See CODEX.⟩

cod•i•cil•la•ry [,kɒdə'sɪləri] *adj.* of the nature of a codicil.

cod•i•fi•ca•tion [,koudəfə'keiʃən] *or* [,kɒdəfə'keiʃən] *n.* **1** the act or process of arranging laws, rules, etc. according to a code or system. **2** the resulting arrangement. **3** the state or fact of being so arranged.

cod•i•fy ['koudə,faɪ] *or* ['kɒdə,faɪ] *v.* **-fied, -fy•ing.** arrange (laws, etc.) according to a system: *The laws of France were codified between 1804 and 1810 by order of Napoleon I.* ⟨< *code* + *-fy*⟩ **—'cod•i,fi•er,** *n.*

cod•lin ['kɒdlɪn] *n.* CODLING[1].

cod•ling[1] ['kɒdlɪŋ] *n.* **1** a small, unripe apple. **2** a kind of long, tapering apple. ⟨ME *querd(e)lying(e)* apple with a hard core, apparently < AF *quer de lion* heart of lion⟩

cod•ling[2] ['kɒdlɪŋ] *n.* **1** a young or small cod. **2** hake.

codling moth a small moth (*Carpocapsa pomonella*) whose larvae destroy apples, pears, etc.

cod–liv•er oil ['kɒd 'lɪvər] the oil extracted from the liver of cod or of related species of fish, used as a source of vitamins A and D.

co•dom•i•nant [kou'dɒmənənt] *adj. Genetics.* referring to a pair of allelic genes that are both expressed in the phenotype.

co•don ['koudɒn] *n. Genetics.* **1** a group of three nucleotides found in DNA or messenger RNA, which is the genetic code for a particular amino acid in protein synthesis. **2** the three-letter code representing such a group.

cod•piece ['kɒd,pis] *n.* a pouch or flap attached to the front of men's breeches or pants to cover the genitals, worn especially in the 15th and 16th centuries in Europe and Britain. ⟨OE *codd* bag, husk, scrotum + *piece*⟩

co–ed or **co•ed** ['kou 'ɛd] *n., adj. —n. Informal.* a student at a co-educational school, college, or university.
—adj. **1** co-educational. **2** for, by, or composed of both sexes: *a co-ed dorm.*

co–ed•u•ca•tion [,kou ɛdʒə'keiʃən] *n.* the education of boys and girls or men and women together in the same school or classes. **—,co-ed•u'ca•tion•al,** *adj.* **—,co-ed•u'ca•tion•al•ly,** *adv.*

co•ef•fi•cient [,kouə'fɪʃənt] *n., adj. —n.* **1** *Mathematics.* a number or symbol put before and multiplying another. In 3*x*, 3 is the coefficient of *x*; in *axy*, *a* is the coefficient of *xy.* **2** *Physics.* a ratio used as a multiplier to calculate the behaviour of a substance under different conditions of heat, light, etc.: *coefficient of expansion.*
—adj. co-operating.

coe•la•canth ['silə,kænθ] *n.* any of an order (Crossopterygii) of fishes having rounded scales and lobed, limblike pectoral fins. They were thought to have been long extinct until a living specimen (*Latimeria chalumnae*) was found near the S coast of Africa in 1938. Other specimens have been found since then. ⟨< NL *coelacanthus* < Gk. *koilos* hollow + *akantha* thorn, spine⟩

coe•len•ter•ate [sɪ'lɛntərɪt] *or* [sɪ'lɛntə,reit] *n., adj. —n.* any of a phylum (Coelenterata) of mostly marine invertebrates having a saclike body with a single opening. The phylum includes the jellyfishes, corals, hydras, and sea anemones. Also called **cnidarian.**
—adj. of or belonging to this phylum. ⟨< NL *coelenterata,* pl. < Gk. *koilos* hollow + *enteron* intestine⟩

coe•len•ter•on [sɪ'lɛntə,rɒn] *n.* the body cavity of a coelenterate.

coe•li•ac ['sili,æk] *adj.* See CELIAC.

coe•lom ['siləm] *n.* the body cavity of most many-celled animals, containing the heart, lungs, etc. Also, **celom.** ⟨< Gk. *koiloma* cavity < *koilos* hollow⟩

coe•lo•stat ['silə,stæt] *n.* an optical apparatus enabling one to view the same area of sky indefinitely. The apparatus consists of a mounted telescope with a mirror driven by clockwork and fixed at the same angle as the earth's rotational axis. ⟨< L *caelum* sky, heavens + Gk. *-states* < *histanai* make stand⟩

coe•no•bite ['sinə,bəit] *or* ['sɛnə,bəit] See CENOBITE.

coe•no•cyte ['sinə,səit] *n.* an organism consisting of a mass of protoplasm with many nuclei, enclosed in a single cell wall. Some algae are coenocytes. ⟨< Gk. *koinos* common + *kytos* a hollow⟩ **—,coe•no'cyt•ic** [-'sɪtɪk], *adj.*

co•en•zyme [kou'ɛnzaɪm] *n.* an organic substance, usually containing a mineral or vitamin, capable of attaching itself to and supplementing a specific protein to form an enzyme system.

co–e•qual [kou 'ikwəl] *adj., n. —adj.* equal in rank, degree, etc.
—n. one that is co-equal. **—co-'e•qual•ly,** *adv.* **—,co-e'qual•i•ty,** *n.*

co•erce [kou'ɜrs] *v.* **co•erced, co•erc•ing. 1** compel; force: *The prisoner was coerced into confessing to the crime.* **2** control or restrain by force. ⟨< L *coercere* < *co-* together + *arcere* restrain⟩ **—co'erc•er,** *n.*

co•er•cion [kou'ɜrʃən] *n.* **1** the use of force; compulsion; constraint. **2** government by force.

co•er•cive [kou'ɜrsɪv] *adj.* **1** compelling; forcing. **2** restraining. **—co'er•cive•ly,** *adv.* **—co'er•cive•ness,** *n.*

coes•ite ['kouzəit] *or* ['kousəit] *n.* a very dense form of silica, produced when quartz is subjected to very high pressure. It can be found in large meteor craters. ⟨after L. *Coes,* Jr. (b. 1915), American mineralogist⟩

co–e•val [kou 'ivəl] *adj., n. —adj.* **1** of the same age, date, or duration. **2** contemporary.
—n. a contemporary. ⟨< LL *coaevus* < *co-* equal + *aevum* age⟩ **—co'e•val•ly,** *adv.*

co–ex•ec•u•tor [,kou ɛg'zɛkjətər] *n.* a person who, along with another, is an executor of a will.

co–ex•ist [,kou ɛg'zɪst] *v.* **1** exist together or at the same time: *Orange trees have co-existing fruit and flowers.* **2** passively tolerate each other; live together without antagonism.

co–ex•ist•ence [,kou ɛg'zɪstəns] *n.* **1** existence together or at the same time. **2** living together in peace in spite of recognized differences. **—,co-ex'ist•ent,** *adj.*

co–ex•tend [,kou ɛk'stɛnd] *v.* extend equally or to the same limits.

co–ex•ten•sion [,kou ɛk'stɛnʃən] *n.* **1** extension over the same space or an equal amount of space. **2** extension over exactly the same time.

co–ex•ten•sive [,kou ɛk'stɛnsɪv] *adj.* extending equally; extending over the same space or time. **—,co-ex'ten•sive•ly,** *adv.*

C. of E. CHURCH OF ENGLAND.

cof•fee ['kɒfi] *n.* **1** a dark brown drink or flavouring made from the roasted and ground beans, or seeds, of the coffee tree.

2 coffee beans, especially when roasted and ground: *a kilogram of coffee.* 3 COFFEE TREE. 4 a medium to dark brown colour. 5 a cup of coffee: *They ordered two coffees.* 6 a social gathering at which coffee is served.
–adj. medium to dark brown. ⟨< Turkish *qahveh* < Arabic *qahwa*⟩

coffee bean the seed of the coffee tree, which may be roasted and ground to make coffee.

coffee break a pause in work, usually mid-morning and mid-afternoon, for coffee or other refreshments, and for a rest from work.

cof•fee•cake ['kɒfi,keik] *n.* 1 a small cake or bun eaten with coffee during a coffee break. 2 a cake flavoured with coffee.

coffee house 1 a small, informal restaurant that serves coffee and other refreshments and usually has some live entertainment: *She got her start as a folk singer by singing in coffee houses.* 2 formerly, in 18th-century London, England, a place where coffee and refreshments were sold, that served as a gathering place for people with similar interests.

coffee klatsch or **klatch** [klɑtʃ], [klʌtʃ], *or* [klætʃ] *n.* a get-together at which coffee is served. ⟨*coffee* + G *Klatsch* chitchat⟩

coffee maker a small electrical appliance which makes coffee, usually by dripping hot water through ground coffee in a filter.

coffee mill a machine for grinding coffee.

coffee pot a covered container for making or serving coffee.

coffee shop an informal restaurant, as in a hotel, where coffee and other refreshments and light meals are sold, usually one in which customers are served at a counter or in which they select their food at a counter and take it to tables to eat.

coffee table a low table, usually placed in front of a chesterfield and used for serving coffee and other refreshments, etc.

coffee–table book ['kɒfi ,teibəl] a book, usually large, expensive, and lavishly illustrated, designed mainly for display, as on a coffee table, and for casual browsing.

coffee tree any of several tall tropical evergreen shrubs (genus *Coffea*) of the madder family, the seeds of which are used to make coffee; especially, *C. arabica*, probably native to Ethiopia, but cultivated in many tropical parts of the world and accounting for the bulk of commercial coffee production.

cof•fer ['kɒfər] *n., v. –n.* 1 a box, chest, or trunk, especially one used to hold money or other valuable things. 2 an ornamental panel in a ceiling, etc. 3 cofferdam. 4 a lock in a canal. 5 **coffers,** *pl.* treasury; funds.
–v. 1 deposit or enclose in or as if in a coffer. 2 build or ornament with coffers: *a coffered ceiling.* ⟨ME < OF *cofre* < L < Gk. *kophinos* basket. See COFFIN.⟩

cof•fer•dam ['kɒfər,dæm] *n.* 1 a watertight enclosure built in a shallow river, lake, etc. It is pumped dry so that the foundations of a bridge, etc. may be built. 2 a space between two compartments of a ship's hold.

cof•fin ['kɒfən] *n., v. –n.* 1 a box into which a dead person is put to be buried or cremated; a casket. 2 the termination of the COFFIN BONE in a horse's hoof.
–v. 1 put into a coffin. 2 shut up tightly. ⟨ME < OF *cofin* < L *cophinus* < Gk. *kophinos* basket⟩

coffin bone the last section of the leg bone in horses and similar animals, enclosed in the hoof.

coffin corner *Football.* a corner of a football field delimited by a goal line and a side line.

cog[1] [kɒg] *n.* 1 one of a series of teeth on the edge of a wheel that transfer motion by locking into the teeth of a similar wheel. 2 a wheel with such a row of teeth on it. 3 a person who plays a small but necessary part in a large and complex organization.
slip a cog, *Informal.* make a mistake. ⟨ME *cogge* < Scand.; cf. Swedish *kugge*⟩

cog[2] [kɒg] *n.* a projection, or tenon, on a wooden beam, etc. that fits into a hole, or mortise, in another beam to form a joint. ⟨origin uncertain⟩

co•gen•cy ['koudʒənsi] *n.* a forcible quality; power of convincing.

co•gen•er•a•tion [,koudʒɛnə'reiʃən] *n.* the production of electricity from steam not completely used in an industrial process.

co•gent ['koudʒənt] *adj.* of reasoning, an argument, etc., forcible; convincing: *The lawyer's cogent arguments convinced the jury.* ⟨< L *cogens, -entis*, ppr. of *cogere* < *co-* together + *agere* drive⟩ **–'co•gent•ly,** *adv.*
☛ *Syn.* See note at VALID.

cogged [kɒgd] *adj.* having cogs.

cog•i•tate ['kɒdʒə,teit] *v.* **-tat•ed, -tat•ing.** think over; consider with care; meditate; ponder. ⟨< L *cogitare* < *co-* (intensive) + *agitare* consider < *agere* discuss⟩ **–'cog•i,ta•tor,** *n.* **–'cog•i•ta•ble,** *adj.*

cog•i•ta•tion [,kɒdʒə'teiʃən] *n.* deep thought; careful consideration; pondering; meditation.

cog•i•ta•tive ['kɒdʒə,teitɪv] *adj.* thoughtful; meditative. **–'cog•i,ta•tive•ly,** *adv.*

co•gnac ['kɒnjæk] *or* ['kounjæk]; *French,* [kɔ'njak] *n.* 1 a fine brandy, originally produced in W France. 2 any other kind of brandy. ⟨< F < *Cognac*, a town and region in France⟩

cog•nate ['kɒgneit] *adj., n. –adj.* 1 related by family or origin. 2 *Linguistics.* **a** of languages, having a common source and hence many closely related words. English, Dutch, and German are cognate languages. **b** of words in different languages, having a common source. 3 having a similar nature or quality.
–n. 1 a person, word, or thing related to another by having a common source. German *Wasser* and English *water* are cognates. 2 a relative on the mother's side. ⟨< L *cognatus* < *co-* together + *gnatus* born⟩

cog•ni•tion [kɒg'nɪʃən] *n.* 1 the mental process by which knowledge is acquired; perception. 2 the resulting knowledge or understanding. ⟨< L *cognitio, -onis* < *cognoscere* < *co-* (intensive) + *gnoscere* known⟩

cog•ni•tive ['kɒgnətɪv] *adj.* 1 of, having to do with, or involving cognition: *cognitive studies.* 2 having to do with factual knowledge and understanding, especially as opposed to emotion.

cog•ni•za•ble ['kɒgnəzəbəl] *or* [kɒg'naɪzəbəl] *adj.* 1 that can be known or perceived; recognizable. 2 within the jurisdiction of a court of law.

cog•ni•zance ['kɒgnəzəns] *for defs. 1 & 3;* ['kɒnəzəns] *for def. 2. n.* 1 knowledge; perception; awareness: *The dictator had cognizance of plots against him.* 2 *Law.* **a** knowledge upon which a judge is bound to act without having it proved in evidence. **b** the right or power to deal with something judicially. **c** an official notice. 3 jurisdiction; responsibility; charge.
take cognizance of, take notice of; give attention to. ⟨ME *conisance* < OF *conoissance* < *conoistre* know < L *cognoscere.* See COGNITION.⟩

cog•ni•zant ['kɒgnəzənt] *or* ['kɒnəzənt] *adj.* 1 aware: *The general was cognizant of the enemy's movements.*

cog•nize ['kɒgnaɪz] *or* [kɒg'naɪz] *v.* **cog•nized, cog•niz•ing.** be aware of; notice.

cog•no•men [kɒg'noumən] *n.* 1 a surname; family name; last name. 2 any name, especially a descriptive nickname. 3 in ancient Rome, the third or family name of a person, as *Cicero* in *Marcus Tullius Cicero.* ⟨< L *cognomen* < *co-* with + *nomen* name; form influenced by *cognoscere* recognize⟩ **–cog'nom•i•nal** [-'nɒmənəl], *adj.*

co•gno•scen•ti [,kɒnjou'ʃɛnti] *or* [,kɒgnə'ʃɛnti] *n.pl., sing.* **co•gno•scen•te** [-tei] *or* [-ti]. People having or claiming to have a keen appreciation of or expert knowledge in a particular field, as in art, literature, or politics. ⟨< obsolete Ital.; ult. < L *cognoscere* to know⟩

co•gon [kou'goun] *n.* a tall, coarse grass (*Imperata cylindrica*) used in the Philippines as cattle food and for thatching. ⟨< Sp. *cogon* < Tagalog⟩

cog railway a railway on a steep slope where traction is provided by a centre rail whose cog engages with a cog on the engine.

cog•wheel ['kɒg,wil] *n.* a wheel with teeth cut in the rim that fit with teeth or grooves in another wheel or in a rack or worm so that one can drive the other; gear.

co•hab•it [kou'hæbɪt] *v.* 1 live together as husband and wife, especially when not legally married. 2 live in the same place or territory; share (a place for living). ⟨< LL *cohabitare* < L *co-* with + *habitare* dwell⟩ **–co,hab•i'ta•tion,** *n.*

co•hab•it•ant [kou'hæbətənt] *n.* a person who or animal that lives together with another or others.

co–heir ['kou 'ɛr] *n.* an heir with another or others.

co–heir•ess ['kou 'ɛrɪs] *n.* an heiress with another or others.

co•here [kou'hir] *v.* **-hered, -her•ing.** 1 stick or hold together as parts of the same mass or substance: *the particles making up a brick cohere.* **2** be connected logically; be consistent. **3** *Physics.* be united by the action of molecular forces. **4** be united in harmony and loyalty. ⟨< L *cohaerere* < *co-* together + *haerere* stick⟩

co•her•ence [kou'hirəns] *n.* **1** a logical connection; consistency. **2** a sticking together; cohesion. **3** *Physics.* the state of being coherent. Also, **coherency**.

co•her•ent [kou'hirənt] *adj.* **1** logically connected; consistent in structure and thought: *A sentence that is not coherent is hard to understand.* **2** sticking together; holding together. **3** making sense by one's speech. **4** *Physics.* of waves, having a high degree of similarity of phase, direction, and amplitude: *Lasers produce coherent light.* **—co'her•ent•ly,** *adv.*

co•he•sion [kou'hiʒən] *n.* **1 a** a sticking together. **b** tendency to hold together: *Wet sand has more cohesion than dry sand.* **2** *Physics.* an attraction between molecules of the same kind, by which the elements of a substance are held together. The tendency of water to form into drops is a result of cohesion. Compare ADHESION (def.4). **3** *Botany.* the union of one part with another. **4** unity; togetherness. ⟨< stem of L *cohaesus* pressed together, pp. of *cohaerere.* See COHERE.⟩

co•he•sive [kou'hisɪv] *adj.* **1** sticking together; tending to hold together. **2** united; close-knit: *The students were a very cohesive group.* **—co'he•sive•ly,** *adv.* **—co'he•sive•ness,** *n.*

co•ho ['kouhou] *n., pl.* **-hoes** or **-ho.** *Cdn.* a Pacific salmon (*Oncorhynchus kisutch*) found along the west coast from S California to Alaska, metallic blue and silver in colour and having red flesh that fades when cooked. The coho is very highly valued as a food and game fish. Also, **cohoe.** ⟨origin uncertain⟩

co•hort ['kouhɔrt] *n.* **1** in ancient Rome, a part of a legion. There were from 300 to 600 soldiers in each cohort, and ten cohorts in each legion. **2** a group or band, especially of soldiers. **3** *Informal.* a companion or associate. **4** *Statistics.* an age group or similarly well-defined group. **5** an accomplice. ⟨< L *cohors, -ortis* court, enclosure. Doublet of COURT.⟩

co•hosh ['kouhɒʃ] *or* [kou'hɒʃ] *n.* either of two eastern American plants, the **black cohosh** (*Cimicifuga racemosa*) of the buttercup family, or the **blue cohosh** (*Caulophyllum thalictroides*) of the barberry family.

co•hous•ing ['kou,haʊzɪŋ] *n.* a design of housing development that allows for independent ownership but also community living.

co•hune [kou'hun] *n.* a palm tree (*Orbignya cohune*) native to Central America, having large nuts that yield an oil similar to coconut oil, which is used to make soap. ⟨< Central American Indian *cohun*⟩

coif [kɔɪf] *for n. 1 and v. 1,* [kwɑf] *for n. 2 and v. 2 & 3. n., v.* *—n.* **1** a cap or hood that fits closely around the head. **2** coiffure. *—v.* **1** provide or cover with a coif or something like a coif. **2** arrange or dress (the hair). **3** style the hair of. ⟨ME < OF *coife* < LL *cofia* < Gmc.⟩

coif•feur [kwɑ'fɜr]; *French,* [kwa'fœʀ] *n.* a male hairdresser. ⟨< F *coiffeur* < *coiffer* coif⟩

coif•feuse [kwɑ'fʊz] *or* [kwɑ'fjuz]; *French,* [kwa'føz] *n.* a female hairdresser.

coif•fure [kwɑ'fjʊr]; *French,* [kwa'fyʀ] *n.* **1** a style of arranging the hair. **2** a covering for the hair; headdress. ⟨< F *coiffure* < *coiffer* coif⟩

coign or **coigne** [kɔɪn] *n.* See QUOIN.
☛ *Hom.* COIN.

coign of vantage a good location for watching or doing something.

coil[1] [kɔɪl] *v., n. —v.* **1** wind around and around in a series of circles to form a spiral or a tube: *The sailor coiled the rope so it would not take up much space.* **2** form or lie in a series of circles: *The snake coiled around a branch.* **3** move in a winding or spiralling course.
—n. **1** one of a series of circles forming a spiral: *One coil of the rope was smaller than the others.* **2** a series of such circles: *The coil of hose was hung on the wall.* **3** a series of connected pipes arranged in a coil or row, as in a radiator. **4** a spiral of wire for conducting electricity, used as an inductor. **5** a twist of hair. **6** a small pile of hay rounded on top; cock. **7** a roll of postage stamps. ⟨< OF *coillir* < L *colligere.* See COLLECT[1].⟩ **—'coil•er,** *n.*

coil[2] [kɔɪl] *n. Archaic.* disturbance; trouble. ⟨origin uncertain⟩

coin [kɔɪn] *n., v. —n.* **1** a piece of metal stamped by a government for use as money. Nickels, dimes, quarters, and loonies are coins. **2** metal money: *The Mint makes coin by stamping metal.* **3** *Slang.* money.

pay (someone) back in (his or her) **own coin,** treat (someone) as he or she treated oneself or others.

the other side of the coin, the opposite view, aspect, or opinion.
—v. **1** make (money) by stamping metal; mint. **2** make (metal) into money. **3** make up; invent (a word or phrase): *The word* chortle *was coined by Lewis Carroll.*

coin money, *Informal.* become rich; have a prospering business: *He's coining money in the oil industry.* ⟨ME < OF *coin* corner < L *cuneus* wedge⟩
☛ *Hom.* COIGN, QUOIN.

coin•age ['kɔɪnɪdʒ] *n.* **1** the making of coins. **2** coins; metal money. **3** a system of coins: *Canada has a decimal coinage.* **4** a word or phrase that has been made up, or invented. **5** the right to coin money. **6** the act or process of making up; inventing: *the coinage of new words.*

co•in•cide [,kouɪn'saɪd] *v.* **-cid•ed, -cid•ing.** **1** occupy the same place in space: *If these triangles* Δ Δ *were placed one over the other, they would coincide.* **2** occupy the same time; occur at the same time: *The working hours of the two friends coincide.* **3** correspond exactly; agree: *Her opinion coincides with mine.* ⟨< Med.L *coincidere* < L *co-* together + *in* upon + *cadere* fall⟩
☛ *Syn.* **3.** See note at AGREE.

co•in•ci•dence [kou'ɪnsədəns] *n.* **1** the chance occurrence of two things together in such a way as to seem remarkable, fitting, etc. **2** the act or condition of coinciding. **3** an exact correspondence; agreement.

co•in•ci•dent [kou'ɪnsədənt] *adj.* **1** coinciding; happening at the same time. **2** occupying the same place or position. **3** in exact agreement (*used with* **with**). **—co'in•ci•dent•ly,** *adv.*

co•in•ci•den•tal [kou,ɪnsə'dɛntəl] *adj.* involving or resulting from coincidence. **—co,in•ci'den•tal•ly,** *adv.*

coin•er ['kɔɪnər] *n.* **1** a person who makes coins. **2** a maker of counterfeit coins. **3** a maker; inventor, especially of words.

coin–op ['kɔɪn ,ɒp] *adj. Informal.* coin-operated.

coin–op•er•at•ed ['kɔɪn 'ɒpə,reitɪd] *adj.* worked by the insertion of a coin or coins: *Machines that sell candy, cigarettes, etc. are coin-operated.*

co–insure [,kou ɪn'ʃʊr] *v.* **-ured, -ur•ing.** insure jointly with another or others. **—,co-in'sur•ance,** *n.*

Coin•treau [kwɑn'trou]; *French,* [kwɑ̃tʀo] *n. Trademark.* a clear, orange-flavoured liqueur, a French brand of curaçao.

coir [kɔɪr] *n.* a fibre obtained from the outer husks of coconuts, used to make rope, mats, etc. ⟨< Malayalam *kayar* cord⟩

co•i•tus ['kouɪtəs], ['kɔɪtəs], *or* [kou'itəs] *n.* sexual intercourse. ⟨< *coitio,* pp. of *coire* go in company⟩

coke[1] [kouk] *n., v.* **coked, cok•ing.** *—n.* **1** a fuel made from coal by heating it in a closed oven until the gases have been removed. Coke burns with much heat and little smoke; it is used in furnaces, for melting metal, etc. **2** the solid waste left after the purification of petroleum.
—v. change into coke. ⟨? var. of *colk* core⟩

coke[2] [kouk] *n., v. —n. Slang.* cocaine.
—v. use cocaine (*used with* **out** *or* **up**).

col [kɒl] *n.* **1** a gap or depression in a range of mountains or hills, usually providing a pass through the range. **2** *Meteorology.* the point of lowest pressure between two anticyclones. ⟨< L *collum* neck⟩
☛ *Hom.* CALL, CAUL.

col– *prefix.* together or altogether; the form of **com-** occurring before *l,* as in *collapse.*

col. 1 column. **2** colony.

Col. or **Col** colonel.

co•la ['koulə] *n.* **1** any of various carbonated soft drinks flavoured with kola nuts, coca, etc. **2** See KOLA.

col•an•der ['kɒləndər], ['kʌləndər], *or* [kə'lændər] *n.* a vessel or dish with many small holes for draining off liquids from foods. ⟨< VL *colator* or Med.L *colatorium* < L *colare* strain⟩

Col•by ['koulbi] *n.* a soft, mild cheese, made by stirring curd as the whey drains off instead of allowing it to settle.

col•can•non [kəl'kænən] *or* ['kɒl,kænən] *n.* an Irish dish consisting of cabbage and potatoes, boiled and mashed together. ⟨< Irish *cal ceannan* white-headed cabbage⟩

col•chi•cine ['kɒltʃə,sin] *n.* a drug used to treat warts and gout. *Formula:* $C_{22}H_{25}NO_6$

col•chi•cum ['kɒltʃəkəm] *n.* **1** any of a genus (*Colchicum*) of Old World plants of the lily family having crocuslike flowers that bloom in autumn. Some colchicums are grown as garden plants. **2** the dried corms or seeds of a colchicum, from which colchicine is extracted. ⟨< L < Gk. *kolchikon* < *Colchis*⟩

Col•chis ['kɒlkɪs] *n.* an ancient country on the eastern shore of the Black Sea. In Greek legend it is the country where the Golden Fleece was found by Jason and the Argonauts. **—'Col•chi•an,** *adj.*

col•co•thar ['kɒlkəθər] *or* ['kɒlkə,θɑr] *n. Chemistry.* a reddish brown iron oxide made by heating ferrous sulphate, used as a polishing agent and as pigment in paints and theatrical cosmetics; jewellers' rouge. ⟨< Sp. *colcotar* < Arabic *qulqutar* < Gk. *chalkanthos* solution of blue vitriol < *chalkos* copper + *anthos* flower⟩

cold [kould] *adj., n. —adj.* **1** much less warm than the body: *Snow and ice are cold.* **2** feeling not enough warmth; feeling uncomfortable because of lack of warmth: *He's always complaining that he's cold.* **3** having a relatively low temperature; less warm than desired: *This coffee is cold.* **4** lacking a proper warm-up period: *The engine is cold.* **5** not kind and sympathetic; indifferent or unfriendly: *a cold person, a cold greeting.* **6** sexually unresponsive. **7** not influenced by emotion; objective: *cold logic.* **8** not cheering; dispiriting: *cold reality, the cold light of day.* **9** faint; weak; not fresh: *a cold trail, a cold scent.* **10** suggesting coolness: *Blue and green are called cold colours.* **11** unconscious: *She was out cold.*
cold comfort, poor consolation.
in cold blood. See BLOOD.
leave (one) **cold,** arouse no interest in one.
throw or **pour cold water on,** actively discourage or belittle: *to throw cold water on someone's plans.*
—n. **1** the lack of heat or warmth; low temperature: *the cold of winter.* **2** a common viral infection that produces a stuffy or running nose and, often, a cough or sore throat. **3** the bodily sensation of not being warm enough. **4** cold weather.
catch cold or **take cold,** become sick with a cold.
come in from the cold, be restored to one's usual status, activity, etc.
(out) in the cold, all alone; neglected; ignored. ⟨OE *cald*⟩
☛ *Syn. adj.* **1, 2. Cold,** CHILLY, COOL = having a low temperature, especially in comparison with body heat. **Cold** = having a low temperature, judged by the standard of normal body heat: *A cold wind is blowing.* **Chilly** = cold enough to be uncomfortable and make a person shiver a little: *Without my coat I feel chilly.* **Cool** = neither hot nor cold, but closer to cold, often pleasantly so: *After the hot day the evening seems cool.*

cold–blood•ed ['kould ,blʌdɪd] *or* ['kould 'blʌdɪd] *adj.* **1** having blood whose temperature varies with that of the surroundings. Snakes and turtles are called cold-blooded, but their blood temperature is actually very close to that of the air or water around them. **2** feeling the cold because of poor circulation. **3** characterized by a lack of normal feelings of consideration, pity, or kindness; emotionless and cruel: *deliberate, cold-blooded murder. The cold-blooded pirates sold all their captives into slavery.* **—'cold-'blood•ed•ly,** *adv.* **—'cold-'blood•ed•ness,** *n.*

cold cash ready money, as distinct from credit.

cold chisel a strong, steel chisel for cutting cold metal.

cold cream a creamy, soothing, oil-based salve for softening or cleansing the skin.

cold cuts cooked or prepared meats or fowl, such as beef, chicken, salami, ham, etc., sliced and served cold.

Cold Duck or **cold duck** a drink made from sparkling Burgundy and champagne. ⟨translation of German *kalte Ente*⟩

cold feet sudden fear or timidity; loss of courage: *He suddenly got cold feet and refused to go on stage.*

cold frame a low box with a clear glass or plastic top, built on the ground outdoors and used to protect young or delicate plants from cold while allowing them exposure to sunlight.

cold front *Meteorology.* the front edge of a cold air mass advancing into and replacing a warm one.

cold–heart•ed ['kould ,hɑrtɪd] *adj.* lacking in feeling; unsympathetic; unkind. **—'cold-,heart•ed•ly,** *adv.* **—'cold-,heart•ed•ness,** *n.*

cold light light without heat. Phosphorescence and fluorescence are kinds of cold light.

cold•ly ['kouldli] *adv.* in a cold manner; without friendliness, warmth, or sympathy.

cold•ness ['kouldnɪs] *n.* **1** the state or quality of being cold. **2** a lack of warmth of feeling or friendliness; indifference.

cold pack 1 something cold put on the body for medical purposes. **2** a method of canning fruits or vegetables in which they are heated only after being placed in the container.

cold–pack ['kould ,pæk] *v.* **1** put a cold pack on. **2** can (food) by cold pack.

cold rubber a tough, synthetic rubber formed at a low temperature.

cold shoulder *Informal.* deliberately unfriendly or indifferent treatment; conscious neglect: *to give someone the cold shoulder, to turn a cold shoulder.*

cold–shoul•der ['kould 'ʃouldər] *v. Informal.* treat in an unfriendly or indifferent way.

cold snap a sudden spell of cold weather.

cold sore a sore on or near the lips, often accompanying a cold or fever, consisting of a group of small blisters that break and form a crust before they begin to heal. It is a form of herpes simplex.

cold steel a steel weapon, such as a knife or sword.

cold storage storage in a very cold place. Perishable foods are put in cold storage to keep them from spoiling.

cold sweat perspiration caused by fear, nervousness, pain, or shock, often accompanied by a cold or clammy feeling: *She broke out in a cold sweat just thinking about her narrow escape.*

cold turkey *Slang.* **1** sudden, total withdrawal from a drug to which one has become addicted: *She said the only way she could quit smoking was cold turkey.* **2** by means of such withdrawal: *He decided to quit cold turkey.* **3** without preparation beforehand; without preliminaries: *He approached the manager cold turkey and asked for a raise.* **4** bluntly: *talk cold turkey to a person.*

cold type any method of typesetting other than by hot-cast metal, such as computer or photo composition.

cold war a prolonged contest for national advantage, conducted by diplomatic, economic, and psychological rather than military means. Compare HOT WAR.

cold–wa•ter flat ['kould,wɒtər] a humble apartment having no hot water or, sometimes, a bathroom.

cold wave 1 a period of very cold weather. **2** a process by which hair is pressed into permanent waves or curls by the application of chemicals rather than heat.

cole [koul] *n. Rare.* any of various plants of the genus *Brassica,* especially rape or cabbage. Also called **colewort.** ⟨OE *cāl,* var. of *cāw(e)l* < L *caulis* cabbage⟩
☛ *Hom.* COAL, KOHL.

co•lec•to•my [kə'lɛktəmi] *n.* surgical removal of the colon.

cole•man•ite ['koulmə,nəit] *n.* a white or clear crystal-forming mineral, used in glass production. *Formula:* $Ca_2B_6O_{11}•5H_2O$ ⟨< after W. T. *Coleman* (1824-1893), American manufacturer of borax⟩

co•le•op•ter•an [,kouli'ɒptəræn] *or* [,kɒli'ɒptərən] *n., adj. —n.* any insect of the order Coleoptera; BEETLE[1].
—adj. of, having to do with, or belonging to the order Coleoptera. ⟨< NL < Gk. *koleopteros* < *koleos* sheath + *pteron* wing⟩

co•le•op•ter•ous [,kouli'ɒptərəs] *or* [,kɒli'ɒptərəs] *adj.* coleopteran.

co•le•op•tile [,kouli'ɒptəl] *or* [,kɒli'ɒptəl] *n.* a tubular sheath covering the terminal bud of grasses for a short time after germination of the grains. ⟨< Gk. *koleos* sheath + *ptilon* feather⟩

cole•slaw ['koul,slɒ] *n.* a salad made of shredded raw cabbage. ⟨< Du. *kool sla* cabbage salad⟩

co•les•ti•pol [kə'lɛstəpəl] *n.* a drug used to treat high cholesterol.

co•le•us ['kouliəs] *n.* any of a genus (*Coleus*) of tropical plants of the mint family, grown for their showy, colourful leaves. ⟨< NL < Gk. *kileos* sheath; from the union of the filaments⟩

cole•wort ['koul,wɜrt] *n.* **1** cole. **2** any kind of cabbage having a loosely packed head of curly leaves, such as kale.

col•ic ['kɒlɪk] *n., adj. —n.* **1** severe pains in the abdomen resulting from muscular spasms. **2** a condition in young babies characterized by constant crying due to various physical complaints.
—adj. **1** of colic. **2** of or having to do with the colon or bowels. ⟨< LL < Gk. *kolikos* of the colon⟩

col•ick•y ['kɒlɪki] *adj.* **1** of colic. **2** having colic.

col•ic•root ['kɒlɪk,rut] *n.* **1** a plant of the genus *Aletris,* either *Aletris farinosa* or *Aletris aurea,* of the lily family, having small white or yellow flowers, and a root supposed to cure colic. **2** any of several other plants, such as the butterfly weed, whose roots are thought to cure colic.

col•ic•weed ['kɒlɪk,wid] *n.* any of a number of plants similar to the Dutchman's-breeches, native to North America.

co•li•form ['koulə,fɔrm] *or* ['kɒlə,fɔrm] *adj.* of, like, or designating any of various bacilli normally found in the colon of vertebrates and excreted in the feces. Coliform bacteria from human and animal feces may contaminate water and cause disease.

col•in ['kɒlɪn] *n.* any American bird of the quail family, such as the bobwhite. ⟨< Am.Sp. < Nahuatl⟩

col•i•se•um [,kɒlə'siəm] *n.* **1** a large building or stadium for games, contests, etc. **2 Coliseum.** See COLOSSEUM. ⟨< Med.L var. of LL *colosseum.* See COLOSSEUM.⟩

co•lis•tin [kə'lɪstɪn] *n.* a drug used to treat certain ear infections. *Formula*: $C_{45}H_{85}O_{10}N_{13}$

co•li•tis [kə'ləitɪs] *n.* inflammation of the colon, often causing severe pain in the abdomen. ⟨< NL *colitis* < Gk. *kolon* colon + *-itis*⟩

coll. **1** college. **2** collection; collector. **3** colleague. **4** colloquial. **5** collegiate.

col•lab•o•rate [kə'læbə,reit] *v.* **-rat•ed, -rat•ing. 1** work together: *Two authors collaborated on that book.* **2** aid or co-operate with someone traitorously. ⟨< L *collaborare* < *com-* with + *laborare* work⟩

col•lab•o•ra•tion [kə,læbə'reiʃən] *n.* the act of collaborating.

col•lab•o•ra•tion•ist [kə,læbə'reiʃənɪst] *n.* someone who collaborates traitorously with enemy occupiers.

col•lab•o•ra•tive [kə'læbərətɪv] *or* [kə'læbə,reitɪv] *adj.* of or resulting from collaboration.

col•lab•o•ra•tor [kə'læbə,reitər] *n.* **1** a person who works with another, usually in literary work. **2** a person who aids or co-operates with someone traitorously.

col•lage [kə'lɑʒ] *n.* **1** a picture made by pasting on a background an arrangement of items with different textures, colours and shapes, such as portions of photographs, newspapers, fabric, string, etc. **2** anything made of odd parts or pieces; composite. **3** a photograph or film scene made of assorted pictures. ⟨< MF *collage* a gluing < OF *colle* < VL *colla* < Gk. *kolla* glue⟩

col•la•gen ['kɒlədʒən] *n.* any of a group of fibrous proteins found in connective tissue, as skin, ligaments, tendons, bone, and cartilage. It forms gelatin when dissolved in boiling water. ⟨< Gk. *kolla* glue + -GEN⟩ **—,col•la'gen•ic,** *adj.*

col•lapse [kə'læps] *v.* **-lapsed, -laps•ing;** *n.* *—v.* **1** fall suddenly down or in as a result of outside pressure or loss of support; cave in: *They escaped from the burning building just before it collapsed. A football will collapse if the air leaks out.* **2** of lungs, become deflated. **3** break down; fail suddenly: *Both his health and his business collapsed within a year.* **4** fold or push together: *to collapse a telescope. This playpen collapses into a very compact package.*
—n. **1** a falling in; sudden shrinking together: *A heavy flood caused the collapse of the bridge.* **2** a breakdown; failure: *She is suffering from a nervous collapse.* ⟨< L *collapsus,* pp. of *collabi* < *com-* (intensive) + *labi* fall⟩

col•laps•i•ble [kə'læpsəbəl] *adj.* made so that it can be folded or pushed into a smaller format. **—col,laps•i'bil•i•ty,** *n.*

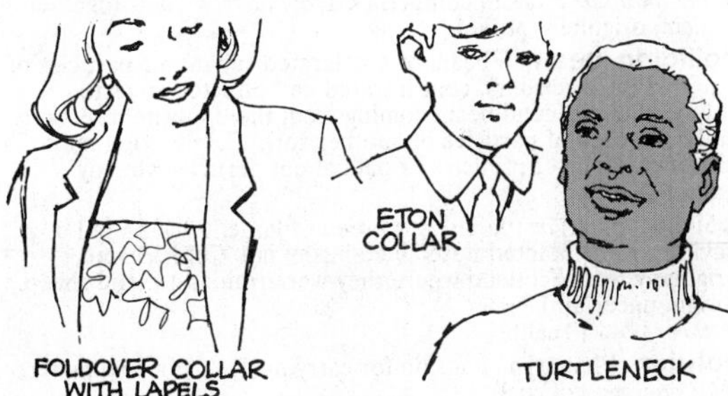

col•lar ['kɒlər] *n., v.* *—n.* **1** a piece or band of cloth that finishes or is attached to the neckline of a garment, designed to stand up around the neck or lie folded over at the base of the neck, sometimes extending over the shoulders. **2** a piece of jewellery resembling a collar worn around the neck or over the chest and shoulders. **3** a band of leather, metal, etc. for the neck of a dog or other pet animal. **4** a thick, padded oval ring that forms part of the harness of a draft animal, fitting around the neck and resting against the shoulders and chest: *A horse's collar bears the weight of the load it is pulling.* See HARNESS for picture. **5** a distinctive marking around the neck of an animal or bird, suggesting a collar: *The cliff swallow has a dark blue head and back and a grey collar around the back of the neck.* **6** the white foam at the top of a freshly poured glass of beer. **7** a ring, disk, or flange on a rod, shaft, etc. that keeps a part from moving to the side. **8** a short pipe connecting two other pipes. **9** *Informal.* an arrest.
—v. **1** put a collar on. **2** seize by the collar; capture or arrest. **3** *Informal.* lay hold of; take. ⟨ME < AF < L *collare* < *collum* neck⟩ **—'col•lar•less,** *adj.* **—'col•lar,like,** *adj.*
☛ *Hom.* CALLER, CHOLER.

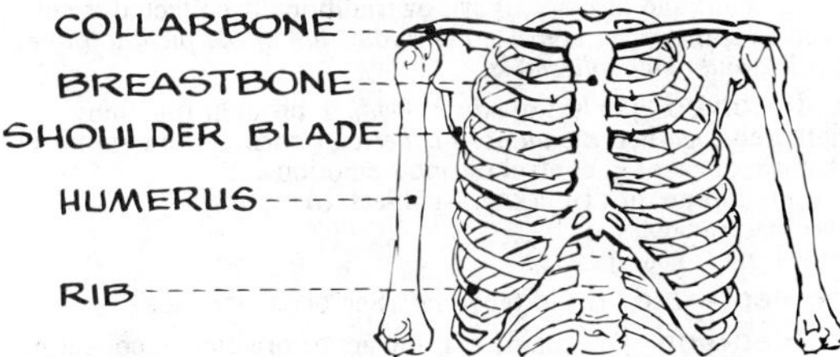

Part of the upper human skeleton, shown from the front

col•lar•bone ['kɒlər,boun] *n.* the bone connecting the breastbone and the shoulder blade; clavicle.

collar cell a cell found inside the body of a sponge, having a projecting rim to which food particles stick when the surrounding water is agitated by the flagellum of the cell.

col•lard ['kɒlərd] *n.* **1** a kind of kale. **2** Usually, **collards** or **collard greens,** *pl.* the fleshy leaves of this plant, cooked as a vegetable. ⟨alteration of *colewort*⟩

col•late ['kouleit], ['kɒleit], *or* [kə'leit] *v.* **-lat•ed, -lat•ing. 1** examine and compare carefully in order to note similarities and differences, check for accuracy, etc.: *to collate a copy of a document with the original, to collate the data from several experiments.* **2** arrange in proper order; put together in sequence: *to collate the pages of a report, to collate the sections of a book for binding.* ⟨< L *collatus,* pp. to *conferre* < *com-* together + *ferre* bring⟩

col•lat•er•al [kə'lætərəl] *adj., n.* *—adj.* **1** parallel; side by side. **2** related but less important; secondary; indirect. **3** in a parallel line of descent; descended from the same ancestors, but in a different line: *Cousins are collateral relatives.* **4** corresponding in rank, importance, or time. **5** additional. **6** secured by stocks, bonds, etc.
—n. **1** a collateral relative. **2** stocks, bonds, etc. pledged as security for a loan. ⟨< Med.L *collateralis* < *com-* together + L *lateralis* lateral⟩ **—col'lat•er•al•ly,** *adv.* **—col'lat•er•al,ize,** *v.*

collateral damage a wartime euphemism for civilian casualties and damage to civilian property near a military installation under attack.

collating sequence *Computer technology.* the order of the internal representations of all the characters in a computer. The collating sequence determines the results of any sorting process done on data stored internally as characters.

col•la•tion [kə'leiʃən] *or* [kou'leiʃən] *n.* **1** the act or process of collating. **2** a light meal; originally, in Benedictine monasteries, a light meal following readings of the Lives of the Fathers *(collationes patrum).* **3** a listing of the physical features of a book, such as number of pages, measurements, etc. ⟨ME < OF < L *collatio, -onis* a putting together⟩

col•la•tor ['kouleitər], ['kɒleitər], *or* [kə'leitər] *n.* a person who collates.

col•league ['kɒlig] *n.* an associate; a fellow worker: *The doctor invited a colleague to examine the patient.* ⟨< F *collègue* < L *collega* < *com-* together + *legare* send or choose as deputy⟩

col•lect[1] [kə'lɛkt] *v., adj., adv.* *—v.* **1** gather (something) together; pick up from different spots: *The teacher collected the questionnaires.* **2** come together in one place; assemble: *A crowd soon collects at the scene of an accident.* **3** pile up; form into a mass; accumulate: *Drifting snow collects behind snow fences.* **4** gather (something) as a hobby: *to collect stamps.* **5** ask and

receive payment for (bills, debts, dues, taxes, etc.) 6 regain control of (oneself, one's wits, etc.): *After the shock he needed to collect himself.*
—adj. or adv. to be paid for by the receiver: *a collect telegram, to telephone collect.* ⟨< L *collectus*, pp. of *colligere* < *com-* together + *legere* gather⟩
☛ *Syn. v.* **1, 2, 4.** See note at GATHER.

col•lect² [ˈkɒlɛkt] *n.* a short prayer used in certain Christian church services. ⟨ME < OF *collecte* < Med.L, short for *oratio ad collectam* prayer on assembly < L *collecta* a gathering in or gathering together < *colligere.* See COLLECT¹.⟩

col•lect•a•ble or **col•lect•i•ble** [kəˈlɛktəbəl] *adj., n.* *—adj.* that may be collected; suitable for collection.
—n. anything having a current attraction for collectors; an item that might be part of a collection, especially something other than an antique or work of art, or traditionally collected items such as coins or stamps: *a store window full of old picture frames, bottles, and other collectables.*

col•lect•ed [kəˈlɛktɪd] *adj., v.* *—adj.* **1** brought together; gathered together: *the author's collected works.* **2** not confused or disturbed; calm; in control of one's emotions.
—v. pt. and pp. of COLLECT¹. **—col'lect•ed•ly,** *adv.* **—col'lect•ed•ness,** *n.*
☛ *Syn.* **2.** See note at CALM.

col•lect•i•ble [kəˈlɛktəbəl] *adj.* See COLLECTABLE.

col•lec•tion [kəˈlɛkʃən] *n.* **1** the act or practice of collecting. **2** a group of things gathered from many places and belonging together: *The library has a large collection of books.* **3** a collecting of money, especially for church expenses or charity. **4** the money collected: *The collection was larger than expected.* **5** something that has come together in one place; accumulation; heap: *There was a collection of debris on the porch.*

col•lec•tive [kəˈlɛktɪv] *adj., n.* *—adj.* **1** of a group; as a group; made or done by all together: *a collective effort, a collective decision.* **2** formed by collecting. **3** functioning or operating on the principle of collectivism.
—n. **1** COLLECTIVE NOUN. **2** a farm, factory, or other organization with collectivistic management. **3** the people working on a collective farm, factory, etc. **—col'lec•tive•ly,** *adv.*

collective bargaining negotiation about wages, hours, and other working conditions between workers organized as a group and their employer or employers.

collective farm a farm operated and worked by a group co-operatively. The farm, its buildings, and its machinery may be owned communally by the group, by an institution, or, as in communist countries, by the state.

collective noun a noun that is singular in form but refers to a collection of things or persons. *Crowd, team, bunch,* and *orchestra* are collective nouns.
☛ *Usage.* A collective noun is used with a singular verb when it refers to a group as a whole (*The committee was silent*), but may be used with a plural verb when it refers to a group in which the individuals are thought of as acting separately (*The committee were asked to prepare separate reports.*).

collective security the guarantee by a group of countries of the security of each country in the group and the maintenance of peace by collective action against a country attacking any nation in the group.

col•lec•tiv•ism [kəˈlɛktɪˌvɪzəm] *n.* the control of the production of goods and services, and the distribution of wealth, by people as a group or by a government.

col•lec•tiv•ist [kəˈlɛktɪvɪst] *n., adj.* *—n.* a person who favours or supports collectivism.
—adj. collectivistic.

col•lec•tiv•is•tic [kəˌlɛktɪˈvɪstɪk] *adj.* of collectivism or collectivists.

col•lec•tiv•i•ty [ˌkɒlɛkˈtɪvəti] *n.* **1** people collectively, especially as forming a community or state. **2** the whole so formed.

col•lec•ti•vize [kəˈlɛktəˌvaɪz] *v.* **-vized, -viz•ing.** make (a state, economy, agricultural community, etc.) collective; transfer ownership of, from an individual or individuals to the state or all the people collectively. **—col,lec•ti•vi'za•tion,** *n.*

collect on delivery payment upon delivery of a parcel or shipment. *Abbrev.:* C.O.D. or c.o.d.

col•lec•tor [kəˈlɛktər] *n.* **1** a person who collects things as a hobby: *a coin collector.* **2** something that collects or appears to collect: *All these ornaments are just dust collectors.* **3** a person hired to collect money owed. **4** in a vacuum tube, the positive electrode that attracts electrons from the emitter.

col•lec•tor•ship [kəˈlɛktərˌʃɪp] *n.* **1** the office of a collector. **2** the district covered by a collector.

collector's item something worth adding to a collection.

col•leen [ˈkɒlin] *or* [kɒˈlin] *n. Irish.* girl. ⟨< Ir. *cailín*, dim. of *caile* girl⟩

col•lege [ˈkɒlɪdʒ] *n.* **1** an institution that offers training or instruction in one or more particular occupations or professions and gives degrees or diplomas, or pre-university education: *the Victoria College of Art. My cousin is taking a course in computer programming at a community college.* **2** *Esp. U.S. Informal.* university: *She's planning to go to college in the fall.* **3** one of the main academic divisions of a university, offering courses of study leading to a degree in a particular academic or professional field; faculty. All universities have a college of arts and sciences, and most have several professional colleges such as engineering, agriculture, medicine, or education. **4** an institution within a university, either offering undergraduate courses in particular subject areas or organized as a social, administrative, and residential unit with courses in a limited range of subjects: *Students at Erindale College get their degree from the University of Toronto.* **5** an organized association of persons having certain powers, rights, duties, and purposes: *the electoral college.* **6** a building or buildings used by a college. **7** (*adjl.*) of or associated with college or university. ⟨ME < OF *colege* < L *collegium* < *collega.* See COLLEAGUE.⟩

collège classique [kɔˈlɛʒ klaˈsik] *Cdn. French.* CLASSICAL COLLEGE.

Collège Mi•li•taire Ro•yale [kɔˈlɛʒ miliˈtɛʀ ʀwaˈjal] one of Canada's three military colleges, located in St. Jean, Québec, but disbanded in 1995.

College of Cardinals the cardinals of the Roman Catholic Church collectively. They elect and advise the Pope.

col•le•gi•al [kəˈlidʒəl] *adj.* **1** of or having to do with a COLLEGE (esp. def. 5). **2** characterized by equal sharing of power or authority among colleagues: *a collegial system of cabinet government.*

col•le•gi•al•i•ty [kəˌlidʒiˈæləti] *n.* the sharing of authority and power among colleagues; especially, in the Roman Catholic Church, the sharing of authority by the Pope and bishops.

col•le•giate [kəˈlidʒɪt] *or* [kəˈlidʒiɪt] *adj., n.* *—adj.* **1** *Cdn.* of or like a high school or high-school students. **2** of or like a college or college students.
—n. Cdn. **1** COLLEGIATE INSTITUTE. **2** *Informal.* any large high school.

collegiate church **1** a church that has a chapter or college but no bishop's see. **2** *U.S.* an association of churches administered by several pastors jointly. **3** a church belonging to such an association. **4** in Scotland, a church served by two or more ministers of equal rank.

collegiate institute *Cdn.* in some provinces, a secondary school providing specified facilities or programs, or having a set minimum number of specialist teachers, over and above those required in a high school.

col•le•gium [kəˈlidʒiəm] *n., pl.* **col•le•gia** [kəˈlidʒiə]. a group of officials acting as a ruling body.

col•lide [kəˈlaɪd] *v.* **-lid•ed, -lid•ing. 1** come violently into contact; come together with force; crash: *Two large ships collided in the harbour.* **2** clash; conflict. ⟨< L *collidere* < *com-* together + *laedere*, originally, strike⟩

colliding beam a beam of accelerated subatomic particles of one sort (as electrons), concentrated and directed so as to collide with a second beam coming from the opposite direction and composed of particles of another sort. The collision may yield new kinds of particles or data about particles already known to exist.

col•lie [ˈkɒli] *or* [ˈkouli] *n.* a breed of large, thick-haired dog having a long, pointed nose and a bushy tail. Collies came originally from Scotland where they were trained to tend sheep. ⟨origin uncertain⟩
☛ *Hom.* COLY [ˈkouli].

col•lier [ˈkɒljər] *n.* **1** a ship for carrying coal. **2** a coal miner. ⟨ME *colier* < *col* coal⟩

col•lier•y [ˈkɒljəri] *n., pl.* **-lier•ies.** a coal mine and its buildings and equipment.

col•lig•a•tive [kəˈlɪgətɪv] *or* [ˈkɒləˌgeitɪv] *adj. Chemistry.* of or having to do with the number of particles present, as in a solution, and not with the nature of the particles: *colligative properties.* ⟨< L *com-* together + *ligare* bind⟩ **—ˌcol•li'ga•tion,** *n.*

col•li•mate ['kɒlə,meit] *v.* **-mat•ed, -mat•ing. 1** bring into line; make parallel. **2** adjust accurately the line of sight of (a surveying instrument, telescope, etc.) ⟨< L *collimare*, misreading for *collineare*, ult. < *com-* together + *linea* line⟩
—,col•li'ma•tion, *n.*

col•li•ma•tor ['kɒlə,meitər] *n. Optics.* **1** a small, fixed telescope used for adjusting the line of sight of other instruments. **2** in a spectroscope, a tube used to throw parallel rays of light on the prism. **3** the lens of this tube.

col•lin•e•ar [kə'lɪniər] *adj. Geometry.* lying in the same straight line: *collinear points.* **—col'lin•e•ar•ly,** *adv.*

Col•lins or **col•lins** ['kɒlɪnz] *n.* a cocktail made with spirits and fruit juice or soda water and sugar.

col•lin•sia [kə'lɪnsiə] *or* [kə'lɪnziə] *n.* any plant of the genus *Collinsia* of the figwort family, having whorled leaves and flower clusters in various colours. ⟨< NL, after Z. *Collins* (1764–1831), American botanist⟩

col•li•sion [kə'lɪʒən] *n.* **1** a violent rushing against; hitting or striking violently together. **2** a clash; conflict. ⟨< LL *collisio, -onis* < L *collidere.* See COLLIDE.⟩

col•lo•cate ['kɒlə,keit] *v.* **-cat•ed, -cat•ing. 1** place together. **2** arrange.
collocate (with), of a word, be used regularly together with (another word or words): *The word* circumstances *collocates with* under *or* in. ⟨< L *collocare* < *com-* together + *locare* place⟩
—,col•lo'ca•tion, *n.*

col•lo•di•on [kə'loudiən] *n.* a gluelike solution of cellulose nitrate in ether and alcohol that dries very rapidly, leaving a tough, waterproof, transparent film. Collodion is used for covering burns and wounds. ⟨< Gk. *kollōdēs* gluey < *kolla* glue⟩

col•loid ['kɒlɔɪd] *n.* **1** a solid, liquid, or gaseous substance made up of very small particles, such as single large molecules or groups of smaller molecules, that will remain suspended without dissolving in a different medium. A colloid may be suspended in a solid, liquid, or gas. **2** a state of matter consisting of such a substance together with the medium in which it is suspended. Fog and the protoplasm of plant and animal cells are colloids. **3** the jellylike protein stored in the thyroid, containing iodine. ⟨< Gk. *kolla* glue⟩

col•loi•dal [kə'lɔɪdəl] *adj.* **1** in the form of a colloid. **2** of, like, or containing a colloid.

col•lop ['kɒləp] *n.* **1** a small slice of meat. **2** a small slice or piece of anything. **3** a fold of flesh or skin on the body. ⟨ME *colope*; origin uncertain⟩

colloq. colloquial; colloquialism.

col•lo•qui•al [kə'loukwiəl] *adj.* **1** used in everyday informal talk, but not in formal speech or writing. *They've had it* and *It's a cinch* are colloquial expressions. Compare INFORMAL. **2** oral; to do with conversation. ⟨< L *colloquium* conversation < *com-* together + *loqui* speak⟩ **—col'lo•qui•al•ly,** *adv.*

☛ *Usage.* **Colloquial** = conversational, used in speaking. Since the speech of people varies with their education, work, and social status, there are obviously many different types of colloquial English. Since the bulk of conversation is informal, **colloquial** suggests informal rather than formal English. It need not, however, mean the speech of uneducated people. As used in many dictionaries, **colloquial** refers to informal, cultivated English; the equivalent label in this dictionary is *Informal.*

col•lo•qui•al•ism [kə'loukwiə,lɪzəm] *n.* **1** a colloquial word or phrase. **2** colloquial style or usage.

col•lo•quist ['kɒləkwɪst] *n.* one who takes part in a colloquium or colloquy.

col•lo•qui•um [kə'loukwiəm] *n., pl.* **-qui•ums** or **-qui•a. 1** a meeting or conference, especially of scholars, scientists, etc. on a particular subject. **2** seminar. ⟨< L *colloquium* conversation⟩

col•lo•quy ['kɒləkwi] *n., pl.* **-quies. 1** a talking together; conversation; conference. **2** a written dialogue: *Erasmus' Colloquies.* ⟨< L *colloquium* < *colloqui* < *com-* with + *loqui* speak⟩

col•lude [kə'lud] *v.* **-lud•ed, -lud•ing.** act together through a secret understanding; conspire. ⟨< L *colludere* < *com-* with + *ludere* play⟩

col•lu•sion [kə'luʒən] *n.* a secret agreement, especially for some wrong purpose.
in collusion, acting secretly together. ⟨< L *collusio, -onis* < *colludere.* See COLLUDE.⟩

col•lu•sive [kə'lusɪv] *adj.* involving collusion; fraudulent.
—col'lu•sive•ly, *adv.*

col•lyr•ium [kə'liriəm] *n.* any medicine for the eyes; eyewash. ⟨< Gk. *kollyrion* eye salve⟩

col•o•bus ['kɒləbəs] *n.* any large monkey of the genus *Colobus*, native to Africa, having no thumbs, and having long, silky, black and white fur.

col•o•cynth ['kɒlə,sɪnθ] *n.* **1** a plant (*Citrullus colocynthis*) of the gourd family, native to warmer Asian and Mediterranean regions, bearing a round yellow or green fruit. **2** the fruit of this plant, having a bitter pulp. **3** the purgative drug made from this fruit. ⟨< L < Gk. *kolokynthis* < *kolokynthē* gourd⟩

co•logne [kə'loun] *n.* a fragrant liquid, not so strong as perfume. ⟨< F *eau de Cologne* water of Cologne < *Cologne*, Germany, where it was first made⟩

Co•lom•bia [kə'lʌmbiə] *n.* a country in NW South America.

Co•lom•bi•an [kə'lʌmbiən] *n., adj. —n.* a native or inhabitant of Colombia.
—adj. of or having to do with Colombia or its people.

co•lon[1] ['koulən] *n.* **1** a mark (:) of punctuation used after an introductory sentence to show that a list, explanation, illustration, long quotation, etc. follows. **2** *pl.* **co•la.** in Classical Greek, a prosodic unit composed of two to six feet, bearing one main accent. Two or more cola form a period. ⟨< L < Gk. *kōlon* limb, clause⟩

co•lon[2] ['koulən] *n., pl.* **co•lons** or **co•la** ['koulə]. the main part of the large intestine, from the caecum to the rectum. See ALIMENTARY CANAL for picture. ⟨ME < L < Gk. *kolon*⟩
—co'lon•ic [kə'lɒnɪk], *adj.*

co•lon[3] [kou'loun] *or* [kə'loun]; *Spanish,* [ko'lon] *n., pl.* **co•lons** or **co•lo•nes** [ko'lones]. **1** the basic unit of money in El Salvador, divided into 100 centavos. **2** the basic unit of money in Costa Rica, divided into 100 centimos. See table of money in the Appendix. **3** a coin worth one colon. ⟨< Sp. *colón* < Cristóbal *Colón* Christopher Columbus⟩

co•lon[4] [kɔ'lɔ̃] *n. French.* a French settler or the descendant of a French settler; a colonial.

colo•nel ['kɜrnəl] *n.* an officer in the armed forces ranking next above a lieutenant-colonel and below a brigadier-general. See chart of ranks in the Appendix. *Abbrev.*: Col. or Col ⟨earlier also *coronel* < F *coronel* var. of *colonel* < Ital. *colonnello* commander of a regiment, ult. < *colonna* column < L *columna*⟩
☛ *Hom.* KERNEL.
☛ *Spelling.* **Colonel** is a spelling that has survived a change of pronunciation. The word, from the French, has two parallel forms, **colonel, coronel,** each pronounced in three syllables. For 150 years the word has been pronounced ['kɜrnəl], from the **coronel** form, but the spelling has survived as **colonel.**

Colonel Blimp See BLIMP.

colo•nel•cy ['kɜrnəlsi] *n., pl.* **-cies.** the rank, commission, or authority of a colonel.

co•lo•ni•al [kə'louniəl] *adj., n. —adj.* **1** of, having to do with, or inhabiting a colony or colonies. **2** possessing or made up of colonies: *the British colonial empire.* **3** Often, **Colonial,** having to do with, prevailing in, or characteristic of the colonies of the British Empire, especially the 13 colonies that became the United States: *colonial furniture, colonial architecture.* **4** having to do with a group of similar bacteria or of similar plants or animals.
—n. a person or organism living in a colony. **—co'lo•ni•al•ly,** *adv.*

co•lo•ni•al•ism [kə'louniə,lɪzəm] *n.* **1** the practice or policy of a nation that rules or seeks to rule over other countries as colonies. **2** the state of being a colony.

co•lo•ni•al•ist [kə'louniəlɪst] *n., adj. —n.* a person who supports or practises colonialism.
—adj. **1** of or having to do with colonialism or colonialists. **2** supporting or practising colonialism.

col•o•nist ['kɒlənɪst] *n.* **1** a person who helps to found a colony. **2** a person who lives in a colony during the period of settlement; settler.

colonist car *Cdn.* formerly, a railway coach having wooden seats and rough berths for sleeping, sometimes also having cooking facilities.

col•o•ni•za•tion [,kɒlənə'zeiʃən] *or* [,kɒlənaɪ'zeiʃən] *n.* the establishment of a colony or colonies: *the colonization of North America.*

colonization company *Cdn.* formerly, a company acting as an agent in bringing colonists to their destination in Canada.

colonization road *Cdn.* formerly, a road built by the government into an unsettled area to make it accessible for settlement.

col•o•nize ['kɒlə,naɪz] *v.* **-nized, -niz•ing.** establish a colony or colonies in: *French fishers colonized this coast. France colonized parts of Canada before Britain did.* **—'col•o,niz•er,** *n.*

col•on•nade [,kɒlə'neid] *n. Architecture.* a series of columns set the same distance apart. ⟨< F < Ital. *colonnata* < *colonna* column < L *columna*⟩

col•on•nad•ed [,kɒlə'neidɪd] *adj.* having a colonnade.

col•o•ny ['kɒləni] *n., pl.* **-nies. 1** a group of people who leave their own country and go to settle in another land, but who still remain citizens of their original country. **2** the settlement made by such a group of people. **3** a territory distant from the country that governs it. **4** a group of people of one country, faith, or occupation living as a group: *There is a large Chinese colony in Vancouver. There are several Doukhobor colonies in British Columbia. There is an artists' colony in Paris.* **5** *Biology.* a group of animals or plants of the same kind, living or growing together: *A coral island is a colony.* **6** *Bacteriology.* a mass of bacteria arising from a single cell, living on or in a solid or partially solid medium. **7 the Colonies, a** the thirteen British colonies that became the United States of America: New Hampshire, Massachusetts, Rhode Island, Connecticut, New York, New Jersey, Pennsylvania, Delaware, Maryland, Virginia, North Carolina, South Carolina, and Georgia. **b** the colonies, as opposed to self-governing dominions, within the British Empire. **8** a group of ants. ⟨< L *colonia* < *colonus* cultivator, settler < *colere* cultivate⟩

col•o•phon ['kɒlə,fɒn] *or* ['kɒləfən] *n.* **1** the words or inscription formerly placed at the end of a book, telling the name of the publisher, the date of publication, etc. Nowadays, much of this information is usually found on the title page or reverse title page. **2** a small design or device of a publisher placed on the last page or on the title page of a book. ⟨< LL < Gk. *kolophōn* summit, final touch⟩

color ['kʌlər] *n., v.* See COLOUR.

Col•o•ra•do [,kɒlə'rædou] *or* [,kɒlə'rɑdou] *n.* a western state of the United States, in the Rocky Mountains.

Colorado potato beetle [,kɒlə'rædou] *or* [,kɒlə'rɑdou] potato beetle.

col•or•ant ['kʌlərənt] *n.* a colouring agent, such as a pigment or dye. ⟨< F *colorant*, ppr. of *colorer* to colour < L *colorare*⟩

col•or•a•tion [,kʌlə'reiʃən] *n.* a colouring; way in which something is coloured: *The coloration of some animals is like that of their surroundings.*

col•o•ra•tu•ra [,kʌlərə'tjurə], [,kʌlərə'turə], *or* [,kɒlərə'turə] *n.* **1** *Music.* ornamental passages such as trills, runs, etc. **2** (*adj.*) characterized by or suitable for such ornamental passages. **3** a vocal composition containing such passages. **4** a soprano who specializes in singing such music. ⟨< Ital. < L *color* colour⟩

col•or•im•e•ter [,kʌlə'rɪmətər] *n.* **1** an instrument or device for measuring the shade, tint, brightness and purity of a colour. **2** a device used in chemical analysis for comparing the colour of a liquid with a standard colour.

col•or•im•e•try [,kʌlə'rɪmətri] *n.* the measuring of colour by means of a colorimeter.

co•los•sal [kə'lɒsəl] *adj.* **1** huge; gigantic; vast. **2** *Informal.* remarkable; outstanding: *a colossal blunder. Her new film is colossal.* ⟨< *colossus*⟩ **—co'los•sal•ly,** *adv.*

Col•os•se•um [,kɒlə'siəm] *n.* in Rome, a large, outdoor theatre, completed in A.D. 80. The Colosseum was used for games and contests. Also, **Coliseum.** ⟨< LL *colosseum*, neut. of L *colosseus* gigantic < *colossus* < Gk. *kolossos* gigantic statue⟩

co•los•sus [kə'lɒsəs] *n., pl.* **-los•sus•es** or **-los•si** [-'lɒsaɪ] *or* [-'lɒsi]. **1** a huge statue. **2** anything huge; gigantic person or thing. ⟨< L < Gk. *kolossos*⟩

Colossus of Rhodes [roudz] a huge statue of Apollo made on the island of Rhodes about 280 B.C. It was one of the seven wonders of the ancient world.

co•los•to•my [kə'lɒstəmi] *n., pl.* **-mies.** the making of an artificial opening in the colon. ⟨< *colon*[2] + Gk. *stoma* opening⟩

co•los•trum [kə'lɒstrəm] *n.* the thin, yellowish milk secreted by a mammal for the first few days after the birth of young. It is especially rich in protein and helps establish both digestion and natural immunity. ⟨< L⟩

co•lot•o•my [kə'lɒtəmi] *n., pl.* **-mies.** a surgical incision into the colon. ⟨< *colon*[2] + Gk. *-tomia* -cutting⟩

col•our or **col•or** ['kʌlər] *n., v.* —*n.* **1** the sensation produced by the different effects of waves of light striking the retina of the eye. Different colours are produced by rays of light having different wavelengths. **2** any colour other than black, white, or grey; chromatic colour: *Most of the photographs are in colour.* **3** a paint, dye, or pigment: *oil colours.* **4** the natural, healthy colour of a person's face: *The colour drained from his face and we thought he would faint.* **5** a flush caused by blushing: *The colour rushed to her face when her mistake was pointed out.* **6** the colour of a person's skin due to pigment. **7** an outward appearance; show: *His lies had some colour of truth.* **8** a distinguishing quality; vividness: *His gift for description adds colour to his stories.* **9** character; type: *a horse of a different colour.* **10** *Music.* **a** a quality of tone by which any musical instrument or combination of instruments can be recognized, used especially in orchestration; tone colour; timbre. **b** the quality of expression in a musical performance or style of musical interpretation which may produce an emotional reaction in the listener or audience: *Her playing has colour and vigour.* **c** the timbre or tone of a voice: *vocal colour.* **11** *Physics.* a theoretical property of quarks which governs the ways in which they interact and combine in larger subatomic particles. **12 colours** or **colors,** *pl.* a badge, ribbon, dress, etc. worn to show allegiance. **13 the colours** or **colors, a** the flag of a nation, regiment, etc.: *He carried the colours in the parade.* **b** the ceremony of raising the flag in the morning and lowering it in the evening. **c** the army, navy, or air force: *Soldiers, sailors, and flyers serve the colours.*

change colour (or **color**), react by becoming either pale or red in the face: *She took the news calmly and didn't even change colour.*

give or **lend colour** (or **color**) **to,** cause to seem true or likely.

lose colour (or **color**), become pale: *He lost a lot of colour during his illness.*

of colour (or **color**), having skin of a colour other than white: *people of colour.*

show (one's) **true colours** (or **colors**), **a** show oneself as one really is. **b** declare one's opinions or plans.

with flying colours (or **colors**), with great success; triumphantly: *She passed the examination with flying colours.*

—*v.* **1** give colour to; put colour on; change the colour of. **2** become red in the face; blush. **3** take on colour; become coloured: *My face coloured in the sun.* **4** present so as to give a wrong idea; put in a false light: *The general coloured his report of the battle to make his own mistakes seem the fault of his officers.* **5** give a distinguishing quality to; affect: *Love of nature coloured all of Sir Charles Roberts' writing.* **6** draw or colour pictures with crayons, markers, etc., as a pastime: *Shelley will sit and colour for hours.* ⟨ME < OF < L⟩ **—'col•our•er** or **'col•or•er,** *n.*

☛ *Syn. n.* **1. Colour,** HUE, SHADE = a sensation produced by the effect of waves of light striking the retina of the eye. **Colour** is the general word: *Her dress is the colour of grass.* **Hue** is poetic in the general meaning of colour. Technically, **hue** = the quality of a colour that gives the name: red, blue, etc. It is also used to suggest partial alteration of a colour: *This pottery is blue with a greenish hue.* **Shade** applies to a degree of intensity of colour: *I like a blue car, but of a lighter shade than navy.*

col•our•a•ble or **col•or•a•ble** ['kʌlərəbəl] *adj.* **1** capable of being coloured. **2** apparently plausible but actually specious or deceptive.

colour bar or **color bar** the denial of rights, privileges, and opportunities on the grounds of skin colour.

col•our•bear•er or **col•or•bear•er** ['kʌlər,bɛrər] *n.* a person who carries the flag or colours; standard bearer.

col•our–blind or **col•or–blind** ['kʌlər ,blaɪnd] *adj.* **1** unable to tell certain colours apart; unable to perceive certain colours or, in certain cases, any colours. **2** not racist.

colour blindness or **color blindness 1** inability to see some colours, usually caused by a genetic defect and inherited in an X-linked recessive pattern. See DEUTAN, PROTAN. **2** freedom from racism.

colour•cast or **col•or•cast** ['kʌlər,kæst] *v., n.* —*v.* broadcast (a television program) in colour.
—*n.* a television broadcast in colour.

col•our–code or **col•or–code** ['kʌlər ,koud] *v.* **-cod•ing.** use standard colours as a means of identification: *The wires in the electrical system are colour-coded.*

col•oured or **col•ored** ['kʌlərd] *adj., n., v.* —*adj.* **1** having colour; not black, white, grey, or clear: *coloured water. He prefers coloured shirts to white ones.* **2** having a certain colour (used in compounds): *red-coloured leaves.* **3 a** *Esp. U.S.* BLACK (*adj.* 3a). **b** *South African.* of racially mixed descent. **4** tinged by emotion, prejudice, desire for effect, etc: *The newspaper published a coloured account of the political convention.* **5** *Cdn.* of leaves, having turned colour in the fall.
—*n.* **1** *Esp. U.S.* BLACK (n. 4). **2** *South African.* a person of racially mixed descent.
—*v.* pt. and pp. of COLOUR.

col•our•fast or **col•or•fast** ['kʌlər,fæst] *adj.* resistant to loss or change of colour by fading or washing.

colour film or **color film** **1** a film for making photographs in colour. **2** a movie made with such film.

colour filter or **color filter** a coloured medium, such as gelatin, through which light is shone to give coloured light for stage effects or photography.

col•our•ful or **col•or•ful** ['kʌlərfəl] *adj.* **1** abounding in colour. **2** picturesque; vivid. **—'col•our•ful•ly,** or **'col•or•ful•ly,** *adv.* **—'col•our•ful•ness** or **'col•or•ful•ness,** *n.*

colour guard or **color guard** the honour guard of a military unit that carries or accompanies the flag during ceremonies, reviews, etc.

col•our•ing or **col•or•ing** ['kʌlərɪŋ] *n., v. —n.* **1** the pattern, kind, or degree of colour or colours that a person or thing has: *His colouring is much better since his health improved.* **2** a substance used to colour something; pigment. **3** a false appearance: *His lies have a colouring of truth.*
—v. ppr. of COLOUR.

colouring book or **coloring book** a book, often in a large format, containing outline drawings for children to colour.

colouring matter or **coloring matter** a substance used to colour; pigment.

col•our•ist or **col•or•ist** ['kʌlərɪst] *n.* **1** an artist who is skilful in painting with colours. **2** a user of colour.

col•our•less or **col•or•less** ['kʌlərlɪs] *adj.* **1** without colour. **2** without excitement or variety; uninteresting: *a colourless personality.* **—'col•our•less•ly** or **'col•or•less•ly,** *adv.* **—'col•our•less•ness** or **'col•or•less•ness,** *n.*

colour line or **color line** a distinction in social, economic, or political privileges between members of different races.

colour phase or **color phase** **1** a change in the colouring of an animal's fur or feathers, as for a season. **2** an individual or group of individual animals with different colouring from the rest of the same species: *The panther is a black colour phase of the leopard.*

colour photography or **color photography** photography using colour film.

colourpoint shorthair or **colorpoint shorthair** a breed of domestic cat, a cross between a Siamese and a shorthair, having blue eyes and white fur shading to dark at the ears, feet, and tail.

colour vision or **color vision** the ability to perceive objects in colour, mediated by the cones of the retina of the eye.

col•pi•tis [kɒl'pəitɪs] *n.* inflammation of the vagina. ⟨< Gk. *kolpos* womb + *-itis*⟩

col•por•teur [,koulpɔr'tɜr], ['koul,pɔrtər], *or* ['kɒl,pɔrtər] *n.* **1** a person who travels about and distributes Bibles, tracts, etc. **2** a hawker of books, broadsides, newspapers, etc. ⟨< F *colporteur* < *colporter* hawk, carry for sale (on the neck) < *col* neck (< L *collum*) + *porter* carry (< L *portare*)⟩

col•po•scope ['kɒlpə,skoup] *n.* a medical instrument used to examine the vagina and cervix, especially for detecting cancer. ⟨< Gk. *kolpos* womb + E *scope*⟩ **—col'pos•co•py** [kɒl'pɒskəpi], *n.*

colt [koult] *n.* **1** a young horse, donkey, etc., especially a male horse under four or five years old. **2** a young or inexperienced person. ⟨OE⟩

col•ter ['koultər] See COULTER.

colt•ish ['koultɪʃ] *adj.* like a colt; lively and frisky. **—'colt•ish•ly,** *adv.*

colts•foot ['koults,fʊt] *n.* a common European perennial plant (*Tussilago farfara*) of the composite family having heart-shaped leaves and yellow, daisylike flowers. ⟨from the shape of the leaves, resembling the imprint of a colt's foot⟩

col•u•brid ['kɒljə,brɪd] *n., adj. —n.* any harmless snake of the family Colubridae, having no vestigial limbs and a face bare of scales. The family includes garter snakes, bull snakes, and water snakes, and most other species ranging from temperate to tropical.
—adj. of or having to do with the family Colubridae.

col•u•brine ['kɒljə,braɪn] *adj.* **1** of or having to do with a snake. **2** of or having to do with the colubrid family of snakes. ⟨< L *colubrinus* < *coluber* serpent⟩

Co•lum•ba [kə'lʌmbə] *n.* the Dove, a southern constellation near Canis Major.

Co•lum•bi•a [kə'lʌmbiə] *n.* a name for the United States of America. Columbia is often represented as a woman dressed in red, white, and blue. ⟨after Christopher *Columbus*⟩

col•um•bine ['kɒləm,baɪn] *n.* **1** any of a genus (*Aquilegia*) of perennial plants of the buttercup family having showy, drooping flowers with five petals, each forming a wide-mouthed tube ending in a hooked spur pointing upward. Several species of columbine grow wild in Canada. **2 Columbine,** in traditional Italian comedy and in pantomime, a girl who is the sweetheart of Harlequin. ⟨ME < OF < LL *columbina* < L *columbina*, fem., dovelike < *columba* dove⟩

co•lum•bite [kə'lʌmbəit] *n.* a black, crystalline mineral, iron niobate, the principal ore of niobium. *Formula*: $(Fe,Mn)Nb_2O_6$

co•lum•bi•um [kə'lʌmbiəm] *n.* See NIOBIUM. ⟨< NL < *Columbia*, the United States⟩

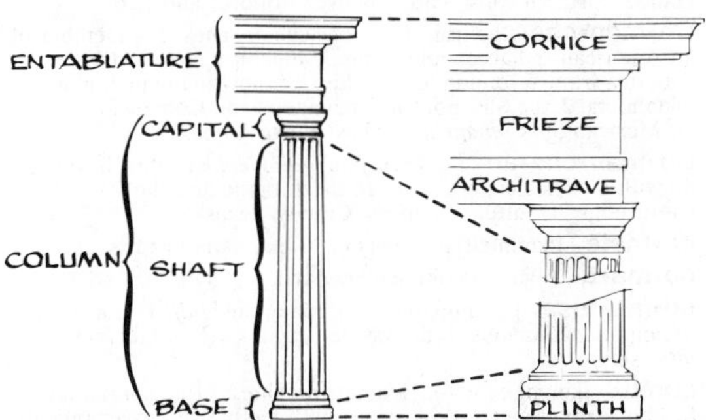

col•umn ['kɒləm] *n.* **1** *Architecture.* a slender, upright structure; pillar. Columns are usually made of stone, wood, or metal, and are used mainly as supports or ornaments to a building. Sometimes a column stands alone as a monument. **2** anything that seems slender and upright like a column: *a column of smoke, a long column of figures, the spinal column.* **3** *Military.* a formation in which troops, units, armoured vehicles, etc. follow one behind the other. **4** a line of ships or aircraft, one behind the other. **5** any similar line of persons, things, etc.: *A long column of cars followed the procession down the street.* **6** a narrow division of a page reading from top to bottom, kept separate by a line or a blank space. A newspaper often has eight columns on a page. **7** a part of a newspaper or periodical used for a special subject or written by a special writer. **8** a line or series of letters, figures, etc., arranged vertically. ⟨< L *columna*⟩
☛ *Pronun.* **column.** In senses 6 and 7, **column** is occasionally pronounced ['kɒljəm] although this pronunciation is considered by most to be substandard. This pronunciation is also used humorously.

co•lum•nar [kə'lʌmnər] *adj.* **1** like a column. **2** made of columns. **3** written or printed in columns.

col•umned ['kɒləmd] *adj.* **1** having columns. **2** formed into columns.

co•lum•ni•a•tion [kə,lʌmni'eiʃən] *n.* the use or arrangement of columns in a building.
☛ *Hom.* CALUMNIATION.

col•um•nist ['kɒləmnɪst] *or* ['kɒləmɪst] *n.* a person who writes or selects and edits the material for a special column in a newspaper.
☛ *Pronun.* **Columnist** is occasionally pronounced ['kɒljəmɪst]. See note at COLUMN.

co•lure [kou'lur] *or* ['koulur] *n.* either of two huge circles of the celestial sphere which cross at a 90° angle at the celestial poles, the first passing through the solstices and the second through the equinoxes. ⟨< L *coluri* < Gk. *kolouroi* the colures, pl. of *kolouros* < *kolos* docked + *oura* tail⟩

co•ly ['kouli] *n., pl.* **co•lies.** any bird of the family Colidae, native to Africa, having a long tail and greyish brown plumage, and the habit of creeping around in trees; mousebird. ⟨< Mod.L *colius* < Gk. *kolios* green woodpecker⟩
☛ *Hom.* COLLIE ['kouli].

col•za ['kɒlzə] *or* ['koulzə] *n.* **1** cole seed. **2** an oil made from these seeds, used as a fuel in lamps, as a lubricant, etc. ⟨< Du. *koolsaad*, literally, cabbage seed⟩

com– *prefix.* **1** with; together: *commingle = mingle with one another. Compress = press together.* **2** altogether; completely: *comprehend = grasp the meaning completely.* Used before *b, m, p,* and, occasionally, before *f* and vowels. Also: **co-** before vowels and *h*; **col-** before *l*; **cor-** before *r*; **con-** before all other consonants. ⟨< L *com-* < *cum*, prep.⟩

com. 1 comedy. 2 commerce. 3 common; commonly. 4 communication.

Com. 1 Commander. 2 Commodore. 3 Commissioner. 4 committee. 5 Communist.

COM *Computer technology.* computer-output microfilm.

co•ma[1] ['koumə] *n., pl.* **co•mas.** a prolonged unconsciousness caused by disease, injury, or poison; stupor. ⟨< Gk. *kōma*⟩

co•ma[2] ['koumə] *n., pl.* **co•mae** [-mi] *or* [-maɪ]. 1 a cloudlike mass around the nucleus of a comet. 2 *Botany.* a tuft of hairs at the end of a seed. ⟨< L < Gk. *komē* hair⟩

Co•ma Be•re•ni•ces ['koumə ,bɛrə'naisiz] *n.* Berenice's Hair, a northern constellation between Boötes and Leo.

Co•man•che [kə'mæntʃi] *n., pl.* **-che** or **-ches. 1** a member of an American Indian people formerly inhabiting W North America from Wyoming to New Mexico, now living mainly in Oklahoma. 2 the Shoshonean language of the Comanche. ⟨< Mexican Sp. *Comanche* < Shoshonean *Komanchi*⟩

Co•man•che•an [kə'mæntʃiən] *adj. Geology.* of or having to do with a geological era between the Jurassic and the Cretaceous. ⟨< after *Comanche* County, Texas⟩

co•mate ['koumeit] *adj. Botany.* having hairs or tufts.

co•ma•tik ['koumə,tɪk] See KOMATIK.

co•ma•tose ['koumə,tous] *or* ['kɒmə,tous] *adj.* 1 in a stupor or coma; unconscious. 2 drowsy; lethargic. ⟨< F < Gk. *kōma*, *-atos* sleep⟩

comb[1] [koum] *n., v.* —*n.* 1 a narrow, short, often somewhat flexible strip of metal, rubber, etc. with teeth, used to arrange or clean the hair or to hold it in place. 2 anything shaped or used like a comb. One kind of comb cleans and takes out the tangles in wool or flax. 3 a currycomb. 4 the thick, red, fleshy crest on the top of the head in some fowls. 5 HONEYCOMB (def. 1). 6 the top of a wave rolling over or breaking.
—*v.* 1 arrange, clean, or take out tangles in, with a comb.
2 search through; look everywhere in: *We had to comb the whole city before we found our lost dog.* 3 of waves, roll over or break at the top. ⟨OE⟩ **—'comb,like,** *adj.*

comb[2] [kum] *or* [koum] See COMBE.

com•bat *v., n.* ['kɒmbæt]; *v. also* [kəm'bæt] *v.* **-bat•ted** or **-bat•ed, -bat•ting** or **-bat•ing;** *n.* —*v.* 1 fight; struggle. 2 fight against; struggle with: *Doctors combat disease.*
—*n.* 1 fighting between opposing armed forces; battle: *Bombers flew over us as we entered combat. My grandfather was wounded in combat.* 2 (*adjl.*) designed for or used in combat: *combat training, combat boots.* 3 any fight or struggle. ⟨< F *combattre* < LD < L *com-* (intensive) + *battuere* beat⟩
☛ *Syn. n.* See note at FIGHT.

com•bat•ant [kəm'bætənt] *or* ['kɒmbətənt] *n., adj.* —*n.* a fighter, especially a member of the armed forces who takes part in the actual combat.
—*adj.* 1 battling; fighting: *combatant forces.* 2 ready to fight or fond of fighting.

combat fatigue a state of mental exhaustion that sometimes occurs among soldiers as a result of warfare in the front lines.

com•bat•ive [kəm'bætɪv] *or* ['kɒmbətɪv] *adj.* ready to fight or oppose; fond of fighting. **—com'bat•ive•ly,** *adv.* **—com'bat•ive•ness,** *n.*

combat team two or more units of different military branches acting together in battle.

combe or **comb** [kum] *or* [koum] *n.* a narrow valley; deep hollow surrounded on three sides by hills. Also, **coomb.** ⟨OE *cumb*, probably < Celtic⟩

comb•er ['koumər] *n.* 1 a person who or thing that combs wool, flax, etc. 2 a wave that rolls over or breaks; breaker.

com•bi•na•tion [,kɒmbə'neiʃən] *n.* 1 a combining or being combined; union: *The combination of flour and water makes paste.* 2 one whole made by combining two or more different things. 3 persons or groups joined together for some common purpose. 4 a series of numbers or letters used in opening a COMBINATION LOCK. 5 the mechanism of such a lock. 6 an undergarment consisting of an undershirt and underpants in one piece. 7 *Mathematics.* **a** the arrangement of individual items of a set into groups of a certain size, without regard to order. **b** a group formed in this way. The possible combinations of *a*, *b*, and *c*, taken two at a time, are *ab*, *ac*, *ba*, *bc*, *ca*, and *cb*. 8 *Chemistry.* the union of substances to form a compound.
—,com•bi'na•tion•al, *adj.*

combination lock a lock that is opened either by turning a dial through a pre-selected sequence of numbers or by setting a series of dials at pre-selected numbers. Turning the dial or dials to the correct position aligns the tumblers inside so that the locking mechanism can be released.

combination square a carpenter's measuring instrument, usually in the shape of a scalene triangle, which is a combination of an adjustable TRY SQUARE with a SPIRIT LEVEL. Combination squares are used to check mitre joints and surface levels. See SQUARE for picture.

com•bine *v. 1, 2* [kəm'baɪn]; *v. 3* ['kɒmbaɪn], *n.* ['kɒmbaɪn] *v.* **-bined, -bin•ing;** *n.* —*v.* 1 join together; unite; mix. 2 *Chemistry.* unite to form a compound. Two atoms of hydrogen combine with one of oxygen to form water. 3 use a combine: *We combined the wheat last week.*
—*n.* 1 a group of people joined together for business or political purposes; combination: *The companies formed a combine to keep prices up.* 2 a machine that cuts and threshes grain in one operation. It separates the seeds from the stalks as it moves across a field. ⟨< LL *combinare* < *com-* together + *bini* two by two⟩ **—com'bin•a•ble,** *adj.* **—com'bin•er,** *n.*
☛ *Syn. v.* 1. See note at JOIN.

com•bined [kəm'baɪnd] *adj., v.* —*adj.* 1 joined or mixed together; united. 2 done by groups, persons, etc. acting together: *a combined effort.*
—*v.* pt. and pp. of COMBINE.

combined operations 1 military operations carried on by two or more allies acting together. 2 military operations in which land, sea, and air forces co-operate; amphibious operations.

comb•ings ['koumɪŋz] *n.pl.* the hairs removed by a comb.

combining form a form of a word used for combining with other words or word elements, or with suffixes or prefixes. *Examples*: *multi-*, as in *multilingual* and *multimillionaire*; *-phone*, as in *telephone* and *Anglophone.*

comb jelly ctenophore.

com•bo ['kɒmbou] *n., pl.* **-bos.** 1 *Informal.* a small group of jazz musicians playing together regularly. 2 a combination, especially of entrees offered on a menu: *I'll have the chicken and rib combo, please.* ⟨shortened form of *combination*⟩

com•bust [kəm'bʌst] *v.* burn up. ⟨back-formed < *combustion*⟩

com•bus•ti•bil•i•ty [kəm,bʌstə'bɪləti] *n.* a combustible quality or condition; flammability.

com•bus•ti•ble [kəm'bʌstəbəl] *adj., n.* —*adj.* 1 capable of taking fire and burning; easily burned: *Gasoline is highly combustible.* 2 easily excited; fiery.
—*n.* a combustible substance. **—com'bus•ti•bly,** *adv.*

com•bus•tion [kəm'bʌstʃən] *n.* 1 the act or process of burning: *The explosion in the coal mine was caused by the combustion of gases.* 2 *Chemistry.* a rapid oxidation accompanied by high temperature and, usually, by light. 3 a slow oxidation not accompanied by high temperature and light. The cells of the body transform food into energy by combustion. 4 violent excitement; tumult. ⟨< LL *combustio, -onis* < L *comburere*, a blend of *co-urere* burn together or simultaneously and *amburere* burn on both sides⟩ **—com'bust•ive,** *adj.*

combustion chamber that part of an engine, such as a jet engine, where combustion occurs.

combustion tube a glass or ceramic tube in which substances can be burned, used mainly in a furnace.

Comdr. Commander.

Comdt. Commandant.

come [kʌm] *v.* **came, come, com•ing.** *interj.* —*v.* 1 move toward the speaker; approach: *Come this way.* 2 reach a particular place in space or time; arrive: *We come now to a different kind of poem. The time has come for us to decide. The girls come home today.* 3 appear: *Light comes and goes.* 4 reach; extend: *The dress comes to her knees.* 5 progress (*often used with* **along**): *She's coming along well now. How is your project coming?* 6 arrive, happen, or belong at a certain position in a series: *She came second in the high jump.* 7 happen; take place; occur: *Come what may.* 8 be caused; result: *You see what comes of meddling.* 9 be derived; originate: *He comes from a poor family. Milk comes from cows.* 10 turn out to be; become: *His dream came true.* 11 enter or be brought into a particular state or condition: *to come into use. My shoelace came undone. When will you come to your senses?* 12 *Informal.* reach sexual orgasm. 13 occur to the mind: *The solution of the problem has just come to me.* 14 be available or obtainable: *This sweater comes in white and yellow.* 15 amount or add up (*to*): *The bill comes to $100.* 16 be due (*to*) (*progressive*

tenses): *I hope you get what is coming to you.* **17** be inherited by: *The jewellery came to me on my mother's death.*
as good (strong, friendly, etc.) as they come, one of the best (strongest, friendliest, etc.).
come about, a take place; happen: *Their meeting came about by accident.* **b** *Nautical.* turn around; change direction.
come across, a meet or find by chance: *We came across some of my old toys when we were cleaning out the basement yesterday.* **b** have the desired effect; succeed: *The actor's attempt to portray terror didn't come across.* **c** *Informal.* give an impression of being; appear: *He comes across very tough, but he's nice when you get to know him. She came across as having a bad temper.* **d** *Slang.* give in to a demand, a persistent request, etc.; hand over money, information, etc.: *She came across with a $100 donation.*
come again, *Informal.* repeat what you have just said. (*imperative only*)
come along, a arrive. **b** accompany someone. **c** make progress.
come around or **round, a** return to consciousness or health; recover. **b** give in; yield; agree. **c** turn around; change direction. **d** come for a visit.
come at, a reach; get. **b** rush toward; attack.
come back, a return. **b** be remembered: *The forgotten name came back to him the next day.* **c** *Informal.* return to a former prominent position or condition: *She's making an effort to come back by appearing as a guest artist on television shows.* **d** make a witty retort.
come between, cause separation or unfriendly feeling between: *The two friends vowed not to let anything come between them.*
come by, a get; obtain; acquire: *How did you come by that black eye?* **b** come for a visit.
come down, a lose position, money, rank, etc.: *He has certainly come down in the last year.* **b** be handed down or passed along: *Many fables have come down through the ages.* **c** *Informal.* become ill (*with*): *He came down with a bad cold.*
come down on, a *Informal.* scold; blame. **b** attack suddenly.
come forward, offer oneself for work or duty; volunteer.
come from, a be born in or to; be descended from; descend from (*simple tenses only*): *She comes from a large family.* **b** be a native or former resident of (*simple tenses only*): *They come from Manitoba.*
come in, a enter: *Please come in.* **b** begin to be used; be brought into use or fashion: *Steamboats came in soon after the invention of the steam engine.* **c** of trains, planes, etc., arrive: *We got there just as the train came in.* **d** of an oil well, begin producing: *This was the first oil well in the area to come in.* **e** win a particular place in a competition, race, examination, etc.: *She came in third in the high jump and first in the 100 m race.*
come in for, get; receive: *He came in for a lot of criticism on his handling of the deal.*
come into, acquire, especially by inheriting: *She has come into a lot of money.*
come off, a happen; take place; occur: *When is the final game going to come off?* **b** finish; emerge, as from a contest: *She tried out for the team yesterday and came off with flying colours.* **c** become detached: *The label came off when I soaked the jar in water.* **d** *Informal.* turn out to be effective or successful: *His jokes didn't come off at all.*
come off it!, *Slang.* you can't be serious.
come on, a develop; progress: *Our garden is coming on fine.* **b** meet by chance; find: *When I turned the corner, I came on a strange sight.* **c** *Theatre.* make an entrance onto the stage: *The murderer comes on in the second act.* **d** *Slang.* make a given impression: *He comes on too strong.*
come on!, *Informal.* **a** hurry: *Come on! We're going to be late!* **b** stop behaving that way: *Oh, come on! You know he didn't mean it that way.* **c** an expression of disbelief: *Four hundred and eighty thousand dollars for that house? Come on!* **d** please!
come on to, make sexual overtures to by suggestive behaviour and talk.
come out, a be revealed or made public: *The details of the scandal never came out.* **b** be offered to the public: *A new model came out last year.* **c** result; end up: *How did your pictures come out?* **d** put in an appearance; offer to take part: *Quite a few students came out for drama this year.* **e** state one's opinion publicly: *She came out strongly in favour of the expressway.* **f** be introduced to society; make a debut. **g** allow one's homosexual preferences to be known.
come out for, support; endorse.
come out with, a *Informal.* say openly: *That child comes out with the strangest questions.* **b** offer to the public: *The publisher has come out with a new edition.*
come over, a happen to; influence or possess: *A strange feeling came over me. I don't know what's come over her; she's so grumpy lately.* **b** *Informal.* visit: *When are you coming over?*
come through, a be successful; win. **b** endure successfully. **c** *Slang.* hand over or pay what is required. **d** do what one promised. **e** be released by an administration: *We can't leave for Nepal till our visas come through.* **f** wear through. **g** show through.
come to, a return to consciousness: *The boxer came to in the dressing room.* **b** turn a ship's bow toward the wind. **c** drop anchor.
come up, a arise: *The question is sure to come up in class.* **b** advance; attain higher status: *The student came up in his esteem. That actor has come up in the world.*
come upon, meet or find by chance: *We came upon them at the plaza this morning.*
come up to, a be as high as: *That fence only comes up to my elbow.* **b** accost; approach: *She came up to me with a big smile on her face.*
come up with, provide; produce, especially in working on a problem: *He couldn't come up with the right answer.*
have (something) **coming to one,** deserve something.
see (something) **coming,** anticipate or foresee something.
—interj. here! look! stop! (*used to express irritation or impatience*). ⟨OE *cuman*⟩

☛ *Usage.* **Come,** ARRIVE, REACH. In the sense of getting to a point or place, **come** is followed by **to, arrive** is followed by **at,** and **reach** requires no preposition: *We came to a conclusion. We arrived at a decision. We reached an agreement.*

come–all–ye ['kʌm ɒl ˌji] *n.* a folk song or ballad especially of Atlantic Canada. ⟨< *Come all ye,* frequent first words.⟩

come•back ['kʌmˌbæk] *n. Informal.* **1** a return to a former prominent or thriving condition or position: *The singer is making a comeback. These animals, once near extinction, are now making a comeback.* **2** a clever or sharp reply: *She's always ready with a good comeback.* **3** a cause for complaint: *When you buy an appliance 'as is', you have no comeback if it doesn't work.*

co•me•di•an [kə'midiən] *n.* **1** a professional entertainer who tells jokes or funny stories, sings funny songs, etc.; a comic. **2** an actor in comedies; an actor of comic parts. **3** *Archaic.* a writer of comedies. **4** a person who amuses others with his or her funny talk and actions. ⟨< F *comédien*⟩

co•me•dic [kə'midɪk] *adj.* of or having to do with comedy.

co•me•di•enne [kəˌmidi'ɛn] *n.* **1** a professional female entertainer who tells jokes or funny stories, sings funny songs, etc.; a comic. **2** an actress in comedies; an actress of comic parts. ⟨< F *comédienne,* fem. of *comédien*⟩

come•down ['kʌmˌdaʊn] *n. Informal.* a loss of position, rank, money, etc.

com•e•dy ['kɒmədi] *n., pl.* **-dies. 1** an amusing play or show having a happy ending. **2** such plays or shows as a class; the branch of drama concerned with such plays. **3** an amusing happening; funny incident. **4** the comic element of drama or literature, or of life in general: *the human comedy.* **5** any literary work having a theme suited to comedy or using the methods of comedy. ⟨ME < OF < L *comoedia* < Gk. *kōmōidia* + *kōmōidos* comedian < *kōmos* merrymaking + *aoidos* singer⟩

comedy of manners a play or narrative ridiculing the manners of high society.

come–hither ['kʌm 'hɪðər] *adj. Informal.* enticing; flirtatious: *a come-hither look.*

come•li•ness ['kʌmlinɪs] *n.* **1** pleasant appearance. **2** fitness; suitableness; propriety.

come•ly ['kʌmli] *adj.* **-li•er, -li•est. 1** having a pleasant appearance; attractive. **2** fitting; suitable; proper. ⟨OE *cȳmlic*⟩

come–on ['kʌm ˌɒn] *n. Slang.* something offered to attract, especially something extra promised in a sales promotion; gimmick: *The offer of a free sample is just a come-on.*

com•er ['kʌmər] *n.* **1** a person who comes. **2** a person who has recently come. **3** *Informal.* a person who shows promise or seems likely to succeed.

co•mes•ti•ble [kə'mɛstəbəl] *n., adj. —n.* something to eat; an article of food.
—adj. eatable. ⟨< LL *comestibilis* < L *comestus,* var. of *comesus,* pp. of *comedere* < *com-* with + *edere* eat⟩

com•et ['kɒmɪt] *n. Astronomy.* a starlike object that travels in an oval orbit around the sun, having a head consisting of an icy nucleus of frozen gases, ice, and dust surrounded by a hazy cloud, and, often, a long, shining tail. Some comets are visible to the naked eye when they are near the sun. ⟨ME *comete* < OF < L *cometa* < Gk. *komētēs* wearing long hair < *komē* hair⟩ **—'com•e,tar•y,** *adj.* **—co'met•ic** [kə'mɛtɪk], *adj.*

come•up•pance [ˌkʌm'ʌpəns] *n. Informal.* whatever penalty, change of luck, etc. one deserves; one's just deserts.

com•fit ['kʌmfɪt] *or* ['kɒmfɪt] *n.* a piece of candy; sweetmeat. ⟨ME < OF *confit* < L *confectus* prepared, pp. of *conficere* < *com-* together + *facere* make⟩

com•fort ['kʌmfərt] *v., n.* —*v.* **1** ease the grief or sorrow of (someone); cheer. **2** give ease to. **3** *Archaic or formal.* help; support.
—*n.* **1** anything that makes trouble or sorrow easier to bear. **2** freedom from pain or hardship; ease; a feeling of being well and contented. **3** a person or thing that makes life easier or takes away hardship. **4** *Archaic or formal.* help or support: *giving aid and comfort to the enemy.* **5** *Esp. U.S.* a comforter for a bed. ⟨ME < OF *confort* < LL *confortare* strengthen < *com-* together + *fortis* strong⟩ —**'com•fort•ing•ly,** *adv.*

☛ *Syn. v.* **1. Comfort,** CONSOLE = ease sorrow, trouble, or pain. **Comfort** = ease the grief or sorrow of a person by making him or her more cheerful and giving him or her hope or strength: *Neighbours comforted the mother of the burned child.* **Console** = make grief or trouble easier to bear by doing something to lighten it or making the person forget it temporarily: *Her music consoled the widow.* —*n.* **2.** See note at EASE.

com•fort•a•ble ['kʌmfərtəbəl] *adj.* **1** giving a feeling of ease: *That's a very comfortable chair. A soft, warm bed is comfortable.* **2** in comfort; at ease; free from pain or hardship. **3** easy; tranquil; undisturbed: *a comfortable sleep.* **4** *Informal.* enough for one's needs; adequate: *She has a comfortable income.*
—**'com•fort•a•ble•ness,** *n.* —**'com•fort•a•bly,** *adv.*

com•fort•er ['kʌmfərtər] *n.* **1** a person who or thing that gives comfort. **2** a padded or quilted covering for a bed. **3** *Brit.* a long, woollen scarf. **4 the Comforter,** *Christianity.* the Holy Spirit.

com•fort•less ['kʌmfərtlɪs] *adj.* **1** bringing no comfort or ease of mind: *comfortless words.* **2** without the comforts of life: *a bare and comfortless room.*

comfort station a public lavatory.

com•frey ['kʌmfri] *n.* **1** any Eurasian herb of the genus *Symphytum,* of the borage family. **2** the common comfrey (*Symphytum officinale*), having hairy leaves and clusters of small white, pink, or purple flowers, formerly used in medicine to congeal wounds. ⟨ME and OF *confirie* < L *conferva* a water plant⟩

com•fy ['kʌmfi] *adj.* **-fi•er, -fi•est.** *Informal.* comfortable.

com•ic ['kɒmɪk] *adj., n.* —*adj.* **1** of comedy or in comedies: *a comic actor.* **2** amusing; funny.
—*n.* **1** the amusing or funny side of literature, life, etc. **2** *Informal.* COMIC BOOK. **3** *Informal.* COMIC STRIP. **4** comedian. **5 comics,** *pl.* the page or section of a newspaper containing comic strips. ⟨< L *comicus* < Gk. *kōmikos* < *kōmos* merrymaking⟩

com•i•cal ['kɒməkəl] *adj.* **1** amusing; funny. **2** *Informal.* queer; strange; odd. —**'com•i•cal•ly,** *adv.* —**'com•i•cal•ness,** *n.*

comic book a book or magazine made up of one or more comic strips.

comic opera an amusing opera having a happy ending.

comic relief any episode in a serious work, especially a drama, that is introduced to relieve tension. The gravedigger's scene in *Hamlet* is an example of comic relief.

comic strip a series of drawings, especially cartoons, that tell a funny story, an adventure, or a series of incidents.

Com•in•form ['kɒmɪn,fɔrm] *n.* an international Communist organization intended to co-ordinate the propaganda of Communist parties throughout the world, formed in 1947 by the signatories of the Warsaw Pact and dissolved in 1956. ⟨< *Com*munist *Inform*ation Bureau⟩

com•ing ['kʌmɪŋ] *n., adj., v.* —*n.* the approach; arrival.
—*adj.* **1** now approaching; next: *this coming spring.* **2** *Informal.* on the way to importance or fame.
—*v.* ppr. of COME.

Com•in•tern ['kɒmɪn,tɜrn] *n.* the Third Communist International, an organization to spread communism, founded at Moscow in 1919 and dissolved in 1943. ⟨< *Com*munist *Intern*ational⟩

co•mi•tia [kə'mɪʃiə] *or* [kə'mɪʃə] *n.pl.* in ancient Rome, a meeting of citizens to pass laws, elect officials, etc. ⟨< L *comitia,* pl. of *comitium* meeting place⟩ —**co'mi•ti•al,** *adj.*

com•i•ty ['kɒməti] *n., pl.* **-ties.** courtesy; civility. ⟨< L *comitas* < *comis* friendly⟩

comity of nations **1** respect shown by one nation for the laws and customs of another. **2** the nations practising such a respect.

com•ma ['kɒmə] *n.* a mark (,) of punctuation, used to show a slight separation of elements within a sentence. Commas are generally used where a slight pause or rise in the voice could be made in speaking, as after an introductory word or phrase, between words in a list, or before and after non-essential phrases or clauses inserted into the middle of a sentence. ⟨< L < Gk. *komma* piece cut off < *koptein* to cut⟩

comma bacillus a comma-shaped bacterium (*Vibrio comma*) that causes cholera in human beings.

comma fault or **comma splice** *Grammar.* a comma between related main clauses not connected by a co-ordinate conjunction. Example: *He said he would come, however, he broke his promise.*

com•mand [kə'mænd] *v., n.* —*v.* **1** give an order to; direct: *The captain commanded the men to fire.* **2** give orders; be commander. **3** have authority or power over; be in control of: *The captain commands his ship.* **4** have a position of control over by virtue of height or elevation; overlook: *A hilltop commands the plain around it.* **5** have ready for use: *With the political knowledge that she commands, she can answer almost any question on current affairs.* **6** ask for and get; force to be given: *Food commands a higher price when it is scarce.*
—*n.* **1** an order; direction: *They obeyed the captain's command.* **2** authority; power; control: *You are under the squad leader's command.* **3** the position of a person who has the right to command: *The general is in command of the army.* **4** the soldiers, ships, district, etc. under an officer who is appointed to command them: *The captain knew every soldier in her command.* **5 Command,** one of the main tactical formations of the Canadian Forces: *Maritime Command.* **6** mastery or control by elevated position: *The hill fort had command of the plain below.* **7** outlook (over); range of vision. **8** the ability to use; mastery: *An effective speaker or writer must have a good command of the language.* **9** a royal invitation. **10** *Computer technology.* an instruction, usually given to an operating system or a software package, directing it to perform some operation: *He used the 'Move' command to rearrange several paragraphs of his letter.*
at (one's) **command,** at one's disposal; available: *He always seems to have the right words at his command.* ⟨ME < OF *comander* < LL *commandare* < L *com-* with + *mandare* commit, command⟩

com•man•dant [,kɒmən'dænt] *or* [,kɒmən'dɑnt] *n.* **1** the officer in command of a military base, camp, etc. **2** the officer in charge of a military college or training school. *Abbrev.:* Comdt. ⟨< F, originally ppr. of *commander* command⟩

com•man•deer [,kɒmən'dir] *v.* **1** seize (private property) for military or public use: *All the automobiles in the town were commandeered by the army.* **2** force into military service. **3** *Informal.* take by force. ⟨< Afrikaans *commandeeren* < F *commander*⟩

com•mand•er [kə'mændər] *n.* **1** a person who commands. **2** *Canadian Forces.* in Maritime Command, the equivalent of a lieutenant-colonel. *Abbrev.:* Cdr. or Cdr See chart of ranks in the Appendix. **3** a naval officer of similar rank in other countries. **4** a member of a high rank in an order of knighthood or a society.

com•mand•er-in-chief [kə'mændər ɪn 'tʃif] *n., pl.* **com•mand•ers-in-chief.** a person who has complete command of the armed forces of a country in a theatre of war, a garrison, etc. *Abbrev.:* C. in C.

com•mand•ing [kə'mændɪŋ] *adj., v.* —*adj.* **1** in command: *a commanding officer.* **2** controlling; powerful: *commanding influences.* **3** authoritative; impressive: *a commanding voice.* **4** having a position of control.
—*v.* ppr. of COMMAND. —**com'mand•ing•ly,** *adv.*

command language *Computer technology.* the complete set of commands available to give directions to an operating system, software package, etc.

com•mand•ment [kə'mændmənt] *n.* **1** an order; law. **2** in the Bible, one of the ten laws that God gave to Moses.

command module the main section of a spacecraft, designed to carry the crew and equipment for communication, flight, and re-entry. A smaller section may be detached from the command module for short, independent flights or landing on a planet or the moon.

com•man•do [kə'mændou] *n., pl.* **-dos** or **-does. 1** a soldier who makes brief, daring raids in enemy territory and does close-range fighting. **2** a group of such soldiers. **3** (*adj.*) having to do with, involving, or designating a commando: *a commando raid.* ⟨< Afrikaans < Pg.⟩

command performance a stage performance, etc. given before royalty by request or order.

command post the centre of operations of a military commander.

comma splice See COMMA FAULT.

com•me•dia dell'ar•te [kɒ'meidjə dɛl 'ɑrtei]; *Italian,* [kɔm'mɛdja dɛl 'lartɛ] *Italian.* a form of comedy originating in the 16th century in Italy, in which a company of professional actors play stock characters in conventional situations but improvise their speeches and comic actions. ⟨< Ital. comedy of art⟩

comme il faut [,kʌm il 'fou]; *French,* [kɔmil'fo] *French.* as it should be; proper; in accordance with etiquette.

com•mem•o•rate [kə'mɛmə,reit] *v.* **-rat•ed, -rat•ing.** **1** preserve the memory of: *Roman emperors built arches to commemorate their victories.* **2** honour the memory of by some ceremony: *Christmas commemorates Christ's birth.* ⟨< L *commemorare* < *com-* together + *memorare* remind⟩ **—com'mem•o,rat•or,** *n.*

com•mem•o•ra•tion [kə,mɛmə'reiʃən] *n.* **1** the act of commemorating. **2** a service, celebration, etc. in memory of some person or event.
in commemoration of, in honour of the memory of.

com•mem•o•ra•tive [kə'mɛmərətɪv] *or* [kə'mɛmə,reitɪv] *adj., n. —adj.* calling to remembrance; honouring the memory of someone or something.
—n. a postage stamp issued to commemorate some person, event, etc. **—com'mem•o•ra•tive•ly,** *adv.*

com•mence [kə'mɛns] *v.* **-menced, -menc•ing.** begin; start. ⟨ME < OF *comencer* < VL < L *com-* together + *initiare* begin (ult. < *inire* begin < *in-* in + *ire* go)⟩ **—com'menc•er,** *n.*
☛ *Syn.* See note at BEGIN.

com•mence•ment [kə'mɛnsmənt] *n.* **1** a beginning; start. **2** the day when a school or college gives diplomas, certificates, etc. to students who have completed the required course of study; graduation day. **3** the ceremonies held on this day.

com•mend [kə'mɛnd] *v.* **1** praise. **2** mention favourably; recommend. **3** hand over for safekeeping: *She commended the child to her friend's care.* ⟨ME < L *commendare* < *com-* (intensive) + *mandare* commit, command. Cf. COMMAND.⟩
☛ *Syn.* **1.** See note at PRAISE.

com•mend•a•ble [kə'mɛndəbəl] *adj.* worthy of praise; deserving approval. **—com'mend•a•bly,** *adv.*

com•men•da•tion [,kɒmən'deiʃən] *n.* **1** the act of commending, especially recommendation or praise. **2** a handing over to another for safekeeping; entrusting.

com•mend•a•to•ry [kə'mɛndə,tɔri] *adj.* **1** praising; expressing approval. **2** mentioning favourably; recommending.

com•men•sal [kə'mɛnsəl] *n., adj. —n.* **1** one who habitually eats meals with another. **2** *Biology.* an organism involved in commensalism.
—adj. of or having to do with commensalism or a commensal. ⟨ME < Med.L *commensalis* < L *com-* with + *mensa* table⟩

com•men•sal•ism [kə'mɛnsə,lɪzəm] *n.* a form of SYMBIOSIS; a relationship between organisms in which one organism benefits while the other is neither helped nor harmed. Compare with AMENSALISM, MUTUALISM, and PARASITISM.

com•men•su•ra•ble [kə'mɛnʃərəbəl] *or* [kə'mɛnsərəbəl] *adj.* **1** measurable by the same set of units: *Greenness and mass are not commensurable.* **2** corresponding in size, amount, or degree; proportionate: *He was a big man, very tall and of commensurable mass.* **—com,men•su•ra'bil•i•ty,** *n.* **—com'men•su•ra•bly,** *adv.*

com•men•su•rate [kə'mɛnʃərɪt] *or* [kə'mɛnsərɪt] *adj.* **1** in the proper proportion; proportionate: *The pay should be commensurate with the work.* **2** of the same size, extent, etc.; equal. **3** measurable by the same set of units; commensurable. ⟨< LL *commensuratus,* pp. of *commensurare* < L *com-* together + *mensurare* measure < *mensura* a measure⟩ **—com'men•su•rate•ly,** *adv.* **—com'men•su•rate•ness,** *n.* **—com,men•su'ra•tion,** *n.*

com•ment ['kɒmɛnt] *n., v. —n.* **1** a short statement, note, or remark that explains, praises, or finds fault with something that has been written, said, or done. **2** a remark. **3** talk; gossip.
—v. **1** make a comment or comments: *Everyone commented on his strange behaviour.* **2** talk; gossip. ⟨ME < LL *commentum* < *commentus,* pp. of L *comminisci* < *com-* with + *minisci* think⟩

com•men•tar•y ['kɒmən,tɛri] *n., pl.* **-tar•ies. 1** a series of notes for explaining the hard parts of a book; explanation or interpretation: *Bibles are often provided with commentaries.* **2** anything that explains or illustrates; comment: *The way she dresses is usually a commentary on her mood.* **3** an explanatory essay or treatise. **4** a description of a sporting event, ceremony, etc., especially one given on radio or television. **5** formerly, an account of historical events seen from one person's point of view: *Caesar's Commentaries.*

com•men•tate ['kɒmən,teit] *v.* **-at•ed, -at•ing. 1** provide a commentary (on). **2** act as commentator. ⟨back formation from *commentator*⟩

com•men•ta•tor ['kɒmən,teitər] *n.* **1** a person who describes and discusses news events, etc. while they are in progress, especially for radio or television: *a sports commentator, a fashion-show commentator.* **2** a person who gives a commentary. ⟨< L⟩

com•merce ['kɒmərs] *n.* **1** buying and selling in large amounts between different places; business. **2** communication between people: *After a rude remark like that, there can be no more commerce between us.* ⟨< F < L *commercium,* ult. < *com-* with + *merx, mercis* wares⟩
☛ *Syn.* See note at TRADE.

com•mer•cial [kə'mɜrʃəl] *adj., n. —adj.* **1** of, for, or having to do with commerce: *commercial law, a piece of commercial property.* **2** made, done, or operating mainly for profit, especially at the expense of quality, artistic merit, etc.: *Her recent plays are very commercial. Their restaurant is very small and not at all commercial.* **3** supported or subsidized by an advertiser: *commercial television.* **4** for business purposes, especially in advertising: *commercial art.* **5** of chemicals, etc., being of average or inferior quality for use in large quantities in industry.
—n. an advertisement on radio or television, broadcast between programs or during a program. **—com'mer•cial•ly,** *adv.*

commercial art the profession of drawing pictures for advertising, books, etc. **—commercial artist.**

commercial bank an ordinary bank as distinguished from a savings bank or other specialized bank.

com•mer•cial•ism [kə'mɜrʃə,lɪzəm] *n.* the aims, methods, and spirit of commerce, especially as showing too great a concern for profit and success: *Commercialism has almost ruined him as an artist.* **—com'mer•cial•ist,** *n.*

com•mer•cial•ize [kə'mɜrʃə,laɪz] *v.* **-ized, -iz•ing.** make (something) a matter of business or trade; apply the methods and goals of business to, often suggesting the loss of some quality or standard: *It's a pity her photography has become so commercialized.* **—com,mer•cial•i'za•tion,** *n.*

commercial paper 1 a bill of exchange or any other negotiable paper used in business. **2** *Finance.* promissory notes sold by corporations in the open market.

commercial traveller or **traveler** sales representative.

com•mie or **Com•mie** ['kɒmi] *n. Slang.* a communist, or anyone with socialist leanings.

com•mi•na•tion [,kɒmə'neiʃən] *n.* **1** in Anglican churches, a recital of divine threats against sinners as part of the Ash Wednesday liturgy. **2** a threat; denunciation. ⟨< L *comminatio, -onis* < *comminari* < *com-* with + *minari* threaten⟩ **—'com•mi•na,to•ry** ['kɒmənə,tɔri], *adj.*

com•min•gle [kə'mɪŋgəl] *v.* **-gled, -gling.** mingle together; blend.

com•mi•nute ['kɒmə,njut] *or* ['kɒmə,nut] *v.* **-nut•ed, -nut•ing.** reduce to a powder or to small fragments; pulverize. In a **comminuted fracture** part of the bone is broken into small fragments. ⟨< L *comminutus,* pp. of *comminuere* < *com-* intensive + *minuere* make smaller < *minus* less⟩ **—,com•mi'nu•tion,** *n.*

com•mis•er•ate [kə'mɪzə,reit] *v.* **-at•ed, -at•ing.** feel or express sorrow for; sympathize; pity (*used with* **with**). ⟨< L *com-* with *miserari* < *com-* + *miser* wretched⟩

com•mis•er•a•tion [kə,mɪzə'reiʃən] *n.* pity; sympathy.

com•mis•sar ['kɒmə,sɑr] *n.* **1** formerly, the head of a government department in the Soviet Union. **2** formerly, a Soviet government official representing the Communist Party in the army, etc. ⟨< Russian *kommisar* < F *commissaire*⟩

com•mis•sar•i•at [,kɒmə'sɛriət] *n.* **1** the department of an army that provides food and daily supplies for soldiers. **2** a food supply. **3** formerly, a department of the Soviet government. ⟨< F < Med.L *commissarius.* See COMMISSARY.⟩

com•mis•sar•y ['kɒmə,sɛri] *n., pl.* **-sar•ies. 1** a store handling food and supplies in a mining camp, lumber camp, military camp, etc. **2** a restaurant in a film studio. **3** a deputy; representative. ⟨< Med.L *commissarius* < L *commissus* entrusted, pp. of *committere.* See COMMIT.⟩

com•mis•sion [kə'mɪʃən] *n., v. —n.* **1** a written paper giving certain powers, privileges, and duties. **2 a** an official certificate giving rank and authority as an officer in the armed forces: *My*

brother has received his commission as a lieutenant in the infantry. **b** the military rank and authority given. **3** **a** a giving of any authority. **b** the authority, power, or right given. **4** the thing for which authority is given; task entrusted to a person. **5** a group of people appointed or elected with authority to do certain things. **6** a government agency with a particular purpose: *housing commission; liquor commission.* **7** a municipal government where power is held by a group of five or more elected municipal department heads, rather than by a mayor and council. **8** a doing or committing, as a crime: *People are punished for the commission of crimes.* **9** pay based on a percentage of the amount of business done: *She gets a commission of 10 percent on all the sales she makes.*
in commission, a in service or use. **b** ready for service or use; in working order.
out of commission, a not in service or use. **b** not ready for use; not in working order.
—*v.* **1** give a commission to. **2** give authority to; give (a person) the right or power (to do something): *Some entrepreneurs commission others to buy or sell property for them.* **3** put in service or use; make ready for service or use. A new warship is commissioned when it has the officers, sailors, and supplies needed for a voyage. **4** pay for (something) to be done: *This painting was commissioned by a local supporter of the arts.* ⟨ME < OF < L *commissio, -onis* < *committere.* See COMMIT.⟩

com•mis•sion•aire [kə,mɪʃə'nɛr] *n.* **1** a person whose job is to open doors, carry bags, etc. at the entrance of a hotel or a club. **2** a member of the CORPS OF COMMISSIONAIRES. Some Canadian cities employ commissionaires to check parking meters and to issue parking tickets to persons whose cars are parked overtime. ⟨< F⟩

com•mis•sioned [kə'mɪʃənd] *adj., v. —adj.* having a commission: *a commissioned officer.*
—*v.* pt. and pp. of COMMISSION.

com•mis•sion•er [kə'mɪʃənər] *n.* **1** a member of a COMMISSION (def. 7). **2** an official in charge of some department of a government: *a police commissioner.* **3** one of a group of persons elected or appointed to govern a city or a county. **4 Commissioner,** *Cdn.* **a** the highest ranking officer of the Royal Canadian Mounted Police. **b** the chief executive officer of the Yukon Territory or the Northwest Territories. **5** a person who directs the operation of a professional sport or sport league.

commission merchant a person who buys or sells goods for others who pay him or her a commission.

com•mis•sure ['kɒmə,ʃur] *n.* **1** a joint or seam where two parts come together. **2** the place where the two hemispheres of the brain join. ⟨ME and OF < L *commissura* < *commissus,* pp. of *committere* to bring together, commit⟩

com•mit [kə'mɪt] *v.* **-mit•ted, -mit•ting. 1** hand over for safekeeping; deliver: *He committed himself to the doctor's care.* **2** put officially in the care of an institution, such as a psychiatric hospital or prison: *The judge committed the accused for psychiatric assessment.* **3** refer (a matter) to a committee for consideration. **4** do (something that is an offence): *to commit a crime, to commit a sin.* **5** reveal one's opinion (*used reflexively*). **6** involve; pledge: *He would not commit himself in any way.* **7** consign; deliver for disposal, etc.: *Hedda committed her manuscript to the fire.* **8** oblige; bind: *His campaign promises committed him to a policy of rapid disarmament.*
commit to memory, learn by heart.
commit to paper or **writing,** write down. ⟨ME < L *committere* < *com-* with + *mittere* send, put⟩ **—com'mit•ta•ble,** *adj.*

☛ *Syn.* **1. Commit,** CONSIGN, ENTRUST = hand over a person or thing. **Commit** = hand over to be kept safe or taken care of: *The court committed the financial affairs of the orphan to a guardian.* **Consign** often suggests formally handing over control: *He consigned his share of the bonds to his sister.* However, it can also mean specifically handing over to an undesirable condition or fate: *consigned to everlasting mediocrity, consigned to the wrecker's ball.* **Entrust** = commit with trust and confidence in the receiver: *I entrusted my door key to my neighbour.*

com•mit•ment [kə'mɪtmənt] *n.* **1** a committing or being committed. **2** a pledge; promise: *She made a commitment to look after her younger brother.* **3** an official order sending a person to prison or to a psychiatric institution. **4** an agreement to assume a future financial obligation. **5** something pledged or committed. **6** dedication; willingness to stick to things over the long term: *Becoming a skilled musician takes commitment. Their relationship suffered from a lack of commitment.*

com•mit•tal [kə'mɪtəl] *n.* the act of committing or the state of being committed.

com•mit•tee [kə'mɪti] *n.* a group of persons appointed or elected by a legislature, club, etc. to consider, investigate, or act on certain matters and report to the main body.
in committee, under consideration by a committee: *The bill is still in committee.* ⟨< AF *committee* committed⟩

☛ *Usage.* **Committee** is a collective noun, to be used with a singular or plural verb depending on whether the group or the individuals are meant: *The committee meets today at four. The committee get together with difficulty. See note at* COLLECTIVE NOUN.

committee of the whole a committee made up of all the members present of a legislature, club, etc.

com•mix [kə'mɪks] *v. Rare.* mix together.

com•mix•ture [kə'mɪkstʃər] *n. Rare.* mixture.

com•mode [kə'moud] *n.* **1** chest of drawers. **2** a stand in a bedroom, to hold a washbasin, pitcher of water, chamber pot, etc.; washstand. **3** a special chair housing a chamber pot. **4** a toilet. ⟨< F < L *commodus* convenient < *com-* with + *modus* measure⟩

com•mo•di•ous [kə'moudiəs] *adj.* **1** roomy. **2** convenient; handy. ⟨< Med.L *commodiosus* < L *commodus.* See COMMODE.⟩ **—com'mo•di•ous•ly,** *adv.* **—com'mo•di•ous•ness,** *n.*

com•mod•i•ty [kə'mɒdəti] *n., pl.* **-ties. 1** anything that is bought and sold; an article of trade or commerce: *Groceries are commodities.* **2** a useful thing. ⟨ME and OF *commodité* benefit, profit < L *commoditas,* fitness, adaptation < *commodus* suitable⟩

com•mo•dore ['kɒmə,dɔr] *n.* **1** *Canadian Forces.* in Maritime Command, the equivalent of a brigadier-general. See chart of ranks in the Appendix. **2** a naval officer of similar rank in other countries. *Abbrev.*: Cmdre. or Cmdre **3** the chief officer of a merchant fleet, yacht club, power squadron, etc. ⟨earlier *commandore,* ? < Du. *kommandeur* < F *commandeur* < *commander* to command⟩

com•mon ['kɒmən] *adj., n. —adj.* **1** belonging equally to each or all of a group; shared by all; joint: *The two cousins soon discovered that they had a lot of common interests. The house was the common property of the three sisters.* **2** widespread; general: *common knowledge, a common nuisance.* **3** generally accepted; usual; popular as opposed to scientific or technical: *The common name for* Equus caballus *is* horse. **4** often met with; usual; familiar: *Snow is common in cold countries. The dandelion is a common weed.* **5** of the most familiar or abundant kind: *common salt.* **6** of or having to do with the community as a whole; public: *the common good.* **7** without special rank or title: *the common people. A common soldier is a private.* **8** no more or greater than ordinary or average: *common courtesy.* **9** below ordinary; of poor quality; inferior: *a common grade of cloth.* **10** coarse; vulgar: *That was a common thing to say.* **11** *Grammar.* **a** designating gender that may be either masculine or feminine. The word *parent* is of common gender; *mother* is of feminine gender. **b** See COMMON NOUN. **12** *Mathematics.* belonging equally to two or more quantities: *a common factor, a common multiple.*
—*n.* **1 the Commons,** the HOUSE OF COMMONS. **2** Also, **commons,** *pl.* land owned or used by all the people of a town, village, etc. **3** *Law.* the right to use and take profit from land belonging to another, such as the right to fish or pasture animals, which a person shares with the owner or others. **4** *Archaic.* **commons,** *pl.* the common people. **5 commons,** a dining hall, especially one attached to a college, etc. **6 commons,** *pl.* food or rations served to all members of a group (*sometimes used with a singular verb*).
in common, equally with another or others; owned, used, done, etc. by both or all.
short commons, too little food: *The prisoners were kept on short commons.* ⟨ME < OF *comun* < L *communis*⟩
—'com•mon•ly, *adv.* **—'com•mon•ness,** *n.*

☛ *Syn. adj.* **2.** See note at GENERAL. **4. Common** ORDINARY = usual. **Common** = often met with or usual because shared by many people or things: *Colds are common in winter.* **Ordinary** = usual because in agreement with the normal standards and order of things: *I use ordinary gasoline.*

☛ *Usage.* **Common,** MUTUAL. Formal English distinguishes between **common** = belonging equally to each or all, and **mutual** = each to the other: *The estate is the common property of the five brothers. Bud and Mary felt a mutual dislike.*

com•mon•age ['kɒmənɪdʒ] *n.* **1** the right to pasture animals on land owned by the town, village, etc. **2** the ownership of land in common. **3** land owned in common. **4** the common people.

com•mon•al•i•ty [,kɒmə'næləti] *n., pl.* **-ties. 1** the quality of being shared; possession in common: *a commonality of purpose.* **2** COMMONALTY (def. 1).

com•mon•al•ty ['kɒmənəlti] *n., pl.* **-ties. 1** the common people; persons without rank or title; the middle and lower classes of society. **2** the members of any group generally and collectively. **3** the members of a corporation.

common blue violet a spring wildflower (*Viola papilionacea*) blooming in damp woodland and having edible purple flowers. The blue violet is the provincial flower of New Brunswick.

common camas BLUE CAMAS.

common carrier a person or company whose business is conveying goods or people for pay. A railway company or airline is a common carrier.

common cold COLD (def. *n.* 2).

common council the lawmaking group of a city, town, etc.

common denominator **1** *Mathematics.* a denominator that is a COMMON MULTIPLE of the denominators of a group of fractions. A common denominator of 1/2, 2/3, and 3/4 is 12, because these three fractions can also be expressed as 6/12, 8/12, and 9/12. **2** a quality, attribute, opinion, etc. shared by all the persons or things in a group.

common difference *Mathematics.* in an arithmetic progression, the constant added to each member of the series.

common divisor *Mathematics.* a number that will divide two or more other numbers without a remainder. A common divisor of 4, 6, 8, and 10 is 2.

com•mon•er ['kɒmənər] *n.* **1** one of the common people; a person who is not a noble. **2** a member of the House of Commons.

Common Era CHRISTIAN ERA.

common fraction *Mathematics.* a fraction in which both the numerator and the denominator are whole numbers; simple fraction. *Examples*: 5/8, 213/500, 8/15. Compare COMPLEX FRACTION.

common gender *Grammar.* **1** a classification consisting of nouns that are considered to be either masculine or feminine, so that they may be replaced in different contexts by *he* or *she*. *Examples*: *friend, person, writer.* **2** a classification consisting of nouns that are considered to be masculine, feminine, or neuter, so that they may be replaced by *he, she* or *it*. *Examples*: *baby, dog.*

common law the body of law based on custom and usage dating from the ancient unwritten laws of England, and recognized and confirmed by the judgments of the courts. It is distinguished from civil law and canon law and law created by statute.

com•mon–law ['kɒmən ˌlɒ] *adj., adv.* —*adj.* **1** of, having to do with, or based on a COMMON-LAW MARRIAGE: *a common-law wife.* **2** of, having to do with, or based on common law.
—*adv.* in a common-law marriage: *They have been living common-law for a year.*

common–law marriage a marriage that has not been solemnized by any civil or church ceremony, but is legally recognized for certain purposes, such as allowances for widow or dependants, inheritance rights, etc. For a relationship to be recognized as a common-law marriage, each of the two partners must agree to the arrangement, and both must be legally able to marry.

common logarithm *Mathematics.* a logarithm having a base of 10.

common market **1** an association of countries to promote mutual free trade. **2 Common Market,** the EUROPEAN ECONOMIC COMMUNITY.

common measure *Music.* 4/4 time, where the beat falls on the quarter note; common time.

common milkweed milkweed.

common multiple *Mathematics.* a number that can be divided by two or more other numbers without a remainder: 12 *is a common multiple of* 2, 3, 4, *and* 6.

common nightshade nightshade.

common noun *Grammar.* any noun that is not a proper noun. A common noun refers to a condition, quality, idea, etc., or to a person, animal, or thing as a member of a class. In the sentence *The dog's name is Sam, dog* and *name* are common nouns; *Sam* is a proper noun. Compare PROPER NOUN.

☛ *Usage.* Common nouns are not usually capitalized unless they are used to begin a sentence.

com•mon–or–gar•den ['kɒmən ər 'gɑrdən] *adj. Informal.* ordinary; familiar; everyday: *common-or-garden pencils.*

com•mon•place ['kɒmənˌpleis] *n., adj.* —*n.* **1** an ordinary or everyday thing: *Sixty years ago broadcasting was a novelty; today it is a commonplace.* **2** an ordinary or obvious remark. **3** one of a collection of notable passages written down for reference.
—*adj.* not new or interesting; everyday; ordinary: *We thought the speech rather commonplace.* **—'com•monˌplace•ness,** *n.*

commonplace book a notebook in which one jots down quotations that appeal to one, together with one's own thoughts.

common pleas lawsuits between private individuals that do not involve criminal cases.

common room a room in a school, college, etc. for students or teachers to socialize and relax. Also, **commons room.**

com•mons ['kɒmənz] *n.pl.* See COMMON (defs. 1, 2, 4-6).

common school in the United States and formerly in Canada, an elementary public school.

common sense ordinary good judgment; practical intelligence: *It's just common sense to carry a spare tire in the car.* **—'com•mon-'sense,** *adj.* **—'com•mon-'sen•si•cal,** *adj.*

common stock ordinary stock in a company, without a definite dividend rate. A holder of common stock is entitled to dividends only if there is any profit left after all other claims have been paid. Compare PREFERRED STOCK.

common thistle thistle.

common time *Music.* 4/4 time; four quarter notes to the measure.

com•mon•weal ['kɒmənˌwil] *n.* **1** the general welfare; public good. **2** *Archaic.* commonwealth.

com•mon•wealth ['kɒmənˌwɛlθ] *n.* **1 the Commonwealth,** BRITISH COMMONWEALTH OF NATIONS. **2** the people who make up a nation; citizens of a state. **3** a democratic state; republic. **4** a group of persons, nations, etc. united by some common interest. **5 Commonwealth,** the government of England under Oliver Cromwell and his son Richard, lasting from 1649 to 1660.

Commonwealth of Independent States a union of Armenia, Belarus, Kazakhstan, Kirghizia, Moldavia, Russia, Turkmenistan, Tajikistan, Ukraine, and Uzbekistan.

Commonwealth of Nations See BRITISH COMMONWEALTH OF NATIONS.

com•mo•tion [kə'mouʃən] *n.* **1** confusion; agitation; violent movement: *We saw a great commotion in the water and then a dolphin surfaced.* **2** public disturbance; insurrection. ⟨< L *commotio, -onis* < *commovere* < *com-* with + *movere* move⟩

com•mu•nal [kə'mjunəl] *or* ['kɒmjənəl] *adj.* **1** of a community; public. **2** owned jointly by all; used or participated in by all members of a group or community. **3** of a commune. ⟨ME and OF < LL *communalis*⟩ **—com'mu•nal•ly,** *adv.*

com•mu•nal•ism [kə'mjunəˌlɪzəm] *or* ['kɒmjənəˌlɪzəm] *n.* **1** a theory or system of government according to which each commune is virtually an independent state and the nation is merely a federation of communes. **2** communal ownership.

com•mu•nard ['kɒmjuˌnɑrd] *n.* **1** a person who belongs to or lives in a commune. **2 Communard,** a person who took part in the Commune of Paris (1871). ⟨< F⟩

com•mune[1] *v.* [kə'mjun]; *n.* ['kɒmjun] *v.* **-muned, -mun•ing;** *n.* —*v.* **1** talk intimately. **2** have thoughts in a relationship (*with*): *to commune with nature.* **3** receive Holy Communion.
—*n.* intimate talk; communion. ⟨< OF *communer* < *comun.* See COMMON.⟩

com•mune[2] ['kɒmjun] *n.* **1** a community of people sharing living accommodation, possessions, and responsibilities. **2** the smallest division for local government in France, Belgium, Switzerland, and Italy. **3** the government or inhabitants of such a division. **4** a local unit of collective farms in China. **5** a collective farm in a Communist country. **6 Commune,** in France: **a** a revolutionary group that governed Paris 1792-1794. **b** a similar group that governed Paris from March 18 to May 28, 1871. ⟨< F *commune*, alteration of OF *comugne* < VL *communia*, originally neut. pl. of L *communis.* See COMMON.⟩

com•mu•ni•ca•ble [kə'mjunəkəbəl] *adj.* that can be communicated: *Ideas are communicable by words. Scarlet fever is a communicable disease.* **—com'mu•ni•ca•bly,** *adv.*

com•mu•ni•cant [kə'mjunɪkənt] *n., adj.* —*n.* **1** a person who receives Holy Communion. **2** a regular attender at a church. **3** a person who gives information by talking, writing, etc.
—*adj.* communicating.

com•mu•ni•cate [kə'mjunɪˌkeit] *v.* **-cat•ed, -cat•ing.** **1** exchange (information or signals) by talk, writing, gestures, etc.; send and receive (messages): *The searchers communicated by two-way radio.* **2** pass along; transmit: *A stove communicates heat to a room. He didn't say anything, but he soon communicated his uneasiness to the rest of us.* **3** get in touch with; get through to: *It was impossible to communicate with my family during the storm.*

The teacher could not communicate with some of the pupils. **4** of rooms or passages, be connected: *The dining room communicates with the kitchen.* **5** receive Holy Communion. ⟨< L *communicare* < *communis.* See COMMON.⟩ **—com'mu•ni,ca•tor,** *n.*

☛ *Syn.* **1. Communicate,** IMPART = pass knowledge, ideas, or information along. **Communicate,** the general word, emphasizes the idea of passing something along from one person or thing to another: *He has not communicated his wishes to me.* **Impart** emphasizes the idea of giving to another a share of what one has: *A teacher imparts knowledge.*

com•mu•ni•ca•tion [kə,mjunə'keiʃən] *n.* **1** the act or fact of passing along; transmitting. **2** a giving or exchanging of information by talking, writing, etc.: *The government leaders are in close communication on this issue.* **3** information given in this way; message: *A communication has been received from the embassy.* **4** a means of going from one place to the other; connection; passage: *There is no communication between these two rooms.* **5 communications,** *pl.* **a** a system for sending or receiving messages, as by telephone, television, or radio. **b** (*used with a singular verb*) the art and technology of communicating, especially by mechanical or electronic means. **c** the movement of troops and supplies in war.

communications satellite an artificial satellite used for radio and television communication. It reflects or relays radio and television signals.

com•mu•ni•ca•tive [kə'mjunɪkətɪv] *or* [kə'mjunə,keitɪv] *adj.* **1** ready to give information; talkative. **2** of or having to do with communication. **—com'mu•ni•ca•tive•ly,** *adv.* **—com'mu•ni•ca•tive•ness,** *n.*

com•mu•ni•ca•tor [kə'mjunə,keitər] *n.* a person or thing that communicates, as, in a large company.

com•mun•ion [kə'mjunjən] *n.* **1** the act of sharing; a having in common. **2** an exchange of thoughts and feelings; intimate talk; fellowship. **3** a close spiritual relationship. **4** a group of people having the same religious beliefs. **5 Communion,** *Christianity.* the commemoration of Christ's Last Supper, in which bread and wine are consecrated and taken as the body and blood of Christ or as symbols of them; the Eucharist; Holy Communion. **6** the bread and wine used in this commemoration. ⟨ME < L *communio, -onis* < *communis.* See COMMON.⟩

com•mu•ni•qué [kə,mjunə'kei] *or* [kə'mjunə,kei] *n.* an official bulletin, statement, or other communication. ⟨< F⟩

com•mu•nism ['kɒmjə,nɪzəm] *n.* **1** the political, social, and economic system of certain countries, such as the People's Republic of China, in which the state, governed by a single party without formal opposition, owns all property, controls the production and distribution of goods and services, and, to a great extent, controls the social and cultural life of the people. **2** Often, **Communism,** a philosophy or system derived from Marxism, advocating state ownership of land and property and seeking the overthrow of non-communist societies on behalf of the working people, or proletariat, of the world. **3** any economic system based on ownership of all property and the means of production and distribution by the community or state. Compare CAPITALISM and SOCIALISM. **4** *Informal.* to a right-wing person, any leftist tendency. ⟨< F *communisme* < *commun,* OF *comun.* See COMMON.⟩

com•mu•nist ['kɒmjənɪst] *n., adj. —n.* **1** a person who favours and supports communism. **2 Communist,** a member of the Communist Party. **3** *Informal.* to a right-wing person, anyone with leftist tendencies.
—adj. of, having to do with, or characteristic of communism or communists; communistic: *communist doctrine.*

com•mu•nis•tic [,kɒmjə'nɪstɪk] *adj.* **1** of or having to do with communists or communism. **2** favouring communism. **—,com•mu'nis•ti•cal•ly,** *adv.*

Communist Party a political party that is dedicated to the establishment of communism, especially as derived from the principles of Marxism.

com•mu•ni•ty [kə'mjunəti] *n., pl.* **-ties. 1** a group of people having common ties or interests and living in the same locality or district and subject to the same laws: *a farming community. This lake provides water for six communities.* **2** the place where they live. **3** a group of people living together: *a community of monks.* **4** any group of people, nations, etc. with a common bond, independent of geography or immediate circumstance: *the worldwide community of artists. The British Commonwealth is a community.* **5** the public: *the approval of the community.* **6** ownership together; sharing together: *community of food supplies, community of ideas.* **7** *Ecology.* a group of animals and plants living in a particular region under similar conditions and interacting with one another, especially in food relationships. **8** likeness, similarity; identity: *Community of interests causes people to work together.* ⟨ME *com(m)unete* < OF < L *communitas* < *communis.* See COMMON.⟩

community centre 1 a hall used for recreation, entertainment, public meetings, etc. in a community. **2** *Cdn.* an arena run by the community as a centre for sporting events, skating, dancing, and other forms of entertainment.

community chest a fund of money contributed voluntarily by people, usually once a year, to support various charitable organizations in their community. The United Way is a kind of community chest.

community college *Cdn.* an institution for post-secondary and adult education, especially for training in particular occupations and skills. Community colleges offer diploma courses, usually two-year programs, in many trades and also have courses for the personal interest of people in the community, ranging from philosophy and art appreciation to orienteering.

Community Doukhobors *Cdn.* SONS OF FREEDOM.

com•mu•nize ['kɒmjə,naɪz] *v.* **-nized, -niz•ing. 1** subject (all property) to state ownership. **2** enforce the practice or adoption of communism in or by (a people, nation, etc.). **—,com•mu•ni'za•tion,** *n.*

com•mu•tate ['kɒmjə,teit] *v.* **-tat•ed, -tat•ing.** *Electricity.* reverse the direction of (current). ⟨back formation from *commutation*⟩

com•mu•ta•tion [,kɒmjə'teiʃən] *n.* **1** an exchange; substitution. **2** the reduction of an obligation, penalty, etc. to a less severe one: *The prisoner obtained a commutation of her sentence from death to life imprisonment.* **3** *Electricity.* a reversal of the direction of a current by a commutator. **4** regular, daily travel back and forth to work by train, bus, automobile, etc. ⟨ME, OF < L *commutatio* < *commutatus,* pp. of *commutare.* See COMMUTE.⟩

com•mu•ta•tive [kə'mjutətɪv] *or* ['kɒmjə,teitɪv] *adj.* **1** of, having to do with, or involving substitution or exchange. **2** *Mathematics.* designating an operation in which the ordering of the elements does not affect the result. Addition and multiplication are commutative because it does not matter which quantity is placed first; subtraction and division are not commutative because reversing the order of the quantities will produce a different answer.

com•mu•ta•tor ['kɒmjə,teitər] *n. Electricity.* **1** a device for reversing the direction of an electric current. **2** a revolving part in a dynamo or motor that carries the current to or from the brushes. See GENERATOR for picture.

com•mute [kə'mjut] *v., n. —v.* **-mut•ed, -mut•ing. 1** change (an obligation, penalty, etc.) to an easier one: *The prisoner's sentence of death was commuted to one of life imprisonment.* **2** travel as a commuter. **3** *Electricity.* reverse the direction of (a current) by a commutator. **4** exchange; substitute; change: *to commute foreign currency into Canadian dollars.*
—n. Informal. a journey made by a commuter: *Vancouver to Victoria can be a long commute!* ⟨< L *commutare* < *com-* (intensive) + *mutare* change⟩

com•mut•er [kə'mjutər] *n.* a person who regularly travels a long distance between his or her home in one community and his or her work in another, especially one who travels by train, bus, etc. from a small community or suburb into a city to work.

Co•mo•ros ['kɒmə,rouz] *n.* a country of islands off the E coast of Africa.

comp. 1 compound. **2** compare; comparative. **3** composition. **4** compositor. **5** composer; composed. **6** complimentary ticket. **7** comprehensive examination. **8** compiler; compiled.

com•pact[1] *adj.* ['kɒmpækt] *or* [kəm'pækt]; *n.* ['kɒmpækt]; *v.* [kəm'pækt] *adj., n., v. —adj.* **1** firmly packed together; closely joined: *The leaves of the cabbage were folded into a compact head.* **2** using few words; brief, well organized, and to the point: *a compact style of writing.* **3** having the parts neatly or tightly arranged within a small space: *a compact portable TV set.* **3** *Poetic.* composed or made (*of*): *It was a tale compact of moonstruck fancy.* **4** of, being, or having to do with the second smallest of the four basic sizes of automobile: *a compact sedan.* *—n.* **1** the second smallest of the four basic sizes of automobile, generally larger than a subcompact and smaller than an intermediate. Compare SUBCOMPACT, INTERMEDIATE, and STANDARD. **2** a small case for carrying face powder or rouge, having a hinged lid with a mirror.

—*v.* **1** pack firmly together; join closely. **2** make by putting together firmly. **3** condense. ⟨< L *compactus,* pp. of *compingere* < *com-* together + *pangere* fasten⟩ **—com'pact•ly,** *adv.* **—com'pact•ness,** *n.*

com•pact[2] ['kɒmpækt] *n.* agreement: *We made a compact not to tell anyone what we had heard.* ⟨< L *compactum* < *compacisci* < *com-* (intensive) + *pacisci* contract⟩

compact disc a kind of RECORD (def. 5) with a pitted surface instead of grooves, on which music, a computer program, or other data has been digitally encoded. It is about 11 cm across and played by means of a laser beam and not a needle: *A compact disc gives sound of a very high quality.*

com•pact•or [kəm'pæktər] *or* ['kɒmpæktər] *n.* an electrically powered device that compacts or crushes garbage and rubbish to a fraction of its original volume.

com•pan•ion[1] [kəm'pænjən] *n., v.* —*n.* **1** a person who goes along with or accompanies another; a person who shares in what another is doing; comrade. **2** anything that matches or goes with another in kind, size, colour, etc. **3** a person paid to live or travel with another as a friend and helper. **4 Companion, a** in certain orders of knighthood, a member of the lowest rank. **b** *Cdn.* a member of the highest rank of the Order of Canada. **5** (*adjl.*) being another member of a set; matching: *the companion volume.*
—*v.* be a companion to; go along with. ⟨ME < OF *compaignon* < LL *companio, -onis* < L *com-* together + *panis* bread⟩ **—com'pan•ion•less,** *adj.*

com•pan•ion[2] [kəm'pænjən] *n.* **1** a covering over the top of a companionway. **2** companionway. ⟨< Du. *kompanje* quarterdeck < OF *compagne* steward's room in a galley < VL *compania* < L *com-* together + *panis* bread⟩

com•pan•ion•a•ble [kəm'pænjənəbəl] *adj.* suited to companionship; agreeable; pleasant; sociable: *a companionable disposition, a companionable evening.*
—com'pan•ion•a•ble•ness, *n.* **—com'pan•ion•a•bly,** *adv.*

com•pan•ion•ate [kəm'pænjənɪt] *adj.* of or like companions.

companionate marriage a non-binding marriage in which childbearing is delayed until later finalization of the marriage and neither member is legally obligated to the other in the event of a divorce.

companion cell any of the small cells with large nuclei adjacent to the sieve tube in the phloem of vascular plants.

com•pan•ion•ship [kəm'pænjən,ʃɪp] *n.* an association as companions; fellowship.

com•pan•ion•way [kəm'pænjən,wei] *n.* a stairway leading from one deck to another on a ship.

com•pa•ny ['kʌmpəni] *n., pl.* **-nies. 1** a group of people joined together for some purpose: *a business company, a company of actors.* **2** in the Middle Ages, an association for the protection of members of a trade; guild. **3** a gathering of persons for social purposes: *He's quite shy in company.* **4** a companion or companions: *You are known by the company you keep.*
5 companionship: *They enjoy each other's company. The dog gives her company.* **6** a guest or guests: *We had company last night.* **7** a group of people. **8** a part of an army commanded by a captain. **9** a troop of Girl Guides. **10** a ship's crew; the officers and sailors of a ship. **11** partners not named in the title of a firm. **12** a unit of firefighters.
bear (someone) **company,** accompany.
keep company, go together; go out with; carry on courtship: *They have been keeping company for several months.*
keep (someone) **company,** stay with for companionship; accompany: *My friend kept me company while I was sick.*
part company, a go separate ways. **b** end companionship. ⟨ME < OF *compagnie* < *compagne* companion < LL *companio.* See COMPANION[1].⟩

Company man *Cdn.* formerly, an employee of the Hudson's Bay Company.

Company of New France a company founded in 1627 in Paris by Cardinal Richelieu to foster immigration to New France and to maintain loyalty to the French Crown and the Catholic Church. The company, which was granted the monopoly of all French commerce in North America and sovereignty over the territories of the New World, ceased to function in 1657.

company town a town built by a company for its workers, to whom it rents houses, provides services, etc.

company union 1 a union of workers in one factory, store, etc., that is not part of a larger union. **2** a union of workers dominated by the employers.

compar. comparative.

com•pa•ra•ble ['kɒmpərəbəl], [kəm'pærəbəl], *or* [kəm'pɛrəbəl] *adj.* **1** able to be compared; having qualities in common: *A fire is comparable with the sun; both give light and heat.* **2** fit to be compared: *A cave is not comparable to a house as a comfortable place to live in.* **—'com•pa•ra•ble•ness,** *n.* **—'com•pa•ra•bly,** *adv.*

☛ *Pronun.* Although many people avoid the pronunciation [kəm'pærəbəl] or [kəm'pɛrəbəl], the form has wide currency among educated Canadians.

com•par•a•tive [kəm'pærətɪv] *or* [kəm'pɛrətɪv] *adj., n.* —*adj.* **1** that compares; of or having to do with comparison: *the comparative method of study.* **2** measured by comparison with something else; relative; not absolute: *Screens give us comparative freedom from flies.* **3** *Grammar.* of or designating the second degree of comparison of an adjective or adverb. *Better* is the comparative form of *good.*
—*n.* **1** *Grammar.* the second degree of comparison of an adjective or adverb. **2** a form or combination of words that shows this degree. *Fairer, better,* and *more slowly* are the comparatives of *fair, good,* and *slowly.*

comparative literature a study of the narratives, plays and poems of different cultures, showing their similarities, differences, and influences.

com•par•a•tive•ly [kəm'pærətɪvli] *or* [kəm'pɛrətɪvli] *adv.* **1** by comparison; relatively. **2** rather; somewhat. **3** in a comparative manner.

com•par•a•tor [kəm'pærətər] *or* [kəm'pɛrətər] *n.* a device for making direct comparisons, as of measurements in different systems. There are comparators for comparing quantities in the metric and imperial systems.

com•pare [kəm'pɛr] *v.* **-pared, -par•ing;** *n.* —*v.* **1** examine (two or more things) to find similarities and differences; find or point out similarities and differences between (*often used with* **with**): *Compare this speech with your own. I compared the two books to see which one had the better bibliography.* **2** think, speak, or write of as similar; liken (*to*): *to compare life to a river.* **3** be considered as an equal: *Artificial light cannot compare with daylight.* **4** *Grammar.* change the form of (an adjective or adverb) to show the comparative and superlative degrees; name the positive, comparative, and superlative degrees of.
not to be compared with, a very different from. **b** not nearly as good as.
—*n.* comparison: *beauty beyond compare.* ⟨< F < L *comparare* < *com-* with + *par* equal⟩

☛ *Usage.* **Compare,** CONTRAST. **Compare** is commonly used in two senses: **a** to point out likenesses (used with *to*): *She compared his poetry to a meandering stream.* **b** to examine two or more objects to find both likenesses and differences (used with *with*): *The teacher compared her poem with one of Al Purdy's.* **Contrast** means to point out differences between: *I contrasted the two federal leaders to show which one was better.*

com•par•i•son [kəm'pærəsən] *or* [kəm'pɛrəsən] *n.* **1** the act or process of comparing; finding the likenesses and differences: *The teacher's comparison of the heart to a pump helped the student to understand its action.* **2** likeness; similarity: *There is no comparison between these two cameras; one is much better than the other.* **3** *Grammar.* a change in an adjective or adverb to show differences of degree. The three degrees of comparison are positive, comparative, and superlative. *Examples: good, better, best; cold, colder, coldest; helpful, more helpful, most helpful.*
in comparison with, compared with: *Even a large lake is small in comparison with an ocean.* ⟨ME < OF *comparison* < L *comparatio* < *comparare.* See COMPARE.⟩

com•par•i•son–shop [kəm'pærəsən ,ʃɒp] *or* [kəm'pɛrəsən ,ʃɒp] *v.* **-shopped, -shop•ping.** compare the prices and quality of an item in different stores in order to determine the lowest available price and the best quality.

com•part•ment [kəm'pɑrtmənt] *n.* **1** a separate division or section of anything; part of an enclosed space set off by walls or partitions: *a storage compartment. The human heart has four compartments.* **2** a separate category or aspect: *the compartments of the mind.* ⟨< F *compartiment* < Ital. *compartimento* < *compartire* divide < LL < L *com-* with + *partiri* share⟩

com•part•men•tal•ize [,kɒmpɑrt'mɛntə,laɪz] *or* [kəm,pɑrt'mɛntə,laɪz] *v.* **-ized, -iz•ing.** divide (things) into isolated compartments or categories, especially in a way that denies or obscures important relationships: *She has a tendency to compartmentalize.* **—,com•part,men•tal•i'za•tion,** *n.*

A compass (def. 1). The needle always points to the north, even when the instrument is turned.

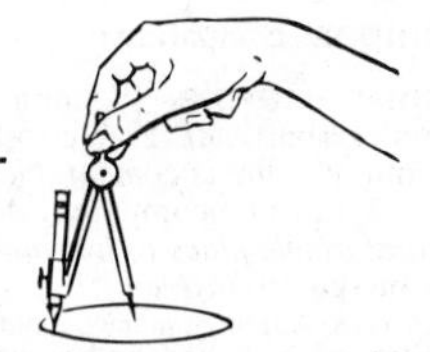
A compass (def. 11). The pointed arm remains fixed so that the other arm moves in a circle.

com•pass ['kʌmpəs] *n., v.* *—n.* **1** an instrument for showing directions, consisting of a magnetized needle suspended by the middle so that it is free to point to the North Magnetic Pole, which is near the North Pole. **2** Sometimes, **compasses,** *pl.* an instrument for drawing circles and curved lines and for measuring distances, consisting of two arms, joined at one end so that they may be moved closer or farther apart, with one arm ending in a point, for use as a pivot, and the other holding a pencil, etc. **3** a boundary or circumference: *The castle had a large dungeon within the compass of its walls.* **4** the extent within limits; scope; range: *The old sailor had had many adventures within the compass of his lifetime.* **5** the range of a voice or musical instrument. **6** a circuit; going around.
box the compass, a name the points of the compass in order. **b** go all the way around and end where one started.
—v. **1** make a circuit of; go around; move around: *The astronaut compassed the earth many times.* **2** form a circle around; hem in; surround: *a farmhouse compassed by trees.* **3** do; accomplish; get. **4** plot; scheme. **5** grasp with the mind; understand completely. ⟨ME < OF *compas* < *compasser* divide equally < VL *compassare* measure off < *compassus* equal step < L *com-* with + *passus* step⟩
☛ *Syn. n.* **3, 4.** See note at RANGE.

compass card a circular card set beneath the needle of a compass showing the 32 points of direction and the degrees of the circle.

com•pas•sion [kəm'pæʃən] *n.* feeling for another's sorrow or hardship that leads one to help the sufferer; sympathy; pity. ⟨ME < OF < L *compassio, -onis* < *compati* < *com-* with + *pati* suffer⟩
☛ *Syn.* See note at PITY.

com•pas•sion•ate [kəm'pæʃənɪt] *adj.* **1** desiring to relieve another's suffering; sympathetic; merciful. **2** of military leave, etc., granted to a person on the basis of unusual circumstances such as family illness or death. **—com'pas•sion•ate•ly,** *adv.*

compass plant any plant, such as *Silphium lacianatum,* whose leaves tend to lie in a north-south direction.

compass saw a handsaw with a very narrow, straight blade for cutting curves.

com•pat•i•ble [kəm'pætəbəl] *adj.* **1** able to exist together in harmony; that can get on well together: *My two brothers are always arguing; they don't seem to be compatible.* **2** *Television.* having to do with or designating the type of colour broadcasting that permits reception in black and white on sets that are not built for colour reception. **3** *Computer technology.* of a computer, able to use the software of another make: *This computer is not compatible with the central one at the bank.* **4** able to be combined without loss of effectiveness or danger to health: *compatible chemicals.* **5** *Electronics.* **a** suitable for use together. **b** able to be played or received on a range of equipment. ⟨< Med.L *compatibilis* < L *compati* suffer with. See COMPASSION.⟩ **—com'pat•i•bly,** *adv.* **—com,pat•i'bil•i•ty,** *n.*

com•pa•tri•ot [kəm'peitriət] *or* [kəm'pætriət] *n., adj.* *—n.* **1** a person from or in the same country as oneself. **2** *Informal.* colleague.
—adj. of the same country. ⟨< LL *compatriota* < *com-* with + *patriota* fellow countryman < Gk. *patriōtēs* < *patria* clan < *patēr* father⟩

com•peer [kəm'pir] *or* ['kɒmpir] *n.* **1** an equal; peer. **2** a comrade; companion. ⟨ME < OF *comper* < L *compar* < *com-* with + *par* equal⟩

com•pel [kəm'pɛl] *v.* **-pelled, -pel•ling. 1** force or oblige; urge irresistibly: *The cold finally compelled her to surrender. The gunmen compelled the employees to lie face down on the floor.* **2** cause or get by force: *Her tone of voice compelled obedience. Such brave actions compel our respect.* **3** *Archaic.* drive or herd together. ⟨< L *compellere* < *com-* (intensive) + *pellere* drive⟩ **—com'pell•er,** *n.*
☛ *Syn.* **1. Compel,** IMPEL = force. **Compel** = force a person to do something: *It is impossible to compel people to love their fellow men.* **Impel** = force to move forward, but is most often used figuratively to mean 'drive by strong inner desire': *Hunger impelled him to beg.*

com•pel•ling [kəm'pɛlɪŋ] *adj., v.* *—adj.* **1** forcing attention or interest: *She has compelling beauty.* **2** strongly persuasive or convincing: *a compelling argument.*
—v. ppr. of COMPEL. **—com'pel•ling•ly,** *adv.*

com•pen•di•ous [kəm'pɛndiəs] *adj.* brief but comprehensive; concise. ⟨ME < LL *compendiosus* < *compendium.* See COMPENDIUM.⟩ **—com'pen•di•ous•ly,** *adv.*

com•pen•di•um [kəm'pɛndiəm] *n., pl.* **-di•ums, -di•a** [-diə]. a summary that gives much information in a little space; concise treatise. ⟨< L *compendium* a saving, shortening < *compendere* < *com-* together + *pendere* weigh⟩

com•pen•sa•ble [kəm'pɛnsəbəl] *adj.* able to be compensated; entitled to compensation: *compensable injuries.*

com•pen•sate ['kɒmpən,seit] *v.* **-sat•ed, -sat•ing. 1** make an equivalent or satisfactory return to or for; reimburse or pay (for): *The hunter agreed to compensate the farmer for shooting her cow. Here is a cheque to compensate your loss.* **2** balance by equal weight, power, etc.; make up; offset (*usually used with* **for**): *A hockey player who is not a very fast skater can sometimes compensate for lack of speed by good positional play.* **3** *Mechanics.* adjust so as to offset variations or produce equilibrium; counterbalance: *Watches and clocks are compensated in order to keep the wheels and springs properly balanced.* **4** make amends. **5** *Psychology.* use COMPENSATION (def. 5). **6** *Biology.* effect a COMPENSATION (def. 4). ⟨< L *compensare* < *com-* with + *pensare* weigh < *pendere*⟩ **—'com•pen,sa•tor,** *n.*
☛ *Syn.* **1.** See note at PAY[1].

com•pen•sa•tion [,kɒmpən'seiʃən] *n.* **1** something given (or received) as an equivalent; a satisfactory return for a loss or injury, or for a service: *He received compensation from the government for the injury he suffered during the robbery.* **2** an offsetting or counterbalancing by an equivalent power, weight, etc.; the act of compensating. **3** anything regarded as an equivalent or reasonable advantage offsetting disadvantages: *Age has its compensations.* **4** *Biology.* the counterbalancing of an organic defect or malfunction by increased development or activity of another organ or part. **5** *Psychology.* the attempt to counterbalance a real or imagined defect or failure by increasing achievement in some other field: *I think his aggressive behaviour is just a compensation for shyness.*

com•pen•sa•tive [kəm'pɛnsətɪv] *or* ['kɒmpən,seitɪv] *adj.* compensating.

com•pen•sa•to•ry [kəm'pɛnsə,tɔri] *adj.* compensating.

com•père or **com•pere** ['kɒmpɛr] *n.* a master or mistress of ceremonies, especially of a radio or television show. ⟨< F *compère* godfather⟩

com•pete [kəm'pit] *v.* **-pet•ed, -pet•ing. 1** try hard to obtain something wanted by others; be rivals; contend. **2** take part (in a contest): *An injury kept her from competing in the final race.* ⟨< L *competere* < *com-* together + *petere* seek⟩
☛ *Syn.* **1.** See note at CONTEND.

com•pe•tence ['kɒmpətəns] *n.* **1** the quality or state of being competent: *No one doubted the guide's competence.* **2** enough money or property to provide a comfortable living. **3** *Linguistics.* a person's internal knowledge of a language (usually his or her native tongue) which enables him or her to speak and understand the language. Compare PERFORMANCE. Also, **competency.**

com•pe•tent ['kɒmpətənt] *adj.* **1** able; fit: *a competent cook.* **2** *Law.* legally qualified: *The court ruled that the witness was not competent to judge the sanity of the accused.* **3** rightfully belonging; proper or permissible (*to*): *It is not competent to the jury to pronounce the sentence.* **4** adequate; sufficient: *a competent knowledge of mathematics.* ⟨< L *competens, -entis* being fit, ppr. of *competere* meet. See COMPETE.⟩ **—'com•pe•tent•ly,** *adv.*
☛ *Syn.* **1.** See note at ABLE.
☛ *Usage.* See note at ABLE.

com•pe•ti•tion [,kɒmpə'tɪʃən] *n.* **1** an effort to obtain something wanted by others; rivalry: *the spirit of competition. There is competition among business firms for trade.* **2** a contest, especially one in which there is a prize for the winner. **3** significant opposition or its source: *He's no competition.* **4** one's rivals in business: *We must outsell the competition.* **5** the struggle between organisms in an environment with limited resources.

in competition with, competing against: *She was in competition with five other dancers.*

com•pet•i•tive [kəm'pɛtətɪv] *adj.* **1** of, based on, or determined by competition: *a competitive examination for a job.* **2** characterized by a drive to excel; concerned with trying to do better than others: *A first-rate athlete must possess a competitive spirit.* **—com'pet•i•tive•ly,** *adv.* **—com'pet•i•tive•ness,** *n.*

com•pet•i•tor [kəm'pɛtətər] *n.* a person who competes.

com•pi•la•tion [ˌkɒmpə'leiʃən] *n.* **1** the act of compiling. **2** a book, list, etc., that has been compiled.

com•pile [kəm'paɪl] *v.* **-piled, -pil•ing. 1** collect and bring together in one list or account. **2** make (a book, report, etc.) out of various materials. **3** *Computer technology.* translate (words and numbers) into MACHINE LANGUAGE for a computer. ⟨ME < OF *compiler* < L *compilare* steal, originally, pile up < *com-* together + *pilare* press⟩

com•pi•ler [kəm'paɪlər] *n.* **1** one who compiles. **2** *Computer technology.* a program that allows a computer to translate words and numbers into MACHINE LANGUAGE.

com•pla•cence [kəm'pleisəns] *n.* complacency.
☛ *Hom.* COMPLAISANCE.

com•pla•cen•cy [kəm'pleisənsi] *n., pl.* **-cies. 1** the state or condition of being pleased with oneself; self-satisfaction: *The defendant's complacency during the trial angered the jury.* **2** undue contentment.

com•pla•cent [kəm'pleisənt] *adj.* **1** pleased with oneself; self-satisfied: *The winner's complacent smile annoyed some people.* **2** obliging; complaisant. ⟨< L *complacens, -entis,* ppr. of *complacere* < *com-* with + *placere* please⟩ **—com'pla•cent•ly,** *adv.*
☛ *Hom.* COMPLAISANT.

com•plain [kəm'plein] *v.* **1** say that something is unsatisfactory; find fault. **2** talk about one's pains, troubles, etc. **3** make an accusation or charge: *She complained to the police about her neighbour's dog.* ⟨ME < OF *complaindre* < VL *complangere* < L *com-* (intensive) + *plangere* lament⟩ **—com'plain•er,** *n.* **—com'plain•ing•ly,** *adv.*
☛ *Syn.* **1. Complain,** GRUMBLE = find fault, express discontent. **Complain** = say one is discontented with some situation: *He is always complaining about the weather.* **Grumble** = mutter complaint in a bad-tempered way: *He is grumbling about the food.*

com•plain•ant [kəm'pleinənt] *n.* a person who complains, especially one who brings a lawsuit or lays a criminal charge against another; plaintiff: *The complainant accused the defendant of cheating him.*

com•plaint [kəm'pleint] *n.* **1** a voicing of dissatisfaction; complaining; finding fault: *Her letter is filled with complaints about her new job.* **2** a cause for complaining. **3** a formal accusation. **4** a sickness or ailment: *Influenza is a common complaint.*

com•plai•sance [kəm'pleizəns] *or* [kəm'pleisəns], ['kɒmpləˌzæns] *or* ['kɒmpləˌsæns] *n.* **1** willingness to please or oblige; agreeableness; courtesy. **2** an obliging or courteous act. ⟨< F⟩
☛ *Hom.* COMPLACENCE [kəm'pleisəns].

com•plai•sant [kəm'pleizənt] *or* [kəm'pleisənt], ['kɒmpləˌzænt] *or* ['kɒmpləˌsænt] *adj.* inclined to do what is asked; willing to please; obliging; courteous. ⟨< F *complaisant,* ppr. of *complaire* acquiesce < L *complacere* < *com-* (intensive) + *placere* please⟩ **—com'plai•sant•ly,** *adv.*
☛ *Hom.* COMPLACENT [kəm'pleisənt].

com•pleat [kəm'plit] *adj. Archaic.* complete.

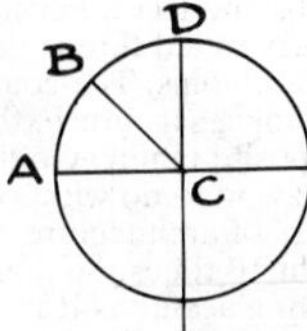

THE ARC BD IS THE COMPLEMENT OF THE ARC AB, AND THE ANGLE BCD IS THE COMPLEMENT OF THE ANGLE ACB

com•ple•ment *n.* ['kɒmpləmənt]; *v.* ['kɒmpləˌmɛnt] *n., v.* —*n.* **1** something that completes or makes perfect; something necessary to make a whole. **2** the full quantity or number; the required amount: *The ship now had its full complement of sailors.* **3** *Grammar.* a word or group of words used after a verb to complete the predicate. A complement can be an adjective, a noun, a noun phrase or clause, a prepositional phrase, etc., and is structurally necessary. *Examples: president* in *She is president; on the table* in *Put the book on the table; that she was angry* in *I sensed that she was angry; ready* in *I will be ready.* **4** *Geometry.* either one of a pair of COMPLEMENTARY ANGLES. The complement of a 70° angle is a 20° angle. **5** *Mathematics.* the subset which added to another subset yields all the elements of the set. **6** either of a pair of COMPLEMENTARY COLOURS. The complement of red is green. **7** *Music.* either of two intervals which together make up an octave. **8** either of two parts of anything that complete each other. **9** a substance found in normal blood serum and protoplasm which combines with antibodies to destroy bacteria and other foreign bodies.
—*v.* supply a lack of any kind in; complete: *My furniture just complemented my sister's, so that together we had what we needed.* ⟨ME < L *complementum* < *complere.* See COMPLETE.⟩
☛ *Hom.* COMPLIMENT.
☛ *Syn. v.* **Complement,** SUPPLEMENT = add to something to complete or enhance it. **Complement** = complete by supplying something that is missing but necessary to make a perfect whole: *The information from the encyclopedia complemented what he already had, and he was ready to write his essay.* **Supplement** = add something to make better or bigger or richer in some way: *Extra-curricular school activities supplement one's education.*
☛ *Usage.* **Complement,** COMPLIMENT (*n.*). **Complement** = something that completes or makes perfect: *She has her full complement of good looks.* **Compliment** means something said in praise: *He paid her a nice compliment.*

com•ple•men•tal [ˌkɒmplə'mɛntəl] *adj.* complementary.

com•ple•men•ta•ri•ty [ˌkɒmpləmɛn'tɛrəti] *n.* the act or state of being complementary; correspondence; relationship.

com•ple•men•ta•ry [ˌkɒmplə'mɛntəri] *adj.* forming a complement; completing something; supplying what is lacking or needed.
☛ *Hom.* COMPLIMENTARY.

complementary angles two angles which together total 90°.

complementary colours or **colors 1** any two colours of the spectrum which, when combined in the right proportions, produce white light. Red and blue-green are complementary colours. **2** any two pigments which, when combined in the right proportions, produce dark grey or black. Red and green are complementary colours in paint.

complementary distribution *Linguistics.* the relationship between linguistic forms (sounds, word forms, etc.) such that one occurs only where the other does not. Aspirated [k] as in *kin* [kʰɪn] and unaspirated [k] as in *skin* [skɪn] in English are in complementary distribution, and so can be represented by the same phonemic symbol.

complementary DNA *Genetics.* synthetic DNA transcribed from a specific messenger RNA through the action of the enzyme RNA transcriptase. Compare GENOMIC DNA. *Abbrev.:* cDNA

com•plete [kəm'plit] *adj., v.* **-plet•ed, -plet•ing.** —*adj.* **1** with all the parts; lacking nothing; whole; full: *a complete set of Dickens' novels.* **2** thorough; total; utter: *complete surprise, complete confidence.* **3** ended; finished; done: *My homework is complete.* **4** consummate; proficient; expert: *She is the complete recorder player.*
—*v.* **1** make up all the parts of; make whole or entire: *She completed her set of dishes by buying a sugar bowl.* **2** make perfect or thorough: *The good news completed my happiness.* **3** get done; end; finish: *She completed her homework early in the evening.* ⟨ME < OF *complet* < L *completus,* pp. of *complere* < *com-* (intensive) + *plere* fill⟩ **—com'plete•ly,** *adv.* **—com'plete•ness,** *n.*
☛ *Syn. adj.* **1. Complete,** ENTIRE = with all the parts. **Complete** = with all the parts needed to make something whole or full: *I have the complete story now.* **Entire** = with no parts taken away: *He gave the entire day to his work, not even taking time for lunch.*

com•ple•tion [kəm'pliʃən] *n.* **1** the act of completing; finishing. **2** the condition of being completed: *The work is near completion.*

com•plex *adj.* ['kɒmplɛks] *or* [kɒm'plɛks]; *n.* ['kɒmplɛks] *adj., n.* —*adj.* **1** not simple; involved; complicated: *The instructions for building the radio were too complex for us to follow.* **2** made up of a number of connected or interwoven parts; composite. A complex sentence has one or more clauses besides the main clause. **3** formed by the union of several or many simpler substances: *a complex carbohydrate.*
—*n.* **1** an interconnected or complicated whole: *The whole complex of charges and countercharges had to be sorted out before they could begin to work on a settlement of the dispute.* **2** a group of related or connected units such as buildings or roads: *The new civic complex includes a library, museum, and auditorium.* **3** *Psychology.* a system of related ideas, feelings, memories, etc.,

of which a person is usually not aware, which strongly influence his or her behaviour in certain ways. **4** *Informal.* an exaggerated mental tendency; obsession: *He's got such a complex about fresh air that he can hardly stay in a room with the windows closed.* **5** *Chemistry.* CO-ORDINATION COMPOUND. ⟨< L *complexus*, pp. of *complecti* embrace < *com-* together + *plectere* twine⟩ **—'com•plex•ly,** *adv.* **—'com•plex•ness,** *n.*

complex fraction a fraction having a fraction in the numerator, in the denominator, or in both; compound fraction. Compare COMMON FRACTION. *Examples*: $1\frac{3}{4}/3$, $1/3\frac{1}{3}$, $\frac{3}{4}/1\frac{7}{8}$

com•plex•ion [kəm'plɛkʃən] *n.* **1** the colour, quality, and general appearance of the skin, particularly of the face. **2** general appearance; nature; character. **3** in medieval physiology, the combination of the four humours (cold, heat, dryness, and moisture) in certain proportions, believed to determine the nature of an animal, plant, or human body. ⟨ME < LL *complexio*, *-onis* constitution < L *complexio* combination < *complexus.* See COMPLEX.⟩

com•plex•ioned [kəm'plɛkʃənd] *adj.* having a certain kind of complexion: *dark-complexioned.*

com•plex•i•ty [kəm'plɛksəti] *n., pl.* **-ties. 1** the state or quality of being complex: *The complexity of the road map made it hard to read.* **2** something complex; a difficulty or complication.

complex number the sum of a real number and an imaginary number. *Example*: $2 + 3\sqrt{-1}$

complex sentence *Grammar.* a sentence having one main clause and one or more subordinate clauses. *Example*: *When the engineer pulls the cord, the whistle blows.* Compare COMPOUND SENTENCE.

com•pli•ance [kəm'plaɪəns] *n.* **1** the act of complying or doing as another wishes; act of yielding to a request or command. **2** a tendency to yield to others. Also, **compliancy.**
in compliance with, complying with; in accordance with.

com•pli•ant [kəm'plaɪənt] *adj.* complying; yielding; obliging: *A compliant person gives in to other people.* ⟨< COMPLY + -ANT⟩ **—com'pli•ant•ly,** *adv.*
☛ *Syn.* See note at OBEDIENT.

com•pli•cate *v.* ['kɒmplə,keit]; *adj.* ['kɒmpləkɪt] *v.* **-cat•ed, -cat•ing;** *adj. —v.* **1** make hard to understand, settle, cure, etc.; mix up; confuse: *You are only complicating the issue.* **2** make worse or more mixed up: *a headache complicated by eye trouble.* *—adj. Biology.* folded lengthwise, as certain types of leaf or insect wing. ⟨< L *complicare* < *com-* together + *plicare* fold⟩

com•pli•cat•ed ['kɒmplə,keitɪd] *adj., v. —adj.* made up of many parts; involved; intricate.
—v. pt. and pp. of COMPLICATE.

com•pli•ca•tion [,kɒmplə'keiʃən] *n.* **1** a complex or confused condition that is hard to understand, settle, cure, etc. **2** a difficulty or problem added to one or more already existing: *Pneumonia was the complication they most feared.* **3** the act or process of complicating. **4** an element in a story or play which complicates the plot.

com•plic•i•ty [kəm'plɪsəti] *n., pl.* **-ties.** a partnership in wrongdoing; the fact or state of being an accomplice: *Knowingly receiving stolen goods is complicity in theft.* ⟨< F *complice* a confederate < LL *complex, -plicis* interwoven < L *complicare* < *com-* together + *plicare* fold⟩

com•pli•ment *n.* ['kɒmpləmənt]; *v.* ['kɒmplə,mɛnt] *n., v. —n.* **1** something good said about a person; something said in praise or congratulation. **2 compliments,** *pl.* greetings: *In the box of flowers was a card reading "With the compliments of a friend."* **3** a courteous act: *The town paid the old artist the compliment of a large attendance at her exhibit.*
with compliments, free of charge.
(with) compliments of, as a gift from: *Pens and paper at the conference are compliments of the hotel management. Take this copy with my compliments.*
—v. **1** praise or congratulate; pay a compliment to. **2** give something to (a person) as a polite attention: *He complimented her with a single long-stemmed rose.* ⟨< F < Ital. < Sp. *cumplimiento* fulfilment of courtesy < *cumplir* fulfil < L *complere* fill up⟩ **—'com•pli•ment•er,** *n.*
☛ *Hom.* COMPLEMENT.
☛ *Usage.* See note at COMPLEMENT.

com•pli•men•ta•ry [,kɒmplə'mɛntəri] *adj.* **1** giving or containing a compliment; expressing courtesy, admiration, or praise. **2** given free: *a complimentary ticket to a concert.*
☛ *Hom.* COMPLEMENTARY.

com•plin ['kɒmplɪn] *n. Christianity.* **1** the last of the seven canonical hours. **2** in some churches, the service for it, now usually following vespers. Also, **compline** ['kɒmplɪn] *or* ['kɒmplaɪn]. ⟨ME < OF *complie* < L *completa (hora)* completed hour⟩

com•ply [kəm'plaɪ] *v.* **-plied, -ply•ing.** act in agreement (*with* a request or a command): *We should comply with the doctor's orders.* ⟨< Ital. *complire* < Sp. *cumplir* < L *complere* complete; influenced by *ply*[1]⟩ **—com'pli•er,** *n.*

com•po•nent [kəm'pounənt] *n., adj. —n.* **1** a part; a constituent element: *A chemist can separate a medicine into its components.* **2** one of the main units or parts of an electrical, electronic, or mechanical system. A printer is one of the components of a computer system. **3** *Physics.* one of a set of vectors whose resultant sum is a given vector.
—adj. **1** forming a part; constituent: *Blade and handle are the component parts of a knife.* **2** made up of separate units, or components: *In a component stereo system, the amplifier and speakers are separate units.* ⟨< L *componens, -entis*, ppr. of *componere* < *com-* together + *ponere* put⟩
☛ *Syn. n.* See note at ELEMENT.

com•port[1] ['kɒmpɔrt] *n.* compote.

com•port[2] [kəm'pɔrt] *v.* **1** behave (*used with a reflexive pronoun*): *She comported herself with dignity throughout the trial.* **2** agree or suit (*used with* **with**): *His silliness at the meeting did not comport with what we had heard of him.* ⟨< F *comporter* < L *comportare* < *com-* together + *portare* carry⟩

com•port•ment [kəm'pɔrtmənt] *n.* behaviour.

com•pose [kəm'pouz] *v.* **-posed, -pos•ing. 1** make up; form the substance or the parts of (*usually used in the passive*): *The ocean is composed of salt water. The Commonwealth is composed of a large number of countries.* **2** create, especially in music or in words: *to compose a symphony, to compose a poem.* **3** create works of music, literature, etc.: *She composes only early in the morning.* **4** get (oneself) ready; put into a proper state: *She composed herself for a long wait.* **5** make (oneself or one's mind) calm and quiet; put into a state of repose: *He tried to compose himself before entering the room.* **6** arrange the parts or elements of; put together in a pleasing or artistic way: *He composes his photographs very carefully.* **7** put into a proper or effective order or arrangement: *to compose pieces of evidence into a coherent argument.* **8** arrange or set up (type) for printing. **9** settle; adjust: *to compose a dispute.* ⟨ME < OF *composer* < *com-* together + *poser* place (see POSE[1])⟩
☛ *Usage.* See note at COMPRISE.

com•posed [kəm'pouzd] *adj., v. —adj.* calm; quiet; self-controlled; tranquil.
—v. pt. and pp. of COMPOSE.
☛ *Syn.* See note at CALM.

com•pos•ed•ly [kəm'pouzɪdli] *adv.* in a composed manner.

com•pos•er [kəm'pouzər] *n.* a person who composes, especially a writer of music.

composing room a room in a printer's works where typesetting is done.

composing stick a small holder, held in the hand, in which monotype metal letters are assembled into words for printing.

com•pos•ite ['kɒmpəzɪt] *or* [kəm'pɒzɪt] *adj., n. —adj.* **1** made up of various parts; compound: *The photographer made a composite picture by putting together parts of several others.* **2** designating a very large plant family (Compositae; also called Asteraceae), consisting mainly of herbs but including a few shrubs and trees, having flower heads made up of many tiny flowers called florets bunched together so that they appear to be single blooms. The composite family includes the dandelion, artichoke, sagebrush, thistles, and daisies. **3** belonging to the composite family. Goldenrod is a composite plant. **4** *Architecture.* of, having to do with, or designating one of the five classical orders of architecture. The characteristic Composite column is in height 10 times the diameter of the base, and has a capital showing acanthus leaves like the Corinthian, but topped by large volutes similar to those of the Ionic. See ORDER for picture.
—n. **1** a composite plant: *Many common weeds are composites.* **2** any composite thing; something made up of distinct parts. ⟨< L *compositus*, pp. of *componere* < *com-* together + *ponere* put. Doublet of COMPOST.⟩ **—'com•pos•ite•ly,** *adv.* **—'com•pos•ite•ness,** *n.*

composite number ['kɒmpəzɪt] *Mathematics.* a number that can be exactly divided by some number other than itself or 1; a number that has more than 2 factors. Thus 8 is a composite number with four factors: 1, 2, 4, and 8; 5 is not a composite number; its only factors are 5 and 1. Compare PRIME NUMBER.

composite school *Cdn.* a secondary school in which a student may receive academic, commercial, or industrial training.

com•po•si•tion [ˌkɒmpəˈzɪʃən] *n.* **1** the make-up of anything or the way it is put together; constitution: *We are studying the composition of light.* **2** the act of composing. Writing sentences, painting pictures, and setting type in printing are all forms of composition. **3** the thing composed, such as a piece of music, writing, etc. **4** the way in which parts of a painting or photograph are arranged to form a balanced whole. **5** a short essay written as a school exercise. **6** a substance formed by a mixture of different ingredients, used especially in various industries and trades to refer to a particular mixed substance regularly used or manufactured: *The table top is of a composition resembling marble.* **7** (*adjl.*) made of such a substance. Shoes can have leather soles or composition soles. Composition picture frames are usually a mixture of wood flakes or chips and a plastic binding agent, shaped and hardened in a mould. **8** an agreement; settlement. **—ˌcom•poˈsi•tion•al,** *adj.* **—ˌcom•poˈsi•tion•al•ly,** *adv.*

com•pos•i•tor [kəmˈpɒzətər] *n.* typesetter.

com•pos men•tis [ˈkɒmpous ˈmɛntɪs] *Latin.* of sound mind; sane. The negative is **non compos mentis.**

com•post [ˈkɒmpoust] *n., v. —n.* **1** a mixture of decayed vegetable or animal matter, such as leaves or manure, used to fertilize and condition soil. **2** mixture.
—v. **1** fertilize with compost. **2** convert into compost. ⟨ME < OF < L *compositus*, pp. of *componere.* See COMPOSITE.⟩

com•po•sure [kəmˈpouʒər] *n.* calmness; quietness; self-control.

com•pote [ˈkɒmpout] *n.* **1** a dish with a supporting stem, used for fruit, candy, etc. **2** stewed fruit. ⟨< F < OF *composte* < L *compos(i)ta*, fem. of *compositus.* See COMPOSITE.⟩

com•pound¹ *adj.* [ˈkɒmpaʊnd] *or* [kɒmˈpaʊnd]; *n.* [ˈkɒmpaʊnd]; *v.* [kɒmˈpaʊnd] *n., adj., v. —n.* **1** a word made by joining together two or more separate words. The words *highway* and *landlocked* are compounds. **2** *Chemistry.* a substance formed by the chemical combination of two or more elements in fixed proportions. The elements lose their individual chemical properties and the compound has new properties. Water is a compound of hydrogen and oxygen. Compare MIXTURE (def. 3). **3** something made by combining or mixing parts; combination or mixture: *Her success in business was due to a compound of common sense and long experience.*
—adj. having more than one distinct part: *a compound sentence. A clover leaf is a compound leaf.*
—v. **1** increase or complicate by adding a new element: *The weekend visitors compounded the space problem at our cottage by bringing along their Saint Bernard.* **2** calculate (interest) on a sum of money borrowed plus the accumulated unpaid interest: *The interest is compounded semi-annually.* **3** *Law.* accept or agree to accept payment not to prosecute: *It is unlawful to compound an indictable offence.* **4** mix or combine: *to compound ingredients.* **5** make by mixing or combining: *to compound a medicine.* **6** settle (a quarrel or a debt) by a compromise. ⟨ME *compoune* < OF *compondre* < L *componere* < *com-* together + *ponere* put⟩ **—comˈpound•a•ble,** *adj.* **—comˈpound•er,** *n.*

com•pound² [ˈkɒmpaʊnd] *n.* an enclosed yard with buildings in it. ⟨probably < Malay *kampong*⟩

compound animal *Biology.* an animal composed of several organisms which have sprung from one parent and are so united as to be indistinguishable. Coral, hydroids, and bryozoans are compound animals.

compound eye *Biology.* an eye made up of many elements, each of which is sensitive to light and forms a part of the total image. Most insects and some crustaceans have compound eyes.

compound flower *Botany.* a flower head made up of many small flowers that appear to be a single bloom. The dandelion, aster, and dahlia are examples of plants that have compound flowers.

compound fraction COMPLEX FRACTION.

compound fracture a fracture in which a broken bone cuts through the flesh and sticks out. Compare SIMPLE FRACTURE.

compound het•e•ro•zy•gote [ˌhɛtərəˈzaɪgout] *Genetics.* an individual having two different abnormal alleles at a given place.

compound interest the interest paid on both the original sum of money borrowed and on the unpaid interest that has accumulated. Compare SIMPLE INTEREST.

compound leaf a leaf composed of two or more leaflets on a common stalk.

compound microscope a microscope having more than one lens, such as one with an eyepiece and an objective.

compound number a quantity expressed in two or more kinds of related units. *Examples*: 63° 30′; 12 h 30 min.

compound sentence *Grammar.* a sentence made up of co-ordinate independent clauses. *Examples*: *He ran away from home, but he soon came back. The winds blew, the rains fell, and the water covered the earth.* Compare COMPLEX SENTENCE.

compound time *Music.* a time signature in which the upper figure is 3 or a multiple of three, such as 3/4, 6/8, etc.

com•pre•hend [ˌkɒmprɪˈhɛnd] *v.* **1** understand fully with the mind: *They did not at first comprehend the significance of the new government bill.* **2** include; contain: *Her report comprehended all the facts.* ⟨ME < L *comprehendere* < *com-* (intensive) + *prehendere* seize)⟩ **—ˌcom•preˈhend•er,** *n.* **—ˌcom•preˈhend•ing•ly,** *adv.*
☛ *Syn.* **2.** See note at INCLUDE.
☛ *Syn.* **Comprehend,** APPREHEND = take hold of something with the mind; grasp. **Comprehend** = take complete hold of the meaning of something and understand it fully and perfectly: *She comprehends atomic energy.* **Apprehend** = take hold of a fact or idea but without necessarily seeing its relationships or implications: *He dimly apprehended what the foreign sailors were talking about.*

com•pre•hen•si•ble [ˌkɒmprɪˈhɛnsəbəl] *adj.* understandable. **—ˌcom•preˈhen•si•bly,** *adv.* **—ˌcom•preˌhen•siˈbil•i•ty,** *n.*

com•pre•hen•sion [ˌkɒmprɪˈhɛnʃən] *n.* **1** the act or power of understanding; ability to get the meaning: *Calculus is beyond his comprehension. The children did well on reading comprehension tests.* **2** the understanding reached after thought on some topic. **3** the act or fact of including. **4** comprehensiveness. ⟨< L *comprehensio, -onis* < *comprehendere.* See COMPREHEND.⟩

com•pre•hen•sive [ˌkɒmprɪˈhɛnsɪv] *adj., n. —adj.* **1** including much; covering everything or nearly everything: *The term's work ended with a comprehensive review.* **2** able to understand many things: *a comprehensive mind.* **3** of or having to do with property insurance that provides coverage for a variety of risks.
—n. a graduate examination. **—ˌcom•preˈhen•sive•ly,** *adv.* **—ˌcom•preˈhen•sive•ness,** *n.*

comprehensive school *Cdn.* COMPOSITE SCHOOL.

com•press *v.* [kəmˈprɛs]; *n.* [ˈkɒmprɛs] *v., n. —v.* **1** make smaller and more compact by pressure or as if by pressure: *Paper is compressed into bales for recycling. She had to compress her speech because the meeting was running late.* **2** squeeze together: *We could see he was angry by the way he compressed his lips.*
—n. **1** a pad of cloth applied to some part of the body to stop bleeding or to provide medication, etc. **2** a machine for compressing material for packing. ⟨ME < F *compresse, compresser* < LL *compressare*, frequentative of L *comprimere* < *com-* together + *premere* press⟩

com•pressed [kəmˈprɛst] *adj., v. —adj.* **1** squeezed together. **2** made smaller by pressure. **3** *Biology.* not thick or rounded; appearing flattened: *A puffin has a deep, compressed bill. A halibut has a compressed body.*
—v. pt. and pp. of COMPRESS.

compressed air air put under extra pressure so that it has a great deal of force when released. Compressed air is used to inflate tires and to operate certain kinds of brakes and guns.

com•press•i•ble [kəmˈprɛsəbəl] *adj.* that can be compressed. **—comˌpress•iˈbil•i•ty,** *n.*

com•pres•sion [kəmˈprɛʃən] *n.* **1** the act or process of compressing. **2** a compressed condition. **3** the reduction in volume of a gas by the application of pressure: *A car with worn piston rings will have poor compression.*

compression ratio the ratio of the maximum volume of a piston chamber to the volume when the piston is fully inserted, used as a measure of the efficiency of an internal-combustion engine, compressor, etc.

com•pres•sive [kəmˈprɛsɪv] *adj.* compressing; tending to compress. **—comˈpres•sive•ly,** *adv.*

com•pres•sor [kəmˈprɛsər] *n.* **1** a person who or thing that compresses, especially a machine for compressing air, gas, etc. See JET ENGINE for picture. **2** *Anatomy.* a muscle that compresses a part of the body. ⟨< L⟩

com•prise [kəmˈpraɪz] *v.* **-prised, -pris•ing.** consist of; include: *Canada comprises ten provinces and two territories.* ⟨ME

< OF *compris*, pp. of *comprendre* < L *comprehendere.* See COMPREHEND.⟩
☛ *Syn.* See note at INCLUDE.
☛ *Usage.* **Comprise** is often confused with COMPOSE. A whole *comprises* its parts or *is composed of* its parts. It is incorrect to write 'is comprised of'.

com•pro•mise ['kɒmprə,maɪz] *v.* **-mised, -mis•ing;** *n.* —*v.* **1** settle a dispute by agreeing that the person or group on each side will give up a part of what he or she demands. **2** put in danger or under suspicion, especially one's reputation or character: *You will compromise your good name if you go along with such a cheap trick.* **3** sacrifice (one's principles, ideals, etc.) to get ahead or to please others.
—*n.* **1** the act of settling a dispute by a partial yielding on both sides. **2** the result of such a settlement. **3** anything halfway between two different things. **4** an exposing to danger, suspicion, etc.; an endangering: *Such a compromise of public safety was most unwise.* **5** the sacrifice of principles or ideals to get ahead or to please others: *moral compromise.* ⟨ME < OF *compromis* < L *compromissum* < *compromittere* < *com-* together + *promittere* promise⟩ **—'com•pro,mis•er,** *n.*

Comp•tom•e•ter [kɒmp'tɒmətər] *n. Trademark.* a machine that adds, subtracts, divides, and multiplies.

comp•trol•ler [kən'troulər] See CONTROLLER (def. 1).

comp•trol•ler•ship [kən'troulər,ʃɪp] See CONTROLLERSHIP.

com•pul•sion [kəm'pʌlʃən] *n.* **1** a compelling or being compelled, or forced: *She claimed that she had signed the confession under compulsion.* **2** *Psychology.* **a** an irresistible impulse to behave or act in a certain way, regardless of whether it is reasonable to do so. **b** an act resulting from such an impulse. ⟨ME < LL *compulsio, -onis* < L *compellere.* See COMPEL.⟩

com•pul•sive [kəm'pʌlsɪv] *adj., n.* —*adj.* **1** of, having to do with, or caused by obsession or compulsion: *a compulsive liar. He was compulsive about cleanliness.* **2** using compulsion.
—*n.* a person who has an obsession, or compulsion.
—com'pul•sive•ly, *adv.*

com•pul•so•ry [kəm'pʌlsəri] *adj.* **1** required; obligatory: *Attendance at school is compulsory for children.* **2** compelling; using force. **—com'pul•so•ri•ly,** *adv.* **—com'pul•so•ri•ness,** *n.*

com•punc•tion [kəm'pʌŋkʃən] *n.* **1** the pricking of conscience; remorse: *The murderer did his work cruelly and without compunction.* **2** a slight or passing regret: *She had no compunction about declining the offer.* ⟨ME < LL *compunctio, -onis* pricking, remorse < L *compungere* < *com-* (intensive) + *pungere* prick⟩ **—com'punc•tious,** *adj.*

com•pu•ta•tion [,kɒmpjə'teiʃən] *n.* **1** a reckoning; calculation. Addition and subtraction are forms of computation. **2** the result of such a calculation; the amount computed.

com•pute [kəm'pjut] *v.* **-put•ed, -put•ing. 1** find out by mathematical work; reckon; calculate. **2** calculate by using a computer. **3** use a computer. ⟨< L *computare* < *com-* up + *putare* reckon. Doublet of COUNT[1].⟩ **—com'put•a•ble,** *adj.*

com•put•er [kəm'pjutər] *n.* **1** an electronic machine that can store large amounts of coded data and can be set, or programmed, to perform mathematical and logical operations at high speed, without the intervention of a human operator during the operation. See also ANALOG COMPUTER, DIGITAL COMPUTER. **2** a person skilled or trained in computing.

computer–aided design *Computer technology.* the use of computer hardware and software to assist in designing buildings, machine parts, etc. Also called **computer-assisted design.** *Abbrev.*: CAD

computer–aided learning a method of learning in which the material to be learned is programmed into a computer in such a way that users can teach themselves, step by step, and test their knowledge after each step.

com•put•er•ese [kəm,pjutə'riz] *n.* the specialized language of computer programming and technology.

computer game *Computer technology.* a game that has been written as computer software so that one plays the game by interacting with a computer system.

computer graphics the use of a computer, especially one that shows colours, to produce designs, portraits, scenes, etc.

com•put•er•ize [kəm'pjutə,raɪz] *v.* **-ized, -iz•ing. 1** perform, regulate, or produce by means of an electronic computer: *computerized bookkeeping, computerized exam results.* **2** store in a computer: *to computerize data.* **3** furnish or equip with a computer or computers. **—com'put•er,iz•a•ble,** *adj.* **—com,put•er•i'za•tion,** *n.*

computerized axial tomography a method of imaging the soft tissues of the body, used to perform scans, especially of the brain, to aid in diagnosis. It is a computerized combination of many tomograms, each being a photograph of a single plane, and all the planes having a common axis. Usually abbreviated to CAT.

computer literacy familiarity with computers and the techniques and vocabulary needed to operate them. **—computer literate.**

computer science *Computer technology.* the science dealing with the design and use of computer hardware and software.

computer terminal a device with a keyboard, like that of a typewriter, on which information or commands are given to a computer, and a screen similar to a television screen, on which the output from the computer is displayed.

com•rade ['kɒmræd], ['kɒmrəd], *or* ['kɒmreid] *n.* **1** a companion and friend; partner. **2** a person who shares in what another is doing; partner; fellow worker. **3** a fellow member of a union, political party, etc., especially of the Communist Party. ⟨< F < Sp. *camarada* room-mate < L *camera.* See CHAMBER.⟩

com•rade–in–arms ['kɒmræd ɪn 'ɑrmz] *n.* a fellow soldier.

com•rade•ly ['kɒmrædli] *or* ['kɒmrədli] *adj.* of, characteristic of, or like a comrade or comrades: *They sat around the fire in comradely silence.* **—'com•rade•li•ness,** *n.*

com•rade•ship ['kɒmræd,ʃɪp] *or* ['kɒmrəd,ʃɪp] *n.* **1** the condition of being a comrade. **2** the relation between comrades; friendship; fellowship.

comte [kɔ̃t] *n. French.* a count or earl.

Com•te•an or **Com•ti•an** ['kɒmtiən] *or* ['koumtiən] *adj.* of or having to do with the philosophy of Auguste Comte (1798-1857), the founder of positivism.

com•tesse [kɔ̃'tɛs] *n. French.* countess.

con[1] [kɒn] *adv., n.* —*adv.* against: *The two debating teams argued the question pro and con.*
—*n.* a reason against. The pros and cons of a question are the arguments for and against it. ⟨short for L *contra* against⟩

con[2] [kɒn] *v.* **conned, con•ning. 1** learn well enough to remember; study. **2** examine carefully; pore over. ⟨var. of *can*[1]⟩

con[3] [kɒn] *v.* **conned, con•ning;** *n.* —*v.* direct the steering of: *She conned the ship between the rocks.*
—*n.* **1** the act or process of conning. **2** the post or station from which this is done. ⟨var. of *cond* < OF *conduire* lead, guide < L *conducere* conduct⟩

con[4] [kɒn] *v.* **conned, con•ning;** *n. Slang.* —*v.* trick; swindle: *He was conned into buying a used car that was worthless.*
—*n.* **1** a swindle: *The whole thing was just a con, but I fell for it.* **2** (*adj.*) of or designating a swindle or a swindler: *a con game, a con artist.* ⟨< *con(fidence)* game, man, etc.⟩

con[5] [kɒn] *n. Slang.* a convict.

con– *prefix.* together or altogether; the form of **com-** occurring before all consonants except *b*, *m*, and *p* and, sometimes, *f*, as in *conclusion*, *confederation.*

con. 1 conclusion. **2** contra (against). **3** concession road. **4** *Music.* concerto. **5** continued.

Con. 1 Conservative. **2** Consul.

con a•mo•re [,kɒn ə'mɔrei]; *Italian,* [,kɔn a'mɔre] *Italian.* **1** with love; with tenderness. **2** heartily; with enthusiasm. **3** *Music.* with feeling.

con artist *Slang.* a person who uses the CONFIDENCE GAME.

co•na•tion [kou'neiʃən] *n. Psychology.* any wish or drive to do something. ⟨< L *conatio* an attempt⟩

con brio [kɔn 'brio] *Italian. Music.* to be played spiritedly.

con•cat•e•nate [kən'kætə,neit] *v.* **-nat•ed, -nat•ing;** *adj.* —*v.* link together.
—*adj.* linked together. ⟨< L *concatenare* < *com-* together + *catena* chain⟩

con•cat•e•na•tion [kən,kætə'neiʃən] *n.* **1** a linking or being linked together. **2** a connected series of things or events.

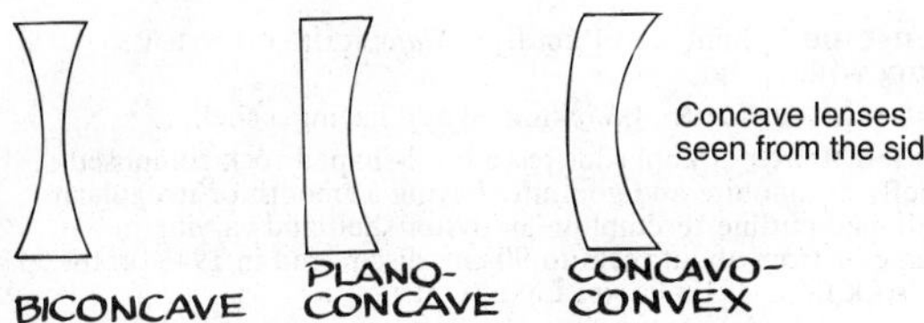

con•cave *adj.* [kɒn'keiv], ['kɒnkeiv], *or* ['kɒŋkeiv]; *n., v.* ['kɒnkeiv] *or* ['kɒŋkeiv]. *adj., n., v.* **-caved, -cav•ing.** *—adj.* hollow and curved like the inside of a circle or sphere.
—n. a concave surface or thing.
—v. make (a lens, surface, line, etc.) concave. ⟨< L *concavus* < *com-* (intensive) + *cavus* hollow⟩ **—con'cave•ly,** *adv.*

con•cav•i•ty [kɒn'kævəti] *n., pl.* **-ties. 1** a concave condition or quality. **2** a concave surface or thing.

con•ca•vo–con•cave [kɒn'keivou kɒn'keiv] *adj.* of a lens which is concave on both sides.

con•ca•vo–con•vex [kɒn'keivou kɒn'vɛks] *adj.* concave on one side and convex on the other. In a concavo-convex lens, the concave side has the greater curvature. See CONCAVE for picture.

con•ceal [kən'sil] *v.* **1** hide. **2** keep secret. ⟨ME < OF *conceler* < L *concelare* < *com-* (intensive) + *celare* hide⟩ **—con'ceal•er,** *n.*
☛ *Syn.* **1.** See note at HIDE[1].

con•ceal•ment [kən'silmənt] *n.* **1** a concealing or being concealed. **2** a means or place for hiding.

con•cede [kən'sid] *v.* **-ced•ed, -ced•ing. 1** admit as true; admit: *We conceded that she was right.* **2** give (what is asked or claimed); grant; yield: *He conceded us the right to walk through his land.* **3** acknowledge defeat in an election. ⟨< L *concedere* < *com-* together + *cedere* yield⟩

con•ceit [kən'sit] *n.* **1** too high an opinion of oneself or of one's ability, importance, etc: *In his conceit the track star thought no one could outrun him.* **2** a fanciful notion; witty thought or expression, often a far-fetched one. **3** *Literature.* in Metaphysical poetry, a long, elaborate image or metaphor. ⟨< *conceive,* on analogy with *deceit*⟩
☛ *Syn.* **1.** See note at PRIDE.

con•ceit•ed [kən'sitɪd] *adj.* having too high an opinion of oneself or one's ability, importance, etc.; vain. **—con'ceit•ed•ly,** *adv.* **—con'ceit•ed•ness,** *n.*

con•ceiv•a•ble [kən'sivəbəl] *adj.* that can be conceived or thought of; imaginable: *We should take every conceivable precaution against fire.* **—con'ceiv•a•ble•ness,** *n.* **—con'ceiv•a•bly,** *adv.*

con•ceive [kən'siv] *v.* **-ceived, -ceiv•ing. 1** form in the mind; think up, plan, or devise: *The plan was poorly conceived. She has conceived a better design for a house that uses solar heating.* **2** develop (an idea, feeling, etc.); begin to have in one's mind: *He conceived a strong dislike for his aunt.* **3** have as an idea or opinion; imagine or believe (*often used with* **of**): *It's hard to conceive of such things ever happening. They conceived themselves to be under the protection of the embassy.* **4** become pregnant. **5** become pregnant with: *She conceived a child.* **6** put in words; express: *The warning was conceived in the plainest language.* ⟨ME < OF *conceveir* < L *concipere* take in < *com-* (intensive) + *capere* take⟩ **—con'ceiv•er,** *n.*
☛ *Syn.* **1.** See note at IMAGINE.

con•cen•trate ['kɒnsən,treit] *v.* **-trat•ed, -trat•ing;** *n.* *—v.* **1** bring or come together to one place: *A convex lens is used to concentrate rays of light.* **2** pay close attention; focus the mind: *She concentrated on the problem.* **3** increase the proportion of a substance in (a solution or mixture): *We concentrated the solution by boiling off some of the water.* **4** *Mining.* remove rock, sand, etc., from (metal or ore). **5** focus: *We will concentrate our efforts on the containment of this terrible disease.*
—n. something that has been concentrated: *lemon juice concentrate.* ⟨< *con-* together + L *centrum* centre⟩ **—'con•cen,tra•tor,** *n.*

con•cen•trat•ed ['kɒnsən,treitɪd] *adj., v. —adj.* **1** brought together in one place. **2** of liquids and solutions, made stronger. **3** focussed or concerted: *a concentrated effort.*
—v. pt. and pp. of CONCENTRATE. **—'con•cen,trat•ed•ly,** *adv.*

con•cen•tra•tion [,kɒnsən'treiʃən] *n.* **1** a concentrating or being concentrated. **2** close attention: *He gave the problem his full concentration.* **3** the strength of a solution.

concentration camp a prison camp where political enemies, prisoners of war, and interned foreigners are held.

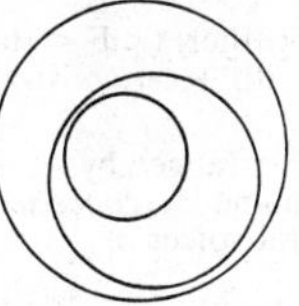
Eccentric circles

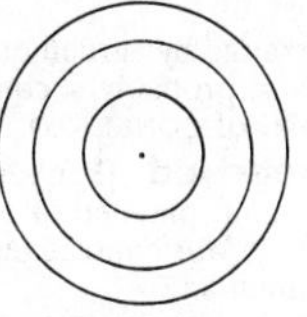
Concentric circles

con•cen•tric [kən'sɛntrɪk] *adj.* having the same centre. Concentric circles are different-sized circles with the same centre. Compare ECCENTRIC (def. 2). Also, **concentrical. —con'cen•tri•cal•ly,** *adv.* **—,con•cen'tri•ci•ty** [,kɒnsɛn'trɪsəti], *n.*

con•cept ['kɒnsɛpt] *n.* a general notion; an idea of a class of objects; idea: *the concept of equality, basic concepts of chivalry.* ⟨< L *conceptus,* pp. of *concipere.* See CONCEIVE.⟩

con•cep•tion [kən'sɛpʃən] *n.* **1** a thought; idea; impression: *Her conception of the problem is different from mine.* **2** the act or power of conceiving. **3** the state of being conceived. **4** becoming pregnant. **5** a design, plan, or concept. **6** the start of a process or a series of events.

con•cep•tu•al [kən'sɛptʃuəl] *adj.* having to do with concepts or general ideas. **—con'cep•tu•al•ly,** *adv.*

conceptual art art in which the artist intends to communicate a mental concept that contributed to the process of creating the art object itself.

con•cep•tu•al•ize [kən'sɛptʃuə,laɪz] *v.* **-ized, -iz•ing.** form an idea of; interpret or think about in terms of concepts. **—con'cep•tu•al,iz•er,** *n.* **—con,cep•tu•al•i'za•tion,** *n.*

con•cep•tus [kən'sɛptəs] *n., pl.* **-tus, -tus•es** or **-ti** [-taɪ] *or* [-ti]. that which has been conceived; embryo. ⟨< L⟩

con•cern [kən'sɜrn] *v., n. —v.* **1** have to do with; relate to: *The letter concerns the proposal for a new bridge. Nine students from our class are concerned with the play.* **2** involve the interests of; be the proper business or affair of: *The message is private; it concerns nobody but me.* **3** trouble; make anxious: *He didn't want to concern his friends with the details of the accident.*
as concerns, about; with reference to.
concern (oneself), a take an interest; be busy: *She will concern herself with the water sports program.* **b** be troubled or worried; be anxious or uneasy: *Don't concern yourself; I have everything ready.*
—n. **1** whatever has to do with a person or thing; matter; business; affair: *Keeping the books is her partner's concern.* **2** a troubled state of mind; worry; anxiety; uneasiness: *The father's concern over his sick child kept him awake all night.* **3** interest; care: *I have some concerns about the environment.* **4** a business company; firm: *He works for a big manufacturing concern in Toronto.* **5** relation; reference: *The special concern of her new book on Saskatchewan history is with the period just after the Depression.*
of concern, of importance; of interest: *a matter of concern to the ratepayers.* ⟨< Med.L *concernere* relate to < LL *concernere* mingle with, mix < L *concretus,* pp. of *concrescere* < *com-* together + *crescere* grow⟩
☛ *Syn. n.* **2.** See note at CARE.
☛ *Usage.* **Concern** (*v.*) used with *with* means 'involve with': *They could not prove she was concerned with the crime.* **Concern** used with *about* or *for* means 'worry': *Are you concerned about his escape? Naturally we were concerned for him when we heard of the accident.*

con•cerned [kən'sɜrnd] *adj., v. —adj.* **1** interested; caring: *Concerned citizens will attend the meeting on pollution.* **2** involved; having a connection: *All the students concerned with the school play were given time off for the dress rehearsal.* **3** troubled; worried; anxious.
—v. pt. and pp. of CONCERN. **—con'cern•ed•ly,** *adv.*

con•cern•ing [kən'sɜrnɪŋ] *prep., v., —prep.* having to do with; with regard to; regarding; relating to; about: *The police officer asked many questions concerning the accident.*
—v. ppr. of CONCERN.

con•cern•ment [kən'sɜrnmənt] *n.* **1** importance; interest. **2** worry; anxiety. **3** affair.

con•cert *n.* ['kɒnsərt]; *v.* [kən'sɜrt] *n., v. —n.* **1** a musical performance. **2** a dance performance or other entertainment. **3** agreement; harmony; union. **4** (*adjl.*) used in concerts; for concerts. **5** (*adjl.*) performing in a concert or concerts: *a concert pianist.*
in concert, a all together; in harmony or agreement. **b** performing publicly: *Hear Gordon Lightfoot in concert at Massey Hall!*

—*v.* arrange by agreement; plan or make together. ⟨< F < Ital. *concerto*, probably < *concertare* < L *com-* with + *certare* strive. Doublet of CONCERTO.⟩

con•cert•ed [kən'sɜrtɪd] *adj., v.* —*adj.* **1** arranged by agreement; planned or made together; combined: *a concerted attack.* **2** *Music.* arranged in parts for several voices or instruments.
—*v.* pt. and pp. of CONCERT. **—con'cert•ed•ly,** *adv.*

concert grand a grand piano having the volume and brilliancy of tone required for use in a large hall or with an orchestra.

con•cer•ti•na [ˌkɒnsər'tinə] *n.* a small musical instrument resembling an accordion. ⟨< *concert*⟩

con•cer•ti•no [ˌkɒntʃɛr'tinou] *n. Music.* **1** a short, single-movement concerto. **2** the soloists in a CONCERTO GROSSO.

con•cert•ize ['kɒnsərˌtaɪz] *v.,* **-ized, -iz•ing. 1** play as a soloist in a concert. **2** make a concert tour.

con•cert•mas•ter ['kɒnsərtˌmæstər] *n.* the leader, usually the first violinist, of an orchestra, ranking next to the conductor.

con•cert•meis•ter ['kɒnsərtˌmaɪstər] *n.* concertmaster. ⟨< G⟩

con•cer•to [kən'tʃɛrtou] *n., pl.* **-tos** or (Italian) **-ti** [-ti]. a musical composition, usually in three movements and usually written for one or more solo instruments, such as a violin, piano, etc., accompanied by an orchestra. ⟨< Ital. Doublet of CONCERT.⟩

concerto gros•so [kən'tʃɛrtou 'grousou] *pl.* **con•cer•ti gros•si** [kən'tʃɛrti 'grousi] a concerto for a group of solo instruments and a full orchestra. ⟨< Ital.⟩

concert pitch 1 *Music.* the standard pitch of orchestral and other instruments, in which the A above middle C = 440 hertz. **2** *Music.* a slightly heightened pitch, often used for tuning instruments for concert use. **3** the height of fitness, readiness, co-ordination, etc.: *Our Olympic runners were at concert pitch.*

con•ces•sion[1] [kən'sɛʃən] *n.* **1** the act of conceding; granting; yielding: *Concession to popular demands was the monarch's weakness.* **2** anything yielded or conceded; admission; acknowledgment: *As a concession, Dad let me stay up an hour longer.* **3** something conceded or granted by a government or controlling authority; grant. Land, privileges, etc., given by a government to a business company are called concessions. **4** a privilege or space granted or leased for a particular use within specified premises: *There is a soft-drink concession at the ball park.* ⟨< L *concessio, -onis* < *concedere.* See CONCEDE.⟩

con•ces•sion[2] [kən'sɛʃən] *n. Cdn.* **1** mainly in Ontario and Québec, a subdivision of land in township surveys, formerly one of the rows of thirty-two 200-acre lots (8.094 hectares) into which each new township was divided. **2** CONCESSION ROAD. **3 concessions,** *pl.* rural or bush districts: *He relies on the concessions for his political support.* ⟨< Cdn.F⟩

con•ces•sion•aire [kənˌsɛʃə'nɛr] *n.* a person, business company, etc., to whom a concession has been granted. ⟨< F *concessionnaire*⟩

con•ces•sion•ar•y [kən'sɛʃəˌnɛri] *adj., n.* —*adj.* of, having to do with, or obtained by a concession.
—*n.* CONCESSIONAIRE.

concession road *Cdn.* especially in Ontario, a rural road following the road allowance between concessions, running as a rule north and south and connected to other concession roads by east-west side roads. Concession roads are usually 2 km apart.

con•ces•sive [kən'sɛsɪv] *adj.* **1** yielding; making or implying concession. **2** *Grammar.* expressing concession. *Though* and *although* introduce concessive clauses.

conch [kɒntʃ] *or* [kɒŋk] *n., pl.* **conch•es** ['kɒntʃɪz] or **conchs** [kɒŋks]. **1** any of various large marine snails having a spiral shell with the outermost spiral roughly triangular in outline and with a wide lip often curled back, revealing a smooth, pearly lining; especially, any member of the plant-eating genera *Strombus* and *Cassis* found mainly in the Caribbean. **2** the shell of a conch, used as an ornament, as a sound-maker, or for making cameos. **3** *Roman Mythology.* this shell, which the Tritons used as a trumpet. **4** concha. ⟨< L *concha* < Gk. *konchē*⟩
☛ *Hom.* CONK [kɒŋk].

con•cha ['kɒŋkə] *n.* **1** *Anatomy.* any of various shell-shaped structures, such as the external ear or a thin bone in the nose. **2** *Architecture.* the half-dome of an apse. ⟨< L *concha* conch⟩

con•chie ['kɒntʃi] *or* ['kɒnʃi] *n. Slang.* CONSCIENTIOUS OBJECTOR.

con•chif•er•ous [kɒŋ'kɪfərəs] *adj.* having a shell.

con•chi•lite ['kɒŋkəˌləit] *n.* a bowl-shaped rock composed chiefly of limonite and goethite, having a smooth or irregularly scalloped outline resembling an oyster shell and varying in diameter from about 3 cm to 90 cm, discovered in 1943 on the bedrock floor of Finlayson Lake (Ont.).

conchoid ['kɒŋkɔɪd] *n.* a path traced by the end point of a line segment on a line which rotates about a fixed point, while the segment's other end point follows a straight line not intersecting the fixed point. ⟨< Gk. *kon choeides* literally, mussel-like⟩

con•cho•log•i•cal [ˌkɒŋkə'lɒdʒəkəl] *adj.* of or having to do with conchology.

con•chol•o•gist [kɒŋ'kɒlədʒɪst] *n.* a person trained in conchology, especially one whose work it is.

con•chol•o•gy [kɒŋ'kɒlədʒi] *n.* the branch of zoology that deals with shells and shellfish. ⟨< Gk. *konchē* shell + E *-logy*⟩

con•ci•erge [ˌkɒnsi'ɛrʒ] *or* [kɒn'sjɛrʒ]; *French,* [kɔ̃'sjɛʀʒ] *n.* **1** doorkeeper. **2** janitor. ⟨< F⟩

con•cil•i•ar [kən'sɪliər] *adj.* of or having to do with a council or councils.

con•cil•i•ate [kən'sɪliˌeit] *v.* **-at•ed, -at•ing. 1** win over; soothe: *She conciliated her angry little sister by promising to take her to the zoo.* **2** gain or regain (good will, regard, favour, etc.) by friendly acts. **3** reconcile; bring into harmony. ⟨< L *conciliare* < *concilium.* See COUNCIL.⟩ **—con'cil•i,at•ing•ly,** *adv.* **—con'cil•i•a•ble,** *adj.*

con•cil•i•a•tion [kənˌsɪli'eiʃən] *n.* conciliating or being conciliated.

con•cil•i•a•tive [kən'sɪliətɪv] *or* [kən'sɪliˌeitɪv] *adj.* conciliatory.

con•cil•i•a•tor [kən'sɪliˌeitər] *n.* a person who conciliates; arbitrator; peacemaker.

con•cil•i•a•to•ry [kən'sɪliəˌtɔri] *adj.* tending or calculated to win over, soothe, or reconcile: *They hoped the apology would have a conciliatory effect on the angry tenants. She spoke to the crowd in a conciliatory tone of voice.*

con•cise [kən'səis] *adj.* expressing much in a few words; brief but full of meaning. ⟨< L *concisus*, pp. of *concidere* < *com-* (intensive) + *caedere* cut⟩ **—con'cise•ly,** *adv.* **—con'cise•ness,** *n.*

con•ci•sion [kən'sɪʒən] *n.* the quality or state of being concise; conciseness.

con•clave ['kɒnkleiv] *or* ['kɒŋkleiv] *n.* **1** a private meeting. **2** a large professional gathering; convention. **3** *Roman Catholic Church.* **a** a meeting of the cardinals for the election of a pope. **b** the rooms where the cardinals meet in private for this purpose. **c** the cardinals as a group. ⟨ME < OF < L *conclave* a room that can be locked < *com-* with + *clavis* key⟩

con•clude [kən'klud] *v.* **-clud•ed, -clud•ing. 1** end; finish: *She concluded her speech with a funny story. The soap opera concluded at last.* **2** arrange; settle: *The two countries concluded a trade agreement.* **3** find out by thinking; reach or arrive at a decision, judgment, or opinion by reasoning; infer: *From the clues we found, we concluded that the thief must have left in a hurry.* **4** decide; resolve: *I concluded not to go.* ⟨< L *concludere* < *com-* (intensive) + *claudere* close⟩ **—con'clud•er,** *n.*
☛ *Syn.* **1.** See note at END.
☛ *Usage.* **Conclude** is used: **a** with *by* before the *-ing* form of the verb: *He concluded his remarks by quoting a passage from Chaucer.* **b** (def. 1) with *with* before a noun: *I will conclude my remarks with a plea addressed to your president.* **c** (def. 3) with *from* when it means 'infer': *I must conclude from what you say that you are dissatisfied.*

con•clu•sion [kən'kluʒən] *n.* **1** an end. **2** the last main division of a speech, essay, etc. **3** a final result; outcome. **4** an arrangement; settlement: *the conclusion of a peace treaty between enemies.* **5** a decision, judgment, or opinion reached by reasoning.
in conclusion, finally; lastly; to conclude.
try conclusions, *Archaic.* engage in a struggle *(with).* ⟨ME < L *conclusio, -onis* < *concludere.* See CONCLUDE.⟩

con•clu•sive [kən'klusɪv] *adj.* decisive; convincing; definite: *conclusive evidence.* **—con'clu•sive•ly,** *adv.* **—con'clu•sive•ness,** *n.*

con•coct [kən'kɒkt] *or* [kɒn'kɒkt] *v.* **1** prepare by putting together ingredients: *The chef has concocted a delicious new dessert.* **2** make up, especially something complicated; invent; devise: *What fantastic money-making scheme have you concocted this time? She concocts really clever mystery stories.* ⟨< L *concoctus*, pp. of *concoquere* < *com-* together + *coquere* cook⟩ **—con'coct•er,** *n.*

con•coc•tion [kən'kɒkʃən] *or* [kɒn'kɒkʃən] *n.* **1** the act of concocting. **2** the thing concocted.

con•com•i•tant [kən'kɒmətənt] *or* [kɒn'kɒmətənt] *adj., n.* *—adj.* accompanying; attending: *a concomitant result.*
—n. an accompanying thing, quality, or circumstance; accompaniment. ⟨< L *concomitans, -antis,* ppr. of *concomitari* < *com-* (intensive) + *comitari* accompany⟩
—con'com•i•tant•ly, *adv.* **—con'com•i•tance,** *n.*

con•cord ['kɒnkɔrd] *or* ['kɒŋkɔrd] *n.* **1** agreement; harmony. **2** *Music.* a harmonious combination of tones sounded together. **3** treaty. **4** *Grammar.* agreement in person, number, gender, tense, etc. *Example: eggs* and *are* in *The eggs are in the basket.* ⟨ME < OF < L *concordia,* ult. < *com-* together + *cor, cordis* heart⟩

con•cord•ance [kən'kɔrdəns] *n.* **1** an agreement; harmony. **2** an alphabetical list of the principal words or all the words occurring in a particular body of writing, with identification of the passages in which they occur: *a concordance of Shakespeare.*

con•cord•ant [kən'kɔrdənt] *adj.* **1** agreeing; harmonious. **2** *Genetics.* referring to twins who are alike with respect to a particular trait. **—con'cord•ant•ly,** *adv.*

con•cor•dat [kən'kɔrdæt] *or* [kɒn'kɔrdæt] *n.* **1** an agreement; compact. **2** a formal agreement between the Pope and a government about church affairs. **3** a similar agreement between any religious body and a government. ⟨< F < LL *concordatum,* pp. neut. of *concordare* make harmonious⟩

Concord grape ['kɒnkɔrd] *or* ['kɒŋkərd] a large, sweet, bluish black variety of grape used for making jelly, juice, or wine.

con•course ['kɒnkɔrs] *or* ['kɒŋkɔrs] *n.* **1** a running, flowing, or coming together; confluence: *The fort was built at the concourse of two rivers.* **2** a crowd. **3** a place where crowds gather or wait: *the main concourse of a railway station. There is a concourse below our office building.* ⟨ME < OF *concours* < L *concursus* < *concurrere* < *com-* together + *currere* run⟩

con•cres•cence [kən'krɛsəns] *n.* **1** a growing together of parts. **2** an increase by the adding of particles. ⟨< L *concrescentia* < *concrescere.* See CONCRETE.⟩

con•crete *adj. 1-3, n. and v. 1* ['kɒnkrit], ['kɒŋkrit], *or* [kɒn'krit]; *adj., 4 and v. 2* [kən'krit] *adj., n., v.* **-cret•ed, -cret•ing.**
—adj. **1** existing of itself in the material world, not merely as an idea or as a quality; real: *All actual objects are concrete. A painting is concrete; its beauty is abstract.* **2** not abstract or general; specific; particular: *The lawyer gave concrete examples of the prisoner's cruelty.* **3** naming a thing, especially something perceived by the senses. *Sugar* and *people* are concrete nouns; *sweetness* and *humanity* are *abstract nouns.* **4** formed into a mass; solid; hardened.
—n. **1** a mixture of crushed stone or gravel, sand, cement, and water that hardens as it dries. **2** the hard substance resulting from the hardening of this mixture: *He fell and hurt his head on the concrete.* **3** (*adjl.*) made of concrete: *a concrete sidewalk.*
—v. **1** cover with concrete. **2** form or mix into a mass; harden into a mass. ⟨< L *concretus,* pp. of *concrescere* < *com-* together + *crescere* grow⟩ **—con'crete•ly,** *adv.* **—con'crete•ness,** *n.*

concrete music music consisting of natural sounds, etc., electronically distorted, and composed directly on magnetic tape.

concrete poetry words arranged on a page or with special typography so as to reflect visually the meaning of the poem.

con•cre•tion [kən'kriʃən] *n.* **1** a forming into a mass; a solidifying. **2** a solidified mass; hard formation. Gallstones are concretions.

con•cret•ism [kɒn'kritɪzəm] *or* [kɒŋ'kritɪzəm] *n.* the endowing of abstract ideas with a tangible form.

con•cu•bi•nage [kən'kjubənɪdʒ] *n.* **1** the condition of living together without legal marriage. **2** the condition of being a concubine.

con•cu•bine ['kɒŋkjə,baɪn] *or* ['kɒnkjə,baɪn] *n.* **1** a woman who lives with or has a continuing sexual relationship with a man without being legally married to him; mistress. Concubine was the usual word for a mistress before about the 17th century. **2** in certain polygamous societies, such as that of the ancient Hebrews, a wife having an inferior social and legal status; a secondary wife. ⟨< L *concubina* < *com-* with + *cubare* lie⟩

con•cu•pis•cence [kən'kjupəsəns] *n.* sensual desire; lust.

con•cu•pis•cent [kən'kjupəsənt] *adj.* **1** eagerly desirous. **2** lustful; sensual. ⟨< L *concupiscens, -entis,* ppr. of *concupiscere* < *com-* (intensive) + *cupere* desire⟩

con•cur [kən'kɜr] *v.* **-curred, -cur•ring. 1** be of the same opinion; agree: *The judges all concurred in giving Alma the prize.* **2** work together: *The events of the week concurred to make it a great holiday.* **3** come together; happen at the same time. ⟨< L *concurrere* < *com-* together + *currere* run⟩ **—con'cur•rer,** *n.*
☛ *Syn.* **1.** See note at CONSENT.

con•cur•rence [kən'kɜrəns] *n.* **1** the holding of the same opinion; agreement. **2** a working together. **3** a happening at the same time. **4** a coming together; a meeting at a point.

con•cur•rent [kən'kɜrənt] *adj., n.* *—adj.* **1** existing side by side; happening at the same time. **2** co-operating. **3** having equal authority or jurisdiction; co-ordinate. **4** agreeing; consistent; harmonious. **5** coming together; meeting in a point.
—n. a concurrent thing or event. **—con'cur•rent•ly,** *adv.*

concurring opinion the opinion of one or more of a group of judges, which agrees with the majority opinion, but gives different reasons for doing so.

con•cuss [kən'kʌs] *v.* **1** agitate or shake violently by or as if by a blow. **2** *Medicine.* injure (the brain) by concussion. ⟨< L *concussus* < *concutere.* See CONCUSSION.⟩

con•cus•sion [kən'kʌʃən] *n.* **1** a sudden, violent shaking; shock: *The concussion caused by the explosion broke many windows.* **2** an injury to the brain, spine, etc., caused by a blow, fall, or other shock. ⟨< L *concussio, -onis* < *concutere* shake violently < *com-* (intensive) + *quatere* shake⟩

con•cus•sive [kən'kʌsɪv] *adj.* **1** of or having to do with concussion. **2** tending to cause concussion.

con•demn [kən'dɛm] *v.* **1** express strong disapproval of: *We should condemn cruelty wherever we find it.* **2** show or judge to be guilty of crime or wrong; convict: *The prisoner is sure to be condemned. Her letters are enough to condemn her.* **3** pass sentence on; doom: *He was condemned to death.* **4** assign to an unpleasant fate or condition: *Poverty condemned them to a life of frustration.* **5** declare not sound or suitable for use: *This bridge has been condemned because it is no longer safe for traffic.* **6** *U.S.* expropriate. ⟨ME < OF *condem(p)ner* < L *condemnare* < *com-* (intensive) + *damnare* cause loss to, condemn < *damnum* loss⟩
—con'demn•er, *n.*

con•dem•na•ble [kən'dɛmnəbəl] *adj.* that should be condemned; blamable.

con•dem•na•tion [,kɒndɛm'neiʃən] *or* [,kɒndəm'neiʃən] *n.* **1** strong disapproval: *He expressed his condemnation of the new plan.* **2** condemning or being condemned: *the condemnation of a prisoner by a judge, the condemnation of an unsafe bridge.* **3** a cause or reason for being condemned: *Her refusal to help was her condemnation.*

con•dem•na•to•ry [kən'dɛmnə,tɔri] *adj.* condemning; expressing condemnation.

con•demned [kən'dɛmd] *adj., v.* *—adj.* **1** pronounced guilty of a crime or wrong. **2** declared to be unfit for use: *a condemned house.*
—v. pt. and pp. of CONDEMN.

con•den•sate ['kɒndən,seit] *or* [kən'dɛnseit] *n.* something formed or produced by condensation.

con•den•sa•tion [,kɒndən'seiʃən] *n.* **1** a condensing or being condensed: *the condensation of a story, the condensation of steam into water.* **2** something condensed; a condensed mass: *A cloud is a condensation of water vapour in the atmosphere. There is a condensation of the book in that magazine.* **3** *Chemistry.* a reaction in which two or more molecules unite to form a larger, denser, and more complex molecule, often with the separation of water or some other simple substance.

con•dense [kən'dɛns] *v.* **-densed, -dens•ing. 1** make or become denser or more compact; reduce the volume of: *Milk is condensed before it is canned.* **2** make stronger; concentrate: *Light is condensed by means of lenses.* **3** change from a gas or vapour to a liquid. If steam comes in contact with cold surfaces, it condenses or is condensed into water. **4** put into fewer words; express more briefly: *She condensed the paragraph into one line.* ⟨< L *condensare* < *com-* together + *densus* thick⟩
—con'den•sa•ble, *adj.*

condensed milk sweetened evaporated milk.

con•dens•er [kən'dɛnsər] *n.* **1** whatever condenses something. **2** a device for receiving and holding a charge of electricity. **3** an apparatus for changing gas or vapour into a liquid. **4** a strong lens or lenses for concentrating light upon a small area. See MICROSCOPE for picture.

con•de•scend [,kɒndɪ'sɛnd] *v.* **1** come down willingly or graciously to the level of one's inferiors in rank: *The king condescended to eat with the beggars.* **2** grant a favour in a haughty or patronizing way. **3** stoop or lower oneself: *She would*

not condescend to taking a bribe. ⟨ME < OF *condescendre* < LL *condescendere* < L *com-* together + *descendere* descend⟩
☛ *Usage.* Note that definition 1 is used with an infinitive (*to eat*) and definition 3 is used with a gerund (*taking*).

con•de•scend•ing [ˌkɒndɪ'sɛndɪŋ] *adj., v. —adj.* showing condescension; patronizing; being helpful in a way that shows a feeling of superiority to others.
—v. ppr. of CONDESCEND. **—ˌcon•de'scend•ing•ly,** *adv.*

con•de•scen•sion [ˌkɒndɪ'sɛnʃən] *n.* **1** the act or an instance of condescending. **2** a patronizing attitude: *I could feel the condescension of the hotel clerk in the way he looked at my old luggage.* ⟨< LL *condescensio, -onis* < *condescendere.* See CONDESCEND.⟩

con•dign [kən'daɪn] *adj.* deserved; adequate; fitting: *a condign punishment.* ⟨ME < OF *condigne* < L *condignus* very worthy < *com-* (intensive) + *dignus* worthy⟩ **—con'dign•ly,** *adv.*
☛ *Usage.* Because **condign** is so often coupled with *punishment*, it is sometimes misunderstood and used incorrectly as a synonym for *severe*.

con•di•ment ['kɒndəmənt] *n.* anything, such as pepper and spices, used to give flavour and relish to food. ⟨< L *condimentum* spice < *condire* to spice, preserve⟩

con•di•tion [kən'dɪʃən] *n., v. —n.* **1** the state in which a person or thing is: *The accident victim was in critical condition in the hospital. Her car is several years old, but still in very good condition.* **2** physical fitness; good health: *People who take part in sports must keep in condition.* **3** rank; social position: *The premier's parents were people of humble condition.* **4** anything on which something else depends; that without which something else cannot occur or exist: *Available oxygen is a condition of human life. A condition of employment as a sales representative is a willingness to travel.* **5** *Grammar.* a clause that expresses or contains such a condition. **6** something demanded as an essential part of an agreement. **7** *Law.* a clause in a legal document, the requirements of which can be revoked or altered in the event of some future happening. **8** an ailment or disease: *My uncle has a heart condition.* **9 conditions,** *pl.* circumstances that affect an activity or situation: *poor driving conditions. The working conditions here are excellent.* **10** *Mathematics.* a requirement expressed by an open sentence. **11** *Logic.* a proposition which determines the truth or falsehood of another proposition.
on condition that, if; provided that: *I'll go on condition that you will too.*
on no condition, not at all; never: *On no condition will I do your homework for you.*
—v. **1** put in good condition: *Exercise conditions your muscles.* **2** be a condition of: *Ability and effort condition success.* **3** make depend on a condition; subject to a condition: *The gift to the boy was conditioned on his good behaviour.* **4** *Archaic.* make conditions; make it a condition. **5 a** shape behaviour of (a person or animal) by repeated exposure to particular conditions, with which responses become associated: *This dog has been conditioned to expect food when it obeys a command.* **b** shape (behaviour) in this way: *Its obedience is a conditioned response.* **6** make accustomed: *Many years of running the store had conditioned her to hard work.* ⟨< L *condicio, -onis* agreement < *condicere* < *com-* together + *dicere* say⟩
☛ *Syn. n.* **1.** See note at STATE.

con•di•tion•al [kən'dɪʃənəl] *adj., n. —adj.* **1** depending on something else; not absolute; limited. *You may go if the sun shines* is a conditional promise. **2** expressing or containing a condition. "If the sun shines" is a conditional clause.
—n. Grammar. a word, phrase, clause, mood, or tense that expresses a condition. **—con'di•tion•al•ly,** *adv.*
—conˌdi•tion'al•i•ty, *n.*

conditional discharge a sentence given to a guilty person, assuring him or her that there will be no record of a conviction, but he or she must fulfil certain conditions such as meeting a probation officer. Compare ABSOLUTE DISCHARGE.

con•di•tioned [kən'dɪʃənd] *adj., v. —adj.* **1** that has been put under a condition; subject to certain conditions. **2** in a given condition. **3** *Psychology.* of or designating a response produced by repeated exposure to particular conditions; learned: *a conditioned reflex.* **4** accustomed (*to*): *conditioned to cold.*
—v. pt. and pp. of CONDITION.

conditioned response or **reflex** *Psychology.* a learned response which is predictable as a result of the subject having been repeatedly subjected to a certain stimulus or set of stimuli.

con•di•tion•er [kən'dɪʃənər] *n.* **1** a lotion or cream used to improve the condition of the hair, skin, etc. **2** any person who or thing that conditions.

con•do ['kɒndou] *n., pl.* **-dos** or **-does.** *Informal.* CONDOMINIUM (defs. 1 and 2).

con•dole [kən'doul] *v.* **-doled, -dol•ing.** express sympathy; sympathize (*used with* **with**): *The widow's friends condoled with her at the funeral.* ⟨< L *condolere* < *com-* with + *dolere* grieve, suffer⟩

con•do•lence [kən'douləns] *or* ['kɒndələns] *n.* an expression of sympathy: *Her friends sent her their condolences.*

con do•lo•re [ˌkɒn də'lɔrei]; *Italian,* [ˌkɔn dɔ'lɔre] *Music.* in a sorrowful manner. ⟨< Ital., with sorrow⟩

con•dom ['kɒndəm] *or* ['kʌndəm] *n.* a thin, usually rubber sheath worn over the penis during sexual intercourse to prevent venereal infection or AIDS and as a contraceptive. ⟨origin unknown⟩

con•do•min•i•um [ˌkɒndə'mɪniəm] *or* [ˌkɒndə'mɪnjəm] *n.* **1** a residential structure in which apartments or townhouses are individually owned as pieces of real estate while the land and common facilities are jointly owned. **2** a unit in such a structure. **3** a joint control, especially by two or more countries over the government of another country. **4** a country whose government is controlled jointly by two or more others: *The Anglo-Egyptian Sudan was a condominium.* ⟨< NL < L *com-* with + *dominium* lordship⟩

con•do•na•tion [ˌkɒndə'neiʃən] *n.* the excusing of an offence, especially by ignoring or overlooking it.

con•done [kən'doun] *v.* **-doned, -don•ing.** ignore or overlook (an offence or fault): *His parents had always condoned his temper tantrums when he was small.* ⟨< L *condonare* < *com-* (intensive) + *donare* give⟩

con•dor ['kɒndɔr] *or* ['kɒndər] *n.* either of two very large New World vultures, now in danger of extinction. The Andean condor (*Vultur gryphus*), found in the high Andes Mountains of South America, has black plumage with a white neck ruff and white wing patches. The California condor (*Gymnogyps californianus*) of the mountains of California, has black plumage with white wing bands. ⟨< Sp. *cóndor* < Peruvian *cuntur*⟩

con•duce [kən'djus] *or* [kən'dus] *v.* **-duced, -duc•ing.** lead; contribute; be favourable (*to*): *Darkness and quiet conduce to sleep.* ⟨< L *conducere* < *com-* together + *ducere* lead⟩

con•du•cive [kən'djusɪv] *or* [kən'dusɪv] *adj.* helpful; favourable: *Exercise is conducive to health.* **—con'du•cive•ly,** *adv.*

con•duct *n.* ['kɒndʌkt]; *v.* [kən'dʌkt] *n., v. —n.* **1** behaviour; way of acting: *Her rude conduct was inexcusable. He won a medal for good conduct.* **2** direction; management: *the conduct of an office.* **3** a leading; escorting: *Give the messenger safe conduct to the king.*
—v. **1** act or behave in a certain way (*used reflexively*): *The way she conducted herself throughout the crisis showed that she had great courage.* **2** direct; manage. **3** direct (an orchestra, choir, etc.) as leader. **4** go along with and show the way to; guide: *The butler conducted him to the library.* **5** transmit (heat, electricity, etc.); be a channel for. ⟨< L *conductus,* pp. of *conducere* < *com-* together + *ducere* lead⟩
☛ *Syn. n.* **1. Conduct,** BEHAVIOUR = way of acting. **Conduct,** the more formal word, applies to a person's general manner of acting, especially in relation to others and to the principles of right and wrong set up by society: *Her conduct is always admirable.* **Behaviour,** used of people and animals, applies to the way of acting toward and in front of others, especially in certain situations: *His behaviour shows his lack of consideration for others. —v.* **2.** See note at MANAGE. **4.** See note at GUIDE.

con•duct•ance [kən'dʌktəns] *n.* **1** the power of conducting electricity as affected by the shape, length, etc., of the conductor. **2** the ease with which a substance or a solution of the substance permits the passage of an electrical current. Its unit of measurement is the siemens.

con•duct•i•ble [kən'dʌktəbəl] *adj.* **1** capable of conducting heat, electricity, etc. **2** capable of being conducted.
—conˌduct•i'bil•i•ty, *n.*

con•duc•tion [kən'dʌkʃən] *n.* **1** *Physics.* the transmission of heat, electricity, etc., by the transferring of energy from one particle to another. **2** *Physiology.* the transmission of sound waves, heat, or nerve impulses by a nerve or nerves. **3** a conveying or being conveyed.

con•duc•tive [kən'dʌktɪv] *adj.* **1** having conductivity. **2** of conduction.

con•duc•tiv•i•ty [ˌkɒndʌk'tɪvəti] *n.* **1** the power of conducting heat, electricity, etc. **2** the ability of a given substance to conduct electricity between opposite faces of a unit cube of the substance, expressed in siemens per metre. **3** the rate of transfer of heat by conduction between opposite faces of a one-centimetre cube of a substance, having unit temperature difference between opposite faces.

con•duc•tor [kən'dʌktər] *n.* **1** a person who conducts; director; manager; leader; guide. **2** the director of an orchestra, chorus, etc. The conductor of an orchestra trains the musicians to work together, selects the music to be used, and directs the players during a performance. **3** the person in charge of a streetcar, bus, railway train, etc. The conductor usually collects the tickets or fares from the passengers. **4** anything that transmits heat, electricity, light, sound, etc. Copper is a good conductor of heat and electricity. **—,con•duc'tor•i•al** [,kɒndʌk'tɔriəl], *adj.* **—con'duc•tor,ship,** *n.*

con•duit ['kɒndwɪt], ['kɒndjuɪt], ['kɒnduɪt], *or* ['kɒndɪt] *n.* **1** a channel or pipe for carrying liquids over long distances. **2** a tube or underground passage for electric wires. ⟨ME < OF *conduit* < Med.L *conductus* a leading, a pipe < L *conductus* contraction < *conducere* < *com-* together + *ducere* draw⟩

con•dy•lo•ma [,kɒndə'loumə] *n., pl.* **-ma•ta** [-mətə]. an inflamed growth on the skin, usually near the anus or genitals. ⟨< L < Gk. *kondyloma* < *kondylos* lump, knob⟩

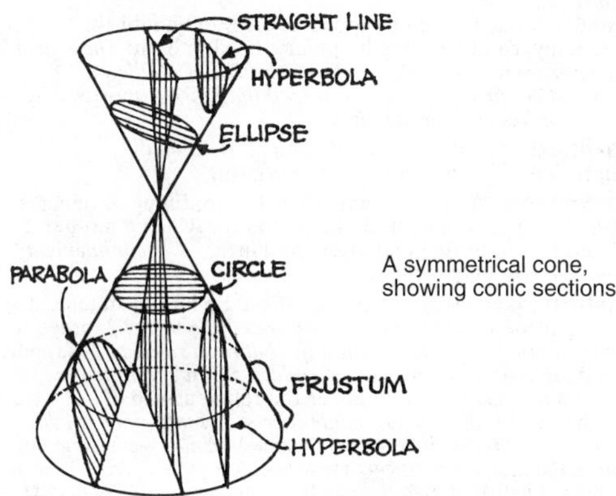

A symmetrical cone, showing conic sections

cone [koun] *n.* **1** *Geometry.* a surface traced by a moving straight line, one point or end of which is fixed, the opposite end passing through all the points of a closed fixed curve. When the fixed curve is a circle and the line from the vertex to the centre of this circle forms a right angle with it, making a symmetrically tapered shape, the surface is called a **right circular cone. 2** a solid figure bounded by such a surface. See SOLID for picture. **3** anything shaped somewhat like a cone with evenly tapered sides: *an ice-cream cone, the cone of a volcano.* **4** *Botany.* **a** the reproductive structure of trees of the pine family, consisting of clusters of overlapping woody scales arranged along an axis, with the ovules contained between the scales. **b** a similar reproductive structure in various other plants, such as horsetails or club mosses. **5** any of the conical cells in the retina of the eye that are sensitive to light and colour. ⟨ME < L *conus* < Gk. *kōnos* pine cone, cone⟩ **—cone'less,** *adj.*

cone•flow•er ['koun,flaʊər] *n.* any of various North American plants of the composite family having flower heads with a raised or cone-shaped central disk surrounded by ray flowers, especially the **prairie coneflower** (*Ratibida columnifera*) or any of several plants of the genera *Rudbeckia* and *Echinacea.*

cone•nose ['koun,nouz] *n.* any of a family (Reduviidae) of bloodsucking insects, especially one of the genus *Triatoma*, that carry parasitic diseases such as Chagas' disease.

cone shell any of a genus (*Conus*) of tropical marine snails, having a brightly coloured, flattened conical shell, and capable of inflicting a poisonous bite.

con•es•to•ga wagon [,kɒnɪ'stougə] a covered wagon with broad wheels, formerly used, especially by American pioneers, for travelling on soft ground or on the prairie. ⟨< *Conestoga*, Pa., where such wagons were first built⟩

co•ney[1] ['kouni] See CONY.

co•ney[2] ['kɒni] *n. Cdn.* inconnu. Also, **connie, cony.**

con•fab *n.* ['kɒn,fæb]; *v.* [kən'fæb] *or* ['kɒnfæb] *n., v.* **-fabbed, -fab•bing.** *Informal.* *—n.* a conversation or conference. *—v.* have a conversation or conference. ⟨shortening of *confabulation*⟩

con•fab•u•late [kən'fæbjə,leit] *v.* **-lat•ed, -lat•ing.** talk together informally and intimately; chat. ⟨< L *confabulari* < *com-* together + *fabula* fable⟩

con•fab•u•la•tion [kən,fæbjə'leiʃən] *n.* an informal, intimate talking together; chat.

con•fect [kən'fɛkt] *v.* make (up); concoct; contrive: *to confect a story.* ⟨< L *confectus*, pp. of *conficere.* See CONFECTION.⟩

con•fec•tion [kən'fɛkʃən] *n.* **1** a piece of candy, candied fruit, jam, etc. **2** an elaborate hat or dress. **3** anything elaborate, such as a sculpture. ⟨< F < L *confectio*, *-onis* < *conficere* prepare < *com-* with + *facere* make⟩

con•fec•tion•er [kən'fɛkshənər] *n.* a person whose business is making or selling candies, ice cream, etc.

confectioners' sugar *Esp. U.S.* ICING SUGAR.

con•fec•tion•er•y [kən'fɛkʃə,nɛri] *or* [kən'fɛkʃənəri] *n., pl.* **-er•ies. 1** candies, sweets, etc.; confections. **2** the business of making or selling confections. **3** a place where confections, ice cream, etc., are made or sold; candy shop.

con•fed•er•a•cy [kən'fɛdərəsi] *n., pl.* **-cies. 1** a union of countries or states; group of people joined together for a special purpose. **2** a league; alliance. **3** conspiracy. **4 Confederacy,** CONFEDERATE STATES OF AMERICA.

con•fed•er•ate *adj., n.* [kən'fɛdərɪt]; *v.* [kən'fɛdə,reit] *adj., n., v.* **-at•ed, -at•ing.** *—adj.* **1** joined together for a special purpose; allied. **2 Confederate,** of or belonging to the CONFEDERATE STATES OF AMERICA: *the Confederate uniform.*
—n. **1** a country, person, etc., joined with another for a special purpose; ally; companion. **2** an accomplice; partner in crime: *The thief was arrested, but her confederate escaped.* **3 Confederate,** *U.S.* a person who lived in and supported the CONFEDERATE STATES OF AMERICA.
—v. **1** enter a union or alliance: *Newfoundland confederated with Canada in 1949. Four provinces of Canada confederated in 1867.* **2** join together for a special purpose; ally. ⟨< L *confoederatus*, pp. of *confoederare* unite in a league < *com-* together + *foedus*, *-deris* league⟩
☛ *Syn. n.* **2.** See note at ACCOMPLICE.

Confederate States of America the group of eleven southern states that seceded from the United States in 1860 and 1861. Their secession lasted until the end of the Civil War in 1865.

con•fed•er•a•tion [kən,fɛdə'reiʃən] *n.* **1** a confederating; the act of joining together in a league; state of being united in a league or alliance: *The conference devised a scheme for the confederation of the foreign colonies.* **2** a group of countries, states, etc., joined together for a special purpose; league. **3 Confederation,** *Cdn.* **a** the name given to the federation of Ontario, Quebec, Nova Scotia, and New Brunswick in 1867. Six other provinces have joined Confederation since 1867. **b** the name of the event by which the original federation was formed in 1867. **4 the Confederation, a** *Cdn.* the ten provinces of Canada. **b** the confederation of the American states from 1781 to 1789.

Confederation Day *Cdn.* a former name for CANADA DAY.

con•fed•er•a•tive [kən'fɛdərətiv] *or* [kən'fɛdə,reitɪv] *adj.* **1** of confederates. **2** of a confederation.

con•fer [kən'fɜr] *v.* **-ferred, -fer•ring. 1** consult together; exchange ideas; talk things over: *The prime minister often confers with her advisers.* **2** give; award; bestow (*on*): *The general conferred a medal on the brave soldier.* ⟨< L *conferre* < *com-* together + *ferre* bring⟩
☛ *Syn.* **1.** See note at CONSULT. **2.** See note at GIVE.

con•fer•ee [,kɒnfə'ri] *n.* **1** a person who takes part in a conference. **2** a person on whom something is conferred.

con•fer•ence ['kɒnfərəns] *n.* **1** a meeting of interested persons to discuss a particular subject: *A conference was called to discuss getting a playground for the school.* **2** the act of taking counsel; the act of talking something over; consultation with a person or a group of persons: *You cannot see Mr. Smith just now; he is in conference.* **3** an association of schools, churches, etc., joined together for some purpose. **4** *Sports.* a league or division of a league. **—,con•fer'en•tial** [-fə'rɛnʃəl], *adj.*

conference call a telephone call involving three or more people, often in different places.

con•fer•ral [kən'fɜrəl] *n.* a conferring; bestowal. Also, **conferment.**

con•fess [kən'fɛs] *v.* **1** acknowledge; admit; own up. **2** concede; grant: *I confess you are right on one point.* **3** admit

one's guilt. **4** *Christianity.* tell (one's sins), especially to a priest in order to obtain forgiveness. **5** *Christianity.* of a priest, hear (a person) tell his or her sins in order to obtain forgiveness; act as a confessor (to). **6 a** state (one's faith or religious beliefs) openly. **b** state one's faith in: *Do you confess Christ?* ⟨ME < OF *confesser* < LL *confessare* < L *confiteri* < *com-* (intensive) + *fateri* confess⟩
☛ *Syn.* **1.** See note at ADMIT.

con•fessed [kən'fɛst] *adj., v.* —*adj.* acknowledged; admitted. —*v.* pt. and pp. of CONFESS.

con•fess•ed•ly [kən'fɛsɪdli] *adv.* by acknowledgment; admittedly.

con•fes•sion [kən'fɛʃən] *n.* **1** acknowledgment; admission; owning up. **2** admission of guilt. **3** *Christianity.* the telling of one's sins, especially to a priest in order to obtain forgiveness. **4** the thing confessed. **5** an acknowledgment of belief; profession of faith. **6** the belief acknowledged; creed. **7** a group sharing a creed; COMMUNION (def. 4). **8** (often pl.) an introspective and critical autobiographical account or one written to seem autobiographical: *Rousseau's confessions.*

con•fes•sion•al [kən'fɛʃənəl] *n., adj.* —*n. Christianity.* **1** a small booth inside a church where a priest hears confessions. **2** the practice of confessing sins to a priest.
—*adj.* of or having to do with confession.

confession of faith **1** a public, usually formal acknowledgment of belief. **2** the belief acknowledged; creed.

con•fes•sor [kən'fɛsər] *n.* **1** a person who confesses. **2** *Christianity.* a priest who has the authority to hear confessions. **3** a person who acknowledges belief.

con•fet•ti [kən'fɛti] *n.* bits of coloured paper (formerly, candies) thrown about at carnivals, weddings, etc. ⟨< Ital. *confetti*, pl., sweetmeats⟩

con•fi•dant [,kɒnfə'dænt] *or* ['kɒnfə,dænt], [,kɒnfə'dɑnt] *or* ['kɒnfə,dɑnt] *n.* a person entrusted with one's secrets, private affairs, etc.; a close friend.

con•fi•dante [,kɒnfə'dænt] *or* ['kɒnfə,dænt], [,kɒnfə'dɑnt] *or* ['kɒnfə,dɑnt] *n.* a woman or girl entrusted with one's secrets, etc.; a close female friend.

con•fide [kən'faɪd] *v.* **-fid•ed, -fid•ing. 1** tell as a secret: *He confided his troubles to his brother.* **2** hand over (a task, person, etc.) in trust; give to another for safekeeping: *The collection of dues is confided to the treasurer.*
confide in, a entrust a secret to: *She always confides in her sister.* **b** put trust in: *to confide in God.* ⟨< L *confidere* < *com-* (intensive) + *fidere* trust⟩ **—con'fid•er,** *n.*

con•fi•dence ['kɒnfədəns] *n.* **1** a firm belief; trust. **2** a firm belief in oneself and one's abilities. **3** boldness; too much boldness: *Although he could not swim, he dived into the water with confidence.* **4** a feeling of trust; assurance that a person will not tell others what is said: *The story was told to me in strict confidence.* **5** something told as a secret. **6** political support for the actions or policy of the cabinet, as expressed by the majority vote of a legislature: *A government that loses a vote of confidence must resign.*
☛ *Syn. n.* **2. Confidence,** ASSURANCE = a firm belief in oneself. **Confidence** emphasizes its basic meaning of faith or trust, and means 'a strong belief in oneself and one's abilities': *Earlier successes gave him confidence for the new venture.* **Assurance** emphasizes its basic meaning of certainty, and means 'sureness of oneself and lack of fears or doubts about one's abilities': *She went into the contest with the assurance of a winner.*

confidence game a type of fraud in which a swindler works on the victim after gaining his or her confidence.

confidence man a swindler who uses a CONFIDENCE GAME.

con•fi•dent ['kɒnfədənt] *adj., n.* —*adj.* **1** firmly believing; certain; sure. **2** sure of oneself and one's abilities. **3** too bold; too sure.
—*n.* a close, trusted friend; confidant. **—'con•fi•dent•ly,** *adv.*
☛ *Syn. adj.* **1.** See note at SURE.

con•fi•den•tial [,kɒnfə'dɛnʃəl] *adj.* **1** intended for or restricted to secret or private use: *The detective's report to her superior was confidential.* **2** showing trust or intimacy: *She spoke in a confidential tone of voice.* **3** trusted with secrets, private affairs, etc.: *a confidential secretary.* **—,con•fi'den•tial•ly,** *adv.* **—,con•fi'den•tial•ness,** *n.*
☛ *Syn.* **3.** See note at FAMILIAR.

con•fi•den•ti•al•i•ty [,kɒnfə,dɛnʃi'ælәti] *n.* the fact or quality of being confidential.

con•fid•ing [kən'faɪdɪŋ] *adj., v.* —*adj.* trustful; trusting. —*v.* ppr. of CONFIDE. **—con'fid•ing•ly,** *adv.*

con•fig•u•ra•tion [kən,fɪgjə'reiʃən] *or* [kən,fɪgə'reiʃən] *n.* **1** the relative position of parts; manner of arrangement; form; shape; outline: *Geographers study the configuration of the earth's surface.* **2** *Astronomy.* **a** the relative position of heavenly bodies, especially of the sun, moon, and planets. **b** any grouping of stars. **3** the relative spatial positions of atoms in a molecule. **4** *Computer technology.* **a** a set of hardware devices and their arrangement in a computer system. **b** during the set-up of a computer system, the set of options selected to make the system perform in a particular way. ⟨< L *configuratio, -onis* < *configurare* form after some pattern < *com-* with + *figura* a form⟩

con•fig•u•ra•tive [kən'fɪgjərətɪv] *or* [kən'fɪgərətɪv] *adj.* of or having to do with configuration.

con•fig•ure [kən'fɪgjər] *or* [kən'fɪgər] *v.,* **-ured, -ur•ing. 1** arrange in a special way. **2** *Computer technology.* choose (and usually implement) the configuration for (a computer system).

con•fine *v.* [kən'faɪn]; *n.* ['kɒnfaɪn] *v.* **-fined, -fin•ing;** *n.* —*v.* **1** keep within limits; restrict. **2** keep indoors; shut in. **3** imprison.
be confined, begin or undergo the process of childbirth.
—*n.* Usually, **confines,** *pl.* a boundary; border; limit: *These people have never been beyond the confines of their own valley.* ⟨< F *confiner* < *confins*, pl., bounds < L *confinium* < *com-* together + *finis* end, border⟩ **—con'fin•er,** *n.*

con•fined [kən'faɪnd] *adj., v.* —*adj.* **1** restricted. **2** imprisoned. —*v.* pt. and pp. of CONFINE.

con•fine•ment [kən'faɪnmənt] *n.* **1** a confining or being confined. **2** imprisonment. **3** the period for which a mother is confined to bed during and after childbirth. ⟨< F *confinement* < *confiner.* See CONFINE.⟩

con•firm [kən'fɜrm] *v.* **1** make official by formal statement; approve; consent to: *Parliament confirmed the treaty.* **2** prove to be true or correct; make certain: *to confirm a rumour.* **3** support; strengthen in an opinion, etc.: *A sudden storm confirmed my decision not to leave.* **4** administer the religious rite of confirmation to. ⟨ME < OF *confermer* < L *confirmare* < *com-* (intensive) + *firmus* firm⟩ **—con'firm•a•ble,** *adj.* **—con'firm•er,** *n.*
☛ *Syn.* **2. Confirm,** CORROBORATE, AUTHENTICATE = prove to be true or genuine. **Confirm** = make certain that something is true or correct, by facts or a statement that cannot be doubted: *The mayor confirmed the report that she had resigned.* **Corroborate** = make more certain that something suspected is true, by a statement or new evidence: *Finding the weapon corroborates the police theory.* **Authenticate** = prove something is genuine or reliable, by the evidence of someone who knows: *Handwriting experts authenticated the will.*

con•fir•ma•tion [,kɒnfər'meiʃən] *n.* **1** the act or process of confirming. **2** something that confirms; proof: *The lab has sent confirmation of the diagnosis.* **3** an assurance (i.e., that one's plans have not been changed): *The airline requires confirmation of your reservation.* **4** *Christianity.* a rite in many churches in which a baptized person is confirmed in his or her faith and admitted to full church membership. **5** *Judaism.* a ceremony in which a young person is confirmed in the Jewish faith.

con•firm•a•tive [kən'fɜrmətɪv] *adj.* confirmatory.

con•firm•a•to•ry [kən'fɜrmə,tɔri] *adj.* confirming.

con•firmed [kən'fɜrmd] *adj., v.* —*adj.* **1** firmly established; proved: *confirmed results.* **2** habitual; constant; permanent: *a confirmed bachelor.* **3** having received the religious rite of confirmation.
—*v.* pt. and pp. of CONFIRM.

con•fis•ca•ble [kən'fɪskəbəl] *adj.* able to be confiscated.

con•fis•cate ['kɒnfə,skeit] *v.* **-cat•ed, -cat•ing. 1** seize for the public treasury: *The government confiscated the property of all traitors.* **2** seize by authority; take and keep: *The customs officer confiscated the smuggled cigarettes.* ⟨< L *confiscare*, originally, lay away in a chest < *com-* (intensive) + *fiscus* chest, public treasury⟩ **—'con•fis,ca•tor,** *n.*

con•fis•ca•tion [,kɒnfə'skeiʃən] *n.* a confiscating or being confiscated: *the confiscation of wealth.*

con•fis•ca•to•ry [kən'fɪskə,tɔri] *adj.* of the nature of confiscation or tending to confiscate.

con•fit [koun'fi]; *French*, [kɔ̃'fi] *n.* a dish comprising meat, duck or goose cooked and congealed within its own fat. ⟨< OF, pp. of *confire* prepare⟩

con•fi•ture ['kɒnfɪ,tʃʊr] *n.* a confection such as a candy or conserve. ⟨< F < OF *confit*⟩

con•fla•gra•tion [,kɒnflə'greiʃən] *n.* a great, destructive fire: *A conflagration destroyed most of the city.* ⟨< L *conflagratio, -onis* < *conflagrare* < *com-* (intensive) + *flagrare* burn⟩

con•flate [kən'fleit] *v.* **-flat•ed, -flat•ing** merge; combine. ⟨< L *conflatus* pp. of *conflare* fuse together⟩

con•fla•tion [kən'fleiʃən] *n.* **1** the act or process of conflating; combination. **2** the merging of two variant texts into a new one. **3** the new thing or text thus produced.

con•flict *n.* ['kɒnflɪkt]; *v.* [kən'flɪkt] *n., v.* —*n.* **1** a prolonged fight or struggle. **2** direct opposition; a disagreement; clash: *A conflict of opinions divided the members into two groups.* **3** an inner struggle.
—*v.* **1** be directly opposed; disagree; clash: *The date conflicts with his vacation plans. Their stories of the accident conflict.* **2** *Archaic.* fight; do battle. ⟨< L *conflictus*, pp. of *confligere* < *com-* together + *fligere* strike⟩
☛ *Syn. n.* **1.** See note at FIGHT.

con•flict•ing [kən'flɪktɪŋ] *adj., v.* —*adj.* that conflicts; disagreeing; clashing.
—*v.* ppr. of CONFLICT.

conflict of interest a clash, or opposition, between the private interests and the public responsibilities of a person in a position of trust, such as a government official.

con•flu•ence ['kɒnfluəns] *n.* **1** a flowing together: *the confluence of two rivers.* **2** the place where two or more rivers, streams, etc., come together: *They pitched camp at the confluence of the two streams.* **3** a coming together of people or things; throng.

con•flu•ent ['kɒnfluənt] *adj., n.* —*adj.* **1** flowing or running together; blending into one: *confluent rivers.* **2** *Medicine.* **a** tending to join or run together: *confluent eruptions of the skin.* **b** characterized by such eruptions.
—*n.* **1** a stream which unites and flows with another of nearly equal size. **2** a smaller stream flowing into a larger one. ⟨< L *confluens, -entis*, ppr. of *confluere* < *com-* together + *fluere* flow⟩

con•flux ['kɒnflʌks] *n.* confluence. ⟨< L *confluxus*, pp. of *confluere* flow together⟩

con•fo•cal [kɒn'foukəl] *adj. Mathematics.* sharing a focus or foci.

con•form [kən'fɔrm] *v.* **1** act according to law or rule; adapt to or accept the normal standards of business, conduct, worship, etc. **2** be similar in form or character: *The path conforms to the shoreline of the lake.* **3** make similar in form or character: *to conform the path to the shoreline. The stranger never conformed her ways to theirs.* **4** be in agreement with: *The textbook conforms to Ministry guidelines.* **5** *Brit.* formerly, comply with the usages of the Church of England. ⟨ME < OF *conformer* < L *conformare* < *com-* with + *formare* shape⟩ **—con'form•er,** *n.*

con•form•a•ble [kən'fɔrməbəl] *adj.* **1** similar. **2** adapted; adjusted. **3** in agreement; agreeable; harmonious: *The committee felt that the proposal was not conformable to their interests.* **4** obedient; submissive: *The boy was usually conformable to his father's wishes.* **5** *Geology.* of strata, uniformly parallel without a break. **—con'form•a•bly,** *adv.* **—con'form•a•ble•ness,** *n.*

con•for•mal [kən'fɔrməl] *adj.* **1** having the same scale in all directions at any given point: *a conformal map projection.* **2** *Mathematics.* preserving the size of all angles.

con•form•ance [kən'fɔrməns] *n.* the act of conforming; conformity.

con•for•ma•tion [,kɒnfɔr'meiʃən] *n.* **1** a structure; shape; the form of a thing resulting from the arrangement of its parts. **2** a symmetrical arrangement of the parts of a thing. **3** a conforming; adaptation.

con•form•ist [kən'fɔrmɪst] *n., adj.* —*n.* **1** a person who tends to conform to generally accepted and conventional usage in behaviour, dress, etc. **2** *Brit.* formerly, a person who complied with the usages of the Church of England.
—*adj.* of or having to do with conformity or conformists; conventional. **—con'form•ism,** *n.*

con•form•i•ty [kən'fɔrməti] *n., pl.* **-ties. 1** a similarity; correspondence; agreement. **2** behaviour in agreement with generally accepted standards of business, law, conduct, or worship; fitting oneself and one's thoughts or actions to the ideas of others; compliance. **3** obedience; submission. **4** *Brit.* formerly, compliance with the usages of the Church of England.

con•found [kən'faʊnd] *for 1-4;* [kɒn'faʊnd] *for 5 v.* **1** confuse; bewilder: *The shock confounded her.* **2** be unable to tell apart: *He confounds "deprecate" and "depreciate."* **3** make uneasy and ashamed. **4** *Archaic.* defeat; overthrow. **5** damn. *Confound* is used as a mild oath. ⟨ME < OF *confondre* < L *confundere* < *com-* together + *fundere* pour⟩ **—con'found•er,** *n.*

con•found•ed [kɒn'faʊndɪd] *or* [kən'faʊndɪd] *adj., v.* —*adj.* **1** damned. *Confounded* is used as a mild oath: *The confounded cat stays out all night.* **2** hateful; detestable.
—*v.* pt. and pp. of CONFOUND. **—con'found•ed•ly,** *adv.*

con•fra•ter•ni•ty [,kɒnfrə'tɜrnəti] *n., pl.* **-ties. 1** brotherhood. **2** a group of men united for some purpose or in a profession. ⟨ME *confraternite* < Med.L *confraternitas* < *confrater.* See CONFRERE.⟩

con•frère or **con•frere** ['kɒnfrɛr] *or* [kɒn'frɛr] *n.* a fellow member; colleague. ⟨< F *confrère* < OF < Med.L *confrater* < L *com-* together + *frater* brother⟩

con•front [kən'frʌnt] *v.* **1** meet face to face, especially as an opponent; stand facing. **2** face boldly; oppose. **3** bring face to face; force to recognize something: *The lawyer confronted the prisoner with the forged cheque. We finally confronted them with their cheating.* **4** compare. ⟨< F *confronter* < Med.L *confrontare* < L *com-* together + *frons, frontis* forehead⟩ **—con'front•al,** *adj.*

con•fron•ta•tion [,kɒnfrən'teiʃən] *n.* **1** meeting or being met face to face. **2** an open facing or conflict of opposing groups, parties, or individuals: *She doesn't believe in confrontation, and would rather try to talk things out reasonably. He keeps his grievances to himself because he is afraid of confrontation.* **3** (*adjl.*) designating tactics or a strategy based on open clashes: *confrontation politics.* **—,con•fron'ta•tion•al,** *adj.*

con•fron•ta•tion•ist [,kɒnfrʌn'teiʃənɪst] *n.* a person who advocates or practises tactics or a strategy of confrontation.

Con•fu•cian [kən'fjuʃən] *adj., n.* —*adj.* of or having to do with Confucius, his teachings, or his followers.
—*n.* a follower of Confucius or his teachings.

Con•fu•cian•ism [kən'fjuʃə,nɪzəm] *n.* a philosophical system based on the belief in the natural goodness of all human beings, that for more than 2000 years dominated the social and political order in China. Confucianism teaches that the greatest virtues are love, justice, reverence, wisdom, and sincerity, and emphasizes respect for parents and ancestors.

Con•fu•cian•ist [kən'fjuʃənɪst] *n., adj.* —*n.* a supporter or follower of Confucianism.
—*adj.* of or having to do with Confucianism.

Con•fu•cius [kən'fjuʃəs] *n.* ? 551-478 B.C., a Chinese philosopher and teacher whose teachings form the basis of Confucianism. ⟨Latinized form of *Kung Fu-tse* Kung the master⟩

Confucius

con•fuse [kən'fjuz] *v.* **-fused, -fus•ing. 1** mix up; throw into disorder. **2** bewilder: *So many people talking to me at once confused me.* **3** be unable to tell apart; mistake (one thing for another): *Even their own mother sometimes confused the twins.* **4** make uneasy and ashamed; embarrass: *Confused by her blunder, she could not say anything for a moment.* ⟨< *confused* < F *confus* < L *confusus*, pp. of *confundere.* See CONFOUND.⟩ **—con'fus•ing•ly,** *adv.*
☛ *Syn.* **4. Confuse,** EMBARRASS, DISCONCERT = disturb a person. **Confuse** = make a person so uneasy and bewildered that he or she cannot think clearly or act sensibly: *Honking at the driver who had stalled his car only confused him.* **Embarrass** = make one so uneasy and self-conscious that he or she cannot talk or act naturally: *Meeting strangers embarrasses her.* **Disconcert** = disturb someone so suddenly or badly that for a moment he or she loses his or her poise and ability to handle the situation: *Forgetting the words disconcerted the singer.*

con•fused [kən'fjuzd] *adj., v.* —*adj.* **1** mixed up; disordered. **2** bewildered.
—*v.* pt. and pp. of CONFUSE.

con•fus•ed•ly [kən'fjuzɪdli] *or* [kən'fjuzdli] *adv.* in a confused manner.

con•fu•sion [kən'fjuʒən] *n.* **1** the act or fact of confusing or being confused. **2** a confused condition; disorder: *There was confusion in the busy street after the accident.* **3** a failure to distinguish clearly: *confusion between red and orange.* **4** bewilderment; inability to think clearly: *In her confusion she quite forgot her appointment.* **5** uneasiness and shame.
covered in or **with confusion,** mortified; embarrassed.

con•fu•ta•tion [,kɒnfjə'teiʃən] *n.* **1** the act of confuting. **2** the thing that confutes. **—con'fu•ta•tive,** *adj.*

con•fute [kən'fjut] *v.* **-fut•ed, -fut•ing. 1** prove (an argument, testimony, etc.) to be false or incorrect: *The lawyer confuted the testimony of the witness by showing actual photographs of the accident.* **2** prove (a person) to be wrong; overcome by argument: *The speaker confuted his opponents by facts and logic.* ⟨< L *confutare*⟩ **—con'fut•er,** *n.*

☛ *Syn.* **Confute,** REFUTE = prove (an adversary, etc.) to be wrong. But **confute** is more intensive and has the force of "silencing or overcoming" a person by refutation.

con•ga ['kɒŋgə] *n., v.* **con•gaed** or **con•ga'd, con•ga•ing.** *—n.* **1** a Cuban dance of African origin, usually performed by a group of people moving one behind the other in a single line. **2** music for this dance, having a strong, syncopated rhythm in 4/4 time. **3** a tall, narrow, low-toned drum that is beaten with the hands. Also called **conga drum.** See DRUM for picture.
—v. dance the conga. ⟨< Sp.⟩

con•gé ['kɒnʒei] *or* [kɒn'ʒei]; *French,* [kɔ̃'ʒe] *n.* **1** dismissal; permission to leave. **2** formal leave-taking or departure. **3** *Architecture.* a moulding with a concave surface. ⟨< F < L *commeatus* going to and fro < *com-* (intensive) + *meare* wander⟩

con•geal [kən'dʒil] *v.* **1** harden or make solid by cold; freeze. **2** thicken; jell: *The blood around the wound had congealed.* ⟨ME < OF *congeler* < L *congelare* < *com-* (intensive) + *gelare* freeze⟩ **—con'geal•er,** *n.* **—con'geal•ment,** *n.*

con•gel•a•tion [,kɒndʒə'leiʃən] *n.* **1** the act or process of congealing. **2** the thing congealed; the product of congealing.

con•ge•ner ['kɒndʒənər] *n.* a person or thing of the same kind or class. ⟨< L *congener* of the same kind < *com-* (intensive) + *genus, -neris* kind⟩ **—,con•ge'ne•ric** [,kɒndʒə'nɛrɪk], *adj.*

con•ge•ni•al [kən'dʒinjəl] *or* [kən'dʒiniəl] *adj.* **1** having similar tastes and interests; getting on well together: *congenial companions.* **2** agreeable; suitable: *congenial work.* ⟨< NL **congenialis* < L *com-* together + *genialis* < *genius* spirit⟩ **—con'gen•ial•ly,** *adv.*

con•ge•ni•al•i•ty [kən,dʒini'æləti] *or* [kən,dʒin'jæləti] *n.* a congenial quality.

con•gen•i•tal [kən'dʒɛnətəl] *adj.* **1** existing at birth, but not necessarily inherited: *A clubfoot is a congenital deformity.* Compare HEREDITARY. **2** inborn; deep-seated; being so since or as if since birth: *congenital dislikes, a congenital liar.* ⟨< L *congenitus* born with < *com-* with + *genitus* born⟩ **—con'gen•i•tal•ly,** *adv.*

congenital defect a defect present at birth. Compare BASIC DEFECT.

con•ger eel ['kɒŋgər] *n.* **1** a large, scaleless marine eel (*Conger conger*) found along the coasts of Europe, Asia, and Africa, and the Atlantic coast of America. The conger eel is an important food fish of Europe. **2** any other eel of the same family (Congridae, the conger eel family). Also called **conger.** ⟨ME < OF *congre* < L < Gk. *gongros*⟩

con•ge•ries [kən'dʒiriz], [kɒn'dʒiri,iz], *or* ['kɒndʒə,riz] *n.sing. and pl.* a collection; heap; mass. ⟨< L *congeries* < *congerere.* See CONGEST.⟩

con•gest [kən'dʒɛst] *v.* **1** fill too full; overcrowd; clog: *The rush-hour traffic congested the streets.* **2** cause too much blood or other fluid to gather in (a part of the body): *An infection of the mucous membrane in the nose will congest the nasal passages.* **3** become congested. ⟨< L *congestus,* pp. of *congerere* < *com-* together + *gerere* carry⟩

con•gest•ed [kən'dʒɛstɪd] *adj., v. —adj.* **1** overcrowded; clogged: *congested hallways.* **2** of a body organ or tissue, containing too much blood or other fluid: *congested mucous membranes, congested lungs.*
—v. pt. and pp. of CONGEST.

con•ges•tion [kən'dʒɛstʃən] *n.* the quality or state of being congested: *traffic congestion. Congestion of the lungs may lead to pneumonia.*

con•ges•tive [kən'dʒɛstɪv] *adj.* accompanied by congestion; produced by congestion; causing congestion.

con•glom•er•ate *adj. and n.* [kən'glɒmərɪt]; *v.* [kən'glɒmə,reit] *adj., n., v.* **-at•ed, -at•ing.** *—adj.* **1** gathered into a rounded mass; clustered. **2** made up of miscellaneous materials gathered from various sources. **3** *Geology.* of or forming a conglomerate.
—n. **1** a mass formed of fragments. **2** *Geology.* a kind of sedimentary rock consisting of waterworn boulders, pebbles, etc. held together by a natural cementing material. **3** a large, widely diversified corporation consisting of a number of companies dealing in different products or services.
—v. collect together or accumulate into a mass or cluster. ⟨< L *conglomerare* < *com-* together + *glomus, -meris* ball⟩ **—con,glom•er'at•ic** [kən,glɒmə'rætɪk], *adj.*

con•glom•er•a•tion [kən,glɒmə'reiʃən] *n.* **1** a mixed-up mass of various things or persons; mixture. **2** a conglomerating or being conglomerated.

Con•go ['kɒŋgou] *n.* **1** a country in west central Africa. **2** the former name of Zaire.

Congo colour or **Congo dye** a dyestuff derived from benzidine, used to colour vegetable fabrics such as cotton.

Con•go•lese [,kɒŋgə'liz] *n., adj. —n.* a native or inhabitant of the Congo region, the former French Congo, the former Belgian Congo, or either of the Congo republics.
—adj. of or having to do with any of these.

Congo red a red powder used as a dye and an indicator of acids; it turns blue in the presence of acid. *Formula:* $C_{32}H_{22}O_6N_6S_2Na_2$

congo snake or **eel** a snakelike amphibian (*Amphiuma means*) found in swampy regions of the SE United States, having gill slits and two pairs of very small, weak legs.

con•grat•u•late [kən'grætʃə,leit] *v.* **-lated, -lat•ing. 1** express one's pleasure to (someone) at his or her happiness or good fortune. **2** consider (oneself) lucky, righteous, smart, great, etc.: *You won, but don't congratulate yourselves; the other team was three players short.* ⟨< L *congratulari* < *com-* with + *gratulari* show joy⟩ **—con'grat•u,la•tor,** *n.*

con•grat•u•la•tion [kən,grætʃə'leiʃən] *n.* **1** a congratulating or wishing a person joy: *a letter of congratulation.* **2 congratulations,** *pl.* an expression of pleasure at another's happiness or good fortune: *Congratulations on winning the tournament.*

con•grat•u•la•to•ry [kən'grætʃələ,tɔri] *adj.* expressing pleasure at another's happiness or good fortune.

con•gre•gate *v.* ['kɒŋgrə,geit]; *adj.* ['kɒŋgrəgɪt] *or* ['kɒŋgrə,geit] *v., adj. —v.* **-gat•ed, -gat•ing.** come together into a crowd or mass; assemble.
—adj. assembled. ⟨< L *congregare* < *com-* together + *grex, gregis* flock⟩

con•gre•ga•tion [,kɒŋgrə'geiʃən] *n.* **1** a coming together into a crowd or mass; assembling. **2** a gathering of people or things; assembly. **3** a group of people gathered together for worship or religious instruction. **4** *Roman Catholic Church.* **a** a committee of cardinals or other clergy. **b** a religious community or order having a common rule and with or without solemn vows.

con•gre•ga•tion•al [,kɒŋgrə'geiʃənəl] *adj.* **1** of a congregation; done by a congregation. **2** of a local Christian church, self-governing; autonomous. **3 Congregational,** of or belonging to Congregationalism or Congregationalists.

con•gre•ga•tion•al•ism [,kɒŋgrə'geiʃənə,lɪzəm] *n.* **1** a system of Christian church government in which each individual church governs itself. **2 Congregationalism,** a Protestant movement embodying the principles and system of organization in which each individual church governs itself.

Con•gre•ga•tion•al•ist [,kɒŋgrə'geiʃənəlɪst] *n., adj. —n.* **1** a member of a congregational church. **2** a believer in Congregationalism.
—adj. of or having to do with Congregationalism.

con•gress ['kɒŋgrɪs] *or* ['kɒŋgrɛs] *n.* **1** a formal meeting of representatives of interested groups to discuss some subject: *They attended an international congress on conservation.* **2** an organization of people for the purpose of promoting a common interest or concern: *the Canadian Labour Congress.* **3** the lawmaking body of a nation, especially of a republic. **4 Congress,** in the United States: **a** the national lawmaking body, consisting of the Senate and House of Representatives, with members from each state. **b** its session. **5** the act or action of meeting or coming together socially or sexually. ⟨< L *congressus* < *congredi* < *com-* together + *gradi* go⟩

con•gres•sion•al [kən'grɛʃənəl] *adj.* **1** of or having to do with a congress. **2 Congressional,** of or having to do with Congress. **—con'gres•sion•al•ly,** *adv.*

con•gress•man ['kɒŋgrɪsmən] *n., pl.* **-men.** Often, **Congressman.** in the United States: **1** a member of Congress. **2** a member of the House of Representatives.

con•gress•wom•an ['kɒŋgrɪs,wʊmən] *n., pl.* **-wom•en.** Often, **Congresswoman,** in the United States, a female member of Congress or of the House of Representatives.

con•gru•ence ['kɒŋgruəns] *or* [kən'gruəns] *n.* **1** agreement;

harmony. **2** the condition of being exactly the same in size and shape, so that all parts match: *Check the congruence of these two triangles.* Also, **congruency.**

con•gru•ent ['kɒŋgruənt] *or* [kən'gruənt] *adj.* **1** agreeing; harmonious. **2** *Geometry.* exactly coinciding: *congruent triangles.* ⟨< L *congruens, -entis,* ppr. of *congruere* agree⟩
—'con•gru•ent•ly, *adv.*

con•gru•i•ty [kən'gruəti] *n., pl.* **-ties. 1** agreement; harmony. **2** suitability. **3** *Geometry.* the exact coincidence of lines, angles, figures, etc. **4** a point of agreement.

con•gru•ous ['kɒŋgruəs] *adj.* **1** agreeing; harmonious. **2** fitting; appropriate. **3** *Geometry.* exactly coinciding. ⟨< L *congruus* < *congruere* agree⟩ **—'con•gru•ous•ly,** *adv.*
—'con•gru•ous•ness, *n.*

Con•i•bear trap ['kouni,bɛr] *Cdn.* a heavy steel trap that kills large animals, such as beavers, instantly. ⟨after F. *Conibear,* a Canadian expert on trapping⟩

con•ic ['kɒnɪk] *adj., n. —adj.* **1** of or having to do with a cone. **2** like a cone; conical.
—n. Geometry. **1** a curve forming the edge of the plane surface produced when a piece is cut from a right circular cone. Depending on the angle at which the cut is made, the conic will be a circle, ellipse, parabola, or hyperbola. See CONE for picture. **2 conics,** the branch of geometry dealing with circles, ellipses, parabolas, and hyperbolas (*used with a singular verb*).

con•i•cal ['kɒnəkəl] *adj.* **1** like a cone; cone-shaped: *The wizard wore a conical hat.* **2** conic. **—'con•i•cal•ly,** *adv.*

conic projection a map projection based on an image of the earth's surface as a cone which is then unrolled to a plane surface.

conic section *Geometry.* **1** a conic. See CONE for picture. **2 conic sections,** a branch of geometry; conics (*used with a singular verb*).

co•nid•i•um [kou'nɪdiəm] *n., pl.* **-nid•ia** [-'nɪdiə]. a single-celled, asexual spore produced in certain fungi. ⟨< Gk. *konis* dust⟩

con•i•fer ['kɒnəfər] *or* ['kounəfər] *n.* any tree or shrub of the order Coniferales, most species having small, needle-shaped, evergreen leaves and all bearing their seeds in cones. Pines, spruces, firs, hemlocks, junipers, and cypresses are conifers. ⟨< L *conifer* cone-bearing < *conus* cone (< Gk. *kōnos*) + *ferre* to bear⟩

co•nif•er•ous [kə'nɪfərəs] *or* [kou'nɪfərəs] *adj.* **1** bearing cones. **2** belonging to or having to do with the conifers.

co•ni•ine ['kouni,in] *or* ['kouniɪn] *n.* a very poisonous alkaloid derived from the poison hemlock. *Formula:* $C_8H_{17}N$ ⟨< *conium* + *-ine*⟩

co•ni•um ['kouniəm] *or* [kou'naɪəm] *n.* **1** any plant of the genus *Conium,* of the umbel family, having feathery leaves and round fruits. **2** POISON HEMLOCK (*Conium maculatum*). ⟨< NL < Gk. *koneion* hemlock⟩

conj. 1 conjunction. **2** conjugation.

con•jec•tur•al [kən'dʒɛktʃərəl] *adj.* **1** involving conjecture. **2** inclined to conjecture. **—con'jec•tur•al•ly,** *adv.*

con•jec•ture [kən'dʒɛktʃər] *n., v.* **-tured, -tur•ing.** *—n.* **1** the formation of an opinion admittedly without sufficient evidence for proof; guessing. **2** such an opinion: *There were many conjectures about how she died, but no one knew for certain.* *—v.* form an opinion based on guesswork; guess. ⟨ME < L *conjectura* < *conjicere* < *com-* together + *jacere* throw⟩ **—con'jec•tur•a•ble,** *adj.* **—con'jec•tur•a•bly,** *adv.* **—con'jec•tur•er,** *n.*
☛ *Syn. v.* See note at GUESS.

con•join [kən'dʒɔɪn] *v.* join together; unite; combine. ⟨ME *conjoignen* < OF *conjoindre* < L *conjungere* < *com-* together + *jungere* join⟩ **—con'join•er,** *n.*

con•joint [kən'dʒɔɪnt] *or* ['kɒndʒɔɪnt] *adj.* **1** joined together; united; combined. **2** formed, done, etc. by two or more in combination; joint. ⟨< F *conjoint,* pp. of *conjoindre.* See CONJOIN.⟩ **—con'joint•ly,** *adv.*

con•ju•gal ['kɒndʒəgəl] *adj.* of or having to do with marriage or the relationship between husband and wife: *conjugal happiness.* ⟨< L *conjugalis* < *com-* with + *jugum* yoke⟩
—'con•ju•gal•ly, *adv.* **—,con•ju'gal•i•ty** [,kɒndʒə'gæləti], *n.*

con•ju•gate *v.* ['kɒndʒə,geit]; *adj., n.* ['kɒndʒə,gɪt] *or* ['kɒndʒəgeit] *v.* **-gat•ed, -gat•ing;** *adj., n. —v.* **1** *Grammar.* give the forms of (a verb) according to a systematic arrangement. **2** of a verb, be conjugated. **3** join together; couple.
—adj. **1** joined together; coupled. **2** *Grammar.* derived from the same root. **3** *Chemistry.* of acids and bases, related by the presence or absence of a proton.
—n. **1** *Grammar.* a word derived from the same root as another. **2** *Chemistry.* a chemically conjugate substance. ⟨< L *conjugare* < *com-* with + *jugum* yoke⟩

con•ju•ga•tion [,kɒndʒə'geiʃən] *n.* **1** *Grammar.* **a** a systematic arrangement of the forms of a verb. **b** a group of verbs having similar forms in such an arrangement. **c** the act of giving the forms of a verb according to such an arrangement. **2** a joining together; coupling. **3** *Biology.* **a** a kind of reproduction in which two single-celled organisms unite temporarily to exchange nuclear material and then separate, as with various protozoa. **b** the fusion of male and female gametes to form a zygote.

con•junct *adj.* ['kɒndʒʌŋkt] *or* [kən'dʒʌŋkt]; *n.* ['kɒndʒʌŋkt] *adj., n. —adj.* joined together; joint; associated; combined.
—n. a person or thing joined to another. ⟨< L *conjunctus,* pp. of *conjungere.* See CONJOIN.⟩

con•junc•tion [kən'dʒʌnkʃən] *n.* **1** a joining or being joined together; union; combination: *A severe illness in conjunction with the hot weather has left the baby very weak.* **2** *Grammar.* a word that expresses a particular connection between similar grammatical units. *And, but,* and *or* are **co-ordinating conjunctions;** *if, as, because,* etc., are **subordinating conjunctions;** *either…or, both…and* are **correlative conjunctions. 3** *Astronomy.* the apparent nearness of two or more heavenly bodies.
☛ *Usage.* **Conjunctions** are used to connect words or phrases of similar function, clauses, or sentences. Some conjunctions also serve the double purpose of introducing a clause and connecting it with the rest of the sentence. Conjunctions are classified as follows: **a Co-ordinating:** those that connect words, phrases, clauses, or sentences of equal rank: *and, but, for, nor, or, so, yet.* **b Correlative:** co-ordinating conjunctions that are used in pairs: *both…and, either…or, neither…nor, not only…but also, whether…or.* **c Subordinating:** those that serve to introduce and to connect subordinate clauses or clause substitutes with the main clauses of sentences: *after, although, as, because, before, if, since, when, whenever, where, while,* and so on. **d** See **conjunctive adverbs,** under CONJUNCTIVE.

con•junc•ti•va [,kɒndʒʌŋk'taɪvə] *or* [kən'dʒʌŋktɪvə] *n., pl.* **-vas, -vae** [-vi] *or* [-vaɪ]. *Anatomy.* the mucous membrane that covers the front of the eyeball and the inner surface of the eyelids. ⟨< NL *(membrana) conjunctiva* connecting membrane⟩
—,con•junc'ti•val, *adj.*

con•junc•tive [kən'dʒʌŋktɪv] *adj., n. —adj.* **1** joining together; connecting; uniting; combining. **2** joined together; joint; united; combined. **3** *Grammar.* **a** like a conjunction; like that of a conjunction. *Then* and *moreover* are conjunctive adverbs. **b** being a conjunction. *And, for,* and *while* are conjunctive terms.
—n. a conjunctive word; conjunction. **—con'junc•tive•ly,** *adv.*
☛ *Usage.* **Conjunctive adverbs.** A number of words that are ordinarily used as adverbs are sometimes used also to connect independent clauses or sentences. They are called **conjunctive adverbs.** Even though they serve as connectives, their adverbial meaning remains important. The most common are: *accordingly, also, anyhow, anyway* (informal), *besides, consequently, furthermore, hence, however, indeed, likewise, moreover, namely, nevertheless, then, therefore.* In a compound sentence, it is normal to use a semicolon before a clause introduced by a conjunctive adverb: *He is extremely conceited; however, he is so charming that people overlook it.* Failure to do so results in a COMMA FAULT.

con•junc•ti•vi•tis [kən,dʒʌŋktə'vəitɪs] *n.* an inflammation of the conjunctiva. ⟨< NL *conjunctivitis* < *conjunctiva* + *-itis* (< Gk.)⟩

con•junc•ture [kən'dʒʌŋktʃər] *n.* **1** a combination of events or circumstances. **2** a critical state of affairs; crisis.

con•jun•to [kɒn'hʊntou] *n.* a style of music in Texas, making much use of trumpets and trombones. ⟨< Sp.⟩

con•ju•ra•tion [,kɒndʒə'reiʃən] *n.* **1** the act of invoking by a sacred name. **2** a magic form of words used in conjuring; magic spell. **3** the practice of magic: *In the fairy tale, the princess was changed into a toad by conjuration.* **4** *Archaic.* a solemn appeal.

con•jure ['kɒndʒər] *or* ['kʌndʒər] *for 1-5;* [kən'dʒʊr] *for 6. v.* **-jured, -jur•ing. 1** compel to appear by or as if by incantation (*often used with* **up**): *The wizard conjured a dragon. Grandma conjured up a bag of toys from the attic.* **2** summon a devil, spirit, etc., by incantation: *The wizard began to conjure.* **3** practise magic; be a conjurer. **4** cause to appear in the mind; evoke (*used with* **up**): *The song conjured up many memories.* **5** perform tricks by sleight of hand. **6** make a solemn appeal to; entreat: *I conjure you not to betray your country.*
(a person or thing) **to conjure with,** one that has great importance or influence: *Since her last novel, she has become a name to conjure with.* ⟨ME < OF < L *conjurare* make a compact < *com-* together + *jurare* swear⟩

con•jur•er or **con•jur•or** ['kɒndʒərər] *or* ['kʌndʒərər] *n.*

1 a sorcerer or wizard. 2 a person who performs tricks by sleight of hand; magician or juggler. 3 shaman or medicine man.

conk [kɒŋk] *n., v. Slang. —n.* **1** a punch or hit, especially on the head. **2** the head.
—v. punch or hit (someone), especially on the head.
conk out, a *Informal.* of a car, machine, etc., break down suddenly: *The car conked out in the middle of an intersection.* **b** *Informal.* be overcome with fatigue or weakness; collapse: *I'm so tired, I'm about ready to conk out.* **c** *Slang.* die. ⟨prob. < E *conch*⟩
☛ *Hom.* CONCH.

con•ker ['kɒŋkər] *n.* **1 conkers,** a game played by children with chestnuts on strings, to see which can shatter the other when knocked together. **2** a horse chestnut used in this game.
☛ *Hom.* CONQUER.

con man *Slang.* CONFIDENCE MAN.

con mo•to [kɒn 'moutou]; *Italian,* [kɔn 'mɔto] *Italian. Music.* with spirited movement (used as a direction).

con•nate ['kɒneit] *or* [kə'neit] *adj.* **1** existing from birth or origin. **2** having the same origin. **3** *Biology.* united into one body, as leaves at the base. ⟨< L *connatum* born with⟩

con•nect [kə'nɛkt] *v.* **1** join, fasten, or link (one thing to another or two things together); unite: *to connect plumbing pipes.* **2** join in some business or interest; bring into some relation: *This store is connected with a major chain.* **3** think of as being associated: *We usually connect spring with sunshine and flowers.* **4** be or become connected. **5** relate in a meaningful way; be in rapport: *She spoke to us, but did not really connect.* **6** put in communication through a telephone system (*used with* **with**): *Could you please connect me with Mr. LeBlanc's office?* **7** of an airline flight, bus run, etc., be so arranged that passengers can change to another aircraft, bus, etc., without delay. **8** *Informal.* achieve one's aim; be successful, especially in hitting or throwing: *to connect for a home run. His first punch went wild, but the second one connected.* **9** link to an electrical power supply: *See if the lamp is connected before you change the bulb.* ⟨< L *connectere* < *com-* together + *nectere* tie⟩ **—con'nect•er** or **con'nec•tor,** *n.*

con•nect•ed [kə'nɛktɪd] *adj., v. —adj.* **1** joined together; fastened together. **2** joined in orderly sequence or by association: *connected ideas.* **3** having ties and associates: *She is well connected socially.* **4** consanguineous.
—v. pt. and pp. of CONNECT. **—con'nect•ed•ly,** *adv.*
☛ *Usage.* **Connected with** and **in connection with** are wordy expressions, usually for *in* or *with: The social life in connection with a college residence* (in a college residence) *will be something you have never experienced before.*

Con•nec•ti•cut [kə'nɛtəkət] *n.* an east coast state of the United States.

connecting rod a bar connecting two or more moving parts in a machine.

con•nec•tion [kə'nɛkʃən] *n.* **1** the act of connecting or state of being connected. **2** something that connects; a connecting part: *There is a loose connection in the wiring.* **3** any kind of practical relation with another thing or person: *He has no connection with his brother's firm.* **4** Usually, **connections,** *pl.* a group of people with whom one is associated in business dealings, etc.: *He'll probably be able to get tickets through his connections in the city.* **5** mental association; thinking of persons or things together; linking together of words or ideas in a logical order. **6** the scheduled meeting of trains, ships, airplanes, etc., so that passengers can change from one to the other without delay. **7** the train, ship, plane, etc., that connects in this way: *I mustn't miss my connection.* **8** a line of communication between two points in a telephone system: *We had a bad connection and couldn't hear her very well.* **9** a related person; relative: *She is a connection of ours by marriage.* **10** a religious denomination. **11** an electrical circuit.
in connection with, in regard or reference to.
in this (or **that**) **connection,** as regards this (or that) matter.
☛ *Usage.* See note at CONNECTED.

con•nec•tive [kə'nɛktɪv] *adj., n. —adj.* that connects.
—n. **1** something that connects. **2** *Grammar.* a word used to connect words, phrases, and clauses. Conjunctions and relative pronouns are connectives. **3** *Botany.* the tissue joining the two lobes of the anther, that splits open to release pollen.

connective tissue tissue that connects, supports, or encloses other tissues and organs in the body.

con•nie or **co•ny** ['kɒni] *n. Cdn.* inconnu. Also, **coney.**

con•ning tower ['kɒnɪŋ] **1** on a submarine, a small tower on the deck, used as an entrance and as a place for observation. See SUBMARINE for picture. **2** an armoured control station on the deck of a warship, occupied by the captain during battle. **3** any similar observation tower from which supervision can be carried out. ⟨*conning,* ppr. of *con* direct the steering of (a ship), var. of earlier *cond,* shortened from ME *condue, condye* guide < OF *conduire* < L *conducere.* See CONDUCT.⟩

con•nip•tion [kə'nɪpʃən] *n. Informal.* Often, **conniptions,** *pl.* a fit of rage, hysteria, etc.; tantrum. Also, **conniption fit.** ⟨coined in pseudo-Latin⟩

con•niv•ance [kə'naɪvəns] *n.* **1** the act of conniving; pretended ignorance or secret encouragement of wrongdoing. **2** *Law.* guilty assent to or knowledge or encouragement of wrongdoing, without participation in it.

con•nive [kə'naɪv] *v.* **-nived, -niv•ing. 1** shut one's eyes to something wrong; give aid to wrongdoing by not telling of it (*used with* **at**): *The mayor was accused of conniving at the misuse of public funds.* **2** co-operate secretly; conspire (*with*): *The general connived with the enemies of his country.* ⟨< L *connivere* shut the eyes, wink < *com-* together + *niv-* press (related to *nictere* wink)⟩ **—con'niv•er,** *n.*

con•niv•ent [kə'naɪvənt] *adj. Biology.* of wings, petals, etc., converging; pointing toward each other.

con•nois•seur [,kɒnə'sɜr] *n.* a person having thorough knowledge and able to make fine distinctions and critical judgments, especially in art and matters of taste: *a connoisseur of wine, a connoisseur of antique furniture.* ⟨< F *connoisseur* (now *connaisseur*), ult. < L *cognoscere* < *co-* (intensive) + *gnoscere* recognize⟩ **—,con•nois'seur•ship,** *n.*

con•no•ta•tion [,kɒnə'teiʃən] *n.* **1** what is suggested by a word or expression in addition to its basic meaning. The connotations associated with words can determine the emotional effect of a statement, etc., and often indicate the attitude of the speaker or writer. The word *slender,* for instance, usually has a more favourable connotation than *thin.* Compare DENOTATION. **2** the suggestion of a meaning in addition to the basic meaning; the act of connoting.

con•no•ta•tive ['kɒnə,teitɪv] *or* [kə'noutətɪv] *adj.* **1** connoting; having connotation. **2** having to do with connotation. **—'con•no,ta•tive•ly,** *adv.*

con•note [kə'nout] *v.* **-not•ed, -not•ing.** suggest in addition to the literal meaning; imply. *Portly, corpulent,* and *obese* all mean 'fleshy'; but *portly* connotes dignity; *corpulent,* bulk; and *obese,* an unpleasant excess of fat. ⟨< Med.L *connotare* < L *com-* with + *notare* to note⟩

con•nu•bi•al [kə'njubiəl] *or* [kə'nubiəl] *adj.* of or having to do with marriage. ⟨< L *connubialis* < *connubium* marriage < *com-* (intensive) + *nubere* marry⟩ **—con'nu•bi•al•ly,** *adv.*

co•no•dont ['kounə,dɒnt] *or* ['kɒnə,dɒnt] *n.* a very small Paleozoic fossil, shaped like a tooth, and being the remains of an extinct marine animal of the order Conodonta. ⟨< G *konodont* < Gk. *konos* cone + *odous, odontos* tooth⟩

co•noid ['kounɔɪd] *adj., n. —adj.* shaped like a cone.
—n. **1** *Geometry.* a surface formed by the revolution of a conic section about its axis. **2** something shaped like a cone, such as the end of a bullet. ⟨< Gk. *kōnoeidēs* < *kōnos* cone + *eidos* form⟩

co•noi•dal [kə'nɔɪdəl] *adj.* conoid.

con•quer ['kɒŋkər] *v.* **1** get by fighting; win in war: *to conquer a country.* **2** overcome by force; defeat; get the better of: *to conquer an enemy, to conquer a bad habit.* **3** be victorious; be the conqueror: *The general said he would conquer or die.* ⟨ME < OF *conquerre* < L *conquaerere* < *com-* (intensive) + *quaerere* seek⟩ **—'con•quer•a•ble,** *adj.*
☛ *Syn.* See note at DEFEAT.
☛ *Hom.* CONKER.

con•quer•or ['kɒŋkərər] *n.* **1** a person who conquers, especially in war. **2 the Conqueror,** King William I of England. As Duke of Normandy, he conquered England in 1066, and reigned as king till his death in 1087.

con•quest ['kɒŋkwɛst] *or* ['kɒnkwɛst] *n.* **1** the act of conquering. **2** the thing conquered; land, people, etc., conquered. **3** a person whose love or favour has been won. **4 the Conquest, a** the gaining of the English throne by William, Duke of Normandy, in 1066. **b** *Cdn.* the British takeover of French possessions in North America with the signing of the Treaty of Paris in 1763. ⟨ME < OF *conqueste* < *conquest,* pp. of *conquerre.* See CONQUER.⟩
☛ *Syn.* **1.** See note at VICTORY.

A Spanish conquistador of the 16th century

con•quis•ta•dor [kɒn'kistə,dɔr], [kɒn'kwɪstə,dɔr] *or* [kɒŋ'kwɪstə,dɔr] *n., pl.* **-dors** or **-dores** [-'dɔriz] *or* [-'dɔreis]. **1** one of the Spanish conquerors who came to South America and the southern parts of North America in the 16th century to look for gold. The conquistadors conquered the Indian civilizations of Mexico and South America in their search for treasure. **2** any conqueror. ⟨< Sp. *conquistador* < *conquistar* conquer⟩

con•san•guin•e•ous [,kɒnsæŋ'gwɪniəs] *adj.* descended from the same parent or ancestor; related by blood. ⟨< L *consanguineus* < *com-* together + *sanguis, -guinis* blood⟩ **—,con•san'guin•e•ous•ly,** *adv.*

con•san•guin•i•ty [,kɒnsæŋ'gwɪnəti] *n.* **1** relationship by descent from the same parent or ancestor; relationship by blood; genetic relationship: *Siblings and cousins are united by ties of consanguinity.* **2** any close relationship or connection.

con•science ['kɒnʃəns] *n.* **1** the sense or awareness of moral right and wrong with respect to one's own conduct or intentions, including the feeling that one ought to do what is right: *Her conscience prompted her to return the book she had stolen.* **2** habitual obedience to the dictates of conscience: *A person of conscience would not have acted in that way.*
in (all) conscience, a honourably; fairly. **b** surely; certainly.
on (one's) **conscience,** troubling one's conscience; making one feel guilty: *Her theft of the book had been on her conscience for a long time.* ⟨ME < OF < L *conscientia* < *conscire* < *com-* with + *scire* know⟩ **—'con•science•less,** *adj.*

conscience money money paid voluntarily by a person whose conscience bothers him or her because of some dishonest act or a feeling of moral responsibility for an accident, etc.

con•science–strick•en ['kɒnʃəns ,strɪkən] *adj.* suffering from a feeling of having done wrong.

con•sci•en•tious [,kɒnʃi'ɛnʃəs] *adj.* **1** careful to do what one knows is right; controlled by conscience. **2** done carefully and properly: *Conscientious work is careful and exact.* **—,con•sci'en•tious•ly,** *adv.* **—,con•sci'en•tious•ness,** *n.*

conscientious objector a person whose beliefs do not let him or her act as a combatant in time of war.

con•scion•a•ble ['kɒnʃənəbəl] *adj.* according to conscience; just. **—'con•scion•a•bly,** *adv.*

con•scious ['kɒnʃəs] *adj.* **1** aware; knowing: *conscious of a sharp pain.* **2** capable of thought, will, or feeling: *A human being is a conscious animal.* **3** mentally awake: *After about five minutes he became conscious again.* **4** known to oneself; felt: *conscious guilt.* **5** meant; intended; deliberate: *a conscious lie. She's making a conscious effort to improve her writing.* **6** self-conscious; preoccupied with oneself. **7** attentive to or concerned with (*often used in compounds*): *clothes-conscious.* ⟨< L *conscius* < *conscire* < *com-* (intensive) + *scire* know⟩ **—'con•scious•ly,** *adv.*

☛ *Syn.* **1. Conscious,** AWARE = knowing that something exists. **Conscious** emphasizes the idea of realizing or knowing in one's mind that one sees, feels, hears, etc., something either physically or emotionally: *She was conscious of a great uneasiness.* **Aware** emphasizes the idea of noticing something one sees, smells, hears, tastes, feels, or is told: *I was conscious that someone was talking, but not aware of what was being said.*

con•scious•ness ['kɒnʃəsnɪs] *n.* **1** the state of being conscious; awareness. People and animals have consciousness; plants and stones do not. **2** all the thoughts and feelings of a person or group of people: *the moral consciousness of our generation.* **3** awareness of what is going on about one; being awake: *A severe shock often makes a person lose consciousness for a time.* **4** *Philosophy.* the power of the mind, whether rational or not, to be aware of acts, sensations, emotions, etc. **5** *Psychology.* the mental activity of which the individual is aware, in contrast to unconscious mental activity.

con•scious•ness–rais•ing ['kɒnʃəsnɪs,reizɪŋ] *n.* the process of making a person aware of his or her condition, needs, potential, etc., in order to bring about change: *The main thrust of the campaign was consciousness-raising about mental illness.*

con•script *v.* [kən'skrɪpt]; *adj. and n.* ['kɒnskrɪpt] *v., adj., n.* *—v.* **1** compel by law to enlist in the armed forces; draft. **2** take for government use: *The dictator proposed to conscript both capital and labour.* **3** *Informal.* compel to help or participate; enlist by force: *We were conscripted to do the dishes.*
—adj. conscripted; drafted.
—n. a person who has been conscripted. ⟨< L *conscriptus*, pp. of *conscribere* < *com-* (intensive) + *scribere* write⟩

conscript fathers ['kɒnskrɪpt] **1** in ancient Rome, the senators. **2** *Poetic.* the senators or legislators of any nation.

con•scrip•tion [kən'skrɪpʃən] *n.* **1** the compulsory enlistment of people in the armed forces; draft. **2** the act or system of forcing contributions of money, labour, or other service to the government or as the government directs.

con•se•crate ['kɒnsə,kreit] *v.* **-crat•ed, -crat•ing;** *adj. —v.* **1** set apart as sacred; make holy: *A church is consecrated to God.* **2** ordain (someone) to a sacred office, especially that of bishop. **3** make an object of veneration or cherished regard; hallow: *Time has consecrated these customs.* **4** devote to a purpose; dedicate: *He has consecrated his life to music.*
—adj. Archaic. consecrated. ⟨< L *consecrare* < *com-* (intensive) + *sacer* sacred⟩ **—'con•se,cra•tor,** *n.*

☛ *Syn. v.* **1, 4.** See note at DEVOTE.

con•se•crat•ed ['kɒnsə,kreitɪd] *adj., v. —adj.* set apart as sacred; made holy.
—v. pt. and pp. of CONSECRATE.

con•se•cra•tion [,kɒnsə'kreiʃən] *n.* **1** the act of consecrating or the condition of being consecrated. **2** an ordination to a sacred office, especially to that of bishop.

con•sec•u•tive [kən'sɛkjətɪv] *adj.* **1** following without interruption; successive: *Monday, Tuesday, and Wednesday are consecutive days.* **2** characterized by logical order; proceeding from one part to another in logical sequence: *consecutive reasoning.* **3** *Music.* of or designating intervals of the same kind following each other: *consecutive thirds, fifths, octaves, etc.* ⟨< F *consécutif* < L *consecutivus* < *consecutus* following closely, pp. of *consequi* < *com-* (intensive) + *sequi* follow⟩ **—con'sec•u•tive•ly,** *adv.* **—con'sec•u•tive•ness,** *n.*

☛ *Syn.* **1.** See note at SUCCESSIVE.

con•sen•su•al [kən'sɛnʃuəl] *adj.* **1** existing or done by mutual consent. **2** of or having to do with a consensus.

con•sen•sus [kən'sɛnsəs] *n.* general agreement. The consensus of opinion means the opinion of all or most of the people consulted. ⟨< L *consenus* < *consentire.* See CONSENT.⟩

con•sent [kən'sɛnt] *v., n. —v.* agree; give approval or permission: *My mother would not consent to my leaving school.*
—n. agreement; approval; permission. ⟨ME < OF *consentir* < L *consentire* < *com-* together + *sentire* feel, think⟩

☛ *Syn. v.* **Consent,** ASSENT, CONCUR = agree. **Consent** = agree *to* something asked for, by giving approval or permission willingly or by giving in to the wishes of others: *She consented to run for president.* **Assent** = agree with something stated or put forward for consideration, by accepting it or expressing agreement: *He assented to the suggested change in plans.* **Concur** = agree with others, by having the same opinion: *The majority concurred in the decision to raise the dues.*

con•sen•ti•ent [kən'sɛnʃənt] *adj.* having the same opinion; agreeing. ⟨< L *consentiens* ppr. of *consentire* < *com-* with + *sentire* to feel⟩

con•se•quence ['kɒnsə,kwɛns] *or* ['kɒnsəkwəns] *n.* **1** a result of some previous action or occurrence; effect: *The consequence of breaking his leg was the loss of his job.* **2** a logical result; deduction; inference. **3** importance: *This matter is of little consequence.* **4** importance in rank or position: *She is a person of consequence in the community.* **5** the relationship between cause and effect; the quality or fact of being consequent.
in consequence (of), as a result (of).
take the consequences, accept any undesirable results of one's actions: *Do it your way if you like, but you'll have to take the consequences if it doesn't work out.*

☛ *Syn.* **1.** See note at EFFECT. **3.** See note at IMPORTANCE.

con•se•quent ['kɒnsəkwənt] *or* ['kɒnsə,kwɛnt] *adj., n. —adj.* **1** following as a natural result or effect; resulting: *His illness and consequent absence put him behind in his work.* **2** following logical sequence; logically consistent: *the consequent development of an idea.*
consequent on or **upon, a** resulting from. **b** inferable from.
—n. **1** anything that follows something else; result; effect. **2** *Mathematics.* the second term of a ratio. In the ratio 1:4, 4 is the consequent, and 1 the antecedent. **3** *Logic.* the second term, or conclusion, of a conditional proposition. **4** *Logic.* an inference. ⟨< L *consequens, -entis,* ppr. of *consequi.* See CONSECUTIVE.⟩

con•se•quen•tial [,kɒnsə'kwɛnʃəl] *adj.* **1** following as an effect; resulting. **2** having importance. **3** self-important; pompous. **—,con•se'quen•tial•ly,** *adv.* **—,con•se'quen•tial•ness,** *n.*

con•se•quent•ly ['kɒnsə,kwɛntli] *or* ['kɒnsəkwəntli] *adv.* as a result; therefore.
☛ *Syn.* See note at THEREFORE.

con•serv•an•cy [kən'sɜrvənsi] *n., pl.* **-cies.** an organization or area designed to conserve and protect natural resources, wildlife, etc.

con•ser•va•tion [,kɒnsər'veiʃən] *n.* **1** a preserving from harm or decay; protecting from loss or from being used up: *the conservation of natural resources.* **2** the official protection and care of forests, rivers, wildlife, etc. **3** CONSERVATION AREA.

conservation area a forest, etc., or a part of it, under official protection and care and usually open for outdoor recreational use. Also, **conservation.**

con•ser•va•tion•ist [,kɒnsər'veiʃənɪst] *n.* a person who believes in and advocates conservation of the forests, rivers, wildlife, etc., of a country.

conservation of energy *Physics.* the principle that the total amount of energy in the universe does not vary, although energy can be changed from one form into another.

conservation of mass or **matter** *Physics.* the principle that the total mass of any closed system remains unchanged by reactions within the system. Thus, in a chemical reaction, matter is neither created nor destroyed but changed from one form to another.

conservation of momentum *Physics.* the principle that the total momentum in any closed system remains unchanged by interactions within the system.

conservation of number *Education.* the principle that a number of items remains constant whether they are spread out or bunched together. Understanding this principle is a cognitive milestone in children.

conservation of volume *Education.* the principle that a volume of liquid remains constant whatever the shape of the container. Understanding this principle is a cognitive milestone in children.

con•serv•a•tism [kən'sɜrvə,tɪzəm] *n.* **1** an inclination to keep things as they are; opposition to change. **2** Often, **Conservatism,** the principles and practices of a conservative political party.

con•serv•a•tive [kən'sɜrvətɪv] *adj., n. —adj.* **1** inclined to keep things as they are or were in the past; opposed to change. **2** Often, **Conservative, a** of or referring to a political party that opposes changes in national institutions. **b** of Conservatives or their policies. **c** of or belonging to a branch of Judaism which accepts moderate adaptation to the modern mainstream. **3** cautious; moderate: *conservative business methods, a conservative estimate.* **4** free from novelties and fads: *It is economical to choose suits of a conservative style.* **5** having the power to preserve from harm or decay; conserving; preserving.
—n. **1** a conservative person. **2** Often, **Conservative, a** a member of a conservative political party. **b** in Canada, a member of the Progressive Conservative Party, one of the principal political groups; a person who supports the views and principles of this party. **c** in the United Kingdom, a member of the Conservative Party. **3** a means of preserving. **—con'serv•a•tive•ly,** *adv.* **—con'serv•a•tive•ness,** *n.*

Conservative Party 1 in the United Kingdom, a political party that favours existing national institutions or a return to some of those recently existing. **2** in Canada, the Progressive Conservative Party.

con•serv•a•tize [kən'sərvə,taɪz] *v.* **-tized, -tiz•ing.** cause to be conservative, politically or socially.

con•serv•a•toire [kən,sɜrvə'twɑr] *n.* a school for instruction in music; conservatory. ⟨< F⟩

con•serv•a•tor [kən'sɜrvə,tɔr], [kən'sɜrvətər], *or* ['kɒnsər,veitər] *n.* **1** a preserver; guardian. **2** one who undertakes the preservation and restoration of art works.

con•serv•a•to•ry [kən'sɜrvə,tɔri] *n., pl.* **-ries. 1** a greenhouse or glass-enclosed room for growing and displaying plants. **2** a school for instruction in music.

con•serve *v.* [kən'sɜrv]; *n.* ['kɒnsɜrv] *or* [kən'sɜrv] *v.* **-served, -serv•ing;** *n. —v.* **1** keep from harm or decay; protect from loss or from being used up. **2** preserve (fruit) with sugar.
—n. Often, **conserves,** *pl.* preserves or jam, especially when made from a mixture of different fruits. ⟨ME < OF *conserve, conserver* < L *conservare* < *com-* (intensive) + *servare* preserve⟩ **—con'serv•a•ble,** *adj.* **—con'serv•er,** *n.*

con•sid•er [kən'sɪdər] *v.* **1** think about in order to decide; examine: *Take time to consider the problem.* **2** think to be; think of as: *We consider E.J. Pratt a great Canadian poet.* **3** allow for; take into account: *This watch runs very well, if you consider how old it is.* **4** be thoughtful of (others and their feelings). **5** think carefully; reflect: *She considered for a while before answering.* **6** think highly of; esteem. **7** look at carefully; gaze at. **8** conclude upon reflection. **9** entertain in the mind as a possibility or option: *Would you consider home-schooling?* ⟨< L *considerare,* originally, examine the stars < *com-* (intensive) + *sidus* star; with reference to augury⟩
☛ *Syn.* **1. Consider,** STUDY, WEIGH = think about something in order to decide. **Consider** = think something over, to give it some careful thought before making a decision about it: *He considered going to college.* **Study** = think out, to consider with serious attention to details: *He studied ways to support himself.* **Weigh** = balance in the mind, to consider carefully both or all sides of an idea or action: *He weighed the idea of going to the local junior college.*

con•sid•er•a•ble [kən'sɪdərəbəl] *adj., n. —adj.* **1** rather large in amount, extent, number, etc.: *a considerable sum of money. She has considerable influence in political circles.* **2** worthy of regard; important: *the most considerable poet of the age.*
—n. Dialect or informal. a large quantity or amount: *We paid considerable for it.*
☛ *Usage.* **Considerable,** CONSIDERABLY. In formal and informal writing, it is important to distinguish between the adverb **considerably** and the adjective **considerable:** *The teacher's explanation helped them considerably* (modifies verb *helped*). *The teacher's explanation was of considerable help to them* (modifies noun *help*).

con•sid•er•a•bly [kən'sɪdərəbli] *adv.* a good deal; much.
☛ *Usage.* See note at CONSIDERABLE.

con•sid•er•ate [kən'sɪdərɪt] *adj.* thoughtful of others and their feelings. **—con'sid•er•ate•ly,** *adv.* **—con'sid•er•ate•ness,** *n.*
☛ *Syn.* See note at THOUGHTFUL.

con•sid•er•a•tion [kən,sɪdə'reiʃən] *n.* **1** careful thought about something before making a decision: *Please give careful consideration to this question.* **2** something thought of as a reason; something to be considered: *Price and quality are two important considerations in buying anything.* **3** money or other payment: *She said she would cut the grass for a small consideration.* **4** thoughtfulness for others and their feelings. **5** importance.
in consideration of, a in view of: *In consideration of his wife's poor health, he moved to a milder climate.* **b** in return for: *She gave him a present in consideration of his helpfulness.*
on no consideration, not at all; never.
take into consideration, allow for; take into account; consider: *The judge took the boy's age into consideration.*
under consideration, being thought about.

con•sid•ered [kən'sɪdərd] *adj., v. —adj.* **1** carefully thought out: *in my considered opinion.* **2** honoured; respected: *She is highly considered as a poet.*
—v. pt. and pp. of CONSIDER.

con•sid•er•ing [kən'sɪdərɪŋ] *prep., adv., v. —prep.* taking into account; making allowance for: *Considering her age, she reads well.*
—adv. taking everything into account: *He does very well, considering.*
—v. ppr. of CONSIDER.

con•sign [kən'saɪn] *v.* **1** hand over; deliver: *The man was consigned to prison. The father consigned the child to her sister's care.* **2** transmit; send: *The order will be consigned to them by express.* **3** set apart; assign. ⟨< F *consigner* < L *consignare* furnish with a seal < *com-* with + *signum* seal⟩ **—con'sign•a•ble,** *adj.* **—,con•sig'na•tion** [,kɒnsɪg'neiʃən], *n.*
☛ *Syn.* **1.** See note at COMMIT.

con•sign•ee [,kɒnsaɪ'ni] *or* [kən'saɪni] *n.* the person or company to whom goods are consigned.

con•sign•er [kən'saɪnər] *n.* consignor.

con•sign•ment [kən'saɪnmənt] *n.* **1** the act of consigning. **2** a shipment sent to a person or company for safekeeping or sale.
on consignment, of goods, sent to a retailer under an arrangement by which the retailer does not pay the distributor until the goods have been sold.

con•sign•or [kən'saɪnər] *or* [ˌkɒnsaɪ'nɔr] *n.* a person or company who consigns goods to another. Also, **consigner.**

con•sist [kən'sɪst] *v., n.* —*v.* **1** be made up; be formed: *A week consists of seven days.* **2** agree; be in harmony.
consist in, have a basis in or be defined by; have its existence in: *Happiness for me consists in being left alone.*
—*n. Cdn.* **1** the way in which a train is made up; the arrangement of cars, etc., in a train. **2** the billing of goods being carried in a train. ⟨< L *consistere* come to a stand, exist, consist < *com-* together + *sistere* stand⟩

con•sist•en•cy [kən'sɪstənsi] *n., pl.* **-cies. 1** holding together; firmness or density. **2** degree of firmness or density: *Icing for a cake must be of the right consistency to spread easily without dripping.* **3** adherence to a single set of principles, course of action, etc.: *He was much admired for his consistency of purpose.* **4** harmony; agreement; accordance: *It's not always easy to maintain consistency between principles and practice.* Also, **consistence.**

con•sist•ent [kən'sɪstənt] *adj.* **1** keeping or inclined to keep to the same principles, course of action, etc.: *What a consistent person says or does today agrees with what he or she said or did yesterday.* **2** in agreement; in accord; compatible: *Driving an automobile at very high speed is not consistent with safety. So much noise is not consistent with comfort.* **3** of uniformly good quality. **4** *Mathematics.* having at least one common solution, as of two or more equations or inequalities. **—con'sist•ent•ly,** *adv.*

con•sis•to•ry [kən'sɪstəri] *n., pl.* **-ries.** *Christianity.* **1** a church council or court, especially, **a** one composed of the Pope and cardinals; the College of Cardinals. **b** the minister and elders or deacons of a congregation in any of various Reformed traditions. **2** a meeting of such a council or court. **3** the place where it meets. ⟨< ONF *consistorie* < L *consistorium* place of assembly < *consistere.* See CONSIST.⟩ **—ˌcon•sis'to•ri•al** [ˌkɒnsɪ'stɔriəl], *adj.*

con•so•la•tion [ˌkɒnsə'leiʃən] *n., adj.* —*n.* **1** comfort. **2** a comforting person, thing, or event.
—*adj.* between losers in an earlier round of a tournament: *a consolation match.*

consolation prize a prize given to a person or team that has not won but has done well.

con•sol•a•to•ry [kən'sɒlə,tɔri] *adj.* consoling; comforting.

con•sole¹ [kən'soul] *v.* **-soled, -sol•ing.** comfort. ⟨< L *consolari* < *com-* (intensive) + *solari* soothe⟩ **—con'sol•a•ble,** *adj.* **—con'sol•er,** *n.* **—con'sol•ing•ly,** *adv.*
☛ *Syn.* See note at COMFORT.

con•sole² ['kɒnsoul] *n.* **1** the desklike part of an organ, containing the keyboard, stops, and pedals. **2** a cabinet for a television set, record player, or radio made to stand on the floor. **3** a panel of buttons, switches, dials, etc., used to control electrical or other apparatus; control panel. **4** *Architecture.* a heavy, ornamental bracket. **5** a panel between the bucket seats of a car, containing controls or storage. ⟨< F⟩

con•sole table ['kɒnsoul] **1** a table supported against a wall by one or more consoles, or brackets. **2** any narrow table designed to be placed against a wall, often having curved or carved legs at the front that resemble consoles.

con•sol•i•date [kən'sɒlə,deit] *v.* **-dat•ed, -dat•ing. 1** unite; combine; merge: *The two territories were consolidated by the government into one administrative district.* **2** make secure; strengthen: *to consolidate an empire. The army spent a day in consolidating its gains by digging trenches.* **3** make or become solid. ⟨< L *consolidare* < *com-* (intensive) + *solidus* solid⟩ **—con'sol•i,dat•or,** *n.*

con•sol•i•dat•ed [kən'sɒlə,deitɪd] *adj., v.* —*adj.* united; combined.
—*v.* pt. and pp. of CONSOLIDATE.

Consolidated Revenue Fund *Cdn.* the pooled income of the Federal Government.

consolidated school a school for pupils from several school districts; a school built to replace two or more smaller ones, especially in country districts, so as to provide a greater range of facilities.

con•sol•i•da•tion [kən,sɒlə'deiʃən] *n.* **1** a consolidating or being consolidated. **2** a business merger.

con•sols ['kɒnsɒlz] *or* [kən'sɒlz] *n.pl.* bonds of the government of the United Kingdom. ⟨short for *consolidated annuities*⟩

con•som•mé ['kɒnsə,mei] *or* [ˌkɒnsə'mei] *n.* a clear soup made by boiling meat with seasoning and, sometimes, vegetables in water. It gels when cooled. ⟨< F *consommé,* pp. of *consommer* < L *consummare* finish. See CONSUMMATE.⟩

con•so•nance ['kɒnsənəns] *n.* **1** harmony; agreement; accordance. **2** *Music.* harmony of sounds; a simultaneous combination of tones that is agreeable to the ear. Compare DISSONANCE. **3** a partial rhyme in which the consonant sounds are alike but the vowels are different. *Examples: lame/loam, seed/side.* Also, **consonancy.**

con•so•nant ['kɒnsənənt] *n., adj.* —*n.* **1** a speech sound formed by completely or partially blocking the breath; a sound that is not a vowel. All languages have both consonants and vowels. The first and last sounds in *tab* are consonants. **2** a symbol, including any letter of the alphabet, that represents such a sound.
—*adj.* **1** harmonious; in agreement; in accord. **2** *Music.* characterized by consonance; agreeing in sound. **3** consonantal. ⟨< L *consonans, -antis,* ppr. of *consonare* < *com-* together + *sonare* sound⟩ **—'con•so•nant•ly,** *adv.*

con•so•nan•tal [ˌkɒnsə'næntəl] *adj.* having to do with a consonant or its sound.

consonant shift a historical phonological change affecting one or more consonants in a language or in a related group of languages. The change from velar to palatal in the Satem languages is the result of a consonant shift, as is the development of Indo-European [p] into [f] in the Germanic languages.

con•sort *n.* ['kɒnsɔrt]; *v.* [kən'sɔrt] *n., v.* —*n.* **1** a husband or wife, especially of a monarch. **2** an associate. **3** a ship accompanying another; an escort vessel. **4** *Music.* a group of instruments of the same kind but different sizes: *a consort of viols, a recorder consort.*
—*v.* **1** keep company; associate: *Do not consort with thieves.* **2** agree; accord. **3** accompany; escort. ⟨< MF < L *consors, -ortis* sharer < *com-* with + *sors* lot⟩

con•sor•ti•um [kən'sɔrʃəm] *or* [kən'sɔrtiəm] *n., pl.* **-ti•a** [-ʃə] *or* [-tiə]. **1** a partnership; association. **2** an agreement among bankers of several nations to give financial aid to another nation. **3** a group, association, etc., formed by such an agreement. **4** an alliance of companies for a specific business undertaking. **5** *Law.* the legal right of a married couple to support and companionship from each other. ⟨< L *consortium* partnership⟩

con•spe•ci•fic [ˌkɒnspə'sɪfɪk] *adj., n.* —*adj.* belonging to the same species.
—*n.* an organism which is of the same species as another.

con•spec•tus [kən'spɛktəs] *n.* **1** a general or comprehensive view. **2** a short summary or outline of a subject; digest; résumé. ⟨< L *conspectus* < *com-* + *specere* look at⟩

con•spic•u•ous [kən'spɪkjuəs] *adj.* **1** easily seen; obvious or showy: *A traffic sign should be conspicuous.* **2** attracting attention; striking or remarkable: *conspicuous gallantry, a conspicuous lack of tact.* ⟨< L *conspicuus* visible < *conspicere* < *com-* (intensive) + *specere* look at⟩ **—con'spic•u•ous•ly,** *adv.* **—con'spic•u•ous•ness,** *n.*
☛ *Syn.* **1.** See note at PROMINENT.

conspicuous consumption lavish spending, especially with the purpose of impressing others.

con•spir•a•cy [kən'spirəsi] *n., pl.* **-cies. 1** a secret scheming or planning together to do something treacherous or evil. **2** the plot or scheme itself: *The conspiracy was revealed as a result of a neighbour's complaint.* **3** the people taking part in such a plot or scheme. **4** *Law.* an agreement between two or more persons to commit an illegal act: *The four contractors were charged with conspiracy to commit fraud.* **5** a happening or acting together as if by design: *It was a conspiracy of the elements to ruin our camping trip.*

con•spir•a•tor [kən'spirətər] *n.* a person who conspires; plotter: *A group of conspirators planned to kill the dictator.*

con•spir•a•to•ri•al [kən,spirə'tɔriəl] *adj.* having to do with conspiracy or conspirators.

con•spire [kən'spaɪr] *v.* **-spired, -spir•ing. 1** plan secretly with others to do something wrong; plot. **2** act together, as if by design: *The rain, the cold, and the mosquitoes conspired to ruin the concert in the park. All things conspired to make her birthday a*

happy one. ⟨ME < OF *conspirer* < L *conspirare* < *com-* together + *spirare* breathe⟩ **—con'spir•er,** *n.*
☛ *Syn.* **1.** See note at PLOT.

con spi•ri•to [kɒn 'spiri,tou] *Music.* to be played with spirit and verve.

const. *Mathematics.* constant.

Const. Constable.

con•sta•ble ['kɒnstəbəl] *n.* **1** a police officer, especially a police officer of the lowest rank. **2** especially in medieval England and France, the chief officer of a royal household. **3** the keeper of a royal fortress or castle. ⟨ME < OF *conestable* < LL *comes stabuli* count of the stable; later, chief household officer⟩

con•stab•u•lar•y [kən'stæbjə,lɛri] *n., pl.* **-lar•ies;** *adj. —n.* **1** the constables of a district. **2** a police force organized like an army; provincial police.
—adj. of the constables of a district; of police officers or a police force.

con•stan•cy ['kɒnstənsi] *n.* **1** the condition of being always the same; absence of change. **2** firmness in belief or feeling; faithfulness; loyalty. **3** unceasingness.

con•stant ['kɒnstənt] *adj., n. —adj.* **1** always the same; not changing: *If you walk due north, your direction is constant.* **2** never stopping; incessant; continuous or continual: *three days of constant rain, a constant smoker. The clock makes a constant ticking sound.* **3** faithful; loyal; steadfast: *A constant friend helps you when you are in trouble.* **4** *Mathematics and physics.* retaining the same value; remaining the same in quantity, size, etc.: *a constant force.*
—n. **1** something that is always the same; a number or quantity that does not change. **2** *Mathematics.* a quantity assumed to be invariable throughout a given calculation or discussion. See ABSOLUTE CONSTANT and ARBITRARY CONSTANT. **3** *Physics.* a numerical quantity expressing a relation or value, as of a physical property of a substance, that remains unchanged under certain conditions. ⟨ME < OF < L *constans, -antis,* ppr. of *constare* stand firm < *com-* (intensive) + *stare* stand⟩ **—'con•stant•ly,** *adv.*
☛ *Syn. adj.* **3.** See note at FAITHFUL.

con•stan•tan ['kɒnstən,tæn] *n.* an alloy of copper and nickel, used in rheostats and thermocouples. It resists expansion.

con•stel•late ['kɒnstə,leit] *v.* **-lat•ed, -lat•ing.** cluster together in or as if in a constellation.

con•stel•la•tion [,kɒnstə'leiʃən] *n.* **1** *Astronomy.* **a** any of the 88 recognized groups of stars traditionally thought of as forming outlines of animals, objects, or persons: *The Big Dipper is in the constellation Ursa Major.* **b** the part of the heavens occupied by such a group. **2** *Astrology.* the relative position of the planets at the time of a person's birth. **3** a brilliant gathering: *There was a constellation of ministers and ambassadors at the reception.* **4** *Psychology.* a cluster of associated thoughts and impressions which can be grouped around one basic idea. ⟨< LL *constellatio, -onis* < L *com-* together + *stella* star⟩

con•ster•nate ['kɒnstər,neit] *v.* **-nat•ed, -nat•ing,** fill with consternation; dismay.

con•ster•na•tion [,kɒnstər'neiʃən] *n.* great dismay; paralysing or bewildering terror: *To our consternation the train rushed on toward the burning bridge.* ⟨< L *consternatio, -onis* < *consternare* terrify, var. of *consternere* lay low < *com-* (intensive) + *sternere* strew⟩
☛ *Syn.* See note at DISMAY.

con•sti•pate ['kɒnstə,peit] *v.* **-pat•ed, -pat•ing.** cause constipation in. ⟨< L *constipare* < *com-* together + *stipare* press. Doublet of COSTIVE.⟩

con•sti•pat•ed ['kɒnstə,peitɪd] *adj., v. —adj.* having constipation.
—v. pt. and pp. of CONSTIPATE.

con•sti•pa•tion [,kɒnstə'peiʃən] *n.* a condition in which the bowels are sluggish or inactive, so that it is difficult or impossible to discharge solid waste from the body.

con•stit•u•en•cy [kən'stɪtʃuənsi] *n., pl.* **-cies. 1** a district represented by a single member in a legislature. Each federal constituency, or riding, in Canada is represented by a member of parliament. **2** the body of voters in such a district. **3** the people who support or are served by a business, institution, etc.

con•stit•u•ent [kən'stɪtʃuənt] *adj., n. —adj.* **1** forming a necessary part; necessary in the composition; composing: *Flour, liquid, salt, and yeast are constituent parts of bread.* **2** appointing; electing. **3** having the power to make or change a political constitution: *a constituent assembly.*
—n. **1** a necessary part of a whole; ingredient; component. **2** a person who has the right to vote or appoint; a voter in a constituency: *Many of the MP's constituents protested her stand on the issue.* **3** *Linguistics.* part of a word, phrase, or sentence. ⟨< L *constituens, -entis,* ppr. of *constituere.* See CONSTITUTE.⟩
☛ *Syn. n.* **1.** See note at ELEMENT.

con•sti•tute ['kɒnstə,tjut], ['kɒnstə,tut], *or* ['kɒnstə,tʃut] *v.* **-tut•ed, -tut•ing. 1** make up; form: *Seven days constitute a week. Hailstorms constitute a serious threat to standing crops.* **2** be in fact; be equivalent to: *Failure to pay constitutes a debt. Your remarks constitute blackmail.* **3** appoint; elect: *Mr. Chang was constituted president of the Home and School Association.* **4** set up; found; establish: *Our association has been constituted as a social and recreational organization.* **5** make by combining parts; frame: *The cabin is well constituted and will withstand the severest weather.* **6** give legal form to: *to constitute a lease.* ⟨< L *constitutus,* pp. of *constituere* < *com-* (intensive) + *statuere* set up⟩ **—'con•sti,tu•tor,** *n.*

con•sti•tu•tion [,kɒnstə'tjuʃən], [,kɒnstə'tuʃən], *or* [,kɒnstə'tʃuʃən] *n.* **1** a person's physical or mental nature or make-up: *A person with a good constitution is strong and healthy.* **2** the way in which anything is organized; structure: *The constitution of the world is the arrangement of all the things in it.* **3** the system of fundamental principles according to which a nation, state, or group is governed: *Our club has a written constitution.* **4** a document stating these principles. **5 the Constitution,** the fundamental rules by which Canada is governed. **6** an appointing; making. **7** a setting up; establishment. **8** a law; decree.

Constitution Act 1867 since 1981, the name of the BRITISH NORTH AMERICA ACT.

con•sti•tu•tion•al [,kɒnstə'tjuʃənəl] *or* [,kɒnstə'tuʃənəl] *adj., n. —adj.* **1** of or in the constitution of a person or thing: *A constitutional weakness makes him subject to colds.* **2** of, in, or according to the constitution of a nation, state, or group: *Some lawyers are experts in constitutional law.* **3** adhering to or supporting a constitution. **4** for one's health.
—n. Informal. a walk or other exercise taken for one's health. **—,con•sti'tu•tion•al•ly,** *adv.*

con•sti•tu•tion•al•i•ty [,kɒnstə,tjuʃə'næləti], [,kɒnstə,tuʃə'næləti], *or* [,kɒnstə,tʃuʃə'næləti] *n.* accordance with the constitution of a nation, state, or group: *The constitutionality of the new law was disputed.*

constitutional monarchy a monarchy in which the ruler has only the powers given to him or her by the constitution and laws of the nation.

con•sti•tu•tive ['kɒnstə,tjutɪv] *or* ['kɒnstə,tutɪv] *adj.* **1** having power to establish or enact. **2** making a thing what it is; formative; constituent; essential. **—'con•sti,tu•tive•ly,** *adv.*

con•strain [kən'strein] *v.* **1** force or compel physically or by moral means: *She was constrained to accept her employer's decision or leave her job.* **2** confine; imprison. **3** repress; restrain. ⟨ME < OF *constreindre* < L *constringere* < *com-* together + *stringere* pull tightly⟩ **—con'strain•er,** *n.*

con•strained [kən'streind] *adj., v. —adj.* forced and stiff; unnatural: *a constrained smile.*
—v. pt. and pp. of CONSTRAIN. **—con'strain•ed•ly,** *adv.*

con•straint [kən'streint] *n.* **1** confinement. **2** restraint. **3** a holding back of natural feelings; forced or unnatural manner; embarrassed awkwardness. **4** force; compulsion. ⟨ME < OF *constreinte,* fem. pp. of *constreindre.* See CONSTRAIN.⟩

con•strict [kən'strɪkt] *v.* draw together; contract; compress: *A tourniquet stops the flow of blood by constricting the blood vessels.* ⟨< L *constrictus,* pp. of *constringere.* See CONSTRAIN.⟩

con•stric•tion [kən'strɪkʃən] *n.* **1** the act of drawing together; contraction; compression. **2** a feeling of tightness: *He coughed and complained of a constriction in his chest.* **3** a constricted part. **4** something that constricts.

con•stric•tive [kən'strɪktɪv] *adj.* drawing together; contracting; compressing. **—con'stric•tive•ly,** *adv.*

con•stric•tor [kən'strɪktər] *n.* **1** any snake, such as a boa or python, that kills its prey by squeezing it with its coils. **2** *Anatomy.* a muscle that constricts some part of the body. **3** a person who or thing that constricts.

con•struct *v.* [kən'strʌkt]; *n.* ['kɒnstrʌkt] *v., n. —v.* **1** put together; build. **2** *Mathematics.* draw (a geometrical figure) so as to fulfil given conditions.
—n. **1** something systematically put together or constructed. **2** an idea or concept that integrates or systematizes a variety of facts or perceptions. ⟨< L *constructus,* pp. of *construere* < *com-* together + *struere* pile⟩
☛ *Syn.* **1.** See note at MAKE.

con•struc•tion [kən'strʌkʃən] *n.* **1** the act of constructing, building, or putting together: *Construction will begin in May.* **2** the way in which a thing is constructed. **3** the thing constructed; building. **4** a meaning; interpretation; the act or result of construing: *He put an unfair construction on what she said.* **5** *Grammar.* **a** the arrangement, connection, or relation of words in a sentence, clause, phrase, etc. **b** any meaningful sequence or grouping. **6** an abstract sculpture using various materials.

con•struc•tion•al [kən'strʌkʃənəl] *adj.* having to do with construction; structural. **—con'struc•tion•al•ly,** *adv.*

con•struc•tion•ist [kən'strʌkʃənɪst] *n.* a person who gives a certain interpretation to laws, a constitution, etc.: *a strict constructionist.*

construction paper a type of thick, coloured paper with a texture resembling felt, used for making cutouts or posters, or for drawing.

con•struc•tive [kən'strʌktɪv] *adj.* **1** building up so as to improve; helpful: *People appreciate constructive suggestions, not destructive criticisms.* **2** having to do with construction; structural. **3** *Law.* not done or expressed directly but inferred or construed as such: *constructive fraud.* **—con'struc•tive•ly,** *adv.* **—con'struc•tive•ness,** *n.*

con•struc•tiv•ism [kən'strʌktə,vɪzəm] *n.* an art movement originating in the former Soviet Union in the 1920s, characterized by the abstract arrangement of planes and masses, using materials such as glass and plastic.

con•struc•tiv•ist [kən'strʌktəvɪst] *n., adj. —n.* an artist who follows the principles of constructivism.
—adj. of or having to do with constructivism or constructivists.

con•struc•tor [kən'strʌktər] *n.* a person who constructs; builder.

con•strue [kən'stru] *v.* **-strued, -stru•ing. 1** show the meaning of; explain; interpret: *Different lawyers may construe the same law differently.* **2** put a particular interpretation on: *Her inability to hold a job can only be construed as indifference.* **3** translate. **4** *Grammar.* analyse the arrangement of words in (a sentence, clause, phrase, etc.). **5** *Grammar.* combine in a collocation: *The word* commune, *meaning 'to talk', is construed with* with. ⟨< L *construere.* See CONSTRUCT.⟩ **—con'stru•a•ble,** *adj.*

con•sue•tude ['kɒnswə,tjud] *or* ['kɒnswə,tud] *n.* custom, especially one considered as having the force of law. ⟨ME < L *consuetudo* < *consuescere* to accustom⟩

con•sul ['kɒnsəl] *n.* **1** an official appointed by the government of a country to look after its business interests in a foreign city and also to assist citizens of his or her country living there. **2** in ancient Rome, either of the two chief magistrates of the republic. **3** any of the three chief magistrates of the First Republic of France (1799-1804). ⟨< L *consul,* probably originally, one who consults the senate⟩

con•su•lar ['kɒnsjələr] *or* ['kɒnsələr] *adj.* **1** of or belonging to a consul. **2** serving as a consul; having the duties of a consul.

con•su•late ['kɒnsjəlɪt] *or* ['kɒnsəlɪt] *n.* **1** the official residence or offices of a consul. **2** the duties, authority, and position of a consul. **3** a consul's term of office. **4** government by consuls.

consul general *pl.* **consuls general.** a consul of the highest rank. He or she is stationed at an important place or has authority over several other consuls.

con•sul•ship ['kɒnsəl,ʃɪp] *n.* **1** the duties, authority, and position of a consul. **2** a consul's term of office.

con•sult [kən'sʌlt] *v.* **1** seek information or advice from; refer to: *Consult a dictionary for the meaning of a word.* **2** exchange ideas; talk things over: *He is consulting with his lawyer.* **3** take into consideration; have regard for: *A good ruler consults the interests and feelings of the people.* **4** act as a consultant: *She consults for several companies.* ⟨< L *consultare* < *consulere* take counsel, consult⟩

☛ *Syn.* **2. Consult,** CONFER = talk something over with someone in order to make a decision. **Consult** = talk over something of importance with another or others who are in a position to give wise advice: *He decided to consult with his attorney before buying the property.* **Confer** = exchange ideas, opinions, or information with another, usually as equals: *The manager conferred with the committee of employees.*

con•sul•tan•cy [kən'sʌltənsi] *n.* **1** consultation, especially the work done by a professional consultant. **2** the position of a consultant. *They offered her a consultancy with the Board of Education.*

con•sult•and [kən'sʌltənd] *n.* an individual seeking advice from a consultant.

con•sult•ant [kən'sʌltənt] *n.* a person who gives professional or technical advice: *a medical consultant.*

con•sul•ta•tion [,kɒnsəl'teiʃən] *n.* **1** the act of consulting; act of seeking information or advice. **2** a meeting to exchange ideas or talk things over.

con•sult•a•tive [kən'sʌltətɪv] *adj.* having to do with consultation; advisory.

con•sult•ing [kən'sʌltɪŋ] *adj., v. —adj.* **1** that consults or asks advice. **2** employed in giving professional advice: *a consulting engineer.*
—v. ppr. of CONSULT.

con•sum•a•ble [kən'sjuməbəl] *or* [kən'suməbəl] *adj., n.*
—adj. intended to be used up: *consumable supplies.*
—n. an article that is intended to be used up: *Government offices have been told to cut expenditures on paper, pencils, and other consumables.*

con•sume [kən'sjum] *or* [kən'sum] *v.* **-sumed, -sum•ing. 1** eat or drink up. **2** purchase (goods) for one's own consumption. **3** destroy; burn up. **4** use up; spend: *A student consumes much time in studying.* **5** waste (time, money, etc.). **6** take up the complete attention of: *Model trains consume him.* **7** waste away; be destroyed.
consumed with, absorbed by: *consumed with envy.* ⟨ME < L *consumere* < *com-* (intensive) + *sumere* take up⟩

con•sum•ed•ly [kən'sjumɪdli] *or* [kən'sumɪdli] *adv.* very much; too much.

con•sum•er [kən'sjumər] *or* [kən'sumər] *n.* **1** a person who buys and uses food, clothing, or anything grown or made by producers. **2** a person or thing that uses up, makes away with, or destroys. **3** heterotroph.

consumer credit credit granted to an approved person for the purchase of consumer goods, and paid off in instalments or on a charge card.

con•sum•er–friend•li•ness [kən'sjumər 'frɛndlinɪs] *or* [kən'sumər-] *n.* the state of being consumer-friendly.

con•sum•er–friend•ly [kən'sjumər 'frɛndli] *or* [kən'sumər-] *adj.* easy for the consumer to use, enjoy, or understand.

consumer goods *Economics.* goods that people use or consume to satisfy their wants: *Food and clothing are two kinds of consumer goods.* Compare CAPITAL GOODS.

con•sum•er•ism [kən'sjumə,rɪzəm] *or* [kən'sumə,rɪzəm] *n.* **1** support for the rights of the consumer. **2** the consumption of goods and services. **3** the theory that a continued increase in the consumption of goods is economically desirable for a society.

con•sum•er•ist [kən'sjumərɪst] *or* [kən'sumərɪst] *n.* a person who supports or practises consumerism.

consumer price index a measure of the change in the cost of living relative to a particular period in the past, represented as a percentage increase over, or decrease from, the cost of selected goods in the base period.

con•sum•mate *v.* ['kɒnsə,meit]; *adj.* [kən'sʌmɪt] *or* ['kɒnsəmɪt] *v.* **-mat•ed, -mat•ing;** *adj. —v.* **1** complete; fulfil: *Her ambition was consummated when she won the first prize.* **2** complete (marriage) by sexual intercourse.
—adj. **1** complete; perfect; in the highest degree: *The paintings of great artists show consummate skill.* **2** accomplished; supremely qualified: *a consummate artist.* ⟨< L *consummare* bring to a peak < *com-* (intensive) + *summa* highest degree⟩ **—con'sum•mate•ly,** *adv.* **'con•sum,mat•or,** *n.*

con•sum•ma•tion [,kɒnsə'meiʃən] *n.* **1** the act of consummating. **2** the thing that consummates.

con•sump•tion [kən'sʌmpʃən] *n.* **1** the act of using or using up: *We took along some food for consumption on our trip. The science of economics deals with the production, distribution, and consumption of wealth.* **2** the amount used up: *Our hydro consumption was up again last month.* **3** a rate of using up: *Gas consumption with this car is about 10 l per 100 km.* **4** a wasting disease of the lungs or of some other part of the body; tuberculosis of the lungs. ⟨< L *consumptio, -onis* < *consumere.* See CONSUME.⟩

con•sump•tive [kən'sʌmptɪv] *adj., n. —adj.* **1** having or likely to have tuberculosis of the lungs. **2** of tuberculosis of the lungs. **3** tending to consume; destructive; wasteful.
—n. a person who has tuberculosis of the lungs.
—con'sump•tive•ly, *adv.* **—con'sump•tive•ness,** *n.*

cont. 1 continue; continued. **2** continent; continental. **3** contents; containing. **4** contract. **5** control.

Cont. Continental.

con•tact ['kɒntækt] *n., adj., v.* —*n.* **1** the condition of touching; touching together: *This insecticide should not come in contact with the skin. When two balls are in contact, one can be moved by touching the other.* **2** the state of being in communication; connection; association: *She has kept in contact with her school friends. The control tower lost contact with the pilot.* **3** a person with whom one can get in touch, especially for business purposes: *She has a useful contact in an advertising agency.* **4** *Electricity.* **a** the connection between two conductors of electricity through which a current passes. **b** a device or component for producing such a connection: *The light went out when the wire broke off at the contact.* **5** *Medicine.* **a** exposure to a contagious disease. **b** a person who has been exposed to a contagious disease. **6** *Geology.* the surface forming the boundary between adjacent rocks. **7 contacts,** *pl. Informal.* CONTACT LENSES. **8** a liaison, usually anonymous, in a covert operation.
—*adj. Aeronautics.* within sight of the ground; of or involving CONTACT FLYING: *a contact approach.*
—*v.* **1** get in touch with; communicate with; call: *There's been an accident! Contact the doctor immediately!* **2** cause to touch. **3** be in contact (with). ⟨< L *contactus* a touching < *contingere* < *com-* with + *tangere* touch⟩

contact flying flying an aircraft within sight of the ground. In contact flying, the pilot directs the aircraft by referring to known points or objects on the ground. Compare INSTRUMENT FLYING.

contact lens a small, thin plastic lens ground to an optical prescription and worn directly over the pupil of the eye to correct defective vision. A contact lens fits the curve of the cornea and floats on a thin layer of tears.

con•tac•tor ['kɒntæktər] *or* [kɒn'tæktər] *n.* an electrical device which alternately makes and breaks contact.

contact potential *Electricity.* the electrical potential between two distinct materials in contact, owing to the different numbers of electrons in their atomic structures.

contact print a photographic print made by placing the negative and photographic paper in direct contact over a light.

con•ta•gion [kən'teidʒən] *n.* **1** the spreading of disease by contact. **2** a disease spread in this way; contagious disease. **3** a means by which disease is spread. **4** the tendency of any influence or emotional or mental state to spread from one person to another: *the contagion of a smile, the contagion of political graft.* **5** a spreading influence or emotional state, especially one that is unpleasant or destructive: *A contagion of fear swept through the crowd and caused a panic.* ⟨< L *contagio, -onis* a touching < *contingere.* See CONTACT.⟩

con•ta•gious [kən'teidʒəs] *adj.* **1** of a disease, communicable by direct contact with a person who has a disease, or with the person's clothing, etc. Compare INFECTIOUS. **2** carrying a disease-producing agent; liable to transmit an infectious disease: *She has not completely recovered, but she is no longer contagious.* **3** used for patients with contagious diseases: *the contagious ward in a hospital.* **4** tending to spread rapidly from one person to another; infectious: *Yawning is contagious.* **—con'ta•gious•ly,** *adv.* **—con'ta•gious•ness,** *n.*

con•tain [kən'tein] *v.* **1** have within itself; hold as contents; include: *This purse contains plenty of money.* **2** be capable of holding: *That pitcher contains a litre.* **3** be equal to (a given number of smaller units): *A metre contains 100 centimetres.* **4** control; hold back; restrain: *He contained his anger.* **5** in warfare, control or restrain (enemy forces) by stopping, holding, or surrounding: *The British fleet under Admiral Nelson contained Napoleon's ships at Trafalgar.* **6** *Mathematics.* be exactly divisible by; be divisible by without a remainder: 12 *contains* 2, 3, 4, *and* 6. ⟨ME < OF *contenir* < L *continere* < *com-* together + *tenere* hold⟩ **—con'tain•a•ble,** *adj.*

☛ *Syn.* **1, 2. Contain,** HOLD, ACCOMMODATE = have within itself or be capable of having and keeping. **Contain** emphasizes the idea of actually having something within itself as contents or parts: *The house contains five rooms.* **Hold** emphasizes the idea of being capable of taking in and keeping or of having room, but is often used interchangeably with **contain:** *A paper bag won't hold water. My car holds six people.* **Accommodate** = hold comfortably: *Most hotel rooms accommodate two people.*

con•tain•er [kən'teinər] *n.* **1** a thing that contains, especially a box, tin, jar, basket, etc., used to hold something for storage or transport. **2 a** a very large, boxlike, standard-sized receptacle for transporting an assortment of cargo. **b** (*adjl.*) of or having to do with the use of such containers: *a container flatcar, a container service.* **3** the amount that a container holds or can hold.

container car a railway flatcar adapted for carrying CONTAINERS (def. 2a).

con•tain•er•iz•ation [kən,teinərə'zeiʃən] *or* [kən,teinərai'zeiʃən] *n.* **1** the system of using CONTAINERS (def. 2a) to transport goods. **2** adaptation to such a system.

con•tain•er•ize [kən'teinə,raɪz] *v.* **-ized, -iz•ing.** pack (cargo) in very large standardized containers.

container port a port with facilities for moving CONTAINERS (def. 2a): *Vancouver is a container port.*

container ship a ship adapted to hold CONTAINERS (def. 2a) for moving cargo.

con•tain•ment [kən'teinmənt] *n.* **1** the act or process of holding or confining. **2** the confinement of a hostile or potentially hostile force within its existing geographical boundaries. **3** (*adjl.*) designating a policy, method, or place of holding or confining: *Containment labs are used in biological research to ensure that micro-organisms used in experiments cannot escape.*

con•tam•i•nant [kən'tæmənənt] *n.* something that contaminates.

con•tam•i•nate [kən'tæmə,neit] *v.* **-nat•ed, -nat•ing.** make impure by contact; defile; pollute: *Flies can contaminate food.* ⟨< L *contaminare* < *contamen* contamination < *com-* with + *tag-*, root of *tangere* touch⟩ **—con'tam•i,na•tor,** *n.* **—con'tam•i•na•tive,** *adj.*

con•tam•i•na•tion [kən,tæmə'neiʃən] *n.* **1** a contaminating or being contaminated; pollution: *Food should be kept covered to avoid contamination by flies.* **2** anything that contaminates; an impurity.

contd. continued.

conte [kount]; *French,* [kɔ̃t] *n.* a short story, especially an imaginative one.

con•temn [kən'tɛm] *v.* view with contempt; despise; scorn. ⟨< L *contemnere* < *com-* (intensive) + *temnere* disdain, originally, cut⟩ **—con'tem•ner** or **con'tem•nor** [kən'tɛmər] *or* [kən'tɛmnər], *n.*

con•tem•plate ['kɒntəm,pleit] *v.* **-plat•ed, -plat•ing. 1** look at for a long time; gaze at: *to contemplate the evening sky.* **2** think about for a long time; consider thoughtfully: *He contemplated his past life, with its successes and failures.* **3** meditate: *I sometimes like to sit and contemplate.* **4** have in mind; consider; intend: *She contemplated going to Europe after graduation. She is contemplating a change of work.* ⟨< L *contemplari* survey < *com-* with + *templum* restricted area marked off for the taking of auguries⟩ **—'con•tem,plat•or,** *n.*

con•tem•pla•tion [,kɒntəm'pleiʃən] *n.* **1** the act of looking at or thinking about something for a long time. **2** deep thought; meditation: *sunk in contemplation.* **3** expectation or intention.

con•tem•pla•tive [kən'tɛmplətɪv] *or* ['kɒntəm,pleitɪv] *adj., n.* —*adj.* **1** thoughtful; meditative. **2** devoted to religious meditation and prayer.
—*n.* a person who leads a contemplative life, especially a monk or a nun. **—con'tem•pla•tive•ly,** *adv.* **—con'tem•pla•tive•ness,** *n.*

con•tem•po•ra•ne•i•ty [kən,tɛmpərə'niəti] *or* [-'neiəti] *n.* the quality or state of being contemporaneous.

con•tem•po•ra•ne•ous [kən,tɛmpə'reiniəs] *adj.* belonging to the same period of time. ⟨< L *contemporaneus* < *com-* with + *tempus, -poris* time⟩ **—con,tem•po'ra•ne•ous•ly,** *adv.* **—con,tem•po'ra•ne•ous•ness,** *n.*

con•tem•po•rar•y [kən'tɛmpə,rɛri] *adj., n., pl.* **-rar•ies.** —*adj.* **1** belonging to or living in the same period of time. **2** of or having to do with the present time; current: *contemporary theatre, contemporary attitudes.* **3** of the same age or date.
—*n.* **1** a person who belongs to the same period of time as another or others: *Shakespeare and Ben Jonson were contemporaries.* **2** a person, magazine, etc., of the same age or date: *We all tend to seek the society of our contemporaries.* ⟨< *com-* together + L *temporarius* belonging to time < *tempus, -poris* time⟩

con•tem•po•rize [kən'tɛmpə,raɪz] *v.* **-rized, -riz•ing,** make or become contemporary.

con•tempt [kən'tɛmpt] *n.* **1** the feeling that a person, act, or thing is mean, low, or worthless; scorn; a despising: *We feel contempt for a liar.* **2** *Law.* disobedience to or open disrespect for the rules or decisions of a court, lawmaking body, etc. A person can be put in jail for **contempt of court.**
hold in contempt, scorn; despise; disgrace: *A traitor is held in contempt.* ⟨< L *contemptus* < *contemnere.* See CONTEMN.⟩
☛ *Syn.* **1.** See note at SCORN.

con•tempt•i•ble [kən'tɛmptəbəl] *adj.* deserving contempt or

scorn; mean; low; worthless: *a contemptible act.* **—con'tempt•i•ble•ness,** *n.* **—con'tempt•i•bly,** *adv.*
☛ *Usage.* See note at CONTEMPTUOUS.

con•temp•tu•ous [kən'tɛmptʃuəs] *adj.* showing contempt; scornful: *a contemptuous look.* **—con'temp•tu•ous•ly,** *adv.* **—con'temp•tu•ous•ness,** *n.*
☛ *Usage.* **Contemptuous** and CONTEMPTIBLE are sometimes confused. The distinction will be clear if one observes that **contemptible** has the suffix **-ible,** meaning 'deserving'.

con•tend [kən'tɛnd] *v.* **1** fight; struggle: *The Arctic explorers had to contend with extreme cold, hunger, and loneliness.* **2** take part in a contest; compete: *Five runners were contending in the first race.* **3** argue; dispute. **4** declare to be a fact; maintain as true in the face of opposition: *Columbus contended that the earth was round.* ⟨< L *contendere* < *com-* (intensive) + *tendere* stretch⟩ **—con'tend•er,** *n.*
☛ *Syn.* **2. Contend,** COMPETE = take part in a contest for something. **Contend** emphasizes the idea of trying hard and struggling against opposition: *Our football team is contending with one from the next town for the championship.* **Compete** emphasizes the idea of rivalry and trying hard to win: *Only two girls are competing for the cup.*

con•tent[1] ['kɒntɛnt] *n.* **1** Usually, **contents,** *pl.* what is contained in anything; all things inside. **2** the facts or ideas stated; what is written in a book or said in a speech, etc., as opposed to the way it is expressed: *The content of her speech was good, but the form was not.* **3** the proportion of a certain substance contained in something else: *Cream has a higher fat content than milk.* **4** the power of containing; capacity: *What is the content of the gas tank of this car?* **5** the subject matter or range of any field of study: *the content of our mathematics course.* ⟨< L *contentum,* pp. neut. of *continere.* See CONTAIN.⟩

con•tent[2] [kən'tɛnt] *v., adj., n.* *—v.* **1** satisfy the requirement or desires of: *Nothing contents her; she is always complaining.* **2** limit (oneself) to a particular action, etc.: *He contented himself with writing a letter to the editor.*
—adj. **1** not desiring anything more than or anything different from what one has; satisfied: *We'll have to be content with whatever accommodations we get.* **2** willing; ready. **3** pleased.
—n. contentment; satisfaction; ease of mind.
to (one's) **heart's content,** to one's full satisfaction; as much as one pleases: *When exams are over you'll be able to play tennis to your heart's content.* ⟨< Med.L *contentare* < L *contentus* satisfied, pp. of *continere.* See CONTAIN.⟩ **—con'tent•ment,** *n.*
☛ *Syn. v.* **1.** See note at SATISFY.

con•tent•ed [kən'tɛntɪd] *adj., v.* *—adj.* satisfied; pleased; easy in mind: *She is a contented person, happy with what she has.*
—v. pt. and pp. of CONTENT. **—con'tent•ed•ly,** *adv.* **—con'tent•ed•ness,** *n.*

con•ten•tion [kən'tɛnʃən] *n.* **1** a statement or point that one has argued for; statement maintained as true in the face of opposition: *Columbus's contention that the earth was round proved to be true.* **2** the act of arguing; disputing; quarrelling: *The main subject of contention was the proposed change in the school curriculum.* **3** an argument or dispute. **4** a struggle; contest. ⟨< L *contentio, -onis* < *contendere.* See CONTEND.⟩

con•ten•tious [kən'tɛnʃəs] *adj.* **1** quarrelsome; fond of arguing; given to disputing: *A contentious person argues and disputes about trifles.* **2** characterized by contention; arousing or provoking contention; controversial: *a contentious election campaign.* **—con'ten•tious•ly,** *adv.* **—con'ten•tious•ness,** *n.*

con•ter•mi•nous [kən'tɜrmənəs] *adj.* coterminous. **—con'ter•min•ous•ly,** *adv.*

con•test *n.* ['kɒntɛst]; *v.* [kən'tɛst] *n., v.* *—n.* **1** a game or competition, especially one in which the entries are rated by judges: *a ploughing contest, a baking contest, a contest to find a name for a new park.* **2** a fight or struggle. **3** an argument or dispute.
—v. **1** try to win. **2** fight or struggle (for): *The soldiers contested every spot of ground.* **3** argue against; dispute about: *The lawyer contested the claim and tried to prove that it was false.* **4** take part in a contest. ⟨< F *contester* < L *contestari* call to witness < *com-* (intensive) + *testis* witness⟩ **—con'test•a•ble,** *adj.*

con•test•ant [kən'tɛstənt] *n.* a person who contests, especially a person who takes part in a game or competition: *The contestant whose name is selected will win a trip to Paris.*

con•text ['kɒntɛkst] *n.* **1** the spoken or written text in which a particular word or group of words occurs: *It's unfair to judge his statement without knowing the context in which he made it.* **2** the immediate environment; attendant circumstances or conditions; background: *the political context of her speech.* ⟨< L *contextus* < *contexere* < *com-* together + *texere* weave⟩

con•tex•tu•al [kən'tɛkstʃuəl] *adj.* having to do with the context; depending on the context. **—con'tex•tu•al•ly,** *adv.*

con•tex•tu•al•ize [kən'tɛkstʃuə,laɪz] *v.* **-ized, -izing.** adapt to a particular (cultural) context. **—con,tex•tu•al•i'za•tion,** *n.*

con•tex•ture [kən'tɛkstʃər] *n.* **1** a making by weaving. **2** something woven; cloth. **3** the way in which something is made; structure.

con•ti•gu•i•ty [,kɒntə'gjuəti] *n., pl.* **-ties. 1** nearness: *The contiguity of the house and garage was a convenience in bad weather.* **2** the state of being in contact. **3** a continuous mass; unbroken stretch.

con•tig•u•ous [kən'tɪgjuəs] *adj.* **1** in actual contact; touching: *A fence showed where the two farms were contiguous.* **2** adjoining; near. ⟨< L *contiguus* < *com-* with + *tag-,* root of *tangere* touch. Related to CONTACT.⟩ **—con'tig•u•ous•ly,** *adv.* **—con'tig•u•ous•ness,** *n.*

con•ti•nence ['kɒntənəns] *n.* **1** self-control; self-restraint; moderation. **2** chastity. **3** ability to control one's bladder and bowel movements. Also, **continency.**

con•ti•nent[1] ['kɒntənənt] *n.* **1** one of the seven great masses of land on the earth. The continents are Asia, Africa, North America, South America, Europe, Australia, and Antarctica. **2** the mainland. **3 the Continent,** the mainland of Europe. It does not include the British Isles. ⟨< L *continens,* short for *terra continens* land held together. See CONTINENT[2].⟩

con•ti•nent[2] ['kɒntənənt] *adj.* **1** showing restraint with regard to the desires or passions; using self-control; temperate. **2** chaste. **3** able to control one's bladder and bowel movements. ⟨< L *continens, -entis,* ppr. of *continere.* See CONTAIN.⟩ **—'con•ti•nent•ly,** *adv.*

con•ti•nen•tal [,kɒntə'nɛntəl] *adj., n.* *—adj.* **1** of, having to do with, or characteristic of a continent: *continental rivers.* **2** Usually, **Continental,** of, having to do with, or characteristic of the mainland of Europe; of or like that of the Continent: *Continental customs differ from those of England.* **3 Continental,** in the United States, of or having to do with the thirteen colonies at the time of the American Revolution.
—n. **1** Usually, **Continental,** a person living on the Continent. **2 Continental,** in the United States: **a** a soldier of the American army during the American Revolution. **b** a piece of paper money issued during the American Revolution. It was considered almost worthless by the time the war was over. **—,con•ti'nen•tal•ly,** *adv.*

continental bed a bed that has no headboard or footboard, being made up of a spring mattress set on top of a box-spring base that has short legs. It is usually slightly narrower than the corresponding standard size.

Continental breakfast a breakfast of rolls, croissants, and other breads, with coffee or tea and, sometimes, cheese, cold cuts, or other bread coverings.

continental code the code adapted from the first Morse code; international code.

Continental Divide a ridge in western North America, in the Rockies, which separates streams flowing toward the Pacific Ocean from those flowing toward the Atlantic or Arctic Oceans; Great Divide.

continental drift *Geology.* the theory that the earth's land masses move gradually over the surface of the earth on a substratum of magma. See also PLATE TECTONICS.

con•ti•nen•tal•ism [,kɒntə'nɛntə,lɪzəm] *n. Cdn.* a policy advocating economic and political union of the countries of a continent, especially the union of Canada and the United States.

con•ti•nen•tal•ist [,kɒntə'nɛntəlɪst] *n., adj. Cdn.* *—n.* an advocate or supporter of continentalism.
—adj. having to do with, reflecting, or favouring continentalism: *a continentalist businessman, a continentalist bias.*

con•ti•nen•tal•i•za•tion [,kɒntɪ,nɛntəlaɪ'zeiʃən] *or* [,kɒntɪ,nɛntələ'zeiʃən] *n.* economic union of countries in a continent, such as Canada and the United States.

continental shelf the submerged shelf of land that borders most continents and ends in a steep slope (the **continental slope**) to deep water.

con•tin•gen•cy [kən'tɪndʒənsi] *n., pl.* **-cies. 1** uncertainty of occurrence; dependence on chance. **2** an accidental happening; unexpected event; chance. **3** a happening or event depending on something that is uncertain; possibility: *The explorer carried supplies for every contingency.* **4** a happening or event depending on or accompanying something else: *the contingencies of foreign travel.* **5** the fact of being contingent.

con•tin•gent [kən'tɪndʒənt] *adj., n.* *—adj.* **1** conditional;

depending on something not certain: *Our plans for a picnic tomorrow are contingent upon pleasant weather.* **2** equally likely to happen or not to happen; possible; uncertain: *The traveller set aside twenty dollars a day for contingent expenses.* **3** happening by chance; accidental; unexpected. **4** *Law.* dependent on events or circumstances that may or may not occur.
—n. **1** a share of soldiers, workers, etc., furnished to a force from other sources: *Canada sent a large contingent of troops to France in World War I.* **2** a group that is part of a larger group: *The Kingston contingent had seats together at the convention.* **3** an accidental or unexpected event. ⟨< L *contingens, -entis* touching, ppr. of *contingere.* See CONTACT.⟩ **—con'tin•gent•ly,** *adv.*

con•tin•u•al [kən'tɪnjuəl] *adj.* **1** repeated many times; very frequent: *continual interference.* **2** never stopping: *the continual flow of the river.* **—con'tin•u•al•ly,** *adv.*

☛ *Usage.* **Continual,** CONTINUOUS. **Continual** in most instances (def. 1) means 'repeated frequently or at close intervals': *Dancing requires continual practice.* It may also mean (def. 2) 'without a break in time': *a continual noise.* **Continuous** means 'ceaseless, without interruption in time or space': *a continuous procession of cars.*

con•tin•u•ance [kən'tɪnjuəns] *n.* **1** staying; remaining: *A public official is paid during his or her continuance in office.* **2** a continuing: *We admired his continuance of work in spite of illness.* **3** the time during which anything lasts; duration. **4** a continuation; sequel: *the continuance of a story.* **5** *Law.* an adjournment or postponement.

con•tin•u•ant [kən'tɪnjuənt] *n. Phonetics.* a speech sound that can be prolonged until the breath runs out, as distinct from a STOP in which the breath is interrupted. Continuants in English are [f], [v], [ʃ], [ʒ], [s], [z], [θ], [ð], [m], [n], [ŋ], [r], [l], [h], and all vowels.

con•tin•u•a•tion [kən,tɪnju'eiʃən] *n.* **1** the going on with an activity or process: *He was looking forward to university as a continuation of his education.* **2** going on with a thing after stopping; beginning again: *They voted for a continuation of the discussion at the next meeting.* **3** anything by which a thing is continued; an added part: *The continuation of the story will appear in next month's magazine.* **4** the act or fact of not stopping.

continuation school *Cdn.* formerly in Ontario, a small secondary school administered by an elementary school board.

con•tin•u•a•tive [kən'tɪnjuətɪv] *or* [kən'tɪnju,eitɪv] *adj., n.* *—adj.* **1** continuing; causing continuation. **2** expressing a continuing thought. **3** *Grammar.* **a** expressing something that follows. *Example:* In "I came, I saw, I conquered," "I saw" and "I conquered" are continuative. **b** of a verb or verb aspect, expressing continuation; progressive.
—n. **1** something that follows. **2** *Grammar.* **a** a continuative word, phrase or clause. **b** the continuative aspect. ⟨< L *continuativus*⟩

con•tin•ue [kən'tɪnju] *v.* **-tin•ued, -tin•u•ing. 1** keep up; keep on; go on in space or time; go on with: *The road continues for quite a distance. We continued our work at the hospital with no break until evening.* **2** go on, or go on with (something), after stopping; begin again: *He ate lunch and then continued his work.* **3** last; endure: *The queen's reign continued for twenty years.* **4** cause to last. **5** extend in space: *The farmer continued her fence from the pasture to the highway.* **6** stay: *The children must continue in school till the end of June.* **7** allow to stay in a position; maintain; retain: *The club continued the president in office for another term.* **8** put off until a later time; postpone; adjourn: *The judge has continued the case until next month.* ⟨ME < OF *continuer* < L *continuare* < *continere* hold together. See CONTAIN.⟩ **—con'tin•u•a•ble,** *adj.*

☛ *Syn.* **1, 3. Continue,** LAST, ENDURE = go on for a long time. **Continue** emphasizes the idea of an activity going on and on without an end, usually without a break: *The heavy snow continued all winter.* **Last** emphasizes the idea of a thing holding out, either in good condition or full strength or for an unusually long time: *These flowers lasted for two weeks.* **Endure** emphasizes the idea of going on, remaining, or surviving, in spite of difficulties, dangers, or pressures of any kind: *These monuments will endure for centuries.*

continued fraction *Mathematics.* a number plus a fraction whose denominator is also a number plus a fraction. *Example:* $a + \cfrac{b}{c + \cfrac{d}{e + f}}$

con•ti•nu•i•ty [,kɒntə'njuəti] *or* [,kɒntə'nuəti] *n., pl.* **-ties. 1** the quality of being a connected whole or an unbroken series: *The story lacked continuity because there were too many unconnected happenings.* **2** a detailed plan of the sequence of scenes in a film. **3** *Radio or television.* **a** any connecting comments or announcements between the parts of a program. **b** a script for such comments or announcements. **4** the story line of a comic strip. **5** the way in which film scenes are connected with no perceptible break.

con•tin•u•o [kən'tɪnju,ou] *n. Music.* a part for an accompanying keyboard instrument, often giving only a figured bass, common in baroque music. ⟨< Ital.⟩

con•tin•u•ous [kən'tɪnjuəs] *adj.* **1** without a stop or break; connected; unbroken: *a continuous line, a continuous sound, continuous work, a continuous line of cars.* **2** *Mathematics.* of or having to do with a function whose value at each point is almost identical to its values at nearby points. **—con'tin•u•ous•ly,** *adv.* **—con'tin•u•ous•ness,** *n.*

☛ *Usage.* See note at CONTINUAL.

continuous forms *Computer technology.* forms (cheques, invoices, etc.) produced in a long strip, separated by perforations, for use on a computer printer.

con•tin•u•um [kən'tɪnjuəm] *n., pl.* **-tin•u•a.** [-'tɪnjuə] **1** a continuous whole; an unbroken series, etc. **2** a line representing a range between extremes, on which a point can show the extent to which something is nearer one or the other extreme. **3** *Mathematics.* a compact connected set. The set of real numbers (rational and irrational) is a continuum. ⟨< L⟩

con•to ['kɒntou] *n.* a money of account in Portugal and Cape Verde, equal to 1000 escudos. ⟨< Pg., literally, account⟩

con•tort [kən'tɔrt] *v.* twist or bend out of shape; distort: *The clown contorted her face. A bad collision contorts the shape of the vehicle.* ⟨< L *contortus,* pp. of *contorquere* < *com-* (intensive) + *torquere* twist⟩

con•tor•tion [kən'tɔrʃən] *n.* **1** a twisting or bending out of shape; a distorting. **2** a contorted condition; distorted form or shape.

con•tor•tion•ist [kən'tɔrʃənɪst] *n.* a person who can twist or bend his or her body into odd and unnatural positions.

con•tour ['kɒntur] *n., v.* *—n.* **1** the outline of a figure, land mass, body of water, etc.: *The contour of the Atlantic coast of Canada is very irregular.* **2** a line representing such an outline or shape. **3** (*adjl.*) showing the outlines of hills, valleys, etc., at regular intervals above sea level: *a contour map.* **4** (*adjl.*) following the contours of uneven ground in such a way as to minimize erosion: *In contour ploughing, the furrows are made horizontally around the slopes of a hill instead of from top to bottom.* **5** (*adjl.*) shaped to fit the contour of a particular object: *a contour chair.*
—v. **1** build (a road, etc.) to follow natural contours. **2** shape to fit the contour of something: *bucket seats contoured to fit the body.* **3** mark with contour lines. **4** make an outline of. ⟨< F < Ital. *contorno* < *contornare* encircle < L *com-* with + *tornus* turning lathe < Gk. *tornos*⟩

☛ *Syn. n.* See note at OUTLINE.

contour interval the difference between two adjacent contour lines on a map.

contour line a line on a map, showing the outline from above of a section of the earth's surface at a particular height above sea level. A 3000 m contour line on a map of a mountain shows what its outline would look like from the top if a horizontal cross section were made at that height.

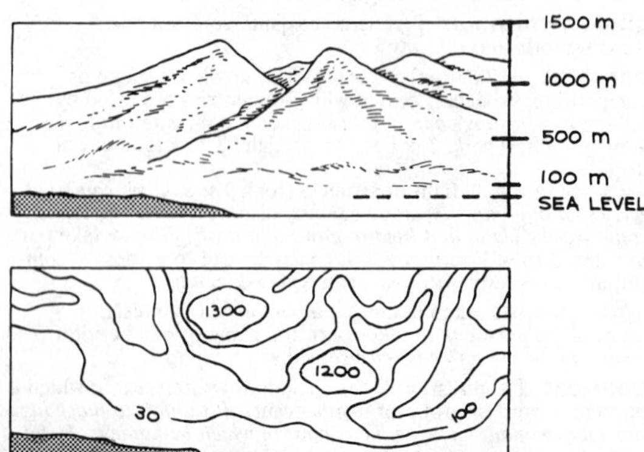

A contour map of the mountains shown in the sketch above

contour map a map showing elevations and depressions of

the earth's surface by means of a series of contour lines made at regular intervals above or below sea level.

contr. 1 contract; contracted. 2 contraction. 3 contralto. 4 contrary. 5 control.

con•tra ['kɒntrə] *n.* a guerrilla or rebel, especially one in Central America, fighting a government established by revolution; counterrevolutionary. ⟨< Sp., short for *contrarrevolucionario*⟩

contra– *prefix.* 1 in opposition; against: *contradistinction = distinction by opposition or contrast.* 2 *Music.* lower in pitch: *contrabass.* ⟨< L *contra-* < *contra* against, adv., prep.⟩

con•tra•band ['kɒntrə,bænd] *n., adj. —n.* 1 goods that may not legally be imported or exported: *The plumage of endangered species of birds, such as the ostrich or egret, is contraband in Canada. Some goods, such as firearms, are contraband except under certain circumstances.* 2 trading contrary to law; smuggling. 3 smuggled goods: *The customs official was looking for contraband.* 4 *U.S.* a black slave who escaped to or was brought within the Union lines during the Civil War. 5 CONTRABAND OF WAR.
—adj. against the law; prohibited: *contraband trade.* ⟨< Sp. < Ital. *contrabando* < *contra-* against (< L) + *bando* < LL *bandum* ban < Gmc.⟩

contraband of war any materials supplied to warring nations by neutral countries and subject to seizure by the opposite side according to international law: *Ammunition is always contraband of war.*

con•tra•bass [,kɒntrə'beis] *n.* 1 the lowest bass instrument of a family of instruments, especially the double bass of the violin family. 2 (*adjl.*) having a pitch an octave lower than normal bass.

con•tra•bass•ist [,kɒntrə'beisɪst] *n.* one who plays a contrabass, especially a skilled player.

con•tra•bas•soon [,kɒntrəbə'sun] *n.* a large bassoon, an octave lower in pitch than the ordinary bassoon; double bassoon.

con•tra•bas•soon•ist [,kɒntrəbə'sunɪst] *n.* one who plays the contrabassoon, especially a skilled player.

con•tra•cep•tion [,kɒntrə'sɛpʃən] *n.* the intentional prevention of conception. ⟨< *contra-* + (*con*)*ception*⟩

con•tra•cep•tive [,kɒntrə'sɛptɪv] *n., adj. —n.* a substance or device for preventing pregnancy or conception.
—adj. of or for contraception.

con•tract *v.* [kən'trækt] *for 1-4 and 7,* ['kɒntrækt] *or* [kən'trækt] *for 5 and 6; n.* ['kɒntrækt] *v., n. —v.* 1 make or become narrower or shorter; make or become smaller; draw together; shrink: *Wrinkling the forehead contracts the brows. Rubber stretches and contracts.* 2 *Grammar.* shorten (a word, etc.) by omitting some of the letters or sounds: *In talking we contract* do not *to* don't. 3 form; enter upon; bring on oneself: *to contract a bad habit.* 4 get; catch (a disease): *She contracted malaria in the tropics.* 5 make a contract; enter into a legal agreement: *The builder contracted to build the new library.* 6 hire (someone) on contract for a specific job: *I've contracted a professional to renovate the kitchen.* 7 *Anatomy.* draw together and thicken (muscle fibre) to move a part of the body.
contract out, subcontract.
—n. 1 an agreement, especially a written agreement that can be enforced by law: *All professional hockey players sign contracts each year, agreeing to play for a certain salary.* 2 a formal agreement of marriage. 3 CONTRACT BRIDGE. 4 in contract bridge, the tricks that the declarer undertakes to win. ⟨< L *contractus,* pp. of *contrahere* < *com-* together + *trahere* draw⟩
—con'tract•i•ble, *adj.*

contract bridge a card game played by four people divided into two opposing pairs. The highest bidder can score toward a game only as many points as he or she promises to make in his or her bid.

con•trac•tile [kən'træktaɪl] *or* [kən'træktəl] *adj.* 1 capable of contracting: *Muscle is contractile tissue.* 2 producing contraction: *Cooling is a contractile force.*

contractile vacuole a vacuole in single-celled organisms that discharges its fluid by contracting.

con•trac•til•i•ty [,kɒntræk'tɪləti] *n.* the ability to contract.

con•trac•tion [kən'trækʃən] *n.* 1 a contracting or being contracted: *Cold causes the contraction of liquids, gases, and metals, whereas heat causes expansion.* 2 something contracted; shortened form: Can't *is a contraction of* cannot. 3 *Anatomy.* the drawing together and thickening of muscle fibre. 4 one episode of shortening of the muscles in the uterus during childbirth, by means of which the cervix is dilated and the baby is expelled from the uterus.

con•trac•tive [kən'træktɪv] *adj.* 1 capable of contracting. 2 producing contraction. 3 of contraction.

contract murder murder which is arranged and paid for by someone else.

con•trac•tor ['kɒntræktər] *or* [kən'træktər] *for 1 and 2;* [kən'træktər] *for 3. n.* 1 a person who agrees to furnish materials or to do a piece of work for a certain price, especially for the construction of buildings: *A contractor normally contracts out work to specialists such as electricians.* 2 any party represented in a contract. 3 *Anatomy.* a muscle that draws together some part or parts of the body.

con•trac•tu•al [kən'træktʃuəl] *adj.* 1 of or having to do with a contract. 2 having the nature of a contract.
—con'trac•tu•al•ly, *adv.*

con•tra•dict [,kɒntrə'dɪkt] *v.* 1 express the opposite of (a statement); declare to be false or untrue: *She contradicted his version of the accident.* 2 deny the statement of (another person): *To contradict a guest is rude.* 3 be contrary to; be inconsistent with: *His quick anger contradicted his previous statement that he never lost his temper.* ⟨< L *contradictus,* pp. of *contradicere,* earlier *contra dicere* say in opposition⟩
☛ *Syn.* **1.** See note at DENY.

con•tra•dic•tion [,kɒntrə'dɪkʃən] *n.* 1 the act of denying what has been said. 2 a statement or act that contradicts another; denial: *His statement was a clear contradiction of what his father had said.* 3 a contrary condition; disagreement; opposition: *a contradiction in terms.* 4 inconsistency.

con•tra•dic•to•ry [,kɒntrə'dɪktəri] *adj., n. —adj.* 1 contradicting; contrary; in disagreement: *First reports of the election were so contradictory that we could not tell who had won.* 2 inclined to contradict.
—n. an opposite.

con•tra•dis•tinc•tion [,kɒntrədɪ'stɪŋkʃən] *n.* a distinction made by opposition or contrast: *The author emphasizes the importance of quality control in contradistinction to speed of production.*

con•trail ['kɒntreil] *n.* the trail of vapour left by an aircraft flying at a high altitude; vapour trail. ⟨< *con*(*densation*) + *trail*⟩

con•tra–in•di•cate [,kɒntrə 'ɪndə,keit] *v.* **-cat•ed, -cat•ing.** *Medicine.* make or declare to be unsafe or imprudent (usually in the passive): *Alcohol is contra-indicated during pregnancy.*

con•tral•to [kən'træltou] *n.* **-tos;** *adj. —n.* 1 the lowest female singing voice; alto. 2 a singer who has such a voice. 3 the part sung by a contralto.
—adj. having to do with, having the range of, or designed for a contralto. ⟨< Ital. *contralto* < *contra-* counter to (< L) + *alto* high < L *altus*⟩

con•tra•po•si•tion [,kɒntrəpə'zɪʃən] *n.* a placing over against; opposite position; contrast.

con•trap•tion [kən'træpʃən] *n. Informal.* a contrivance; device; gadget. ⟨? < *contrive*⟩

con•tra•pun•tal [,kɒntrə'pʌntəl] *adj. Music.* 1 of or having to do with counterpoint. 2 according to the rules of counterpoint. ⟨< Ital. *contrapunto* (now *contrappunto*) counterpoint⟩ **—,con•tra'pun•tal•ly,** *adv.*

con•tra•pun•tist [,kɒntrə'pʌntɪst] *n.* a person skilled in the rules and execution of counterpoint.

con•tra•ri•e•ty [,kɒntrə'raɪəti] *n., pl.* **-ties.** 1 the state or quality of being contrary. 2 something contrary; a contrary fact or statement.

con•tra•ri•wise ['kɒntrɛri,waɪz] *for 1 and 2;* ['kɒntrɛri,waɪz] *or* [kən'trɛri,waɪz] *for 3. adv.* 1 in the opposite way or direction. 2 on the contrary. 3 perversely.

con•tra•ry ['kɒntrɛri] *for adj. 1, 2, 3, n., and adv.;* ['kɒntrɛri] *or* [kən'trɛri] *for adj. 4. adj., n., pl.* **-ries;** *adv. —adj.* 1 opposed in purpose, character, etc.; opposite; completely different: *Contrary to all expectations, the party was a great success. The plan is contrary to government policy.* 2 opposite in direction, position, etc. 3 unfavourable: *a contrary wind.* 4 arbitrarily opposing others; stubborn; perverse.
—n. 1 a fact or quality that is the opposite of something else; the opposite: *What she has just told us is the contrary of what we heard yesterday.* 2 *Logic.* either of two propositions so linked that only one may be true although both may be false.
on the contrary, exactly opposite to what has been said: *He didn't go straight home; on the contrary, he stopped at three different stores and even visited a friend.*
to the contrary, with the opposite effect.

—adv. in opposition; in an opposite way. ⟨ME < AF *contrarie* < L *contrarius* < *contra* against⟩ **—'con•tra•ri•ly,** *adv.* **—'con•tra•ri•ness,** *n.*
☛ *Syn. adj.* **1.** See note at OPPOSITE.

con•trast *n.* ['kɒntræst]; *v.* [kən'træst] *n., v.* *—n.* **1** a great difference; difference; striking difference: *the contrast between black and white.* **2** anything that shows a striking difference when put side by side with something else: *Black hair is a sharp contrast to light skin.* **3** *Arts.* the use of varied colours, shapes, sounds, etc., to heighten the effect of a composition.
—v. **1** compare (two things) so as to show their differences: *My project was to contrast the climate of the Mackenzie Valley and that of the District of Keewatin.* **2** show differences when compared or put side by side: *Blue and yellow contrast prettily in a design.* **3** form a contrast to; set off (*used with* **with**): *The strained language of his speeches contrasts oddly with the ease and naturalness of his letters.* **4** put close together to heighten an effect by emphasizing differences. ⟨< F < Ital. *contrasto* < *contrastare* < VL *contrastare* < L *contra-* against + *stare* stand⟩ **—con'trast•a•ble,** *adj.* **—con'trast•ing•ly,** *adv.*
☛ *Usage.* See note at COMPARE.

con•trast•ive [kən'træstɪv] *adj.* having to do with or involving contrast: *A contrastive study of English and French grammar would show the ways in which the structures of the two languages are different.*

con•trast•y ['kɒntræsti] *or* [kən'træsti] *adj.* of photographs, having very marked contrast between light and dark areas.

con•tra•val•la•tion [,kɒntrəvə'leiʃən] *n.* a military defence work designed to protect besiegers against attack by the besieged or by outside forces.

con•tra•vene [,kɒntrə'vin] *v.* **-vened, -ven•ing. 1** conflict with; oppose: *A dictatorship contravenes the liberty of individuals.* **2** contradict. **3** violate; infringe. ⟨< LL *contravenire* < L *contra-* against + *venire* come⟩ **—,con•tra'ven•er,** *n.*

con•tra•ven•tion [,kɒntrə'vɛnʃən] *n.* **1** a conflict; opposition. **2** contradiction. **3** a violation; infringement.

con•tre•danse ['kɒntrə,dæns]; *French,* [kɔ̃tʀə'dɑ̃s] *n. French.* **1** a dance in which the partners stand in two lines facing each other. **2** the music written for such a dance. ⟨< E *country-dance*⟩

con•tre•temps ['kɒntrə,tɑ̃]; *French,* [kɔ̃ntʀə'tɑ̃] *n., pl.* **-temps** [-,tɑ̃z] *French.* an unfortunate accident; embarrassing or awkward happening. ⟨< OF *contrestant,* ppr. of *contrester* oppose < VL *contrastare* (see CONTRAST); influenced by F *temps* time < L *tempus*⟩

con•trib•ut•a•ble [kən'trɪbjətəbəl] *adj.* **1** capable of being contributed; payable as a contribution. **2** of persons, subject to contribution; obliged to contribute.

con•trib•ute [kən'trɪbjut] *v.* **-ut•ed, -ut•ing. 1** give (money, help, etc.) along with others; furnish as a share: *We should also contribute to the Red Cross. Everyone was asked to contribute suggestions for the party.* **2** write (articles, stories, etc.) for a newspaper or magazine.
contribute to, help bring about: *Poor food contributed to the child's illness.* ⟨< L *contributus,* pp. of *contribuere* bring together, collect < *com-* together + *tribuere* bestow, assign, originally, divide among the tribes < *tribus* tribe⟩

con•tri•bu•tion [,kɒntrə'bjuʃən] *n.* **1** the act of contributing; giving of money, help, etc., along with others. **2** the money, help, etc., given; gift. **3** an article, story, etc., written for a newspaper or magazine. **4** a tax; levy.

con•trib•u•tive [kən'trɪbjətɪv] *adj.* contributing; helping to bring about. **—con'trib•u•tive•ly,** *adv.* **—con'trib•u•tive•ness,** *n.*

con•trib•u•tor [kən'trɪbjətər] *n.* **1** a person or thing that contributes. **2** a person who writes articles, stories, etc., for a newspaper or magazine.

con•trib•u•to•ry [kən'trɪbjə,tɔri] *adj., n.* *—adj.* contributing; helping to bring about: *The worker's carelessness was a contributory cause of the accident.*
—n. a person or thing that contributes.

con•trite ['kɒntrəit] *or* [kən'trəit] *adj.* **1** sad and humbled by a sense of having done wrong; penitent. **2** showing deep regret and sorrow: *She wrote an apology in contrite words.* ⟨< L *contritus* crushed, pp. of *conterere* < *com-* (intensive) + *terere* rub, grind⟩ **—con'trite•ly,** *adv.* **—con'trite•ness,** *n.*

con•tri•tion [kən'trɪʃən] *n.* **1** sorrow for one's sins; being contrite; sincere penitence. **2** deep regret.

con•triv•ance [kən'traɪvəns] *n.* **1** something invented; a mechanical device. **2** the act or manner of planning or designing: *By careful contrivance he managed to fit all his appointments into one afternoon.* **3** the power or ability of contriving. **4** a plan; scheme.

con•trive [kən'traɪv] *v.* **-trived, -triv•ing. 1** invent; design: *to contrive a new kind of engine.* **2** scheme; plot: *to contrive a robbery.* **3** manage; arrange to have something happen: *I will contrive to be there by ten o'clock.* **4** bring about. ⟨ME < OF *controver* < *con-* (< L *com-*) (intensive) + *trover* find < L *turbare* stir up < *turba* commotion⟩ **—con'triv•er,** *n.*

con•trived [kən'traɪvd] *adj., v.* *—adj.* produced by contrivance; not natural; artificial.
—v. pt. and pp. of CONTRIVE.

con•trol [kən'troul] *n., v.* **-trolled, -trol•ling.** *—n.* **1** power or authority; command: *He has no control over his feelings. The rebels are in control of the capital.* **2** restraint: *She showed great control in not losing her temper.* **3** regulation: *birth control, gun control.* **4** a means of regulation or restraint; check: *They argued that the new law was not effective as a control against price increases.* **5** a device that regulates the working of a machine: *The control for our furnace is in the front hall.* **6 controls,** the instruments and devices by which a car, locomotive, etc., is operated: *After the crash, the pilot was found dead at the controls.* **7** *Statistics.* **a** a standard of comparison for testing the results of scientific experiments. **b** verification of the results of an experiment by repeating it, changing one variable at a time, and comparing the result with such a standard. **8** a spirit that directs a medium in a spiritualistic séance. **9** (*adjl.*) serving as a control: *a control experience.* **10** (*adjl.*) equipped with a control or controls: *a control room.*
—v. **1** exercise power or authority over; command or direct: *A ship's captain controls the ship and its crew.* **2** hold back; keep down; restrain: *to control an impulse, to control a forest fire.* **3** regulate: *to control prices and wages.* **4** check or verify (an experiment, the effects of a drug, testimony, etc.) by some standard of comparison or by independent investigation. **5** *Accounting.* check, verify, or regulate (expenditures, accounts, etc.). ⟨< F *contrôler* < OF *contreroller* < *contrerolle* register < *contre* against (< L *contra*) + *rolle* roll < L *rotulus,* dim. of *rota* wheel⟩ **—con'trol•ling•ly,** *adv.*
☛ *Syn. n.* **1.** See note at AUTHORITY.

control experiment an experiment in which each variable is controlled in turn, allowing the experimenter to determine the effect of each.

con•trol•la•ble [kən'trouləbəl] *adj.* that can be controlled; capable of being checked or restrained.

con•trolled–ac•cess [kən'trould 'æksɛs] *adj.* of a road, having a limited number of entries from other roads, which do not cross the traffic: *a controlled-access highway.*

controlled atmosphere a method of preserving fruit such as apples in a regulated temperature, for later marketing. *Abbrev.:* CA

con•trol•ler [kən'troulər] *n.* **1** a person employed to supervise expenditures or to manage financial affairs. Also, **comptroller. 2** a person who controls, directs, or regulates: *an air traffic controller.* **3** a device that controls or regulates something on a machine. **4** in certain city councils, a member of the BOARD OF CONTROL. **5** *Computer technology.* a device that controls one or more peripheral devices (disks, terminals, etc.) and connects them to a computer.

con•trol•ler•ship [kən'troulər,ʃɪp] *n.* the position or office of a controller.

control panel a panel containing all the instruments necessary for the control and operation of a complex mechanism such as a computer or an aircraft.

control rod 1 in a nuclear reactor, a mechanism, containing fuel or other matter, used to control the rate of a chain reaction. **2** in an aircraft, a rod for transmitting movements from the controls in the cockpit to the rudder, ailerons, etc.

control room 1 in a radio or television studio, a soundproof room from which the transmission of a broadcast can be controlled. **2** a room containing all the instruments necessary to control a complex operation, such as the launching of a rocket.

control stick the lever that controls the direction of an aircraft's movement.

control tower at an airfield, the building from which the taking off and landing of aircraft is controlled.

con•tro•ver•sial [,kɒntrə'vɜrʃəl] *or* [,kɒntrə'vɜrsiəl] *adj.* **1** of, open to, or arousing controversy: *a controversial question. She is a controversial politician.* **2** fond of controversy. **—,con•tro'ver•sial•ly,** *adv.*

con•tro•ver•sial•ist [ˌkɒntrəˈvɜrʃəlɪst] *n.* a person who takes part in, enjoys, or is skilled in controversy.

con•tro•ver•sy [ˈkɒntrəˌvɜrsi] *n., pl.* **-sies. 1** the act of arguing an important issue about which differences of opinion exist; debate; dispute: *The controversy between the company and the union ended in a strike.* **2** a quarrel; wrangle. ⟨< L *controversia* < *controversus* < *contro-* against + *versus*, pp. of *vertere* turn⟩

☛ *Syn.* **1.** See note at ARGUMENT.

con•tro•vert [ˈkɒntrəˌvɜrt] *or* [ˌkɒntrəˈvɜrt] *v.* **1** dispute; deny; oppose: *The statement of the last witness controverts the evidence of the first two.* **2** dispute about; discuss; debate. ⟨< L *contro-* against + *vertere* turn⟩ **—ˈcon•troˌvert•er,** *n.*

con•tro•vert•i•ble [ˌkɒntrəˈvɜrtəbəl] *adj.* that can be controverted; debatable. **—ˌcon•troˈvert•i•bly,** *adv.*

con•tu•ma•cious [ˌkɒntjəˈmeiʃəs] *or* [ˌkɒntəˈmeiʃəs] *adj.* stubbornly rebellious; obstinately disobedient.
—ˌcon•tuˈma•cious•ly, *adv.* **—ˌcon•tuˈma•cious•ness,** *n.*

con•tu•ma•cy [ˈkɒntjəməsi] *or* [ˈkɒntəməsi] *n., pl.* **-cies.** stubborn resistance to authority; obstinate disobedience. ⟨< L *contumacia* < *contumax* insolent < *tumere* swell up⟩

con•tu•me•li•ous [ˌkɒntjəˈmiliəs] *or* [ˌkɒntəˈmiliəs] *adj.* contemptuously insolent; insulting. **—ˌcon•tuˈme•li•ous•ly,** *adv.* **—ˌcon•tuˈme•li•ous•ness,** *n.*

con•tu•me•ly [ˈkɒntjəməli], [ˈkɒntəməli], [kənˈtjuməli], *or* [kənˈtuməli] *n., pl.* **-lies. 1** insolent contempt; insulting words or actions; humiliating treatment. **2** a humiliating insult. ⟨< L *contumelia*, originally, insolent action < *tumere* swell up⟩

con•tuse [kənˈtjuz] *or* [kənˈtuz] *v.* **-tused, -tus•ing.** injure without breaking the skin; bruise. ⟨< L *contusus*, pp. of *contundere* < *com-* (intensive) + *tundere* pound⟩

con•tu•sion [kənˈtjuʒən] *or* [kənˈtuʒən] *n.* **1** a bruising or being bruised. **2** a bruise.

co•nun•drum [kəˈnʌndrəm] *n.* **1** a riddle; a puzzling question whose answer involves a pun or play on words. *When is a door not a door?* is a conundrum. The answer to this conundrum is *When it's ajar.* **2** any puzzling problem. ⟨origin unknown⟩

con•ur•ba•tion [ˌkɒnərˈbeiʃən] *n.* a number of urban communities that have expanded and thus grown so close together that they can be considered as one large community. ⟨< *con-* + *urb(an)* + *-ation*⟩

con•va•lesce [ˌkɒnvəˈlɛs] *v.* **-lesced, -lesc•ing.** regain strength after illness; make progress toward health. ⟨< L *convalescere* < *com-* (intensive) + *valescere* grow strong < *valere* be strong⟩

con•va•les•cence [ˌkɒnvəˈlɛsəns] *n.* **1** a gradual recovery of health and strength after illness. **2** the time during which a person is convalescing.

con•va•les•cent [ˌkɒnvəˈlɛsənt] *adj., n. —adj.* recovering health and strength after illness: *Such exercise is too strenuous for a convalescent person.*
—n. **1** a person recovering after illness. **2** (*adjl.*) of or for persons who are convalescing: *the convalescent ward of a hospital, a convalescent diet.*

con•vec•tion [kənˈvɛkʃən] *n.* **1** *Physics.* the transfer of heat from one place to another by the circulation of heated particles of a gas or liquid. A forced-air furnace system heats a room by convection. **2** the act or process of conveying. ⟨< L *convectio*, *-onis* < *convehere* < *com-* together + *vehere* carry⟩

con•vec•tion•al [kənˈvɛkʃənəl] *adj.* of or characterized by convection.

convection oven a small, portable oven that heats and cooks food by convection, reducing cooking time. Most kinds produce their own heat by electricity, gas, or microwave energy; others may be placed on a stove element.

con•vec•tive [kənˈvɛktɪv] *adj.* **1** capable of conveying; transporting. **2** having to do with or resulting from convection.

con•vec•tive•ly [kənˈvɛktɪvli] *adv.* by means of convection.

con•vec•tor [kənˈvɛktər] *n.* a convective agent or device.

con•ven•ance [ˈkɒnvənəns]; *French,* [kɔ̃vˈnɑ̃s] *n.* normal social custom. ⟨< F < *convenir* be in accord, fit⟩

con•vene [kənˈvin] *v.* **-vened, -ven•ing. 1** meet for some purpose; gather together; assemble: *Parliament convenes in Ottawa at least once a year.* **2** call together (members of an organization, etc.) ⟨< L *convenire* < *com-* together + *venire* come⟩

con•ven•er [kənˈvinər] *n.* convenor.

con•ven•ience [kənˈvinjəns] *n.* **1** the fact or quality of being convenient: *Many people appreciate the convenience of frozen foods.* **2** comfort; advantage: *Many provincial parks have camping places for the convenience of tourists.* **3** anything handy or easy to use; something that increases comfort and saves trouble or work: *A folding table is a convenience in a small room. Their house is filled with electrical appliances and other modern conveniences.* **4** Often, **conveniences,** *pl.* toilet or washroom. **5** (*adjl.*) intended or prepared for people's convenience: *They live on convenience foods.* Also (defs. 1, 2), **conveniency**.
at (one's) **convenience,** so as to suit one as to time, place, or other conditions: *Write at your convenience.*
marriage of convenience, a marriage undertaken to gain citizenship or other benefit, and not as a personal relationship.

convenience food dried or frozen food that can be stored and used at one's convenience with a minimum of preparation, such as soup mixes, frozen pizzas, TV dinners, etc.

convenience store a small store, often a franchise or one of a chain of stores, that is open every day until late evening or 24 hours a day, and specializes in selling basic food items, such as milk and bread, and a variety of small dry-goods items.

con•ven•ient [kənˈvinjənt] *adj.* **1** saving trouble; well arranged; easy to use: *to use a convenient tool, to take a convenient bus, to live in a convenient house.* **2** within easy reach; handy: *to meet at a convenient place.* **3** easily done; not troublesome: *Would it be convenient for you to give me a lift to the meeting?*
convenient to, *Informal.* near; easy to reach from: *The library is convenient to our apartment.* ⟨< L *conveniens, -entis*, ppr. of *convenire* meet, agree, be suitable. See CONVENE.⟩
—conˈven•ient•ly, *adv.*

con•ven•or or **con•ven•er** [kənˈvinər] *n.* a person who is responsible for calling together the members of a committee, club, etc., and who often acts as their chairperson.

con•vent [ˈkɒnvɛnt] *or* [ˈkɒnvənt] *n.* **1** a community of persons dedicated to a religious life; in modern usage, a community of nuns. **2** the building or buildings in which they live. ⟨ME < AF *covent* < L *conventus* assembly < *convenire.* See CONVENE.⟩

con•ven•ti•cle [kənˈvɛntəkəl] *n.* **1** a secret or unauthorized meeting, especially for religious worship. **2** a secret religious meeting or assembly of certain Protestants who dissented from the doctrines and forms of the Church of England during the 16th and 17th centuries. **3** the place of such a meeting. ⟨< L *conventiculum*, dim. of *conventus* assembly. See CONVENT.⟩

con•ven•tion [kənˈvɛnʃən] *n.* **1** a meeting for some purpose; gathering; assembly. A political party holds a convention to choose candidates for public offices. **2** the delegates to a meeting or assembly. **3** an agreement. A convention signed by two or more countries is usually about less important matters than those in a treaty. **4** general agreement; common consent; custom. **5** a custom approved by general agreement; rule based on common consent: *Using the right hand to shake hands is a convention.* **6** *Arts.* a procedure or stylistic or formal detail used routinely in a given genre or art form and accepted by the beholder, reader, etc., as fitting and as having a certain significance: *It is a convention of the theatre to treat asides spoken by a character as though they were not heard by other persons on stage.* ⟨< L *conventio, -onis* < *convenire.* See CONVENE.⟩

con•ven•tion•al [kənˈvɛnʃənəl] *adj.* **1** depending on conventions; customary: *"Good morning" is a conventional greeting.* **2** acting or behaving according to commonly accepted and approved ways. **3** ordinary; not interesting; not original: *conventional furniture, conventional thought.* **4** *Art.* following custom rather than nature. Flowers and leaves are often drawn in a conventional design without any idea of making them look real. **5** of weapons, warfare, etc., not nuclear or biological. **6** of or having to do with a convention. **—conˈven•tion•al•ly,** *adv.*

☛ *Syn.* **1.** See note at FORMAL.

con•ven•tion•al•ism [kənˈvɛnʃənəˌlɪzəm] *n.* **1** a tendency to follow conventional usages; adherence to custom. **2** something conventional; formal usage, word, phrase, etc.
—conˈven•tion•al•ist, *n.*

con•ven•tion•al•i•ty [kənˌvɛnʃəˈnæləti] *n., pl.* **-ties. 1** a conventional quality or character: *the conventionality of modern life.* **2** conventional behaviour; adherence to custom. **3** a conventional custom or rule: *The girls at boarding school were required to observe the conventionalities very strictly.*

con•ven•tion•al•ize [kənˈvɛnʃənəˌlaɪz] *v.* **-ized, -iz•ing. 1** make conventional. **2** draw or design according to a particular or conventional style, rather than according to nature; stylize or simplify. **—conˌven•tion•al•iˈza•tion,** *n.*

conventional wisdom popular belief: *Conventional wisdom has it that one catches a cold as a result of being cold.*

con•ven•tion•eer [kən,vɛnʃə'nir] *n.* one who attends a convention, usually as a delegate.

con•ven•tu•al [kən'vɛntʃuəl] *adj., n. —adj.* of or like a convent.
—n. a member of a convent.

con•verge [kən'vɜrdʒ] *v.* **-verged, -verg•ing. 1** meet or tend to meet in a point. *The freeways converge just before the bridge.* **2** turn toward each other: *If you look at the end of your nose, your eyes converge.* **3** come together; centre: *The interest of all the students converged on the celebration.* **4** tend toward the same character or effect: *Our opinions converge on this issue despite our different premises.* **5** cause to converge. **6** *Linguistics.* of dialects, merge; become more alike. Compare DIVERGE. **7** *Mathematics.* draw near to some finite limit. A series converges when the sum of a number of its terms approaches a limiting value. ⟨< LL *convergere* < L *com-* together + *vergere* incline⟩

con•ver•gence [kən'vɜrdʒəns] *n.* **1** the act, process, or fact of converging; a meeting, or tendency to meet, in a point. **2** the point of meeting. **3** the turning inward of the eyes in focussing on something very close to them. **4** a tendency toward a common character or effect: *the convergence of cultures of peoples who have lived together for a long time.* **5** *Biology.* the tendency in animals or plants not closely related to develop similar characteristics when living under the same conditions. **6** *Linguistics.* of dialects, a merging; becoming more alike. Compare DIVERGENCE. Also, **convergency.**

con•ver•gen•cy [kən'vɜrdʒənsi] *n., pl.* **-cies.** convergence.

con•ver•gent [kən'vɜrdʒənt] *adj.* tending to converge; inclining toward each other or toward a common point.

con•vers•a•ble [kən'vɜrsəbəl] *adj.* **1** easy or pleasant to talk to. **2** fond of talking. **3** having to do with or proper for social intercourse. **—con'vers•a•bly,** *adv.*

con•ver•sant [kən'vɜrsənt] *or* ['kɒnvərsənt] *adj.* familiar by use or study; acquainted: *He is not conversant with the history of philosophical thought.* **—con'ver•sant•ly,** *adv.*

con•ver•sa•tion [,kɒnvər'seiʃən] *n.* **1** informal or friendly talk; the exchange of thoughts by talking informally: *There is much pleasure in good conversation.* **2** a talk; a meeting for the purpose of informal talk: *The professor invited his students to his home for a conversation.*

con•ver•sa•tion•al [,kɒnvər'seiʃənəl] *adj.* **1** of or having to do with conversation. **2** fond of conversation; good at conversation. **3** characteristic of conversation.

con•ver•sa•tion•al•ist [,kɒnvər'seiʃənəlɪst] *n.* a person who is fond of or good at conversation; one who cultivates the art of conversation.

con•ver•sa•tion•al•ly [,kɒnvər'seiʃənəli] *adv.* in a conversational, informal manner.

conversation piece an object which attracts comment by its unusual or exotic nature.

con•ver•sa•zi•o•ne [,kɒnvər,sætsi'ounei]; *Italian,* [,kɔnvɛr,satsi'ɔne] *n.* a social circle for the discussion of artistic and literary matters. ⟨< Ital.⟩

con•verse[1] *v.* [kən'vɜrs]; *n.* ['kɒnvərs] *v.* **-versed, -vers•ing;** *n.* *—v.* talk informally together: *The two old veterans liked conversing about their experiences during the war.*
—n. conversation. ⟨ME < OF *converser* < L *conversari* live with < *com-* with + *versari* live, be busy < *verti* turn⟩ **—con'vers•er,** *n.*

con•verse[2] *adj.* [kən'vɜrs] *or* ['kɒnvɜrs]; *n.* ['kɒnvɜrs] *adj., n.* *—adj.* **1** opposite; contrary. **2** reversed in order; turned about.
—n. **1** something that is opposite or contrary. **2** something that is turned around: *"Honest but poor" is the converse of "Poor but honest."* ⟨< L *conversus* turned around, pp. of *convertere.* See CONVERT.⟩

con•verse•ly [kən'vɜrsli] *or* ['kɒnvɜrsli] *adv.* if or when turned the other way around: *Six is more than five; conversely, five is less than six.*

con•ver•sion [kən'vɜrʒən] *or* [kən'vɜrʃən] *n.* **1** the act of converting or the process of being converted: *the conversion of real estate into liquid assets. Heat causes the conversion of water into steam.* **2** the act or experience of adopting a religion: *He told them about his conversion several years before.* **3** *Football.* the act or fact of kicking a point after a touchdown. **4** *Logic.* an operation involving the transposition of the subject and predicate of a proposition. The conversion of *No truly creative person is bored* is *No one who is bored is truly creative.* **5 a** an exchange of one currency for another. **b** the cost of this: *The buyer will pay the conversion.* **6** a taking and using unlawfully: *conversion of the club's funds to his own use.* **7 a** *Mathematics.* a single instance of the compounding of interest; calculation of a new sum by adding accrued interest to the preceding principal. Frequency of conversion means the number of times a year that interest is compounded. **b** a change in the expression of a value without a change in the value itself, as converting a length in inches to its counterpart in centimetres. **8** *Psychology.* the process by which an inner conflict manifests itself as a physical ailment.

con•vert *v.* [kən'vɜrt]; *n.* ['kɒnvɜrt] *v., n. —v.* **1** change; turn: *These machines convert pulp into paper. One last effort converted defeat into victory.* **2** change or cause to change from one religion, political party, etc., to another: *The missionaries converted many people to Christianity.* **3** cause to adopt a religion: *She was converted at a prayer meeting.* **4** take and use unlawfully: *The dishonest treasurer converted the club's money to her own use.* **5** turn the other way around; invert; transpose. **6** exchange for an equivalent: *He converted his Canadian dollars into French francs before he left.* **7** exchange (a bond or other security) for another type of security, as common stock. **8** *Law.* change (real property) to personal property or vice versa. **9** *Logic.* modify (a proposition) by interchanging its terms, as by conversion. **10** *Football.* kick a goal after a touchdown.
—n. **1** a person who has been converted. **2** *Cdn. Football.* **a** a goal kicked after a touchdown. **b** the point made by successfully kicking such a goal. ⟨< L *convertere* < *com-* (intensive) + *vertere* turn⟩
☛ *Syn. v.* **1.** See note at TRANSFORM.

con•vert•er [kən'vɜrtər] *n.* **1** a device for changing alternating electrical current into direct current. **2** a device for adapting a television set to receive more channels than it was designed for. **3** a device in a radio receiver for changing frequencies from higher to lower. **4** a furnace in which pig iron is changed into steel by the Bessemer process. **5** any person or thing that converts.

con•vert•i•ble [kən'vɜrtəbəl] *adj., n. —adj.* **1** capable of being converted: *Wood is convertible into paper. A two-dollar bill is convertible into coins.* **2** of an automobile, having a top that may be folded down. **3** of securities, that can be exchanged for others of the same value.
—n. an automobile with a cloth roof that can be folded down behind the rear seat. **—con'vert•i•bly,** *adv.* **—con,vert•i'bil•i•ty,** *n.*

con•vert•i•plane [kən'vɜrtə,plein] *n.* an aircraft that operates like a conventional airplane in level flight, but that takes off and lands like a helicopter. ⟨< *convert*ible + air*plane*⟩

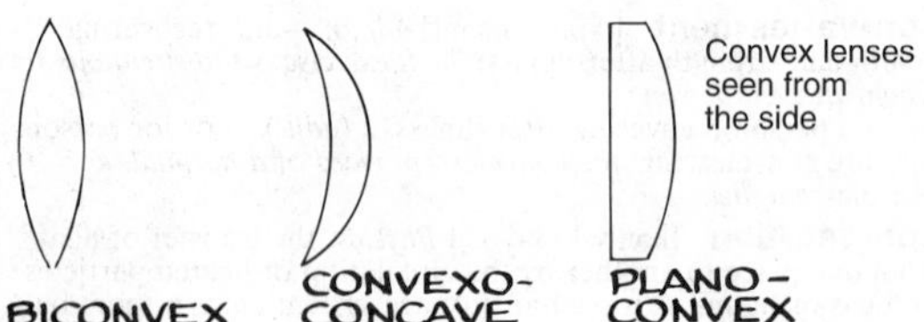

con•vex [kɒn'vɛks] *or* ['kɒnvɛks] *adj., n. —adj.* curved out, like the outside of a circle or sphere: *The crystal of a watch is slightly convex.*
—n. a convex surface or thing. ⟨< L *convexus* vaulted, probably < *com-* around + *vac-* bend (related to *vacillare* totter, sway)⟩ **—con'vex•ly,** *adv.*

con•vex•i•ty [kɒn'vɛksəti] *or* [kən'vɛksɪti] *n., pl.* **-ties. 1** a convex condition or quality. **2** a convex surface or thing.

con•vex•o–con•cave [kɒn'vɛksou kɒn'keiv] *or* [kən'vɛksou kən'keiv] *adj.* convex on one side and concave on the other. In a convexo-concave lens, the convex side has the greatest curvature. See CONVEX for picture.

con•vex•o–con•vex [kɒn'vɛksou kɒn'vɛks] *or* [kən'vɛksou-] *adj.* convex on both sides, like a lens; biconvex.

con•vex•o–plane [kɒn'vɛksou ,plein] *or* [kən'vɛksou-] *adj.* having a flat side and a convex side; plano-convex.

con•vey [kən'vei] *v.* **1** carry; transport: *A bus conveys passengers.* **2** transmit; conduct: *A wire conveys an electric current.* **3** express; make known; communicate: *Her words convey no meaning to me.* **4** *Law.* transfer the ownership of (property) from one person to another: *The old farmer conveyed his farm to his daughter.* ⟨ME < OF *conveier* < VL < L *com-* with + *via* road. Doublet of CONVOY.⟩ **—con'vey•a•ble,** *adj.*
☛ *Syn.* **1.** See note at CARRY.

con•vey•ance [kən'veiəns] *n.* **1** the act of carrying; transportation; transmission. **2** anything that carries people and goods; vehicle. **3** communication. **4** *Law.* **a** transfer of the ownership of property from one person to another. **b** a written statement that shows such a transfer; deed.

con•vey•anc•er [kən'veiənsər] *n.* a lawyer or lawyer's assistant who investigates the ownership of property and prepares contracts, deeds, etc., for its transfer from one person to another.

con•vey•anc•ing [kən'veiənsɪŋ] *n.* the preparation of deeds, etc., for the transfer of the ownership of property from one person to another.

con•vey•or or **con•vey•er** [kən'veiər] *n.* **1** a person or thing that conveys. **2** a mechanical device that carries things from one place to another by means of a moving endless belt or a series of rollers: *Grain is carried from one level of an elevator to another by means of a conveyor.*

conveyor belt CONVEYOR (def. 2).

con•vict *v.* [kən'vɪkt]; *n.* ['kɒnvɪkt] *v., n.* —*v.* **1** prove guilty. **2** declare guilty: *The jury convicted the prisoner of murder.* **3** impress with a sense of guilt: *a person convicted of sin.*
—*n.* **1** a person convicted by a court. **2** a person serving a prison sentence for some crime. ⟨< L *convictus,* pp. of *convincere.* See CONVINCE.⟩

con•vic•tion [kən'vɪkʃən] *n.* **1** convicting or being convicted: *a conviction for theft. She was overcome with conviction and remorse.* **2** the appearance or condition of being convinced: *She spoke with conviction on the benefits of regular exercise.* **3** a firm belief. **4** *Rare.* the act of convincing a person.
☛ *Syn.* **3.** See note at BELIEF.

con•vict•ive [kən'vɪktɪv] *adj.* **1** able to convince. **2** able to convict.

con•vince [kən'vɪns] *v.* **-vinced, -vinc•ing. 1** make (a person) feel sure; cause to believe; persuade by argument or proof: *The mistakes Nan made convinced the teacher that she had not studied her lesson.* **2** *Informal.* cause to consent (*to* do something) by persuasive argument: *They finally convinced me to sell the motorcycle.* ⟨< L *convincere* < *com-* (intensive) + *vincere* overcome⟩
☛ *Syn.* See note at PERSUADE.
☛ *Usage.* **Convince,** in formal English, is always followed by *of* plus a noun or by a *that*-clause: *I can easily convince you of his innocence. You will soon be convinced that I am right.* The construction *convince someone to do something* is strictly confined to informal English.

con•vin•ci•ble [kən'vɪnsəbəl] *adj.* capable of being convinced.

con•vinc•ing [kən'vɪnsɪŋ] *adj., v.* —*adj.* **1** that convinces: *a convincing argument.* **2** plausible; credible; realistic.
—*v.* ppr. of CONVINCE. **—con'vinc•ing•ly,** *adv.* **—con'vinc•ing•ness,** *n.*

con•viv•i•al [kən'vɪviəl] *adj.* **1** fond of eating and drinking with friends; jovial; sociable. **2** of or suitable for a feast or banquet; festive. ⟨< LL *convivialis* < L *convivium* feast < *com-* with + *vivere* live⟩ **—con'viv•i•al•ly,** *adv.*

con•viv•i•al•i•ty [kən,vɪvi'æləti] *n., pl.* **-ties. 1** a fondness for eating and drinking with friends; sociability. **2** eating and drinking with friends; festivity; good fellowship.

con•vo•ca•tion [,kɒnvə'keiʃən] *n.* **1** a calling together; an assembling by a summons. **2** an assembly; a number of persons gathered in answer to a summons: *The convocation of clergy passed a resolution condemning war.* **3** at certain universities: **a** the officials and graduates as a legislative, advisory, or electoral body. **b** a meeting of this body. **4** at other universities: **a** an assembly of the members of a university for a specific purpose. **b** a ceremony at which degrees are conferred. **—,con•vo'ca•tion•al,** *adj.*

con•voke [kən'vouk] *v.* **-voked, -vok•ing.** call together; summon to assemble. ⟨< L *convocare* < *com-* together + *vocare* call⟩ **—con'vok•er,** *n.*

con•vo•lute [,kɒnvə'lut] *adj., v.* **-lut•ed, -lut•ing.** —*adj.* coiled; rolled up into a spiral shape with one part over another.
—*v.* coil. ⟨< L *convolutus,* pp. of *convolvere* < *com-* together + *volvere* roll⟩ **—,con•vo'lute•ly,** *adv.*

con•vo•lut•ed [,kɒnvə'lutɪd] *adj., v.* —*adj.* **1** having convolutions; coiled; twisted. **2** complicated; intricate, especially excessively so: *a convoluted theory.*
—*v.* pt. and pp. of CONVOLUTE.

con•vo•lu•tion [,kɒnvə'luʃən] *n.* **1** a coiling, winding, or twisting together. **2** a coil; winding; twist. **3** *Anatomy.* an irregular fold or ridge on the surface of the brain. **4** the quality of being convoluted.

con•volve [kən'vɒlv] *v.,* **-volved, -volv•ing,** coil; twist; roll together. ⟨< L *convolvere.* See CONVOLUTE.⟩

con•vol•vu•lus [kən'vɒlvjələs] *n., pl.* **-lus•es, -li** [-,lai] *or* [-,li] any of a genus (*Convolvulus*) of plants, usually vines, having flowers shaped like trumpets. The morning glory is a convolvulus. ⟨< L *convolvulus* bindweed < *convolvere* roll around; with reference to its twining stems. See CONVOLUTE.⟩

con•voy ['kɒnvɔi] *v., n.* —*v.* accompany in order to protect; escort: *Warships convoy merchant ships in wartime.*
—*n.* **1** an escort; protection: *The gold was moved from the truck to the vault under convoy of armed guards.* **2** warships, soldiers, etc., that convoy; a protecting escort. **3** the ship, fleet, supplies, etc., accompanied by a protecting escort. **4** any vehicles together with their escort. **5** the act of escorting for protection: *The convoy of merchant ships was continued throughout the war.* ⟨ME < OF *convoier, conveier.* Doublet of CONVEY.⟩

con•vul•sant [kən'vʌlsənt] *adj., n.* —*adj.* that causes convulsions.
—*n.* a drug or other agent that causes convulsions.

con•vulse [kən'vʌls] *v.* **-vulsed, -vuls•ing. 1** shake violently: *An earthquake convulsed the island.* **2** cause violent disturbance in; disturb violently: *Rage convulsed his face.* **3** throw into convulsions; affect with muscular spasms: *The sick child was convulsed before the doctor came.* **4** throw into a fit of laughter; cause to shake with laughter: *The clown convulsed the audience with her funny acts.* ⟨< L *convulsus,* pp. of *convellere* tear away *com-* (intensive) + *vellere* tear⟩

con•vul•sion [kən'vʌlʃən] *n.* **1** Often, **convulsions,** *pl.* a violent, involuntary contracting and relaxing of the muscles; spasm. **2** a fit of laughter. **3** a violent disturbance: *The country was undergoing a political convulsion.*

con•vul•sive [kən'vʌlsɪv] *adj.* **1** sudden, violent, etc., like a convulsion: *The dog made convulsive efforts to free itself from the chain.* **2** having convulsions. **3** producing convulsions. **—con'vul•sive•ly,** *adv.*

co•ny[1] or **co•ney** ['kouni] *n., pl.* **-nies. 1** rabbit. **2** rabbit fur. **3** pika. **4** a fish (*Epinephelus fulvus*) of the grouper family, native to tropical Atlantic waters. **5** in the King James Version of the Bible, the hyrax. ⟨< ME *coni* < OF *conin, conil* < L *cuniculus* rabbit⟩

co•ny[2] ['kɒni] *Cdn.* inconnu. Also, **connie, coney.**

coo [ku] *n., v.* **cooed, coo•ing.** —*n.* a soft, murmuring sound made by doves or pigeons.
—*v.* **1** make a soft, murmuring sound. **2** murmur softly; speak in a soft or loving manner. **3** of a baby, make the voluntary open vowel sounds that are the first precursors of language. ⟨imitative⟩ **—'coo•er,** *n.*
☛ *Hom.* COUP.

coo•ee ['kui] *n., pl.* **-ees;** *interj., v.* —*n. or interj.* in Australia, a long, shrill signal call of the aborigines, adopted by the colonists.
—*v.* make this call. Also, **cooey.**

cook [kʊk] *v., n.* —*v.* **1** prepare (food) for eating by applying heat, as in boiling, baking, frying, or broiling: *We use coal, wood, gas, oil, or electricity for cooking.* **2** undergo cooking; be cooked. **3** act as cook; work as cook: *He cooked for the whole camp.* **4** apply heat or fire to. **5** *Informal.* subject or be subjected to heat or fire: *I am just cooking in this heavy coat! She cooked the engine when her radiator failed in the middle of a heavy traffic jam.* **6** *Informal.* tamper with (accounts, etc.); doctor; falsify: *She was caught cooking the company's books, and was charged with theft.*
cook someone's goose. See GOOSE.
cook up, *Informal.* **a** make up; prepare. **b** prepare falsely: *The young liar had cooked up a story to explain his absence.*
what's cooking, *Slang.* what's happening.
—*n.* a person who cooks. ⟨OE *cōc* < LL *cocus* < L *coquus*⟩

cook•book ['kʊk,bʊk] *n.* a book containing directions for cooking various kinds of food; book of recipes.

cook•ee, cook•ie, or **cook•y** ['kʊki] *n. Cdn.* a cook or assistant cook in a lumber camp.

cook•er ['kʊkər] *n.* an apparatus or container to cook things in.

cook•er•y ['kʊkəri] *n., pl.* **-er•ies. 1** the art or occupation of cooking. **2** *Cdn.* a cookhouse at a lumber camp or mine. **3** a place for cooking.

cook•house ['kʊk,hʌus] *n.* a room or place for cooking, especially in a large camp.

cook•ie ['kʊki] *n.* **1** any of various kinds of small, sweet, more or less flat, crisp cake. Sometimes, **cooky.** **2** *Slang.* person: *a shrewd cookie.* ⟨< Du. *koekje* little cake⟩

cook–off ['kʊk ,ɒf] *n.* a public cooking competition.

cook•out ['kʊk,ʌut] *n.* the cooking and eating of a meal out-of-doors; a picnic, etc., where the food is cooked outdoors.

cook•shop ['kʊk,ʃɒp] *n.* a place where food is cooked and sold; small restaurant.

cook•stove ['kʊk,stouv] *n.* a stove for cooking.

cook•ware ['kʊk,wɛr] *n.* utensils needed for cooking, such as pots, pans, cake tins, casseroles, etc.

cook•y ['kʊki] *n., pl.* **cook•ies.** See COOKIE.

cool [kul] *adj., n., v.* —*adj.* **1** somewhat cold; more cold than hot: *We sat in the shade where it was cool.* **2** allowing or giving a cool feeling: *cool clothes.* **3** not excited; calm and unemotional. **4** having or showing little enthusiasm or interest; not cordial: *a cool greeting.* **5** bold; impudent: *a cool customer.* **6** *Informal.* without exaggeration or qualification: *a cool million dollars.* **7** of colours, suggesting coolness: *Blue and green are called cool colours. The chesterfield and chair were a cool grey.* **8** *Slang.* admirable; excellent. **9** *Slang.* relaxed and restrained in a sophisticated way: *cool jazz.*
—*n.* **1** a cool part, place, or time: *the cool of the evening.* **2** *Slang.* control of one's actions, feelings, etc.; self-control: *Keep your cool.*
—*v.* **1** become cool: *Let the cake cool before you put on the icing.* **2** make cool.
cool down or **off,** *Informal.* **a** lose one's enthusiasm, especially for a person. **b** calm down, especially after being very angry.
cool it, *Slang.* calm down; regain one's self-control: *He told his excited little sister to cool it.*
cool (one's) **heels,** *Informal.* be kept waiting for a long time.
stay or **keep cool,** *Slang.* keep calm. ⟨OE *cōl*⟩ —**'cool•ly,** *adv.* —**'cool•ness,** *n.*
☛ *Syn. adj.* **1.** See note at COLD.

cool•ant ['kulənt] *n.* a cooling agent, used for machinery, etc.

cool•er ['kulər] *n.* **1** an apparatus or container that cools foods or drinks, or keeps them cool. **2** anything that cools, such as a cool drink. **3** *Slang.* a jail: *He got drunk and landed in the cooler.* **4** a carbonated fruit drink containing a small amount of wine or other alcohol.

cool–head•ed ['kul 'hɛdɪd] *adj.* calm; not easily excited. —**'cool-,head•ed•ly,** *adv.* —**'cool-,head•ed•ness,** *n.*

coo•lie ['kuli] *n.* **1** an unskilled labourer in parts of Asia. **2** any labourer who does hard work for very little pay. Also, **cooly.** ⟨probably < Tamil *kuli* hire, hired servant⟩
☛ *Hom.* COULEE.

cool•ish ['kulɪʃ] *adj.* rather cool.

coo•ly ['kuli] *n., pl.* **-lies.** See COOLIE.

coomb [kum] *or* [koum] See COMBE.

coon [kun] *n. Informal.* raccoon.

coon•skin ['kun,skɪn] *n.* **1** the skin of a raccoon, used in making caps, coats, etc. **2** (*adjl.*) made of coonskin.

coon•tie ['kunti] *n.* a tropical tree resembling a palm tree (*Zamia floridana*), native to Florida and having an underground trunk yielding starch. ⟨< Seminole *kunti* coontie flour, starch⟩

coop [kup] *n., v.* —*n.* **1** a small cage or pen for chickens, rabbits, etc. **2** *Slang.* jail.
fly the coop, *Slang.* escape.
—*v.* **1** keep or put in a coop. **2** confine, especially in a very small space (*often used with* **up**): *The children were cooped up indoors on account of the rain.* ⟨ME *cupe* basket < L *cupa* cask⟩
☛ *Hom.* COUPE.

co–op ['kou ,ɒp] *or* [,kou 'ɒp] *n., adj. Informal.* co-operative.

coop•er ['kupər] *n., v.* —*n.* a person who makes or repairs barrels, casks, etc.
—*v.* make or repair (barrels, casks, etc.). ⟨? < MDu., MLG *kuper* < L *cuparius* < *cupa* cask⟩

coop•er•age ['kupərɪdʒ] *n.* **1** the work done by a cooper. **2** the price paid for such work. **3** the shop where such work is done.

co–op•er•ate [kou 'ɒpə,reit] *v.* **-at•ed, -at•ing.** work together; unite in producing a result. ⟨< LL *cooperari* < *co-* together + *operari* to work < L *opera* effort, work⟩ —**co-'op•er,a•tor,** *n.*

co–op•er•a•tion [kou ,ɒpə'reiʃən] *n.* **1** the act of working together; united effort or labour. **2** a co-operative combination of persons or groups. **3** *Ecology.* an interaction between individuals or organisms in a community, colony, etc., that is on the whole beneficial to all. —**co-,op•er'a•tion•ist,** *n.*

co–op•er•a•tive or **co•op•er•a•tive** [kou 'ɒpərətɪv] *or* [kou 'ɒpə,reitɪv] *adj., n.* —*adj.* **1** wanting or willing to work together with others. **2** of, having to do with, or being a co-operative. **3** of or designating an educational program at the secondary or post-secondary level in which students work at jobs related to their studies for academic credit instead of pay.
—*n.* an enterprise owned jointly by a group of people and operated for their mutual benefit. Co-operatives may take the form of stores, farm marketing agencies, housing units, etc. —**co-'op•er•a•tive•ly,** *adv.* —**co-'op•er•a•tive•ness,** *n.*

Co–operative Commonwealth Federation a Canadian political party, the CCF, established in 1932. The federal CCF ceased to exist on a national level after the New Democratic Party was formed in 1961. See also NEW DEMOCRATIC PARTY.

co–operative federalism a system in which constituent members, such as provinces, can vote to accept or reject a federal suggestion.

co–operative store a store where merchandise is sold to members who share in the profits and losses according to the amount they buy.

Cooper's hawk a hawk (*Accipiter cooperii*) of medium size, with rounded wings and tail.

co–opt [kou 'ɒpt] *v.* **1** of a committee, etc., add or elect (a new member). **2** persuade or oblige to join one's own system, culture, side in a dispute, etc.; take over. ⟨< L *cooptare* to choose < *co-* with + *optare* to choose⟩ —**co-'op•tion,** *n.*

co–or•di•nate or **co•or•di•nate** *adj. and n.* [kou 'ɔrdənɪt] *or* [kou 'ɔrdə,neit]; *v.* [kou 'ɔrdə,neit] *adj., n., v.* **-nat•ed, -nat•ing.** —*adj.* **1** equal in importance; of equal rank. **2** made up of co-ordinate parts. **3** *Grammar.* grammatically equivalent. A compound sentence contains two or more co-ordinate clauses. **4** *Mathematics.* Usually, **coordinate,** having to do with or involving the use of co-ordinates. **5** *Chemistry.* in which one atom shares two electrons with another atom: *a co-ordinate bond.*
—*n.* **1** a co-ordinate person or thing. **2 co-ordinates,** *pl.* **a** matching items of clothing, luggage, or furniture: *This skirt and this sweater are co-ordinates.* **b** in geography, a pair of references, such as latitude or longitude, which fixes a position on a map. **3** *Mathematics.* Usually, **coordinate,** any of two or more magnitudes that define the position of a point, line, or plane by reference to a fixed figure, system of lines, etc.
—*v.* **1** make co-ordinate; make equal in importance. **2** arrange in proper order or relation; harmonize; adjust; orchestrate: *To be a good swimmer you should co-ordinate the movements of your arms and legs. They had good topics and speakers at the conference, but the whole thing was very poorly co-ordinated and I ended up in the wrong seminar.* **3** *Chemistry.* combine by a bond in which two electrons from only one atom form the bonding pair. ⟨< *co-* with + L *ordinatus,* pp. of *ordinare* regulate < *ordo, -inis* rank, order⟩ —**co-'or•di•nate•ly,** *adv.* —**co-'or•di•nate•ness,** *n.* —**co-'or•di,na•tor,** *n.*

coordinate geometry the use of algebra and coordinates to solve problems in geometry; analytic geometry.

co–ordinating conjunction *Grammar.* a conjunction used to join clauses of equal importance. *Examples:* and, but, or.

co–or•di•na•tion or **co•or•di•na•tion** [kou ,ɔrdə'neiʃən] *n.* **1** the condition of working together smoothly and easily, often used with reference to muscles: *She became a better swimmer as her co-ordination improved.* **2** arrangement in the proper order or proper relation: *She made an outline for her composition to help in the co-ordination of her ideas.* **3** a putting or being put into the same order or rank.

co–ordination chemistry the area of inorganic chemistry involving co-ordination compounds.

co–ordination complex a compound in which an atom or group of atoms forms a co-ordinate bond with another atom or group of atoms.

co–ordination compound a compound that consists of a central metallic ion, usually a transition element, co-ordinated with several surrounding ions called ligands; complex ion.

co–or•di•na•tive [kou 'ɔrdənətɪv] *or* [kou 'ɔrdə,neitɪv] *adj.* co-ordinating.

Coos [kus] *n.* **1** a member of an American Indian people now living in Oregon. **2** the language of this people.

coot [kut] *n.* **1** any of a genus (*Fulica*) of dark grey inland marsh birds of the rail family, resembling ducks, but having a smaller bill and toes with scalloplike lobes of skin along the sides; mud hen. **2** a North American scoter. **3** *Informal.* a foolish or simple person: *The poor coot couldn't even remember where his hotel was.* ⟨? < Du. *koet*⟩

coot•ie ['kuti] *n. Slang.* louse. ⟨< Malay *kutu* dog tick⟩

cop[1] [kɒp] *n. Slang.* a police officer. ⟨short for *copper*[2]⟩

cop[2] [kɒp] *v.* **copped, cop•ping. 1** *Slang.* steal. **2** capture; seize; nab.
cop a plea, plead guilty to one charge in order to avoid being tried for a more serious one.
cop out, *Slang.* **a** avoid responsibility, commitment, challenge, etc., by withdrawing from the situation or by simply failing to act. **b** confess to a crime by implicating others. ⟨OE *coppian*⟩

cop. **1** copper. **2** copyright; copyrighted.

co•pa•cet•ic [,koupə'sɛtɪk] *or* [,koupə'sitɪk] *adj. Slang.* completely satisfactory: *checking to see that everything was copacetic.* ⟨origin unknown; 20c.⟩

co•pai•ba [kou'peibə] *or* [kou'paɪbə] *n.* a resin obtained from several tropical South American trees of the genus *Copaifera*, of the legume family, formerly used in medicine and now in varnishes. ⟨< Sp. and Pg. < Tupi *cupaiba*⟩

co•pal ['koupəl] *n.* a hard, lustrous resin from various tropical trees, used chiefly in making varnish. ⟨< Sp. < Nahuatl *kopalli*⟩

co•palm ['koupɒm] *or* ['koupɑm] *n.* **1** the sweet gum tree (*Liquidambar styraciflua*), having palmate leaves. **2** a yellow, aromatic resin obtained from this tree.

co–part•ner [kou 'pɑrtnər] *n.* a fellow partner; associate.

co–part•ner•ship [kou 'pɑrtnər,ʃɪp] *n.* partnership.

cope[1] [koup] *v.* **coped, cop•ing.** strive or fight, with some degree of success; struggle on even terms; deal successfully: *He said he just couldn't cope any more. She was too weak to cope with the extra work.* ⟨ME < OF *coper* strike < *coup.* See COUP.⟩
—'cope•less, *adj.*

cope[2] [koup] *n., v.* **coped, cop•ing.** *—n.* **1** *Christianity.* a long cape worn by some clergy during certain religious rites.
2 anything like a cope; a cloaklike covering, such as a canopy, a high, arched roof, or the sky. **3** *Architecture.* a coping.
—v. **1** cover with a cope or something like a cope. **2** provide with a coping or something like a coping. ⟨OE **cāpe* < Med.L *capa* cloak, var. of LL *cappa* hood, apparently < L *caput* head⟩

COPE *Cdn.* Committee for Original Peoples' Entitlement.

co•peck ['koupɛk] See KOPECK.

co•pe•pod ['koupə,pɒd] *n.* any of a large subclass (Copepoda) of mostly very tiny crustaceans found as a constituent of plankton in water. ⟨< NL *Copepoda* < Gk. *kōpē* oar + *pous, podos* foot⟩

Co•per•ni•can [kə'pɜrnəkən] *adj.* of or having to do with Nikolaus Copernicus (1473-1543), a Polish astronomer, or his system of astronomy. The Copernican system is the theory that the earth revolves on its axis and the planets move in orbits around the sun.

cope•stone ['koup,stoun] *n.* **1** the top stone of a wall; a stone used for or in a coping. **2** a finishing touch; climax. ⟨< *cope*[2] + *stone*⟩

cop•i•er ['kɒpiər] *n.* **1** a person who copies; imitator. **2** a person who makes written copies; copyist. **3** a machine that makes copies; duplicator.

co–pi•lot ['kou ,paɪlət] *n.* the assistant or second pilot in an aircraft.

cop•ing ['koupɪŋ] *n.* the top layer of a brick or stone wall. It is usually built with a slope to shed water. ⟨< *cope*[2]⟩

coping saw a saw with a narrow blade set in a U-shaped frame, used for cutting curves in wood. A coping saw has between three and five teeth per centimetre. Compare FRET SAW.

co•pi•ous ['koupiəs] *adj.* **1** plentiful; abundant: *copious rainfall; a copious harvest.* **2** containing or providing much. **3** containing many words; wordy: *a copious argument.* ⟨< L *copiosus* < *copia* plenty < *copis* well supplied < *co-* with + *ops* resources⟩ **—'co•pi•ous•ly,** *adv,* **—'co•pi•ous•ness,** *n.*

co•pla•nar [kou'pleinər] *adj. Mathematics.* (of points, lines, figures) lying in the same plane. A circle is a set of coplanar points. ⟨< *co-* + *plane* + *-ar*⟩

co•pol•y•mer [kou'pɒlɪmər] *n.* a chemical compound made up of large molecules, formed by the polymerization of two or more different compounds (monomers). **—co,pol•y'mer•ic** [-'mɛrɪk], *adj.*

co•pol•y•mer•ize [kou'pɒlɪmə,raɪz] *v.* **-ized, -iz•ing.** polymerize (two different compounds) to produce a copolymer.

cop–out ['kɒp ,ʌut] *n. Slang.* **1** an avoidance of responsibility, commitment, etc. **2** an excuse for such behaviour: *What kind of a cop-out is that?* **3** a person who avoids responsibility.

cop•per[1] ['kɒpər] *n., v., adj. —n.* **1** a tough, reddish brown metallic chemical element that is easily shaped into thin sheets or fine wire and resists rust. Copper is an excellent conductor of heat and electricity. *Symbol:* Cu; *at.no.* 29; *at.mass* 63.55. **2** a copper or bronze coin, especially a penny. **3** a large boiler or cauldron. **4** a reddish brown. **5** a small, copper-coloured butterfly of the family Lycaenidae, native to temperate climates.
—v. cover with copper.
—adj. **1** made of copper. **2** having the colour copper. ⟨OE *coper* < L *cuprum*, for earlier *aes Cyprium* metal of Cyprus⟩

cop•per[2] ['kɒpər] *n. Slang.* a police officer; cop. ⟨< *cop*[2]⟩

cop•per•as ['kɒpərəs] *n.* a green sulphate of iron, used in dyeing, photography, making ink, etc. *Formula:* $FeSO_4 \cdot 7H_2O$ ⟨ME < OF *couperose* < Med.L *(aqua) cuprosa* (water) of copper < L *cuprum.* See COPPER.⟩

Copper Eskimo a member of a group of Inuit living along the Arctic coast near the Coppermine River. ⟨with reference to their use of copper tools⟩

cop•per•head ['kɒpər,hɛd] *n.* a poisonous snake (*Agkistrodon contortrix*) of the eastern and central United States having a copper-coloured head. It is closely related to the water moccasin.

cop•per•plate ['kɒpər,pleit] *n.* **1** a thin, flat piece of copper on which a design, writing, etc., is engraved or etched. **2** an engraving, picture, or print made from a copperplate. **3** the art of copperplate printing or engraving. **4** a type of elegant handwriting.

copper pyrites *n.* a copper ore formed of iron and copper sulphide. *Formula:* $CuFeS_2$

copper red•horse ['rɛd,hɔrs] a fish (*Moxostoma hubbsi*) of the sucker family, found in the Richelieu River, just east of Montréal. It is a threatened species.

cop•per•smith ['kɒpər,smɪθ] *n.* a person who makes things out of copper.

copper sulphate or **sulfate** a sulphate of copper that is white in its powdery anhydrous form and blue in its crystalline hydrous form. It is used chiefly in the dyeing of textiles, in electroplating, and as a fungicide. *Formula:* $CuSO_4$

cop•per•y ['kɒpəri] *adj.* **1** of or containing copper. **2** like copper. **3** copper-coloured.

cop•pice ['kɒpɪs] *n.* copse. ⟨ME *copis* < OF *copeis* < *coper*, *colper* to strike⟩

cop•ra ['kɒprə] *or* ['kouprə] *n.* the dried meat of ripe coconuts, which yields coconut oil, the basic cooking oil of the tropics, and coconut meal, a valuable high-protein food for livestock. ⟨< Pg. < Malayalam *koppara*⟩

co–processor [kou 'prousɛsər] *n. Computer technology.* a computer component that provides additional functions beyond those of the main processor or increases the speed of certain operations: *a math co-processor.*

cop•ro•lite ['kɒprə,lɔit] *n. Archaeology.* fossilized animal feces. ⟨< Gk. *kopros* dung + E *-lite*⟩

cop•rol•o•gy [kə'prɒlədʒi] *n.* **1** preoccupation with feces. **2** the scientific examination of feces, for diagnostic purposes, as in medicine, or for archaeological purposes, in the case of fossilized excrement. ⟨< Gk. *kopros* dung + E *-logy*⟩

cop•roph•a•gous [kə'prɒfəgəs] *adj.* eating excrement, as certain beetles. ⟨< Gk. *kopros* dung + *-phagos* < *phagein* to eat⟩

copse [kɒps] *n.* a thicket of small trees, bushes, shrubs, etc.; BLUFF[1] (def. 2). ⟨< OF *copeiz* a cut-over forest < *couper* cut, ult. < L < Gk. *kolaphos* a blow⟩

Copt [kɒpt] *n.* **1** a native of Egypt descended from the ancient Egyptians. **2** a member of the Coptic Church. ⟨< NL *Coptus* < Arabic *Quft, Qubt* the Copts⟩

cop•ter ['kɒptər] *n. Informal.* helicopter.

Cop•tic ['kɒptɪk] *adj., n. —adj.* of or having to do with the Copts.
—n. the language formerly spoken by the Copts. Coptic is now used only in the rituals of the Coptic Church. ⟨< NL *coptus* < Arabic *Quft, Qift* the Copts < Coptic *Gyptios* < Gk. *Aigyptios* Egyptian⟩

Coptic Church the national Christian church of Egypt and of Ethiopia.

cop•u•la ['kɒpjələ] *n., pl.* **-las, -lae** [-,li] *or* [-,laɪ]. **1** a linking verb such as *is, seemed.* **2** *Logic.* the word or words in a proposition which connect(s) the subject and the predicate. In *the sky is blue, is* is the copula, *sky* is the subject, and *blue* is the predicate. **3** something that serves to connect or link. ⟨< L *copula* bond. Doublet of COUPLE.⟩ **—'cop•u•lar,** *adj.*

cop•u•late ['kɒpjə,leit] *v.* **-lat•ed, -lat•ing.** of human beings or animals, come together in sexual union. ⟨< L *copulare* < *copula.* See COPULA.⟩

cop•u•la•tion [,kɒpjə'leiʃən] *n.* **1** sexual union between male and female human beings or animals. **2** *Grammar or logic.* a joining or being joined together; connection.

cop•u•la•tive ['kɒpjələtɪv] *or* ['kɒpjə,leitɪv] *adj., n. —adj.* **1** serving to couple or connect. **2** *Grammar.* **a** serving to connect words or clauses of equal rank: And *is a copulative conjunction.* **b** being a copula: Be *is a copulative verb.*
—n. a copulative word. In *He became captain, became* is a copulative. **—'cop•u•la•tive•ly,** *adv.*

cop•y ['kɒpi] *n., pl.* **cop•ies;** *v.* **cop•ied, cop•y•ing.** *—n.* **1** anything made to be just like another; anything made on the pattern or model of another; duplicate; reproduction: *One written page, picture, dress, or chair can be an exact copy of another.* **2** *Archaic.* something to be followed as a pattern or model, especially for penmanship. **3** one of a number of books, newspapers, magazines, pictures, etc., made at the same printing. **4** the material to be set up in type for a book, newspaper, magazine, advertisement, etc. **5** *Journalism.* source material for an article, news report, etc.: *She's always good copy, with her unusual ideas and colourful way of talking.*
—v. **1** make a copy or copies; make a copy of: *Copy this page. She has no ideas of her own, all she can do is copy.* **2** be like; follow as a pattern or model; imitate: *The little boy copied his father's way of walking.* **3** steal from; plagiarize: *You must not copy the poet's words and pass them off as your own.* ⟨ME < OF *copier* < Med.L *copia* transcript < L *copia* plenty. See COPIOUS.⟩
☛ *Syn. v.* **1, 2. Copy,** IMITATE = try to make a thing like something else by following a pattern or model. **Copy** = follow a model as closely and exactly as possible: *She copied all the pictures in her book.* **Imitate** = try to make or do something in the style of a pattern or model: *Sometimes a teacher asks a class to imitate something written by a great author.*

cop•y•book ['kɒpi,bʊk] *n., adj. —n.* a book with models of handwriting to be copied in learning to write.
a blot on one's copybook, a serious error.
don't blot your copybook, be very careful.
—adj. commonplace; conventional; ordinary: *a copybook speech.*

co•py•cat ['kɒpi,kæt] *n.* a person who slavishly imitates another in dress, behaviour, etc.

copy desk the desk in a newspaper office where news stories and articles are edited before being set up for printing.

copy editor a person who edits written material and prepares it for publication. **—'cop•y-,ed•it,** *v.*

cop•y•hold ['kɒpi,hould] *n. Brit.* formerly, **a** ownership of land proved by a copy of the roll of a manorial court. **b** the land held in this way.

cop•y•hold•er ['kɒpi,houldər] *n.* **1** a person who reads manuscripts aloud to a proofreader. **2** *Law.* a person who owns land by copyhold. **3** a device for holding copy, as that used by a compositor in setting type.

cop•y•ist ['kɒpiɪst] *n.* **1** a person who makes written copies. **2** a person who copies; imitator.

copy–pro•tect ['kɒpi prə,tɛkt] *Computer technology.* prevent the unauthorized creation of usable copies of (software).

copy protection *Computer technology.* features in software, designed to prevent usable copies of it from being created without authorization.

cop•y•read•er ['kɒpi,ridər] *n.* a person who reads and edits copy for a newspaper.

cop•y•right ['kɒpi,rəit] *n., v., adj. —n.* a right to copy, granted by law to an author, composer, artist, etc., making him or her for a certain number of years the only person who can sell, print, publish, or copy a particular work, or who can authorize others to do so: *Because Shakespeare's plays are not under copyright, anyone can produce them on stage without paying a fee.*
—v. protect by getting a copyright: *Books, pieces of music, plays, etc., are usually copyrighted.*
—adj. protected by copyright: *This material is copyright.*

cop•y•writ•er ['kɒpi,rəitər] *n.* a person whose work is writing advertisements and other publicity material to be used in newspapers, magazines, radio, or television.

coq au vin [kɒk ou 'vɛ̃]; *French,* [kɔko'vɛ̃] *n.* a French dish consisting of chicken cooked in a casserole with red wine, vegetables and seasonings.

co•quet [kou'kɛt] *v.* **-quet•ted, -quet•ting,** *adj. —v.* **1** flirt. **2** trifle.
—adj. coquettish. ⟨< F *coqueter* < *coquet,* dim. of *coq* cock⟩

co•quet•ry ['koukətri] *or* [kou'kɛtri] *n., pl.* **-ries. 1** the act or an instance of flirting. **2** a trifling.

co•quette [kou'kɛt] *n., v.* **-quet•ted, -quet•ting.** *—n.* a woman who tries to attract men merely to please her vanity; flirt.
—v. of a woman, behave flirtatiously. ⟨< F *coquette,* fem. of *coquet.* See COQUET.⟩

co•quet•tish [kou'kɛtɪʃ] *adj.* **1** of a coquette. **2** like a coquette; like a coquette's. **—co'quet•tish•ly,** *adv.* **—co'quet•tish•ness,** *n.*

co•quil•la nut [kou'kijə] the hard brown nut of a South American palm tree (*Attalea funifera*), used in carving and cabinetmaking. ⟨< Sp. *coquillo,* dim. of *coco* coconut⟩

co•quille [kou'kil]; *French,* [kɔ'kij] *n.* **1** a dish of seafood or chicken baked in a sauce and served in a scallop shell. **2** the scallop shell itself. ⟨< F, shell⟩

coquille St. Jacques [sɛ̃ 'ʒak] a French dish of scallops minced in a wine sauce and served in scallop shells, topped with grated cheese browned under the broiler.

co•qui•na [kou'kinə] *n.* **1** a soft, whitish rock composed of fragments of seashells and corals. **2** a small clam of the genus *Donax,* especially *Donax variabilis,* native to E and S U.S. tidal waters. ⟨< Sp. *coquina* shellfish. Akin to CONCH.⟩

co•qui•to [kou'kitou] *n.* a palm tree (*Jubaea spectabilis* or *Jubaea chilensis*) native to Chile, whose nuts yield oil. ⟨< Sp. dim. of *coco* coco palm⟩

cor– *prefix.* together or altogether; the form of **com-** occurring before *r,* as in *correspond.*

cor. 1 corner. **2** coroner. **3** correction; corrected. **4** corresponding. **5** correspondence. **6** correspondent.

Cor. Coroner.

cor•a•cle ['kɔrəkəl] *n.* a light, bowl-shaped boat used for many centuries in the British Isles for river fishing, originally made of woven reeds, grasses, or branches with a covering of hides. The coracles used today in Wales and Ireland have a covering of canvas and tar. ⟨< Welsh *corwgl* < *corwg* round body or vessel, torso, carcass⟩

cor•a•coid ['kɔrə,kɔɪd] *n., adj. —n.* **1** in birds and reptiles, the bone between the shoulder blade and the breastbone. **2** in mammals, a bony process extending from the shoulder blade to or toward the breastbone.
—adj. of this bone or bony process. ⟨< NL < Gk. *korakoeidēs* < *korax, -akos* crow + *eidos* form⟩

cor•al ['kɔrəl] *n., adj. —n.* **1** any of various marine polyps (class Anthozoa) having a stony, horny, or leathery external or internal skeleton. Most corals live in colonies, with their bodies joined together by membranes and their skeletons cemented together. **2** the stony or horny substance that forms the skeleton of certain of these animals, especially any of the order Madreporaria, colonies of which form coral reefs and islands. **3** a colony of certain of these animals which, together with the skeletons of dead individual animals, form a single mass. **4** a piece of the skeletal material of certain of these animals, especially any of several corals of the genus *Corallium,* whose pink or red internal skeleton is used for jewellery. **5** a deep, somewhat yellowish, pink. **6** a lobster's full-grown ovaries.
—adj. **1** having the colour coral. **2** made of coral: *a coral necklace.* ⟨ME < OF < L *corallum* < Gk. *koral(l)ion*⟩
☛ *Hom.* CHORAL.

coral bells a North American plant (*Heuchera sanguinea*), having small red or white flowers and an astringent root.

cor•al•ber•ry ['kɔrəl,bɛri] *n.* a North American shrub (*Symphoricarpos orbiculatus*) of the honeysuckle family, having hairy leaves, small white flowers, and reddish purple fruit; Indian currant.

cor•al•line ['kɔrə,laɪn] *or* ['kɔrəlɪn] *adj., n. —adj.* **1** made of or like coral. **2** coral-coloured.
—n. **1** any animal like a coral. **2** any of various red algae (family Corallinaceae) that produce limestone. ⟨< NL *corallina* < LL *corallinus* coral-red⟩

cor•al•loid ['kɔrə,lɔɪd] *adj.* like coral in looks or structure.

coral reef a reef consisting mainly of coral produced by many colonies of coral polyps over a period of centuries, with new animals building on the skeletons left behind by animals that have died.

cor•al•root ['kɔrəl,rut] *n.* any of a genus (*Corallorhiza*) of orchids found in northern temperate regions, having leafless stems, pink, purple, or greenish flowers, and branched underground stems resembling coral.

coral snake **1** any of a genus (*Micrurus*) of poisonous snakes of tropical and subtropical America typically marked with red, black, and yellow or white bands around the body. Coral snakes are related to the cobras and mambas. **2** any of various brightly coloured African and Asian snakes belonging to the same family (Elapidae).

cor ang•lais ['kɔr ɑŋ'glei]; *French,* [,kɔRã'glɛ] *n.* ENGLISH HORN. ⟨< F⟩

cor•bel ['kɔrbəl] *n., v.* **-belled** or **-beled, -bel•ling** or **-bel•ing.** *—n. Architecture.* a bracket of stone, wood, etc., on the side of a wall. It helps support a projecting ledge above.
—v. furnish with corbels; support by corbels. ⟨ME < OF *corbel,* dim. of *corp* raven < L *corvus*⟩

cor•bie ['kɔrbi] *n. Scottish.* a raven or crow. ⟨alteration of ME *corbin* < OF < L *corvinus* of a raven < *corvus* raven⟩

cord [kɔrd] *n., v. —n.* **1** heavy, thick string of several strands or fibres twisted together; thin rope. **2** a thin, flexible, insulated cable having a plug at one end, used to connect an electrical appliance to a source of power. **3** a similar cable for connecting a desk telephone to the main telephone line, or a telephone handset to its base. **4** *Anatomy.* a structure in an animal body that resembles a cord. The spinal cord is in the backbone. The vocal cords are in the throat. **5** any force or influence that ties or restrains: *a cord of affection.* **6** a ridge on cloth. **7** cloth made with such ridges. **8 cords,** *pl.* pants made of corduroy or other cloth with ridges. **9** a unit for measuring cut firewood, equal to 128 cubic feet (about 3.6 m^3). A standard cord is a stack of wood measuring 8 feet long by 4 feet high by 4 feet deep (about 2.4 m × 1.2 m × 1.2 m). A **face cord** is only 1 to 1½ feet deep (about 30 to 45 cm).
—v. **1** fasten or tie with heavy string or cord, or provide with cord. **2** pile (wood) in cords. ⟨ME < OF *corde* < L < Gk. *chordē* gut. Doublet of CHORD[2].⟩ **—'cord•less,** *adj.*
☛ *Hom.* CHORD.

cord•age ['kɔrdɪdʒ] *n.* **1** cords; ropes. The cordage of a ship is also called its rigging. **2** a quantity of wood measured in cords.

cor•date ['kɔrdeit] *adj.* heart-shaped. ⟨< NL *cordatus* < L *cor, cordis* heart⟩ **—'cor•date•ly,** *adv.*

cord•ed ['kɔrdɪd] *adj., v. —adj.* **1** having ridges on it; ribbed. **2** fastened with a cord; bound with cords. **3** made of cords; furnished with cords. **4** of wood, piled in cords. **5** of a muscle, looking like a tight cord.
—v. pt. and pp. of CORD.

cor•delle [kɔr'dɛl] *or* ['kɔrdɛl] *n., v.* **-elled, -el•ling.** *Cdn. —n.* a towline.
—v. tow (a canoe, etc.) with a cordelle. ⟨< Cdn.F < F *cordelle,* dim. of OF *corde.* See CORD.⟩

cord foot a unit for measuring cut firewood, having the height and depth of a cord and a length of one foot, thus equalling 16 cubic feet. A standard cord equals 8 cord feet. *Abbrev.*: cd.ft.

cord•grass ['kɔrd,græs] *n.* any marsh grass of the genus *Spartina,* native to coastal regions and growing as tall as 3 m.

cor•di•al ['kɔrdiəl] *or* ['kɔrdʒəl] *adj., n., —adj.* **1** warm; friendly: *His host gave him a cordial welcome.* **2** strengthening; stimulating: *a cordial drink.* **3** heartfelt; sincere: *a cordial dislike of cats.*
—n. **1** a food, drink, or medicine that strengthens or stimulates. **2** liqueur. ⟨ME < Med.L *cordialis* < L *cor, cordis* heart⟩ **—'cor•di•al•ly,** *adv.* **—'cor•di•al•ness,** *n.*

cor•di•al•i•ty [,kɔrdi'æləti] *or* [kɔr'dʒæləti] *n., pl.* **-ties.** a cordial quality or feeling; warmth: *The cordiality of her welcome made Tomasina feel at home.*

cor•di•er•ite ['kɔrdiə,rəit] *n.* a blue crystalline mineral, a silicate of magnesium and aluminum, containing some iron. *Formula*: $(MgFe_2)Al_4Si_5O_{18}$ ⟨< after P.L.A. *Cordier* (1777-1861), F geologist⟩

cor•di•form ['kɔrdɪ,fɔrm] *adj.* shaped like a heart. ⟨< L *cor, cordis* heart⟩

cor•dil•le•ra [kɔr'dɪlərə], [,kɔrdə'lɛrə], *or* [,kɔrdəl'jɛrə] *n.* **1** a long mountain range; chain of mountains. **2 Cordilleras, a** the main mountain system of a continent: *the Cordilleras of the Andes.* **b** a system of mountain ranges extending from Alaska to Cape Horn. ⟨< Sp., ult. < L *chorda* rope, cord. See CORD.⟩

Cor•dil•le•ran [kɔr'dɪlərən], [,kɔrdə'lɛrən], *or* [,kɔrdɪl'jɛrən] *adj.* **1** of the Cordilleras, a mountain system in W North America and South America. **2** living or growing in the Cordilleras.

cord•ing ['kɔrdɪŋ] *n.* the surface of a ribbed cloth, as corduroy.

cord•ite ['kɔrdəit] *n.* a smokeless gunpowder composed chiefly of nitroglycerin and guncotton. ⟨< *cord,* n.⟩

cord•less ['kɔrdləs] *adj.* **1** without a cord. **2** of mechanical devices, battery-operated, as opposed to those that must be plugged into an outlet: *a cordless telephone.*

cor•do•ba ['kɔrdəbə] *n.* **1** the basic unit of money in Nicaragua, divided into 100 centavos. See table of money in the Appendix. **2** a coin or note worth one cordoba. ⟨< Francisco de *Córdoba* (1475-1526), a Spanish explorer⟩

cor•don ['kɔrdən] *n., v. —n.* **1** a line or circle of soldiers, police, ships, forts, etc., placed at intervals around an area to guard it. **2** a cord, braid, or ribbon worn as an ornament or badge of honour.
—v. put a protective line or barrier around (*usually used with* **off**): *The area around the famous painting was cordoned off.* ⟨< F *cordon* < *corde* cord⟩

cor•don bleu ['kɔrdɔ̃ 'blʊ]; *French,* [kɔRdɔ̃'blø] **1** a high honour or great distinction. **2** a person highly honoured or greatly distinguished in his or her field, especially a chef of great skill. **3** French cooking of a fine style. ⟨< F blue ribbon, because the highest order of French knights wore it as a badge⟩

cor•don sa•ni•taire [kɔr'dɔ̃ sænə'tɛr]; *French,* [kɔR'dɔ̃sani'tɛR] *n.* **1** a line of guards about a quarantined area. **2** a buffer zone.

cor•do•van ['kɔrdəvən] *or, for n. 1, 2 and adj. 1,* [kɔr'douvən] *n., adj. —n.* **1** a kind of soft, fine-grained leather first made in Córdoba, Spain. Cordovan was originally made of goatskin, but now is usually made of split horsehide. **2** a shoe made of this leather. **3 Cordovan,** a native or inhabitant of Córdoba.
—adj. **1** made of cordovan. **2 Cordovan,** of or having to do with Córdoba. ⟨< Sp. *cordobán* < *Córdoba,* a city in S Spain⟩

cor•du•roy ['kɔrdə,rɔɪ] *n., v. —n.* **1** cloth, usually of cotton, in a plain or twill weave, having a thick, velvetlike cut pile in wide or narrow ridges called wales. **2** (*adjl.*) having ridges like corduroy. **3** *Cdn.* a corduroy road or bridge. **4 corduroys,** *pl.* corduroy pants. **5** (*adjl.*) made of corduroy.
—v. surface or bridge with logs laid crosswise: *They corduroyed the muddy portage road.* ⟨< *cord* + obs. *duroy,* a kind of woollen cloth produced formerly⟩

corduroy bridge *Cdn.* a bridge built over a stream or river and having a surface of logs laid crosswise.

corduroy road *Cdn.* a road or stretch of road surfaced with logs laid crosswise, usually across low-lying, swampy or muddy land.

cord•wain ['kɔrdwein] *n. Archaic.* Cordovan leather. ⟨ME < AF *cordewan,* OF *cordouan* < Sp. *cordobán.* See CORDOVAN.⟩

cord•wood ['kɔrd,wʊd] *n.* **1** wood sold or stacked in cords. **2** wood or standing timber suitable for use as firewood.

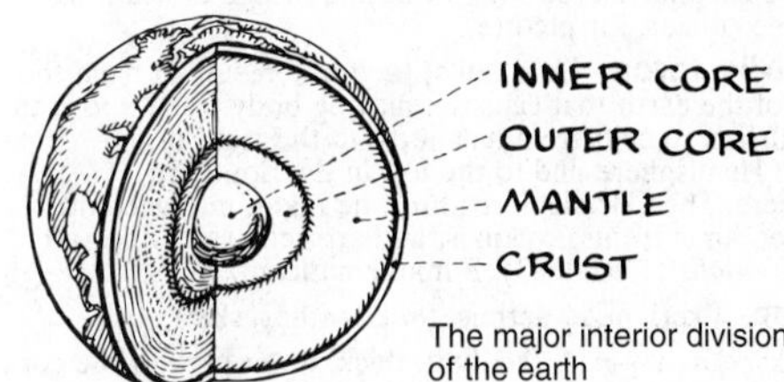

The major interior divisions of the earth

core [kɔr] *n., v.* **cored, cor•ing.** *—n.* **1** the tough central part of some fruits, such as apples and pears, that contains seeds. **2** the central part of the earth, beginning at a depth of about 2880 km and having a radius of about 3400 km, believed by most geologists to consist of iron with a small amount of nickel. **3** a base layer of low-grade wood, plywood, etc., to which veneers or plastic laminates are glued: *The wall units are constructed of elm veneers on a plywood core.* **4** *Electricity.* **a** the conducting wire and its insulation in a subterranean or submarine cable. **b** a bar of soft iron, bundle of iron wires, etc., forming the centre of an electromagnet, induction coil, etc., and serving to increase and concentrate the induced magnetic field. **5** *Metallurgy.* an inner mould made of sand and other ingredients filling the space

intended to be left hollow in a hollow casting. **6 a** the heartwood of a tree. **b** the lumber from this wood, usually soft and inexpensive, used as a base for veneers. **7** a central strand around which other strands are wound or woven in making certain kinds of rope, cord, or thread. **8** a cylindrical portion of rock or other material extracted from the centre of a mass by cutting or drilling. **9** the area in the centre of a nuclear reactor where the reaction takes place. **10** the central or most important part: *the core of a boil, the core of a hurricane, the core of an argument.*
—v. take out the core of: *The cook cored the apples.* ⟨ME; origin uncertain⟩ **—'cor•er,** *n.*
☛ *Hom.* CORPS.

co•re•li•gion•ist [ˌkourəˈlɪdʒənɪst] *n.* one who has the same religious affiliation.

co•re•op•sis [ˌkɔriˈɒpsɪs] *n.* **1** any of a genus (*Coreopsis*) of plants of the composite family having yellow, red-and-yellow, or reddish flowers shaped like daisies. **2** the flower of this plant. ⟨< NL < Gk. *koris* bedbug + *opsis* appearance; from the shape of the seed⟩

co•re•spond•ent or **co–re•spond•ent** [ˌkourɪˈspɒndənt] *or* [ˌkɔrəˈspɒndənt] *n. Law.* a person accused of adultery with one who is being sued for divorce.
☛ *Hom.* CORRESPONDENT [ˌkɔrəˈspɒndənt].

Cor•fam [ˈkɔrfæm] *n. Trademark.* a porous, leatherlike, synthetic plastic used especially for the manufacture of footwear. ⟨arbitrary coinage⟩

cor•gi [ˈkɔrgi] *n.* WELSH CORGI. ⟨< Welsh *corgi* < *corr* dwarf + *ci* dog⟩

A corgi

co•ri•a•ceous [kɔriˈeiʃəs] *adj.* of or having to do with leather; like leather. ⟨< LL *coriaceus* < L *corium* leather, skin⟩

co•ri•an•der [ˌkɔriˈændər] *or* [ˈkɔriˌændər] *n.* **1** an annual herb (*Coriandrum sativum*) of the parsley family native to the Mediterranean region, but widely cultivated for its tiny, seedlike, sweet-smelling fruits. **2** its fruit, used as a spice and as a flavouring in liqueurs and medicines. ⟨< F *coriandre* < L < Gk. *koriandron,* var. of *koriannon,* the name of this plant⟩

Co•rin•thi•an [kəˈrɪnθiən] *n., adj. —n.* **1** a native or inhabitant of Corinth, a seaport in S Greece. **2** a lover of fine living.
—adj. **1** of or having to do with Corinth or its people. **2** loving fine living. **3** *Architecture.* of, having to do with, or designating the latest of the three orders of ancient Greek architecture. The characteristic Corinthian column is 10 times the diameter of the base in height, and has a slender, deeply fluted shaft with a bell-shaped capital carved with an ornate design of acanthus leaves. See ORDER for picture.

Co•ri•o•lis force [ˌkɔriˈoulɪs] the force resulting from the rotation of the earth that causes a moving body on or above the earth's surface to drift from its course to the right in the Northern Hemisphere and to the left in the Southern Hemisphere. The Coriolis force must be taken into account in plotting ocean currents, cyclones, and artificial satellites. ⟨after G.G. de *Coriolis* (1792-1843), F mathematician⟩

co•ri•um [ˈkɔriəm] *n.* dermis. ⟨< L leather, skin⟩

cork [kɔrk] *n., v. —n.* **1** the light, thick, outer bark of the cork oak, used for bottle stoppers, floats for fishing lines, inner soles of shoes, floor and wall coverings, etc. **2** anything made of cork, especially a stopper for a bottle: *Bottles of wine are usually closed with a cork.* **3** any stopper made of other material such as glass, rubber, etc. **4** (*adj.*) made of cork or with cork. **5** *Botany.* the outer bark of woody plants, consisting of layers of dead tissue produced by the *cork cambium.*
blow one's cork, *Informal.* explode with rage.
—v. **1** stop up with a cork. **2** confine; restrain; check. **3** blacken with burnt cork. ⟨< Sp. *alcorque* < Arabic < L *quercus* oak⟩

cork•age [ˈkɔrkɪdʒ] *n.* a charge made by a hotel or restaurant for uncorking and serving wine supplied by a client.

cork•board [ˈkɔrkˌbɔrd] *n.* material made of small bits of cork pressed together. A single sheet may be mounted and used as a notice board; the material may also be used as a floor or wall covering.

cork cambium *Botany.* a layer of tissue outside the cambium, forming cork; phellogen.

corked [kɔrkt] *v., adj. —v.* pt. and pp. of CORK.
—adj. **1** of wine, having the flavour adversely affected by the cork having too much tannin in it. **2** *Slang.* drunk.

cork elm a tall tree of the genus *Ulmus* with a ridged bark, native to the eastern U.S.; wahoo.

cork•er [ˈkɔrkər] *n. Esp. Brit. Slang.* a person or thing of surpassing quality or size.

cork•ing [ˈkɔrkɪŋ] *adj., v. —adj. Esp. Brit. Slang.* excellent; outstanding; fine.
—v. ppr. of CORK.

cork oak an evergreen oak (*Quercus suber*) of the Mediterranean from whose inner bark cork is obtained. Cork oaks are also cultivated in India and the S United States.

cork•screw [ˈkɔrkˌskru] *n., v. —n.* **1** a tool with a screw, or spiral, for pulling out the corks of bottles. **2** (*adj.*) shaped like a corkscrew; spiral: *The plane did a corkscrew dive.*
—v. move or advance in a spiral or zigzag course.

cork•wood [ˈkɔrkˌwʊd] *n.* **1** a shrub (*Leitneria floridana*) having light wood, deciduous leaves, and a fruit structured like a raspberry. **2** any other tree or shrub whose wood is light, such as the balsa. **3** the wood of any of these trees or shrubs.

cork•y [ˈkɔrki] *adj.* **cork•i•er, cork•i•est.** *Informal.* **1** of cork. **2** like a cork: *a corky flavour.* **—'cork•i•ness,** *n.*

corm [kɔrm] *n. Botany.* a fleshy, bulblike underground stem, such as that of the gladiolus, that has leaves and buds on the upper surface and roots usually on the lower. ⟨< NL *cormus* < Gk. *kormos* stripped tree trunk < *keirein* shear⟩

cor•mo•rant [ˈkɔrmərənt] *n.* **1** any of a family (Phalacrocoracidae) of large, mainly black, web-footed sea birds having a long, hooked bill and an often bright-coloured pouch of naked skin under the mouth. Cormorants are used in the Far East for catching fish. **2** a greedy person. ⟨ME < OF *cormaran* < *corp* raven (< L *corvus*) + *marenc* of the sea < L *mare*⟩

corn¹ [kɔrn] *n., v. —n.* **1** a tall cereal plant (*Zea mays*) having seeds, or kernels, that grow in rows along a thick, woody axis called a cob; maize; Indian corn. **2** the kernels, used for food or fodder. **3** any small, hard seed or grain, especially of cereal plants. **4** *Brit.* grain in general, especially wheat or oats. **5** any small, hard particle, as of sand or salt. **6** CORN SNOW. **7** *Slang.* anything trite, too sentimental, or unsophisticated.
—v. **1** preserve (meat) with strong salt water or by dry salt. **2** form into grains, as gunpowder; granulate. ⟨OE⟩

corn² [kɔrn] *n.* a hardening and thickening of the skin, usually on a toe. Corns are caused by pressure or rubbing and are often very painful. ⟨ME < OF *corn* horn < L *cornu*⟩

corn•ball [ˈkɔrnˌbɒl] *adj., n. Slang. —adj.* corny: *cornball humour.*
—n. an unsophisticated person.

corn boil CORN ROAST.

corn borer the larva of any of various moths, such as *Pyrausta nubilalis,* that attacks corn plants.

corn bread a type of bread made of cornmeal instead of flour.

corn chip a chip similar to a potato chip, but made with cornflour.

corn•cob [ˈkɔrnˌkɒb] *n.* **1** the central, woody part of an ear of corn, on which the kernels grow. **2** a tobacco pipe with a bowl hollowed out of a piece of dried corncob.

corn coc•kle [ˈkɒkəl] a European annual plant (*Agrostemma githago*) of the pink family having purplish red flowers and poisonous seeds. It is now naturalized in North America, where it has become a weed in grainfields.

corn crake a short-billed rail (*Crex crex*) native to Europe and Asia, commonly found in European grainfields.

corn•crib [ˈkɔrnˌkrɪb] *n.* a bin or small, ventilated building for storing unshelled corn.

corn dog *Informal.* a wiener dipped in cornmeal batter and deep fried, usually on a stick.

cor•ne•a [ˈkɔrniə] *n.* the transparent part of the outer coat of the eyeball. The cornea covers the iris and the pupil. See EYE for picture. ⟨< Med.L *cornea (tela)* horny (web) < L *cornu* horn⟩

cor•ne•al [ˈkɔrniəl] *adj.* of or having to do with the cornea.

corn ear•worm [ˈirˌwɜrm] the larva of a moth (*Heliothis zea*) that feeds on ears of corn.

corned [kɔrnd] *adj., v. —adj.* **1** preserved with strong salt water or dry salt: *corned beef.* **2** *Slang.* drunk.
—v. pt. and pp. of CORN.

cor•nel ['kɔrnəl] *n.* dogwood. ⟨< G < Med.L *cornolius,* ult. < L *cornu*⟩

cor•nel•ian [kɔr'niljən] *n.* carnelian.

cor•ne•ous ['kɔrniəs] *adj.* horny; of or like horn. ⟨< L *corneus* < *cornu* horn⟩

cor•ner ['kɔrnər] *n., v. —n.* **1** the point or place where lines or surfaces meet: *A diagonal joins two opposite corners of a rectangle.* **2** the space between two lines or surfaces near where they meet; angle: *There was a bookcase in the far corner of the room.* **3** the place where two streets meet. **4** (*adjl.*) at a corner: *the corner drugstore.* **5** (*adjl.*) for a corner: *a corner shelf.* **6** something that forms, protects, or decorates a corner: *The leather wallet has gold corners.* **7** a secret or secluded place. **8** a place that is far away; region; part: *People have searched in all corners of the earth for gold.* **9** an awkward or difficult position; a place from which escape is impossible: *a tight corner.* **10** *Business.* a buying up of the available supply of some stock or article to raise its price: *a corner in cotton.* **11** a monopoly: *Nobody has a corner on truth.*
around the corner, imminent.
cut corners, a shorten the way by going across corners. **b** save money, effort, time, etc., often at the expense of quality.
turn the corner, pass the worst or most critical point.
—v. **1** put in a corner; drive into a corner. **2** force into an awkward or difficult position; drive into a place from which escape is impossible. **3** *Business.* buy up all or nearly all that can be had of (something) to raise its price: *Some speculators have tried to corner wheat.* **4** drive (a car) around a sharp corner. **5** of an automobile, round corners, especially sharp corners and at relatively high speeds: *It corners well.* ⟨ME < AF var. of OF *cornere* < L *cornu* horn, tip⟩

cor•ner•back ['kɔrnər,bæk] *n. Football.* a defensive back who plays behind the linebackers and covers offensive plays run toward the sidelines.

cor•nered ['kɔrnərd] *v., adj. —v.* pt. and pp. of CORNER.
—adj. **1** without hope of escape or relief: *A cornered animal will fight.* **2** having corners of a given kind or number: *three-cornered, sharp-cornered.*

corner kick *Soccer.* a free kick from the corner of the field by an offensive player after a defensive player has allowed the ball past his or her own goal line.

cor•ner•stone ['kɔrnər,stoun] *n.* **1** a stone at the corner of two walls which it holds together. **2** such a stone built into the corner of a building as its formal beginning. The laying of a cornerstone is often accompanied with ceremonies. **3** a main part on which something else rests; foundation; basis: *Clear thinking is the cornerstone of good writing.*

cor•ner•wise ['kɔrnər,waɪz] *adv., adj.* **1** with the corner in front; so as to form a corner. **2** from corner to corner; on a diagonal. Also, **cornerways.**

cor•net¹ [kɔr'nɛt] *for 1;* ['kɔrnɪt] *or* [kɔr'nɛt] *for 2 and 3. n.* **1** a valved brass wind instrument resembling a trumpet, now used mostly in brass bands. The cornet was very popular for all orchestral music in the late 19th century, before the valve trumpet was adopted. **2** a piece of paper rolled into a cone and twisted at one end, used to hold candy, nuts, etc. **3** a cone-shaped pastry holding a filling such as whipped cream. ⟨ME < OF, ult. < L *cornu* horn⟩

cor•net² ['kɔrnɪt] *or* [kɔr'nɛt] *n.* **1** a large, spreading, white cap worn by the Sisters of Charity. **2** formerly, an officer in a British cavalry troop who carried the flag. ⟨< F *cornette,* dim. of *corne,* ult. < L *cornu* horn⟩

cor•net•tist or **cor•net•ist** [kɔr'nɛtɪst] *n.* a person who plays the cornet, especially a skilled player.

corn•fed ['kɔrn,fɛd] *adj.* **1** of an animal, fed on corn or some other grain. **2** *Informal.* robust, plump, and unsophisticated: *a cornfed country lass.*

corn•field ['kɔrn,fild] *n.* a field of growing corn.

corn•flakes ['kɔrn,fleiks] *n.* a dry breakfast cereal, made of crisp flakes of corn, usually served in a bowl with milk.

corn•flour ['kɔrn,flaʊər] *n.* **1** flour made from corn rather than wheat. **2** *Esp. Brit.* cornstarch.
☛ *Hom.* CORNFLOWER.

corn•flow•er ['kɔrn,flaʊər] *n.* BACHELOR'S-BUTTON.
☛ *Hom.* CORNFLOUR.

corn•husk ['kɔrn,hʌsk] *n.* the husk of an ear of corn.

cor•nice ['kɔrnɪs] *n., v.* **-niced, -nic•ing.** *—n.* **1** *Architecture.* the moulded, projecting, topmost part of the upper section of a wall or storey supported on columns or pilasters; the top part of an entablature. See COLUMN for picture. **2** an ornamental moulding around the top of a wall. **3** any of various other ornamental mouldings, as for concealing a curtain rod or otherwise decorating the top of a window. **4** an overhanging ledge of snow or ice on the ridge of a mountain.
—v. furnish or decorate with a cornice. ⟨< F < Ital. < Med.Gk. *korōnis* copestone < Gk. *korōnis* something bent⟩

cor•niche [kɔr'niʃ] *n.* a winding mountain or coastal road. ⟨< F, cornice⟩

cor•nic•u•late [kɔr'nɪkjʊlɪt] *or* [kɔr'nɪkjə,leit] *adj.* having horns or protuberances like horns. ⟨< L *corniculus* dim. of *cornu* horn⟩

Cor•nish ['kɔrnɪʃ] *adj., n. —adj.* of or having to do with Cornwall, a county in SW England, its people, or the language formerly spoken by them.
—n. **1** the ancient, extinct Celtic language of Cornwall. **2** ROCK CORNISH; Cornish hen.

Cornish hen ROCK CORNISH.

Cor•nish•man ['kɔrnɪʃmən] *n., pl.* **-men.** a native or inhabitant of Cornwall.

Cor•nish•wo•man ['kɔrnɪʃ,wʊmən] *n., pl.* **Cor•nish•wo•men.** a female native or inhabitant of Cornwall, a county in SW England.

corn•meal ['kɔrn,mil] *n.* meal made from ground-up corn.

corn picker a machine for cutting corn and removing the husks.

corn pone in the S United States, a flat loaf of cornmeal shaped by hand; corn bread made without milk or eggs.

corn poppy a variety of European and Asian poppy (*Papaver rhoeas*) which often grows in grainfields.

corn roast a picnic held usually in the early fall, at which corn is roasted or boiled for eating off the cob.

corn salad a plant (*Valerianella locusta*) which often grows in European grainfields, having edible leaves and pink, white, or blue flowers.

corn silk the long, glossy styles that emerge in a silky tuft from the tip of an ear of corn.

corn smut a disease of corn, characterized by black swellings. It is caused by a fungus (*Ustilago maydis*).

corn snow snow consisting of granular particles suggesting cornmeal, formed by alternate periods of thawing and freezing.

corn•stalk ['kɔrn,stɒk] *n.* a stalk of a corn plant.

corn•starch ['kɔrn,stɑrtʃ] *n.* a starchy flour made from corn, used to thicken puddings, sauces, etc.

corn stook a stack of cornstalks cut and set up on end together in a field.

corn sugar sugar made from cornstarch.

corn syrup syrup made from corn.

cor•nu•co•pi•a [,kɔrnjə'koupiə] *n.* **1** a horn-shaped container or ornament. **2** a decorated curved horn overflowing with fruits and flowers, used as a symbol of a good harvest or any time of prosperity. **3** an overflowing supply; abundance. **4** *Greek mythology.* the magical horn of the goat which suckled the infant Zeus. This horn had the property of filling with whatever the goat's owner commanded. ⟨< LL *cornucopia,* for L *cornu copiae* horn of plenty, originally a horn of the goat that suckled Zeus⟩

corn whisky whisky distilled from corn.

corn•y ['kɔrni] *adj.* **corn•i•er, corn•i•est.** *Informal.* too trite, sentimental, or unsophisticated: *corny jokes. That movie has some corny scenes.*

co•rol•la [kə'roulə] *or* [kə'rɒlə] *n.* the internal envelope or floral leaves of a flower, usually of some colour other than green; the petals. The corolla can consist of separate petals, as in the rose, or fused petals, as in the morning glory. See ANTHOPHORE for picture. ⟨< L *corolla* garland, dim. of *corona* crown⟩ **—'cor•ol,late** ['kɔrə,leit], *adj.*

cor•ol•lar•y [kə'rɒləri] *or* ['kɔrə,lɛri] *n., pl.* **-lar•ies.** **1** something proved incidentally in proving something else. **2** an inference; deduction. **3** a natural consequence or result: *He believes his good health is a corollary of his simple way of life.* **4** (*adjl.*) like a corollary; resulting. ⟨< LL *corollarium* < L *corollarium* gift < *corolla* garland. See COROLLA.⟩

cor•o•man•del [,kɔrə'mændəl] *n.* **1** a tropical Asian tree

(*Diospyros melanoxylon*). 2 the hard, brown wood of this tree. 3 a type of lacquer decoration, used in China for screens, etc. ⟨< after the *Coromandel* Coast of southeast India⟩

co•ro•na [kə'rounə] *n., pl.* **-nas, -nae** [-ni]. 1 a crown or crownlike object. 2 *Meteorology.* a ring of usually coloured light visible around a shining body such as the sun or moon when it is seen through a thin cloud of water droplets or, sometimes, dust particles in the atmosphere. Compare HALO (def. 1), PARHELIC CIRCLE. 3 *Astronomy.* a layer of gases forming the outer part of the sun's atmosphere. The corona is visible to the naked eye only when the direct rays of the sun are blocked during a total eclipse. 4 an upper or crownlike part. 5 *Botany.* the trumpet-shaped inner part of the corolla of some flowers, such as the daffodil. 6 a kind of cigar. 7 *Architecture.* the top part of a cornice. ⟨< L *corona* crown. Doublet of CROWN.⟩

Corona Aus•tral•is [ɒ'strælɪs] *or* [ɒ'streilɪs] a southern constellation near Sagittarius; the Southern Crown; Wreath. ⟨< L *Corona australis* the Southern Crown⟩

Corona Bo•re•al•is [ˌbɔri'ælɪs] *or* [ˌbɔri'eilɪs] a northern constellation; the Northern Crown. ⟨< L *Corona borealis* the Northern Crown⟩

cor•o•nach ['kɔrənəx] *n. Scottish and Irish.* a dirge. ⟨< Irish *coranach* < *comh-* together + *ranach* a weeping < *ran* weep⟩

co•ro•na•graph [kə'rounəˌgræf] *n.* a telescope for observing the corona of the sun by means of lenses that produce an artificial solar eclipse.

cor•o•nal *n.* ['kɔrənəl]; *adj.* [kə'rounəl] *or* ['kɔrənəl] *n., adj.* —*n.* 1 a crown or coronet. 2 garland. 3 *Linguistics.* a sound articulated with the blade of the tongue.
—*adj.* 1 of or having to do with a crown or a corona. 2 *Anatomy.* **a** of or having to do with the corona of the skull. **b** of or having to do with the **coronal suture**, which joins the frontal and parietal bones of the skull. 3 *Linguistics.* articulated with the blade of the tongue.

cor•o•nar•y ['kɔrəˌnɛri] *adj., n.* —*adj.* 1 *Anatomy.* of or designating either or both of the two arteries branching from the aorta that supply blood to the muscular tissue of the heart. 2 having to do with or resembling a crown.
—*n.* CORONARY THROMBOSIS. ⟨< L *coronarius* encircling < *corona* crown⟩

coronary artery either of two arteries leading from the aorta and providing the heart with blood.

coronary care unit a hospital facility dealing specifically with the intensive care of heart disease patients.

coronary insufficiency failure of the coronary arteries to provide the heart with sufficient amounts of blood, giving rise to angina and heart failure.

coronary thrombosis the stopping up, or occlusion, of a coronary artery by a blood clot (thrombus), usually as a result of atherosclerosis and usually leading to the destruction of muscle tissue in the heart. Compare MYOCARDIAL INFARCTION.

cor•o•na•tion [ˌkɔrə'neiʃən] *n.* 1 the ceremony of crowning a monarch. 2 (*adjl.*) of or having to do with a coronation: *coronation robes.*

cor•o•ner ['kɔrənər] *n.* a person, usually a medical doctor, appointed by a provincial government for a particular community or area to investigate the cause of any sudden or unexpected death that may be the result of a crime or of a situation that could be dangerous to other people. ⟨ME < AF *corouner* officer of the crown < *coroune.* See CROWN.⟩

coroner's inquest an inquiry by a coroner, usually with a jury, into the cause of a death that is not clearly due to natural causes.

coroner's jury a group of persons chosen to witness a coroner's investigation and to determine the cause of any death not clearly due to natural causes.

cor•o•net ['kɔrəˌnɛt], ['kɔrənɪt], *or* [ˌkɔrə'nɛt] *n.* 1 a small crown worn as a mark of noble rank below that of a monarch. A monarch wears a crown; princes and nobles wear coronets. 2 a circle of gold, jewels, or flowers worn around the head as an ornament. 3 the part of a horse's foot above the hoof. ⟨< MF *coronete*, dim. of OF *corone* crown < L *corona*⟩

Corp. 1 Corporation. 2 Corporal.

cor•po•ra ['kɔrpərə] *n.* pl. of CORPUS.

cor•po•ral[1] ['kɔrpərəl] *adj.* of or having to do with the body: *corporal punishment.* ⟨< L *corporalis* < *corpus* body⟩ **—'cor•po•ral•ly,** *adv.*

cor•po•ral[2] ['kɔrpərəl] *n.* 1 *Canadian Forces.* a non-commissioned officer ranking next above a private and below a master corporal. See chart of ranks in the Appendix. 2 a non-commissioned officer of similar rank in the armed forces of other countries. 3 in the RCMP, a non-commissioned officer senior to a first constable and junior to a staff sergeant. *Abbrev.:* Corp., Cpl. or Cpl ⟨< F *corporal*, former var. of *caporal* < Ital. *caporale* < *capo* head < L *caput*⟩

cor•po•ral•cy ['kɔrpərəlsi] *n.* the rank or position of a corporal.

cor•po•ral•i•ty [kɔrpə'ræləti] *n.* the state of having a body; physical existence.

corporal punishment physical punishment; punishment given by striking the body, as in spanking, strapping, beating, or whipping.

cor•po•rate ['kɔrpərɪt] *adj.* 1 forming a corporation; incorporated. 2 belonging to a corporation; having to do with a corporation. 3 united; combined; joint. ⟨< L *corporatus*, pp. of *corporare* form into a body < *corpus* body⟩

cor•po•rate•ly ['kɔrpərɪtli] *adv.* 1 in a corporate capacity; as a body. 2 bodily; in the body.

cor•po•ra•tion [ˌkɔrpə'reiʃən] *n.* 1 a group of persons having a charter that gives them as a group certain legal rights and privileges distinct from those of the individual members of the group. A corporation can buy and sell, own property, etc., as if it were a single person. 2 a group of persons with authority to act as a single person. The mayor and councillors of a city are a corporation. 3 *Informal.* a prominent abdomen.

cor•po•ra•tive ['kɔrpərətɪv] *or* ['kɔrpəˌreitɪv] *adj.* 1 of or having to do with a corporation. 2 of or having to do with a state in which economic industries such as banking are organized as corporations.

cor•po•re•al [kɔr'pɔriəl] *adj.* 1 of or for the body; bodily: *Food and water are corporeal nourishment.* 2 of a material nature; tangible: *Land, trees, and buildings are corporeal things.* ⟨< L *corporeus* < *corpus* body⟩ **—cor'po•re•al•ly,** *adv.*

cor•po•re•al•i•ty [kɔrˌpɔri'æləti] *n.* the quality or condition of being corporeal.

corps [kɔr] *n., pl.* **corps** [kɔrz]. 1 a military formation made up of more than one division. 2 a branch of the armed forces that provides special services: *the Signal Corps.* 3 a group of people organized for working together: *a corps of volunteers.* 4 CORPS DE BALLET. ⟨< F < OF *corps* < L *corpus* body. Doublet of CORPSE, CORPUS, CORSE.⟩
☛ *Hom.* CORE.

corps de bal•let ['kɔr də bæ'lei]; *French,* [kɔRdba'lɛ] all the dancers in a ballet company not classed as soloists. The members of the corps de ballet usually dance as a group. ⟨< F⟩

corpse [kɔrps] *n.* 1 a dead body, especially of a human being. 2 anything that was once lively but is now defunct. ⟨ME < OF *cors* < L *corpus* body. Doublet of CORPS, CORPUS, CORSE.⟩

corps•man ['kɔrmən] *n.* 1 an enlisted man in the U.S. navy or army who performs medical duties or helps with the wounded. 2 a member of any corps.

Corps of Commissionaires an organization of former members of the Canadian armed forces who can be hired as gatekeepers, guards, night watchmen, etc. Members of the Corps of Commissionaires, who wear dark blue uniforms, are often employed to protect property.

cor•pu•lence ['kɔrpjələns] *n.* fatness. Also, **corpulency.**

cor•pu•lent ['kɔrpjələnt] *adj.* fat. ⟨< L *corpulentus* < *corpus* body⟩ **—'cor•pu•lent•ly,** *adv.*

cor pul•mo•na•le [ˌkɔr ˌpʊlmə'næli], [ˌpʊlmə'neili], *or* [ˌpulmə'nɑli] *n.* a rare lung condition affecting miners, leading to heart disease. ⟨< NL, pulmonary heart⟩

cor•pus ['kɔrpəs] *n., pl.* **-po•ra** [-pərə]. 1 a complete collection of writings on some subject, or of some period, or of laws, etc. 2 any body of material, data, etc., especially as the object of study or research. 3 a body, especially the dead body of a person or animal. 4 part of a body; the main part of an organ; specialized tissue. ⟨< L *corpus* body. Doublet of CORPS, CORPSE, CORSE.⟩

cor•pus cal•lo•sum ['kɔrpəs kə'lousəm] *pl.* **cor•po•ra cal•lo•sa** ['kɔrpərə kə'lousə]. a bundle of nerves in the brain that connects the left and right cerebral hemispheres. ⟨< NL, literally, callous body⟩

Cor•pus Chris•ti ['kɔrpəs 'krɪsti] *Christianity, esp. Roman Catholic Church.* the feast in honour of the Eucharist, celebrated on the Sunday following Trinity Sunday. ⟨< L *corpus Christi* body of Christ⟩

cor•pus•cle [ˈkɔrpʌsəl] *or* [ˈkɔrpəsəl] *n.* **1** any of the cells that float in the blood, lymph, etc. Red corpuscles carry oxygen and carbon dioxide; some white corpuscles destroy disease germs. **2** a very small particle. ⟨< L *corpusculum,* dim. of *corpus* body⟩

cor•pus•cu•lar [kɔrˈpʌskjələr] *adj.* of corpuscles; consisting of corpuscles; like that of corpuscles.

cor•pus de•lic•ti [ˈkɔrpəs dɪˈlɪktaɪ] *or* [dɪˈlɪkti] **1** *Latin.* the actual facts which prove a crime or offence against the law has been committed. **2** *Informal.* the body of a murdered person. ⟨< L *corpus delicti* body of the crime⟩

cor•pus ju•ris [ˈkɔrpəs ˈdʒʊrɪs] a complete collection of laws. ⟨< L⟩

cor•pus lu•te•um [ˈkɔrpəs ˈlutiəm], *pl.* **cor•po•ra lu•te•a** [ˈkɔrpərə ˈlutiə]. a yellow endocrine mass formed in the ovary from the ruptured sac left behind after the release of a mature ovum. ⟨< NL, yellow body⟩

cor•pus stri•a•tum [ˌkɔrpəs straɪˈeitəm] either of the two masses of white and grey matter located in front of the thalamus in each hemisphere of the brain. ⟨< NL, striated body⟩

corr. **1** correspondent; corresponding; correspondence. **2** correct; corrected.

cor•rade [kəˈreid] *v.* **-rad•ed, -rad•ing.** wear or be worn away by the abrasive action of water containing sand, etc. ⟨< L *corradere* to scrape together < *com-* together + *radere* to scrape⟩ **—cor'ra•sive** [kəˈreisɪv], *adj.* **—cor'ra•sion** [kəˈreiʒən], *n.*

cor•ral [kəˈræl] *n., v.* **-ralled, -ral•ling.** *—n.* **1** an enclosed space for keeping horses, cattle, etc. **2** a circular camp formed by wagons, carts, etc., for defence against attack. **3** a trap for game, fish, etc.
—v. **1** drive into or keep in a corral. **2** hem in; surround; capture. **3** form (wagons) into a circular camp. **4** *Slang.* catch; get; collect: *Our club has corralled several new members.* ⟨< Sp. *corral* < *corro* ring. Doublet of CRAWL[2].⟩

cor•rect [kəˈrɛkt] *adj., v. —adj.* **1** agreeing with fact or reason; free from mistakes or faults; right: *the correct answer.* **2** agreeing with a general standard of good taste; proper: *correct manners.*
—v. **1** change to what is right; remove mistakes or faults from: *Correct any wrong spellings that you find.* **2** alter or adjust to agree with some standard: *to correct the reading of a barometer.* **3** point out or mark the errors of: *The teacher corrects the test papers and returns them to the students.* **4** set right by disciplining; find fault with in order to improve; reprove: *The mother corrected the child.* **5** counteract (something hurtful); cure; overcome: *to correct a bad habit. He was given medicine to correct his stomach trouble.* ⟨< L *correctus,* pp. of *corrigere* make straight < *com-* + *regere* direct⟩ **—cor'rect•a•ble,** *adj.* **—cor'rect•ly,** *adv.* **—cor'rect•ness,** *n.* **—cor'rec•tor,** *n.*

☛ *Syn. adj.* **1. Correct,** ACCURATE, EXACT = without error or mistake. **Correct,** the most general word, suggests only the absence of mistakes or errors: *They gave correct answers to the questions.* **Accurate** emphasizes the suggestion of careful effort to make something agree with facts or a model: *He gave an accurate account of the incident.* **Exact** emphasizes the suggestion of complete agreement in every detail with the facts or model: *Her painting is an exact copy of the original.*

cor•rect•ed [kəˈrɛktɪd] *adj., v. —adj.* made free from mistakes or faults.
—v. pt. and pp. of CORRECT.

cor•rec•tion [kəˈrɛkʃən] *n.* **1** the act or process of correcting. **2** something put in place of an error or mistake. **3** a punishment; rebuke; scolding. **4** an amount added or subtracted to correct a result. **5** the counteracting or neutralizing of harmful or unpleasant effects, as of a medicine. **6** a brief reversal of an economic trend.

cor•rec•tion•al [kəˈrɛkʃənəl] *adj.* **1** of or having to do with correction; corrective. **2** of or having to do with prison.

correctional centre prison.

correctional officer a prison warden.

correction line *Cdn.* on the Prairies, a surveyor's line that runs north and south every six miles (about 10 km) on the surveyor's original east-west base line, to mark townships and municipalities. Both lines are often used as trails or roads.

cor•rec•tive [kəˈrɛktɪv] *adj., n. —adj.* tending to correct; setting right; making better: *Corrective exercises will make weak muscles strong.*
—n. something that tends to correct or set right anything that is wrong or hurtful. **—cor'rec•tive•ly,** *adv.*

cor•re•late *v.* [ˈkɔrəˌleit]; *n.* [ˈkɔrəlɪt] *v.* **-lat•ed, -lat•ing;** *n.* *—v.* **1** be related one to the other; have a mutual relation: *The results of the study on television advertising correlate closely with earlier findings.* **2** place in or bring into proper relation with one another; show the connection or relation between: *Try to correlate your conclusions with the facts.*
—n. either of two related things, especially when one implies the other. ⟨< *cor-* together + *relate*⟩

cor•re•lat•ed [ˈkɔrəˌleitɪd] *adj., v. —adj.* related one to another.
—v. pt. and pp. of CORRELATE.

cor•re•la•tion [ˌkɔrəˈleiʃən] *n.* **1** the mutual relation of two or more things: *There is a close correlation between climate and vegetation.* **2** a correlating or being correlated. **3** *Statistics.* an interdependence between random variables or between sets of numbers.

correlation coefficient *Statistics.* a number between 1 and –1 which indicates the degree of positive or negative correlation of two quantities or sets of data. Numbers close to 0 indicate little or no correlation.

cor•rel•a•tive [kəˈrɛlətɪv] *adj., n. —adj.* **1** mutually dependent; so related that each implies the other. **2** *Grammar.* having a mutual relation and commonly used together. Conjunctions used in pairs, such as *either...or* and *both...and,* are correlative words.
—n. **1** either of two closely related things. **2** *Grammar.* a correlative word. **—cor'rel•a•tive•ly,** *adv.*

cor•re•spond [ˌkɔrəˈspɒnd] *v.* **1** be in harmony; agree: *His friendly manner corresponded with what they had been told of him.* **2** be similar; have the same function, value, effect, etc., in its own context: *The human arm corresponds to a bird's wing.* **3** agree in amount, proportion, or position. **4** exchange letters; write letters to each other. ⟨< Med.L *correspondere* < L *com-* together, with + *respondere* answer⟩

☛ *Syn.* **1-3.** See note at AGREE.

cor•re•spond•ence [ˌkɔrəˈspɒndəns] *n.* **1** an agreement; harmony: *There was no correspondence between the two accounts of the events.* **2** a similarity; resemblance: *Historians have noted a correspondence between the careers of the two women.* **3** an exchange of letters; letter writing. **4** letters: *She found a pile of correspondence on her desk when she returned from her holidays.* **5** *Mathematics.* a matching of the members of one set of objects with the members of a second set of objects.

correspondence course a set of lessons on a certain subject given by a correspondence school.

correspondence school a school that gives lessons by mail. Instructions, explanations, and questions are sent to the student, and he or she returns his or her written answers for correction or approval.

cor•re•spond•ent [ˌkɔrəˈspɒndənt] *n., adj. —n.* **1** a person who exchanges letters with another. **2** a person employed by a newspaper, a radio or television network, etc., to send news from a distant place. A foreign correspondent is a reporter who gathers news in another country. **3** a person or company that has regular business with another in a distant place: *This important bank has correspondents in all the large cities of the world.* **4** anything that corresponds to something else.
—adj. corresponding; in agreement.

☛ *Hom.* CORESPONDENT.

cor•re•spond•ing [ˌkɔrəˈspɒndɪŋ] *adj., v. —adj.* **1** agreeing; in harmony. **2** similar; matching. **3** handling or carrying on correspondence: *The club has a recording secretary and a corresponding secretary.*
—v. ppr. of CORRESPOND. **—ˌcor•re'spond•ing•ly,** *adv.*

corresponding angles *Geometry.* pairs of angles made by a transversal line cutting two or more other lines. See ANGLE for picture.

cor•ri•da [kəˈridə]; *Spanish,* [kɔˈriða] *n.* **1** bullfight. **2** a running: *The annual running of the bulls in Pamplona is called a corrida.* ⟨< Sp., a running race⟩

cor•ri•dor [ˈkɔrəˌdɔr] *or* [ˈkɔrədər] *n.* **1** a long hallway; passage in a large building from which doors lead into separate rooms. **2** a narrow strip of land connecting two parts of a country or an inland country with a seaport. **3** part of a city, especially a long, narrow area such as a major street, or a street bounded with tall buildings. ⟨< F < Provençal *corredor* < *correr* run < L *currere*⟩

cor•rie [ˈkɔri] *n. Scottish.* a circular hollow on a mountainside; cirque. ⟨< Scots Gaelic *coire,* literally, cauldron⟩

Cor•rie•dale [ˈkɒriˌdeil] *n.* a New Zealand breed of sheep with white faces, bred for both their wool and their meat.

cor•ri•gen•dum [ˌkɔrəˈdʒɛndəm] *n., pl.* **-da** [-də]. **1** an error in a book, manuscript, etc., to be corrected. **2 corrigenda,** *pl.* a list of errors with their corrections, in a book. ⟨< L *corrigendum* (thing) to be corrected < *corrigere.* See CORRECT.⟩

cor•ri•gi•ble ['kɔrədʒəbəl] *adj.* **1** that can be corrected. **2** yielding to correction; willing to be corrected. ⟨< Med.L *corrigibilis* < L *corrigere.* See CORRECT.⟩ **—ˌcor•ri•gi'bil•i•ty,** *n.* **—'cor•ri•gi•bly,** *adv.*

cor•rob•o•rate [kə'rɒbəˌreit] *v.* **-rat•ed, -rat•ing.** make more certain; confirm: *Witnesses corroborated the officer's statement.* ⟨< L *corroborare* strengthen < *com-* + *robur* oak⟩ **—cor'rob•oˌra•tor,** *n.*
☛ *Syn.* See note at CONFIRM.

cor•rob•o•ra•tion [kəˌrɒbə'reiʃən] *n.* **1** confirmation by additional proof. **2** something that corroborates; additional proof.

cor•rob•o•ra•tive [kə'rɒbərətɪv] *or* [kə'rɒbəˌreitɪv] *adj.* corroborating; confirming. **—cor'rob•o•ra•tive•ly,** *adv.*

cor•rob•o•ra•to•ry [kə'rɒbərəˌtɔri] *adj.* corroborative.

cor•rob•o•ree [kə'rɒbəˌri] *n.* **1** a tribal dance of Australian aborigines, held at night. **2** *Esp. Australian.* a noisy gathering or celebration. **3** *Esp. Australian.* a noise; tumult. ⟨< Australian native name⟩

cor•rode [kə'roud] *v.* **-rod•ed, -rod•ing. 1** eat or wear away gradually, especially by chemical action: *Rust had corroded the steel rails.* **2** become corroded: *Iron corrodes quickly.* **3** destroy or cause to deteriorate gradually: *natural generosity corroded by ambition.* ⟨< L *corrodere* < *com-* + *rodere* gnaw⟩

cor•rod•i•ble [kə'roudəbəl] *adj.* capable of being corroded. **—corˌrod•i'bil•i•ty,** *n.*

cor•ro•sion [kə'rouʒən] *n.* **1** the act or process of corroding. **2** a corroded condition. **3** a product of corroding, such as rust. ⟨< LL *corrosio, -onis* < *corrodere.* See CORRODE.⟩

cor•ro•sive [kə'rousɪv] *adj., n.* *—adj.* **1** producing corrosion; corroding; eating away. **2** harsh and critical in speech.
—n. a substance that corrodes: *Most acids are corrosives.*
—cor'ro•sive•ly, *adv.*

corrosive sublimate MERCURIC CHLORIDE.

cor•ru•gate ['kɔrəˌgeit] *v.* **-gat•ed, -gat•ing.** bend or shape (a surface or a thin sheet of material) into wavelike folds; make wrinkles in; furrow. ⟨< L *corrugare* < *com-* (intensive) + *ruga* wrinkle⟩

Corrugated iron

corrugated iron sheet iron or steel, usually galvanized, that is shaped into curved ridges. It is sometimes used for roofs, walls, etc.

corrugated paper paper or cardboard that is bent into a row of wavelike ridges, used in wrapping packages, etc.

cor•ru•ga•tion [ˌkɔrə'geiʃən] *n.* **1** a corrugating or being corrugated. **2** one of a series of wavelike ridges; a wrinkle; furrow.

cor•rupt [kə'rʌpt] *adj., v.* *—adj.* **1** dishonest; especially, influenced by or involving bribes: *a corrupt judge.* **2** depraved or wicked. **3** of a text or manuscript, debased or made meaningless by errors, alterations, insertions, etc. **4** of a dialect, etc., considered inferior to the standard form of the language because of changes that have taken place in structure, vocabulary, or pronunciation: *Dante's writings helped Italian to become accepted as a literary language rather than just a corrupt form of Latin.* **5** rotten; decayed.
—v. **1** make or become dishonest. **2** deprave. **3** alter (a text, word, etc.) from its original or correct form. **4** make or become tainted or rotten. ⟨< L *corruptus,* pp. of *corrumpere* < *com-* + *rumpere* break⟩ **—cor'rupt•er** or **cor'rupt•or,** *n.* **—cor'rupt•ly,** *adv.* **—cor'rupt•ness,** *n.*
☛ *Syn. adj.* **1, 2. Corrupt,** DEPRAVED = made morally bad. **Corrupt** emphasizes the idea that the person or thing was good, pure, honourable and has been made bad by evil influences: *The Medical Association took away the licence of the doctor because of his corrupt practices.* **Depraved** emphasizes the idea that a person's morals have become worse and worse until his or her character, desires, pleasures, etc., are thoroughly evil: *This murder was committed by a depraved criminal.*

cor•rupt•i•ble [kə'rʌptəbəl] *adj.* **1** that can be corrupted. **2** liable to be corrupted; perishable. **—corˌrupt•i'bil•i•ty** or **cor'rupt•i•ble•ness,** *n.* **—cor'rupt•i•bly,** *adv.*

cor•rup•tion [kə'rʌpʃən] *n.* **1** the act or fact of being corrupt or making corrupt. **2** moral deterioration; depravity. **3** dishonesty or a dishonest practice, especially bribery. **4** alteration of a text or manuscript from its correct form. **5** an altered, or corrupt, form **6** rot; decay. **7** *Archaic.* a corrupting influence.

cor•rup•tive [kə'rʌptɪv] *adj.* tending to corrupt; causing corruption. **—cor'rup•tive•ly,** *adv.*

cor•sage [kɔr'sɑʒ] *or* [kɔr'sɑdʒ] *n.* **1** a single flower or a small bouquet to be worn on a woman's dress, blouse, jacket, etc. **2** the upper part of a dress; bodice. ⟨< F < OF < *cors* body < L *corpus*⟩

cor•sair ['kɔrsɛr] *n.* **1** a privateer, especially a Saracen or Turkish privateer of the Barbary Coast. **2** pirate. **3** the ship of a pirate or a privateer. ⟨< F *corsaire* < Ital. < VL *cursarius* runner < L *cursus* a run. Doublet of HUSSAR.⟩

corse [kɔrs] *n. Archaic and poetic.* corpse. ⟨ME < OF *cors* < L *corpus* body. Doublet of CORPS, CORPSE, CORPUS.⟩
☛ *Hom.* COARSE, COURSE.

corse•let ['kɔrslɪt] *for 1;* [ˌkɔrsə'lɛt] *for 2. n.* **1** a piece of armour for the body. Also, **corslet. 2** a light corset, with few or no stays. ⟨< F *corselet,* double of dim. of OF *cors* body. See CORPSE.⟩

cor•set ['kɔrsɪt] *n., v.* *—n.* **1** a firm, close-fitting undergarment stiffened and reinforced by stays, formerly worn especially by women to support or shape the torso. **2** a similar garment worn by men or women because of injury, weakness, or deformity. **3** a medieval outer garment for the upper body, worn by either sex.
—v. **1** dress in or fit with a corset. **2** control or restrict as if by a corset. ⟨< F *corset,* dim. of OF *cors* body. See CORPSE.⟩

cor•se•tiere [ˌkɔrsə'tir] *or* [ˌkɔrsə'tjɛr] *n.* a maker or seller of corsets and other undergarments.

cor•se•try ['kɔrsətri] *n.* **1** the art or trade of making corsets and other foundation garments. **2** corsets as a group.

Cor•si•can ['kɔrsəkən] *n., adj.* *—n.* **1** a native or inhabitant of Corsica, a French island in the Mediterranean Sea. **2 the Corsican,** Napoleon Bonaparte.
—adj. of or having to do with Corsica or its people.

cors•let ['kɔrslɪt] See CORSELET (def. 1).

cor•tege or **cor•tège** [kɔr'tɛʒ] *or* [kɔr'teiʒ] *n.* **1** a procession: *a funeral cortege.* **2** a group of followers, attendants, etc.; retinue. ⟨< F < Ital. *corteggio* < *corte* court⟩

Cor•tes ['kɔrtɛz] *or* ['kɔrteis]; *Spanish,* [kɔr'tes] *n.* in Spain, the national legislature. ⟨< Sp., pl. of *corte* court⟩

cor•tex ['kɔrtɛks] *n., pl.* **-ti•ces** [-təˌsiz]. **1** *Botany.* a complex layer of tissue between the epidermis or corky layer and the vascular tissue of a stem or root, made up mainly of parenchyma cells. **2** the bark or rind of a plant used as medicine. **3** *Anatomy.* **a** the outer part of an internal organ such as the kidneys or the adrenal glands. **b** the thin layer of grey matter that covers the cerebrum of the brain: *the cerebral cortex.* ⟨< L *cortex* bark⟩

cor•ti•cal ['kɔrtəkəl] *adj.* **1** of or having to do with a cortex. **2** consisting of cortex. **—'cor•ti•cal•ly,** *adv.*

cor•ti•cate ['kɔrtəkɪt] *or* ['kɔrtəˌkeit] *adj.* having a cortex; covered with bark. Also, **corticated.** ⟨< L *corticatus* < *cortex* bark⟩

cor•ti•co•ster•oid [ˌkɔrtɪkou'stɛrɔɪd] *n.* any of a group of steroid hormones produced by the adrenal cortex or made synthetically. They regulate blood sugar and sodium levels and are anti-inflammatory agents.

cor•ti•co•ster•one [ˌkɔrtɪkou'stɛroun] *or* [ˌkɔrtɪ'kɒstəˌroun] *n.* a steroid which helps to increase muscle mass, the metabolism of carbohydrates, etc. *Formula:* $C_{21}H_{30}O_4$

cor•ti•co•tro•pin [ˌkɔrtɪkou'troupɪn] *n.* a drug used to test the production of cortisol by the adrenal glands; ACTH.

cor•ti•sone ['kɔrtəˌzoun] *n.* one of the hormones produced by the cortex of the adrenal glands, necessary for the regulation of many functions of the body. Cortisone is used in the treatment of various diseases, including arthritis and leukemia. *Formula:* $C_{21}H_{28}O_5$

cor•tin ['kɔrtɪn] *n.* a secretion from the cortex of the adrenal glands containing cortisone and other hormones.

cor•ti•sol ['kɔrtɪˌsɒl] *n.* hydrocortisone.

co•run•dum [kə'rʌndəm] *n.* an extremely hard mineral, aluminum oxide, sometimes containing iron, magnesia, or silica. Dark-coloured corundum is used for polishing and grinding.

Sapphires and rubies are transparent varieties of corundum. *Formula*: Al_2O_3 ⟨< Tamil *kurundam*; cf. Skt. *kuruvinda* ruby⟩

cor•us•cate ['kɔrə,skeit] *v.* **-cat•ed, -cat•ing.** give off flashes of light; sparkle; glitter. ⟨< L *coruscare* < *coruscus* darting, flashing⟩ **—co'rus•cant** [kə'rʌskənt], *adj.*

cor•us•ca•tion [,kɔrə'skeiʃən] *n.* **1** a flash of light; sparkle. **2** a flashing; sparkling. **3** a mental flash; sudden brilliance or wit.

cor•vée [kɔr'vei] *n.* **1** unpaid work done by a peasant for his feudal lord. **2** unpaid or partly unpaid labour imposed by authorities on the residents of a district. ⟨< F < Med.L *corrogata (opera)* (work) requisitioned < L *corrogare* < *com-* together + *rogare* ask⟩

cor•vette or **cor•vet** [kɔr'vɛt] *n.* **1** formerly, a warship equipped with sails and only one tier of guns. **2** a small, fast warship for use in antisubmarine and convoy work. ⟨? < MDu. *korf*, a kind of ship < L *corbis* basket⟩

cor•vi•na [kɔr'vinə] *n.* **1** a fish (*Menticirrhus undulatus*) found in the Pacific coastal waters of North America. **2** any similar food fish of the genus *Cynoscion.* ⟨< Sp. originally fem. of *corvino* ravenlike < L *corvinus* < *corvus* raven⟩

cor•vine ['kɔrvaɪn] *or* ['kɔrvɪn] *adj.* of or like a crow. ⟨< L *corvinus* < *corvus* crow⟩

Cor•y•bant ['kɔrə,bænt] *n., pl.* **Cor•y•ban•tes** [,kɔrə'bæntiz] or **Cor•y•bants. 1** one of the attendants of Cybele, an ancient nature goddess of Asia Minor. The Corybantes followed her over the mountains by torchlight with wild music and dancing. **2** a priest of Cybele. **—,Cor•y'ban•tian** [,kɔrə'bænʃən], *adj.*

Cor•y•ban•tic [,kɔrə'bæntɪk] *adj.* **1** of the Corybantes. **2** resembling the Corybantes or their rites.

co•ryd•a•lis [kɔ'rɪdəlɪs] *n.* PALE CORYDALIS. ⟨< NL < Gk. *korydallis* crested lark < *korys* helmet⟩

cor•ymb ['kɔrɪmb] *or* ['kɔrɪm] *n. Botany.* a flat cluster of flowers in which the outer flowers blossom first. Small flowers on short stems grow from a longer, central stem to form a round, rather flat cluster. Cherry blossoms are corymbs. ⟨< L *corymbus* < Gk. *korymbos* top, cluster⟩

co•rym•bose [kə'rɪmbous] *adj.* **1** growing in corymbs. **2** of or like a corymb.

cor•y•phae•us [,kɔrə'fiəs] *n.* **1** in ancient Greek drama, the leader of the chorus. **2** a leader of a chorus or other group. ⟨< L < Gk. *koryphaios* < *koryphe* head, top⟩

cor•y•phée [,kɔrə'fei] *n. Ballet.* a leading member of the CORPS DE BALLET. A coryphée dances in the front row of the corps de ballet or in a small group. ⟨< F < L < Gk. *koryphaios* leader < *koryphē* head⟩

co•ry•za [kə'raɪzə] *n.* a cold in the head. ⟨< LL < Gk. *koryza* catarrh⟩

cos[1] or **cos lettuce** [kɒs] *n.* romaine. ⟨< the island of *Cos* in the Aegean Sea⟩

cos[2] cosine.

cos. 1 companies. **2** countries.

Co•sa Nos•tra ['kouzə 'noustrə] a secret criminal society; the Mafia. ⟨< Ital.; literally, "our affair"⟩

cosec cosecant.

co•se•cant [kou'sikænt] *or* [kou'sikənt] *n. Trigonometry.* in a right triangle, the ratio of the length of the hypotenuse to the length of the opposite side; the secant of the complement of a given angle or arc. See SINE for picture.

co•seis•mal [kou'saɪzməl] *or* [kou'səismal] *adj.* of or having to do with points on the earth's surface affected by the same earthquake. Also, **coseismic.**

co•sign ['kousaɪn] *or* [kou'saɪn] *v.* **1** sign (a contract) along with the maker, thereby becoming responsible for meeting the obligation if the maker fails to pay. **2** sign jointly.
—'co•sign•er, *n.*
☛ *Hom.* COSINE.

co•sig•na•to•ry [kou'sɪgnə,tɔri] *adj., n., pl.* **-ries.** *—adj.* signing along with another or others.
—n. a person who signs something along with another or others.

co•sine ['kousaɪn] *n. Trigonometry.* in a right triangle, the ratio of the length of the adjacent side to the length of the hypotenuse; the sine of the complement of a given angle or arc. See SINE for picture. ⟨< NL *co. sinus* short for *complementi sinus,* sine of the complement⟩
☛ *Hom.* COSIGN.

co•si•ness ['kouzinɪs] *n.* the state or quality of being cosy. Also, **coziness.**

cos•met•ic [kɒz'mɛtɪk] *n., adj. —n.* a preparation for beautifying the skin, hair, nails, etc. Powder, lipstick, and face creams are cosmetics.
—adj. **1** beautifying to the skin, hair, nails, etc. **2** of or having to do with cosmetics. **3** meant to improve something superficially: *Instead of the promised repairs, we found that only cosmetic repainting had been done to the old car.* ⟨< Gk. *kosmētikos* of order, adornment < *kosmos* order⟩ **—cos'met•i•cal•ly,** *adv.*

cos•me•ti•cian [,kɒzmə'tɪʃən] *n.* an expert in the choosing and applying of make-up.

cosmetic surgery surgery performed to improve a person's appearance, especially of the face.

cos•me•tol•o•gy [,kɒzmə'tɒlədʒi] *n.* the work of a beautician; art of applying cosmetics. **—,cos•me'tol•o•gist,** *n.*

cos•mic ['kɒzmɪk] *adj.* **1** of or belonging to the cosmos; having to do with the whole universe: *Cosmic forces produce stars and meteors.* **2** of the universe except the earth. **3** vast. ⟨< Gk. *kosmikos* < *kosmos* order, world⟩

cos•mi•cal•ly ['kɒzmɪkli] *adv.* **1** according to cosmic laws. **2** on a vast or cosmic scale.

cosmic dust fine particles of matter falling upon the earth from outer space or forming interstellar clouds.

cosmic noise radio-frequency radiation from the Milky Way that may be detected by radio receivers.

cosmic rays streams of mostly electrically charged particles that travel through space at speeds nearly equal to that of light; some of these enter the earth's atmosphere, where they collide with atoms in the air, producing secondary cosmic rays of enormous energy which are eventually converted into heat. The radiation from cosmic rays in outer space is a hazard for space travellers.

cos•mo•drome ['kɒzmə,droum] *n.* a launching site for Russian spaceships and satellites.

cos•mo•gon•ic [,kɒzmə'gɒnɪk] *adj.* of or having to do with cosmogony. Also, **cosmogonal** [kɒz'mɒgənəl].

cos•mog•o•nist [kɒz'mɒgənɪst] *n.* a person who studies cosmogony or who advocates a particular cosmogony.

cos•mog•o•ny [kɒz'mɒgəni] *n., pl.* **-nies. 1** the creation or origin of the universe: *Cosmogony has puzzled philosophers throughout history.* **2** any theory of its creation or origin. ⟨< Gk. *kosmogonia* < *kosmos* world + *gonos* birth⟩

cos•mog•ra•pher [kɒz'mɒgrəfər] *n.* a person trained in cosmography, especially one whose work it is.

cos•mo•graph•ic [,kɒzmə'græfɪk] *adj.* of or about cosmography. **—,cos•mo'graph•ic•al•ly,** *adv.*

cos•mog•ra•phy [kɒz'mɒgrəfi] *n.* **1** the science that describes and maps the general appearance and structure of the universe. Cosmography includes astronomy, geography, and geology. **2** a general description of the universe or the earth. ⟨< Gk. *kosmographia* < *kosmos* world + *graphein* write⟩

cos•mo•log•i•cal [,kɒzmə'lɒdʒəkəl] *adj.* of or having to do with cosmology. **—,cos•mo'log•i•cal•ly,** *adv.*

cos•mol•o•gist [kɒz'mɒlədʒɪst] *n.* a person trained in cosmology, especially one whose work it is.

cos•mol•o•gy [kɒz'mɒlədʒi] *n.* **1** the branch of learning that deals with the description of the universe as an ordered whole made up of parts and subject to laws by which it functions. Cosmology may be considered as a branch of philosophy or of natural science. **2** a particular theory or account of the structure and workings of the universe. ⟨< Gk. *kosmos* world + E *-logy*⟩

cos•mo•naut ['kɒzmə,nɒt] *n.* a Russian astronaut. ⟨< Russian *kosmonaut* < Gk. *kosmos* universe + *nautes* sailor⟩

cos•mop•o•lis [kɒz'mɒpəlɪs] *n.* a cosmopolitan city.

cos•mo•pol•i•tan [,kɒzmə'pɒlətən] *adj., n. —adj.* **1** made up of elements or people from many parts of the world: *a cosmopolitan art collection. Montréal is a cosmopolitan city.* **2** familiar with and feeling at home in many parts of the world: *a cosmopolitan person.* **3** sophisticated and urbane. **4** of animals or plants, found in almost all parts of the world.
—n. **1** a person who feels at home in many parts of the world. **2** an organism found in almost all parts of the world.

cos•mo•pol•i•tan•ism [,kɒzmə'pɒlətə,nɪzəm] *n.* the quality or condition of being cosmopolitan.

cos•mop•o•lite [kɒz'mɒpə,lɔit] *n.* **1** a cosmopolitan person. **2** an animal or plant found in all or many parts of the world. ⟨< Gk. *kosmopolitēs* < *kosmos* world + *politēs* citizen < *polis* city⟩ **—cos'mop•o•lit,ism,** *n.*

cos•mos ['kɒzmɒs], ['kɒzmous], *or* ['kɒzməs] *n.* **1** the universe thought of as an orderly, harmonious system. **2** any complete system that is orderly and harmonious. **3** order; harmony. Cosmos is the opposite of chaos. **4** any of a genus (*Cosmos*) of garden plants of the composite family, especially a tall plant (*C. bipinnatus*) with much-divided leaves and white, pink, purple, or orange flowers that bloom from midsummer through fall. ⟨< NL < Gk. *kosmos* order, world⟩

cos•mo•tron ['kɒzmə,trɒn] *n.* a proton accelerator. ⟨apparently < *cosmic* + (*cycl*)*otron*⟩

co•spon•sor [kou'spɒnsər] *n., v.* —*n.* one who sponsors or supports, jointly with another party.
—*v.* sponsor or support jointly.

Cos•sack ['kɒsæk] *or* ['kɒsək] *n., adj.* —*n.* a member of a people living in Ukraine in communes, traditionally famous as horsemen. They fought in the Russian cavalry under the czarist régime.
—*adj.* of, having to do with, or characteristic of the Cossacks. ⟨< Russian *kozak, kazak*⟩

cos•set ['kɒsɪt] *n., v.* —*n.* a pet, especially a pet lamb.
—*v.* make a pet of; treat as a pet; pamper. ⟨OE **cossettan* kiss < *coss* a kiss⟩

cost [kɒst] *n., v.* **cost** (defs. 1, 2, 4) or **costed** (def. 3), **cost•ing.** —*n.* **1** the price paid or demanded: *The cost of these gloves was $18.* **2** a loss or sacrifice: *The fox escaped from the trap at the cost of a leg.* **3** outlay or expenditure of time, labour, trouble, effort, etc. **4 costs,** *pl.* the expenses of a lawsuit or case in court. **5** a price equalling the cost of production, without mark-ups by distributor or retailer: *to sell something at cost.*
at all costs or **at any cost,** regardless of expense; by all means; no matter what must be done: *They had to catch the next boat at all costs, or lose their chance to escape.*
—*v.* **1** have a price of: *This hat costs $18.* **2** require spending of (money, effort, suffering, etc.): *The other hat costs a lot more. The school play cost much time and effort.* **3** estimate the expenditure required for the production or completion of: *The company is costing a new project.* **4** cause someone the loss or sacrifice of: *The accident almost cost him his life. Her many absences finally cost her her job.* ⟨ME < OF *cost* < *coster* < L *constare* < *com-* with + *stare* stand⟩
☛ *Syn. n.* **1.** See note at PRICE.

cos•ta ['kɒstə] *n.* a rib or riblike structure or marking of a plant or animal. ⟨< NL < L a rib⟩ —**'cos•tate,** *adj.*

cost accounting 1 a system of accounting that records all expenses, including overhead, incurred in making and distributing a product. **2** the keeping of such accounts. —**cost accountant.**

cos•tal ['kɒstəl] *adj.* near, on, or having to do with a rib or the ribs. ⟨< LL *costalis* < L *costa* rib⟩

co–star ['kou ,stɑr] *n., v.* **-starred, -star•ring.** —*n.* an actor of equal prominence with another (or others) playing a leading role in a movie, play, etc.
—*v.* be, cause to be, or feature as a co-star.

cos•tard ['kɒstərd] *n.* a variety of large English apple. ⟨earlier meaning, 'a ribbed apple'; probably < OF *coste* rib < L *costa*⟩

Cos•ta Ri•ca ['kɒstə 'rikə] *or* ['koustə] *n.* a country in Central America.

Cos•ta Ri•can ['kɒstə 'rikən] *or* ['koustə] *n., adj.* —*n.* a native or inhabitant of Costa Rica.
—*adj.* of or having to do with Costa Rica or its people.

cost–ef•fec•tive ['kɒst ɪ'fɛktɪv] *adj.* bringing good results or profit for little expenditure; economical.
—**'cost-ef'fec•tive•ness,** *n.*

cos•ter•mon•ger ['kɒstər,mʌŋgər] *or* [-,mɒŋgər] *n. Brit.* a person who sells fruit, vegetables, fish, etc., from a handcart or stand in the street. Also, **coster.** ⟨earlier *costardmonger* < *costard* + *monger* dealer, trader⟩

cos•tive ['kɒstɪv] *adj.* **1** constipated. **2** producing constipation. **3** stingy. **4** tending to withhold opinions or feelings, etc. ⟨ME < OF *costive* < L *constipatus,* pp. of *constipare.* Doublet of CONSTIPATE.⟩ —**'cos•tive•ly,** *adv.* —**'cos•tive•ness,** *n.*

cost•ly ['kɒstli] *adj.* **-li•er, -li•est. 1** of great value: *costly jewels.* **2** costing much: *costly mistakes.* **3** costing too much. —**'cost•li•ness,** *n.*
☛ *Syn.* See note at EXPENSIVE.

cost•ma•ry ['kɒst,mɛri] *n.* a plant (*Chrysanthemum balsamita*) of the composite family, with aromatic edible leaves.

cost of living the average price paid by a person, family, etc., for the necessities such as food, rent, clothing, transportation, etc., within a given period.

cost of living index CONSUMER PRICE INDEX.

cost plus an arrangement or contract under which the selling price is based on the cost of production plus an agreed profit. —**'cost-'plus,** *adj.*

cos•tume *n.* ['kɒstjum] *or* ['kɒstʃum]; *v.* ['kɒstjum] *or* ['kɒstʃum], [kɒs'tjum] *or* [kɒs'tʃum] *n., v.* **-tumed, -tum•ing.** —*n.* **1** a style of dress of a particular time, place, occupation, or social class, including garments, hairstyles, jewellery or other ornaments, etc. **2** dress belonging to another time or place, worn on the stage, at masquerades, etc.: *The actors wore Spanish costumes.* **3** a complete set of outer garments: *a street costume, a hunting costume.*
—*v.* provide a costume or costumes for; dress. ⟨< F < Ital. < VL *consuetumen* custom. Doublet of CUSTOM.⟩

costume jewellery dress ornaments made of ordinary materials, without precious stones.

cos•tum•er ['kɒstjumər] *or* ['kɒstʃumər] *n.* **1** a person who makes, sells, or rents costumes or dresses. **2** a rack for hanging clothes.

cos•tum•i•er [kɒs'tjumiər]; *French,* [kɔsty'mje] *n.* costumer.

cos•tu•mi•ère [kɒs,tjumi'ɛr]; *French,* [kɔstjy'mjɛʀ] *n.* a female costumier.

co•sy ['kouzi] *adj.* **co•si•er, co•si•est;** *n., pl.* **co•sies;** *v.* **co•sied, co•sy•ing** —*adj.* **1** warm and comfortable; snug: *She liked to read in a cosy corner by the fire.* **2** familiar or intimate, especially excessively so.
—*n.* a cover, usually of padded or knitted cloth, used to keep a teapot warm.
—*v.*
cosy up to, *Informal.* ingratiate oneself with. Also, **cozy.** ⟨< Scand., origin uncertain⟩ —**'co•si•ly,** *adv.* —**'co•si•ness,** *n.*
☛ *Syn. adj.* See note at SNUG.

co•syn•tro•pin [kou'sɪntrəpɪn] *n.* a drug used to test the functioning of the adrenal glands.

cot[1] [kɒt] *n.* **1** a narrow bed, sometimes made of canvas stretched on a frame that folds together. **2** *Brit.* a baby's crib. ⟨< Anglo-Indian < Hind. *khāt*; cf. Skt. *khatvā*⟩
☛ *Hom.* CAUGHT.

cot[2] [kɒt] *n.* **1** a cottage; small house. **2** something small built for shelter or protection. **3** a protective covering; sheath: *a cot for an injured finger.* ⟨OE⟩
☛ *Hom.* CAUGHT.

cot[3] cotangent.

co•tan•gent [kou'tændʒənt] *n. Trigonometry.* in a right triangle, the ratio of the length of the adjacent side (not the hypotenuse) to the length of the opposite side; the tangent of the complement of a given angle or arc. ⟨< NL *cotangens* < *co. tangens* short for *complementi tangens* tangent of the complement⟩

COTC or **C.O.T.C.** Canadian Officers Training Corps.

cote [kout] *n.* a shelter or shed for small animals, birds, etc.: *a dovecote.* ⟨OE. Related to COT[2].⟩
☛ *Hom.* COAT.

co•teau [kə'tou]; *French,* [kɔ'to] *n.* **1** a small hill; hillock. **2** a line of hills or ridges, often functioning as a watershed. ⟨< Cdn.F.⟩

Côte d'Ivoire [kotdi'vwaʀ] *French.* the French name of Ivory Coast.

co•ten•ant [kou'tɛnənt] *n.* one of a group of tenants of the same place; joint tenant.

co•te•rie ['koutəri] *or* [,koutə'ri] *n.* a set or circle of acquaintances; group of people who often meet socially. ⟨< F *coterie,* originally, an association for tenants of the same farm owner < OF *cotier* cotter[2] < *cote* hut < MDu. *kote*⟩

co•ter•mi•nous [kou'tɜrmənəs] *adj.* **1** having a common boundary; bordering; meeting at their ends. **2** having the same boundaries or limits; co-extensive. Also, **conterminous.** ⟨< L *conterminus* < *com-* with + *terminus* boundary⟩

co•til•lion [kou'tɪljən] *n.* **1** a dance with complicated steps and frequent changing of partners, led by one couple. **2** a society ball, often a debutante ball. **3** quadrille. **4** a piece of music for a cotillion. ⟨< F *cotillon,* originally, petticoat, dim. of *cotte* coat⟩

co•to•ne•as•ter [kə,touni'æstər] *or* [kə'tɒni,æstər] *n.* any of a genus (*Cotoneaster*) of widely cultivated flowering shrubs of the rose family. ⟨< NL < L *cotonea* quince + *-aster* dim. suffix⟩

Cots•wold ['kɒtswould] *or* ['kɒtswəld] *n.* a breed of large sheep having long wool. ⟨< *Cotswolds,* hills in SW England⟩

cot•tage ['kɒtɪdʒ] *n.* **1** a small, usually simply built and often uninsulated house for summer holiday use, as at a resort. **2** a small house, especially in a rural or wooded area. **3** any of various individual houses or cabins, at a camp, school, etc., which house a small group of residents. ⟨< *cot*[2]⟩

cottage cheese a soft, white cheese made from the curds of sour skim milk.

cottage country a region away from a city, where city people and locals have cottages.

cottage industry a system of production in which workers make products at home with their own equipment for someone who agrees to sell them.

cottage pudding cake covered with a sweet sauce.

cot•tag•er ['kɒtɪdʒər] *n.* **1** a person who lives in a cottage. **2** a summer resident in a rural or resort area.

cot•ter[1] ['kɒtər] *n.* **1** a wedge or other tapered piece used to hold parts of a structure together. **2** COTTER PIN. ⟨origin uncertain⟩

cot•ter[2] or **cot•tar** ['kɒtər] *n.* in Scotland, a man who works for a farmer and is allowed to use a small cottage and a plot of land. ⟨< Med.L *cotarius* < *cota* < OE *cot* cot[2]⟩

A cotter pin

cotter pin a long metal strip, round on one side and flat on the other, that is bent double and used for inserting into a slot or hole to hold small parts of machinery together. The two ends of the cotter pin are flared out after it is inserted, to keep it in place.

A cotton plant

cot•ton ['kɒtən] *n., v.* —*n.* **1** soft, downy white or yellowish fibres obtained from the seed pods of any of several plants (genus *Gossypium*) of the mallow family, and used in making fabrics, threads, etc. The cotton is attached to the seeds in a fluffy mass. **2** any of the plants that produce these fibres: *Cotton grows in warm climates.* **3** the crop of such plants. **4** thread or cloth made from cotton fibres. **5** (*adjl.*) made of cotton. **6** any downy substance resembling cotton fibres, growing on other plants.
—*v. Informal.* **1** agree; get along. **2** take a liking (*to*): *I cottoned to her at once.*
cotton on (to), *Informal.* understand: *He still hasn't cottoned on that it was only a joke.*
cotton up to, *Informal.* flatter: *Did you see the way he was cottoning up to the coach?* ⟨ME < OF *coton* < Ital. *cotone* < Arabic *qutn*⟩

cotton batting soft, fluffy cotton formed into balls, large wads, or thin layers, used as padding in quilting, for dressing wounds, etc.

cotton candy a light, fluffy candy made by spinning melted sugar.

cotton flannel a soft cotton cloth, with a texture like that of woollen flannel.

cotton gin a machine for separating the fibres of cotton from the seeds.

cotton grass any of a genus (*Eriophorum*) of sedges found in north temperate and arctic regions, having spikes of flowers that resemble tufts of cotton.

cotton gum a tall tree (*Nyssa aquatica*) native to Florida, having leaves with a texture like that of cotton.

cot•ton•mouth ['kɒtən,mʌuθ] *n.* WATER MOCCASIN.

cotton sedge *Cdn.* COTTON GRASS.

cot•ton•seed ['kɒtən,sid] *n., pl.* **-seed** or **-seeds.** the seed of cotton, used for making cottonseed oil, fertilizer, cattle food, etc.

cottonseed oil oil pressed from cottonseed, used for cooking, for making soap, etc.

cotton stainer any of various insects of the genus *Dysdercus*, that enter and discolour cotton bolls.

cot•ton•tail ['kɒtən,teil] *n.* any of several species of rabbit (genus *Sylvilagus*), the common wild rabbit of North America, having brownish or greyish fur and a fluffy tail with a white or light grey underside.

cot•ton•weed ['kɒtən,wid] *n.* any of a number of European perennial plants (*Otanthus maritimus*) bearing downy leaves.

cot•ton•wood ['kɒtən,wʊd] *n.* **1** any of various North American poplars, such as the **eastern cottonwood** (*Populus deltoides*) and the **black cottonwood** (*P. trichocarpa*), both of which are native to Canada. They are named for the cottony tufts of hairs on the seeds, characteristic of poplars. **2** the wood of any of these trees.

cotton wool **1** COTTON BATTING. **2** unprocessed cotton.

cot•ton•y ['kɒtəni] *adj.* **1** of cotton. **2** like cotton; soft; fluffy; downy. **3** covered with fine hairs that feel like cotton.

cot•y•le•don [,kɒtə'lidən] *n.* an embryo leaf in the seed of a plant; the first leaf, or either of the first pair of leaves, growing from a seed. See EMBRYO for picture. ⟨< L < Gk. *kotylēdōn* cup-shaped hollow < *kotylē* small vessel⟩

cot•y•le•don•ous [,kɒtə'lidənəs] *adj.* having cotyledons.

couch [kʌutʃ] *n., v.* —*n.* **1** chesterfield; sofa. **2** any long piece of furniture for reclining or sitting on, especially one that is upholstered. **3** any place to sleep or rest: *The deer sprang up from its grassy couch.* **4** *Poetic.* bed. **5** *Archaic.* the burrow or den of a wild animal. **6** a frame on which barley is spread to be malted. **7** the grain spread in this way. **8** a priming coat put on before painting.
—*v.* **1** put on a couch. **2** lie down on a couch. **3** put in words; express: *Some poets couch their ideas in beautiful language.* **4** lower; bring down; put in a level position ready to attack: *The knights couched their lances and prepared to charge.* **5** lie hidden ready to attack. **6** spread (grain) to germinate for malting. ⟨ME < OF *couche* < *coucher* lay in place < L *collocare* < *com-* (intensive) + *locus* a place⟩ —**'couch,like,** *adj.*

couch•ant ['kʌutʃənt] *adj. Heraldry.* (*used after the noun*) lying down, but with the head raised. ⟨< F *couchant*, ppr. of *coucher* lie⟩

cou•chette [ku'ʃɛt] *n.* a berth on a train, containing a seat that folds out into a bed. ⟨< F, dim. of *couche* bed⟩

couch grass [kutʃ] a coarse, perennial grass (*Agropyron repens*) that is native to Europe but has become a common weed in North America, having long, wiry, white or yellowish underground stems by which it spreads; quack grass.

couch potato *Informal.* someone who is sedentary and watches television a lot.

cou•gar ['kugər] *n.* a large, usually sand-coloured wild animal (*Felis concolor*) of the cat family found in many parts of North and South America, having short, black ears and a very long, black-tipped tail; mountain lion. ⟨< F *couguar* < NL < Tupi-Guarani *guaçu ara*⟩

cough [kɒf] *v., n.* —*v.* force air from the lungs suddenly with a short, harsh noise or series of noises.
cough up, a expel from the throat or lungs by coughing. **b** *Slang.* give; bring out; produce; pay (what is due).
—*n.* **1** the act of coughing. **2** the sound of coughing. **3** repeated acts of coughing. **4** a condition marked by frequent coughing: *She has a bad cough.* ⟨ME *coghen*, related to OE *cohhetan*⟩
☛ *Hom.* QOF.

cough drop a small candy containing medicine to relieve coughs, hoarseness, etc.

could [kʊd]; *unstressed,* [kəd] *v.* **1** pt. and conditional tense of CAN. **2** a modal auxiliary used in: **a** asking permission: *Could I turn the light out now?* **b** making a polite request: *Could you wait just five minutes until I'm ready?* **c** conveying doubt: *It could be* *true.* ⟨OE *cūthe*; the *l* was inserted on analogy with *should, would.*⟩

could•n't ['kʊdənt] could not.

couldst [kʊdst] *v. Archaic or poetic.* 2nd pers. sing. of COULD. *Thou couldst* means *You* (sing.) *could.*

cou•lee ['kuli] *n.* **1** *Cdn., esp. Prairies.* a deep, narrow ravine that is usually dry in summer. **2** a stream of lava. ⟨< F *coulée*, fem. pp. of *couler* flow < L *colare* strain⟩
☛ *Hom.* COOLIE.

cou•loir [kul'wɑr] *or* ['kulwɑr]; *French,* [ku'lwaʀ] *n.* a deep gorge or gully on the side of a mountain. ⟨< F < OF *couloir* passage, literally, a slide, glide < *couler* flow. See COULEE.⟩

cou•lomb [ku'lɒm] *or* ['kulɒm] *n.* an SI unit for measuring the quantity, or charge, of electricity flowing past a given section of an electric circuit within a given time. One coulomb is the electric charge furnished by a current of one ampere in one second. *Symbol*: C ⟨after Charles A. de *Coulomb* (1736-1806), a French physicist⟩

cou•lom•bic force [ku'lɒmbɪk] a force of attraction or repulsion between electrostatically charged particles, proportional to the magnitudes of the charges and inversely proportional to the square of the distance between the particles.

coul•ter or **col•ter** ['koultər] *n.* a sharp blade or disc on a plough to cut the earth ahead of the ploughshare. ⟨ME *culter* < OF *coltre* or OE *culter* both < L *culter* ploughshare⟩

cou•ma•rin ['kumərɪn] *n.* a fragrant but toxic white crystalline substance, obtained from the tonka bean or made synthetically, used in soaps and perfumes but no longer permitted in food. *Formula*: $C_9H_6O_2$ ⟨< F *coumarine* < *coumarou* tonka bean < Pg. < Tupi *cumaru*⟩

cou•ma•rone ['kumə,roun] *n.* a colourless liquid obtained from coal tar and used to make resins for paints and varnishes. *Formula*: C_8H_6O ⟨< G *kumaron* < *kumarin* (< F *coumarine* (see COUMARIN)) + *on* -one⟩

coun•cil ['kaʊnsəl] *n.* **1** a group of people called together to give advice, talk things over, or settle questions: *council of war.* **2** a small group of people elected by citizens to make laws for and govern a township, city, municipal district, etc. **3** a group of people appointed to advise a monarch, governor, etc.: *the Privy Council.* **4** the deliberation or consultation that takes place at the meeting of a council.
in council, a at a meeting of a council. **b** in consultation; deliberating together: *The family is in council planning a vacation.* ⟨ME < OF *concile* < L *concilium* < *com-* together + *calare* call⟩
☛ *Hom.* COUNSEL.
☛ *Usage.* **Council,** COUNSEL. **Council** is a noun: *They called together a council* (group) *of the town's industrial leaders.* **Counsel** may be a noun or a verb: *Mrs. Smith could always be counted on for good counsel* (advice). *Each side tried to get Mr. Avery as its counsel* (adviser). *I do not like to counsel* (advise) *you on that point.*

coun•cil•lor or **coun•cil•or** ['kaʊnsələr] *n.* **1** an elected member of a council of a town, village, etc.; alderman. **2** *Cdn.* in Prince Edward Island, a member of the Legislative Assembly elected by the property owners. **—'coun•cil•lor,ship,** *n.*
☛ *Hom.* COUNSELLOR.

Council of the Northwest Territories the legislative body responsible for local government in the Northwest Territories, consisting of 15 elected members. It has powers similar to those of a provincial legislature, but all natural resources except game are under federal control.

Council of Trent the council of the Roman Catholic Church held at Trent, Italy, from time to time between 1545 and 1563. It formulated many of the present Catholic doctrines, corrected certain abuses within the church, and organized the Catholic opposition to the Protestant movement.

council of war **1** a conference of high officers of the armed forces to give advice and talk over matters of special importance. **2** an important conference to decide on a plan of action in any conflict.

coun•ci•lor ['kaʊnsələr] See COUNCILLOR.

coun•sel ['kaʊnsəl] *n., v.* **-selled** or **-seled, -sel•ling** or **-sel•ing.** *—n.* **1** the act of talking things over; consultation or deliberation: *There was little time for counsel.* **2** advice: *A wise person gives good counsel.* **3** a lawyer or group of lawyers: *She is acting as counsel for the defence.* **4** *Archaic.* wisdom; prudence. **5** *Archaic.* deliberate purpose; design; plan; scheme.
hold or **take counsel,** talk things over; consult or deliberate: *The stranded travellers held counsel to decide what they should do next. He took counsel with his friends.*
keep (one's) **own counsel,** keep quiet about one's ideas and plans; not tell one's secrets.
—v. **1** give advice to; advise, often in a professional capacity: *She counsels high school students.* **2** recommend: *She counselled immediate action.* **3** exchange ideas; consult together; deliberate. ⟨ME < OF *conseil* < L *consilium* < *consulere* consult, originally, convoke < *com-* together + *sel-* take⟩
☛ *Hom.* COUNCIL.
☛ *Syn. n.* **2.** See note at ADVICE.
☛ *Usage.* See note at COUNCIL.

coun•sel•lor or **coun•sel•or** ['kaʊnsələr] *n.* **1** a person who gives advice; adviser, especially a professional one, often a psychologist. **2** lawyer. **3** a person who supervises, especially at a summer camp. **4** in the Mormon church, an adviser to the leader.
☛ *Hom.* COUNCILLOR.

count[1] [kaʊnt] *v., n. —v.* **1** name numbers in order: *Wait till I count to ten.* **2** add; find how many: *She counted the books and found there were fifty.* **3** include in counting; take into account: *Let's not count that game.* **4** be included in counting; be taken into account: *Your first race is only for practice; it won't count.* **5** have value, significance, or influence: *She's one of the people who count in the company. His promise doesn't count much.* **6** depend; rely; trust (*used with* **on**): *Can I count on you to help?* **7** plan or expect (*used with* **on**): *You should count on spending at least $50 for dinner.* **8** consider; think of as: *I count myself lucky to have married you.* **9** *Music.* keep track of (beats): *Count four measures before coming in. Count carefully.*
count for, be worth.
count in, *Informal.* include: *Count me in for the party!*
count off, divide into equal groups by counting: *Count off in fours, from the left.*
count out, a not include in a plan: *If you go skiing, count me out.* **b** *Boxing.* declare (a fallen fighter) the loser when he cannot get up after ten seconds have been counted: *He was counted out in the third round of the fight.*
—n. **1** the act of counting or adding up: *They made a careful count to see that none of the pupils were missing.* **2** the total number of individuals or units in a given sample: *a low blood count.* **3** *Law.* a separate charge in an indictment: *three counts of theft.* **4** a point in a critique, argument, etc.: *You are right on three counts.* **5** ability to keep track in counting: *I've lost count.* **6** *Boxing.* the act of calling off up to ten seconds to give a fallen fighter time to get up before he is declared the loser. ⟨ME < OF *conter* < L *computare* < *com-* up + *putare* reckon. Doublet of COMPUTE.⟩ **—'count•a•ble,** *adj.*

count[2] [kaʊnt] *n.* a European nobleman having a rank about the same as that of a British earl. ⟨< OF *conte* < L *comes, -itis* companion < *com-* with + *ire* go⟩

count•down or **count–down** ['kaʊnt ,daʊn] *n.* **1** the period of time immediately preceding the firing or launching of a missile, rocket, etc. **2** the calling out of the minutes (and seconds, in the last stage) of this period as they pass.

coun•te•nance ['kaʊntənəns] *n., v.* **-nanced, -nanc•ing.** *—n.* **1** an expression of the face: *His angry countenance frightened us all.* **2** face; features: *The queen had a noble countenance.* **3** approval; sanction: *He gave countenance to our plan, but no active help.* **4** calmness; composure.
keep (one's) **countenance, a** be calm; not show feeling. **b** keep from smiling or laughing.
lose countenance, a get excited. **b** be embarrassed or humiliated.
put out of countenance, embarrass and confuse; make uneasy and ashamed.
—v. tolerate; sanction: *A dictator will not countenance opposition.* ⟨ME < OF *contenance* < Med.L *continentia* demeanour < L *continentia* self-control < *continere.* See CONTAIN.⟩ **—'coun•te•nanc•er,** *n.*
☛ *Syn. n.* **1, 2.** See note at FACE.

count•er[1] ['kaʊntər] *n.* **1** something used for counting. **2** an imitation coin. **3** a fixture in a store, restaurant, etc., having a long, flat, relatively narrow top surface for displaying goods, serving food, etc., and closed sides, usually with shelves or drawers: *a lunch counter.* **4** a similar fixture built in against one wall in a kitchen or bathroom and usually including a sink or washbasin.
over the counter, directly to the public, without a prescription: *Patent medicines can be sold over the counter.*
under the counter, secretly, often illegally. ⟨< AF *counteour* < *conter.* See COUNT[1].⟩

count•er[2] ['kaʊntər] *n.* a person or thing that counts. ⟨< *count*[1]⟩

coun•ter[3] ['kaʊntər] *adv., adj., v., n. —adv.* in the opposite

direction; opposed; contrary: *His wild idea runs counter to common sense.*
—adj. opposite; contrary.
—v. **1** go, say or act counter to; oppose: *He did not like our plan, so he countered it with one of his own.* **2** meet or answer (a blow or move) with another in return.
—n. **1** that which is opposite or contrary to something else. **2** a blow or move to answer or meet another. **3** *Boxing.* a blow given while deflecting one's opponent's punch; counterpunch. **4** *Fencing.* a deflecting of one's opponent's foil by a circular motion with one's own. **5** *Football.* a move in which the player with the ball runs to the side of the field, away from the movement of the lineman of the offence. **6** a stiff piece inside the back of a shoe around the heel. **7** the part of a ship's stern from the water line up to the end of the curved part. **8** the depressed part of the face of a type, coin, medal, etc. ⟨< F < L *contra* against⟩

counter– *combining form.* **1** against; in opposition to, as in *counteract.* **2** in return, as in *counterattack.* **3** corresponding or complementary, as in *counterpart.* ⟨See COUNTER[3]⟩
☛ *Usage.* **Counter-.** As with many such combining forms, usage is divided as to whether or not **counter** should be followed by a hyphen when used in combinations. In this dictionary a hyphen is used before a following 'r' and in most nouns, adjectives, and adverbs in which the primary stress falls on the second element of the compound: *counter-revolution, counter-espionage;* but *counterattack, counterpane,* etc.

coun•ter•act [ˌkaʊntərˈækt] *v.* act against; neutralize the action or effect of; hinder.

coun•ter•ac•tion [ˌkaʊntərˈækʃən] *n.* an action opposed to another action; hindrance.

coun•ter•ac•tive [ˌkaʊntərˈæktɪv] *adj., n. —adj.* tending to counteract.
—n. something that counteracts.

coun•ter•at•tack [ˈkaʊntərəˌtæk] *n., v. —n.* an attack made to counteract an attack.
—v. attack in return.

coun•ter•bal•ance *n.* [ˈkaʊntərˌbæləns]; *v.* [ˌkauntərˈbæləns] *n., v.* **-anced, -anc•ing.** *—n.* **1** a mass balancing another mass. **2** an influence, power, etc., balancing or offsetting another.
—v. act as a counterbalance to; offset; neutralize: *The two friends' different personalities seem to counterbalance each other.*

coun•ter•blow [ˈkaʊntərˌblou] *n.* a retaliatory blow, especially in boxing.

coun•ter•charge [ˈkaʊntərˌtʃɑrdʒ] *n., v.* **-charged, -charg•ing.** *—n.* a charge or accusation made to oppose one made by an accuser.
—v. charge or accuse (someone) after being oneself charged or accused.

coun•ter•check [ˈkaʊntərˌtʃɛk] *n., v. —n.* **1** something that restrains or opposes; an obstacle. **2** a check made upon a check; double check for verification.
—v. **1** restrain or oppose by some obstacle. **2** make a second check of; check again.

counter cheque a blank, unpersonalized cheque obtainable for use in a bank or at a store.

coun•ter•claim [ˈkaʊntərˌkleim] *n., v. —n.* an opposing claim; claim made by a person to offset a claim made against him or her.
—v. ask for or make a counterclaim. **—ˈcoun•terˌclaim•ant,** *n.*

coun•ter•clock•wise [ˌkaʊntərˈklɒkˌwaɪz] *adv. or adj.* in the direction opposite to that in which the hands of a clock move.

coun•ter•cul•ture [ˈkaʊntərˌkʌltʃər] *n.* a movement or group that rejects the values and mores of the prevailing culture in a particular society and pursues a quite different lifestyle: *the hippie counterculture of the Sixties.* **—ˌcoun•terˈcul•tur•al,** *adj.*

coun•ter•cur•rent [ˈkaʊntərˌkɜrənt] *n., adv. —n.* a current running in the opposite direction; an opposing current.
—adv. in an opposite manner or direction; contrary.

coun•ter–es•pi•o•nage [ˌkaʊntər ˈɛspiəˌnɑʒ] *or* [ˌkaʊntər ˈɛspiənɪdʒ] *n.* the taking of measures to prevent or confuse enemy espionage.

coun•ter•feit [ˈkaʊntərfɪt] *v., n., adj. —v.* **1** copy (money, handwriting, pictures, etc.) in order to deceive or defraud: *He was sent to prison for counterfeiting five-dollar bills.* **2** resemble closely. **3** pretend; dissemble: *She counterfeited a grief she did not feel.*
—n. a copy made to deceive or defraud and passed as genuine; forgery: *The store manager refused to accept the fifty-dollar bill because she suspected it was a counterfeit.*
—adj. **1** not genuine; sham; forged. **2** pretended; dissembled. ⟨ME < OF *contrefait* imitated, pp. of *contrefaire* < *contre-* against (< L *contra-*) + *faire* make < L *facere*⟩ **—ˈcoun•terˌfeit•er,** *n.*
☛ *Syn. adj.* **1.** See note at FALSE.

coun•ter•foil [ˈkaʊntərˌfɔɪl] *n.* the part of a cheque, receipt, etc., kept as a record. ⟨< *counter-* + *foil* leaf⟩

coun•ter•in•sur•gen•cy [ˌkaʊntərɪnˈsɜrdʒənsi] *n., pl.* **-cies.** defense and counterattack against guerrilla warfare and infiltration.

coun•ter–in•tel•li•gence [ˌkaʊntər ɪnˈtɛlədʒəns] *n.* **1** a government or military department whose work is to track down and prevent espionage, sabotage, etc. **2** the system or methods used by such a department.

coun•ter–ir•ri•tant [ˌkaʊntər ˈirətənt] *n.* an agent used to produce superficial irritation or inflammation on a part of the body in order to relieve a deep-seated congestion or inflammation by bringing blood to the surface.

coun•ter•mand *v.* [ˌkaʊntərˈmænd] *or* [ˈkaʊntərˌmænd]; *n.* [ˈkaʊntərˌmænd] *v., n. —v.* **1** withdraw or cancel (an order, command, etc.). **2** recall or stop by a contrary order; order back.
—n. an order that cancels or is contrary to a previous order. ⟨ME < OF *contremander* < L *contra-* against + *mandare* order⟩

coun•ter•march [ˈkaʊntərˌmɑrtʃ] *v. or n.* march in the opposite direction; march back.

coun•ter•meas•ure [ˈkaʊntərˌmɛʒər] *n.* a measure or move taken to offset another.

coun•ter•mine *n.* [ˈkaʊntərˌmaɪn]; *v.* [ˈkaʊntərˌmaɪn] *or* [ˌkaʊntərˈmaɪn] *n., v.* **-mined, -min•ing.** *—n.* **1** a submarine mine intended to set off enemy mines prematurely. **2** a counterplot.
—v. **1** place countermines (against). **2** counterplot.

coun•ter•mis•sile [ˈkaʊntərˌmɪsaɪl] *or* [-ˌmɪsəl] *n.* a missile designed to intercept and destroy another missile.

coun•ter•move [ˈkaʊntərˌmuv] *n., v.* **-moved, -mov•ing.** *—n.* an opposing move; a move made in response to another's move.
—v. make an opposing move; move in response to another's action.

coun•ter•of•fen•sive [ˈkaʊntərəˌfɛnsɪv] *or* [ˌkaʊntərəˈfɛnsɪv] *n.* an attack on a large scale undertaken by a defending force to take the initiative back from an attacking force.

coun•ter•of•fer [ˈkaʊntərˌɒfər] *n.* an offer made in response to an unacceptable offer.

coun•ter•pane [ˈkaʊntərˌpein] *n.* an outer covering for a bed; bedspread. ⟨alteration of *counterpoint* < OF *contrepoint* bed covering < Med.L *culcita puncta* quilt, stitched mattress. The latter part of the English word was altered to *pane* from association with ME *pane* piece of cloth < OF *pan.* See PANE.⟩

coun•ter•part [ˈkaʊntərˌpɑrt] *n.* **1** a person or thing closely resembling another. **2** a person or thing that corresponds to another; equivalent: *The federal energy minister is holding talks with his provincial counterparts.* **3** a person or thing that complements another: *Night is the counterpart of day.* **4** a copy or duplicate, especially of a legal document.

coun•ter•plot *n.* [ˈkaʊntərˌplɒt]; *v.* [ˈkaʊntərˌplɒt] *or* [ˌkaʊntərˈplɒt] *n., v.* **-plot•ted, -plot•ting.** *—n.* a plot to defeat another plot.
—v. resist or oppose (a plot) with a counterplot.

coun•ter•point [ˈkaʊntərˌpɔɪnt] *n., v. —n.* **1** *Music.* **a** a melody added to another as an accompaniment. **b** the art of combining two or more melodies so that they form a harmonious unit but the individual melodies can still be distinguished. **c** the style of composition in which more or less individual melodies are combined according to fixed rules. **2** an element, theme, item, etc., that contrasts with or complements another; foil.
—v. arrange in counterpoint. ⟨< F *contrepoint*⟩

coun•ter•poise *n.* [ˈkaʊntərˌpɔɪz]; *v.* [ˈkaʊntərˌpɔɪz] *or* [ˌkaʊntərˈpɔɪz] *n., v.* **-poised, -pois•ing.** counterbalance.

coun•ter–pro•duc•tive [ˌkaʊntər prəˈdʌktɪv] *adj.* acting against or hindering the achievement of a goal; not productive or useful.

coun•ter•pro•po•sal [ˈkaʊntərprəˌpouzəl] *n.* a proposal made in response to an unacceptable proposal.

coun•ter–ref•or•ma•tion [ˌkaʊntər ˌrɛfərˈmeiʃən] *n.* **1** a reform movement opposed to a previous reform movement. **2 Counter-Reformation,** the movement in the Roman Catholic Church during the 16th and 17th centuries to correct certain abuses within the church, formulate many doctrines of the church, and organize Catholic opposition to Protestantism.

coun•ter–rev•o•lu•tion [ˌkaʊntər ˌrɛvəˈluʃən] *n.* a revolution against a government established by a previous revolution.

coun•ter–rev•o•lu•tion•ary [ˌkaʊntər ˌrɛvəˈluʃəˌnɛri] *adj., n. —adj.* of or having to do with a counter-revolution. *—n.* one who supports a counter-revolution.

coun•ter•scarp [ˈkaʊntərˌskɑrp] *n.* the outer slope or wall of a moat, ditch, etc., in a fortification. ⟨< F *contrescarpe*⟩

coun•ter•shaft [ˈkaʊntərˌʃæft] *n.* a shaft that transmits motion from the main shaft to the working parts of a machine.

coun•ter•sign [ˈkaʊntərˌsaɪn]; *n., v. —n.* **1** a password given in answer to the challenge of a sentinel: *The soldier had to give the countersign before he could pass the sentry.* **2** a secret sign or signal given in answer to another. **3** a signature added to another signature to confirm it.
—v. sign (something already signed by another) to confirm it. ⟨< F *contresigne*⟩ **—ˌcoun•terˈsig•na•ture** [-ˈsɪgnətʃər], *n.*

coun•ter•sink [ˈkaʊntərˌsɪŋk] *v.* **-sunk, -sink•ing;** *n.*
—v. **1** enlarge the upper part of (a hole) to make room for the head of a screw, bolt, etc. **2** sink the head of (a screw, bolt, etc.) into such a hole so that it is even with or below the surface.
—n. **1** a countersunk hole. **2** a tool for countersinking holes.

coun•ter•spy [ˈkaʊntərˌspaɪ] *n.* a spy who works to uncover or oppose the activities of enemy spies.

coun•ter•ten•or [ˈkaʊntərˌtɛnər] *n.* **1** the highest adult male singing voice, above tenor. Countertenor usually involves falsetto in its upper range. **2** a singer who has such a voice. **3** the part sung by a countertenor. **4** (*adjl.*) having to do with, having the range of, or designed for a countertenor.

coun•ter•vail [ˈkaʊntərˌveil] *or* [ˌkaʊntərˈveil] *v.* **1** counteract; avail against. **2** compensate; offset; make up for. ⟨ME < AF *countrevaloir* < L *contra valere* be of worth against⟩

coun•ter•weigh [ˌkaʊntərˈwei] *v.* act as a counterbalance to; offset the balance of.

coun•ter•weight [ˈkaʊntərˌweit] *n.* a mass that balances another mass.

counter word a word of approval or disapproval commonly used without reference to its exact meaning; as *terrific, wonderful, ghastly.*

coun•ter•work [ˈkaʊntərˌwɜrk] *n.* something constructed in opposition, as a wall or fortification.

count•ess [ˈkaʊntɪs] *n.* **1** the wife or widow of an earl or count. **2** a woman whose rank is equal to that of an earl or count. ⟨ME < OF *contesse* < Med.L *comitissa,* fem. of L *comes.* See COUNT[2].⟩

counting house a building or office used for keeping accounts and doing business.

counting room an office used for keeping accounts and doing business.

count•less [ˈkaʊntlɪs] *adj.* too many to count; very many; innumerable: *the countless grains of sand on the seashore, the countless stars.*

count noun a word denoting a thing which can have a plural. *Bottle* is a count noun; *milk* is not. *Formality* can be used as a count noun (= 'formal thing') or not (as when it means 'formalness').

coun•tri•fy [ˈkʌntrəˌfaɪ] *v.* **-fied, -fy•ing.** cause to conform to a rural way of life. **2** make typical of a rural way of life: *I don't like their kitchen; it's too countrified.*

coun•try [ˈkʌntri] *n., pl.* **-tries. 1** an expanse of land characterized by a particular geography, population, etc.; a region or district: *Cossack country. They live in the hill country to the north.* **2** a nation; state: *They came from France, a country across the sea.* **3** the people of a nation. **4** the land where a person was born or is a citizen: *In my own country the customs are very different.* **5** land with few houses, away from cities or industrial areas; uncultivated land or farmland: *We drove out into the country.* **6** (*adjl.*) of, in, or like the country as opposed to the city; rural: *She likes country food and country air.* **7** COUNTRY MUSIC. **8** (*adjl.*) of or having to do with country music.
across country. See ACROSS. ⟨ME < OF *contree* < VL *contrata* region lying opposite < L *contra* against⟩

country and western COUNTRY MUSIC.

country club a club in the country near a city, or in the suburbs, having a clubhouse and facilities for outdoor sports, especially golf.

country cousin a person from the country who finds the city confusing, exciting, or frightening.

coun•try–dance [ˈkʌntri ˌdæns] *n.* a dance in which partners face each other in two long lines. The Virginia reel is a country-dance.

coun•try•folk [ˈkʌntriˌfouk] *n.* the people who live in the country.

country food a good, simple, hearty, plentiful meal.

country gentleman a gentleman who lives on his estate in the country.

country house a home in the country.

coun•try•man [ˈkʌntrimən] *n., pl.* **-men. 1** a man of one's own country; compatriot: *They met many of their countrymen in their travels through Europe.* **2** a man who lives in the country; a rustic.

country marriage *Cdn.* formerly, among fur traders and pioneers, a common-law marriage between a white man and a First Nations or Métis woman.

country mile a very long distance.

country music a style of music that developed from the traditional folk music of white people in the S United States, having very simple rhythm and harmony. Modern country music has spread throughout North America and other countries and contains many elements of blues, popular music, and rock.

coun•try•seat [ˈkʌntriˌsit] *n.* a residence or estate in the country, especially a fine one.

coun•try•side [ˈkʌntriˌsaɪd] *n.* **1** land outside cities and towns, especially with reference to its features such as trees, flowers, hills and valleys, and its general appearance: *The countryside looked beautiful in the fall sun.* **2** a certain section of the country. **3** its people: *The whole countryside was up in arms.*

coun•try–wide [ˈkʌntri ˌwaɪd] *adj.* nationwide.

country wife *Cdn.* formerly, a First Nations or Métis common-law wife of a white fur trader or pioneer.

coun•try•wom•an [ˈkʌntriˌwʊmən] *n., pl.* **-wom•en. 1** a woman of one's own country; compatriot. **2** a woman living in the country; a rustic.

count•ship [ˈkaʊntʃɪp] *n.* **1** the title or rank of a count. **2** the territory owned by or under the control of a count.

coun•ty [ˈkaʊnti] *n., pl.* **-ties. 1** an administrative district of a country, province, state, etc. The county form of municipal government is used in Nova Scotia, New Brunswick, Québec, Ontario, and Alberta. **2** in Great Britain and Ireland, one of the districts into which the country is divided for administrative, judicial, and political purposes. **3** the people of a county. **4** the government of a county. ⟨ME < AF *counte* < *counte,* var. of OF *conte.* See COUNT[2].⟩

county court a court having limited jurisdiction in the county or district where it is held.

county seat a town or city where the county government is located.

county town *Brit.* COUNTY SEAT.

coup [ku] *n., pl.* **coups** [kuz]. **1** a sudden, brilliant action; an unexpected, clever move; master stroke. **2** a stroke or blow. **3** a cleverly organized crime. **4** COUP D'ÉTAT. ⟨< F < L < Gk. *kolaphos*⟩
☛ *Hom.* COO.

coup de grâce [ˈku də ˈgrɑs]; *French,* [kudˈgʀɑs] **1** an action that gives a merciful death to a suffering animal or person. **2** a finishing stroke: *The runner's final sprint gave the coup de grâce to his opponents.* ⟨< F *coup de grâce,* literally, stroke of grace⟩

coup de main [ˈku də ˈmɛ̃]; *French,* [kudˈmɛ̃] a sudden, unexpected attack. ⟨< F, blow of the hand⟩

coup de maître [ˈku də ˈmɛtrə]; *French,* [kudˈmɛtʀ] an act of genius; a master stroke. ⟨< F, stroke of a master⟩

coup d'é•tat [ˈku deiˈtɑ]; *French,* [kudeˈta] *Politics.* a sudden and decisive use of force by a small group of people, especially in the violent overthrow of a government. ⟨< F *coup d'état,* literally, stroke of state⟩

coup de thé•â•tre [ˈku də teiˈɑtrə]; *French,* [kudteˈatʀ] **1** a pivotal event in a dramatic work. **2** an action or event designed to create sensation. ⟨< F, stroke of theatre⟩

coup d'oeil [kuˈdœj] *French.* a view taken in at a glance.

coupe [kup] *n.* a closed, two-door automobile, usually seating two to five people. ⟨< *coupé*⟩
☛ *Hom.* COOP.

cou•pé [ku'pei] *for 1,* [ku'pei] *or* [kup] *for 2. n.* **1** a closed carriage with a seat for two people inside and a seat for the driver outside. **2** coupe. ⟨< F *coupé*, pp. of *couper* cut⟩

cou•ple ['kʌpəl] *n., v.* **-pled, -pling.** *—n.* **1** two things of the same kind that go together; a pair. **2** *Mechanics.* two balanced forces which create rotation by their movement in opposite but parallel directions. **3** two people who are married, engaged, or paired together for a dance, party, game, etc. **4** *Informal.* a few; several (*used with* **of**): *It shouldn't take longer than a couple of days.*
—v. **1** join together; join together in pairs. **2** copulate. **3** *Electricity.* connect by a coupler. ⟨ME < OF *cople* < L *copula* bond. Doublet of COPULA.⟩
☛ *Syn. n.* **1.** See note at PAIR.
☛ *Usage.* **Couple** = strictly, two persons or things associated in some way: *a married couple.* In everyday speech **couple** is equivalent to the numeral two: *She borrowed a couple of pencils.*

cou•pler ['kʌplər] *n.* **1** in an organ, a device for coupling keys or keyboards so they can be played together. **2** a device used to join together two railway cars. **3** a device used to connect electric circuits in order to transfer energy from one to the other. **4** that part of the body of an animal between the hipbones and the ribs. **5** any person or thing that couples.

cou•plet ['kʌplɪt] *n.* **1** two successive lines of verse that rhyme and have the same number of metrical feet. *Example*: Be not the first by whom the new is tried/Nor yet the last to lay the old aside. **2** a couple; pair. ⟨< F *couplet*, dim. of *couple* couple⟩

cou•pling ['kʌplɪŋ] *n., v. —n.* **1** the act or process of joining or copulating. **2** a device for joining parts of machinery. **3** a device used to join two railway cars. **4** a device or arrangement for transferring electrical energy from one circuit to another.
—v. ppr. of COUPLE.

cou•pon ['kupɒn] *or, often,* ['kjupɒn] *n.* **1** a part of a ticket, advertisement, package, etc., that entitles the person who holds it to get something in exchange: *She saved the coupons that came with each box of soap to get free cups and saucers.* **2** a printed statement of interest due on a bond, which can be cut from the bond and presented for payment. ⟨< F *coupon* < *couper* cut⟩

cour•age ['kɜrɪdʒ] *n.* bravery; the strength of mind to control fear and act firmly in the face of danger or difficulties.
have the courage of (one's) **convictions,** act as one believes one should. ⟨ME < OF *corage*, *curage* < *cuer* heart < L *cor*⟩
☛ *Syn.* **1. Courage,** BRAVERY = fearlessness. **Courage** applies to moral strength that makes a person face any danger, trouble, or pain steadily and in spite of fear: *Although blinded by the explosion, he faced the future with courage.* **Bravery** applies to a kind of courage that is shown by bold, fearless, daring action in the presence of danger: *The Commandos are famous for their bravery.*

cou•ra•geous [kə'reidʒəs] *adj.* full of courage; brave. **—cou'ra•geous•ly,** *adv.* **—cou'ra•geous•ness,** *n.*

cou•rante [ku'rɑnt]; *French,* [ku'ʀɑ̃t] *n.* **1** an old French dance with fast steps. **2** the music for this dance. **3** such music used as a movement in a classical composition. ⟨< F < fem. of *courant*, ppr. of *courir* run, glide < L *currere* run⟩

cou•reur de bois [ku'rɜr də 'bwɑ]; *French,* [kuʀœʀdə'bwa] *pl.* **coureurs de bois.** [ku'rɜr də 'bwɑ]; *French,* [kuʀœʀdə'bwa] *Cdn.* formerly, in the North and Northwest, a French or Métis fur trader or woodsman. Radisson and Groseilliers were two famous coureurs de bois. ⟨< Cdn.F⟩

cour•gette [kʊr'ʒɛt] *n. Brit.* zucchini. ⟨< F dim. of *courge* gourd⟩

cour•i•er ['kɜriər] *or* ['kʊriər] *n.* **1** a person or agency whose work is carrying messages, especially official government messages. **2** a secret agent who transfers information to and from other agents. **3** a person who goes with a group of travellers and takes care of hotel reservations, tickets, etc. **4** an agency that undertakes to deliver letters and parcels very rapidly. ⟨< F *courrier* < Ital. < L *currere* run⟩
☛ *Hom.* CURRIER ['kɜriər].

course [kɔrs] *n., v.* **coursed, cours•ing.** *—n.* **1** an onward movement; progress: *the course of events. She gets little rest in the course of her daily work.* **2** a direction taken: *The ship's course was east.* **3** a line of action or conduct: *The only sensible course was to go home.* **4** a way; path or track; channel: *the course of a stream.* **5** a series of similar things, acts, or events arranged in some regular order: *a course of medical treatment, a course of lectures in history.* **6** the regular order; the ordinary way of proceeding: *the course of nature.* **7** duration; period of time: *in the course of the day; in the course of his career as prime minister.* **8** in a university, college, or school: **a** a body of presented studies that make up a curriculum leading to a degree or diploma: *a two-year hairdressing course.* **b** a unit within such a body of studies; subject: *How many courses are you taking next year?* **9** a part of a meal served at one time: *Soup was the first course.* **10** an area marked out for a game or sport: *a racecourse, a golf course.* **11** a layer of bricks, stones, shingles, etc.; row. **12** the lowest square sail on any mast of a square-rigged ship.
a matter of course, a normal way of proceeding.
in due course, at the proper or usual time; after a while.
of course, a as might be expected; needless to say; naturally: *Of course it will rain on the weekend.* **b** certainly; without question: *Of course I'll do it.*
off course, straying from the right direction.
on course, going in the planned direction: *The automatic pilot keeps the plane on course.*
run or **take its course,** of something, come to the end of its natural development.
—v. **1** race; run: *The blood courses through the arteries.* **2** hunt with hounds. **3** cause (hounds) to hunt for game. ⟨< F *cours* < L *cursus* a running, and < F *course* < Ital. *corsa* a running < L *currere* run⟩
☛ *Hom.* COARSE, CORSE.

cours•er[1] ['kɔrsər] *n.* **1** *Poetic.* a swift horse. **2** a warhorse. ⟨ME < OF *coursier* < *cours* a running < L *cursus*⟩

cours•er[2] ['kɔrsər] *n.* a bird of the family Glareolidae, native to arid regions and noted for fast running. ⟨< NL *Cursorius* genus name < LL, having to do with running⟩

cours•er[3] ['kɔrsər] *n.* **1** a person or thing that courses. **2** a hound used for hunting. ⟨< *course* + *-er*[1]⟩

course•ware ['kɔrs,wɛr] *Computer technology.* computer software that presents instruction in a variety of subjects: *Our school uses courseware to help with the teaching of chemistry.*

cours•ing ['kɔrsɪŋ] *n., v. —n.* **1** the act of a person or thing that courses. **2** hunting with hounds, by sight rather than scent.
—v. ppr. of COURSE.

court [kɔrt] *n., v. —n.* **1** a space partly or wholly enclosed by walls or buildings. **2** a short street, especially a wide lane opening off a street and having buildings on three sides, or ending in a circle. **3** a place marked or walled off for any of various games: *a tennis court, a squash court.* **4** the residence of a king, queen, or other sovereign; a royal palace. **5** the family, household, or followers of a sovereign. **6** a sovereign and his or her advisers as a ruling power. **7** a formal assembly held by a sovereign. **8** *Law.* **a** a place where justice is administered. **b** the persons who are chosen to administer justice; a judge or judges. **c** an assembling of such persons to administer justice. **d** a session of a judicial body. **9** attention paid to get favour; effort to please. **10** the act of wooing; seeking to marry. **11** *Cdn.* **a** a single act or number in the program of a skating review or carnival. **b** the skater or skaters performing this act.
hold court, a of a sovereign, hold a formal assembly. **b** receive or entertain people in a lordly way.
out of court, a without a trial or other legal proceedings; privately: *The case was settled out of court.* **b** not important enough to be considered.
pay court to, a pay attention to (a person) to get his or her favour; try to please. **b** woo.
—v. **1** pay attention to (a person) to get his or her favour; try to please. **2** try to gain the love of, especially with the intention of marrying; woo. **3** try to get; act so as to get (danger, disaster, death, etc.); seek: *It is foolish to court danger.* ⟨ME < OF *cort* < L *cohors* enclosure, retinue. Doublet of COHORT.⟩

court bouillon liquid for cooking food such as fish, made by boiling white wine together with herbs and certain vegetables.

court card *Esp. Brit.* the king, queen, or jack of any suit of playing cards; face card.

cour•te•ous ['kɜrtiəs] *adj.* polite; thoughtful of others: *It is a courteous act to hold the door open for someone loaded with parcels.* ⟨ME < OF *corteis* < *cort.* See COURT.⟩
—'cour•te•ous•ly, *adv.* **—'cour•te•ous•ness,** *n.*
☛ *Syn.* See note at POLITE.

cour•te•san ['kɔrtə,zæn], ['kɔrtəzən], [,kɔrtə'zæn], *or* [,kɜrtə'zæn] *n.* **1** a prostitute whose clients are men of high rank, especially men at court. **2** any prostitute. Also, **courtezan.** ⟨< F *courtisane* < Ital. *cortigiana* woman of the court < *corte* < L *cohors.* Related to COURT.⟩

cour•te•sy ['kɜrtəsi] *n., pl.* **-sies. 1** polite or gracious behaviour; thoughtfulness for others. **2** Usually, **courtesies,** *pl.* a polite or thoughtful act or expression: *They exchanged courtesies and each went his way.*
by courtesy, as a favour, rather than as something rightfully owing.

by courtesy of or **through the courtesy of,** with the consent of; with the permission or approval of: *The poem is included in the book by courtesy of the author.*
courtesy of, free of charge by: *Soap, shampoo, and toothpaste are provided courtesy of the hotel.* ⟨ME < OF *cortesie* < *corteis.* See COURTEOUS.⟩
☛ *Hom.* CURTESY.

courtesy car a car lent free of charge, as by a garage while repairing one's own car.

courtesy card a card issued by a bank, store, etc., granting the holder certain privileges.

cour•te•zan ['kɔrtə,zæn], ['kɔrtəzən], [,kɔrtə'zæn], *or* [,kɜrtə'zæn] See COURTESAN.

court•house ['kɔrt,hʌus] *n.* a building where law courts are held.

cour•ti•er ['kɔrtiər] *n.* **1** a person often present at the court of a king, queen, etc.; court attendant. **2** a person who tries to win the favour of another by flattering and pleasing him or her.

court•li•ness ['kɔrtlinɪs] *n.* politeness; elegance; polish.

court•ly ['kɔrtli] *adj.* **-li•er, -li•est. 1** suitable for a royal court; polite; elegant: *courtly manners, courtly hospitality.* **2** of or having to do with a royal court. **3** trying hard to please one's superior.

court–mar•tial ['kɔrt 'mɑrʃəl] *n., pl.* **courts-mar•tial;** *v.* **-tialled** or **-tialed, -tial•ling** or **-tial•ing.** *—n.* **1** a court made up of commissioned officers in the armed forces for the purpose of trying armed forces personnel accused of breaking military law. **2** a trial by such a court: *The captain's court-martial will be held next week.*
—v. try by such a court.

court of law a place where justice is administered; law court.

Court of St. James's the official name for the British court, which gets its name from St. James's Palace in London, where royal receptions were formerly held.

court plaster formerly, cloth with a sticky substance on one side, used for covering and protecting slight cuts.

court•room ['kɔrt,rum] *or* [-,rʊm] *n.* a room where a law court is held.

court•ship ['kɔrtʃɪp] *n.* the condition or time of courting with the intention of marrying; wooing.

court shoe 1 a shoe for playing court games such as tennis. **2** *Esp. Brit.* a low shoe; pump.

court tennis a game in which a ball is hit back and forth over a low net. It is played on an enclosed court, as distinguished from lawn tennis which is played outdoors.

court•yard ['kɔrt,jɑrd] *n.* a space enclosed by walls in or near a large building.

cous•cous ['kuskus] *n.* a North African food made from steamed wheat and usually served with cooked chicken. Couscous is cooked and used in much the same way that rice is. ⟨< F < Berber *kuskus* < *Arabic* < *kaskasa* grind, pound⟩

cous•in ['kʌzən] *n.* **1** the son or daughter of one's uncle or aunt. **First cousins** have two of the same grandparents; **second cousins** have two of the same great-grandparents; and so on for third and fourth cousins. Your father's, mother's, or child's first cousin is your **first cousin once removed. 2** a distant relative. **3** a person who is related by culture, race, etc.: *our English cousins.* **4** any person or thing thought of as related to another: *A good swimmer is first cousin to a beaver.* **5** *Formal.* a title used by a sovereign in addressing another sovereign or a great nobleman. ⟨ME < OF *cosin, cusin* < L *consobrinus* mother's sister's child < *com-* together + *soror* sister⟩
☛ *Hom.* COZEN.

cous•in–ger•man ['kʌzən 'dʒɜrmən] *n., pl.* **cous•ins-ger•man.** a son or daughter of one's uncle or aunt; first cousin. ⟨< F *cousin-germain; germain* < L *germanus*⟩

cous•in•ly ['kʌzənli] *adj., adv. —adj.* of, like, or characteristic of a cousin.
—adv. in a cousinly manner.

cous•in•ry ['kʌzənri] *n.* all one's cousins or other relations, as a group.

cous•in•ship ['kʌzən,ʃɪp] *n.* the relationship of a cousin or cousins.

couth [kuθ] *adj., n. Facetious. —adj.* sophisticated; refined.
—n. sophistication; refinement: *His writing style is colourful but lacks couth.* ⟨back formation from *uncouth*⟩

cou•ture [ku'tur] *or* [ku'tʃur]; *French,* [ku'tyʀ] *n.* the business of dressmaking and fashion design. ⟨< F < L *com-* together + *suere* sew⟩

cou•tu•ri•er [ku'turi,ei] *or* [ku'turiər]; *French,* [kutyʀ'je] *n.* a male dressmaker or women's fashion designer. ⟨< F *couturier* tailor < *couture* sewing < VL < L *consuere* < *com-* together + *suere* sew⟩

cou•tu•ri•ère [ku,turi'ɛr]; *French,* [kuty'ʀjɛʀ] *n.* a woman dressmaker or women's fashion designer. ⟨< F. See COUTURIER.⟩

cou•vade [ku'vɑd] *n.* the custom among certain peoples in which the father imitates the experience of childbirth, and shares the mother's social and ritual role. ⟨< F < *couver* < L *cubare* lie down⟩

co•va•lence [kou'veiləns] *n. Chemistry.* **1** a bond in which two atoms share a pair of electrons. **2** the ability to form such a bond. **3** the total of the pairs of electrons which one atom can share with surrounding atoms. Also, **covalency**.

co•va•lent [kou'veilənt] *adj.* of or having to do with covalence.

covalent bond a chemical bond in which two or more electrons are shared by two atoms.

co•var•i•ance [kou'vɛriəns] *n. Statistics.* a calculation of the relationship between two variables whose values are measured at the same time. Covariance is measured by calculating the product of the average values of the variables and subtracting that from the average of the product of both variables.

cove [kouv] *n.* **1** a small, sheltered bay; an inlet on the shore; the mouth of a creek. **2** a sheltered nook. **3** a concave moulding, such as a hollow curve between a wall and the ceiling. Also (def. 3), **coving.** ⟨OE *cofa* chamber⟩

cov•en ['kʌvən] *n.* **1** a gathering of witches. **2** a company or community of witches; especially, traditionally, a group of thirteen. ⟨< OF *covin* group, ult. < L *convenīre* to come together⟩

cov•e•nant ['kʌvənənt] *n., v. —n.* **1** a solemn agreement between two or more persons or groups to do or not to do a certain thing; compact. **2 Covenant, a** the agreement signed by Scottish Presbyterians and members of the English Parliament in 1643. It set up the Presbyterian Church in England. **b** an earlier agreement signed by Scottish Presbyterians in 1638, for the defence of the Presbyterian faith. **c** the COVENANT OF THE LEAGUE OF NATIONS. **3** in the Bible, the solemn promises of God to people; a compact between God and people. **4** a legal contract or agreement.
—v. **1** solemnly agree (to do certain things). **2** enter into a covenant or formal agreement. ⟨ME < OF *covenant* < *covenir* < L *convenire.* See CONVENE.⟩ **—,cov•e'nant•al** [,kʌvə'næntəl], *adj.*

cov•e•nan•tee [,kʌvənən'ti] *n.* the person with whom a covenant is made; the recipient of the promises in a compact.

cov•e•nant•er ['kʌvənəntər]; *also* [,kʌvə'næntər] *for 2. n.* **1** a person who makes a solemn agreement. **2 Covenanter,** a person who signed and supported either of the Covenants of the Scottish Presbyterians in the 17th century.

Covenant of the League of Nations the constitution of the League of Nations. It comprises the first part of the Treaty of Versailles that was signed in 1919.

cov•e•nan•tor ['kʌvənəntər] *n. Law.* a person who makes a covenant and assumes its obligations.

Cov•en•try ['kʌvəntri] *or* ['kɒvəntri] *n.*
send to Coventry, refuse to associate with; ostracize. ⟨< *Coventry,* city in central England where prisoners were sent in the Civil War⟩

cov•er ['kʌvər] *v., n. —v.* **1** put something over or around so as to protect, keep warm, hide, etc.: *She covered the sleeping child with his coat. Pull the blind to cover the window.* **2** lie thickly on the surface of; be spread or scattered over: *Dust covered her shoes. Snow covered the ground.* **3** clothe; wrap up: *People in the Arctic cover themselves with furs.* **4** extend over; occupy: *Their farm covers 300 hectares.* **5** invest (oneself or one's reputation) with some quality: *She covered herself with glory.* **6** hide; conceal: *to cover a mistake.* **7** protect, screen, or shelter: *to cover someone's retreat.* **8** go over; travel: *We covered more than 500 km on the first day of our trip.* **9** deal with; take in: *The review covered everything we learned last term.* **10** be enough for; provide for: *I had just enough money to cover the cost of the meal plus a tip.* **11** aim straight at: *to cover a person with a pistol.* **12** have or keep within range: *The guns of the fort on the hill covered the territory down to the sea.* **13** put one's hat or cap on: *Cover your*

head when you are in the sun. **14** protect by insurance; insure against a particular risk: *The house is covered but not the contents.* **15** *Journalism.* act as a reporter or photographer of (an event or subject): *She covers the city police court.* **16** work in; be responsible for (a territory): *One of our sales staff covers the whole of Manitoba and Saskatchewan.* **17** be covered; wear a hat: *Never cover in the presence of your king.* **18** *Sports.* watch over and try to thwart (an opposing player). **19** *Football.* try to stop (an opposing player) from catching the ball or stop (a punted ball) from being thrown back. **20** *Card games.* put a higher-ranking card on (a card played earlier). **21** stand behind; support: *The shortstop covered the second baseman in case the ball got by him.* **22** *Informal.* act as a substitute while someone is absent: *He is covering for the manager while she's away.* **23** ensure that (someone's) guilt is not found out (*used with* **for**): *Please cover for me until I can put the missing money back.* **24** deposit the equivalent of (money deposited by another in betting); accept the conditions of (a bet). **25** *Business.* buy commodities, securities, etc., for future delivery as a protection against (loss). **26** of a male animal, copulate with (the female). **27** brood or sit on (eggs or chicks).
cover up, a cover completely; hide; conceal: *He did his best to cover up his error.* **b** hide knowledge or an act in order to protect oneself or someone else: *He's obviously trying to cover up. She will always cover up for a colleague.* **c** seek to cover or protect oneself: *The boxer covered up under the onslaught of blows.*
—*n.* **1 a** anything that covers: *She always puts covers on her school books.* **b** specifically, a bedcovering; blanket: *He hogs the covers all night!* **2** protection; shelter: *We took cover in an old barn during the storm. The soldiers attacked under cover of dark.* **3** *Hunting.* a COVERT (def. 2). **4** something that hides or disguises, such as a false identity: *Her job as newspaper reporter was just a cover for her activities as a spy.* **5** *Sports.* a player who watches over and tries to thwart an opposing player. **6** a place for one person at a table, set with a plate, knife, fork, spoon, napkin, etc. **7** COVER CHARGE. **8** funds adequate to cover or meet a liability or secure against possible loss. **9** *Philately.* **a** an envelope or wrapper with stamp and any postal markings affixed. **b** a letter addressed on the reverse side after folding to form an envelope.
blow (someone's) **cover** or **disguise,** expose someone's false identity: *The spy posed as a bookseller until an alert scholar blew his cover.*
break cover, come out of hiding, especially suddenly: *She broke cover and ran for the house.*
take cover, find a shelter from attack.
under cover, a hidden; secret; disguised. **b** secretly. ⟨ME < OF *covrir* < L *cooperire* < *co-* up + *operire* cover⟩ **—'cov•er•er,** *n.* **—'cov•er•less,** *adj.*

cov•er•age ['kʌvərɪdʒ] *n.* **1** the scope and manner of presenting information by a reporter, newspaper, etc. **2** in insurance, the risks covered by a policy. **3** the maximum amount payable by the insurer under a policy: *We have $50 000 coverage in case of accidental death.* **4** an amount held to meet liabilities: *a 60 percent gold coverage of paper money.* **5** the section of the potential buying public presumably reached by a given advertising campaign, medium, etc.

cov•er•alls ['kʌvər,ɒlz] *n.pl.* a sturdy outer garment that includes shirt and pants in a single unit, usually worn to protect other clothing. Mechanics usually wear coveralls.

cover charge a charge made in some nightclubs, discothèques, restaurants, etc., for service, entertainment, etc., in addition to the charge for food or drink.

cover crop a crop sown in a field or orchard to protect the soil, especially in winter.

cov•ered ['kʌvərd] *adj., v.* —*adj.* **1** having a cover or covering. **2** wearing one's hat or cap.
—*v.* pt. and pp. of COVER.

covered bridge a bridge with a protective roof over the roadway: *There are many covered bridges in New Brunswick.*

covered wagon a large wagon having a removable, arched canvas cover.

A covered wagon

cover glass a piece of thin glass used to cover a microscopic preparation on a slide; coverslip.

cov•er•ing ['kʌvərɪŋ] *n., v.* —*n.* anything that covers.
—*v.* ppr. of COVER.

covering letter a letter sent together with other material, such as a résumé, giving an outline or explanation.

cov•er•let ['kʌvərlɪt] *n.* **1** an outer covering for a bed; bedspread. **2** any covering. ⟨ME *coverlite,* apparently < OF *covrir* (see COVER) + *lit* bed < L *lectus*⟩

cov•er•lid ['kʌvərlɪd] *n.* coverlet.

co•versed sine ['kouvərst] *Trigonometry.* a function equalling the sine of a particular angle subtracted from one; versed cosine. ⟨< *co(sine)* + NL *versus* + E *sine*⟩

cov•er•slip ['kʌvər,slɪp] *n.* COVER GLASS.

cover story 1 an article in a magazine dealing with a topic shown on the cover. **2** a false alibi: *The spy took care to preserve his cover story.*

cov•ert ['kʌvərt] *or* ['kouvərt] *adj., n.* —*adj.* secret; hidden; disguised: *covert glances.*
—*n.* **1** a shelter; hiding place. **2** a thicket in which animals hide. **3 coverts,** *pl.* the smaller and weaker feathers of a bird that cover the bases of the larger feathers of the wings and tail. ⟨ME < OF *covert,* pp. of *covrir.* See COVER.⟩ **—'cov•ert•ly,** *adv.* **—'cov•ert•ness,** *n.*
☛ *Syn. adj.* See note at SECRET.

co•vert cloth ['kouvərt] *or* ['kʌvərt] cloth of wool, silk and wool, or rayon, usually brownish, used for coats.

cov•er•ture ['kʌvər,tʃʊr] *or* ['kʌvərtʃər] *n.* **1** a cover; a covering. **2** a shelter; hiding place. **3** a hiding or keeping secret.

cov•er–up ['kʌvər ,ʌp] *n.* **1** a strategem, action, or device designed to conceal something, especially a serious mistake or a crime. **2** a garment which covers another garment such as a swimsuit.

cov•et ['kʌvɪt] *v.* desire eagerly (something that belongs to another). ⟨ME < OF *coveitier,* ult. < L *cupere* desire⟩ **—'cov•et•er,** *n.*
☛ *Syn.* See note at ENVY.

cov•et•ous ['kʌvətəs] *adj.* desiring things that belong to others. **—'cov•et•ous•ly,** *adv.* **—'cov•et•ous•ness,** *n.*

cov•ey ['kʌvi] *n., pl.* **-eys. 1** a small flock or brood of partridges, quail; etc. **2** a small group of people: *surrounded by a covey of reporters.* ⟨ME < OF *covée* < *cover* incubate < L *cubare* lie⟩

cov•ing ['kouvɪŋ] *n.* COVE (def. 3).

cow[1] [kaʊ] *n., pl.* **cows** or (*archaic or dialect*) **kine. 1** the full-grown female of any bovine animal, especially of domestic cattle. **2** the female of various other large mammals: *an elephant cow, a buffalo cow, a cow moose.* ⟨OE *cū*⟩ **—'cow,like,** *adj.*

cow[2] [kaʊ] *v.* make afraid; frighten: *Don't let their threats cow you.* ⟨? < ON *kúga*⟩

cow•age ['kaʊɪdʒ] *n.* cowhage.

cow•ard ['kaʊərd] *n.* **1** a person who lacks courage or gives in to fear; a person who runs from danger, trouble, etc. **2** (*adjl.*) lacking courage; cowardly. ⟨ME < OF *coart* < *coe* tail < L *coda,* dial. var. of *cauda;* with reference to an animal with its tail between its legs⟩

cow•ard•ice ['kaʊərdɪs] *n.* **1** lack of courage; the quality of being easily overcome by fear in the face of danger, pain, etc. **2** a group of curs.

cow•ard•li•ness ['kaʊərdlinɪs] *n.* the state or quality of being cowardly.

cow•ard•ly ['kaʊərdli] *adj., adv.* —*adj.* **1** lacking courage. **2** of a coward; suitable for a coward.
—*adv.* in a cowardly manner.
☛ *Syn.* **1.** See note at TIMID.

cow•bane ['kaʊ,bein] *n.* any of several poisonous plants of the parsley family, especially a North American species (*Oxypolis rigidior*).

cow•bell ['kaʊ,bɛl] *n.* a bell hung around a cow's neck to indicate the cow's location.

cow•ber•ry ['kaʊ,bɛri] *n.* **1** a shrub (*Vaccinium vitis-idaea*), often found in cattle pastures, having pink or white flowers and bearing dark red fruit. **2** the fruit of this plant or similar plants.

cow•bind ['kaʊ,baɪnd] *n.* a toxic vine (*Bryonia alba* or *Bryonia dioica*) bearing black or red fruit, whose roots were once used therapeutically as a laxative.

cow•bird ['kaʊ,bərd] *n. Cdn.* a small North American blackbird (*Molothrus ater*), the adult male having mainly black plumage with a brown head and neck, the female having brownish grey plumage. Cowbirds are parasitic, laying their eggs in the nests of other small birds.

cow•boy ['kaʊ,bɔɪ] *n.* especially in western Canada and the

United States, a rider who looks after cattle on a ranch and on the range. A cowboy performs many duties on horseback.

cow•catch•er ['kaʊ,kætʃər] *n.* a metal apron at the bottom of the front of a locomotive, designed to roll to one side any obstruction on the tracks.

cow•er ['kaʊər] *v.* **1** crouch in fear or shame. **2** draw back tremblingly from another's threats, blows, etc. ⟨ME *couren* < Scand.⟩

cow•fish ['kaʊ,fɪʃ] *n., pl.* **-fish** or **-fish•es. 1** any of several small tropical fishes (family Ostraciidae) having hornlike projections above the eyes, such as *Lactophrys quadricornis.* **2** any of various sea mammals, such as a sea cow. **3** a Pacific dolphin (*Tursiops gilli*).

cow•girl ['kaʊ,gɜrl] *n.* a woman or girl who looks after cattle on a ranch.

cow•hage ['kaʊɪdʒ] *n.* **1** a tropical vine (*Mucuna pruriens*), bearing reddish or blackish pods. **2** the pod of this vine, whose bristles can penetrate skin and cause itching. Also, **cowage.** ⟨< Hind. *kawanch*; influenced by *cow*⟩

cow•hand ['kaʊ,hænd] *n.* a cowboy or cowgirl.

cow•herb ['kaʊ,hɜrb] *or* ['kaʊərb] *n.* an annual weed (*Saponaria vaccaria*) of the pink family, native to Europe, having pink flowers.

cow•herd ['kaʊ,hɜrd] *n.* a person whose work is looking after cattle while they are at pasture.

cow•hide ['kaʊ,haɪd] *n., v.* **-hid•ed, -hid•ing.** *—n.* **1** the hide of a cow. **2** leather made from it. **3** a whip made of braided leather.
—v. whip with a cowhide; flog.

Cow•i•chan ['kaʊɪtʃən] *n.* **1** a member of a Salishan people of the First Nations living mainly on Vancouver Island, noted for their knitting of distinctively patterned sweaters. **2** COWICHAN SWEATER.

Cowichan sweater *Cdn., esp. West Coast.* a heavy sweater of unbleached wool, knitted by the Cowichans of Vancouver Island, distinguished by symbolic knitted designs, originally black and white, now sometimes multicoloured.

cow killer the wingless female of a species of ant (*Dasymutilla occidentalis*) of the S and E U.S., having a poisonous sting.

cowl [kaʊl] *n., v. —n.* **1** a monk's cloak with a hood. **2** the hood itself. **3** anything shaped like a hood. **4** the part of an automobile body that includes the windshield and the dashboard. **5** a cowling. **6** a covering for the top of a chimney, designed to increase the draft.
—v. **1** put a monk's cowl on. **2** cover with a cowl or something resembling a cowl. ⟨OE *cūle, cug(e)le* < LL *cuculla*, var. of L *cucullus* hood⟩

cowled [kaʊld] *adj., v. —adj.* **1** having a cowl. **2** shaped like a cowl.
—v. pt. and pp. of COWL.

cow•lick ['kaʊ,lɪk] *n. Informal.* a small tuft of hair that will not lie flat, usually just above the forehead.

cowl•ing ['kaʊlɪŋ] *n., v. —n.* a metal covering over an aircraft engine.
—v. ppr. of COWL.

cowl neck a wide neck on a woman's knit garment, consisting of loose folds of fabric vaguely resembling a lowered hood.

cow•man ['kaʊmən] *n., pl.* **-men. 1** an owner of cattle; ranchman. **2** one who works with cattle; cowboy.

co–work•er ['kou ,wɜrkər] *or* [,kou 'wɜrkər] *n.* one who works with a person; fellow worker: *She's one of his co-workers.*

cow parsnip *Cdn.* any of several tall perennial plants of the genus *Heracleum*, of the parsley family, such as *H. sphondylium* or *H. lanatum*, having large, flat clusters of white or purple flowers.

cow•pea ['kaʊ,pi] *n.* **1** a plant (*Vigna unguicalata*) of the pea family that has very long pods, widely grown in S U.S. for use as cattle feed, fertilizer, etc. **2** the seed of this plant, sometimes used as food for humans; black-eyed pea.

Cowper's glands ['kʌpərz] *or* ['kupərz] two small glands in the human male that secrete a mucous substance into the urethra during sexual excitement. ⟨after William *Cowper* (1666-1709), English anatomist⟩

cow pilot a small fish (*Abudefduf saxatilis*) vertically striped with green and black, and found in warm Atlantic waters.

cow•poke ['kaʊ,pouk] *n. Cdn. Informal.* cowboy.

cow pony any horse used in the herding of cattle.

cow•pox ['kaʊ,pɒks] *n.* a disease of cows causing small pustules on their udders. The vaccine for smallpox is obtained from cows that have cowpox.

cow•punch•er ['kaʊ,pʌntʃər] *n. Cdn. Informal.* cowboy.

cow•rie or **cow•ry** ['kaʊri] *n.* **1** a glossy yellow sea shell, used as money in some parts of Africa and Asia. **2** the mollusc that forms this shell, any of various gastropods of the family Cypraeidae. ⟨< Hind. *kauri*⟩

cow shark any of several sharks of the family Hexanchidae, having six or seven gills on each side.

cow•shed ['kaʊ,ʃɛd] a building in which cows are kept for shelter or during milking.

cow•skin ['kaʊ,skɪn] *n.* cowhide.

cow•slip ['kaʊ,slɪp] *n.* **1** any of various North American plants (genus *Dodecatheon*) from the primrose family, bearing flowers with turned-back petals; shooting star. **2** a wild plant (*Mertensia virginica*) found in Eastern North America and bearing purple or blue flowers; Virginia cowslip. **3** a European primrose (*Primula veris*) having crinkled leaves and clusters of bright yellow flowers that bloom in spring. **4** MARSH MARIGOLD. ⟨OE *cūslyppe* < *cū* cow + *slyppe* slime⟩

cow•town ['kaʊ,taʊn] *n. Cdn.* in western Canada and the United States, a town that is largely dependent on the cattle business; a market or shipping centre for cattle.

cow vetch a climbing plant (*Vicia cracca*) having vivid purple flowers along one side of the stem. It is a European plant which has become naturalized in North America, especially in the east. Also called **tufted vetch.**

cox [kɒks] *n., v. —n.* coxswain.
—v. **1** act as a coxswain. **2** be the coxswain of.

cox•a ['kɒksə] *n., pl.* **cox•ae** ['kɒksi] *or* ['kɒksaɪ]. **1** the hipbone or hip joint. **2** the short segment of the leg of an arthropod by which the leg is joined to the body. ⟨< L, hip⟩ **—'cox•al,** *adj.*

cox•al•gia [kɒk'sældʒiə] *or* [kɒk'sældʒə] *n.* pain in the hip. ⟨< NL < L *coxa* hip, angle + Gk. *algos* pain < *algein* to feel pain⟩

cox•comb ['kɒks,koum] *n.* **1** a vain, empty-headed man; a conceited dandy. **2** See COCKSCOMB (def. 2). ⟨var. of *cock's comb*⟩

cox•comb•ry ['kɒks,koumri] *n., pl.* **-ries. 1** silly vanity; empty-headed conceit. **2** an example of this.

cox•swain ['kɒksən] *or* [-,swein] *n.* a person who steers a boat, racing shell, etc., and is in charge of the crew. Also, **cockswain.** ⟨< *cock* cockboat + *swain*⟩

coy [kɔɪ] *adj.* **1** shy; modest; bashful. **2** pretending to be shy: *The flirt wore a coy smile.* ⟨ME < OF *coi* < L *quietus* at rest. Doublet of QUIET and QUIT, adj.⟩ **—'coy•ly,** *adv.* **—'coy•ness,** *n.*

coy•o•te [kaɪ'outi], ['kaɪout], *or* ['kaɪut] *n., pl.* **-otes** or (*esp. collectively*) **-ote.** a North American wild animal (*Canis latrans*) of the dog family found throughout the continent, but especially on the plains, resembling a small wolf, having a buff coat and a bushy black-tipped tail, and noted for its nighttime calls that range from long mournful howls to short barks. Coyotes feed mainly on small wild animals such as gophers, rats, mice, and hares. ⟨< Mexican Sp. < Nahuatl *koyotl*⟩

co•yo•til•lo [,kɔɪə'tɪlou] *n.* a shrub (*Karwinskia humboldtiana*) of the buckthorn family, native to SW U.S. and Mexico, and bearing poisonous berries which can cause paralysis. ⟨< Am.Sp. dim. of *coyote*⟩

coy•pu ['kɔɪpu] *n., pl.* **-pus** or (*esp. collectively*) **-pu.** a large beaverlike water rodent (*Myocastor coypus*) native to South America, having an undercoat of soft, reddish brown fur called nutria that is commercially valuable. ⟨< Sp. *coipu* < Araucanian (S Am.Ind. linguistic stock) *koypu*⟩

coz [kʌz] *n. Informal.* cousin.

coz•en ['kʌzən] *v.* **1** cheat; defraud (*usually used with* **out of** *or* **of**): *The child was cozened out of his inheritance.* **2** deceive; beguile: *They cozened her into signing the papers.* ⟨origin unknown⟩ **—'coz•en•er,** *n.*
☛ *Hom.* COUSIN.

coz•en•age ['kʌzənɪdʒ] *n.* a cozening; fraud; deception.

co•zy ['kouzi] See COSY. **—'co•zi•ly,** *adv.* **—'co•zi•ness,** *n.*

cp 1 candlepower. **2** chemically pure.

cp. 1 compare. **2** coupon(s).

CP 1 Canadian Pacific. **2** Canadian Press. **3** Command Post.

C.P. 1 Common Prayer. 2 Communist Party. 3 *Cdn. French.* **a** Conseil privé (Privy Council). **b** Conseiller privé (Privy Councillor). 4 *French.* case postale (post office box).

C.P.A. *U.S.* Certified Public Accountant.

cpd. compound(s).

cpi *Computer technology*. characters per inch.

CPI *Cdn.* Consumer Price Index.

Cpl. or **Cpl** corporal.

cpm or **c.p.m.** cycles per minute.

CPO or **C.P.O.** chief petty officer.

CPR 1 Canadian Pacific Railway. 2 cardiopulmonary resuscitation.

cps 1 cycles per second; Hz. 2 *Computer technology.* characters per second.

CPU *Computer technology*. central processing unit.

CQ a call put out by amateur radio operators seeking response. ⟨< *I seek you*⟩

cr. 1 credit; creditor. 2 crown.

Cr chromium.

Cr. 1 Crescent. 2 Creek.

C.R. *Cdn. French.* Conseiller de la reine (Queen's Counsel).

crab[1] [kræb] *n., v.* **crabbed, crab•bing.** *—n.* **1** any decapod crustacean having a short abdomen, or 'tail', that is carried tucked up under a short, broad shell and having the first pair of legs modified into pincers. Most of the approximately 4500 species are marine, but some are found in fresh water and even on land. **2** any of several other crustaceans resembling the true crab, such as the hermit crab. **3** the flesh of a crab, eaten as food. Also called **crabmeat. 4** a machine or apparatus for raising or moving heavy weights. **5 Crab,** *Astronomy or astrology.* Cancer. **6** the path of an aircraft heading into a crosswind, which is sideways to the ground.
catch a crab, make a faulty stroke in rowing.
—v. catch crabs for eating. ⟨OE *crabba*⟩ **—'crab•ber,** *n.*

crab[2] [kræb] *n., v.* **crabbed, crab•bing.** *—n.* **1** CRAB APPLE. **2** a cross, sour, ill-natured person; one who is always complaining or finding fault.
—v. **1** find fault; complain; criticize: *It doesn't do any good to crab about the weather.* **2** *Informal.* interfere with; spoil: *His lack of enthusiasm crabbed the deal.* ⟨origin uncertain⟩

crab apple **1** any of several small trees (genus *Malus*) of the rose family having fragrant white, pink, or red flowers and small, very tart applelike fruit. **2** the fruit of any of these trees, used especially for jellies and preserves.

crab•bed ['kræbɪd] *or* [kræbd] *adj., v. —adj.* **1** crabby; bad-tempered. **2** hard to understand; perplexing. **3** hard to read or decipher because cramped and irregular: *The teacher objected to crabbed handwriting.*
—v. [kræbd] pt. and pp. of CRAB. ⟨< *crab*[1] with influence from *crab*[2]⟩ **—'crab•bed•ly,** *adv.* **—'crab•bed•ness,** *n.*

crab•by ['kræbi] *adj.* **-bi•er, -bi•est.** *Informal.* cross, peevish, or ill-natured. ⟨< *crab*[2]⟩ **—'crab•bi•ly,** *adv.* **—'crab•bi•ness,** *n.*

crab cactus a house plant (*Schlumbergera bridgesii*) with dark green, fleshy leaves and red flowers; Christmas cactus.

crab grass any of various coarse grasses (genus *Digitaria*) that spread rapidly. Crab grass is considered a lawn pest.

crab louse a parasitic louse (*Phthirus pubis*) that infests the pubic area of the human body. Also called **crabs**.

crab•meat ['kræb,mit] *n.* the flesh of a crab, eaten as food.

Crab nebula *Astronomy.* a cloud of gas believed to be the remnant of a supernova explosion, observed in 1054, in the constellation Taurus.

crabs [kræbz] *n.* CRAB LOUSE.

crab's eyes **1** a tropical climbing plant (*Albrus precatorius*) of the pea family, bearing poisonous red and black seeds; jequirity. **2** the seeds of this plant, used for beads.

crab spider any spider of the family Thomisidae, characterized by sideways movement.

crab•stick ['kræb,stɪk] *n.* a staff or club made of crab apple wood.

crab•wise ['kræb,waɪz] *adv. or adj.* moving sideways like a crab: *The car went out of control and slid crabwise into the fence.*

crack[1] [kræk] *n., v. —n.* **1** an uneven place, line, or opening in a surface made by breaking without separating into parts: *a crack in a cup.* **2** a sudden, sharp noise: *the crack of a whip.* **3** *Informal.* a blow that makes a sudden, sharp noise. **4** a narrow space: *There were cracks between the boards of the old floor.* **5** *Informal.* an instant; moment. **6** *Slang.* a try; effort; attempt: *Let me take a crack at opening the jar.* **7** *Slang.* a joke. **8** *Slang.* a nasty or sharp remark: *What do you mean by that crack?* **9** *Informal.* a superior person or thing: *She is a crack at skiing.* **10** (*adj.*) *Informal.* very good, excellent; first-rate: *a crack shot, a crack regiment.*
fall between/through the cracks, of a person or thing, be ignored, overlooked, etc., in a particular system or process.
—v. **1** break without separating into parts: *to crack a window.* **2** open (a door, window, etc.) by a slit. **3** break with a sudden, sharp noise: *The tree cracked and fell.* **4** make or cause to make a sudden, sharp noise: *The whip cracked. He cracked the whip.* **5** *Informal.* hit with a sudden, sharp noise. **6** of the voice, change or cause to change sharply in pitch or quality because of hoarseness or emotion. **7** *Slang.* give way or cause to give way; break down: *Not even torture could crack him.* **8** *Slang.* break into: *to crack a safe.* **9** *Chemistry.* separate (petroleum, coal tar, etc.) into various substances. **10** solve; decipher: *to crack a code.* **11** of the voice, change downwards in pitch in male adolescents.
crack a bottle, *Informal.* open a bottle and drink what is in it.
crack a joke, tell a joke; say something funny.
crack a smile, smile, especially reluctantly.
crack down, *Informal.* take stern disciplinary measures.
crack up, a crash or smash. **b** *Informal.* suffer a breakdown in mental or physical health. **c** *Informal.* respond or cause to respond with a fit of laughter: *I almost cracked up when she said that. This TV program always cracks her up.* **d** *Informal.* praise; tout (*used in the passive*): *That book is not what it's cracked up to be.*
get cracking, *Informal.* get started quickly: *We'd better get cracking if we want to catch that bus.* ⟨OE *cracian*, v., and ME *crak*, n., both < Gmc.⟩

crack[2] *n. Slang.* an extremely addictive illegal form of cocaine which has been purified for smoking and is in the shape of small rocks. ⟨origin uncertain⟩

crack–brained ['kræk,breind] *adj. Informal.* crazy; insane.

crack•down ['kræk,daʊn] *n. Informal.* swift disciplinary action: *The police intensified their crackdown on drunken drivers.*

cracked [krækt] *adj., v. —adj.* **1** broken without separating into parts. **2** of the voice, lacking evenness; broken; having harsh notes. **3** *Informal.* crazy; insane.
—v. pt. and pp. of CRACK.

crack•er ['krækər] *n.* **1** a thin, crisp, unleavened biscuit or wafer: *a soda cracker, a graham cracker.* **2** a small paper roll used as a party favour containing a motto, a paper cap, etc. A cracker explodes when it is pulled at both ends. **3** a person or instrument that cracks.

cracker barrel an open barrel for salted crackers, formerly common in grocery and country stores.

crack•er–bar•rel ['krækər ˌbærəl] *or* [-ˌbɛrəl] *adj.* of or having the informality and simplicity of country people; down-to-earth: *cracker-barrel humour.*

crack•er•jack ['krækər,dʒæk] *n., adj. Slang. —n.* an especially fine person or thing.
—adj. of superior ability or quality.

crack•ers ['krækərz] *adj. Slang.* crazy (*not used before the noun*).

crack house a place where CRACK[2] is bought and sold.

crack•ing ['krækɪŋ] *n., v., adj., adv. —n.* the process of changing certain hydrocarbons in petroleum and other oils into lighter hydrocarbons by heat and pressure. Gasoline may be produced by cracking.
—v. ppr. of CRACK.
—adj. Slang. first-rate; great.
—adv. Slang. very (used with *good*): *a cracking good book.*

crack•le ['krækəl] *v.* **-led, -ling;** *n. —v.* **1** make slight, sharp, repeated sounds: *A fire crackled on the hearth.* **2** of china, glass, etc., become minutely cracked.
—n. **1** a slight, sharp, repeated sound, such as paper makes when it is crushed. **2** very small cracks on the surface of some kinds of china, glass, etc. **3** china, glass, etc., made with such a surface; crackleware. ⟨< *crack*⟩

crack•le•ware ['krækəl,wɛr] *n.* ceramic ware made with a crackled glaze.

crack•ling ['kræklɪŋ] *n., v. —n.* **1** Usually, **cracklings,** *pl.* the crisp remains of rendered animal fat, especially from pork. **2** the crisp, browned skin of roasted pork.
—v. ppr. of CRACKLE.

crack•ly ['krækli] *adj.* **-li•er, -li•est.** that crackles; making a crackle: *crackly paper.*

crack•nel ['kræknəl] *n.* **1** a hard, brittle biscuit. **2 cracknels,** *pl.* **a** small pieces of fat pork fried crisp. **b** cracklings. ⟨< F *craquelin* < MDu. *crakelinc*⟩

crack of dawn the very instant of dawn; the first appearance of the sun over the horizon.

crack of doom **1** the signal for the Last Judgment. **2** a signal for the end of everything.

crack•pot ['kræk,pɒt] *Slang. n., adj.* *—n.* a very eccentric or crack-brained person.
—adj. eccentric; crack-brained; impractical.

cracks•man ['kræksmən] *n., pl.* **-men.** a burglar, especially a safecracker.

crack–up ['kræk ,ʌp] *n.* **1** a smash-up; crash: *That pilot has been in more than one crack-up.* **2** *Informal.* a mental or physical collapse.

cra•dle ['kreidəl] *n., v.* **-dled, -dling.** *—n.* **1** a baby's little bed, usually on rockers or swinging on a frame. **2** the first period of one's life; babyhood. **3** the place where a thing begins its growth: *The authorities seem to disagree on where we should look for the cradle of civilization.* **4** a frame to support a ship, aircraft, or other large object while it is being built, repaired, lifted, etc. **5** the part of a telephone that supports the receiver. **6** a box on rockers designed to wash gold from earth. **7** a frame attached to a scythe for laying grain evenly as it is cut. **8** CRADLE SCYTHE. **9** a frame to keep bedclothes from touching an injured or burnt leg.
rob the cradle, *Informal.* choose as a companion, or marry, a person much younger than oneself.
—v. **1** hold as in a cradle: *She cradled the child in her arms.* **2** put or rock in a cradle. **3** shelter or train in early life. **4** support (a ship, etc) in a cradle. **5** wash (gold from earth) in a cradle. **6** cut with a CRADLE SCYTHE. ⟨OE *cradol*⟩ **—'cra•dle,like,** *adj.*

cra•dle–board ['kreidəl ,bɔrd] *n. Cdn.* a First Nations peoples' device for carrying a baby, consisting of a thin, rectangular board to which a kind of bag is fastened, formerly widely used throughout North America except in the Arctic.

cradle hill *Cdn., esp. Maritimes.* a small mound such as might have originally been formed at the base of an uprooted tree.

cradle scythe a scythe with a frame attached to it for laying grain evenly as it is cut.

cra•dle•song or **cradle song** ['kreidəl,sɒŋ] *n.* lullaby.

craft [kræft] *n., pl.* **crafts** (defs. 2-4), **craft** (def. 6); *v.* *—n.* **1** skill or art, especially in handwork: *The craft of the artist is evident in the fine detail of the carving.* **2** a trade or a kind of work, other than one of the fine arts, requiring special skill: *Carpentry and weaving are crafts.* **3** the group of persons practising a skilled trade: *Carpenters compose a craft or guild of workers.* **4** an article made by hand, especially one with practical as well as aesthetic value. **5** skill in deceiving others; slyness; trickiness: *He used craft to get all their money from them.* **6** a boat, ship, aircraft, or spacecraft. **7** (*adjl.*) of or for a craft or crafts: *craft supplies, a craft sale.*
—v. construct or form, usually by hand and with special skill: *The store is featuring oak furniture crafted in England. This quilt was crafted by hand.* ⟨OE *cræft*⟩
☛ *Syn.* **5.** See note at CUNNING.

crafts•man ['kræftsmən] *n., pl.* **-men. 1** a man who practises a trade or handicraft. **2** a man who is highly skilled in the techniques of a craft or art: *a craftsman in wood. His latest work shows he is a craftsman.* **3** a private in the Royal Canadian Electrical and Mechanical Engineers.

crafts•man•like ['kræftsmən,lɔik] *adj.* showing craftsmanship: *a craftsmanlike piece of work.*

crafts•man•ship ['kræftsmən,ʃɪp] *n.* skill in artistic or exacting work; skilled workmanship.

crafts•peo•ple ['kræfts,pipəl] *n.pl.* people who practise a trade or handicraft.

crafts•wom•an ['kræfts,wʊmən] *n., pl.* **crafts•wom•en. 1** a woman who practises a trade or handicraft. **2** a woman who is highly skilled in the techniques of a craft or art.

craft union a labour union made up of persons in the same craft. Unions of carpenters, plumbers, bricklayers, etc. are craft unions.

craft•y ['kræfti] *adj.* **craft•i•er, craft•i•est.** skilful in deceiving others; sly; tricky: *The crafty thief escaped by disguising himself as a waiter.* **—'craft•i•ly,** *adv.* **—'craft•i•ness,** *n.*

crag [kræg] *n.* a steep, rugged rock or cliff; a projecting rock. ⟨< Celtic (compare Welsh *craig*)⟩

crag•ged ['krægɪd] *adj.* craggy.

crag•gy ['krægi] *adj.* **-gi•er, -gi•est. 1** with many crags; rocky: *a craggy hillside.* **2** suggesting the hardness and unevenness of a crag; rugged; rough: *a craggy face.* **—'crag•gi•ly,** *adv.* **—'crag•gi•ness,** *n.*

crags•man ['krægzmən] *n., pl.* **-men.** someone who is very good at climbing crags.

crake [kreik] *n.* any of various short-billed rails, especially of Europe. ⟨ME < ON *kráka* crow⟩

cram ['kræm] *v., n.* *—v.* **crammed, cram•ming. 1** force; stuff: *She crammed all her clothes quickly into the bag.* **2** fill too full: *The hall was crammed with people.* **3** eat too fast or too much. **4** feed (someone) too fast or too much. **5** *Informal.* stuff with knowledge or information. **6** *Informal.* learn or study a great amount in a short time: *He is cramming for his history examination.*
—n. **1** a crammed or crowded condition; crush. **2** the act of cramming, especially in preparation for an examination. **3** information acquired by cramming. **4** a person who crams. ⟨OE *crammian* < *crimman* insert⟩ **—'cram•mer,** *n.*

cram•bo ['kræmbou] *n.* a game in which a player must think up a rhyme for a word or line given by another. ⟨< earlier *crambe* < L *crambe (repetita)* cabbage (served up again)⟩

cramp[1] [kræmp] *n., v.* *—n.* **1** a painful, involuntary contracting of muscles from a sudden chill, strain, etc.: *The swimmer was seized with a cramp.* **2** a temporary paralysis of particular muscles as a result of overexercising them: *Writer's cramp can be brought on by excessive writing.* **3 cramps,** *pl.* sharp, continuous pains in the abdomen.
—v. cause a painful numbness or stiffness in: *I was cramped from sitting in one position so long.* ⟨< F < Frankish **crampo* crampon (def. 1). Akin to CRAMPON.⟩

cramp[2] [kræmp] *n., v., adj.* *—n.* **1** a small metal bar with both ends bent, used in building to hold timbers, stone or concrete blocks, etc., permanently in place. **2** a clamp. **3** something that confines or hinders; limitation; restriction.
—v. **1** fasten together with a cramp. **2** confine in a small space; limit; restrict: *If the flowerpot is too small, it will cramp the roots of the plant. The three girls were cramped up in one little tent. Cramped handwriting is small and hard to read.* **3** turn (the wheels of an automobile, etc.) sharply.
cramp (one's) **style,** *Slang.* restrict or interfere with one's natural or usual behaviour.
—adj. cramped. ⟨< MDu.; cf. MLG *krampe*⟩

cramp•fish ['kræmp,fɪʃ] *n.* ELECTRIC RAY.

cram•pon ['kræmpən] *n.* **1** a strong iron bar with hooks at one end, used to lift heavy things; grappling iron. **2** an iron plate set with spikes, that is fastened to the bottom of a shoe to prevent slipping when climbing, walking on ice, etc. ⟨< F < Frankish **crampo* crampon (def. 1). Akin to CRAMP[1].⟩

cran•ber•ry ['kræn,bɛri] *n., pl.* **-ries. 1** a firm, sour, dark red berry produced by any of several climbing or trailing plants (genus *Vaccinium*) of the heath family. Cranberries are used for jelly, sauces, etc.: *Cranberry sauce is often eaten with turkey.* **2** a plant that produces these berries. **3** any of several species of viburnum often grown for ornament. The **highbush cranberry** (*Viburnum trilobum*) has edible fruit. ⟨< LG *kraanbere*⟩

cranberry bog a marsh where cranberries grow.

crane [krein] *n., v.* **craned, cran•ing.** *—n.* **1** a machine with a long, swinging arm, for lifting and moving heavy weights. **2** any of several devices usually consisting of a horizontal arm swinging on a vertical axis, such as a metal arm in a fireplace used to hold a kettle over the fire, or a boom for holding a film or television camera. **3** any of a family (Gruidae) of tall, grey, brown, or white wading birds having long legs, a long neck and bill, and a partly naked head. Cranes resemble herons but they fly with the neck stretched out while herons fly with the neck curved back. **4** any of various herons, especially the great blue heron.
—v. **1** move by, or as if by, a crane. **2** stretch (the neck) as a crane does: *He craned his neck, trying to see over the crowd.* ⟨OE *cran*⟩ **—'crane,like,** *adj.*

crane fly any of a family (Tipulidae) of flies having a long, slender body, two narrow wings, and very long legs. Crane flies look like large mosquitoes but do not bite.

cranes•bill ['kreinz,bɪl] *n.* GERANIUM (def. 2), especially any of several wild species, so called from the long, slender, beaklike projection of the fruit. Also, **crane's-bill.**

cran•i•al ['kreiniəl] *adj.* of, from, or having to do with the skull, or cranium. **—'cra•ni•al•ly,** *adv.*

cranial index CEPHALIC INDEX.

cranial nerve any of the nerves beginning in the lower part of the brain, which control certain bodily senses and movements. Mammals, birds, and reptiles have twelve pairs of cranial nerves.

cranial vault the roof of the skull.

cra•ni•ate ['kreiniɪt] *or* ['kreini,eit] *adj., n. —adj.* having a skull.
—n. an animal with a skull.

cra•ni•o•fa•cial [,kreiniə'feiʃəl] *adj.* referring to the combination of features of the cranium and face.

cra•ni•ol•o•gist [,kreini'ɒlədʒɪst] *n.* a person trained in craniology, especially one whose work it is.

cra•ni•ol•o•gy [,kreini'ɒlədʒi] *n.* the science that deals with the size, shape, and other characteristics of skulls. ⟨< Gk. *kranion* skull + E *-logy*⟩

cra•ni•om•e•ter [,kreini'ɒmətər] *n.* an instrument for measuring the outside of a skull.

cra•ni•om•e•try [,kreini'ɒmətri] *n.* the science of measuring skulls; measurement of skulls. ⟨< Gk. *kranion* skull + E *-metry*⟩

cra•ni•ot•o•my [,kreini'ɒtəmi] *n.* a surgical operation that involves the opening of the skull. ⟨< Gk. *kranion* skull + *-tomia* a cutting⟩

cra•ni•um ['kreiniəm] *n., pl.* **-ni•ums, -ni•a** [-niə]. **1** the skull of a vertebrate. **2** the part of the skull enclosing the brain. **3** all of the skull except the lower jaw. ⟨< LL < Gk. *kranion*⟩

crank [kræŋk] *n., v., adj. —n.* **1** a part or handle of a machine connected at right angles to a shaft to transmit motion. **2** *Informal.* a person with queer notions or habits, especially one possessed by some idea: *The police got a few calls from cranks when they asked for information about the missing girl.* **3** (*adjl.*) from or by a crank or a person thought to be a crank: *a crank call.* **4** *Informal.* a cross or ill-tempered person; grouch: *I wouldn't ask any favours of that old crank.* **5** a fanciful turn of speech: *quips and cranks.* **6** a fantastic or queer idea or action.
turn (someone's) **crank,** *Slang.* be or do just the thing that excites someone.
—v. **1** work or start by means of a crank: *to crank a window open.* **2** turn a crank. **3** bend into the shape of a crank. **4** twist; wind. **5** *Slang.* hit hard; slam: *She cranked a shot into the net.*
crank up, *Informal.* increase by or as if by turning a control knob: *crank up the volume, crank up production.*
—adj. of machinery, loose and unsteady. ⟨OE *cranc*⟩

crank•case ['kræŋk,keis] *n.* a heavy, metal case forming the bottom part of an internal-combustion engine. The crankcase of a gasoline engine encloses the crankshaft, connecting rods, etc.

crank•shaft ['kræŋk,ʃæft] *n.* a shaft turning or turned by a crank.

crank•y ['kræŋki] *adj.* **crank•i•er, crank•i•est. 1** cross; irritable; ill-natured. **2** odd; queer. **3** liable to capsize; loose; shaky. **—'crank•i•ly,** *adv.* **—'crank•i•ness,** *n.*

cran•nied ['krænid] *adj.* full of crannies.

cran•nog ['krænəg] *n.* **1** in ancient Ireland and Scotland, a lake dwelling built on an artificial island. **2** in ancient Ireland and Scotland, a fortified artificial island. ⟨< Irish *crann* tree, mast, beam⟩

cran•ny ['kræni] *n., pl.* **-nies.** a small, narrow opening; crack; crevice. ⟨< F *cran* fissure, ult. < Med.L *crena* notch⟩

crap [kræp] *n.* **1** *Slang.* nonsense. **2** *Slang.* dirt or garbage. ⟨ME chaff, siftings < OF *crape* scale, ordure or Med.L *crappa* chaff⟩ **—'crap•py,** *adj.*

crape [kreip] *n.* See CREPE (defs. 1 and 5).

crape myrtle a tall Chinese shrub (*Lagerstroemia indica*) of the loosestrife family, having pink or purple flowers, now widely grown in S and W U.S. as an ornamental.

crap•pie ['kræpi] *n.* either of two small North American freshwater fishes (*Pomoxis annularis* or *P. nigromaculatus*) of the sunfish family that are edible. ⟨< Cdn.F *crapet*⟩

craps [kræps] *n.* **1** a gambling game played with two dice. **2** a first throw at craps with a low number. ⟨< Louisiana F *craps* the game of hazard < F *craps, crabs* < E *crabs* the lowest throw in hazard⟩

crap•shoot•er ['kræp,ʃutər] *n.* a person who plays craps.

crap•u•lence ['kræpjələns] *n.* sickness from overeating or over-drinking.

crap•u•lent ['kræpjələnt] *adj.* sick from overeating or over-drinking. ⟨< LL *crapulentus* < L *crapula* drunkenness⟩

crap•u•lous ['kræpjələs] *adj.* **1** habitually given to overeating or over-drinking. **2** sick from overeating or over-drinking.

crash[1] ['kræʃ] *n., v. —n.* **1** a sudden, very loud noise like many dishes falling and breaking, or like sudden, loud band music: *a crash of thunder. There was a crash as the platform collapsed. The huge tree fell with a crash.* **2** a hitting, colliding, or breaking with force and a loud noise; a violent impact or fall: *the crash of an airplane. There was a serious car crash at this intersection last night.* **3** a sudden and severe decline or failure, as in business: *a stock market crash.* **4** *Computer technology.* failure of a computer system or of one of its components: *Yesterday's computer crash caused the bank's automatic teller machines to go down.* **5** (*adjl.*) *Informal.* characterized by great hurry or speed and by concentrated effort: *a crash course in Italian, a crash campaign to raise money.*
—v. **1** make a sudden, loud noise: *The thunder crashed.* **2** fall, hit, or break with force and a loud noise: *The dishes crashed to the floor.* **3** go or move with force and a loud noise: *A bullet crashed through the window. He crashed into the room.* **4** collide or cause to collide: *The two cars crashed right in front of our house.* **5** of a pilot or aircraft, make a CRASH LANDING. **6** fail or decline suddenly: *The stock market crashed.* **7** *Computer technology.* of a computer system, cease to function due to some hardware or software error. **8** *Informal.* enter or attend without an invitation, ticket, etc.: *to crash a party.* **9** *Informal.* sleep: *Can I crash in your apartment?* **10** *Slang.* return quickly to a normal emotional state after a drug-induced high. ⟨blend of *craze* shatter and *mash*⟩ **—'crash•er,** *n.*

crash[2] [kræʃ] *n.* a coarse linen cloth, used for towels, curtains, upholstering, etc. ⟨probably < Russian; cf. Russian *krashenina* coloured linen⟩

crash dive 1 a fast descent made by a submarine in an emergency. **2** a downward plunge by an aircraft, ending in a crash.

crash–dive ['kræʃ ,daɪv] *v.* **-dived, -div•ing. 1** of a submarine, make a fast descent in an emergency. **2** of an aircraft, make a downward plunge that ends in a crash.

A crash helmet as worn by a motorcyclist

crash helmet a heavily padded helmet worn by automobile racers, motorcycle riders, etc.

crash•ing ['kræʃɪŋ] *adj., v. —adj.* complete, utter: *a crashing bore.*
—v. ppr. of CRASH.

crash–land ['kræʃ 'lænd] *v.* of an aircraft or its pilot, make a forced landing in an emergency, usually with damage to the aircraft.

crash landing a forced landing made by an aircraft in an emergency, usually with damage to the aircraft.

crash pad *Slang.* temporary accommodation.

crass [kræs] *adj.* **1** gross; stupid; vulgar. **2** thick; coarse. ⟨< L *crassus* thick⟩ **—'crass•ly,** *adv.* **—'crass•ness,** *n.*

crate [kreit] *n., v.* **crat•ed, crat•ing.** *—n.* **1** a large frame, box, basket, etc., used to pack furniture, glass, fruit, etc., for shipping or storage. **2** *Slang.* an aircraft or car, especially one that is old or worn out.
—v. pack in a crate. ⟨< L *cratis* wickerwork⟩

cra•ter[1] ['kreitər] *n.* **1** a depression around the opening at the top of a volcano. **2** a bowl-shaped hole: *The battlefield was full of craters made by exploding shells.* **3** a round, ringlike elevation on the surface of the moon, resembling the crater of a volcano. **4** in ancient Greece and Rome, a large mixing bowl with a wide mouth and two handles. Also, **krater. 5 Crater,** the Cup, a small southern constellation between Corvus and Hydra. ⟨< L < Gk. *kratēr* bowl < *kra-* mix⟩

crat•er[2] ['kreitər] *n.* a person or thing that packs or stores goods in a crate.

cra•ton ['kreitɒn] *n. Geology.* a stable unit of Precambrian rock. ⟨< G *kraton,* based on Gk. *kratos* power⟩ **—cra'ton•ic,** *adj.*

cra•vat [krə'væt] *n.* **1** a scarf or cloth formerly worn around the neck. A cravat was wound around the neck several times outside the standing collar of the shirt. **2** ascot. ⟨< F *cravate,* special use of *Cravate* Croat⟩

crave [kreiv] *v.* **craved, crav•ing. 1** long for; yearn for; desire strongly: *The thirsty man craved water.* **2** ask earnestly; beg: *to crave a favour.* ⟨OE *crafian* demand⟩

cra•ven ['kreivən] *adj., n. —adj.* cowardly: *a craven act.*
—n. coward.
cry craven, surrender; admit defeat. ⟨ME *cravant;* origin uncertain⟩ **—'cra•ven•ly,** *adv.* **—'cra•ven•ness,** *n.*

crav•ing ['kreivɪŋ] *n., v. —n.* a longing or yearning; strong desire.
—v. ppr. of CRAVE.
☛ *Syn.* See note at DESIRE.

craw [krɒ] *n.* **1** the crop of a bird or insect. **2** the stomach of any animal.
stick in one's craw, be difficult to accept; be disagreeable or unsatisfactory. ⟨ME *crawe* < OE **craga* neck⟩

craw•fish ['krɒ,fɪʃ] *n., pl.* **-fish** or **-fish•es;** *v. —n.* crayfish.
—v. Informal. move backward; back out of something; retreat. ⟨var. of *crayfish*⟩

crawl[1] [krɒl] *v., n. —v.* **1** move with the body close to or dragging on the ground. Worms, snakes, and insects crawl. **2** move on hands and knees; creep: *to crawl through a hole in a fence. Babies usually crawl before they learn to walk.* **3** move slowly: *The traffic crawled on the icy roads.* **4** swarm with crawling things: *The ground was crawling with ants.* **5** feel creepy: *My flesh crawled at the thought of the huge snakes.* **6** behave or move slavishly or abjectly; fawn. **7** swim with alternate overarm strokes and a continuous kicking motion.
make (one's) **flesh/skin crawl,** fill one with fear or disgust, as though bugs were crawling on one's skin.
—n. **1** a slow pace; crawling: *The traffic was moving at a crawl.* **2** a fast way of swimming, using alternate overarm strokes and a continuous kicking motion. ⟨ME ? < ON *krafla*⟩ **—'crawl•er,** *n.*

crawl[2] [krɒl] *n.* an enclosure made with stakes in shallow water, used to hold turtles, fish, etc. ⟨< Du. *kraal* < Sp. *corral.* Doublet of CORRAL.⟩

crawler tractor a tractor that can travel over very rough ground on its two continuous tracks.

crawl space a low, narrow space in a house or other building, which gives access to wiring, pipes, etc., especially under a house which has no basement.

crawl•y ['krɒli] *adj.* **crawl•i•er, crawl•i•est.** feeling as if things are crawling over one's skin; creepy.

cray•fish ['krei,fɪʃ] *n., pl.* **-fish** or **-fish•es. 1** any of numerous freshwater decapod crustaceans, especially of the genera *Astacus* and *Cambarus,* resembling small lobsters, found almost throughout the world, having a segmented body with a long abdomen ending in a fanlike part, and having four pairs of legs, one pair of pincers, and two pairs of feelers. Crayfish often move backward. **2** any spiny lobster of the family Palinuridae. ⟨ME *crevise* < OF *crevice* crab < OHG *krebiz,* influenced by E *fish.* Akin to CRAB[1].⟩

cray•on ['kreiɒn] *or* ['kreiən] *n., v.* **-oned, -on•ing.** *—n.* **1** a stick or pencil of chalk, charcoal, or any of various coloured substances, for drawing or writing. **2** a drawing made with crayons.
—v. draw or colour with a crayon or crayons. ⟨< F *crayon* < *craie* chalk < L *creta*⟩

craze [kreiz] *n., v.* **crazed, craz•ing.** *—n.* **1** something everybody is very much interested in for a short time; a fad. **2** a tiny crack in the glaze of pottery, etc.
—v. **1** make crazy: *She was nearly crazed with the pain.* **2** make tiny cracks all over the surface of (earthenware, pottery, etc.) **3** of pottery, etc., develop a mesh of tiny cracks. ⟨ME *crase(n)* break; ? < ON **krasa*⟩

cra•zy ['kreizi] *adj.* **-zi•er, -zi•est;** *n., pl.* **-zies.** *—adj.* **1** affected with madness; insane. **2** distracted or temporarily out of control as a result of some violent emotion: *crazy with fear, a thrill-crazy mob.* **3** *Informal.* very foolish or wild; not sensible: *a crazy driver. He has some crazy idea about walking from Dawson to Whitehorse.* **4** *Informal.* very enthusiastic; excessively preoccupied (*used with* **about**): *She's crazy about cars.* **5** *Informal.* extremely fond; infatuated (*used with* **about**): *He's crazy about her.* **6** *Informal.* unusual and conspicuous; odd; bizarre: *She likes crazy jewellery.* **7** not strong or sound; shaky and frail: *a crazy old bridge.* **8** having uneven cracks: *crazy paving.*
—n. Slang. an insane, wild, or very eccentric person.
like crazy, *Informal.* to an extreme degree; extremely hard, fast, etc.: *laughing like crazy. He took off on his bike, pedalling like crazy.* ⟨< *craze.* 16c.⟩ **—'cra•zi•ly,** *adv.* **—'cra•zi•ness,** *n.*
☛ *Syn.* **1-3.** See note at MAD.

crazy bone FUNNY BONE.

crazy paving paving arranged in an irregular pattern to achieve a decorative effect.

crazy quilt 1 a quilt made of pieces of cloth of various shapes, colours, and sizes, sewn together with no definite pattern. **2** anything with an irregular pattern.

cra•zy•weed ['kreizi,wid] *n.* any of various wild plants (genera *Astragalus* and *Oxytropis*) related to the pea, native to Mexico and the southwest of the United States, and causing the loco disease in horses, cattle, etc.; locoweed.

creak [krik] *v., n. —v.* make a prolonged, loud squeak: *The hinges on our doors creak because they need oiling.*
—n. a creaking noise. ⟨ME *creke(n);* apparently imitative⟩
☛ *Hom.* CREEK.

creak•y ['kriki] *adj.* **creak•i•er, creak•i•est.** likely to creak; creaking. **—'creak•i•ly,** *adv.* **—'creak•i•ness,** *n.*

cream [krim] *n., v., adj. —n.* **1** the yellowish part of milk that contains fat. The cream rises to the top when milk that is not homogenized is allowed to stand. Butter is made from cream. **2** (*adjl.*) containing or made of cream or milk: *cream sauce, cream soup.* **3** food made of cream; food like cream: *ice cream, chocolate creams.* **4** an oily preparation put on the skin to make it smooth and soft or to treat a skin condition. **5** a yellowish white. **6 the cream,** the best part of anything: *the cream of the crop. The cream of a class is made up of the best students.* **7** a thick, sweet liqueur; crème.
the cream rises to the top, the best person or idea will succeed.
—v. **1** put cream into. **2** take or skim cream from. **3** take away the choicest part of (something) for later use. **4** form like cream on the top; foam; froth. **5** allow (milk) to form cream. **6** cook with cream, milk, or a sauce made of cream or milk with butter and flour. **7** beat into a smooth mixture like cream: *to cream butter and sugar together in making a cake.* **8** *Cdn. Slang.* **a** *Sports.* defeat soundly or decisively. **b** hurt or damage severely, especially as a result of hard blows or forceful impact.
cream off, *Informal.* select the best part of.
—adj. **1** having the colour cream. **2** creamy. ⟨ME *creme* < OF *cresme* < LL *crama* cream < Gaulish, and < Ecclesiastical L *chrisma* ointment < Gk. *chrisma* < *chriein* anoint⟩

cream cheese a soft, white cheese made from cream or milk and cream.

cream–col•oured ['krim ˌkʌlərd] *adj.* off-white; whitish yellow.

cream•cups ['krim,kʌps] *n.* a Californian annual plant (*Platystemon californicus*) of the poppy family, having small, pale yellow flowers.

cream•er ['krimər] *n.* **1** a small pitcher for holding cream. **2** a machine for separating cream from milk; separator. **3** a refrigerator in which milk is placed while the cream is rising. **4** a liquid or powder manufactured from any of various edible oils, used especially as a substitute for cream or milk in coffee or tea.

cream•er•y ['krimәri] *n., pl.* **-er•ies. 1** a place where butter and cheese are made. **2** a place where cream, milk, and butter are sold or bought. **3** a place where milk is set for cream to rise.

cream of tar•tar ['tɑrtər] a very sour, white powder used in cooking and in medicine; potassium bitartrate. Cream of tartar is obtained from the deposit in wine casks. *Formula:* $KHC_4H_4O_6$

cream puff a light pastry usually filled with whipped cream or custard.

cream sauce a sauce made of cream or milk with flour and butter.

cream soda a vanilla-flavoured carbonated soft drink.

cream•y ['krimi] *adj.* **cream•i•er, cream•i•est. 1** like cream; smooth and soft. **2** having much cream in it. **3** having the colour of cream; yellowish white. **—'cream•i•ly,** *adv.* **—'cream•i•ness,** *n.*

crease [kris] *n., v.* **creased, creas•ing.** *—n.* **1** a ridge or groove in a pliable substance, made by or as if by folding and pressing; a fold or wrinkle. **2** *Cdn. Hockey and lacrosse.* a small area marked off in front of each goal. The crease is reserved for the goal tender and prohibited to attacking players except when the puck or ball is inside it. **3** *Cricket.* **a** either of two lines at each end of the pitch that define the positions of the bowler and the batsman. **b** the space enclosed by these two lines.
—v. **1** make a crease or creases in. **2** become creased or wrinkled: *This skirt creases badly.* **3** graze with a bullet. ⟨origin unknown⟩ **—'creas•er,** *n.* **—'crease•less,** *adj.*
☛ *Hom.* CREESE, KRIS.

cre•ate [kri'eit] *v.* **-at•ed, -at•ing. 1** make a thing that has not existed before: *The Bible says that God created all things.* **2** make something original by intelligence and skill: *She created this garden in the desert.* **3** invest as: *He was created a knight.* **4** produce or bring about: *to create a disturbance, to create new jobs.* **5** be the first to act (a particular part or role) in a play. ⟨< L *creare*⟩

cre•a•tine ['kriə,tin] *or* ['kriətɪn] *n.* a colourless, crystalline compound, found chiefly in the muscle tissue of vertebrate animals, which is involved with supplying energy for voluntary muscle contraction. *Formula*: $C_4H_9N_3O_2$ ⟨< F *créatin* < Gk. *kreat* flesh⟩

cre•at•i•nine [kri'ætə,nin] *or* [kri'ætənɪn] *n.* a crystalline product of creatine metabolism, found in blood, muscle, and urine, where it is excreted and can be used to measure kidney function. *Formula*: $C_4H_7N_3O$

cre•a•tion [kri'eiʃən] *n.* **1** a creating or being created. **2** all things created; the world and everything in it; the universe. **3** a thing produced by intelligence and skill, usually something important or original: *That painting is a magnificent creation.* **4 the Creation,** the creating of the universe by God.

cre•a•tion•ism [kri'eiʃə,nɪzəm] *n.* **1** the theory that the universe and everything in it were specially created by God and are not the result of accident or evolution. **2** the doctrine that God creates a new soul for each human being at birth.

cre•a•tion•ist [kri'eiʃənɪst] *n.* a person who believes in creationism. **—cre,a•tion'is•tic,** *adj.*

creation science a theory of the beginning of the universe which discounts Darwinism and tries to show that a scientific analysis of the data supports the biblical account of creation by God. **—creation scientist.**

cre•a•tive [kri'eitɪv] *adj.* **1** having the power to create; inventive; productive: *Sculptors are creative artists.* **2** showing originality or imagination; artistic: *creative engineering, creative writing.* **3** stimulating creativity: *creative toys.* **4** deceptive in an imaginative way: *creative bookkeeping.* **—cre'a•tive•ly,** *adv.* **—cre'a•tive•ness,** *n.*

cre•a•tiv•i•ty [,kriei'tɪvəti] *n.* creative ability; the quality of being creative.

cre•a•tor [kri'eitər] *n.* **1** a person who creates. **2 the Creator,** God.

crea•ture ['kritʃər] *n.* **1** anything created. **2** a living being; an animal or person. **3** a person who is completely under the influence of another; a person who is ready to do anything that another asks. **4 the creature.** *Informal.* whisky. ⟨< L *creatura* < *creare* create⟩

creature comforts the things that give bodily comfort. Food, clothing, and shelter are creature comforts.

crèche [krɛʃ] *or* [kreiʃ] *n.* **1** a place where children are taken care of while their mothers are at work; day nursery. **2** a model showing the Christ child in the manger, with attendant figures, that is often displayed in homes, churches, etc., at Christmas. **3** especially formerly, an asylum or hospital for foundlings; orphanage. **4** a group of penguins or other animals that are raised by the whole community. ⟨< F < Gmc. Akin to CRIB.⟩

cre•dence ['kridəns] *n.* **1** belief: *Never give credence to gossip.* **2** an introduction or recommendation of confidence; credential: *a letter of credence.* ⟨< Med.L *credentia* < L *credere* believe⟩

cre•den•tial [krə'dɛnʃəl] *n.* **1** something that gives or recommends credit or confidence. **2 credentials,** letters of introduction, entitling the bearer to credit or confidence; references: *After showing her credentials, the new inspector was allowed to see the bank's records.*

cre•den•za [krə'dɛnzə] *n.* **1** a sideboard or buffet. **2** a piece of office furniture, similar to a low cupboard with doors. ⟨< Ital. < ML *credentia* credence⟩

cred•i•bil•i•ty [,krɛdə'bɪləti] *n.* the fact or quality of being credible.

credibility gap 1 a discrepancy between one's words and one's actions. **2** a difficulty in making people believe one.

cred•i•ble ['krɛdəbəl] *adj.* believable; reliable; trustworthy: *It seems hardly credible that Bill has grown so tall in one year.* ⟨ME < L *credibilis* < *credere* believe⟩ **—'cred•i•ble•ness,** *n.* **—'cred•i•bly,** *adv.*
☛ *Usage.* **Credible,** CREDITABLE, and CREDULOUS are sometimes confused. **Credible** = believable: *Her story is too full of coincidences to be credible.* **Creditable** = bringing honour or praise: *He turned in a creditable performance, though his heart was no longer in his acting.* **Credulous** = too ready to believe: *I was credulous enough to think I would really be given the job.*

cred•it ['krɛdɪt] *n., v.* *—n.* **1** belief in the truth of something; faith; trust: *They placed little credit in his story of having been robbed.* **2** confidence or trust in a person's ability and intention to pay later for something he or she wishes to buy now: *to get credit for a purchase.* **3** the time allowed for delayed payment: *They give only short-term credit.* **4** the amount of money a person has in an account: *He had a credit of $5000 in his savings account.* **5** an amount of money lent by a bank: *We will give you $3000 credit.* **6** *Accounting.* **a** an entry of money paid on an account. **b** the right-hand side of an account where such entries are made. **c** the amount entered or shown on this side. **7** reputation with respect to payment of debts: *If you pay your bills on time, your credit will be good.* **8** good reputation: *a person of credit.* **9** recognition; honour: *The person who does the work should get the credit.* **10** a source of honour or praise: *The author's latest novel is a credit to her.* **11** an acknowledgment of the authorship, source, etc., of material used in a publication, work done on a dramatic show, radio or television program, etc.: *He was promised a credit for his contribution to the documentary.* **12** Usually, **credits,** *pl.* a listing of the producers, directors, actors, technicians, and others who have contributed their skills to a film, radio or television program, or a play. **13** an entry on a student's record showing that a course of study has been satisfactorily completed. **14** a unit of work entered in this way: *I need three credits to graduate.*
do credit to, bring honour or recognition to: *Her quick action did credit to her courage.*
give (someone) **credit for,** believe or acknowledge that a person has: *Give him credit for some intelligence and let him try the job himself.*
give credit to, believe; have faith in; trust.
on credit, on a promise to pay later: *She bought her car on credit.*
to one's credit, in one's favour or honour: *To her credit, she refused to betray her friend.*
—v. **1** believe in the truth of something; have faith in; trust: *It was difficult to credit the boy's strange explanation for his absence.* **2** add an amount to (an account) as a deposit. **3** enter on the credit side of an account. **4** assign to as a credit. **5** put an entry on the record of (a student) showing that he or she has passed a course of study. **6** give recognition to; attribute something to (*used with* **with**): *He credited her with the original idea.* ⟨< F < Ital. < L *creditum* a loan < *credere* trust, entrust⟩
☛ *Syn.* **6. Credit,** ACCREDIT = believe someone or something responsible for saying, doing, feeling, or causing something. **Credit** emphasizes the idea of believing, not always with enough reason or evidence: *She credits me with doing things I never thought of.* **Accredit** emphasizes the idea of accepting because of some proof: *We accredit Peary with having discovered the North Pole.*

cred•it•a•ble ['krɛdətəbəl] *adj.* bringing credit or honour: *a creditable record of attendance.* **—'cred•it•a•ble•ness,** *n.* **—'cred•it•a•bly,** *adv.*
☛ *Usage.* See note at CREDIBLE.

credit bureau a business that collects information regarding the credit ratings of individuals or companies and offers this information as a service to subscribers.

credit card an identification card entitling its holder to charge the cost of goods or services.

Cred•i•tiste [,krɛdɪ'tist] *adj., n. Cdn.* *—adj.* of or having to do with the Social Credit Rally, a political party.
—n. a member of this party. ⟨< Cdn.F *Créditiste*⟩

Creditiste Party *Cdn.* SOCIAL CREDIT RALLY.

credit line 1 the limit of borrowing offered by a bank; line of credit. **2** mention of one's name among the credits for a film, play, etc.

cred•i•tor ['krɛdətər] *n.* a person to whom money or goods are due; one to whom a debt is owed.

credit rating the financial standing and reputation of a company or individual, used to set the amount of money or credit that one may borrow or obtain.

credit union a co-operative association that makes loans to its members at low rates of interest.

cre•do ['kreidou] *or* ['kridou] *n., pl.* **-dos. 1** a creed: *Her credo in art was purity of form.* **2** Also, **Credo,** *Christianity.* **a** the Apostles' Creed or the Nicene Creed. **b** any of various musical settings for either of these Creeds. ⟨< L *credo* I believe. Doublet of CREED.⟩

cre•du•li•ty [krə'djuləti] *or* [krə'duləti] *n.* an excessive readiness to believe.

cred•u•lous ['krɛdʒələs] *adj.* too ready to believe; easily deceived. ⟨< L *credulus* < *credere* believe⟩ **—'cred•u•lous•ly,** *adv.* **—'cred•u•lous•ness,** *n.*
☛ *Usage.* See note at CREDIBLE.

Cree [kri] *n., pl.* **Cree** or **Crees;** *adj.* *—n.* **1** a member of a people of the First Nations living mainly in the Prairie Provinces. **2** the Algonquian language of the Cree.
—adj. of or having to do with the Cree or their language.

creed [krid] *n.* **1** a formal statement of the essential points of religious belief. **2** a set of beliefs, principles, or opinions: *It was his creed that work should come before play.* **3 the Creed,** *Christianity.* the Apostles' Creed or the Nicene Creed. ⟨OE *crēda* < L *credo* I believe. Doublet of CREDO.⟩

creek [krik] *or, often,* [krɪk] *n.* **1** a small freshwater stream. **2** a narrow bay, running inland for some distance.
up the creek, *Slang.* in difficulty. ⟨ME *creke;* cf. MDu. *creke*⟩
☛ *Hom.* CREAK [krik], CRICK [krɪk].
☛ *Pronun.* Most Canadians pronounce **creek** the same as **creak,** but in some regions, especially in parts of the West, the pronunciation (krɪk) is common.

Creek [krik] *n., pl.* **Creek** or **Creeks. 1** a member of a group of American Indian peoples formerly living in Alabama, Georgia, and N Florida, now living in Oklahoma. **2** their language.
☛ *Hom.* CREAK, CREEK [krik].

creel [kril] *n.* **1** a basket for holding fish that have been caught. **2** a basketlike trap for fish, lobsters, etc. **3** a framework for holding the bobbins in a spinning machine or loom. ⟨ME *crele* ? < OF *creil,* ult. < L *cratis* wickerwork⟩

creep [krip] *v.* **crept, creep•ing;** *n.* *—v.* **1** move with the body close to the ground or floor or other walking surface; crawl: *The cat crept along the branch. A baby creeps on its hands and knees.* **2** move slowly. **3** grow along the ground or over a wall by means of clinging stems: *a creeping plant. Ivy had crept up the wall of the old house.* **4** move or behave in a timid, stealthy, or servile manner: *The robbers crept toward their victims.* **5** develop gradually but persistently: *creeping materialism.* **6** slip slightly out of place: *The hall rug creeps so we always have to put it back in place.* **7** feel as if things were creeping over the skin; shiver; shudder: *I could feel my flesh creep, and my hair stood on end.*
creep up on, approach slowly and silently: *Darkness was creeping up on the forest. The soldiers crept up on the enemy sentry.*
—n. **1** a creeping; slow movement. **2** *Geology.* slow movement of soil or disintegrated rock down a slope, due to gravity, frost, or ground water: *tangential creep, continental creep.* **3** *Physics.* the process of softening, flexing, or melting of material with accompanying changes in shape and dimension that result from increased stress or temperature. **4 the creeps,** *Informal.* a feeling of fear or disgust, as if things were creeping over one's skin. **5** *Slang.* a person who gives one the creeps; an undesirable or unlikable person. ⟨OE *crēopan*⟩

creep•age ['kripɪdʒ] *n.* the extent of movement or of melting of a material.

creep•er ['kripər] *n.* **1** a person who or thing that creeps. **2** any plant that grows along a surface, sending out rootlets from the stem, such as the Virginia creeper and ivy. **3** any of a family (Certhiidae) of small, mostly brownish birds that climb along the trunk and branches of trees, looking for insects. The one North American species is the **brown creeper** (*Certhia familiaris*). **4** a piece of canvas or other material that is attached to the bottom of a ski for better gripping in climbing uphill. **5** CLIMBING IRON. **6 creepers,** *pl.* a one-piece garment combining top and pants, worn by babies. **7** a low frame on small wheels, on which a mechanic can lie to repair a vehicle from underneath. **8** the lowest gear in a large truck, for climbing or descending steep hills. Also called **creeper gear.**

creeping bent grass a kind of BENT GRASS (*Agrostis stolonifera*) used on golf greens.

creep•y ['kripi] *adj.* **creep•i•er, creep•i•est. 1** having a feeling of horror, as if things were creeping over one's skin: *The ghost story made us feel creepy.* **2** causing such a feeling: *a creepy howl.* **3** creeping; moving slowly. **—'creep•i•ly,** *adv.* **—'creep•i•ness,** *n.*

creep•y–crawl•y ['kripi 'krɒli] *adj., n., pl.* **creep•y-crawl•ies.** *—adj.* making one feel shivery or afraid: *I had a nightmare in which there were creepy-crawly things all over me.*
—n. **1** a small insect or other creature, especially when thought of as frightening. **2 the creepy-crawlies,** *pl.* the feeling of fear such insects or scary movies may give: *That scene always gives me the creepy-crawlies.*

creese [kris] *n. Rare.* See KRIS.
☛ *Hom.* CREASE.

cre•mate [krɪ'meit] *or* ['krimeit] *v.* **-mat•ed, -mat•ing.** burn (something, especially a dead body) to ashes. ⟨< L *cremare* burn⟩

cre•ma•tion [krɪ'meiʃən] *n.* the burning of a dead body to ashes instead of burying it.

cre•ma•tor [krɪ'meitər] *or* ['krimeitər] *n.* **1** a person who cremates. **2** a furnace for cremating. ⟨< LL⟩

cre•ma•to•ri•um [ˌkrɛmə'tɔriəm] *or* [ˌkrimə'tɔriəm] *n., pl.* **-ums** or **-ria** [-riə]. **1** a furnace for cremating. **2** an establishment that has a furnace for cremating.

cre•ma•to•ry ['krɛməˌtɔri] *or* ['kriməˌtɔri] *adj., n., pl.* **-ries.** *—adj.* of or having to do with cremation.
—n. Esp. U.S. crematorium.

crème [kʀɛm] *n. French.* **1** cream. **2** a thick, sweet liqueur.

crème brûlée ['krɛm bru'lei]; *French,* [kʀɛmbʀy'le] *n.* a caramel custard with a skin of burnt sugar. ⟨< F literally, burnt cream⟩

crème de ca•ca•o ['krɛm də kə'keiou], [kə'kaʊ] *or* ['kouˌkou]; *French,* [kʀɛmdəka'kao] chocolate-flavoured liqueur. ⟨< F⟩

crème de la crème ['krɛm də lə 'krɛm]; *French,* [kʀɛmdəla'kʀɛm] *French.* the very best; most select. ⟨literally, cream of the cream⟩

crème de menthe ['krɛm də 'mɒnt] *or* ['mɛnθ]; *French,* [kʀɛmdə'mɑ̃t] *French.* a liqueur flavoured with mint.

Cre•mo•na [krɪ'mounə] *n.* any of the fine violins made in Cremona, Italy, by the Amati, Guarneri, and Stradivari families during the 16th, 17th, and 18th centuries.

cre•nate ['krineit] *adj.* with a scalloped edge. Also, **crenulate.** ⟨< NL *crenatus* < Med.L *crena* notch⟩ **—'cre•nate•ly,** *adv.*

cre•na•tion [krɪ'neiʃən] *n.* **1** the condition of being crenate. **2** a crenate formation. **3** the shrivelled, scalloped appearance of a red blood cell, especially resulting from exposure to a salty solution.

cre•na•ture ['krɛnətʃər] *or* ['krinətʃər] *n.* **1** a small bulge on an edge. **2** the indentation between such bulges.

cre•nel ['krɛnəl] *n.* an arrow-slit or loophole in the top of a battlement. ⟨< F *crenel* notch, ult. < Med.L *crena*⟩

cren•el•ate ['krɛnəˌleit] See CRENELLATE.

cren•el•late ['krɛnəˌleit] *v.* **-lat•ed, -lat•ing.** furnish with battlements. **—ˌcren•el'la•tion,** *n.*

cren•u•late ['krɛnjəlɪt] *or* ['krɛnjəˌleit] *adj.* crenate.

cren•u•la•tion [ˌkrɛnjə'leiʃən] *n.* a scallop, bulge, or indentation. **2** the condition of having scallops.

cre•o•dont ['kriəˌdɒnt] a small, extinct, carnivorous animal of the suborder Creodonta, having a small brain. ⟨< NL *creodonta* < Gk. *kreas* flesh + *odous* tooth⟩

Cre•ole ['krioul] *or* ['kreioul] *n., adj.* *—n.* **1** a person who is a descendant of the original French settlers of Louisiana, and who has preserved their language and culture. **2** a person of French or Spanish ancestry born in Spanish America or the West Indies. **3** a black person or one of mixed black and European ancestry born in Spanish America or the West Indies. **4** the dialect of French spoken by many Blacks in Louisiana. **5** HAITIAN CREOLE. **6 creole,** a language that is based on two or more languages and, unlike a pidgin, that is the mother tongue of a community of speakers. Creoles develop from extended contact between peoples speaking different languages.
—adj. **1** of or having to do with Creoles. **2 creole,** of, having to do with, or characteristic of a creole. **3** cooked in a sauce made of stewed tomatoes, peppers, etc. ⟨< F *créole* < Sp. < Pg. *crioulo* < *criar* bring up < L *creare* create⟩

cre•o•lized ['kriəˌlaɪzd] *adj.* designating a language that is a creole, or that, together with another or others, forms the basis of a creole.

cre•o•sol ['kriə,soul] *or* ['kriə,sɒl] *n.* a colourless, oily liquid obtained from wood tar and a resin of the guaiacum tree, used as an antiseptic. *Formula:* $C_8H_{10}O_2$ ⟨< *creosote*⟩

cre•o•sote ['kriə,sout] *n., v.* **-sot•ed, -sot•ing.** *—n.* **1** an oily liquid with a penetrating odour, obtained by distilling wood tar. It is used to preserve wood and in cough medicine. **2** a similar substance obtained from coal tar.
—v. treat with creosote. ⟨originally, a meat preservative; < Gk. *kreo-* (for *kreas* flesh) + *sōtēr* saviour < *sōzein* save⟩

creosote bush an evergreen shrub with a smell like that of creosote, found in New Mexico and other parts of the southwestern U.S.

crepe or **crêpe** [kreip] *n.* **1** a kind of cloth woven with a crinkled surface. **2** CREPE PAPER. **3** CREPE RUBBER. **4** *(adjl.)* made of crepe: *a crepe dress, crepe soles.* **5** a piece of black crepe used as a sign of mourning: *The officers at the funeral all wore crepes on their sleeves.* **6** Usually, **crêpe,** a large, very thin pancake usually served folded or rolled up with a filling. ⟨< F *crêpe* < L *crispa* curled⟩

crepe de Chine ['kreip də 'ʃin] a soft, thin, medium-weight, silk crepe. ⟨< F *crêpe de Chine* China crepe⟩

crepe paper thin, crinkled, stretchy paper used for making party decorations, etc.

crepe rubber crude or synthetic rubber, made with a crinkled surface and used especially for the soles of shoes.

crêpe su•zette [su'zɛt]; *French,* [kʀɛpsy'zɛt] *n., pl.* **crêpes suzette.** a thin pancake, usually rolled in fruit juice and brandy, and set ablaze when served. ⟨< F⟩

cre•pey ['kreipi] *adj.* crinkled like crepe paper.

crep•i•tant ['krɛpətənt] *adj.* crackling; rattling.

crep•i•tate ['krɛpə,teit] *v.* **-tat•ed, -tat•ing.** crackle; rattle. ⟨< L *crepitare* crackle < *crepare* crack⟩ **—,crep•i'ta•tion,** *n.*

crept [krɛpt] *v.* pt. and pp. of CREEP.

cre•pus•cu•lar [krɪ'pʌskjələr] *adj.* **1** of twilight; resembling twilight; dim; indistinct. **2** of certain birds, insects, etc., appearing or flying by twilight.

cre•pus•cule [krɪ'pʌskjul] *n.* twilight. ⟨< F *crépuscule* < L *crepusculum*⟩

cres. or **cresc.** crescendo.

Cres. Crescent (in street names).

cre•scen•do [krə'ʃɛndou] *n., pl.* **-dos;** *adj., adv., v. —n.* **1** *Music.* **a** a gradual increase in loudness. **b** a symbol (<) indicating this, placed over the affected passage of music. **c** a passage to be played or sung with a crescendo. **2** any gradual increase in force, loudness, etc.: *a crescendo of cheers.* **3** the peak of such an increase; climax: *Complaints reached a crescendo.*
—adj. or adv. gradually increasing in volume, etc.
—v. increase gradually in volume, etc. *Abbrev.:* cres. or cresc. ⟨< Ital. *crescendo,* ppr. of *crescere* increase < L⟩

cres•cent ['krɛsənt] *n., adj. —n.* **1** the shape of the moon as seen from the earth in its first or last quarter. **2** anything having this or a similar shape. A curved street or a curved row of houses is sometimes called a crescent. **3** a light roll, made of yeast dough, shaped like a crescent moon. **4** the emblem of the former Turkish Empire and of the present republic of Turkey. **5** Turkish or Islamic power.
—adj. **1** shaped like the moon in its first or last quarter. **2** growing; increasing. ⟨< L *crescens, -entis,* ppr. of *crescere* grow⟩ **—'cres•cent,like,** *adj.* **—cre'scen•tic** [krɪ'sɛntɪk], *adj.*

cre•sol ['krisoul] *or* ['krisɒl] *n.* an oily liquid obtained from tar, used as a disinfectant. *Formula:* C_7H_8O ⟨var. of *creosol*⟩

cress [krɛs] *n.* any of various plants (family Cruciferae, the mustard family) having leaves with a peppery taste used in salads and as garnish. ⟨OE *cresse*⟩

cres•set ['krɛsɪt] *n.* a metal container for burning oil, wood, etc., to give light. Cressets are mounted on poles or hung from above. ⟨ME < OF *cresset,* earlier *craisset* < *crois* cross < L *crux* (with reference to light from the Cross of Christ); influenced by *craisse* grease⟩

crest [krɛst] *n., v. —n.* **1** a tuft of hair or feathers, or a growth of skin on the head of a bird or animal. **2** the narrow top of the neck, in a horse, lion, etc. **3** a raised edge on a bone. **4** a decoration, plumes, etc., on the top of a helmet. **5** a decoration at the top of a coat of arms. A family crest is sometimes put on silverware, dishes, stationery, etc. **6** the top of a helmet. **7** an emblem, usually of felt cloth, worn by members of various organizations, athletic teams, etc.: *a hockey crest. The soldier wore his regimental crest on the breast pocket of his blue blazer.* **8** a similar emblem awarded as a sign of merit in studies, athletics, etc. **9** the top part; the top of a hill, wave, ridge, etc.; peak; summit. **10** among peoples of the First Nations on the West Coast: **a** the symbol of a particular clan or similar social group. **b** the social group identified by this symbol.
—v. **1** furnish with a crest. **2** of waves, form or rise into a crest. **3** of a river, etc., reach its highest point. **4** serve as a crest to; top; crown. **5** reach the crest or summit of (a hill, wave, etc.). ⟨ME < OF *creste* < L *crista* tuft⟩ **—'crest,like,** *adj.*

crest•ed ['krɛstɪd] *adj., v. —adj.* having a crest: *a crested bird, a crested shield.*
—v. pt. and pp. of CREST.

crested fly•catch•er ['flaɪ,kætʃər] any of several flycatchers (genus *Tyrannidae*) having a large crest.

crested hon•ey•creep•er ['hʌnɪ,kripər] a rare bird (*Palmeria dolei*) found only on the island of Maui in Hawaii, having a crest of feathers above the bill. It is about 18 cm long. It is an endangered species.

crest•fall•en ['krɛst,fɒlən] *adj.* **1** dejected; discouraged. **2** with head lowered or crest hanging. **—'crest,fall•en•ly,** *adv.*

crest•ing ['krɛstɪŋ] *n., v. —n.* a decorative strip along a wall or roof.
—v. ppr. of CREST.

cre•syl•ic [krɪ'sɪlɪk] *adj.* **1** of or having to do with creosol or creosote. **2** of or having to do with any of various phenols used in the manufacture of plastics, etc. ⟨< *cres(ol)* + *-yl* + *-ic*⟩

cre•ta•ceous [krɪ'teiʃəs] *adj., n. —adj.* **1** like chalk; containing chalk. **2 Cretaceous,** of or having to do with the geological period when most of the chalk deposits were made; of or having to do with rocks formed in this period.
—n. **Cretaceous,** *Geology.* **a** the period, beginning approximately 130 million years ago, when most of the chalk deposits were made. **b** the group of rocks formed in this period. See geological time chart in the Appendix. ⟨< L *cretaceus* < *creta* chalk < *Creta,* the island of Crete⟩

Cre•tan ['kritən] *n., adj. —n.* a native or inhabitant of Crete.
—adj. of or having to do with Crete or its people.
☛ *Hom.* CRETIN ['kritən].

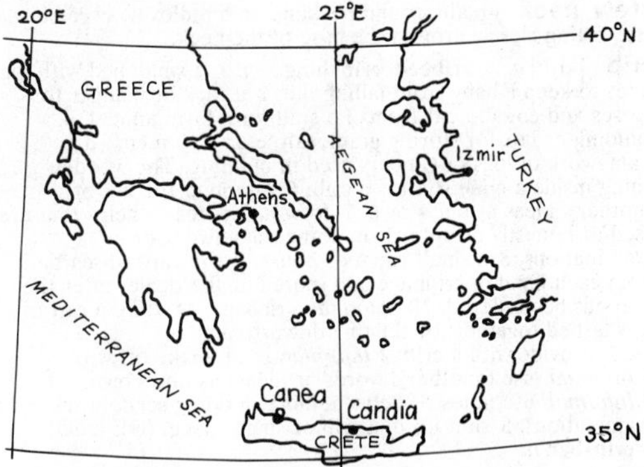

Crete shown in relationship to Greece and Turkey

Crete [krit] *n.* a Greek island in the Mediterranean Sea, SE of Greece.

cre•tin ['krɛtən] *or* ['kritən] *n.* a person who is severely mentally retarded, especially one afflicted with cretinism. ⟨< F *crétin* < Swiss dial. < OF *chrestien* < L *Christianus* Christian; came to mean "man," then "fellow," then "poor fellow"⟩
☛ *Hom.* CRETAN ['kritən], CRETON ['krɛtən].

cre•tin•ism ['krɛtə,nɪzəm] *or* ['kritə,nɪzəm] *n.* an abnormal condition, usually present from birth, in which physical and mental growth is stunted because the thyroid gland cannot produce enough thyroid hormone.

cre•ton ['krɛtən]; *French,* [kʀɛ'tɔ̃] *n. Cdn.* a pâté of pork, fat, and spices, especially popular in Québec. ⟨< Cdn.F⟩
☛ *Hom.* CRETIN ['krɛtən].

cre•tonne [krɪ'tɒn] *or* [kri'tɒn] *n.* a strong cotton cloth with designs printed in colours on one or both sides, used for curtains, furniture covers, etc. ⟨< F *cretonne,* probably < *Creton,* a village in Normandy, France, noted for its cloth⟩

Creutz•feldt–Ja•kob disease ['krɔɪts,fɛlt 'jɑkoup] *or* ['jɑkoub] a disease of the nervous system thought to be caused by a rare virus and characterized by dementia, loss of sight, and uncontrolled body movements. Creutzfeldt-Jakob disease is usually fatal and has no known cure. ⟨< after H.G. *Creutzfeldt* (1885-1964) and A. *Jakob* (1884-1931), German physicians⟩

cre•valle [krə'væli] *or* [krə'vælə] *n.* **1** a food fish of the family Carangidae, found in tropical waters and having silvery scales and a widely forked tail. **2 crevalle jack**, a similar fish (*Caranx hippos*), found in the tropical Atlantic. ⟨< altered from Pg. *cavalla* < L *caballus* horse⟩

cre•vasse [krə'væs] *n., v.* —*n.* **1** a deep crack or crevice in the ice of a glacier. **2** a break in a levee, dike, or dam.
—*v.* make crevasses in. ⟨< F *crevasse* < OF *crevace.* Doublet of CREVICE.⟩

crev•ice ['krɛvɪs] *n.* a narrow split or crack. ⟨ME *crevace* < OF < VL *crepacia* < L *crepare* crack. Doublet of CREVASSE.⟩

crew[1] [kru] *n., v.* —*n.* **1** a group of people who work together; gang: *A camera crew looks after the filming of a television program. A repair crew is working on the hydro lines.* **2** the people who operate a ship, sometimes including the officers and captain. **3** the people who operate an aircraft. **4** a team of people who operate a boat or a racing shell. **5** a team of people who do the physical work in a theatre. **6** *Informal.* a group or crowd: *The whole crew came to our place for dinner.*
—*v.* **1** staff (a ship) with a crew; provide a crew. **2** act as a crew or as a member of a crew. ⟨ME *crue* < MF *creüe* increase, reinforcement < *creistre* grow < L *crescere*⟩

crew[2] [kru] *v.* a pt. of CROW[1].

crew cut a close-cropped haircut for men.

crew•el ['kruəl] *n.* **1** a loosely twisted woollen yarn, used for embroidery. **2** embroidery done with this yarn. ⟨origin uncertain⟩
☛ *Hom.* CRUEL.

crew•el•work ['kruəl,wɜrk] *n.* embroidery done with crewel yarn.

crew•man ['krumən] *n., pl.* **-men.** a member of a crew.

crew neck a plain, round neckline on a pullover, sweatshirt, etc., fitting closely around the base of the neck.

crib [krɪb] *n., v.* **cribbed, crib•bing.** —*n.* **1** a small bed with high sides to keep a baby from falling out. **2** a rack or manger for horses and cows to eat from. **3** a stall for a farm animal. **4** a building or box for storing grain, salt, etc.: *a corn crib.* **5** a framework of logs or timbers used in building. The wooden lining inside a mine shaft is a crib. **6** *Informal.* the use of another's ideas as one's own. **7** *Informal.* notes or helps that are used dishonestly or unfairly in doing schoolwork or in examinations. **8** a small room or house. **9** the cards discarded from each hand in cribbage and scored by the dealer after the deal has been played. **10** *Informal.* cribbage. **11** *Cdn.* a raft of logs lashed together for floating downstream.
—*v.* **1** provide with a crib. **2** *Informal.* steal; make off with. **3** *Informal.* use (another's words or ideas) as one's own. **4** *Informal.* use notes or helps unfairly in doing schoolwork or in examinations. **5** shut up in a crib or small space. ⟨OE *cribb*⟩ **—'crib•ber,** *n.*

crib•bage ['krɪbɪdʒ] *n.* a card game for two, three, or four people. The players keep score with a narrow board (**cribbage board**) having holes into which movable pegs fit. ⟨ME and OE, oxstall + E *-age*⟩

crib•bing [krɪbɪŋ] *n., v.* —*n. Mining.* **1** the lining of timber in a shaft; crib. **2** the pieces of timber used in a crib. **3** CRIB BITING.
—*v.* ppr. of CRIB.

crib biting the bad habit that certain horses have of gnawing at the wood of their stalls while swallowing air.

crib death SUDDEN INFANT DEATH SYNDROME.

crib•ri•form ['krɪbrɪ,fɔrm] *adj.* having holes in the manner of a sieve. ⟨< L *cribrum* sieve, related to *cervere* separate + E *-form*⟩

cri•ce•tid [krəi'sitɪd] *or* [krəi'sɛtɪd] *n.* any rodent of the family Cricetidae, which includes gerbils, hamsters, muskrats, and many species of mice and rats.

crick[1] [krɪk] *n., v.* —*n.* a sudden muscular cramp; painful stiffness of muscles, as, a crick in the neck.
—*v.* cause such a cramp in. ⟨origin uncertain⟩
☛ *Hom.* CREEK [krɪk].

crick[2] [krɪk] *n. Dialect.* CREEK (def. 1).

crick•et[1] ['krɪkɪt] *n.* **1** any of a large family (Gryllidae) of insects resembling grasshoppers, having long, threadlike antennae, long hind legs for jumping, and two pairs of wings. Male crickets produce the characteristic chirping noise by rubbing a kind of scraper on one of the leathery forewings against a row of teeth on the other. **2** a small metal object with a spring, that makes a clicking noise when pressed, used as a toy or for signalling. ⟨ME < OF *criquet;* imitative⟩

crick•et[2] ['krɪkɪt] *n., v.* —*n.* **1** an outdoor game played by two teams of eleven players each, with ball, bats, and wickets. **2** *Informal.* fair play; good sportsmanship (only in the negative).
—*v.* play the game of cricket. ⟨< OF *criquet* goal post, stick, probably < MDu. *cricke* stick to lean on⟩

crick•et[3] ['krɪkɪt] *n.* a small, low, wooden stool. ⟨origin uncertain⟩

crick•et•er ['krɪkətər] *n.* a person who plays cricket.

cri de coeur [kʀid'kœʀ] *French.* a heartfelt appeal; a loud cry of protest, etc.

cried [kraɪd] *v.* pt. and pp. of CRY.

cri•er ['kraɪər] *n.* **1** an official who shouts out public announcements; town crier. **2** a person who shouts out announcements of goods for sale. **3** a person who cries.

cries [kraɪz] *n., v.* —*n.* pl. of CRY.
—*v.* 3rd person singular, present tense of CRY.

crime [kraɪm] *n.* **1** an act that is against the law. **2** the activity of criminals; violation of law. **3** a wrong act; SIN (def. 2). **4** *Informal.* something regretted or deplored: *It's a crime that her abilities are so underused.* ⟨ME < OF < L *crimen* accusation, offence⟩
☛ *Syn.* **1. Crime,** OFFENCE = an act that breaks a law. **Crime** applies particularly to an act that breaks a law that has been made by people for the public good: *Murder and swindling are crimes.* **Offence** is more general, and applies to an act, not always serious, that breaks any moral, public, or social law: *Lying and cruelty are offences.*

Cri•me•an [kraɪ'miən] *adj.* of or having to do with the Crimea, a peninsula in S Ukraine, extending into the Black Sea.

crime pas•si•o•nel ['krim,pæsjə'nɛl]; *French,* [kʀimpasjɔ'nɛl] a crime of passion, such as murder for personal reasons, often to do with sex.

crim•i•nal ['krɪmənəl] *n., adj.* —*n.* a person guilty of a crime.
—*adj.* **1** guilty of crime. **2** having to do with crime: *criminal court, criminal law.* **3** being a crime or like crime; wrong; deplorable. ⟨< L *criminalis* < *crimen.* See CRIME.⟩

Criminal Code in Canada, the list of crimes.

crim•i•nal•ist•ics [,krɪmɪnə'lɪstɪks] *n.* the police science which includes ballistics, fingerprints and how to catch a murderer by examining the remains of his or her victim.

crim•i•nal•i•ty [,krɪmə'næləti] *n., pl.* **-ties. 1** the fact or quality of being a crime or criminal; guilt. **2** a criminal act.

crim•i•nal•ize ['krɪmɪnə,laɪz] *v.,* **-lized, -liz•ing.** make (something) criminal; put (an action) into the Criminal Code: *Some people want abortion to be criminalized.*

criminal law that branch of law which deals with crimes and is limited to the Criminal Code. Compare CIVIL LAW.

criminal lawyer a lawyer who specializes in criminal law, especially in the defence of anyone charged with a crime.

crim•i•nal•ly ['krɪmənəli] *adv.* **1** in a criminal manner. **2** according to criminal law.

crim•i•nate ['krɪmə,neit] *v.* **-nat•ed, -nat•ing. 1** accuse of a crime. **2** furnish evidence as to the guilt of (someone). ⟨< L *criminare* < *crimen.* See CRIME.⟩

crim•i•na•to•ry ['krɪmənə,tɔri] *adj.* criminating.

crim•i•no•log•i•cal [,krɪmənə'lɒdʒəkəl] *adj.* of or having to do with criminology. **—,crim•i•no'log•i•cal•ly,** *adv.*

crim•i•nol•o•gist [,krɪmə'nɒlədʒɪst] *n.* a person trained in criminology, especially one whose work it is.

crim•i•nol•o•gy [,krɪmə'nɒlədʒi] *n.* the scientific study of crime and criminals, and of the treatment of criminals. ⟨< L *crimen, -minis* crime + E *-logy*⟩

crimp[1] [krɪmp] *v., n.* —*v.* **1** press into small, narrow folds; make wavy: *The girl crimped her hair before going to the party.* **2** pinch, fold, or bend into shape. **3** pinch together: *Crimp the edges of the pastry before baking the pie.* **4** hinder; cramp.
—*n.* **1** a crimping. **2** something crimped; fold; wave. **3** a waved or curled lock of hair. **4** the natural curl or wave in wool fibre.
put a crimp in, *Slang.* interfere with; hinder. ⟨OE *(ge)crympan*⟩ **—'crimp•er,** *n.*

crimp[2] [krɪmp] *n., v.* —*n.* formerly, a person who made a

business of forcing or tricking men into becoming sailors, soldiers, etc.
—v. force or trick (someone) into becoming a sailor, a soldier, etc. ⟨origin uncertain⟩

crim•ple ['krɪmpəl] *v.* **-pled, -pling.** wrinkle; crumple; curl. ⟨< *crimp*[1]⟩

crimp•y ['krɪmpi] *adj.* **crimp•i•er, crimp•i•est.** having small, narrow folds; wavy. **—'crimp•i•ness,** *n.*

crim•son ['krɪmzən] *n., adj., v. —n.* **1** a deep red. **2** a deep red pigment or dye.
—adj. **1** having a deep red colour: *a crimson rose.* **2** covered with blood: *his crimson hands.*
—v. turn deep red: *His face crimsoned with shame.* ⟨< Ital. *cremesion* < *cremisi, chermisi* the colour crimson < Arabic *qirmazi* < *qirmiz* the kermes insect (from which a red dye was derived) < Skt. *Krmis* worm, insect⟩

crimson clover a European annual clover (*Trifolium incarnatum*) of the legume family, having deep red flowers, cultivated in the S U.S. for forage.

cringe [krɪndʒ] *v.* **cringed, cring•ing;** *n. —v.* **1** shrink from danger or pain; crouch in fear. **2** bow down timidly; try to get favour or attention by servile behaviour: *The beggar cringed as he put out his hand for money.*
—n. a cringing. ⟨ME *crengen* < OE *cringan* give way⟩
—'cring•er, *n.* **—'cring•ing•ly,** *adv.*

crin•gle ['krɪŋgəl] *n.* a small loop or ring of rope on the edge of a sail. The sail can be fastened by putting a rope through the cringle. ⟨apparently < LG *kringel,* dim. of *kring* ring⟩

cri•nite[1] ['kraɪnəit] *adj.* **1** hairy. **2** *Botany.* having tufts like hair. ⟨< L *crinitus,* pp. of *crinire* provide with hair⟩

cri•nite[2] ['kraɪnəit] *or* ['krɪnəit] *n.* a fossil crinoid. ⟨< Gk. *krinon* lily + ITE⟩.

crin•kle ['krɪŋkəl] *v.* **-kled, -kling;** *n. —v.* **1** become or cause to be wrinkled: *Her suit was crinkled from lying on the floor.* **2** rustle: *Paper crinkles when it is crushed.*
—n. **1** a wrinkle; ripple. **2** a rustle. ⟨ME *crenkle(n)* < OE *crincan* bend⟩

crin•kle•root ['krɪŋkəl,rut] *n.* a plant (*Dentaria diphylla*) of the toothwort family, having purple or white flowers and a strong-smelling root.

crin•kly ['krɪŋkli] *adj.* **-kli•er, -kli•est.** full of crinkles.

cri•noid ['kraɪnɔɪd] *or* ['krɪnɔɪd] *n., adj. —n.* any of a class (Crinoidea) of sea animals resembling flowers, with a more or less cup-shaped body and long, feathery arms. Some crinoids, such as the sea lilies, have long stalks by which they are attached to the sea bottom; others swim about freely.
—adj. **1** of or designating the class Crinoidea. **2** shaped like a lily. ⟨< Gk. *krinoeidēs* < *krinon* lily⟩

crin•o•line ['krɪnəlɪn] *or* ['krɪnə,lin] *n.* **1** a stiff cloth used as a lining to hold a skirt out, make a coat collar stand up, etc. **2** a petticoat of crinoline to hold a skirt out. **3** HOOP SKIRT. ⟨< F < Ital. *crinolino* < *crino* horsehair (< L *crinis* hair) + *lino* thread < L *linum*⟩

cri•num ['kraɪnəm] *n.* any plant of the genus *Crinum,* of the amaryllis family, native to tropical and subtropical regions and having umbels of large pink, red, or white flowers. ⟨< NL < Gk. *krinon* lily⟩

cripes [krəips] *interj. Slang.* a mild expression of irritation, surprise, etc. ⟨euphemism for Christ⟩

crip•ple ['krɪpəl] *n. v.* **-pled, -pling.** *—n.* a person or animal that is partly disabled, especially one that is lame.
—v. **1** make a cripple of. **2** damage; disable; weaken: *The ship was crippled by the storm.* ⟨OE *crypel.* Related to CREEP.⟩
—'crip•pler, *n.*
☛ *Usage.* **Cripple** is now almost completely confined to metaphorical use; **disable** is preferred in the context of physical or mental conditions of human beings.

cri•sis ['krəisɪs] *n., pl.* **-ses** [-siz]. **1** the turning point in a serious illness, after which it is known whether the patient is expected to live or die. **2** an important or deciding event. **3** a time or state of danger or anxious waiting: *England faced a crisis during the Battle of Britain.* ⟨< L < Gk. *krisis* < *krinein* decide⟩
☛ *Syn.* **3.** See note at EMERGENCY.

crisp [krɪsp] *adj., v., n. —adj.* **1** firm and stiff, but breaking or snapping easily and sharply: *Dry toast and fresh celery are crisp.* **2** fresh; sharp and clear; bracing: *The air was cool and crisp.* **3** clear-cut; decisive: *"Don't talk; fight" is a crisp sentence.* **4** brisk; snappy; full of energy: *crisp repartee.* **5** curly and wiry: *crisp hair.* **6** new or clean and pressed or as if pressed: *a crisp blouse, a crisp $20 bill.* **7** crinkled.
—v. make or become crisp.
—n. **1** something crisp, such as a thin cookie. **2** *Brit.* a potato chip. **3** a dessert with a crumb topping: *apple crisp.*
burnt to a crisp, of food, badly overcooked. ⟨< L *crispus* curled⟩
—'crisp•ly, *adv.* **—'crisp•ness,** *n.*

crisp•er ['krɪspər] *n.* a compartment in a refrigerator for storing fresh vegetables and fruit.

crisp•y ['krɪspi] *adj.* **crisp•i•er, crisp•i•est.** crisp.
—'crisp•i•ness, *n.*

criss•cross ['krɪs,krɒs] *adj., adv., v., n. —adj.* marked or made with crossed lines; crossed; crossing: *Plaids have a crisscross pattern.*
—adv. crosswise.
—v. **1** mark or cover with crossed lines. **2** come and go across: *Buses and cars crisscross the city.* **3** lie across (one another): *In New York, streets and avenues crisscross (one another).*
—n. a mark or pattern made of crossed lines. ⟨alteration of *Christ's cross*⟩

cris•ta ['krɪstə] *n., pl.* **-tae** [-ti]. a folded ridge formed from the inner membrane of a mitochondrion and important to the respiration of a cell. ⟨< L, tuft, crest, comb⟩

cris•tate ['krɪsteit] *adj.* of a bird, having a crest.

cri•te•ri•a [krəi'tiriə] *n.* a pl. of CRITERION.

cri•te•ri•on [krəi'tiriən] *n.* **-te•ri•a** *or* **-te•ri•ons.** a rule or standard for making a judgment; test: *Wealth is only one criterion of success.* ⟨< Gk. *kritērion* < *krinein* judge⟩
☛ *Syn.* See note at STANDARD.

crit•ic ['krɪtɪk] *n.* **1** a person who makes judgments of the merits and faults of books, music, films, plays, acting, etc. **2** a person whose profession is preparing such judgments for a newspaper, magazine, radio or television program, etc. **3** a person who carefully examines and analyses anything for its merits and faults: *In a democracy all citizens are called upon to be critics of government policy.* **4** a person who disapproves or finds fault; faultfinder. ⟨< L *criticus* < Gk. *kritikos* critical < *krinein* to judge⟩

crit•i•cal ['krɪtəkəl] *adj.* **1** inclined to find fault or disapprove: *a critical disposition.* **2** skilled as a critic. **3** coming from one who is skilled as a critic; involving careful analysis and examination: *a critical judgment, critical thinking.* **4** belonging to the work of a critic: *critical essays.* **5** of a crisis; important in a situation of danger or difficulty; crucial: *the critical moment.* **6** full of danger or difficulty; causing a crisis: *Her delay was critical.* **7** of supplies, labour, or resources, necessary for some work or project but existing in inadequate supply. **8** *Physics and mathematics.* of or having to do with a point at which some action, property, or condition undergoes a change. **9** *Nuclear physics.* having to do with, or capable of producing, a chain reaction: *critical mass.* **10** of or involving the operation of an atomic reactor: *a critical experiment.* **11** *Medicine.* dangerous: *She is in critical condition in the hospital.* **—'crit•i•cal•ly,** *adv.* **—'crit•i•cal•ness,** *n.*

critical angle **1** *Optics.* the smallest possible angle of incidence that gives total reflection. **2** *Aeronautics.* the angle of attack of a wing at which maximum lift is momentarily reached and above which turbulence occurs, drag is greatly increased, lift is destroyed, and the airfoil tends to stall.

critical density the density of a substance when its critical temperature and pressure have been reached.

critical mass *n.* **1** the smallest amount needed to start something off. **2** *Nuclear physics.* the minimum quantity of fissionable material required in a reactor to produce or maintain a chain reaction.

critical point the physical point at which a substance which has reached its critical temperature can maintain itself as liquid and gas in equilibrium.

critical pressure the least pressure at which a gas can be liquefied at its critical temperature.

critical temperature the highest temperature at which a gas can be liquefied by pressure alone.

critical volume the volume of a mass when its critical temperature and pressure have been reached.

crit•i•cism ['krɪtə,sɪzəm] *n.* **1** a criticizing; faultfinding. **2** the making of judgments; the act of approving or disapproving; an analysis of merits and faults. **3** the rules and principles used in making careful judgments of the merits and faults of books, music, films, plays, acting, etc. **4** a critical comment, essay, review, etc. **5** a scholarly examination of a text to date or reconstruct it or to evaluate its style.
☛ *Syn.* **4.** See note at REVIEW.

☛ *Usage.* Note that **criticism** (defs. 2-4) involves the making of judgments (favourable or unfavourable) after careful consideration; it does not necessarily involve faultfinding (def. 1).

crit•i•cize ['krɪtə,saɪz] *v.* **-cized, -ciz•ing. 1** express disapproval (of); find fault (with): *Do not criticize him until you know all the facts.* **2** judge as a critic; discuss the merits and faults of. **3** act or speak as a critic. **—'crit•i,ciz•er,** *n.*

cri•tique [krɪ'tik] *n., v.,* **cri•tiqued, cri•tiqu•ing.** *—n.* **1** a critical essay or review. Some newspapers regularly publish critiques of new books. **2** the art of criticism; criticism.
—v. write or give a review of; criticize. ⟨< F < Gk. *kritikē (technē)* the critical art, fem. of *kritikos.* See CRITIC.⟩

crit•ter ['krɪtər] *n. Dialect.* **1** any living creature. **2** an animal, especially a cow, raised as livestock. ⟨alteration of *creature*⟩

croak [krouk] *n., v. —n.* a deep, hoarse sound, made by a frog, crow, raven, etc.
—v. **1** make a deep, hoarse sound. **2** utter in a deep, hoarse voice. **3** be always prophesying misfortune; be dissatisfied; grumble. **4** *Slang.* die. ⟨OE **crācian*; related to *crācettan* of the same meaning⟩ **—'croak•er,** *n.*

croak•y ['krouki] *adj.* **croak•i•er, croak•i•est. 1** deep and hoarse; making a croaking sound. **2** having a tendency to croak. **—'croak•i•ly,** *adv.* **—'croak•i•ness,** *n.*

Cro•at ['krouæt] *or* [krout] *n.* a native or inhabitant of Croatia.

Cro•a•tia [krou'eiʃə] *n.* a republic in E Europe, part of the former Yugoslavia.

Cro•a•tian [krou'eiʃən] *n., adj. —n.* **1** Croat. **2** a Slavic language spoken by the Croats, identical to Serbian except that Croatian is written with the Latin alphabet while Serbian uses the Cyrillic alphabet. See SERBO-CROATIAN.
—adj. of or having to do with Croatia, the Croats, or their language.

croc [krɒk] *n. Informal.* crocodile.
☛ *Hom.* CROCK.

cro•chet [krou'ʃei] *or* ['krouʃei] *n., v.* **-cheted** [-'ʃeid], **-chet•ing** [-'ʃeiɪŋ]. *—n.* a kind of lacy needlework made by interlocking loops of a single thread, using a hooked needle. Crochet may be fine or heavy, and is used for making sweaters, shawls, doilies, tablecloths, etc.
—v. **1** make of crochet: *to crochet a shawl.* **2** do crochet: *I like to crochet.* ⟨< F *crochet*, dim. of *croc* hook < Gmc. Doublet of CROCKET, CROTCHET.⟩ **—cro'chet•er** [-'ʃeiər], *n.*

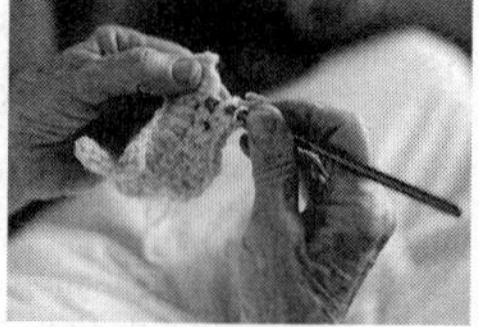
Crochet

crochet hook the hooked needle used in crochet. Crochet hooks come in many sizes.

cro•cid•o•lite [krou'sɪdə,ləit] *n.* a blue-green kind of asbestos; blue asbestos. ⟨< Gk. *krokis, krokidos* var. of *krokys* nap on woollen cloth + -LITE⟩

crock [krɒk] *n.* **1** a pot or jar made of baked clay. **2** such a pot or jar filled with something: *a crock of jam.* **3** *Slang.* a bottle of liquor. **4** *Slang.* a worthless, old, or decrepit person, horse, car, etc. **5** *Slang.* a piece of nonsense; something patently false. **6 a** a game of marbles. **b** a group of six marbles. ⟨OE *crocc(a)*⟩
☛ *Hom.* CROC.

crocked [krɒkt] *adj. Slang.* drunk.

crock•er•y ['krɒkəri] *n.* dishes, jars, etc., made of baked clay; earthenware.

crock•et ['krɒkɪt] *n. Architecture.* an ornament, usually made to resemble foliage, along the edges of a spire, pinnacle, gable, etc. ⟨< AF *croket*, var. of OF *crochet*, dim. of *croc* hook < Gmc. Doublet of CROCHET, CROQUET, CROTCHET.⟩

Crock•pot ['krɒk,pɒt] *n. Trademark.* an electric earthenware pot used for slow cooking of meats, stews, etc.

croc•o•dile ['krɒkə,daɪl] *n.* **1** any of a family (Crocodylidae) of large, tropical, aquatic reptiles having a thick, scaly skin, a long, round body, four short legs, and a powerful tail. Crocodiles closely resemble alligators, to which they are related, but they are faster moving and have a narrower snout. **2** leather from the hide of a crocodile. ⟨ME < OF < LL *crocodilus* < Gk. *krokodilos*, earlier, lizard < *krokē* pebble + *drilos* worm⟩

crocodile tears pretended or insincere grief.

croc•o•dil•i•an [,krɒkə'dɪliən] *adj., n. —adj.* **1** of or like a crocodile. **2** of or like any crocodilian.
—n. any of an order of reptiles that includes crocodiles, alligators, etc.

cro•co•ite ['kroukou,əit] *n.* a red, orange, or yellow mineral, lead chromate. *Formula*: $PbCrO_4$ ⟨< Gk. *krokos* saffron + E *-ite*[1]⟩

cro•cus ['kroukəs] *n., pl.* **cro•cus•es** or **cro•ci** [-saɪ] *or* [-si].
1 any of a large genus (*Crocus*) of small plants of the iris family, growing from a fleshy underground stem and having long, slender leaves and a single large, cup-shaped flower that may be white, yellow or purple. Crocuses bloom early in spring and are popular garden plants. **2** *Cdn.* a small wildflower (*Anemone patens*) of central North America, a species of anemone having fine silky hairs on the stem and leaves and a single large, mauve, cup-shaped flower that blooms very early in spring; pasqueflower. The crocus is the floral emblem of Manitoba. **3** the flower of a crocus. **4** a deep-yellow colour; saffron. **5** a polishing powder consisting of iron oxide: *jeweller's crocus.* ⟨< L < Gk. *krokos* < Semitic⟩

Croe•sus ['krisəs] *n.* **1** King of Lydia from 560 to 546 B.C., famous for his great wealth. **2** any very rich person.

croft [krɒft] *n. Brit.* **1** a small enclosed field. **2** a very small rented farm. ⟨OE⟩

croft•er ['krɒftər] *n. Brit.* a person who cultivates a small farm.

Crohn's disease [krounz] a chronic inflammation of the lower bowel that causes thickening of the walls of the colon. ⟨after B.B. *Crohn* (1884-1983), American doctor who described the disease in 1932⟩

crois•sant [krə'sɒnt]; *French,* [kʀwa'sɑ̃] *n.* a small roll of bread shaped like a crescent. ⟨< F *croissant* ppr. of *croître* grow < L *crēscere.* See CRESCENT.⟩

croix de guerre [,krwɑ də 'gɛr]; *French,* [kʀwad'gɛʀ] in France, a medal given to servicemen for bravery under fire. ⟨< F, war cross⟩

cro•ki•nole ['kroukə,noul] *n.* a table game for two or four players in which each player tries to flick polished wooden or plastic disks into or near the centre of a round board, at the same time trying to knock out the disks of the opposing player or players. ⟨< F *croquignole* a flick, fillip⟩

Cro–Mag•non [krou 'mægnən] *or* [krou 'mænjən] *n.* an early type of human being generally considered to be a race of modern people (*Homo sapiens*), known from skeletal remains found in S Europe, along with artifacts of bone and stone. ⟨< *Cro-Magnon* cave, near Dordogne, SW France, where their remains have been found⟩

crom•lech ['krɒmlək] *n.* **1** a circle of upright stones erected in prehistoric times. **2** upright stones with a large, flat stone laid horizontally on them. ⟨< Welsh *cromlech* < *crom* bent + *llech* flat stone⟩

A cromlech

Crom•well current ['krɒmwɛl] an equatorial counter-current flowing east across the Pacific under the prevailing westerly current. ⟨< T. *Cromwell*, U.S. oceanographer⟩

crone [kroun] *n.* a shrivelled, wrinkled, old woman. ⟨< MDu. *croonje* < OF *carogne* carcass, hag. Doublet of CARRION.⟩

Cro•nus ['krounəs] *n. Greek mythology.* a Titan who was ruler of the universe until overthrown by his son Zeus. Cronus corresponds to the Roman god Saturn.

cro•ny ['krouni] *n., pl.* **-nies.** a very close friend; chum. ⟨origin uncertain⟩

crook [krʊk] *n., v.* **crooked** [krʊkt], **crook•ing;** *adj. —n.* **1** something having a hooked or bent form or part, such as a shepherd's staff or a bishop's crosier. **2** a hooked or bent part of something: *the crook of a hockey stick, the crook of an umbrella handle.* **3** a bend or curve: *a crook in a stream.* **4** *Informal.* a thief or swindler.
—v. bend or curve: *She beckoned to the children by crooking her finger at them.*
—adj. Austral. Slang. **1** bad, unpleasant, or unsatisfactory. **2** bad-tempered. **3** sick. ⟨ME *crōc* < ON *krókr*⟩

crook•ed ['krʊkɪd] *for defs. 1-3*; [krʊkt] *for def. 4. adj.* **1** not straight; bent, curved, or twisted: *narrow, crooked streets, a crooked piece of lumber. Your skirt is crooked.* **2** not perpendicular or parallel; slanted: *The picture on the wall is crooked.*

3 dishonest: *a crooked politician, a crooked deal.* 4 having a crook in it, especially by design. **—'crook•ed•ly,** *adv.* **—'crook•ed•ness,** *n.*

crooked canoe [krʊkt] *Cdn.* a canoe designed by the Eastern James Bay Cree, having a keel forming an arc, often more than 30 cm higher at the ends than amidships.

crooked knife ['krʊkɪd] *Cdn.* a woodworking knife having a blade that ends in a hook, used widely in the North, especially by people of the First Nations, in making snowshoe frames, pelt stretchers, canoes, etc. ⟨translation of Cdn.F *couteau croché*⟩

crook•neck ['krʊk,nɛk] *n.* a variety of squash having a long, curved neck.

crook•necked ['krʊk,nɛkt] *adj.* having a hooked or curved neck.

croon [krun] *v., n.* *—v.* **1** murmur; hum; sing in a low tone: *The mother was crooning to her baby.* **2** sing in a low voice with exaggerated emotion.
—n. a low singing; humming or murmuring. ⟨ME < MDu. *kronen* murmur⟩ **—'croon•er,** *n.*

crop [krɒp] *n., v.* **cropped, crop•ping.** *—n.* **1** a product grown or gathered for use, especially for use as food or fibre: *Wheat is the main crop of the Prairie Provinces.* **2** the total amount of a grain, vegetable, or fruit produced in one season: *The potato crop was very small this year.* **3** anything like a crop; group; collection: *a crop of new paperbacks in the bookstore.* **4** the act of clipping or cutting off short. **5** a short haircut. **6** a piece cut off or a notch cut in the ear of an animal. **7 a** the baglike swelling in a bird's food passage where food is prepared for digestion. **b** a similar organ in other animals or in insects. **8** a short whip having a loop instead of a lash: *a riding crop.* **9** the handle of a whip. **10** *Mining.* an outcrop of a vein or seam.
—v. **1** plant and cultivate a crop. **2** bear a crop or crops. **3** cut or bite off the top of: *Sheep crop grass very short.* **4** clip; cut short (the tail, ear, hair, edge of a book, etc.). **5** *Mining.* come to the surface of the ground, as a vein of ore.
crop out, appear or come to the surface: *Great ridges of rock cropped out all over the hillside.*
crop up, appear or occur unexpectedly: *All sorts of difficulties cropped up.* ⟨OE *cropp* sprout, craw⟩
☛ *Syn. n.* **1, 2. Crop,** YIELD, HARVEST = a product of the land, grown or gathered for use. **Crop** is the general word, applying to the product while growing and when gathered: *The tomato crop was damaged by frost.* **Yield** applies to the quantity or amount of a crop produced: *The yield from those trees was poor this year.* **Harvest,** more formal, emphasizes the idea of gathering and applies to the process or time of gathering or to the amount gathered in one season: *The wheat is ready for harvest.*

crop–dust•ing ['krɒp ,dʌstɪŋ] *n.* the practice of spraying pesticides from a low-flying plane over growing crops. **—'crop-,dust•er,** *n.*

crop–eared ['krɒp ,ird] *adj.* of an animal, having the ears cut short.

crop•land ['krɒp,lænd] *n.* land under cultivation for crops. Also, **croplands.**

crop•per ['krɒpər] *n.* **1** a person who or thing that crops. **2** a person who raises a crop or crops, especially a sharecropper. **3** a plant that furnishes a crop: *The soybean is a hardy cropper.*
come a cropper, *Informal.* **a** fall heavily. **b** fail; collapse.

crop rotation *Agriculture.* a way of conserving the fertility of soil by successively planting on the same ground different crops with varying food requirements.

cro•quet [krou'kei] *n., v.* **-quet•ed** [-keid], **-quet•ing** [-'keiɪŋ]. *—n.* **1** an outdoor game played by driving wooden balls through small wire arches by means of mallets. **2** a driving away of an opponent's ball by striking one's own when the two are in contact.
—v. drive away (an opponent's ball) by striking one's own ball when the two are in contact. ⟨< F *croquet,* dial. var. of *crochet.* See CROCHET.⟩

cro•quette [krou'kɛt] *n.* a small ball or cake of chopped or ground cooked meat, fish, vegetable, etc., coated with crumbs and fried. ⟨< F *croquette* < *croquer* crunch⟩

crore [krɔr] *n.* in India and Pakistan, ten million. ⟨< Hind.⟩

cro•sier or **cro•zier** ['krouʒər] *n.* **1** an ornamental staff carried by or before bishops, abbots, and abbesses. **2** *Botany.* the curled top of a young fern. ⟨ME < OF *crossier* crook bearer < VL *croccia* crook < Gmc.⟩

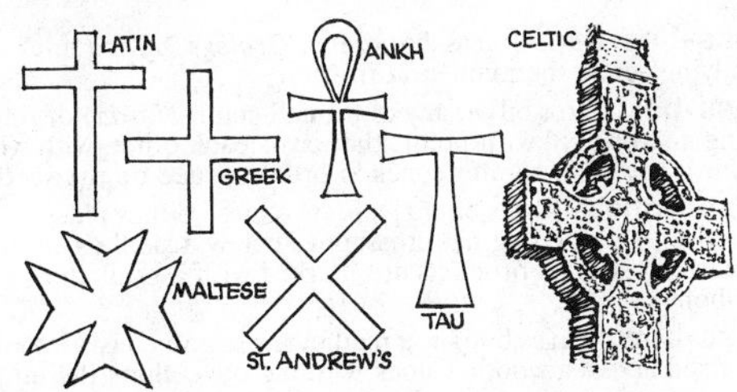

Crosses (def. 3); at the far right, a 5th-century Irish stone cross

cross [krɒs] *n., v., adj.* *—n.* **1** an upright post with another across it near the top, upon which condemned persons were executed by the ancient Romans. **2 the Cross, a** the cross on which Jesus died. **b** the sufferings and death of Jesus; the Atonement. **3** any object, design, or mark shaped somewhat like a cross, consisting of at least two lines which cross. A cross is the main symbol of the Christian religion. A person who cannot write his or her name represents his or her signature with a cross. **4** a crossing; a lying or going across. **5** a burden of duty; suffering or trouble that must be endured. **6** the act of crossing breeds, varieties, or species of animals or plants. **7** the result of such crossing: *Our dog is a cross between chihuahua and fox terrier.* **8** something that is like a combination of two different things or is intermediate between them: *Documentary drama is a cross between theatre and journalism.* **9** *Boxing.* a countering blow crossing over the opponent's lead. **10 Cross,** the SOUTHERN CROSS.
take the cross, join a crusade.
—v. **1** draw a line across: *In writing you cross the letter* t. **2** cancel by drawing a line or lines through (*used with* **off** *or* **out**): *Cross my name off your list. She crossed out the wrong word.* **3** set or lay crosswise one over the other; put one thing across (another): *He crossed his arms.* **4** go across; go to the other side of: *to cross a bridge.* **5** lie or extend across; form a cross (with): *Lansdowne Avenue crosses Main Street. The two streets cross.* **6** pass, each thing having as its destination the other's origin: *Our letters crossed in the mail, and I got hers the same day she got mine.* **7** trace the form of a cross on (something or someone) with the right hand as an act of Christian devotion: *He knelt and crossed himself.* **8** oppose or hinder; thwart: *crossed in love. If anyone crosses him, he gets very angry.* **9** cause (two different breeds, varieties, or species of animals or plants) to mate in order to produce a new kind: *Canadian breeders have crossed domestic cattle with buffalo to produce the cattalo.* **10** cause to touch, passing electricity where it is not wanted: *These wires are crossed.*
cross (one's) **fingers, a** put one finger over another in a superstitious gesture intended to keep trouble away, or when saying something but keeping back part of one's thoughts. **b** hope for the best.
cross (one's) **heart,** make the sign of the cross over one's heart when swearing that something is true.
cross (one's) **mind,** occur to one; be thought: *It never crossed my mind that he might forget.*
cross (someone's) **palm,** pay (someone) money: *Cross the Gypsy's palm with silver.*
cross (someone's) **path,** meet (a person).
cross swords, a fight with swords in single combat. **b** engage in controversy.
cross the floor, of a member of a legislature, leave one's party by moving from one's assigned seat with that party to a seat in another section of the chamber.
—adj. **1** in a bad temper; grumpy. **2** lying across: *a cross timber.* **3** moving or going across: *cross traffic.* **4** crossbred.
at cross purposes, in conflict or opposition. ⟨OE *cros* < OIrish *cros* < L *crux.* Doublet of CRUX.⟩ **—'cross•ly,** *adv.* **—'cross•ness,** *n.*
☛ *Hom.* CROSSE.

cross– *combining form.* **1** cross-shaped: *cross-stitch = a stitch crossed over another.* **2** moving across: *crossfire = lines of fire crossing one another.* **3** counter: *cross-check = counter-check.* **4** across regular lines of affinity: *cross-fertilization = fertilization of one plant by pollen from another.*

cross•bar ['krɒs,bɑr] *n.* a bar, line, or stripe going crosswise.

cross•beam ['krɒs,bim] *n.* a large beam that crosses another or extends from wall to wall.

cross–bed•ded ['krɒs ,bɛdɪd] *adj. Geology.* having lines of rock lying across the main stratification.

cross•bill ['krɒs,bɪl] *n.* any of a small genus (*Loxia*) of finches having a strong bill with points that cross each other, with which the birds pry open conifer cones in order to feed on the seeds.

cross•bones ['krɒs,bounz] *n.pl.* two large bones placed crosswise. A pirate flag has crossbones below a skull as a symbol of death. Poisonous products are marked with a skull and crossbones.

cross•bow ['krɒs,bou] *n.* a medieval weapon consisting of a bow fixed across a wooden stock with a groove along the middle to direct an arrow or a stone.

cross•bow•man ['krɒs,boumən] *n., pl.* **-men.** formerly, a soldier who used a crossbow.

cross•brace ['krɒs,breis] *n.* crossbeam.

cross•bred ['krɒs,brɛd] *adj., n. —adj.* produced by crossbreeding.
—n. an animal or plant produced by crossbreeding.

cross•breed ['krɒs,brid] *v.* **-bred, -breed•ing;** *n. —v.* breed by mixing kinds, breeds, or races.
—n. an individual or breed produced by crossbreeding. A mule is a crossbreed, developed by crossing a horse and a donkey.

cross bun a bun marked with a cross on the top. Hot cross buns are traditionally eaten on Good Friday.

cross–check ['krɒs ,tʃɛk] *v., n. —v.* **1** check again, or check against another source. **2** *Hockey or lacrosse.* give (an opponent) an illegal check by holding one's stick in both hands and thrusting it in front of the opponent's face or body.
—n. **1** the act of cross-checking something. **2** *Hockey or lacrosse.* an illegal check made by cross-checking.

cross–coun•try ['krɒs 'kʌntri] *adj., adv., n. —adj.* **1** across fields or open country instead of by road or over a track: *a cross-country race.* **2** that crosses a country: *a cross-country flight.* **3** of or designating the sport of skiing over relatively flat country, using long, narrow skis. Also called **Nordic.** Compare DOWNHILL. **4** for use in cross-country skiing: *cross-country skis.*
—adv. across a country: *to fly cross-country.*
—n. a cross-country team footrace.

cross cousin *Anthropology.* the son or daughter of one's paternal aunt or maternal uncle.

cross–cul•tu•ral ['krɒs 'kʌltʃərəl] *adj.* having to do with interchange or comparison between different cultures: *a cross-cultural study.* **—'cross-'cul•tur•al•ly,** *adv.*

cross•cur•rent ['krɒs,kɜrənt] *n.* **1** a current of air blowing across another. **2** a contradictory tendency or trend: *the crosscurrents of political thought.*

cross•cut ['krɒs,kʌt] *adj., n., v.* **-cut, -cut•ting.** *—adj.* **1** of a cut, incision, etc., made across or obliquely. **2** made or used for cutting across: *crosscut teeth on a saw.*
—n. **1** a cut, course, or path across. **2** CROSSCUT SAW. **3** a section of a film that shows contrasting scenes by turns.
—v. **1** cut or go across. **2** show (contrasting scenes in a film) by turns.

crosscut saw a saw used or made for cutting across the grain of wood.

cross dressing wearing the clothes of the opposite sex so as to appear to be a member of that sex.

crosse [krɒs] *n.* a lacrosse stick. ⟨< Cdn.F < F *crosse* a hooked stick⟩
☛ *Hom.* CROSS.

cross–ex•am•i•na•tion [,krɒs ɛg,zæmə'neiʃən] *n.* **1** *Law.* examination to check a previous examination, especially the questioning of a witness by the lawyer for the opposing side to test the truth of the witness's evidence. **2** a close or severe questioning.

cross–ex•am•ine ['krɒs ɛg'zæmən] *v.* **-ined, -in•ing. 1** *Law.* question closely to test the truth of evidence given. **2** question closely or severely. **—,cross-ex'am•in•er,** *n.*

cross–eye ['krɒs ,aɪ] *n.* a strabismus, especially the form in which both eyes are turned in toward the nose.

cross–eyed ['krɒs ,aɪd] *adj.* having one eye or both eyes turned in toward the nose.

cross–fer•tile ['krɒs 'fɜrtaɪl] *or* ['krɒs 'fɜrtəl] *adj.* able to be cross-fertilized.

cross–fer•ti•li•za•tion [,krɒs ,fɜrtəlaɪ'zeiʃən] *or* [,krɒs ,fɜrtələ'zeiʃən] *n.* **1** *Botany.* the fertilization of one flower by pollen from another. **2** *Zoology.* the fertilization of one species by another, or one hermaphrodite by another.

cross–fer•ti•lize ['krɒs 'fɜrtə,laɪz] *v.* **-lized, -liz•ing. 1** cause the cross-fertilization of. **2** be subjected to cross-fertilization.

cross•fire ['krɒs,faɪr] *n.* **1** gunfire coming from two or more opposite directions so as to cross. **2** a verbal attack from two or more sources or directions.

cross fox a colour phase of the red fox in which there is a dark stripe down the back and across the shoulders.

cross–grained ['krɒs ,greind] *adj.* **1** of wood, having the grain running across the regular grain; having an irregular or gnarled grain. **2** hard to get along with; contrary.

cross hairs fine strands stretched across the focal plane of an optical instrument for accurately defining the line of sight.

cross•hatch ['krɒs,hætʃ] *v.* mark or shade with two sets of parallel lines crossing each other.

cross•hatch•ing ['krɒs,hætʃɪŋ] *n.* shading made with intersecting sets of parallel lines.

cross–in•dex ['krɒs 'ɪndɛks] *v., n. —v.* in an index, accompany (an item) by a direction referring the reader to another place in the same index.
—n. such a cross-reference.

cross•ing ['krɒsɪŋ] *n., v. —n.* **1** a place where things cross each other. **2** a place at which a street, river, etc., may be crossed. **3** the act of crossing, especially a voyage across water. **4** crossbreeding.
—v. ppr. of CROSS.

crossing guard a member of a school patrol, or other individual, who escorts children across busy streets.

cross•ing-over ['krɒsɪŋ 'ouvər] *n.* CROSSOVER (def. 4).

cross•jack ['krɒs,dʒæk] *n.* a square sail on the lower yard of a mizzenmast.

cross–leg•ged ['krɒs ,lɛgɪd] *or* ['krɒs ,lɛgd] *adv.* **1** with the ankles crossed and the knees bent and spread wide apart: *We all sat cross-legged on the floor.* **2** with one leg crossed in front of the other: *standing cross-legged.*

cross•let ['krɒslɪt] *n.* a small cross.

Cross of Valour *Cdn.* Canada's highest award for bravery, given for extraordinary heroism in circumstances of extreme peril. It is the highest of a series of three bravery decorations, the other two being the Star of Courage and the Medal of Bravery. *Abbrev.:* CV Also, **Cross of Valor.**

cros•sop•te•ryg•ian [krɒ,sɒptə'rɪdʒən] *or* [krə,sɒptə'rɪdʒən] *n.* any of various fish of the Crossopterygii group of which all but the coelacanth are extinct, thought to be the ancestors of amphibians and land animals. ⟨< NL *Crossopterygii* name of the group < Gk. *krosso*; fringe + *pteryx* wing, fin⟩

cross•o•ver ['krɒs,ouvər] *n.* **1** a place at which a crossing is made. **2** anything that crosses over or connects, as a bridge over a highway. **3** a transferring or crossing over. **4** *Genetics.* the interchange of segments between paired chromosomes during the first meiotic division in the process of forming reproductive cells.

cross•patch ['krɒs,pætʃ] *n. Informal.* a cross, bad-tempered person.

cross•piece ['krɒs,pis] *n.* a piece that is placed across something.

cross–pol•li•nate ['krɒs 'pɒlə,neit] *v.* **-nat•ed, -nat•ing. 1** cause cross-pollination in. **2** be subjected to cross-pollination.

cross–pol•li•na•tion [,krɒs ,pɒlə'neiʃən] *n.* the transfer of pollen from the anther of one flower to the stigma of another. Insects and wind are agents of cross-pollination.

cross–product ['krɒs ,prɒdəkt] *n.* a vector which is at right angles to two other vectors, with a magnitude equal to the product of the magnitude of the two vectors and the sine of the angle between the two; vector product.

cross–ques•tion *v.* ['krɒs 'kwɛstʃən]; *n.* ['krɒs ,kwɛstʃən] *v., n. —v.* question closely or severely; cross-examine.
—n. a question asked in cross-examining.

cross•rail ['krɒs,reil] *n.* a piece of wood, metal, etc., that lies across something.

cross–re•fer [,krɒs rɪ'fɜr] *v.* **-ferred, -fer•ring. 1** refer from one part to another. **2** make a cross reference.

cross–ref•er•ence ['krɒs 'rɛfərəns] *n., v.* **-er•enced, -er•enc•ing.** *—n.* a reference or instruction in one part of a book, index, etc., to another part for more information. Under **crupper,** the instruction "See HARNESS for picture" is a

cross-reference. In this dictionary, cross-references are printed in SMALL CAPITALS.
—*v.* cross-refer.

cross•road ['krɒs,roud] *n.* **1** a road that crosses another. **2** a road connecting main roads. **3 crossroads, a** a place where roads cross (*used with a singular or plural verb*): *We said we would wait for them at the crossroads.* **b** a critical point, especially where a decision has to be made (*used with a singular verb*): *The country is now at an economic crossroads.* **c** a centre of activity for a region.

cross•ruff ['krɒs,rʌf] *n., v.* —*n. Card games.* a play in which each of two partners leads a card that the other can trump.
—*v.* trump cards in this way.

cross section 1 a cutting across; a cutting made at right angles to an axis: *Tomatoes are usually sliced by making a series of cross sections.* **2** a part cut off in this way. **3** a drawing, etc., of the surface exposed by such a cutting. **4** a small selection of people, things, etc., thought to be typical of all the members of a larger, whole group to which they belong, and chosen to stand for the whole group; a representative sample: *The newspaper wanted to get the views of a cross section of the community.* **5** *Physics.* a measure of the probability that a given interaction will occur, especially between subatomic particles, expressed as the geometric area that must be attributed to individual particles to account for the frequency of occurrence.

cross–staff ['krɒs ,stæf] *n. Surveying.* an instrument for measuring distances at right angles to the main line.

cross–stitch ['krɒs ,stɪtʃ] *n., v.* —*n.* **1** one stitch crossed over another, forming an X. **2** embroidery made with this stitch. See EMBROIDERY for picture.
—*v.* embroider or sew with cross-stitches.

cross street 1 a street that crosses another. **2** a street connecting main streets.

cross talk 1 *Radio and Telephone.* interference from another frequency or line. **2** idle chatter. **3** *Esp. Brit.* witty dialogue between comedians. **—'cross-,talk,** *adj.*

cross•tie ['krɒs,taɪ] *n.* a heavy piece of timber or iron placed crosswise to form a foundation or support. The rails of a railway track are fastened to crossties about 30 cm apart.

cross•town ['krɒs,taʊn] *adj., adv.* —*adj.* that runs across the town or city: *a crosstown bus.*
—*adv.* across the town.

cross•trees ['krɒs,triz] *n.pl.* two horizontal bars of wood near the top of a sailing ship's mast. See MAST for picture.

cross•walk ['krɒs,wɒk] *n.* a street crossing marked with white or yellow lines: *In some cities approaching vehicles must stop when pedestrians are using a crosswalk.*

cross•way ['krɒs,wei] *n.* CROSSROAD (defs. 1, 2).

cross•ways ['krɒs,weiz] *adv.* crosswise.

cross•wind ['krɒs,wɪnd] *n.* a wind blowing across the intended flight path of an aircraft, or the sailing route of a ship: *Crosswinds caused the captain to change course.*

cross•wise ['krɒs,waɪz] *adv.* **1** so as to cross; across. **2** in the form of a cross. **3** opposite to what is required; wrongly.

cross•word puzzle ['krɒs,wɜrd] a puzzle with numbered clues to certain words and with sets of blank squares to be filled in, one letter to a square, with the answers. Some of the words read across and some downwards so that some letters belong to two words that cross each other.

cross•yard ['krɒs,jɑrd] *n.* on a ship, a pole or spar fastened crosswise.

cro•ta•mi•ton [krou'tæmə,tɒn] *n.* a drug used to relieve itching and cure scabies.

crotch [krɒtʃ] *n.* **1** a forked piece or part; place where a tree, bough, etc., divides into two limbs or branches. **2** the place where the human body divides into its two legs. **3** the seam at the join of the legs of a pair of pants, shorts, or underpants. ⟨var. of *crutch*⟩

crotched [krɒtʃt] *adj.* having a crotch; forked.

crotch•et ['krɒtʃɪt] *n.* **1** an odd notion; unreasonable whim. **2** a small hook or hooklike part. **3** *Brit. Music.* a quarter note. ⟨ME < OF *crochet,* dim. of *croc* hook < Gmc. Doublet of CROCHET, CROCKET.⟩

crotch•et•y ['krɒtʃəti] *adj.* full of odd notions or unreasonable whims. **—'crotch•et•i•ness,** *n.*

crot•on ['kroutən] *n.* **1** any of a genus (*Codiaeum*) of shrubs of the spurge family, especially a tropical shrub (*C. variegatum*) native to Malaysia, widely cultivated for its showy, many-coloured leaves that may be flat or crinkled and may have smooth or deeply lobed edges. **2** any of a genus (*Croton*) of mostly tropical shrubs, trees, and herbs also of the spurge family, especially one (*C. tigilium*) whose seeds yield croton oil. ⟨< NL < Gk. *krotōn* tick[2]⟩

croton bug a small, winged cockroach (*Blatella germanica*).

cro•ton•ic acid [krou'tɒnɪk] a colourless crystalline solid used to make resins, etc. *Formula*: $C_4H_6O_2$

croton oil a thick, bitter oil obtained from the seeds of the CROTON (def. 2), used as a counter-irritant and formerly also used internally as a strong cathartic.

crouch [krʌutʃ] *v., n.* —*v.* **1** stoop low with legs bent like an animal ready to spring, or in hiding, or shrinking in fear. **2** bow down in a timid or slavish manner; cower. **3** bend low.
—*n.* **1** the act or state of crouching. **2** a crouching position. A baseball catcher's squatting stance is called a crouch. ⟨ME < OF *crochir* < *croc* hook < Gmc.⟩

croup[1] [krup] *n.* an inflammation or diseased condition of the throat and windpipe characterized by a hoarse cough and difficult breathing. ⟨< *croup*, v., ? blend of *croak* and *whoop*⟩

croup[2] [krup] *n.* the rump of a horse, etc. See HORSE for picture. ⟨ME < OF *croupe* < Gmc.⟩

crou•pi•er ['krupiər] *n.* the attendant at a gambling table who rakes in the money and pays the winners. ⟨< F *croupier* < *croupe*; see CROUP[2]; originally, one who rides behind⟩

croup•y ['krupi] *adj.* **1** sick with croup. **2** hoarse and having difficulty in breathing. **3** of croup; resembling croup.

crou•stade [kru'stɑd] *n.* a dish comprising a shell of bread, pastry, rice or potatoes, filled with something savoury, such as ragout, mushrooms, etc. ⟨< F < Provençal *crustado* < L *crustatus* pp. of *crustare* to encrust < *crusta* crust⟩

crou•ton ['krutɒn] *or* [kru'tɒn] *n.* a small piece of toasted or fried bread, often served in soup and salads. ⟨< F *croûton* < *croûte* crust < L *crusta*⟩

crow[1] [krou] *n., v.* **crowed** (or **crew** for 1), **crowed, crow•ing.**
—*n.* **1** a loud cry made by a rooster. **2** a happy sound made by a baby. **3** an exultant or triumphant cry. **4 Crow,** Corvus, a southern constellation between Virgo and Hydra.
—*v.* **1** make the cry of a rooster. **2** make the happy sound of a baby. **3** show happiness and pride; boast: *The winning team crowed over its victory.* ⟨OE *crāwan*; imitative⟩

crow[2] [krou] *n.* **1** any of various large, glossy-black birds (genus *Corvus*) that are somewhat smaller than most ravens, having a loud, harsh call. The common crow of North America is *Corvus brachyrhynchos.* **2** any of various other birds of the same family (Corvidae). **3** crowbar.
as the crow flies, in a straight line: *It's about 5 km away as the crow flies, but nearly 10 km by road.*
eat crow, *Informal.* be forced to do something very disagreeable and humiliating. ⟨OE *crāwe*⟩

Crow [krou] *n., pl.* **Crow** or **Crows. 1** member of an American Indian people living in Montana and Wyoming. **2** the Siouan language of this people.

crow•bar ['krou,bɑr] *n.* a strong iron or steel bar with a bent, forked, flattened end, used as a lever.

crow•ber•ry ['krou,bɛri] *n., pl.* **-ries. 1** a low-growing evergreen shrub (*Empetrum nigrum*) of the cool regions of the northern hemisphere having a small, black, berrylike fruit that is edible but insipid in taste. **2** any of various other plants of the same family (Empetraceae). **3** the fruit of any of these plants.

crow–boot ['krou ,but] *n. Cdn.* a mukluk, usually made of muskrat fur and having a thick moosehide sole.

crowd [kraʊd] *n., v.* —*n.* **1** a large number of people together: *A crowd gathered to hear the speaker.* **2** the common people; people in general; the masses: *Many newspapers appeal to the crowd.* **3** *Informal.* group; set: *The boy went out with his crowd to the dance.* **4** a large number of things together.
—*v.* **1** collect in large numbers. **2** fill; fill too full with people, etc.: *to crowd a bus.* **3** squeeze; cram into too small a space: *They crowded three motorbikes into one parking space.* **4** push; shove, especially in a mass or crowd. **5** press forward; of a large group, force its way: *to crowd into a building.* **6** *Slang.* pressure someone, as by harassing or tormenting.
crowd on sail, raise more sails to make a ship go faster.
crowd out, exclude because of lack of space. ⟨OE *crūdan* press⟩

☛ *Syn. n.* **1. Crowd,** THRONG, SWARM[1] = a large number of people together. **Crowd** applies to a large number of people pressed closely together without much order: *A crowd was waiting in the lobby.* **Throng** suggests still larger numbers and more movement of pressing together and pushing forward: *At Christmas there are throngs in the streets.* **Swarm** emphasizes the idea of a large, confused, moving mass: *A swarm of students gathered.*

crowd•ed ['kraʊdɪd] *adj., v.* —*adj.* **1** filled with a crowd. **2** filled; filled too full; packed. **3** close together; too close together.
—*v.* pt. and pp. of CROWD. —**'crowd•ed•ly,** *adv.*
—**'crowd•ed•ness,** *n.*

crow•foot ['krou,fʊt] *n., pl.* **-foots** *for 1,* **-feet** *for 3, 4, 5.* **1** any of several plants (genus *Ranunculus*) having yellow or white flowers and deeply lobed leaves that look somewhat like a bird's foot. See also BUTTERCUP. **2** (*adjl.*) designating the family (Ranunculaceae) that includes the crowfoots, buttercups, columbines, and anemones, more often called the buttercup family. **3** an arrangement of small ropes used to suspend awnings, etc., on a ship. **4** a piece of zinc used as one of the poles or electrodes in some kinds of batteries. **5** formerly, an iron ball having four spikes, thrown on the ground to hinder the advance of enemy cavalry.

crown ['kraʊn] *n., v.* —*n.* **1** a head covering of precious metal and jewels, worn by a monarch. **2 the Crown, a** the power and authority of a monarch, or of the officials who exercise that authority; royal power. **b** a monarch acting in his or her official capacity. **3** a monarch; a king, queen, etc. **4** (*adjl.*) of a crown; having to do with a crown: *the crown jewels.* **5** a design or thing shaped like a crown. **6** a wreath for the head: *The winner of the race received a crown.* **7** an honour; reward. **8** the head. **9** the top; highest part: *the crown of the head, the crown of a hat.* **10** the highest state or quality of anything. **11 a** the part of a tooth outside the gum. **b** the chewing surface of a tooth. **c** an artificial substitute for either of these. **12** a former British silver coin, worth 5 shillings. **13** a coin or unit of money in various countries, translated as 'crown', such as the krone. **14** the end of an anchor between the arms. **15** *Botany.* **a** the corona of a flower or seed. **b** the top of a root of a plant, from which the stem arises. **c** the leaves and branches of a tree or shrub. **16** the crest of a bird. **17** the tip of a deer's horn. **18** a size of printing paper, usually 38.1 × 50.8 cm.
—*v.* **1** put a crown on; make king, queen, etc. **2** honour; reward. **3** be on top of; cover the highest part of: *A fort crowns the hill.* **4** make perfect or complete; add the finishing touch to: *Success crowned her efforts.* **5** supply (a tooth) with a crown. **6** *Checkers.* make a king of (a piece that has been moved across the checkerboard). **7** *Informal.* hit on the head. **8** of forest fires, spread rapidly from treetop to treetop. ⟨ME < AF *coroune* < L *corona* garland, wreath, crown. Doublet of CORONA.⟩
☛ *Syn. n.* **9, 10.** See note at TOP.

A crown: the Empress Wu of China (A.D.690-705)

Crown attorney *Cdn.* a lawyer who represents the Crown (the government) in a trial.

crown cap a type of bottle top whose edges are pinched together to hold the glass.

crown colony a colony under the power and authority of the British government.

Crown corporation *Cdn.* a legal agency or company through which the Government of Canada or one of the provincial governments carries on certain activities. Air Canada, the CBC, and the St. Lawrence Seaway Authority are Crown corporations.

crown court *Brit.* a court of criminal jurisdiction holding periodic sessions in towns of England and Wales.

crown fire *Cdn.* a forest fire that spreads from treetop to treetop.

crown gear a gear that transmits power from the drive shaft to the axle of an automobile. See DIFFERENTIAL for picture.

crown glass 1 a very clear glass used in optical instruments. **2** an old kind of window glass that is in round sheets with a thick part in the middle.

crown jewels jewels that are a traditional part of the regalia of a royal family: *The British crown jewels are kept in the Tower of London.*

crown land 1 public land; land belonging to a government whose official head of state is a monarch. **2** land that is the personal property of a monarch.

crown prince the eldest living son of a king, queen, etc.; the heir apparent to a kingdom.

crown princess 1 the wife of a crown prince. **2** a woman or girl who is heir apparent to a kingdom.

Crown prosecutor *Cdn.* CROWN ATTORNEY.

crown roast a roast of ribs, usually lamb, tied in a circle with paper coverings on the tips.

crown vetch a plant (*Coronilla varia*) of the legume family, native to Europe, having clusters of pink or white flowers, and often grown in the New World to control erosion on roadsides. Also called **axseed.**

Crow rate *Cdn.* the fee charged by the government for transportation of grain. ⟨after *Crow's Nest Pass*, on the border between Alberta and British Columbia⟩

crow's–foot ['krouz ,fʊt] *n., pl.* **-feet. 1** Usually, **crow's-feet,** *pl.* wrinkles at the outer corners of the eyes. **2** a three-pointed embroidered design used to finish the ends of seams, openings, etc. **3** CROWFOOT (def. 3).

crow's–nest or **crows–nest** ['krouz ,nɛst] *n.* **1** a small, enclosed platform near the top of a ship's mast, used by the lookout. **2** any similar platform ashore.

cro•zier ['krouʒər] See CROSIER.

CRT *n., pl.* **CRT's** or **CRTs.** CATHODE-RAY TUBE.

CRTC CANADIAN RADIO-TELEVISION AND TELECOMMUNICATIONS COMMISSION.

cru•cial ['kruʃəl] *adj.* **1** very important; critical; decisive. **2** *Rare.* very trying; severe. **3** *Medicine.* having the form of a cross; cross-shaped. ⟨< NL (medical) *crucialis* < L *crux, crucis* cross; with reference to the fork of a road⟩ —**'cru•cial•ly,** *adv.*

cru•ces ['krusiz] *n.* a pl. of CRUX.

cru•ci•ate ['kruʃiɪt] *or* ['kruʃi,eit] *adj.* **1** shaped like a cross. **2** *Botany.* having leaves or flowers shaped like a cross with equal arms, such as mustard. **3** *Zoology.* of wings, especially of insects, crossing diagonally when folded. ⟨< NL *cruciatus*, pp. of *cruciare* crucify⟩

cru•ci•ble ['krusəbəl] *n.* **1** a container in which metals, ores, etc., can be melted. **2** a severe test or trial. ⟨< Med.L *crucibulum* originally, night lamp⟩

crucible steel good quality steel melted in a crucible and used for making knives.

cru•ci•fer ['krusɪfər] *n., adj.* —*n.* **1** a person who carries the cross in a Christian procession. **2** a cruciferous plant.
—*adj.* cruciferous. ⟨< Ecclesiastical LL < L *crux* cross + *ferre* to bear⟩

cru•ci•fer•ous [kru'sɪfərəs] *adj.* of or having to do with the family Cruciferae of plants, including the mustards, cabbage, broccoli and other plants with cross-shaped leaves or flowers.

cru•ci•fix ['krusə,fɪks] *n.* **1** a cross with a figure of the crucified Christ on it. **2** a cross. ⟨< LL *crucifixus*, alteration of L *cruci fixus* fixed to a cross < *crux* cross and *fixus*, pp. of *figere* fasten⟩

cru•ci•fix•ion [,krusə'fɪkʃən] *n.* **1** the act of crucifying or being crucified. **2 the Crucifixion, a** the crucifying of Christ. **b** a picture, statue, etc., of Christ's death on the cross.

cru•ci•form ['krusə,fɔrm] *adj.* shaped like a cross. ⟨< L *crux, crucis* cross + E *-form* shaped (< L *-formis*)⟩

cru•ci•fy ['krusə,faɪ] *v.* **-fied, -fy•ing. 1** put to death by nailing or binding the hands and feet to a cross. **2** treat severely; persecute; torture. **3** blame and punish for the errors and crimes of someone else: *The newspapers crucified the mayor for a mistake made by his secretary.* ⟨ME < OF *crucifier* < LL *crucifigere* (alteration of L *cruci figere*; see CRUCIFIX); influenced by OF verbs ending in *-fier* (< L *-ficare*)⟩ —**'cru•ci,fi•er,** *n.*

crude [krud] *adj.* **crud•er, crud•est;** *n.* —*adj.* **1** in a natural or raw state; not yet prepared for use; unprocessed; unanalysed: *crude rubber, crude statistics.* **2** not skilfully or carefully made or done; rough, careless, or unfinished: *a crude shack, a crude attempt.* **3** lacking taste, grace, or tact; rude or vulgar: *a crude remark.* **4** bare and undisguised or unadorned: *the crude truth.* **5** *Archaic.* immature; unripe.
—*n. Informal.* CRUDE OIL; petroleum. ⟨< L *crudus* raw⟩
—**'crude•ly,** *adv.* —**'crude•ness,** *n.*
☛ *Syn.* **1.** See note at RAW.

crude oil petroleum as it comes from the well, before it is refined.

cru•di•tés [ˌkrudɪ'tei]; *French,* [kʀydi'te] *n.pl.* small pieces of raw vegetable, eaten as an appetizer or snack, usually with dip. ⟨< F, raw things⟩

cru•di•ty ['krudəti] *n., pl.* **-ties. 1** a crude quality or condition; roughness; lack of finish. **2** a crude action, thing, etc.

cru•el ['kruəl] *adj.* **1** fond of causing much pain to others and delighting in their suffering; not caring about the pain and suffering of others: *a cruel master.* **2** showing a cruel nature: *cruel acts.* **3** causing much pain and suffering: *a cruel war.* ⟨ME < OF < L *crudelis* rough. Related to CRUDE.⟩ **—'cru•el•ly,** *adv.* **—'cru•el•ness,** *n.*

☛ *Hom.* CREWEL.

☛ *Syn.* **1. Cruel,** BRUTAL, PITILESS = unfeeling in treatment of people and animals. **Cruel** emphasizes the idea of being completely untouched by the suffering of others and suggests taking pleasure in watching it or in causing pain: *Most people abhor cruel behaviour.* **Brutal** suggests the cruelty of a wild animal, shown by unrestrained force and fury: *The brutal captors beat their prisoners.* **Pitiless** means completely without pity or willingness to show mercy to those who are suffering: *The pitiless woman refused to help the poor sick girl.*

cru•el•ty ['kruəlti] *n., pl.* **-ties. 1** the state or condition of being cruel; readiness to give pain to others or to delight in their suffering. **2** a cruel act. **3** *Law.* behaviour by a spouse that causes physical harm or mental suffering.

cru•et ['kruɪt] *n.* **1** a glass bottle to hold vinegar, oil, etc., for the table. **2** a set of such bottles on a stand. ⟨ME < OF *cruet,* dim. of *cruie* pot < Gmc.⟩

cruise [kruz] *v.* **cruised, cruis•ing;** *n.* —*v.* **1** sail about from place to place on pleasure or business; sail over or about: *He bought a yacht so that he could cruise along the coast. They spent the summer cruising the Caribbean.* **2** journey or travel from place to place (in), with or without a special destination: *The taxi cruised about in search of passengers. Many police cars are cruising the streets.* **3** travel in an aircraft or automobile at the speed of maximum mechanical efficiency. **4** *Logging. Cdn.* examine (a tract of forest) to estimate the value of the timber on it, especially for a logging company.
—*n.* **1** the act of sailing about from place to place on pleasure or business. **2** *(adjl.)* having to do with a cruise: *a cruise ship.* **3** *Informal.* CRUISE MISSILE. ⟨< Du. *kruisen* move, especially, sail crosswise < *kruis* cross < L *crux*⟩

☛ *Hom.* CRUSE.

cruise control in a vehicle, a device to maintain engine speed at a constant rate.

cruise missile a guided missile that may be sent off from an aircraft or ship and that travels at low altitudes in order to escape detection by radar.

cruis•er ['kruzər] *n.* **1** a warship with less armour and more speed than a battleship. **2** an aircraft, taxi, power boat, etc., that cruises. **3** a police car connected with headquarters by radio; a patrol car or scout car used for patrolling streets and highways. **4** *Cdn.* a person employed by a logging company to estimate the volume of timber standing on a particular acreage. **5** a person who goes on a cruise. **6** CABIN CRUISER.

cruis•er•weight ['kruzərˌweit] *n. Brit.* a boxer weighing no more than 86.18 kg.

cruising radius the maximum distance that an aircraft, ship, etc., can travel from its base and back without refuelling.

crul•ler ['krʌlər] *n.* a kind of doughnut made by twisting together pieces of rich, sweet dough and frying them in fat. Also, **kruller.** ⟨apparently < Du. *kruller* < *krullen* curl⟩

crumb [krʌm] *n., interj., v.* —*n.* **1** a very small piece of bread, cake, etc., broken from a larger piece. **2** the soft, inside part of bread. **3** a little bit: *a crumb of comfort.* **4** *Informal.* a worthless person; a person of no importance. Also, **crumbum.**
—*interj.* a mild exclamation of disappointment, frustration, etc.
—*v.* **1** break into crumbs. **2** cover with crumbs for frying or baking. **3** *Informal.* brush or wipe the crumbs from (a tablecloth, etc.). ⟨OE *cruma*⟩

crum•ble ['krʌmbəl] *v.* **-bled, -bling.,** *n.* —*v.* **1** break into very small pieces or crumbs. **2** fall to pieces; decay: *The old wall was crumbling away at the edges.*
—*n.* a dessert dish consisting of fruit with a crisp crumb topping: *peach crumble.* ⟨earlier *crimble* < OE *(ge)crymman* < *cruma* crumb⟩

crum•bly ['krʌmbli] *adj.* **-bli•er, -bli-est.** tending to crumble; easily crumbled. **—'crum•bli•ness,** *n.*

crum•bum ['krʌmbəm] *n.* CRUMB (def. 4).

crumb•y ['krʌmi] *adj.* **crumb•i•er, crumb•i•est. 1** full of crumbs. **2** soft like the inside part of bread. **3** *Slang.* crummy. **—'crumb•i•ness,** *n.*

☛ *Hom.* CRUMMY.

crum•horn ['krʌmˌhɔrn] *n.* an early musical instrument having a double reed and a tube which is bent at the end. Also, **krummhorn, krumhorn.** ⟨< G *krumm* bent⟩

crum•my ['krʌmi] *adj.* **-mi•er, -mi•est;** *n., pl.* **-mies.** *Slang.* —*adj.* cheap; shoddy; inferior.
—*n. Logging. Cdn.* an old truck or van used to take loggers to and from their work site. ⟨var. of *crumby*⟩ **—'crum•mi•ness,** *n.*

☛ *Hom.* CRUMBY.

crump [krʌmp] *v. or n. Brit.* crunch.

crum•pet ['krʌmpɪt] *n.* a round, flat cake, thicker than a pancake, baked on a griddle. Crumpets are usually toasted and eaten with butter while hot. ⟨OE *crompeht* full of crumples⟩

crum•ple ['krʌmpəl] *v.* **-pled, -pling;** *n.* —*v.* **1** crush together; wrinkle: *She crumpled the letter into a ball.* **2** fall down; collapse: *The boxer crumpled to the floor.* **3** make (something or someone) collapse: *The blow crumpled him.* **4** become crumpled.
—*n.* a wrinkle made by crushing something together. ⟨OE *crump* bent⟩

crunch [krʌntʃ] *v., n.* —*v.* **1** crush noisily with the teeth. **2** produce a noise like that of teeth crushing something hard: *The hard snow crunched under our feet.* **3** proceed with such a noise: *The children crunched through the snow.*
—*n.* **1** the act or sound of crunching. **2** *Informal.* a crucial stage or turning point; crisis. **3** *Informal.* shortage; squeeze: *the oil crunch.* ⟨earlier *cra(u)nch;* apparently influenced by *crush, munch*⟩

crunch•y ['krʌntʃi] *adj.* **crunch•i•er, crunch•i•est.** brittle and crackling. **—'crunch•i•ness,** *n.*

crun•nick ['krʌnɪk] *n. Cdn. Maritimes* a dry, twisted piece of wood for a fire. ⟨? < O Irish *crann* tree⟩

crup•per ['krʌpər] *n.* **1** a strap attached to the back of a harness and passing under a horse's tail. See HARNESS for picture. **2** the rump of a horse. ⟨ME < OF *cropier* < *crope* croup[2] < Gmc.⟩

cru•ral ['krʊrəl] *adj. Anatomy.* of the leg. ⟨< L *cruralis* < *crus, cruris* leg⟩

crus [krʌs] *or* [krʊs] *n.* **1** the calf of the leg. **2** any leglike appendage. ⟨< L, leg, shank⟩

cru•sade [kru'seid] *n., v.* **-sad•ed, -sad•ing.** —*n.* **1** Often, **Crusade,** any one of the Christian military expeditions between the years 1096 and 1272 whose aim was to recover the Holy Land from the Muslims. **2** a war having a religious purpose and approved by religious authorities. **3** an evangelistic campaign; a revival. **4** a vigorous campaign against a public evil or in favour of some new idea: *the crusade against tuberculosis.*
—*v.* take part in a crusade. ⟨anglicization of earlier *crusada* < Sp. *cruzada,* ult. < L *crux* cross⟩

cru•sad•er [kru'seidər] *n.* **1** a person who takes part in a crusade. **2 Crusader,** a person who took part in any of the Crusades to recover the Holy Land from the Muslims.

cruse [kruz] *or* [krus] *n. Archaic.* a jug, pot, or bottle made of earthenware. ⟨< MDu. *croes*⟩

☛ *Hom.* CRUISE [kruz].

crush [krʌʃ] *v., n.* —*v.* **1** squeeze together so violently as to break or bruise. **2** wrinkle or crease by wear or rough handling: *His hat was crushed when the girl sat on it.* **3** break into fine pieces or reduce to pulp by grinding, pounding, or pressing. **4** flatten by heavy pressure. **5** subdue with force; conquer. **6** oppress or burden; overwhelm with disappointment, humiliation, etc.: *He was crushed by her refusal to marry him.* **7** crowd (*usually used with* **into,** etc.): *Too many people crushed into the auction room.*
—*n.* **1** a crushing or being crushed. **2** a violent pressure like grinding or pounding. **3** a mass of people crowded close together. **4** *Slang.* **a** a sudden, strong liking for a person. **b** the object of a sudden, strong liking. ⟨ME *crusch(en),* apparently < OF *croissir* < Gmc.⟩ **—'crush•a•ble,** *adj.* **—'crush•er,** *n.*

crust [krʌst] *n., v.* —*n.* **1** the hard, outside part of bread, rolls, etc. **2** a piece of this; any hard, dry piece of bread, etc. **3** the baked outside covering of a pie. **4** any hard outside covering: *The snow had a crust that was thick enough to walk on.* **5** *Geology.* the outer layer of the earth, about 30-50 km thick, composed of rock. See CORE for picture. **6** *Slang.* nerve; impudence; gall: *She has a lot of crust to come barging in here like that.*
—*v.* **1** cover or become covered with a crust. **2** form or collect into a crust. ⟨< L *crusta* rind⟩ **—'crust,like,** *adj.*

crus•ta•cean [krʌ'steiʃən] *n., adj.* —*n.* any of a large class (Crustacea) of arthropods, most of them water animals, having

hard shells, jointed bodies with appendages, and two pairs of antennae. Barnacles, crabs, lobsters, shrimps, and wood lice are crustaceans.
–adj. of or having to do with crustaceans. ⟨< NL < L *crusta* shell, rind⟩

crus•ta•ceous [krʌ'steiʃəs] *adj.* **1** crustacean. **2** having a shell or crust. **3** of or like a crust.

crus•tal ['krʌstəl] *adj.* of or having to do with a crust, especially of the earth or moon.

crust•y ['krʌsti] *adj.* **crust•i•er, crust•i•est. 1** having a crust; crustlike: *crusty bread.* **2** bad-tempered or harsh in manner, speech, etc. **–'crust•i•ly,** *adv.* **–'crust•i•ness,** *n.*

crutch [krʌtʃ] *n. v.* *–n.* **1** a support to help a lame or disabled person walk, usually consisting of a long, rubber-tipped staff with a padded crosspiece at the top that fits under the armpit, and a handgrip lower down. **2** a support or brace with a forked top. **3** anything that serves as a prop or support: *She is such a poor manager that she has to use her assistant as a crutch.*
–v. support with or as if with a crutch; prop. ⟨OE *crycc*⟩

crux [krʌks]. *n., pl.* **crux•es** or **cru•ces** ['krusiz]. **1** the essential or crucial part; the most important point. **2** a puzzling or perplexing question; difficult point to explain. **3 Crux,** *Astronomy.* Southern Cross. **4** *Heraldry.* a cross. ⟨< L, *crux, crucis* cross. Doublet of CROSS.⟩

crux an•sa•ta ['krʌks æn'seitə] *n.* a cross with a loop rather than a vertical branch at the top; ankh. ⟨< L, cross with a handle⟩

crwth [kruθ] *n.* an ancient Celtic musical instrument like a violin, but rectangular, and played with a bow. ⟨< Welsh⟩

cry [kraɪ] *v.* **cried, cry•ing;** *n., pl.* **cries.** *–v.* **1** make a sound that shows pain, fear, sorrow, etc. **2** shed tears; weep. **3** bring (oneself) to a particular state by continuous crying: *The infant cried itself into a frenzy.* **4** of an animal, make its usual noise or call. **5** call loudly; shout. **6** announce in public: *Peddlers cried their wares in the street. The king ordered the news cried in the streets.*
cry down, make little of; speak of as unimportant or of little value; depreciate.
cry off, break an agreement; refuse to do something.
cry (one's) **eyes** or **heart out,** shed many tears.
cry out, a call loudly; shout. **b** scream; yell. **c** complain.
cry (out) for, a ask earnestly for; beg for. **b** need very much.
cry up, praise; speak of as important or valuable.
–n. **1** a sound made by a person or animal that shows some strong feeling, such as pain, fear, anger, or sorrow; noise that shows grief, pain, etc. **2** a spell of shedding tears; fit of weeping. **3** the noise or call of an animal: *a gull's cry, the cry of the wolf.* **4** a loud call; shout: *a cry for help, cries of joy.* **5** a call to action; slogan: *"Forward" was the army's cry as it attacked.* **6** a public announcement; proclamation: *a peddler's cry.* **7** an opinion generally expressed; public voice. **8** an appeal; entreaty. **9 a** the yelping of hounds in the chase. **b** a pack of hounds.
a far cry, a a long way (*from*). **b** very different (*from*).
in full cry, in close pursuit. ⟨ME < OF *crier* < L *quiritare,* originally, implore the aid of the *Quirites* or Roman citizens⟩

cry•ba•by ['kraɪ,beibi] *n., pl.* **-bies. 1** a person, especially a child, who cries easily or pretends to be hurt. **2** someone who makes a fuss over a loss or defeat.

cry•ing ['kraɪɪŋ] *adj., v.* *–adj.* **1** that cries. **2** demanding attention; very bad: *a crying evil.*
–v. ppr. of CRY.

cryo– *combining form.* cold; frost or freezing. ⟨< Gk. *kryos* frost⟩

cry•o•bi•ol•o•gist [,kraɪoubaɪ'ɒlədʒɪst] *n.* a person trained in cryobiology, especially one whose work it is.

cry•o•bi•ol•o•gy [,kraɪoubaɪ'ɒlədʒi] *n.* the branch of biology dealing with the effects of very low temperatures on organisms, especially warm-blooded animals.

cry•o•gen ['kraɪədʒən] *n.* a substance for producing low temperatures.

cry•o•gen•ic [,kraɪə'dʒɛnɪk] *n., adj.* *–n.* **cryogenics,** the branch of physics dealing with the production of extremely low temperatures, approaching absolute zero, and the effect of such temperatures on matter (*used with a singular verb*).
–adj. of or having to do with cryogens or cryogenics.

cry•o•hy•drate [,kraɪou'haɪdreit] *n.* a mixture of ice and another substance, such as salt, designed to reduce the minimum freezing temperature.

cry•o•lite ['kraɪə,ləit] *n.* a fluoride of sodium and aluminum found in Greenland. It is used in making soda, aluminum, etc. *Formula:* Na_3AlF_6

cry•om•e•ter [kraɪ'ɒmətər] *n.* a thermometer designed to measure lower temperatures than a mercury thermometer can.

cry•on•ics [kraɪ'ɒnɪks] *n.* the rapid freezing of a body immediately after death, in an attempt to preserve it so that it might be brought back to life in the future. ⟨< Gk. *kryos* frost + E *-onics*⟩ **–cry'on•ic,** *adj.*

cry•o•phyte ['kraɪə,fəit] *n.* a plant, such as algae or some mosses, that can grow on ice or snow.

cry•o•probe ['kraɪə,proub] *n.* a surgical instrument designed to convey intense cold to a diseased part of the body, in order to destroy it.

cry•o•sur•gery [,kraɪou'sɜrdʒəri] *n.* surgery that uses very low temperatures to destroy diseased tissue. **–,cry•o'sur•gi•cal,** *adj.*

cry•o•ther•a•py [,kraɪou'θɛrəpi] *n.* the use of low temperatures in the treatment of disease or injury.

crypt [krɪpt] *n.* **1** an underground room or vault. The crypt beneath the main floor of a church was formerly often used as a burial place. **2** *Anatomy.* any small cavity in the body, as a follicle or glandular hollow. ⟨< L *crypta* < Gk. *kryptē* vault < *kryptos* hidden. Doublet of GROTTO.⟩

crypt•a•nal•y•sis [,krɪptə'næləsɪs] *n.* the deciphering of messages written in a code for which the key is not known.

cryp•tic ['krɪptɪk] *adj.* **1** having a hidden meaning; secret; mysterious: *a cryptic message, a cryptic reply.* **2** *Zoology.* designed to camouflage, as the shape or colour of some animals. Sometimes, **cryptical.** ⟨< LL *crypticus* < Gk. *kryptikos* < *kryptos* hidden⟩ **–'cryp•ti•cal•ly,** *adv.*

crypto– *combining form.* secret or hidden, as in *cryptogram.* Also, before vowels, **crypt-.** ⟨< Gk. *kryptos* hidden⟩

cryp•to•gam ['krɪptə,gæm] *n.* any plant that does not produce flowers or seeds, but reproduces by means of spores, including algae, fungi, ferns, and mosses. ⟨< NL *cryptogamia* < Gk. *kryptos* hidden + *gamos* marriage⟩ **–,cryp•to'gam•ic, cryp'tog•a•mous** [krɪp'tɒgəməs], *adj.*

cryp•to•gram ['krɪptə,græm] *n.* something written in secret code or cipher. **–,cryp•to'gram•mic,** *adj.*

cryp•to•graph ['krɪptə,græʃ] *n.* **1** cryptogram. **2** a device for encoding or decoding cipher.

cryp•to•graph•ic [,krɪptə'græfɪk] *adj.* of or having to do with cryptography. **–,cryp•to'graph•ic•al•ly,** *adv.*

cryp•tog•ra•phy [krɪp'tɒgrəfi] *n.* the art or process of writing or deciphering secret codes or ciphers.
–cryp'tog•ra•pher or **cryp'tog•ra•phist,** *n.*

cryp•to•me•ria [,krɪptə'miriə] *n.* a tall tree (*Cryptomeria japonica*) of the bald-cypress family, native to Asia and bearing cones; Japanese cedar.

cryp•to•pine ['krɪptə,pin] *or* ['krɪptə,pɪn] *n.* a poisonous alkaloid found in opium in very small quantities. *Formula:* $C_{21}H_{23}NO_5$

crypt•o•xan•thin [,krɪptə'zænθɪn] *n.* a pigment found in butter, eggs, and certain plants, which the human body can change into vitamin A. *Formula:* $C_{40}H_{56}O$ ⟨< Gk. *kryptos* hidden + *xanthos* yellow + E *-in*⟩

crys•tal ['krɪstəl] *n., adj.* *–n.* **1** a clear, transparent mineral, a kind of quartz, that looks like ice. **2** a piece of crystal cut to a special shape for use or ornament. Crystals are sometimes used as beads, and hung around lights. **3 a** glass of great brilliance and transparency, used especially in making drinking glasses, serving dishes, etc.: *The wine glasses were made of crystal.* **b** glasses, dishes, etc., made of crystal: *Crystal glistened on the dinner table.* **4** the glass over the face of a watch. **5** a regularly shaped mass with angles and flat surfaces, into which a substance solidifies: *Crystals of sugar can be distinguished from crystals of snow by their difference in form.* **6** a piece of quartz used to control the frequency of a radio-frequency oscillator or filter.
–adj. **1** made of crystal: *crystal ornaments.* **2** clear and transparent like crystal. ⟨ME < OF < L *crystallus* < Gk. *krystallos* clear ice, ult. < *kryos* frost⟩

crystal ball a ball of crystal or glass, used in crystal gazing.

crys•tal–clear ['krɪstəl 'klir] *adj.* **1** as clear as crystal; extremely clear and transparent. **2** very easy to understand; simple and lucid.

crystal detector *Electronics.* a device used in early radios for rectifying alternating currents, consisting of a crystal embedded in soft metal.

crystal gazing 1 the act or practice of staring into a crystal ball, supposedly to induce a vision of remote events, future happenings, etc. 2 *Informal.* speculation about the future. **—crystal gazer.**

crystal lattice a regular three-dimensional pattern of points in space indicating the positions of atoms, molecules, or ions in a crystal.

crys•tal•line ['krɪstə,laɪn], ['krɪstə,lin], *or* ['krɪstəlɪn] *adj.* 1 consisting of crystals; solidified in the form of crystals: *Sugar and salt are crystalline.* 2 of rocks, composed of crystals. 3 of or having to do with crystals and their formation. 4 made of crystal. 5 clear and transparent like crystal.

crystalline lens the lens of the eye.

crys•tal•lite ['krɪstə,ləit] *n.* 1 a mineral in igneous rock which is beginning to turn crystalline. The new crystals are very small. 2 such a very small crystal.

crys•tal•li•za•tion [,krɪstələ'zeiʃən] *or* [,krɪstəlaɪ'zeiʃən] *n.* 1 a crystallizing or being crystallized. 2 a crystallized substance or formation. 3 the taking on of a real, concrete, or permanent form: *The meeting resulted in the crystallization of our plans.*

crys•tal•lize ['krɪstə,laɪz] *v.* **-lized, -liz•ing.** 1 form into crystals; solidify into crystals: *Water crystallizes to form snow.* 2 form into definite shape: *His vague ideas crystallized into a clear plan.* 3 coat with sugar. **—'crys•tal,liz•er,** *n.*

crys•tal•log•ra•pher [,krɪstə'lɒgrəfər] *n.* a person trained in crystallography, especially one whose work it is.

crys•tal•log•ra•phy [,krɪstə'lɒgrəfi] *n.* the science that deals with the form, structure, and properties of crystals. ⟨< Gk. *krystallos* crystal + E *-graphy*⟩ **—,crys•tal•lo'graph•ic,** *adj.*

crys•tal•loid ['krɪstə,lɔɪd] *adj., n.* *—adj.* 1 like crystal. 2 like a crystalloid.
—n. 1 *Chemistry.* a substance (usually capable of crystallization) that, when dissolved in a liquid, will diffuse readily through vegetable or animal membranes. 2 a very small particle of protein, found in seeds, etc. ⟨< Gk. *krystalloeidēs* < *krystallos* crystal + *eidos* form⟩

crystal set an early type of radio receiver in which radio signals were demodulated by means of a crystal detector. Earphones were needed for listening to it because it had no amplifier.

crystal system a system of classification of crystals according to their shape.

crystal violet a dye used as a bacterial stain in Gram's method, also as an antiseptic; gentian violet. *Formula*: $C_{25}H_{30}ClN_3$

Cs 1 cesium. 2 cirro-stratus.

C.S. 1 CIVIL SERVICE. 2 CHRISTIAN SCIENCE.

csc cosecant.

CSC 1 Civil Service Commission. 2 Canadian Services College.

CSIS Canadian Security and Intelligence Service, the intelligence branch of the Canadian government.

ct. 1 cent. 2 county. 3 court. 4 one hundred (for L *centum*).

cte•noid ['tɛnɔɪd] *or* ['tinɔɪd] *adj.* having marginal projections like the teeth of a comb, as the scales of certain fishes. ⟨< Gk. *ktenos* comb⟩

cten•o•phore ['tɛnə,fɔr] *or* ['tinə,fɔr] *n.* any of a phylum (Ctenophora) of marine invertebrates having a jellyfishlike body with eight bands of cilia by means of which they swim. Also called **comb jelly.** ⟨< NL *ctenophora* the class name < Gk. *kteis, ktenos* comb + *phorein* to bear⟩ **—cten'oph•o•ran** [tɛ'nɒfərən], *adj.*

ctn cotangent.

ctn. carton(s).

CT scan CAT SCAN. **—CT scanner.**

CTV Canadian Television (Canadian Television Network, Ltd.).

cu. cubic.

Cu 1 copper. 2 cumulus.

cub [kʌb] *n.* 1 a young bear, fox, lion, etc. 2 **Cub,** a member of the Cubs, a program of the Scouts. 3 an inexperienced or awkward boy. 4 a boy who behaves badly. ⟨origin uncertain⟩

Cu•ba ['kjubə] *n.* an island country in the West Indies. See HAITI for map.

Cu•ban ['kjubən] *n., adj.* *—n.* a native or inhabitant of Cuba. *—adj.* of or having to do with Cuba or its people.

Cuban heel a medium-height heel with a tapering end, used on women's shoes.

cu•ba•ture ['kjubətʃər] *n.* 1 the determination of the cubic content of anything. 2 cubic content; volume.

cub•by•hole ['kʌbi,houl] *n.* 1 a small, enclosed space. 2 a small open space for putting something, such as in a desk; pigeonhole. ⟨< *cubby* (dim. of Brit. dial. word *cub* shed, coop) + *hole*⟩

cube[1] [kjub] *n., v.* **cubed, cub•ing.** *—n.* 1 a solid with six equal square sides. See SOLID for picture. 2 *Mathematics.* the product obtained when a number is cubed: *The cube of* 4 *is* 64. 3 anything shaped like a cube, as, an ice cube or sugar cube.
—v. 1 make or form into the shape of a cube: *The beets we had for supper were cubed instead of sliced.* 2 *Mathematics.* use (a number) three times as a factor: 5 *cubed is* 125, *since* 5 × 5 × 5 = 125. 3 measure the cubic capacity of (something). 4 score (meat) in a pattern of squares, to tenderize it. ⟨< L *cubus* < Gk. *kybos* cube, die⟩ **—'cube,like,** *adj.*

cube[2] ['kjubei] *or* ['kubei] *n.* a tropical plant of the genus *Lonchocarpus*, of the legume family, used to make insecticides. ⟨< Sp. *quibey* < native name⟩

cu•beb ['kjubɛb] *n.* 1 the dried, unripe berry of a tropical shrub (*Piper cubeba*) of the pepper family, used as a spice and in medicine. Cubebs were formerly crushed and smoked in pipes or cigarettes for the treatment of catarrh. 2 a cigarette made from these berries. ⟨< F *cubèbe* < Arabic *kabāba*⟩

cube root *Mathematics.* a number used as the factor of a cube: *The cube root of* 125 *is* 5.

cu•bic ['kjubɪk] *adj.* 1 shaped like a cube. 2 having length, breadth, and thickness. A cubic centimetre is the volume of a cube whose edges are one centimetre long. The cubic content of a room is the number of cubic metres it contains. 3 *Mathematics.* having to do with or involving the cubes of numbers. *Abbrev.*: cu.

cu•bi•cal ['kjubəkəl] *adj.* shaped like a cube.
☛ *Hom.* CUBICLE.

cu•bi•cle [kjubəkəl] *n.* a small room or compartment, especially one of the divisions of a large dormitory, a carrel-like compartment in a library, or a private compartment in a public washroom. ⟨< L *cubiculum* bedroom < *cubare* lie⟩
☛ *Hom.* CUBICAL.

cubic measure a unit or series of units for measuring volume or capacity:
1000 cubic millimetres = 1 cubic centimetre
1000 cubic centimetres = 1 cubic decimetre
1000 cubic decimetres = 1 cubic metre

cu•bi•form ['kjubə,fɔrm] *adj.* shaped like a cube; cubic.

cub•ism ['kjubɪzəm] *n. Art.* a style (developed in the early part of the 20th century) in which people, objects, etc., are represented by means of geometric forms, including squares, triangles, etc., as well as cubes.

cub•ist ['kjubɪst] *n., adj.* *—n.* an artist or sculptor whose art is in the style of cubism.
—adj. of or having to do with cubism or cubists. **—cu'bis•tic,** *adj.* **—cu'bis•tic•al•ly,** *adv.*

cu•bit ['kjubɪt] *n.* an ancient unit for measuring length, varying from about 45 cm to 50 cm. The cubit was based on the length of the arm from the elbow to the tip of the middle finger. ⟨< L *cubitum* elbow, cubit⟩

Cub•mas•ter ['kʌb,mæstər] *n.* PACK SCOUTER.

cu•boid ['kjubɔɪd] *adj., n.* *—adj.* 1 shaped like or nearly like a cube. 2 *Anatomy.* of or having to do with the cuboid.
—n. 1 something shaped like a cube. 2 a solid having six flat sides, each one a rectangle: *A cube is a special kind of cuboid. A brick is a cuboid.* 3 *Anatomy.* a bone between the heel and the instep.

cub reporter a young, inexperienced newspaper reporter.

cuck•old ['kʌkəld] *n., v.* *—n.* the husband of an unfaithful wife.
—v. make a cuckold of. ⟨ME *cukeweld* < OF *cucuault* < *coucou* cuckoo; from the cuckoo's habit of laying its eggs in another bird's nest⟩

cuck•old•ry ['kʌkəldri] *n.* a cuckolding or being cuckolded.

cuck•oo *n., v.* ['kuku] *or, sometimes,* ['kʊku]; *adj.* ['kuku] *n., pl.* **-oos;** *adj., v.* *—n.* 1 any of a family (Cuculidae) of birds having a long, slender body, greyish brown and white plumage, and pointed wings. Many species, including the well-known European cuckoo (*Cuculus canorus*), lay their eggs in the nests of other

birds, which then hatch them and raise the baby cuckoos. **2** the two-note call of a cuckoo, that resembles its name. **3** an imitation of this call. **4** *Slang.* an eccentric or mildly crazy person.
—*adj. Slang.* foolish or crazy.
—*v.* make the sound of a cuckoo or an imitation of it. ⟨imitative⟩

cuckoo clock a clock with a toy bird that pops out of a little door at regular intervals and makes a sound like that of a European cuckoo to mark the hour, half-hour, etc.

cuck•oo•flo•wer ['kuku,flaʊər] *n.* **1** lady's-smock, a form of cress (*Cardamine pratensis*) having pink or white flowers. **2** RAGGED ROBIN. ⟨so called because these plants are in bloom when the cuckoo first calls⟩

cuck•oo•pint ['kuku,paɪnt] *n.* a common European plant (*Arum maculatum*), also called **lords-and-ladies**, with large leaves.

cuckoo spit **1** a frothy substance produced on plants by the young of certain insects such as the froghopper or spittlebug, to protect the larvae. **2** any insect that produces this secretion.

cu•cul•late ['kjukə,leit] *or* [kjə'kʌleit] *adj.* **1** shaped like a hood: *a cucullate leaf.* **2** having a hoodlike part. ⟨< LL *cucullatus* < L *cucullus* cap⟩

cu•cum•ber ['kjukʌmbər] *n.* **1** the long, fleshy fruit of a vine (*Cucumis sativus*) of the gourd family, having a green skin and white flesh, commonly used as a vegetable. Cucumbers are eaten raw, often in salads, and are also pickled. **2** the vine it grows on.
cool as a cucumber, a very cool. **b** calm and unruffled; not excited. ⟨ME < OF *cocombre* < L *cucumis*⟩

cucumber tree **1** an American magnolia tree (*Magnolia acuminata*) having large green flowers and dark red conical fruit like a cucumber. **2** any similar tree, such as an East Indian tree of the genus *Averrhoa.*

cu•cur•bit [kju'kɜrbɪt] *n.* a gourd or any plant of the gourd family. ⟨< L *cucurbita*⟩ **—cu,cur•bi'ta•ceous,** *adj.*

cud [kʌd] *n.* **1** food that has been brought up into the mouth from the first and second stomachs of cattle, deer, camels, and other ruminants to be chewed before being swallowed again. **2** *Dialect.* a quid of tobacco.
chew the cud, think or ponder something; ruminate. ⟨OE *cudu,* var. of *cwidu*⟩

cud•dle ['kʌdəl] *v.* **-dled, -dling;** *n.* —*v.* **1** hold closely and lovingly in one's arms or lap: *The father cuddled his baby.* **2** lie close and snug; curl up: *The two puppies cuddled together in front of the fire.* **3** hug.
—*n.* **1** a spell of cuddling. **2** a hug. ⟨origin uncertain⟩

cud•dle•some ['kʌdəlsəm] *adj.* cuddly; inviting cuddling; huggable.

cud•dly ['kʌdli] *adj.* **cud•dli•er, cud•dli•est. 1** given to cuddling. **2** pleasing to cuddle.

cud•dy ['kʌdi] *n., pl.* **-dies. 1** a small cabin on a boat. **2** the cook's galley on a small boat. **3** a small room or cupboard. ⟨origin uncertain⟩

cudg•el ['kʌdʒəl] *n., v.* **-elled** or **-eled, -el•ling** or **-el•ing.**
—*n.* a short, thick stick used as a weapon; club.
take up the cudgels for, defend strongly.
—*v.* beat with a cudgel.
cudgel (one's) **brains,** try very hard to think. ⟨OE *cycgel*⟩

cud•weed ['kʌd,wid] *n.* any composite plant of the genus *Gnaphalium*, having simple woolly leaves.

cue[1] [kju] *n., v.* **cued, cu•ing** or **cue•ing.** —*n.* **1** a hint or suggestion as to what to do or when to act: *When the host or hostess sits down, that is your cue to begin dessert.* **2** an action or speech on or behind the stage, which gives the signal for an actor, singer, musician, etc., to enter or to begin. In a play the last word or words of one actor's speech is the cue for another to come on the stage, begin speaking, etc. **3** the part one is to play; course of action. **4** *Archaic.* frame of mind; mood.
on cue, a at the right moment: *They started on cue.* **b** in response to a cue.
take (one's) **cue from,** be guided by: *Being a stranger, he took his cue from the actions of the natives.*
—*v.* give a cue to or for; give a suggestion, hint or signal to or for: *Don't forget to cue him when to start the song. She never sounds spontaneous; all her responses seem cued.*
cue in, introduce (music, sound effects, etc.) at a specific point on cue. ⟨probably < F *queue* tail, end < L *coda,* dial. var. of *cauda*; with reference to the end of a preceding actor's speech⟩
☛ *Hom.* QUEUE.

cue[2] [kju] *n.* **1** queue; pigtail. **2** *Billiards, etc.* a long, tapering stick used for striking the ball. **3** in shuffleboard, a long stick for pushing the disks. ⟨var. of *queue*⟩
☛ *Hom.* QUEUE.

cue ball *Billiards, etc.* the ball, usually white, which is struck by the cue.

cue card a card showing the words to be spoken or sung by a television performer, which is usually attached to the camera out of sight of the audience. It is the forerunner of the TELEPROMPTER.

cues•ta ['kwɛstə] *n.* a ridge or hill that has a steep face on one side and a gentle slope on the other. ⟨< Sp. < L *costa* side, rib⟩

cuff[1] [kʌf] *n.* **1** the part of a sleeve or glove that goes around the wrist. **2** a turned-up fold around the bottom of a trouser leg. **3** the part of a long glove or gauntlet that covers the wrist or part of the arm. **4** handcuff. **5** the part of a blood pressure instrument that wraps round the arm and is inflated.
off the cuff, without preparation; impromptu: *She had no notes but spoke off the cuff.*
on the cuff, on credit. ⟨ME *cuffe* glove; origin uncertain⟩
—'cuff•less, *adj.*

cuff[2] [kʌf] *v. or n.* hit with the hand; slap. ⟨origin uncertain⟩

cuff link a device for linking together the open ends of a shirt cuff.

cu. ft. cubic foot (feet).

cui bo•no ['kwi 'bounou], ['kui 'bounou], *or* ['kuaɪ 'bounou] *Latin.* **1** for whose benefit? **2** of what good? for what use?

cu. in. cubic inch(es).

cui•rass [kwɪ'ræs] *n.* **1** a piece of armour for the body consisting of a breastplate fastened to another plate protecting the back. See ARMOUR for picture. **2** the breastplate alone. **3** the armour plate of a warship. **4** *Zoology.* the protective bony plates on some animals. ⟨ME < OF *cuirasse* < Ital. *corazza* < VL < LL *coriacea (vestis)* (garment) of leather < L *corium* leather; form influenced by F *cuir* leather < L *corium*⟩

cui•ras•sier [,kwirə'sir] *n.* a cavalry soldier wearing a cuirass. ⟨< F⟩

Cui•se•naire rods ['kwizə,nɛr] *Trademark.* a set of sticks marked with a mathematical value according to length, used in early childhood education. ⟨named after their inventor⟩

cui•sine [kwɪ'zin] *n.* **1** a style of cooking or preparing food: *French cuisine, casual cuisine.* **2** food. **3** a kitchen. ⟨< F < L *cocina*, var. of *coquina* < *coquus* a cook⟩

cuisse [kwɪs] *n.* a piece of armour to protect the thigh. ⟨< F *cuisse* thigh < L *coxa* hip⟩

cuke [kjuk] *n. Informal.* cucumber.

cul–de–sac ['kʌl də ,sæk] *or* ['kʊl də ,sæk]; *French,* [kyd'sak] *n.* **1** a street or passage open at only one end; blind alley. **2** any part of the anatomy, such as the caecum, that is closed at the end. **3** a situation that is impossible to get out of. ⟨< F *cul-de-sac* bottom of the sack⟩

cu•lex ['kjulɛks] *n., pl.* **-li•ces** [-lə,siz]. any of a genus (*Culex*) of mosquitoes found throughout the world, including the common mosquito (*C. pipiens*) of North America and Europe. ⟨< L *culex* gnat⟩ **—'cu•li•cine,** *adj.*

cu•li•nar•y ['kʌlə,nɛri] *or* ['kjulə,nɛri] *adj.* **1** having to do with cooking or the kitchen: *Judy is often praised for her culinary skill.* **2** used in cooking. ⟨< L *culinarius* < *culina* kitchen⟩

cull [kʌl] *v., n.* —*v.* **1** pick out; select: *The lawyer culled a few important facts from the mass of evidence.* **2** pick over; make selections from. **3** select, or select certain members of, for slaughter: *The herd is culled to keep the numbers down to a point where the remainder have a good chance of survival through the winter.*
—*n.* something picked out as being inferior or worthless. Poor fruit, stale vegetables, and lumber and animals not up to standard are called culls. ⟨ME < OF *cuillir* < L *colligere.* See COLLECT.⟩ **—'cull•er,** *n.*

cul•let ['kʌlɪt] *n.* broken or waste glass used to speed up the melting process in the manufacture of new glass. ⟨< F *collet* dim. of *col* neck, referring to the bits of glass at the neck of a bottle after blowing⟩

culm[1] [kʌlm] *n.* **1** coal dust. **2** hard coal of poor quality. ⟨? related to COAL⟩

culm[2] [kʌlm] *n., v.* —*n. Botany.* the jointed stem characteristic of grasses, usually hollow.
—*v.* grow or develop into a culm. ⟨< L *culmus* stalk⟩

cul•mi•nant ['kʌlmənənt] *adj.* **1** at the highest point; topmost. **2** culminating.

cul•mi•nate ['kʌlmə,neit] *v.* **-nat•ed, -nat•ing. 1** rise to, reach, or form a highest point or endpoint: *The church tower had a long winding staircase that culminated in a lookout platform.* **2** reach the decisive point or climax: *The dramatic action of the play culminates in a murder.* **3** bring (something) to its climax. ⟨< LL *culminare* < L *culmen* top⟩

cul•mi•na•tion [,kʌlmə'neiʃən] *n.* **1** the highest point; climax. **2** a reaching of the highest point or endpoint.

cu•lottes [ku'lɒts], [kju'lɒts], *or* [kə'lɒts] *n.pl.* a divided skirt; a woman's garment that looks like a flared skirt but is divided and sewn in the manner of pants. ⟨< F⟩

cul•pa•bil•i•ty [,kʌlpə'bɪləti] *n.* the fact or condition of being culpable.

cul•pa•ble ['kʌlpəbəl] *adj.* deserving blame. ⟨ME < OF < L *culpabilis* < *culpa* fault⟩ **—'cul•pa•ble•ness,** *n.* **—'cul•pa•bly,** *adv.*

cul•prit ['kʌlprɪt] *n.* **1** a person guilty of a fault or a crime; offender. **2** a prisoner in court who has been accused of a crime. **3** someone or something that is the cause of trouble: *When her tire went flat, she found the nail that was the culprit.* ⟨apparently < AF *cul. prit.* earlier *cul. prist,* short for *culpable,* deserving punishment < L *culpabilis* and *prist,* var. of OF *prest* ready (for trial), ult. < L *praesto* on hand⟩

cult [kʌlt] *n.* **1** a system of religious worship. **2** an unorthodox religious group under the domination of a leader, given to extreme practices. **3** great admiration for a person, thing, idea, etc.; worship or devotion: *In the former Soviet Union, the cult of Stalin was discouraged after his death.* **4** a group showing such admiration; worshippers. **5** (*adjl.*) greatly admired by a small group: *a cult film.* ⟨< L *cultus* worship < *colere* worship⟩ **—'cult•ic,** *adj.* **—'cult•ism,** *n.*

cul•ti•gen ['kʌltɪdʒən] *n.* **1** a cultivated plant of unknown origin and having no wild counterpart, such as the cabbage. **2** cultivar. ⟨< *culti(vated)* + *-gen*⟩

cult•ish ['kʌltɪʃ] *adj.* of, having to do with, or characteristic of cults: *the cultish aspects of astrology.*

cult•ist ['kʌltɪst] *n.* a person who tends to follow or practise a cult.

cul•ti•va•ble ['kʌltəvəbəl] *adj.* that can be cultivated.

cul•ti•var ['kʌltɪ,vɑr] *n.* a variety of plant produced from a known natural species by cultivation. ⟨< *culti(vated) var(iety)*⟩

cul•ti•vat•a•ble ['kʌltə,veitəbəl] *or* [,kʌltə'veitəbəl] *adj.* cultivable.

cul•ti•vate ['kʌltə,veit] *v.* **-vat•ed, -vat•ing. 1** prepare and use (land) to raise crops by ploughing it, planting seeds, and taking care of the growing plants. **2** help (plants) grow by labour and care. **3** loosen the ground around (growing plants) to kill weeds, etc. **4** promote the growth, development, or improvement of by time, thought, and effort: *to cultivate one's mind. Artists cultivate their craft. Friendships cultivated in school often last a lifetime.* **5** seek better acquaintance with; try to win the friendship of. ⟨< Med.L *cultivare* < *cultivus* under cultivation < L *cultus,* pp. of *colere* till⟩

cul•ti•vat•ed ['kʌltə,veitɪd] *adj., v.* —*adj.* **1** prepared and used to raise crops: *A field of wheat is cultivated land; a pasture is not.* **2** produced by cultivation; not wild: *All hybrid tea roses are cultivated flowers.* **3** improved; developed. **4** cultured; refined. —*v.* pt. and pp. of CULTIVATE.

cul•ti•va•tion [,kʌltə'veiʃən] *n.* **1** the act or practice of cultivating. **2** the result of improvement or growth through education or experience; culture: *a man of cultivation.*
under cultivation, of land, planted with crops or prepared for planting: *Most of their land is now under cultivation.*

cul•ti•va•tor ['kʌltə,veitər] *n.* **1** a tool or machine used to loosen the ground and destroy weeds. A cultivator is pulled or pushed between rows of growing plants. **2** a person or thing that cultivates.

cul•trate ['kʌltreit] *adj.* having a sharp point and sharp edges. ⟨< L *cultratus* knifelike⟩

cul•tur•al ['kʌltʃərəl] *adj.* **1** of or having to do with culture: *Music and art are cultural studies.* **2** the result of cultivation or breeding. **—'cul•tur•al•ly,** *adv.*

cultural anthropology the study of peoples of the past and present, emphasizing language and customs.

cultural evolution the process of change in a culture, especially in ways that affect its adaptation to the environment. The invention of agriculture was part of human cultural evolution.

cultural lag or **culture lag** *Sociology.* delay in the adaptation of one aspect of a culture to accommodate changes in another aspect, especially, delay in the adaptation of social institutions to technological advances.

cul•tu•ra•ti [,kʌltʃə'rɑti] *n.* the artistic community. ⟨< *culture* + *-ati* on the analogy of *literati*⟩

cul•ture ['kʌltʃər] *n., v.* **-tured, -tur•ing.** —*n.* **1** the arts, beliefs, habits, institutions, and other human endeavours considered together as being characteristic of a particular community, people, or nation. Modern Canadian culture is strongly influenced by television and other mass media. **2** a people or group sharing such endeavours. **3** fineness of feelings, thoughts, tastes, manners, etc. **4** the development of the mind or body by education, training, etc. **5** behaviour that is socially taught, rather than instinctive or individual. **6** the preparation of land to raise crops by ploughing, planting, and the necessary care; cultivation. **7** the raising of bees, fish, silkworms, etc. **8** *Biology.* **a** the growth of living micro-organisms, such as bacteria, in a special medium for scientific study or medicinal use. **b** a group or colony of micro-organisms produced in this way.
—*v.* **1** cultivate; refine. **2** *Biology.* grow (bacteria, etc.) in a special nutrient medium for scientific study, medicinal use, etc. ⟨< F < L *cultura* a tending < *colere* cultivate⟩
☛ *Syn. n.* 3, 4. See note at EDUCATION.

cul•tured ['kʌltʃərd] *adj., v.* —*adj.* **1** having or showing culture; refined. **2** produced or raised under artificial conditions, as in a laboratory, etc.: *cultured pearls.*
—*v.* pt. and pp. of CULTURE.

cultured pearl a natural pearl artificially cultivated by introducing a foreign body into an oyster, so causing the oyster to secrete a protective substance that hardens around the irritant.

culture lag CULTURAL LAG.

culture medium a substance, often a liquid, specially prepared for the growth in a laboratory of micro-organisms or cells.

culture shock the feeling of confusion, alienation, etc., from being suddenly exposed to a culture that is markedly different from one's own.

culture vulture *Slang.* one who declares great interest in artistic and intellectual matters.

cul•tur•ist ['kʌltʃərɪst] *n.* **1** a person who cultivates plants or breeds animals. **2** a person who advocates cultural education.

cul•tus[1] ['kʌltəs] *n.* a religious cult. ⟨< L. See CULT.⟩

cul•tus[2] ['kʌltəs] *adj. Cdn. West coast.* worthless; unimportant; bad. ⟨< Chinook jargon < Chinook *cultus* worthless⟩

cul•ver•in ['kʌlvərɪn] *n.* **1** a musket used in the Middle Ages. **2** a long, heavy cannon used in the 16th and 17th centuries. ⟨ME < OF *coulevrine* < *couleuvre* < L *colubra* serpent⟩

cul•vert ['kʌlvərt] *n.* a small channel or drain that allows water to run under a road, railway, etc. ⟨origin uncertain⟩

cum [kʌm] *or* [kʊm] *prep.* combined with or together with (*used especially to form nonce compounds*): *an antique-cum-junk shop.* ⟨< L *cum* with⟩

cum•ber ['kʌmbər] *v., n.* —*v.* **1** burden; trouble: *Household cares cumber a busy mother.* **2** hinder; hamper: *The logger's heavy boots cumbered him in walking.*
—*n.* hindrance. ⟨ME, probably < OF *combrer* impede < *combre* barrier < Celtic⟩ **—'cum•ber•er,** *n.*

cum•ber•some ['kʌmbərsəm] *adj.* clumsy; unwieldy; burdensome: *The armour worn by medieval knights seems cumbersome to us today. Long, badly constructed sentences are cumbersome.* **—'cum•ber•some•ly,** *adv.* **—'cum•ber•some•ness,** *n.*

cum•brance ['kʌmbrəns] *n.* a burden; something that causes problems.

cum•brous ['kʌmbrəs] *adj.* cumbersome. **—'cum•brous•ly,** *adv.* **—'cum•brous•ness,** *n.*

cum•in or **cum•min** ['kʌmən] *n.* **1** a small, Mediterranean annual herb (*Cuminum cyminum*) of the parsley family widely cultivated for its aromatic seeds, which are used as a spice. **2** the seeds of this plant. ⟨OE *cymen* < L *cuminum* < Gk. *kyminon*⟩

cum lau•de [kʊm 'laʊdei] *Latin.* **1** with praise or honour. To graduate *cum laude* is to graduate with high rank. **2** a person who has graduated from a high school or university with high honours.

cum•mer•bund ['kʌmər,bʌnd] *n.* a broad sash worn around the waist, now especially with a tuxedo. Also, **kummerbund.**

⟨< Hind. *kamarband* < Persian *kamar* waist, loins (< Arabic) + *band* band, bandage⟩

cum•quat ['kʌmkwɒt] See KUMQUAT.

cu•mu•late *v.* ['kjumjə,leit]; *adj.* ['kjumjəlɪt] *or* ['kjumjə,leit] *v.* **-lat•ed, -lat•ing;** *adj.* *—v.* heap up; accumulate. *—adj.* heaped up. ⟨< L *cumulare* < *cumulus* heap⟩

cu•mu•la•tion [,kjumjə'leiʃən] *n.* **1** a heaping up; an accumulating. **2** a heap; accumulation.

cu•mu•la•tive ['kjumjələtɪv] *or* ['kjumjə,leitɪv] *adj.* heaped up; accumulated; increasing or growing in amount, force, etc., by additions: *a cumulative argument.* A cumulative dividend is one that must be added to future dividends if not paid when due. **—'cu•mu•la•tive•ly,** *adv.* **—'cu•mu•la•tive•ness,** *n.*

cumulative voting a system of electing members of a legislature in which each voter may vote as many times as there are positions to be filled and cast more than one vote per candidate.

cu•mu•li•form ['kjumjələ,fɔrm] *adj.* shaped like a cumulus cloud.

cu•mu•lo–cir•rus [,kjumjəlou 'sirəs] *n., pl.* **-cir•ri** [-'siraɪ] *or* [-'siri]. a cloud that is part cumulus, part cirrus.

cu•mu•lo–nim•bus [,kjumjəlou 'nɪmbəs] *n., pl.* **-bus•es** or **-bi** [-baɪ] *or* [-bi]. a massive cloud formation combining features of both cumulus and nimbus clouds and having peaks that resemble mountains.

cu•mu•lo–stra•tus [,kjumjəlou 'streitəs] *or* ['strætəs] *n.* a cumulus cloud with its base spread out horizontally like a stratus cloud.

cu•mu•lous ['kjumjələs] *adj.* of or like cumulus clouds.
☛ *Hom.* CUMULUS.

cu•mu•lus ['kjumjələs] *n., pl.* **-li** [-,laɪ] *or* [-,li]. **1** a cloud formation of rounded heaps having a flat base. **2** a heap. ⟨< L *cumulus* heap⟩
☛ *Hom.* CUMULOUS.

cu•ne•ate ['kjuniɪt] *or* ['kjuni,eit] *adj.* tapering to a point at the base; wedge-shaped. ⟨< L *cuneatus* < *cuneus* wedge⟩ **—'cu•ne•ate•ly,** *adv.*

A section of a cuneiform inscription in Old Persian carved on the rock face of a mountain in Iran by order of the Persian king, Darius I, c. 500 B.C. The inscription describes the first year of his reign, during which he put down several rebellions against his rule. The part shown means "this is Ciçatakhma. He lied thus—he said, 'I am king'."

cu•ne•i•form ['kjuniɪ,fɔrm], ['kjunɪ,fɔrm], *or* [kju'nii,fɔrm] *n., adj.* *—n.* **1** the wedge-shaped characters used in the writing of ancient Babylonia, Assyria, Persia, etc. **2** a wedge-shaped bone, especially one of the three bones of the human ankle. *—adj.* **1** wedge-shaped. **2** of or having to do with cuneiform characters. **3** of or denoting any wedge-shaped bone. ⟨< L *cuneus* wedge + E *-form* shaped (< L *-formis*)⟩

cu•nit ['kjunɪt] *n.* a measure of wood equal to 1.3 cords, formerly 100 cubic feet (about 9.3 cubic metres) of solid wood. ⟨? < *cu(bic)* + *(u)nit*⟩

cun•ner ['kʌnər] *n.* a small fish (*Tautogolabrus adspersus*), a kind of wrasse, found off the Atlantic coast of North America, from Newfoundland south to New England. ⟨origin unknown⟩

cun•ning ['kʌnɪŋ] *adj., n.* *—adj.* **1** clever in getting what one wants or in deceiving one's enemies; crafty; wily: *a cunning rogue.* **2** showing craftiness or wiliness: *a cunning plot.* **3** having or showing skill or cleverness: *cunning hands, cunning workmanship.* **4** *Rare, Informal.* attractively small, delicate, quaint, etc.; cute: *a cunning baby.*
—n. **1** craftiness; wiliness: *A fox has a great deal of cunning.* **2** *Archaic.* skill or cleverness. ⟨OE *cunning* < *cunnan* know (how). Related to CAN[1].⟩ **—'cun•ning•ly,** *adv.* **—'cun•ning•ness,** *n.*
☛ *Syn. adj.* **1.** See note at SLY. *—n.* **1. Cunning,** CRAFT = skill in getting what one wants. **Cunning** suggests slyness and the use of clever tricks or false appearances to hide one's real purpose and get the better of others: *He has the cunning of a cat chasing a mouse.* **Craft** suggests skill in deceiving others by clever and artful plans, devices, and underhand methods: *He has the craft of a successful swindler.*

cup [kʌp] *n., v.* **cupped, cup•ping.** *—n.* **1** a small but rather deep dish to drink from, usually having one curved handle. **2** as much as a cup holds; a cupful: *She ordered a cup of tea.* **3** a unit for measuring capacity or volume, used especially in cooking. One cup is equal to about 250 mL. **4** something resembling a cup in shape or function. **5** an ornamental cup, vase, etc., given to the winner of a contest; a trophy. **6** a hole in golf. **7** a mixed drink: *a claret cup.* **8** any dish served in a cup: *a fruit cup.* **9** *Christianity.* **a** the chalice or other vessel used in Communion. **b** the consecrated wine, etc., contained in this vessel. **10** one of the two breast supports of a bra, or the size of this: *a C cup.* **11** something to be experienced or endured; one's lot or fate: *It was a bitter cup for her.* **12** *Medicine.* formerly, a CUPPING GLASS.
in (one's) **cups,** drunk.
(one's) **cup of tea,** *Informal.* something or someone that pleases one.
—v. **1** curve or shape (one's hands, etc.) to resemble a cup: *She cupped her hands to catch the ball. The old man cupped a hand behind one ear.* **2** put into or take in or as in a cup: *She cupped her chin in her hand.* **3** *Medicine.* formerly, bleed (a person) by means of a cupping glass. ⟨OE *cuppe* < LL *cuppa*; cf. L *cupa* tub⟩ **—'cup,like,** *adj.*

cup•bear•er ['kʌp,bɛrər] *n.* **1** a person who fills and passes around the cups in which drinks are served. **2** formerly, in royal households, a noble who tasted the wine before handing it to his master or mistress.

cup•board ['kʌbərd] *n.* **1** a closet or cabinet with shelves for dishes, food, etc. **2** a closet for storing clothing, linens, etc.

cupboard love insincere expressions of love for selfish reasons; affection offered for the sake of something, such as food and care, to be received in return.

cup•cake ['kʌp,keik] *n.* a small cake baked in a cup-shaped container.

cu•pel ['kjupəl] *or* [kju'pɛl] *n., v.* **cu•pelled, cu•pel•ling. 1** a small porous container in the shape of a cup, used to assay precious metals. **2** a furnace bottom for refining silver, etc. *—v.* assay or refine in a cupel. ⟨< F *coupelle* < Med.L *cupella,* dim. < L *cupa* tub⟩

cup•fer•ron ['kjupfə,rɒn] *or* ['kupfə,rɒn] *n.* a white soluble crystalline substance used as a reagent to identify copper, iron, etc. *Formula:* $C_6H_9N_3O_2$ ⟨< *cup(ric)* + *ferr(o)* + *-on*⟩

cup•ful ['kʌpfʊl] *n., pl.* **-fuls.** as much as a cup can hold.

Cu•pid ['kjupɪd] *n.* **1** *Roman mythology.* the god of sexual love, the son of Venus, corresponding to the Greek god Eros. Cupid was usually represented as a winged boy with bow and arrows. **2 cupid,** a figure of a naked winged boy used as a symbol of sexual love: *Valentine cards often have cupids on them.*

cu•pid•i•ty [kju'pɪdəti] *n.* eager desire, especially to possess something; greed. ⟨< L *cupiditas* < *cupidus* desirous < *cupere* long for, desire⟩

cu•pid's–bow ['kjupɪdz ,bou] *adj.* shaped like the bow usually depicted as held by a cupid: *a cupid's-bow mouth.*

cu•po•la ['kjupələ] *n.* **1** a round dome forming the roof of a building or part of a building. **2** a small structure on top of a roof. **3** a domelike thing or part. **4** a small furnace for melting metals. ⟨< Ital. < LL *cupula*, dim. of L *cupa* tub⟩

A cupola

cup•ping ['kʌpɪŋ] *n. Medicine.* formerly, the practice of bleeding a patient, using a cupping glass.

cupping glass *Medicine.* formerly, a kind of glass cup in which a partial vacuum could be created by suction or heat; it was applied to a person's skin to draw blood to the surface for slow bloodletting.

cu•pre•ous ['kjupriəs] *adj.* **1** of or containing copper. **2** copper-coloured. ⟨< L *cupreus* < *cuprum* copper⟩

cu•pric ['kjuprɪk] *adj. Chemistry.* of or containing divalent copper.

cupric sulphate or **sulfate** BLUE VITRIOL. *Formula*: $CuSO_4 \cdot 5H_2O$

cu•prif•er•ous [kju'prɪfərəs] *adj.* containing copper.

cu•prite ['kjuprəit] *n.* a reddish brown mineral that is an important ore of copper. *Formula*: Cu_2O

cu•pro•nick•el ['kjuprou,nɪkəl] *n.* an alloy of copper and up to 40 percent nickel, used to make coins and some hardware.

cu•prous ['kjuprəs] *adj. Chemistry.* of or containing monovalent copper.

cu•prum ['kjuprəm] *n.* copper. ⟨< L. See COPPER.⟩

cu•pule ['kjupjul] *n.* **1** a cup-shaped membranous cover surrounding a fruit, as in the acorn. **2** any cup-shaped organ or part. ⟨< L *cupula* cupola⟩

cur [kɜr] *n.* **1** a worthless dog; mongrel. **2** an ill-bred, despicable person. ⟨ME *curre*⟩

cur•a•ble ['kjurəbəl] *adj.* that can be cured. **—,cur•a'bil•i•ty** or **'cur•a•ble•ness,** *n.* **—'cur•a•bly,** *adv.*

cu•ra•çao [,kjʊrə'sou], [,kjʊrə'saʊ], *or* ['kjʊrə,sou] *n.* a liqueur or cordial flavoured with orange peel. ⟨< *Curaçao*, a Dutch island in the West Indies⟩
Hom. CURASSOW ['kjʊrə,sou].

cu•ra•cy ['kjʊrəsi] *n., pl.* **-cies.** the position, rank, or work of a curate.

cu•ra•re [kju'rɑri] *or* [ku'rɑri] *n.* **1** a poisonous, blackish, resinlike extract of certain tropical American plants, especially *Chondrodendron* genus of the family Menispermaceae and *Strychnos* genus of the family Loganiaceae, which causes paralysis of the muscles. It is used medicinally as a muscle relaxant and has long been used by Indian peoples of South America as an arrow poison in hunting game. Also, **curari. 2** any of the plants, such as the moonseed (*Chondrodendron tomentosum*), which yield curare. ⟨< Sp. *curaré* or Portuguese *curare* < Tupi⟩

cu•ras•sow ['kjʊrə,sou] *or* [kjə'ræsou] *n.* a bird of the family Cracidae, especially *Crax rubra*, native to South and Central America, and having dark feathers. Although it is related to chickens, it nests in trees. ⟨< Curaçao⟩
Hom. CURAÇAO ['kjurə,sou].

cu•rate *n.* ['kjʊrɪt]; *v.* ['kjʊreit] *n., v.* **cu•rat•ed, cu•rat•ing.**
—n. a member of the clergy who is an assistant to a pastor, rector, or vicar.
—v. act as curator for (an exhibition, etc.) ⟨< Med.L *curatus* < *cura* CURE (def. 5) < L *cura* care. Doublet of CURÉ.⟩

cur•a•tive ['kjʊrətɪv] *adj., n. —adj.* having the power to cure; curing; tending to cure.
—n. a means of curing. **—'cur•a•tive•ly,** *adv.* **—'cur•a•tive•ness,** *n.*

cu•ra•tor [kjə'reitər] *or* ['kjʊreitər] *n.* **1** a person in charge of all or part of a museum, library, etc. **2** the guardian of a minor. ⟨< L *curator* < *curare* care for < *cura* care⟩

curb [kɜrb] *n., v. —n.* **1** a raised border of concrete or stone along the edge of a street, driveway, etc. **2** an enclosing framework or border supporting the base or outer edge of a dome, shaft, etc. **3** a chain or strap fastened to a horse's bit and passing under its lower jaw. When the reins are pulled tight, the curb checks the horse. **4** anything that checks or restrains. **5** a market that deals in stocks and bonds not listed on the regular stock exchange. The name comes from the fact that such markets originally conducted their business on the streets.
—v. **1** hold in check; restrain. **2** provide with a curb. **3** cause (a driver) to pull his or her car over to the curb, usually because of a traffic violation. **4** lead (a dog) to the curb, gutter, or other place away from a sidewalk where it may defecate. ⟨ME < OF *courbe* < L *curvus* bent⟩
☛ *Syn. v.* **1.** See note at CHECK.

curb bit a horse's bit having a curb.

curb•ing ['kɜrbɪŋ] *n., v. —n.* **1** material for making a curb. **2** a raised border of concrete, etc.; curb.
—v. ppr. of CURB.

curb roof a roof having two slopes on each side.

curb•stone ['kɜrb,stoun] *n.* a stone or stones forming a curb; a raised border of concrete, etc., along the sides of a street, driveway, etc.

cur•cu•li•o [kər'kjuli,ou] *n., pl.* **-li•os.** any of various American weevils, especially any that are pests of fruit trees, such as *Conotrachelus nenuphar.* ⟨< L⟩

cur•cu•ma ['kɜrkjəmə] *n.* a plant of the genus *Curcuma*, of the ginger family, native to the Old World, and having showy flowers and thick, tuberous roots that yield starch. ⟨< NL < Arabic *kurkum* saffron, crocus⟩

curd [kɜrd] *n., v. —n.* **1** Often, **curds,** *pl.* the thick part of milk that separates from the watery part when milk sours. **2** any food that resembles this: *bean curd.*
—v. form into curds; curdle. ⟨ME *curd, crud*⟩

cur•dle ['kɜrdəl] *v.* **-dled, -dling. 1** form into curds. Milk curdles when it is kept too long. **2** thicken.
curdle the blood of, horrify; terrify. ⟨< *curd*⟩

curd•y ['kɜrdi] *adj.* **curd•i•er, curd•i•est. 1** full of curds. **2** like curdled milk.

cure [kjʊr] *v.* **cured, cur•ing;** *n. —v.* **1** bring back to health or to a normal, sound, or proper condition: *The sick child was soon cured. The punishment was meant to cure her of lying.* **2** get rid of (some undesirable condition): *to cure a cold, to cure a bad habit.* **3** prepare for keeping; preserve: *They cured the meat by drying and salting it.* **4** treat (a substance) by chemical or physical means in order to prepare it for use: *Rubber is cured by vulcanizing it. Tobacco is cured by drying it.* **5** become cured.
—n. **1** recovery from a disease; bringing or being brought back to health: *Her cure took a long time.* **2** a period or course of treatment for a disease: *a rest cure.* **3** something that restores to health; a successful medical treatment, drug, etc.: *Researchers have not yet found a cure for cancer.* **4** anything that permanently relieves or corrects a problem or a harmful situation: *a cure for laziness. The tax cuts are not a cure for inflation, but merely a stopgap.* **5** spiritual charge; religious care. **6** a method or process of curing meat, fish, etc. ⟨ME < OF *curer* < L *curare* care for < *cura* care⟩ **—'cure•less,** *adj.* **—'cur•er,** *n.*
☛ *Syn. v.* **2. Cure,** HEAL, REMEDY = make well or right. **Cure** applies particularly to bringing back to health after sickness and disease: *The new treatment cured his skin disease.* **Heal** = make whole, and is used particularly of wounds, burns, etc.: *This medicine will heal that cut.* **Remedy** = put right, and applies to curing or relieving any unhealthy condition, physical or otherwise: *The operation remedied his twisted foot. These measures will hopefully remedy government inefficiency.*

cu•ré [kjʊ'rei]; *French,* [ky'ʀe] *n.* a parish priest. ⟨< F < Med.L *curatus.* Doublet of CURATE.⟩

cure–all ['kjʊr,ɒl] *n.* a remedy supposed to cure all diseases or evils.

cur•et•tage [kjʊ'rɛtɪdʒ] *or* [,kjʊrə'tɑʒ] *n.* a scraping or cleaning of tissues in a body cavity with a small, scoop-shaped surgical instrument. ⟨< F *curetage*⟩

cu•rette [kjʊ'rɛt] *n.* a scoop-shaped surgical instrument for performing curettage. Also, **curet.**

cur•few ['kɜrfju] *n.* **1** the giving of a signal, such as a bell ringing, at a fixed time every evening. In the Middle Ages, it announced the time to put out lights and cover fires. More recently it has been used as a direction for persons to leave streets and public places. **2** the signal given: *"The curfew tolls the knell of parting day."* **3** the time when it is given: *Everyone was indoors before curfew.* **4** a time set by parents, camp or boarding school authorities, etc., at or before which children must be indoors or in bed. **5** a formal regulation forbidding persons to be on the streets after a certain hour. ⟨ME < AF *coeverfu* < *covrir* cover (< L *cooperire*) + *feu* fire < L *focus* hearth⟩

cu•ri•a ['kjʊriə] *n., pl.* **cu•ri•ae** ['kjʊri,i] *or* ['kjʊri,aɪ]. **1** in ancient Rome: **a** the meeting place of the senate. **b** one of the ten divisions of each of the three tribes into which all Roman citizens were divided. **c** the meeting place of one of these divisions. **2** a medieval council or court of law. **3 Curia,** *Roman Catholic Church.* a group of high officials who assist the Pope in the government and administration of the Church; the papal court. ⟨< L⟩ **—'cu•ri•al,** *adj.*

cu•rie ['kjʊri] *or* [kjʊ'ri] *n.* a unit for measuring radioactivity, equal to 37 gigabecquerels. *Symbol:* Ci ⟨after Mme. Marie *Curie* (1867-1934), a French physicist and chemist, born in Poland⟩

Cu•rie's law [kjʊ'riz] *or* ['kjʊriz] the principle that the magnetic susceptibility of a paramagnetic substance varies inversely with its absolute temperature. ⟨< after Pierre *Curie* (1859-1906), French physicist⟩

cu•ri•o ['kjʊri,ou] *n., pl.* **cu•ri•os.** an object valued as a curiosity: *The traveller brought back many curios from foreign lands.* ⟨short for *curiosity*⟩

cu•ri•o•sa [,kjʊri'ousə] *n.pl.* exotic things, especially books dealing with unusual topics. ⟨< L, literally, curious objects⟩

cu•ri•os•i•ty [,kjʊri'ɒsəti] *n., pl.* **-ties. 1** an eager desire to know: *Her curiosity made her open the forbidden door.* **2** the condition of being too eager to know; inquisitiveness: *Curiosity killed the cat.* **3** a strange, rare, or novel object or feature. **4** an odd, unusual, or interesting quality: *He was intrigued with the curiosity of the place.*

cu•ri•ous ['kjʊriəs] *adj.* **1** eager to know: *a curious student.* **2** too eager to know; prying: *That old man is curious about other people's business.* **3** strange; odd; unusual: *a curious old book.* **4** *Archaic.* very careful; exact: *a curious inquiry into the customs of the Blackfoot.* **5** *Informal.* very odd; eccentric: *curious notions.* ⟨ME < OF *curios* < L *curiosus* inquisitive, full of care, ult. < *cura* care⟩ **—'cu•ri•ous•ly,** *adv.* **—'cu•ri•ous•ness,** *n.*

☛ *Syn.* **1, 2. Curious,** INQUISITIVE, PRYING = eager to find out about things. **Curious** = eager to learn things, but sometimes suggests being too eager to know about other people's business: *A normal child is curious about how things work.* **Inquisitive** suggests constantly asking questions to find out what one wants to know, especially about personal matters: *She is too inquisitive about my dates.* **Prying** adds to *inquisitive* the idea of peeping and of busying oneself about other people's business: *I had a prying landlord.*

cu•ri•um ['kjʊriəm] *n.* a radioactive chemical element produced by the bombardment of plutonium and uranium by helium ions. *Symbol:* Cm; *at.no.* 96; *at.mass* 247.07; *half-life* 1.6×10^7 years. ⟨after Mme. Marie *Curie* (1867-1934), a French physicist and chemist, born in Poland⟩

curl [kɜrl] *v., n.* *—v.* **1** twist or roll into a coil or coils (*sometimes used with* **up**): *to curl up a piece of paper. She uses a curling iron to curl her hair.* **2** take the form of ripples, coils, or twists (*often used with* **up**): *Paper curls when it burns.* **3** grow in coils or spirals: *My hair curls naturally.* **4** move or progress in curves or twists: *smoke curling from the chimney. A stream curled through the woods.* **5** form into a curve; twist: *Her lip curled in a sneer.* **6** *Curling.* **a** slide (a stone) down the ice. **b** engage in the game of curling.

curl up, a take a comfortable position sitting or lying down with one's legs drawn up: *The child curled up in the big chair and went to sleep.* **b** *Informal.* collapse; break down.

—n. **1** a curled lock of hair. **2** something shaped like this. **3** a curling or being curled. **4** a disease of plants which makes the leaves curl up.

in curl, curled: *keeping hair in curl.* ⟨ME *curle(n), crulle(n)* < *crul* curly⟩

curl•er ['kɜrlər] *n.* **1** a person who takes part in the game of curling. **2** a device on which hair is twisted to make it curl.

cur•lew ['kɜrlu] *or* ['kɜrlju] *n., pl.* **-lew** or **-lews.** any of a genus (*Numenius*) of medium-sized or large wading birds related to the sandpipers, having a long, thin, downward-curving bill. They breed in temperate and subarctic regions of the northern hemisphere and migrate to the southern hemisphere for winter. ⟨ME < OF *courlieu;* imitative⟩

A curlew

curl•i•cue ['kɜrlɪ,kju] *n.* a fancy twist, curl, flourish, etc.: *curlicues in handwriting.* ⟨< *curly* + *cue*[2]⟩

curl•ing ['kɜrlɪŋ] *n., v.* *—n.* a game played on ice, in which large, heavy, round stones are slid toward a target at the end of the rink.

—v. ppr. of CURL.

curling iron an instrument for curling hair by means of heat and, sometimes, steam, consisting of a usually metal rod that is heated and around which a strand of hair to be curled is wound.

curling stone or **rock** the object, usually made of granite, that is slid down the ice in the game of curling.

curling tongs CURLING IRON.

curl•pa•per ['kɜrl,peipər] *n.* a piece of folded paper over which a lock of hair is rolled up tightly to curl it.

curl–up ['kɜrl ,ʌp] *n.* a modified sit-up; a conditioning exercise that consists of lying on one's back with knees bent, and raising the head, neck, and shoulders from the floor so as to bring the chin as near as possible to the chest. Compare SIT-UP.

curl•y ['kɜrli] *adj.* **curl•i•er, curl•i•est. 1** curling; having a tendency to curl; wavy: *curly hair.* **2** having curls: *a curly head.* **3** of wood, having a wavy grain. **—'curl•i•ness,** *n.*

cur•mudg•eon [kər'mʌdʒən] *n.* a rude, stingy, bad-tempered man. ⟨origin unknown⟩ **—cur'mudg•eon•ly,** *adj.*

cur•rach or **cur•ragh** ['kʌrəx] *or* ['kʌrə] *n.* coracle. ⟨< Irish and Scots Gaelic *currach;* 15c.⟩

cur•rant ['kɜrənt] *n.* **1** a small, seedless raisin, used in cakes, etc. **2** a small, sour, edible berry that is the fruit of any of several shrubs (genus *Ribus*) of the saxifrage family. Currants may be red, white, or black and are used for jelly, wine, preserves, etc. **3** a shrub that produces these berries. ⟨ME *(raysons of) Coraunte* < AF *(raisins de) Corauntz* raisins of Corinth⟩

☛ *Hom.* CURRENT.

cur•ren•cy ['kɜrənsi] *n., pl.* **-cies. 1** the money in actual use in a country: *Canadian currency cannot be used in Mexico.* **2** a passing from person to person; circulation: *The town gossips gave the rumour currency.* **3** general use or acceptance; common occurrence: *The word* fire-reels, *which was the common term for a fire engine in Toronto and Montréal, has now passed out of currency.*

cur•rent ['kɜrənt] *n., adj.* *—n.* **1** a flow or stream of water or air in one direction, especially within a larger body of water or air: *Stay near the shore so you don't get caught in the current.* **2** a flow of electricity along a wire, etc. **3** the rate or amount of such a flow, usually expressed in amperes: *Heating requires much more current than lighting does.* **4** a course or tendency of events, ideas, etc.; a general direction or drift: *the current of public opinion.*

—adj. **1** of or at the present time: *current fashions, the current month. His current job involves a lot of travelling.* **2** most recent: *The current issue of a magazine is the one most recently published.* **3** generally used or accepted; common or prevalent: *Many slang expressions of the seventies are no longer current.* **4** going around; passing from person to person: *A rumour is current that prices will go up.* ⟨ME < OF < L *current, -entis,* ppr. of *currere* run⟩

☛ *Hom.* CURRANT.

☛ *Syn. n.* **1.** See note at STREAM. *—adj.* **1, 3. Current,** PRESENT, PREVAILING = generally used or occurring at a certain time. **Current** emphasizes the notion of continuity in circulation or use at a given time: *English usage current in the 17th century.* **Present** means here and now: *This apartment meets my present needs.* **Prevailing** emphasizes relative predominance or vogue: *This bathing suit agrees with the prevailing fashion.*

current density a measure of the electric current flowing through a cross-section of the conductor of a right angle to the direction of the current. Current density is measured in amperes per square centimetre.

cur•rent•ly ['kɜrəntli] *adv.* **1** at the present time or in the present period: *The prime minister is currently vacationing in the Maritimes. Her songs are currently very popular.* **2** generally; commonly.

cur•ri•cle ['kɜrəkəl] *n.* a two-wheeled carriage drawn by two horses. ⟨< L *curriculum.* See CURRICULUM.⟩

cur•ric•u•lar [kə'rɪkjələr] *adj.* having to do with a curriculum.

cur•ric•u•lum [kə'rɪkjələm] *n., pl.* **-lums** or **-la** [-lə]. **1** the whole range of studies offered in a school, college, etc., or in a type of school: *the university curriculum. Our high-school curriculum includes English, mathematics, science, history, and modern languages.* **2** the prescribed content of any one course of study: *The English curriculum at this school changes every few years.* **3** a program of studies leading to a particular degree, certificate, etc.: *the curriculum of the Law School.* ⟨< L *curriculum* race course, chariot, dim. of *currus* chariot < *currere* run⟩

curriculum vi•tae ['vitaɪ] *pl.* **curricula vitae.** a summary of one's life, listing schools, colleges, etc. attended, jobs held, prizes

or other distinctions gained, etc., used especially to accompany job applications. *Abbrev.*: c.v. ⟨< L; literally, course of life⟩
☛ *Syn.* **Curriculum vitae,** RÉSUMÉ = summary of one's life, qualifications, etc. In Canadian usage, **résumé** is the general term; **curriculum vitae** is used mainly in academic and professional situations.

cur•ri•er ['kɜriər] *n.* **1** a person who curries tanned leather. **2** a person who curries horses, etc. ⟨ME < OF *corier* < L *coriarius* tanner < *corium* leather⟩
☛ *Hom.* COURIER.

cur•rish ['kɜrɪʃ] *adj.* of or like a cur; snarling; ill-bred; worthless. **—'cur•rish•ly,** *adv.* **—'cur•rish•ness,** *n.*

cur•ry[1] ['kɜri] *v.* **-ried, -ry•ing. 1** rub and clean (a horse, etc.) with a brush or currycomb. **2** prepare (tanned leather) for use by soaking, scraping, beating, colouring, etc. **3** beat or whip.
curry favour (with someone), seek (a person's) favour by flattery, constant attentions, etc. ⟨ME < OF *correier* put in order < *con-* (intensive) + *reier* arrange < Gmc.⟩

cur•ry[2] ['kɜri] *n., pl.* **-ries;** *v.* **-ried, -ry•ing.** *—n.* **1** a spicy dish consisting especially of meat, fish, or eggs prepared with a sauce seasoned with pungent spices such as cayenne, ginger, coriander, etc. Curries are common in S Asia, the West Indies, etc. **2** a sauce seasoned with such spices. **3** CURRY POWDER.
—v. prepare with curry sauce or powder: *curried lamb.* ⟨< Tamil *kari*⟩

cur•ry•comb ['kɜri,koum] *n., v.* *—n.* a brush with metal teeth for rubbing and cleaning a horse.
—v. use a currycomb on; brush with a currycomb.

curry powder a finely ground mixture of spices, such as turmeric, cumin, coriander, cayenne, ginger, etc., used especially to make curries.

curse [kɜrs] *v.* **cursed** or **curst, curs•ing;** *n.* *—v.* **1** call on a supernatural or divine being to bring evil or harm to: *to curse one's enemies.* **2** bring evil or harm to; torment or afflict: *cursed with poverty, cursed by the gods.* **3** rail at by using blasphemous words; revile: *to curse one's fate, to curse the gods.* **4** use blasphemous or obscene words to express anger, hatred, frustration, etc.; swear or swear at: *He cursed when he hit his thumb with the hammer. She cursed her servant for his clumsiness.* **5** excommunicate.
be cursed with, have and suffer from: *Richard is cursed with a weak stomach.*
—n. **1** the words that a person says when he or she curses someone or something. **2** a person or thing that is or ought to be cursed; a source of evil or harm: *The stolen money proved to be a curse to them. Malaria was the curse of the expedition.* **3** harm or evil that comes as if in answer to a curse or as a retribution: *They claimed that there was a curse on the diamond.* **4** a blasphemous or obscene word used to express anger, hatred, frustration, etc.: *Their talk was full of curses.* **5 the curse,** *Slang.* **a** menstruation. **b** an occurrence of menstruation; period. **6** a sentence of excommunication. ⟨OE *cūrs,* n., *cursian,* v.⟩ **—'curs•er,** *n.*
☛ *Syn. v.* **3, 4. Curse,** SWEAR = use profane or foul language. **Curse** emphasizes anger or hatred: *He cursed the poor waitress who had spilled soup on him.* **Swear** (def. 1) suggests using the names of holy persons or things or similar words to punctuate one's speech or express feelings: *He swore horrible oaths when he hurt himself.*

curs•ed ['kɜrsɪd] *or* [kɜrst] *adj., v.* *—adj.* **1** under a curse. **2** deserving a curse; evil; hateful.
—v. [kɜrst] a pt. and a pp. of CURSE. **—'curs•ed•ly,** *adv.* **—'cur•sed•ness,** *n.*

cur•sive ['kɜrsɪv] *adj., n.* *—adj.* written with the letters joined together. Ordinary handwriting is cursive.
—n. **1** a letter made to join other letters. **2** a style of printing type imitating handwriting. **3** cursive script. ⟨< Med.L *cursivus* < *cursus,* pp. of L *currere* run⟩ **—'cur•sive•ly,** *adv.*

cur•sor ['kɜrsər] *n.* **1** *Computer technology.* a mark on the video display of a computer that indicates where the next character will be placed. **2** the sliding glass of a slide rule or optical instrument, having a fine hairline on it, used to facilitate computing or sighting. ⟨< L, runner⟩

cur•so•ri•al [kər'sɔriəl] *adj.* **1** for running. **2** having legs fitted for running: *The ostrich is a cursorial bird.*

cur•so•ry ['kɜrsəri] *adj.* hasty; superficial; without attention to details: *Even a cursory reading of the letter showed many errors.* ⟨< LL *cursorius* of a race < *currere* run⟩ **—'cur•so•ri•ly,** *adv.* **—'cur•so•ri•ness,** *n.*

curst [kɜrst] *adj., v. Archaic.* *—adj.* cursed.
—v. a pt. and a pp. of CURSE.

curt [kɜrt] *adj.* short; rudely brief; abrupt: *Her curt answer made him angry.* ⟨< L *curtus* cut short⟩ **—'curt•ly,** *adv.* **—'curt•ness,** *n.*
☛ *Syn.* See note at BLUNT.

cur•tail [kər'teil] *v.* cut short; cut off part of; reduce; lessen. ⟨< *curtal,* adj., cut short (especially of tails) < OF *curtald* < L *curtus;* influenced by *tail*⟩
☛ *Syn.* See note at SHORTEN.

cur•tail•ment [kər'teilmənt] *n.* a curtailing; diminution.

cur•tain ['kɜrtən] *n., v.* *—n.* **1** a piece of cloth or other similar material hung at windows or in doorways to protect from sun, wind, or rain, to separate, conceal, or darken, or to decorate. **2** *Theatre.* **a** a movable hanging screen that separates the stage from the part where the audience sits. **b** the opening or rising of the curtain at the beginning of an act or scene, or the fall or closing of the curtain at the end of an act or scene. **3** anything that hides or acts as a barrier: *a curtain of fog. They had placed a curtain of secrecy over all their movements.* **4** the part of a wall between two bastions, towers, or the like. **5 curtains,** *pl. Slang.* death: *One false move and it's curtains for all of you.*
bring or **ring down** or **lower the curtain on,** terminate; end: *The merger brought down the curtain on the company's independence.*
draw the curtain over or **on,** conceal.
raise the curtain on, a disclose; reveal. **b** be or mark the beginning of.
ring up the curtain, a raise or open a theatre curtain. **b** begin something.
—v. **1** provide with or as if with a curtain. **2** hide or cover with or as if with a curtain.
curtain off, separate or divide by means of a curtain or curtains. ⟨ME < OF *curtine* < LL *cortina*⟩ **—'cur•tain•less,** *adj.*

curtain call 1 a call for an actor, musician, etc., to return to the stage and acknowledge the applause of the audience. **2** the reappearance by the performer(s).

curtain lecture a scolding given by a wife to her husband. ⟨originally with reference to the old-fashioned curtained bed⟩

curtain raiser 1 *Theatre.* a short play given before the main play. **2** a little thing used to introduce something bigger: *The walkout of a few workers was the curtain raiser to a major strike.*

curtain speech a speech, usually by a performer and often in front of the theatre curtain, given after a play.

curtain wall a wall between columns or piers of a frame or skeleton of a building, which supports no load other than its own weight, and is not supported by girders or beams.

cur•te•sy ['kɜrtəsi] *n., pl.* **-sies.** *Law.* the right a husband has, under certain conditions, in the land left by his dead wife. ⟨var. of *courtesy*⟩
☛ *Hom.* COURTESY.

curt•sey ['kɜrtsi] *n., pl.* **-seys;** *v.* **-seyed, -sey•ing.** See CURTSY.

curt•sy ['kɜrtsi] *n., pl.* **-sies;** *v.* **-sied, -sy•ing.** *—n.* a bow of respect or greeting by women, made by bending the knees and lowering the body slightly.
—v. make a curtsy. ⟨var. of *courtesy*⟩

cu•rule chair ['kjʊrul] a special folding seat used by the highest civil officials in ancient Rome. It was upholstered, backless, armless, and had thick curved legs. ⟨< L *curulis* < *currus* chariot⟩

cur•va•ceous [kər'veiʃəs] *adj. Informal.* of a girl or woman, having a full figure, attractively well-developed.

cur•va•ture ['kɜrvətʃər] *or* ['kɜrvə,tʃʊr] *n.* **1** a curving or bending. **2** a curved condition, especially an abnormal one: *a curvature of the spine.* **3** a curved piece or part; curve. **4** the degree of curving; curve: *the curvature of the earth's surface.*

curve [kɜrv] *n., v.* **curved, curv•ing.** *—n.* **1** a line that has no straight part. **2** something having the shape of a curve; bend: *The driver had to slow down for the curves in the road.* **3** *Baseball.* a ball pitched with a spin that causes it to swerve just before it reaches the batter: *A good curve is difficult to hit.* **4** the degree to or manner in which something curves. **5** *Mathematics.* a line whose course can be defined by an equation, such as a parabola or a straight line. **6** a line on a graph, representing statistical data, such as economic trends, average achievement of a group, etc.: *the cost-of-living curve.*
—v. **1** bend so as to form a curve. **2** move in the course of a curve. **3** pitch a curve in baseball. **4** *Informal.* adjust (marks or grades) so as to conform to a standard curve. ⟨< L *curvus* bending⟩

curve•ball ['kɜrv,bɒl] *n.* CURVE (def. 3).

curved [kɜrvd] *adj., v.* *—adj.* bent so as to form a curve.
—v. pt. and pp. of CURVE.

cur•vet *n.* ['kɜrvɪt]; *v.* [kər'vɛt] *or* ['kɜrvɪt] *n., v.* **-vet•ted** or **-vet•ed, -vet•ting** or **-vet•ing.** *—n.* a leap in the air made by a

horse. The forelegs are first raised and then the hind legs, so that all legs are off the ground for a second.
—v. **1** of a horse, make a leap in the air. **2** make (a horse) leap in the air. ⟨< Ital. *corvetta,* dim. of *corvo* curve < L *curvus* bending. Doublet of CAVORT.⟩

cur•vi•lin•e•al [ˌkɜrvəˈlɪniəl] *adj.* curvilinear.

cur•vi•lin•e•ar [ˌkɜrvəˈlɪniər] *adj.* consisting of a curved line or lines; enclosed by curved lines. Also, **curvilineal**. **—ˌcur•viˈlin•e•ar•ly,** *adv.*

curv•y [ˈkɜrvi] *adj.* **1** *Informal.* curvaceous. **2** having a curve or curves.

cus•cus [ˈkʌskəs] *n.* a marsupial of the genus *Phalanger,* native to NE Australia and having pointed ears and a bushy prehensile tail. It lives in trees. ⟨< native name⟩

cush•at [ˈkʌʃət] *or* [ˈkʊʃət] *n.* a wood pigeon (*Columba palumbus*).

cu•shaw [kəˈʃɒ] *n.* a kind of squash (*Cucurbita moschata*) with a long, curved neck. ⟨< Algonquian⟩

Cush•ing's disease [ˈkʊʃɪŋz] a disease caused by malfunction of the adrenal gland and characterized by obesity, fatigue, hypertension, and osteoporosis. ⟨after Harvey *Cushing* (1869-1939), American neurosurgeon⟩

cush•ion [ˈkʊʃən] *n., v. —n.* **1** a soft pillow or pad used to sit, lie, or kneel on. **2** anything used or shaped like a cushion. Air or steam forms a cushion in some machines to protect them from sudden shocks or jars. **3** anything that lessens the effects of distress or adversity, relieves a burden, or makes for greater comfort or ease: *a cushion of savings against sickness or retirement.* **4** *Cdn.* the enclosed ice surface, especially an outdoor one, on which hockey is played. **5** the elastic lining of the sides of a billiard table. **6** the layer of soft rubber in the casing of a pneumatic tire.
—v. **1** put or seat on a cushion; support with cushions. **2** supply with a cushion. **3** protect from sudden shocks or jars with a cushion of steam. **4** protect: *His family's wealth had always cushioned him against failure.* **5** ease the effects of: *The presence of caring friends cushioned her grief.* **6** hide or suppress, as if under a cushion. ⟨ME < OF *coussin,* probably < VL *coxinum* < L *coxa* hip⟩ **—ˈcush•ionˌlike,** *adj.*

cush•y [ˈkʊʃi] *adj.* **cush•i•er, cush•i•est.** *Slang.* luxuriously comfortable and easy: *a cushy job, a cushy life.* ⟨< Hind. *khush* pleasant⟩ **—ˈcush•i•ness,** *n.*

cusk [kʌsk] *n., pl.* **cusk** or **cusks.** a large food fish (*Brosme brosme*) of the cod family found along the North American and European coasts of the Atlantic, having a barbel on the chin, a single, long dorsal fin, and a single, long anal fin. ⟨origin unknown⟩

CUSO formerly, Canadian Universities Service Overseas, an organization sending people, especially young people, to work in the Third World.

cusp [kʌsp] *n.* **1** a pointed end; point: *A crescent has two cusps.* **2** a blunt or pointed protuberance on the crown of a tooth. **3** *Astrology.* the time when two signs are adjacent.
on the cusp of, ready for; about to experience: *on the cusp of fame.* ⟨< L *cuspis, -pidis*⟩

cus•pid [ˈkʌspɪd] *n.* a tooth having one cusp; a canine tooth. ⟨< L *cuspid-, cuspis* point, cusp⟩

cus•pi•dal [ˈkʌspədəl] *adj.* **1** of or having to do with a cusp. **2** having a pointed end.

cus•pi•date [ˈkʌspəˌdeit] *adj.* having a sharp, pointed end.

cus•pi•da•tion [ˌkʌspəˈdeiʃən] *n. Architecture.* the use of pointed designs for ornament.

cus•pi•dor [ˈkʌspəˌdɔr] *n.* a container to spit into; spittoon. ⟨< Pg. *cuspidor* spitter < *cuspir* spit < L *conspuere* spit on < *com-* + *spuere* spit⟩

cuss [kʌs] *n., v. Informal. —n.* **1** a curse. **2** an odd or troublesome person or animal: *Tell that cuss to get over here now.*
—v. curse (*often used with* **out**): *He cussed me out for a whole half minute.* ⟨var. of *curse*⟩ **—ˈcus•ser,** *n.*

cuss•ed [ˈkʌsɪd] *adj. Informal.* **1** cursed. **2** stubborn. **—ˈcuss•ed•ly,** *adv.* **—ˈcuss•ed•ness,** *n.*

cus•tard [ˈkʌstərd] *n.* a baked, boiled, or frozen food made of eggs and milk, usually sweetened. ⟨var. of *crustade* < F < Provençal *croustado* pasty[2] < L *crustare* encrust < *crusta* crust⟩

custard apple **1** any of various shrubs or small trees (genus *Annona*) of tropical America, especially *A. reticulata* of the West Indies, having dark brown fruit with a sweet, reddish yellow, very soft pulp. **2** the fruit of this tree. **3** (*adjl.*) **custard-apple,** designating a family (Annonaceae) of shrubs and trees that includes the custard apple, pawpaw, and soursop.

cus•to•di•al [kʌˈstoudiəl] *adj.* having to do with custody or custodians.

cus•to•di•an [kʌˈstoudiən] *n.* **1** the person in charge; guardian or keeper: *the custodian of a museum, the legal custodian of a child.* **2** caretaker; janitor.

cus•to•di•an•ship [kʌˈstoudiənˌʃɪp] *n.* the position or duties of a custodian.

cus•to•dy [ˈkʌstədi] *n., pl.* **-dies. 1** a keeping; charge; care: *Parents have custody of their young children.* **2** a being confined or detained; imprisonment.
in custody, in the care of the police; in prison.
take into custody, arrest. ⟨< L *custodia* < *custos, -odis* guardian⟩

cus•tom [ˈkʌstəm] *n., adj. —n.* **1** a usual action; habit: *It was her custom to rise early.* **2** a habit maintained for so long that it has almost the force of law. **3** the accepted way of acting in a community or other group; convention; tradition. **4** the regular business given by a customer: *She threatened to take her custom to another store.* **5** customers collectively. **6 customs,** *pl.* **a** a duty paid to the government on things brought in from a foreign country. **b** the office at a seaport, international airport, or border crossing where imported goods are checked. **c** the department of the government that collects duty. **7** in feudal times, a tax or service regularly due from tenants to their lord.
—adj. **1** made or done specially for an individual customer; made or done to order: *a car with custom fenders, custom threshing.* **2** making or doing things to order; not selling mass-produced goods or services: *a custom tailor.* ⟨ME < OF *custume* < VL *consuetumen* < L *consuescere.* Doublet of COSTUME.⟩
☛ *Syn. n.* **1.** See note at HABIT.

cus•tom•ar•y [ˈkʌstəˌmɛri] *adj.* **1** according to custom; as a habit; usual. **2** holding or held by custom; established by custom: *customary law.* **—ˌcus•tomˈar•i•ly,** *adv.*
☛ *Syn.* See note at USUAL.

cus•tom–built [ˈkʌstəm ˈbɪlt] *adj.* built according to the specifications of an individual customer: *a custom-built bedroom suite.*

cus•tom•er [ˈkʌstəmər] *n.* **1** a person who buys, especially a regular patron of a particular store. **2** *Informal.* a person; fellow: *Don't get mixed up with him; he's a rough customer.*

cus•tom•ize [ˈkʌstəˌmaɪz] *v.* **-ized, -iz•ing.** make or alter according to individual requirements; make or alter to order: *to customize a van.* **—ˈcus•tomˌiz•er,** *n.*

cus•tom–made [ˈkʌstəm ˈmeid] *adj.* made according to the specifications of an individual customer: *custom-made draperies.*

customs house a government building or office where taxes on things brought into a country are collected.

customs officer a government official who examines goods being brought into a country and charges any taxes that may be payable.

customs union a group of countries which eliminate customs duty on goods travelling between them, and impose the same duty on other nations.

cut [kʌt] *v.* **cut, cut•ting;** *adj., n. —v.* **1** open, remove part of, or divide with something sharp: *to cut meat, timber, grass, one's nails, etc.* **2** make, shape, or prepare by cutting: *He cut a hole through the wall with an axe. I cut two left shirtfronts by mistake.* **3** take off or remove by cutting: *She cut a large slice from the loaf.* **4** make a cut, opening, channel, etc.: *This knife cuts well. The river has cut deep through the rock.* **5** be cut; admit of being cut: *Stale bread cuts better than fresh bread.* **6** pierce or wound with something sharp: *She cut her finger on the broken glass.* **7** grow (a new tooth): *The baby is fretful because she is cutting her teeth.* **8** geld (a stallion or bullock). **9** reduce; decrease: *to cut expenses.* **10** dilute (alcohol): *whisky cut with water.* **11** prepare (a stencil) for mimeographing or the like: *to cut a stencil.* **12** engrave: *Their names were cut on the inside of the ring.* **13** go by a more direct way; go: *He cut across the field to save time.* **14** cross; divide by crossing: *A brook cuts that field.* **15** make a recording on: *to cut a record, tape, etc.* **16** edit (film): *A good movie can be ruined by being badly cut.* **17** remove (part of a film, play, or book): *We'll have to cut that scene.* **18** in film, move suddenly to another scene: *Now let's cut to the street scene.* **19** shape (a diamond): *The value of a diamond depends on how well it is cut.* **20** work as a cutter. **21** hit or strike sharply: *The cold wind cut me to the bone.* **22** *Sports.* hit with a slicing stroke: *He cut the ball so that it bounded almost backward.* **23** hurt the feelings of: *His mean remarks cut me.* **24** *Informal.* refuse to recognize socially: *Everyone in the class cut the boy who came first in the test by* *cheating.* **25** *Informal.* be absent from (a class, lecture, etc.) without authorization: *He wanted to cut history when he heard there was going to be a test.* **26** make less sticky or stiff; dissolve: *Gasoline cuts grease and tar.* **27** draw (a card) at random from a pack. **28** divide (a pack of cards) at random. **29** *Informal.* do; perform; make: *to cut a caper.* **30** shorten by omitting some part or parts: *Your speech will be more effective if you cut it in several places.* **31** come to an end; conclude; stop (especially as an order to stop cameras filming a motion picture or television scene). **32** change direction suddenly: *She had to cut to the right to avoid the oncoming car.*

cut across, go straight across or through.
cut a figure, a look good. **b** invite attention by one's appearance, conversation, etc.
cut and run, depart hastily.
cut back, a go back suddenly. **b** shorten (a plant) by cutting off the end. **c** reduce output, expenditure, etc. **d** return to an earlier part of a film, book, etc.
cut both ways, have disadvantages or bad effects as well as advantages or good effects.
cut corners, a take a short way around a square. **b** find a short way to do something. **c** do a job not very thoroughly. **d** shortchange someone.
cut down, a cause to fall by cutting. **b** reduce; decrease. **c** kill. **d** humiliate.
cut down to size, *Informal.* **a** humiliate (someone). **b** *Informal.* lessen the importance or prestige of (something or someone considered to be important); belittle.
cut in, a go in suddenly. **b** break in; interrupt. **c** interrupt a dancing couple to take the place of one of them. **d** move a vehicle suddenly into a line of moving traffic. **e** connect, join, etc., especially to a machine or working part. **f** mix (shortening, butter, etc.) into flour by working it in with a knife.
cut it, be up to par; be satisfactory: *Her work just doesn't cut it.*
cut it out, cease whatever irritating activity one is engaged in.
cut loose, *Informal.* speak or act in an uncontrolled way.
cut no ice (with), *Informal.* fail to impress; fail to accomplish anything.
cut off, a remove from the outside of something by cutting: *to cut off the bark of a tree.* **b** shut off: *Our power was cut off for an hour.* **c** stop suddenly. **d** break; interrupt. **e** disinherit. **f** block. **g** in driving, force (another) to brake by moving unexpectedly into the space immediately in front of his or her vehicle.
cut one's teeth on, learn or use (something) when very young.
cut out, a remove from the inside by cutting: *She cut the core out of the apple.* **b** take out; leave out. **c** usurp the place of; get the better of. **d** make by cutting; make; form: *Her cousin showed her how to cut out paper dolls.* **e** *Slang.* stop doing, using, making, etc.: *to cut out candy. He was told to cut out the teasing.* **f** move out of an assigned or expected position: *The reckless driver suddenly cut out from his own lane.* **g** of an engine, suddenly stop working. **h** *Slang.* depart unexpectedly.
cut out for, suited to: *She's not cut out for a musical career.*
cut short. See SHORT.
cut (someone) **dead,** be obvious about refusing to recognize socially.
cut teeth. See TEETH.
cut up, a cut into small pieces. **b** *Informal.* hurt. **c** *Informal,* show off or behave like a clown.
cut up rough, a become physically violent. **b** make difficulties. **c** misbehave badly.
—adj. **1** that has been cut: *a cut pie.* **2** *Botany.* of a leaf or petal, with incised edges. **3** shaped or formed by cutting. **4** reduced: *at cut prices.* **5** gelded.
cut and dried, a arranged in advance. **b** too predictable; dull; uninteresting.
—n. **1** a wound or opening made by cutting. **2** a passage, channel, etc., made by cutting or digging. **3** a piece cut off or cut out: *a cut of meat.* **4** the way in which a thing is cut; style; fashion. **5** a decrease, reduction. **6** a way straight across or through; shortcut. **7** the edge or surface of something that has been cut: *a ragged cut, a clean cut.* **8** a sharp blow or stroke. **9** *Sports.* a slicing stroke. **10** an action or speech that hurts feelings. **11** *Informal.* refusal to recognize socially. **12** *Informal.* an unauthorized absence from a class, lecture, etc. **13** *Logging.* the amount of wood cut: *Nearly half the cut is pulpwood.* **14** *Printing.* **a** a block or plate with a picture engraved on it. **b** a picture made from such a block or plate. **15** *Informal.* a share: *Each partner has a cut of the profits.* **16** one of the sections of a recording. **17** in film, **a** a sudden change to another scene. **b** a whole movie in its edited form: *a rough cut.* **18 a** a random division of a pack of playing cards. **b** the random selection of one card. **19** haircut. **20** the act of cutting: *She made a quick cut into the cardboard.* **21** *Cdn.* a natural gully or ravine, serving as a pass through a mountainous region.
a cut above, *Informal.* somewhat superior to: *He's a cut above the average politician, but he's no statesman.* ⟨ME *cutte(n)*; origin uncertain⟩

☛ *Syn. v.* **1. Cut,** CHOP, HACK = separate or remove with something sharp. **Cut** is the general word: *He cut some branches for kindling.* **Chop** = cut by hitting: *to chop wood.* **Hack** = cut or chop roughly and unevenly: *She hacked desperately at the rope to free herself.*

cut–and–dried ['kʌt ən 'draɪd] *adj.* **1** ready for use; prepared in advance: *a cut-and-dried scheme.* **2** dull; routine; lacking suspense or vitality: *a cut-and-dried lecture.*

cut and fill a system by which material excavated to make a road, canal, etc., is used to form an adjacent embankment.

cut and paste 1 a method of editing text by using scissors and tape. **2** *Computer technology.* remove a portion of a picture or text (in a document, spreadsheet, etc.) from one location and place it at another location. **—'cut-and-'paste,** *adj.*

cut and thrust 1 hand to hand fighting, especially with swords. **2** *Fencing.* the action of cutting and thrusting. **3** vigorous and lively interchange: *the cut and thrust of debate.*

cu•ta•ne•ous [kju'teiniəs] *adj.* of, on, or having to do with the skin. ⟨< Med.L *cutaneus* < L *cutis* skin⟩

cut•a•way ['kʌtə,wei] *n., adj.* *—n.* **1** a coat having the lower part cut back in a curve or slope from the waist in front to the tails in back. Cutaways are used by men for formal wear in the daytime. Some women wear tailored cutaways as formal evening wear. **2** a cutaway model. **3** (in film or television) a fast change from one shot to the next.
—adj. of or designating a drawing or model of a building, machine, etc., having part of the outside wall or surface cut away to show its internal structure or workings.

cut•back ['kʌt,bæk] *n.* **1** a reduction in output, expenditure, etc.: *The company has had to make cutbacks in expenditures because of a slump in sales.* **2** a flashback of past happenings in a novel, movie, etc.

cut•bank ['kʌt,bæŋk] *n.* the outer side of a curve in a stream or river where the force of the current has cut away the earth, leaving an overhanging bank.

cutch [kʌtʃ] *n.* a brown, resinous substance taken from the wood of an Oriental acacia, (*Acacia catechu*) used as an astringent and in dyeing and tanning; catechu. ⟨< Malay *kachu*⟩

cut•down ['kʌt,daʊn] *n. Medicine.* a procedure in which a vessel or cavity is opened so as to insert a catheter.

cute [kjut] *adj.* **cut•er, cut•est.** *Informal.* **1** pleasing or attractive, especially in a pretty, lovable, dainty, or delicate way: *a cute puppy, a cute dress, a cute girl.* **2** *Informal.* handsome; good-looking: *a cute guy.* **3** clever; shrewd; cunning: *a cute trick.* **4** consciously stylish or mannered: *cute dialogue.* ⟨var. of *acute*⟩ **—'cute•ly,** *adv.* **—'cute•ness,** *n.*

cute•sy ['kjutsi] *adj.* **cute•si•er, cute•si•est.** *Informal.* cute, especially in an affected or deliberate way.

cu•tey ['kjuti] See CUTIE.

cut glass glass shaped or decorated by grinding and polishing.

cut–grass ['kʌt ,græs] *n.* any of several grasses, such as *Leersia oryzoides*, which have leaves with sharp or hooked edges that can cut skin.

cu•ti•cle ['kjutəkəl] *n.* **1** the outer layer of skin of vertebrates; epidermis. **2** the strip of hardened or dead skin at the base and sides of a fingernail or toenail. **3** *Botany.* a very thin film covering the surface of a plant. **4** *Zoology.* the hard, dead, outer tissue of many invertebrates, secreted by the epidermis. ⟨< L *cuticula*, dim. of *cutis* skin⟩

cu•tie ['kjuti] *n.* **1** *Informal.* a cute person. Also, **cutey.** **2** *Slang.* a clever, shrewd person or plan.

cut–in ['kʌt ,ɪn] *n. Film.* a still or close-up added to a moving sequence to break up the action.

cu•tin ['kjutən] *n. Botany.* a waxy substance that is the chief ingredient of the outer skin of many plants. ⟨< L *cutis* skin⟩

cu•tin•ize ['kjutɪ,naɪz] *v.* **cu•tin•ized, cu•tin•iz•ing.** of outer plant cells, make or become waterproof with a layer of cutin. **—,cu•tin•i'za•tion,** *n.*

cu•tis ['kjutɪs] *n., pl.* **cutes** ['kjutiz]. **1** the skin beneath the epidermis; derma. **2** the two layers of vertebrate skin, the dermis and the epidermis. ⟨< L⟩

cut•lass ['kʌtləs] *n.* a short, heavy, slightly curved sword with a single-edged blade. ⟨< F *coutelas* < L *culter* knife⟩

cutlass fish any fish of the genus *Trichiurus*, having a long, compressed body and sharp teeth, native to tropical waters.

cut–leaved tooth•wort ['kʌt ,livd 'tuθwərt] a woodland plant (*Dentaria laciniata*) having divided leaves and clusters of white or pale purple flowers with four petals.

cut•ler ['kʌtlər] *n.* a person who makes, sells, or repairs knives, scissors, and other cutting instruments. ⟨ME < OF *coutelier* < *coutel* small knife < L *cultellus*, dim. of *culter* knife⟩

cut•ler•y ['kʌtləri] *n.* **1** knives, forks, and spoons for table use. **2** knives, scissors, and other cutting instruments. **3** the business of a cutler.

cut•let ['kʌtlɪt] *n.* **1** a slice of meat from the leg or ribs for broiling or frying: *a veal cutlet.* **2** a flat, fried cake of chopped meat or fish; croquette. ⟨< F *côtelette*, dim. of *côte* < L *costa* rib⟩

cut•line ['kʌt,laɪn] *n.* **1** a caption to an illustration, cartoon, etc. **2** *Cdn.* a survey or other line cut through bush.

cut•off ['kʌt,ɒf] *n., adj.* **1** the act of cutting off. **2** the point at which something is cut off, especially the limit set for an activity, process, etc. **3** an exit ramp or lane from a highway: *Take the Islington cutoff and go north.* **4** a short way across or through; a road or passage shorter than the one normally used. **5 a** a new passage cut by a river across a bend. **b** the water in the old channel, thus cut off. **6** a stopping of the passage of steam or working fluid to the cylinder of an engine. **7** the mechanism or device that does this. **8** the point in an electrical circuit at which a mechanism prevents the flow of current of certain frequencies to or from the circuit. **9** *Baseball.* the interception of a ball thrown to a base from the outfield. **10 cutoffs,** *pl. Informal.* jeans or other pants that have been cut without hemming to serve as shorts.
—*adj.* at or in which anything is cut off: *a cutoff date.*

cut•out ['kʌt,ʌut] *n.* **1** a shape or design that has been cut out or is to be cut out: *Some books for children have cutouts.* **2** a device that allows the exhaust gases of an internal-combustion engine to pass straight into the air instead of going through a muffler. **3** a device for breaking an electric current.

cut–o•ver ['kʌt 'ouvər] *adj.* from which the trees have been cut: *cut-over land.*

cut–price ['kʌt 'prəis] *adj. Brit.* CUT-RATE.

cut•purse ['kʌt,pərs] *n.* thief; pickpocket. ⟨from the former practice of stealing purses by cutting them from belts, where they used to be hung⟩

cut–rate ['kʌt 'reit] *adj.* having or featuring a price or prices below what is usual: *cut-rate merchandise, a cut-rate store.*

cut•tage ['kʌtɪdʒ] *n.* the technique of growing plants from cuttings.

cut•ter ['kʌtər] *n.* **1** a person who cuts, especially one whose work is cutting cloth to be made up into clothes. **2** a tool or machine for cutting: *a meat cutter.* **3** *Cdn.* a small, light sleigh, usually pulled by one horse. See SLEIGH for picture. **4** a kind of sleigh pulled as a trailer by a snowmobile. **5** a small sailboat with one mast. **6** a boat belonging to a warship, used to carry people and supplies to and from the ship. **7** a small, armed ship used for patrolling coastal waters.

cut•throat ['kʌt,θrout] *n., adj.* —*n.* **1** murderer. **2** CUTTHROAT TROUT.
—*adj.* **1** murderous. **2** relentless; merciless: *cutthroat competition.*

cutthroat trout *Cdn.* a large trout (*Salmo clarki*) distinguished by bright red streaks under the lower jaw, found mainly in the Rocky Mountain region and highly valued as a game fish.

cut time *Music.* 2/2 time, where the beat falls on the half note instead of the quarter note; alla breve.

cut•ting ['kʌtɪŋ] *n., adj., v.* —*n.* **1** something cut off or out, especially: **a** a small shoot cut from a plant to grow a new plant. **b** a newspaper or magazine clipping. **2** a place or way cut through high ground for a road, track, etc. **3** the act of one that cuts. **4** (*adjl.*) designed to cut; sharp or keen: *the cutting edge of a knife.* **5** (*adjl.*) on which things can be cut: *a cutting table.* **6** *Cdn.* a stand of timber.
—*adj.* **1** that hurts the feelings; sarcastic: *a cutting remark.* **2** cold and piercing: *a cutting wind.*
—*v.* ppr. of CUT. —**'cut•ting•ly,** *adv.*

cutting edge **1** the forefront, especially in reference to technological advance: *on the cutting edge of computer technology.* **2** the most effective or crucial part: *Our excellent sales force is the cutting edge of this company.*

cutting horse *Cdn.* a saddle horse trained to be used in separating an individual cow, etc., from a herd.

cut•tle ['kʌtəl] *n.* cuttlefish.

cut•tle•bone ['kʌtəl,boun] *n.* the hard internal shell of cuttlefish, used as a food supplement for caged birds and, in powder form, as a polishing agent.

cut•tle•fish ['kʌtəl,fɪʃ] *n., pl.* **-fish** or **-fish•es.** any of various marine molluscs (order Sepioidea) characterized by a broad, flattened body and a thick, calcified internal shell and having ten sucker-bearing arms, two of which are longer tentacles used in capturing prey. Cuttlefish belong to the same class (Cephalopoda) as octopuses and squids. ⟨*cuttle*, OE *cudele* cuttlefish⟩

cut–up ['kʌt ,ʌp] *n. Informal.* a person who shows off or behaves like a clown.

cut•wa•ter ['kʌt,wɒtər] *n.* **1** the front part of a ship's prow. **2** the wedge-shaped edge of a bridge pier, designed to break the force of the current.

cut•work ['kʌt,wɜrk] *n.* openwork embroidery in which part of the cloth is cut away.

cut•worm ['kʌt,wɜrm] *n.* the larva of any of various moths (family Noctuidae) that feeds on young plant stems at night, cutting them off near ground level. Cutworms are pests in gardens.

cu•vée [ku'vei]; *French.* [ky've] *n.* a mixture of various wines to produce a specific flavour, especially of champagne.

cu•vette [kju'vɛt] *n.* **1** a narrow glass tube used in laboratories. **2** a jewel with a bas-relief design. ⟨< F, basin, dim. of *cuve* vat < L *cupa* tub⟩

cu. yd. cubic yard(s).

CV *Cdn.* CROSS OF VALOUR.

C.V. CURRICULUM VITAE.

C.V.O. Commander (of the Royal) Victorian Order.

CVS CHORIONIC VILLUS SAMPLING.

C.V.S.M. Canadian Volunteer Service Medal.

C.W.A.C. or **CWAC** Canadian Women's Army Corps.

C.W.O. or **CWO** chief warrant officer.

cwt. hundredweight.

–cy *noun-forming suffix.* **1** the office, position, or rank of, as in *captaincy.* **2** the quality, state, condition, or fact of being, as in *bankruptcy.* ⟨(directly or < F *-cie*) < L *-cia*, Gk. *-keia*; (directly or < F *-cie* or *-tie*) < L *-tia*, Gk. *-tia*, *-teia*⟩

cy•an [saɪ'æn] *n., adj.* greenish blue. ⟨< Gk. *kyanos* blue substance⟩

cy•an•a•mide [saɪ'ænə,maɪd] *or* [saɪ'ænəmɪd] *n.* **1** a white or colourless crystalline chemical compound. *Formula*: CH_2N_2 **2** a salt of this compound.

cy•a•nate ['saɪə,neit] *n.* a salt of cyanic acid.

cy•an•ic [saɪ'ænɪk] *adj.* **1** of cyanogen; containing cyanogen. **2** blue. ⟨< Gk. *kyanos* dark blue⟩

cyanic acid a colourless, poisonous liquid. *Formula*: HOCN

cy•a•nide ['saɪə,naɪd] *or* ['saɪənɪd] *n., v.* **cy•an•id•ed, cy•an•id•ing.** —*n.* a salt of hydrocyanic acid, especially potassium cyanide (a powerful poison).
—*v.* treat with a cyanide.

cyanide process a method of refining gold or silver from coarse ore by treating it with sodium cyanide or potassium cyanide, followed by electrolysis.

cy•a•nine ['saɪə,nin] *or* ['saɪənɪn] *n.* a blue liquid dye which makes photographic plates more sensitive to colour. *Formula*: $C_{29}H_{35}N_2I$

cy•a•nite ['saɪə,nəit] *n.* a silicate of aluminum usually occurring in blue, blade-shaped crystals. *Formula*: Al_2SiO_5 Also, **kyanite.** ⟨< Gk. *kyanos* blue substance + E- *ite*[1]⟩

cy•a•no•co•bal•a•min [,saɪənoukou'bæləmɪn] *or* [,saɪənoukou'bɒləmɪn] *n.* vitamin B_{12}.

cy•an•o•gen [saɪ'ænədʒən] *n.* **1** a colourless, poisonous, flammable gas having the odour of bitter almonds. *Formula*: C_2N_2 **2** a univalent radical (-CN) consisting of one atom of carbon and one of nitrogen. ⟨< F *cyanogène* < Gk. *kyanos* dark blue substance + *-genēs* born, produced⟩

cy•a•no•sis [,saɪə'nousɪs] *n.* blueness or lividness of the skin, caused by lack of oxygen in the blood. ⟨< NL < Gk. *kyanōsis* dark blue colour < *kyanos* dark blue⟩

cy•a•not•ic [,saɪə'nɒtɪk] *adj.* of, having to do with, or affected with cyanosis.

cy•a•nu•ric acid [,saɪə'njʊrɪk] a white, soluble acid derived from urea and used in the manufacture of plastic, bleach, etc. *Formula*: $C_3N_3(OH)_3$

Cy•be•le ['sɪbə,li] *n.* a goddess of nature of ancient Asia Minor, parallel to the Greek goddess Rhea.

cy•ber– *combining form.* **1** having to do with computers: *cyberphobe.* **2** existing in cyberspace: *cyberart.*

cy•ber•nate ['saɪbər,neit] *v.* **-nat•ed, -nat•ing.** operate or control (a process, industry, etc.) by cybernation: *a cybernated bakery, a cybernated world.* ⟨< *cybern(etics)* + *-ate*[1]⟩

cy•ber•na•tion [,saɪbər'neiʃən] *n.* automation in manufacturing, etc., by means of computers.

cy•ber•net•ics [,saɪbər'nɛtɪks] *n.* the comparative study of communication and control mechanisms in living organisms and machines. ⟨< Gk. *kybernētikos* of a pilot < *kybernētēs* pilot < *kybernan* to steer⟩ **—,cy•ber'net•ic,** *adj.*

cy•ber•pho•bia [,saɪbər'foubiə] *n.* an abnormal fear of computers. **—'cy•ber,phobe,** *n.* **—,cy•ber'pho•bic,** *adj.*

cy•ber•space ['saɪbər,speis] *n. Computer technology.* major computer networks, activity on them, and products of such activity, especially when thought of as a special dimension or 'universe' in which things may exist which have no existence in the tangible world

cy•borg ['saɪbɔrg] *n.* a person or animal whose bodily functions are regulated or monitored by mechanical or electrical devices in a scientific experiment. ⟨< *cyb(ernetic)* + *org(anism)*⟩

cy•cad ['səikæd] *n.* any of an order (Cycadales) of large, palmlike, tropical or subtropical plants having long, fernlike leaves at the top of a thick, unbranched stem that resembles a column. There is only one surviving family (Cycadaceae) of cycads, which includes the sago palm. ⟨< NL *cycas, -adis* < Gk. *kykas*, scribal mistake for *koïkas*, pl. of *koïx* palm⟩

cy•cas ['səikæs] *n.* any Old World tropical plant of the genus *Cycas*, having dark green leaves and grown in warm climates for its decorative effect.

cy•cla•mate ['səiklə,meit] *n.* any of a group of salts of sodium or calcium formerly extensively used as substitutes for sugar. ⟨< *cycl(ohexyl-sulph)amate.* 20c.⟩

cyc•la•men ['səikləmən] *or* ['sɪkləmən] *n.* any of a genus (*Cyclamen*) of plants of the primrose family, having heart-shaped leaves and showy white, purple, pink, or crimson flowers, whose five petals bend backward. ⟨< NL < L < Gk. *kyklaminos*⟩

A cyclamen

cy•clan•de•late [səi'klændə,leit] *n.* a drug used to treat diseases of the vascular system.

cy•cla•zo•cine [,səiklə'zousin] *or* [,səiklə'zousɪn] *n.* an analgesic drug used to treat morphine or heroin addiction. Although not addictive itself, it blocks the action of morphine or heroin. *Formula*: $C_{18}H_{25}NO$

cy•cle ['səikəl] *n., v.* **-cled, -cling.** *—n.* **1** a period of time or complete process of growth or action that repeats itself in the same order: *The seasons of the year—spring, summer, fall, and winter—are a cycle.* **2** a complete set or series. **3** all the stories, poems, legends, etc., about a great hero or event: *There is a cycle of stories about the adventures of King Arthur and his knights.* **4** a very long period of time; age. **5** a bicycle, tricycle, or motorcycle. **6** *Electricity.* a complete or double alternation or reversal of an alternating current. The number of cycles per second is the measure of frequency. **7** an alternating sound wave: *The tone A above middle C is at 440 cycles per second, or hertz.* **8** *Biology.* a recurring series of changes. **9** *Botany.* a closed circle or whorl of leaves. **10** *Astronomy.* an orbit or circle in the heavens: *the cycle of a planet.* **11** *Physics.* a series of operations by which a substance or operation is finally brought back to the initial state. **12** the series of strokes of a piston in the cylinder of an engine. *—v.* **1** pass through a cycle; occur over and over again in the same order. **2** ride a cycle, especially a bicycle. ⟨< LL *cyclus* < Gk. *kyklos* wheel⟩

cy•clic ['səiklɪk] *or* ['sɪklɪk] *adj.* **1** of a cycle. **2** moving or occurring in cycles. **3** *Chemistry.* **a** containing a ring of atoms. **b** of or having to do with an arrangement of atoms in a ring or closed chain. Also, **cyclical. —'cy•clic•al•ly,** *adv.*

cy•clist ['səɪklɪst] *n.* the rider of a cycle, especially a bicycle or motorcycle.

cy•cli•zine ['səiklə,zin] *n.* an antihistamine drug used to treat nausea, including motion sickness. *Formula*: $C_{18}H_{22}N_2$

cyclo– *combining form.* **1** circle or circular, as in *cycloid.* **2** cyclic, as in *cyclopropane.* ⟨< Gk. *kyklos* wheel⟩

cy•clo•ben•za•prine [,səiklou'bɛnzə,prin] *n.* a muscle relaxant drug.

A cycloid (*n.* def.)

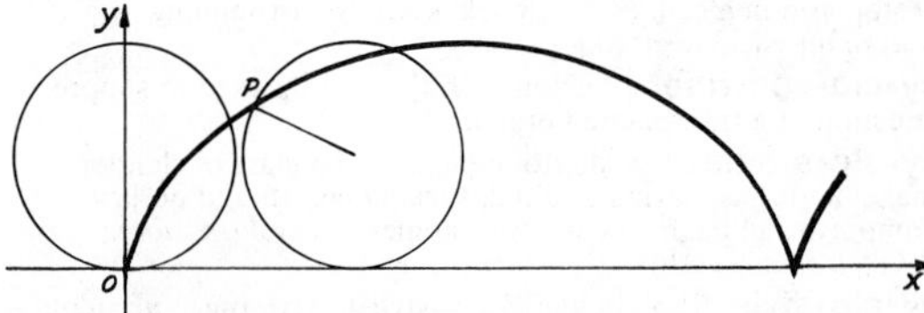

cy•cloid ['səiklɔɪd] *adj., n. —adj.* **1** like a circle. **2** of the scales of certain fishes, somewhat circular, with smooth edges. **3** of a fish, having cycloid scales. **4** of or having to do with a person who has cyclothymia.
—n. Geometry. a curve traced by a point on the circumference, on a radius, or on a prolonged radius of a circle when the circle is rolled along a straight line and kept in the same plane.

cy•clom•e•ter [səi'klɒmətər] *n.* **1** an instrument that records the number of revolutions that a wheel makes, used to measure the distance that a vehicle travels. **2** an instrument for measuring the arcs of circles.

cy•clone ['səikloun] *n.* **1** a severe windstorm resulting from a condition of low pressure, with winds moving in a spiral toward the centre, where the air pressure is lowest. Hurricanes and typhoons are cyclones. **2** a low-pressure condition or weather system that can produce such storms. Cyclones are sometimes thousands of kilometres across. **3** any violent windstorm with spiralling winds, such as a tornado. **4** in blast furnaces, a cylindrical vessel into which a gas is injected at a tangent, causing the gas to swirl around the cylinder. ⟨< Gk. *kyklōn*, ppr. of *kykloein* move around in a circle⟩

cyclone cellar a deep cellar in which people can shelter from cyclones.

Cyclone fence *Trademark.* a type of chain-link fence, often with barbed wire running along the top of it.

cy•clon•ic [səi'klɒnɪk] *adj.* **1** of a cyclone. **2** like a cyclone. Also, **cyclonical. —cy'clon•i•cal•ly,** *adv.*

cy•clo•nite ['səiklə,nəit] *n.* a crystalline compound, insoluble in water, used in the manufacture of rat poisons and explosives. *Formula*: $C_3H_6N_6O_6$

cy•clo•pae•di•a [,səiklə'pidiə] See CYCLOPEDIA.

cy•clo•pae•dic [,səiklə'pidɪk] See CYCLOPEDIC.

cy•clo•par•af•fin [,səiklou'pærəfɪn] *or* [,səiklou'pɜrəfɪn] *n.* any saturated, alicyclic hydrocarbon, containing at least three carbon atoms and having the basic formula C_nH_{2n}.

Cy•clo•pe•an [,səiklə'piən] *or* [səi'kloupiən] *adj.* **1** of or having to do with the Cyclopes. **2** Usually, **cyclopean,** huge; gigantic.

cy•clo•pe•di•a or **cy•clo•pae•di•a** [,səiklə'pidiə] *n.* a book giving information on all branches of one subject. A cyclopedia is different from an encyclopedia in that it usually does not go beyond one field or classification of knowledge. ⟨shortened form of *encyclopedia*⟩

cy•clo•pe•dic or **cy•clo•pae•dic** [,səiklə'pidɪk] *adj.* **1** wide and varied. **2** having to do with a cyclopedia.

cy•clo•pen•tane [,səiklou'pɛntein] *n.* a clear fluid cycloparaffin. *Formula*: C_5H_{10}

cy•clo•pen•to•late [,səiklou'pɛntə,leit] *n.* a drug used to dilate the pupil of the eye.

cy•clo•phos•pha•mide [,səiklou'fɒsfə,maɪd] *n.* a drug used to treat certain forms of cancer. *Formula*: $C_7H_{15}N_2O_2P$

cy•clo•ple•gia [,səiklou'plidʒiə] *or* [,səiklou'plidʒə] *n.* a defect in visual accommodation, caused by the paralysis of certain eye muscles. ⟨< NL < Gk. *kyklos* a circle + *-plegia* < *plege* a stroke⟩ **—,cy•clo'ple•gic,** *adj.*

cy•clo•pro•pane [,səiklou'proupein] *n.* a colourless, flammable gas used as an anesthetic. *Formula*: C_3H_6

Cy•clops ['səiklɒps] *n., pl.* **Cy•clo•pes** [səi'kloupiz]. *Greek* *mythology.* one of a group of one-eyed giants. ⟨< L < Gk. *Kyklōps* < *kyklos* circle + *ōps* eye⟩

cy•clo•ram•a [ˌsəiklə'ræmə] *n.* **1** a large picture of a landscape, battle, etc., on the wall of a circular room. **2** *Theatre.* a curved screen crossing the width of a stage and used as a background for the scenery. ⟨< *cyclo-* + Gk. *horama* spectacle⟩

cy•clo•sis [səi'klousɪs] *n.* the streaming movement of protoplasm in a cell. ⟨< NL < Gk. *kyklosis* surrounding < *kykloun* encircle < *kyklos* circle⟩

cy•clo•spo•rine [ˌsəiklou'spɔrin] *n.* a drug used to suppress rejection of a transplanted organ.

cy•clo•stome ['səikləˌstoum] *n.* any of a class of slender, snakelike fishes, having a round, sucking mouth and no jaws. Lampreys and hagfishes are cyclostomes. ⟨< *cyclo* + *stome* < Gk. *stoma* mouth⟩

cy•clo•style ['səikləˌstaɪl] *n., v.* **-styled, -styl•ing.** *—n.* an old method of duplicating by means of stencils.
—v. duplicate by this method.

cy•clo•thy•mia [ˌsəiklə'θaɪmiə] *n.* a mental illness in which the patient alternates between depression and high spirits; a mild form of manic-depressive psychosis. ⟨< NL < Gk. *kyklos* circle + *thymos* spirit⟩ **—ˌcy•clo'thy•mic,** *adj.*

cy•clo•tron ['səikləˌtrɒn] *n.* a type of accelerator in which charged particles are accelerated in a spiral inside two hollow, D-shaped metal electrodes. ⟨< *cyclo-* + *-tron* (as in *electron*)⟩

cyg•net ['sɪgnɪt] *n.* a young swan. ⟨ME < OF *cygne* < L *cygnus*, earlier *cycnus* < Gk. *kyknos*⟩
☛ *Hom.* SIGNET.

Cyg•nus ['sɪgnəs] *n. Astronomy.* a northern constellation in the Milky Way, thought of by the ancients as being arranged in the shape of a swan. ⟨< L *cygnus* swan⟩

cyl. cylinder; cylindrical.

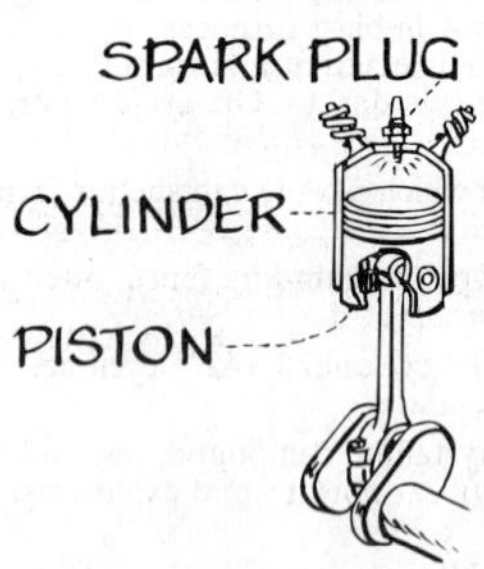

A cylinder of an internal-combustion engine

cyl•in•der ['sɪləndər] *n.* **1** a solid bounded by two equal, parallel circles and a curved surface, formed by moving a straight line of fixed length so that its ends always lie on the two parallel circles. See SOLID for picture. **2** the surface of such a solid. **3** any long, round object, solid or hollow, with flat ends: *Rollers and tin cans are cylinders.* **4** the part of a revolver that contains chambers for cartridges. **5** the piston chamber of an engine. See STEAM ENGINE for another picture. **6 a** a vessel or container having the form of a cylinder. **b** its contents. **7** a pump barrel. **8** any cylindrical roller on a printing press. **9** in the ancient Middle East, a big clay cylinder bearing cuneiform writing or a similar stone worn as a bracelet. ⟨< L *cylindrus* < Gk. *kylindros* < *kylindein* to roll⟩

cylinder head in an internal-combustion engine, the closed end of a cylinder.

cy•lin•dri•cal [sə'lɪndrəkəl] *adj.* shaped like a cylinder; having the form of a cylinder. Sometimes, **cylindric**.
—cy'lin•dri•cal•ly, *adv.* **—cyˌlin•dri'cal•i•ty,** *n.*

cyl•in•droid ['sɪlɪnˌdrɔɪd] *n., adj.* *—n.* a cylinder having oval instead of round ends.
—adj. like a cylinder.

cym•bal ['sɪmbəl] *n.* one of a pair of slightly concave metal plates, usually brass, used as a percussion instrument in music. Cymbals are struck together to make a ringing sound. A cymbal can also be struck with a drumstick, hammer, or wire brush. ⟨OE < L *cymbalum* < Gk. *kymbalon* < *kymbē* hollow of a vessel⟩
—'cym•bal•ist, *n.*
☛ *Hom.* SYMBOL.

cym•ba•lom ['sɪmbələm] *n.* See CIMBALOM.

cym•bid•ium [sɪm'bɪdiəm] *n.* an orchid of the genus *Cymbidium*, native to Asia and Australia, having long clusters of large yellow, pink, cream, or white flowers. ⟨< NL < L *cymba* a boat, skiff (< Gk. *kymbe* boat) + NL *-idium* dim. suffix⟩

cyme [saɪm] *n. Botany.* a flower cluster in which there is a flower at the top of the main stem and of each branch of the cluster. The flower in the centre opens first. The sweet william has cymes. See INFLORESCENCE for picture. ⟨< F < L *cyma* < Gk. *kyma* something swollen, sprout < *kyein* be pregnant⟩

cy•mene ['saɪmin] *n.* a colourless, sweet-smelling substance derived from cumin and other plants, and used to make paints. It exists in three forms: **orthocymene, metacymene,** and **paracymene.** *Formula*: $C_{10}H_{14}$ ⟨< Gk. See CUMIN.⟩

cy•mo•gene ['saɪməˌdʒin] *n.* a flammable by-product of petroleum, containing a high proportion of butane, used under pressure for freezing. ⟨< *cym(ene)* + F *-gène* < Gk. *-genes* born⟩

cym•o•phane ['saɪməˌfein] *n.* an iridescent type of chrysoberyl. ⟨< Gk. *kyma* something swollen (< *kyein* to be pregnant) + *phainein* to appear⟩

cy•mose ['saɪmous] *or* [saɪ'mous] *adj. Botany.* **1** having a cyme or cymes. **2** like a cyme. **—cy'mose•ly,** *adv.*

Cym•ric ['kɪmrɪk] *n., adj.* *—n.* **1** Welsh. **2** the group of Celtic languages that includes Breton, Cornish, and Welsh; the Brythonic languages.
—adj. **1** of or having to do with the Brythons or their languages. **2** of or having to do with the Welsh people or Welsh.

Cym•ry ['kɪmri] *n.* **1** the branch of the Celts that includes the Welsh, Cornish, and Bretons. **2** the Welsh people. ⟨< Welsh *Cymry* Welshmen, pl. of *Cymru*⟩

cyn•ic ['sɪnɪk] *n., adj.* *—n.* **1** a person inclined to believe that the motives for people's actions are insincere and selfish. **2** a sneering, sarcastic person. **3 Cynic,** in ancient Greece, a member of a group of philosophers who taught that self-control is the essential part of virtue. They despised pleasure, money, and personal comfort.
—adj. **1** cynical. **2 Cynic,** of or having to do with the Cynics or their doctrines. ⟨< L *cynicus* < Gk. *kynikos* doglike < *kyōn* dog⟩

cyn•i•cal ['sɪnəkəl] *adj.* **1** doubting the sincerity and goodness of others. **2** sneering; sarcastic. **—'cyn•i•cal•ly,** *adv.*
—'cyn•i•cal•ness, *n.*
☛ *Syn.* **1. Cynical,** PESSIMISTIC = doubting and mistrustful. **Cynical** emphasizes the idea of doubting the honesty, sincerity, and disinterestedness of people and their motives for doing things: *People cannot make friends with a person who is cynical about friendship.* **Pessimistic** emphasizes the idea of always looking on the dark side of things and expecting the most unpleasant or worst things to happen: *She has a very pessimistic attitude toward her work.*

cyn•i•cism ['sɪnəˌsɪzəm] *n.* **1** a cynical quality or disposition. **2** a cynical remark. **3 Cynicism,** the doctrines of the Cynics.

cy•no•pho•bia [ˌsaɪnə'foubiə] *n.* an abnormal fear of dogs. ⟨< Gk. *kyon, kynos* dog + E *-phobia*⟩

cy•no•sure ['saɪnəˌʃʊr] *or* ['sɪnəˌʃʊr] *n.* **1** something that is the centre of attraction or interest: *She was the cynosure of all eyes.* **2 Cynosure,** *Astronomy.* **a** the constellation containing the North Star, now usually called Ursa Minor, or Little Bear. **b** the North Star. **3** something used for guidance or direction. ⟨< L *Cynosura* (def. 2) < Gk. *kynosoura* dog's tail < *kyōn* dog + *oura* tail⟩

Cyn•thi•a ['sɪnθiə] *n.* **1** Artemis, the goddess of the moon. **2** the moon.

cy•pher ['səifər] See CIPHER.

cy•press ['səiprəs] *n.* **1** any of a genus (*Cupressus*) of evergreen trees found in North America, S Europe, and Asia, having small, scalelike, overlapping leaves and round, upright cones. There are no cypresses native to Canada. **2** any of several related trees, such as the yellow cypress. **3** (*adjl.*) designating the family (Cupressaceae) of coniferous trees that includes the true cypresses, junipers, and arborvitae. **4** any of various other coniferous trees, such as the bald cypress. **5** the wood of any of these trees, used for boards, shingles, and doors. ⟨ME < OF < L *cupressus* < Gk. *kyparissos*⟩

cypress vine an annual, tropical American vine (*Ipomoea quamoclit* or *Quamoclit pennata*) of the morning-glory family, having finely divided leaves and large, trumpet-shaped, red or white flowers.

Cyp•ri•an ['sɪpriən] *n., adj.* *—n.* a native or inhabitant of Cyprus.
—adj. of or having to do with Cyprus or its people.

cyp•ri•nid ['sɪprənɪd] *n., adj.* *—n.* any of a family (Cyprinidae) of mainly soft-finned freshwater fishes found in North America,

Africa, Europe, and Asia, having toothless jaws, sometimes with barbels. Carps, minnows, and goldfish are cyprinids.
—adj. of, having to do with, or designating this family of fishes. The cyprinid family is also called the minnow family. Also, **cyprinoid**. ⟨< L *cyprinus* carp (< Gk.) + E *-oid* resembling (< Gk. *eidos* form)⟩

Cyp•ri•ot ['sɪpriət] *n., adj. —n.* **1** a native or inhabitant of Cyprus. **2** the dialect of Greek spoken in Cyprus.
—adj. of or having to do with Cyprus or its people.

cyp•ri•pe•di•um [,sɪprə'pidiəm] *n., pl.* **-di•a** [-diə]. **1** any of a genus (*Cypripedium*) of orchids having large, drooping flowers with a pouchlike lip. See also LADY'S-SLIPPER. **2** any of a genus (*Paphiopedilum*) of tropical Old World orchids which have been much used by orchid breeders to produce cultivated varieties and hybrids. This genus is closely related to the genus *Cypripedium*, and is included in that genus by some authorities. ⟨< NL *cypripedium*, apparently, alteration of *cypripodium* < Gk. *Kypris* Aphrodite + *podion,* dim. of *pous*, *podos* foot⟩

cy•pro•hep•ta•dine [,saiprou'hɛptə,din] *n.* an antihistamine drug. *Formula*: $C_{21}H_{21}N$

cy•pro•te•rone [sai'prɒtə,roun] *n.* a drug used to treat prostate cancer.

Cy•prus ['saiprəs] *n.* an island country in the E Mediterranean Sea, south of Turkey. See LEBANON for map.

Cy•ril•lic [sɪ'rɪlɪk] *adj.* of, having to do with, or designating an ancient Slavic alphabet from which the Russian, Bulgarian, and Serbian alphabets have developed. See table of alphabets in the Appendix. ⟨< St. *Cyril*, an apostle to the Slavs in the 9c., who is traditionally supposed to have invented it⟩

cyst [sɪst] *n.* **1** an abnormal, saclike growth in animals or plants that usually contains fluid and has no outside opening. **2** any saclike structure in animals or plants. **3** a thick, round, resistant covering serving to protect various organisms at rest. ⟨< NL *cystis* < Gk. *kystis* pouch, bladder⟩

cys•tec•to•my [sɪ'stɛktəmi] *n.* **1** surgical removal of a cyst. **2** surgical removal of the gall bladder or part of the bladder.

cys•te•ine ['sɪstiɪn] *or* ['sisti,in] *n.* an amino acid found in most proteins and derived from cystine. *Formula*: $HSCH_2CH(NH_2)COOH$

cyst•ic ['sɪstɪk] *adj.* **1** of or like a cyst. **2** having or characterized by a cyst or cysts. **3** enclosed in a cyst.

cys•ti•cer•cus [,sɪstə'sɜrkəs] *n., pl.* **-cer•ci** [-'sɜrsaɪ] *or* [-'sɜrsi]. the larva of certain tapeworms, having a bladder around the head; bladderworm.

cystic fibrosis [faɪ'brousɪs] a congenital disease of some children, causing frequent respiratory infections and malfunction of the pancreas.

cys•tine ['sɪstin] *or* ['sɪstɪn] *n.* a crystalline amino acid found in many proteins, especially keratin. *Formula*: $C_6H_{12}N_2O_4S_2$ ⟨< Gk. *kystis* bladder, sac + E *-ine*²⟩

cys•ti•tis [sɪ'stəitɪs] *n.* inflammation of the urinary bladder.

cys•to•cele ['sɪstə,sil] *n.* a hernia of the urinary bladder protruding into the vagina. ⟨< Gk. *kystos* bladder + *kele* tumour, hernia⟩

cys•to•lith ['sɪstə,lɪθ] *n.* a calcium carbonate deposit found on the ends of stalks on the epidermal cells of certain plants. ⟨< Gk. *kystos* bladder, circle + *lithos* stone⟩

cys•to•scope ['sɪstə,skoup] *n.* an instrument for examining the inside of the urinary bladder. **—,cys•to'scop•ic** [-'skɒpɪk], *adj.*

cys•tos•co•py [sɪ'stɒskəpi] *n.* exploration of the bladder or urinary tract with the help of a cystoscope. ⟨< Gk. *kystos* bladder, sac + *-skopia* < *skopein* to see⟩

cys•tot•o•my [sɪ'stɒtəmi] *n.* a surgical incision made into the bladder or gall bladder.

cy•ta•ra•bine [səi'tærə,bin] *or* [səi'tɛrə,bin] *n.* a drug used to treat leukemia. *Formula*: $C_9H_{13}N_3O_5$

-cyte *combining form.* cell: *leucocyte = a white (blood) cell.* ⟨< Gk. *kytos* anything hollow⟩

Cyth•er•e•a [,sɪθə'riə] *n. Greek mythology.* Aphrodite, the goddess of sexual love and beauty.

cyto- *combining form.* cell; cells: *cytology = the study of cells.* Also, **cyt-** before vowels. ⟨< Gk. *kytos* anything hollow⟩

cy•to•chrome ['səitə,kroum] *n.* any of various pigments concerned with cellular respiration, important as catalysts in the oxidation process.

cy•to•ge•net•ics [,səitoudʒə'nɛtɪks] *n. Biology.* the study of chromosomes and their abnormalities. **—,cy•to•ge'net•ic,** *adj.*

cy•to•ki•nin [,səitou'kaɪnɪn] *n.* any of a group of hormones synthesized in plant cells and important to cell division, rooting, and the health of leaves. ⟨< *cyto-* + *kinin* (< *kin(etic)* + *-in*)⟩

cy•tol•o•gist [saɪ'tɒlədʒɪst] *n.* a person trained in cytology, especially one whose work it is.

cy•tol•o•gy [səi'tɒlədʒi] *n.* the branch of biology that deals with the formation, structure, and function of the cells of animals and plants. ⟨< Gk. *kytos* receptacle, cell + E *-logy*⟩ **—,cy•to'log•ic•al,** *adj.*

cy•tol•y•sin [səi'tɒləsɪn] *n.* any substance that causes cytolysis.

cy•tol•y•sis [səi'tɒləsɪs] *n.* the breakdown of cells.

cy•to•meg•a•lo•vi•rus [,səitou,mɛgəlou'vaɪrəs] *n.* any of various DNA viruses (family Herpitoviridae) whose symptom is enlarged epithelial cells. These viruses are generally harmless except in newborns and people with weak immune systems, where they may cause severe problems.

cy•to•plasm ['səitə,plæzəm] *n. Biology.* the living substance or protoplasm of a cell, exclusive of the nucleus. See CELL for picture. **—,cy•to'plas•mic,** *adj.*

cy•to•sine ['səitə,sin] *n.* a substance present in nucleic acid in cells. It is one of the pyrmidine bases of both DNA and RNA. *Formula*: $C_4H_5N_3O$ ⟨< *cyto-* + *-ose*² + *-ine*²⟩

CZ Canal Zone.

czar or **tsar** [zɑr] *n.* **1** emperor. It was the title of the former emperors of Russia. **2** autocrat; a person with absolute power: *Al Capone was a czar of crime.* ⟨< Russian *tsar* < Old Church Slavic < Gothic < L *Caesar* Caesar⟩

czar•das ['tʃɑrdɑʃ] *n.* **1** a Hungarian national dance having a slow first section followed by a fast one. **2** the music for such a dance. ⟨< Hungarian *csárdás*⟩

czardom or **tsar•dom** ['zɑrdəm] *n.* **1** the position or power of a czar. **2** the territory ruled by a czar.

czar•e•vitch or **tsar•e•vitch** ['zɑrə,vɪtʃ] *n.* **1** the eldest son of a Russian czar. **2** the son of a Russian czar. ⟨< Russian *tsarevich*⟩

cza•rev•na or **tsa•rev•na** [zɑ'rɛvnə] *n.* **1** the daughter of a Russian czar. **2** the wife of a czarevitch. ⟨< Russian *tsarevna*⟩

cza•ri•na or **tsa•ri•na** [zɑ'rinə] *n.* the wife of a czar; a Russian empress. ⟨< G *Zarin* (earlier *Czarin*), fem. of *Zar* < Russian *tsar.* See CZAR.⟩

czar•ism or **tsar•ism** ['zɑrɪzəm] *n.* **1** the Russian government under the czars. **2** autocratic government; despotism.

czar•ist or **tsar•ist** ['zɑrɪst] *n., adj. —n.* a supporter of the government of the czars in Russia.
—adj. **1** of or having to do with the czars or Russia under the czars. **2** characteristic of czarism.

Czech [tʃɛk] *n., adj. —n.* **1** a native or inhabitant of the Czech Republic. **2** the Slavic language of the Czechs.
—adj. of or having to do with the Czech Republic, its people, or their language.

Czech Republic a country in central Europe, comprising Bohemia and Moravia, the western provinces of the former Czechoslovakia.

D d *D d*

d or **D** [di] *n., pl.* **d's** or **D's. 1** the fourth letter of the English alphabet. **2** any speech sound represented by this letter. **3** a person or thing identified as *d*, especially the fourth in a series. **4 D, a** a grade rating a person's work or performance as being below average and barely acceptable. **b** a person or thing receiving this rating. **5** *Music.* **a** the second tone in the scale of C major. **b** a symbol representing this tone. **c** a key, etc. of a musical instrument that produces this tone. **d** the scale or key that has D as its keynote. **6 D,** the Roman numeral for 500. **7 D,** something shaped like the letter D. **8** (*adjl.*) of or being a D or d. **9** any device, such as a printer's type, a lever, or a key on a keyboard, that produces a d or D.

d 1 day. **2** deci- (an SI prefix). **3** ***d*** diameter.

d. 1 died; dead. **2** formerly, in the United Kingdom and some other countries, penny or pence. (L *denarius*) **3** dime. **4** dollar. **5** day. **6** date. **7** delete. **8** daughter. **9** degree. **10** dyne. **11** departs; departure.

D 1 deuterium. **2** sometimes, **d,** *Physics.* density.

D. 1 Doctor (in academic degrees). **2** December. **3** *U.S. Politics.* Democrat; Democratic. **4** Dutch. **5** Duke. **6** Duchess. **7** Don (Spanish title). **8** God (L *deus*). **9** Lord (L *dominus*).

da deca- (an SI prefix).

D.A. *U.S.* DISTRICT ATTORNEY.

dab[1] [dæb] *v.* **dabbed, dab•bing;** *n.* *—v.* **1** touch lightly; pat with something soft or moist; tap (*used with* **at**): *He dabbed at the spot with his napkin.* **2** put on with light strokes: *She dabbed some powder on her nose.*
—n. **1** a quick, light touch or blow; pat; tap. **2** a small, soft or moist mass: *a dab of butter.* **3** a little bit. ⟨ME⟩ **—'dab•ber,** *n.*

dab[2] [dæb] *n.* any of various flounders, especially any of a genus (*Limanda*) of fishes found in the North Pacific and North Atlantic Oceans. ⟨origin uncertain⟩

dab[3] [dæb] *n. Informal.* expert. Sometimes, **dab hand.** ⟨origin uncertain⟩

dab•ble ['dæbəl] *v.* **-bled, -bling. 1** dip (hands, feet, etc.) in and out of water; splash. **2** work a little; do something in a half-hearted or superficial way: *to dabble at painting, to dabble in stocks.* ⟨< Flemish *dabbelen*⟩ **—'dab•bler,** *n.*

da capo [dɑ 'kɑpou]; *Italian,* [da 'kapo] *Music.* **1** from the beginning (a direction to repeat a passage). **2** the passage to be repeated. *Abbrev.*: D.C. ⟨< Ital. literally, from the head⟩

dab•chick ['dæb,tʃɪk] *n.* any of various small grebes of Europe. ⟨?< OE *dop* dive + *chick*⟩

da•car•ba•zine [də'kɑrbə,zin] *n.* a drug used to treat skin cancer. *Formula*: $C_6H_{10}N_6O$

dace [deis] *n., pl.* **dace** or **daces. 1** any of several small freshwater cyprinid fishes of North America, such as the **pearl dace** (*Semotilus margarita*), common in Canadian waters from the Maritimes to the Rocky Mountains. **2** a small, slender freshwater cyprinid fish (*Leuciscus leuciscus*) of Europe. ⟨ME *darse* < OF *dars* dart < Med.L *darsus*⟩

da•cha ['dɑtʃə] *n.* a Russian summer cottage. ⟨< Russian⟩

dachs•hund ['dæʃ,hʊnd], ['dɑks,hʊnd], *or* ['dɑks,hʊnt]; *German,* ['daxs,hʊnt] *n.* a breed of small dog having a long body, long, drooping ears, a slender muzzle, and very short legs. The dachshund was originally developed in Germany for hunting badgers. ⟨< G *Dachshund* < *Dachs* badger + *Hund* dog⟩

da•coit [də'kɔɪt] *n.* in India or Burma, a member of a gang of robbers. ⟨< Hind. *dakait* < *daka* gang-robbery⟩

dac•quoise [dæ'kwɑz] *n.* a dessert comprising layers of meringue with nuts, alternating with a cream or mocha filling, and sometimes fruit, served chilled. ⟨< F, fem. of *dacquois* of Dax (a city in France)⟩

Da•cron ['deikrɒn] *or* ['dækrɒn] *n. Trademark.* a synthetic polyester fibre used for dress fabrics, carpets, etc.

dac•tin•o•my•cin [,dæktənou'məisɪn] *n.* a drug used to treat certain forms of cancer. *Formula*: $C_{62}H_{86}N_{12}O_{16}$

dac•tyl ['dæktəl] *n.* **1** a metrical foot consisting of one strongly stressed syllable followed by two weakly stressed syllables or one long syllable followed by two short syllables. *Example*: "Táke hĕr ŭp téndĕrlÿ." **2** *Zoology.* a finger or toe. ⟨< L < Gk. *daktylos* finger. Doublet of DATE[2].⟩

dac•tyl•ic [dæk'tɪlɪk] *adj.* **1** of dactyls. **2** consisting of dactyls. **—dac'tyl•i•cal•ly,** *adv.*

dac•tyl•o•gram [dæk'tɪlə,græm] *n.* a fingerprint.

dac•ty•lol•o•gy [,dæktə'lɒlədʒi] *n.* a language of signs made with fingers, such as used by the deaf. ⟨< Gk. *daktylos* finger + E *-logy*⟩

dad [dæd] *n. Informal.* father.

Da•da or **da•da** ['dɑdɑ] *or* ['dɑdə] *n.* Dadaism.

Da•da•ism or **da•da•ism** ['dɑdə,ɪzəm] *n.* a style in art and literature developed during World War I, characterized by the use of unconventional materials and techniques, by witty satire of all previous art forms and methods, and by an attitude of revolt against existing standards. ⟨< F *dada* horse, hobbyhorse (a child's word) + E *-ism*⟩

Da•da•ist or **da•da•ist** ['dɑdəɪst] *n., adj. —n.* a follower of Dadaism.
—adj. of or having to do with Dadaism. **—,Da•da'ist•ic** or **,da•da'ist•ic,** *adj.*

dad•dy ['dædi] *n., pl.* **-dies.** *Informal.* father. ⟨< *dad*⟩

dad•dy–long•legs ['dædi 'lɒŋ,lɛgz] *n.sing. or pl.* **1** any of an order (Opiliones) of arachnids resembling spiders but having a rounded body without a 'waist' and four pairs of very long, thin, bent legs. **2** *Brit.* CRANE FLY.

da•do ['deidou] *n., pl.* **-does** or **-dos. 1** *Architecture.* the part of a pedestal between the base and the cap. **2** the lower part of an inside wall when covered with a special finish of wood, wallpaper, etc. **3** this special decoration. **4 a** a rectangular groove cut into the side of a plank to receive another set at right angles to it. **b** a joint made in this fashion. ⟨< Ital. *dado* die[2] < L *datus* given⟩

dae•dal ['didəl] *adj. Poetic.* **1** ingenious; skilful: *the sculptor's daedal hand.* **2** intricately made; with complex ornamentation. **3** like a maze; complex. ⟨< L < Gk. *daidalos* skilful; skilfully wrought < *daidallein* work cunningly⟩

Dae•da•li•an or **Dae•da•le•an** [dɪ'deiliən] *or* [dɪ'deiljən] *adj.* **1** skilful; ingenious. **2** intricate; mazelike. **3** having to do with Daedalus.

Daed•al•us ['dɛdələs] *or* ['didələs] *n. Greek mythology.* a skilful builder who built the Labyrinth in Crete and who invented wings by means of which he and his son Icarus escaped from imprisonment in the Labyrinth.

dae•mon ['dimən] *n.* **1** an attendant or guardian spirit. **2** *Greek mythology.* a supernatural being halfway between a god and a human being. ⟨< L < Gk. *daimon*⟩
☛ *Hom.* DEMON.

daf•fo•dil ['dæfə,dɪl] *n., adj. —n.* **1** any of various plants (genus *Narcissus*) of the amaryllis family having long, slender leaves and yellow or yellow and white flowers with a trumpet-shaped corona growing out from the centre of its petals. **2** the flower of any of these plants. **3** a bright yellow.
—adj. bright yellow. ⟨var. of *affodill* < VL *affodillus* < L < Gk. *asphodelos*⟩

daff•y ['dæfi] *adj.* **daff•i•er, daff•i•est.** *Informal.* **1** foolish; silly. **2** crazy; insane. ⟨< ME *daffe* fool⟩ **—'daf•fi•ness** *n.*
daffy on, crazy about: *The girl was daffy on the young soldier.*

daft [dæft] *adj.* **1** silly; foolish. **2** crazy; insane. ⟨OE *(ge)dæfte* gentle⟩ **—'daft•ly,** *adv.* **—'daft•ness,** *n.*

dag [dæg] *n. Cdn.* a heavy, flat, double-edged triangular blade, used by the First Nations people as a weapon and tool. ⟨< Cdn.F < F *dague* dagger⟩

D.A.G. Deputy Adjutant General.

dag•ger ['dægər] *n., v. —n.* **1** a small weapon with a short, pointed blade, used for stabbing. **2** *Printing.* a sign (†) to refer the reader to a footnote, a note at the back of the book, etc.
look daggers at, look at (someone or something) with hatred or anger.
—v. **1** stab with a dagger. **2** mark with a dagger sign. ⟨probably < obs. *dag* stab⟩

da•guerre•o•type [də'gɛrə,təip] *or* [də'gɛriə,təip] *n.* **1** an early photographic process. In daguerreotype, the pictures were made on light-sensitive, silver-coated metal plates. **2** a picture made in this way. ⟨after L. *Daguerre* (1789-1851), its inventor⟩

Dag•wood sandwich ['dæg,wʊd] a large sandwich composed of several layers of varied and, often, unusual fillings.

⟨after the comic strip character *Dagwood* Bumstead, who makes himself such sandwiches⟩

dah [dɑ] *n.* the name corresponding to a dash in Morse code. Compare DIT.

dahl [dɑl] *n.* **1** any of various legumes, as lentils, chick peas, etc., used in Indian cooking. ⟨< Hind. *daal* split pulse⟩

dahl•ia ['deiljə], ['dæljə], *or* ['dɑljə] *n.* **1** any of a genus (*Dahlia*) of tall perennial plants of the composite family native to Mexico and Central America, including many cultivated varieties grown for their large, showy flower heads that appear in late summer and fall. **2** the flower head of a dahlia. ⟨< NL; after A. *Dahl*, Swedish botanist⟩

A dahlia

Dail Eir•eann ['dɒl 'eirən] *or* ['dɔɪl 'ɛrɪn] the lower house of parliament of Ireland. ⟨< Irish *dáil* assembly, and *Éireann*, gen. of *Éire* Ireland⟩

dai•ly ['deili] *adj., n., pl.* **-lies;** *adv.* *—adj.* **1** done, happening, or appearing every day, or every day but Sunday: *a daily paper, a daily visit.* **2 evaluated each day:** *daily interest rates.*
—n. **1** a newspaper appearing every day, or every day but Sunday. **2 dailies,** *pl. Film.* prints of the first shot of a scene or scenes; rushes.
—adv. every day; day by day.

daily double *Horse racing.* a bet or a form of betting in which a person bets on two horses at once in two separate races, usually the first two races of the day. To win the daily double, the better must have picked the winning horse in each of the two races.

dai•mio ['daɪmjou] *n., pl.* **-mio** or **-mios.** in Japan, one of the great feudal nobles who, from the 14th to the 19th century, were vassals of the emperor. Also, **daimyo.** ⟨< Japanese < Chinese *dai* great + *mio* name⟩

dain•ty ['deinti] *adj.* **-ti•er, -ti•est;** *n., pl.* **-ties.** *—adj.* **1** having delicate beauty; pretty and graceful: *a dainty flower.* **2** having or showing delicate and refined tastes and feelings; particular: *She is dainty about her eating.* **3** overly refined and delicate; too particular. **4** good to eat; delicious: *a dainty morsel.*
—n. something very good to eat; a delicious bit of food. ⟨< OF *deinte* < L *dignitas* worthiness. Doublet of DIGNITY.⟩
—'dain•ti•ly, *adv.* **—'dain•ti•ness,** *n.*
☛ *Syn. adj.* **1.** See note at DELICATE.

dai•qui•ri ['dækəri] *or* ['dəikəri] *n.* a cocktail made from rum, lime juice, and sugar. ⟨< *Daiquiri* Cuba⟩

dair•y ['dɛri] *n., pl.* **dair•ies;** *adj.* *—n.* **1** a room or building where milk and cream are kept and made into butter and cheese. **2** a business that processes and sells or distributes milk and milk products. **3** DAIRY FARM. **4** dairy products: *I don't eat dairy.*
—adj. of milk and its products. ⟨ME *deierie* < *deie* maid (OE *dæge* breadmaker)⟩

dairy cattle cows kept to give milk for human consumption.

dairy farm a farm where milk and milk products are produced. **—dairy farmer, —dairy farming.**

dair•y•ing ['dɛriɪŋ] *n.* the business of raising cows to produce milk and cream, or of making butter and cheese.

dair•y•maid ['dɛri,meid] *n.* a girl or woman who works in a dairy.

dair•y•man [,dɛrimən] *n., pl.* **-men. 1** a man who owns or manages a dairy farm. **2** a man who works in a dairy.

da•is ['deiɪs], ['daɪəs], *or* [deis] *n.* a raised platform at one end of a hall or a large room. A throne, seats of honour, a lecture desk, etc. are set on a dais. ⟨ME < OF *deis* < L *discus* quoit, dish < Gk. *diskos.* Doublet of DESK, DISCUS, DISH, and DISK.⟩

dai•sy ['deizi] *n., pl.* **-sies. 1** any of several plants (genus *Chrysanthemum*) of the composite family, especially the **ox-eye daisy** or the **Shasta daisy.** Daisies have tall, leafy stems and showy flower heads consisting of a yellow central disk surrounded by usually white, petal-like ray flowers. **2** any of various other plants of the composite family having similar flowers, such as the **English daisy** (*Bellis perennis*) or the **Michaelmas daisies** (genus *Aster*). **3** the flower of any of these plants. **4** *Slang.* a first-rate person or thing.
pushing up the daisies, *Slang.* dead and buried. ⟨OE *dæges ēage* day's eye⟩ **—'dai•sy,like,** *adj.*

daisy chain **1** a string of daisies attached together. **2** any chain of linked objects or events.

daisy wheel a rotatable wheel that produces the printing in an electronic typewriter or computer printer.

daisy wheel printer *Computer technology.* a printer in which the print characters are positioned at the ends of spokes on a daisy wheel.

Da•ko•ta [də'koutə] *n., pl.* **-tas** or **-ta;** *adj.* *—n.* **1** a member of a group of American Indians living on the plains of southern Canada and the N United States. **2** the Siouan language of the Dakotas and Assiniboines. **3 the Dakotas,** North and South Dakota.
—adj. of or having to do with the Dakotas and Assiniboines or their language. ⟨< Dakota *dakota* allies < *da* to think of as + *koda* friend⟩

Da•lai La•ma ['dɑlaɪ 'lɑmə] *or* [dɑ'laɪ 'lɑmə] the chief priest of the religion of Lamaism in Tibet and Mongolia and the political leader of Tibet. ⟨< Mongolian *dalai* ocean; see LAMA.⟩

da•la•si [də'lɑsi] *or* ['dɑlɑ,si] *n., pl.* **dalasi.** the basic unit of money in The Gambia, divided into 100 butut. See table of money in the Appendix. ⟨< Mandingo, complete; short for *dalasi fano* a complete pane⟩

dale [deil] *n.* valley. ⟨OE *dæl*⟩

da•let ['dɑlət] *or* ['dɑləd] *n.* the fifth letter of the Hebrew alphabet. See table of alphabets in the Appendix.

dalle [dæl] *n.* dalles.

dalles [dælz] *or* ['dæləs] *n.pl. Cdn.* a narrow stretch of river between high rock walls, characterized by whirlpools, rapids, and treacherous currents. ⟨< Cdn.F < F *dalle* gutter < Gmc.⟩

dal•li•ance ['dæliəns] *or* ['dæljəns] *n.* **1** flirtation; dallying. **2** playing; trifling. ⟨< ME *daliaunce*⟩

Dall sheep [dɒl] *Cdn.* a white North American sheep (*Ovis dalli*) of the western mountains found from northern British Columbia to the Arctic Ocean. ⟨after W.H. *Dall* (1845-1927), American naturalist⟩

Dall's sheep DALL SHEEP.

dal•ly ['dæli] *v.* **-lied, -ly•ing. 1** loiter; linger idly; waste time: *He was late because he dallied along the way. She dallied away the whole afternoon.* **2** play or toy (*with*). **3** behave in a playful manner, especially flirt with a person. ⟨< OF *dalier* chat⟩
—'dal•ly•ing•ly, *adv.* **—'dal•li•er,** *n.*
☛ *Syn.* **2.** See note at TRIFLE.

Dal•ma•tian [dæl'meiʃən] *n., adj.* *—n.* **1** a breed of medium-sized, short-haired dog, usually white with black spots; coach dog. **2** a native or inhabitant of Dalmatia, a region in the former Yugoslavia. **3** a Romance language formerly spoken in Dalmatia.
—adj. of or having to do with Dalmatia or its people.

A Dalmatian

dal segno [dæl 'sɛnjou] *Music.* from the sign (a direction to repeat the section starting at the sign). ⟨< Ital.⟩

dal•ton ['dɒltən] *n.* *Biochemistry.* a unit of mass equal to 1/16 of the mass of an atom of hydrogen. ⟨after John *Dalton* (1766-1844), English physicist⟩

Dal•to•ni•an [dɒl'tounian] *adj., n.* *—adj.* **1** of or having to do with John Dalton (1766-1844), an English chemist and physicist who described colour-blindness and who was himself colour-blind. **2** of or suggestive of his writings and theories. **3** of or having to do with colour-blindness.
—n. a person who is colour-blind.

Dal•ton•ism or **dal•ton•ism** ['dɒltə,nɪzəm] *n.* colour-blindness, especially the inability to distinguish red from green. ⟨< F *daltonisme* < John Dalton + *-isme* ism. See DALTON.⟩

dam[1] [dæm] *n., v.* **dammed, dam•ming.** *—n.* **1** a wall built to hold back flowing water. **2** the water held back by a dam. **3** anything resembling a dam. **4** on the Prairies, a reservoir of water collected from the spring thaw and from rainfall, used for watering cattle, etc.; dugout; pothole.
—v. **1** provide with a dam; hold back by means of a dam: *Beavers*

had dammed the stream. **2** hold back; block: *He tried to dam back his tears.* ⟨ME < MLG or MDu. *dam;* akin to OE *fordemman* dam up⟩ **—'dam,like,** *adj.*
☛ *Hom.* DAMN.

dam² [dæm] *n.* **1** the female parent of four-footed animals. **2** *Archaic.* mother. ⟨var. of *dame*⟩
☛ *Hom.* DAMN.

dam•age ['dæmɪdʒ] *n., v.* **-aged, -ag•ing.** *—n.* **1** injury or harm that lessens value or usefulness. **2** *Slang.* cost; price: *What's the damage?* **3 damages,** *pl.* money claimed by law or paid to make up for some harm done to a person or his or her property.
—v. injure or harm so as to lessen value or usefulness; harm; hurt: *I damaged my sweater in football practice.* ⟨ME < OF < *dam* < L *damnum* loss, hurt⟩ **—'dam•age•a•ble,** *adj.* **—'dam•ag•ing•ly,** *adv.*
☛ *Syn. v.* See note at HARM.

da•mar ['dæmɑr] See DAMMAR.

dam•a•scene ['dæmə,sin] *or* [,dæmə'sin] *v.* **-scened, -scen•ing;** *n., adj. —v.* ornament (metal) with inlaid gold or silver or with a wavy design.
—n. **1** ornamentation of this kind. **2** a small plum; damson.
—adj. of, having, or resembling such ornament. ⟨< L *Damascenus* < Gk. *Damaskēnos* of Damascus⟩

Dam•a•scene ['dæmə,sin] *or* [,dæmə'sin] *adj., n. —adj.* of or having to do with the city of Damascus.
—n. a native or inhabitant of Damascus.

Dam•as•cus steel [də'mæskəs] a kind of ornamented steel, used in making swords, etc.

dam•ask ['dæməsk] *n., adj., v. —n.* **1** reversible linen, silk, or cotton fabric with woven designs. **2** a linen material of this type, used especially for tablecloths and serviettes. **3** damascened metal. **4** the wavy designs on such metal. **5** a rose colour; pink.
—adj. **1** made of or like damask. **2** pink; rose-coloured: *damask cheeks.* **3** of or named after the city of Damascus.
—v. **1** damascene. **2** weave with the design of damask fabric. ⟨< L *Damascus* < Gk. *Damaskos* Damascus⟩

damask rose a fragrant, pink rose (*Rosa damascena*) from which hybrid roses were developed and attar is obtained.

dame [deim] *n.* **1 Dame, a** in the United Kingdom, the title of a woman who belongs to an order of knighthood. It is used before the given name. **b** the legal title of the wife or widow of a knight or baronet. **2** *Archaic.* the woman in authority in a household. **3** *Archaic.* lady. **4** an elderly woman. ⟨ME < OF < L *domina* mistress⟩

dame•hood ['deim,hʊd] *n.* the quality or condition of being a dame: *She received her damehood in 1974.*

dame's violet a Eurasian plant (*Hesperis matronalis*) of the mustard family, having clusters of four-petalled white or purple flowers in late spring. Also called **dame's rocket.**

dam•mar ['dæmɑr] *n.* a resin obtained from evergreen trees of the genus *Agathis,* of southern Asia and Australia, used to make a colourless varnish. Also, **dammer, damar.** ⟨< Malay *damar* evergreen resins⟩

dam•mit ['dæmɪt] *Slang.* damn it.

damn [dæm] *v., n., adj., adv., interj. —v.* **1** declare to be bad or inferior; condemn: *The throne speech was damned by the press.* **2** cause to fail; ruin. **3** swear at; curse. **4** doom to eternal punishment; condemn to hell. **5** prove the guilt of (a person): *damning evidence.*
damn with faint praise, praise with so little enthusiasm as to condemn.
—n. **1** an utterance of *damn* as a curse. **2** *Slang.* the smallest amount or degree: *not worth a damn. He didn't care a damn.*
—adj. or adv. Slang. damned (*used as an intensifier*): *It's a damn shame. She's a damn good writer.*
—interj. Slang. an exclamation of anger, frustration, etc. ⟨ME < OF *damner* < L *damnare* condemn < *damnum* loss⟩
☛ *Hom.* DAM.

dam•na•ble ['dæmnəbəl] *adj.* **1** abominable; outrageous; detestable. **2** deserving damnation. **—'dam•na•ble•ness,** *n.* **—'dam•na•bly,** *adv.*

dam•na•tion [dæm'neiʃən] *n., interj. —n.* **1** damning or being damned; condemnation. **2** a condemnation to eternal punishment. **3** a curse.
—interj. an expression of annoyance; a curse.

dam•na•to•ry ['dæmnə,tɔri] *adj.* damning; assigning to damnation; condemnatory.

damned [dæmd] *adj., adv., v. —adj.* **1** condemned to eternal punishment. **2** condemned as bad or inferior: *This damned pen won't write.* **3** (*noml.*) **the damned,** *pl.* all the souls condemned to

eternal punishment. **4** *Slang.* detestable or abominable (*used as an intensifier*): *That's a damned lie! When we got there the damned place was closed.* **5** *Slang.* extraordinary (*used in the superlative*): *It was the damnedest thing I ever saw.*
do (one's) **damnedest,** *Informal.* do one's best or utmost: *She'll do her damnedest to get the job done on time.*
—adv. Slang. very: *He should be damned glad to get the work.*
—v. pt. and pp. of DAMN.

Dam•o•cles ['dæmə,kliz] *n.* a flatterer and courtier of Dionysius, King of Syracuse. Damocles thought Dionysius must be the happiest of men, but Dionysius asked him to share the happiness of a king. He gave a banquet for Damocles, seating his guest beneath a naked sword that hung above his head by a single hair. By this means Damocles was made aware of the dangers surrounding kings.
sword of Damocles, any imminent danger.

dam•oi•selle [,dæmə'zɛl] *n. Archaic.* damsel.

Da•mon ['deimən] *n. Legend.* a man who pledged his life for his friend Pythias (or Phintias), who had been sentenced to death.
Damon and Pythias, any loyal and devoted friends.

dam•o•sel or **dam•o•zel** [,dæmə'zɛl] *or* ['dæmə,zɛl] *n. Archaic.* damsel.

damp [dæmp] *adj., n., v. —adj.* slightly wet; moist.
—n. **1** moisture: *One could feel the damp in the morning air.* **2** something that checks or deadens: *His ill-humoured objections put a damp on our spirits.* **3** any foul or explosive gas that collects in mines, such as chokedamp or firedamp: *The mine disaster was caused by exploding damp.*
—v. **1** moisten; dampen. **2** slow down the combustion of (a fire) by cutting off most of the air supply: *She damped down the fire for the night.* **3** discourage; check. **4** *Music.* stop the vibrations of (a string, etc.).
damp off, of a young plant, die because of mildew. ⟨< MDu. or MLG *damp* vapour⟩ **—'damp•ly,** *adv.* **—'damp•ness,** *n.*
☛ *Syn. adj.* **Damp,** MOIST, HUMID = rather wet. **Damp** describes an unpleasant degree of wetness: *This house is damp in rainy weather.* **Moist** describes wetness that is desirable: *Keep the soil moist.* **Humid** is literary or scientific, but is used commonly to describe a high degree of moisture in the air: *In the East the air is humid in summer.*

damp–dry ['dæmp ,draɪ] *v.* **-dried, -dry•ing,** *adj. —v.* dry (laundry) to a point where it is still slightly damp, ready for ironing.
—adj. of or having to do with such laundry.

damp•en ['dæmpən] *v.* **1** make moist or slightly wet: *We dampen clothes before ironing them.* **2** deaden; depress; discourage. **3** become damp. **—'damp•en•er,** *n.*

damp•er ['dæmpər] *n.* **1** a person or thing that discourages or depresses. **2** a movable plate to control the draft in a stove or furnace. **3** *Music.* **a** a device for checking vibration and reducing the volume of sound, especially of piano strings. **b** a mute for muffling the sound of a horn, etc. **4** *Electricity.* **a** a device for checking the vibration of a magnetic needle. **b** a piece of copper in or near the poles of a synchronous machine to decrease oscillation.
put a damper on, suppress; curb; curtail; squelch: *The chairperson put a damper on every suggestion the committee made.*

damp•ing–off ['dæmpɪŋ 'ɒf] *n.* the decaying of newly planted seedlings, cuttings, etc. at the surface of the ground.

dam•sel ['dæmzəl] *n.* a maiden or a young girl. ⟨ME *dameisele* < OF, ult. < L *domina* lady, mistress. Doublet of DEMOISELLE.⟩

dam•sel•fish ['dæmzəl,fɪʃ] *n.* any tropical, brightly coloured fish of the family Pomacentridae, living in coral reefs.

damsel fly any of a suborder (Zygoptera) of insect resembling dragonflies but smaller and having the wings closed together vertically over the back when at rest.

dam•son ['dæmzən] *n.* **1** a small Asiatic tree (*Prunus institia*) of the rose family, cultivated for its small, dark purple, edible plums. **2** the fruit of this tree, having an acid taste and used especially in jams and preserves. ⟨< L *(prunum) damascenum* (plum) of Damascus⟩

dan [dæn] *n. Cdn.* in the North: **1** a sealskin used as a container for oil. **2** a buoy made of inflated sealskin or sheepskin sewn airtight, used as a mark in deep-sea fishing. ⟨origin uncertain⟩

Dan [dæn] *n.*
from Dan to Beersheba, from one end of the country to the

other. ⟨< the names of two towns in ancient Palestine, *Dan,* at the northern boundary, and *Beersheba,* at the southern boundary⟩

Da•na•id or **Da•na•ïd** ['dænid] *n.* one of the Danaides.

Da•na•i•des or **Da•na•ï•des** [də'neiə,diz] *n.pl. Greek mythology.* the fifty daughters of Danaus, King of Argus. All but one killed their husbands on their wedding night, and were condemned to draw water with a sieve forever in Hades.

da•na•zol ['dænə,zɒl] *n.* a drug used to treat endometriosis. *Formula:* $C_{22}H_{27}NO_2$

dance [dæns] *v.* **danced, danc•ing;** *n.* —*v.* **1** move in rhythm, usually in time with music. **2** do or take part in (a dance). **3** jump up and down; move in a lively way. **4** bob up and down. **5** cause to dance; lead or conduct by dancing: *He danced his partner across the ballroom floor.*
dance attendance on, wait on often and attentively; be excessively polite and obedient to.
dance to another tune, change one's actions in response to changing circumstances.
—*n.* **1** a movement in rhythm, usually in time with music. **2** some special groups of steps, etc: *The waltz and fox trot were the dances she knew best.* **3** the art of dancing. **4** one round of dancing. **5** a piece of music for dancing or in a dance rhythm. **6** a party where people dance. **7** a movement up and down; lively movement. **8 the dance,** ballet. **9** (*adjl.*) of or for dancing.
lead someone a dance, cause a person trouble, especially by luring him or her into a vain pursuit. ⟨ME < OF *danser,* probably < Gmc.⟩ —**'danc•ing•ly,** *adv.*

dance hall 1 a public hall or room for dancing. **2** *Cdn.* an area where prairie chickens perform courtship dances.

dance of death a representation of a medieval dance in which a skeleton, symbolizing Death, dances with people to remind them of human mortality.

danc•er ['dænsər] *n.* **1** a person who dances. **2** a person whose occupation is dancing.

danc•er•cise ['dænsər,saiz] *n.* exercise through dancing.

D and C dilatation and curettage; dilatation of the cervix and curettage of the uterus, a surgical procedure used to diagnose or treat uterine disorders.

dan•de•li•on ['dændə,laiən] *or* ['dændi,laiən] *n.* any of a genus (*Taraxacum*) of plants of the composite family, native to Europe and Asia but now found throughout the temperate regions of North America, having long, often toothed leaves radiating from the base of the plant and a single, bright yellow head made up of many ray flowers. The common dandelion (*T. officinale*) occurs as a weed throughout Canada and is also grown for its edible leaves and flowers. ⟨< F *dent de lion* lion's tooth; from its toothed leaves⟩

dan•der ['dændər] *n.* **1** allergy-causing fragments of skin, hair, etc. **2** *Informal.* temper; anger.
get (one's) **dander up,** get angry; lose one's temper. ⟨origin uncertain⟩

Dan•die Din•mont ['dændi 'dınmɒnt] a breed of small terrier originally developed in the border country of England and Scotland, having a long body, long ears, short legs, and a rough coat, with silky hair on the top of the head. ⟨< *Dandie Dinmont* (a character in Sir W. Scott's *Guy Mannering*), who owned such terriers⟩

A Dandie Dinmont

dan•di•fy ['dændə,fai] *v.,* **-fied, -fy•ing.** make trim or smart like a dandy.

dan•dle ['dændəl] *v.* **-dled, -dling. 1** move (a child, etc.) up and down on one's knee or in one's arms. **2** pet; pamper. ⟨? < earlier Ital. *dandolare,* var. of *dondolare* swing⟩ —**'dan•dler,** *n.*

dan•druff ['dændrəf] *n.* small, whitish scales that flake off the scalp. ⟨< earlier *dander* + *hurf* scab < ON *hrufa*⟩

dan•dy ['dændi] *n., pl.* **-dies;** *adj.* **-di•er, -di•est.** —*n.* **1** a man who is too careful of his dress and appearance. **2** *Slang.* anything that is excellent or pleasing.
—*adj.* **1** of a dandy; too carefully dressed. **2** excellent; first-rate: *Everything is just dandy.* ⟨originally Scottish, ? < *Dandy,* a Scottish var. of *Andrew*⟩

dandy roll a cylinder used in papermaking, which impresses the watermark on paper.

Dane [dein] *n.* **1** a native or inhabitant of Denmark. **2** a person of Danish descent. **3** formerly, a person from any part of what is now Scandinavia: *King Alfred fought many battles against the Danes.*
☛ *Hom.* DEIGN.

Dane•geld or **dane•geld** ['dein,gɛld] *n.* from the 10th to 12th centuries, an annual tax levied in Britain to buy off the Danish invaders, later continued as a land tax. ⟨ME *Dane* Dane (< ON) + ON *gjeld* payment⟩

Dane•law ['dein,lɒ] *n.* **1** a set of laws enforced by the Danes when they held NE England in the 9th and 10th centuries A.D. **2** the part of England under these laws.

dan•ger ['deindʒər] *n.* **1** a chance of harm; nearness to harm; risk or peril: *A mountain climber's life is full of danger.* **2** anything that may cause harm: *Hidden rocks are a danger to ships.*
in danger of, liable to (with the accompanying threat of injury, harm, or death): *The old bridge is in danger of collapsing. The sick man is in danger of dying.* ⟨ME < OF *dangier* < L *dominium* sovereignty < *dominus* master⟩
☛ *Syn.* **1. Danger,** PERIL = threat of harm. **Danger** is the general word, always suggesting there is a definite chance of harm, but the harm is not always near or certain: *Miners at work are always in danger.* **Peril** suggests great harm is very near at hand and probable: *When a mine caves in, the miners are in peril.*

dan•ger•ous ['deindʒərəs] *adj.* likely to cause harm; not safe; risky. —**'dan•ger•ous•ly,** *adv.* —**'dan•ger•ous•ness,** *n.*

dan•gle ['dæŋgəl] *v.* **-gled, -gling. 1** hang and swing loosely: *The curtain cord dangles.* **2** hold or carry (something) so that it swings loosely: *The nurse dangled the toys in front of the baby.* **3** be a hanger-on or follower: *He was always dangling after the older boys.* **4** hold before a person as a temptation or inducement: *to dangle false hopes before a person.* ⟨< Scand.; cf. Danish *dangle*⟩ —**'dan•gler,** *n.*

dan•gle•ber•ry ['dæŋgəl,bɛri] *n.* a kind of huckleberry (*Gaylussacia frondosa*) found in eastern North America.

dangling participle a participle, past or present, that is not logically or grammatically attached to the noun or pronoun it is intended to modify. Also called **unattached participle.**
☛ *Usage.* The **dangling participle** can have ambiguous and often ludicrous effects. Thus, in *Swimming in the pond, the car was out of sight,* the participle *swimming* seems to refer to the car, which is logically ludicrous. Such a faulty sentence can be improved in several ways. The **dangling participle** can be attached to a noun or pronoun capable of modification: *Swimming in the pond, I could not see the car.* The **participial phrase** can be replaced by a clause: *When I was swimming in the pond, the car was out of sight.* Do not confuse a phrase containing a dangling or unattached participle with an **absolute phrase** (see ABSOLUTE, def. 8).

Dan•iel ['dænjəl] *n.* an upright judge or other person of great wisdom. ⟨< Daniel, in the Bible, a Hebrew prophet whose great faith in God kept him unharmed in the lion's den⟩

Dan•ish ['deinıʃ] *adj., n.* —*adj.* of or having to do with Denmark, the Danes, or their language.
—*n.* **1** the Germanic language of the Danes. **2 the Danish,** *pl.* the people of Denmark. **3** *Informal.* DANISH PASTRY: *Let's have a Danish for dessert.* ⟨OE *Denisc*⟩

Danish pastry 1 a rich, flaky pastry made with yeast, sometimes filled, and iced. **2** a piece of such pastry.

dank [dæŋk] *adj.* unpleasantly damp; moist; wet: *The cave was dark, dank, and chilly.* ⟨ME; cf. Swedish *dank* marshy spot⟩ —**'dank•ly,** *adv.* —**'dank•ness,** *n.*

danse ma•ca•bre [dɑ̃sma'kabʀ] *French.* dance of death.

dan•seur [dɑ̃'sœʀ] *French.* a male dancer, especially one in a ballet company. ⟨< OF *danser.* See DANCE.⟩

dan•seuse [dɑ̃'søz] *n., pl.* **-seuses** [-'søez]. a female dancer, especially in a ballet. ⟨< F⟩

Dan•te•an ['dæntiən] *or* ['dɑntiən] *adj.* of or having to do with Dante Alighieri (1265-1321), Italian poet.

dan•thron ['dænθrɒn] *n.* a laxative drug.

dan•tro•lene ['dæntrə,lin] *n.* a drug used to control spasms due to diseases such as multiple sclerosis. *Formula:* $C_{14}H_{10}N_4O_5$

Dan•u•bi•an [dæn'jubiən] *adj.* of or having to do with the Danube River, in S Europe, or the people living near it.

Daph•ne ['dæfni] *n.* **1** *Greek mythology.* a nymph, pursued by Apollo, who was saved by being changed into a laurel tree. **2 daphne,** a laurel tree or any evergreen shrub of the genus *Daphne.* ⟨< Gk., laurel tree⟩

daph•ni•a ['dæfniə] *n., pl.* **daph•ni•a.** a freshwater crustacean used as food for aquarium fish.

dap•per ['dæpər] *adj.* **1** neat; trim; spruce. **2** small and active. ⟨ME < MDu. *dapper* agile, strong⟩ —**'dap•per•ly,** *adv.* —**'dap•per•ness,** *n.*

dap•ple ['dæpəl] *adj., n., v.* **-pled, -pling.** *—adj.* spotted: *a dapple horse.*
—n. **1** a spotted appearance or condition. **2** an animal with a spotted or mottled skin.
—v. mark or become marked with spots. ⟨cf. ON *depill* spot⟩

dap•pled ['dæpəld] *adj., v. —adj.* spotted.
—v. pt. and pp. of DAPPLE.

dap•ple–grey ['dæpəl 'grei] *adj., n. —adj.* grey with spots of darker grey. Also, **dapple-gray.**
—n. a dapple-grey horse.

dap•sone ['dæpsoun] *n.* a drug used to treat Hodgkin's disease and some forms of dermatitis. *Formula:* $C_{12}H_{12}N_2O_2S$

darb [dɑrb] *n. Cdn. Slang.* any thing or person thought to be especially large, good, etc. ⟨origin uncertain⟩

Dar•by and Joan ['dɑrbi ən 'dʒoun] any old and devoted married couple. ⟨from characters in an English ballad of the 18th century⟩

Dard [dɑrd] *n.* a group of Indo-European languages spoken in Kashmir, NW Pakistan, and NE Afghanistan. **—'Dar•dic,** *adj.*

dare [dɛr] *v.* **dared** or *(archaic)* **durst, dared, dar•ing;** *n. —v.* **1** have courage; be bold; be bold enough to: *He doesn't dare to dive from the bridge.* **2** have courage to face; not be afraid of; face or meet boldly: *The explorer dared the dangers of the Arctic.* **3** meet and resist; face and defy. **4** challenge: *I dare you to jump.*
I dare say, probably; maybe; perhaps: *I dare say her success was due to hard work.*
—n. a challenge. ⟨OE *dearr* infinitive, *durran*)⟩ **—'dar•er,** *n.*

☛ *Syn. v.* **1. Dare,** VENTURE = be courageous or bold enough to do something. **Dare** emphasizes the idea of meeting fearlessly any danger or trouble, especially in doing something that is or seems important: *Only one man dared to enter the burning building.* **Venture** emphasizes the idea of being willing to take chances: *She decided to venture into a new business.*

☛ *Usage.* **Dare** can be used without *do* in negatives and questions: *How dare you? How dare he? I dare not try it.* **Dare** can be used with another verb in the infinitive without *to: I dare say. He doesn't dare dive from the bridge.*

dare•dev•il ['dɛr,dɛvəl] *n., adj. —n.* **1** a recklessly adventurous person; one who does bold and dangerous things that are unnecessary. **2** a stuntman or stuntwoman.
—adj. reckless: *a daredevil stunt.* **—'dare,dev•il•ry,** *n.*

dare•say ['dɛr'sei] *v.,* **-said, -say•ing.** believe (used only in the first person singular): *I daresay it will rain soon.*

dar•ing ['dɛrɪŋ] *n., adj., v. —n.* the courage to take risks; boldness.
—adj. courageous; bold.
—v. ppr. of DARE. **—'dar•ing•ly,** *adv.* **—'dar•ing•ness,** *n.*

Dar•jeel•ing [dɑr'dʒilɪŋ] *n.* a fine quality Indian tea. ⟨< *Darjeeling* in NE India⟩

dark [dɑrk] *adj., n. —adj.* **1** without light or with very little light: *the dark side of the moon. It was a dark, moonless night. I thought he must be in bed, because his window was dark.* **2** allowing only some light to pass through: *She was wearing her dark glasses.* **3** not light-complexioned: *a dark skin, dark good looks.* **4** deep in shade; closer in colour to black than white: *dark green, a dark background, dark hair.* **5** secret; hidden: *He kept his past dark.* **6** evil; wicked: *a dark deed.* **7** gloomy and sad; dismal: *Those were dark days. Don't always look on the dark side of things.* **8** sullen or angry: *She gave him a dark look.* **9** hard to understand; obscure: *dark sayings.* **10** ignorant; unenlightened: *a culturally dark age.* **11** of radio or television stations, not broadcasting. **12** of a voice, deep and plummy, sometimes also sad. **13** *Phonetics.* of the sound [l], articulated at the velum. In English, this [l] occurs only in the coda position of a syllable, such as in *bull.*
keep dark, keep silent; not tell about.
—n. **1 the dark,** the absence of light; darkness: *He's afraid of the dark. It was a shock to step from the dark of the cave into the sunlight.* **2** the time when the dark of night begins; nightfall: *The children are not allowed out after dark. They waited until dark to continue their journey.* **3** a dark colour: *the darks and lights in a painting.* **4** obscurity; secrecy.
in the dark, not knowing or understanding; in ignorance: *I'm still in the dark about what I'm supposed to do on the project.* ⟨OE *deorc*⟩ **—'dark•ly,** *adv.* **—'dark•ness,** *n.*

☛ *Syn. adj.* **1. Dark,** DIM = without light. **Dark** = without any light or with very little light: *The house is dark, not a light is on.* **Dim** = without enough light to see clearly or distinctly: *With only the fire burning, the room was dim.*

dark adaptation adaptation of the eyes to dim light, involving dilation of the pupils and other changes.

Dark Ages 1 the Middle Ages, especially the early part (from the 5th to the 10th centuries) so named from the idea that it was a time of economic and intellectual poverty in most parts of Europe. **2** any similar period.

Dark Continent formerly, Africa, because so little was known about it by Europeans.

dark•en ['dɑrkən] *v.* make or become dark or darker.
not darken the door of, not come to the home of.
—'dark•en•er, *n.*

dark horse *Informal.* **1** an unexpected winner about which little is known. **2** a person who is unexpectedly nominated for a political or other office.

dark•ish ['dɑrkɪʃ] *adj.* rather dark. **—'dark•ish•ness,** *n.*

dark lantern a lantern whose light can be hidden by a cover or dark glass.

dark•ling ['dɑrklɪŋ] *adv., adj. —adv. Poetic.* in the dark.
—adj. dark; dim; obscure: *the darkling plain.* ⟨< *dark* + OE *-ling,* an adverbial suffix indicating state or manner⟩

dark reactions chemical reactions that are part of photosynthesis but do not require light for energy.

dark•room ['dɑrk,rum] *or* [-,rʊm] *n.* a room arranged for developing or printing photographs, having no light or a light of a colour that will not affect light-sensitive photographic materials.

dark•some ['dɑrksəm] *adj. Poetic.* **1** dark. **2** gloomy.

dar•ling ['dɑrlɪŋ] *n., adj. —n.* **1** a person very dear to another; a person much loved. **2** a favourite: *She's the darling of the jet set.* **3** a term of address for one's near and dear, or, often inappropriately, for anyone regarded as small or cute.
—adj. **1** very dear; much loved. **2** *Informal.* very attractive; pleasing; charming: *a darling little shop.* ⟨OE *dēorling* < *dēore* dear⟩ **—'dar•ling•ly,** *adv.* **—'dar•ling•ness,** *n.*

darn[1] [dɑrn] *v., n. —v.* mend by weaving rows of thread or yarn across (a hole or torn place).
—n. **1** the act of darning. **2** a place mended by darning. ⟨< dial. F *darner* mend < *darne* piece < Breton *darn*⟩

darn[2] [dɑrn] *interj., adj., adv., or n. Informal.* a mild form of the word **damn,** used to express annoyance, anger, surprise, etc.: *Darn! The window's frozen shut. He's a darn fool.* ⟨< *damn;* influenced by *tarnal* (informal for *eternal*)⟩

darned [dɑrnd] *adj., adv. Informal.* damned.

dar•nel ['dɑrnəl] *n.* any of several species of ryegrass, especially *Lolium temulentum,* a noxious weed found in grainfields in Europe and Asia. **Persian darnel** (*L. persicum*) is a common and troublesome Canadian weed introduced from Asia. ⟨ME; cf. F dial. *darnelle*⟩

darn•er ['dɑrnər] *n.* **1** a person who darns. **2** DARNING NEEDLE.

darn•ing ['dɑrnɪŋ] *n., v. —n.* **1** the act of mending with interwoven rows of stitches. **2** the articles darned or to be darned.
—v. ppr. of DARN[1].

darning needle 1 a long needle with an eye large enough to take the heavy thread used for darning. **2** *Informal.* dragonfly.

dar•shan ['dɑrʃən] *n.* **1** *Hinduism.* the feeling of exaltation which one gets in the presence of a great man. **2** *Judaism.* a teacher in a synagogue. ⟨< Hind. *darasan* < Skt. *darsana* a seeing⟩

dart [dɑrt] *n., v. —n.* **1** a small, slender, pointed weapon usually having feathers at the back, for throwing by hand or shooting from a tube or gun. **2 darts,** an indoor game in which players throw darts at a round board marked off in concentric circles and numbered radiating sections (*used with a singular verb).* **3** a sudden quick movement: *She made a dart for the window.* **4** a sharp look, word, etc. **5** a tapered fold, or tuck, in a garment to shape it to a part of the body or to make it hang better: *Long, narrow sleeves usually have darts at the elbow.* **6** the stinger of an insect.
—v. **1** throw or shoot suddenly and quickly. **2** move suddenly and quickly: *She darted across the street.* **3** direct or send suddenly: *She darted an angry glance at her sister.* **4** sew darts in (a garment or part of one). ⟨ME < OF < Gmc.⟩

dart•er ['dɑrtər] *n.* **1** any of a subfamily (Etheostomidae) of small, slender, freshwater fishes of E North America, some of which are brightly coloured. **2** snakebird. **3** an animal, person, or thing that darts.

Dar•win•i•an [dɑr'wɪniən] *adj., n. —adj.* **1** of or having to do with Charles Darwin (1809-1882), an English scientist. **2** of or having to do with his theory of evolution.
—n. a person who believes in Darwinism.

Dar•win•ism ['dɑrwə,nɪzəm] *n.* **1** Charles Darwin's theory of evolution, that in successive generations all plants and animals tend to develop slightly varying forms. Through natural selection the forms that survive are those which have adapted themselves to their environment better than the forms that become extinct. According to the theory, this process is the origin of all the species. **2** belief in Darwin's theory.

dash [dæʃ] *v., n., interj.* —*v.* **1** throw: *We dashed water over her.* **2** splash: *She dashed some paint on the canvas.* **3** rush: *They dashed by in a car.* **4** strike violently against something. *The boat was dashed against the cliff.* **5** smash: *He dashed the bowl to bits on a rock.* **6** ruin: *Our hopes were dashed.* **7** depress; discourage. **8** mix with a small amount of something else. **9** abash; confound: *She was dashed by the sudden questioning of the teacher.*
dash off, a do, make, write, etc., quickly: *He dashed off a short letter to his friend.* **b** rush away.
—*n.* **1** a splash. **2** a rush. **3** a smash. **4** anything that depresses or discourages; a check. **5** a small amount. **6** a short race: *the hundred-metre dash.* **7** a blow; a stroke. **8** a mark (—) used in writing or printing, especially to show a break in sense or in the structure of a sentence. **9** *Telegraphy.* a long sound or signal that represents a letter or part of a letter: *Morse code uses dots and dashes.* **10** DASHBOARD (def. 1). **11** energy; spirit; liveliness. **12** showy appearance or behaviour.
cut a dash, dress showily.
—*interj.* a mild curse; a euphemism for *damn.* ⟨ME *dasche(n)*; cf. Danish *daske* slap⟩

dash•board ['dæʃ,bɔrd] *n.* **1** a panel with controls and gauges, below the windshield and in front of the operator in an automobile, aircraft, etc. **2** a screen on the front of a wagon, boat, etc., to provide protection from splashing mud or water.

dashed [dæʃt] *adj., adv.* damned.

dash•er ['dæʃər] *n.* **1** one that dashes. **2** a device with blades for stirring the cream in a churn or ice-cream freezer. **3** *Cdn.* the fence surrounding the ice of a hockey rink; the boards. **4** *Informal.* a spirited person.

da•shi•ki [dɑ'ʃiki] *or* [də'ʃiki] *n.* a loose-fitting, collarless, pullover robe or tunic, usually made of a brightly coloured and patterned cotton. ⟨of West African origin⟩

dash•ing ['dæʃɪŋ] *adj., v.* —*adj.* **1** full of energy and spirit; lively. **2** having or showing a sense of style; showy.
—*v.* ppr. of DASH. —**'dash•ing•ly,** *adv.*

dash light a small light that illuminates the dashboard in a motor vehicle.

das•sie ['dæsi] *n.* hyrax. ⟨< Afrikaans⟩

das•tard ['dæstərd] *n.* **1** a mean coward; sneak. **2** (*adj.*) mean and cowardly; sneaking. ⟨ME, originally, a dullard, apparently < *dazed*, pp. of *daze* + *-ard*, as in *dullard*, etc.⟩ —**'das•tard•ly,** *adj.* —**'das•tard•li•ness,** *n.*

das•y•me•ter [də'sɪmətər] *n.* an instrument which measures the density of a gas. ⟨< Gk. *dasys* dense + *-meter*⟩

das•y•ure ['dæsi,jur] *n.* **1** a carnivorous marsupial of the family Dasyuridae, native to Australia, having a red or brown coat with white spots. **2** any related animal, such as the Tasmanian devil. ⟨< NL *dasyurus* < Gk. *dasys* thick, hairy + *oura* tail⟩

dat. dative.

DAT digital audio tape.

da•ta ['deitə] *or* ['dætə] *n.* pl. of **datum. 1** facts or concepts presented in a form suitable for processing in order to draw conclusions: *All the data indicate the beginning of an economic boom.* **2** *Computer technology.* values, characters, or symbols on which a computer carries out various operations.
☛ *Usage.* **Data** is the plural of the seldom-used singular *datum.* Since its meaning is often collective, referring to a group of facts as a unit, **data** is often used with a singular verb in informal English: *The data you have collected is not enough to convince me.* Formal English continues to regard **data** as a plural rather than as a collective noun: *We will analyse the data that have been obtained.*

data bank a body of information stored and available for processing in a computer.

data base or **da•ta•base** ['deitə,beis] *or* ['dætə,beis] *n.* information stored, usually in a computer, for easy access and retrieval.

data centre *Computer technology.* a central computer installation: *Our data centre is on the fifth floor.*

data dipper *Computer technology.* a program which allows the user to retrieve data from a remote database.

data entry *Computer technology.* a process in which a human operator enters data into a computer system, usually in large quantities.

data processing the operations performed on data, especially by a computer, in order to derive information or to organize files. —**,da•ta-'pro•cess•ing,** *adj.*

data processor a computer which does data processing.

date¹ [deit] *n., v.* **dat•ed, dat•ing.** —*n.* **1** the time when something happens. **2** a statement of time: *There is a date stamped on every piece of Canadian money.* **3** a period of time. **4 dates,** *pl.* the years of a person's birth and death: *What are Mozart's dates?* **5** the number of a day of the month: *What is today's date?* **6** an appointment for a certain time, especially for a social engagement with a person of the opposite sex: *She's made a date with him for Saturday.* **7** the social engagement itself: *She said it was a boring date. He's out on a date.* **8** *Informal.* the person with whom one has such an engagement: *Who's your date for the dance?*
bring up to date, a revise so as to reflect current information. **b** give current information to (a person).
out of date, old-fashioned; not in present use: *That dress looks out of date.*
to date, till now; up to the present moment; yet: *There have been no replies to date.*
up to date, a to the present time. **b** modern; according to the latest style or idea; in fashion: *Her clothes are always up to date.* **c** having current information: *Be sure to use up-to-date sources for your research. Are you up to date on the Grinberg affair?*
—*v.* **1** mark with a date; put a date on. **2** find out the date of; give a date to: *The scientist was unable to date the fossil.* **3** belong to a certain period of time; have its origin: (*usually used with* **from**): *That house dates from the late 18th century.* **4** cause to seem old-fashioned: *That expression dates you—it's no longer used.* **5** make a social appointment with (a person of the opposite sex): *He's been trying for months to date her.* **6** go out regularly with (a particular person of the opposite sex); go on dates: *They've been dating for a long time. She dates a fellow from another school.* **7** be or become out of date. ⟨ME < MF < Med.L *data*, pp. fem. of L *dare* give⟩ —**'dat•a•ble** or **'date•a•ble,** *adj.*
☛ *Usage.* **Dates.** The usual Canadian method of writing dates is: *July 1, 1867; November 3, 1985.* However, in military use, and increasingly among scientists, the day of the month is placed first: *3 Nov. 1985.* Names of months having more than four letters are often abbreviated. In numeric dating, Canadian and British practice has been to indicate the day, month, and year in that order: 3/11/85. American practice is to put the month before the day: 11/3/85. To avoid confusion between these two systems, the preferred international system of numeric dating puts year, month, and day: *1985 11 03, 85 11 03,* or *85-11-03.* If required, such dates can be followed by the time, using the 24-hour clock: 85 11 03 21 05.

date² [deit] *n.* **1** the oblong, fleshy, edible fruit of the date palm. **2** DATE PALM. ⟨ME < OF < L *dactylus* < Gk. *daktylos* date, finger. Doublet of DACTYL.⟩

dat•ed ['deitɪd] *adj., v.* —*adj.* **1** marked with a date; showing a date. **2** out of date.
—*v.* pt. and pp. of DATE. —**'dat•ed•ly,** *adv.* —**'dat•ed•ness,** *n.*

date•less ['deitlɪs] *adj.* **1** without a date; not dated. **2** endless; unlimited. **3** so old that it cannot be given a date. **4** old but still admirable, in good style, etc. **5** classic; not likely to become outdated.

date line **1** an imaginary line agreed upon as the place where each calendar day first begins. It runs north and south through the Pacific, mostly along the 180th meridian. When it is Sunday just east of the date line, it is Monday just west of it. **2** a line in a letter, newspaper, etc., giving the date and place of writing.

date palm a tall palm tree (*Phoenix dactylifera*) that bears dates. It is native to Syria but widely cultivated in tropical regions of the world.

date stamp **1** a rubber stamp for recording dates, having a series of numbers and, often, the names of the months on separate parallel rings of rubber that can be rotated to bring the desired numbers and names into alignment for any given date. **2** an inked impression made by such a stamp. —**'date-,stamp,** *v.*

da•tive ['deitɪv] *adj., n.* —*adj. Grammar.* of, having to do with, or being the grammatical case found in some languages (such as German and Latin), that shows that a noun, pronoun, or adjective is an indirect object of a verb or an object of any of certain prepositions. English has no dative case, but expresses such a grammatical relationship by prepositions such as *to* or *for* and through word order.
—*n.* **1** the dative case. **2** a word or construction in the dative case. *Abbrev.:* dat. ⟨< L *dativus* of giving < *datus*, pp. of *dare* give⟩

da•tum ['deitəm] *or* ['dætəm] *n., pl.* **da•ta. 1** a fact from which conclusions can be drawn. **2** *Surveying.* a hypothetical or actual

level, height, etc., from which measurements are made. ⟨< L *datum* (thing) given, pp. neut. of *dare.* Doublet of DIE[3].⟩
☛ *Usage.* See note at DATA.

da•tu•ra [dəˈtjurə] *or* [dəˈturə] *n.* any plant of the genus *Datura*, of the nightshade family, having hallucinogenic or poisonous leaves and seeds. ⟨< NL < Hind. *dhatura*⟩

daub [dɒb] *v., n. —v.* **1** coat or cover with plaster, clay, mud, etc. **2** apply (greasy or sticky stuff). **3** make dirty; soil; stain. **4** paint unskilfully.
—n. **1** something used to daub. **2** a mark made by daubing; smear. **3** a crudely painted picture. **4** the act of daubing. ⟨ME < OF *dauber* < L *dealbare* < *de-* + *albus* white⟩ **—ˈdaub•er,** *n.*

daugh•ter [ˈdɒtər] *n., adj. —n.* **1** a female child (immediate descendant of her parents). **2** a female descendant. **3** a girl or woman thought of as related to something in the same way that a child is related to its parents: *a daughter of France.* **4** anything thought of as a daughter in relation to its origin: *Skill is the daughter of hard work.* **5** DAUGHTER ELEMENT.
—adj. **1** of, being, or like a daughter. **2** resulting from a primary division, segmentation, or replication: *a daughter cell.* ⟨OE *dohtor*⟩

daughter element *Physics.* an element produced by the decay of a radioactive element.

daugh•ter–in–law [ˈdɒtər ɪn ˌlɒ] *n., pl.* **daugh•ters-in-law.** the wife of one's son.

daugh•ter•ly [ˈdɒtərli] *adj.* **1** of a daughter. **2** like that of a daughter. **3** proper for a daughter.

dau•no•ru•bi•cin [ˌdɒnouˈrubɪsɪn] *n.* an antibiotic drug used to treat certain forms of leukemia. Also called **daunomycin.**

daunt [dɒnt] *v.* dismay or discourage. ⟨ME < OF *danter* < L *domitare* < *domare* tame⟩

daunt•less [ˈdɒntlɪs] *adj.* not to be frightened or discouraged; brave; fearless. **—ˈdaunt•less•ly,** *adv.* **—ˈdaunt•less•ness,** *n.*

dau•phin [ˈdɒfən]; *French,* [doˈfɛ̃] *n.* the title given to the oldest son of the king of France, from 1349 to 1830. ⟨< F *dauphin*, originally a family name⟩

dau•phine [ˈdɒfin]; *French,* [doˈfin] *n.* the wife of a dauphin. ⟨< F. See DAUPHIN.⟩

dau•phin•ess [ˈdɒfənɪs] *or* [ˈdɒfəˌnɛs] *n.* dauphine.

da•ven [ˈdɑvən] *v. Judaism.* intone the words of the liturgy.

dav•en•port [ˈdævənˌpɔrt] *n.* **1** a large chesterfield, or sofa. **2** *Brit.* a writing desk with drawers and a hinged shelf to write on. ⟨origin uncertain⟩

Da•vid [ˈdeivɪd] *n.*
David and Jonathan, any pair of devoted friends. ⟨in the Bible, two devoted friends⟩

dav•it [ˈdævɪt] *or* [ˈdeivɪt] *n.* **1** one of a pair of cranelike devices projecting over the side of a ship, used especially for raising or lowering lifeboats or cargo. **2** a crane projecting over the bow of a ship, used for raising or lowering an anchor. ⟨ME < AF *daviot*⟩

Da•vy Jones [ˈdeivi ˈdʒounz] the evil spirit of the sea; the sailor's devil.

Davy Jones's locker the sea, especially as the grave of those who have drowned or been buried at sea.

Davy lamp a lamp for miners, worn on the helmet, and enclosed in wire to protect the miner from firedamp. ⟨after the name of its inventor, Sir H. *Davy* (1778-1829)⟩

daw [dɒ] *n.* jackdaw. ⟨ME *dawe*⟩

daw•dle [ˈdɒdəl] *v.* **-dled, -dling;** *n. —v.* waste time; idle; loiter: *Don't dawdle over your work.*
—n. **1** a person who dawdles. **2** the act of dawdling. ⟨origin uncertain⟩ **—ˈdawd•ler,** *n.*

dawn [dɒn] *n., v. —n.* **1** the break of day; the first light in the east. **2** the beginning: *before the dawn of history.*
—v. **1** grow light: *The day dawned bright and clear.* **2** grow clear to the eye or mind: *It dawned on me that she was expecting a gift.* **3** begin; appear: *A new era is dawning.* ⟨ME *dawnen* < *dawning* daybreak, probably < ON; replacing ME *dawen* < OE *dagian* become day⟩
☛ *Hom.* DON [dɒn].

dawn redwood a large coniferous tree (*Metasequoia glyptostroboides*) of the baldcypress family, native to China but naturalized in the United States. It looks like the California redwood, but is deciduous.

day [dei] *n.* **1** the time between sunrise and sunset. **2** the light of day; daylight. **3** the 24 hours of day and night; the time it takes the earth to turn once on its axis: *There are 31 days in January.* **4** *Astronomy.* the time needed by any celestial body to turn once on its axis: *The Martian day is a little longer than Earth's.* **5** a certain day on which something happens, set aside for a particular purpose or for celebration: *Christmas Day.* **6** the hours for work: *She works a seven-hour day.* **7** a certain period of time: *the present day, in days of old.* **8** an indefinite time in the past or, usually, future: *one of these days.* **9 days,** *pl.* a lifetime: *to spend one's days in contemplating nature.* **10** a period of life, activity, power, or influence: *He has had his day.* **11** the conflict or contest of a particular day: *Our team won the day. The day is ours.*
call it a day, *Informal.* stop work: *I'm tired; let's call it a day.*
day after day, every day for many days.
day by day, each day; one day at a time.
day in, day out, every day.
from day to day, each day; one day at a time.
have (one's) **day in court,** have a chance to give (one's) side of a story.
pass the time of day, take part in small talk.
right from day one, from the very beginning.
the time of day, a the time. **b** a greeting; salutation. ⟨OE *dæg*⟩
☛ *Hom.* DEY.

day bed or **day•bed** [ˈdei ˌbɛd] *n.* a bed, usually narrow, having a low headboard and a footboard of equal height, and, usually, a rail or support of some kind along one side that can function as a backrest: a day bed can be used as a couch by day.

day book **1** *Bookkeeping.* a book in which a record is kept of each day's business. **2** diary.

day•break [ˈdeiˌbreik] *n.* dawn; the time when it first begins to get light in the morning.

day camp a summer camp for children in which they have daytime activities as at a regular camp but return home for the night.

day care **1** the care and training of babies and preschool children outside the home during the day: *The ratepayers were asking for more funds for day care.* **2** a similar arrangement for the social life of old, physically disabled, or mentally ill people. **—ˈday-ˌcare,** *adj.*

day–care centre a place where small children may be cared for during the day while their parents are at work.

day coach a railway passenger car which is not a dining car or sleeping car.

day•dream [ˈdeiˌdrim] *n., v.* **-dreamed** or **-dreamt, -dream•ing.** *—n.* **1** a dreamy thought about pleasant things. **2** a pleasant plan or fancy, unlikely to come true.
—v. think dreamily about pleasant things. **—ˈdayˌdream•er,** *n.*

day•flow•er [ˈdeiˌflaʊər] *n.* any plant of the genus *Commelina*, of the spiderwort family, having small blue flowers that last for a single day.

day•fly [ˈdeiˌflaɪ] *n.* the adult mayfly.

day labourer or **laborer** an unskilled or manual worker who is paid by the day.

day letter a telegram sent during the day for delivery later the same day. Service is slower for a day letter than for a regular telegram but cheaper.

day•light [ˈdeiˌləit] *n.* **1** the light of day. **2** the daytime. **3** dawn; daybreak. **4** publicity; openness. **5** open space; a gap.
scare/beat/knock the daylights out of, *Slang.* frighten or beat (someone) severely.
see daylight, *Informal.* **a** understand. **b** approach the end of a hard or tiresome job.

daylight–saving time time that is one hour in advance of standard time and gives more daylight after working hours. Clocks are set ahead one hour in the spring and back one hour in the fall. Compare STANDARD TIME.

day lily **1** any of a genus (*Hemerocallis*) of plants of the lily family native to Europe and Asia but widely cultivated for their large yellow, orange, or red flowers that last about a day. **2** PLANTAIN LILY.

day•lin•er [ˈdeiˌlaɪnər] *n.* a railway train which runs express between two cities, or between suburbs and a city during the day.

day•long [ˈdeiˌlɒŋ] *adj. or adv.* through the whole day.

day nursery a nursery for the care of small children during the day.

Day of Atonement YOM KIPPUR.

Day of Judgment according to the Christian Bible, the day of God's final judgment of humankind at the end of the world.

day room a room in a hospital, army camp, etc., set aside for social activities or reading.

days [deiz] *adv.* during the day; in the daytime; every day: *to work nights and sleep days.*

day school 1 a school held in the daytime. 2 a private school for students who live at home. 3 an elementary school held on weekdays.

days of grace the extra days (usually three) allowed for payment after a bill or note falls due.

day•spring ['dei,sprɪŋ] *n. Poetic.* the dawn; daybreak.

day•star ['dei,stɑr] *n.* 1 MORNING STAR. 2 *Poetic.* sun.

day student a non-resident student at a residential high school or college.

day•time ['dei,taɪm] *n.* the time when it is day.

day–to–day ['dei tə 'dei] *adj.* ordinary or regular; everyday: *Civil servants are involved in the day-to-day operation of government.*

day trip a leisure trip lasting no longer than a day. **—'day-,trip•per,** *n.*

day•work ['dei,wɜrk] *n.* work, especially domestic, contracted and remunerated on a daily basis.

daze [deiz] *v.* **dazed, daz•ing;** *n.* —*v.* 1 confuse; bewilder; cause to feel stupid; stun: *She was so dazed by her fall that she didn't know where she was.* 2 dazzle.
—*n.* a confused state of mind; bewilderment. ⟨ME *dase(n)* < ON; cf. Icelandic *dasask* become weary⟩

daz•ed•ly ['deizɪdli] *adv.* in a dazed, confused, or stupid manner.

daz•zle ['dæzəl] *v.* **-zled, -zling;** *n.* —*v.* 1 confuse, dim, or overpower (the eyes) with too bright light or with quick-moving lights. 2 overcome (the senses or the mind) by brightness, display, etc.: *The young pianist's performance dazzled the critics.*
—*n.* the act or fact of dazzling; a bewildering brightness. ⟨< *daze*⟩ **—'daz•zler,** *n.* **—'daz•zling•ly,** *adv.*

db decibel.

D.B.E. Dame (Commander of the Order) of the British Empire.

dbl. double.

d.c. *Music.* da capo.

DC, D.C., or **d.c.** direct current.

D.C. 1 *Music.* return to beginning (for Ital. *da capo*). 2 District of Columbia.

D.C.M. Distinguished Conduct Medal.

D.C.V.O. Distinguished Commander of the Victorian Order.

D–day ['di ,dei] *n.* 1 the day when the Allies landed in France in World War II; June 6, 1944. 2 the day on which a previously planned military attack is to be made, or on which an operation, as, in business, is to be started. ⟨< *D*, first letter of *day*⟩

DDC or ddC dideoxycytinide.

DDE a poisonous residue of DDT which stops calcium production, causing birds to lay eggs with extremely fragile shells.

DDI didanosine.

DDT ['di'di'ti] *n.* a colourless, odourless crystalline compound that is a very powerful and long-lasting poison, formerly much used as an insecticide. *Formula:* $C_{14}H_9Cl_5$ ⟨short for *d*ichloro - *d*iphenyl - *t*richloroethane⟩

de– *prefix.* 1 do the opposite of, as in *decamp, deforest, decentralize, demobilize.* 2 down, as in *depress, descend.* 3 away; off, as in *deport, detract.* 4 cause to leave something, as in *derail.* 5 entirely; completely (intensive), as in *despoil.* 6 remove, as in *defrost.* ⟨< L *de-* < *de* from, away⟩

de•ac•ces•sion or **de-ac•ces•sion** [,diæk'sɛʃən] *v.* remove (an item) from the collection in an art gallery, museum, or library, and sell it.

dea•con ['dikən] *n.* 1 an officer of a Christian church who helps the minister in church duties other than preaching. 2 a member of the Christian clergy immediately below a priest in rank. ⟨OE *diacon* < L *diaconus* < Gk. *diakonos* servant⟩

dea•con•ess ['dikənɪs] *or* ['dikə,nɛs] *n.* a woman deacon.

dea•con•ry ['dikənri] *n., pl.* **-ries.** 1 the position of deacon. 2 deacons collectively.

de•ac•ti•vate [di'æktə,veit] *v.* **-at•ed, -at•ing.** make inoperative or inactive: *to deactivate a bomb, to deactivate a military base.* **—de,ac•ti'va•tion,** *n.* **—de'ac•ti,va•tor,** *n.*

dead [dɛd] *adj., adv., n.* —*adj.* 1 no longer living; that has died. 2 without life; inanimate. 3 like death: *in a dead faint.* 4 not active or productive; dull, stagnant, quiet, etc. 5 without force, power, spirit, or feeling: *a dead handshake. She spoke in a dead voice.* 6 no longer having significance, power, or effect: *a dead issue.* 7 no longer active: *a dead fire, a dead volcano.* 8 no longer in use; obsolete: *a dead language.* 9 no longer functioning or producing: *a dead battery.* 10 out of play; not in the game: *a dead ball.* 11 no longer bouncy: *a dead ball.* 12 *Informal.* very tired; worn-out. 13 sure; certain: *a dead shot, a dead certainty.* 14 complete; absolute: *a dead loss, dead silence.* 15 precise; exact: *dead centre.* 16 not connected to a source of power: *a dead circuit. The telephone line is dead.* 17 *Printing.* of type, etc., already used or no longer needed. 18 completely uninterested by or unconscious of (*used with* **to**): *dead to science.* 19 not resonant.
dead in the water, *Slang.* finished; done for.
dead to the world, fast asleep.
—*adv.* 1 completely; absolutely: *The forecast was dead wrong. I'm dead tired.* 2 directly; straight: *dead ahead.*
—*n.* 1 **the dead,** *pl.* those who are dead; all who no longer have life: *We remembered the dead of our wars on Remembrance Day.* 2 the time of greatest darkness, quiet, cold, etc.: *the dead of night.* ⟨OE *dēad*⟩ **—'dead•ness,** *n.*
☛ *Syn. adj.* **1, 2. Dead,** DECEASED, LIFELESS = without life. **Dead** applies particularly to someone or something that was living or alive, but no longer is: *The flowers in my garden are dead.* **Deceased,** a technical word, applies only to a dead person: *The deceased man left no will.* **Lifeless** is used both of what now is or seems to be without life and of things that never had life: *He lifted the lifeless body.*

dead air 1 air that is trapped between two walls for insulation. 2 *Radio and television.* a period of no broadcasting.

dead•beat ['dɛd,bit] *n.* 1 *Informal.* **a** a person who purposefully avoids paying for what he or she gets. **b** a lazy person; loafer. 2 (*adjl.*) of a needle on a meter, etc., showing a steady reading; not oscillating.

dead•bolt ['dɛd,boult] *n.* a type of lock having a bolt that is turned with the key.

dead centre 1 in an engine, the position of the crank and connecting rod at which the connecting rod has no power to turn the crank. Dead centre occurs at each end of a stroke, when the crank and the connecting rod are in the same straight line. 2 the stationary centre of a revolving object.

dead duck *Informal.* 1 a person or thing that is completely exhausted and without further strength or usefulness. 2 one whose fate is sealed: *The boss said, "Make another mistake like that, and you're a dead duck."*

dead•en ['dɛdən] *v.* 1 make dull or weak; lessen the intensity or force of. 2 reduce the sound of. 3 make insensitive to; harden emotionally: *Life in the army deadened them to cruelty.* 4 insulate (a wall, floor, etc.) so that sound does not penetrate; soundproof. **—'dead•en•er,** *n.*

dead end 1 a street, passage, etc., closed at one end. 2 a point in a discussion, plan, etc. beyond which progress is impossible: *When the committee reached a dead end, they decided to drop the plan.*

dead–end ['dɛd 'ɛnd] *adj.* 1 closed at one end. 2 having no opportunity for progress, advancement, etc.; fruitless: *a dead-end job.* 3 of the slums; tough; *a dead-end gang.*

dead•en•ing ['dɛdənɪŋ] *n.* soundproofing material.

dead•eye ['dɛd,aɪ] *n.* 1 a round, flat, wooden block used to fasten the shrouds of a ship. 2 *Slang.* one who is an accurate shot.

dead•fall ['dɛd,fɒl] *n.* 1 a trap for animals made so that a heavy weight falls upon and holds or kills the animal. 2 a mass of fallen trees and underbrush. 3 a dead tree that has been blown to the ground.

dead•head ['dɛd,hɛd] *n., v.* —*n.* 1 *Informal.* a person who rides on a bus, sees a game, etc. without paying. 2 *Informal.* a train, railway car, bus, etc. travelling without passengers or freight. 3 *Slang.* a stupid or dull person. 4 *Cdn.* a log or fallen tree partly or entirely submerged in a lake, etc., usually with one end embedded in the bottom.
—*v.* 1 *Informal.* drive a train, bus, truck, etc. without passengers or freight. 2 travel on free tickets.

dead heat a race that ends in a tie.

dead letter 1 an unclaimed letter; a letter that cannot be delivered or returned to the sender because the address is wrong, impossible to read, or incomplete. 2 a law, rule, etc. that is not enforced.

dead–letter office a department of the Post Office to which dead letters are sent to be opened or destroyed.

dead lift a lift of something heavy by unaided manual strength.

dead•light ['dɛd,ləit] *n.* **1** a cover for a ship's porthole in bad weather. **2** a thick window in the side of a ship. **3** a skylight which does not open.

dead•line ['dɛd,laɪn] *n.* **1** a time limit; the latest possible time to do something. **2** a line or boundary that must not be crossed.

dead load the constant, invariable load that a structure such as a bridge carries, that is due to the weight of the supported structures, permanent attachments, etc. Also called **dead weight.** Compare LIVE LOAD.

dead•lock ['dɛd,lɒk] *n., v.* —*n.* a position in which it is impossible to act or continue because of disagreement: *Employers and strikers were at a deadlock.*
—*v.* bring or come to such a position: *The talks were deadlocked for weeks.*

dead•ly ['dɛdli] *adj.* **-li•er, -li•est;** *adv.* —*adj.* **1** causing death; liable to cause death; fatal: *a deadly wound.* **2** like death: *deadly paleness.* **3** filled with hatred that lasts till death: *deadly enemies.* **4** causing death of the spirit: *deadly sin.* **5** *Informal.* extreme; intense. **6** dull: *The party was a deadly affair.* **7** absolutely accurate: *a deadly aim.*
—*adv.* **1** *Informal.* extremely. **2** like death. **3** as if dead.
—'dead•li•ness, *n.*
☛ *Syn. adj.* **1.** See note at FATAL.

deadly nightshade 1 BLACK NIGHTSHADE. **2** belladonna.

deadly sins in certain Christian theologies, the seven sins that can lead to damnation: pride, covetousness, lust, anger, gluttony, envy, and sloth.

dead march funeral march.

dead•pan ['dɛd,pæn] *adj., adv., n., v.* **-panned, -pan•ning.**
—*adj.* showing no expression or emotion: *a deadpan face, deadpan humour.*
—*adv.* in a deadpan manner: *She told the whole ridiculous story deadpan.*
—*n.* **1** a deadpan face or manner. **2** someone who assumes such a face or manner.
—*v.* express or act in a deadpan manner: *to deadpan a joke.*

dead point DEAD CENTRE.

dead reckoning 1 the calculation of the location of a ship or aircraft without observations of the sun, stars, etc., by using a compass and studying the record of the voyage. **2** calculation of one's location by using natural landmarks.

Dead Sea Scrolls the name given to a number of parchment, leather, and copper scrolls found in 1947 and later in caves near the Dead Sea. They date approximately from between 100 B.C. and A.D. 100, and contain Hebrew and Aramaic texts of Biblical writings, explanation, etc.

dead set 1 the position of a hunting dog which remains still when it has found a quarry. **2** a determined effort or attack.
dead set against, refusing to give ground on (an issue which one opposes).

dead•stock ['dɛd,stɒk] *n.* the carcass of an animal, ready for butchering. Compare LIVESTOCK.

dead weight 1 the heavy weight of anything inert. **2** a very great or oppressive burden. **3** the mass of a vessel or vehicle without a load. **4** freight chargeable by mass rather than by volume, or bulk. **5** DEAD LOAD. **—'dead-,weight,** *adj.*

dead•wood ['dɛd,wʊd] *n.* **1** dead branches or trees. **2** useless people or things. **3** wording that adds nothing to the meaning of a sentence. **4** strengthening timbers at the bow or stern of a wooden ship.

deaf [dɛf] *adj.* **1** not able to hear. **2** not able to hear well. **3** not willing to hear; heedless: *A miser is deaf to all requests for money.* ⟨OE *dēaf*⟩ **—'deaf•ly,** *adv.* **—'deaf•ness,** *n.*

deaf•en ['dɛfən] *v.* **1** make deaf. **2** stun with noise. **3** drown out by a louder sound. **4** make soundproof. **—'deaf•en•ing•ly,** *adv.*

deaf–mute ['dɛf ,mjut] *n., adj.* —*n.* a person who is unable to hear or speak because of congenital deafness.
—*adj.* unable to hear or speak.

deal[1] [dil] *v.* **dealt, deal•ing;** *n.* —*v.* **1** have to do (*with*): *Arithmetic deals with numbers.* **2** occupy oneself; take action: *The courts deal with those who break the laws.* **3** act; behave: *Deal fairly with everyone.* **4** take positive action; struggle successfully (*with*): *I don't know how to deal with the problem.* **5** do business; buy and sell: *A butcher deals in meat.* **6** give: *One fighter dealt the other a blow.* **7** give a share of to each; distribute. **8** distribute (playing cards). **9** sell (illegal drugs).
deal out, to give out or distribute.
—*n.* **1** *Informal.* a business arrangement; bargain. **2** *Informal.* a set-up; arrangement; plan: *a new deal. What's the deal here?* **3** a kind of treatment: *a rough deal.* **4** *Card games.* **a** the distribution of cards. **b** a player's turn to deal. **c** the time during which one deal of cards is being played. **d** the cards held by a player; hand. **5** a quantity; amount: *I took a deal of trouble.* **6** a dealing; distributing.
a good deal or **a great deal, a** a large part, portion, or amount: *She spends a great deal of her money on holiday trips.* **b** to a great extent or degree; much: *He smokes a good deal.*
a square deal, an honest business transaction; a fair arrangement.
big deal, *Slang.* an expression of disparagement.
make a big deal out of, *Informal.* treat (something) as important; fuss over. ⟨OE *dælan*⟩

deal[2] [dil] *n.* **1** a board of pine or fir wood, usually about 18 cm × 180 cm × 7.6 cm. **2** pine or fir wood in the form of deals. **3** (*adj.*) made of deal: *a deal table.* ⟨< MLG or MDu. *dele* plank⟩

deal•er ['dilər] *n.* **1** a person or group that trades; one engaged in buying and selling: *a car dealer.* **2** *Card games.* the person who distributes the cards to the players. **3** a person who deals, or acts, in a particular way: *a plain dealer.*

deal•er•ship ['dilər,ʃɪp] *n.* the business, franchise, or territory of a DEALER (def. 1).

deal•ing ['dilɪŋ] *n., v.* —*n.* **1** a way of doing business: *The storekeeper is respected for his honest dealing.* **2** a way of acting; behaviour toward others. **3** the act or process of distributing.
4 dealings, *pl.* **a** business relations: *The fur trader was honest in his dealings with the trappers.* **b** actions; behaviour: *The teacher tried to be fair in all his dealings with students.*
—*v.* ppr. of DEAL[1].

dealt [dɛlt] *v.* pt. and pp. of DEAL[1].

de•am•i•nate [di'æmə,neit] *v.,* **-at•ed, -at•ing.** alter (a compound) by removing the amino group $-NH_2$.
—de,am•i'na•tion, *n.*

dean [din] *n.* **1** the head of a school or faculty in a university or college. **2** a member of the faculty of a university or college who has charge of the behaviour or studies of the students. **3** a high official of a Christian church, often in charge of a cathedral. **4** the member who has belonged to a group longest. **5** the most illustrious member of a profession, literary association, organization, etc.: *Robertson Davies was considered by many to be the dean of Canadian novelists.* ⟨ME < OF *deien* < LL *decanus* master of ten < *decem* ten⟩

dean•er•y ['dinəri] *n., pl.* **-er•ies. 1** the position or authority of a dean. **2** the residence of a dean.

dea•nol ['dinɒl] *n.* a drug used to treat learning-disabled or hyperactive children.

dean•ship ['dinʃɪp] *n.* the position, office, or rank of a dean.

dear [dir] *adj., n., adv., interj.* —*adj.* **1** much loved; precious. **2** much valued; highly esteemed. *Dear* is used as a form of polite address at the beginning of letters: *Dear Sir, Dear Isabel.* **3** high-priced; costly; expensive.
—*n.* a dear one.
—*adv.* at a high price; at a great cost.
hold dear, value highly.
—*interj.* an exclamation of surprise, trouble, etc. ⟨OE *dēore*⟩
—'dear•ly, *adv.* **—'dear•ness,** *n.*
☛ *Hom.* DEER.
☛ *Syn. adj.* **3.** See note at EXPENSIVE.

dear•ie or **dear•y** ['diri] *n., pl.* **dear•ies.** *Informal.* a dear one; darling.

Dear John letter *Informal.* a letter written to terminate a romantic involvement, engagement, etc., especially one written to a man by his girlfriend.

dearth [dɜrθ] *n.* **1** a scarcity; lack. **2** a scarcity of food; famine. ⟨ME *derthe* < *dere* hard, grievous < OE *dēor*⟩

death [dɛθ] *n.* **1** the act or fact of dying; the end of life in human beings, animals, or plants. **2** the state or condition of being dead. **3** Often, **Death,** a personalization of the power that destroys life, often represented as a skeleton dressed in black and carrying a scythe. **4** any ending that is like dying; total destruction: *the death of an empire, the death of all our hopes.* **5** any condition like being dead. **6** a cause of death: *Alcoholism was the death of her.* **7** bloodshed; murder.
at death's door, dying; about to die; almost dead.

be death on, be very strongly opposed to: *He's death on all drugs.*
do to death, a kill; murder. **b** do, act, or say (the same thing) so often that it becomes boring.
like death warmed over, *Informal.* extremely sick or appearing to be so.
put to death, kill or execute.
to death, almost beyond endurance; extremely: *She said she was bored to death.*
to the death, a to the last resource; to the last extreme: *a fight to the death.* **b** until the end of one's life: *Honour to the death is his motto.* ⟨OE *dēath*⟩ **—'death,like,** *adj.*

death•bed ['dɛθ,bɛd] *n.* **1** a bed on which a person dies. **2** the last hours of life. **3** (*adjl.*) occurring during the last hours of life: *The murderer made a deathbed confession.*

death•blow ['dɛθ,blou] *n.* **1** a blow that kills. **2** anything that puts an end to something else.

death•cam•as ['dɛθ,kæməs] *n.* **1** a plant of the genus *Zigadenus* of the hyacinth family, having leaves like grass, that is poisonous to sheep. **2** the root of this plant, poisonous to many animals.

death cap DEATH CUP.

death cup a very poisonous mushroom (*Amanita phalloides*) having a white, green, or brown cap and a bulbous base and appearing in woods in summer or early autumn.

death duty SUCCESSION DUTY; inheritance tax.

death•ful ['dɛθfəl] *adj.* **1** deadly. **2** like death. **3** like that of death. **4** mortal.

death house part of a prison housing the execution chamber and prisoners awaiting execution.

death knell 1 a bell tolled to announce a death. **2** something which signals the end of something, as, a business operation.

death•less ['dɛθlɪs] *adj.* never dying; living or lasting forever; immortal; eternal. **—'death•less•ness,** *n.* **—'death•less•ly,** *adv.*

death•ly ['dɛθli] *adj., adv.* *—adj.* **1** like that of death: *Her face was a deathly white.* **2** causing death; deadly. **3** *Poetic.* of death.
—adv. **1** as if dead. **2** extremely: *deathly ill.*

death mask a clay, wax, or plaster likeness of a person's face made from a cast taken after his or her death.

death penalty punishment by death, now abolished in Canada.

death rate the proportion of the number of deaths per year to the total population or to some other stated number.

death rattle a rattling sound coming from the mouth of a dying person.

death row a section of prison cells housing prisoners awaiting execution.

death sand *Military.* radioactive dust that may be scattered over vast areas. It would kill all, or most, of the life it touched.

death's–head ['dɛθs,hɛd] *n.* a human skull, used as a symbol of death.

death's–head moth a large European moth (*Acherontia atropos*) whose markings resemble a human skull.

death squad a group hired by an oppressive political regime to liquidate its opponents.

death tax DEATH DUTY.

death•trap ['dɛθ,træp] *n.* **1** an unsafe building or structure where the risk of fire or other hazard is great. **2** a very dangerous situation.

death warrant 1 an official order for a person's death. **2** anything that spells the demise or fall of a person, era, event, etc.: *Talking pictures were the death warrant for silent movies.*
sign the death warrant of cause the destruction of (a person or thing).

death•watch ['dɛθ,wɒtʃ] *n.* **1** a watch kept beside a dying or dead person. **2** a guard for a person about to be put to death. **3** a small, destructive beetle that lives in wood and makes a ticking sound that is supposed to be an omen of death.

death wish *Psychiatry.* a conscious or unconscious desire for one's own death; suicidal tendency.

deb [dɛb] *n. Informal.* debutante.

de•ba•cle [dɪ'bɑkəl] *or* [dɪ'bækəl]; *French,* [de'bakl] *n.* **1** a disaster; overthrow; downfall. **2** the breaking up of ice in a river. **3** a violent rush of waters carrying debris. ⟨< F *débâcle* < *débâcler* free *dé-* un- + *bâcler* to bar⟩

de•bar [di'bɑr] *or* [dɪ'bɑr] *v.* **-barred, -bar•ring.** bar out; shut out; prevent; prohibit. ⟨< F *débarrer* < LL *debarrare* < L *de-* from + *barrare* bar⟩ **—de'bar•ment,** *n.*

de•bark¹ [di'bɑrk] *or* [dɪ'bɑrk] *v.* go or put ashore from a ship or aircraft; disembark. ⟨< *débarquer* < *dé-* from + *barque* bark³ < LL *barca*⟩

de•bark² [,di'bɑrk] *v.* remove bark from (a tree). ⟨< *de-* + *bark¹*⟩ **—de'bark•er,** *n.*

de•bar•ka•tion [,dibɑr'keiʃən] *n.* a debarking or being debarked; a landing from a ship or aircraft.

de•base [dɪ'beis] *v.* **-based, -bas•ing. 1** make low in quality or character; dishonour or cheapen: *to debase oneself by a mean act.* **2** lower the exchange value of (currency): *Poor management by a country of its financial affairs will generally debase its currency on world markets.* **3** lower the content value of (a coin or coinage) by increasing the proportion of base metal in it. ⟨< *de-* down + *(a)base*⟩ **—de'base•ment,** *n.* **—de'bas•er,** *n.*

de•bat•a•ble [dɪ'beitəbəl] *adj.* **1** capable of being debated; open to debate. To be debatable, a topic must have at least two sides. **2** not decided; in dispute.

de•bate [dɪ'beit] *v.* **-bat•ed, -bat•ing;** *n.* *—v.* **1** discuss reasons for and against (something). **2** argue about (a question, topic, etc.) in a public meeting. **3** think over in one's mind; consider the pros and cons of, etc.
—n. **1** a discussion of reasons for and against. **2** a public argument for and against a question in a meeting. A formal debate is a contest between two sides to see which one has more skill in speaking and reasoning. **3** in Parliament, the discussion of a motion that is to be voted on. ⟨ME < OF *débatre* < VL *debattere* < L *de-* (intensive) + *battuere* beat⟩ **—de'bat•er,** *n.*
☛ *Syn. v.* **1.** See note at DISCUSS.

de•bauch [dɪ'bɒtʃ] *v., n.* *—v.* **1** lead away from virtue or morality; corrupt morally or seduce: *debauched by bad companions.* **2** corrupt or spoil (the senses, taste, judgment, etc.): *a mind debauched by prejudice.* **3** cause to indulge excessively in sensual pleasures, eating, drinking, etc.
—n. **1** a bout or period of debauchery. **2** debauchery. ⟨< F *débaucher* entice from duty⟩ **—de'bauch•er,** *n.* **—de'bauch•ment,** *n.*

deb•au•chee [də,bɒ'tʃi], [,dɛbɒ'ʃi], *or* [də'bɒtʃi] *n.* an intemperate, dissipated, or depraved person.

de•bauch•er•y [dɪ'bɒtʃəri] *n., pl.* **-er•ies. 1** too much indulgence in sensual pleasures; dissipation. **2** a seduction from virtue or morality.

de•ben•ture [dɪ'bɛntʃər] *n.* **1** a bond, especially one issued by a corporation rather than a government and backed by the general assets of the corporation. **2** a written acknowledgment of a debt. ⟨ME < L *debentur* there are owing, 3rd person pl., present passive, of *debere*⟩

de•bil•i•tate [dɪ'bɪlə,teit] *v.* **-tat•ed, -tat•ing.** enfeeble; weaken: *A hot, wet climate is often debilitating to people not accustomed to it.* ⟨< L *debilitare* < *debilis* weak⟩ **—de,bil•i'ta•tion,** *n.*

de•bil•i•ty [dɪ'bɪləti] *n., pl.* **-ties.** weakness. ⟨ME < OF *débilité* < L *debilitas* < *debilis* weak⟩

deb•it ['dɛbɪt] *n., v.* *—n.* **1** *Accounting.* **a** the entry of something owed in an account. **b** the left-hand side of an account where such entries are made. **c** the amount entered or shown on this side. **2** the money owed by a person on an account. **3** a liability.
—v. **1** charge with or as a debt: *Debit her account $500.* **2** enter as a debit in a bank account, etc. ⟨< L *debitum* (thing) owed, pp. neut. of *debere.* Doublet of DEBT.⟩

deb•o•nair or **deb•o•naire** [,dɛbə'nɛr] *adj.* **1** especially of a man, suave; elegant and refined. **2** light-hearted and cheerful. **3** having pleasant manners; courteous. ⟨ME < OF *debonaire* < *de bon aire* of good disposition⟩ **—,deb•o•'nair•ly,** *adv.*

de•bouch [dɪ'buʃ] *v.* **1** come out from a narrow or confined place into open country: *The soldiers debouched from the gorges into the plain.* **2** come out; emerge; issue: *A horde of children debouched from the bus.* ⟨< F *déboucher* < *dé-* from + *bouche* mouth < L *bucca*⟩

de•bouch•ment [dɪ'buʃmənt] *n.* **1** an act of debouching. **2** a mouth; outlet: *the debouchment of a river.*

de•bride•ment [dɪ'bridmənt] *or* [dei'bridmənt]; *French,* [debʀid'mɑ̃] *n.* the surgical removal of dead tissue or foreign matter from a wound. ⟨< F⟩

de•brief [di'brif] *or* [dɪ'brif] *v.* question (a combat pilot, intelligence agent, etc.) immediately on return from a mission to find out the results of the mission and anything else the person learned while on the mission.

de•brief•ing [di'brifɪŋ] *or* [dɪ'brifɪŋ] *n., v. —n.* the action or process of questioning a combat pilot, etc., on return from a mission.
—v. ppr. of DEBRIEF.

de•bris or **dé•bris** [də'bri], [dei'bri], *or* ['dɛbri]; *French,* [de'bRi] *n.* **1** scattered fragments; ruins; rubbish: *Debris from the explosion was scattered all over the street.* **2** *Geology.* a mass of fragments of rock, etc.: *the debris left by a glacier.* ⟨< F *débris* < OF *débrisier* < *de-* away + *brisier* break⟩

de•bri•so•quine [də'brɪsə,kwin] *n.* a drug used to treat high blood pressure.

debt [dɛt] *n.* **1** something owed to another. **2** a liability or obligation to pay or render something: *struggling under a load of debt.* **3** the state or condition of being under such an obligation: *in debt.* **4** a sin. **5** *Cdn.* **a** credit given at a trading post to hunters and trappers in the form of supplies to be paid for out of the next season's catch. **b** the amount of credit given. **c** in the North, credit taken at any store. ⟨ME < OF *dette* < L *debitum* (thing) owed, pp. neut. of *debere.* Doublet of DEBIT.⟩

debt of honour or **honor** a betting or gambling debt.

debt•or ['dɛtər] *n.* **1** a person who owes something to someone else. **2** *Cdn.* a person owing or taking debt at a trading post, store, etc.

de•bug [di'bʌg] *or* [dɪ'bʌg] *v.* **-bugged, -bug•ging. 1** locate and remove errors or malfunctions in: *to debug a computer program.* **2** locate and remove hidden microphones in (a room, etc.). **3** remove insects from.

de•bunk [dɪ'bʌŋk] *v.* **1** expose as false, exaggerated, empty, etc.: *to debunk a theory. She wrote an article debunking the manufacturer's claims.* **2** expose the false reputation of: *to debunk a hero.* **3** remove nonsense or sentimentality from.
—de'bunk•er, *n.*

de•but or **dé•but** ['deibju] *or* [dei'bju] *n., v. —n.* **1** a first public appearance: *an actor's debut on the stage; the debut of a new magazine.* **2** a first formal appearance in society. **3** the start of a career or involvement.
—v. start off in some career or path: *Her political life debuted in the 1960s.* ⟨< F *début* < *débuter* make the first stroke < *de-* from + *but* mark (in game or sport)⟩

deb•u•tante or **dé•bu•tante** ['dɛbjə,tɑnt] *or* [,dɛbjə'tɑnt], ['deibjə,tɑnt] *or* [,deibjə'tɑnt]; *French,* [deby'tɑ̃t] *n.* **1** a young woman making her debut into upper-class or upper-middle-class society, especially at a formal ball. **2** one who makes a beginning, especially in any public career. ⟨< F *débutante,* ppr. fem. of *débuter.* See DEBUT.⟩

dec. **1** deceased. **2** declension. **3** decrease.

Dec. December.

deca– *SI prefix.* ten: *A decagram is ten grams. Symbol:* da ⟨< Gk. combining form *deka-* < *deka* ten⟩

dec•ade ['dɛkeid] *n.* **1** a period of ten years. **2** a group of ten. ⟨< F < LL *decas, decadis* < Gk. *dekas* group of ten < *deka* ten⟩

de•ca•dence ['dɛkədəns] *n.* a falling off; decline; decay: *the decadence of manners.* ⟨< F < Med.L *decadentia* < L *de-* down + *cadere* fall⟩

de•ca•dent ['dɛkədənt] *adj., n. —adj.* **1** falling off; declining, especially in moral quality; growing worse. **2** *Informal.* self-indulgent; hedonistic; appealing to the self-indulgent or hedonistic: *a decadent chocolate cake.*
—n. a decadent person. **—'de•ca•dent•ly,** *adv.*

de•caf•fein•ate [dɪ'kæfə,neit] *v.* **-at•ed, -at•ing.** remove the caffeine from: *They drink only decaffeinated coffee.*

dec•a•gon ['dɛkə,gɒn] *n.* a polygon having ten sides. ⟨< Med.L *decagonum* < Gk. *dekagonon* < *deka* ten + *gōnia* corner, angle⟩ **—dec'a•gon•al** [dɛ'kægənəl], *adj.*

dec•a•gram ['dɛkə,græm] *n.* a unit of mass equal to ten grams.

dec•a•he•dron [,dɛkə'hidrən] *n., pl.* **-drons, -dra** [-drə]. a polyhedron having ten faces. ⟨< NL < Gk. *deka* ten + Gk. *hedra* base⟩ **—,dec•a'he•dral,** *adj.*

de•cal ['dɛkəl], ['dikæl], *or* [dɪ'kæl] *n.* decalcomania.
☛ *Hom.* DECKLE ['dɛkəl].

de•cal•ci•fy [di'kælsə,faɪ] *v.,* **-fied, -fy•ing.** remove lime or calcium from (bone, etc.). **—de,cal•ci•fi'ca•tion,** *n.* **—de'cal•ci,fi•er,** *n.*

de•cal•co•ma•ni•a [dɪ,kælkə'meiniə] *n.* **1** a design or picture treated so that it will stick to glass, wood, etc. **2** a process of decorating glass, wood, etc., by applying these designs or pictures. ⟨< F *décalcomanie* < *décalquer* transfer a tracing + *manie* mania⟩

de•ca•les•cence [,dɛkə'lɛsəns] *n.* absorption of heat without a corresponding rise in temperature, when a metal has been heated to a certain point (795°C for iron). ⟨< L *decalescere* become warm < *de-* intensifying prefix + *calescere* grow warm < *calere* be warm⟩

dec•a•li•tre ['dɛkə,litər] *n.* a unit of volume equal to ten litres. Also, **decaliter.**

Dec•a•logue ['dɛkə,lɒg] *n.* **1** in the Bible, the Ten Commandments. Also, **Decalog. 2 decalogue** or **decalog,** any set of ten rules. ⟨< F *décalogue* < LL < Gk. *dekalogos* < *deka* ten + *logos* word⟩

dec•a•me•tre ['dɛkə,mitər] *or* [dɛ'kæmɪtər] *n.* a unit of length equal to ten metres. Also, **decameter.**

de•camp [di'kæmp] *v.* **1** depart quickly, secretly, or without ceremony. **2** leave a camp. ⟨< F *décamper* < *dé-* departing from + *camp* camp⟩ **—de'camp•ment,** *n.*

de–Can•a•dian•iz•a•tion [,di kə,neidiənaɪ'zeiʃən] *or* [,di kə,neidiənə'zeiʃən] the making of something into non-Canadian; removal of the Canadian character of something.

dec•a•nal ['dɛkənəl] *or* [dɪ'keinəl] *adj.* of a dean or deanery. ⟨< LL *decanus* dean⟩

de•cant [dɪ'kænt] *v.* **1** pour off (liquor or a solution) gently without disturbing the sediment. **2** pour from one container to another. ⟨< Med.L *decanthare* < *de-* from + *canthus* lip (of container) < Gk. *kanthos* corner of the eye⟩ **—,de•can'ta•tion,** *n.*

de•cant•er [dɪ'kæntər] *n.* a glass bottle with a stopper, used for serving wine or liquor.

de•cap•i•tate [dɪ'kæpə,teit] *v.* **-tat•ed, -tat•ing.** cut off the head of; behead. ⟨< LL *decapitare* < L *de-* away + *caput, capitis* head⟩ **—de'cap•i,ta•tor,** *n.* **—de,cap•i'ta•tion,** *n.*

dec•a•pod ['dɛkə,pɒd] *n.* **1** any of an order (Decapoda) of crustaceans having five pairs of appendages with one or more pair modified into pincers. Lobsters, shrimps, and crabs are decapods. **2** any of an order (Decapoda) of cephalopod molluscs having ten arms, including squid and cuttlefish. **3** (*adjl.*) of, having to do with, or designating a decapod. ⟨< *deca-* ten + Gk. *pous, podos* foot⟩ **—de'cap•o•dal,** *adj.*

de•car•bon•ate [di'kɑrbə,neit] *v.* **-at•ed, -at•ing.** remove carbon dioxide or carbonic acid from. **—de'car•bon,a•tor,** *n.*

de•car•bon•ize [di'kɑrbə,naɪz] *v.* **-ized, -iz•ing.** remove carbon from: *Iron is decarbonized in making steel.*
—de'car•bon,iz•er, *n.* **—de,car•bon•iz'a•tion,** *n.*

de•car•bur•ize [di'kɑrbə,raɪz] *v.,* **-ized, -iz•ing.** decarbonize.
—de,car•bu•ri'za•tion, *n.*

dec•a•stere ['dɛkə,stir] *n.* a unit of volume equal to ten steres, each equal to one cubic metre.

dec•a•syl•lab•ic [,dɛkəsə'læbɪk] *adj., n. —adj.* having ten syllables.
—n. decasyllable.

dec•a•syl•la•ble [,dɛkə'sɪləbəl] *n.* a line of verse having ten syllables.

de•cath•lete [dɪ'kæθlit] *n.* an athlete who competes in the decathlon.

de•cath•lon [dɪ'kæθlɒn] *n.* an athletic contest consisting of ten separate events for the competitor, in which the winner is the person who has the highest total of points from all the events. The decathlon consists of the 100 m, 400 m, and 1500 m runs, and the long jump, high jump, pole vault, shot-put, javelin and discus throws, and 110 m hurdles. ⟨< *deca-* + Gk. *athlon* contest⟩

de•cay [dɪ'kei] *v., n. —v.* **1** become rotten: *The fruit and vegetables began to decay.* **2** cause to rot. **3** grow less in power, strength, wealth, beauty, etc. **4** of radioactive substances, undergo transformation through the disintegration of component nuclei. **5** of subatomic particles, disintegrate into other subatomic particles. **6** of an orbiting earth satellite, slow down because of atmospheric friction.
—n. **1** a rotting condition. **2** a loss of power, strength, wealth, beauty, etc. **3** *Physics.* a loss in quantity of a radioactive substance through disintegration of its component nuclei. **4** disintegration of subatomic particles into other subatomic particles. **5** reduction in speed of an orbiting earth satellite, caused by atmospheric friction. **6** a rotting or rotted thing or part. ⟨ME < OF *decair* < *de-* down + *cair* < L *cadere* fall⟩
☛ *Syn. v.* **1. Decay,** ROT, DECOMPOSE = change from a good or healthy condition to a bad one. **Decay** emphasizes the idea of changing little by little through natural processes: *Some diseases cause the bones to decay.* **Rot,** more emphatic, emphasizes the idea of spoiling, and applies especially to plant and animal matter: *The fruit rotted on the vines.*

Decompose emphasizes the idea of breaking down into original parts, by natural or chemical processes: *Bodies decompose after death.*

de•cease [dɪ'sis] *n., v.* **-ceased, -ceas•ing.** *—n.* death: *His decease was unexpected.*
—v. die. ⟨ME < OF *deces* < L *decessus* < *decedere* < *de-* away + *cedere* go⟩

de•ceased [dɪ'sist] *adj., n., v. —adj.* dead (*used of persons*).
—n. **the deceased,** a particular person or persons who have died recently: *a memorial service for the deceased.*
—v. pt. and pp. of DECEASE.
☛ *Syn. adj.* See note at DEAD.

de•ce•dent [dɪ'sidənt] *n. Law. Esp. U.S.* deceased person: *The decedent's will was read in court.* ⟨< L *decedens, -entis,* ppr. of *decedere.* See DECEASE.⟩

de•ceit [dɪ'sit] *n.* **1** the act or practice of making a person believe as true something that is false. **2** a dishonest trick; a lie spoken or acted. **3** the quality of being deceitful; deceitfulness: *He was so full of deceit that he believed his own lies.* **4** a group of lapwings. ⟨ME < OF *deceite* < *deceveir.* See DECEIVE.⟩
☛ *Syn.* **1. Deceit,** DECEPTION, GUILE = false or misleading representation. **Deceit** suggests a habit of trying to mislead others by covering up or twisting the truth and giving wrong ideas of things: *The trader was truthful and without deceit.* **Deception** applies to the act that gives a false or wrong idea, but does not always suggest a malevolent purpose: *A magician uses deception.* **Guile** suggests craftiness and slyness and deception by means of tricks: *He got what he wanted by guile, not work.*

de•ceit•ful [dɪ'sitfəl] *adj.* **1** ready or willing to deceive or lie: *a deceitful person.* **2** meant to deceive: *a deceitful friendliness.* **3** tending to deceive; deceptive: *a deceitful mildness in the air.* **—de'ceit•ful•ly,** *adv.* **—de'ceit•ful•ness,** *n.*

de•ceive [dɪ'siv] *v.* **-ceived, -ceiv•ing. 1** cause to accept as true something that is not true; mislead. **2** use deceit. ⟨ME < OF *deceveir* < L *decipere* < *de-* away + *capere* take⟩ **—de'ceiv•a•ble,** *adj.* **—de'ceiv•er,** *n.* **—de'ceiv•ing•ly,** *adv.*
☛ *Syn.* See note at CHEAT.

de•cel•er•ate [di'sɛlə,reit] *v.* **-at•ed, -at•ing.** decrease the velocity of; slow down. ⟨< *de-* + *(ac)celerate*⟩ **—de,cel•er'a•tion,** *n.* **—de'cel•er,a•tor,** *n.*

de•cel•er•on [di'sɛlə,rɒn] *n.* an aileron used to slow down an aircraft while it is flying; speed brake. ⟨*de-* + *accelerate* + *aileron*⟩

De•cem•ber [dɪ'sɛmbər] *n.* the twelfth and last month of the year. It has 31 days. ⟨ME < OF *decembre* < L *December* < *decem* ten; because it was the tenth month in the early Roman calendar⟩

de•cem•vir [dɪ'sɛmvər] *n., pl.* **-virs, -vi•ri** [-və,raɪ] *or* [-və,ri]. **1** in ancient Rome, a member of a council of ten men. The decemvirs in 451 and 450 B.C. prepared the earliest Roman law code. **2** a member of a council of ten. ⟨< L *decemvir,* sing. of *decemviri* < *decem* ten + *viri* men⟩

de•cem•vi•rate [dɪ'sɛmvərɪt] *or* [dɪ'sɛmvə,reit] *n.* **1** the office or government of decemvirs. **2** a group or council of ten men or decemvirs.

de•cen•cy ['disənsi] *n., pl.* **-cies. 1** the quality or state of being decent; conformity to accepted standards of behaviour, good taste, courtesy, etc.: *Common decency requires that you pay for the window you broke.* **2** modesty; respectability. **3 decencies,** *pl.* **a** the generally accepted standards of behaviour; proper and suitable actions: *She tried hard to observe the decencies although the situation was unfamiliar to her.* **b** things needed for a proper standard of living.

de•cen•ni•al [dɪ'sɛniəl] *adj., n. —adj.* **1** of or for ten years. **2** happening every ten years.
—n. a tenth anniversary. ⟨< L *decennium* decade < *decem* ten + *annus* year⟩ **—de'cen•ni•al•ly,** *adv.*

de•cent ['disənt] *adj.* **1** proper and right: *a decent burial. The decent thing to do is apologize.* **2** not vulgar, immodest, or obscene: *decent language. His stories are usually decent.* **3** conforming to generally accepted standards of honesty, goodness, sincerity, etc.: *decent people.* **4** meeting at least the minimum standards of quality, etc.; reasonably good; adequate: *a decent wage. You can't even get a decent meal in this town.* **5** not severe; rather kind: *His boss was very decent about his being late for work.* **6** *Informal.* properly dressed to be seen in public: *Are you decent, or shall I wait outside?* ⟨< L *decens, -entis* becoming, fitting, ppr. of *decere*⟩ **—'de•cent•ly,** *adv.* **—'de•cent•ness,** *n.*

de•cen•tral•i•za•tion [di,sɛntrəlaɪ'zeiʃən] *or* [di,sɛntrələ'zeiʃən] *n.* the act of decentralizing or the state of being decentralized.

de•cen•tral•ize [di'sɛntrə,laɪz] *v.* **-ized, -iz•ing. 1** spread or distribute (authority, power, etc.) among several groups or local governments. **2** reorganize (a large industry, business, etc.) into smaller units of management and operation: *decentralize a department store.*

de•cep•tion [dɪ'sɛpʃən] *n.* **1** the act of deceiving. **2** the state of being deceived. **3** something that deceives; an illusion. **4** a trick meant to deceive; fraud; sham. ⟨< LL *deceptio, -onis* < *decipere.* See DECEIVE.⟩
☛ *Syn.* See note at DECEIT.

de•cep•tive [dɪ'sɛptɪv] *adj.* **1** tending to deceive; misleading: *a deceptive calm before the storm.* **2** meant to deceive; deceiving: *The deceptive mildness of his manner did not fool them for long.* **—de'cep•tive•ly,** *adv.* **—de'cep•tive•ness,** *n.*

de•cer•e•brate [di'sɛrə,breit] *v.* **-at•ed, -at•ing,** *n., adj. —v.* surgically remove the cerebrum.
—n. **1** a decerebrated animal. **2** a person with brain damage who acts like a decerebrate animal.
—adj. of or having to do with a decerebrate.

de•cer•ti•fy [di'sɛrtə,faɪ] *v.* **-fied, -fy•ing. 1** remove a certificate or licence from (usually, someone). **2** declare (someone) to be no longer insane. **—de,cer•ti•fi'ca•tion,** *n.*

décharge [dei'ʃɑrʒ]; *French,* [de'ʃaʀʒ] *n. Cdn.* a shallow stretch in a water course, where it is necessary to unload a canoe, etc., in order to make way by tracking or paddling.
make a décharge, unload in order to pass through a shallow stretch of water. ⟨< Cdn.F < *décharger* unload⟩

deci– *SI prefix.* tenth: *A decimetre is one tenth of a metre. Symbol:* d ⟨< F *déci-* < L *decimus* tenth < *decem* ten⟩

dec•i•bel ['dɛsə,bɛl] *or* ['dɛsəbəl] *n.* a unit for expressing the loudness of a sound. ⟨< *deci-* + *bel,* a unit of measure in physics, after A. G. *Bell* (1847-1922), the inventor of the telephone⟩

de•cide [dɪ'saɪd] *v.* **-cid•ed, -cid•ing. 1** settle (a question, dispute, etc.) by giving victory to one side; give a judgment or the decision. **2** make up one's mind; resolve. **3** cause (a person) to reach a decision. ⟨< L *decidere* cut off < *de-* away + *caedere* cut⟩ **—de'cid•er,** *n.*
☛ *Syn.* **2. Decide,** DETERMINE, RESOLVE = make up one's mind. **Decide** emphasizes the idea of coming to a conclusion after some talk or thinking over: *I decided to take the position at the bank.* **Determine** suggests fixing one's mind firmly and unalterably on doing something: *I am determined to make a success of it.* **Resolve** = make up one's mind positively to do or not to do something: *She resolved to do good work.*

de•cid•ed [dɪ'saɪdɪd] *adj., v. —adj.* **1** clear; definite; unquestionable. **2** firm; determined.
—v. pt. and pp. of DECIDE. **—de'cid•ed•ness,** *n.*
☛ *Usage.* **Decided,** DECISIVE. There is a distinction between **decided,** meaning definite or unquestionable, and **decisive,** meaning having or giving a clear result: *His height gave him a decided advantage. In World War II the Battle of El Alamein was a decisive victory.*

de•cid•ed•ly [dɪ'saɪdɪdli] *adv.* **1** clearly; definitely; unquestionably. **2** firmly; in a determined manner.

de•cid•ua [dɪ'sɪdʒuə] *n.* the lining of the uterus during pregnancy, expelled with the placenta during birth. ⟨< NL *(membrana) decidua* deciduous membrane⟩ **—de'cid•u•al,** *adj.*

de•cid•u•ous [dɪ'sɪdʒuəs] *adj.* **1** falling off at a particular season or stage of growth: *deciduous leaves, deciduous horns.* **2** of trees, shrubs, etc., shedding leaves annually. Maples, elms, and most oaks are deciduous trees. ⟨< L *deciduus* < *decidere* < *de-* + *cadere* fall⟩ **—de'cid•u•ous•ly,** *adv.* **—de'cid•u•ous•ness,** *n.*

dec•i•gram ['dɛsɪ,græm] *n.* a unit of mass, equal to 1/10 gram.

dec•ile ['dɛsaɪl] *or* ['dɛsəl] *n. Statistics.* **1** any value dividing a frequency distribution into ten groups having identical frequency. **2** any one of these ten groups.

dec•i•li•tre ['dɛsɪ,litər] *n.* a unit of volume equal to 1/10 litre. Also, **deciliter.**

de•cil•lion [dɪ'sɪljən] *n.* **1** in Canada, the United States, and France, a number represented by the numeral consisting of 1 with 33 zeros following it. **2** in the British and German numerical systems, a number represented by the numeral consisting of 1 with 60 zeros following it. ⟨< *deci-* < *(mi)llion*⟩

dec•i•mal ['dɛsəməl] *adj., n. —adj.* based on or having to do with the number 10. The metric system is a decimal system of measurement.
—n. **1** a numeral having a decimal point; decimal number: *The numerals 23.6, 3.09, and 0.728 are decimals.* **2** DECIMAL POINT: *Put the decimal between the units and the tenths.* ⟨< L *decimus* tenth⟩

decimal classification a system of classifying books in a library, by numbers with decimals. See DEWEY DECIMAL SYSTEM.

decimal fraction 1 DECIMAL NUMBER. 2 a decimal number less than one.

dec•i•mal•ize ['dɛsəmə,laɪz] *v.* **-ized, -iz•ing.** change (a number, system, etc.) to a decimal form or system: *The United Kingdom decimalized its currency in the early 1970s.* **—,dec•i•mal•iz'a•tion,** *n.*

dec•i•mal•ly ['dɛsəməli] *adv.* 1 by means of decimals. 2 by tens.

decimal number a number including a fraction whose denominator is 10, 100, 1000, etc., usually written in decimal form. *Examples*: 0.2, 9.93, 4.1.

decimal point the period between the units and the tenths of a decimal fraction. The decimal point separates the whole number from the fractional part of a decimal number.

decimal system a system of numeration which is based on units of ten.

dec•i•mate ['dɛsə,meit] *v.* **-mat•ed, -mat•ing.** 1 destroy much of; kill a large part of: *Pollution had decimated the species.* 2 formerly, select by lot and execute every tenth member of. 3 take or destroy one tenth of. ⟨< L *decimare* take a tenth, ult. < *decem* ten⟩ **—,dec•i'ma•tion,** *n.* **—'dec•i,ma•tor,** *n.*

dec•i•me•tre ['dɛsə,mitər] *n.* an SI unit for measuring length, equal to one tenth of a metre or ten centimetres. One cubic decimetre is equal to one litre. *Symbol*: dm Also, **decimeter.**

de•ci•pher [dɪ'saɪfər] *v.* 1 make out the meaning of (something that is not clear): *trying to decipher poor handwriting, to decipher a mystery.* 2 interpret (secret writing) by using a key; change (something in cipher or code) to ordinary language. **—de'ci•pher•a•ble,** *adj.* **—de'ci•pher•er,** *n.*

de•ci•sion [dɪ'sɪʒən] *n.* 1 the act of making up one's mind; resolution. 2 the deciding or settling of a question, dispute, etc., by giving judgment to one side. 3 a judgment reached or given. 4 firmness; determination: *A man of decision makes up his mind what to do and then does it.* 5 *Boxing.* the winning of a match on points or by the verdict of the referee and judges, rather than by a knockout. ⟨< L *decisio, -onis* < *decidere.* See DECIDE.⟩ **—de'ci•sion•al,** *adj.*

de•ci•sive [dɪ'saisɪv] *adj.* 1 having or giving a clear result; settling something beyond question. 2 having or showing decision: *a decisive answer.* 3 crucially important: *a decisive moment in her life.* **—de'ci•sive•ly,** *adv.* **—de'ci•sive•ness,** *n.*
☛ *Usage.* See note at DECIDED.

dec•i•stere ['dɛsə,stir] *n.* a unit of volume equal to 1/10 of a stere (a cubic metre).

deck [dɛk] *n., v.* *—n.* 1 a floor or platform extending from side to side of a ship. Often the upper deck has no roof over it. 2 a raised floor or platform against an outside wall of a house or cottage, usually having no roof, used for barbecues, etc. 3 any floor, platform, or shell resembling the deck of a ship. 4 a pack of playing cards. 5 TAPE DECK.
below decks, downstairs on a ship.
clear the deck or **decks,** a remove unnecessary objects from the decks of a warship to prepare for action. b make ready for any action.
hit the deck, *Slang.* a drop to the ground. b prepare for action. c get out of bed.
on deck, *Informal.* a ready for work, etc.; on hand: *We were all on deck for the cleanup.* b next in line, especially for batting in baseball.
stack the deck, *Informal.* a arrange a pack of cards dishonestly. b prepare circumstances in advance.
—v. 1 provide with a deck. 2 decorate or trim: *The hall was decked with flags.* 3 *Slang.* knock down: *He decked his opponent with a telling blow.*
deck out, dress; adorn: *Grace was decked out in white linen.* ⟨< MDu. *dek* roof⟩

deck chair a light folding chair, usually having a canvas cover, for use in the open air.

deck•er ['dɛkər] *n. Cdn. Baseball. Slang.* a catcher's mitt.

deck hand a sailor who works on deck; an ordinary sailor.

deck•house ['dɛk,hʌus] *n.* a cabin or compartment built on the deck of a ship.

deck•le ['dɛkəl] *n.* 1 a detachable frame around the outside of a mould used in making paper by hand. 2 either of two bands along the edge of the wire of a papermaking machine that regulate the width of the web. 3 DECKLE EDGE. 4 the crust of meat and fat on a roast. ⟨< G *Deckel,* dim. of *Decke* cover⟩
☛ *Hom.* DECAL ['dɛkəl].

deckle edge 1 the rough edge of untrimmed paper made on a deckle. 2 an imitation of it. **—'deck•le-,edged,** *adj.*

deck tennis a game similar to tennis, usually played on board a passenger ship, in which a ring of rope, rubber, etc., is tossed back and forth over a net.

de•claim [dɪ'kleim] *v.* 1 recite (a poem, etc.) in public; make a formal speech or recitation. 2 speak or say in a loud and emotional manner; speak or write for effect. ⟨< L *declamare* < *de-* (intensive) + *clamare* cry⟩ **—de'claim•er,** *n.*

dec•la•ma•tion [,dɛklə'meiʃən] *n.* 1 the act or art of reciting in public; the making of a formal speech or speeches. 2 a selection of poetry, prose, etc. for reciting; formal speech. 3 the act of talking loudly and emotionally. 4 loud and emotional talk.

de•clam•a•to•ry [dɪ'klæmə,tɔri] *adj.* 1 having to do with declamation. 2 loud and emotional.

dec•la•ra•tion [,dɛklə'reiʃən] *n.* 1 the act of declaring: *a declaration of love.* 2 a public statement or formal announcement: *a declaration of war.* 3 a document containing such a statement or announcement. 4 a statement acknowledging possession of income, goods, etc., for purposes of taxation, customs charges, etc. 5 a strong statement. 6 *Bridge.* a bid, especially the winning bid. 7 *Cricket.* a tactical decision by one side to close its innings.

Declaration of Independence in the United States, the public statement adopted by the Continental Congress on July 4, 1776, in which the American colonies were declared free and independent of Britain.

de•clar•a•tive [dɪ'klærətɪv] *or* [dɪ'klɛrətɪv] *adj.* making a statement. **—de'clar•a•tive•ly,** *adv.*
☛ *Usage.* **Declarative sentences,** as opposed to imperative, interrogative, and exclamatory sentences, make statements: *That was the most delicious breakfast we had ever tasted.*

de•clar•a•to•ry [dɪ'klærə,tɔri] *or* [dɪ'klɛrə,tɔri] *adj.* declarative.

de•clare [dɪ'klɛr] *v.* **-clared, -clar•ing.** 1 announce publicly and formally; make known; proclaim: *Parliament has the power to declare war. That company has just declared a dividend on its stock.* 2 say strongly; assert: *She declared that she would solve the problem if it took her all night.* 3 state one's opinion or decision; proclaim oneself for or against something (*used with a pronoun ending in* **-self**): *They declared themselves against the use of violence.* 4 announce one's vote, decision, etc. (*used with* **for** *or* **against**): *One minister declared for economic sanctions, while the other declared for military action.* 5 acknowledge being in possession of (income, assets, goods, etc.) for income tax, customs charges, etc. 6 *Bridge.* announce what suit will be played as trumps. 7 *Cricket.* make a tactical decision to close one's side's innings. 8 to state that (a dividend) is forthcoming. 9 demonstrate evidence of (something): *The tools declare her interest in carpentry.*
declare oneself, a make one's opinion felt. b show one's true self.
I declare! I am amazed. ⟨ME < L *declarare* < *de-* (intensive) + *clarare* make clear < *clarus* clear⟩ **—de'clar•er,** *n.*
☛ *Syn.* **1.** See note at ANNOUNCE. **2.** Declare, ASSERT = say something positively. **Declare** = state something openly, strongly, and confidently, sometimes in spite of possible contradiction: *The weather bureau declares that the rain will stop.* **Assert** = state something positively, usually without proof and sometimes in spite of proof that one is wrong: *He asserts that he was not there, but ten people saw him.*

de•clar•ed•ly [dɪ'klærɪdli] *or* [dɪ'klɛrɪdli] *adv.* openly; avowedly.

dé•clas•sé or **de•clas•se** [,deiklæ'sei] *or* [,deiklɑ'sei] *French,* [dekla'se] *adj.* reduced in rank or social position; degraded. ⟨< F⟩

de•clas•si•fy [di'klæsə,faɪ] *v.* **-fied, -fy•ing.** remove (documents, codes, etc.) from the list of restricted, confidential, or secret information. **—de,clas•si•fi'ca•tion,** *n.*

de•clen•sion [dɪ'klɛnʃən] *n.* 1 *Grammar.* in certain languages: a a variation in the form of nouns, pronouns, and adjectives according to their case. b a class of nouns, etc., having similar forms for the different cases. Latin nouns are usually grouped in five declensions. c the act of giving the variant forms of a word. 2 a downward movement, bend, or slope. 3 a sinking or falling into a lower or inferior condition; deterioration or decline. 4 deviation from a standard. 5 a polite refusal. ⟨irregularly < OF < L *declinatio, -onis* < *declinare.* See DECLINE.⟩ **—de'clen•sion•al,** *adj.*

de•clin•a•ble [dɪ'klaɪnəbəl] *adj.* that can be declined;

especially, in grammar, having different forms to show different cases: *English personal pronouns are declinable.*

dec•li•na•tion [ˌdɛklə'neiʃən] *n.* **1** a downward bend or slope. **2** a polite refusal. **3** the deviation of the needle of a compass from true north or south. **4** *Astronomy.* the angular distance of a star, planet, etc. from the celestial equator. The declination of a star is used to locate its north or south position in the heavens. **5** a turning aside; deviation from a standard.

de•cline [dɪ'klaɪn] *v.* **-clined, -clin•ing;** *n.* *—v.* **1** refuse, especially politely, to accept or to do (something): *The woman declined my offer of help.* **2** bend or slope down: *The hill declines to a fertile valley.* **3** make (something) bend or slope down. **4** grow less in strength, power, value, etc.; grow worse; decay: *Great nations have risen and declined.* **5** of the sun, sink in the west. **6** of the day, approach night. **7** sink to a low moral level. **8** *Grammar.* give or list the cases or case endings of (a noun, pronoun, or adjective).
—n. **1** falling or sinking to a lower level: *the decline of the sun to the horizon, a decline in prices.* **2** growing worse; a losing of strength, power, value, etc.: *the decline of a person's strength, the decline of the Roman Empire.* **3** the last part of anything: *in the decline of a person's life.* **4** *Archaic.* a wasting disease; consumption; tuberculosis of the lungs. **5** a downward slope. ⟨< L *declinare* < *de-* from + *clinare* bend⟩ **—de'clin•er,** *n.*
☛ *Syn. v.* **1.** See note at REFUSE[1].

de•cliv•i•tous [dɪ'klɪvətəs] *adj.* rather steep.

de•cliv•i•ty [dɪ'klɪvəti] *n., pl.* **-ties.** a downward slope. ⟨< L *declivitas* < *declivus* sloping downward < *de-* down + *clivus* slope⟩

de•clutch [di'klʌtʃ] *v.* disengage the clutch of a car, truck, etc.

de•co ['dɛkou] *adj.* of or having to do with ART DECO.

de•coct [dɪ'kɒkt] *v.* extract desired substances from (herbs, etc.) by boiling. ⟨< L *decoctus,* pp. of *decoquere* < *de-* away + *coquere* cook⟩

de•coc•tion [dɪ'kɒkʃən] *n.* **1** the act of boiling to extract some desired substance. **2** a preparation made by boiling a substance in water or other liquid; an extract obtained by boiling.

de•code [di'koud] *or* [dɪ'koud] *v.* **-cod•ed, -cod•ing.** **1** translate (coded messages) into ordinary language. **2** get the meaning of (any symbol or series of symbols): *A dyslexic person may be very articulate and have an excellent vocabulary, and still have difficulty decoding written words.*

de•cod•er [di'koudər] *n.* **1** someone who deciphers messages. **2** a machine that decodes scrambled signals, as, on a telephone or cable television. **3** *Computer technology.* in a computer, a circuit which produces a single output when fed by certain inputs.

dé•colle•tage [ˌdeikɒlə'tɑʒ]; *French,* [dekɔl'taʒ] *n.* **1** the neckline of a dress, blouse, etc., that is cut revealingly low. **2** a dress, blouse, etc., cut with such a neckline. ⟨< F⟩

dé•colle•té [ˌdeikɒlə'tei]; *French,* [dekɔl'te] *adj.* **1** of a dress, blouse, etc., low-necked. **2** wearing a low-necked dress, blouse, etc. ⟨< F *décolleté,* pp. of *décolleter* bare the neck of⟩

de•col•o•nize [di'kɒləˌnaɪz] *v.* **-ized, -iz•ing.** give independence to (a colony). **—deˌcol•o•niz'a•tion,** *n.*

de•col•or•ant [di'kʌlərənt] *adj., n.* *—adj.* able to decolorize. *—n.* a substance that decolorizes.

de•col•or•ize [di'kʌləˌraɪz] *v.* **-ized, -iz•ing.** remove colour from, as by bleaching. **—deˌcol•or•iz'a•tion,** *n.*

de•col•our or **de•col•or** [di'kʌlər] *v.* decolorize.

de•com•mis•sion [ˌdikə'mɪʃən] *v.* **1** take out of active service; retire: *to decommission a ship.* **2** revoke the commission of (an officer).

de•com•pose [ˌdikəm'pouz] *v.* **-posed, -pos•ing. 1** decay; rot or become rotten. **2** separate (a substance) into what it is made of: *A prism decomposes sunlight into its many colours.* **3** of a substance, become separated into its parts.
☛ *Syn.* **1.** See note at DECAY.

de•com•pos•er [ˌdikəm'pouzər] *n.* **1** one that decomposes. **2** an organism that feeds on the wastes and dead tissues of other organisms, converting these materials to simpler forms. Many fungi and bacteria are decomposers.

de•com•po•si•tion [ˌdikɒmpə'zɪʃən] *or* [diˌkɒmpə'zɪʃən] *n.* **1** the act or process of decomposing. **2** decay; rot.

de•com•press [ˌdikəm'prɛs] *v.* **1** release from pressure. **2** remove pressure from (a diver, etc.) gradually by means of an air lock or decompression chamber.

de•com•pres•sion [ˌdikəm'prɛʃən] *n.* **1** the removal or lessening of pressure, especially of air pressure. **2** surgical relief of pressure, as in the brain.

decompression chamber an airtight compartment used for the gradual readjustment of persons from abnormal to normal air pressure or for the simulation of low air pressure in training flyers for high-altitude flight.

decompression sickness a disorder characterized by severe headache, pain in muscles and joints, cramp, and difficulty in breathing, due to the formation of nitrogen bubbles in body tissues and caused by too sudden and substantial a decrease in atmospheric pressure, as when a person returns too rapidly to normal atmospheric pressure from high underwater pressure or when a person ascends too rapidly to a high altitude in an unpressurized aircraft; the bends.

de•con•ges•tant [ˌdikən'dʒɛstənt] *n.* a drug used to relieve congestion of the mucous membranes in the nose.

de•con•struc•tion [ˌdikən'strʌkʃən] *n.* a movement in literary criticism, begun in France in the 1960s, stating that no text has meaning in reality, but only in relation to other words. **—ˌde•con'struc•tion•ist,** *adj., n.*

de•con•tam•i•nate [ˌdikən'tæməˌneit] *v.* **-nat•ed, -nat•ing. 1** make free from poison gas or harmful radioactive agents. **2** free from any sort of contamination. **—ˌde•conˌtam•i'na•tion,** *n.*

de•con•trol [ˌdikən'troul] *v.* **-trolled, -trol•ling;** *n.* *—v.* remove controls from: *to decontrol the price of meat.*
—n. a removing of controls.

dé•cor or **de•cor** [dei'kɔr] *n.* **1** decoration. **2** the overall style and arrangement of the furnishings of a room, etc. **3** a stage setting. ⟨< F *décor* < *décorer* decorate⟩

dec•o•rate ['dɛkəˌreit] *v.* **-rat•ed, -rat•ing. 1** furnish with ornamental things, especially for a particular occasion: *to decorate a Christmas tree. The room was decorated with flowers for the reception.* **2** plan the style, colour, and arrangement of (interior furnishings, wallpaper, etc.). **3** paint or paper (a room, house, etc.). **4** give a medal, ribbon, etc., to (a person) as a mark of honour: *The firefighter was decorated for bravery.* ⟨< L *decorare* < *decus, decoris* adornment⟩
☛ *Syn.* **1. Decorate,** ORNAMENT, ADORN = add something to give or increase beauty. **Decorate** = put on ornaments or other trimming to add finish, colour, or a festive appearance to something: *We decorated the Christmas tree.* **Ornament** suggests adding, often permanently, something that especially suits a thing and adds to its general effect and beauty: *Stained glass windows ornament the church.* **Adorn** suggests adding something that is beautiful itself and therefore increases the beauty of a thing or person: *She adorned her hair with flowers.*

dec•o•ra•tion [ˌdɛkə'reiʃən] *n.* **1** the act or process of decorating. **2** anything used to add beauty; ornament. **3** a medal, ribbon, etc., awarded as a mark of honour: *The general wore many decorations.*

dec•o•ra•tive ['dɛkərətɪv] *or* ['dɛkəˌreitɪv] *adj.* decorating; helping to adorn; ornamental: *The flowered curtains were highly decorative.* **—'dec•o•ra•tive•ly,** *adv.* **—'dec•o•ra•tive•ness,** *n.*

dec•o•ra•tor ['dɛkəˌreitər] *n.* **1** a person who decorates, especially one who specializes in designing colour schemes and the style and arrangement of furnishings for rooms, etc. **2** (*adjl.*) designed for use in the decoration of rooms, etc.: *decorator fabrics, decorator colours.*

dec•o•rous ['dɛkərəs] *or* [dɪ'kɔrəs] *adj.* well-behaved; acting properly; in good taste; dignified. ⟨< L *decorus* < *decor* seemliness, comeliness⟩ **—'dec•o•rous•ly,** *adv.* **—'dec•o•rous•ness,** *n.*

de•cor•ti•cate [di'kɔrtɪˌkeit] *v.* **-cat•ed, -cat•ing.** peel; shuck; debark. **—deˌcor•ti'ca•tion,** *n.* **—de'cor•tiˌca•tor,** *n.*

de•co•rum [dɪ'kɔrəm] *n.* **1** propriety of action, speech, dress, etc.: *You behave with decorum when you do what is proper.* **2** an observance or requirement of polite society. ⟨< L *decorum,* neut. of *decorus* seemly⟩

de•cou•page or **dé•cou•page** [ˌdeiku'pɑʒ]; *French,* [deku'paʒ] *n.* the technique of decorating a surface by gluing down paper cutouts and then coating the surface with a finish such as varnish. ⟨< F *découpage* act of cutting out⟩

de•cou•ple [di'kʌpəl] *v.* **-pled, -pling. 1** separate; uncouple. **2** disconnect (circuits, etc.).

de•coy *v.* [dɪ'kɔɪ]; *n.* ['dikɔɪ] *or* [dɪ'kɔɪ] *v., n.* *—v.* **1** lure wild birds, animals, etc. into a trap or within gunshot. **2** lead or tempt into danger. **3** *Cdn.* deke.
—n. **1** an artificial bird used to lure real birds into a trap or within range of a hunter's gun. **2** a bird or other animal trained to lure others of its kind into a trap. **3** any place into which wild birds or animals are lured. **4** any person or thing used to lead or

tempt into danger. ⟨< MDu. *de kooi* the cage < L *cavea* cave⟩ **—de'coy•er,** *n.*

de•crease *v.* [dɪ'kris]; *n.* ['dikris] *or* [dɪ'kris] *v.* **-creased, -creas•ing;** *n.* *—v.* **1** become less: *Hunger decreases as one eats.* **2** make less: *to decrease prices.*
—n. **1** the process of becoming less: *A decrease in humidity made the hot weather more bearable.* **2** the amount by which a thing becomes or is made less.
on the decrease, decreasing. ⟨ME < OF *de(s)creiss-*, a stem of *descreistre* < L *decrescere* < *de-* down + *crescere* grow⟩ **—de'creas•ing•ly,** *adv.*
☛ *Syn. v.* **Decrease,** DIMINISH, DWINDLE = become less. **Decrease** suggests steadily going down little by little: *The output of the factory is decreasing.* **Diminish** suggests becoming smaller in size, amount, or importance because someone or something keeps taking away a part: *The renovations on the house have diminished his savings.* **Dwindle** emphasizes the idea of wasting away, or becoming smaller and smaller until almost nothing is left: *Our savings have dwindled.*

de•cree [dɪ'kri] *n., v.* **-creed, -cree•ing.** *—n.* **1** a decision or order made by a government, court, church, etc. **2** something foreordained.
—v. order or determine by or as if by decree: *The government decreed that the election would take place July 8.* ⟨ME < OF *decre*, var. of *decret* < L *decretum*, pp. neut. of *decernere* < *de-* from + *cernere* sift, decide⟩ **—de'cre•er,** *n.*

decree ni•si ['nəisaɪ] *or* ['nisi] *Law.* a conditional granting of a divorce. The decree becomes final, or absolute, after a given period unless cause to the contrary is shown in the interim. ⟨< L *nisi* unless⟩

dec•re•ment ['dɛkrəmənt] *n.* **1** a gradual decrease; slow loss. **2** the amount lost by gradual decrease. **3** *Mathematics.* the amount by which a variable decreases. ⟨< L *decrementum* < *decrescere.* See DECREASE; compare INCREMENT.⟩

de•crep•it [dɪ'krɛpɪt] *adj.* broken down or weakened by old age; old and feeble: *a decrepit old house. He has become old and decrepit.* ⟨< L *decrepitus* broken down < *de-* + *crepare* creak⟩ **—de'crep•it•ly,** *adv.*

de•crep•i•tude [dɪ'krɛpə,tjud] *or* [dɪ'krɛpə,tud] *n.* feebleness, usually from old age; a decrepit condition; weakness.

decresc. decrescendo.

de•cre•scen•do [,dikrə'ʃɛndou] *or* [,deikrə'ʃɛndou] *n., pl.* **-dos;** *adj., adv. Music. —n.* **1** a gradual decrease in force or loudness; diminuendo. The sign for a decrescendo is >. **2** a passage to be played or sung with a decrescendo.
—adj. or adv. with a gradual decrease in force or loudness. *Abbrev.*: decresc. ⟨< Ital.⟩

de•cres•cent [di'krɛsənt] *adj.* of the moon, waning in its last quarter.

de•cre•tal [dɪ'kritəl] *n., adj. —n. Roman Catholic Church.* a papal decree or reply settling some question of doctrine or ecclesiastical law.
—adj. of or having to do with a decree. ⟨ME < OF < Med.L *decretale*, ult. < L *decretum.* See DECREE.⟩

de•cre•tive [dɪ'kritɪv] *adj.* having the nature or force of a decree. **—de'cre•tive•ly,** *adv.*

de•cre•to•ry ['dɛkrə,tɔri] *or* [dɪ'kritəri] *adj.* **1** established by a decree. **2** of or having to do with a decree.

de•cri•al [dɪ'kraɪəl] *n.* the act of decrying.

de•crim•i•nal•ize [di'krɪmənə,laɪz] *v.* **-ized, -iz•ing.** remove (a specific act, etc.) from the category of criminal offence: *to decriminalize the possession of marijuana.*
—de,crim•i•nal•i'za•tion, *n.*

de•cry [dɪ'kraɪ] *or* [di'kraɪ] *v.* **-cried, -cry•ing. 1** condemn: *The minister decried gambling in all its forms.* **2** make little of; try to lower the value of: *The lumber dealer decried the use of concrete for houses.* **3** devalue (money) officially. ⟨< F *decrier* < *de-* away, apart + *crier* cry < L *quiritare*⟩ **—de'cri•er,** *n.*

de•crypt [di'krɪpt] *v.* convert a coded message into readable form; decipher. **—de'cryp•tion,** *n.*

de•cum•bent [dɪ'kʌmbənt] *adj.* **1** of stems, branches, etc., lying or trailing on the ground with the end tending to climb. **2** lying down; reclining. ⟨< L *decumbens*, *-entis*, ppr. of *decumbere* lie down⟩ **—de'cum•ben•cy,** *n.*

dec•u•ple ['dɛkjʊpəl] *adj.* ten times more; tenfold.

de•cur•rent [dɪ'kɜrənt] *adj. Botany.* especially of a leaf, extending downward from the base as two wings along the stem. The common thistle (*Cirsium vulgare*) has decurrent leaves. ⟨< L *decurrens*, *-entis*, ppr. of *decurrere* < *de-* down + *currere* run⟩

de•cus•sate [dɛ'kʌsɪt], [dɪ'kʌseit], *or* ['dɛkə,seit] *adj.* **1** crossed; intersecting. **2** of leaves, etc., arranged along the stem in pairs, each pair at right angles to the pair next above or below. ⟨< L *decussatus*, pp. of *decussare* to cross in the shape of an X < *decussis* the figure ten (X) < *decem* ten⟩
—de'cus•sate•ly, *adv.*

ded•i•cate ['dɛdə,keit] *v.* **-cat•ed, -cat•ing. 1** set apart for a sacred or solemn purpose; consecrate: *The new altar was dedicated at a special service.* **2** give up wholly or earnestly to some person or purpose: *The minister dedicated her life to the service of God.* **3** address (a book, poem, etc.) to a friend or patron as a mark of affection, respect, gratitude, etc. **4** celebrate the opening of (a bridge, institution, meeting, etc.) with an official ceremony. ⟨< L *dedicare* proclaim, affirm < *de-* (intensive) + *dicare* proclaim⟩ **—'ded•i,ca•tor,** *n.*
☛ *Syn.* **2.** See note at DEVOTE.

ded•i•cat•ed ['dɛdə,keitɪd] *adj., v. —adj.* **1** wholly committed; faithful. **2** of a computer, program, etc., performing one function only.
—v. pt. and pp. of DEDICATE.

ded•i•ca•tion [,dɛdə'keiʃən] *n.* **1** setting apart or being set apart for a sacred or solemn purpose: *the dedication of a church.* **2** very great and constant interest or commitment; close attachment; complete loyalty (to some person or purpose): *a dedication to music, a dedication to one's country.* **3** the words dedicating a book, poem, etc., to a friend or patron. **4** a ceremony attending the official opening of something, as a building, institution, or convention: *the dedication of a new library wing.*

ded•i•ca•tive ['dɛdəkətɪv] *or* ['dɛdə,keitɪv] *adj.* dedicatory.

ded•i•ca•to•ry ['dɛdəkə,tɔri] *adj.* of dedication; as a dedication.

de•dif•fer•en•ti•a•tion [di,dɪfə,rɛnʃi'eiʃən] *n.* a process in which cells, tissues, etc., lose their special form or function; loss of specialization.

de•duce [dɪ'djus] *or* [dɪ'dus] *v.* **-duced, -duc•ing. 1** infer from a general rule or principle; reach (a conclusion) by reasoning: *After looking at the evidence, the firefighters deduced the cause of the fire.* **2** trace the course, descent, or origin of. ⟨< L *deducere* < *de-* down + *ducere* lead⟩

de•duc•i•ble [dɪ'djusəbəl] *or* [dɪ'dusəbəl] *adj.* capable of being deduced or inferred.

de•duct [dɪ'dʌkt] *v.* take away; subtract. ⟨< L *deductus*, pp. of *deducere.* See DEDUCE.⟩
☛ *Syn.* See note at SUBTRACT.

de•duct•i•ble [dɪ'dʌktəbəl] *adj., n. —adj.* that can be deducted: *Your contribution is deductible from your taxable income.*
—n. an amount paid by the insured when a claim is made: *I had to pay the $50 deductible.*

de•duc•tion [dɪ'dʌkʃən] *n.* **1** the act of taking away; subtraction: *No deduction in pay is made for absence due to illness.* **2** the amount deducted. **3** *Logic.* the act or process of reaching a conclusion by reasoning; inference. A person using deduction reasons from general laws to particular cases. *Example*: *All animals die; a cat is an animal; therefore, a cat will die.* **4** a conclusion reached by this method of reasoning.
☛ *Usage.* **Deduction** and INDUCTION are the names of two opposite processes of logical reasoning. **Deduction** is the process by which one starts with a general principle, or premise, applies it to a particular case, and arrives at a conclusion that is true provided the premise is true: *All animals die; this is an animal; therefore, this will die.* **Induction** applies to the process by which one collects many particular cases, finds out what is common to all of them, and forms a general rule or principle that is probably true of the whole class: *Every animal I have tested died; therefore, all animals die.*

de•duc•tive [dɪ'dʌktɪv] *adj.* of or using deduction; reasoning by deduction. **—de'duct•ive•ly,** *adv.*

deed [did] *n., v. —n.* **1** something done; act. **2** a brave, skilful, or unusual act. **3** an action; doing; performance. **4** a written or printed document, sealed and signed, containing some contract. A buyer of real estate receives a deed legally transferring the ownership.
—v. transfer by deed. ⟨OE *dǣd*⟩

deed poll *Law.* a deed involving only one party, consisting of a formal declaration of an act. A legal name change is made by deed poll. ⟨from the original practice of 'polling', or cutting even, the edge of such a deed, rather than indenting it, as was done for deeds made in two or more copies. 16c.⟩

dee•jay ['di,dʒei] *n. Informal.* DISC JOCKEY. ⟨abbrev. of *d*isc *j*ockey⟩

deem [dim] *v.* think; believe; consider: *The lawyer deemed it unwise to take the case to court.* ⟨OE *dēman* < *dōm* judgment⟩
☛ *Hom.* DEME.

de–em•pha•size [di 'ɛmfə,saɪz] *v.* **-ized, -iz•ing.** reduce emphasis on; make less prominent; play down: *They agreed to de-emphasize the contentious points.*

deep [dip] *adj., adv., n. —adj.* **1** going far down or back: *a deep cut, a deep well, a deep recess.* **2** from far down or back: *Take a deep breath.* **3** far on or in: *deep in the forest.* **4** in depth: *a tank 2 m deep.* **5** low in pitch: *a deep voice.* **6** strong and dark in colour: *a deep red.* **7** strong; great; intense: *deep sorrow, a deep sleep.* **8** requiring or showing much thought and study: *a deep book.* **9** immersed or involved: *deep in thought, deep in debt.* **10** going below the surface: *a speech of deep importance.* **11** wise; shrewd. **12** sly; crafty. **13** extreme: *He's in deep trouble.* **14** from front to back: *The lot on which the house stands is 40 m deep.* **15** closely kept: *a deep secret.*
in deep water, in difficulty or danger.
—adv. **1** far down or back: *The men dug deep before they found water.* **2** far on or in: *She studied deep into the night.*
deep down, in one's inmost feelings: *Deep down, she regrets her behaviour.*
in (too) deep, (over)involved in a dangerous or compromising situation.
—n. **1** a deep place. **2** the most intense part: *the deep of winter.* **3 the deep,** the sea. ⟨OE *dēop*⟩ **—'deep•ly,** *adv.* **—'deep•ness,** *n.*

deep–chest•ed ['dip 'tʃɛstɪd] *adj.* having a barrel chest.

deep cover **1** a careful disguise, as for a spy. **2** in cricket, a fielding position.

deep–dish ['dip 'dɪʃ] *adj.* baked in a container with high sides; thick: *a deep-dish pie, a deep-dish pizza.*

deep–dyed ['dip 'daɪd] *adj.* **1** having a strong colour. **2** thorough; complete: *a deep-dyed villain.*

deep•en ['dipən] *v.* make or become deeper.

deep–freeze *n.* ['dip ,friz]; *v.* ['dip 'friz] *or* ['dip ,friz] *n., v.* **-froze** or **-freezed, -fro•zen** or **-freezed, -freez•ing.** *—n.* **1** a freezer cabinet or chest for freezing foods rapidly and storing them frozen for long periods. **2** the state of being deep-frozen: *The government kept the controversial report in deep-freeze.*
—v. **1** freeze (food) rapidly for storage in a deep-freeze. **2** keep as if frozen: *to deep-freeze a plan.* **—'deep-'freez•er,** *n.*

deep–fry ['dip ,fraɪ] *v.* **-fried, -fry•ing.** fry in deep fat or oil. **—'deep-,fry•er,** *n.*

deep–laid ['dip 'leid] *adj.* planned secretly and carefully: *deep-laid schemes.*

deep–root•ed ['dip 'rutɪd] *adj.* **1** deeply rooted. **2** firmly fixed: *deep-rooted traditions, a deep-rooted dislike.*

deep–sea ['dip 'si] *adj.* of or in the deeper parts of the sea: *a deep-sea diver.*

deep–seat•ed ['dip 'sitɪd] *adj.* **1** far below the surface. **2** firmly fixed: *The disease was so deep-seated that it could not be cured.*

deep–set ['dip 'sɛt] *adj.* **1** set deeply. **2** firmly fixed.

deep–six ['dip 'sɪks] *v., n. Slang. —v.* eliminate; reject.
—n.
give (something) **the deep six,** *Slang.* reject (something) completely.

deep South or **Deep South** in the United States, generally, Georgia, Alabama, Mississippi, Louisiana, and part of South Carolina.

deep space space beyond the earth's atmosphere; outer space.

deep structure *Linguistics.* **1** the underlying pattern of relationships linking the elements of meaning of a sentence. **2** a formal representation of this, showing the relationships symbolically but without the grammatical indicators used to show them in the actual sentence. Compare SURFACE STRUCTURE.

deep•wat•er ['dip,wɒtər] *adj.* of or having to do with deep water; deep-sea.

deepwater cisco ['sɪskou] a freshwater fish (*Coregonus johannae*) native to the Great Lakes and having silvery, iridescent scales. Also called **deepwater chub.**

deepwater sculpin ['skʌlpɪn] a freshwater or saltwater fish (*Myoxocephalus quadricornis*) native to Europe, Asia, and the Great Lakes, and having a greyish brown back with lighter underparts.

deer [dir] *n., pl.* **deer. 1** any of various cud-chewing animals (family Cervidae) having long, slender legs with small, split hoofs, the males (and, in some species, some females) having solid, bony antlers that are shed each year. See WHITE-TAILED DEER, MULE DEER, FALLOW DEER, RED DEER, ROE DEER, MUSK DEER. **2** any member of the family Cervidae, including the moose, elk, and caribou. **3** *Cdn. North.* caribou. ⟨OE *dēor* animal⟩
☛ *Hom.* DEAR.

deer fly any of a genus (*Chrysops*) of small horseflies having dark markings on the wings.

deer•hound ['dir,haʊnd] *n.* a breed of large dog resembling a greyhound, but larger and having shaggy hair; it comes from Scotland, where it was originally bred for hunting deer.

deer lodge a lodge or camp to accommodate deer hunters, especially one that may be rented by hunters visiting the area during the open season.

deer mouse any of several New World mice (genus *Peromyseus*) usually having brownish fur with white underparts and feet.

deer•skin ['dir,skɪn] *n.* **1** the hide of a deer. **2** leather made from it. **3** (*adjl.*) made from this leather: *deerskin moccasins.* **4 deerskins,** *pl.* clothing made from this leather.

deer•stalk•er ['dir,stɒkər] *n.* **1** a person who hunts deer by stalking. **2** a close-fitting cap with earflaps, originally worn by hunters and popularized in Conan Doyle's Sherlock Holmes stories.

de–es•ca•late [di 'ɛskə,leit] *v.* **-lat•ed, -lat•ing.** stop or reverse growth or expansion of: *to de-escalate a war.* **—de-,es•ca'la•tion,** *n.*

def. 1 definition; defined. **2** defendant; defence. **3** deferred. **4** defective.

de•face [dɪ'feis] *v.* **-faced, -fac•ing.** spoil the appearance of; mar. ⟨< obs. F *defacer* < *de-* away, apart + *face* face < L *facies* form⟩ **—de'fac•er,** *n.*
☛ *Syn.* **Deface,** DISFIGURE = spoil the appearance of someone or something. **Deface** = spoil the surface of something by blotting out an important detail, by scratching something in, etc.: *Scribbled pictures and remarks defaced the pages of the library book.* **Disfigure** suggests spoiling the beauty of a person or thing by permanent injury too deep or serious to remove: *Open pit mines disfigured the landscape.*

de•face•ment [dɪ'feismənt] *n.* **1** the act of defacing. **2** the state of being defaced. **3** anything that defaces.

de fac•to [dɪ 'fæktou] *or* [dei 'fæktou] **1** in fact; in reality. **2** actually existing, whether legal or not: *a de facto government.* ⟨< L *de facto* from the fact⟩

de•fal•cate [dɪ'fælkeit] *or* [dɪ'fɒlkeit] *v.* **-cat•ed, -cat•ing.** steal or misuse money trusted to one's care. ⟨< Med.L *defalcare,* literally, to cut off with a sickle < *de-* away + *falx, -cis* sickle⟩ **—de'fal•ca•tor,** *n.*

de•fal•ca•tion [,difæl'keiʃən] *or* [,difɒl'keiʃən] *n.* **1** the theft or misuse of money entrusted to one's care. **2** the amount stolen or misused.

def•a•ma•tion [,dɛfə'meiʃən] *n.* a defaming or being defamed; slander; libel.

de•fam•a•to•ry [dɪ'fæmə,tɔri] *adj.* defaming; slanderous.

de•fame [dɪ'feim] *v.* **-famed, -fam•ing.** attack the good name of; harm the reputation of; speak evil of; slander; libel: *Those in public life are sometimes defamed by opponents.* ⟨ME < OF *diffamer* < L *diffamare* damage by rumour < *de-* down, from (confused with *dis-*) + *fama* rumour⟩ **—de'fam•er,** *n.*

def. art. DEFINITE ARTICLE.

de•fault [dɪ'fɒlt] *n., v. —n.* **1** a failure to do something or to appear somewhere when due; neglect. If, in any contest, one side does not appear, it loses by default. **2** a failure to pay when due. **3** *Law.* a failure to appear in court at the time specified for a legal proceeding. **4** (*adjl.*) that results from failure to take (alternative) action. **5** *Computer technology.* an action taken or value assigned automatically by a computer in the absence of explicit instructions. **6** (*adjl.*) *Computer technology.* determined according to the default: *The default data type for this field is numeric.*
in default of, in the absence of; lacking: *In default of tools, she used a hairpin and a needle.*
—v. **1** fail to do something or appear somewhere when due. **2** lose (a match, etc.) by default. **3** fail to pay when due. **4** *Law.* **a** fail to appear in court at a specified time. **b** declare (a person) in default. **c** lose a case by default. **5** *Computer technology.* be determined according to the default: *In the airline's personnel database, the 'Pilot-in-command hours' field defaults to zero if it is left blank.* ⟨ME < OF *defaute* < *defaillir* < *de-* de- + *faillir,* ult. < L *fallere* deceive⟩

de•fault•er [dɪ'fɒltər] *n.* **1** a person who defaults. **2** a person who steals or misuses money trusted to his or her care.

de•feat [dɪ'fit] *v., n.* —*v.* **1** win a victory over; overcome: *to defeat an opposing team, to defeat an enemy.* **2** bring to nothing; prevent the success of; frustrate or thwart: *to defeat someone's plans, to defeat a bill in Parliament.* **3** *Law.* make null and void; annul.
—*n.* **1** the act of defeating or state of being defeated: *the defeat of all our hopes, the defeat of an army.* **2** an instance of defeating or being defeated: *It was a humiliating defeat.* ⟨ME < OF *de(s)fait,* pp. of *desfaire* < LL *diffacere* < L *dis-* un- + *facere* do⟩
—de'feat•er, *n.*
☛ *Syn. v.* **1. Defeat,** CONQUER, OVERCOME = win a victory over someone or something. **Defeat** = win a victory, at least for the moment: *We defeated Laurier Collegiate in basketball yesterday.* **Conquer,** more formal, emphasizes the idea of winning control over people, things, or feelings: *Some countries may be defeated, but never conquered.* **Overcome** emphasizes the idea of getting the better of things or, especially, feelings, regarded as problems, obstacles, or weaknesses: *He could not overcome his dislike for that man.*

de•feat•ism [dɪ'fitɪzəm] *n.* the attitude or behaviour of a defeatist.

de•feat•ist [dɪ'fitɪst] *n., adj.* —*n.* a person who tends to expect or readily accepts defeat.
—*adj.* characteristic of a defeatist: *a defeatist attitude.*

def•e•cate ['dɛfə,keit] *v.* **-cat•ed, -cat•ing.** have a movement of the bowels. ⟨< L *defaecare* < *de-* from + *faeces,* pl. dregs, solid excrement⟩ **—,def•e'ca•tion,** *n.*

de•fect *n.* ['difɛkt] *or* [dɪ'fɛkt]; *v.* [dɪ'fɛkt] *n., v.* —*n.* **1** a fault; blemish; imperfection. **2** *Genetics.* See BASIC DEFECT, CONGENITAL DEFECT. **3** the lack of something essential to completeness; a falling short.
—*v.* forsake one's own country, group, etc. for another, especially another that is opposed to it in political or social doctrine. ⟨< L *defectus* want < *deficere* fail. See DEFICIENT.⟩ **—de'fect•or,** *n.*
☛ *Syn.* **1. Defect,** FLAW[1] = an imperfection or fault. **Defect** is the general word, applying to any imperfection on the surface or in the make-up of a person or thing: *A hearing aid helps to overcome defects in hearing. No person is without defects.* **Flaw** applies to a defect in structure, suggesting a crack or break when used literally, a fault in character or an error or shortcoming when used figuratively: *That bubble is a flaw in the glass. Jealousy is the great flaw in his character. She performed the long sonata without a single flaw.*

de•fec•tion [dɪ'fɛkʃən] *n.* **1** a falling away from loyalty, duty, religion, etc.; desertion. **2** failure. **3** the act of defecting from one's country.

de•fec•tive [dɪ'fɛktɪv] *adj.* **1** having a serious flaw or blemish; faulty: *Her hearing is defective. We returned the toaster because it was defective.* **2** *Grammar.* lacking one or more of the usual forms of inflection. *Ought* is a defective verb.
—*n.* a defective person or thing. **—de'fect•ive•ly,** *adv.* **—de'fect•ive•ness,** *n.*

de•fence [dɪ'fɛns] *or, for def. 4,* ['difɛns] *n.* **1** the act of defending or protecting; a guarding against attack or harm: *The armed forces are responsible for the defence of the country.* **2** anything that defends or protects; something used to guard against attack or harm: *A wall around a city used to be a defence against enemies. A well-built house or a warm coat is a defence against cold weather.* **3** *Boxing or fencing.* the act of defending oneself. **4** the team or players defending a goal in a game. **5** an action, speech, or writing in favour of something. **6** *Law.* **a** the arguments, etc., presented by a defendant or his or her lawyer in contesting a case. **b** a defendant and his or her lawyers collectively. Also, **defense.** ⟨ME < OF < L *defensa* < *defendere* ward off⟩

de•fence•less [dɪ'fɛnslɪs] *adj.* having no defence; unprotected; helpless against attack or harm: *A baby is defenceless.* Also, **defenseless. —de'fence•less•ly,** *adv.* **—de'fence•less•ness,** *n.*

de•fence•man [dɪ'fɛnsmən] *n., pl.* **-men.** *Sports.* a player whose job is to prevent the opposing players from approaching the goal. Also, **defenseman.**

defence mechanism **1** any self-protective reaction by an organism. **2** *Psychology.* an unconscious adjustment of behaviour or mental attitude designed to shut out unpleasant emotions.

de•fend [dɪ'fɛnd] *v.* **1** guard from attack or harm; protect. **2** *Sports.* **a** try to keep an opponent away from: *to defend a goal.* **b** maintain (one's position as champion) by playing or fighting against a challenger: *He will forfeit his title unless he defends it within a year.* **3** justify or maintain against opposition, criticism, etc.: *to defend one's argument. She defended their conduct in a letter to the editor.* **4** *Law.* **a** act as counsel for in a court of law: *He has hired a well-known lawyer to defend him.* **b** resist or deny (the claim of a plaintiff); contest (a lawsuit or charge): *Is she going to defend the speeding charge?* ⟨ME < OF < L *defendere* ward off⟩
☛ *Syn.* **1.** See note at GUARD.

de•fen•da•ble [dɪ'fɛndəbəl] *adj.* defensible.

de•fend•ant [dɪ'fɛndənt] *n.* **1** a person against whom an action is brought in a court of law. Compare ACCUSED. **2** a person charged with a criminal offence in a court of law.

de•fend•er [dɪ'fɛndər] *n.* **1** a protector or guardian. **2** *Sports.* the holder of a championship who is defending it by playing or fighting against a challenger.

de•fen•es•trate [di'fɛnɪ,streit] *v.* **-trat•ed, -trat•ing.** throw (someone) out of a window. ⟨< L *de-* out of + *fenestra* window⟩ **—de,fen•es'tra•tion,** *n.*

de•fense [dɪ'fɛns] See DEFENCE.

de•fense•less [dɪ'fɛnslɪs] See DEFENCELESS.

de•fense•man [dɪ'fɛnsmən] *n., pl.* **-men.** See DEFENCEMAN.

de•fen•si•bil•i•ty [dɪ,fɛnsə'bɪləti] *n.* the quality or state of being defensible.

de•fen•si•ble [dɪ'fɛnsɪbəl] *adj.* **1** capable of being defended. **2** justifiable; proper. **—de'fen•si•bly,** *adv.*

de•fen•sive [dɪ'fɛnsɪv] *adj., n.* —*adj.* **1** ready to defend; defending. **2** for defence: *Their team had a good defensive strategy.* **3** of defence; too ready to justify or explain; tending to think of oneself as attacked: *a defensive attitude.*
—*n.* **1** a position or attitude of defence. **2** anything that defends.
on the defensive, having a defensive attitude: *She has been criticized so much that she is always on the defensive.*
—de'fen•sive•ly, *adv.* **—de'fen•sive•ness,** *n.*

de•fer[1] [dɪ'fɜr] *v.* **-ferred, -fer•ring.** put off; delay. ⟨< L *differe.* Doublet of DIFFER.⟩ **—de'fer•ra•ble,** *adj.* **—de'fer•rer,** *n.*
☛ *Syn.* See note at DELAY.

de•fer[2] [dɪ'fɜr] *v.* **-ferred, -fer•ring.** yield; submit to another's judgment, opinion, or wishes: *He deferred to his sister's wishes.* ⟨< F *déférer* < L *deferre* < *de-* down + *ferre* carry⟩

def•er•ence ['dɛfərəns] *n.* **1** a yielding to the judgment or opinion of another; courteous submission. **2** respect; regard.
in deference to, out of respect or regard for: *In deference to his mother's wishes, he worked hard at his studies.*
☛ *Syn.* **2.** See note at HONOUR.

def•er•ent[1] ['dɛfərənt] *adj.* deferential. ⟨< *defer*[1]⟩

def•er•ent[2] ['dɛfərənt] *adj. Anatomy.* drawing down or out. ⟨< *defer*[2]⟩

def•er•en•tial [,dɛfə'rɛnʃəl] *adj.* showing deference; respectful. **—,def•er'en•tial•ly,** *adv.*

de•fer•ment [dɪ'fɜrmənt] *n.* a putting off; delay.

de•fer•ox•a•mine [,dɛfə'rɒksə,min] *n.* a drug used to treat iron intoxication.

de•ferred [dɪ'fɜrd] *adj., v.* —*adj.* **1** postponed. **2** with benefits withheld for a certain time. **3** *Esp. U.S.* exempted for a time from induction into the armed forces.
—*v.* pt. and pp. of DEFER.

de•fi•ance [dɪ'faɪəns] *n.* **1** the act or an instance of openly resisting or opposing: *Rebellion always involves defiance against authority.* **2** intent or willingness to openly resist or oppose: *Her defiance showed clearly on her face. He shouted his defiance.*
in defiance of, a in open opposition to; showing contempt or disregard for: *She took the car in defiance of her father's wishes.* **b** in spite of: *In defiance of the good weather forecast, it began to rain.*

de•fi•ant [dɪ'faɪənt] *adj.* showing defiance; challenging; openly resisting or offering a challenge; hostile. ⟨< F *défiant,* ppr. of *défier* defy⟩ **—de'fi•ant•ly,** *adv.* **—de'fi•ant•ness,** *n.*

de•fib•ril•late [di'fɪbrə,leit] *v.,* **-lat•ed, -lat•ing.** arrest fibrillation of (the heart muscle) by applying electric shock. **—de,fib•ril'la•tion,** *n.* **—de'fib•ril,la•tor,** *n.*

de•fi•cien•cy [dɪ'fɪʃənsi] *n., pl.* **-cies. 1** a lack or absence of something needed or required; incompleteness. **2** the amount by which something falls short or is too small.

deficiency disease disease caused by a diet lacking in one or more vitamins, minerals, or essential nutrients.

de•fi•cient [dɪ'fɪʃənt] *adj., n.* —*adj.* **1** incomplete; defective. **2** not sufficient in quantity, force, etc.; lacking: *Her diet is deficient in protein.*
—*n.* a person or thing that is deficient: *a mental deficient.* ⟨< L

deficiens, -entis failing, ppr. of *deficere* < *de-* from + *facere* make, do⟩ **—de'fi•cient•ly,** *adv.*

def•i•cit ['dɛfəsɪt] *n., adj.* *—n.* the amount by which a sum of money falls short; shortage: *Since the club owed $15 and had only $10 in the treasury, there was a deficit of $5.*
—adj. Economics. of financing, spending, etc., conducted with borrowed funds: *deficit spending.* ⟨< L *deficit* it is wanting. See DEFICIENT.⟩

de•fi•er [dɪ'faɪər] *n.* a person who defies.

de•file[1] [dɪ'faɪl] *v.* **-filed, -fil•ing. 1** make filthy or dirty; make disgusting in any way. **2** destroy the purity or cleanness of; corrupt. **3** violate the sanctity or ceremonial or ritual cleanness of: *During the war many shrines and churches were defiled by marauding raiders. For strict Brahmins, food is defiled if touched with the left hand.* **4** stain; dishonour: *Charges of corruption defiled the reputation of the government.* ⟨alteration of ME *defoul* (< OF *defouler* trample down, violate) after obs. *file* befoul < OE *fȳlan* < *fūl* foul⟩ **—de'fil•er,** *n.*

de•file[2] [dɪ'faɪl] *or* ['difaɪl] *v.* **-filed, -fil•ing;** *n.* *—v.* march in a line.
—n. **1** a narrow way or passage through which troops can march only in narrow columns. **2** a steep and narrow valley. **3** a march in a line. ⟨< F *défilé,* special use of pp. of *défiler* march by files < *dé-* off + *file* file[1]⟩

de•file•ment [dɪ'faɪlmənt] *n.* **1** the act of defiling. **2** the state of being defiled. **3** something that defiles. ⟨< *defile*[1]⟩

de•fine [dɪ'faɪn] *v.* **-fined, -fin•ing. 1** make clear the meaning of; explain: *A dictionary defines words.* **2** write definitions of words: *I've spent all morning defining.* **3** make clear; make distinct. **4** fix; settle. **5** settle the limits of. **6** be a distinguishing feature of; characterize: *Perseverance usually defines success.* ⟨ME < OF < L *definire* to limit < *de-* from + *finis* boundary⟩ **—de'fin•a•ble,** *adj.* **—de'fin•er,** *n.*

def•i•nite ['dɛfənɪt] *adj.* **1** clear and exact in meaning or expression; free of ambiguity or doubt: *He wouldn't give a definite answer. She was very definite about the time of the shot. Is it definite that we're going?* **2** precisely defined; having exact limits; fixed: *a definite area, a definite number of players.* **3** See DEFINITE ARTICLE. ⟨< L *definitus,* pp. of *definire.* See DEFINE.⟩ **—'def•i•nite•ness,** *n.*

☛ *Usage.* **Definite,** DEFINITIVE are not synonyms, although both suggest 'leaving no doubt'. **Definite** is a synonym of *distinct* and means 'perfectly clear and exact', leaving no doubt about either what is meant or what is not meant: *I expect a definite answer, either yes or no.* **Definitive** is a synonym of *decisive,* and means 'final and complete', putting an end to doubt or uncertainty: *We have appealed to the Supreme Court for a definitive answer.*

definite article *Grammar.* **1** in English, the word *the,* used before nouns to designate a specific or previously identified person, thing, etc. **2** its equivalent(s) in any other language.

definite integral *Mathematics.* the sum of an infinite number of infinitesimally small amounts, summed between stated (definite) bounds. It has a value equal to the area under a curve, bounded by the curve, the x-axis, and the lower and upper bounds.

def•i•nite•ly ['dɛfənɪtli] *adv.* **1** in a definite manner. **2** certainly: *Will you go? Definitely.*

def•i•ni•tion [ˌdɛfə'nɪʃən] *n.* **1** the act or process of explaining or making clear the meaning of a word or group of words. **2** a statement that makes clear the meaning of a word or group of words; explanation. **3** the power of making clear and distinct. The capacity of a lens to give a clear, distinct image of an object is called its definition. **4** clearness or distinctness of detail, etc., in the reproduction of sound or images on a recording, photograph, television screen, etc. **5** the state or quality of being clearly defined; definiteness.

def•i•ni•tion•al [ˌdɛfə'nɪʃənəl] *adj.* of or having to do with definition.

de•fin•i•tive [dɪ'fɪnətɪv] *adj., n.* *—adj.* **1** conclusive; final. **2** authoritative; completely reliable: *That book is the definitive work on marine biology.* **3** designating a type of postage stamp issued in various denominations and available for a certain length of time in all post offices for regular use. Canadian definitive stamps usually feature the Queen or a series of related designs for the various denominations. **4** limiting; defining; distinguishing.
—n. **1** *Grammar.* a word that limits or defines a noun, such as, in English, *the, this, all,* and *none.* **2** a definitive stamp. **—de'fin•i•tive•ly,** *adv.* **—de'fin•i•tive•ness,** *n.*

☛ *Usage.* See note at DEFINITE.

def•la•grate ['dɛfləˌgreit] *v.,* **def•la•grat•ed, def•la•grat•ing.** burn with great heat. ⟨< L *deflagratus,* pp. of *deflagrare* to burn, consume < *de-* intensifier + *flagrare* to burn⟩ **—ˌdef•la'gra•tion,** *n.*

de•flate [dɪ'fleit] *v.* **-flat•ed, -flat•ing. 1** let air or gas out of (a balloon, tire, football, etc.). **2** reduce the amount of; reduce: *to deflate prices, to deflate currency.* **3** become reduced. **4** injure or destroy the conceit or confidence of: *Our laughter soon deflated him.* ⟨< L *deflare* < *de-* off + *flare* blow⟩ **—de'flat•or,** *n.*

de•fla•tion [dɪ'fleiʃən] *n.* **1** the act of deflating: *the deflation of a tire, the deflation of a prig.* **2** a reduction. **3** the reduction of the amount of available money in circulation so that prices go down. Compare INFLATION. **4** *Geology.* the removal of solid particles by the wind, leaving the rocks exposed to the weather.

de•fla•tion•ar•y [dɪ'fleiʃəˌnɛri] *or* [dɪ'fleiʃənri] *adj.* of or having to do with deflation.

de•flect [dɪ'flɛkt] *v.* bend or turn aside; change the direction of. ⟨< L *deflectere* < *de-* away + *flectere* bend⟩ **—de'flec•tor,** *n.*

de•flec•tion [dɪ'flɛkʃən] *n.* **1** a bending or turning aside. **2** the amount of bending or turning. **3** a bending downward. **4** *Physics.* the movement of the needle or indicator of a scientific instrument from its zero or normal position.

de•flec•tive [dɪ'flɛktɪv] *adj.* **1** causing deflection. **2** tending to deflect.

de•flo•ra•tion [ˌdiflə'reiʃən] *or* [ˌdɛflə'reiʃən] *n.* the act of deflowering. ⟨ME *defloracioun* < OF *desfloracion* < LL *defloratio*⟩

de•flow•er [di'flaʊər] *v.* **1** end the virginity of (a girl or woman). **2** mar the beauty or innocence of; spoil. **3** strip flowers from. **—de'flow•er•er,** *n.*

de•fog [di'fɒg] *v.* **-fogged, -fog•ging. 1** remove moisture from (a car window, etc.) **2** make (an issue, one's thinking, etc.) clear. **—de'fog•ger,** *n.*

de•fo•li•ant [di'fouliənt] *n.* a chemical agent that defoliates.

de•fo•li•ate [di'fouliˌeit] *v.* **-at•ed, -at•ing.** remove the leaves from (a plant or plants), especially by means of a chemical spray. **—deˌfo•li'a•tion,** *n.* **—de'fo•liˌa•tor,** *n.*

de•for•est [di'fɔrɪst] *v.* clear of trees: *The land had to be deforested before the settlers could farm it.* **—deˌfor•est'a•tion,** *n.* **—de'for•est•er,** *n.*

de•form [dɪ'fɔrm] *v.* **1** spoil the form or shape of: *Shoes that are too tight deform the feet.* **2** make ugly; disfigure: *a face deformed by rage.* **3** become altered in shape or form. **4** *Physics.* change the shape of by stress. **—de'form•er,** *n.*

de•for•ma•tion [ˌdifɔr'meiʃən] *or* [ˌdɛfər'meiʃən] *n.* **1** deforming or being deformed. **2** a change of form. **3** a changed form. **4** *Physics.* a change in the shape or dimensions of a body, resulting from stress; strain. **5** *Geology.* **a** any change in the original state or size of rock masses, especially as produced by faulting. **b** an instance of this.

de•formed [dɪ'fɔrmd] *adj., v.* *—adj.* especially of the body or a part of it, not properly formed; distorted or misshapen: *a deformed foot.*
—v. pt. and pp. of DEFORM.

de•form•i•ty [dɪ'fɔrməti] *n., pl.* **-ties. 1** a part that is not properly formed. **2** the condition of being improperly formed. **3** an improperly formed person or thing. **4** ugliness.

de•fraud [dɪ'frɒd] *v.* take money, rights, etc., away from by fraud; cheat: *The dishonest man defrauded the widow of her savings.* ⟨ME < MF < L *defraudare* < *de-* completely + *fraus, fraudis* fraud⟩ **—de'fraud•er,** *n.* **—ˌde•fraud'a•tion,** *n.*

de•fray [dɪ'frei] *v.* pay (costs or expenses): *The expenses of national parks are defrayed by the taxpayers.* ⟨< F *défrayer* < *de-* (intensive) + *frai* cost⟩ **—de'fray•er,** *n.* **—de'fray•al** or **de'fray•ment,** *n.*

de•frock [di'frɒk] *v.* unfrock.

de•frost [di'frɒst] *v.* **1** remove frost or ice from. **2** thaw out (frozen foods). **3** of frozen foods, thaw: *The peas are still defrosting.*

de•frost•er [di'frɒstər] *n.* a device that removes ice, either through heat or mechanically. Defrosters are used on automobile windshields and in refrigerators.

deft [dɛft] *adj.* skilful; nimble: *the deft fingers of a violinist or a surgeon.* ⟨var. of *daft*⟩ **—'deft•ly,** *adv.* **—'deft•ness,** *n.*

☛ *Syn.* See note at DEXTEROUS.

de•funct [dɪ'fʌŋkt] *adj., n.* *—adj.* dead; extinct.
—n. **the defunct,** the dead person. ⟨< L *defunctus,* pp. of *defungi* finish < *de-* (intensive) + *fungi* perform⟩

de•fuse [dɪ'fjuz] *or* [di'fjuz] *v.* **-fused, -fus•ing. 1** remove the fuse or triggering device from (a bomb, etc.). **2** remove or neutralize a potential source of trouble or friction in: *to defuse a tense situation.*
☛ *Hom.* DIFFUSE [dɪ'fjuz].
☛ *Usage.* See note at DIFFUSE.

de•fy [dɪ'faɪ] *v.* **-fied, -fy•ing. 1** resist boldly or openly. **2** withstand; resist: *This strong fort defies capture.* **3** challenge (a person) to do or prove something. ⟨ME < OF *de(s)fier* < VL < L *dis-* away, apart + *fidus* faithful⟩

deg. degree(s).

dé•ga•gé [ˌdeigɑ'ʒei]; *French,* [dega'ʒe] *adj.* **1** easy in manner or style. **2** detached; uninvolved. **3** *Ballet.* with leg and foot extended.

de•gauss [di'gʌus] *or* [di'gɒs] *v.* **1** neutralize the magnetic field of (a steel ship) by means of electric coils carrying currents producing an opposing magnetic field, as a defence against magnetic mines. **2** demagnetize. ⟨< Karl Friedrich *Gauss* (1777-1855), a German mathematician⟩ **—de'gaus•ser,** *n.*

de•gen•er•a•cy [di'dʒɛnərəsi] *or* [dɪ'dʒɛnrəsi] *n., pl.* **-cies.** a degenerate condition, process, or action.

de•gen•er•ate *v.* [dɪ'dʒɛnə,reit]; *adj. and n.* [dɪ'dʒɛnərɪt] *v.* **-at•ed, -at•ing;** *adj., n.* *—v.* **1** decline in physical, mental, or moral qualities; grow worse. **2** *Biology.* **a** of an organism, become less specialized and simpler in structure. **b** of a structure or part in an organism, become functionally useless.
—adj. **1** that has degenerated. **2** *Biology.* that has lost the normal or more highly developed characteristics of its type.
—n. a person who shows degraded and debased physical, mental, or moral qualities: *Only a degenerate could have committed such a horrible crime.* ⟨< L *degenerare,* ult. < *de-* down + *genus* race, kind⟩ **—de'gen•er•ate•ly,** *adv.*

de•gen•er•a•tion [dɪ,dʒɛnə'reiʃən] *n.* **1** the process of degenerating. **2** a degenerate condition. **3** *Medicine.* a deterioration in tissues or organs caused by disease, injury, etc. **4** *Biology.* evolution or development toward simpler structures or toward the disappearance of structures or functions.

de•gen•er•a•tive [dɪ'dʒɛnərətɪv] *or* [dɪ'dʒɛnə,reitɪv] *adj.* **1** tending to degenerate. **2** characterized by degeneration; showing degeneration. **—de'gen•er•a•tive•ly,** *adv.*

de•glam•or•ize [di'glæmə,raɪz] *v.* **-ized, -iz•ing.** make (something) less glamorous, appealing, attractive, etc.: *an article that deglamorizes show business.*

de•glu•ti•nate [di'glutɪ,neit] *v.* **-at•ed, -at•ing.** remove gluten from.

de•glu•ti•tion [ˌdiglu'tɪʃən] *or* [ˌdɛglu'tɪʃən] *n.* the act or power of swallowing. ⟨< F *déglutition* < L *deglutire* swallow down⟩

deg•ra•da•tion [ˌdɛgrə'deiʃən] *n.* **1** degrading or being degraded: *Failure to obey orders caused the captain's degradation to the rank of private.* **2** a degraded condition: *The drunkard, filthy and half-starved, lived in degradation.* **3** *Geology.* the wearing down of land, rocks, etc., by erosion.

de•grade [dɪ'greid] *v.* **-grad•ed, -grad•ing. 1** reduce to a lower rank; take away a position, an honour, etc. from. **2** make bad; lower in value; debase; dishonour: *You degrade yourself when you tell a lie.* **3** *Geology.* wear down by erosion. **4** *Biology.* reduce to a lower classification. **5** *Chemistry.* reduce systematically the molecule of (a compound) into others of less complex structure. ⟨ME < OF *degrader* < LL *degradare* < L *de-* down + *gradus* step, grade⟩ **—de'grad•a•ble,** *adj.* **—de'grad•er,** *n.*

de•grad•ing [dɪ'greidɪŋ] *adj., v.* *—adj.* that degrades or debases.
—v. ppr. of DEGRADE. **—de'grad•ing•ly,** *adv.*

de•grease [di'gris] *v.* **-greased, -greas•ing.** remove grease from; give a thorough cleaning to (esp. steel before it is electroplated).

de•gree [dɪ'gri] *n.* **1** a stage or step in a scale or process. **2** a step in direct line of descent: *a cousin two degrees removed.* **3** the amount, intensity, or extent of an action or condition: *To what degree is she interested in reading?* **4** a unit for measuring temperature. The boiling point of water is 100°C. *Symbol*: ° **5** a line marking a degree on a thermometer. **6** a unit used with the SI for measuring plane angles, especially in navigation, surveying, etc. There are 360 degrees in a circle and 90 degrees in a right angle. One degree is equal to (π ÷ 180) radians. *Symbol*: ° **7** a position on the earth's surface as measured by degrees of latitude or longitude. **8** rank: *A princess is a lady of high degree.* **9** a rank or title given by a university or college to a student whose work fulfils certain requirements, or to a person as an honour: *an M.A. degree, a D.D. degree.* **10** *Grammar.* one of the three stages in the comparison of adjectives or adverbs. *Fast* is the positive degree; *faster,* the comparative degree; *fastest,* the superlative degree. **11** *Algebra.* the rank as determined by an exponent or sum of exponents. a^3 and a^2b are terms of the third degree. $x^2y^2z^3$ is a term of the seventh degree. **12** *Law.* a measure of the seriousness of a crime: *first-degree murder.* **13** a measure of the seriousness of a burn. **14** *Music.* **a** an interval between any note of the scale and the next note. **b** a line or space on the staff showing the position of the notes. **c** the interval between two of these. **15** a relative condition, manner, way, or respect: *A bond and a stock may both be wise investments, each in its degree.* **16** a rank in the hierarchy of a fraternal society.
by degrees, gradually.
to a degree, a by a large amount; to a great extent. **b** somewhat; rather. ⟨ME < OF *degre* < VL *degradus* < *degradare* divide into steps < L *de-* down + *gradus* step, grade⟩
☛ *Usage.* **Degrees.** Academic degrees, when given with a person's name, are separated from the name by a comma: *Harry James, M.A.; Harry Paynter, B.Sc.* When the institution granting the degree is named or when the year of granting is given, the following forms are used: *George Smith, B.A. (Alberta), M.A. (McGill), Ph.D. (Toronto); Parmeshwar Jha, B.A. '85, M.A. '88.*

degree Celsius a unit used with the SI for measuring temperature. On a thermometer, zero degrees Celsius (0°C) is the temperature at which water freezes, and one hundred degrees Celsius (100°C) is the temperature at which water boils. A temperature interval of one degree Celsius is equal to one kelvin (1°C = 1 K). *Symbol*: °C

degree–day [dɪ'gri ,dei] *n.* a unit representing one degree of deviation (usually 18°C) in the mean outdoor temperature for one day. It is used to determine fuel requirements.

degree of freedom 1 *Statistics.* any of the independent variables that make up a frequency distribution. **2** *Physics. Chemistry.* any one of the limited set of ways in which a thing or system may move or change, each expressible independently.

de•gres•sion [dɪ'grɛʃən] *n.* **1** a lowering. **2** a lowering of the tax rate on successively smaller sums. ⟨< Med.L *degressio* < L *degressus,* pp. of *degredi* go down < *de-* down + *gradi* to step⟩ **—de'gres•sive,** *adj.*

de•gus•ta•tion [ˌdigə'steiʃən] *n.* **1** a sampling of foods, wines, etc. **2** a variety, as of foods or wines, provided for sampling.

de•hire [di'haɪər] *v.* **-hired, -hir•ing.** terminate the employment of; fire (someone).

de•hisce [di'hɪs] *v.* **-hisced, -hisc•ing.** of a mature fruit, anther, etc., burst open along a definite line, discharging seeds or pollen. ⟨< L *dehiscere,* ult. < *de-* down + *hiare* gape⟩

de•his•cence [di'hɪsəns] *n.* the bursting open of a mature fruit, anther, etc. to discharge seeds or pollen.

de•his•cent [di'hɪsənt] *adj.* of certain fruits, anthers, etc., splitting or bursting open along one or more definite lines when mature to release seeds or pollen.

de•horn [di'hɔrn] *v.* remove the horns from.

de•hu•man•ize [di'hjumə,naɪz] *v.* **-ized, -iz•ing.** deprive of human qualities, interest, sympathy, etc. **—de,hu•man•i'za•tion,** *n.*

de•hu•mid•i•fy [ˌdihju'mɪdə,faɪ] *v.* **-fied, -fy•ing.** remove moisture from (the air, etc.) **—,de•hu,mid•i•fi'ca•tion,** *n.* **—,de•hu'mid•i,fi•er,** *n.*

de•hy•drate [di'haɪdreit] *v.* **-drat•ed, -drat•ing. 1** deprive (a chemical compound) of water or the elements of water. **2** remove water or moisture from; dry. **3** lose water or moisture.

de•hy•dra•tion [ˌdihaɪ'dreiʃən] *n.* **1** the removal or loss of water from a chemical compound or from vegetables, fruits, etc. **2** an excessive loss of body fluids.

dehydration synthesis a chemical reaction in which molecules unite into a larger molecule, giving off water in the process.

de•hy•dro•gen•ase [di'haɪdrədʒə,neis] *or* [ˌdihaɪ'drɒdʒə,neis] an enzyme that activates hydrogen and causes its removal, as from body tissue.

de•hy•dro•gen•ate [di'haɪdrədʒə,neit] *or* [ˌdihaɪ'drɒdʒə,neit] *v.* **-at•ed, -at•ing.** remove hydrogen from (a compound). **—de,hy•dro•gen'a•tion,** *n.*

de–ice [di 'əis] *v.* **-iced, -ic•ing.** prevent formation of ice on; remove ice from (an aircraft, etc.). **—de'ic•er,** *n.*

deic•tic ['dəiktɪk] *adj. Grammar.* being or relating to a word whose referent depends on the context, such as *these, us.* ⟨< Gk. *deiktikos* < *deiktos* capable of proof < *deiknynai* to prove⟩

de•i•fi•ca•tion [ˌdiəfə'keiʃən] *n.* a deifying or being deified.

de•i•fy ['diəˌfaɪ] *v.* **-fied, -fy•ing. 1** make a god of. **2** worship or regard as a god. **3** treat as a god; hero-worship. ⟨ME < OF *deifier* < LL *deificare* < *deus* god + *facere* make⟩ **—'de•iˌfi•er,** *n.*

deign [dein] *v.* **1** condescend; think fit: *So conceited a man would never deign to notice us.* **2** condescend to give (an answer, a reply, etc.). ⟨ME < OF *deignier* < L *dignari* < *dignus* worthy⟩
☛ *Hom.* DANE.

De•i gra•ti•a [ˌdeii 'grɑtiə] *or* [ˌdiaɪ 'greiʃii] *Latin.* by the grace of God.

Dei•mos ['dimɔs] *or* ['deimɔs] *n.* the smaller satellite of Mars.

de•in•dus•tri•al•ize [ˌdiɪn'dʌstriəˌlaɪz] *v.* **-ized, -iz•ing. 1** make less industrial in nature or force. **2** take away the potential for industrial growth in (a conquered nation). **3** become less industrial. **—ˌde•inˌdus•tri•al•i'za•tion,** *n.*

de•in•sti•tu•tion•al•ize [ˌdiɪnstɪ'tjuʃənəˌlaɪz] *or* [ˌdiɪnstɪ'tuʃənəˌlaɪz] *v.* **-ized, -iz•ing. 1** release (someone) from a psychiatric hospital or other institution. **2** provide care for (someone mentally or physically handicapped) in the community instead of in an institution. **3** free from the depersonalizing nature or effects of an institution. **4** lose the nature of an institution. **—ˌde•in•stiˌtu•tion•al•i'za•tion,** *n.*

de•i•on•ize [di'aɪəˌnaɪz] *v.* **-ized, -iz•ing.** purify (water) by removing salt ions. **—deˌi•on•i'za•tion,** *n.*

de•ism ['diɪzəm] *n.* **1** a belief that God exists entirely apart from our world and does not influence the lives of human beings. **2** a belief in God without accepting any particular religion. ⟨< L *deus* god⟩

de•ist ['diɪst] *n.* a person who believes in deism.
—de'ist•ic, *adj.*

de•i•ty ['diɪti] *n., pl.* **-ties. 1** a god or goddess. **2** a divine nature; the state of being a god. **3 the Deity,** God. ⟨ME < OF *deite* < L *deitas* < *deus* god⟩

dé•jà vu [ˌdeiʒɑ 'vu]; *French,* [deʒa'vy]. **1** the feeling or sense that one has already experienced something that is in fact a new situation or happening. **2** the condition or fact of being tiresomely reminded (by some current event, etc.) of something past: 'Déjà vu: *Revival of the Cold War*'.

de•ject [dɪ'dʒɛkt] *v.* lower the spirits of; discourage.

de•ject•ed [dɪ'dʒɛktɪd] *adj., v. —adj.* in low spirits; sad; discouraged.
—v. pt. and pp. of DEJECT. **—de'ject•ed•ly,** *adv.*
—de'ject•ed•ness, *n.*
☛ *Syn.* See note at SAD.

de•jec•tion [dɪ'dʒɛkʃən] *n.* lowness of spirits; sadness; discouragement: *Her face showed her dejection at missing the party.* ⟨< L *dejectio, -onis* < *dejicere* < *de-* down + *jacere* throw⟩

dé•jeu•ner [ˌdeiʒə'nei]; *French,* [deʒœ'ne] *n. French.* **1** breakfast. **2** luncheon.

de ju•re [di 'dʒuri], [dei 'dʒurei], *or* [de 'jure] *Latin.* by right; according to law.

deka– *U.S.* See DECA-.

deke [dik] *n., v.* **deked, dek•ing.** *—n. Hockey. Cdn. Slang.* a fake shot or movement intended to draw a defending player out of position.
—v. **1** draw (a defending player) out of position by faking a shot or movement (often used with **out**) **2** manoeuvre (oneself or the puck) by feinting so as to outsmart a defending player. ⟨< *decoy*⟩

del. 1 delete. **2** delegate. **3** delivery. **4** deliver.

de•lam•i•nate [di'læməˌneit] *v.* **-at•ed, -at•ing.** divide or be divided into layers. **—deˌlam•i'na•tion,** *n.*

Del•a•ware ['dɛləˌwɛr] **1** an east coast state of the United States. **2** a member of a group of American Indians who lived in the Delaware River valley. **3** their Algonquian language. **4** a small, sweet, red American grape.

de•lay [dɪ'lei] *v., n. —v.* **1** put off till a later time: *We will delay the party for a week.* **2** make late; keep waiting; hinder the progress of: *The accident delayed the train for two hours. Ignorance delays progress.* **3** go or act slowly or with pauses, etc.: *Don't delay; they're waiting for you.*
—n. **1** the act of delaying. **2** the fact of being delayed. **3** the time occupied in delay: *a delay of three hours.* ⟨ME < OF *delaier* postpone < *de-* away + *laier* leave, let, probably < Celtic⟩
—de'lay•er, *n.* **—de'lay•ing•ly,** *adv.*
☛ *Syn. v.* **1. Delay,** DEFER, POSTPONE = put off doing something. **Delay** emphasizes the idea of putting off, and suggests either holding off for some reason but planning to act at some later time or, often, putting off indefinitely: *I delayed seeing the dentist.* **Defer** usually suggests deciding to put off until a better time, with the intention of acting then: *I deferred going until I had more time.* **Postpone** suggests deferring until a definite time, after something has been done, learned, etc.: *I postponed going until next week.*

de•le ['dili] *v., n. —v.* **-led, -le•ing.** *Printing.* cross out; delete.
—n. a delete mark. ⟨< L *dele,* imperative of *delere* delete⟩

de•lec•ta•ble [dɪ'lɛktəbəl] *adj.* very pleasing; delightful. ⟨ME < OF < L *delectabilis* < *delectare.* See DELIGHT.⟩
—de'lec•ta•ble•ness, *n.* **—de'lec•ta•bly,** *adv.*

de•lec•ta•tion [ˌdilɛk'teiʃən] *n.* delight; pleasure; entertainment: *The magician did many tricks for our delectation.*

del•e•ga•cy ['dɛləgəsi] *n., pl.* **-cies.** delegation.

del•e•gate *n.* ['dɛləˌgeit] *or* ['dɛləgɪt]; *v.* ['dɛləˌgeit] *n., v.* **-gat•ed, -gat•ing.** *—n.* a person given power or authority to act for others; representative.
—v. **1** appoint or send (a person) as a delegate: *Each club delegated one member to attend the provincial meeting.* **2** give over (one's power or authority) to another as agent or deputy: *The provinces have delegated some of their rights to the Federal Government.* ⟨< L *delegatus,* pp. of *delegare* < *de-* (intensive) + *legare* send with a commission⟩

del•e•ga•tion [ˌdɛlə'geiʃən] *n.* **1** a delegating or being delegated: *the delegation of authority.* **2** a group of delegates: *Each province sent a delegation to the national convention.*

de•lete [dɪ'lit] *v.* **-let•ed, -let•ing. 1** strike out or take out (anything written or printed); remove; cross out. **2** erase; wipe out: *Shock deleted all recollection of the accident from her mind.* ⟨< L *deletus,* pp. of *delere* destroy⟩

del•e•te•ri•ous [ˌdɛlə'tiriəs] *adj.* harmful; injurious. ⟨< NL *deleterius* < Gk. *dēlētērios,* ult. < *dēleesthai* hurt⟩
—ˌdel•e'te•ri•ous•ly, *adv.* **—ˌdel•e'te•ri•ous•ness,** *n.*

de•le•tion [dɪ'liʃən] *n.* **1** the act of deleting. **2** the fact of being deleted. **3** a deleted part. **4** *Genetics.* the loss of a segment of DNA, of any size from a single base pair to an entire chromosome.

delft [dɛlft] *n.* **1** a kind of earthenware made in the Netherlands, having an opaque white glaze and decorated, usually, in blue. **2** any pottery having a similar glaze and colour. ⟨< *Delft,* a city in the SW Netherlands⟩

delft•ware ['dɛlftˌwɛr] *n.* delft.

del•i ['dɛli] *n., adj. —n. Informal.* DELICATESSEN (def. 1).
—adj. of foods, of the kind sold in a delicatessen: *deli meats.*

de•lib•er•ate *adj.* [dɪ'lɪbərɪt]; *v.* [dɪ'lɪbəˌreit] *adj., v.* **-at•ed, -at•ing.** *—adj.* **1** carefully thought out; made or done on purpose: *His excuse was a deliberate lie.* **2** slow and careful in deciding what to do: *A deliberate person takes a long time to make up her mind.* **3** slow, but firm and purposeful: *They advanced with deliberate steps.*
—v. **1** think (something) over carefully; consider. **2** discuss reasons for and against something; debate. ⟨< L *deliberatus,* pp. of *deliberare* < *de-* (intensive) + *librare* weigh⟩ **—de'lib•er•ate•ly,** *adv.* **—de'lib•er•ate•ness,** *n.* **—de'lib•erˌa•tor,** *n.*
☛ *Syn.* See note at SLOW.

de•lib•er•a•tion [dɪˌlɪbə'reiʃən] *n.* **1** careful thought. **2** a discussion of reasons for and against something; debate: *the deliberations of the Legislative Assembly.* **3** slowness and care: *The hunter aimed his gun with great deliberation.*

de•lib•er•a•tive [dɪ'lɪbərətɪv] *or* [dɪ'lɪbəˌreitɪv] *adj.* **1** for deliberation; having to do with deliberation; discussing reasons for and against something: *Parliament is a deliberative body.* **2** characterized by deliberation; coming as a result of deliberation. **—de'lib•er•a•tive•ly,** *adv.*

del•i•ca•cy ['dɛləkəsi] *n., pl.* **-cies. 1** a delicate quality or nature; slightness and grace: *the delicacy of lace, the delicacy of a flower, the delicacy of a baby's skin.* **2** fineness of feeling for small differences; sensitiveness: *delicacy of hearing or touch.* **3** need of care, skill, or tact: *a matter of great delicacy.* **4** thought or regard for the feelings of others. **5** a shrinking from what one considers offensive or not modest. **6** weakness; the condition of being easily hurt or made ill: *The child's delicacy was a worry to her parents.* **7** a choice kind of food; a dainty.

del•i•cate ['dɛləkɪt] *adj.* **1** light or fine and pleasant to taste or smell: *delicate foods, a delicate fragrance.* **2** soft or fine in structure or make: *delicate features, delicate silks for blouses.* **3** easily crushed, broken, or torn; fragile: *a delicate flower, a delicate china cup.* **4** requiring skill and care in handling: *a* *delicate situation, a delicate heart operation.* **5** of a colour, pale; not intense: *a delicate shade of green.* **6** capable of responding to very slight changes of condition; very sensitive: *delicate instruments, a delicate sense of touch.* **7** easily hurt or made ill: *a delicate child. He has a delicate constitution.* **8** very subtle; marked by fine distinctions: *delicate shades of meaning, delicate irony.* **9** having or showing consideration for the feelings of others: *a delicate approach.* **10** excessively refined or sensitive. ⟨ME < L *delicatus* pampered⟩ **—'del•i•cate•ly,** *adv.* **—'del•i•cate•ness,** *n.*

☛ *Syn.* **1, 2. Delicate,** DAINTY = fine in quality and pleasing to the senses and taste. **Dainty** emphasizes smallness: *The child wore a dainty dress.* **Delicate** suggests fineness of quality without regard to size: *a delicate perfume from a dainty flower. He does delicate woodcarving.*

del•i•ca•tes•sen [ˌdɛlɪkə'tɛsən] *n.* **1** a store that sells fine prepared foods, such as cooked meats, smoked fish, cheese, salads, pickles, etc. **2** the foods sold at such a store. ⟨< G *Delikatessen*, pl. of *Delikatesse* delicacy < F *délicatesse*⟩

☛ *Usage.* **Delicatessen** = a store that sells prepared foods, is singular in use: *The delicatessen closes at nine o'clock.* When *delicatessen* means the foods sold at such a store, it is usually plural in use: *Delicatessen usually require little preparation for serving.*

de•li•cious [dɪ'lɪʃəs] *adj.* **1** very pleasing to taste or smell. **2** very pleasing; delightful: *a delicious colour combination, a whole delicious hour of free time.* **3 Delicious,** a kind of red or yellow eating apple having a fine and very sweet flavour. ⟨ME < OF *delicieus* < LL *deliciosus* < *delicae* delight < *delicere* entice. See DELIGHT.⟩ **—de'li•cious•ly,** *adv.* **—de'li•cious•ness,** *n.*

☛ *Syn.* **1. Delicious,** LUSCIOUS = delighting the senses. **Delicious** is used chiefly to mean pleasing in flavour, less often in fragrance or aroma: *This dessert is delicious. The coffee smells delicious.* **Luscious** adds to *delicious* the suggestion of richness or sweetness and, when applied to fruit, ripeness or juiciness: *She makes luscious apple pie.*

de•light [dɪ'ləit] *n., v.* *—n.* **1** great pleasure; joy. **2** something that gives great pleasure.
—v. **1** please greatly. **2** have great pleasure (*in*): *Children delight in surprises.* ⟨ME < OF *delit* < *delitier* < L *delectare* to charm < *delicere* entice < *de-* (intensive) + *lacere* entice; spelling influenced by *light*⟩ **—de'light•er,** *n.*

☛ *Syn. n.* **1.** See note at PLEASURE.

de•light•ed [dɪ'ləitɪd] *adj., v.* *—adj.* greatly pleased; joyful; glad.
—v. pt. and pp. of DELIGHT. **—de'light•ed•ly,** *adv.*

de•light•ful [dɪ'ləitfəl] *adj.* very pleasing; giving joy. **—de'light•ful•ly,** *adv.* **—de'light•ful•ness,** *n.*

de•light•some [dɪ'ləitsəm] *adj.* delightful. **—de'light•some•ly,** *adv.* **—de'light•some•ness,** *n.*

De•lil•ah [dɪ'laɪlə] *n.* any false, treacherous woman. ⟨< *Delilah,* in the Bible, the Philistine woman who was loved by Samson and who betrayed him⟩

de•lim•it [dɪ'lɪmɪt] *v.* fix the limits of; mark the boundaries of. **—deˌlim•i'ta•tion,** *n.* **—de'lim•iˌta•tive,** *adj.*

de•lim•it•er [dɪ'lɪmɪtər] *n. Computer technology.* a boundary marker that sets off commands, data input, etc.

de•lin•e•ate [dɪ'lɪniˌeit] *v.* **-at•ed, -at•ing. 1** trace the outline of. **2** draw; sketch. **3** describe in words. ⟨< L *delineare* < *de-* (intensive) + *linea* line⟩ **—de'lin•eˌa•tor,** *n.* **—de'lin•e•a•tive,** *adj.*

de•lin•e•a•tion [dɪˌlɪni'eiʃən] *n.* **1** a drawing; sketch. **2** description.

de•lin•quen•cy [dɪ'lɪŋkwənsi] *n., pl.* **-cies. 1** the failure to do what is required by law or duty; guilt. **2** a fault; offence. **3** the condition or habit of behaving unlawfully: *Juvenile delinquency is greatly increased by wartime conditions.* **4** a debt that should have been paid.

de•lin•quent [dɪ'lɪŋkwənt] *adj., n.* *—adj.* **1** failing to do what is required by law or duty; guilty of a fault or an offence. **2** due and unpaid; overdue: *The owners lost their house when it was sold for delinquent taxes.* **3** having to do with delinquents.
—n. a delinquent person; offender; criminal: *a juvenile delinquent.* ⟨< L *delinquens, -entis,* ppr. of *delinquere* fail < *de-* down + *linquere* leave⟩ **—de'lin•quent•ly,** *adv.*

del•i•quesce [ˌdɛlə'kwɛs] *v.* **-quesced, -quesc•ing. 1** become liquid by absorbing moisture from the air. **2** melt away. **3** *Biology.* **a** become soft or liquid as a stage of growth. **b** branch into many smaller sections, as veins in a leaf. ⟨< L *deliquescere* < *de-* + *liquescere* become fluid < *liquere* be liquid⟩

del•i•ques•cence [ˌdɛlə'kwɛsəns] *n.* the act or process of deliquescing. **—ˌdel•i'ques•cent,** *adj.*

de•lir•i•ous [dɪ'lɪriəs] *adj.* **1** temporarily out of one's senses; wandering in mind; raving. **2** wildly excited: *delirious with joy.* **3** caused by delirium.
—de'lir•i•ous•ly, *adv.* **—de'lir•i•ous•ness,** *n.*

de•lir•i•um [dɪ'lɪriəm] *n., pl.* **-lir•i•ums, -lir•i•a** [-'lɪriə]. **1** a temporary disorder of the mind that occurs during fevers, insanity, drunkenness, etc. Delirium is characterized by excitement, irrational talk, and hallucinations. **2** any wild excitement that cannot be controlled. ⟨< L *delirium* < *delirare* rave, be crazy < *de lira (ire)* (go) out of the furrow (in ploughing)⟩

delirium tre•mens ['trimənz] delirium characterized by violent tremblings and terrifying hallucinations, usually caused by prolonged excessive consumption of alcoholic drinks. *Abbrev.:* d.t.'s ⟨< NL *delirium tremens* trembling delirium⟩

de•list [di'lɪst] *v.* remove from a list, catalogue, etc.

de•liv•er [dɪ'lɪvər] *v.* **1** carry and give out; distribute: *to deliver mail.* **2** hand over; give up: *to deliver a fort to the enemy.* **3** make a delivery. **4** give forth in words: *The traveller delivered an interesting talk about her journey. The jury delivered its verdict.* **5** strike; throw: *to deliver a blow.* **6** set free; rescue; save from evil or trouble: *Deliver us from evil.* **7** help give birth: *The farmer delivered his prize cow of a calf.* **8** help in the birth of: *The doctor delivered the baby at noon.* **9** give birth. **10** yield or emit as a product: *These trees deliver 60 L of maple syrup.*
be delivered of, give birth to.
deliver oneself of, a speak; give out: *He delivered himself of a carefully prepared statement to the press.* **b** unburden oneself of (ideas, feelings, etc.) ⟨ME < OF *delivrer* < L *deliberare* set free < *de-* (intensive) + *liber* free⟩ **—de'liv•er•a•ble,** *adj.*
—de'liv•er•er, *n.*

☛ *Syn.* **6.** See note at RESCUE.

de•liv•er•ance [dɪ'lɪvərəns] *n.* **1** the act of setting free or the state of being set free; a rescue; release. **2** a formal opinion or judgment.

de•liv•er•y [dɪ'lɪvəri] *n., pl.* **-er•ies. 1** the act of carrying and handing over letters, goods, etc.; the act of distributing: *The mail delivery was late today.* **2** a giving up; handing over: *The captive was released upon the delivery of his ransom.* **3** a manner of speaking; way of giving a speech, lecture, etc.: *The minister has an excellent delivery.* **4** an act or way of striking, throwing, etc. **5** a rescue; release. **6** the act of giving birth; childbirth: *a difficult delivery.* **7** the act of assisting at a birth. **8** anything that is delivered; goods to be delivered. **9** *Law.* the formal handing over of property to another. **10** yield or emission; production.

dell [dɛl] *n.* a small, sheltered glen or valley, usually with trees in it. ⟨OE⟩

Del•mon•i•co steak [dɛl'mɒnɪˌkou] CLUB STEAK.

de•louse [di'lʌus] *or* [di'laʊz] *v.* **-loused, -lous•ing.** remove lice from. **—de'lous•er,** *n.*

Del•phi ['dɛlfaɪ] *n.* a town in ancient Greece where a famous oracle of Apollo was located.

Del•phi•an ['dɛlfiən] *adj.* Delphic.

Del•phic ['dɛlfɪk] *adj.* **1** having to do with the oracle of Apollo at Delphi. **2** obscure; having a double meaning. **3** of or having to do with Delphi.

Delphic oracle the oracle of Apollo at Delphi. The oracle often gave ambiguous answers to questions.

del•phin•i•um [dɛl'fɪniəm] *n.* any of a genus (*Delphinium*) of annual and perennial herbs of the buttercup family found in temperate regions of the northern hemisphere. Many species are cultivated in gardens for their tall spikes of blue, purple, pink, or white flowers. ⟨< NL < Gk. *delphinion* < *delphin* dolphin; from the shape of the nectar gland of the flower⟩

Del•phi•nus [dɛl'faɪnəs] *n.* a northern constellation between Aquila and Pegasus.

del•ta ['dɛltə] *n.* **1** a deposit of earth and sand, usually three-sided, that collects at the mouths of some rivers. **2** the fourth letter of the Greek alphabet (δ, Δ). **3** any triangular space or figure. ⟨< Gk.⟩ **—del'ta•ic** [dɛl'teiɪk], *adj.*

delta ray an electron emitted when a fast-moving, charged particle, such as an alpha particle, penetrates matter.

delta wave or **rhythm** a type of brain wave which oscillates at about 2 to 4 cycles per second. It is associated with a state of deep sleep or brain disease.

A deltawing aircraft

del•ta•wing ['dɛltə,wɪŋ] *adj., n.* —*adj.* of an aircraft, having wings in the shape of a Greek delta or triangle.
—*n.* such an aircraft or its structure.

del•ti•ol•o•gy [,dɛlti'ɒlədʒi] *n.* the collecting of postcards as a hobby. ⟨< Gk. *deltion,* dim. of *deltos* writing tablet + *-logy*⟩ **—,del•ti'ol•o•gist,** *n.*

del•toid ['dɛltɔɪd] *adj., n.* —*adj.* **1** shaped like the Greek delta (Δ); triangular. **2** of or having to do with the deltoid muscle.
—*n.* DELTOID MUSCLE. ⟨< NL *deltoides* < Gk. *deltoeidēs* < *delta* delta + *eidos* form⟩

deltoid muscle *Physiology.* a large, triangular muscle of the shoulder. It lifts the arm away from the side of the body.

de•lude [dɪ'lud] *v.* **-lud•ed, -lud•ing.** mislead; deceive: *He deluded himself into believing he would pass his examinations without studying.* ⟨< L *deludere* < *de-* (to the detriment of) + *ludere* play⟩ **—de'lud•er,** *n.* **—de'lud•ing•ly,** *adv.*

del•uge ['dɛljudʒ] *n., v.* **-uged, -ug•ing.** —*n.* **1** a great flood. **2** a heavy fall of rain. **3** any overwhelming rush: *a deluge of work. Most stores have a deluge of orders just before Christmas.* **4 the Deluge,** in the Bible, the great flood in the days of Noah.
—*v.* **1** flood. **2** overwhelm as if by a flood: *The movie star was deluged with requests for her autograph.* ⟨ME < OF < L *diluvium* < *diluere* < *dis-* away + *luere* wash⟩
☛ *Syn. n.* **1.** See note at FLOOD.

de•lu•sion [dɪ'luʒən] *n.* **1** the act of deluding or the state of being deluded: *In his delusion, he had expected his friends to come to his rescue.* **2** a false notion or belief: *The voyages of Columbus disproved the common delusion of his time that the earth was flat.* **3** *Psychiatry.* a fixed belief maintained in spite of all evidence from one's own senses and the objective world that the belief is false: *The old man suffered from the delusion that his food was being poisoned.* ⟨ME < LL *delusio, -onis* < *deludere.* See DELUDE.⟩ **—de'lu•sion•al,** *adj.*
☛ *Syn.* See note at ILLUSION.

de•lu•sive [dɪ'lusɪv] *adj.* misleading; deceptive; false. **—de'lu•sive•ly,** *adv.* **—de'lu•sive•ness,** *n.*

de•lu•so•ry [dɪ'lusəri] *adj.* delusive; deceptive.

de•luxe or **de luxe** [də'lʌks] *or* [də'lʊks]; *French,* [də'lyks] *adj.* of exceptionally fine or luxurious quality; elegant and costly. ⟨< F⟩

delve [dɛlv] *v.* **delved, delv•ing. 1** search carefully for information: *The scholar delved in many libraries for facts.* **2** *Archaic, poetic, or dialect.* dig. ⟨OE *delfan*⟩ **—'delv•er,** *n.*

de•mag•net•ize [di'mægnə,taɪz] *v.* **-ized, -iz•ing.** deprive of magnetism. **—de,mag•net•i'za•tion,** *n.* **—de'mag•net,iz•er,** *n.*

dem•a•gog ['dɛmə,gɒg] *Esp. U.S.* See DEMAGOGUE.

dem•a•gog•ic [,dɛmə'gɒdʒɪk] *or* [,dɛmə'gɒgɪk] *adj.* **1** of or having to do with a demagogue. **2** like a demagogue or demagogues. **—,dem•a'gog•ic•al•ly,** *adv.*

dem•a•gogue ['dɛmə,gɒg] *n.* a popular leader who stirs up the people by appealing to their emotions and prejudices, especially a person whose aim is personal advancement or power. ⟨< Gk. *dēmagōgos* < *dēmos* people + *agōgos* leader < *agein* lead⟩

dem•a•gogu•er•y [,dɛmə'gɒgəri] *or* ['dɛmə,gɒgəri] *n.* **1** the principles and practices of a demagogue. **2** government by a demagogue. **3** demagogues as a group.

dem•a•go•gy ['dɛmə,gɒdʒi], ['dɛmə,goudʒi], *or* ['dɛmə,gɒgi] *n.* demagoguery.

de•mand [dɪ'mænd] *v., n.* —*v.* **1** ask for with authority or claim as a right: *to demand a trial, to demand payment of a debt. The police officer demanded her driver's licence.* **2** ask urgently or insistently: *"What have you done with my hockey stick?" she demanded.* **3** call for; require; need: *Training a puppy demands patience.*
—*n.* **1** an urgent or insistent request: *a demand for an answer.* **2** the thing demanded: *Her demand was the immediate release of all the prisoners.* **3** a claim; call: *With two jobs to look after, he has many demands on his time.* **4** a seeking or being sought after; request or need: *Because of the large crop, the supply of apples was greater than the demand. Taxis are in great demand on rainy days.* **5** (*adjl.*) payable on demand without advance notice: *a demand loan, demand bill.*
in demand, wanted by many people.
on demand, as and when requested: *a loan payable on demand.* ⟨ME < OF < L *demandare* < *de-* from + *mandare* to order⟩
—de'mand•er, *n.*
☛ *Syn. v.* **1, 3. Demand,** CLAIM, REQUIRE = ask or call for something as a right or need. **Demand** emphasizes insisting, sometimes in a domineering way, on getting something a person or thing has the authority, right, or need to call for: *I demand an answer immediately.* **Claim** emphasizes having, or stating one has, the right to get what is demanded: *She claimed the inheritance.* **Require** emphasizes the need for what is demanded: *This letter requires an answer.*

demand deposit a non-interest-bearing bank account from which the depositor can withdraw money at any time without prior notice; chequing account.

demand feeding the feeding of an infant when he or she seems hungry rather than at scheduled times.

de•mand•ing [dɪ'mændɪŋ] *adj., v.* —*adj.* exacting; requiring a great deal of attention, effort, etc.; making many demands: *a demanding person, a demanding job.*
—*v.* ppr. of DEMAND. **—de'mand•ing•ly,** *adv.*

demand–pull inflation a kind of inflation in which prices rise due to an excess demand for goods; buyers' inflation.

de•man•toid [dɪ'mæntɔɪd] *n.* a bright green variety of garnet; a semiprecious stone. ⟨< MHG *demant* < OF *diamant* diamond + E *-oid*⟩

de•mar•cate ['dimɑr,keit] *or* [dɪ'mɑrkeit] *v.* **-cat•ed, -cat•ing. 1** set and mark the limits of. **2** separate; distinguish. ⟨< *demarcation*⟩ **—'de•mar,ca•tor,** *n.*

de•mar•ca•tion [,dimɑr'keiʃən] *or* [,dɛmɑr'keiʃən] *n.* **1** the act of setting and marking the limits. **2** a separation; distinction. **3** a limit; boundary. ⟨< Sp. *demarcación* < *de-* off + *marcar* mark⟩

de•marche or **dé•marche** [dei'mɑrʃ] *n.* **1** a plan of action. **2** a diplomatic manoeuvre, step, or protest. **3** a change of plans. ⟨< F *démarche* literally, gait⟩

deme [dim] *n.* within a species, a small group of interbreeding organisms. ⟨< Gk. *demos* people, district⟩
☛ *Hom.* DEEM.

de•mean[1] [dɪ'min] *v.* lower in dignity or standing; humble: *Arrogant politicians are often demeaned following an election loss.* ⟨< *de-* down + *mean*[2]; formed after *debase*⟩
☛ *Hom.* DEMESNE [dɪ'min].

de•mean[2] [dɪ'min] *v.* behave or conduct oneself (in a certain manner): *He demeaned himself well.* ⟨ME < OF *demener* < *de-* (intensive) + *mener* lead < L *minare* drive⟩
☛ *Hom.* DEMESNE [dɪ'min].

de•mean•ing [dɪ'minɪŋ] *adj., v.* —*adj.* that demeans.
—*v.* ppr. of DEMEAN. **—de'mean•ing•ly,** *adv.*

de•mean•our or **de•mean•or** [dɪ'minər] *n.* the way a person looks and acts; behaviour; conduct; manner. ⟨ME *demenure* < *demenen* behave < OF *demener.* See DEMEAN[2].⟩

dem•e•clo•cy•cline [,dɛməklou'səiklin] *n.* an antibiotic drug. *Formula:* $C_{21}H_{21}ClN_2O_8$

de•ment•ed [dɪ'mɛntɪd] *adj.* insane; crazy. ⟨< L *dementare* < *demens* mad < *de-* out of + *mens, mentis* mind⟩
—de'ment•ed•ly, *adv.* **—de'ment•ed•ness,** *n.*

de•men•tia [dɪ'mɛnʃə] *n.* a condition characterized by a partial or complete deterioration of mental powers, the ability to reason, etc.

Dem•e•ra•ra sugar [,dɛmə'rɑrə] *or* [,dɛmə'rɛrə] *n.* a brown sugar with large grains. ⟨< the *Demerara River* in Guyana⟩

de•mer•it [dɪ'mɛrɪt] *n.* **1** a fault; defect. **2** a mark against a person's record given for unsatisfactory performance or behaviour or for violation of a rule or law, and entailing a loss of privileges or other punishment upon accumulation of a certain number of marks. Many provinces have a system of demerits for certain driving offences. **3** (*adjl.*) of, having to do with, or designating a system that uses demerits to record offences.

de•mer•sal [dɪˈmɜrsəl] *adj.* native to sea or lake bottoms. ⟨< L *demersus* pp. of *demergere* to submerge < *de-* intensifier + *mergere* to sink⟩

de•mesne [dɪˈmein] *or* [dɪˈmin] *n.* **1** *Law.* the possession of land as one's own. **2** the land or land and buildings possessed as one's own; real estate. **3** the house and land belonging to a lord and used by him. **4** domain; realm. **5** region. ⟨ME < AF *demesne,* a respelling of OF *demeine* domain. Doublet of DOMAIN.⟩
☛ *Hom.* DEMEAN [dɪˈmin].

De•me•ter [dɪˈmitər] *n. Greek mythology.* the mother of Persephone and wife to the King of the Underworld, goddess of agriculture and of the fruitful earth, corresponding to the Roman goddess Ceres.

demi– *prefix.* **1** half: *demigod = half god.* **2** smaller than usual in size, power, etc.: *demitasse = a small cup.* ⟨< F *demi* half < VL < L *dimidius* < *dis-* apart + *medius* middle⟩

dem•i•god [ˈdɛmi,gɒd] *n.* **1** *Mythology.* **a** a god that is partly human; the offspring of a god or goddess and a human being: *Hercules was a demigod.* **b** a minor or lesser god. **2** a person who is so outstanding in some way as to seem godlike: *The famous hockey player was a demigod to his young fans.*

dem•i•god•dess [ˈdɛmi,gɒdɛs] *n. Mythology.* **1** a goddess that is partly human; the offspring of a god or goddess and a human being. **2** a woman who has been deified.

dem•i•john [ˈdɛmi,dʒɒn] *n.* a large bottle of glass or earthenware enclosed in wicker. ⟨< F *dame-jeanne* Lady Jane, playful personification⟩

de•mil•i•tar•ize [diˈmɪlətə,raɪz] *v.* **-ized, -iz•ing. 1** free from military control. **2** remove the military power of.
—de,mil•i•ta•ri'za•tion, *n.*

dem•i•mon•daine [,dɛmimɒnˈdein] *n.* a woman of the demimonde.

dem•i•monde [ˈdɛmi,mɒnd] *or* [,dɛmiˈmɒnd]; *French,* [dəmiˈmɔ̃d] *n.* **1** in French literature, a class of women who, though not socially respectable, maintain a position on the fringes of society because they are supported by wealthy lovers. **2** any social group considered not entirely respectable. **3** prostitutes collectively. ⟨< F *demi-monde* half-world⟩

de•mise [dɪˈmaiz] *n., v.* **-mised, -mis•ing.** *—n.* **1** death. **2** *Law.* the transfer of an estate by a will or lease. **3** the transfer of royal power by death or abdication.
—v. **1** *Law.* transfer (an estate) by a will or lease. **2** transfer (royal power) by death or abdication. ⟨apparently < AF *demise,* pp. of *desmettre* put away < *des-* away + *mettre* put < L *mittere* let go, send⟩

dem•i•sem•i•qua•ver [,dɛmiˈsɛmi,kweivər] *n. Esp. Brit. Music.* a thirty-second note.

dem•i•tasse [ˈdɛmi,tæs] *n.* **1** a small cup for serving black coffee. **2** a small cup of black coffee. ⟨< F *demi-tasse* half-cup⟩

dem•i•urge [ˈdɛmi,ɜrdʒ] *n.* in various philosophical systems, especially of the ancient Greeks, a creative or ruling force subordinate to deity. ⟨< Gk. *demiourgos* craftsman < *demos* people + *ergon* work⟩ **—,dem•i'urg•ic,** *adj.*

dem•i•volte [ˈdɛmi,voult] *n. Dressage.* a half-turn with the horse's front legs in the air. ⟨< F *demi* half + *volte* leap⟩

dem•o [ˈdɛmou] *n., pl.* **dem•os.** *Informal.* **1** a demonstration or display: *a cooking demo.* **2** a political demonstration or protest. **3** an automobile, machine, or other product used in demonstration; demonstrator. **4** a compact disc or tape recording used to demonstrate a new song, the talent of a musician, etc.

de•mo•bi•lize [diˈmoubə,laɪz] *v.* **-lized, -liz•ing. 1** disband: *After the war, it took several months to demobilize the armed forces.* **2** discharge from one of the armed forces.
—de,mo•bi•li'za•tion, *n.*

de•moc•ra•cy [dɪˈmɒkrəsi] *n., pl.* **-cies. 1** a government that is periodically elected and thus controlled by the people who live under it. Under a democracy, the people rule either by direct vote at public meetings or indirectly through the election of certain representatives to govern them. **2** the ideals and principles of such a government, such as equality of rights and opportunities and the rule of the majority. **3** a country, state, or community having such a government. **4** the treatment of others as one's equals. **5** the common people or their political power. ⟨< F *démocratie* < Gk *dēmokratia* < *dēmos* people + *kratos* rule⟩

dem•o•crat [ˈdɛmə,kræt] *n.* **1** a person who believes that a government should be elected by the people who live under it. **2** a person who treats all other people as equals. **3** a light, four-wheeled carriage drawn by two horses, having two double seats, one behind the other. **4 Democrat,** *U.S.* a member of the Democratic Party.

dem•o•crat•ic [,dɛməˈkrætɪk] *adj.* **1** of or like a democracy. **2** treating other people as one's equals: *She was very democratic in her treatment of the employees.* **3** appealing to large numbers of people. **4 Democratic,** *U.S.* of or having to do with the Democratic Party. **—,dem•o'crat•i•cal•ly,** *adv.*

Democratic Party one of the two main political parties of the United States.

de•moc•ra•tize [dɪˈmɒkrə,taɪz] *v.* **-tized, -tiz•ing.** make or become democratic. **—de,moc•ra•ti'za•tion,** *n.*

dé•mo•dé [,deimouˈdei]; *French,* [demoˈde] *adj.* outmoded; old-fashioned.

de•mod•u•late [diˈmɒdʒə,leit] *v.* **-lat•ed, -lat•ing.** *Electronics.* separate (an output signal) from a modulated carrier wave.

de•mod•u•la•tion [di,mɒdʒəˈleiʃən] *n. Electronics.* the process of separating information (the output signal) from a modulated carrier wave.

de•mod•u•la•tor [diˈmɒdʒə,leitər] *n. Electronics.* a device used for demodulation.

de•mo•graph•ic [,dɛməˈgræfɪk] *or* [,diməˈgræfɪk] *adj.* of or having to do with demography. **—,de•mo'graph•i•cal•ly,** *adv.*

de•mo•graph•ics [,dɛməˈgræfɪks] *or* [,diməˈgræfɪks] *n.* **1** the statistical data of a population, such as distribution, age, sex, average income, etc., derived from a census. **2** demography.

de•mog•ra•phy [dɪˈmɒgrəfi] *n.* the science dealing with the statistics of births, deaths, diseases, etc. of a community. ⟨< Gk. *demos* people + *-graphy*⟩ **—de'mog,ra•pher,** *n.*

dem•oi•selle [,dɛmwɒˈzɛl]; *French,* [dəmwaˈzɛl] *n.* **1** damsel. **2** a crane of Asia, Europe, and N Africa, having long white plumes behind the eyes. **3** a type of dragonfly. **4** HOODOO (def. 3). ⟨< F < OF *dameisele.* Doublet of DAMSEL.⟩

de•mol•ish [dɪˈmɒlɪʃ] *v.* **1** pull or tear down; wreck; raze: *The old train station will be demolished this summer.* **2** break into pieces; smash or crush: *The whole pile of books fell on the glass table and demolished it.* **3** show to be false or weak; ruin or discredit: *The government's arguments for the new bill were demolished by the opposition.* ⟨< F *démolis-,* a stem of *démolir* < L *demoliri* tear down < *de-* down + *moles* mass⟩
—de'mol•ish•er, *n.* **—de'mol•ish•ment,** *n.*
☛ *Syn.* See note at DESTROY.

dem•o•li•tion [,dɛməˈlɪʃən] *or* [,diməˈlɪʃən] *n.* **1** destruction, especially by explosives; ruin. **2 demolitions,** *pl.* explosives for destruction, especially in war.

demolition bomb a bomb with a relatively large explosive charge, used especially for destroying buildings and other objects.

demolition derby a contest involving smashing up old cars with another old car, to see which can do the most damage.

de•mon [ˈdimən] *n.* **1** an evil spirit; devil; fiend. **2** a very wicked or cruel person. **3** an evil or undesirable influence or condition: *The demon of greed ruined the miser's happiness.* **4** a person who has great energy, vigour, or skill: *She's a demon for work.* **5** an enthusiast: *a speed demon.* **6** Usually spelled **daemon, a** an attendant or guardian spirit. **b** *Greek mythology.* a supernatural being halfway between a god and a human being. ⟨< L < Gk. *daimonion* divine (thing); in Christian writings, evil spirit < *daimōn* divinity, spirit⟩
☛ *Hom.* DAEMON.

de•mon•e•tize [diˈmɒnə,taɪz] *or* [diˈmʌnə,taɪz] *v.* **-tized, -tiz•ing. 1** deprive of its standard value as money. **2** withdraw from use as money. **—de,mon•e•ti'za•tion,** *n.*

de•mo•ni•ac [dɪˈmouni,æk] *or* [dɪˈmɒni,æk] *adj., n. —adj.* **1** of demons. **2** devilish; fiendish. **3** raging; frantic. **4** possessed by an evil spirit.
—n. a person possessed by an evil spirit.

de•mo•ni•a•cal [,diməˈnaɪəkəl] *adj.* demoniac.
—,de•mo'ni•a•cal•ly, *adv.*

de•mon•ic [dɪˈmɒnɪk] *adj.* **1** of evil spirits; caused by evil spirits. **2** influenced by a guiding spirit; inspired.
—de'mon•ic•al•ly, *adv.*

de•mon•ism [ˈdimə,nɪzəm] *n.* **1** belief in demons. **2** the worship of demons.

de•mon•ize [ˈdimə,naɪz] *v.* **-ized, -iz•ing.** subject to demonic activity or influence.

de•mon•ol•a•try [ˌdimə'nɒlətri] *n.* the worship of demons. ⟨< Gk. *daimono-* < *daimon* + Ecclesiastical Gk. *latreia* hired service < *latreuein* to serve, worship < *latris* hired servant⟩ **—ˌde•mon'o•lat•er,** *n.*

de•mon•ol•o•gy [ˌdimə'nɒlədʒi] *n.* the study of demons or of beliefs about demons. **—ˌde•mon'ol•o•gist,** *n.*

de•mon•stra•ble [dɪ'mɒnstrəbəl] *or* ['dɛmənstrəbəl] *adj.* capable of being proved. **—deˌmon•stra'bil•i•ty,** *n.*

de•mon•stra•bly [dɪ'mɒnstrəbli] *or* ['dɛmənstrəbli] *adj.* **1** in a manner that can be proved; clearly. **2** by demonstration.

dem•on•strate ['dɛmənˌstreit] *v.* **-strat•ed, -strat•ing.** **1** establish the truth of; prove. **2** show how (something) happens or is done; explain and illustrate with the aid of visual examples, experiments, etc.: *We watched the lab instructor demonstrate the process of electrolysis.* **3** try to prove the quality, usefulness, etc. of (a product) to a prospective buyer or buyers by showing it in use: *The sales rep demonstrated the electric drill for her by drilling holes in thick steel.* **4** show clearly and openly: *She demonstrated her love for her niece by giving her a big hug.* **5** show feeling or views about a particular person, issue, etc., publicly and en masse: *An angry crowd demonstrated in front of the city hall.* ⟨< L *demonstrare* < *de-* (intensive) + *monstrare* show⟩

dem•on•stra•tion [ˌdɛmən'streiʃən] *n.* **1** a clear proof: *a demonstration of the defendant's guilt, a demonstration that the earth is round.* **2** a showing how something happens or is done; an explanation with the use of visual examples, experiments, etc.: *a demonstration of weaving techniques.* **3** a showing of a product in use to illustrate its merits to a prospective buyer or buyers: *the demonstration of a new overhead projector.* **4** an open show or expression of feeling: *a demonstration of joy.* **5** a public show of feelings or views about something by many people in a parade or meeting. **6** a display of military power or potential. **7** *Logic.* an argument or series of propositions that leads necessarily to a certain conclusion. **8** *Mathematics.* the process of proving that certain assumptions necessarily produce a certain result.

de•mon•stra•tive [dɪ'mɒnstrətɪv] *adj., n.* *—adj.* **1** expressing one's affections freely and openly: *The girl's demonstrative greetings embarrassed her shy brother.* **2** showing clearly; illustrative; explanatory. **3** giving proof; conclusive. **4** *Grammar.* pointing out the one or ones referred to as distinct from others of the same group or class. The adjective *this* in *this book* is a demonstrative adjective which serves to distinguish one particular book from all others.
—n. Grammar. a pronoun or adjective that points out: *That* and *these* are demonstratives. **—de'mon•stra•tive•ly,** *adv.* **—de'mon•stra•tive•ness,** *n.*

☛ *Usage. This, that, these, those* are called **demonstrative adjectives** or **pronouns** according to their use in a sentence. Adjective: *We bought this car in May.* Pronoun: *This costs a good bit more than those.*

dem•on•stra•tor ['dɛmənˌstreitər] *n.* **1** a person who demonstrates a process, procedure, or product for an audience, such as one who shows a medical or dental procedure or conducts a laboratory experiment for students, or one who shows how a machine or apparatus is used. **2** a person who takes part in a public demonstration of protest or demand: *Several demonstrators were hurt in a scuffle with guards.* **3** a sample product used by a seller to demonstrate the merits of the product: *She got a very good deal on her new car because it was a demonstrator.*

de•mor•al•ize [dɪ'mɔrəˌlaɪz] *or* [di'mɔrəˌlaɪz] *v.* **-ized, -iz•ing.** **1** corrupt the morals of: *The drug habit demoralizes people.* **2** weaken the morale, spirit, courage, or discipline of; dishearten: *Lack of food and ammunition demoralized the besieged soldiers.* **3** throw into confusion or disorder because of unease or anxiety: *Threats of war demoralized the stock market.* **—deˌmor•al•i'za•tion,** *n.* **—de'mor•aˌliz•er,** *n.*

de•mote [dɪ'mout] *v.* **-mot•ed, -mot•ing.** put back to a lower grade; reduce in rank. ⟨< *de-* + *(pro)mote*⟩

de•mot•ic [dɪ'mɒtɪk] *adj., n.* *—adj.* **1** of the common people; popular. **2** of the Egyptian form of simplified writing, using characters derived from hieratic writing.
—n. **1** the standard spoken form of modern Greek. **2** a simplified form of ancient Egyptian writing, hieratic and not hieroglyphic. ⟨< Gk. *demotikos* < *dēmos* the people⟩

de•mo•tion [dɪ'mouʃən] *n.* **1** the act of demoting. **2** the fact of being demoted.

de•mount [di'maʊnt] *v.* remove from a mounting.

de•mount•a•ble [di'maʊntəbəl] *adj.* that can be removed: *a demountable wheel rim.*

de•mul•cent [dɪ'mʌlsənt] *adj., n.* *—adj.* soothing: *Certain herbs are known for their demulcent qualities.*
—n. a soothing ointment or medicine. ⟨< L *demulcens, -entis,* ppr. of *demulcere* < *de-* + *mulcere* soothe⟩

de•mur [dɪ'mɜr] *v.* **-murred, -mur•ring;** *n.* *—v.* **1** object: *The clerk demurred at working overtime.* **2** *Law.* present a demurrer.
—n. objection. ⟨< OF *demurer* < L *demorari* < *de-* (intensive) + *morari* delay⟩ **—de'mur•ral,** *n.*

de•mure [dɪ'mjur] *adj.* **-mur•er, -mur•est.** **1** quiet and modest in behaviour: *a demure young lady.* **2** artificially proper; assuming an air of modesty; coy: *the demure smile of a flirt.* ⟨< obs. *mure,* adj., demure < OF *meür* < L *maturus* mature⟩ **—de'mure•ly,** *adv.* **—de'mure•ness,** *n.*

☛ *Syn.* See note at MODEST.

de•mur•rage [dɪ'mɜrɪdʒ] *n.* **1** the failure to load or unload a ship, railway car, etc. within the time specified. **2** the payment made for this failure. ⟨< *demur*⟩

de•mur•rer [dɪ'mɜrər] *n.* **1** a person who objects. **2** *Law.* an objection by one party to a lawsuit that although the facts are as presented by the opposite party, the first party does not have to answer the claim. A person sued for an old debt might present a demurrer, claiming that the statute of limitations prohibits the suit.

de•mys•ti•fy [di'mɪstəˌfaɪ] *v.* **-fied, -fy•ing.** take away the mystery from; make (something) seem ordinary. **—deˌmys•ti•fi'ca•tion,** *n.*

de•my•thol•o•gize [ˌdimɪ'θɒləˌdʒaɪz] *v.* **-ized, -iz•ing.** **1** remove from (the Bible, etc.) elements regarded as mythological in order to get a more rationalistic or naturalistic interpretation. **2** remove mythical or mystical elements from; make rational, realistic, or commonplace: *to demythologize Hollywood.*

den [dɛn] *n., v.* **denned, den•ning.** *—n.* **1** a wild animal's home; lair: *The bear's den was in a cave.* **2** a room in a home where a person can read, work, or think in privacy: *There is a small, cosy den off the living room.* **3** a small, dirty, unattractive room, house, etc.: *The beggars lived in dens along the waterfront.* **4** a place used as a hideout or for secret activities: *a den of thieves.* **5** in Scouts, a group of eight to ten Cubs.
—v. **1** live in or retire to a den. **2** escape into or hide in a den. ⟨OE *denn*⟩ **—'denˌlike,** *adj.*

de•nar [də'nɑr] *n.* the basic unit of currency in Macedonia, divided into 100 deni. See table of money in the Appendix.

de•nar•i•us [dɪ'nɛriəs] *n.* **-nar•i•i** [-'nɛriˌaɪ] *or* [-'nɛriˌi]. in ancient Rome: **1** a silver coin. **2** a gold coin. ⟨< L *denarius* containing ten (here, ten times the value of an *as*[2]) < *deni* ten at a time. Doublet of DINAR, DENIER[2].⟩

den•a•ry ['dɛnəri] *or* ['dinəri] *adj.* of ten; containing ten; decimal. ⟨See DENARIUS⟩

de•na•tion•al•ize [di'næʃənəˌlaɪz] *or* [di'næʃnəˌlaɪz] *v.* **-ized, -iz•ing.** **1** deprive of national rights, scope, or character. **2** of industries, return from national to private control or ownership. **—deˌna•tion•al•i'za•tion,** *n.*

de•nat•u•ral•ize [di'nætʃərəˌlaɪz] *or* [di'nætʃrəlaɪz] *v.* **-ized, -iz•ing.** **1** make unnatural. **2** withdraw citizenship from (a naturalized citizen). **—deˌnat•u•ral•i•'za•tion,** *n.*

de•na•tur•ant [di'neitʃərənt] *n.* a denaturing substance or agent.

de•na•ture [di'neitʃər] *v.* **-tured, -tur•ing.** **1** change the nature of. **2** make (alcohol, food, etc.) unfit for drinking or eating without destroying its usefulness for other purposes. **3** change the properties of (a protein) by changing its structure, as by heat or the addition of chemicals. **4** add an isotope to (fissionable material) to stop the whole from being used in nuclear weapons. **—deˌna•tur'a•tion,** *n.*

de•na•zi•fy [di'nɑtsəˌfaɪ] *or* [di'nætsəˌfaɪ] *v.* **-fied, -fy•ing.** rid of Nazi doctrines or Nazi influences. **—deˌna•zi•fi'ca•tion,** *n.*

den•dri– or **den•dro–** *combining form.* of trees ⟨< Gk. *dendron* tree⟩

den•dri•form ['dɛndrɪˌfɔrm] *adj.* tree-shaped.

den•drite ['dɛndraɪt] *n.* **1** *Geology.* **a** a stone or mineral with branching, treelike markings. **b** a treelike marking. **2** *Anatomy.* the branching part at the receiving end of a nerve cell. See NEURON for picture. ⟨< Gk. *dendritēs* of a tree < *dendron* tree⟩ **—den'drit•ic,** *adj.*

den•dro•chro•no•log•i•cal [ˌdɛndrouˌkrɒnə'lɒdʒəkəl] *adj.* of or having to do with dendrochronology.

den•dro•chro•nol•o•gy [ˌdɛndroukrə'nɒlədʒi] *n.* the science or technique of dating past events, archaeological sites, etc. by studying the growth rings of timber.

den•droid ['dɛndrɔɪd] *adj.* having a form like that of a tree.

den•dro•log•i•cal [,dɛndrə'lɒdʒəkəl] *adj.* of or having to do with dendrology. **—,den•dro'log•i•cal•ly,** *adv.*

den•drol•o•gist [dɛn'drɒlə,dʒɪst] *n.* a person trained in dendrology, especially one whose work it is.

den•drol•o•gy [dɛn'drɒlədʒi] *n.* the branch of botany dealing with trees and shrubs.

De•ne ['dɛni] *or* ['dɛnei] *n.pl., adj. —n.* the Athapascan First Nations peoples of the Northwest Territories.
—adj. of, having to do with, or designating the Dene. ⟨< F *déné* < Athapascan *dene* people, men⟩

Den•eb ['dɛnɛb] *n.* a very bright first magnitude star in the constellation Cygnus. ⟨< Arabic *dhanab* tail⟩

den•e•ga•tion [,dɛnə'geiʃən] *n.* denial; a denying or contradicting. ⟨< F *dénégation* < L *denegatio* < *denegare* to deny < *de-* intensifier + *negare* to deny⟩

Dene Nation *Cdn.* the official organization representing the Athapascan peoples of the Northwest Territories. The Dene Nation was formerly called the Northwest Territories Indian Brotherhood.

de•neu•tral•ize [di'njutrə,laɪz] *or* [di'nutrə,laɪz] *v.* **-ized, -iz•ing.** abolish the neutral status of (a country, territory, etc.). **—de,neu•tral•i'za•tion,** *n.*

den•gue ['dɛŋgei] *or* ['dɛŋgi] *n.* an infectious tropical fever with skin rash and severe pain in the joints and muscles. ⟨< Sp. < Swahili *kidinga*⟩

den•i ['dɛni] *n.* a unit of currency in Macedonia, equal to 1/100 of a denar. See table of money in the Appendix.

de•ni•a•ble [dɪ'naɪəbəl] *adj.* that can be denied. **—de'ni•a•bly,** *adv.*

de•ni•al [dɪ'naɪəl] *n.* **1** an assertion that something is not true or real: *a denial that goblins exist.* **2** an assertion that one does not believe or accept something; renunciation or disavowal: *Galileo was required to give a public denial of his theories.* **3** the act of refusing to satisfy a request, etc. **4** refusal to acknowledge a person or thing; a disowning. **5** self-denial.

de•ni•er[1] [dɪ'naɪər] *n.* a person who denies. ⟨< *deny*⟩

den•ier[2] ['dɛnjər] *or* [də'nir] *for 1;* [də'nir] *for 2; French,* [də'nje] *n.* **1** a unit of mass for measuring the fineness of silk, rayon, or nylon yarn. One denier equals a yarn weighing 1 g for each 9000 m. **2** formerly, a small coin of France and other W European countries. ⟨< OF < L *denarius.* Doublet of DINAR, DENARIUS.⟩

den•i•grate ['dɛnə,greit] *v.* **-grat•ed, -grat•ing. 1** defame; blacken the reputation of (someone). **2** make black; blacken. ⟨< L *denigrare* blacken thoroughly < *de-* (intensive) + *nigrare* blacken < *niger* black⟩ **—'den•i•grat•or,** *n.* **—,den•i'gra•to•ry,** *adj.*

den•i•gra•tion [,dɛnə'greiʃən] *n.* the act of blackening a reputation; defamation.

den•im ['dɛnəm] *n.* **1** a heavy, coarse cotton cloth with a diagonal weave, usually woven with a coloured warp and white filling threads. Denim is used mainly for work and casual clothes, upholstery, etc. **2 denims,** *pl.* pants or overalls made of denim, usually blue. ⟨short for F *serge de Nîmes* serge of Nîmes⟩

de•ni•tri•fy [di'naitrə,faɪ] *v.* **-fied, -fy•ing.** *Chemistry.* **1** remove nitrogen or its compounds from. **2** change (nitrates) by reduction into nitrites, nitrogen, or ammonia. **—de,ni•tri•fi'ca•tion,** *n.*

den•i•zen ['dɛnəzən] *n.* **1** an inhabitant; occupant: *Fish are denizens of the sea.* **2** one who often goes to a place; frequenter. **3** a foreigner who is given certain rights of citizenship. **4** a foreign word, plant, animal, etc. that has been naturalized: *The common English sparrow is a denizen of North America; it was first brought from Europe about 1850.* ⟨ME < AF *denzein* < *denz* within < LL < L *de* from + *intus* within⟩

Den•mark ['dɛnmɑrk] *n.* a country in N Europe, between the Baltic Sea and the North Sea.

den mother a woman who supervises a den of Cubs.

de•nom•i•nate *v.* [dɪ'nɒmə,neit]; *adj.* [dɪ'nɒmənɪt] *or* [-'nɒmə,neit] *v.* **-na•ted, -nat•ing;** *adj. —v.* give a specific name to.
—adj. designating a number that represents a quantity in terms of a unit of measurement. *7* and *18* in 7 m and 18 kg are denominate numbers. ⟨< L *denominare* < *de-* (intensive) + *nomen* name⟩

de•nom•i•na•tion [dɪ,nɒmə'neiʃən] *n.* **1** a name for a group or class of things; name. **2** a religious group, usually represented by a number of local churches. Presbyterian and Baptist are two large Protestant denominations. **3** a class or kind of units: *The Canadian coin of lowest denomination is a cent.* **4** the act of naming. **5** *Mathematics.* a class or kind of units: *Reducing 5/12, 1/3, and 1/6 to the same denomination gives 5/12, 4/12, and 2/12.*

de•nom•i•na•tion•al [dɪ,nɒmə'neiʃənəl] *adj.* having to do with some religious denomination or denominations; controlled by a religious denomination; sectarian.
—de,nom•i'na•tion•al•ly, *adv.*

de•nom•i•na•tion•al•ism [dɪ,nɒmə'neiʃənə,lɪzəm] *n.* **1** denominational principles or a system based on them. **2** support of such principles or of such a system; preference for or insistence on the views of a particular denomination. **3** a division into denominations.

de•nom•i•na•tive [dɪ'nɒmənətɪv] *or* [dɪ'nɒmə,neitɪv] *adj., n.* *—adj.* **1** giving a distinctive name; naming. **2** *Grammar.* formed from a noun or an adjective. *Centre* and *whiten* are denominative verbs.
—n. Grammar. a word formed from a noun or an adjective.
—de'nom•i•na•tive•ly, *adv.*

de•nom•i•na•tor [dɪ'nɒmə,neitər] *n.* **1** *Mathematics.* the number below the line in a fraction, stating the size of the parts in their relation to the whole. In 3/4, 4 is the denominator, and 3 is the numerator. **2** a person or thing that names.

de•no•ta•tion [,dinou'teiʃən] *n.* **1** a meaning, especially the exact, literal meaning. Compare CONNOTATION. **2** an indication; a denoting or marking out. **3** a name, mark, or sign; symbol. **4** *Logic.* **a** the class, type, or number of things included in a given term; extension. **b** a value, quantity, etc. represented by a symbol. **5** the act of denoting.

de•no•ta•tive [dɪ'noutətɪv] *or* ['dinou,teitɪv] *adj.* having the quality of denoting; indicative.

de•note [dɪ'nout] *v.* **-not•ed, -not•ing. 1** be the sign of; indicate: *A fever usually denotes sickness.* **2** be a name for; mean. **3** stand for as a symbol: *The sign × denotes multiplication.* ⟨< F *dénoter* < L *denotare* < *de-* down + *nota* mark⟩

de•noue•ment or **dé•noue•ment** [,deinu'mɑ̃]; *French,* [denu'mɑ̃] *n.* the solution or unravelling of a plot in a play, a story, etc.; outcome; end. ⟨< F *dénouement* < *dénouer* untie < L *de* down from + *nodare* tie⟩

de•nounce [dɪ'naʊns] *v.* **-nounced, -nounc•ing. 1** condemn publicly; express strong disapproval of. **2** inform against; accuse: *He denounced his own brother to the military police as a spy.* **3** give formal notice of the termination of (a treaty, etc.). ⟨ME < OF *denouncier* < L *denuntiare* < *de-* (intensive) + *nuntius* messenger⟩ **—de'nounc•er,** *n.* **—de'nounce•ment,** *n.*

de nou•veau *French,* [dənu'vo] again; afresh; anew.

de no•vo [di 'nouvou] *or* [dei'nouvou]; *Latin* [dei'nowo] *Latin.* anew; starting again.

dense [dɛns] *adj.* **den•ser, dens•est. 1** closely packed together; thick: *a dense fog.* **2** profound; intense; impenetrable: *dense ignorance.* **3** stupid; dull; slow-thinking: *His dense look showed he did not understand the problem.* **4** *Photography.* (of a developed negative) relatively opaque, with strong contrasts of light and shade. ⟨< L *densus*⟩ **—'dense•ly,** *adv.* **—'dense•ness,** *n.*

den•sim•e•ter [dɛn'sɪmətər] *n.* an instrument for measuring density or specific gravity.

den•si•tom•e•ter [,dɛnsɪ'tɒmətər] *n.* an instrument to measure optical density. ⟨< F *densité* (< L *densitas*) + *-meter*⟩

den•si•ty ['dɛnsəti] *n., pl.* **-ties. 1** a dense condition or quality; having parts very close together; compactness; thickness: *The density of the forest prevented us from seeing more than a little way ahead.* **2** the quantity of anything per unit area: *population density.* **3** *Physics.* the quantity of matter in a particular unit of volume; the ratio of the mass of a given volume of a substance to that of an equal volume of a standard substance. A cubic metre of lead has more mass than a cubic metre of wood, so we say lead has a greater density than wood. Water is the standard of density for solids and liquids, and air for gases. **4** *Electricity.* **a** the quantity of electricity per unit of area on a charged surface. **b** current density. **5** *Photography.* the relative opaqueness of a developed negative. **6** *Computer technology.* the quantity of data that may be stored per unit of space on auxiliary storage (disk, tape, etc.): *This tape has a recording density of 6250 bits per inch.* **7** stupidity.

dent[1] [dɛnt] *n., v. —n.* **1** a hollow made by a blow or pressure; a dint: *Bullets had made dents in the soldier's steel helmet.* **2** an

effect, especially one that lessens, weakens or damages: *The new TV set made a bad dent in our bank account.*
—*v.* **1** make a dent in. **2** become dented. ⟨ME *dente,* var. of *dint*⟩

dent² [dɛnt] *n.* **1** a toothlike part, as in a gearwheel, comb, etc. **2** a notch; indentation. ⟨< OF *dent* tooth < L *dens, dentis*⟩

dent. **1** dentist. **2** dentistry.

den•tal ['dɛntəl] *adj., n.* —*adj.* **1** of or for the teeth. **2** of, by, or for dentistry. **3** *Phonetics.* of speech sounds, produced by placing the tip of the tongue against or near the back of the upper front teeth: *French speakers pronounce the consonants* [t] *and* [d] *as dental sounds, whereas in English* [t] *and* [d] *are alveolar.*
—*n. Phonetics.* a consonantal sound produced by placing the tip of the tongue against or near the back of the upper front teeth. ⟨< L *dens, dentis* tooth⟩ **—'dent•al•ly,** *adv.*

dental floss a thin, strong, smooth thread, waxed or unwaxed, used to remove plaque and food particles from between the teeth.

dental hygiene care of the teeth, such as brushing, flossing, and having regular cleanings.

dental hygienist a licensed technician who assists a dentist by performing such duties as examining and cleaning a person's teeth, taking X-rays, etc.

den•ta•li•um [dɛn'teiliəm] *n.* any of a genus (*Dentalium*) of burrowing molluscs found along seashores, having an elongated, tapering shell that is open at both ends. Dentalium shell was traditionally used by North American First Nations peoples of the West Coast to make decorations for clothing, etc.

den•tate ['dɛnteit] *adj.* **1** having teeth or pointed, toothlike projections. **2** of leaves, having a toothed margin. ⟨< L *dentatus* < *dens, dentis* tooth⟩ **—'den•tate•ly,** *adv.*

den•ti•care ['dɛntə,kɛr] *n.* a government-sponsored program of dental insurance for all people. ⟨< *dent*al + med*icare*⟩

den•ti•cle ['dɛntɪkəl] *n. Zoology.* a small, toothlike projection or scale. ⟨< L *denticulus* dim. of *dens, dentis* tooth⟩
—den'tic•u•late, *adj.*

den•ti•form ['dɛntɪ,fɔrm] *adj.* shaped like a tooth.

den•ti•frice ['dɛntəfrɪs] *n.* a paste, powder, or liquid for cleaning the teeth. ⟨< F < L *dentifricium* < *dens, dentis* tooth + *fricare* rub⟩

den•tin ['dɛntɪn] *n.* dentine.

den•tine ['dɛntin], ['dɛntɪn], *or* [dɛn'tin] *n.* the hard, bony material beneath the enamel, forming the main part of a tooth. ⟨< L *dens, dentis* tooth⟩

den•tist ['dɛntɪst] *n.* a person who is qualified to practise the prevention and treatment of problems and diseases of the teeth and gums. ⟨< F *dentiste* < *dent* tooth < L *dens, dentis*⟩

den•tist•ry ['dɛntɪstri] *n.* the art or profession of a dentist.

den•ti•tion [dɛn'tɪʃən] *n.* **1** the growth of teeth; teething. **2** the kind, number, and arrangement of the teeth: *Dogs and wolves have the same dentition.* ⟨< L *dentitio, -onis* < *dens, dentis* tooth⟩

den•toid ['dɛntɔɪd] *adj.* like a tooth. ⟨< L *dens, dentis* tooth + *-oid*⟩

den•ture ['dɛntʃər] *n.* Usually, **dentures,** *pl.* a group of false teeth set in a plate to fit over the gum, especially a full set of upper and lower teeth. ⟨< F *denture* < *dent* tooth < L *dens, dentis*⟩

den•tur•ist ['dɛntʃərɪst] *n.* a person trained to make and fit dentures.

de•nu•cle•ar•ize [di'njukliə,raɪz] *or* [di'nukliə,raɪz] *v.* **-ized, -iz•ing.** make (a place) free of nuclear weapons.
—de,nu•cle•ar•i'za•tion, *n.*

de•nu•da•tion [,dinjʊ'deiʃən] *or* [,dɛnjʊ'deiʃən] *n.* **1** a denuding. **2** a denuded condition. **3** *Geology.* the laying bare of rock, especially by erosion.

de•nude [dɪ'njud] *or* [dɪ'nud] *v.* **-nud•ed, -nud•ing. 1** make bare; strip of clothing, covering, etc.: *trees denuded of leaves.* **2** *Geology.* lay (rock) bare by removing what lies above, especially by erosion. ⟨< L *denudare* < *de-* (intensive) + *nudus* bare⟩

de•nu•mer•a•ble [dɪ'njumərəbəl] *or* [dɪ'numərəbəl] *adj.* countable; designating a set, each element of which can be associated with a natural integer.

de•nun•ci•a•tion [dɪ,nʌnsi'eiʃən] *n.* **1** public condemnation; expression of strong disapproval. **2** the act of informing against someone; accusation. **3** a formal notice of the intention to end a treaty, etc. **4** a declaration of a curse, revenge, etc.; warning; threat. ⟨< L *denuntiatio, -onis* < *denuntiare.* See DENOUNCE.⟩
—de'nun•ci,a•tor, *n.*

de•nun•ci•a•to•ry [dɪ'nʌnsiə,tɔri] *or* [dɪ'nʌnʃə,tɔri] *adj.* condemning; accusing; threatening.

Den•ver sandwich ['dɛnvər] WESTERN SANDWICH. ⟨< *Denver,* the capital of Colorado⟩

de•ny [dɪ'naɪ] *v.* **-nied, -ny•ing. 1** declare (something) is not true: *The prisoner denied the charges against him. They denied the existence of disease in the town.* **2** say that one does not hold to or accept: *to deny a political party.* **3** refuse (someone something): *I could not deny her so small a favour.* **4** refuse to acknowledge as one's own; disown: *He denied his signature.*
deny (oneself), do without the things one wants for the sake of others or of some cause.
deny (oneself) to, refuse to see: *Illness forced Mrs. Pasquale to deny herself to all callers.* ⟨< F *dénier* < L *denegare* < *de-* completely + *negare* say no⟩

☛ *Syn.* **1. Deny,** CONTRADICT = declare something not true. **Deny** = state definitely or emphatically that something is untrue or cannot be true: *She denied the accusation.* **Contradict** suggests saying or arguing the opposite of what has been said, whether it is true or not: *He contradicts everything I say, even if he has to insist that black is white.*

de•o•dar ['diə,dɑr] *n.* **1** a cedar of the Himalayas, having drooping branches. It is cultivated for shade. **2** the wood of this tree. ⟨< Hind. < Skt. *devadaru* wood of the gods⟩

de•o•dor•ant [di'oudərənt] *n., adj.* —*n.* a preparation that destroys, prevents, or masks an undesirable odour, especially a powder, liquid, or salve used on the body.
—*adj.* capable of destroying, preventing, or masking undesirable odours.

de•o•dor•ize [di'oudə,raɪz] *v.* **-ized, -iz•ing.** remove undesirable odours from: *to deodorize a bathroom.*
—de,o•dor•i'za•tion, *n.*

de•o•dor•iz•er [di'oudə,raɪzər] *n.* a substance, or a device releasing a substance, used to destroy or mask odours, especially in a room, on articles of furniture, etc.: *She bought some deodorizer for the dog's bed. We need to recharge this deodorizer.*

De•o gra•ti•as [,diou 'grɑʃiəs] *or* ['deiou 'grɑtiəs] *Latin.* thanks to God.

de•on•tol•o•gy [,diɒn'tɒlədʒi] *n.* the branch of ethics that deals with moral obligation and right action according to a rule rather than by results. ⟨< Gk. *deon, deontos* that which is binding, necessity (< *dein* to bind) + *-logy*⟩
—de,on•to'log•i•cal, *adj.*

De•o vo•len•te ['diou və'lɛnti] *or* ['deiou vou'lɛntei] *Latin.* if God is willing. *Abbrev.:* D.V.

de•ox•i•dize [di'ɒksə,daɪz] *v.* **-dized, -diz•ing.** remove oxygen from. **—de,ox•i•di'za•tion,** *n.* **—de'ox•i,diz•er,** *n.*

de•ox•y•cho•lic acid [,diɒksɪ'kɒlɪk] a drug used to treat certain digestive conditions.

de•ox•y•gen•ate [dɪ'ɒksədʒə,neit] *v.* **-at•ed, -at•ing.** remove oxygen from; deoxidize. **—de,ox•y•gen'a•tion,** *n.*

de•ox•y•ri•bo•nu•cle•ase [,diɒksɪ,raɪbou'njuklieis] *or* [-'nuklieis] *n.* a drug used in the treatment of wounds.

de•ox•y•ri•bo•nu•cle•ic acid [di,ɒksə,raɪbounju'kliɪk] *or* [-nu'kliɪk] DNA, an essential component of all living matter, that in higher organisms contains the genetic codes determining heredity. ⟨< *de-* from, away + *oxy*(*gen*) + *ribonucleic acid*⟩

de•ox•y•ri•bose [di,ɒksə'raɪbous] *n.* the sugar constituent of DNA. *Formula*: $C_5H_{10}O_4$

dep. **1** deputy. **2** department. **3** deponent. **4** deposit. **5** depot. **6** departs. **7** departure.

de•part [dɪ'pɑrt] *v.* **1** go away; leave: *The train departs at 6:15.* **2** set out; start: *It's time to depart on my long journey.* **3** turn away; make a change (*from*): *to depart from one's usual way of doing things.* **4** die. ⟨ME < OF < LL *departire* divide < L *de-* away + *pars, partis* part⟩
depart this life, quit or leave: *She departed this life at the age of seventy.*

☛ *Syn.* **1. Depart,** WITHDRAW, RETIRE = go away or leave; all are more or less formal words in this sense. **Depart** suggests parting or separating oneself from a person, place, or thing, especially for a long time: *He departed from his home.* **Withdraw** and **retire** = go out or remove oneself from a place, activity, or someone's presence, often only temporarily and usually for reasons of time, privacy, need for rest, etc.: *I withdrew (retired) while they discussed my qualifications.*

de•part•ed [di'pɑrtɪd] *or* [dɪ'pɑrtɪd] *adj., v.* —*adj.* **1** dead. **2** gone; past. **3** (*noml.*) a dead person or persons.
—*v.* pt. and pp. of DEPART.

de•part•ment [dɪ'pɑrtmənt] *n.* **1** a separate part or division of a larger unit, such as a government, business, school, store, etc.: *the city fire department, the furniture department of a store, the department of external affairs of the federal government, the English department of a school.* **2** a field or range of activity or influence: *He said that handling complaints from customers was not his department.* **3** in France and some Latin American countries, an administrative district similar to a province. **4** a regular section of a magazine. ⟨ME and OF *departement* < *departir* < VL *departire* to divide, separate, for L *dispartire* < *dis-* apart + *partire* to divide⟩

de•part•men•tal [ˌdipɑrt'mɛntəl] *or* [dɪpɑrt'mɛntəl] *adj., n.* *—adj.* **1** having to do with a department. **2** divided into departments. **3** having to do with a departmental examination. *—n. Cdn.* short for **departmental examination,** a standardized examination formerly held prior to high-school matriculation. **—ˌde•part'men•tal•ly,** *adv.*

de•part•men•tal•ize [ˌdipɑrt'mɛntəˌlaɪz] *or* [dɪˌpɑrt'mɛntəˌlaɪz] *v.* **-ized, -iz•ing. 1** divide into departments. **2** arrange, classify, or restrict as if in departments. **—ˌde•partˌmen•ta•li'za•tion,** *n.*

department store a store that is organized into departments where many different kinds of merchandise and services are sold.

de•par•ture [dɪ'pɑrtʃər] *n.* **1** the act of going away; the act of leaving. **2** a turning away; change: *a departure from our old custom.* **3** a starting on a new course of action or thought. **4** death. **5** *Nautical.* the distance travelled east or west from a starting point.

de•pend [dɪ'pɛnd] *v.* **1** rely; trust: *You can depend on this timetable from the depot.* **2** be dependent; rely for needed help or support: *Children depend on their parents.* **3** be a result of; be controlled or influenced by: *The success of our picnic depends partly on the weather.* **4** hang down.
that depends or **it depends,** the answer will be determined by certain conditions or actions that are not yet definitely known or understood: *"That depends," answered the cook.* ⟨ME < OF *dependre* < L *dependere* < *de-* from + *pendere* hang⟩ **—de'pend•er,** *n.*
☛ *Syn.* **1, 2.** See note at RELY.

de•pend•a•bil•i•ty [dɪˌpɛndə'bɪləti] *n.* reliability; trustworthiness.

de•pend•a•ble [dɪ'pɛndəbəl] *adj.* reliable; trustworthy. **—de'pend•a•ble•ness,** *n.* **—de'pend•a•bly,** *adv.*

de•pend•ant [dɪ'pɛndənt] *n., adj. —n.* a person who depends on someone else for support: *He has a younger brother living with him as a dependant.*
—adj. Rare. See DEPENDENT.
☛ *Usage.* See note at DEPENDENT.

de•pend•ence [dɪ'pɛndəns] *n.* **1** reliance on another for support or help. **2** reliance; trust. **3** the condition of being a result of another thing; the fact of being controlled or influenced by something else: *the dependence of crops on the weather.* Also, **dependance.**

de•pend•en•cy [dɪ'pɛndənsi] *n., pl.* **-cies. 1** a country or territory controlled by another country: *Gibraltar is a dependency of the United Kingdom.* **2** dependence. **3** a thing that depends on another for existence or help. **4** addiction, as to drugs, alcohol, etc. Also, **dependancy.**

de•pend•ent [dɪ'pɛndənt] *adj., n. —adj.* **1** relying on another for support or help: *A child is dependent on its parents.* **2** resulting from another thing; controlled or influenced by something else: *Good crops are dependent on the right kind of weather.* **3** addicted, as to drugs, alcohol, etc. **4** hanging down. **5** *Grammar.* subordinate: *a dependent clause.*
—n. See DEPENDANT. **—de'pend•ent•ly,** *adv.*
☛ *Usage.* DEPENDANT, **dependent.** Although some people use these two forms interchangeably, most writers use *dependant* for the noun and *dependent* for the adjective.

dependent clause *Grammar.* a clause in a complex sentence that cannot act alone as a sentence; subordinate clause. In "If I go home, my dog will follow me," *If I go home* is a dependent clause.

dependent variable *Mathematics.* in a statement, a variable whose value depends on the value assigned to the independent variable. *Example*: in $y = fx$, y is the dependent variable.

de•per•son•al•ize [di'pɜrsənəˌlaɪz] *v.* **-ized, -iz•ing. 1** take away subjective or personal elements from; make impersonal: *Too much bureaucracy depersonalizes the relationship between government and the people. The song tells of his own experience, but the experience has been depersonalized.* **2** deprive (someone) of individuality; treat as a thing or as merely a member of a class. **—deˌper•son•al•i'za•tion,** *n.*

de•pict [dɪ'pɪkt] *v.* **1** represent by drawing, painting, or carving; picture. **2** describe in words: Who Has Seen the Wind *depicts life on the Prairies during the Depression.* ⟨< L *depictus*, pp. of *depingere* < *de-* + *pingere* paint⟩ **—de'pict•er,** *n.*

de•pic•tion [dɪ'pɪkʃən] *n.* **1** the act or process of depicting. **2** a picture, sculpture, description, etc.

dep•i•late ['dɛpəˌleit] *v.* **-lat•ed, -lat•ing.** remove hair from. ⟨< L *depilare* < *de-* from + *pilus* hair⟩ **—ˌdep•i'la•tion,** *n.* **—'dep•iˌla•tor,** *n.*

de•pil•a•to•ry [dɪ'pɪləˌtɔri] *adj., n.* **-ries.** *—adj.* capable of removing hair.
—n. a paste, liquid, or other preparation for removing hair.

de•plane [di'plein] *v.* **-planed, -plan•ing.** leave an airplane: *It was raining when we deplaned at Dorval Airport.*

de•plete [dɪ'plit] *v.* **-plet•ed, -plet•ing.** empty; exhaust: *The traveller went home because her funds were depleted.* ⟨< L *depletus*, pp. of *deplere* empty < *de-* + *-plere* fill⟩

de•ple•tion [dɪ'pliʃən] *n.* **1** a depleting. **2** the state of being depleted.

de•plor•a•ble [dɪ'plɔrəbəl] *adj.* **1** to be deplored; regrettable; lamentable: *a deplorable accident.* **2** wretched; miserable. **—de'plor•a•ble•ness,** *n.* **—de'plor•a•bly,** *adv.*

de•plore [dɪ'plɔr] *v.* **-plored, -plor•ing. 1** be very sorry about; regret deeply; lament. **2** treat as miserable or wretched. **3** censure; disapprove of: *I deplore your behaviour last night.* ⟨< L *deplorare* < *de-* (intensive) + *plorare* weep⟩

de•ploy [dɪ'plɔɪ] *v.* **1** spread out (troops, military units, etc.) from a column into a long battle line. **2** distribute (personnel, resources, etc.) in convenient positions for future use. **3** use: *to deploy one's talents to the best advantage.* ⟨< F *déployer* < *dé-* + *ployer* < L *plicare* fold⟩ **—de'ploy•ment,** *n.*

de•po•lar•ize [di'pouləˌraɪz] *v.* **-ized, -iz•ing.** destroy or neutralize the polarity or polarization of. **—deˌpo•lar•i'za•tion,** *n.* **—de'po•larˌi•zer,** *n.*

de•pone [dɪ'poun] *v.* **-poned, -pon•ing.** testify in writing under oath. ⟨< L *deponere* put down (in Med.L, testify) < *de-* down + *ponere* put⟩

de•po•nent [dɪ'pounənt] *n., adj. —n.* **1** a person who testifies, especially in writing, under oath. **2** *Greek and Latin grammar.* a verb passive in form but active in meaning, such as *sequi.*
—adj. having passive form but active meaning. ⟨< L *deponens, -entis*, ppr. of *deponere* < *de-* away, down + *ponere* put⟩

de•pop•u•late [di'pɒpjəˌleit] *v.* **-lat•ed, -lat•ing.** deprive of inhabitants: *The conquerors depopulated the enemy's country, driving the inhabitants away or killing them.* **—de'pop•uˌla•tor,** *n.*

de•pop•u•la•tion [diˌpɒpjə'leiʃən] *n.* depopulating or being depopulated.

de•port [dɪ'pɔrt] *v.* **1** banish; expel; remove. When an alien is deported, he or she is sent out of the country, usually back to his or her native land. **2** behave or conduct (oneself) in a particular manner: *The boys were trained to deport themselves like gentlemen.* ⟨< F *déporter* < L *deportare* < *de-* away + *portare* carry⟩ **—de'port•er,** *n.*
☛ *Syn.* **1.** See note at BANISH.

de•port•a•ble [dɪ'pɔrtəbəl] *adj.* **1** liable to expulsion. **2** punishable by banishment.

de•por•ta•tion [ˌdipɔr'teiʃən] *n.* banishment; expulsion, removal: *Deportation of criminals from Britain to Australia was once common.*

de•por•tee [ˌdipɔr'ti] *or* [dɪpɔr'ti] *n.* a person who is or has been deported.

de•port•ment [dɪ'pɔrtmənt] *n.* **1** the way a person acts; behaviour; conduct: *A gentleman is known by his deportment.* **2** good bearing; graceful movement: *Young ladies once took lessons in deportment as a part of their regular studies.*

de•pos•al [dɪ'pouzəl] *n.* **1** deposing. **2** deposition.

de•pose [dɪ'pouz] *v.* **-posed, -pos•ing. 1** put out of office or a position of authority: *The queen was deposed by the revolution.* **2** *Law.* declare under oath, especially when making a statement for later use as evidence in court; testify: *She deposed that she had seen the prisoner on the day of the murder.* ⟨ME < OF *deposer* < *de-* down (< L) + *poser* put. See POSE[1].⟩ **—de'pos•able,** *adj.* **—de'pos•er,** *n.*

de•pos•it [dɪ'pɒzɪt] *v., n. —v.* **1** put down; lay down; leave lying: *The flood deposited a layer of mud in the streets.* **2** put in a place for safekeeping: *People deposit money in banks.* **3** pay as a pledge to do something or to pay more later. If you deposit part

of the price, most stores will keep an article for you until you can pay the rest.
—*n.* **1** the material laid down or left lying by natural means: *a deposit of mud and sand at the mouth of a river.* **2** something put in a place for safekeeping: *Money put in a bank is a deposit.* **3** a sum of money paid as a pledge or security: *In the election, one of the candidates lost her deposit.* **4** the act of depositing. **5** a mass of some mineral in rock or in the ground.
on deposit, a in a place for safekeeping. **b** in a bank. ⟨< L *depositus*, pp. of *deponere* < *de-* away + *ponere* put⟩

de•pos•i•tar•y [dɪ'pɒzə,tɛri] *n., pl.* **-aries. 1** a person or company that receives something for safekeeping; trustee. **2** depository; storehouse.

dep•o•si•tion [,dɛpə'zɪʃən] *or* [,dipə'zɪʃən] *n.* **1** the act of putting out of office or a position of authority. **2** *Law.* **a** the act of testifying under oath. **b** testimony given under oath; especially, such testimony taken down in writing to be used as evidence later in court: *The witness made a deposition because she was not able to testify in court.* **3** the act or process of depositing: *the deposition of sediment at the mouth of a river.* **4** something deposited; deposit.

de•pos•i•tor [dɪ'pɒzətər] *n.* a person who deposits, especially one who deposits money in a bank.

de•pos•i•to•ry [dɪ'pɒzə,tɔri] *n., pl.* **-ries. 1** a place where a thing is put for safekeeping or storage; storehouse. **2** depositary; trustee.

dep•ot ['dipou] *or* ['dɛpou] *n.* **1** a bus or railway station. **2** a storehouse, especially for military supplies. **3** a military recruiting and distribution centre. ⟨< F *dépôt* < L *depositum* < *deponere.* See DEPOSIT.⟩

de•prave [dɪ'preiv] *v.* **-praved, -prav•ing.** pervert; make bad; corrupt: *Too much liquor often depraves a person's character.* ⟨ME < L *depravare* < *de-* + *pravus* crooked, wrong⟩
—,de•pra'va•tion, *n.* **—de'prav•er,** *n.*

de•praved [dɪ'preivd] *adj., v.* —*adj.* corrupt; perverted.
—*v.* pt. and pp. of DEPRAVE.
☛ *Syn.* See note at CORRUPT.

de•prav•i•ty [dɪ'prævəti] *n., pl.* **-ties. 1** wickedness; corruption. **2** a corrupt act; bad practice.

dep•re•cate ['dɛprə,keit] *v.* **-cat•ed, -cat•ing. 1** express strong disapproval of; plead against; protest against: *Lovers of peace deprecate war.* **2** belittle. ⟨< LL *deprecari* plead in excuse, avert by prayer < *de-* + *precari* pray⟩ **—'dep•re,cat•ing•ly,** *adv.*
—'dep•re,ca•tor, *n.*
☛ *Usage.* **Deprecate,** DEPRECIATE. Do not confuse **deprecate** = express strong disapproval of, with **depreciate** =lessen in value or price: *I feel I must deprecate the course the club is following. Naturally a car depreciates after a number of years of service.*

dep•re•ca•tion [,dɛprə'keiʃən] *n.* a strong expression of disapproval; a pleading or protesting against something.

dep•re•ca•to•ry ['dɛprəkə,tɔri] *adj.* **1** deprecating. **2** *Informal.* apologetic.

de•pre•ci•a•ble [dɪ'priʃiəbəl] *or* [dɪ'priʃəbəl] *adj.* that can be lessened in value.

de•pre•ci•ate [dɪ'priʃi,eit] *v.* **-at•ed, -at•ing. 1** lessen the value or price of. **2** lessen in value: *Certain goods depreciate if they are kept very long.* **3** speak slightingly of; belittle: *She depreciates the value of exercise.* ⟨< L *depretiare* < *de-* + *pretium* price⟩ **—de'pre•ci,at•ing•ly,** *adv.* **—de'pre•ci,a•tor,** *n.*
☛ *Usage.* See note at DEPRECATE.

de•pre•ci•a•tion [dɪ,priʃi'eiʃən] *n.* **1** a lessening or lowering in value: *Machinery undergoes depreciation as it is used or becomes obsolete.* **2** the amount of such loss of value, or the allowance made for it in accounting. **3** a reduction in the value of money. **4** a speaking slightingly of; a belittling.

de•pre•ci•a•to•ry [dɪ'priʃə,tɔri] *adj.* tending to depreciate, disparage, or undervalue.

dep•re•da•tion [,dɛprə'deiʃən] *n.* the act or an instance of plundering; robbery; a ravaging. ⟨< L *depraedatio, -onis* < *depraedare* pillage < *de-* + *praeda* booty⟩

de•press [dɪ'prɛs] *v.* **1** make sad or gloomy; cause to have low spirits: *She was depressed by the bad news from home.* **2** press down; push down; lower: *depress the keys of a piano.* **3** lower in amount or value. **4** reduce the activity of; weaken: *Some medicines depress the action of the heart.* **5** *Music.* lower the pitch of. ⟨< OF *depresser* < L *depressus*, pp. of *deprimere* < *de-* + *premere* press⟩ **—de'press•ing•ly,** *adv.*

de•pres•sant [dɪ'prɛsənt] *adj., n.* —*adj.* decreasing the rate of vital activities; quieting.
—*n.* a substance that lessens pain or excitement or that decreases the rate of vital activities; sedative or tranquillizer.

de•pressed [dɪ'prɛst] *adj., v.* —*adj.* **1** gloomy; low-spirited; sad. **2** *Psychiatry.* affected by clinical depression. **3** pressed down; lowered. **4** of a place, poor and underprivileged; having little employment or good housing: *a depressed area.* **5** *Botany. Zoology.* flattened down; broader than it is high.
—*v.* pt. and pp. of DEPRESS.
☛ *Syn.* **1.** See note at SAD.

depressed area a region characterized by unemployment, poverty, etc.

de•pres•sion [dɪ'prɛʃən] *n.* **1** the state of feeling sad or gloomy; low spirits. **2** *Psychiatry.* a long-term clinical condition in which a person has continual feelings of sadness or hopelessness not directly caused by real events. **3** the action of pressing down: *Depression of the gas pedal causes an automobile to accelerate.* **4** a lowering of amount, force, activity, or quality: *A rapid depression of the mercury in a barometer usually indicates a storm.* **5** a low place or part; hollow: *Depressions in the lawn were filled with water after the rain.* **6** a period of low economic activity, accompanied by high levels of unemployment. **7 the Depression,** the severe economic depression of the 1930s. **8** *Meteorology.* an area of low barometric pressure; low. **9** *Astronomy.* the angular distance of a celestial body below the horizon.

de•press•ive [dɪ'prɛsɪv] *adj., n.* —*adj.* tending to produce or characterized by depression: *He's in a depressive mood again.*
—*n.* a person who often feels depressed for no reason; a person affected by clinical depression.

de•pres•so•mo•tor [dɪ,prɛsou'moutər] *adj.* of a drug or substance that inhibits muscle movement.

de•press•or [dɪ'prɛsər] *n.* **1** a person or thing that depresses. **2** a muscle that pulls down a part. Compare LEVATOR. **3** an instrument for pressing down some part or organ: *a tongue depressor.*

de•priv•al [dɪ'praɪvəl] *n.* deprivation.

dep•ri•va•tion [,dɛprə'veiʃən] *n.* **1** the act of depriving. **2** the state of being deprived; loss; privation. Also, **deprival.**
—,dep•ri'va•tion•al, *adj.*

de•prive [dɪ'praɪv] *v.* **-prived, -priv•ing. 1** take something away from by force: *The people deprived the cruel tyrant of his power.* **2** keep from having or doing something: *Worrying deprived her of sleep.* ⟨ME < OF *depriver* < *de-* (intensive) + *priver* deprive < L *privare*, originally, exempt⟩ **—de'priv•er,** *n.*

de•prived [dɪ'praɪvd] *adj., v.* —*adj.* suffering from or characterized by a lack of comfort, income, etc.; poor: *She had a deprived childhood.*
—*v.* pt. and pp. of DEPRIVE.

de pro•fun•dis [,di prou'fʌndɪs] *or* [,dei prou'fʊndɪs] *Latin.* from the depths (of sorrow, misery, despair, etc.).

de•pro•gram [di'prougræm] *v.* **-grammed, -gram•ming.** teach (someone) to cast off beliefs inculcated by brainwashing.

dept. 1 department. **2** deputy.

depth [dɛpθ] *n.* **1** the quality of being deep; deepness. **2** the distance from top to bottom: *the depth of a hole.* **3** the distance from front to back: *The depth of our house is 40 m.* **4** a deep place. **5** the deepest part: *in the depths of the earth.* **6** the most central part; middle: *in the depth of the forest.* **7** the middle of a period of time: *the depth of winter.* **8** intensity (of feelings, etc.). **9** profoundness: *A philosopher should have depth of mind.* **10** lowness of pitch. **11** intensity of colour, etc. **12** often, **depths,** *pl.* **a** most profound degree: *the depths of despair.* **b** low moral condition: *to sink to such depths.* **13** in painting, architecture, etc., perspective.
in depth, in a thorough or detailed manner: *to study a subject in depth.*
out of (one's) **depth, a** in water so deep that one cannot touch bottom. **b** in a situation too difficult to understand or cope with: *He was out of his depth in the mathematics class.* ⟨ME *depth(e)* < OE *dēop* deep⟩

depth bomb DEPTH CHARGE.

depth charge an explosive charge dropped from a ship or airplane and set to explode at a certain depth under water.

depth of field *Photography.* the range of space which is reproduced in clear detail in a photograph. It varies with the focal length and aperture size of the camera, and with the distance from the camera to the subject.

depth perception the capacity of an observer to perceive and estimate the distance between faraway objects, and the distance between the observer and those objects.

depth psychology any psychological approach which concerns the workings of the unconscious.

dep•u•ta•tion [ˌdɛpjəˈteiʃən] *n.* **1** the act of deputing. **2** a group of persons appointed to act for others.

de•pute [dɪˈpjut] *v.* **-put•ed, -put•ing. 1** appoint (someone) to do one's work or to act in one's place: *The teacher deputed a pupil to take charge of the room while she was gone.* **2** give (work, authority, etc.) to another. ⟨ME < OF < LL *deputare* assign < L *deputare* consider as < *de-* + *putare* think, count⟩

dep•u•tize [ˈdɛpjəˌtaɪz] *v.* **-tized, -tiz•ing. 1** appoint as deputy. **2** act as deputy. **—ˌdep•u•tiˈza•tion,** *n.*

dep•u•ty [ˈdɛpjəti] *n., pl.* **-ties. 1** a person appointed to do the work of or to act in the place of another: *A deputy minister is an assistant to a minister in the Cabinet and acts in the minister's place in case of absence.* **2** a representative to or in certain assemblies. In Québec, the members of the National Assembly are often called deputies. **3** (*adjl.*) acting as a deputy. ⟨< F *député*, originally pp. of *députer* < LL *deputare.* See DEPUTE.⟩

deputy minister in Canada, a senior civil servant who acts as assistant to or representative of a Cabinet minister in the federal or provincial Parliaments.

deputy returning officer in Canada, an official appointed by the returning officer of a constituency to look after the procedure of voting at a particular polling station: *The deputy returning officer is in charge of counting the ballots. Abbrev.*: DRO

de•qua•li•ni•um [ˌdɛkwəˈlɪniəm] *n.* an antiseptic drug used to treat mouth and throat infections.

der. 1 derivation; derivative; derived.

de•rac•i•nate [diˈræsəˌneit] *or* [dɪˈræsəˌneit] *v.* **-at•ed, -at•ing. 1** tear up by the roots. **2** displace from one's home or one's normal environment: *deracinated refugees.* ⟨< F *déraciner* < *dé-* from + *racine* root < LL *radicina* < L *radix, radicis* root⟩ **—deˌrac•iˈna•tion,** *n.*

de•rail [diˈreil] *or* [dɪˈreil] *v.* **1** cause (a train, etc.) to run off the rails. **2** run off the rails. **—deˈrail•ment,** *n.*

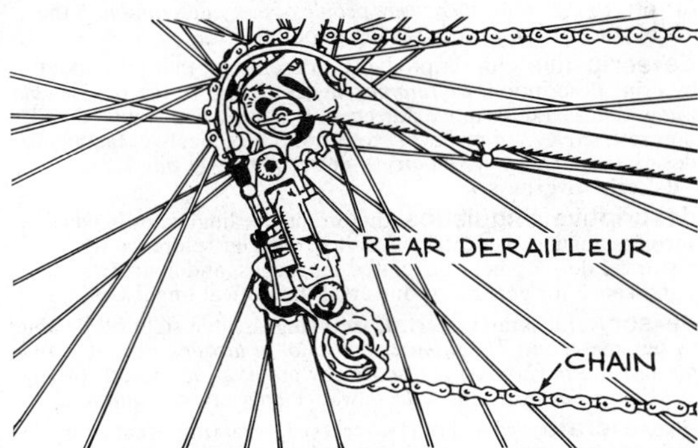

The rear hub of a bicycle showing the derailleur

de•rail•leur [dɪˈreilər] *n.* **1** a spring-driven mechanism on a bicycle that changes gears by causing the drive chain to move from one sprocket wheel to another. **2** a bicycle equipped with a derailleur. ⟨< F *dérailleur*⟩

de•range [dɪˈreindʒ] *v.* **-ranged, -rang•ing. 1** disturb the order or arrangement of; throw into confusion. **2** make insane. ⟨< F *déranger* < *dé-* away + *ranger* range⟩

de•range•ment [dɪˈreindʒmənt] *n.* **1** a disturbance of order or arrangement. **2** a mental disorder; insanity.

der•by [ˈdɜrbi]; *Esp. Brit.* [ˈdɑrbi] *for 1a. n., pl.* **-bies. 1 Derby, a** a famous horse race in England, founded by the Earl of Derby in 1780 and run every year at Epsom Downs, near London. **b** any of several annual horse races of similar importance: *the Kentucky Derby.* **2** any contest or race: *a fishing derby, a dog derby, a bicycle derby.* **3** a man's stiff hat having a rounded crown and narrow brim; bowler. See HAT for picture.

de•reg•u•late [diˈrɛgjəˌleit] *v.* **-lat•ed, -lat•ing.** remove restrictions from; decontrol: *to deregulate air fares.* **—deˌreg•uˈla•tion,** *n.*

der•e•lict [ˈdɛrəˌlɪkt] *adj., n. —adj.* **1** abandoned; deserted; forsaken: *a derelict ship.* **2** failing in one's duty; negligent.
—n. **1** a ship abandoned at sea. **2** any despised, deserted person or thing: *The unemployed alcoholic quickly became a derelict.* **3** land from which water has receded. ⟨< L *derelictus*, pp. of *derelinquere* abandon < *de-* (intensive) + *re-* behind + *linquere* leave⟩

der•e•lic•tion [ˌdɛrəˈlɪkʃən] *n.* **1** a failure in one's duty; negligence. **2** an abandonment; desertion; forsaking. **3** the gaining of land by the receding of water.

de•ride [dɪˈraɪd] *v.* **-rid•ed, -rid•ing.** make fun of; laugh at in scorn; ridicule with contempt. ⟨< L *deridere* < *de-* down + *ridere* laugh⟩ **—deˈrid•er,** *n.* **—deˈrid•ing•ly,** *adv.*
☛ *Syn.* See note at RIDICULE.

de ri•gueur [dəʀiˈgœʀ] *French.* required by etiquette; according to custom; proper.

de•ri•sion [dɪˈrɪʒən] *n.* **1** scornful laughter; ridicule; contempt. **2** an object of ridicule. ⟨< L *derisio, -onis* < *deridere.* See DERIDE.⟩

de•ri•sive [dɪˈrəisɪv] *adj.* **1** mocking; ridiculing. **2** ridiculous; inspiring derision. **—deˈri•sive•ly,** *adv.* **—deˈri•sive•ness,** *n.*

de•ri•so•ry [dɪˈrəisəri] *or* [dɪˈraɪzəri] *adj.* **1** derisive. **2** laughable; deserving contempt.

deriv. derivation; derivative; derived.

der•i•va•tion [ˌdɛrəˈveiʃən] *n.* **1** the act or process of deriving. **2** the state of being derived. **3** the source; origin: *The celebration of Halloween is of Scottish derivation. Many English words are of French derivation.* **4** the formation of a new word from an existing word or base, especially by the addition of an affix other than an inflectional ending. *Example*: *quickness = quick + -ness* (a suffix). **5** a statement of how a word was formed. **6** in generative grammar, the process of forming a sentence. **—ˌder•iˈva•tion•al,** *adj.*

de•riv•a•tive [dɪˈrɪvətɪv] *adj., n. —adj.* **1** derived; not original. **2** derivational; having to do with derivation.
—n. **1** something derived. Words formed by adding prefixes and suffixes, etc. to other words are called derivatives. **2** *Chemistry.* a substance obtained from another by modification or by partial substitution of components. **3** *Mathematics.* the rate of change of one quantity with respect to another. **—deˈriv•a•tive•ly,** *adv.*

de•rive [dɪˈraɪv] *v.* **-rived, -riv•ing. 1** receive or obtain from a particular source: *She derives a great pleasure from music. Gasoline is derived from petroleum.* **2** come from a source or origin; originate or develop: *Our word* table *derives from Latin* tabula. **3** make or create (new words) by adding suffixes or prefixes: *The words* kindness, kinder, *and* unkind *are derived from* kind. **4** trace the development or origin of (a custom, condition, word, etc.): *Scholars derive many modern English words from Old French. He derives all his present troubles from the loss of his job years ago.* **5** obtain by reasoning; deduce: *He derived his conclusion from the large amount of data he had collected.* **6** obtain (a chemical compound) from another by substituting a different element. ⟨< MF < LL *derivare* lead off, draw off < L *de-* from + *rivus* stream⟩ **—deˈriv•a•ble,** *adj.* **—deˈriv•er,** *n.*

derived word a word formed by adding one or more prefixes or suffixes to an existing word or root.

der•ma [ˈdɜrmə] *n.* dermis.

der•ma•bra•sion [ˌdɜrməˈbreiʒən] *n.* the use of a rotating brush or sandpaper on skin to remove acne scars or other blemishes.

der•mal [ˈdɜrməl] *adj.* of the skin.

der•ma•ti•tis [ˌdɜrməˈtəitɪs] *n.* inflammation of the skin.

der•ma•to– *combining form.* skin. Also, **dermat-, dermo-, derm-.**

der•ma•to•glyph•ics [ˌdɜrmətouˈglɪfɪks] *n.* the pattern of lines on the fingers and palm of the hand or the toes and sole of the foot, used in medical diagnosis. ⟨< Gk. *derma, dermatos* skin + *glyphe* a carving < *glyphein* to carve, cut⟩

der•ma•to•log•i•cal [ˌdɜrmətəˈlɒdʒəkəl] *adj.* of or having to do with dermatology.

der•ma•tol•o•gist [ˌdɜrməˈtɒlədʒɪst] *n.* a person trained in dermatology, especially one whose work it is.

der•ma•tol•o•gy [ˌdɛrməˈtɒlədʒi] *n.* the science that deals with the skin and its diseases.

der•ma•to•phyte [dərˈmætəˌfəit] *or* [ˈdɜrmətouˌfəit] *n.* a fungal parasite found on the skin, such as the fungus which causes ringworm. ⟨< Gk. *derma, dermatos* skin + *phyton* a plant⟩

der•ma•to•plas•ty [ˌdɜrmətouˈplæsti] *or* [dərˈmætouˌplæsti] *n.* skin grafts used for plastic surgery of the skin. ⟨< Gk. *derma, dermatos* skin + *-plastia* formed < *plassein* to form⟩

der•ma•to•sis [ˌdɜrmə'tousɪs] *n.* any skin disease. ⟨< Gk. *derma, -atos* skin + E *-osis*⟩

der•mis ['dɜrmɪs] *n.* **1** the sensitive layer of skin beneath the epidermis. See EPIDERMIS for picture. **2** the skin. ⟨< Gk. *derma* skin⟩

der•moid ['dɜrmɔɪd] *adj.* of certain benign tumours, composed of material such as hair, skin, and teeth. ⟨< Gk. *derma* skin + *-oid*⟩

der•nier cri [ˌdɛrnjei 'kri]; *French,* [dɛrnje'kʀi] the latest word in fashion. ⟨< F last cry⟩

der•o•gate ['dɛrəˌgeit] *v.* **-gat•ed, -gat•ing. 1** take away; detract: *The king felt that summoning a parliament would derogate from his authority.* **2** become worse; degenerate; deviate from a norm or standard (*used with* **from**). ⟨< L *derogare* < *de-* down from + *rogare* ask⟩

der•o•ga•tion [ˌdɛrə'geiʃən] *n.* **1** a lessening or impairment (of power, law, position, etc.); detraction. **2** the act or state of becoming worse; deterioration; debasement.

de•rog•a•tive [dɪ'rɒgətɪv] *adj.* derogatory. **—de'rog•a•tive•ly,** *adv.*

de•rog•a•to•ry [dɪ'rɒgəˌtɔri] *adj.* **1** disparaging; belittling; showing an unfavourable opinion of some person or thing: *The word* skinny *has a derogatory connotation, but* slender *does not.* **2** lessening the value; detracting. **—de'rog•aˌto•ri•ly,** *adv.*

der•rick ['dɛrɪk] *n.* **1** a machine for lifting and moving heavy objects. A derrick has a long arm that swings at an angle from the base of an upright post or frame. **2** a towerlike framework over an oil well, gas well, etc., which holds the drilling and hoisting machinery. ⟨after *Derrick,* a 17c. hangman at Tyburn in London, England⟩

der•ri•ère or **der•ri•ere** [ˌdɛri'ɛr] *n.* buttocks. ⟨< F, lit. behind⟩

der•ring–do ['dɛrɪŋ 'du] *n. Archaic.* heroic daring; daring deeds. ⟨alteration of ME *dorryng don* daring to do⟩

der•ris ['dɛrɪs] *n.* any of a genus (*Derris*) of tropical woody climbing plants of the pea family, including some species whose roots yield the compound rotenone, used as an insecticide and fish poison. ⟨< NL < Gk. *derris* leather cover⟩

der•vish ['dɜrvɪʃ] *n.* a member of any of several Muslim religious orders dedicated to a life of poverty and chastity. The dervishes of some orders practise religious rites that include whirling, dancing, etc. ⟨< Turkish *dervīsh* < Persian *darvīsh* beggar⟩

DES diethylstilbestrol, a hormone formerly given to pregnant women to prevent miscarriage, but now associated with cancer in the daughters of those women.

de•sal•i•nate [di'sæləˌneit] *v.* **-nat•ed, -nat•ing.** remove salt from, especially from seawater. **—deˌsal•i'na•tion,** *n.*

de•salt [di'sɒlt] *v.* remove salt from: *to desalt seawater.* **—de'salt•er,** *n.*

des•cant *n.* ['dɛskænt]; *v.* [dɛs'kænt] *n., v.* *—n.* **1** *Music.* **a** a separate melody or counterpoint sung above the basic melody. **b** the highest part or melody in harmonic music; soprano or treble. **2** any song or melody. **3** an extended comment; discourse. **4** (*adjl.*) playing high notes: *a descant recorder.*
—v. **1** talk at great length; discourse freely: *to descant upon the wonders of nature.* **2** *Music.* sing or play a descant. ⟨ME < OF *deschanter* < Med.L *discantare* < L *dis-* away + *cantus* song < *canere* sing⟩

de•scend [dɪ'sɛnd] *v.* **1** go or come down from a higher place to a lower place: *The river descends to the sea.* **2** pass from an earlier to a later time: *We still have many superstitions descended from the Middle Ages.* **3** go in sequence from greater to smaller, or higher to lower: *The numerals* 100, 75, 50, 25 *form a series arranged in descending order.* **4** extend or slope downward: *The road descended in a winding path to the sea.* **5** make a sudden appearance or attack (*used with* **on** or **upon**): *Many tourists descended upon the town during the exhibition.* **6** be handed down from parent to child; pass by inheritance: *The land has descended in the family for 150 years.* **7** come down from a source, especially an ancestor (*usually used in the passive*): *Melanie is descended from a pioneer family.* **8** lower oneself; stoop: *She descended to cheating in an effort to win the scholarship.* **9** *Music.* go down note by note: *to descend the scale; a descending minor third.* **10** *Astronomy.* travel, or seem to travel, in the direction of the horizon. ⟨ME < OF < L *descendere* < *de-* down + *scandere* climb⟩

de•scend•ant [dɪ'sɛndənt] *n., adj.* *—n.* **1** a person tracing his or her parentage to a certain individual family, or group: *a descendant of the United Empire Loyalists; a descendant of the great Chief Dan George.* **2** something derived from an earlier form: *Grand opera is the descendant of opéra bouffe.*
—adj. descending; going or coming down.

de•scend•ent [dɪ'sɛndənt] *adj.* descending.

de•scend•er [dɪ'sɛndər] *n.* that part of a written or printed letter, such as p or g, that goes below the line. Compare ASCENDER.

de•scent [dɪ'sɛnt] *n.* **1** the act or process of coming down or going down from a higher to a lower place: *the balloon made a rapid descent.* **2** a downward slope: *the sharp descent of the ground to the sea.* **3** a way or passage down; a means of descending: *We took the steep descent carefully.* **4** a family line; ancestry: *Our family is of Turkish descent. They can trace their descent back to the 18th century.* **5** a transmitting or handing down of property, qualities, etc., from parent to child; transmission through inheritance: *The estate was acquired by descent. We can trace the descent of red hair in our family through five generations.* **6** one generation. **7** a sinking to a lower condition or quality; a decline: *a descent to bigotry and racism.* **8** a sudden attack or unexpected appearance: *The descent of the invaders on the town led to the slaughter of many people.* **9** a group of woodpeckers. ⟨ME < OF *descente* < *descendre* < L *descendere.* See DESCEND.⟩
☛ *Hom.* DISSENT.

de•scram•ble [di'skræmbəl] *v.* **-bled, -bling.** restore (a signal) to an intelligible state, such as in cable television. **—de'scram•bler,** *n.*

de•scribe [dɪ'skraɪb] *v.* **-scribed, -scrib•ing. 1** tell or write about: *The reporter described the accident in detail.* **2** give a picture of in words, music, etc. **3** draw the outline of; trace: *The skater described a figure 8.* ⟨< L *describere* < *de-* from + *scribere* write⟩ **—de'scrib•a•ble,** *adj.* **—de'scrib•er,** *n.*

de•scrip•tion [dɪ'skrɪpʃən] *n.* **1** the act of describing; the act of giving a picture or account in words. **2** a composition or account that describes. **3** a picture in words, music, etc. **4** a kind or sort: *In the crowd there were people of every description.* **5** the act of tracing; the act of drawing in outline.

de•scrip•tive [dɪ'skrɪptɪv] *adj.* **1** describing; that tells about by using description. **2** *Grammar.* **a** describing. In the phrase *cold water, cold* is a descriptive adjective. **b** adding descriptive detail; non-restrictive. **3** of or having to do with an objective, factual description: *descriptive biology.* **—de'scrip•tive•ly,** *adv.* **—de'scrip•tive•ness,** *n.*

descriptive linguistics that branch of linguistics in which a specific language is described as it is, without reference to historical development or related languages, and apart from its significance for general or universal theoretical linguistics.

de•scry [dɪ'skraɪ] *v.* **-scried, -scry•ing. 1** catch sight of; be able to see; make out: *The shipwrecked sailor at last descried an island far away on the horizon.* **2** discover by observation; detect. ⟨ME < MF *descrier* proclaim < *des-* away + *crier* cry < L *quiritare*⟩

des•e•crate ['dɛsəˌkreit] *v.* **-crat•ed, -crat•ing.** treat or use without respect; disregard the sacredness of: *The enemy desecrated the church by using it as a stable.* ⟨< *de-* (do the opposite of) + *(con)secrate*⟩ **—'des•eˌcrat•er** or **'des•eˌcrat•or,** *n.*

des•e•cra•tion [ˌdɛsə'kreiʃən] *n.* **1** the act of desecrating: *The Puritans thought that work or amusement on Sundays was a desecration of the Sabbath.* **2** the fact or state of being desecrated.

de•seg•re•gate [di'sɛgrəˌgeit] *v.* **-gat•ed, -gat•ing.** abolish any law or practice in (a place) that requires the members of a particular race or particular races to be isolated for any purpose from the rest of the population: *to desegregate the schools.*

de•seg•re•ga•tion [diˌsɛgrə'geiʃən] *n.* **1** the act or process of desegregating. **2** the state of being desegregated.

de•sen•si•tize [di'sɛnsəˌtaɪz] *v.* **-tized, -tiz•ing. 1** make less sensitive. **2** *Photography.* make less sensitive to light. **3** *Medicine.* make (someone) no longer allergic to a substance. **—deˌsen•si•ti'za•tion,** *n.* **—de'sen•siˌtiz•er,** *n.*

des•er•pi•dine [dɛ'sɜrpəˌdin] *n.* a drug used to treat high blood pressure.

des•ert[1] ['dɛzərt] *n.* **1** a dry, barren region, usually sandy and without trees. **2** (*adjl.*) dry; barren. **3** a region that is not inhabited or cultivated; wilderness. **4** (*adjl.*) not inhabited or cultivated; wild: *Robinson Crusoe was shipwrecked on a desert island.* **5** a place or environment that provides no stimulus to the intellect or imagination. ⟨ME < OF < LL *desertum* (thing) abandoned, pp. neut. of *deserere.* See DESERT[2].⟩
☛ *Syn.* **1, 3. Desert,** WILDERNESS = an uninhabited or uncultivated region. **Desert** emphasizes dryness and barrenness and applies to a region

that is usually sandy and without water, trees, or inhabitants: *Great sections of desert in Arizona and California have been turned into rich agricultural areas by irrigation.* **Wilderness** emphasizes lack of trails and roads and applies particularly to a region where few people have ever been and that is covered with dense vegetation: *Large areas in northern Ontario are wilderness.*

de•sert² [dɪ'zɜrt] *v.* **1** go away and leave; abandon; forsake: *The man was guilty of deserting his family.* **2** run away from (duty, one's post, etc.). **3** leave military service without permission and with no intention of returning: *The soldier who had deserted was caught and court-martialled.* **4** fail; leave: *The boy's courage deserted him when he met the angry dog.* ⟨< F < LL *desertare* < L *deserere* abandon < *de-* dis- + *serere* join⟩ **—de'sert•er,** *n.*

☛ *Hom.* DESERT³, DESSERT.

☛ *Syn.* **1. Desert,** FORSAKE, ABANDON = leave someone or something completely. **Desert** emphasizes breaking a promise, oath, etc., or running away from a duty, and therefore implies blame: *He deserted his country and helped the enemy.* **Forsake** emphasizes breaking off sentimental attachments and thus has emotional connotations, but does not necessarily suggest blame: *She forsook the country village for a career in banking.* **Abandon** emphasizes that the action is final and complete, though it may be voluntary or involuntary, necessary or resulting from a desire to avoid duty: *They abandoned the wrecked plane.*

de•sert³ [dɪ'zɜrt] *n.* **1** Usually, **deserts,** *pl.* what is deserved; a suitable reward or punishment: *The robber got his just deserts when he was sentenced to five years in prison.* **2** the fact of meriting reward; a deserving: *This privilege is not of our own desert.* ⟨ME < OF *deserte,* pp. of *deservir* < L *deservire.* See DESERVE.⟩

☛ *Hom.* DESERT², DESSERT.

de•sert•i•fi•ca•tion [dɪ,zɜrtəfə'keiʃən] *n.* the deterioration of arid land into desert, caused by a change in climate or by overuse by people and animals.

de•ser•tion [dɪ'zɜrʃən] *n.* **1** deserting or being deserted. **2** *Law.* a deliberate abandoning of one's husband or wife and of the related moral and legal obligations. **3** a running away from duty. **4** the leaving of military service without permission.

de•serve [dɪ'zɜrv] *v.* **-served, -serv•ing. 1** have a claim or right to; be worthy of: *Good work deserves good pay.* **2** be worthy: *She deserves well.* ⟨ME < OF < L *deservire* serve well < *de-* (intensive) + *servire* serve⟩ **—de'serv•er,** *n.*

de•serv•ed•ly [dɪ'zɜrvɪdli] *adv.* according to what is deserved; justly; rightly: *deservedly punished.*

de•serv•ing [dɪ'zɜrvɪŋ] *adj., v.* —*adj.* **1** that deserves; worthy (*of* something). **2** good; having merit of some kind.
—*v.* ppr. of DESERVE. **—de'serv•ing•ly,** *adv.*

de•sex [di'sɛks] *v.* **1** remove the sex organs of. **2** lessen the sexual characteristics of. Also, **desexualize.**

des•ha•bille [,dɛzə'bil] *or* [deizɑ'bi]; *French,* **déshabillé** [dezabi'je] *n.* dishabille.

des•ic•cant ['dɛsəkənt] *n., adj.* —*n.* an agent or drug that dries or dessicates.
—*adj.* drying or desiccating.

des•ic•cate ['dɛsə,keit] *v.* **-cat•ed, -cat•ing. 1** dry thoroughly; make dry. **2** preserve by drying thoroughly, as raisins or coconut. **3** make or become intellectually or emotionally dry. ⟨< L *desiccare* < *de-* out + *siccus* dry⟩ **—,des•ic'ca•tion,** *n.*
—'des•ic,ca•tor, *n.*

☛ *Usage.* **Desiccate.** Because desiccated foods have often been cut into small pieces, people sometimes erroneously suppose that *desiccate* means 'cut up or shred'.

de•sid•er•a•ta [dɪ,sɪdə'rætə], [dɪ,sɪdə'reitə], *or* [dɪ,zɪdə'rætə] *n.* pl. of DESIDERATUM.

de•sid•er•a•tive [dɪ'sɪdərətɪv] *or* [dɪ'sɪdə,reitɪv] *adj., n.* —*adj.* expressing, implying, or having desire.
—*n. Grammar.* that which expresses the desire to perform the action signified by another verb from which it is derived.

de•sid•er•a•tum [dɪ,sɪdə'rætəm], [dɪ,sɪdə'reitəm], *or* [dɪ,zɪdə'rætəm] *n., pl.* **-ta.** [-tə]. something desired or needed: *Her consent is a desideratum.* ⟨< L *desideratum,* pp. neut. of *desiderare* long for⟩

de•sign [dɪ'zaɪn] *n., v.* —*n.* **1** a drawing, plan, or sketch made to serve as a pattern from which to work: *a design for a machine, a dress design.* **2** in painting, weaving, building, etc., an arrangement of detail, form, and colour: *a wallpaper design in tan and brown.* **3** the art of making designs, patterns, or sketches: *Architects are skilled in design.* **4** a non-representational piece of artistic work. **5** a plan in mind to be carried out; purpose, aim, or intention. **6** a scheme of attack; evil plan: *The thief had designs upon the safe.* **7** the underlying plan or conception; organization of parts in relation to the whole and to its purpose: *the evidence of design in a communication satellite, unity of design in a novel.*
by design, on purpose; intentionally: *Whether by accident or by design, he knocked over the lamp.*

—*v.* **1** make a first sketch of; plan out; arrange the form and colour of; draw in outline: *to design a dress.* **2** make drawings, sketches, plans, etc.: *He designs for a firm of dressmakers.* **3** plan out; form in the mind; contrive: *The author designed an exciting plot.* **4** make so as to suit a given purpose, user, etc.; intend: *a kitchen designed for disabled persons. That stand is not designed to support such heavy music books.* **5** have in mind to do; purpose: *Did you design this, or did it just happen?* **6** *Archaic.* set apart; intend: *His parents designed him for the ministry.* ⟨< MF *desseign,* n., and F *désigner,* v., both < earlier *desseigner* < L *designare* < *de-* (intensive) + *signum* mark⟩

☛ *Syn. n.* **5.** See note at PLAN. **7.** See note at INTENTION.

des•ig•nate *v.* ['dɛzɪg,neit]; *adj.* ['dɛzɪgnɪt] *or* ['dɛzɪg,neit] *v.* **-nat•ed, -nat•ing;** *adj.* —*v.* **1** mark out; point out; indicate definitely: *Red lines designate main roads on this map. His uniform designates his rank.* **2** name; entitle: *The ruler of the country was designated king.* **3** select for duty, office, etc.; appoint: *That is the woman designated as the new Governor General.*
—*adj.* appointed; selected. ⟨< L *designare.* See DESIGN.⟩
—'des•ig,na•tor, *n.*

des•ig•nat•ed ['dɛzɪg,neitɪd] *adj., v.* —*adj.* specially chosen: *a designated driver, the designated hitter, designated imports.*
—*v.* pt. and pp. of DESIGNATE.

des•ig•na•tion [,dɛzɪg'neiʃən] *n.* **1** the act of marking out; the act of pointing out; a definite indication: *The designation of places on a map should be clear.* **2** a descriptive title; name: Your Majesty *is a designation given to the Queen.* **3** the appointment or selection for a duty, office, position, etc.: *The designation of Cabinet officers is one of the powers of the prime minister.*

de•sign•ed•ly [dɪ'zaɪnɪdli] *adv.* purposely; intentionally.

des•ig•nee [,dɛzɪg'ni] *n.* one who is designated.

de•sign•er [dɪ'zaɪnər] *n.* **1** a person who designs: *The dress designer completed his patterns and sketches for his spring showing of women's clothes.* **2** plotter; schemer. **3** (*adjl.*) designed by and named after a prestigious couturier: *designer jeans.*

de•sign•ing [dɪ'zaɪnɪŋ] *adj., n., v.* —*adj.* **1** that designs. **2** scheming; plotting: *a designing rogue.* **3** showing plan or forethought.
—*n.* the art of making designs, patterns, sketches, etc.: *She studies dress designing at school.*
—*v.* ppr. of DESIGN. **—de'sign•ing•ly,** *adv.*

de•si•pra•mine [dɛ'zɪprə,min] *n.* a drug used to treat depression. *Formula:* $C_{18}H_{22}N_2$

de•sir•a•bil•i•ty [dɪ,zaɪrə'bɪləti] *n.* the state or quality of being desirable.

de•sir•a•ble [dɪ'zaɪrəbəl] *adj.* worth wishing for; worth having; pleasing; good; excellent. **—de'sir•a•ble•ness,** *n.*
—de'sir•a•bly, *adv.*

de•sire [dɪ'zaɪr] *v.* **-sired, -sir•ing;** *n.* —*v.* **1** long for; wish strongly for. **2** wish or long (to do something). **3** express a wish for; ask for or request, especially in a formal manner: *The Governor General desires your presence.* **4** want (someone) sexually.
—*n.* **1** a strong wish; a longing: *Her desire is to travel.* **2** an expressed wish; request. **3** something desired: *Grant me this desire.* **4** sensual appetite; lust. ⟨ME < OF *desirer* < L *desiderare* long for⟩ **—de'sir•er,** *n.*

☛ *Syn. v.* **1, 2.** See note at WISH. *n.* **1. Desire,** LONGING, CRAVING = a strong wish. **Desire** applies to any strong wish, good or bad, for something a person thinks or hopes he or she can get: *Her desire is to travel.* **Longing** applies to an earnest desire, sometimes for something a person thinks he or she can get if he or she tries or wishes hard enough, but often for something that seems beyond reach: *His longing for a BMW is pathetic.* **Craving** applies to a desire so strong that it amounts to a need or hunger: *She has a craving for candy.*

de•sir•ous [dɪ'zaɪrəs] *adj.* having or showing desire or longing; strongly wishing: *desirous of fame, desirous to learn all one can. He was desirous that his true identity be concealed.*

de•sist [dɪ'sɪst] *or* [dɪ'zɪst] *v.* stop; cease: *The judge ordered him to desist from fighting.* ⟨< MF *desister* < L *desistere* < *de-* from + *sistere* stop⟩

desk [dɛsk] *n.* **1** a piece of furniture with, often, one or more drawers and a flat or sloping top on which to write or to rest books, papers, etc. **2** a department of work at a certain location or at a desk: *the information desk of a library, the copy desk of a newspaper office.* **3** in an orchestra, the place or status of a musician: *She has held the first desk for years.* ⟨< Med.L *desca* < Ital. *desco* < L *discus* quoit, dish < Gk. *diskos.* Doublet of DAIS, DISCUS, DISH, and DISK.⟩

desk•top ['dɛsk,tɒp] *n., adj.* —*n.* **1** the top of a desk. **2** *Computer technology.* a screen, in certain operating systems, from which one opens files or applications.
—*adj.* of a computer, small enough to sit on a desk.

desktop publishing the preparation of camera-ready copy for printing, using a computer.

des•lan•o•side [dɛz'lænə,said] *n.* a drug containing digitalis, used to treat certain heart conditions.

des•mo•pres•sin ['dɛzmə,prɛsɪn] *or* [,dɛzmə'prɛsɪn] *n.* an antidiuretic drug used to treat diabetes. *Formula*: $C_{46}H_{64}N_{14}O_{12}S_2$

des•o•late *adj.* ['dɛsəlɪt] *or* ['dɛzəlɪt]; *v.* ['dɛsə,leit] *or* ['dɛzə,leit] *adj., v.* **-lat•ed, -lat•ing.** —*adj.* **1** laid waste; devastated; barren: *desolate land.* **2** not lived in; deserted: *a desolate house.* **3** left alone; solitary; lonely. **4** unhappy; wretched; forlorn: *The ragged, hungry child looked desolate.* **5** dreary; dismal: *a desolate life.*
—*v.* **1** make unfit to live in; lay waste: *The Vikings desolated the land they attacked.* **2** deprive of inhabitants. **3** make lonely, unhappy, or forlorn: *He was desolated to hear that his old friend was going away.* ⟨ME < L *desolatus*, pp. of *desolare* < *de-* completely + *solus* alone⟩ —**'des•o•late•ly,** *adv.*
—**'des•o•late•ness,** *n.* —**'des•o,lat•er, 'des•o,la•tor,** *n.*

☛ *Syn. adj.* **4. Desolate,** DISCONSOLATE = unhappy and forlorn. **Desolate** = unhappy because feeling left alone, deserted by everyone or, especially, separated from someone: *She was desolate when he went away.* **Disconsolate** = wretched because broken-hearted, without hope, and unable to be consoled or comforted: *She was disconsolate when her former boyfriend married another woman.*

des•o•la•tion [,dɛsə'leiʃən] *or* [,dɛzə'leiʃən] *n.* **1** the action of making desolate: *the desolation of a vast area by fire.* **2** the condition of being desolated; devastation: *the desolation left by the forest fire.* **3** the condition of being solitary, deserted, or uninhabited: *the desolation of the Barren Ground.* **4** a lonely or isolated place. **5** lonely sorrow or misery; grief: *There was desolation in the eyes of the condemned man.*

des•o•nide ['dɛsə,naɪd] *n.* a drug in cream form used to treat certain skin conditions.

de•sorb [di'zɔrb] *or* [di'sɔrb] *v.* treat a substance so as to remove (material that has been adsorbed or absorbed). ⟨*de-* + ab*sorb*⟩ —**de'sorp•tion,** *n.*

de•spair [dɪ'spɛr] *n., v.* —*n.* **1** a complete loss of hope; the state of being without hope; a feeling that nothing good can happen: *Despair seized us as we felt the boat sinking. In despair, he took his own life.* **2** a person or thing that causes hopelessness: *She was the despair of her parents.*
—*v.* lose or give up hope: *The doctors despaired of saving the sick woman's life.* ⟨ME < OF *despeir* < *desperer* < L *desperare* < *de-* out of, without + *sperare* to hope⟩

☛ *Syn. n.* **1. Despair,** DESPERATION = hopelessness. **Despair** emphasizes loss of hope and usually suggests sinking into a state of discouragement: *In his despair over losing his job he sold all his precious possessions and left town.* **Desperation** suggests a recklessness that is caused by despair and is expressed in rash or frantic action as a last resort: *He had no job and no money, and in desperation he robbed a bank.*

de•spair•ing [dɪ'spɛrɪŋ] *adj., v.* —*adj.* feeling, showing, or expressing despair; hopeless.
—*v.* ppr. of DESPAIR. —**de'spair•ing•ly,** *adv.*
—**de'spair•ing•ness,** *n.*

☛ *Syn.* See note at HOPELESS.

des•patch [dɪ'spætʃ] See DISPATCH.

des•patch•er [dɪ'spætʃər] See DISPATCHER.

des•per•a•do [,dɛspə'rɑdou] *or* [,dɛspə'reidou] *n., pl.* **-does** or **-dos.** a bold or reckless criminal; a dangerous outlaw. ⟨< OSp. *desperado* < L *desperatus.* Doublet of DESPERATE.⟩

des•per•ate ['dɛspərɪt] *or* ['dɛsprɪt] *adj.* **1** having lost all hope: *She would have to be desperate before she asked for help.* **2** made reckless or violent through loss of hope: *a desperate criminal.* **3** resulting from loss of hope; showing recklessness caused by despair: *a last, desperate bid for freedom.* **4** giving little or no hope of improvement; very dangerous or serious: *a desperate illness. The situation is desperate.* **5** having an extreme need or desire: *desperate for affection. After a week of being cooped up in the cabin, she was desperate for something to do.* **6** extreme: *in desperate need of assistance.* ⟨ME < L *desperatus*, pp. of *desperare.* See DESPAIR. Doublet of DESPERADO.⟩
—**'des•per•ate•ly,** *adv.* —**'des•per•ate•ness,** *n.*

☛ *Syn.* **1-4.** See note at HOPELESS.

des•per•a•tion [,dɛspə'reiʃən] *n.* **1** recklessness caused by despair; willingness to do anything, regardless of risks or consequences: *Desperation finally made her give herself up. He saw that the stairs were on fire and in desperation he jumped out of the window.* **2** a despairing; desperate state.

☛ *Syn.* See note at DESPAIR.

des•pic•a•ble ['dɛspɪkəbəl] *or* [dɪ'spɪkəbəl] *adj.* fit to be despised; contemptible: *Cowards and liars are despicable.* ⟨< LL *despicabilis* < L *despicari* despise⟩ —**des'pic•a•ble•ness,** *n.*
—**des'pic•a•bly,** *adv.*

de•spise [dɪ'spaɪz] *v.* **-spised, -spis•ing. 1** look down on; feel contempt for; scorn: *Most people despise a traitor.* **2** dislike or feel an aversion to. ⟨ME < OF *despis-*, a stem of *despire* < L *despicere* < *de-* down + *specere* look at⟩ —**de'spis•er,** *n.*

de•spite [dɪ'spəit] *prep., n.* —*prep.* in spite of: *The girls went for a walk despite the rain.*
—*n.* **1** insult; injury. **2** *Archaic.* malice; spite. **3** *Archaic.* contempt; scorn.
in despite of, a in spite of. **b** in defiance of. ⟨ME < OF *despit* < L *despectus* a looking down upon < *despicere* < *de-* down + *specere* look at⟩

de•spite•ful [dɪ'spəitfəl] *adj. Archaic.* spiteful; malicious.
—**de'spite•ful•ly,** *adv.* —**de'spite•ful•ness,** *n.*

de•spoil [dɪ'spɔɪl] *v.* rob; plunder. ⟨ME < OF *despoillier* < L *despoliare* < *de-* completely + *spolium* armour, booty⟩
—**de'spoil•er,** *n.* —**de'spoil•ment,** *n.*

de•spo•li•a•tion [dɪ,spouli'eiʃən] *n.* robbery; pillage.

de•spond [dɪ'spɒnd] *v., n.* —*v.* lose heart, courage, or hope.
—*n. Archaic.* despondency. ⟨ME < L *despondere* < *de-* away + *spondere* lose heart⟩ —**de'spond•ing•ly,** *adv.*

de•spond•en•cy [dɪ'spɒndənsi] *n., pl.* **-cies.** loss of courage or hope; discouragement; dejection. Also, **despondence.**

de•spond•ent [dɪ'spɒndənt] *adj.* without courage or hope; discouraged; dejected. —**de'spond•ent•ly,** *adv.*

des•pot ['dɛspət] *or* ['dɛspɒt] *n.* **1** a tyrant; oppressor. **2** a monarch having unlimited power; an absolute ruler. **3** any person who uses his or her power to get his or her own way: *Some fathers are despots in the eyes of their children.* **4** in medieval Italy, a noble, prince, or military leader in a city. ⟨< MF < Gk. *despotēs* master⟩

des•pot•ic [dɛ'spɒtɪk] *adj.* of a despot; tyrannical; having unlimited power. —**des'pot•i•cal•ly,** *adv.*

des•pot•ism ['dɛspə,tɪzəm] *n.* **1** tyranny; oppression. **2** government by a monarch having unlimited power. **3** despotic rule or control. **4** a country having such rule.

des•sert [dɪ'zɜrt] *n.* **1** a sweet course served at the end of a meal. **2** a food, such as fruit, cake, or ice cream, served at this course. ⟨< F *dessert* < *desservir* clear the table < *des-* from + *servir* serve < L *servire*⟩

☛ *Hom.* DESERT[2], DESERT[3].

des•sert•spoon [dɪ'zɜrt,spun] *n.* a spoon larger than a teaspoon and smaller than a tablespoon.

des•sert•spoon•ful [dɪ'zɜrt,spunfʊl] *or* [-fəl] *n., pl.* **-fuls.** the amount that a dessertspoon can hold.

de•sta•bil•ize [di'steibə,laɪz] *v.* **-ized, -iz•ing.** deprive of stability; make unstable: *to destabilize a country's economy.*
—**de,sta•bi•li'za•tion,** *n.*

de Stijl [də 'staɪl] *or* [də 'steil] a 20th-century abstract art movement whose work is characterized by rectangular designs and the use of black, grey, and the primary colours. ⟨< Du., the Style, after the journal founded by Mondrian and van Doesburg in 1917⟩

des•ti•na•tion [,dɛstə'neiʃən] *n.* **1** a place to which a person or thing is going or is being sent. **2** a setting apart for a particular purpose or use; intention. ⟨ME < L *destinatio*⟩

des•tine ['dɛstən] *v.* **-tined, -tin•ing. 1** set apart for a particular purpose or use; intend: *The prince was destined from birth to be a king.* **2** cause by fate: *My letter was destined never to reach her.*
destined for, a intending to go to; bound for: *ships destined for England.* **b** intended for: *My brother is destined for the ministry.* ⟨ME < OF < L *destinare* make fast < *de-* (intensive) + *stare* stand⟩

des•ti•ny ['dɛstəni] *n., pl.* **-nies. 1** one's lot or fortune; what becomes of a person or thing in the end. **2** what is predetermined to happen in spite of all efforts to change or prevent it. **3** the power that foreordains; overruling necessity; fate: *Do you believe in destiny?*

☛ *Syn.* See note at FATE.

des•ti•tute ['dɛstə,tjut] *or* ['dɛstə,tut] *adj.* **1** lacking necessities such as food, clothing, and shelter: *The family is destitute and needs help.* **2** not having; being without, especially something desirable or needed (*used with* **of**): *a region destitute of trees. The tyrant was destitute of pity.* ⟨< L *destitutus*, pp. of *destituere* forsake < *de-* away + *statuere* put, place⟩

des•ti•tu•tion [ˌdɛstəˈtjuʃən] *or* [ˌdɛstəˈtuʃən] *n.* **1** a destitute condition; extreme poverty. **2** the state of being without; lack. ⟨< ME < L *destitutio* putting away⟩

☛ *Syn.* **1.** See note at POVERTY.

de•stroy [dɪˈstrɔɪ] *v.* **1** ruin or wreck by tearing down, breaking, etc., or as if by tearing down, breaking, etc.; demolish: *Hail destroyed their crop. Many paintings were destroyed in the flood. His reputation has been destroyed by his involvement in the scandal.* **2** defeat completely: *The enemy was destroyed.* **3** put an end to; bring to nothing: *A heavy rain destroyed all hope of a picnic. Repeated failures have destroyed her confidence.* **4** kill: *The injured dog had to be destroyed.* **5** counteract the effect of; make void. ⟨ME < OF *destruire* < VL < L *destruere* < *de-* un- + *struere* pile, build⟩

☛ *Syn.* **1. Destroy,** DEMOLISH = ruin. **Destroy** suggests bringing to nothing or making useless by breaking to pieces, taking apart, killing, or other means: *Some children destroy all their toys.* **Demolish** = tear down, and applies only to things thought of as having been built up, such as buildings or, figuratively, arguments and theories: *The city demolished many buildings to make room for the speedway.*

de•stroy•er [dɪˈstrɔɪər] *n.* **1** a person or thing that destroys. **2** a small, fast warship equipped with guns, torpedoes, and other weapons: *In wartime, the Royal Canadian Navy used destroyers for hunting submarines.*

destroying angel either of two highly poisonous mushrooms (*Amanita verna* or *Amanita virosa*) which grow in warm, damp woodlands.

de•struct [dɪˈstrʌkt] *v., n.* —*v.* **1** blow up (a rocket or other missile) that fails to function properly. **2** destroy. **3** (of a rocket or other missile) be destroyed, especially automatically.
—*n.* the destructing of a rocket or missile. ⟨back formation < *destruction*⟩

de•struct•i•ble [dɪˈstrʌktəbəl] *adj.* capable of being destroyed. **—deˌstruct•iˈbil•i•ty** or **deˈstruct•i•ble•ness,** *n.*

de•struc•tion [dɪˈstrʌkʃən] *n.* **1** the act or process of destroying. **2** the condition or fact of being destroyed; ruin. **3** anything that destroys; the causes or means of destruction: *That letter was the destruction of all her hopes.* ⟨ME < OF < L *destructio, -onis* < *destruere* destroy. See DESTROY.⟩

☛ *Syn.* See note at RUIN.

de•struc•tive [dɪˈstrʌktɪv] *adj.* **1** tending to destroy; liable to cause destruction: *Termites are destructive insects.* **2** destroying; causing destruction. **3** guilty of destroying; in the habit of causing destruction: *Destructive children should be corrected.* **4** not helpful; merely discrediting; not constructive: *His criticism was destructive because it showed what was wrong, but did not show how to correct it.* **—deˈstruc•tive•ly,** *adv.* **—deˈstruc•tive•ness,** *n.*

destructive distillation the decomposition of a substance, such as wood or coal, by strong heat in a closed container, and the collection of the volatile products.

de•struc•tor [dɪˈstrʌktər] *n.* **1** a furnace or incinerator for the burning of refuse. **2** something that destructs.

des•ue•tude [ˈdɛswəˌtjud] *or* [ˈdɛswəˌtud]; *French,* [desweˈtyd] *n.* disuse: *Many words once commonly used have fallen into desuetude.* ⟨< F < L *desuetudo* < *de-* dis- + *suescere* accustom⟩

de•sul•phur•ize [diˈsʌlfəˌraɪz] *v.* **-ized, -iz•ing.** remove sulphur from. **—deˌsul•phur•iˈza•tion,** *n.*

des•ul•to•ry [ˈdɛsəlˌtɔri] *or* [ˈdɛzəlˌtɔri] *adj.* **1** jumping from one thing to another at random; without aim or method: *The careful and systematic study of a few books is better than the desultory reading of many.* **2** irrelevant; unconnected; accidental: *desultory thoughts.* ⟨< L *desultorius* of a leaper, ult. < *de-* down + *salire* leap⟩ **—ˈdes•ulˌto•ri•ly,** *adv.* **—ˈdes•ulˌto•ri•ness,** *n.*

de•tach [dɪˈtætʃ] *v.* **1** loosen and remove; unfasten; separate: *She detached a charm from her bracelet.* **2** separate (a number of men, ships, tanks, etc.) from the main body for some special duty: *One squad of soldiers was detached to guard the camp.* **3** make uninvolved; make aloof; set apart: *He tried to detach himself from the situation.* ⟨< F *détacher*, formed with *dé-* away + OF *tache* nail⟩ **—deˈtach•a•ble,** *adj.* **—deˈtach•er,** *n.*

de•tached [dɪˈtætʃt] *adj., v.* —*adj.* **1** separate from others; isolated: *A detached house is not in a solid row with others.* **2** not influenced by one's interests and prejudices, or those of others; impartial; aloof.
—*v.* pt. and pp. of DETACH. **—deˈtach•ed•ly** [dɪˈtætʃɪdli], *adv.* **—deˈtach•ed•ness** [dɪˈtætʃɪdnɪs], *n.*

de•tach•ment [dɪˈtætʃmənt] *n.* **1** separation. **2** standing apart; aloofness. **3** a freedom from prejudice or bias; impartial attitude: *Students were surprised at the professor's air of detachment in talking about her own books.* **4** *Military.* **a** troops, ships, tanks, etc. sent on or assigned to some special duty: *He belonged to the machine-gun detachment.* **b** the state of being on special duty: *a platoon of soldiers on detachment.* **5** the smallest unit in the organization of the Royal Canadian Mounted Police or other police force. Some rural detachments of the RCMP have only one or two officers.

de•tail [ˈditeil] *or* [dɪˈteil] *n., v.* —*n.* **1** a small part of something; a particular item that is not of great importance in itself: *Their stories were alike in every detail.* **2** dealing with or showing things individually or one by one: *She doesn't care for the detail involved in accounting. This new map has more detail than the old one.* **3** any of the small parts that go to make up a painting, etc.: *The details are beautifully painted, but the general effect is dull.* **4** a reproduction of a part of a painting or other work of art: *The picture on the card is a detail of a painting by Leonardo da Vinci.* **5** *Esp. Military.* **a** a small group selected for or sent on some special duty: *The captain sent a detail of six soldiers to guard the road.* **b** the task or duty itself.
go into detail, give all the parts or particulars separately: *There was no time to go into detail, so she just gave them a general outline of the situation.*
in detail, part by part; giving all the particulars: *She described the inside of the airplane in detail.*
—*v.* **1** give the particulars of; report or tell in full: *She detailed all the things she had seen and done on her trip. The particulars are detailed in the enclosed brochure.* **2** select for or send on special duty: *Police were detailed to hold back the crowd watching the parade.* ⟨< F *détail* < *détaillir* cut in pieces < *de-* completely + *tailler* cut⟩ **—ˈde•tail•er,** *n.*

☛ *Syn. n.* **1.** See note at ITEM.

☛ *Pronun.* **Detail.** The noun may be pronounced in two ways: [ˈditeil] *or* [dɪˈteil]. The second is older; the first especially common in situations where the word is used a great deal (army life, architecture, etc.). The pronunciation [ˈditeil] is also more frequently used for the verb.

de•tailed [ˈditeild] *or* [dɪˈteild] *adj., v.* —*adj.* having much detail: *a detailed description, a detailed map.*
—*v.* pt. and pp. of DETAIL.

de•tain [dɪˈtein] *v.* **1** hold back; keep from going; delay. **2** keep in custody; confine: *The police detained the suspected thief for further questioning.* **3** *Archaic.* withhold. ⟨ME < OF *detenir* < L *detinere* < *de-* away + *tenere* hold⟩

de•tain•ee [ˌditeiˈni] *n.* a person held in custody; prisoner.

de•tain•ment [dɪˈteinmənt] *n.* detention.

de•tas•sel [diˈtæsəl] *v.* **-selled, -sel•ling.** remove tassels from (corn) in order to assist cross-pollination and the production of hybrid seed.

de•tect [dɪˈtɛkt] *v.* **1** find out; discover or reveal: *to detect a crime.* **2** discover the existence or presence of: *to detect an odour. She detected a note of sadness in his voice.* **3** *Electronics.* demodulate. ⟨< L *detectus*, pp. of *detegere* < *de-* un- + *tegere* cover⟩

de•tect•a•ble or **de•tect•i•ble** [dɪˈtɛktəbəl] *adj.* capable of being detected.

de•tec•tion [dɪˈtɛkʃən] *n.* **1** the act or process of detecting or the fact of being detected: *the detection of a crime.* **2** *Electronics.* demodulation.

de•tec•tive [dɪˈtɛktɪv] *n.* **1** a police officer whose work is investigating crimes. **2** a person who works for a company or organization as an investigator. **3** (*adjl.*) having to do with detectives and their work: *detective stories.* **4** (*adjl.*) designed for or used in detecting something: *detective devices.*

de•tec•tor [dɪˈtɛktər] *n.* **1** a device or instrument for detecting or measuring the presence of electricity, radioactivity, heat, etc. **2** *Electronics.* demodulator. **3** any person or thing that detects.

de•tent [dɪˈtɛnt] *n.* a pawl or catch in a mechanical device such as a clock, which regularly checks and releases movement. ⟨See DÉTENTE⟩

dé•tente [deiˈtɒnt]; *French,* [deˈtɑ̃t] *n. French.* the easing of tensions, especially between nations or political groups: *a détente in the cold war.* ⟨< F < *détendre* relax < *dé-* + *tendre* stretch⟩

de•ten•tion [dɪˈtɛnʃən] *n.* **1** the act of detaining or holding back; especially, keeping in custody: *A jail is used for the detention of persons who have been arrested.* **2** the state of being detained; delay. **3** a form of school punishment in which a student is kept behind after school or during recess. ⟨< LL *detentio, -onis* < L *detinere.* See DETAIN.⟩

de•ter [dɪ'tɜr] *v.* **-terred, -ter•ring.** discourage, keep back, or hinder by the prospect of something unpleasant or frightening: *The extreme heat deterred us from going downtown.* ⟨< L *deterrere* < *de-* from + *terrere* frighten⟩

de•ter•gen•cy [dɪ'tɜrdʒənsi] *n.* a detergent quality; cleansing power.

de•ter•gent [dɪ'tɜrdʒənt] *n., adj.* —*n.* **1** a chemical compound that acts like a soap, used for cleansing: *Detergents are usually preferred to soap for most laundry and for dishes because they keep dirt particles suspended in the water.* **2** any substance for cleansing: *Soap is a detergent.*
—*adj.* cleansing: *the detergent action of suds.* ⟨< L *detergens*, *-entis*, ppr. of *detergere* < *de-* off + *tergere* wipe⟩

de•te•ri•o•rate [dɪ'tiriə,reit] *v.* **-rat•ed, -rat•ing. 1** become worse; lessen in value or effectiveness; depreciate: *Machinery deteriorates if it is not given good care.* **2** make worse. ⟨< L *deteriorare* < *deterior* worse⟩

de•te•ri•o•ra•tion [dɪ,tiriə'reiʃən] *n.* **1** a deteriorating. **2** the condition of having deteriorated.

de•ter•ment [dɪ'tɜrmənt] *n.* **1** a deterring. **2** something that deters.

de•ter•mi•na•ble [dɪ'tɜrmənəbəl] *adj.* **1** capable of being settled or decided. **2** capable of being found out exactly. **3** capable of being ended or of having limits set to it.

de•ter•mi•na•cy [dɪ'tɜrmɪnəsi] *n.* **1** the state or quality of being determinate. **2** the state or fact of being determined; having a foreseeable outcome.

de•ter•mi•nant [dɪ'tɜrmənənt] *n., adj.* —*n.* **1** something that determines. **2** *Mathematics.* the sum of all the products that can be formed according to special laws from a certain number of quantities arranged in a square matrix.
—*adj.* determining.

de•ter•mi•nate [dɪ'tɜrmənɪt] *adj.* **1** with exact limits; fixed; definite. **2** settled; positive. **3** determined; resolute. **4** *Botany.* designating an inflorescence in which each floral stem ends in a single flower; cymose. **—de'ter•mi•nate•ly,** *adv.* **—de'ter•mi•nate•ness,** *n.*

de•ter•mi•na•tion [dɪ,tɜrmə'neiʃən] *n.* **1** the act of formally settling or deciding a question, problem, controversy, etc.: *the determination of the boundary lines of the provinces.* **2** the result of settling or deciding; settlement or decision: *They were unable to come to any determination on the question of inheritance.* **3** the act of finding out the exact amount, position, or kind by calculating, measuring, etc.: *the determination of the amount of gold in a sample of ore.* **4** the result of finding out by calculating, etc.; conclusion or solution: *Their research was based on earlier scientific determinations.* **5** the result of coming to a decision; a fixed purpose: *She left with the determination to find out who her real parents were.* **6** great firmness in carrying out a purpose; the quality of being determined; resoluteness or resolve: *The boy's determination was not weakened by the difficulties he met.* **7** *Logic.* **a** the making of an idea, concept, etc. more concise in its outline by the addition of restrictive attributes or other qualifying features. **b** the defining of a concept by specifying its parts.

de•ter•mi•na•tive [dɪ'tɜrmənətɪv] *or* [dɪ'tɜrmə,neitɪv] *adj., n.* —*adj.* determining.
—*n.* something that determines. **—de'ter•mi•na•tive•ly,** *adv.* **—de'ter•mi•na•tive•ness,** *n.*

de•ter•mine [dɪ'tɜrmən] *v.* **-mined, -min•ing. 1** make up one's mind firmly; resolve: *He determined to become the best Scout in his troop.* **2** settle; decide. **3** find out exactly; fix: *The captain determined the latitude and longitude of the ship's position.* **4** *Geometry.* fix the position of. **5** be the deciding factor in reaching a certain result; bring about a certain result: *Tomorrow's events will determine whether we are to go or stay.* **6** fix or settle beforehand. **7** give an aim to; direct; impel: *Let hope determine your thinking.* **8** limit; define: *The meaning of a word is partly determined by its use in a particular sentence.* **9** put an end to; conclude. **10** come to an end. **11** *Mathematics.* find a value for: *to determine the roots of a function.* ⟨ME < OF < L *determinare* set limits to < *de-* completely + *terminus* end⟩ **—de'ter•mi,na•tor,** *n.*
☛ *Syn.* **1.** See note at DECIDE.

de•ter•mined [dɪ'tɜrmənd] *adj., v.* —*adj.* **1** with one's mind firmly made up; resolved: *The determined explorer kept on her way in spite of the storm.* **2** firm; resolute: *His determined look showed that he had made up his mind.*
—*v.* pt. and pp. of DETERMINE.

de•ter•mined•ly [dɪ'tɜrməndli] *or* [dɪ'tɜrmənɪdli] *adv.* in a determined manner.

de•ter•min•er [dɪ'tɜrmənər] *n.* a person or thing that determines; especially, in grammar, a specifying word such as *the*, *a*, *her*, or *this*, that comes before a noun or before an adjective followed by a noun.

de•ter•min•ism [dɪ'tɜrmə,nɪzəm] *n.* **1** the doctrine that human actions, including the act of choosing, are the necessary results of antecedent causes. **2** the doctrine that all events are determined by antecedent causes. **—de,ter•mi'nis•tic,** *adj.* **—de,ter•mi'nis•ti•cal•ly,** *adv.*

de•ter•min•ist [dɪ'tɜrmənɪst] *n.* a person who believes in determinism.

de•ter•rence [di'tɜrəns] *or* [dɪ'tɜrəns] *n.* **1** the act or process of deterring. **2** something that deters; a restraint. **3** the amassing of nuclear weapons to deter another country from attacking.

de•ter•rent [dɪ'tɜrənt] *adj., n.* —*adj.* deterring; restraining.
—*n.* something that deters: *Fear of consequences is a common deterrent from wrongdoing.*

de•test [dɪ'tɛst] *v.* dislike very much; hate. ⟨< F *détester* < L *detestari* curse while calling the gods to witness < *de-* (intensive) + *testari* to witness⟩ **—de'test•er,** *n.*
☛ *Syn.* See note at HATE.

de•test•a•ble [dɪ'tɛstəbəl] *adj.* deserving to be detested; hateful. **—de'test•a•ble•ness,** *n.* **—de'test•a•bly,** *adv.*

de•tes•ta•tion [,ditɛs'teiʃən] *n.* **1** a very strong dislike; hatred. **2** a detested person or thing.

de•throne [di'θroun] *v.* **-throned, -thron•ing, 1** deprive of the power to rule; remove from a throne; depose. **2** remove (someone) from any high office.

de•throne•ment [di'θrounmənt] *n.* dethroning or being dethroned.

det•o•nate ['dɛtə,neit] *v.* **-nat•ed, -nat•ing. 1** cause to explode with violence: *The workers detonated the dynamite.* **2** explode with violence: *The bomb detonated.* ⟨< L *detonare* < *de-* (intensive) + *tonare* thunder⟩

det•o•na•tion [,dɛtə'neiʃən] *n.* **1** an explosion with violence. **2** a loud noise.

det•o•na•tor ['dɛtə,neitər] *n.* **1** a fuse, percussion cap, etc. used to set off an explosive. **2** any explosive.

de•tour ['ditur] *or* [dɪ'tur] *n., v.* —*n.* **1** a road that is used when the main road or direct road cannot be travelled. **2** a roundabout way.
—*v.* **1** use a roundabout way; make a detour: *We detoured around the flooded part of the highway.* **2** cause to use a detour. **3** circumvent by using a detour; bypass. ⟨< F *détour* < *détourner* turn aside < *de-* away from + *tourner* turn⟩

de•tox ['ditɒks] *n. Informal.* **1** detoxification. **2** a unit in a hospital dealing with drug and alcohol detoxification.

de•tox•i•cate [di'tɒksə,keit] *v.* **-cat•ed, -cat•ing.** detoxify. **—de,tox•i'ca•tion,** *n.*

de•tox•i•fy [di'tɒksə,faɪ] *v.* **-fied, -fy•ing.** remove a poison or toxic substance, or its effect from: *to detoxify an alcoholic.* ⟨< *de-* + *toxin* + *-fy*⟩ **—de,tox•i•fi'ca•tion,** *n.*

de•tract [dɪ'trækt] *v.* **1** take away quality, value, etc. (*from*): *The ugly frame detracts from the picture.* **2** deflect; draw away: *The children detracted his attention from weightier matters.* ⟨< L *detractus*, pp. of *detrahere* < *de-* away + *trahere* draw⟩

de•trac•tion [dɪ'trækʃən] *n.* **1** the act of speaking evil; belittling. **2** a taking away; detracting.

de•trac•tive [dɪ'træktɪv] *adj.* **1** tending to detract. **2** speaking evil; belittling. **—de'trac•tive•ly,** *adv.*

de•trac•tor [dɪ'træktər] *n.* a person who speaks evil of or belittles another.

de•train [di'trein] *v.* **1** get off a railway train. **2** put off from a railway train. **—de'train•ment,** *n.*

de•tri•bal•ize [di'traɪbə,laɪz] *v.* **-ized, -iz•ing.** take away the tribal character or organization of; lose tribal character or organization. **—de,tri•ba•li'za•tion,** *n.*

det•ri•ment ['dɛtrəmənt] *n.* **1** damage; injury; harm: *He continued working long hours, apparently without detriment to his health.* **2** something that causes damage or harm. ⟨ME < L *detrimentum* < *deterere* < *de-* away + *terere* wear⟩

det•ri•men•tal [,dɛtrə'mɛntəl] *adj.* damaging; injurious; harmful: *Lack of sleep is detrimental to one's health.* **—,det•ri'men•tal•ly,** *adv.*

de•tri•tion [dɪ'trɪʃən] *n.* a wearing away by friction. ⟨< Med.L *detritio*⟩

de•tri•tus [dɪ'traitəs] *n.* **1** particles of rock or other material worn away from a mass. **2** any disintegrated material; debris: *The detritus left by the flood covered the highway.* ⟨< L *detritus* a rubbing away⟩ **—de'tri•tal,** *adj.*

de trop [də 'trou]; *French,* [də'tʀo] *French.* **1** too much; too many. **2** unwelcome; in the way.

de•tu•mes•cence [,ditju'mɛsəns] *n.* a shrinking of tissue; the collapse of an erection. **—,de•tu'mes•cent,** *adj.*

deuce[1] [djus] *or* [dus] *n.* **1** a playing card marked with a 2. **2** *Dice.* **a** the side of a die having two spots. **b** a throw of two. **3** *Tennis.* a tie score at 40 each in a game. ⟨< OF *deus* two < L *duos,* accus. of *duo* two⟩

deuce[2] [djus] *or* [dus] *interj. Informal.* a mild oath used to express annoyance or surprise: *What the deuce does he want now?* ⟨probably < LG *duus* deuce[1], an unlucky throw at dice⟩

deu•ced [djust] *or* [dust], ['djusɪd] *or* ['dusɪd] *adj., adv. Informal. —adj.* devilish; excessive.
—adv. devilishly; excessively.

deu•ced•ly ['djusɪdli] *or* ['dusɪdli] *adv. Informal.* devilishly; excessively.

de•us ex ma•chi•na [,diəs ɛks 'mækənə] *Latin.* **1** a person, god, or event that comes just in time to solve a difficulty in a story, play, etc. **2** a person or event that solves any difficulty in a dramatic manner. ⟨literally, god from the machinery (with reference to a stage device in the ancient theatre)⟩

deu•tan ['djutæn] *or* ['dutæn] *n. Genetics.* a type of red-green colour blindness, with X-linked recessive inheritance. ⟨< *deuteran*opia⟩

deu•ter•an•ope ['djutərə,noup] *or* ['dutərə,noup] *n.* one who has deuteranopia.

deu•ter•an•o•pi•a [,djutərə'noupiə] *or* [,dutərə'noupiə] a red-green colour blindness. ⟨< Gk. *deuteros* second + *a-* + *opia* < *ops* eye⟩

deu•ter•at•ed ['djutə,reitəd] *or* ['dutə,reitəd] *adj.* **1** of or having to do with a compound in which deuterium atoms replace some or all of the hydrogen atoms. **2** including deuterium as a component.

deu•te•ri•um [dju'tiriəm] *or* [du'tiriəm] *n.* an isotope of hydrogen having a mass double that of ordinary hydrogen; heavy hydrogen. *Symbol*: D or $^{2}_{1}H$ ⟨< NL < Gk. *deutereion,* neut., having second place < *deuteros* second⟩

deuterium oxide HEAVY WATER. *Formula*: D_2O

deu•ter•o•ca•non•i•cal [,djutəroukə'nɒnɪkəl] *or* [,dutəroukə'nɒnɪkəl] *adj.* of or having to do with those books of the Apocrypha held to be legitimate by the Roman Catholic Church but not by the Protestant churches. ⟨< Gk. *deuteros* second + ME *canonical* < Ecclesiastical Med.L *canonicalis*⟩

deu•ter•og•a•my [,djutə'rɒgəmi] *or* [,dutə'rɒgəmi] *n.* a second marriage after divorce, or after the death of the first spouse; digamy. ⟨< Med.L *deuterogamia* < Gk. *deuteros* second + *-gamia* < *gamos* marriage⟩

deu•ter•on ['djutə,rɒn] *or* ['dutə,rɒn] *n. Chemistry.* the nucleus of a deuterium atom, consisting of one proton and one neutron. ⟨< *deuterium* + *-on,* as in *proton*⟩

deu•to•plasm ['djutə,plæzəm] *or* ['dutə,plæzəm] *n. Biology.* the yolk or other material that provides nourishment for the embryo in an egg or cell. ⟨< Gk. *deuteros* second + *plasma.* See PLASMA.⟩ **—,deu•to'plas•mic,** *adj.*

Deutsche mark ['dɔɪtʃə ,mɑrk] **1** the basic unit of money in Germany, divided into 100 pfennigs. See table of money in the Appendix. **2** a coin worth one Deutsche mark. Also, **deutsche mark.**

deut•zi•a ['djutsiə] *or* ['dutsiə] *n.* a shrub of the genus *Deutzia,* of the saxifrage family, having showy pink, purple, or white flowers, grown as an ornamental. ⟨after Jean *Deutz,* 18c. Dutch botanist⟩

de•va ['deivə] *n.* **1** *Hinduism, Buddhism.* a god. **2** *Zoroastrianism.* an evil spirit. ⟨< Sanskrit *deva* god⟩

de•val•u•ate [di'vælju,eit] *v.* **-at•ed, -at•ing.** devalue.

de•val•u•a•tion [di,vælju'eiʃən] *n.* devaluating or being devaluated.

de•val•ue [di'vælju] *v.* **-val•ued, -val•uing. 1** officially reduce the value of (currency) in relation to other currencies or to gold. **2** lessen or take away the importance or value of; belittle or depreciate.

De•va•na•ga•ri [,dɛvə'nɑgəri] *n.* the Sanskrit alphabet; also that of many north Indic languages. ⟨< Skt. *devanagari* city of the gods < *deva* gods + *nagara* city⟩

dev•as•tate ['dɛvə,steit] *v.* **-tat•ed, -tat•ing. 1** make desolate; destroy; ravage: *A long war devastated the border towns.* **2** overwhelm; crush: *The playwright was devastated by the critic's bad review.* ⟨< L *devastare* < *de-* (intensive) + *vastus* waste⟩ **—'dev•as,tat•or,** *n.* **—'dev•as,tat•ing•ly,** *adv.*

dev•as•tat•ing ['dɛvə,steitɪŋ] *adj., v. —adj.* **1** causing destruction or devastation: *a devastating earthquake.* **2** very telling, effective, or crushing: *a devastating criticism.*
—v. ppr. of DEVASTATE.

dev•as•ta•tion [,dɛvə'steiʃən] *n.* a devastating or being devastated: *The people were shocked at the devastation caused by the forest fire.*

de•vein [di'vein] *v.* clean (shrimp and other shellfish) by removing the vein, or intestine.

de•vel•op [dɪ'vɛləp] *v.* **1** come into being gradually through successive stages of growth and change: *Many plants develop from seeds. Land animals are believed to have developed from sea animals.* **2** bring into being through successive stages: *The modern power loom was developed from a simple hand loom.* **3** go from earlier to later stages, especially by a natural process of growth and change; become gradually bigger, fuller, more mature, etc.: *She is developing into a fine, healthy child. The idea had been developing in his mind for some time.* **4** cause to grow and mature: *Exercise and wholesome food develop healthy bodies.* **5** come to have; acquire bit by bit: *to develop an aversion for seafood. She has developed an interest in stamp collecting.* **6** work out in more and more detail; make bigger, better, fuller, etc.: *to develop an argument. Gradually they developed their plans for the Boys' Club.* **7** make or become known; reveal: *No new facts developed from the detective's inquiry.* **8** occur; transpire: *Let's see what develops before investing in that company.* **9** change, especially by means of construction work, from a natural or near natural state to one that serves another purpose: *The plan to develop the park area was strongly opposed by the public. The government is developing the water power of the northern rivers for industry.* **10** make more urban, more up to date, or more industrialized: *They have developed the old downtown area.* **11** become more industrialized, etc.: *Some nations are only just developing.* **12** *Photography.* **a** treat with chemicals to bring out the image recorded on a photographic plate or film: *The film was developed commercially but she made the prints herself.* **b** of an image, be brought out; become visible: *We watched the picture develop.* **13** *Music.* elaborate (a theme or motive) by variation of rhythm, melody, harmony, etc. **14** *Geometry.* expand in the form of a series. **15** *Mathematics.* project (a surface) onto a plane without stretching or shrinking any element of the surface. ⟨< F *développer* unwrap⟩

de•vel•op•er [dɪ'vɛləpər] *n.* **1** a person whose business is developing real estate on a large scale: *A developer buys a tract of land and builds an office complex, an apartment building, houses, etc. on it for the purpose of selling them.* **2** *Photography.* a chemical used to bring out the picture on an exposed film, plates, etc. **3** any person or thing that develops.

de•vel•op•ing [dɪ'vɛləpɪŋ] *adj., v. —adj.* advancing in production, technology, medicine, and overall standard of living after becoming self-governing: *the developing nations.*
—v. ppr. of DEVELOP.

de•vel•op•ment [dɪ'vɛləpmənt] *n.* **1** the act of working out in detail: *The development of a feasible plan took many hours of work.* **2** the process of developing; growth: *The parents followed their child's development with pride.* **3** a happening; an outcome or result; news: *Newspapers give information about the latest developments in world affairs.* **4** the process of bringing into being through successive stages: *the development of a new kind of motor.* **5** progression through successive stages by a natural process of growth and change: *the development of a caterpillar into a butterfly.* **6** the process of changing something from a natural or older state for a particular purpose: *the development of the waterfront for industry.* **7** the product or result of developing in this way: *The old farm is now a large housing development.* **8** a group of buildings constructed by the same person or company: *The new development will have business offices and stores.* **9** *Photography.* the developing of a film. **10** *Music.* any of the sections in a piece of music having variation on a theme.

de•vel•op•men•tal [dɪ,vɛləp'mɛntəl] *adj.* having to do with development. **—de,vel•op'men•tal•ly,** *adv.*

development road *Cdn.* in the North, a road or one of a system of access roads intended to help the exploitation of natural resources.

De•vi ['deivi] *n. Hinduism.* a goddess, the wife of Siva. ⟨< Skt. goddess < *deva* god⟩

de•vi•ance ['diviəns] *n.* **1** the quality or state of being deviant. **2** deviant behaviour: *the problem of controlling deviance.*

de•vi•ant ['diviənt] *adj., n. —adj.* deviating from an accepted standard.
—n. a person who is deviant, especially in sexual behaviour.

de•vi•ate *v.* ['divi,eit]; *n.* ['diviət] *or* ['divi,eit]; *adj.* ['diviət] *v.* **-at•ed, -at•ing;** *n., adj. —v.* **1** turn aside (from a norm, course, rule, truth, etc.); diverge: *His statements sometimes deviated slightly from the truth.* **2** cause to turn aside.
—n. an individual who shows a marked deviation from the norm.
—adj. **1** characterized by a marked deviation from the norm. **2** deviant. ⟨< LL *deviare* < *de-* aside + *via* way⟩ **—'de•vi,a•tor,** *n.*
☛ *Syn.* See note at DIVERGE.

de•vi•a•tion [,divi'eiʃən] *n.* **1** a turning aside from a norm, course, rule, truth, etc.; divergence: *No deviation from the rules was allowed. The deviation of the compass needle was caused by the iron on the ship.* **2** *Statistics.* **a** the difference between the mean of a set of values and one value in the set, used to measure variation from the norm. **b** the amount of such difference.

de•vi•a•tion•ism [,divi'eiʃə,nɪzəm] *n.* a turning aside from strict principles, especially from official Communist policy.

de•vi•a•tion•ist [,divi'eiʃənɪst] *n.* a person who turns aside from strict principles, especially from official Communist policy.

de•vice [də'vəis] *n.* **1** a mechanical invention used for a special purpose; machine; apparatus: *a device for lighting a gas stove.* **2** a plan; scheme; trick: *By some device or other he got the boy to let him into the house.* **3** a drawing or figure used in a pattern or as an ornament. **4** *Literature or music.* a stylistic or technical feature introduced to achieve a particular effect. **5** a picture or design on a coat of arms, often accompanied by a motto. **6** motto.
leave to (one's) **own devices,** leave to do as one thinks best: *The teacher left us to our own devices in choosing a book for our report.* ⟨fusion of ME *devis* separation, talk + *devise* design, emblem, plan; both < OF < L *divisus,* pp. of *dividere* divide⟩
☛ *Usage.* **Device,** DEVISE. Do not confuse **device,** meaning a mechanical invention or a scheme or trick, with **devise,** meaning 'think out': *By one unfair device after another, he amassed a huge fortune. Ann devised a new plan for the organization.*

dev•il ['dɛvəl] *n., v.* **-illed** or **-iled, -il•ling** or **-il•ing;** *interj. —n.* **1 the Devil,** the chief spirit of evil; the enemy of goodness; Satan. **2** an evil spirit; fiend; demon. **3** a wicked or cruel person. **4** a very dashing, energetic, or reckless person. **5** an unfortunate or wretched person: *The poor devil didn't even hear the warning.* **6** *Informal.* something that is hard to handle, solve, understand, etc.: *That last problem was a real devil.* **7** something very bad; an evil influence or power: *the devil of greed.* **8** formerly, PRINTER'S DEVIL. **9** a person who does literary work for another, for which the latter gets the credit or pay. **10** any of various machines for tearing or shredding paper, rags, etc.
between the devil and the deep (blue) sea, between two equally dangerous and unpleasant alternatives; in a dilemma.
devil of a, *Informal.* **a** very difficult, awkward, complicated, etc.: *We had the devil of a time getting the piano into the basement.* **b** very: *She's done a devil of a fine job.*
give the devil his due, be fair even to a bad or disliked person.
go to the devil, go to ruin; degenerate, especially morally.
like the devil, with great force; energetically: *They drove like the devil.*
play the devil with, *Informal.* upset; cause to go wrong.
raise the devil, *Slang.* make a great disturbance.
the devil take the hindmost, do not worry about what happens to the slowest or last one.
the devil to pay, much trouble ahead.
—v. **1** tease; bother; harass. **2** prepare (food) with hot seasoning: *to devil ham, devilled eggs.* **3** tear (rags, etc.) to pieces with a devil; subject to the cleaning action of a devil.
—interj. **the devil!** exclamation used to express disgust, anger, surprise, etc. ⟨OE *deofol* < L < Gk. *diabolos* slanderer < *diaballein* slander < *dia-* across, against + *ballein* throw⟩

dev•il•fish ['dɛvəl,fɪʃ] *n., pl.* **-fish** or **-fish•es. 1** any of a family (Mobulidae) of very large rays found in warm seas. **2** any large cephalopod, especially an octopus.

de•vil•ish ['dɛvəlɪʃ] *adj., adv. —adj.* **1** of, having to do with, like, or worthy of a devil or devils; cruel, wicked, mischievous, etc.: *a devilish scheme for getting the inheritance.* **2** *Informal.* very great; extreme: *She's always in such a devilish hurry.*
—adv. Informal. very; extremely: *They worked devilish hard.*
—'dev•il•ish•ly, *adv.* **—'dev•il•ish•ness,** *n.*

dev•il–may–care ['dɛvəl mei 'kɛr] happy-go-lucky or reckless: *She showed a devil-may-care attitude toward authority.*

dev•il•ment ['dɛvəlmənt] *n.* **1** an evil action; wicked behaviour. **2** daring behaviour. **3** mischief.

Devil of the Woods *Cdn.* wolverine.

devil ray devilfish.

dev•il•ry ['dɛvəlri] *n., pl.* **-ries.** deviltry.

devil's advocate **1** in the Roman Catholic Church, an official appointed to argue against a proposed beatification or canonization. **2** a critic who argues either against a popular cause or for an unpopular cause. **3** *Informal.* one who argues against something, often perversely.

devil's club a spiny shrub (*Oplopanax horridum*) of the same family as ivies and ginseng, found in W North America, having very large, maplelike leaves, small, greenish white flowers, and scarlet berries.

A devil's club

devil's darning needle dragonfly.

devil's food cake a rich, dark, smooth chocolate cake.

devil's paintbrush a perennial weed (*Hieracium aurantiacum*) originating in Europe but now common in many parts of North America, having orange flowers on a long stem.

dev•il•try ['dɛvəltri] *n., pl.* **-tries. 1** an evil action; wicked behaviour. **2** daring behaviour. **3** mischief. **4** great cruelty or wickedness.

dev•il•wood ['dɛvəl,wʊd] *n.* a small olive tree (*Osmanthus americanus*) found in SE U.S., having glossy leaves and hard wood.

de•vi•ous ['diviəs] *adj.* **1** winding; twisting; roundabout: *We took a devious route through side streets and alleys to avoid the crowded main streets.* **2** straying from the right course; not straightforward; going astray: *His devious nature was shown in half lies and acts of petty dishonesty.* ⟨< L *devius* < *de-* out of + *via* the way⟩ **—'de•vi•ous•ness,** *n.* **—'de•vi•ous•ly,** *adv.*

de•vise [dɪ'vaɪz] *v.* **-vised, -vis•ing;** *n. —v.* **1** think out; plan; contrive; invent: *The girls devised a scheme for earning money during the summer vacation.* **2** *Law.* give or leave (land, buildings, etc.) by a will.
—n. Law. **1** a giving or leaving of land, buildings, etc., by a will. **2** a will or part of a will doing this. **3** land, buildings, etc., given or left in this way. ⟨ME < OF *deviser* dispose in portions, arrange, ult. < L *dividere* divide⟩ **—de'vis•a•ble,** *adj.* **—de'vis•al,** *n.*
☛ *Usage.* See note at DEVICE.

de•vis•ee [dɪ,vaɪ'zi] *or* [,dɛvə'zi] *n. Law.* a person to whom land, buildings, etc., are given or left by a will.

de•vis•er [dɪ'vaɪzər] *n.* one who devises; an inventor.

de•vi•sor [dɪ'vaɪzər] *or* [dɪ'vaɪzɔr] *n. Law.* a person who gives or leaves land, buildings, etc. by a will.

de•vi•tal•i•za•tion [di,vəitəlaɪ'zeiʃən] *or* [di,vəitələ'zeiʃən] *n.* devitalizing or being devitalized.

de•vi•tal•ize [di'vəitə,laɪz] *v.* **-ized, -iz•ing. 1** kill; take the life of. **2** weaken; exhaust; make less vital.

de•vit•ri•fy [di'vɪtrɪ,faɪ] *v.* **-fied, -fy•ing.** make (glass, vitreous rock, etc.) opaque and crystalline by intense heat.
—de,vit•ri•fi'ca•tion, *n.*

de•voice [di'vɔɪs] *v.* **-voiced, -voic•ing.** take away the voicing from: *Voiced consonants such as* [d] *at the end of German words are devoiced;* [d] becomes [t].

de•void [dɪ'vɔɪd] *adj.* not having; lacking (*used with* **of**): *a speech completely devoid of humour.* ⟨ME; originally *devoided,* pp. of *devoid* cast out < OF *desvoidier* < *des-* away + *voidier* to empty < *voide* empty, ult. < var. of L *vacuus*⟩

de•voir [də'vwɑr] *n.* **1** Usually, **devoirs,** *pl.* formal acts of courtesy or respect. **2** *Archaic.* duty. ⟨ME < OF, to owe < L *debere*⟩

dev•o•lu•tion [,dɛvə'luʃən] *or* [,divə'luʃən] *n.* **1** a progression from stage to stage. **2** the transmitting or passing of property from person to person; the passing on to a successor of an unexercised right. 3 the delegating (of duty, responsibility, etc.) to another. 4 *Biology.* evolution toward simpler structures or toward the disappearance of structures or functions; degeneration. 5 the decentralizing of authority; transfer of power from a central government to regional or local governments. ⟨< Med.L *devolutio, -onis* < *devolvere.* See DEVOLVE.⟩ **—ˌde•vo'lu•tion•ary,** *adj.* **—ˌde•vo'lu•tion•ist,** *n.*

de•volve [di'vɒlv] *or* [dɪ'vɒlv] *v.* **-volved, -volv•ing. 1** transfer (duty, work, etc.) to someone else. **2** be handed down to someone else; be transferred: *If the president is unable to handle her duties, they devolve upon the vice-president.* ⟨< L *devolvere* < *de-* down + *volvere* roll⟩

Dev•on ['dɛvən] *n.* a breed of beef cattle with red hides. ⟨< the county of *Devonshire* in England, where this breed originated⟩

De•vo•ni•an [də'vouniən] *adj., n. —adj.* **1** of or having to do with Devonshire, a county in SW England. **2** *Geology.* of or having to do with a period of the Paleozoic era.
—n. **1** a native of Devonshire, England. **2** *Geology.* **a** the period of the Paleozoic era coming between the Carboniferous and the Silurian. See geological time chart in the Appendix. **b** the rocks formed during this period.

Devonshire cream ['dɛvənʃər] a rich, thickened cream; clotted cream, usually served with scones.

de•vote [dɪ'vout] *v.* **-vot•ed, -vot•ing. 1** give up (oneself, one's money, time, or efforts) to some person, purpose, or service: *The mother devoted herself to her children.* **2** set apart and consecrate to God or to a sacred purpose. **3** set apart for any particular purpose: *That museum devotes one wing to modern art.* ⟨< L *devotus,* pp. of *devovere* < *de-* entirely + *vovere* vow. Doublet of DEVOUT.⟩
☛ *Syn.* **Devote,** DEDICATE, CONSECRATE = give something or someone up to a purpose. **Devote** emphasizes giving up seriously to a single purpose, shutting out everything else: *He devoted his time to study.* **Dedicate** emphasizes giving up or setting apart earnestly or solemnly for a serious or sacred use: *He dedicated his life to science. They dedicated the hospital.* **Consecrate** = set a person or thing apart as sacred or glorified, by a solemn vow or ceremony: *A bishop consecrated the burial ground.*

de•vot•ed [dɪ'voutɪd] *adj., v. —adj.* **1** loyal; faithful: *a devoted friend.* **2** set apart for some purpose; dedicated; consecrated.
—v. pt. and pp. of DEVOTE. **—de'vot•ed•ly,** *adv.* **—de'vot•ed•ness,** *n.*

dev•o•tee [ˌdɛvə'ti] *n.* **1** a person deeply devoted to something. **2** a person earnestly devoted to religion.

de•vo•tion [dɪ'vouʃən] *n.* **1** a deep, steady affection; a feeling of loyalty; faithfulness: *the devotion of a lifelong friend.* **2** the act of devoting or the state of being devoted: *the devotion of much time to study.* **3** earnestness in religion; devoutness. **4** religious worship or observance; divine worship. **5 devotions,** *pl.* religious worship; private prayers: *He was at his devotions.*

de•vo•tion•al [dɪ'vouʃənəl] *adj., n.* **1** having to do with devotion; used in worship. **2** a short service of Christian worship. **3** a short homily at an informal Christian gathering. **—de'vo•tion•al•ly,** *adv.*

de•vour [dɪ'vaʊr] *v.* **1** of animals, eat. **2** eat hungrily or greedily: *They devoured their meal in about ten minutes.* **3** consume; destroy: *The fire quickly devoured the whole building.* **4** swallow up; engulf. **5** take in with eyes or ears in a hungry, greedy way: *devour a new book.* **6** completely absorb the attention or emotions of: *devoured by curiosity, devoured by envy.* ⟨ME < OF *devorer* < L *devorare* < *de-* down + *vorare* gulp⟩ **—de'vour•er,** *n.* **—de'vour•ing•ly,** *adv.*

de•vout [dɪ'vʌut] *adj.* **1** active in worship and prayer; sincerely religious. **2** showing devotion: *a devout prayer.* **3** earnest; sincere; hearty: *devout thanks, a devout follower.* ⟨ME < OF *devot* < L *devotus,* pp. of *devovere.* Doublet of DEVOTE.⟩ **—de'vout•ly,** *adv.* **—de'vout•ness,** *n.*
☛ *Syn.* **1.** See note at PIOUS.

dew [dju] *or* [du] *n., v. —n.* **1** the moisture from the air that condenses and collects in small drops on cool surfaces during the night. **2** moisture in small drops. **3** anything fresh like dew.
—v. make wet with dew; moisten. ⟨OE *dēaw*⟩ **—'dew•less,** *adj.*
☛ *Hom.* DO[1], DUE [du].

Dewar flask ['djuər] *or* ['duər] a vacuum flask used to store gases. ⟨after John *Dewar* (1848-1923), Scottish chemist⟩

dew•ber•ry ['dju,bɛri] *or* ['du-] *n., pl.* **-ries. 1** any trailing blackberry, including numerous species and cultivated varieties. The northern dewberry (*Rubus flagellarius*) is a North American species found from Nova Scotia and Québec west to Minnesota and south to Texas. **2** the fruit of any of these plants.

dew•claw ['dju,klɒ] *or* ['du,klɒ] *n.* a small, useless hoof or toe on the feet of deer, pigs, dogs, cats, etc.

dew•drop ['dju,drɒp] *or* ['du-] *n.* a drop of dew.

Dew•ey decimal system ['djui] *or* ['dui] one of the two main systems for classifying books, pamphlets, etc. in libraries. Each subject and its subdivisions are assigned specific numbers and decimals. *Examples*: Literature 800, History 900, Canadian History 971, Canadian Northwest History 971.2. ⟨< Melvil *Dewey* (1851-1931), an American librarian who devised the system⟩

dew•fall ['dju,fɒl] *or* ['du,fɒl] *n.* **1** the formation or deposition of dew. **2** the time in the evening when this begins.

dew•lap ['dju,læp] *or* ['du-] *n.* **1** a loose fold of skin under the throat of cattle and some other animals. **2** a similar fold of skin under the throat of certain birds or people. ⟨< *dew* (origin and meaning uncertain) + *lap* < OE *læppa* pendulous piece⟩ **—'dew,lapped,** *adj.*

dew point the temperature at which the water vapour in air that is cooling begins to condense as dew.

dew–worm ['dju,wɜrm] *or* ['du-] *n. Cdn.* any large earthworm that comes to the surface at night when there is dew on the grass. Dew-worms are often used as fishing bait.

dew•y ['djui] *or* ['dui] *adj.* **dew•i•er, dew•i•est. 1** wet with dew. **2** of dew. **3** like dew; refreshing; sparkling; coming gently; vanishing quickly. **—'dew•i•ly,** *adv.* **—'dew•i•ness,** *n.*

dew•y–eyed ['djui ˌaɪd] *or* ['dui ˌaɪd] *adj.* trusting; naive; untainted by cynicism.

dex•a•meth•a•sone [ˌdɛksə'mɛθə,soun] *n.* a corticosteroid drug used to treat certain allergies, etc. *Formula*: $C_{22}H_{29}FO_5$

dex•brom•phe•ni•ra•mine [ˌdɛks,brɒmfə'nirə,min] *n.* an antihistamine drug used to treat nasal congestion.

dex•chlor•phe•ni•ra•mine [ˌdɛks,klɔrfə'nirə,min] *n.* an antihistamine drug used to treat hay fever, etc.

dex•ter ['dɛkstər] *adj.* **1** of or on the right-hand side. **2** *Heraldry.* situated on that part of an escutcheon to the right of the bearer, and hence to the left of the observer. ⟨< L *dexter* right⟩

dex•ter•i•ty [dɛk'stɛrəti] *n.* **1** skill in using the body, especially the hands. **2** skill in using the mind; cleverness.

dex•ter•ous ['dɛkstərəs] *or* ['dɛkstrəs] *adj.* **1** having or showing skill in using the body, especially the hands. **2** having or showing skill in using the mind; clever. Also, **dextrous. —'dex•ter•ous•ly** or **'dex•trous•ly,** *adv.* **—'dex•ter•ous•ness** or **'dex•trous•ness,** *n.*
☛ *Syn.* **1. Dexterous,** DEFT, ADROIT (def. 2) = skilful in using the hands and body. **Dexterous** suggests easy, quick, smooth movements and lightness and sureness of touch coming from practice: *Mary is a dexterous pianist.* **Deft** adds to **dexterous** the idea of neatness and exceptional lightness and swiftness: *A surgeon has to be deft.* **Adroit** adds to **dexterous** the idea of being quick-witted and is sometimes reserved for mental skill or resourcefulness: *The adroit lawyer got the truth out of the witness.*

dex•tral ['dɛkstrəl] *adj.* **1** of the right hand; right-hand. **2** right-handed. **3** having the spire or whorl rising counterclockwise from the bottom right, as with most snail shells.

dex•tral•i•ty [dɛk'strælәti] *n.* **1** the state of being on the right side rather than the left. **2** right-handedness.

dex•tran ['dɛkstræn] *n. Chemistry.* a white, slimy carbohydrate, produced in sugar solutions by bacterial action. It is used to examine the uterus. ⟨< L *dexter* right hand, from its plane of polarization⟩

dex•tra•no•mer ['dɛkstrə,noumər] *n.* a drug used as a wound cleansing agent.

dex•trin ['dɛkstrɪn] *n.* a gummy substance obtained from starch, used as an adhesive, for sizing paper, etc. ⟨< F⟩

dex•trine ['dɛkstrɪn] *or* ['dɛkstrin] *n.* dextrin. ⟨< F *dextrine,* so called for its rightward rotation of the plane of polarization⟩

dextro– *combining form.* toward the right.

dex•tro•am•phet•a•mine [ˌdɛkstrouæm'fɛtə,min] *or* [-mɪn] *n.* a form of amphetamine used in medicine as a stimulant, etc. *Formula*: $C_9H_{13}N$

dex•tro•me•thor•phan [ˌdɛkstroumə'θɔrfən] *n.* a drug used to suppress coughing.

dex•tro•ro•ta•to•ry [ˌdɛkstrə'routə,tɔri] *adj.* **1** turning or causing to turn toward the right or in a clockwise direction. **2** *Physics. Chemistry.* characterized by turning the plane of polarization of light to the right, as a crystal, lens, or compound in solution.

dex•trorse ['dɛkstrɔrs] *adj.* rising spirally from left to right: *the dextrorse stem of a vine.*

dex•trose ['dɛkstrous] *n.* a sugar that is less sweet than cane sugar; a form of glucose. *Formula*: $C_6H_{12}O_6$ ⟨< *dexter* + *(gluc)ose*⟩

dex•tro•thy•rox•ine [,dɛkstrouθaɪ'rɒksin] *n.* a drug used to lower cholesterol.

dex•trous ['dɛkstrəs] *adj.* dexterous.

dey [dei] *n., pl.* **deys.** formerly, a title for rulers of Algiers, Tunis, and Tripoli. ⟨< F < Turkish *dāī*, originally, maternal uncle⟩
☛ *Hom.* DAY.

D.F. Defender of the Faith.

D.F.C. Distinguished Flying Cross.

D.F.M. Distinguished Flying Medal.

D.G. 1 DEI GRATIA. 2 DEO GRATIAS.

dhar•ma ['dɑrmə] *n.* **1** *Buddhism.* law. **2** *Hinduism.* virtue; righteousness; correct behaviour. ⟨< Skt. *dharma* decree, custom, right course of conduct⟩

Dhar•ma•pa•da [,dɑrmə'pʌdə] *n. Buddhism.* a sacred book covering almost every aspect of Buddhist teaching about truth, duty, and enlightenment.

dhar•na ['dɑrnə] *n. Hinduism.* a method of seeking redress in which the wronged party fasts on the wrongdoer's property until satisfaction is given. ⟨< Hind. persistence⟩

dho•bi ['doubi] *n.* in India, a washerperson. ⟨< Hind. *dhob* washing⟩

dhole [doul] *n., pl.* **dholes** or **dhole.** an Asian wild animal (*Cuon alpinus*) of the dog family having a reddish brown coat and rounded ears. Dholes usually hunt in packs. ⟨origin uncertain⟩

dho•ti ['douti] *n.* **1** a garment for the lower body worn especially by Hindu men, consisting of a single, large, unstitched piece of cloth passing between the legs, secured at the waist and loosely wrapping the legs down to the mid-calf or ankle. **2** a fabric used for dhotis. ⟨< Hind.⟩

dhow [daʊ] *n.* a lateen-rigged sailing ship that is used along the coasts of the Arabian peninsula and E Africa. ⟨cf. Arabic *dāw*⟩
☛ *Hom.* TAO.

dhur•rie ['dɜri] *n.* an Indian mat woven in cotton or wool. ⟨< Hind.⟩

di–[1] *prefix.* **1** twice; double; twofold, as in *dicotyledon.* **2** having two atoms, etc., of the substance specified, as in *dioxide.* Also, **dis-**, before *s.* ⟨< Gk. *di-* < *dis*⟩

di–[2] the form of **dis-**[1] before *b, d, l, m, n, r, s, v,* and sometimes before *g* and *j,* as in *direct, divert.*

di–[3] the form of **dia-** before vowels, as in *diorama.*

dia– *prefix.* through; across; thoroughly, as in *diaphragm, diameter.* Also, **di-** before vowels. ⟨< Gk. *dia-* < *dia*, prep.⟩

di•a•be•tes [,daɪə'bitɪs] *or* [,daɪə'bitiz] *n.* any of several diseases characterized by an excessive quantity of urine and abnormal thirst, especially diabetes mellitus. ⟨< NL < Gk. *diabētēs* a passer-through < *dia-* through + *bainein* go⟩

diabetes in•sip•i•dus [ɪn'sɪpɪdəs] a form of diabetes characterized by an excessive quantity of urine and abnormal thirst.

diabetes mel•li•tus [mə'ləitəs] *or* [mə'litəs] a form of diabetes characterized by excessive sugar in the urine and by the inability of the body to absorb normal amounts of sugar and starch, caused by failure to produce insulin, or resistance to insulin. ⟨< NL *diabetes mellitus* honey diabetes⟩

di•a•bet•ic [,daɪə'bɛtɪk] *or* [,daɪə'bitɪk] *adj., n. —adj.* **1** of or having to do with diabetes. **2** having diabetes.
—n. a person having diabetes.

di•a•ble•rie [di'ɑbləri]; *French,* [djablə'ʀi] *n.* **1** diabolic magic or art; sorcery; witchcraft. **2** deviltry; reckless mischief. **3** a domain or realm of devils. **4** the study of devils and deviltry. ⟨< F⟩

di•a•bol•ic [,daɪə'bɒlɪk] *adj.* **1** devilish; like the Devil; very cruel or wicked; fiendish. **2** having to do with the Devil or devils. ⟨< LL *diabolicus* < Gk. *diabolikos* < *diabolos.* See DEVIL.⟩ **—,di•a'bol•i•cal•ly,** *adv.*

di•a•bol•i•cal [,daɪə'bɒləkəl] *adj.* diabolic.

di•ab•o•lism [daɪ'æbə,lɪzəm] *n.* **1** sorcery; witchcraft. **2** a diabolical action; deviltry. **3** belief in or worship of a devil or devils. **4** the character or condition of a devil. **—di'ab•o•list,** *n.*

di•a•ce•tyl•mor•phine [,daɪə,sitɪl'mɔrfin] *n.* a narcotic analgesic drug.

di•a•chron•ic [,daɪə'krɒnɪk] *adj.* of or concerned with the occurrence and development of phenomena, especially of language, over time: *diachronic linguistics.* Compare SYNCHRONIC.

di•a•chron•i•cal•ly [,daɪə'krɒnɪkli] *adv.* in a diachronic manner; chronologically.

diachronic linguistics the study of a language as it has changed over a course of time.

di•ac•o•nal [daɪ'ækənəl] *or* [di'ækənəl] *adj.* of or having to do with a deacon. ⟨< Med.L *diaconalis* < L *diaconus.* See DEACON.⟩

di•ac•o•nate [daɪ'ækə,neit], [daɪ'ækənɪt], *or* [di'ækə,neit] *n.* **1** the rank or position of a deacon. **2** a group of deacons.

di•a•crit•ic [,daɪə'krɪtɪk] *adj., n. —adj.* diacritical.
—n. a diacritical mark. ⟨< Gk. *diakritikos* < *diakrinein* < *dia-* apart + *krinein* separate⟩

di•a•crit•i•cal [,daɪə'krɪtəkəl] *adj.* **1** serving to distinguish; marking a distinction. **2** capable of seeing distinctions: *a woman of superior diacritical powers.* **—,di•a'crit•i•cal•ly,** *adv.*

diacritical mark a mark like ¨ ˆ ¯ ¸ ´ or ` placed over or under a letter to indicate pronunciation, etc.

di•a•del•phous [,daɪə'dɛlfəs] *adj.* **1** of stamens, occurring in two clusters. **2** of a plant, having such stamens. ⟨< *di-*[1] + Gk. *adelphos* brother⟩

di•a•dem ['daɪə,dɛm] *n.* **1** a crown. **2** an ornamental band of cloth formerly worn as a crown. **3** royal power, authority, or dignity. ⟨< L < Gk. *diadēma* < *diadeein* < *dia-* across + *deein* bind⟩

di•ad•ro•mous [daɪ'ædrəməs] *adj.* of fish, such as salmon, travelling between fresh water and salt water. ⟨< *dia-* through + Gk. *-dromos* < *dramein* to run⟩

di•aer•e•sis [daɪ'ɛrəsɪs] *n., pl.* **-ses** [-,siz]. See DIERESIS.

di•a•ge•ot•ro•pism [,daɪədʒi'ɒtrə,pɪzəm] *n.* the tendency of certain plants to grow horizontally along the surface of the ground. **—,di•a,ge•o'tro•pic,** *adj.*

di•ag•nose [,daɪəg'nous] *or* [,daɪəg'nouz] *v.* **-nosed, -nos•ing. 1** make a diagnosis of; find out the nature of by an examination: *The doctor diagnosed the child's disease as measles.* **2** examine (a person) and so arrive at a diagnosis: *She was diagnosed as having cancer.*

di•ag•no•sis [,daɪəg'nousɪs] *n., pl.* **-ses** [-siz]. **1** the act or process of finding out what disease a person or animal has by examination and careful study of the symptoms: *The doctor used X-rays and blood tests in her diagnosis.* **2** a careful study of the facts about something to find out its essential features, faults, etc. **3** a decision reached after a careful study of symptoms or facts. **4** *Biology.* a description that classifies precisely; the scientific determination of a genus, species, etc. ⟨< NL < Gk. *diagnōsis* < *diagignōskein* < *dia-* apart + *gignōskein* learn to know⟩

di•ag•nos•tic [,daɪəg'nɒstɪk] *adj., n. —adj.* **1** of or having to do with diagnosis: *a diagnostic survey of the problem.* **2** helping in diagnosis: *diagnostic tests.*
—n. **1 diagnostics,** *pl.* (*with a singular verb*) the art of making medical diagnoses. **2** a characteristic sign; piece of evidence: *Frequent turnover is a good diagnostic of employee dissatisfaction.* **—,di•ag'nos•ti•cal•ly,** *adv.*

di•ag•nos•ti•cian [,daɪəgnɒ'stɪʃən] *n.* a person who is expert in making diagnoses.

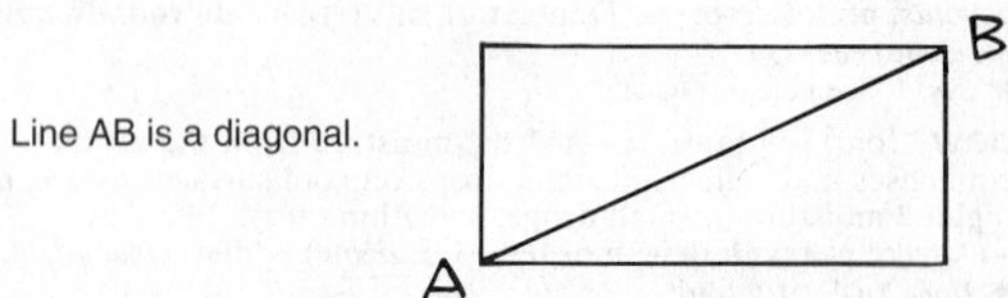

Line AB is a diagonal.

di•ag•o•nal [daɪ'ægənəl] *adj., n. —adj.* **1** *Geometry.* joining any two non-adjacent angles or vertices of a polygon or polyhedron. **2** slanting; oblique. **3** having slanting parts, lines, etc.: *a diagonal weave.*
—n. **1** *Geometry.* a diagonal line or plane. **2** a diagonal direction, course, line, pattern, etc. **3** something set or placed on a slant. **4** a short, slanting line between two words, as in *and/or.* ⟨< L

diagonalis < Gk. *diagōnios* from angle to angle < *dia-* across + *gōnia* angle⟩

di•ag•o•nal•ly [daɪ'ægənəli] *adv.* in a diagonal direction.

di•a•gram ['daɪə,græm] *n., v.* **-grammed** or **-gramed, -gram•ming** or **-gram•ing.** *—n.* **1** a drawing or sketch showing important parts of a thing. A diagram may be an outline, a plan, a drawing, a figure, a chart, or a combination of any of these, made to show clearly what a thing is or how it works: *He drew a diagram to show us how to get to his house. The engineer drew a diagram of the bridge.* **2** *Mathematics.* a figure used to aid in the proof of a geometrical proposition or as a mathematical representation.
—v. put on paper, a chalkboard, etc. in the form of a drawing or sketch; make a diagram of. ⟨< L < Gk. *diagramma* < *dia-* apart, out + *graphein* mark⟩

di•a•gram•mat•ic [,daɪəgrə'mætɪk] *adj.* **1** in the form of a diagram. **2** in outline only; sketchy. **—,di•a•gram'mat•ic•al•ly,** *adv.*

di•a•gram•mat•i•cal [,daɪəgrə'mætəkəl] *adj.* diagrammatic.

di•a•ki•ne•sis [,daɪəkɪ'nisɪs] *n.* a late prophase stage in cell division in which homologous chromosomes have completely separated and crossed over. ⟨< NL *dia* through + Gk. *kinesis* motion⟩

di•al ['daɪəl] *or* [daɪl] *n., v.* **-alled** or **-aled, -al•ling** or **-al•ing.** *—n.* **1** a marked surface on which a moving pointer indicates a measurement of some kind. The face of a clock or of a compass is a dial. A dial may show the amount of water in a tank or the amount of steam pressure in a boiler. **2** the plate or disk on a radio or television set marked with numbers to identify the station frequencies, and having a movable indicator connected to a tuning knob for tuning in different stations. **3** a disk on a telephone that is rotated in order to make connection with another telephone line. **4** the control knob in the centre of the face of a combination lock that must be rotated through a particular sequence of numbers in order to open the lock. **5** a sundial.
—v. use a dial in order to operate, select, etc.: *to dial a combination on a lock, to dial a favourite program. Dial carefully when you use the phone. He dialled a wrong number.*
dial direct, make a telephone call without using an operator: *I dialled direct but got a wrong number.* ⟨apparently < Med.L *(rota) dialis* daily (wheel) < L *dies* day⟩

dial. dialect; dialectal.

dial–a–bus ['daɪəl ə ,bʌs] *n.* a system of public transportation in which a bus arrives in response to a phone call.

di•a•lect ['daɪə,lɛkt] *n.* **1** a form of speech characteristic of a fairly definite region or class: *the Scottish dialect, the dialect spoken in Lunenberg, Nova Scotia.* **2** one of a group of closely related languages: *Some of the Romance dialects* (*all descended from Latin*) *are French, Italian, Spanish, Romanian, Romansch, and Portuguese.* **3** the JARGON (def. 3) of a profession or other group: *thieves' dialect.* **4** (*adjl.*) of or having to do with a dialect or dialects: *a dialect dictionary, a dialect atlas.* ⟨< L *dialectus* < Gk. *dialektos,* ult. < *dia-* between + *legein* speak⟩

☛ *Syn.* **1.** See note at LANGUAGE.

☛ *Usage.* **Dialects** exist because of the separation of groups of speakers either regionally or socially. Where several regional dialects exist, one may attain the highest status because it may be spoken in the area which contains the centre of government, education, or trade. A dialect is a valid form of a language; it is not to be confused with a misuse of a standard form.

di•a•lec•tal [,daɪə'lɛktəl] *adj.* of or having to do with a dialect; like that of a dialect. **—,di•a'lec•tal•ly,** *adv.*

di•a•lec•tic [,daɪə'lɛktɪk] *n., adj.* *—n.* **1** the art or practice of logical discussion employed in finding out the truth of a theory or opinion. **2** logical argumentation; a discussion of the logical truth of an opinion or theory. **3** *Logic.* a branch that consists of formal rhetorical reasoning. **4** *Logic.* a method based on the resolution of contradictory opposites, thesis and antithesis, leading to synthesis.
—adj. **1** having to do with logical discussion: *dialectic criticism.* **2** dialectal.

di•a•lec•ti•cal [,daɪə'lɛktəkəl] *adj.* dialectic. **—,di•a'lec•ti•cal•ly,** *adv.*

dialectical materialism a socialist doctrine formulated by Karl Marx and Friedrich Engels, using the philosopher Hegel's dialectic method, that advocates a classless society emerging as the result of a long struggle between economic classes.

di•a•lec•ti•cian [,daɪəlɛk'tɪʃən] *n.* **1** a person skilled in dialectic; logician. **2** dialectologist.

di•a•lec•tics [,daɪə'lɛktɪks] *n.* dialectic.

di•a•lec•tol•o•gist [,daɪəlɛk'tɒlədʒɪst] *n.* a person trained in dialectology, especially one whose work it is.

di•a•lec•tol•o•gy [,daɪəlɛk'tɒlədʒi] *n.* the study of dialects, regional and social.

di•a•log ['daɪə,lɒg] *Esp. U.S.* See DIALOGUE.

di•al•o•gist [daɪ'ælədʒɪst] *or* ['daɪə,lɒgɪst] *n.* **1** a person who writes dialogues. **2** a person who dialogues.

di•a•logue ['daɪə,lɒg] *n., v.* **-logued, -logu•ing.** *—n.* **1** conversation between two or more persons. **2** the element of a story, play, film, etc. that consists of conversation: *The play has clever dialogue. Dialogue is difficult for some novelists.* **3** communication or interchange of ideas or opinions, especially between individuals or groups having opposing or very different viewpoints. **4** *Music.* a composition for two voices or instruments or two groups of voices or instruments, thought of as resembling a conversation. **5** a literary work in the form of a conversation.
—v. **1** take part in a dialogue. **2** express in the form of a dialogue. ⟨ME < OF *dialoge* < L < Gk. *dialogos* < *dia-* between + *logos* speech⟩

dial tone the humming sound that is heard in a telephone receiver when the receiver is lifted, indicating that the line is in service and open for use.

di•a•lyse or **di•a•lyze** ['daɪə,laɪz] *v.* **-lysed** or **-lyzed, -lys•ing** or **-lyz•ing.** *Chemistry.* **1** apply dialysis to. **2** separate or procure by dialysis. **—'di•a,lys•er,** or **'di•a,lyz•er,** *n.*

di•al•y•sis [daɪ'æləsɪs] *n., pl.* **-ses** [-,siz]. **1** *Chemistry.* the separation of crystalloids from colloids in solution by the application of the principle that crystalloids diffuse readily through a membrane, and colloids not at all or very slightly. **2** *Medicine.* the separation of waste matter from the blood in an artificial kidney, using this process. ⟨< Gk. *dialysis* < *dia-* apart + *lyein* loose⟩

di•a•lyt•ic [,daɪə'lɪtɪk] *adj.* having to do with or like dialysis. **—,di•a'lyt•ic•al•ly,** *adv.*

di•a•lyze ['daɪə,laɪz] *v.* **-lyzed, -lyz•ing.** See DIALYSE.

di•a•lyz•er ['daɪə,laɪzər] *n.* a machine for dialysis, such as an artificial kidney.

diam. diameter.

di•a•mag•net•ic [,daɪəmæg'nɛtɪk] *adj., n.* *—adj.* repelled by a magnet; taking a position at right angles to the lines of force of a magnet.
—n. a diamagnetic body or substance. **—,di•a•mag'net•i•cal•ly,** *adv.*

di•a•mag•net•ism [,daɪə'mægnə,tɪzəm] *n.* **1** a diamagnetic quality. **2** diamagnetic phenomena. **3** diamagnetic force. **4** the science dealing with diamagnetic phenomena.

dia•man•té [,diəmɒn'tei] *or* [diə'mɒntei]; *French,* [djamɑ̃'te] *n., adj.* *—n. French.* a fabric set with rhinestones, etc., so that it sparkles.
—adj. set with diamonds, artificial diamonds, or diamond chips: *diamanté buttons.* ⟨< F, pp. of *diamanter* set with diamonds < *diamant* diamond⟩

di•am•e•ter [daɪ'æmətər] *n.* **1** a straight line passing from one side to the other through the centre of a circle, sphere, etc. See CIRCLE for picture. **2** the length of such a line, especially a measurement of width or thickness through the centre of a round object such as a ball, tree trunk, etc. **3** *Optics.* the unit of measure of lens magnification. ⟨< OF *diametre* < L < Gk. *diametros* < *dia-* across + *metron* measure⟩

di•a•met•ric [,daɪə'mɛtrɪk] *adj.* **1** of or along a diameter. **2** of an opposite or opposites, direct, absolute, or exact.

di•a•met•ri•cal [,daɪə'mɛtrəkəl] *adj.* diametric.

di•a•met•ri•cal•ly [,daɪə'mɛtrɪkli] *adv.* **1** as a diameter. **2** directly; exactly; entirely.
diametrically opposed, directly opposite; exactly contrary.

dia•mond ['daɪmənd] *or* ['daɪəmənd] *n.* **1** a colourless or tinted precious stone, formed of pure carbon in crystals. Diamond is the hardest substance known. **2** a piece of this stone, or a gem made from it. Inferior diamonds are used to cut glass. **3** (*adjl.*) made of or containing diamond or a diamond: *a diamond ring.* **4** a tool with a diamond tip for cutting. **5** a plane figure shaped like this ♦. **6 a** a playing card with one or more red diamond-shaped designs on it. **b diamonds,** *pl.* the suit of cards marked with this design. **7** *Baseball.* the space inside the lines that connect the bases.
diamond cut diamond, a dispute or struggle between two well-matched opponents.

diamond in the rough or **rough diamond,** a person who has good qualities but poor manners. ⟨ME < OF *diamant* < Med.L *diamas, -antis,* alteration of L *adamas, -antis* adamant⟩

diamond anniversary a 60th or, sometimes, 75th anniversary in a series.

dia•mond•back ['daımәndbæk] *or* ['daıәmәnd-] *n.* **1** a large, very dangerous rattlesnake (*Crotalus adamanteus*) of the S United States, having cream and grey diamond-shaped markings. **2 diamondback terrapin,** an edible turtle (*Malaclemys terrapin*), having a shell marked with diamond shapes, found in salt water in North America. **3** a moth (*Plutella xylostella*), having brown and white wings that fold into a diamond shape.

diamond hitch a hitch used in fastening a load to a pack animal, in which the rope is thrown back and forth across the animal in such a way that it forms a diamond pattern on top of the pack.

diamond jubilee the celebration of a 60th or, sometimes, 75th anniversary in a series.

diamond wedding the 60th or, sometimes, 75th anniversary of a wedding.

diamond willow *Cdn.* willow wood having a diamond-patterned grain, resulting from an abnormal growth of the stems that may occur in any species of willow. It is prized for making lamps, walking sticks, ornaments, etc.

Di•an•a [daı'ænә] *n.* **1** *Roman mythology.* the goddess who was the protector and helper of women. She was also the goddess of the moon and of hunting and corresponds to the Greek goddess Artemis. **2** *Poetic.* moon.

di•an•drous [daı'ændrәs] *adj.* that has two stamens. ⟨< *di-*[1] + Gk. *aner, andr-* man⟩

di•an•thus [daı'ænθәs] *n.* any of a genus (*Dianthus*) of annual and perennial herbs of the pink family, including the carnation, sweet william, and pink. ⟨< NL *Dianthus* < Gk. *Dios,* genitive of *Zeus* Zeus + *anthos* flower⟩

di•a•pa•son [,daıә'peizәn] *or* [,daıә'peisәn] *n.* **1** *Poetic.* harmony. **2** melody; strain. **3** a swelling musical sound. **4** the whole range of a voice or instrument. **5** range; gamut; entire scope: *the diapason of emotional experience.* **6** a fixed standard of pitch. **7** a tuning fork. **8** in an organ, either of two principal stops: **a open diapason,** a stop giving full, majestic tones. **b stopped diapason,** a stop giving powerful flutelike tones. **9** *Greek music.* octave. ⟨< L < Gk. *diapasōn* octave < *dia pasōn (chordōn)* across all (the notes of the scale)⟩

di•a•pause ['daıә,pɒz] *n.* in the life cycle of some insects and other animals, a period of suspended development and inactivity.

di•a•pen•sia [,daiә'pɛnsiә] *n.* a northern wildflower (*Diapensia lapponica*) blooming in the summer in arctic regions, and having small, white flowers with yellow centres.

Diaper (def. 3)

di•a•per ['dәipәr] *or* ['daıәpәr] *n., v.* —*n.* **1** a piece of cloth folded up, or a pad of other absorbent material, as underpants for a baby; napkin. **2** an allover pattern of small, repeated geometric figures, especially diamonds. **3** a white cotton or linen cloth woven with such a pattern. Babies' diapers were originally made of such material.
—*v.* **1** put a diaper on: *to diaper a baby.* **2** ornament with a diaper pattern. ⟨ME < OF *diapre,* var. of *diaspre* < Med.Gk. *diaspros* < *dia-* (intensive) + *aspros* white⟩

di•aph•a•nous [daı'æfәnәs] *adj.* **1** transparent: *Gauze is a diaphanous fabric.* **2** hazy; vague. ⟨< Med.L *diaphanus* < Gk. *diaphanēs* < *dia-* through + *phainein* show⟩ **—di'aph•a•nous•ly,** *adv.* **—di'aph•a•nous•ness,** *n.*

di•a•phone ['daıә,foun] *n. Linguistics.* the set of speech sounds which includes all the variants of any phoneme.

di•a•pho•re•sis [,daıәfә'risis] *n. Medicine.* perspiration, especially when artificially induced. ⟨< LL < Gk. *diaphorēsis* < *dia-* through + *phorein* carry⟩

di•a•pho•ret•ic [,daıәfә'rɛtık] *adj., n.* —*adj.* causing perspiration.
—*n.* a drug, herb, or other agent causing perspiration.

di•a•phragm ['daıә,fræm] *n.* **1** a partition of muscles and tendons separating the cavity of the chest from the cavity of the abdomen. See LIVER for picture. **2** a thin partition in some shellfish, etc. **3** a similar partition in plants. **4** a thin disk or cone that moves rapidly to and fro when sounds or electrical signals are directed at it, used in telephone receivers, microphones, earphones, and in similar instruments. **5** a device for controlling the amount of light entering a camera, microscope, etc. **6** a contraceptive device for women, consisting of a flexible, moulded cap, usually made of thin rubber, that is fitted over the entrance to the uterus to prevent the entry of sperm. ⟨< LL < Gk. *diaphragma* < *dia-* across + *phragma* fence < *phrassein* to fence⟩

di•a•phrag•mat•ic [,daıәfræg'mætık] *adj.* having to do with a diaphragm; like a diaphragm. **—,di•a•phrag'mat•ic•al•ly,** *adv.*

di•ar•chy ['daıarki] *n., pl.* **-chies.** government by two people or two ruling authorities. Also, **dyarchy.** ⟨< Gk. *di-* twice + *archos* ruler (< *archein* to rule) + E *-y*[3]⟩

di•a•rist ['daıәrıst] *n.* a person who keeps a diary.

di•ar•rhe•a or **di•ar•rhoe•a** [,daıә'riә] *n.* the condition of having too many and too loose movements of the bowels. ⟨< LL *diarrhoea* < Gk. *diarrhoia* < *dia-* through + *rheein* flow⟩ **—,di•ar'rhe•al,** *adj.*

di•a•ry ['daıәri] *or* ['daıri] *n., pl.* **-ries. 1** an account, written down each day, of what one has done, thought, etc. during the day. **2** a book for keeping such an account. ⟨< L *diarium* < *dies* day⟩

Di•as•po•ra [daı'æspәrә] *n.* **1** the scattering of the Jews after their captivity in Babylon. **2** the Jews thus scattered. **3** the places where they settled. **4** the early Jewish Christians living outside Palestine. **5** Jews living outside modern Israel. **6** often, **diaspora,** any scattered people with a common bond. ⟨< Gk. *diaspora* a scattering < *dia-* through + *speirein* sow⟩

di•a•stase ['daıә,steis] *n.* an enzyme that changes starch into dextrine and maltose during digestion, germination of seeds, etc. ⟨< F < Gk. *diastasis* separation < *dia-* apart + *sta-* stand⟩ **—di•a'stat•ic** [,daıә'stætık], *adj.*

di•as•to•le [daı'æstәli] *n.* the normal, rhythmical dilation of the heart, especially that of the ventricles. Compare SYSTOLE. ⟨< LL < Gk. *diastolē* expansion < *dia-* apart + *stellein* send⟩

di•as•tol•ic [,daıә'stɒlık] *adj.* having to do with diastole.

diastolic pressure the blood pressure measured when the heart is refilling after pumping blood. Diastolic pressure is lower than SYSTOLIC PRESSURE.

di•as•tro•phism [daı'æstrә,fızәm] *n.* the action of the forces that have caused the deformation of the earth's crust, producing mountains, continents, etc. ⟨< Gk. *diastrophe* distortion⟩ **—,di•a'stroph•ic,** *adj.*

di•a•ther•mic [,daıә'θɜrmık] *adj.* **1** having to do with diathermy. **2** allowing heat rays to penetrate. ⟨< F *diathermique* < Gk. *dia-* through + *thermē* heat⟩

di•a•ther•my ['daıә,θɜrmi] *n.* a method of treating disease by heating the tissues beneath the skin with an electric current.

di•ath•e•sis [daı'æθәsıs] *n.* a tendency to contract certain diseases. ⟨< NL < Gk. *diathesis* arrangement < *diatithenai* to arrange < *dia-* apart + *tithenai* to put⟩ **—,di•a'thet•ic** [,daıә'θɛtık], *adj.*

di•a•tom ['daıә,tɒm] *n.* any of numerous microscopic, unicellular, aquatic algae that have hard shells composed mostly of silica. ⟨< NL *Diatoma,* genus name < Gk. *diatomos* cut in half < *diatemnein* cut through⟩

di•a•to•ma•ceous [,daıәtә'meiʃәs] *adj.* of or having to do with diatoms; consisting of or containing diatoms or their fossil remains: *diatomaceous earth.*

di•a•tom•ic [,daıә'tɒmık] *adj. Chemistry.* **1** containing only two atoms. **2** containing two replaceable atoms. **3** bivalent.

di•at•o•mite [daı'ætә,mәit] *n.* earth consisting of the fossil remains of diatoms; diatomaceous earth. It is used as an abrasive, insulator, filter, etc.

di•a•ton•ic [,daıә'tɒnık] *adj. Music.* of or using only the eight tones of a standard major or minor scale. ⟨< L *diatonicus* < Gk. *diatonikos* < *dia-* through + *tonos* tone⟩ **—,di•a'ton•ic•al•ly,** *adv.*

diatonic scale *Music.* a standard major or minor scale of eight tones in the octave.

di•a•tribe ['daıә,traıb] *n.* a bitter and violent denunciation of some person or thing. ⟨< L *diatriba* < Gk. *diatribē* pastime, study, discourse < *dia-* away + *tribein* wear⟩

di•a•tri•zo•ate [ˌdaɪəˈtrɪzouˌeit] *n.* a drug used in radiography of the gastrointestinal tract.

di•a•ze•pam [daɪˈæzəˌpæm] *n.* a drug used to relieve anxiety; a minor tranquillizer. *Formula:* $C_{16}H_{13}ClN_2O$

di•az•i•non [daɪˈæzəˌnɒn] *n.* a colourless, liquid insecticide, used against flies, on fruit trees, etc. *Formula:* $C_{12}H_{21}N_2O_3PS$

di•a•zox•ide [ˌdaɪəˈzɒksaɪd] *n.* a drug used to lower blood pressure. *Formula:* $C_8H_7ClN_2O_2S$

dib [dɪb] *n., interj.* —*n.* **1** a small marble, usually made of clay: *She bought some dibs at the store.* **2 dibs,** *pl.* the game played with such marbles. **3 dibs,** *pl. Slang.* **a** money made, especially in small amounts. **b** one's share or shares in any profitable venture. **4 dibs,** *pl. Informal.* a stated claim to a desired object: *I have first dibs on the ice cream.*
—*interj.* a word used in assertion of such a claim: *Dibs on the ice cream!* ⟨origin uncertain⟩

di•ba•sic [daɪˈbeisɪk] *adj. Chemistry.* **1** having two hydrogen atoms that can be replaced by two atoms or radicals of a base in forming salts. **2** having two atoms of a monovalent metal.

dib•ble [ˈdɪbəl] *n., v.* **-bled, -bling.** —*n.* a pointed tool that makes holes in the ground for seeds, young plants, etc.
—*v.* **1** make a hole in (the soil) with or as if with a dibble. **2** sow or plant (seeds, etc.) in this way. ⟨origin uncertain⟩

di•brach [ˈdaɪˌbræk] *n. Prosody.* PYRRHIC[2]. ⟨< *di-*[1] + Gk. *brachion* arm⟩

di•bu•caine [daɪˈbjukein] *n.* a drug used in a cream form as a topical anesthetic. *Formula:* $C_{20}H_{29}N_3O_2$

dice [dəis] *n.* pl. of **die**[3]; *v.* **diced, dic•ing.** —*n.* **1** small cubes with a different number of spots (one to six) on each side, used, usually in pairs, in playing games and gambling. **2** *Informal.* a single one of these cubes; DIE[3]. **3** a game of chance played with such cubes (*used with a singular verb*). **4** small cubes of food.
load the dice, *Informal.* decide or ensure the outcome for or against something unfairly in advance.
no dice, *Slang.* **a** a failing or lack of success. **b** no (in answer to a request).
—*v.* **1** play dice, tossing them to see how many spots there will be on the sides turned up. **2** lose by gambling with dice (*used with* **away**): *She diced away her inheritance.* **3** take serious risks: *dicing with death.* **4** cut (vegetables, etc.) into small cubes: *to dice carrots.* **5** ornament with a pattern of cubes or squares.
—**ˈdic•er,** *n.*

di•ceph•a•lous [dəiˈsɛfələs] *adj.* having two heads, as with certain animal abnormalities.

dic•ey [ˈdəisi] *adj. Slang.* **1** chancy; risky; uncertain. **2** on the point of erupting into a dangerous situation.

di•chlor•a•ce•tic acid [ˌdəiklɔrəˈsitɪk] a chemical used in medicine to cauterize calluses and verrucas.

di•chlo•ride [dəiˈklɔraɪd] *or* [-ˈklɔrɪd] *n.* a compound composed of chlorine and one other element or a radical, with two atoms of chlorine for every atom of the other element or radical.

di•chon•dra [dəiˈkɒndrə] *n.* any vine of the genus *Dichondra,* of the morning-glory family, often grown as a ground cover instead of grass. ⟨< NL < Gk. *di-* twice + *chondros* grain⟩

di•chot•o•mous [dəiˈkɒtəməs] *adj.* **1** divided or dividing into two parts. **2** *Botany.* branching by repeated divisions into two.
—**diˈchot•o•mous•ly,** *adv.*

dichotomous classification a system of classifying objects by repeatedly categorizing into one of two possible sets.

di•chot•o•my [dəiˈkɒtəmi] *n., pl.* **-mies. 1** a division into two parts. Compare POLYCHOTOMY. **2** *Botany.* branching by repeated divisions into two parts. **3** *Zoology.* a form of branching in which each successive axis divides into two. **4** *Logic.* classification by division, or by successive subdivison, into two categorically opposed groups or sections: *the dichotomy in the universe of the living and the non-living.* ⟨< Gk. *dichotomia* a cutting in half < *dicha* in two + *temnein* cut⟩ —**diˈchot•o•mize,** *v.*

di•chro•ic [dəiˈkrouɪk] *adj.* **1** having or showing two colours. **2** of a crystal, showing two different colours according to the direction of transmitted light, due to a difference in the amount of absorption of the rays. **3** of a solution, showing different colours for different concentrations, as a solution of chlorophyl. ⟨< Gk. *dichroos* of two colours < *di-* + *chros* colour⟩

di•chro•ism [ˈdəikrouˌɪzəm] *n.* **1** the property of certain crystals which give off different colours when viewed from two different directions. **2** the showing of different colours by certain solutions in different strengths. **3** the characteristic of certain substances in showing different colours according to whether light is reflected or transmitted.

di•chro•mate [dəiˈkroumeit] *n.* a chromate whose molecules have two atoms of chromium; bichromate.

di•chro•mat•ic [ˌdəikrouˈmætɪk] *adj.* **1** having two colours. **2** *Zoology.* showing two colour phases independent of phases correlated with age, sex, or season. **3** of, having to do with, or affected with DICHROMATISM (def. 2).

di•chro•ma•tism [dəiˈkrouməˌtɪzəm] *n.* **1** a dichromatic quality or condition. **2** colour blindness in which a person can distinguish only two of the primary colours. ⟨See DI-[1], CHROMATIC⟩

dick [dɪk] *n. Slang.* detective. ⟨shortened form of *detective*⟩

dick•cis•sel [dɪkˈsɪsəl] *n.* a brownish grey finch (*Spiza americana*) that breeds in central North America and winters in N South America. The adult male in breeding plumage looks like a tiny meadowlark. ⟨imitative⟩

dick•ens [ˈdɪkənz] *n., interj.* —*n.* the devil; deuce.
—*interj.* **the dickens!** an exclamation expressing surprise or annoyance.

Dick•en•si•an [dɪˈkɛnziən] *or* [dɪˈkɛnsiən] *adj., n.* —*adj.* **1** of or having to do with Charles Dickens (1812-1870), an English novelist. **2** of or suggestive of his style, writings, characters, etc.
—*n.* a person who studies or admires Charles Dickens or his works.

dick•er [ˈdɪkər] *v., n.* —*v.* trade by barter or by petty bargaining.
—*n.* **1** a petty bargain. **2** the act of bargaining. ⟨< *dicker,* n., a lot of ten hides⟩

dick•ey[1] [ˈdɪki] *n., pl.* **-eys. 1** a shirt front that can be detached. **2** a high collar on a shirt. **3** a child's bib or pinafore. **4** a false shirt or blouse front worn under a cardigan, jacket, low-cut dress, etc. **5** the driver's seat on the outside of a carriage. **6** a seat at the back of a carriage for servants. **7** a small bird. **8** donkey. ⟨< *Dick,* proper name⟩

dick•ey[2] [ˈdɪki] *n., pl.* **-eys.** *Cdn.* a pullover garment for the upper body, having a hood and made of duffel or skins; parka; ATIGI (def. 2). Also, **dickie, dicky.** ⟨< Inuktitut *atigi*⟩

dick•ie [ˈdɪki] *n., pl.* **-ies.** See DICKEY[2].

dick•y [ˈdɪki] *n., pl.* **-ies.** See DICKEY[2].

di•cli•nous [dəiˈklaɪnəs] *or* [ˈdəiklənəs] *adj. Botany.* **1** having pistils and stamens in separate flowers, either on one plant or on separate plants. **2** containing only pistils or only stamens. ⟨< *di-*[1] + Gk. *kline* bed⟩

di•clo•fe•nac [ˌdəiklouˈfɛnək] *n.* a drug used to treat rheumatoid arthritis and osteoarthritis.

di•clox•a•cil•lin [ˌdəiklɒksəˈsɪlɪn] *n.* an antibiotic drug.

di•cot [ˈdəikɒt] *n.* dicotyledon.

di•cot•y•le•don [dəiˌkɒtəˈlidən] *or* [ˌdaɪkɒtəˈlidən] *n. Botany.* any flowering plant having two seed leaves (cotyledons) in the embryo, including the hardwood trees and most cultivated plants. Dicotyledons and monocotyledons constitute the two main groups of angiosperms. See also MONOCOTYLEDON.

di•cot•y•le•don•ous [dəiˌkɒtəˈlidənəs] *or* [ˌdaɪkɒtəˈlidənəs] *adj. Botany.* having two seed leaves; belonging to the dicotyledons.

di•crot•ic [dəiˈkrɒtɪk] *adj.* having two pulse beats per heart beat. ⟨< Gk. *dikrotos* double-beating < *di-* double + *krotos* rattling noise⟩

dict. 1 dictionary. **2** dictator.

dic•ta [ˈdɪktə] *n.* a pl. of DICTUM.

Dic•ta•phone [ˈdɪktəˌfoun] *n. Trademark.* an instrument that records and reproduces sounds, used for dictating and transcribing. ⟨< *dicta(te)* + *-phone*⟩

dic•tate *v.* [ˈdɪkteit] *or* [dɪkˈteit]; *n.* [ˈdɪkteit] *v.* **-tat•ed, -tat•ing;** *n.* —*v.* **1** say or read (something) aloud for another person or other persons to write or type: *to dictate a letter, to dictate a spelling list.* **2** command with authority; give (orders that must be obeyed): *No one is going to dictate to me.*
—*n.* a direction or order that is to be carried out or obeyed: *An honest man follows the dictates of his conscience.* ⟨< L *dictare* say often < *dicere* tell, say⟩

dic•ta•tion [dɪkˈteiʃən] *n.* **1** the act of saying or reading (something) aloud for another person or other persons to write or type: *The pupils wrote to the teacher's dictation.* **2** the words said or read aloud to be written down: *I did not catch the first sentence of the dictation.* **3** the act of commanding with authority;

act of giving orders that must be obeyed: *The servant acted at the dictation of his master.*

dic•ta•tor ['dɪkteitər] *or* [dɪk'teitər] *n.* **1** a person exercising absolute authority; especially, a person who, without having any claim through inheritance or free popular election, seizes control of a government: *The dictator of the country had complete power over its people.* **2** a person whose authority is widely accepted in some special field: *a dictator of men's fashions.* **3** a person who dictates words or sentences for someone else to record. **4** in Roman history, an official given absolute authority over the state in times of emergency.

dic•ta•to•ri•al [,dɪktə'tɔriəl] *adj.* **1** of or like that of a dictator: *dictatorial government.* **2** imperious; domineering; overbearing: *The soldiers disliked the dictatorial manner of the new officer.* **—,dic•ta'to•ri•al•ly,** *adv.*

dic•ta•tor•ship [dɪk'teitər,ʃɪp] *or* ['dɪkteitər,ʃɪp] *n.* **1** the position or rank of a dictator. **2** the period during which a dictator rules. **3** absolute authority; the power to give orders that must be obeyed. **4** a country under the rule of a dictator.

dic•tion ['dɪkʃən] *n.* **1** the manner of expressing ideas in words; style of speaking or writing. Good diction implies grammatical correctness, a wide vocabulary, and skill in the choice and arrangement of words. **2** pronunciation and enunciation in speaking or singing: *clear diction.* ⟨< L *dictio, -onis* saying < *dicere* say⟩

☛ *Syn.* **Diction,** PHRASEOLOGY, WORDING = words and the way of using them. **Diction** applies to words and emphasizes the choice of words used to express ideas and feelings and the way in which they convey meaning: *John's diction is poor; he uses too much slang and too many colourless words.* **Phraseology** applies to the grouping of words, particularly in the way peculiar to a person, group, profession, etc.: *I don't understand legal phraseology.* **Wording** applies to words and grouping but emphasizes their special suitability for a purpose: *I like the wording of that greeting.*

dic•tion•ar•y ['dɪkʃə,nɛri] *n., pl.* **-ar•ies. 1** a book of words arranged alphabetically, with information about their meanings, forms, and, usually, pronunciation and history. Some dictionaries also give information on how words are used in sentences and idiomatic expressions. **2** a book of names or words of some special subject or activity, arranged alphabetically, with information on meanings, uses, etc.: *a law dictionary, a dictionary of trademarks.* **3** a book of alphabetically arranged words of one language with equivalent words or meanings in another language: *an English-Czech dictionary, a French-English dictionary.* ⟨< Med.L *dictionarium* < L *dictio.* See DICTION.⟩

Dic•to•graph ['dɪktə,græf] *n. Trademark.* a telephone with a very sensitive transmitter, used for secretly listening to or obtaining a record of conversation. ⟨< L *dictum* (thing) said + E *-graph*⟩

dic•tum ['dɪktəm] *n., pl.* **-tums** or **-ta** [-tə]. **1** a formal comment; an authoritative opinion: *The dictum of the critics was that the play was excellent.* **2** maxim; saying. ⟨< L *dictum* (thing) said, pp. neut. of *dicere* say⟩

di•cy•clo•mine [dəi'səiklə,min] *n.* a drug used to relieve muscle spasm of the gastrointestinal tract.

did [dɪd] *v.* pt. of DO[1].

di•dact ['daɪdækt] *n.* a didactic person. ⟨back-formation from *didactic*⟩

di•dac•tic [daɪ'dæktɪk] *or* [dɪ'dæktɪk] *adj.* **1** intended to instruct: *The fables of Aesop are didactic stories; each one has an instructive moral.* **2** inclined to instruct others; teacherlike: *The older brother was called "Professor" because of his didactic manner.* ⟨< Gk. *didaktikos* < *didaskein* teach⟩ **—di'dac•ti•cal•ly,** *adv.*

di•dac•ti•cal [daɪ'dæktəkəl] *or* [dɪ'dæktəkəl] *adj.* didactic.

di•dac•ti•cism [daɪ'dæktə,sɪzəm] *or* [dɪ'dæktə,sɪzəm] *n.* a didactic quality, character, or manner.

di•dac•tics [daɪ'dæktɪks] *or* [dɪ'dæktɪks] *n.* the science or art of giving instruction.

di•da•no•sine [daɪ'dænə,sin] *n.* dideoxynosine.

did•dle ['dɪdəl] *v.* **-dled, -dling.** *Informal.* **1** cheat; swindle. **2** waste (time). **3** ruin. **4** fiddle with; fool around with. ⟨origin uncertain⟩

di•de•ox•y•cy•ti•dine [,dɪdi,ɒksɪ'səitə,din] *n.* a drug used experimentally in the treatment of AIDS. *Formula*: $C_9H_{13}N_3O_3$

di•de•ox•y•no•sine [,dɪdi,ɒksɪ'nou,sin] *n.* an antiviral drug used experimentally in the treatment of AIDS. *Formula*: $C_{10}H_{12}N_4O_3$

did•n't ['dɪdənt] contraction of did not.

di•do ['daɪdou] *n., pl.* **-dos** or **-does.** *Informal.* a prank; trick; a mischievous or disorderly action.
cut up didos, *Informal.* get into mischief. ⟨origin uncertain⟩

didst [dɪdst] *v. Archaic or poetic.* 2nd pers. sing. past tense of **do**[1]. *Thou didst* means *You* (sing.) *did.*

did•y•mous ['dɪdəməs] *adj. Botany.* paired or having two parts. ⟨< Gk. *didymos* twin, two⟩

die[1] [daɪ] *v.* **died, dy•ing. 1** cease to live; stop living; become dead. **2** come to an end; lose force or strength; stop. **3** *Informal.* want very much; long keenly (*used in a progressive tense, followed by* **to** *or* **for**): *I'm dying to go to the Rockies. She was dying for a cold drink.* **4** cease to care about something; lose one's sensitivity (*to*): *He had died to books long before entering high school.* **5** suffer great agony: *to die of embarrassment. I'll just die if I don't get this job.*
die away or **down,** stop or end little by little; lose force or strength gradually: *The music died away.*
die hard, struggle until death; resist to the very end; refuse to give in.
die off, die one after another until all are dead: *The whole herd of cattle died off in the epidemic.*
die out, a stop or end little by little. **b** cease or end completely. ⟨OE *dīegan*⟩

☛ *Hom.* DYE.

☛ *Syn.* **1, 2. Die,** PERISH = stop living or existing. **Die,** the general word meaning 'to stop living', is also used figuratively of things that have been active in any way: *The noisy conversation of the class died down suddenly when the teacher came into the room.* **Perish,** more formal or literary than **die,** emphasizes losing life through violence or hardship, and used figuratively means 'to go out of existence permanently': *Many perished in the great fire. The forces of evil may cause civilization to perish.*

☛ *Usage.* **Die** is generally used with *of* before an illness: *He died of* (not *from* or *with) cancer.*

die[2] [daɪ] *n., pl.* **dies,** *v.* **—***n.* **1** any tool or apparatus for shaping, cutting, or stamping things, usually under pressure. A die is usually a metal block or plate cut in a certain way. **2** a tool for cutting threads on pipes, bolts, etc.
—*v.* cut, stamp, or shape with a die. ⟨< *die*[3]⟩

☛ *Hom.* DYE.

die[3] [daɪ] *n., pl.* **dice.** a small cube marked with a different number of spots (from one to six) on each face, used for gambling and playing certain games: *Dice are often used in pairs.* See also DICE.
the die is cast, the decision is made and cannot be changed. ⟨ME < OF *de* < L *datum* (thing) given (i.e., by fortune), pp. neut. of *dare* give. Doublet of DATUM.⟩

☛ *Hom.* DYE.

die•back ['daɪ,bæk] *n.* a disease of trees and other woody plants in which the twigs and tips of branches die first.

die–cast ['daɪ 'kæst] *adj.* made by the process of die-casting: *a die-cast engine block.*

die caster a person who makes die castings.

die casting 1 a process by which metal is cast to a desired shape by being forced into a mould, or die, when molten. **2** a metal object made in this way.

di•e•cious [daɪ'iʃəs] See DIOECIOUS.

dief•fen•bach•ia [,difən'bækiə] *or* [,difən'bɑxiə] *n.* a tropical plant of the genus *Dieffenbachia,* of the arum family, native to tropical America, having large, glossy, poisonous leaves. ⟨< Ernst *Dieffenbach,* a German botanist (1811-1855)⟩

die–hard ['daɪ ,hɑrd] *adj., n.* **—***adj.* resisting to the very end; refusing to give in.
—*n.* a person who refuses to give in.

diel•drin ['dildrən] *n.* a very poisonous insecticide obtained by the oxidation of aldrin with certain acids. *Formula*: $C_{12}H_8OCl_6$ ⟨< O. *Diels,* German chemist (1876-1954) + *aldrin*⟩

di•e•lec•tric [,daɪɪ'lɛktrɪk] *adj., n.* **—***adj.* non-conducting.
—*n.* a dielectric substance, such as glass, rubber, or wood.

di•en•ceph•a•lon [,daɪən'sɛfə,lɒn] *n.* that part of the brain housing the thalamus and hypothalamus; the rear end of the forebrain.

di•en•es•trol [,daɪə'nɛstrəl] *n.* a hormone cream used to treat vaginitis.

die–off ['daɪ ,ɒf] *n.* the gradual destruction of animals or birds.

di•er•e•sis or **di•aer•e•sis** [daɪ'ɛrəsɪs] *n., pl.* **-ses** [-,siz]. **1** two dots (¨) placed over the second of two consecutive vowels to indicate that the second vowel is to be pronounced in a separate syllable. *Example*: naïve. **2** the separation of adjacent vowel sounds, as shown by this mark. ⟨< L *diaeresis* < Gk.

diairesis separation, division < *diaireein* divide < *dia-* apart + *haireein* take⟩ **—ˌdi•er'et•ic,** *adj.*

die•sel ['dizəl] *or* ['disəl] *n., v.* *—n.* **1** DIESEL ENGINE. **2** a vehicle powered by a diesel engine. **3** (*adjl.*) powered by a diesel engine: *a diesel train.* **4** (*adjl.*) of or for diesel engines: *diesel fuel.* *—v.* of gasoline engines, continue running after the ignition is switched off, with fuel ignited by compressive heat from remaining piston motion.

diesel engine an internal-combustion engine that burns fuel oil which is ignited by heat from compressed air instead of by an electric spark, as in a gasoline engine. ⟨after R. *Diesel* (1858-1913), its inventor⟩

die•sel•ize or **Die•sel•ize** ['dizəˌlaɪz] *or* ['disəˌlaɪz] *v.* **-ized, -iz•ing.** equip with a diesel engine or engines.

diesel motor DIESEL ENGINE.

diesel oil a light fuel oil burned by diesel engines and obtained from crude oil after the distillation of gasoline and kerosene.

die•sink•er ['daɪˌsɪŋkər] *n.* a person who makes dies for shaping or stamping.

Di•es I•rae ['daiiz 'aɪri] *or* ['dieis 'iraɪ] **1** a medieval Latin hymn describing the Day of Judgment and usually sung at Christian masses for the dead. **2** a musical setting for such a hymn. ⟨< L *dies irae* day of wrath⟩

di•e•sis ['daɪəsɪs] *n., pl.* **-ses** [-ˌsiz]. a printer's mark (‡) used for reference purposes; double dagger. ⟨< L < Gk. *diienai* to send through⟩

die•stock ['daɪˌstɒk] *n.* a frame which holds dies steady for cutting threads on screws, etc.

di•es•trus [daɪ'ɛstrəs] *n.* the interval between periods of sexual heat in female mammals. Compare ESTRUS.
—di'es•trous, *adj.*

di•et¹ ['daɪət] *n., v.* **-et•ed, -et•ing.** *—n.* **1** the usual food and drink for a person or animal. **2** a special selection of food and drink eaten during illness or in an attempt to lose or gain weight. **3** something provided or used habitually or repeatedly: *a steady diet of good advice.*
—v. eat or cause to eat special food and drink. ⟨ME < OF *diete(r)* < L < Gk. *diaita* way of life⟩ **—'di•et•er,** *n.*

di•et² ['daɪət] *n.* **1** a formal assembly. **2** the national lawmaking body in certain countries. ⟨< Med.L *dieta* day's work, session of councillors, ult. identical with *diet¹* but influenced by L *dies* day⟩

di•e•tar•y ['daɪəˌtɛri] *adj., n., pl.* **-tar•ies.** *—adj.* of or having to do with diet: *Dietary rules tell what food to eat for healthy living and how to prepare it.*
—n. **1** a system of rules for eating and drinking. **2** a daily allowance of food in a prison, hospital, etc.

di•e•tet•ic [ˌdaɪə'tɛtɪk] *adj.* of or having to do with diet or with a particular diet. **—ˌdi•e'tet•i•cal•ly,** *adv.*

di•e•tet•ics [ˌdaɪə'tɛtɪks] *n.* the science that deals with the amount and kinds of food needed by the body (*used with a singular verb*).

di•eth•yl•a•mine [ˌdaɪɛ'θɪləˌmin] *n.* a drug used as a topical analgesic rub for sore muscles.

di•eth•yl•car•ba•ma•zine [daɪˌɛθəlkɑr'bæməˌzin] *n.* a drug used to treat various tropical parasitic diseases. *Formula*: $C_{10}H_{21}N_3O$

di•eth•yl•pro•pi•on [daɪˌɛθəl'proupiən] *n.* a drug used to treat obesity. *Formula*: $C_{13}H_{19}NO$—HCl

di•eth•yl•stil•bes•trol [daɪˌɛθəlstɪl'bɛstrɒl] *n.* a synthetic hormone once used to prevent miscarriage. *Formula*: $C_{18}H_{20}O_2$ See also DES.

di•e•ti•tian or **di•e•ti•cian** [ˌdaɪə'tɪʃən] *n.* a person trained to plan meals that have the proper proportion of various kinds of food; a specialist in dietetics.

dif– the form of **dis-¹** before *f*, as in *diffuse.*

diff. difference; different.

dif•fer ['dɪfər] *v.* **1** be unlike; be different. **2** have or express a different opinion; disagree. ⟨ME < OF < L *differre* set apart, differ < *dis-* apart + *ferre* carry. Doublet of DEFER¹.⟩

☛ *Usage.* **Differ** is followed by *from* when it means 'be unlike or different': *My answers to the algebra problems differed from Gina's.* When the meaning is 'disagree', *differ* is followed by *with* or *from: I differed from him in the solution he offered. She never differs with my plans.*

dif•fer•ence ['dɪfrəns] *or* ['dɪfərəns] *n.* **1** the condition of being different. **2** the way of being different; point in which people or things are different. **3** what is left after subtracting one number from another: *The difference between 6 and 15 is 9.* **4** the amount or extent by which one thing differs from another: *The difference in size between Nova Scotia and Ontario is great.* **5** the condition of having a different opinion; disagreement. **6** the matter which is disagreed about. **7** a dispute.
make a difference, a give or show different treatment; show partiality. **b** matter; be important; have an effect or influence.
same difference, *Slang.* it makes no difference.
split the difference, a divide what is left in half. **b** meet halfway; compromise.
what's the difference? it doesn't matter.

☛ *Syn.* **Difference,** DISCREPANCY, DISPARITY = unlikeness between two things. **Difference** applies to lack of sameness or any unlikeness, large or small, in a detail, quality, etc.: *There is a difference in John's and Mary's heights.* **Discrepancy** applies to a lack of agreement between things that should be alike or balance: *There was a discrepancy between the two reports of the accident.* **Disparity** applies to a lack of equality: *There is a disparity between my expenses and my income.*

dif•fer•ent ['dɪfrənt] *or* ['dɪfərənt] *adj.* **1** not alike; not like. **2** not the same; separate; distinct: *I saw her three different times today.* **3** not like others or most others; unusual. **4** sundry; miscellaneous: *She told me different things about her country.*
—'dif•fer•ent•ly, *adv.*

☛ *Usage.* **Different.** In formal English, the standard idiom is *different from: His second book was entirely different from his first.* Informal usage is divided, using *from,* sometimes *to* (which is a common British idiom), and often *than*: *She was different than any other girl he had ever known. Different than* is becoming more common when the object is a clause: *The house was a good deal different than he remembered it.*

dif•fer•en•ti•a [ˌdɪfə'rɛnʃiə] *n., pl.* **-ti•ae** [-ʃiˌi] *or* [-ʃiˌaɪ]. *Logic.* the quality or condition that distinguishes one species from all the others of the same genus or class. ⟨< L *differentia* difference⟩

dif•fer•en•tial [ˌdɪfə'rɛnʃəl] *adj., n.* *—adj.* **1** of a difference; showing a difference; depending on a difference: *Differential duties, rates, charges, etc. are those that differ according to circumstances.* **2** distinguishing; distinctive. **3** having to do with distinguishing characteristics or specific differences: *A differential diagnosis attempts to distinguish between two similar diseases or objects of natural history.* **4** *Mathematics.* having to do with or involving differentials. **5** *Physics and mechanics.* concerning the difference of two or more motions, pressures, etc. **6** *Geology.* producing different or selective effects on formations or constituents of rocks, soils, etc.: *differential erosion, differential weathering.*
—n. **1** a differential duty or rate, or the difference involved. **2** *Mathematics.* **a** an infinitesimal difference between consecutive values of a variable quantity. **b** a function in which this difference varies with some other variable. **3** in an automobile, an arrangement of gears that allows one of the rear wheels to turn faster than the other in going round a corner or curve. **4** *Statistics.* a derivative of a function times the increase in the independent variable. **—ˌdif•fer'en•tial•ly,** *adv.*

differential calculus the branch of mathematics dealing with differentials and their relations. Compare INTEGRAL CALCULUS.

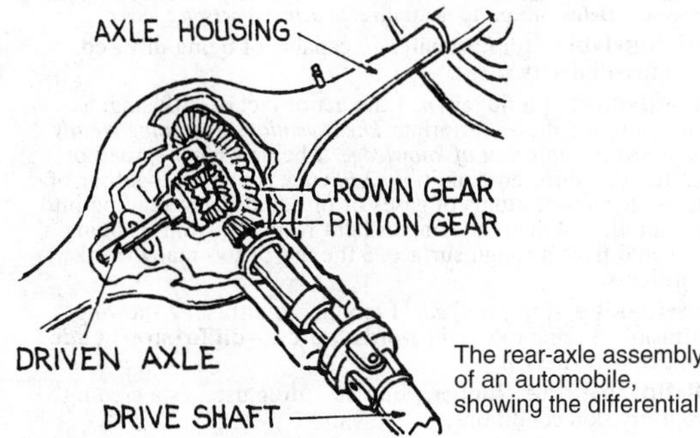

The rear-axle assembly of an automobile, showing the differential

differential gear DIFFERENTIAL (def. *n.* 3).

dif•fer•en•ti•ate [ˌdɪfə'rɛnʃiˌeit] *v.* **-at•ed, -at•ing. 1** show or constitute a difference between or in: *an act of kindness that differentiates real consideration for others from mere politeness.* **2** recognize or see a distinction; discriminate: *The twins were so much alike that it was almost impossible to differentiate between them.* **3** make different. **4** become different in character: *The words* metal *and* mettle *have the same origin but have*

differentiated over the centuries to become two separate words. 5 *Biology.* make different in the process of growth or development; make unlike by modification. 6 *Mathematics.* find the derivative of. 7 *Biology.* become differentiated or specialized: *The cells of an embryo differentiate into organs and parts as it grows.* **—,dif•fer'en•ti,a•tor,** *n.*
☛ *Syn.* 1, 2. See note at DISTINGUISH.

dif•fer•en•ti•a•tion [,dɪfə,rɛnʃi'eiʃən] *n.* **1** the act or process of differentiating; alteration; modification; distinction. **2** *Biology.* change in the structure, etc. due to specialization. **3** *Mathematics.* the calculation of the differential or derivative.

dif•fi•cult ['dɪfə,kʌlt] *or* ['dɪfəkəlt] *adj.* **1** hard to do or understand: *Cutting down the tree was difficult. Mathematics is difficult for some people.* **2** hard to deal with, get along with, or please: *The secretary found his new employer difficult.*

dif•fi•cul•ty ['dɪfə,kʌlti] *or* ['dɪfəkəlti] *n., pl.* **-ties. 1** the fact, degree, or condition of being difficult: *the difficulty of a job.* **2** hard work; much effort. **3** trouble. **4** financial trouble. **5** something that is difficult; something in the way; an obstacle. **6** a disagreement; quarrel.
in difficulties, in trouble, especially money trouble: *Our spendthrift friend is in difficulties again.*
make difficulties, cause trouble; hinder by raising objections: *We will get the meeting finished quickly if no one makes difficulties.* ⟨ME < L *difficultas* < *difficilis* hard < *dis-* not + *facilis* easy⟩

dif•fi•dence ['dɪfədəns] *n.* lack of self-confidence; shyness.

dif•fi•dent ['dɪfədənt] *adj.* lacking in self-confidence; shy. ⟨< L *diffidens, -entis,* ppr. of *diffidere* < *dis-* away + *fidere* trust⟩ **—'dif•fi•dent•ly,** *adv.*

dif•fract [dɪ'frækt] *v.* break up by diffraction. ⟨< L *diffractus,* pp. of *diffringere* < *dis-* up + *frangere* break⟩

dif•frac•tion [dɪ'frækʃən] *n. Physics.* **1** a breaking up of a ray of light into a series of light and dark bands or into the coloured bands of the spectrum. **2** a similar breaking up of sound waves, electricity, etc.

diffraction grating *Physics.* a plate of glass or polished metal with very fine and close parallel lines, used to produce spectra by diffraction.

dif•frac•tive [dɪ'fræktɪv] *adj.* having to do with diffraction; tending to diffract. **—dif'frac•tive•ly,** *adv.* **—dif'frac•tive•ness,** *n.*

dif•fuse *v.* [dɪ'fjuz]; *adj.* [-'fjus] *v.* **-fused, -fus•ing;** *adj.*
—v. **1** spread out so as to cover a larger space or surface; scatter widely; disperse; dissipate. **2** *Physics.* mix together by spreading into one another, as one gas with another or one liquid with another; spread by diffusion.
—adj. **1** not concentrated at a single point; spread out: *diffuse light.* **2** using many words where a few would do: *a diffuse writer.* ⟨ME < L *diffusus,* pp. of *diffundere* < *dis-* in every direction + *fundere* pour⟩ **—dif'fuse•ly,** *adv.* **—dif'fuse•ness,** *n.* **—dif'fus•er** or **dif'fus•or,** *n.*
☛ *Hom.* DEFUSE [dɪ'fjuz].
☛ *Usage.* Do not confuse **diffuse** with DEFUSE in figurative use. **Diffuse** means to spread: *His constant complaining diffused frustration throughout the camp.* **Defuse** means to neutralize: *to defuse a person's anger.*

dif•fus•i•ble [dɪ'fjuzəbəl] *adj.* capable of being diffused. **—dif,fus•i'bil•i•ty,** *n.*

dif•fu•sion [dɪ'fjuʒən] *n.* **1** the act or fact of diffusing; a spreading widely; a scattering: *The invention of printing greatly increased the diffusion of knowledge.* **2** being widely spread or scattered; a diffused condition. **3** *Physics.* a mixing together of the molecules or atoms of gases or of liquids by spreading into one another. **4** the scattering of light resulting from its being reflected from a rough surface. **5** the use of too many words; wordiness.

dif•fu•sive [dɪ'fjusɪv] *adj.* **1** tending to diffuse. **2** showing diffusion. **3** using too many words; wordy. **—dif'fu•sive•ly,** *adv.* **—dif'fu•sive•ness,** *n.*

di•flo•ra•sone [dɪ'flɔrə,soun] *n.* a drug used as a cream to treat dry skin conditions.

di•flu•cor•to•lone [,dɪflu'kɔrtə,loun] *n.* a drug used as a cream to treat certain skin conditions.

di•flu•ni•sal [dɪ'flunə,sæl] *n.* a drug used as an analgesic and anti-inflammatory agent in the treatment of rheumatoid arthritis, etc. *Formula:* $C_{13}H_8F_2O_3$

dig [dɪg] *v.* **dug** or *(archaic)* **digged, dig•ging;** *n. —v.* **1** use a spade, hands, claws, or snout to make a hole or to turn over ground: *After digging for three hours, they were still only 1 m down. She's out in the garden digging for earthworms.* **2** make or form by removing earth or other material: *to dig a hole, to dig a basement.* **3** prepare by turning over ground: *to dig a garden.* **4** make a way by digging: *to dig through a snowbank, to dig under a fence.* **5** get by digging: *to dig potatoes, to dig clams.* **6** make a careful search or inquiry for information, or into a book, etc.: *We will really have to dig for that information.* **7** make a thrust or stab with; prod: *The rider dug her spurs into the horse.* **8** *Slang.* understand or appreciate: *Do you dig what they're talking about?* **9** *Slang.* like or admire: *I don't dig country music.* **10** *Slang.* notice; observe: *Dig that jacket!*
dig in, a work hard. **b** make a protective trench. **c** secure one's position: *He has really dug in at the factory.* **d** *Informal.* eat heartily.
dig into, *Informal.* work hard at or partake heartily of.
dig up, a unearth. **b** excavate. **c** find out by active inquiry.
—n. **1** the act of digging. **2** *Informal.* an archaeological excavation. **3** *Informal.* a thrust or poke: *a dig in the ribs.* **4** *Informal.* a sarcastic remark: *He made several nasty little digs about their escapade.* **5 digs,** *pl. Esp. Brit. Informal.* lodgings; quarters; DIGGINGS (def. 3). ⟨ME *dygge(n),* probably < MF *diguer* < Gmc.⟩

di•gam•ma [daɪ'gæmə] *n.* a letter in the early Greek alphabet (*F*), with the phonetic value of English (w).

dig•a•my ['dɪgəmi] *n.* a second marriage after divorce, or after the death of the first spouse: deuterogamy. **—'dig•a•mous,** *adj.*

Dig•by chicken ['dɪgbi] *Cdn.* a small, smoke-cured herring. ⟨< *Digby,* N.S.⟩

di•gen•e•sis [daɪ'dʒɛnəsɪs] *n. Biology.* sexual reproduction in one generation which is followed by asexual reproduction in the next generation. **—,di•gen'e•tic** [,daɪdʒə'nɛtɪk], *adj.*

di•gest [daɪ'dʒɛst] *or* [dɪ'dʒɛst] *v.*; *n.* ['daɪdʒɛst] *v., n. —v.* **1** change (food) in the stomach and intestines so that it can be taken into the blood and used as nourishment. **2** undergo this process; be digested: *Some foods digest more quickly than others.* **3** understand and absorb mentally; arrange in the mind: *It often takes a long time to digest new ideas.* **4** condense and arrange according to some system; summarize. **5** endure; tolerate: *I find it difficult to digest his bad manners.* **6** *Chemistry.* soften or decompose by means of heat, moisture, or chemicals.
—n. **1** information condensed according to some system; a summary: *a digest of law.* **2** a periodical, etc., containing a collection of summaries or condensed versions: *a book-review digest.* ⟨ME < L *digestus,* pp. of *digerere* separate, dissolve < *dis-* apart + *gerere* carry⟩
☛ *Syn. n.* See note at SUMMARY.

di•gest•er [daɪ'dʒɛstər] *or* [dɪ'dʒɛstər] *n.* **1** a person who makes a digest. **2** a heavy, covered kettle, etc. for softening or dissolving a substance by heat and moisture. **3** a machine vat used in a pulp mill.

di•gest•i•bil•i•ty [daɪ,dʒɛstə'bɪləti] *or* [dɪ,dʒɛstə'bɪləti] *n.* the quality of being digestible.

di•gest•i•ble [daɪ'dʒɛstəbəl] *or* [dɪ'dʒɛstəbəl] *adj.* capable of being digested; easily digested. **—di'gest•i•ble•ness,** *n.* **—di'gest•i•bly,** *adv.*

di•ges•tif [diʒɛ'stif] *n.* an after-dinner liqueur meant to help digestion. ⟨< F⟩

di•ges•tion [daɪ'dʒɛstʃən] *or* [dɪ'dʒɛstʃən] *n.* **1** the digesting of food. **2** the ability to digest food. **3** the act of digesting books, ideas, etc. **4** the decomposition action of bacteria on waste matter.

di•ges•tive [daɪ'dʒɛstɪv] *or* [dɪ'dʒɛstɪv] *adj., n. —adj.* **1** of or for digestion: *Saliva is one of the digestive juices.* **2** helping digestion: *digestive biscuits.*
—n. something that aids digestion. **—di'gest•ive•ly,** *adv.*

digged [dɪgd] *v. Archaic* pt. of DIG.

dig•ger ['dɪgər] *n.* **1** a person that digs. **2** the part of a machine that turns up the ground. **3** any tool for digging. **4** Usually, **Digger,** *Informal.* an Australian or New Zealander. **5 Digger,** a member of any of the First Nations peoples who dug roots for food.

digger wasp any of various solitary wasps (family Sphecidae) that dig into the ground to make their nests, stocking the nests with paralysed insects or spiders for their larvae to feed on.

dig•gings ['dɪgɪŋz] *n.pl.* **1** a mine or place where digging is being done: *The archaeologists examined the new diggings.* **2** the material that is dug out. **3** *Informal.* a place to live, usually a sleeping room in a house where, sometimes, meals are also provided.

dight [dəit] *v.* **dight** or **dight•ed, dight•ing.** *Archaic.* **1** dress; adorn. **2** equip. ⟨OE *dihtan* compose, arrange < L *dictare* dictate⟩

dig•it ['dɪdʒɪt] *n.* **1** a finger or toe. **2** any of the figures 1, 2, 3, 4, 5, 6, 7, 8, 9. 0 is not, strictly speaking, called a digit but is known as a cipher. ⟨ME < L *digitus* finger⟩

dig•it•al ['dɪdʒətəl] *adj., n.* —*adj.* **1** of or having to do with the fingers or toes. **2** performed with a finger. **3** of or having to do with numerals (digits) or calculation by numerals. **4** of, having to do with, or providing information in the form of numerals. A digital clock shows the time in the form of changing numerals rather than by hands moving over a dial. **5** of or by means of a DIGITAL COMPUTER. **6** of a method of recording where sounds are stored as binary digits on a magnetic medium. These digits are then interpreted electronically.
—*n.* **1** a finger. **2** a key of an organ, piano, etc., played with the finger. **—'dig•it•al•ly,** *adv.*

digital audio tape a cassette tape produced by the methods of digital recording. Digital audio tapes are distortion-free. *Abbrev.*: DAT

digital computer *Computer technology.* a computer that represents and processes data internally as digits of some number system (usually binary). Compare ANALOGUE COMPUTER.

dig•i•tal•in [ˌdɪdʒə'tælɪn] *or* [ˌdɪdʒə'teilɪn] *n.* a glucoside or a mixture of glucosides obtained from the foxglove. *Formula*: $C_{36}H_{56}O_{14}$ ⟨< *digitalis* + *-in*⟩

dig•i•tal•is [ˌdɪdʒə'tælɪs] *or* [ˌdɪdʒə'teilɪs] *n.* **1** a medicine used for stimulating the heart, obtained from the dried leaves of the purple foxglove (*Digitalis purpurea*). **2** foxglove (genus *Digitalis*). ⟨< L *digitalis* pertaining to the finger < *digitus* finger; from the shape of the corolla⟩

dig•i•tal•ize ['dɪdʒətəˌlaɪz] *v.* **-ized, -iz•ing.** treat with enough digitalis to effect a reverse of the condition.
—ˌdig•i•tal•i'za•tion, *n.*

dig•i•tate ['dɪdʒəˌteit] *adj.* **1** having fingers or toes. **2** *Botany.* having radiating divisions like fingers. **3** *Zoology.* having digits or digitlike parts. **—'dig•iˌtate•ly,** *adv.*

dig•i•ti•grade ['dɪdʒətəˌgreid] *n., adj.* —*n.* an animal having feet shaped so that the toes are on the ground, but not the heels. Dogs, cats, and horses are digitigrades.
—*adj.* having feet like this. ⟨< F < L *digitus* finger, toe + *gradi* walk⟩

dig•i•tize ['dɪdʒəˌtaɪz] *v.* **-ized, -iz•ing.** *Computer technology.* convert (pictures, data, etc.) to digital form for processing by a computer. **—ˌdig•i•ti'za•tion,** *n.* **—'dig•iˌtiz•er,** *n.*

dig•i•tox•in [ˌdɪdʒɪ'tɒksɪn] *n.* a preparation of digitalis, used to treat certain heart conditions. *Formula*: $C_{41}H_{64}O_{13}$

di•glos•si•a [daɪ'glɒsiə] *n.* the existence within a language of two distinct forms, usually formal and informal, which are used for different purposes or by people on differing social levels. ⟨< *di-*[1] + Gk. *glossa* tongue, language⟩

dig•ni•fied ['dɪgnəˌfaɪd] *adj., v.* —*adj.* having or showing dignity; noble or stately.
—*v.* pt. and pp. of DIGNIFY. **—'dig•niˌfied•ly,** *adv.*

dig•ni•fy ['dɪgnəˌfaɪ] *v.* **-fied, -fy•ing. 1** give dignity to; make noble, worthwhile, or worthy: *The little farmhouse was dignified by the great elms around it.* **2** give a high-sounding name to. ⟨< OF *dignifier* < LL *dignificare* < L *dignus* worthy + *facere* make⟩

dig•ni•tar•y ['dɪgnəˌtɛri] *n., pl.* **-tar•ies.** a person who has a position of honour: *A bishop is a dignitary of the church.*

dig•ni•ty ['dɪgnəti] *n., pl.* **-ties. 1** a proud and self-respecting manner; stateliness and formality: *He replied with dignity that he was not interested in their scheme. She had great dignity of bearing.* **2** self-respect; self-esteem: *She maintained that lying about the matter would be beneath her dignity.* **3** high rank, office, or position or the honour or esteem attached to it: *He felt that casual dress was not in keeping with the dignity of his position as director.* **4** the quality of being worthy of honour or esteem; true worth, nobility, or excellence: *the dignity of labour.* **5** *Archaic.* dignitary. **6** a stately appearance: *the dignity of a castle.* ⟨ME < OF *dignete* < L *dignitas* < *dignus* worthy. Doublet of DAINTY.⟩

dig•ox•in [dɪ'dʒɒksən] *n.* a preparation of digitalis used to treat congestive heart failure. *Formula*: $C_{41}H_{64}O_{14}$

di•graph ['daɪgræf] *n.* two letters used together to spell a single sound. *Examples*: *ea* in *each, th* in *with, sh* in *shop.* Compare LIGATURE. ⟨< *di-*[1] double, twice + Gk. *graphē* a writing⟩ **—di'graph•ic,** *adj.*

di•gress [daɪ'grɛs] *or* [dɪ'grɛs] *v.* **1** turn aside; get off the main subject in talking or writing. **2** swerve. ⟨< L *digressus*, pp. of *digredi* deviate < *dis-* aside < *gradi* to step⟩ **—di'gress•er,** *n.*
☛ *Syn.* See note at DIVERGE.

di•gres•sion [daɪ'grɛʃən] *or* [dɪ'grɛʃən] *n.* **1** a turning aside; a getting off the main subject in talking or writing. **2** that portion of the speech or writing which digresses. **—di'gres•sion•al,** *adj.*

di•gres•sive [daɪ'grɛsɪv] *or* [dɪ'grɛssɪv] *adj.* tending to digress; digressing. **—di'gres•sive•ly,** *adv.* **—di'gres•sive•ness,** *n.*

di•he•dral [daɪ'hidrəl] *adj., n.* —*adj.* **1** having or formed by two intersecting planes: *a dihedral angle.* **2** of aircraft wings, not horizontal, but inclined to each other so as to form a dihedral angle. **3** of an aircraft, having such wings.
—*n.* **1** a figure formed by two intersecting planes; a dihedral angle. **2** the angle between an upwardly or downwardly inclined aircraft wing and the horizontal plane of its axis. ⟨< *di-*[1] two + Gk. *hedra* seat; base + E *-al*[1]⟩

di•hy•brid [daɪ'haɪbrɪd] *adj., n.* —*adj.* having parents whose genetic makeup differs in two pairs of inheritable traits.
—*n.* a dihybrid organism.

di•hy•dro•er•got•a•mine [daɪˌhaɪdrouər'gɒtəˌmin] *n.* a drug used to treat migraine headaches. *Formula*: $C_{33}H_{37}N_5O_5$

di•hy•dro•mor•phi•none [daɪˌhaɪdrou'mɔrfəˌnoun] *n.* a narcotic analgesic drug. *Formula*: $C_{17}H_{19}O_3N$

di•hy•dro•strep•to•my•cin [daɪˌhaɪdrouˌstrɛptə'maɪsɪn] *n.* an antibiotic drug. *Formula*: $C_{21}H_{41}N_7O_{12}$

Dijon mustard [di'ʒɒn]; *French,* [di'ʒɔ̃] a good quality mustard containing white wine, made in Dijon, France.

dik–dik ['dɪk ˌdɪk] *n.* any small antelope of the genera *Madoqua* or *Rhynchotragus*, native to E Africa, only 40 cm high at the shoulder. ⟨< Ethiopian native name⟩

dike [dəɪk] *n., v.* **diked, dik•ing.** —*n.* **1** a bank of earth or a dam built as a defence against flooding. **2** a ditch or channel for water. **3** a bank of earth thrown up in digging. **4** a low wall of earth or stone; causeway. **5** a barrier; obstacle. **6** *Geology.* a long, usually narrow mass of igneous rock that was thrust, while molten, into a fissure in older rock.
—*v.* **1** provide with a dike or dikes. **2** drain with a ditch or channel for water. Also, **dyke.** ⟨ME < ON *dík.* Akin to DITCH.⟩

dike•land ['dəiklənd] *n.* land, usually below sea level, that is protected from flooding by a system of embankments.

dik•tat [dɪk'tɑt] *n.* a dogmatic or uncompromising statement of opinion, policy, demands, etc. ⟨< G⟩

di•lap•i•date [dɪ'læpəˌdeit] *v.* **-at•ed, -at•ing.** fall into ruin through neglect.

di•lap•i•dat•ed [dɪ'læpəˌdeitɪd] *adj., v.* —*adj.* falling to pieces; partly ruined or decayed through neglect: *a dilapidated house.*
—*v.* pt. and pp. of DILAPIDATE. ⟨< L *dilapidatus*, pp. of *dilapidare* demolish, destroy (with stones) < *dis-* (intensive) + *lapis, lapidis* stone⟩

di•lap•i•da•tion [dɪˌlæpə'deiʃən] *n.* a falling to pieces; decay; ruin; tumble-down condition: *The house was in the last stage of dilapidation.*

di•lat•ant [daɪ'leitənt] *or* [də'leitənt] *adj., n.* —*adj.* dilating or able to dilate.
—*n.* anything that causes dilation.

dil•a•ta•tion [ˌdaɪlə'teiʃən] *or* [ˌdɪlə'teiʃən] *n.* **1** dilation. **2** an enlargement, expansion, or stretched condition of a part or opening of the body.

dilatation and curettage a procedure in which the cervix is dilated and the walls of the uterus are scraped to remove tissue. *Abbrev.*: D and C

di•late [daɪ'leit], [dɪ'leit], *or* ['daɪleit] *v.* **-lat•ed, -lat•ing.**
1 make or become larger or wider: *The pupils of Anne's eyes dilated when the light dimmed.* **2** speak or write in a very complete or detailed manner. ⟨< L *dilatare* < *dis-* apart + *latus* wide⟩
☛ *Syn.* **1.** See note at EXPAND.

di•lat•ed [daɪ'leitɪd], [dɪ'leitɪd], *or* ['daɪleitɪd] *adj., v.* —*adj.* widened; expanded.
—*v.* pt. and pp. of DILATE.

di•la•tion [daɪ'leiʃən] *or* [dɪ'leiʃən] *n.* **1** the act of dilating; enlargement; widening. **2** a dilated condition. **3** a dilated part.

di•la•tor [daɪ'leitər], [dɪ'leitər], *or* ['daɪleitər] *n.* **1** a person or thing that dilates. **2** *Physiology.* a muscle that dilates some part of the body. **3** a surgical instrument for dilating wounds, canals of the body, etc.

dil•a•to•ry ['dɪlə,tɔri] *adj.* **1** tending to delay; not prompt. **2** causing delay. ⟨< L *dilatorius* < *dilator* delayer < *dilatus*, pp. of *differre* defer, delay. See DIFFER.⟩ **—'dil•a,to•ri•ly,** *adv.* **—'dil•a,to•ri•ness,** *n.*

dil•do ['dɪldou] *n.* a device shaped like an erect penis, used for sexual stimulation. ⟨of unknown origin. 17c.⟩

di•lem•ma [dɪ'lɛmə] *n.* **1** a situation requiring a choice between two things when either one is unpleasant or undesirable; a difficult choice: *Her dilemma was that she would have to give up her holiday trip or miss playing in the basketball finals.* **2** an argument forcing an opponent to choose one of two alternatives equally unfavourable to him or her. **3** a grave predicament. ⟨< LL < Gk. *dilemma* < *di-* two + *lemma* premise⟩

☛ *Syn.* **1, 3.** See note at PREDICAMENT.

dil•et•tan•te [,dɪlə'tænti], [,dɪlə'tɑnt], ['dɪlə,tɑnt], *or* ['dɪlə,tænt] *n., pl.* **-tes** [-tiz] or **-ti** [-ti]; *adj.* *—n.* **1** a person who is interested in some art or other subject only as an amusement; a dabbler or trifler. **2** a lover of the fine arts.
—adj. of or like a dilettante. ⟨< Ital. *dilettante* < *dilettare* < L *delectare.* See DELIGHT.⟩

dil•et•tan•te•ism [,dɪlə'tɑnti,ɪzəm] *or* [,dɪlə'tænti,ɪzəm] *n.* dilettantism.

dil•et•tan•ti [,dɪlə'tænti] *or* [,dɪlə'tɑnti] *n.* a pl. of DILETTANTE.

dil•et•tant•ism [,dɪlə'tæntɪzəm] *or* [,dɪlə'tɑntɪzəm] *n.* the quality or practice of a dilettante.

dil•i•gence¹ ['dɪlədʒəns] *n.* the quality of being diligent; careful effort; the ability to work hard and steadily; industry: *The student's diligence was rewarded with high marks.* ⟨< F < L *diligentia* < *diligere.* See DILIGENT.⟩

dil•i•gence² ['dɪlədʒəns] *n.* a public stagecoach formerly used in some parts of Europe. ⟨< F *carrosse de diligence* express coach⟩

dil•i•gent ['dɪlədʒənt] *adj.* **1** hard-working; industrious: *a diligent student.* **2** careful and steady: *diligent effort.* ⟨< L *diligens, -entis,* ppr. of *diligere* value highly, love < *dis-* apart + *legere* choose⟩ **—'dil•i•gent•ly,** *adv.*

☛ *Syn.* **1.** See note at BUSY.

dill [dɪl] *n.* **1** a tall herb (*Anethum graveolens*) of the parsley family having finely divided leaves and flat clusters of small, yellow flowers. The aromatic leaves, immature flower clusters, and seeds are used to flavour soups, stews, salads, and cucumber pickles. **2** the seeds or leaves of this plant. **3** DILL PICKLE: *Dills are my favourite pickles.* ⟨OE *dile*⟩

dill pickle a cucumber pickle flavoured with dill.

dil•ly ['dɪli] *n., pl.* **-lies.** *Slang.* a person or thing thought of as extraordinary, unique, odd, outstanding, etc.: *a dilly of a game.* ⟨apparently < *del*ightful + *-y²*⟩

dil•ly–dal•ly ['dɪli ,dæli] *v.* **-lied, -ly•ing.** waste time; loiter; trifle. ⟨reduplication of *dally*⟩

dil•ti•a•zem [dɪl'taɪə,zɛm] *n.* a drug used to treat angina pectoris. *Formula*: $C_{22}H_{26}N_2O_4S$

dil•u•ent ['dɪljuənt] *adj., n.* *—adj.* used to dilute or causing dilution.
—n. anything used to dilute or to cause dilution.

di•lute [dɪ'lut] *or* [daɪ'lut] *v.* **-lut•ed, -lut•ing;** *adj.* *—v.* **1** make weaker or thinner by adding water or some other liquid. **2** lessen the force, effect, or value of. **3** become diluted.
—adj. **1** diluted. **2** present in solution, especially a weak solution: *a dilute acid.* ⟨< L *dilutus*, pp. of *diluere* < *dis-* apart + *luere* wash⟩

di•lut•ed [dɪ'lutɪd] *or* [daɪ'lutɪd] *adj., v.* *—adj.* weakened; thinned.
—v. pt. and pp. of DILUTE.

di•lu•tion [dɪ'luʃən] *or* [daɪ'luʃən] *n.* **1** the act of diluting. **2** the fact or state of being diluted. **3** something diluted.

di•lu•vi•al [dɪ'luviəl] *or* [daɪ'luviəl] *adj.* **1** of or having to do with a flood. **2** made up of debris left by a flood or glacier. ⟨< L *diluvialis* < *diluvium.* See DELUGE.⟩

di•lu•vi•an [dɪ'luviən] *or* [daɪ'luviən] *adj.* diluvial.

dim [dɪm] *adj.* **dim•mer, dim•mest;** *v.* **dimmed, dim•ming.**
—adj. **1** not bright, clear, or distinct: *a dim light, a dim outline.* **2** not clearly or completely perceived or distinguished; vague: *She had a dim memory of the event.* **3** not able to see or perceive clearly and distinctly: *Her eyesight was getting dim.* **4** not likely to have a good result or outcome: *Her future looks dim.* **5** without lustre; dull. **6** *Informal.* unfavourable: *His chances of winning the race are pretty dim.* **7** *Informal.* stupid; dull.
take a dim view of, disapprove of; look on with disfavour: *He takes a dim view of practical jokes.*
—v. **1** make or become dim or dimmer: *The theatre lights were dimmed.* **2** change (the headlights of a motor vehicle) to the low beam.
dim out, lower the brightness of (lights), by allowing light to appear only through slits, by use of blue bulbs, etc.: *to dim out the lights on stage.* ⟨OE *dimm*⟩ **—'dim•ly,** *adv.* **—'dim•ness,** *n.*

☛ *Syn. adj.* **1.** See note at DARK.

dim. **1** diminuendo. **2** diminutive.

dime [daɪm] *n.* a coin of Canada or the United States, equal to one tenth of a dollar; a ten-cent coin.
a dime a dozen, *Informal.* cheap and commonplace: *Those comic T-shirts are a dime a dozen.*
on a dime, precisely; within very limited time or space: *to turn on a dime, to stop on a dime.* ⟨< OF *disme* < L *decima (pars)* tenth (part) < *decem* ten⟩

di•men•hy•dri•nate [,daɪmɛn'haɪdrə,neit] *n.* a drug used to prevent motion sickness. *Formula*: $C_{17}H_{22}NO{\bullet}C_7H_6ClN_4O_2$ ⟨< *dim*ethyl + diphen*hydramine* + *-ate*⟩

dime novel a sensational or melodramatic novel, usually published as a cheap paperback: *Dime novels are all he ever reads.*

di•men•sion [dɪ'mɛnʃən] *or* [daɪ'mɛnʃən] *n.* **1** the measurement of length, breadth, or thickness: *The dimensions of my room are 4.2 m by 3.1 m.* **2** the size; extent: *It was a project of large dimensions.* **3** element, factor, or characteristic: *Her latest work adds a new dimension to the art of film.* **4** a measurable property, such as time, mass, or temperature. **5** *Mathematics.* a property of length, area, and volume. A figure having length only is of one dimension (a line); having area, is of two dimensions (e.g., a rectangle); having volume, is of three dimensions (e.g., a cube). **6** *Physics.* any basic quantity, such as distance, time, mass, through which one can define all other quantities. Distance divided by time are the dimensions for velocity. **7** (*adjl.*) of any material, cut to a specified size: *dimension lumber.* ⟨ME < MF < L *dimensio, -onis* < *dis-* out + *metiri* measure⟩ **—di'men•sion•less,** *adj.*

di•men•sion•al [dɪ'mɛnʃənəl] *or* [daɪ'mɛnʃənəl] *adj.* **1** having to do with dimension or dimensions. **2** having, exploiting, etc. a stated number of dimensions: *a three-dimensional movie.* **—di'men•sion•al•ly,** *adv.* **—di,men•sion'al•i•ty,** *n.*

di•mer ['daɪmər] *n. Chemistry.* a compound in which two molecules of the same substance are present, especially as produced by polymerization. ⟨< *di-¹* two + Gk. *meros* part⟩

di•mer•cap•rol [,daɪmər'kæprɒl] *n.* a drug used to treat gold, mercury, or arsenic poisoning. *Formula*: $C_3H_8OS_2$

dim•er•ous ['dɪmərəs] *adj.* consisting of two parts, divisions, or members.

dime store a store selling a large variety of articles in a low price range.

dim•e•ter ['dɪmətər] *n., adj.* *—n.* a line of verse having two metrical feet. *Examples*: The hóoded bát/Twirls sóftly bý (Walter de la Mare).
—adj. having two metrical feet. ⟨< L *dimetrus* < Gk. *dimetros* < *di-* two + *metron* meter⟩

di•meth•o•thi•a•zine [daɪ,mɛθou'θaɪə,zin] *n.* an antihistamine drug.

di•meth•yl•pol•y•sil•ox•ane [daɪ,mɛθɪl,pɒli'sɪlɒk,sein] *n.* a drug used to treat skin inflammation caused by irritants, such as diaper rash.

di•meth•yl•sulph•ox•ide [daɪ,mɛθɪl,sʌl'fɒksaɪd] *n.* a drug used to treat certain skin conditions.

dimin. **1** diminuendo. **2** diminutive.

di•min•ish [dɪ'mɪnɪʃ] *v.* **1** make or become smaller in size, amount, or importance; lessen; reduce: *The heat diminished as the sun went down.* **2** *Music.* reduce (a major or minor interval) by a half-tone. **3** *Architecture.* taper or cause to taper. ⟨blend of *diminue* (< L *diminuere* < *dis-* (intensive) + *minuere* lessen) and *minish* (< OF *menuisier* make small < VL *minutiare*, ult. < L *minutus* small)⟩ **—di'min•ish•ing•ly,** *adv.*

☛ *Syn.* See note at DECREASE.

diminished chord a chord of two or more notes, including a diminished (flattened) interval.

diminishing returns the increase of profit in a smaller

proportion than the increase in capital, labour, etc.; progressively smaller increases in output from equal increases in input.

di•min•u•en•do [dɪ,mɪnju'ɛndou] *n., pl.* **-dos;** *adj., adv., v. Music.* —*n.* **1** a gradual decrease of volume. The sign in music for a diminuendo is >. **2** a passage to be played or sung with a diminuendo.
—*adj. or adv.* with a diminuendo.
—*v.* decrease gradually in force or volume. *Abbrev.:* dim. or dimin. ⟨< Ital. *diminuendo,* ppr. of *diminuire* diminish⟩

dim•i•nu•tion [,dɪmə'njuʃən] *or* [,dɪmə'nuʃən] *n.* **1** diminishing; lessening; reduction; decrease. **2** *Music.* a shortening of a variation of a piece, brought about by halving the time values. ⟨ME < OF < L *diminutio, -onis*⟩

di•min•u•tive [dɪ'mɪnjətɪv] *adj., n.* —*adj.* **1** small; little; tiny. **2** expressing smallness.
—*n.* **1** a small person or thing. **2** *Grammar.* a word or part of a word expressing smallness, as the suffixes *-let* and *-kin* in English. ⟨< Med.L *diminutivus* < L *diminutus,* pp. of *diminuere* lessen⟩ **—di'min•u•tive•ly,** *adv.* **—di'min•u•tive•ness,** *n.*
☛ *Syn. adj.* **1.** See note at LITTLE.

dim•i•ty ['dɪməti] *n., pl.* **-ties.** a thin cloth, usually of cotton, woven with heavy threads at intervals in a striped or cross-barred arrangement, used for dresses, curtains, etc. ⟨ME < Ital. *dimito* < Gk. *dimitos* of double thread < *di-* double + *mitos* warp thread⟩

dim•mer ['dɪmər] *n.* **1** a device for dimming an electric light: *We have a dimmer for the light in our dining room.* **2** a switch for changing the headlights of a motor vehicle to the low beam. **3** any person or thing that dims.

di•mor•phic [daɪ'mɔrfɪk] *adj.* occurring in two distinct forms: *Some aquatic plants have dimorphic leaves; the floating leaves are different from the lower, submerged leaves.*

di•mor•phism [daɪ'mɔrfɪzəm] *n.* **1** the occurrence within one type, species, etc., of two distinct forms or two distinct types of individual. **2** the property of certain substances of crystallizing in two distinct forms. ⟨< *di-*[1] + Gk. *morphe* form + *-ism*⟩

di•mor•phous [daɪ'mɔrfəs] *adj.* **1** of a chemical compound, crystallizing in two distinct forms. **2** dimorphic.

dim•out ['dɪm,ʌut] *n.* a lessening or concealing of artificial light at night, especially in wartime, to make cities less noticeable by the enemy from the air.

dim•ple ['dɪmpəl] *n., v.* **-pled, -pling.** —*n.* **1** a small, natural hollow on the surface of a plump part of the body, such as on the cheek, the chin, or the back of the hand. **2** any small, hollow place: *A golf ball has dimples.*
—*v.* **1** make dimples in: *The rain dimpled the smooth surface of the pond.* **2** have or form dimples: *Her cheeks dimple when she smiles.* ⟨ME *dympull,* cognate with MHG *tümpfil* pool⟩

dim sum ['dɪm 'sʌm] Chinese food consisting of small, steamed dumplings filled with meat, fish, etc. Dim sum are served from a passing cart, and not ordered in advance.

dim•wit ['dɪm,wɪt] *n. Informal.* a stupid person; fool or simpleton.

dim•wit•ted ['dɪm,wɪtəd] *adj. Informal.* not intelligent; stupid: *a dimwitted person.* **—,dim'wit•ted•ly,** *adv.* **—,dim'wit•ted•ness,** *n.*

din [dɪn] *n., v.* **dinned, din•ning.** —*n.* a loud, confused noise that lasts for some time.
—*v.* **1** make a din. **2** subject to a din. **3** say over and over: *She was always dinning into our ears the importance of hard work.* ⟨OE *dynn;* cf. ON *dynr*⟩
☛ *Syn. n.* See note at NOISE.

di•nar [di'nɑr] *n.* **1** the basic unit of money in certain countries: in Algeria, divided into 100 centimes; in Bahrain, Iraq, Jordan, Kuwait, and the People's Republic of Yemen, divided into 1000 fils; in Libya, divided into 1000 dirhams; in Serbia divided into 100 paras; in Sudan, divided into 10 pounds; in Tunisia, divided into 100 millim. See money table in the Appendix. **2** a unit of money in Iran, equal to 1/100 of a rial. **3** a coin worth one dinar. **4** any of various gold coins used in ancient Arab countries. ⟨< Arabic or Persian < LGk. *denarion* < L *denarius.* Doublet of DENARIUS, DENIER[2].⟩

dine [daɪn] *v.* **dined, din•ing. 1** eat dinner. **2** give a dinner to or for.
dine out, eat dinner away from home. ⟨ME < OF *disner* < VL *disjejunare* to breakfast < *dis* apart (cessation) + *jejunium* fast[2]⟩
☛ *Hom.* DYNE.

din•er ['daɪnər] *n.* **1** a person who is eating dinner. **2** DINING CAR. **3** a restaurant shaped and decorated like such a car. **4** a small eating place, usually near a main highway.

di•nette [daɪ'nɛt] *n.* **1** a small dining room. **2** a set of chairs and a table for such a room.

ding [dɪŋ] *v., n.* —*v.* **1** make a sound like a bell; ring continuously. **2** *Informal.* say over and over. **3** damage or destroy by striking or knocking. **4** dent, as by striking: *That red car dinged mine in the parking lot.*
—*n.* **1** the sound made by a bell. **2** a dent. ⟨imitative⟩

ding–a–ling ['dɪŋ ə ,lɪŋ] *n. Slang.* fool; nitwit; oaf.

ding•bat ['dɪŋ,bæt] *n. Slang.* **1** a stupid, silly, or crazy person. **2** any thing, gadget, or device; dingus. **3** *Printing.* any of a font of ornamental characters, used as at the opening of a paragraph, etc. ⟨origin uncertain⟩

ding–dong ['dɪŋ ,dɒŋ] *n., adj.* —*n.* **1** the sound made by a bell or anything like a bell with alternating strokes; any persistent or monotonous ringing. **2** a jingle; rhyme in verse or song.
—*adj.* **1** ringing with alternating strokes. **2** *Informal.* in which each side has the advantage in turns; closely contested: *a ding-dong contest, a ding-dong race.* ⟨imitative⟩

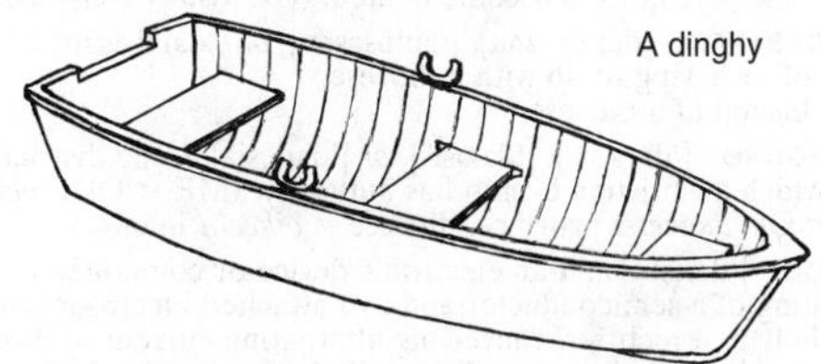
A dinghy

din•ghy ['dɪŋi] *or* ['dɪŋgi] *n., pl.* **-ghies. 1** a small rowboat. **2** a small boat used as a tender or lifeboat by a large boat. **3** a small sailboat. **4** an inflatable boat or raft. ⟨< Hind. *dingi*⟩

din•gle ['dɪŋgəl] *n.* a small, deep, shady valley. ⟨origin uncertain⟩

din•go ['dɪŋgou] *n., pl.* **-goes.** a wolflike wild dog (*Canis dingo*) of Australia. ⟨< native Australian name⟩

ding•us ['dɪŋəs] *n. Slang.* a thing, gadget, or device of which the name is unknown, unfamiliar, or forgotten. ⟨< Du. *dinges* < *ding* thing, object⟩

din•gy ['dɪndʒi] *adj.* **-gi•er, -gi•est. 1** dirty-looking; not bright and fresh; dull. **2** shabby; decrepit. ⟨origin uncertain⟩ **—'din•gi•ly,** *adv.* **—'din•gi•ness,** *n.*

dining car a railway car in which meals are served.

dining room a room in which dinner and other meals are served.

Din•ka ['dɪŋkɑ] *or* ['dɪŋkə] *n.* **1** a member of a group of peoples living in S Sudan. **2** their Nilotic language.

dink•ey ['dɪŋki] *n., pl.* **-eys.** *Informal.* a small locomotive, used for pulling freight cars around in a railway yard, for hauling logs, etc. ⟨< *dinky*⟩

dink•y ['dɪŋki] *adj.* **dink•i•er, dink•i•est.** *Slang.* small; insignificant; cute. ⟨< Scottish or N English dial. *dink* trim + *-y*[2]⟩

din•ner ['dɪnər] *n.* **1** one of the three main meals of the day, especially the largest meal. Some people have dinner at noon; others have a lunch at noon and dinner or supper in the evening. **2** a formal social event including dinner: *They're having a dinner to celebrate their parents' wedding anniversary.* **3** the food served at dinner. **4** a packaged, prepared meal, designed for quick and convenient preparation: *a TV dinner.* **5** a complete meal in a restaurant; prix fixe. ⟨ME < OF *disner* dine; infinitive used as noun⟩ **—'din•ner•less,** *adj.*

dinner jacket TUXEDO (def. 1).

dinner theatre a restaurant in which a dramatic performance is presented during or after dinner.

din•ner•time ['dɪnər,taɪm] *n.* the time at which dinner is eaten.

din•ner•ware ['dɪnər,wɛr] *n.* plates, serving dishes, etc. for serving dinner.

dino– *prefix.* of or having to do with a dinosaur or dinosaurs. ⟨< Gk. *deinos* terrible⟩

di•no•flag•el•late [,daɪnə'flædʒə,leit] *or* [-lɪt] *n.* a member of an order of marine organisms, some of which are very toxic.

di•no•pros•tone [,daɪnou'prɒstoun] *n.* a drug used to induce labour.

di•no•saur ['daɪnə,sɔr] *n.* **1** any of a group of extinct reptiles constituting two separate orders, the reptilelike Saurischia and the birdlike Ornithischia, which dominated the earth during the Mesozoic era. Some of the later dinosaurs were gigantic, the largest land animals that have ever lived on earth. **2** a person or thing that is hopelessly old-fashioned. ⟨< NL *dinosaurus* < Gk. *deinos* terrible + *sauros* lizard⟩

di•no•sau•ri•an [ˌdaɪnəˈsɔriən] *adj., n.* *—adj.* of or like a dinosaur.
—n. dinosaur.

di•no•there [ˈdaɪnouˌθir] *n.* any of an extinct genus (*Dinotherium*) of mammals of the Miocene. They resembled elephants with tusks that curved down and back. ⟨< *dino-* + Gk. *ther* beast⟩

dint [dɪnt] *n., v.* *—n.* a hollow made by the force of a blow or by pressure; dent.
by dint of, by the force of; by means of: *By dint of hard work the job was completed on schedule.*
—v. **1** make a dent in. **2** become dented. ⟨OE *dynt*; cf. ON *dyntr*⟩

di•oc•e•san [daɪˈɒsəzən], [daɪˈɒsəsən], *or* [ˌdaɪəˈsisən] *adj., n.* *—adj.* of or having to do with a diocese.
—n. a bishop of a diocese.

di•o•cese [ˈdaɪəˌsis], [ˈdaɪəsɪs], *or* [ˈdaɪəˌsiz] *n.* the district over which a Christian bishop has authority. ⟨ME < OF *diocise* < L < Gk. *dioikēsis* province, diocese < *oikeein* inhabit⟩

di•ode [ˈdaɪoud] *n.* **1** an electronic device or component consisting of a semiconductor and two attached electrodes, used especially as a rectifier, converting alternating current to direct current. Also called **semiconductor diode. 2** a simple electron tube having only two electrodes (an anode and a cathode), formerly widely used as a rectifier but now largely replaced by the semiconductor diode. ⟨< *di-*[1] + electr*ode.* 20c.⟩

di•oe•cious [daɪˈiʃəs] *adj. Botany.* having male and female flowers in separate plants. Also, **diecious.** ⟨< NL *dioecia*, genus name < Gk. *di-* double + *oikos* house⟩

Di•o•ne [daɪˈouni] *n.* one of Saturn's ten satellites.

Di•o•ny•si•a [ˌdaɪəˈnɪʃiə] *or* [ˌdaɪəˈnɪsiə] *n.pl.* a set of festivals in honour of the Greek god Dionysus.

Di•o•nys•i•ac [ˌdaɪəˈnɪsiˌæk] *adj.* Dionysian.

Di•o•ny•sian [ˌdaɪəˈnɪʃən] *or* [ˌdaɪəˈnɪsiən] *adj.* **1** of or having to do with Dionysus. **2** highly exuberant; frenzied.

Di•o•ny•sus [ˌdaɪəˈnaɪsəs] *n. Greek mythology.* the god of wine, corresponding to the Roman god Bacchus.

di•o•ram•a [ˌdaɪəˈræmə] *n.* **1** a picture to be looked at through a small opening. It is lighted in such a way as to be very realistic. **2** a scene to be viewed through a windowlike opening, showing a painted background and a foreground occupied by sculptured figures (life-size or smaller) of animals, people, etc., and appropriate accessory objects. **3** a display representing a scene from nature, with stuffed or sculptured animals in a realistic habitat, as shown in a museum. ⟨< F < Gk. *dia-* through + *horama* sight⟩ **—ˌdi•oˈram•ic,** *adj.*

di•o•rite [ˈdaɪəˌrəit] *n.* a coarse-grained igneous rock consisting essentially of hornblende and feldspar. ⟨< F *diorite* < Gk. *diorizein* distinguish (< *dia-* through + *orizein* mark a boundary) + F *-ite* ite[1]⟩

Di•os•cu•ri [ˌdaɪəsˈkjʊraɪ] *or* [ˌdaɪəsˈkjʊri] *n.pl.* the twins Castor and Pollux. ⟨< Gk. *Dioskouroi* < *Dios*, gen. of *Zeus* Zeus + *kouros* boy, son⟩

di•ox•ide [daɪˈɒksaɪd] *or* [-ˈɒksɪd] *n. Chemistry.* an oxide having two atoms of oxygen per molecule.

di•ox•in [daɪˈɒksən] *n.* any of a family of 75 aromatic hydrocarbons, some of which are highly toxic, that are produced as industrial by-products in the manufacture of chlorinated phenols and are also believed to be formed through combustion; especially, one such hydrocarbon, the most toxic manufactured chemical. Dioxins, known chemically as chlorinated dibenzo-*p*-dioxins, have the general formula $C_{12}H_nCl_{8-n}O_2$; the most toxic form is 2,3,7,8-tetrachlorodibenzo-*p*-dioxin.

dip [dɪp] *v.* **dipped** or **dipt, dip•ping;** *n.* *—v.* **1** put under water or any liquid and lift quickly out again: *Jane dipped her hand into the pool.* **2** go under water and come quickly out again. **3** dye by dipping in a liquid. **4** wash or clean by dipping in a liquid. **5** disinfect (a sheep or pig) by immersing in disinfectant. **6** immerse in a solution for plating or galvanizing. **7** make (a candle) by putting a wick into hot tallow or wax. **8** take up in the hollow of the hand or with a pail, pan, or other container: *to dip water from a well, to dip up a sample of wheat.* **9** put (one's hand, a spoon, etc.) into to take out something: *to dip into a pot. She dipped the scoop into the barrel.* **10** take a small amount from (*used with* **into**): *We had to dip into our savings.* **11** lower and raise again quickly: *The ship's flag was dipped as a salute.* **12** sink or drop down: *The bird dipped in its flight.* **13** slope downward: *The road dips.* **14** of an aircraft, make a short, sudden dive to gain momentum for a climb. **15** read or look at for a short time (*used with* **into**): *to dip into a magazine while waiting.* **16** inquire into superficially; dabble (*used with* **into**): *to dip into the arts for a time.* **17** decrease for a short time: *Production dipped last month.*
—n. **1** a dipping of any kind, especially a plunge into and out of a tub of water, the ocean, etc. **2** a liquid in which to dip something: *sheep dip.* **3** a candle made by dipping. **4** that which is taken out or up by dipping. **5** a creamy mixture of foods eaten by dipping into it with a cracker, piece of bread, raw vegetable, etc.: *a cheese dip.* **6** a sudden drop. **7** the degree of slope down. **8** a sinking down and out of sight; setting: *the dip of the sun.* **9** the angular distance of the visible horizon below the horizontal plane through the observer's eye. **10** the downward inclination of the magnetic needle at any particular place; the angle which the direction of the needle makes with the horizontal. **11** *Slang.* pickpocket. **12** a gymnastic exercise consisting of lowering the body between parallel bars, before raising it again. **13** *Slang.* a person. ⟨OE *dyppan.* Cognate with DEEP.⟩

☛ *Syn. v.* **1. Dip,** PLUNGE, IMMERSE = put into a liquid. **Dip** emphasizes taking right out again after putting or lowering partly in or wholly under: *I dipped my handkerchief in the cool water.* **Plunge** emphasizes throwing or putting completely under, suddenly or with force: *I plunged the vegetables into boiling water.* **Immerse** emphasizes keeping completely under long enough to get thoroughly soaked: *I immersed my clothes in the soapy water.*

di•phen•i•dol [dəiˈfɛnɪˌdɒl] *n.* a drug used to control vertigo and motion sickness.

di•phen•ox•y•late [ˌdaɪfɛnˈɒksɪˌleit] *n.* a drug used to control diarrhea.

di•phos•gene [dəiˈfɒsdʒin] *n.* a highly poisonous liquid related to phosgene and used in chemical warfare. *Formula*: $ClCO_2CCl_3$

diph•the•ri•a [dɪfˈθiriə] *or* [dɪpˈθiriə] *n.* an acute, infectious disease of the throat, usually accompanied by a high fever and by the formation of membranes that hinder breathing. ⟨< F *diphthérie* < Gk. *diphthera* hide, leather; with reference to the tough membrane developed on the affected parts⟩

diph•the•ri•al [dɪfˈθiriəl] *or* [dɪpˈθiriəl] *adj.* having to do with diphtheria; diphtheritic.

diph•the•rit•ic [ˌdɪfθəˈrɪtɪk] *or* [ˌdɪpθəˈrɪtɪk] *adj.* **1** of diphtheria; like diphtheria. **2** having diphtheria. Also, **diphtheric** [dɪfˈθɛrɪk].

diph•thong [ˈdɪfθɒŋ] *or* [ˈdɪpθɒŋ] *n.* **1** *Phonetics.* a vowel sound made up of two identifiable vowel sounds in immediate sequence and pronounced in one syllable, as *ou* in *house, oi* in *noise.* **2** loosely, two vowel letters representing a single vowel sound, properly called a digraph, as *ea* in *eat.* **3** loosely, several letters joined together in printing, such as *ffi,* æ, and œ, properly called a LIGATURE. ⟨< F *diphthongue* < LL < Gk. *diphthongos* < *di-*[1] double + *phthongos* sound⟩

☛ *Spelling, Pronun.* Sometimes a **diphthong** is represented by only one letter, as *i* in *ice* or *u* in *abuse.* The commonest Canadian English diphthongs are: [aɪ], [əi], [ɔɪ], [aʊ], [ʌu], [ou], [ei], and [ju].

diph•thon•gal [dɪfˈθɒŋgəl], [dɪpˈθɒŋgəl], [dɪfˈθɒŋəl], *or* [dɪpˈθɒŋəl] *adj.* of or like a diphthong.

diph•thong•ize [ˈdɪfθɒŋˌaiz] *or* [ˈdɪpθɒŋˌaɪz] *v.* **-ized, -iz•ing. 1** change (a vowel or vowels) into a diphthong. **2** become a diphthong. **—ˌdiph•thong•iˈza•tion,** *n.*

di•piv•e•frin [dəiˈpɪvəfrɪn] *n.* a drug used to treat glaucoma.

di•pleg•ia [dəiˈplidʒə] *n.* parallel paralysis on both sides of the body. ⟨< *di-* + Gk. *plegia* stroke⟩

di•plex [ˈdaɪplɛks] *adj.* of transmission or reception of two signals simultaneously with a single circuit. Compare DUPLEX[2], SIMPLEX[2].

dip•lo•coc•cus [ˌdɪplouˈkɒkəs] *n.* any of various parasitic bacteria growing in pairs. Pneumococcus, which causes lobar pneumonia, is a diplococcus. ⟨< NL < Gk. *diploos* twofold + *kokkos* grain, seed⟩

di•plod•o•cus [dɪˈplɒdəkəs] *or* [dɪˈploudəkəs] *n.* a dinosaur of North America that lived by eating plants. ⟨< NL < Gk. *diploos* twofold + *dokos* main supporting beam. Coined by O.C. Marsh (1831-1899), American paleontologist.⟩

dip•loid [ˈdɪplɔɪd] *adj., n.* *—adj.* **1** double or twofold. **2** designating a nucleus, cell, or organism having paired

homologous chromosomes (twice the haploid number of chromosomes).
—*n.* a diploid nucleus, cell, or organism. Compare HAPLOID. ⟨< Gk. *diploos* double + E *-oid*, or taken from G. 20c. cf. HAPLOID⟩

di•plo•ma [də'ploumə] *n., pl.* **-mas** or **-ma•ta** [-mətə]. **1** a certificate given by a school, college, or university to its graduating students. **2** any certificate that bestows certain rights, privileges, honours, etc. **3** a charter given to a state. ⟨< L < Gk. *diplōma* paper folded double, ult. < *diploos* double⟩

di•plo•ma•cy [də'plouməsi] *n., pl.* **-cies. 1** the management of relations between nations. The making of treaties, international agreements, etc. is an important part of diplomacy. **2** skill in managing such relations. **3** skill in dealing with others; tact: *Our son showed diplomacy in being very helpful at home the day he wanted to use the car.* ⟨< F *diplomatie* < *diplomate* diplomat⟩

diploma mill *Informal.* a substandard or non-accredited educational establishment which grants diplomas of little value.

dip•lo•mat ['dɪplə,mæt] *n.* **1** a person employed in diplomacy, especially a representative of a nation who is located in a foreign country with the duty of looking after the interests of his or her own nation in the foreign country. **2** a person who is skilful in dealing with others; a tactful person. ⟨back formation < F *diplomatique.* See DIPLOMATIC.⟩

dip•lo•mate ['dɪplə,meit] *n.* a doctor who is certified as a specialist in a branch of medicine after examination by a board.

dip•lo•mat•ic [,dɪplə'mætɪk] *adj.* **1** of or having to do with the management of relations between nations or with the people conducting such relations: *diplomatic immunity. Ambassadors and high commissioners are the highest-ranking members of the diplomatic service.* **2** having or showing skill in dealing with others; tactful: *a diplomatic police officer. He gave a diplomatic answer to avoid hurting his friend's feelings.* ⟨< NL *diplomaticus*, F *diplomatique* < Gk. *diplōma, -atos.* See DIPLOMA.⟩

dip•lo•mat•i•cal•ly [,dɪplə'mætɪkli] *adv.* in a diplomatic manner; with diplomacy.

diplomatic corps all of the ambassadors, ministers, etc., of foreign nations at the capital of a country.

diplomatic immunity special privileges accorded to diplomats and their families and staffs by international agreement, including freedom from arrest, search, and taxation.

di•plo•ma•tist [də'ploumətɪst] *n.* diplomat.

di•plo•pi•a [dɪ'ploupiə] *n.* a visual disorder or defect in which single objects are seen in duplicate; double vision. ⟨< NL < *diplo-* double + Gk. *ōps eye*⟩

di•plop•ic [dɪ'plɒpɪk] *or* [dɪ'ploupɪk] *adj.* of or having to do with diplopia.

dip•lo•pod ['dɪplə,pɒd] *n.* any of a class of elongated, cylindrical arthropods having one pair of short antennae and many body segments, with two pairs of legs on most segments; millipede. ⟨< NL *diplopoda* < Gk. *diplo-* double + *pous, podos* foot⟩

dip needle DIPPING NEEDLE.

dip•no•an ['dɪpnouən] *or* [dɪp'nouən] *n.* any fish that breathes with lungs as well as gills. ⟨< Gk. *dipnoos* double-breathed < *di-* two + *pnoe* breath⟩

di•po•lar [daɪ'poulər] *adj.* of, having to do with, or being a dipole.

di•pole ['daɪ,poul] *n.* **1** two opposite, equal electric charges or magnetic poles separated by a small distance. **2** a molecule in which the centres of positive and negative charge are separated. **3** a radio or television antenna consisting of a straight metal rod divided at the centre point, with the connecting wire fixed at this point; also, **dipole antenna.**

dip•per ['dɪpər] *n.* **1** a long-handled utensil for dipping liquids, similar to a ladle but having a larger, deeper, usually flat-bottomed cup. **2** any of a genus (*Cinclus*) of diving birds that feed on insects, etc. in fast-flowing streams. The American dipper (*C. mexicanus*) is a fairly small, grey bird found around western mountain streams from Alaska and the Yukon south to Panama. **3 Dipper,** *Astronomy.* See BIG DIPPER and LITTLE DIPPER. **4** any person or thing that dips.

dipping needle a magnetic needle balanced to swing vertically and indicate by its dip the direction of the earth's magnetic field.

dip•py ['dɪpi] *adj.* **-pi•er, -pi•est.** *Slang.* **1** foolish; half-witted. **2** light-headed; giddy; intoxicated.

dip•so•ma•ni•a [,dɪpsə'meiniə] *n.* an abnormal,

uncontrollable craving for alcoholic liquor. ⟨< NL < Gk. *dipsa* thirst + *mania* mania⟩

dip•so•ma•ni•ac [,dɪpsə'meini,æk] *n.* a person who has dipsomania.

dip–stick or **dip•stick** ['dɪp ,stɪk] *n.* **1** a rod for measuring the level of liquid in a container, such as the oil in the crankcase of a car. **2** *Slang.* a foolish or eccentric person.

dipt [dɪpt] *v.* a pt. and a pp. of DIP.

dip•ter•an ['dɪptərən] *n., adj.* —*n.* any dipterous insect. —*adj.* dipterous.

dip•ter•ous ['dɪptərəs] *adj.* **1** of, having to do with, or belonging to a large order (Diptera) of insects characterized by a single pair of wings and sucking or piercing mouthparts. Members of this order are also called **two-winged flies** and include houseflies, mosquitoes, and midges. **2** having two wings or winglike parts. ⟨< NL *dipterus* two-winged < Gk. *dipteros* < *di-* two + *pteron* wing⟩

dip•tych ['dɪptɪk] *n.* **1** an ancient writing tablet consisting of two pieces of wood or ivory hinged together along one side, like a book, and having the inner surfaces waxed for writing on with a stylus. **2** a pair of paintings or carvings on two panels hinged together. **3** anything folded so as to have two matching parts. ⟨< LL *diptycha*, neut. pl. < Gk. *diptychos* folded double < *di-* twice + *ptychē* fold⟩

di•pyr•id•a•mole [dəi'pirɪdə,moul] *n.* a drug used to treat angina pectoris. *Formula*: $C_{24}H_{40}N_8O_4$

dire [daɪr] *adj.* **dir•er, dir•est. 1** causing great fear or suffering; terrible: *a dire flood, a dire enemy.* **2** desperate; urgent; extreme: *dire poverty. They were in dire distress.* ⟨< L *dirus*⟩ **—'dire•ly,** *adv.* **—'dire•ness,** *n.*

di•rect [dɪ'rɛkt] *or* [daɪ'rɛkt] *v., adj., adv.* —*v.* **1** manage; control; guide: *The teacher directs the work of the pupils.* **2** plan, guide, and rehearse the staging of (a play, opera, film, television or radio program, etc.). See DIRECTOR (def. 3). **3** order; command: *The captain directed her men to advance.* **4** tell or show the way; give information about where to go, what to do, etc.: *Can you direct me to the railway station?* **5** put the address on (a letter, package, etc.). **6** address (words, etc.) to a person: *to direct a request to the king.* **7** point, aim, or project (something) in a particular direction or course or toward a certain objective or target: *We should direct our efforts to a useful end. The firefighter directed the hose at the flames.* **8** act as conductor in the rehearsals and performances of (a choir, band, or orchestra).
—*adj.* **1** proceeding in a straight line; without a stop or turn; straight: *a direct route.* **2** in an unbroken line of descent: *a direct descendant of Queen Victoria.* **3** immediate; prompt; swift: *She took direct action on hearing of the matter.* **4** without anyone or anything in between; by oneself or itself; not through others: *a direct tax.* **5** straightforward; frank; plain; truthful: *a direct answer. She made a direct denial of the charge of cheating.* **6** exact; absolute: *the direct opposite.* **7** of or produced by the action of the people as voters, without intermediaries or representatives: *a direct election.* **8** *Astronomy.* moving from west to east.
—*adv.* directly. ⟨< L *directus*, pp. of *dirigere* set straight < *dis-* apart + *regere* guide⟩ **—di'rect•ing•ly,** *adv.* **—di'rect•ness,** *n.*

☛ *Syn. v.* **1.** See note at MANAGE. *adj.* **Direct,** IMMEDIATE = proceeding from one to another without a break. **Direct** = going straight from one to another in an unbroken line, though there may be many steps between: *Overwork and too much strain were the direct cause of his death.* **Immediate** = going from one thing to the next, without anything between: *A heart attack was the immediate cause of his death.*

☛ *Usage.* **Direct address.** The name or descriptive term by which one addresses a person or persons: *My friends, I wish you would forget this night. It's all right, Mrs. Williams, for you to come in now.* As these examples show, the term denoting the person or persons addressed is set off from the rest of the sentence by a comma, or, if it is in the middle of the sentence, by two commas.

direct access *Computer technology.* a method of access to any item of data (in a computer storage device) without searching through all of the preceding data: *A disk allows direct access to the records stored on it.* Also called **random access. —direct-access,** *adj.*

direct current a steady electric current that flows in one direction. *Abbrev.*: DC., D.C., or d.c.

direct discourse discourse in which the exact words of a speaker are quoted. *Example*: *"I'll think it over," he replied.* Compare INDIRECT DISCOURSE.

di•rec•tion [dɪ'rɛkʃən] *or* [daɪ'rɛkʃən] *n.* **1** guidance; management; control: *The school is under the direction of a good principal.* **2** an order; command. **3** a knowing or telling what to do, how to do, where to go, etc.; instruction: *Can you give me directions how to reach Montréal?* **4** the address on a letter or package. **5** the course taken by a moving body, such as a ball or a bullet. **6** any way in which one may face or point. **7** a line of action, tendency, etc.: *The town shows improvement in many directions.* **8** *Music.* a word, phrase, or sign indicating the tempo or style in which a score or part of a score should be played. **9** the work of directing musical or theatrical performances.

☛ *Syn.* **7. Direction,** TREND, TENDENCY = line or course of action. **Direction** applies to the line followed in the course of progress or an aim guiding the course of action: *The crime investigation has taken a new direction.* **Trend** applies particularly to a general direction of custom or preference: *The trend is toward fewer required subjects in school.* **Tendency** applies to natural movement in a certain direction or an inclination to act in a definite direction: *The tendency is toward higher taxes.*

di•rec•tion•al [dɪˈrɛkʃənəl] *or* [daɪˈrɛkʃənəl] *adj.* **1** of or having to do with direction in space. **2** *Radio.* fitted for determining the direction from which signals come, or for sending signals in one direction only. **3** having to do with direction: *a directional tendency, directional signals.*

direction finder a receiving device, usually having a loop aerial, by which the direction of incoming radio signals may be determined.

di•rec•tive [dɪˈrɛktɪv] *or* [daɪˈrɛktɪv] *n., adj. —n.* an order or instruction as to procedure.
—adj. directing. **—di'rec•tive•ly,** *adv.* **—di'rec•tive•ness,** *n.*

di•rect•ly [dɪˈrɛktli] *or* [daɪˈrɛktli] *adv.* **1** in a direct line or manner; straight. **2** exactly; absolutely: *directly opposite.* **3** immediately; at once. **4** without intermediate agency: *The secretary is directly responsible to the editor.*

direct mail advertising material sent directly to large numbers of people at their home or business addresses, in order to solicit orders for products, contributions to charities, etc.

direct object *Grammar.* a term for a word showing the person or thing directly undergoing the action expressed by the verb. In 'The car struck me', *me* is the direct object. Verbs which take a direct object are transitive verbs. Compare INDIRECT OBJECT.

Di•rec•toire [dirɛkˈtwɑr]; *French,* [diʀɛkˈtwaʀ] *n., adj.*
—n. the Directory.
—adj. **1** of the time of the Directory (1795-1799). **2** of or resembling the ornate styles of the Directory period: *a Directoire table, Directoire dresses.*

di•rec•tor [dɪˈrɛktər] *or* [daɪˈrɛktər] *n.* **1** a person who leads or controls; manager: *the director of a private school, the director of a building restoration project.* **2** one of a group of persons chosen to direct the overall affairs of a company or institution: *She is on the board of directors of a large corporation.* **3** a person who plans, guides, and rehearses the staging of a play, opera, film, etc. **4** *Music.* a person who leads a choir, orchestra, etc.; conductor.

☛ *Usage.* **Director** (def. 3), PRODUCER. Usually, the **producer** initiates a show and controls the business side of the production, while the **director** has overall responsibility for the creative side. The **producer** is sometimes called an *impresario.*

di•rec•tor•ate [dɪˈrɛktərɪt] *or* [daɪˈrɛktərɪt] *n.* **1** the position of a director. **2** a group of directors.

di•rec•to•ri•al [dɪrɛkˈtɔriəl] *or* [ˌdaɪrɛkˈtɔriəl] *adj.* having to do with a director or directorate.

director's chair a folding chair with a canvas back and seat and a wooden frame.

di•rec•tor•ship [dɪˈrɛktərˌʃɪp] *or* [daɪˈrɛktərˌʃɪp] *n.* the position or term of office of a director.

di•rec•to•ry [dɪˈrɛktəri] *or* [daɪˈrɛktəri] *n., pl.* **-ries;** *adj.*
—n. **1** a list of names and addresses: *A telephone book is one kind of directory.* **2** a book of rules or instructions. **3** a group of directors; directorate. **4 Directory,** a group of five men that governed France, 1795-1799. **5** *Computer technology.* an index of files in storage. A directory typically contains the file names and file-related information (file sizes, creation dates, etc.).
—adj. directing; advisory: *legislation of a directory character.*

direct question a question quoted directly and enclosed in quotation marks. *Example*: She asked, *"When did they arrive?"* Compare INDIRECT QUESTION.

di•rec•trix [daɪˈrɛktrɪks] *n. Geometry.* a line providing a constant ratio of the distance of a moving point from a fixed point to its distance from the line.

direct tax a tax which the government collects directly from the persons who must pay it. Income taxes, property taxes, and succession duties are direct taxes. The federal sales tax is an indirect tax; consumers pay it but the government collects it from merchants.

dire•ful [ˈdaɪrfəl] *adj.* dire; dreadful; terrible. **—'dire•ful•ly,** *adv.* **—'dire•ful•ness,** *n.*

dirge [dɜrdʒ] *n.* **1** a song or hymn of lamentation for a person's death, especially one that is part of a funeral rite. **2** any slow, sad, solemn song, tune, or poem. ⟨contraction of L *dirige* direct (imperative of *dirigere*), first word in the office for the dead⟩

dir•ham [dəˈræm] *n.* **1** the basic unit of money in Morocco, divided into 100 centimes. **2** the basic unit of money in the United Arab Emirates, divided into 100 fils. **3** a unit of currency of Qatar. One hundred dirhams equal one riyal. See table of money in the Appendix. **4** a unit of money in Libya, ¹⁄₁₀₀₀ of a dinar. **5** a coin or note worth one dirham. Also, (def. 3) **dirhem.** ⟨< Arabic *dirham* < L < Gk. *drachmē*⟩

dir•i•gi•bil•i•ty [ˌdirədʒəˈbɪləti] *n.* the fact or quality of being dirigible.

dir•i•gi•ble [dɪˈrɪdʒəbəl] *or* [ˈdirədʒəbəl] *n., adj. —n.* a kind of aircraft having a long, gas-filled hull that keeps it up in the air and a steering and propelling mechanism underneath the hull; airship. Some dirigibles have a rigid hull; in others the hull is non-rigid.
—adj. capable of being steered. ⟨< L *dirigere* direct⟩

dirk [dɜrk] *n., v. —n.* dagger.
—v. stab with a dirk. ⟨origin unknown⟩

dirn•dl [ˈdɜrndəl] *n.* **1** an Alpine peasant woman's costume consisting of a blouse, a tight, usually laced bodice, and a full, bright-coloured skirt, gathered at the waist. **2** a dress imitating such a costume. **3** a skirt of this type. ⟨< South G dial. *Dirndl* girl, dim. of *Dirne* maid⟩

dirt [dɜrt] *n.* **1** mud, dust, earth, or anything of this nature. Dirt soils whatever it gets on. **2** loose earth; soil. **3** lewd or obscene words, images, or thoughts. **4** nastiness, meanness, or corruption. **5** *Informal.* anything worthless or contemptible: *She had treated them like dirt.* **6** malicious gossip: *He delighted in spreading all the latest dirt.* **7** *Mining.* the earth, gravel, or other material from which gold is separated by washing.
eat dirt, *Informal.* submit to a humiliating experience, such as making an apology or taking back something one has said. ⟨ME *drit* < ON *drit* excrement⟩ **—'dirt•less,** *adj.*

dirt bike a small motorcycle that is designed for riding over rough ground and that cannot be licensed for use on roads.

dirt–cheap [ˈdɜrt ˈtʃip] *adj.* very cheap.

dirt farmer *Informal.* a person who does his or her own farming.

dirt–poor [ˈdɜrt ˈpur] *adj.* lacking the necessities of life, such as food, clothing, and shelter; poverty-stricken.

dirt•y [ˈdɜrti] *adj., adv.* **dirt•i•er, dirt•i•est;** *v.* **dirt•ied, dirt•y•ing.** *—adj.* **1** soiled by dirt; unclean. **2** that makes dirty; soiling: *a dirty job.* **3** unpleasant; disagreeable: *to hire someone to do the dirty work.* **4** not clear or pure in colour; clouded: *a dirty red.* **5** low; mean; vile. *a dirty trick.* **6** not decent; lewd or obscene: *a dirty joke.* **7** stormy; windy: *dirty weather.* **8** causing a great amount of radioactive fallout: *a dirty bomb.* **9** cheating; unsporting: *dirty tactics in the rink.* **10** showing displeasure or annoyance (usually in the expression **dirty look**).
dirty end of the stick, the difficult or unsavoury part of a venture.
do the dirty on (someone) or **do** (someone) **dirty,** behave unscrupulously toward (someone), as by swindling, libelling, etc.
—adv. in a dirty way: *to fight dirty, talk dirty.*
—v. **1** make dirty; soil. **2** become dirty. **—'dirt•i•ness,** *n.*

☛ *Syn. adj.* **1. Dirty,** FILTHY, FOUL = unclean. **Dirty** = soiled in any way: *Children playing in mud get dirty.* **Filthy,** often expressing a disgusted attitude toward a person or thing, emphasizes the idea of being too dirty: *In some cities and towns the streets are filthy.* **Foul,** expressing a strong reaction of disgust, suggests being filled or covered with filth or something unhealthy, impure, or rotten: *The water in the swamp is foul.*

dirty linen private or intimate matters that are slightly shameful or reprehensible, causing embarrassment if made public.
air or **hang** or **wash** (one's) **dirty linen in public,** make a public spectacle of family quarrels, etc.

dirty pool conduct or an action that is mean, dishonest, or unfair.

Dirty Thirties or **dirty thirties** the drought years of the 1930s, which coincided with the Great Depression. ⟨from the dust storms resulting from the prairie drought⟩

Dis [dɪs] *n.* **1** *Roman mythology.* the god of the lower world, corresponding to the Greek god Pluto. **2** the lower world; Hades. ⟨< L, contraction of *dives* rich, translation of Gk. *Plouton* Pluto⟩

dis–[1] *prefix.* **1** the opposite of, as in *discontent.* **2** do the reverse of, as in *disentangle.* **3** apart; away, as in *dispel.* **4** not, as in *dishonest.* **5** completely (intensive), as in *disturb.* Also, **di-,** before *b, d, l, m, n, r, s, v,* and sometimes before *g* and *j*; **dif-** before *f.* ⟨< L⟩

dis–[2] a form of **di-**[1] before *s*, as in *dissyllable.*

dis•a•bil•i•ty [ˌdɪsəˈbɪləti] *n., pl.* **-ties. 1** a physical or mental condition consisting in the absence or impairment of a specific faculty, ability, etc.: *a hearing disability, an accident resulting in permanent disability.* **2** something that disables: *Paralysis is a physical disability.* **3** *Law.* something that disqualifies: *Her relationship to the accused was a disability that disqualified her from serving on the jury at his trial.* **4** disadvantage; hindrance: *Not knowing French would be a real disability in that job.*

dis•a•ble [dɪˈseibəl] *v.* **-bled, -bling. 1** deprive of effectiveness, ability, or power; make useless; cripple: *Pulling this lever disables the whole system.* **2** cause to have a physical or mental disability: *The accident disabled her.* **3** disqualify legally. **—disˈa•ble•ment,** *n.*

☛ *Syn.* **1.** See note at CRIPPLE.

dis•a•bled [dɪˈseibəld] *adj., v.* —*adj.* **1** deprived of effectiveness, ability, or power; crippled. **2** having a physical or mental disability (often in compounds): *a learning-disabled pupil. The ramp provides access for disabled customers.*
—*v.* pt. and pp. of DISABLE.

dis•a•buse [ˌdɪsəˈbjuz] *v.* **-bused, -bus•ing.** make free (of deception or error): *Education should disabuse people of prejudice.*

dis•ac•cord [ˌdɪsəˈkɔrd] *v., n.* —*v.* disagree; be out of harmony.
—*n.* disagreement; lack of harmony.

dis•ad•van•tage [ˌdɪsədˈvæntɪdʒ] *n.* **1** a lack of advantage; unfavourable condition: *The new child was at a disadvantage in school.* **2** harm; loss: *The candidate's enemies spread rumours to his disadvantage.*

dis•ad•van•taged [ˌdɪsədˈvæntɪdʒd] *adj.* **1** suffering from severe economic or social disadvantage. **2** (*noml.*) **the disadvantaged,** *pl.* all those who are disadvantaged.

dis•ad•van•ta•geous [dɪsˌædvənˈteidʒəs] *or* [ˌdɪsədvənˈteidʒəs] *adj.* causing disadvantage; unfavourable. **—disˌad•vanˈta•geous•ly,** *adv.* **—disˌad•vanˈta•geous•ness,** *n.*

dis•af•fect [ˌdɪsəˈfɛkt] *v.* alienate the affections, loyalty, commitment, etc. of.

dis•af•fect•ed [ˌdɪsəˈfɛktɪd] *adj., v.* —*adj.* **1** unfriendly; discontented. **2** no longer loyal; disloyal: *a disaffected Communist.*
—*v.* pt. and pp. of DISAFFECT.

dis•af•fec•tion [ˌdɪsəˈfɛkʃən] *n.* **1** unfriendliness; discontent: *Lack of food and supplies caused disaffection among the soldiers.* **2** disloyalty; desertion: *The government party was seriously weakened by the disaffection of many of its members.*

dis•af•fil•i•ate [ˌdɪsəˈfɪli,eit] *v.* **-at•ed, -at•ing.** end an affiliation; dissociate. **—ˌdis•afˌfil•iˈa•tion,** *n.*

dis•af•firm [ˌdɪsəˈfɜrm] *v.* contradict; repudiate, reverse, or deny (a previous statement, decision, etc.) **—ˌdis•af•firˈma•tion,** *n.*

dis•a•gree [ˌdɪsəˈgri] *v.* **-greed, -gree•ing. 1** fail to agree; differ: *The witness disagreed with the lawyer about the time of the accident.* **2** quarrel; dispute. **3** have a bad effect; be harmful: *Strawberries disagree with her.*

dis•a•gree•a•ble [ˌdɪsəˈgriəbəl] *adj.* **1** not to one's liking; unpleasant. **2** bad-tempered; cross. **—ˌdis•aˈgree•a•ble•ness,** *n.* **—ˌdis•aˈgree•a•bly,** *adv.*

dis•a•gree•ment [ˌdɪsəˈgrimənt] *n.* **1** a failure to agree; difference of opinion. **2** a quarrel or dispute. **3** a difference; unlikeness: *There is a striking disagreement between the two species.*

dis•al•low [ˌdɪsəˈlaʊ] *v.* **1** refuse to allow; deny the truth or value of. **2** *Law.* reject: *The request for a new trial was disallowed.* **3** *Cdn.* of the Federal Government, nullify an Act of a provincial legislature.

dis•al•low•ance [ˌdɪsəˈlaʊəns] *n.* **1** a disallowing: *The trial proceeded after the disallowance of the Crown Attorney's request.* **2** *Cdn.* the power of the Federal Government to annul provincial legislation. **3** *Cdn.* an Act of the Federal Government exercising this power.

dis•am•big•u•ate [ˌdɪsæmˈbɪgju,eit] *v.* **-at•ed, -at•ing.** make clear by eliminating the ambiguity; rephrase (an utterance) so as to avoid ambiguity.

dis•ap•pear [ˌdɪsəˈpir] *v.* **1** pass from sight. **2** pass from existence; be lost. **—ˌdis•apˈpear•er,** *n.*

☛ *Syn.* **1. Disappear,** VANISH, FADE = pass from sight. **Disappear** is the general word, meaning pass out of sight, whether slowly or quickly, gradually or suddenly: *She disappeared into the night.* **Vanish** = disappear without a trace, usually suddenly, often in some strange or mysterious way: *The stranger vanished from the town.* **Fade** = disappear slowly: *The ship faded into the fog.*

dis•ap•pear•ance [ˌdɪsəˈpirəns] *n.* the act of disappearing.

dis•ap•point [ˌdɪsəˈpɔɪnt] *v.* **1** fail to satisfy or please; leave (one) wanting or expecting something. **2** fail to keep a promise to (someone). **3** keep from happening; oppose and defeat. **—ˌdis•apˈpoint•er,** *n.*

dis•ap•point•ment [ˌdɪsəˈpɔɪntmənt] *n.* **1** the state of being or feeling disappointed. **2** a person or thing that causes disappointment. **3** the act or fact of disappointing.

dis•ap•pro•ba•tion [ˌdɪsæprəˈbeiʃən] *or* [dɪsˌæprəˈbeiʃən] *n.* disapproval.

dis•ap•prov•al [ˌdɪsəˈpruvəl] *n.* **1** an opinion or feeling against; an expression of an opinion against; dislike. **2** a refusal to consent; rejection.

dis•ap•prove [ˌdɪsəˈpruv] *v.* **-proved, -prov•ing. 1** have or express an opinion against. **2** show dislike (of): *The boy disapproved of going to school in the summer.* **3** refuse consent to; reject: *The judge disapproved the verdict.* **—ˌdis•apˈprov•ing•ly,** *adv.*

dis•arm [dɪsˈɑrm] *v.* **1** take weapons away from: *The police captured the bandits and disarmed them.* **2** stop having armed forces; reduce or limit the size of the armed forces. **3** remove suspicion from; make friendly; calm the anger of: *The speaker's frankness disarmed the angry mob, and they soon began to cheer him.* **4** make harmless: *The soldiers disarmed the big bomb.* **—disˈarm•er,** *n.* **—disˈarm•ing•ly,** *adv.*

dis•ar•ma•ment [dɪsˈɑrməmənt] *n.* **1** the act of disarming. **2** the reduction or limitation of armed forces and their equipment.

dis•ar•range [ˌdɪsəˈreindʒ] *v.* **-ranged, -rang•ing.** disturb the arrangement of; put out of order: *The wind disarranged her hair.* **—ˌdis•arˈrange•ment,** *n.* **—ˌdis•arˈrang•er,** *n.*

dis•ar•ray [ˌdɪsəˈrei] *n., v.* —*n.* **1** a disorder; confusion. **2** a disorder of clothing.
—*v.* **1** put into disorder or confusion. **2** *Archaic.* undress; strip.

dis•ar•tic•u•late [ˌdɪsɑrˈtɪkju,leit] *v.* **-lat•ed, -lat•ing.** separate or become separated at a joint, as, especially, bones. **—ˌdis•arˌtic•uˈla•tion,** *n.*

dis•as•sem•ble [ˌdɪsəˈsɛmbəl] *v.* **-bled, -bling.** take apart.

dis•as•so•ci•ate [ˌdɪsəˈsouʃi,eit] *or* [ˌdɪsəˈsousi,eit] *v.* **-at•ed, -at•ing.** dissociate.

dis•as•ter [dɪˈzæstər] *n.* **1** an event that causes much suffering or loss; great misfortune: *A destructive fire, flood, earthquake, or shipwreck is a disaster.* **2** a complete failure or flop: *His latest movie is a disaster. Their trip to Europe was a disaster; everything possible went wrong.* ⟨< F *désastre* < Ital. *disastro* (lack of a lucky star) < L *dis-* without + *astrum* star < Gk. *astron*⟩

☛ *Syn.* **1. Disaster,** CALAMITY, CATASTROPHE = a great misfortune. **Disaster** applies to an event that happens suddenly or unexpectedly and causes much loss and suffering: *The lack of rain for so many weeks was a disaster for the farmers.* **Calamity** applies to a disaster that causes intense suffering and grief, often to a great number: *The flooding of the river last year was a calamity.* **Catastrophe** suggests a disaster that is final and complete, causing loss that can never be made up: *A nuclear war would be a catastrophe.*

disaster area 1 an area that has suffered a disaster. **2** an area that, having suffered some severe disaster, becomes entitled to special government assistance: *The flooded section of the province was designated a disaster area.*

dis•as•trous [dɪˈzæstrəs] *adj.* **1** bringing disaster; causing great danger, suffering, loss, pain, or sorrow. **2** marked by complete failure. **—disˈas•trous•ly,** *adv.*

dis•a•vow [ˌdɪsəˈvaʊ] *v.* deny that one knows about, approves of, or is responsible for; disclaim: *The prisoner disavowed the confession bearing his signature.*

dis•a•vow•al [ˌdɪsəˈvaʊəl] *v.* a disavowing; denial of knowledge, approval, or responsibility.

dis•band [dɪsˈbænd] *v.* **1** dismiss from service: *Most of the army was disbanded after the war.* **2** break ranks; become scattered. **—disˈband•ment,** *n.*

dis•bar [dɪsˈbɑr] *v.* **-barred, -bar•ring.** deprive (a lawyer) of the right to practise his or her profession. **—disˈbar•ment,** *n.*

dis•be•lief [ˌdɪsbɪ'lif] *n.* a lack of belief; inability or refusal to believe.
☛ *Syn.* See note at UNBELIEF.

dis•be•lieve [ˌdɪsbɪ'liv] *v.* **-lieved, -liev•ing.** refuse or be unable to believe. **—ˌdis•be'liev•er,** *n.*

dis•bur•den [dɪs'bɜrdən] *v.* relieve of an emotional burden: *The boy disburdened his mind to his sister by confessing what he had done.*

dis•burse [dɪs'bɜrs] *v.* **-bursed, -burs•ing.** pay out; expend. ⟨< MF < OF *desbourser* < *des-* away from + *bourse* purse < LL *bursa* < Gk. *byrsa* leather, wineskin⟩ **—dis'burs•er,** *n.*
☛ *Syn.* See note at SPEND.

dis•burse•ment [dɪs'bɜrsmənt] *n.* **1** the act of paying out: *Our treasurer attends to the disbursement of funds.* **2** the money paid out; expenditure.

disc [dɪsk] *n., v. —n.* **1** a phonograph record or compact disc. **2** any of the round, concave blades of a disc harrow. **3** DISC HARROW. **4** See DISK.
—v. cultivate with a disc harrow. Also, **disk.** ⟨See DISK⟩

disc. **1** discount. **2** discovered.

dis•card *v.* [dɪ'skɑrd]; *n.* ['dɪskɑrd] *v., n. —v.* **1** give up as useless or worn out; throw aside. **2** *Card games.* **a** get rid of (useless or unwanted playing cards) by throwing them aside or playing them. **b** play (a card) that is neither a trump nor of the suit led.
—n. **1** the act of throwing aside as useless. **2** something thrown aside as useless or not wanted: *That old book is a discard from the library.* **3** *Card games.* the unwanted cards thrown aside; a card played as useless. ⟨< *dis-*[1] + *card*[1]⟩ **—dis'card•er,** *n.*

disc brake a brake in a motor vehicle in which flat pads are pressed against both sides of a disc attached to a wheel. Also, **disk brake.**

dis•cern [dɪ'sɜrn] *or* [dɪ'zɜrn] *v.* perceive; see clearly; distinguish; recognize. ⟨ME < OF *discerner* < L *discernere* < *dis-* off + *cernere* separate⟩ **—dis'cern•er,** *n.*

dis•cern•i•ble [dɪ'sɜrnəbəl] *or* [dɪ'zɜrnəbəl] *adj.* capable of being discerned. **—dis'cern•i•bly,** *adv.*

dis•cern•ing [dɪ'sɜrnɪŋ] *or* [dɪ'zɜrnɪŋ] *adj., v. —adj.* shrewd; perceptive; insightful; acute; discriminating.
—v. ppr. of DISCERN. **—dis'cern•ing•ly,** *adv.*

dis•cern•ment [dɪ'sɜrnmənt] *or* [dɪ'zɜrnmənt] *n.* **1** keenness in perceiving and understanding; good judgment; shrewdness. **2** the act of discerning.
☛ *Syn.* **1.** See note at INSIGHT.

dis•charge *v.* [dɪs'tʃɑrdʒ]; *n.* [dɪs'tʃɑrdʒ] *or* ['dɪstʃɑrdʒ] *v.* **-charged, -charg•ing;** *n. —v.* **1** unload (a ship); unload (cargo) from a ship; unload. **2** fire; shoot: *to discharge a gun.* **3** release; let go; dismiss: *to discharge a patient from a hospital, to discharge a committee.* **4** dismiss from a job; fire: *He was discharged for incompetence.* **5** give off; let out: *The clouds discharge electricity in the form of lightning.* **6** come or pour forth: *The river discharged into a bay.* **7** rid of an electric charge; withdraw electricity from: *to discharge a battery.* **8** lose an electric charge. **9** pay; settle: *to discharge a debt.* **10** release from an obligation; exempt: *to discharge a debtor from her debts.* **11** perform; carry out: *to discharge one's duty.* **12** *Law.* cancel or set aside (a court order or an obligation). **13** of a wound or diseased place, ooze (pus or other waste matter). **14** of dye or colouring, spread. **15** remove or bleach (a dye or colour) from a textile, cloth, etc.
—n. **1** an unloading. **2** a firing off of a gun, a blast, etc.: *The noise of the discharge could be heard for blocks.* **3** a release; the act of letting go; a dismissing: *the discharge of a convict from prison.* **4** a piece of writing that shows a person's release or dismissal; certificate of release: *Members of the armed services got discharges when the war ended.* **5** a giving off; a letting out: *His mother explained that lightning is a discharge of electricity from the clouds.* **6** something given off or let out: *the watery discharge from a sore.* **7** the rate of flow: *The discharge from the pipe is 45* dm^3/s. **8** the transference of electricity between two charged bodies when placed in contact or near each other. **9** payment: *the discharge of a debt.* **10** carrying out; performance: *A public official should be honest in the discharge of his or her duties.* ⟨< *dis-*[1] + *charge*⟩ **—dis'charg•er,** *n.*
☛ *Syn. v.* **11.** See note at PERFORM.

discharge tube a clear tube containing gas or vapour which emits light when an electric current is passed through it. Neon signs are discharge tubes.

A disc harrow

disc harrow a harrow that turns and loosens soil by means of one or more rows of revolving saucer-shaped blades set at an angle.

dis•ci•ple [də'saɪpəl] *n., v.* **-pled, -pling.** *—n.* **1** a person who believes in and helps to spread the ideas and teachings of another; follower. **2** one of the followers of Jesus, especially one of the twelve Apostles. **3 Disciple,** a member of the Disciples of Christ.
—v. train (someone) as a disciple.
⟨ME < OF < L *discipulus* pupil (*discere* learn)⟩
☛ *Syn.* **1.** See note at FOLLOWER.

dis•ci•ple•ship [di'saɪpəlˌʃɪp] *n.* **1** the state of being a disciple. **2** the time during which one is a disciple. **3** the life, qualities or conduct of a disciple.

Disciples of Christ a religious sect founded in the U.S. in 1809, that rejects all creeds and seeks to unite Christians on the basis of the New Testament alone.

dis•ci•plin•a•ble ['dɪsəplɪnəbəl] *adj.* **1** that can be disciplined. **2** deserving discipline.

dis•ci•pli•nar•i•an [ˌdɪsəplə'nɛriən] *n., adj. —n.* a person who enforces discipline or who believes in strict discipline.
—adj. disciplinary.

dis•ci•pli•nar•y ['dɪsəpləˌnɛri] *adj.* **1** of or having to do with discipline. **2** for discipline; intended to improve discipline: *disciplinary measures.*

dis•ci•pline ['dɪsəplɪn] *n., v.* **-plined, -plin•ing.** *—n.* **1** training, especially of the mind or character. **2** the training effect of experience, misfortune, etc. **3** a trained condition of order and obedience. **4** order among school pupils, members of the armed forces, or members of any group. **5** the methods or rules for regulating the conduct of members of any group; the control exercised over members of a group. **6** punishment; chastisement. **7** a branch of instruction or education; a field of study: *the discipline of science.*
—v. **1** train; bring to a condition of order and obedience; bring under control: *A good officer must know how to discipline soldiers.* **2** punish: *The rebellious convicts were severely disciplined.* ⟨ME < OF < L *disciplina* < *discipulus.* See DISCIPLE.⟩
—'dis•ci•plin•er, *n.*

disc jockey a person who chooses, plays, and introduces recorded music for a radio program, dance, or other social function, etc. Also, **disk jockey.**

dis•claim [dɪs'kleim] *v.* **1** refuse to recognize as one's own; deny connection with: *The motorist disclaimed responsibility for the accident.* **2** give up all claim to: *She disclaimed any share in the profits.*

dis•claim•er [dɪs'kleimər] *n.* **1** denial or repudiation. **2** a written statement of denial or repudiation. **3** a person who disclaims.

dis•cli•max [dɪs'klaɪmæks] *n. Ecology.* a climax community changed by constant disruption by humans or their animals.

dis•close [dɪ'sklouz] *v.* **-closed, -clos•ing.** **1** open to view; uncover. **2** make known; reveal. **—dis'clos•er,** *n.*
☛ *Syn.* **2.** See note at REVEAL.

dis•clo•sure [dɪ'sklouʒər] *n.* **1** the act of disclosing. **2** the thing disclosed.

dis•co ['dɪskou] *n., v. —n.* **1** discothèque. **2** the style of music or dancing characteristic of discothèques. **3** (*adjl.*) of, having to do with, or characteristic of discothèques or their styles of music or dancing.
—v. go to or dance at a discothèque. Also, **disco dance.**

dis•cog•ra•pher [dɪ'skɒgrəfər] *n.* a person who compiles discographies.

dis•cog•ra•phy [dɪ'skɒgrəfi] *n.* **1** a list of musical recordings, classified according to performer, musical category, date of release, etc. **2** the history or study of musical recordings.

dis•coid ['dɪskɔɪd] *adj., n. —adj.* **1** like a disk in shape. **2** *Botany.* of a composite flower head, composed of only disk flowers.
—n. a disklike object. **—dis'coid•al,** *adj.*

dis•col•or•a•tion [dɪsˌkʌlə'reiʃən] *n.* **1** discolouring or being discoloured. **2** a discoloured spot: *There was a slight discoloration at the bottom of the curtain.*

dis•col•our or **dis•col•or** [dɪs'kʌlər] *v.* **1** change or spoil the colour of; stain: *Smoke had discoloured the new paint work.* **2** become changed in colour.

dis•com•bob•u•late [ˌdɪskəm'bɒbjəˌleit] *v.* **-lat•ed, -lat•ing.** *Informal.* disconcert; confuse. ⟨fanciful alteration and extension, perhaps of *discomfit*⟩ **—ˌdis•comˌbob•u'la•tion,** *n.*

dis•com•fit [dɪs'kʌmfɪt] *v.* **1** overthrow completely; defeat; rout. **2** defeat the plans or hopes of; frustrate. **3** embarrass greatly; confuse; disconcert. ⟨ME < OF *desconfit,* pp. of *desconfire* < *des-* away + *confire* make, accomplish < L *conficere*⟩ **—dis'com•fit•er,** *n.*

dis•com•fi•ture [dɪs'kʌmfɪtʃər] *n.* **1** a complete overthrow; defeat; rout. **2** the defeat of plans or hopes; frustration. **3** confusion; embarrassment.

dis•com•fort [dɪs'kʌmfərt] *n., v.* *—n.* **1** a lack of comfort; a feeling of uneasiness; mild pain: *She felt considerable discomfort after the operation.* **2** a feeling of embarrassment, confusion, etc.: *Her discomfort increased as her guilt became more and more evident.* **3** something that causes discomfort.
—v. make uncomfortable or uneasy.

dis•com•mode [ˌdɪskə'moud] *v.* **-mod•ed, -mod•ing.** put to inconvenience. ⟨< *dis* not + F *commode* convenient⟩

dis•com•pose [ˌdɪskəm'pouz] *v.* **-posed, -pos•ing.** disturb the self-possession of; make uneasy; bring into disorder.

dis•com•po•sure [ˌdɪskəm'pouʒər] *n.* the state of being disturbed; uneasiness; embarrassment.

dis•con•cert [ˌdɪskən'sɜrt] *v.* **1** disturb the self-possession of; embarrass greatly; confuse: *The police officer was disconcerted at finding that he had arrested the wrong man.* **2** upset; disorder: *The chairperson's plans were disconcerted by the late arrival of the speaker.* **—ˌdis•con'cert•ing•ly,** *adv.*
☛ *Syn.* **1.** See note at CONFUSE.

dis•con•cert•ed [ˌdɪskən'sɜrtɪd] *adj., v.* *—adj.* disturbed; confused.
—v. pt. and pp. of DISCONCERT. **—ˌdis•con'cert•ed•ly,** *adv.* **—ˌdis•con'cert•ed•ness,** *n.*

dis•con•form•i•ty [ˌdɪskən'fɔrmɪti] *n., pl.* **-ties.** *Geology.* the surface separating two parallel strata of rock and showing that the lower stratum underwent considerable erosion before the higher one was laid down.

dis•con•nect [ˌdɪskə'nɛkt] *v.* undo or break the connection of; unfasten; separate: *She disconnected the electric fan by pulling out the plug.*

dis•con•nect•ed [ˌdɪskə'nɛktɪd] *adj., v.* *—adj.* **1** not connected; separate. **2** without order or connection; incoherent; broken: *The injured man could give only a disconnected account of the accident.*
—v. pt. and pp. of DISCONNECT. **—ˌdis•con'nect•ed•ly,** *adv.* **—ˌdis•con'nect•ed•ness,** *n.*

dis•con•nec•tion [ˌdɪskə'nɛkʃən] *n.* **1** the act of disconnecting. **2** the state of being disconnected; separation.

dis•con•so•late [dɪs'kɒnsəlɪt] *adj.* without hope; forlorn; unhappy; cheerless. ⟨ME < Med.L *disconsolatus* < L *dis-* not + *consolatus,* pp. of *consolari* < *com-* together + *solari* soothe⟩ **—dis'con•so•late•ly,** *adv.* **—dis'con•so•late•ness,** *n.*
☛ *Syn.* See note at DESOLATE.

dis•con•tent [ˌdɪskən'tɛnt] *n., adj., v.* *—n.* lack of contentment; restlessness or dissatisfaction.
—adj. discontented.
—v. make discontented.

dis•con•tent•ed [ˌdɪskən'tɛntɪd] *adj., v.* *—adj.* not contented; not satisfied; displeased and restless; disliking what one has and wanting something different: *She was discontented with life in the country.*
—v. pt. and pp. of DISCONTENT. **—ˌdis•con'tent•ed•ly,** *adv.* **—ˌdis•con'tent•ed•ness,** *n.*

dis•con•tent•ment [ˌdɪskən'tɛntmənt] *n.* discontent.

dis•con•tin•u•ance [ˌdɪskən'tɪnjuəns] *n.* a stopping or being stopped.

dis•con•tin•u•a•tion [ˌdɪskənˌtɪnju'eiʃən] *n.* **1** a breaking off; stopping; ceasing. **2** a break; interruption.

dis•con•tin•ue [ˌdɪskən'tɪnju] *v.* **-tin•ued, -tin•u•ing.** **1** cause to cease; put an end or stop to: *The morning train service has been discontinued. After the patient got well, the doctor discontinued her visits.* **2** cease from; cease to take, use, etc. **3** *Law.* terminate (a lawsuit) at the request of the plaintiff or by his or her failure to continue it. **—ˌdis•con'tin•u•er,** *n.*

dis•con•ti•nu•i•ty [ˌdɪskɒntə'njuəti] *or* [-kɒntə'nuəti], [dɪsˌkɒntə'njuəti] *or* [dɪsˌkɒntə'nuəti] *n., pl.* **-ties.** **1** lack of connection and unity, or an instance of this: *The discontinuity of the plot made the novel clumsy and hard to understand.* **2** *Mathematics.* the value of the independent variable at the point where a function is interrupted.

dis•con•tin•u•ous [ˌdɪskən'tɪnjuəs] *adj.* not continuous; broken, interrupted. **—ˌdis•con'tin•u•ous•ly,** *adv.*

dis•co•phile ['dɪskəˌfail] *n.* a connoisseur and collector of phonograph records or compact discs.

dis•cord ['dɪskɔrd] *n., v.* *—n.* **1** a difference of opinion; unfriendly relations; a disagreement. **2** *Music.* **a** a lack of harmony in tones sounded at the same time. **b** an inharmonious combination of tones. **3** harsh, clashing sounds.
—v. conflict; jar; be discordant. ⟨ME < OF *discord* < *discorder* < L *discordare* < *discors, -cordis* discordant < *dis-* apart + *cor, cordis* heart⟩

dis•cord•ance [dɪ'skɔrdəns] *n.* **1** a discord of sounds. **2** disagreement.

dis•cord•an•cy [dɪ'skɔrdənsi] *n.* discordance.

dis•cord•ant [dɪ'skɔrdənt] *adj.* **1** not in harmony: *a discordant note in music.* **2** not in agreement; not fitting together: *Many discordant views were expressed.* **3** harsh; clashing: *The sound of some automobile horns is discordant.* **4** *Genetics.* referring to a pair of twins, only one of whom has a particular trait. **—dis'cord•ant•ly,** *adv.*

disc•o•thèque ['dɪskəˌtɛk] *n.* a type of night club where one may listen and dance to recorded music. ⟨< F; originally, record library⟩

dis•count *v.* [dɪs'kaʊnt] *or* ['dɪskaʊnt]; *n.* ['dɪskaʊnt] *v., n.*
—v. **1** deduct (a certain percentage) of the amount or cost: *The store discounts 3 percent on all bills paid when due.* **2** allow for exaggeration, prejudice, or inaccuracy in; believe only part of. **3** make less effective by anticipation: *The price of the stock fell before its dividend was reduced, for the reduction had already been discounted.* **4** buy, sell, or lend money on (a note, bill of exchange, etc.), deducting a certain percentage to allow for unpaid interest. **5** lend (money), deducting the interest in advance. **6** sell (goods) at a discount. **7** leave out of account; disregard: *In her plans she discounted the expense.* **8** reject; discard as unimportant or false: *She discounts the whole theory. Just discount those rumours.*
—n. **1** a deduction from the amount or cost: *During the sale the dealer allowed a 10 percent discount on all cash purchases.* **2** (*adjl.*) having or referring to a price less than the current average retail price: *discount merchandise, discount prices.* **3** a percentage charged for buying, selling, or lending money on a note, bill of exchange, etc. **4** the interest deducted in advance. **5** the act of discounting.
at a discount, a at less than the regular price; below par. **b** easy to get because not in demand. ⟨< MF *desconter* < *des-* away + *conter* count < L *computare*⟩ **—dis'count•a•ble,** *adj.* **—dis'count•er,** *n.*

dis•coun•te•nance [dɪs'kaʊntənəns] *v.* **-nanced, -nanc•ing.** **1** refuse to approve; discourage: *This school discountenances secret societies.* **2** abash; disconcert.

discount house **1** DISCOUNT STORE. **2** *Esp. Brit.* a financial firm which trades in discounted rates, loans, etc.

discount rate **1** the percentage charged for discounting notes. **2** sale price; cheaper rate.

discount store a retail store that sells merchandise for less than the current average retail price, making its profit from a big sales volume with low overhead.

dis•cour•age [dɪ'skɜrɪdʒ] *v.* **-aged, -ag•ing.** **1** take away the courage of; lessen the hope or confidence of: *Repeated failures discouraged him.* **2** try to prevent by disapproving; frown upon. **3** prevent or hinder through fear, loss of incentive, etc.: *Lack of recognition discouraged him from writing more novels.* **4** make unattractive; make to seem not worthwhile: *The chill of winter soon discouraged our picnics.* ⟨ME < OF *descoragier* < *des-* away + *corage.* See COURAGE.⟩ **—dis'cour•ag•er,** *n.* **—dis'cour•ag•ing•ly,** *adv.*

dis•cour•age•ment [dɪ'skɜrɪdʒmənt] *n.* **1** the state of being or feeling discouraged. **2** the thing that discourages. **3** the act of discouraging.

dis•course *n.* ['dɪskɔrs]; *v.* [dɪ'skɔrs] *n., v.* **-coursed, -cours•ing.** *—n.* **1** a formal speech or writing: *Lectures and sermons are discourses.* **2** a conversation; talk. **3** *Linguistics.* **a** all the linked utterances which constitute the script of a spoken or written text; such a text as a linguistic unit. **b** such texts collectively, or the characteristic manner in which they are formed in a given language: *English discourse is different from French discourse.* **c** the study of this: *a specialist in discourse.*
—v. **1** speak or write formally. **2** converse; talk. ⟨< F *discours*

< Med.L < L *discursus* < *dis-* in different directions + *currere* run〉 **—dis'cours•er,** *n.*

dis•cour•te•ous [dɪs'kɜrtiəs] *adj.* not courteous; rude; impolite. **—dis'cour•te•ous•ly,** *adv.* **—dis'cour•te•ous•ness,** *n.*

dis•cour•te•sy [dɪs'kɜrtəsi] *n., pl.* **-sies. 1** lack of courtesy; rudeness; impoliteness. **2** a rude or impolite act.

dis•cov•er [dɪ'skʌvər] *v.* **1** see or learn of for the first time; find out. **2** *Archaic.* make known; reveal. **3** bring (someone with talent) from obscurity into public prominence. 〈ME < OF *descovrir* < *des-* away + *covrir* cover < L *cooperire*〉 **—dis'cov•er•a•ble,** *adj.* **—dis'cov•er•er,** *n.*

dis•cov•er•y [dɪ'skʌvəri] *n., pl.* **-er•ies. 1** the act of discovering. **2** the thing discovered. **3** a person whose special talent has just been discovered, especially an actor, writer, athlete, etc.

discovery claim *Cdn.* the first gold-bearing area on a creek to be officially registered.

dis•cred•it [dɪs'krɛdɪt] *v., n.* —*v.* **1** destroy trust in; show to be unworthy of belief or trust: *to discredit a witness. Science has discredited the theory that the earth is flat.* **2** refuse to believe; give no credit to: *I see no reason to discredit his statement.* **3** damage the reputation of; disgrace.
—*n.* **1** reason for disbelief; doubt; distrust: *The new evidence throws discredit on her testimony.* **2** loss of good name or standing: *His conduct brought discredit on his firm.* **3** a person or thing that causes loss of good name or standing; disgrace: *Her behaviour was a discredit to the school.*

dis•cred•it•a•ble [dɪs'krɛdətəbəl] *adj.* bringing discredit. **—dis'cred•it•a•bly,** *adv.*

dis•creet [dɪ'skrit] *adj.* **1** prudent and tactful in speech or behaviour; restrained: *a discreet servant. A lawyer must be discreet and not violate the confidence of a client.* **2** showing prudence and tact; polite: *The salesclerk maintained a discreet distance while they discussed their finances. Her criticism was so discreet that he was not offended.* **3** not lavish or ostentatious; modest: *discreet elegance.* 〈ME < OF *discret* < Med.L < L *discretus* separated, pp. of *discernere.* Doublet of DISCRETE. See DISCERN.〉 **—dis'creet•ly,** *adv.* **—dis'creet•ness,** *n.*
☛ *Hom.* DISCRETE.

dis•crep•an•cy [dɪ'skrɛpənsi] *n., pl.* **-cies. 1** lack of consistency; difference; disagreement. **2** an example of inconsistency or disagreement: *The lawsuit was lost because of discrepancies in the statements of the witnesses.*
☛ *Syn.* **1.** See note at DIFFERENCE.

dis•crep•ant [dɪ'skrɛpənt] *adj.* differing; disagreeing; different; inconsistent. 〈< L *discrepans, -antis,* ppr. of *discrepare* < *dis-* differently + *crepare* sound〉 **—dis'crep•ant•ly,** *adv.*

dis•crete [dɪ'skrit] *adj.* **1** separate; distinct. **2** consisting of distinct parts. 〈ME < L *discretus,* separated, pp. of *discernere.* Doublet of DISCREET. See DISCERN.〉 **—dis'crete•ly,** *adv.* **—dis'crete•ness,** *n.*
☛ *Hom.* DISCREET.

dis•cre•tion [dɪ'skrɛʃən] *n.* **1** the freedom to judge or choose: *Making final plans was left to the president's discretion.* **2** the quality of being discreet; good judgment; carefulness in speech or action; wise caution.
age of discretion, the age at which one is legally able to manage one's affairs; adulthood.
at one's discretion, as one sees fit.

dis•cre•tion•ar•y [dɪ'skrɛʃə,nɛri] *adj.* with freedom to decide or choose; left to one's own judgment.

dis•crim•in•a•ble [dɪ'skrɪmənəbəl] *adj.* that can be discriminated or distinguished: *discriminable colours.*

dis•crim•i•nate *v.* [dɪ'skrɪmə,neit]; *adj.* [dɪ'skrɪmənɪt] *v.* **-nat•ed, -nat•ing;** *adj.* —*v.* **1** note or see a difference; make a distinction (*between*): *It is often difficult to discriminate between a mere exaggeration and a deliberate falsehood.* **2** make a distinction in treatment: *The law ought not to discriminate against any race, creed, or colour.* **3** see the difference in or between; distinguish with the mind: *The study of literature helps a person discriminate good writing from poor writing.* **4** be the identifying mark of; differentiate: *The broad brush strokes discriminate the original painting from the fake.*
—*adj.* having discrimination, making careful distinctions. 〈< L *discriminare* < *discrimen* separation < *discernere.* See DISCERN.〉 **—dis'crim•i•nate•ly,** *adv.* **—dis'crim•i,na•tor,** *n.*
☛ *Syn. v.* **1, 3.** See note at DISTINGUISH.

dis•crim•i•nat•ing [dɪ'skrɪmə,neitɪŋ] *adj., v.* —*adj.* **1** having or showing the ability to discriminate well: *a discriminating judgment. A discriminating buyer will be able to see that this fabric is inferior.* **2** that discriminates: *The discriminating mark of measles is a rash on the skin.* **3** *Business.* differential: *Manufacturers wanted a discriminating duty on imports.*
—*v.* ppr. of DISCRIMINATE. **—dis'crim•i,nat•ing•ly,** *adv.*

dis•crim•i•na•tion [dɪ,skrɪmə'neiʃən] *n.* **1** the act of making or recognizing differences and distinctions. **2** the ability to make fine distinctions: *Her discrimination in such matters is well-known.* **3** the act or practice of making or showing a difference in treatment based on prejudice: *He was happy to work for a firm in which there was no discrimination.*

dis•crim•i•na•tive [dɪ'skrɪmənətɪv] *or* [dɪ'skrɪmə,neitɪv] *adj.* **1** that distinguishes; discriminating. **2** discriminatory; biassed: *a discriminative tax.*

dis•crim•i•na•to•ry [dɪ'skrɪmənə,tɔri] *adj.* marked by or showing partiality or prejudice; biassed: *discriminatory laws.*

dis•crown [dɪs'kraʊn] *v.* deprive of royal power; depose.

dis•cur•sive [dɪ'skɜrsɪv] *adj.* **1** wandering or shifting from one subject to another; rambling: *Her carefully planned speech was not discursive, but developed one topic.* **2** founded on deliberate reasoning instead of intuition. 〈< Med.L *discursivus* < L *discursus* discourse〉 **—dis'cur•sive•ly,** *adv.* **—dis'cur•sive•ness,** *n.*

dis•cus ['dɪskəs] *n., pl.* **-cus•es** or **-ci** [-kaɪ] *or* [-ki]. **1** a heavy, circular plate of stone or metal, used in athletic games as a test of skill and strength in throwing. **2** the event of throwing the discus. 〈< L < Gk. *diskos* quoit. Doublet of DAIS, DESK, DISH, and DISK.〉

dis•cuss [dɪ'skʌs] *v.* **1** talk about together, bringing in various points of view; talk over informally. **2** explain in detail; expound in speech or writing: *Her new book discusses the future of the publishing industry in Canada.* 〈ME < L *discussus,* pp. of *discutere* < *dis-* apart + *quatere* shake〉 **—dis'cuss•er,** *n.*
☛ *Syn.* **Discuss,** ARGUE, DEBATE = talk something over with others. **Discuss** emphasizes considering all sides of a question: *We discussed the best road to take.* **Argue** suggests taking one side and bringing forward facts and reasons for it and against the others: *I argued for taking the new highway.* **Debate** suggests more formal arguing, often publicly, between clearly drawn up sides: *The Oxford students debated against two Canadian students in Toronto last week.*

dis•cus•sant [dɪ'skʌsənt] *n.* a person who takes part in a panel discussion, symposium, etc.

dis•cus•sion [dɪ'skʌʃən] *n.* **1** talking about together; going over the reasons for and against; the act of discussing things informally. **2** a formal, detailed presentation of a topic in speech or writing; discourse: *He concluded his talk with a discussion of the social implications of a guaranteed annual wage.*

dis•dain [dɪs'dein] *v., n.* —*v.* look down on; consider beneath oneself; scorn: *He took his bicycle, disdaining to go by bus.*
—*n.* contempt; scorn. 〈ME < OF *desdeignier* < *des-* away + *deignier* deign < L *dignari*〉
☛ *Syn. n.* See note at SCORN.

dis•dain•ful [dɪs'deinfəl] *adj.* feeling or showing disdain. **—dis'dain•ful•ly,** *adv.* **—dis'dain•ful•ness,** *n.*

dis•ease [dɪ'ziz] *n.* **1** a condition in which an organ, system, or part does not function properly; sickness; illness: *People, animals, and plants are all liable to suffer from disease.* **2** any particular illness: *Chicken pox is an infectious disease.* **3** a disordered or bad condition of mind, morals, public affairs, etc. 〈ME < OF *desaise* < *des-* away + *aise* ease, opportunity < VL *adjacens* neighbourhood < L *adjacens* adjacent〉 **—dis'ease•less,** *adj.*

dis•eased [dɪ'zizd] *adj.* **1** having a disease; showing signs of sickness or illness; being diseased: *a diseased hand.* **2** disordered: *a diseased mind.*

dis•em•bark [,dɪsɪm'bɑrk] *v.* **1** go ashore from a ship or leave an aircraft: *We disembarked at Montréal.* **2** unload from a ship or aircraft: *to disembark passengers.*

dis•em•bar•ka•tion [,dɪsɪmbɑr'keiʃən] *n.* a disembarking or being disembarked.

dis•em•bar•rass [,dɪsɪm'bærəs] *or* [,dɪsɪm'bɛrəs] *v.* **1** free from something that holds back or entangles; disengage. **2** relieve; rid. **3** free from embarrassment or uneasiness.

dis•em•bod•y [,dɪsɪm'bɒdi] *v.* **-bod•ied, -bod•y•ing.** separate (a soul, spirit, etc.) from the body: *Ghosts are usually thought of as disembodied spirits.* **—,dis•em'bod•i•ment,** *n.*

dis•em•bow•el [,dɪsɪm'baʊəl] *v.* **-elled** or **-eled, -el•ling** or **-el•ing.** take or rip out the bowels of. **—,dis•em'bow•el•ment,** *n.*

dis•en•chant [,dɪsɪn'tʃænt] *v.* **1** free from a magic spell or illusion. **2** free from unrealistically favourable ideas about something; disillusion: *The bad weather disenchanted us with the*

Rockies. —ˌdis•en'chant•er, *n.* —ˌdis•en'chant•ing•ly, *adv.* —ˌdis•en'chant•ment, *n.*

dis•en•chant•ed [ˌdɪsɪn'tʃæntɪd] *adj., v.* —*adj.* disappointed; disillusioned: *After a few weeks, Tim felt disenchanted with his new job.*
—*v.* pt. and pp. of DISENCHANT.

dis•en•cum•ber [ˌdɪsɪn'kʌmbər] *v.* free from a burden, annoyance, or trouble.

dis•en•fran•chise [ˌdɪsɪn'fræntʃaɪz] *v.* **-chised, -chis•ing.** disfranchise. —ˌ**dis•en'fran•chise•ment,** *n.*

dis•en•gage [ˌdɪsɪn'geidʒ] *v.* **-gaged, -gag•ing. 1** free from an engagement, pledge, obligation, etc. **2** detach; loosen: *The mother disengaged her hand from that of the sleeping child.* **3** *Military.* go away from combat or contact with (an enemy).
—ˌ**dis•en'gage•ment,** *n.*

dis•en•gaged [ˌdɪsɪn'geidʒd] *adj., v.* —*adj.* **1** not busy or in use; free from appointments. **2** released; detached.
—*v.* pt. and pp. of DISENGAGE.

dis•en•tan•gle [ˌdɪsɪn'tæŋgəl] *v.* **-tan•gled, -tan•gling.** free from tangles or complications; untangle.
—ˌ**dis•en'tan•gle•ment,** *n.*

dis•en•throne [ˌdɪsɪn'θroun] *v.* **-throned, -thron•ing.** dethrone.

dis•en•twine [ˌdɪsɪn'twaɪn] *v.* **-twined, -twin•ing.** disentangle.

dis•e•qui•lib•ri•um [dɪsˌikwə'lɪbriəm] *or* [ˌdɪsikwə'lɪbriəm] *n.* loss of equilibrium.

dis•es•tab•lish [ˌdɪsɪ'stæblɪʃ] *v.* deprive of the character of being established; especially, withdraw state recognition or support from (a church). —ˌ**dis•es'tab•lish•ment,** *n.*

dis•es•teem [ˌdɪsɪ'stim] *v. or n.* scorn; dislike.

di•seur [di'zɜr]; *French,* [di'zœʀ] *n.* a male performer of songs, monologues, impersonations, etc. ⟨< F⟩

di•seuse [di'zuz]; *French,* [di'zœz] *n.* a female performer of songs, monologues, impersonations, etc. ⟨< F⟩

dis•fa•vour or **dis•fa•vor** [dɪs'feivər] *n., v.* —*n.* **1** unfavourable opinion; disapproval: *The employees looked with disfavour on any attempt to change their cafeteria.* **2** the state or condition of having lost favour or trust or of being regarded with disapproval: *The ambassador was in disfavour with the government at home.* **3** an injurious act: *He did me a disfavour by selling me that broken television set.*
—*v.* view with disapproval; withhold favour from.

dis•fig•ure [dɪs'fɪgjər] *or* [dɪs'fɪgər] *v.* **-ured, -ur•ing.** spoil the appearance of; mar the beauty of: *Large billboards disfigured the countryside.* —**dis'fig•ur•er,** *n.*
☛ *Syn.* See note at DEFACE.

dis•fig•ure•ment [dɪs'fɪgjərmənt] *or* [dɪs'fɪgərmənt] *n.* **1** the act of disfiguring. **2** a disfigured condition. **3** something that disfigures; a defect.

dis•fran•chise [dɪs'fræntʃaɪz] *v.* **-chised, -chis•ing. 1** take the rights of citizenship away from. A disfranchised person cannot vote or hold office. **2** take a right or privilege from. Also, **disenfranchise.**

dis•fran•chise•ment [dɪs'fræntʃɪzmənt] *n.* disfranchising or being disfranchised. Also, **disenfranchisement.**

dis•gorge [dɪs'gɔrdʒ] *v.* **-gorged, -gorg•ing. 1** throw up (what has been swallowed); vomit forth. **2** pour forth; discharge: *Swollen streams disgorged their waters into the river.* **3** give up unwillingly: *The robbers were forced to disgorge their plunder.* ⟨ME < OF *desgorger* < *des-* reverse of + *gorge* gorge < LL *gurges* throat, jaws < L *gurges* abyss, whirlpool⟩ —**dis'gorg•er,** *n.*

dis•grace [dɪs'greis] *n., v.* **-graced, -grac•ing.** —*n.* **1** a loss of respect or honour: *The boy's disgrace was deeply felt by his family.* **2** a person or thing that causes dishonour or shame: *To be put in prison is usually considered a disgrace.* **3** the state or condition of having fallen from honour and good repute: *The girl was in disgrace with her teachers and friends for having cheated on an exam.*
—*v.* **1** cause to lose honour or respect; bring shame upon: *He disgraced his family by his behaviour.* **2** treat with disfavour; humiliate: *The cowardly officer was disgraced for failing to do his duty.* ⟨< F *disgrâce* < Ital. *disgrazia* < *dis-* opposite of + *grazia* grace < L *gratia*⟩ —**dis'grac•er,** *n.*
☛ *Syn. n.* **1. Disgrace,** DISHONOUR, IGNOMINY = loss of good name or respect. **Disgrace** suggests losing the respect and approval of others: *He was in disgrace after his ungentlemanly behaviour.* **Dishonour** suggests losing one's honour or reputation, or having them taken from one: *For neglect of duty he was stripped of his rank with dishonour.* **Ignominy** means public disgrace or dishonour and suggests being put to shame and held in contempt: *He brought on himself the ignominy of being caught cheating in the game.*

dis•grace•ful [dɪs'greisfəl] *adj.* causing loss of honour or respect; shameful. —**dis'grace•ful•ly,** *adv.* —**dis'grace•ful•ness,** *n.*

dis•grun•tle [dɪs'grʌntəl] *v.* **-tled, -tling.** put in bad humour; dissatisfy: *the customer was disgruntled by the poor service.* ⟨< *dis-*[1] apart + obs. *gruntle,* frequentative of *grunt*⟩
—**dis'grun•tle•ment,** *n.*

dis•grun•tled [dɪs'grʌntəld] *adj., v.* —*adj.* in bad humour; discontented; disgusted; displeased.
—*v.* pt. and pp. of DISGRUNTLE. ⟨< *dis-* + obs. *gruntle* grunt, grumble⟩

dis•guise [dɪs'gaɪz] *v.* **-guised, -guis•ing;** *n.* —*v.* **1** make changes in clothes or appearance of (someone) for concealment or for looking like someone else: *The spy disguised himself as an old man.* **2** hide what (something) really is; make (something) seem like something else: *The pirates had disguised their ship. He disguised his handwriting. He disguised his hate by a show of friendliness.*
—*n.* **1** the use of a changed or unusual dress and appearance in order not to be recognized: *The criminal resorted to disguise to escape from jail.* **2** clothes, actions, etc. used to hide who one really is or to make a person look like someone else: *Woman's clothes and a wig formed his disguise.* **3** a false or misleading appearance; deception; concealment. **4** the state or condition of being disguised: *in disguise.* ⟨ME < OF *desguisier* < *des-* down + *guise* guise < Gmc.⟩ —**dis'guis•ed•ly,** *adv.* —**dis'guise•ment,** *n.*
—**dis'guis•er,** *n.*

dis•gust [dɪs'gʌst] *n., v.* —*n.* **1** a strong, sickening dislike; loathing: *Bad odours or tastes can arouse disgust. Many people wrote to express their disgust at the newspaper's sensational account of the murder trial.* **2** weary indignation or dissatisfaction: *His excuses for not helping out were so silly that she finally hung up in disgust.*
—*v.* **1** arouse loathing in; be very offensive to. **2** cause weary indignation or dissatisfaction in. ⟨< MF *desgoust,* n., *desgouster,* v. < *des-* apart + *goust* taste < L *gustus*⟩ —**dis'gust•ing•ly,** *adv.*
☛ *Syn. n.* See note at DISLIKE.

dis•gust•ed [dɪs'gʌstɪd] *adj., v.* —*adj.* **1** filled with disgust. **2** *Informal.* fed up; tired: *She said she was disgusted with their constant quarrelling.*
—*v.* pt. and pp. of DISGUST. —**dis'gust•ed•ly,** *adv.*
—**dis'gust•ed•ness,** *n.*

dis•gust•ing [dɪs'gʌstɪŋ] *adj., v.* —*adj.* that disgusts; unpleasant; distasteful.
—*v.* ppr. of DISGUST. —**dis'gust•ing•ly,** *adv.*

dish [dɪʃ] *n., v.* —*n.* **1** any vessel or container, usually shallow and flat-bottomed, used for holding or serving food. **2 dishes,** *pl.* cups, saucers, glasses, plates, bowls, etc. together: *It's your turn to wash the dishes.* **3** the amount of food served in a dish. **4** a particular kind of food: *My favourite dish is sliced peaches and cream.* **5** something shallow and hollow like a dish. **6** an antenna shaped like a dish or having a dish-shaped reflector. **7** *Slang.* an attractive person. **8** *Slang.* something that one really likes; a favourite thing: *That kind of music is just my dish.*
—*v.* **1** put (food) into a dish ready for serving or eating (*often used with* **out** *or* **up**): *You may dish the dinner now.* **2** shape like a dish; make concave. **3** ruin or defeat. **4** present (facts, etc.) neatly and attractively (*used with* **up**): *to dish up a good argument.* **5** *Informal.* give or dispense, especially very freely or indiscriminately (*used with* **out**): *to dish out punishment, dishing out compliments.*
dish it out, *Slang.* abuse or punish someone physically or verbally: *She can dish it out, but she can't take it.* ⟨OE *disc* < L *discus* dish, discus < Gk. *diskos.* Doublet of DAIS, DESK, DISCUS, and DISK.⟩

dis•ha•bille [ˌdɪsə'bil] *n.* **1** informal, careless dress. **2** a garment or costume worn carelessly. **3** the condition of being only partly dressed. Also, **deshabille.** ⟨< F *déshabillé,* pp. of *déshabiller* < *dés-* away + *habiller* dress⟩

dish antenna a radio or television antenna composed of leads and a reflector shaped like a dish.

dis•har•mo•ny [dɪs'hɑrməni] *n., pl.* **-nies.** lack of harmony; discord.

dish•cloth ['dɪʃˌklɒθ] *n.* a cloth to wash dishes with.

dis•heart•en [dɪs'hɑrtən] *v.* discourage; depress: *A long drought disheartens a farmer.* —**dis'heart•en•ing•ly,** *adv.*
—**dis'heart•en•ment,** *n.*

di•shev•el [dɪ'ʃɛvəl] *v.* **-elled** or **-eled, -el•ling** or **-el•ing.** disarrange or rumple (hair, clothing, etc.).

di•shev•elled or **di•shev•eled** [dɪ'ʃɛvəld] *adj., v.* —*adj.* **1** rumpled; mussed; disordered; untidy: *a dishevelled appearance.* **2** hanging loosely or in disorder: *dishevelled hair.*
—*v.* pt. and pp. of DISHEVEL. ⟨ME < OF *descheveler* < *des-* away + *chevel* hair < L *capillus*⟩

dish•ful ['dɪʃfʊl] *n., pl.* **-fuls.** as much as a dish can hold.

dis•hon•est [dɪs'ɒnɪst] *adj.* **1** lacking honesty or integrity; inclined to cheat, steal, deceive, etc.: *You cannot expect a fair deal from a dishonest merchant.* **2** showing falseness or deceit: *a dishonest advertisement, a dishonest account of the accident.* **3** arranged to work or function in an unfair way: *a dishonest card game, dishonest scales.* **—dis'hon•est•ly,** *adv.*

dis•hon•es•ty [dɪs'ɒnɪsti] *n., pl.* **-ties. 1** lying, cheating, or stealing; lack of honesty. **2** a dishonest act.

dishonor [dɪs'ɒnər] *n., v.* See DISHONOUR.

dis•hon•or•able [dɪs'ɒnərəbəl] *adj.* See DISHONOURABLE.

dis•hon•our or **dis•hon•or** [dɪs'ɒnər] *n., v.* —*n.* **1** a loss of honour or reputation; shame; disgrace. **2** the cause of dishonour. **3** a refusal or failure to pay a cheque, bill, etc.
—*v.* **1** cause or bring dishonour to. **2** refuse or fail to pay (a cheque, bill, etc.). **3** behave disrespectfully toward.
—dis'hon•our•er or **dis'hon•or•er,** *n.*
☛ *Syn. n.* **1.** See note at DISGRACE.

dis•hon•our•a•ble or **dis•hon•or•a•ble** [dɪs'ɒnərəbəl] *adj.* **1** causing loss of honour; shameful; disgraceful. **2** without honour. **—dis'hon•our•a•ble•ness** or **dis'hon•or•a•ble•ness,** *n.* **—dis'hon•our•a•bly** or **dis'hon•or•a•bly,** *adv.*

dish•pan ['dɪʃ,pæn] *n.* **1** a large pan or basin in which to wash dishes. **2** (*adj.*) of hands, etc., showing signs of having been in hot water a lot: *dishpan hands.*

dish•rag ['dɪʃ,ræg] *n.* dishcloth.

dish•tow•el ['dɪʃ,taʊəl] *n.* a cloth for drying dishes; tea towel.

dish•wash•er ['dɪʃ,wɒʃər] *n.* **1** a machine for washing, rinsing, and drying dishes in one continuous operation. **2** a person who washes dishes, especially one employed by a restaurant, hospital, etc. **3** *Slang.* a pearl diver.

dish•wa•ter ['dɪʃ,wɒtər] *n.* water in which dishes are being or have been washed.

dis•il•lu•sion [,dɪsɪ'luʒən] *v., n.* —*v.* free from illusion; destroy the idealism of; disappoint: *He thought he could trust everyone; but soon he was disillusioned.*
—*n.* a freeing or being freed from illusion; a destruction of idealism.

dis•il•lu•sion•ment [,dɪsɪ'luʒənmənt] *n.* disillusioning or being disillusioned.

dis•in•cen•tive [,dɪsɪn'sɛntɪv] *n.* deterrent.

dis•in•cli•na•tion [dɪs,ɪnklə'neiʃən] *or* [,dɪsɪnklə'neiʃən] *n.* unwillingness; averseness.

dis•in•cline [,dɪsɪn'klaɪn] *v.* **-clined, -clin•ing.** make or be unwilling or averse.

dis•in•clined [,dɪsɪn'klaɪnd] *adj., v.,* —*adj.* unwilling or averse.
—*v.* pt. and pp. of DISINCLINE.

dis•in•fect [,dɪsɪn'fɛkt] *v.* destroy potentially harmful micro-organisms in or on: *Surgical instruments are disinfected before they are used.* **—,dis•in'fec•tor,** *n.*

dis•in•fect•ant [,dɪsɪn'fɛktənt] *n., adj.* —*n.* an agent that disinfects, especially a chemical substance such as alcohol, chlorine, or carbolic acid.
—*adj.* that disinfects.

dis•in•fec•tion [,dɪsɪn'fɛkʃən] *n.* the destruction of disease germs.

dis•in•fla•tion [,dɪsɪn'fleiʃən] *n.* a lowering of prices, not accompanied by deflation, and meant to increase buying power.

dis•in•for•ma•tion [dɪs,ɪnfər'meiʃən] *or* [,dɪsɪnfər'meiʃən] *n.* false information, intended to mislead.

dis•in•gen•u•ous [,dɪsɪn'dʒɛnjuəs] *adj.* insincere; not frank. **—,dis•in'gen•u•ous•ly,** *adv.* **—,dis•in'gen•u•ous•ness,** *n.*

dis•in•her•it [,dɪsɪn'hɛrɪt] *v.* prevent from inheriting; deprive of an inheritance or heritage: *to disinherit one's children.*

dis•in•her•it•ance [,dɪsɪn'hɛrətəns] *n.* the act of disinheriting or the state of being disinherited.

dis•in•te•grate [dɪs'ɪntə,greit] *v.* **-grat•ed, -grat•ing. 1** break up; separate into small parts or bits: *Time had caused the old books to disintegrate into a pile of fragments and dust.* **2** *Physics.* change in nuclear structure through bombardment by charged particles.

dis•in•te•gra•tion [dɪs,ɪntə'greiʃən] *n.* **1** a breaking up; separation into small parts or bits: *Rain and frost had caused the gradual disintegration of the rock.* **2** *Physics.* the emission of an alpha or beta particle by the nucleus of a radioactive element.

dis•in•te•gra•tor [dɪs,ɪntə'greitər] *n.* **1** a person or thing that causes disintegration. **2** a machine for disintegrating a substance.

dis•in•ter [,dɪsɪn'tɜr] *v.* **-terred, -ter•ring. 1** take out of a grave or tomb; dig up. **2** bring to light; discover and reveal.

dis•in•ter•est [dɪs'ɪntrɪst] *or* [-'ɪntərɪst] *n.* lack of interest; indifference.

dis•in•ter•est•ed [dɪs'ɪntrɪstɪd] *or* [-'ɪntə,rɛstɪd] *adj.* not having or showing selfish motives; not concerned with one's own interests; impartial; fair. **—dis'in•ter•est•ed•ly,** *adv.* **—dis'in•ter•est•ed•ness,** *n.*

☛ *Usage.* **Disinterested** and UNINTERESTED should not be confused. **Disinterested** = having no selfish interest or personal feelings in a matter and therefore having no reason or desire to be anything but strictly impartial and fair: *A judge should be disinterested.* **Uninterested** = not interested in any way, having no concern or feelings about the matter and paying no attention: *An uninterested student can spoil a class.*

dis•in•ter•ment [,dɪsɪn'tɜrmənt] *n.* **1** the act of disinterring or the state of being disinterred. **2** something disinterred.

dis•join [dɪs'dʒɔɪn] *v.* separate; keep from joining; prevent from being joined.

dis•joint [dɪs'dʒɔɪnt] *v.* **1** take apart at the joints: *disjoint a chicken.* **2** break up; disconnect; put out of order: *Don't disjoint your speech with too many irrelevant asides.* **3** put out of joint; dislocate. **4** come apart; be put out of joint.

dis•joint•ed [dɪs'dʒɔɪntɪd] *adj., v.* —*adj.* **1** taken apart at the joints. **2** broken up; disconnected; incoherent: *The girl's essay was rambling and disjointed.* **3** out of joint.
—*v.* pt. and pp. of DISJOINT. **—dis'joint•ed•ly,** *adv.* **—dis'joint•ed•ness,** *n.*

disjoint set *Mathematics.* one of two or more sets having no numbers in common.

dis•junct [dɪs'dʒʌŋkt] *adj.* **1** not joined; disjoined; separated. **2** having the body separated by deep clefts into head, thorax, and abdomen: *Wasps are disjunct insects.* ⟨< L *disjunctum* < *dis* apart + *jungere* join⟩

dis•junc•tion [dɪs'dʒʌŋkʃən] *n.* **1** the act of disjoining or state of being disjoined; a separation. **2** *Logic.* the relation between the terms of a disjunctive proposition.

dis•junc•tive [dɪs'dʒʌŋktɪv] *adj., n.* —*adj.* **1** causing separation; separating. **2** *Grammar.* showing a choice or contrast between two ideas, words, etc. *Either…or, but, yet,* etc. are disjunctive conjunctions. *Otherwise, else,* etc. are disjunctive adverbs. **3** *Grammar.* in some languages, designating a form of pronoun that is used alone or following a preposition instead of immediately next to the verb, e.g. the series *moi, toi,* etc. in French. **4** *Logic.* involving alternatives. A disjunctive proposition asserts that one or the other of two things is true but both cannot be true.
—*n.* **1** *Logic.* a statement involving alternatives. **2** *Grammar.* a disjunctive conjunction or pronoun. **—dis'junc•tive•ly,** *adv.*

disk [dɪsk] *n., v.* —*n.* **1** a round, thin, flat object. **2** a round, flat or apparently flat, surface: *the sun's disk.* **3** the round, central part of the flower head of most composite plants: *The daisy has a yellow disk.* **4** *Anatomy.* any round, flat part or structure, especially any of the masses of fibrous cartilage between the bodies of the vertebrae. **5** *Computer technology.* a round, thin, flat plate on which a computer stores data through the use of optical or magnetic technology. **6** See DISC.
—*v.* See DISC. Also, **disc.** ⟨< L *discus* discus < Gk. *diskos.* Doublet of DAIS, DESK, DISCUS, and DISH.⟩ **—'disk,like** or **'disc,like,** *adj.* **—'disk•er** or **'disc•er,** *n.*

disk brake DISC BRAKE.

disk drive an electronic device in a computer that reads data stored on disks.

disk•ette [dɪs'kɛt] *n.* a small, flexible, plastic disk on which data for a computer can be stored.

disk flower any of the tiny flowers that make up the central disk of the flower head of a composite plant. The ox-eye daisy has yellow disk flowers and white ray flowers. See COMPOSITE for picture.

disk harrow See DISC HARROW.

disk jockey See DISC JOCKEY.

disk operating system *Computer technology.* the program that runs the computer's internal functions and enables the user to manage the computer's operations. *Abbrev.*: DOS

disk wheel a spokeless wheel, solid between the rim and the centre.

dis•like [dɪs'ləik] *n., v.* **-liked, -lik•ing.** *—n.* a feeling of not liking; a feeling against.
—v. not like; object to; have a feeling against.
☛ *Syn. n.* **Dislike,** DISTASTE, DISGUST = a feeling of not liking someone or something. **Dislike** is the general word, applying to any degree of this feeling: *Barbara has a dislike for study and would rather play baseball.* **Distaste** applies to a fixed dislike for something one finds unpleasant or disagreeable: *She has a distaste for chocolate.* **Disgust** applies to a strong dislike for something that is disagreeable, sickening, or bad: *We feel disgust for bad odours and tastes.*

dis•lo•cate ['dɪslou,keit] *or* [,dɪslou'keit] *v.* **-cat•ed, -cat•ing.** **1** cause one or more of the bones of (a joint) to be shifted out of place: *The football player dislocated his shoulder when he fell.* **2** put out of order; disturb; upset: *Our plans for the picnic were dislocated by the bad weather.* **—'dis•lo,ca•tor,** *n.*

dis•lo•ca•tion [,dɪslou'keiʃən] *n.* the act of dislocating or the state of being dislocated.

dis•lodge [dɪs'lɒdʒ] *v.* **-lodged, -lodg•ing.** **1** drive or force out of a place, position, etc.: *The worker used a crowbar to dislodge a heavy stone from the wall. Heavy gunfire dislodged the enemy from the fort.* **2** leave a lodging place.

dis•lodg•ment [dɪs'lɒdʒmənt] *n.* the act of dislodging or the state of being dislodged.

dis•loy•al [dɪs'lɔɪəl] *adj.* not loyal; unfaithful: *A disloyal servant let the thieves into the house.* **—dis'loy•al•ly,** *adv.*

dis•loy•al•ty [dɪs'lɔɪəlti] *n., pl.* **-ties.** **1** lack of loyalty; unfaithfulness: *The traitor was shot for disloyalty to his country.* **2** a disloyal act.
☛ *Syn.* **1. Disloyalty,** TREACHERY, TREASON = faithlessness. **Disloyalty** = unfaithfulness, felt or shown, to anyone or anything to whom one owes allegiance or is bound by promises, love, or friendship: *Refusing to defend parents, school, or country is disloyalty.* **Treachery** = dishonest faithlessness, and suggests some definite act of betraying trust while pretending to be loyal: *Secretly working to the detriment of a friend is treachery.* **Treason** applies to treachery to one's country, shown by doing something specifically to help the enemy: *Deliberately broadcasting enemy propaganda to our troops is treason.*

dis•mal ['dɪzməl] *adj.* **1** dark; gloomy: *Damp caves or rainy days are dismal.* **2** dreary; miserable: *Sickness often makes a person feel dismal.* ⟨ME *dismall* < AF *dis mal* evil days < L *dies mali*⟩ **—'dis•mal•ly,** *adv.*

dis•man•tle [dɪs'mæntəl] *v.* **-tled, -tling.** **1** strip of covering, equipment, furniture, guns, rigging, etc.: *The warship was dismantled before the hull was sold for scrap metal.* **2** pull down or take apart: *We had to dismantle the bookcases to move them.* ⟨< MF *desmanteler* < *des-* away + *mantel* mantle < L *mantellum*⟩

dis•mast [dɪs'mæst] *v.* take the mast or masts from; break down the mast or masts of: *The storm dismasted the ship.*

dis•may [dɪ'smei] *n., v.* *—n.* **1** a loss of courage because of fear of what is about to happen. **2** lack of confidence because of unexpected difficulty; sudden apprehension.
—v. trouble greatly; make afraid: *The thought that she might fail the history test dismayed her.* ⟨ME < OF **desmaier* < VL *dismagare* deprive of strength < L *dis-* (reverse) + Frankish **magan* have strength⟩ **—dis'may•ing•ly,** *adv.*
☛ *Syn. n.* **Dismay,** CONSTERNATION = a feeling of being unnerved or overwhelmed by the thought of what is going to happen next. **Dismay** suggests loss of ability to face or handle something frightening, baffling, or upsetting that comes as a surprise or shock: *The mother was filled with dismay when her son confessed he had robbed a store.* **Consternation** = dismay and dread so great that a person cannot think clearly or, sometimes, move: *To our consternation the child darted out in front of the speeding car.*

dis•mem•ber [dɪs'mɛmbər] *v.* **1** pull apart; cut to pieces; separate or divide into parts: *The Austro-Hungarian Empire was dismembered after the First World War.* **2** cut or tear the limbs from. **—dis'mem•ber•ment,** *n.*

dis•miss [dɪ'smɪs] *v.* **1** send away; allow to go: *At noon the teacher dismissed the class.* **2** remove from a position or office; discharge; fire: *The clerk was dismissed because he was always late for work.* **3** put out of mind; stop thinking about or considering: *Dismiss your troubles and be happy. She dismissed the magazine article with a laugh.* **4** *Law.* refuse to consider (a complaint, plea, etc.) in a court: *to dismiss a charge.* ⟨< L *dismissus*, var. of *dimissus* < *dis-* away + *missus,* pp. of *mittere* send⟩

dis•miss•al [dɪ'smɪsəl] *n.* **1** the act of dismissing or the state or fact of being dismissed. **2** a written or spoken order dismissing someone.

dis•mis•sion [dɪ'smɪʃən] *n.* dismissal.

dis•mis•sive [dɪ'smɪsɪv] *adj.* dismissing or showing dismissal: *a dismissive gesture.* **—dis'mis•sive•ly,** *adv.*

dis•mount [dɪs'maʊnt] *v.* **1** get off a horse, bicycle, etc. **2** knock, throw, or otherwise remove from a horse; unhorse. **3** take (a thing) from its setting or support: *The cannon was dismounted for shipping to another fort.* **4** take apart; take to pieces. **5** deprive (troops) of horses or mounts: *The enemy dismounted the troops by stealing their horses.*

dis•o•be•di•ence [,dɪsə'bidiəns] *or* [,dɪsə'bidjəns] *n.* a refusal to obey; failure to obey.

dis•o•be•di•ent [,dɪsə'bidiənt] *or* [,dɪsə'bidjənt] *adj.* refusing to obey; failing to obey. **—,dis•o'be•di•ent•ly,** *adv.*

dis•o•bey [,dɪsə'bei] *v.* fail to follow orders or rules; refuse to obey. **—,dis•o'bey•er,** *n.*

dis•o•blige [,dɪsə'blaɪdʒ] *v.* **-bliged, -blig•ing.** **1** neglect to oblige; refuse to oblige; refuse to do a favour for. **2** give offence to. **3** inconvenience (someone).

dis•op•er•a•tion [,dɪsɒpə'reiʃən] *or* [dɪs,ɒpə'reiʃən] *n.* *Ecology.* mutually harmful interaction between two independent organisms.

di•so•pyr•a•mide [,daɪsou'pirə,maɪd] *n.* a drug used to treat certain heart conditions. *Formula*: $C_{21}H_{29}N_3O$

dis•or•der [dɪs'ɔrdər] *n., v.* *—n.* **1** a lack of order or system; confusion: *The room was in such disorder that it was impossible to find anything.* **2** a public disturbance; riot. **3** a sickness; disease: *a disorder of the stomach.*
—v. **1** destroy the order of; throw into confusion. **2** upset the functions of; cause sickness in: *Such food is likely to disorder the stomach.*

dis•or•dered [dɪs'ɔrdərd] *adj., v.* *—adj.* **1** not in order; disturbed. **2** sick.
—v. pt. and pp. of DISORDER.

dis•or•der•ly [dɪs'ɔrdərli] *adj., adv.* *—adj.* **1** not orderly; in confusion: *The books and papers lay in a disorderly pile on the floor.* **2** causing disorder; making a disturbance; breaking rules; unruly: *a disorderly mob.* **3** *Law.* acting against public peace and order: *disorderly conduct.*
—adv. Archaic. in a disorderly manner. **—dis'or•der•li•ness,** *n.*

dis•or•gan•ize [dɪs'ɔrgə,naɪz] *v.* **-ized, -iz•ing.** throw into confusion and disorder; upset the order and arrangement of: *Heavy snowstorms disorganized the train schedule.*
—dis,or•gan•i'za•tion, *n.*

dis•or•gan•ized [dɪs'ɔrgə,naɪzd] *adj., v.* *—adj.* disorderly; messy; untidy; lacking in system.
—v. pt. and pp. of DISORGANIZE.

dis•o•ri•ent [dɪs'ɔri,ɛnt] *or* [dɪs'ɔriənt] *v.* cause to lose sense of direction or time; mix up; disconcert: *His sudden rise to fame and fortune disoriented him at first.* ⟨< F *désorienter*⟩
—dis,o•ri•en'ta•tion, *n.*

dis•o•ri•en•tate [dɪs'ɔriɛn,teit] *v.* disorient. ⟨< *dis* + ORIENTATE⟩

dis•own [dɪs'oun] *v.* refuse to recognize as one's own; cast off: *He disowned his disobedient daughter. The politician disowned her former views on the subject.*

dis•par•age [dɪ'spærɪdʒ] *or* [dɪ'spɛrɪdʒ] *v.* **-aged, -ag•ing.** **1** speak slightingly of; try to lessen the importance or value of; belittle: *The coward disparaged the hero's brave attempt to rescue the drowning child.* **2** lower the reputation of; discredit. ⟨ME < OF *desparagier* match unequally < *des-* apart + *parage* rank, lineage < L *par* equal⟩ **—dis'par•ag•er,** *n.* **—dis'par•ag•ing•ly,** *adv.*

dis•par•age•ment [dɪ'spærɪdʒmənt] *or* [dɪ'spɛrɪdʒmənt] *n.* **1** the act of disparaging; detraction; belittlement. **2** something that lowers a thing or person in worth or importance. **3** a lessening in esteem or standing: *Say nothing that will be to Anna's disparagement.*

dis•pa•rate ['dɪspərɪt] *adj.* distinct in kind; essentially different; unlike; dissimilar. ⟨< L *disparatus*, pp. of *disparare* < *dis-* apart + *parare* get⟩ **—'dis•pa•rate•ly,** *adv.*
—'dis•pa•rate•ness, *n.*

dis•par•i•ty [dɪ'spærəti] *or* [dɪ'spɛrəti] *n., pl.* **-ties.** inequality; difference: *There will be disparities in the accounts of the same event given by several people.*
☛ *Syn.* See note at DIFFERENCE.

dis•pas•sion [dɪs'pæʃən] *n.* freedom from emotion or prejudice; calmness; impartiality.

dis•pas•sion•ate [dɪs'pæʃənɪt] *adj.* free from emotion or prejudice; calm; impartial: *To a dispassionate observer, the drivers of both cars seemed equally at fault.* **—dis'pas•sion•ate•ly,** *adv.* **—dis'pas•sion•ate•ness,** *n.*

dis•patch or **des•patch** *v.* [dɪ'spætʃ]; *n.* [dɪ'spætʃ] *or* ['dɪspætʃ] *v., n.* *—v.* **1** send off to some place or for some purpose: *She dispatched a messenger to tell the general what had happened.* **2** get (something) done promptly or speedily. **3** give the death blow to; kill. **4** *Informal.* eat up. **5** dismiss; send away; get rid of: *The homemaker dispatched the sales representative.*
—n. **1** a sending off (of a letter, a messenger, etc.): *Please hurry up the dispatch of this telegram.* **2** a written message such as a news report or a report to a government by an ambassador or other official: *This dispatch has been two days on the way.* **3** promptness; speed. **4** a putting to death; killing. **5** an agency for conveying goods, etc.
mention in dispatches, *Military.* **a** commend (someone) for bravery, distinguished service, etc., in the official report of an action. **b** the fact of being commended in this way: *She was promoted twice and received three mentions in dispatches.* ⟨< Ital. *dispacciare* hasten or Sp. *despachar*⟩

dispatch box DISPATCH CASE.

dispatch case a usually flat, stiff case for carrying documents or other papers.

dis•patch•er or **des•patch•er** [dɪ'spætʃər] *or* ['dɪspætʃər] *n.* a person who dispatches: *She is a dispatcher for a taxi company.*

dis•pel [dɪ'spɛl] *v.* **-pelled, -pel•ling.** drive away and scatter; disperse: *The captain's cheerful laugh dispelled our fears.* ⟨< L *dispellere* < *dis-* away + *pellere* drive⟩ **—dis'pel•ler,** *n.*
☛ *Syn.* See note at SCATTER.

dis•pen•sa•ble [dɪ'spɛnsəbəl] *adj.* **1** that may be done without; unimportant. **2** capable of being dispensed or administered. **—dis'pen•sa•ble•ness,** *n.*

dis•pen•sa•ry [dɪ'spɛnsəri] *n., pl.* **-ries. 1** a place where medicines and medical advice are given free or for a small charge. **2** that part of a hospital where medicines are prepared and stored.

dis•pen•sa•tion [ˌdɪspən'seiʃən] *n.* **1** the act of giving out; act of distributing: *the dispensation of charity to the poor.* **2** the thing given out or distributed: *They gave thanks for the dispensations of Providence.* **3** rule; management: *England under the dispensation of Elizabeth I.* **4** the management or ordering of the affairs of the world by God or Nature. **5** a religious system: *the Christian dispensation.* **6** *Roman Catholic Church.* **a** official permission to disregard a law, obligation, etc., without penalty. **b** the writing giving such permission.

dis•pen•sa•to•ry [dɪ'spɛnsəˌtɔri] *n., pl.* **-ries. 1** a book that tells how to prepare and use medicines. **2** *Archaic.* dispensary.

dis•pense [dɪ'spɛns] *v.* **-pensed, -pens•ing. 1** give out; distribute: *The Red Cross dispensed food and clothing to the refugees.* **2** carry out; put in force; apply: *Judges and courts of law dispense justice.* **3** prepare and give out: *Druggists dispense medicines.* **4** exempt or excuse (from): *They were dispensed from their oath.*
dispense with, a get rid of; make unnecessary: *The new evaluation system dispenses with oral examinations.*
b get along without; do without: *He found he could dispense with rich food when he began to eat properly.* ⟨ME < OF *despenser* < L *dispensare* weigh out < *dis-* out < *pendere* weigh⟩
☛ *Syn.* **1.** See note at DISTRIBUTE.

dis•pens•er [dɪ'spɛnsər] *n.* **1** a device, often automatic and often coin-operated, which is made to release its contents one at a time or in measured amounts: *There are dispensers for gum, chocolate bars, coffee, sandwiches, cigarettes, paper cups, etc.* **2** a container, such as a spray bottle or aerosol can, that sprays or feeds out its contents in a convenient form and amount. **3** a person who or thing that dispenses.

dis•peo•ple [dɪs'pipəl] *v.* **-pled, -pling.** deprive of all or many people or inhabitants.

dis•per•sal [dɪ'spɜrsəl] *n.* a dispersion; the act of scattering or state of being scattered: *the dispersal of a crowd.*

dis•perse [dɪ'spɜrs] *v.* **-persed, -pers•ing. 1** send in different directions; scatter: *The police dispersed the rioters.* **2** go in different directions: *The crowd dispersed when the game was over.* **3** distribute; circulate: *Children went through the crowd dispersing handbills.* **4** disappear or cause to disappear; dispel; dissipate: *The swelling on her arm was dispersed by cold compresses.* **5** *Physics.* divide (white light) into its coloured rays. **6** *Chemistry.* scatter (the particles of a colloid) throughout another substance or a mixture. ⟨ME < MF *disperser* < L *dispersus,* pp. of *dispergere* < *dis-* in every direction + *spargere* scatter⟩
☛ *Syn.* **1.** See note at SCATTER.

dis•per•si•ble [dɪ'spɜrsəbəl] *adj.* capable of being dispersed.

dis•per•sion [dɪ'spɜrʒən] *or* [dɪ'spɜrʃən] *n.* **1** dispersing or being dispersed. **2** *Physics.* **a** the separation of light into its different colours. **b** a similar separation of electromagnetic waves, etc. **3** *Chemistry.* **a** a substance that has been dispersed. **b** the system consisting of the dispersed colloidal particles and the medium in which they are dispersed. **4** *Statistics.* the scatter of data around some central value. **5** Diaspora.

dis•per•sive [dɪ'spɜrsɪv] *adj.* dispersing; tending to disperse.

dis•pir•it [dɪ'spirɪt] *v.* depress; discourage; dishearten. **—dis'pir•it•ed•ly,** *adv.* **—dis'pir•it•ed•ness,** *n.*

dis•place [dɪs'pleis] *v.* **-placed, -plac•ing. 1** put something else in the place of; take the place of: *The automobile has displaced the horse and buggy.* **2** remove from a position of authority. **3** put out of place; move from its usual place or position: *A floating body displaces its own weight of liquid.*

displaced person a person forced out of his or her own country by war, famine, political disturbance, etc.; refugee. *Abbrev.:* DP or D.P.

dis•place•ment [dɪs'pleismənt] *n.* **1** displacing or being displaced. **2** the volume or mass of a fluid displaced by something floating in it; especially, the volume or mass of water displaced by a ship. **3** the volume in a pump or engine cylinder displaced by a stroke of the piston. **4** *Geology.* the distance of movement of rock or strata on one side of a fault in relation to the corresponding rock or strata on the other side. **5** *Psychiatry.* an unconscious defensive process in which the focus of an emotion is transferred to another object or person.

dis•play [dɪ'splei] *v., n.* *—v.* **1** expose to view, especially in such a way as to show to advantage: *Many ancient weapons are displayed in the museum.* **2** be or give evidence of; show: *He displayed great tact in his handling of a delicate situation.* **3** spread out; unfold or unfurl: *to display a flag, to display a newspaper.* **4** *Electronics.* present (electronic signals) in visual form, as on a computer screen. **5** *Zoology.* of a bird, etc., make a breeding display.
—n. **1** a planned showing of something for some special purpose; exhibit: *Our class had a display of drawings at the exhibition.* **2** an obvious showing or revealing; making plain or clear: *a shocking display of bad temper, a display of courage.* **3** a showing off; ostentation: *Her fondness for display led her to buy showy clothes.* **4** *Printing.* the choice and arrangement of type so as to make certain words or parts prominent. **5** *Electronics.* **a** a device for presenting computerized information or electronic signals visually, such as a computer monitor. **b** the information so presented. **6** *Zoology.* especially among certain birds, a pattern of movement resembling a kind of dance, performed by the males just prior to breeding. **7** a spurious and exaggerated show (of emotion, etc.); pretence: *a display of affection.* ⟨ME < OF *despleier* < L *displicare* scatter < *dis-* apart + *plicare* fold⟩
☛ *Syn. v.* **1. Display,** EXHIBIT, EVINCE = show. **Display** = put out in view for others, especially the public, to look at: *The stores are displaying new spring clothes.* **Exhibit** = show as something especially worth looking at in a way that draws attention: *She exhibited her wedding presents on the table.* **Evince** = show in some way something that cannot be seen with the eyes, such as a feeling or quality: *He evinced obvious displeasure when he learned he would have to stay after school.*
n. **1.** See note at SHOW.

dis•please [dɪs'pliz] *v.* **-pleased, -pleas•ing.** offend, annoy, or be disagreeable to: *She was displeased by their apparent lack of respect. The new furnishings displeased him.* **—dis'pleas•ing•ly,** *adv.*

dis•pleas•ure [dɪs'plɛʒər] *n.* **1** the feeling of being displeased; annoyance or disapproval. **2** *Archaic.* discomfort; uneasiness. **3** *Archaic.* offence; injury.

dis•port [dɪ'spɔrt] *v., n.* *—v.* amuse (oneself); sport; play: *People laughed at the polar bears disporting themselves in the water.*
—n. Archaic. a pastime; amusement. ⟨ME < OF *desporter* < *des-* away from + *porter* carry < L *portare*⟩

dis•pos•a•ble [dɪ'spouzəbəl] *adj., n.* *—adj.* **1** that may be disposed of; usable. **2** at one's disposal; available. **3** designed to be thrown away after a single use.
—n. **disposables,** *pl.* disposable consumer goods.

dis•pos•al [dɪ'spouzəl] *n.* **1** the act or process of getting rid of something: *The city looks after the disposal of garbage.* **2** the act or process of selling or giving away to another: *She arranged for the disposal of her property in her will.* **3** a final arranging of matters; a settling of affairs: *The lawyer's disposal of the difficulty satisfied everybody.* **4** the act or process of putting in a certain order or

position: *The disposal of the chairs around the sides of the room left plenty of space in the middle.* **5** sale.
at (someone's) **disposal,** ready for one's use or service at any time; under one's control or management: *She put all her books at her guests' disposal. Does he have a car at his disposal?*

dis•pose [dɪ'spouz] *v.* **-posed, -pos•ing. 1** put in a certain order or position; arrange: *The battleships were disposed in a straight line.* **2** arrange (matters); settle (affairs); determine. **3** make ready or willing; incline: *More pay and shorter hours of work disposed her to take the new job.* **4** make liable or subject: *Getting your feet wet disposes you to catching cold.*
dispose of, a get rid of: *to dispose of a lot of old papers.* **b** sell or give away: *to dispose of one's property.* **c** eat or drink up: *We disposed of a whole watermelon.* **d** arrange; settle: *The club disposed of its business in an hour.* ⟨ME < OF *disposer* < *dis-* variously + *poser* place. See POSE[1].⟩ **—dis'pos•er,** *n.*

dis•posed [dɪ'spouzd] *adj., v. —adj.* having a particular disposition or attitude: *How were they disposed toward the plan? He was a well-disposed young man—friendly and sympathetic.*
—v. pt. and pp. of DISPOSE.
disposed to, inclined; tending: *She is always disposed to get angry at the least little thing.*

dis•po•si•tion [ˌdɪspə'zɪʃən] *n.* **1** one's habitual ways of acting toward others or of thinking about things; nature: *a cheerful disposition, a selfish disposition.* **2** a tendency; inclination: *a disposition to argue.* **3** the act or process of putting in order or position; orderly arrangement: *the disposition of troops in battle.* **4** final arrangement; settlement: *the satisfactory disposition of a difficult problem.* **5** the act or process of getting rid of, giving away, selling, etc.: *the disposition of nuclear wastes. The court will look after the disposition of the property of the deceased.*
☛ *Syn.* **1. Disposition,** TEMPERAMENT, TEMPER = the qualities that characterize a person as an individual. **Disposition** applies to the controlling mental or emotional quality that determines a person's natural or usual way of thinking and acting: *He has a quarrelsome disposition.* **Temperament** applies to the combined physical, emotional, and mental qualities that determine a person's whole nature: *She has an artistic temperament.* **Temper** applies to the combined natural and acquired qualities that determine the state of mind in which a person meets problems and troubles: *He is calm in temper.* **Temper** may also be applied to a more temporary state: *I found him in a good temper.* It can also mean a fit of anger: *The girl was in a temper again.*

dis•pos•sess [ˌdɪspə'zɛs] *v.* **1** force to give up the possession of a house, land, etc.; oust: *The farmer was dispossessed for not paying her rent.* **2** deprive: *Fear dispossessed him of his senses.* **—ˌdis•pos'ses•sion,** *n.* **—ˌdis•pos'ses•sor,** *n.*

dis•praise [dɪs'preiz] *v.* **-praised, -prais•ing;** *n. —v.* express disapproval of; speak against; blame.
—n. an expression of disapproval; blame. **—dis'prais•er,** *n.*

dis•prize [dɪs'praɪz] *v.* **-prized, -priz•ing.** *Archaic.* disdain.

dis•proof [dɪs'pruf] *n.* **1** a disproving; refutation. **2** a fact, reason, etc. that disproves something.

dis•pro•por•tion [ˌdɪsprə'pɔrʃən] *n., v. —n.* **1** a lack of proportion; lack of proper proportion; lack of symmetry. **2** something out of proportion.
—v. make disproportionate.

dis•pro•por•tion•al [ˌdɪsprə'pɔrʃənəl] *adj.* not in proportion; disproportionate.

dis•pro•por•tion•al•ly [ˌdɪsprə'pɔrʃənəli] *adv.* without proportion; unequally.

dis•pro•por•tion•ate [ˌdɪsprə'pɔrʃənɪt] *adj.* out of proportion; lacking in proper proportion: *a disproportionate amount of time spent on details.*

dis•pro•por•tion•ate•ly [ˌdɪsprə'pɔrʃənɪtli] *adv.* in a disproportionate degree; inadequately or excessively.

dis•prove [dɪs'pruv] *v.* **-proved, -prov•ing.** prove false or incorrect; refute. **—dis'prov•a•ble,** *adj.*

dis•put•a•ble [dɪ'spjutəbəl] *or* ['dɪspjətəbəl] *adj.* liable to be disputed; uncertain; questionable.

dis•pu•tant [dɪ'spjutənt] *or* ['dɪspjətənt] *n., adj. —n.* a person who takes part in a dispute or debate.
—adj. in a dispute; disputing.

dis•pu•ta•tion [ˌdɪspjə'teiʃən] *n.* **1** a debate; controversy. **2** a dispute. **3** a formal exercise in which opposing parties attack or defend a thesis.

dis•pu•ta•tious [ˌdɪspjə'teiʃəs] *adj.* fond of disputing; inclined to argue. **—ˌdis•pu'ta•tious•ly,** *adv.* **—ˌdis•pu'ta•tious•ness,** *n.*

dis•put•a•tive [dɪ'spjutətɪv] *adj.* disputatious.

dis•pute [dɪ'spjut] *v.* **-put•ed, -put•ing;** *n. —v.* **1** discuss; argue; debate. **2** quarrel. **3** disagree with (a statement); declare not true; call into question: *The insurance company disputed her claim for damages.* **4** fight against; oppose; resist: *disputing the enemy troops' advance.* **5** fight or contend for; try to win: *The sisters were disputing ownership of the house. The troops had to dispute every patch of ground as they advanced.*
—n. **1** an argument; debate. **2** a quarrel.
beyond dispute, a not to be disputed. **b** final; settled.
in dispute, being disputed. ⟨< L *disputare* examine, discuss, argue < *dis-* item by item + *putare* calculate⟩ **—dis'put•er,** *n.*
☛ *Syn. n.* **1.** See note at ARGUMENT.

dis•qual•i•fi•ca•tion [dɪsˌkwɒləfə'keiʃən] *n.* **1** disqualifying or being disqualified. **2** something that disqualifies.

dis•qual•i•fy [dɪs'kwɒləˌfaɪ] *v.* **-fied, -fy•ing. 1** make unfit; make unable to do something: *His injury disqualified him from playing football.* **2** declare unfit or unable to do something; deprive of a right or privilege because some criterion is not met: *He was disqualified from voting because he was in jail.* **3** *Sports, etc.* deprive of the right to play or the right to win a competition: *The hockey team was disqualified by the referee for refusing to come out on the ice.*

dis•qui•et [dɪs'kwaɪət] *v., n. —v.* make uneasy or anxious; disturb: *Rumours of a revolution disquieted the dictator.*
—n. uneasiness; anxiety.

dis•qui•et•ing [dɪs'kwaɪətɪŋ] *adj., v. —adj.* disturbing.
—v. ppr. of DISQUIET.

dis•qui•e•tude [dɪs'kwaɪəˌtjud] *or* [-'kwaɪəˌtud] *n.* uneasiness; anxiety.

dis•qui•si•tion [ˌdɪskwɪ'zɪʃən] *n.* a long or formal speech or writing about a subject. ⟨< L *disquisitio, -onis,* ult. < *dis-* (intensive) + *quaerere* seek⟩

dis•re•gard [ˌdɪsrɪ'gɑrd] *v., n. —v.* **1** pay no attention to; take no notice of: *Disregarding his clothing, he jumped into the lake to save the child.* **2** treat without proper regard or respect; slight.
—n. **1** lack of attention; neglect: *a disregard for fame and fortune, disregard of traffic laws.* **2** a lack of proper regard or respect: *Her action showed a shocking disregard for the feelings of others.*
—ˌdis•re'gard•er, *n.*

dis•re•gard•ful [ˌdɪsrɪ'gɑrdfəl] *adj.* lacking in regard; neglectful; careless.

dis•rel•ish [dɪs'rɛlɪʃ] *v. or n.* dislike.

dis•re•mem•ber [ˌdɪsrɪ'mɛmbər] *v. Informal.* fail to remember; forget.

dis•re•pair [ˌdɪsrɪ'pɛr] *n.* a bad condition; need of repairs: *The house was in disrepair.*

dis•rep•u•ta•ble [dɪs'rɛpjətəbəl] *adj.* **1** having a bad reputation; shady: *a disreputable dance hall.* **2** not respectable; dishonourable: *disreputable conduct, a disreputable politician.* **3** shabby; much worn: *a disreputable old hat.*
—dis'rep•u•ta•bly, *adv.*

dis•re•pute [ˌdɪsrɪ'pjut] *n.* disgrace; discredit; disfavour: *Many remedies formerly used are now in disrepute.*

dis•re•spect [ˌdɪsrɪ'spɛkt] *n.* a lack of respect; rudeness; impoliteness: *Older people disliked the boy because of his disrespect toward his parents.*

dis•re•spect•ful [ˌdɪsrɪ'spɛktfəl] *adj.* rude; showing no respect; lacking in courtesy to elders or superiors.
—ˌdis•re'spect•ful•ly, *adv.* **—ˌdis•re'spect•ful•ness,** *n.*

dis•robe [dɪs'roub] *v.* **-robed, -rob•ing.** undress.
—dis'rob•er, *n.*

dis•rupt [dɪs'rʌpt] *v.* **1** break up; split; shatter: *Their relationship was disrupted by a violent dispute.* **2** destroy the order or continuity of: *to disrupt a classroom or a meeting, to disrupt telephone service.* ⟨< L *disruptus,* pp. of *disrumpere* < *dis-* apart + *rumpere* break⟩ **—dis'rup•tion,** *n.*

dis•rup•tive [dɪs'rʌptɪv] *adj.* tending to break up; causing disruption: *a disruptive influence.*

dis•sat•is•fac•tion [ˌdɪssætɪs'fækʃən] *or* [dɪsˌsætɪs'fækʃən] *n.* discontent; displeasure.

dis•sat•is•fac•to•ry [ˌdɪssætɪs'fæktəri] *or* [dɪsˌsætɪs'fæktəri] *adj.* causing discontent; unsatisfactory.

dis•sat•is•fied [dɪs'sætɪsˌfaɪd] *adj.* **1** discontented; displeased. **2** showing discontent or displeasure.

dis•sat•is•fy [dɪs'sætɪsˌfaɪ] *v.* **-fied, -fy•ing.** fail to satisfy; make discontented; displease.

dis•sect [dɪ'sɛkt] *or* [daɪ'sɛkt] *v.* **1** cut in pieces; divide into parts. **2** cut up or separate the parts of (an animal, plant, etc.) in order to examine or study the structure. **3** examine carefully part by part; analyse: *The lawyer dissected the testimony to show where the witnesses had contradicted themselves.* ⟨< L *dissectus,* pp. of *dissecare* < *dis-* apart + *secare* cut⟩

dis•sect•ed [dɪ'sɛktɪd] *or* [dəi'sɛktɪd] *adj., v. —adj.* cut or divided into many parts: *These plants have dissected leaves.* —*v.* pt. and pp. of DISSECT.

dis•sec•tion [dɪ'sɛkʃən] *or* [dəi'sɛkʃən] *n.* **1** the act of separating or dividing an animal or plant into parts in order to examine or study its structure. **2** an animal, plant, etc. that has been dissected. **3** a fine or thorough analysis; consideration of something in detail or point by point.

dis•sec•tor [dɪ'sɛktər] *or* [dəi'sɛktər] *n.* **1** a person who dissects. **2** an instrument used in dissecting.

dis•sem•ble [dɪ'sɛmbəl] *v.* **-bled, -bling. 1** disguise or hide (one's real feelings, thoughts, plans, etc.): *She dissembled her anger with a smile.* **2** conceal one's motives, etc.; be a hypocrite. **3** pretend; feign: *The bored listener dissembled an interest she didn't feel.* **4** pretend not to see or notice; disregard; ignore. ⟨alteration, after *resemble,* of obs. *dissimule* dissimulate < OF *dissimuler* < L *dissimulare*⟩ **—dis'sem•bler,** *n.* **—dis'sem•bling•ly,** *adv.*

dis•sem•i•nate [dɪ'sɛmə,neit] *v.* **-nat•ed, -nat•ing.** scatter or spread widely: *to disseminate knowledge.* ⟨< L *disseminare* < *dis-* in every direction + *semen* seed⟩ **—dis,sem•i'na•tion,** *n.* **—dis'sem•i,na•tor,** *n.*

dis•sen•sion [dɪ'sɛnʃən] *n.* a disputing; quarrelling; hard feelings caused by a difference of opinion: *Their political disagreement caused dissension.*

dis•sent [dɪ'sɛnt] *v., n. —v.* **1** differ in opinion; disagree: *Two of the judges dissented from the decision of the other three.* **2** refuse to conform to the rules and beliefs of an established religious institution or political system. **3** withhold consent.
—*n.* **1** a difference of opinion; disagreement: *Dissent among the members broke up the club meeting.* **2** a formal declaration of disagreement of opinion about something. **3** a refusal to conform to the rules and beliefs of an established religious institution or political system: *Some of the Puritans' dissent caused their separation from the Church of England.* ⟨ME < L *dissentire* < *dis-* differently + *sentire* think, feel⟩ **—dis'sent•ing•ly,** *adv.*
☛ *Hom.* DESCENT.

dis•sent•er [dɪ'sɛntər] *n.* **1** a person who dissents. **2 Dissenter,** in England and Scotland, a Protestant who belongs to some church other than the state church.

dis•sen•tient [dɪ'sɛnʃənt] *adj., n. —adj.* dissenting, especially from the opinion of the majority.
—*n.* a person who dissents.

dis•ser•ta•tion [,dɪsər'teiʃən] *n.* a formal discussion of a subject, especially a thesis submitted by a candidate for a doctoral or other higher degree; treatise. ⟨< L *dissertatio, -onis* < *dissertare,* frequentative of *disserere* < *dis-* apart (distribution) + *serere* join words⟩

dis•serv•ice [dɪs'sɜrvɪs] *or* [dɪ'sɜrvɪs] *n.* a bad treatment; harm; injury.

dis•sev•er [dɪ'sɛvər] *v.* sever; separate; divide. **—dis'sev•er•ance,** *n.*

dis•si•dence ['dɪsədəns] *n.* disagreement; dissent.

dis•si•dent ['dɪsədənt] *adj., n. —adj.* disagreeing; dissenting.
—*n.* a person who disagrees or dissents. ⟨< L *dissidens, -entis,* ppr. of *dissidere* < *dis-* apart + *sedere* sit⟩

dis•sim•i•lar [dɪ'sɪmələr] *or* ['dɪsɪmələr] *adj.* not similar; unlike; different. **—dis'sim•i•lar•ly,** *adv.*

dis•sim•i•lar•i•ty [dɪ,sɪmə'lærəti] *or* [dɪ,sɪmə'lɛrəti] *n., pl.* **-ties.** lack of similarity; unlikeness; difference.

dis•sim•i•late [dɪ'sɪmə,leit] *v.* **-lated, -lat•ing.** make or become unlike. ⟨< *dis-* + *assimilate*⟩

dis•sim•i•la•tion [dɪ,sɪmə'leiʃən] *n.* **1** the act or process of making or becoming unlike. **2** *Biology.* the breaking down of organic substances into simpler ones; catabolism. **3** *Phonetics.* the changing of one of two similar, neighbouring speech sounds so that one becomes unlike the other. *Example:* The Latin word *peregrinus* became Italian *pellegrino,* changing the first *r* to *l.* ⟨See PEREGRINE and PILGRIM⟩

dis•si•mil•i•tude [,dɪssə'mɪlətjud] *or* [-sə'mɪlə,tud] *n.* unlikeness; difference.

dis•sim•u•late [dɪ'sɪmjə,leit] *v.* **-lat•ed, -lat•ing.** disguise or hide under a pretence; dissemble. ⟨< L *dissimulare*⟩ **—dis'sim•u,la•tor,** *n.*

dis•sim•u•la•tion [dɪ,sɪmjə'leiʃən] *n.* **1** the act of dissembling; hypocrisy; pretence; deceit. **2** a group of birds.

dis•si•pate ['dɪsə,peit] *v.* **-pat•ed, -pat•ing. 1** spread in different directions; scatter: *The crowd soon dissipated.* **2** disappear: *The fog had dissipated by mid-morning.* **3** cause to disappear; dispel: *The sun dissipated the mists.* **4** spend foolishly; waste on things of little value: *The extravagant son soon dissipated his father's fortune.* **5** indulge too much in foolish or harmful pleasures. ⟨< L *dissipare* < *dis-* in different directions + *sipare* throw⟩

dis•si•pat•ed ['dɪsə,peitɪd] *adj., v. —adj.* **1** indulging too much in harmful or foolish pleasures; dissolute: *a dissipated youth.* **2** scattered. **3** wasted.
—*v.* pt. and pp. of DISSIPATE.

dis•si•pa•tion [,dɪsə'peiʃən] *n.* **1** dissipating or being dissipated. **2** an amusement; diversion, especially harmful amusements. **3** too much indulgence in foolish pleasures; intemperance. **4** a wasting by misuse.

dis•so•ci•ate [dɪ'souʃi,eit] *or* [dɪ'sousi,eit] *v.* **-at•ed, -at•ing. 1** break the connection or association of; separate: *When the man discovered that his companions were dishonest, he soon dissociated himself from them.* **2** *Chemistry.* separate or decompose by dissociation. ⟨< L *dissociare* < *dis-* apart + *socius* ally⟩

dis•so•ci•a•tion [dɪ,souʃi'eiʃən] *or* [dɪ,sousi'eiʃən] *n.* **1** the act of dissociating or state of being dissociated. **2** *Chemistry.* **a** the separation of molecules of an electrolyte into constituent ions; ionization. Sodium and chlorine ions are formed by the dissociation of sodium chloride molecules in water. **b** reversible decomposition. Dissociation occurs when water is heated so that it decomposes into hydrogen and oxygen; when the temperature is lowered again, the elements recombine into water. **3** *Psychiatry.* the separation of an idea or feeling from the main stream of consciousness, sometimes leading to multiple personality.

dis•so•ci•a•tive [dɪ'souʃətɪv], [dɪ'souʃi,eitɪv], *or* [dɪ'sousi,eitɪv] *adj.* having to do with or causing dissociation.

dis•sol•u•bil•i•ty [dɪ,sɒljə'bɪləti] *n.* the fact or quality of being dissoluble.

dis•sol•u•ble [dɪ'sɒljəbəl] *adj.* capable of being dissolved. **—dis'sol•u•ble•ness,** *n.*

dis•so•lute ['dɪsə,lut] *adj.* living an immoral life. ⟨< L *dissolutus,* pp. of *dissolvere.* See DISSOLVE.⟩ **—'dis•so•lute•ly,** *adv.*

dis•so•lu•tion [,dɪsə'luʃən] *n.* **1** a breaking up; termination: *The partners arranged for the dissolution of their partnership.* **2** the ending of an assembly, especially of a parliament prior to an election. **3** ruin; destruction. **4** death. **5** a breaking down; decomposition: *the dissolution of water by electrolysis.* **6** the act or process of changing into a liquid state. **7** the state of being liquid.

dis•solve [dɪ'zɒlv] *v.* **-solved, -solv•ing;** *n. —v.* **1** make or become liquid, especially by putting or being put into a liquid; form into a solution in a liquid: *Salt and sugar will dissolve in water.* **2** break up; end: *to dissolve a partnership.* **3** dismiss or end (an assembly, especially a parliament before an election). **4** fade or cause to fade away: *The dream dissolved when she woke up. His friendly smile dissolved her anger.* **5** solve; explain; clear up. **6** separate into parts; decompose. **7** *Film and television.* fade or cause to fade gradually from the screen while the succeeding scene slowly appears.
dissolve in (or **into**) **tears,** give way to weeping; shed many tears.
—*n. Film and television.* the gradual disappearing of the figures of a scene while those of a succeeding scene slowly take their place. ⟨ME < L *dissolvere* < *dis-* (intensive) + *solvere* loose⟩ **—dis'solv•a•ble,** *adj.* **—dis'solv•er,** *n.*
☛ *Syn. v.* **1.** See note at MELT.

dis•so•nance ['dɪsənəns] *n.* **1** a combination of sounds that is not harmonious; harshness and unpleasantness of sound; discord. Compare CONSONANCE. **2** disagreement; lack of harmony. **3** *Music.* the relationship or sound of two or more tones in a combination which is conventionally considered to be in a condition of unrest needing resolution or completion; discord.

dis•so•nant ['dɪsənənt] *adj.* **1** harsh in sound; clashing; not harmonious. **2** out of harmony with other views or persons; disagreeing: *Her dissonant views always made the meetings unpleasant.* ⟨ME < L *dissonans, -antis,* ppr. of *dissonare* < *dis-* differently + *sonare* sound⟩ **—'dis•so•nant•ly,** *adv.*

dis•suade [dɪ'sweid] *v.* **-suad•ed, -suad•ing.** persuade not to do something (*used with* **from**): *The father dissuaded his son from leaving school.* ⟨ME < L *dissuadere* < *dis-* against + *suadere* to urge⟩

dis•sua•sion [dɪ'sweizən] *n.* the act of dissuading.

dis•sua•sive [dɪ'sweisɪv] *adj.* attempting to dissuade; tending to dissuade. **—dis'sua•sive•ly,** *adv.* **—dis'sua•sive•ness,** *n.*

dis•syl•lab•ic [ˌdɪssəˈlæbɪk], [ˌdɪsəˈlæbɪk], *or* [ˌdaɪsəˈlæbɪk] *adj.* disyllabic.

dis•syl•la•ble [ˌdɪsˈsɪləbəl] *or* [dɪˈsɪləbəl] *n.* disyllable. ⟨< F *dissylabe* < L < Gk. *disyllabos* < *di-* two + *syllabē* syllable⟩

dis•sym•met•ry [dɪsˈsɪmətri] *or* [dɪˈsɪmətri] *n.* **1** asymmetry. **2** symmetry of two separate objects, each of which is the mirror image of the other, as in feet.

dist. **1** district. **2** distance. **3** distinguish; distinguished.

dis•taff [ˈdɪstæf] *n.* **1** a stick, split at the tip, to hold wool, flax, etc., so that it may be spun into thread. **2** the staff on a spinning wheel for holding flax. **3** women's work or affairs. **4** the female sex; woman or women. **5** the female branch of a family. ⟨OE *distæf* < *dis-* (akin to MLG *dise* bunch of flax on a distaff) + *stæf* staff⟩

distaff side the maternal side or branch of a family. Compare SPEARSIDE.

dis•tain [dɪˈstein] *v. Archaic.* **1** discolour; stain. **2** dishonour; disgrace. ⟨ME < OF *desteindre* < *des-* apart + *teindre* dye, colour < L *tingere*⟩

dis•tal [ˈdɪstəl] *adj. Anatomy.* away from the place of attachment or origin; terminal: *Fingernails are at the distal ends of fingers.* Compare PROXIMAL. ⟨< *distant*⟩

dis•tance [ˈdɪstəns] *n., v.* **-tanced, -tanc•ing.** *—n.* **1** the space in between; the extent of separation in space: *Is the theatre within walking distance? The distance from here to town is 5 km.* **2** a long way; far away: *The farm is situated quite a distance from the highway.* **3** a place or time far away: *a light in the distance. At this distance it is hard to remember the details.* **4** the time in between; interval. **5** remoteness in time. **6** *Music.* the interval or difference between two tones. **7** a lack of friendliness or familiarity; coolness of manner; reserve. **8** *Painting.* **a** the distant part of a landscape: *One sees cattle grazing in the distance.* **b** the part of a picture that represents this: *There is no distance in his paintings, which are all flat and two-dimensional.* **9** *Horse racing.* a space measured back from the winning post. In order to qualify for further heats, a horse must be within this space when the winner finishes. **10** the dichotomy or divide between two concepts, ideas, etc. at different points on, or at either end of, a continuum: *the distance between health and illness.*
go the distance, *Sports.* **a** play an entire game without substitution. **b** of a boxer, fight or last an entire match without being knocked out. **c** endure anything to the end.
keep at a distance, refuse to be friendly or familiar with; treat with reserve: *We tried to be friendly but she kept us at a distance.*
keep (one's) **distance, a** remain some distance away: *The dog might be dangerous, so keep your distance.* **b** be not too friendly or familiar; be or stay aloof: *She prefers to keep her distance with her employees.*
—v. **1** leave far behind; do much better than. **2** *Horse racing.* beat by a distance. **3** keep (oneself) at an emotional distance (from); choose to have no connection with: *The British government has tried to distance itself from the controversial author and his novel.*

dis•tant [ˈdɪstənt] *adj.* **1** far away in space: *Vancouver is distant from Québec City. The moon is distant from the earth.* **2** away: *The town is 3 km distant.* **3** far apart in time, relationship, likeness, etc.; not close: *A third cousin is a distant relative.* **4** not friendly: *She gave him only a distant nod.* **5** faraway; absent; dreamy: *There was a distant look in her eyes.* ⟨ME < MF < L *distans, -antis,* ppr. of *distare* < *dis-* off + *stare* stand⟩ **—ˈdis•tant•ly,** *adv.*
☛ *Syn.* **1, 2. Distant,** FAR, REMOTE = not near. **Distant** = standing away in space, and suggests a considerable space unless the exact measure is stated: *He lives in a distant city. Kingston is 255 km distant from Toronto.* **Far** = a long way off; **remote** = far removed, especially from the centre of things: *The far North is not so remote as it used to be.*

dis•taste [dɪsˈteist] *n.* dislike; aversion: *His distaste showed plainly on his face.*
☛ *Syn.* See note at DISLIKE.

dis•taste•ful [dɪsˈteistfəl] *adj.* unpleasant; disagreeable; offensive. **—disˈtaste•ful•ly,** *adv.* **—disˈtaste•ful•ness,** *n.*

dis•tem•per¹ [dɪsˈtɛmpər] *n., v. —n.* **1** an infectious disease of dogs and other animals, accompanied by a short, dry cough and a loss of strength. **2** any sickness of the mind or body; disorder; disease. **3** disturbance.
—v. make unbalanced; disturb; disorder. ⟨ME < LL *distemperare* mix improperly < L *dis-* not + *temperare* mix in proper proportion⟩

dis•tem•per² [dɪsˈtɛmpər] *n., v. —n.* **1** a method or process of painting in which powdered colours are mixed with glue or other sizing, used especially for painting interior walls, scenes for theatre sets, etc. Distemper is a kind of tempera. **2** the paint used in distemper painting. **3** a painting done in distemper.
—v. **1** mix (ingredients) to produce distemper. **2** paint with such a mixture. ⟨< OF *destemprer* soak < LL *distemperare* mix thoroughly < L *dis-* completely + *temperare* mix⟩

dis•tend [dɪsˈtɛnd] *v.* stretch out; swell out; expand: *His cheeks distended when he blew his bugle. The pouter pigeon can distend its crop.* ⟨< L *distendere* < *dis-* apart + *tendere* stretch⟩

dis•ten•si•ble [dɪsˈtɛnsəbəl] *adj.* capable of being distended.

dis•ten•sion or **dis•ten•tion** [dɪsˈtɛnʃən] *n.* the act of distending or the state of being distended.

dis•tich [ˈdɪstɪk] *n., pl.* **-tichs.** two lines of verse forming a stanza, and usually making complete sense; couplet. *Example:*
Those who in quarrels interpose
Must often wipe a bloody nose.
⟨< L < Gk. *distichon* < *di-* two + *stichos* line⟩

dis•tich•ous [ˈdɪstɪkəs] *adj. Botany.* of leaves, arranged in two vertical rows, one on each side of the stem.

dis•til or **dis•till** [dɪˈstɪl] *v.* **-tilled, -til•ling. 1** heat (a liquid or other substance) and condense the vapour given off. Distilled water is pure because the impurities in the original water do not vaporize when the water does. **2** obtain by distilling: *Gasoline is distilled from crude oil.* **3** condense. **4** extract; refine: *A jury must distil the truth from the testimony of the witnesses.* **5** give off in drops: *Flowers distil nectar.* **6** fall or let fall in drops; drip. **7** undergo distillation. ⟨< L *distillare* < *de-* down + *stilla* drop⟩

dis•til•late [ˈdɪstəlɪt] *or* [ˈdɪstəˌleit] *n.* **1** a distilled liquid; something obtained by distilling. **2** anything that is concentrated or abstracted like a distillate: *The book was a distillate of the author's major ideas over the years.*

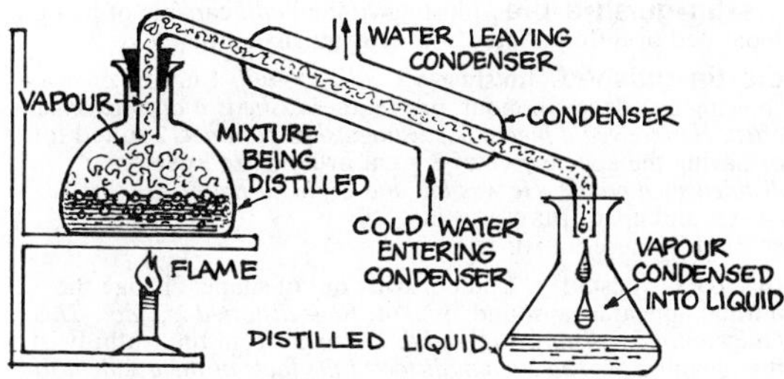

dis•til•la•tion [ˌdɪstəˈleiʃən] *n.* **1** the act or process of distilling. **2** something distilled; extract; essence: *Kerosene is a distillation of petroleum.*

dis•tilled [dɪˈstɪld] *adj., v. —adj.* obtained by distilling.
—v. pt. and pp. of DISTIL.

dis•till•er [dɪˈstɪlər] *n.* a person who or thing that distils, especially one that makes whisky, rum, brandy, etc.

dis•till•er•y [dɪˈstɪləri] *or* [dɪˈstɪlri] *n., pl.* **-er•ies.** a place where distilling is done, especially of whisky, rum, brandy, etc.

dis•tinct [dɪˈstɪŋkt] *adj.* **1** not the same; separate: *There are two distinct questions to be considered.* **2** different in quality or kind: *Mice are distinct from rats.* **3** clear; plain: *distinct writing.* **4** unmistakable; definite; decided: *a distinct lisp, a distinct advantage.* ⟨< L *distinctus,* pp. of *distinguere.* See DISTINGUISH.⟩ **—disˈtinct•ness,** *n.*

dis•tinc•tion [dɪˈstɪŋkʃən] *n.* **1** the act of making a difference; distinguishing from others: *She treated all alike, without distinction.* **2** the quality or state of being distinguishable; difference: *Is there any distinction between ducks and geese?* **3** a point of difference; a distinguishing quality or feature: *There are only minor distinctions between our house and the others on the block.* **4** honour or esteem: *The title is given as a mark of distinction.* **5** a mark or sign of honour. **6** excellence that distinguishes one from others; superiority: *a man of distinction. The novel has true distinction. The soldier had served with distinction.*
distinction without a difference, a false distinction; artificial difference.

dis•tinc•tive [dɪˈstɪŋktɪv] *adj.* **1** serving to distinguish clearly from others; special; characteristic: *Police officers wear a distinctive uniform.* **2** designating one of a set of speech sounds in a given language that serve to distinguish words. The difference between *p* and *b* is distinctive in English because it alone distinguishes words such as *pat* from *bat.* **—disˈtinc•tive•ly,** *adv.* **—disˈtinc•tive•ness,** *n.*

distinctive feature *Linguistics.* any one of the phonetic characteristics that distinguish phonemes. *Example*: the distinctive features of the English phoneme /i/ include [+ high], [– back], and [+ tense]. [– back] distinguishes /i/ from /u/, which is [+ high], [+ back], and [+ tense]. Similarly, its other distinctive features cause /i/ to contrast with other vowels.

dis•tinct•ly [dɪ'stɪŋktli] *adv.* **1** clearly; plainly: *Speak distinctly.* **2** unmistakably; decidedly: *The prisoner was distinctly unhappy.*

dis•tin•gué [,dɪstæŋ'gei] *or* [dɪ'stæŋgei]; *French,* [distɛ̃'ge] *adj.* looking important or superior; distinguished. ⟨< F⟩

dis•tin•guish [dɪ'stɪŋgwɪʃ] *v.* **1** tell apart; see or show the difference between. **2** see or show the difference (*often used with* **between** or **among**): *I find it hard to distinguish between Maria's handwriting and her sister's.* **3** see or hear clearly; make out plainly: *It is much too dark for me to distinguish the outline of the house.* **4** make different; be a special quality or feature of: *The ability to talk distinguishes human beings from animals.* **5** make famous or well-known: *She distinguished herself by winning all three prizes.* **6** separate into different groups; classify. ⟨< L *distinguere* mark with a prick < *dis-* between + *stinguere* to prick⟩

☛ *Syn.* **1-3. Distinguish,** DIFFERENTIATE, DISCRIMINATE = see or show the differences in or between things. **Distinguish** = see and know the qualities and features of a thing that give it its special character and set it off from others: *She distinguished the violins in the orchestra.* **Differentiate** = show the exact differences between one thing and others of the same class: *The teacher differentiated between Shakespeare's sonnets and Milton's.* **Discriminate** = see the fine shades of difference *between* things: *Sometimes only experts can discriminate between counterfeit bills and genuine money.*

dis•tin•guish•a•ble [dɪ'stɪŋgwɪʃəbəl] *adj.* capable of being separated or differentiated. **—dis'tin•guish•a•bly,** *adv.*

dis•tin•guished [dɪ'stɪŋgwɪʃt] *adj., v. —adj.* **1** having or showing excellence, honour, or greatness: *She is a distinguished artist. He received a medal for distinguished conduct.* **2** suited for or having the appearance of a great or honoured person: *a distinguished profile. He was tall and distinguished.*
—v. pt. and pp. of DISTINGUISH.

☛ *Syn.* **1.** See note at EMINENT.

dis•tort [dɪ'stɔrt] *v.* **1** pull or twist out of shape; change the normal appearance, sound, etc., of: *Rage distorted his face. This faulty amplifier distorts the sound.* **2** change from the truth; twist the meaning of: *The woman distorted the facts of the accident to escape blame.* ⟨< L *distortus,* pp. of *distorquere* < *dis-* (intensive) + *torquere* twist⟩

dis•tor•tion [dɪ'stɔrʃən] *n.* **1** the act of distorting: *Distortion by the media makes for a poorly informed public.* **2** the result of distorting; anything distorted: *The article contains many distortions. They laughed at the distortions produced by the curved mirrors.*

dis•tract [dɪ'strækt] *v.* **1** draw away the mind, attention, etc., of: *The nurse distracted the baby while the doctor gave the injection. The music distracted him from his studies.* **2** confuse the attention of; disturb; bewilder: *Several people talking at once can distract a listener.* **3** put out of one's mind; make frantic or crazed (*used only after the verb* **be**): *He was nearly distracted by the thought of his brother trapped in the mine.* ⟨< L *distractus,* pp. of *distrahere* < *dis-* away + *trahere* draw⟩ **—dis'tract•ible,** *adj.* **—dis'tract•ing•ly,** *adv.*

dis•tract•ed [dɪ'stræktɪd] *adj., v. —adj.* **1** confused; bewildered: *She looked about her in a distracted way, trying to remember what she had come into the room for.* **2** in a frenzy; frantic; crazed: *He stood on the roof of the burning building, distracted with terror.*
—v. pt. and pp. of DISTRACT. **—dis'tract•ed•ly,** *adv.*

dis•trac•tion [dɪ'strækʃən] *n.* **1** a distracting or being distracted: *In their distraction, the parents of the missing child hardly knew what they were doing.* **2** anything that draws away the attention, mind, etc.: *Noise can be a distraction when you are studying.* **3** something that relieves the mind or spirit; a relief from continued thought, effort, grief, etc.: *Movies are a convenient and popular distraction.* **4** insanity; madness.

dis•trac•tive [dɪ'stræktɪv] *adj.* distracting; tending to distract.

dis•train [dɪ'strein] *v. Law.* seize (goods) for unpaid rent or other debts. ⟨ME < OF *destreindre* < L *distringere* < *dis-* apart + *stringere* draw⟩ **—dis'train•er** or **dis'train•or,** *n.*

dis•traint [dɪ'streint] *n. Law.* an act of distraining.

dis•trait [dɪ'streit] *adj.* not paying attention; absent-minded. ⟨< F *distrait,* pp. of *distraire* distract⟩

dis•traught [dɪ'strɒt] *adj.* **1** in a state of mental conflict and confusion. **2** crazed. ⟨var. of obs. *distract,* adj. See DISTRACT.⟩

dis•tress [dɪ'strɛs] *n., v. —n.* **1** great mental or physical pain; trouble. **2** misfortune: *economic distress.* **3** a dangerous or desperate situation: *A ship sinking or burning at sea is in distress.*
—v. **1** cause pain, grief, peril, or suffering to; make miserable or troubled. **2** subject to pressure, stress, or strain. ⟨ME < OF *distrece,* ult. < L *districtus,* pp. of *distringere* < *dis-* apart + *stringere* draw⟩ **—dis'tress•ing•ly,** *adv.*

☛ *Syn. n.* **1.** See note at SORROW.

dis•tressed [dɪ'strɛst] *adj., v. —adj.* **1** troubled; anxious; agitated; in great mental pain. **2** in difficulty: *a distressed ship. Several distressed firms went bankrupt.* **3** damaged: *distressed furniture, distressed produce.*
—v. pt. and pp. of DISTRESS.

distressed area a region characterized by an abnormally low standard of living because of unemployment, poverty, etc.

dis•tress•ful [dɪ'strɛsfəl] *adj.* **1** causing distress; painful. **2** feeling or showing distress; suffering. **—dis'tress•ful•ly,** *adv.* **—dis'tress•ful•ness,** *n.*

dis•trib•u•tar•y [dɪs'tribjʊ,tɛri] *n., pl.* **-ta•ries.** a branch of a river that flows away from, rather than into, the main stream and never rejoins it.

dis•trib•ute [dɪ'strɪbjut] *or* ['dɪstrɪ,bjut] *v.* **-ut•ed, -ut•ing.** **1** give (some of) to each; divide and give out in shares: *to distribute candy.* **2** spread; scatter: *Distribute the paint evenly over the wall.* **3** divide into parts: *The children were distributed into three groups for the tour.* **4** sell (goods) to a particular market. **5** arrange; classify. **6** *Logic.* use (a term) so that it includes every member of a class. *Example*: *dogs* in the sentence *All dogs are animals.* **7** *Printing.* take apart and return (composed type) to the proper compartments in the case. ⟨< L *distributus,* pp. of *distribuere* < *dis-* individually + *tribuere* assign⟩

☛ *Syn.* **1. Distribute,** DISPENSE = give out shares. **Distribute** = divide the amount one has into shares, usually definite but not necessarily equal, and give them out according to some plan: *The teacher distributed paper to the class.* **Dispense** = give to each of a group the amount that has been measured out as his or her right or proper share: *The club dispensed new clothing to the children in the orphanage.*

dis•tri•bu•tion [,dɪstrə'bjuʃən] *n.* **1** the act or process of distributing: *Everyone was waiting for the distribution of the prizes.* **2** the position, arrangement, or spread of anything over an area or space or a period of time: *an even distribution of paint. Caribou have a wide distribution in the North.* **3** anything distributed. **4** *Economics.* the marketing of products; the process by which goods get to the consumers: *She is in charge of distribution for the company.* **5** division and arrangement; classification. **6** *Statistics.* the arrangement of numerical data with respect to some isolated feature, value, etc.

dis•tri•bu•tion•al [,dɪstrə'bjuʃənəl] *adj.* of or having to do with distribution.

dis•trib•u•tive [dɪ'strɪbjətɪv] *adj., n. —adj.* **1** of or having to do with distribution; distributing. **2** *Mathematics.* designating a property of an operation by which the operation has the same result when applied to a set of quantities as it has when applied to individual members of the set. Multiplication is distributive over addition since $a(b + c)$ is the same as $ab + ac$. **3** *Grammar.* designating each individual of a group considered separately. *Each, every, either,* and *neither* are distributive words.
—n. a distributive word. **—dis'trib•u•tive•ly,** *adv.* **—dis'trib•u•tive•ness,** *n.*

distributive curve *Statistics.* a graph showing how the frequencies expressed are distributed.

dis•trib•u•tor [dɪ'strɪbjətər] *n.* **1** a person or thing that distributes. **2** a person or company that distributes to consumers the goods grown or made by producers. **3** a part of a gasoline engine that distributes electric current to the spark plugs. **—dis'trib•u•tor•ship,** *n.*

dis•trict ['dɪstrɪkt] *n., v. —n.* **1** a part of a larger area; region: *Northern Ontario is the leading gold-mining district in Canada. They lived in a fashionable district of the city.* **2** a part of a country, a province, or a city marked off for a special purpose, such as providing schools, electing officials, etc.: *a school district, a local improvement district. The Northwest Territories are divided into three districts: Mackenzie, Keewatin, and Franklin.*
—v. divide into districts. ⟨< LL *districtus* district < L *distringere.* See DISTRESS.⟩

district attorney *U.S.* a lawyer who is the prosecuting officer for a federal or state judicial district.

District of Co•lum•bia [kə'lʌmbiə] the federal district of the United States, corresponding to the city of Washington, which is the national capital. *Abbrev.*: D.C.

dis•trust [dɪs'trʌst] *v., n.* —*v.* not trust; have no confidence in; be suspicious of.
—*n.* a lack of trust or confidence; suspicion: *She could not overcome her distrust of the stranger.*
☛ *Syn. n.* See note at SUSPICION.

dis•trust•ful [dɪs'trʌstfəl] *adj.* not trusting; suspicious. **distrustful of,** lacking confidence in. **—dis'trust•ful•ly,** *adv.* **—dis'trust•ful•ness,** *n.*

dis•turb [dɪ'stɜrb] *v.* **1** destroy the peace, quiet, or rest of: *The noise of the road construction disturbed us so much that we couldn't sleep.* **2** break in upon with noise or change; interrupt: *Don't disturb him now; he's studying.* **3** put out of order: *Someone has disturbed all my papers.* **4** make uneasy; trouble: *The party officials were disturbed by the results of the survey.*
5 inconvenience: *Don't disturb yourself; I can do it.* **6** *Psychology.* cause to be emotionally unbalanced (*usually in the past participle*): *Disturbed children often do poorly in school.* ⟨< L *disturbare* < *dis-* (intensive) + *turba* commotion⟩ **—dis'turb•er,** *n.* **—dis'turb•ing•ly,** *adv.*

dis•turb•ance [dɪ'stɜrbəns] *n.* **1** a disturbing or being disturbed. **2** anything that disturbs. **3** confusion; disorder: *The police were called to quell the disturbance.* **4** uneasiness; trouble; worry.

di•sul•fir•am [,daɪsʌl'firəm] *n.* a drug used to treat alcoholism. *Formula*: $C_{10}H_{20}N_2S_4$

di•sul•phide or **di•sul•fide** [daɪ'sʌlfaɪd] *or* [-'sʌlfɪd] *n. Chemistry.* a compound consisting of two atoms of sulphur combined with another element or radical. Also, **bisulphide.**

dis•un•ion [dɪs'junjən] *n.* **1** a separation; division. **2** a lack of unity; disagreement.

dis•u•nite [,dɪsjə'naɪt] *v.* **-nit•ed, -nit•ing. 1** separate; divide. **2** destroy the unity of; cause to disagree.

dis•u•ni•ty [dɪs'junəti] *n.* lack of unity; disunion.

dis•use *n.* [dɪs'jus]; *v.* [dɪs'juz] *n., v.* **-used, -us•ing.** —*n.* lack of use; not being used: *The old tools were rusted from disuse. Many words common in Shakespeare's time have fallen into disuse.*
—*v.* stop using.

di•syl•lab•ic [dəisɪ'læbɪk], [,dɪsɪ'læbɪk], *or* [,daɪsɪ'læbɪk] *adj.* having two syllables: Ditto *is a disyllabic word.* Also, **dissyllabic.**

di•syl•la•ble ['dəɪ'sɪləbəl], [dəɪ'sɪləbəl], *or* [,daɪ'sɪləbəl], ['dɪsɪləbəl] *or* [dɪ'sɪləbəl] *n.* a word having two syllables. Also, **dissyllable.**

dit [dɪt] *n.* the name corresponding to a dot in Morse code. Compare DAH. ⟨echoic⟩

ditch [dɪtʃ] *n., v.* —*n.* a long, narrow trench dug in the earth, usually used to carry off water.
—*v.* **1** make a ditch or ditches. **2** make a ditch or ditches in. **3** drive (a vehicle) into a ditch: *He ditched his car.* **4** land (an aircraft not equipped for the purpose) on water. **5** abandon (especially an aircraft in flight): *The pilot ditched the airplane because two engines were on fire.* **6** *Slang.* **a** get rid of. **b** leave in the lurch. ⟨OE *dīc*⟩ **—'ditch•er,** *n.*

ditch•dig•ger ['dɪtʃ,dɪgər] *n.* a person or machine that digs ditches.

ditch•dig•ging ['dɪtʃ,dɪgɪŋ] *n., adj.* —*n.* the job of digging ditches.
—*adj.* of or for the digging of ditches.

dith•er ['dɪðər] *n., v.* —*n. Informal.* a state of quivering excitement or hesitation: *We were all in a dither, waiting for the results of the competition.*
—*v. Informal.* act nervously or indecisively; hesitate. ⟨origin uncertain⟩

dith•y•ramb ['dɪθə,ræm] *or* ['dɪθə,ræmb] *n.* **1** a Greek choral song in honour of Dionysus. **2** a poem that is full of wild emotion, enthusiasm, etc. **3** any speech or writing like this. ⟨< L < Gk. *dithyrambos*⟩

dith•y•ram•bic [,dɪθə'ræmbɪk] *adj.* **1** of or like a dithyramb. **2** wildly enthusiastic.

dit•to ['dɪtou] *n., pl.* **-tos;** *adv., v.* **-toed, -to•ing;** *interj.* —*n.* **1** the same; exactly the same as appeared before. **2** inverted commas or apostrophes (") that stand for ditto; DITTO MARK. **3** a copy; duplicate.
—*adv. Informal.* as said or done before; likewise.
—*v.* **1** copy or repeat: *She simply dittoed what I had said.* **2** make a copy or copies of on a duplicating machine: *to ditto a memo.*
—*interj. Informal.* the same; "I agree!" ⟨< Ital. *ditto* said < L *dictus*, pp. of *dicere* say⟩

ditto mark a small mark (") used in lists, tables, etc., directly under something written to show that it is repeated. *Example*:

10 copies at 10¢ each = $1.00
40 " " 5¢ " = $2.00

dit•ty ['dɪti] *n., pl.* **-ties.** a short, simple song or poem. ⟨ME < OF *dite* < L *dictatum* (thing) dictated, pp. neut. of *dictare* dictate⟩

ditty bag a small bag, used especially by sailors, to hold sewing things and other odds and ends. ⟨origin uncertain⟩

ditty box a small box used as a ditty bag.

di•u•re•sis [,daɪə'risɪs] *n.* excessive or frequent urination. ⟨< NL < Gk. *diourein* < *dia* through + *ourein* to urinate⟩

di•u•ret•ic [,daɪjə'rɛtɪk] *or* [,daɪə'rɛtɪk] *adj., n.* —*adj.* causing an increase in the flow of urine.
—*n.* any drug or other agent, such as coffee, that causes an increase in the flow of urine. ⟨ME < LL *diureticus* < Gk. *diourētikos* < *dia-* through + *ourein* urinate⟩

di•ur•nal [daɪ'ɜrnəl] *adj.* **1** occurring every day; daily. **2** of or belonging to the daytime. **3** *Zoology.* active during the day and not at night: *Most birds are diurnal.* **4** *Botany.* opening during the day and closing at night. **5** lasting a day. ⟨ME < LL *diurnalis* < L *dies* day. Doublet of JOURNAL.⟩ **—di'ur•nal•ly,** *adv.*

div. **1** dividend. **2** division; divided.

di•va ['divə] *n., pl.* **-vas.** a prima donna; famous woman opera singer. ⟨< Ital. < L *diva* goddess⟩

di•va•gate ['daɪvə,geit] *or* ['dɪvə,geit] *v.* **-gat•ed, -gat•ing.** wander; stray. ⟨< L *divagari* < *dis-* about + *vagari* wander⟩

di•va•ga•tion [,daɪvə'geiʃən] *or* [,dɪvə'geiʃən] *n.* a wandering.

di•va•lent [daɪ'veilənt] *adj. Chemistry.* having a valence of two.

Di•va•li [dɪ'vali] *n.* a Hindu festival celebrated in the fall. It is dedicated to Lakshmi and is also known as the Festival of Lights. Also, **Diwali, Dewali.** ⟨< Hind.⟩

di•van [dɪ'væn] *or* ['daɪvæn] *n.* **1** a long, low, usually backless and armless couch. **2** in Turkey and other Middle Eastern countries: **a** a court or council. **b** a council chamber. **3** a smoking room. ⟨< Turkish *divān* < Persian *dēvān* (now *dīwān*) collection of written sheets, book or set of accounts, hence accounting office, treasury, council chamber; 16c.⟩

dive [daɪv] *v.* **dived** or **dove, dived, div•ing;** *n.* —*v.* **1** plunge headfirst, usually into the water. **2** go down or out of sight suddenly: *She dived into an alley.* **3** plunge the hand suddenly into anything: *He dived into his pocket and fished out a dollar.* **4** of an aircraft, missile, etc., plunge downward at a steep angle. **5** of a submarine, submerge. **6** penetrate with the mind; investigate in depth: *Tina has been diving into the history of the Incas.*
—*n.* **1** the act of diving. **2** the downward plunge of an aircraft, missile, submarine, etc. **3** *Informal.* a cheap, disreputable place for drinking and gambling. **4** *Informal.* cheap, poor lodgings.
take a dive, *Informal.* suffer an apparent knockout in a boxing match by deliberately falling to the canvas, usually as part of some illegal gambling arrangement. ⟨OE *dȳfan*⟩
☛ *Usage.* **Dived,** DOVE[2]. Both forms are used in Canadian English for the past tense, though **dived** seems to be more widely preferred in writing and in formal English. However, **dove** (< OE *dūfan*) is the standard preferred form for many people.

dive–bomb ['daɪv ,bɒm] *v.* bomb at close range using a dive bomber.

dive bomber a bomber that releases its bomb load just before it pulls out of a dive toward the target.

div•er ['daɪvər] *n.* **1** a person or thing that dives. **2** a person whose occupation is working under water. **3** a diving bird: *The loon is a well-known Canadian diver.*

di•verge [dɪ'vɜrdʒ] *or* [daɪ'vɜrdʒ] *v.* **-verged, -verg•ing. 1** move or lie in different directions from one point; branch off: *Their paths diverged at the fork in the road.* **2** differ or vary: *They usually agreed, but their opinions diverged on this matter.* **3** become dissimilar gradually: *Her opinions diverged from mine as we grew older. Dialects diverge when people are isolated from each other.* **4** turn away from a set course; deviate. **5** cause to diverge. **6** *Mathematics.* (of a series) increase indefinitely as more terms are added. ⟨< LL *divergere* < *dis-* in different directions + *vergere* slope⟩
☛ *Syn.* **1. Diverge,** DEVIATE, DIGRESS = turn or move in a different direction. **Diverge** = branch out in different directions like a Y from a main or old path or way: *Our paths diverged when we left school.* **Deviate** = turn aside in one direction from a normal or regular path, way of thinking or acting, rule, etc.: *The teacher deviated from her custom and gave us no homework.* **Digress** applies chiefly to turning aside from the main subject while speaking or writing: *I lose interest if an author digresses too much.*

di•ver•gence [dɪ'vɜrdʒəns] *or* [daɪ'vɜrdʒəns] *n.* **1** the act or state of diverging; difference: *The committee couldn't come to any agreement because of the wide divergence of opinion among its members.* **2** *Mathematics.* the fact of diverging.

di•ver•gen•cy [dɪ'vɜrdʒənsi] *or* [daɪ'vɜrdʒənsi] *n., pl.* **-cies.** divergence.

di•ver•gent [dɪ'vɜrdʒənt] *or* [daɪ'vɜrdʒənt] *adj.* **1** diverging; different. **2** causing divergence. **3** *Botany.* of a plant, having a part sticking out. **4** heading in a different or original direction: *divergent thinking.* **—di'ver•gent•ly,** *adv.*

di•vers ['daɪvərz] *adj. Formal or archaic.* several different; various: *at divers times in the history of humankind.* ⟨ME < OF < L *diversus*, pp. of *divertere.* See DIVERT.⟩

di•verse [dɪ'vɜrs], [daɪ'vɜrs], *or* ['daɪvərs] *adj.* **1** different; completely unlike. **2** varied: *A person of diverse interests can talk on many subjects.* ⟨var. of *divers*; now regarded as immediately from L *diversus*⟩ **—di'verse•ness,** *n.*

di•verse•ly [dɪ'vɜrsli] *or* [daɪ'vɜrsli] *adv.* in different ways or directions; differently; variously.

di•ver•si•fi•ca•tion [dɪ,vɜrsəfə'keiʃən] *or* [daɪ,vɜrsəfə'keiʃən] *n.* the act or process of diversifying or the state of being diversified.

di•ver•si•fy [dɪ'vɜrsə,faɪ] *or* [daɪ'vɜrsə,faɪ] *v.* **-fied, -fy•ing.** **1** give variety to; vary: *He joined a travel club to diversify his interests.* **2** expand or extend (business activities) into different fields: *The company has recently diversified and now produces a whole range of cleaning products.* **3** distribute (investments, etc.) among several different securities in order to reduce risk. ⟨< Med.L *diversificare* < L *diversus* diverse + *facere* make⟩ **—di'ver•si,fi•er,** *n.*

di•ver•sion [dɪ'vɜrʒən] *or* [daɪ'vɜrʒən] *n.* **1** a manoeuvre intended to draw attention away from a planned activity or attack; feint. **2** an amusement; entertainment; pastime: *Golf is my mother's favourite diversion.* **3** a turning aside: *High tariffs often cause a diversion of trade from one country to another.*

di•ver•sion•ar•y [dɪ'vɜrʒə,nɛri], [daɪ'vɜrʒə,nɛri], *or* [dɪ'vɛrʒənəri] *adj.* of, like, or being a diversion or feint, especially in military tactics.

di•ver•sion•ist [dɪ'vɜrʒə,nɪst] *n.* one who practises diversionary tactics for strategic reasons.

di•ver•si•ty [dɪ'vɜrsəti] *or* [daɪ'vɜrsəti] *n., pl.* **-ties. 1** complete difference; unlikeness. **2** variety: *Diversity of opinion is encouraged in a democracy.*

☛ *Syn.* **2.** See note at VARIETY.

di•vert [dɪ'vɜrt] *or* [daɪ'vɜrt] *v.* **1** turn aside: *A ditch diverted water from the stream into the fields.* **2** amuse; entertain: *She browsed through the bookstore, looking for something to divert her during the flight.* **3** defect the concentration of; distract: *Her jokes diverted me from my work.* ⟨< MF *divertir* < L *divertere* < *dis-* aside + *vertere* turn⟩

di•ver•tic•u•li•tis [,daɪvər,tɪkjə'ləɪtɪs] *n.* the inflammation of a diverticulum, especially the rupture of one or more in the colon, allowing leakage of fecal matter into the abdominal cavity.

di•ver•tic•u•lum [,daɪvər'tɪkjələm] *n., pl.* **-la** [-lə]. *Anatomy.* an abnormal tubular sac or process branching off from a canal or cavity. ⟨< L⟩

di•ver•ti•men•to [dɪ,vɛrti'mɛntou] *n., pl.* **-ti** [-ti]. *Music.* **1** an instrumental composition, usually in several movements, intended to amuse and entertain. **2** an instrumental composition, usually light and entertaining, consisting of variations on a previously existing theme. ⟨< Ital.⟩

di•ver•tisse•ment [dɪ'vɜrtɪsmənt]; *French,* [divɛrtis'mɑ̃] *n. French.* **1** an amusement; entertainment. **2** a short ballet. **3** *Music.* **a** a collection of songs and dances inserted into an opera, ballet, etc. **b** divertimento. **c** a light, entertaining composition for use between the acts of an opera, ballet, etc. ⟨< F⟩

Dives ['daɪviz] *n.* any rich man. ⟨in the Bible, the rich man in the parable of the rich man and the beggar, from interpretation of L *dives* rich, in the Vulgate, as a proper noun⟩

di•vest [dɪ'vɛst] *or* [daɪ'vɛst] *v.* **1** strip; rid; free: *The police divested the impostor of his stolen uniform and fake decorations.* **2** force to give up; deprive: *Citizens were divested of their right to vote.* **3** *Law.* take away (property). ⟨< Med.L *divestire* < OF *desvestir* < *des-* away + *vestir* < L *vestire* clothe⟩ **—di'vest•i•ture, di'vest•ure,** or **di'vest•ment,** *n.*

di•vide [dɪ'vaid] *v.* **-vid•ed, -vid•ing;** *n.* *—v.* **1** separate into parts: *A brook divides the field. The river divides and forms two streams.* **2** *Mathematics.* separate into equal parts: *Divide* 8 *by* 2, *and you get* 4. *Symbol*: ÷ **3** do a mathematical division: *She knew how to divide and multiply by the age of six.* **4** give some of to each; share: *The children divided the candy among them.* **5** disagree or cause to disagree; differ or cause to differ in feeling, opinion, etc.: *The school divided on the choice of a motto. Jealousy divided us.* **6** separate or cause to separate into two groups in voting. **7** mark off in parts; graduate (a scale, instrument, etc.). **8** distinguish by kinds; sort out; classify. **9** keep (two things) apart with a physical boundary or separator.
—n. a ridge of land separating the regions drained by two different river systems. ⟨ME < L *dividere*⟩

☛ *Syn. v.* See note at SEPARATE.

di•vid•ed [dɪ'vaɪdɪd] *adj., v.* *—adj.* **1** separated. **2** of a leaf, cut to the base so as to form distinct portions. **3** disagreeing in feeling, opinion, etc. **4** having a partition or dividing strip between opposite lanes: *a divided highway.*
—v. pt. and pp. of DIVIDE.

☛ *Usage.* **Divided usage.** Usage is said to be *divided* when two or more forms of a word are used more or less equally by the members of a speech community. **Divided usage** is not applied, for example, to localisms, like *coulee, gulch, ravine* (when referring to the same object), nor to differences, such as *ain't* and *isn't*, that belong to separate levels of the language. It applies to standard spellings, pronunciations, or constructions on which speakers and writers of similar education might differ. The two pronunciations of *either* ['iðər] and ['aɪðər], the two spellings of *honour* (*honour* and *honor*), and the two past tenses of *dive* (*dived* and *dove*) are examples of divided usage.

divided highway a road, such as an expressway, having a median strip or boulevard between lanes of traffic going in opposite directions.

divided skirt a woman's garment that looks like a flared skirt but is divided and sewn in the manner of trousers.

div•i•dend ['dɪvə,dɛnd] *n.* **1** *Mathematics.* a number or quantity to be divided by another: *In* 8 ÷ 2, 8 *is the dividend.* **2** money to be shared by those to whom it belongs. If a company makes a profit, it declares a dividend to the owners of the company. **3** a share of such money. **4** a part of the profits of an insurance company given to a person holding an insurance policy. **5** return; benefit: *An active lifestyle brings important dividends.* ⟨< L *dividendum* (thing) to be divided⟩

di•vid•er [dɪ'vaɪdər] *n.* **1** a person or thing that divides. **2** a device for partitioning an indoor area into several sections. **3** a piece of cardboard for separating sections of a notebook, or a similar thing in a diskette storage box, card index, etc. **4 dividers,** *pl.* an instrument for measuring distances, dividing lines, etc.; compasses.

div•i•na•tion [,dɪvə'neiʃən] *n.* **1** the art or act of foreseeing the future or revealing the unknown by supernatural means. **2** a skilful guess or prediction.

di•vin•a•to•ry [də'vɪnə,tɔri] *adj.* of or having to do with divination.

di•vine [dɪ'vaɪn] *adj., n., v.* **-vined, -vin•ing.** *—adj.* **1** of God or a god. **2** by or from God. **3** to or for God; sacred; holy. **4** like God or a god; heavenly. **5** *Informal.* delightful; excellent; unusually good: *"What a divine hat!" cried Sue.*
—n. a person who knows much about theology, especially a minister or priest.
—v. **1** find out or foretell by supernatural means. **2** find out by intuition or by guessing: *She divined their plan and immediately set out to stop them.* **3** locate (water, minerals, etc.) underground by using a divining rod. ⟨ME < OF (v., MF < L *divinare*) < L *divinus* of a deity < *divus* deity⟩ **—di'vine•ness,** *n.*

di•vine•ly [dɪ'vaɪnli] *adv.* **1** in a divine or godlike manner. **2** by the agency or influence of God. **3** *Informal.* superbly: *The orchestra played divinely at its first concert.*

di•vin•er [dɪ'vaɪnər] *n.* **1** a person who divines, especially one who foresees the future or perceives the unknown, or professes to do these things. **2** a person who locates water, minerals, etc. underground by using a divining rod: *a water diviner.*

divine right of kings the right to rule, alleged to be given to kings by God rather than by people.

diving bell a large, hollow, bell-shaped container open at the bottom, used since ancient times as a chamber for people to work in underwater. A diving bell is supplied with air through a hose; the pressure of the air keeps the water out.

diving board a board fixed with a spring, mounted over the deep end of a swimming area and used for diving from.

diving suit a waterproof suit with a helmet into which air can be pumped through a tube. Diving suits are worn by persons working under water.

divining rod a forked stick, usually of willow or hazel, used to indicate the location of water or metal underground. It is supposed to bend downward where these are present.

di•vin•i•ty [dɪ'vɪnəti] *n., pl.* **-ties. 1** a divine being; a god or goddess. **2 the Divinity,** God. **3** divine nature or quality: *The divinity of Jesus is accepted by Christians.* **4** theology: *a student of divinity.* **5** a creamy fudge.

di•vis•i•ble [dɪ'vɪzəbəl] *adj.* **1** capable of being divided. **2** capable of being divided without leaving a remainder: *Any even number is divisible by* 2. **—di,vis•i'bil•i•ty,** *n.*

di•vi•sion [dɪ'vɪʒən] *n.* **1** a dividing or being divided. **2** the act or process of giving some to each; distribution: *a division of labour.* **3** *Mathematics.* the process of dividing one number by another. **4** something that divides, such as a boundary or a partition. **5** one of the parts, sections, or groups into which something is divided. **6** *Military.* a major formation or unit under single command, including administrative services, arms, etc. **7** *Biology.* a major category in the classification of plants, corresponding to the phylum in the classification of animals. This category is more specific than the kingdom and more general than the class. See classification chart in the Appendix. **8** a difference of opinion or interest; disagreement. **9** the process of separating into two groups for voting in a legislative body. ⟨< L *divisio, -onis* < *dividere* divide⟩

di•vi•sion•al [dɪ'vɪʒənəl] *adj.* of, having to do with, or belonging to a division: *a divisional commander, divisional court.*

division of labour or **labor 1** a condition under which the work of a society is divided among various trades and professions, as those of priest, soldier, shoemaker, etc. **2** a distribution of separate small parts of a process among many workers, as in a modern factory.

di•vi•sive [dɪ'vaisɪv] *or* [dɪ'vɪzɪv] *adj.* tending or serving to divide, disunite, etc. **—di'vi•sive•ly,** *adv.* **—di'vi•sive•ness,** *n.*

di•vi•sor [dɪ'vaɪzər] *n.* **1** a number or quantity by which another is divided: *In* 8 ÷ 2, 2 *is the divisor.* **2** a number or quantity that divides another without a remainder.

di•vorce [dɪ'vɔrs] *n., v.* **-vorced, -vorc•ing.** *—n.* **1** the legal ending of a marriage. **2** complete separation: *The pamphlet advocated the divorce of church and state.*
—v. **1** legally dissolve the marriage contract between. **2** end marriage with (one's spouse) by getting a divorce: *Mrs. Chung divorced her husband. The Chungs divorced.* **3** separate or detach (something) *from*: *She led a lonely life, divorced from all her childhood friends and pleasures.* ⟨ME < OF < L *divortium* separation < *divertere.* See DIVERT.⟩ **—di'vorc•er,** *n.*

di•vor•cé [dɪ,vɔr'sei] *or* [dɪ'vɔrsei] *n.* a divorced man.

di•vor•cee [dɪ,vɔr'si] *or* [dɪ'vɔrsi] *n.* a divorced person.

di•vor•cée [dɪ,vɔr'sei] *n.* a divorced woman.

di•vorce•ment [dɪ'vɔrsmənt] *n.* divorce.

div•ot ['dɪvət] *n.* a small piece of turf or earth dug up by a golf club in making a stroke. ⟨origin uncertain⟩

di•vulge [dɪ'vʌldʒ] *or* [daɪ'vʌldʒ] *v.* **-vulged, -vulg•ing.** reveal (something secret); make known; make public: *The traitor divulged secret plans to the enemy.* ⟨< L *divulgare* publish < *dis-* away + *vulgus* common people⟩ **—di'vulg•er,** *n.* **—di'vulg•ence,** *n.*

div•vy ['dɪvi] *v.* **div•vied, div•vy•ing;** *n. Slang. —v.* divide or share.
divvy up, make a division into shares.
—n. a share or portion. ⟨var. of *divide*⟩

dix [dis] *n.* **1** in bezique and some other card games, the lowest trump. **2** in pinochle, a score of ten points. ⟨< F *dix* ten⟩

Dix•ie ['dɪksi] *n.* the southern states of the United States, especially those that united to form the Confederacy in 1860-1861. ⟨< *Dixie's Land*, title of a song by Daniel D. Emmett (1815-1904), American songwriter, after *Dixie*, name of a black character in a minstrel play (1850)⟩

Dix•ie•land or **dix•ie•land** ['dɪksi,lænd] *n.* a style of orchestral jazz with a strong rhythm in 4/4 time, usually played by a small band, with improvisation often by several instruments at the same time.

diz•en ['dɪzən] *or* ['daɪzən] *v. Archaic.* bedizen. ⟨Cf. MDu. *disen* wind up flax, MLG *dise* bunch of flax on distaff⟩

di•zy•got•ic twins [,daɪzaɪ'gɒtɪk] a pair of twins derived from two zygotes. Also called **fraternal twins**.

diz•zy ['dɪzi] *adj.* **-zi•er, -zi•est;** *v.* **-zied, -zy•ing.** *—adj.* **1** having a sensation that things about one are whirling or spinning around and that one is about to fall: *Most of the midway rides make me dizzy.* **2** confused; bewildered. **3** causing or likely to cause dizziness: *The mountaineer climbed to a dizzy height.* **4** *Informal.* foolish; silly: *What a dizzy thing to do!*
—v. make dizzy: *The ride on the merry-go-round had dizzied her.* ⟨OE *dysig* foolish⟩ **—'diz•zi•ly,** *adv.* **—'diz•zi•ness,** *n.*

DJ or **D.J. 1** disc jockey. **2** dinner jacket.

djel•la•ba or **djel•la•bah** [dʒə'lɑbə] *n.* a long, loose gown worn by men in Arabic countries. ⟨< Arabic *jallaba*, contraction of *jallabiya*⟩

Dji•bou•ti [dʒɪ'buti] *n.* a country in E Africa.

djinn [dʒɪn] See JINN.
☛ *Hom.* GIN[1-3].

D–layer D REGION.

dm decimetre(s).

DM Deutsche Mark.

DNA any of various acids that are an essential component of all living matter and that in higher organisms contain the genetic codes determining heredity. ⟨abbrev. of *d*eoxyribo*n*ucleic *a*cid⟩

DNA fingerprint the unique pattern of DNA bands obtained by the use of DNA probes that detect highly variable repeat sequences, used for identification, especially for forensic purposes.

DNB Dictionary of National Biography.

DND or **D.N.D.** Department of National Defence.

do[1] [du] *v. pres. sing.* 1 **do,** 2 **do,** 3 **does;** *pl.* **do;** *pt.* **did;** *pp.* **done;** *ppr.* **do•ing;** *n. —v.* **1** carry out; perform: *That's easier said than done. She did her work.* **2** act; work: *Do or die.* **3** complete; finish; end: *My assignment is done.* **4** make; produce: *Walt Disney did a movie about wildlife in the Arctic.* **5** be the cause of; bring about: *Do good. Your work does you credit.* **6** act; behave: *Do wisely.* **7** have as a livelihood or professional occupation: *What does his mother do? She does legal work for the immigration department.* **8** render: *to do homage, to do justice.* **9** deal with as the case may require; take care of: *to do the dishes, to do one's hair. Does he do windows?* **10** get along; manage; fare: *How are they doing?* **11** be satisfactory; be enough; serve: *He said any kind of paper would do.* **12** work out; solve: *to do a puzzle, to do a sum.* **13** cook: *The roast will be done in an hour.* **14** cover; traverse: *We did 100 km in an hour.* **15** *Informal.* travel at a speed of: *That police car was doing at least 120 km/h.* **16** *Informal.* cheat; trick. **17** *Informal.* spend (time) in jail as an inmate: *He's doing time. She's doing three months.* **18** *Slang.* consume; use (a substance, especially a drug): *He decided never to do drugs. I don't do Brussels sprouts or spinach.* **19** occur; happen: *What's doing at the SkyDome tonight?* **20 Do** is also used in certain constructions where it has a grammatical function (as an auxiliary verb) but no special meaning in itself: **a** in asking questions: *Do you like milk?* **b** to emphasize a verb: *I do want to go.* **c** to stand for a verb already used: *My dog goes where I do.* **d** in negative statements that contain **not:** *I do not think they will come. He enjoyed the movie but she did not.* **e** in inverted constructions after the adverbs *rarely, hardly, little,* etc.: *Rarely did she laugh.*
do away with, a abolish: *do away with a rule.* **b** kill.
do by, act or behave toward; treat.
do for, a look after the needs of, as housekeeper, etc: *Who did for her while she was sick?* **b** *Informal.* ruin, destroy, or kill: *That job almost did for me.*
do in, *Informal.* **a** ruin or kill: *That exercise is enough to do anybody in.* **b** tire out: *I'm all done in.*
do (one's) **bit.** See BIT[2].
do over, *Informal.* **a** redo. **b** renovate or redecorate: *They did the den over last summer.*
do up, a close or fasten (a zipper, buttons, laces, etc.): *Do up your shoelaces. He had trouble doing up the top button.* **b** close the fastenings of: *to do up a coat.* **c** wrap up: *to do up a package.* **d** clean and get ready for use: *to do up a room.* **e** *Informal.* wear out; exhaust. **f** *Informal.* style (one's hair) in a bun or roll so that it is off the neck.
do with, enjoy or use (*preceded by* **can** *or* **could**): *I could do with a hammer and nails—would you hand them to me? I could do with a mug of hot chocolate.*
do without, get along without the thing mentioned or implied: *We can do without luxuries if we have to.*
have to do with, relate to; deal with: *Abstract art has little to do with everyday experience.*
how do you do? Pleased to meet you. (*used in formal introductions*)
it isn't done, it is not considered good manners, good taste, etc.
—n. **1** *Informal.* celebration: *They had a big do for us when we got back.* **2** *Informal.* something that is expected or prescribed: *the do's and don'ts of etiquette.* ⟨OE dōn⟩
☛ *Hom.* DEW, DUE.

☛ *Syn.* **1. Do,** PERFORM, ACCOMPLISH = carry out work, etc. **Do** is the general word and may be used, at least informally, of every kind of act: *She did nothing today.* **Perform,** the formal word, often interchangeable with **do,** particularly emphasizes doing by going through a process, and may suggest regular activities: *He performed all of his duties in a perfunctory way. This update will allow your computer to perform a variety of new functions.* **Accomplish** = carry out successfully to the desired end: *She worked hard but accomplished very little.*

The eight-tone musical scale

do[2] [dou] *n. Music.* **1** the first and last tones of an eight-tone scale: *do, re, mi, fa, sol, la, ti, do.* **2** the tone C. ⟨< Italian *do* as used for the *ut* of *gamut*⟩

☛ *Hom.* DOE, DOUGH.

do. ditto.

DOA dead on arrival.

do•a•ble ['duəbəl] *adj.* that can be done; practicable.

dob•bin ['dɒbən] *n.* a farm horse, especially a quiet, plodding one. ⟨var. of *Robin,* traditional name for a farm horse⟩

Do•ber•man pin•scher ['doubərmən 'pɪnʃər] *or* ['pɪntʃər] a breed of fairly large, slender, short-haired dog originally developed in Germany. Doberman pinschers are often trained as watchdogs. ⟨< Ludwig *Doberman,* a German dog breeder + G *Pinscher* terrier⟩

A Doberman pinscher

do•bra ['doubrə] *n.* the currency of Sao Tome and Principe. See table of money in the Appendix.

Do•bro ['doubrou] *n. Trademark.* an acoustic steel guitar having an aluminum resonator. A Dobro is used mainly in country music, and played flat upon the lap. ⟨< *Do*pera *bro*thers, its inventors; probably influenced by Czech *debro* good⟩

dob•son•fly ['dɒbsən,flaɪ] *n., pl.* **-flies.** any of a family (Corydalidae) of insects found in many parts of the world, especially *Corydalis cornutus,* whose large, carnivorous, aquatic larva, called a hellgrammite, is used as fishing bait. Also, **dobson fly.** ⟨origin uncertain⟩

do•bu•ta•mine [dou'bjutə,min] *n.* a drug used to treat certain heart conditions.

do•cent ['dousənt] *n.* **1** a person trained as a guide and lecturer to conduct groups through a picture gallery, museum, etc. **2** *U.S.* a lecturer, especially at a college or university. ⟨< G *Dozent* < L *docens, -entis,* ppr. of *docere* teach⟩

do•cile ['dousaɪl], ['dɒsaɪl], *or* ['dɒsəl] *adj.* **1** easily managed; meekly obedient. **2** easily taught; willing to learn. ⟨ME < L *docilis* < *docere* teach⟩ **—'do•cile•ly,** *adv.*

☛ *Syn.* **1.** See note at OBEDIENT.

do•cil•i•ty [dɒ'sɪləti] *or* [dou'sɪləti] *n.* a docile quality.

dock[1] [dɒk] *n., v.* *—n.* **1** a platform, wharf, etc. for loading or unloading cargo or freight. **2** the water between two piers, permitting the entrance of ships. **3** a large basin equipped with floodgates to receive ships for loading, unloading, and repairs. **4** drydock.

—v. **1** bring (a ship) alongside a dock: *The sailors docked the ship and began to unload it.* **2** come into a dock. **3** join (spacecraft) together in space. ⟨< MDu. or MLG *docke*⟩

dock[2] [dɒk] *n., v.* *—n.* **1** the solid, fleshy part of an animal's tail. **2** the part of a tail left after cutting or clipping.

—v. **1** cut short; cut the end off: *Horses' and dogs' tails are sometimes docked.* **2** cut down; take away part of: *The company docked the employees' wages when they came late to work.* ⟨OE *-docca,* as in *finger-docca* finger muscle⟩

dock[3] [dɒk] *n.* the place where an accused person stands in criminal court. ⟨Cf. Flemish *dok* pen⟩

dock[4] [dɒk] *n.* any of numerous herbs (genus *Rumes*) of the buckwheat family, some of which are troublesome weeds. ⟨OE *docce*⟩

dock•age[1] ['dɒkɪdʒ] *n.* **1** a place to dock a ship. **2** a charge for using a dock. **3** the docking of ships. ⟨< *dock*[1]⟩

dock•age[2] ['dɒkɪdʒ] *n.* **1** an act of cutting down or cutting off. **2** a cut or deduction made, as from wages. **3** easily removable foreign material that is added to grain in processing. ⟨< *dock*[2]⟩

dock•er[1] ['dɒkər] *n. Esp. Brit.* a labourer who works on a dock; longshoreman.

dock•er[2] ['dɒkər] *n.* a person who or thing that docks, cuts off, or cuts short.

dock•et ['dɒkɪt] *n., v.* *—n.* **1** a list of cases to be tried by a court: *There are 12 cases on this morning's docket.* **2** a summary or list of decisions made in a court of law. **3** any list of matters to be considered by some group of people; agenda. **4** a label or ticket giving the contents of a package, document, etc.

—v. **1** enter on a docket. **2** make a summary or list of (judgments, documents, etc.). **3** mark with a docket. ⟨origin uncertain⟩

dock•work•er ['dɒk,wɜrkər] *n.* a worker who loads and unloads cargo at the side of a ship; shorehand; stevedore.

dock•yard ['dɒk,jɑrd] *n.* a place where ships are built, equipped, and repaired. A dockyard contains docks, workshops, and warehouses for supplies.

doc•tor ['dɒktər] *n., v.* *—n.* **1** a person who is licensed to treat diseases. **2** any person who treats diseases by magic: *a witch doctor.* **3** a person who has received the highest degree possible in a university: *a Doctor of Laws, a Doctor of Philosophy.* **4** *Archaic.* a learned man; teacher. **5** any of various mechanical devices, especially one designed to remedy something. **6** a brightly coloured artificial fishing fly. *Abbrevs.*: Dr. (defs. 1 and 3, as a title); D. (def. 3, for Latin names of degrees).

—v. **1** give medical treatment to; try to heal: *She doctors her children when they have colds or stomach aches.* **2** *Informal.* practise medicine. **3** tamper with: *The dishonest cashier doctored the accounts.* **4** alter: *The whisky had been doctored with water. You can doctor your own tea. With a little doctoring you can use the same resumé for both job applications.* **5** mend; repair, especially machinery, etc. ⟨ME < OF *doctour* < L *doctor* teacher < *docere* teach⟩

doc•tor•al ['dɒktərəl] *adj.* of or having to do with a doctor or doctorate.

doc•tor•ate ['dɒktərɪt] *n.* the degree of Doctor given by a university.

doc•tri•naire [,dɒktrə'nɛr] *n., adj.* *—n.* an impractical theorist; a person who tries to apply a theory rigidly, without considering the actual circumstances or consequences.

—adj. characteristic of a doctrinaire; theoretical and impractical: *a doctrinaire approach.*

doc•tri•nal [,dɒk'traɪnəl] *or* ['dɒktrənəl] *adj.* of, characterized by, or having to do with doctrine: *a doctrinal sermon.*
—doc'tri•nal•ly, *adv.*

doc•trine ['dɒktrən] *n.* **1** what is taught as the belief of a church, nation, or group of persons. **2** what is taught; teachings collectively. **3** a belief, especially a religious one. ⟨ME < OF < L *doctrina* < *doctor.* See DOCTOR.⟩

doc•u•dra•ma or **doc•u–dra•ma** ['dɒkju,dræmə] *or* ['dɒkju,drɑmə] *n.* a film that is basically factual but which contains fictional elements for added dramatic interest. ⟨*docu*mentary + *drama*⟩

doc•u•ment *n.* ['dɒkjəmənt]; *v.* ['dɒkjə,mɛnt] *n., v.* *—n.* **1** something written, printed, etc. that gives information or proof of some fact; any original or official paper that can be used as evidence. Letters, maps, and pictures are documents. **2** *Computer technology.* a text file in its entirety.

—v. **1** provide with original or official papers. **2** prove or support by means of such papers. **3** provide with references to authoritative material and original sources that support a claim, argument, or theory: *Her article on the effects of artificial lighting is well-documented.* **4** demonstrate or illustrate in a book, film, etc.: *The film documents the changing face of the North.* ⟨< L *documentum* example, proof < *docere* show⟩

doc•u•men•ta•rist [,dɒkjə'mɛntərɪst] *n.* a maker of documentary films.

doc•u•men•ta•ry [,dɒkjə'mɛntəri] *or* [,dɒkjə'mɛntri] *adj., n., pl.* **-ries.** *—adj.* **1** consisting of documents; in writing, print, etc.: *The man's own letters were documentary evidence of his guilt.* **2** presenting or recording factual information in an artistic fashion: *a documentary film.*

—n. a documentary book, film, radio, or television program.

doc•u•men•ta•tion [,dɒkjəmən'teiʃən] *n.* **1** printed material that explains the use of some equipment, piece of computer software, etc.: *There was no documentation to help us understand our new microwave.* **2** the production of such material: *She does documentation for a software design firm.*

do•cu•sate ['dɒkjʊ,seit] *n.* a laxative drug containing calcium.

dod•der¹ ['dɒdər] *v.* **1** shake; tremble. **2** move unsteadily; totter: *The man dodders about as if he were ninety years old.* ⟨origin uncertain⟩ **—'dod•der•er,** *n.*

dod•der² ['dɒdər] *n.* any of a genus (*Cuscuta*) of annual plants of the morning-glory family, having no leaves, chlorophyl, or roots when mature, and living as parasites by twining around other plants and drawing food from them through suckers. ⟨ME *doder*⟩

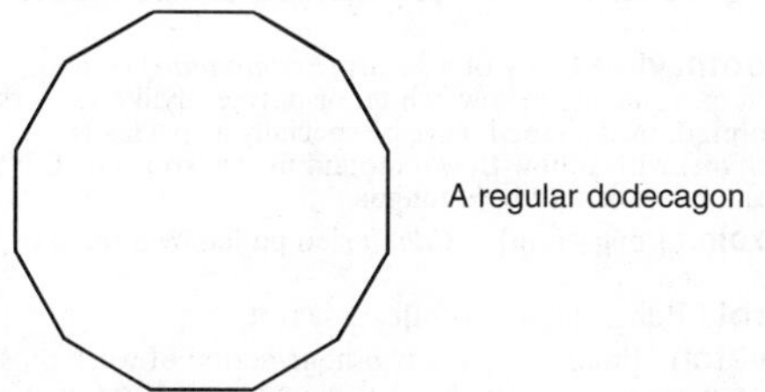

A regular dodecagon

do•dec•a•gon [dou'dɛkə,gɒn] *n.* a polygon having 12 sides. ⟨< Gk. *dōdekagonon* < *dōdeka* twelve + *gōnia* angle⟩

do•dec•a•he•dron [,doudɛkə'hidrən] *or* [dou,dɛkə'hidrən] *n., pl.* **-drons, -dra** [-drə]. a polyhedron having 12 faces. The faces of a regular dodecahedron are regular pentagons. ⟨< Gk. *dōdekaedron* < *dōdeka* twelve + *hedra* seat, base⟩

do•dec•a•phon•ic [,doudɛkə'fɒnɪk] *or* [dou,dɛkə'fɒnɪk] *adj. Music.* of a system, introduced by the U.S. composer Arnold Schönberg, in which the twelve notes of the chromatic scale are re-sorted into some arbitrary order. The resulting **tone row** then forms the basis for further composition. ⟨< Gk. *dodeka* twelve + *phone* sound⟩

dodge [dɒdʒ] *v.* **dodged, dodg•ing;** *n.* *—v.* **1** move quickly to one side: *She dodged into the shadow of the house.* **2** move quickly in order to get away from (a person, a blow, or something thrown): *He dodged the ball as it came flying toward his head.* **3** get away from or avoid (an obligation, problem, etc.) by trickery, cunning, or evasion; evade: *She is trying to dodge her responsibilities as leader by not taking a stand on the issue.*
—n. **1** a sudden movement to one side. **2** *Informal.* a trick or scheme: *a clever dodge.* ⟨origin uncertain⟩

dodge•ball ['dɒdʒ,bɒl] *n.* a game, usually played by children, in which players forming a circle or two opposite lines try to hit opponents in the centre with a large, inflated ball.

dodg•er ['dɒdʒər] *n.* **1** a person who dodges, especially one who uses tricky or cunning devices. **2** a small handbill.

do•do ['doudou] *n., pl.* **-dos** or **-does. 1** either of two extinct species of large, heavy bird (genus *Raphus*) having a large, hooked bill, short legs, and small wings that were useless for flying. The dodos, believed to be most closely related to the pigeon family, were found on islands in the Indian Ocean. **2** *Informal.* a person who is hopelessly old-fashioned. **3** *Informal.* a stupid person; dolt.
dead as a dodo, defunct or obsolete, with no chance of revival: *That issue is dead as a dodo.* ⟨< Pg. *doudo* fool⟩

doe [dou] *n.* the female of a deer, antelope, rabbit, hare, and of most other animals whose male is called a buck. See also HIND². ⟨OE dā⟩
☛ *Hom.* DO², DOH, DOUGH.

Doe [dou] *n.* See JOHN DOE.

doe•eyed ['dou,aɪd] *adj.* having eyes as naïve, shy, and soft as those of a doe.

do•er ['duər] *n.* a person who does something, especially with energy and enthusiasm.

does [dʌz] *v.* 3rd pers. sing., present tense, of DO¹.

doe•skin ['dou,skɪn] *n.* **1** the skin of a female deer. **2** a very soft leather made from this skin. **3** a smooth, soft, woollen cloth with a short nap, used for suits, sportswear, etc.

does•n't ['dʌzənt] *v.* contraction of does not.

do•est ['duɪst] *v. Archaic.* 2nd pers. sing., present tense, of DO¹. *Thou doest* means *you* (sing.) *do.*

do•eth ['duɪθ] *v. Archaic.* 3rd pers. sing., present tense, of DO¹. *She doeth* means *she does.*

doff [dɒf] *v.* **1** take off; remove: *to doff one's clothes.* **2** take off or lift (one's hat) in greeting: *He doffed his hat to her.* **3** get rid of; throw aside. ⟨originally a 14c. contraction of *do off* take or put off, remove⟩

dog [dɒg] *n., v.* **dogged, dog•ging.** *—n.* **1** a domesticated, meat-eating mammal (*Canis familiaris*), kept as a pet or used for such purposes as guarding people or property, hunting, or leading the blind. Two breeds of dog are the cocker spaniel and the greyhound. **2** (*adjl.*) designating the family (Canidae) of meat-eating animals that includes the dog as well as wolves, coyotes, jackals, and foxes. **3** a male dog, fox, wolf, etc. **4** any of various animals resembling a dog in some way, such as the prairie dog. **5** *Informal.* a mean, contemptible man. **6** *Informal.* a person or thing that is inferior or unattractive. **7** *Informal.* a man; fellow: *You're a lucky dog.* **8** any of various simple mechanical devices for holding or gripping. **9** a firedog; andiron. **10 Dog,** either of two constellations, **Canis Major** (Great Dog) or **Canis Minor** (Little Dog).
a dog's age, a long while; a very long time: *I haven't spoken to her in a dog's age.*
every dog has his day, everyone gets some attention or luck sometime in his or her life.
go to the dogs, be ruined; deteriorate rapidly.
let sleeping dogs lie, don't stir up unnecessary trouble; let well enough alone.
put on the dog, *Informal.* behave or dress in a showy, affected manner.
teach an old dog new tricks, get an older person to accept new ideas or ways of doing things.
—v. **1** hunt or follow like a dog: *The police dogged the thief's footsteps until they caught him.* **2** worry as if by a dog; beset: *The company was dogged by financial crises for several years.* **3** fasten or secure (a log, etc.) by means of a DOG (def. 8). ⟨OE *docga*⟩
—'dog,like, *adj.*

dog•bane ['dɒg,bein] *n.* **1** any of a genus (*Apocynum*) of mainly tropical plants having clusters of small, white or pink, bell-shaped flowers. Some dogbanes are poisonous. **2** (*adjl.*) designating the family (Apocynaceae) of herbs, shrubs, and trees that includes dogbanes and periwinkles.

dog•ber•ry ['dɒg,bɛri] *n., pl.* **-ries. 1** any of various plants having berrylike fruit, such as the European dogwood, mountain ash, or wild gooseberry. **2** the fruit of any of these plants.

dog•cart ['dɒg,kɑrt] *n.* **1** a small cart pulled by a dog or dogs. **2** a small, open, usually two-wheeled carriage with two seats that are back to back.

dog•catch•er ['dɒg,kætʃər] *n.* a person whose job is to pick up stray dogs and take them to the pound.

dog collar 1 a collar for a dog. **2** *Informal.* a clerical collar. **3** *Informal.* a CHOKER (def. 1 or 2).

dog days in the northern hemisphere, a period of very hot, humid, and uncomfortable weather during July and August. ⟨with reference to the rising of Sirius, the Dog Star⟩

doge [doudʒ]; *Italian,* ['dɔdʒe] *n.* the chief magistrate of Venice or Genoa when they were republics. ⟨< Venetian Ital. < L *dux* leader. Doublet of DUCE, DUKE.⟩

dog–ear ['dɒg ,ir] *n., v.* *—n.* a folded-down corner of a page in a book: *I made a dog-ear to mark the page where I stopped reading.* Also, **dog's-ear.**
—v. fold down the corner of.

dog–eared ['dɒg ,ird] *adj., v.* *—adj.* **1** having a dog-ear: *Find the dog-eared page.* **2** having many pages with dog-ears: *a dog-eared old schoolbook.* **3** looking much used; shabby: *Almost everything in the room is dog-eared.*
—v. pt. and pp. of DOG-EAR.

dog–eat–dog ['dɒg ,it 'dɒg] *adj.* marked by ruthless or vicious competition: *a dog-eat-dog society.*

dog•fight ['dɒg,fəit] *n., v.* **-fought, -fight•ing.** *Informal.* *—n.* **1** a fight between dogs. **2** any rough fight or uproar. **3** a combat between individual fighter planes.
—v. engage in a dogfight.

dog•fish ['dɒg,fɪʃ] *n., pl.* **-fish** or **-fishes. 1** any of several species of small shark found in temperate and warm seas, especially the **spiny dogfish** (*Squalus acanthias*), having a spine in front of each back fin. **2** bowfin.

dog•ged ['dɒgɪd] *adj.* stubborn; persistent; not giving up: *In spite of failures, she kept on with dogged determination.* ⟨< *dog*⟩ **—'dog•ged•ly,** *adv.* **—'dog•ged•ness,** *n.*

dog•ger¹ ['dɒgər] *n.* **1** a person who dogs. **2** *Logging.* a worker who ties dogs or hooks to a log for hauling by cable.

dog•ger² ['dɒgər] *n.* a broad boat with two masts, used by fishers in the North Sea. ⟨ME; origin uncertain⟩

dog•ger•el ['dɒgərəl] *n., adj. —n.* poor poetry; poetry that is trivial and not well written: *Doggerel is often written for a comic effect.*
—adj. having to do with or designating such poetry. ⟨ME; origin uncertain⟩

dog•gie ['dɒgi] *n.* a child's word or a pet name for a dog.

doggie bag a bag supplied to a patron by a restaurant for the purpose of carrying home food untouched from the patron's meal. ⟨from the idea of taking leftover food, especially meat, home to one's pet⟩

dog•gone ['dɒg'gɒn] *adj., adv., v., interj.* **-goned, -gon•ing.** *Slang. —adj.* darned; damned.
—adv. very; much.
—v., interj. darn; damn. ⟨euphemistic alteration of *God damn*⟩

dog•gy ['dɒgi] *adj.* **-gi•er, -gi•est;** *n., pl.* **-gies.** *—adj.* **1** of or like a dog: *There's a doggy smell in the car.* **2** *Informal.* outwardly showy.
—n. See DOGGIE.

dog•house ['dɒg,hʌus] *n.* a small house or shelter for a dog. **in the doghouse,** *Slang.* in disfavour with somebody.

do•gie ['dougi] *n.* in the western parts of Canada and the United States, a motherless calf on the range or in a range herd. Also, **dogy.** ⟨origin uncertain⟩

dog in the manger a person who prevents others from using or enjoying something of no value to himself or herself (from Aesop's fable of the dog that would not let the ox eat the hay in the manger). **—dog-in-the-'man•ger,** *adjl.*

dog•leg ['dɒg,lɛg] *n., v.* **-legged, -leg•ging.** *—n.* **1** a sharp angle or bend like that of a dog's hind leg: *a dogleg in a road.* **2** something having a sharp angle or bend. **3** (*adjl.*) of or shaped like a dogleg.
—v. follow or have a course with a sharp angle: *The street doglegs before it crosses the railway.*

dog•ma ['dɒgmə] *n., pl.* **-mas, -ma•ta** [-mətə]. **1** a belief or body of beliefs authorized by a church. **2** a doctrine or belief, or a system of such beliefs. **3** opinion asserted in a positive manner as if it were authoritative. ⟨< L < Gk. *dogma* opinion < *dokeein* think⟩

dog•mat•ic [dɒg'mætɪk] *adj.* **1** having to do with dogma; doctrinal. **2** asserting opinions as if one were the highest authority; positive; overbearing. **3** asserted in such a way. **—dog'mat•i•cal•ly,** *adv.*

dog•mat•i•cal [dɒg'mætəkəl] *adj.* dogmatic.

dog•ma•tism ['dɒgmə,tɪzəm] *n.* **1** a positive or authoritative assertion of opinion. **2** overly strict insistence upon dogma.

dog•ma•tist ['dɒgmətɪst] *n.* **1** a person who asserts opinions as if they were authoritative. **2** a person who states, explains, or insists upon dogma.

dog•ma•tize ['dɒgmə,taɪz] *v.* **-tized, -tiz•ing. 1** assert opinions in a positive or authoritative manner. **2** express as a dogma.

dog•nap ['dɒg,næp] *v.* **-napped, -nap•ping.** steal (a dog or dogs) for ransom or resale. ⟨< *dog* + kid*nap*⟩

do–good•er ['du ,gʊdər] *n. Informal.* a person who is too eager to correct or set things right.

dog paddle an unsophisticated swimming stroke in which the body remains more or less vertical, the arms pump up and down one at a time, and the legs move as in a running position.

Dog•rib ['dɒgrɪb] *n., pl.* **-rib** or **-ribs;** *adj. —n.* **1** a member of a First Nations people who live in the Northwest Territories. The Dogrib traditionally occupied the region between Great Bear Lake and Great Slave Lake. **2** the Athapascan language of the Dogrib.
—adj. of or having to do with the Dogrib or their language.

dog rose a wild rose (*Rosa canina*) native to Europe, having white or pink flowers.

dog salmon CHUM³.

dog's–ear ['dɒgz ,ir] *n.* DOG-EAR.

dog•sled ['dɒg,slɛd] *n. Cdn.* a sled that is pulled by dogs.

dog–sledge ['dɒg ,slɛdʒ] *n. Cdn.* dogsled.

dog's life a miserable life.

Dog Star 1 Sirius. **2** Procyon.

dog's–tooth violet ['dɒgz ,tuθ] *n.* DOGTOOTH VIOLET.

dog tag *Informal.* **1** an identification disk worn on a neck chain by a member of the armed forces. **2** a metal disk attached to a dog's collar, showing that a licence has been paid, and often giving the name and address of the dog.

dog–team ['dɒg ,tim] *n.* a number of dogs trained as a team for use in pulling a vehicle, especially a sled: *They had travelled the entire distance by dog-team.*

dog–tired ['dɒg 'taɪrd] *adj.* very tired.

dog•tooth ['dɒg,tuθ] *n., pl.* **-teeth. 1** a canine tooth. **2** HOUND'S TOOTH. **3** an early English architectural ornament consisting of a series of pointed projections around a raised centre.

dog•tooth violet any of a genus (*Erythronium*) of plants of the lily family, having yellow, white, or purple lilylike flowers and long, pointed, oval-shaped leaves; especially a species (*E. americanum*) with yellow flowers found in the woods of E North America, also called **adder's-tongue.**

dog–train ['dɒg ,trein] *n. Cdn.* a sled pulled by a team of dogs.

dog•trot ['dɒg,trɒt] *n.* a gentle, easy trot.

dog•watch ['dɒg,wɒtʃ] *n.* a two-hour period of work on a ship. There are two dogwatches a day, one from 4 to 6 p.m. and the other from 6 to 8 p.m.

dog•wood ['dɒg,wʊd] *n.* **1** any of a genus (*Cornus*) of trees, shrubs, and herbs having clusters of small flowers, often surrounded by showy, petal-like bracts, and red, dark blue, or white fruit. The blossom of the **western flowering dogwood** is the floral emblem of British Columbia. **2** the heavy, hard wood of any of these trees or shrubs. **3** (*adjl.*) designating a family (Cornaceae) of shrubs, trees, or herbs found throughout the world. The dogwood family consists of about 100 species, including the flowering dogwoods and the bunchberry.

do•gy ['dougi] *n., pl.* **-gies.** See DOGIE.

doh [dou] See DO².
☛ *Hom.* DOE, DOUGH.

doi•ly ['dɔɪli] *n., pl.* **-lies. 1** a small, decorative piece of linen, lace, or paper used on or under plates, vases, etc. **2** a small dessert napkin. ⟨after a 17c. London dry-goods dealer⟩

do•ings ['duɪŋz] *n.pl.* **1** things done; actions. **2** social activities or behaviour.

doit [dɔɪt] *n.* **1** a former Dutch copper coin worth about ¼ cent. **2** a small sum; trifle; bit: *No one cares a doit what he thinks.* ⟨< Du. *duit*⟩

do–it–your•self ['du ɪt jər'sɛlf] *adj.* designed for use, construction, or assembly by amateurs: *a do-it-yourself construction kit.*

do•jo ['doudʒou] *n.* a gymnasium or studio where karate, judo, etc. are taught. ⟨< Japanese *dōjō*⟩

dol•ce ['doultʃei] *adj. Italian.* sweet; soft.

dol•ce far nien•te ['doultʃei fɑr 'njɛntei]; *Italian,* ['doltʃe far 'njɛnte] *Italian.* pleasant idleness (literally, sweet to do nothing).

dol•ce vi•ta ['doltʃe 'vita] *Italian.* an easy life, often depraved.

dol•drums ['dɒldrəmz] *or* ['doul-] *n.pl.* **1** certain regions of the ocean near the equator where the wind is very light or constantly shifting. Sailing ships caught in the doldrums were often unable to move for days. **2** the calm or windless weather characteristic of these regions. **3** dullness; a gloomy feeling; low spirits: *The whole family was in the doldrums because of the rainy weather.* ⟨probably related to *dull*⟩

dole¹ [doul] *n., v.* **doled, dol•ing.** *—n.* **1** a portion of money, food, etc. given in charity. **2** a small portion. **3** the relief money given by a government to unemployed people: *Many people received the dole during the Depression.* **4** *Archaic.* lot; fate. **go** or **be on the dole,** receive relief money from the government.
—v. **1** deal out in portions to the poor. **2** give in small portions. ⟨OE *dāl* part. Related to DEAL¹.⟩

dole² [doul] *n. Archaic.* sorrow; grief. ⟨ME < OF *doel* < VL *dolus* grief < L *dolere* grieve⟩

dole•ful ['doulfəl] *adj.* sad; mournful; dreary; dismal. **—'dole•ful•ly,** *adv.* **—'dole•ful•ness,** *n.*

dol•er•ite ['dɒlə,rəit] *n.* a dark igneous rock, a variety of basalt. ⟨< F *dolérite* < Gk. *doleros* deceptive (because it looks like diorite)⟩

dole•some ['doulsəm] *adj. Archaic.* doleful.

dol•i•cho•ce•phal•ic [ˌdɒləkousə'fælɪk] *adj.* having a skull whose breadth is less than 80 percent of its length; long-headed. Compare BRACHYCEPHALIC. ⟨< Gk. *dolichos* long + *kephalikos* < *kephale* head⟩

doll [dɒl] *n., v.* —*n.* **1** a child's plaything made to look like a baby, child, or grown person. **2** a pretty child, girl, or woman. **3** *Slang.* a very attractive or likable person.
—*v. Slang.* dress in a stylish or showy way. (*used with* **up**): *They were all dolled up for the party.* ⟨pet name for *Dorothy*⟩
—'doll-ˌlike, *adj.*

dol•lar ['dɒlər] *n.* **1** the basic unit of money in Australia, Bahamas, Barbados, Bermuda, Canada, Cayman Islands, Grenada, Guyana, Hong Kong, Jamaica, Liberia, New Zealand, Singapore, Trinidad and Tobago, United States, West Indies (Leeward Islands, Windward Islands), and Zimbabwe, divided into 100 cents. *Symbol*: $ See table of money in the Appendix. All dollars are not worth the same amount. **2** a note or coin worth one dollar. **3** *Informal.* money: *be paid top dollar.* ⟨earlier *daler* < LG < G *(Joachims)thaler* coin of St. Joachim's valley (in Bohemia)⟩

dollar crisis the situation arising when a country's reserve of (U.S.) dollars becomes dangerously low through failure to balance its imports from the United States by its exports.

dollar diplomacy *Informal.* a rich country's use of economic aid to needy nations in order to advance its own financial interests or to gain allies for its foreign policy.

dollar gap the shortage of dollars (for exchange) in a country suffering from a dollar crisis.

dollar imperialism the extending of control and authority into foreign countries through the buying power of the (U.S.) dollar.

dollar sign or **mark** the symbol $, meaning dollar or dollars: *Five dollars can be written $5.*

doll•house a miniature house for dolls, used as a toy: *Our mother made all the wooden furniture for our dollhouse.* Also, **doll's house.**

dol•lop ['dɒləp] *n., v.* —*n.* a portion or serving, large or small, of something soft or liquid: *a dollop of ice cream.*
—*v.* apply or spread on heavily. ⟨? < Scand.; cf. Norwegian *dolp* lump⟩

doll•y ['dɒli] *n., pl.* **doll•ies;** *v.,* **dol•lied, dol•ly•ing.** —*n.* **1** a child's name for a doll. **2** a small, low frame on wheels, used to move heavy objects: *the fridge was moved on a dolly.* **3** a small truck on which a movie or television camera can be moved about. **4** a small locomotive run on narrow-gauge tracks, used in switching, construction jobs, etc. **5** *Mining.* a device for shaking and washing ore in a vessel. **6** a bar with a flat or cup-shaped piece set at an angle on one end, used to form or hold the head of a rivet. **7** a block placed on the top of a pile while it is being driven.
—*v.* move (a camera) on a dolly: *The cinematographer dollied in for the final scene.* ⟨< *doll*⟩

Dolly Var•den ['vɑrdən] **1** a char (*Salvelinus malma*) native to NW North America and NE Asia, having small red, orange, or yellow spots on the sides and back. **2** formerly, a long flower-printed dress having the skirt tied in loops to show the petticoat. **3** formerly, a woman's wide-brimmed hat trimmed with flowers and turned down at one side. ⟨< *Dolly Varden*, a character in Dickens' *Barnaby Rudge*⟩

dol•ma ['doulmə] *n.* a Turkish or Greek dish of vine leaves, eggplants, peppers, etc. stuffed with minced meat, rice, and spices. ⟨< Turkish something stuffed < *dol* fill + *ma* noun suffix⟩

dol•man ['doulmən] *or* ['dɒlmən] *n., pl.* **-mans. 1** a woman's coat with capelike flaps instead of sleeves. **2** a long Turkish robe, open at the front. **3** a hussar's gold-braided uniform jacket worn like a cape with the sleeves hanging free. ⟨ult. < Turkish *dōlāmān*⟩
☛ *Hom.* DOLMEN.

dolman sleeve a sleeve that tapers from narrow at the wrist to wide at the shoulder, fitting into the whole side of the bodice rather than just an armhole.

dol•men ['doulmən] *or* ['dɒlmən] *n.* a prehistoric monument, generally regarded as a tomb, consisting of a large, flat stone laid across upright stones. ⟨< F < Breton *tol* table + *men* stone⟩
☛ *Hom.* DOLMAN.

dol•o•mite ['dɒləˌməit] *or* ['douləˌməit] *n.* **1** a rock consisting mainly of calcium and magnesium carbonate. Much so-called white marble is really dolomite. **2** calcium and magnesium carbonate. *Formula*: $CaMg(CO_3)_2$ ⟨after D.G. de *Dolomieu* (1750-1801), a French geologist⟩

dol•o•mit•ic [ˌdɒlə'mɪtɪk] *adj.* containing or consisting of dolomite.

do•lor ['doulər] See DOLOUR.

do•lo•ro•so [ˌdoulə'rousou] *adj. Music.* plaintive, soft, sorrowful. ⟨< Ital.⟩

dol•or•ous ['dɒlərəs] *or* ['doulərəs] *adj.* **1** mournful; sorrowful. **2** grievous; painful. **—'dol•or•ous•ly,** *adv.*
—dol'or•ous•ness, *n.*

do•lour or **do•lor** ['doulər] *n. Poetic.* sorrow; grief. ⟨ME < OF < L *dolour*⟩

dol•phin ['dɒlfən] *n.* **1** any of various small, highly intelligent, toothed whales (family Delphinidae) having a snout shaped like a beak. Dolphins are often trained to perform in aquariums. **2** (*adjl.*) designating the family that includes the dolphins and the killer whale. **3** porpoise. **4** either of two large, edible, saltwater fishes (genus *Coryphaena*) remarkable for their changes of colour when taken from the water. **5** a buoy or piling used to mark a channel for ships. ⟨ME < OF *daulphin* < L < Gk. *delphis*⟩

dolphin striker on a ship, a small spar under the bowsprit that helps support the jib boom.

dolt [doult] *n.* a dull, stupid person. ⟨apparently a var. of obs. *dold*, pp. of ME **dole(n)* to dull, OE *dol* dull⟩

dolt•ish ['doultɪʃ] *adj.* dull and stupid. **—'dolt•ish•ly,** *adv.*
—'dolt•ish•ness, *n.*

-dom *noun-forming suffix.* **1** the position, rank, or realm of a —: *kingdom = realm of a king.* **2** the condition of being —: *martyrdom = condition of being a martyr.* **3** all those who are —: *fandom = all those who are fans.* ⟨OE *-dōm* state, condition < *dōm.* See DOOM.⟩

dom. **1** domestic. **2** dominion.

Dom. **1** Dominion. **2** Dominican.

do•main [də'mein] *n.* **1** the territory under the control of one ruler or government. **2** the land owned by one person; an estate. **3** a field of thought, action, etc.: *the domain of science, the domain of politics.* **4** *Mathematics.* the set of values taken on by the independent variable of a function. ⟨< F *domaine* < OF < L *dominium* < *dominus*, lord, master < *domus* house. Doublet of DEMESNE.⟩

dome [doum] *n., v.* **domed, dom•ing.** —*n.* **1** *Architecture.* a rounded roof or ceiling on a circular or many-sided base. **2** anything that is or appears high and rounded: *the dome of the sky, the dome of a hill.* **3** any domed building, especially a sports stadium. **4** *Crystallography.* a prism whose faces meet in a horizontal edge, like the roof of a house. **5** *Geology.* an anticlinal formation, circular or elliptical in structure, characteristic of oil and salt deposits, extrusions of volcanic lava, etc. **6** *Slang.* the head.
—*v.* **1** cover with a dome. **2** form into the shape of a dome. **3** rise or swell like a dome. ⟨< F *dôme* < Provençal *doma* < LL *doma* roof, house < Gk.⟩ **—'dome,like,** *adj.*

dome car a railway car having a glass-enclosed upper level that resembles a dome and affords a wide view.

dome fastener *Cdn.* a metal or plastic fastener consisting of two parts, one with a small, rounded projection in the centre that snaps into a socket in the centre of the other.

Domesday Book ['dumzˌdei] a record of the value and ownership of the lands in England, made in 1086 at the order of William the Conqueror.

do•mes•tic [də'mɛstɪk] *adj., n.* —*adj.* **1** of the home, household, or family affairs: *domestic cares, a domestic scene.* **2** fond of home and family life. **3** of animals, not wild; tame: *Cats, dogs, cows, horses, sheep, and pigs are domestic animals.* **4** of one's own country; not foreign: *domestic news, domestic affairs.* **5** made in one's own country; native: *domestic cheese.*
—*n.* a servant in a household: *Cooks, butlers, and maids are domestics.* ⟨< L *domesticus* < *domus* house⟩
—do'mes•ti•cal•ly, *adv.*

do•mes•ti•cate [də'mɛstəˌkeit] *v.* **-cat•ed, -cat•ing. 1** change (animals or plants) from a wild to a tame or cultivated state; tame. **2** make fond of home and family life. **3** bring (a foreign word, custom, etc.) into accepted use in a region or country; adopt. **4** transfer (foreign organisms) to another area, region, etc.; naturalize.

do•mes•ti•ca•tion [dəˌmɛstə'keiʃən] *n.* domesticating or being domesticated.

do•mes•tic•i•ty [ˌdoumə'stɪsəti] *n., pl.* **-ties. 1** home and family life. **2** fondness for home and family life. **3 domesticities,** *pl.* domestic affairs.

domestic science HOME ECONOMICS.

dom•i•cile ['dɒmə,saɪl] *or* ['dɒməsəl] *n., v.* **-ciled, -cil•ing.**
—n. **1** a dwelling place; home; residence. **2** *Law.* a place of permanent residence. One may have several residences, but only one legal domicile at a time.
—v. settle in a domicile. ⟨ME < MF < L *domicilium* < *domus* house⟩

dom•i•cil•i•ar•y [,dɒmə'sɪli,ɛri] *adj.* having to do with a domicile.

dom•i•nance ['dɒmənəns] *n.* a being dominant; rule; control. Also, **dominancy.**

dom•i•nant ['dɒmənənt] *adj., n. —adj.* **1** controlling, ruling, or governing; strongest and most influential: *The dominant influence in her life has been her grandmother.* **2** rising high above its surroundings; towering: *The window looked out on the dominant hills to the west.* **3** *Music.* based on or having to do with the fifth note in a standard major or minor scale. **4** *Genetics.* of or designating a gene in one of a pair of chromosomes that dominates over the corresponding gene in the other chromosome and is therefore expressed as a trait in an organism; the gene of an allelic pair that is phenotypically expressed in the heterozygote. If one of such a pair of genes inherited by a person is for brown eyes and the other is for blue, the person will have brown eyes because that gene is dominant. Compare RECESSIVE.
—n. **1** *Music.* the fifth tone in an eight-tone scale. G is the dominant in the key of C. **2** *Genetics.* dominant character. **3** *Ecology.* the most extensive and characteristic species in a plant or animal community, determining the type and abundance of other species in the community. ⟨< F < L *dominans, -antis,* ppr. of *dominari.* See DOMINATE.⟩ **—'dom•i•nant•ly,** *adv.*

☛ *Syn. adj.* **1. Dominant,** PREDOMINANT, PARAMOUNT = uppermost. **Dominant** = ruling, and therefore having the most influence, power, or authority: *Efficiency is the dominant idea in many businesses.* **Predominant** = before others in influence, power, authority, and therefore principal or superior: *Love of liberty is predominant in struggles for independence.* **Paramount** = first in importance, authority, or rank, and therefore supreme: *It is of paramount importance that we finish the work on time.*

dominant inheritance *Genetics.* inheritance of a trait determined by a dominant gene. In **autosomal dominant inheritance,** the gene concerned is on an autosome, and affected individuals are heterozygous. Each offspring of an affected individual has a 50 percent chance of inheriting the gene. In **X-linked dominant inheritance,** affected males transmit the trait to none of their sons and all of their daughters, whereas affected females transmit to half their offspring of either sex.

dom•i•nate ['dɒmə,neit] *v.* **-nat•ed, -nat•ing. 1** control or rule by strength, numbers, or power: *A person of strong will often dominates others. Dandelions will dominate over lawn grass if they are not kept out.* **2** rise high above; tower over: *The mountain dominates the harbour.* **3** have the foremost place or the greatest influence in: *The new hockey team already dominates the league. Their products dominate the market.* ⟨< L *dominari* < *dominus* lord, master⟩ **—'dom•i,na•tor,** *n.* **—'dom•i•na•tive,** *adj.*

dom•i•na•tion [,dɒmə'neiʃən] *n.* a dominating or being dominated; control; rule: *The country was under the domination of a tyrant for many years.*

dom•i•neer [,dɒmə'nir] *v.* rule (over) at one's own will; tyrannize; be overbearing in asserting one's authority. ⟨< Du. *domineren* < F < L *dominari.* See DOMINATE.⟩

dom•i•neer•ing [,dɒmə'nirɪŋ] *adj., v. —adj.* inclined to domineer; overbearing: *a domineering attitude, a domineering person.*
—v. ppr. of DOMINEER. **—,dom•i'neer•ing•ly,** *adv.*

Do•mi•ni•ca [,dɒmə'nikə] *or* [də'mɪnɪkə] an island country in the Caribbean Sea.

Do•min•i•can [də'mɪnəkən] *adj., n. —adj.* **1** of Saint Dominic or the religious orders founded by him. **2** of or having to do with the Dominican Republic.
—n. **1** a friar or nun belonging to the Dominican order. **2** a native or inhabitant of the Dominican Republic.

Dominican Republic a country in the Caribbean. See HAITI for map.

dom•i•nie ['dɒməni] *for 1;* ['dɒməni] *or* ['douməni] *for 2.*
n. **1** *Esp. Scottish.* schoolmaster. **2** *Informal.* member of the clergy. ⟨< L *domine* (vocative) lord, master⟩

do•min•ion [də'mɪnjən] *n.* **1** supreme authority; rule; control. **2** a territory or country under the control of one ruler or government: *The old king divided his dominion between his sons.* **3 Dominion, a** a name formerly used for certain self-governing countries in the British Commonwealth of Nations: *the Dominion of Canada, the Dominion of New Zealand.* **b** (*adjl.*) formerly, in Canada, under the control or authority of the federal government: *the Dominion Fire Commissioner.* **c** (*adjl.*) formerly, in Canada, relating to the country as a whole; national in scope: *the Dominion Drama Festival.* ⟨< obs. F < Med.L *dominio, -onis,* alteration of L *dominium* ownership⟩

Dominion Day old name for a national holiday commemorating the establishment of the Dominion of Canada on July 1, 1867; now called **Canada Day.**

dom•i•no ['dɒmə,nou] *n., pl.* **-noes** or **-nos. 1 dominoes,** a game played with flat, usually black, oblong pieces of wood, bone, etc. that are either blank or marked with dots on one side (*used with a singular verb*). **2** one of the pieces used in playing this game. **3** a long, loose, hooded cloak and a mask for the upper part of the face, worn as a disguise, especially at masquerades. **4** a mask, usually black, for the upper part of the face. **5** a person wearing a domino. ⟨< F < L *domino* (dative of *dominus* master), short for some such phrase, jestingly used, as *benedicamus Domino* let us praise the Lord⟩

domino theory 1 the theory that the fall of one nation will cause adjoining nations to fall, as do dominoes standing in a row when one is toppled. **2** this theory as applied to any similar chain of events.

dom•pe•ri•done [dɒm'pɛrɪ,doun] *n.* a drug used to treat certain gastric disorders.

don[1] [dɒn]; *Spanish,* [don] *n.* **1 Don,** a Spanish title meaning Mr. or Sir: *Don Felipe.* **2** a Spanish gentleman; Spaniard. **3** in the United Kingdom, a university teacher, especially a head, fellow, or tutor of a college of Oxford or Cambridge. **4** in some Canadian universities and colleges, an official in charge of a student residence. **5** *Archaic.* a person of rank or distinction. **6** an important Mafia figure. ⟨< Sp. < L *dominus* lord, master⟩
☛ *Hom.* DAWN.

don[2] [dɒn] *v.* **donned, don•ning.** put on. ⟨contraction of *do on*⟩
☛ *Hom.* DAWN.

do•nate ['douneit] *or* [dou'neit] *v.* **-nat•ed, -nat•ing.** give; contribute, especially to an institution or public service: *My mother donates blood regularly. He donated fifty dollars to the church.* ⟨< L *donare* < *donum* gift⟩ **—do'nat•or,** *n.*

do•na•tion [dou'neiʃən] *n.* **1** the act of giving or contributing. **2** a gift; contribution.

done [dʌn] *adj., v. —adj.* **1** completed; finished; ended; through. **2** *Informal.* worn out; exhausted. **3** cooked; cooked enough: *Are the potatoes done?* **4** proper; fitting; conforming to custom or convention: *This is the done thing. Eating peas with a knife is not done.*
done for, *Informal.* finished; destined to die; ruined.
done with, *Informal.* finished; completed: *I'd like to get this done with.*
—v. pp. of DO[1].
☛ *Hom.* DUN.

do•nee [dou'ni] *n.* a person who has been given something as a gift.

dong [dɒŋ] *n., pl.* **dong. 1** the basic unit of money in Vietnam, divided into 10 hao. See table of money in the Appendix. **2** a note worth one dong.

don•jon ['dʌndʒən] *or* ['dɒndʒən] *n.* the large, strongly fortified inner tower of a castle; keep. ⟨var. of *dungeon*⟩
☛ *Hom.* DUNGEON ['dʌndʒən].

Don Juan [,dɒn 'wɒn], [,dɒn 'xwɒn], *or* [,dɒn 'dʒuən] **1** a legendary Spanish nobleman who led a dissolute and immoral life. **2** any person leading an immoral life; libertine.
☛ *Pronun.* **Don Juan.** This name is usually pronounced [dɒn 'wɒn] or [dɒn 'xwɒn] in imitation of the Spanish pronunciation [don 'xwan], but Byron's poem *Don Juan* and its hero are always pronounced [,dɒn 'dʒuən].

don•key ['dɒŋki] *or* ['dʌŋki] *n., pl.* **-keys. 1** a domestic animal descended from the wild ass of Africa (*Equus asinus*), resembling a horse but smaller and having longer ears, a shorter neck and mane, and smaller hooves. **2** a stubborn person. **3** a silly or stupid person. **4** DONKEY ENGINE. ⟨? a nickname form of *Duncan*⟩

donkey engine a small steam engine. Donkey engines are used on ships for hoisting anchor, etc. **—donkey engineer.**

donkey's years *Informal.* a very long time: *We haven't had a family reunion in donkey's years.*

don•key–work ['dɒŋki ,wɜrk] *n.* hard work, usually of a monotonous or humble nature.

don•na ['dɒnə]; *Italian,* ['donna] *n.* **1** lady. **2 Donna,** an Italian title meaning Lady or Madam. ⟨< Ital. < L *domina* mistress⟩

don•née [də'nei]; *French,* [də'ne] *n.* the idea used as point of departure for the plot of a literary work. ⟨< F⟩

don•nish ['dɒnɪʃ] *adj.* of or like a university don; pedantic; formal. **—'don•nish•ly,** *adv.* **—'don•nish•ness,** *n.*

Don•ny•brook ['dɒni,brʊk] *n. Informal.* a riot; a brawl: *The players engaged in a terrific Donnybrook after the hockey game.* Also, **donnybrook.** ⟨< *Donnybrook,* a town in Ireland, site of an annual fair. The 1855 fair was suppressed because of wild brawls.⟩

do•nor ['dounər] *n.* **1** a person who contributes; giver. **2** *Medicine.* a person who donates blood for transfusion, or an organ or tissue for transplantation: *The Canadian Red Cross Society welcomes blood donors.* **3** *Physics.* in a covalent bond, the atom which provides the shared pair of electrons. ⟨ME < AF *donour* < L *donator* < *donare.* See DONATE.⟩

do–noth•ing ['du ,nʌθɪŋ] *n., adj.—n.* **1** one who does nothing; idler. **2** a person unwilling to take action because it may upset the existing order.
—adj. lazy, lacking initiative, or reluctant to upset existing conditions by acting.

Don Qui•xo•te [,dɒn ki'houti] *or, occasionally,* [,dɒn 'kwɪksət]; *Spanish,* [don ki'xote] **1** the hero of a story by Cervantes that satirizes chivalric romances, published in two parts in 1605 and 1615. Don Quixote is chivalrous and idealistic but ridiculously impractical. **2** any person of high but impractical ideas.

don't [dount] contraction of do not.
☛ *Usage.* **Don't** is universally used in conversation and often in informal writing when *do not* would seem too emphatic or when rhythm seems more comfortable with the shorter form. The use of **don't** in place of *does not* with a third person singular subject is not standard English.

doo•dad ['dudaed] *n.* **1** *Informal.* a fancy, trifling ornament. **2** doohickey.

doo•dle ['dudəl] *v.* **-dled, -dling;** *n. —v.* make drawings or marks of any kind while thinking of something else; draw absent-mindedly: *He doodled while he was talking on the telephone.*
—n. a drawing or mark made absent-mindedly. ⟨< G *dudeln* to play the bagpipe < Polish *dudlic* < *dudy* a bagpipe < Turkish *duduk* a flute⟩

doo•dle•bug ['dudəl,bʌg] *n.* **1** *Informal.* a small car or other vehicle. **2** any of various devices with which it is claimed mineral and oil deposits can be located. **3** *Informal.* BUZZ BOMB. **4** *U.S.* **a** the larva of the ant lion. **b** any of various similar larvae.

doo•hick•ey ['du,hɪki] *n. Informal.* **1** any small mechanical device; gadget. **2** any small device, whose name has been temporarily forgotten: *Pass that doohickey for opening windows.* ⟨a humorous coinage based on *do*⟩

doom [dum] *n., v. —n.* **1** fate. **2** an unhappy or terrible fate; ruin; death: *The soldiers marched to their doom in battle.* **3** judgment; sentence: *The judge pronounced the guilty man's doom.* **4** the end of the world; God's final judgment of people.
—v. **1** make a bad or undesirable outcome certain: *The weather doomed our hopes for a picnic.* **2** destine to an unhappy or terrible fate: *the doomed men.* **3** condemn (to punishment): *The prisoner was doomed to death.* ⟨OE *dōm* law, judgment⟩
☛ *Syn. n.* **1.** See note at FATE.

doom•say•er ['dum,seiər] *n.* one who habitually forecasts disastrous happenings.

dooms•day ['dumz,dei] *n.* **1** the end of the world; day of God's final judgment of people. **2** any day of disaster or of settlement of accounts.

Doomsday Book DOMESDAY BOOK.

door [dɔr] *n.* **1** a movable structure of wood, metal, glass, etc. intended for closing up an entrance to a building or room: *Doors usually swing or slide open and shut.* **2** a similar structure designed to close off an opening giving access to a cupboard, closet, etc.: *a bookcase with sliding glass doors.* **3** an opening where a door is; doorway: *I saw him just as he came through the door.* **4** the room or building to which a particular door belongs: *Her house is the third door from the corner.* **5** any means by which to go in or out; a way to get something; access: *an open door to the Yukon.*
close, shut, or **slam the door,** reject or exclude; make something impossible: *The car accident slammed the door on our hopes of a summer trip.*
darken the door of, visit.
lay (something) **at the door of** (someone), blame someone for something.
out of doors, outside; not in a house or other building.
show (someone) **the door,** ask or order a person to leave. ⟨OE *duru*⟩ **—'door,like,** *adj.*
☛ *Hom.* DOR.

door•bell ['dɔr,bɛl] *n.* a bell inside the house to be rung by pressing a button or pulling a handle on the outside of a door as a signal that someone has arrived.

do–or–die ['du ər 'daɪ] *adj.* showing evidence of an unstoppable determination, or a great need, to succeed; urgent: *a do-or-die endeavour.*

door•jamb ['dɔr,dʒæm] *n.* the upright piece forming the side of a doorway.

door•keeper ['dɔr,kipər] *n.* **1** a person who guards a door or entrance. **2** doorman.

door•knob ['dɔr,nɒb] *n.* a knob on a door that releases the latch of the door when turned.

door•man ['dɔrmən] *or* [-,mæn] *n., pl.* **-men. 1** a person whose work is opening the door of a hotel, store, apartment building, etc. for people going in or out. **2** a person who guards a door.

door•mat ['dɔr,mæt] *n.* **1** a mat for wiping dirt off shoes, usually placed by an outside door of a house. **2** *Informal.* a person who is easily imposed upon. **3** knotgrass.

door•nail ['dɔr,neil] *n.* a nail with a large head.
dead as a doornail, entirely dead.

door•plate ['dɔr,pleit] *n.* a metal plate on a door with a name, number, etc. on it.

door•post ['dɔr,poust] *n.* doorjamb.

door prize a prize whose winner is drawn at random from those present at a public function.

door•sill ['dɔr,sɪl] *n.* threshold.

door•step ['dɔr,stɛp] *n.* a step leading from an outside door to the ground.

door•stop ['dɔr,stɒp] *n.* a device to hold a door open or to prevent it from opening too far.

door–to–door ['dɔr tə 'dɔr] *adj., adv. —adj.* **1** making a call, often uninvited, at each residential or business address in turn in a particular area or district: *a door-to-door salesperson, a door-to-door canvasser.* **2** made or done by going from one address to the next: *door-to-door selling.* **3** going from the original starting point to the final destination: *The courier service offers door-to-door delivery.*
—adv. **1** at or to each address in turn: *She went door-to-door, campaigning for the election.* **2** from starting point to destination: *The taxi cost us sixteen dollars door-to-door.*

door•way ['dɔr,wei] *n.* **1** an entrance to be closed by a door. **2** a way to get something; access.

door•yard ['dɔr,jɑrd] *n.* a yard near the door of a house; yard around a house.

doo•zer ['duzər] *n. Slang.* doozy.

doo•zy ['duzi] *n. Slang.* an outstanding person or thing: *Their new camper is a doozy.* ⟨originally a variant of *daisy,* later associated with *Duesenberg* (automobile) as a standard of excellence⟩

do•pa ['doupə] *n.* an amino acid which changes into dopamine through the action of an enzyme. One of its isomers, L-Dopa, is used as a drug to treat patients with Parkinson's disease. *Formula:* $C_9H_{11}NO_4$

do•pa•mine ['doupə,min] *n.* **1** a drug used to treat shock resulting from certain heart conditions. **2** a neurotransmitter in the brain. ⟨*d*(ihydr)*o*(xy)*p*(henyl) + *amine*⟩

dop•ant ['doupənt] *n.* a substance added to something to effect a desired change. ⟨< *dope*⟩

dope [doup] *n., v.* **doped, dop•ing.** *—n.* **1** *Slang.* a harmful narcotic drug, such as heroin or opium. **2** oil, grease, etc. used to make machinery run smoothly. **3** a varnish formerly put on the cloth parts of an airplane to make them stronger, waterproof, and airtight. **4** *Slang.* facts; information: *What's the latest dope on the scandal?* **5** *Slang.* a forecast; prediction. **6** *Slang.* a very stupid person. **7** *Slang.* a stimulating drug illegally given to a horse before a race.
—v. **1** *Slang.* apply or give an anesthetic to: *The doctor doped her before setting her broken leg.* **2** use dope. **3** adulterate (something) with another substance in order to change it in some way.
dope out, *Slang.* figure out; work out. ⟨< Du. *doop* dipping sauce < *doopen* dip⟩ **—'dop•er,** *n.*

dope fiend *Slang.* a drug addict.

dope–sheet ['doup ˌʃit] *n.* a sheet with the program of a horse racing event, complete with names of horses and jockeys, and records of previous races.

dope•ster ['doupstər] *n. Slang.* a person who claims to be in the know, especially in sports, politics, etc., and makes forecasts about future events.

dope•y or **dop•y** ['doupi] *adj. Slang.* **1** drugged; drowsy; as if affected by drugs. **2** very stupid.

dop•pel•gäng•er ['dʌpəlˌgɛŋər]; *German,* ['dɔpəlgɛŋə] *n.* a ghostly double of a living person. ⟨< G < *doppel* double + *Gänger* goer⟩

dop•pler or **Dop•pler** ['dɒplər] *adj.* of or having to do with the Doppler effect.

Doppler effect *Physics.* the apparent shift in the frequency of sound, light, and other waves caused by relative movement between the source and the observer. ⟨< Christian *Doppler* (1803-1853), an Austrian physicist⟩

Doppler shift DOPPLER EFFECT.

dor [dɔr] *n.* a kind of large beetle. ⟨OE *dora*⟩
☛ *Hom.* DOOR.

do•ra•do [də'rɑdou] *n.* either one of two DOLPHINS (def. 4) valued as game fish. ⟨Sp., gilded⟩

Do•ra•do [dɔ'rɑdou] *or* [də'rɑdou] *n. Astronomy.* a southern constellation between Pictor and Reticulum. The constellation Dorado includes part of the Magellanic Cloud.

do•ré ['dɔrei] *or* ['dɔri] *for def. 1;* [dɔ'rei] *for def. 2. n.* **1** *Cdn.* WALLEYE (def. 7). **2** gilded. ⟨< Cdn.F *doré* golden⟩

Do•ri•an ['dɔriən] *adj., n. —adj.* of or having to do with Doris, an ancient region of Greece, or its inhabitants; Doric.
—n. a native or inhabitant of Doris.

Dorian mode *Music.* an ascending or descending scale from D to D played only on the white keys of a keyboard instrument.

Dor•ic ['dɔrɪk] *adj., n. —adj.* **1** *Architecture.* of, having to do with, or designating the earliest of the three orders of ancient Greek architecture. The characteristic Doric column is eight times the diameter in height, and has a tapering shaft with shallow flutes and a plain, rounded capital. The Parthenon in Athens, dedicated to the goddess Athena, is a Doric temple. See ORDER for picture. **2** of or having to do with Doris, a small, region in the central part of ancient Greece, its people, or their language.
—n. a dialect of ancient Greek spoken especially in the Peloponnesus.

Dor•king ['dɔrkɪŋ] *n.* a breed of chicken having a long, heavy body and five toes on each foot. ⟨after *Dorking,* a town in Surrey, England⟩

dorm [dɔrm] *n. Informal.* dormitory.

dor•man•cy ['dɔrmənsi] *n.* a dormant condition.

dor•mant ['dɔrmənt] *adj.* **1** sleeping or apparently sleeping: *Bears are dormant during the winter.* **2** in a state of rest or inactivity: *a dormant volcano. Plant bulbs are dormant during the cold of winter.* **3** *Heraldry.* lying with the head resting on the paws (*used after the noun*): *a lion dormant.* ⟨ME < OF *dormant,* ppr. of *dormir* sleep < L *dormire*⟩
☛ *Syn.* **1, 2.** See note at INACTIVE.

Dormers on a 19th-century mansion designed by Sir Charles Barry, in Guelph, Ontario

dor•mer ['dɔrmər] *n.* **1** a small, gablelike structure projecting from a sloping roof, having a window set vertically into the outer end. **2** the window itself. ⟨originally, a sleeping room; < OF *dormeor* < L *dormitorium.* Doublet of DORMITORY.⟩

dormer window dormer.

dor•mi•to•ry ['dɔrməˌtɔri] *n., pl.* **-ries. 1** a sleeping room containing a number of beds. **2** a building with sleeping and living accommodation for many people; a residence, as for students at a university. **3** (*adjl.*) of or designating a community serving as a residential satellite to a nearby city. ⟨< L *dormitorium* < *dormire* sleep. Doublet of DORMER.⟩

dor•mouse ['dɔrˌmʌus] *n., pl.* **-mice.** any of numerous small, mouselike rodents of the Old World, especially *Muscardinus avellanarius,* having fine, soft fur, large black eyes, and a very long, furry tail. ⟨apparently < E dial. *dorm* sleep, doze (< F *dormir* < L *dormire*) + mouse⟩

dor•my or **dor•mie** ['dɔrmi] *adj. Golf.* of a player, beating an opponent by as many holes as remain to be played.

dor•sal ['dɔrsəl] *adj.* **1** *Zoology.* of, on, or near the back: *a dorsal fin.* See SPINAL COLUMN for picture. **2** *Botany.* of the side of a leaf, branch, etc. away from the axis. **3** *Phonetics.* of a consonant or vowel, articulated with the back of the tongue. ⟨< LL *dorsalis* < L *dorsum* back⟩ **—'dor•sal•ly,** *adv.*

Dor•set ['dɔrsɪt] *n.* **1** an Inuit culture of northeastern Canada and N Greenland, lasting from approximately 900 B.C. to A.D. 1000, characterized by skill in carving and by the hunting of seal and caribou. **2** a medium-sized breed of sheep, formerly with both male and female having horns, but now polled. ⟨< Cape *Dorset,* Baffin Island⟩

dor•so•ve•lar [ˌdɔrsou'vilər] *adj., n. Phonetics —adj.* pronounced with the back of the tongue touching the soft palate. *—n.* a dorsovelar consonant, such as [k] or [g]. ⟨< *dorsal* + *velar*⟩

do•ry¹ ['dɔri] *n., pl.* **-ries.** a rowboat with a flat bottom and high sides, often used by ocean fishers. ⟨< Central Am.Ind. *dóri* dugout⟩

do•ry² ['dɔri] *n., pl.* **-ries.** *Cdn.* **1** John Dory, an edible sea fish. **2** WALLEYE (def. 7); doré. ⟨< doré⟩

DOS DISK OPERATING SYSTEM.

dos–à–dos, do–si–do, or **do–se–do** ['dou zə 'dou] *or* ['dou si 'dou] *n.* a figure in many folk dances in which two partners start out facing, revolve round each other back to back, and return to their initial positions.

dos•age ['dousɪdʒ] *n.* **1** the size and frequency of a dose. **2** the giving of medicine in doses. **3** the intensity or length of application of X-rays in certain methods of therapy. **4** the measured addition of ingredients to a substance to give it a certain strength or flavour.

dosage compensation *Genetics.* the compensation in mammalian cells for the presence of two X chromosomes in females and only one in males, by inactivation of one X chromosome in the female.

dose [dous] *n., v.* **dosed, dos•ing.** *—n.* **1** the amount of a medicine to be taken at one time. **2** a portion; the amount of anything given at one time as a remedy, treatment, etc.: *a dose of flattery.* **3** a certain amount of brandy, sugar, etc. added to wine to give it strength or flavour. **4** anything unpleasant to take or endure: *a dose of hard work.*
—v. **1** give medicine to in doses; treat with medicine: *The doctor dosed the boy with quinine.* **2** add syrup, etc. to (wine) during bottling to increase flavour or strength. ⟨< F < LL < Gk. *dosis* a giving < *didonai* give⟩ **—'dos•er,** *n.*

do•sim•e•ter [dou'sɪmətər] *n.* a device for measuring the dosage or amount of radiation received over a given period of time. ⟨< Gk. *dosis* dose + E *-meter*⟩

doss [dɒs] *n., v. —n. Slang.* **1** a bed in a cheap lodging house. **2** DOSS HOUSE. **3** sleep.
—v. bed down in any convenient spot; sleep. ⟨probably < F *dos* the back < VL *dossum* < L *dorsum*⟩

dos•sal ['dɒsəl] *n.* a cloth hung behind an altar. ⟨< Med.L *dossale* < L *dorsalis* dorsal⟩

doss house *Slang.* a cheap lodging house.

dos•si•er ['dɒsiei] *or* ['dɒsiər] *n.* a collection of papers or documents about some subject or person. ⟨< F⟩

dost [dʌst] *v. Archaic.* the form of DOEST used as an auxiliary: *Dost thou know?*
☛ *Hom.* DUST.

dot¹ [dɒt] *n., v.* **dot•ted, dot•ting.** *—n.* **1** a tiny, round mark; a very small spot; point. **2** a small, round spot: *a blue necktie with white dots.* **3** *Music.* **a** a tiny, round mark after a note or rest that makes it half again as long. **b** a similar mark placed over or under a note to indicate that it is to be played or sung staccato. **4** a short sound used in sending messages by telegraph or radio.
on the dot, *Informal.* at exactly the right time; at the specified time.
on the dot of, *Informal.* at exactly (a given hour): *She arrived on the dot of six.*
—v. **1** mark with a dot or dots: *He never dots his i's when he writes.*

2 be here and there in; give variety to: *Trees and bushes dotted the broad lawn.*
dot (one's) **i's and cross** (one's) **t's** or **dot the i's and cross the t's,** be very accurate or meticulous. ⟨< OE *dott* head of a boil⟩

dot² [dɒt] *n.* dowry. ⟨< F < L *dos, dotis*⟩

DOT or **D.O.T.** Department of Transport.

dot•age ['doutɪdʒ] *n.* an enfeebled and childish mental condition that sometimes accompanies old age. ⟨< *dote*⟩

do•tard ['doutərd] *n.* a person who is mentally enfeebled and childish because of old age; one in his or her dotage. ⟨< *dote*⟩

dote [dout] *v.* **dot•ed, dot•ing. 1** be feeble-minded and childish because of old age. **2** be foolishly fond of; be too fond (*used with* **on** or **upon**): *He dotes on his daughter.* ⟨ME *doten*⟩ **—'dot•er,** *n.*

doth [dʌθ] *v. Archaic.* the form of DOETH used as an auxiliary.

dot•ing ['doutɪŋ] *adj., v.—adj.* **1** foolishly fond; too fond. **2** in his or her dotage.
—v. ppr. of DOTE. **—'dot•ing•ly,** *adv.*

dot matrix printer a computer printer which prints letters made up of dots. This printing is not as clear as letter-quality printing.

dot•ted ['dɒtɪd] *adj., v.—adj.* **1** marked with or as with a dot or dots. **2** formed of dots: *Sign on the dotted line.* **3** *Music.* of a note or rest, followed by a dot, thus making it half again as long: *a dotted eighth.*
—v. pt. and pp. of DOT.

dotted swiss SWISS MUSLIN.

dot•ter•el ['dɒtərəl] *n.* **1** a rare Eurasian plover (*Eudromias morinellus*) having a mottled brown back and reddish brown belly. **2** any of various other birds of the same family (Charadriidae, especially genus *Charadrius*). **3** *Brit. Dialect.* a stupid person who is easily fooled or cheated. ⟨< *dote*⟩

dot•tle ['dɒtəl] *n.* the plug of tobacco left in a pipe after smoking. ⟨ME *dottel* a plug, ? dim. of *dot* small piece⟩

dot•ty ['dɒti] *adj.* **-ti•er, -ti•est. 1** *Informal.* feeble-minded or mentally unbalanced. **2** *Informal.* unsteady; shaky; feeble. **3** *Informal.* very enthusiastic. **4** full of dots. **—'dot•ti•ness,** *n.*

Dou•ay Bible ['duei] an English translation of the Latin Vulgate Bible, made by a group of Roman Catholic scholars. The New Testament was published at Reims in 1582, the Old Testament at Douai in 1609-1610. The Douay Bible is the version traditionally used by English-speaking Roman Catholics. ⟨< *Douai,* a town in N France⟩

Douay Version DOUAY BIBLE. *Abbrev.:* D.V.

dou•ble ['dʌbəl] *adj., adv., n., v.* **-bled, -bling.** *—adj.* **1** twice as much, as many, as large, as strong, etc.: *double pay, a double letter.* **2** for two: *a double bed.* **3** made of two similar parts; in a pair: *double doors.* **4** made of two unlike parts; combining two in one. *Bear* has a double meaning: *carry* and *a certain animal.* **5** insincere; deceitful; false: *a double tongue.* **6** *Botany.* having more than one set of petals: *Some roses are double, others are single.* **7** *Music.* **a** having two beats or a multiple of two beats to the measure. **b** (of an instrument) producing a tone an octave lower than the ordinary instrument: *a double trumpet.*
—adv. **1** twice. **2** two (of everything) instead of one: *The blow made him see double.* **3** as a pair or by pairs: *They rode double on the motorcycle.*
—n. **1** a number or amount that is twice as much. **2** a person or thing just like another: *I saw your double in the streetcar yesterday.* **3** a fold; bend. **4** a sharp backward bend or turn; shift. **5** *Baseball.* a hit by which the batter gets to second base. **6** *Bridge.* the act of doubling a bid. **7 doubles,** *pl.* a game with two players on each side. **8** an understudy. **9** in a film or play, a substitute: *She always uses a double to do the stunts for her in her films.*
on the double, a quickly; at a run. **b** in double time.
—v. **1** make twice as much or twice as many. **2** become twice as much or as many. **3** be used in place of (another); be the double of. **4** take another's place: *Tom doubled for me when I couldn't get to the meeting.* **5** serve two purposes; play (two parts): *The maid doubled as cook. In a production of* Hamlet, *it is traditional for an actor to double the parts of the Ghost and the First Gravedigger.* **6** fold; bend: *He doubled his fists in anger.* **7** turn suddenly and sharply; turn back on one's own trail: *The fox doubled back on its track to get away from the dogs.* **8** go around: *The ship doubled the Cape.* **9** *Bridge.* increase the points or penalties of (an opponent's bid). **10** move at a run: *We doubled over to the barracks.* **11** make move at a run: *The corporal doubled his men around the building.* **12** *Baseball.* make a two-base hit. **13** *Music.* play or sing the upper or lower octave to (another instrument or voice): *The soprano doubles the tenor.*
double back, a fold over: *She doubled back the cloth to make a hem.* **b** go back the same way that one came: *He decided he must have passed the house, so he doubled back.*
double up, a fold back; fold up: *He doubled up the five-dollar bill and put it in his pocket.* **b** draw the knees up toward the chest; bend the upper part of the body toward the lower part: *She doubled up in pain.* **c** share a room, a bed, etc. with another: *When guests came, the two brothers had to double up.* **d** move at the double; run. ⟨ME < OF < L *duplus.* Doublet of DUPLE.⟩
—'dou•bler, *n.*

☛ *Usage.* **Double letter.** In abbreviations, a double letter often indicates plurality: *pp.* = *pages; LL.B.* = *Bachelor of Laws.*

☛ *Usage.* **Double negative.** The use of two negatives for one is no longer acceptable in formal or informal educated usage, though it is often found in non-standard speech and writing. Non-standard: *There wasn't no answer to my call.* Formal and informal: *There was no answer to my call. There wasn't any answer to my call.*

double agent a person who is ostensibly working as a secret agent for one side but is in fact working for the other. A double agent may even be deceiving both sides.

double bar *Music.* a double line on a staff that marks the end of a movement or of an entire piece of music.

dou•ble–bar•relled or **dou•ble–bar•reled** ['dʌbəl 'bærəld] *or* ['dʌbəl 'bɛrəld] *adj.* **1** having two barrels: *a double-barrelled shotgun.* **2** having a twofold purpose. **3** having a double meaning: *a double-barrelled question.*

double bass a stringed instrument with a deep bass tone, the largest member of the modern violin family, played upright on the floor with the player standing or sitting behind it. The double bass, which has five or six strings, is derived directly from one of the 17th-century viols, not from the violins.

A double bass

double bassoon a large bassoon, an octave lower in pitch than the ordinary bassoon.

double bill two plays, movies, etc. presented on one program.

double bind a catch-22; dilemma; situation in which two opposing things are expected or required of a person, neither of which will be an acceptable course of action.

double–blind ['dʌbəl 'blaɪnd] *adj.* of or having to do with an experiment in which neither the subject nor the researcher knows which treatment the subject is receiving. This technique is commonly used in comparing the effect of a new drug with that of a placebo.

double boiler a pair of pans, one of which fits down into the other. The food in the upper pan is cooked gently by the heat from the boiling water in the lower pan.

double bond *Chemistry.* a bond in which two atoms in a molecule share two pairs of electrons.

dou•ble–breast•ed ['dʌbəl 'brɛstɪd] *adj.* of clothing, overlapping enough to make two thicknesses cross the breast and having two rows of buttons.

dou•ble–check ['dʌbəl ˌtʃɛk] *v., n. —v.* check twice: *The police double-checked the vagrant's story before releasing him.*
—n. a checking of something twice.

double chin a soft fold of flesh under the chin.

double–click ['dʌbəl ˌklɪk] *v. Computer technology.* click twice in rapid succession.

dou•ble–clutch ['dʌbəl 'klʌtʃ] *v.* change gear in a motor vehicle by releasing the clutch between gears, or between neutral and another gear.

double cross *Informal.* an act of treachery.

dou•ble–cross ['dʌbəl ˌkrɒs] *v. Informal.* promise to do one thing and then do another; be treacherous to.
—'dou•ble-ˌcros•ser, *n.*

double dagger a mark (‡) used for reference from one place in a book to another.

double date a DATE (def. 7) for two couples. **—double-date,** *v.*

dou•ble–deal•er ['dʌbəl 'dilər] *n.* a person guilty of double-dealing.

dou•ble–deal•ing ['dʌbəl 'dilɪŋ] *n. or adj.* pretending to do one thing and then doing another; deceiving.

double–deck ['dʌbəl ˌdɛk] *adj., v. —adj.* having or consisting of two decks, floors, levels, sections, etc.: *double-deck beds.* *—v.* arrange or construct in two decks, floors, etc.

dou•ble–deck•er ['dʌbəl 'dɛkər] *n.* **1** a structure having two decks, floors, levels, sections, etc.: *Some railway cars are double-deckers.* **2** a sandwich having two layers of filling between three slices of bread.

double decomposition *Chemistry.* a reaction in which the molecules of two different compounds exchange radicals to form new compounds.

dou•ble–dig•it ['dʌbəl 'dɪdʒɪt] *adj.* usually of a percentage, ranging from 10 to 99: *double-digit inflation.*

double Dutch a children's skipping game in which each turner swings two ropes at a time in a crossing pattern for the person jumping.

dou•ble–edged ['dʌbəl 'ɛdʒd] *adj.* **1** two-edged. **2** as much against as for: *a double-edged compliment.*

dou•ble–en•ten•dre ['dʌbəl ɒn'tɒndrə]; *French,* [dublɑ̃'tɑ̃dʀ] *n.* a word or expression with two meanings. One is often indelicate or improper. ⟨< obs. F *double entendre,* literally, to be taken two ways⟩

double entry a system of bookkeeping in which each transaction is written down twice, once on the credit side of one account and once on the debit side of another. Compare SINGLE ENTRY.

double exposure *Photography.* **1** the exposing of a piece of film twice. **2** two negatives superimposed onto the same print.

dou•ble–faced ['dʌbəl 'feist] *adj.* **1** having two faces or aspects. **2** of cloth, having a nap or finish on both sides. **3** two-faced.

double fault *Tennis, etc.* failure to serve correctly twice in succession, resulting in loss of a point.

double feature a cinema program with two full-length films.

double flat *Music.* a sign (𝄫) to indicate that a note must be lowered two half tones below the natural pitch.

dou•ble–glazed ['dʌbəl 'gleizd] *adj.* having two layers of glass for better insulation in windows, etc.

double glazing windows having two layers of glass for insulation.

dou•ble–head•ed ['dʌbəl 'hɛdɪd] *adj.* **1** twofold; double. **2** having two heads: *a double-headed tool.* **3** having both good and bad qualities.

dou•ble–head•er ['dʌbəl 'hɛdər] *n.* **1** two baseball games between the same teams on the same day, one right after the other. **2** a railway train pulled by two engines.

double helix the spiral character of each molecule of DNA, the base sequence on one strand being complementary to the sequence on the other strand.

double indemnity in life insurance, a clause binding the insurance company to pay twice the face value of the policy in case of the accidental death of the insured.

dou•ble–joint•ed ['dʌbəl 'dʒɔɪntɪd] *adj.* having very flexible joints that allow fingers, arms, legs, etc., to bend in unusual ways.

double kayak *Cdn.* a kayak to seat two people.

double knit a knitted fabric made on a machine with a double set of needles to produce a double thickness of cloth: *Double knits are often reversible.*

double–knit ['dʌbəl 'nɪt] *adj.* knitted on a machine with a double set of needles: *double-knit jersey.*

double negative the use of two negatives in a sentence desired to be negative. *Example: There wasn't no butter in the store.* = *There was no butter* or *There wasn't any butter.* Double negatives are regarded as non-standard.

dou•ble–park ['dʌbəl 'pɑrk] *v.* park (a car, etc.) beside another car that is occupying the area where parking is allowed: *It is usually illegal to double-park.*

double play *Baseball.* a play in which two base runners are put out. **—'double-ˌplay,** *adj.*

double pneumonia pneumonia in which both lungs are affected.

dou•ble–quick ['dʌbəl 'kwɪk] *n., adj., adv., v. —n.* in marching, the next quickest step to a run. *—adj.* very quick. *—adv.* in double-quick time. *—v.* march in double-quick step.

dou•ble–reed ['dʌbəl 'rid] *adj. Music.* having two reeds bound together and made to vibrate against each other. The oboe and the bassoon are double-reed instruments.

double sharp *Music.* a sign (×) to indicate that a note must be raised two half tones above the natural pitch.

dou•ble–space ['dʌbəl ˌspeis] *v.* **-spaced, -spac•ing.** skip a line between lines of written or printed text.

dou•ble•speak ['dʌbəlˌspik] *n.* DOUBLE TALK.

double standard rules governing behaviour (especially sexual) which are more liberal for men than for women.

double star two stars so closely aligned that they look like one to the naked eye.

dou•ble–stop ['dʌbəl ˌstɒp] *v.* **-stopped, -stop•ping.** play two notes at once on a stringed instrument by stroking the bow across two strings simultaneously.

dou•blet ['dʌblɪt] *n.* **1** a short, close-fitting jacket with or without sleeves, worn by European men from about the 15th to the 17th century. **2** a pair of two similar or equal things. **3** one of a pair. **4** one of two or more words in a language, derived from the same original source but coming by different routes. *Example: fragile* and *frail.* ⟨ME < OF dim. of *double* originally something folded, a type of material⟩

double tackle a pulley with two grooved wheels.

dou•ble–take ['dʌbəl 'teik] *n.* a delayed reaction to a situation, joke, etc., often used for comic effect by actors.

double talk talk that is purposely made confusing so as to cloak ignorance or deceit.

dou•ble•think ['dʌbəlˌθɪŋk] *n.* the simultaneous acceptance or putting forth of ideas, concepts, or principles that are in fact contradictory. Doublethink may be unconscious, or it may be deliberate and intended to mislead. ⟨coined by George Orwell in his novel *1984,* pub. 1949⟩

double time **1** payment at twice the normal rate: *They get double time for working on Sundays or holidays.* **2** a rate of marching in which 180 paces, each of about 90 cm, are taken in a minute. **3** double-quick. **4** *Music.* **a** two beats to the bar. **b** of tempo, twice as fast as the previous tempo. **—'double-ˌtime,** *v.*

dou•ble•tree ['dʌbəlˌtri] *n.* a crossbar on a carriage, wagon, plough, etc. When two horses are used, the singletrees of their harness are attached to this crossbar.

double vision diplopia.

double window a window together with a storm window, made either in one piece or as separate structures.

doubling dose *Biology.* the amount of ionizing radiation that doubles the spontaneous mutation rate in the organism.

dou•bloon [dʌ'blun] *n.* **1** a former Spanish gold coin. Its value varied from about $5 to about $16. **2** toonie. ⟨< F *doublon* or < Sp. *doblón* < *doble* double⟩

dou•bly ['dʌbli] *adv.* **1** twice; twice as. **2** two at a time. **3** *Archaic.* deceitfully.

doubt [dʌut] *v., n. —v.* **1** not believe; not be sure (of); feel uncertain (about). **2** be uncertain. **3** *Archaic.* be afraid; fear; suspect: *They doubted a sinister motive in the queen's friendliness.* *—n.* **1** a lack of belief or sureness; uncertainty. **2** a feeling of uncertainty. **3** an uncertain condition or situation: *In such a case, the defendant is entitled to the benefit of the doubt.*

beyond doubt, surely; certainly.

in doubt, not sure; uncertain.

no doubt, a surely; certainly: *No doubt we will win in the end.* **b** probably: *Even if he had money, he'd no doubt expect me to pay the bill.*

without doubt, without question; certainly: *She will pass the test without doubt.* ⟨ME < OF *douter* < L *dubitare*⟩ **—'doubt•er,** *n.* **—'doubt•ing•ly,** *adv.*

☛ *Syn. n.* **1.** See note at SUSPICION.

☛ *Usage.* In negative statements the verb **doubt** is followed by **that:** *I don't doubt that she is clever.* In positive statements use **whether** (in formal use) or **if** (informal) to show uncertainty: *I doubt whether she can pass the exam.* To show real lack of belief, use **that:** *I doubt that she can answer this one.*

doubt•ful ['dʌutfəl] *adj.* **1** unclear; not distinct; not certain: *a doubtful advantage. It is doubtful whether he ever saw his friend again.* **2** full of doubt; feeling uncertain: *He looked doubtful.* **3** open to question or suspicion: *Her sly answers made her sincerity doubtful.* **—'doubt•ful•ly,** *adv.* **—'doubt•ful•ness,** *n.*

doubting Thomas ['tɒməs] a person who doubts everything. ⟨< St. *Thomas,* the disciple who doubted Christ's resurrection⟩

doubt•less ['dʌutlɪs] *adv., adj.* *—adv.* **1** surely; certainly. **2** probably.
—adj. sure; certain. **—'doubt•less•ly,** *adv.* **—'doubt•less•ness,** *n.*

douche [duʃ] *n., v.* **douched, douch•ing.** *—n.* **1** a jet of water applied on or into any part of the body: *A douche of salt water up my nose helped relieve my head cold.* **2** an application of a douche. **3** a spray, syringe, or other device for applying a douche.
—v. **1** apply a douche to. **2** take a douche. ⟨< F < Ital. *doccia,* ult. < L *ducere* lead⟩

dough [dou] *n.* **1** a soft, thick mixture of flour, liquid, and other ingredients for baking. Bread, biscuits, cake, pie crust, etc. are made from dough. **2** any soft, thick mass like this. **3** *Informal.* money. ⟨OE *dāg*⟩ **—'dough,like,** *adj.*
☛ *Hom.* DO[2], DOE.

dough•boy ['dou,bɔɪ] *n. U.S. Informal.* an infantryman in the United States army.

dough•nut ['dou,nʌt] *n.* a small cake, often ring-shaped, fried in deep fat.

dough•ty ['dʌuti] *adj.* **-ti•er, -ti•est.** brave; valiant; strong: *doughty knights.* ⟨OE *dohtig* < *dugan* be good⟩ **—'dough•ti•ly,** *adv.* **—'dough•ti•ness,** *n.*

dough•y ['doui] *adj.* **dough•i•er, dough•i•est.** of or like dough; soft and thick or pale and flabby.

Doug•las fir ['dʌgləs] **1** any of a small genus (*Pseudotsuga*) of trees of the pine family native to W North America and E Asia; especially, *P. menziesii,* one of the most important timber trees of North America, having long, narrow, hanging cones and flat needles growing singly along the stem. This species occurs in two forms: a very tall coastal form with yellowish green needles, usually growing to more than 50 m high, and a smaller, inland form with bluish green needles. **2** the hard, strong wood of this tree. ⟨after David *Douglas* (1798-1834), a Scottish botanist and explorer⟩

Douglas maple a variety of maple (*Acer glabrum*) growing on cliffs and rocky ledges along the northern Pacific coast, in sheltered valleys in the Rockies, and in the foothills of Alberta.

Douk•ho•bour or **Douk•ho•bor** ['dukə,bɔr] *n.* a member of a 200-year-old Christian sect originally from Russia, that traditionally believes that every person knows what is right and must be guided by this knowledge rather than by any outside authority. Several thousand Doukhobours left Russia in 1898 and settled in western Canada. ⟨< Russian *dukhoborcy* < *dukh* spirit + *borcy* wrestlers⟩

Dou•ma ['dumɑ] See DUMA.

dour [dur], [daʊr], *or* ['daʊər] *adj.* **1** gloomy; sullen. **2** stern; severe. **3** stubborn. ⟨< L *durus* hard, stern⟩ **—'dour•ly,** *adv.* **—'dour•ness,** *n.*
☛ *Hom.* DOWER ['daʊər].

douse [dʌus] *v.* **doused, dous•ing. 1** plunge or be plunged into water or any other liquid. **2** throw water over; drench. **3** *Informal.* put out (a light); extinguish: *We doused the candles.* **4** lower or slacken (a sail) in haste. **5** close (a porthole). ⟨origin uncertain⟩ **—'dous•er,** *n.*

dove[1] [dʌv] *n.* **1** any of various species of pigeon, especially any of several of the smaller, wild species. **2 Dove,** the Holy Ghost. **3** a person who tends to favour compromise or conciliation in disputes or controversial issues, especially one who opposes war or a policy of military strength. Compare HAWK[1] (def. 3). **4** a gentle, innocent, or loving person. ⟨OE *dūfe.* Related to DIVE.⟩

dove[2] [douv] *v.* a pt. of DIVE.
☛ *Usage.* See note at DIVE.

dove•cot ['dʌv,kɒt] *n.* dovecote.

dove•cote ['dʌv,kout] *n.* a small house or shelter for doves or pigeons.

dove•kie ['dʌvki] *n.* **1** a small, black and white auk (*Plautus alle*) of the North Atlantic, which breeds in the Arctic and winters farther south. It is common as a migrant along the eastern Canadian coasts from Baffin Island south to the Maritimes. Also, **dovekey. 2** the black guillemot. See GUILLEMOT. ⟨< Scottish dim. of *dove[1]*⟩

dove•tail ['dʌv,teil] *n., v.* *—n.* **1** a wedge-shaped projection at the end of a piece of wood, metal, etc. that can be fitted into a corresponding opening at the end of another piece to form a joint. **2** the joint formed in this way. See JOINT for picture.
—v. **1** fasten, join, or fit together with projections that fit into openings. **2** fit together exactly: *The various bits of evidence dovetailed so completely that the mystery was solved at once. Their complementary strengths dovetailed to make them a great team.*

dov•ish ['dʌvɪʃ] *adj.* **1** like a dove. **2** favouring a peaceful solution to any conflict; opposing war.

dow•a•ger ['daʊədʒər] *n.* **1** a woman who holds some title or property from her dead husband: *The queen and her mother-in-law, the queen dowager, were both present.* **2** *Informal.* a dignified, elderly woman. ⟨< OF *douagere* < *douage* dower < *douer* endow < L *dotare*⟩

dow•dy ['daʊdi] *adj.* **-di•er, -di•est;** *n., pl.* **-dies.** *—adj.* **1** dressed in a dull or unimaginative way: *a dowdy person.* **2** not stylish; shabby: *The old woman wore a dowdy coat and a shapeless hat.*
—n. a woman whose clothes are dowdy. ⟨origin uncertain⟩ **—'dow•di•ly,** *adv.* **—'dow•di•ness,** *n.*

dow•el ['daʊəl] *n., v.* **-elled** or **-eled, -el•ling** or **-el•ing.** *—n.* a cylindrical peg or pin fitted into corresponding holes in two pieces of wood, etc. so as to form a joint holding the two pieces or parts together. See JOINT for picture.
—v. fasten or furnish with dowels. ⟨probably akin to MLG *dovel,* G *Döbel* plug, tap (of a cask)⟩

dow•el•ling or **dow•el•ing** ['daʊəlɪŋ] *n.* wood in long, slender, cylindrical rods that can be cut up to make dowels.

dow•er ['daʊər] *n., v.* *—n.* **1** *Law.* a widow's share of her dead husband's property. **2** *Archaic or poetic.* dowry. **3** a natural gift, talent, or quality; endowment.
—v. provide with a dower; endow. ⟨ME < OF *douaire* < Med.L *dotarium* < L *dotare* endow < *dos, dotis* dowry⟩ **—'dow•er•less,** *adj.*
☛ *Hom.* DOUR.

dow•itch•er ['daʊətʃər] *n.* either of two very similar and closely related species (*Limnodromus griseus* and *L. scolopaceus*) of shore bird belonging to the same family as sandpipers and snipes, having a very long, straight bill and a white lower back and rump. They breed in arctic and subarctic regions of North America and winter as far south as Central and South America. ⟨< Iroquois⟩

down[1] [daʊn] *adv., prep., adj., v., n.* *—adv.* **1** from a higher to a lower place or condition: *They ran down from the top of the hill.* **2** in a lower place or condition: *Down in the valley the fog still lingers.* **3** to a sitting or lying position: *She sat down. He lay down.* **4** to or in a place or condition thought of as lower: *down river; down East. She lives in the Yukon, but goes down to Vancouver every winter.* **5** to a position or condition that prevents evasion, loss, etc.: *to track something down, to pin someone down. The dogs ran the fox down.* **6** from an earlier to a later time or person: *The house was handed down from father to son.* **7** to a less excited condition: *Settle down!* **8** from a larger to a smaller amount, degree, station, etc.: *everyone from the hotel manager down to the bellhop. The temperature has gone down.* **9** actually; really: *Stop talking, and get down to work.* **10** on paper; in writing: *Take down what I say.* **11** in cash when bought: *You can pay part of the price down and the rest later.* **12** into a heavier or more concentrated form: *to boil down to a thick syrup.* **13** *Computer technology.* from an operational state to a non-operational state: *The bank employee took the ATM down in order to replenish its cash supply.* **14** in or into a subservient or humiliated state: *These laws are meant to keep the electorate down. His jokes are not funny; they usually consist in putting others down.*
come down with, succumb to (a disease).
down to the ground, thoroughly; completely: *She's a Conservative down to the ground.*
down with (someone or something)! an exclamation used to express a strong desire for the removal or end of somebody or something: *Down with the President! Down with TV!*
—prep. downward along, through, or into: *to ride down a hill, to walk down a street, to sail down a river.*
—adj. **1** in a lower place or condition. **2** going or pointed down: *the down escalator.* **3** sick; ill: *She is down with a cold.* **4** sad; discouraged: *He felt down about his failure.* **5** *Football.* no longer in play. **6** behind by a certain amount: *The Redskins are down two points. We are down $10.* **7** *Baseball.* out. **8** *Computer technology.* not operational; out of service: *The system has been down since noon.* **9** of one or more tasks in a series, completed: *One exam down, two to go!*
down and out, a completely without health, money, friends, etc. **b** *Boxing.* knocked out.
down on, *Informal.* **a** angry at; having a grudge against. **b** attacking; criticizing.
—v. **1** put down; get down: *She downed the medicine at one swallow.* **2** defeat: *to down the favourite team.* **3** lie down: *Down, Fido!*
—n. **1** a downward movement. **2** a period of bad luck or

unhappiness: *the ups and downs of life.* **3** *Football.* a chance to move the ball forward. In Canadian football, a team is allowed three downs in which to move the ball forward ten yards. **4** *Informal.* a grudge: *to have a down on someone.* ⟨var. of *adown,* OE *adūne,* earlier *of dūne* from (the) hill. Cf. DOWN³.⟩

down² [daʊn] *n.* **1** the short, soft, fluffy feathers beneath the outer feathers of adult birds and forming the plumage of young birds. Down is used in pillows and as a lightweight insulation for winter clothing, etc. **2** soft hair or fluff; fuzz: *The down on a boy's chin develops into a beard.* ⟨ME < ON *dúnn*⟩

down³ [daʊn] *n.* Usually **downs,** *pl.* a stretch of high, rolling, grassy land. ⟨OE *dūn* hill. Akin to DUNE.⟩

down–and–out•er ['daʊn ən 'ʌutər] *n.* a person who has no money and is in poor health or desperate circumstances.

down•beat ['daʊn,bit] *n., adj.* —*n. Music.* **1** the first beat in a measure. **2** the downward gesture of the conductor's hand to indicate this beat.
—*adj. Informal.* **1** casual and relaxed: *an official tour with a downbeat approach.* **2** depressing or depressed.

down–bow ['daʊn ,bou] *n. Music.* a bow stroke on a stringed instrument, in which the bow is drawn its full length, from the frog to the other end, across the strings.

down•cast ['daʊn,kæst] *adj., n.* —*adj.* **1** directed downward: *Ashamed of his mistake, he stood with downcast eyes.* **2** dejected; sad; discouraged: *She was downcast after her failure to make the team.*
—*n.* a ventilation shaft in a mine.

down•draft ['daʊn,dræft] *n.* a gust of air coming down (usually a chimney).

down East BACK EAST.

down•er ['daʊnər] *n. Slang.* **1** a depressant drug, such as a tranquillizer or barbiturate. **2** a depressing experience or situation: *That interview was a downer.*

down•fall ['daʊn,fɒl] *n.* **1** a coming to ruin; sudden overthrow of a great person, institution, or nation through a change in fortune: *the downfall of a hero, the downfall of an empire.* **2** a heavy fall of rain or snow; a downpour.

down•fall•en ['daʊn,fɒlən] *adj.* fallen; overthrown; ruined.

down–filled ['daʊn 'fɪld] *adj.* filled or insulated with down from birds: *Down-filled pillows are very soft. Down-filled clothing is very light and warm.*

down•fold ['daʊn,fould] *n. Geology.* a downward fold or depression; syncline.

down•grade ['daʊn,greid] *n., v.* **-grad•ed, -grad•ing;** *adj., adv.* —*n.* **1** a downward slope. **2** a going down toward an inferior state or condition: *He's been on the downgrade since he missed that promotion.*
—*v.* **1** lower the status and rate of pay of a job or person: *The position has been downgraded.* **2** reduce in value or esteem: *a downgraded reputation.* **3** think of or refer to in a slighting way; belittle: *Don't downgrade the novel; it was a first attempt.*
—*adj., adv.* downward.

down•heart•ed ['daʊn'hɑrtɪd] *adj.* discouraged; dejected; depressed. **—,down'heart•ed•ly,** *adv.* **—,down'heart•ed•ness,** *n.*

down•hill ['daʊn,hɪl] *adv., adj., n.* —*adv.* **1** down the slope of a hill; toward the bottom of a hill. **2** toward a worse condition or state (*used especially in the expression* **go downhill**): *Her business has been going downhill for some time.*
—*adj.* **1** sloping or going downward: *a downhill run.* **2** of or designating the sport of skiing down hillsides or mountainsides, usually on prepared slopes, the top of which are reached by means of some sort of mechanical lift. Downhill skiing requires more rigid boots and bindings than cross-country skiing. Also called **alpine. 3** for use in downhill skiing: *downhill skis.* **4** *Informal.* proceeding smoothly and without effort; easy: *After we got the members signed up, the rest of the planning was all downhill.*
—*n.* a downhill skiing race.

Down•ing Street ['daʊnɪŋ] **1** in London, a street where several important offices of the British government are located, including the official residence (at No. 10) of the prime minister. **2** the British government.

down•link ['daʊn,lɪŋk] *n.* **1** the sending of signals from a satellite or spaceship to a receiver on earth. **2** such a receiver.

down•load ['daʊn,loud] *v. Computer technology.* transfer (files, programs, etc.) from a larger or central computer to a smaller or remote computer via a telecommunications link: *The pricing data was downloaded to the branch-office computer for their point-of-sale system.* Compare UPLOAD.

down payment in instalment buying, a deposit or initial payment made at the time of a purchase.

down•play ['daʊn,plei] *v.* play down; belittle; treat (something) as not very important.

down•pour ['daʊn,pɔr] *n.* a heavy rainfall.

down•range ['daʊn,reindʒ] *adj., adv.* along a range in the direction away from the starting point: *The missile soared 2000 km downrange.*

down•right ['daʊn,rəit] *adj., adv.* —*adj.* **1** thorough; complete: *a downright thief, a downright lie.* **2** plain; positive: *His downright answer left no doubt as to what he thought.* **3** plain and direct in speech or behaviour: *a downright person.*
—*adv.* **1** thoroughly; completely: *He was downright rude to me.* **2** plainly; definitely. **—'down,right•ly,** *adv.* **—'down,right•ness,** *n.*

down•scale *adj.* ['daʊn,skeil]; *v.* [,daʊn'skeil] *adj., v.* **-scaled, -scal•ing.** —*adj.* not of or for the wealthy, prestigious, etc.
—*v.* **1** decrease the size of. **2** make less opulent.

down•shift ['daʊn,ʃɪft] *v., n.* —*v.* shift from a higher to a lower gear.
—*n.* a shifting from a higher to a lower gear.

down•side ['daʊn,saɪd] *n.* **1** a lower part. **2** a loss on an investment. **3** disadvantage; negative aspect: *It's a good plan but the downside of it is that Gail won't be there that day.*

down•size ['daʊn,saɪz] *v.* make (something, such as a company) smaller: *The Powell River Mill was downsized and automated.*

down•spout ['daʊn,spʌut] *n.* a vertical pipe attached to an eavestrough for carrying rainwater down to the ground.

down•stage ['daʊn,steidʒ] *or* [,daʊn'steidʒ] *adj. or adv.* in a theatre, toward or at the front of the stage.

down•stairs [,daʊn'stɛrz] *adv., adj., n.* —*adv.* **1** down the stairs: *Tomasina slipped and fell downstairs.* **2** on a lower floor: *I looked downstairs but couldn't find it.* **3** to a lower floor: *I went downstairs for breakfast.*
—*adj.* on a lower floor: *The downstairs rooms are dark.*
—*n.* the lower floor or floors: *The downstairs is usually much warmer.*

down•start ['daʊn,stɑrt] *n.* someone who descends from a higher social level. Compare UPSTART.

down•stream ['daʊn,strim] *or* [,daʊn'strim] *adv., adj.* —*adv.* in the direction of the current of a stream or river.
—*adj.* farther along in the direction of a stream or river: *The sawmill was downstream from the town.*

down•swing ['daʊn,swɪŋ] *n.* **1** a downward movement or trend: *a sharp downswing in sales.* **2** a swinging down.

Down syndrome [daʊn] a condition of mental retardation accompanied by certain abnormal physical characteristics, such as a broad, short skull, skin folds on the upper eyelids, a thick tongue, and broad hands with short fingers: *Down Syndrome is not inherited, but exists from birth because it is caused by an abnormal development of one of the 46 chromosomes in some or all cells.* ⟨after Langdon *Down* (1828-1896), English physician⟩

down•throw ['daʊn,θrou] *n. Geology.* the downward movement of one side of a fault.

down time **1** a period when work has to stop, often because of failure of equipment, or power cut. **2** a period of rest and relaxation: *I need some down time from the pressures of work.* Also, **downtime.**

down–to–earth ['daʊn tə 'ɜrθ] *adj.* practical; realistic: *She would rather have down-to-earth planning than visionary theories.*

down•town [,daʊn'taʊn] *adv., adj., n.* —*adv. or adj.* **1** to, toward, or in the lower part of a town. **2** to or in the main part or business section of a town: *His office is in downtown Vancouver. She likes working downtown.*
—*n.* the business section or main part of a town.

down•trend ['daʊn,trɛnd] *n.* a decline in business.

down•trod ['daʊn,trɒd] *adj.* downtrodden.

down•trod•den ['daʊn,trɒdən] *adj.* **1** tyrannized over; oppressed. **2** trodden down.

down•turn ['daʊn,tɜrn] *n.* downtrend.

down under the region of Australia, New Zealand, etc. ⟨with reference to the antipodes, in relation to the British Isles⟩

down•ward ['daʊnwərd] *adv. or adj.* **1** toward a lower place or condition. **2** from an earlier to a later time: *downward through history.* **3** toward a lower or worse condition or state: *There is a* *downward trend in the economy.* **—'down•ward•ly,** *adv.* **—'down•ward•ness,** *n.*

down•wards ['daʊnwərdz] *adv.* downward.

down•wind ['daʊn,wɪnd] *or* [,daʊn'wɪnd] *adj., adv.* **1** in the same direction as that in which the wind is blowing. **2** on the leeward side: *Be sure to keep downwind of the animal you are tracking, then it can't smell you.*

down•y ['daʊni] *adj.* **down•i•er, down•i•est. 1** of soft feathers or hair. **2** covered with soft feathers or hair. **3** like down; soft; fluffy. **—'down•i•ly,** *adv.* **—'down•i•ness,** *n.*

downy woodpecker a small black and white woodpecker with a broad, white stripe down the middle of its back.

dow•ry ['daʊri] *n., pl.* **-ries. 1** the money, property, etc. that a bride brings to her husband. **2** a natural gift, talent, or quality; endowment from nature: *a dowry of good health and intelligence.* Also, **dower.** ⟨ME < AF *dowarie* < OF *douaire.* See DOWER.⟩

dowse [daʊz] *v.* **dowsed, dows•ing.** use a divining rod to locate water, minerals, etc. ⟨< Brit. dial. (SW England) ? < ME *dushen* push down; 17c.⟩ **—'dows•er,** *n.*

dox•a•pram [,dɒksə,præm] *n.* a drug used to stimulate respiration.

dox•e•pin ['dɒksə,pɪn] *n.* a drug used to treat depression. *Formula*: $C_{19}H_{21}NO$

dox•ol•o•gy [dɒk'sɒlədʒi] *n., pl.* **-gies.** a Christian hymn or statement praising God. One of the best-known doxologies begins: "Glory to God in the highest." ⟨< Med.L < Gk. *doxologia* < *doxologos* < *doxa* glory, praise + *logos* speaking⟩

dox•o•ru•bi•cin [,dɒksə'rubəsɪn] *n.* a drug used to treat various forms of cancer. *Formula*: $C_{27}H_{29}NO_{11}$

dox•y[1] ['dɒksi] *n. Informal.* a doctrine or belief. ⟨abstracted from *orthodoxy, heterodoxy*, etc.⟩

dox•y[2] ['dɒksi] *n. Slang.* a prostitute or mistress. ⟨origin uncertain⟩

dox•y•cy•cline [,dɒksɪ'səiklin] *or* [,dɒksɪ'səiklɪn] *n.* an antibiotic drug. *Formula*: $C_{22}H_{24}N_2O_8$

dox•y•la•mine [dɒk'sɪlə,min] *n.* a drug used to treat morning sickness.

doy•en ['dɔɪən] *or* ['dwɑjən]; *French,* [dwa'jɛ̃] *n.* a leader or senior member of a group. ⟨< F *doyen* dean < OF *deien.* See DEAN.⟩

doy•enne [dɔɪ'jɛn] *or* [dwɑ'jɛn]; *French,* [dwa'jɛn] *n.* a woman who is a leader or senior member of a group: *the doyenne of popular singers.*

doy•ley ['dɔɪli] See DOILY.

doz. dozen; dozens.

doze [douz] *v.* **dozed, doz•ing;** *n.* *—v.* **1** sleep lightly; be half asleep: *I was dozing on the chesterfield when I heard a light knock on the door.* **2** fall into a light sleep (*used with* **off**): *He dozed off during the news broadcast.*
—n. a light sleep; a nap. ⟨< Scand.; cf. Danish *döse* make dull⟩ **—'doz•er,** *n.*

doz•en ['dʌzən] *n., pl.* **-ens** or (*after a number*) **-en.** a group of 12. ⟨ME < OF *dozeine* < *douse* twelve < L *duodecim*⟩

doz•enth ['dʌzənθ] *adj., n.* twelfth.

doz•er ['douzər] *n. Informal.* bulldozer.

doz•y ['douzi] *adj.* **doz•i•er, doz•i•est. 1** drowsy; sleepy. **2** stupid; mentally not very alert. **—'doz•i•ly,** *adv.* **—doz•i•ness,** *n.*

DP or **D.P. 1** displaced person. **2** data processing.

DPH Department of Public Health.

dpt. 1 department. **2** deponent.

dr. 1 dram(s). **2** debtor. **3** drawer. **4** debit. **5** drachma.

Dr. or **Dr 1** Doctor. **2** Drive.

drab[1] [dræb] *adj.* **drab•ber, drab•best;** *n.* *—adj.* **1** dull; monotonous; unattractive: *the drab houses of the mining town.* **2** dull brownish grey.
—n. **1** a dull brownish grey. **2** a khaki drill uniform: *The soldiers wore drab on manoeuvres.* ⟨apparently var. of *drap* cloth < F. See DRAPE.⟩ **—'drab•ly,** *adv.* **—'drab•ness,** *n.*

drab[2] [dræb] *n.* **1** a dirty, untidy woman. **2** prostitute. ⟨cf. Irish *drabóg* slattern⟩

drab[3] [dræb] *n.* See DRIBS AND DRABS.

drachm [dræm] See DRAM[1].

drach•ma ['drækmə] *or* ['drɑkmə] *n., pl.* **-mas** or **-mae** [-mi]. **1** the basic unit of money in Greece, divided into 100 lepta. See table of money in the Appendix. **2** a coin worth one drachma. **3** an ancient Greek silver coin. **4** an ancient Greek unit of mass. ⟨< L *drachma* < Gk. *drachmē* handful⟩

Dra•co ['dreikou] *n.* a northern constellation, a part of which forms a semicircle around the Little Dipper; dragon. ⟨< L *Draco* dragon⟩

dra•co•ni•an [drei'kouniən] *or* [drə'kouniən] *adj.* Often, **Draconian. 1** of or having to do with Draco, an Athenian legislator of the 7th century B.C., or his harsh code of laws. **2** harsh or cruel: *draconian security procedures.*

dra•con•ic [drei'kɒnɪk] *or* [drə'kɒnɪk] *adj.* Sometimes, **Draconic,** draconian. **—dra'con•i•cal•ly,** *adv.*

drae•ger•man ['drægərmən] *or* ['dreigər-] *n., pl.* **-men.** *Cdn.* especially in the Maritimes, a coal miner trained in underground rescue work and the use of special oxygen equipment effective in gas-filled mines. ⟨< Alexander B. *Dräger* (1870-1928), a German scientist who devised the special equipment used by these men + *man*⟩

draft [dræft] *n., v.* *—n.* **1** a current of air inside a building or other enclosed space. **2** a device for regulating a current of air: *When I opened the draft of the furnace the fire burned faster.* **3** a plan; sketch. **4** a rough, unpolished version of a piece of writing. The first draft of an essay is often quite different from the finished work. **5** (*adjl.*) *Computer technology.* describing a quality of print produced by a printer. Draft quality is usually the lowest print quality available on the printer, suitable for non-final drafts of a document: *She printed early versions of her résumé in draft mode.* **6** a selection of persons or things from a group for some special purpose, such as choosing new players for a sports team. **7** the persons or things selected. **8** *Esp. U.S.* **a** a system for selecting persons for compulsory military service. **b** a group of persons selected in this way. **9** the act of pulling loads. **10** the quantity or thing pulled. **11** (*adjl.*) used for pulling loads: *Draft horses are bigger and stronger than horses used for riding.* **12** the act of pulling in a net to catch fish. **13** the quantity of fish caught in a net at one time. **14** a written order requiring the payment of a stated amount of money, especially a cheque drawn by one branch of a bank on another. **15** a heavy demand or drain on anything: *Her long illness was a draft on her resources.* **16** the depth of water that a ship draws or needs for floating, especially when loaded. **17** the act or an instance of drinking or inhaling: *He emptied the glass at one draft.* **18** the amount drunk or inhaled: *She took in a large draft of fresh air.* **19** the act of drawing beer, ale, etc. from a keg or other container. **20** the amount drawn at one time: *a draft of ale.* **21** (*adjl.*) drawn from a keg, etc. when ordered: *Some people prefer draft beer to bottled beer.* **22** beer, ale, etc. drawn from a keg, etc. when ordered. *Do they sell draft there?*
on draft, of beer, ale, etc., available for drawing directly from a keg, etc. when ordered: *Most taverns have beer on draft.*
—v. **1** make up or prepare a plan, sketch, or rough version of: *to draft new legislation. She drafted the letter to the editor on the bus on her way home.* **2** select from a group for some special purpose, such as for military service or for special duty within the armed forces: *Ten men from the battalion were drafted for guard duty.* **3** draw off or away. Also, **draught.** ⟨var. of *draught*⟩ **—'draft•er,** *n.*
☛ *Spelling.* **Draft** has become the preferred spelling for all senses, though **draught** is still widely used for such meanings as in *a draught of fish, a ship's draught,* or *beer on draught.*

draft–dodg•er ['dræft ,dɒdʒər] *n.* a person who evades compulsory military service, especially in the United States.

draft•ee [dræf'ti] *n. U.S.* a person who is drafted for military service.

draft horse a large, strong, heavily built horse used for hauling heavy loads, pulling a plough, etc. Draft horses are now bred mainly for show.

drafts•man ['dræftsmən] *n., pl.* **-men. 1** a person who makes plans or sketches. A draftsman draws designs or diagrams from which buildings and machines are made. **2** a person who draws up legal or official documents. **3** an artist who is especially skilled in drawing. Also, **draughtsman.**
☛ *Spelling.* See notes at DRAFT and DRAUGHT.

drafts•man•ship ['dræftsmən,ʃɪp] *n.* the work of a draftsman. Also, **draughtsmanship.**

draft•y ['dræfti] *adj.* **draft•i•er, draft•i•est.** having, letting in, or exposed to currents of air: *a drafty room, a drafty window.* Also, **draughty. —'draft•i•ly,** *adv.* **—'draft•i•ness,** *n.*

drag [dræg] *v.* **dragged, drag•ging;** *n.* *—v.* **1** pull or move along heavily or slowly; pull or draw along the ground: *A team of horses dragged the big log out of the forest.* **2** go too slowly: *Time drags* *when you have nothing to do.* **3** trail along the ground: *Your scarf is dragging.* **4** pull a net, hook, harrow, etc. over or along for some purpose: *to drag a lake for fish or for a drowned person's body.* **5** use a drag. **6** *Slang.* take part in a drag race. **7** *Slang.* puff on a cigarette, etc. **8** *Computer technology.* move (an object displayed on a computer screen) from one location to another, usually using a mouse. **9** go or cause to go wearily and slowly: *She didn't feel like dragging around town all day. I dragged myself out of bed at six.* **10** forcibly involve (someone) in a situation; oblige to be present: *I don't want to be dragged into that mess! She dragged me to the ballet.*

drag in, bring (something irrelevant) into a discussion: *Whatever we talk about, you drag in hockey.*

drag (one's) **feet** or **heels,** *Informal.* act or work slowly on purpose.

drag out or **on,** make or be too slow or long: *She dragged her story out to take up the whole coffee break.*

—n. **1** a net, hook, etc., used in dragging. **2** the act of dragging. **3** anything dragged. **4** any person or thing that holds back; an obstruction or hindrance: *outworn ideas that are a drag on progress. A lazy player is a drag on a hockey team.* **5** a low, strong sled for carrying heavy loads; stoneboat. **6** a big coach with seats inside and on top. **7** a heavy harrow or other implement drawn over land to level it and break up clods. **8** a device used to retard motion or action, such as a sea anchor or a brake on a fishing reel or the wheel of a vehicle. **9** the force acting on a body in motion through a fluid in a direction opposite to the body's motion and produced by friction. **10** a pull on a fishing line caused by a water current. **11** *Hunting.* **a** an animal's trail or scent. **b** an artificial scent dragged on the ground to leave a trail for hounds. **c** DRAG HUNT. **12** *Slang.* social or political influence: *He's got a lot of drag at city hall.* **13** *Slang.* a puff on a cigarette, etc.: *She took a final drag and put out the cigarette.* **14** *Slang.* a boring person or situation: *That party was a drag.* **15** *Slang.* street: *That's the main drag.* **16** *Slang.* women's clothing worn by a man (*used especially in the phrase* **in drag**). ⟨ME < ON *draga,* if not a dial. var. of *draw,* OE *dragan*⟩ **—'drag•gy,** *adj.*

☛ *Syn. v.* **1.** See note at DRAW.

dra•gée [dra'ʒei]; *French,* [dRa'ʒe] *n.* **1** a lozenge or throat drop. **2** a sugar-coated nut. ⟨< F⟩

drag•ger ['drægər] *n.* **1** a person or thing that drags. **2** a boat used in fishing; trawler.

drag•gle ['drægəl] *v.* **-gled, -gling. 1** make or become wet or dirty by dragging through mud, water, dust, etc. **2** trail along the ground. **3** follow slowly; lag behind; straggle.

drag•hound ['dræg,haʊnd] *n.* a hound trained to follow an artificial scent or drag.

drag hunt a hunt using an artificial scent or drag.

drag•line ['dræg,laɪn] *n.* **1** a rope dragging from something, such as the guide line on a dirigible. **2** an excavating or dredging machine having an endless belt of scoops or buckets that are drawn toward the machine in the digging operation. **3** a rope for pulling anything.

drag•net ['dræg,nɛt] *n.* **1** a net pulled over the bottom of a river, pond, etc. or along the ground: *Fish and small birds can be caught in a dragnet.* **2** an extensive search or hunt to catch or round up criminals, etc.: *They were arrested in the police dragnet.*

drag•o•man ['drægəmən] *n., pl.* **-mans** or **-men.** in the Near East, an interpreter. ⟨< F < Med.Gk. *dragomanos* < Arabic *targumān*⟩

A dragon in the traditional Chinese style

drag•on ['drægən] *n.* **1** *Folklore and legend.* a monster, usually conceived of as a huge, fierce, lizardlike, or snakelike creature, often having wings like a bat and often capable of breathing out fire and smoke. **2** a fierce, belligerent, or extremely stern person, especially a woman. **3** any of numerous small, brilliantly coloured tree lizards (genus *Draco*) of S Asia and the East Indies having winglike membranes. **4** the constellation Draco. ⟨ME < OF < L *draco* < Gk. *drakōn. Doublet of* DRAKE.⟩ **—'drag•on,like,** *adj.*

drag•on•fly ['drægən,flaɪ] *n., pl.* **-flies.** any of a suborder (Anisoptera) of insects having a long, slender body, large head with large eyes, and four long, iridescent, membranous wings which are held straight out from the body when at rest. Dragonflies are harmless and even beneficial to people because they eat many other insects considered harmful.

drag•on•nade [,drægə'neid] *n.* **1** the persecution of the French Protestants by the troops of Louis XIV. **2** any persecution by soldiers. ⟨< F *dragonnade* < *dragon.* See DRAGOON.⟩

dra•goon [drə'gun] *n., v.* *—n.* **1** formerly, a soldier who was mounted on a horse and was armed with a heavy musket. **2** a soldier in any of several cavalry regiments. Most dragoon regiments are now equipped with tanks or other armoured vehicles.

—v. **1** oppress or persecute by dragoons. **2** force by violence; bully or oppress (*into* something): *She was dragooned into signing a false statement.* ⟨< F *dragon* dragon, pistol, (later) soldier⟩

drag race a contest with motor vehicles to see which can accelerate fastest.

drag•ster ['drægstər] *n. Slang.* a car used in a drag race.

drag strip a straight stretch of asphalt or concrete road set aside or built for drag races.

drain [drein] *v., n.* *—v.* **1** draw (a liquid) off slowly: *A ditch drains water from a swamp.* **2** flow off gradually: *The water drains into a river.* **3** draw water or other liquid from; empty or dry by draining: *They drained the swamp to get more land for crops.* **4** dry; lose moisture by dripping or flowing: *I left the umbrella outside to drain.* **5** take away from slowly; deprive little by little: *The long war had drained the country of its young people and its resources.* **6** use up little by little; gradually exhaust: *This business has drained all the money out of my savings account.* **7** use up the strength, vitality, etc. of (a person): *I was completely drained by the experience.* **8** ebb, little by little; vanish slowly: *Her high spirits drained away.* **9** empty by drinking; drink dry: *He drained his glass.* **10** of a river, flow (*into*): *The Mackenzie River drains into the Arctic Ocean.* **11** of a large body of water, receive the waters of (another): *Lake Ontario drains the Niagara River.*

—n. **1** a means, such as a channel or pipe, for carrying off water or other liquid. **2** a slow taking away or withdrawing; a gradual outflow or lessening: *Lack of opportunity at home caused a serious drain of talent to other regions.* **3** anything that causes such an overflow or lessening: *The big car soon became a drain on her budget.*

down the drain, to nothing: *His savings went down the drain on a bad investment.* ⟨OE *drēahnian.* Related to DRY.⟩

drain•age ['dreinɪdʒ] *n.* **1** the act or process of draining; a gradual flowing off. **2** a system of channels or pipes for carrying off water or waste of any kind. **3** what is drained off. **4** the area that is drained.

drainage basin the area that is drained by a river and its tributaries.

drain•board ['drein,bɔrd] *n.* **1** a board set at a downward angle into one side of a sink for draining off the water from washed dishes. **2** a rubber mat or tray used for the same purpose.

drain•er ['dreinər] *n.* **1** a person who makes channels or lays pipes for draining land. **2** a pan, vat, etc. for draining off liquid.

drain•pipe ['drein,pəip] *n.* a pipe for carrying off water or other liquid. See EAVES for picture.

drake [dreik] *n.* the adult male of a duck. Compare DUCK. ⟨OE *draca* < L *draco.* Doublet of DRAGON.⟩

dram[1] [dræm] *n.* **1** in apothecaries' weight, a unit equal to 60 grains or ⅛ ounce (about 3.89 g). **2** in avoirdupois weight, a unit equal to 27.34 grains or 1/16 ounce (about 1.77 g). **3** a small drink of alcoholic liquor. **4** a small amount of anything. Also, *Brit.* **drachm.** ⟨ME < OF *drame* < L *drachma.* Doublet of DRACHMA.⟩

dram[2] [dræm] *n. Cdn. Logging.* formerly, a section of a timber raft, made up of several cribs lashed together. ⟨origin uncertain⟩

dram[3] [dræm] *n.* the basic unit of currency in Armenia, divided into 100 lumma. See table of money in the Appendix.

dra•ma ['dræmə] *or* ['dramə] *n.* **1** a story written to be acted out by actors on a stage or on film, etc.; a play, especially one that is not a comedy or that is very moving. **2** a series of happenings suggesting such a play: *The history of Arctic exploration is a great and thrilling drama.* **3** the art of writing, acting, or producing plays; the branch of literature having to do with plays: *She is studying drama.* **4** acting; playing in role: *creative drama.* **5** a dramatic quality; action, pathos, or excitement: *the drama of a rescue at sea.* ⟨< LL < Gk. *drama* play, deed < *draein* do⟩

dra•ma•tic [drə'mætɪk] *adj.* **1** of or having to do with plays. **2** seeming like a drama or play; full of action or feeling; exciting: *There was a dramatic pause and then he leaped onto the stage.* **3** vibrant; colourful: *a dramatic evening dress, a dramatic personality.* **—dra'mat•i•cal•ly,** *adv.*

☛ *Syn.* **2. Dramatic,** THEATRICAL, MELODRAMATIC, as applied to situations in real life, mean 'having qualities suitable to plays or the stage'. **Dramatic** emphasizes genuineness, and suggests exciting the imagination as well as moving the feelings: *The reunion of the veterans with their wives was dramatic.* **Theatrical** emphasizes show and unreality, and suggests artificial or cheap effects calling directly on the feelings: *Her show of gratitude was theatrical.* **Melodramatic** emphasizes sensationalism and exaggeration, especially in trying to stir up the feelings: *The paper gave a melodramatic account of the child's murder.*

dra•mat•ics [drə'mætɪks] *n.pl.* **1** the art or practice of acting or producing plays (*usually used with a singular verb*): *She is studying dramatics.* **2** dramatic productions. **3** exaggerated emotional behaviour or expression: *Don't pay any attention to his dramatics.*

dram•a•tis per•so•nae ['dræmətɪs pər'souni] *or* [pər'sounaɪ] the characters or actors in a play. ⟨< L⟩

dram•a•tist ['dræmətɪst] *n.* a writer of plays; playwright.

dram•a•ti•za•tion [,dræmətaɪ'zeiʃən] *or* [,dræmətə'zeiʃən] *n.* **1** the act of dramatizing. **2** what is dramatized.

dram•a•tize ['dræmə,taɪz] *v.* **-tized, -tiz•ing. 1** make a drama of; arrange in the form of a play: *to dramatize a novel.* **2** show or express in a dramatic way; make exciting and thrilling. **3** lend itself to being dramatized: *His novels do not dramatize well.* **—'dram•a,tiz•er,** *n.*

dram•a•turge ['dræmə,tɜrdʒ] *n.* **1** a dramatist, especially one employed by a theatre company. **2** a person who advises a theatre company, especially about new scripts, which he or she chooses and edits.

dram•a•tur•gic [,dræmə'tɜrdʒɪk] *adj.* having to do with dramaturgy. **—,dram•a'tur•gi•cal•ly,** *adv.*

dram•a•tur•gy ['dræmə,tɜrdʒi] *n.* the art of writing or producing dramas. ⟨< Gk. *dramatourgia* < *drama* drama + *-ourgos* making < *ergon* work⟩

drank [dræŋk] *v.* pt. of DRINK.

drape [dreip] *v.* **draped, drap•ing;** *n.* *—v.* **1** cover or hang with cloth falling loosely in graceful folds, especially as a decoration: *The buildings were draped with red, white, and blue bunting.* **2** arrange (clothes, hangings, etc.) in graceful folds: *The designer draped the robe around the model's shoulders.* **3** fall in graceful folds: *Soft fabrics drape well.* **4** stretch out loosely or lazily: *He draped his legs over the arm of the chesterfield.*
—n. **1 drapes,** *pl.* large curtains that are made to hang in folds; draperies: *There are drapes on the large windows in the living room.* **2** arrangement of cloth in folds: *The bodice of the dress has a soft drape.* **3** the way a garment hangs on the body: *I don't like the drape of the skirt.* ⟨ME < OF *draper* < *drap* cloth < LL *drappus*⟩

drap•er ['dreipər] *n.* **1** *Esp. Brit.* a dealer in cloth or dry goods. **2** one who drapes.

drap•er•y ['dreipəri] *n., pl.* **-per•ies. 1** clothing or hangings arranged in graceful folds, especially on figures in paintings or sculpture. **2** the graceful arrangement of hangings or clothing. **3** cloth or fabric. **4 draperies,** *pl.* drapes.

dras•tic ['dræstɪk] *adj.* **1** acting with force or violence; forceful and violent: *The general was a drastic man who showed no mercy.* **2** extreme; severe; harsh: *The police took drastic measures to put a stop to the crime wave.* ⟨< Gk. *drastikos* effective < *draein* do⟩ **—'dras•ti•cal•ly,** *adv.*

drat [dræt] *interj. Informal.* a mild oath expressing annoyance. ⟨< *'od rot* < *God rot*⟩

drat•ted ['drætɪd] *adj. Informal.* confounded; darned.

draught [dræft] See DRAFT. ⟨ME *draht* < OE *dragan* draw⟩ **—'draught•er,** *n.*

☛ *Spelling.* See note at DRAFT. Compounds and derivatives beginning with **draught-** are entered under their **draft-** form.

draughts [dræfts] *n.pl. Brit.* the game of checkers.

Dra•vid•i•an [drə'vɪdiən] *n., adj.* *—n.* **1** a family of about twenty languages spoken by the original inhabitants of central and S India, N Sri Lanka, and some parts of Pakistan. **2** a member of any of the Dravidian-speaking peoples.
—adj. of, having to do with, or designating the Dravidian-speaking peoples or their languages. ⟨< *Dravida* name of a region in S India⟩

draw [drɒ] *v.* **drew, drawn, draw•ing;** *n.* *—v.* **1** pull; drag: *The horse drew the wagon.* **2** pull out; pull up; pull back: *He drew the cork from the bottle.* **3** bring out; take out; get out: *Draw a pail of water from the well. The blow drew blood.* **4** pull (a curtain) across or (a blind) down. **5** take out (a pistol, sword, etc.) for action. **6** pull (a violin bow) across strings. **7** pull (a bow) ready to shoot an arrow. **8** take; get; receive: *I drew another idea from the story. He draws his pay each Friday.* **9** make; cause; bring: *Your actions draw praise or blame on yourself.* **10** move; come; go: *We drew near the fire to get warm.* **11** attract; cause to come: *A parade draws a crowd.* **12** *Sports.* make (a ball) move in a particular way. **13** make a picture or likeness of with pencil, pen, chalk, crayon, etc.; represent by lines. **14** make pictures or likenesses with pen, pencil, chalk, crayon, etc.; make drawings: *He draws very well for a six-year-old.* **15** describe; depict: *The characters in this novel are not fully drawn; they seem unreal.* **16** cause (the enemy's fire) to be directed toward oneself. **17** write out in proper form; frame; draft (*usually used with* **up**): *The will was drawn up by a lawyer.* **18** write (an order to pay money): *to draw a cheque.* **19** obtain resources or assistance, etc. (*used with* **on**): *You can always draw on your savings if you have to. He had a vast store of knowledge to draw on.* **20** make a current of air to carry off smoke: *A chimney draws.* **21** breathe in; inhale; take in: *to draw a breath.* **22** of time, etc., come or go gradually but steadily: *The day drew to a close. Night draws on. Death was drawing nigh her.* **23** make the same score in (a game); finish with either side winning. **24** pull out to make tense; extend completely; stretch: *The men drew the rope taut.* **25** make or become small or smaller; shrink. **26** of a ship or boat, sink to a depth of; need for floating: *A ship draws more water when it is loaded than when it is empty. The big ship draws 8.5 m of water.* **27** take out the insides of; eviscerate. **28** cause (a body fluid) to move to the outside of the body: *This special ointment will draw the pus.* **29** of tea, be made by extraction of an essence; steep. **30** suck (*on*): *to draw on a pipe.* **31** temper (steel) by reheating. **32** find out by reasoning; infer: *to draw a conclusion.* **33** draw by lot; get by chance. **34** empty; drain: *to draw a lake.* **35** *Curling.* slide (a stone) so that it comes to rest within the target area without hitting another stone. **36** of sails, fill with wind.
draw a blank, fail completely to get what one wants: *He tried to get information from their neighbours but drew a blank.*
draw and quarter, a submit or subject to a medieval execution in which the limbs of the victim are tied, each to a different horse, and the horses sent in various directions. **b** disembowel and cut up after hanging. **c** berate; punish; tongue-lash.
draw in, of evening or night, approach slowly.
draw on, a of evening or night, approach slowly. **b** take money or resources from: *to draw on the company for expenses.*
draw (oneself) **up, a** stand up straight. **b** become annoyed.
draw out, a extend too much; prolong: *Don't draw out the story so much. The movie was long and drawn out.* **b** persuade to talk; get to respond freely: *We tried to draw him out because we knew he was just shy.*
draw the line, set a limit, especially for behaviour: *He doesn't know where to draw the line in playing pranks.*
draw up, a arrange in order: *to draw up a squad on the parade square.* **b** come or bring to a stop: *A taxi drew up at the entrance.* **c** write out in proper form: *The will was drawn up by a lawyer.*
—n. **1** the act or result of drawing. **2** anything that attracts. **3** *Sports and games.* tie: *If neither side wins, it is a draw.* **4** a lottery; a drawing of lots. **5** the lot drawn. **6** the cards dealt to a player. **7** a part of a drawbridge that can be moved. **8** a small land basin into or through which water drains; valley: *The rancher found her strayed cattle grazing in a draw.* **9** *Curling.* a shot in which the stone comes to rest within the target area without hitting another stone.
beat to the draw, be quicker than someone else: **a** in drawing a gun. **b** in doing anything else.
quick on the draw, a quick to draw one's weapon. **b** quick to say or do the thing called for by the occasion. ⟨OE *dragan*⟩

☛ *Syn. v.* **1. Draw,** DRAG, HAUL = pull. **Draw** suggests smoothness or ease of movement: *She drew a chair to the table.* **Drag** suggests resistance and means to pull with force, sometimes slowly: *He dragged the couch across the room.* **Haul** suggests pulling or dragging something very heavy, slowly and with great effort: *Two engines are needed to haul trains over the mountains.*

draw•back ['drɒ,bæk] *n.* **1** something that lessens satisfaction or success; a disadvantage or hindrance: *Our trip was interesting, but the rainy weather was a drawback.* **2** a refund of duty paid on imported goods that are later exported or used to produce something for export.

draw•bridge ['drɒ,brɪdʒ] *n.* a bridge that can be wholly or partly lifted, lowered, or moved to one side in order to prevent passage across it or to enable large boats to pass along the river beneath it. See CASTLE for picture.

draw•ee [drɒ'i] *n.* a person for whom an order to pay money is written.

draw•er ['drɒər] *for 1-4;* [drɔr] *for 5;* [drɔrz] *for 6. n.* **1** a person who draws liquor, as at a bar. **2** draftsman. **3** a person who writes an order to pay money. **4** any person who or thing that draws. **5** a box built to slide in and out of a table, dresser, desk, etc.: *He kept his shirts in a drawer in the dresser.* **6 drawers,** *pl.* an undergarment for the lower part of the body, fitting around the waist and having long or short legs; underpants.

draw•ing ['drɒɪŋ] *n., v.* —*n.* **1** the art or act of making a picture or design with lines drawn on a surface, especially without the use of colour. **2** a picture or design made in this way. **3** a lottery.
—*v.* ppr. of DRAW.

drawing board **1** a board used as a support for drawing or drafting on paper. **2** the planning stage: *The new rapid transit line is still on the drawing board. The scheme failed completely and they were forced to go back to the drawing board.*

drawing card an attractive event or performer, intended to draw people to a show.

drawing knife drawknife.

draw•ing–pin ['drɒɪŋ ,pɪn] *n. Brit.* thumbtack.

drawing room **1** a room for receiving or entertaining guests; parlour. **2** a private compartment in a passenger car of a train, including beds for one or more persons, toilet, etc., and often specially made up to order for a person or group. **3** formerly, a levee or formal reception, especially at court. ⟨for *withdrawing room*⟩

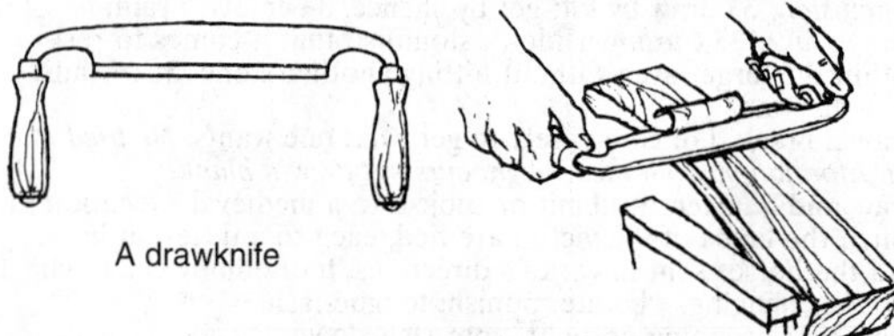

A drawknife

draw•knife ['drɒ,naif] *n., pl.* **-knives.** a tool for shaving wood, consisting of a long blade with a handle at either end, set at right angles to the blade. The blade is always drawn toward the user.

drawl [drɒl] *v., n.* —*v.* talk in a slow way, making the vowels of words very long: *He drawled a lazy answer.*
—*n.* a way of speaking in which the vowels of words are made long: *English speakers in some regions speak with a drawl.* ⟨apparently related to *draw*⟩ **—'drawl•er,** *n.* **—'drawl•ing•ly,** *adv.*

draw•mas•ter ['drɒ,mæstər] *n. Curling.* the official in charge of organizing a bonspiel, drawing teams, arranging schedules of play, etc.

drawn [drɒn] *adj., v.* —*adj.* distorted with pain or fear; tense; anxious: *His face looked tired and drawn.*
—*v.* pp. of DRAW.

drawn butter butter which is melted for use as a sauce.

drawn work ornamental work done by drawing threads from a fabric, the remaining portions usually being formed into patterns by needlework.

draw•shave ['drɒ,ʃeiv] *n.* drawknife.

draw•string ['drɒ,strɪŋ] *n.* a cord, ribbon, or string running through a hem, eyeholes, etc. so that it can be drawn tight: *a hood with a drawstring, a drawstring at the top of a duffel bag.*

dray [drei] *n., v.* —*n.* **1** a low, strong cart for hauling heavy loads. **2** a group of squirrels.
—*v.* transport or carry on a cart. ⟨OE *dræge* dragnet < *dragan* draw⟩

dray•age ['dreiɪdʒ] *n.* **1** the act of hauling a load on a dray. **2** a charge for hauling a load on a dray.

dray•man ['dreimən] *n., pl.* **-men.** a man who drives a dray.

DRB or **D.R.B.** Defence Research Board.

dread [drɛd] *v., n., adj.* —*v.* **1** look forward to with fear or extreme uneasiness or reluctance: *He dreaded the long walk back home in the dark. She dreaded the interview.* **2** feel great fear. **3** *Archaic.* regard with awe.
—*n.* **1** fear, especially of something that will or may happen: *The old woman lived in dread of winter.* **2** a person or thing inspiring fear. **3** *Archaic.* awe.
—*adj.* **1** dreaded; dreadful: *a dread tyrant.* **2** held in awe; awe-inspiring. ⟨OE *drædan*⟩
☛ *Syn. n.* **1.** See note at FEAR.

dread•ful ['drɛdfəl] *adj.* **1** causing dread; terrible or awe-inspiring: *The dragon was a dreadful creature.* **2** *Informal.* very bad; very unpleasant: *I have a dreadful cold.*
—'dread•ful•ness, *n.*

dread•ful•ly ['drɛdfəli] *adv.* **1** in a dreadful manner. **2** *Informal.* very; exceedingly: *She was dreadfully upset.*

dread•locks ['drɛd,lɒks] *n.pl.* very thin braids all over the head, as worn by Rastafarians.

dread•nought or **dread•naught** ['drɛd,nɒt] *n.* a big, powerful battleship with heavy armour and large guns. ⟨< *Dreadnought*, the first such ship, built in 1906⟩

dream [drim] *n., v.* **dreamed** or **dreamt, dream•ing.** —*n.* **1** something imagined during sleep. **2** an aspiration; a lofty hope: *The boy had dreams of being a hero.* **3** the state in which a person has dreams. **4** something having great beauty or charm. **5** a daydream; reverie. **6** (*adjl.*) perfect; ideal: *a dream holiday.*
like a dream, very easily, smoothly, etc.; without any problems, complications, setbacks, etc.: *My new typewriter works like a dream. The interview went like a dream.*
—*v.* **1** have (a dream or dreams): *to dream dreams. He dreamed he was a Mountie.* **2** have daydreams: *The girl dreamed of being a queen.* **3** have an aspiration or lofty hope: *She dreams of becoming a famous marine biologist.* **4** think of (something) as possible; suppose in a vague way; imagine (*usually negative*): *We never dreamed that he'd actually believe it.* **5** spend in dreaming (*usually used with* **away**): *She dreamed the afternoon away.*
dream of, (*usually negative*) consider: *I wouldn't dream of hurting an animal.*
dream on! *Informal.* that is only wishful thinking!
dream up, *Informal.* devise or conceive (an idea, invention, etc.) in the mind; think up: *She was always dreaming up fanciful machines.* ⟨OE *drēam* joy, music; meaning influenced by ON *draumr* dream⟩ **—'dream•less,** *adj.* **—'dream,like,** *adj.*

dream•boat ['drim,bout] *n. Slang.* **1** a very imaginative invention, idea, etc.: *Today's commonplaces are often yesterday's dreamboats.* **2** a very attractive person.

dream•er ['drimər] *n.* **1** a person who has dreams. **2** a person whose ideas do not fit real conditions; impractical person; visionary. **3** a daydreamer.

dream•land ['drim,lænd] *n.* **1** a place where a person seems to be when he or she is dreaming. **2** a beautiful and desirable place. **3** an ideal place existing only in the imagination. **4** sleep.
in dreamland, asleep.

dreamt [drɛmt] *v.* a pt. and a pp. of DREAM.

dream world a world in one's imagination, in which everything is perfect but unreal.

dream•y ['drimi] *adj.* **dream•i•er, dream•i•est. 1** like something in a dream; vague; dim: *a dreamy recollection.* **2** full of dreams: *a dreamy sleep.* **3** fond of thinking about pleasant things that are unreal; impractical: *a dreamy person.* **4** soft and soothing: *dreamy songs.* **5** *Informal.* wonderful, delightful, attractive, etc.
—'dream•i•ly, *adv.* **—'dream•i•ness,** *n.*

drear [drir] *adj. Poetic.* dreary.

drear•y ['driri] *adj.* **drear•i•er, drear•i•est. 1** dull; gloomy; cheerless; depressing. **2** *Archaic.* sad; sorrowful. **3** uninteresting; boring: *We heard a dreary speech last Thursday.* ⟨OE *drēorig*⟩
—'drear•i•ly, *adv.* **—'drear•i•ness,** *n.*

dreck [drɛk] *n.* anything worthless or rubbishy; garbage. ⟨< Yiddish *drek* < German *Dreck* filth⟩

dredge[1] [drɛdʒ] *n., v.* **dredged, dredg•ing.** —*n.* **1** a machine with a scoop, series of buckets, etc. for removing mud, sand, or other materials from the bottom of a river, harbour, etc. **2** an apparatus with a net, used for gathering oysters, etc. It is dragged along the bottom of the sea. **3** a boat equipped for dredging.
—*v.* **1** clean out or deepen (a channel, harbour, etc.) with a dredge; use a dredge. **2** bring up or gather with a dredge. **3** dig up; gather: *The lawyer dredged up all the facts he could find to support his case.* ⟨ME *dreg.* Related to DRAG.⟩ **—'dredg•er,** *n.*

dredge[2] [drɛdʒ] *v.* **dredged, dredg•ing.** sprinkle: *to dredge meat with flour.* ⟨apparently < *dredge*, n., grain mixture < OF *dragie* < L < Gk. *tragēmata* spices⟩ **—'dredg•er,** *n.*

DREE [dri] *Cdn.* Department of Regional Economic Expansion.

D region the lowest layer of the ionosphere, about 55 to 90 km above the earth.

dregs [drɛgz] *n.pl.* **1** the solid bits of matter that settle to the bottom of a liquid: *After pouring the tea, she rinsed the dregs out of the teapot.* **2** the lowest or worst part: *the dregs of society.* ⟨ME < Scand.; cf. Icel. *dreggjar*⟩

drei•del ['dreidəl] *or* ['draɪdəl] *n.* a kind of four-sided top with Hebrew letters on each side, used by Jewish children in a game, especially at Hanukkah. ⟨< Yiddish *dreydl* < *drey(en)* to rotate, turn⟩

drench [drɛntʃ] *v., n.* —*v.* **1** wet thoroughly; soak: *We were drenched in the cloudburst.* **2** give a dose of medicine to (an animal).
—*n.* **1** a thorough wetting; soaking. **2** a dose of liquid medicine put down the throat of an animal. ⟨OE *drencan* < *drincan* drink⟩ **—'drench•er,** *n.* **—'drench•ing•ly,** *adv.*
☛ *Syn. v.* **1.** See note at WET.

Dresden ['drɛzdən] *n.* **1** a kind of fine porcelain, noted for its delicacy of design. **2** something made of this porcelain.
⟨< *Dresden,* a city in Germany, near which this ware was originally made⟩

dress [drɛs] *n., v.* **dressed** or **drest, dress•ing.** —*n.* **1** an outer garment consisting of a bodice and skirt, in one piece, worn by women and girls. **2** (*adjl.*) of or for a dress: *dress fabric.* **3** an outer covering or appearance: *The trees were in their summer dress.* **4** clothes: *They care very little about dress.* **5** formal clothes. **6** (*adjl.*) of or characterized by formal dress: *It was a dress occasion.* **7** (*adjl.*) worn on formal occasions: *a dress suit.* **8** clothes suitable for or characteristic of a certain time or occasion: *formal dress, casual dress. The play was performed in modern dress.*
—*v.* **1** put clothes on: *to dress a doll. She dressed and went down to play.* **2** wear clothes properly and attractively: *Her sister really knows how to dress.* **3** provide clothing for: *He dresses his little girl in handmade clothes.* **4** put formal clothes on: *They always dress for dinner.* **5** decorate; trim; adorn: *The store windows were dressed for Christmas.* **6** make ready for use; prepare: *The butcher dressed the chickens by pulling out the feathers, cutting off the head and feet, and taking out the insides.* **7** arrange (the hair) by curling, combing, etc.: *She just had her hair dressed.* **8** put a medicine, bandage, etc. on (a wound or sore): *The nurse dressed the wound every day.* **9** form in a straight line: *The captain ordered the soldiers to dress their ranks.* **10** smooth or finish: *to dress leather.*
dress down, a scold or rebuke severely. **b** wear old or casual clothes so as not to be conspicuous.
dress up, a put on one's best clothes. **b** put on formal clothes. **c** wear a costume. **d** make (an object, concept, etc.) seem newer, more exciting: *They dressed up last year's design and presented it as a new one.* ⟨ME < OF *dresser* arrange, ult. < L *directus* straight. See DIRECT.⟩
☛ *Syn. n.* **4. Dress,** APPAREL, ATTIRE = clothing. **Dress** is the general word for outer clothing, dresses and suits, etc.: *I can't go camping without the proper dress.* **Apparel,** more formal and impersonal, applies to outer clothing for men, women, or children: *You can't buy underwear in that store; it carries only apparel.* **Attire,** rather formal, emphasizes the general impression made by clothes: *We need neat, not fine, attire.* —*v.* **1.** See note at CLOTHE.

dres•sage [drɛ'sɑʒ] *or* ['drɛsɪdʒ]; *French,* [dʀɛ'saʒ] *n.* the process of guiding a horse without reins through various manoeuvres, the rider using barely perceptible signals of leg pressure, body weight, etc. ⟨< F⟩

dress circle an expensive section of seats in a theatre, usually upstairs.

dress coat a man's coat with an open front and two long tails, worn on formal occasions, especially in the evening.

dress•er¹ ['drɛsər] *n.* **1** a person who dresses another person, especially one whose work is helping actors or entertainers dress for their performances. **2** a person whose work is decorating and arranging displays in store windows. **3** a person who dresses attractively or in a particular way: *He's a smart dresser.* **4** a tool or machine to prepare things for use. ⟨< *dress*⟩

dress•er² ['drɛsər] *n.* **1** a piece of furniture with drawers for clothes and, usually, a mirror. **2** a piece of furniture with shelves for dishes. **3** a table on which to get food ready for serving. ⟨ME < OF. See DRESS.⟩

dress•ing ['drɛsɪŋ] *n., v.* —*n.* **1** what is put on or in something to prepare it for use. **2** a sauce for salads, fish, meat, etc. **3** a stuffing of bread crumbs, seasoning, etc. for roast chicken, turkey, etc. **4** the medicine, bandage, etc. put on a wound or sore. **5** fertilizer. **6** formation: *The soldiers are noted for their dressing on parade.* **7** the act of one that dresses: *the dressing of a store window. She took care with her dressing before the dance.*
—*v.* ppr. of DRESS.

dress•ing–down ['drɛsɪŋ 'daʊn] *n.* a severe scolding.

dressing gown a loose robe worn while dressing or resting.

dressing room a room for getting dressed in, especially a room behind the stage in a theatre, in which actors dress.

dressing table a table with a mirror at which one can sit to put on cosmetics, brush or arrange the hair, etc.

dress•mak•er ['drɛs,meikər] *n.* **1** a person whose work is making clothes, especially for women. **2** (*adjl.*) of women's clothing, having soft or flowing lines and fine decoration: *a dressmaker suit.* Compare TAILORED.

dress•mak•ing ['drɛs,meikɪŋ] *n.* the act or occupation of making dresses, etc.

dress parade a formal military parade in dress uniform.

dress rehearsal a rehearsal of a play with costumes and scenery just as for a regular performance.

dress shield a cloth pad worn under the armpit, to prevent the garment from being stained with perspiration.

dress suit a suit worn by men on formal occasions, especially in the evening.

dress uniform military wear for formal occasions.

dress•y ['drɛsi] *adj.* **dress•i•er, dress•i•est. 1** stylish and formal; not casual: *That outfit is too dressy for a wiener roast.* **2** fond of wearing showy clothes. **—'dress•i•ness,** *n.*

drest [drɛst] *v.* a pt. and a pp. of DRESS.

drew [dru] *v.* pt. of DRAW.

drib•ble ['drɪbəl] *v.* **-bled, -bling;** *n.* —*v.* **1** flow or let flow in drops, small amounts, etc.; trickle: *Gasoline dribbled from the leak in the tank.* **2** let saliva run from the mouth. **3** move (a ball) along by bouncing it or giving it short kicks.
—*n.* **1** a dropping; dripping; trickle. **2** a very light rain. **3** the act of dribbling a ball. ⟨< *drib,* var. of *drip*⟩ **—'drib•bler,** *n.*

drib•let ['drɪblɪt] *n.* a small amount: *She paid off the debt in driblets, a dollar or two a week.*

dribs and drabs *Informal.* small and incomplete amounts.

dried [draɪd] *v.* pt. and pp. of DRY.

dri•er ['draɪər] *adj., n.* —*adj.* comparative of DRY.
—*n.* **1** Also, **dryer,** a substance added to oil paint, varnish, etc. to make it dry faster. **2** See DRYER.

drift [drɪft] *v., n.* —*v.* **1** carry or be carried along by currents of water or air: *The wind drifted the boat onto rocks. A raft drifts if it is not steered.* **2** move or appear to move aimlessly: *People drifted in and out of the meeting.* **3** go along without knowing or caring where one is going: *Some people have a purpose in life; others just drift.* **4** pass without special intention. **5** move or appear one at a time or in small groups as drift does on a beach: *The students drifted into class.* **6** heap or be heaped up by the wind: *The wind is so strong it's drifting the snow. The snow is drifting badly.* **7** move little by little or effortlessly from a given position.
drift apart, gradually cease to be close friends: *We drifted apart after our university days.*
—*n.* **1** a drifting: *the drift of an iceberg.* **2** the direction of drifting. **3** a tendency; trend: *The drift of opinion was against war.* **4** the meaning; direction of thought: *I caught the drift of her speech, but I couldn't understand all the details.* **5** snow, sand, etc. heaped up by the wind. **6** floating matter driven by currents of water, as a log or a mass of wood. **7** a slow current of water, especially a slow ocean current. **8** the sideways movement of an aircraft or ship off its projected course due to crosscurrents of air or water. **9** the distance that a ship or aircraft is off its course because of currents. **10** *Geology.* sand, gravel, rocks, etc. moved from one place and left in another by a river, glacier, etc. **11** an almost horizontal passageway in a mine along a vein of ore, coal, etc. **12** *Mechanics.* an instrument for making holes larger or altering their shape. **13** a group of hogs. ⟨ME *drift* a driving < OE *drīfan* drive. Related to DRIVE.⟩ **—'drift•ing•ly,** *adv.*

drift•age ['drɪftɪdʒ] *n.* **1** a drifting. **2** the distance drifted. **3** what has drifted; material that drifts around in water or is washed up on the shore.

drift fence 1 a snow fence. **2** a deer fence; converging lines of stone or turf used by Inuit to drive caribou into a slaughtering area.

drift–ice ['drɪft ,əis] *n. Cdn.* small masses of ice drifting in the sea.

drift net a fishing net with floats at the top and sinkers at the bottom, that flows with the current or tide.

drift•wood ['drɪft,wʊd] *n.* wood drifting in the water or washed ashore.

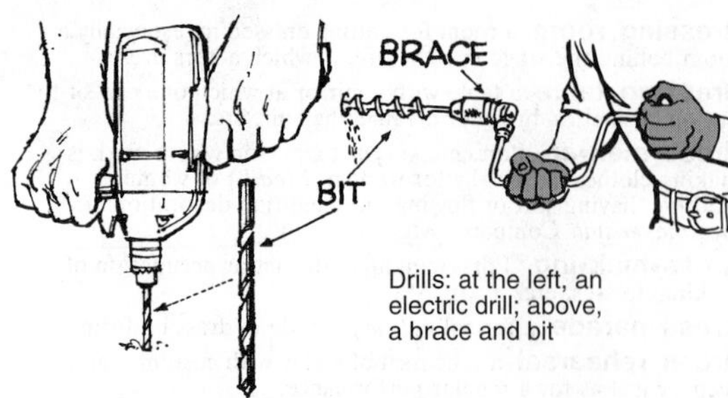

Drills: at the left, an electric drill; above, a brace and bit

drill[1] [drɪl] *n., v.* —*n.* **1** an implement or machine for boring holes. **2** group instruction and training in physical fitness, handling a rifle, grammar, or anything else by repetitive exercises; the process of teaching or training by having the learners do a thing over and over again: *The teacher gave the class plenty of drill in arithmetic.* **3** *Informal.* a correct or approved procedure for doing something: *This leaflet gives the drill for putting the machine together.* **4** a snail that bores into and destroys oysters.
—*v.* **1** bore a hole in; pierce with a drill. **2** make with a drill: *to drill a hole.* **3** teach or train by having learners do a thing over and over again. **4** be taught or trained in this way. ⟨< MDu. *dril* (n.) < *drillen* (v.) bore⟩ —**'drill•er,** *n.*
☛ *Syn. n.* **2.** See note at EXERCISE.

drill[2] [drɪl] *n., v.* —*n.* **1** a machine for planting seeds in rows. It makes a small furrow, drops the seed, and then covers the furrow. **2** a small furrow to plant seeds in. **3** a row of planted seeds.
—*v.* plant in small furrows. ⟨origin uncertain⟩

drill[3] [drɪl] *n.* a strong, twilled cotton cloth similar to denim, used for overalls, uniforms, ticking, etc. ⟨short for *drilling* < G *Drillich* < L *trilix* of three threads < *tri-* three + *licium* thread⟩

drill[4] [drɪl] *n.* a baboon (*Mandrillus leucophaeus*) of W Africa, closely related to the mandrill but smaller. ⟨probably < West African name⟩

drill•ing ['drɪlɪŋ] *n.* DRILL[3].

drill•mas•ter ['drɪl,mæstər] *n.* an instructor who teaches by drilling, especially one who drills soldiers in marching, handling guns, etc.

drill press a machine for drilling holes, especially in metal, ready for rivets.

dri•ly ['draɪli] See DRYLY.

drink [drɪŋk] *v.* **drank, drunk, drink•ing;** *n.* —*v.* **1** swallow (liquid). **2** swallow the liquid contents of: *She drank the whole glass.* **3** take and hold; absorb: *The dry ground drank up the rain.* **4** use liquor: *Does he drink?* **5** consume liquor to excess. **6** drink in honour of; toast: *They drank his health.* **7** put (oneself) in a particular state by drinking: *They're always drinking themselves silly.* **8** waste (time or money) on liquor: *He drank his weekend away. She drinks up every pay cheque.*
drink deep(ly) of, feel (an emotion or experience) intensely.
drink in, take in eagerly with the senses or mind.
drink to, drink in honour of; drink with good wishes for.
—*n.* **1** any liquid swallowed or to be swallowed: *Can I have a drink of milk?* **2** liquor. **3** excessive drinking of liquor: *He's taken to drink.* **4** *Slang.* **the drink,** a body of water; ocean, lake, pool, etc. ⟨OE *drincan*⟩ —**'drink•less,** *adj.*
☛ *Syn. v.* **1. Drink,** SIP, IMBIBE = swallow a liquid. **Drink** is the general word: *A person or animal must drink water in order to stay alive.* **Sip** = drink little by little in very small quantities: *One should sip, not gulp, very cold or hot liquids.* **Imbibe,** formal, is now for the most part used humorously in the literal sense of drinking; used figuratively, it means 'absorb': *Her one desire is to imbibe more knowledge.*
☛ *Usage.* **Drunk, drank.** Although **drunk** is the usual past participle, some educated North Americans use **drank** in speech, especially to avoid associations with *drunken* or *drunkenness*: *He's drank several glasses of milk already.* In writing, **drunk** should be used, except perhaps when writing dialogue. **Drank** is the proper form for the past tense.

drink•a•ble ['drɪŋkəbəl] *adj., n.* —*adj.* fit to drink.
—*n.* something to drink.

drink•er ['drɪŋkər] *n.* a person who drinks, especially one who drinks liquor as a habit or to excess.

drinking fountain a public water supply, outdoors or in a building such as a school or office, which delivers a jet of drinking water when a control is pressed or turned.

drip [drɪp] *v.* **dripped** or **dript, drip•ping;** *n.* —*v.* **1** fall or let fall in drops. **2** be so wet that drops fall.
—*n.* **1** a falling in drops. **2** the liquid that falls in drops. **3** a part that projects to keep water off the parts below. **4** *Slang.* a person considered to be objectionable. **5** *Medicine.* the constant dispensing of fluids and medicine intravenously. ⟨OE *dryppan* < *dropa* a drop⟩

drip–dry ['drɪp ,draɪ] *adj., v.* **-dried, -dry•ing.** —*adj.* made to be dried by being let drip after washing, then needing little or no ironing: *drip-dry curtains.*
—*v.* let drip until dry.

drip•ping ['drɪpɪŋ] *n., v.* —*n.* **1** liquid that has dripped down. **2** sometimes, **drippings,** *pl.* the melted fat and juice that drip down from meat while roasting: *Some people like beef dripping spread on bread.*
—*v.* ppr. of DRIP.

dripping pan a pan put under roasting meat to catch the dripping.

drip•py ['drɪpi] *adj.* **1** leaking water in drips: *a drippy shower fixture.* **2** *Slang.* soppy; foolish.

dript [drɪpt] *v.* a pt. and a pp. of DRIP.

drive [draɪv] *v.* **drove, driv•en, driv•ing;** *n.* —*v.* **1** make go; cause to move: *Drive the dog away.* **2** make go by hitting; propel: *to drive a spike.* **3** force into or out of some place, condition, act, etc.: *That dog's barking drives me crazy. Hunger drove him to steal.* **4** manage; operate; guide by steering: *to drive a car, to drive a motorboat.* **5** go or travel in a car or other vehicle: *We drove out into the country for the afternoon.* **6** travel over or across in a car, etc.; cover: *We drove 300 km without stopping.* **7** carry or transport in a car or other vehicle: *The truck driver drove the girls all the way to Toronto.* **8** bring about or obtain by being clever, shrewd, forceful, etc.: *He drove a good bargain when he bought his bicycle.* **9** compel (oneself or another) to work very hard: *He drove himself to complete the project on schedule.* **10** dash or rush with force: *The ship drove on the rocks.* **11** set in motion; supply power for: *The wind drives the windmill.* **12** *Mining.* excavate horizontally; make a drift. **13** go through an area and herd or direct (game) toward waiting hunters with guns. **14** *Sports.* hit very hard and fast: *to drive a golf ball.* **15** aim; strike. **16** get or make by drilling, boring, etc.: *to drive a well.* **17** move (logs) in large numbers down a river: *The loggers drove the logs to the mill.* **18** have a licence to operate a motor vehicle: *Does he drive?* **19** have as one's motor vehicle: *What are you driving these days?*
drive at, mean; intend: *I didn't understand what she was driving at.*
drive in, *Baseball.* of a player at bat, cause (a run) to be scored or (another player) to score by hitting and getting on base.
let drive, aim; strike: *The boxer let drive a left to the jaw.*
—*n.* **1** a trip taken in a car or other vehicle: *a Sunday drive.* **2** a road (*used mainly in street names*): *Winona Drive.* **3** DRIVEWAY (def. 1): *He left his car in the drive all night.* **4** capacity for hard work; forceful action; energy: *Her success was largely due to her great drive.* **5** an impelling force; pressure: *The craving for approval is a strong drive in people.* **6** a special effort of a group for some purpose: *The town had a drive to get money for charity.* **7** a very hard, fast hit. **8** a military attack, often a large-scale, forceful attack. **9** the act or process of moving a herd of cattle or sheep overland. **10** the act or process of floating a great many logs down a river: *Drives are held when the ice melts in spring.* **11** a great many logs floating down a river. **12** a thing or things driven: *a drive of logs.* **13** a part that drives machinery: *a chain drive.* **14** the special way in which a motor, transmission, etc. generates or controls a vehicle's power or motion: *fluid drive, four-wheel drive.* **15** *Mining.* a horizontal or inclined tunnel or passage. **16** *Golf.* the act of hitting a ball from a tee: *I'd like to improve my drive.* **17** *Computer technology.* a device that contains or accepts a volume of computer storage (disk, reel of tape, etc.) for purposes of reading or writing data. ⟨OE *drīfan*⟩
☛ *Syn. n.* **1.** See note at RIDE.

drive–in ['draɪv ,ɪn] *n., adj.* —*n.* a place where customers may make purchases, eat, or attend movies, etc. while seated in their cars.
—*adj.* of or being such a place: *a drive-in bank.*

driv•el ['drɪvəl] *v.* **-elled** or **-eled, -el•ling** or **-el•ing;** *n.* —*v.* **1** let saliva run from the mouth. **2** flow like saliva running from the mouth. **3** talk or say in a stupid, foolish manner; talk silly nonsense. **4** waste (time, energy, etc.) in a stupid, foolish way (*usually with* **away**).
—*n.* **1** saliva running from the mouth. **2** stupid, foolish talk. ⟨OE *dreflian*⟩

driv•el•ler or **driv•el•er** ['drɪvələr] *n.* a person who drivels.

driv•en ['drɪvən] *v., adj.* —*v.* pp. of DRIVE.
—*adj.* **1** carried along and gathered into heaps by the wind;

drifted: *driven snow.* **2** of a person, compelled by a strong feeling of urgency, competitiveness, etc.

driv•er ['draɪvər] *n.* **1** a person or thing that drives. **2** a person who directs the movement of an engine, automobile, horses, etc. **3** a person who makes the people under him or her work very hard. **4** a golf club with a large, wooden head, used in hitting the ball from the tee. **5** a part of a machine, such as a gear or wheel, that transmits the motion to another part or parts.
the driver's seat, the position of power. **—'driv•er•less,** *adj.*

drive shaft a shaft that transmits power or motion, such as the shaft in a motor vehicle that connects the transmission to the axle of the driving wheels. See UNIVERSAL JOINT for picture.

drive•train ['draɪv,trein] *n.* the mechanism that sends the turning power of an automobile to the wheels.

drive•way ['draɪv,wei] *n.* **1** a private road. A driveway usually leads from a house to the public street or road. **2** *Cdn.* a road, especially one that is lined with trees and lawns.

driv•ing ['draɪvɪŋ] *adj., v. —adj.* urgent; forceful; rhythmic: *the driving beat of the drums, a driving rain.*
—v. ppr. of DRIVE.

driving boat *Logging.* a shallow-draft rowboat used in driving logs.

driz•zle ['drɪzəl] *v.* **-zled, -zling;** *n. —v.* **1** rain in very small drops resembling mist, especially intermittently or over a prolonged period. **2** fall in very small drops. **3** shed or let fall in very small drops or bits: *Drizzle the shaved chocolate over the cake.*
—n. rain that falls in very small drops. ⟨? < ME *drese* to fall < OE *drysnian* to fall⟩

driz•zly ['drɪzli] *adj.* drizzling.

DRO deputy returning officer.

drogue [droug] *n.* **1** a device shaped like a large funnel at the end of the hose used to refuel airplanes in flight. The pilot of the plane being refuelled guides the nose of his or her plane into the drogue. **2** a small parachute that springs open when a parachute pack is opened and helps to draw out the main parachute. **3** a similar device attached to a space capsule, etc. to stabilize it or slow it down. **4** SEA ANCHOR. ⟨? var. of *drag,* n.⟩

droit [drɔɪt]; *French,* [dʀwa] *n.* **1** *Law.* a right or claim. **2** something to which a person has a right or claim; a due.

droll [droul] *adj., n., v. —adj.* amusingly odd; humorously quaint; laughable: *We smiled at the monkey's droll tricks.*
—n. a funny person; jester; buffoon.
—v. joke; jest. ⟨< F *drôle* (originally n.) good fellow < Du. *drol* little fat fellow⟩ **—'drol•ly,** *adv.* **—'droll•ness,** *n.*

droll•er•y ['droulәri] *n., pl.* **-er•ies. 1** something odd and amusing; a laughable trick. **2** quaint humour. **3** jesting.

drom•e•dar•y ['drɒmə,dɛri] *or* ['drʌmə,dɛri] *n., pl.* **-dar•ies.** a swift camel raised for racing and riding, especially the one-humped Arabian camel. ⟨ME < OF *dromedaire* < LL *dromedarius* < Gk. *dromas, -ados* runner⟩

dro•na•bi•nol [drou'næbɪ,nɒl] *n.* a narcotic drug used to treat severe nausea and vomiting resulting from cancer chemotherapy.

drone[1] [droun] *n., v.* **droned, dron•ing.** *—n.* **1** a male bee, especially a male honeybee. Drones do not sting, gather honey, or help in the upkeep of a hive; their sole function is to mate with the queen. **2** a person not willing to work; idler; loafer. **3** a pilotless aircraft, missile, or vessel directed by remote control.
—v. spend time idly; loaf. ⟨OE *drān*⟩

drone[2] [droun] *v.* **droned, dron•ing;** *n. —v.* **1** make a deep, continuous, humming sound: *Bees droned among the flowers.* **2** talk or say in a monotonous voice: *to drone a series of instructions.*
—n. **1** a deep, continuous, humming sound: *the drone of airplane motors.* **2** any of the pipes on a bagpipe that sound a continuous tone. ⟨related to DRONE[1]⟩

drool [drul] *v., n. —v.* **1** let saliva run from the mouth as a baby does. **2** *Informal.* make an excessive show of pleasure or enthusiasm (*often used with* **over**): *drooling over the rock group's latest recording.*
—n. **1** saliva running from the mouth. **2** *Slang.* foolish talk. ⟨contraction of *drivel*⟩

droop [drup] *v., n. —v.* **1** hang down; bend down. **2** become weak; lose strength and energy. **3** become discouraged or depressed; be sad and gloomy.
—n. **1** a bending position; the act or condition of hanging down. **2** discouragement or depression; gloom: *The droop of his spirits showed in his face.* ⟨ME < ON *drúpa*⟩ **—'droop•ing•ly,** *adv.* **—'droop•y,** *adj.*

drop [drɒp] *n., v.* **dropped, drop•ping.** *—n.* **1** a small, roundish mass of liquid, usually formed in falling: *a drop of rain, a drop of blood.* **2** something small and roundish, resembling such a mass: *a cough drop, a lemon drop. Some earrings are called drops.* **3** a very small amount of liquid: *Drink a drop of this.* **4** a very small amount of anything: *a drop of kindness.* **5** a sudden fall or decrease: *a drop in temperature, a drop in prices.* **6** the distance down; the length of fall: *a drop of 10 m.* **7** something arranged to fall or let fall: *A letter drop is a slot, usually with a hinged cover.* **8** *Baseball.* a pitch that suddenly dips downward as it reaches the plate. **9** the act of letting bombs, supplies, etc. fall from an aircraft. **10 drops,** *pl.* liquid medicine given in drops. **11 a** a secret place where illegal goods, drugs, etc. are left. **b** these goods.
at the drop of a hat, a when a signal is given. **b** at once; willingly.
drop in the bucket or **ocean,** a very small amount compared to the rest.
get or **have the drop on,** *Slang.* **a** point a gun at (a person) before he or she can point one at you. **b** get or have an advantage over.
—v. **1** fall or let fall in small masses of liquid: *Rain drops from the sky. He had to drop some medicine into his sore eye.* **2** take a sudden fall or decrease: *They used to think you could drop off the edge of the earth. The price of tomatoes always drops in August.* **3** let fall, either deliberately or accidentally: *He dropped the package.* **4** cause to fall: *The boxer dropped his opponent with one hard punch.* **5** fall dead or wounded: *The soldier dropped when the bullet hit him.* **6** fall from exhaustion: *I'm so tired, I could drop.* **7** cause to fall dead or wounded; kill: *The hunter dropped the deer with one shot.* **8** go lower; sink: *The sun dropped below the horizon.* **9** make lower; cause to become lower: *Drop your voice.* **10** pass into a less active or worse condition: *She finally dropped into a coma.* **11** let go; dismiss: *Members who do not pay will be dropped from the club.* **12** leave out; omit: *Drop the 'e' in 'drive' before adding 'ing'.* **13** stop; end; close: *They agreed to let the quarrel drop. Drop the subject.* **14** write and send (a letter, etc.): *Drop me a note when you get there.* **15** pay a casual or unexpected visit (*used with* **in, by, over,** *etc.*): *We dropped in at my sister's last night.* **16** give or express casually: *to drop a hint.* **17** go along gently with the current or tide: *The raft dropped down the river.* **18** set down from a ship, automobile, carriage, etc. (*often with* **off**): *The taxi driver dropped his passengers at the corner.* **19 a** *Rugger.* make (a goal) by a drop kick. **b** *Football.* drop-kick (a ball). **20** *Slang.* lose: *The team dropped four straight games.* **21** give birth (to): *Has the cow dropped her calf yet? She looks ready to drop any day now.* **22** spend (money), especially in a wasteful manner: *They just dropped three hundred bucks for a chair!*
drop a brick, make a tactless or tasteless comment.
drop a curtsy, curtsy.
drop behind or **back,** lag behind; fall behind: *He started out strongly in the race but soon dropped back to fourth place.*
drop off, a go to sleep. **b** become less; decrease: *sales of chewing gum have dropped off.* **c** stop: *I think I'll drop off at the grocery store.*
drop out, leave school, a training program, etc., without completing the course.
wait for the other shoe to drop, *Informal.* wait for the next logical happening in a series. ⟨OE *dropa*⟩ **—'drop,like,** *adj.*

drop cake 1 a small, sweet cake for which the batter is dropped onto a greased pan or into boiling oil. **2** a small, sweet cake baked in a muffin tin as an individual serving.

drop•cloth ['drɒp,klɒθ] *n.* when painting walls or objects, a large piece of plastic, cloth, etc., used to protect the floor or the furnishings from paint drips.

drop cookie a cookie for which the dough is dropped by spoonfuls onto a flat sheet for baking, instead of being rolled out and cut.

drop curtain a stage curtain which rises or descends, rather than being drawn across.

dro•per•i•dol [drou'pɛri,dɒl] *n.* a drug used as a tranquillizing adjunct to anesthesia, or to treat nausea and vomiting. *Formula:* $C_{22}H_{22}FN_3O_2$

drop–forge ['drɒp ,fɔrdʒ] *v.* **-forged, -forg•ing.** beat (hot metal) into shape with a very heavy hammer or weight. **—'drop-,forg•er,** *n.*

drop–front ['drɒp ,frʌnt] *adj.* of furniture, having a front that opens out on hinges and lies flat to form a shelf or writing surface: *a drop-front desk.*

drop goal *Rugger.* a goal scored by a drop kick.

drop hammer a very heavy weight lifted by machinery and then dropped on the metal that is to be beaten into shape.

drop–in centre ['drɒp ˌɪn] an informal place, often run by a church or social service organization, for young people, parents with preschoolers, street people, or other groups with special needs to come to for help, recreation, or companionship.

drop kick a kick given to a football just as it touches the ground after being dropped from the hands.

drop–kick ['drɒp ˌkɪk] *v.* give (a football) a drop kick. **—'drop-ˌkick•er,** *n.*

drop leaf a hinged section of the surface of a table. Such a leaf can be folded down when not in use.

drop–leaf ['drɒp 'lif] *adj.* having a drop leaf: *a drop-leaf dining table.*

drop•let ['drɒplɪt] *n.* a tiny drop.

drop light an electric or gas lamp connected with a fixture above by a tube or wire.

drop–off ['drɒp ˌɒf] *n.* **1** a lessening or decline: *a drop-off in sales.* **2** a sudden, sharp slope.

drop–out ['drɒp ˌʌut] *n.* **1** a person who leaves school, a training program, etc., without completing the course. **2** the act or fact of dropping out. **3** (*adjl.*) of or having to do with drop-outs or dropping out: *the drop-out generation, a low drop-out rate.*

drop pass in hockey, a type of passing play in which the player in possession of the puck draws opposing players out of position and drops the puck back for a teammate.

drop•per ['drɒpər] *n.* **1** a person who or thing that drops. **2** a small glass or plastic tube with a hollow rubber cap at one end and a small opening at the other end from which a liquid can be made to fall in drops.

drop•pings ['drɒpɪŋz] *n.pl.* **1** what is dropped. **2** the dung of animals and birds.

drop shot **1** *Tennis.* a shot in which the ball barely clears the net before bouncing slightly on the other side. **2** a gun pellet made by dropping molten metal into water to solidify it.

drop•si•cal ['drɒpsəkəl] *adj.* **1** of or like dropsy. **2** having dropsy.

drop•sy ['drɒpsi] *n.* an abnormal accumulation of watery fluid in certain tissues or cavities of the body; edema. ⟨ME, var. of *hydropsy* < OF *idropisie* < L *hydropisis* < Gk. *hydrōps* < *hydōr* water⟩

dropt [drɒpt] *v.* a pt. and a pp. of DROP.

drosh•ky or **dros•ky** ['drɒʃki] *n., pl.* **-kies.** a low, open, four-wheeled Russian carriage. ⟨< Russian *drozhki,* dim. of *drogi* wagon⟩

dro•soph•i•la [drou'sɒfələ] *n., pl.* **-lae** [-ˌli] *or* [-ˌlaɪ]. any of a genus (*Drosophila*) of small, two-winged flies, most of which feed on ripe or rotting fruit, etc. Some species, especially *D. melanogaster*, are widely used in laboratory genetic research. ⟨< NL < Gk. *drosos* dew + *philos* loving⟩

dross [drɒs] *n.* **1** the waste or scum that comes to the surface of molten metals; slag. **2** waste material; rubbish. ⟨OE *drōs*⟩

drought [drʌut] *n.* **1** a long period of dry weather; continued lack of rain. **2** a prolonged shortage of anything. **3** *Archaic or dialect.* thirst. ⟨OE *drūgath.* Related to DRY.⟩

☛ *Usage.* **Drought,** DROUTH. Both forms are in good use, though **drought** is more usual in formal English.

drought•y ['drʌuti] *adj.* **1** showing or suffering from drought. **2** lacking moisture; dry.

drouth [drʌuθ] *n.* drought.

☛ *Usage.* See note at DROUGHT.

drouth•y ['drʌuθi] *adj.* droughty.

drove¹ [drouv] *v.* pt. of DRIVE.

drove² [drouv] *n.* **1** a group of cattle, sheep, pigs, etc., moving or driven along together; a herd or flock. **2** a large group of people moving along together; a crowd. ⟨OE *drāf*⟩

dro•ver ['drouvər] *n.* **1** a person who drives cattle, sheep, pigs, etc., to market. **2** a dealer in cattle.

drown [draʊn] *v.* **1** suffocate under water or other liquid. **2** kill by keeping under water or some other liquid. **3** cover with water; flood. **4** be stronger or louder than; keep from being heard (*usually used with* **out**): *The boat's whistle drowned out what she was trying to tell us.* **5** get rid of: *He tried to drown his sorrow in drink.* ⟨OE *druncnian.* Related to DRINK.⟩ **—'drown•er,** *n.* **—'drown•ing•ly,** *adv.*

drowse [draʊz] *v.* **drowsed, drows•ing;** *n.* —*v.* **1** be sleepy or half asleep; doze: *drowsing in a hammock.* **2** make or be inactive or dull, as if asleep. **3** pass (time) in drowsing (*used with* **away**): *He drowsed the day away.*

—*n.* the state of being sleepy or half asleep. ⟨OE *drūs(i)an* sink, become slow⟩

drow•sy ['draʊzi] *adj.* **-si•er, -si•est. 1** half asleep; sleepy. **2** done sleepily; caused or characterized by sleepiness. **3** causing sleepiness or half-sleep; lulling. **4** inactive; lethargic. **—'drow•si•ly,** *adv.* **—'drow•si•ness,** *n.*

☛ *Syn.* **1.** See note at SLEEPY.

drub [drʌb] *v.* **drubbed, drub•bing. 1** beat with a stick; thrash; whip soundly. **2** in a fight, game, contest, etc., defeat by a large margin. ⟨? < Arabic *daraba* beat⟩ **—'drub•ber,** *n.*

drub•bing ['drʌbɪŋ] *n., v.* —*n.* **1** a beating. **2** a thorough defeat. —*v.* ppr. of DRUB.

drudge [drʌdʒ] *n., v.* **drudged, drudg•ing.** —*n.* a person who does hard, tiresome, or disagreeable work.

—*v.* do hard, tiresome, or disagreeable work. ⟨ME *drugge(n)*; probably related to OE *drēogan* work, suffer⟩

drudg•er•y ['drʌdʒəri] *n., pl.* **-er•ies.** hard, uninteresting, or disagreeable work.

drug [drʌg] *n., v.* **drugged, drug•ging.** —*n.* **1** a substance (other than food) used as a medicine or as a component of a medicine, especially one listed in an official pharmacopoeia. Such a substance increases or decreases the activity of the cells, organs, etc. that it affects. **2** a substance that brings drowsiness or sleep, lessens pain by dulling the nerves, or causes euphoria; narcotic: *Opium is a habit-forming drug.*

drug on the market, an article that is too abundant, is no longer in demand, or has too slow a sale.

—*v.* **1** give drugs to, particularly drugs that are harmful or cause sleep. **2** put a harmful or poisonous drug in (food or drink). **3** affect or overcome (the body or senses) as if by a drug: *The wine drugged him. She was drugged by the soothing music.* ⟨ME < MF *drogue* < MLG *droge-fate* dry barrels, with *droge-* wrongly taken as the name of the contents⟩ **—'drug•less,** *adj.*

drug abuse the use of a drug, usually illegal but sometimes a prescription drug, to an extent that harms the body, and causes addiction. **—drug abuser.**

drug culture **1** the people who take illegal drugs, regarded as a distinct segment of society. **2** their lifestyle.

drug•get ['drʌgɪt] *n.* **1** a coarse, thick woollen fabric used for rugs. **2** a rug or carpet made of this fabric. **3** a woollen or mixed fabric used for clothing. ⟨< F *droguet*⟩

drug•gie ['drʌgi] *n. Slang.* a person who is hooked on drugs.

drug•gist ['drʌgɪst] *n.* **1** a person who sells drugs, medicines, etc. **2** a person licensed to fill prescriptions; pharmacist.

drug•store ['drʌgˌstɔr] *n.* a store where drugs and other medicines are sold. A drugstore often sells soft drinks, cosmetics, magazines, etc., as well as drugs.

Dru•id or **dru•id** ['druɪd] *n.* a member of a religious order of priests, prophets, poets, etc., among the ancient Celts of Great Britain, Ireland, and Gaul where they were powerful as leaders and judges until the advent of the Christian religion. ⟨< F *druide* < L *druidae*, pl. < Gaulish; cf. Old Irish *drui* sorcerer⟩

Dru•id•ic or **dru•id•ic** [dru'ɪdɪk] *adj.* of or having to do with the Druids.

dru•id•i•cal [dru'ɪdəkəl] *adj.* druidic.

Dru•id•ism ['druəˌdɪzəm] *n.* the religion of the Druids, or their beliefs and practices.

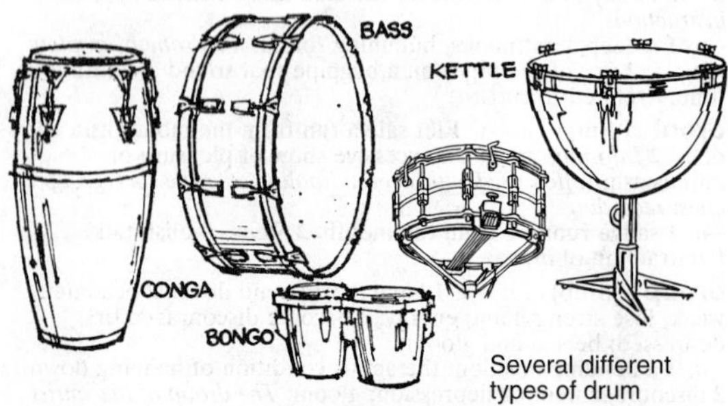

Several different types of drum

drum [drʌm] *n., v.* **drummed, drum•ming.** —*n.* **1** a musical

percussion instrument that makes a sound when it is beaten, tapped, or brushed. A drum is usually a hollow cylinder with a covering stretched tightly over each end. **2** the sound made when a drum is beaten; any sound like this. **3** anything shaped somewhat like a drum. **4** the part around which something is wound in a machine. **5** a drum-shaped container to hold oil, food, etc. **6** eardrum. **7** *Architecture.* **a** a circular or polygonal structure upon which a dome is erected. **b** the block of stone making up one section of the shaft of a column. **8** a natural organ by which an animal produces a loud or bass sound. **9** drumfish.
beat the drums for, *Informal.* support vigorously; promote; advocate.
—*v.* **1** beat or play a drum; make a sound like this. **2** beat, tap, or strike again and again: *Stop drumming on the table with your fingers. She drummed her pen on the edge of the desk while thinking.* **3** force into one's mind by repeating over and over: *Algebra was just drummed into me because I didn't understand it.* **4** sound like a drum; resound: *The noise drummed in his ears.* **5** (of birds and insects) make a hollow, reverberating sound, as by quivering the wings: *The gnats drummed around her.* **6** call or summon by or as if by beating a drum.
drum out of, send away from in disgrace.
drum up, a call together: *We could not drum up enough players for our game.* **b** get by asking again and again: *to drum up support for a project.* ⟨< *drumslade* drummer < Du. or LG *trommelslag* drumbeat⟩ —**'drum,like,** *adj.*

drum•beat ['drʌm,bit] *n.* the sound made when a drum is beaten.

drum dance *Cdn.* **1** an Inuit dance consisting of expressive body movements and gestures, performed to the accompaniment of drums and with the dancer or dancers singing as they dance. **2** any of various dances of the First Nations, accompanied by drums. —**drum dancer.**

drum•fish ['drʌm,fɪʃ] *n., pl.* **-fish** or **-fish•es.** any of various carnivorous fishes (family Sciaenidae) found mainly along the warm and tropical western shores of the Atlantic. Most drumfishes can make a drumming sound by moving certain muscles attached to the air bladder.

drum•head ['drʌm,hɛd] *n.* the parchment or membrane stretched tightly over the end of a drum.

drumhead court–martial a court-martial on the battlefield or while troops are moving, held in order to try offenders without delay.

drum•lin ['drʌmlən] *n.* a ridge or oval hill formed by deposit from a glacier. ⟨for *drumling,* dim. of *drum* ridge < Irish and Scots Gaelic *druim* ridge⟩

drum major the leader or director of a marching band.

drum ma•jo•rette [,meidʒə'rɛt] a girl or woman who accompanies a marching band, twirling a baton.

drum•mer ['drʌmər] *n.* **1** a person who plays a drum, especially a skilled player. **2** *Informal.* sales representative.

drum•stick ['drʌm,stɪk] *n.* **1** a stick for beating a drum. **2** the lower, meaty part of the leg of a cooked chicken, turkey, or other edible bird.

drunk [drʌŋk] *adj., n., v.* —*adj.* **1** overcome by liquor; intoxicated. **2** very much excited or affected: *drunk with success.* **3** drunken: *drunk driving.*
—*n. Slang.* **1** a person who is drunk or often drunk; a drunkard. **2** a spell of drinking liquor; drinking spree: *a three-day drunk.*
—*v.* pp. and archaic pt. of **drink:** *She had drunk all the milk.*
☛ *Usage.* **Drunk,** DRUNKEN. As an adjective standing before the noun, the form **drunken** is preferred, except in the set phrases *drunk driver, drunk driving.*

drunk•ard ['drʌŋkərd] *n.* a person who is often drunk; a person who frequently drinks too much liquor.

drunk•en ['drʌŋkən] *adj., v.* —*adj.* **1** drunk. **2** caused or affected by being drunk. **3** often drinking too much liquor.
—*v. Archaic.* a pp. of DRINK. —**'drunk•en•ly,** *adv.* —**'drunk•en•ness,** *n.*
☛ *Usage.* See note at DRUNK.

drunk•om•e•ter [drʌŋk'ɒmətər] *n.* breathalyser.

dru•pa•ceous [dru'peiʃəs] *adj. Botany.* **1** like a drupe. **2** producing drupes.

drupe [drup] *n.* a soft, fleshy fruit having a thin, skinlike covering and, in the centre, a hard pit or stone containing the seed. Cherries and peaches are drupes. See FRUIT for picture. ⟨< NL *drupa* < L < Gk. *dryppa* very ripe olive⟩

drupe•let ['druplɪt] *n.* a small fissure drupe. A raspberry or blackberry is a mass of drupelets.

druse [druz] *n.* encrusted crystals, as of quartz, lining a small fissure in rock. ⟨< G < OHG *druos* lump, swelling⟩

Druse or **Druze** [druz] *n.* a member of a sect in Syria and Lebanon whose basically Muslim religion contains Christian elements. ⟨< Arabic *Durūz,* pl.⟩

druth•ers ['drʌðərz] *n.pl. Informal or dialect.* a free choice or one's own way: *If I had my druthers, I'd quit tomorrow.* ⟨< shortening of *I'd rather,* influenced by *other*⟩

dry [draɪ] *adj.* **dri•er, dri•est;** *v.* **dried, dry•ing;** *n., pl.* **drys.**
—*adj.* **1** not wet or moist. **2** having little or no rain: *a dry climate.* **3** not giving milk: *That cow has been dry for a month.* **4** containing no water or other liquid. **5** too lacking in moisture; parched; brittle; shrivelled: *dry skin.* **6** not shedding tears or accompanied by tears: *a dry sob.* **7** not involving mucus: *a dry cough.* **8** wanting a drink; thirsty. **9** not under, in, or on water: *dry land.* **10** not liquid; solid: *dry measure.* **11** causing thirst: *Cutting the lawn is dry work.* **12** apparently matter-of-fact but actually ironic: *dry humour.* **13** not interesting; dull: *a dry speech.* **14** without butter: *dry toast.* **15** stale: *dry bread.* **16** free from sweetness or fruity flavour: *dry wine.* **17** *Informal.* having or favouring laws against making and selling alcoholic beverages. **18** abstaining from drinking alcoholic beverages. **19** bald; plain; unadorned: *a list of dry facts.* **20** yielding nothing: *After writing five novels in as many years, she was suddenly dry.*
not dry behind the ears, *Informal.* inexperienced, naïve; young.
suck dry, exhaust the vitality or productivity of.
—*v.* **1** make or become dry. **2** preserve by dehydrating.
dry out, a make or become completely dry: *He laid his socks on a rock to dry out.* **b** *Informal.* take or cause to take treatment for alcoholism.
dry up, a of water or a body of water, etc., disappear as a result of evaporation, drainage, or cutting off of the source of supply: *The creek dried up last summer.* **b** make or become completely dry; dry out: *The paint dried up because someone left the top off the jar.* **c** *Slang.* stop talking: *Why don't you dry up?* **d** *Informal.* make or become uncreative or unproductive.
—*n. Informal.* a person who favours laws against making and selling alcoholic drinks. ⟨OE *drȳge*⟩ —**'dry•ness,** *n.*
☛ *Syn. adj.* **1. Dry,** ARID = without moisture. **Dry** is the general word, meaning 'not wet or moist': *This bread is dry.* **Arid** = completely dry or dried out, and adds the idea of barrenness, particularly when applied to land: *No crops will grow in this arid soil.*

dry•a•ble ['draɪəbəl] *adj.* capable of being dried in a clothes dryer without coming to harm.

dry•ad or **Dry•ad** ['draɪæd] *or* ['draɪəd] *n., pl.* **-ads, -a•des** [-ə,diz]. *Greek mythology.* a nymph that lives in a tree; wood nymph. ⟨< L < Gk. *Dryades,* pl. < *drys* tree⟩ —**dry'ad•ic,** *adj.*

dry•as ['draɪəs] *n., pl.* **dry•as.** any small alpine plant of the genus *Dryas,* of the rose family, resembling a strawberry plant and having single creamy to yellow flowers, and fruit like anemone fruit. The mountain avens are dryas.

dry battery **1** a set of dry cells connected to produce electric current. **2** DRY CELL.

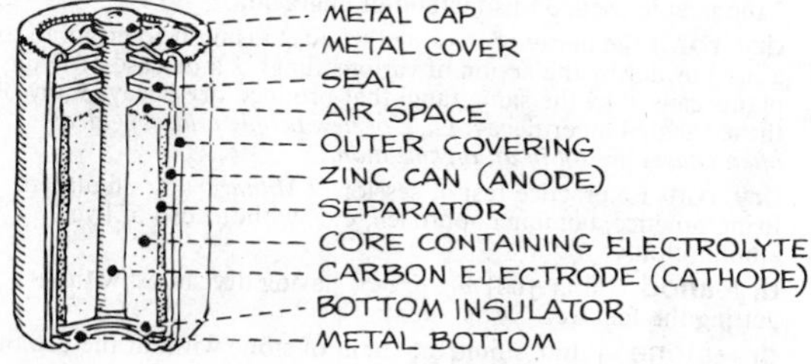

A carbon-zinc dry cell: a flashlight battery. The electrolyte, a paste of ammonium chloride, zinc chloride, manganese dioxide, and carbon, reacts with the zinc, causing it to become negatively charged. When the zinc anode and the carbon cathode are connected by a conducting wire, electrons flow from the anode to the cathode, producing an electric current.

dry cell an electrochemical cell in which the electrolyte is in the form of a paste so that it cannot spill.

dry cereal any breakfast cereal that does not require cooking and is sold ready for eating.

dry–clean ['draɪ ˌklin] *v.* clean clothes, drapes, etc. by dry cleaning.

dry–clean•a•ble ['draɪ ˌklinəbəl] *adj.* that can be dry-cleaned: *Most fabrics are dry-cleanable.*

dry cleaner a person or company that does dry cleaning.

dry cleaning 1 the cleaning of fabrics without water, using a solvent. Most commercial dry cleaning today is done with synthetic or petroleum-based solvents. **2** something that is to be or has been dry-cleaned: *I have to pick up the dry cleaning on my way home today.*

dry dock an area set between two piers, built watertight so that water may be pumped out or kept high. Dry docks are used for building or repairing ships.

dry–dock ['draɪ ˌdɒk] *v.* **1** place in a dry dock. **2** go into dry dock.

dry•er ['draɪər] *n.* **1** an appliance or machine for drying things quickly, especially by heat or blowing air: *A clothes dryer dries clothes by blowing air over them as they are tumbled in a revolving drum.* Also, **drier. 2** a stand or rack for hanging clothes up to dry. **3** See DRIER (def. 1). **4** any person who or thing that dries.

dry–eyed ['draɪ 'aɪd] *adj.* not weeping; not shedding tears: *He remained dry-eyed at the funeral.*

dry–farm ['draɪ ˌfɑrm] *v.* farm (land) where there is no irrigation and little rain.

dry farmer a person who engages in dry farming.

dry farming a way of farming land in dry regions where there is no irrigation, using methods that save soil moisture and raising crops that survive drought.

dry fly an artificial fishing lure made to resemble a fly or other insect floating on the water. Compare WET FLY.

dry goods cloth, ribbon, lace, etc.

Dry Ice *Trademark.* a very cold, white solid formed when carbon dioxide is compressed and then cooled. It is used for cooling because it changes from solid back to gas without becoming liquid. It is used in the theatre to create an illusion of fog.

dry law a law prohibiting the making and selling of alcoholic liquor.

dry•ly or **dri•ly** ['draɪli] *adv.* in a DRY (def. 12) manner: *He spoke dryly of his experiences at election time.*

dry measure a system of units for measuring such things as grain, flour, or fruit.

2 pints = 1 quart (1.14 dm^3)
8 quarts = 1 peck (9.09 dm^3)
4 pecks = 1 bushel (36.4 dm^3)

dry nurse a nurse who takes care of a baby, but does not suckle it.

dry–nurse ['draɪ ˌnɜrs] *v.* **-nursed, -nurs•ing.** act as dry nurse to.

dry point 1 a picture made from a copper plate into which lines have been engraved with a hard needle without using acid. **2** the needle used. **3** this method of engraving.

dry rot 1 the decay of seasoned wood, causing it to crumble to a dry powder by the action of various fungi. **2** a disease of living plants caused by the same fungi that produce dry decay. **3** any of these fungi. **4** inner decay: *Lack of new people and new ideas often causes dry rot in an organization.*

dry run 1 a practice test or session. **2** *Military.* any simulated firing practice, bombing approach, etc., without use of live ammunition.

dry–shod ['draɪ ʃɒd] *adj. or adv.* having dry shoes; without getting the feet wet.

dry–stone ['draɪ ˌstoun] *adj.* built of stone without the use of mortar: *a dry-stone wall.*

dry•wall ['draɪˌwɒl] *n., v. —n.* **1** a construction method for interior walls, using plasterboard instead of wet plaster. **2** plasterboard. **3** (*adjl.*) made of plasterboard: *drywall panelling.* —*v.* construct the walls of with plasterboard instead of wet plaster.

dry wash clothes, linens, etc. that have been washed and dried, but not ironed.

d.s. 1 daylight-saving. **2** *Business.* days after sight.

DS *Typing.* double space.

D.S. or **d.s.** *Music.* repeat from the point indicated (for Ital. *dal segno* from the sign).

D.S.C. Distinguished Service Cross.

D.S.M. Distinguished Service Medal.

D.S.O. Distinguished Service Order.

d.t.'s DELIRIUM TREMENS.

Du. Dutch.

du•al ['djuəl] *or* ['duəl] *adj., n. —adj.* **1** of two; showing two. **2** consisting of two parts; double; twofold: *The airplane had dual controls, one set for each pilot.* **3** *Grammar.* signifying or denoting reference to two. Some languages have a **dual number** for nouns, pronouns, verbs, etc., distinct in form from singular and plural. —*n. Grammar.* **1** the dual number. **2** a word or construction in the dual number. ⟨< L *dualis* < *duo* two⟩
☛ *Hom.* DUEL.

du•al•ism ['djuəˌlɪzəm] *or* ['duəˌlɪzəm] *n.* **1** a dual condition; duality. **2** *Philosophy.* the doctrine that all the phenomena of the universe can be explained by two independent and distinct forces, substances, or principles, such as mind and matter, or good and evil. **3** *Christian theology.* **a** the doctrine that Christ consisted of two personalities. **b** the doctrine that two distinct elements are constituted in people, as body and spirit.

du•al•ist ['djuəlɪst] *or* ['duəlɪst] *n.* a believer in dualism.
☛ *Hom.* DUELLIST.

du•al•is•tic [ˌdjuə'lɪstɪk] *or* [ˌduə'lɪstɪk] *adj.* **1** having to do with dualism; based on dualism. **2** dual. **—ˌdu•al'is•ti•cal•ly,** *adv.*

du•al•i•ty [dju'æləti] *or* [du'æləti] *n., pl.* **-ties. 1** a dual condition or quality. **2** something that is a combination of two distinct things or principles.

du•al–pur•pose ['djuəl 'pɜrpəs] *or* ['duəl 'pɜrpəs] *adj.* having, serving, or designed for two functions, such as sheep that are raised for both wool and meat.

dub¹ [dʌb] *v.* **dubbed, dub•bing. 1** make (a person) a member of an order of knighthood by striking his shoulder lightly with a sword: *He was dubbed a knight.* **2** give a title to; call; name: *Because of his very blond hair, the boys dubbed him 'Whitey'.* **3** smooth or dress (wood, leather, etc.) by rubbing, scraping, etc. ⟨OE *dubbian*⟩

dub² [dʌb] *n., v.* **dubbed, dub•bing.** *Slang. —n.* **1** a clumsy, unskilful person. **2** *Sports.* an awkward, clumsy player. —*v.* do or play awkwardly; bungle. ⟨? related to *dub¹*⟩

dub³ [dʌb] *v.* **dubbed, dub•bing;** *n. —v.* **1** push; thrust. **2** beat a drum. —*n.* **1** a thrust or push. **2** the beat of a drum. ⟨origin uncertain⟩

dub⁴ [dʌb] *v.* **dubbed, dub•bing;** *n. —v.* **1** add music, voices, or sound effects to (a film, a radio or television broadcast, a recording, etc.) by making or replacing a sound track: *The Italian film was dubbed with English dialogue.* **2** add (sounds) to a film, recording, etc. (*usually used with* **in**). **3** rerecord (a previously made recording). —*n.* **1** the sounds added. **2** a copy of a recording. ⟨short for *double*⟩

dub•bin ['dʌbɪn] *n.* a waxy substance used to preserve and waterproof shoes, leather, etc.

du•bi•e•ty [dju'baɪəti] *or* [du'baɪəti] *n., pl.* **-ties. 1** doubtfulness; uncertainty. **2** something that is doubtful. ⟨< LL *dubietas*⟩

du•bi•ous ['djubiəs] *or* ['dubiəs] *adj.* **1** that is or can be doubted; uncertain: *a dubious compliment, dubious authorship, a dubious friend.* **2** having doubt. **3** of questionable character, probably bad: *a dubious scheme for making money.* ⟨< L *dubiosus* < *dubius* doubtful < *du-* two⟩ **—'du•bi•ous•ly,** *adv.* **—'du•bi•ous•ness,** *n.*

du•bi•ta•ble ['djubətəbəl] *or* ['dubətəbəl] *adj.* liable to doubt or question. ⟨< L *dubitabilis* < *dubitare* doubt⟩

du•cal ['djukəl] *or* ['dukəl] *adj.* of or having to do with a duke or dukedom. ⟨< LL *ducalis* < L *dux, ducis* leader⟩ **—'du•cal•ly,** *adv.*

duc•at ['dʌkət] *n.* **1** a gold or silver coin formerly used in some European countries. **2** *Slang.* a ticket. ⟨ME < Ital. *ducato* < Med.L < L *dux, ducis* leader⟩

du•ce ['dutʃei] *n. Italian.* **1** leader. **2 Il Duce,** the title given to Benito Mussolini (1883-1945), dictator of Italy from 1922 to 1943. ⟨< Ital. < L *dux, ducis* leader. Doublet of DOGE, DUKE.⟩

duch•ess ['dʌtʃɪs] *n.* **1** the wife or widow of a duke. **2** a woman with a rank equal to that of a duke. ⟨ME < OF *duchesse* < *duc* duke. See DUKE.⟩

duch•y ['dʌtʃi] *n., pl.* **duch•ies.** the territory under the rule of a duke or duchess; a dukedom. ⟨ME and OF *duchee* < LL *ducatus* territory of a duke⟩

duck[1] [dʌk] *n.* **1** any of numerous small or medium-sized aquatic birds (family Anatidae) having a thick body, short neck and legs, flat bill, and webbed feet. **2** the adult female of a duck. Compare DRAKE. **3** the flesh of a duck used for food. **4** *Informal.* darling; pet. **5** *Slang.* a person, especially one considered strange but harmless: *He's a queer old duck.*
like water off a duck's back, without having any effect. ⟨OE *dūce.* Related to DUCK[2].⟩ **—'duck,like,** *adj.*

duck[2] [dʌk] *v., n.* —*v.* **1** dip or plunge suddenly under water and out again. **2** lower the head or bend the body suddenly to keep from being hit, seen, etc. **3** lower (the head) or bend (the body) suddenly. **4** *Informal.* get or keep away from; avoid: *He is always ducking his responsibilities.* **5** *Informal.* escape; make off (*often used with* **out**): *She ducked out when she heard they were coming.*
—*n.* the act or an instance of ducking. ⟨ME *duke(n)*⟩
—'duck•er, *n.*

duck[3] [dʌk] *n.* **1** a strong cotton or linen cloth with a lighter and finer weave than canvas. Duck is used to make small sails, and clothes for sailors or people living in hot climates. **2 ducks,** *pl. Informal.* trousers made of duck. ⟨< Du. *doek* cloth⟩

duck[4] [dʌk] *n.* a military vehicle that resembles a truck, but has a watertight body so that it may move through the water like a boat. ⟨for DUKW, its code name⟩

duck•bill ['dʌk,bɪl] *n.* platypus.

duckbilled platypus platypus.

duck•board ['dʌk,bɔrd] *n.* Usually, **duckboards,** *pl.* a platform of slats laid on a muddy, wet, or cold surface to form a floor or path.

ducking stool formerly, a stool on which a person was tied and ducked into water as a punishment.

duck•ling ['dʌklɪŋ] *n.* a young duck.

duck•pins ['dʌk,pɪnz] *n.* **1** a game that resembles bowling but is played with smaller balls and pins. **2** the pins used in this game.

ducks and drakes the game of skipping flat stones on water.
make ducks and drakes of or **play ducks and drakes with,** handle recklessly; squander foolishly.

duck soup *Slang.* something that is easily done; a cinch: *This job will be duck soup to us.*

duck•tail ['dʌk,teil] *n.* a haircut in which the sides are grown long, brushed back, and cut to look like a duck's tail.

duck•weed ['dʌk,wid] *n.* **1** any of a genus (*Lemna*) of tiny, floating, aquatic plants found in ponds and also in stagnant water. **2** (*adjl.*) designating a family (Lemnaceae) of tiny, stemless, aquatic plants, including the duckweeds, that float freely on or in the water, having no real foliage, but consisting only of a frond or fronds, with one or more roots growing from the bottom, and minute flowers from the top or edge. Members of the duckweed family are the simplest flowering plants.

duc•ky ['dʌki] *adj. Informal.* charming; cute; lovely (*often used ironically*).

duct [dʌkt] *n.* **1** a tube, pipe, or channel for carrying liquid, air, wires, etc. **2** a tube in the body for carrying a bodily fluid: *tear ducts.* ⟨< L *ductus* < *ducere* lead⟩ **—'duct•less,** *adj.*

duc•tile ['dʌktaɪl] *or* ['dʌktəl] *adj.* **1** capable of being hammered out thin or drawn out into a wire: *Gold and copper are ductile metals.* **2** easily moulded or shaped: *Wax is ductile.* **3** easily managed or influenced; docile. ⟨< F < L *ductilis* < *ducere* lead⟩

duc•til•i•ty [dʌk'tɪləti] *n., pl.* **-ties.** a ductile quality.

ductless gland a gland without a duct whose secretion passes directly into the blood or lymph circulating through it; endocrine gland. The thyroid, the spleen, and the thymus are ductless glands.

dud [dʌd] *n., adj. Informal.* —*n.* **1** a person or thing that is useless or unsatisfactory; a failure, misfit, etc.: *The novel proved to be a dud.* **2** a shell or bomb that fails to explode. **3 duds,** *pl.* **a** clothes. **b** possessions; personal belongings.
—*adj.* worthless, useless, or unsatisfactory: *a dud cheque.* ⟨ME *dudde*; of unknown origin⟩

dude [djud] *or* [dud] *n.* **1** in the western parts of Canada and the United States, a city-bred person, especially one who spends a holiday on a ranch. **2** a man who pays too much attention to his clothes; dandy. **3** *Slang.* any person. ⟨origin unknown⟩

dude ranch a ranch that is run as a tourist resort.

dudg•eon ['dʌdʒən] *n. Archaic.* anger; resentment.
in high dudgeon, very angry; resentful. ⟨origin unknown⟩

dud•ish ['djudɪʃ] *or* ['dudɪʃ] *adj.* like that of a dude.

due [dju] *or* [du] *adj., n., adv.* —*adj.* **1** owed as a debt; to be paid or given to as a right: *Money is due to him for his work. Respect is due to older people.* **2** proper; suitable; rightful: *Good deeds deserve due reward; bad deeds deserve due punishment.* **3** as much as needed; enough: *Use due care when crossing streets.* **4** promised to come or be ready; looked for; expected: *The train is due at noon. Your report is due tomorrow.* **5** of notes, bills, etc., becoming payable; having reached maturity; mature. **6** of dates, on which notes, bills, etc., become mature.
become due, be required to be paid.
due to, a caused by: *The accident was due to her careless use of the gun.* **b** *Informal.* on account of: *The rally was postponed due to the bad weather.*
fall due, be required to be paid.
—*n.* **1** something owed as a debt or to be paid or given as a right: *Courtesy is a person's due as long as he or she is your guest.* **2 dues,** *pl.* **a** the amount of money owed or to be paid; a fee; tax. **b** the amount of money owed or to be paid to a club, etc. by a member.
give a person his or her due, be fair to a person.
pay (one's) **dues, a** pay a fee for belonging to an organization. **b** *Slang.* suffer the initial hardships which earn (one) certain privileges or rights.
—*adv.* straight; directly; exactly: *The wind is due east.* ⟨ME < OF *deü*, pp. of *devoir* owe < L *debere*⟩
☛ *Hom.* DEW [du], DO[1].
☛ *Usage.* **due to: Due** was originally used only as an adjective, and therefore in formal English many writers use **due to** only to introduce an adjective phrase (one modifying a noun): *Her success was due to her hard work* (modifies *success*). In informal English **due to** is often used to introduce an adverb phrase: *Due to her hard work, she succeeded.* However, many people do not approve of this construction. To avoid it, use **because of** or **on account of:** *She succeeded because of her hard work. On account of her hard work, she succeeded.*

du•el ['djuəl] *or* ['duəl] *n., v.* **-elled** or **-eled, -el•ling** or **-el•ing.** —*n.* **1** a formal fight between two men armed with swords or firearms. Duels were arranged to settle quarrels, avenge insults, etc., and were fought in the presence of witnesses, called seconds. **2** any fight or contest between two opponents: *a duel of wits.*
—*v.* fight or compete in a duel or duels. ⟨< Med.L *duellum* a combat between two < L *duellum* (early form of *bellum*) war⟩
☛ *Hom.* DUAL.

du•el•list or **du•el•ist** ['djuəlɪst] *or* ['duəlɪst] *n.* a person who fights a duel or duels.
☛ *Hom.* DUALIST.

du•en•de [du'ɛndei] *n.* a special personal magnetism or charm that makes one attractive. ⟨< Spanish *duende* ghost or demon⟩

du•en•na [dju'ɛnə] *or* [du'ɛnə] *n.* **1** an elderly woman who is the governess and chaperone of young girls in a Spanish or Portuguese family. **2** a governess; chaperone. ⟨< Sp. *dueña* < L *domina* mistress⟩

du•et [dju'ɛt] *or* [du'ɛt] *n.* **1** a piece of music to be sung or played by two people. **2** two singers or players performing together. ⟨< Ital. *duetto*, dim. of *duo.* See DUO.⟩

duff[1] [dʌf] *n.* a flour pudding boiled in a cloth bag: *plum duff.* ⟨var. of *dough*⟩

duff[2] [dʌf] *n.* the decaying vegetable matter that covers the ground in a forest. ⟨origin uncertain⟩

duff[3] [dʌf] *n. Slang.* buttocks. ⟨origin uncertain⟩

duf•fel or **duf•fle** ['dʌfəl] *n.* **1** a coarse woollen cloth having a thick nap. **2** the personal belongings of a hunter, camper, soldier, etc. **3** DUFFEL SOCK. **4** DUFFEL BAG. **5** DUFFEL COAT. ⟨< Du. < *Duffel*, a town near Antwerp⟩

duffel bag or **duffle bag 1** a large bag of heavy cloth or canvas, used by campers, hunters, soldiers, etc. for carrying personal belongings. **2** any bag of stout material.

duffel coat or **duffle coat** a knee-length, usually hooded coat made of duffel.

duffel sock or **duffle sock** in the North: **1** one of a pair of wrap-around leggings made of long strips of duffel or blanketing, worn as a protection against intense cold. **2** an outer sock or liner made of duffel, worn between a sock and a boot or mukluk, etc.

duff•er ['dʌfər] *n.* **1** *Informal.* a useless, clumsy, or stupid person. **2** a person who plays a game, such as golf, poorly. **3** *Slang.* a term of endearment or familiar term of address for a male baby or child or an old man: *And how is the little duffer? Is the old duffer still hale and hearty?* ⟨origin uncertain⟩

duf•fle ['dʌfəl] See DUFFEL.

dug[1] [dʌg] *v.* pt. and pp. of DIG.

dug[2] [dʌg] *n.* a teat or nipple of a female animal. ⟨< Scand.; cf. Danish *dægge*, Swedish *dägga* suckle⟩

du•gong ['dugɒŋ] *n.* a large, whalelike marine mammal (*Dugong dugon*) found in shallow coastal waters off E Africa, the Philippines, New Guinea, and N Australia, having flipperlike forelimbs and a paddlelike, slightly forked tail. The dugong is the only living member of the family Dugongidae. ⟨< Malay *dūyong*⟩

dug•out ['dʌg,ʌut] *n.* **1** a rough shelter made by digging into the side of a hill, trench, etc. During war, soldiers use dugouts for protection against bullets and bombs. **2** a small shelter at the side of a baseball field, used by players who are not at bat or not in the game. **3** a boat made by hollowing out a large log. **4** *Cdn.* especially on the Prairies, a large excavation used to hold water collected there from the spring thaw and from rainfall: *Some dugouts are used for watering livestock; others are used for watering land.*

du•i ['djui] *or* ['dui] *n.* a pl. of DUO.

dui•ker ['dəikər] *n.* a small African antelope of the genera *Cephalophus* or *Sylvicapra*, having short horns in the male and often the female, common south of the Sahara. Some species are endangered. ⟨< Du. *duiker* a diver < *duiken* to duck⟩

du jour [du 'ʒur]; *French,* [dy'ʒuʀ] of items on a menu, served on this day: *quiche du jour.* ⟨< F of the day⟩

duke [djuk] *or* [duk] *n.* **1** a nobleman ranking next below a prince and above a marquis. **2** a prince who rules a small state or country called a duchy. **3 dukes,** *pl. Slang.* hands; fists. **4** a variety of cherry, a hybrid of sour and sweet cherry. ⟨ME < OF *duc* < L *dux, ducis* leader. Doublet of DOGE, DUCE.⟩

duke•dom ['djukdəm] *or* ['duk-] *n.* **1** the territory under the rule of a duke or duchess; duchy. **2** the title or rank of a duke.

Duk•ho•bor ['dukə,bɔr] *n.* Doukhobour.

dul•cet ['dʌlsɪt] *adj.* soothing, especially to the ear; sweet; pleasing. ⟨< F *doucet,* dim. of *doux,* earlier *dulz* sweet < L *dulcis*⟩

dul•ci•mer ['dʌlsəmər] *n.* **1** a musical instrument with metal strings, played by striking the strings with two hammers. **2** a similar instrument of the southern Appalachians, held in the lap and played by plucking. ⟨< MF *doulcemer,* var. of *doulcemele* < L *dulcis* sweet + *melos* song (< Gk.)⟩

Dul•cin•e•a or **dul•cin•ea** [dʌl'sɪniə] *or* [,dʌlsə'niə] *n.* any idolized sweetheart. ⟨< *Dulcinea,* the peasant girl who is Don Quixote's sweetheart and whom he idolizes as a fine and beautiful lady; from Sp. *dulce* sweet⟩

dule [djul] *n.* a group of doves.

dull [dʌl] *adj., v.* —*adj.* **1** not sharp or pointed: *a dull knife.* **2** not bright or clear: *dull eyes, a dull day.* **3** slow in understanding; stupid: *a dull mind.* **4** showing a lack of liveliness in the senses or feelings. **5** not interesting; tiresome; boring: *a dull book.* **6** having little life, energy, or spirit; not active: *Business is dull these days.* **7** not felt sharply: *a dull pain.* —*v.* make or become dull. ⟨ME *dul*⟩ —**'dul•ly,** *adv.* —**'dull•ness** or **'dul•ness,** *n.*

☛ *Syn. adj.* **1. Dull,** BLUNT = with the edge or point not sharp. **Dull** suggests that the object described has lost the sharpness it had or is not as sharp as it should be: *This knife is dull.* **Blunt** suggests that the edge or point is not intended to be sharp or keen: *The blunt side of a knife will not cut meat. The weapon used by the murderer was a blunt instrument, possibly a poker.* **3.** See note at STUPID.

dull•ard ['dʌlərd] *n.* a person who is stupid and who learns very slowly.

dull•ish ['dʌlɪʃ] *adj.* rather dull.

dulls•ville or **Dulls•ville** ['dʌlz,vɪl] *n. Slang.* a place, activity, social function, etc. that is very boring.

dul•ly ['dʌli] *adv.* in a dull manner.

dulse [dʌls] *n.* a large, edible, reddish seaweed (*Rhodymenia palmata*) found along the American and European coasts of the North Atlantic. ⟨< Irish and Scots Gaelic *duileasg*⟩

du•ly ['djuli] *or* ['duli] *adv.* **1** according to what is due; properly; rightfully: *The documents were duly signed before a lawyer.* **2** as much as is needed; enough. **3** when due; at the proper time: *The debt was duly paid.*

Du•ma ['dumɑ] *n.* in Imperial Russia, the national lawmaking body, established in 1905 and discontinued in 1917. Also, **Douma.** ⟨< Russian *duma* thought, counsel, ult. < Gmc. Related to DEEM, DOOM.⟩

dumb [dʌm] *adj.* **1** not having the power of speech: *Animals are dumb.* **2** *Archaic.* suffering from an inability to speak as a result of sickness, injury, etc.; mute: *deaf and dumb.* **3** silenced for the moment by fear, surprise, shyness, etc.: *The poor child was dumb with embarrassment.* **4** not expressed in words: *dumb astonishment, dumb grief.* **5** unwilling to speak; silent: *They questioned him repeatedly, but he remained dumb.* **6** not producing sound. **7** *Informal.* stupid; unintelligent, or foolish: *He's too dumb to catch on to this. Locking your keys in the car is a dumb thing to do.* ⟨< (defs. 1-6) OE *dumb*; (def. 7) influenced by G *dumm* stupid⟩ —**'dumb•ly,** *adv.* —**'dumb•ness,** *n.*

☛ *Syn.* **1. Dumb,** MUTE, SPEECHLESS = without the power of speech. **Dumb** = being by nature without the power of speech, and although sometimes used interchangeably with **mute** and **speechless,** it is the term applied particularly to animals: *Even intelligent animals are dumb.* **Mute** emphasizes being silent as the result of an injury or disorder, and applies particularly to people who have never been able to speak because they were born deaf or became deaf in very early life and have never or almost never heard sounds: *Many mute children are now taught to speak.* **Speechless** = deprived of speech, usually temporarily and as the result of emotion, surprise, etc.: *I was speechless with rage.*

dumb–bell ['dʌm ,bɛl] *n.* **1** a short bar of wood or iron with large, heavy, round ends. Dumb-bells are generally used in pairs and are lifted or swung around to exercise the muscles of the arms, back, etc. **2** *Slang.* a stupid person. Also, **dumbbell.**

dumb•found [,dʌm'faʊnd] *or* ['dʌm,faʊnd] See DUMFOUND.

dumb show gestures without words; pantomime: *She indicated by dumb show that she wanted to speak to me privately.*

dumb•struck ['dʌm,strʌk] *adj.* made speechless through amazement.

dumb•wait•er ['dʌm,weitər] *n.* **1** a small box with shelves, pulled up and down a shaft like an elevator to send dishes, food, rubbish, etc. from one floor to another. **2** a small stand placed near a dining table, for holding dishes, etc.

dum•dum ['dʌm,dʌm] *n.* **1** a soft-nosed bullet that spreads out when it strikes, causing a large, jagged wound. **2** a stupid person; fool; also, **dumb-dumb.** ⟨< *Dum Dum,* a town near Calcutta, India, where the bullet was first made⟩

dumdum bullet dumdum.

dum•found [,dʌm'faʊnd] *or* ['dʌm,faʊnd] *v.* amaze to the point of making unable to speak; bewilder utterly. ⟨< *dumb* + con*found*⟩

dum•my ['dʌmi] *n., pl.* **-mies;** *adj.* —*n.* **1** a figure of a person, used to display clothing in store windows, to take the place of passengers in crash-testing cars, to tackle in football, etc. **2** an empty or imitation package or article used for display or advertisement: *All the articles in this window are dummies.* **3** *Informal.* a stupid person; blockhead. **4** an imitation; counterfeit. **5** a person supposedly acting for himself or herself, but really acting for another. **6** a person who has nothing to say or who takes no active part in affairs. **7** *Card games.* **a** a player whose cards are laid face up on the table and played by his or her partner. **b** a hand of cards played in this way. **8** *Printing.* **a** a sample volume bound or unbound, and usually either blank or only partly printed, to show the size and general appearance of a book, etc. in preparation. **b** a format for parts or the whole of a magazine, book, etc., made up of printer's proofs pasted down upon empty pages to show the general arrangement of the material; layout.
—*adj.* **1** made to resemble the real thing; make-believe; imitation; counterfeit: *The children played soldier with dummy swords made of wood.* **2** acting for another while supposedly acting for oneself. **3** *Card games.* played with a hand of cards exposed. ⟨< *dumb* + *-y*[1]⟩

dump [dʌmp] *v., n.* —*v.* **1** empty out; throw down; unload in a mass: *The truck backed up to the curb and dumped the topsoil on the driveway.* **2** unload rubbish: *No dumping.* **3** put (goods) on the market in large quantities and at a low price; especially, do so in a foreign country at a price below that in the home country. **4** *Slang.* get rid of; abandon; reject: *to dump an unpopular candidate.* **5** *Computer technology.* **a** copy (data in memory) to another location. **b** print out (data in memory).
dump on, *Slang.* **a** express strong disapproval or contempt; disparage or malign: *She dumped on the government's foreign policy in a letter to the editor.* **b** *Slang.* make a scapegoat of or vent one's ill feeling on: *So you lost the race! Don't dump on me!*
—*n.* **1** a place for unloading rubbish. **2** a heap of rubbish. **3** a place for storing military supplies: *an ammunition dump.* **4** *Slang.* a shabby, ill-kept, untidy, or otherwise depressing house, town, or locality: *Life in this dump is unbearable.* **5** *Computer technology.* the act, process, or product of dumping stored data. **6** *Logging.* a place at water's edge where cut logs are piled before being rolled into the water and driven downstream. **7** *Placer mining.* a pile of dirt waiting to be put through the sluice box to

separate any gold that may be there. ⟨ME ? < Scand; cf. Danish *dumpe* fall with a thud⟩

dump•ling ['dʌmplɪŋ] *n.* **1** a rounded piece of dough, boiled or steamed and served with meat or in soup. **2** a small pudding made by enclosing fruit in a piece of dough and baking or steaming it. **3** a dumpy animal or person, short and of rounded outlines. ⟨< *dump* a badly shaped piece + *-ling*⟩

dumps [dʌmps] *n.pl. Informal.* low spirits; gloomy feelings. **(down) in the dumps,** feeling gloomy or sad. ⟨prob. < Du. *domp* haze, dullness. Related to DAMP.⟩

Dump•ster ['dʌmpstər] *n. Trademark.* a big metal trash container used to hold large quantities of garbage, as for apartment buildings, construction sites, etc.

dump truck a vehicle that opens at the bottom or tips to dump its contents.

dump•y ['dʌmpi] *adj.* **dump•i•er, dump•i•est.** short and fat. **—'dump•i•ly,** *adv.* **—'dump•i•ness,** *n.*

dun¹ [dʌn] *v.* **dunned, dun•ning;** *n.* *—v.* demand payment of a debt from (someone) again and again.
—n. **1** a demand for payment, especially of a debt. **2** a person constantly demanding payment of a debt. ⟨var. of *din,* with reference to making a din for money due⟩
☛ *Hom.* DONE.

dun² [dʌn] *adj., n.* *—adj.* dull greyish brown.
—n. **1** a dull greyish brown colour. **2** a dull greyish brown horse. ⟨OE *dunn*⟩
☛ *Hom.* DONE.

Duncan Phyfe ['dʌŋkən 'fəif] **1** of, like, or having to do with a style of gracefully proportioned and soundly constructed furniture. **2** this style of furniture. **3** a piece of furniture of this style. ⟨after *Duncan Phyfe* (1768-1854), an American furniture designer⟩

dunce [dʌns] *n.* **1** a child slow at learning his or her lessons in school. **2** a stupid person. ⟨< *Duns(man),* name applied by his attackers to any follower of John *Duns Scotus,* a medieval theologian⟩

dunce cap or **dunce's cap** a tall, cone-shaped cap formerly worn as a punishment by a child who was slow in learning his or her lessons in school.

dun•der•head ['dʌndər,hɛd] *n.* a stupid, foolish person; dunce; blockhead. ⟨*dunder* of uncertain origin⟩
—'dun•der,head•ed•ness, *n.*

dune [djun] *or* [dun] *n.* a mound or ridge of loose sand heaped up by the wind. ⟨< F < MDu. *dune.* Akin to DOWN³.⟩

dune buggy a small, usually roofless vehicle, often a converted car, for use on sand dunes or rough terrain.

dung [dʌŋ] *n., v.* *—n.* animal excrement; manure: *Dung is much used as a fertilizer.*
—v. put dung on. ⟨OE⟩

dun•ga•ree [,dʌŋgə'ri] *or* ['dʌŋgə,ri] *n.* **1** a coarse cotton cloth, used for work clothes, sails, etc., especially blue denim. **2 dungarees,** *pl.* trousers or clothing made of this cloth. ⟨< Hind. *dungrī* a coarse calico cloth. 17c.⟩

dung beetle **1** any of various scarab beetles that feed on dung both as adults and larvae. **2** any of various other dung-eating beetles.

dun•geon ['dʌndʒən] *n., v.* *—n.* **1** a dark underground room to keep prisoners in. **2** donjon.
—v. confine in a dungeon; imprison. ⟨ME < OF *donjon* < Gmc.⟩
☛ *Hom.* DONJON.

dung•hill ['dʌŋ,hɪl] *n.* **1** a heap of dung. **2** a vile place or person.

dunk [dʌŋk] *v.* **1** dip (something) into a liquid: *to dunk doughnuts in coffee.* **2** *Informal.* push (somebody) under water. **3** *Basketball.* score by jumping up and dropping (the ball) through the basket. ⟨< LG *dunken* dip⟩ **—'dunk•er,** *n.*

dunk shot *Basketball.* a shot in which a player jumps up and scores by dropping the ball through the basket.

dun•lin ['dʌnlən] *n., pl.* **-lin** or **-lins.** a small sandpiper (*Calidris alpina*) having a downward-curving bill and grey plumage that in breeding season becomes reddish on the back and black on the belly. Dunlins breed in the Arctic and winter on seacoasts farther south. ⟨dim. of *dun²*⟩

dun•nage ['dʌnɪdʒ] *n.* **1** personal belongings; kit; baggage. **2** branches, mats, etc. placed around a cargo to protect it from damage by water or chafing. ⟨origin uncertain⟩

du•o ['djuou] *or* ['duou] *n., pl.* **duos, dui. 1** *Music.* a duet. **2** *Informal.* a pair. ⟨< Ital. < L *duo* two⟩

du•o•dec•i•mal [,djuou'dɛsəməl] *or* [,duou-] *adj., n.* *—adj.* having to do with twelfths or twelve; proceeding by twelves.
—n. **1** a twelfth part. **2 duodecimals,** *pl. Mathematics.* a system of numbering or computing, using twelve as a base instead of ten as in the decimal system.

du•o•dec•i•mo [,djuou'dɛsə,mou] *or* [,duou-] *n., pl.* **-mos. 1** the page size of a book in which each leaf is one-twelfth of a printer's whole sheet of paper, or about 12.5 cm × 19 cm. **2** a book having pages of this size. ⟨< L *in duodecimo* in a twelfth⟩

du•o•de•nal [,djuou'dinəl] *or* [,duou-] *adj.* of or in the duodenum: *a duodenal ulcer.*

du•o•de•num [,djuou'dinəm] *or* [,duou-] *n., pl.* **-na** [-nə]. the first part of the small intestine, just below the stomach. See ALIMENTARY CANAL for picture. ⟨ME < Med.L < L *duodeni* twelve each; with reference to its length, about twelve finger breadths⟩

du•op•o•ly [dju'ɒpəli] *or* [du'ɒpəli] *n. Economics.* domination of a market by two parties, as sellers, suppliers, etc. ⟨< L *duo* two + mono*poly*⟩

du•o•tone ['djuə,toun] *or* ['duə,toun] *adj., n.* *—adj. Printing.* printed in two tones of the same colour.
—n. a method by which illustrations are reproduced in two tones of the same colour. ⟨< L *duo* two + E *tone*⟩

dup. duplicate.

dupe [djup] *or* [dup] *n., v.* **duped, dup•ing.** *—n.* **1** a person easily deceived or tricked. **2** one who is being deluded or tricked: *The young politician's inexperience is making her the dupe of some unscrupulous schemers.*
—v. deceive; trick. ⟨< F < OF *duppe,* earlier *d'uppe* < L *upupa* hoopee (a bird thought to be stupid)⟩ **—'dup•er,** *n.*

du•ple ['djupəl] *or* ['dupəl] *adj.* **1** double. **2** *Music.* having two or a multiple of two beats to the measure. ⟨< L *duplus* double. Doublet of DOUBLE.⟩

du•plet ['djuplɪt] *or* ['duplɪt] *n. Chemistry.* a pair of electrons that is shared by two atoms.

duple time *Music.* two-part time.

du•plex ['djuplɛks] *or* ['duplɛks] *adj., n.* *—adj.* **1** double; twofold. **2** of or having to do with a telegraphic system in which two messages can be transmitted in both directions at once over one circuit. Compare DIPLEX, SIMPLEX (def. 2).
—n. **1** *Cdn.* a building consisting of two dwellings under one roof, either side by side or one above the other: *Most of the houses on this street are duplexes.* **2** *Cdn.* one of the dwellings in such a building. **3** *U.S.* DUPLEX APARTMENT. ⟨< L *duplex* < *du-* two + *plicare* fold⟩

duplex apartment *U.S.* a self-contained apartment with rooms on two floors.

du•pli•cate *adj., n.* ['djupləkɪt] *or* ['dupləkɪt]; *v.* ['djuplə,keit] *or* ['duplə,keit] *adj., n., v.* **-cat•ed, -cat•ing.** *—adj.* **1** exactly alike; corresponding exactly: *We have duplicate keys for the front door.* **2** having or consisting of two similar or corresponding parts: *A person's lungs are duplicate.* **3** designating a card game in which identical hands are played by a second set of players in order to compare scores: *duplicate bridge.*
—n. **1** an exact copy; reproduction; replica: *She made a duplicate of her letter to the editor of the newspaper.* **2** a counterpart; double: *This chair is a duplicate of one we have at home.*
in duplicate, in two copies exactly alike: *This application must be made out in duplicate.*
—v. **1** make an exact copy of; repeat exactly. **2** make double or twofold; double. ⟨< L *duplicatus,* pp. of *duplicare* to double < *du-* two + *plicare* fold⟩ **—'du•pli•ca•tive,** *adj.*

du•pli•ca•tion [,djuplə'keiʃən] *or* [,duplə'keiʃən] *n.* **1** duplicating or being duplicated. **2** a duplicate copy.

du•pli•ca•tor ['djuplə,keitər] *or* ['duplə,keitər] *n.* a machine for making many exact copies of anything written or typed; a duplicating machine.

du•plic•i•ty [dju'plɪsəti] *or* [du'plɪsəti] *n., pl.* **-ties.** deceitfulness; treachery; secretly acting one way and openly acting another in order to deceive. ⟨< LL *duplicitas* doubleness < L *duplex.* See DUPLEX.⟩ **—du'plic•i•tous,** *adj.*

du•ra•bil•i•ty [,djʊrə'bɪləti] *or* [,dʊrə'bɪləti] *n., pl.* **-ties.** lasting quality; ability to stand wear.

du•ra•ble ['djʊrəbəl] *or* ['dʊrəbəl] *adj.* able to last a long time; not soon injured or worn out. ⟨ME < OF < L *durabilis* < *durare* to last, harden < *durus* hard⟩ **—'du•ra•ble•ness,** *n.*
—'du•ra•bly, *adv.*

durable goods goods that last a long time, such as furniture or appliances.

Du•ral•u•min [dju'ræljəmɪn] *or* [du'ræljəmɪn] *n. Trademark.* a light, strong, hard metal that is an alloy of aluminum containing copper, manganese, and magnesium. ⟨< *durable* + *alumin*um⟩

du•ra ma•ter ['djʊrə 'meitər] *or* ['dʊrə 'meitər] the outer covering of the brain and spinal cord, formed of tough, fibrous membrane. ⟨< ML, literally hard mother⟩ **—'du•ral,** *adj.*

du•rance ['djurəns] *or* ['durəns] *n.* imprisonment, especially in the phrase **durance vile.** ⟨< MF *durance* duration⟩

du•ra•tion [djʊ'reiʃən] *or* [dʊ'reiʃən] *n.* length of time; the time during which something lasts: *The strike was expected to be of short duration.*
for the duration, until the end. ⟨ME < LL *duratio, -onis* < L *durare* to last⟩

dur•bar ['dɜrbɑr] *n.* in India: **1** an official court or audience chamber. **2** any formal reception or assembly held by a governmental authority. **3** formerly, in British India, a formal assembly held to mark special occasions such as the proclamation of Queen Victoria as Empress of India. ⟨< Hind., Persian *darbār* court⟩

du•ress [djʊ'rɛs] *or* [dʊ'rɛs], ['djʊrɛs] *or* ['dʊrɛs] *n.* **1** compulsion. A person cannot be legally forced to fulfil a contract signed under duress. **2** imprisonment. ⟨ME < OF *duresse* < L *duritia* hardness < *durus* hard⟩

Dur•ham ['dɜrəm] *n.* shorthorn. ⟨< *Durham,* a county in England, where this breed originated⟩

Durham boat a large boat much used in the early 19th century on the St. Lawrence River and its tributaries for carrying freight and passengers. It could be propelled by sails or poles. ⟨after Robert *Durham,* an 18c. American boat builder⟩

Durham report the *Report on the Affairs of British North America,* issued in 1839 by Lord Durham (1792-1840), Governor-in-Chief of British North America from May to December, 1838. The report led to the union of Upper and Lower Canada in 1841 and to the introduction of responsible government and municipal government in Canada.

dur•ian ['djuriən], ['duriən], *or* ['dɜriən] *n.* **1** a tree (*Durio zibethinus*) of the East Indies, bearing a pungent but edible fruit. **2** this fruit, oval in shape and having a hard, prickly rind covering cream-coloured pulp. ⟨< Malay *duri* thorn⟩

dur•ing ['djʊrɪŋ] *or* ['dʊrɪŋ] *prep.* **1** throughout; through the entire time of: *The old woman stays in the house during the day, but usually goes for a walk in the evening. The children played tag during recess.* **2** at some time in; in the course of: *They're going to drop in and see us sometime during the day.* ⟨ppr. of obs. *dure* endure < OF < L *durare*⟩

dur•mast ['dɜrmæst] *n.* a large oak (*Quercus petraea*) native to Eurasia, whose resilient, heavy wood is much used in carpentry. ⟨probably < *dun*[2] + *mast*[2]⟩

Du•roc ['djʊrɒk] *or* ['dʊrɒk] *n.* a breed of large, red pig developed in the United States. ⟨after the name of a horse owned by the developer of this breed. 19c.⟩

Du•roc–Jer•sey ['djʊrɒk 'dʒɜrzi] *or* ['dʊrɒk-] *n.* Duroc.

dur•ra ['durə] *n.* a variety of sorghum raised for grain. ⟨< Arabic *dhura*⟩

durst [dɜrst] *v.* a pt. of DARE.

du•rum ['djʊrəm], ['dʊrəm] *or,* especially on the Prairies, ['dɜrəm] *n.* a species of wheat (*Triticum durum*) having a high gluten content, used especially in making pastas, such as macaroni and spaghetti. ⟨< L *durum,* neut. of *durus* hard⟩

durum wheat durum.

dusk [dʌsk] *n., adj., v.* *—n.* **1** the time just before dark; twilight. **2** shade; gloom.
—adj. Poetic. dusky.
—v. make or become dusky or shadowy. ⟨var. of OE *dux, dox* dark⟩

dusk•y ['dʌski] *adj.* **dusk•i•er, dusk•i•est. 1** somewhat dark; dark coloured. **2** dim; obscure. **3** gloomy; sorrowful. **—'dusk•i•ly,** *adv.* **—'dusk•i•ness,** *n.*

☛ *Syn.* **1. Dusky,** SWARTHY = rather dark. **Dusky,** the general word, means rather dark and dim, but not completely without light or colour: *It was dusky in the old warehouse. They painted the door a dusky brown.* **Swarthy** = very dark coloured, and applies only to complexion: *He has a swarthy skin.*

dust [dʌst] *n., v.* *—n.* **1** fine, dry earth. **2** any fine powder. **3** the earth, especially as a place of burial. **4** what is left of a dead body after decay. **5** a low or humble condition. **6** a worthless thing. **7** a cloud of dust floating in the air: *The car raised a great dust.* **8** confusion; disturbance; turmoil: *to raise a dust about nothing.* **9** *Brit.* ashes or refuse. **10** pollen.
bite the dust, a *Slang.* fall dead or wounded: *A shot rang out and one of the outlaws bit the dust.* **b** *Sports.* be defeated.
lick the dust, humble oneself slavishly.
make the dust fly, be quick or energetic.
shake the dust off (one's) **feet,** go away feeling angry or scornful.
throw dust in (someone's) **eyes,** deceive or mislead a person: *The escape plan depended on his success in throwing dust in the eyes of the police.*
—v. **1** remove dust from (furniture, etc.): *Be careful when you dust the figurines. I spent two hours dusting.* **2** make free of dust or other loose dirt (*used with* **off**): *He picked up his fallen hat, dusted it off, and left.* **3** sprinkle (plants) with insecticide powder: *Dust the roses once a month. Farmers have to dust the crops.* **4** bring back to use; revive (*used with* **off**): *She dusted off an old manuscript and sent it to a publisher.* **5** sprinkle with something in powder form: *Dust each cupcake with icing sugar.* **6** of a bird, bathe in dust. **7** *Archaic.* soil with dust. ⟨OE *dūst*⟩
—'dust,like, *adj.*
☛ *Hom.* DOST.

dust•bin ['dʌst,bɪn] *n. Brit.* a receptacle for refuse or trash; garbage can.

dust bowl especially in the western parts of Canada and the United States, a region that suffers from severe dust storms due to long periods of drought.

dust devil a small whirlwind that stirs up a column of dust, leaves, etc. as it moves along.

dust•er ['dʌstər] *n.* **1** a person who or thing that dusts, especially a cloth, brush, etc., used to get dust off things. **2** a contrivance for removing dust by sifting; sieve. **3** an apparatus for sifting or blowing dry poisons onto plants to kill insects. **4** a light dress or robe that fastens down the front, usually without a belt and worn especially when doing light household chores. **5** a lightweight coat worn over the clothes to protect them from dust. **6** *Informal.* DUST STORM. **7** a dusty avalanche. **8** a dry or unproductive well hole.

dust•fall ['dʌst,fɒl] *n.* the amount of lead dust found to have dropped on the ground from the polluted atmosphere.

dusting powder 1 an antiseptic powder for dusting over wounds, etc. **2** a fine, usually perfumed powder for dusting on the body after a bath, etc.

dust jacket 1 a removable paper cover for a book, folded over the cover to protect it and to display the book effectively for selling purposes. **2** a record sleeve.

dust•less ['dʌstlɪs] *adj.* **1** without dust. **2** not causing dust.

dust•pan ['dʌst,pæn] *n.* a flat pan, shaped like a short, broad shovel with a straight edge, for sweeping dust or debris into from the floor.

dust•proof ['dʌst,pruf] *adj.* impervious to dust.

dust ruffle a decorative trim extending all around the bottom of a bed mattress to the floor.

dust sheet a large sheet to protect articles of furniture from dust.

dust storm a strong wind carrying clouds of dust across or from a dry region.

dust•up ['dʌst,ʌp] *n. Slang.* a violent quarrel; commotion; disturbance.

dust•y ['dʌsti] *adj.* **dust•i•er, dust•i•est. 1** covered with or full of dust. **2** like dust; dry and powdery. **3** having the colour of dust; greyish: *a dusty pink.* **—'dust•i•ly,** *adv.* **—'dust•i•ness,** *n.*

dusty miller a plant (*Centaurea cineraria*) having leaves covered with white fluff.

Dutch [dʌtʃ] *n., adj.* *—n.* **1 the Dutch,** *pl.* **a** the people of the Netherlands. **b** *Esp. U.S.* the Pennsylvania Dutch. **2** the official language of the Netherlands.
beat the Dutch, *Informal.* be very strange or surprising; outdo anything considered remarkable.
in Dutch, *Slang.* in trouble or disgrace: *He's in Dutch with his sister.*
—adj. **1** of or having to do with the Netherlands, its people, or their language. **2** *Esp. U.S.* PENNSYLVANIA DUTCH.
go Dutch, *Informal.* have each person pay for himself or herself. ⟨< MDu. *dutsch* Dutch, German⟩
☛ *Usage.* The numerous derogatory expressions compounded of **Dutch,** such as **Dutch courage** are a legacy from the Dutch-British commercial rivalry of the 17th and 18th centuries.

Dutch Belted a breed of black dairy cattle originating in the Netherlands, with a white band around the body.

Dutch courage *Informal.* courage brought on by alcohol.

Dutch door a door that is divided into an upper and lower section, each of which may be opened separately.

Dutch elm disease a killing disease of elm trees, caused by a fungus (*Ceratocystis ulmi*) and carried by insects.

Dutch•man ['dʌtʃmən] *n., pl.* **-men. 1** a native or inhabitant of the Netherlands. **2** a Dutch ship. **3** in carpentry, a piece of wood used to close a hole, such as in an improperly made joint.

Dutch•man's–breech•es ['dʌtʃmənz 'brɪtʃɪz] *n.sing. or pl.* a spring-flowering perennial herb (*Dicentra cucullaria*) of the eastern woodlands of North America, closely related to the bleeding heart, having fernlike leaves and hanging or nodding, double-spurred flowers that resemble upside-down breeches.

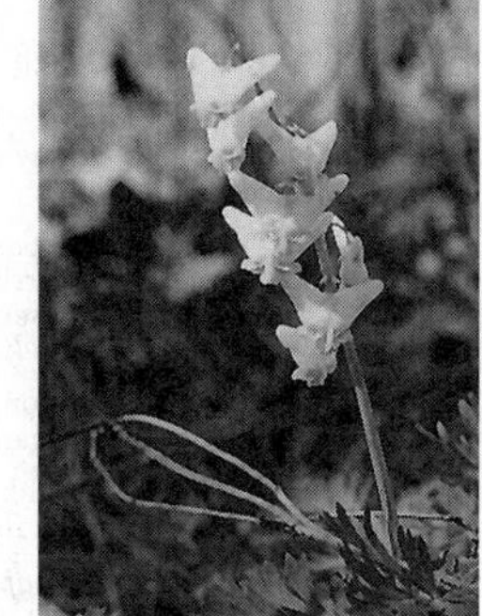
Dutchman's-breeches

Dutchman's–pipe a climbing vine (*Aristolochia durior*) of the birthwort family, having large brownish or purple leaves and a curved flower resembling a tobacco pipe.

Dutch oven 1 a large, heavy metal pot with a high, rounded lid, used for cooking roasts, etc. in the oven. **2** a metal box with an open side, used for roasting meat, etc. before an open fire: *The open side of the Dutch oven faces toward the fire.* **3** a brick oven in which the walls are first heated, and food is put in to cook after the fire goes out or is removed.

Dutch treat *Informal.* a meal or entertainment in which each person pays for himself or herself.

Dutch•wo•man ['dʌtʃ,wʊmən] *n., pl.* **-wom•en** [-,wɪmən]. a female native or inhabitant of the Netherlands.

du•te•ous ['djutiəs] *or* ['dutiəs] *adj.* dutiful; obedient. **—'du•te•ous•ly,** *adv.* **—'du•te•ous•ness,** *n.*

du•ti•a•ble ['djutiəbəl] *or* ['dutiəbəl] *adj.* on which a duty or tax must be paid: *Perfumes imported into Canada are dutiable goods.*

du•ti•ful ['djutəfəl] *or* ['dutəfəl] *adj.* **1** doing the duties required of one; obedient: *a dutiful daughter.* **2** required by duty; proceeding from or expressing a sense of duty: *dutiful words.* **—'du•ti•ful•ly,** *adv.* **—'du•ti•ful•ness,** *n.*

du•ty ['djuti] *or* ['duti] *n., pl.* **-ties. 1** the thing that a person ought to do; something that is right to do: *It is your duty to obey the laws.* **2** the feeling of having to do what is right: *She acted out of duty, although she was afraid.* **3** the thing that a person has to do in his or her work; action required by one's occupation or position: *One of her duties as a reporter is to cover the meetings of the city council.* **4** the proper behaviour owed to an older or superior person; obedience; respect. **5** a tax due to the government, especially on goods brought into or taken out of a country. **6** a tax on the performance of certain transactions, the execution of various deeds and documents, etc. **7** the efficiency of a machine; its work done or needed; relative power.
do duty for, serve in place of.
in duty bound, compelled to do something as a duty.
off duty, away from one's work or occupation: *He's off duty till six o'clock.*
on duty, at or to one's work or occupation: *She goes on duty at midnight.* ⟨ME < AF *duete* < *du,* var. of OF *deü.* See DUE.⟩
☛ *Syn.* **1. Duty,** OBLIGATION = what a person ought to do. **Duty** applies to what a person ought to do because conscience, piety, or law demands it: *I have a duty to help my parents.* **Obligation** applies to something incidental to social living, to specific actions demanded by usage, customs, etc.: *I have obligations to my neighbours.*

duty–bound ['djuti 'baʊnd] *or* ['duti] *adj.* bound by duty; obligated: *He was duty-bound to pay his share of the cost.*

duty–free ['djuti 'fri] *or* ['duti] *adj.* exempt from custom duty.

du•um•vir [dju'ʌmvər] *or* [du'ʌmvər] *n., pl.* **-virs, -vi•ri** [-və,raɪ] *or* [-və,ri]. in ancient Rome, either of two men who shared the same governmental position. ⟨< L *duumvir* man of two⟩

du•um•vir•ate [dju'ʌmvərɪt] *or* [du'ʌmvərɪt] *n.* **1** a governmental position shared by two men simultaneously: *The consulship in ancient Rome was a duumvirate.* **2** a union or partnership of two men.

du•vet [dju'vei] *or* [du'vei] *n.* a down-filled quilt or comforter with a removable cover, used instead of a top sheet and blanket.

du•ve•tyn ['duvə,tin] *n.* a soft, closely woven, woollen cloth having a velvety finish. ⟨< *duvet* down quilt < F⟩

D.V. 1 DEO VOLENTE. **2** DOUAY VERSION.

DVA Department of Veterans Affairs.

dwarf [dwɔrf] *n., pl.* **dwarfs** or **dwarves** [dwɔrvz]; *v.* *—n.* **1** a person, animal, or plant much smaller than the usual size for its kind. **2** in fairy tales, a tiny, often ugly person who has magic powers. **3** (*adjl.*) much smaller than the usual size of its kind; checked in growth. **4** DWARF STAR.
—v. **1** keep from growing large; check in growth. **2** cause to seem small by contrast or by distance: *That tall building dwarfs the other.* ⟨OE *dweorg*⟩ **—'dwarf•ism,** *n.*
☛ *Syn. n.* **1. Dwarf,** MIDGET, PYGMY = a person very much smaller than average. **Dwarf** applies particularly to a very small person whose growth has been stunted, usually by glandular deficiency, and who often has a head large enough for a normal person of his or her age, or larger, or a body deformed in some way. **Dwarf** may also be applied to a stunted animal or plant; however, it usually refers not to the individual but to a *kind* or *variety* smaller than related varieties, either because of natural differentiation or because of breeding: *dwarf marigolds, the dwarf birch.* **Midget** applies to a tiny person who is perfectly shaped and normal in every way except size. A **pygmy** is one of a diminutive race found in Africa; but the word may be used as a synonym for both **dwarf** and **midget.**

dwarf•ish ['dwɔrfɪʃ] *adj.* like a dwarf; smaller than usual. **—'dwarf•ish•ly,** *adv.* **—'dwarf•ish•ness,** *n.*

dwarf star a star of relatively low mass and brightness.

dweeb [dwib] *n. Slang.* a show-off who likes to claim membership in a small group of intellectuals who are enthusiastic about things no one else understands. ⟨origin unknown⟩

dwell [dwɛl] *v.* **dwelt** or **dwelled, dwell•ing. 1** *Formal or poetic.* make one's home; live. **2** keep the attention fixed; think, write, or speak at length or insistently (*used with* **on** *or* **upon**): *to dwell on one's misfortunes.* ⟨OE *dwellan* delay⟩

dwell•er ['dwɛlər] *n.* a person who lives in a given place: *a city dweller.*

dwell•ing ['dwɛlɪŋ] *n., v.* *—n. Formal or poetic.* a place used, or meant to be used, to live in; residence; abode: *a two-family dwelling.*
—v. ppr. of DWELL.

dwelling place *Poetic.* dwelling.

dwelt [dwɛlt] *v.* a pt. and a pp. of DWELL.

dwin•dle ['dwɪndəl] *v.* **-dled, -dling.** make or become smaller and smaller; shrink; diminish. ⟨dim. of obs. *dwine* < OE *dwīnan* waste away⟩
☛ *Syn.* See note at DECREASE.

dwt. pennyweight(s).

DWT or **dwt** dead-weight tonnage.

DX or **D.X.** *Radio.* distance; distant.

Dy dysprosium.

dy•ad ['daɪæd] *n.* **1** a whole composed of two parts; a pair. **2** *Biology.* a pair of chromosomes formed during the division of a tetrad. **3** *Chemistry.* any atom, radical, etc. having a valence of two. **4** *Sociology.* two people in an interdependent and ongoing relationship. **—dy'ad•ic,** *adj.* ⟨< LL *dyas, dyadis* < Gk. *dyo* two⟩

Dy•ak ['daɪæk] *n.* **1** a member of an Indonesian people living in central Borneo. **2** their language.

dy•arch•y ['daɪɑrki] *n.* See DIARCHY.

dyb•buk ['dɪbək] *n. Jewish folklore.* a spirit, either a demon or the soul of a dead person, that takes possession of a living human being. Also, **dibbuk.** ⟨< Hebrew *dibbuq,* originally, cement, glue⟩

dye [daɪ] *n., v.* **dyed, dye•ing.** *—n.* **1** a colouring matter used to colour cloth, hair, etc., or a liquid containing it: *Some dyes are vegetable, others chemical.* **2** a colour produced by treatment with such colouring matter; tint; hue: *A good dye will not fade.*
of deepest or **blackest dye,** of the lowest or vilest kind.
—v. **1** colour (cloth, hair, etc.) by dipping into or treating with a liquid containing colouring matter: *to have a dress dyed.* **2** colour; stain: *The spilled grape juice dyed the tablecloth purple.* **3** become coloured when treated with a dye: *This material dyes evenly.* ⟨OE *dēag*⟩
☛ *Hom.* DIE.

dyed–in–the–wool ['daɪd ɪn ðə 'wʊl] *adj.* **1** of people, thoroughgoing, especially in an ideological sense; unchanging: *a dyed-in-the-wool conservative.* **2** of materials, dyed before being woven into cloth.

dye•ing ['daıɪŋ] *n., v.* *—n.* the colouring of fabrics with dye.
—v. ppr. of DYE.
☛ *Hom.* DYING.

dy•er ['daıər] *n.* a person whose business is dyeing fabrics.

dye•stuff ['daı,stʌf] *n.* any substance, such as indigo or cochineal, yielding a dye or used as a dye.

dye•wood ['daı,wʊd] *n.* any wood, such as logwood, from which pigment is obtained.

dy•ing ['daıɪŋ] *adj., n., v.* *—adj.* **1** about to die. **2** coming to an end. **3** of death; at death.
—n. death.
—v. ppr. of DIE[1].
dying for, *Informal.* wanting very much: *I'm dying for a cup of coffee.*
dying to, *Informal.* wanting to very much: *I'm dying to see Jane again.*
☛ *Hom.* DYEING.

dyke [dəik] *n., v.* **dyked, dyk•ing.** See DIKE[1].

dy•nam•e•ter [daı'næmətər] *n.* a device for measuring the degree of magnification of a telescope. ⟨< *dyna-* (< Gk. *dynamis* power) + *-meter*⟩

dy•nam•ic [daı'næmık] *adj., n.* *—adj.* **1** of or having to do with energy or force in motion. **2** of or having to do with dynamics. **3** active; energetic; forceful: *Many successful salespeople have dynamic personalities.*
—n. **1 dynamics, a** the branch of physics that deals with the study of the motion of bodies (kinematics) and the relation between motion and the forces producing it (kinetics). **b** kinetics. **c** MECHANICS (def. 1), including kinetics, kinematics, and statics. **2** Often, **dynamics,** *pl.* a force or set of forces producing change, growth, or interaction: *the dynamics of glacier motion, the dynamics of family life, the values that constitute the dynamics of a civilization.* **3** Usually, **dynamics,** *pl.* a branch of study dealing with such forces: *She is an expert on population dynamics.* **4 dynamics,** *pl. Music.* the effect of variation and contrast in force or loudness. ⟨< Gk. *dynamikos* < *dynamis* power⟩ **—dy'nam•i•cal•ly,** *adv.*

dy•nam•i•cal [daı'næməkəl] *adj.* dynamic.

dy•na•mism ['daınə,mızəm] *n.* **1** any of various doctrines or philosophical systems which seek to explain the phenomena of nature by the action of some force. **2** dynamic quality; energetic quality.

dy•na•mist ['daınəmıst] *n.* a person who believes in dynamism. **—,dy•na'mist•ic,** *adj.*

dy•na•mite ['daınə,məit] *n., v.* **-mit•ed, -mit•ing;** *adj.* *—n.* **1** a powerful explosive often used in blasting rock, tree stumps, etc., made of nitroglycerin mixed with an absorbent material and pressed into round sticks. **2** *Informal.* anything dramatic, impressive, or likely to have resounding consequences: *A speech like that is potential dynamite in Canadian politics.*
—v. **1** blow up or destroy with dynamite. **2** mine or charge with dynamite.
—adj. spectacular; fantastic; exciting; effective: *What a dynamite idea! Hire Carol—she's dynamite!* ⟨< Gk. *dynamis* power; named by Alfred Nobel (1833-1896), the inventor⟩ **—'dy•na,mit•er,** *n.*

dy•na•mo ['daınə,mou] *n., pl.* **-mos. 1** GENERATOR (def. 1). **2** a very energetic and forceful person. ⟨short for *dynamo-electric machine*⟩

dy•na•mo–e•lec•tric ['daınəmou ı'lɛktrık] *adj.* having to do with the transformation of mechanical energy into electric energy, or electric energy into mechanical energy. ⟨< *dynamo-* (< Gk. *dynamis* power) + *electric*⟩

dy•na•mom•e•ter [,daınə'mɒmətər] *n.* an apparatus for measuring force or power, especially one for measuring the power of an engine. ⟨< F *dynamomètre*⟩ **—,dy•na•mo'met•ric,** *adj.*

dy•na•mom•e•try [,daınə'mɒmətri] *n.* the art or process of measuring forces.

dy•na•mo•tor ['daınə,moutər] *n.* a combined electric motor and dynamo for changing the voltage of an electric current.

dy•nast ['daınæst] *or* ['dınæst] *n.* **1** a member of a dynasty; hereditary ruler. **2** any ruler. ⟨< L < Gk. *dynastēs* < *dynasthai* be powerful⟩

dy•nas•tic [daı'næstık] *or* [dı'næstık] *adj.* of or having to do with a dynasty. **—dy'nas•tic•al•ly,** *adv.*

dy•nas•ty ['daınəsti] *or* ['dınəsti] *n., pl.* **-ties. 1** a succession of rulers who belong to the same family: *The Bourbon dynasty ruled France for more than 200 years.* **2** the period of time during which a dynasty rules.

dy•na•tron ['daınə,trɒn] *n.* **1** a vacuum tube that uses the secondary emission of electrons caused by an increase in the plate voltage to decrease the plate current. Dynatrons are often used in radio as oscillators. **2** *Physics.* meson. ⟨< Gk. *dyna*mis + elec*tron.* See DYNAMIC, ELECTRIC.⟩

dyne [daın] *n.* a unit of force equal to ten micronewtons. ⟨< F < Gk. *dynamis* power < *dynasthai* be powerful⟩
☛ *Hom.* DINE.

dys– *prefix.* bad or abnormal: *dysfunction.* ⟨< Gk.⟩

dys•cra•sia [dıs'kreiʒə] *or* [dıs'kreiziə] *n.* an abnormal imbalance in the blood or any other part of the body. ⟨< Gk. *dyskrasia* bad temperament⟩

dys•en•ter•y ['dısən,tɛri] *or* ['dısəntri] *n.* a painful disease of the intestines, producing diarrhea with blood and mucus. ⟨ME < OF *dissenterie* < L Gk. *dysenteria* < *dys-* bad + *entera* intestines⟩ **—,dys•en'ter•ic,** *adj.*

dys•func•tion [dıs'fʌŋkʃən] *n.* a functional abnormality or impairment, as of a body organ. ⟨< Gk. *dys-* bad + E *function*⟩

dys•func•tion•al [dıs'fʌŋkʃənəl] *adj.* **1** having to do with dysfunction. **2** performing badly or improperly; malfunctioning.

dys•gen•ic [dıs'dʒɛnık] *adj.* having to do with or causing degeneration in the offspring. Compare EUGENIC. ⟨< Gk. *dys-* bad + *gen-* produce⟩

dys•gen•e•sis [dıs'dʒɛnəsıs] *n.* defective development.

dys•graph•ia [dıs'græfiə] *n.* inability to write, resulting from a brain lesion. **—dys'graph•ic,** *adj.* ⟨< Gk. *dys* bad + *graphia* writing < *graphein* to write⟩

dys•lex•i•a [dıs'lɛksiə] *n.* an impairment of the ability to read. ⟨< NL < Gk. *dys-* faulty, bad + lexia < Gk. *lexis* speech. 19c.⟩

dys•lex•ic [dıs'lɛksık] *adj., n.* *—adj.* **1** of or having to do with dyslexia. **2** having dyslexia.
—n. a person who has dyslexia.

dys•men•or•rhea [,dısmɛnə'riə] *n.* painful menstruation. ⟨< Gk. *dys* -bad + *men* month + *rhein* to flow⟩

dys•morph•ic [dıs'mɔrfık] *adj.* structurally abnormal as a result of defective prenatal development. ⟨< Gk. *dys* bad + *morphe* form⟩

dys•morph•ism [dıs'mɔrfızəm] *n.* structural abnormality or abnormalities resulting from a defect in early development; congenital malformation.

dys•morph•o•lo•gy [,dısmɔr'fɒlədʒi] *n.* the field of medical genetics concerned with the diagnosis and interpretation of patterns of structural abnormality.

dys•pep•si•a [dıs'pɛpsiə] *or* [dıs'pɛpʃə] *n.* poor digestion; indigestion. Compare EUPEPSIA. ⟨< L < Gk. *dyspepsia* < *dys-* bad + *pep-* cook, digest⟩

dys•pep•tic [dıs'pɛptık] *adj., n.* *—adj.* **1** having to do with or causing dyspepsia. **2** suffering from dyspepsia. **3** gloomy; pessimistic.
—n. a person who has dyspepsia. **—dys'pep•ti•cal•ly,** *adv.*

dys•pha•si•a [dıs'feiʒə] *or* [dıs'feiziə] *n.* difficulty in speaking or in understanding speech, as a result of brain damage. ⟨< NL < Gk. *dys-* bad + *-phasis.* See APHASIA.⟩ **—dys'pha•sic,** *adj.*

dys•pho•nia [dıs'founiə] *n.* inability to make speech sounds, as from extreme hoarseness. ⟨< NL < Gk. *dysphonia* < *dys* bad + *phone* voice⟩ **—dys'phon•ic** [dıs'fɒnık], *adj.*

dys•pho•ri•a [dıs'fɔriə] *n. Medicine.* a chronic feeling of general discontent and illness. ⟨< Gk. *dysphoria* discomfort, ult. < *dys-* ill, bad + *phorein* to bear, suffer⟩

dys•pla•sia [dıs'pleiʒə] *or* [dıs'pleiziə] *n.* abnormal development or growth of a part. ⟨< Gk. *dys* bad + *plasis* a moulding⟩ **—dys'plas•tic** [dıs'plæstık], *adj.*

dysp•nea [dısp'niə] *n.* difficulty in breathing. ⟨< L *dispnoea* < Gk. *dyspnoia* < *dys* bad + *pnoe* breathing < *pnein* breathe⟩

dys•pro•si•um [dıs'prouziəm] *or* [dıs'prousiəm] *n.* a rare chemical element, the most magnetic substance known. *Symbol:* Dy; *at.no.* 66; *at.mass* 162.50. ⟨< NL < Gk. *dysprositos* hard to get at⟩

dys•rhyth•mia [dıs'rıðmiə] *n.* a lack of rhythm, such as in speech or brain waves.

dys•to•nia [dɪs'touniə] *n.* a lack of muscle tone due to disease or abnormality in the nervous system.

dys•to•pi•a [dɪs'toupiə] *n.* an imaginary place or state where everything is bad and people lead a wretched life. Compare UTOPIA. ⟨< NL *dys-* bad + *-topia* as in *utopia.* Coined by English philosopher J.S. Mill. 19c.⟩ **—dys'to•pi•an,** *adj.*

dys•troph•ic [dɪs'trɒfɪk] *or* [dɪs'troufɪk] *adj.* **1** having to do with or resulting from dystrophy. **2** *Ecology.* having to do with a body of water derived from a bog. Dystrophic ponds are highly acidic, host few plants or animals, and contain large amounts of humic matter.

dys•tro•phy ['dɪstrəfi] *n. Medicine.* **1** defective nutrition. **2** defective development or degeneration: *muscular dystrophy.* ⟨< Gk. *dys-* bad + *trophē* nourishment⟩

dys•u•ria [dɪs'jʊriə] *n.* painful urination. ⟨< *dys-* + *-uria* < NL < Gk. *-ouria* < *ouron* urine⟩

dz. dozen(s).

E e *E e*

e or **E** [i] *n., pl.* **e's** or **E's.** **1** the fifth letter of the English alphabet. **2** any speech sound represented by this letter. **3** a person or thing identified as *e*, especially the fifth in a series. **4** *Music.* **a** the third tone of the scale of C major. **b** a symbol representing this tone. **c** a key or string that produces this tone. **d** the scale or key that has E as its keynote. **5** **E,** something shaped like the letter E. **6** *Mathematics.* the base of the system of natural logarithms, having an approximate numerical value of 2.718 28. **7** a grade or mark indicating work below average. **8** (*adjl.*) of or being an E or e. **9** a printed or written form of the letter E or e. **10** anything, such as a printer's type, a lever, or a key on a keyboard, that produces an e or E.

e **1** *Physics.* erg. **2** *Baseball.* error.

e– *prefix.* out of; from, as in *educe, emerge, erase, evoke.* It is the form of **ex-**[1] used before consonants except *c, f, p, q, s, t.*

E **1** excellent. **2** *Physics.* energy. **3** *Electricity.* electromotive force.

E or **E.** **1** east; eastern. **2** English. **3** earth.

E. **1** Earl. **2** engineer; engineering.

ea. each.

EA educational age.

each [itʃ] *adj., pron., adv.* *—adj.* every one of two or more persons or things considered separately or one by one: *Each dog has a name.*
—pron. **1** every single one: *She gave a pencil to each.* **2** all of a group, thought of as individuals: *We each have our work to do.*
—adv. for each; to each; apiece: *These pencils cost ten cents each.*
⟨OE *ǣlc* < *ā* ever + *gelīc* alike⟩

☛ *Syn. adj.* **Each,** EVERY = one and all (of a number or group). **Each** emphasizes that one and all of a number, or one and the other of two, are thought of singly, as individuals: *Each dog has a name* means that, as individuals, all the dogs in the group have names of their own. **Every,** relating to a group, means that one and all are included, with no exceptions: *Every dog has a name* = none of the dogs was left without a name. In a more inclusive sense, **every** refers to one and all everywhere: *Every dog has his day.*

☛ *Usage.* Because many people think it is awkward to write *Each (person) gives his or her opinion*, the use of *their opinion* is quite frequent. The verb remains singular to agree with *each*, but a plural pronoun (*their*) is used.

each other **1** each of two in an action or relation that is reciprocal: *They struck each other* (that is, they struck, *each* striking *the other*). **2** one another: *The three boys struck at each other.*

☛ *Usage.* See note at ONE ANOTHER.

ea•ger ['igər] *adj.* **1** wanting very much; desiring strongly; impatient to do or get something: *The child is eager to have the candy.* **2** characterized by or showing keenness of desire or feeling: *eager looks.* ⟨ME < OF *aigre* keen < L *acer, acris*⟩
—'ea•ger•ly, *adv.* **—'ea•ger•ness,** *n.*

☛ *Syn.* **1. Eager,** KEEN, ANXIOUS = desirous, or wanting very much. **Eager** suggests enthusiasm with a touch of impatience: *The girls were eager to start building the clubhouse.* **Keen** suggests intensity of desire and quickness in action: *keen on learning golf.* **Anxious** implies desire overhung with fear about what may happen if the desire is not fulfilled: *They were anxious to do their best.*

☛ *Hom.* EAGRE.

eager beaver *Informal.* an especially or excessively enthusiastic and hard-working person.

ea•gle ['igəl] *n.* **1** any of a number of large, strong birds of prey (family Accipitridae), having very keen eyes and powerful wings. Eagles eat small animals, fish, or other birds. **2** a standard bearing the figure of an eagle as an emblem. **3** *Golf.* two strokes less than par for any hole on a course. **4** *Astronomy.* an equatorial constellation between Sagitta and Serpens; Aquila. ⟨ME < OF *aigle* < L *aquila*⟩

eagle eye **1** keen vision. **2** careful watch; lookout: *keeping an eagle eye on the prisoners, keeping an eagle eye out for bargains.*

ea•gle–eyed ['igəl ,aɪd] *adj.* able to see far and clearly.

eagle ray any of several rays (family Myliobatidae) having eyes under heavy brows and a tail with a jagged spine.

Eagle Scout **1** the highest rank in the American Scouts. **2** a boy with such a rank.

ea•glet ['iglɪt] *n.* a young eagle. ⟨< F *aiglette*, dim. of *aigle* eagle⟩

ea•gle•wood ['igəl,wʊd] *n.* the wood of a tree (*Aquileria agallocha*) of the aloe family.

ea•gre ['igər] *or* [eigər] *n.* a flood resulting from a tidal bore. ⟨Brit. dial. form, probably < OE *eagor* flood, high tide, akin to ON *ægir* ocean⟩

☛ *Hom.* EAGER ['igər].

eal•dor•man ['ɒldərmən] *n.* in Old English times, the chief officer of a shire.

Eames chair [imz] *Trademark.* a swivel chair, upholstered and on rubber casters.

-ean *suffix.* belonging to: *European.*

E and OE errors and omissions excepted.

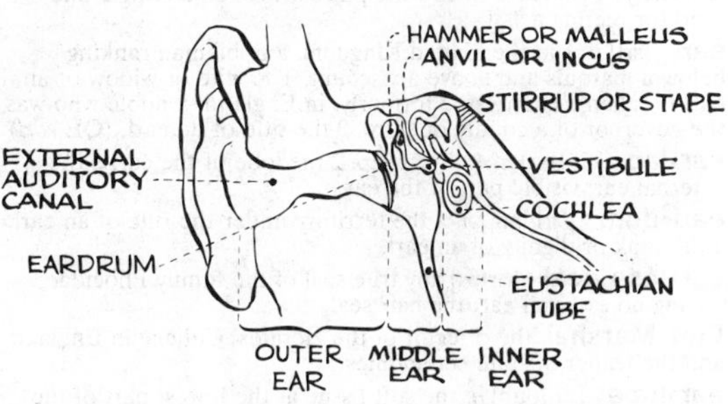

The human ear

ear[1] [ir] *n.* **1** the organ of hearing and balance in the higher vertebrates. In humans and other mammals it consists typically of three parts: the **external ear, middle ear,** and **inner ear. 2** the external, visible part of the ear in humans and most mammals. **3** the sense of hearing. **4** the ability to distinguish small differences in sounds: *That musician has a very good ear for pitch and tone.* **5** attention, especially favourable attention; heed: *to give ear to a request. She has the ear of the director.* **6** something resembling an external ear in shape or position, such as the handle of a cup.
all ears, *Informal.* listening attentively or eagerly.
believe (one's) **ears,** credit what one hears.
bend (someone's) **ear,** *Slang.* talk to someone at great length.
by ear, without reading or memorizing written music: *He can't read music but he can play almost anything by ear.*
fall on deaf ears, receive no attention; be ignored.
go in one ear and out the other, be heard but make no impression: *Their warning to her simply went in one ear and out the other.*
have or **keep an ear to the ground.** *Informal.* pay attention to what people are thinking and saying so that one can act accordingly.
have the ear of, be in a favourable position to influence (someone).
lend an ear, listen; pay attention.
play it by ear, *Informal.* proceed instinctively or spontaneously, without a plan.
prick up one's ears, a listen more attentively. **b** eavesdrop.
set by the ears, cause to disagree or quarrel; stir up trouble between.
set (something) **on its ear,** *Informal.* put into a state of excitement or upheaval: *a young designer setting the fashion world on its ear.*
turn a deaf ear, refuse to listen; pay no attention.
up to the ears, *Informal.* deeply taken up; thoroughly involved; almost overcome.
wet behind the ears, *Informal.* inexperienced; not yet able to cope; quite immature. ⟨OE *ēare*⟩ **—'ear•less,** *adj.* **—'ear,like,** *adj.*

ear[2] [ir] *n., v.* *—n.* the mature spike of cereal plants, containing the seeds, or kernels. An ear of corn consists of rows of kernels surrounding the outside of a long, thick, woody cob.
—v. of such plants, develop ears; mature: *Soon the corn will ear.* ⟨OE *ēar*⟩

ear•ache ['ir,eik] *n.* pain in the ear.

ear•drop ['ir,drɒp] *n.* **1** earring, especially one with a hanging ornament. **2** **eardrops,** *pl.* any medication placed in the ear drop by drop.

ear•drum ['ir,drʌm] *n.* the thin membrane that stretches across the middle ear and vibrates when sound waves strike it; tympanic membrane. See EAR[1] for picture.

eared [ird] *adj.* **1** having ears or earlike parts. **2** having an ear or ears of a specific number or kind (*used in compounds*): *a mangy, one-eared dog.*

eared seal any of a family (Otariidae) of seals having short, pointed external ears, thick fur, and hind limbs that can turn forward to support the body for locomotion on land.

ear•flap ['ir,flæp] *n.* a part of a cap that can be turned down over the ear to keep it warm.

ear•ful ['irfʊl] *n.* **1** enough of what is being said. **2** a scolding. **3** gossip.

ear•ing ['iriŋ] *n.* a small rope placed through a cringle and used for reefing a sail.

earl [ɜrl] *n.* **1** in the United Kingdom, a nobleman ranking below a marquis and above a viscount. The wife or widow of an earl is called a countess. **2** formerly, in England, a noble who was the governor of a county or shire. **3** the title of an earl. ⟨OE *eorl*⟩

ear•lap ['ir,læp] *n.* **1** an earflap. **2** the lobe of the ear. **3** the external ear; visible part of the ear.

earl•dom ['ɜrldəm] *n.* **1** the territory under the rule of an earl. **2** the rank or dignity of an earl.

ear•less seal ['irləs] any true seal of the family Phocidae, having no external ear; the hair seal.

Earl Marshal the director of the Heralds' College in England and the leader of state ceremonies.

ear•lobe ['ir,loub] *n.* the soft tissue at the lowest part of the external ear.

ear•ly ['ɜrli] *adv., adj.* **-li•er, -li•est.** *—adv.* **1** near the beginning: *The sun is not hot early in the day.* **2** before the usual, normal, or expected time: *We got there 15 minutes early.* **3** long ago; far back in time; in ancient times: *The plough was invented early in the history of humans.* **4** before very long; in the near future; soon.

early on, at an early stage: *They learned early on not to push her.*

—adj. **1** that happens or arrives before the usual, normal, or expected time: *an early dinner, an early spring.* **2** of or occurring in the first part: *In his early years he liked ships.* **3** happening far back in time. **4** occurring in the near future: *Let us have an early reply.* ⟨OE *ǣrlīce* < *ǣr* ere + *-līce* -ly[1]⟩ **—'ear•li•ness,** *n.*

Early American of or characteristic of the style of furniture of the Colonial Period in U.S. history.

early bird *Informal.* a person who gets up or arrives early.

Early Modern English the English language from about 1450 to 1750, including the language of Shakespeare and the King James Bible.

ear•mark ['ir,mɑrk] *n., v. —n.* **1** *Informal.* a mark made on the ear of an animal to show who owns it. **2** a special mark, quality, or feature that identifies or gives information about a person or thing; sign.

—v. **1** make an earmark on. **2** identify or distinguish: *Careful work earmarks a good student.* **3** set aside for some special purpose: *Five hundred dollars is earmarked to buy books for the library.*

ear•muffs ['ir,mʌfs] *n.pl.* a pair of coverings, attached to a headband, to put over the ears to keep them warm.

earn [ɜrn] *v.* **1** receive for work or service; be paid: *She earns ten dollars an hour.* **2** do enough work for; deserve; be worth: *He is paid more than he really earns.* **3** bring or get as deserved: *Her unselfish acts earned her the respect of all who knew her.* **4** gain as a profit or return: *Money well invested earns good interest.* **5** *Baseball.* score (a run) that is not due to an opponent's error: *an earned run.* ⟨OE *earnian*⟩ **—'earn•er,** *n.*

☛ *Hom.* ERNE, URN.

earned run average *Baseball.* the average number of runs scored by a player in nine innings. *Abbrev.:* ERA

ear•nest[1] ['ɜrnɪst] *adj., n. —adj.* **1** sincerely zealous; strong and firm in purpose; serious. **2** important; to be taken seriously: *"Life is real, life is earnest."*

—n.

in earnest, a serious or seriously: *I speak in earnest.* **b** sincerely or zealously; with or as if with determination and purpose: *It began to rain in earnest.* ⟨OE *eornost*⟩ **—'ear•nest•ly,** *adv.* **—'ear•nest•ness,** *n.*

ear•nest[2] ['ɜrnɪst] *n.* **1** the part given or done in advance as a pledge for the rest: *Take this as an earnest of what is to come.* **2** anything that shows what is to come; pledge; token; foretaste. ⟨ME *ernes,* apparently alteration (by association with *-ness*) of *erres* < OF *erres,* pl. < L *arra* < Gk. *arrhabōn* < Hebrew *'ērābōn*⟩

earnest money money paid as a pledge.

earn•ings ['ɜrnɪŋz] *n.pl.* money earned from work or investment; wages from a job; profits.

ear•phone ['ir,foun] *n.* a receiver for a radio, telephone, hearing aid, etc. that fits over or is inserted into the ear: *Many portable radios have earphones for private listening.*

ear•piece ['ir,pis] *n.* **1** a part of something that is connected to, held to, or supported by the ear: *the earpiece of a telephone.* **2** earflap.

ear•plug ['ir,plʌg] *n.* a round piece of pliable material such as wax, rubber, or plastic, for insertion into the outer ear to keep out water or noise.

ear•ring ['ir,rɪŋ] *n.* an ornament for the lobe of the ear, held in place either by a wire or post passed through a hole pierced in the lobe or by a screw or clip.

ear•shell ['ir,ʃɛl] *n.* **1** the abalone. **2** the ear-shaped shell of the abalone.

ear•shot ['ir,ʃɒt] *n.* the distance at which a sound can be heard; range of hearing: *She was out of earshot and could not hear our shouts.*

ear•split•ting ['ir,splɪtɪŋ] *adj.* of a noise, painfully deafening.

ear•stone ['ir,stoun] *n.* any calcareous particle found in the inner ear of certain vertebrates.

earth [ɜrθ] *n., v. —n.* **1 Earth,** the planet on which we live; the third planet from the sun, and the fifth in size. **2** all the people who live on this planet. **3** this world (often in contrast to heaven and hell). **4** dry land. **5** ground; soil; dirt: *The earth in the garden is soft.* **6** the ground: *The arrow fell to earth 100 m away.* **7** the hole of a fox or other burrowing animal. **8** worldly matters. **9** *Chemistry.* a metallic oxide from which it is difficult to remove the oxygen, such as alumina. **10** *Electricity.* the connection of a conductor with the earth.

come back to earth, stop dreaming and get back to practical matters.

down to earth, a seeing things as they really are. **b** practical.

go to earth, hide.

on earth, ever (*an intensifier used with* **how, what,** etc.): *How on earth can we get all this in the car? What on earth is he talking about?*

run to earth, a hunt or chase until caught. **b** look for until found.

—v. **1** connect (an electrical wire or other conductor) with the earth; ground. **2** cover with soil: *to earth up a plant or its roots.* **3** drive (a fox, etc.) to its burrow. **4** of a hunted fox, etc., hide in its burrow. ⟨OE *eorthe*⟩

☛ *Syn. n.* **1, 3. Earth,** WORLD, GLOBE = the planet on which we live. **Earth** applies to this planet in contrast to the other planets and sun, stars, etc. or, sometimes, to heaven and hell. **World** applies to the earth as the home of people, usually suggesting all humans and human affairs. In the works of older writers, **world** sometimes means the visible universe, including sun, stars, etc. **Globe** applies to the earth as our world, and emphasizes its roundness: *everyone on earth, the people of the world, travelling all over the globe.*

earth•born ['ɜrθ,bɔrn] *adj.* **1** sprung from the earth. **2** human; mortal.

earth•bound ['ɜrθ,baʊnd] *adj.* **1** bound or limited to this earth. **2** headed for the earth: *earthbound meteors.*

earth–con•scious ['ɜrθ ,kɒnʃəs] *adj.* environmentally aware.

Earth Day since 1970, the day (April 22) on which people are urged to protect the environment.

earth•en ['ɜrθən] *adj.* **1** made of earth. **2** made of baked clay. **3** of the earth; earthly.

earth•en•ware ['ɜrθən,wɛr] *n.* **1** an opaque, somewhat porous type of pottery fired at a relatively low temperature. Earthenware must be glazed to make it non-porous. Compare PORCELAIN, STONEWARE. **2** any pottery. **3** articles made of earthenware. **4** (*adjl.*) made of earthenware: *an earthenware jug.*

earth–friend•ly ['ɜrθ ,frɛndli] *adj.* environmentally sound; not harmful to nature.

earth•light ['ɜrθ,lɔit] *n.* earthshine.

earth•ling ['ɜrθlɪŋ] *n.* **1** an inhabitant of the earth; human being. **2** a worldly person.

earth•ly ['ɜrθli] *adj.* **-li•er, -li•est. 1** having to do with the earth, the natural world, and not with heaven. **2** possible; conceivable: *That rubbish is of no earthly use.* **—'earth•li•ness,** *n.*

☛ *Syn.* **1. Earthly,** TERRESTRIAL, WORLDLY = having to do with the earth. **Earthly** describes things connected with life in this world, in contrast to heavenly things: *He thinks only of earthly affairs.* **Terrestrial** is the formal word, contrasted with CELESTIAL, and is used particularly to describe things on the earth regarded as a planet: *Of all terrestrial beings people are the most adaptable.* **Worldly,** in contrast to **spiritual,** emphasizes thinking only in a secular way, especially of pleasures, success, vanity, etc.: *She enjoys wealth, power, and other worldly pleasures.*

earth•man [ˈɜrθ,mæn] *or* [ˈɜrθmən] *n.* **-men.** a person considered as an inhabitant of the planet earth; human being.

Earth Mother the planet Earth regarded as the mother of matter or source of life.

earth movement **1** an earthquake. **2** a raising of environmental consciousness; a group devoted to preservation of natural ecological balance.

earth•mov•er [ˈɜrθ,muvər] *n.* bulldozer.

earth•nut [ˈɜrθ,nʌt] *n.* **1** the underground part of certain plants, such as root, tuber, or underground pod: *Peanuts are earthnuts.* **2** a plant producing such a root, tuber, etc. **3** a truffle. **4** *Informal.* a very zealous environmentalist. Also (def. 4), **earth nut**.

earth•quake [ˈɜrθ,kweik] *n.* a shaking of the earth's surface, caused by shock waves generated by the movement of rocks beneath the earth's surface.

earth science any of a group of sciences concerned with the origin and physical features of the earth. Geology, geography, and seismology are earth sciences.

earth–shak•ing [ˈɜrθ ˌʃeikɪŋ] *adj.* of extreme importance or significance.

earth•shine [ˈɜrθ,ʃaɪn] *n.* the faint illumination of the part of the earth not lit by sunlight, caused by the reflection of light.

earth•star [ˈɜrθ,stɑr] *n.* a fungus of the genus *Geaster*, whose outer layer splits into a starlike shape.

earth station a receiving station, usually a concave dish, for electronic signals transmitted from an artificial satellite, especially one transmitting television programs.

earth tide a modification of the earth's crust, similar to the ocean tide, due to gravitation. The rigidity of the earth can be calculated from the distortions thus caused in solid rock.

earth tone any of the colours beige, tan, brown, etc., being found in soil or vegetation.

earth•ward [ˈɜrθwərd] *adv. or adj.* toward the earth. Also (adv.), **earthwards**.

earth•work [ˈɜrθ,wɜrk] *n.* **1** a bank of earth piled up for a fortification. **2** the moving of earth in engineering operations. **3** a very large work of art making use of the natural features of a place.

earth•worm [ˈɜrθ,wɜrm] *n.* any of various round, segmented worms (class Oligochaeta) that live in soil, especially any of the genus *Lumbricus*, which are valued in gardens, etc. because they help to aerate and fertilize the soil.

earth•y [ˈɜrθi] *adj.* **earth•i•er, earth•i•est. 1** of earth or soil. **2** like earth or soil. **3** not spiritual; worldly. **4** not refined; coarse. **5** natural; simple and frank; unsophisticated. **—ˈearth•i•ly,** *adv.* **—ˈearth•i•ness,** *n.*

ear trumpet formerly, a trumpet-shaped instrument held to the ear as an aid in hearing.

ear•wax [ˈir,wæks] *n.* the sticky, yellowish substance that collects in the canal of the outer ear; cerumen.

ear•wig [ˈir,wɪg] *n.* any of numerous insects (order Dermaptera) having long, jointed antennae and a long, slender body, with a pair of appendages at the tail end that are like forceps. ⟨OE *ēarwicga* < *ēare* ear + *wicga* beetle, worm⟩

ease [iz] *n., v.* **eased, eas•ing.** *—n.* **1** freedom from pain or trouble; comfort. **2** freedom from trying hard; lack of effort: *He enjoyed the ease of his part-time job.* **3** freedom from constraint; natural or easy manner.
at ease, a free from pain, trouble, or constraint; comfortable. **b** with the hands behind the back, the feet apart, and the body somewhat relaxed: *The soldiers stood at ease.*
take (one's) **ease,** make oneself comfortable; rest.
with ease, without having to try hard; with little effort: *She learned to spell with ease.*
—v. **1** make free from pain or trouble; give relief or comfort to. **2** lessen; lighten: *This medicine eased my pain.* **3** make easy; loosen: *The belt is too tight; ease it a little.* **4** move slowly and carefully: *She eased the big box through the narrow door.* **5** become less rapid, less tense, etc. **6** make (money, credit, etc.) available at low rates of interest. **7** of securities, goods, etc., tend to decline in prices.
ease in, break in with light work.
ease off or **up, a** lessen; lighten. **b** loosen.
ease out of, dismiss from or leave (a job, an office, etc.) quietly or by degrees. ⟨ME < OF *aisier* < *aise* comfort, elbow-room < VL *adjacens* neighbourhood < L *adjacens* adjacent. Doublet of ADJACENT.⟩
☛ *Syn. n.* **1. Ease,** COMFORT = freedom from strain. **Ease** = freedom from hard work, trouble, pain, or any pressure, and suggests being relaxed or at rest: *When the holidays come, I am going to live a life of ease.* **Comfort** = freedom from all strain, pain, hardship, and unhappiness, and emphasizes feeling well and perfectly content: *Let others have money and fame; I want only comfort.*

ease•ful [ˈizfəl] *adj.* restful; free from anxiety or tension: *half in love with easeful death.*

ea•sel [ˈizəl] *n.* a support or frame for holding an artist's canvas, a chalkboard, etc. upright. ⟨< Du. *ezel* easel, literally, ass < L *asinus*⟩

ease•ment [ˈizmənt] *n.* **1** *Law.* a right held by one person or party in land owned by another. **2** an easing; relief: *an easement of political tension.* **3** convenience.

eas•i•ly [ˈizəli] *adv.* **1** in an easy manner; without difficulty or great effort: *She solved the puzzle easily.* **2** without pain or trouble; comfortably: *The patient was resting easily.* **3** smoothly; freely. **4** by far; beyond question: *She is easily the best singer in the choir.* **5** very likely: *A war may easily begin.*

eas•i•ness [ˈizinɪs] *n.* **1** the quality, condition, or state of being easy. **2** carelessness; indifference.

east [ist] *n., adj., adv. —n.* **1** the direction of the sunrise; point of the compass to the right as one faces north. **2** Also, **East,** the part of any country toward the east. **3 the East, a** the eastern part of Canada and the United States. **b** the countries in Asia; the Orient. **c** the Eastern Roman Empire.
back East or **down East,** *Cdn.* **a** any point to the east of Winnipeg, especially that part east of Québec: *He's from down East.* **b** in or toward any place east of Winnipeg, especially that part east of Québec: *Western Canadians speak of Ontario as being back East.*
—adj. **1** toward the east. **2** from the east: *an east wind.* **3** in the east. **4 East,** of the part of a country, city, etc. in the East. **5** of the part of a Christian church where the altar is situated; in the direction of the church altar.
east of, farther east than.
—adv. toward the east: *They travelled east.* ⟨OE *ēast*⟩

east•bound [ˈist,baʊnd] *adj.* going toward the east.

East•er [ˈistər] *n., adj. —n.* **1** the yearly Christian celebration commemorating Christ's rising from the dead. In most churches, Easter comes between March 21 and April 26, on the first Sunday after the first full moon after March 21. **2** the season of Easter.
—adj. of or for Easter: *Easter music.* ⟨OE *ēastre*, originally, the name of a dawn goddess < *ēast* east⟩

Easter egg a coloured egg, either real or made of chocolate, glass, etc. used as a gift or ornament at Easter.

Easter lily any of several cultivated lilies having large, waxy, white trumpet-shaped flowers, especially *Lilium longiflorum*, often grown for Easter.

east•er•ly [ˈistərli] *adj. or adv., n., pl.* **-lies.** *—adj. or adv.* **1** toward the east. **2** from the east: *an easterly wind.*
—n. a windstorm from the east.

east•ern [ˈistərn] *adj.* **1** toward the east. **2** from the east. **3** of or in the east; of or in the eastern part of the country. **4** of or in the Orient, or Asia; Oriental. **5** of or having to do with the Eastern Orthodox Church.

Eastern Church **1** formerly, the Christian church in the eastern Roman Empire that separated from the Western Church in the 9th century. **2** EASTERN ORTHODOX CHURCH. **3** Uniat.

East•ern•er [ˈistərnər] *n.* a native or inhabitant of the eastern part of the country: *In the West, Ontario people are referred to as Easterners. In Ontario, Maritimers are referred to as Easterners.*

Eastern hemisphere that part of the world that includes the continents of Europe, Asia, Africa, and Australia.

east•ern•i•za•tion [ˌistərnaɪˈzeiʃən] *or* [ˌistərnəˈzeiʃən] *n.* the process of introducing or adapting eastern ideas, institutions, culture, etc.

east•ern•ize [ˈistər,naɪz] *v.* **-ized, -iz•ing.** cause to introduce or adopt eastern ideas, customs, culture, etc. **—ˈeast•ern,iz•er,** *n.*

east•ern•most [ˈistərn,moust] *adj.* farthest east.

Eastern Orthodox Church the Greek and Russian orthodox Christian churches, derived from the Byzantine church and acknowledging as head the Patriarch of Constantinople (Istanbul).

eastern red cedar RED CEDAR (def. 1).

Eastern rite the liturgy and organization of the Eastern Orthodox Church or any of the Uniat churches.

Eastern Roman Empire BYZANTINE EMPIRE.

Eastern Townships *Cdn.* most of that part of Québec lying south of the St. Lawrence River Valley and west of a line drawn southeast from Québec City to the United States border. The Eastern Townships were first settled by United Empire Loyalists and were then predominantly English-speaking.

eastern white cedar a medium-sized arborvitae (*Thuja occidentalis*) found especially in eastern Canada and the United States, having a tapered trunk and a dense, narrow, conical crown. Because the wood of this tree is extremely light in mass and resistant to decay, it is valuable for poles, shingles, canoes, etc.

eastern white pine a pine tree (*Pinus strobus*) of eastern Canada, a tall conifer up to 75 m high, bearing needles and cylindrical cones. It produces valuable softwood lumber.

East•er•tide ['istər,taɪd] *n.* Easter time, the 50 days between Easter and Pentecost.

East Germanic a subdivision of the Germanic languages. The only East Germanic language of which there are written records is Gothic.

East Indian *n., adj. —n.* **1** a native or inhabitant of the Indian subcontinent. **2** a person of East Indian descent. **3** formerly, a native or inhabitant of the East Indies.
—adj. of or having to do with the Indian subcontinent, the East Indies, or East Indians.

East Indies formerly, the name that was given to the region of S Asia that includes India and SE Asia, to distinguish it from the newly discovered West Indies: *Indonesia was once called the Dutch East Indies.*

east•ing ['istɪŋ] *n.* **1** an easterly direction. **2** the distance covered by a vessel east of its point of origin.

East•main ['ist,mein] *n. Cdn.* the eastern shore of Hudson Bay.

east–north•east ['ist ,nɔrθ'ist] *n., adj., adv. —n.* a direction or compass point midway between east and northeast.
—adj. or adv. in, toward, or from this direction.

east–south•east ['ist ,sʌuθ'ist] *n., adj., adv. —n.* a direction or compass point midway between east and southeast.
—adj. or adv. in, toward, or from this direction.

east•ward ['istwərd] *adj., adv., n. —adj.* toward the east; east: *an eastward slope.*
—adv. toward the east; east: *to ride eastward.*
—n. an eastward part, direction, or point. Also (adv.), **eastwards.**

east•ward•ly ['istwərdli] *adj. or adv.* **1** toward the east. **2** in an easterly direction. **3** of winds, from the east.

east•wards ['istwərds] *adv.* eastward.

eas•y ['izi] *adj.* **eas•i•er, eas•i•est;** *adv. —adj.* **1** requiring little effort; not hard: *easy work.* **2** free from pain, discomfort, trouble, or worry: *an easy life.* **3** giving comfort or rest: *an easy chair.* **4** fond of comfort or rest; lazy. **5** not harsh; not severe; not strict: *easy terms.* **6** *Informal.* not hard to influence; ready to agree with, believe in, or help anyone: *Choose whichever one you wish: I'm easy.* **7** smooth and pleasant; not awkward: *easy manners.* **8** not tight; loose: *an easy fit.* **9** not fast; slow: *an easy pace.* **10** not much in demand; not hard to get. **11** of a money market, favourable to borrowers. **12** of aces or honours in card games, divided evenly between the competing sides.
easy does it! *Informal.* relax; don't work so hard.
easy on the eyes, *Informal.* beautiful; good to look at.
on easy street, in comfortable circumstances.
—adv. Informal. in an easy manner; with ease.
easy come, easy go, *Informal.* ephemeral; easily lost.
go easy on, *Informal.* **a** treat gently. **b** use sparingly.
take it easy, relax. ⟨ME < OF *aisie*, pp. of *aisier* set at ease. See EASE.⟩
☛ *Syn. adj.* **1. Easy,** SIMPLE, EFFORTLESS = requiring little effort. **Easy** = not hard because not too much work is needed: *Dinner was easy to prepare.* **Simple** = not complicated: *I can work out simple crossword puzzles.* **Effortless** = performed without effort, but suggests seeming to be easy or simple either by nature or by training: *Watch the effortless movements of a cat.*

easy chair a comfortable chair, usually having arms and cushions.

eas•y•go•ing ['izi,gouɪŋ] *adj.* **1** usually taking matters easily; tending not to worry: *an easygoing person.* **2** rather too lenient.

easy mark *Informal.* a person who is easily imposed on.

easy virtue laxity in moral behaviour.

eat [it] *v.* **ate, eat•en, eat•ing. 1** take into the mouth and swallow, especially solid food that needs at least some chewing: *She ate slowly. I don't eat meat.* **2** have a meal: *Where shall we eat?* **3** destroy, use up, or waste by or as if by eating (*usually used with* **up, through, into,** *etc.*): *Termites have eaten through the posts. Extravagant spending soon ate up his inheritance. The acid has eaten into the metal.* **4** make by or as if by eating: *Moths had eaten holes in the sweater.* **5** *Informal.* make annoyed or anxious: *What's eating her?* **6** bring (oneself) into a particular state by eating: *She ate herself sick on the rich food.*
eat crow, *Informal.* be humbled.
eat (one's) **heart out,** be consumed with longing or envy; pine.
eat (one's) **words,** *Informal.* take back what one has said; retract.
eat out, have a meal in a restaurant.
eat out of (someone's) **hand,** be completely submissive to someone.
eat up, a eat all of: *The dog still hasn't eaten up the food we put out.* **b** *Informal.* finish eating: *Eat up, we've got to go.* **c** *Informal.* receive eagerly or greedily: *They showered him with attention and he just ate it up.* ⟨OE *etan*⟩ **—'eat•er,** *n.*

eat•a•ble ['itəbəl] *adj., n. —adj.* fit to eat; edible.
—n. Usually, **eatables,** *pl.* food.

eat•en ['itən] *v.* pp. of EAT.

eat•er•y ['itəri] *n., pl.* **-er•ies.** *Informal.* restaurant.

eat•ing ['itɪŋ] *n., adj., v. —n.* something edible: *His homemade pie is good eating.*
—adj. for eating: *eating apples.*
—v. ppr. of EAT.

eats [its] *n. Informal.* food; a meal.

eau de Co•logne [ou də kə'loun] cologne. ⟨< F *eau de Cologne* water of Cologne, Germany, where it was first made⟩

eau de toilette [ou də twɑ'lɛt]; *French* [odətwa'lɛt]. a fragrant liquid, weaker than perfume, used after bathing, as a cologne in grooming, etc.

eau de vie [odə'vi]. *French.* brandy. ⟨literally, water of life⟩

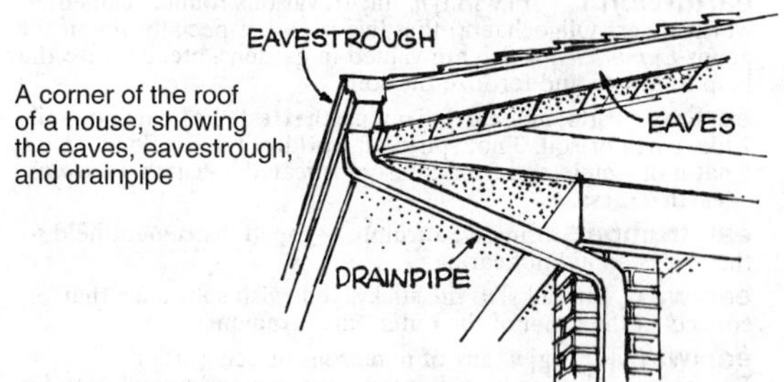

A corner of the roof of a house, showing the eaves, eavestrough, and drainpipe

eaves [ivz] *n.pl.* the lower edges of a roof projecting beyond the wall of a building. ⟨OE *efes*⟩
☛ *Usage.* **Eaves,** originally singular, is now understood as plural, and a new singular, *eave,* is sometimes found.

eaves•drop ['ivz,drɒp] *v.* **-dropped, -drop•ping.** listen to what one is not supposed to hear; listen secretly to private conversation. ⟨OE *efesdrype* the dripping of water from the eaves, the ground on which the water drips; hence to stand there, especially to listen to private conversation⟩ **—'eaves,drop•per,** *n.*

eaves•trough ['ivz,trɒf] *n.* a channel placed along the eaves of a roof to catch rainwater and carry it away. See EAVES for picture.

ebb [ɛb] *n., v. —n.* **1** a flowing of the tide away from the shore; fall of the tide. **2** a growing less or weaker; decline. **3** a point of decline: *His fortunes were at their lowest ebb.*
—v. **1** of the tide, flow out; fall: *We waded farther out as the tide ebbed.* **2** grow less or weaker; decline: *His courage began to ebb as he neared the haunted house.* ⟨OE *ebba*⟩

ebb and flow 1 the falling and rising of the tide. **2** constantly changing circumstances; good times and bad times: *the ebb and flow of business.*

ebb tide the flowing of the tide away from the shore.

Eb•lis ['ɛblɪs] *n.* in Islamic theology, an evil spirit, the leader of the jinns, a class of beings lower than angels.

eb•on ['ɛbən] *n. Archaic or poetic.* ebony.

eb•on•ite ['ɛbə,nəit] *n.* a hard, black substance made by heating rubber together with a large quantity of sulphur; vulcanite. Ebonite is used in making combs and buttons and for electric insulation. ⟨< *ebony* + *-ite*[1]⟩

eb•on•ize ['ɛbə,naɪz] *v.* **-ized, -iz•ing.** make to look like ebony by staining black.

eb•on•y ['ɛbəni] *n., pl.* **-on•ies. 1** the hard, heavy, usually almost black wood of any of various tropical Old World trees (genus *Diospyros*), used especially for decorative woodwork, carvings, etc. **2** any tree that yields ebony. **3** (*adjl.*) made of or resembling ebony. **4** (*adjl.*) designating a family (Ebonaceae) of tropical trees and shrubs, including the ebonies and persimmons. ⟨ME *hebeny* < L *ebeninus* of ebony < Gk. < Egyptian⟩

e•bul•lience [ɪ'bʊljəns], [ɪ'bʌljəns], *or* [ɪ'bʌliəns] *n.* **1** an overflow of excitement, liveliness, etc.; great enthusiasm. **2** a bubbling up like a boiling liquid: *the ebullience of the river below the falls.*

e•bul•lient [ɪ'bʊljənt], [ɪ'bʌljənt], *or* [ɪ'bʌliənt] *adj.* **1** overflowing with excitement, liveliness, etc.; very enthusiastic. **2** a boiling; a bubbling. ⟨< L *ebulliens, -entis,* ppr. of *ebullire* < *ex-* out + *bullire* boil⟩ **—e'bul•lient•ly,** *adv.*

eb•ul•li•tion [,ɛbə'lɪʃən] *n.* **1** a boiling; a bubbling up. **2** an outburst (of feeling, etc.).

eb•ur•na•tion [,ɛbər'neiʃən] *n.* the process that forms bone into a mass like ivory. ⟨< L *eburnus* of ivory (< *ebur* ivory) + *-ation*⟩

ec– the form of EX-[2] before consonants, as in *eccentric, eclectic, ecstasy.*

é•car•té [,eikɑr'tei] *n.* a card game for two people, played with 32 cards. ⟨< F *écarté,* pp. of *écarter* discard < *é-* out + *carte* card[1]⟩

ec•bol•ic [ɛk'bɒlɪk] *adj., n. —adj.* promoting childbirth by increasing the contractions of the uterus.
—n. any substance that does this. ⟨< Gk. *ekbole* a throwing out < *ek-* out + *ballein* to throw⟩

ECC Economic Council of Canada.

ec•ce ho•mo ['ɛksi 'houmou], ['ɛkei], *or* ['ɛtʃei] **1** Latin for "Behold the man!" **2** a picture, statue, etc. of Christ crowned with thorns.

ec•cen•tric [ɛk'sɛntrɪk] *adj., n. —adj.* **1** out of the ordinary; odd, peculiar: *eccentric clothes, eccentric habits.* **2** of circles, spheres, etc., not having the same centre. Compare CONCENTRIC. See CONCENTRIC for picture. **3** not having a perfectly circular path or shape: *the eccentric orbit of a planet.* **4** off centre; having its axis set off centre: *an eccentric wheel.*
—n. **1** a person who behaves in an unusual manner. **2** a disk or wheel set off centre so that it can change circular motion into back-and-forth motion. ⟨< Med.L *eccentricus* < L *eccentrus* < Gk. *ekkentros* < *ek-* out + *kentron* centre⟩
—ec'cen•tri•cal•ly, *adv.*

ec•cen•tric•i•ty [,ɛksɛn'trɪsəti] *n., pl.* **-ties. 1** something queer or out of the ordinary; oddity; peculiarity. **2** an eccentric condition; the state of being unusual or out of the ordinary. **3** the length of the back-and-forth stroke of an ECCENTRIC (def.2). **4** *Astronomy.* the amount of deviation of the orbit of a planet from a perfect circle.

ec•chy•mo•sis [,ɛkɪ'mousɪs] *n.* a discoloration, as with a bruise, caused by blood coming to the surface. ⟨NL < Gk. *ekchymosis* < *ekchymousthai* pour out < *ek-* + *cheein* pour⟩
—,ec•chy'mot•ic [,ɛkɪ'mɒtɪk], *adj.*

ec•cle•sia [ɪ'kliziə] *or* [ɪ'kliʒə] *n.* **1** the assembly of citizens of an ancient Greek state for political purposes. **2** a Christian church or its members. ⟨< Gk. *ekklesia* church⟩

ec•cle•si•as•tic [ɪ,klizi'æstɪk] *n., adj. —n.* a member of the clergy.
—adj. ecclesiastical. ⟨< LL *ecclesiasticus* < Gk., ult. < *ekklesia* church⟩

ec•cle•si•as•ti•cal [ɪ,klizi'æstəkəl] *adj.* **1** of or having to do with the church or the clergy. **2** having to do with early writings on Christianity. **—ec,cle•si'as•ti•cal•ly,** *adv.*

ec•cle•si•as•ti•cism [ɪ,klizi'æstə,sɪzəm] *n.* **1** all ecclesiastical beliefs and practices. **2** an excessive adherence to ecclesiastical form.

ec•cle•si•ol•o•gy [ɪ,klizi'ɒlədʒi] *n.* the study of the art of decoration and the architecture of churches.

ec•crine ['ɛkrin], ['ɛkraɪn], *or* ['ɛkrɪn] *adj.* of a gland, secreting externally, as the sweat glands of humans. ⟨< Gk. *ekkrinein* to separate, secrete⟩

ec•dys•i•ast [ɛk'dɪzi,æst] *n.* a dancer who gradually removes clothing. ⟨coined by H.L. Mencken < Gk. See ECDYSIS.⟩

ec•dy•sis ['ɛkdəsɪs] *n.* of snakes, crustaceans, etc., the shedding of the outer covering. ⟨< Gk. *ekdysis* a getting out, stripping < *ekdein* strip off < *ek-* out of + *dyein* enter⟩

ec•dy•sone ['ɛkdə,zoun] *n.* a hormone that produces growth in insects or crustaceans. ⟨< NL < Gk. *ekdysis* a getting out, stripping + E *-one*⟩

e•ce•sis [ɪ'sisɪs] *n.* the establishment of an organism in a new environment. ⟨< Gk. *oikesis* a dwelling or residing < *oikein* inhabit (< *oikos* house) + *-sis* action suffix⟩

ECG electrocardiogram.

ech•e•lon ['ɛʃə,lɒn] *n., adj., v. —n.* **1** an arrangement of troops, ships, etc. in a steplike formation. **2** a level of command. **3** a unit performing a special task or stationed in a certain position: *a maintenance echelon, a support echelon.* **4** the personnel of a military or naval force.
—adj. of, having to do with, or in the form of an echelon.
—v. form into a steplike arrangement. ⟨< F *échelon* rung of a ladder < *échelle* ladder < L *scala*⟩

ech•e•ve•ria [,ɛtʃə'viriə] *or* [,ɛkə'viriə] *n.* any of various tropical American plants (genus *Echeveria*) with succulent leaves in a rosette. ⟨after *Echeveri,* 19c. Mexican botanical illustrator⟩

e•chid•na [ɪ'kɪdnə] *n., pl.* **-nas, -nae** [-ni] *or* [-naɪ]. either of two species of egg-laying mammal (*Zaglossus bruijni* of New Guinea and *Tachyglossus aculeatus* of Australia), both having a spine-covered back, a long, narrow snout, and a long, sticky tongue for catching ants and termites, on which they feed. The echidnas constitute the family Tachyglossidae. ⟨< L < Gk. *echidna* viper⟩

e•chi•nate [ɪ'kaɪneit] *or* [ɪ'kaɪnɪt], ['ɛkɪ,neit] *or* ['ɛkɪnɪt] *adj.* having spines; prickly.

e•chi•no•coc•cus [ɪ,kaɪnou'kɒkəs] *or* [,ɛkɪnou'kɒkəs] *n.* any parasitic tapeworm (genus *Echinococcus*) whose larvae infect animals, with fatal results.

e•chi•no•derm [ɪ'kaɪnə,dɜrm] *or* ['ɛkənə,dɜrm] *n.* any of a phylum (Echinodermata) of invertebrate animals that live on the sea bottom, including starfish, sea urchins, and sea cucumbers. Echinoderms have a radially symmetrical body. ⟨< NL *Echinodermata* < Gk. *echinos* sea urchin, originally, hedgehog + *derma* skin⟩ **—e,chi•no'derm•al** or **e,chi•no'derm•a•tous,** *adj.*

e•chi•noid [ɪ'kaɪnɔɪd] *or* ['ɛkɪ,nɔɪd] *n.* one of the class Echinoides, which includes sea urchins and sand dollars.

e•chi•nus [ɪ'kaɪnəs] *n., pl.* **-ni** [-naɪ] *or* [-ni]. **1** any of a genus (*Echinus*) of sea urchins, such as an edible species (*E. esculentus*) of the Mediterranean. **2** *Architecture.* the rounded moulding forming part of the capital of a Doric column. See ORDER for picture. ⟨< L < Gk. *echinos* sea urchin, originally hedgehog⟩

ech•o ['ɛkou] *n., pl.* **ech•oes;** *v.* **ech•oed, ech•o•ing.** *—n.* **1** a sounding again; repeating of a sound. An echo is heard when a sound is sent back by a wall, cliff, or hill. **2** a person who repeats the words or imitates the feelings, acts, etc. of another. **3** the act of repeating the words or imitating the feelings, acts, etc. of another. **4** a sympathetic response: *Patriotic sentiments evoke an echo in every breast.* **5** *Music.* **a** a very soft repetition of a phrase. **b** a stop of an organ for producing soft or echolike tones. **6** a cardplayer's response to a signal from his or her partner or by a signal to his or her partner's lead. **7** a radio wave which has been reflected. Such echoes are the basis of radar, sonar, etc.
—v. **1** send back or repeat (sound): *The hills echoed the sound of the explosion.* **2** be repeated in sound; resound: *The boom echoed through the valley.* **3** repeat (the words) or imitate (the feelings, acts, etc.) of (another): *That girl is always echoing her mother. I wish she would stop echoing my every remark.* ⟨ME < L < Gk.; cf. *ēchē* sound⟩ **—'ech•o•er,** *n.* **—'ech•o,like,** *adj.*

Echo ['ɛkou] *n. Greek legend.* a nymph who pined away with love for Narcissus until only her voice was left.

ech•o•car•di•o•graph•y [ˌɛkouˌkɑrdi'ɒgrəfi] *n.* the study of the structure of the heart using an image formed by high-frequency sound waves. **—ˌech•o'car•di•oˌgram,** *n.* **—ˌech•oˌcar•di•o'graph•ic,** *adj.* **—ˌech•oˌcar•di'ol•o•gy,** *n.*

echo chamber in recording and broadcasting, a room or microphone which produces hollow sound effects.

ech•o•gram ['ɛkouˌgræm] *n.* the image produced on an oscilloscope by ultrasound waves reflected from tissue.

e•cho•ic [ɛ'kouɪk] *adj.* **1** like an echo. **2** in imitation of natural sounds; onomatopoeic. *Buzz, caw,* and *moo* are echoic words.

ech•o•ism ['ɛkouˌɪzəm] *n.* onomatopoeia.

ech•o•la•lia [ˌɛkou'leiliə] *n.* an involuntary repetition of the speech of others, including words and pauses. ⟨< *echo* + Gk. *lalia* speech⟩

ech•o•lo•ca•tion [ˌɛkoulou'keiʃən] *n.* the determination of the position of a distant or invisible object by means of the reflection of sound waves from it, based on the determination of the length of time required for the sound waves, or echo, to return and the direction from which they return. Bats use echolocation to navigate.

echo ranging ECHO SOUNDING.

echo sounder a device that measures the time for a sound wave to be reflected from the bottom of a body of water or from an object in the water.

echo sounding the determining of the depth of water or the location of an underwater object by means of an echo sounder.

ech•o•thi•o•phate i•o•dide [ˌɛkou'θaɪəˌfeit 'aɪəˌdaɪd] *n.* a drug used in the form of eye drops to treat glaucoma.

echt [ɛxt] *adj.* authentic. Compare ERSATZ. ⟨< G⟩

é•clair [ei'klɛr] *or* [ɪ'klɛr] *n.* an oblong piece of puff pastry filled with whipped cream or custard and covered with icing. ⟨< F *éclair,* literally, lightning < *éclairer* lighten < L *exclarare* < *ex-* out + *clarus* clear⟩

é•clair•cis•se•ment [eiˌklɛrsis'mɑ̃]; *French,* [eklɛʀsis'mɑ̃] *n.* **1** a clarification. **2 Eclaircissement,** the Enlightenment.

ec•lamp•sia [ɪ'klæmpsiə] *n.* toxemia of pregnancy, characterized by convulsions. ⟨NL < Gk. *eklampsis* a beaming forth < *ek-* out + *lampein* shine⟩

é•clat [ei'klɑ]; *French,* [e'kla] *n.* **1** a brilliant success. **2** fame; glory. **3** a burst of applause or approval. **4** an elaborate display. ⟨< F *éclat* < *éclater* burst out⟩

ec•lec•tic [ɪ'klɛktɪk] *adj., n. —adj.* **1** selecting and using what seems best from various sources. **2** made up of such selections. *—n.* a follower of an eclectic method. ⟨< Gk. *eklektikos* < *eklegein* < *ek-* out of + *legein* pick⟩ **—ec'lec•ti•cal•ly,** *adv.*

ec•lec•ti•cism [ɪ'klɛktəˌsɪzəm] *n.* **1** the use or advocacy of an eclectic method. **2** an eclectic system of philosophy, medicine, etc.

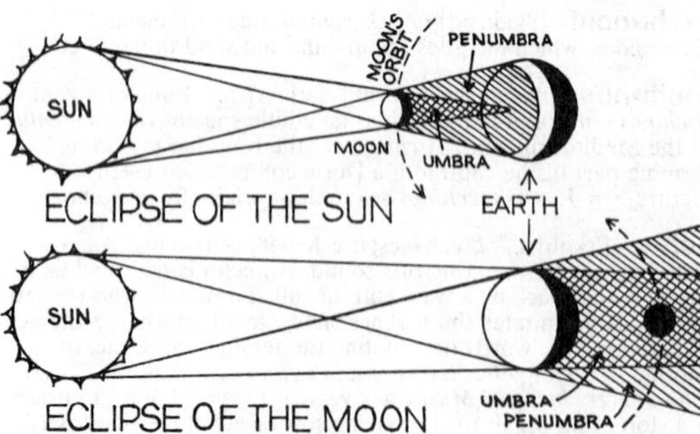

e•clipse [ɪ'klɪps] *n., v.* **e•clipsed, e•clips•ing.** *—n.* **1** a darkening of the sun, moon, etc. when some other heavenly body is in a position that partly or completely cuts off its light as seen from some part of the earth's surface. A **solar eclipse** occurs when the moon passes between the sun and the earth. A **lunar eclipse** occurs when the moon enters the earth's shadow. **2** any blocking out of light. **3** a loss of importance or reputation; failure for a time: *The former champion has suffered an eclipse.*
—v. **1** cut off or obscure the light from; darken. **2** obscure the importance or reputation of; make less outstanding by comparison; surpass: *Napoleon eclipsed all the other generals of his time.* ⟨ME < OF < L < Gk. *ekleipsis* < *ek-* out + *leipein* leave⟩ **—e'clips•er,** *n.*

eclipse chaser someone who travels in order to witness a solar eclipse.

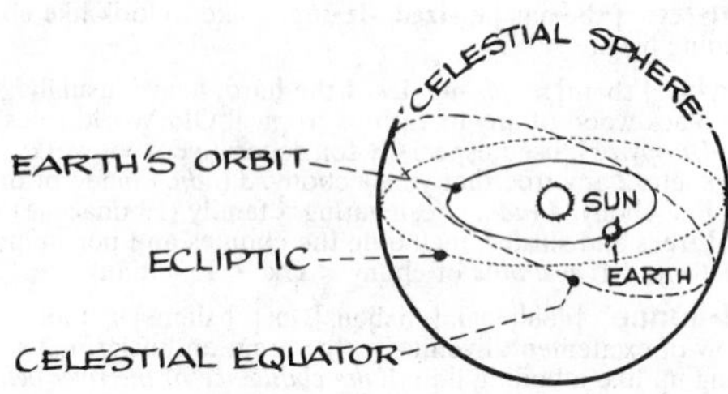

e•clip•tic [ɪ'klɪptɪk] *n., adj. —n.* the great circle on the celestial sphere that is the apparent annual path of the sun around the earth. It is the plane that contains the orbit of the earth.
—adj. of or having to do with the ecliptic or an eclipse. Also (adj.), **ecliptical.**

ec•logue ['ɛklɒg] *n.* a short poem about country life, often written as a dialogue between shepherds. ⟨< L *ecloga* < Gk. *eklogē* a selection < *eklegein.* See ECLECTIC.⟩

e•clo•sion [ɪ'klouʒən] *n.* **1** the emergence of an adult insect from its pupal case. **2** the emergence of an insect larva from the egg. ⟨< F *éclosion* < *éclore* to hatch, be hatched < OF *esclore* < VL **exclaudere* hatch out, alter < L *excludere* to hatch, drive out⟩

ECM EUROPEAN COMMON MARKET.

eco– *combining form.* of or having to do with the environment or habitat; ecological: *ecosystem.*

ec•o•cide ['ikəˌsaɪd] *or* ['ɛkəˌsaɪd] *n.* the destruction of the earth's ecology by industrial waste.

ec•o•ge•net•ics [ˌikoudʒə'nɛtɪks] *or* [ˌɛkoudʒə'nɛtɪks] *n. Genetics.* the study of the influence of genetics on variation in response to environmental agents.

e•col. **1** ecology. **2** ecological.

é•cole [ei'koul]; *French,* [e'kɔl] *n. French.* school.

E. coli [i 'koulaɪ] *Escherichia coli,* a species of bacteria found in human intestines, and responsible for water pollution. ⟨after T. *Escherich* (1857-1911), G physician + L *coli* of the colon⟩

ec•o•log•i•cal [ˌikə'lɒdʒəkəl] *or* [ˌɛkə'lɒdʒəkəl] *adj.* of or having to do with ecology. **—ˌec•o'log•i•cal•ly,** *adv.*

e•col•o•gist [ɪ'kɒlədʒɪst] *n.* a person trained in ecology, especially one whose work it is.

e•col•o•gy [ɪ'kɒlədʒi] *n.* **1** the branch of biology that deals with the relation of living organisms to their environment and to each other. **2** the branch of sociology that deals with the relations between human beings and their environment. ⟨< Gk. *oikos* house + E *-logy*⟩

econ. economic; economics; economy.

e•con•a•zole nitrate [ɪ'kɒnəˌzoul] *n.* an antifungal drug.

e•con•o•met•ric [ɪˌkɒnə'mɛtrɪk] *adj.* of or having to do with econometrics. **—eˌcon•o'met•ri•cal•ly,** *adv.*

e•con•o•met•rics [ɪˌkɒnə'mɛtrɪks] *n.* (*used with a singular verb*) the use of mathematics and statistics to verify economic theories, make economic forecasts, etc.

e•co•nom•ic [ˌɛkə'nɒmɪk] *or* [ˌikə'nɒmɪk] *adj.* **1** having to do with economics. Economic problems have to do with the production, distribution, and consumption of wealth in a society. **2** having to do with the management of the income, supplies, and expenses of a household, community, government, etc. **3** having to do with the material welfare of a community or nation; practical; utilitarian. **4** economical; saving; thrifty.

☛ *Usage.* **Economic,** ECONOMICAL. Although the meanings and uses of these two words often overlap, careful speakers and writers distinguish between them, using **economic** to refer to economics and the economy, and **economical** to refer to saving, or thrift: *There is danger of an economic crisis. We are going to buy a more economical car.*

e•co•nom•i•cal [ˌɛkə'nɒməkəl] *or* [ˌikə'nɒməkəl] *adj.* **1** avoiding waste; saving; thrifty: *An efficient engine is economical in its use of fuel.* **2** having to do with economics.

☛ *Syn.* **1. Economical,** FRUGAL, THRIFTY = saving. **Economical** = avoiding waste of money, time, work, or any other resources by careful planning and making the best and fullest possible use of what is spent: *He does more than others because he is economical of time and energy.* **Frugal** emphasizes saving by living simply and needing or using little: *The frugal widow bought and used food carefully.* **Thrifty** = avoiding waste by planning well, spending carefully, improvising, and working hard: *Successful farmers are thrifty.*

☛ *Usage.* See note at ECONOMIC.

e•co•nom•i•cal•ly [ˌɛkəˈnɒmɪkli] *or* [ˌikəˈnɒmɪkli] *adv.* **1** in an economical manner. **2** from the point of view of economics.

economic geography the study of the economy as determined by natural resources.

e•co•nom•ics [ˌɛkəˈnɒmɪks] *or* [ˌikəˈnɒmɪks] *n.* the science of the production, distribution, and consumption of wealth. Economics deals with the material welfare of people and the problems of capital, labour, wages, prices, tariffs, taxes, etc.

economies of scale economic conditions which favour mass production of a product by causing its price to lower as production increases.

e•con•o•mist [ɪˈkɒnəmɪst] *n.* **1** a person trained in economics, especially one whose work it is. **2** *Archaic.* an economical person.

e•con•o•mize [ɪˈkɒnəˌmaɪz] *v.* **-mized, -miz•ing. 1** manage (a resource) so as to avoid waste; use to the best advantage. **2** cut down expenses. **—e'con•o,miz•er,** *n.*

e•con•o•my [ɪˈkɒnəmi] *n., pl.* **-mies. 1** making the most of what one has; freedom from waste in the use of anything; thrift. **2** an instance of this; saving: *Many little economies were necessary.* **3** the managing of affairs and resources to the best advantage; management. **4** an efficient arrangement of parts; organization; system. **5** a system of managing the production, distribution, and consumption of goods: *feudal economy.* **6** (*adjl.*) offered at a price lower than normal: *an economy flight*. ⟨< L < Gk. *oikonomia* < *oikos* house + *nemein* manage⟩

e•co•spe•cies [ˈikouˌspisiz] *or* [ˈɛkou-], [ˈikouˌspiʃiz] *or* [ˈɛkou-] *n., pl.* **-cies.** a species that includes a number of distinct ecotypes. ⟨< *eco(logy)* + *species.* 20c.⟩ **—ˌe•co•spe'cif•ic** [-spəˈsɪfɪk], *adj.*

e•co•sphere [ˈikouˌsfir] *or* [ˈɛkouˌsfir] *n.* the parts of the universe that can support life, especially the biosphere of the earth.

e•co•sys•tem [ˈikouˌsɪstəm] *or* [ˈɛkouˌsɪstəm] *n.* the system formed by the interaction of all the living things of a particular environment with one another and with their habitat.

e•co•tone [ˈikəˌtoun] *or* [ˈɛkəˌtoun] *n.* the zone between two different ecosystems.

e•co•type [ˈikəˌtəip] *or* [ˈɛkəˌtəip] *n.* a group of organisms within a taxonomic species that have become modified structurally and physiologically by their environment but that can still interbreed with other groups in the species to produce fertile offspring. **—ˌe•co'typ•ic** [ˌikəˈtɪpɪk], *adj.* **—ˌe•co'typ•i•cal•ly,** *adv.*

ec•ru or **é•cru** [ˈɛkru], [ˈeikru], *or* [eiˈkru] *n. or adj.* very pale brown; the colour of unbleached linen. ⟨< F *écru* raw, unbleached, var. of *cru* raw < L *crudus*⟩

ec•sta•sy [ˈɛkstəsi] *n., pl.* **-sies. 1** a state of great joy; thrilling or overwhelming delight; rapture: *Speechless with ecstasy, the audience listened to the glorious music.* **2** any strong feeling that completely absorbs the mind; uncontrollable emotion; transports. **3** trance. ⟨< L *extasis* < Gk. *ekstasis* trance, distraction < *existanai* < *ek-* out + *histanai* to place⟩

ec•stat•ic [ɛkˈstætɪk] *adj., n. —adj.* **1** full of ecstasy; showing ecstasy. **2** caused by ecstasy. **3** likely to experience or show ecstasy.
—n. **1** a person subject to fits of ecstasy. **2 ecstatics,** *pl.* fits of ecstasy; raptures. **—ec'stat•i•cal•ly,** *adv.*

ECT or **E.C.T.** ELECTRO-CONVULSIVE THERAPY.

ecto– *combining form.* to or on the outside: *Ectoderm = the outer cellular layer of an embryo.* ⟨< Gk. *ekto-* < *ektos* outside⟩

ec•to•blast [ˈɛktəˌblæst] *n.* **1** ectoderm. **2** epiblast. ⟨< *ecto-* + Gk. *blastos* sprout⟩

ec•to•derm [ˈɛktəˌdɜrm] *n. Biology.* the outer layer of cells formed during the development of the embryos of animals. Skin, hair, nails, the enamel of teeth, and essential parts of the nervous system grow from the ectoderm. ⟨< *ecto-*+*-derm* skin (< Gk. *derma*)⟩ **—ˌec•to'derm•al** or **ˌec•to'derm•ic,** *adj.*

ec•to•gen•e•sis [ˌɛktouˈdʒɛnəsɪs] *n.* the development of an embryo outside its natural environment, as in a test tube.

ec•tog•e•nous [ɛkˈtɒdʒənəs] *adj.* of a parasite, growing outside the organism that provides food. Also, **ectogenic** [ˌɛktouˈdʒɛnɪk].

ec•to•mere [ˈɛktəˌmir] *n.* one of the blastomeres that take

part in the development of the ectoderm. **—ˌec•to'mer•ic** [-ˈmɛrɪk], *adj.*

ec•to•morph [ˈɛktəˌmɔrf] *n.* **1** a human body type characterized by a light frame, medium to tall stature, long limbs, and long, thin, tight muscles. It is one of three basic body types. Compare ENDOMORPH, MESOMORPH. **2** a person having such a body structure. ⟨< *ecto-* + Gk. *morphe* form, shape⟩

ec•to•mor•phic [ˌɛktəˈmɔrfɪk] *adj.* of, having to do with, or being an ectomorph. **—ˌec•to'morph•i•cal•ly,** *adv.*

-ectomy *combining form.* surgical removal of a part or organ of the body, as in *tonsillectomy.* ⟨< NL *-ectomia* < Gk. *ek-* out + *-tomia* a cutting⟩

ec•to•par•a•site [ˌɛktouˈpærəˌsəit] *or* [-ˈpɛrəˌsəit] *n.* an external parasite. **—ˌec•toˌpar•a'sit•ic** [-ˈsɪtɪk], *adj.*

ec•to•pia [ɛkˈtoupiə] *n.* an abnormal position of an organ in part of the body. ⟨NL < Gk. *ektopos* away from a place < *ek-* out of + *topos* place⟩ **—ec'top•ic** [ɛkˈtɒpɪk], *adj.*

ectopic pregnancy the lodging of the embryo in a Fallopian tube, where it cannot develop into a fetus and must be removed surgically.

ec•to•plasm [ˈɛktəˌplæzəm] *n.* **1** *Biology.* the outer portion of the cytoplasm of a cell. **2** a supposed emanation from the body of a medium in a trance. ⟨< *ecto-*+ Gk. *plasma* something moulded⟩ **—ˌec•to'plas•mic,** *adj.*

ec•to•proct [ˈɛktəˌprɒkt] *n.* any of the various tiny water animals (phylum Bryozoa) found in salt water and fresh water and growing in mosslike colonies; bryozoan. ⟨< NL *Ektoprocta* < Gk. *ektos* outside + *proktos* anus⟩

ec•to•sarc [ˈɛktouˌsɑrk] *n.* the ectoplasm of a protozoan. ⟨< *ecto-* + Gk. *sarx* flesh⟩

ec•to•therm•al [ˌɛktouˈθɜrməl] *adj.* of an animal, as a fish or reptile, with a body temperature that varies with the temperature of its surroundings; cold-blooded. Compare ENDOTHERMAL.

ec•type [ˈɛktəip] *n.* an imitation; copy. ⟨< Gk. *ektypos* engraved < *ek-* out + *typos* figure⟩

é•cu [eiˈkju]; *French,* [eˈky] *n., pl.* **é•cus** [eiˈkjuz]; *French,* [eˈky] *French.* **1** in the Middle Ages, a short, triangular shield carried by a mounted soldier. **2** any of several French gold or silver coins of varying value, in use from the 13th century on, especially a silver coin of the 17th and 18th centuries.

ECU European Currency Unit; the currency of the European Communities, used in international finance.

Ec•ua•dor [ˈɛkwəˌdɔr] *n.* a country in NW South America.

Ec•ua•do•re•an or **Ec•ua•do•ri•an** [ˌɛkwəˈdɔriən] *n., adj. —n.* a native or inhabitant of Ecuador.
—adj. of or having to do with Ecuador or its people.

ec•u•mene [ˈɛkjəˌmin] *n.* the permanently settled portion of a country, continent, etc.; inhabited land. The Canadian ecumene consists of three separate blocs of fairly densely populated land connected by a continent-wide band of less continuously settled land called a **broken ecumene.** ⟨< Gk. *oikoumenē* inhabited, ult. < *oikos* dwelling, habitation⟩

ec•u•men•i•cal [ˌɛkjəˈmɛnəkəl] *adj.* **1** general; universal. **2** of or representing the whole Christian Church. **3** promoting unity among all Christians or Christian denominations. Also, **ecumenic, oecumenical.** ⟨< L < Gk. *oikoumenikos* < *oikoumenē (gē)* inhabited (world), ult. < *oikos* dwelling⟩ **—ˌec•u'men•i•cal•ly,** *adv.*

ec•u•men•i•cal•ism [ˌɛkjəˈmɛnəkəˌlɪzəm] *n.* the beliefs and practices of the ecumenical movement.

ecumenical movement a Protestant group aiming at universal Christian unity.

ec•u•me•nism [ˈɛkjəməˌnɪzəm] *or* [ɪˈkjuməˌnɪzəm] *n.* ecumenical principles or a church movement in support of them.

ec•ze•ma [ˈɛksəmə], [ɛgˈzimə], *or* [ˈɛgzəmə] *n.* an inflammation of the skin with redness, itching, and the formation of patches of scales. ⟨< NL < Gk. *ekzema* < *ek-* out + *zeein* to boil⟩ **—ec'ze•ma•tous,** *adj.*

-ed[1] *suffix.* forming the past tense of most English verbs. ⟨OE *-de, -ede, -ode, -ade*⟩

☛ *Pronun.* **-ed.** Pronounced as a separate syllable [ɪd] after [t] or [d]: *wanted, loaded*; otherwise, as [d] after a vowel or voiced consonant: *vowed, lagged*; and as [t] after a voiceless consonant: *dressed, washed.*

-ed[2] *suffix.* **1** forming the past participle. **2** with various meanings: **a** having; supplied with, as in *bearded, long-legged,* *pale-faced, tender-hearted.* **b** having the characteristics of, as in *honeyed.* ⟨OE *-ed, -od, -ad*⟩

☛ *Pronun.* **-ed.** Pronunciation as for **-ed**[1] except that, in certain participles used adjectivally, **-ed**[2] may be pronounced [ɪd] instead of [d] or [t]: *aged* ['eidʒɪd], *learned* ['lɜrnɪd], *crooked* ['krʊkɪd].

ed. **1** editor; edition; edited. **2** educated at.

E.D. (Canadian) Efficiency Decoration (for officers of Military Auxiliary Forces).

e•da•cious [ɪ'deiʃəs] *adj.* voracious. ⟨< L *edax, edacis* < *edere* eat⟩ **—e'da•ci•ty** [ɪ'dæsəti], *n.*

E•dam ['eidəm] *or* ['idəm] *n.* EDAM CHEESE.

Edam cheese **1** a round, yellow cheese made in the Netherlands, and usually having red wax on the outside. **2** any cheese resembling this. ⟨< a village in the Netherlands⟩

e•daph•ic [ɪ'dæfɪk] *adj.* resulting from particular soil conditions such as drainage. ⟨< Gk. *edaphos* soil, ground + *-ic*⟩

E.D.C. or **EDC** **1** European Defence Community (France, Italy, Germany, and Benelux united for mutual defence). **2** *Cdn.* Export Development Corporation.

Ed•da ['ɛdə] *n., pl.* **Ed•das.** either of two Icelandic literary works written about 1200 to 1230, one in prose, the other in verse. They relate some of the old Norse myths and legends and give rules for the writing of poetry. ⟨< ON *ōthr* poetry < Gmc. **wōth-* exaltation of spirits, poetry, song⟩

ed•do ['ɛdou] *n.* the root of the taro, eaten as food. ⟨probably < a West African name⟩

ed•dy ['ɛdi] *n., pl.* **-dies;** *v.* **-died, -dy•ing.** *—n.* **1** water, air, etc. moving against the main current, especially when having a whirling motion; small whirlpool or whirlwind. **2** any similar current, as of fog or dust, or of thought or opinion: *Eddies of controversy grew around the new theory.*
—v. **1** move against the main current in a whirling motion; whirl: *The water eddied down the drain.* **2** move in circles. ⟨? < OE *ed-* turning + *ēa* stream⟩

e•del•weiss ['eidəl,vəis] *n.* a small Alpine plant (*Leontopodium alpinum*) of the composite family, having heads of very small, white flowers in the centre of star-shaped clusters of fuzzy leaves. ⟨< G *Edelweiss* < *edel* noble + *weiss* white⟩

e•de•ma [ɪ'dimə] *n., pl.* **-ma•ta** [-mətə]. **1** a swelling caused by an abnormal accumulation of watery fluid in the tissues of the body. **2** excessive swelling in plants as a result of excess water. ⟨< NL < Gk. *oidēma* < *oidos* tumour⟩ **—e'dem•a•tous** [ɪ'dɛmətəs], *adj.*

E•den ['idən] *n.* a delightful spot; paradise. ⟨< Hebrew *'edēn,* literally, pleasure, delight; in the Bible, the garden where Adam and Eve lived at first.⟩ **—E'den•ic** [i'dɛnɪk], *adj.*

e•den•tate [ɪ'dɛnteit] *n., adj. —n.* any of an order (Edentata) of New World mammals having only cheek teeth or no teeth at all, including sloths, anteaters, and armadillos.
—adj. **1** of, having to do with, or belonging to the order Edentata. **2** lacking teeth. ⟨< L *edentatus* < *ex-* without + *dens, dentis* tooth⟩

e•den•tu•lous [ɪ'dɛntʃələs] *or* [ɪ'dɛntjələs] *adj.* toothless. ⟨< L *edentulus* < *e-* out + *dens, dentis* tooth⟩

edge [ɛdʒ] *n., v.* **edged, edg•ing.** *—n.* **1** a line or place where something ends; part farthest from the middle; side. **2** a brink; verge. **3** a thin, sharp side that cuts. The blade of a knife, axe, or razor has an edge. **4** *Geometry.* a line at which two surfaces of a solid meet: *the edge of a box.* **5** sharpness; keenness. **6** *Informal.* an advantage: *We have a slight edge on the second team in the league.*
on edge, a disturbed; nervous; tense. **b** tense with eagerness; anxious; impatient: *We were all on edge until we arrived at the station.*
set on edge, a disturb; cause to feel excited or irritable. **b** make eager, anxious, or impatient.
set (one's) **teeth on edge,** irritate one extremely.
take the edge off, deprive of force, strength, bitterness, harshness, or enjoyment.
—v. **1** put an edge on; form an edge on; decorate or trim the edge of. **2** move in a sideways manner: *She edged through the crowd.* **3** move little by little: *He edged his chair nearer to the fire.* **4** *Informal.* win a narrow victory over: *Our team edged the visitors 3-2.* **5** tilt (a ski) so that the edge cuts the snow.
edge in, manage to get in.
edge out, *Informal.* defeat by a narrow margin: *Montréal edged out Toronto in the playoffs.* ⟨OE *ecg*⟩ **—'edg•er,** *n.*

edged [ɛdʒd] *adj.* sharp.

edge tool a tool with a sharp cutting edge.

edge•ways ['ɛdʒ,weiz] *adv.* with the edge forward; in the direction of the edge. Also, **edgewise.**
get a word in edgeways, manage to say something to a talkative person or in a talkative group.

edg•ing ['ɛdʒɪŋ] *n., v. —n.* **1** anything forming an edge or put along an edge. **2** a border or trimming for an edge.
—v. ppr. of EDGE.

edg•y ['ɛdʒi] *adj.* **edg•i•er, edg•i•est.** **1** having an edge; sharp; sharply defined: *edgy outlines.* **2** impatient; irritable. **—'edg•i•ly,** *adv.* **—'edg•i•ness,** *n.*

edh [ɛð] *n.* **1** in the old English alphabet, a letter (ð) used to represent a voiceless or voiced interdental fricative. **2** a symbol [ð] used in some phonetic alphabets (such as IPA, used in this book) to represent the voiced interdental fricative, as in *th*en. Also, **eth.**

ed•i•ble ['ɛdəbəl] *adj., n. —adj.* fit to eat; eatable: *Not all mushrooms are edible.*
—n. Usually, **edibles,** *pl.* things fit to eat; food. ⟨< LL *edibilis* < L *edere* eat⟩ **—,ed•i'bil•i•ty,** *n.*

e•dict ['idɪkt] *n.* **1** a public order or command by some authority; decree. **2** any order or injunction. ⟨< L *edictum* < *edicere* < *ex-* out + *dicere* say⟩
☛ *Syn.* See note at PROCLAMATION.

Edict of Nantes the decree signed at Nantes in 1598 by Henry IV of France, giving religious freedom to the French Protestants. It was repealed in 1685 by Louis XIV, causing wholesale emigration of Protestants, such as the Huguenots, from France.

ed•i•fi•ca•tion [,ɛdəfə'keiʃən] *n.* moral improvement; spiritual benefit; instruction.

ed•i•fice ['ɛdəfɪs] *n.* **1** a building, especially a large or imposing building. **2** any elaborate construction or organization. ⟨ME < OF *edifice* < L *aedificium* < *aedificare* build < *aedis* temple (pl., house) + *facere* make⟩
☛ *Syn.* See note at BUILDING.

ed•i•fy ['ɛdə,faɪ] *v.* **-fied, -fy•ing.** improve morally; benefit spiritually; instruct. ⟨ME < OF *edifier* < L *aedificare* build (up). See EDIFICE.⟩

e•dile ['idaɪl] See AEDILE.

ed•it ['ɛdɪt] *v.* **1** prepare, especially for publication, correcting errors, checking facts, etc. **2** have charge of (a newspaper, magazine, dictionary, etc.) and decide what shall be printed in it. **3** revise or give final form to (film, tape recordings, etc.) by such means as cutting and splicing. **4** *Computer technology.* compile or modify (a computer file or program). ⟨< L *editus,* pp. of *edere* < *ex-* out + *dare* give; partly < *editor*⟩

edit. edition; edited; editor.

e•di•tion [ɪ'dɪʃən] *n.* **1** all the copies of a book, newspaper, etc. printed alike and issued at or near the same time: *In the second edition of the book many of the errors in the first edition had been corrected.* **2** the form in which a book is printed or published: *The reading matter in the cheap one-volume edition was exactly the same as in the three-volume edition. Some books appear in pocket editions.* **3** an issue of the same newspaper, book, etc. published at different times with additions, changes, etc.: *the afternoon edition, a foreign edition.* **4** the published work of a literary or classical author, known by its publishing house, editor, or translator: *the Riverside edition of Shakespeare, the Lattimore edition of* The Iliad. **5** a single copy of a book. **6** a special printing of a book. **7** a limited set of identical collectible items.

ed•i•tor ['ɛdətər] *n.* **1** a person who edits, especially one whose occupation is preparing material for publication or broadcasting. **2** a person who is responsible for the content of a periodical or newspaper, or for a particular section or department of one: *a sports editor.* **3** a device used for editing movies, magnetic tape, etc., including a splicer, etc. **4** a person who edits a movie. ⟨< L⟩

ed•i•to•ri•al [,ɛdə'tɔriəl] *n., adj. —n.* an article in a newspaper or magazine, or a comment in a radio or television broadcast, giving the opinion or attitude of the publisher, editor, speaker, etc. regarding some subject.
—adj. of, having to do with, or characteristic of an editor or editorials.

ed•i•to•ri•al•ist [,ɛdə'tɔriəlɪst] *n.* a person who writes editorials.

ed•i•to•ri•al•ize [,ɛdə'tɔriə,laɪz] *v.* **-ized, -iz•ing.** **1** write (news articles) as if they were editorials, including comment and criticisms in the articles. **2** write an editorial. **3** express opinions as though one were writing an editorial.
—,ed•i,to•ri•al•i'za•tion, *n.* **—,ed•i'to•ri•al,iz•er,** *n.*

ed•i•to•ri•al•ly [ˌɛdəˈtɔriəli] *adv.* **1** in an editorial manner. **2** in an editorial.

ed•i•tor–in–chief [ˈɛdətər ɪn ˈtʃif] *n., pl.* **ed•i•tors-in-chief.** the person who is the head of the editorial staff of a publication or publishing house.

ed•i•tor•ship [ˈɛdətərˌʃɪp] *n.* the position, duties, or authority of an editor.

E•do [ˈidou] *n.* **1** a people living in Nigeria, in the Benin region. **2** the Kwa language of these people.

E.D.P. or **EDP** electronic data processing.

ed•ro•pho•ni•um chloride [ˌɛdrəˈfouniəm] *n.* a drug used to reverse the effect of muscle relaxant drugs.

eds. **1** editions. **2** editors.

EDTA a clear, crystal-forming solid useful for its chelating ability. EDTA is used in industry as a food preservative, and in medicine as an anticoagulant and as a treatment for lead poisoning and other types of metal poisoning. *Formula*: $C_{10}H_{16}N_2O_8$ ⟨< *e*thylene*d*iamine*t*etraacetic *a*cid⟩

ed•u•ca•ble [ˈɛdʒəkəbəl] *adj.* capable of being educated, taught, or trained.

ed•u•cate [ˈɛdʒəˌkeit] *v.* **-cat•ed, -cat•ing. 1** develop in knowledge, skill, ability, or character by training, study, or experience; teach; train. **2** send to school. ⟨< L *educare* bring up, raise; related to *educere.* See EDUCE.⟩

educated guess an estimate based on experience.

ed•u•ca•tion [ˌɛdʒəˈkeiʃən] *n.* **1** the process of development in knowledge, skill, ability, or character by teaching, training, study, or experience; teaching; training. **2** the knowledge, skill, ability, or character developed by teaching, training, study, or experience. **3** the science and art that deals with the principles, problems, etc. of teaching and learning. ⟨< L *educatio*⟩

☛ *Syn.* **2. Education,** ENLIGHTENMENT, CULTURE = the qualities and knowledge a person gets from study, teaching, and experience. **Education** emphasizes the training, knowledge, and abilities a person gets through teaching and study: *A person with education knows how to speak, write, and read well.* **Enlightenment** emphasizes the insight and understanding that make a person free from prejudice and ignorance: *A person with enlightenment knows the value of education.* **Culture** applies to the combination of enlightenment and fineness of feeling and taste that results from complete education: *A person of culture appreciates music and art.*

ed•u•ca•tion•al [ˌɛdʒəˈkeiʃənəl] *adj.* **1** of or having to do with education: *an educational association.* **2** giving education; tending to educate: *an educational film.* **—ˌed•uˈca•tion•al•ly,** *adv.*

ed•u•ca•tion•al•ist [ˌɛdʒəˈkeiʃənəlɪst] *n.* an expert on the methods and principles of education; educator. Also, **educationist.**

ed•u•ca•tive [ˈɛdʒəkətɪv] *or* [ˈɛdʒəˌkeitɪv] *adj.* **1** that educates; instructive. **2** of or having to do with education.

ed•u•ca•tor [ˈɛdʒəˌkeitər] *n.* **1** a person whose profession is education; teacher. **2** a leader in education; authority on methods and principles of education.

e•duce [ɪˈdjus] *or* [ɪˈdus] *v.* **e•duced, e•duc•ing.** bring out; draw forth; elicit; develop. ⟨< L *educere* < *ex-* out + *ducere* lead⟩ **—eˈdu•ci•ble,** *adj.* **—eˈduc•tion** [ɪˈdʌkʃən], *n.*

Ed•war•di•an [ɛdˈwɔrdiən] *or* [ɛdˈwɑrdiən] *adj.* **1** of or having to do with King Edward VII or his reign (1901-1910). **2** like or characteristic of this age, especially as marked by material wealth, luxury, and complacency. **3** of or having to do with the style of architecture common during the reigns of the first three King Edwards of England (1239-1377).

–ee *suffix.* **1** a person who is ——: *absentee = person who is absent.* **2** a person who is ——ed: *appointee = person who is appointed.* **3** a person to whom something is ——ed: *mortgagee = person to whom something is mortgaged.* **4** a person who ——s: *standee = a person who stands.* ⟨< F *-é*, masc. pp. ending⟩

E.E. Electrical Engineer.

EEC EUROPEAN ECONOMIC COMMUNITY.

EEG *Medicine.* electroencephalogram.

eel [il] *n.* **1** any of an order (Apodes) of long, snakelike, usually scaleless fishes having a smooth, slimy skin and no pelvic fins. **2** any of various other fishes that are similar in shape, such as the electric eel or the lamprey. ⟨OE *ǣl*⟩ **—ˈeel-ˌlike,** *adj.*

eel•grass [ˈilˌgræs] *n.* **1** a perennial marine plant (*Zostera marina*) growing under water along the Atlantic and Pacific coasts of North America, having very long, tapelike leaves. **2** TAPE GRASS.

eel•pout [ˈilˌpʌut] *n.* **1** a small, eel-like saltwater fish. **2** burbot. ⟨OE *ǣlepūte*⟩

eel•worm [ˈilˌwɜrm] *n.* any small nematode of the family Anganillidae.

e'en [in] *adv. Poetic.* **1** even. **2** evening.

e'er [ɛr] *adv. Poetic.* ever.
☛ *Hom.* AIR, ERE, ERR [ɛr], EYRE, HEIR.

–eer *suffix.* **1** a person who is concerned with, works with, or deals with: *auctioneer, charioteer.* **2** a person who produces: *pamphleteer, sonneteer.* **3** be concerned or deal with (*sometimes pejorative*): *electioneer.* ⟨< F *-ier*⟩

EER energy efficiency ratio, a formula to show the efficiency of a machine by giving its output of work as a ratio of the input of energy to achieve it.

ee•rie [ˈiri] *adj.* **-ri•er, -ri•est. 1** causing fear; strange; weird: *an eerie scream.* **2** *Archaic.* timid because of superstition. ⟨ME *eri*, var. of *erg*, OE *earg* cowardly⟩ **—ˈee•ri•ness,** *n.*
☛ *Hom.* EYRIE.
☛ *Syn.* **1.** See note at WEIRD.

ee•ri•ly [ˈirəli] *adv.* in an eerie way; in a way that causes fear: *The shutters in the old, deserted house creaked eerily.*

ee•ry [ˈiri] *adj.* **-ri•er, -ri•est.** See EERIE.

ef– the form of EX-[1] before *f*, as in *effect.*

EFC Eastern Football Conference.

ef•face [ɪˈfeis] *v.* **-faced, -fac•ing. 1** rub out; blot out; do away with; destroy; wipe out: *The inscriptions on many ancient monuments have been effaced by time. It takes many years to efface the unpleasant memories of a war.* **2** keep (oneself) from being noticed; make inconspicuous: *The shy boy effaced himself by staying in the background.* **3** of the tissue forming the cervix, thin out or cause to thin out to permit dilation during childbirth: *The cervix will efface during the first stage of labour. The pressure of the baby's head effaces the cervix.* ⟨< F *effacer* < *es-* away + *face* face < L *facies* form⟩ **—efˈface•a•ble,** *adj.* **—efˈfac•er,** *n.* **—efˈface•ment,** *n.*
☛ *Syn.* **1.** See note at ERASE.

ef•fect [ɪˈfɛkt] *n., v. —n.* **1** whatever is produced by a cause; something made to happen by a person or thing; result. **2** the power to produce results; force; validity. **3** something that produces an impression: *sound effects.* **4** influence: *The medicine had an immediate effect.* **5** the impression produced by something. **6** the combination of elements in a picture, piece of music, etc.: *Sunshine coming through leaves creates a lovely effect.* **7** purport; intent; meaning. **8 effects,** *pl.* personal property; belongings; goods.
for effect, for show; to impress or influence others.
give effect to, put in operation; make active.
in effect, a in result; in fact; really. **b** in operation; active: *The new rules are now in effect.*
into effect, into operation; into action; into force.
of or **to no effect,** with no results; useless(ly).
take effect, begin to operate; become active: *The new prices will take effect on January 1st.*
to the effect, with the meaning or purpose (*that*).
—v. **1** produce as an effect; make happen; get done; bring about. **2** *Rare.* make; construct. ⟨ME < L *effectus* < *efficere* < *ex-* out + *facere* make⟩ **—efˈfect•less,** *adj.*
☛ *Syn. n.* **1. Effect,** CONSEQUENCE, RESULT = something produced by a cause. **Effect** applies to whatever is produced by a cause, particularly what happens or occurs directly and immediately: *The effect of raising the speed limit was a number of bad accidents.* **Consequence** applies to something that follows, but is not always closely or directly connected with the cause: *As a consequence, there was a provincial investigation of highway conditions.* **Result** applies to what happens as a final effect or consequence: *The result was a new set of traffic regulations.* **8.** See note at PROPERTY.
☛ *Usage.* **Effect,** AFFECT[1]. Because these words sound similar, they are often confused in writing. Most commonly, **effect** is a noun, meaning 'result', and **affect** is a verb, meaning 'to influence': *We don't know what effect the new rule will have. The new rule will affect everybody.* However, in formal English **effect** is also used as a verb meaning 'get done, bring about': *She effected an improvement in the working conditions.* Thus to *affect a proposal* means to influence it or make a change in it, while *to effect a proposal* means to get it done or bring it to completion.

ef•fec•tive [ɪˈfɛktɪv] *adj., n. —adj.* **1** producing an effect. **2** producing the desired effect. **3** in operation; active: *These laws will become effective on New Year's Day.* **4** striking; impressive. **5** actual or real, not theoretical or nominal (*used only before a noun*): *one's effective income after deductions.* **6** of a soldier, military force, etc., equipped and ready for action.
—n. a soldier, military unit, etc. equipped and ready for action. **—efˈfec•tive•ly,** *adv.* **—efˈfec•tive•ness,** *n.*

☛ *Syn. adj.* **1. Effective,** EFFECTUAL, EFFICIENT = producing an effect. **Effective,** usually describing things, emphasizes producing a wanted or expected effect: *Several new drugs are effective in treating serious diseases.* **Effectual,** describing people or things, emphasizes having produced or having the power to produce the exact effect or result intended: *Her efforts are more energetic than effectual.* **Efficient,** often describing people, emphasizes being able to produce the effect wanted or intended without wasting energy, time, etc.: *A skilled surgeon is highly efficient.*

ef•fec•tor [ɪ'fɛktər] *n. Physiology.* **1** a muscle or gland capable of responding to a nerve impulse. **2** the part of a nerve that transmits an impulse.

ef•fec•tu•al [ɪ'fɛktʃuəl] *adj.* **1** producing the effect desired; capable of producing the effect desired: *Quinine is an effectual preventive of malaria.* **2** valid. **—ef'fec•tu•al•ness** or **ef,fec•tu'al•i•ty,** *n.*
☛ *Syn.* **1.** See note at EFFECTIVE.

ef•fec•tu•al•ly [ɪ'fɛktʃuəli] *adv.* with a desired effect; thoroughly.

ef•fec•tu•ate [ɪ'fɛktʃu,eit] *v.* **-at•ed, -at•ing.** cause; make happen; bring about; accomplish. ⟨< F *effectuer* < L *effectus.* See EFFECT.⟩ **—ef,fec•tu'a•tion,** *n.*

ef•fem•i•na•cy [ɪ'fɛmənəsi] *n.* **1** lack of manly qualities; unmanly weakness or delicacy. **2** lack of force or vigour.

ef•fem•i•nate [ɪ'fɛmənɪt] *adj.* **1** lacking in manly qualities; showing weakness or delicacy. **2** of ideas, art, etc., without force or vigour. ⟨< L *effeminatus*, pp. of *effeminare* make a woman out of < *ex-* out + *femina* woman⟩ **—ef'fem•i•nate•ly,** *adv.* **—ef'fem•i•nate•ness,** *n.*

ef•fen•di [ɪ'fɛndi] *n., pl.* **-dis.** in Turkey: **1** a title of respect similar to 'Sir' or 'Master'. **2** a person having this title; doctor, official, scholar, etc. ⟨< Turkish *efendī* < Gk. *authentēs* master, doer < *auto-* by oneself + *hentēs* one who acts⟩

ef•fer•ent ['ɛfərənt] *adj., n. —adj.* of nerves, blood vessels, etc., conveying outward from a central organ or point. Efferent nerves carry impulses from the brain to the muscles. Compare AFFERENT.
—n. an efferent nerve. ⟨< L *efferens*, *-entis*, ppr. of *efferre* < *ex-* out + *ferre* carry⟩

ef•fer•vesce [,ɛfər'vɛs] *v.* **-vesced, -vesc•ing. 1** give off bubbles of gas; bubble: *Ginger ale effervesces.* **2** be lively and happy; be excited. ⟨< L *effervescere* boil up < *ex-* out + *fervescere* begin to boil < *fervere* be hot⟩

ef•fer•ves•cence [,ɛfər'vɛsəns] *n.* **1** the act or process of bubbling, or the state of being bubbly. **2** liveliness; gaiety.

ef•fer•ves•cent [,ɛfər'vɛsənt] *adj.* **1** giving off bubbles of gas; bubbling. **2** lively; merry. **—,ef•fer'ves•cent•ly,** *adv.*

ef•fete [ɪ'fit] *adj.* **1** no longer able to produce; worn out; exhausted. **2** lacking in character. ⟨< L *effetus* worn out by bearing < *ex-* out + *fe-* breed, bear⟩ **—ef'fete•ly,** *adv.* **—ef'fete•ness,** *n.*

ef•fi•ca•cious [,ɛfə'keiʃəs] *adj.* producing the desired results; effective: *Vaccination for typhoid is efficacious.* **—,ef•fi'ca•cious•ly,** *adv.* **—,ef•fi'ca•cious•ness,** *n.*

ef•fi•ca•cy ['ɛfəkəsi] *n., pl.* **-cies.** the power to produce a desired effect or result; effectiveness. ⟨< L *efficacia* < *efficere* accomplish. See EFFICIENT.⟩

ef•fi•cien•cy [ɪ'fɪʃənsi] *n., pl.* **-cies. 1** the ability to produce the effect wanted without waste of time, energy, etc. **2** efficient operation: *Friction lowers the efficiency of a machine.* **3** the ratio of work done to the energy used in producing it, expressed as a percentage. **4** EFFICIENCY APARTMENT.

efficiency apartment a one-room apartment with kitchenette and bathroom; bachelor apartment.

efficiency expert a person whose profession is to devise more effective, economical methods of doing things in factories, offices, etc.

ef•fi•cient [ɪ'fɪʃənt] *adj.* **1** able to produce the effect wanted without waste of time, energy, etc. **2** actually producing the effect in question: *Heat is the efficient cause in changing water to steam.* ⟨< L *efficiens*, *-entis*, ppr. of *efficere* < *ex-* out of + *facere* do, make⟩ **—ef'fi•cient•ly,** *adv.*
☛ *Syn.* **1.** See note at EFFECTIVE.

ef•fi•gy ['ɛfədʒi] *n., pl.* **-gies.** a statue, etc. of a person; image: *The dead man's monument bore his effigy.*
burn or **hang** (someone) **in effigy,** burn or hang an image of a person to show hatred or contempt. ⟨< F *effigie* < L *effigies* < *effingere* < *ex-* out + *fingere* form⟩

ef•flo•resce [,ɛflə'rɛs] *v.* **-resced, -resc•ing. 1** burst into bloom; blossom out. **2** *Chemistry.* **a** change to a powder either throughout or on the surface by loss of water of crystallization when exposed to air. **b** become covered with a crusty deposit when water evaporates. ⟨< L *efflorescere* < *ex-* out + *flos, floris* flower⟩

ef•flo•res•cence [,ɛflə'rɛsəns] *n.* **1** the act or process of blooming; flowering. **2** the period or state of flowering: *The efflorescence of Romantic music occurred during the 19th century.* **3** a mass of flowers. **4** anything resembling a mass of flowers. **5** *Chemistry.* **a** a change that occurs when crystals lose their water of crystallization and become powder. **b** a powder formed in this way. **c** the formation of a crusty deposit when water evaporates from a solution. **d** a deposit formed in this way. **6** an eruption on the skin; rash.

ef•flo•res•cent [,ɛflə'rɛsənt] *adj.* **1** blooming; flowering. **2** *Chemistry.* that undergoes or has undergone efflorescence.

ef•flu•ence ['ɛfluəns] *n.* **1** an outward flow. **2** the thing that flows out; emanation.

ef•flu•ent ['ɛfluənt] *adj., n. —adj.* flowing out or forth.
—n. **1** a stream flowing out of another stream, lake, etc. **2** liquid industrial waste, sewage, etc., especially when causing pollution. **3** something that flows out or forth; effluence; emanation. ⟨< L *effluens*, *-entis*, ppr. of *effluere* < *ex-* out + *fluere* flow⟩

ef•flu•vi•um [ɪ'fluviəm] *n., pl.* **-vi•a** or **-vi•ums. 1** an unpleasant vapour or odour. **2** a vapour; odour. ⟨< L *effluvium* a flowing out < *effluere.* See EFFLUENT.⟩ **—ef'flu•vi•al,** *adj.*

ef•flux ['ɛflʌks] *n.* **1** the outward flow of a liquid. **2** something that flows out.

ef•fort ['ɛfərt] *n.* **1** the use of energy and strength to do something; a trying hard: *Climbing a steep hill takes effort.* **2** a hard try; strong attempt. **3** the result of effort; anything done with effort; achievement. Works of literature, music, or art are often called literary or artistic efforts. **4** *Physics.* the amount of energy required to perform a physical task: *To lift a mass of one kilogram requires effort equivalent to ten newtons.* ⟨< F < OF *esfort* < *esforcier* force, exert < L *ex-* out + *fortis* strong⟩
☛ *Syn.* **1. Effort,** ENDEAVOUR, APPLICATION = active use of physical or mental power to do something. **Effort** emphasizes using energy and strength and trying hard, but usually suggests a single act or action: *Gilles made an effort to finish his work today.* **Endeavour,** more formal, applies to sincere and serious effort continued over some time: *By constant endeavour, he realized his ambition.* **Application** emphasizes continued, concentrated effort and close attention to what one is doing: *By application to his work he makes good grades.*

ef•fort•less ['ɛfərtlɪs] *adj.* requiring or involving no effort; easy. **—'ef•fort•less•ly,** *adv.* **—'ef•fort•less•ness,** *n.*
☛ *Syn.* See note at EASY.

ef•fron•ter•y [ɪ'frʌntəri] *n., pl.* **-ter•ies.** shameless boldness; impudence: *The politician had the effrontery to ask the people he had insulted to vote for him.* ⟨< F *effronterie* < OF < LL *effrons* barefaced, shameless < *ex-* without + *frons, frontis* forehead, ability to blush, hence, without blushing⟩

ef•ful•gence [ɪ'fʌldʒəns] *n.* brightness; radiance.

ef•ful•gent [ɪ'fʌldʒənt] *adj.* shining brightly; radiant. ⟨< L *effulgens*, *-entis*, ppr. of *effulgere* < *ex-* forth + *fulgere* shine⟩ **—ef'ful•gent•ly,** *adv.*

ef•fuse *v.* [ɪ'fjuz]; *adj.* [ɪ'fjus] *v.* **-fused, -fus•ing,** *adj.*
—v. pour out; spill; shed.
—adj. Biology loosely spread out. ⟨< L *effusus*, pp. of *effundere* < *ex-* out + *fundere* pour⟩

ef•fu•sion [ɪ'fjuʒən] *n.* **1** a pouring out: *the effusion of blood.* **2** an unrestrained expression of feeling, etc. in talking or writing. **3** the seeping of a fluid into a cavity. **4** the fluid that seeps.

ef•fu•sive [ɪ'fjusɪv] *adj.* **1** showing too much feeling; too emotional in expression. **2** having to do with igneous rocks that have solidified near to or on the earth's surface. **—ef'fu•sive•ly,** *adv.* **—ef'fu•sive•ness,** *n.*

Ef•ik ['ɛfɪk] *n.* **1** a member of a people of SE Nigeria. **2** the language of these people, related to Bantu.

eft [ɛft] *n.* **1** a newt in the land stage. **2** formerly, a small newt or lizard. ⟨OE *efete.* Cf. NEWT.⟩

EFT *Computer technology.* electronic fund transfer, a method of transferring money electronically from one bank or one account to another.

EFTA European Free Trade Association, established in 1960 and including as original members Austria, Denmark, Norway, Portugal, Sweden, Switzerland, and the United Kingdom.

e.g. for example (for L *exempli gratia*).
☛ *Usage.* **E.g.** is not usually italicized, that is, not underlined in writing, but should always have abbreviation periods. In all but expository prose or technical writing, the English phrase "for example" is stylistically preferable. In formal writing *e.g.* is preceded by some punctuation mark.

e•gad [ɪ'gæd] *interj.* a mild oath, like "by Jove." ⟨alteration of a God! *Oh God!*⟩

e•gal•i•tar•i•an [ɪ,gælə'tɛriən] *n., adj.* —*n.* a person who believes in equality, especially in social equality.
—*adj.* of or relating to equality, especially social equality.

e•gal•i•tar•i•an•ism [ɪ,gælə'tɛriə,nɪzəm] *n.* belief in equality, especially in social equality.

E•ge•ria [ɪ'dʒiriə] *n.* a woman adviser. ⟨< *Egeria*, the Roman goddess of fountains and childbirth, and adviser to a king⟩

e•gest [ɪ'dʒɛst] *v.* discharge from the body in solid form.
—e'ges•tion, *n.*

e•ges•ta [ɪ'dʒɛstə] *n.* excrement.

egg¹ [ɛg] *n.* **1** a roundish body, covered with a shell or membrane, that is laid by the female of birds, fishes, and other animals that do not bring forth live young. **2** *Biology.* a female reproductive cell. **3** specifically, a hen's egg as used for food. **4** anything shaped like a hen's egg. **5** *Slang.* an aerial bomb.
bad egg, a person or plan that comes to no good.
good egg, a good or promising person or thing.
have egg on one's face, *Informal.* be completely embarrassed.
have or **put all** (one's) **eggs in one basket,** risk everything that one has on one chance.
lay an egg, commit a public blunder; make a shocking mistake.
⟨ME < ON⟩ **—'egg•less,** *adj.* **—'egg,like,** *adj.* **—'eg•gy,** *adj.*

egg² [ɛg] *v.* urge; encourage (*on*): *The other boys egged him on to fight.* ⟨ME < ON *eggja* < *egg* edge, point⟩

egg and dart in architecture, a decorative moulding of egg-shaped figures alternating with figures shaped like a dart, an anchor, or a tongue. Also, **egg and anchor, egg and tongue.**

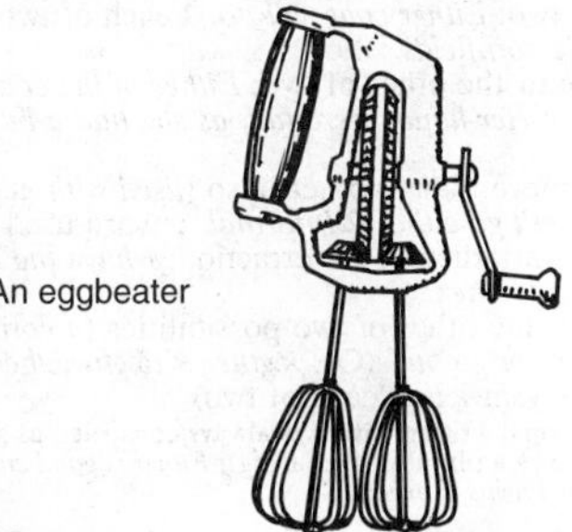
An eggbeater

egg•beat•er ['ɛg,bitər] *n.* **1** a kitchen utensil for beating or whipping eggs, cream, etc., especially a hand-operated one with rotary blades. **2** *Slang.* helicopter.

egg cell a mature female reproductive cell; ovum.

egg coal anthracite coal having a diameter of 5-10 cm.

egg foo yong [,ɛg fu 'jʌŋ] a dish of Chinese-American origin, made with beaten, cooked eggs, bean sprouts, diced shrimp, onions, etc.

egg•head ['ɛg,hɛd] *n. Informal.* an intellectual, especially one who is committed to cultural and intellectual interests and who pays no attention to popular fads; highbrow.

egg•nog ['ɛg,nɒg] *n.* a drink made of eggs beaten up with milk and sugar and spices such as nutmeg, often containing whisky, brandy, or wine. ⟨< *egg¹* + dialect *nog* strong ale⟩

egg•plant ['ɛg,plænt] *n.* **1** a plant (*Solanum melongena*) of the nightshade family, bearing a large, egg-shaped fruit, used as a vegetable and having a glossy purple skin when ripe. **2** the fruit of this plant.

An eggplant

egg roll a small, filled, unraised, egg-based pastry containing bean sprouts or other vegetables and, often, pieces of chicken, shrimp, etc. Egg rolls are fried in deep fat.

eggs Benedict a dish of poached eggs on slices of ham and toast, covered with hollandaise sauce.

egg•shell ['ɛg,ʃɛl] *n., adj.* —*n.* **1** the shell covering an egg. **2** a yellowish white colour: *They chose the eggshell for the living room walls.*
—*adj.* **1** like an eggshell; very thin and delicate. **2** a semi-mat finish on paint when dry: *eggshell paint, eggshell finish.* **3** yellowish white, as an eggshell.

egg timer a measuring device, usually shaped like a miniature hourglass, for timing the boiling of an egg to the desired firmness.

egg tooth a small projection in the upper beak of a bird, or the jaw of a reptile, used by the embryo to break the shell when hatching.

e•gis ['idʒɪs] *n.* aegis.

eg•lan•tine ['ɛglən,taɪn] *or* ['ɛglən,tin] *n.* sweetbrier. ⟨< F *eglantine*, dim. of OF *aiglent* < VL *aculentus* < L *acus* needle⟩

e•go ['igou] *or* ['ɛgou] *n., pl.* **e•gos. 1** the individual as a whole in his or her capacity to think, feel, and act; self. **2** *Informal.* conceit. **3** *Philosophy.* the element of being that consciously and continuously enables an individual to think, feel, and act. **4** *Psychoanalysis.* the part of the personality that is conscious of the environment and adapts itself to it. ⟨< L *ego* I⟩

e•go•cen•tric [,igou'sɛntrɪk] *or* [,ɛgou-] *adj., n.* —*adj.* **1** looking upon oneself as the focus and object of all experience and events; seeing everything in relation to oneself; self-centred; egoistic. **2** *Philosophy.* real only when perceived by the mind.
—*n.* an egocentric person.

ego ideal 1 a person's total identification with loving parents. **2** an ideal for which one strives.

e•go•ism ['igou,ɪzəm] *or* ['ɛgou,ɪzəm] *n.* **1** the state of seeking the welfare of oneself only; selfishness. **2** talking too much about or thinking too well of oneself; conceit. **3** *Philosophy.* the ethical doctrine that morality lies in the pursuit of individual self-interest, and that self-interest motivates all conduct.
☛ *Syn.* See note at EGOTISM.

e•go•ist ['igouɪst] *or* ['ɛgouɪst] *n.* **1** a person who seeks the welfare of himself or herself only; selfish person. **2** a person who talks too much about or thinks too well of himself or herself; a conceited person. **3** *Philosophy.* a believer in egoism as a principle of human conduct.

e•go•is•tic [,igou'ɪstɪk] *or* [,ɛgou'ɪstɪk] *adj.* **1** seeking the welfare of oneself only; selfish. **2** talking too much about or thinking too well of oneself; conceited. **3** *Philosophy.* of or having to do with egoism. **—,e•go'is•ti•cal•ly,** *adv.*

e•go•ma•ni•a [,igou'meiniə] *or* [,ɛgou-] *n.* the quality or state of being extremely self-centred and conceited.

e•go•ma•ni•ac [,igou'meini,æk] *or* [,ɛgou-] *n.* a person characterized by egomania.

e•go•ma•ni•a•cal [,igoumə'naɪəkəl] *or* [,ɛgou-] *adj.* of, having to do with, or characterized by egomania.
—,e•go•ma'ni•a•cal•ly, *adv.*

ego psychology the study of the ego and its functions, and how these relate to emotional maturation and disorders.

e•go•tism ['igə,tɪzəm] *or* ['ɛgə,tɪzəm] *n.* **1** the excessive use of *I, my,* and *me;* habit of thinking, talking, or writing too much of oneself. **2** self-conceit. **3** selfishness. ⟨< *ego* + *-t* + *-ism*⟩
☛ *Syn.* **Egotism,** EGOISM = a habit of thinking too much about self. **Egotism** emphasizes conceit, boasting, and selfishness, and means always talking about oneself and one's own affairs and trying to get attention: *Henry's egotism drives away friends.* **Egoism** emphasizes being self-centred and looking at everyone and everything only as it affects oneself and one's own welfare, but does not suggest boasting or annoying conceit, nor always selfishness: *We forget the natural egoism of a genius if she is successful.*

e•go•tist ['igətɪst] *or* ['ɛgətɪst] *n.* **1** a person who thinks and talks about himself or herself a great deal; conceited, boastful person. **2** a selfish person.

e•go•tis•tic [,igə'tɪstɪk] *or* [,ɛgə'tɪstɪk] *adj.* **1** characterized by egotism; conceited. **2** selfish. Also, **egotistical.** —**,e•go'tis•ti•cal•ly,** *adv.*

ego trip *Informal.* an experience or act whose primary value or purpose is to enhance the self-satisfaction and feeling of power of the person involved: *His newspaper column was just an ego trip.*

e•go–trip ['igou ,trɪp] *or* ['ɛgou-] *v.* **-tripped, -trip•ping.** *Informal.* indulge in an ego trip. —**'e•go-,trip•per,** *n.*

e•gre•gious [ɪ'gridʒəs] *adj.* **1** remarkably or extraordinarily bad; outrageous; flagrant: *an egregious lie.* **2** remarkable; extraordinary. ⟨< L *egregius* < *ex-* out + *grex, gregis* herd, flock⟩ —**e'gre•gious•ly,** *adv.*

e•gress ['igrɛs] *n.* **1** a going out: *The enemy blocked the narrow pass so that no egress was possible for our soldiers.* **2** a way out; exit. **3** the right to go out. ⟨< L *egressus* < *egredi* < *ex-* out + *gradi* step, go⟩ —**e'gres•sion,** *n.* —**e'gres•sive,** *adj.*

e•gret ['igrɛt] *or* ['ɛgrɛt], ['igrɪt] *or* ['ɛgrɪt] *n.* **1** any of various herons that in mating season grow tufts of beautiful, long plumes, which were formerly much used as ornaments for the head. **2** an aigrette. ⟨< F *aigrette*⟩

E•gypt ['idʒɪpt] *n.* a country in NE Africa, properly called the Arab Republic of Egypt. See LEBANON and SUDAN for maps.

E•gyp•tian [ɪ'dʒɪpʃən] *n., adj.* —*n.* **1** a native or inhabitant of Egypt. **2** the Afro-Asiatic language of the ancient Egyptians. —*adj.* of or having to do with Egypt or its people.

Egyptian cotton a type of high-quality cotton having long fibres, much grown in Egypt.

E•gyp•tol•o•gist [,idʒɪp'tɒlədʒɪst] *n.* a person trained in Egyptology, especially one whose work it is.

E•gyp•tol•o•gy [,idʒɪp'tɒlədʒi] *n.* the science or study of the monuments, history, language, etc. of ancient Egypt.

eh [ei] *interj.* **1** an exclamation expressing doubt, surprise, or failure to hear exactly. **2** *Can. Informal.* an all-purpose tag question: *He didn't make it, eh? So that's what you think, eh?* **3** *Cdn. Informal.* a filler, like 'you know' or 'you see', inviting the listener to identify with what one is saying: *I was just minding my own business, eh, when along comes some guy and pushes me off the sidewalk. It's my father's birthday, eh, so I'd better be there.*

EHF or **ehf** EXTREMELY HIGH FREQUENCY.

EIB Export-Import Bank.

ei•der ['aɪdər] *n.* **1** any of several large sea ducks (especially of genus *Somateria*) that breed in the Arctic. Also, **eider duck.** **2** eiderdown. ⟨< Icel. *ǣthr*⟩

ei•der•down ['aɪdər,daʊn] *n.* **1** the soft feathers from the breasts of eiders, used to stuff pillows and bed quilts, as trimming, etc. **2** a quilt stuffed with these feathers.

eider duck EIDER (def. 1).

ei•det•ic [aɪ'dɛtɪk] *adj.* of mental images, almost photographically accurate and vivid. ⟨< Gk. *eidetikos* constituting a figure < *eidos* what is seen, shape⟩ —**ei'det•i•cal•ly,** *adv.*

ei•do•lon ['aɪdə,lɒn] or [aɪ'doulən] *n.* **1** a ghost. **2** an image of an ideal. ⟨< Gk., image < *eidos* what is seen, shape. Related to IDOL.⟩

eight [eit] *n., adj.* —*n.* **1** one more than seven; 8. **2** the numeral 8: *He makes his eights with two circles.* **3** the eighth in a set or series; especially, a playing card having eight spots: *the eight of diamonds.* **4** *Rowing.* **a** a crew of eight rowers. **b** the boat they use. **5** any set or series of eight persons or things: *The computer was programmed to count in eights.* **6** something shaped like a figure eight.
—*adj.* **1** being one more than seven. **2** being eighth in a set or series (*used mainly after the noun*): *Section Eight is missing.* ⟨OE *eahta*⟩

eight ball *Pool.* **1** a black ball bearing a figure 8, which in certain varieties of the game carries a penalty if hit or pocketed. **2** a form of pool in which one side must pocket all other balls before the one numbered 8.
behind the eight ball, *Slang.* in an unfavourable position; in an awkward or threatening situation.

eight•een ['eit'tin] *n., adj.* —*n.* **1** eight more than ten; 18. **2** the numeral 18: *The 18 is not in line with the other figures in the column.* **3** the eighteenth in a set or series. **4** a set or series of eighteen persons or things.
—*adj.* being eighteenth in a set or series (*used after the noun*): *Chapter Eighteen.* ⟨OE *eahtatēne*⟩

eight•een•mo ['eit'tinmou] *n.* in bookbinding, octodecimo, a size of page.

eight•eenth ['eit'tinθ] *adj. or n.* **1** next after the 17th; last in a series of eighteen; 18th. **2** one, or being one, of 18 equal parts.

eight•fold ['eit,fould] *adj., adv.* —*adj.* **1** having eight parts. **2** eight times as much.
—*adv.* in eightfold measure; eight times as much.

eighth [eitθ] *adj., n.* —*adj.* **1** next after the seventh; last in a series of eight; 8th. **2** being one of 8 equal parts.
—*n.* **1** the next after the seventh; last in a series of eight; 8th. **2** one of 8 equal parts. **3** *Music.* one octave. —**'eighth•ly,** *adv.*

eighth note *Music.* a short note, one eighth of a whole note. See NOTE for picture.

eighth rest *Music.* a rest, or sign for silence, equal in duration to an eighth note.

eight•i•eth ['eitiɪθ] *adj. or n.* **1** next after the 79th; last in a series of 80; 80th. **2** one, or being one, of 80 equal parts.

eight•mo ['eitmou] *n.* in bookbinding, octavo, a size of page.

eight•y ['eiti] *n., pl.* **eight•ies;** *adj.* —*n.* **1** eight times ten; 80. **2 eighties,** *pl.* the years from eighty through eighty-nine, especially of a century or of a person's life: *My great-grandmother is in her eighties.*
—*adj.* eight times ten; 80. ⟨OE *eahtatig*⟩

ei•kon ['əikɒn] See ICON.

ein•korn ['aɪnkɔrn] *n.* a variety of wheat (*Triticum monosecum*) grown in arid regions. ⟨< G *ein* one + *Korn* grain⟩

Einstein equation ['aɪnstaɪn] an equation expressing the relation of mass and energy: $E = mc^2$. E is the energy in joules; m is the mass in grams; c is the speed of light in a vacuum in metres per second.

Ein•stein•i•an [aɪn'staɪniən] *adj.* having to do with Albert Einstein (1879-1955), German physicist, especially his theory of relativity.

ein•stein•i•um [aɪn'staɪniəm] *n.* a rare, artificial chemical element that is radioactive and is produced as a by-product of nuclear fission. *Symbol*: Es; *at.no.* 99; *at.mass* 254.09; *half-life* 276 days. ⟨after Albert *Einstein* (1879-1955)⟩

eis•tedd•fod [aɪ'stɛðvɒd] *n., pl.* **eis•tedd•fod•au** [,aɪstɛð'vɒdaɪ] an annual assembly of Welsh poets and musicians. ⟨< Welsh *eisteddfod* session < *eistedd* sit, akin to E *sit*⟩

ei•ther ['iðər] *or* ['aɪðər] *adj., pron., adv., conj.* —*adj.* **1** one or the other of two: *Either coat will do.* **2** each of two: *On either side of the river lie cornfields.*
—*pron.* **1** one or the other of two: *Either of the coats will do.* **2** each of two: *Her hands were full, as she had a bag of groceries in either.*
—*adv.* **1** any more than another; also (*used with negatives*): *If you don't go, I won't go either.* **2** *Informal.* a word used to strengthen a negative in contradiction or retraction: *I have the keys with me—no, I don't either.*
—*conj.* one or the other of two possibilities (*a correlative with* **or**): *Either come in or go out.* ⟨OE *ǣgther* < *ǣghwæther* each of two < *ā* always + *gehwæther* each of two⟩
☛ *Usage.* In formal writing, **either** is always construed as singular (though its informal use as a plural is increasing): *Either is good enough for me. Either Grace or Phyllis is expected.*

e•jac•u•late [ɪ'dʒækjə,leit] *v.* **-lat•ed, -lat•ing. 1** say suddenly and briefly; exclaim. **2** eject; discharge. **3** of a man, eject semen. ⟨< L *ejaculari* < *ex-* out + *jaculum* javelin < *jacere* throw⟩

e•jac•u•la•tion [ɪ,dʒækjə'leiʃən] *n.* **1** something said suddenly and briefly; exclamation. **2** an ejection; discharge. **3** the ejection of semen by a man. **4** *Roman Catholic Church.* a brief, spontaneous prayer.

e•jac•u•la•to•ry [ɪ'dʒækjələ,tɔri] *adj.* **1** said suddenly and briefly; containing exclamations. **2** ejecting; discharging.

e•ject [ɪ'dʒɛkt] *v.* **1** throw out: *The volcano ejected lava and ashes.* **2** force out; expel: *The landlord ejected the tenant who did not pay her rent.* **3** force (someone) out of an aircraft by means of an ejection seat or capsule. **4** escape from an aircraft using an ejection seat: *The pilot ejected when the cockpit caught fire.* ⟨< L *ejectus*, pp. of *ejicere* throw out < *ex-* out + *jacere* throw⟩

e•jec•ta [ɪ'dʒɛktə] *n.* matter ejected, such as lava from a volcano.

e•jec•tion [ɪ'dʒɛkʃən] *n.* **1** ejecting or being ejected. **2** something ejected: *Lava is a volcanic ejection.*

ejection capsule a cockpit or cabin that can be ejected from an airplane and parachuted to earth.

ejection seat in an aircraft, a seat that, with its occupant, can be instantly ejected and parachuted to earth.

e•ject•ment [ɪ'dʒɛktmənt] *n.* **1** an ejecting; a dispossessing; an ousting. **2** *Law.* an action to regain possession of real estate.

e•jec•tor [ɪ'dʒɛktər] *n.* a person who or thing that ejects.

eke¹ [ik] *v.* **eked, ek•ing.** *Archaic or dialect.* increase; enlarge; lengthen.
eke out, a supply what is lacking to; supplement: *The clerk eked out her regular wages by working evenings and Sundays.* **b** barely make (a living) by various schemes or makeshifts. **c** use (something) very thriftily to make it go as far as possible. ⟨dial. var. of obs. *eche* augment, OE *ēcan* < OE *ēaca* addition⟩

eke² [ik] *adv. or conj. Archaic.* also; moreover. ⟨OE *ēac*⟩

EKG electrocardiogram.

e•kis•tics [ɪ'kɪstɪks] *n.* (*used with a singular verb*) the study of the ecology of human beings in settlements or communities. ⟨< Gk. *oikistiké* (< *oikistés* settler < *oikos* house) + E *-ics.* 20c.⟩ **—e'kis•tic** or **e'kis•ti•cal,** *adj.*

el [ɛl] *n.* **1** *Informal.* an elevated railway. **2** the letter L (or l) or something shaped like a capital L. **3** See ELL².

e•lab•o•rate *adj.* [ɪ'læbərɪt]; *v.* [ɪ'læbə,reit] *adj., v.* **-rat•ed, -rat•ing.** *—adj.* worked out with great care; having many details; complicated.
—v. **1** work out with great care; add details to: *The inventor spent months in elaborating her plans for a new engine.* **2** talk, write, etc. in great detail; give added details: *The witness was asked to elaborate upon one of his statements.* **3** make with labour; produce. **4** make (basic substances) into more complex ones for the body's use as part of digestion. ⟨< L *elaboratus*, pp. of *elaborare* < *ex-* out + *labor* work⟩ **—e'lab•o•rate•ly,** *adv.* **—e'lab•o•rate•ness,** *n.* **—e'lab•o,rat•or,** *n.*

☛ *Syn. adj.* **Elaborate,** STUDIED, LABOURED = worked out in detail. **Elaborate** emphasizes the idea of details, and means having many details all worked out with great care and exactness: *The scientists made elaborate preparations for studying the eclipse.* **Studied** emphasizes care in working out details, and means being thought out beforehand and done on purpose: *His studied politeness was insulting.* **Laboured** emphasizes great effort to work out details, and means showing effort by being strained and unnatural: *The boy gave a laboured excuse for arriving late at school.*

e•lab•o•ra•tion [ɪ,læbə'reiʃən] *n.* **1** an elaborating or being elaborated. **2** something elaborated.

E•lam•ite ['ilə,məit] *n.* **1** a native or inhabitant of Elam, an ancient country in what is now W Iran, just east of ancient Babylonia. **2** the language once spoken by the Elamites, now extinct.

é•lan [ei'lɑn]; *French,* [e'lɑ̃] *n.* liveliness or enthusiasm combined with flair. ⟨< F *élan* < *élancer* throw forth⟩

e•land ['ilənd] *n.* either of two large, oxlike antelopes (*Taurotragus oryx* and *T. derbianus*) of central and southern Africa, having straight, spiral horns. ⟨< Du. *eland* elk⟩

élan vital [elɑ̃ vi'tal] *French.* in Bergsonian philosophy, a creative force that produces growth and does not depend on physical action.

el•a•pid ['ɛləpɪd] *n., adj. —n.* any of the poisonous snakes of the family Elapidae, such as the cobra.
—adj. having to do with that family. ⟨< NL *Elapidae* < Med.Gk. *elaps* fish, sea serpent⟩

e•lapse [ɪ'læps] *v.* **e•lapsed, e•laps•ing.** slip away; glide by; pass: *Hours elapsed while she slept like a log.* ⟨< L *elapsus*, pp. of *elabi* < *ex-* away + *labi* glide⟩

e•las•mo•branch [ɪ'læsmə,bræŋk] *or* [ɪ'læzmə,bræŋk] *n., adj. —n.* any of a subclass (Elasmobranchii; also called Euselachii) of fishes having a cartilaginous skeleton and five to seven pairs of gill slits opening directly to the outside from the pharynx.
—adj. of the Elasmobranchii. ⟨< NL *Elasmobranchii*, pl. < Gk. *elasmos* metal plate + *branchia* gills⟩

e•las•tic [ɪ'læstɪk] *adj., n. —adj.* **1** having the quality of springing back to its original size, shape, or position after being stretched, squeezed, bent, etc.: *Toy balloons, sponges, and steel springs are elastic.* **2** springing back; springy: *an elastic step.* **3** being able to recover quickly from weariness, low spirits, or misfortune; buoyant: *His elastic spirits never let him be discouraged for long.* **4 a** easily altered to suit changed conditions; flexible; adaptable. **b** *Economics.* adjusting readily to fluctuations in the market.
—n. **1** tape or fabric woven partly of rubber threads. **2** RUBBER BAND. ⟨< NL *elasticus* < Gk. *elastikos* driving, propulsive < *elaunein* drive⟩ **—e'las•ti•cal•ly,** *adv.*

e•las•tic•i•ty [ɪlæ'stɪsəti] *or* [,ilæ'stɪsəti] *n.* **1** an elastic quality: *Rubber has great elasticity.* **2** flexibility: Good *and* evil *are words having great elasticity of meaning.* **3** *Economics.* the ability to adjust to market conditions.

e•las•ti•cize [ɪ'læstɪ,saɪz] *v.* **-cized, -ciz•ing.** weave or make with elastic: *The dress has an elasticized belt.*

elastic tissue elastic, yellow, fibrous connective tissue found in the inner walls of arteries and veins.

e•las•tin [ɪ'læstɪn] *n.* the albuminoid base of elastic tissue such as cartilage, made up of protein.

e•las•to•mer [ɪ'læstəmər] *n.* an elastic substance, such as natural rubber, synthetic rubber, or any of various rubberlike plastics. ⟨< *elastic* + Gk. *meros* part⟩ **—e,las•to'mer•ic** [-'merɪk], *adj.*

e•late [ɪ'leit] *v.* **e•lat•ed, e•lat•ing.** put in high spirits; make joyful or proud. ⟨< L *elatus* < *ex-* out, away + *latus*, pp. of *ferre* carry⟩

e•lat•ed [ɪ'leitɪd] *adj., v. —adj.* in high spirits; joyful; proud. *—v.* pt. and pp. of ELATE. **—e'lat•ed•ly,** *adv.* **—e'lat•ed•ness,** *n.*

el•at•er ['ɛlətər] *n.* **1** *Botany.* an elastic filament that dispenses spores. **2** elaterid. ⟨NL < Gk *elater* driver < *elaunein* drive⟩

e•lat•er•id [ɪ'lætərɪd] *n., adj. —n.* a beetle of the family Elateridae.
—adj. belonging to that family.

e•lat•er•ite [ɪ'lætə,rəit] *n.* a natural asphalt that is rubbery.

el•a•te•ri•um [,ɛlə'tiriəm] *n.* a greyish green solid used as a cathartic, obtained from the juice of the squirting cucumber (*Eballium elaterium*).

e•la•tion [ɪ'leiʃən] *n.* high spirits; joyous pride; exultant gladness.
☛ *Hom.* ILLATION.

E layer the HEAVISIDE LAYER.

el•bow ['ɛlbou] *n., v. —n.* **1** the joint between the upper arm and forearm. **2** the outer part of this joint, especially the point formed when the arm is bent. See ARM for picture. **3** a joint in the forelimb of a four-legged animal that corresponds to the human elbow. **4** the part of a sleeve covering the elbow. **5** something resembling a bent elbow, such as a sharp bend in a road or river or a short, sharply bent piece of pipe used to join pipes at an angle.
at (someone's) **elbow,** near at hand; close by: *When John did his homework, his dictionary was always at his elbow.*
out at (the) **elbows,** ragged or very poor.
rub elbows with, mingle with (people, especially of a different social level).
up to the elbows in, deeply involved in or occupied with.
—v. **1** push with the elbow: *Somebody elbowed her off the sidewalk.* **2** make (one's way) by pushing with the elbows: *He elbowed his way through the crowd.* **3** be at an angle. ⟨OE *elnboga* < *eln* length of lower arm + *boga* bow²⟩

elbow grease *Informal.* hard work; energy.

el•bow•ing ['ɛlbouɪŋ] *n., v. —n. Hockey.* the offence, resulting in a penalty, of jabbing one's elbows into an opponent's body. *—v.* ppr. of ELBOW.

el•bow•room or **elbow room** ['ɛlbou,rum] *or* [-,rʊm] *n.* plenty of room; enough space to move or work in.

eld [ɛld] *n. Archaic.* **1** old age. **2** old times; former times. ⟨OE *eldo* < *eald* old⟩

eld•er¹ ['ɛldər] *adj., n. —adj.* **1** born, produced, or formed before something else; older; senior: *my elder sister, an elder statesman.* **2** prior in rank, validity, etc.: *an elder title to an estate.* **3** earlier; former: *in elder times.*
—n. **1** an older person: *The children showed respect for their elders.* **2** an aged person. **3** an ancestor. **4** one of the older and more influential men of a group or community; a chief, ruler, member of council, etc. **5** any of various important officers of certain churches. ⟨OE *eldra*, comparative of *eald* old⟩

☛ *Usage.* **Elder,** ELDEST. These forms of *old* survive in formal English and are used, when speaking of persons, chiefly for members of the same family: *the elder brother, our eldest daughter;* and in some phrases: *the elder statesman.*

el•der² ['ɛldər] *n.* any of a genus (*Sambucus*) of shrubs or small trees of the honeysuckle family having clusters of small, white or pink flowers and edible red, purple, or black berries. ⟨OE *ellærn*⟩

el•der•ber•ry ['ɛldər,bɛri] *n., pl.* **-ries. 1** the edible fruit of an elder, used for jam, wine, etc. **2** ELDER[2].

eld•er•ly ['ɛldərli] *adj., n.* —*adj.* **1** somewhat old; beyond middle age; near old age. **2** having to do with old people.
—*n.*
the elderly, people who are old. —**'eld•er•li•ness,** *n.*
☛ *Syn.* See note at OLD.

eld•er•ship ['ɛldər,ʃɪp] *n.* **1** the office or position of an elder in a church. **2** a group or court of elders; presbytery.

elder statesman any influential person whose political advice is deeply respected.

eld•est ['ɛldɪst] *adj.* oldest. ⟨OE *eldest(a)*, superlative of *eald* old⟩
☛ *Usage.* See note at ELDER.

El•do•ra•do [,ɛldə'rɑdou] *n., pl.* **-dos. 1** a legendary city of great wealth sought by early explorers in South America. **2** any fabulously wealthy place. Also, **El Dorado.** ⟨< Sp. *El Dorado* the gilded⟩

eld•ritch ['ɛldrɪtʃ] *adj.* weird. ⟨probably < ME *elf, elve* elf + *-rice* kingdom⟩

El•e•at•ic [,ɛli'ætɪk] *adj.* having to do with a philosophy that considered change to be of no value, and immutability all that can be known. ⟨< L *Eleaticus* after *Elea* (Velia), ancient Gk. colony in Italy⟩ —**,El•e'at•i,cism,** *n.*

elec. or **electr.** electricity; electrical; electrician.

el•e•cam•pane [,ɛlɪkæm'pein] *n.* a tall plant (*Inula helenium*) with yellow flowers, native to Eurasia.

e•lect [ɪ'lɛkt] *v., adj.* —*v.* **1** choose or select for an office by voting: *The club members elect a new president each year.* **2** choose; select: *We elected to play baseball.* **3** *Christian theology.* of God, select for salvation and eternal life.
—*adj.* **1** elected but not yet in office (*used after a noun*): *the chair elect.* **2** specially chosen; selected or elite. **3** *Christian theology.* chosen by God for salvation and eternal life. **4** (*noml.*) **the elect,** *pl.* **a** a group of people who have special rights and privileges. **b** *Christian theology.* those who have been chosen by God for salvation and eternal life. ⟨< L *electus*, pp. of *eligere* < *ex-* out + *legere* choose⟩

e•lec•tion [ɪ'lɛkʃən] *n.* **1** a choice. **2** a choosing by vote. **3** *Christian theology.* a selection by God for salvation. **4** GENERAL ELECTION.

e•lec•tion•eer [ɪ,lɛkʃə'nir] *v.* work for the success of a candidate or party in an election. —**e,lec•tion'eer•er,** *n.*

e•lec•tive [ɪ'lɛktɪv] *adj., n.* —*adj.* **1** chosen by an election: *Councillors are elective officials.* **2** filled by an election: *an elective office.* **3** having the right to vote in an election. **4** having to do with the principle of electing to office. **5** *Chemistry.* tending to combine with certain substances in preference to others. **6** open to choice; not required: *elective surgery. German is an elective subject in many high schools.*
—*n.* a subject or course of study that may be taken, but is not required. —**e'lec•tive•ly,** *adv.* —**e'lec•tive•ness,** *n.*

e•lec•tor [ɪ'lɛktər] *n.* **1** a person who has the right to vote in an election. **2** *U.S.* a member of the ELECTORAL COLLEGE. **3** formerly, one of the princes who had the right to elect the emperor of the Holy Roman Empire.

e•lec•tor•al [ɪ'lɛktərəl] *or* [,ilɛk'tɔrəl] *adj.* **1** of electors. **2** of or having to do with an election. —**e'lec•tor•al•ly,** *adv.*

electoral college *U.S.* a group of people chosen by the voters to elect the President and Vice-President of the United States.

e•lec•tor•ate [ɪ'lɛktərɪt] *n.* **1** the persons having the right to vote in an election. **2** formerly, a territory under the rule of an elector of the Holy Roman Empire. **3** formerly, the rank of an elector of the Holy Roman Empire.

electr. electrical; electricity; electrician.

E•lec•tra [ɪ'lɛktrə] *n. Greek legend.* the daughter of Agamemnon and Clytemnestra. Electra urged her brother, Orestes, to kill their mother and her lover in order to avenge the murder of their father.

Electra complex *Psychiatry.* the repressed desire of a daughter for her father, parallel to the Oedipus complex in males.

el•ec•tret [ɪ'lɛktrɪt] *n.* any of various permanently magnetized materials, used in telephones and microphones.

e•lec•tric [ɪ'lɛktrɪk] *adj., n.* —*adj.* **1** of or having to do with electricity: *an electric current.* **2** producing or carrying an electric current: *an electric wire, an electric generator.* **3** produced by electricity: *an electric shock, an electric fire.* **4** operated by electricity: *an electric shaver.* **5** of a musical instrument, using electronic amplification: *an electric guitar.* **6** thrilling or exciting: *an electric atmosphere, an electric performance.* **7** of colours, very bright: *electric blue.*
—*n.* **1** *Informal.* an electric train, car, etc. **2** *Archaic.* a non-conducting substance, such as amber or glass, used to excite or store electricity. ⟨< NL *electricus* < LGk. *ēlektron* amber (which, under friction, has the property of attracting)⟩
—**e'lec•tri•cal•ly,** *adv.*

e•lec•tri•cal [ɪ'lɛktrəkəl] *adj.* **1** electric. **2** having to do with or working by electricity.

electrical engineering the branch of engineering which deals with electricity, especially in its practical application to communications, power supplies, etc.

electrical storm ELECTRIC STORM.

electrical transcription 1 the system of radio broadcasting from a special phonograph record. **2** a special phonograph record used for such broadcasting.

electric brain ELECTRONIC BRAIN; computer.

electric cell BATTERY (def. 2).

electric chair 1 a chair used in electrocuting criminals. **2** the penalty of death by legal electrocution: *He was sentenced to the electric chair.*

electric charge CHARGE (*n.* def. 4).

electric eel a large, eel-like, freshwater fish (*Electrophorus electricus*) of South America, having an electric organ in its tail which can produce a shock strong enough to stun a person.

electric eye PHOTO-ELECTRIC CELL.

electric field the space surrounding an electrically charged body, within which electric force is produced.

electric furnace 1 a furnace which produces heat by electricity. **2** a furnace heated by electricity to high temperatures, used to melt metals, smelt, make steel, etc.

electric heater a portable device that furnishes heat by means of small electric coils.

e•lec•tri•cian [ɪlɛk'trɪʃən] *or* [,ilɛk'trɪʃən] *n.* a person whose work is installing or repairing electric wires, lights, motors, etc.

e•lec•tric•i•ty [ɪlɛk'trɪsəti] *or* [,ilɛk'trɪsəti] *n.* **1** a form of energy that can produce light, heat, magnetism, and chemical changes, and that can be generated by friction, induction, or chemical changes. **2** an electric current; flow of electrons. **3** electricity as a public utility, provided for heating, lighting, etc.: *They charge a lot for electricity.* **4** the branch of physics that deals with electricity. **5** an electric charge. **6** excitement.

electric light bulb a glass bulb enclosing a filament by which electricity is converted to light for illumination.

electric needle in surgery, an electrode in the form of a needle, used to cauterize.

electric ray any of a family (Torpedinidae) of rays found in warm seas, having an electric organ in each wing which can produce shocks to stun prey or other predators.

electric storm or **electrical storm** a storm accompanied by thunder and lightning.

e•lec•tri•fi•ca•tion [ɪ,lɛktrəfə'keiʃən] *n.* an electrifying or being electrified.

e•lec•tri•fy [ɪ'lɛktrə,faɪ] *v.* **-fied, -fy•ing. 1** charge with electricity. **2** equip to use electricity: *Some railways once operated by steam are now electrified.* **3** give an electric shock to. **4** excite; thrill. **5** provide with electric power service: *Many rural areas will soon be electrified.* —**e'lec•tri,fi•able,** *adj.* —**e'lec•tri,fi•er,** *n.*

electro– before vowels **electr–** *combining form.* **1** electric, as in *electromagnet.* **2** electrically, as in *electropositive.* **3** electricity. ⟨< Gk. *ēlektron* amber⟩

e•lec•tro–ac•ous•tics [ɪ,lɛktrou ə'kustɪks] *n.* the science dealing with the interaction of electric and acoustic phenomena.

e•lec•tro–an•al•y•sis [ɪ,lɛktrou ə'næləsɪs] *n.* chemical analysis using electrolytic techniques.

e•lec•tro•bi•ol•o•gy [ɪ,lɛktroubaɪ'ɒlədʒi] *n.* the branch of biology that deals with electrical phenomena in living organisms.

e•lec•tro•car•di•o•gram [ɪ,lɛktrou'kɑrdiə,græm] *n.* a tracing made by an electrocardiograph. *Abbrev.*: ECG, EKG

e•lec•tro•car•di•o•graph [ɪ,lɛktrou'kɑrdiə,græf] *n.* an instrument that records the electric current produced by the action of the heart muscle, used in the diagnosis and treatment of heart disease. —**e,lec•tro,car•di•o'graph•ic,** *adj.*

—e,lec•tro,car•di•o'graph•i•cal•ly, *adv.*
—e,lec•tro,car•di'og•ra•phy, *n.*

e•lec•tro•chem•i•cal [ɪ,lɛktrou'kɛməkəl] *adj.* of, having to do with, or involving the principles or processes of electrochemistry. **—e,lec•tro'chem•i•cal•ly,** *adv.*

electrochemical cell a device capable of producing an electric current by means of chemical action, consisting of a container with two electrodes of different metals in a paste or liquid that will conduct electricity. An electrochemical cell generates a current when the electrodes are connected by a conducting wire. A flashlight battery is an electrochemical cell.

e•lec•tro•chem•is•try [ɪ,lɛktrou'kɛmɪstri] *n.* the branch of chemistry that deals with chemical changes produced by electricity and the production of electricity by chemical changes.

e•lec•tro–con•vul•sive therapy [ɪ,lɛktrou kən'vʌlsɪv] the treatment of mental disorders, especially depression, through shock induced by electrical means.

e•lec•tro•cute [ɪ'lɛktrə,kjut] *v.* **-cut•ed, -cut•ing.** kill by an electric current. ⟨< *electro-* + *(exe)cute*⟩ **—e,lec•tro'cu•tion,** *n.*

e•lec•trode [ɪ'lɛktroud] *n.* a conductor through which an electric current enters or leaves a conducting medium such as an electrolyte, gas, or vacuum in a battery, electron tube, etc. ⟨< *electro-* + Gk. *hodos* way⟩

e•lec•tro•de•pos•it [ɪ,lɛktroudɪ'pɒzɪt] *v., n.* —*v.* deposit (a suspended substance) on an electrode.
—*n.* the substance deposited. **—e,lec•tro,dep•o'si•tion** [-,dɛpə'sɪʃən], *n.*

e•lec•tro•di•al•y•sis [ɪ,lɛktroudaɪ'æləsɪs] *n.* dialysis speeded by the application of an electric current over a membrane.

e•lec•tro•dy•nam•ic [ɪ,lɛktroudaɪ'næmɪk] *adj.* **1** of or having to do with the force of electricity in motion. **2** of or having to do with electrodynamics.
—e,lec•tro•dy'nam•i•cal•ly, *adv.*

e•lec•tro•dy•nam•ics [ɪ,lɛktroudaɪ'næmɪks] *n.* the branch of physics that deals with the action of electricity or with electric currents.

e•lec•tro•dy•na•mom•e•ter [ɪ,lɛktrou,daɪnə'mɒmətər] *n.* an instrument used to measure voltage, power, or current by the interaction between two magnetic fields.

e•lec•tro•en•ceph•a•lo•gram [ɪ,lɛktrouɛn'sɛfələ,græm] *n.* a tracing made by an electroencephalograph. *Abbrev.*: EEG

e•lec•tro•en•ceph•a•lo•graph [ɪ,lɛktrouɛn'sɛfələ,græf] *n.* an instrument for measuring the electrical activity of the brain, used in the diagnosis and treatment of brain disorders.
—e,lec•tro•en,ceph•a•lo'graph•ic, *adj.*
—e,lec•tro•en,ceph•a'log•raph•y, *n.*

e•lec•tro•form•ing [ɪ'lɛktrə,fɔrmɪŋ] *n.* the process of forming a metallic object by electroplating a removable matrix.

e•lec•tro•graph [ɪ'lɛktrə,græf] *n.* **1** a graph produced electrically. **2** the equipment used to produce this graph.

e•lec•tro•jet [ɪ'lɛktrə,dʒɛt] *n.* a current of ions in the upper atmosphere that causes the Northern Lights.

e•lec•tro•ki•net•ics [ɪ,lɛktroukɪ'nɛtɪks] *n.* the branch of physics that deals with electricity in motion.

e•lec•tro•lier [ɪ,lɛktrə'lir] *n.* a chandelier or other support for electric lights. ⟨< *electro-* + *(chande)lier*⟩

e•lec•trol•o•gist [ɪlɛk'trɒlədʒɪst] *or* [,ilɛk'trɒlədʒɪst] *n.* one skilled in the use of electrolysis for removing warts, moles, etc.

e•lec•tro•lu•mi•nes•cence [ɪ,lɛktrou,lumɪ'nɛsəns] *n.* light produced by an electric current in a dielectric phosphor.

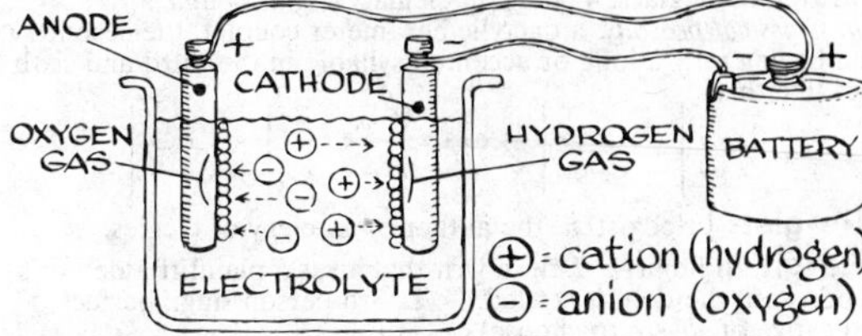

The electrolysis (def. 1) of water. The electrolyte is water with salt (or sulphuric acid, etc.) added to ionize it.

e•lec•trol•y•sis [ɪlɛk'trɒləsɪs] *or* [,ilɛk'trɒləsɪs] *n.* **1** the chemical decomposition of an electrolyte (a conducting solution or salt solution) by the passage of an electric current through it. Electrolysis is used for electroplating metals and also to produce chemicals, such as chlorine. **2** the destruction of unwanted body tissues, such as hair roots or moles, by means of an electric current. ⟨< *electro-* + Gk. *lysis* a loosing < *lyein* loose⟩

e•lec•tro•lyte [ɪ'lɛktrə,ləit] *n.* **1** a solution or molten substance that conducts an electric current, becoming decomposed in the process. In an electrolyte the current is carried by ions moving in the electric field between electrodes, not by free electrons as in metals. See DRY CELL and ELECTROLYSIS for pictures. **2** a compound which, in solution or in the molten state, will conduct an electric current. **3** an active substance in the brain, such as potassium or sodium. ⟨< *electro-* + Gk. *lytos* loosed < *lyein* loose⟩

e•lec•tro•lyt•ic [ɪ,lɛktrə'lɪtɪk] *adj.* of or having to do with electrolysis or with an electrolyte. **—e,lec•tro'lyt•i•cal•ly,** *adv.*

electrolytic cell any device which uses electrolysis to produce chemical changes or an electric current.

e•lec•tro•lyze [ɪ'lɛktrə,laɪz] *v.* **-lyzed, -lyz•ing.** decompose by electrolysis. **—e,lec•tro•ly'za•tion,** *n.* **—e'lec•tro,lyz•er,** *n.*

e•lec•tro•mag•net [ɪ'lɛktrou,mægnɪt] *n.* a strong temporary magnet made by coiling wire around an iron core and passing an electric current through the wire. The current causes the iron to become magnetized.

e•lec•tro•mag•net•ic [ɪ,lɛktroumæg'nɛtɪk] *adj.* of, having to do with, or caused by electromagnetism.
—e,lec•tro•mag'net•i•cal•ly, *adv.*

electromagnetic force a force arising from an electric charge in motion.

electromagnetic pulse a surge of electromagnetic energy resulting from a nuclear explosion and often causing great damage to electronic equipment.

electromagnetic radiation radiation consisting of electromagnetic waves. *Abbrev.*: EMR

electromagnetic spectrum the whole range of wavelengths (or frequencies) of electromagnetic waves, from the longest radio waves (wavelength 10^5 metres) to the shortest cosmic rays (wavelength 10^{-17} metre).

electromagnetic unit any of a system of units for measuring electricity or magnetism. *Abbrev.*: EMU, e.m.u., emu, or E.M.U.

electromagnetic wave a wave of energy resulting from periodic variations in the intensity of electric and magnetic fields vibrating at right angles to each other. Electromagnetic waves can travel through space or matter and include radio waves, infrared radiation, light waves, X-rays, gamma rays, and cosmic rays.

e•lec•tro•mag•net•ism [ɪ,lɛktrou'mægnə,tɪzəm] *n.* **1** the magnetism produced by a current of electricity. **2** the branch of physics that deals with this.

e•lec•tro•me•chan•i•cal [ɪ,lɛktroumə'kænəkəl] *adj.* of, having to do with, or being a mechanical device or process that is electrically activated or controlled.

e•lec•tro•met•al•lur•gy [ɪ,lɛktrou'mɛtə,lɜrdʒi] *or* [ɪ,lɛktroumə'tælərdʒi] *n.* the branch of metallurgy dealing with the use of electricity to process metals.

e•lec•trom•e•ter [ɪlɛk'trɒmətər] *or* [,ilɛk'trɒmətər] *n.* an instrument for measuring differences in electrical charge or potential.

e•lec•tro•mo•tive [ɪ,lɛktrə'moutɪv] *adj.* **1** producing a flow of electricity. **2** of or having to do with ELECTROMOTIVE FORCE.

electromotive force the amount of energy derived from an electric source in one second when one unit of current is passing through the source, commonly measured in volts. Electromotive force is produced by differences in electric charge or potential. *Abbrev.*: EMF, e.m.f., or emf

electromotive series *Chemistry.* an ordering of the metallic elements so that each is positive with reference to those that follow it and negative with reference to those that precede it.

e•lec•tro•mo•tor [ɪ'lɛktrə,moutər] *n.* **1** a machine producing electric current. **2** a motor run by electricity.

e•lec•tro•my•o•graph [ɪ,lɛktrou'maɪə,græf] *n.* an instrument used to diagnose muscle and nerve disease. An electromyograph measures voltage levels in the muscles and records them by means of graphic tracings. ⟨< Gk. *elektron* electric + *mys, myos* muscle + *graphe* writing⟩

e•lec•tron [ɪ'lɛktrɒn] *n.* an elementary particle present in all atoms, consisting of a negative electric charge of about 1.602×10^{-19} coulombs. It has a mass of about 9.11×10^{-31} kilograms when at rest. ⟨< Gk. *ēlektron.* See ELECTRIC.⟩

electron beam a stream of electrons moving in the same direction at the same speed. The electron beam inside the picture tube of a television set produces the picture on the screen.

electron cloud the electrons around an atomic nucleus, regarded as a cloud.

e•lec•tro•neg•a•tive [ɪ,lɛktrou'nɛgətɪv] *adj.* **1** charged with negative electricity. **2** tending to pass to the positive pole in electrolysis. **3** non-metallic; acid. **—e,lec•tro,neg•a'tiv•i•ty,** *n.*

electron gun a device that guides the flow and greatly increases the speed of atomic particles. Electron guns are used in oil refining and in various other industries.

e•lec•tron•ic [ɪlɛk'trɒnɪk] *or* [,ilɛk'trɒnɪk] *adj.* **1** of or having to do with an electron, electrons, or electronics. **2** of or having to do with computers; computerized. **—e,lec'tron•i•cal•ly,** *adv.*

electronic banking banking activities, such as deposits and withdrawals, performed at a machine.

electronic brain COMPUTER (def. 1). Also, **electric brain.**

electronic mail messages sent from one terminal to another or others by users of a computer network system; e-mail. Electronic mail does not require the use of a modem or fax.

electronic music music created, usually on magnetic tape, from sound made by electronic generators and filters.

electronic organ a type of electric organ that does not use pipes, but includes various electronic devices such as synthesizers and amplifiers.

e•lec•tron•ics [ɪlɛk'trɒnɪks] *or* [,ilɛk'trɒnɪks] *n.* the branch of physics that deals with the production, activity, and effects of electrons in motion (*used with a singular verb*). Radar, radio, television, etc. are based on the principles of electronics.

electron lens in an electron microscope, the conductors that set up fields to convert electrons to light rays.

electron microscope a microscope that uses beams of electrons instead of beams of light, and has much higher power than any ordinary microscope. Its enlarged images are not observable directly by the eye, but are projected upon a fluorescent surface or photographic plate. Compare OPTICAL MICROSCOPE.

electron multiplier a vacuum tube which produces a large number of secondary electrons by bringing an electron into contact with an anode.

electron optics the control of electrons in motion by means of electron lenses.

electron telescope a telescope that converts an infrared image to a visible picture.

electron tube a device for producing a controlled flow of electrons, consisting of a sealed glass or metal tube, etc., either having a vacuum inside or containing a gas at low pressure through which the electrons can move readily to carry current between the electrodes inside the tube. Microwave tubes and cathode-ray tubes are two kinds of electron tube.

e•lec•tron•volt [ɪ'lɛktrɒn,voult] *n.* a unit used with the SI for measuring the kinetic energy of electrons. One electronvolt is equal to the energy acquired by an electron when it is accelerated through a potential difference of one volt (equivalent to 1.602×10^{-19} joules). *Symbol*: eV

e•lec•tro•phil•ic [ɪ,lɛktrou'fɪlɪk] *adj.* able to accept additional electrons as in an electron multiplier.

e•lec•tro•pho•re•sis [ɪ,lɛktroufə'risɪs] *n.* **1** the movement of charged particles produced by electrodes immersed in a liquid. **2** a laboratory technique used to separate substances by differences in their rate of mobility in an electric field. ⟨< *electro-* + (*cata*)*phoresis* < *cata-* down + Gk. *phoresis* bearing < *pherein* bear⟩

e•lec•troph•o•rus [ɪlɛk'trɒfərəs] *or* [,ilɛk'trɒfərəs] *n., pl.* **-ri** [-,raɪ] *or* [-,ri]. a simple device for producing charges of electricity by means of induction. ⟨< NL *electrophorus* < *electro-* + Gk. *-phoros* bearing⟩

e•lec•tro•phys•i•ol•o•gy [ɪ,lɛktrou,fɪzi'ɒlədʒi] *n.* **1** the study of the electrical characteristics of live cells. **2** the study of the production of electricity by animal and plant organisms.

e•lec•tro•plate [ɪ'lɛktrə,pleit] *v.* **-plat•ed, -plat•ing;** *n.* *—v.* cover with a coating of metal by means of electrolysis. *—n.* **1** silverware, etc., covered in this way. **2** *Printing.* a plate made by this process. **—e'lec•tro,plat•er,** *n.*

e•lec•tro•pos•i•tive [ɪ,lɛktrou'pɒzətɪv] *adj., n.* *—adj.* **1** charged with positive electricity. **2** tending to pass to the negative pole (cathode) in electrolysis. **3** metallic; basic. *—n.* an electropositive substance.

e•lec•tro•scope [ɪ'lɛktrə,skoup] *n.* any of various devices or instruments for detecting the presence of a minute electric charge on a body and showing whether the charge is positive or negative. **—e,lec•tro'scop•ic** [-'skɒpɪk], *adj.*

e•lec•tro•stat•ic [ɪ,lɛktrou'stætɪk] *adj.* **1** having to do with electricity at rest or with stationary electric charges. **2** concerning electrostatics. **—e,lec•tro'stat•i•cal•ly,** *adv.*

electrostatic generator any of several devices that generate high voltages by storing electric charges.

e•lec•tro•stat•ics [ɪ,lɛktrou'stætɪks] *n.* the branch of physics that deals with objects charged with electricity.

electrostatic unit any of a system of units for measuring electricity or magnetism. *Abbrev.*: esu

e•lec•tro•sur•ge•ry [ɪ,lɛktrou'sɜrdʒəri] *n.* in surgery, the use of an electrical device such as a laser.

e•lec•tro•ther•a•py [ɪ,lɛktrou'θɛrəpi] *n.* the treatment of disease by electricity. **—e,lec•tro'ther•a•pist,** *n.*

e•lec•tro•ther•mal [ɪ,lɛktrou'θɜrməl] *adj.* having to do with the production of heat by electricity.

e•lec•trot•o•nus [ɪlɛk'trɒtənəs] *or* [,ilɛk'trɒtənəs] *n.* the altered state of the sensitivity of a nerve caused by passage of an electric current. ⟨< *electro-* + L *tonus* tone⟩

e•lec•tro•type [ɪ'lɛktrə,taip] *n., v.* **-typed, -typ•ing.** *—n.* **1** *Printing.* a metal or composition plate made by electroplating material onto it. **2** a print made from such a plate. *—v.* make such a plate or plates of. **—e'lec•tro,typ•er,** *n.* **—e,lec•tro'typ•ic** [-'tɪpɪk], *adj.*

e•lec•tro•va•lence [ɪ,lɛktrou'veiləns] *n.* the number of electrons gained or lost by an atom when it becomes an ion in a compound. **—e,lec•tro'va•lent,** *adj.*

electrovalent bond a bond created by the transfer of electrons from one atom to another; ionic bond.

e•lec•tro•weak [ɪ'lɛktrou,wik] *n.* a force combining electromagnetic force and the WEAK FORCE.

e•lec•trum [ɪ'lɛktrəm] *n.* a pale yellow alloy of gold and silver, used in former times. ⟨< L < Gk. *ēlektron*⟩

e•lec•tu•ar•y [ɪ'lɛktʃu,ɛri] *n., pl.* **-ar•ies.** a medicinal paste of powdered drugs and syrup or honey. ⟨ME < LL *electuarium* < Gk. *ekleikton* < *ekleichein* lick out < *ex-* out + *leichein* lick⟩

el•ee•mos•y•nar•y [,ɛlə'mɒsə,nɛri] *or* [,ɛli'mɒsə,nɛri], [,ɛlə'mɒzə,nɛri] *or* [,ɛli'mɒzə,nɛri] *adj.* **1** of or for charity; charitable. **2** provided by charity; free. **3** dependent on charity; supported by charity. ⟨< LL *eleemosynarius* < L *eleemosyna* < Gk. *eleēmosynē* compassion < *eleos* mercy⟩

el•e•gance ['ɛləgəns] *n.* **1** refined grace and richness; luxury free from coarseness. **2** something elegant. Also, **elegancy.**

el•e•gant ['ɛləgənt] *adj.* **1** having or showing good taste; gracefully and richly refined: *The palace had elegant furnishings.* **2** expressed with taste; correct and polished in expression or arrangement: *an elegant speech.* **3** *Informal.* fine; excellent; superior. **4** exact and simple as a solution. ⟨< F < L *elegans, -antis*⟩ **—'el•e•gant•ly,** *adv.*

☛ *Syn.* **1.** See note at FINE[1].

el•e•gi•ac [,ɛlə'dʒaɪək], [,ɛlə'dʒiək], *or* [ɪ'lidʒɪ,æk] *adj., n.* *—adj.* **1** of or suitable for an elegy. **2** sad; mournful; melancholy. **3** written in elegiacs. **4** being an elegiac: *elegiac couplet.* *—n.* *Classical prosody.* a dactylic hexameter couplet, the second line having only a long or accented syllable in the third and sixth feet like this:

— ◡ ◡ | — ◡ ◡ | — ◡ ◡ | — ◡ ◡ | — ◡ ◡ | — ◡
— ◡ ◡ | — ◡ ◡ | — | — ◡ ◡ | — ◡ ◡ | —

el•e•gist ['ɛlədʒɪst] *n.* the author of an elegy or elegies.

e•le•git [ɪ'lidʒɪt] *n. Law.* a writ that gives a plaintiff a debtor's goods until the debt is settled. ⟨< L, 3rd person sing., perfect indicative of *eligere* to choose⟩

el•e•gize ['ɛlə,dʒaɪz] *v.* **-gized, -giz•ing. 1** write an elegy about. **2** write an elegy; lament.

el•e•gy ['ɛlədʒi] *n., pl.* **-gies. 1** a mournful or melancholy poem; poem that is a lament for the dead. Milton's *Lycidas* and Shelley's *Adonais* are elegies. **2** a poem written in elegiac verse. ⟨< F *élégie* < L < Gk. *elegeia,* ult. < *elegos* mournful poem⟩

elem. 1 element(s); elementary.

el•e•ment ['ɛləmənt] *n.* **1** one of the simple substances, such as gold, iron, carbon, sulphur, oxygen, and hydrogen, that have not yet been separated into simpler parts by chemical means; a substance composed of atoms that are chemically alike. See Periodic Table in the Appendix. **2** one of the parts of which anything is made up: *Honesty, industry, and kindness are elements of good living.* **3** one of the four substances—earth, water, air, and fire—that were once thought to make up all other things. **4** the place, condition, activities, etc. best suited to or preferred by a person or thing: *She was in her element tinkering with old clocks.* **5** a unit, such as a military formation, that is part of a larger group. **6 the elements,** *pl.* **a** the simple, necessary parts to be learned first; first principles. **b** the atmospheric forces: *The storm seemed a war of the elements.* **c** bread and wine used in the Eucharist. **7** any member of a set. **8** in an electric oven, stove burner, heater, etc., the metal coil which reddens with heat. **9** *Mathematics.* any of the parts of a configuration, as a side or an angle of a triangle. **10** any fundamental assumption. **11** *Mathematics.* the expression that follows the integral sign(s) in a definite integral. **12** a small metal ball in certain electric typewriters, with raised characters that print as the appropriate keys are pressed. **13** *Computer technology.* any piece of data in an array. ⟨< L *elementum* rudiment, first principle⟩

☛ *Syn.* **2. Element,** COMPONENT, CONSTITUENT = one of the parts of which something is made up. **Element** is the general word, applying to a part of any thing, but sometimes suggests an essential or basic part: *Kindness is an element of courtesy.* **Component** = a part of something that is put together as a compound or mixture: *Nutmeg is a component of this sauce.* **Constituent,** often used interchangeably with *component*, differs in that it suggests an intrinsic, definitive, or necessary part instead of just any part: *Syrup is one of the constituents of a sundae; ice cream the other.*

el•e•men•tal [,ɛlə'mɛntəl] *adj.* **1** of the four elements – earth, water, air, and fire. **2** of the forces of nature: *Many indigenous peoples worship elemental gods, such as the sun, earth, thunder, etc.* **3** as found in nature; simple but powerful: *Survival is an elemental instinct.* **4** being a necessary or essential part. **5** ELEMENTARY (def. 2); **—,el•e'men•tal•ly,** *adv.*

el•e•men•ta•ry [,ɛlə'mɛntəri] *adj.* **1** of or dealing with the simple, necessary parts to be learned first; having to do with first principles; introductory; basic. **2** *Chemistry.* **a** made up of only one chemical element; not a compound: *Silver is an elementary substance.* **b** having to do with a chemical element or elements. **3** ELEMENTAL (defs. 3, 4). **4** of or having to do with elementary schools. **—,el•e'men•tar•i•ly,** *adv.*

☛ *Syn.* **1. Elementary,** RUDIMENTARY, PRIMARY = having to do with the beginnings of something. **Elementary** emphasizes the idea of basic things and means having to do with the first steps or beginning facts and principles of anything: *John learned simple addition and subtraction when he began elementary arithmetic.* **Rudimentary** is a formal word emphasizing the idea of an undeveloped beginning and used particularly to mean 'consisting of the first parts and principles of knowledge or of a subject studied': *She has only a rudimentary knowledge of mathematics.* **Primary** emphasizes coming first in order or time: *Children attend primary school before high school.*

elementary particle *Physics.* one of the basic components of matter, sharing the properties of an energy wave and a particle. Electrons, positrons, and photons are some elementary particles.

elementary school a school of six, seven, or eight grades for children aged six and over, which is followed by high school or junior high school. Some elementary schools also include kindergarten. Elementary schools vary from province to province. **—,el•e'men•ta•ry ,school,** *adj.*

el•e•men•toid [,ɛlə'mɛntɔɪd] *adj.* having the appearance of an element: *an elementoid compound.*

el•e•mi ['ɛləmi] *n.* any of various resins used in making varnishes. ⟨< F *élémi* < Sp *elemi* < Arabic *al-lami*⟩

e•len•chus [ɪ'lɛŋkəs] *n. Logic.* the refutation of a person's conclusion. ⟨L < Gk. *elenchos* refutation < *elenchien* refute, shame⟩ **—e'lenc•tic,** *adj.*

el•e•op•tene [,ɛli'ɒptin] *n. Chemistry.* the liquid part of a volatile oil, distinct from the solid part. ⟨< Gk. *elaion* olive oil + *ptenos* having wings⟩

el•e•phant ['ɛləfənt] *n., pl.* **-phants** or *(esp. collectively)* **-phant.** either of two huge mammals (family Elephantidae) of Africa and Asia having thick, tough, almost hairless, grey skin, a thickset body, thick legs, and a flexible, muscular proboscis called a trunk, that is a prolongation of the nose and upper lip and is used for conveying food and water to the mouth. These animals, the **African elephant** (*Loxodonta africana*) and the **Indian elephant** (*Elephas maximus*), are the only living representatives of the order Proboscidea. ⟨ME < OF *olifant* < L < Gk. *elephas, -antis* elephant, ivory, probably < Egyptian⟩

An Indian elephant

el•e•phan•ti•a•sis [,ɛləfən'taɪəsɪs] *n.* a disease in which parts of the body, usually the legs, become greatly enlarged and the skin thickened and broken. It is caused by parasitic worms that block the flow of lymph. ⟨< L < Gk. *elephantiasis* < *elephas, -antis* elephant⟩

el•e•phan•tine [,ɛlə'fæntaɪn], [,ɛlə'fæntɪn], *or* ['ɛləfən,taɪn] *adj.* **1** like an elephant; huge; heavy; clumsy; slow. **2** of elephants.

elephant seal either of two enormous hair seals, the **northern elephant seal** (*Mirounga angustirostris*) and the **southern elephant seal** (*M. leonina*), having a thick, heavy body and a large head with a long, broad snout, the adult male also having a long proboscis which, when inflated, curves downward into the mouth. Elephant seals are the largest pinnipeds.

el•e•phant's–ear ['ɛləfənts ,ir] *n.* **1** any of a genus (*Colocasia*) of tropical Old World plants of the arum family, having very large, heart-shaped leaves, especially *C. esculenta*, cultivated in several varieties as an ornamental plant and also (especially in the Far East and the South Pacific) for its starchy rootstocks. See also TARO. **2** any of several domestic begonias with large, ornamental leaves.

elephant's head a type of lousewort (*Pedicularis groenlandica*) found blooming in summer in high or Arctic regions, having many small pink flowers on a stem about half a metre long.

El•eu•sin•i•an mysteries [,ɛlju'sɪniən] in ancient Greece, the secret, religious ceremonies held yearly at the city of Eleusis, near Athens, in honour of the goddesses Demeter and Persephone.

elev. elevation.

el•e•vate ['ɛlə,veit] *v.* **-vat•ed, -vat•ing. 1** lift up; raise. **2** raise in rank or station: *The soldier was elevated to knighthood for bravery.* **3** raise in quality: *Good books elevate the mind.* **4** put in high spirits; make joyful or proud; elate. ⟨< L *elevare* < *ex-* out + *levare* lighten, raise⟩

☛ *Syn.* See note at RAISE.

el•e•vat•ed ['ɛlə,veitɪd] *adj., n., v.* —*adj.* **1** lifted up; raised; high. **2** dignified; lofty; noble. **3** in high spirits; joyful; proud.
—*n. Informal.* ELEVATED RAILWAY.
—*v.* pt. and pp. of ELEVATE.

elevated railway a railway raised above the ground on a supporting frame high enough for streetcars, automobiles, etc. to pass underneath.

el•e•va•tion [,ɛlə'veiʃən] *n.* **1** a raised place; high place: *A hill is an elevation.* **2** height above the earth's surface: *The airplane fell from an elevation of 1000 m.* **3** height above sea level: *The elevation of Calgary is 1045 m.* **4** dignity; loftiness; nobility. **5** the act of elevating: *the elevation of Caesar to be the ruler of Rome.* **6** the state of being elevated. **7** a flat drawing of the front, rear, or side of a building. **8** *Astronomy.* the altitude of any heavenly body above the horizon. **9** *Surveying.* the angular distance of an object above the horizontal plane through the point of observation. **10** *Ballet.* **a** the technique that allows a ballet dancer to leap high enough to remain in midair for a while. **b** the height to which he or she so leaps. **11** the angle made by a large gun with the horizontal to ensure accurate aim.

el•e•va•tor ['ɛlə,veitər] *n.* **1** anything that raises or lifts. **2** a moving platform or cage to carry people and freight up and down in a building, mine, etc. **3** a building for storing grain. **4** a horizontal, flat, hinged piece on an aircraft, usually on the tail, that is lowered or raised to make the aircraft climb or descend. ⟨< LL⟩

elevator shaft a vertical passageway for an ELEVATOR (def. 2).

e•lev•en [ɪ'lɛvɪn] *n., adj.* —*n.* **1** one more than ten; 11. **2** the numeral 11: *That looks like an 11.* **3** the eleventh in a set or series. **4** *Cricket, soccer, etc.* a team of eleven players: *This year our school has the best eleven ever.* **5** any set or series of eleven persons or things.
—*adj.* **1** being one more than ten. **2** being eleventh in a set or series (*used after the noun*): *Chapter Eleven.* ⟨OE *endleofan* one left (over ten)⟩

e•lev•en•ses [ɪ'lɛvənzɪz] *n. Brit. Informal.* a snack with a beverage, served in the morning around 11 o'clock.

e•lev•enth [ɪ'lɛvənθ] *adj., adv., or n.* **1** next after the 10th; last in a series of 11. **2** one, or being one, of 11 equal parts.

eleventh hour the latest possible moment; time just before it is too late.

e•lev•on ['ɛlə,vɒn] *n.* on an aircraft, a control that is both aileron and elevator. ⟨< *elev(ator)* + *(ailer)on*⟩

elf [ɛlf] *n., pl.* **elves. 1** a tiny, mischievous fairy. **2** a small, mischievous person. ⟨OE *ælf*⟩ **—'elf,like,** *adj.*

elf•in ['ɛlfən] *adj., n. —adj.* **1** of or suitable for elves; like an elf's in mischievousness, delicacy, etc.: *elfin grace. The child's elfin smile was very charming.* **2** having to do with fairies. **3** tiny. *—n.* elf.

elf•ish ['ɛlfɪʃ] *adj.* elflike; elfin; mischievous. **—'elf•ish•ly,** *adv.* **—'elf•ish•ness,** *n.*

elf•lock ['ɛlf,lɒk] *n.* a tangled lock of hair, supposedly caused by elves.

el•hi ['ɛlhaɪ] *adj.* for use in grades 1 through 12: *elhi reading material.* ⟨< *el(ementary)* + *hi(gh)* school⟩

e•lic•it [ɪ'lɪsɪt] *v.* draw forth: *to elicit a reply, to elicit applause, to elicit the truth.* ⟨< L *elicitus,* pp. of *elicere* < *ex-* out + *lacere* entice⟩ **—e'lic•it•or,** *n.*
☛ *Hom.* ILLICIT.

e•lic•i•ta•tion [ɪ,lɪsə'teiʃən] *n.* **1** a drawing forth or being drawn forth. **2** the thing elicited.

e•lide [ɪ'laɪd] *v.* **e•lid•ed, e•lid•ing. 1** omit or slur over (a syllable or vowel) in pronunciation. The *e* in *the* is elided in *th' Immortal dies.* **2** omit or cancel (a written word, passage, etc.). **3** ignore or suppress. **—e'lid•i•ble,** *adj.* ⟨< L *elidere* < *ex-* out + *laedere* dash⟩

el•i•gi•bil•i•ty [,ɛlədʒə'bɪləti] *n., pl.* **-ties.** fitness; a being qualified; desirability.

el•i•gi•ble ['ɛlədʒəbəl] *adj., n. —adj.* **1** fit or proper to be chosen; desirable: *an eligible bachelor.* **2** properly qualified; meeting all requirements set by law or rule: *Players had to pass in all subjects to be eligible for the school team.* **3** *Football.* allowed to receive a forward pass.
—n. an eligible person. ⟨< F < LL < L *eligere* pick out, choose. See ELECT.⟩ **—'el•i•gi•ble•ness,** *n.* **—'el•i•gi•bly,** *adv.*

e•lim•i•nate [ɪ'lɪmə,neit] *v.* **-nat•ed, -nat•ing. 1** get rid of; remove: *The new bridge over the railway tracks eliminated the danger in crossing.* **2** pay no attention to; leave out of consideration; omit: *The architect eliminated furniture, rugs, etc. in figuring the cost of the house.* **3** *Mathematics.* get rid of (an unknown quantity) by combining algebraic equations. **4** put out of a championship competition by reason of defeat: *The Toronto team was eliminated in the first round of the hockey playoffs.* **5** expel (waste) from the body; excrete. ⟨< L *eliminare* < *ex-* out + *limen* threshold⟩ **—e'lim•i,na•tor,** *n.* **—e'lim•i•na,to•ry** or **e'lim•i•na•tive,** *adj.*
☛ *Syn.* See note at EXCLUDE.

e•lim•i•na•tion [ɪ,lɪmə'neiʃən] *n.* an eliminating or being eliminated.
elimination round, that part of a competition which eliminates a competitor from the championship round.

E•lis ['ilɪs] *n.* an ancient division of W Greece. Olympic games were held on the plains of Olympia in Elis.

e•li•sion [ɪ'lɪʒən] *n.* **1** the slurring or suppression of a vowel or a syllable in pronouncing. Elision is often used in poetry for euphony or rhythm, and generally consists in cutting off a vowel at the end of one word when the next begins with a vowel. **2** omission or cancellation. ⟨< L *elisio, -onis* < *elidere.* See ELIDE.⟩

e•lite or **é•lite** [ɪ'lit] *or* [ei'lit] *n., adj. —n.* **1** the part of a community or group regarded as being the most distinguished, gifted, intelligent, rich, etc. (*sometimes used as a plural*). **2** a size of typewriter type having 12 characters to 1 inch.
—adj. **1** of or having to do with an elite. **2** choice; superior; distinguished. **3** of or having to do with elite type. ⟨< F OF *eslite,* fem. pp. of *eslire* pick out < L *eligere.* See ELECT.⟩

e•lit•ism or **é•lit•ism** [ɪ'litɪzəm] *or* [ei'litɪzəm] *n.* **1** control or leadership by an elite. **2** belief in or support of such control or leadership. **3** awareness of belonging to an elite.

e•lit•ist or **é•lit•ist** [ɪ'litɪst] *or* [ei'litɪst] *adj., n. —adj.* of, having to do with, or characterized by elitism.
—n. a person who believes in elitism or considers himself or herself a member of an elite.

e•lix•ir [ɪ'lɪksər] *n.* **1** a substance supposed to have the power of changing lead, iron, etc. into gold or of lengthening life indefinitely, sought by the alchemists of the Middle Ages. **2** a universal remedy; cure-all. **3** a medicine made of drugs or herbs mixed with alcohol and syrup. **4** the quintessence of a thing; chief principle. ⟨ME < Med.L < Arabic *al-iksīr* (def. 1), probably < Gk. *xērion* drying powder used on wounds < *xēros* dry⟩

Eliz. Elizabethan.

E•liz•a•be•than [ɪ,lɪzə'biθən] *adj., n. —adj.* of or having to do with the time of Queen Elizabeth I (1533-1603).
—n. a person, especially a writer, of the time of Queen Elizabeth I.

Elizabethan sonnet a type of sonnet used by Shakespeare and many other Elizabethans. It has a rhyme scheme *abab cdcd efef gg.*

elk [ɛlk] *n., pl.* **elks** or *(esp. collectively)* **elk. 1** a large North American mammal (*Cervus canadensis*), the second largest member of the deer family, having a light or dark brown coat with a light coloured rump patch, long, shaggy, dark brown hair covering the neck and shoulders, and, in the adult male, large antlers, usually with five tines; wapiti. Some authorities consider the elk to be of the same species as the European red deer. **2** a large deer (*Alces alces*) of Europe and Asia, considered by many authorities to be of the same species as the North American moose. The elk closely resembles the moose, but is considerably smaller. **3** any of several other large deer of Asia. **4** a soft leather made from elk hide, or from calfskin or cowhide in imitation of this. ⟨apparently < AF form of OE *eolh*⟩

elk•hound ['ɛlk,haʊnd] *n.* NORWEGIAN ELKHOUND.

ell¹ [ɛl] *n.* an old measure of length, chiefly used in measuring cloth. In England it was equal to about 115 cm. ⟨OE *eln* length of lower arm⟩

ell² [ɛl] *n.* **1** an extension of a building at one end and usually at right angles to it, forming a letter L. **2** a pipe or tube with a right-angled bend. Also, **el.**

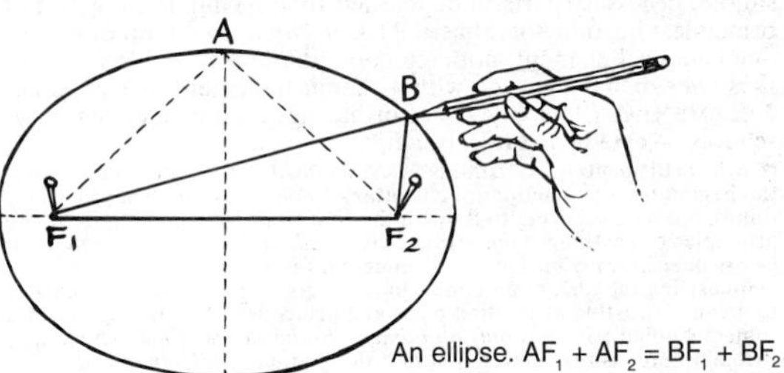

An ellipse. $AF_1 + AF_2 = BF_1 + BF_2$.

el•lipse [ɪ'lɪps] *n. Geometry.* an oval having both ends alike. It is the path of a point that moves so that the sum of its distances from two fixed points remains the same. Any conic section formed by a cutting plane inclined to the base but not passing through the base is an ellipse. See CONE for picture. ⟨< L *ellipsis.* See ELLIPSIS.⟩

el•lip•ses [ɪ'lɪpsɪz] *for 1;* [ɪ'lɪpsiz] *for 2. n.* **1** pl. of ELLIPSE. **2** pl. of ELLIPSIS.

el•lip•sis [ɪ'lɪpsɪs] *n., pl.* **-ses** [-siz]. **1** *Grammar.* the omission of a word or words that could complete the construction of a sentence. *Example: In* She is as tall as her brother, *there is a permissible ellipsis of* is tall *after* brother. **2** in writing or printing, marks (. . .or * * *) used to show an omission. ⟨< L < Gk. *elleipsis* < *elleipein* come short, leave out⟩

el•lip•soid [ɪ'lɪpsɔɪd] *n., adj. —n. Mathematics.* **1** a solid of which all plane sections are ellipses or circles. **2** its surface. *—adj.* of or in the form of an ellipsoid. Also, **ellipsoidal.**

el•lip•tic [ɪ'lɪptɪk] *adj.* elliptical.

el•lip•ti•cal [ɪ'lɪptəkəl] *adj.* **1** having to do with or shaped like an ellipse. **2** having to do with or marked by ellipsis. **3** of speech or writing, extremely concise or economical of words, often to the point of obscurity. **—el'lip•ti•cal•ly,** *adv.*

el•lip•ti•ci•ty [,ɛlɪp'tɪsɪti] *n.* **1** deviation from the form of a sphere to an ellipsoidal form. **2** the amount of such deviation.

elm [ɛlm] *n.* **1** any of a genus (*Ulmus*) of tall trees native mainly to north temperate regions, valued as shade and timber trees. **2** the hard wood of an elm. **3** (*adjl.*) designating the family (Ulmaceae) of trees that includes the elms and hackberries. ⟨OE⟩

elm bark beetle a beetle (*Scolytus multistriatus*) whose diet consists of elm tree bark. The elm bark beetle is the carrier of Dutch elm disease.

elm leaf beetle a beetle (*Pyrrhalta luteola*) whose diet, in its larval and mature stages, consists of elm tree leaves.

El Niño [ɛl 'ninjou] a warm current sometimes occurring off the west coast of North America, having influence on the weather. ⟨< Sp. the (Christ) child⟩

el•o•cu•tion [ˌɛlə'kjuʃən] *n.* **1** the art of speaking or reading clearly and effectively in public; art of public speaking, including the correct use of the voice, gestures, etc. **2** a manner of speaking or reading in public. ⟨< L *elocutio, -onis* < *eloqui* < *ex-* out + *loqui* speak⟩

el•o•cu•tion•ar•y [ˌɛlə'kjuʃəˌnɛri] *adj.* of or having to do with elocution.

el•o•cu•tion•ist [ˌɛlə'kjuʃənɪst] *n.* **1** a person skilled in elocution. **2** a teacher of elocution.

e•lo•dea [ɪ'loudiə] *or* [ˌɛlə'diə] *n.* any of various grasslike underwater plants of the genus *Elodea.* Elodea is a favourite aquarium plant because it gives off large quantities of oxygen. ⟨< NL < Gk. *helodes* swampy < *helos* a swamp⟩

E•lo•him [ɪ'louhɪm], [ɪ'louhim], ['ɛlouˌhim], *or* ['ɛlouhɪm] *n.* a Hebrew name for God. ⟨< Hebrew *elohim,* pl.⟩

e•lon•gate [ɪ'lɒŋgeit] *or* ['ilɒŋˌgeit] *v.* **-gat•ed, -gat•ing;** *adj.* *—v.* lengthen; extend; stretch: *A rubber band can be elongated to several times its normal length.*
—adj. **1** lengthened. **2** long and thin: *the elongate leaf of a willow.* ⟨< L *elongare* < *ex-* out + *longus* long⟩

e•lon•ga•tion [ˌilɒŋ'geiʃən] *n.* **1** a lengthening; extension. **2** a lengthened part; continuation. **3** *Astronomy.* the angular distance between the sun and any planet or the moon, measured from the earth.

e•lope [ɪ'loup] *v.* **e•loped, e•lop•ing. 1** run away with a lover. **2** run away; escape. ⟨< AF *aloper,* ? < ME *lope(n)* run, probably < ON *hlaupa* leap⟩ **—e'lope•ment,** *n.* **—e'lop•er,** *n.*

el•o•quence ['ɛləkwəns] *n.* **1** a flow of speech that has grace and force: *The eloquence of the speaker moved all hearts.* **2** the power to win by speaking; the art of speaking so as to stir the feelings. **3** expressiveness: *the eloquence of tears.*

el•o•quent ['ɛləkwənt] *adj.* **1** speaking or spoken with eloquence. **2** highly expressive: *an eloquent gesture. Her frown was eloquent of her displeasure.* ⟨ME < OF < L *eloquens, -entis,* ppr. of *eloqui* < *ex-* out + *loqui* speak⟩ **—'el•o•quent•ly,** *adv.*

El Sal•va•dor [ɛl 'sælvəˌdɔr] a country in NW Central America.

else [ɛls] *adj., adv. —adj.* **1** other; different; instead: *What else could I say?* **2** in addition: *The Browns are here; do you expect anyone else?*
—adv. **1** differently: *How else can it be done?* **2** otherwise; if not: *Hurry, else you will be late.*
or else, *Informal.* or suffer for it; or pay a penalty: *You'd better return my bike, or else.* ⟨OE *elles*⟩
☛ *Usage.* The possessive ending is transferred to **else** when this word follows a pronoun: *someone else's, who else's* (not *whose else*).

else•where ['ɛlsˌwɛr] *adv.* somewhere else; in or to some other place.

else•whith•er ['ɛlsˌwɪðər] *adv. Archaic.* to some other place.

e•lu•ci•date [ɪ'lusəˌdeit] *v.* **-dat•ed, -dat•ing.** make clear; explain: *The scientist elucidated her theory by a few simple experiments.* ⟨< LL *elucidare* < L *ex-* out + *lucidus* bright⟩ **—e'lu•ciˌda•tor,** *n.* **—e'lu•ciˌda•tive,** *adj.*

e•lu•ci•da•tion [ɪˌlusə'deiʃən] *n.* a making clear; explanation.

e•lude [ɪ'lud] *v.* **e•lud•ed, e•lud•ing. 1** slip away from; avoid or escape by cleverness, quickness, etc.: *The sly fox eluded the dogs.* **2** escape discovery by; baffle: *The cause of cancer will not long elude research.* ⟨< L *eludere* < *ex-* out + *ludere* play⟩ **—e'lud•er,** *n.*
☛ *Syn.* **1.** See note at ESCAPE.

E•lul [ɛ'lul] *or* ['ɛlul] *n.* in the Hebrew calendar, the sixth month of the ecclesiastical year and the twelfth month of the civil year.

e•lu•sion [ɪ'luʒən] *n.* an eluding; clever avoidance. ⟨< Med.L *elusio, -onis* < *eludere.* See ELUDE.⟩
☛ *Hom.* ILLUSION.

e•lu•sive [ɪ'lusɪv] *adj.* **1** hard to describe or understand; baffling. **2** tending to elude: *The elusive fox got away from the hunters.* **—e'lu•sive•ly,** *adv.* **—e'lu•sive•ness,** *n.*
☛ *Hom.* ILLUSIVE.

e•lu•so•ry [ɪ'lusəri] *adj.* elusive.
☛ *Hom.* ILLUSORY.

e•lute [ɪ'lut] *v.* **e•lut•ed, e•lut•ing.** remove by dissolving. ⟨< L *elutus,* pp. of *eluere* to wash out < *e-* out + *luere* var. of *lavare* to wash⟩ **—e'lu•tion,** *n.*

e•lu•tri•ate [ɪ'lutriˌeit] *v.* **-at•ed, -at•ing.** purify by washing or decanting, as with ore in water. ⟨< L *elutriare* < *eluere.* See ELUTE.⟩ **—eˌlu•tri'a•tion,** *n.*

e•lu•vi•al [ɪ'luviəl] *adj.* having to do with eluviation.

e•lu•vi•a•tion [ɪˌluvi'eiʃən] *n.* **1** the movement of soil below the surface as a result of heavy rain. **2** erosion of rocks in which the eroded material remains in the same place.

e•lu•vi•um [ɪ'luviəm] *n., pl.* **-vi•a** [-viə]. *Geology.* a deposit of debris and dust, produced by the erosion and disintegration of rock, that has remained in its place of origin. ⟨< NL < L *ex* out + *luere* wash⟩

el•ver ['ɛlvər] *n.* a young eel, just past the larval stage. ⟨var. of *eelfare,* the passing of young eels up a stream < *eel* + *fare* journey (blend of OE *fær* and *faru*)⟩

elves [ɛlvz] *n.* pl. of ELF.

elv•ish ['ɛlvɪʃ] *adj.* elfish; elflike. **—'elv•ish•ly,** *adv.*

E•lys•i•an [ɪ'lɪziən] *or* [ɪ'lɪʒən] *adj.* **1** of or having to do with Elysium. **2** happy; delightful.

E•lys•i•um [ɪ'lɪziəm] *or* [ɪ'lɪʒəm] *n.* **1** *Greek mythology.* a place where heroes and virtuous people lived after death. **2** any place or condition of perfect happiness; paradise. Also (def. 1), **Elysian Fields.** ⟨< L < Gk. *Elysion (pedion)* Elysian (field)⟩

el•y•tron ['ɛlɪˌtrɒn] *n., pl.* **-tra.** either of the hardened front wings of beetles and some other insects, that form a protective covering for the hind pair. ⟨< NL < Gk. *elytron* sheath < *elyein* roll around⟩ **—'el•yˌtroid,** *adj.*

em[1] [ɛm] *n., pl.* **ems. 1** the letter M, m. **2** *Printing.* the square of any size of type; unit for measuring the amount of print in a line, page, etc. It was originally the portion of a line occupied by the letter *m.* **3** pica.

'em or **em**[2] [əm] *pron.pl. Informal.* them (*in connected discourse where elision occurs frequently*). ⟨probably < OE *hem* them⟩

em–[1] the form of **en-**[1] before *b, p,* and sometimes *m,* as in *embark, employ.*

em–[2] the form of **en-**[2] before *b, m, p, ph,* as in *emblem, emphasis.*

E.M. 1 Efficiency Medal. **2** Edward Medal.

e•ma•ci•ate [ɪ'meisiˌeit] *or* [ɪ'meiʃiˌeit] *v.* **-at•ed, -at•ing.** make unnaturally thin; cause to lose flesh or waste away: *A long illness had emaciated the invalid.* ⟨< L *emaciare* < *ex-* (intensive) + *macies* leanness⟩

e•ma•ci•at•ed [ɪ'meisiˌeitɪd] *or* [ɪ'meiʃiˌeitɪd] *adj., v. —adj.* thin from losing flesh: *The invalid was pale and emaciated.*
—v. pt. and pp. of EMACIATE.

e•ma•ci•a•tion [ɪˌmeisi'eiʃən] *or* [ɪˌmeiʃi'eiʃən] *n.* an unnatural thinness from loss of flesh; wasting away.

e–mail ELECTRONIC MAIL.

em•al•an•ge•ni ['ɛməlɒŋˌgeini], [ɪ'mæləŋˌgeini], *or* [ˌɛməlɒŋ'geini] *n.* pl. of LILANGENI.

em•a•nate ['ɛməˌneit] *v.* **-nat•ed, -nat•ing. 1** come forth: *Fragrance emanated from the flowers. The rumour emanated from Ottawa.* **2** give out; emit. ⟨< L *emanare* < *ex-* out + *manare* flow⟩
☛ *Syn.* See note at ISSUE.

em•a•na•tion [ˌɛmə'neiʃən] *n.* **1** a coming forth. **2** anything that comes forth from a source: *Light and heat are emanations from the sun.* **3** *Chemistry.* a gas given off by a disintegrating radioactive substance. **—'em•a•na•tive,** *adj.*

e•man•ci•pate [ɪ'mænsəˌpeit] *v.* **-pat•ed, -pat•ing. 1** release from slavery or restraint; set free. **2** in Roman law, terminate parental control over. ⟨< L *emancipare* < *ex-* away + *manceps* purchaser < *manus* hand + *capere* take⟩ **—eˌman•ci'pa•tion,** *n.* **—e'man•ciˌpa•tor,** *n.*

e•mar•gin•ate [ɪ'mɑrdʒənɪt] *or* [ɪ'mardʒəˌneit] *adj.* **1** notched at the margin. **2** *Botany.* of a leaf or flower, notched at the apex.

e•mas•cu•late *v.* [ɪ'mæskjəˌleit]; *adj.* [ɪ'mæskjəlɪt] *or* [ɪ'mæskjəˌleit] *v.* **-lat•ed, -lat•ing;** *adj. —v.* **1** remove the male glands of; castrate. **2** destroy the force of; weaken: *The editor emasculated the speech by cutting out its strongest passages.*
—adj. deprived of vigour; weakened; effeminate. ⟨< L *emasculare* < *ex-* away + *masculus* male⟩ **—eˌmas•cu'la•tion,** *n.*

—e'mas•cu,la•tor, *n.* —e'mas•cu•la•tive or e'mas•cu•la,to•ry, *adj.*

em•balm [ɛm'bɒm] *or* [ɛm'bɑm] *v.* **1** treat (a dead body) with drugs, chemicals, etc. to keep it from decaying. **2** keep in memory; preserve: *Many fine sentiments are embalmed in poetry.* **3** fill with sweet scent; perfume: *Roses embalmed the June air.* Also, **imbalm.** ⟨ME < OF *embaumer* < *en-* in + *baume* balm < L *balsamum*⟩ **—em'balm•er,** *n.* **—em'balm•ment,** *n.*

em•bank [ɛm'bæŋk] *v.* protect, enclose, or confine with a raised bank of earth, stones, etc.

em•bank•ment [ɛm'bæŋkmənt] *n.* **1** a raised bank of earth, stones, etc., used to hold back water, support a roadway, etc. **2** a protecting, enclosing, or confining with a bank of this kind.

em•bar•go [ɛm'bɑrgou] *n., pl.* **-goes;** *v.* **-goed, -go•ing.** *—n.* **1** an order of a government forbidding ships to enter or leave its ports: *During the war, an embargo was placed on certain vessels.* **2** any restriction put on commerce by law. **3** a restriction; restraint; hindrance.
—v. lay an embargo on; forbid to enter or leave port. ⟨< Sp. *embargo* < *embargar* restrain < VL *in-* in + *barra* bar⟩

em•bark [ɛm'bɑrk] *v.* **1** go on board ship: *Many people embark for Europe in Montréal.* **2** enter a plane, bus, train, etc. as a passenger. **3** put on board ship: *The general embarked his troops.* **4** engage in an enterprise. **5** involve (a person) in an enterprise; invest (money) in an enterprise: *She foolishly embarked much money in the swindler's scheme and so lost it all.*
embark on, begin or enter upon: *After leaving university, the young woman embarked on a business career.* ⟨< F *embarquer* < *en-* in + *barque* bark³⟩ **—,em•bar'ka•tion,** *n.*

em•bar•rass [ɛm'bærəs] *or* [ɛm'bɛrəs] *v.* **1** humiliate (a person); make self-conscious: *Meeting strangers embarrassed the shy boy so that he blushed and stammered.* **2** complicate; mix up; make difficult: *She embarrasses discussion of the simplest subject by use of technical terms.* **3** involve in difficulties; hinder: *Heavy equipment embarrassed the army's movements.* **4** burden with debt; involve in financial difficulties. ⟨< F *embarrasser*, literally, to block < Ital. *imbarazzare* (< VL *barra* bar), literally, put a block into⟩ **—em'bar•rass•ing•ly,** *adj.*
☛ *Syn.* **1.** See note at CONFUSE.

em•bar•rassed [ɛm'bærəst] *or* [ɛm'bɛrəst] *adj., v. —adj.* in a state of embarrassment.
—v. pt. and pp. of EMBARRASS.

em•bar•rass•ment [ɛm'bærəsmənt] *or* [ɛm'bɛrəsmənt] *n.* **1** an embarrassing or being embarrassed. **2** something that embarrasses: *The ill-mannered boy was an embarrassment to his parents.* **3** an excessive amount: *an embarrassment of riches.*

em•bas•sy ['ɛmbəsi] *n., pl.* **-sies. 1** an ambassador and his or her staff of assistants. An embassy ranks next above a legation. **2** the official residence, office, etc. of an ambassador in a foreign country. **3** the position or duties of an ambassador. **4** a person or group officially sent to a foreign government with a special errand. **5** a special errand; important mission; official message. ⟨< OF *ambassee* < Ital. < Provençal < Gmc; cf. Gothic *andbahti* service⟩

em•bat•tle¹ [ɛm'bætəl] *v.* **-tled, -tling. 1** prepare for battle; form into battle order. **2** fortify (a town, etc.). **3** involve in or beset with conflict; cause to be the scene or centre of much strife. ⟨ME < OF *embatailler* < *en-* into + *bataille* battle < L *battuere* beat⟩

em•bat•tle² [ɛm'bætəl] *v.* **-tled, -tling.** provide with battlements; fortify. ⟨< *em-¹* + obs. *battle*, v., furnish with battlements⟩

em•bay [ɛm'bei] *v.* **1** put or bring into a bay for shelter; force into a bay. **2** shut in; surround.

em•bay•ment [ɛm'beimənt] *n.* **1** a bay. **2** the physical process of the formation of a bay.

em•bed [ɛm'bɛd] *or* [ɪm'bɛd] *v.* **-bed•ded, -bed•ding. 1** plant in a bed: *She embedded the bulbs in a box of sand.* **2** fix or enclose in a surrounding mass: *Precious stones are found embedded in rock.* **3** fix firmly (in the mind): *Every detail of the accident is embedded in my memory.* **4** *Linguistics.* express in a subordinate clause of a sentence. Also, **imbed. —em'bed•ment,** *n.*

em•bel•lish [ɛm'bɛlɪʃ] *v.* **1** decorate; adorn; ornament. **2** make more interesting by adding real or imaginary details; elaborate: *She embellished the old stories so that they sounded new.* ⟨ME < OF *embelliss-*, a stem of *embellir* < *en-* in (intensive) + *bel* handsome < L *bellus*⟩

em•bel•lish•ment [ɛm'bɛlɪʃmənt] *n.* **1** the act of embellishing or state of being embellished. **2** a decoration; adornment; ornament. **3** a detail, often imaginary, added to make a story, account, etc. more interesting.

em•ber¹ ['ɛmbər] *n.* **1** a piece of wood or coal still glowing in the ashes of a fire. **2 embers,** *pl.* ashes in which there is still some fire. ⟨OE *ǣmerge*⟩

em•ber² ['ɛmbər] *adj. Roman Catholic and Anglican Churches.* having to do with the EMBER DAYS. ⟨OE *ymbren, ymbryne* course, literally, running around < *ymb* around + *ryne* a running⟩

Ember days *Roman Catholic and Anglican Churches.* one of four series of three days each, set apart for fasting and prayer. The Ember days are the Wednesday, Friday, and Saturday following the first Sunday in Lent, following Whitsunday, and including or following September 14 and December 13.

em•bez•zle [ɛm'bɛzəl] *v.* **-zled, -zling.** steal by putting to one's own use (money held in trust for some other person or group of persons): *The treasurer embezzled $2000 from the club's funds.* ⟨< AF *enbesiler* < OF *besillier* maltreat, of uncertain origin⟩ **—em'bez•zle•ment,** *n.* **—em'bez•zler,** *n.*

em•bit•ter [ɛm'bɪtər] *v.* make bitter; make more bitter: *The old man was embittered by the loss of his money.*
—em'bit•ter•ment, *n.*

em•bla•zon [ɛm'bleizən] *v.* **1** display conspicuously; picture in bright colours. **2** decorate; adorn: *The knight's shield was emblazoned with his coat of arms.* **3** praise highly; honour publicly; make known the fame of: *King Arthur's exploits were emblazoned in song and story.* ⟨< *en¹-* + blazon⟩
—em'bla•zon•er, *n.* **—em'bla•zon•ment,** *n.*

em•bla•zon•ry [ɛm'bleizənri] *n., pl.* **-ries. 1** a brilliant decoration; adornment; conspicuous display. **2** a display of coats of arms, etc.; heraldic decoration.

em•blem ['ɛmbləm] *n.* **1** an object or representation that stands for an invisible quality, idea, etc. by some connection of thought; sign of an idea; symbol: *The dove is an emblem of peace.* **2** a heraldic device. **3** a picture suggesting a moral, often with an accompanying explanation, proverb, etc. ⟨< L *emblema* inlaid work < Gk. *emblēma* insertion < *en-* in + *ballein* throw⟩
☛ *Syn.* **1. Emblem,** SYMBOL = an object or sign that represents something else. The two words are interchangeable in current usage; but **symbol** strictly means something naturally associated in the mind with the thing symbolized: *The crown is the symbol of kingship.* **Emblem** is usually something that is chosen arbitrarily to represent the nature of the object in mind: *The beaver and the maple leaf are both emblems of Canada.*

em•blem•at•ic [,ɛmblə'mætɪk] *adj.* used as an emblem; symbolic: *The Cross is emblematic of Christianity.* Also, **emblematical. —,em•blem'at•i•cal•ly,** *adv.*

em•blem•a•tize [ɛm'blɛmə,taɪz] *v.* **-ized, -iz•ing. 1** be an emblem of. **2** represent by or as by an emblem.

em•ble•ments ['ɛmbləmənts] *n. Law.* the product or profit from land that has been planted. ⟨ME *emblaymentez* < OF *emblaement* < *emblaer* < *en* + *blee* grain⟩

em•bod•i•ment [ɛm'bɒdimənt] *n.* **1** an embodying or being embodied. **2** that in which something is embodied; person or thing symbolizing some idea, quality, etc. **3** something embodied.

em•bod•y [ɛm'bɒdi] *v.* **-bod•ied, -bod•y•ing. 1** put into visible form; express in definite form: *The building embodied the idea of the architect.* **2** bring together and include in a single book, law, system, etc.; organize: *The Constitution Act, 1967, embodies the conditions of Confederation.* **3** make part of an organized book, law, system, etc.; incorporate: *The new engineer's suggestions were embodied in the revised plan of the bridge.*

em•bold•en [ɛm'bouldən] *v.* make bold; encourage.
—em'bold•en•er, *n.*

em•bol•ec•to•my [,ɛmbə'lɛktəmi] *n.* the surgical removal of an embolus from an artery that it is obstructing.

em•bol•ic [ɛm'bɒlɪk] *adj.* **1** of or caused by an embolus or embolism. **2** *Biology.* pushing or growing inward. **3** *Pathology.* of or during emboly.

em•bo•lism ['ɛmbə,lɪzəm] *n.* **1** the obstruction of a blood vessel by an embolus. **2** embolus. **3** the insertion of an extra day or days into a calendar. **4** the period of time inserted. ⟨< L < Gk. *embolismos* < *emballein* < *en-* in + *ballein* throw⟩

em•bo•lus ['ɛmbələs] *n., pl.* **-li** [-,laɪ] *or* [-,li]. a particle of foreign matter, such as a detached blood clot, air bubble, or mass of bacteria, that has been carried along in the bloodstream until it has become lodged so as to obstruct the flow of blood. ⟨< L < Gk. *embolos* peg; < *emballein* put in. See EMBOLISM.⟩

em•bo•ly ['ɛmbəli] *n. Pathology.* the growth of one part into another. ⟨< Gk. *embole* < *emballein*. See EMBOLUS.⟩

em•bon•point [ɑ̃bɔ̃'pwɛ̃] *n. French.* fatness; plumpness.

em•bos•om [ɛm'bʊzəm] *or* [ɛm'buzəm] *v.* **1** surround; enclose; envelop. **2** embrace; cherish.

em•boss [ɛm'bɒs] *v.* **1** decorate with a design, pattern, etc. that stands out from the surface, made by pressing or moulding: *Canadian coins are embossed with letters and figures.* **2** cause to stand out from the surface: *She ran her finger over the letters to see if they had been embossed.* ⟨ME < OF *embocer* < *en-* in + *boce* swelling, BOSS[2]⟩

em•boss•ment [ɛm'bɒsmənt] *n.* **1** an embossing. **2** a figure carved or moulded in relief. **3** a part that sticks out; bulge.

em•bou•chure [,ɑmbu'ʃʊr]; *French,* [ɑ̃bu'ʃyʀ] *n.* **1** the mouth of a river. **2** the widening of a river valley into a plain. **3** *Music.* **a** the mouthpiece of a wind instrument. **b** the shaping and use of the lips, tongue, etc. in playing such an instrument; lip. ⟨< F *embouchure* < *emboucher* put into or discharge from a mouth < *en-* in + *bouche* mouth < L *bucca*⟩

em•bow [ɛm'bou] *v.* curve into the shape of an arch or bow.

em•bow•er [ɛm'baʊər] *v.* enclose in a shelter of leafy branches.

em•brace[1] [ɛm'breis] *v.* **-braced, -brac•ing;** *n.* —*v.* **1** clasp or hold in the arms to show love or friendship; hug. **2** hug one another: *The two lovers embraced.* **3** take up or accept, especially willingly or gladly: *to embrace an opportunity, to embrace a cause.* **4** include as an integral part: *The collection embraces all her early writings.* **5** surround; enclose: *A high wall embraced the garden.*
—*n.* **1** the act of clasping or holding in the arms. **2** encirclement or grasp: *The small firm now found itself in the embrace of a multinational corporation.* **3** close association. **4** the act of taking up or accepting: *Rajiv's sudden embrace of foreign ideology distressed his parents.* ⟨ME < OF *embracer* take into one's arms < VL < L *in-* in + *brachium* arm < Gk. *brachion*⟩
—em'brace•a•ble, *adj.*

em•brace[2] [ɛm'breis] *v.* **-braced, -brac•ing.** *Law.* try to influence (the jury) by corrupt means. ⟨< ME *embrasen* < OF *embraser*; ignite, incite < *en-* in + *braise* glowing coals⟩

em•branch•ment [ɛm'bræntʃmənt] *n.* **1** a branching out, as of a river. **2** a ramification.

em•bran•gle [ɛm'bræŋgəl] *v.* **-bran•gled, -brang•ling.** confuse. ⟨< *em-* + E dialect *brangle* argue⟩

em•bra•sure [ɛm'breiʒər] *n.* **1** an opening in a wall for a gun, with sides that spread outward to permit the gun to swing through a greater arc. **2** *Architecture.* a slanting of the wall at an oblique angle on the inner sides of a window or door. ⟨< F *embrasure* < *embraser* widen an opening⟩

em•bro•cate ['ɛmbrə,keit] *v.* **-cat•ed, -cat•ing.** bathe and rub with liniment or lotion. ⟨< LL *embrocare* < *embroc(h)a* < Gk. *embrochē* lotion < *en-* in + *brechein* wet⟩

em•bro•ca•tion [,ɛmbrə'keiʃən] *n.* **1** a bathing and rubbing with liniment or lotion. **2** the liniment or lotion used.

em•broi•der [ɛm'brɔidər] *v.* **1** ornament (cloth, leather, etc.) with a raised design or pattern made with a needle and thread. **2** make (a design, pattern, etc.) on cloth, leather, etc. with stitches: *She embroidered flowers around the edge of the collar.* **3** do embroidery. **4** add imaginary details to; exaggerate: *He didn't exactly tell lies, but he did embroider his stories.* ⟨< *em-*[1] + *broider* embroider < OF *broder*⟩ **—em'broi•der•er,** *n.*

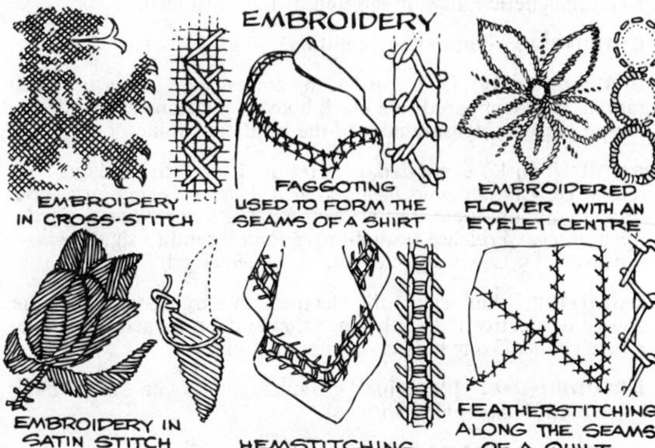

em•broi•der•y [ɛm'brɔidəri] *n., pl.* **-der•ies. 1** the act or art of embroidering. **2** raised and ornamental designs in cloth, leather, etc. sewn with a needle; embroidered work or material. **3** imaginary details; exaggeration. **4** any lavish ornamentation.

em•broil [ɛm'brɔil] *v.* **1** involve (a person, country, etc.) in an argument or quarrel: *She did not wish to become embroiled in the dispute.* **2** throw (affairs, etc.) into a state of confusion. ⟨< F *embrouiller* < *en-* in + *brouiller* to disorder⟩ **—em'broil•er,** *n.* **—em'broil•ment,** *n.*

em•brown [ɛm'braʊn] *v.* tan; darken.

em•brue [ɛm'bru] *v.* **-brued, -bru•ing.** imbrue.

em•bry•ec•to•my [,ɛmbri'ɛktəmi] *n.* the surgical removal of an embryo outside the uterus.

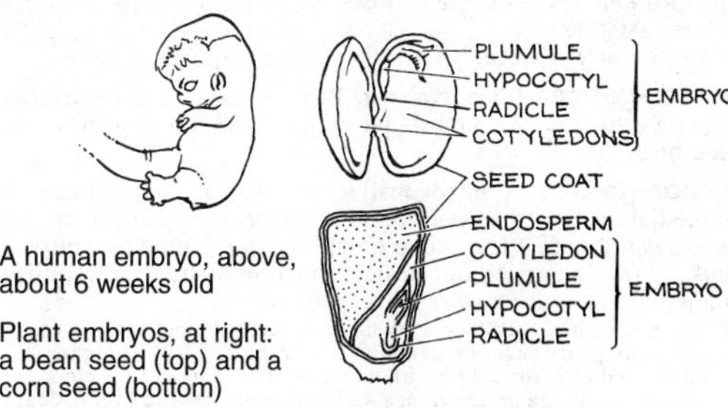

A human embryo, above, about 6 weeks old

Plant embryos, at right: a bean seed (top) and a corn seed (bottom)

em•bry•o ['ɛmbriou] *n., pl.* **-bry•os. 1** the unborn young of a vertebrate, especially during the earliest stage of its development; the term is used for a human offspring in the womb up to about the end of the ninth week after conception. Compare FETUS. **2** the undeveloped plant within a seed, usually consisting of a radicle, plumule, and cotyledons. **3** a beginning or undeveloped state of something. **4** (*adjl.*) embryonic.
in embryo, in an undeveloped state. ⟨< Med.L < Gk. *embryon* < *en-* in + *bryein* swell⟩

em•bry•og•en•y [,ɛmbri'ɒdʒəni] *n.* the formation and development of an embryo. Also, **embryogenesis** [,ɛmbriou'dʒɛnəsɪs]. **—,em•bry•o'gen•ic,** *adj.*

em•bry•o•log•i•cal [,ɛmbriə'lɒdʒəkəl] *adj.* of or having to do with embryology. Also, **embryologic. —,em•bry•o'log•ic•al•ly,** *adv.*

em•bry•ol•o•gist [,ɛmbri'ɒlədʒɪst] *n.* a person trained in embryology, especially one whose work it is.

em•bry•ol•o•gy [,ɛmbri'ɒlədʒi] *n.* the branch of biology that deals with the formation and development of embryos.

em•bry•on•ic [,ɛmbri'ɒnɪk] *adj.* **1** of the embryo. **2** undeveloped; not mature. **—,em•bry'on•i•cal•ly,** *adv.*

embryonic membrane any of various membranes involved in the maturation of a vertebrate embryo, as the yolk sac or the amnion.

em•bry•o•phyte ['ɛmbriə,fəit] *n.* any of various plants of the subkingdom Embryobionta, having an embryo enclosed within a seed or archegonium. Bryophites, ferns, and angiosperms are embryophytes. ⟨< Gk. *embryon* embryo, fetus + *phyton* plant⟩

embryo sac *Botany.* a structure made by the female gametophyte of a seed plant to hold the embryo.

embryo transfer the transfer of an embryo that has begun development in the uterus, or in the laboratory, to a different uterus to complete its development.

em•cee ['ɛm'si] *n., v.* **-ceed, -cee•ing.** *Informal.*
—*n.* master of ceremonies.
—*v.* act as master of ceremonies of; be master of ceremonies. Also, **M.C.** ⟨< the initials *M.C.*⟩

-eme *Linguistics.* a suffix identifying a structural part of a language, such as a morpheme. ⟨< (*phon*)*eme*⟩

e•mend [ɪ'mɛnd] *v.* make changes, as the result of scholarly criticism, to free (a faulty text, document, etc.) from errors; correct. ⟨< L *emendare* < *ex-* out of + *mendum, menda* fault. Doublet of AMEND.⟩ **—e'mend•a•ble,** *adj.* **—e'mend•er,** *n.*

e•men•date ['imən,deit], ['ɛmən,deit], *or* [ɪ'mɛndeit] *v.* **-dat•ed, -dat•ing.** emend. **—'e•men,da•tor,** *n.*

e•men•da•tion [,imɛn'deiʃən] *or* [,ɛmɛn'deiʃən] *n.* **1** a correction; improvement. **2** a change, as a result of scholarly criticism, to free a faulty text, document, etc. from errors.

em•er•ald ['ɛmərəld] *n., adj. —n.* **1** a bright green precious stone; transparent green beryl. **2** a piece of this stone or a gem made from it. **3** a kind of corundum with a similar appearance. **4** a bright green. **5** *Printing.* a size of type; 6½ point. *—adj.* bright green. ⟨ME < OF *esmeralde* < L < Gk. *smaragdos*⟩

Emerald Isle, the *Poetic.* Ireland.

emerald shiner a fish (*Notropis atherinoides*) native to the upper St. Lawrence River and the Great Lakes, having green back and sides, with a white belly. Average size: 6-8 cm long.

e•merge [ɪ'mɜrdʒ] *v.* **e•merged, e•merg•ing. 1** come out; come up; come into view: *The sun emerged from behind a cloud.* **2** become known: *Many facts emerged as a result of the investigation.* ⟨< L *emergere* < *ex-* out + *mergere* dip⟩

☛ *Hom.* IMMERGE.

☛ *Syn.* See note at ISSUE.

e•mer•gence [ɪ'mɜrdʒəns] *n.* **1** the act or fact of emerging; a coming into view. **2** a superficial outgrowth, such as a thorn on a rose bush.

e•mer•gen•cy [ɪ'mɜrdʒənsi] *n., pl.* **-cies. 1** a sudden need for immediate action: *I keep a fire extinguisher in my car for use in an emergency.* **2** (*adjl.*) for a time of sudden need: *an emergency brake.* **3** (*adjl.*) carried out or performed in a situation requiring immediate action: *an emergency operation.*

☛ *Syn.* **Emergency,** CRISIS = a trying or dangerous time or state of affairs. **Emergency** suggests a sudden or unexpected happening or situation that calls for action without delay: *The failure of the city's electric power caused an emergency.* **Crisis** emphasizes the life-or-death nature of a happening or situation that marks a turning point in the life of a person, country, etc.: *The floods brought a crisis into the lives of the valley's inhabitants.*

emergency brake an auxiliary brake, usually hand-operated, to hold a vehicle in place when parked, stopped on a hill, etc.

e•mer•gent [ɪ'mɜrdʒənt] *adj.* **1** emerging. **2** becoming politically and economically independent. **3** newly arising as the result of a recent change or improvement.

e•mer•i•tus [ɪ'mɛrətəs] *adj., n. —adj., pl.* **e•mer•i•ti** [-,ti] *or* [-,taɪ]. retired from an office or position but retaining one's rank and title as an honour: *a professor emeritus, professors emeriti.* *—n., pl.* **e•mer•i•ti** [-,ti] *or* [-,taɪ]. a person holding such an honorary title and rank. ⟨< L *emeritus*, pp. of *emerere* + *ex-* to the end + *merere* serve⟩

e•mer•sion [ɪ'mɜrʒən] *or* [ɪ'mɜrʃən] *n.* an emerging. ⟨< L *emersio, -onis* < *emergere.* See EMERGE.⟩

☛ *Hom.* IMMERSION.

em•er•y ['ɛməri] *n.* a hard, dark mineral, an impure corundum, used for grinding, smoothing, and polishing. ⟨< F *émeri* < Ital. < VL *smericulum* < Med.Gk. *smēris* < Gk. *smyris* abrasive powder⟩

emery board a flat strip of cardboard coated with powdered emery, used as a file.

emery cloth cloth coated with powdered emery, used for removing light rust.

emery paper a fine grade of sandpaper, used for final smoothing.

emery wheel SANDER (def. 3).

e•me•sis [ɪ'misɪs] *n.* vomiting.

e•met•ic [ɪ'mɛtɪk] *adj., n. —adj.* causing vomiting. *—n.* something that causes vomiting. ⟨< L < *emeticus* < Gk. *emetikos* < *emeein* vomit⟩

em•e•tine ['ɛmə,tin] *or* ['ɛmətɪn] *n.* an alkaloid derived from ipecac root and used as an emetic.

e•meu ['imju] See EMU.

EMF, emf, or **e.m.f.** ELECTROMOTIVE FORCE.

–emia *suffix.* blood; condition of the blood: *leukemia.*

em•i•grant ['ɛməgrənt] *n., adj. —n.* a person who leaves his or her own country or region to settle in another. Compare IMMIGRANT. *—adj.* **1** leaving one's own country or region to settle in another. **2** migratory. **3** of or having to do with emigration or emigrants.

em•i•grate ['ɛmə,greit] *v.* **-grat•ed, -grat•ing.** leave one's own country or region to settle in another: *Many people emigrated from Russia during the revolution.* Compare IMMIGRATE. ⟨< L *emigrare* < *ex-* out + *migrare* move⟩

em•i•gra•tion [,ɛmə'greiʃən] *n.* **1** the act of leaving one's own country or region to settle in another. **2** a movement of emigrants: *In recent years there has been much emigration from Europe to Canada.* Compare IMMIGRATION.

é•migré ['ɛmə,greі]; *French,* [emi'gʀe] *n., pl.* **-grés** [-,greiz]; *French,* [-'gʀe] *French.* **1** an emigrant. **2** a royalist refugee from France during the French Revolution. **3** a refugee from Russia during and after the Russian Revolution.

em•i•nence ['ɛmənəns] *n.* **1** a rank or position above all or most others; high standing; greatness; fame. **2** a high place; lofty hill. **3 Eminence,** *Roman Catholic Church.* the title of honour given to a cardinal: *his Eminence, your Eminence.* **4** *Anatomy.* a projection, especially on a bone.

é•mi•nence grise [eminɑ̃s 'gʀiz] *n., pl.* **é•mi•nences grises** [eminɑ̃s 'gʀiz] *French.* a person who exercises power unofficially or behind the scenes. ⟨literally, grey eminence, a nickname of Père Joseph (died 1638), a French monk who was private secretary of Cardinal Richelieu⟩

em•i•nent ['ɛmənənt] *adj.* **1** distinguished; exalted: *The Governor General is an eminent woman.* **2** conspicuous; noteworthy: *The judge was a woman of eminent fairness.* **3** high; lofty. **4** prominent; projecting. ⟨< L *eminens, -entis*, ppr. of *eminere* be prominent < *ex-* out + *minere* jut⟩ **—'em•i•nent•ly,** *adv.*

☛ *Syn.* **2. Eminent,** PROMINENT, DISTINGUISHED = well-known. **Eminent** = standing high among or above all others of the same kind because of excellence in something: *Wolfe and Montcalm were eminent generals.* **Prominent** = standing out from the crowd, and suggests being well-known at least locally: *The president of that bank is a prominent woman in her home town.* **Distinguished** = set off from others of the same kind because of outstanding qualities, and suggests being well-known to the public: *Lieutenant-generals are distinguished officers.*

eminent domain *Law.* the right of the government to take private property for public use such as roads. The owner must be paid the fair market value for the property taken.

e•mir [ə'mir] *n.* **1** a Muslim title given to rulers, governors, and military and naval commanders. **2** a title of dignity given to the descendants of Mohammed. Also, **amir.** ⟨< Arabic *amir* commander⟩

e•mir•ate [ə'mirɪt] *n.* **1** the rank or authority of an emir. **2** the territory governed by an emir.

em•is•sar•y ['ɛmə,sɛri] *n., pl.* **-sar•ies.** a person sent on a mission or errand, especially one sent secretly. ⟨< L *emissarius* < *emittere.* See EMIT.⟩

e•mis•sion [ɪ'mɪʃən] *n.* **1** the act or fact of emitting. **2** the thing emitted. **3** *Electronics.* **a** the streaming out of electrons from the heated cathode of a vacuum tube. **b** the streaming out of electrons from an electrode subjected to irradiation or to the impact of electrons or ions. ⟨< L *emissio, -onis* < *emittere.* See EMIT.⟩

emission control a device attached to a vehicle to reduce pollution from the exhaust system.

emission spectrum the spectrum of bright bands, unique to a substance, created by passing through a spectrometer the electromagnetic radiation emitted by the substance.

e•mis•sive [ɪ'mɪsɪv] *adj.* emitting.

e•mis•siv•i•ty [,ɛmɪ'sɪvɪti] *n.* the ability of an object to reflect radiant heat compared to a black body of the same size and temperature; a measurement of the insulation value of glass.

e•mit [ɪ'mɪt] *v.* **e•mit•ted, e•mit•ting. 1** give off; send out; discharge: *The sun emits light and heat. Volcanoes emit lava.* **2** put into circulation; issue. **3** utter; express: *The trapped lion emitted roars of rage.* **4** release (radiation). **5** *Radio.* send (a signal) via airwaves. ⟨< L *emittere* < *ex-* out + *mittere* send⟩

e•mit•ter [ɪ'mɪtər] *n.* **1** the electrode in a transistor that is the source of electrons. **2** a substance that emits radioactive particles: *a beta emitter.* **3** any person or thing that emits.

Em•man•u•el [ɪ'mænju,ɛl] *n.* Immanuel. ⟨< Gk. *Emmanouel* < Hebrew *imanuel* God with us⟩

em•men•a•gogue [ə'mɛnə,gɒg] *or* [ə'minə,gɒg] *n.* a medication that stimulates menstrual flow. ⟨< Gk. *emmena* menses (< *en-* in + *men* month) + E-*agogue* < Gk. *agogos* leading < *agein* lead⟩

Em•men•ta•ler ['ɛmən,tɑlər] *n.* a pale yellow Swiss cheese made from whole milk. ⟨< G *Emmentaler* < *Emmenthal,* a town in Switzerland⟩

Emmentaler cheese

Em•men•thal ['ɛmən,tɑl] *n.* Emmentaler.

em•mer ['ɛmər] *n.* a species of wheat (*Triticum dicoccum*) grown for forage. ⟨G < OHG *amari*⟩

em•met ['ɛmɪt] *n. Archaic.* ant. ⟨OE *æmete*⟩

em•me•tro•pia [,ɛmə'troupiə] *n.* the condition of an eye which is able to focus light rays on the retina for perfect vision. ⟨NL < Gk. *emmetros* proportionate, fit (< *en-* in + *metron* measure) + *-opia* < *ops* eye⟩ **—,em•me'trop•ic** [-'trɒpɪk], *adj.*

Em•my ['ɛmi] *n., pl.* **-mies.** an annual award presented in the United States by the Academy of Television Arts and Sciences for outstanding achievement in the field of television. The Emmy is a gold-plated statuette. ⟨< *Immy,* slang shortening of *image orthicon*⟩

e•mol•lient [ɪ'mɒljənt], [ɪ'mɒliənt], *or* [ɪ'mouliənt] *adj., n.* *—adj.* softening; soothing.
—n. something that softens and soothes: *Cold cream is an emollient for the skin. His encouragement was an emollient to her troubled mind.* ⟨< L *emolliens, -entis,* ppr. of *emollire* soften < *ex-* (intensive) + *mollis* soft⟩

e•mol•u•ment [ɪ'mɒljəmənt] *n.* the profit from a job, office, or position; salary; fee. ⟨< L *emolumentum* profit, ult. < *ex-* out + *molere* grind⟩

e•mote [ɪ'mout] *v.* **e•mot•ed, e•mot•ing.** *Informal.* **1** act a role in an exaggerated manner. **2** show emotion. **—e'mot•er,** *n.*

e•mo•ti•con [ɪ'moutə,kɒn] *n. Computer technology.* an icon conveying the emotion of the communication, made up of punctuation marks intended to be seen when the head is tilted to the left side. Tip your head to the side to see the icon **:-)** for a smile, **:-(** for a frown. ⟨< *emot*(*ion*) + *icon*⟩

e•mo•tion [ɪ'mouʃən] *n.* **1** feeling as opposed to reason: *Fear, anger, passion, joy, and grief are emotions.* **2** a strong feeling; a subjective reaction involving psychological and physical changes; excitement or agitation: *a voice choked with emotion, an emotion-charged meeting.* ⟨< F *émotion* (after *motion*) < *émouvoir* stir up < L *emovere* < *ex-* out + *movere* move⟩
☛ *Syn.* See note at FEELING.

e•mo•tion•al [ɪ'mouʃənəl] *adj.* **1** of or having to do with the emotions. **2** showing emotion. **3** appealing to the emotions: *The guest speaker made an emotional plea for money to help disabled children.* **4** easily affected by emotion: *Emotional people are likely to cry if they hear sad music or read sad stories.*
—e'mo•tion•al•ly, *adv.*

e•mo•tion•al•ism [ɪ'mouʃənə,lɪzəm] *n.* **1** an emotional quality or character. **2** an appeal to the emotions. **3** a tendency to display emotion too easily. **4** an ethical theory basing high value on emotion as a guide to behaviour.

e•mo•tion•al•ist [ɪ'mouʃənəlɪst] *n.* **1** a person whose emotions are easily aroused. **2** a person who uses the emotions to try to influence others. **3** a person who bases theories of conduct on the emotions.

e•mo•tion•al•ity [ɪ,mouʃə'nælәti] *n.* the state of being emotional.

e•mo•tion•al•ize [ɪ'mouʃənə,laɪz] *v.* **-ized, -iz•ing.** attribute an emotional character to (something).
—e,mo•tion•al•i'za•tion, *n.*

e•mo•tion•less [ɪ'mouʃənlɪs] *adj.* devoid of emotion.
—e'mo•tion•less•ly, *adv.* **—e'mo•tion•less•ness,** *n.*

e•mo•tive [ɪ'moutɪv] *adj.* **1** showing or causing emotion. **2** having to do with the emotions. **—e'mo•tive•ly,** *adv.* **—e'mo•tive•ness,** *n.*

em•pale [ɛm'peil] *v.* **-paled, -pal•ing.** impale.

em•pa•na•da [,ɛmpə'nɑdə]; *Spanish* [,ɛmpa'nadə] *n.* a Spanish or Latin-American turnover, stuffed with seasoned ground meat and vegetables or fruit, and deep-fried. ⟨< Am.Sp. stuffed in bread⟩

em•pan•el [ɛm'pænəl] *v.* **-elled** or **-eled, -el•ling** or **-el•ing.** impanel.

em•pa•thet•ic [,ɛmpə'θɛtɪk] *adj.* of, having to do with, or characterized by empathy. **—,em•pa'thet•i•cal•ly,** *adv.*

em•path•ic [ɛm'pæθɪk] *adj.* empathetic.

em•pa•thize ['ɛmpə,θaɪz] *v.* **-thized, -thiz•ing.** feel empathy (*with*): *to empathize with someone's aspirations.*

em•pa•thy ['ɛmpəθi] *n. Psychology.* the quality or process of entering fully, through imagination, into another's feelings or motives, into the meaning of a work of art, etc. ⟨< Gk. *empatheia* < *en-* in + *pathos* feeling⟩

em•pen•nage [ɛm'pɛnɪdʒ] *or* ['ɛmpənɪdʒ]; *French,* [ɑ̃pɛ'naʒ] *n. Aeronautics.* the tail assembly of an aircraft. ⟨< F *empennage* feathering of an arrow < OF *empenner* to feather (an arrow)⟩

em•per•or ['ɛmpərər] *n.* **1** a man who is the sovereign ruler of an empire. Compare EMPRESS. **2** any brilliantly coloured butterfly of the family Nymphalidae. ⟨ME < OF *empereor* < L *imperator* commander < *imperare* command < *in-* in + *parare* order⟩

emperor penguin a large penguin (*Aptenodytes forsteri*) of the Antarctic.

em•per•y ['ɛmpəri] *n. Archaic or poetic.* absolute dominion. ⟨< AF *emperie* < L *imperium* empire⟩

em•pha•sis ['ɛmfəsɪs] *n., pl.* **-ses** [-,siz]. **1** special force; stress; importance: *emphasis on scientific studies.* **2** special force or loudness given to particular syllables, words, or phrases; stress. ⟨< L < Gk. < *emphainein* indicate < *en-* in + *phainein* show⟩

em•pha•size ['ɛmfə,saɪz] *v.* **-sized, -siz•ing. 1** give special force to; stress; make important: *She emphasized that word by saying it very loudly.* **2** call attention to: *Accidents emphasize the need for careful driving.*

em•phat•ic [ɛm'fætɪk] *adj., n.* *—adj.* **1** spoken or done with force or stress; strongly expressed: *Her answer was an emphatic "No!"* **2** speaking with force or stress; expressing oneself strongly: *The emphatic speaker kept pounding the table and shouting.* **3** attracting attention; very noticeable; striking: *The club made an emphatic success of their party.* **4** *Grammar.* **a** of the present or past tense auxiliary of the verb *do,* used to convey emphasis and usually bearing heavy stress: *I do think that governments should be held responsible for their actions.* **b** designating the form of the past or present tense that uses this auxiliary.
—n. Grammar. **a** an auxiliary verb, usually *do,* that emphasizes the main verb: *Do stay longer.* **b** a verb form or verb phrase that makes use of such an auxiliary. ⟨< Gk. *emphatikos* < *emphainein.* See EMPHASIS.⟩ **—em'phat•i•cal•ly,** *adv.*

em•phy•se•ma [,ɛmfə'zimə] *or* [,ɛmfə'simə] *n.* a condition of the lungs which causes impaired breathing because of abnormal distension of the air sacs. ⟨< NL < Gk. *emphysēma* bodily inflation⟩ **—,em•phy•se'mat•ic** [,ɛmfəzə'mætɪk] or **,em•phy'se•ma•tous,** *adj.*

em•pire ['ɛmpaɪr] *n.* **1** a group of countries or states under the same ruler or government, one country having some measure of control over the rest: *the Roman Empire.* **2** a country ruled by an emperor or empress: *the Japanese Empire.* **3** the time during which such a government holds sway: *The Second Empire lasted from 1852 until the deposing of Napoleon III in 1870.* **4** absolute power; supreme authority. **5** a very large business conglomerate controlled by one person or group. ⟨ME < OF < L *imperium*⟩

Em•pire ['ɛmpaɪr] *adj.* **1** of or having to do with the first French Empire (1804-1815). **2 a** of, like, or having to do with a style of massive, ornate furniture in fashion during this period. **b** of, like, or having to do with a style of high-waisted, short-sleeved woman's dress in fashion during this period.

em•pir•ic [ɛm'pɪrɪk] *n., adj.* *—n.* a person who lacks theoretical or scientific knowledge and relies entirely on practical experience.
—adj. empirical. ⟨< L *empiricus* < Gk. *empeirikos* < *en-* in + *peira* experience, experiment⟩

em•pir•i•cal [ɛm'pirəkəl] *adj.* **1** based on experiment and observation: *Chemistry is largely an empirical science.* **2** based entirely on practical experience, without regard to science or theory: *The doctor's assistant had only an empirical knowledge of medicine.* Also, **empiric. —em'pir•i•cal•ly,** *adv.*

empirical formula *Chemistry.* a formula designating the elements of a compound and their properties.

em•pir•i•cism [ɛm'pirə,sɪzəm] *n.* **1** the use of methods based on experiment and observation, especially as practised in the natural sciences. **2** *Philosophy.* the theory that all knowledge is based on sense experience. **3** reliance on experience without the aid of science.

em•pir•i•cist [ɛm'pirəsɪst] *n.* a person who practises or advocates empiricism.

em•place [ɛm'pleis] *v.* **-placed, -plac•ing.** put in position.

em•place•ment [ɛm'pleismənt] *n.* **1** a space or platform for a heavy gun or guns. **2** a placing in position: *the emplacement of windows into a wall.*

em•plane [ɛm'plein] *v.* **-planed, -plan•ing. 1** get on an airplane. **2** put (someone or something) on an airplane.

em•ploy [ɛm'plɔɪ] *v., n.* —*v.* **1** use the services of; give work and pay to: *That big factory employs many workers.* **2** use: *You employ a knife, fork, and spoon in eating.* **3** engage the attention of; keep busy; occupy: *Instead of wasting time, she employed herself in reading.*
—*n.* a being employed; service for pay; employment: *There are many workers in the employ of the government.* ⟨< F *employer* < L *implicare* < *in-* in + *plicare* fold. Doublet of IMPLICATE, IMPLY.⟩ **—em'ploy•a•ble,** *adj.*
☛ *Syn. v.* **1. Employ,** HIRE = give work and pay to someone. **Employ** emphasizes a certain regularity and dignity in the work: *The steel mill employs most of the men in the town.* **Hire,** the more everyday word, means 'employ on a temporary or occasional basis': *She hired a man to mow the lawn.* **2.** See note at USE.

em•ploy•ee [ɛm'plɔɪi] *or* [ɛmplɔɪ'i] *n.* a person who works for some person or firm for pay. ⟨< F *employé,* pp. of *employer* employ⟩

em•ploy•er [ɛm'plɔɪər] *n.* **1** a person or firm that employs one or more persons. **2** user.

em•ploy•ment [ɛm'plɔɪmənt] *n.* **1** an employing or being employed. **2** what a person does for a living; work. **3** the percentage or number of people working at a paid job: *Employment went down this month.* **4** manner of using: *There is a clever employment of colour in that painting.*
☛ *Syn.* **2.** See note at OCCUPATION.

em•poi•son [ɛm'pɔɪzən] *v.* **1** corrupt. **2** embitter.

em•po•ri•um [ɛm'pɔriəm] *n., pl.* **-ri•ums, -ri•a** [-riə]. **1** a centre of trade; marketplace. **2** a large store selling many different things. ⟨< L < Gk. *emporion* < *emporos* merchant, traveller < *en-* on + *poros* voyage⟩

em•pow•er [ɛm'paʊər] *v.* **1** give power or authority to: *The secretary was empowered to sign certain contracts.* **2** enable; permit: *Training a person who is receiving social assistance empowers that person to gain control of his or her life.* Also, **impower. —em'pow•er•ment,** *n.*

em•press ['ɛmprɪs] *n.* **1** the wife of an emperor. **2** a woman who is the sovereign ruler of an empire. **3** an influential or powerful woman.

em•presse•ment [,ɑmprɛs'mɑ̃]; *French,* [ɑ̃pʀɛs'mɑ̃] *n.* too much cordiality.

em•prise or **em•prize** [ɛm'praɪz] *n. Archaic.* **1** an adventure; daring undertaking. **2** knightly daring. ⟨ME < OF *emprise,* originally fem. pp. of *emprendre* undertake < *en-* in + *prendre* take < L *prehendere*⟩

emp•ty ['ɛmpti] *adj.* **-ti•er, -ti•est;** *v.* **-tied, -ty•ing;** *n., pl.* **-ties.** —*adj.* **1** with nothing or no one in it: *The birds had gone and their nest was empty.* **2** vacant; unoccupied: *an empty room or house.* **3** having no cargo; unloaded: *an empty ship.* **4** not real; meaningless: *an empty promise, an empty threat.* **5** lacking knowledge or sense; foolish; frivolous. **6** *Informal.* hungry. **empty of,** without; lacking.
—*v.* **1** pour out or take out the contents of; make empty: *Empty the cup into the sink.* **2** pour out (something) until its container is empty: *She emptied the undrinkable coffee into a nearby flowerpot.* **3** become empty: *The hall emptied as soon as the concert was over.* **3** flow out; discharge: *The St. Lawrence River empties into the Gulf of St. Lawrence.*
—*n. Informal.* something that is empty; an empty bottle, container, freight car, etc. ⟨OE *ǣmtig* < *ǣmetta* leisure⟩ **—'emp•ti•ly,** *adv.* **—'emp•ti•ness,** *n.*

emp•ty–hand•ed ['ɛmpti 'hændɪd] *adj.* having nothing in the hands; bringing or taking nothing: *We expected our uncle to bring a present for each of us, but he arrived empty-handed.*

emp•ty–head•ed ['ɛmpti 'hɛdɪd] *adj.* silly; stupid.

empty nester one whose children have become independent and left home.

empty nest syndrome depression felt by a mother or father whose children have left home to be independent.

empty set *Mathematics.* a set that has no members.

em•pur•pled [ɛm'pɜrpəld] *adj.* made purple; coloured with purple.

em•py•e•ma [,ɛmpaɪ'imə] *n.* a collection of pus in a body cavity, especially in the lungs. ⟨altered < ME *empima* < Med.L *empyema* < Gk. *empyema* < *empyein* to suppurate < *en-* in + *pyon* pus⟩ **—,empy'e•mic,** *adj.*

em•pyr•e•al [ɛm'pɪriəl], [,ɛmpaɪ'riəl], *or* [,ɛmpə'riəl] *adj.* of the empyrean; celestial; heavenly.

em•py•re•an [ɛm'pɪriən], [,ɛmpaɪ'riən], *or* [,ɛmpə'riən] *n., adj.* —*n.* **1** the highest heaven; region of pure light. **2** the sky; firmament; the vault of the heavens.
—*adj.* empyreal. ⟨< LL *empyreus* < Gk. *empyrios, empyros* < *en-* in + *pyr* fire⟩

EMR ELECTROMAGNETIC RADIATION.

e•mu ['imju] *n.* a very large, flightless bird (*Dromaius novae hollandiae*) of Australia, the only living member of the family Dromaiideae, resembling an ostrich but smaller. Also, **emeu.** ⟨< Pg. *ema* ostrich, crane⟩

EMU, e.m.u., emu, or **E.M.U.** ELECTROMAGNETIC UNIT.

em•u•late ['ɛmjə,leit] *v.* **-lat•ed, -lat•ing. 1** try to equal or excel: *The proverb tells us to emulate the industry of the ant.* **2** try to equal with some success. **3** be a rival to (someone). **4** be an imitation or takeoff of: *This program emulates software produced by another major company.* ⟨< L *aemulari* < *aemulus* striving to equal⟩ **—'em•u,la•tor,** *n.*

em•u•la•tion [,ɛmjə'leiʃən] *n.* **1** imitation in order to equal or excel; ambition or desire to equal or excel. **2** a product that emulates another.

em•u•la•tive ['ɛmjələtɪv] *or* ['ɛmjə,leitɪv] *adj.* **1** tending to emulate. **2** of or caused by emulation. **—'em•u•la•tive•ly,** *adv.*

em•u•la•tor ['ɛmjə,leitər] *n. Computer technology.* the software or hardware that makes two computers compatible.

em•u•lous ['ɛmjələs] *adj.* **1** wishing to equal or excel. **2** caused by emulation. ⟨< L *aemulus*⟩ **—'em•u•lous•ly,** *adv.* **—'em•u•lous•ness,** *n.*

e•mul•si•fi•ca•tion [ɪ,mʌlsəfə'keiʃən] *n.* an emulsifying or being emulsified.

e•mul•si•fy [ɪ'mʌlsə,faɪ] *v.* **-fied, -fy•ing.** form or make into an emulsion. **—e'mul•si,fi•er,** *n.*

e•mul•sion [ɪ'mʌlʃən] *n.* **1** a mixture of liquids that do not dissolve in each other. In an emulsion very fine drops of one of the liquids are evenly distributed throughout the other. **2** *Pharmacy.* a milky liquid containing very tiny drops of fat, oil, etc. Cod-liver oil is made into an emulsion to improve its taste. **3** a light-sensitive coating on a camera film, plate, etc. ⟨< NL *emulsio, -onis* < L *emulgere* < *ex-* out + *mulgere* milk⟩ **—e'mul•sive,** *adj.*

e•mul•soid [ɪ'mʌlsɔɪd] *adj.* having a liquid disperse phase.

e•munc•to•ry [ɪ'mʌŋktəri] *n.* a part or an organ of the body that excretes something, such as the skin or kidneys. ⟨< NL *emunctorium* < L *emungere* clean out⟩

en [ɛn] *n.* **1** the letter N, n. **2** *Printing.* half the width of an em.

en–[1] *prefix.* **1** cause to be; make, as in *enable, enfeeble.* **2** put in; put on, as in *encircle, enthrone.* **3** cause to have, as in *encourage, empower.* **4** other meanings, as in *enact, entwine.* The addition of *en-* rarely changes the meaning of a verb except to make it more emphatic. Also, **em-,** before *b, p,* and sometimes *m.* ⟨< OF < L *in-* < *in* in, into⟩

en–[2] *prefix.* in; on, as in *encephalon.* Also, **em-,** before *b, m, p, ph.* ⟨< Gk.⟩

–en[1] *suffix.* **1** cause to be; make, as in *blacken, sharpen.* **2** cause to have, as in *heighten, strengthen.* **3** become, as in *sicken, soften.* **4** come to have; gain, as in *lengthen.* ⟨OE *-nian*⟩

–en[2] *suffix.* made of, as in *silken, wooden, woollen.* ⟨OE⟩

–en[3] *suffix.* *-en* (or *-n*) ends the past participles of many so-called strong verbs, as in *fallen, shaken, written, sworn.* ⟨OE⟩

–en[4] *suffix.* *-en* is used to form the plural of a few nouns, as in *children, oxen.* ⟨OE *-an*⟩

en•a•ble [ɛ'neibəl] *v.* **-bled, -bling. 1** give ability, power, or means to; make able: *Airplanes enable people to travel through the air.* **2** make possible or easy.

en•act [ɛ'nækt] *v.* **1** pass (a bill) giving it validity as law; make into a law. **2** decree; order. **3** play the part of; act out; play: *In her time, the famous actor had enacted many characters from Shakespeare.* **—en'ac•tor,** *n.*

en•act•ive [ɛ'næktɪv] *adj.* able to establish as a law.

en•act•ment [ɛ'næktmənt] *n.* **1** an enacting or being enacted. **2** law.

en•al•a•pril mal•e•ate [ɛ'nælə,prɪl 'mæli,eit] *n.* a drug used to treat high blood pressure.

e•nam•el [ɪ'næməl] *n., v.* **-elled** or **-eled, -el•ling** or **-el•ing.** —*n.* **1** a glasslike substance melted and then cooled to make a

smooth, hard surface. Different colours of enamel are used to cover or decorate metal, pottery, etc. **2** a paint or varnish used to make a smooth, hard, glossy surface. **3** the smooth, hard, glossy outer layer of the teeth. **4** anything covered or decorated with enamel. **5** any smooth, hard, shiny coating or surface.
—v. **1** cover or decorate with enamel. **2** form an enamel-like surface upon. **3** adorn with various colours; decorate as if with enamel. ⟨ME < AF *enamayller* < *en-* on + *amayl* enamel < Gmc.⟩ **—e'nam•el•ler** or **e'nam•el•er,** *n.* **—e'nam•el•list** or **e'nam•el•ist,** *n.*

e•nam•el•ware [ɪ'næməl,wɛr] *n.* pots, pans, etc. that are made of metal coated with enamel.

en•am•our or **en•am•or** [ɛ'næmər] *v.* arouse to love; cause to fall in love; charm: *Her beauty enamoured the prince.* ⟨< OF *enamourer* < *en-* in + *amour* love < L *amor*⟩

en•am•oured or **en•am•ored** [ɛ'næmərd] *adj., v.*
—adj. very much in love; captivated; charmed (*usually used with* **of**): *He was enamoured of the boss's daughter.*
—v. pt. and pp. of ENAMOUR.

e•nan•ti•o•morph [ɪ'næntiou,mɔrf] *n.* a crystal that is a mirror image of another. ⟨< G < Gk. *enantios* opposite (< *en-* in + *anti* against) + *morphe* form⟩ **—e,nan•ti•o'morph•ic,** *adj.* **—e,nan•ti•o'morph•ism,** *n.*

en ar•ri•ère [ɑ̃na'ʀjɛʀ] *French.* backward.

en•ar•thro•sis [,ɛnɑr'θrousɪs] *n.* a ball-and-socket joint like the one at the shoulder. ⟨< NL < Gk. *enarthrosis* < *enarthros* jointed < *en-* in + *arthron* joint⟩

en a•vant [ɑ̃na'vɑ̃] *French.* forward.

en bloc [,ɛn 'blɒk] *or* [,ɒn 'blɒk]; *French,* [ɑ̃'blɔk] all together; in one lump. ⟨< F⟩

en broch•ette [ɑ̃ bʀɔ'ʃɛt] *French.* broiled on a skewer like a shish kebab.

en brosse [ɑ̃'bʀɔs] *French.* of a haircut, so short as to stand on end like the bristles of a brush. ⟨< F, like a brush⟩

enc. **1** enclosed. **2** enclosure.

en•cae•nia [ɛn'siniə] *n.pl.* **1** the ceremonies in honour of the founding of a city or the blessing of a church. **2 Encaenia,** a ceremony at the University of Oxford in memory of its founding. ⟨altered < ME *encenia* < L *encaenia* < Gk. *enkainia* < *en-* in + *kainos* new⟩

en•cage [ɛn'keidʒ] *v.* **-caged, -cag•ing.** coop up; put in a cage.

en•camp [ɛn'kæmp] *v.* **1** make a camp: *It took the soldiers only an hour to encamp.* **2** stay in a camp: *They encamped there for three weeks.* **3** put in a camp: *They were encamped in tents.*

en•camp•ment [ɛn'kæmpmənt] *n.* **1** the act of forming a camp. **2** camp.

en•cap•su•late [ɛn'kæpsə,leit] *or* [ɛn'kæpsjə,leit] *v.* **-lat•ed, -lat•ing. 1** enclose in or as if in a capsule: *The book encapsulates a vanishing way of life.* **2** condense; abridge. Also, **encapsule.** **—en,cap•su'la•tion,** *n.*

en•car•nal•ize [ɛn'kɑrnə,laɪz] *v.* **-ized, -iz•ing.** make carnal by investing with a bodily form or a worldly character.

en•case [ɛn'keis] *v.* **-cased, -cas•ing. 1** put into a case. **2** cover completely; enclose: *Armour encased the knight's body.* Also, **incase.** **—en'case•ment,** *n.*

en cas•se•role [ɒn ,kæsə'roul]; *French,* [ɑ̃kas'ʀɔl] cooked in a casserole. ⟨< F⟩

en•caus•tic [ɛn'kɒstɪk] *n., adj. Ceramics, etc. —n.* **1** the method or process of burning in colours. **2** a work produced by this method.
—adj. decorated by burning in colours. Encaustic tile is decorated by burning in coloured clays. **—en'caus•ti•cal•ly,** *adv.*

-ence *suffix.* **1** the act, fact, quality, or state of ——ing: *abhorrence, dependence, indulgence.* **2** the quality or state of being ——ent: *absence, confidence, competence, independence, prudence.* See also -ENCY. ⟨< L *-entia*⟩

en•ceinte[1] [ɒn'sænt]; *French,* [ɑ̃'sɛ̃t] *adj.* pregnant. ⟨< F < Med.L *incincta, incinctus* ungirt < *in-* not + *cinctus* pp. of *cingere* gird⟩

en•ceinte[2] [ɒn'sænt]; *French,* [ɑ̃'sɛ̃t] *n.* **1** the wall enclosing a fortified place. **2** the place enclosed. ⟨< F < pp. of *enceindre* < L *incingere* gird about, surround < *in-* in + *cingere* gird⟩

En•cel•a•dus [ɛn'sɛlədəs] *n. Astronomy.* a moon of the planet Saturn. Enceladus reflects more light than any other celestial body.

en•ce•phal•ic [,ɛnsə'fælɪk] *adj.* of or having to do with the brain. ⟨< Gk. *enkephalos* brain⟩

en•ceph•a•lit•ic [ɛn,sɛfə'lɪtɪk] *adj.* having to do with or having encephalitis.

en•ceph•a•li•tis [ɛn,sɛfə'ləitɪs] *n.* an inflammation of the brain caused by injury, infection, poison, etc. ⟨< NL < Gk. *enkephalos* brain + Gk. *-itis*⟩

encephalitis le•thar•gi•ca [lɪ 'θɑrdʒəkə] a kind of encephalitis prevalent between 1915 and 1926; sleeping sickness.

en•ceph•a•lo•gram [ɛn'sɛfələ,græm] *n.* an X-ray photograph of the brain.

en•ceph•a•lo•my•e•li•tis [ɛn,sɛfəlou,maɪə'ləitɪs] *n.* an inflammation of the brain and spine, found in humans and certain animals, especially horses.

en•ceph•a•lon [ɛn'sɛfə,lɒn] *n.* brain. ⟨< NL < Gk. *enkephalos* < *en-* in + *kephalē* head⟩

en•ceph•a•lop•ath•y [ɛn,sɛfə'lɒpəθi] *n.* any of several diseases of the brain. **—en,ceph•a•lo'path•ic** [ɛn,sɛfəlou'pæθɪk], *adj.*

en•chain [ɛn'tʃein] *v.* **1** put in chains; fetter. **2** attract and fix firmly; hold fast: *The speaker's earnestness enchained the attention of her audience.*

en•chant [ɛn'tʃænt] *v.* **1** use magic on; put under a spell: *The witch enchanted the princess.* **2** delight greatly; charm. ⟨< F *enchanter* < L *incantare* < *in-* against + *cantare* chant⟩ **—en'chant•er,** *n.*

en•chant•ing [ɛn'tʃæntɪŋ] *adj., v. —adj.* **1** very delightful; charming. **2** bewitching.
—v. ppr. of ENCHANT. **—en'chant•ing•ly,** *adv.*

en•chant•ment [ɛn'tʃæntmənt] *n.* **1** the use of magic; the act of putting under a spell. **2** the condition of being put under a magic spell. **3** a magic spell. **4** delight; rapture. **5** something that delights or charms; charm.

en•chan•tress [ɛn'tʃæntrɪs] *n.* **1** a woman who makes magic spells; witch. **2** a very delightful, charming woman.

en•chase [ɛn'tʃeis] *v.* **-chased, -chas•ing. 1** engrave: *Her initials were enchased on the back of the watch.* **2** ornament with engraved designs; decorate with gems, inlay, etc.: *The shield was enchased with gold and silver.* **3** place in a setting; mount; frame. ⟨< F *enchâsser* < *en-* in + *châsse* frame, case < L *capsa* box⟩

en•chi•la•da [,ɛntʃɪ'lɑdə] *n.* a tortilla rolled around a filling of meat, cheese, etc., served with a peppery sauce.
the whole enchilada, *Slang.* the whole thing. ⟨< Mexican Sp., ult. < Sp. *en-* in + Nahuatl *chili* chili⟩

en•ci•na [ɛn'sinə] *n.* an oak tree native to the southwest of the United States. ⟨< Sp. < VL *ilicina* holm oak⟩

en•ci•pher [ɛn'səifər] *v.* put (a message) into code.

en•cir•cle [ɛn'sɜrkəl] *v.* **-cled, -cling. 1** form a circle around; surround: *Trees encircled the pond.* **2** go in a circle around: *The moon encircles the earth.*

en•cir•cle•ment [ɛn'sɜrkəlmənt] *n.* an encircling or being encircled.

en clair [ɒn 'klɛr]; *French* [ɑ̃'klɛʀ] of a message, not in code: *information en clair.* ⟨< F in clear⟩

en•clasp [ɛn'klæsp] *v.* enfold in one's arms; embrace.

en•clave ['ɛnkleiv] *or* ['ɒnkleiv]; *French,* [ɑ̃'klav] *n.* **1** a country or district surrounded by the territory of another country. **2** a separate or distinct unit enclosed within a larger one. **3** a small, cohesive, locally concentrated group distinguished by its culture, religion, ethnicity, etc. from the dominant group which surrounds it: *an enclave of White Russians in Paris, an enclave of Muslims in Bosnia.* ⟨< F *enclave* < *enclaver* enclose⟩

en•clit•ic [ɛn'klɪtɪk] *n.* a word or contraction that, having no stress, is pronounced as part of the preceding word. *Examples*: *not* in *I cannot tell*; *s* in *Bert's here* (= Bert is here). ⟨< LL *encliticus* < Gk. *enklitikos* < *enklinein* lean on < *en-* in, on + *klinein* lean, incline⟩

en•close [ɛn'klouz] *v.* **-closed, -clos•ing. 1** shut in on all sides; surround. **2** put a wall or fence around. **3** include in an envelope or package along with something else: *A cheque was enclosed with the letter.* Also, **inclose.** ⟨< *en-*[1] in + *close*, v., ME, after OF *enclos*, pp. of *enclore*⟩

en•clo•sure [ɛn'klouʒər] *n.* **1** an enclosing or being enclosed. **2** something that encloses, such as a wall or fence. **3** an enclosed place or area: *The cows were herded into the enclosure.*
4 something enclosed, especially additional material enclosed in an envelope with a letter. Also, **inclosure.**

en•code [ɛn'koud] *v.* **-cod•ed, -cod•ing. 1** put into code: *The spy encoded her message before mailing it.* **2** express verbally; put into words. **—en'cod•er,** *n.*

en•co•mi•ast [ɛn'koumi,æst] *or* [ɛn'koumiəst] *n.* a writer or speaker of encomiums; eulogist. ⟨< Gk. *enkōmiastēs* < *enkōmion.* See ENCOMIUM.⟩

en•co•mi•um [ɛn'koumiəm] *n., pl.* **-mi•ums, -mi•a** [-miə]. an elaborate expression of praise; high praise; eulogy. ⟨< LL < Gk. *enkōmion*, neut., laudatory < *en-* in + *kōmos* revelry⟩

en•com•pass [ɛn'kʌmkpəs] *v.* **1** surround completely; shut in on all sides; encircle: *The atmosphere encompasses the earth.* **2** include; contain. **—en'com•pass•ment,** *n.*

en•core ['ɒŋkɔr] *or* ['ɒnkɔr], [ɒŋ'kɔr] *or* [ɒn'kɔr] *interj., n., v.* **-cored, -cor•ing.** *—interj.* once more; again.
—n. **1** an extra performance or appearance by a musician, entertainer, etc. at the end of a concert in response to audience demand. **2** a demand by an audience for such a performance or appearance.
—v. **1** call for a repetition of (a song, etc.), or the reappearance of (a performer, etc.): *The audience encored the singer by applauding.* **2** *Informal.* play or perform an encore: *The orchestra encored with Gershwin's* Rhapsody in Blue. ⟨< F⟩

en•coun•ter [ɛn'kaʊntər] *v., n. —v.* **1** meet unexpectedly: *I encountered an old friend on the train.* **2** meet with (difficulties, opposition, etc.); be faced with. **3** meet as an enemy; meet in a fight or battle.
—n. **1** a meeting; unexpected meeting. **2** a confrontation; a meeting of two opposed forces, teams, etc.; a fight; battle. ⟨ME < OF *encontrer* < VL < L *in-* in + *contra* against⟩

encounter group a group of people engaged in training to enhance emotional sensitivity and the release of feelings through exercises with members of the group.

en•cour•age [ɛn'kɜrɪdʒ] *v.* **-aged, -ag•ing. 1** give courage to; increase the hope or confidence of; urge on: *Success encourages you to go ahead and do better.* **2** be favourable to; help; promote; be an incentive to: *High prices for farm products encourage farming. Exercise encourages muscle tone.* **3** urge; recommend (to); advise: *Students are encouraged to register as early as possible. We do not encourage you to try this at home.* ⟨ME < OF *encoragier* < *en-* in + *corage* courage, ult. < L *cor* heart⟩ **—en'cour•ag•er,** *n.* **—en'cour•ag•ing•ly,** *adv.*

en•cour•age•ment [ɛn'kɜrɪdʒmənt] *n.* **1** the act of encouraging. **2** the state of being or feeling encouraged. **3** something that encourages.

en•croach [ɛn'kroutʃ] *v.* **1** go beyond proper or usual limits: *The sea encroached upon the shore and submerged the beach.* **2** trespass upon the property or rights of another; intrude: *He is a good sales rep and will not encroach upon his customer's time.* ⟨< OF *encrochier* < *en-* in + *croc* hook < Gmc.⟩ **—en'croach•er,** *n.*
☛ *Syn.* **2.** See note at INTRUDE.

en•croach•ment [ɛn'kroutʃmənt] *n.* **1** encroaching. **2** something taken by encroaching.

en croûte [ɒn 'krut]; *French,* [ɑ̃'kRut] of food, especially meat, enclosed in pastry and baked: *poulet en croûte.* ⟨< F in a crust⟩

en•crust [ɛn'krʌst] *v.* **1** cover with a crust or hard coating: *The inside of a kettle is encrusted with lime.* **2** form a crust (*on*); form into a crust: *The extremely cold weather during the night had encrusted the snow so that it was able to bear our weight.* **3** decorate with a layer of costly material: *The gold crown was encrusted with precious gems.* Also, **incrust**. ⟨< L *incrustare* < in- + on + *crusta* crust⟩ **—,en•crus'ta•tion,** *n.*

en•cum•ber [ɛn'kʌmbər] *v.* **1** hold back (from running, doing, etc.); hinder; hamper: *Heavy shoes encumber the wearer in the water.* **2** make difficult to use; fill; obstruct: *Rubbish and old boxes encumbered the fire escape.* **3** weigh down; burden: *The doctor is encumbered with the care of too many patients.* **4** of property, put under a mortgage or a legal claim. See ENCUMBRANCE (def. 4): *The farm was encumbered with a heavy mortgage.* Also, **incumber**. ⟨ME < OF *encombrer* < *en-* in + *combre* barrier, probably < Celtic⟩

en•cum•brance [ɛn'kʌmbrəns] *n.* **1** anything that encumbers; a hindrance; obstruction. **2** an annoyance; trouble; burden. **3** a dependent person; child. **4** *Law.* a claim, mortgage, etc. on property. Also, **incumbrance.**

–ency suffix. **1** the act, fact, quality, or state of ——ing: *dependency.* **2** the quality or state of being ——ent: *clemency, frequency.* **3** other meanings: *agency, currency.* See also -ENCE. ⟨< L *-entia*⟩

encyc. or **ency.** encyclopedia.

en•cyc•li•cal [ɛn'sɪkləkəl] *or* [ɛn'səiklәkəl] *n., adj. —n. Roman Catholic Church.* a letter from the Pope to his clergy.
—adj. intended for wide circulation. ⟨< LL *encyclicus* < Gk. *enkyklios* < *en-* in + *kyklos* circle⟩

en•cy•clo•pe•di•a or **en•cy•clo•pae•di•a** [ɛn,səiklə'pidiə] *n.* **1** a book or series of books giving information, usually arranged alphabetically, on all branches of knowledge. **2** a book treating one subject very thoroughly, with its articles arranged alphabetically: *a medical encyclopedia.* ⟨< LL *encyclopaedia* < Gk. *enkyklopaideia*, for *enkyklios paideia* well-rounded education⟩

en•cy•clo•pe•dic or **en•cy•clo•pae•dic** [ɛn,səiklə'pidɪk] *adj.* **1** covering a wide range of subjects; possessing wide and varied information. **2** of or having to do with an encyclopedia. **—en,cy•clo'pe•di•cal•ly,** *adv.*

en•cy•clo•pe•dist or **en•cy•clo•pae•dist** [ɛn,səiklə'pidɪst] *n.* **1** a person who makes or compiles an encyclopedia. **2 the Encyclopedists,** *pl.* the contributors to *L'Encyclopédie* (1751-1772) edited by Diderot and D'Alembert. *L'Encyclopédie* is renowned for its attempt to provide rational explanations of the universe. Voltaire and Rousseau were two Encyclopedists.

en•cyst [ɛn'sɪst] *v.* enclose or become enclosed in a cyst or sac. **—en'cyst•ment,** *n.*

end [ɛnd] *n., v. —n.* **1** the last part; conclusion: *She read through to the end of the book.* **2** the edge or outside limit of an object or area; boundary: *Those trees mark the end of their property.* **3** the point where something that has length stops or ceases to be: *Every stick has two ends.* **4** a purpose; object: *The end of work is to get something done.* **5** a result; outcome: *It is hard to tell what the end will be.* **6** death; destruction: *He met his end in the accident.* **7** a cause of death or destruction. **8** a part left over; remnant; fragment. **9** *Football.* **a** the player at either end of the line of scrimmage. **b** the position of either of these players. **10** *Curling.* one of the divisions of a game: *Our team was beaten in the last end.*
at loose ends, a not settled or established. **b** in confusion or disorder.
end to end, with the end of one object set next to the end of another; endways: *The dominoes were arranged end to end on the table.*
in the end, finally; at last: *Everything will turn out all right in the end.*
jump or **go off the deep end,** *Slang.* act suddenly and rashly without deliberation.
keep or **hold** (one's) **end up,** sustain one's part or bear one's share fully in an undertaking or performance.
make an end of, stop; do no more.
make (both) ends meet, a spend no more than one has. **b** just manage to live on what one has.
no end (of), *Informal.* very much; very many: *We had no end of trouble with that car. That annoyed her no end.*
on end, a upright in position: *She stood the dominoes on end.* **b** one after another: *It snowed for days on end.*
put an end to, stop; do away with; destroy; kill.
the ends of the earth, the most distant areas: *Victor Frankenstein pursued his monster to the ends of the earth.*
—v. **1** have a boundary: *Their property ends here.* **2** bring or come to an end; stop; finish: *when the summer ends. Let us end this fight.* **3** form the end of; be the end of: *This chapter ends the book.* **4** destroy; kill. **5** surpass: *It was a holiday to end all holidays.* **6** arrive at a particular final stage, condition, rank, etc. (*often used with* **up**): *She ended up a judge. You'll end up in the water if you keep rocking the boat. He tried one scheme after another but ended by losing all his savings.* ⟨OE *ende*⟩ **—'end•er,** *n.*
☛ *Syn. v.* **2. End,** CONCLUDE, FINISH = bring or come to a close. **End** suggests a sudden stop or natural close: *My holidays ended when school started.* **Conclude** is a formal word and suggests a formal ending of a speech, essay, action, piece of business, etc.: *Singing the national anthem will conclude the meeting.* **Finish** suggests completion, ending only after getting everything done that should be done: *I never finish my homework on time.*

end–all ['ɛnd ,ɒl] *n.* the ultimate; the end of everything.

en•dan•ger [ɛn'deindʒər] *v.* cause danger to; expose to loss or injury: *Fire endangered the hotel's guests, but no lives were lost.*

endangered species any species of life that is threatened with extinction.

end•arch ['ɛndɑrk] *adj. Botany.* of a plant, with the xylem growing from the middle of the stem toward the outside, Compare EXARCH[2]. ⟨< Gk. *endon* within + *arche* beginning⟩

end•ar•ter•ec•to•my [ɛn,dɑrtə'rɛktəmi] *n.* the surgical or chemical removal of plaque deposits or of the lining of a vein or artery to increase circulation. ⟨< Gk. *endon* within + *arteria* artery + E *-ectomy*⟩

en•dear [ɛn'dir] *v.* make dear: *Her kindness endeared her to all of us.* **—en'dear•ing•ly,** *adv.*

en•dear•ing [ɛn'dirɪŋ] *adj., v. —adj.* **1** affectionate: *an endearing gaze.* **2** that endears.
—v. ppr. of ENDEAR.

en•dear•ment [ɛn'dirmənt] *n.* **1** the act of endearing or state of being endeared. **2** the thing that endears. **3** an act or word showing love or affection; caress.

en•deav•our or **en•deav•or** [ɛn'dɛvər] *v., n. —v.* try hard; attempt earnestly; make an effort; strive.
—n. an earnest attempt; effort. ⟨ME < *-en-*[1] + *devoir* < *dever* duty < OF *deveir* < L *debere* owe⟩ **—en'deav•our•er** or **en'deav•or•er,** *n.*
☛ *Syn. v.* See note at TRY. *—n.* See note at EFFORT.

en•dem•ic [ɛn'dɛmɪk] *adj., n. —adj.* regularly found in a particular people or locality: *Cholera is endemic in India.* Compare ENZOOTIC.
—n. **1** an endemic disease. **2** an animal or plant that is endemic to a particular region. ⟨< Gk. *endēmos* native < *en-* in + *dēmos* people⟩ **—en'dem•i•cal•ly,** *adv.*

en•der•mic [ɛn'dɜrmɪk] *adj.* of or having to do with substances, as medicine, absorbed through the skin.

en dés•ha•bil•lé [ɑ̃dezabi'je] *French.* partly or carelessly dressed.

end•game ['ɛnd,geim] *n.* **1** *Chess.* the last stage of a chess game, when most pieces have been taken. **2** the last stage of anything.

end•ing ['ɛndɪŋ] *n., v. —n.* **1** the last part; end. **2** death. **3** *Grammar.* a letter or syllable added to a word or stem to change its meaning or to show how it is used in relation to other words. The common plural ending in English is *-s* or *-es*, as in *kings, dresses.*
—v. ppr. of END.

en•dive ['ɛndaɪv] *or* ['ɒndiv]; *French,* [ɑ̃'div] *n.* **1** a kind of chicory having finely divided, curly leaves, used for salads. **2** a kind of chicory that has broad leaves and looks like smooth white celery, also used for salads; escarole. ⟨ME < OF < Med.L *endivia* < L *intibus* < Gk. *entybon*⟩

end•less ['ɛndlɪs] *adj.* **1** having no end; never stopping; lasting or going on forever: *the endless motion of the stars.* **2** appearing to have no end; seeming never to stop: *an endless task.* **3** with the ends joined; continuous: *A bicycle chain is an endless chain.* **—'end•less•ly,** *adv.* **—'end•less•ness,** *n.*

end line *Basketball, Football.* one of the two lines at either end of the court or playing field, marking the boundaries of the playing area.

end man **1** the person at the end of a row or line. **2** in a minstrel show, a person at either end of a line of performers, who engages in comic dialogue.

end•most ['ɛnd,moust] *adj.* nearest to the end; last; farthest.

end•note ['ɛnd,nout] *n.* a footnote placed at the end of a paper, book, etc. rather than at the bottom of the page.

endo– *combining form.* within; inside; inner: *endocarp, endoderm, endogamy.* ⟨< Gk. *endo-* < *endon*⟩

en•do•blast ['ɛndou,blæst] *n.* endoderm. ⟨< *endo-* + Gk. *blastos* sprout⟩

en•do•car•di•al [,ɛndou'kɑrdiəl] *adj.* **1** in the heart. **2** of or having to do with the endocardium.

en•do•car•di•um [,ɛndou'kɑrdiəm] *n.* the delicate, smooth membrane that lines the chambers of the heart. ⟨< NL *endocardium* + Gk. *endon* within + *kardia* heart⟩

en•do•carp ['ɛndou,kɑrp] *n. Botany.* the inner layer of a fruit or ripened ovary of a plant. A peach stone is an endocarp. ⟨< *endo-* + Gk. *karpos* fruit⟩

en•do•cra•ni•um [,ɛndou'kreiniəm] *n.* the structure below the brain in an insect's head capsule. ⟨< Gk. *endon* within + *cranium*⟩

en•do•crine ['ɛndou,kraɪn], ['ɛndoukrɪn], *or* ['ɛndou,krin] *adj., n. —adj.* **1** producing secretions that pass directly into the blood or lymph instead of into a duct. The thyroid is an endocrine gland. **2** of or having to do with the endocrine glands or the hormones they secrete. Compare EXOCRINE.
—n. **1** ENDOCRINE GLAND. **2** its secretion. ⟨< *endo-* + Gk. *krinein* separate⟩

endocrine gland any of various ductless glands that secrete hormones that influence other organs in the body.

en•do•cri•nol•o•gy [,ɛndoukrə'nɒlədʒi] *n.* the study of endocrine glands. **—,en•do•cri'nol•o•gist,** *n.*

en•do•derm ['ɛndou,dɜrm] *n. Biology.* the inner layer of cells formed during development of animal embryos. The lining of the organs of the digestive system develops from the endoderm. ⟨< *endo-* + Gk. *derma* skin⟩ **—,en•do'der•mal** or **,en•do'der•mic,** *adj.*

en•do•der•mis [,ɛndou'dɜrmɪs] *n. Botany.* in stems and roots, the deepest layer of cortex cells.

en•do•don•tics [,ɛndou'dɒntɪks] *n.* (*used with a singular verb*) the branch of dentistry dealing with the diagnosis and treatment of disorders of the pulp of the teeth. ⟨< NL *endodontia* < Gk. *endo-* within + *odōn* tooth. 19c.⟩
—,en•do'don•tic, *adj.*

en•do•don•tist [,ɛndou'dɒntɪst] *n.* a dentist who specializes in endodontics; a root-canal specialist.

en•do•en•zyme [,ɛndou'ɛnzaɪm] *n.* an enzyme that operates within a cell.

end of steel *Cdn.* **1** the limit to which tracks have been laid for a railway. **2** a town at the end of a railway line; the terminus of a northern railway: *A road will soon connect us with the end of steel.*

en•dog•a•mous [ɛn'dɒgəməs] *adj.* of or having to do with endogamy. Also, **endogamic** [,ɛndou'gæmɪk].

en•dog•a•my [ɛn'dɒgəmi] *n.* **1** the custom of marrying within one's own group, etc. **2** pollination of a flower by pollen from another flower on the same plant.

en•dog•e•nous [ɛn'dɒdʒənəs] *adj. Biology.* **1** growing from the inside, originating within. Compare EXOGENOUS. **2** having to do with the nitrogenous parts of cells and tissues and their growth.

en•dog•e•ny [ɛn'dɒdʒəni] *n. Biology.* a growing from within, as in cell formation.

en•do•lymph ['ɛndou,lɪmf] *n.* the fluid of the inner ear.

en•do•me•tri•o•sis [,ɛndou,mitri'ousɪs] *n.* inflammation of the endometrium.

en•do•me•tri•um [,ɛndou'mitriəm] *n., pl* **en•do•me•tri•a** [-triə]. the mucous membrane lining the uterus. ⟨< *endo-* + Gk. *metra* uterus⟩ **—,en•do'me•tri•al,** *adj.*

en•do•morph ['ɛndou,mɔrf] *n.* **1** a human body type characterized by a heavy frame, relatively short stature with short limbs, and the capacity for great muscular development. It is one of three basic body types. Compare ECTOMORPH, MESOMORPH. **2** a person having such a body structure. **3** a mineral included within another, as tourmaline is in quartz. ⟨< *endo-* + Gk. *morphe* form⟩

en•do•mor•phic [,ɛndou'mɔrfɪk] *adj.* of, having to do with, or being an endomorph.

en•do•morph•ism [,ɛndou'mɔrfɪzəm] *n.* the change resulting from the cooling of igneous rock as it joins the wall rock of a lode or vein.

end–on ['ɛnd 'ɒn] *adj.* of or on the end: *an end-on collision.*

en•do•pa•ra•site [,ɛndou'pærə,səit] *or* [,ɛndou'pɛrə,səit] *n.* a parasite that lives within an organ, such as a tapeworm.

en•do•pep•ti•dase [,ɛndou'pɛptə,deis] *n.* an enzyme that causes the hydrolysis of peptide bonds inside a peptide chain. ⟨< Gk. *endon* within + *peptide* + *-ase* (abstracted from *diastase*)⟩

en•doph•a•gous [ɛn'dɒfəgəs] *adj.* of some parasites, nourishing themselves from the inside of an organism. ⟨< *endo-* + Gk. *-phagos* < *phagein* to eat⟩

en•do•phyte ['ɛndou,fəit] *n.* a plant that grows within another plant. Also, **entophyte. —,en•do'phyt•ic** [-'fɪtɪk], *n.*

en•do•plasm ['ɛndou,plæzəm] *n. Biology.* the inner portion of the cytoplasm of a cell. ⟨< *endo-* + Gk. *plasma* something formed or moulded⟩ **—,en•do'plas•mic,** *adj.*

endoplasmic reticulum the network of membranes inside most living cells.

end organ the end of a working nerve, sensory or motor, in tissue.

en•dor•phin [ɛn'dɔrfɪn] *n.* in the central nervous system, any polypeptide produced internally to relieve pain. ⟨< F *endorphine* < *endo(gène)* endogenous + *(m)orphine*⟩

en•dor•sa•tion [ˌɛndɔr'seiʃən] *n. Cdn.* approval; support: *The mayor's proposals received wide endorsation.*

en•dorse [ɛn'dɔrs] *v.* **-dorsed, -dors•ing. 1** write one's name, instructions, etc. on the back of (a cheque, money order, or other document): *She had to endorse the cheque before the bank would cash it.* **2** approve; support: *Parents heartily endorsed the plan for a school playground.* **3** publicly and officially declare that one approves or supports. Also, **indorse.** ⟨alteration of ME *endoss(n)* < OF *endosser* < *en-* on + *dos* back < L *dorsum*⟩ **—en'dors•a•ble,** *adj.* **—en'dors•er,** *n.*

en•dor•see [ɛnˌdɔr'si] *or* [ˌɛndɔr'si] *n.* a person to whom a cheque, note, or other document is assigned by endorsement. Also, **indorsee.**

en•dorse•ment [ɛn'dɔrsmənt] *n.* **1** the act of writing on the back of a cheque or other document. **2** a name, comment, or instructions, etc. written on the back of a cheque or other document. **3** approval; support: *The proposal for a new stadium has our endorsement.* **4** an additional provision or clause in an insurance contract by which the coverage described in the contract may be increased or diminished. **5** a contract under which a celebrity, for a fee, publicly endorses a product or service or its supplier. Also, **indorsement.**

en•do•scope ['ɛndouˌskoup] *n.* a slender instrument for examining a hollow body organ. **—ˌen•do'scop•ic** [-'skɒpɪk], *adj.* **—en'dos•co•py** [ɛn'dɒskəpi], *n.* **—en'dos•co•pist** [ɛn'dɒskəpɪst], *n.*

en•do•skel•e•ton [ˌɛndou'skɛlətən] *n.* the internal supporting structure of all vertebrates and some other groups of animals such as starfish, sea urchins, and some varieties of coral. Compare EXOSKELETON. **—ˌen•do'skel•e•tal,** *adj.*

en•dos•mo•sis [ˌɛndɒz'mousɪs] *or* [ˌɛndɒs'mousɪs] *n. Physical chemistry.* **1** reverse osmosis from the outside to the inside. **2** the flow of a liquid to one of greater concentration. **—ˌen•dos'mot•ic** [ˌɛndɒs'mɒtɪk], *adj.* **—ˌen•dos'mot•i•cal•ly,** *adv.*

en•do•sperm ['ɛndouˌspɜrm] *n. Botany.* nourishment for the embryo enclosed with it in the seed of a plant. See EMBRYO for picture.

en•do•spore ['ɛndouˌspɔr] *n.* **1** an asexual spore as formed by certain bacteria. **2** the inner wall of such a spore.

en•dos•te•um [ɛn'dɒstiəm] *n.* the membrane lining the medullary hollow of a bone. ⟨< *endo-* + Gk. *osteon* bone⟩ **—en'dos•te•al,** *adj.*

en•do•the•ci•um [ˌɛndou'θiʃiəm] *or* [ˌɛndou'θisiəm] *n. Botany.* **1** the lining of the hollow of an anther. **2** the inner layer of a capsule of a moss. ⟨< *endo-* + NL *thecium* case < Gk. *thekion*⟩

en•do•the•li•um [ˌɛndou'θiliəm] *n.* a layer of flat cells lining vessels that contain fluid, such as lymph vessels and veins. ⟨< *endo-* + *(epi)thelial*⟩ **—ˌen•do'the•li•al,** *adj.*

en•do•ther•mal [ˌɛndou'θɜrməl] *adj.* of an animal, as a mammal or bird, having a constant body temperature; warm-blooded. Compare ECTOTHERMAL.

en•do•therm•ic [ˌɛndou'θɜrmɪk] *adj.* causing the absorption of heat.

en•do•tox•in [ˌɛndou'tɒksɪn] *n.* a toxin released when the cell producing it in a micro-organism is destroyed.

en•dow [ɛn'daʊ] *v.* **1** give money or property to provide an income for: *The rich man endowed the college he had attended.* **2** furnish at birth; provide with some ability, quality, or talent; favour: *Nature endowed her with both beauty and brains.* **3** attribute certain qualities to (something not actually having them): *endow storms with anger.* ⟨ME < OF *endouer* < *en-* in + *douer* endow < L *dotare*⟩ **—en'dow•er,** *n.*

en•dow•ment [ɛn'daʊmənt] *n.* **1** the money or property given to provide an income: *This college has a large endowment.* **2** a gift from birth; ability; talent: *A good sense of rhythm is a natural endowment.* **3** the act of endowing; a state of being endowed.

endowment insurance life insurance that is guaranteed to the beneficiary or to the holder after the date of maturity.

end•pa•per ['ɛndˌpeipər] *n.* a folded sheet of paper half of which is pasted to the inside of either cover of a book, the other half acting as a flyleaf.

end plate the terminal of a motor nerve activating muscles.

end product 1 the part remaining after something is processed. **2** *Nuclear physics.* the last stable member of a series of isotopes, each produced by the radioactive decay of the preceding isotope.

end rhyme the rhyme at the ends of lines of verse.

end run *Football.* a play in which the ball carrier tries to score a touchdown by outflanking the opposite defensive players.

end•stopped ['ɛndˌstɒpt] *adj.* of a line of verse, having the sense end with the end of the line.

end table a small table set beside a chair or at either end of a chesterfield.

en•due [ɛn'dju] *or* [ɛn'du] *v.* **-dued, -du•ing. 1** provide with a quality or power; furnish; supply: *The wisest man is not endued with perfect wisdom.* **2** put on; don. **3** clothe. Also, **indue.** ⟨ME < OF *enduire* < L *inducere* lead into; confused with L *induere* put on⟩

en•dur•able [ɛn'djʊrəbəl] *adj.* **1** likely to last. **2** that may be tolerated.

en•dur•ance [ɛn'djʊrəns] *or* [ɛn'dʊrəns] *n.* **1** the power to last or keep on: *A person must have great endurance to run in a marathon.* **2** the power to put up with, bear, or stand: *Her endurance of the pain was remarkable.* **3** an act or instance of enduring pain, hardship, etc. **4** a period of time.

en•dure [ɛn'djʊr] *or* [ɛn'dʊr] *v.* **-dured, -dur•ing. 1** keep on; last: *These statues have endured for a thousand years.* **2** undergo; bear; tolerate: *Those brave people endured much pain.* ⟨ME < OF *endurer* < L *indurare* make hard < *in-* in (causative) + *durus* hard⟩ **—en'dur•a•ble,** *adj.* **—en'dur•a•bly,** *adv.* **—en'dur•er,** *n.*
☛ *Syn.* **2.** See note at BEAR[1].

en•dur•ing [ɛn'djʊrɪŋ] *or* [ɛn'dʊrɪŋ] *adj., v.* —*adj.* lasting; permanent.
—*v.* ppr. of ENDURE. **—en'dur•ing•ly,** *adv.*
☛ *Syn.* See note at LASTING.

end use the particular function that a manufactured product ultimately serves or to which it is limited.

end user *Computer technology.* a person who makes use of computer systems created by others but is often not personally skilled at developing them. Also, **end-user.** Also called **user.** **—'end-'us•er,** *adj.*

end•ways ['ɛndˌweiz] *adv.* **1** on end; upright. **2** with the end forward; in the direction of the end. **3** lengthwise. **4** end to end.

end•wise ['ɛndˌwaɪz] *adv.* endways.

En•dym•i•on [ɛn'dɪmiən] *n. Greek mythology.* a beautiful youth loved by Selene, the goddess of the moon.

end zone 1 *Football.* the part of the field between each goal line and the corresponding end of the field. **2** *Hockey.* the ice between each blue line and the corresponding end of the rink.

–ene a suffix indicating lack of saturation of an organic compound: *ethylene.* ⟨< L *-enus*⟩

ENE or **E.N.E.** east-northeast, a direction halfway between east and northeast.

en•e•ma ['ɛnəmə] *n., pl.* **-mas, -ma•ta** [-mətə]. **1** an injection of liquid into the rectum to flush the bowels. **2** the liquid or apparatus used. ⟨< Gk. *enema* < *en-* in + *hienai* send⟩

en•e•my ['ɛnəmi] *n., pl.* **-mies 1** a person or group that hates and tries to harm another. **2** a hostile force, nation, fleet, army, or air force; person, ship, etc. of a hostile nation. **3** anything harmful: *Frost is an enemy of plants.* **4** (*adjl.*) of an enemy: *enemy planes.* ⟨ME < OF *enemi* < L *inimicus* < *in-* not + *amicus* friendly⟩
☛ *Syn. n.* **1, 2. Enemy,** FOE = a hostile person, group, country, army, etc. **Enemy** is the common and general word, applying to any person or group who wants or tries to harm another person or group in any way: *Because of his unfair methods that businessman has many enemies.* **Foe,** now chiefly poetic or literary, means a very dangerous and actively opposed enemy.

enemy alien an alien living in a country at war with the alien's own country.

en•er•get•ic [ˌɛnər'dʒɛtɪk] *adj.* **1** full of energy; eager to work. **2** full of force; active. **—ˌen•er'get•i•cal•ly,** *adv.*

en•er•get•ics [ˌɛnər'dʒɛtɪks] *n. sing.* the branch of physics dealing with energy. **ˌen•er•ge'tis•tic,** *adj.* **—ˌen•er'get•i•cist,** *n.*

en•er•gid ['ɛnərˌdʒɪd] *or* [ɛ'nɜrdʒɪd] *n. Biology.* a nucleus surrounded by cytoplasm, that is not a cell.

en•er•gize ['ɛnərˌdʒaɪz] *v.* **-gized, -giz•ing. 1** give energy to; make active. **2** *Electricity.* charge.

en•er•giz•er ['ɛnərˌdʒaɪzər] *n.* **1** any one of several drugs used to give energy or to relieve severe mental depression. **2** a device that stores chemical energy and can operate small mechanisms.

en•er•gu•men [ˌɛnər'gjumən] *n.* **1** a fanatic. **2** one possessed by the devil. ⟨< LL *energumenos* < Gk. *energoumenos,* passive participle of *energin* work on⟩

en•er•gy ['ɛnərdʒi] *n., pl.* **-gies. 1** active strength or force; healthy power; vigour: *Young people usually have more energy than old people.* **2** strength; force; power. **3** *Physics.* the capacity for doing work, such as lifting or moving an object. Energy is measured in joules. **4** natural resources such as oil, coal, hydro-electric power needed to make things work, especially industrial machinery, heating and lighting systems: *We must conserve energy.* ⟨< LL < Gk. *energeia* < *energos* active < *en-* in + *ergon* work⟩

energy level *Physics.* one of a measurable series of states of energy in which matter exists.

en•er•vate *v.* ['ɛnər,veit]; *adj.* [ɪ'nɜrvɪt] *v.* **-vat•ed, -vat•ing,** *adj.* *—v.* lessen the vigour or strength of; weaken: *A hot, damp climate enervates people who are not used to it.*
—adj. devitalized; weakened; enervated. ⟨< L *enervare* < *ex-* away + *nervus* sinew, nerve⟩ **—,en•er'va•tion,** *n.* **—'en•er,va•tor,** *n.*

en fa•mille [ɑ̃fa'mij] *French.* with one's family; at home; informally.

en•fant [ɑ̃'fɑ̃] *n. French.* child.

en•fant ter•ri•ble [ɑ̃'fɑ̃'tɛ'ʀibl] *French.* **1** a child whose behaviour, questions, remarks, etc. embarrass older people. **2** a person who shocks or embarrasses the establishment by flouting convention.

en•fee•ble [ɛn'fibəl] *v.* **-bled, -bling.** make feeble; weaken. **—en'fee•ble•ment,** *n.* **—en'fee•bler,** *n.*

en•feoff [ɛn'fif] *v.* give (someone) land freehold.

en•fet•ter [ɛn'fɛtər] *v.* fasten with or as if with fetters.

en•fi•lade [,ɛnfə'leid] *or* [,ɒnfə'lɑd]; *French,* [ɑ̃fi'lad] *n., v.* **-lad•ed, -lad•ing.** *—n.* **1** gunfire directed from the side at a line of troops or a position held by them. **2** the placing of troops under enfilade.
—v. fire guns at (a line of troops or the position held by them) from the side. ⟨< F *enfilade* < *enfiler* thread, pierce < *en-* on + *fil* thread < L *filum*⟩

en•fleur•age [,ɒnflə'rɑʒ]; *French,* [ɑ̃flœ'ʀaʒ] *n.* in making perfume, the method of endowing odourless oils with the fragrance of flowers.

en•flu•rane ['ɛnflə,rein] *n.* a drug used as an inhalant anesthetic.

en•fold [ɛn'fould] *v.* **1** fold in; wrap up: *The old lady was enfolded in a shawl.* **2** embrace; clasp: *The mother enfolded her baby in her arms.* Also, **infold. —en'fold•ment,** *n.*

en•force [ɛn'fɔrs] *v.* **-forced, -forc•ing. 1** force obedience to; put into force: *Police and judges enforce the laws.* **2** force; compel: *The robbers enforced obedience to their demand by threats of violence.* **3** urge with force; emphasize: *The teacher enforced the principle by examples.* ⟨ME < OF *enforcier,* ult. < L *in-* + *fortis* strong⟩ **—en'force•a•ble,** *adj.* **—en'forc•er,** *n.*

en•force•ment [ɛn'fɔrsmənt] *n.* an enforcing; putting into force: *Strict enforcement of the laws against speeding will reduce automobile accidents.*

en•fran•chise [ɛn'fræntʃaɪz] *v.* **-chised, -chis•ing. 1** give the right to vote: *For federal elections, Canadian citizens are enfranchised at the age of 18.* **2** set free; release from slavery or restraint. **—en'fran•chis•er,** *n.*

en•fran•chise•ment [ɛn'fræntʃɪzmənt] *n.* an enfranchising or being enfranchised.

eng. 1 engine. **2** engineer; engineering. **3** engraving; engraved; engraver.

Eng. 1 England; English. **2** Engineer. **3** engine.

ENG electronic news gathering; the reporting of current events, often for live coverage, by means of portable television cameras, tape recorders, transmission equipment, etc.

en•gage [ɛn'geidʒ] *v.* **-gaged, -gag•ing. 1** keep busy; occupy: *Work engages much of her time.* **2** keep oneself busy; be occupied; be active; take part: *He engages in politics. His wife engages in social work.* **3** hire; employ: *She engaged a cook for the summer.* **4** arrange to secure for occupation or use; reserve: *We engaged a room in the hotel.* **5** bind (oneself or another) by a promise or contract; pledge: *I will engage to be there on time.* **6** promise or pledge to marry: *Nico and Olga are engaged. Olga is engaged to Nico.* **7** catch and hold; attract: *Bright colours engaged the baby's attention.* **8** fit into; lock together; interlock: *The teeth of one gear engage with the teeth of another. The teeth engage each other.* **9** come into contact with in battle; attack: *Our soldiers engaged the enemy.* **10** secure the participation of (someone) in a conversation or activity: *He resisted all attempts to engage him in conversation.* **11** activate; make (system or machine, or part of one) operative.
engage in, a take part in; be active in: *She engages in many sports.* **b** occupy with: *They were engaged in repairing the car.* ⟨< F *engager* < *en gage* under pledge⟩ **—en'gag•er,** *n.*

en•ga•gé¹ [ɑ̃ga'ʒe] *n. Cdn. French.* formerly, one hired by a fur company for inland service in the trade. ⟨< Cdn.F < F *engagé* enlisted⟩

en•ga•gé² [ɑ̃ga'ʒe] *adj. French.* **1** involved; not aloof. **2** of art, artists, intellectuals, etc., committed to a cause or ideal, usually political: *Sartre was an engagé writer.* Guernica *is an engagé painting.*

en•gaged [ɛn'geidʒd] *adj., v. —adj.* **1** promised or pledged to marry. **2** busy; occupied: *Engaged in conversation, they did not see us.* **3** taken for use or work; hired. **4** fitted together. **5** involved in a fight or battle. **6** in operation. **7** booked; reserved.
—v. pt. and pp. of ENGAGE.

en•gage•ment [ɛn'geidʒmənt] *n.* **1** the act of engaging. **2** the fact or condition of being engaged. **3** a promise; pledge: *An honest person fulfils all her engagements.* **4** the time between becoming pledged to marry and the actual wedding: *They got married after an engagement of six months.* **5** a meeting with someone at a certain time; appointment. **6** a scheduled performance of some kind: *a speaking engagement at the Business Luncheon. The band had several engagements in local nightclubs.* **7** the period of being hired; time of use or work. **8** a fight; battle.
☛ *Syn.* **7.** See note at BATTLE.

en•gag•ing [ɛn'geidʒɪŋ] *adj., v. —adj.* very attractive; pleasing; charming.
—v. ppr. of ENGAGE. **—en'gag•ing•ly,** *adv.* **—en'gag•ing•ness,** *n.*

en garde [ɑ̃'gaʀd] *French. Fencing.* a warning to an opponent to prepare for action.

en•gar•land [ɛn'gɑrlənd] *v.* encircle with or as if with garlands.

En•gel•mann spruce ['ɛŋgəlmən] **1** a tall spruce tree (*Picea engelmannii*) found throughout the interior mountain regions of British Columbia and Alberta, having oval cones and curved, bluish-green needles often covered with a whitish, powdery coating called a bloom. **2** the light, soft wood of this tree. ⟨< George *Engelmann* (1809-1884), a German-born physicist and botanist⟩

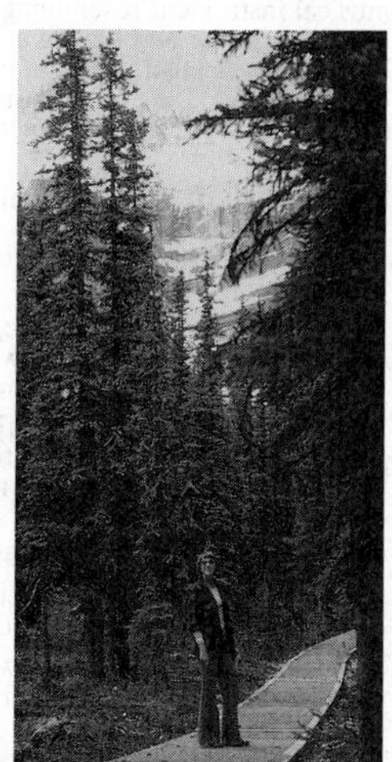
Engelmann spruce

en•gen•der [ɛn'dʒɛndər] *v.* bring into existence; produce; cause: *Filth engenders disease.* ⟨ME < OF *engendrer* < L *ingenerare* < *in-* in + *generare* create⟩

en•gine ['ɛndʒən] *n.* **1** a machine that applies power to some work, especially a machine that can start others moving. **2** a machine that pulls a railway train. **3** a machine; device; instrument: *Those big guns are engines of war.* **4** FIRE ENGINE. ⟨ME < OF *engin* < L *ingenium* inborn qualities, talent < *in-* in + *gen-,* root of *gignere* create, produce, beget. Related to GENIUS.⟩

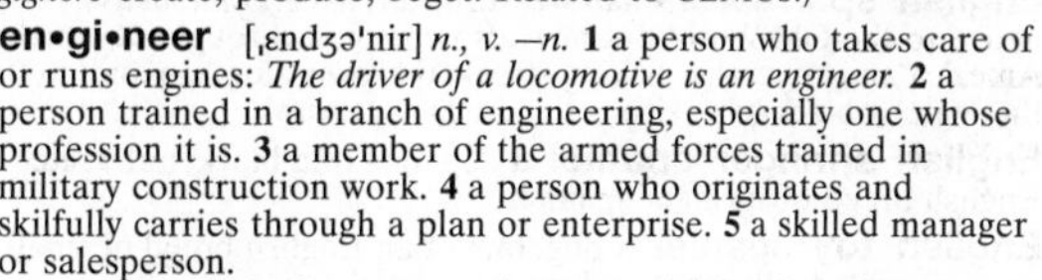

en•gi•neer [,ɛndʒə'nir] *n., v. —n.* **1** a person who takes care of or runs engines: *The driver of a locomotive is an engineer.* **2** a person trained in a branch of engineering, especially one whose profession it is. **3** a member of the armed forces trained in military construction work. **4** a person who originates and skilfully carries through a plan or enterprise. **5** a skilled manager or salesperson.
—v. **1** plan, build, direct, or work as a professional engineer. **2** manage; guide: *Although many opposed his plan, he engineered it through to final approval.*

en•gi•neer•ing [,ɛndʒə'nirɪŋ] *n., v. —n* **1** the application of science to such practical uses as the design and building of structures and machines, and the making of many products of modern technology: *Knowledge of engineering is needed in building railways, bridges, and dams.* **2** the act of managing, contriving, or manoeuvring.
—v. ppr. of ENGINEER.

engine house a station for a fire engine.

en•gine•ry ['ɛndʒənri] *n.* engines; machines.

en•gird [ɛn'gɜrd] *v.* **-girt** or **-gird•ed, -gird•ing.** encircle.

en•gla•cial [ɛn'gleiʃəl] *adj. Geology.* within the ice of a glacier: *an englacial river.*

Eng•land ['ɪŋglənd] *n.* a country occupying the largest of the British Isles which, together with Wales and Scotland, constitutes Great Britain.

Eng•lish ['ɪŋglɪʃ] *n., adj., v.* —*n.* **1 the English,** *pl.* **a** the people of England. **b** *Cdn.* English Canadians. **2** the English language, belonging to the West Germanic branch of the Indo-European language family; it is the traditional and official language of England, one of the two official languages of Canada, and also the official language of most other Commonwealth countries and the United States. It is usually divided into three main historical periods: Old English or Anglo-Saxon (before 1100), Middle English (about 1100-1500), and Modern English (from about 1500). **3** a large size of type formerly used in printing, about equal to 14 point. **4** Often, **english,** a spinning motion imparted to a ball by hitting on one side of its centre.
—*adj.* **1** of or having to do with England, its people, or the language English. **2** *Cdn.* of or having to do with Canadian English or English Canadians.
—*v.* **1** translate into or express in English. **2** Often, **english,** give a spinning motion to (a billiard ball, etc.). ⟨OE *Englisc* < *Engle* the English people⟩ **—'Eng•lish•ness,** *n.*

English Canadian a Canadian of English ancestry or one whose principal language is English, especially as opposed to French. **—'Eng•lish–Ca'na•di•an,** *adj.*

English cocker spaniel a breed of hunting dog, resembling the cocker spaniel but larger, as an adult weighing between 12-15 kg.

English horn a wooden musical instrument resembling an oboe, but larger and having a lower tone. ⟨a mistranslation of F *cor anglé* angled, cornered horn, *anglé* being confused with *anglais* English⟩

An English horn

Eng•lish•ism ['ɪŋglɪˌʃɪzəm] *n.* **1** an attachment to what is English. **2** an English custom or expression.

English ivy a climbing vine (*Hedera helix*), an evergreen with yellow flowers and black berries.

Eng•lish•man ['ɪŋglɪʃmən] *n., pl.* **-men. 1** a man who is a native or inhabitant of England. **2** a man of English descent.

English muffin a muffin of yeast dough, cooked on a griddle.

Eng•lish•ry ['ɪŋglɪʃri] *n.* **1** the condition of being English by birth. **2** the part of a population having English ancestry.

English saddle a saddle with a padded leather seat and side flaps. It does not have the horn of the Western saddle, and the stirrups are kept short.

English setter a breed of setter having black and white markings and, sometimes, tan spots.

English sonnet ELIZABETHAN SONNET.

English sparrow a small weaverbird (*Passer domesticus*) native to the Old World but now also common throughout North America and Australia, having streaked brown plumage and, in the male, a black bib. Also called **house sparrow.**

English springer spaniel a dog, one of a black and white, English breed of springer spaniel.

English toy spaniel a dog, one of an English breed of small spaniels with a silky coat and rounded head.

English walnut 1 a Eurasian walnut tree (*Juglans regia*) long cultivated in England before being introduced to North and South America, valued as an ornamental tree and for its edible nuts and its timber. **2** the nut of this tree, often used pickled.

Eng•lish•wom•an ['ɪŋglɪʃˌwʊmən] *n., pl.* **-wom•en. 1** a woman who is a native or inhabitant of England. **2** a woman of English descent.

en•gorge [ɛn'gɔrdʒ] *v.* **-gorged, -gorg•ing. 1** swallow greedily. **2** glut; gorge; feed greedily. **3** *Medicine.* congest with blood or other fluid. **—en'gorge•ment,** *n.*

engr. 1 engineer. **2** engraved; engraver; engraving.

en•graft [ɛn'græft] *v.* **1** insert or graft a shoot from (one tree) or plant into or on another: *Peach trees can be engrafted on plum trees.* **2** add permanently; implant: *Honesty and thrift are engrafted in her character.* Also, **ingraft.**

en•grail [ɛn'greil] *v.* **1** decorate (an edge) with notches or ridges. **2** decorate the outer edge of (a medal or coin) with raised marks. ⟨< ME *engrelen* (only in pp.) < OF *engresler* < *en-* in + *gresle* slender < L *gracilis* scanty⟩

en•gram ['ɛngræm] *n.* **1** *Biology.* the permanent alteration caused by a stimulus in a protoplasm. **2** the trace, in neural tissue, of an individual memory. **—en'gram•mic,** *adj.*

en•grave [ɛn'greiv] *v.* **-graved, -grav•ing. 1** cut in; carve artistically: *The jeweller engraved the boy's initials on the back of the watch.* **2** decorate by engraving: *Will you have the watch engraved?* **3** *Printing.* **a** cut in lines on a metal plate, block of wood, etc. for printing. **b** print from such a plate, block, etc. **4** impress deeply; fix firmly: *His mother's face was engraved on his memory.* **5** photoengrave. ⟨< *en-*[1] + *grave*[3]⟩

en•grav•er [ɛn'greivər] *n.* a person who engraves metal plates, blocks of wood, etc. for printing.

engraver beetle a beetle that lives in the trunks of trees and engraves channels that weaken the tree.

en•grav•ing [ɛn'greivɪŋ] *n., v.* —*n.* **1** the art of an engraver; cutting lines in metal plates, blocks of wood, etc. for printing. **2** a picture printed from an engraved plate, block, etc. **3** an engraved plate, block, etc.; engraved design or pattern.
—*v.* ppr. of ENGRAVE.

en•gross [ɛn'grous] *v.* **1** occupy wholly; take up all the attention of: *She was engrossed in a story.* **2** copy or write in large letters; write a beautiful copy of. **3** write out in formal style; express in legal form. **4** *Business.* buy all or much of (the supply of some commodity) so as to control prices. ⟨(defs. 1, 4) < *in gross* < F *en gros* in a lump, in large amounts; (defs. 2, 3) < AF *engrosser* < *en-* in + *grosse* large writing, document⟩ **—en'gross•er,** *n.* **—en'gross•ment,** *n.*

en•gros•sing [ɛn'grousɪŋ] *adj., v.* —*adj.* **1** absorbing. **2** controlling.
—*v.* ppr. of ENGROSS.

en•gulf [ɛn'gʌlf] *v.* swallow up; overwhelm; submerge: *A wave engulfed the small boat.* Also, **ingulf.**

en•hance [ɛn'hæns] *v.* **-hanced, -hanc•ing.** improve; add to; heighten: *The gardens enhanced the beauty of the house.* ⟨ME < AF *enhauncer* raise, ult. < L *altus* high. Related to HAWSER.⟩ **—en'hance•ment,** *n.* **—en'hanc•er,** *n.*

en•har•mon•ic [ˌɛnhɑr'mɒnɪk] *adj. Music.* **1** having to do with or designating a scale, a style of music, or an instrument employing intervals smaller than a semitone, especially quarter tones. **2** of different notes on the scale that have the same tone or key on an instrument. *Example*: *C sharp and D flat.* **—ˌen•har'mon•i•cal•ly,** *adv.*

en haut [ɑ̃'o] *French.* above; on high.

e•nig•ma [ɪ'nɪgmə] *n.* **1** a puzzling statement; riddle: *To most of the audience the philosopher seemed to speak in enigmas.* **2** a baffling or puzzling problem, situation, person, etc.: *The queer behaviour of the child was an enigma even to her parents.* ⟨< L < Gk. *ainigma* < *ainissesthai* speak darkly < *ainos* fable⟩

en•ig•mat•ic [ˌɛnɪg'mætɪk] *or* [ˌinɪg'mætɪk] *adj.* like a riddle; baffling; puzzling; mysterious. Also, **enigmatical.** **—ˌen•ig'mat•i•cal•ly,** *adv.*

en•jamb•ment or **en•jambe•ment** [ɛn'dʒæmmənt] *or* [ɛn'dʒæmbmənt]; *French,* [ɑ̃ʒɑ̃b'mɑ̃] *n. Prosody.* the continuation of a sentence without pause from one line or couplet to the next. ⟨< F *enjambement* < MF *enjamber* encroach, stride < *en-* on + OF *jambe* leg < L *gamba*⟩

en•join [ɛn'dʒɔɪn] *v.* **1** order; direct; urge: *Parents enjoin good behaviour on their children.* **2** *Law.* issue an authoritative command. Through an injunction a judge may enjoin a person not to do some act. ⟨ME < OF *enjoindre* < L *injungere* attack, charge < *in-* on + *jungere* join⟩ **—en'join•er,** *n.* **—en'join•ment,** *n.*

en•joy [ɛn'dʒɔɪ] *v.* **1** have or use with joy; be happy with; take pleasure in. **2** have as an advantage or benefit: *She enjoyed good health.* **3** be happy; have a good time (*used with a reflexive pronoun*): *Did you enjoy yourself at the party?* ⟨ME < OF *enjoir* < *en-* in (intensive) + *joir* rejoice < L *gaudere*⟩ **—en'joy•er,** *n.*

en•joy•a•ble [ɛn'dʒɔɪəbəl] *adj.* capable of being enjoyed; giving enjoyment; pleasant. **—en'joy•a•bly,** *adv.* **—en'joy•a•ble•ness,** *n.*

en•joy•ment [ɛn'dʒɔɪmənt] *n.* **1** the act of enjoying. **2** something enjoyed. **3** joy; happiness; pleasure. **4** the condition of having as an advantage or benefit; possession; use: *Laws protect the enjoyment of our rights.*

en•keph•a•lin [ɛn'kɛfəlɪn] *n.* an endorphin. ⟨< Gk. *enkephalon* brain + E *-in*⟩

en•kin•dle [ɛn'kɪndəl] *v.* **-dled, -dling. 1** set on fire. **2** arouse; excite; stir up. **3** light up; brighten.

en•lace [ɛn'leis] *v.* **-laced, -lac•ing. 1** bind or encircle as with lace. **2** wind about; encircle; enfold. **3** twine together; interlace. **4** drape with lace or netting. ⟨< F *enlacer*⟩

en•large [ɛn'lɑrdʒ] *v.* **-larged, -larg•ing. 1** make or become larger; increase in size: *Enlarge the photograph.* **2** talk or write in greater detail; elaborate (*used with* **on** *or* **upon**): *The reporter asked him to enlarge on his earlier statement.* ⟨ME < OF *enlarger* < *en-* in (causative) + *large* large < L *largus* copious⟩ **—en'larg•er,** *n.*

☛ *Syn.* **1.** See note at INCREASE.

en•large•ment [ɛn'lɑrdʒmənt] *n.* **1** an enlarging or being enlarged. **2** anything that is an enlarged form of something else. **3** *Photography.* a print that is made larger than the negative. **4** anything that enlarges something else; an addition.

en•light•en [ɛn'ləitən] *v.* **1** instruct. **2** give the light of truth and knowledge to; make free from prejudice, ignorance, etc. **—en'light•en•er,** *n.*

en•light•en•ment [ɛn'ləitənmənt] *n.* **1** an enlightening of the mind. **2** the fact or state of being enlightened. **3 Enlightenment,** a philosophical movement in Europe in the 18th century, characterized by rationalism, by scepticism about existing political and social beliefs, and by emphasis on intellectual freedom.

☛ *Syn.* See note at EDUCATION.

en•list [ɛn'lɪst] *v.* **1** get (someone) to join a branch of the armed forces. **2** enrol in some branch of the armed forces. **3** induce to join in some cause or undertaking; secure the help or support of: *The mayor enlisted the churches of our city to work for more parks.* **4** join in some cause or undertaking; give help or support. **5** ask for and get (help, etc.): *The mayor enlisted the support of the churches.* ⟨< *en-*[1] + list[1]⟩ **—en'list•er,** *n.*

en•list•ment [ɛn'lɪstmənt] *n.* **1** an enlisting or being enlisted. **2** the time for which a person enlists.

en•liv•en [ɛn'laɪvən] *v.* make lively, active, gay, or cheerful: *The speaker enlivened her talk with humour. Bright curtains enliven a room.* **—en'liv•en•er,** *n.* **—en'liv•en•ing•ly,** *adv.* **—en'liv•en•ment,** *n.*

en masse [ˌɒn 'mæs] *or* [ˌɛn 'mæs]; *French,* [ɑ̃'mas] in a group; all together. ⟨< F⟩

en•mesh [ɛn'mɛʃ] *v.* catch in or as if in a net; enclose in meshes; entangle. **—en'mesh•ment,** *n.*

en•mi•ty ['ɛnməti] *n., pl.* **-ties.** the feeling that enemies have for each other; hatred. ⟨ME < OF *ennemistie* < VL < L *inimicus.* See ENEMY.⟩

en•ne•ad ['ɛniˌæd] *or* ['ɛniəd] *n.* a group of nine people or things. ⟨< G *enneas, enneados* < *ennea* nine⟩

en•no•ble [ɛn'noubəl] *v.* **-bled, -bling. 1** give a title or rank of nobility to; raise to the rank of noble. **2** raise in the respect of others; dignify; exalt: *A good deed ennobles the person who does it.* **3** make finer or more noble in nature: *Her character had been ennobled through suffering.* **—en'no•ble•ment,** *n.* **—en'no•bler,** *n.*

en•nui [ɒn'wi]; *French,* [ɑ̃'nyi] *n.* a feeling of weariness and discontent from lack of occupation or interest; boredom. ⟨< F. Related to ANNOY.⟩

en•ol ['inɒl] *or* ['inoul] *n. Chemistry.* an organic compound consisting of a hydroxyl group and two carbon atoms. ⟨< *-ene* + *-ol*⟩ **—e'nol•ic,** *adj.*

e•nor•mi•ty [ɪ'nɔrməti] *n., pl.* **-ties. 1** extreme wickedness; outrageousness: *The murderer finally realized the enormity of his crime.* **2** an extremely wicked crime; outrageous offence. **3** great magnitude: *He was daunted by the sheer enormity of the task.*

e•nor•mous [ɪ'nɔrməs] *adj.* **1** extremely large; huge: *Long ago enormous animals lived on the earth.* **2** extremely wicked; outrageous. ⟨< L *enormis* < *ex-* out of + *norma* pattern⟩ **—e'nor•mous•ness,** *n.*

☛ *Syn.* **1.** See note at HUGE.

e•nor•mous•ly [ɪ'nɔrməsli] *adv.* in or to an enormous degree; extremely; vastly; beyond measure.

e•no•sis [ɛ'nousɪs] *n.* union; in particular, the hypothetical joining of Greece and Cyprus. ⟨< Mod.Gk.⟩

e•nough [ɪ'nʌf] *adj., n., adv., interj.* —*adj.* as much or as many as needed or wanted: *Buy enough food for the picnic.*
—*n.* an adequate quantity or number: *I have had enough to eat.*
—*adv.* **1** sufficiently; adequately: *Have you played enough?* **2** quite; fully: *He is willing enough to take a tip.* **3** rather; fairly: *She talks well enough for a two-year-old.*
—*interj.* stop! no more! ⟨OE *genōg*⟩

☛ *Syn. adj.* **Enough,** SUFFICIENT, ADEQUATE = as much as is needed. **Enough** is the general word, and is often used interchangeably with **sufficient,** but it means 'as much as is needed to satisfy a desire': *A growing child never has enough time to play.* **Sufficient** = as much as is required to satisfy a need: *She is not getting sufficient food.* **Adequate** = as much as is needed to meet a specific, especially a minimum, requirement: *To be healthy one must have an adequate diet.*

☛ *Usage.* **Enough.** There is a tendency among some speakers to place the adjective **enough** after a noun it modifies; the adverb **enough** must be placed after an adjective or adverb it modifies: *We have enough room. We have room enough. Martha's sewing is good enough for me. You don't get up early enough.*

e•nounce [ɪ'naʊns] *v.* **e•nounced, e•nounc•ing. 1** proclaim; make a public or formal statement of. **2** speak; pronounce; enunciate.

e•now [ɪ'naʊ] *adj., n., or adv. Archaic.* enough.

en pas•sant [ɑ̃pa'sɑ̃] *French.* **1** in passing; by the way; incidentally. **2** *Chess.* referring to a play used to take, with one's own pawn, an opponent's pawn that has just made its first move of two spaces, but is treated as though it had only moved one.

en•phy•tot•ic [ˌɛnfə'tɒtɪk] *adj.* having to do with a disease that affects but does not destroy plants. ⟨< *en-*[2] in, on + Gk. *phyton* plant + *-ic*⟩

en•plane [ɛn'plein] *v.* enter an aircraft.

en prise [ɒn 'priz]; *French,* [ɑ̃'pʀiz] *Chess.* likely to be taken by an opponent.

en•quire [ɛn'kwaɪr] *v.* **-quired, -quir•ing.** inquire.

en•quir•y [ɛn'kwaɪri] *or* ['ɛnkwəri] *n., pl.* **-quir•ies.** inquiry.

en•rage [ɛn'reidʒ] *v.* **-raged, -rag•ing.** put into a rage; make very angry; make furious. **—en'rag•ed•ly,** *adv.* **—en'rage•ment,** *n.* ⟨< OF *enrager* < *en-* in (causative) + *rage* rage < VL *rabia* < L *rabies*⟩

en rap•port [ɑ̃ʀa'pɔʀ] *French.* in sympathy; in agreement.

en•rapt [ɛn'ræpt] *adj.* rapt; filled with great delight.

en•rap•ture [ɛn'ræptʃər] *v.* **-tured, -tur•ing.** fill with great delight; entrance: *The audience was enraptured by the singer's beautiful voice.*

en•rav•ish [ɛn'rævɪʃ] *v.* enrapture.

en•reg•ist•er [ɛn'rɛdʒɪstər] *v.* record.

en•rich [ɛn'rɪtʃ] *v.* **1** make rich or richer: *An education enriches your mind. Decorations enrich a room. Fertilizers enrich the soil.* **2** raise the nutritive value of (a food) by adding vitamins and minerals in processing. **3** make (a radioactive element) more fissionable by increasing the content of fissionable material. Uranium that has its content of the isotope U-235 increased is called enriched uranium. **4** *Education.* expand the range or content of (a course of study): *an enriched program.* ⟨ME < OF *enrichir* < *en-* in (causative) + *riche* rich⟩ **—en'rich•er,** *n.*

en•rich•ment [ɛn'rɪtʃmənt] *n.* **1** an enriching or being enriched. **2** anything that enriches. **3** *Education.* a stream or, more commonly, a withdrawal program for very able students, using an enriched curriculum.

en•robe [ɛn'roub] *v.* **-robed, -rob•ing.** dress; attire.

en•rol or **en•roll** [ɛn'roul] *v.* **-rolled, -rol•ling. 1** write in a list. **2** have one's name written in a list. **3** make a member. **4** become a member. ⟨ME < OF *enroller* < *en-* in + *rolle* roll, n., ult. < L *rota* wheel⟩

en•rol•ee or **en•rol•lee** [ɛnˌrou'li] *or* [ˌɛnrou'li] *n.* a person enrolled in a school, university, or course of study.

en•rol•ment or **en•roll•ment** [ɛn'roulmənt] *n.* **1** an enrolling. **2** the number enrolled: *The school has an enrolment of 200 students.* **3** a record; entry.

en•root [ɛn'rut] *v.* IMPLANT (def. 3).

en route [ɒn 'rut]; *French,* [ɑ̃'ʀut] on the way: *We shall stop at Toronto en route from Montréal to Winnipeg.* ⟨< F⟩

ens [ɛnz] *or* [ɛns] *n. Metaphysics.* an entity. ⟨< LL *ens, entis* a being < ppr. of *esse* to be⟩

en•sam•ple [ɛn'sæmpəl] *n. Archaic.* example.

en•san•guine [ɛn'sæŋgwɪn] *v.* **-guined, -guin•ing.** stain with blood.

en•sconce [ɛn'skɒns] *v.* **-sconced, -sconc•ing. 1** shelter safely; hide: *The soldiers were ensconced in strongly fortified trenches.* **2** settle comfortably and firmly: *The cat ensconced itself in the armchair.* ⟨ < *en-*[1] + *sconce* fortification, probably < Du. *schans*⟩

en•sem•ble [ɒn'sɒmbəl]; *French,* [ɑ̃'sɑ̃bl] *n.* **1** all the parts of a thing considered together. **2** *Music.* **a** a united performance by the full number of singers, instrumentalists, dancers, etc.: *After the solo all the singers joined in the ensemble.* **b** a group of musicians or the musical instruments used in taking part in such a performance: *Two violins, a cello, and a harp made up the string ensemble.* **3** a group of dancers, actors, etc. **4** a set of clothes of which each item is chosen to match or complement the others; a complete, harmonious costume. ⟨< F < VL < L *in-* + *simul* at the same time⟩

en•sheathe [ɛn'ʃið] *v.* **-sheathed, -sheath•ing.** sheathe.

en•shrine [ɛn'ʃraɪn] *v.* **-shrined, -shrin•ing. 1** enclose in a shrine: *A fragment of the Cross is enshrined in the cathedral.* **2** keep sacred; cherish: *Memories of happier days were enshrined in the old woman's heart.*

en•shrine•ment [ɛn'ʃraɪnmənt] *n.* **1** an enshrining. **2** anything that enshrines or surrounds.

en•shroud [ɛn'ʃraʊd] *v.* cover; hide; veil: *Fog enshrouded the ship, but we could hear its siren.*

en•si•form ['ɛnsɪ,fɔrm] *adj. Biology.* shaped like a sword. ⟨< L *ensis* sword + E *-form*⟩

en•sign ['ɛnsən] *for 1–3,* ['ɛnsaɪn] *for 4 n.* **1** a flag; banner: *the Red Ensign.* **2** the lowest commissioned officer in the United States navy. **3** formerly, a British army officer whose duty was carrying the flag. **4** the sign of one's rank, position, or power; symbol of authority. ⟨ME < OF *enseigne* < L *insignia* insignia. Doublet of INSIGNIA.⟩

en•sign•ship ['ɛnsən,ʃɪp] *n.* the rank or position of an ensign.

en•si•lage ['ɛnsəlɪdʒ] *n.* **1** the preservation of green fodder by packing it in a silo or pit. **2** green fodder preserved in this way. Ensilage is used to feed cattle in winter. ⟨< F⟩

en•sile [ɛn'saɪl] *or* ['ɛnsaɪl] *v.* **-siled, -sil•ing.** make green fodder into silage.

en•slave [ɛn'sleiv] *v.* **-slaved, -slav•ing.** reduce to slavery; subjugate or dominate: *an enslaved people. She was enslaved by alcohol.* **—en'slav•er,** *n.*

en•slave•ment [ɛn'sleivmənt] *n.* an enslaving or being enslaved.

en•snare [ɛn'snɛr] *v.* **-snared, -snar•ing.** catch in a snare; trap. **—en'snare•ment,** *n.* **—en'snar•er,** *n.* Also, **insnare.**

en•sor•cel or **en•sor•cell** [ɛn'sɔrsəl] *v.* **-celled** or **-celed, -cell•ing** or **-cel•ing.** enchant; bewitch. ⟨< F *ensorceler*⟩

en•soul [ɛn'soul] *v.* hold dear in the soul.

en•sphere [ɛn'sfir] *v.* **-sphered, -spher•ing. 1** enclose in a sphere. **2** shape into a sphere. Also, **insphere.**

en•stat•ite ['ɛnstə,təit] *n. Mineralogy.* a fibrous magnesium silicate found in igneous rocks. ⟨< G *enstatit* < Gk. *enstates* opponent⟩

en•sue [ɛn'su] *or* [ɛn'sju] *v.* **-sued, -su•ing. 1** come after; follow: *the ensuing year.* **2** happen as a result: *In his anger he hit the man, and a fight ensued.* ⟨ME < OF *ensuivre* < L *insequi* < *in-* upon + *sequi* follow⟩

☛ *Syn.* See note at FOLLOW.

en suite [ɒn 'swit] **1** in a set. **2** forming part of a whole: *master bedroom with en suite bathroom.* ⟨< F⟩

en•sure [ɛn'ʃur] *v.* **-sured, -sur•ing. 1** make sure or certain: *Careful planning and hard work ensured the success of the party.* **2** make sure of getting; secure: *A letter of introduction will ensure you an interview.* **3** make safe; protect: *Proper clothing ensured us against the cold.* ⟨< AF *enseurer* < *en-* in (causative) + *seür* sure < L *securus*⟩

☛ *Usage.* **Ensure,** INSURE. **Ensure** is the usual spelling for 'make sure or certain'; **insure,** for 'arrange for money payment in case of loss, accident, or death': *Check your work to ensure its accuracy. They insured their house against fire.*

en•swathe [ɛn'swɒð] *or* [ɛn'sweið] *v.* **-swathed, -swath•ing.** envelop in or as in a bandage.

-ent *suffix.* **1** ——ing: *absorbent, indulgent, coincident.* **2** one that ——s: *correspondent, president, superintendent.* **3** other meanings: *competent, confident.* ⟨< L *-ens, -entis*⟩

en•tab•la•ture [ɛn'tæblətʃər] *or* [ɛn'tæblə,tʃur] *n. Architecture.* a horizontal band forming the top of a wall or storey, supported by columns or pilasters. In classical architecture, the entablature consists of a cornice, a frieze, and an architrave. See COLUMN for picture. ⟨< Ital. *intavolatura* < *in-* on + *tavola* board, tablet < L *tabula*⟩

en•ta•ble•ment [ɛn'teibəlmənt] *n.* the pedestal supporting a statue.

en•tail [ɛn'teil] *v., n. —v.* **1** impose; require: *Owning an automobile entailed greater expense than he had expected.* **2** limit the inheritance of (property, etc.) to a specified line of heirs so that it cannot be left to anyone else. An entailed estate usually passes to the eldest son.
—n. **1** the act of entailing. **2** an entailed inheritance. **3** the order of descent specified for an entailed estate. ⟨ME < *en-*[1] + OF *taille* cutting, tax < *taillier* cut⟩ **—en'tail•er,** *n.*

en•tail•ment [ɛn'teilmənt] *n.* an entailing or being entailed.

en•tan•gle [ɛn'tæŋgəl] *v.* **-gled, -gling. 1** catch in a net; cause to get tangled up. **2** get twisted up and caught; tangle: *Loose string is easily entangled.* **3** cause to get into difficulty; involve: *The villain tried to entangle the hero in an evil scheme.* **4** perplex; confuse. **—en'tan•gler,** *n.* **—en'tan•gling•ly,** *adv.*

en•tan•gle•ment [ɛn'tæŋgəlmənt] *n.* **1** an entangling or being entangled. **2** anything that entangles: *The trench was protected by a barbed-wire entanglement.*

en•ta•sis ['ɛntəsɪs] *n., pl.* **-ses** [-,siz]. *Architecture.* the convex shape given to a column or tower. ⟨< NL < Gk. *entasis* a stretching < *enteinein* to stretch tight < *en-* in + *teinein* to stretch⟩

en•tel•ech•y [ɛn'tɛləki] *n. Philosophy.* a vital force urging one to fulfilment. ⟨< ME *entelechia* < L < Gk. *entelecheia* actuality < *en-* in + *telei* (*telos*) end + *echein* hold⟩

en•tente [ɑn'tɑnt]; *French,* [ɑ̃'tɑ̃t] *n.* **1** an understanding; agreement between two or more governments. **2** the parties to an understanding; governments that have made an agreement.

en•tente cor•diale [ɑ̃tɑ̃t kɔʀ'djal] *French.* a friendly understanding or agreement.

en•ter ['ɛntər] *v.* **1** go or come into: *She entered the house. They entered the yard.* **2** go or come in: *Let them enter.* **3** become a part or member of; join: *He entered the armed forces when he was 18.* **4** cause to join; enrol; obtain admission for: *Parents enter their children in school.* **5** begin; start (*often used with* **on** *or* **upon**): *to enter the practice of law.* **6** become involved (in); begin to take part (*often used with* **into**): *to enter a contest, to enter into the spirit of the game, to enter into conversation with someone.* **7** write or print in a book, list, etc.: *Words are entered in a dictionary in alphabetical order.* **8** come into or take possession of (*usually used with* **upon**). **9** put formally on record; register: *to enter a complaint in court, to enter a claim for a piece of public property.* **10** form a part of; be a consideration in (*used with* **into**): *The possibility of failure didn't even enter into her calculations.* **11** consider (*used with* **into**): *The book does not enter into the issue of morality at all.* **12** *Theatre.* come on stage (*used as a stage direction*): *Enter Ghost.* **13** report (a ship or its cargoes) at the custom house. **14** *Computer technology.* input (data or instructions) into a computer.

enter into, a begin to take part in: *He entered into conversation with the woman.* **b** be a consideration in: *That question doesn't enter into the problem.* **c** consider; discuss: *enter into a question of law.*

enter on or **upon, a** begin; start: *Nina entered on her professional duties as soon as she finished law school.* **b** take possession of. ⟨ME < OF *entrer,* ult. < L *intra* within⟩ **—'en•ter•er,** *n.*

en•ter•ic [ɛn'tɛrɪk] *adj.* intestinal. Also, **enteral** ['ɛntərəl]. ⟨< Gk. *enterikos* < *entera* intestines⟩

enteric fever TYPHOID FEVER.

en•ter•i•tis [,ɛntə'rəitɪs] *n.* an inflammation of the intestines, usually accompanied by diarrhea, fever, etc. ⟨< Gk. *entera* intestines + E *-itis*⟩

en•ter•o– *combining form.* intestine. ⟨< Gk. *enteron*⟩

en•ter•o•bi•a•sis [,ɛntərou'baɪəsɪs] *n.* the condition of being infested with pinworms. ⟨< NL < *Enterobius* name of genus < *entero-* + Gk. *bios* life⟩

en•ter•o•coc•cus [,ɛntərou'kɒkəs] *n., pl.* **en•ter•o•coc•ci** [-saɪ]. a streptococcus found in human intestines.

en•ter•o•gas•trone [,ɛntərou'gæstroun] *n.* a hormone that slows the secretion of gastric juice and thus of digestive capacity.

en•ter•o•ki•nase [,ɛntərou'kaɪneis] *n.* an enzyme in the intestines that changes trypsinogen to trypsin.

en•ter•on ['ɛntə,rɒn] *n.* ALIMENTARY CANAL.

en•ter•os•to•my [,ɛntə'rɒstəmi] *n.* a surgical incision made into the intestines.

en•ter•o•vi•rus [,ɛntərou'vaɪrəs] *n.* any of various viruses of the genus *Enterovirus,* responsible for gastrointestinal infections and other disorders. Poliomyelitis is caused by an enterovirus.

en•ter•prise ['ɛntər,praɪz] *n.* **1** an important, difficult, or dangerous undertaking. **2** an undertaking; project: *a business enterprise.* **3** readiness to start projects; courage and energy in starting projects. **4** the carrying on of enterprises; taking part in enterprises. See PRIVATE ENTERPRISE. ⟨ME < OF *entreprise* < *entre-* between + *prise,* fem. pp. of *prendre* take < L *prehendere*⟩ **—'en•ter,pris•er,** *n.*

en•ter•pris•ing ['ɛntər,praɪzɪŋ] *adj.* ready to try new, important, difficult, or dangerous plans; courageous and energetic in starting projects. **—'en•ter,pris•ing•ly,** *adv.*

en•ter•tain [,ɛntər'tein] *v.* **1** amuse; please; interest: *The circus entertained the children.* **2** have as a guest: *She entertained ten people at dinner.* **3** have guests; invite people to one's home: *She entertains a great deal.* **4** take into the mind; consider: *to entertain an idea.* **5** hold in the mind; maintain: *Even after failing twice, we still entertained a hope of success.* ⟨< F *entretenir* < *entre-* among + *tenir* hold < L *tenere*⟩ **—,en•ter'tain•a•ble,** *adj.*

☛ *Syn.* **1.** See note at AMUSE.

en•ter•tain•er [,ɛntər'teinər] *n.* **1** a person who entertains. **2** a singer, musician, reciter, etc. who takes part in public entertainments.

en•ter•tain•ing [,ɛntər'teinɪŋ] *adj., v.* *—adj.* very interesting; pleasing; amusing.
—v. ppr. of ENTERTAIN. **—,en•ter'tain•ing•ly,** *adv.*

en•ter•tain•ment [,ɛntər'teinmənt] *n.* **1** an entertaining or being entertained. **2** something that interests, pleases, or amuses. A show or play is an entertainment. **3** hospitality; the act or practice of paying attention to the comfort and desires of guests: *The hostess devoted herself to the entertainment of her guests.*

en•thal•py [ɛn'θælpi] *or* ['ɛnθəlpi] *n. Physics.* the heat content per unit mass of substance. ⟨< Gk. *enthalpein* to warm in⟩

en•thral or **en•thrall** [ɛn'θrɒl] *v.* **-thralled, -thrall•ing.** **1** captivate; fascinate; charm: *The explorer enthralled the audience with the story of his exciting adventures.* **2** make a slave of; enslave. Also, **inthral** or **inthrall. —en'thral•ment** or **en'thrall•ment,** *n.*

en•throne [ɛn'θroun] *v.* **-throned, -thron•ing.** **1** set on a throne. **2** place highest of all; exalt: *"Mercy is enthroned in the hearts of men."* **3** invest with authority, especially as a sovereign or as a bishop. Also, **inthrone. —en'throne•ment,** *n.*

en•thuse [ɛn'θuz] *or* [ɛn'θjuz] *v.* **-thused, -thus•ing.** *Informal.* **1** show enthusiasm. **2** fill with enthusiasm. ⟨< *enthusiasm*⟩

☛ *Usage.* Although many people object to **enthuse,** it is now often heard in the U.S. and, less often, in Canada. It is wise to avoid the word in formal writing.

en•thu•si•asm [ɛn'θuzi,æzəm] *or* [ɛn'θjuzi,æzəm] *n.* **1** eager interest; zeal: *The great leader filled her followers with enthusiasm.* **2** an activity that creates interest. ⟨< LL *enthusiasmus* < Gk. *enthousiasmos* < *entheos* god-possessed < *en-* in + *theos* god⟩

en•thu•si•ast [ɛn'θuzi,æst] *or* [ɛn'θjuzi,æst], [ɛn'θuziəst] *or* [ɛn'θjuziəst] *n.* **1** a person who is filled with ardent interest or zeal: *a baseball enthusiast.* **2** a person who is carried away by his or her feelings for a cause.

en•thu•si•as•tic [ɛn,θuzi'æstɪk] *or* [ɛn,θjuzi'æstɪk] *adj.* full of enthusiasm; eagerly interested. **—en,thu•si'as•ti•cal•ly,** *adv.*

en•thy•meme ['ɛnθə,mim] *n. Logic.* a syllogism in which one of the premises is implied but not stated. ⟨< L *enthymema* < Gk. *enthymema* < *enthymesthai* to consider, reflect upon < *en-* in + *thymos* mind⟩

en•tice [ɛn'təis] *v.* **-ticed, -tic•ing.** tempt by arousing hopes or desires; attract by offering some pleasure or reward: *The robber enticed his victims into a cave by promising to show them a gold mine.* ⟨ME < OF *enticier* stir up, incite ? < *en-* in + L *titio* firebrand⟩ **—en'tic•er,** *n.* **—en'tic•ing•ly,** *adv.*

☛ *Syn.* See note at LURE.

en•tice•ment [ɛn'təismənt] *n.* **1** an enticing or being enticed. **2** anything that entices.

en•tire [ɛn'taɪr] *adj., n.* *—adj.* **1** having all the parts or elements; whole; complete: *The entire platoon was wiped out.* **2** not broken; in one piece. **3** of leaves, not indented. **4** thorough; total; absolute: *entire trust.* **5** not castrated or gelded: *an entire horse.*
—n. an uncastrated horse. ⟨ME < OF *entier* < L *integer* < *in-* not + *tag-* a base of *tangere* touch. Doublet of INTEGER.⟩

☛ *Syn.* **1.** See note at COMPLETE.

en•tire•ly [ɛn'taɪrli] *adv.* **1** wholly; completely; fully. **2** solely.

en•tire•ty [ɛn'taɪrti] *or* [ɛn'taɪrəti] *n., pl.* **-ties. 1** wholeness; completeness. **2** a complete thing; whole. **3** *Law.* possession by one person only; undivided possession.
in its entirety, wholly; as a whole: *She enjoyed the concert in its entirety.*

en•ti•tle [ɛn'təitəl] *v.* **-tled, -tling. 1** give the title of; call by the name of: *She read a poem entitled "Trees."* **2** give a claim or right to; provide with a reason to ask or get something: *Their age and experience entitle old people to the respect of young people.* **3** bestow a title of an honorary nature on. Also, **intitle.** ⟨ME < OF *entituler* < LL *intitulare* < L *in-* in + *titulus* title⟩

en•ti•tle•ment [ɛn'təitəlmənt] *n.* **1** the state of being entitled. **2** something to which one is entitled. Also, **intitlement**.

en•ti•ty ['ɛntəti] *n., pl.* **-ties. 1** something that has a real and separate existence either actually or in the mind; anything real in itself. Persons, mountains, languages, and beliefs are entities. **2** a state of being; existence. ⟨< LL *entitas* < L *ens, entis,* ppr. of *esse* be⟩

en•to•blast ['ɛntə,blæst] *n.* endoblast.

en•tomb [ɛn'tum] *v.* **1** place in a tomb; bury. **2** shut up as if in a tomb. **3** serve as a tomb for. Also, **intomb.** ⟨ME < OF *entomber* < *en-* in + *tombe* tomb < LL *tumba* < Gk. *tymbos*⟩ **—en'tomb•ment,** *n.*

en•to•mo•log•i•cal [,ɛntəmə'lɒdʒəkəl] *adj.* of or having to do with entomology. Also, **entomologic. —,en•to•mo'log•ic•al•ly,** *adv.*

en•to•mol•o•gist [,ɛntə'mɒlədʒɪst] *n.* a person trained in entomology, especially one whose work it is.

en•to•mol•o•gy [,ɛntə'mɒlədʒi] *n.* the branch of zoology that deals with insects. ⟨< Gk. *entomon* insect (< *entomos* cut, notched < *en-* in + *temnein* cut) + E *-logy*⟩

en•to•moph•a•gous [,ɛntə'mɒfəgəs] *adj.* having a diet consisting mainly of insects. ⟨< Gk. *entomon* insect (see ENTOMOLOGY) + *phagos* < *phagein* to eat⟩

en•to•moph•i•lous [,ɛntə'mɒfələs] *adj.* pollinated by insects. ⟨< Gk. *entomon* insect + E *-philous*⟩

en•to•mos•tra•can [,ɛntə'mɒstrəkən] *adj., n.* *—adj.* belonging to the order Entomostraea.
—n. any small crustacean of that order. ⟨< Gk. *entomon* insect (see ENTOMOLOGY) + *ostrakon* shell⟩

en•to•phyte ['ɛntə,fəit] *n.* endophyte.

en•to•proct ['ɛntə,prɒkt] *n.* any of the various small, mossy water invertebrates of the phylum Entoprocta, having a ring of tentacles encircling the anus and mouth. ⟨< Gk. *entos* within + *proctos* anus⟩

en•tou•rage ['ɒntʊ,rɑʒ] *or* [,ɒntʊ'rɑʒ] *n.* **1** environment; surroundings. **2** a group of attendants or people usually accompanying a person. ⟨< F *entourage* < *entourer* surround⟩

en•to•zo•on [,ɛntə'zouən] *n., pl.* **en•to•zoa** [-'zouə]. any parasite living inside a creature. ⟨< Gk. *entos* within + *zoion* animal⟩ **—,en•to'zo•al,** *adj.*

en•tr'acte [ɑn'trækt]; *French,* [ɑ̃'tʀakt] *n.* **1** an interval between two acts of a play, ballet, opera, etc. **2** the music, dancing, or any entertainment performed during this interval. ⟨< F *entr'acte* between-act⟩

en•trails ['ɛntreilz] *or* ['ɛntrəlz] *n.pl.* **1** the inner parts of a human or animal. **2** the intestines; bowels. **3** any inner parts. ⟨ME < OF *entrailles* < LL *intralia* < L *interanea* < *inter* within⟩

en•train[1] [ɛn'trein] *v.* **1** get on a train. **2** put on a train: *The soldiers were entrained at night.* ⟨*en-* + *train*⟩

en•train[2] [ɛn'trein] *v. Chemistry.* **1** during distillation or evaporation, carry as liquid drops. **2** trap (bubbles) in a liquid that is chemically turbulent in a reaction. ⟨< F *entraîner* draw or drag along < *en-* away, along + OF *trahiner*⟩

en•trance[1] ['ɛntrəns] *n.* **1** the act of entering: *The actor's entrance was greeted with applause.* **2** a place by which to enter; door, passageway, etc. **3** the freedom or right to enter; permission to enter. ⟨< MF *entrance* < *entrer* enter < L *intrare.* See ENTER.⟩

en•trance[2] [ɛn'træns] *v.* **-tranced, -tranc•ing. 1** put into a trance. **2** fill with joy; delight; charm. ⟨< *en-*[1] + *trance*⟩ **—en'tranc•ing•ly,** *adv.*

en•trance•ment [ɛn'trænsmənt] *n.* **1** an entrancing or being entranced. **2** something that entrances.

en•trance•way ['ɛntrəns,wei] *n.* a place by which to enter.

en•trant ['ɛntrənt] *n.* **1** a person who enters. **2** a new member in a profession, club, association, etc. **3** a person who takes part in a contest. ⟨< F *entrant,* ppr. of *entrer* enter⟩

en•trap [ɛn'træp] *v.* **-trapped, -trap•ping. 1** catch in a trap. **2** bring into difficulty or danger by or as if by trickery: *By clever questioning, the lawyer entrapped the witness into contradicting* *himself.* ⟨< MF *entrapre* < *en-* in (intensive) + *trape* trap⟩ **—en'trap•ment,** *n.*

en•treat [ɛn'trit] *v.* ask earnestly; beg and pray; implore: *The captives entreated the pirates not to kill them.* Also, **intreat.** ⟨ME < OF *entraitier* < *en-* in (intensive) + *traitier* treat < L *tractare*⟩ **—en'treat•er,** *n.* **—en'treat•ing•ly,** *adv.* **—en'treat•ment,** *n.*

en•treat•y [ɛn'triti] *n., pl.* **-treat•ies.** an earnest request; prayer: *The pirates paid no attention to their captives' entreaties for mercy.*

en•tre•chat [ɑ̃tʀə'ʃa] *n. Ballet.* a vertical leap in which the dancer's calves are beaten together as the feet, pointed downwards, cross. Several beats may be performed in one leap. ⟨< F *entrechat*, a respelling of Ital. *(capriola) intrecciata* complicated (leap) < *intrecciare* intertwine < *in-* in + *treccia* tress, plait⟩

en•tre•côte [,ɒntrə'kout] *or* ['ɒntrə,kout]; *French,* [ɑ̃tʀə'kot] *n.* a piece of steak from between the ribs. ⟨< F, between the ribs⟩

en•tree or **en•trée** [ɒn'trei] *or* ['ɒntrei]; *French,* [ɑ̃'tʀe] *n.* **1** the act of entering. **2** the freedom or right to enter; access. **3** the main dish of food at dinner or lunch. **4** a dish of food served before the roast or between the main courses at dinner. ⟨< F *entrée*, fem. pp. of *entrer* enter⟩

en•tre•mets [,ɒntrə'mei] *or* ['ɒntrə,mei]; *French,* [ɑ̃tʀə'mɛ] *n.* food served between courses or as a dessert.

en•trench [ɛn'trɛntʃ] *v.* **1** surround with a trench; fortify with trenches. **2** establish firmly: *Exchanging gifts at Christmas is a custom entrenched in people's minds.* **3** trespass; encroach; infringe: *Do not entrench upon the rights of others.* Also, **intrench.**

en•trench•ment [ɛn'trɛntʃmənt] *n.* **1** an entrenching. **2** an entrenched position. **3** a defence consisting of a trench and a rampart of earth or stone. Also, **intrenchment.**

en•tre nous [ɑ̃trə'nu] *French.* between ourselves; confidentially.

en•tre•pôt [,ɒntrə'pou] *or* ['ɒntrə,pou]; *French,* [ɑ̃tʀə'po] *n.* **1** a place where goods are stored; warehouse. **2** a place where goods are sent for distribution; commercial centre. ⟨< F⟩

en•tre•pre•neur [,ɒntrəprə'nɜr] *n.* a person who organizes and manages a business or industrial enterprise, attempting to make a profit but taking the risk of a loss. ⟨< F *entrepreneur* < *entreprendre* undertake⟩

en•tre•pre•neur•i•al [,ɒntrəprə'njʊriəl], [-'nʊriəl], *or* [-'nɜriəl] *adj.* of or having to do with an entrepreneur or entrepreneurs, especially when involving strong initiative and opportunism.

en•tre•pre•neur•ship [,ɒntrəprə'nɜrʃɪp] *n.* **1** the existence or activity of entrepreneurs. **2** the qualities or function of an entrepreneur.

en•tre•sol ['ɒntrə,sɒl]; *French,* [ɑ̃tʀə'sɔl] *n.* a low storey between the first two floors of a building; mezzanine. ⟨< F⟩

en•tro•py ['ɛntrəpi] *n.* **1** *Physics.* **a** in a thermodynamic system, a measure of the energy that is not available for conversion to mechanical work. **b** a measure of the degree of molecular disorder in a system. **2 a** the tendency of the universe toward increasing disorder. **b** the probable outcome of this tendency. **3** *Communications.* a statistical measure of the predictable accuracy of a system in transmitting information. ⟨< G *Entropie*, probably influenced by Gk. *entropia* a turning in < *en-* + *tropē* a turning < *trepein* to turn⟩

en•trust [ɛn'trʌst] *v.* **1** charge with a trust; trust: *The club entrusted the newly elected treasurer with all its money.* **2** give the care of; hand over for safekeeping: *While travelling, they entrusted their son to his grandparents.* Also, **intrust. —en'trust•ment,** *n.*
☛ *Syn.* **2.** See note at COMMIT.

en•try ['ɛntri] *n., pl.* **-tries. 1** the act of entering. **2** a place by which to enter; a way to enter. A vestibule is an entry. **3** the right to enter. **4** something written or printed in a book, list, etc. Each word explained in a dictionary is an entry. A bookkeeper makes entries in a ledger. **5** a person or thing that takes part in a contest. **6** *Law.* the act of taking possession of lands or buildings by entering or setting foot on them. **7** a giving of an account of a ship's cargo at a customs house to obtain permission to land the goods. **8** in bridge, a winning card. ⟨ME < OF *entree* < *entrer.* See ENTER.⟩

en•try•way ['ɛntrɪ,wei] *n.* an opening or passage that gives entrance.

entry word 1 in a dictionary, one of the words listed in alphabetical order and followed by information concerning its pronunciation, meanings, etc. Entry words are printed in heavy black type in this dictionary. **2** in other reference books, a word giving the subject of the following article. **3** the word under which a book, pamphlet, etc. is entered in a list or catalogue.

en•twine [ɛn'twaɪn] *v.* **-twined, -twin•ing. 1** twine together. **2** twine around: *Roses entwined the little cottage.* **—en'twine•ment,** *n.*

en•twist [ɛn'twɪst] *v.* twist together.

e•nu•cle•ate [ɪ'njukli,eit] *or* [ɪ'nukli,eit] *v.* **-at•ed, -at•ing. 1** remove by surgery from its enclosing cover. **2** deprive of its nucleus.

e•nu•mer•ate [ɪ'njumə,reit] *or* [ɪ'numə,reit] *v.* **-at•ed, -at•ing. 1** name one by one; give a list of: *She enumerated the provinces of Canada.* **2** count. **3** *Cdn.* make up a list of (voters in an area) or enter (a person) in such a list. ⟨< L *enumerare* < *ex-* out + *numerus* number⟩

e•nu•mer•a•tion [ɪ,njumə'reiʃən] *or* [ɪ,numə'reiʃən] *n.* **1** an enumerating; listing; counting. **2** a list.

e•nu•mer•a•tive [ɪ'njumərətɪv] *or* [ɪ'numərətɪv], [ɪ'njumə,reitɪv] *or* [ɪ'numə,reitɪv] *adj.* that enumerates; having to do with enumeration.

e•nu•mer•a•tor [ɪ'njumə,reitər] *or* [ɪ'numə,reitər] *n.* **1** *Cdn.* a person appointed to list, prior to an election, the eligible voters in a polling area. **2** any person or thing that lists or counts.

e•nun•ci•a•ble [ɪ'nʌnsiəbəl] *adj.* able to be enunciated.

e•nun•ci•ate [ɪ'nʌnsi,eit] *or* [ɪ'nʌnʃi,eit] *v.* **-at•ed, -at•ing. 1** pronounce (words) clearly and articulately: *She is a well-trained actor and enunciates very distinctly.* **2** state definitely; announce: *After performing many experiments, the scientist enunciated a new theory.* ⟨< L *enuntiare* < *ex-* out + *nuntius* messenger⟩ **—e'nun•ci,a•tor,** *n.* **—e'nun•ci•a•tive,** *adj.*

e•nun•ci•a•tion [ɪ,nʌnsi'eiʃən] *n.* **1** one's manner of pronouncing words. **2** a definite statement; announcement: *the enunciation of a set of rules.*

en•ure [ɛ'njur] See INURE.

en•u•re•sis [,ɛnjə'risɪs] *n.* involuntary passing of urine, especially during sleep. ⟨< NL < Gk. *enourein* to urinate in < *en-*in + *ourein* urinate⟩ **—,en•u'ret•ic** [-'rɛtɪk], *adj., n.*

en•vel•op [ɛn'vɛləp] *v.* **-oped, -op•ing. 1** wrap; cover. **2** surround: *Our soldiers enveloped the enemy and captured them.* **3** hide; conceal: *Fog enveloped the village.* ⟨ME < OF *enveloper* < *en-* in (intensive) + *voloper* wrap⟩

en•ve•lope ['ɛnvə,loup] *or* ['ɒnvə,loup] *n.* **1** a paper cover in which a letter or anything flat and fairly thin can be mailed, filed, etc. It can usually be folded over and sealed by wetting a gummed edge. **2** a covering; wrapper. **3** *Botany.* a surrounding or enclosing part, as of leaves. **4** *Biology.* any enclosing covering, such as membrane or shell; integument. **5** *Geometry.* a curve or surface touching a continuous series of curves or surfaces. **6** *Astronomy.* a nebulous mass surrounding the nucleus of a comet on the side nearest the sun. **7** a bag that holds the gas in a balloon or airship. **8** the outer covering of a rigid airship. **9** the set of constraints within which a vehicle, system, etc. may operate safely. ⟨< F *enveloppe* < *envelopper* envelop⟩

en•vel•op•ment [ɛn'vɛləpmənt] *n.* **1** an enveloping or being enveloped. **2** something that envelops; wrapping; covering.

en•ven•om [ɛn'vɛnəm] *v.* **1** make poisonous. **2** fill with bitterness, hate, etc: *The wicked boy envenomed his father's mind against his half brother.* ⟨ME < OF *envenimer* < *en-* in + *venim* venom < L *venenum*⟩

en•vi•a•ble ['ɛnviəbəl] *adj.* to be envied; desirable; worth having: *She has an enviable school record.* **—'en•vi•a•ble•ness,** *n.* **—'en•vi•a•bly,** *adv.*

en•vi•ous ['ɛnviəs] *adj.* full of envy; feeling or showing envy. ⟨ME < AF *envious*, var. of OF *envieus* < *envie.* See ENVY.⟩ **—'en•vi•ous•ly,** *adv.* **—'en•vi•ous•ness,** *n.*

en•vi•ron [ɛn'vaɪrən] *v.* surround; enclose. ⟨ME < OF *environner* < *environ* around < *en-* in + *viron* circle⟩

en•vi•ron•ment [ɛn'vaɪərnmənt] *or* [ɛn'vaɪrənmənt] *n.* **1** all the surrounding conditions and influences that affect the development of a living thing. Differences in environment often account for differences in the same kind of plant found in different places. **2** surroundings: *an environment of poverty. Banff has a beautiful environment.* **3 the environment,** the earth as natural surroundings; the air, water, land around us.

en•vi•ron•men•tal [ɛn,vaɪərn'mɛntəl] *or* [ɛn,vaɪrən'mɛntəl] *adj.* having to do with environment. **—en,vi•ron'men•tal•ly,** *adv.*

en•vi•ron•men•tal•ism [ɛn,vaɪərn'mɛntə,lɪzəm] *or*

[ɛn,vaɪrən'mɛntə,lɪzəm] *n.* **1** *Psychology.* the theory that environment is more influential than heredity in the development of an individual. **2** emphasis on the protection of the natural environment and the preservation of ecological balance.

en•vi•ron•men•tal•ist [ɛn,vaɪərn'mɛntəlɪst] *or* [ɛn,vaɪrən'mɛntəlɪst] *n., adj.* —*n.* **1** a person who believes in and advocates the protection of the natural environment against pollution, etc. and the preservation of ecological balance. **2** *Psychology.* an advocate of the theory of environmentalism. —*adj.* of or having to do with environmentalists or environmentalism.

environmental resistance the resistance of environmental factors, such as food supply, to population expansion.

en•vi•rons [ɛn'vaɪrənz] *n.pl.* surrounding districts; suburbs.

envisage [ɛn'vɪzɪdʒ] *v.* **-aged, -ag•ing. 1** foresee; visualize: *I envisage no difficulty with our plans.* **2** *Archaic.* look in the face of; confront: *He finally envisaged the realities of the situation.* ⟨< F *envisager* < *en-* in + *visage* face⟩

en•vi•sion [ɛn'vɪʒən] *v.* have a mental picture of; imagine, especially something that does not yet exist; picture to oneself; look forward to: *It is difficult to envision a state of permanent peace.*

en•voi ['ɛnvɔɪ]; *French,* [ɑ̃'vwa] *n.* ENVOY².

en•voy¹ ['ɛnvɔɪ] *or* ['ɒnvɔɪ] *n.* **1** messenger. **2** a diplomat ranking next below an ambassador and next above a minister. ⟨< F *envoyé,* pp. of *envoyer* send < OF *envoier.* See ENVOY².⟩

en•voy² ['ɛnvɔɪ] *n.* **1** a short stanza ending a poem. **2** a postscript to a literary work, often addressed to a friend or patron of the author. Also, **envoi.** ⟨ME < OF *envoy* < *envoier* send < VL < L *in via* on the way⟩

envoy extraordinary a diplomat ranking below an ambassador.

en•vy ['ɛnvi] *n., pl.* **-vies;** *v.* **-vied, -vy•ing.** —*n.* **1** discontent or ill will at another's good fortune because one wishes it were one's own. **2** the object of such feeling: *She was the envy of the younger girls in the school.*
—*v.* **1** feel envy toward: *Some people envy the rich.* **2** feel envy (toward) because of: *James envied his friend's success. I don't envy you your promotion; I wouldn't want the responsibility.* ⟨ME < OF *envie* < L *invidia,* ult. < *invidere* look with enmity at < *in-* against + *videre* see⟩ —**'en•vi•er,** *n.* —**'en•vy•ing•ly,** *adv.,*

☛ *Syn.* **Envy,** COVET. **Envy** = feel discontent, jealousy, or sometimes, hatred or resentment toward a person because of something he or she has that one wishes one had oneself: *Joan envies famous people. She envies their fame.* **Covet** = feel a great desire for something, especially something belonging to someone else: *He covets his neighbour's new car.*

en•wind [ɛn'waɪnd] *v.* **en•wound, en•wind•ing.** encircle or envelop by winding.

en•womb [ɛn'wum] *v.* enclose in, or as if in, a womb.

en•wrap [ɛn'ræp] *v.* **-wrapped, -wrap•ping.** enclose; envelop; wrap. Also, **inwrap.**

en•wreathe [ɛn'rið] *v.* **-wreathed, -wreath•ing.** wreathe around; encircle; surround. Also, **inwreathe.**

en•zo•ot•ic [,ɛnzou'ɒtɪk] *adj., n.* —*adj.* having to do with diseases affecting animals in only one locality or season. Compare ENDEMIC, EPIZOOTIC.
—*n.* a disease of that type. ⟨< *en* + Gk. *zoion* animal⟩

en•zy•mat•ic [,ɛnzaɪ'mætɪk] *or* [,ɛnzə'mætɪk] *adj.* of, having to do with, or produced by enzymes. Also, **enzymic** [ɛn'zaɪmɪk].

en•zyme ['ɛnzaɪm] *n.* a chemical substance, usually protein, produced in living cells, that can cause changes in other substances within the body, such as speeding up a biochemical reaction, without being changed itself. Pepsin is an enzyme. ⟨< Med.Gk. *enzymos* leavened < *en-* in + *zymē* leaven⟩

en•zy•mol•o•gist [,ɛnzaɪ'mɒlədʒɪst] *or* [,ɛnzə'mɒlədʒɪst] *n.* a person trained in enzymology, especially one whose work it is.

en•zy•mol•o•gy [,ɛnzaɪ'mɒlədʒi] *or* [,ɛnzə'mɒlədʒi] *n.* the study of enzymes.

eo– *combining form:* primeval: *Eocene. eohippus.* ⟨< Gk. *ēōs* dawn⟩

E•o•cene ['iə,sin] *n., adj. Geology.* —*n.* **1** the second division or epoch of the Tertiary period, in the Cenozoic era, beginning approximately 60 million years ago, when the lowest rocks were formed, and mammals were the dominant species. **2** the rocks formed during this period. See geological time chart in the Appendix.
—*adj.* having to do with this period or group of rocks. ⟨< Gk. *ēōs* dawn + *kainos* recent⟩

e•o•hip•pus [,iou'hɪpəs] *n.* any of an extinct genus (*Hyracotherium*) of animals of the Eocene epoch, the earliest known stage in the evolution of the horse. These dog-sized animals had forefeet with four toes and hind feet with two. ⟨< NL *Eohippus* < Gk. *ēōs* dawn + *hippos* horse⟩

E•o•li•an [i'ouliən] See AEOLIAN. Also, **Eolic.**

e•o•lith ['iəlɪθ] *n.* a roughly shaped stone tool belonging to a very early stage of human culture. ⟨< Gk. *ēōs* dawn + *lithos* stone⟩

e•o•lith•ic or **E•o•lith•ic** [,iə'lɪθɪk] *adj., n.* —*adj.* of or having to do with a very early stage of human culture, characterized by the use of the most primitive stone instruments. —*n.* this stage, the earliest part of the Stone Age.

e.o.m. end of month.

e•on ['iən] *or* ['iɒn] *n.* **1** the longest period of geological time. **2** a very long period of time; many thousands of years: *Eons passed before life existed on the earth.* Also, **aeon.** ⟨< L *aeon* < Gk. *aiōn* lifetime, age⟩

e•o•ni•an [i'ouniən] *adj.* ageless.

E•os ['iɒs] *n. Greek mythology.* the goddess of the dawn. Eos corresponds to the Roman goddess Aurora. ⟨< L < Gk.⟩

e•o•sin ['iəsɪn] *n.* **1** a rose-red dye or stain made from coal tar. *Formula*: $C_{20}H_8Br_4O_5$ **2** its reddish brown potassium or sodium salt. **3** any of various similar red dyes. ⟨< Gk. *ēōs* dawn⟩

e•o•sin•o•phil [,iou'sɪnə,fɪl] *n. Biology.* any cell, tissue, etc., that can be stained with eosin. ⟨< *eosin* + *-phile*⟩

ep– form of EPI- before vowels and *h,* as in *epode, ephemeral.*

EP of phonograph records, tapes, etc., extended play.

e•pact ['ipækt] *n.* **1** the difference (11 days) between the solar year and the lunar year. **2** the age of the moon at the beginning of the calendar year. **3** the difference in time between a lunar month and a calendar month. ⟨< F *épacte* < LL *epactae* < Gk. *epaktai (hemerai)* intercalary (days) < *epagein* intercalate < *epi-* on, in + *agein* bring⟩

ep•arch ['ɛpɑrk] *n.* **1** the chief administrator of an eparchy. **2** *Greek Orthodox Church.* a bishop. ⟨< Gk. *eparchos* < *epi-* over + *archos* ruler⟩

ep•ar•chy ['ɛpɑrki] *n.* **1** in Greece, a subdivision of a province. **2** *Greek Orthodox Church.* a diocese.

ep•au•lette or **ep•au•let** [,ɛpə'lɛt] *or* ['ɛpə,lɛt] *n.* an ornamental tab or piece on the shoulder of a uniform. ⟨< F *épaulette,* dim. of *épaule* shoulder⟩

é•pée [ei'pei] *n.* a sword used in fencing, especially one with a sharp point and no cutting edge. ⟨< F *épée* < OF *espee* < L *spatha* < Gk. *spathē* blade, sword⟩ —**é'pée•ist,** *n.*

e•pei•rog•e•ny [,ɛpaɪ'rɒdʒəni] *n. Geology.* movement of the earth's crust over a broad area to form continents. Also, **epirogeny.** ⟨< Gk. *epeiros* mainland + *-geneia* < *-genes* born⟩ —**e,pei•ro'gen•ic** or **e,pei•ro•ge'net•ic,** *adj.*

ep•en•ceph•a•lon [,ɛpɛn'sɛfə,lɒn] *n.* the hindbrain.

ep•en•dy•ma [,ɛ'pɛndəmə] *n.* the membrane lining the ventricles of the brain and the spinal cord. ⟨< NL < Gk. *ependyma* an upper garment < *ependyein* to put on over < *epi-* over + *endyein* < *en-* over + *dyein* to put on⟩

e•pen•the•sis [ɪ'pɛnθəsɪs] *n.* the insertion of an extra sound in a word, with no historical basis, as a schwa [ə] after the first syllable of *athletic.* ⟨< *epi-* + Gk. *en-* in + *thesis* a placing⟩ —**,ep•en'thet•ic** [,ɛpɛn'θɛtɪk], *adj.*

e•pergne [ɪ'pɜrn] *or* [ei'pɛrn] *n.* an ornamental serving dish used as a centrepiece on a dining table. ⟨probably < F *épargne* a saving < *épargner* to save⟩

e•pex•e•ge•sis [ɛ,pɛksə'dʒisɪs] *n.* **1** the adding of an explanation to text. **2** the added explanation itself. ⟨< Gk. *epexegesis* detailed account < *epexegeisthai* to recount in detail < *epi-* on, in + *exegeisthai* to point out < *ex-* out + *hegeisthai* to lead, guide⟩

e•phah ['ifə] *n.* an ancient Hebrew unit of dry measure equal to about 35 L. ⟨< Hebrew⟩

e•phe•be [ɛ'fib] *or* ['ɛfib] *n.* a young man; a young Athenian man in classical times. Also, **ephebus.** ⟨< L *ephebus* ephebus < Gk. *ephebos* < *epi-* upon + *hebe* manhood⟩

e•phed•rine [ɪ'fɛdrɪn]; *Chemistry,* ['ɛfə,drin] *or* ['ɛfədrɪn] *n.* a drug used to relieve hay fever, asthma, head colds, etc. It is a plant alkaloid. *Formula:* $C_{10}H_{15}ON$ Also, **ephedrin.** ⟨< NL *ephedra* < L *ephedra* horsetail (a plant) < Gk.⟩

e•phem•er•a [ɪ'fɛmərə] *n., pl.* **-er•ae** [-ə,ri] *or* [-ə,raɪ] or

-er•as. **1** any short-lived person or thing: *Of the many books published in a year, the majority are ephemerae.* **2** an emphemerid; mayfly. **3** ephemeral things collectively. **4** printed matter intended for short-term use, such as a playbill, sought by collectors. **5** a brief fever. ⟨< Gk. *ephēmeros* living only a day < *epi-* upon + *hēmera* day⟩

e•phem•er•al [ɪ'fɛmərəl] *adj., n.* *—adj.* lasting for only a day; lasting for only a very short time; very short-lived.
—n. any organism with a short life cycle.

e•phem•er•id [ɪ'fɛmərɪd] *n.* mayfly.

e•phem•e•ris [ɪ'fɛmərɪs] *n., pl.* **e•phe•mer•i•des** [ˌɛfɪ'mɛrɪˌdiz] a chart showing the daily positions of a celestial body.

E•phe•sian [ɪ'fiʒən] *n., adj.* *—n.* a native or inhabitant of Ephesus, an ancient Greek city in W Asia Minor.
—adj. of Ephesus or its people.

e•phod ['ifɒd] *or* ['ɛfɒd] *n.* a vestment worn in ancient times by Hebrew priests when performing sacred duties. ⟨< Hebrew, 'to put on'⟩

eph•or ['ɛfɔr] *or* ['ɛfər] *n., pl.* **-ors, -o•ri** [-əˌraɪ] *or* [-əˌri]. in ancient Sparta, one of the five leading magistrates, elected yearly by the people to advise the king. ⟨< L < Gk. *ephoros* < *epi-* over + *horaein* see⟩

epi– *prefix.* on; over; upon; in addition; to; among: *epidemic.* Also, **ep-**, before vowels and *h.* ⟨< Gk. *epi-* < *epi*, prep., adv.⟩

ep•i•blast ['ɛpəˌblæst] *n. Embryology.* the ectoderm. ⟨< *epi-* + Gk. *blastos* sprout⟩

e•pib•o•ly [ɪ'pɪbəli] *Embryology.* the growth of one cell over another. ⟨< Gk. *epibole* throwing upon < *epiballein* throw upon < *epi-* on + *ballein* throw⟩ **—ˌep•i'bol•ic** [ˌɛpɪ'bɒlɪk], *adj.*

ep•ic ['ɛpɪk] *n., adj.* *—n.* **1** a long poem that tells of the adventures of one or more great heroes. An epic is written in a dignified, majestic style, and often gives expression to the ideals of a nation or race. *Beowulf*, the *Iliad*, and *Paradise Lost* are epics. **2** any piece of writing having the qualities of an epic. **3** any story or series of events worthy of being the subject of an epic. **4** *Informal.* a spectacular motion picture or other entertainment.
—adj. **1** of or having to do with an epic. **2** like an epic; grand in style; heroic. Also, (adj.), **epical.** ⟨< L *epicus* < Gk. *epikos* < *epos* word, story⟩ **—'ep•i•cal•ly,** *adv.*

ep•i•ca•lyx [ˌɛpə'keilɪks] *or* [-'kælɪks] *n. Botany.* a ring of bracts at the base of a flower that looks like an outer calyx.

ep•i•can•thus [ˌɛpə'kænθəs] *n.* a fold in the upper eyelid, associated with many Mongolian peoples; the **epicanthic fold**, covering the inner corner of the eye. ⟨< Gk. *epi-* on, in + *kanthos* canthus, the corner of the eye⟩

ep•i•car•di•um [ˌɛpə'kardiəm] *n.* the inner layer of the pericardium.

ep•i•carp ['ɛpəˌkarp] *n.* the outer layer of the pericarp of a fruit. The epicarp forms the skin of a pear or peach. ⟨< *epi-* on + Gk. *karpos* fruit⟩

ep•i•ce•di•um [ˌɛpə'sidiəm] *or* [ˌɛpəsə'daɪəm] *n., pl.* **ep•i•ce•di•a** [-diə] *or* [-'daɪə]. a funeral hymn. ⟨< L < Gk. *epikedeion* < *epikedeios* funereal < *epi-* on, in + *kedos* grief, funeral rites⟩

ep•i•cene ['ɛpəˌsin] *adj., n.* *—adj.* **1** *Grammar.* **a** having only one gender for both sexes. The Latin noun *leo* is epicene, as it is masculine in gender but stands for both *lion* and *lioness.* **b** of common gender. English nouns such as *fish, mouse*, etc. are epicene. **2** belonging to or having the characteristics of both sexes. **3** not clearly of either sex; sexless. **4** effeminate.
—n. **1** an epicene person. **2** an epicene noun. ⟨< L < Gk. *epikoinos* common gender < *epi-* upon + *koinos* common⟩

ep•i•cen•tre ['ɛpəˌsɛntər] *n.* **1** the point from which earthquake waves seem to go out. It is situated directly above the true centre of the earthquake. **2** any focal point of great tension, disturbance, etc.: *the epicentre of a revolt.* Also, **epicenter. —ˌep•i'cen•tral,** *adj.*

ep•i•cot•yl [ˌɛpə'kɒtəl] *n.* the part of a plant embryo stem above the cotyledons.

ep•i•cra•ni•um [ˌɛpə'kreiniəm] *n.* **1** *Zoology*. the structures which cover the skull. **2** *Entomology*. the upper part of an insect's head. ⟨< *epi-* + *cranium*⟩

ep•i•crit•ic [ˌɛpə'krɪtɪk] *adj.* having to do with that part of the nervous system that is responsible for the detection of heat and movement.

ep•i•cure ['ɛpəˌkjʊr] *n.* a person who has a refined taste in eating and drinking and cares much about foods and drinks. ⟨Anglicized var. of *Epicurus*⟩

ep•i•cu•re•an [ˌɛpəkjə'riən] *or* [ˌɛpə'kjʊriən] *adj., n.*
—adj. **1** like an epicure; fond of pleasure and luxury. **2** fit for an epicure. **3 Epicurean,** of Epicurus or his philosophy.
—n. **1** a person fond of pleasure and luxury; epicure. **2 Epicurean,** a believer in the philosophy of Epicurus.

Ep•i•cu•re•an•ism [ˌɛpəkjə'riəˌnɪzəm] *or* [ˌɛpə'kjʊriəˌnɪzəm] *n.* **1** the philosophy or principles of Epicurus (342?-270 B.C.), a Greek philosopher who taught that pleasure is the highest good and that virtue alone produces pleasure. **2** Also, **epicureanism,** the belief in or practice of this philosophy. **3** epicurism.

ep•i•cur•ism ['ɛpəkjəˌrɪzəm] *n.* the lifestyle followed by an epicure.

ep•i•cy•cle ['ɛpəˌsəikəl] *n.* **1** in the cosmology of Ptolemy, a small circle on the circumference of another circle, with the earth or another planet at its centre. The movement of such a circle around the larger one explained the motion of the planets. **2** *Geometry*. a circle which rolls around the outside or inside of another circle's circumference, resulting in an epicycloid or hypocycloid. **—ˌep•i'cy•clic,** *adj.*

epicyclic train a system of gears in which the axis of one wheel revolves around another.

ep•i•cy•cloid [ˌɛpə'səiklɔɪd] *n. Geometry.* a curve made by the motion of a point on the circumference of a circle rolling around the outside of a stationary circle.

ep•i•dem•ic [ˌɛpə'dɛmɪk] *n., adj.* *—n.* **1** a rapid spreading of a disease so that many people have it at the same time: *All the schools in the city were closed because of an epidemic of scarlet fever.* **2** the rapid spread of an idea, fashion, etc. **3** the disease, attitude, behaviour, etc. so spread: *Grumbling is an epidemic in this office.*
—adj. affecting many people at the same time; widespread or spreading rapidly: *an epidemic disease. The wild rumours had reached epidemic proportions.* Also (adj.) **epidemical.** ⟨< F *épidémique* < *épidémie* < Med.L < Gk. *epidēmia* stay, visit, prevalence (of a disease) < *epi-* among + *dēmos* people⟩ **—ˌep•i'dem•i•cal•ly,** *adv.*

ep•i•de•mi•o•log•ic•al [ˌɛpəˌdimiə'lɒdʒəkəl] *or* [ˌɛpəˌdɛmi-] *adj.* **1** of or having to do with epidemiology. **2** like an epidemic. Also, **epidemiologic. —ˌep•iˌde•mi•o'log•i•cal•ly,** *adv.*

ep•i•de•mi•ol•o•gist [ˌɛpəˌdimi'ɒlədʒɪst] *or* [ˌɛpəˌdɛmi-] *n.* a person trained in epidemiology, especially one whose work it is.

ep•i•de•mi•ol•o•gy [ˌɛpəˌdimi'ɒlədʒi] *or* [ˌɛpəˌdɛmi-] *n.* the branch of medicine dealing with the occurrence, transmission, and control of infectious and epidemic diseases.

ep•i•den•drum [ˌɛpə'dɛndrəm] *n* any of various American orchids of the genus *Epidendrum*, bearing small flowers and growing in tropical climates. ⟨< NL < Gk. *epi-* over + *dendron* tree⟩

ep•i•der•mal [ˌɛpə'dɜrməl] *adj.* of or having to do with the epidermis. Also, **epidermic.**

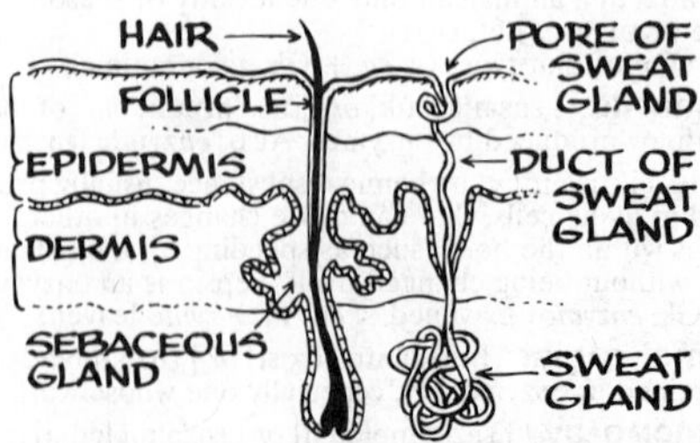

The layers of human skin as seen through a microscope

ep•i•der•mis [ˌɛpə'dɜrmɪs] *n.* **1** the outer layer of the skin of vertebrates. **2** the outer covering on the shells of many molluscs. **3** any of various other outer layers of invertebrates. **4** a skinlike layer of cells in seed plants and ferns.

ep•i•di•a•scope [ˌɛpə'daɪəˌskoup] *n.* a device for projecting transparencies onto a screen.

ep•i•did•y•mis [ˌɛpə'dɪdəməs] *n., pl.* **ep•i•di•dym•i•des** [ˌɛpədə'dɪməˌdiz]. that part of the spermatic duct that is on the side of the testis. ⟨< NL < Gk. *epi-* on + *didymoi* testicles, orig. pl. of *didymos* double⟩

ep•i•dote ['ɛpə,dout] *n.* a mineral consisting chiefly of aluminum, iron, and lime silicate. ⟨< F *épidote* < Gk. *epididonai* to increase < *epi-* over + *didonai* give (because it is longer in the base of the crystal than allied materials)⟩
—**,ep•i'dot•ic** [-'dɒtɪk], *adj.*

ep•i•fo•cal [,ɛpə'foukəl] *adj.* epicentral.

ep•i•gas•tric [,ɛpə'gæstrɪk] *adj.* having to do with the epigastrium.

ep•i•gas•tri•um [,ɛpə'gæstriəm] *n.* the middle region of the abdomen, lying over the stomach.

ep•i•ge•al [,ɛpə'dʒiəl] **1** *Biology.* living in, on, or near the surface of the ground. **2** *Botany.* having cotyledons above the surface of the ground. ⟨< Gk. *epigeios* on the earth < *epi-* upon + *ge* the earth⟩

ep•i•gene ['ɛpə,dʒin] *adj.* **1** *Geology.* formed or originating on or just below the surface of the earth. **2** *Crystallography.* not natural in the material in which it occurs. ⟨< F *épigène* < Gk. *epigenes* born late < *epi-* at, over + *-genes* born⟩

ep•i•gen•e•sis [,ɛpə'dʒɛnəsɪs] *n.* **1** *Biology.* the hypothesis that an embryo results from changes that produce completely new structures not originally existing in any form in the egg. **2** *Geology.* **a** a body of ore formed after being enclosed. **b** metamorphism. **3** *Medicine.* **a** the development of secondary symptoms or effects. **b** such a symptom or effect.

ep•i•ge•net•ic [,ɛpədʒə'nɛtɪk] *adj.* produced by epigenesis.

e•pig•e•nous [ɪ'pɪdʒənəs] *adj. Botany.* growing, as a fungus does, on the upper surface of a plant.

ep•i•glot•tis [,ɛpə'glɒtɪs] *n.* a thin, triangular plate of cartilage that covers the entrance to the windpipe during swallowing, so that food, etc. does not get into the lungs. See WINDPIPE for picture. ⟨< LL < Gk. *epiglottis* < *epi-* on + *glotta* tongue⟩ —**,ep•i'glot•tal** or **,ep•i'glot•tic,** *adj.*

ep•i•gone ['ɛpə,goun] *n.* a poor imitator of a writer or artist. ⟨< Gk. *epigonos* one born after⟩ —**,ep•i'gon•ic** [-'gɒnɪk], *adj.* —**e'pig•on•ism** [ɪ'pɪgə,nɪzəm], *n.*

ep•i•gram ['ɛpə,græm] *n.* **1** a short, pointed, witty saying. *Example*: *"The only way to get rid of temptation is to yield to it."* **2** a short poem ending in a witty or clever turn of thought. *Example*:

Here lies our Sovereign Lord the King
Whose word no man relies on,
Who never said a foolish thing,
Nor ever did a wise one.

⟨< L < Gk. *epigramma* < *epigraphein* < *epi-* on + *graphein* write⟩

☛ *Syn.* **Epigram,** PARADOX, APHORISM, PROVERB. An **epigram** is a short, pointed, witty saying. A special type of epigram is the **paradox**, which makes a statement that, as it stands, contradicts fact or common sense or itself, and yet suggests a truth or at least a half-truth: *All generalizations are false, including this one.* Closely related to epigrams are **aphorisms**—pithy statements but more likely to be abstract and not necessarily witty: *A living dog is better than a dead lion.* **Proverbs** are the often quoted, concrete expressions of popular wisdom. They are likely to make observations on character or conduct: *Still waters run deep.*

ep•i•gram•mat•ic [,ɛpəgrə'mætɪk] *adj.* **1** of epigrams; full of epigrams. **2** like an epigram; terse and witty.
—**,ep•i•gram'mat•i•cal•ly,** *adv.*

ep•i•gram•mat•ism [,ɛpə'græmə,tɪzəm] *n.* the style of epigrams or the use of epigrams. —**,ep•i'gram•ma•tist,** *n.*

ep•i•gram•mat•ize [,ɛpə'græmə,taɪz] *v.,* **-ized, -iz•ing.** **1** speak or write in epigrams. **2** characterize (a person or thing) in an epigram.

ep•i•graph ['ɛpə,græf] *n.* **1** an inscription on a building, monument, tomb, etc. **2** a quotation or motto at the beginning of a book or chapter. ⟨< Gk. *epigraphē* inscription < *epigraphein* < *epi-* on + *graphein* write⟩ —**,ep•i'graph•ic,** *adj.*

e•pig•ra•phy [ɪ'pɪgrəfi] *n.* **1** inscriptions collectively. **2** the branch of knowledge that deals with the deciphering and interpretation of inscriptions. ⟨< *epigraph* inscription < Gk. *epigraphē* < *epigraphein.* See EPIGRAM.⟩ —**e'pig•ra•pher** or **e'pig•ra•phist,** *n.*

e•pig•y•nous [ɪ'pɪdʒɪnəs] *adj. Botany.* of a flower, having its floral parts near the top of the ovary.

ep•i•lep•sy ['ɛpə,lɛpsi] *n.* a chronic disorder of the central nervous system characterized by attacks involving partial or complete loss of consciousness and, usually, mild or severe convulsions. ⟨< LL < Gk. *epilepsia* seizure, ult. < *epi-* on + *lambanein* take⟩

ep•i•lep•tic [,ɛpə'lɛptɪk] *adj., n.* —*adj.* **1** of or having to do with epilepsy: *Most epileptic seizures can be controlled with drugs.* **2** affected with epilepsy.
—*n.* a person affected with epilepsy.

ep•i•lim•ni•on [,ɛpə'lɪmniən] *or* [,ɛpə'lɪmni,ɒn] *n.* in an unfrozen lake, the layer of water above the thermocline. The epilimnion is warm and rich in oxygen. ⟨< NL < Gk. *epi-* over + *limnion* dim. of *limne* marshy lake⟩

ep•i•logue ['ɛpə,lɒg] *n.* **1** a concluding section added to a novel, poem, etc. and serving to round out or interpret the work. **2** a speech or poem after the end of a play, addressed to the audience and spoken by one of the actors. **3** the actor who speaks an epilogue. **4** any concluding act or event. ⟨< F *épilogue* < L < Gk. *epilogos*, ult. < *epi-* in addition + *legein* speak⟩

ep•i•mere ['ɛpə,mir] *n. Zoology.* in most vertebrate embryos, the dorsal part of the mesoderm which will develop into skeletal muscle. ⟨< *epi-* + Gk. *meros* part⟩

ep•i•my•si•um [,ɛpə'mɪsiəm] *n.* the fibrous sheath enclosing a muscle. ⟨< NL < Gk. *epi-* on + *mys* muscle + NL *-ium*⟩

ep•i•nas•ty ['ɛpə,næsti] *n.* the excessive growth of a plant that bends down the leaves or stems. ⟨< *epi-* + Gk. *nastos* pressed, squeezed close + *-y*[3]⟩

ep•i•neph•rine [,ɛpə'nɛfrɪn] *or* [,ɛpə'nɛfrin] *n.* adrenalin. ⟨< *epi-* + Gk. *nephros* kidney + E *-ine*[2]⟩

ep•i•neu•ri•um [,ɛpɪ'njʊriəm] *or* [,ɛpɪ'nʊriəm] *n.* the sheath around a nerve, containing veins and lymph ducts. ⟨< NL < Gk. *epi-* on, in + *neuron* nerve⟩

E•piph•a•ny [ɪ'pɪfəni] *n.* **1** the yearly Christian celebration commemorating the coming of the Wise Men to Christ at Bethlehem; in most Christian churches, January 6. **2 epiphany,** a moment or experience of revelation. ⟨ME < OF < LL < LGk. *epiphania*, ult. < Gk. *epi-* to + *phainein* show⟩ —**,ep•i'phan•ic** [,ɛpə'fænɪk], *adj.*

ep•i•phe•nom•en•al•ism [,ɛpəfə'nɒmənə,lɪzəm] *n.* the hypothesis that mental activity is nothing in itself but only a secondary phenomenon accompanying neural processes.

ep•i•phe•nom•e•non [,ɛpəfə'nɒmənən] *n., pl.* **-na** [-nə]. any secondary phenomenon, such as a complication in an illness.

ep•i•phy•sis [ɪ'pɪfəsɪs] *n., pl.* **-ses** [-,siz]. part of a bone, usually at the end, that originally develops by means of cartilage that is then ossified. ⟨< NL < Gk. *epiphysis* a growth upon < *epiphyein* to grow upon < *epi-* upon + *phyein* grow⟩

ep•i•phyte ['ɛpə,fəit] *n.* **1** any plant, such as Spanish moss or certain orchids, that grows on or is attached to another plant for support but does not derive its nourishment from its host; air plant. **2** a parasitic plant that lives on the outer surface of an animal. ⟨< *epi-* on + Gk. *phyton* plant⟩

ep•i•phyt•ic [,ɛpə'fɪtɪk] *adj.* being an epiphyte; having the characteristics of an epiphyte. —**,ep•i'phyt•i•cal•ly,** *adv.*

ep•i•phy•tol•o•gy [,ɛpəfəi'tɒlədʒi] *n. Botany.* the study of epidemics in plants.

ep•i•phy•tot•ic [,ɛpəfəi'tɒtɪk] *adj.* describing a disease which affects a lot of plants at the same time.

ep•i•ru•bi•cin [,ɛpə'rubɪsɪn] *n.* a drug used to treat certain forms of cancer.

e•pis•cia [ɪ'pɪʃə] *or* [ɪ'pɪʃiə] *n.* any of various American plants of the genus *Episcia*, found in tropical climates, bearing furry leaves and red or white flowers. ⟨< NL < Gk. *episkia* shaded < *epi-* on, in + *skia* shadow⟩

e•pis•co•pa•cy [ɪ'pɪskəpəsi] *n., pl.* **-cies. 1** the government of a church by bishops. **2** bishops as a group. **3** the position, rank, or term of office of a bishop; episcopate.

e•pis•co•pal [ɪ'pɪskəpəl] *adj.* **1** of or having to do with bishops. **2** governed by bishops. **3 Episcopal,** of or having to do with the Church of England, the Anglican Church of Canada, the Protestant Episcopal Church in the United States, etc. ⟨< LL *episcopalis* < L *episcopus* bishop < Gk. *episkopos* overseer < *epi-* on, over + *skopos* watcher. See BISHOP.⟩ —**e'pis•co•pal•ly,** *adv.*

E•pis•co•pa•lian [ɪ,pɪskə'peiliən] *or* [ɪ,pɪskə'peiljən] *n., adj.* —*n.* **1** a member of the Protestant Episcopal Church. **2** a believer in the episcopal form of church government.
—*adj.* **1** Episcopal. **2** following the episcopal form of church government.

E•pis•co•pa•lian•ism [ɪ,pɪskə'peiljə,nɪzəm] *n.* **1** the doctrines, ceremonies, etc. of Episcopalians. **2** adherence to the Episcopal Church or Episcopal principles.

e•pis•co•pal•ism [ɪ'pɪskəpə,lɪzəm] *n.* the theory that gives church government to bishops and not to one individual.

e•pis•co•pate [ɪ'pɪskəpɪt] *or* [ɪ'pɪskə,peit] *n.* **1** the position, rank, or term of office of a bishop. **2** a district under the charge of a bishop; bishopric. **3** bishops as a group.

e•pi•si•ot•om•y [ɪ,pizi'ɒtəmi] *n.* surgical incision of the perineum to allow room for birth. ⟨< Gk. *epision* pubic region + *tome* a cutting⟩

ep•i•sode ['ɛpə,soud] *n.* **1** an incident or experience that stands out from others: *The time Emily Carr spent in France was an important episode in the artist's life.* **2 a** a set of events or actions within the main plot of a novel, story, etc. but complete in itself. **b** *Music.* a similar digression in a composition. **3** in classical Greek tragedy, the part between two choric songs. **4** a portion of a serial play, film, etc.: *The concluding episode will be shown next week.* **5** an incident or series of incidents complete in itself but belonging to a larger event: *an episode in the Reformation.* ⟨< Gk. *episodion*, neut., coming in besides, ult. < *epi-* on + *eis* into + *hodos* way⟩

ep•i•sod•ic [,ɛpə'sɒdɪk] *adj.* **1** like an episode; incidental; occasional. **2** consisting of a series of episodes: *Her new novel is loosely episodic.* Also, **episodical.** **–,ep•i'sod•i•cal•ly,** *adv.*

ep•i•some ['ɛpɪ,soum] *n.* a small piece of DNA independent of the life of the cell, which may replicate separately. ⟨< Gk. *epi-* + *soma* body⟩

e•pis•ta•sis [ɪ'pɪstəsɪs] *Genetics.* the dominance of one set of genes over the other; the action of a gene in preventing the expression of another gene at a different place. ⟨< NL < Gk. a stopping < *epistanai* to stop < *epi-* at + *histanai* to stand⟩ **–,epi'stat•ic** [,ɛpə'stætɪk], *adj.*

ep•i•stax•is [,ɛpə'stæksɪs] *n.* a nosebleed. ⟨< NL < Gk. *epistazein* bleed at the nose < *epi-* upon + *stazein* drip⟩

ep•i•ste•mic [,ɛpə'stɛmɪk] *adj.* of or having to do with knowledge or how knowledge is acquired. ⟨< Gk. *episteme* knowledge⟩

e•pis•te•mo•log•i•cal [ɪ,pɪstəmə'lɒdʒəkəl] *adj.* of or having to do with epistemology. **–e,pis•te•mo'log•i•cal•ly,** *adv.*

e•pis•te•mol•o•gist [ɪ,pɪstə'mɒlədʒɪst] *n.* a person knowledgeable about or studying epistemology.

e•pis•te•mol•o•gy [ɪ,pɪstə'mɒlədʒi] *n.* the part of philosophy that deals with the origin, nature, and limits of knowledge. ⟨< Gk. *epistēmē* knowledge + E *-logy*⟩

ep•i•ster•num [,ɛpə'stɜrnəm] *n.* **1** the front part of the sternum in mammals. **2** in some reptiles and amphibians, a bony membrane between and beneath the clavicles.

e•pis•tle [ɪ'pɪsəl] *n.* **1** a letter, especially an instructive or a formal one. **2** a literary work, usually in verse, written in the form of a letter. **3 Epistle, a** a letter written by one of Christ's Apostles. The Epistles make up 21 books of the New Testament. **b** a selection from one of these, read as part of certain Christian church services. ⟨OE *epistole* < L < Gk. *epistolē*, ult. < *epi-* to + *stellein* send⟩

☛ *Syn.* **1.** See note at LETTER.

e•pis•to•lar•y [ɪ'pɪstə,lɛri] *adj.* **1** carried on by letters; contained in letters. **2** of letters; suitable for writing letters. **3** composed in the form of letters, like some novels.

e•pis•to•ler [ɪ'pɪstələr] *n.* **1** the writer of an epistle. **2** the person who reads the epistle in Communion. Also, **epistler.**

ep•i•style ['ɛpə,staɪl] *n. Architecture.* the part of a building resting directly on top of columns; architrave. ⟨< L < Gk. *epistylion* < *epi-* on + *stylos* pillar⟩

ep•i•taph ['ɛpə,tæf] *n.* **1** a short statement in memory of a dead person, usually put on his or her tombstone. **2** any brief writing resembling such an inscription. ⟨< L < Gk. *epitaphion* funeral oration < *epi-* at + *taphos* tomb⟩ **–,ep•i'taph•ic** or **,ep•i'taph•i•al,** *adj.*

e•pit•a•sis [ɪ'pɪtəsɪs] *n.* that part of a classical drama just before the climax. ⟨< Gk. a stretching; tension < *epiteinein* < stretch < *epi-* + *teinein* stretch⟩

ep•i•tha•la•mi•on [,ɛpəθə'leimiən] *n., pl.* **-mi•a** [-miə]. a poem or song in honour of a bride, bridegroom, or newly married couple. Also, **epithalamium.** ⟨< L < Gk. *epithalamion* < *epi-* at + *thalamos* bridal chamber⟩

ep•i•the•li•oid [,ɛpə'θili,ɔɪd] *adj.* like the epithelium.

ep•i•the•li•o•ma [,ɛpə,θili'oumə] *n.* a carcinoma deriving from the epithelium.

ep•i•the•li•um [,ɛpə'θiliəm] *n., pl.* **-li•ums, -li•a** [-liə]. *Biology.* a thin layer of cells forming a tissue that covers surfaces and lines hollow organs. ⟨< NL < Gk. *epi-* on + *thēlē* nipple⟩ **–,ep•i'the•li•al,** *adj.*

ep•i•thet ['ɛpə,θɛt] *or* ['ɛpəθət] *n.* **1** a descriptive expression; an adjective or noun, or sometimes a clause, expressing some quality or attribute. In *crafty Ulysses* and *Richard the Lion-Hearted* the epithets are *crafty* and *the Lion-Hearted.* **2** a word or phrase (sometimes highly insulting) used in place of a person's name. **3** that part of the scientific name of an animal or plant which denotes a species, variety, or other division of a genus. ⟨< L < Gk. *epitheton* added < *epi-* on + *tithenai* place⟩ **–,ep•i'thet•ic** or **,ep•i'thet•ic•al,** *adj.*

e•pit•o•me [ɪ'pɪtəmi] *n.* **1** a condensed account; summary. An epitome contains only the most important points of a literary work, subject, etc. **2** a person or thing that is typical or representative of a quality; an ideal or typical example: *Solomon is spoken of as the epitome of wisdom.* ⟨< L < Gk. *epitomē* < *epitemnein* cut short < *epi-* into + *temnein* cut⟩

e•pit•o•mize [ɪ'pɪtə,maɪz] *v.* **-mized, -miz•ing.** make or be an epitome of; summarize.

ep•i•zo•ic [,ɛpə'zouɪk] *adj.* living on the surface of an animal but not parasitic. **–,ep•i'zo•ite,** *n.*

ep•i•zo•on [,ɛpə'zouɒn] *n.* an external parasite.

ep•i•zo•ot•ic [,ɛpəzou'ɒtɪk] *adj., n.* *–adj. Veterinary Medicine.* temporarily prevalent among animals. Compare ENZOOTIC. *–n.* an epizootic disease. ⟨< *epi-* among < Gk. *zōion* animal⟩

ep•i•zo•ot•i•ol•o•gy [,ɛpəzou,ɒti'ɒlədʒi] *n.* the study of epidemics in animals. ⟨< NL < F *épizootie* (formed by analogy from *épidémie*) + E *-logy*⟩

e•poch ['ipɒk] *or* ['ɛpək] *n.* **1** a period of time; era. **2** a period of time in which striking things happened. **3** the starting point of such a period: *The invention of the steam engine marked an epoch in the evolution of industry.* **4** one of the divisions of time into which a geological period is divided: *the Holocene epoch of the Quaternary period.* **5** a date marking the start of an epoch. **6** *Astronomy.* an arbitrary point in time used as a reference. ⟨< Med.L < Gk. *epochē* a stopping, fixed point in time < *epechein* < *epi-* up + *echein* hold⟩

ep•och•al ['ɛpəkəl] *or* ['ipɒkəl] *adj.* **1** having to do with an epoch. **2** epoch-making.

e•poch–mak•ing ['ipɒk ,meikɪŋ] *or* ['ɛpək-] *adj.* beginning an epoch; causing important changes.

ep•ode ['ɛpoud] *n. Greek prosody.* **1** a lyric poem in which a long line is followed by a shorter one. **2** a part of a lyric ode following the strophe and antistrophe. ⟨< F < L *epodos* < Gk. *epoidos* < *epi-* after + *aidein* sing⟩

ep•o•nym ['ɛpə,nɪm] *n.* **1** a person from whom a nation, group, place, etc. gets or is reputed to get its name: *Romulus is the eponym of Rome.* **2** a person whose name is a synonym for something: *Ananias is the eponym of liar.* ⟨< Gk. *epōnymos* < *epi-* to + (dial.) *onyma* name⟩

e•pon•y•mous [ɪ'pɒnəməs] *adj.* giving one's name to a nation, group, place, book, etc.

e•pon•y•my [ɪ'pɒnəmi] *n.* the derivation of the name of a country or a city from the name of a person, as *Russia* is derived from *Rus* 'a Viking'.

ep•o•pee ['ɛɪpə,pei] *or* [,eipə'pei] *n.* **1** an epic poem. **2** epic poetry as a literary genre. ⟨< F *épopée* < Gk. *epopoiia* the making of epics < *epopoios* epic poet < *epos* song + *poiein* to make⟩

ep•os ['ɛpɒs] *n.* an epic poem preserved orally.

e•pox•ide [ɛ'pɒksaɪd] *n. Chemistry.* a compound composed of two linked carbon atoms and an oxygen atom.

e•pox•y [ɛ'pɒksi] *or* [ɪ'pɒksi] *adj., n., pl.* **-ox•ies.** *–adj.* containing oxygen as a bond between two different atoms already united in another way. Epoxy resins are extremely durable plastics used for adhesives, varnishes, etc. *–n.* an epoxy resin. ⟨< *ep-* + *oxy(gen)*⟩

EPROM ['iprɒm] *Computer technology.* a kind of PROM chip that can be erased by ultraviolet light and reprogrammed. ⟨< *e*rasable PROM⟩

E–proposition *Logic.* a negative proposition about all members of a class. *Example*: *No men are immortal.*

ep•si•lon ['ɛpsə,lɒn] *or* [ɛp'saɪlən] *n.* the fifth letter of the Greek alphabet (Ε, ε), corresponding to *e* (as in *get*) in English. ⟨< Med.Gk. *epsilon* < Gk. *e psilon* simple *e*⟩

Epsom Downs ['ɛpsəm] the track near the town of Epsom where England's famous horse race, the Derby, is run.

Epsom salt or **salts** hydrated magnesium sulphate, a bitter, white, crystalline powder used in medicine, especially as a laxative. *Formula*: $MgSO_4 \cdot 7H_2O$ ⟨< *Epsom*, a town in SE England⟩

Epstein–Barr virus ['ɛpstaın 'bɑr] a kind of virus causing infectious mononucleosis and, possibly, chronic fatigue syndrome as well as certain cancers. ⟨after M.A. *Epstein* (born 1921), British pathologist, and Y.M. *Barr*, British virologist⟩

eq. **1** equal; equation. **2** equivalent. **3** equator.

eq•ua•bil•i•ty [,ɛkwə'bıləti] *or* [,ikwə-] *n.* an equable condition or quality.

eq•ua•ble ['ɛkwəbəl] *or* ['ikwəbəl] *adj.* **1** changing little; uniform. **2** even; tranquil: *an equable temperament.* ⟨< L *aequabilis* < *aequare* make uniform < *aequus* even, just⟩
—'eq•ua•bly, *adv.* **—'eq•ua•ble•ness,** *n.*
☛ *Syn.* See note at EVEN.

e•qual ['ikwəl] *adj., n., v.* **e•qualled** or **e•qualed, e•qual•ling** or **e•qual•ing.** *—adj.* **1** the same in amount, size, number, value, degree, rank, nature, quality, etc.: *Ten dimes are equal to one dollar. The two roasts were almost equal in size.* **2** the same throughout; even; uniform. **3** evenly matched; with no advantage on either side: *an equal contest.* **4** having the strength, capacity, ability, etc. necessary for a task or situation (*used with* **to**): *She proved to be equal to the task.* **5** *Archaic.* just; fair.
—n. a person or thing that is equal to another: *We are all equals here. In swimming she had no equal.* $7 + 3$ *is the equal of* 5×2.
—v. **1** be the same as: *Four times five equals twenty. Symbol*: =
2 make or do something equivalent to; match: *He tried hard to equal the scoring record.* ⟨< L *aequalis* < *aequus* even, just⟩
—'e•qual•ly, *adv.*
☛ *Syn. adj.* **1. Equal,** EQUIVALENT, TANTAMOUNT = as much as another or each other. **Equal** = exactly the same in size, amount, value, or any quality that can be measured or weighed: *The pieces of pie are equal.* **Equivalent,** applying to things otherwise different, means equal in value or in a quality that cannot be physically measured, such as meaning, importance, effect, etc.: *A CEGEP course may be regarded as equivalent to the first two years of university.* **Tantamount,** applying only to immaterial things, means equivalent to another in effect: *His answer was tantamount to an insult.*
☛ *Usage.* **Equally,** when used with an adjective or adverb, is not followed by *as*: *Spring is a lovely season, but I find fall equally beautiful.* **Equally** is redundant in a comparison of equals using *as…as*: *She is as bright as her brother,* **not** *She is equally as bright as her brother*.

equal–area projection ['ikwəl 'ɛriə] a map projection that shows the area of regions accurately as to size.

e•qual•i•tar•ian [ı,kwɒlə'tɛriən] *adj., n.* *—adj.* egalitarian; of or following the doctrine that all people are equal.
—n. a follower of that doctrine.

e•qual•i•ty [ı'kwɒləti] *n., pl.* **-ties.** the condition of being equal; sameness in amount, size, number, value, degree, rank, etc.

e•qual•i•za•tion [,ikwəlaı'zeiʃən] *or* [,ikwələ'zeiʃən] *n.* **1** the act of equalizing or the state of being equalized. **2** *Cdn.* the principle or practice of the federal government paying money to the less wealthy provinces in order to bring their standard of living nearer to that of the resource-rich provinces.

e•qual•ize ['ikwə,laız] *v.* **-ized, -iz•ing. 1** make equal. **2** make even or uniform.

e•qual•iz•er ['ikwə,laızər] *n.* **1** a person or thing that equalizes. **2** a device for equalizing strain, pressure, etc. **3** *Electricity.* **a** any network of coils, resistors, or capacitors introduced into a circuit to change its response, especially its audio frequency response so as to reduce distortion. **b** a conductor of low resistance used to equalize voltages.

equal opportunity **1** the principle or practice of giving everyone the same chance or treatment regardless of sex, religion, colour, etc. **2** of a company, etc., operating on such a principle: *an equal opportunity employer.*

e•qual sign Also, **equals sign.** the sign (=), used in equations.

e•qua•nim•i•ty [,ikwə'nıməti] *or* [,ɛkwə-] *n.* evenness of mind or temper; calmness: *A wise person bears misfortune with equanimity.* ⟨< L *aequanimitas* < *aequus* even + *animus* mind, temper⟩

e•quan•i•mous [ı'kwænıməs] *adj.* even-tempered; calm; mentally and emotionally composed or controlled.
—e'quan•i•mous•ly, *adv.*

e•quat•a•ble [ı'kweitəbəl] *adj.* that can be equated.
—e,quat•a'bil•i•ty, *n.*

e•quate [ı'kweit] *v.* **e•quat•ed, e•quat•ing. 1** state to be equal (*with*); put in the form of an equation. **2** consider, treat, or represent as equal (*with*). **3** make equal (*with*). **4** reduce to an average. ⟨< L *aequare* make equal < *aequus* equal⟩

e•qua•tion [ı'kweiʒən] *or* [ı'kweiʃən] *n.* **1** a statement of equality between two quantities. *Examples*: $(4 \times 8) + 12 = 44$; $C = 2\pi r$. **2** an expression using chemical formulas and symbols showing the substances used and produced in a chemical reaction. *Example*: $HCl + NaOH \rightarrow NaCl + H_2O$
3 an equating or being equated.

equation of time *Astronomy.* the ever-varying difference between apparent solar time and mean solar time. The two may differ by as much as 16 min.

e•qua•tor [ı'kweitər] *n.* **1** an imaginary circle around the middle of the earth, halfway between the North Pole and the South Pole. **2** a similarly situated circle on any heavenly body. **3** CELESTIAL EQUATOR. **4** a circle separating a surface into two congruent parts. ⟨< Med.L *aequator (diei et noctis)* equalizer (of day and night) < L *aequare* make equal. See EQUATE.⟩

e•qua•to•ri•al [,ikwə'tɔriəl] *or* [,ɛkwə-] *adj., n.* *—adj.* **1** of, at, or near the equator: *equatorial countries.* **2** similar to conditions at or near the equator. **3** of a telescope, having a mount or support with two axes, one of which is parallel with the earth's surface.
—n. a telescope mount with two axes, one of which forms an angle with the other and is parallel to the earth's surface.

Equatorial Gui•nea ['gıni] a country in west central Africa.

eq•uer•ry ['ɛkwəri] *n., pl.* **-ries. 1** an officer of a royal or noble household who has charge of the horses or who accompanies his master's carriage. **2** an attendant on a royal or noble person. ⟨short for *groom of the equerry* < F *écurie* stable < Gmc.; influenced by L *equus* horse⟩

e•ques•tri•an [ı'kwɛstriən] *adj., n.* *—adj.* **1** of riders or ridership; having to do with horseback riding: *Jockeys need to have equestrian skill.* **2** on horseback; mounted on horseback. An equestrian statue shows a person riding a horse. **3** of or having to do with the equites of ancient Rome. **4** of or having to do with knights.
—n. a rider or performer on horseback. ⟨< L *equestris* of a horseman < *equus* horse⟩

e•ques•tri•enne [ı,kwɛstri'ɛn] *n.* a woman rider or performer on horseback. ⟨< F⟩

equi– *combining form.* **1** equal, as in *equivalence.* **2** equally, as in *equiangular, equidistant.* ⟨< L *aequus* equal⟩

e•qui•an•gu•lar [,ikwi'æŋgjələr] *adj.* having all angles equal: *A square is equiangular.*

e•qui•dis•tant [,ikwə'dıstənt] *adj.* equally distant: *All points of the circumference of a circle are equidistant from the centre.*
—,e•qui'dis•tant•ly, *adv.* **—,e•qui'dis•tance,** *n.*

e•qui•lat•er•al [,ikwə'lætərəl] *adj., n.* *—adj.* designating a geometric figure having all its sides equal in length.
—n. **1** a geometric figure having all its sides equal in length. See TRIANGLE for picture. **2** a side equal in length to others. ⟨< LL *aequilateralis* < L *aequus* equal + *latus, lateris* side⟩
—,e•qui'lat•er•al•ly, *adv.*

e•quil•i•brant [ı'kwıləbrənt] *n. Physics.* a force able to balance a specified force or set of forces.

e•quil•i•brate [ı'kwılə,breit] *or* [,ikwə'laıbreit] *v.* **-brat•ed, -brat•ing.** balance. ⟨< LL *aequilibratus* in equilibrium < L *aequus* equal + *libra* balance⟩ **—e'quil•i'bra•tion,** *n.*
—e'quil•i,bra•tor, *n.*

e•quil•i•brist [ı'kwılə,brıst] *n.* one who performs feats of balance, such as a tightrope walker.

e•qui•lib•ri•um [,ikwə'lıbriəm] *or* [,ɛkwə-] *n.* **1** a state of balance; condition in which opposing forces exactly balance or equal each other: *Scales are in equilibrium when the weights on each side are equal.* **2** the state of a chemical system when no further change occurs in it. **3** a condition of balance between things of any kind. **4** mental poise: *She is a sensible person and will not let petty annoyances upset her equilibrium.* ⟨< L *aequilibrium*, ult. < *aequus* equal + *libra* balance⟩

e•qui•mo•lec•u•lar [ˌikwəmə'lɛkjələr] *adj.* having an equal number of molecules.

e•quine ['ikwaɪn] *or* ['ɛkwaɪn] *adj., n. —adj.* of horses; like a horse; like that of a horse.
—n. a horse. ⟨< L *equinus* < *equus* horse⟩

e•qui•noc•tial [ˌikwə'nɒkʃəl] *or* [ˌɛkwə-] *adj., n. —adj.* **1** having to do with either equinox. Equinoctial points are the two imaginary points in the sky where the sun crosses the celestial equator. **2** occurring at or near the equinox: *equinoctial gales.* **3** at or near the earth's equator: *Borneo is an equinoctial island.*
—n. **1** CELESTIAL EQUATOR. **2** a storm occurring at or near the equinox.

equinoctial line or **circle** CELESTIAL EQUATOR.

equinoctial point a point on the celestial sphere where the sun crosses the equator.

equinoctial year LUNAR YEAR.

e•qui•nox ['ikwəˌnɒks] *or* ['ɛkwə-] *n.* **1** either of the two times in the year when the centre of the sun crosses the celestial equator, and day and night are of equal length all over the earth. The **vernal** (spring) **equinox** occurs in the northern hemisphere about March 21, the **autumnal equinox** about September 22. **2** either of two equinoctial points. ⟨< Med.L *equinoxium* < L *aequinoctium* < *aequus* equal + *nox* night⟩

e•quip [ɪ'kwɪp] *v.* **e•quipped, e•quip•ping. 1** furnish with all that is needed; fit out; provide: *The fort was equipped with guns, ammunition, and food. She was equipped with a good mind and a keen sense of humour.* **2** train; instruct. **3** attire (oneself) for a particular purpose. ⟨< F *équipper* < OF *esquiper* < ON *skipa* man (a ship) < *skip* ship. Akin to SHIP.⟩
☛ *Syn.* **1.** See note at FURNISH.

eq•ui•page ['ɛkwəpɪdʒ] *n.* **1** a carriage. **2** a carriage with its horses, driver, and servants. **3** equipment; outfit.

e•quip•ment [ɪ'kwɪpmənt] *n.* **1** the act of equipping. **2** the state of being equipped. **3** what a person or thing is equipped with; outfit, supplies, tools, facilities, etc. **4** knowledge or skill; ability. **5** the rolling stock of a transportation business such as a railway. **6** materials used to provide service, usually in transportation.

e•qui•poise ['ikwəˌpɔɪz] *or* ['ɛkwə-] *n.* **1** a state of balance. **2** a balancing force; counterbalance.

e•qui•pol•lent [ˌikwɪ'pɒlənt] *adj., n. —adj.* **1** equal in power. **2** *Logic.* of two propositions each of which may be deduced from the other.
—n. an equivalent. ⟨ME < OF *equipolent* < L *aequipollens* < *aequus* equal + *pollens*, ppr. of *pollere* be strong⟩

e•qui•pon•der•ance [ˌikwɪ'pɒndərəns] *n.* equality in weight; equipoise. **—ˌeq•ui'pon•der•ant,** *adj.*

e•qui•pon•der•ate [ˌikwɪ'pɒndəˌreit] *v.* **-at•ed, -at•ing.** be equal in weight (to); counterbalance.

e•qui•po•ten•tial [ˌikwɪpə'tɛnʃəl] *adj. Physics.* having the same potential at every point.

eq•ui•se•tum [ˌɛkwə'sitəm] *n., pl.* **-tums, -ta** [-tə]. **1** a genus of plants with jointed, green, cylindrical stems, either simple or branched, rough to the touch, and having leaves reduced to scales. **2** horsetail. ⟨< NL < L *equisaetum* < *equus* horse + *saeta* (coarse) hair⟩

eq•ui•ta•ble ['ɛkwətəbəl] *adj.* **1** fair; just: *Paying a person what she has earned is equitable.* **2** *Law.* having to do with or dependent upon equity; valid in equity, as distinguished from common law and statute law. **—'eq•ui•ta•ble•ness,** *n.* **—'eq•ui•ta•bly,** *adv.*

eq•ui•tant ['ɛkwɪtənt] *adj. Botany.* of some plants, having leaves that overlap at the base, like a fan. ⟨< L *equitans* ppr. of *equitare* to ride⟩

eq•ui•ta•tion [ˌɛkwə'teiʃən] *n.* horseback riding; ridership. ⟨< L *equitatio, -onis*, ult. < *equus* horse⟩

eq•ui•tes ['ɛkwəˌtiz] *n.pl.* in ancient Rome: **1** originally, the class of citizens serving in the cavalry. **2** later, a privileged class of citizens. ⟨< L *equites*, pl. of *eques* horseman, knight < *equus* horse⟩

eq•ui•ty ['ɛkwəti] *n., pl.* **-ties. 1** fairness; justice. **2** what is fair and just. **3** *Law.* **a** a system of rules and principles based on fairness and justice. Equity covers cases in which fairness and justice require a settlement not covered by common law. **b** a claim or right according to equity. **4** the amount that a property, business, etc. is worth beyond what is owed on it. ⟨< L *aequitas* < *aequus* even, just⟩

equity of redemption *Law.* the right to redeem property even if a mortgage payment is late.

e•quiv•a•lence [ɪ'kwɪvələns] *n.* **1** a being equivalent; equality in value, force, significance, etc. **2** *Chemistry.* **a** the quality of having equal valence. **b** valence. **3** *Geometry.* the fact of being equal in extent, but not in form.

e•quiv•a•lent [ɪ'kwɪvələnt] *adj., n. —adj.* **1** equal in value, measure, force, effect, meaning, etc.: *Nodding one's head is equivalent to saying yes.* **2** *Chemistry.* equal in combining or reacting value to a (stated) quantity of another substance. **3** *Geometry.* having the same extent: *A triangle and a square that are equivalent have the same area.*
—n. **1** something equivalent: *He accepted the equivalent of his wages in groceries.* **2** a word, expression, sign, etc. of equal meaning or import. ⟨< LL *aequivalens, -entis*, ppr. of *aequivalere* < L *aequus* equal + *valere* be worth⟩ **—e'quiv•a•lent•ly,** *adv.*
☛ *Syn.* **1.** See note at EQUAL.

equivalent weight *Chemistry.* the combining power by weight of an element to replace the equivalent of half the atomic weight of oxygen, that is, 8 g of oxygen.

e•quiv•o•cal [ɪ'kwɪvəkəl] *adj.* **1** having two or more meanings; intentionally vague or ambiguous: *His equivocal answer left us uncertain as to his real opinion.* **2** undecided; uncertain: *The result of the experiment was equivocal.* **3** questionable; rousing suspicion: *The stranger's equivocal behaviour made everyone distrust her.* ⟨< LL *aequivocus* ambiguous < L *aequus* equal + *vocare* call⟩ **—e'quiv•o•cal•ly,** *adv.* **—e'quiv•o•cal•ness,** *n.*

e•quiv•o•cate [ɪ'kwɪvəˌkeit] *v.* **-cat•ed, -cat•ing. 1** use expressions of double meaning in order to mislead. **2** avoid taking a stand. ⟨< LL *aequivocare* call by the same name < *aequivocus* ambiguous. See EQUIVOCAL.⟩ **—e'quiv•oˌcat•ing•ly,** *adv.* **—e'quiv•oˌcat•or,** *n.*

e•quiv•o•ca•tion [ɪˌkwɪvə'keiʃən] *n.* **1** the use of equivocal expressions in order to mislead. **2** an equivocal expression. **3** the avoidance of an issue at hand.

e•qui•voke or **e•qui•voque** ['ɛkwəˌvouk] *or* [ˌɛkwə'vouk] *n.* **1** a pun. **2** a double meaning.

E•quu•le•us [ɪ'kwuliəs] *n. Astronomy.* a northern constellation in the equatorial region. ⟨< L, little horse⟩

er [ɜr] *interj.* an expression of hesitation in speech.

-er[1] *suffix.* **1** a person or thing that ——s: *admirer = a person who admires; burner = a thing that burns.* **2** a native or inhabitant of ——: *Newfoundlander = a native or inhabitant of Newfoundland; villager = a native or inhabitant of a village.* **3** a person that makes or works with ——: *hatter = a person who makes hats.* **4** a person or thing that is or has ——: *six-footer = a person who is six feet tall.* ⟨OE *-ere*, ult. < L *-arius*⟩
☛ *Usage.* **-er, -or.** Names of persons or things performing an act (nouns of agent) and some other nouns are generally formed in English by adding **-er** to a verb (*doer, killer, painter, heater, thinker*), but many, chiefly nouns taken from Latin or French (*assessor, prevaricator*), end in **-or.** With a few words (*exhibitor* or *exhibiter, adviser* or *advisor*) either ending may be used.

-er[2] *suffix.* a person or thing connected with ——: *officer.* ⟨< AF, OF < L *-arius, -arium*⟩

-er[3] *suffix.* forming the comparative degree: **1** of certain adjectives: *softer, smoother.* **2** of certain adverbs: *faster.* ⟨OE *-ra* (masc.), *-re* (fem., neut.), adj. OE *-or*, adv.⟩
☛ *Usage.* See notes at ADJECTIVE and ADVERB.

-er[4] *suffix.* a frequentative: *flicker, patter.* ⟨OE *-rian*⟩

Er erbium.

E.R. Queen Elizabeth (for L *Elizabeth Regina*).

e•ra ['ɛrə] *or* ['irə] *n.* **1** a historical period distinguished by certain important or significant happenings; an age in history. The decade from 1929 to 1939 is often called the Depression Era. **2** a period of time starting from some important or significant happening, date, etc.: *the A-bomb era.* **3** a system of reckoning time from some important or significant happening, given date, etc. The Christian era is the period of time reckoned from about four years after the birth of Christ. **4** one of five very extensive expanses of time in geological history. See geological time chart in the Appendix. ⟨< LL *era*, var. of *aera* number, epoch; probably same word as L *aera* counters (for reckoning), pl. of *aes* brass⟩

ERA *Baseball.* EARNED RUN AVERAGE.

e•ra•di•ate [ɪ'reidiˌeit] *v.* **-at•ed, -at•ing.** radiate. **—eˌrad•i'a•tion,** *n.*
☛ *Hom.* IRRADIATE.

e•rad•i•ca•ble [ɪ'rædəkəbəl] *adj.* that can be eradicated.

e•rad•i•cate [ɪ'rædə,keit] *v.* **-cat•ed, -cat•ing. 1** get rid of entirely; destroy completely: *Yellow fever has been eradicated in many countries.* **2** pull out by the roots: *to eradicate weeds from a garden.* ⟨< L *eradicare* < *ex-* out + *radix, radicis* root⟩ **—e'rad•i,ca•tor,** *n.* **—e'rad•i•ca•tive,** *adj.*

e•rad•i•ca•tion [ɪ,rædə'keiʃən] *n.* an eradicating; complete destruction.

e•rase [ɪ'reis] *v.* **e•rased, e•ras•ing. 1** rub out; scrape out: *She erased the wrong answer and wrote in the right one.* **2** remove all trace of; blot out: *The blow on his head erased from his memory the details of the accident.* **3** remove marks or recorded information from: *Please erase the chalkboard. She accidentally erased the whole tape while recording. Please erase the entire disk.* ⟨< L *erasus,* pp. of *eradere* < *ex-* out + *radere* scrape⟩ **—e'ras•a•ble,** *adj.*

☛ *Syn.* **1, 2. Erase,** EXPUNGE, EFFACE = remove everything from a record of some kind. **Erase** = remove all trace of something by scraping or rubbing, literally as from paper or figuratively as from memory: *I erased him from my mind.* **Expunge** = blot out so that the thing seems never to have existed: *The judge ordered certain charges expunged from the record.* **Efface** = wipe out identity or existence by or as if by rubbing away the face: *Rain and wind effaced the inscription on the monument.*

e•ras•er [ɪ'reisər] *n.* a piece of rubber or any other substance for erasing marks made with pencil, ink, chalk, etc.

e•ra•sion [ɪ'reiʒən] *n. Surgery.* **1** the excision of a joint. **2** the scraping away of tissue.

E•ras•ti•an [ɪ'ræstiən] *adj., n. —adj.* of or having to do with Thomas Erastus (1524–1583) or his teachings.
—n. an advocate of Erastianism.

E•ras•ti•an•ism [ɪ'ræstiə,nɪzəm] *n.* the doctrine of the supremacy of the state over the church.

e•ra•sure [ɪ'reiʃər] *or* [ɪ'reiʒər] *n.* **1** the act of erasing. **2** an erased word, letter, etc. **3** a place where a word, letter, etc. has been erased.

Er•a•to ['ɛrə,tou] *n. Greek mythology.* the Muse of love poetry.

er•bi•um ['ɜrbiəm] *n.* a rare metallic chemical element of the yttrium group. *Symbol:* Er; *at.no.* 68; *at.mass* 167.26. ⟨< NL *erbium* < *(Ytt)erby,* a town in Sweden⟩

ere [ɛr] *prep., conj. Poetic or archaic. —prep.* before.
—conj. **1** before. **2** sooner than; rather than. ⟨OE *ǣr*⟩

☛ *Hom.* AIR, E'ER, ERR, EYRE, HEIR.

Er•e•bus ['ɛrəbəs] *n. Greek mythology.* a dark, gloomy place through which the dead passed on their way to Hades.

e•rect [ɪ'rɛkt] *adj., v. —adj.* **1** straight up; upright: *That flagpole stands erect.* **2** raised; bristling; sticking out straight: *The cat faced the dog with fur erect.*
—v. **1** put straight up; set upright: *They erected a television antenna on the roof. The mast was erected on a firm base.* **2** build; put up: *That house was erected forty years ago.* **3** put together; set up: *When the missing parts arrived, we erected the machine.* **4** *Geometry.* construct on a given base. **5** *Physiology.* cause to become rigid. ⟨ME < L *erectus,* pp. of *erigere* < *ex-* up + *regere* direct⟩ **—e'rect•ly,** *adv.* **—e'rect•ness,** *n.* **—e'rect•or,** *n.*

☛ *Syn. adj.* **1.** See note at UPRIGHT.

e•rec•tile [ɪ'rɛktail] *adj.* of body tissue or an organ, capable of becoming rigid or erect when filled with blood.

e•rec•tion [ɪ'rɛkʃən] *n.* **1** the act of erecting or the state of being erected; construction: *the erection of a building.* **2** something erected; a building or other structure. **3** the enlarged, rigid state or condition of erectile tissue or an organ, especially of the penis or clitoris when filled with blood due to sexual excitement. **4** an erect penis.

E region a region of the ionosphere containing the E layer or Heaviside layer. Compare F REGION.

ere•long [,ɛr'lɒŋ] *adv. Poetic or archaic.* before long; soon.

er•e•mite ['ɛrə,məit] *n. Archaic.* hermit. ⟨ME < L *eremita* < Gk. *erēmitēs* dweller in a desert < *erēmos* uninhabited. Doublet of HERMIT.⟩ **—,er•e'mit•ic** [,ɛrə'mɪtɪk] or **,er•e'mit•i•cal,** *adj.*

er•e•mu•rus [,ɛrə'mjurəs] *n.* any of various perennial plants of the genus *Eremurus,* known for their long flower spikes. ⟨< NL < Gk. *eremos* desolate + NL *-urus* < Gk. *oura* tail⟩

e•rep•sin [ɪ'rɛpsɪn] *n.* a mixture of peptidases producing amino acids in the small intestine.

er•e•thism ['ɛrə,θɪzəm] *n.* the excessive response of any part of the body to a stimulus. ⟨< F *éréthisme* < Gk. *erethismos* irritation < *erethizein* to irritate⟩

ere•while [,ɛr'waɪl] *adv. Archaic.* a while before; a short time ago.

erg¹ [ɜrg] *n.* a unit for measuring work or energy, equal to 0.1 microjoules. *Abbrev.:* e ⟨< Gk. *ergon* work⟩

erg² [ɜrg] *n.* a large area of sand dunes in the desert. ⟨< F < Arabic *'irq*⟩

er•go ['ɛrgou] *or* ['ɜrgou] *adv. or conj. Latin.* therefore.

er•go•cal•cif•e•rol [,ɜrgoukæl'sɪfə,rɒl] *n.* Vitamin D_2, obtained by ultraviolet irradiation of ergosterol. ⟨< *ergot* + *calciferous* + *-ol*⟩

er•go•graph ['ɜrgə,græf] *n.* a device for measuring the extent of a muscle to gauge its capacity. ⟨< Gk. *ergon* work + E *-graph*⟩

er•go•loid mes•y•lates ['ɜrgə,lɔɪd 'mɛsə,leits] *n.* a drug used to treat certain cases of dementia in elderly patients.

er•gom•e•ter [ər'gɒmətər] *n.* an instrument for measuring the work done, or energy produced, by a muscle or group of muscles. ⟨< Gk. *ergon* work + E *-meter.* 20c.⟩

er•go•nom•ic [,ɜrgə'nɒmɪk] *adj.* of or having to do with ergonomics.

er•go•nom•ics [,ɜrgə'nɒmɪks] *n. (used with a singular verb) Biotechnology.* the scientific study of the relationship between human beings and their working environment with a view to increasing efficiency. ⟨< Gk. *ergon* work + E econ*omics.* 20c.⟩

er•gon•o•mist [ər'gɒnəmɪst] *n.* a person trained in ergonomics, especially one whose work it is.

er•gos•te•rol [ər'gɒstə,rɒl] *n. Biochemistry.* a sterol that is not soluble in water, found in ergot and yeast, and converted to Vitamin D_2. *Formula:* $CH_{22}H_{44}O$ ⟨< F *ergot* (< OF *argot* a rooster's spur) + chole*sterol*⟩

er•got ['ɜrgət] *or* ['ɜrgɒt] *n.* **1** a disease of rye and other cereals in which the grains are replaced by blackish fungous growths. **2** any fungus producing this disease. **3** the growth produced by this disease. **4** a medicine made from these growths, used to stop bleeding and to contract muscles. ⟨< F < OF *argot* cock's spur⟩

er•got•a•mine [ər'gɒtə,min] *n.* a drug used to treat migraine headaches.

er•got•ism ['ɜrgə,tɪzəm] *n.* **1** poisoning by ergot-infected grain. **2** a condition resulting from medicinal overuse of ergot.

er•i•ca•ceous [,ɛrɪ'keiʃəs] *adj.* belonging to the plant family Ericaceae, which includes heather, azaleas, and rhododendrons.

E•rid•a•nus [ɪ'rɪdənəs] *n. Astronomy.* the River, a large southern constellation between Cetus and Orion.

E•rie ['iri] *n., pl.* **E•rie** or **E•ries. 1** Native American people living along the southern and eastern shores of Lake Erie. **2** the language of the Erie, one of the Iroquoian family.

Er•in ['ɛrɪn] *n. Poetic.* Ireland.

E•rin•y•es [ɪ'rɪni,iz] *n.pl., sing.* **E•rin•ys** [ɪ'rɪnɪs] *or* [ɪ'raɪnɪs]. *Greek mythology.* the Furies, also called Eumenides.

er•is•tic [ɛ'rɪstɪk] *adj.* **1** having to do with argument and discord. **2** fond of argument. ⟨< Gk. *eristikos* < *erizein* to strive, dispute < *eris* strife⟩

Er•i•tre•a [,ɛrɪ'triə] *n.* a country in E Africa.

Er•i•tre•an [,ɛrɪ'triən] *adj.* of or having to do with Eritrea.

Er•len•mey•er flask ['ɜrlən,maɪər] a laboratory flask with a broad base and a narrow neck, shaped like a cone. ⟨after Emil *Erlenmeyer* (1825-1909), German chemist⟩

erl•king ['ɜrl,kɪŋ] *n. Germanic mythology.* a spirit or personification of natural forces, such as cold, storm, etc., that does harm, especially to children. ⟨< G *Erlkönig* alder-king, a mistranslation of Danish *ellerkonge* king of the elves⟩

er•mine ['ɜrmɪn] *n., pl.* **-mines** or *(esp. collectively)* **-mine. 1** a small carnivorous mammal (*Mustela erminea*) of northern and arctic regions, closely related to the weasels, having thick, soft fur which in summer is brown on the upper parts of the body and creamy white on the under parts, but which in winter in the most northerly regions changes to pure white except for the tip of the tail, which remains black. **2** any northern weasel in its white winter coat. **3** the highly valued fur of an ermine, traditionally used to trim the ceremonial or official robes of a judge, monarch, etc. **4** the position or rank of a judge, noble, or monarch. **5** *Heraldry.* a stylized representation of fur shown by black spots on a white background. ⟨ME < OF < Gmc. or < L *Armenius (mus)* Armenian (rat)⟩

er•mined ['ɜrmɪnd] *adj.* adorned with ermine.

Er•mite ['ɜrməit] *n. Cdn.* a type of sharp, salty blue cheese made in the Eastern townships of Québec. ⟨< Cdn.F < F *ermite* hermit, because made by Benedictine monks.⟩

erne [ɜrn] *n.* a sea eagle, especially *Haliaetus albicilla* of Europe. ⟨OE *earn*⟩
☛ *Hom.* EARN, URN.

e•rode [ɪ'roud] *v.* **e•rod•ed, e•rod•ing. 1** eat into; eat or wear away gradually: *Running water erodes soil and rocks.* **2** form by a gradual eating or wearing away: *The stream eroded a channel in the solid rock.* **3** be eaten or worn away gradually; be formed in this way: *The cliffs are eroding. The channel had probably eroded for a million years.* **4** make (something) decay: *to erode traditional values.* **5** undergo such decay: *Some say the educational system is eroding.* ⟨< L *erodere* < *ex-* away + *rodere* gnaw⟩

e•rog•e•nous [ɪ'rɒdʒənəs] *adj.* of or designating any area of the body that can produce sexual excitement when stimulated. ⟨< L *eros* sexual love + E *-genous*⟩

E•ros ['irɒs] *or* ['ɛrɒs] *n.* **1** *Greek mythology.* the god of love, son of Aphrodite. Eros corresponds to the Roman god Cupid. **2 eros,** sexual desire. **3 eros,** *Psychology.* **a** all the instincts for self-preservation. **b** libido.

e•rose [ɪ'rous] *adj.* **1** uneven. **2** *Botany.* of a leaf, having irregularly notched edges. ⟨< L *erosus* pp. of *erodere* < *e-* out, off + *rodere* to gnaw⟩

e•ro•sion [ɪ'rouʒən] *n.* **1** a gradual eating or wearing away by glaciers, running water, waves, or wind: *By absorbing water, trees help prevent the erosion of soil.* **2** the condition of being eaten or worn away. **3** gradual decay: *the erosion of the justice system.* **—e'ro•sion•al,** *adj.* ⟨< L *erosio, -onis* < *erodere.* See ERODE.⟩

e•ro•sive [ɪ'rousɪv] *adj.* eroding; causing erosion.

e•rot•ic [ɪ'rɒtɪk] *adj., n.* *—adj.* **1** of, having to do with, or arousing sexual desire. **2** characterized by strong sexual desire or sensitivity to sexual stimulation.
—n. an erotic person. ⟨< Gk. *erōtikos* of Eros⟩
—e'rot•i•cal•ly, *adv.*

e•rot•i•ca [ɪ'rɒtɪkə] *n.* erotic literature, art, etc.

e•rot•i•cism [ɪ'rɒtɪ,sɪzəm] *n.* **1** an erotic quality, theme, or character. **2** sexual arousal or desire. **3** preoccupation with sex. Also, **erotism** ['ɛrə,tɪzəm].

e•ro•to•gen•ic [,ɛrətə'dʒɛnɪk] *or* [ɪ,rɒtə'dʒɛnɪk] *adj.* erogenous.

e•ro•to•ma•nia [,ɛrətə'meiniə] *or* [ɪ,rɒtə'meiniə] *n.* *Psychiatry.* an abnormal and persistent desire for sex.

err [ɛr] *or* [ɜr] *v.* **1** go wrong; make mistakes: *Everyone errs at some time or other.* **2** be wrong; be mistaken or incorrect. **3** do wrong; sin: *To err is human; to forgive, divine.* ⟨ME < OF < L *errare* wander⟩
☛ *Hom.* AIR, E'ER, ERE, EYRE, HEIR [ɛr].
☛ *Pronun.* **Err.** In the past regularly pronounced [ɜr]; but there is a growing preference for the pronunciation [ɛr], probably by analogy with *error* ['ɛrər] and *errant* ['ɛrənt].

er•ran•cy ['ɛrənsi] *n.* the behaviour or lifestyle of a KNIGHT ERRANT.

er•rand ['ɛrənd] *n.* **1** a trip to do something, often for someone else: *The little boy goes to the store and runs errands for his parents.* **2** the purpose or object of a trip. ⟨OE *ǣrende*⟩

errand boy 1 a boy who does errands. **2** *Informal.* a man who acts entirely under others, without using his own initiative or intelligence.

er•rant ['ɛrənt] *adj.* **1** travelling in search of adventure; wandering; roving: *a knight errant.* **2** of thoughts, conduct, etc., straying from the regular path. **3** of a wind, changing frequently. ⟨< F *errant,* ppr. of OF *errer* travel (< L *iterare*), blended with F *errant,* ppr. of *errer* err (< L *errare*)⟩
☛ *Hom.* ARRANT.

er•rant•ry ['ɛrəntri] *n., pl.* **-ries.** the conduct or action of a KNIGHT ERRANT.

er•ra•ta [ɪ'rɑtə] *or* [ɪ'reitə] *n.* pl. of ERRATUM.

er•rat•ic [ɪ'rætɪk] *adj., n.* *—adj.* **1** not steady; uncertain; irregular: *An erratic mind jumps from one idea to another.* **2** odd; unusual: *erratic behaviour.*
—n. **1** *Geology.* a boulder or mass of rock transported from its original site, especially by glacial action. **2** an erratic person or thing. ⟨< L *erraticus* < *errare* err⟩ **—er'rat•i•cal•ly,** *adv.*

er•ra•tum [ɪ'rɑtəm] *or* [ɪ'reitəm] *n., pl.* **-ta. 1** an error in printing or writing. **2** Usually, **errata,** *pl.* a list of errors in a printed work, included with the work on a separate page. ⟨< L *erratum,* neut. pp. of *errare* err⟩

er•ro•ne•ous [ɪ'rouniəs] *adj.* of ideas, statements, etc., wrong; mistaken; incorrect: *Years ago many people held the erroneous belief that the earth was flat.* ⟨< L *erroneus* < *errare* err⟩ **—er'ro•ne•ous•ly,** *adv.* **—er'ro•ne•ous•ness,** *n.*

er•ror ['ɛrər] *n.* **1** something wrong; what is incorrect; a mistake: *A false belief is an error.* **2** wrongdoing; sin. **3** *Baseball.* a faulty play that permits the batter to remain at bat or allows a runner to advance who should have been put out. **4** in measurements or calculations, the difference between the observed or approximate amount and the correct amount. **5** *Law.* a mistake in fact or law.
in error, a wrong or mistaken: *The teacher was in error.* **b** by mistake: *She got on the westbound bus in error.* ⟨ME < OF < L *error* < *errare* err⟩
☛ *Syn.* **1. Error,** MISTAKE = something incorrect or wrong. **Error** implies a straying or deviation from a rule or course of action: *I failed my test because of errors in spelling.* **Mistake** applies to an error in judging or understanding, usually due to taking one thing for another: *I used your towel by mistake.*

er•satz ['ɛrzɑts], ['ɛrzæts], *or* [ɛr'zɑts] *adj. or n.* substitute, often poor in quality. Compare ECHT. ⟨< G⟩

Erse [ɜrs] *n., adj.* *—n.* **1** the Celtic language of the Scottish Highlanders. **2** the Celtic language of Ireland or of the Isle of Man.
—adj. of either of these languages. ⟨ME *Erish* Irish⟩
☛ *Usage.* The terms **Gaelic** (for the Scottish language), **Irish,** and **Manx** are now preferred to **Erse.**

erst [ɜrst] *adv. Archaic.* formerly; long ago. ⟨OE *ǣrst,* superlative of *ǣr* ere⟩

erst•while ['ɜrst,waɪl] *adv., adj.* *—adv. Archaic.* some time ago; in time past; formerly.
—adj. former; past.

e•ru•cic acid [ɪ'rusɪk] a fatty acid found especially in some varieties of rapeseed oil. *Formula:* $C_{22}H_{42}O_2$

e•ruct [ɪ'rʌkt] *v.* belch. ⟨< L *eructare* < *ex-* out + *ructare* belch⟩

e•ruc•tate [ɪ'rʌkteit] *v.* **-tat•ed, -tat•ing.** belch.

e•ruc•ta•tion [ɪrʌk'teiʃən] *or* [,irʌk'teiʃən] *n.* **1** a belching. **2** that which is belched up.

er•u•dite ['ɛrjə,dəit] *or* ['ɛrə,dəit] *adj.* scholarly; learned. ⟨< L *eruditus,* pp. of *erudire* instruct < *ex-* away + *rudis* rude⟩ **—'er•u,dite•ly,** *adv.* **—'er•u,dite•ness,** *n.*

er•u•di•tion [,ɛrjə'dɪʃən], [,ɛrə'dɪʃən], *or* [,ɛru'dɪʃən] *n.* acquired knowledge; scholarship; learning.

e•rum•pent [ɪ'rʌmpənt] *adj.* **1** *Botany.* appearing to burst through the epidermis. **2** bursting out. ⟨< L *erumpens* ppr. of *erumpere* burst forth⟩

e•rupt [ɪ'rʌpt] *v.* **1** burst forth: *Hot water erupted from the geyser.* **2** throw forth lava, hot water, etc.: *The volcano erupted.* **3** break out in a rash: *Her skin erupted when she had measles.* **4** break through the gums: *When the baby was seven months old, his teeth started to erupt.* **5** eject with force; throw forth. ⟨< L *eruptus,* pp. of *erumpere* < *ex-* out + *rumpere* burst⟩
☛ *Hom.* IRRUPT.

e•rup•tion [ɪ'rʌpʃən] *n.* **1** a bursting forth. **2** a throwing forth of lava, etc. from a volcano or of hot water from a geyser. **3** *Medicine.* **a** a breaking out in a rash: *The skin of a person with measles is in a state of eruption.* **b** red spots on the skin; rash: *Scarlet fever causes an eruption on the body.* **4** of the teeth, the process of breaking through the gums. **5** an outbreak; outburst: *eruptions of racial or national hatred.*
☛ *Hom.* IRRUPTION.

e•rup•tive [ɪ'rʌptɪv] *adj., n.* *—adj.* **1** bursting forth; tending to burst forth. **2** causing the skin to break out: *Measles is an eruptive disease.* **3** *Geology.* of or formed by volcanic eruptions.
—n. Geology. a rock formed or forced up by eruption.
—e'rup•tive•ly, *adv.*
☛ *Hom.* IRRUPTIVE.

-ery *suffix.* **1** a place for ——ing: *cannery, hatchery.* **2** a place for ——s: *nunnery.* **3** the occupation or business of a ——: *cookery.* **4** the state or condition of a ——: *slavery.* **5** the qualities, actions, etc. of a ——: *knavery.* **6** ——s as a group: *machinery.* ⟨< OF *-erie* < *-ier* (< L *-arius*) + *-ie* (< LL *-ia* < Gk. *-ia*)⟩

e•ryn•go [ɪ'rɪŋgou] *n.* any plant of the genus *Eryngium,* having clusters of small flowers. ⟨< L *eryngion* kind of thistle < Gk. *erungion* dim. of *erungos* thistle⟩

er•y•sip•e•las [,ɛrə'sɪpələs] *or* [,irə'sɪpələs] *n.* **1** an acute infectious disease characterized by fever and a deep red inflammation of the skin. **2** an acute or chronic bacterial disease of swine, and less commonly of turkeys and sheep, characterized by enteritis, red patches on the skin, and arthritis. ⟨< Gk. < *erythros* red + *pelas* skin⟩ **—,er•y•si'pel•a•tous** [,ɛrəsə'pɛlətəs], *adj.*

er•y•sip•e•loid [ˌɛrəˈsɪpəˌlɔɪd] *or* [ˌɪrəˈsɪpəˌlɔɪd] *n.* an infectious disease of the hands, showing red lesions.

er•y•the•ma [ˌɛrəˈθimə] *n.* a rash on the skin, caused by poison or sunburn. ⟨< NL < Gk. *erythema* < *erythainein* to redden, blush < *erythros* red⟩ **—ˌer•y•theˈmat•ic** [-θəˈmætɪk] or **ˌer•yˈthe•ma•tous,** *adj.*

er•y•thrism [ˈɛrɪˌθrɪzəm] *n.* colouring (of fur or feathers) that is unusually red. ⟨< Gk. *erythros* red + E *-ism*⟩

er•y•thrite [ˈɛrɪˌθrəit] *n.* a red, hydrated arsenate of cobalt, found in veins of cobalt and used for colouring glass. ⟨< Gk. *erythros* red + E *-ite*⟩

e•ryth•ro•blast [əˈrɪθrouˌblæst] *n.* any of the cells in bone marrow that become erythrocytes. ⟨< Gk. *erythros* red + *blastos* sprout⟩

e•ryth•ro•blast•o•sis [əˌrɪθroublæˈstousɪs] *n.* **1** the abnormal presence of erythroblasts in the blood. **2** such a condition in a fetus or newborn baby, caused by a blood incompatibility with the mother.

e•ryth•ro•cyte [əˈrɪθrouˌsəit] *n.* one of the red blood cells that carry oxygen to cells and tissues, and carbon dioxide back to the lungs. ⟨< Gk. *erythros* red + E *-cyte*⟩ **—eˌryth•roˈcyt•ic** [-ˈsɪtɪk], *adj.*

er•y•throid [ˈɛrɪˌθrɔɪd] *adj.* **1** having a reddish colour. **2** having to do with erythrocytes or the cells from which they grow.

e•ryth•ro•my•cin [ɪˌrɪθrouˈməisɪn] *n.* an antibiotic drug related to streptomycin, used for treating infections caused by certain gram-positive bacteria. *Formula*: $C_{37}H_{67}NO_{13}$ ⟨< Gk. *erythros* red + *mykēs* fungus⟩

e•ryth•ro•poi•e•sis [ˌɛrɪθroupɔɪˈisɪs] *n.* a hormone which stimulates the production of red blood cells, and is used to treat certain forms of anemia. ⟨< *erythro*(*cyte*) + Gk. *poiesis* making⟩

Es einsteinium.

–es[1] *noun plural suffix.* a form of -s[1] used for nouns ending in *s, z, sh, ch,* or a final *y* that changes to *i* in the plural, for some nouns ending in a vowel, and for nouns ending in *f* that changes to *v* in the plural: *masses, fuzzes, bushes, churches, families, tomatoes, scarves.*

–es[2] *verb suffix.* a form of -s[2] used for verbs ending in *s, z, sh, ch,* or a final *y* that changes to *i,* and for some verbs ending in a vowel: *blesses, buzzes, flashes, teaches, flies, goes.*

es•ca•drille [ˈɛskəˌdrɪl] *or* [ˌɛskəˈdrɪl] *n.* formerly: **1** a squadron of usually six aircraft, especially in the French armed forces in World War I. **2** a small fleet of ships. ⟨< F *escadrille,* dim. of *escadre* squadron; form influenced by Sp. *escuadrilla,* dim. of *escuadra*⟩

es•ca•lade [ˌɛskəˈleid] *n., v.* **—***n.* **-lad•ed, -lad•ing.** the climbing of the walls of a fortified place with the help of ladders. —*v.* scale or attack over (a wall, rampart, etc.) by means of ladders. ⟨< F < Ital. *scalata,* ult. < L *scala* ladder⟩

es•ca•late [ˈɛskəˌleit] *v.* **-lat•ed, -lat•ing.** increase or expand by stages in amount, intensity, extent, etc.: *escalating costs. Small battles can easily escalate into major wars.* ⟨back formation < *escalator*⟩ **—ˌes•caˈla•tion,** *n.*

es•ca•la•tor [ˈɛskəˌleitər] *n.* a continuous moving stairway. Many department stores have escalators to carry the customers from one floor to another. ⟨< *Escalator,* a blend of *escalade* and *elevator,* formerly a trademark⟩

escalator clause a provision in a contract allowing an increase or decrease in wages, royalties, etc. under specified conditions.

es•cal•lop [ɛˈskɒləp] *or* [ɛˈskæləp] *v., n.* —*v.* bake in a cream sauce or with bread crumbs.
—*n.* **1** food cooked in this way: *escallop of veal.* **2** SCALLOP (def. 1). ⟨(originally n.) < OF *escalope* shell < Gmc.⟩

es•ca•pade [ˈɛskəˌpeid] *or* [ˌɛskəˈpeid] *n.* **1** a breaking loose from rules or restraint. **2** a wild adventure or prank. ⟨< F < Ital. *scappata* < *scappare* escape⟩

es•cape [ɛˈskeip] *v.* **-caped, -cap•ing;** *n., adj.* —*v.* **1** get free; get out and away: *to escape from prison.* **2** get free from: *He thinks he will never escape hard work.* **3** keep free or safe from; avoid: *We all escaped the measles.* **4** avoid capture, trouble, etc.: *The thief has escaped.* **5** come out (of unintentionally): *A cry escaped her lips. A wonderful smell was escaping from the kitchen.* **6** fail to be noticed or remembered by: *I knew his face, but his name escaped me.* **7** of a cultivated plant, start to grow wild.
—*n.* **1** an act of escaping. **2** a way of escaping: *There was no escape from the trap.* **3** relief from boredom, trouble, etc.: *to find escape in mystery stories.* **4** an outflow or leakage of gas, water, etc. **5** a cultivated plant grown wild.
—*adj.* providing a way of escape or avoidance. ⟨ME < AF *escaper,* ult. < L *ex-* out of + *cappa* cloak⟩

☛ *Syn. v.* **3. Escape,** EVADE, ELUDE = keep free from someone or something. **Escape** = miss possible or threatened unpleasantness or danger by being out of its way or by managing to keep free: *He escaped being killed in the blast because he had not gone to work.* **Evade** emphasizes cleverness or trickery in managing to stay free: *Some children try to evade doing chores around the home.* **Elude** suggests slipperiness and quickness in getting away from trouble that is close or in keeping free: *The bandit eluded the posse that was following him.*

escape artist a performer whose skill consists in getting free from chains or other confinement. Also, **escapologist.**

escape clause a clause that frees a signer of a contract from certain responsibilities under specified circumstances.

es•cap•ee [ɛˌskeiˈpi] *or* [ɛˈskeipi] *n.* a person who has escaped, especially one who has escaped from prison.

escape mechanism **1** *Psychiatry.* a thought or action, usually unconscious, that permits avoidance of an unpleasant reality. **2** any device or apparatus, such as an ejection seat in an aircraft, designed to permit escape or release in an emergency.

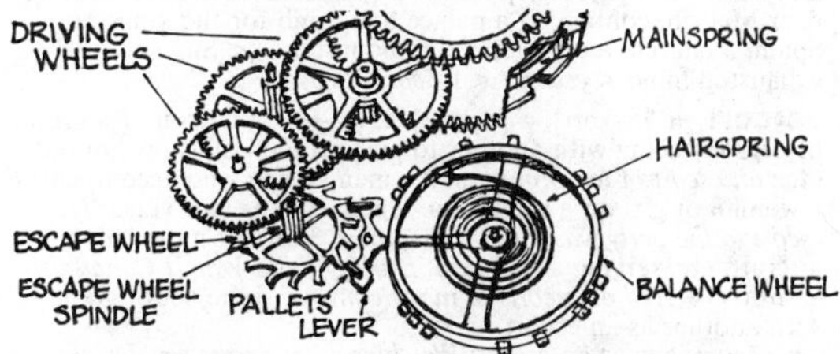

The balance wheel and lever escapement of a mainspring-driven mechanical watch. The mainspring turns the escape wheel through a series of driving wheels. The balance wheel and lever control the movement of the escape wheel by allowing it to turn through only one notch at a time.

es•cape•ment [ɛˈskeipmənt] *n.* **1** a device in a timepiece consisting of a notched wheel and a lever or catch, by which the clockwork is controlled and which transmits energy from the source of power to the pendulum or balance wheel. **2** a ratchet mechanism, such as the one that controls the horizontal movement of a typewriter carriage.

escape velocity *Physics.* the minimum speed an object must attain to get free of a gravitational field. An escape velocity of approximately 40 320 km/h is needed to overcome the gravitational pull of the earth.

es•cap•ism [ɛˈskeipɪzəm] *n.* a habitual avoidance of unpleasant realities by recourse to imagination or to entertainment.

es•cap•ist [ɛˈskeipɪst] *n., adj.* —*n.* a person who seeks escape from reality in daydreams, amusements, etc.
—*adj.* providing a way of escaping from reality: *escapist literature.*

es•cap•ol•o•gist [ɛˌskeiˈpɒlədʒɪst] *n.* ESCAPE ARTIST.

es•car•got [ˌɛskɑrˈgou] *or* [ɛˈskɑrgou]; *French,* [ɛskaʀˈgo] *n.* an edible snail. ⟨< F⟩

es•ca•role [ˈɛskəˌroul] *n.* a kind of endive that has broad leaves, used for salads. ⟨< F⟩

es•carp•ment [ɛˈskɑrpmənt] *n.* **1** a steep slope; cliff. **2** the ground made into a steep slope as part of a fortification. Also (def. 2), **escarp.** ⟨< F *escarpement* < *escarper* form into a steep slope < *escarpe* a steep slope < Ital. *scarpa* < Gmc.⟩

–esce *suffix.* forming verbs that refer to actions which are just beginning: *coalesce, effervesce.* ⟨< L *-escere*⟩

–escence *suffix.* forming nouns of state or quality derived from adjectives ending in *-escent: obsolescence, luminescence.* ⟨< L *-escentia* < *-escens*⟩

–escent *suffix.* **1** forming adjectives and nouns derived from verbs ending in *-esce*: *effervescent.* **2** forming adjectives and nouns having to do with some state, condition, or process that is just beginning: *adolescent, pubescent.* ⟨< L *-escens*⟩

es•char [ˈɛskɑr] *or* [ˈɛskər] *n.* a hard crust on the skin, often from a burn. ⟨altered (after L) < ME *escare* < OF < LL *eschara* < Gk. *escharos* fireplace, brazier. Doublet of SCAR.⟩
☛ *Hom.* ESKER [ˈɛskər].

es•cha•rot•ic [ˌɛskəˈrɒtɪk] *adj.* producing an eschar.

es•cha•to•log•i•cal [ˌɛskətəˈlɒdʒəkəl] *adj.* of or having to do with eschatology.

es•cha•tol•o•gy [ˌɛskəˈtɒlədʒi] *n.* **1** the body of doctrines concerning the four last things: death, judgment, heaven, and hell. **2** the branch of theology that deals with these things. ⟨< Gk. *eschatos* last, final + E *-logy*⟩

es•cheat [ɛsˈtʃit] *n., v. —n. Law.* **1** a reverting of the ownership of property to the state or to the lord of a manor when there are no legal heirs. **2** the property whose ownership has so reverted.
—v. Law. **1** revert to the state or the lord of the manor.
2 confiscate; transfer (the ownership of property) to the state. ⟨ME < OF *eschete*, ult. < L *ex-* out + *cadere* fall⟩

es•chew [ɛsˈtʃu] *v.* avoid; shun; keep away from using, doing, etc.: *A wise person eschews bad company. A dieter eschews rich desserts.* ⟨ME < OF *eschiver* < Gmc.⟩ **—es'chew•er,** *n.*

es•co•lar [ˈɛskəˌlɑr] *n.* any slender fish of the family Gempylidae. ⟨< Sp., literally, scholar, because it has rings around the eyes reminiscent of spectacles⟩

Es•co•ri•al [ɛˈskɔriəl]; *Spanish,* [ˌɛskɔriˈal] *n.* a huge structure near Madrid, containing a palace and tomb for the kings of Spain, a church, a college, and a monastery. ⟨< Sp., site of exhausted mine < *escoria* < L *scoria* dross⟩

es•cort *n.* [ˈɛskɔrt]; *v.* [ɛˈskɔrt] *n., v. —n.* **1** a person or a group of persons going with another to give protection, show honour, etc.: *an escort of ten Mounties.* **2** a man or boy who accompanies a woman or girl on a walk, to a dance, etc., or vice versa: *Her escort to the party was a tall young man.* **3** one or more ships, aircraft, etc. serving as a guard: *During World War II Canada's destroyers served as escorts to many convoys.* **4** the act of going with another as an escort.
—v. accompany as an escort: *Warships escorted the royal yacht. Four police officers escorted the dangerous criminal to prison. Ward escorted Mary to the movies.* ⟨< F *escorte* < Ital. *scorta* < *scorgere* guide < L *ex-* out + *corrigere* set right⟩
☛ *Syn. v.* See note at ACCOMPANY.

es•cri•toire [ˌɛskrəˈtwɑr] *or* [ˈɛskrəˌtwɑr] *n.* a writing desk. ⟨< F < LL *scriptorium* < L *scribere* write⟩

es•crow [ˈɛskrou] *or* [ɛˈskrou] *n. Law.* a deed, bond, or other written agreement put in the charge of a third person until certain conditions are fulfilled by two other parties.
in escrow, held by a third party in accordance with an agreement. ⟨< AF var. of OF *escroue* scrap, scroll < Gmc.⟩

es•cu•do [ɛˈskudou] *n., pl.* **-dos. 1** the basic unit of money in Portugal and Cape Verde, divided into 100 centavos. See table of money in the Appendix. **2** a unit of money in Chile, equal to 1/100 of a peso. **3** a coin worth one escudo. **3** any of various gold or silver coins formerly used in Spain, Portugal, and their colonies. ⟨< Pg. < L *scutum* shield⟩

es•cu•lent [ˈɛskjələnt] *adj., n. —adj.* suitable for food; edible.
—n. something edible, especially a vegetable. ⟨< L *esculentus* < *esca* food⟩

Es•cu•ri•al [ɛˈskjʊriəl] *n.* Escorial.

es•cutch•eon [ɛˈskʌtʃən] *n.* **1** a shield or shield-shaped surface on which a coat of arms is put. **2** a protective metal plate around a keyhole. **3** the panel on a ship's stern bearing its name.
blot on the escutcheon, a disgrace to honour or reputation. ⟨< ONF *escuchon* < L *scutum* shield⟩

-ese *suffix.* **1** of, belonging to, or having to do with: *Japanese = of, belonging to, or having to do with Japan.* **2** a native or inhabitant of: *Portuguese = a native or inhabitant of Portugal.*
3 the language of: *Chinese = a language of China.* **4** a typical style or vocabulary: *journalese = newspaper style.* ⟨< OF *-eis* < L *-ensis*⟩

ESE or **E.S.E.** east-southeast, a direction halfway between east and southeast.

es•ker [ˈɛskər] *n.* a winding ridge of sand, gravel, etc. believed to have been deposited by meltwater streams flowing inside the retreating glaciers of the Ice Age. Also, **eskar.** ⟨< Irish *eiscir*⟩
☛ *Hom.* ESCHAR.

Es•ki•mo [ˈɛskəˌmou] *n., pl.* **-mos** or **-mo. 1** See INUIT. **2** See INUKTITUT. ⟨origin uncertain⟩
☛ *Usage.* See note at INUIT.

Eskimo curlew a bird (*Numenius borealis*) of N North America, wintering in South America. It is an endangered species.

Eskimo dog *Cdn.* a breed of large, very strong dog native to the North, long used by the Inuit for pulling sleds and for hunting. An Eskimo dog can go for several days without food and still pull a load of 50 kg.

An Eskimo dog

Eskimo pie a chocolate-coated ice-cream bar.

ESL English as a second language.

e•so•phag•e•al [ˌisəˈfædʒiəl] *or* [ɪˌsɒfəˈdʒiəl] *adj.* of, having to do with, or connected with the esophagus.

e•soph•a•gus [ɪˈsɒfəgəs] *n., pl.* **-gi** [-ˌdʒaɪ] *or* [-ˌgaɪ]. the passage for food from the mouth to the stomach; gullet. Also, **oesophagus.** See ALIMENTARY CANAL and WINDPIPE for pictures. ⟨< NL < Gk. *oisophagos* < *oiso-* carry + *phagein* eat⟩

es•o•ter•ic [ˌɛsəˈtɛrɪk] *adj.* **1** understood only by the select few; intended for an inner circle of disciples, scholars, etc.
2 private; secret; confidential; opposed to EXOTERIC. ⟨< Gk. *esōterikos*, ult. < *esō* within⟩ **—,es•o'ter•i•cal•ly,** *adv.*

es•o•ter•i•ca [ˌɛsəˈtɛrɪkə] *n.* esoteric items.

es•o•tro•pia [ˌɛsouˈtroupiə] *n.* a disorder in which one eye is able to focus on an object while the other eye looks inward. Compare EXOTROPIA. ⟨< NL < Gk. *eso* within + NL *-tropia* < Gk. *trope* a turn⟩

esp. or **espec.** especially.

E.S.P. or **ESP** EXTRASENSORY PERCEPTION.

es•pa•drille [ˈɛspəˌdrɪl] *or* [ˌɛspəˈdrɪl] *n.* a sandal with a canvas upper attached to a rope sole. ⟨< F altered by metathesis < *espardille* < dial. Gascon *espartilho* dim. < Sp. *esparto* < L *spartum* < Gk. *sparton, spartos* a kind of long, coarse grass⟩

es•pal•ier [ɛˈspæljər] *or* [ɛˈspæljei] *n., v. —n.* **1** a framework of stakes upon which fruit trees and shrubs are trained. **2** a plant or row of plants trained to grow in this way.
—v. train as or furnish with an espalier. ⟨< F < Ital. *spalliera* support < *spalla* shoulder⟩

Es•pa•ña [ɛˈspanja] *n. Spanish.* Spain.

es•par•to [ɛˈspɑrtou] *n.* either of two grasses (*Stipa tenacissima* or *Lygeum spartum*) native to Spain and N Africa, used for making baskets, rope, and paper. Also, **esparto grass.** ⟨< Sp. < L < Gk. *spartos*⟩

espec. especially.

es•pe•cial [ɛˈspɛʃəl] *adj.* special; particular; exceptional: *my especial friend, of no especial value.* ⟨ME < OF < L *specialis* belonging to a particular species. Doublet of SPECIAL.⟩

es•pe•cial•ly [ɛˈspɛʃəli] *adv.* particularly; chiefly; unusually.
☛ *Syn.* **Especially,** PARTICULARLY, PRINCIPALLY = in a special manner or degree, first or most of all. **Especially** emphasizes the idea of over and above all others: *This book is designed especially for young students.* **Particularly** singles out the foremost case or example from others of the same class or kind: *All my arithmetic problems are hard, but particularly this one.* **Principally** emphasizes the idea of before all others or for the most part: *Robberies occur principally at night.*
☛ *Usage.* **Especially,** SPECIALLY. **Especially** = pre-eminently or exceptionally. **Specially** = for that purpose and no other. You should say, *I came specially to see John* if you came only for the purpose of seeing John; but, *I came especially to see John* if you would see others after seeing John, or if you have other business in mind besides visiting. A parallel distinction exists between **especial** and **special,** although the latter word now replaces **especial** for most purposes.

Es•pe•ran•to [ˌɛspəˈrɑntou] *or* [ˌɛspəˈræntou] *n.* an artificial language for international use, whose vocabulary and grammar are based on forms common to the principal European languages. ⟨< the pseudonym 'Dr. *Esperanto*' ('he who hopes') used by its inventor, the Polish philologist Dr. L.L. Zamenhof⟩

es•pi•al [ɛˈspaɪəl] *n.* **1** the act of spying. **2** the act of watching. **3** discovery. ⟨< *espy*⟩

es•pi•o•nage [ˈɛspiəˌnɑʒ] *or* [ˈɛspiənɪdʒ] *n.* the use of spies, especially the use of spies by one country to find out the military, political, etc. secrets of another; spying. ⟨< F *espionnage* < *espionner* to spy < *espion* spy < Ital. *spione* < *spia* spy < Gmc.⟩

es•pla•nade [ˌɛspləˈneid] *or* [ˌɛspləˈnɑd] *n.* **1** any open, level space used for public walks or drives. **2** an open space separating a fortress from the houses of a town. ⟨< F < Sp. *esplanada* < *esplanar* < L *explanare* < *ex-* out + *planus* level⟩

es•pous•al [ɛˈspaʊzəl] *n.* **1** the act of espousing; adoption (of a cause, etc.). 2 the ceremony of becoming engaged or married. 3 **espousals,** *pl.* **a** a betrothal; betrothal ceremony. **b** a marriage; wedding. ⟨ME < OF *espousailles*, pl. < L *sponsalia*, neut. pl. of *sponsalis* having to do with betrothal < *sponsus* betrothed. See ESPOUSE.⟩

es•pouse [ɛ'spaʊz] *v.* **-poused, -pous•ing. 1** marry. **2** give (a woman) in marriage. **3** take up or make one's own: *Late in life she espoused a new religion.* ⟨ME < OF *espouser* < L *sponsare* < *sponsus* betrothed, pp. of *spondere* betroth⟩ **—es'pous•er,** *n.*

es•pres•so [ɛ'sprɛsou] *n., pl.* **-sos.** a very strong coffee made from dark-roasted, finely powdered beans and brewed under steam pressure. ⟨< Ital. *espresso*, pp. of *esprimere* < L *exprimere.* See EXPRESS.⟩

espresso bar a coffee shop that specializes in espresso.

es•prit [ɛ'spri] *n.* lively wit; spirit. ⟨< F *esprit* < L *spiritus* spirit, originally, breath < *spirare* breathe. Doublet of SPIRIT, SPRITE.⟩

esprit de corps [ɛ'spri də 'kɔr]; *French,* [ɛspʀid'kɔʀ] a sense of union and of common interests and responsibilities in some group: *The regiment has a strong esprit de corps.*

es•py [ɛ'spaɪ] *v.* **-pied, -py•ing.** see or catch sight of something, especially something far away, small, or partly hidden. ⟨ME < OF *espier* < Gmc.⟩

Esq. Esquire.

☛ *Usage.* **Esq., Esquire.** Written after a man's name in the inside and outside address of a letter, **Esq.** or **Esquire** is formal and is no longer widely used in Canada except in official and professional circles. Many people consider the usage British, archaic, or both. No other title (such as *Mr., Dr., Hon.*) should be used with the word: *Harry A. Kinne, Esq.*

-esque *suffix.* **1** in the ——style; resembling the ——style: *Romanesque.* **2** like a ——; like that of a ——: *statuesque.* ⟨< F < Ital. *-esco* < Gmc. Akin to -ISH.⟩

es•quire [ɛ'skwaɪr] *or* ['ɛskwaɪr] *n.* **1** in the Middle Ages, a young man of noble family who attended a knight until he himself was made a knight. **2** an Englishman ranking next below a knight. **3** *Archaic.* an English country gentleman; squire. **4 Esquire,** a title of respect (for birth, position, or education) placed after a man's last name instead of placing *Mr.* before the name: *John Jones, Esquire = Mr. John Jones.* ⟨ME < OF *esquier* < L *scutarius* shieldbearer < *scutum* shield⟩

☛ *Usage.* See note at ESQ.

ess [ɛs] *n.* **1** the nineteenth letter of the alphabet (S, s). **2** anything shaped like an S.

-ess *suffix.* female, as in *heiress, hostess, lioness.* ⟨< F *-esse* < L < Gk. *-issa*⟩

☛ *Usage.* This feminine suffix is to be avoided in names of occupations, where it has acquired a quasi-diminutive connotation that is offensively sexist.

es•say *n.* ['ɛsei] *for 1 and 2,* usually [ɛ'sei] *for 3 and 4; v.* [ɛ'sei] *n., v. —n.* **1** a literary composition on a certain subject. An essay is usually shorter, more personal, and less methodical than a treatise. **2** a written composition, theme, term paper, etc. assigned as an exercise in a high school, college, etc. **3** a try; attempt. **4** a draft of a design for a new piece of paper money or a postage stamp.
—v. try; attempt: *She essayed a very difficult jump.* ⟨< OF *essai* < L *exagium* a weighing⟩ **—es'say•er,** *n.*

es•say•ist ['eseiɪst] *n.* a writer of essays.

es•sence ['ɛsəns] *n.* **1** that which makes a thing what it is; the necessary part or parts; important feature or features: *Kindness is the essence of politeness.* **2** any concentrated substance that has the characteristic flavour, fragrance, or effect of the plant, fruit, etc. from which it is obtained. Atropine is the essence of the belladonna plant. **3** a solution of such a substance in alcohol. Essence of peppermint is oil of peppermint dissolved in alcohol. **4** a perfume. **5** *Philosophy.* the intrinsic nature of something, separate from its physical appearance. **6** something that is, especially a spiritual or immaterial entity.
in essence, essentially; fundamentally.
of the essence, most important: *Discretion is of the essence.* ⟨ME < OF < L *essentia* < *esse* be⟩

Es•sene ['ɛsin] *or* [ɛ'sin] *n.* a member of an ascetic Jewish sect from the 2nd century B.C. to the 2nd century A.D. **—Es'se•ni•an** or **Es'sen•ic** [ɛ'sɛnɪk], *adj.*

es•sen•tial [ɪ'sɛnʃəl] *adj., n. —adj.* **1** needed to make a thing what it is; basic; necessary: *Good food and enough rest are essential to good health.* **2** of, like, or constituting the essence of a substance. **3** being or containing the essence, or fragrance, flavour, and medicinal qualities, of a plant or other material: *essential odours.* **4** being such by its essence or very nature, or in the highest sense: *essential happiness, essential poetry.*
—n. an absolutely necessary thing, element, or quality; a basic part; fundamental feature: *Learn the essentials first; then learn the details.* ⟨ME < Med.L *essentialis* < L *essentia.* See ESSENCE.⟩ **—es'sen•tial•ly,** *adv.*

☛ *Syn. adj.* **1.** See note at NECESSARY.

es•sen•tial•ism [ɪ'sɛnʃə,lɪzəm] *n.* **1** *Education.* the doctrine that concepts and skills needed by society must be taught to everybody. **2** *Philosophy.* the theory that every material thing has an essence which is distinct from, and has primacy over, its actual physical characteristics and particular existence. **—es'sen•tial•ist,** *n.*

es•sen•ti•al•i•ty [ɪ,sɛnʃi'æləti] *n., pl.* **-ties. 1** the quality or fact of being essential. **2** an essential feature.

essential oil a volatile oil having the characteristic fragrance or flavour of the plant or fruit from which it is extracted. It is used in making perfumes and in flavouring.

es•son•ite ['ɛsə,naɪt] *n.* a dark reddish brown type of garnet, also called **cinnamon stone.** ⟨< Gk. *hesson* inferior + E *-ite*[1]⟩

-est *suffix.* forming the superlative degree: **1** of adjectives: *warmest.* **2** of adverbs: *fastest.* ⟨OE *-est, -ost*⟩

☛ *Usage.* See notes at ADJECTIVE and ADVERB.

est. **1** established. **2** estate. **3** estuary. **4** estimated.

es•tab•lish [ɪ'stæblɪʃ] *v.* **1** set up permanently: *to establish a government or a business.* **2** settle in a position; set up in a business: *She established herself in the most comfortable chair. He stayed until his sons were established in their new residence.* **3** bring about permanently; cause to be accepted: *to establish a custom.* **4** show beyond dispute; prove: *to establish a fact.* **5** make (a church) a national institution recognized and supported by the government. **6** set down or ordain (a law, system, etc.) on a permanent basis. **7** *Cards.* get control of (a suit) in order to win all subsequent plays with it. ⟨ME < OF *establiss-*, a stem of *establir* < L *stabilire* make stable < *stabilis* stable⟩ **—es'tab•lish•er,** *n.*

☛ *Syn.* See note at FIX.

established church a church that is a national institution, recognized and supported by the government.

es•tab•lish•ment [ɪ'stæblɪʃmənt] *n.* **1** the act of establishing or the state of being established: *the establishment of a scholarship fund.* **2** something established, such as a household, business, church, army, or code of laws. **3 the Establishment, a** the Church of England or the Presbyterian Church of Scotland. **b** the people having the greatest social and political influence in a society and generally being opposed to change and the influence of other groups. **4** the number of people in a regiment, a ship's company, etc., as set by regulations: *The regiment needed three officers to complete its establishment.*

es•tab•lish•men•tar•i•an [ɪ,stæblɪʃmən'tɛriən] *adj., n. —adj.* of, having to do with, or supporting the Establishment. *—n.* a person who belongs to or supports the Establishment. **—es,tab•lish•men'tar•i•an,ism,** *n.*

es•tam•i•net [ɛstami'nɛ] *French. n.* a small café.

es•tan•cia [ɛ'stɑnsiə] *n.* a large estate in Spanish America, often a cattle ranch. ⟨< Sp. a dwelling⟩

es•tate [ɪ'steit] *n.* **1** a large piece of land belonging to a person; landed property: *She has a beautiful estate with a country house and a swimming pool on it.* **2** what a person owns; property; possessions. Land and buildings are real estate. When a person dies, his or her estate is divided up among those to whom he or she has left it. **3** a condition or stage in life: *the estate of womanhood.* **4** a class or order of persons within a nation. The traditional estates (called **the three estates**) making up the body politic in European countries were the nobility, the clergy, and the commons (the third estate), each with different political rights. See also FOURTH ESTATE. **5** *Law.* the extent of an owner's rights to the use of his or her property. ⟨ME < OF *estat* < L *status* state. Doublet of STATE.⟩

Es•tates–Gen•er•al [ɪ'steits 'dʒɛnərəl] *n., pl.* STATES-GENERAL (def. 1).

es•teem [ɪ'stim] *v., n. —v.* **1** have a very favourable opinion of; regard highly: *We esteem people of good character.* **2** think; consider: *People have often esteemed happiness the greatest good.*
—n. a very favourable opinion; high regard: *Courage is held in esteem.* ⟨ME < OF *estimer* < L *aestimare* value⟩

☛ *Syn. v.* **1.** See note at VALUE.

es•ter ['ɛstər] *n.* a compound resulting from the reaction of an acid with an alcohol, so that the acid loses a hydroxyl group and the alcohol loses a hydrogen atom. Animal and vegetable fats and oils are esters. ⟨coined by L. Gmelin (1788-1853), a German chemist, from *es(sig)* vinegar + *(ä)ther* ether⟩

es•ter•ase ['ɛstə,reis] *n. Biochemistry.* any enzyme that converts an ester into an acid and an alcohol by hydrolysis.

es•ter•i•fy [ɛ'stɛrɪ,faɪ] *v.* **-fied, -fy•ing.** *Chemistry.* convert to an ester. **—es,ter•i•fi'ca•tion,** *n.*

es•the•sia [ɛs'θiʒə] *or* [ɛs'θiziə] *n.* sensitivity; ability to feel.

es•the•si•om•e•ter [ɛs,θizi'ɒmətər] *n.* a device to measure the sense of touch, especially one that establishes how far apart two points pressed into the finger have to be in order to be perceived as separate. ⟨< NL *aesthesia* + *meter*⟩

es•thete ['ɛsθit] *or* ['isθit] *n.* See AESTHETE.

es•thet•ic [ɛs'θɛtɪk] *or* [ɪs'θɛtɪk] *adj.* **1** See AESTHETIC. **2** having to do with esthesia. **—es'thet•i•cal•ly,** *adv.*

es•thet•ic•ian [,ɛsθə'tɪʃən] *or* [,isθə'tɪʃən] *n.* See AESTHETICIAN.

es•thet•i•cism [ɛs'θɛtə,sɪzəm] *or* [ɪs'θɛtə,sɪzəm] *n.* See AESTHETICISM.

es•thet•ics [ɛs'θɛtɪks] *or* [ɪs'θɛtɪks] *n.* See AESTHETICS.

Es•tho•ni•an [ɛs'θouniən] *n. or adj.* Estonian.

es•ti•ma•ble ['ɛstəməbəl] *adj.* **1** worthy of esteem; deserving high regard. **2** capable of being estimated or calculated. ⟨< ME and OF < L *aestimabilis* < *aestimare* value, appraise⟩ **—'es•ti•ma•bly,** *adv.*

es•ti•mate *n.* ['ɛstəmɪt]; *v.* ['ɛstə,meɪt] *n., v.* **-mat•ed, -mat•ing.** *—n.* **1** a judgment or opinion about how much, how many, how good, etc.: *My estimate of the length of the room was 7 m; it actually measured 6.56 m.* **2** a statement of what a certain job will cost, made by one willing to do the work: *The painter's estimate for painting the house was $1500.*
—v. **1** form a judgment or opinion about (how much, how many, how good, etc.). **2** fix (the work, size, amount, etc.), especially in a rough way; calculate approximately. **3** draw up or submit a statement of (the cost of doing a specified piece of work or the price at which a contractor is prepared to undertake it). ⟨< L *aestimatus*, pp. of *aestimare* value⟩ **—'es•ti,ma•tor,** *n.*

☛ *Syn. v.* **1. Estimate,** APPRAISE, EVALUATE = judge the measure, weight, or value of someone or something. **Estimate** suggests an opinion based on personal knowledge, experience, or taste, and emphasizes that the result given may not be correct: *Without measuring, I would estimate the length of the room as 5 m.* **Appraise** emphasizes expert opinion, and suggests that the result given is correct or cannot be questioned: *to appraise property for taxation.* **Evaluate** especially suggests trying to find the value or worth of a thing or person in terms that are not necessarily quantifiable, and are usually subjective: *She evaluates people by their clothes.*

es•ti•ma•tion [,ɛstə'meiʃən] *n.* **1** judgment; opinion: *In my estimation, your plan will not work.* **2** esteem; respect; regard: *to hold in high estimation.* **3** the act or process of estimating.

es•ti•ma•tive ['ɛstɪ,meitɪv] *adj.* **1** capable of estimating. **2** estimated.

es•ti•val ['ɛstəvəl] *or* [ɛ'staɪvəl] *adj.* of or having to do with summer. Also, **aestival.** ⟨< L *aestivalis* < *aestivus*, adj. of *aestas* summer⟩

es•ti•vate ['ɛstə,veit] *v.* **-vat•ed, -vat•ing. 1** spend the summer. **2** *Zoology.* spend the summer in a dormant or torpid condition. Some snakes estivate. Compare HIBERNATE. Also, **aestivate.**

es•ti•va•tion [,ɛstə'veiʃən] *n.* **1** *Zoology.* the state of being in a dormant or torpid condition during the summer. **2** *Biology.* the arrangement of the parts of a flower in the bud.

Es•to•ni•a [ɛ'stouniə] *or* [ɪ'stouniə] *n.* a country in north central Europe, on the Baltic Sea. See LATVIA for map.

Es•to•ni•an [ɛ'stouniən] *or* [ɪ'stouniən] *n., adj. —n.* **1** a native or inhabitant of Estonia. **2** a person of Estonian descent. **3** the Finno-Ugric language of the Estonians.
—adj. of or having to do with Estonia, its people, or their language. Also, **Esthonian.**

es•top [ɪ'stɒp] *v.* **-topped, -top•ping. 1** *Law.* prevent from asserting or doing something contrary to a previous assertion or act. **2** *Archaic.* stop; bar; obstruct. ⟨< OF *estoper* < *estoupe* tow < L *stuppa*⟩

es•top•pel [ɪ'stɒpəl] *n.* an estopping.

es•to•vers [ɛ'stouvərz] *n. Law.* things that are needful, such as alimony or an income from an estate to a beneficiary. ⟨< ME < OF *estovoir* to be necessary < L *est opus* it is needed⟩

es•tra•di•ol [,ɛstrə'daɪɒl] *or* [,ɛstrə'daɪoul] *n.* an estrogenic hormone found in the follicle cells of ovaries and used to treat estrogen deficiency. *Formula:* $C_{18}H_{24}O_2$ ⟨< *estrus* + *di-* + *-ol*⟩

es•tra•mus•tine [,ɛstrə'mʌstin] *n.* a drug used to treat certain forms of cancer.

es•trange [ɪ'streindʒ] *v.* **-tranged, -trang•ing. 1** turn (a person) from affection to indifference, dislike, or hatred; make unfriendly; separate: *A quarrel had estranged him from his family.* **2** keep apart; keep away. ⟨ME < OF *estranger* < L *extraneare* < *extraneus* strange, foreign. Related to STRANGE.⟩ **—es'trang•er,** *n.*

es•trange•ment [ɪ'streindʒmənt] *n.* an estranging or being estranged: *A misunderstanding between the two friends had caused their estrangement.*

es•tray [ɪ'strei] *n. Law.* a stray person, animal, or thing.

es•tri•ol ['ɛstri,ɒl] *n.* an estrogenic hormone used in treating estrogen deficiency. ⟨< *estrus* + *tri-* + *-ol*⟩

es•tro•gen ['ɛstrədʒən] *n.* any of three hormones that induce a series of physiological changes in females, especially in the reproductive or sexual organs. ⟨< *estrus* + *-gen* producer⟩

es•tro•gen•ic [,ɛstrə'dʒɛnɪk] *adj. Biochemistry.* producing or promoting estrus.

es•trone ['ɛstroun] *n.* an estrogenic hormone used in treating estrogen deficiency. ⟨< *estrus* + *-one*⟩

es•tro•pip•ate [,ɛstrou'pɪpeit] *n.* an estrogenic hormone used in treating estrogen deficiency.

es•trous ['ɛstrəs] *or* ['istrəs] *adj.* having to do with the estrus.
☛ *Hom.* ESTRUS.

es•trous cycle the hormonally controlled reproductive cycle of the female of all placental mammals except the higher primates, from the beginning of one period of estrus, or heat, to the beginning of the next.

es•trus ['ɛstrəs] *or* ['istrəs] *n.* a condition or period in the sexual cycle of all female placental mammals except the higher primates in which they are receptive to copulation with males and are capable of conceiving; heat. Compare DIESTRUS. ⟨< NL < L *oestrus* gadfly, horsefly, sting, frenzy < Gk. *oistros*⟩
☛ *Hom.* ESTROUS.

es•tu•ar•ine ['ɛstjuərɪn] *or* ['ɛstjuə,rin] *adj.* **1** formed in an estuary. **2** found in an estuary.

es•tu•ar•y ['ɛstʃu,ɛri] *n., pl.* **-ar•ies. 1** a broad mouth of a river flowing into the sea, where its current meets the tide and is influenced by it. **2** an inlet of the sea. ⟨< L *aestuarium* < *aestus* tide⟩ **—,es•tu'ar•i•al,** *adj.*

esu ELECTROSTATIC UNIT.

es•ur•i•ent [ɪ'sʊriənt] *or* [ɪ'sjʊriənt] *adj.* greedy. ⟨< L *esurire* be hungry⟩ **—e'sur•i•ence** or **e'sur•i•en•cy,** *n.* **—e'sur•i•ent•ly,** *adv.*

-et *suffix.* little——: *owlet = little owl; islet = little isle.* ⟨< OF⟩

e•ta ['eitə] *or* ['itə] *n.* the seventh letter of the Greek alphabet (Η, η).

ETA estimated time of arrival.

ét•a•gère [,eitə'ʒɛr]; *French,* [eta'ʒɛʀ] *n.* a piece of furniture with open shelves for showing ornaments.

et al. 1 and others (for L *et alii*). **2** and elsewhere (for L *et alibi*).

e•ta•lon ['eitə,lɒn]; *French,* [eta'lɔ̃] *n.* an optical device consisting of two reflecting glass plates, used to measure wavelengths. ⟨< F < MF *estalon* standard < OF *estal* place⟩

etc. ET CETERA.

et cet•er•a [ɛt'sɛtərə] **1** and others or the rest; and so forth. **2** or the like; or something similar. ⟨ME < L *et* and + *cetera* the other (things)⟩

☛ *Usage.* **Et cetera** is a Latin phrase meaning 'and (the) others'. Since the *et* itself means 'and', there is no need to put *and* before it. It is redundant to write *and et cetera* or *and etc.*

et•cet•er•as [ɛt'sɛtərəz] *n.pl.* usual additions or extra things.

etch [ɛtʃ] *v.* **1** engrave (a drawing or design) by using acid to eat into a metal plate, glass, etc. **2** engrave a drawing or design on (a plate, etc.) by means of acid: *to etch a copper plate.* **3** practise this art. **4** impress vividly: *The scene was etched on her mind.* ⟨< Du. *etsen* < G *ätzen.* Akin to EAT.⟩ **—'etch•er,** *n.*

etch•ant ['ɛtʃənt] *n.* any chemical used in etching.

etch•ing ['ɛtʃɪŋ] *n., v. —n.* **1** a picture or design printed from an etched plate. **2** an etched plate; an etched drawing or design. **3** the art of an etcher; the process of engraving a drawing or design on a metal plate, glass, etc. by means of acid.
—v. ppr. of ETCH.

ETD estimated time of departure.

e•ter•nal [ɪ'tɜrnəl] *adj.* **1** without beginning or ending; existing before, throughout, and beyond all time. **2** always and forever the same. **3** seeming to go on forever; occurring so frequently as to be almost constant. **4** *(noml.)* **the Eternal,** God. **5** *Metaphysics.* not subject to time or change. ⟨ME < OF < L *aeternalis*, ult. < *aevum* age⟩

☛ *Syn. adj.* **1. Eternal,** EVERLASTING = lasting forever. **Eternal** emphasizes having neither a beginning nor an end: *God is eternal.* **Everlasting** emphasizes having no end, but going on and on forever: *We wish for everlasting peace.*

Eternal City, the Rome.

e•ter•nal•ly [ɪ'tɜrnəli] *adv.* **1** without beginning or ending; throughout and beyond all time. **2** always and forever. **3** constantly; incessantly.

eternal triangle a situation involving conflict arising from the emotional, usually sexual, relationships among either two men and one woman or two women and one man.

e•ter•ni•ty [ɪ'tɜrnəti] *n., pl.* **-ties. 1** time without beginning or ending; all time or the absence of time. **2** an eternal quality; timelessness; endlessness. **3** the endless period after death. **4** a seemingly endless period of time. ⟨ME < OF *eternite* < L *aeternitas* < *aeternus* eternal, ult. < *aevum* age⟩

e•ter•nize [ɪ'tɜrnaɪz] *or* ['itər,naɪz] *v.* **-nized, -niz•ing. 1** make eternal; perpetuate. **2** immortalize. **—e,ter•ni'za•tion,** *n.*

e•te•sian [ɪ'tiʒən] *or* [ɪ'tiziən] *adj.* of some winds in the Mediterranean, occurring annually. ⟨< L *etesius* < Gk. *etesios* < *etos* year⟩

eth [ɛð] See EDH.

e•thac•ry•nate [ɪ'θækrə,neit] *n.* a diuretic drug.

eth•am•bu•tol [ɪ'θæmbjə,tɒl] *n.* a drug used to treat tuberculosis.

eth•ane ['ɛθein] *n.* a colourless, odourless, flammable hydrocarbon of the alkane series, present in natural gas and coal gas. *Formula*: C_2H_6 ⟨< *ether*⟩

eth•a•nol ['ɛθə,noul] *or* ['ɛθə,nɒl] *n.* ETHYL ALCOHOL. ⟨< *ethan(e)* + *(alcoh)ol*⟩

eth•chlor•vy•nol [,ɛθklɔr'vaɪnɒl] *or* [,ɛθklɔr'vaɪnəl] *n.* a drug used to treat insomnia.

eth•ene ['ɛθin] *n. Chemistry.* ethylene.

e•ther ['iθər] *n.* **1** *Chemistry.* any of a group of organic compounds formed by the action of acids on alcohols and composed of two hydrocarbon groups connected by an oxygen atom; especially ethyl ether, a colourless, strong-smelling liquid that burns and evaporates readily. Its fumes cause unconsciousness when deeply inhaled and it is used as an anesthetic, a solvent for fats and resins, etc. *Formula*: $(C_2H_5)_2O$ **2** *Poetic.* the upper regions of space beyond the earth's atmosphere; clear sky. **3** the invisible, elastic substance formerly supposed to be distributed evenly through all space and to conduct light waves, electric waves, etc. Also, **aether** (for defs. 2 and 3). ⟨< L *aether* < Gk. *aithēr* upper air⟩

e•the•re•al [ɪ'θiriəl] *adj.* **1** light; airy; delicate: *Her ethereal beauty made her seem more like a spirit than a human being.* **2** not of the earth; heavenly. **3** of or having to do with the upper regions of space. **4** of or having to do with the ether formerly believed to be diffused through space. **5** like or containing ethyl ether. Also (defs. 1-4), **aethereal.** ⟨ < ME < L *aether* < Gk. *aither* < *aithein* to kindle, burn⟩ **—e'the•re•al•ly,** *adv.*

e•the•re•al•ize [ɪ'θiriə,laɪz] *v.* **-ized, -iz•ing.** make ethereal.

e•ther•i•fy ['iθərə,faɪ] *or* [ɪ'θɛrə,faɪ] *v.* **-fied, -fy•ing.** convert (an alcohol) into ether.

e•ther•i•za•tion [,iθərə'zeiʃən] *or* [,iθəraɪ'zeiʃən] *n.* **1** being or becoming etherized. **2** a giving of ether as an anesthetic.

e•ther•ize ['iθə,raɪz] *v.* **-ized, -iz•ing. 1** make unconscious with ether fumes. **2** change into ether.

eth•ic ['ɛθɪk] *adj., n. —adj.* ethical.
—n. **1** a system of ethics. **2** a particular individual value or standard: *the work ethic.* ⟨< L *ethicus* < Gk. *ēthikos* < *ēthos* moral character⟩

eth•i•cal ['ɛθəkəl] *adj.* **1** having to do with standards of right and wrong; of ethics or morality. **2** in accordance with formal or professional rules of right and wrong: *It is not considered ethical for a doctor to disclose a patient's confidences.* **3** of a medication, requiring a doctor's prescription. **—'eth•i•cal•ly,** *adv.*

☛ *Syn.* **1.** See note at MORAL.

eth•i•cist ['ɛθəsɪst] *n.* one concerned with ethical matters and goals or engaged in the formal study of ethics.

eth•ics ['ɛθɪks] *n.* **1** the study of standards of right and wrong; that part of philosophy dealing with moral conduct, duty, and judgment *(used with a singular verb).* **2** formal or professional rules of right and wrong; system of conduct or behaviour *(used with a plural verb): Medical ethics do not permit doctors and surgeons to advertise.*

E•thi•o•pi•a [,iθi'oupiə] *n.* a country in NE Africa, on the Red Sea, formerly called Abyssinia. See SUDAN for map.

E•thi•o•pi•an [,iθi'oupiən] *n., adj. —n.* **1** a native or inhabitant of Ethiopia. **2** *Archaic.* a black African.
—adj. **1** of or having to do with Ethiopia or its people. **2** *Archaic.* black African. **3** belonging to a geographical division including part of Africa and Arabia.

E•thi•op•ic [,iθi'ɒpɪk] *or* [,iθi'oupɪk] *n., adj. —n.* the ancient Semitic language of Ethiopia.
—adj. of or having to do with this language or the church using it.

e•this•te•rone [ɛ'θɪstə,roun] *n.* a hormone used to treat progesterone deficiency.

eth•moid ['ɛθmɔɪd] *adj., n. —adj.* having to do with certain bones situated in the walls and septum of the nose and containing numerous perforations for the filaments of the olfactory nerve.
—n. an ethmoid bone. ⟨< Gk. *ēthmoeidēs* < *ēthmos* sieve + *eidos* form⟩

eth•nic ['ɛθnɪk] *adj., n. —adj.* **1** of or having to do with various groups of people by nationality and their characteristics, customs, and languages. **2** *Cdn. Informal.* of or having to do with immigrants who are not native speakers of English or French: *ethnic dances, the ethnic vote.*
—n. Cdn. Informal. an immigrant who is not a native speaker of English or French; a person of foreign birth or descent: *There are ethnics in Toronto from many parts of Europe.* ⟨< L *ethnicus* < Gk. *ethnikos* < *ethnos* nation⟩ **—'eth•ni•cal•ly,** *adv.*

☛ *Usage.* **Ethnic,** *adj.* (def. 2) and *n.* This strictly informal use of **ethnic** has become established in Canada and is spreading to the United States, though many people consider it unacceptable since it assumes a 'default' or 'normal' ethnicity of English or French. Usually something less potentially offensive, such as *immigrant* or *multicultural*, depending on the context, will serve as well or better.

ethnic cleansing the forced removal or wholesale killing of people of a certain ethnic group from an area.

eth•nic•i•ty [ɛθ'nɪsəti] *n.* ethnic quality, character, or status.

ethno– *combining form.* race; nation: *ethnology.* ⟨< Gk. *ethno-* < *ethnos* nation⟩

eth•no•cen•tric [,ɛθnou'sɛntrɪk] *adj.* characterized by preoccupation with one's own cultural or national group, belief in its superiority over others, or an unconscious assumption that it constitutes the norm. **—,eth•no'cen•tri•cal•ly,** *adv.*

eth•no•cen•tric•i•ty [,ɛθnousɛn'trɪsəti] *n.* ethnocentrism.

eth•no•cen•trism [,ɛθnou'sɛntrɪzəm] *n.* the quality or condition of being ethnocentric.

eth•nog•ra•pher [ɛθ'nɒgrəfər] *n.* a person trained in ethnography, especially one whose work it is.

eth•no•graph•ic [,ɛθnə'græfɪk] *adj.* having to do with ethnography. **—,eth•no'graph•i•cal•ly,** *adv.*

eth•nog•ra•phy [ɛθ'nɒgrəfi] *n.* the scientific description and classification of individual cultural groups of people.

eth•no•ling•ui•stics [,ɛθnoulɪŋ'gwɪstɪks] *n.* the study of a language in relation to its culture.

eth•no•log•i•cal [,ɛθnə'lɒdʒəkəl] *adj.* having to do with ethnology. Also, **ethnologic. —,eth•no'log•i•cal•ly,** *adv.*

eth•nol•o•gist [ɛθ'nɒlədʒɪst] *n.* a person trained in ethnology, especially one whose work it is.

eth•nol•o•gy [ɛθ'nɒlədʒi] *n.* the branch of anthropology that deals with the comparison of various cultural groups of people, their origin, distribution, and characteristics.

eth•no•mu•si•col•o•gy [,ɛθnou,mjuzɪ'kɒlədʒi] *n.* the study of the folk music of various cultures and its relation to its users.

eth•o•log•i•cal [,iθə'lɒdʒəkəl] *adj.* of or having to do with ethology. **—,eth•o'log•i•cal•ly,** *adv.*

e•thol•o•gist [ɪ'θɒlədʒɪst] *n.* a person trained in ethology, especially one whose work it is.

e•thol•o•gy [ɪ'θɒlədʒi] *n.* the scientific study of the behaviour of animals, especially of wild animals in their natural environment. ⟨< L *ethologia* character portrayal < Gk. < *ethos* disposition, character + *logos* word⟩

e•tho•prop•a•zine [,iθou'prɒpə,zin] *n.* a drug used to treat Parkinson's disease and other symptoms.

e•thos ['iθɒs] *n.* the essential and distinctive character or spirit of a race or people, or of a system, culture, institution, etc. ⟨< NL < Gk. *ēthos* character, nature⟩

e•tho•sux•i•mide [,iθou'sʌksə,maɪd] *n.* an anticonvulsant drug used to treat certain forms of epilepsy.

eth•yl ['ɛθəl] *n.* **1** a univalent radical present in many organic compounds. Ordinary alcohol contains ethyl. *Formula*: C_2H_5 **2 Ethyl,** *Trademark.* **a** a poisonous, colourless lead compound once used in gasoline to reduce knocking; tetraethyl lead. *Formula*: Pb $(C_2H_5)_4$ **b** a gasoline containing this compound. ⟨< *ether*⟩

ethyl acetate a liquid ester having a fragrance like fruit. *Formula*: $C_4H_8O_2$

ethyl alcohol ordinary alcohol, made by the fermentation of grain, sugar, etc. *Formula*: C_2H_5OH

eth•yl•ate ['ɛθə,leit] *v.* **-at•ed, -at•ing.** introduce into (a compound) the ethyl group, glycol, or ethylene radical.

ethyl cellulose a white, grainy solid made by soaking wood pulp in sodium hydroxide and then treating it with ethyl chloride. Adhesives and insulation contain ethyl cellulose.

ethyl chloride a substance which remains a gas at ordinary temperatures and becomes a flammable liquid under compression. *Formula*: C_2H_5Cl

ethyl di•hy•drox•y•prop•yl PABA [,daɪhaɪ,drɒksi'prɒpɪl] *n.* a sunscreen with sun protection factor 14.

eth•yl•ene ['ɛθə,lin] *n.* a colourless, flammable gas with an unpleasant odour, used as an anesthetic, in making organic compounds, and for colouring and ripening citrus fruits. *Formula*: C_2H_4

ethylene glycol a colourless, viscous liquid used in cooling systems. *Formula*: $H_6O_2C_2$

ethylene series *Chemistry.* the alkene series.

ethy•no•di•ol di•ac•e•tate [,ɛθə'noudi,ɒl daɪ'æsə,teit] *n.* an oral contraceptive.

e•tid•ron•ate [ɪ'tɪdrə,neit] *n.* a drug used to treat bone mass loss, especially in post-menopausal women.

e•ti•o•late ['itiə,leit] *v.* **-lat•ed, -lat•ing. 1** *Botany.* make (a plant) pale or colourless by depriving it of light; blanch. **2** of a plant, become pale or colourless through lack of sunlight. **3** make weak, dull, colourless: *Her literary style was bland and etiolated.* ⟨< F *étioler* blanch⟩ **—,e•ti•o'la•tion,** *n.*

e•ti•ol•o•gy [,iti'ɒlədʒi] *n.* **1** the assigning of a cause. **2** the branch of philosophy that deals with origins or causes. **3** the origin of a disease. **4** the theory of the causes of disease. Also, **aetiology.** ⟨< L *aetiologia* < Gk. *aitiologia* < *aitia* cause + *-logos* treating of⟩ **—,e•ti•o'log•i•cal** or **,e•ti•o'log•ic,** *adj.* **—,e•ti•o'log•i•cal•ly,** *adv.*

et•i•quette ['ɛtəkɪt] *n.* **1** the conventional rules for conduct or behaviour in polite society. **2** the formal rules or conventions governing conduct in a profession, official ceremony, etc.: *medical etiquette.* ⟨< F < Gmc.⟩

Eton collar ['itən] a broad, stiff collar worn outside the coat collar. See COLLAR for picture. ⟨< *Eton,* a town in S England on the Thames, the site of a famous school⟩

Eton jacket ['itən] a short, black coat with broad lapels. The jacket comes to the waist and is not made to button. ⟨< *Eton.* See ETON COLLAR.⟩

e•top•o•side [ɪ'tɒpə,saɪd] *n.* a drug used to treat certain forms of cancer, especially lung cancer.

e•tret•i•nate [ɪ'trɛtə,neit] *n.* a drug used to treat certain skin conditions.

E•tru•ri•an [ɪ'truriən] *adj. or n.* Etruscan.

E•trus•can [ɪ'trʌskən] *n., adj.* *—n.* **1** a native or inhabitant of Etruria, an ancient country in W Italy. **2** the language of Etruria. *—adj.* of or having to do with Etruria, its people, their language, art, or customs. ⟨< L *Etruscus*⟩

et seq. and the following; and that which follows. ⟨for L *et sequens*⟩

–ette *suffix.* **1** small: *kitchenette, statuette.* **2** a substitute for; imitation: *Leatherette.* ⟨< F *-ette,* fem. of *-et* -et⟩

é•tude [ei'tjud] *or* [ei'tud] *n.* **1** a study. **2 a** a piece of music intended to develop skill in technique. **b** a composition of a similar type, having artistic quality, and intended for public performance: *Chopin's études.* ⟨< F *étude* study < L *studium.* Doublet of STUDIO, STUDY.⟩

e•tui [ei'twi] *or* ['ɛtwi] *n.* a small, decorated case used to contain small articles such as needles. ⟨< F *étui* < OF *estui* < *estuier* to place in a cover, enclose < VL **studiare* to treat with care < L *studium* zeal, study⟩

et•y•mo•log•i•cal [,ɛtəmə'lɒdʒəkəl] *adj.* of or having to do with the origin and history of words. **—,et•y•mo'log•i•cal•ly,** *adv.*

et•y•mol•o•gist [,ɛtə'mɒlədʒɪst] *n.* a person trained in etymology, especially one whose work it is.

et•y•mol•o•gize [,ɛtə'mɒlə,dʒaɪz] *v.* **-gized, -giz•ing. 1** trace the history of (a word). **2** give the etymology of words.

et•y•mol•o•gy [,ɛtə'mɒlədʒi] *n., pl.* **-gies. 1** an explanation of the origin of a word and a description of the changes it has gone through in its history. **2** the branch of linguistics dealing with word origins. ⟨< L < Gk. *etymologia* < *etymon* the original sense or form of a word (neut. of *etymos* true, real) + *-logos* treating of⟩

et•y•mon ['ɛtə,mɒn] *n.* the original form of a word that is the basis of later derivatives. ⟨< Gk. *etymon* (neut. adj.) what is true⟩

eu– *prefix.* good; well: *eulogy, euphony.* ⟨< Gk.⟩

Eu europium.

eu•caine ['jukein] *or* [ju'kein] *n.* a white solid used as an anesthetic. ⟨< *eu-* + *(co)caine*⟩

eu•ca•lypt ['jukə,lɪpt] *n.* eucalyptus.

eu•cal•yp•tol [,jukə'lɪptɒl] *n.* a viscous liquid derived from eucalyptus oil, used in flavourings and in pharmaceuticals. *Formula*: $C_{10}H_{18}O$

eu•ca•lyp•tus [,jukə'lɪptəs] *n.* **-tus•es, -ti** [-taɪ]. any of a genus (*Eucalyptus*) of mainly Australian evergreen trees of the myrtle family cultivated for their wood, gum, and resin, and the oil that can be extracted from the leaves. Also, **eucalypt.** ⟨< NL < Gk. *eu-* well + *kalyptos* covered; with reference to bud covering⟩

eucalyptus oil an oil extracted from eucalyptus leaves, used as an ingredient in expectorants and antiseptics.

eu•ca•ry•ote [ju'kæri,out] *or* [ju'kɛri,out] *n.* an organism with a membrane-bound nucleus and, like all higher organisms, having two kinds of cell, diploid and somatic. A eucaryote has a nuclear membrane, but a procaryote has not. Also, **eukaryote.** Compare PROCARYOTE. ⟨< Gk. *eu-* good, well + *karyon* nut, kernel⟩

eu•char•is ['jukərɪs] *n.* any South American plant of the genus *Eucharis,* cultivated for its fragrant flowers.

Eu•cha•rist ['jukərɪst] *n.* **1** the Christian sacrament of the Lord's Supper; Holy Communion. **2** the consecrated bread and wine used in this sacrament. ⟨< LL < Gk. *eucharistia* thankfulness, the Eucharist⟩ **—,Eu•cha'ris•tic,** *adj.*

eu•chre ['jukər] *n., v.* **-chred, -chring.** *—n.* **1** a simple card game for two, three, or four players, using the 32 (or 28, or 24) highest cards in the pack. **2** a social gathering during which people play euchre. **3** the failure of the side that declared the trump to win three tricks.
—v. **1** defeat (the side that declared the trump) at euchre. **2** *Informal.* outwit; defeat. ⟨origin uncertain⟩

eu•chro•ma•tin [ju'kroumətɪn] *n. Genetics.* the chromatin that contains almost all the genes. It is relatively uncondensed and light-staining in interphase cells.

eu•clase ['jukleis] *n.* a very rare mineral, beryllium aluminum silicate, usually green or blue. *Formula*: $HBeAlSiO_5$ ⟨< F < Gk. *eu-* good + *klasis* a breaking < *klan* break, because it breaks easily⟩

Eu•clid•e•an or **Eu•clid•i•an** [ju'klɪdiən] *adj.* **1** of or having to do with Euclid, a Greek mathematician who wrote a book on geometry about 300 B.C. **2** of or about his principles of geometry.

eu•de•mo•nia [,judə'mouniə] *n.* happiness, especially, in Aristotelian thought, the well-being characterizing a life of a rational activity. ⟨< Gk. *eudaimonia* < *eudaimon* < having a good spirit < *eu-* good + *daimon* spirit, fate, divine power⟩

eu•de•mon•ism [ju'dimə,nɪzəm] *n.* the doctrine that happiness, as distinct from pleasure, is the proper result of all behaviour.

eu•di•om•e•ter [,judi'ɒmətər] *n. Chemistry.* a graduated measuring tube for the analysis of gases. ⟨< Gk. *eudios* clear, fair + E *-meter*⟩

eu•ge•nia [ju'dʒiniə] *or* [ju'dʒinjə] *n.* any of the several evergreen plants found in tropical climates, bearing edible red cherrylike berries.

eu•gen•ic [ju'dʒɛnɪk] *adj.* **1** having to do with improvement of the race; improving the race; improving the offspring produced, especially by curbing reproduction in certain groups: *eugenic breeding.* Compare DYSGENIC. **2** coming of good stock. ⟨< Gk. *eugenēs* well-born < *eu-* well + *genos* birth⟩ **—eu'gen•i•cal•ly,** *adv.*

eu•gen•i•cist [ju'dʒɛnɪsɪst] *n.* an advocate of eugenics.

eu•gen•ics [ju'dʒɛnɪks] *n.sing. or pl.* **1** the science of improving the human race by a careful selection of parents, by encouraging breeding by persons with desirable traits (positive eugenics), and by discouraging breeding by those with undesirable traits such as limited intelligence or hereditary diseases (negative eugenics), in order to develop healthier and more intelligent children. **2** the study of improving offspring.

eu•ge•nol ['judʒə,nɒl] *n.* an aromatic oil found in clover and used in perfumery. *Formula:* $C_{10}H_{12}O_2$

eu•gle•na [ju'glinə] *n.* any one-celled organism of the genus *Euglena,* found in fresh water. ⟨< NL < Gk. *eu-* good, fair + *glene* pupil (of the eye)⟩

Eu•he•mer•ism [ju'himə,rɪzəm] *or* [ju'hɛmə,rɪzəm] the theory of Euhemerus that mythology about gods arises from the deification of human beings. ⟨< *Euhemerus,* Greek writer, 4c. B.C.⟩

eu•ka•ry•ote [ju'kæri,out] *or* [ju'kɛri,out] *n.* See EUCARYOTE.

eu•la•chon ['juləkən] *n.* oolichan.

eu•lo•gia [ju'loudʒiə] *or* [ju'loudʒə] *n. Eastern Church.* the blessed bread given to the congregation during Vespers. ⟨< Med.L food, blessing < Gk. praise < *eulegein* to speak well of, bless < *eu-* good, well + *logos* word⟩

eu•lo•gist ['julədʒɪst] *n.* a person who eulogizes or composes eulogies.

eu•lo•gis•tic [,julə'dʒɪstɪk] *adj.* praising highly. Also, **eulogistical. —,eu•lo'gis•ti•cal•ly,** *adv.*

eu•lo•gi•um [ju'loudʒiəm] *n., pl.* **-gi•ums, -gi•a** [-dʒiə]. eulogy; praise. ⟨< Med.L *eulogium,* var. of L *eulogia* < Gk. *eulogia.* See EULOGY.⟩

eu•lo•gize ['julə,dʒaɪz] *v.* **-gized, -giz•ing.** praise very highly. **—'eu•lo,giz•er,** *n.*

eu•lo•gy ['julədʒi] *n., pl.* **-gies. 1** a speech or writing in praise of a person, action, etc.: *She pronounced a eulogy upon the hero.* **2** high praise. ⟨< Gk. *eulogia* < *eu-* well + *legein* speak⟩

Eu•men•i•des [ju'mɛnə,diz] *n.pl. Greek mythology.* the Furies; Erinyes. Literally, the kindly (goddesses), a name used for the Furies to avoid offending them.

eu•nuch ['junək] *n.* **1** a castrated man. **2** a castrated man in charge of a harem or the household of an Oriental ruler. ⟨< L *eunuchus* < Gk. *eunouchos* < *eunē* bed + *echein* keep⟩

eu•on•y•mus [ju'ɒnəməs] *n.* any small shrub of the genus *Euonymus,* having the seed enclosed in crimson capsules. ⟨< NL < L, spindle tree < Gk. *euonymos* well named < *eu-* good, well + *onyma* name⟩

eu•pa•to•ri•um [,jupə'tɔriəm] *n.* any plant of the genus *Eupatorium.* ⟨< NL < Gk. *eupatorion* hemp agrimony⟩

eu•pat•rid ['jupə,trɪd] *n.* one of the aristocrats of ancient Athens and other Greek states, once a member of the hereditary ruling class. ⟨< Gk. *eupatrides* < *eu-* good, well + *pater* father⟩

eu•pep•si•a [ju'pɛpsiə] *or* [ju'pɛpʃə] *n.* good digestion. Compare DYSPEPSIA. ⟨< NL < Gk. *eupepsia* < *eupeptos* having a good digestion < *eu-* well + *peptein* digest⟩

eu•pep•tic [ju'pɛptɪk] *adj.* **1** having good digestion. **2** aiding digestion. **3** cheerful; in good health.

eu•phe•mism ['jufə,mɪzəm] *n.* **1** the use of a mild or indirect expression instead of one that is harsh or unpleasantly direct. **2** a mild or indirect expression used in this way. *Pass away* is a common euphemism for *die.* The name *Eumenides,* meaning *kindly goddesses,* was a euphemism for the Furies. ⟨< Gk. *euphēmismos* < *euphemizein* speak with fair words < *eu-* good + *phēmē* speaking⟩

eu•phe•mist ['jufəmɪst] *n.* a person who uses euphemisms.

eu•phe•mis•tic [,jufə'mɪstɪk] *adj.* of or showing euphemism; containing a euphemism. **—,eu•phe'mis•ti•cal•ly,** *adv.*

eu•phem•ize ['jufə,maɪz] *v.* **-ized, -iz•ing. 1** describe by means of euphemism. **2** make use of euphemisms.

eu•phon•ic [ju'fɒnɪk] *adj.* **1** having to do with euphony. **2** euphonious. **—eu'phon•i•cal•ly,** *adv.*

eu•pho•ni•ous [ju'founiəs] *adj.* sounding well; pleasing to the ear; harmonious. **—eu'pho•ni•ous•ly,** *adv.* **—eu'pho•ni•ous•ness,** *n.*

eu•pho•ni•um [ju'founiəm] *n.* a brass musical instrument resembling a tuba and having a loud, deep tone. ⟨< NL < Gk. *euphōnos* well-sounding < *eu-* good + *phōnē* sound⟩

A euphonium

eu•pho•ny ['jufəni] *n., pl.* **-nies. 1** agreeableness of sound; pleasing effect to the ear; harmony of speech sounds as uttered or combined in utterance. **2** the tendency, in the development of a language over time, to change sounds so as to favour ease of utterance. **3** a combination of harmonious sounds. ⟨< LL < Gk. *euphōnia* < *eu-* good + *phōnē* sound⟩

eu•phor•bi•a [ju'fɔrbiə] *n.* any of a genus (*Euphorbia*) of plants of the spurge family, including the spurges and poinsettia, all having a milky juice or latex which in some species is poisonous. ⟨< L *euphorbea* < *Euphorbus,* a Greek physician⟩

eu•pho•ri•a [ju'fɔriə] *n. Psychology.* a feeling of exaltation. ⟨< NL < Gk. *euphoria* < *eu-* good + *pherein* bear⟩ **—eu'phor•ic,** *adj.*

eu•phor•iant [ju'fɔriənt] *adj., n. —adj.* producing euphoria. *—n.* a substance that produces euphoria.

eu•phot•ic [ju'fɒtɪk] *adj.* having to do with the topmost layer of water that gets the light needed for photosynthesis. ⟨< Gk. *eu-* good, well + *photos,* gen. of *phos* light⟩

eu•phu•ism ['jufju,ɪzəm] *n.* **1** an affected style of speaking and writing English that was fashionable around 1600, characterized by long series of antitheses, frequent similes, and alliteration. *Example: "...the milk of the Tygresse, that the more salt there is thrown into it the fresher it is."* **2** any affected, elegant style of writing; flowery, artificial language. **3** an instance of such writing. ⟨< *Euphues,* the main character in two works of John Lyly, a 16c. English dramatist and romance writer < Gk. *euphyes* shapely < *eu-* good, well + *phye* growth (< *phyein* grow)⟩

eu•phu•ist ['jufjuɪst] *n.* a person who uses euphuism.

eu•phu•is•tic [,jufju'ɪstɪk] *adj.* using or containing euphuism; like euphuism. **—,eu•phu'is•ti•cal•ly,** *adv.*

eu•plas•tic [ju'plæstɪk] *adj.* quick to heal. ⟨< Gk. *eu-* good, well + *plastikos* forming < *plassein* form⟩

eu•ploid ['juplɔɪd] *adj. Genetics.* of any chromosome number that is an exact multiple of the haploid number present in a gamete of the species. Compare ANEUPLOID, HETEROPLOID. ⟨< Gk. *eu-* good, well + *ploos* fold + E *-oid*⟩

Eur. Europe; European.

Eur•a•sia [jʊ'reiʒə] *n.* the continents of Europe and Asia.

Eur•a•sian [jʊ'reiʒən] *adj., n. —adj.* **1** of or having to do with Europe and Asia or its people. **2** of mixed European and Asian parentage.
—n. a person of mixed European and Asian parentage.

Eur•a•tom ['jʊrə,tɒm] *or* [jʊ'rætəm] *n.* an organization to pool the nuclear power research and developments of six European countries (France, Germany, Italy, Belgium, the Netherlands, and Luxembourg); European Atomic Energy Community.

eu•re•ka [jʊ'rikə] *interj.* an exclamation of triumph about a discovery or a solution to a problem. ⟨< Gk. *heurēka* I have found (it) < *heuriskein* to find; the exclamation traditionally attributed to the ancient Greek mathematician Archimedes, on making a discovery⟩

eu•rhyth•mic [jʊ'rɪðmɪk] *adj.* **1** of or having to do with eurhythmics. **2** pleasingly proportioned. Also, **eurythmic. —eu'rhyth•mi•cal•ly,** *adv.*

eu•rhyth•mics [jʊ'rɪðmɪks] *n.* a system for the development of rhythm and grace by the performing of bodily movements in response to music. Also, **eurythmics.**

eu•rhyth•my [jʊ'rɪðmi] *n.* **1** harmony in proportion. **2** harmony in motion. Also, **eurythmy.**

eu•ri•pus [jʊ'raɪpəs] *n.* a strait having a violent flow of water. ⟨< L < Gk. *euripos* < *eu-* good, well + *rhipe* rush, impetus⟩

eu•ro ['jʊrou] *n. Australian.* wallaroo. ⟨< aboriginal language⟩

Euro– *combining form.* **1** Europe or European: *Eurodollar.*

2 Europe, or European, and ——: *Eurasian.* Also, before vowels, **Eur-.**

Eu•ro•bond ['jurou,bɒnd] *n.* a corporate bond sold on the European market and repaid in its original currency.

Eu•roc•ly•don [jʊ'rɒklə,dɒn] *n.* a stormy or northeast wind. ⟨< Gk. *euroklydon* < *euros* east wind + **akylon* north wind < L *aquilo*⟩

Eu•ro•crat ['jʊrə,kræt] *n.* a member of the administration of the European Economic Community. ⟨< *Euro-* + (*bureau*)*crat*⟩

Eu•ro•cur•ren•cy ['jʊrou,kɜrənsi] *n.* money deposited in a European bank but in the currency of the country of origin.

Eu•ro•dol•lar ['jʊrou,dɒlər] *n.* a United States dollar held in a bank, etc. in Europe.

Eu•ro•mart ['jʊrou,mɑrt] *n.* EUROPEAN ECONOMIC COMMUNITY. Also, **Euromarket.**

Eu•ro•pa [jʊ'roupə] *n.* **1** a Phoenician princess loved by Zeus in the guise of a bull. **2** a satellite of Jupiter.

Europe ['jʊrəp] *n.* a continent in the west part of Eurasia, bounded by the Ural Mountains, the Caucasus Mountains, and the Black Sea in the east, the Atlantic Ocean in the west, and the Mediterranean Sea in the south.

Eu•ro•pe•an [,jʊrə'piən] *adj., n. —adj.* **1** of or having to do with Europe or its inhabitants. **2** *Archaic.* of or designating a major race of people that includes the traditional inhabitants of Europe, the Middle East, and N Africa, distinguished by a combination of biological characteristics, including generally lighter skin than any other major racial group.
—n. **1** a native or inhabitant of Europe. **2** a person whose recent ancestors came from Europe. **3** *Archaic.* a member of the European race.

European Common Market EUROPEAN ECONOMIC COMMUNITY.

European Economic Community a trading and political association of W European countries for eliminating tariffs between each other and working toward a complete economic union. The original member countries, all joining in 1958, were Belgium, France, Italy, Luxembourg, the Netherlands, and Germany. The United Kingdom, the Irish Republic, and Denmark joined in 1973, Greece in 1981, and Spain and Portugal in 1986. *Abbrev.*: EEC

Eu•ro•pe•an•ize [,jʊrə'piə,naɪz] *v.* **-ized, -iz•ing. 1** make European in appearance, habit, way of life, etc. **2** integrate (a country) into the EEC.

European plan a hotel system by which guests pay for only room and service, meals being extra. Compare AMERICAN PLAN.

eu•ro•pi•um [jʊ'roupiəm] *n.* a rare, metallic chemical element of the same group as cerium. *Symbol*: Eu; *at.no.* 63; *at.mass* 151.96. ⟨< NL < L *Europa* Europe < Gk.⟩

eu•ry•ha•line [,jʊrə'heilaɪn] *or* [,jʊrə'hælaɪn] *adj. Biology.* capable of living in waters of widely varying salinity. ⟨< Gk. *eurys* wide + *halinos* saline < *hals* salt⟩

eu•ry•hy•gric [,jʊrə'haɪgrɪk] *adj. Biology.* adapting to a wide range of humidity. ⟨< Gk. *eurys* wide + *hygros* wet, moist⟩

eu•ryph•a•gous [jʊ'rɪfəgəs] *adj. Biology.* having a varied diet. ⟨< Gk. *eurys* wide + *phagos* < *phagein* to eat⟩

eu•ry•therm ['jʊrə,θɜrm] *n.* an organism capable of living in widely varying temperatures. ⟨< Gk. *eurys* wide + *therme* heat⟩ **—,eu•ry'ther•mic,** *adj.*

eu•ryth•mic [jʊ'rɪðmɪk] See EURHYTHMIC.

eu•ryth•mics [jʊ'rɪðmɪks] See EURHYTHMICS.

Eu•sta•chi•an tube [ju'steiʃən] a slender canal between the pharynx and the middle ear, which equalizes the air pressure on the two sides of the eardrum. See EAR[1] for picture.
⟨< Bartolommeo *Eustachio*, a 16c. Italian anatomist⟩

eu•sta•sy ['justəsi] *n. Geology.* a change in sea level all over the world, caused by continental glaciers advancing or retreating. ⟨< NL *eustasia* < Gk. *eu-* good, well + *stasis* a standing < *histanai* stand⟩ **—eu'stat•ic** [ju'stætɪk], *adj.*

eu•tec•tic [ju'tɛktɪk] *adj.* of alloys, formed at the lowest temperature for solidifying. ⟨< Gk. *eutektos* easily fused < *eu-* good, well + *tekein* to melt⟩

eu•tec•toid [ju'tɛktɔɪd] *n.* a eutectic alloy.

eu•tha•na•sia [,juθə'neiʒə] *n.* **1** an easy, painless death. **2** a painless killing, especially to end a painful and incurable disease; mercy killing. ⟨< Gk. *euthanasia* < *eu-* easy + *thanatos* death⟩

eu•then•ics [ju'θɛnɪks] *n.* the science of biologically improving the human race by controlling the environment or living conditions. ⟨< Gk. *euthēnia* well-being⟩

eu•troph•ic [ju'trɒfɪk] *or* [ju'troufɪk] *adj.* of a lake or river, having excessive plant growth due to a high concentration of nutrients (such as phosphates), resulting in a decrease in oxygen, and hence a decrease in the number of fish, etc. Compare OLIGOTROPHIC. ⟨< Gk. *eu-* good, well + *trophikos* nourishing < *trophē* food, nourishment⟩ **—eu,troph•i'ca•tion,** *n.*

eu•troph•y ['jutrəfi] *n.* the condition of being eutrophic.

eux•e•nite ['juksə,nəit] *n.* a shiny black mineral made of cerbium, uranium, titanium, and yttrium. ⟨< G *euxenit* < Gk. *euxenos* hospitable < *eu-* good + *xenos* stranger, so called because it has many strange elements in it.⟩

eV electronvolt.

EVA extravehicular activity; spacewalk.

e•vac•u•ant [ɪ'vækjuənt] *adj., n. —adj. Medicine.* producing evacuation; cathartic; purgative.
—n. an evacuant medicine, drug, etc., especially a purgative.

e•vac•u•ate [ɪ'vækju,eit] *v.* **-at•ed, -at•ing. 1** leave empty; withdraw from: *The soldiers evacuated the fort.* **2** withdraw; remove: *to evacuate all foreign residents from the war zone.* **3** make empty: *to evacuate the bowels.* ⟨< L *evacuare* < *ex-* out + *vacuus* empty⟩ **—e'vac•u,a•tor,** *n.*

e•vac•u•a•tion [ɪ,vækju'eiʃən] *n.* **1** the act of evacuating or being evacuated. **2** something discharged in evacuation; excrement. **—e'vac•u•a•tive,** *adj.*

e•vac•u•ee [ɪ,vækju'i] *or* [ɪ'vækju,i] *n.* one who is removed to a place of greater safety.

e•vade [ɪ'veid] *v.* **e•vad•ed, e•vad•ing. 1** get away from by trickery; avoid by cleverness. **2** avoid (the truth, a commitment, an issue, etc.) by indefinite or misleading statements; be evasive. **3** be impenetrable to the efforts or thinking of; baffle: *The solution evades me.* ⟨< L *evadere* < *ex-* away + *vadere* go⟩
☛ *Syn.* **1.** See note at ESCAPE.

e•vad•er [ɪ'veidər] *n.* one who evades: *an income tax evader.*

e•vag•i•nate [ɪ'vædʒə,neit] *v.* **-nat•ed, -nat•ing. 1** turn inside out. **2** cause to protrude. ⟨< L *evaginatus* pp. of *evaginare* to unsheathe < *e-* from + *vagina* sheath⟩ **—e,vag•i'na•tion,** *n.*

e•val•u•ate [ɪ'vælju,eit] *v.* **-at•ed, -at•ing. 1** judge the worth, quality, or importance of: *to evaluate a statement, to evaluate a new data processing system.* **2** find or decide the value of: *An expert evaluated the old clock at $900.* **3** *Mathematics.* obtain the numerical value of (a function). ⟨< F *évaluer*⟩ **—e'val•u,a•tor,** *n.*
☛ *Syn.* See note at ESTIMATE.

e•val•u•a•tion [ɪ,vælju'eiʃən] *n.* **1** an evaluating. **2** an estimate of worth or quality: *The coach made too high an evaluation of the centre's ability to score.*

e•val•u•a•tive [ɪ'væljuətɪv] *or* [ɪ'vælju,eitɪv] *adj.* of or having to do with evaluation.

ev•a•nesce [,ɛvə'nɛs] *v.* **-nesced, -nes•cing.** disappear gradually; fade away; vanish. ⟨< L *evanescere* < *ex-* out + *vanescere* vanish < *vanus* insubstantial⟩

ev•a•nes•cence [,ɛvə'nɛsəns] *n.* **1** a gradual disappearance; a fading away; vanishing. **2** a tendency to disappear or fade away; inability to last long.

ev•a•nes•cent [,ɛvə'nɛsənt] *adj.* tending to disappear or fade away; able to last only a short time. **—,ev•a'nes•cent•ly,** *adv.*

e•van•gel [ɪ'vændʒəl] *n.* **1** *Christianity.* the Gospel; good news of the saving of people through Christ. **2** good news. **3** evangelist. **4 Evangel,** in the Bible, one of the four gospels; Matthew, Mark, Luke, or John. ⟨< L *evangelium* < Gk. *euangelion* good tidings, ult. < *eu-* good + *angellein* announce⟩

e•van•gel•i•cal [,ivæn'dʒɛləkəl] *or* [,ɛvən'dʒɛləkəl] *adj.* **1** of, concerning, or according to the four Gospels of the New Testament. **2** of or having to do with the Protestant churches that emphasize Christ's atonement and salvation by faith as the most important parts of Christianity. Methodists and Baptists are evangelical; Unitarians and Universalists are not. **3** evangelistic. **4 Evangelical, a** designating those Protestant churches deriving from Lutheranism, rather than Calvinism. Compare REFORMED. **b** (in some parts of Europe) Protestant.
—,e•van'gel•i•cal•ly, *adv.*

e•van•gel•i•cal•ism [,ivæn'dʒɛləkə,lɪzəm] *or* [,ɛvən'dʒɛləkə,lɪzəm] *n.* **1** the doctrines of evangelical churches. **2** the adherence to such doctrines.

e•van•gel•ism [ɪ'vændʒə,lɪzəm] *n.* **1** a preaching of the Gospel; earnest effort for the spread of the Gospel. **2** the work of an evangelist. **3** the belief in the doctrines of an evangelical church or party. **4** a missionary zeal for any cause.

e•van•gel•ist [ɪ'vændʒəlɪst] *n.* **1** a preacher of the Gospel. **2** a travelling preacher who urges people to make a religious commitment in revival services or camp meetings. **3 Evangelist,** any one of the four apostles, Matthew, Mark, Luke, or John, who wrote the Gospels bearing their names. **4** a zealous proponent of any doctrine.

e•van•gel•is•tic [ɪ,vændʒə'lɪstɪk] *adj.* **1** of or by evangelists. **2** of, for, or having to do with evangelism. **3** of the Evangelists. **—e,van•gel'is•ti•cal•ly,** *adv.*

e•van•gel•ize [ɪ'vændʒə,laɪz] *v.* **-ized, -iz•ing. 1** preach the Gospel (to). **2** convert to Christianity by preaching. **—e,van•gel•i'za•tion,** *n.*

e•vap•o•ra•ble [ɪ'væpərəbəl] *adj.* able to be evaporated.

e•vap•o•rate [ɪ'væpə,reit] *v.* **-rat•ed, -rat•ing. 1** change into a vapour: *The heat of the sun evaporated the puddles. Some solids, such as moth balls and dry ice, evaporate without melting.* **2** remove moisture, especially water, from: *Heat is used to evaporate milk.* **3** give off moisture. **4** vanish; disappear; fade away: *Her good resolutions evaporated soon after New Year's Day.* **5** cause (a metal) to be deposited by sublimating it. **6** eject (electrons, neutrons, etc.) ⟨< L *evaporare* < *ex-* out + *vapor* vapour⟩ **—e,vap•o'ra•tion,** *n.* **—e'vap•o•ra•tive,** *adj.*

evaporated milk whole milk that has been concentrated, by evaporation of some of its water, to one half or less of its original bulk, sealed in tins, and sterilized by heating.

e•vap•o•ra•tor [ɪ'væpə,reitər] *n.* an apparatus for evaporating water or other liquid.

e•vap•o•tran•spi•ra•tion [ɪ,væpou,trænspə'reiʃən] *n. Meteorology.* the process of evaporation and plant transpiration by which water vapour returns to the atmosphere.

e•va•sion [ɪ'veiʒən] *n.* **1** a getting away from something by trickery; act of avoiding by cleverness: *Evasion of one's duty is contemptible.* **2** an attempt to escape an argument, a charge, a question, etc.: *The prisoner's evasions of the lawyer's questions convinced the jury of his guilt.* **3** a means of evading; trick or excuse used to avoid something. ⟨ME < OF < LL *evasio, -onis* < L *evadere.* See EVADE.⟩

e•va•sive [ɪ'veisɪv] *or* [ɪ'veizɪv] *adj.* tending or trying to evade: Perhaps *is an evasive answer.* **—e'va•sive•ly,** *adv.* **—e'va•sive•ness,** *n.*

eve [iv] *n.* **1** the evening or day before a holiday or some other special day: *New Year's Eve.* **2** the time just before: *Everything was quiet on the eve of the battle.* **3** *Poetic.* evening. ⟨var. of *even²*⟩

Eve [iv] *n.*
daughter of Eve, any woman or girl. ⟨in the Bible, the first woman. Tempted by Satan, she ate the forbidden fruit and afterwards induced Adam, her husband, to do the same⟩

e•vec•tion [ɪ'vɛkʃən] *n. Astronomy.* a periodic disturbance in the moon's orbit due to the attraction of the sun. ⟨< L *evectio* a going up, carrying out < *evectus* pp. of *evehere* < *e-* out + *vehere* to carry⟩

e•ven¹ ['ivən] *adj., v., adv. —adj.* **1** level; flat; smooth: *Even country has no hills.* **2** at the same level; in the same plane or line: *The snow was even with the window.* **3** always the same; regular; uniform: *An even motion does not change.* **4** equal: *They divided the money into even shares.* **5** See EVEN NUMBER. **6** of a round number, neither more nor less; exact: *Twelve apples make an even dozen. Tax brought the total to six dollars even.* **7** owing nothing and owed nothing: *When he had paid all of his debts, he was even.* **8** not easily disturbed or angered; calm: *A person with an even temper is seldom excited.* **9** not favouring one more than another; fair: *Justice is even treatment.*
be even, a owe nothing. **b** have revenge.
get even, a settle a debt. **b** get revenge.
—v. **1** make equal; tie: *to even the score.* **2** make level or of similar extent: *She evened the edges by trimming them.*
even out, become more even: *After a while the path evened out and the going became easier.*
—adv. **1** in an even manner. **2** just; exactly: *She left even as you came.* **3** indeed: *He is ready, even eager, to go.* **4** fully; quite: *He was faithful even unto death.* **5** though one would not expect it; as one would not expect: *Even the least noise disturbs her.* **6** still; yet: *You can do even better if you try.*
break even, *Informal.* have equal gains and losses.
even if, in spite of the fact that; although.
even though, although. ⟨OE *efen*⟩ **—'e•ven•er,** *n.* **—'e•ven•ly,** *adv.* **—'e•ven•ness,** *n.*

☛ *Syn. adj.* **3. Even,** UNIFORM, EQUABLE = always the same. **Even** emphasizes being regular and steady, never changing in motion, action, quality, etc.: *The even hum of the motor stopped.* **Uniform** emphasizes being always the same in form or character, never changing from the normal or regular: *We should have uniform traffic laws.* **Equable** is a formal word used interchangeably with **even,** but suggesting a quality in the thing or person that makes it likely to be even or uniform: *She has an equable temperament.*

e•ven² ['ivən] *n. Poetic.* evening. ⟨OE *ǣfen*⟩

e•ven•fall ['ivən,fɒl] *n. Poetic.* the beginning of the evening.

e•ven–hand•ed ['ivən 'hændɪd] *adj.* impartial; fair; just: *The judge meted out even-handed justice to all.* **—'e•ven-'hand•ed•ly,** *adv.* **—'e•ven-'hand•ed•ness,** *n.*

eve•ning ['ivnɪŋ] *n., adj. —n.* **1** the last part of day and early part of night; the time between day and night. **2** the time between sunset and bedtime. **3** the last part: *Old age is the evening of life.* **4** a reception or entertainment held in the evening.
—adj. in the evening; of the evening; for the evening. ⟨OE *ǣfnung* < *ǣfnian* become evening < *ǣfen* evening⟩

evening dress formal clothes worn in the evening.

evening gown a woman's evening dress, usually long.

evening primrose 1 any of a genus (*Oenothera*) of New World herbs having spirally arranged leaves and fragrant flowers, especially a common wildflower (*O. biennis*) whose yellow flowers open in the evening. The oil from its seeds has medicinal properties. **2** (*adjl.*) **evening-primrose,** designating the family (Onagraceae) of plants that includes the fireweed, fuchsia, and evening primrose.

eve•nings ['ivnɪŋz] *adv.* in the evenings; every evening.

evening star a bright planet seen in the western sky after sunset. Venus is often the evening star.

even money in a wager, equal odds.

even number a number that has no remainder when divided by 2: *The even numbers are* 2, 4, 6, 8, *etc.*

e•ven–pin•nate ['ivən 'pɪnɪt] *or* ['ivən 'pɪneit] *adj. Botany.* having leaflets in symmetrical pairs.

e•ven•song ['ivən,sɒŋ] *n.* **1** in certain Christian churches, a service said or sung in the late afternoon or early evening; vespers. **2** *Archaic.* evening. ⟨OE *ǣfensang*⟩

e•vent [ɪ'vɛnt] *n.* **1** a happening; *current events.* **2** an important happening: *The discovery of oil in Alberta was certainly an event.* **3** the result; outcome: *We made careful plans and awaited the event.* **4** an item or contest in a program of sports or other planned happenings: *The broad jump was the last event.* **5** something that is planned: *a social event.*
at all events or **in any event,** in any case; whatever happens.
in the event of, in case of; if there is; if there should be: *In the event of rain the party will be held indoors.*
in the event that, if it should happen that; supposing: *In the event that the roads are icy, we will not come.* ⟨< L *eventus* < *evenire* < *ex-* out + *venire* come⟩

☛ *Syn.* **1. Event,** INCIDENT, OCCURRENCE = happening. **Event** applies particularly to a happening of some importance, usually resulting from what has gone before: *Graduation from high school is an event that most students eagerly look forward to.* **Incident** applies to a less important happening taking place between events, but not always in connection with them: *The unexpected meeting with a girl I used to know was an amusing incident.* **Occurrence** is the general word for any happening, event, or incident: *Going to school is an everyday occurrence.*

e•ven–tem•pered ['ivən 'tɛmpərd] *adj.* not easily disturbed or angered; calm.

e•vent•ful [ɪ'vɛntfəl] *adj.* **1** full of events; having many unusual events: *Our day at the fall fair was highly eventful.* **2** having important results; important: *July 1, 1867, Dominion Day, was an eventful day for Canada.* **—e'vent•ful•ly,** *adv.* **—e'vent•ful•ness,** *n.*

e•ven•tide ['ivən,taɪd] *n. Poetic.* evening.

e•ven•tu•al [ɪ'vɛntʃuəl] *adj.* coming in the end; final: *Her eventual success after several failures surprised us.* **—e'ven•tu•al•ly,** *adv.*

e•ven•tu•al•i•ty [ɪ,vɛntʃu'ælәti] *n., pl.* **-ties.** a possible occurrence or condition; possibility: *We hope for rain but are ready for the eventuality of drought.*

e•ven•tu•ate [ɪ'vɛntʃu,eit] *v.* **-at•ed, -at•ing.** come out in the end; happen finally; result. **—e,ven•tu'a•tion,** *n.*

ev•er ['ɛvər] *adv.* **1** at any time: *Is she ever at home?* **2** at all times; always: *ever at your service.* **3** at all; by any chance; in any case: *What did you ever do to make her so angry?* **4** *Informal.* so; very: *Am I ever hungry!*
ever so, *Informal.* very.
for ever and a day, always.

for ever and ever, always; eternally. ⟨OE *æfre*⟩

ev•er•glade ['ɛvər,gleid] *n.* **1** *U.S.* a large tract of low, wet ground partly covered with tall grass; a large swamp or marsh. **2 the Everglades,** a large swamp in S Florida, now a U.S. national park.

ev•er•green ['ɛvər,grin] *adj., n.* —*adj.* **1** remaining green all year: *evergreen leaves.* **2** having leaves or needles all year: *evergreen tree.* **3** enduring: *an evergreen hope.*
—*n.* **1** an evergreen tree, shrub, or herb. **2 evergreens,** *pl.* evergreen twigs or branches used for decoration, especially at Christmas.

ev•er•last•ing [,ɛvər'læstɪŋ] *adj., n.* —*adj.* **1** lasting forever; never ending or stopping. **2** lasting a long time. **3** lasting too long; repeated too often; tiresome: *his everlasting complaints.*
—*n.* **1** an eternity. **2** any of numerous plants of the composite family having papery flowers that are used for winter bouquets and decorations because they keep their form and in many cases their colour when they are dry. One of the most widely grown of the everlastings is the strawflower. **3** any of various other plants with similar characteristics, such as amaranths or any of several grasses with showy spikes or panicles. **4** the flower of any such plants. **5 the Everlasting,** God. **—,ev•er'last•ing•ly,** *adv.* **—,ev•er'last•ing•ness,** *n.*

☛ *Syn. adj.* **1.** See note at ETERNAL.

ev•er•more [,ɛvər'mɔr] *adv. or n.* always; forever.
for evermore, always.

e•ver•si•ble [ɪ'vɜrsɪbəl] *adj.* able to be everted.

e•ver•sion [ɪ'vɜrʒən] *or* [ɪ'vɜrʃən] *n.* **1** a turning of an organ, structure, etc. inside out. **2** a being turned inside out. ⟨< L *eversio, -onis* < *evertere.* See EVERT.⟩

e•vert [ɪ'vɜrt] *v.* turn (something) inside out; turn to the outside. ⟨< L *evertere* < *ex-* out + *vertere* turn⟩

e•vert•or [ɪ'vɜrtər] *n. Anatomy.* a muscle that turns a part of the body to the outside.

eve•ry ['ɛvri] *adj.* **1** all, regarded singly or separately; each and all: *Every written word is made of letters.* **2** all possible; complete: *We showed her every consideration.* **3** at a regular interval of: *A bus leaves every two hours.*
every now and then, from time to time: *Every now and then we have a frost that ruins the crop.*
every other, each first, third, fifth, etc., or second, fourth, sixth, etc.; each alternating: *The courier makes deliveries every other day.*
every so often, from time to time.
every which way, *Informal.* in all directions; helter-skelter: *He had packed his suitcase every which way.* ⟨OE *æfre* ever + *ælc* each⟩

☛ *Syn.* **1.** See note at EACH.

eve•ry•bod•y ['ɛvri,bʌdi] *or* [-,bɒdi] *pron.* every person; everyone: *Everybody likes the new teacher.*

☛ *Usage.* **Everybody,** EVERYONE. **a** Both these pronouns are grammatically singular: *Everybody was thrilled when our troops marched past. Everyone who wishes to attend is invited.* Sometimes, however, a following pronoun may be plural: *Everyone was dressed in their best clothes.* In this example, **everyone** is thought of as referring to a number of people, and the use of **their** avoids distinguishing between **his** and **her.** To make such expressions accord with formal written usage, it is often better to change the **everybody** or **everyone** to a more specific plural or collective than to change the later pronoun. **b** The pronoun **everybody** is always written as one word.

eve•ry•day ['ɛvri'dei] *or* ['ɛvri,dei] *adj.* **1** of every day; daily: *Accidents are everyday occurrences.* **2** for every ordinary day; not for Sundays or holidays: *She wears everyday clothes to work.* **3** not exciting or unusual; ordinary: *He's just an everyday writer.*

☛ *Usage.* **Everyday** is written as one word when it is an adjective, but as two words when **day** is a noun modified by **every:** *This was an everyday occurrence. Every day seemed a year.*

Every•man ['ɛvri,mæn] *n.* **1** an early 16th-century morality play symbolizing the journey through life. **2** the chief character in this play, personifying humanity. **3** the average person; a typical human being.

eve•ry•one ['ɛvri,wʌn] *or* ['ɛvriwən] *pron.* every person; everybody: *Everyone took his or her purchases home.*

☛ *Usage.* **Everyone. a** See note at EVERYBODY. **b Everyone** is written as one word when it is a pronoun, but as two words when **one** is a pronoun modified by **every:** *Everyone wants to attend the concert. Winning this game depends upon every one of you.*

eve•ry•thing ['ɛvri,θɪŋ] *pron., n.* —*pron.* every thing; all things.
—*n.* something extremely important; a very important thing: *This news means everything to us.*

☛ *Usage.* **Everything** is written as one word when it is a noun or pronoun, but as two words when **thing** is a noun modified by **every:** *Everything has its proper place. There is a noun for every thing or idea you can name.*

eve•ry•where ['ɛvri,wɛr] *adv.* in or to every place; in or to all places: *We looked everywhere for our lost dog.*

e•vict [ɪ'vɪkt] *v.* **1** expel by a legal process from land, a building, etc.; eject (a tenant): *Because he had not paid his rent, the tenant was evicted by the sheriff.* **2** expel or put out by force: *The soldiers evicted the enemy from the occupied building.* **3** regain (property) by court injunction or greater claim. ⟨< L *evictus,* pp. of *evincere.* See EVINCE.⟩ **—e'vic•tor,** *n.*

e•vic•tion [ɪ'vɪkʃən] *n.* an evicting or being evicted; explusion.

ev•i•dence ['ɛvədəns] *n., v.* **-denced, -denc•ing.** —*n.* **1** whatever makes clear the truth or falsehood of something: *The evidence showed that she had not been near the place of the crime.* **2** *Law.* **a** facts established and accepted in a court of law. Before deciding a case, the judge or jury hears all the evidence given by both sides. **b** a person who gives testimony in a court of law: *He was queen's evidence.* **3** an indication; sign: *A smile gives evidence of pleasure.* **4** the quality of being evident; obviousness.
in evidence, easily seen or noticed: *A crying baby is much in evidence.*
—*v.* make easy to see or understand; show clearly; prove: *His smiles evidenced his pleasure.*

☛ *Syn. n.* **1. Evidence,** TESTIMONY, PROOF = something that makes clear that a thing is true or false. **Evidence** applies to any facts that point toward, but do not fully prove, the truth or falsehood of something: *Running away was evidence of his guilt.* **Testimony** = something said or done to show or prove something true or false: *His speech was clear testimony of his good intentions.* **Proof** = complete evidence that leaves no doubt: *His actions were proof that he was telling the truth.*

ev•i•dent ['ɛvədənt] *adj.* easy to see or understand; clear; plain: *He has brought Betty a kitten, to her evident joy.* ⟨< L *evidens, -entis* < *ex-* out + *videns,* ppr. of *videre* see⟩

☛ *Syn.* See note at OBVIOUS.

ev•i•den•tial [,ɛvə'dɛnʃəl] *adj.* **1** serving as evidence; of evidence; based on evidence. **2** like evidence; giving evidence. **—,ev•i'dent•ial•ly,** *adv.*

ev•i•dent•ly ['ɛvədəntli] *or* ['ɛvɪ,dɛntli] *adv.* **1** plainly; clearly. **2** apparently; presumably; seemingly.

e•vil ['ivəl] *adj., n.* —*adj.* **1** morally bad; wrong; sinful; wicked, especially profoundly so: *an evil life, an evil character.* **2** causing or bringing harm or injury: *an evil plan, an evil day.* **3** unfortunate: *an evil fate.* **4** due to bad character or conduct: *an evil reputation.* **5** offensive; corrupt: *evil-smelling.*
—*n.* **1** something bad; sin; wickedness. **2** something that causes harm or injury; something that takes away happiness and prosperity: *War is a great evil.* ⟨OE *yfel*⟩ **—'e•vil•ly,** *adv.* **—'e•vil•ness,** *n.*

e•vil•do•er ['ivəl,duər] *n.* a person who does evil.

e•vil•do•ing ['ivəl,duɪŋ] *n.* the doing of evil.

evil eye 1 the power that some people are supposed to have of causing harm or bringing bad luck to others by looking at them. **2** such a look. **—'e•vil-,eyed,** *adj.*

e•vil–mind•ed ['ivəl 'maɪndɪd] *adj.* **1** having an evil mind; wicked; malicious. **2** inclined to interpret anything in a lewd way. **—'ev•il-'mind•ed•ly,** *adv.* **—'ev•il-'mind•ed•ness,** *n.*

Evil One the Devil; Satan.

e•vince [ɪ'vɪns] *v.* **e•vinced, e•vinc•ing. 1** show clearly: *The dog evinced its dislike of strangers by growling.* **2** show that one has (a certain quality, trait, etc.). ⟨< LL *evincere* claim for oneself < *ex-* out + *vincere* conquer⟩ **—e'vince•ment,** *n.*

☛ *Syn.* See note at DISPLAY.

e•vin•ci•ble [ɪ'vɪnsəbəl] *adj.* able to be proved; demonstrable.

e•vin•cive [ɪ'vɪnsɪv] *adj.* indicative.

e•vis•cer•ate [ɪ'vɪsə,reit] *v.* **-at•ed, -at•ing. 1** remove the bowels from; disembowel. **2** weaken by depriving of some vital part: *The abridgment leaves the book somewhat eviscerated.* **3** *Surgery.* **a** remove the entrails of. **b** remove the contents of (an organ). ⟨< L *eviscerare* < *ex-* out + *viscera* viscera⟩ **—e,vis•cer'a•tion,** *n.*

ev•i•ta•ble ['ɛvətəbəl] *adj.* able to be avoided.

ev•oc•a•ble ['ɛvəkəbəl] *or* [ɪ'vɒkəbəl] *adj.* able to be evoked.

ev•o•ca•tion [,ɛvə'keiʃən] *n.* an evoking.

e•voc•a•tive [ɪ'vɒkətɪv] *adj.* tending to produce or arouse an emotional response, a vivid mental image, etc. **—e'voc•a•tive•ly,** *adv.* **—e'voc•a•tive•ness,** *n.*

ev•o•ca•tor ['ɛvə,keitər] *n.* **1** a person who makes an evocation. **2** *Embryology.* the chemical substance that causes development.

e•voke [ɪ'vouk] *v.* **e•voked, e•vok•ing.** call forth; bring out: *A* *good joke evokes a laugh.* ⟨< L *evocare* < *ex-* out + *vocare* call⟩ **—e'vok•er,** *n.*

ev•o•lute ['ɛvə,lut] *n. Mathematics.* the locus of the centres of curvature of a given curve (the INVOLUTE).

ev•o•lu•tion [,ɛvə'luʃən] *or* [,ivə'luʃən] *n.* **1** any process of formation or growth; gradual development: *the evolution of the modern steamship from the first crude boat.* **2** something evolved; a product of development; not a sudden discovery or creation. **3** *Biology.* the theory that all living things developed from a few simple forms of life or from a single form. **4** the theory that the human race makes constant progress socially, politically, spiritually, etc. **5** *Biology.* the adaptation of a species to its environment by the agency of selection. **6** a movement of ships or soldiers, planned beforehand. **7** a movement that is a part of a definite plan, design, or series: *the graceful evolutions of a ballet dancer.* **8** a releasing; giving off; setting free: *the evolution of heat from burning coal.* **9** *Mathematics.* the extraction of roots from powers. ⟨< L *evolutio, -onis* < *evolvere.* See EVOLVE.⟩

ev•o•lu•tion•al [,ɛvə'luʃənəl] *or* [,ivə'luʃənəl] *adj.* evolutionary. **—,ev•o'lu•tion•al•ly,** *adv.*

ev•o•lu•tion•ar•y [,ɛvə'luʃə,nɛri] *or* [,ivə'luʃə,nɛri] *adj.* **1** having to do with evolution or development. **2** in accordance with a theory of evolution. **3** performing evolutions; having to do with evolutions.

ev•o•lu•tion•ist [,ɛvə'luʃənɪst] *or* [,ivə'luʃənɪst] *n.* a student of, or believer in, a theory of evolution. **—,ev•o'lu•tion,ism,** *n.*

e•volve [ɪ'vɒlv] *v.* **e•volved, e•volv•ing. 1** develop or be developed gradually by a process of evolution: *The girls evolved a plan for earning money during their summer vacation. We are learning how the different species evolved. Languages evolve.* **2** release (heat, gas, etc.); give off; set free. ⟨< L *evolvere* < *ex-* out + *volvere* roll⟩ **—e'volv•er,** *n.*

e•volve•ment [ɪ'vɒlvmənt] *n.* evolving or being evolved.

ev•zone ['ɛvzoun] *n.* a member of an elite Greek infantry corps that is famous for its valour. ⟨< Gk. *euzōnos* dressed for exercise < *eu-* well + *zōnē* girdle⟩

ewe [ju] *n.* a female sheep. ⟨OE *ēowu*⟩
☛ *Hom.* YEW, YOU.

E•we ['eiwei] *or* ['eivei] *n.* **1** a people of Togo, Ghana, and Dahomey. **2** the Kwa language of these people.

ewe–neck ['ju ,nɛk] *n.* of a horse's neck, one that is thin and does not form an arch. **—'ewe-,necked,** *adj.*

ew•er ['juər] *n.* a large water jug with a wide mouth and spout. ⟨ME < AF var. of OF *eviere, aiguiere* < VL *aquaria* < L *aquarius* of or for water < *aqua* water⟩

ex[1] [ɛks] *prep.* **1** out of. *Ex elevator* means free of charges until the time of removal from the grain elevator. **2** without; not including. *Ex-dividend stocks* are stocks on which the purchaser will not receive the next dividend to be paid. ⟨< L⟩

ex[2] [ɛks] *n.* **1** the twenty-fourth letter of the alphabet (X, x). **2** anything shaped like an X.

ex[3] [ɛks] *n. Informal.* a former spouse, boyfriend, girlfriend, etc.: *She saw her ex downtown yesterday.*

Ex [ɛks] *n. Informal.* an exhibition, especially the Canadian National Exhibition held annually in Toronto.

ex–[1] *prefix.* **1** out of, from, or out, as in *express, exit, export.* **2** utterly or thoroughly, as in *exterminate, exasperate.* **3** former or formerly, as in *ex-president, ex-member.* Also: **e-,** before voiced *c* or *s.* **ef-,** before *f.* ⟨< L *ex-* < *ex* out of⟩

ex–[2] *prefix.* from, out, as in *exodus.* Also, **ec-,** before *c* or *s.* ⟨< Gk.⟩

ex. 1 example. **2** examined. **3** exchange. **4** exercise.

exa- *combining form.* the factor 10^{18}; quintillion: *exametre, exajoule.*

ex•ac•er•bate [ɛg'zæsər,beit] *or* [ɛk'sæsər,beit] *v.* **-bat•ed, -bat•ing. 1** make worse; aggravate (pain, disease, anger). **2** irritate (a person). ⟨< L *exacerbare* < *ex-* completely + *acerbus* harsh, bitter⟩

ex•ac•er•ba•tion [ɛg,zæsər'beiʃən] *or* [ɛk,sæsər'beiʃən] *n.* **1** a making worse; aggravation. **2** irritation.

ex•act [ɛg'zækt] *adj., v. —adj.* **1** without any error, mistake or vagueness; strictly correct; accurate; precise: *an exact measurement, the exact amount.* **2** strict; severe; rigorous. **3** characterized by or using strict accuracy: *A scientist should be an exact thinker.*
—v. **1** demand and get; force to be given: *If he does the work, he can exact payment for it.* **2** call for; need; require: *A hard piece of work exacts effort and patience.* ⟨< L *exactus,* pp. of *exigere* weigh accurately < *ex-* out + *agere* weigh⟩ **—ex'act•a•ble,** *adj.* **—ex'act•ness,** *n.* **—ex'act•or,** *n.*
☛ *Syn. adj.* **1.** See note at CORRECT.

ex•act•ing [ɛg'zæktɪŋ] *adj., v. —adj.* **1** requiring much; making severe demands; hard to please: *an exacting employer.* **2** requiring effort, care, or attention: *Flying an airplane is exacting work.*
—v. ppr. of EXACT. **—ex'act•ing•ly,** *adv.* **—ex'act•ing•ness,** *n.*

ex•ac•tion [ɛg'zækʃən] *n.* **1** an exacting or being exacted; a demanding and getting; an enforcing of a payment considered arbitrary: *The ruler's exactions of money left the people very poor.* **2** the thing exacted. Taxes, fees, etc., forced to be paid, are exactions.

ex•act•i•tude [ɛg'zæktə,tjud] *or* [ɛg'zæktə,tud] *n.* exactness.

ex•act•ly [ɛg'zæktli] *adv.* **1** in an exact manner; accurately; precisely. **2** just so; quite right.

exact science a science in which facts can be accurately observed and results can be accurately predicted. Mathematics and physics are exact sciences.

ex•ag•ger•ate [ɛg'zædʒə,reit] *v.* **-at•ed, -at•ing. 1** make (something) seem greater than it is; overstate: *She exaggerated the dangers of the trip in order to frighten them into not going.* **2** say or think something is greater than it is; go beyond the truth: *He always exaggerates when he tells about things he has done.* **3** increase, intensify, or enlarge (features, emotions, gestures, etc.) abnormally. ⟨< L *exaggerare* < *ex-* out, up + *agger* heap⟩ **—ex'ag•ger,a•tor,** *n.*

ex•ag•ger•a•tion [ɛg,zædʒə'reiʃən] *n.* **1** a statement that goes beyond the truth; overstatement: *It is an exaggeration to say that you would rather die than touch a snake.* **2** the act of exaggerating or state of being exaggerated: *His constant exaggeration made people distrust him. Her exaggeration of the role weakened its comic effect.* **3** a result or effect of exaggerating; something exaggerated.

ex•alt [ɛg'zɒlt] *v.* **1** place high or raise in rank, honour, power, character, quality, etc.: *Election to high office exalts a person.* **2** fill with pride, joy, or noble feeling. **3** praise; honour; glorify. ⟨< L *exaltare* < *ex-* out, up + *altus* high⟩

ex•al•ta•tion [,ɛgzɒl'teiʃən] *n.* **1** an exalting or being exalted. **2** an elation of mind or feeling; rapture.

ex•am [ɛg'zæm] *n. Informal.* examination.

ex•a•men [ɛg'zeimən] *n.* an examination, especially of conscience, usually every day.

ex•am•i•na•tion [ɛg,zæmə'neiʃən] *n.* **1** a careful test; scrutiny; inspection: *The doctor made a careful examination of my eyes.* **2** a set of questions or tasks to test knowledge or skill; a formal test: *an examination in arithmetic.* **3** a written set of answers given in such a test: *The examinations still have not been marked.* **4** *Law.* an interrogation, especially of a witness. **5** the mode or means of examining. **—ex,am•i'na•tion•al,** *adj.*
☛ *Syn.* **1.** See note at INVESTIGATION.

ex•am•ine [ɛg'zæmən] *v.* **-ined, -in•ing. 1** look at closely and carefully. **2** test the knowledge or qualifications of; ask questions of or set tasks for as a test. **3** question (a witness) formally. ⟨< F *examiner* < L *examinare* < *examen* a weighing < *exigere.* See EXACT.⟩ **—ex'am•in•a•ble,** *adj.* **—ex'am•in•er,** *n.*

ex•am•i•nee [ɛg,zæmə'ni] *n.* a person who is being examined.

ex•am•ple [ɛg'zæmpəl] *n.* **1** one thing taken to show what others are like; a case that shows something; sample: *Vancouver is an example of a busy city.* **2** a model; pattern of something to be imitated or avoided: *That father is a good example to his sons.* **3** an instance or sample that serves to illustrate a way of doing or making something: *The problems in the mathematics textbook were accompanied by examples.* **4** an instance or case, especially of punishment intended as a warning to others: *As an example, the captain made the shirkers clean up the camp.*
for example, as an illustration or illustrations; for instance: *Children play many games; for example, baseball.*
make an example of, treat sternly, or punish, as a sample of the result of misbehaviour or crime.
set an example, behave so that others may profitably imitate; be a model or pattern of conduct.
without example, with nothing like it before. ⟨ME < OF *essample* < L *exemplum,* originally, that which is taken out (i.e., a sample) < *eximere.* See EXEMPT.⟩
☛ *Syn.* **1. Example,** SAMPLE = a part or thing taken to show the nature of something. **Example** applies to an individual thing, fact, happening, situation, etc. that shows what the type or kind is like or how a general rule works: *This chair is an example of period furniture.* **Sample** applies to a part taken out of a thing or class to show the quality of the whole,

which is considered to be exactly like it: *She looked carefully at all the samples of material before buying any. The doctor examined a sample of her blood.* 2. See note at MODEL.

ex•an•i•mate [ɛg'zænɪmɪt] *or* [ɛk'sænəmɪt] *adj.* **1** lifeless. **2** without spirit.

ex•an•them [ɛk'sænθəm] *or* [ɛg'zænθəm] *n.* a disease characterized by fever and eruptions, like measles. ⟨< LL *exanthema* < Gk. *exanthema* efflorescence, eruption < *exanthein* to bloom < *ex-* out + *anthein* to flower < *anthos* flower⟩

ex•arch[1] ['ɛksɑrk] *n. Eastern Orthodox Church.* a bishop who is below a patriarch. ⟨< LL *exarchus* monastic overseer < Gk. *exarchos* leader < *ex-* out + *archos* ruler⟩

ex•arch[2] ['ɛksark] *adj. Botany.* of a plant, with the xylem growing from the outer stem toward the inside. Compare ENDARCH. ⟨*ex-*[2] + Gk. *arche* beginning⟩

ex•arch•ate [ɛks'ɑrkɪt] *n. Eastern Orthodox Church.* the office of exarch.

ex•as•per•ate [ɛg'zæspə,reit] *v.* **-at•ed, -at•ing.** irritate very much; annoy extremely; make angry: *The child's endless questions exasperated her mother.* ⟨< L *exasperare* < *ex-* thoroughly + *asper* rough⟩ **—ex'as•per,at•ed•ly,** *adv.* **—ex'as•per,at•er,** *n.*

☛ *Syn.* See note at IRRITATE.

ex•as•per•a•tion [ɛg,zæspə'reiʃən] *n.* **1** the act of exasperating. **2** extreme annoyance, irritation, or anger.

exc. except.

Exc. Excellency.

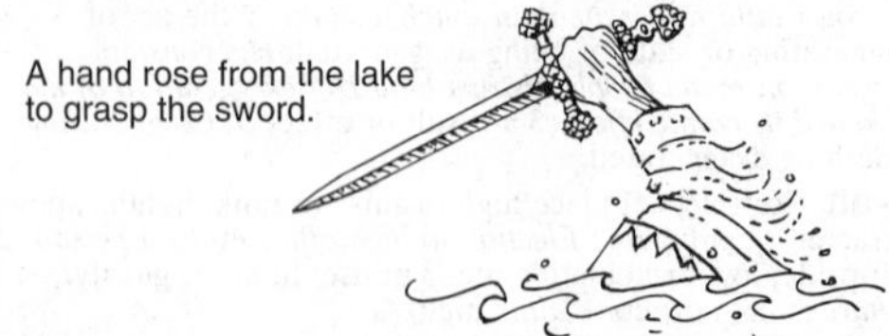
A hand rose from the lake to grasp the sword.

Ex•cal•i•bur [ɛks'kæləbər] *n. Arthurian legend.* the magic sword of King Arthur. ⟨ME < OF *escalibor* < Med.L *Caliburnus,* probably < Celtic⟩

ex ca•the•dra [,ɛks kə'θidrə] *or* [-'kæθədrə] **1** with authority; from the seat of authority. **2** spoken with authority; authoritative. ⟨< L *ex cathedra* from the chair⟩

ex•ca•vate ['ɛkskə,veit] *v.* **-vat•ed, -vat•ing. 1** make a hole by removing dirt, sand, rock, etc.: *The construction company will begin to excavate tomorrow.* **2** make by digging; dig: *The tunnel was excavated through solid rock.* **3** dig out; scoop out: *Steam shovels excavated the dirt.* **4** get or uncover by digging: *They excavated the ancient buried city.* **5** hollow out. ⟨< L *excavare* < *ex-* out + *cavus* hollow⟩

ex•ca•va•tion [,ɛkskə'veiʃən] *n.* **1** a digging; a digging out or up. **2** a hole or hollow made by digging. **3** something dug up or revealed by excavating.

ex•ca•va•tor ['ɛkskə,veitər] *n.* a person who or thing that excavates. A steam shovel is an excavator.

ex•ceed [ɛk'sid] *v.* go beyond; be more or greater than; do more than; surpass: *The sum of 5 and 7 exceeds 10. The success of the party exceeded our best expectations.* ⟨< F < L *exedere* < *ex-* out + *cedere* go⟩

ex•ceed•ing [ɛk'sidɪŋ] *adj., adv., v. —adj.* surpassing; very great; unusual; extreme.
—adv. Archaic. exceedingly.
—v. ppr. of EXCEED.

ex•ceed•ing•ly [ɛk'sidɪŋli] *adv.* extremely; unusually; very: *Yesterday was an exceedingly hot day.*

ex•cel [ɛk'sɛl] *v.* **-celled, -cel•ling. 1** be better than; do better than: *He excelled his classmates in history.* **2** be better than others; do better than others: *excel in wisdom.* ⟨< F < L *excellere*⟩

☛ *Syn.* **1, 2. Excel,** SURPASS, OUTDO = be better in quality or action. **Excel** emphasizes standing out above others in fineness, merit, or doing things: *She excels in mathematics.* **Surpass** = be better in comparison with others or a definite standard: *Mary surpassed all the previous school records for the high jump.* **Outdo,** more informal, emphasizes doing more or better than others: *The runner outdid all other contestants for the athlete-of-the-year award.*

ex•cel•lence ['ɛksələns] *n.* **1** the fact of being or doing better than others or of reaching some very high standard; superiority: *the pursuit of excellence.* **2** an unusually good quality: *The inn was famous for the excellence of its food.* **3** anything in which a person or thing surpasses all others: excellent feature or ability; particular virtue: *Music is only one of her many excellences.* **4 Excellence,** Excellency; Your Excellency.

ex•cel•len•cy ['ɛksələnsi] *n., pl.* **-cies. 1** excellence. **2 Excellency,** a title of honour used in speaking to or of the Governor General, an ambassador, a bishop, etc. *Abbrev.:* Exc.

ex•cel•lent ['ɛksələnt] *adj.* unusually good; better than others; first-class: *She is an excellent golfer.* ⟨< L *excellens, -entis,* ppr. of *excellere* excel⟩ **—'ex•cel•lent•ly,** *adv.*

ex•cel•si•or [ɛk'sɛlsiər] *n.* **1** short, fine, curled shavings of soft wood used as a packing material or as stuffing. **2** a size of printing type, 3 point. ⟨a former trademark < L *excelsior,* comparative of *excelsus* high, pp. of *excellere* excel⟩

ex•cept [ɛk'sɛpt] *prep., conj., v. —prep.* leaving out; but; other or otherwise than: *every day except Sunday. He hardly ever goes out except to visit his sister.*
—conj. **1** *Informal.* only; but; were it not for the fact (*that*): *I'd like to go with you except that I can't swim.* **2** *Archaic.* unless: *except you repent.*
—v. **1** take out or leave out; exclude: *All the children, the baby excepted, were helping to clean up the backyard.* **2** make objection; object (*to* or *against*).
except for, leaving out; other than: *It's a good movie, except for a few boring scenes near the beginning.* ⟨< L *exceptus,* pp. of *excipere* < *ex-* out + *capere* take⟩

☛ *Syn. prep.* **Except,** BUT = leaving out. **Except** emphasizes the idea of leaving out, keeping out, or even shutting out: *Everyone was invited to the party except me.* **But** is unemphatic, and suggests more the idea of not taking in than of keeping out: *Everyone was invited but me.*

☛ *Usage.* See note at ACCEPT.

ex•cept•ing [ɛk'sɛptɪŋ] *prep., conj., v. —prep.* except; leaving out; other than.
—conj. Archaic. unless.
—v. ppr. of EXCEPT.

ex•cep•tion [ɛk'sɛpʃən] *n.* **1** the act of leaving out or excluding: *I like all the paintings, with the exception of this one. They said they could make no exception, and that everyone would have to pay the full fee.* **2** an unusual instance; a case that does not follow the rule: *She usually comes on time; today was an exception.* **3** a person or item excluded: *I loved the books, with one exception.* **4** a disagreement; controversy: *a paper liable to exception.* **5** *Law.* an objection raised in the course of a trial.
take exception, a object or protest (*used with* **to**): *She took exception to the editorial, and wrote a letter to the newspaper about it.* **b** be offended.

ex•cep•tion•a•ble [ɛk'sɛpʃənəbəl] *adj.* liable to objection; objectionable. **—ex'cep•tion•a•bly,** *adv.*

ex•cep•tion•al [ɛk'sɛpʃənəl] *adj.* **1** out of the ordinary; unusual: *This warm weather is exceptional for January.* **2** challenged or gifted physically or mentally: *exceptional children.* **—ex'cep•tion•al•ly,** *adv.*

ex•cep•tive [ɛk'sɛptɪv] *adj.* **1** likely to make an exception. **2** making an exception.

ex•cerpt *n.* ['ɛgzɜrpt] *or* ['ɛksɜrpt]; *v.* [ɪg'zɜrpt] *or* [ɛk'sɜrpt] *n., v.*
—n. a selected passage; quotation; extract: *The article included excerpts from several medical books.*
—v. take out; select (passages) from some source; quote; take extracts. ⟨< L *excerptum,* pp. of *excerpere* < *ex-* out + *carpere* pluck⟩ **—ex'cerp•tion,** *n.*

ex•cess [ɛk'sɛs] *or, esp. for 4,* ['ɛksɛs] *n.* **1** the act or an instance of going beyond what is usual, enough, or right: *The excesses of the last city council were exposed in the report. He was opposed to all excess in eating and drinking.* **2** an amount or degree beyond what is usual, enough, or right: *an excess of grief.* **3** the amount by which one quantity or thing is more than another: *She had to pay for an excess of 5 kg on her luggage.* **4** (*adjl.*) being more than the usual permitted, or proper amount: *Airlines charge for excess baggage.* **5** the part exceeding what is needed; superfluous part; extra: *I cut the material I needed and stored the excess.*
in excess of, more than; over: *They expect the contributions to be in excess of $5000.*
to excess, too much: *He eats candy to excess.* ⟨ME < OF < L *excessus* < *excedere.* See EXCEED.⟩

ex•ces•sive [ɛk'sɛsɪv] *adj.* too much; too great; going beyond what is necessary or right: *She didn't buy the couch because she felt the price was excessive.* **—ex'cess•ive•ly,** *adv.* **—ex'cess•ive•ness,** *n.*

☛ *Syn.* **Excessive,** EXORBITANT, INORDINATE = too much or too great. **Excessive** = going beyond what is right or normal in amount or extent: *Jennifer spends an excessive amount of time on the phone.* **Exorbitant** also

= excessive, beyond what is proper or reasonable, and particularly describes demands, especially quantifiable ones: *He asked an exorbitant rent for the house.* **Inordinate** = going beyond what is in order, and suggests a lack of restraint: *He has an inordinate appetite.*

ex•change [ɛks'tʃeindʒ] *v.* **-changed, -chang•ing;** *n.* *—v.* **1** give for something else: *She would not exchange her house for a palace.* **2** give in trade for something regarded as equivalent: *I will exchange ten dimes for a dollar.* **3** give and receive (things of the same kind): *to exchange letters.* **4** switch or reverse the positions of; substitute. **5** replace or have replaced (a purchase): *We cannot exchange swimsuits.* **6** make an exchange. **7** *Finance.* pass or be taken in exchange or as an equivalent.
—n. **1** an exchanging: *Ten dimes for a dollar is a fair exchange. He switched around the desk and the bookshelf, but she did not notice the exchange till he told her.* **2** something that has been given, received, or offered in an exchange. **3** a place where things are exchanged or traded. Stocks are bought, sold, and traded in a stock exchange. **4** a central telephone office. **5** an arrangement whereby each of two students or teachers from different institutions, sometimes in different countries, studies or teaches for a time at the other institution or in the other country. **6** a conversation; dialogue. **7** a system of settling accounts in different places by exchanging bills of exchange that represent money instead of exchanging money itself. **8** the changing of the money of one country into the money of another. **9** a fee charged for settling accounts or changing money. **10** the rate of exchange; varying rate or sum in one currency given for a fixed sum in another currency. **11** BILL OF EXCHANGE. **12** **exchanges,** *pl.* the cheques or drafts sent to a clearing house for settlement and exchange. ⟨ME < OF *eschangier* < VL *excambiare* < *ex-* out + *cambiare* change (< Celtic)⟩ **—ex'chang•er,** *n.*
☛ *Syn. v.* **3. Exchange,** INTERCHANGE = give and take. **Exchange** emphasizes the idea of trading, or giving one thing and getting back another: *We exchanged souvenirs.* **Interchange** emphasizes the idea of a more complicated exchange, often by several parties taking turns giving and receiving or giving back something equal in value or amount, usually something abstract: *Delegates from different countries interchanged ideas.*

ex•change•a•ble [ɛks'tʃeindʒəbəl] *adj.* capable of being exchanged. **—ex,change•a'bil•i•ty,** *n.*

exchange rate the ratio at which the currency of one country can be exchanged for that of another.

exchange reaction *Chemistry.* a process in which atoms of the same element exchange positions within a molecule or between molecules.

exchange student a high school or university student who takes part in an EXCHANGE (def. 5).

ex•cheq•uer [ɛks'tʃɛkər] *n.* **1** a treasury, especially the treasury of a state or nation. **2** *Informal.* finances; funds.
3 Exchequer, a the department of the British government in charge of its finances and the public revenues. **b** the offices of this department of the British government. **c** the funds of the British government. ⟨ME < OF *eschequier* chessboard; because accounts were kept on a table marked in squares⟩

Exchequer Court a court having jurisdiction to hear legal actions brought by or against the Federal Government, absorbed in 1971 by the Federal Court of Canada.

ex•ci•mer laser ['ɛksəmər] a kind of gas laser that gives off radioactive ultraviolet rays which are used in medicine, in industry, and in the making of nuclear weapons.

ex•cip•i•ent [ɛk'sɪpiənt] *n.* any inert substance used to form a medication into a tablet. ⟨< L *excipiens* ppr. of *excipere* < *ex-* out + *capere* to take⟩

ex•cis•a•ble [ɛk'saɪzəbəl] *or, esp. for def. 1,* ['ɛksaɪzəbəl] *adj.* **1** subject to excise duty. **2** that can be excised or cut out: *an excisable tumour.*

ex•cise[1] ['ɛksaɪz] *or* [ɛk'saɪz] *n., v.* **-cised, -cis•ing.** *—n.* **1** a tax or duty on the manufacture, sale, or use of certain articles made, sold, or used within a country. There is an excise on tobacco.
2 formerly, any tax. **3** the fee paid to obtain a licence for fishing, hunting, etc.
—v. impose an excise on. ⟨apparently < MDu. *excijs* < OF *acceis* tax, ult. < L *ad-* to + *census* tax⟩

ex•cise[2] [ɛk'saɪz] *v.* **-cised, -cis•ing.** remove by or as if by cutting out: *to excise a tumour, to excise a passage from a book.* ⟨< L *excisus*, pp. of *excidere* < *ex-* out + *caedere* cut⟩

ex•ci•sion [ɛk'sɪʒən] *n.* the action or process of excising.

ex•cit•a•ble [ɛk'səitəbəl] *adj.* **1** easily stirred up and aroused: *Our dog is excitable and will bark at anything.* **2** capable of responding to stimuli: *an excitable nerve.* **—ex,cit•a'bil•i•ty** or **ex'cit•a•ble•ness,** *n.* **—ex'cit•a•bly,** *adv.*

ex•cit•ant [ɛk'səitənt] *or* ['ɛksətənt] *n., adj.* *—n.* **1** something that arouses or excites; stimulant. **2** the liquid that produces a magnetic field in an electric cell.
—adj. stimulating; tending to arouse or excite.

ex•ci•ta•tion [,ɛksəi'teiʃən] *or* [,ɛksə'teiʃən] *n.* an exciting or being excited, especially the production of a magnetic field by means of electricity or the raising of an atom or nucleus to a higher level of energy.

ex•cite [ɛk'səit] *v.* **-cit•ed, -cit•ing. 1** stir up the feelings of; move to strong emotion: *It excited her just to think of what she would do with the money.* **2** arouse; provoke (a response): *His new jacket excited envy in some of the other boys.* **3** stir to action or activity: *Don't excite the dogs. Oppression by the aristocracy excited the peasants to rebellion.* **4** produce or increase a response in (an organ, tissue, organism, etc.); stimulate: *to excite a nerve.*
5 produce a magnetic field in (the coils of a generator, etc.).
6 raise (an atom, nucleus, or molecule) to a higher level of energy. **7** supply with electricity to produce a magnetic field or electrical activity. ⟨ME < L *excitare*, ult. < *ex-* out + *ciere* set in motion⟩

ex•cit•ed [ɛk'səitɪd] *adj., v.* *—adj.* **1** stirred up; aroused: *He was so excited he couldn't sleep.* **2** *Physics.* raised to a higher level of energy: *an excited atom.* **3** of a nerve, etc., stimulated.
—v. pt. and pp. of EXCITE. **—ex'cit•ed•ly,** *adv.*

ex•cite•ment [ɛk'səitmənt] *n.* **1** an exciting; act of arousing: *the excitement of nations to war.* **2** the state of being excited.
3 something that excites. **4** noisy activity; commotion; ado: *What's all the excitement?*

ex•cit•er [ɛk'səitər] *n.* **1** a person or thing that excites.
2 *Electricity.* **a** a dynamo, battery, etc. used to produce a magnetic field in another dynamo or motor. **b** a device for producing Hertzian waves.

ex•cit•ing [ɛk'səitɪŋ] *adj., v.* *—adj.* producing excitement: *an exciting piece of news, an exciting game.*
—v. ppr. of EXCITE. **—ex'cit•ing•ly,** *adv.*

ex•ci•ton [ɛk'səitɒn] *or* ['ɛksə,tɒn] *n.* in a crystal, an electrically caused state consisting of an excited electron bound to a positive hole made by its excitation.

ex•ci•tor [ɛk'səitər] *n.* a nerve that leads to greater action when stimulated.

ex•claim [ɛk'skleim] *v.* say or speak suddenly in surprise or strong feeling; cry out. ⟨< F < L *exclamare* < *ex-* + *clamare* cry out⟩

ex•cla•ma•tion [,ɛksklə'meiʃən] *n.* **1** the act of exclaiming.
2 something exclaimed. *Ah!* and *oh!* are exclamations.
☛ *Usage.* An exclamation may be any statement or command that would be spoken with special force or emphasis. It may also be a sentence in which a special structure or word order indicates force or emphasis: *What a fine house you have! How comfortable it looks!*

exclamation mark or **exclamation point** a mark of punctuation (!) used after a word or sentence to show that it is an exclamation. The exclamation mark is also used, within square brackets or, informally, parentheses, to suggest that some statement or situation is remarkable, absurd, or the like.
☛ *Usage.* Take care not to overuse exclamation marks. If too many are used in a piece of writing, they quickly lose their effectiveness. Except in very familiar writing, don't use more than one exclamation mark after any one word, phrase, or sentence.

ex•clam•a•to•ry [ɛk'sklæmə,tɔri] *adj.* using, containing, or expressing exclamation: *an exclamatory sentence.*

ex•clave ['ɛkskleiv] *n.* part of a country that is isolated by foreign territory. ⟨*ex-*[2] + (*en*)*clave*⟩

ex•clo•sure [ɛk'sklouʒər] *n.* any area protected against intruders.

ex•clude [ɛk'sklud] *v.* **-clud•ed, -clud•ing. 1** shut out; keep out: *Blinds exclude light. Love excludes fear.* **2** keep from a place, privilege, activity, etc.; keep from including or considering: *Professional players are excluded from the competition. The invitation excludes children.* **3** EXPEL (def. 2). ⟨ME < L *excludere* < *ex-* out + *claudere* shut⟩ **—ex'clud•er,** *n.*
☛ *Syn.* **1. Exclude,** ELIMINATE = keep out. **Exclude** emphasizes keeping someone or something from coming into a place, thought, rights, etc.: *Closing the windows excludes street noises.* **Eliminate** emphasizes putting out something already in, by getting rid of it or shutting it off from attention: *He eliminated fear from his thinking.*

ex•clud•ing [ɛk'skludɪŋ] *prep., v.* *—prep.* except for; with the exception of; not counting: *All the neighbours, excluding those away on holidays, will be at the picnic.*
—v. ppr. of EXCLUDE.

ex•clu•sion [ɛk'skluʒən] *n.* **1** the act of excluding or the state of being excluded. **2** an object or item excluded.

to the exclusion of, so as to exclude: *She worked away at her science project to the exclusion of everything else.* ⟨< L *exclusio, -onis* < *excludere.* See EXCLUDE.⟩ **—ex'clu•sion,ar•y,** *adj.*

ex•clu•sion•ism [ɛk'skluʒə,nɪzəm] *n.* the practice of denying rights or privileges to all but certain people. **—ex'clu•sion•ist,** *n.*

exclusion principle *Physics.* the theory that no pair of neutrons, electrons, or protons can exist in a system with the same quantum number.

ex•clu•sive [ɛk'sklusɪv] *or* [ɛk'skluzɪv] *adj., n.* *—adj.* **1** each shutting out the other. *Baby* and *adult* are exclusive terms since a person cannot be both. **2** shutting out all or most other things, considerations, etc.: *He demanded our exclusive attention. She has an exclusive interest in sports.* **3** not divided or shared with others; single; sole: *A patent gives an inventor the exclusive right for a certain number of years to make what he or she has invented.* **4** excluding certain people or groups for social, financial, or other reasons: *an exclusive club, an exclusive school.* **5** selling only expensive items: *an exclusive boutique.* **6** not available elsewhere or to anyone else: *an exclusive design, an exclusive interview.* **7** *Grammar.* of a first person plural pronoun, excluding the person(s) spoken to. In *We will go if you will, we* is exclusive; in *We are two of a kind, you and I,* it is not. In some languages, these are distinct pronouns. Compare INCLUSIVE.
exclusive of, excluding; leaving out; not counting or considering: *There are 26 days in that month, exclusive of Sundays. The label says the dress is all cotton, exclusive of trimmings.*
—n. something exclusive, especially an article, news story, etc. published by only one periodical. **—ex'clu•sive•ness,** *n.*

ex•clu•sive•ly [ɛk'sklusɪvli] *adv.* with the exclusion of all others: *That selfish girl looks out for herself exclusively.*

ex•clu•siv•i•ty [,ɛksklu'sɪvəti] *n.* **1** the quality or state of being exclusive; exclusiveness. **2** exclusive rights.

ex•cog•i•tate [ɛks'kɒdʒə,teit] *v.* **-tat•ed, -tat•ing. 1** think through. **2** create by such thinking; devise.

ex•com•mu•ni•cate *v.* [,ɛkskə'mjunə,keit]; *adj., n.* [,ɛkskə'mjunəkɪt] *or* [,ɛkskə'mjunə,keit] *v.* **-cat•ed, -cat•ing;** *adj., n.* *—v.* cut off from membership in a church; expel formally from the fellowship of a church; prohibit from participating in any of the rites of a church.
—adj. excommunicated; denied the sacraments of the church.
—n. an excommunicated person. ⟨< LL *excommunicare,* literally, put out of the fellowship (of the Church) < L *ex-* out of + *communis* common⟩

ex•com•mu•ni•ca•tion [,ɛkskə,mjunə'keiʃən] *n.* **1** a formal expulsion from the fellowship of a church; prohibition from participating in any of the rites of a church. **2** the formal, official statement announcing excommunication. **3** the condition or state of a person who has been excommunicated.

ex•co•ri•ate [ɛk'skɔri,eit] *v.* **-at•ed, -at•ing. 1** strip or rub off the skin of; make raw and sore. **2** denounce violently. ⟨< LL *excoriare* < *ex-* off + *corium* hide, skin⟩ **—ex,co•ri'a•tion,** *n.*

ex•cre•ment ['ɛkskrəmənt] *n.* waste matter discharged from the bowels; feces. ⟨< L *excrementum,* ult. < *excernere* < *ex-* out + *cernere* sift⟩ **—,ex•cre'ment•al,** *adj.*

ex•cres•cence [ɛk'skrɛsəns] *n.* **1** an unnatural or disfiguring growth or addition, such as a wart or bunion. **2** any abnormal increase or outgrowth. **3** a normal outgrowth, such as a beard.

ex•cres•cen•cy [ɛk'skrɛsənsi] *n.* **1** something that is excrescent. **2** the state of being excrescent.

ex•cres•cent [ɛk'skrɛsənt] *adj.* **1** forming an unnatural growth or a disfiguring addition. **2** *Phonetics.* of a sound, present for no historical or grammatical reason, as *b* in *thimble,* derived from Old English *thymle.* ⟨< L *excrescens, -entis,* ppr. of *excrescere* < *ex-* out + *crescere* grow⟩

ex•cre•ta [ɛk'skritə] *n.pl.* waste matter discharged from the body, such as sweat or urine. ⟨< L *excreta,* neut. pl. of *excretus,* pp. of *excernere.* See EXCREMENT.⟩ **—ex'cre•tal,** *adj.*

ex•crete [ɛk'skrit] *v.* **-cret•ed, -cret•ing. 1** discharge (waste matter) from the body; separate (waste matter) from the blood or tissues. The skin excretes sweat. **2** *Botany.* get rid of (waste) from the cells. ⟨< L *excretus,* pp. of *excernere.* See EXCREMENT.⟩

ex•cre•tion [ɛk'skriʃən] *n.* **1** the discharge of waste matter from the body; the separation of waste matter from the blood or tissues. **2** the waste matter discharged from the body; waste matter separated from the blood or tissues. Sweat is an excretion.

ex•cre•tive [ɛk'skritɪv] *adj.* excreting; serving to excrete.

ex•cre•to•ry ['ɛkskrə,tɔri] *or* [ɛks'kritəri] *adj.* of or having to do with excretion; that excretes: *The kidneys are excretory organs.*

ex•cru•ci•ate [ɛk'skruʃi,eit] *v.* **-at•ed, -at•ing.** torture. ⟨< L *excruciare* < *ex-* utterly + *cruciare* torture, crucify < *crux, crucis* cross⟩

ex•cru•ci•at•ing [ɛk'skruʃi,eitiŋ] *adj.* **1** very painful; torturing; causing great suffering. **2** intense; so extreme as to be unbearable: *excruciating care, in excruciating detail.* **—ex'cru•ci,at•ing•ly,** *adv.*

ex•cru•ci•a•tion [ɛk,skruʃi'eiʃən] *n.* **1** the act or an instance of excruciating. **2** the state of being excruciated.

ex•cul•pate ['ɛkskəl,peit] *or* [ɛk'skʌlpeit] *v.* **-pat•ed, -pat•ing.** free from blame; prove innocent. ⟨< Med.L **exculpare* < L *ex-* out + *culpa* guilt⟩ **—ex'cul•pa•ble,** *adj.*

ex•cul•pa•tion [,ɛkskəl'peiʃən] *n.* **1** a freeing from blame; a proving innocent. **2** something that vindicates or that proves innocence; excuse.

ex•cul•pa•to•ry [ɛk'skʌlpə,tɔri] *adj.* tending to exculpate or capable of exculpating.

ex•cur•rent [ɛk'skɜrənt] *adj.* **1** running out. **2** *Biology.* giving passage outward. **3** *Botany.* having a stem or trunk that is not divided.

ex•cur•sion [ɛk'skɜrʒən] *or* [ɛk'skɜrʃən] *n.* **1** a short journey made with the intention of returning; a pleasure trip: *Our club went on an excursion to the mountains.* **2** a round trip at a reduced fare, usually involving a restriction on the length of time spent on the trip, dates of travel, etc. **3** a group of people who go on an excursion. **4** a wandering from the subject; deviation; digression. **5** *Physics.* **a** a single movement of something from a centre by oscillation. **b** the distance of this movement. **6** an increase in the power of a reactor. **7** *Medicine.* the degree of movement from some central point, as of the chest during breathing. ⟨< L *excursio, -onis* < *excurrere* < *ex-* out + *currere* run⟩

ex•cur•sion•ist [ɛk'skɜrʒənɪst] *or* [ɛk'skɜrʃənɪst] *n.* a person who goes on an excursion.

ex•cur•sive [ɛk'skɜrsɪv] *adj.* off the subject; wandering; rambling. **—ex'cur•sive•ly,** *adv.* **—ex'cur•sive•ness,** *n.*

ex•cur•sus [ɛk'skɜrsəs] *n.* a long explanation of some matter in a book, usually given as a note at the end.

ex•cus•a•ble [ɛk'skjuzəbəl] *adj.* that can or ought to be excused: *Her anger was excusable since they had been so rude.* **—ex'cus•a•bly,** *adv.*

ex•cu•sa•to•ry [ɛk'skjuzə,tɔri] *adj.* designed or functioning as an excuse.

ex•cuse *v.* [ɛk'skjuz]; *n.* [ɛk'skjus] *v.* **-cused, -cus•ing;** *n.* *—v.* **1** overlook (a fault, etc.); pardon (a person); forgive. **2** give a reason or apology for (something); try to clear (someone) of blame: *She excused her own faults by blaming others.* **3** be a reason or explanation for; clear of blame: *Sickness excused his absence from school.* **4** free from duty or obligation; let off: *Those who passed the first test are excused from the second one.* **5** not demand or require; dispense with: *We will excuse your presence.* **6** seek or obtain exemption or release for.
excuse me, a I apologize. **b** please may I leave? or, I am afraid I must leave.
excuse oneself, a ask to be pardoned. **b** ask permission to leave.
—n. **1** a real or pretended reason or explanation. **2** an apology given. **3** the act of excusing.
a poor excuse for, a substandard example of: *That was a poor excuse for a paper that you handed in.*
make one's excuses, regretfully decline an invitation to attend some gathering. ⟨ME < OF < L *excusare* < *ex-* away + *causa* cause⟩ **—ex'cus•er,** *n.*

☛ *Syn. v.* **1. Excuse,** PARDON, FORGIVE = free from blame or punishment. **Excuse** = overlook, or let off with only disapproval, less important errors and faults: *This time she excused my carelessness.* **Pardon,** more formal in tone, means free from punishment due for serious faults, wrongdoing, or crimes: *The governor pardoned the thief.* **Forgive** suggests more personal feeling, and emphasizes giving up all wish to punish for a wrong done: *He forgave his brother for leaving home.* *—n.* **2. Excuse,** APOLOGY = something said to explain an offence or failure. **Excuse** suggests trying to justify a mistake or failure or to make it seem less serious, in order to escape being blamed or punished: *She is always late, and always has an excuse.* **Apology** suggests admitting that one has, or seems to have, done or been wrong and expressing regret: *He offered his apology for damaging my car.*

☛ *Usage.* **Excuse,** PARDON. **Pardon me** is sometimes considered more elegant than **Excuse me** in upper-class social situations. **I beg (your) pardon** is a standard formula meaning "I didn't hear what you said"; it can also be a sarcastic retort to a stupid or incredible statement. **Excuse** has the special meaning of 'give permission to leave'.

ex–dividend [ɛks 'dɪvədənd] *adj., adv.* not including a dividend that was previously declared.

exec. executive; executor.

ex•e•cra•ble ['ɛksəkrəbəl] *adj.* **1** abominable; detestable: *an execrable crime.* **2** *Informal.* very bad: *execrable taste in art.* ⟨< L *execrabilis*⟩ **—'ex•e•cra•ble•ness,** *n.* **—'ex•e•cra•bly,** *adv.*

ex•e•crate ['ɛksə,kreit] *v.* **-crat•ed, -crat•ing. 1** express or feel extreme loathing for; abhor: *The former leader's cruelty was execrated by his disillusioned followers.* **2** curse. ⟨< L *ex(s)ecrare* < *ex-* completely + *sacer* accursed⟩ **—'ex•e,crat•or,** *n.* **—,ex•e'cra•tion,** *n.* **—'ex•e,cra•tive** or **'ex•e•cra,to•ry,** *adj.*

ex•e•cra•tion [,ɛksə'kreiʃən] *n.* **1** an imprecation. **2** the object that is execrated. **3** the act of execrating.

ex•ec•u•tant [ɛg'zɛkjətənt] *n.* a performer, especially in the arts.

ex•e•cute ['ɛksə,kjut] *v.* **-cut•ed, -cut•ing. 1** carry out; do: *The nurse executed the doctor's orders.* **2** put into effect; enforce: *to execute a law.* **3** put to death according to law: *The convicted murderer was executed.* **4** make according to a plan or design: *The tapestry was executed with great skill.* **5** perform or play (a piece of music). **6** *Law.* make (a deed, lease, contract, will, etc.) complete or valid by signing, sealing, or doing whatever is necessary. **7** *Computer technology.* follow (an instruction); cause (a program) to be in action. ⟨ME < OF < Med.L *ex(s)ecutare* < L *ex(s)ecutus,* pp. of *exsequi* < *ex-* out + *sequi* follow⟩

☛ *Syn.* **1.** See note at PERFORM.

ex•e•cu•tion [,ɛksə'kjuʃən] *n.* **1** the act of executing: *the execution of one's duties, the execution of a law, the execution of a statue in marble.* **2** the manner of executing: *The pianist's execution was flawless.* **3** a written order from a court directing a judgment to be carried out.

ex•e•cu•tion•er [,ɛksə'kjuʃənər] *n.* **1** a person who carries out the death penalty according to law. **2** any person who puts another to death.

ex•ec•u•tive [ɛg'zɛkjətɪv] *adj., n. —adj.* **1** having to do with carrying out or managing affairs: *an executive committee. The head of a school has an executive position.* **2** suitable or designed for executives: *an executive suite, executive toys.* **3** having the duty and power of putting the laws into effect: *The Cabinet is the executive branch of our government.* **4** involving or having to do with a group of people responsible for running the affairs of a society, association, or club: *There's an executive meeting this afternoon.*
—n. **1** a person who carries out or manages affairs: *The president of a company is an executive.* **2** a person, group, or branch of government that has the duty and power of putting the laws into effect. **3** a group of people responsible for running the affairs of a society, association, or club. **—ex'ec•u•tive•ly,** *adv.*

Executive Council in Canada, the Cabinet of a provincial government, consisting of the premier and his or her ministers.

executive officer the manager of a company.

executive session a meeting held *in camera.*

ex•ec•u•tor [ɛg'zɛkjətər] *for 1;* ['ɛksə,kjutər] *for 2. n.* **1** a person named in a will to carry out the provisions of the will. Compare ADMINISTRATOR (def. 2). **2** a person who performs or carries out things. ⟨ME < AF *executour* < L *ex(s)ecutor* < *exsequi.* See EXECUTE.⟩ **—ex,ec•u'tor•i•al,** *adj.*

ex•ec•u•to•ry [ɛg'zɛkjə,tɔri] *adj.* **1** *Law.* to be carried out. **2** executive.

ex•e•dra ['ɛksədrə] *or* [ɪk'sidrə] *n.* **1** *Architecture.* a portico with a bench. **2** a bishop's throne. **3** an outdoor bench of stone with a back. ⟨< L < Gk. *exedra* < *ex-* out + *hedra* seat⟩

ex•e•ge•sis [,ɛksə'dʒisɪs] *n., pl.* **-ses** [-siz]. **1** a scholarly explanation or interpretation of written work, especially of the Bible or of a passage in the Bible: *The translator studied several exegeses of the parable of the Good Samaritan before translating it.* **2** an explanation or interpretation of a word, sentence, etc.; explanatory note. ⟨< Gk. *exēgēsis* < *ex-* out + *hēgeesthai* lead, guide⟩

ex•e•gete ['ɛksɪ,dʒit] *n.* one skilled in exegesis.

ex•e•get•i•cal [,ɛksə'dʒɛtəkəl] *adj.* having to do with exegesis; expository. Also, **exegetic.**

ex•e•get•ics [,ɛksə'dʒɛtɪks] *n.* the study, science, or art of exegesis.

ex•em•plar [ɛg'zɛmplər] *or* [ɛg'zɛmplɑr] *n.* **1** a person or thing worth imitating; an ideal model or pattern: *They looked on him as the exemplar of courage.* **2** a typical case; example: *She was belligerent and defensive, the exemplar of the insecure child.* **3** a copy of any published material, as a book or pamphlet. ⟨ME < L *exemplar* < *exemplum.* See EXAMPLE.⟩

ex•em•pla•ry [ɛg'zɛmpləri] *or* ['ɛgzəm,plɛri] *adj.* **1** worth imitating; being a good model or pattern: *exemplary conduct. She showed exemplary courage.* **2** of a penalty or punishment, serving as a warning or deterrent: *a sentence of exemplary severity.* **3** serving as an example; typical: *exemplary passages from a book.* ⟨< L *exemplaris* < *exemplum.* See EXAMPLE.⟩ **—ex'em•pla•ri•ly,** *adv.* **—ex'em•pla•ri•ness,** *n.*

exemplary damages *Law.* damages awarded to the plaintiff which exceed the value of actual loss, meant to serve as punishment to the defendant.

ex•em•pli•fi•ca•tion [ɛg,zɛmpləfə'keiʃən] *n.* **1** the act of showing by example. **2** something that serves to illustrate; example: *The sudden price increases were an exemplification of the law of supply and demand.* **3** *Law.* a copy of a document attested by an official seal.

ex•em•pli•fy [ɛg'zɛmplə,faɪ] *v.* **-fied, -fy•ing. 1** show by example; be an example of: *The knights exemplified courage and courtesy.* **2** *Law.* make a sworn copy of (a document). ⟨< Med.L *exemplificare* < L *exemplum* example + *facere* make⟩

ex•em•pli gra•ti•a [ɛg'zɛmplaɪ 'greiʃiə] *or* [ɛg'zɛmpli 'grɑtiə] *Latin.* for example; for instance. *Abbrev.:* e.g.

ex•em•plum [ɛg'zɛmpləm] *n.* **1** an example. **2** in old sermons, an illustrative parable.

ex•empt [ɛg'zɛmpt] *v., adj., n. —v.* make free from a duty, obligation, rule, etc.; release: *Students who get very high marks will be exempted from the final examination.*
—adj. free from a duty, obligation, rule, etc.; released: *Food is exempt from sales tax.*
—n. a person who has been exempted. ⟨ME < OF < L *exemptus,* pp. of *eximere* < *ex-* out + *emere* take⟩ **—ex'emp•ti•ble,** *adj.*

ex•emp•tion [ɛg'zɛmpʃən] *n.* **1** an exempting or being exempted; freedom from a duty, obligation, rule, etc.; immunity: *Churches have exemption from taxes.* **2** someone who or something that is exempted, especially a part of a person's income that does not have to be taxed: *There is a basic tax exemption that can be claimed by everyone. The teacher read the list of exemptions to the class.*

☛ *Syn.* **1. Exemption,** IMMUNITY = freedom from obligation or duty. **Exemption** emphasizes freeing a person or thing from some obligation, rule, etc. required of or applied to others: *Churches have exemption from taxes.* **Immunity** emphasizes being protected from obligations, restrictions, and penalties to which other people are liable: *Members of Parliament have immunity from jury duty.*

ex•en•ter•ate [ɛk'sɛntə,reit] *v.* **-at•ed, -at•ing. 1** eviscerate. **2** *Surgery.* remove the contents of (an organ). ⟨< L *extenteratus* pp. of *exenterare* < Gk. *exenterizein* < *ex-* out + *enteron* bowel⟩

ex•e•qua•tur [,ɛksə'kweitər] *n.* **1** the document that a host country gives to a consul as authority to serve there. **2** the authority of a bishop to perform his or her office.

ex•e•quies ['ɛksə,kwiz] *n.* funeral rites; obsequies. ⟨< ME *exequies, pl.* < OF < L *exequiae* < *exequi* to follow up, pursue⟩

ex•er•cise ['ɛksər,saɪz] *n., v.* **-cised, -cis•ing.** *—n.* **1** activity to train or develop the body or keep it healthy: *Running and playing volleyball are forms of exercise.* **2** a particular activity or series of activities designed to develop or train the body or mind or develop some skill or faculty: *She does aerobic exercises every morning. There is an exercise at the end of each lesson.* **3** active use or practice; a putting into action: *the exercise of one's right to vote, the exercise of care to promote safety.* **4** the performance (of duties, functions, etc.). **5 exercises,** *pl.* a formal activity; ceremony: *the opening exercises in Parliament, graduation exercises.*
—v. **1** take part or cause to take part in an activity to keep fit or to train or develop some part of the body or to improve skill: *singing scales to exercise the voice. She exercises every other day at a fitness club.* **2** use actively; employ: *to exercise one's mind or imagination, to exercise care in crossing the street.* **3** carry out in action; perform or fulfil: *to exercise the duties of one's office.* **4** have as an effect: *What others think exercises a great influence on most of us.* **5** occupy the attention of, especially so as to worry, trouble, or annoy (*usually used in the passive*): *The city council has been greatly exercised by the problem of inflation.* ⟨ME < OF *exercice* < L *exercitium* < *exercere* not allow to rest < *ex-*[2] + *arcere* keep away⟩

☛ *Syn. n.* **1. Exercise,** PRACTICE, DRILL[1] = active use of physical or mental power for training or improvement. **Exercise** emphasizes repeated use of mental or physical powers to develop strength, health, and energy: *Exercise of the mind increases its power.* **Practice** applies to action repeated often and regularly to develop skill or gain perfection, especially in the use of a particular power: *Learning to play the piano well takes much practice.* **Drill** = constant repetition of a particular kind of exercise to discipline the body or mind and develop correct habits: *Some children need drill in spelling.*

ex•er•cis•er ['ɛksər,saɪzər] *n.* **1** one who exercises. **2** a machine for exercising the body.

ex•ergue ['ɛksɜrg] *or* [ɛg'zɜrg] *n.* on a coin or medal, the space below the design. ⟨< F that which is out of the work < NL *exergum* < Gk. *ex-* out, outside of + *ergon* work⟩

ex•ert [ɛg'zɜrt] *v.* **1** put forth; exercise or bring to bear: *to exert an influence, to exert effort, to exert one's authority.* **2** try hard; strive (*used with a reflexive pronoun*): *We're going to have to exert ourselves to make the deadline.* ⟨< L *ex(s)ertus,* pp. of *ex(s)erere* thrust out < *ex-* out + *serere* attach⟩ **—ex'ert•ive,** *adj.*

ex•er•tion [ɛg'zɜrʃən] *n.* **1** effort: *The exertion of moving the piano was too much for him and he collapsed. It was through the exertions of many volunteers that the fair succeeded.* **2** a putting into action; active use; use: *an exertion of authority.*

ex•e•unt ['ɛksiənt] *or* ['ɛksiʊnt] *v. Latin.* in stage directions, the signal for actors to leave the stage. It is the plural of EXIT and means "They go out."

ex•fo•li•ate [ɛks'fouli,eit] *v.* **-at•ed, -at•ing. 1** cast or be cast off as flakes or scales. **2** *Geology.* of some minerals, split. ⟨< LL *exfoliatus* pp. of *exfoliare* to strip of leaves < L *ex-* out + *folium* leaf⟩

ex gratia [ɛks 'greiʃə] *or* [ɛks 'grɑtiə] *Latin.* not required but as a favour.

ex•hal•ant [ɛks'heilənt] *adj., n.* —*adj.* exhaling.
—*n.* that which exhales.

ex•ha•la•tion [,ɛkshə'leiʃən] *n.* **1** the act of exhaling. Breathing out is an exhalation of air. **2** something exhaled; air, vapour, smoke, odour, etc.

ex•hale [ɛks'heil] *v.* **-haled, -hal•ing. 1** breathe out: *to exhale air from the lungs. The doctor told her to exhale completely.* **2** give off (air, vapour, smoke, odour, etc.). **3** pass off as vapour; rise like vapour: *Sweet odours exhale from the flowers.* ⟨< F < L *exhalare* < *ex-* out + *halare* breathe⟩

ex•haust [ɛg'zɒst] *v., n.* —*v.* **1** empty completely: *to exhaust a well.* **2** use up: *to exhaust one's money.* **3** tire very much: *The climb up the hill exhausted us.* **4** drain of strength, resources, etc.: *The long war exhausted the country.* **5** draw off or be drawn off; discharge: *to exhaust the air in a jar. Gases from an automobile exhaust through a pipe.* **6** leave nothing important to be found out or said about; study or treat thoroughly: *Her book about tulips exhausted the subject.* **7** deprive wholly of useful or essential properties: *to exhaust the soil.* **8** deprive of ingredients by the use of solvents. **9** empty of all content, leaving a vacuum.
—*n.* **1** the escape of used steam, gasoline, etc. from a machine. **2** a means or way for used steam, gasoline, etc. to escape from an engine. **3** the used steam, gasoline, etc. that escapes. ⟨< L *exhaustus,* pp. of *exhaurire* < *ex-* out, off + *haurire* draw⟩
—ex'haust•er, *n.*

ex•haust•ed [ɛg'zɒstɪd] *adj., v.* —*adj.* **1** used up. **2** worn out; very tired.
—*v.* pt. and pp. of EXHAUST. **—ex'haust•ed•ly,** *adv.*
☛ *Syn.* **2.** See note at TIRED.

ex•haust•i•bil•i•ty [ɛg,zɒstə'bɪləti] *n.* the quality of being exhaustible; capability of being exhausted.

ex•haust•i•ble [ɛg'zɒstəbəl] *adj.* capable of being exhausted.

ex•haus•tion [ɛg'zɒstʃən] *n.* **1** an exhausting or being exhausted. **2** extreme fatigue.

ex•haus•tive [ɛg'zɒstɪv] *adj.* leaving out nothing important; thorough; comprehensive: *Her conclusions are based on an exhaustive study of the subject.* **—ex'haust•ive•ly,** *adv.*
—ex'haust•ive•ness, *n.*
☛ *Usage.* Do not confuse **exhaustive,** meaning 'thorough', with **exhausting,** meaning 'very tiring'. An *exhaustive* lecture on Vitamin A would be *exhausting* to a grade eight class, but appropriate in a medical school.

ex•haust•less [ɛg'zɒstlɪs] *adj.* that cannot be exhausted.

exhaust manifold in an internal-combustion engine, the metal part that moves used gases from the cylinders to the exhaust.

exhaust pipe in an internal-combustion engine, the tube that leads gases out of the engine.

ex•hib•it [ɛg'zɪbɪt] *v., n.* —*v.* **1** show; display. **2** show formally and publicly. **3** show in court as evidence; submit for consideration or inspection. **4** put one's artwork or crafts on display: *He is exhibiting at the craft show next month.*
—*n.* **1** a show; display. **2** the thing or things shown publicly. **3** a small exhibition or a part of a large exhibition: *Have you seen the art exhibit in the Jubilee Building?* **4** a document or other thing shown in court and referred to in written evidence. ⟨< L *exhibitus,* pp. of *exhibere* < *ex-* out + *habere* hold⟩
☛ *Syn. v.* **1.** See note at DISPLAY. *n.* **2, 3. Exhibit,** EXHIBITION = a public show. **Exhibit** applies particularly to an object or collection of things put on view as one part of a fair, exhibition, or other public show: *Her lambs were part of the school's exhibit at the county fair.* **Exhibition** applies to a public show of works of art, rare objects of any kind, commercial objects, etc.: *The city holds an exhibition of all its different products every year.*

ex•hi•bi•tion [,ɛksə'bɪʃən] *n.* **1** the act of showing; display: *He said he had never seen such an exhibition of bad manners.* **2** a public show: *The art school holds an exhibition every year.* **3** a thing or things shown publicly. **4** a public showing of livestock, produce, manufactured goods, etc., accompanied by amusements such as sideshows, rides, games, and other forms of entertainment; a big fair: *the Canadian National Exhibition.*
☛ *Syn.* **2, 3.** See note at EXHIBIT.

ex•hi•bi•tion•ism [,ɛksə'bɪʃə,nɪzəm] *n.* **1** an excessive tendency to seek attention or to show off one's abilities. **2** a compulsive tendency to expose the genitals in public. **3** an instance of such exposure.

ex•hi•bi•tion•ist [,ɛksə'bɪʃənɪst] *n.* **1** a person who tends to seek attention or show off his or her abilities excessively. **2** a person given to compulsive exposure of the genitals in public.
—,ex•hi,bi•tion'is•tic, *adj.*

ex•hi•bi•tive [ɛg'zɪbɪtɪv] *adj.* **1** disposed to exhibit. **2** used for exhibition.

ex•hib•i•tor [ɛg'zɪbətər] *n.* a person, company, or group that exhibits. Also, **exhibiter**.

ex•hi•bi•to•ry [ɛg'zɪbə,tɔri] *adj.* exhibitive.

ex•hil•ar•ant [ɛg'zɪlərənt] *adj., n.* —*adj.* exhilarating.
—*n.* something that exhilarates.

ex•hil•a•rate [ɛg'zɪlə,reit] *v.* **-rat•ed, -rat•ing. 1** refresh; invigorate: *The girls were exhilarated by their early-morning swim.* **2** make merry or lively; put into high spirits: *She was exhilarated by the prospect of getting home a day early.* ⟨< L *exhilarare* < *ex-* thoroughly + *hilaris* merry⟩ **—ex'hil•a,rat•or,** *n.*

ex•hil•a•ra•tion [ɛg,zɪlə'reiʃən] *n.* **1** an exhilarated feeling or condition; high spirits; stimulation. **2** the act of exhilarating.

ex•hort [ɛg'zɔrt] *v.* urge strongly; advise or warn earnestly: *The preacher exhorted his congregation to live out their faith.* ⟨< L *exhortari* < *ex-*[2] + *hortari* urge strongly⟩ **—ex'hort•er,** *n.*

ex•hor•ta•tion [,ɛgzɔr'teiʃən] *or* [,ɛksɔr'teiʃən] *n.* **1** a strong urging; earnest advice or warning. **2** a speech, sermon, etc. that exhorts.

ex•hor•ta•tive [ɛg'zɔrtətɪv] *adj.* exhortatory.

ex•hor•ta•to•ry [ɛg'zɔrtə,tɔri] *adj.* urging; intended to exhort; admonitory.

ex•hu•ma•tion [,ɛkshju'meiʃən] *n.* an exhuming.

ex•hume [ɛks'hjum] *or* [ɛg'zjum] *v.* **-humed, -hum•ing. 1** take out of a grave or out of the ground; dig up. **2** reveal. ⟨< Med.L *exhumare* < L *ex-* out of + *humus* ground⟩

ex•i•gen•cy [ɛg'zɪdʒənsi] *or* ['ɛksəjənsi] *n., pl.* **-cies. 1** the state or quality of being urgent: *The exigency of the case justified his rudeness.* **2 exigencies,** *pl.* urgent needs; requirements of a particular situation: *The exigencies of business kept her from attending the conference.* **3** a situation demanding immediate action or attention; urgent case. Also, **exigence** ['ɛksədʒəns].

ex•i•gent ['ɛksədʒənt] *adj.* **1** demanding immediate action or attention; urgent: *The exigent pangs of hunger sent her on a search for food.* **2** demanding a great deal; exacting. ⟨< L *exigens, -entis,* ppr. of *exigere.* See EXACT.⟩ **—'ex•i•gent•ly,** *adv.*

ex•i•gi•ble ['ɛksədʒəbəl] *adj.* required; exactable.

ex•i•gu•i•ty [,ɛgzə'gjuəti] *or* [,ɛksə'gjuəti] *n.* scantiness; smallness.

ex•ig•u•ous [ɛg'zɪgjuəs] *or* [ɛk'sɪgjuəs] *adj.* scanty; small. ⟨< L *exiguus* scanty, originally, weighed out (sparingly) < *exigere.* See EXACT.⟩ **—ex'ig•u•ous•ly,** *adv.* **—ex'ig•u•ous•ness,** *n.*

ex•ile ['ɛgzaɪl] *or* ['ɛksaɪl] *v.* **-iled, -il•ing;** *n.* —*v.* force (a person) to leave his or her country or home; banish: *After the revolution many people were exiled from the country.*
—*n.* **1** the condition of being exiled; banishment: *Napoleon's exile to Elba was brief.* **2** an exiled person. **3** any prolonged absence from one's own country. **4 the Exile,** the captivity of the Jews in Babylon during the 6th century B.C. ⟨ME < OF *exilier* < LL *exiliare* < L *ex(s)ilium*⟩
☛ *Syn. v.* See note at BANISH.

ex•il•ic [ɛg'zɪlɪk] *or* [ɛk'sɪlɪk] *adj.* having to do with exile.

ex–im•port ['ɛks 'ɪmpɔrt] *n. Cdn.* in professional football, a non-Canadian who, after playing in the country for a certain number of years, qualifies as a Canadian player.

ex•ist [ɛg'zɪst] *v.* **1** have actual existence; be; be real. **2** live; have life: *A person cannot exist without air.* **3** occur or be recorded: *Such cases exist in medicine, but they are rare.* ⟨< F *exister* < L *ex(s)istere* < *ex-* forth + *sistere* stand⟩

ex•ist•ence [ɛg'zɪstəns] *n.* **1** real or actual being; being: *to come into existence, to question the existence of ghosts.* **2** way of life; life: *Many bush pilots lead a dangerous existence.* **3** occurrence; presence. **4** all that exists. **5** something that exists.

ex•ist•ent [ɛg'zɪstənt] *adj.* **1** existing. **2** existing now; of the present time.

ex•is•ten•tial [ˌɛgzɪ'stɛnʃəl] *or* [ˌɛksɪ'stɛnʃəl] *adj.* **1** of or having to do with actual existence or experience. **2** of or having to do with existentialism: *an existential play.*
—ˌex•is'ten•tial•ly, *adv.*

ex•is•ten•tial•ism [ˌɛgzɪ'stɛnʃəˌlɪzəm] *or* [ˌɛksɪ'stɛnʃəˌlɪzəm] *n.* a system of philosophy that avoids highly abstract theories on life and emphasizes personal experience, holding that humans are free and responsible, and that reality consists in living.

ex•is•ten•tial•ist [ˌɛgzɪ'stɛnʃəlɪst] *or* [ˌɛksɪ'stɛnʃəlɪst] *adj., n.* *—adj.* having to do with, supporting, or resembling existentialism. *—n.* a person who supports or follows the philosophy of existentialism.

ex•it ['ɛgzɪt] *or* ['ɛksɪt] *n., v.* *—n.* **1** a way out: *The theatre had five exits.* **2** a going out; departure. **3** *Theatre.* the departure of an actor from the stage: *a graceful exit.* **4** death.
—v. **1** make an exit; go out or away, or die. **2** *Theatre.* go off stage (*used as a stage direction*): *Exit Hamlet.* ⟨< L *exit* goes out; also < L *exitus* a going out; both < *ex-* out + *ire* go⟩

exit poll a survey of voters leaving a polling booth.

ex li•bris [ˌɛks 'libɾɪs] *or* [ˌɛks 'laɪbrɪs] *Latin.* **1** from the books (*of*); an inscription used on a bookplate, followed by the name of the book's owner. **2** bookplate.

ex ni•hi•lo [ˌɛks 'nihəˌlou] *or* [ˌɛks 'naɪəˌlou] from nothing: *Epics are not created ex nihilo.* ⟨< L⟩

ex•o– *prefix.* outside: *exogenous.* ⟨< Gk. *exo-* outside < *ex-* out⟩

ex•o•bi•ol•o•gist [ˌɛksoubaɪ'ɒlədʒɪst] *n.* a person trained in exobiology, especially one whose work it is.

ex•o•bi•ol•o•gy [ˌɛksoubaɪ'ɒlədʒi] *n.* the study of life on other planets or celestial bodies.

ex•o•carp ['ɛksouˌkɑrp] *n.* epicarp. ⟨< Gk. *exō-* outside + *karpos* fruit⟩

ex•o•cen•tric [ˌɛksou'sɛntrɪk] *adj. Linguistics.* of a construction, having a syntactic function different from that of any of its parts.

ex•o•crine ['ɛksoukrɪn], ['ɛksouˌkraɪn], *or* ['ɛksouˌkrin] *adj.* **1** of a gland, secreting by means of a duct. **2** having to do with such a process. Compare ENDOCRINE. ⟨< Gk. *exo-* without + *(endo)crine*⟩

ex•o•don•tics [ˌɛksou'dɒntɪks] *n.* the branch of dentistry dealing with extractions. Also, **exodontia** [ˌɛksou'dɒnʃiə]. ⟨< *ex-* + Gk. *odon, odontos* tooth⟩ **—ˌex•o'don•tist,** *n.*

ex•o•dus ['ɛksədəs] *n.* **1** a going out; departure, especially of a large number of people: *Every summer there is an exodus from the city.* **2** Often, **Exodus,** the departure of the Israelites from Egypt under Moses, as recorded in the Old Testament book of the same name. ⟨< L < Gk. *exodos* < *ex-* out + *hodos* way⟩

ex of•fi•ci•o [ˌɛks ə'fɪʃiˌou] because of one's office: *The secretary is, ex officio, a member of all committees.* ⟨< L⟩

ex•og•a•my [ɛk'sɒgəmi] *n.* **1** the custom or practice of marriage to a person outside one's own group, tribe, clan, etc. **2** reproduction by the fusion of gametes from distantly related or unrelated parents. ⟨< Gk. *exo-* without + *gamia* < *gamos* marriage⟩ **—ex'og•a•mous** or **ˌex•o'gam•ic** [ˌɛksə'gæmɪk], *adj.*

ex•og•e•nous [ɛk'sɒdʒənəs] *adj.* **1** of, having to do with, or originating from external causes: *an exogenous infection.* Compare ENDOGENOUS. **2** of or having to do with external circumstances, such as food or climate, which affect an organism. **3** *Botany.* designating stems that increase in thickness by the addition of annual layers on the outside of the wood, inside the bark. ⟨< NL *exogenus* growing on the outside < Gk. *exō-* outside + *genēs* born, produced⟩

ex•on ['ɛksɒn] *n.* an expressed sequence of a gene. A gene may contain many exons, separated by introns.

ex•on•er•ate [ɛg'zɒnəˌreit] *v.* **-at•ed, -at•ing.** **1** free from blame; prove or declare innocent: *Witnesses to the accident completely exonerated the driver of the truck.* **2** relieve of a duty, task, obligation, etc. ⟨< L *exonerare* < *ex-* off + *onus, oneris* burden⟩ **—exˌon•er'a•tion,** *n.* **—ex'on•erˌa•tor,** *n.* **—ex'on•er•a•tive,** *adj.*

ex•o•nu•mia [ˌɛksə'njumiə] *or* [ˌɛksə'numiə] *n.pl.* items made to look like money, as tokens or medals, which do not circulate as money. ⟨< Gk. *exō-* outside + *num(ismatics)*⟩

ex•o•pep•ti•dase [ˌɛksou'pɛptɪˌdeis] *n.* any of various enzymes that remove terminal amino acids from a protein chain.

ex•oph•thal•mic goitre [ˌɛksɒf'θælmɪk] a disease caused by excessive production of thyroid hormone, causing protruding eyeballs.

ex•oph•thal•mos [ˌɛksɒf'θælməs] *n.* abnormal protruding of the eyeball. Also, **exophthalmus** or **exophthalmia.** ⟨< NL < Gk. with prominent eyes < *ex-* out + *ophthalmos* eye⟩
—ˌex•oph'thal•mic, *adj.*

ex•or•a•ble ['ɛksərəbəl] *or* ['ɛgzərəbəl] *adj.* easily persuaded by an earnest request. ⟨< L *exorabilis* < *exorare* to move by entreaty < *ex-* out + *orare* to speak⟩

ex•or•bi•tance [ɛg'zɔrbətəns] *n.* the quality of being exorbitant.

ex•or•bi•tant [ɛg'zɔrbətənt] *adj.* going far beyond what is customary, right, or reasonable; grossly excessive: *exorbitant prices, an exorbitant demand.* ⟨< L *exorbitans, -antis,* ppr. of *exorbitare* go out of the track < *ex-* out of + *orbita* track⟩
☛ *Syn.* See note at EXCESSIVE.

ex•or•bi•tant•ly [ɛg'zɔrbətəntli] *adv.* **1** extravagantly. **2** in an excessive degree or amount; beyond reasonable limits.

ex•or•cise ['ɛksɔrˌsaɪz] *v.* **-cised, -cis•ing.** **1** drive out (an evil spirit) by prayers, ceremonies, etc. **2** free (a person or place) from an evil spirit. ⟨< LL *exorcizare* < Gk. *exorkizein* bind by oath, conjure, exorcise < *ex-* + *horkos* oath⟩ **—'ex•orˌcis•er,** *n.*

ex•or•cism ['ɛksɔrˌsɪzəm] *n.* **1** the act of exorcising. **2** the prayers, ceremonies, etc. used in exorcising.

ex•or•cist ['ɛksɔrsɪst] *n.* a person who exorcises.

ex•or•cize ['ɛksɔrˌsaɪz] *v.* **-cized, -ciz•ing.** See EXORCISE.

ex•or•di•um [ɛg'zɔrdiəm] *or* [ɛk'sɔrdiəm] *n., pl.* **-di•ums, -di•a** [-diə]. **1** the beginning. **2** the introductory part of a speech, treatise, etc. ⟨< L *exordium* < *ex-*[2] + *ordiri* begin, originally, begin a web⟩ **—ex'or•di•al,** *adj.*

ex•o•skel•e•tal [ˌɛksou'skɛlətəl] *adj.* of or having to do with the exoskeleton.

ex•o•skel•e•ton [ˌɛksou'skɛlətən] *n.* the hard, external structure that protects and supports the bodies of many invertebrates, such as oysters, lobsters, and insects. Compare ENDOSKELETON.

ex•o•sphere ['ɛksouˌsfir] *n.* the outermost rim of the earth's atmosphere; the layer of the atmosphere in which the ionosphere begins to merge with interplanetary space.

ex•o•spore ['ɛksouˌspɔr] *n. Botany.* the outer covering of a spore. **—ˌex•o'spor•ous,** *adj.*

ex•os•to•sis [ˌɛksɒ'stousɪs] *n.* an abnormal growth on a bone or tooth. ⟨< NL < Gk. *exostosis* < *ex-* outside + *osteon* a bone⟩

ex•o•ter•ic [ˌɛksə'tɛrɪk] *adj.* **1** capable of being understood by the general public. Compare ESOTERIC. **2** not restricted to an inner circle of disciples, scholars, etc. **3** external. **4** mundane; simple; common. ⟨< LL *exotericus* < Gk. *exōterikos* < *exō-* outside < *ek* out of⟩ **—ˌex•o'ter•ic•al•ly,** *adv.*

ex•o•therm•ic [ˌɛksou'θɜrmɪk] *adj. Chemistry.* having to do with a chemical change that generates heat.

ex•ot•ic [ɛg'zɒtɪk] *adj., n.* *—adj.* **1** foreign; not native: *Many exotic plants are grown in Canada as house plants.* **2** strange or unusual in a way that is fascinating or beautiful; strikingly unusual: *an exotic glamour.* **3** *Informal.* beautiful or fascinating because of strangeness. **4** *Physics, chemistry.* resulting from complicated technical procedures: *exotic compounds.*
—n. something exotic. ⟨< L *exoticus* < Gk. *exōtikos* < *exō-* outside < *ek* out of⟩ **—ex'ot•i•cal•ly,** *adv.*

ex•ot•i•ca [ɛg'zɒtɪkə] *n.pl.* exotic things, especially things that are different, strange, or unusual in an intriguing or exciting way: *He has interested himself in such exotica as undersea aquariums and geodesic houseboats.* ⟨< neuter plural of L *exoticus* < Gk. *exotikos* foreign⟩

exotic dancer a striptease dancer.

ex•ot•i•cism [ɛg'zɒtəˌsɪzəm] *n.* **1** the state or quality of being exotic. **2** something unusual, such as a foreign word or phrase.

ex•o•tox•in [ˈɛksou,tɒksɪn] *n. Biochemistry.* a soluble toxin from a micro-organism.

ex•o•tro•pia [,ɛksouˈtroupiə] *n.* a disorder in which one eye is able to focus on an object while the other eye looks outward. Compare ESOTROPIA. ⟨< NL < Gk. *exō-* outside + NL *-tropia* < Gk. *trope* a turn⟩

exp. 1 export; exportation. 2 express. 3 expenses. 4 expired.

ex•pand [ɛkˈspænd] *v.* **1** increase in size; enlarge; swell: *The balloon expanded as it filled with air.* **2** spread out; open out; unfold; extend: *A bird expands its wings before flying.* **3** speak or write (*on*) in greater detail; enlarge (*upon*): *She expanded on the theme in the second chapter.* **4** *Mathematics.* express (a quantity) as a sum of terms, product of terms, etc. ⟨< L *expandere* < *ex-* out + *pandere* spread. Doublet of SPAWN.⟩ **—exˈpand•er,** *n.* **—exˈpand•ing•ly,** *adv.*

☛ *Syn.* **1, 2. Expand,** SWELL, DILATE = make or become larger. **Expand** emphasizes spreading out or opening out in any or all directions: *Our interests expand as we grow.* **Swell** emphasizes growing bigger, getting higher or bigger around than normal, usually from pressure inside or from having something added: *His abscessed tooth made his face swell.* **Dilate** = widen, and applies particularly to circular or hollow things: *The pupils of her eyes dilated in the darkness.*

ex•pan•da•ble [ɛkˈspændəbəl] *adj.* expansible.

expanded metal sheet metal partially cut into strips and then stretched so as to form a mesh, used to reinforce concrete.

ex•panse [ɛkˈspæns] *n.* **1** a large, unbroken space or stretch; wide, spreading surface: *The Pacific Ocean is a vast expanse of water.* **2** the extent of expansion. ⟨< L *expansum*, pp. neut. of *expandere.* See EXPAND.⟩

ex•pan•si•ble [ɛkˈspænsəbəl] *adj.* capable of being expanded. **—ex,pan•siˈbil•ity,** *n.*

ex•pan•sile [ɛkˈspænsaɪl] *or* [ɛkˈspænsəl] *adj.* **1** capable of expanding; of such a nature as to expand. **2** of or having to do with expansion.

ex•pan•sion [ɛkˈspænʃən] *n.* **1** the act or process of expanding or the fact of being expanded: *Heat caused the expansion of the gas in the balloon. The expanding gas caused the expansion of the balloon. The expansion of the factory doubled the amount of goods it produced.* **2** the amount or degree of expansion. **3** a part or thing that is the result of expanding: *The thesis is an expansion of a paper she wrote last year.* **4** the development of a topic. **5** in an engine, the increase in volume of the working fluid which takes place in a cylinder. **6** *Mathematics.* the expression of a quantity as a sum of terms, product of terms, etc. ⟨< LL *expansio, -onis* < *expandere.* See EXPAND.⟩

ex•pan•sion•ar•y [ɛkˈspænʃə,nɛri] *adj.* **1** having to do with or tending toward expansion or expansionism. **2** inflationary.

expansion bolt a bolt with an attachment that expands as the bolt enters a surface, anchoring it.

ex•pan•sion•ism [ɛkˈspænʃə,nɪzəm] *n.* a policy of territorial or commercial expansion, usually at the expense of weaker rivals.

ex•pan•sion•ist [ɛkˈspænʃənɪst] *n., adj. —n.* a supporter or advocate of expansionism.
—adj. of, having to do with, or favouring expansionism. **—ex,pan•sionˈis•tic,** *adj.*

ex•pan•sive [ɛkˈspænsɪv] *adj.* **1** capable of expanding or tending to expand. **2** wide; spreading. **3** taking in much or many things; broad; extensive. **4** showing one's feelings freely and openly; demonstrative: *He is a very expansive and hospitable person.* **5** of an engine, working by expansion. **6** *Psychiatry.* having delusions of grandeur, often taking the form of inordinate generosity or confidence, euphoria, etc.; manic. **—exˈpan•sive•ly,** *adv.* **—exˈpan•sive•ness,** *n.*

ex par•te [,ɛks ˈpɑrti] *Latin.* **1** *Law.* of a legal proceeding, from or in the interest of one side or party only. **2** partisan.

ex•pa•ti•ate [ɛkˈspeiʃi,eit] *v.* **-at•ed, -at•ing. 1** write or talk much (*on*): *She expatiated on the thrills of her trip.* **2** roam or wander freely. ⟨< L *ex(s)patiari* walk about < *ex-* out + *spatium* space⟩ **—exˈpa•ti,a•tor,** *n.*

ex•pa•ti•a•tion [ɛk,speiʃiˈeiʃən] *n.* **1** the act of writing or talking much. **2** an extended talk, description, etc. **3** freedom of movement.

ex•pa•tri•ate *v.* [ɛksˈpeitri,eit]; *adj., n.* [ɛksˈpeitriɪt] *or* [ɛksˈpeitri,eit] *v.* **-at•ed, -at•ing;** *adj., n. —v.* **1** banish; exile. **2** withdraw (oneself) from one's country; renounce one's citizenship.
—adj. expatriated: *There are many expatriate Canadians in New York.*
—n. an expatriated person; exile or emigrant. ⟨< LL *expatriare* < L *ex-* out of + *patria* fatherland⟩

ex•pa•tri•a•tion [ɛks,peitriˈeiʃən] *n.* **1** a banishment; exile. **2** a withdrawal from one's country; renunciation of one's citizenship.

ex•pect [ɛkˈspɛkt] *v.* **1** look forward to; think likely to come or happen. **2** look forward to with reason or confidence; desire and feel sure of getting: *They expect to be married in April. He's expecting a bonus from his company.* **3** count on as reasonable, necessary, or right: *A soldier is expected to be properly dressed. She expected a reward for finding and returning the dog.* **4** *Informal.* think; suppose; guess: *I expect they'll be coming by car.* **5** look forward to the arrival of: *We'll expect you for dinner on Thursday. I expected her last night.* **6** await the birth of: *My sister is expecting her first baby.* ⟨< L *ex(s)pectare* < *ek-* out + *specere* look⟩ **—exˈpect•a•ble,** *adj.* **—exˈpect•a•bly,** *adv.*

ex•pect•ance [ɛkˈspɛktəns] *n.* expectation.

ex•pect•an•cy [ɛkˈspɛktənsi] *n., pl.* **-cies. 1** a showing or feeling of expectation. **2** what is expected, especially the expected amount based on statistical information: *a life expectancy of 67 years.*

ex•pect•ant [ɛkˈspɛktənt] *adj., n. —adj.* **1** having or showing expectation: *He opened his birthday present with an expectant smile.* **2** awaiting the birth of a child.
—n. a person who expects something. **—exˈpect•ant•ly,** *adv.*

ex•pec•ta•tion [,ɛkspɛkˈteiʃən] *n.* **1** the act or state of expecting something to come or happen; anticipation: *Their eager expectation was almost palpable.* **2** something expected; the thing looked forward to: *Contrary to expectation, he turned out to be an excellent student.* **3** Usually, **expectations,** *pl.* a reason for expecting something; a prospect, especially of advancement or prosperity: *They say she has great expectations.* **4** *Statistics.* the expected value of any random variable.
in expectation (of), expecting: *It was only in expectation of a reward that he returned the wallet.* **—exˈpec•ta•tive,** *adj.*

expectation of life the average number of years that a person of a certain age can expect to live.

ex•pect•ing [ɛkˈspɛktɪŋ] *adj., v. —adj. Informal.* pregnant.
—v. ppr. of EXPECT.

ex•pec•to•rant [ɛkˈspɛktərənt] *adj., n. —adj.* causing or helping the discharge of phlegm, etc.
—n. a medicine that promotes expectoration.

ex•pec•to•rate [ɛkˈspɛktə,reit] *v.* **-rat•ed, -rat•ing.** cough up and spit out (phlegm, etc.); spit. ⟨< L *expectorare* < *ex-* out of + *pectus, pectoris* breast⟩ **—exˈpec•to,ra•tor,** *n.*

ex•pec•to•ra•tion [ɛk,spɛktəˈreiʃən] *n.* **1** the act of expectorating. **2** the expectorated matter.

ex•pe•di•en•cy [ɛkˈspidiənsi] *n., pl.* **-cies. 1** usefulness; suitability for bringing about a desired result; desirability or fitness under the circumstances. **2** personal advantage; self-interest: *Her offer to help was prompted by expediency, not kindness.* **3** an expedient. Also (defs. 1, 2), **expedience.** ⟨< ME < OF < L *expediens* ppr. of *expedire* hasten, dispatch⟩

ex•pe•di•ent [ɛkˈspidiənt] *adj., n. —adj.* **1** fit for bringing about a desired result; desirable or suitable under the circumstances; useful: *She decided it would be expedient to take an umbrella.* **2** prompted by a concern for personal advantage; based on self-interest; politic.
—n. a means of bringing about a desired result: *Having no ladder or rope, the prisoner tied sheets together and escaped by this expedient.* ⟨< L *expediens, -entis*, ppr. of *expedire* free from a net, set right < *ex-* out + *pes, pedis* foot⟩ **—exˈpe•di•ent•ly,** *adv.*

ex•pe•di•ent•ial [,ɛkspidiˈɛnʃəl] *adj.* decided by expediency.

ex•pe•dite [ˈɛkspə,dəit] *v.* **-dit•ed, -dit•ing. 1** make easy and quick; speed up: *If everyone will help, it will expedite matters.* **2** do quickly. **3** dispatch. ⟨< L *expeditus*, pp. of *expedire.* See EXPEDIENT.⟩

ex•pe•dit•er [ˈɛkspə,dəitər] *n.* a person who expedites, especially one employed to look after supplying raw materials or delivering finished products on schedule.

ex•pe•di•tion [,ɛkspəˈdɪʃən] *n.* **1** a journey for some special purpose. A voyage of discovery or a military march against the enemy is an expedition. **2** the group of people, ships, etc. that make such a journey. **3** efficient and prompt action; speed: *He completed his work with expedition.*

ex•pe•di•tion•ar•y [,ɛkspəˈdɪʃə,nɛri] *adj.* of, concerning, or making up an expedition.

ex•pe•di•tious [,ɛkspəˈdɪʃəs] *adj.* quick; speedy; efficient and prompt. **—,ex•peˈdi•tious•ly,** *adv.* **—,ex•peˈdi•tious•ness,** *n.*

ex•pel [ɛkˈspɛl] *v.* **-pelled, -pel•ling. 1** force out; force to leave:

When the gunpowder exploded, the bullet was expelled from the gun. **2** put out; dismiss permanently: *A troublesome pupil may be expelled from school.* ⟨< L *expellere* < *ex-* out + *pellere* drive⟩ **—ex'pel•ler,** *n.*

ex•pel•lant or **ex•pel•lent** [ɛk'spɛlənt] *adj., n. —adj.* tending to force out or expel.
—n. an expellant medicine.

ex•pel•lee [ˌɛkspɛ'li] *or* [ɛkˌspɛ'li] *n.* **1** one who is deported from a country. **2** one who is expelled.

ex•pend [ɛk'spɛnd] *v.* spend; use up. ⟨< L *expendere* < *ex-* out + *pendere* weigh, pay. Doublet of SPEND.⟩ **—ex'pend•er,** *n.*
☛ *Syn.* See note at SPEND.

ex•pend•a•ble [ɛk'spɛndəbəl] *adj., n. —adj.* **1** normally consumed or used up in service; not able to be used again: *Pencils, paper, stamps, etc. are expendable items.* **2** that may be sacrificed if necessary; more convenient, economical, etc. to sacrifice in certain situations than to rescue or protect: *People don't usually like to think of themselves as being expendable in their jobs.*
—n. Usually, **expendables,** *pl.* expendable persons or things.

ex•pend•i•ture [ɛk'spɛndətʃər] *or* [ɛk'spɛndəˌtʃʊr] *n.* **1** a spending; a using up: *Such a complicated enterprise requires the expenditure of much money, time, and effort.* **2** the amount of money, time, energy, etc. spent or used up: *Limit your expenditures to what is necessary.*

ex•pense [ɛk'spɛns] *n.* **1** the cost; charge: *The expense of the trip was slight. He travelled at his uncle's expense.* **2** a cause of spending: *Running a car is an expense.* **3** an expending; the paying out of money; outlay: *Her time at university put her father to considerable expense.* **4** loss; sacrifice. **5 expenses,** *pl.* **a** the charges incurred in running one's business or doing one's job. **b** the money to repay such charges: *Because she has to travel a lot as a consultant, she gets expenses besides her salary.*
at the expense of, a paid by. **b** with the loss or sacrifice of: *He achieved the prosperity he had desired, but it was at the expense of his health.* **c** to the detriment of. **d** exploiting; with (someone) as the object: *They had many a laugh at his expense.* ⟨ME < AF < LL *expensa* < L *expensus,* pp. of *expendere.* See EXPEND.⟩

expense account a statement of expenses incurred in the course of duty, that will be repaid.

ex•pen•sive [ɛk'spɛnsɪv] *adj.* costly; high-priced.
—ex'pen•sive•ly, *adv.* **—ex'pen•sive•ness,** *n.*
☛ *Syn.* **Expensive,** COSTLY, DEAR = costing much. **Expensive,** the general word, means 'high-priced', sometimes suggesting more than a person can afford, sometimes more than a thing is worth, and applies to cost in money or in time, effort, etc.: *He had a very expensive pocketknife.* **Costly** = of very high price, but usually because rare, precious, luxurious, etc., and is often used to refer to great effort, sacrifice, etc.: *a costly jewel, a costly victory.* **Dear** = too expensive: *Meat is dear this week.*

ex•pe•ri•ence [ɛk'spiriəns] *n., v.* **-enced, -enc•ing.** *—n.* **1** something that has happened to one; what is or has been met with, felt, done, seen, etc. on a particular occasion: *The expedition through the jungle was an exciting experience for her.* **2** a living through something; observing or taking part in events: *He has learned a lot by experience.* **3** everything gone through that makes up the life of a person, community, race, etc.: *No parallel for such wickedness can be found in human experience.* **4 a** skill, practical knowledge, or wisdom gained by observing, doing, or living through things: *a person of wide experience. Applicants must have a B.Sc. or equivalent experience.* **b** the time spent gaining this: *They require a minimum of three years' experience.*
—v. have happen to one; meet with; feel; live through: *Visiting the Calgary Stampede was the greatest thrill I ever experienced.* ⟨ME < OF < L *experientia* < *experiri* test, try out⟩
—ex'pe•ri•enc•er, *n.*
☛ *Syn. v.* **Experience,** UNDERGO = go through some event. **Experience** emphasizes having something happen to one, but does not suggest whether it is pleasant or unpleasant, brief or long-lasting, important or unimportant: *Visiting the Calgary Stampede was the greatest thrill I ever experienced.* **Undergo** often suggests having to suffer or live through something unpleasant, painful, or dangerous: *I had to undergo many disappointments and failures before experiencing success.* Also, **experience** implies perception and so is generally used only of sentient beings; **undergo** can have any subject: *These chemicals undergo a powerful reaction when combined.*

ex•pe•ri•enced [ɛk'spiriənst] *adj., v. —adj.* skilful or wise because of much experience in a particular field or activity; expert; practised: *an experienced nurse, an experienced driver.*
—v. pt. and pp. of EXPERIENCE.

ex•pe•ri•en•tial [ɛkˌspiri'ɛnʃəl] *adj.* having to do with experience; based on or coming from experience.
—exˌpe•ri'en•tial•ly, *adv.*

ex•per•i•ment *v.* [ɛk'spɛrəˌmɛnt]; *n.* [ɛk'spɛrəmənt] *v., n.*
—v. try in order to find out; make trials or tests: *He has been experimenting with dyes to get the colour he wants.*
—n. **1** a test or trial to find out something new or to demonstrate something that is known: *a cooking experiment to test a new kind of flour. We did an experiment in school today to show how electricity produces magnetism.* **2** a conducting of such tests or trials; experimentation: *Scientists test out theories by experiment.* ⟨< L *experimentum* < *experiri.* See EXPERIENCE.⟩
—ex'per•iˌment•er, *n.*
☛ *Syn. n.* **1.** See note at TRIAL.

ex•per•i•men•tal [ɛkˌspɛrə'mɛntəl] *adj.* **1** based on experiments: *Chemistry is an experimental science.* **2** used for or specializing in experimentation: *an experimental farm.* **3** based on experience, not on theory or authority. **4** for testing or trying out: *They are growing an experimental variety of wheat at the university farm.* **5** tentative: *The new drug is still in the experimental stage.*
—exˌper•i'men•tal•ly, *adv.*

ex•per•i•men•tal•ism [ɛkˌspɛrə'mɛntəˌlɪzəm] *n.* the use or advocacy of experimentation.

ex•per•i•men•tal•ist [ɛkˌspɛrə'mɛntəlɪst] *n.* a person who conducts scientific or artistic experiments or tries to introduce something new in a field.

ex•per•i•men•ta•tion [ɛkˌspɛrəmən'teiʃən] *n.* the act or process of experimenting or making experiments: *More experimentation is needed to confirm the results.*

ex•pert *n.* ['ɛkspərt]; *adj.* ['ɛkspərt] *or* [ɛk'spɜrt] *n., adj. —n.* a very skilful person; person who knows a great deal about some special thing or topic.
—adj. **1** very skilful; knowing a great deal about some special field of knowledge. **2** from an expert; requiring or showing knowledge about some special field of knowledge. ⟨< L *expertus,* pp. of *experiri* test. See EXPERIENCE.⟩ **—'ex•pert•ly** *adv.*
—'ex•pert•ness, *n.*
☛ *Syn. adj.* **1. Expert,** PROFICIENT, SKILLED = having the training and knowledge to do a special thing well. **Expert** = having mastery or unusual ability as the result of experience in addition to training and practice: *He is an expert chemist.* **Proficient** = very good at doing something, especially as the result of training and practice: *He is proficient at sewing.* **Skilled** = knowing thoroughly how to do something and being unusually proficient at doing it: *She is a skilled mechanic.*

ex•per•tise [ˌɛkspər'tiz] *n.* **1** an overall grasp of a subject, process, etc., produced by ability, experience, and skill. **2** the state or quality of being an expert; skill. ⟨< F⟩

expert system *Computer technology.* a computer system designed to solve problems by imitating the knowledge, judgment, and experience of a human expert in some field.

ex•pi•a•ble ['ɛkspiəbəl] *adj.* that can be expiated.

ex•pi•ate ['ɛkspiˌeit] *v.* **-at•ed, -at•ing.** make amends for (a wrong, sin, etc.); atone for: *The young king tried to expiate the injustices of his uncle's rule.* ⟨< L *expiare* < *ex-* completely + *piare* appease < *pius* devout⟩ **—'ex•piˌa•tor,** *n.*

ex•pi•a•tion [ˌɛkspi'eiʃən] *n.* **1** making amends for a wrong, sin, etc.; atonement: *He made a public apology in expiation of his error.* **2** amends; a means of atonement; something that wipes out wrong or sin.

ex•pi•a•to•ry ['ɛkspiəˌtɔri] *adj.* intended to expiate; expiating; atoning.

ex•pi•ra•tion [ˌɛkspə'reiʃən] *n.* **1** coming to an end: *the expiration of a lease.* **2** breathing out: *the expiration of used air from the lungs.* **3** the sound made in breathing out. **4** what is breathed out. **5** the process of dying; death.

ex•pir•a•to•ry [ɛk'spaɪrəˌtɔri] *adj.* having to do with breathing out air from the lungs.

ex•pire [ɛk'spaɪr] *v.* **-pired, -pir•ing. 1** come to an end; cease to be valid or in effect: *You must obtain a new automobile licence before your old one expires.* **2** die. **3** breathe out: *to expire used air from the lungs.* ⟨< L *ex(s)pirare* < *ex-* out + *spirare* breathe⟩
—ex'pir•er, *n.*

ex•pi•ry [ɛk'spaɪri] *or* ['ɛkspəri] *n., pl.* **-ries.** EXPIRATION (defs. 1, 5).

ex•plain [ɛk'splein] *v.* **1** make clear or understandable; tell what something means or how something is done, organized, formed, used, etc.: *The teacher explained how a generator works. Can you explain what refraction is? I explained the paragraph to her.* **2** tell the significance of; interpret: *to explain a dream. Nobody could explain his strange behaviour.* **3** give an acceptable reason for; excuse or justify: *She couldn't explain her absence.* **4** give an explanation: *Wait! Let me explain!* **5** be the explanation of or for: *That explains why she hasn't arrived yet.*
explain away, get rid of or make insignificant by giving reasons

or as if by giving reasons: *to explain away someone's fears. There is a lot of evidence against her that cannot be explained away.*
explain oneself, a make one's meaning clear: *I guess I didn't explain myself very well because nobody understood.* **b** justify or give reasons for one's conduct: *Why did you go off and leave your little brother alone? Explain yourself.* ⟨< L *explanare* < *ex-* out + *planus* flat⟩ **—ex'plain•a•ble,** *adj.* **—ex'plain•er,** *n.*

☛ *Syn.* **Explain,** INTERPRET = make plain or understandable. **Explain** = make clear and plain something that is not understood: *She explained all the difficult mathematical problems to me.* **Interpet** = explain or bring out the meaning of something especially difficult, by using special knowledge or, sometimes, unusual understanding or imagination: *She interpreted the symbolism of the poem for us.*

ex•pla•na•tion [,ɛksplə'neiʃən] *n.* **1** the act or process of explaining: *His explanation of electricity was easy to follow. Their attitude toward the new members requires explanation.* **2** something that explains: *That book was a good explanation of the principle of atomic fission.*

ex•plan•a•to•ry [ɛk'splænə,tɔri] *adj.* explaining; serving or helping to explain: *Read the explanatory part of the lesson before you try to do the problems.* Also, **explanative.**
—ex,plan•a'to•ri•ly, *adv.*

ex•plant [ɛks'plænt] *v., n.* *—v.* take (material) from an organism and place it in a culture.
—n. a piece of tissue removed from an organism, to be cultured for analysis or experimentation. **—,ex•plan'ta•tion,** *n.*

ex•ple•tive [ɛk'splitɪv] *or* ['ɛksplətɪv] *n., adj.* *—n.* **1** an oath or exclamation that has no meaning other than as an expression of surprise, anger, annoyance, etc.: *The expressions* Damn! *and* My goodness! *are expletives.* **2** a syllable, word, or phrase added to fill out a line of verse, etc. without adding anything to the sense. **3** *Grammar.* **a** in English, a word used in a sentence to take the normal place of the subject or object, which is identified later. *There* and *it* in the following sentences are expletives: *There is a book on the table. It is too bad that the book has no pictures. They thought it terrible that the book should cost so much.* **b** in some other languages, a word required by the grammar but having no independent meaning. *Ne* is often an expletive in French.
—adj. serving to fill out, without adding meaning. ⟨< LL *expletivus* < *expletus,* pp. of *explere* < *ex-* out + *plere* fill⟩

ex•pli•ca•ble ['ɛkspləkəbəl] *or* [ɛk'splɪkəbəl] *adj.* capable of being explained. ⟨< L *explicabilis* < *explicare.* See EXPLICIT.⟩

ex•pli•cate ['ɛksplə,keit] *v.* **-cat•ed, -cat•ing. 1** develop the meaning or implication of (a principle, doctrine, etc.); analyse logically. **2** explain. ⟨< L *explicare.* See EXPLICIT.⟩
—'ex•pli,ca•tor, *n.* **—ex'plic•a•tive,** *adj.*

ex•pli•ca•tion [,ɛksplə'keiʃən] *n.* **1** explanation. **2** a detailed statement or description.

explication de texte [ɛksplikasjɔ̃ də 'tɛkst] *French.* a detailed textual analysis of a literary work, involving an examination of the style, content, and language, and how these relate to meaning.

ex•pli•ca•to•ry ['ɛkspləkə,tɔri] *or* [ɛk'splɪkə,tɔri] *adj.* that explains.

ex•plic•it [ɛk'splɪsɪt] *adj.* **1** clearly expressed; distinctly stated; definite and unambiguous: *an explicit statement of intentions. He gave such explicit directions that everyone understood them.* Compare IMPLICIT (def. 2). **2** clear and unreserved in expression; frank; outspoken: *The description of the accident victim's injuries was so explicit that it shocked some people.* **3** obvious; evident. ⟨< L *explicitus,* pp. of *explicare* unfold, explain < *ex-* un- + *plicare* fold⟩ **—ex'plic•it•ly,** *adv.* **—ex'plic•it•ness,** *n.*

ex•plode [ɛk'sploud] *v.* **-plod•ed, -plod•ing. 1** burst violently and noisily because of pressure from within; blow up: *The building was destroyed when the defective boiler exploded.* **2** undergo an uncontrolled chemical or nuclear reaction that produces a violent expansion of gases, along with noise, heat, light, etc.: *The bomb exploded.* **3** cause to explode; set off: *to explode a bomb, to explode dynamite.* **4** react suddenly with noise or violence: *The speaker's mistake was so funny the audience exploded with laughter.* **5** cause to be utterly rejected; destroy belief in: *Columbus helped to explode the theory that the earth was flat.* **6** increase rapidly in an uncontrolled way: *an exploding population.* **7** *Phonetics.* **a** end the articulation of (a stop) by audibly releasing the breath. The first *p* in *pop* is always exploded, the final *p* is often not. **b** of a stop, be articulated with such a release of breath. ⟨< L *explodere* drive out by clapping < *ex-* out + *plaudere* clap⟩ **—ex'plod•er,** *n.*

ex•plod•ed [ɛk'sploudəd] *adj., v.* *—adj.* designating a diagram showing the parts of a machine, apparatus, etc. separated from each other, as if by an explosion, but in the correct position in relation to each other: *The manual has an exploded view of the universal joint.*
—v. pt. and pp. of EXPLODE.

ex•ploit *n.* ['ɛksplɔɪt] *or* [ɛk'splɔɪt]; *v.* [ɛk'splɔɪt] *n., v.* *—n.* a bold, unusual act; daring deed: *Old stories tell about the exploits of famous heroes.*
—v. **1** make use of; turn to practical account: *A mine is exploited for its minerals.* **2** make unfair or selfish use of: *Nations sometimes exploit their colonies, taking as much wealth out of them as they can.* **3** promote through public relations. ⟨ME < OF *esploit* < VL *explicitum* achievement < L *explicitum,* pp. neut. of *explicare* unfold, settle. See EXPLICIT.⟩ **—ex'ploit•a•ble,** *adj.*
—ex'ploit•er, *n.*

☛ *Syn. n.* **Exploit,** FEAT, ACHIEVEMENT = a great or unusual deed. **Exploit** emphasizes daring or great courage or bravery in accomplishing something in the face of danger or against odds: *The pilot won the Victoria Cross for his exploits in the Battle of Britain.* **Feat** emphasizes use of great skill or strength in accomplishing something unusual: *Climbing Mount Everest is a tremendous feat.* **Achievement** emphasizes continued hard work in spite of difficulties and obstacles in accomplishing something outstanding: *Two Canadians, F.G. Banting and J.J.R. Macleod, won the Nobel Prize in 1923 for their achievements in medicine.*

ex•ploi•ta•tion [,ɛksplɔɪ'teiʃən] *n.* **1** use. **2** selfish or unfair use.

ex•ploit•a•tive [ɛk'splɔɪtətɪv] *adj.* of, having to do with, or characterized by exploitation, especially when selfish or unfair. Also, **exploitive.**

ex•plo•ra•tion [,ɛksplə'reiʃən] *n.* the act or an instance of exploring: *exploration for oil, the exploration of new territory.*

ex•plor•a•tive [ɛk'splɔrətɪv] *adj.* **1** exploratory. **2** inclined to make explorations.

ex•plor•a•to•ry [ɛk'splɔrə,tɔri] *adj.* of, having to do with, or related to exploration: *exploratory surgery, exploratory travels.*

ex•plore [ɛk'splɔr] *v.* **-plored, -plor•ing. 1** go or travel over (land or water) for the purpose of finding out about geographical features, natural resources, etc.: *Champlain explored the Ottawa River and Georgian Bay.* **2** go or search through (a place, etc.), in order to find out about it: *to explore one's surroundings. They explored the abandoned house.* **3** look into closely and carefully; investigate: *We will have to explore all the possibilities before deciding on a course of action.* **4** examine carefully, especially by touch: *She explored the wall with her fingers, searching for the light switch. The doctor explored the wound.* ⟨< L *explorare* investigate, spy out; originally, cry out (at sight of game or enemy) < *ex-* out + *plorare* weep⟩ **—ex'plor•ing•ly,** *adv.*

☛ *Syn.* **1, 2.** See note at SEARCH.

ex•plor•er [ɛk'splɔrər] *n.* **1** a person who explores. **2** any instrument for exploring a wound, a dental cavity, etc.

ex•plo•sion [ɛk'splouʒən] *n.* **1** the act of blowing up; a bursting with a loud noise: *the explosion of a bomb.* **2** a loud noise caused by something blowing up: *People 10 km away heard the explosion.* **3** a noisy bursting forth: *an explosion of laughter, an explosion of anger.* **4** *Phonetics.* the sudden, audible release of the breath at the end of the articulation of a stop. **5** an outbreak or bursting forth of anything capable of development: *an explosion of economic activity, the population explosion.* ⟨< L *explosio, -onis* < *explodere.* See EXPLODE.⟩

ex•plo•sive [ɛk'splousɪv] *or* [ɛk'splouzɪv] *adj., n.* *—adj.* **1** capable of exploding; likely to explode: *Gunpowder is explosive.* **2** tending to burst forth noisily: *The irritable old man had an explosive temper.* **3** *Phonetics.* plosive. **4** of or having to do with sudden outbursts: *explosive evolution, an explosive situation.*
—n. **1** a substance that is capable of exploding: *Explosives are used in making fireworks.* **2** a projectile, firework, etc. containing such a substance and designed to explode under certain conditions. **3** *Phonetics.* plosive. **—ex'plo•sive•ly,** *adv.*
—ex'plo•sive•ness, *n.*

ex•po ['ɛkspou] *n. Informal.* exposition: *Expo 86.*

ex•po•nent [ɛk'spounənt] *n.* **1** a person or thing that explains, interprets, etc. **2** a person who favours or speaks for (*used with* **of**): *She is an exponent of the guaranteed annual wage.* **3** a person or thing that stands as an example, type, or symbol of something: *This woman is a famous exponent of self-education.* **4** *Algebra.* an index or small number written above and to the right of a symbol or quantity to show how many times the symbol or quantity is to be used as a factor. *Examples*: $2^2 = 2 \times 2$; $a^3 = a \times a \times a$. ⟨< L *exponens, -entis,* ppr. of *exponere.* See EXPOUND.⟩

ex•po•nen•tial [,ɛkspə'nɛnʃəl] *adj.* **1** having to do with algebraic exponents; involving unknown or variable quantities as exponents. **2** of any growth or increase, occurring more and more rapidly or by greater and greater quantities.
—,ex•po'nen•tial•ly, *adv.*

ex•port *v.* [ɛk'spɔrt] *or* ['ɛkspɔrt]; *n.* ['ɛkspɔrt] *v., n.* *—v.* send (articles or goods) out of one country for sale and use in another: *Canada exports millions of tonnes of wheat each year.* *—n.* **1** the act of selling or shipping articles or goods to another country. **2** the goods or articles so sold and shipped: *Clothing is an important export of Québec.* **3** (*adjl.*) of a kind or quality suitable for export: *export liquors. Export quality is usually higher than the regular domestic quality.* **4** (*adjl.*) of or having to do with exports or exporting: *export duty.* ⟨< L *exportare* < *ex-* away + *portare* carry⟩ **—,ex•por'ta•tion,** *n.*

ex•port•er [ɛk'spɔrtər] *or* ['ɛkspɔrtər] *n.* a person or company whose business is exporting goods.

ex•pose [ɛk'spouz] *v.* **-posed, -pos•ing. 1** lay open; leave unprotected; uncover; make vulnerable or liable: *The soldiers in the open field were exposed to the enemy's gunfire. His foolish actions exposed him to ridicule.* **2** lay open to view, especially something that was hidden; display or make visible: *to expose a card in a card game. They stripped off the paint around the fireplace, exposing the original tile surface.* **3** make known; show up; reveal: *to expose a murderer. The investigators exposed the takeover plot.* **4** *Photography.* allow light to reach and act on (a sensitive film, plate, or paper). **5** put out without shelter; abandon: *The ancient Spartans used to expose babies that they did not want.* ⟨< OF *exposer* < *ex-* forth (< L *ex-*) + *poser* put. See POSE[1].⟩ **—ex'pos•er,** *n.*

ex•po•sé [,ɛkspou'zei] *or* ['ɛkspou,zei] *n.* **1** the showing up of a crime, of dishonesty, fraud, etc. **2** something, as an article, film, etc., that does this. ⟨< F *exposé,* originally pp. of *exposer* expose⟩

ex•po•si•tion [,ɛkspə'zɪʃən] *n.* **1** a public show or exhibition. The Canadian National Exhibition in Toronto is a well-known annual exposition. **2** a detailed explanation: *the exposition of a scientific theory.* **3** a speech or a piece of writing explaining a process or idea. **4** *Music.* **a** the first section of a movement, as of a sonata, in which the principal and secondary subjects are presented. **b** the first entry, in a fugue, of the theme or themes in each part or voice. **5** *Literature.* the part which sets out the story, especially of a drama. ⟨< ME *exposicioun* < OF *exposition* < L *expositio* < *expositus,* pp. of *exponere.* See EXPOUND.⟩

ex•pos•i•tor [ɛk'spɒzətər] *n.* a person who explains or expounds; interpreter or commentator. ⟨< LL < L *exponere.* See EXPOUND.⟩

ex•pos•i•to•ry [ɛk'spɒzə,tɔri] *adj.* of, having to do with, or including exposition: *expository writing.* Also, **expositive.**

ex post fac•to ['ɛks 'poust 'fæktou] made or done after something, but applying to it. An **ex post facto law** applies to actions done before the law was passed. ⟨< Med.L *ex post facto* from what is done afterward⟩

ex•pos•tu•late [ɛk'spɒstʃə,leit] *v.* **-lat•ed, -lat•ing.** reason earnestly with a person, protesting against something he or she means to do or has done; remonstrate (*with*): *They expostulated with their son about the foolishness of leaving school.* ⟨< L *expostulare* < *ex-* (intensive) + *postulare* demand⟩ **—ex'pos•tu,la•tor,** *n.*

ex•pos•tu•la•tion [ɛk,spɒstʃə'leiʃən] *n.* an earnest protest; remonstrance: *Expostulations having failed, the boss resorted to threats.*

ex•pos•tu•la•to•ry [ɛk'spɒstʃələ,tɔri] *adj.* of or characteristic of expostulation.

ex•po•sure [ɛk'spouʒər] *n.* **1** the act or instance of exposing: *The exposure of the real criminal cleared the innocent man. We would all dread public exposure of our faults.* **2** the condition or an instance of being exposed: *Years of exposure to the rain had ruined the machinery.* **3** appearance in public, as on television, etc.: *His campaign manager thought he needed more television exposure.* **4** a position in relation to the sun and wind. A house with a southern exposure is open to sun and wind from the south. **5** *Photography.* **a** the time during which light reaches and acts on a film or plate. **b** the part of a film used for one picture. **c** the total amount of light on a film in making a picture.
die of exposure, die from hypothermia due to lack of shelter or adequate clothing.

exposure meter *Photography.* a device for measuring the intensity of light, used to indicate the correct exposure needed for taking a photograph under particular light conditions. Some cameras have a built-in exposure meter.

ex•pound [ɛk'spaʊnd] *v.* **1** make clear; explain or interpret. **2** set forth or state in detail. ⟨ME < OF *espondre* < L *exponere* < *ex-* forth + *ponere* put⟩

ex•press [ɛk'sprɛs] *v., adj., n.* *—v.* **1** put into words: *Express your ideas clearly.* **2** show by look, voice, or action; reveal: *Your smile expresses joy.* **3** show by a sign, figure, etc.; indicate: *The sign × expresses multiplication.* **4** say what one thinks (*used as a reflexive verb*): *She is a good speaker and expresses herself clearly.* **5** send by express. **6** press out; squeeze out: *The juice is expressed from grapes to make wine.* **7** *Genetics.* cause or allow (a gene) to produce some substance or have a particular effect.
—adj. **1** clear; explicit; definite: *It was his express wish that we should go without him.* **2** particular; special: *She came for the express purpose of seeing you.* **3** exact: *He is the express image of his father.* **4** having a particular purpose: *an express visit.*
—n. **1** a special messenger or message sent for a particular purpose. **2** a quick or direct means of sending things. Packages and money can be sent by express in trains or airplanes. **3** a system or company for sending parcels, money, etc.: *Canadian National Express.* **4** (*adjl.*) having to do with express: *an express agency or company, the express business.* **5** things sent by express. **6** (*advl.*) by express; directly. **7** a train, bus, elevator, etc. travelling fast and making few stops. **8** (*adjl.*) travelling fast and making few stops: *an express train.* **9** (*adjl.*) for fast travelling: *an express highway.* **10** EXPRESS RIFLE. ⟨< L *expressus,* pp. of *exprimere* < *ex-* out + *premere* press⟩ **—ex'press•er,** *n.*

ex•press•age [ɛk'sprɛsɪdʒ] *n.* **1** the business of carrying parcels, money, etc. by express. **2** a charge for carrying parcels, etc. by express.

ex•press•i•ble [ɛk'sprɛsəbəl] *adj.* capable of being expressed.

ex•pres•sion [ɛk'sprɛʃən] *n.* **1** a putting into words: *Clarity of expression is important in style.* **2** a word or group of words used as a unit: *'Wise guy' is a slang expression.* **3** a showing by look, voice, or action: *Her sigh was an expression of sadness.* **4** something that indicates feeling, spirit, character, etc.; look that shows feeling: *He had a silly expression on his face.* **5** a bringing out the meaning or beauty of something read, spoken, played, sung, etc.: *Try to read with more expression.* **6** a showing by a sign, figure, etc. **7** a symbol or group of symbols expressing some mathematical process or quantity. **8** a pressing out: *the expression of oil from plants.* **9** *Genetics.* **a** the action of a gene. **b** the phenotype resulting from the action of a gene.

ex•pres•sion•ism [ɛk'sprɛʃə,nɪzəm] *n.* **1** a movement in art and literature in the late 19th and 20th centuries, marked by the attempt to express the artist's subjective feelings without regard for accepted forms or tradition. It began as a revolt against naturalism and impressionism. **2** a similar movement in music.

ex•pres•sion•ist [ɛk'sprɛʃənɪst] *n., adj.* *—n.* a writer, artist, etc. who follows the principles of expressionism.
—adj. of, like, or having to do with expressionism.

ex•pres•sion•is•tic [ɛk,sprɛʃə'nɪstɪk] *adj.* of or having to do with expressionism or expressionists.
—ex,pres•sion'is•ti•cal•ly, *adv.*

ex•pres•sion•less [ɛk'sprɛʃənlɪs] *adj.* without expression: *an expressionless face, an expressionless voice.*
—ex'pres•sion,less•ly, *adv.* **—ex'pres•sion•less•ness,** *n.*

ex•pres•sive [ɛk'sprɛsɪv] *adj.* **1** serving as a sign or indication; representing (*used with* **of**): Alas *is a word expressive of sadness.* **2** full of expression; having or showing much feeling, meaning, etc.: *an expressive pause. She has a very expressive face.* **3** of or having to do with expression: *She is a writer of great expressive power.* **—ex'pres•sive•ly,** *adv.* **—ex'pres•sive•ness,** *n.*
☛ *Syn.* **2. Expressive,** SIGNIFICANT, SUGGESTIVE = full of meaning. **Expressive** emphasizes showing a meaning or feeling in a strikingly clear or lively way: *An expressive shrug revealed her contempt.* **Significant** emphasizes being full of meaning, which may be expressed, but often is only pointed to: *He wondered why she ended every remark with such a significant smile.* **Suggestive** emphasizes conveying meaning in an indirect way, as by expressing part of the meaning or by hinting: *The teacher gave an interesting and suggestive list of composition topics.*

ex•pres•siv•i•ty [,ɛksprɛ'sɪvəti] *n.* **1** expressive quality. **2** *Genetics.* the range of intensity seen in the expression of some genetic traits, which may vary from slight to intense in different individuals. Compare PENETRANCE.

ex•press•ly [ɛk'sprɛsli] *adv.* **1** clearly; explicitly; definitely: *You were expressly forbidden to touch it.* **2** specially; for the particular purpose: *She came expressly to see you.*

express rifle a rifle used to kill animals at short distances. It has a large charge and a light bullet.

ex•press•way [ɛk'sprɛs,wei] *n.* a divided highway for fast driving; a highway that stretches for long distances with few intersections. Most interchanges on expressways are built on two levels so that vehicles do not have to cross in front of each other on the highway.

ex•pro•pri•ate [ɛks'proupri,eit] *v.* **-at•ed, -at•ing. 1** take (property) away from an owner, especially for public use: *The provincial government expropriated 50 000 m² of land for a public* *housing development.* **2** put (a person) out of possession; dispossess. ⟨< Med.L *expropriare* < *ex-* away from + *proprius* one's own⟩ **—ex,pro•pri'a•tion,** *n.* **—ex'pro•pri,a•tor,** *n.*

ex•pul•sion [ɛk'spʌlʃən] *n.* an expelling or being expelled: *expulsion of air from the lungs. The threat of expulsion from school did not help.* ⟨< L *expulsio, -onis* < *expellere.* See EXPEL.⟩

ex•pul•sive [ɛk'spʌlsɪv] *adj.* expelling or having the power to expel: *the expulsive power of steam under pressure.*

ex•punc•tion [ɛk'spʌŋkʃən] *n.* **1** the act of expunging. **2** something expunged. ⟨< LL *expunctio* < L *expunctus,* pp. of *expungere.* See EXPUNGE.⟩

ex•punge [ɛk'spʌndʒ] *v.* **-punged -pung•ing.** remove completely; blot out; erase: *The secretary was directed to expunge certain accusations from the record.* ⟨< L *expungere* < *ex-* out + *pungere* prick⟩ **—ex'pung•er,** *n.*

☛ *Syn.* See note at ERASE.

ex•pur•gate ['ɛkspər,geit] *v.* **-gat•ed, -gat•ing. 1** remove objectionable passages or words from (a book, letter, etc.); purify. **2** remove (objectionable passages). ⟨< L *expurgare* < *ex-* out + *purgare* purge⟩ **—'ex•pur,ga•tor,** *n.* **—ex'pur•ga,to•ry,** *adj.*

ex•pur•ga•tion [,ɛkspər'geiʃən] *n.* the removing or removal from a book, etc. of something that seems objectionable.

ex•quis•ite [ɛk'skwɪzɪt] *or* ['ɛkskwɪzɪt] *adj., n.—adj.* **1** very lovely in a delicate way: *exquisite lace. Violets are exquisite flowers.* **2** of great elegance. **3** of highest excellence; most admirable: *an exquisite painting technique, exquisite taste.* **4** keenly sensitive: *an exquisite ear for music.* **5** sharp; intense: *exquisite pain, exquisite joy.*

—n. one who is exaggeratedly refined in matters of etiquette and taste. ⟨< L *exquisitus,* pp. of *exquirere* < *ex-* out + *quaerere* seek⟩ **—ex'quis•ite•ly,** *adv.* **—ex'quis•ite•ness,** *n.*

ex•san•guine [ɛks'sæŋgwɪn] *adj.* bloodless; anemic.

ex•scind [ɛk'sɪnd] *v.* tear away. ⟨< L *exscindere* < *ex-* out + *scindere* to cut⟩

ex•sect [ɛk'sɛkt] *v.* cut away. ⟨< L *exsectus,* pp. of *exsecare* < *ex-* out + *secare* to cut⟩ **—ex'sect•ile,** *adj.*

ex•sert [ɛk'sɜrt] *v.* force out. ⟨< L *exsertus,* pp. of *exserere* to stretch out⟩ **—ex'sert•ile,** *adj.*

ex–serv•ice [,ɛks 'sɜrvɪs] *adj.* having formerly served in the armed forces.

ex•sic•cate ['ɛksɪ,keit] *v.* **-cat•ed, -cat•ing.** dry out. ⟨< ME *exsiccaten* < L *exsiccatus* pp. of *exsiccare* to make dry < *ex-* out + *siccare* to dry < *siccus* dry⟩ **—ex'sic•ca•tive,** *adj.*

ex•stip•u•late [ɛk'stɪpjəlɪt] *adj. Botany.* without stipules.

ex•stro•phy ['ɛkstrəfi] *n. Medicine.* a congenital turning inside out of an organ, such as the bladder.

ex•tant ['ɛkstənt] *or* [ɛk'stænt] *adj.* still in existence; currently existing: *Some of Captain Vancouver's charts are extant.* ⟨< L *ex(s)tans, -antis,* ppr. of *ex(s)tare* < *ex-* out, forth + *stare* stand⟩

ex•tem•po•ral [ɛks'tɛmpərəl] *adj. Archaic.* extemporaneous.

ex•tem•po•ra•ne•ous [ɛk,stɛmpə'reiniəs] *adj.* **1** spoken or done without preparation; impromptu: *an extemporaneous speech.* **2** of a speech, planned, but delivered with few notes. **3** made for the occasion; makeshift: *an extemporaneous shelter against a storm.* **4** inclined and able to make speeches without preparation: *an extemporaneous speaker.* ⟨< LL *extemporaneus* < L *ex tempore* according to the moment⟩ **—ex,tem•po'ra•ne•ous•ly,** *adv.* **—ex,tem•po'ra•ne•ous•ness,** *n.*

ex•tem•po•rar•y [ɛk'stɛmpə,rɛri] *adj.* extemporaneous. **—ex,tem•po'rar•i•ly,** *adv.*

ex•tem•po•re [ɛk'stɛmpəri] *or* [ɛk'stɛmpərei] *adj. or adv.* on the spur of the moment; without preparation; offhand or impromptu: *Each pupil will be called on to speak extempore.* ⟨< L *ex tempore* according to the moment⟩

ex•tem•po•rize [ɛk'stɛmpə,raɪz] *v.* **-rized, -riz•ing. 1** speak, play, sing, or dance, composing as one proceeds: *The pianist was extemporizing.* **2** compose offhand; make for the occasion: *The campers extemporized a shelter for the night.* **—ex,tem•po•ri'za•tion,** *n.* **—ex'tem•po,riz•er,** *n.*

ex•tend [ɛk'stɛnd] *v.* **1** stretch out: *She extended her hand to the visitor.* **2** continue in time, space, or direction: *The beach extended for more than a kilometre in each direction.* **3** straighten out: *Extend your arms in front of you.* **4** lengthen: *to extend a meeting. They have extended the ski trail another 3 km.* **5** enlarge or broaden: *to extend a gym, to extend one's knowledge.* **6** become longer or larger. **7** give; grant: *to extend help to someone in need, to extend credit.* **8** exert (oneself); strain. **9** cause to put out greater or maximum effort: *The competition was not strong enough to extend her.* **10** increase the quantity of (a substance) by adding a cheaper or less pure variety. **11** *Bookkeeping.* transfer from one column to another. **12** prolong payment of (a debt). ⟨< L *extendere* < *ex-* out + *tendere* stretch⟩ **—ex'tend•er,** *n.*

☛ *Syn.* **4.** See note at LENGTHEN.

ex•tend•ed [ɛk'stɛndɪd] *adj., v. —adj.* **1** extensive; widespread. **2** long; lengthened; prolonged. **3** widened. **4** spread out; outstretched.

—v. pt. and pp. of EXTEND.

extended care hospital treatment over a long period.

extended family a family whose members are of several generations and branches.

ex•tend•er [ɛk'stɛndər] *n.* a thinner added to paint.

ex•tend•i•ble [ɛk'stɛndəbəl] *adj.* that can be extended. **—ex,tend•i'bil•i•ty,** *n.*

ex•ten•si•ble [ɛk'stɛnsəbəl] *adj.* of a bodily or mechanical part, capable of being protruded, stretched, or opened out: *an extensible tongue.*
—ex,ten•si'bil•i•ty, *n.*

ex•ten•sile [ɛk'stɛnsaɪl] *or* [ɛk'stɛnsəl] *adj.* extensible.

ex•ten•sion [ɛk'stɛnʃən] *n.* **1** an extending or being extended: *The extension of one's right hand is a sign of friendship.* **2** a part that extends something; addition: *The new extension to the school will have several classrooms and a gym.* **3** an extra telephone connected to a line: *He heard it all because he was listening in on the extension.* **4** an increase in time, especially in the time allowed for something: *I got an extension on my essay because I had been sick.* **5** an educational program provided by a university for people who cannot take regular courses: *People who have full-time jobs can upgrade their education by taking evening classes through extension.* **6** (*adjl.*) of, in, or designating such a program: *She's taking an extension course.* **7** range; extent. **8** *Physics.* that property of a body by which it occupies a portion of space. **9** the straightening of a part by the action of an extensor muscle. **10** the condition of being straightened in this way. **11** the pulling or stretching of a fractured or dislocated part to enable the bones to be restored to their natural relative positions. **12** *Logic.* the class to which a given term applies. ⟨< LL *extensio, -onis* < L *extendere.* See EXTEND.⟩ **—ex'ten•sion•less,** *adj.*

extension cord an electrical cord having a plug at one end and a socket at the other, used to lengthen the cord attached to an electrical appliance.

extension ladder a ladder having a movable part or parts enabling it to be extended to varying heights as needed.

ex•ten•si•ty [ɛk'stɛnsəti] *n.* **1** EXTENSION (def. 8). **2** *Psychology.* the sensory ability to judge spatial dimension.

ex•ten•sive [ɛk'stɛnsɪv] *adj.* **1** of great extent; wide; broad; large: *an extensive park. She has extensive knowledge in several branches of science.* **2** far-reaching; affecting many things; comprehensive: *extensive change.* **3** depending on the use of large areas: *extensive agriculture.* **—ex'ten•sive•ly,** *adv.*
—ex'ten•sive•ness, *n.*

ex•ten•som•e•ter [,ɛkstɛn'sɒmətər] *n.* an instrument to determine degrees of contraction or expansion in a material.

ex•ten•sor [ɛk'stɛnsər] *or* [ɛk'stɛnsɔr] *n. Physiology.* a muscle that extends or straightens out a limb or other part of the body. ⟨< LL *extensor* one who stretches⟩

ex•tent [ɛk'stɛnt] *n.* **1** the size, space, length, amount, or degree to which a thing extends: *Railways carry people and goods through the whole extent of the country. The extent of a judge's power is limited by law.* **2** something extended; an extended space: *a vast extent of prairie.* **3** *Physics.* anything that has extension; an object or body having length, area, or volume. **4** *Logic.* extension. ⟨< AF *extente, estente,* fem. pp., used as a noun, of *estendre* extend < L *extendere.* See EXTEND.⟩

ex•ten•u•ate [ɛk'stɛnju,eit] *v.* **-at•ed, -at•ing. 1** make (guilt, a fault, an offence, etc.) seem less; excuse in part: *She claimed there were extenuating circumstances for their rude behaviour.* **2** make less or weaker. ⟨< L *extenuare* < *ex-* out + *tenuis* thin⟩ **—ex'ten•u,at•ing•ly,** *adv.* **—ex'ten•u,a•tor,** *n.*

ex•ten•u•a•tion [ɛk,stɛnju'eiʃən] *n.* **1** an extenuating: *The lawyer pleaded her client's youth in extenuation of the crime.* **2** extenuated condition. **3** something that lessens the seriousness of guilt, a fault, an offence, etc.; a partial excuse.

ex•te•ri•or [ɛk'stiriər] *n., adj. —n.* **1** an outer surface or part; outward appearance; outside: *The exterior of the house was of brick. The gruff old man has a harsh exterior but a kind heart.* **2** an outdoor scene on the stage. **3** a motion picture made outdoors. *—adj.* **1** on the outside; outer: *The skin of an apple is its exterior* *covering.* **2** coming from without; happening outside: *exterior influences.* **3** suitable for use outside: *exterior paint.* ⟨< L *exterior*, comparative of *exterus* outside < *ex-* out of⟩ **—ex'te•ri•or•ly,** *adv.* **—ex,te•ri'or•i•ty** [-'ɔrəti], *n.*

exterior angle *Geometry.* **1** any of the four angles formed on the outer sides of two lines by a straight line cutting through them. See TRIANGLE for picture. **2** the angle formed on the outside of a polygon between one of its sides and an extension of a side next to it. Compare INTERIOR ANGLE.

ex•te•ri•or•ize [ɛk'stiriə,raɪz] *v.* **-ized, -iz•ing. 1** externalize. **2** in surgery, expose for treatment.

ex•ter•mi•nate [ɛk'stɜrmə,neit] *v.* **-nat•ed, -nat•ing.** destroy completely: *This poison will exterminate rats.* ⟨< LL *exterminare* destroy < L *exterminare* drive out < *ex-* out of + *terminus* boundary⟩ **—ex,ter•mi'na•tion,** *n.*

ex•ter•mi•na•tor [ɛk'stɜrmə,neitər] *n.* a person who or thing that exterminates, especially a person whose business is exterminating cockroaches, bedbugs, rats, etc.

ex•tern ['ɛkstɜrn] *n.* a medical student who is not a resident of a hospital. Compare INTERN[2]. ⟨< F *externe* < L *externus*⟩

ex•ter•nal [ɛk'stɜrnəl] *adj., n.* *—adj.* **1** of or on the outside; outer: *the external wall of a house.* **2** to be used on the outside of the body: *Liniment and rubbing alcohol are external remedies.* **3** entirely outside; coming from without: *external air. External influences affect our lives.* **4** having existence outside one's mind: *external reality.* **5** for outward appearance; superficial: *Her politeness is only external.* **6** not essential or basic; extraneous: *Her decision was influenced too much by external factors.* **7** having to do with international affairs; foreign: *external affairs. War affects a nation's external trade.*
—n. **1** an outer surface or part; outside. **2 externals,** *pl.* clothing, manners, outward acts, or appearances: *He judges people by such externals as clothing and length of hair.* ⟨< L *externus* outside < *exterus* outside < *ex-* out of⟩ **—ex'ter•nal•ly,** *adv.*

external–combustion engine an engine in which the fuel is burned outside the engine, as a steam engine.

external degree a university degree granted to students who take courses by correspondence or through an affiliated institution.

external ear the fleshy part of the ear attached to the head, including the opening to the vestibule.

external galaxy any galaxy other than our own, that is, other than the Milky Way.

ex•ter•nal•ism [ɛk'stɜrnə,lɪzəm] *n.* excessive attention to matters of form in religion.

ex•ter•nal•i•ty [,ɛkstər'næləti] *n., pl.* **-ties. 1** the quality of being external. **2** an external thing.

ex•ter•nal•ize [ɛk'stɜrnə,laɪz] *v.* **-ized, -iz•ing.** give objective shape or form to (things in the mind or emotions); make external.

ex•ter•o•cep•tor ['ɛkstərou,sɛptər] *n. Physiology.* a receptor responding to a stimulus outside the body. ⟨< L *exter* on the outside + *receptor*⟩ **—,ex•ter•o'cep•tive,** *adj.*

ex•ter•ri•to•ri•al [,ɛkstɛrɪ'tɔriəl] *adj.* EXTRA-TERRITORIAL.

ex•tinct [ɛk'stɪŋkt] *adj.* **1** no longer in existence: *The dinosaur is an extinct animal.* **2** no longer active; extinguished: *an extinct volcano.* ⟨< L *ex(s)tinctus*, pp. of *ex(s)tinguere.* See EXTINGUISH.⟩

ex•tinc•tion [ɛk'stɪŋkʃən] *n.* **1** an extinguishing or being extinguished: *The sudden extinction of the lights left the room in darkness.* **2** a being or becoming extinct: *The caribou was once threatened with extinction.* **3** a suppression; a doing away with completely; wiping out; destruction: *The war caused the extinction of many organizations.*

ex•tinct•ive [ɛk'stɪŋktɪv] *adj.* for the purpose of extinguishing.

ex•tin•guish [ɛk'stɪŋgwɪʃ] *v.* **1** put out; quench: *Water extinguished the fire.* **2** put an end to; do away with; wipe out; destroy: *One failure after another extinguished her hope.* **3** eclipse or obscure by superior brilliance. **4** discharge (a debt). ⟨< L *ex(s)tinguere* < *ex-* out + *stinguere* quench⟩ **—ex'tin•guish•a•ble,** *adj.*
☛ *Syn.* **2.** See note at ABOLISH.

ex•tin•guish•er [ɛk'stɪŋgwɪʃər] *n.* **1** a person who or thing that extinguishes. **2** a device for quenching fires.

ex•tir•pate ['ɛkstər,peit] *or* [ɛk'stɜrpeit] *v.* **-pat•ed, -pat•ing. 1** remove or destroy completely; abolish or exterminate: *to extirpate a prejudice.* **2** tear up by the roots. ⟨< L *ex(s)tirpare* < *ex-* out + *stirps* root⟩ **—'ex•tir,pa•tor,** *n.* **—ex'tir•pa•tive,** *adj.*

ex•tir•pa•tion [,ɛkstər'peiʃən] *n.* **1** complete removal or destruction. **2** a tearing up by the roots.

ex•tir•pa•to•ry [ɛk'stɜrpə,tɔri] *adj.* extirpating; serving to root out or destroy.

ex•tol or **ex•toll** [ɛk'stoul] *v.* **-tolled, -tol•ling.** praise highly. ⟨< L *extollere* < *ex-* up + *tollere* raise⟩

ex•tort [ɛk'stɔrt] *v.* **1** obtain (something, such as money, a favour, or a promise) from a person by threats, criminal accusations, or violence. **2** obtain (something) by persistent demands or arguments, cajoling, etc.: *children extorting a promise of a picnic from their parents.* ⟨< L *extortus*, pp. of *extorquere* < *ex-* out + *torquere* twist⟩ **—ex'tort•er,** *n.* **—ex'tort•ive,** *adj.*
☛ *Syn.* See note at EXTRACT.

ex•tor•tion [ɛk'stɔrʃən] *n.* **1** the act or an instance of inducing or attempting to induce someone to do something by threats, real or false criminal accusations, or violence: *Extortion is an indictable offence in Canada.* **2** the demanding of an exorbitant price. **3** the thing extorted.

ex•tor•tion•ar•y [ɛk'stɔrʃə,nɛri] *adj.* characterized by or given to extortion.

ex•tor•tion•ate [ɛk'stɔrʃənɪt] *adj.* **1** characterized by extortion: *extortionate demands.* **2** much too great; exorbitant: *an extortionate price.* **—ex'tor•tion•ate•ly,** *adv.*

ex•tor•tion•er [ɛk'stɔrʃənər] *n.* a person who is guilty of extortion. Also, **extortionist**.

ex•tra ['ɛkstrə] *adj., n., adv.* *—adj.* **1** more, greater, or better than what is usual, expected, or needed: *extra pay, an extra workload. Do you have an extra pencil?* **2** not included in the overall price: *Bread is extra in this restaurant.*
—n. **1** something for which an additional charge is made: *The sunroof is an extra. Her bill for extras was $30.* **2** something in addition to what is usual, expected, or needed: *If you don't have enough, ask us; we have extra.* **3** a special edition of a newspaper. **4** an extra worker, especially a person hired by the day to act in crowd scenes, etc. in a motion picture. **5** BYE[1].
—adv. more than usually: *The quality is extra fine. They like their coffee extra strong.* ⟨probably short for *extraordinary*⟩

extra– *prefix.* outside, beyond, besides, as in *extraordinary.* ⟨< L⟩

ex•tra–base hit ['ɛkstrə 'beis] *Baseball.* a double, triple, or home run.

ex•tra–bil•ling ['ɛkstrə 'bɪlɪŋ] *n.* a charge made by a doctor beyond what is covered under the government health insurance plan: *Extra-billing is illegal in Canada.*

ex•tra•ca•non•i•cal [,ɛkstrəkə'nɒnɪkəl] *adj.* not belonging to the canon; of a text, lacking legitimacy.

ex•tra•cel•lu•lar [,ɛkstrə'sɛljələr] *adj. Biology.* located outside a cell.

ex•tract *v.* [ɛk'strækt]; *n.* ['ɛkstrækt] *v., n.* *—v.* **1** pull out or draw out, usually with some effort: *to extract a tooth.* **2** obtain by pressing, distilling, etc., or by a chemical process: *to extract oil from olives.* **3** draw out or obtain against a person's will: *to extract payment, to extract a confession.* **4** deduce: *to extract a principle from a collection of facts.* **5** derive: *to extract pleasure from a situation.* **6** take out; select (a passage) from a book, speech, etc. **7** *Mathematics.* calculate or find (the root of a number).
—n. **1** something drawn out or taken out; a passage taken from a book, speech, etc. **2** a concentrated preparation of a substance. Vanilla extract, made from vanilla beans, is often used as a flavouring in ice cream. ⟨< L *extractus*, pp. of *extrahere* < *ex-* out + *trahere* draw⟩ **—ex'tract•a•ble** or **ex'tract•i•ble,** *adj.*
☛ *Syn. v.* **3. Extract,** EXTORT = draw out of someone with force. **Extract** emphasizes getting something out with great effort of persuasion, emotional manipulation, etc.: *She finally extracted a promise from him not to do it again.* **Extort** suggests the use of brute force, fraud, etc.: *Not even torture could extort from him the names of his companions.*

ex•trac•tion [ɛk'strækʃən] *n.* **1** an extracting or being extracted: *the extraction of a tooth.* **2** descent; origin: *Ms. Del Rio is of Spanish extraction.* **3** something extracted.

ex•trac•tive [ɛk'stræktɪv] *adj.* **1** extracting; tending to extract. **2** capable of being extracted. **3** having the nature of an extract. **4** of production in which materials are derived directly from nature, as in mining or farming.

ex•trac•tor [ɛk'stræktər] *n.* **1** something or someone that extracts. **2** in a firearm, the mechanism that removes an empty cartridge.

ex•tra–cur•ric•u•lar [,ɛkstrə kə'rɪkjələr] *adj.* outside the regular course of study: *Football and debating are extra-curricular activities in high school.*

ex•tra•dit•a•ble ['ɛkstrə,dəitəbəl] *adj.* **1** that can be extradited. A person accused of murder in the United States is extraditable if he or she is caught in Canada. **2** for which a person can be extradited: *Murder is an extraditable offence.*

ex•tra•dite ['ɛkstrə,dəit] *v.* **-dit•ed, -dit•ing. 1** give up or deliver (a fugitive or prisoner) to another nation or legal authority for trial or punishment: *If an escaped prisoner from Canada is caught in the United States, he or she can be extradited to Canada.* **2** obtain the extradition of (such a person). ⟨< *extradition*⟩

ex•tra•di•tion [,ɛkstrə'dɪʃən] *n.* the surrender of a fugitive or prisoner by one state, nation, or legal authority to another for trial or punishment. ⟨< F < L *ex-* out + *traditio* a delivering up < *tradere* hand over⟩

ex•tra•dos [ɛk'streidɒs] *n. Architecture.* the exterior surface of an arch or vault. ⟨< OF < L *extra* beyond + F *dos* < L *dorsum* back⟩

ex•tra•gal•ac•tic [,ɛkstrəgə'læktɪk] *adj.* outside the Milky Way.

ex•tra•ju•dic•ial [,ɛkstrədʒʊ'dɪʃəl] *adj.* beyond the authority of a court. **—,ex•tra•ju'dic•ial•ly,** *adv.*

ex•tra–le•gal [,ɛkstrə 'ligəl] *adj.* beyond the control or influence of law. **—,ex•tra–'le•gal•ly,** *adv.*

ex•tra•mar•i•tal [,ɛkstrə'mærətəl] *or* [-'mɛrətəl] *adj.* outside the limits or bonds of marriage.

ex•tra•mun•dane [,ɛkstrəmʌn'dein] *adj.* outside the physical world.

ex•tra•mu•ral [,ɛkstrə'mjʊrəl] *adj.* **1** occurring or done outside the boundaries of a school or college: *extramural activities.* **2** between schools or colleges: *extramural hockey.* **3** of, having to do with, or taking part in studies outside the normal program of a university, college, etc. **4** beyond the boundaries or walls of a city. ⟨< L *extra muros* outside the walls + E *-al*⟩

ex•tra•ne•ous [ɛk'streiniəs] *adj.* **1** coming from outside; foreign: *Sand or some other extraneous matter had got into the butter.* **2** not essential to what is under consideration; irrelevant: *In her talk on conservation, she made several interesting but extraneous remarks about wildlife photography.* ⟨< L *extraneus* < *extra* outside < *ex-* out of. Doublet of STRANGE.⟩ **—ex'tra•ne•ous•ly,** *adv.* **—ex'tra•ne•ous•ness,** *n.*

ex•tra•nu•cle•ar [,ɛkstrə'njukliər] *or* [,ɛkstrə'nukliər] *adj. Biology.* having to do with the parts of a cell outside the nucleus.

ex•tra•or•di•naire [ɛk,strɔrdi'nɛr]; *French,* [ɛkstʀaɔʀdi'nɛʀ] *adj.* (*placed after the noun*) extraordinary; striking; unusual: *a comedian extraordinaire.*

ex•tra•or•di•nar•i•ly [ɛk'strɔrdə,nɛrəli] *or* [,ɛkstrə'ɔrdə,nɛrəli] *adv.* in an extraordinary manner; to an extraordinary degree; most unusually.

ex•tra•or•di•nar•y [ɛk'strɔrdə,nɛri] *or* [,ɛkstrə'ɔrdə,nɛri] *adj.* **1** far beyond what is ordinary; most unusual; very remarkable: *Two metres is an extraordinary height for a woman. She is an extraordinary child.* **2** outside of or additional to the regular class of officials; special (*placed after the noun*). An **envoy extraordinary** is an envoy sent on a special mission; he or she ranks below an ambassador. **3** unplanned; deviating from the customary routine: *An extraordinary session of Parliament was called to deal with the crisis.* ⟨< L *extraordinarius* < *extra ordinem* out of the (usual) order⟩

ex•trap•o•late [ɛk'stræpə,leit] *v.* **-lat•ed, -lat•ing. 1** *Mathematics.* project (new values or terms of a series) from those already known. **2** infer (something) by projecting from known facts on the assumption that they form part of a series. ⟨< *extra* + *interpolate*⟩ **—ex,trap•o'la•tion,** *n.* **—ex'trap•o,la•tor,** *n.*

ex•tra•sen•so•ry [,ɛkstrə'sɛnsəri] *adj.* beyond the normal scope or range of the senses: *Mental telepathy is one kind of extrasensory perception.*

extrasensory perception the perceiving of things in other than a sensory fashion; mental telepathy.

ex•tra•sys•to•le [,ɛkstrə'sɪstəli] *n.* a derangement in the rhythm of the heart, causing an extra contraction between beats.

ex•tra–ter•res•tri•al [,ɛkstrə tə'rɛstriəl] *adj., n. —adj.* coming from or existing beyond the limits of the earth's atmosphere: *extra-terrestrial life.*
—n. a supposed creature from another planet.

ex•tra–ter•ri•to•ri•al [,ɛkstrə ,tɛrə'tɔriəl] *adj.* **1** outside the laws of the country that a person is living in. Any ambassador to a foreign country has certain extra-territorial privileges. **2** beyond territorial limits or jurisdiction. **—,ex•tra–,ter•ri'to•ri•al•ly,** *adv.*

ex•tra–ter•ri•to•ri•al•ity [,ɛkstrə ,tɛrɪ,tɔri'æləti] *n.* **1** freedom from local laws, as given to an ambassador. **2** the jurisdiction of a country over its citizens abroad.

ex•tra•u•ter•ine [,ɛkstrə'jutərɪn] *adj.* outside the uterus: *an extrauterine pregnancy.*

ex•trav•a•gance [ɛk'strævəgəns] *n.* **1** careless and lavish spending; wastefulness: *His extravagance kept him always in debt.* **2** highly exaggerated quality; a going beyond the bounds of reason; excess: *The extravagance of the sales rep's claims caused us to doubt the worth of his product.* **3** an extravagant action, idea, purchase, etc.

ex•trav•a•gant [ɛk'strævəgənt] *adj.* **1** spending carelessly and lavishly; wasteful: *An extravagant person usually has expensive tastes and habits.* **2** highly exaggerated; beyond the bounds of reason; excessive: *People laughed at the inventor's extravagant praise of her invention. He refused to buy the ring because of its extravagant price.* **3** costing more than is fit and proper: *They spent a whole day's pay on an extravagant dinner.* ⟨< Med.L *extravagans, -antis,* ppr. of *extravagari* < L *extra-* outside + *vagari* wander⟩ **—ex'trav•a•gant•ly,** *adv.*

ex•trav•a•gan•za [ɛk,strævə'gænzə] *n.* a lavish or spectacular play, piece of music, literary composition, party, etc. Musical comedies having elaborate scenery, gorgeous costumes, etc. are extravaganzas. ⟨< Ital. *stravaganza* peculiar behaviour, influenced by E *extravagant*⟩

ex•trav•a•gate [ɛk'strævə,geit] *v.* **-gat•ed, -gat•ing. 1** stray. **2** go beyond reasonable limits.

ex•trav•a•sate [ɛk'strævə,seit] *v.* **-sat•ed, -sat•ing. 1** *Geology.* eject (lava). **2** *Pathology.* force (blood) from surrounding tissue. **3** flow out; escape or be exuded. ⟨< L *extra* beyond + *vas* a vessel + *-ate*[1]⟩ **—ex,trav•a'sa•tion,** *n.*

ex•tra•vas•cu•lar [,ɛkstrə'væskjələr] *adj.* **1** outside a vessel of the vascular system. **2** without blood vessels.

ex•tra•ve•hic•u•lar [,ɛkstrəvɪ'hɪkjələr] *adj.* having to do with the activity of an astronaut outside his or her spacecraft.

ex•tra•ver•sion [,ɛkstrə'vɜrʒən] *or* [-'vɜrʃən] *n.* See EXTROVERSION.

ex•tra•vert ['ɛkstrə,vɜrt] *n.* See EXTROVERT.

ex•treme [ɛk'strim] *adj.* **-trem•er, -trem•est;** *n. —adj.* **1** much more than usual; very great; very strong; the most, greatest, etc. possible. **2** very severe or harsh: *The government took extreme measures to crush the revolt.* **3** farthest from the centre; outermost: *the extreme outlying districts of the city.* **4** farthest from the centre in political opinion, etc.; in favour of strong measures; not moderate: *She's a member of the extreme right.* **5** far from the usual or ordinary: *an extreme mode of dress.*
—n. **1** something extreme; one of two things, places, parts, etc. (often with the other only implied) as far or as different as possible from each other: *Love and hate are two extremes of feeling. Cape Town is at the southern extreme of Africa.* **2** an extreme degree or condition: *Joy is happiness in the extreme.* **3** *Mathematics.* the first or last term in a proportion or series: *In the proportion,* 2 *is to* 4 *as* 8 *is to* 16, 2 *and* 16 *are the extremes;* 4 *and* 8 *are the means.* **4** an extreme act, attitude, statement, etc.; something very immoderate.
go to extremes, do or say too much; resort to extreme measures. ⟨< L *extremus,* superlative of *exterus* outside < *ex-* out of⟩ **—ex'treme•ness,** *n.*

☛ *Usage.* **Extreme.** Although *extremer* and *extremest* are used as the comparative and superlative of *extreme, more extreme* and *most extreme* are found more frequently in general usage.

ex•treme•ly [ɛk'strimli] *adv.* much more than usual; very.

extremely high frequency the highest range of frequencies in the radio spectrum, between 30 and 300 gigahertz. Extremely high frequency is the range next above superhigh frequency.

extremely low frequency the lowest range of frequencies in the radio spectrum, between 30 and 300 hertz.

extreme unction *Roman Catholic Church.* the sacrament given by a priest to a dying person or one in danger of death.

ex•trem•ism [ɛk'strimɪzəm] *n.* **1** a tendency to go to political or ideological extremes. **2** an instance of extremism.

ex•trem•ist [ɛk'strimɪst] *n., adj. —n.* a person who goes to extremes, especially one who has extreme views; a radical.
—adj. having or showing extreme views or ideas; radical: *an extremist position. She is too extremist ever to get elected in this riding.*

ex•trem•i•ty [ɛk'strɛməti] *n., pl.* **-ties. 1** the very end; the farthest possible place; the last part or point. **2** an extreme need, danger, suffering, etc.: *In their extremity the people on the sinking ship bore themselves bravely.* **3** the highest degree; the ultimate form: *Joy is the extremity of happiness.* **4** an extreme action: *The soldiers were forced to the extremity of firing their rifles to scatter the angry mob.* **5 the extremities,** *pl.* the hands and feet.

ex•tri•ca•ble ['ɛkstrəkəbəl] *adj.* capable of being extricated.

ex•tri•cate ['ɛkstrə,keit] *v.* **-cat•ed, -cat•ing.** set free (from entanglements, difficulties, embarrassing situations, etc.); release: *Tom extricated his younger brother from the barbed-wire fence.* ⟨< L *extricare* < *ex-* out of + *tricae* perplexities⟩ **—,ex•tri'ca•tion,** *n.*

ex•trin•sic [ɛk'strɪnzɪk] *or* [ɛk'strɪnsɪk] *adj.* **1** not essential or inherent; caused by external circumstances. **2** being, coming, or acting from outside of a thing: *extrinsic aid, an extrinsic stimulus.* Compare INTRINSIC. ⟨< later L *extrinsecus* outer < earlier L *extrinsecus* from outside < OL **extrim* from outside + *secus* following⟩ **—ex'trin•si•cal•ly,** *adv.*

extrinsic factor Vitamin B_{12}.

extro– *prefix.* outward or outside, as in *extrovert.* ⟨var. of L *extra-*⟩

ex•trorse [ɛk'strɔrs] *adj. Botany.* turned or facing outward. ⟨< LL *extrorsus* in an outward direction < *extra-* outside + *versus* toward⟩ **—ex'trorse•ly,** *adv.*

ex•tro•ver•sion [,ɛkstrə'vɜrʒən] *or* [-'vɜrʃən] *n.* **1** the tendency to be more interested in other persons and in what is going on around one than in one's thoughts and feelings. Compare INTROVERSION. **2** extrophy. Also (def. 1), **extraversion.** ⟨altered < G *Extraversion* < L *extra* outside + ML *versio* turning⟩

ex•tro•vert ['ɛkstrə,vɜrt] *n., adj.* *—n.* a person more interested in other persons and in what is going on around him or her than in his or her thoughts and feelings; a person who is active and talkative rather than thoughtful. Compare INTROVERT.
—adj. characterized by extroversion. Also, **extravert.** ⟨< *extro-* outside (var. of *extra-*) + L *vertere* turn⟩

ex•tro•vert•ed ['ɛkstrə,vɜrtɪd] *adj.* extrovert.

ex•trude [ɛk'strud] *v.* **-trud•ed, -trud•ing. 1** squeeze, force, or push out. **2** shape (metal, plastic, etc.) by forcing through a die. **3** protrude; project. ⟨< L *extrudere* < *ex-* out + *trudere* thrust⟩

ex•tru•sion [ɛk'struʒən] *n.* **1** the act or process of extruding. **2** something produced by this process: *plastic extrusions.* **3** a being extruded. **4** an extrusive rock formation. ⟨< L *extrudere.* See EXTRUDE.⟩

ex•tru•sive [ɛk'strusɪv] *adj.* **1** tending to extrude. **2** of a rock, formed on the surface of the earth after being extruded, while molten, through the crust. Compare INTRUSIVE (def. 2).

ex•u•ber•ance [ɛg'zubərəns] *or* [ɛg'zjubərəns] *n.* **1** the fact, quality, state, or condition of being exuberant. **2** great abundance. **3** luxurious growth. **4** an instance of exuberance. Also, **exuberancy.**

ex•u•ber•ant [ɛg'zubərənt] *or* [ɛg'zjubərənt] *adj.* **1** having or showing high spirits and unrestrained joy: *She gave us an exuberant welcome.* **2** elaborate or lavish: *an exuberant use of bright colours.* **3** very abundant; overflowing: *exuberant good health.* **4** profuse in growth; luxuriant: *the exuberant vegetation of the jungle.* ⟨< L *exuberans, -antis,* ppr. of *exuberare* grow luxuriantly < *ex-* thoroughly + *uber* fertile⟩ **—ex'u•ber•ant•ly,** *adv.*

ex•u•ber•ate [ɛg'zubə,reit] *or* [ɛg'zjubə,reit] *v.* **-at•ed, -at•ing. 1** overflow. **2** display exuberance. ⟨< ME *exuberaten* < L *exuberatus,* pp. of *exuberare*⟩

ex•u•date ['ɛksjədɪt] *or* ['ɛgzjədɪt], ['ɛksjə,deit] *or* ['ɛgzjə,deit] *n.* any substance exuded.

ex•u•da•tion [,ɛksjə'deiʃən] *or* [,ɛgzjə'deiʃən] *n.* **1** an exuding. **2** something exuded, such as sweat.

ex•ude [ɛg'zud] *or* [ɛg'zjud] *v.* **-ud•ed, -ud•ing. 1** come or send out in drops; ooze: *Sweat exudes from the skin.* **2** show conspicuously or abundantly: *She exudes self-confidence.* ⟨< L *ex(s)udare* < *ex-* out + *sudare* sweat⟩

ex•ult [ɛg'zʌlt] *v.* be very glad; rejoice greatly: *The winners exulted in their victory.* ⟨< L *ex(s)ultare,* frequentative of *exsilire* leap out or up < *ex-* forth + *salire* leap⟩ **—ex'ult•ing•ly,** *adv.*

ex•ult•ant [ɛg'zʌltənt] *adj.* rejoicing greatly; exulting; triumphant: *He gave an exultant shout.* **—ex'ult•ant•ly,** *adv.*

ex•ul•ta•tion [,ɛgzʌl'teiʃən] *or* [,ɛksʌl'teiʃən] *n.* the act of exulting; great rejoicing; triumph: *There was exultation over the army's victory.* Also, **exultancy** [ɛg'zʌltənsi].

ex•urb ['ɛksɜrb] *n.* an exurban area. ⟨< *ex-*[1] out of + *(sub)urb,* coined in 1955 by A.C. Spectorsky (1910-1972), U.S. author and editor⟩

ex•ur•ban [ɛks'ɜrbən] *adj.* of, having to do with, or in a residential region or area outside the suburbs of a major city, especially one inhabited by well-to-do or wealthy people.

ex•ur•ban•ite [ɛks'ɜrbə,nəit] *adj., n.* *—adj.* working in a city but living outside it.
—n. a person who works in a city but lives outside it.

ex•urb•ia [ɛks'ɜrbiə] *n.* a small area outside a city, usually inhabited by wealthy people.

ex•u•vi•ae [ɛk'suvii] *or* [ɛg'zuvii], [ɛk'sjuvii] *or* [ɛg'zjuvii] *n.* pl. of **exuvia.** the outer covering of some creatures, such as shell or skin, that has been sloughed off. ⟨< L what is stripped off < *exuere* to strip off⟩ **—ex'u•vi•al,** *adj.*

ex•u•vi•ate [ɛk'suvi,eit], [ɛg'zuvi,eit], [ɛk'sjuvi,eit], *or* [ɛg'zjuvi,eit] *v.* **-at•ed, -at•ing.** shed (a skin, coat, shell, etc.); moult. ⟨< L *exuviae* stuffed skins⟩

–ey *adjective-forming suffix.* full of; containing; like: *clayey, skyey,* etc. ⟨var. of *-y*[1] used after -y⟩

ey•as ['aɪəs] *n.* **1** a young hawk taken from the nest for training as a falcon. **2** nestling. ⟨ME *a nyas* (mistaken as *an eyas*) < OF *niais,* literally, fresh from the nest; ult. < L *nidus* nest⟩

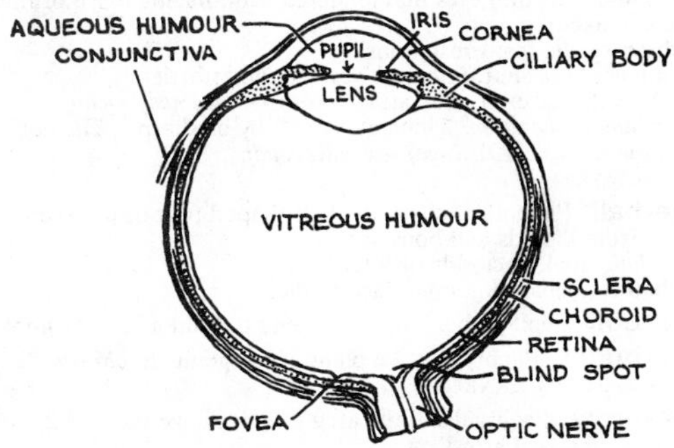

A diagram of the human eye, shown from above

eye [aɪ] *n., v.* **eyed, eye•ing** or **ey•ing.** *—n.* **1** either of the two organs of the body by which people and animals see; organ of sight. **2** the coloured part of this organ; iris: *She has brown eyes.* **3** this organ and all the visible structures on and around it, including the eyelids, eyelashes, etc.: *The blow gave him a black eye.* **4** any organ or machine that is sensitive to light. **5** Often, **eyes,** *pl.* the sense of seeing; vision; sight: *She has very good eyes.* **6** the ability to see small differences in things: *A good artist must have an eye for colour.* **7** a look; glance: *He cast an eye in her direction.* **8** a watchful look. **9** Often, **eyes,** *pl.* a way of thinking or considering; view; opinion; judgment: *She can do no wrong in his eyes. Beauty is in the eye of the beholder.* **10** something like or suggesting an eye: *the eye of a needle, the eye of a potato.* **11** the calm, clear area at the centre of a hurricane, cyclone, etc. **12** *Slang.* PRIVATE EYE; investigator; detective.
an eye for an eye, punishment or revenge as severe as the offence or injury.
be all eyes, watch eagerly and attentively: *The children were all eyes as he began to open the box.*
catch (someone's) **eye,** attract (someone's) attention: *A notice in the newspaper caught his eye.*
cry (one's) **eyes out,** *Informal.* sob tempestuously: *The little boy cried his eyes out at his mother's departure.*
eyes right or **eyes left,** a military order to turn the head to the right or to the left as a salute while marching.
feast (one's) **eyes on,** admire (something attractive or splendid): *Feast your eyes on the most beautiful mountain in Canada!*
give (someone) **the eye,** *Slang.* ogle; look at in a flirtatious manner.
have an eye for, be a sound and appreciative judge of: *She has an eye for a good painting.*
have an eye to, look out for; pay attention to.
have eyes for, *Informal.* admire; be interested in.
in a pig's eye, *Slang.* on no account; not ever.
in the eye of the wind, *Nautical.* against the direction of the wind.
in the eye(s) of, in the judgment, opinion, or view of: *In the eyes of most doctors, smoking is dangerous to health.*
in the public eye, often seen in public or often mentioned in

newspaper or magazine articles, etc.: *She is very much in the public eye since her record-breaking swim.*
keep an eye on, watch; take care of: *Keep an eye on the baby.*
keep an eye out for, be vigilant for; be wary of: *You had better keep an eye out for pickpockets in the crowd.*
keep (one's) **eyes open** (or **peeled,** or **skinned**), be attentive (to); watch (for): *Keep your eyes peeled for bargains at the flea market.*
look (someone) **in the eye,** look directly at someone's eyes.
make eyes at, look at in a flirtatious or loving way.
my eye, *Informal.* an exclamation used to express disagreement or contradiction: *Tired, my eye! She's just lazy.*
open (someone's) **eyes,** make (a person) see what is really happening: *That experience opened our eyes to what he was really like.*
run (one's) **eye(s) over,** give a cursory glance at: *She quickly ran her eyes over the report.*
see eye to eye, agree entirely; have exactly the same opinion: *They often don't see eye to eye, but they never actually fight.*
set (or **lay** or **clap**) **eyes on,** see; look at: *I knew who he was the minute I set eyes on him.*
shut (one's) **eyes to,** refuse to see or consider: *You can't shut your eyes to the problem forever.*
under the eye of, supervised by: observed by.
up to one's (or **the**) **eyes in,** inundated with; having more of than one can handle.
with an eye to, for; considering.
with one's eyes shut, *Informal.* very easily; effortlessly.
—*v.* **1** fix the gaze on; look at: *He sat there, curiously eyeing everything in the room.* **2** look at watchfully or sharply: *The dog eyed the stranger.* ⟨OE ēage⟩ **—'eye,like,** *adj.*
☛ *Hom.* AYE², I.

eye•ball ['aɪ,bɒl] *n., v.* —*n.* the ball-shaped part of the eye apart from the lids and bony socket.
—*v. Slang.* look at closely or intently.
eyeball to eyeball, *Informal.* face to face.

eye bolt a bolt with a loop at one end to hold a rope or hook.

eye•bright ['aɪ,brəit] *n.* **1** a plant of the genus *Euphrasia.* **2** SCARLET PIMPERNEL.

eye•brow ['aɪ,braʊ] *n.* **1** the arch of hair above the eye. **2** the bony ridge that it grows on.
raise an eyebrow or (one's) **eyebrows,** look surprised: *She raised her eyebrows at his outburst.*
raise eyebrows or **an eyebrow,** arouse interest or excitement; cause a mild sensation: *His outlandish get-up raised a few eyebrows, but that was all.*

eye–catch•er ['aɪ ,kætʃər] *n. Informal.* anything striking; an attraction.

eye–catch•ing ['aɪ ,kætʃɪŋ] *adj. Informal.* **1** striking; appealing. **2** conspicuous; clearly visible.

eye contact the act of looking someone in the eye, or meeting someone's gaze with one's own: *If you don't want him to notice you, don't make eye contact.*

eye•cup ['aɪ,kʌp] *n.* a small cup with a rim shaped to fit over the eye, used in washing the eyes or putting medicine in them.

eyed [aɪd] *adj., v.* —*adj.* **1** having an eye or eyes. **2** having an eye or eyes of a specific kind, colour, number, etc. (*used in compounds*): *a one-eyed pirate, a dark-eyed girl.* **3** having markings that resemble eyes, such as a peacock's tail.
—*v.* pt. and pp. of EYE.

eye dialect in some writings, the use of spellings supposed to represent a dialect.

eye•drop•per ['aɪ,drɒpər] *n.* DROPPER (def. 2).

eye•ful ['aɪfʊl] *n.* **1** as much as the eye can see at one time. **2** *Informal.* a good look. **3** *Slang.* a person who is unusually good-looking. **4** an amount of some substance, as drops, applied to the eye.

eye•glass ['aɪ,glæs] *n.* **1** a lens for aiding or correcting vision, especially a monocle. **2** eyecup. **3** eyepiece. **4 eyeglasses,** *pl.* a pair of glass or plastic lenses held in a frame and worn in front of the eyes to aid or correct vision; spectacles.

eye•hole ['aɪ,houl] *n.* **1** the bony socket for the eyeball. **2** a hole to look through. **3** a round opening for a pin, hook, rope, etc. to go through.

eye•lash ['aɪ,læʃ] *n.* **1** one of the hairs on the edge of the eyelid or below the eye. **2** one row or fringe of such hairs.
by an eyelash, by a narrow margin; by very little.

eye•less ['aɪlɪs] *adj.* blind or without eyes.

eye•let ['aɪlɪt] *n., v.* —*n.* **1** a small eye. **2** a small, round hole for a lace or cord to go through. **3** a metal ring that is set around such a hole to strengthen it; grommet. **4** a small, round hole edged with fine stitches, used as a decorative pattern in embroidery. **5** cloth having an allover pattern of such eyelets. **6** a hole to look through.
—*v.* make an eyelet in. ⟨< OF *œillet,* dim. of *œil* eye < L *oculus;* influenced by E *eye* and *-let*⟩
☛ *Hom.* ISLET.

eye•lid ['aɪ,lɪd] *n.* the movable fold of skin over the eye.

eye•lin•er ['aɪ,laɪnər] *n.* a coloured cosmetic applied as a fine line on the eyelids along the base of the lashes to emphasize the contour of the eyes.

eye–o•pen•er ['aɪ ,oupənər] *n.* **1** a happening or discovery that comes as a revelation: *Her behaviour during the trial was an eye-opener; I had no idea she could be so cool-headed.* **2** a drink of liquor taken early in the day.

eye–o•pen•ing ['aɪ ,oupənɪŋ] *adj.* enlightening or revealing: *an eye-opening experience.*

eye•piece ['aɪ,pis] *n.* the lens or set of lenses nearest to the eye of the user in a telescope, microscope, etc. See MICROSCOPE and TELESCOPE for pictures.

eye rhyme the final words of lines of verse that appear to rhyme because of their similar spelling, but have different pronunciations. The words *cough, tough,* and *though* are eye rhymes.

eye•shade ['aɪ,ʃeid] *n.* **1** a visor to shield the eyes in bright light. **2** EYE SHADOW.

eye shadow a cosmetic in any of various colours applied to the eyelids to accent the eye.

eye•shot ['aɪ,ʃɒt] *n.* the range of vision.

eye•sight ['aɪ,səit] *n.* **1** the power of seeing; sight. **2** the range of vision; view.

eye socket the bony cavity in which the eyeball is set.

eye•sore ['aɪ,sɔr] *n.* something unpleasant to look at: *An untidy garbage heap is an eyesore.*

eye splice a loop made at the end of a rope by turning it back and splicing it with the main piece of rope.

eye•spot ['aɪ,spɒt] *n.* **1** the simplest kind of organ for seeing, found in many invertebrates, consisting of a spot of pigment that is sensitive to light. **2** a spot resembling an eye, as in a peacock's tail.

eye•stalk ['aɪ,stɒk] *n. Zoology.* the stalk or peduncle upon which the eye is borne in lobsters, shrimp, etc.

eye•strain ['aɪ,strein] *n.* a tired or weak condition of the muscles of the eye caused by overuse or by an uncorrected defect, such as shortsightedness.

eye•tooth ['aɪ,tuθ] *n., pl.* **-teeth.** either of the two pointed, upper teeth between the incisors and the bicuspids; upper canine tooth.
give (one's) **eyeteeth for,** *Informal.* go to great lengths to get or achieve: *I'd give my eyeteeth for a piano like that.*

eye•wash ['aɪ,wɒʃ] *n.* **1** a liquid preparation to clean or heal the eyes. **2** *Slang.* deceiving flattery. **3** *Slang.* nonsense.

eye•wit•ness ['aɪ,wɪtnɪs] *n.* a person who actually sees or has seen some act or happening, and thus can give testimony concerning it.

eyre [ɛr] *Law.* formerly, in England, a session of the court held in different counties. ⟨< ME and Anglo-F *eire* < OF *erre* < *errer* to travel⟩
☛ *Hom.* AIR, E'ER, ERE, ERR, HEIR.

ey•rie ['iri], ['ɛri], *or* ['aɪri] *n., pl.* **-ries. 1** the nest of an eagle or other bird of prey high on a mountain or cliff. **2** a house, castle, etc. built in a high place. Also, **aerie.** ⟨< Med.L *aeria* < OF *aire* air < L *ager* field; different spellings influenced by L *aer* air and ME *ey* egg⟩
☛ *Hom.* EERIE ['iri].

ey•rir ['eirir] *n., pl.* **au•rar** ['aʊrɑr] a unit of money in Iceland, equal to 1/100 of a krona. ⟨< ON, prob. < L *aureus* a gold coin⟩

F f *F f*

f or F [ɛf] *n., pl.* **f's** or **F's.** **1** the sixth letter of the English alphabet. **2** any speech sound represented by this letter. **3** a person or thing identified as *f*, especially the sixth in a series. **4** **F, a** a grade rating a person's work or performance as too poor to be accepted; failing grade. **b** a person receiving such a rating. **5** *Music.* **a** the fourth tone in the scale of C major. **b** a symbol representing this tone. **c** a key, string, etc. that produces this tone. **d** the scale or key that has F as its keynote. **6** something shaped like the letter F. **7** any device, such as a printer's type, a lever, or a key on a keyboard, that produces an f or F. **8** (*adjl.*) of or being an F or f.

f. **1** female; feminine. **2** forte. **3** franc. **4** *Mathematics.* function. **5** *Photography.* F NUMBER (focal length). **6** folio. **7** frequency. **8** the following page, line, etc.: *p. 83f. means page 83 and the following page.* **9** frame.

F fluorine.

F. or **F** **1** Fahrenheit. **2** French. **3** Friday. **4** February. **5** Father. **6** fine. **7** farad.

F1 *Genetics.* the first-generation offspring of a mating.

F2 *Genetics.* the second generation, produced by mating two members of the F1.

fa [fɑ] *n. Music.* **1** the fourth tone of an eight-tone major scale. **2** the tone F. See DO² for picture. ⟨See GAMUT⟩

fab [fæb] *adj. Slang.* fabulous.

fa•ba•ceous [fə'beiʃəs] *adj.* belonging to the bean family of plants. ⟨< L *fabaceus* < *faba* bean⟩

Fa•bi•an ['feibiən] *adj., n.* —*adj.* **1** using or designating a strategy of delay and avoidance of direct confrontation to wear out an opponent; cautious and circumspect. **2** of or having to do with the FABIAN SOCIETY.
—*n.* a member or supporter of the FABIAN SOCIETY. ⟨< *Fabius Maximus*, a Roman general who successfully harassed Hannibal's army without risking a battle⟩

Fa•bi•an•ism ['feibiə,nɪzəm] *n.* **1** especially in politics, the practice of using delay and avoidance of direct confrontation to wear out an opponent. **2** a moderate form of socialism; the principles and methods of the Fabian Society.

Fabian Society an English socialist society, founded in 1884, that favours the adoption of socialism by gradual reform rather than by revolution.

fa•ble ['feibəl] *n., v.* **-bled, -bling.** —*n.* **1** a story made up to teach a lesson. **2** an untrue story; falsehood. **3** a legend; myth.
—*v.* **1** tell or write (fables). **2** tell or write about in fables: *He is fabled to be one of the greatest frontiersmen of all time.* ⟨< ME < OF < L *fabula* < *fari* speak⟩
☛ *Syn.* See note at ALLEGORY.

fa•bled ['feibəld] *adj., v.* —*adj.* **1** told about in fables, legends, or myths: *the fabled Paul Bunyan.* **2** having no real existence; made up; fictitious.
—*v.* pt. and pp. of FABLE.

fab•li•au ['fæbli,ou] *n., pl.* **-aux** [-ouz]. a medieval poem, usually French or English, relating a short tale that deals with real or possible (often comic) incidents of ordinary human life. ⟨< F *fabliau*, dim. of *fable* fable⟩

fab•ric ['fæbrɪk] *n.* **1** any woven, knitted, or pressed material; cloth. Velvet, canvas, linen, felt, and flannel are fabrics. **2** the texture or quality of such material. Cloth may have a smooth or rough fabric. **3** an interwoven structure; something constructed of combined and interdependent parts; framework: *the fabric of society.* ⟨< F *fabrique* < L *fabrica* workshop. Doublet of FORGE¹.⟩

fab•ri•cate ['fæbrə,keit] *v.* **-cat•ed, -cat•ing.** **1** build; construct; manufacture. **2** make by fitting together standardized parts: *Automobiles are fabricated from parts made in different factories.* **3** make up; invent (stories, lies, excuses, etc.). **4** forge (a document). ⟨< L *fabricare* build < *fabrica* workshop⟩
—**'fab•ri,ca•tor,** *n.*

fab•ri•ca•tion [,fæbrə'keiʃən] *n.* **1** manufacture; the act of fabricating. **2** something fabricated, especially a story, lie, excuse, etc.

fab•rique [fə'brik]; *French,* [fa'bʀik] *n. Cdn.* formerly, in French Canada, a local parish body responsible for the maintenance and management of church property; vestry. ⟨< Cdn.F⟩

fab•u•list ['fæbjəlɪst] *n.* **1** a person who tells, writes, or makes up fables. **2** liar. ⟨< F *fabuliste* < L *fabula* a story⟩

fab•u•lous ['fæbjələs] *adj.* **1** not believable; amazing; exaggerated: *That antique shop charges fabulous prices.* **2** of or belonging to a fable; imaginary: *The phoenix is a fabulous bird.* **3** like a fable. **4** *Informal.* wonderful; exciting: *We had a fabulous time at the party.* ⟨< L *fabulosus* < *fabula.* See FABLE.⟩
—**'fab•u•lous•ly,** *adv.* —**'fab•u•lous•ness,** *n.*

fa•çade [fə'sɑd] *n.* **1** the front part of a building. **2** any side of a building that faces a street or other open space. **3** a front or outward part or appearance of anything, especially when thought of as concealing something: *a façade of honesty.* Also, **facade.** ⟨< F *façade* < *face.* See FACE.⟩

face [feis] *n., v.* **faced, fac•ing.** —*n.* **1** the front part of the head, from forehead to chin: *a beautiful face, a wide face.* **2** an expression or look: *His face was sad.* **3** a distortion of the face, usually expressing annoyance, disgust, etc. or meant to amuse: *He made a face and said he didn't like the coat. A little girl on the bus was making faces at people.* **4** outward appearance or aspect: *On the face of it, she seems to have a good chance to win. We have new information that puts a different face on the matter.* **5** the upper or outer surface of something: *the face of the earth.* **6** the front or main side of something: *the face of a clock, the face of a playing card.* **7** *Mathematics.* one of the plane surfaces of a solid: *A cube has six faces.* **8** *Mining.* the surface at the end of a tunnel, drift, or excavation where work is in progress. **9** *Printing.* typeface. **10** dignity, self-respect, or prestige: *To some people, loss of face is a disaster. She tried to save face by changing the subject.* **11** gall; nerve; impudence: *I didn't think she would have the face to come back after being asked to leave.*
face down (or **up**), with the face or main surface downward (or upward): *The photograph fell face down into the puddle.*
face to face, a with faces toward each other: *The skaters were lined up face to face.* **b** in person; personally: *I never expected to meet him face to face.* **c** in the actual presence (*used with* **with**): *The wounded soldier knew he was face to face with death.*
fly in the face of, oppose.
in the face of, a in the presence of: *She showed no fear in the face of danger.* **b** in spite of: *He has succeeded in the face of tremendous difficulties.*
lose face, lose dignity or prestige.
on the face of it, as it appears.
pull a long face, look unhappy or disapproving.
put a good (or **brave,** etc.) **face on,** make the best of; face cheerfully, bravely, etc.
put (one's) **face on,** *Informal.* apply makeup to one's face.
set (one's) **face against,** oppose and resist: *He has set his face against any kind of change.*
show (one's) **face,** appear; be seen.
to (someone's) **face,** boldly or impudently, in the presence of: *She repeated the gossip to the teacher's face.*
—*v.* **1** have the face turned toward: *The dancers stood facing each other. Our house faces east.* **2** turn the face toward: *He was told to face the wall.* **3** be opposite to: *Look at the picture facing page 60.* **4** meet bravely or boldly; confront: *The mayor went out to face the angry demonstrators. She has the courage to face her problems.* **5** present itself to: *Another problem now faced us. They were faced with a difficult decision.* **6** cover the surface of with a layer of different material: *a wooden house faced with brick.* **7** apply a facing to (a garment), etc. **8** smooth the surface of (stone, etc.).
face down, disconcert.
face off, *Cdn. Hockey.* put (a puck) into play by dropping it between the sticks of two players facing each other: *The referee starts a hockey game by facing off the puck at centre ice.*
face up to, meet bravely and boldly: *to face up to a difficult situation, to face up to an enemy.*
face with, present with (a problem): *They faced her with an impossible request.* ⟨< F *face* < VL *facia* < L *facies* form⟩
☛ *Syn. n.* **1. Face,** COUNTENANCE, VISAGE = the front part of the head. **Face** is the common word, but especially emphasizes the physical nature or the features: *That girl has a pretty face.* **Countenance** is formal and emphasizes the looks, especially as they show a person's thoughts, feelings, or character: *He has a cheerful countenance.* **Visage** is a literary word meaning either face or countenance, but emphasizing the general look of the face: *The people were awed by the emperor's sombre visage.*

face card a playing card that is a king, queen, or jack.

face•cloth ['feis,klɒθ] *n.* a small cloth, usually made of towelling, for washing the face or body; washcloth.

face cord a stack of firewood about 1.2 m × 2.4 m, cut in 60 cm lengths.

–faced having a specific kind of face or number of faces: *sad-faced, round-faced, two-faced, satin-faced.*

face•down ['feis,daʊn] *n.* a confrontation; a facing someone down.

face–harden ['feis ,hardən] *v.* harden the surface of metal by chilling; caseharden.

face•less ['feislɪs] *adj.* **1** without a face: *a faceless clock.* **2** anonymous; without individual character.

face•lift ['feis,lɪft] *n., v.* *–n.* **1** an operation designed to improve the appearance of a face by tightening the skin, removing wrinkles, etc. **2** *Informal.* a change in appearance or manner of operation, designed to improve or bring up to date: *The whole company needs a facelift.*
–v. give a facelift to. **–'face,lift•er,** *n.*

face–off ['feis ,ɒf] *n.* **1** *Cdn. Hockey.* the act of putting the puck into play by dropping it between the sticks of two opposing players facing each other; a facing off: *The last goal was scored from the face-off.* **2** an unfriendly disagreement; confrontation.

face•plate ['feis,pleit] *n.* **1** a perforated plate on a spindle, to which the work is fastened. **2** any of various protective platelike covers.

face powder a cosmetic powder for the face.

fac•er ['feisər] *n.* **1** one that faces. **2** a blow in the face. **3** a violent check; a sudden serious difficulty.

face–sav•ing ['feis ,seivɪŋ] *adj.* that preserves or is intended to preserve one's dignity, self-respect, etc.: *That was just a face-saving gesture.*

fac•et ['fæsɪt] *n., v.* **-et•ted** or **-et•ed, -et•ting** or **-et•ing.** *–n.* **1** any of the small, flat, polished surfaces of a cut gem. **2** the surface of any of the segments of a compound eye of an insect, etc. **3** the flat, narrow surface between the flutes of a column. **4** a view or aspect, as of a character or personality: *Selfishness was a facet of his character that we seldom saw.*
–v. cut facets on. ⟨< F *facette,* dim. of *face.* See FACE.⟩

fa•ce•ti•ae [fə'siʃi,i] *n. pl.* witty remarks or writings. ⟨< L *facetia* jest⟩

fa•ce•tious [fə'siʃəs] *adj.* **1** attempting to be humorous. **2** said in fun; not to be taken seriously. ⟨< L *facetia* jest < *facetus* witty⟩ **–fa'ce•tious•ly,** *adv.* **–fa'ce•tious•ness,** *n.*

face–to–face ['feis tə 'feis] *adj.* involving direct personal interaction: *a face-to-face interview.*

face value **1** the value stated on a bond, cheque, coin, bill, insurance policy, etc.: *He paid much more than the face value for the silver quarters in his collection.* **2** the apparent worth, intention, or meaning: *She took the compliment at face value and did not worry about any hidden meaning.*

fa•cia ['feiʃiə] *or* ['feiʃə] See FASCIA.

fa•cial ['feiʃəl] *adj., n.* *–adj.* **1** of the face: *facial features, facial expression.* **2** for the face: *a facial treatment, facial tissue.*
–n. Informal. a massage or cosmetic treatment of the face. **–'fa•cial•ly,** *adv.*

facial angle the angle formed by two intersecting lines, one from the base of the nose to the forehead, the other from the base of the nose to the ear.

facial index the ratio of the length of the face to its breadth.

–fac•i•ent *suffix.* that causes something: *febrifacient,* causing fever. ⟨< L⟩

fa•ci•es ['feiʃiz] *or* ['feisiz], ['feiʃi,iz] *or* ['feisi,iz] *n., pl.* **1** *Ecology.* the general appearance of members of a group. **2** *Medicine.* facial appearance. **3** *Geology.* the distinctive features of a rock, as its components, appearance, etc. ⟨< L *face.* See FACE.⟩

fac•ile ['fæsaɪl] *or* ['fæsəl] *adj.* **1** easily done, used, etc.: *a facile task, facile methods.* **2** moving, acting, working, etc. with ease; fluent or ready: *a facile hand, a facile tongue, a facile pen.* **3** showing little thought, effort, depth, etc.; superficial or insincere: *facile answers to complex questions, facile repentance.* **4** of easy manners or temper; agreeable; mild: *Her facile nature adapted itself to any company.* ⟨< L *facilis* easy < *facere* do⟩ **–'fac•ile•ly,** *adv.* **–'fac•ile•ness,** *n.*

fa•cil•i•tate [fə'sɪlə,teit] *v.* **-tat•ed, -tat•ing. 1** make easy; lessen the labour of; help forward; assist: *A vacuum cleaner facilitates housework.* **2** lead (a discussion); help (a meeting) to go well. ⟨< F *faciliter* < Ital. *facilitare* < L *facilis* < *facere* to do⟩ **–fa'cil•i,ta•tive,** *adj.* **–fa'cil•i,ta•tor,** *n.* **–fa,cil•i'ta•tion,** *n.*

fa•cil•i•ty [fə'sɪləti] *n., pl.* **-ties. 1** the absence of difficulty; ease: *The facility of communication is far greater now than it was a hundred years ago.* **2** the ability to do anything easily, quickly, or smoothly; fluency or skill. **3** Usually, **facilities,** *pl.* something, such as equipment, furnishings, etc., that makes an action or activity possible or easier: *The library provides facilities for studying. The school has excellent sports facilities.* **4** a building or part of one used for a special purpose: *a research facility in the biology block.* **5** *Archaic.* the quality of being mild or easygoing.

fac•ing ['feisɪŋ] *n., v.* *–n.* **1** a layer of different material covering a surface, used for protection or ornament: *The front of the courthouse has a marble facing.* **2** the material used for this layer. **3** a lining along the inside edges of the front opening, neckline, etc. of a garment, in the same or a contrasting fabric: *A facing is often meant to be turned back, as a collar or cuff.* **4** the material used for this lining. **5** **facings,** *pl.* the cuffs, collar, and trimmings of a military or military-style coat, usually in a contrasting colour.
–v. ppr. of FACE.

facsim. facsimile.

fac•sim•i•le [fæk'sɪməli] *n., v.* **-led** [-lid], **-le•ing.** *–n.* **1** an exact copy or likeness; a perfect reproduction. **2** (*adjl.*) being a facsimile: *a facsimile edition.* **3** an electronic process for transmitting printed matter and photographs by telephone and reproducing them on paper at the receiving set; fax.
in facsimile, exactly.
–v. make a facsimile of. ⟨< L *fac* (imperative) make + *simile* (neut.) like⟩

facsimile machine FAX MACHINE.

fact [fækt] *n.* **1** anything known to be true or to have really happened; something that has or had actual existence: *historical facts, the fact of gravity. It is a fact that he was there, because several people identified him. Space travel is a fact.* **2** the quality of being real; the state of things as they are or have happened; reality; truth: *The fact of the matter is, she never wanted to go. I want fact, not fantasy.* **3** something said or believed to be true or to have really happened: *Check your facts before you present your argument.* **4** an actual deed or act, especially a criminal act: *She was charged with being an accessory after the fact.* **5** *Law.* anything that is known or alleged to have occurred in connection with a case (as distinguished from a principle or rule): *A question of fact is decided by the jury, a question of law by the court.*
as a matter of fact, in fact, or **in point of fact,** in truth; actually: *He hasn't had much education; in fact, he never got past grade five.*
facts and figures, factual information: *You need facts and figures to prove your theory.* ⟨< L *factum* (thing) done, pp. neut. of *facere* do. Doublet of FEAT.⟩

☛ *Usage.* **Fact.** *The fact that* is very often a circumlocution for which *that* alone would be more direct and more acceptable stylistically: *He was quite conscious (of the fact) that his visitor had some special reason for coming.*

fact–find•ing ['fækt ,faɪndɪŋ] *n.* **1** the determination of the facts or realities of a case or situation. **2** (*adjl.*) engaged in or having the purpose of finding out facts: *a fact-finding committee, an arbitrator engaged on a fact-finding mission.* **–'fact-,find•er,** *n.*

fac•tion ['fækʃən] *n.* **1** a group of people in a political party, church, club, etc. acting together, usually in opposition to another such group or the main body: *A faction often seeks to promote only its own interests at the expense of the group as a whole.* **2** strife or quarrelling among the groups within a political party, church, club, etc. ⟨< L *factio, -onis* party, originally, a doing < *facere* do. Doublet of FASHION.⟩

fac•tion•al ['fækʃənəl] *adj.* **1** of or having to do with a faction or factions; partisan. **2** causing faction. **–'fac•tion•al•ly,** *adv.*

fac•tion•al•ism ['fækʃənə,lɪzəm] *n.* **1** a condition or situation characterized by faction: *a democracy threatened by regional, linguistic, and religious factionalism.* **2** alignment with a particular faction. **–'fac•tion•al•ist,** *n., adj.*

fac•tion•al•ize ['fækʃənə,laɪz] *v.,* **-ized, -iz•ing.** cause strife (in) through faction. **–,fac•tion•al•i'za•tion,** *n.*

fac•tious ['fækʃəs] *adj.* **1** causing strife or faction. **2** of or caused by strife or faction. ⟨< L *factiosus* < *factio.* See FACTION.⟩ **–'fac•tious•ly,** *adv.* **–'fac•tious•ness,** *n.*

fac•ti•tious [fæk'tɪʃəs] *adj.* developed by effort; not natural; artificial: *Extensive advertising can cause a factitious demand for an article.* ⟨< L *facticius* artificial < *facere* do, make. Doublet of FETISH.⟩ **–fac'ti•tious•ly,** *adv.* **–fac'ti•tious•ness,** *n.*

☛ *Usage.* **Factitious,** FICTITIOUS. Because 'artificial' is one of the ingredients of the meaning of **factitious** it is sometimes confused with **fictitious**. It helps to remember that **factitious** contrasts not with 'real', but with 'natural' or 'spontaneous'.

fac•ti•tive ['fæktətɪv] *adj. Grammar.* **1** denoting a verb that takes a direct object and an objective complement. *Examples*: They *made* him captain. They *called* him a fool. **2** of or having to do with such a verb. ⟨< NL *factitivus* < L *factitare* make or declare to be < *factare* make (frequentative) < *facere* make, do⟩ **—'fac•ti•tive•ly,** *adv.*

fact of life **1** a part of life or existence that cannot be changed or ignored, especially an unpleasant or harsh part. **2 facts of life,** *pl. Informal.* information about human sexual functions.

fac•tor ['fæktər] *n., v.* *—n.* **1** any element, condition, quality, etc. that helps to bring about a result: *Endurance is an important factor of success in sports.* **2** *Mathematics.* any of the numbers, algebraic expressions, etc. that produce a given number or quantity when multiplied together: 5, 3, *and* 4 *are factors of* 60. **3** *Cdn.* a person who acts as a representative of a company; agent: *The Hudson's Bay Company formerly employed many factors, now usually called managers, in its fur-trading posts throughout the Northland.* **4** a finance company, bank, etc. that buys the debts owing to another firm at a discount in order to make a profit by collecting them.
—v. **1** *Mathematics.* separate into factors. **2** act or enter (*into* something) as a factor.
factor in, include as a variable.
factor out, exclude or isolate as a variable. ⟨< L *factor* doer < *facere* do⟩

fac•tor•age ['fæktərɪdʒ] *n.* **1** the business of a factor or agent; buying and selling on commission. **2** a commission paid to a factor or agent.

fac•tor•i•al [fæk'tɔriəl] *n., adj.* *—n. Mathematics.* the product of a given integer and all the positive integers below it down to 1. *Example*: 4 factorial = 4 × 3 × 2 × 1 = 24 *Symbol*: *n*! or $\underline{n|}$ (where *n* is the given integer).
—adj. of or having to do with factors or factorials.

fac•tor•ize ['fæktə,raɪz] *v.* **-rized, -riz•ing.** *Mathematics.* separate into factors. **—,fac•tor•i'za•tion,** *n.*

factor of safety the ratio of maximum resistance of some object or material to the estimated maximum stress applied to it.

fac•to•ry ['fæktəri] *n., pl.* **-ries.** **1** a building or group of buildings where things are manufactured. **2** formerly, a trading post: *Moose Factory, Ontario.* ⟨< Med.L *factoria* < L *factor.* See FACTOR.⟩

fac•to•tum [fæk'toutəm] *n.* a person employed to do all kinds of work. ⟨< Med.L < L *fac* (imperative) do + *totum* the whole⟩

fac•tu•al ['fæktʃuəl] *adj.* of, containing, or consisting of fact or facts: *The newspaper simply gave a factual report on the fire, without speculating on possible causes.* **—'fac•tu•al•ly,** *adv.* **—'fac•tu•al•ness,** *n.*

fac•tu•a•lism ['fæktʃuə,lɪzəm] *n.* the theory that only factual information is of value; dependence on the factual. **—'fac•tu•al•ist,** *n.*

fact•u•al•i•ty [,fæktʃu'æləti] *n.* the condition or quality of being a fact.

fac•ture ['fæktʃər] *n.* **1** the process of manufacturing. **2** the thing manufactured. **3** the manner or quality of production ⟨< L *factura* a making⟩

fac•u•la ['fækjələ] *n., pl.* **faculae** [-,li] *or* [-,laɪ]. a very bright spot on the surface of the sun. ⟨< L dim. of *fax* torch⟩

fa•cul•ta•tive ['fækəltətɪv] *or* ['fækəl,teitɪv] *adj.* **1** giving permission. **2** optional. **3** of an animal or plant, able to survive in several modes or environments. **4** contingent; possible; not certain to happen. ⟨< F *facultatif* < L *facultas* < *facilis* < *facere* to do⟩

fac•ul•ty ['fækəlti] *n., pl.* **-ties.** **1** a power of the mind or body: *the faculty of hearing, the faculty of memory. She is over ninety years old, but she still has all her faculties.* **2** the power to do some special thing, especially a power of the mind: *Stephanie has a remarkable faculty for arithmetic.* **3** the teaching staff of a university or college. **4** a department of learning in a university: *the faculty of theology, the faculty of law.* **5** the members of a profession: *The medical faculty is made up of physicians, surgeons, etc.* ⟨< L *facultas* < *facilis.* See FACILE.⟩

fad [fæd] *n.* something everybody is very much interested in for a short time; a craze; rage: *Crossword puzzles became a fad several years ago.* ⟨origin uncertain⟩ **—'fad•dy,** *adj.*

fad•dish ['fædɪʃ] *adj.* **1** inclined to follow fads. **2** like a fad. **—'fad•dish•ly,** *adv.* **—'fad•dish•ness,** *n.*

fad•dism ['fædɪzəm] *n.* the following of fads or temporary fashions.

fad•dist ['fædɪst] *n.* a person devoted to a fad or one who readily takes up fads.

fade [feid] *v.* **fad•ed, fad•ing.** **1** lose colour or brightness: *The bedroom curtains have faded a lot.* **2** lose freshness or strength; wither: *Most of the garden flowers had faded by September.* **3** die away; disappear: *The sound of the train faded in the distance. The television picture is fading.* **4** cause to fade: *Sunlight will fade the colours in some fabrics.* **5** *Slang.* make a bet against (the dicer or thrower). **6** of brakes, diminish in power. **7** of a ball, diverge from its course.
fade in, of a screen image or electronic signal, slowly become more distinct or louder.
fade out, of a screen image or electronic signal, slowly become less distinct or quieter. ⟨ME < OF *fader* < *fade* pale, weak < VL *fatidus* < L *fatuus* silly, tasteless; influenced by L *sapidus* (cf. OF *sade*) tasty⟩
☛ *Syn.* **3.** See note at DISAPPEAR.

fade–in ['feid ,ɪn] *n.* in film, radio, or television, a gradual increase in brightness, distinctness, or sound.

fade•less ['feidlɪs] *adj.* not fading; permanent.

fade–out ['feid ,ʌut] *n.* **1** in film, radio, or television, a gradual decrease in brightness, distinctness, or sound. **2** a gradual disappearance.

fa•do ['fɑdu] *n.* in Portugal, a melancholy popular song or dance, usually with guitar accompaniment. ⟨< Pg. literally, fate < L *fatum*⟩

fae•cal ['fikəl] See FECAL.

fae•ces ['fisiz] See FECES.

fa•er•ie ['feiəri] *or* ['fɛri] *n., pl.* **-ies;** *adj. Archaic.*
—n. **1** fairyland. **2** fairy.
—adj. fairy. Also, **faery.** ⟨var. of *fairy*⟩
☛ *Hom.* FAIRY, FERRY ['fɛri].

Faer•oe Islands ['fɛrou] a group of islands in the N Atlantic, belonging to Denmark.

Faer•o•ese [,fɛrou'iz] *n., adj.* *—n.* a native of the Faeroe Islands. *—adj.* the North Germanic language spoken there.

fa•er•y ['feiəri] *or* ['fɛri] See FAERIE.

fag[1] [fæg] *v.* **fagged, fag•ging;** *n. Esp. Brit.* *—v.* **1** work hard or until wearied: *Tom fagged away at his mathematics.* **2** tire by work: *The horse was fagged.*
fagged out, *Informal.* tired out; exhausted.
—n. **1** a hard, uninteresting job; drudgery. **2** a person who does hard work; drudge. ⟨origin uncertain⟩

fag[2] [fæg] *n. Esp. Brit. Slang.* cigarette. ⟨origin uncertain⟩

fag end **1** the last and poorest part of anything; remnant. **2** the coarse, unfinished end of a piece of cloth. **3** an untwisted end of rope.

fag•got or **fag•ot** ['fægət] *n., v.* *—n.* **1** a bundle of sticks or twigs tied together: *She built the fire with faggots.* **2** a bundle of iron rods or pieces of iron or steel to be welded.
—v. **1** tie or fasten together into bundles; make into a faggot. **2** ornament with faggoting. ⟨< OF⟩

fag•got•ing or **fag•ot•ing** ['fægətɪŋ] *n.* **1** a style of embroidery in which a group of crosswise threads is pulled out of a fabric and the lengthwise threads thus exposed are tied together in groups resembling faggots. **2** a decorative openwork method of joining two finished edges. See EMBROIDERY for picture.

fag•ot ['fægət] See FAGGOT.

fag•ot•ing ['fægətɪŋ] See FAGGOTING.

Fahr. Fahrenheit.

Fahr•en•heit ['fɛrən,həit] *or* ['fɛrən,həit] *adj.* of, based on, or according to a scale for measuring temperature, on which 32 degrees marks the freezing point of water and 212 degrees the boiling point. *Abbrev.*: F., F, or Fahr. See THERMOMETER for picture. ⟨< Gabriel Daniel *Fahrenheit* (1686-1736), the German physicist who introduced this scale⟩

fai•ence [faɪ'ɒns]; *French,* [fa'jɑ̃s] *n.* a glazed earthenware or porcelain, usually of fine quality. ⟨< F; said to be named after and to have been invented in *Faenza,* Italy, in 1299⟩

fail [feil] *v., n.* *—v.* **1** not succeed; fall short of success: *She tried hard, but failed.* **2** be unsuccessful in (an examination, course of study, etc.); receive a mark of failure (in): *She failed her first year.* **3** give a mark of failure to: *The teacher failed a third of the class.* **4** fall far short of what is wanted or expected; come to nothing: *to fail in one's duty. The project failed. The crops failed again this*

year. **5** decrease to the point of not being enough; run out: *A rescue party found them just before their supplies failed.* **6** not remember or choose (to do); neglect: *He failed to follow our advice.* **7** not be able (*to*): *I fail to understand why she didn't even show up.* **8** be of no use to, when needed: *Words failed her and she could think of nothing to say. His friends failed him when he was in trouble.* **9** stop performing or operating: *We were still far from home when the engine failed.* **10** lose strength; become weak or weaker: *The sick man's heart was failing.* **11** not make enough profit to stay in business; go bankrupt: *That company will fail.*
—n. Archaic (*except in* **without fail**). failure.
without fail, without failing to do, happen, etc.; surely; certainly. ⟨ME < OF *faillir,* ult. < L *fallere* deceive⟩ **—'fail•er,** *n.*
☛ *Hom.* FAILLE.

fail•ing ['feilɪŋ] *n., prep., adj., v.* *—n.* **1** failure. **2** a fault; weakness; defect.
—prep. in the absence of; in default of; lacking: *Failing good weather, the party will be held indoors.*
—adj. of failure; indicating failure: *a failing grade.*
—v. ppr. of FAIL.
☛ *Syn. n.* **2.** See note at FAULT.

faille [faɪl] *or* [feil]; *French,* [faj] *n.* a soft, ribbed cloth of silk, rayon, acetate, etc. ⟨< F < MDu. *falie* scarf⟩
☛ *Hom.* FAIL [feil], FILE [faɪl].

fail–safe ['feil ˌseif] *adj.* **1** of a mechanism or system, incorporating an element that enables it to return automatically to a safe condition in the event of a breakdown or malfunction. **2** proof against failure: *I have a fail-safe recipe for banana bread.*

fail•ure ['feiljər] *n.* **1** a falling short of success; lack of success. **2** the fact of not being successful in an examination, course, etc. **3** a not doing; neglecting. **4** a falling short of what is wanted or expected: *the failure of crops.* **5** a loss of strength; becoming weak; dying away. **6** the fact or condition of not making enough profit to stay in business; becoming bankrupt: *the failure of a company.* **7** the malfunction or breakdown of a device, machine, etc. **8** a person or thing that has failed: *The picnic was a failure because it rained.*

fain [fein] *adj., adv. Archaic.* *—adj.* willing; eager; ready.
—adv. readily; willingly; eagerly: *I would fain go with you.* ⟨ME < OE *faegen*⟩
☛ *Hom.* FANE, FEIGN.

fai•né•ant ['feiniənt]; *French,* [fɛne'ɑ̃] *n., adj.* *—n.* an idler.
—adj. lazy. ⟨< OF *faignant* idler, ppr. of *faindre* shirk, altered by folk etymology as though < *fai(t)* does + *néant* nothing⟩

faint [feint] *adj., n., v.* *—adj.* **1** not clear or plain; dim: *a faint idea, faint colours. We could see a faint outline of trees through the fog.* **2** weak; exhausted; feeble: *a faint voice.* **3** done feebly or without zest: *a faint attempt.* **4** ready to faint; about to faint: *I feel faint.* **5** lacking courage; cowardly: *Faint heart ne'er won fair lady.* **6** remote: *a faint chance.*
—n. **1** a condition in which a person is unconscious for a short time, caused by an insufficient flow of blood to the brain: *He fell to the floor in a faint.* **2 faints,** *pl.* impure spirits in the first and last stages of distillation.
—v. **1** lose consciousness temporarily. **2** *Archaic.* grow weak; lose courage: *"Ye shall reap, if ye faint not."* ⟨ME < OF *faint, feint,* pp. of *faindre, feindre.* See FEIGN.⟩ **—'faint•ly,** *adv.* **—'faint•ness,** *n.*
☛ *Hom.* FEINT.

faint•heart ['feintˌhɑrt] *n. Archaic or poetic.* a faint-hearted person.

faint–heart•ed ['feint 'hɑrtɪd] *adj.* lacking courage; cowardly; timid. **—'faint-'heart•ed•ly,** *adv.* **—'faint-'heart•ed•ness,** *n.*

fair[1] [fɛr] *adj., adv., n., v.* *—adj.* **1** not favouring one more than the other or others; just; honest: *a fair judge.* **2** according to the rules: *fair play.* **3** pretty good; not bad; average: *She has a fair understanding of the subject. There is only a fair crop of wheat this year.* **4** favourable; likely; promising: *She seems a fair candidate for success.* **5** not dark; blond: *fair hair, a fair complexion.* **6** not cloudy or stormy; clear; sunny: *The weather will be fair today.* **7** pleasing to the eye or mind; beautiful: *a fair lady. He spoke fair words.* **8** of good size or amount; ample: *They own a fair piece of property.* **9** clean or pure; without blemishes or errors; correct: *fair water, a fair copy.* **10** easily read; plain: *fair handwriting.* **11** favourable; helpful, especially to a ship's course: *We had fair winds all the way.* **12** seeming good at first, but not really so: *His fair promises proved false.* **13** clear; unobstructed: *fair passage.*
fair and square, *Informal.* **a** just; honest. **b** justly; honestly.
fair enough, an expression of agreement.
fair to middling, moderately good; average.
in a fair way, likely: *She's in a fair way to be chosen as the valedictorian.*
no fair, *Informal.* unfair (often used by children as an interjection).
—adv. **1** in an honest, straightforward manner; honestly: *fair-spoken, to play fair.* **2** directly; straight: *The stone hit him fair on the head.*
bid fair, seem likely; have a good chance.
—n. Archaic. a woman, especially a sweetheart. ⟨OE *fæger*⟩ **—'fair•ness,** *n.*
—v. smooth the surface of; streamline.
☛ *Hom.* FARE.
☛ *Syn. adj.* **1. Fair,** JUST, IMPARTIAL = not showing favour in making judgments. **Fair** emphasizes putting all on an equal footing: *He is fair even to people he dislikes.* **Just** emphasizes paying attention only to what is right or lawful: *Our teacher is always just in her grading.* **Impartial** emphasizes complete absence of favour or feeling for or against either side: *We need someone impartial to settle this quarrel.*

fair[2] [fɛr] *n.* **1** a gathering of people for the purpose of showing goods, products, etc., often with entertainment or a midway; exhibition: *the Royal Winter Fair. At the county fair last year, prizes were given for the best farm products and livestock.* **2** a gathering of people to buy and sell, often held in a certain place at regular times during the year: *a trade fair.* **3** an entertainment and sale of articles; bazaar: *Our club held a fair to raise money.* ⟨ME < OF *feire* < LL *feria* holiday⟩
☛ *Hom.* FARE.

fair ball *Baseball.* a batted ball that is not a foul.

fair game **1** animals or birds that it is lawful to hunt. **2** a person or thing that is considered a suitable or legitimate object of pursuit or attack: *He was fair game for political cartoonists because of his odd mannerisms.*

fair•ground ['fɛrˌgraʊnd] *n.* an outdoor space, usually having equipment for exhibitions and entertainment, where fairs are held.

fair–haired ['fɛr 'hɛrd] *adj.* having light-coloured hair.

fair–haired boy *Informal.* a favourite.

fair•ing ['fɛrɪŋ] *n.* a structure fitted around a part of an aircraft, spacecraft, motor vehicle, etc. to make a smooth outline and thus reduce drag: *landing gear fairings, a motorcycle fairing.*

fair•ish ['fɛrɪʃ] *adj.* fairly good, well, or large.

Fair Isle **1** a small island of the Shetlands, noted for its knitting industry. **2** (*adjl.*) of a style of knitting characterized by broad bands of coloured wools: *a Fair Isle sweater.* **3** a garment knitted in coloured wools, often in bands.

fair•lead ['fɛrˌlid] *n.* a pulley to help with the rigging of a ship.

fair•ly ['fɛrli] *adv.* **1** in a fair manner; justly; honestly. **2** to a fair degree; rather; somewhat: *The pay was fairly good.* **3** actually or really: *He fairly beamed when he saw his picture in the paper.* **4** clearly.

fair–mind•ed ['fɛr ˌmaɪndɪd] *adj.* not prejudiced; just; impartial. **—'fair,mind•ed•ly,** *adv.* **—'fair,mind•ed•ness,** *n.*

fair play **1** an abiding by the rules of a game; fair dealings in any contest. **2** just and equal treatment of all.

fair sex women, collectively.

fair shake *Esp. U.S. Informal.* an honest arrangement; fair treatment.

fair–spo•ken ['fɛr 'spoukən] *adj.* speaking smoothly and pleasantly; civil; courteous.

fair•way ['fɛrˌwei] *n.* **1** an unobstructed passage or way. The fairway in a harbour is the channel for ships. **2** the part in a golf course where the grass is kept short, between the tee and the putting green.

fair–weath•er ['fɛr 'wɛðər] *adj.* **1** of or fitted for fair weather. **2** weakening or failing in time of need: *He is only a fair-weather friend.*

fair•y ['fɛri] *n., pl.* **fair•ies;** *adj.* *—n.* a supernatural being of folklore and mythology having magical powers and able to help or harm human beings. In recent legend, fairies have been pictured as very small, and sometimes very lovely and delicate. In medieval story, however, fairies were often of full human size.
—adj. **1** of fairies. **2** like a fairy; lovely; delicate: *wings of fairy gossamer.* ⟨ME < OF *faerie* < *fae.* See FAY[1].⟩ **—'fair•y,like,** *adj.*
☛ *Hom.* FAERIE, FERRY.

fair•y•land ['fɛriˌlænd] *n.* **1** the imaginary place where the fairies live. **2** any charming and pleasant place.

fairy ring a ring of mushrooms and darker grass, etc. growing around the edge of a body of underground fungi. It used to be thought that fairy rings were made by fairies dancing.

fairy shoe or **slipper** *Cdn.* a pink orchid (*Calypso bulbosa*).

fairy shrimp a freshwater shrimp of the order Anostraca.

fairy tale **1** a story about fairies or other beings with magic powers. **2** an untrue story, especially one intended to deceive; lie. **—'fair•y-ˌtale,** *adj.*

fait ac•com•pli ['fɛt əkɒm'pli]; *French,* [fɛtakɔ̃'pli] something done and so no longer worth opposing. ⟨< F⟩

faith [feiθ] *n., interj. —n.* **1** a believing without proof; trust. **2** belief in God, religion, or spiritual things. **3** what is believed. **4** a particular religion: *people of many different faiths.*
bad faith, dishonesty or insincerity.
break faith, fail to keep one's word or promise; be treacherous.
good faith, honesty; sincerity: *Although the boys had done the wrong thing, they had acted in good faith.*
in faith, truly; indeed.
keep faith, keep one's promise; be loyal or faithful.
keep the faith, be true to one's principles; uphold a particular order or organization; work for a cause.
—interj. Archaic. truly; indeed. ⟨ME < OF *feid* < L *fides.* Doublet of FAY[2].⟩
☛ *Syn. n.* See note at BELIEF.

faith•ful ['feiθfəl] *adj., n. —adj.* **1** worthy of trust; doing one's duty; keeping one's promise; loyal; constant: *a faithful friend, a faithful servant.* **2** true; accurate; conscientious: *The witness gave a faithful account of what happened.* **3** full of faith.
—n. **the faithful, a** true believers. **b** loyal followers or supporters. **—'faith•ful•ly,** *adv.* **—'faith•ful•ness,** *n.*
☛ *Syn. adj.* **1. Faithful,** LOYAL, CONSTANT = true to a person or thing. **Faithful** emphasizes being true to a person, group, belief, duty, or trust to which one is bound by a promise, pledge, honour, or love: *She is a faithful friend.* **Loyal** adds to **faithful** the idea of wanting to stand by and fight for the person or thing, even against heavy odds: *She was loyal during his trial.* **Constant** emphasizes steadfast devotion to friends or loved ones: *One could not find a more constant friend.*

faith healing supernatural healing by touch alone or a passage of hands, based on faith in God working through the healer. **—faith healer.**

faith•less ['feiθlɪs] *adj.* **1** unworthy of trust; failing in one's duty; breaking one's promise; not loyal: *A traitor is faithless.* **2** not reliable. **3** without faith; unbelieving. **—'faith•less•ly,** *adv.* **—'faith•less•ness,** *n.*

fake[1] [feik] *v.* **faked, fak•ing;** *n., adj. —v.* **1** make to seem satisfactory; falsify; counterfeit: *The picture was faked by pasting together two photographs.* **2** intentionally give a false appearance of; simulate: *to fake an illness.* **3** pretend; give a false appearance: *She's not really surprised, she's only faking.* **4** improvise; contrive plausible behaviour or response: *She got through the exam by faking.*
fake it, bluff; put on a false appearance; improvise: *If you don't know the words to the song, just fake it.*
fake (someone) **out,** *Informal.* get the better of (someone) by some act of deception.
—n. a fraud; deception: *The beggar's limp was a fake.*
—adj. **1** intended to deceive; false: *a fake testimonial.* **2** imitation; simulated: *fake diamonds.* ⟨origin uncertain⟩ **—'fak•er,** *n.*

fake[2] [feik] *v.,* **faked, fak•ing,** *n. —v.* coil (a rope) to run freely. *—n.* a coil of such rope.

fak•er•y ['feikəri] *n.* fraud or deceit.

fa•kir ['feikər] *or* [fə'kir] *n.* **1** a Muslim holy man who lives by begging, such as a dervish. **2** a Hindu ascetic, such as a yogi. **3** any Muslim or Hindu travelling beggar who does tricks to get donations. ⟨< Arabic *faqir* poor⟩

fa–la ['fɑ 'lɑ] *n.* a refrain in some old songs.

fa•la•fel [fə'lɑfəl] *n.* a Middle Eastern dish of seasoned, fried chick peas and other vegetables, stuffed into the pocket of a pita. ⟨< Arabic *falafil*⟩

Fa•lange ['fælændʒ] *or* [fə'lændʒ]; *Spanish,* [fa'laŋxe] *n.* the Fascist party of Spain. ⟨< Sp. < L *phalanx* phalanx < Gk.⟩

Fa•lan•gist [fə'lændʒɪst] *n.* a member of the Falange.

fal•cate ['fælkeit] *adj.* curved like a sickle; hooked. ⟨< L *falcatus* < *falx, falcis* sickle⟩

fal•chion ['fɒltʃən] *or* ['fɒlʃən] *n.* **1** a medieval sword having a broad, short blade with an edge that curves to a point. **2** *Poetic.* any sword. See SWORD for picture. ⟨ME < OF Ital. *falcione,* ult. < L *falx, falcis* sickle⟩

fal•ci•form ['fælsɪˌfɔrm] *adj.* falcate; sickle-shaped. ⟨< L *falx, falcis* sickle + E *form*⟩

fal•con ['fɒlkən], ['fælkən], *or* ['fɒkən] *n.* **1** any of a family (Falconidae) of birds of prey that are active during the day; especially, any of the genus *Falco,* including the peregrine falcon, gyrfalcon, and North American sparrow hawk, having long, pointed wings and a strong, hooked bill with a toothlike projection on the side of the upper part. **2** any of various falcons or hawks trained for use in falconry, especially a female peregrine. Compare TERCEL. **3** a small cannon used in the 15th century. ⟨ME < OF < LL *falco, -onis* for L *falx, falcis* sickle; from the hooked talons⟩

fal•con•er ['fɒlkənər], ['fælkənər], *or* ['fɒkənər] *n.* **1** a person who hunts with falcons. **2** a breeder and trainer of falcons.

fal•con•et [ˌfɒlkə'nɛt], [ˌfælkə'nɛt], *or* [ˌfɒkə'net] *n.* **1** a small Asian falcon. **2** a small, light cannon of the 15th to 17th centuries, smaller than a FALCON (def. 3).

fal•con–gen•tle ['fɒlkən 'dʒɛntəl], ['fælkən-], *or* ['fɒkən-] *n.* the female of the peregrine falcon.

fal•con•ry ['fɒlkənri], ['fælkənri], *or* ['fɒkənri] *n.* **1** the sport of hunting with falcons. **2** the training of falcons to hunt.

fal•de•ral ['fɒldəˌrɒl] *n.* **1** a flimsy thing, a trifle. **2** nonsense; rubbish. **3** a meaningless refrain in songs. Also, **falderol, folderol.** ⟨< origin uncertain; probably nonsense syllables⟩

fald•stool ['fɒldˌstul] *n.* **1** a folding chair used by a bishop away from his or her own church. **2** a desk for the singing or reading of the Litany. ⟨< OE *fealdestol* folding chair⟩

Falk•land Islands ['fɒklənd] *or* ['fɒklənd] a British dependency in the S Atlantic Ocean.

fall [fɒl] *v.* **fell, fall•en, fall•ing;** *n. —v.* **1** drop or come down from a higher place: *The snow is falling fast. The leaves are falling from the trees.* **2** come down suddenly from an erect position: *He fell on his knees.* **3** hang down: *Her curls fell upon her shoulders.* **4** droop; be depressed: *His spirits fell when he heard they weren't going.* **5** yield to temptation: *He was tempted and fell.* **6** lose position, power, dignity, etc.: *The dictator fell from the people's favour.* **7** be captured, overthrown, or destroyed: *The fort fell to the enemy.* **8** drop wounded or dead; especially, be killed in battle: *The plaque carried the names of those who fell in the last war.* **9** pass into a certain condition; become: *She fell asleep. The rent falls due on Monday. She has fallen in love again.* **10** come; arrive: *When night falls, the stars appear.* **11** come by or as if by chance or lot: *Our choice fell on her. My birthday falls on a Sunday this year.* **12** pass by inheritance: *The money fell to the only daughter.* **13** be placed: *The primary stress of* farmer *falls on the first syllable.* **14** become lower or less: *Prices fell sharply. The water in the river has fallen 80 cm. Her voice fell.* **15** be naturally divided: *The story falls into five parts.* **16** look sad or disappointed: *His face fell at the bad news.* **17** slope downward: *The land falls gradually to the beach.* **18** be directed: *The light falls on my book.* **19** *Logging.* cut down; fell. **20** be spoken unintentionally: *The bad news fell from her lips.*
fall across or **among,** come upon or among by chance; meet with.
fall (all) over oneself, be too eager (to help, please, etc.).
fall apart, crumble; break down; disintegrate.
fall away, a withdraw support or allegiance. **b** become bad or worse. **c** be overthrown or destroyed. **d** become thin.
fall back, retreat; go toward the rear: *The soldiers fell back to a stronger position.*
fall back on, a go back to for safety. **b** turn to for help or support: *He knew he could fall back on his father.*
fall behind, a fail to keep up; drop back: *Before the race was half over, the slow runners had fallen a lap behind.* **b** be in arrears in paying.
fall down, fail: *Our plans could fall down if we're not careful.*
fall down on, *Informal.* prove a failure at through neglect or lack of effort.
fall flat, fail completely; have no effect or interest: *The poor performance fell flat.*
fall for, *Slang.* **a** be deceived by. **b** fall in love with.
fall foul (of or **upon), a** become entangled (with). **b** come into conflict (with); quarrel (with). **c** come into collision (with), as ships.
fall from grace, a *Informal.* lose favour. **b** turn aside into sin or evildoing; backslide.
fall heir to, inherit.
fall in, a collapse; cave in: *The roof fell in from the weight of the snow.* **b** *Military.* take one's place in line; line up in the correct formation. **c** join (in doing something): *As they walked along, they fell in together.*
fall in with, a meet by chance: *On our trip, we fell in with some interesting people.* **b** agree with: *They fell in with our plans.* **c** join with.
fall off, a decline; become less: *Attendance at baseball games falls off late in the season.* **b** of health, deteriorate. **c** of a boat or ship, turn to leeward.
fall on or **upon, a** attack: *Thieves fell on the man and stole his*

money. **b** come across; light on. **c** be incumbent on: *It falls on me to thank our speaker.*
fall out, a *Military.* leave one's place in line. **b** stop being friends; quarrel. **c** turn out; happen. **d** of teeth or hair, come loose or come out.
fall (or **bend**) **over backwards,** *Informal.* try very hard (to do something).
fall short (of), a fail to reach some goal or standard. **b** fail to equal: *Income fell short of expenditures.* **c** not suffice; be inadequate: *Their supplies of ammunition fell short.*
fall through, fail: *Her plans fell through.*
fall to, a begin to fight or attack: *The swordsman fell to with great enthusiasm.* **b** begin to eat: *The girls fell to as soon as they sat down.* **c** go into place; close by itself: *The lid of the chest fell to.*
fall under, a belong under; be classified as. **b** come under; be subject to: *to fall under her influence.*
—n. **1** a falling; dropping from a higher place. **2** the amount that falls: *We had a very heavy fall of snow last winter.* **3** an amount of timber felled. **4** the distance that anything falls. **5** waterfall. **6** a coming down suddenly from an erect position: *The child had a bad fall when she tripped on the step.* **7** a hanging down or way of hanging down: *the fall of her skirt.* **8** a giving in to temptation. **9** a loss of position, power, dignity, etc. **10** a capture; overthrow; destruction. **11** the proper place: *the fall of a stress.* **12** a lowering; becoming less. **13** a downward slope. **14** the season of the year between summer and winter; autumn. **15** (*adjl.*) of, having to do with, or particular to the fall season: *fall clothes, the fall semester.* **16** *Wrestling.* **a** being thrown on one's back. **b** a contest. **17 falls,** *pl.* **a** a waterfall; cataract; cascade. **b** an apparatus used in lowering and raising a ship's boat. **18 the Fall,** in the Bible, the sin of Adam and Eve in yielding to temptation and eating the forbidden fruit, resulting in the corruption of the whole earth and the human race. **19** a long, full woman's hairpiece that hangs freely. **20** a group of woodcocks. **21** the loose end of anything that hangs free: *a fall of rope.*
fall from grace, a a coming into disfavour. **b** a turning aside into sin or wrongdoing.
ride for a fall, act so as to be in danger or get into trouble.
the fall of the cards, the way things work out by chance. ⟨OE *feallan*⟩
☛ *Usage.* **Falls** (def. 17 a) is treated as singular and as plural. We ordinarily use it with a plural verb: *The falls are almost dry in August.* On the other hand, it may be used with a singular article (*a falls*), although this is often avoided in favour of *a waterfall.* When *falls* is part of a place name, the name is used with a singular verb: *Niagara Falls is receding.*

fal•la•cious [fəˈleiʃəs] *adj.* **1** deceptive; misleading: *fallacious hopes for a lasting peace.* **2** containing or being a fallacy; logically unsound: *fallacious reasoning.* **—falˈla•cious•ly,** *adv.* **—falˈla•cious•ness,** *n.*

fal•la•cy [ˈfæləsi] *n., pl.* **-cies. 1** a false idea; mistaken belief; error: *It is a fallacy to suppose that riches always bring happiness.* **2** a mistake in reasoning; misleading or unsound argument. **3** unsoundness; falsity; delusive character. ⟨< L *fallacia* < *fallax* deceptive < *fallere* deceive⟩

fal•lal [fælˈlæl] *n.* a useless bit of finery. ⟨coined word⟩

fall•back [ˈfɒl,bæk] *n.* **1** any thing or plan kept in reserve as a backup. **2** a retreating or withdrawal.

fall•en [ˈfɒlən] *v., adj. —v.* pp. of FALL.
—adj. **1** that has dropped: *They picked up some fallen apples.* **2** on the ground; down flat: *a fallen tree.* **3** degraded. **4** overthrown; destroyed. **5** (*noml.*) **the fallen,** *pl.* all those killed in battle: *The memorial commemorates the fallen of the First World War.* **6** shrunken; decreased: *fallen cheeks.*

fall•er [ˈfɒlər] *n.* **1** *Logging.* a person whose work is to fell trees. **2** any device, such as a machine for crushing rocks, that operates by falling.

fall fair *Cdn.* a fair held in the fall in a community for the exhibiting and judging of livestock, produce, and crafts, often with horse races, dances, and other forms of entertainment.

fall•fish [ˈfɒl,fɪʃ] *n.* a minnow (*Semotilis corporalis*) found in the eastern U.S.

fall goose *Cdn.* wavey.

fall guy *Slang.* **1** the member of a comic act who is the butt of all the jokes or pranks. **2** any person left in a difficult situation, especially a scapegoat.

fal•li•bil•i•ty [,fæləˈbɪləti] *n.* a fallible quality or nature.

fal•li•ble [ˈfæləbəl] *adj.* **1** liable to be deceived or mistaken; liable to err. **2** liable to be erroneous, inaccurate, or false. ⟨< Med.L *fallibilis* < *fallere* deceive⟩ **—ˈfal•li•ble•ness,** *n.* **—ˈfal•li•bly,** *adv.*

falling–out [ˈfɒlɪŋ ˈʌut] *n., pl.* **fallings-out.** *Informal.* a quarrel.

falling sickness *Archaic.* epilepsy.

falling star meteor.

fall line 1 a line that marks the end of layers of hard rock of a plateau and the beginning of a softer rock layer of a coastal plain. Many falls and rapids mark this line. **2** the natural line of descent between two points on a ski slope.

fall•off [ˈfɒl,ɒf] *n.* a lessening or decline.

Fal•lo•pi•an tubes [fəˈloupiən] in female mammals, a pair of slender tubes through which ova from the ovaries pass to the uterus. ⟨after *Fallopius,* a 16c. Italian anatomist⟩

fall–out [ˈfɒl ,ʌut] *n.* **1** the radioactive particles or dust that fall to the earth after a nuclear explosion. **2** the falling of such particles. **3** incidental result or side effect of anything.

fal•low[1] [ˈfælou] *or, esp. in the Prairie Provinces,* [ˈfɒlou] *adj., n., v. —adj.* **1** of land, ploughed and left unseeded for a season or more: *a fallow field.* **2** not productive or active; unstimulated: *a fallow imagination.*
lie fallow, a of land, be left ploughed and unseeded. **b** remain inactive, unproductive, etc.: *bonds lying fallow in a safety deposit box.*
—n. land or ground left fallow; SUMMER FALLOW.
—v. plough and harrow (land) and leave unseeded. ⟨OE *fealga, pl.* of *fealh,* fallow land⟩
☛ *Hom.* FOLLOW [ˈfɒlou].

fal•low[2] [ˈfælou] *n. or adj.* pale yellowish brown. ⟨OE *fealu*⟩

fallow deer either of two species of small deer (*Dama dama* of S Europe and *D. mesopotamica* of SW Asia) having flattened, palmate antlers and a coat ranging in colour from pale yellow to reddish, with white or brown spots in summer.

false [fɒls] *adj.* **fals•er, fals•est;** *adv. —adj.* **1** not true; not correct; wrong: *false statements, false testimony.* **2** not truthful; lying. **3** not loyal; not faithful: *a false friend.* **4** not real or natural; artificial or simulated: *a false tooth, false diamonds.* **5** made or done so as to deceive: *The fugitive left a false trail for his pursuers. The dishonest butcher used false scales.* **6** *Music.* not true in pitch: *a false note.* **7** pretended; not genuine or sincere: *false humility, false enthusiasm.* **8** based on wrong notions; ill-founded: *false pride, a false sense of security.* **9** *Biology.* improperly called or named. The false acacia is really a locust tree. **10** not structurally essential; fitted over or in front of another part to strengthen it, disguise it, etc.: *They put in a false ceiling to hide the pipes. The store had a false front.*
—adv. in a false manner.
play false, deceive; cheat; trick; betray. ⟨< L *falsus* < *fallere* deceive⟩ **—ˈfalse•ly,** *adv.* **—ˈfalse•ness,** *n.*
☛ *Syn. adj.* **4. False,** COUNTERFEIT = of concrete things, not real or genuine. **False,** describing something made to look like the real thing, is used of synthetic or manufactured products made to resemble natural ones, and sometimes suggests being intended to deceive others: *Most false teeth really look natural.* **Counterfeit** emphasizes passing as the real thing, and always suggests being meant to deceive for a wrong or harmful purpose, or cheat: *Counterfeit money occasionally gets into circulation.*

false acacia a tree (*Robinia pseudoacacia*), also known as the black locust, naturalized in Canada and grown as an ornamental for its whitish flowers.

false alarm 1 a warning signal, such as a fire alarm, air raid siren, etc., given when no danger exists. **2** a situation that arouses some strong reaction, as of hope, fear, etc., which proves to be unjustified.

false bottom the bottom of a trunk, suitcase, drawer, etc., that forms a secret or a supplementary compartment.

false colours or **colors 1** a flag of another country, used for deception: *The raiding ship was flying false colours.* **2** false pretences.

false face a funny or ugly mask; mask.
put on a false face, assume a certain appearance or behaviour in order to deceive.

false fruit *Botany.* fruit originating elsewhere than from the ovary.

false•heart•ed [ˈfɒlsˈhɑrtəd] *adj.* deceitful; treacherous.

false•hood [ˈfɒlshʊd] *n.* **1** lack of truth or accuracy; falsity. **2** a false idea, theory, etc. **3** the practice of making false statements; lying. **4** a deliberately false statement; lie.
☛ *Syn.* **4.** See note at LIE[1].

false keel an extra keel for stability below the main keel.

false position a position in which one seems to act or is obliged to act against one's own interests or morality.

false pregnancy a condition in which a female body shows signs of pregnancy as a result of other physical or mental causes.

false ribs the ribs not attached to the breastbone. Human beings have five pairs of false ribs.

false Solomon's seal a North American wild flower (*Smilacina stellata*), having clusters of starry white flowers changing to red berries.

false step 1 a wrong step; stumble: *One false step and the climber would fall to her death.* 2 a mistake or blunder: *The police were waiting for the suspect to make a false step.*

false teeth artificial teeth used after the real teeth have been removed; dentures.

fal•set•to [fɒl'sɛtou] *n., pl.* **-tos;** *adv.* *—n.* **1** an adult male voice pitched artificially high, especially a singing voice that goes above the normal full tenor range. **2** a singer who uses falsetto. **3** (*adjl.*) of a speaking or singing voice, in falsetto: *He sang in a falsetto voice.*
—adv. in falsetto: *He sang the part falsetto.* ⟨< Ital. *falsetto*, dim. of *falso* false < L *falsus.* See FALSE.⟩

false•work ['fɒls,wɜrk] *n.* a temporary structure that supports a bridge, etc. until the main structure is completed.

fal•sies ['fɒlsiz] *n.pl. Informal.* **1** a type of padded brassiere, worn to give a full-bosomed appearance. **2** the padding itself.

fal•si•fi•ca•tion [,fɒlsəfə'keiʃən] *n.* **1** a falsifying or being falsified. **2** something that falsifies or is falsified.

fal•si•fy ['fɒlsə,faɪ] *v.* **-fied, -fy•ing. 1** make a false version or copy of; change in order to deceive; misrepresent. **2** make false statements; lie. **3** prove (something) to be false; disprove. ⟨< LL *falsificare* < L *falsificus* acting falsely < *falsus* (see FALSE) + *facere* make⟩ **—'fal•si,fi•er,** *n.* **—'fal•si,fi•able,** *adj.*

fal•si•ty ['fɒlsəti] *n., pl.* **-ties. 1** the quality or fact of being false; incorrectness: *the falsity of his smile. Education showed him the falsity of his superstitions.* **2** something false; lie. **3** untruthfulness; deceitfulness; treachery.

Fal•staff•i•an [fɒl'stæfiən] *adj.* **1** of or having to do with Falstaff, a soldier in Shakespeare's *Henry IV* and *Merry Wives of Windsor*, or his group of ragged soldiers. **2** fat, jolly, and brazen, as Falstaff was.

falt•boat ['fɒlt,bout] *n.* a collapsible canoe. ⟨< G *Faltboot* < *falten* fold + *boot* boat⟩

fal•ter ['fɒltər] *v., n.* *—v.* **1** lose courage; draw back; hesitate; waver: *The soldiers faltered for a moment as their captain fell.* **2** move unsteadily; stumble; totter. **3** speak or say in hesitating, broken words; stammer: *Greatly embarrassed, he faltered out his thanks.* **4** come forth in hesitating, broken sounds: *Her voice faltered.*
—n. **1** the act of faltering. **2** a faltering sound. ⟨ME *faltren*; cf. ON *faltrask* be burdened⟩ **—'fal•ter•er,** *n.* **—'fal•ter•ing•ly,** *adv.*
☛ *Syn. v.* **1.** See note at HESITATE.

fame [feim] *n.* **1** the condition of being very well known; having much said or written about one. **2** what is said about one; reputation. ⟨< obs. F < L *fama* < *fari* speak⟩

famed [feimd] *adj.* famous; celebrated; well-known.

fa•meuse [fə'mjuz]; *French*, [fa'møz] *n. Cdn.* SNOW APPLE. ⟨< F *fameuse*⟩

fa•mil•ial [fə'mɪljəl] *or* [fə'mɪliəl] *adj.* **1** of, having to do with, or characteristic of a family. **2** tending to occur in or be transmitted within a family: *a familial snub nose.*

fa•mil•iar [fə'mɪljər] *adj., n.* *—adj.* **1** often seen or experienced; well-known; common: *a familiar tune, a familiar face. A knife is a familiar tool.* **2** well acquainted: *She is familiar with French culture.* **3** close; personal; intimate: *familiar friends.* **4** not formal; friendly. **5** too friendly; presuming; forward: *They didn't like his familiar manner.* **6** of a tame animal, kept as a pet.
—n. **1** a close friend. **2** a spirit or demon supposed to serve a particular person. A witch is traditionally supposed to have a familiar in the shape of a black cat. **3** *Roman Catholic Church.* a person who belongs to the household of a bishop, and renders domestic, though not menial, service. **4** an officer of the Inquisition whose chief duty was to arrest the accused or suspected. ⟨ME < OF < L *familiaris* < *familia.* See FAMILY.⟩ **—fa'mil•iar•ly,** *adv.*
☛ *Syn. adj.* **3. Familiar,** INTIMATE[1], CONFIDENTIAL = personally near or close. **Familiar** suggests the free and easy relationship that comes when people are closely acquainted or have known each other a long time: *I am not familiar with my cousin.* **Intimate** suggests a close relationship that develops when people know each other and each other's thoughts and feelings very well: *They are intimate friends.* **Confidential** emphasizes the trust people place in each other, and suggests that neither will divulge the other's secrets and private affairs: *She is the manager's confidential secretary.*

fa•mil•iar•i•ty [fə,mɪl'jærəti] *or* [fə,mɪl'jɛrəti], [fə,mɪli'ærəti] *or* [fə,mɪli'ɛrəti] *n., pl.* **-ties. 1** close acquaintance. **2** a freedom of behaviour suitable only to friends; lack of formality or ceremony. **3** an instance of such behaviour: *She dislikes such familiarities as the use of her first name by people she has just met.*

fa•mil•iar•ize [fə'mɪljə,raɪz] *v.* **-ized, -iz•ing. 1** make well acquainted: *Before playing the new game, familiarize yourself with the rules.* **2** make well-known: *The publicity given to nuclear research has familiarized a whole new vocabulary.*
—fa,mil•iar•i'za•tion, *n.*

fam•i•lism ['fæmə,lɪzəm] *n. Sociology.* a social structure in which the demands of the family as a whole supersede those of the individuals in the family. **—,fam•i'lis•tic,** *adj.*

fam•i•ly ['fæməli] *n., pl.* **-lies. 1** a father, mother, and their children; a parent, his or her spouse or partner if any, and his or her child or children. **2** the children of a father and mother: *Do they have a family?* **3** one's spouse or partner and children: *She says her family doesn't want to move.* **4** a group of related people living in the same house. **5** all of a person's relatives. **6** an extended group of related people; clan. **7** *Biology.* a major category in the classification of plants and animals, more specific than the order and more general than the genus. Lions, tigers, and leopards belong to the cat family. The prairie lily, dogtooth violet, and trillium belong to the lily family. See classification chart in the Appendix. **8** *Linguistics.* a group of related languages descending from a single language. English, French, German, Hindi, Italian, and Russian are some of the languages belonging to the Indo-European family. **9** *Ecology.* a community of organisms belonging to the same species. **10** *Mathematics.* a group of curves, functions, etc., that have some property in common. **11** any group of related or similar things.
in the family way, *Informal.* pregnant. ⟨< L *familia* household < *famulus* servant⟩
☛ *Usage.* **Family,** though singular, may take a plural verb when the emphasis is on the individual members: *Her family is opposed to the marriage. The family were gathered in the living room.*

family allowance 1 an allowance paid to members of the armed forces, often to cover living expenses overseas. **2** an allowance paid by a government to parents for each of their children under a stipulated age. **3 Family Allowance,** formerly, in Canada, a fixed allowance paid by the federal government for children up to the age of 16 who are maintained by parents and guardians. It has been replaced by the income-adjusted Child Tax Benefit (or Credit). Provincial governments can vary the rates within certain limits, and a few provinces have their own program to supplement the federal one.

family circle the immediate members of a family; adults and children of a particular household.

Family Compact in Canada, the name applied to the governing class of Upper Canada before 1837, and, in particular, to the executive and legislative councils of Upper Canada.

family doctor or physician a physician in general practice, who looks after the health of everyone in a family.

family name 1 surname; last name. **2** the reputation of a family. **3** the line of descent as reckoned by a given surname: *to trace the family name.*

family planning the idea or policy of limiting the number or timing the birth of children in the family; birth control.

family room a room in a house used informally by members of the family for snacks, conversation, games, etc.

family skeleton a cause of shame that a family tries to keep secret: *They tried to ignore their family skeleton, the desertion of their grandfather to the enemy.*

family style the manner of serving of meals in residences and certain restaurants, where platters of food are passed around the table and people serve themselves.

family tree 1 a diagram showing the relationships and descent of all the members and ancestors of a family; genealogical chart. **2** all the members of a family line.

fam•ine ['fæmɪn] *n.* **1** starvation. **2** a lack of food in a place; time of starving: *Many people have died during famines in India.* **3** a very great shortage of anything: *a coal famine.* ⟨< F *famine* < *faim* hunger < L *fames*⟩

fam•ish ['fæmɪʃ] *v.* be or make extremely hungry; make or become weak from hunger.
be famished or **famishing,** *Informal.* be very hungry: *Let's eat; I'm famished.* ⟨ME *famen* famish < OF *afamer* < L *ad* (intensive) + *fames* hunger; modelled after verbs in *-ish*⟩
—'fam•ish•ment, *n.*
☛ *Syn.* See note at HUNGRY.

fa•mot•i•dine [fə'mɒtə,din] *n.* an antihistamine drug.

fa•mous ['feiməs] *adj.* very well known; noted: *a famous general.* ⟨< AF < L *famosus* < *fama.* See FAME.⟩ **—'fa•mous•ly,** *adv.*

☛ *Syn.* **Famous,** RENOWNED, NOTED = very well-known. **Famous** applies to a person, place, thing, or happening widely known to the public either during or after its lifetime or existence, usually in a good way if still living: *A great crowd of people greeted the famous cosmonaut.* **Renowned** suggests great or long-lasting fame, often great praise and honour: *Shakespeare is renowned.* **Noted** = well-known for a particular thing, but not always for something good or for a long time: *The noted gangster was deported. He was noted for his meanness.*

fam•u•lus ['fæmjələs] *n.* the servant of a magician. ⟨< L slave⟩

fan[1] [fæn] *n., v.* **fanned, fan•ning.** *—n.* **1** an instrument or device with which to stir the air in order to cool or ventilate a room, to cool one's face, or to blow dust away: *A hand fan is narrow at the bottom and opens out to be wide at the top.* **2** anything spread out like an open hand fan. **3** of machinery: **a** any of various devices consisting essentially of a series of radiating flat or curved blades attached to and revolving with a central hublike part. **b** such a device turned by a belt from the driveshaft for cooling the radiator of an automobile. **c** such a device turned by an electric motor for cooling a room. **4** a winnowing machine. **5** a vane on a windmill that maintains the sails at right angles to the wind.

A fan

—v. **1** make a current of (air) with a fan, etc. **2** direct a current of air toward with a fan, etc.: *Fan the fire to make it burn faster.* **3** drive away with a fan, etc.: *She fanned the flies from the sleeping child.* **4** stir up; arouse: *Cruel treatment fanned their dislike into hate.* **5** spread out like an open hand fan. **6** blow gently and refreshingly on; cool: *The breeze fanned their hot faces.* **7** winnow. **8** *Baseball. Slang.* strike out: *He fanned three times in one game. The pitcher fanned five batters.*
fan out, spread out like an open hand fan.
fan the air, fail to hit something with a stick, one's hand, etc.
⟨OE *fann* < L *vannus* fan for winnowing grain⟩ **—'fan,like,** *adj.* **—'fan•ner,** *n.*

fan[2] [fæn] *n. Informal.* **1** a person extremely interested in a sport, one of the performing arts, etc., especially as a spectator: *a hockey fan, a movie fan.* **2** an admirer of an actor, writer, etc. **3** an enthusiastic supporter or user of anything: *a great fan of herbal remedies.* ⟨short for *fanatic*⟩

fa•nat•ic [fə'nætɪk] *n., adj. —n.* a person who is carried away beyond reason by his or her feelings or beliefs.
—adj. fanatical. ⟨< L *fanaticus* inspired by divinity < *fanum* temple⟩

fa•nat•i•cal [fə'nætəkəl] *adj.* unreasonably enthusiastic; extremely zealous. **—fa'nat•i•cal•ly,** *adv.*

fa•nat•i•cism [fə'nætə,sɪzəm] *n.* an unreasonable enthusiasm; extreme zeal.

fan belt the belt that drives the fan to cool an automobile engine or other machine.

fan•cied ['fænsid] *adj.* imagined; imaginary.

fan•ci•er ['fænsiər] *n.* a person who is especially interested in and knowledgeable about something, especially the growing or breeding of particular kinds of plants or animals: *She's a dog fancier.*

fan•ci•ful ['fænsəfəl] *adj.* **1** marked by fancy or caprice; quaint; whimsical: *fanciful designs or decorations.* **2** influenced by fancy; indulging in fancies: *He was in a fanciful mood when he wrote this delightful story.* **3** suggested by fancy; imaginary; unreal: *She gave a fanciful account of the events.* **—'fan•ci•ful•ly,** *adv.* **—'fan•ci•ful•ness,** *n.*

fan•cy ['fænsi] *n., pl.* **-cies;** *v.* **-cied, -cy•ing;** *adj.* **-ci•er, -ci•est.** *—n.* **1** one's power to imagine; imagination, especially of a decorative, whimsical, or playful kind: *Poetic fancy has produced some great works of literature.* **2** something imagined or supposed; something unreal: *Is it just fancy, or do I hear a sound?* **3** an idea or notion: *She had a sudden fancy to go for a swim.* **4** a liking or fondness based mainly on whim: *They took a fancy to each other right away.*
—v. **1** form an idea of; imagine: *Can you fancy yourself living in that house?* **2** have an idea; suppose; guess: *I fancy she is about sixty.* **3** like or be fond of: *He fancied the idea of having a reunion.*
fancy oneself, think too highly of oneself: *That girl really fancies herself.*
—adj. **1** having or showing great technical skill and grace: *He showed us some fancy dancing.* **2** not plain or simple; decorated, ornamental, or elaborate; showy: *a fancy table setting, a fancy costume.* **3** of high quality: *These canned peaches are labelled 'fancy'.* **4** extravagant, especially of prices: *It's a nice place, but they also have fancy prices.* **5** of an animal or plant, bred for special ornamental or odd qualities that have no practical function. ⟨contraction of *fantasy*⟩ **—'fan•ci•ly,** *adv.* **—'fan•ci•ness,** *n.*

☛ *Syn. n.* **1.** See note at IMAGINATION.

fancy dress a costume for a masquerade, especially one representing an animal, a person from history or fiction, etc.

fan•cy–free ['fænsi 'fri] *adj.* **1** not in love. **2** carefree; not restrained.

fan•cy•work ['fænsi,wɜrk] *n.* ornamental needlework; embroidery, crocheting, etc.

F. and A. M. Free and Accepted Masons.

fan•dan•go [fæn'dæŋgou] *n., pl.* **-gos. 1** a lively Spanish dance in three-four time. **2** the music for such a dance. **3** a piece of foolery or nonsense. ⟨< Sp.⟩

fane [fein] *n. Archaic or poetic.* temple; church. ⟨< L *fanum* temple⟩

☛ *Hom.* FAIN, FEIGN.

fan•fare ['fænfɛr] *n.* **1** a short tune or call sounded by trumpets, bugles, hunting horns, etc. **2** a loud show of activity, talk, etc.; showy flourish. ⟨< F *fanfare* < *fanfarer* blow a fanfare < Sp. < Arabic *farfâr* talkative⟩

fan•fa•ro•nade [,fænfərə'neid]; *French,* [fɑ̃faʀɔ'nad] *n.* bluster; pompous verbosity. ⟨< F *fanfarronade* boasting⟩

fan•fold paper ['fæn,fould] a continuous length of paper of a normal width for printing, which folds in alternate directions along perforations at regular page-length intervals as it comes out of a computer printer.

fang [fæŋ] *n.* **1** a long, sharp tooth by which certain animals, such as dogs, wolves, etc., seize and hold prey; canine tooth: *The hungry wolf buried its fangs in the caribou's neck.* **2** a hollow or grooved tooth by which a poisonous snake injects poison into its prey. **3** a long, slender, tapering part of anything, such as the root of a tooth or the prong of a fork. ⟨OE⟩ **—fanged,** *adj.*

fan hitch *Cdn.* a method, first used by the Inuit, of harnessing sled dogs with a lead dog up in front and others on shorter traces fanning out behind it.

fan•jet ['fæn,dʒɛt] *n.* turbojet.

fan•light ['fæn,ləit] *n.* **1** a semicircular window with bars spread out like an open fan. **2** any semicircular or other window over a door.

fan mail the mail received by a celebrity from fans.

fan•ny ['fæni] *n., pl.* **fan•nies.** *Slang.* buttocks.

fanny pack *Slang.* a container for money, etc. in the form of a small pouch worn around the waist.

fan palm any palm with wide, fanlike leaves, rather than long, narrow leaves.

fan•tail ['fæn,teil] *n.* **1** a tail, end, or part spread out like an open fan. **2** a breed of domestic pigeon having a large tail that spreads out like a fan. **3** any of various birds, fish, etc. having a fan-shaped tail, especially the **fantail darter** (*Catonotus flabellaris*), a species of perch. **4** *Architecture.* a fan-shaped structure or part.

fan–tan ['fæn ,tæn] *n.* **1** a Chinese gambling game played by betting on the number of coins under a bowl. **2** a card game in which the player who gets rid of his or her cards first wins the game. ⟨< Chinese *fan t'an* repeated divisions⟩

fan•ta•si•a [fæn'teiʒə] *or* [fæn'teiziə] *n. Music.* **1** a composition in which form depends on the composer's fancy. **2** a medley of popular tunes with interludes. **3** a literary composition of a similar kind. ⟨< Ital. *fantasia* < L < Gk. *phantasia.* Doublet of FANTASY.⟩

fan•ta•sist ['fæntəsɪst] *n.* a person who creates fantasies.

fan•ta•size ['fæntə,saɪz] *v.* **-sized, -siz•ing. 1** indulge in vivid and often extravagant daydreams or fantasies: *She often fantasized about living the life of a rock star.* **2** represent as an unreal scene or history: *The settlement of the West has been fantasized by some novelists.*

fan•tast ['fæntæst] *n.* a visionary. ⟨< Gk. *phantast* boaster⟩

fan•tas•tic [fæn'tæstɪk] *adj.* **1** very fanciful; capricious; eccentric; irrational: *The idea of space travel seemed fantastic a hundred years ago.* **2** existing only in the imagination; unreal: *There are many fantastic creatures in* The Wizard of Oz. **3** very odd or queer; wild and strange in shape; showing or stimulating unrestrained fancy: *The firelight cast weird, fantastic shadows on the walls.* **4** *Informal.* unbelievably good, quick, high, etc.: *That store charges fantastic prices.* Also, **fantastical**. ⟨ME < OF < LL < Gk. *phantastikos* < *phantazesthai* appear⟩
—fan'tas•ti•cal•ly, *adv.*

fan•ta•sy ['fæntəsi] *or* ['fæntəzi] *n., pl.* **-sies. 1** the play of the mind; imagination or fancy: *The idea of space travel was once pure fantasy.* **2** a fanciful or fantastic idea or notion; a caprice or whim: *It was a mere fantasy, not to be taken seriously.* **3** wild imagining or daydreaming; the creation of unrealistic or far-fetched mental images to satisfy desires not fulfilled in real life: *living in a world of fantasy.* **4** such an idea or mental image: *fantasies about sudden wealth and fame.* **5** fiction featuring strange and grotesque characters and fantastic acts or events in a coherent setting: The Lord of the Rings *is a fantasy.* **6** *Music.* fantasia. Also (*esp. Brit.*), **phantasy.** ⟨ME < OF *fantasie* < L < Gk. *phantasia* appearance, image, ult. < *phainein* show. Doublet of FANTASIA.⟩
☛ *Syn.* **1** See note at IMAGINATION.

fan tracery *Architecture.* tracery used in FAN VAULTING.

fan vaulting *Architecture.* a style of vaulting in which the ribs flare out like those of a fan. See VAULT for picture.

fan•wise ['fæn,waɪz] *adv.* as a hand fan; spread out like an open fan.

fan•zine ['fæn,zin] *n. Informal.* a fan magazine. ⟨< *fan* + (*maga*)*zine*⟩

FAO in the United Nations, Food and Agricultural Organization.

far [fɑr] *adj.* **far•ther** or **fur•ther, far•thest** or **fur•thest;** *adv.* *—adj.* **1** distant; not near: *a far country.* **2** more distant: *the far side of the hill.* **3** extending to a great distance; long: *a far look ahead, a far journey.* **4** a long way (*from*): *far from home. She is far from pretty.*
a far cry, a a long way (*from*). **b** completely different (*from*).
—adv. **1** a long way off in time or space: *to look far into the future, to travel far.* **2** very much: *It is far better to be overcautious than to be careless in driving.* **3** to an advanced point, time, or degree: *She studied far into the night. The explorers penetrated far into the jungle.*
as far as, a to the distance, point, or degree that; to a given point: *as far as the crossroads, as far as I can, as far as that is concerned.* **b** with regard to: *There's no problem as far as finances.*
by far, very much: *He was by far the better swimmer.*
far and away, unquestionably: *He was far and away the best student.*
far and near, everywhere.
far and wide, everywhere; even in distant parts.
far be it from me, I do not dare or want.
far from it, by no means; not at all: *Agree with you? Far from it!*
far gone, in an advanced state of decay.
far out, a *Slang.* fine; excellent. **b** *Informal.* very advanced and different; avant-garde: *His taste in art is far out.*
go far, a last long: *That new shampoo doesn't go very far.* **b** tend very much: *A sincere apology goes far toward mending a relationship.* **c** get ahead: *She shows great promise; she should go far.*
how far, to what distance, point, or degree.
in so far as, to the extent that.
so far, a to this or that point: *He accepts teasing just so far and then he gets angry.* **b** until now or then: *Our team has won every game so far this season.* Also, **thus far.**
so far as, to the extent that.
so far so good, until now everything has been safe or satisfactory. ⟨OE *feorr*⟩
☛ *Syn. adj.* **1.** See note at DISTANT.

far•ad ['færəd] *or* ['fɛrəd] *n.* an SI unit of electrical capacity. A farad is the capacity of a condenser having a charge of one coulomb when the potential across the plate is one volt. *Symbol:* F ⟨after Michael *Faraday.* See FARADAY.⟩

far•a•day ['færə,dei] *or* ['fɛrə,dei] *n.* a unit of electricity equal to about 96 500 coulombs. In electrolysis, it is the amount needed to deposit one gram atom of a univalent element. ⟨< Michael *Faraday* (1791-1867), an English physicist and chemist⟩

fa•rad•ic [fə'rædɪk] *adj.* of or having to do with induced currents of electricity.

far•a•dism ['færə,dɪzəm] *n.* the use of faradic current to treat disease.

far•a•dize ['færə,daɪz] *or* ['fɛrə,daɪz] *v.* **-dized, -diz•ing.** treat by faradism.

far•an•dole ['færən,doul] *or* ['fɛrən,doul] *n.* **1** a fast Provençal dance in six-eight time, in which the dancers join hands to form a chain, following a leader in a winding course. **2** the music for this dance. ⟨< F < Provençal *farandoulo*⟩

far•a•way ['fɑrə,wei] *adj.* **1** distant; far away: *faraway countries.* **2** dreamy: *A faraway look in her eyes showed that she was thinking of something else.*

farce [fɑrs] *n., v.* *—n.* **1** a play intended merely to make people laugh, full of ridiculous happenings, absurd actions, and improbable situations. **2** such plays as a class; branch of drama concerned with such plays. **3** the kind of humour found in such plays; broad humour. **4** ridiculous mockery; absurd pretence: *The trial was a mere farce.*
—v. **1** spice (a composition or speech); season: *He farced his essay with anecdotes.* **2** fill out; pad (a composition or speech). ⟨< F *farce,* literally, stuffing < *farcir* < L *farcire* stuff; originally applied to comic interludes⟩

far•ceur [fɑr'sɜr] *n.* **1** a writer or performer of farces. **2** a wag; joker. ⟨< F⟩ **—far'ceuse** [fɑr'sʊz], *n.*

far•ci•cal ['fɑrsəkəl] *adj.* of or like a farce; ridiculous; absurd; improbable. **—'far•ci•cal•ly,** *adv.* **—'far•ci•cal•ness,** *n.* **—,far•ci'cal•i•ty,** *n.*

far•cy ['fɑrsi] *n.* a disease of horses; glanders. ⟨ME *farsine* < OF *farcin,* ult. < L *farcimen* sausage < *farcire. See* FARCE.⟩

far•del ['fɑrdəl] *n. Archaic.* bundle; burden. ⟨ME < OF *fardel,* dim. of *farde* bundle < Arabic *farda*⟩

fare [fɛr] *n., v.* **fared, far•ing.** *—n.* **1** the sum of money paid to ride in an aircraft, a train, car, bus, etc. **2** the passenger on an aircraft, a train, car, bus, etc. **3** food provided or eaten: *dainty fare.*
—v. **1** eat food; be fed. **2** get along; do: *If you fare well, you have good luck or success.* **3** turn out; happen: *It will fare hard with the thief if he is caught.* **4** *Archaic or poetic.* go; travel. ⟨OE *faran*⟩ **—'far•er,** *n.*
☛ *Hom.* FAIR.

Far East China, Japan, and other parts of E Asia.

fare•well [,fɛr'wɛl] *interj., n.* *—interj.* **1** an expression of good wishes at parting. **2** goodbye; good luck.
—n. **1** an expression of good wishes at parting. **2** a departure; leave-taking. **3** (*adjl.*) of farewell; parting; last: *The singer gave a farewell performance.*

far•fel ['fɑrfəl] *n.* a Yiddish noodle used in soup. ⟨< Yiddish *farfel, ferfel* < MHG *varvelen* soup with pieces of dough or beaten egg⟩

far–fetched ['fɑr 'fɛtʃt] *adj.* not likely; hard to believe; forced; strained: *a far-fetched excuse.*

far–flung ['fɑr 'flʌŋ] *adj.* widely spread; covering a large area.

fa•ri•na [fə'rinə] *n.* **1** flour or meal made from any grain or root, especially cornmeal or coarse wheat flour used for puddings or as a breakfast cereal. **2** starch, especially from potatoes. ⟨< L *farina* < *far* grits⟩

far•i•na•ceous [,færə'neiʃəs] *or* [,fɛrə'neiʃəs] *adj.* consisting of flour or meal; starchy; mealy. Cereals, bread, and potatoes are farinaceous foods.

fa•ri•nose ['færə,nous] *or* ['fɛrə,nous] *adj.* producing or like farina.

farm [fɑrm] *n., v.* *—n.* **1** a tract of land together with the buildings on it, where agricultural crops or domestic livestock or birds are raised. **2** a tract of land or water where a specific thing is raised for market. See FISH FARM, OYSTER FARM. **3** *Sports.* FARM CLUB. **4** *Archaic.* **a** a fixed yearly amount payable in the form of rent, taxes, etc. **b** a fixed yearly amount accepted from a person instead of taxes, or the like, that he or she is authorized to collect. **5 a** the letting out of the collection of public taxes. **b** the condition of being let out at a fixed amount: *a district in farm.* **c** a district let out for the collection of taxes.
—v. **1** raise crops or animals on a farm: *Mary and her brother farm for a living.* **2** cultivate (land): *They farm 100 hectares.* **3** take proceeds or profits of (a tax, undertaking, etc.) on paying a fixed sum. **4** let out (taxes, revenues, an enterprise, etc.) to another for a fixed sum or percentage. **5** let the labour or services of (a person) for hire. **6** formerly, contract for the maintenance of (paupers, children, etc.)
farm out, a *Sports.* send (a professional athlete) to a less advanced league so that he or she can gain experience. **b** turn over to a person, company, etc. for a special purpose: *He farms*

out the right to pick berries on his land. **c** subcontract (work) to someone outside the company, shop, etc. **d** ruin the fertility of (soil) by overfarming. ⟨ME < OF *ferme* lease, leased farm < *fermer* make a contract < L *firmare* < *firmus* firm⟩

farm cheese a variety of cottage cheese, pressed and dried.

farm club or **team** *Sports.* a minor-league team that trains players for the major leagues.

farm•er ['fɑrmər] *n.* **1** a person who raises crops or animals on a farm. **2** formerly, a person who took a contract for the collection of taxes by agreeing to pay a certain sum to the government.

farm hand a person employed to work on a farm.

farm•house ['fɑrm,hʌus] *n.* the dwelling on a farm.

farm•ing ['fɑrmɪŋ] *n., v. —n.* **1** the business of raising crops or animals on a farm; agriculture. **2** (*adjl.*) of or having to do with farmers or agriculture: *farming methods, a farming community.* **3** formerly, the practice of letting out land, the collection of a public revenue, etc.
—v. ppr. of FARM.

farm•land ['fɑrm,lænd] *or* ['fɑrmlənd] *n.* land suitable for or used for raising crops or grazing.

farm•out ['fɑrm,ʌut] *n.* an instance of farming out; especially, a sublease for drilling oil, granted by one company to another.

farm•stead ['fɑrm,stɛd] *n.* a farm with its buildings.

farm system *Sports.* an organization of clubs or teams that train players for a major-league club.

farm•yard ['fɑrm,jɑrd] *n.* the yard connected with the buildings of a farm or enclosed by them.

Far North in Canada, the Arctic and sub-Arctic regions; the territories lying north of the provinces.

far•o ['fɛrou] *n.* a gambling game played by betting on the order in which certain cards will appear. ⟨apparently alteration of *Pharaoh,* from the image on the original playing cards⟩
☛ *Hom.* PHARAOH, FARROW.

far–off ['fɑr 'ɒf] *adj.* distant; far away: *far-off lands.*

far•ouche [fə'ruʃ] *adj.* **1** fierce. **2** not sociable. ⟨< F < OF *forasche* ill-tamed < VL *forasticus* out-of-doors < L *foras* outside⟩

far–out ['fɑr 'ʌut] *adj. Informal.* (*before a noun*) avant-garde; bizarrely unconventional: *far-out tastes in dress.*

far•ra•go [fə'reigou] *or* [fə'rɑgou] *n., pl.* **-goes.** a confused mixture; hodgepodge; jumble. ⟨< L *farrago* mixed fodder, ult. < *far* grits⟩ **—far'rag•i•nous** [fə'rædʒɪnəs], *adj.*

far–rang•ing ['fɑr 'reindʒɪŋ] *adj.* **1** able to travel over a great length or distance: *far-ranging missiles.* **2** covering a wide area (of thought, influence, subject matter, etc.): *a far-ranging debate, a far-ranging inspection.*

far–reach•ing ['fɑr 'ritʃɪŋ] *adj.* having a wide influence or effect; extending far.

far•ri•er ['færiər] *or* ['fɛriər] *n.* **1** a blacksmith who shoes horses. **2** *Archaic.* a horse doctor; veterinarian. ⟨< MF *ferrier* < L *ferrarius* < *ferrum* iron⟩

far•ri•er•y ['færiəri] *or* ['fɛriəri] *n., pl.* **-er•ies. 1** the work of a farrier. **2** the place where a farrier works. **3** *Archaic.* the care and treatment of horses.

far•row ['færou] *or* ['fɛrou] *n., v. —n.* a litter of pigs.
—v. give birth to (a litter of pigs): *The sow farrowed yesterday. She farrowed a litter of six.* ⟨OE *fearh*⟩
☛ *Hom.* FARO, PHARAOH ['fɛrou].

far•ru•ca [fə'rukə] *n.* an Andalusian gypsy dance. ⟨< Sp., ult. < a dim. of *Francisco* Francis⟩

far–see•ing ['fɑr 'siɪŋ] *adj.* **1** able to see far. **2** looking ahead; planning wisely for the future.

far–sight•ed ['fɑr ,səitɪd] *adj.* **1** having a condition of the eyes in which the visual images of nearby objects come to a focus behind the retina, so that they are not clear; able to see far. A far-sighted person has better vision for distant objects than for near objects. Compare NEAR-SIGHTED. **2** looking ahead; planning wisely for the future. **—'far,sight•ed•ly,** *adv.* **—'far,sight•ed•ness,** *n.*

far•ther ['fɑrðər] *adj., adv.* (*a comparative of* FAR). *—adj.* more distant; longer in space: *Three kilometres is farther than two.*
—adv. **1** at or to a greater distance: *Go no farther.* **2** at or to a more advanced point: *She has investigated the subject farther than most people.* ⟨ME *ferther*⟩

☛ *Usage.* **Farther,** FURTHER. In formal English **farther** is used for physical distance and **further** for abstract and metaphysical senses: *We have moved our campsite farther from the road. Her criticisms of the school went further than mine.* Informally, **further** is often used in all senses.

far•ther•most ['fɑrðər,moust] *adj.* most distant; farthest.

far•thest ['fɑrðɪst] *adj., adv.* (a superlative of FAR). *—adj.* **1** most distant. **2** longest in space: *His last trip was the farthest he had ever undertaken.*
—adv. **1** to or at the greatest distance or most advanced point. **2** most. ⟨ME *ferthest*⟩

far•thing ['fɑrðɪŋ] *n.* **1** a former British coin worth a fourth of a penny. **2** something having little value. ⟨OE *fēorthung* < *fēortha* fourth⟩

far•thin•gale ['fɑrðɪŋ,geil] *n.* a hoop skirt or framework for extending a woman's skirt at the hip line, worn in England from about 1550 to about 1650. ⟨< MF *verdugale* < Sp. *verdugado* < *verdugo* rod, ult. < L *viridis* green⟩

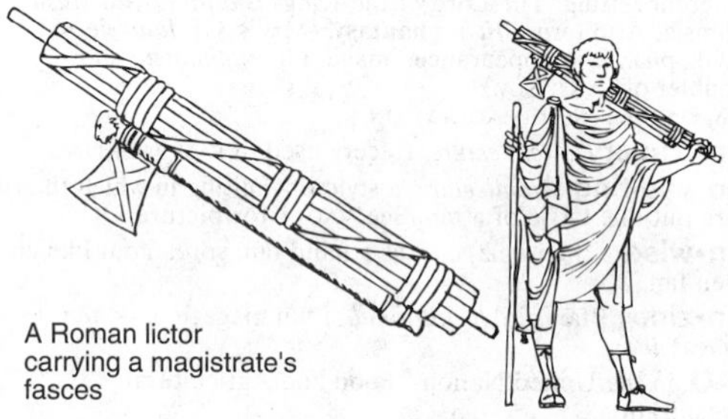

A Roman lictor carrying a magistrate's fasces

fas•ces ['fæsiz] *n.* pl. of **fas•cis** ['fæsɪs]. in ancient Rome, a bundle of rods or sticks containing an axe with the blade projecting, carried before a magistrate as a symbol of authority. ⟨< L *fasces,* pl. of *fascis* bundle⟩

fas•ci•a ['feiʃə] *or* ['feiʃiə] *for 1, 3;* ['fæʃə] *or* ['fæʃiə] *for 2 n., pl.* **-ci•ae** [-i,i] *or* [-i,ai] **1** a long, flat band or surface, such as a horizontal band forming part of a cornice or architrave, or a flat surface above a shop window, often carrying the name of the shop. See FRAME for picture. **2** a sheet of connective tissue beneath the skin, enclosing and separating groups and layers of muscle. **3** *Biology.* a broad band of contrasting colour. Also, **facia.** ⟨< L⟩ **—'fas•ci•al,** *adj.*

fas•ci•ate ['fæʃi,eit] *adj.* **1** bound with a band. **2** *Botany.* **a** made up of or growing in bundles. **b** of stems, pressed together into one; coalescent. **3** *Zoology.* having bands or broad stripes of colour.

fas•ci•a•tion [,fæʃi'eiʃən] *n.* **1** the act of bandaging. **2** *Biology.* a fasciate condition.

fas•ci•cle ['fæsəkəl] *n.* **1** a small bundle; especially, in botany, a small cluster of flowers, leaves, roots, etc. **2** one of the parts of a book published in instalments. ⟨< L *fasciculus,* dim. of *fascis* bundle⟩

fas•ci•cu•late [fə'sɪkjəlɪt] *or* [fə'sɪkjə,leit] *adj.* arranged in bundles. Also, **fascicular.**

fas•ci•cule ['fæsə,kjul] *n.* fascicle.

fas•ci•cu•lus [fə'sɪkjələs] *n., pl.* **fasciculi** [-,li] *or* [-,laɪ]. a bundle of nerve fibres. ⟨< L⟩

fas•ci•nate ['fæsə,neit] *v.* **-nat•ed, -nat•ing. 1** attract very strongly; enchant by charming qualities: *The actress' charm and beauty fascinated everyone.* **2** hold motionless by strange power, terror, etc.: *Snakes are said to fascinate small birds.* ⟨< L *fascinare* < *fascinum* spell⟩

fas•ci•nat•ing ['fæsə,neitɪŋ] *adj., v. —adj.* captivating; enchanting; charming.
—v. ppr. of FASCINATE. **—'fas•ci,nat•ing•ly,** *adv.*

fas•ci•na•tion [,fæsə'neiʃən] *n.* **1** a fascinating or being fascinated. **2** a very strong attraction; charm; enchantment.

fas•ci•na•tor ['fæsə,neitər] *n.* **1** a long, lightweight scarf, usually knitted or crocheted, worn by women over the head or around the neck. **2** a person who fascinates.

fas•cine [fæ'sin] *n.* **1** a bundle of sticks tied together, formerly used to fill ditches, strengthen earthworks, etc. **2** *Cdn.* a large, circular trap, resembling a palisade enclosure, for catching fish. ⟨< F < L *fascina* bundle of sticks < *fascis* bundle⟩

fas•cism ['fæʃɪzəm] *n.* **1** Also, **Fascism,** the doctrines, principles, or methods of Fascists. **2** any system of government in which property is privately owned, but in which all industry and labour are regulated by a strong national government, while all opposition is rigorously suppressed. **3** any expression of extreme right-wing authoritarian or nationalistic views. ⟨< Ital. *fascismo* < *fascio* bundle (as political emblem) < L *fascis.* See FASCES.⟩

☛ *Usage.* **Fascism,** FASCIST are capitalized when they refer to the Italian movement or party, as we capitalize *Liberal* and *Conservative* in this country. When the word refers to a movement in another country in which the party has a different name, it need not be capitalized but often is. When it refers to the general idea of fascist politics, or an unorganized tendency, it is not capitalized. Compare NAZI.

fas•cist ['fæʃɪst] *n., adj.* *—n.* **1 Fascist,** a member of a strongly nationalistic political party that seized control of the Italian government in 1922 under the leadership of Mussolini. **2** Also, **Fascist,** a member of any similar political party in other countries. **3** a person who favours and supports fascism.
—adj. Also, **Fascist,** of or having to do with fascism or fascists.
—fas'cis•tic, *adj.* **—fas'cis•ti•cal•ly,** *adv.*

☛ *Usage.* See note at FASCISM.

fash•ion ['fæʃən] *n., v.* *—n.* **1** a manner; way: *Crabs walk in a peculiar fashion.* **2** the prevailing style; current custom in dress, manners, speech, etc. **3** a garment in the current style: *That shop carries all the latest fashions.* **4** (*adjl.*) of or concerned with fashion or fashions: *a fashion magazine, a fashion designer.* **5** social prominence or standing, as shown by dress or way of life: *a man of fashion.*
after or **in a fashion,** in some way or other; not very well.
set the fashion, fix the fashion, method, etc. for others to follow.
—v. **1** make; shape; form; create: *She fashioned a whistle out of the stick. She fashioned a dress.* **2** adjust; modify to suit a particular use or user.
fashion after or **on,** model after: *Pierre always fashioned himself on his father. My dress is fashioned after the bride's.* ⟨ME < AF *fashion* < L *factio* a doing or making. Doublet of FACTION.⟩

☛ *Syn. n.* **2. Fashion,** STYLE = custom in dress, manners, living, speech, etc. **Fashion** applies to the custom prevailing at a particular time or among a particular group: *She likes to read about the latest fashions.* **Style** is often used in place of *fashion,* but now particularly emphasizes good taste, regardless of the fashion: *That dress is in such good style that it will last for years.* *—v.* See note at MAKE.

fash•ion•a•ble ['fæʃənəbəl] *adj.* **1** following the fashion; in fashion; stylish. **2** of, like, or used by people of fashion.
—'fash•ion•a•ble•ness, *n.* **—'fash•ion•a•bly,** *adv.*

-fashioned *combining form.* in fashion or style: *old-fashioned = old in fashion or style.*

fashion plate **1** a picture of the prevailing style in clothes. **2** a person who wears stylish clothes.

fast[1] [fæst] *adj., adv.* *—adj.* **1** quick; rapid; swift: *a fast runner.* **2** indicating a time ahead of the correct time: *My watch is fast.* **3** too free; wild; not restrained in pleasures: *He led a fast life, drinking and gambling.* **4** firm; secure; tight: *a fast hold on a rope.* **5** loyal; steadfast: *They have been fast friends for years.* **6** not fading easily: *This cloth is dyed with fast colour.* **7** adapted for speed; helping to produce or increase speed: *a fast track.* **8** using greater than average speed, force, etc.: *a fast pitcher.* **9** firmly fixed or attached; tightly shut or locked: *a fast window or door.* **10** *Photography.* (of a film, lens, etc.) making a short exposure possible.
a fast one, a trick or hoax, especially in the expression *pull a fast one.*
—adv. **1** quickly; rapidly; swiftly. **2** firmly; securely; tightly. **3** thoroughly; completely; soundly: *She was fast asleep.* **4** *Poetic.* close; near: *fast by Thistledown.* **5** of a timepiece, ahead of the correct time: *That clock is running fast.*
play fast and loose, be tricky, insincere, or unreliable: *to play fast and loose with the truth.* ⟨OE *fæst*⟩

☛ *Syn. adj.* **1.** See note at QUICK.

fast[2] [fæst] *v., n.* *—v.* go without food; eat little or nothing; go without certain kinds of food. Members of some religious faiths fast on certain days.
—n. **1** a fasting. **2** a day or period of fasting.
break (one's) **fast,** eat food for the first time after fasting. ⟨OE *fæstan*⟩

fast•back ['fæst,bæk] *n.* **1** an automobile roof that slopes downward in a long curve to the back. **2** an automobile with such a roof.

fast•ball ['fæst,bɒl] *n.* **1** a variety of softball having a number of features to add speed and action, making the game more like baseball. **2** *Baseball.* a basic pitch in which the ball travels at great speed in a direct trajectory.

fast break in basketball and lacrosse, an attempt to score before the defending team can get into position.

fast breeder reactor a nuclear reactor in which high-energy neutrons are allowed to set up a chain reaction.

fast buck *Slang.* money made easily and quickly and often in a dubious manner.

fast day a day observed by fasting, especially a day regularly set apart by a religious organization.

fas•ten ['fæsən] *v.* **1** fix firmly in place so as to close; tie, lock, shut, etc.: *to fasten a dress, to fasten a door.* **2** impose; impute: *He tried to fasten the blame upon his companions.* **3** direct; fix (the gaze, etc.): *The dog fastened its eyes on the stranger.* **4** become fixed in place: *The door wouldn't fasten properly.* **5** attach or join (one thing to another).
fasten down, fix to a decision: *We have been unable to fasten the supplier down to a definite date.*
fasten on or **upon, a** take hold of; seize. **b** choose. **c** single out or focus on. ⟨OE *fæstnian* < *fæst* fast[1]⟩

fas•ten•er ['fæsənər] *n.* **1** a person who fastens. **2** an attachment, device, etc. used to fasten a door, garment, etc.

fas•ten•ing ['fæsənɪŋ] *n., v.* *—n.* **1** the act of fitting firmly in place. **2** a device used to fasten things together: *Locks, bolts, clasps, hooks, buttons, etc. are all fastenings.*
—v. ppr. of FASTEN.

fast food restaurant food prepared quickly, often for taking out. **—'fast-'food,** *adj.*

fast forward a mode of operating an audio or video tape recorder, in which the tape is wound on at high speed so as to reach a further point in the recording.

fas•tid•i•ous [fæ'stɪdiəs] *or* [fə'stɪdiəs] *adj.* hard to please; extremely refined or critical; easily disgusted: *a fastidious eater. He's fastidious about clothes.* ⟨< L *fastidiosus* < *fastidium* loathing⟩ **—fas'tid•i•ous•ly,** *adv.* **—fas'tid•i•ous•ness,** *n.*

fas•ti•gi•ate [fæ'stɪdʒiɪt] *or* [fæ'stɪdʒi,eit] *adj. Biology.* **1** tapering. **2** having erect branches. ⟨< L *fastigium* top⟩

fast lane **1** part of the highway reserved for traffic travelling quickly. **2** a hectic, busy life: *life in the fast lane.*

fast•ness ['fæstnɪs] *n.* **1** a strong, safe place; stronghold: *The bandits hid in their mountain fastness.* **2** the quality of being fast.

fast reactor FAST BREEDER REACTOR.

fast talk smooth, persuasive patter, often designed to prevent or overcome suspicion.

fast–talk ['fæst ,tɒk] *v.* gain (something) or persuade (a person) by means of fast talk: *He fast-talked his way into the job.*

fast time *Informal.* DAYLIGHT-SAVING TIME.

fast track **1** a racetrack considered as allowing horses to run quickly. **2** a railway track for express trains. **3** a career path promising rapid promotion. **4** a method of building in which construction is begun before the plans are finished.
on the fast track, being promoted more quickly than usual.
—'fast-,track, *v.*

fast water a rapidly flowing river used for transportation.

fat [fæt] *n., adj.* **fat•ter, fat•test;** *—n.* **1** any of various kinds of white or yellow oily substance formed in the bodies of animals and also in some seeds. **2** any animal tissue mainly composed of such a substance. **3** *Chemistry.* any of a class of organic compounds of which the natural fats are mixtures. **4** the richest, best, or most nourishing part of anything. **5** *Cdn. Seal hunting.* **a** seal blubber. **b** sealskins with attached blubber. **c** seals, especially whitecoats, as the object of the hunt. **6** excessive weight; fatness: *Fat increases the risk of heart attack.* **7** anything surplus or not needed: *Government departments have been asked to trim the fat from their budgets.*
chew the fat, *Slang.* talk casually together; chat.
in or **into the fat,** *Cdn. Seal hunting.* among the seal herd: *The hunt began yesterday, with all 11 ships in the fat.*
live off the fat of the land, have the best of everything.
the fat is in the fire, it is too late to prevent unpleasant results; matters have been made worse.
—adj. **1** consisting of or containing fat; oily: *fat meat.* **2** abounding in some desirable element; fertile: *fat land.* **3** yielding much money; profitable: *a fat job.* **4** affording good opportunities. **5** prosperous: *He grew fat from his vast holdings of land.* **6** full of good things; plentifully supplied; plentiful. **7** fleshy; plump; round and well-fed: *a rosy-cheeked, fat little toddler.* **8** thick; broad. **9** dull; stupid. **10** too fat; corpulent; obese. *She has got quite fat.* **11** *Slang.* not much; little; small: *A fat chance you have of catching him now. A fat lot of help you are to me.* **12** having volatile oil as an ingredient: *fat coal.* ⟨OE *fætt,* originally pp., fatted⟩ **—'fat,like,** *adj.* **—'fat•ly,** *adv.* **—'fat•ness,** *n.*

☛ *Syn. adj.* **7, 10. Fat,** STOUT, PORTLY = having much flesh. **Fat** is the general word, in common use applying to any degree from healthy, well-fed plumpness to ugly, unhealthy obesity: *That girl is too fat.* **Stout** emphasizes thickness and bulkiness, but sometimes suggests firm rather than flabby flesh and is often used as a euphemism for too fat: *She calls herself stylishly stout.* **Portly** = stout and stately: *The retired admiral is a portly old gentleman.*

fa•tal ['feitəl] *adj.* **1** causing death: *fatal accidents.* **2** causing destruction or ruin: *The loss of all our money was fatal to our plans.* **3** decisive; fateful: *At last the fatal day for the contest arrived.* **4** influencing fate: *The Fates, the three goddesses who controlled the fate of humankind, were sometimes called the fatal sisters.* ⟨ME < L *fatalis* < *fatum.* See FATE.⟩ **—'fa•tal•ness,** *n.*

☛ *Syn.* **1. Fatal,** DEADLY, MORTAL, and LETHAL can all mean 'causing death'. **Fatal** is used of something that has caused death or is sure to cause it: *a fatal disease.* **Deadly** refers to something likely to cause death: *a deadly weapon.* **Mortal** is used to refer to a state, event, etc. but not to a weapon: *a mortal wound.* **Lethal** is used of something sure to kill and designed or intended to do so: *a lethal dose.*

fa•tal•ism ['feitə,lɪzəm] *n.* **1** the belief that fate controls everything that happens. **2** submission to everything that happens as inevitable.

fa•tal•ist ['feitəlɪst] *n.* a believer in fatalism.

fa•tal•is•tic [,feitə'lɪstɪk] *adj.* **1** of or having to do with fatalism. **2** believing that fate control everything; accepting things and events as inevitable. **—,fa•tal'is•ti•cal•ly,** *adv.*

fa•tal•i•ty [fə'tæləti] *or* [fei'tæləti] *n., pl.* **-ties. 1** a fatal accident or happening; death: *There were several fatalities on the highways last weekend.* **2** a person killed in such an accident or happening: *Even good drivers can become fatalities.* **3** a fatal influence or effect; deadliness: *The fatality of many types of cancer has been reduced.* **4** the condition of being controlled by fate; inevitable necessity: *a vain struggle against fatality.* **5** fatalism.

fa•tal•ly ['feitəli] *adv.* **1** in a manner leading to death or disaster: *He was fatally wounded.* **2** according to fate.

Fatal Sisters the Fates (see FATE, def. 6).

Fa•ta Mor•ga•na ['fɑtə mɔr'gɑnə] a mirage sometimes seen in the Straits of Messina near Sicily and once held to be caused by Morgan le Fay, the fairy half-sister of King Arthur. ⟨< Ital., literally, Morgan le Fay⟩

fat•back ['fæt,bæk] *n.* salted and dried strips of fat from the back of a hog.

fat cat *Slang.* a person who is rich, privileged, and powerful or influential.

fate [feit] *n., v.* **fat•ed, fat•ing.** *—n.* **1** a power thought to determine and control everything that is or happens; destiny: *Fate is beyond human control. She does not believe in fate.* **2** what is caused by fate. **3** one's lot or fortune. **4** what becomes of a person or thing: *The jury settled the fate of the accused.* **5** death; ruin. **6 the Fates,** *pl. Greek and Roman mythology.* the three goddesses believed to control human life. They were Clotho, who spins the thread of life; Lachesis, who decides how long it shall be; and Atropos, who cuts it off.
—v. preordain by destiny. ⟨ME < L *fatum* (thing) spoken (i.e., by the gods), pp. neut. of *fari* speak⟩

☛ *Hom.* FETE.

☛ *Syn.* **1, 3, 4. Fate,** DESTINY, DOOM = a person's fortune or lot in life. **Fate** suggests some power or force that determines what becomes of a person or thing, and emphasizes an outcome that cannot be avoided, escaped, or changed: *World history describes the fate of many nations.* **Destiny,** often used interchangeably with **fate,** emphasizes a fate all prearranged and not to be altered, often a glorious one: *Stardom was her destiny.* **Doom** applies to an unhappy or awful end: *The condemned man went to his doom.*

fat•ed ['feitɪd] *adj., v. —adj.* **1** controlled by fate. **2** destined; predestined. **3** short-lived; unfortunate; doomed: *a fated social assistance program.*
—v. pt. and pp. of FATE.

fate•ful ['feitfəl] *adj.* **1** controlled by fate. **2** determining what is to happen; decisive. **3** showing what fate decrees; prophetic. **4** causing death, destruction, or ruin; disastrous. **—'fate•ful•ly,** *adv.* **—'fate•ful•ness,** *n.*

fat farm *Informal.* a resort or camp where people go to lose excess weight through special diets and exercise.

fath. fathom(s).

fat•head ['fæt,hɛd] *n.* **1** *Slang.* a dolt; a stupid or slow person. **2** a type of minnow. **—'fat,head•ed,** *adj.*

fa•ther ['fɒðər] *n., v. —n.* **1** a male parent. **2** a person who is like a father; stepfather, adoptive father, or father-in-law. **3** a male ancestor; forefather. **4** a man who helped to make or initiate something; founder, leader, inventor, author, oldest member, etc.: *Fathers of Confederation. Alexander Graham Bell was the father of the telephone.* **5** a title of respect used in addressing priests or other clergymen. **6** a clergyman having this title. **7** a title of respect to an old man. **8** in ancient Rome, a senator. **9 the Father,** God. **10 the fathers,** *pl.* the chief writers and teachers of the Christian Church during the first six centuries A.D.
—v. **1** produce or bring forth, as a father; beget: *He has fathered three children.* **2** take care of as a father does; act as a father to. **3** make; originate. **4** acknowledge oneself as the father of. **5** foist: *They fathered the crime on him.* ⟨OE *fæder*⟩ **—'fa•ther,like,** *adj.*

father confessor **1** a priest who hears confessions. **2** a person to whom one confides everything.

father figure a man regarded as having all the qualities of an ideal father.

fa•ther•hood ['fɒðər,hʊd] *n.* **1** the condition of being a father. **2** the qualities of fathers. **3** fathers as a group.

fa•ther–in–law ['fɒðər ɪn ,lɒ] *n., pl.* **fa•thers-in-law.** the father of one's husband or wife.

fa•ther•land ['fɒðər,lænd] *n.* one's native country; the land of one's ancestors.

fa•ther•less ['fɒðərlɪs] *adj.* **1** without a father living. **2** without a known father.

fa•ther•ly ['fɒðərli] *adj.* **1** of or belonging to a father: *fatherly responsibilities.* **2** like a father; kindly. **—'fa•ther•li•ness,** *n.*

Fathers' Day a day honouring fathers, celebrated on the third Sunday in June.

Fathers of Confederation the men, led by Sir John A. Macdonald, who brought about the confederation of the original provinces of Canada in 1867.

Father Time a personification of time as an old man with a beard and carrying a scythe.

fath•om ['fæðəm] *n., pl.* **fath•oms** or (*esp. collectively*) **fath•om;** *v. —n.* a unit of measure equal to 1.83 m, used mostly in measuring the depth of water and the length of ships' ropes, cables, etc.
—v. **1** measure the depth of; sound. **2** get to the bottom of; understand fully. ⟨OE *fæthm* width of the outstretched arms⟩

fath•om•a•ble ['fæðəməbəl] *adj.* **1** that can be measured. **2** understandable.

Fa•thom•e•ter [fæ'ðɒmətər] *n. Trademark.* a sounder used to measure water depth.

fath•om•less ['fæðəmlɪs] *adj.* **1** too deep to be measured. **2** impossible to be fully understood. **—'fath•om•less•ness,** *n.*

fa•tid•ic or **fa•tid•i•cal** [fə'tɪdɪk] *or* [fə'tɪdɪkəl] *adj.* prophetic. ⟨< L *fatidicum* spoken by fate⟩

fa•ti•ga•ble ['fætəgəbəl] *adj.* easily tired. ⟨< L *fatigabilis*⟩ **—,fat•i•ga'bil•i•ty,** *n.*

fa•tigue [fə'tig] *n., v.* **-tigued, -tigu•ing;** *adj. —n.* **1** physical or mental weariness. **2** any task or exertion producing weariness: *The doctor has not yet recovered from the fatigues of the epidemic.* **3** a weakening (of metal) caused by continuous use or strain. **4** *Physiology.* a temporary decrease in the functional capacity of an organ or cell after excessive activity. **5** FATIGUE DUTY. **6 fatigues,** *pl.* clothes worn during fatigue duty.
—v. **1** cause fatigue in; weary. **2** weaken (metal) by much use or strain.
—adj. having to do with fatigue. ⟨< F *fatigue* < *fatiguer* < L *fatigare* tire⟩

fatigue duty non-military work done by members of the armed forces. Cleaning up the camp or repairing roads is fatigue duty.

Fa•ti•ma [fə'timə] *or* ['fætəmə] *n.* A.D. 606?-632, the favourite daughter of Mohammed.

fat•ling ['fætlɪŋ] *n.* a calf, lamb, kid, or pig fattened to be killed for food.

fat–sol•u•ble ['fæt 'sɒljəbəl] *adj.* soluble in oils or fats.

fat•ten ['fætən] *v.* **1** make (a stock animal, etc.) fat or fleshy (*often used with* **up**): *The hogs were being fattened for market.* **2** enrich (soil). **3** make richer or fuller; swell. **4** become fat or fatter.
fatten on or **upon,** take advantage of in order to live well: *He has been fattening on his sons for years.* **—'fat•ten•er,** *n.* **—'fat•ten•ing,** *adj.*

fat•tish ['fætɪʃ] *adj.* somewhat fat.

fat•ty ['fæti] *adj.* **-ti•er, -ti•est. 1** of fat; containing fat: *fatty tissues.* **2** like fat; oily; greasy. **—'fat•ti•ly,** *adv.* **—'fat•ti•ness,** *n.*

fatty acid *Chemistry.* any of a group of organic acids, some of which, such as stearic acid, are found in animal and vegetable fats and oils. *Formula*: $C_nH_2O_2$

fatty degeneration *Pathology.* the pathological formation of fat in cells, associated with disturbance in the cells's function.

fa•tu•i•ty [fə'tjuɪti] *or* [fə'tuɪti] *n., pl.* **-ties. 1** self-satisfied stupidity; folly; silliness. **2** a foolish remark or act. ⟨< L *fatuitas* < *fatuus* foolish⟩

fat•u•ous ['fætʃuəs] *adj.* stupid but self-satisfied; foolish; silly. ⟨< L *fatuus* foolish⟩ **—'fat•u•ous•ly,** *adv.* **—'fat•u•ous•ness,** *n.*
☛ *Syn.* See note at FOOLISH.

fau•bourg ['foubur]; *French,* [fo'buʀ] *n.* **1** suburb. **2** a district in a city.

fau•cal ['fɒkəl] *adj., n. Phonetics. —adj.* of, having to do with, or produced in the fauces.
—n. a sound produced in the fauces. ⟨< L *fauces* throat + E *-al*[1]⟩

fau•ces ['fɒsiz] *n.pl.* the cavity at the back of the mouth, leading into the pharynx. ⟨< L⟩ **—'fau•cial** ['fɒʃəl], *adj.*

fau•cet ['fɒsɪt] *n.* **1** *Esp. U.S.* a device for controlling the flow of water or other liquid in a pipe, tank, barrel, etc.; tap. **2** the enlarged end of a pipe into which the end of another pipe fits. ⟨< F *fausset* < *fausser* bore through, originally, break < L *falsare* corrupt⟩

faugh [fɒ] *interj.* an exclamation of disgust.

fault [fɒlt] *n., v. —n.* **1** something that is not as it should be; a flaw; defect. **2** a mistake. **3** a cause for blame; responsibility: *Whose fault was it?* **4** *Geology.* a break in a mass of rock, with the segment on one side of the break pushed up or down. **5** *Tennis, etc.* a failure to serve the ball into the right place. **6** an accidental defect in an electric circuit.
at fault, a deserving blame; wrong. **b** puzzled; perplexed.
find fault, pick out faults; complain: *The boy said that his mother was always finding fault.*
find fault with, object to; criticize: *The teacher was always finding fault with badly done homework.*
in fault, deserving blame; wrong.
to a fault, too much; very: *generous to a fault.*
—v. **1** *Tennis, etc.* fail to serve the ball into the right place. **2** find fault with: *Her work could not be faulted.* **3** *Geology.* (of rock strata) develop or cause to develop a fault or faults. ⟨ME < OF *faute,* ult. < L *fallere* deceive⟩
☛ *Syn.* **1. Fault,** FAILING = a defect in character, mental attitude, emotional make-up, conduct, or habits. **Fault** particularly suggests a lack of something essential to perfection, but not necessarily a cause for blame: *Sloppiness is his greatest fault.* **Failing** suggests a falling short of perfection, and applies particularly to a weakness in character, often excusable: *Extravagance is her failing.*

fault•find•er ['fɒlt,faɪndər] *n.* **1** a person who finds fault; complainer. **2** a device for locating defects, as in an electric circuit.

fault•find•ing ['fɒlt,faɪndɪŋ] *n. or adj.* finding fault; complaining; pointing out faults.

fault•less ['fɒltlɪs] *adj.* without a single fault; free from blemish or error; perfect. **—'fault•less•ly,** *adv.* **—'fault•less•ness,** *n.*

fault•y ['fɒlti] *adj.* **fault•i•er, fault•i•est.** having faults; containing blemishes or errors; wrong; imperfect. **—'fault•i•ly,** *adv.* **—'fault•i•ness,** *n.*

faun [fɒn] *n. Roman mythology.* one of a class of minor rural deities originally represented as men with the horns and tail of a goat, but later partially assimilated with the Greek satyrs and, like them, represented as having a goat's hind legs and a lustful character. ⟨ME < L *Faunus* a rural deity⟩
☛ *Hom.* FAWN.

fau•na ['fɒnə] *n.* **1** all the animals of a particular region or time: *the fauna of Australia, the fauna of the carboniferous age.* **2** a book or list dealing with such animals. ⟨< NL *Fauna* a rural goddess, wife of Faunus⟩ **—'faun•al,** *adj.*

Faust [faʊst] *n. German legend.* an old philosopher who sells his soul to the devil in return for having everything that he wants on earth. The story of Faust has inspired many literary and musical works since medieval times. **—'Faust•i•an,** *adj.*

faute de mieux ['fout də 'mjœ]; *French,* [fotdə'mjø] for lack of anything better. ⟨< F⟩

fau•teuil [fou'tœj]; *French,* [fo'tœj] *n.* **1** an upholstered armchair. **2** *Brit.* a seat in the stalls of a theatre. ⟨< F⟩

Fauve [fouv] *n.pl.* any of a group of French painters, including Henri Matisse, whose work in the period from 1905 to 1920 is characteristic of Fauvism. Also, **Fauvist.** ⟨< F *fauve* wild beast⟩

Fau•vism ['fouvɪzəm] *n. Painting.* a style that was an extreme form of expressionism, developed in France in the early 20th century and characterized by simplicity and boldness of design, vivid clashing colours, and individuality of approach.
—'Fau•vist, *n., adj.*

faux [fou]; *French,* [fo] *adj.* imitation; artificial: *faux pearls.* ⟨< F⟩
☛ *Hom.* FOE.

faux–naif [,fou nɑ'if]; *French,* [fona'if] *adj., n. —adj.* **1** putting on an air of childlike simplicity or naiveté. **2** of a style in art or literature that affects childlike simplicity or lack of sophistication in its depictions or themes: *Rousseau painted in the faux-naif style.*
—n. **1** a person who feigns naiveté or simplicity. **2** a faux-naif style. ⟨< F⟩

faux pas [,fou 'pɑ]; *French,* [fo'pɑ] *pl.* **faux pas** [,fou 'pɑz]; *French,* [fo'pɑ] a slip in speech, conduct, manners, etc.; breach of etiquette; blunder. ⟨< F⟩

fa•va bean ['fɑvə] an edible bean (*Vicia faba*) of the pea family, bearing beans in large pods; broad bean. ⟨< Ital. *fava* bean < L *faba*⟩

fav•e•o•late [fə'viəlɪt] *or* [fə'viə,leit] *adj.* like a honeycomb. ⟨< L *faveolus* < *favus* honeycomb⟩

fav•ism ['fɑvɪzəm] *n.* anemia caused by an allergic reaction to the fava bean. It is most common in people of Mediterranean ancestry.

fa•vo•ni•an [fə'vouniən] *adj.* favourable like the west wind. ⟨< L *favonius* west wind⟩

fa•vor ['feivər] See FAVOUR.

fa•vour or **fa•vor** ['feivər] *n., v. —n.* **1** an act of kindness: *Will you do me a favour?* **2** liking; approval: *They are sure to look with favour on your plan.* **3** the condition of being liked or approved: *A fashion in favour this year may be out of favour next year. He is out of favour with the boss.* **4** the favouring of one or some more than others; favouritism. **5** a gift or token: *The knight wore his lady's favour on his arm.* **6** a small gift, especially one given as a souvenir at a party. **7** *Now rare.* a letter; note: *We acknowledge your favour of the 15th.*
find favour with, win the approval of; please.
in favour of, a on the side of; supporting. **b** to the advantage of; helping. **c** to be paid to: *Make the cheque out in favour of the company, not the sales representative.*
in (someone's) **favour,** for (someone's) benefit.
—v. **1** show kindness to. **2** like; approve. **3** treat better than other people. **4** be on the side of; support: *to favour legal reform.* **5** be to the advantage of; help. **6** treat unusually gently: *The dog favours its sore foot when it walks.* **7** look like: *She favours her mother's side of the family.* ⟨ME < OF < L *favor* < *favere* show kindness to⟩ **—'fa•vour•er** or **'fa•vor•er,** *n.*
☛ *Syn. n.* **2. Favour,** GOOD WILL = kindly or friendly feeling. **Favour** emphasizes having kindly or friendly thoughts or giving approval: *The manager looked on the new clerk with favour.* **Good will** emphasizes greater friendliness and desire or effort to be helpful: *The audience showed its good will toward the singer by its applause.*

fa•vour•a•ble or **fa•vor•a•ble** ['feivərəbəl] *adj.* **1** favouring; approving. **2** being to one's advantage; helping: *a favourable wind.* **3** boding well; promising. **—'fa•vour•a•ble•ness** or **'fa•vor•a•ble•ness,** *n.* **—'fa•vour•a•bly** or **'fa•vor•a•bly,** *adv.*
☛ *Syn.* **3. Favourable,** AUSPICIOUS = promising or giving signs of turning out well. **Favourable** = promising because conditions or people having to do with an event or situation show they will be helpful: *It was a favourable time for our trip, since business was light.* **Auspicious** = promising because all the signs (including, often, omens or portents) point to a lucky or successful outcome: *The popularity of his first book was an auspicious beginning to his career.*

fa•voured or **fa•vored** ['feivərd] *adj., v. —adj.* **1** treated with favour. **2** having special advantages; talented. **3** having a certain appearance (*in compounds*): *ill-favoured.*
—v. pt. and pp. of FAVOUR.

fa•vour•ite or **fa•vor•ite** ['feivərɪt] *adj., n. —adj.* liked better than others; liked very much.
—n. **1** a person or thing liked better than others; one liked very much: *Marina is a favourite with everybody.* **2** a person treated with special favour. **3** *Sports.* a person, horse, etc. expected to win a contest. ⟨ME < MF *favorit* (fem. *favourite*) < Ital. *favorito,* ult. < *favore* favour < L *favor*⟩

fa•vour•it•ism or **fa•vor•it•ism** ['feivərə,tɪzəm] *n.* **1** a favouring of one or some more than others; the having of favourites. **2** the state of being a favourite.

fawn[1] [fɒn] *n., adj., v. —n.* **1** a young deer less than a year old. **2** a light, slightly greyish brown colour.
—adj. having the colour fawn.

–*v.* of deer, give birth to (young). ⟨ME < OF *faon*, ult. < L *fetus* fetus⟩ **–'fawn,like,** *adj.*
☛ *Hom.* FAUN.

fawn[2] [fɒn] *v.* **1** cringe and bow to get favour or attention; act slavishly: *Flattering relatives fawned on the rich old woman.* **2** of dogs, etc., show fondness by crouching, wagging the tail, licking the hand, etc. ⟨OE *fagnian* < *fægen* fain⟩ **–'fawn•er,** *n.* **–'fawn•ing•ly,** *adv.*
☛ *Hom.* FAUN.

fawn lily DOGTOOTH VIOLET.

fax [fæks] *n., pl.* **fax•es;** *v.,* **faxed, fax•ing.** *–n.* **1** a system for transmitting printed and other material by electronic means such as telephone or cable. It is received as an exact hard copy at the other end. **2** the equipment used: *Does your office have a fax?* **3** the material sent: *Here is the fax you expected.*
–*v.* send (something) to (someone), using the system: *Your letter will be faxed today. Fax me a reply by Wednesday.* ⟨A shortening/abbreviation and respelling of *facsimile*⟩

fax machine a machine for sending and receiving faxes.

fay[1] [fei] *n.* fairy. ⟨ME < OF *fae, fee,* ult. < L *fatum.* See FATE.⟩
☛ *Hom.* FE, FEY.

fay[2] [fei] *n. Archaic.* faith: *By my fay!* ⟨ME < OF *fei* < L *fides.* Doublet of FAITH.⟩
☛ *Hom.* FE, FEY.

faze [feiz] *v.* **fazed, faz•ing.** *Informal.* disturb; worry; bother; put out. ⟨var. of *feeze,* OE *fēsian* drive⟩
☛ *Hom.* PHASE.
☛ *Usage.* **Faze,** an informal term meaning 'worry, bother, or disturb', is almost always used negatively: *His original failure did not faze him. Nothing we said fazed her — she just carried on.*

FBI *U.S.* FEDERAL BUREAU OF INVESTIGATION.

fbm feet board measure.

F clef *Music.* the bass clef. See CLEF for picture.

F.D. Fire Department.

Fdn Foundation.

fe [fei] *n.* the nineteenth letter of the Hebrew alphabet. See table of alphabets in the Appendix.
☛ *Hom.* FAY, FEY.

Fe iron. ⟨< L *ferrum*⟩

F.E. Forest Engineer.

fe•al•ty ['fiəlti] *or* ['filti] *n., pl.* **-ties. 1** in the Middle Ages, the loyalty and duty owed by a vassal to his feudal lord: *The nobles swore fealty to the king.* **2** loyalty; faithfulness; allegiance. **3** an oath of loyalty. ⟨ME < OF *feaulte* < L *fidelitas.* Doublet of FIDELITY.⟩

fear [fir] *n., v.* *–n.* **1** the state of being afraid; a desire to escape from a danger, pain, or evil that one feels is near; dread: *In spite of his fear, he opened the door and stepped out into the dark.* **2** a cause for fear; danger: *There is no fear of our losing.* **3** an uneasy feeling or anxious thought; concern: *She had no fear of opposition.* **4** a feeling of awe and reverence.
for fear of, in order to prevent: *We went as quietly as we could, for fear of arousing the dog.*
without fear or favour, impartially; justly.
–*v.* **1** feel fear. **2** feel fear of. **3** regret: *I fear I must disagree.* **4** have an uneasy feeling or anxious thought; feel concern. **5** have awe and reverence for: *to fear God.*
fear for, worry about. ⟨OE *fær* peril⟩
☛ *Syn. n.* **1. Fear,** DREAD, ALARM = the disagreeable feeling that comes over a person when danger or harm threatens. **Fear** is the general word, meaning 'a being afraid': *The knight felt no fear in the midst of battle.* **Dread** applies to the fear that comes from knowing something unpleasant or frightening will happen or from expecting danger, often unknown or uncertain: *He has a constant dread of losing his job.* **Alarm** applies to startled or excited fear, coming from the sudden appearance of danger: *The explosion caused widespread alarm.*

fear•ful ['firfəl] *adj.* **1** causing fear; terrible; dreadful: *The conflagration was a fearful sight.* **2** full of fear; afraid: *fearful of the dark.* **3** showing or caused by fear: *She cast a fearful glance about her.* **4** *Informal.* very bad, unpleasant, etc.: *a fearful cold.* **–'fear•ful•ly,** *adv.* **–'fear•ful•ness,** *n.*

fear•less ['firlɪs] *adj.* without fear; afraid of nothing; brave; daring. **–'fear•less•ly,** *adv.* **–'fear•less•ness,** *n.*

fear•nought ['fir,nɒt] *n.* **1** a strong cloth. **2** a coat made of this cloth.

fear•some ['firsəm] *adj.* **1** causing fear; frightful: *a fearsome sight.* **2** timid; afraid: *fearsome of danger.* **–'fear•some•ly,** *adv.* **–'fear•some•ness,** *n.*

fea•sance ['fizəns] *n. Law.* the doing or performance of a condition, obligation, duty, etc. (*often in compounds*): *malfeasance.* ⟨AF *fesance* < F *faire* to do⟩

fea•si•bil•i•ty [,fizə'bɪləti] *n.* the quality of being feasible: *to study the feasibility of project.*

fea•si•ble ['fizəbəl] *adj.* **1** capable of being done or carried out easily; practicable: *The committee selected the plan that seemed most feasible.* **2** likely; probable: *The witness' explanation of the accident sounded feasible.* **3** suitable; convenient: *The road was too rough to be feasible for travel by automobile.* ⟨ME < OF *faisable,* ult. < L *facere* do⟩ **–'fea•si•ble•ness,** *n.* **–'fea•si•bly,** *adv.*
☛ *Syn.* **1.** See note at POSSIBLE.

feast [fist] *n., v.* *–n.* **1** an elaborate meal prepared for a number of guests on some special occasion. **2** an unusually delicious or abundant meal. **3** something that gives pleasure or joy; a special treat: *a feast for the eyes.* **4** a religious festival or celebration: *Christmas and Easter are the most important Christian feasts.*
–*v.* **1** have a feast. **2** provide with a feast: *The queen feasted the ambassadors.* **3** give pleasure or joy to: *We feasted our eyes on the magnificent view.* ⟨ME < OF < L *festa* festal ceremonies⟩ **–'feast•er,** *n.*
☛ *Syn. n.* **1. Feast,** BANQUET = an elaborate meal with many guests. **Feast** emphasizes the abundance, fineness, and richness of the food and drink, served to a large number in celebration of a special occasion: *We went to the family feast.* **Banquet** emphasizes the formality of the celebration and applies particularly to a formal dinner given in rich surroundings: *A banquet was given by the town to honour the returning hero.*

feast day 1 a day set aside as a celebration of some religious festival, or in honour of some person, event, or thing. **2** NAME DAY.

feat [fit] *n.* a great or unusual deed; an act showing great skill, daring, strength, etc. ⟨ME < OF *fait* < L *factum* (thing) done. Doublet of FACT.⟩
☛ *Hom.* FEET.
☛ *Syn.* See note at EXPLOIT.

feath•er ['fɛðər] *n., v.* *–n.* **1** one of the light, thin growths that cover a bird's skin. Because they are soft and light, feathers are often used to fill pillows. **2** something like a feather in shape or lightness. **3** the act of feathering an oar. **4** *Archery.* **a** a bird's feather or something like it attached to the end of an arrow to direct its flight.
feather in one's cap, something to be proud of.
in feather, covered with feathers.
in fine (or **high** or **good**) **feather,** in very good humour; exuberantly happy: *We were all in fine feather the first day on the trail.*
–*v.* **1** supply or cover with feathers. **2** grow like feathers. **3** move like feathers. **4** turn (an oar) after a stroke so that the blade is parallel to the surface of the water, and keep it that way until the next stroke begins. **5** turn (the blade of an airplane propeller) to decrease wind resistance. **6** touch or apply pressure lightly and intermittently: *The driver feathered her brakes to slow down on the slippery road.* **7** touch (the strings of a violin, etc.) very lightly with a bow. **8** cut (hair) in different lengths to give a soft appearance. **9** provide with a featheredge. **10** of a bird, acquire feathers. **11** *Printing.* adjust (the space between lines on a page) so that the page ends neatly.
feather (one's) **nest,** take advantage of chances to get rich. ⟨OE *fether*⟩ **–'feath•er•less,** *adj.* **–'feath•er,like,** *adj.*

feather bed 1 a soft, warm mattress filled with feathers. **2** a bed having such a mattress. **3** *Informal.* an easy way of living.

feath•er–bed ['fɛðər,bɛd] *v.* **-bed•ded, bed•ding. 1** coddle; provide with luxuries. **2** engage in, or subject to, feather-bedding.

feath•er–bed•ding ['fɛðər ,bɛdɪŋ] *n.* the requiring of an employer to pay extra employees or to pay full wages for restricted output, in order to reduce unemployment and create jobs.

feath•er•brain ['fɛðər,brein] *n.* a silly, foolish, weak-minded person.

feath•er•brained ['fɛðər,breind] *adj.* silly; foolish; scatterbrained: *That was a featherbrained thing to do!*

feath•ered ['fɛðərd] *adj., v.* *–adj.* **1** having feathers; covered with feathers. **2** equipped and supplied with feathers: *a feathered dart.* **3** swift; rapid: *birds in their feathered flight.*
–*v.* pt. and pp. of FEATHER.

feath•er•edge ['fɛðər,ɛdʒ] *n., v.* **-edged, -edg•ing.** *–n.* a very thin edge.
–*v.* furnish with such an edge.

feath•er•edged ['fɛðər,ɛdʒd] *adj.* having a very thin edge.

fea•ther•head ['fɛðər,hɛd] *n.* featherbrain.

fea•ther•ing ['fɛðərɪŋ] *n., v. —n.* plumage, or anything suggesting it.
—v. ppr. of FEATHER.

feather palm any palm tree with pinnate leaves.

feather star a crinoid of the order Comatulida that is freeswimming.

feath•er•stitch ['fɛðər,stɪtʃ] *n., v. —n.* a zigzag embroidery stitch. See EMBROIDERY for picture.
—v. **1** make zigzag embroidery stitches. **2** decorate with such stitches.

feath•er•weight ['fɛðər,weit] *n., adj. —n.* **1** a very light thing or person. **2** a boxer who weighs between 55 kg and 57 kg. **3** an unimportant person or thing: *She is a featherweight on the political scene.* **4** the lightest weight a horse can carry in a handicap race.
—adj. **1** very light. **2** of or having to do with featherweights. **3** unimportant.

feath•er•y ['fɛðəri] *adj.* **1** having feathers; covered with feathers. **2** like feathers; soft, light, etc. **—'feath•er•i•ness,** *n.*

feat•ly ['fitli] *adv. Archaic.* **1** nimbly; skilfully. **2** suitably; properly. **3** neatly; elegantly. ⟨< ME *fetli* < *fet* < OF *fait* pp. of *faire* to do < L *facere*⟩

fea•ture ['fitʃər] *n., v.* **-tured, -tur•ing.** *—n.* **1** a part of the face. The eyes, nose, mouth, chin, and forehead are features. **2 features,** *pl.* the face. **3** a distinct part or quality; something that stands out and attracts attention; any characteristic. **4** a main attraction, especially a full-length movie. **5** a special article, comic strip, etc. in a newspaper or magazine.
—v. **1** make a feature of; give special prominence to: *The movie featured an outstanding actor. The store was featuring radios in its sale.* **2** be featured; have a prominent part (*in*): *She features in several recent films.* **3** *Informal.* be like in features. **4** *Informal.* imagine. ⟨ME < OF *feture* < L *factura* < *facere* do⟩

☛ *Syn. n.* **3. Feature,** CHARACTERISTIC, TRAIT = a quality of a person or thing. **Feature** applies to a quality or detail that stands out and attracts attention: *The main features of the resort are its climate and scenery.* **Characteristic** applies to a quality or feature that expresses or shows the character or nature of a person, thing, or class or distinguishes it from others: *Ruggedness was a characteristic of the early pioneers in Canada.* **Trait** applies particularly to a distinguishing feature of the character or mind of a person: *Cheerfulness is her outstanding trait.*

☛ *Usage.* The term **feature article** or **feature story** is often used for a newspaper or magazine article that gives the writer's feelings and opinions about an event or situation, as opposed to a **news story,** which gives the facts without personal comment.

fea•tured ['fitʃərd] *adj., v. —adj.* **1** having a certain kind of facial feature (*used only in compounds*): *a hard-featured man.* **2** shown or advertised as a special feature: *The featured entertainers this week are a group from Winnipeg.*
—v. pt. and pp. of FEATURE.

feature film a full-length fictional film.

feature–length ['fitʃər ,lɛŋθ] *adj.* of the usual length of a feature film or magazine article.

fea•ture•less ['fitʃərlɪs] *adj.* without striking features; not distinctive or impressive: *a featureless landscape.*

Feb. February.

feb•ri•fuge ['fɛbrə,fjudʒ] *n., adj. —n.* **1** a medicine to reduce fever. **2** a cooling drink.
—adj. curing or lessening fever. ⟨< F. Cf. FEVERFEW.⟩

fe•brile ['fibraɪl] *or* ['fibrəl], ['fɛbraɪl] *or* ['fɛbrəl] *adj.* **1** of fever; feverish. **2** caused by fever. ⟨< Med.L *febrilis* < *febris* fever⟩

Feb•ru•ar•y ['fɛbru,ɛri] *or* ['fɛbju,ɛri] *n., pl.* **-ar•ies.** the second month of the year. It has 28 days except in leap years, when it has 29. ⟨< L *Februarius* < *februa,* pl., the Roman feast of purification celebrated on Feb. 15⟩

fe•cal ['fikəl] *adj.* having to do with feces. Also, **faecal.**

fe•ces ['fisiz] *n.pl.* **1** the waste matter discharged from the intestines. Also, **faeces. 2** dregs; sediment. ⟨< L *faeces,* pl., dregs⟩

feck•less ['fɛklɪs] *adj.* **1** futile; ineffective. **2** careless: *feckless behaviour.* **3** worthless. ⟨< *feck* vigour, var. of *fect* < *effect*⟩ **—'feck•less•ly,** *adv.* **—'feck•less•ness,** *n.*

fec•u•lent ['fɛkjələnt] *adj.* **1** muddy; turbid. **2** very filthy; fouled by feces. ⟨< ME < L *faeculentus* < *faecula* dim. < *faex* dregs, lees⟩ **—'fec•u•lence,** *n.*

fe•cund ['fikənd] *or* ['fɛkənd] *adj.* fruitful; productive; fertile: *Edison had a fecund mind.* ⟨< F < L *fecundus*⟩

fe•cun•date ['fikən,deit] *or* ['fɛkən,deit] *v.,* **-dat•ed, -dat•ing.** make fruitful. **—,fe•cun'da•tion,** *n.*

fe•cun•di•ty [fɪ'kʌndəti] *n.* fruitfulness; fertility.

fed¹ [fɛd] *v.* pt. and pp. of FEED.
fed up (with), annoyed; tired; wearied (by).

fed² [fɛd] *n. Slang.* **1** a member or official of the federal government. **2 the feds,** *pl.* the federal government. **3** *U.S.* an agent or official of the FBI. Also, **Fed.**

Fed•a•yeen [,fɛdɑ'jin] *n., pl.* **-yeen.** in Egypt, a commando or guerrilla fighter. ⟨< colloquial Arabic *fidā'iyīn,* pl. of literary Arabic *fidā'i* (literally) one who sacrifices himself < *fida'* redemption; sacrifice⟩

fed•er•al ['fɛdərəl] *adj., n. —adj.* **1** formed by an agreement between groups establishing a central organization to handle their common affairs while the parties to the agreement keep control of local affairs: *The Canadian Federation of Agriculture is a federal organization of farm representatives.* **2** of or having to do with a central government formed in this way: *Parliament is the federal lawmaking body of Canada.* **3** Also, **Federal,** of or having to do with the central government of Canada. **4 Federal,** in the United States: **a** of or having to do with the Federalist Party, in existence from 1789 to 1816. **b** supporting the central government during the Civil War.
—n. **Federal,** in the United States, a supporter or soldier of the central government during the Civil War. ⟨< L *foedus, foederis* compact⟩ **—'fed•er•al•ly,** *adv.*

Federal Bureau of Investigation a United States government bureau that investigates violations of federal laws, except those concerning postal service, currency, taxes, etc., which are under the jurisdiction of other federal agencies.

Federal Court of Canada a court with trial and appeal divisions, that deals with cases involving revenues of the Crown, claims in relation to patent, copyright, or trademark, claims under maritime law, and other specialized matters, and that has exclusive jurisdiction over suits against the Crown in federal affairs.

Federal Government **1** the government of Canada, located in Ottawa. Its responsibilities are specified by the Constitution Act. **2** the prime minister and his or her Cabinet. Also, **federal government.**

fed•er•al•ism ['fɛdərə,lɪzəm] *n.* **1** the federal principle of government. **2** belief in or support of this principle.

fed•er•al•ist ['fɛdərəlɪst] *n.* a person who favours the federal principle of government.

fed•er•al•ize ['fɛdərə,laɪz] *v.* **-ized, -iz•ing. 1** put under the control of the federal government. **2** unite into a federal union. **—,fed•er•al•i'za•tion,** *n.*

fed•er•ate *v.* ['fɛdə,reit]; *adj.* ['fɛdərɪt] *v.* **-at•ed, -at•ing;** *adj.*
—v. join in a league, federal union, etc.
—adj. formed into a federation; federated. ⟨< L *foederare* league together < *foedus, -deris* compact⟩

fed•er•a•tion [,fɛdə'reiʃən] *n.* **1** the act or process of federating, especially the formation of a federal union. **2** a nation formed by such an act; a union of a number of separate provinces, states, etc.: *Canada and the United States are both federations.* **3** a union formed by agreement of organizations, states, or nations; league: *a federation of student groups.*

fed•er•a•tive ['fɛdərətɪv] *or* ['fɛdə,reitɪv] *adj.* of, like, or forming a federation. **—'fed•er•a•tive•ly,** *adv.*

fe•do•ra [fə'dɔrə] *n.* a soft felt hat with a curved brim and a crown creased lengthwise. ⟨apparently from the play *Fédora* by the French playwright Sardou⟩

fee [fi] *n., v.* **feed, fee•ing.** *—n.* **1** a sum of money asked or paid for a service or privilege; charge: *Doctors and lawyers get fees for their services.* **2 fees,** *pl.* the money paid for instruction at a school or university. **3 a** in a feudal society, land held by a vassal on condition of homage and service to a superior lord who has actual ownership of it; fief. **b** the rights or responsibility of the vassal in such an arrangement. **4** an inherited or heritable estate in land. See also FEE SIMPLE and FEE TAIL.
hold in fee, have absolute legal possession of.
—v. Rare. give a fee to. ⟨ME < AF var. of OF *fieu* < Med.L *feudum* fief ? < Gmc.; cf. OE *feoh* money, cattle⟩

fee•ble ['fibəl] *adj.* **-bler, -blest. 1** lacking strength; weak: *a feeble old man.* **2** weak intellectually or morally: *a feeble mind.* **3** lacking in force; ineffective: *a feeble attempt.* **4** lacking in volume, brightness, etc.: *a feeble cry.* ⟨ME < OF *feble* < L *flebilis* lamentable < *flere* weep⟩ **—'fee•ble•ness,** *n.* **—'fee•bly,** *adv.*

fee•ble–mind•ed ['fibəl ,maɪndɪd] *adj.* **1** weak in mind;

lacking normal intelligence. **2** weak-willed; irresolute.
—'fee•ble-,mind•ed•ly, *adv.* **—'fee•ble-,mind•ed•ness,** *n.*

feed [fid] *v.* **fed, feed•ing;** *n.* *—v.* **1** give food to. **2** give as food: *Feed this grain to the chickens.* **3** of animals, eat: *Don't disturb the cows while they're feeding.* **4** be sufficient food for: *One of their burgers feeds two people.* **5** supply with material: *to feed a machine, to feed a furnace.* **6** put or convey (fuel or material) into a machine, etc. in operation: *to feed paper into the printer.* **7** of such fuel, material, etc., pass or be so conveyed: *The paper feeds into the printer from beneath.* **8** relay (radio or television signals) to a transmitting station for broadcast. **9** satisfy; gratify: *Praise fed her vanity.* **10** sustain; support. *He fed his anger with thoughts of revenge.* **11** *Theatre.* supply (another actor) with (cues). **12** *Sports.* pass or give (the puck, ball, etc.) to (a teammate).
fed up, *Slang.* **a** fed too much. **b** annoyed; tired.
feed on or **upon, a** live at the expense of; prey on. **b** derive satisfaction, support, etc. from.
feed to, supply to: *The agency feeds news stories to all the radio stations.*
—n. **1** food for livestock, especially a prepared mixture of grain, etc. **2** an allowance or amount of such food given at one time. **3** *Informal.* a meal, especially a large one: *They gave us a good feed.* **4** the action or process of feeding, especially supplying material to a machine, etc. **5** the material supplied. **6** the mechanism or system by which something is fed, as material for a machine, radio signals, etc. **7** *Theatre.* **a** a line or cue to which a comedian replies with a line that gets a laugh. **b** a person who gives such cues. **8** *Sports.* the act or an instance of passing a puck, ball, etc.
off one's feed, too sick to eat. ⟨OE *fēdan* < *fōda* food⟩
☛ *Syn. —n.* **1. Feed,** FODDER = food for animals and fowls. **Feed** is the general word: *Give the chickens their feed.* **Fodder** applies to coarse or dried feed, like alfalfa, hay, corn, or other plants fed to horses, cattle, pigs, or sheep: *Put some fodder in the bins.*

feed•back ['fid,bæk] *n.* **1** the return to a system, machine, etc. of part of its output, either as an unwanted effect or in order to change or control future output. **2** the modification of a biological or psychological reaction or process by the activity of some of its products. **3** information on the results of one's actions that will influence one's future decisions or actions.

feed•bag ['fid,bæg] *n.* a bag that can be hung over a horse's head for holding oats, etc.; nose bag.
put on the feedbag, *Slang.* eat.

feed•box ['fid,bɒks] *n.* **1** a box used to hold food for livestock. **2** a box containing the mechanism for feeding a machine or the material fed into it.

feed•er ['fidər] *n.* **1** a person who or thing that feeds. **2** a device that supplies food to a person or animal: *a bird feeder.* **3** anything that supplies something else with material. A brook is a feeder for a river. A branch that brings traffic to the main line is a feeder. **4** *Electricity.* a wire or cable used to conduct electricity from a source to a distribution point. **5** a steer, etc. being fattened for slaughter.

feeder line a branch airline, railway, pipeline, etc.

feed•lot ['fid,lɒt] *n.* a plot of land for feeding and fattening livestock for the market.

feed•stock ['fid,stɒk] *n.* raw material, as, petroleum, supplied to manufacturing plants to produce product, as, gasoline.

feel [fil] *v.* **felt, feel•ing;** *n.* *—v.* **1** touch, especially in order to know the texture, temperature, etc.: *Feel this cloth.* **2** try to find or make (one's way) by touch: *He felt his way across the room when the lights went out.* **3** test or examine by touching: *to feel a person's pulse.* **4** search by touch; grope: *He felt in his pockets for a dime.* **5** find out by touching: *Feel how cold my hands are.* **6** be aware of through the sense of touch: *to feel the cool breeze.* **7** have the feeling of being; be: *She feels well, I feel lonely.* **8** give the feeling of being; seem to the sense of touch: *The air feels cold.* **9** have in one's mind, soul, heart, etc.; experience: *She feels joy.* **10** have pity or sympathy: *She feels for all who suffer.* **11** be influenced or affected by: *The ship feels her helm. I am beginning to feel my age.* **12** think; believe; consider: *I feel that we will win.* **13** be capable of sentience; have feelings: *Do insects feel?*
feel for or **with,** sympathize with.
feel like, a have a desire for; want: *I feel like an ice-cream cone.* **b** seem as if there will be: *It feels like rain.* **c** seem like to the sense of touch or to one's emotional nature: *The cat's fur felt like silk. When you are insecure, every criticism feels like a rejection.*
feel out, find out about in a cautious way.
feel up to, feel able to do something.
make (something) **felt,** behave so that others notice (something): *The critic made his displeasure felt.*
—n. **1** the way in which something feels to the touch: *I like the feel of silk. Wet soap has a greasy feel.* **2** the sense of touch. **3** the act of feeling. **4** ambience; atmospheric effect: *I don't like the feel of that dark alley.* **5** a natural appreciation; instinct; talent (*for*): *That tailor has a real feel for leather.*
get the feel of, become used to; become comfortable with: *Get the feel of that car before you drive to Montréal.* ⟨OE *fēlan*⟩

feel•er ['filər] *n.* **1** a special part of an animal's body for touching with. An insect's antennae are its feelers. **2** a suggestion, remark, hint, question, etc. made to find out what others are thinking or planning. **3** a person who or thing that feels.

feel•ing ['filɪŋ] *n., adj., v.* *—n.* **1** the sense of touch: *By feeling we can distinguish between something hard and something soft.* **2** a sensation experienced through this sense: *a feeling of pain.* **3** the ability or power to experience physical sensation: *She had no feeling in her left hand.* **4** emotion: *Joy, sorrow, fear, and anger are feelings.* **5** the capacity for emotion; sensibility; the emotional nature: *She was guided by feeling rather than thought.* **6** sensitivity to the higher or more refined emotions: *His work shows both feeling and taste.* **7** pity; sympathy. **8** an opinion; sentiment: *Her feeling was that right would win.* **9** the quality felt to belong to anything: *There is a weird feeling about the place.* **10 feelings,** *pl.* susceptibilities: *You hurt her feelings with that remark.* **11** a vaguely perceived forewarning; hunch: *I had a feeling this would happen.*
—adj. full of feeling; sensitive; emotional.
—v. ppr. of FEEL. **—'feel•ing•ly,** *adv.*
☛ *Syn. n.* **4. Feeling,** EMOTION, PASSION = a pleasant or painful mental state produced in a person in reaction to a stimulus of some kind. **Feeling** is the general word: *He had a vague feeling of hope.* **Emotion** = a strong and moving feeling, such as love, fear, sorrow, joy, etc.: *She was so overwhelmed with emotion that she couldn't speak for a moment.* **Passion** = violent emotion, usually overcoming the power to think clearly and taking complete possession of a person: *In a passion of rage he smashed the watch.*

fee simple *Law.* an estate in land without any limitation on inheritance or transfer of ownership; in Canada it denotes full ownership, subject to the rights of the Crown.

feet [fit] *n.* pl. of **foot.**
carry or **sweep off one's feet, a** make very enthusiastic. **b** impress.
drag one's feet, work or act slowly on purpose.
feet of clay, ordinary qualities instead of superhuman.
get (or **have**) **cold feet.** See COLD FEET.
get (one's) **feet wet,** *Informal.* try some new experience or activity.
get to (one's) **feet,** stand up.
have (one's) **feet on the ground,** be sensible, practical, clear-headed.
on (one's) **feet, a** of a person, erect. **b** independent; self-sufficient: *She helped her relatives until they were on their feet financially.*
sit at the feet of, be a pupil or admirer of.
stand on one's own feet, be independent.
☛ *Hom.* FEAT.

fee tail *Law.* an estate in land subject to specified restrictions on who may inherit it.

feign [fein] *v.* **1** put on a false appearance of; pretend: *Some animals feign death when in danger.* **2** make up with intent to deceive; invent falsely: *to feign an excuse.* **3** *Archaic.* represent fictitiously. **4** *Archaic.* imagine: *The phoenix is a feigned bird.* ⟨ME < OF *feign-*, a stem of *feindre* < L *fingere* form⟩ **—'feign•er,** *n.*
☛ *Hom.* FAIN, FANE.

feigned [feind] *adj., v.* *—adj.* **1** imagined; not real. **2** pretended: *a feigned attack.* **3** invented to deceive: *a feigned headache.*
—v. pt. and pp. of FEIGN. **—'feign•ed•ly,** *adv.*

feint [feint] *n., v.* *—n.* **1** a movement intended to deceive; pretended blow; sham attack. **2** a false appearance; pretence.
—v. make a pretended blow or sham attack: *The fighter feinted with his right hand and struck with his left.* ⟨< F *feinte* < *feindre* feign⟩
☛ *Hom.* FAINT.

feist•y [fəisti] *adj.,* **feist•i•er, feist•i•est. 1** aggressively energetic and exuberant. **2** touchy or quarrelsome: *My cat is feisty.* ⟨< *feist,* dialect, < originally (literally), a fart < ME *fist* < OE *fisten*⟩ **—'feist•i•ness,** *n.*
☛ *Usage.* **Feisty** tends to be used of people or animals that are small, so that their aggressiveness is unexpected.

feld•spar ['fɛld,spɑr] *n.* any of several crystalline minerals composed mostly of aluminum silicates. Also, **felspar.** ⟨< *feld-*

(< G *Feldspath*, literally, field spar) + *spar*³⟩ **—'feld•spar,oid,** *adj.* **—feld'spath•ic** [fɛld'spæθɪk], *adj.*

fe•li•cif•ic [,fili'sɪfɪk] *adj.* causing happiness. ⟨< L *felix* happy + *fic*⟩

fe•lic•i•tate [fə'lɪsə,teit] *v.* **-tat•ed, -tat•ing.** formally express good wishes to; congratulate: *John's friends felicitated him on his good fortune.* ⟨< LL *felicitare* < *felix* happy⟩

fe•lic•i•ta•tion [fə,lɪsə'teiʃən] *n.* a formal expression of good wishes; congratulation.

fe•lic•i•tous [fə'lɪsətəs] *adj.* **1** well chosen for the occasion; unusually appropriate: *The poem was full of striking and felicitous similes.* **2** having a gift for apt speech. **3** fortunate; happy. **—fe'lic•i•tous•ly,** *adv.* **—fe'lic•i•tous•ness,** *n.*

fe•lic•i•ty [fə'lɪsəti] *n., pl.* **-ties. 1** happiness; bliss. **2** good fortune; blessing. **3** a pleasing aptness; appropriateness; grace: *The famous writer phrased her ideas with felicity.* **4** a happy turn of thought; well-chosen phrase. **5** a fortunate quality or feature. ⟨ME < OF < L *felicitas* < *felix* happy⟩

☛ *Syn.* **1.** See note at HAPPINESS.

fe•lid ['filɪd] *n.* a feline.

fe•line ['filaɪn] *adj., n. —adj.* **1** of or having to do with the cat family. **2** catlike; stealthy; sly: *The hunter stalked the deer with noiseless feline movements.*
—n. any animal belonging to the cat family. Lions, tigers, and panthers are felines. ⟨< L *felis* cat⟩ **—'fe•line•ly,** *adv.* **—fe'lin•i•ty** [fə'lɪnəti], *n.*

fell¹ [fɛl] *v.* pt. of FALL.

fell² [fɛl] *v., n. —v.* **1** cause to fall; knock down: *One blow felled him to the ground.* **2** cut down (a tree). **3** turn down and stitch one edge of (a seam) over the other.
—n. **1** all the trees cut down in one season. **2** a seam finished by felling. ⟨OE *fellan* < *feallan* fall⟩

fell³ [fɛl] *adj.* **1** cruel; fierce; terrible: *a fell blow.* **2** deadly; destructive: *a fell disease.* ⟨ME < OF *fel* < VL *fello.* See FELON¹.⟩ **—'fel•ly,** *adv.* **—'fell•ness,** *n.*

fell⁴ [fɛl] *n.* the skin or hide of an animal with the hair on it. ⟨OE. Related to FILM.⟩

fell⁵ [fɛl] *n.* **1** a stretch of high moorland. **2** a hill; mountain. ⟨< ON *fjall*⟩

fel•la ['fɛlə] *n. Slang.* fellow.

☛ *Hom.* FELLAH.

fel•la•gha [fə'lɑgə] *n., pl.* **-ghas** or **-gha.** an Arab guerrilla. ⟨< Arabic *fallaq* (literally) outlaw⟩

fel•lah¹ ['fɛlə] *n., pl.* **fel•la•hin** ['fɛlə,hin]. in Egypt and other Arabic-speaking countries, a peasant or farm labourer. ⟨< Arabic *fallāh* husbandman⟩

☛ *Hom.* FELLA.

fel•lah² ['fɛlə] *n. Slang.* fellow.

☛ *Hom.* FELLA.

fel•late [fɛ'leit] *v.,* **-lat•ed, -lat•ing.** perform fellatio on.

fel•la•tio [fə'leiʃou] *n.* a form of sexual activity in which the penis is taken into the mouth. ⟨< NL < L *fellatus,* pp. of *fellare* suck⟩

fell•er¹ ['fɛlər] *n.* **1** a person or thing that fells. **2** a part attached to a sewing machine to fell seams.

fell•er² ['fɛlər] *n. Slang.* fellow.

fel•loe ['fɛlou] *n.* the circular rim of a wheel, into which the outer ends of the spokes are inserted. Also, **felly.** ⟨var. of FELLY⟩

☛ *Hom.* FELLOW ['fɛlou].

fel•low ['fɛlou]; *for def. 1, often* ['fɛlə] *n.* **1** *Informal.* a man or boy (*often used as a familiar form of address*): *There were three fellows in the car. Never mind, old fellow!* **2** a companion or associate. **3** one of the same class or rank; equal: *The world has not his fellow.* **4** the other one of a pair; mate. **5** a graduate student who has a fellowship in a university or college. **6** an honoured member of a learned society. **7** (*adjl.*) belonging to the same class; united by the same work, interests, aims, etc.; being in the same or a like condition: *fellow citizens, fellow sufferers.* **8 Fellow,** a member of the governing body of certain British or American universities or colleges: *a Fellow of Balliol College, Oxford.*
hail fellow well met, very friendly. ⟨OE *fēolaga* < ON *felagi* partner (literally, fee-layer)⟩

☛ *Hom.* FELLOE.

fellow feeling sympathy.

fellow man or **fel•low–man** ['fɛlou 'mæn] *n.* a fellow human being; another human being or human beings in general, thought of as one's comrades or peers.

fel•low•ship ['fɛlou,ʃɪp] *n.* **1** companionship; friendliness. **2** a taking part with others; sharing. **3** a group of people having similar tastes, interests, etc.; brotherhood; society. **4** a position or sum of money given to a person, such as a graduate student, to enable him or her to go on with his or her studies. **5** the relationship existing among those holding the same religious beliefs; communion. **6** the position held by a university or college Fellow.

fel•ly ['fɛli] *n., pl.* **-lies.** felloe. ⟨OE *felg*⟩

fel•on¹ ['fɛlən] *n., adj. —n.* a person who has committed a felony.
—adj. Archaic. wicked or cruel. ⟨ME < OF *felon* < L; ultimate origin uncertain⟩

fel•on² ['fɛlən] *n.* a painful, usually pus-filled infection on a finger or toe, especially near the nail; whitlow. ⟨origin uncertain⟩

fe•lo•ni•ous [fə'louniəs] *adj.* **1** that is a felony; criminal. **2** wicked; villainous. **—fe'lo•ni•ous•ly,** *adv.* **—fe'lo•ni•ous•ness,** *n.*

fel•on•ry ['fɛlənri] *n.* felons as a group.

fel•o•ny ['fɛləni] *n., pl.* **-nies.** a crime regarded by the law as grave, or major, such as arson, rape, or murder. The technical equivalent of the U.S. term *felony* in Canadian law is *indictable offence.*

fel•site ['fɛlsəit] *n.* an igneous rock of quartz and feldspar. ⟨< *fels(par)* + *ite*⟩

fel•spar ['fɛl,spɑr] *n.* feldspar.

felt¹ [fɛlt] *v.* pt. and pp. of FEEL.

felt² [fɛlt] *n., v. —n.* **1** a kind of cloth that is not woven but is made by rolling and pressing together wool, hair, or fur, used to make hats, slippers, and pads. **2** something made of felt. **3** (*adjl.*) made of felt: *a felt hat.* **4** *Papermaking.* a belt, usually of textile material, that carries the freshly formed paper through the machine.
—v. **1** make into felt. **2** cover with felt. **3** of fibres, become pressed or matted together like felt. ⟨OE⟩

felt•ing ['fɛltɪŋ] *n., v. —n.* **1** material made of felt. **2** the process of making felt.
—v. ppr. of FELT².

felt pen a pen similar to a ballpoint, but having a point or tip made of felt and using a more liquid ink.

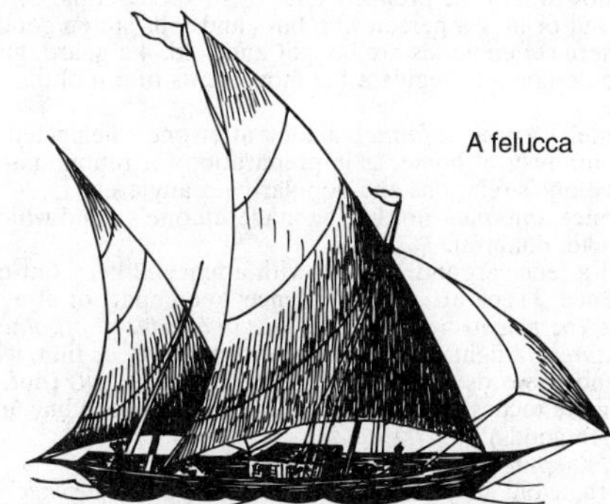

A felucca

fe•luc•ca [fə'lʌkə] *n.* a long, narrow, lateen-rigged ship similar to a galley, formerly used especially by privateers because of its speed. ⟨< Ital. < Arabic *fulk* ship⟩

fem. female; feminine.

fe•male ['fimeil] *n., adj. —n.* **1** a woman or girl. **2** an animal belonging to the sex that gives birth to young or produces eggs. **3** *Botany.* **a** a flower having a pistil or pistils and no stamens. **b** a plant bearing only flowers with pistils.
—adj. **1** of or having to do with women or girls. **2** belonging to the sex that gives birth to young or produces eggs. **3** *Botany.* **a** designating or having to do with any reproductive structure that produces or contains elements that need fertilization from the male element. **b** bearing flowers that contain a pistil or pistils but no stamens: *a female plant.* **c** producing fruit after fertilization. **4** of pipe fittings, etc., having a hollow part into which a corresponding male part fits. ⟨ME < OF < *femelle* < L *femella,* dim. of *femina* woman; form influenced by *male*⟩

fem•i•nine ['fɛmənɪn] *adj., n. —adj.* **1** of or like a woman or women; having qualities considered characteristic of women. **2** suited to women: *feminine fashions.* **3** effeminate. **4** *Grammar.* belonging to or designating the grammatical gender that includes some words for female persons and animals as well as a wide variety of other kinds of referents. In French, the words *femme* (woman), *maison* (house), and *lune* (moon) are feminine; in German, the words *Frau* (woman), *Tür* (door), and *Sonne* (sun) are feminine. Compare MASCULINE, NEUTER. **5** *Music.* of a phrase, ending in a chord or note that does not bear an accent. **6** *Prosody.* designating a rhyme of two syllables of which the second is unstressed (as, *motion, notion*), or of three syllables of which the second and third are unstressed (as, *happily, snappily*).
—n. Grammar. **1** the feminine gender. **2** a word or form in the feminine gender. ⟨ME < OF < L *femininus* < *femina* woman⟩ **—'fem•i•nine•ly,** *adv.* **—'fem•i•nine•ness,** *n.*

fem•i•nin•ity [ˌfɛmə'nɪnəti] *n.* **1** a feminine quality or condition. **2** women collectively.

fem•i•nism ['fɛməˌnɪzəm] *n.* **1** a movement to win increased rights and activities for women. **2** loosely, female chauvinism.

fem•i•nist ['fɛmənɪst] *n., adj. —n.* a person who believes in or favours feminism.
—adj. of or having to do with feminism.

fem•in•ize ['fɛmɪˌnaɪz] *v.,* **-ized, -iz•ing.** make or become feminine. **—ˌfem•in•i'za•tion,** *n.*

femme de chambre [famdə'ʃɑ̃mbʀ] *French.* **1** lady's maid. **2** chambermaid. ⟨< F 'woman of the bedroom'⟩

femme fa•tale [ˌfamfa'tal] *pl.* **femmes fa•tales** [ˌfamfa'tal]. *French.* a disastrously seductive woman; siren.

fem•o•ral ['fɛmərəl] *adj.* of the femur. ⟨< L *femur, femoris* thigh⟩

fe•mur ['fimər] *n., pl.* **fe•murs** or **fem•o•ra** ['fɛmərə] **1** thighbone. See LEG and PELVIS for pictures. **2** *Zoology.* a corresponding leg bone or segment in animals and insects. ⟨< L *femur* thigh⟩

fen[1] [fɛn] *n.* a marsh; swamp; bog. ⟨OE *fenn*⟩

fen[2] [fɛn] *n., pl.* **fen. 1** a unit of money in the People's Republic of China, equal to 1/100 of a yuan or 1/10 of a chiao. See table of money in the Appendix. **2** a coin worth one fen. ⟨< Chinese⟩

fence [fɛns] *n., v.* **fenced, fenc•ing.** *—n.* **1** a railing, wall, wire mesh, or other means of enclosing a yard, garden, field, farm, etc. to show where the property ends or to keep people or animals out or in. **2** a person who buys and sells stolen goods. **3** a place where stolen goods are bought and sold. **4** a guard, guide, or gauge designed to regulate the movements of a tool or machine.
mend (one's) **fences,** *Informal.* **a** look after one's neglected political interests at home, as in preparation for renomination. **b** improve one's relations and popularity in any area.
on the fence, *Informal.* not having made up one's mind which side to take; doubtful.
—v. **1** put a fence around; enclose with a fence. **2** keep out or in with a fence. **3** separate as if by a fence; keep apart or at a distance: *The patents were used to fence in and block off other manufacturers.* **4** fight, now only in sport, theatre, or film, with long, slender swords called foils; compete in FENCING (def. 1). **5** use evasive tactics, as in debate; parry or quibble. **6** buy and sell (stolen goods).
fence in, keep in with a fence: *to fence in the chickens.*
fence with, avoid giving a direct answer to. ⟨var. of *defence*⟩

fenc•er ['fɛnsər] *n.* **1** a person who fences with a sword or foil. **2** a person who makes or mends fences.

fenc•ing ['fɛnsɪŋ] *n., v. —n.* **1** the art of fighting, now only as a sport, or in theatre or film, with swords or foils. **2** the act or practice of parrying the points of one's opponent in a debate, discussion, or argument. **3** the material for making fences. **4** fences.
—v. ppr. of FENCE.

fend [fɛnd] *v.* **1** *Archaic.* defend. **2** *Archaic.* resist.
fend for (oneself), *Informal.* provide for oneself; get along by one's own efforts.
fend off, ward off; keep off. ⟨var. of *defend*⟩

fend•er ['fɛndər] *n.* **1** a curved protective covering over the wheels of an automobile, truck, etc.; mudguard. **2** a guard, made of rubber, rope, plastic, etc., hung over the sides of a boat or attached to a dock to protect the boat in docking. **3** a device such as a frame attached to the front of a locomotive, streetcar, etc. to reduce injury to an animal or person in case of a collision. **4** a metal guard, frame, or screen in front of a fireplace to keep hot coals and sparks from the room. **5** anything that keeps or wards something off. ⟨var. of DEFENDER⟩

fender bender *Informal.* a trivial car accident.

fe•nes•tra [fə'nɛstrə] *n., pl.* **fe•nes•trae** [-tri] *or* [-traɪ]. **1** a natural opening between the middle and inner ear. **2** *Zoology.* a small, clear spot on the wing of certain insects. **3** *Medicine.* the hole resulting from fenestration. ⟨< NL < L, window⟩

fen•es•trate [fə'nɛstrɪt] *or* [fə'nɛstreit] *adj.* **1** having windows. **2** containing fenestrae. Also, **fenestrated** ['fɛnəˌstreitɪd]. ⟨< L *fenestratus*⟩

fen•es•tra•tion [ˌfɛnə'streiʃən] *n.* **1** the placement of windows in a building. **2** *Medicine.* the operation of making an opening into the labyrinth or semicircular canal of the ear to eliminate deafness caused by obstruction of sound waves. ⟨< L *fenestrare* provide with windows < *fenestra* window⟩

fen•flu•ra•mine [fɛn'flʊrəˌmin] *n.* an appetite-suppressing drug, used by people who need to lose weight.

Fe•ni•an ['finiən] *or* ['finjən] *n., adj. —n.* **1** a member of an Irish secret organization founded in the United States about 1858 for the purpose of overthrowing English rule in Ireland. **2** a member of a group of warriors in Irish legend.
—adj. of or having to do with the Fenians. ⟨< OIrish *fēne*, a name of the ancient inhabitants of Ireland, confused with Irish *fianna*, a legendary body of warriors⟩ **—'Fe•ni•anˌism,** *n.*

fen•nec ['fɛnɛk] *n.* a N African fox (*Fennecus zerda*) having large eyes and ears. ⟨< Arabic *fanak*⟩

fen•nel ['fɛnəl] *n.* **1** a perennial European herb (*Foeniculum vulgare*) of the parsley family, cultivated for its aromatic seeds and leaves which are used to flavour food. **2** the aromatic seeds of this plant. ⟨OE *fenol* < VL **fenuclum*, ult. < L *fenum* hay⟩
☛ *Hom.* PHENYL.

fen•ny [fɛni] *adj.* **1** marshy; swampy; boggy. **2** growing or living in fens. ⟨OE *fennig* < *fenn* fen⟩

fen•o•fi•brate [ˌfɛnou'faɪbreit] *n.* a drug used to control cholesterol.

fe•not•e•rol [fə'nɒtəˌrɒl] *n.* a drug used to treat asthma.

fen•u•greek ['fɛnjəˌgrik] *n.* a plant (*Trigonella faenum-graecum*) of southeastern Europe grown for its edible and medicinal seeds and as forage. ⟨< ME *fenugrek* < OF *fenugrec* < L *faenum-graecum* Greek hay⟩

feoff [fif] See FIEF. **—'feoff•ment,** *n.*

fe•ral[1] ['fɛrəl] *or* ['firəl] *adj.* **1** wild; untamed. **2** brutal; savage. **3** of a human being, living in the wild and not brought up by other humans: *Feral children never learn language.* ⟨< L *fera* beast⟩
☛ *Hom.* FERRULE, FERULE ['fɛrəl].

fe•ral[2] ['fɛrəl] *or* ['firəl] *adj.* **1** deadly or fatal: *a feral disease.* **2** gloomy; funereal. ⟨< L *feralis* of the dead, of funeral rites⟩
☛ *Hom.* FERRULE, FERULE ['fɛrəl].

fer–de–lance ['fɛr də ˌlæns] *n.* a large pit viper (*Bothrops atrox*) found in tropical America. It is very poisonous. ⟨< F, literally, iron (tip) of a spear⟩

fer•i•ty ['fɛrəti] *n.* **1** a wild state. **2** ferocity. ⟨< L *feritas* < *ferus* fierce⟩

fer•ma•ta [fər'mɑtə] *n. Music.* PAUSE (def. 5). ⟨< Ital. *fermare* to stop, confirm < L *firmare* to make firm < *firmus* firm⟩

fer•ment *v.* [fər'mɛnt]; *n.* ['fɜrmɛnt] *v., n. —v.* **1** undergo a chemical reaction in which sugar is converted to ethyl alcohol. The fermenting of grapes or other fruit produces wine. If the reaction continues and the alcohol is allowed to evaporate, vinegar results. **2** cause this chemical change in (something). **3** cause unrest in; excite; agitate. **4** be excited; seethe with agitation or unrest.
—n. **1** fermentation. **2** a substance or organism that causes fermentation: *Yeast is used as a ferment in brewing beer.* **3** excitement; agitation; unrest. ⟨< L *fermentare* < *fermentum* leaven < *fervere* boil⟩ **—fer'ment•a•ble,** *adj.* **—fer'ment•a•tive,** *adj.* **—fer'ment•er,** *n.*
☛ *Usage.* **Ferment,** FOMENT. Because **ferment** can mean 'cause or undergo excitement or agitation' it is often confused with **foment. Foment** denotes a similar kind of action but its object is always an effect or event: *to foment rebellion.* The object of **ferment** is the people who experience it or carry it out: *The new atrocities only served to ferment the dissatisfied peasantry.* Also, only **ferment** can be used intransitively.

fer•men•ta•tion [ˌfɜrmɛn'teiʃən] *n.* **1** the act or process of fermenting. **2** excitement; agitation; unrest: *There was a long period of fermentation before the outbreak of revolution.*

fer•mi ['fɛrmi] *or* ['fɜrmi] *n. Physics.* a unit of length, 10^{13} cm. ⟨< Enrico *Fermi* (1901-1954), Italian-born U.S. nuclear physicist⟩

fer•mi•on ['fɜrmi,ɒn] *n. Physics.* any subatomic particle subject to the PAULI EXCLUSION PRINCIPLE. ⟨See FERMI⟩

fer•mi•um ['fɜrmiəm] *n.* an artificial, radioactive, metallic element. *Symbol*: Fm; *at.no.* 100; *at.mass* 257.10; *half-life* approx. 80 days. ⟨See FERMI⟩

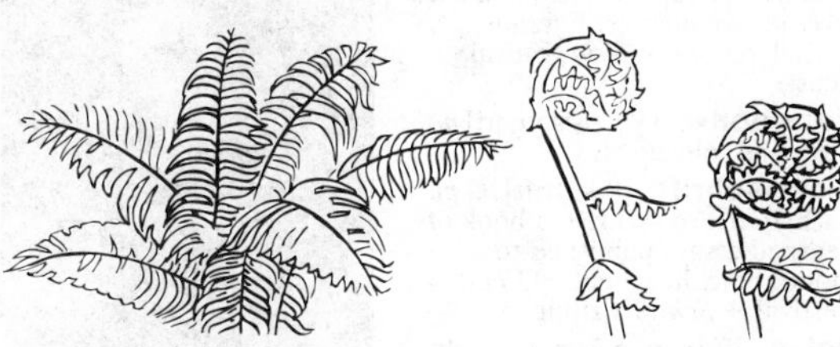

Fern: an ostrich fern, common in the Maritimes

Fiddleheads of this fern

fern [fɜrn] *n.* any of a class (Polypodiopsida, also called Filicinae) of flowerless vascular plants reproducing by means of spores. ⟨OE *fearn*⟩ **—'fern,like,** *adj.*
☛ *Hom.* FIRN.

fern•er•y ['fɜrnəri] *n., pl.* **-er•ies. 1** a place where ferns are grown for ornament. **2** a container in which ferns are grown for ornament. **3** the collection of ferns in either of these.

fern•y ['fɜrni] *adj.* of, like, or overgrown with ferns: *the forest's ferny floor.*

fe•ro•cious [fə'rouʃəs] *adj.* **1** savage; fierce. **2** intense: *a ferocious appetite.* ⟨< L *ferox, -ocis* fierce⟩ **—fe'ro•cious•ly,** *adv.*
☛ *Syn.* See note at FIERCE.

fe•ro•cious•ness [fə'rouʃəsnəs] *n.* ferocity.

fe•roc•i•ty [fə'rɒsəti] *n., pl.* **-ties.** savage behaviour; fierceness. ⟨< L *ferocitas* < *ferox* fierce⟩

–ferous *suffix.* producing; containing; conveying, as in *metalliferous.* ⟨< *-fer* (< L *ferre* bear) + E *-ous*⟩

fer•re•ous ['fɛriəs] *adj.* **1** containing iron. **2** like iron. ⟨< L *ferreus* < *ferrum* iron⟩

fer•ret[1] ['fɛrət] *n., v. —n.* **1** a domesticated albino form of the European polecat used especially for hunting rodents. **2** BLACK-FOOTED FERRET.
—v. **1** hunt with ferrets. **2** drive out of hiding (*usually used with* **out**): *to ferret out a criminal.* **3** find or find out by persistent searching (*usually used with* **out**): *to ferret out the truth of the matter.* **4** search; rummage; dig: *ferreting around in his pockets for a quarter.* ⟨ME < OF *furet,* ult. < L *fur* thief⟩ **—'fer•ret•y,** *adj.*

fer•ret[2] ['fɛrət] *n.* a narrow ribbon for binding. ⟨< Ital. *fioretti* floss silk, pl. of *fioretto* little flower⟩

ferri– *combining form.* iron; *ferriferous.* ⟨< L *ferrum* iron⟩

fer•ri•age ['fɛriɪdʒ] *n.* **1** transportation by ferry. **2** the fare paid for such transportation.

fer•ric ['fɛrɪk] *adj.* of or containing iron, especially trivalent iron. Compare FERROUS. ⟨< L *ferrum* iron⟩

ferric oxide a reddish brown compound of iron and oxygen found naturally as hematite and produced chemically in powder form for use as a pigment, abrasive, etc. *Formula*: Fe_2O_3

fer•rif•er•ous [fə'rɪfərəs] *adj.* FERREOUS (def. 1).

fer•ri•mag•net•ic [,fɛrɪmæg'nɛtɪk] *adj.* of or having to do with a material having weak permanent magnetism. Ferrimagnetic material is used in recording tape. ⟨< L *ferrum* iron + *magnet* + *-ic*⟩ **—,fer•ri'mag•net,ism,** *n.*

Fer•ris wheel ['fɛrɪs] a large, revolving framework of steel like an upright wheel, equipped with swinging seats that hang from its rim: *Ferris wheels are found in the amusement areas of fairs, exhibitions, and carnivals.* ⟨< G.W.G. *Ferris* (1859-1896), an American engineer, the inventor⟩

fer•rite ['fɛrəit] *n.* **1** any of various ferromagnetic crystalline compounds of the formula MFe_2O_4, M being a divalent metal such as zinc. **2** any allotrope of iron, highly susceptible to magnetism and occurring in cast iron, steel, etc. **3** any of a group of iron compounds occurring as microscopic particles in various types of igneous rock. ⟨< *ferri-* + *-ite*⟩

fer•ri•tin ['fɛrətɪn] *n.* an iron-storing protein found in the liver, spleen, and bone marrow. ⟨< *ferrite* + *-in*⟩

ferro– *combining form.* iron; derivation from iron: *ferrochromium.* ⟨< L *ferrum* iron⟩

fer•ro•chro•mi•um [,fɛrou'kroumiəm] *n.* an alloy of iron and chromium.

fer•ro•con•crete [,fɛrou'kɒnkrit] *or* [-kɒn'krit], [,fɛrou'kɒŋkrit] *or* [-kɒŋ'krit] *n.* concrete strengthened by a metal framework embedded in it; reinforced concrete.

fer•ro•e•lec•tric [,fɛrouɪ'lɛktrɪk] *n. Physics.* any crystalline solid having natural polarization of electric fields in the crystal lattice, and exceptional piezoelectric and elastic properties. ⟨< L *ferrum* iron + *electric*⟩ **—,fer•ro,e•lec'tric•i•ty,** *n.*

fer•ro•mag•net•ic [,fɛroumæg'nɛtɪk] *adj.* easily susceptible to magnetization, as iron is. The magnetism in ferromagnetic substances varies in force with the magnetizing field being applied, and may remain even after the field is no longer being applied. **—,fer•ro'mag•net,ism,** *n.*

fer•ro•man•ga•nese [,fɛrou'mæŋgə,niz] *or* [-'mæŋgə,nis] *n.* an alloy of iron, manganese, and sometimes carbon, used for making tough steel.

fer•rous ['fɛrəs] *adj.* of or containing iron, especially divalent iron. Compare FERRIC. ⟨< L *ferrum* iron⟩

ferrous as•cor•bate [ə'skɔrbeit] *n.* a drug used to treat iron deficiency anemia.

ferrous fu•ma•rate ['fjumə,reit] *n.* a drug used to treat anemia.

ferrous glu•co•nate ['glukə,neit] *n.* a drug used to treat anemia.

ferrous suc•ci•nate ['sʌksə,neit] a drug used to treat iron deficiency anemia.

ferrous sulphate or **sulfate** a drug used to treat anemia.

fer•ru•gi•nous [fə'rudʒɪnəs] *adj.* **1** of or containing iron. **2** like that of iron. **3** reddish brown like rust. ⟨< L *ferruginus* < *ferrugo* iron rust < *ferrum* iron⟩

fer•rule ['fɛrul] *or* ['fɛrəl] *n., v.* **-ruled, -rul•ing.** *—n.* **1** a metal ring or cap put around the end of a cane, wooden handle, umbrella, etc. to strengthen and protect it. **2** *Mechanics.* a small tube used to encase and tighten a joint. Also, **ferule.**
—v. provide with a ferrule. ⟨earlier *verrel* < OF *virelle* < L *viriola,* dim. of *viriae* bracelets; form influenced by L *ferrum* iron⟩
☛ *Hom.* FERAL ['fɛrəl], FERULE.

fer•ry ['fɛri] *n., pl.* **-ries;** *v.* **-ried, -ry•ing.** *—n.* **1** a boat that carries people and goods back and forth across a river or narrow stretch of water. **2** this service or the firm or system under which it is provided. **3** a place where a ferry operates. **4** delivery of aircraft to a destination by flying them.
—v. **1** carry (people and goods) back and forth on or as if on a ferry, etc., especially as a regular service: *Hundreds of cars are ferried across Northumberland Strait every day.* **2** cross on a ferry: *They ferried to Wolfe Island last Sunday.* **3** carry back and forth across a wide stretch of water in an aircraft. **4** fly (an aircraft) to a destination for delivery. ⟨OE *ferian* < *fær* fare⟩
☛ *Hom.* FAERIE, FAIRY.

fer•ry•boat ['fɛri,bout] *n.* FERRY (def. 1).

fer•ry•man ['fɛrimən] *n., pl.* **-men. 1** a person who owns or has charge of a ferry. **2** a person who works on a ferry.

fer•tile ['fɜrtaɪl] *or* ['fɜrtəl] *adj.* **1** capable of reproduction; able to produce seeds, fruit, young, etc; fecund. **2** of soil, capable of producing plants, crops, etc.: *Sand is not very fertile.* **3** producing many young; prolific: *Rabbits are fertile creatures; they have litters of young more often than many other animals.* **4** productive of many ideas; inventive: *a fertile mind.* **5** *Biology.* capable of developing into a new individual; fertilized: *Chicks hatch from fertile eggs.* **6** of nuclear material, fissionable by the action of neutrons. ⟨< L *fertilis* < *ferre* bear⟩ **—'fer•tile•ly,** *adv.* **—'fer•tile•ness,** *n.*
☛ *Syn.* **1. Fertile,** PRODUCTIVE = able to produce much. **Fertile** emphasizes containing within itself the things needed to nourish what is brought forth and maintain its life and development, and describes things in which seeds or ideas can take root and grow: *The seed fell on fertile ground. He has a fertile imagination.* **Productive** emphasizes bringing forth, especially in abundance: *Those fruit trees are very productive. She is a productive writer.*

Fertile Crescent a fertile, crescent-shaped strip of land on the eastern shore of the Mediterranean.

fer•til•i•ty [fər'tɪləti] *n.* the condition or degree of being fertile.

fer•ti•li•za•tion [ˌfɜrtəlaɪ'zeiʃən] *or* [ˌfɜrtələ'zeiʃən] *n.* **1** the application of fertilizer. **2** *Biology.* the union of male and female reproductive cells to form a cell that will develop into a new individual.

fer•ti•lize ['fɜrtəˌlaɪz] *v.* **-lized, -liz•ing. 1** make fertile; make able to produce much: *A crop of alfalfa fertilized the soil by adding nitrates to it.* **2** put fertilizer on. **3** *Biology.* of a male reproductive cell or sperm, unite with (a female reproductive cell) in fertilization; impregnate or pollinate.

fer•ti•liz•er ['fɜrtəˌlaɪzər] *n.* a person who or thing that fertilizes, especially a substance put on land to make it able to produce more. Manure is a common fertilizer.

fer•ule[1] ['fɛrul] *or* ['fɛrəl] *n., v.* **-uled, -ul•ing.** *—n.* a stick or ruler formerly used for punishing children by striking them, especially on the hand.
—v. punish with a stick or ruler. ⟨< L *ferula* rod⟩
☛ *Hom.* FERAL ['fɛrəl], FERRULE.

fer•ule[2] ['fɛrul] *or* ['fɛrəl] See FERRULE.
☛ *Hom.* FERAL ['fɛrəl].

fer•ven•cy ['fɜrvənsi] *n.* great warmth of feeling; intensity; ardour.

fer•vent ['fɜrvənt] *adj.* **1** showing warmth of feeling; ardent; intense: *a fervent plea.* **2** hot; glowing. ⟨< F < L *fervens, -entis,* ppr. of *fervere* boil⟩ **—'fer•vent•ly,** *adv.* **—'fer•vent•ness,** *n.*

fervid ['fɜrvɪd] *adj.* **1** showing great warmth of feeling; intensely emotional. **2** intensely hot. ⟨< L *fervidus* < *fervere* boil⟩ **—'fer•vid•ly,** *adv.* **—'fer•vid•ness,** *n.*

fer•vour or **fer•vor** ['fɜrvər] *n.* **1** great warmth of feeling; intense emotion: *The patriot's voice trembled with the fervour of his emotion.* **2** intense heat. ⟨ME < OF < L *fervor* < *fervere* boil⟩

fes•cue ['fɛskju] *n.* **1** any of a genus (*Festuca*) of grasses native to temperate and cold regions of the northern hemisphere, some of which are widely cultivated as pasture and fodder grasses and for use in lawn mixtures. **2** a small stick, etc. used as a pointer in teaching children to read. ⟨ME < OF *festu* < L *festuca*⟩

fess or **fesse** [fɛs] *n. Heraldry.* a wide, horizontal band across the middle of a shield. ⟨ME < OF *fesse, faisse* < L *fascia* band⟩

fess up *Informal.* confess.

-fest *combining form.* a festival: *songfest.* ⟨< G *Fest* festival, celebration⟩

fes•ta ['fɛstə] *n. Italian.* a holiday; feast; festival; party.

fes•tal ['fɛstəl] *adj.* of a feast, festival, or holiday; gay; joyous; festive: *A wedding or a birthday is a festal occasion.* ⟨< MF < LL < L *festum* feast⟩ **—'fes•tal•ly,** *adv.*

fes•ter ['fɛstər] *v., n.* *—v.* **1** form pus: *The neglected wound festered and became very painful.* **2** cause pus to form in. **3** cause pain or bitterness; rankle: *Resentment festered in her heart.* **4** decay; rot.
—n. a sore that forms pus; small ulcer. ⟨ME < OF *festre* < L *fistula* pipe, ulcer. Doublet of FISTULA.⟩

fes•ti•na•tion [ˌfɛstə'neiʃən] *n.* involuntary acceleration in gait, symptomatic of Parkinson's disease. ⟨< L *festinatus,* pp. of *festinare* to hurry⟩

fes•ti•val ['fɛstəvəl] *n.* **1** a day or special time of rejoicing or feasting, often in memory of some great happening or person: *A Mozart festival is held in Salzburg.* **2** a celebration; entertainment: *Every year the city has a music festival during the first week in May.* **3** a competition among drama groups, orchestras, etc. for recognition as the best in the region: *a high-school music festival.* **4** merrymaking; revelry. **5** (*adjl.*) having to do with a festival. ⟨< Med.L *festivalis,* ult. < L *festum* feast⟩

Festival of Lights 1 Hanukkah. **2** Divali.

fes•tive ['fɛstɪv] *adj.* of or for a feast, festival, or holiday; gay; joyous; merry: *A birthday or wedding is a festive occasion.* **—'fes•tive•ly,** *adv.* **—'fes•tive•ness,** *n.*

fes•tiv•i•ty [fɛ'stɪvəti] *n., pl.* **-ties. 1** a festive activity; something done to celebrate: *Are you attending the festivities tonight?* **2** gaiety; merriment. **3** festival.

fes•toon [fɛ'stun] *n., v.* *—n.* **1** a hanging curve of flowers, leaves, ribbons, etc.: *The flags were hung on the wall in colourful festoons.* **2** a carved or moulded ornament like this on furniture, pottery, etc.
—v. **1** decorate with festoons: *The Christmas tree was festooned with tinsel.* **2** form into festoons; hang in curves: *Draperies were festooned over the window.* ⟨< F *feston* < Ital. *festone* < *festa* festival, feast⟩

Festoons

fes•toon•e•ry [fɛ'stunəri] *n.* festoons collectively.

Fest•schrift ['fɛstˌʃrɪft] *n., pl.* **-schrif•ten** or **-schrift.** a book of learned essays published to honour a colleague. ⟨< G *Fest* festival + *Schrift* writing⟩

fet•a ['fɛtə] *n.* a firm, crumbly, white Greek cheese made from sheep's or goat's milk. ⟨< Mod. Gk. *tyri pheta* < *tyri* cheese + *pheta* < Ital. *fetta* a slice⟩

fe•tal ['fitəl] *adj.* of, having to do with, or like a fetus. Also, **foetal.**

fetal alcohol syndrome a syndrome of characteristic congenital malformations and mental retardation, resulting from prenatal exposure to alcohol.

fe•ta•tion [fi'teiʃən] *n.* pregnancy; gestation.

fetch[1] [fɛtʃ] *v., n.* *—v.* **1** go and get; bring. *He's gone to fetch the newspaper.* **2** cause to come; summon: *Someone fetch the doctor!* **3** be sold for: *Eggs were fetching a good price that year.* **4** *Informal.* attract; charm: *Flattery will fetch her.* **5** *Informal.* hit; strike: *He fetched him one on the nose.* **6** give (a groan, sigh, etc.). **7** *Nautical.* reach; arrive at: *They tried to fetch the harbour but the storm broke too soon.* **8** *Nautical.* take a course; move; go: *The boat was fetching to windward.* **9** of a dog, retrieve objects that have been thrown. **10** provoke; bring forth: *to fetch a laugh.*
fetch and carry, do small jobs.
fetch up, *Informal.* arrive; stop.
—n. the act of fetching. ⟨OE *feccan*⟩ **—'fetch•er,** *n.*

fetch[2] [fɛtʃ] *n.* an apparition, usually of one who is to die shortly. ⟨origin uncertain⟩

fetch•ing ['fɛtʃɪŋ] *adj., v.* *—adj. Informal.* attractive; charming: *She wore a fetching hat.*
—v. ppr. of FETCH. **—'fetch•ing•ly,** *adv.*

fete or **fête** [feit] *or* [fɛt]; *French,* [fɛt] *n., v.* **fet•ed** or **fêt•ed, fet•ing** or **fêt•ing.** *—n.* a festival; a gala entertainment or celebration, usually held outdoors: *A large fete was given for the benefit of the town hospital.*
—v. honour with a fete; entertain: *The engaged couple were feted by their friends.* ⟨< F *fête* feast⟩
☛ *Hom.* FATE [feit].

fet•ich ['fɛtɪʃ] *or* ['fitɪʃ] See FETISH.

fet•id ['fɛtɪd] *or* ['fitɪd] *adj.* smelling very bad; stinking. Also, **foetid.** ⟨< L *foetidus* < *foetere* to smell.⟩ **—'fet•id•ly,** *adv.* **—'fet•id•ness,** *n.*

fe•tip•a•rous [fi'tɪpərəs] *adj.* of animals, bearing incompletely developed offspring, as marsupials. ⟨< L *fetus* progeny + *-parus* < *parere* to bring forth, bear⟩

fet•ish ['fɛtɪʃ] *or* ['fitɪʃ] *n.* **1** a material object believed to contain a spirit or to have magical powers. **2** anything regarded with unreasoning reverence or devotion: *Some people make a fetish of style.* **3** a condition in which sexual excitement is derived from an object or a non-sexual part of the body. **4** an object or non-sexual body part giving such excitement. Also, **fetich.** ⟨< F *fétiche* < Pg. *feitiço* charm, originally adj., artificial < L *facticius.* Doublet of FACTITIOUS.⟩

fet•ish•ism ['fɛtɪˌʃɪzəm] *or* ['fitɪˌʃɪzəm] *n.* **1** a belief in fetishes; worship of fetishes. **2** behaviour characterized by a FETISH (def. 3).

fet•ish•ist ['fɛtɪʃɪst] *or* ['fitɪʃɪst] *n.* a person who worships or is obsessed by a fetish; one who practises fetishism.
—ˌfet•ish'is•tic, *adj.*

fet•lock ['fɛtˌlɒk] *n.* **1** the tuft of hair above a horse's hoof on the back part of the leg. **2** the part of a horse's leg where this tuft grows. See HORSE for picture. **3** the joint at this spot. ⟨ME *fetlok*⟩

fe•tol•o•gy [fi'tɒlədʒi] *n.* the branch of medicine concerning the treatment and development of the fetus. ⟨< L *fetus* progeny + E *-logy*⟩

fe•tor ['fitər] *n.* a strong, offensive smell. Also, **foetor.** ⟨< L *foetor* < *foetere* to smell⟩

fe•to•scope ['fitə,skoup] *n.* **1** an endoscope for viewing the fetus through a fibre-optic tube, used to detect fetal abnormalities. **2** a stethoscope for listening to the fetal heartbeat.

fe•tos•co•py [fi'tɒskəpi] *n.* the action of viewing the fetus through a fetoscope. **–,fe•to'scop•ic** [,fitə'skɒpɪk], *adj.*

fet•ter ['fɛtər] *n., v.* *–n.* **1** a chain or shackle for the feet to prevent escape. **2** Usually, **fetters,** *pl.* anything that shackles or binds; restraint.
–v. **1** bind with fetters; chain the feet of. **2** bind; restrain: *The boy had to learn to fetter his temper.* ⟨OE *feter.* Related to FOOT.⟩

fet•tle ['fɛtəl] *n.* condition; trim: *The horse is in fine fettle and should win the race.* ⟨? < ME *fettel(en)* gird up < OE *fetel* belt⟩

fet•tu•ci•ne [,fɛtu'tʃini] *n. sing. and pl.* narrow, flat strips of pasta. Also, **fettuccine, fettucini.** ⟨< Ital.⟩

fe•tus ['fitəs] *n.* the unborn young of a vertebrate, especially a mammal, and especially during the later period of its development when it begins to clearly resemble the newborn of its species; the term is used for a human offspring in the womb from about nine weeks after conception. Compare EMBRYO. Also, **foetus.** ⟨< L. See FETIPAROUS.⟩

feud[1] [fjud] *n., v.* *–n.* **1** a long and deadly quarrel between families, tribes, etc., often passed down from generation to generation. **2** continued strife between two persons, groups, etc. **3** a quarrel.
–v. engage in a quarrel, especially a deadly one, one involving families particularly: *They have been feuding with their neighbours for years.* ⟨var. of ME *fede* < OF *fe(i)de* < OHG *fehida* enmity⟩
☛ *Syn. n.* **3.** See note at QUARREL[1].

feud[2] [fjud] *n.* a feudal estate; fief. ⟨< Med.L *feudum* < Gmc.⟩

feu•dal ['fjudəl] *adj.* **1** of or having to do with feudalism. **2** of or having to do with feuds or fiefs. **3** of or like a feud. ⟨< Med.L *feudalis* < *feudum.* See FEUD[2].⟩

feu•dal•ism ['fjudə,lɪzəm] *n.* **1** the social, economic, and political system of Western Europe in the Middle Ages. Under this system vassals gave military and other services to a lord in return for protection and the use of land owned by the lord. **2** any social, economic, or political system that suggests or resembles this. **–'feu•dal•ist,** *n.*

feu•dal•is•tic [,fjudə'lɪstɪk] *adj.* **1** of or having to do with feudalism. **2** tending toward or favouring feudalism.

feu•dal•i•ty [fju'dæləti] *n., pl.* **-ties. 1** a feudal estate; fief. **2** feudal quality or character.

feudal system feudalism.

feu•da•to•ry ['fjudə,tɔri] *adj., n., pl.* **-ries.** *–adj.* **1** owing feudal services. **2** holding or held as a feudal estate or fief. *–n.* **1** a feudal vassal: *The duke summoned his feudatories to aid him in war.* **2** a feudal estate; fief.

feu de joie [fød'ʒwa] *pl.* **feux de joie.** *French.* a salute made by a line of troops firing their rifles in rapid succession. ⟨< F, literally, fire of joy⟩

feud•ist ['fjudɪst] *n.* **1** a person engaging in a feud. **2** an authority on feudal law.

fe•ver ['fivər] *n., v.* *–n.* **1** an unhealthy condition of the body in which the temperature is higher than normal. **2** any of various diseases that cause fever, such as scarlet fever and typhoid fever. **3** an excited, restless condition. **4** a current fad or enthusiasm for something or for some person.
–v. affect with fever or excite as if with fever. ⟨OE *fefer* < L *febris*⟩ **–'fe•ver•less,** *adj.*

fever blister COLD SORE.

fe•vered ['fivərd] *adj., v.* *–adj.* **1** having fever; hot with fever: *a fevered brow.* **2** excited; restless.
–v. pt. and pp. of FEVER.

fe•ver•few ['fivər,fju] *n.* a perennial European plant (*Chrysanthemum parthenium*) of the composite family having small, daisylike flowers. Feverfew, formerly widely believed to be useful in reducing a fever, is still often cultivated as a garden flower. ⟨OE *fēferfūg(i)e* < LL *febrifug(i)a* < L *febris* fever + *fugare* drive away⟩

fe•ver•ish ['fivərɪʃ] *adj.* **1** having fever, especially a slight fever. **2** caused by fever: *feverish thirst, feverish dreams.* **3** causing fever: *a feverish climate.* **4** infested with fever-causing organisms or diseases: *a feverish swamp.* **5** excited; restless. **–'fe•ver•ish•ly,** *adv.* **–'fe•ver•ish•ness,** *n.*

fe•ver•ous ['fivərəs] *adj.* feverish.

fever pitch a state of intense excitement or frenzied activity.

fe•ver•wort ['fivər,wɜrt] *n.* any of several perennial herbs (genus *Triosteum*) of the honeysuckle family formerly used in medicine. Also called, **fever-root.**

few [fju] *adj., n.* *–adj.* not many: *There are few people more than 200 cm tall.*
–n. **1** a small number: *Only a few of the children had bicycles.* **2 the few,** the minority, especially a small, privileged group.
few and far between, very few or infrequent.
quite a few, *Informal.* a good many: *We caught ten fish, but quite a few got away.* ⟨OE *fēawe*⟩ **–'few•ness,** *n.*
☛ *Hom.* PHEW.
☛ *Usage.* **Fewer,** LESS. **Fewer** refers only to number and to things that are counted: *Fewer cars were on the road. There were fewer than sixty present.* Except in informal usage, **less** refers only to amount or quantity and to things that are measured: *There was a good deal less tardiness in the second term. There was even less hay than the summer before.*

fey [fei] *adj.* strange or unusual in any of many different ways, including visionary, psychic, or otherworldly. ⟨< ME *feie* < OE *fæge* fated, akin to G *feige* cowardly⟩ **–'fey•ly,** *adv.* **–'fey•ness,** *n.*
☛ *Hom.* FAY, FE.

fez [fɛz] *n., pl.* **fez•zes.** a brimless felt cap, usually red, having a high crown with a flat top and ornamented with a long, black tassel. It was formerly the national headdress of Turkish men. See CAP for picture. ⟨< Turkish; after *Fez,* Morocco⟩

ff fortissimo.

ff. **1** and the following pages, sections, etc.: *p. 26 ff. means page 26 and the following few pages.* **2** folios.

F.I. FALKLAND ISLANDS.

fi•a•cre [fi'ɑkər]; *French,* ['fjakʀ] *n.* a small, four-wheeled, horse-drawn hackney coach. ⟨< St. *Fiacre,* the name of the hotel in Paris where they were first hired⟩

fi•an•cé [,fiɑn'sei], [fi'ɑnsei], *or* ['fiɑn,sei] *n.* a man to whom a woman is engaged to be married. ⟨< F *fiancé,* pp. of *fiancer* betroth⟩

fi•an•cée [,fiɑn'sei], [fi'ɑnsei], *or* ['fiɑn,sei] *n.* a woman to whom a man is engaged to be married. ⟨< F⟩

fi•as•co [fi'æskou] *n., pl.* **-cos** or **-coes. 1** a failure; breakdown. **2** a scandalous or embarrassing failure. ⟨< F < Ital. *fiasco,* literally, flask; development of meaning uncertain⟩

fi•at ['fiət] *or* ['fiæt], ['faɪət] *or* ['faɪæt] *n.* **1** any authoritative, often arbitrary order or command; decree. **2** sanction: *He acted under the fiat of the queen.* ⟨< L *fiat* let it be done⟩

fib [fɪb] *n., v.* **fibbed, fib•bing.** *–n.* a lie about some small matter; a trivial lie.
–v. tell such a lie. ⟨? < *fibble-fable* < *fable*⟩ **–'fib•ber,** *n.*
☛ *Syn.* See note at LIE.[1]

fi•ber ['faɪbər] See FIBRE.

Fi•ber•glas ['faɪbər,glæs] *n. Trademark.* a brand of fibreglass.

Fi•bo•nac•ci sequence or **series** [,fibə'nɑtʃi] an infinite sequence of numbers, each number being the sum of the two previous ones. ⟨< L *Fibonacci* 13c. Italian mathematician⟩

fi•bre ['faɪbər] *n.* **1** one of the threadlike cells or structures that combine with others to form certain plant or animal tissues. **2** tissue formed in this way: *muscle fibre. Hemp fibre is used to make rope or cloth.* **3** a slender, threadlike root of a plant. **4** a long, slender filament of wool, cotton, glass, rayon, nylon, etc. used especially for making yarn or cloth. **5** a yarn or cloth made of such fibres. **6** texture: *cloth of coarse fibre.* **7** essential nature or character: *a strong moral fibre. The very fibre of her being was stirred.* **8** ROUGHAGE (def. 2). Also, **fiber.** ⟨< F *fibre* < L *fibra*⟩

fi•bre•board ['faɪbər,bɔrd] *n.* **1** a building material made by compressing fibrous materials, such as wood or cane fibre or straw, into flat, semirigid sheets. It is used in the construction of interior walls, as sheathing for the inside of exterior walls, etc. Also, **fiberboard. 2** a sheet of this board.

fi•bre•fill ['faɪbər,fɪl] *n.* synthetic fibres used as a filling for winter coats, sleeping bags, pillows, etc. Also, **fiberfill.**

fi•bre•glass ['faɪbər,glæs] *n., v.* *–n.* **1** glass drawn and spun into fine threads or fibres. **2** a thick material consisting of matted fibreglass, used for insulation. **3** textile fabric woven from fibreglass, used for curtains, etc. **4** a moulded or pressed material consisting of plastic mixed with fibreglass, used for making boat hulls, automobile bodies, etc. **5** (*adjl.*) made of fibreglass.
–v. form or shape with fibreglass. Also, **fiberglass.**

fibre optics **1** the technology of using a very long, fine, flexible glass or acrylic fibre or a bundle of such fibres for transmitting light or optical images by total internal reflection or refraction. **2** (*adjl.*) designating such a fibre or a bundle of such fibres forming part of a telecommunications system, optical instrument, etc. **—'fi•bre-'op•tic,** *adj.*

fi•bre•scope ['faɪbər,skoup] *n.* a fibre-optic endoscope designed for examining inaccessible areas. Also, **fiberscope.**

fi•bril ['faɪbrəl] *n.* **1** a small or very slender fibre. **2** one of the hairs on the roots of some plants. ⟨< NL *fibrilla* dim. of *fibra* fibre⟩ **—'fi•bril•lar, 'fi•bril,lose,** *adj.*

fi•bril•late ['faɪbrə,leit] *or* ['fɪbrə,leit] *v.* **-lat•ed, -lat•ing. 1** of a muscle or muscle fibre, undergo or exhibit fibrillation. **2** break up or form into fibrils.

fi•bril•la•tion [,faɪbrə'leiʃən] *or* [,fɪbrə'leiʃən] *n.* **1** the act or process of splitting or forming into fibrils. **2** irregular, usually rapid, twitching of individual muscle fibres within a muscle. **3** rapid, irregular contractions or twitchings in the muscular wall of the heart, interfering with or replacing the normal rhythmical contractions of the heart.

fi•brin ['faɪbrɪn] *n.* a tough, elastic, insoluble protein forming the fibrous network of a blood clot. Fibrin is formed from fibrinogen by the action of an enzyme in the blood. ⟨< L *fibra* fibre + E *-in*⟩

fi•brin•o•gen [faɪ'brɪnədʒən] *n.* a soluble protein found especially in blood plasma, that is converted into fibrin by the action of an enzyme when blood clots. ⟨< *fibrin* + *-gen*⟩

fi•brin•o•gen•ic [,faɪbrɪnə'dʒɛnɪk] *adj.* producing fibrin.

fi•bri•nol•y•sin [,faɪbrɪ'nɒləsɪn] *n.* an enzyme which can digest fibrin in the bloodstream, and is used to clean wounds. ⟨< *fibrin* + *lysin*⟩

fi•bri•nol•y•sis [,faɪbrɪ'nɒləsɪs] *n.* the digesting of fibrin by an enzyme in the bloodstream. ⟨< *fibrin* + *lysis*⟩ **—,fi•bri•no'lyt•ic** [,faɪbrɪnə'lɪtɪk], *adj.*

fi•bri•no•sis [,faɪbrə'nousɪs] *n.* a condition marked by too much fibrin in the blood.

fi•brin•ous ['faɪbrənəs] *adj.* **1** of or like fibrin. **2** containing fibrin.

fi•bro•blast ['faɪbrə,blæst] *n.* a type of cell that synthesizes collagen and forms the fibres in connective tissue. It is often used for cell study in cultures; an explant of skin or other tissue gives rise to a layer of fibroblasts, which can be subcultured and grown for up to 30 cell generations. ⟨< L *fibra* fibre + Gk. *blastos* a sprout⟩ **—,fi•bro'blas•tic,** *adj.*

fi•broid ['faɪbrɔɪd] *adj., n.* *—adj.* made up of fibres; of fibrelike structure.
—n. a tumour made up of fibres or fibrous tissue: *The patient has fibroids in her uterus.*

fi•bro•in ['faɪbrouɪn] *n.* the protein from which spiders' webs and raw silk are made. ⟨< L *fibra* fibre + E *-in*⟩

fi•bro•ma [faɪ'broumə] *n.* a fibrous but benign tumour. **—fi'brom•a•tous** [faɪ'brɒmətəs], *adj.*

fi•bro•nec•tin [,faɪbrou'nɛktɪn] *n.* a protein that destroys bacteria in the blood and helps build connective tissue. ⟨< L *fibra* fibre + *nectere* to bind + *-in*⟩

fi•bro•pla•sia [,faɪbrou'pleiʒə] *or* [-'pleiziə] *n.* the growth of connective tissue, as in some diseases or wound healing. ⟨< L *fibra* fibre + NL *-plasia* < Gk. *plasis* a moulding < *plassein* to mould⟩

fi•bro•sis [faɪ'brousɪs] *n.* an excessive growth of fibrous connective tissue in the body. ⟨< NL *fibrosis* < L *fibra* fibre + *-osis* -osis⟩ **—fi'brot•ic** [faɪ'brɒtɪk], *adj.*

fi•bro•si•tis [,faɪbrə'səitɪs] *n.* inflammation of fibrous tissue in the muscle sheaths. ⟨< NL *fibrosus* fibrous + *-itis* < Gk. *-itis* fem. of *-ites*⟩

fi•brous ['faɪbrəs] *adj.* made up of fibres; having fibres; like fibre. **—'fi•brous•ly,** *adv.*

fi•bro•vas•cu•lar [,faɪbrou'væskjələr] *adj. Botany.* made of fibres and ducts for conveying a fluid, such as sap. Leaf veins are fibrovascular bundles.

fib•u•la ['fɪbjələ] *n., pl.* **-lae** [-,li] or [-,laɪ] or **-las. 1** *Anatomy.* the outer, thinner of the two bones in the human lower leg, extending from the knee to the ankle. See LEG for picture. **2** *Zoology.* the corresponding bone in the hind leg of an animal. **3** a clasp or brooch, often highly ornamented, used by the ancient Greeks and Romans. A fibula resembles a decorated safety pin. ⟨< L *fibula* clasp, brooch⟩

fib•u•lar ['fɪbjələr] *adj. Anatomy.* of or having to do with the fibula.

–fic *suffix.* making or causing, as in *scientific, terrific.* ⟨< L *-ficus* < *facere* do, make⟩

–fication *suffix.* a making or doing; corresponding to verbs ending in *-fy*, as in *falsification, purification.* ⟨< L *-ficatio, -onis* < *-ficare* < *facere* do, make⟩

fiche [fiʃ] *n.* microfiche.

fich•u ['fɪʃu]; *French,* [fi'ʃy] *n.* a three-cornered piece of muslin, lace, or other soft material worn by women about the neck, with the ends drawn together or crossed on the breast. ⟨< F, little shawl < *ficher* attach with a pin⟩

fick•le ['fɪkəl] *adj.* likely to change without reason; changing; not constant: *fickle fortune, a fickle friend.* ⟨OE *ficol* deceitful⟩ **—'fick•le•ness,** *n.*

fic•tile ['fɪktaɪl] *or* ['fɪktəl] *adj.* **1** plastic. **2** moulded into a shape. **3** made of clay. **4** having to do with pottery. **5** of a person, easily led. ⟨< L *fictilis* earthen < pp. of *fingere.* See FICTION.⟩

fic•tion ['fɪkʃən] *n.* **1** novels, short stories, and other prose writings that tell about imaginary, and sometimes real, people and happenings. Both characters and events in fiction may sometimes be partly real. **2** what is imagined or made up; imaginary happenings; make-believe: *The explorer exaggerated so much in telling about his adventures that it was impossible to separate fact from fiction.* **3** an imaginary account or statement; made-up story. **4** an inventing of imaginary accounts, stories, etc.; a feigning. **5** something conventionally acted on as a fact for the sake of expedience, in spite of its possible falsity. It is a legal fiction that a corporation is a person. ⟨< L *fictio, -onis* < *fingere* to form, fashion⟩ **—'fic•tion•ist,** *n.*

fic•tion•al ['fɪkʃənəl] *adj.* of or having to do with fiction. **—'fic•tion•al•ly,** *adv.*

fic•tion•al•ize ['fɪkʃənə,laɪz] *v.,* **-ized, -iz•ing.** make into fiction; *The movie gives a highly fictionalized account of frontier life.* **—,fic•tion•al•i'za•tion,** *n.*

fic•ti•tious [fɪk'tɪʃəs] *adj.* **1** not real; imaginary; made-up: *Characters in novels are usually entirely fictitious.* **2** assumed in order to deceive; false: *The criminal used a fictitious name.* ⟨< L *ficticius* artificial < *fingere* form, fashion⟩ **—fic'ti•tious•ly,** *adv.* **—fic'ti•tious•ness,** *n.*

fic•tive ['fɪktɪv] *adj.* **1** imaginary. **2** creative of fiction. ⟨< F *fictif* < Med.L *fictivus*⟩ **—'fic•tive•ly,** *adv.*

fi•cus ['fəɪkəs] *n., pl.* **fi•cus** or **fi•cus•es** a tree of the genus *Ficus*, of the mulberry family, including the rubber plant and *Ficus benjamina*. ⟨< NL < L, fig⟩

fid [fɪd] *n.* **1** a square wooden or iron bar used to support a topmast. **2** a round, tapering pin, usually of hardwood, used for separating strands of rope in splicing. It has a groove along one side for feeding a strand to be tucked between the separated strands. ⟨origin uncertain⟩

–fid *suffix.* split; cleft; lobed, as in *bifid.* ⟨< L *-fidus* < *findere* cleave, split⟩

fid•dle ['fɪdəl] *n., v.* **-dled, -dling.** *—n.* **1** *Informal.* an instrument of the violin or viol family, especially a violin. **2** on a ship, a low railing on the edge of a table to prevent dishes, etc. from sliding off when the ship rolls or pitches. **3** *Slang.* deception or fraud.
fit as a fiddle, in excellent physical condition.
play second fiddle, take a secondary part.
—v. **1** *Informal.* play on a violin. **2** make aimless movements; play nervously or restlessly; toy: *Instead of answering, the embarrassed boy just fiddled with his jacket.* **3** spend time idly or aimlessly: *fiddling around in his workshop.* **4** tamper or interfere: *Don't fiddle with the controls.* **5** *Slang.* swindle; cheat.
fiddle away, waste (time). ⟨OE *fithele* (recorded in *fithelere* fiddler); probably akin to Med.L *vitula.* See VIOL.⟩ **—'fid•dler,** *n.*

fid•dle–de–dee [,fɪdəl di 'di] *n. or interj.* nonsense.

fid•dle–fad•dle ['fɪdəl ,fædəl] *n., interj., v.* **-fad•dled, -fad•dling.** *Informal.* *—n.* trifling speech or action.
—interj. nonsense.
—v. busy oneself about trivial things. ⟨? reduplication of *fiddle*⟩

fid•dle•head ['fɪdəl,hɛd] *n.* **1** one of the young, curled fronds of certain ferns (such as the ostrich fern), eaten as a delicacy. Fiddleheads are eaten especially in Nova Scotia and New Brunswick. See FERN for picture. **2** a scroll-shaped ornament on a ship's bow, resembling the head of a violin. Also, **fiddleneck.**

fiddler crab a small burrowing crab (genus *Uva*) common along the Atlantic coast of the U.S.

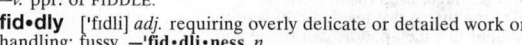

A fiddler crab

fid•dle•stick ['fɪdəl,stɪk] *n., interj. —n.* **1** *Archaic.* a violin bow. **2** a mere nothing; trifle.
—interj. **fiddlesticks,** nonsense! rubbish!

fid•dling ['fɪdlɪŋ] *adj., v. —adj.* trifling; petty.
—v. ppr. of FIDDLE.

fid•dly ['fɪdli] *adj.* requiring overly delicate or detailed work or handling; fussy. **—'fid•dli•ness,** *n.*

Fi•de•i De•fen•sor ['faɪdi,aɪ] *or* ['fidei,i dɪ'fɛnsɔr] *Latin.* Defender of the Faith, one of the titles of the British Sovereign.

fi•de•ism ['fidei,ɪzəm] *or* ['faɪdi,ɪzəm] *n. Philosophy.* the view that all real knowledge is ultimately of the nature of faith and that reason alone is insufficient. ⟨< NL *fideismus* < L *fides* faith + *ismus* < Gk. *-ismos* suffix of action or state⟩ **—'fi•de•ist,** *n.* **—,fi•de'ist•ic,** *adj.*

fi•del•i•ty [fə'dɛləti] *or* [faɪ'dɛləti] *n.* **1** faithfulness to a trust or vow; steadfast faithfulness; loyalty. **2** reliability or thoroughness in the performance of duty: *His fidelity and industry brought him speedy promotion.* **3** exactness, as of a copy; accuracy: *The reporter wrote her story with absolute fidelity.* **4** the ability of a device, as a radio transmitter or receiver, to transmit or reproduce an electric signal or sound accurately. ⟨< L *fidelitas,* ult. < *fides* faith. Doublet of FEALTY.⟩

fidg•et ['fɪdʒɪt] *v., n. —v.* **1** move about restlessly; be uneasy: *A child fidgets if she has to sit still for a long time.* **2** make uneasy.
—n. **1** the condition of being restless or uneasy. **2** a person who moves about restlessly. **3 the fidgets,** *pl.* a fit of restlessness or uneasiness. ⟨< obs. *fidge* move restlessly⟩

fidg•et•y ['fɪdʒəti] *adj.* restless; uneasy. **—'fidg•et•i•ness,** *n.*

fi•du•cial [fɪ'djuʃəl] *or* [fɪ'duʃəl] *adj.* of any line or point, used as a standard or base from which to measure and calculate. ⟨< L *fiducialis* < *fiducia* trust⟩

fi•du•ci•ar•y [fə'djuʃi,ɛri] *or* [fə'duʃi,ɛri] *adj., n., pl.* **-ar•ies.**
—adj. **1** held in trust: *fiduciary estates.* **2** holding in trust. A fiduciary possessor is legally responsible for what belongs to another. **3** of a trustee; of trust and confidence: *A guardian acts in a fiduciary capacity.* **4** depending upon public trust and confidence for its value. Paper money that cannot be redeemed in gold or silver is fiduciary currency.
—n. a trustee. ⟨< L *fiduciarus* < *fiducia* trust⟩

fie [faɪ] *interj. Archaic.* for shame! Shame on you! (*now often used facetiously*) ⟨< ME fi < OF, ultimately imitative⟩
☛ *Hom.* PHI.

fief [fif] *n., v. —n.* in feudal times, a piece of land held from a lord in return for military and other services as required; feudal estate.
—v. invest with a fief. Also, **feoff.** ⟨< F < Gmc.; see FEE⟩ **—'fief•dom,** *n.*

field [fild] *n., v. —n.* **1** a piece of land used for crops or pasture: *a wheat field.* **2** land with few or no trees. **3** a piece of land used for some special purpose: *a playing field.* **4** land yielding some product: *a coal field.* **5** *Military.* **a** the place where a battle is or has been fought. **b** a battle: *The English won the field at Poitiers.* **c** a region where certain military operations are carried on. **6** *Sports.* **a** an area for athletics, games, etc. **b** the part of this area used for contests in jumping, etc. as opposed to races. **c** the sports contested in this area. **d** all those participating in a game, contest, or outdoor sport: *At the halfway mark in the marathon, a Canadian was leading the field.* **e** all those participating in a game or contest except one or more specified: *to bet on one horse against the field.* **f** a defensive football, baseball, etc. team. **7** *Baseball.* **a** the playing field, including both infield and outfield. **b** the outfield. **8** a range of opportunity or interest; sphere of activity or operation: *the field of science.* **9** a place away from the office or laboratory, where a scientist, linguist, anthropologist, etc., collects data, samples, etc. **10** a large, flat space; broad surface: *a field of ice.* **11** the surface on which some emblem is pictured or painted; background: *the field of a coat of arms.* **12** the ground of each division of a flag. **13** *Physics.* the space throughout which a force operates. A magnet has a magnetic field about it. **14** the space or area in which things can be seen through a telescope, microscope, etc. without moving it: *the field of vision.* **15** *Television, film.* the entire screen area occupied by an image. **16** *Mathematics.* **a** a set which is commutative under addition and also under multiplication, e.g., 3+2 = 2+3 and 3 × 2 = 2 × 3. **b** a set such that division, multiplication, addition, or subtraction performed on any two members yields another member. **17** *Computer technology.* **a** a location on a computer screen, on a document, or in a record, where a data item appears or is entered: *the SIN field.* **b** the data so appearing or being entered. **18** (*adjl.*) native to or taking place in the field: *a field assignment, field flowers.*
keep or **hold the field,** maintain activity, as in a military campaign, game, or any other contest.
leave the field, cease activity, as in a military campaign, game, or any other contest.
play the field, a *Informal.* take a broad sphere of action or operation. **b** *Slang.* go out with many different persons of the opposite sex.
take the field, begin a battle, campaign, game, etc.
—v. **1** *Baseball, cricket, etc.* **a** stop or catch and return (a ball). **b** act as a fielder. **2** put into the field; bring in or have as player, candidate, etc.: *to field a good baseball team. The party fielded only a handful of candidates.* **3** protect; defend: *He fielded his political position gracefully.*
field a question, answer a question asked unexpectedly. ⟨OE *feld*⟩

field artillery artillery mounted on carriages for easy movement by armies in the field.

field chickweed a wildflower (*Cerastium arvense*) of North America and Eurasia, having white flowers on a 20 cm stem.

field corn corn grown for fodder.

field day **1** a day set aside for athletic contests and outdoor sports. **2** a day when soldiers perform drills, mock fights, etc. **3** a day of unusual activity, display, or success. **4** a day spent by a scientist, etc., in field work.

field•er ['fildər] *n.* **1** *Baseball.* a player who is stationed around or outside the diamond to stop the ball and throw it in. **2** *Cricket.* a person playing a similar position.

fielder's choice *Baseball.* a fielder's decision to put out a base runner rather than the batter.

field event any one of the events at an athletic meet that are held on the field as opposed to the track. The high jump, the pole vault, the shot put and the discus throw are field events.

field•fare ['fild,fɛr] *n.* a European thrush (*Turdus pilaris*) having a grey head, black tail, and brown and white body. It has appeared occasionally in Canada. ⟨OE *feldefare*⟩

field glasses or **field glass** binoculars.

field goal **1** *Football.* a goal counting three points scored by kicking the ball between the uprights and above the bar of the goal post. **2** *Basketball.* a goal made while the ball is in play.

field gun an artillery gun.

field hockey a game played on a grass field by two teams whose players, except the goalie, use curved sticks and try to drive a ball into the opposing team's goal.

field hospital a temporary hospital near a battlefield.

field house a building near an athletic field, used for storing equipment, for dressing rooms, etc.

field jacket a light, waterproof cotton jacket designed to be worn by soldiers in combat.

field kitchen a portable kitchen that can be set up in the open to cook food for a large number of people, such as an army unit.

field magnet an electromagnet used in a generator or motor to make a strong electrical field.

field marshal an officer of the highest rank in the armies of certain countries, ranking above a general. *Abbrev.:* F.M.

field mouse **1** any of various voles, especially a medium-sized species (*Microtus pennsylvanicus*) found throughout most of Canada and the northern United States. **2** any of a genus (*Apodemus*) of nocturnal, burrowing Old World mice found in Europe, Asia, and N Africa.

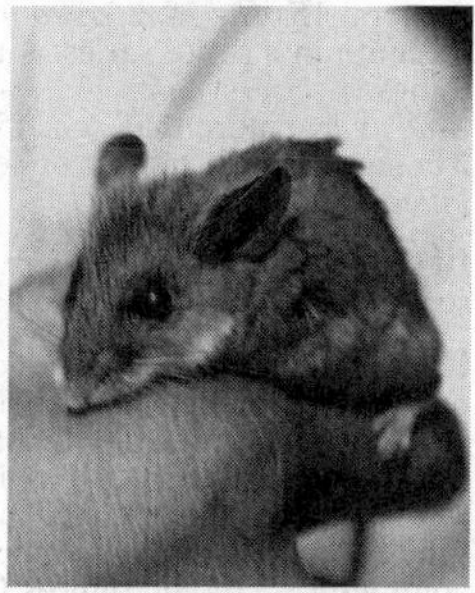
A field mouse

field officer any commissioned officer senior to a captain and junior to a brigadier-general.

field of fire the area that a gun or battery covers effectively.

field•piece ['fild,pis] *n.* FIELD GUN.

field•stone ['fild,stoun] *n., adj.* *—n.* rough stones used for houses, walls, etc. especially when found in the area near the construction site.
—adj. of or resembling fieldstone.

field test a test made of a new product, system, etc. in the environment or by the users for which it is intended, to determine its durability, efficiency, acceptability, etc.
—'field-,test, *v.*

field theory *Physics.* a theory in which physical fields form the basic quantities.

field trial **1** a test of the performance of hunting dogs in the field. **2** FIELD TEST.

field trip a trip away from the school to give students special opportunities for observing facts relating to a particular field of study.

field winding the circuit, usually in coils, that produces a magnetic field in a generator.

field work the scientific or technical work done in the field by surveyors, geologists, linguists, sociologists, etc. gathering data.

field•work ['fild,wɜrk] *n.* a temporary fortification for defence made by soldiers in the field.

field•work•er ['fild,wɜrkər] *n.* one engaged in field work. Also, **field worker.**

fiend [find] *n.* **1** an evil spirit; devil. **2** an extremely wicked or cruel person. **3 the Fiend,** the Devil. **4** *Informal.* a person who indulges excessively in some habit, practice, game, etc.: *She is a fiend for work.* ⟨OE *fēond,* originally ppr. of *fēogan* hate⟩
—'fiend,like, *adj.*

fiend•ish ['findɪʃ] *adj.* **1** extremely cruel or wicked; devilish: *fiendish tortures, a fiendish yell.* **2** *Informal.* very difficult: *a fiendish exam.* **—'fiend•ish•ly,** *adv.* **—'fiend•ish•ness,** *n.*

fierce [firs] *adj.* **fierc•er, fierc•est. 1** savage; wild: *a fierce lion.* **2** raging; violent: *a fierce wind.* **3** very eager or active; ardent: *a fierce determination to win.* **4** *Informal.* intense; extreme: *The heat was fierce.* ⟨ME < OF *fers, fiers* < L *ferus* wild⟩ **—'fierce•ly,** *adv.* **—'fierce•ness,** *n.*

☛ *Syn.* **1. Fierce,** FEROCIOUS, SAVAGE = wild and harsh. **Fierce** emphasizes having a pitiless or unfeeling nature, showing a readiness to harm or kill, or being given to wild rage, especially in manner or actions: *He was a fierce fighter.* **Ferocious** suggests being wildly fierce or cruel, or showing wild force, especially in looks, disposition, or actions: *That man looks ferocious.* **Savage** adds the idea of showing an uncivilized lack of restraint on the emotions or passions and an inhuman lack of feeling for pain caused to others: *She has a savage temper.*

fi•er•y ['faɪri], ['faɪəri] *adj.* **fi•er•i•er, fi•er•i•est. 1** consisting of fire; containing fire; burning; flaming. **2** like fire; very hot, brilliant, or glowing: *a fiery red.* **3** full of feeling or spirit; ardent: *a fiery speech.* **4** easily aroused or excited: *a fiery temper.* **5** inflamed: *a fiery sore.* **—'fi•er•i•ly,** *adv.* **—'fi•er•i•ness,** *n.*

fi•es•ta [fi'ɛstə] *n.* **1** a religious festival; saint's day. **2** a celebration; festivity. ⟨< Sp. *fiesta* feast⟩

fife [fəif] *n., v.* **fifed, fif•ing.** *—n.* a small, shrill musical instrument like a flute: *Fifes and drums are used in playing marches.*
—v. play on a fife. ⟨< G *Pfeife* pipe⟩ **—'fif•er,** *n.*

fif•teen ['fɪf'tɪn] *n., adj.* *—n.* **1** five more than ten; 15. **2** the numeral 15: *The 15 refers to the song number, not the page.* **3** the fifteenth in a set or series. **4** a set or series of fifteen persons or things.
—adj. **1** five more than ten; 15: *Fifteen people answered the ad.* **2** being fifteenth in a set or series (*used after the noun*): *Chapter Fifteen.* ⟨OE *fīftēne*⟩

fif•teenth ['fɪf'tinθ] *adj. or n.* **1** next after the 14th; last in a series of fifteen; 15th. **2** one, or being one, of 15 equal parts.

fifth [fɪfθ] *adj., n.* *—adj.* **1** next after the fourth; last in a series of five; 5th. **2** being one of 5 equal parts.
—n. **1** the next after the fourth; last in a series of five; 5th. **2** one of 5 equal parts. **3** *Music.* **a** the fifth tone from the tonic or keynote of a scale; the dominant. **b** the interval between such tones. **c** a combination of such tones. **4** *Slang.* a bottle of liquor containing 25.6 fluid ounces (about 800 ml), which is one fifth of a U.S. gallon. ⟨alteration of OE *fīfta*⟩

fifth column any group of persons within a country who secretly aid its enemies. Originally, the term was applied to the Franco supporters in Madrid during the Spanish Civil War, who constituted an additional, or fifth, column to the four military columns that attacked the city from outside.

fifth columnist a member of the FIFTH COLUMN.

fifth•ly ['fɪfθli] *adv.* in the fifth place.

fifth wheel *Informal.* **1** a wheel-like device over the front axle of a carriage, used to support the vehicle during turns. **2** a person or thing that is not needed and is in the way. **3** a trailer or camper in which people can travel and live.

fif•ti•eth ['fɪftiɪθ] *adj. or n.* **1** next after the 49th; last in a series of fifty; 50th. **2** one, or being one, of 50 equal parts.

fif•ty ['fɪfti] *n., pl.* **-ties;** *adj.* *—n.* **1** five times ten; 50. **2** the numeral 50. **3** the fiftieth in a set or series. **4** a 50-dollar bill: *She asked the teller for two fifties.* **5 fifties,** *pl.* the years from fifty through fifty-nine, especially of a century or of a person's life: *Her grandfather is in his fifties.* **6** a set or series of fifty persons or things.
—adj. **1** five times ten; 50. **2** being fiftieth in a set or series (*used after the noun*): *Chapter Fifty.* ⟨OE *fiftig*⟩

fif•ty–fif•ty ['fɪfti 'fɪfti] *adv. or adj. Informal.* half-and-half; in or with equal shares.

fig[1] [fɪg] *n.* **1** any of a genus (*Ficus*) of tropical and subtropical trees and shrubs of the mulberry family, bearing seedlike fruits in a fleshy, pear-shaped receptacle. **2** the receptacle enclosing the fruits of any of these trees or shrubs, especially the soft, sweet, edible receptacle, commonly called a fruit, of *F. carica.* Figs are eaten fresh or dried. **3** something of little or no value; trifle (*used with a negative*): *I don't care a fig for your opinion.* ⟨ME < OF *figue* < Provençal *figa,* ult. < L *ficus* fig⟩

fig[2] [fɪg] *n. Informal.* dress; equipment.
in full fig, fully dressed or equipped. ⟨origin uncertain⟩

fig. figure; figurative; figuratively.

fight [fəit] *n., v.* **fought, fight•ing.** *—n.* **1** a struggle; battle; conflict; combat; contest. **2** an angry dispute. **3** the power or will to fight: *There's plenty of fight left in him yet.* **4** a boxing match.
put up a fight, offer vigorous resistance.
show fight, resist; be ready to fight: *The hunted animal was too weary to show fight.*
—v. **1** take part in a fight. **2** take part in a boxing match (against). **3** take part in a fight against; war against. **4** carry on (a fight, conflict, etc.): *to fight a war.* **5** work; struggle (against): *We need to fight racism. She fought against her feelings of discouragement.* **6** get or make by fighting: *She fought her way to the top.* **7** cause (especially an animal) to fight. **8** disagree angrily; quarrel: *The brothers were always fighting about one thing or another.*
fight back, offer resistance; show fight: *They had no heart to fight back.*
fight down, control: *to fight down a feeling of fear.*
fight it out, fight until one side wins.
fight off, a turn back; repel: *Fight off an enemy attack.* **b** overcome; stop the progress of: *to fight off a cold.*
fight on, continue struggling.
fight shy of, keep away from; avoid. ⟨OE *feoht,* n., *feohtan,* v.⟩

☛ *Syn. n.* **1. Fight,** COMBAT, CONFLICT = battle or struggle. **Fight** = a struggle for victory or mastery between two or more people, animals, or forces, and particularly suggests hand to hand fighting: *When children fight, they often hurt one another.* **Combat** applies particularly to a battle between two armed people or forces: *The gladiators were ordered into combat in the arena.* **Conflict** emphasizes clashing, and applies to a battle or fight or to a mental or moral struggle between two beliefs, duties, etc.: *We all undergo mental conflicts.*

fight•er ['fəitər] *n.* **1** one that fights. **2** a professional boxer. **3** FIGHTER PLANE.

fight•er–bomb•er ['fəitər ,bɒmər] *n.* an aircraft used both as a fighter and as a bomber.

fighter pilot the pilot of a fighter plane.

fighter plane a highly manoeuvrable and heavily armed airplane used mainly for attacking enemy aircraft or strafing ground forces.

fighting chance *Informal.* the possibility of success after a long, hard struggle.

fighting cock **1** gamecock. **2** *Informal.* a pugnacious person.

fighting words a statement that provokes opposition or hostility.

fig•ment ['fɪgmənt] *n.* something imagined; a made-up story. ⟨< L *figmentum* < *fingere* form, fashion⟩

fig•ur•al ['fɪgjərəl] *adj.* of painting, sculpture, etc., showing recognizable animal or human figures.

fig•ur•ant ['fɪgjərənt]; *French,* [figy'ʀɑ̃] *n.* a male member of the corps de ballet.

fig•u•rante [,fɪgjə'rɑnt]; *French,* [figy'ʀɑ̃t] *n.* a female member of the corps de ballet.

fig•ur•ate ['fɪgjərɪt] *or* ['fɪgərɪt] *adj.* **1** having a characteristic or well-defined form, shape, or pattern. **2** *Music.* full of embellishments; ornate.

fig•ur•a•tion [,fɪgjə'reiʃən] *or* [,fɪgə'reiʃən] *n.* **1** a form; shape. **2** a forming; shaping. **3** a representation by a likeness or symbol. **4** the act of marking or adorning with figures or designs. **5** *Music.* **a** the use of transitional tones, ornaments, etc. that are not essential to the harmony. **b** the indicating of harmonics with figures above the bass part. **c** the use of a repeated motif or figure in variations.

fig•ur•a•tive ['fɪgjərətɪv] *or* ['fɪgərətɪv] *adj.* **1** of words or their use, going beyond literal meaning to add beauty or force; metaphoric. **2** having many figures of speech. Much poetry is figurative. **3** representing by a likeness or symbol: *A globe is a figurative model of the world.* **4** being or having to do with representational art. **—'fig•ur•a•tive•ly,** *adv.* **—'fig•ur•a•tive•ness,** *n.*

fig•ure ['fɪgər] *or* ['fɪgjər] *n., v.* **-ured, -ur•ing.** *—n.* **1** a symbol for a number. The symbols 1, 2, 3, etc. are called figures. **2** an amount or value given in figures: *The price is too high; ask a lower figure.* **3** a form or shape: *In the darkness she saw dim figures moving.* **4** a form enclosing a surface or space: *Circles, triangles, squares, cubes, and spheres are geometrical figures.* **5** a person; character: *Samuel de Champlain is a great figure in Canadian history.* **6** a human form; a person considered from the point of view of appearance, manner, etc.: *The poor old woman was a figure of distress.* **7** an artificial representation of the human form in sculpture, painting, drawing, etc., usually of the whole or greater part of the body. **8** a picture; drawing; diagram; illustration: *This dictionary makes use of many figures to help explain the meaning of words.* **9** a design; pattern: *Cloth or wallpaper often has figures on it.* **10** *Music.* MOTIF (def. 3). **11** an outline traced by movements: *figures made by an airplane.* **12** *Dancing or skating.* a set of movements. **13** FIGURE OF SPEECH. **14** *Logic.* any of the forms of a syllogism that differ only in the position of the middle term as subject or predicate. **15 figures,** calculations using figures; arithmetic: *She was never very good at figures.*
—v. **1** be conspicuous; appear: *The names of great leaders figure in the story of human progress.* **2** show by a figure; represent in a diagram. **3** decorate with a figure or pattern. **4** *Informal.* think; consider. **5** *Informal.* **a** make sense: *That figures.* **b** be as expected; be true to form: *Late to his own wedding? It figures!* **6** use figures to find the answer to a problem; reckon, compute; show by figures. **7** *Music.* **a** write figures over and under (the bass) to indicate the intended harmony. **b** use transitional tones, ornaments, etc. in; embellish. **8** picture mentally; imagine: *Figure to yourself a happy family, secure in their own home.*
figure in, include as a factor in calculations.
figure on, *Informal.* **a** depend on; rely on. **b** consider as part of a plan or undertaking: *I knew I'd have to pay, but I didn't figure on spending this much.*
figure out, *Informal.* **a** find out by using figures: *She soon figured out how much it would cost.* **b** think out; understand: *She couldn't figure out what was meant.* ⟨< F < L *figura* < *fingere* form⟩ **—'fig•ur•er,** *n.*
☛ *Syn. n.* **3.** See note at FORM.

fig•ured ['fɪgjərd] *or* ['fɪgərd] *adj.* **1** decorated with a design or pattern; not plain. **2** shown by a figure, diagram, or picture. **3** formed; shaped: *figured in bronze.* **4** *Music.* **a** ornamented; florid. **b** having accompanying chords of the bass part indicated by figures.

figure eight the shape of a figure 8, as traced by a skater, plane, etc.

fig•ure•head ['fɪgər,hɛd] *or* ['fɪgjər,hed] *n.* **1** a person who is the head in name only, and has no real authority or responsibility. **2** a statue or carving decorating the bow on a ship.

figure of speech an expression in which words are used out of their literal meaning or in exceptional combinations to add beauty or force. Similes and metaphors are figures of speech.

figure skate an ice skate for use in figure skating.

fig•ure–skate ['fɪgər ,skeit] *or* ['fɪgjər ,skeit] *v.* **-skat•ed, -skat•ing.** engage in figure skating. **—'fig•ure-,skat•er,** *n.*

figure skating the art or practice of performing figures and balletic programs on ice skates, often to music.

fig•ur•ine [,fɪgjə'rin] *or* [,fɪgə'rin] *n.* a small ornamental figure made of stone, pottery, metal, etc.; statuette. ⟨< F < Ital. *figurina,* dim. of *figura* figure⟩

fig•wort ['fɪg,wərt] *n.* **1** any of a genus (*Scrophularia*) of plants found in north temperate regions, having small greenish or purplish flowers. **2** (*adjl.*) designating the family of plants that includes the figworts, speedwells, and mulleins.

Fi•ji ['fidʒi] *n.* **1 the Fiji Islands,** a country in the S Pacific, made up of a group of islands. **2** Fijian.

Fi•ji•an ['fidʒiən] *or* [fɪ'dʒiən] *n., adj. —n.* **1** a native or inhabitant of the Fiji Islands. **2** the Malayo-Polynesian language of the Fijians.
—adj. of or having to do with the Fiji Islands, their people, or their language.

fil•a•ment ['fɪləmənt] *n.* **1** a very fine thread. **2** a very slender, threadlike part. The wire that gives off light in an electric light bulb is a filament. **3** *Botany.* the stalklike part of a stamen that supports the anther. See FLOWER for picture. **4** the wire in a vacuum tube through which current passes to generate the heat necessary for electrons to be emitted. In some vacuum tubes, the filament also acts as the cathode. **5** a continuous strand of yarn of a synthetic, as acetate, which may be used in weaving without spinning. ⟨< LL *filamentum* < L *filum* thread⟩ **—,fil•a'men•ta•ry,** *adj.*

fil•a•men•tous [,fɪlə'mɛntəs] *adj.* **1** threadlike. **2** having filaments.

fi•lar ['faɪlər] *adj.* like a thread. ⟨< L *Filum* thread + E *-ar*⟩

fi•lar•ia [fɪ'lɛriə] *n., pl.* **fi•lar•i•ae** [fɪ'lɛri,i] *or* [fɪ'lɛri,aɪ]. a parasite worm carried by mosquitoes to animals and human beings, causing diseases such as elephantiasis. ⟨< L *filum* thread⟩ **—fi'lar•i•al,** *adj.*

fil•a•ri•a•sis [,fɪlə'raɪəsɪs] *n.* a disease caused by filariae in the lymph vessels, blood, or tissue, and characterized by swelling.

fil•a•ture ['fɪlətʃər] *n.* the spinning of fibres, such as silk, into threads. ⟨< F < pp. of LL *filare* to spin⟩

fil•bert ['fɪlbərt] *n.* **1** hazelnut. **2** any of several hazels cultivated for their edible nuts, especially a European species (*Corylus maxima*). ⟨after St. *Philibert,* because the nuts ripen about the time of his day, August 22⟩

filch [fɪltʃ] *v.* steal (small or petty things); pilfer: *He filched pencils from the teacher's desk.* ⟨origin uncertain⟩ **—'filch•er,** *n.*
☛ *Syn.* See note at STEAL.

file[1] [faɪl] *n., v.* **filed, fil•ing.** *—n.* **1** a folder or special cabinet or drawer for keeping papers, etc. in order. **2** a set of papers, records, data, etc. kept in order. **3** a line of persons, animals, or things one behind another. **4** a small detachment of soldiers. **5** one of the vertical lines of squares on a chessboard, checkerboard, etc., extending from player to player. Compare RANK. **6** a collection of news stories sent by wire. **7** *Computer technology.* a collection of information stored in a computer as a logical unit under a single name or title.
in file, one after another; in succession: *We walked in file.*
on file, kept in order in a file: *All the reports are on file.*
—v. **1** put away (papers, etc.) in order. **2** march or move in a file. **3** make application or suit: *to file for citizenship, to file for divorce.* **4** send (a news story) by wire: *The reporter immediately filed her story of the explosion.* **5** submit or register (an application or suit, income tax return, complaint, etc.). ⟨< F *fil* thread (< L *filum*) and F *file* row (ult. < LL *filare* spin a thread)⟩ **—'fil•er,** *n.*

file[2] [faɪl] *n., v.* **filed, fil•ing.** *—n.* a steel tool with many small ridges or teeth on it: *The rough surface of a file is used to cut through or wear away hard materials or to make rough materials smooth.*
—v. smooth or wear away with a file. ⟨OE *fīl*⟩ **—'fil•er,** *n.*

file clerk a person whose work is taking care of the files in an office.

file•fish ['faɪl,fɪʃ] *n., pl.* **-fish** or **-fish•es.** any of various tropical marine fishes (family Balistidae) having a rough skin and a very long dorsal spine.

fi•let [fɪ'lei] *or* ['fɪlei] *n.* **1** a net or lace having a square mesh. **2** FILLET (def. 3). ⟨< F. See FILLET.⟩

filet mignon [mi'njɔ̃] a small, round, thick piece of choice beef, cut from the tenderloin. ⟨< F⟩

fil•i•al ['fɪliəl] *adj.* of a son or daughter; due from a son or daughter: *The children treated their parents with filial respect.* ⟨< LL *filialis* < L *filius* son, *filia* daughter⟩ **—'fil•i•al•ly,** *adv.*

filial generation See F1, F2.

fil•i•a•tion [ˌfɪli'eiʃən] *n.* **1** descent; derivation, as of succeeding generations, or of branches or offshoots from some original line or stem. **2** the relationship between descendants and ancestors, or between derived forms or products and their origin. ⟨< ME *filiacion* < OF *filiation* < LL *filiatio* < L *filius* son⟩

fil•i•bus•ter ['fɪləˌbʌstər] *n., v.* —*n.* **1 a** the deliberate hindering of the passage of a bill in a legislature by long speeches or other means of delay. **b** a member of a legislature who hinders the passage of a bill by such means. **2** a person who fights against another country without the authorization of his or her government; freebooter.
—*v.* **1** deliberately hinder the passage of a bill by long speeches or other means of delay. **2** fight against another country without the authorization of one's government; act as a freebooter. ⟨< Sp. *filibustero* < F *flibustier,* alteration of *fribustier* < Du. *vrijbuiter.* See FREEBOOTER.⟩ —**'fil•i,bus•ter•er,** *n.*

fil•i•form ['fɪləˌfɔrm] *adj.* like a thread. ⟨< L *filum* a thread + *-form*⟩

fil•i•gree ['fɪləˌgri] *n., v.* **-greed, -gree•ing;** *adj.* —*n.* **1** very delicate, lacelike ornamental work of gold or silver wire. **2** a lacy, delicate, or fanciful pattern in any material: *The frost made a beautiful filigree on the windowpane.*
—*v.* decorate with or form into filigree.
—*adj.* ornamented with filigree; made into filigree. ⟨for *filigrane* < F < Ital. *filigrana* < L *filum* thread + *granum* grain⟩

filing cabinet a steel or wooden cabinet containing drawers for storing files of letters or other papers, records, etc.

fil•ings ['faɪlɪŋz] *n.pl.* the small pieces of iron, wood, etc. that have been removed by a file.

Fil•i•pine ['fɪləˌpin] See PHILIPPINE.

Fil•i•pi•no [ˌfɪlə'pinou] *n., pl.* **-nos;** *fem.* **Filipina** [-'pinə], **-nas;** *adj.* —*n.* a native or inhabitant of the Philippines.
—*adj.* of or having to do with the Philippines or its inhabitants; Philippine.

fill [fɪl] *v., n.* —*v.* **1** put something into until there is room for no more; make full: *to fill a cup.* **2** become full: *The hall filled rapidly.* **3** take up all the space in: *The crowd filled the hall.* **4** put a lot of something into: *fill one's heart with fear.* **5** satisfy the hunger or appetite of. **6** supply what is needed for: *A store fills orders, prescriptions, etc.* **7** stop up or close by putting something in: *A dentist fills decayed teeth.* **8** hold and do the duties of (a position, office, etc.). **9** supply a person for or appoint a person to (a position, office, etc.). **10** pervade; permeate, as a smell or sound: *The smell of burnt garlic filled the kitchen.* **11** fulfil or meet (a need, requirements, standards, etc.) **12** *Nautical.* cause (a sail) to billow; set (a sail) so that it billows.
fill in, a fill with something put in: *Fill in the blanks.* **b** complete by filling: *to fill in the end of a sentence.* **c** put in to complete something: *She filled in the wrong word.* **d** inform; bring up to date: *Could you fill me in as to what happened during my absence?* **e** substitute (*for*): *Joan will be filling in while Mark is away. Can you fill in for me tonight?*
fill out, a make larger; grow larger; swell: *The baby is now three months old and she has really filled out.* **b** make rounder; grow rounder; **c** complete; make fuller, more thorough or comprehensive, etc.: *He added a few examples to fill out his argument.* **d** complete (a questionnaire, etc.); enter (requested information) on a form.
fill the bill, come up to requirements.
fill up, fill; fill completely.
—*n.* **1** enough to fill something. **2** all that is needed or wanted: *Eat and drink your fill; there is plenty for all of us.* **3** something that fills, especially earth or rock used to make uneven land level. ⟨OE *fyllan* < *full* full⟩

filled gold a combination of gold plate with some base metal.

fill•er ['fɪlər] *n.* **1** a person or thing that fills. **2** an implement used to fill something, such as a funnel. **3** anything put in to fill something. A pad of paper for a notebook, a preparation put on wood to fill cracks before painting it, and the tobacco inside cigars are all fillers. **4** something used to fill an empty time or space or to increase bulk: *They used an old film short as a filler between the two programs. All those quotes and anecdotes in his essay are just filler.*

fil•lér ['fillɛr] *n., pl.* **fillér.** a unit of money in Hungary, equal to ¹⁄₁₀₀ of a forint. ⟨< Hungarian⟩

fil•let ['fɪlɪt]; *n. 3 and v. 2, usually* [fɪ'lei] *n., v.* —*n.* **1** a narrow band, ribbon, etc. put around the head to keep the hair in place or as an ornament. **2** a narrow band or strip of any material. Fillets are often used between mouldings, the flutes of a column, etc. **3** a slice of fish, meat, etc. without bones or fat; filet.
—*v.* **1** bind or decorate with a narrow band, ribbon, strip, etc. **2** cut (fish, meat, etc.) into fillets. ⟨< F *filet,* dim. of *fil* < L *filum* thread⟩

fill–in ['fɪl ˌɪn] *n.* **1** a person or thing used to fill a vacancy or omission. **2** an activity that occupies spare time between more important events. **3** information that brings someone up to date on a situation; a briefing.

fill•ing ['fɪlɪŋ] *n., v.* —*n.* **1** anything put in to fill something. A dentist puts a filling in a decayed tooth. **2** the threads running from side to side across a woven fabric. **3** a making full; a becoming full.
—*v.* ppr. of FILL.

filling station a place where gasoline and oil for motor vehicles are sold; gas station.

fil•lip ['fɪləp] *v., n.* —*v.* **1** strike with the fingernail as it is snapped quickly outward after being bent and held back against the thumb. **2** toss or cause to move by striking in this way: *He filliped a coin into the beggar's cup.* **3** make a fillip. **4** rouse; revive; stimulate.
—*n.* **1** the act of snapping the fingernail quickly outward after bending and holding it back against the thumb. **2** anything that rouses, revives, or stimulates: *Relishes serve as fillips to the appetite.* ⟨probably imitative⟩

fil•lis•ter ['fɪlɪstər] *n. Carpentry.* **1** a groove. **2** a tool for making grooves. ⟨origin unknown⟩

fil•ly ['fɪli] *n., pl.* **-lies. 1** a young female horse; a mare that is less than four or five years old. **2** *Informal.* a lively girl. ⟨< ON *fylja.* Akin to FOAL.⟩

film [fɪlm] *n., v.* —*n.* **1** a very thin layer, sheet, surface, or coating: *a film of dew. Oil poured on water will spread and make a film.* **2 a** cellulose material coated on one side with a light-sensitive emulsion and used in making photographic negatives or transparencies. **b** a thin, flexible strip or sheet of this material. **3** movie. **4** a very thin sheet or leaf of metal or other material. **5** films or filmmaking as an industry, art form, object of study, etc. **6** any opacity of the cornea. **7** a delicate net of threads.
—*v.* **1** cover or become covered with a film: *His eyes filmed with tears.* **2** make a movie of or from: *to film a scene, to film a novel.* **3** be suitable for a movie: *Battle scenes usually film well.* **4** make a movie: *They're filming on location next week.*
film over, become covered with or as with a film: *The lens of my microscope is filmed over with moisture.* ⟨OE *filmen.* Related to FELL⁴.⟩ —**'film,like,** *adj.*

film badge a badge containing photographic film that records levels of radiation. *A technician in a laboratory, atomic power plant, etc. wears a film badge to guard against receiving a dangerous level of radiation.*

film•go•er ['fɪlmˌgouər] *n.* a person who goes to see movies, especially one who does so regularly or habitually.

film•ic ['fɪlmɪk] *adj.* of, having to do with, or like a movie or movies, especially with regard to visual features or qualities.

film•mak•er ['fɪlmˌmeikər] *n.* a person who makes movies.

film•mak•ing ['fɪlmˌmeikɪŋ] *n.* the art or process of making movies.

film noir [nwɑr] a movie that is shot in sombre tones, often set in a corrupt urban environment, and characterized by a mood of cynicism, despair, and fatalism. ⟨< F black film⟩

film•og•ra•phy [fɪl'mɒgrəfi] *n.* a list of movies associated with a certain person, genre, etc: *At the back of the movie star's biography was a filmography of the pictures she had made.* ⟨< *film* + (*bibli*)*ography*⟩

film•strip ['fɪlmˌstrɪp] *n.* a series of still pictures on one theme or subject, put on film to be projected in sequence.

film•y ['fɪlmi] *adj.* **film•i•er, film•i•est. 1** of or like a film; very thin: *a filmy nightgown.* **2** covered with or as if with a film. —**'film•i•ly,** *adv.* —**'film•i•ness,** *n.*

fil•ose ['failous] *adj.* threadlike. ⟨< L *filum* a thread + E *-ose* < L *-osus* full of, like⟩

fils¹ [fɪls] *or* [fils] *n., pl.* **fils. 1** a unit of money in Bahrain, Iraq, Jordan, Kuwait, and the People's Democratic Republic of Yemen, equal to ¹⁄₁₀₀₀ of a dinar. See table of money in the Appendix. **2** a unit of money in the United Arab Emirates, equal to ¹⁄₁₀₀ of a dirham. **3** a unit of money in the Yemen Arab Republic, equal to ¹⁄₁₀₀ of a riyal. **4** a coin worth one fils. ⟨Arabic⟩

fils² [fis] *n.* the younger (*used after the surname of a male*): *Dumas fils.* ⟨< F, son⟩

fil•ter ['fɪltər] *n., v.* —*n.* **1** a device for straining out substances from a liquid or gas by passing it slowly through felt, paper, sand, charcoal, etc. A filter is used to remove impurities from drinking water. **2** the felt, paper, sand, charcoal, or other porous material used in such a device: *coffee filters.* **3** a device for controlling certain light rays, electric currents, etc. Putting a yellow filter in front of a camera lens causes less blue light to reach the film. **4** any means of preventing or permitting the passage or progress of certain elements: *This questionnaire acts as a filter for new applicants. All art had to pass through the filter of censorship.*
—*v.* **1** pass through a filter; strain: *filtered coffee.* **2** act as a filter for. **3** pass or flow very slowly: *Water filters through the sandy soil and into the well. The news filtered down eventually to the rank and file.* **4** remove or control by or as if by a filter (*used with* **out**): *Filter out all the dirt before using this water.* ⟨< Med.L *filtrum* felt < Gmc.⟩ —**'fil•ter•er,** *n.*
☛ *Hom.* PHILTRE.

fil•ter•a•ble ['fɪltərəbəl] *adj.* **1** that can be filtered. **2** capable of passing through a filter that arrests bacteria: *a filterable virus.* Also, **filtrable.** —**,fil•ter•a'bil•i•ty,** *n.*

filter bed a tank or reservoir with a sand or gravel bottom, for filtering water or sewage.

filter paper porous paper through which a liquid can be strained, leaving solids behind.

filter tip **1** a cigarette with an attached filter, for removing impurities from the smoke before it is inhaled. **2** the filter itself. —**'fil•ter-,tip** or **'fil•ter-,tipped,** *adj.*

filth [fɪlθ] *n.* **1** foul, disgusting dirt: *The alley was littered with garbage and other filth.* **2** obscene words, images, or thoughts; vileness; moral corruption; pornography. ⟨OE *fȳlth* < *fūl* foul⟩

filth•y ['fɪlθi] *adj.* **filth•i•er, filth•i•est. 1** disgustingly dirty; foul. **2** vile; obscene; pornographic. —**'filth•i•ly,** *adv.* —**'filth•i•ness,** *n.*
☛ *Syn.* See note at DIRTY.

fil•tra•ble ['fɪltrəbəl] *adj.* filterable.

fil•trate ['fɪltreit] *n., v.* **-trat•ed, -trat•ing.** —*n.* liquid that has been passed through a filter.
—*v.* pass through a filter.

fil•tra•tion [fɪl'treiʃən] *n.* a filtering or being filtered.

fi•lum ['faɪləm] *n., pl.* **fi•la** [-lə] *Anatomy.* a filament. ⟨< L, thread⟩
☛ *Hom.* PHYLUM.

fim•bria ['fɪmbriə] *n. Zoology.* a fringe. ⟨< NL < L *fimbriae* threads, fringe⟩

fim•bri•ate ['fɪmbriɪt] *or* ['fɪmbri,eit] *adj. Zoology.* having a border of hair.

fin [fɪn] *n.* **1** a movable, winglike part of a fish's body. Moving the fins enables the fish to swim and to guide and balance itself in the water. **2** something like a fin in shape or use, as: **a** a fixed or movable piece attached to aircraft to provide stability in flight. **b** any of the thin, flat, lateral projections on a radiator, engine cylinder, etc., designed to dissipate heat. **c** FLIPPER (def. 2). ⟨OE *finn*⟩ —**'fin•less,** *adj.* —**'fin,like,** *adj.*
☛ *Hom.* FINN.

fin•able ['faɪnəbəl] *adj.* liable to a fine.

fi•na•gle [fə'neigəl] *v.,* **-gled, -gling.** *Informal.* **1** manage to get craftily or cleverly: *He finagled his way into the job.* **2** cheat; swindle. ⟨var. of Brit. dial. *fainaigue* renege at cards; origin uncertain⟩ —**fi'na•gler,** *n.*

fi•nal ['faɪnəl] *adj., n.* —*adj.* **1** at the end; last; with no more after it: *a final consonant.* **2** deciding; settling the question; not to be changed: *The decisions of the judge will be final.* **3** expressing or having to do with purpose: *a final clause.* **4** ultimate: *The final responsibility is his.*
—*n.* **1** something final: *The last examination of a school term is a final.* **2** **finals,** *pl.* the last or deciding set in a series of contests, examinations, etc. **3** *Music.* a tonic note. ⟨ME < L *finalis* < *finis* end⟩
☛ *Syn. adj.* **1.** See note at LAST¹.

fi•na•le [fə'næli] *or* [fə'nɑli] *n.* **1** the last part of an artistic performance. **2** the last part; end. ⟨< Ital. *finale* final⟩

fi•nal•ist ['faɪnəlɪst] *n.* a person who takes part in the last or deciding set in a series of contests, etc.

fi•nal•i•ty [fə'næləti] *or* [faɪ'næləti] *n., pl.* **-ties. 1** the quality or fact of being final, finished, or settled: *He spoke with an air of finality.* **2** something final; a final act, speech, etc.

fi•nal•ize ['faɪnə,laɪz] *v.* **-ized, -iz•ing.** bring to a conclusion; complete or finish in such a manner as to be final: *The committee hopes to finalize its report next week.*

fi•nal•ly ['faɪnəli] *adv.* **1** at the end; last; lastly. **2** so as to decide or settle the question. **3** at last; eventually, after a long delay or many preliminaries. **4** ultimately: *He says that all wrongdoing can finally be traced to fear or pride.*

fi•nance ['faɪnæns], [fə'næns], *or* [faɪ'næns] *n., v.* **-nanced, -nanc•ing.** —*n.* **1** money matters. **2** the management of large sums of public or private money. **Public finance** is the management of government revenue and expenditure: *Who is the current Minister of Finance?* **3** **finances,** *pl.* money matters; money; funds; revenues.
—*v.* **1** provide or get money for: *His friends helped him finance a new business.* **2** manage the finances of. ⟨ME < OF *finance* ending, settlement of a debt, ult. < *fin* end < L *finis.* Related to FINE².⟩

finance company a firm whose business is lending money for repayment by instalments with interest.

fi•nan•cial [faɪ'nænʃəl] *or* [fə'nænʃəl] *adj.* **1** having to do with money matters. **2** having to do with the management of large sums of public or private money. —**fi'nan•cial•ly,** *adv.*
☛ *Syn.* **1. Financial,** MONETARY, FISCAL = having to do with money. **Financial** = having to do with money matters in general: *His financial affairs are in bad condition.* **Monetary** = of or directly connected with money itself: *His work brought him fame, but little monetary reward. The dollar is a monetary unit.* **Fiscal** = having to do with the funds and financial affairs of a government, institution, or corporation: *The fiscal year of the Canadian government begins on April 1.*

fin•an•cier [,faɪnən'sir], [,fɪnən'sir], *or* [fə'nænsiər] *n.* **1** a person skilled in finance. **2** a person who is active in matters involving large sums of money. ⟨< F⟩

fin•back ['fɪn,bæk] *n.* rorqual.

finch [fɪntʃ] *n.* any of a family (Fringillidae) of songbirds having a short, strong, conical bill for crushing seeds. Some common finches are the goldfinches, grosbeaks, buntings, and cardinals. ⟨OE *finc*⟩

find [faɪnd] *v.* **found, find•ing;** *n.* —*v.* **1** come upon; happen on; meet with: *She found a silver dollar on the road.* **2** look for and get: *Please find my hat for me.* **3** discover; learn: *We found that she could not swim.* **4** see; know; feel; perceive: *He found that he was growing sleepy.* **5** get; get the use of: *Can you find time to do this?* **6** arrive at; reach: *Water finds its level.* **7** *Law.* decide and declare: *The jury found the accused man guilty. The judge found for the defendant.* **8** provide; supply: *to find food and lodging for a friend.* **9** come to have; receive: *The book found many readers.*
find oneself, a become aware of being: *He found himself in trouble.* **b** learn one's abilities and make good use of them; find one's niche. **c** reach one's own conclusions about the basic questions of existence, one's place in the universe, etc.; arrive at a world view.
find out, a learn about; come to know; discover. **b** cause the deeds or true character of (something or someone) to become known: *Their carelessness will find them out.*
—*n.* **1** a finding. **2** something found, especially something exciting or valuable: *This rare old book was quite a find.* ⟨OE *findan*⟩

find•er ['faɪndər] *n.* **1** a person who or thing that finds. **2** a small extra lens on the outside of a camera that shows what is being photographed. **3** a small telescope attached to a larger one to help find objects more easily.

fin de siè•cle [fɛ̃də'sjɛkl] *French.* the end of the century. From about 1880 to 1910, *fin de siècle* was used adjectivally to mean 'up-to-date', connoting also 'over-elegant' or 'decadent'. Nowadays it is being revived to mean 'of the end of the twentieth century'.

find•ing ['faɪndɪŋ] *n., v.* —*n.* **1** a discovering. **2** the thing found. **3** Often, **findings,** *pl.* the decision(s) or conclusion(s) reached after an examination of facts, data, etc. by a commission, judge, scholar, etc.: *The Commission will publish its findings next spring.* **4** **findings,** *pl.* the tools and supplies, other than the main materials, used by a shoemaker, dressmaker, or other artisan: *A jeweller's findings include swivels, clasps, and wire.*
—*v.* ppr. of FIND.

fine¹ [faɪn] *adj.* **fin•er, fin•est;** *adv., v.* **fined, fin•ing.** —*adj.* **1** of very high quality; very good; excellent: *a fine speech, a fine view, a fine young woman.* **2** very small or thin: *fine wire.* **3** in very small particles: *fine sand.* **4** sharp: *a tool with a fine edge.* **5** not coarse or heavy; delicate: *fine linen.* **6** refined; elegant: *fine manners.* **7** subtle: *The law makes fine distinctions.* **8** too highly decorated; showy: *fine language or writing.* **9** handsome; good-looking: *a fine horse.* **10** clear; pleasant; bright: *fine weather.* **11** without

impurities. Fine gold is gold not mixed with any other metal. **12** having a stated proportion of gold or silver in it. A gold alloy that is 925/1000 fine is 92.5 percent gold. **13** well; in good health: *I feel fine.*
—adv. Informal. very well; excellently.
—v. make fine or finer; become fine or finer. ⟨ME < OF *fin*, ult. < L *finire* finish⟩ **—'fine•ly,** *adv.*

☛ *Syn. adj.* **1, 6. Fine,** CHOICE, ELEGANT = very high quality. **Fine** is the general word: *He does fine work.* **Choice** = of fine or the best quality, usually carefully picked by or for a taste that can tell and appreciate differences in quality or value: *He selected a choice piece of jade.* **Elegant** = showing fine taste, rich or luxurious but graceful and refined: *She selected an elegant velvet gown.*

fine² [faɪn] *n., v.* **fined, fin•ing.** *—n.* a sum of money paid as a punishment.
in fine, a finally. **b** in a few words; briefly.
—v. cause to pay a fine. ⟨ME < OF *fin* < L *finis* end; in Med.L, settlement, payment⟩

fi•ne³ ['finei] *n. Music.* a direction marking the end of a passage that has to be repeated. ⟨< Ital.⟩

fine art **1** works of art: *He buys fine art. She is exhibiting her fine art at the gallery.* **2** any of music, dance, drama, literature, or the visual arts. **3** any skill requiring dexterity, creativity, cleverness, etc. (*sometimes used facetiously*): *the fine art of wine-tasting, the fine art of mincing garlic.*

fine–drawn ['faɪn ,drɒn] *adj.* **1** drawn out until very small or thin. **2** very subtle: *Fine-drawn distinctions are difficult to understand.*

fine–grained ['faɪn ,greind] *adj.* having a fine, close grain: *Mahogany is a fine-grained wood.*

fine•ness ['faɪnnɪs] *n.* **1** the quality of being fine. **2** the proportion of gold or silver in an alloy.

fine print details printed in small print on a contract or other document, often in obscure wording: *Be sure to read the fine print.*

fin•er•y ['faɪnəri] *n., pl.* **-er•ies.** showy clothes, ornaments, etc. ⟨< FINE¹⟩

fines [faɪnz] *n.pl.* screened crushed rock.

fine–scaled sucker ['faɪn ,skeild] a freshwater fish (*Catostomus commersoni*) of Canada, having a loose, fleshy-lipped and sucker-shaped mouth.

fine–spun ['faɪn ,spʌn] *adj.* **1** spun or drawn out until very small or thin. **2** very subtle.

fi•nesse [fə'nɛs] *n., v.* **-nessed, -ness•ing.** *—n.* **1** delicacy of execution; skill: *That artist shows wonderful finesse.* **2** the skilful handling of a delicate situation to one's advantage; craft; stratagem: *a master of finesse.* **3** *Bridge, whist, etc.* an attempt to take a trick with a lower card while holding a higher card, in the hope that the card or cards between may not be played.
—v. **1** use finesse; handle with finesse. **2** bring or change by finesse. **3** make a finesse with (a card). ⟨< F *finesse* < *fin* fine¹⟩

fine–toothed ['faɪn 'tuθt] *adj.* having fine, very closely set teeth: *a fine-toothed saw.*
go over with a fine-toothed comb, examine carefully.

fine–tune ['faɪn 'tjun] *or* ['tun] *v.,* **-tuned, -tun•ing. 1** make small adjustments to the tuning of (a radio, TV set, etc.) **2** make small adjustments to (a plan of action, idea, etc.) to make it better.

fin•ger ['fɪŋgər] *n., v. —n.* **1** one of the five end parts of the hand, especially the four besides the thumb. **2** the part of a glove that covers a finger. **3** anything shaped or used like a finger. **4** the breadth of a finger (about 2 cm). **5** the length of a finger (about 9.5 cm).
burn (one's) **fingers,** get into trouble by meddling.
have a finger in the pie, a take part or have a share in doing something. **b** meddle; interfere.
have/keep one's fingers crossed, wish for good luck.
lift a finger, expend the least effort (*used only in the negative*): *He didn't lift a finger to help.*
lay a finger on, touch to any degree (*used only in the conditional or negative*): *If you lay a finger on the child, you'll be sorry! I didn't even lay a finger on her, but she started crying.*
put (one's) **finger on,** point out exactly.
put the finger on, *Slang.* single out for slaying (by a gang).
twist around (one's) **little finger,** manage easily; control completely.
work one's fingers to the bone, work extremely hard, especially at a menial or thankless job.
—v. **1** touch or handle with the fingers; use the fingers on. **2** leave fingerprints on. **3** perform or mark (a passage of music) with a certain fingering. **4** pilfer; filch; steal. **5** *Slang.* point out; betray; inform on. **6** make vague grasping movements with the fingers. **7** point or extend like a finger. ⟨OE⟩ **—'fin•ger•er,** *n.*

finger alphabet SIGN LANGUAGE.

fin•ger•board ['fɪŋgər,bɔrd] **1** a strip of wood on the neck of a violin, guitar, etc. against which the strings are pressed by the fingers of the player. **2** the keyboard on a piano, harpsichord, or organ.

finger bowl a small bowl to hold water for rinsing the fingers during or after a meal.

fin•ger•breadth ['fɪŋgər,brɛdθ] *or* ['fɪŋgər,brɛtθ] *n.* the breadth of a finger, about 2 cm.

finger cymbals a pair of metal plates, like small cymbals, attached to the middle fingers, or the middle finger and thumb, by loops.

finger food snack food or hors d'oeuvres prepared to be eaten with the fingers, such as canapés, raw vegetables and dip, trail mix, etc.

fin•ger•hold ['fɪŋgər,hould] *n.* **1** anything that offers a grip for the fingers. **2** a grip using the fingers only. **3** a weak support or grip.

fin•ger•ing ['fɪŋgərɪŋ] *n., v. —n.* **1** a touching or handling with the fingers. **2** a way of using the fingers. In playing certain musical instruments the fingering is important. **3** the signs marked on a piece of music to show which fingers are to be used in playing particular notes. **4** a fine type of yarn, usually woollen, used in knitting.
—v. ppr. of FINGER.

fin•ger•ling ['fɪŋgərlɪŋ] *n.* **1** a young fish; a fry, especially late in the first year. **2** something very small.

fin•ger•mark ['fɪŋgər,mɑrk] *n.* a smudge or stain left by a finger.

fin•ger•nail ['fɪŋgər,neil] *n.* the hard layer of hornlike substance at the end of a finger.

fin•ger•paint ['fɪŋgər,peint] *v.* paint with the fingers, palms, etc. instead of with brushes.

finger paint any of various thickened water colours used in finger painting.

finger painting **1** a technique of applying paint using fingers, palms, etc. instead of brushes, common with young children and some artists. **2** a design or picture so painted.

finger post a guidepost having a sign shaped like a finger or hand to show the direction.

fin•ger•print ['fɪŋgər,prɪnt] *n., v. —n.* **1** ridges or an impression of the markings on the inner surface of the last joint of a finger or thumb. Fingerprints are unique to an individual and so are used for identification, especially of criminals. **2** loosely, the pattern of markings on the skin itself. **3** any idiosyncratic, identifying feature.
—v. take the fingerprints of.

A fingerprint

fin•ger•stall ['fɪŋgər,stɒl] *n.* a rigid protective covering for an injured finger.

fin•ger•tip ['fɪŋgər,tɪp] *n.* **1** the very end or tip of the finger. **2** a fingerstall used to protect the tip of a finger.
have at one's fingertips, be knowledgeable about or ready with.
(right down) to the (or one's) **fingertips,** to the depth of one's being; through and through: *a perfectionist to the fingertips.*

fin•i•al ['fɪniəl] *or* ['faɪniəl] *n.* **1** *Architecture.* an ornament on the top of a roof, the corner of a tower, the end of a pew in church, etc. **2** the highest point. ⟨< Med.L *finium* final settlement (probably originally, end) < L *finis*⟩

fin•i•cal ['fɪnɪkəl] *adj.* finicky. ⟨apparently < *fine¹*⟩ **—'fin•i•cal•ly,** *adv.* **—,fin•i'cal•i•ty,** *n.*

fin•ick•ing ['fɪnɪkɪŋ] *adj.* finicky.

fin•ick•y ['fɪnɪki] *adj.* too dainty or particular; too precise or fussy: *He's terribly finicky about his food.* ⟨< *finical*⟩

fin•is ['fɪnɪs] *n.* end. ⟨< L⟩

fin•ish [ˈfɪnɪʃ] *v., n.* —*v.* **1** bring (action, speech, etc.) to an end; end: *She finished the performance with a short fugue. That ought to finish their sarcastic comments.* **2** bring (an action, work, affairs, etc.) to completion; complete: *I have not finished eating. He started the race but did not finish it. Have you finished the book yet?* **3** come to an end: *There was so little wind that the sailing race didn't finish until after dark.* **4** achieve a place in a contest: *She finished third.* **5** use up completely: *to finish a spool of thread.* **6** *Informal.* overcome completely: *My answer finished him.* **7** *Informal.* destroy; kill: *to finish a wounded animal.* **8** perfect; polish. **9** prepare the surface of in some way: *to finish cloth with a nap.*
finish off, a complete, esp. something started by someone else or temporarily abandoned. **b** overcome completely; destroy; kill.
finish up, a complete. **b** use up completely.
finish with, a complete. **b** stop being friends with; have nothing to do with. **c** finish using; come to the end of one's need of: *Have you finished with my book yet?*
—*n.* **1** the end. **2** a polished condition or quality; perfection. **3** the way in which a surface is prepared. **4** something used to finish something else. **5** cultivated manners or speech; social polish. **6** the work done on a building after the main structure is finished, such as the window and door trim, etc. **7** the material used for such work. **8** the mode or style of completion of something: *a slow finish, a late finish.* **9** demise or downfall: *This expedition will be the finish of me.*
in at the finish, present at the end. ⟨ME < OF *feniss-*, a stem of *fenir* < L *finire*⟩ —**ˈfin•i•sh•er,** *n.*
☛ *Hom.* FINNISH.
☛ *Syn. v.* **1-3.** See note at END.

fin•ished [ˈfɪnɪʃt] *adj., v.* —*adj.* **1** ended. **2** completed. **3** *Informal.* exhausted; defeated; completely overcome: *By the third round the boxer was finished.* **4** perfected; polished.
—*v.* pt. and pp. of FINISH.

finishing nail a slender nail with a small head.

finishing school a private school that prepares young women for social life rather than for business or a profession.

fi•nite [ˈfaɪnəit] *adj., n.* —*adj.* **1** having limits or bounds; not infinite: *Death ends our finite existence.* **2** *Grammar.* designating a verb inflected for features such as person, number, and tense. In the sentence *Before going to the game, she stopped to mail the letter*, *stopped* is the finite verb, *going* is a participle, and *to mail* is an infinitive. **3** *Mathematics.* **a** of a number, capable of being reached or passed in counting. **b** of a magnitude, less than infinite and greater than infinitesimal. **c** of a set, containing a definite number of elements.
—*n.* something finite. ⟨< L *finitus*, pp. of *finire* finish⟩

fi•ni•tude [ˈfɪnɪˌtjud] *or* [ˈfɪnɪˌtud] *n.* a being finite.

fink [fɪŋk] *n. v.* —*n. Slang.* **1** informer. **2** strikebreaker. **3** any unpleasant person.
—*v.* be a tattletale; inform (*on*). ⟨< G, finch; adopted 1740 by students at Jena to designate those who did not belong to any fraternity; later extended to include someone not in an organization, as a union⟩

Fin•land [ˈfɪnlənd] *n.* a republic in N Europe lying NE of the Baltic Sea.

Finn [fɪn] *n.* **1** a native or inhabitant of Finland. **2** a person of Finnish descent. **3** a member of any of the peoples speaking Finnic languages.
☛ *Hom.* FIN.

fin•nan had•die [ˈfɪnən ˈhædi] smoked haddock. ⟨for *Findon haddock*; from the name of a town in Scotland⟩

finned [fɪnd] *adj.* having a fin or fins.

Finn•ic [ˈfɪnɪk] *n., adj.* —*n.* a branch of the Finno-Ugric family of languages, including Finnish, Estonian, and Lapp.
—*adj.* of or having to do with this group of languages or the Finns.

Finn•ish [ˈfɪnɪʃ] *n., adj.* —*n.* **1** the language of the Finns. **2 the Finnish,** *pl.* the people of Finland.
—*adj.* of or having to do with Finland, its people, or their language.
☛ *Hom.* FINISH.

Finn•mark [ˈfɪnˌmɑrk] *n.* markka.

Fin•no–U•gric [ˈfɪnou ˈjugrɪk] *or* [-ˈugrɪk] *n., adj.* —*n.* a family of languages spoken primarily in N and E Europe and W Asia, including Finnish, Estonian, Hungarian, and Lapp.
—*adj.* of or having to do with these languages or any of the peoples speaking them.

fin•ny [ˈfɪni] *adj.* **1** abounding with or having to do with fish: *The sea is sometimes called the finny deep.* **2** having fins. **3** like a fin.

fin whale rorqual.

fiord [fjɔrd] *n.* a long narrow bay of the sea between high banks or cliffs. Norway has many fiords. Also, **fjord.** ⟨< Norwegian *fiord*, earlier *fjorthr.* Akin to FIRTH.⟩

fip•ple [ˈfɪpəl] *n.* a wedge or plug in the mouthpiece of certain wind instruments, such as recorders, reducing the opening to a narrow slit through which the breath is directed.

fipple flute any wind instrument, such as a recorder, having a fipple.

fir [fɜr] *n.* **1** any of a genus (*Abies*) of evergreen trees of the pine family found throughout the north temperate regions of the world, having leaves shaped like flattened needles and bearing upright cones. The four species of the fir native to Canada are balsam fir, alpine fir, amabilis fir, and grand fir. **2** the wood of any of these trees. **3** any of several other evergreens, as the Douglas fir (genus *Pseudotsuga*). ⟨OE **fyrh* (cf. *furhwudu* fir-wood) or < ON *fyri-*⟩
☛ *Hom.* FUR.

fire [faɪr] *n., v.* **fired, fir•ing.** —*n.* **1** the flame, heat, and light caused by something burning. **2** a burning mass of fuel: *Put more wood on the fire.* **3** fuel arranged for burning: *A fire was laid in the fireplace.* **4** a destructive burning: *A great fire destroyed the furniture factory.* **5** the principle of combustion: *the discovery of fire by early humans.* **6** a preparation that will burn: *Red fire is used in signalling.* **7** something that suggests a fire because it is hot, glowing, brilliant, or light: *the fire of lightning, an insane fire in his eye, the fire in a diamond.* **8** any feeling that suggests fire; passion, fervour, enthusiasm, excitement, etc. **9** a burning pain; fever; inflammation: *the fire of a wound.* **10** a severe trial or trouble. **11** the shooting or discharge of guns, etc.: *enemy fire.* **12** anything similar to gunfire in its rapidity and continuous action: *a fire of recriminations.*
between two fires, attacked from both sides.
build a fire under, *Informal.* induce or force to act more quickly, decisively, etc.
catch fire, begin to burn: *Be careful that the curtains don't catch fire from the lamp.*
fight fires, treat a problem one incident at a time, instead of by structural prevention.
fight fire with fire, respond in kind to an opponent's attack.
go through fire and water, endure many troubles or dangers.
hang fire, a be slow in going off. **b** be slow in acting. **c** be delayed.
lay a fire, arrange fuel so that it is ready to be lit.
on fire, a burning. **b** full of a feeling or spirit like fire; excited: *The troops were on fire with the desire for victory.*
open fire, a begin to shoot. **b** begin a verbal attack.
play with fire, meddle with something dangerous.
set fire to, cause to burn.
set on fire, a cause to burn. **b** fill with a feeling or spirit like fire.
set the world on fire, become brilliant and famous.
take fire, a begin to burn. **b** become excited, enthusiastic, roused, etc. **c** become suddenly and intensely active, successful, or popular; catch on.
under fire, a exposed to shooting from enemy guns. **b** attacked; blamed; criticized.
—*v.* **1** cause to burn. **2** begin to burn; burst into flame. **3** supply fuel to; tend: *The men fired the steamship's huge furnaces.* **4** dry with heat; bake: *Bricks are fired to make them hard.* **5** grow or make hot, red, glowing, etc. **6** arouse; excite; inflame: *Stories of adventure fire the imagination.* **7** discharge (a gun, bomb, gas mine, etc.). **8** discharge or propel (a missile, etc.) from or as if from a gun; shoot: *to fire a rocket. The soldiers fired from the fort. The hunter fired small shot.* **9** be so discharged. **10** direct with force and speed: *to fire off an angry letter. The audience fired questions at the speaker.* **11** *Informal.* dismiss from a job, etc. **12** of grain, turn yellow before ripening as a result of drought or disease. **13** of pottery, etc., respond in a specified manner to baking in a kiln: *This clay fires a deep red.*
fire away, *Informal.* begin; start; go ahead, esp. to speak.
fire up, a start a fire in a furnace, boiler, etc: *The men did not have time to fire up.* **b** make or become angry; lose or cause to lose one's temper. **c** make enthusiastic or excited. **d** set a machine or other device in operation. ⟨OE *fȳr*⟩ —**ˈfir•er,** *n.*

fire alarm **1** the signal that a fire has broken out. **2** a device that gives such a signal.

fire ant a small ant, genus *Solenopsis*, with a burning sting.

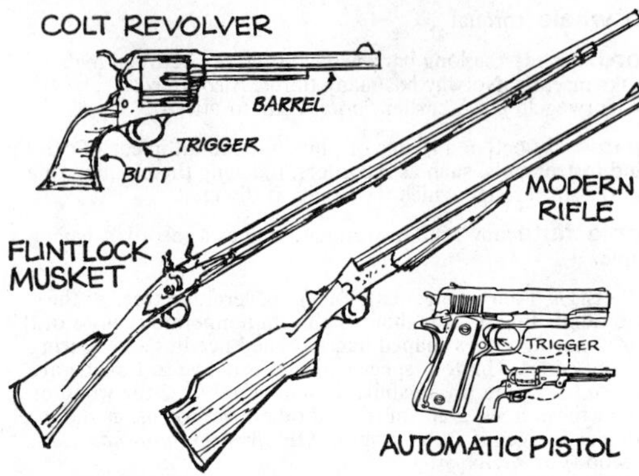

fire•arm ['faɪr,ɑrm] *n.* rifle, pistol, or other weapon to shoot with, usually such as a person can carry.

fire•ball ['faɪr,bɒl] *n.* **1** anything that looks like a ball of fire, such as a ball of lightning. **2** a large, brilliant meteor. **3** the great billowing mass of fire produced by an atomic explosion. **4** formerly, a ball of burning stuff thrown as a weapon. **5** *Baseball.* a very fast pitch to the batter. **6** *Informal.* a person who possesses great energy and enthusiasm.

fire•bird ['faɪr,bɜrd] *n.* **1** the phoenix. **2** any of several birds, such as the Baltimore oriole or the scarlet tanager, having brilliant plumage.

fire blight a disease of trees which blackens the leaves and kills the branches. It is caused by a bacterium (*Erwinia amylovora*).

fire•boat ['faɪr,bout] *n.* a boat equipped with apparatus for putting out fires on a dock, ship, etc.

fire•bomb ['faɪr,bɒm] *n., v.* —*n.* an incendiary bomb. —*v.* **1** attack or destroy with a firebomb or firebombs. **2** attack (a fire) with a water bomber.

fire•bomb•er ['faɪr,bɒmər] *n.* **1** a person who attacks or destroys with firebombs. **2** WATER BOMBER.

fire•bomb•ing ['faɪr,bɒmɪŋ] *n.* **1** the act or an instance of using an incendiary bomb to attack or destroy: *Several people have been arrested in connection with the firebombing.* **2** the use of a water bomber to fight a forest fire.

fire•box ['faɪr,bɒks] *n.* **1** the place for the fire in a furnace, boiler, indoor fireplace, etc. **2** the furnace of a steam boiler, especially that of a steam locomotive. **3** FIRE ALARM (def. 2).

fire•brand ['faɪr,brænd] *n.* **1** a piece of burning wood. **2** a person who stirs up others, for good or ill.

fire•brat ['faɪr,bræt] *n.* bristletail.

fire•break ['faɪr,breik] *n.* a strip of land that has been cleared of trees or on which the sod has been turned over so as to prevent the spreading of a forest fire or a prairie fire.

fire•brick ['faɪr,brɪk] *n.* a brick capable of withstanding great heat, and used to line furnaces and fireplaces. See BLAST FURNACE for picture.

fire brigade 1 a body of people organized, often privately or temporarily, to fight fires. **2** *Esp. Brit.* FIRE DEPARTMENT.

fire•bug ['faɪr,bʌg] *n. Informal.* a person who has a mania for setting houses or property on fire; pyromaniac.

fire cherry a tree (*Prunus pensylvanica*) of deciduous forests in Canada, especially British Columbia. It bears bright red edible fruit; its wood is often used as fuel.

fire chief the head of a fire department.

fire clay clay capable of resisting high temperatures, used for making crucibles, firebricks, etc.

fire company a group of people organized to put out fires.

fire control control of the firing of weapons, often nowadays by computer.

fire•crack•er ['faɪr,krækər] *n.* a paper roll containing gunpowder and a fuse: *A firecracker explodes with a loud noise.*

fire•damp ['faɪr,dæmp] *n.* a mixture of gases, consisting mainly of methane, that forms in coal mines. It is dangerously explosive when mixed with certain proportions of air.

fire department a municipal department in charge of the fighting and preventing of fires.

fire•dog ['faɪr,dɒg] *n.* andiron. See FIREPLACE for picture.

fire door a door made of fireproof material, used to stop a fire from spreading.

fire drill drill for firefighters, a ship's crew, pupils in a school, etc., to train them for duties or for orderly exit in case of fire.

fire–eat•er ['faɪr ,itər] *n.* **1** an entertainer who pretends to eat fire. **2** a person who is too ready to fight or quarrel.

fire engine a truck with a machine for spraying water, chemicals, etc. and with ladders and other equipment to put out fires.

fire escape a stairway, ladder, etc. in or on a building, to use in case of fire.

fire extinguisher a container filled with chemicals that can be sprayed upon fire to extinguish it.

fire•fight ['faɪr,fəit] *n.* a skirmish before a full military attack.

fire•fight•er ['faɪr,fəitər] *n.* **1** a member of a fire department. **2** a person who fights forest fires.

fire•fight•ing ['faɪr,fəitɪŋ] *n.* **1** the act or process of fighting fires. **2** the act of correcting individual problems as they arise, instead of taking general preventive measures.

fire–find•er ['faɪr ,faɪndər] *n.* an instrument consisting of a sighting device and a map, for finding the position of a forest fire.

fire•fly ['faɪr,flaɪ] *n., pl.* **-flies. 1** any of a family (Lampyridae) of small nocturnal beetles having an abdominal organ by means of which they produce flashes of light. Firefly larvae and the adult wingless females of some species are called glow-worms. **2** any of various other beetles having luminescent organs, especially some tropical members of the family Elateridae.

fire•guard ['faɪr,gɑrd] *n.* **1** FIRE SCREEN. **2** firebreak.

fire hall *Cdn.* **1** a building in which firefighting equipment is kept. **2** the headquarters of a fire department: *Permits for burning trash may be obtained at the fire hall.*

fire hydrant a connection to the water main for firefighters, placed at intervals along a street.

fire insurance insurance against damage or loss caused by fire.

fire irons tools, such as a poker, tongs, and shovel, needed for tending a fire.

fire•less ['faɪrlɪs] *adj.* **1** without a fire. **2** without enthusiasm or animation.

fire•light ['faɪr,ləit] *n.* the light from a fire.

fire line 1 firebreak. **2** the front edge of a forest fire or a prairie fire.

fire•lock ['faɪr,lɒk] *n.* an old type of gun, fired by a spark falling on the gunpowder; flintlock.

fire•man ['faɪrmən] *n., pl.* **-men. 1** a male firefighter. **2** a man whose work is taking care of the fire in a furnace, boiler, locomotive, etc.

fire opal an orange-red opal with changing colours.

A fireplace

fire•place ['faɪr,pleis] *n.* a place built in the wall of a room or outdoors to hold a fire.

fire plug FIRE HYDRANT. Also, **fireplug**.

fire pot the part of a stove, furnace, etc. that holds the fire.

fire•pow•er ['faɪr,paʊər] *n.* **1** the amount of fire delivered by a military unit, by a particular weapon, etc. **2** the ability to deliver fire.

fire•proof ['faɪr,pruf] *adj., v.* —*adj.* that will not burn; almost impossible to burn: *A building made entirely of steel and concrete*

is *fireproof.*
—*v.* make fireproof.

fire rang•er ['faɪr ˌreindʒər] *n. Cdn.* a government employee engaged in preventing and putting out forest fires on Crown lands.

fire–reels ['faɪr ˌrilz] *n. Cdn., esp. Ontario. Archaic or dialect.* FIRE ENGINE.

fire sale a sale of goods damaged as a result of a fire.

fire screen a screen to be placed in front of a fire as protection against heat or flying sparks.

fire ship formerly, a ship loaded with explosives and inflammable materials, set adrift among enemy ships.

fire•side ['faɪrˌsaɪd] *n., adj.* —*n.* **1** the space around a fireplace or hearth. **2** the home. **3** home life.
—*adj.* located, happening, etc. beside the fire.

fire–spot•ter ['faɪr ˌspɒtər] *n.* a person who works as an agent of the firefighting authorities by watching for and locating forest fires.

fire station FIRE HALL.

fire•storm ['faɪrˌstɔrm] *n.* **1** a large fire with strong winds, such as started by a nuclear explosion. **2** a violent outburst: *a firestorm of protest.*

Fire Temple *Zoroastrianism.* a temple or shrine in which a sacred fire is always burning.

fire•thorn ['faɪrˌθɔrn] *n.* any plant of the genus *Pyracantha* of the rose family, grown for its brightly coloured ornamental fruits.

fire tower a tower from which to keep watch for forest fires.

fire•trap ['faɪrˌtræp] *n.* **1** a building hard to get out of in case of fire. **2** a building that will burn very easily.

fire•truck ['faɪrˌtrʌk] *n.* FIRE ENGINE.

fire wall **1** a fireproof wall for confining a possible fire. **2** a fireproof plate or shield behind the engine of an automobile or airplane.

fire•ward•en ['faɪrˌwɔrdən] *n.* an official whose duty is preventing and putting out fires in forests, camps, etc.

fire•wa•ter ['faɪrˌwɒtər] *n.* any strong alcoholic drink: *The indigenous peoples of North America called whisky, gin, rum, etc. firewater.*

fire•weed ['faɪrˌwid] *n.* **1** any of several plants (genus *Epilobium*) of the evening-primrose family, especially a tall species (*E. angustifolium*) of north temperate regions, that flourishes mainly in newly burned areas, having long, showy spikes of purplish pink flowers. The fireweed is the floral emblem of the Yukon. **2** any of several other plants that commonly grow in burned areas.

Fireweed

fire•wood ['faɪrˌwʊd] *n.* wood for burning as fuel.

fire•work ['faɪrˌwɜrk] *n.* **1** a firecracker, bomb, rocket, etc. that, on being ignited or exploded, makes a loud noise or a beautiful, fiery or sparkly display, especially at night. **2 fireworks, a** a firework display. **b** any violent altercation, as a quarrel.

firing line **1** any line where soldiers are stationed to shoot at the enemy, a target, etc. **2** the soldiers on such a line. **3** the foremost position in a controversy, campaign for a cause, etc.

firing range **1** an area used for shooting practice. **2** the distance within which specific weapons are effective: *The robber was within firing range.*

firing squad **1** a small detachment of troops assigned to shoot to death a condemned person. **2** a detachment assigned to fire a salute.

fir•kin ['fɜrkən] *n.* **1** a quarter of a barrel, used as a measure of capacity. **2** a small wooden cask for butter, etc. ⟨ME *ferdekyn* < MDu. *verdelkijn,* dim. of *verdel,* literally, fourth part⟩

firm[1] [fɜrm] *adj., v., adv.* —*adj.* **1** not yielding easily to pressure or force; solid; hard: *firm flesh.* **2** not easily moved or shaken; tightly fastened or fixed: *a tree firm in the earth.* **3** steady in motion or action: *a firm step, a firm grasp.* **4** not easily changed; determined; resolute; positive: *a firm purpose.* **5** not changing; staying the same; steady: *a firm price.* **6** finally concluded; settled: *a firm order.*
—*v.*
firm up, a make or become firm **b** *Informal.* arrange definitely: *When can we firm up the date for our meeting?*
—*adv.*
stand or **hold firm,** remain set in one's convictions despite opposition. ⟨< L *firmus*⟩ —**'firm•ly,** *adv.* —**'firm•ness,** *n.*

☛ *Syn. adj.* **1. Firm,** HARD, SOLID = not yielding easily to pressure or force. **Firm** = so strong, tough, or compact in composition or structure that it is not easy to squeeze or pull out of shape, bend, or dig or cut into: *Her muscles are firm.* **Hard** = so strong, stiff, or thick as to be almost impossible to squeeze, pull, etc.: *The ground is too hard to dig.* **Solid** = so strongly built, uniformly dense, firm, or hard as to withstand all pressure or force: *We build houses on solid ground.*

firm[2] [fɜrm] *n.* a company or partnership of two or more persons in business or professional practice together, especially unincorporated: *an old and trusted firm.* ⟨< Ital. < Sp., Pg. *firma* signature, ult. < L *firmus* firm[1]⟩

fir•ma•ment ['fɜrməmənt] *n.* the arch of the heavens; sky. ⟨< L *firmamentum,* ult. < *firmus* firm[1]⟩ —**ˌfir•ma'men•tal,** *adj.*

firm•ware ['fɜrmˌwɛr] *n. Computer technology.* the system programs stored permanently on a computer's ROM chip.

firn [fɜrn] *n.* névé. ⟨< G *firn* of last year⟩
☛ *Hom.* FERN.

first [fɜrst] *adj., adv., n.* —*adj.* **1** coming or happening before all others; 1st: *a baby's first birthday.* **2 a** ranking highest; first in importance; *first vice-president.* **b** surpassing all others in quality, performance, etc.: *Pyotr is first in his class.* **3** of or having to do with the lowest gear of a vehicle or bicycle: *first gear.* **4** *Music.* **a** highest in pitch. **b** playing or singing the part highest in pitch: *first soprano.* **c** being the leading player in a section of an orchestra: *first violin.*
first things first, what is most important must come first.
in the first place, first; firstly; before anything else.
(the) first thing, a at the earliest possible moment: *She is going first thing in the morning.* **b** even the most basic facts (used with a negative): *He doesn't know the first thing about hygiene.*
—*adv.* **1** before all others; before anything else: *Women and children go first.* **2** before some other thing or event: *First bring me the chalk. First, we went to Paris, then to Rome.* **3** for the first time: *when I first visited Italy.* **4** rather; sooner: *I'll go to jail first.* **5** coming before other points; most importantly: *First, it is not safe; second, it isn't even fun.*
—*n.* **1** a person, thing, place, etc. that is first. **2** the winning position in a race, etc. **3** the beginning. **4** in an automobile or similar machine, the first, or lowest, gear; low. **5 firsts,** *pl.* articles of the best quality.
at first, in the beginning: *At first, Henrietta did not like school.*
first and foremost, chiefly; above all.
first and last, taking all together.
from the first, since the beginning. ⟨OE *fyrst*⟩

☛ *Usage.* **First. a** When used with a numeral, **first,** like all other ordinals, precedes the numeral: *For tomorrow I want you to do the first six problems.* **b first, last, latest. First** and **last** refer to items in a series, usually of more than two: *Her first act in office was to appoint a new secretary. We felt let down at the end of the last act.* **Latest** refers to a series that is still continuing: *Have you read the latest instalment of the new serial story?* **Last** refers either to the final item of a completed series or to the most recent item of a continuing series: *His last jump proved fatal. I was pleased with the last election.*

first aid the emergency treatment given to an injured person before a doctor comes. —**'first-'aid,** *adjl.*

first base **1** *Baseball.* the base that must be touched first by a runner. **2** the one playing first base.
get to first base, *Informal.* make the first step toward success: *The new secretary will never get to first base if she is not punctual.*

first–born ['fɜrst ˌbɔrn] *adj., n.* —*adj.* born first; oldest.
—*n.* the first-born child.

first class **1** the highest class or rank or best quality. **2** the class of mail that includes letters, postcards, etc. **3** on a first-class ship, train, airplane, etc.; in or on the first-class section. **4** by first-class mail. —**'first-'class,** *adj.*

first cousin the child of one's father's or mother's sister or brother.

first day Sunday, especially among Quakers. Also, **First Day.**

first–day cover ['fɜrst 'dei] *Philately.* an envelope bearing a commemorative stamp, cancelled on its first day of issue by the post office that issued it.

first finger the finger next to the thumb.

first floor 1 in North America, the ground floor of a building. 2 in Britain and Europe, and sometimes in Québec, the floor above the ground floor.

first fruits 1 the earliest fruits of the season. 2 the first products or results.

first–generation ['fɜrst ˌdʒɛnə'reiʃən] *adj.* of immigrants who came as adults, or their customs.

first–hand ['fɜrst 'hænd] *adj. or adv.* from the original source; direct: *first-hand information. She got the information first-hand.*

first lady the wife of the president of the United States. Also, **First Lady**.

first light dawn.

first•ling ['fɜrstlɪŋ] *n.* 1 the first of its kind. 2 the first product or result. 3 the first offspring of an animal.

first•ly ['fɜrstli] *adv.* in the first place; first.

first magnitude a measure of the brightness of a star. The first magnitude is the brightest.

First Meridian *Cdn.* the basic north-south line from which lands were surveyed in the Northwest Territories and are now surveyed in the Prairie Provinces. The First Meridian is located just west of Winnipeg at 97°W.

first mortgage a mortgage having priority over all other claims on the same property.

first name a person's first given name or, sometimes, the second (or third) given name if that is what the person is usually known by.

First Nations 1 the original peoples of Canada. 2 of or designating these peoples.

first night the night of the opening performance of a play or other live show. **—'first-'night•er,** *n.*

first offender someone convicted of having broken the law for the first time.

first person *Grammar.* **a** the form of a pronoun or verb used to refer to the speaker and those he or she includes with himself or herself. **b** the grammatical category that is marked by such forms. *I, me, mine,* and *we, us, ours* are pronouns of the first person. *Am* is a form of the verb *be* in the first person. **—'first-'per•son,** *adj.*

first quarter 1 the period between the new moon and the first half moon. 2 the phase of moon represented by the first half moon after the new moon.

first–rate ['fɜrst 'reit] *adj., adv. —adj.* 1 of the highest class. 2 *Informal.* excellent; very good.
—adv. Informal. excellently; very well.

first–strike ['fɜrst 'strəik] *adj.* of nuclear armaments or their use, offensive as opposed to defensive.

first string the starting lineup in a sport, as distinct from substitutes. **—'first-'string,** *adj.*

first water the highest grade: *diamonds of the first water.*

firth ['fɜrθ] *n.* especially in Scotland, a narrow arm of the sea; estuary of a river. ⟨< ON *fjörthr.* Akin to FIORD.⟩

fisc [fɪsk] *n.* a royal or state treasury; exchequer. ⟨< L *fiscus* purse⟩

fis•cal ['fɪskəl] *adj., n. —adj.* 1 financial. 2 having to do with a treasury or exchequer: *Important changes were made in the government's fiscal policy.*
—n. in some countries, a public prosecutor. ⟨< L *fiscalis* < *fiscus* purse⟩ **—'fis•cal•ly,** *adv.*
☛ *Syn. adj.* **1.** See note at FINANCIAL.

fiscal year the time between one yearly settlement of financial accounts and another. The fiscal year of the Canadian government ends March 31.

fish [fɪʃ] *n., pl.* **fish** or (*esp. for different species*) **fish•es;** *v.*
—n. 1 any of a large group of cold-blooded aquatic vertebrates that breathe by means of gills and most of which have fins and scales. Living fishes are divided into three taxonomic classes: the jawless fishes (Agnatha), including lampreys and hagfishes; the cartilaginous fishes (Chondrichthyes), including sharks and rays; and the bony fishes (Osteichthyes), including sturgeons, salmon and trout, perches, smelts, tunas, flatfishes, and drumfishes. 2 any of various other aquatic creatures (*usually used in compounds*): *starfish, crayfish, jellyfish.* 3 the flesh of fish used for food. 4 *Informal.* a person, especially when thought of as being disadvantaged or lacking some desirable human trait: *a queer fish. The poor fish was caught red-handed.* 5 a long strip of iron, wood, etc. used to strengthen a joint, etc. 6 **the Fishes,** *pl. Astronomy or astrology.* Pisces. 7 sometimes, **Fish**, a children's card game in which each player tries to collect matching sets of cards from the other players.
a fish out of water, a person who is uncomfortable or ill at ease as a result of being out of his or her usual environment.
drink like a fish, drink a lot of alcohol.
have other fish to fry, *Informal.* have other, especially more important, things to do.
—v. 1 try to catch fish. 2 try to catch fish in: *to fish a pool.* 3 try to pick up as if with a hook, etc. (*used with* **for**): *He fished for the quarter with a bent wire.* 4 search by groping inside something: *She fished in her purse for a coin.* 5 take or pull out, as if fishing: *I fished the map from the back of the drawer.* 6 try to get, especially by indirect means (*used with* **for**): *fishing for compliments.*
fish in troubled waters, take advantage of confusion or trouble to get what one wants.
fish or cut bait, attack a task head-on or abandon it altogether.
fish out, exhaust the supply of fish in (a lake, etc.) by fishing. ⟨OE *fisc*⟩ **—'fish•less,** *adj.* **—'fish,like,** *adj.*

fish and chips pieces of fish fried in a batter and served with French fries.

fish ball FISH CAKE.

fish•bowl ['fɪʃ,boul] *n.* 1 a usually round glass enclosure for keeping small fish. 2 any lifestyle in which one is unusually exposed to public view.

fish cake a patty or ball of ground fish, often combined with mashed potato.

fish eagle osprey.

fish•er ['fɪʃər] *n.* 1 a North American mammal (*Martes pennanti*) of the weasel family, closely related to and resembling the marten, but larger and less arboreal. Fishers are found in the forests of Canada and the N United States. 2 the thick, dark greyish brown fur of a fisher. 3 a person who fishes.
☛ *Hom.* FISSURE.

fish•er•man ['fɪʃərmən] *n., pl.* **-men.** 1 a man who fishes for a living or for pleasure. 2 a ship used in fishing. 3 (*adjl.*) designating a kind of thick sweater knitted in a variety of stitches and usually having a turtleneck.

fish•er•y ['fɪʃəri] *n., pl.* **-er•ies.** 1 the business or industry of farming, catching, and processing fish. 2 a place for catching fish: *Salmon is the main catch in the Pacific fisheries.* 3 a place where fish are farmed or processed.

fish–eye lens ['fɪʃ ,aɪ] a wide-angle photographic lens that covers a field of vision of about 180°, producing a circular image with distortion similar to that of a reflection on a globe.

fish farm a place where fish are bred and raised for the market.

fish flake a slatted platform used for drying fish: *Fish flakes are a familiar sight in Newfoundland fishing villages.*

fish flour a tasteless, odourless, high-protein flour produced by pulverizing dried fish.

fish glue a strong glue made from waste parts of fish.

fish hawk osprey.

fish–hook ['fɪʃ ,hʊk] *n.* a barbed hook used for catching fish.

fish house a hut or small building on the shore, where fishers store their gear, catch, etc. Fish houses are sometimes used also for smoking and curing fish.

fish•ing ['fɪʃɪŋ] *n., v. —n.* the catching of fish for a living or for pleasure.
—v. ppr. of FISH.

fishing ground a place where fish are plentiful.

fishing hole a hole cut through the ice of a lake, river, etc. to catch fish in winter.

fishing hut a small hut which is towed out onto the ice of a lake, to shelter ice fishers.

fishing line a line used in fishing. Also, **fish line**.

fishing lodge 1 a very primitive cabin for fishers. 2 an expensive hotel for fishers.

fishing rod or **pole** a slender rod, made of bamboo, plastics, etc. for fishing, with a line attached. Also, **fish pole**.

fishing smack a small ship used in fishing at sea.

fishing tackle rods, lines, hooks, etc. used in catching fish.

fish joint the point at which two rails or beams are joined by a fishplate.

fish ladder fishway.

fish line FISHING LINE.

fish meal ground-up dried fish used as feed for livestock, etc. or as fertilizer.

fish•mon•ger ['fɪʃ,mʌŋgər] *or* [-,mɒŋgər] *n. Esp. Brit.* a dealer in fish.

fish oil oil obtained from fish.

fish pass fishway.

fish•plate ['fɪʃ,pleit] *n.* a plate used to fasten two rails or beams together end to end. The rails of a railway track are usually joined by fishplates.

fish pole FISHING ROD.

fish•pond ['fɪʃ,pɒnd] *n.* a pond in which there are fish, especially an ornamental pool where fish, such as goldfish, are kept in captivity.

fish•skin disease ['fɪʃ,skɪn] a hereditary skin disease in which the skin becomes dry and scaly; ichthyosis.

fish stick **1** frozen fish fillets packaged in the form of a short, oblong stick for ease in shipping and handling: *Each year, thousands of fish sticks are shipped from the Maritimes to markets in Central Canada.* **2** a portion of fish, often breaded and pre-cooked, frozen and packaged for retail sale.

fish story *Informal.* an exaggerated, unbelievable story.

fish•tail ['fɪʃ,teil] *adj., v.* —*adj.* like a fish's tail in shape or action.
—*v.* **1** swing the tail of an airplane from side to side to reduce its speed. **2** of a motor vehicle, etc., have the rear end swing from side to side out of control.

fish•way ['fɪʃ,wei] *n.* a waterway built as an ascending series of little pools to enable fish to pass over a dam or falls on their way to spawning grounds upstream. Also called **fish ladder** or **fish pass.**

fish wheel a mechanical device for catching fish, consisting of several scoop nets on a circular frame which is driven by the force of the current.

fish•wife ['fɪʃ,wəif] *n., pl.* **-wives** [-,waɪvz]. **1** a woman who sells fish. **2** a woman who uses coarse and abusive language or who berates.

fish•y ['fɪʃi] *adj.* **fish•i•er, fish•i•est. 1** like a fish in smell, taste, or shape. **2** of fish. **3** full of fish. **4** *Informal.* doubtful; unlikely; suspicious. **5** of eyes, without expression or lustre; dull. **—'fish•i•ly,** *adv.* **—'fish•i•ness,** *n.*

fis•sile ['fɪsaɪl] *or* ['fɪsəl] *adj.* **1** easily split. **2** capable of nuclear fission. ⟨< L *fissilis* < *findere* cleave⟩ **—fis'sil•i•ty** [fɪ'sɪləti], *n.*

fis•sion ['fɪʃən] *n., v.* —*n.* **1** a splitting apart; division into parts. **2** *Biology.* a method of reproduction in which the body of the parent divides to form two or more independent individuals. Many simple plants and animals reproduce by fission. **3** *Physics.* the splitting that occurs when the nucleus of an atom under bombardment absorbs a neutron. Nuclear fission releases tremendous amounts of energy when heavy elements, especially plutonium and uranium, are involved.
—*v.* undergo or cause to undergo fission. ⟨< L *fissio, -onis* < *findere* cleave⟩

fis•sion•a•ble ['fɪʃənəbəl] *adj.* capable of nuclear fission.

fission bomb an atomic bomb that derives its force solely from the splitting of atoms. Compare FUSION BOMB.

fis•si•pa•rous [fɪ'sɪpərəs] *adj.* reproducing by fission. ⟨< L *fissus* pp. of *findere* to cleave, split + *-parus* < *parere* to bring forth, bear⟩

fis•si•ped ['fɪsə,pɛd] *adj.* **1** CLOVEN-HOOFED (def. 1). **2** CLOVEN-FOOTED (def. 1). ⟨< L *fissipes, fissipedis* cloven-footed < *fissus* pp. of *findere* to cleave, split + *pes, pedis* foot⟩

fis•si•ros•tral [,fɪsə'rɒstrəl] *adj.* of a bird, having a beak that is deeply cleft. ⟨< L *fissus* pp. of *findere* to cleave, split + *rostrum* beak⟩

fis•sure ['fɪʃər] *n., v.* **-sured, -sur•ing.** —*n.* **1** a split or crack; a long, narrow opening: *a fissure in a rock.* **2** a splitting apart; a division into parts. **3** *Anatomy.* a natural cleft or opening in an organ or part of the body. **4** *Pathology.* an abnormal crack or opening at the juncture of skin and a mucous membrane: *buccal fissure.*
—*v.* split apart; divide into parts; become split. ⟨< F < L *fissura* < *findere* cleave⟩
☛ *Hom.* FISHER.

fist [fɪst] *n., v.* —*n.* **1** the hand closed tightly. **2** *Informal.* the hand. **3** *Informal.* handwriting. **4** the grasp. **5** *Printing.* a symbol (☛).
—*v.* seize or hit with the fist. ⟨OE *fȳst*⟩ **—'fist,like,** *adj.*

-fisted *combining form.* having ——fists: *quick-fisted = having quick fists.*

fist•fight ['fɪst,fəit] *n.* a fight with the fists.

fist•ful ['fɪst,fʊl] *n., pl.* **fist•fuls.** as much as a closed hand can hold.

fist•ic ['fɪstɪk] *adj. Informal.* having to do with fighting with the fists; done with the fists.

fist•i•cuffs ['fɪstə,kʌfs] *n.pl.* blows with the fists: *It soon came to fisticuffs between them.*

fist•note ['fɪst,nout] *n.* in printed texts, a special note preceded by a FIST (def. 5).

fis•tu•la ['fɪstʃələ] *n., pl.* **-las** or **-lae** [-,li]. **1** a tube or pipe. **2** a tubelike sore connecting the surface of the body with an internal organ or cavity. ⟨< L *fistula* pipe, ulcer. Doublet of FESTER, n.⟩

fis•tu•lar ['fɪstʃələr] *adj.* **1** tubelike; tubular. **2** made up of tubelike parts. **3** having to do with a fistula. Also, **fistulous.**

fit[1] [fɪt] *adj.* **fit•ter, fit•test;** *v.* **fit** or (*esp. for 4–6, 8*) **fit•ted, fit•ting;** *n.* —*adj.* **1** suitable or appropriate: *a dress fit for a queen. The movie isn't fit for children. Grass is fit food for cattle; it is not fit for human beings.* **2** having the necessary or proper qualifications: *They were declared fit for active service. He's not fit to run his own business.* **3** prepared to do or undergo something; ready: *fit to receive visitors. I was almost fit to scream.* **4** in good physical condition; healthy: *They exercise daily to keep fit.*
fit to be tied, *Informal.* overcome with frustration.
see or **think fit,** consider it suitable, right, etc. (to): *She may see fit to ignore the whole incident.*
—*v.* **1** be suited or suitable to; be fit for: *Let the punishment fit the crime.* **2** make right, proper, or suitable: *to fit the action to the word.* **3** have the right size or shape (for): *The last piece of the puzzle didn't fit. The dress fits her well.* **4** change (something) to make it the right shape: *I should be able to fit the dress for you.* **5** measure (someone) for something to be fitted: *They fitted him for his artificial leg.* **6** supply with something needed or wanted; equip (*often used with* **out** *or* **up**): *The car is fitted with radial tires.* **7** put (something) on or in, making necessary adjustments: *to fit a slipcover on a chesterfield.* **8** make ready or competent; prepare: *They are receiving preliminary training to fit them for the expedition.* **9** accommodate: *to fit another appointment into a busy schedule. I can't fit another thing in my suitcase.* **10** correspond or agree with: *Her story doesn't fit the facts.* **11** belong; suit: *That girl doesn't fit well in our group.*
fit the bill, meet the requirements exactly.
—*n.* **1** the manner in which one thing fits another: *the fit of a coat, a tight fit.* **2** something that fits: *This coat is a good fit.* ⟨ME *fyt*; origin uncertain⟩
☛ *Syn. adj.* **1. Fit,** SUITABLE, APPROPRIATE = having the right qualities for something. **Fit** = having the qualities needed for the purpose, work, or use of the person or thing: *That shack is not fit to live in.* **Suitable** = having the qualities right or proper for a definite occasion, purpose, position, condition, or situation: *The lawyer found a suitable office.* **Appropriate** = particularly fit or suitable for the particular person, purpose, position, occasion, etc.: *A tailored suit is appropriate for a secretary.*

fit[2] [fɪt] *n.* **1** a sudden, sharp attack of illness: *a fit of colic.* **2** a sudden attack of illness characterized by loss of consciousness or by convulsions: *a fainting fit.* **3** any sudden, sharp attack or outburst: *a fit of laughter, a fit of coughing. In a fit of anger he hit his friend.*
by fits and starts, irregularly; starting, stopping, beginning again, and so on.
have, throw, or **take a fit,** have a violent negative reaction. ⟨OE *fitt* conflict⟩

fitch [fɪtʃ] *n.* **1** the European polecat. **2** the dark brown fur of a polecat. ⟨? < MDu. *fisse*⟩

fitch•et ['fɪtʃɪt] *n.* fitch.

fitch•ew ['fɪtʃu] *n.* fitch.

fit•ful ['fɪtfəl] *adj.* going on and then stopping awhile; irregular: *a fitful sleep, a fitful conversation.* ⟨< *fit*[2]⟩ **—'fit•ful•ly,** *adv.* **—'fit•ful•ness,** *n.*

fit•ly ['fɪtli] *adv.* **1** in a suitable manner. **2** at a proper time.

fit•ness ['fɪtnɪs] *n.* **1** suitability. **2** physical and muscular health. **3** (*adjl.*) for physical health: *a fitness club.* **4** *Biology.* the comparative ability of an individual or genotype to reproduce: *fitness is a major factor in evolution.*

fit•ted ['fɪtɪd] *adj., v.* —*adj.* made to follow the contours of the body, furniture, etc.: *a fitted blouse, a fitted sheet.*
—*v.* pt. and pp. of FIT.

fit•ter [ˈfɪtər] *n.* **1** a person who fits. **2** a person who fits dresses, suits, etc. on people. **3** a person who adjusts parts of machinery. **4** a person who supplies and fixes anything necessary for some purpose: *a pipe fitter.*

fit•ting [ˈfɪtɪŋ] *adj., n., v.* —*adj.* right; proper; suitable.
—*n.* **1** a trying on of unfinished clothes to see if they will fit. **2** a small part used to join other parts. **3 fittings,** *pl.* furnishings; fixtures.
—*v.* ppr. of FIT. —**ˈfit•ting•ly,** *adv.*
☛ *Syn. adj.* **Fitting,** BECOMING, SEEMLY = appropriate; in accord with some standard. **Fitting** = suiting the purpose or nature of a thing, character, or mood of a person, atmosphere or spirit of a time, place, or occasion, etc.: *It is a fitting evening for a dance.* **Becoming** = fitting or suitable in conduct or speech, enhancing a person's character or position, or meeting personal standards: *Gentleness is becoming in a nurse.* **Seemly** = pleasing and fitting or becoming, as judged by rules for conduct or behaviour as well as by good taste: *Swearing is not seemly in a child.*

five [faɪv] *n., adj.* —*n.* **1** one more than four; 5: *I counted only five.* **2** the numeral 5: *I think it's a five, but I'm not sure.* **3** the fifth in a set or series; especially, a playing card or side of a die having five spots: *a pair of fives.* **4** a five-dollar bill: *The cashier gave me two fives.* **5** a set or series of five persons or things: *The Romans counted in fives.* **6** a basketball team. **7 fives,** a British ball game similar to squash, played in a walled court with bats or hands (*used with a singular verb*).
—*adj.* **1** being one more than four; 5: *We ordered five tickets.* **2** being fifth in a set or series (*used mainly after the noun*): *Lesson Five is easier than Lesson Four.* ⟨OE *fīf*⟩

five–and–ten [ˈfaɪv ən ˈtɛn] *n.* a small store selling inexpensive items, formerly ones that cost five or ten cents. Also, **five-and-ten-cent store, five-and-dime.**

five•fold [ˈfaɪv,fould] *adj., adv.* —*adj.* **1** five times as much or as many. **2** having five parts.
—*adv.* five times as much or as many.

Five Nations a former confederacy of Iroquois peoples of the First Nations, consisting of the Mohawks, Oneidas, Onondagas, Cayugas, and Senecas. Members of the Five Nations (now the Six Nations with the inclusion of the Tuscarora) lived in Ontario and Québec.

five o'clock shadow *Informal.* the light growth of hair seen in the evening on the face of a man who shaved that morning.

five•pin [ˈfaɪv,pɪn] *n.* **1 fivepins,** a bowling game in which a heavy ball is rolled along a long indoor alley with the aim of knocking over the five bottle-shaped wooden pins arranged upright at the other end (*used with a singular verb*): *Fivepins is a popular Canadian game.* **2** one of the pins used in this game. **3** (*adjl.*) of this type of bowling: *fivepin bowling, or fivepin alley.*

five–star [ˈfaɪv ˈstɑr] *adj.* of a movie, resort, hotel, etc., of the very best class; excellent; first-rate. ⟨from being marked in reviews with a number of stars, five being the highest⟩

fix [fɪks] *v.* **fixed, fix•ing;** *n.* —*v.* **1** make firm; become firm; fasten tightly; be fastened tightly: *We fixed the post in the ground.* **2** settle; set: *He fixed the price at one dollar.* **3** mend; repair. **4** direct or hold steady (eyes, attention, etc.); be directed or held steadily. **5** attract and hold (the eye, attention, etc.). **6** set one's gaze steadily toward: *She fixed him with an impudent eye.* **7** make or become rigid. **8** put definitely: *She fixed the blame on the leader.* **9** treat to keep from changing or fading: *A dye or photograph is fixed with chemicals.* **10** *Informal.* put in order; arrange. **11** *Informal.* get revenge upon; get even with; punish. **12** *Chemistry.* **a** make stable; change into a more permanent form or state. **b** bring about the combining of (atmospheric nitrogen) with other compounds to creat substances such as nitrates, ammonia, etc. **13** *Informal.* spay or castrate: *Has your cat been fixed?* **14** *Informal.* prearrange or influence the outcome of (a game, race, trial, etc.) by payment or other inducement or manipulation: *The jury had been fixed.* **15** commit to memory: *The boy fixed the spelling lesson in his mind.*
fix on or **upon,** decide on; choose; select.
fix up, *Informal.* **a** mend; repair. **b** put in order; arrange. **c** provide with something needed: *I will fix you up in that house. We fixed him up with a date for Friday's dance.*
—*n. Informal.* **1** a position hard to get out of; awkward state of affairs. **2** the position of a ship, aircraft, radio transmitter, etc. as determined by obtaining radio signals or other signals from two or more given points. **3** an arrangement for dodging the law, especially one made by bribery. **4** money thus paid. **5** a sports contest whose outcome is prearranged. **6** a dose of a narcotic, especially intravenous. ⟨< F *fixer,* ult. < L *fixus,* pp. of *figere* fix⟩ —**ˈfix•a•ble,** *adj.*
☛ *Syn. v.* **1, 2. Fix,** ESTABLISH, SETTLE[1] = set something or someone firmly in position. **Fix** emphasizes setting so firmly, solidly, or definitely in a position, place, or condition that it is hard to change or move: *We fixed the stove in place.* **Establish,** used primarily with abstract nouns, emphasizes making firm, stable, and lasting, and means 'set up or fix firmly or permanently': *They established a partnership.* **Settle** = put in a steady, ordered, or permanent position, place, or condition: *He settled his daughter in a business of her own.*

fix•ate [ˈfɪkseit] *v.* **-at•ed, -at•ing.** (*usually passive*) **1** *Psychoanalysis.* **a** check the development of (the libidinal or aggressive impulse) at an early time in the child's psychosexual maturation. **b** cause (someone) to have a morbid attachment or preoccupation as a result of such a checked development (*used with* **on**). **2** obsess.

fix•a•tion [fɪkˈseiʃən] *n.* **1** the act of fixing or condition of being fixed. **2** a treatment to keep something from changing or fading: *the fixation of a photographic film.* **3** *Chemistry.* the process of changing into a more stable form, such as converting atmospheric nitrogen into molecules containing nitrogen that plants can use. **4** *Psychoanalysis.* **a** a fixating or being fixated. **b** a morbid attachment or prejudice. **5** obsession.

fix•a•tive [ˈfɪksətɪv] *n., adj.* —*n.* a substance used to keep something from fading or changing.
—*adj.* that prevents fading or change.

fixed [fɪkst] *adj., v.* —*adj.* **1** not movable; firm; steady. **2** settled; set; definite: *fixed charges for taxicabs.* **3** made stiff or rigid. **4** not adjusted or indexed over time: *a fixed income.* **5** *Informal.* prearranged privately or dishonestly: *a fixed horse race.* **6** *Chemistry.* **a** entering into a stable compound. **b** not volatile: *a fixed acid.* **7** *Informal.* spayed or castrated. **8** of a heavenly body whose position relative to the earth or other bodies appears unchanging: *a fixed star.* **9** of a persistent idea or thought that cannot be dislodged: *a fixed obsession.*
be fixed for, *Informal.* supplied with; set up: *How are you fixed for the holidays? She is certainly well fixed for dishes.*
—*v.* pt. and pp. of FIX.

fix•ed•ly [ˈfɪksɪdli] *adv.* in a fixed manner; without change; intently: *to stare fixedly.*

fix•ed•ness [ˈfɪksɪdnɪs] *n.* a being fixed; intentness.

fixed oil a natural oil that is not volatile.

fixed–point representation [ˈfɪkst ˈpɔɪnt] the use of a fixed decimal to express numbers, rather than scientific notation, as 900 instead of 9×10^2. Compare FLOATING-POINT REPRESENTATION.

fix•er [ˈfɪksər] *n.* **1** a fixative. **2** *Informal.* a person who arranges deals, negotiations, political favours, drug deals, etc., especially underhandedly or illegally.

fix•ings [ˈfɪksɪŋz] *n.pl. Informal.* **1** furnishings; trimmings. **2** ingredients.

fix•i•ty [ˈfɪksəti] *n., pl.* **-ties. 1** a fixed condition or quality; permanence; steadiness; firmness. **2** something fixed.

fix•ture [ˈfɪkstʃər] *n.* **1** something put in place to stay: *bathroom fixtures, electric light fixtures.* **2** a person or thing that stays in one place, job, etc.: *After twenty-five years of service, he is considered a fixture in the factory.* **3** a game or some other sports event for which a date has been fixed. ⟨var. of obs. *fixure* (< L *fixura* a fastening < *figere* fasten); influenced by *mixture*⟩

fizz [fɪz] *v., n.* —*v.* **1** make a hissing sound. **2** effervesce; give off gas bubbles.
fizz on, *Informal.* of a suggestion, act, etc., provoke a reaction in (someone); excite or arouse (*usually with a negative*): *We nearly killed ourselves laughing about it, but it didn't fizz on him at all.*
—*n.* **1** a hissing sound. **2** a bubbling drink, such as champagne, soda water, etc. **3** *Informal.* bubbles; effervescence: *This ginger ale has no fizz left.* Also, **fiz.** ⟨imitative⟩

fiz•zle [ˈfɪzəl] *v.* **-zled, -zling;** *n.* —*v.* **1** hiss or sputter weakly: *The firecracker fizzled instead of exploding with a bang.* **2** *Informal.* fail.
fizzle out, end in failure.
—*n.* **1** a hissing; sputtering. **2** *Informal.* failure. ⟨< obs. *fise* the breaking of wind; cf. OE *fisting*⟩

fizz•y [ˈfɪzi] *adj.* **fizz•i•er, fizz•i•est.** that fizzes.

fjeld [fjɛld] *or* [fjɛl] *n.* in Scandinavian topography, a plateau with sparse vegetation. ⟨< Norwegian < ON *fiall, fjall*⟩

fjord [fjɔrd] See FIORD.

fl. **1** fluid. **2** flourished. **3** florin. **4** floor. **5** *Music.* flute.

F.L. or **F/L** FLIGHT LIEUTENANT.

flab [flæb] *n.* **1** excess fat or loose flesh on the body, resulting from overeating, poor muscle tone, etc. **2** anything superfluous, especially that hinders efficiency. ⟨back formation from *flabby;* 20c.⟩

flab•ber•gast ['flæbər,gæst] *v. Informal.* make speechless with surprise; astonish greatly; amaze. ⟨? blend of *flap* or *flabby* + *aghast*⟩

flab•by ['flæbi] *adj.* **-bi•er, -bi•est.** lacking firmness or force; soft; weak: *flabby cheeks.* ⟨var. of earlier *flappy* < *flap*⟩ **—'flab•bi•ly,** *adv.* **—'flab•bi•ness,** *n.*
☛ *Syn.* See note at LIMP[2].

flac•cid ['flæksɪd] *or* ['flæsɪd] *adj.* limp; weak: *flaccid muscles, a flaccid will.* ⟨< L *flaccidus* < *flaccus* flabby⟩ **—'flac•cid•ly,** *adv.*

flac•cid•i•ty [flæk'sɪdəti] *n.* a flaccid quality or condition.

flack[1] [flæk] *n., v. Slang. —n.* **1** a publicity or press agent. **2** public relations material; publicity.
—v. **1** act as a publicity agent: *flacking for a well-known author.* **2** put out as publicity material. ⟨origin uncertain⟩

flack[2] [flæk] See FLAK.

flack•er•y ['flækəri] *n. Informal.* publicity.

fla•con [flə'kɒn] *or* ['flækən]; *French,* [fla'kɔ̃] *n., pl.* **flacons.** a small bottle with a stopper, used for perfume, smelling salts, etc. ⟨< F < OF *flascon.* See FLAGON.⟩

flag[1] [flæg] *n., v.* **flagged, flag•ging.** *—n.* **1** a piece of cloth, often rectangular, that shows the emblem of a country, of a unit of the armed forces, or of some other organization: *the Canadian flag, the regimental flag.* **2** a piece of cloth, often rectangular or triangular, and of a bright colour, used as a decoration: *The hall was decorated with many flags.* **3** a piece of cloth of a certain shape, colour, or design that has a special meaning: *A red flag is often a sign of danger, a white flag of surrender, a black flag of disaster.* **4** something that suggests a flag. The tail of a deer or of a setter dog is a flag, as is a paper tab or other marker. **5** a large cloth used to keep lights from interfering with a television camera. **6** *Music.* a line added to the stem of a written note less than a quarter note. An eighth note has one flag, a sixteenth note two, etc. **7 flags,** *pl.* **a** the feathers on the second joint of a bird's wing. **b** the long feathers on the lower parts of the legs of certain birds.
—v. **1** put a flag or flags over or on; decorate with flags. **2** stop or signal, especially by waving a flag: *to flag a train.* **3** communicate by a flag: *to flag a message.* **4** decoy (game) by waving a flag or something like it to excite attention or curiosity. ⟨? < *flag[3]*⟩ **—'flag•ger,** *n.* **—'flag•less,** *adj.*

flag[2] [flæg] *n.* **1** any of various plants having swordlike leaves, such as the blue flag (a wild iris) or the sweet flag (an arum). **2** the leaf of any of these plants. ⟨Cf. Danish *flæg*⟩

flag[3] [flæg] *v.* **flagged, flag•ging.** get tired; grow weak; droop: *After doing the same thing for a long time, one's interest flags.* ⟨Cf. earlier Du. *vlaggheren* flutter⟩

flag[4] [flæg] *n., v.* **flagged, flag•ging.** *—n.* a flagstone.
—v. pave with flagstones. ⟨? var. of *flake*⟩

flag•el•lant ['flædʒələnt] *or* [flə'dʒɛlənt] *n., adj. —n.* **1** a person who whips or is whipped. **2** a person who whips himself or herself for religious discipline or for penance.
—adj. having the habit of whipping.

flag•el•late *v.,* ['flædʒə,leit]; *adj., n.,* ['flædʒəlɪt], ['flædʒə,leit], *or* [flə'dʒɛlɪt]. *v.* **-lat•ed, -lat•ing;** *adj., n. —v.* whip; flog.
—adj. **1** long, slender, and flexible, as a flagellum or whiplash. **2** *Biology, zoology.* having flagella. **3** *Botany.* having runners or runnerlike branches.
—n. a flagellate organism. ⟨< L *flagellare* < *flagellum,* dim. of *flagrum* whip⟩ **—'flag•el,la•tor,** *n.*

flag•el•la•tion [,flædʒə'leiʃən] *n.* a whipping; flogging.

fla•gel•lum [flə'dʒɛləm] *n., pl.* **-la** [-lə] or **-lums. 1** *Biology.* a long, whiplike tail or part, which is an organ of locomotion in certain cells, bacteria, protozoa, etc. **2** a whip. **3** *Botany.* a runner of a plant. **4** *Zoology.* the end of the antennae in certain insects. ⟨< L *flagellum,* dim. of *flagrum* whip⟩

flag•eo•let [,flædʒə'lɛt] *n.* a small musical wind instrument resembling a recorder, with a mouthpiece at one end, six main finger holes, and sometimes keys. ⟨< F *flageolet,* dim. of OF *flajol* flute, ult. < L *flare* blow⟩

flag football a game following the rules of Canadian football but in which tackling is outlawed, the ball carrier being stopped in his or her advance when a handkerchief is snatched from his or her back pocket.

flag•ging[1] ['flægɪŋ] *adj., v. —adj.* drooping; tired; weak.
—v. ppr. of FLAG. ⟨< *flag[3]*⟩

flag•ging[2] ['flægɪŋ] *n.* **1** flagstones. **2** a pavement made of flagstones. ⟨< *flag[4]*⟩

flag•ging[3] ['flægɪŋ] *n.* **1** material for making flags. **2** decorative flags collectively. ⟨< *flag[1]*⟩

fla•gi•tious [flə'dʒɪʃəs] *adj.* scandalously wicked; shamefully vile. ⟨< L *flagitiosus* < *flagitium* shame⟩ **—fla'gi•tious•ly,** *adv.* **—fla'gi•tious•ness,** *n.*

flag•man ['flægmən] *n., pl.* **-men. 1** a person who has charge of or carries a flag. **2** a person who signals with a flag or lantern at a railway crossing, etc.

flag of convenience the flag of a foreign country with which a ship is registered for legal or commercial convenience.

flag officer a naval officer having a rank of rear-admiral or above and entitled to display a flag on his or her ship indicating his or her rank or command.

flag of truce a white flag used as a sign of surrender or of a desire to confer with the enemy.

flag•on ['flægən] *n.* **1** a container for liquids, usually having a handle and a spout, and often a cover. **2** a large bottle, holding about two litres. **3** the contents of a flagon. ⟨ME < OF *flascon.* Akin to FLASK.⟩

flag•pole ['flæg,poul] *n.* a pole from which a flag is flown.

fla•grant ['fleigrənt] *adj.* notorious; glaringly outrageous; scandalous. ⟨< L *flagrans, -antis,* ppr. of *flagrare* burn⟩ **—'fla•gran•cy,** *n.* **—'fla•grant•ly,** *adv.*

fla•gran•te de•lic•to [flə'græntei dɪ'lɪktou] *Law.* in the very act of committing the crime; in the performance of the deed. ⟨< L *in flagrante delicto,* literally, while the crime is blazing⟩

flag•ship ['flæg,ʃɪp] *n.* **1** the ship that carries the officer in command of a fleet or squadron and displays his or her flag. **2** the grandest or most important ship of a shipping company. **3** the most outstanding member of any set or group **4** (*adjl.*) main; leading: *The chain's flagship store is in Toronto.*

flag•staff ['flæg,stæf] *n.* a pole from which a flag is flown.

flag station or **stop** a railway station where trains stop only when a signal is given.

flag•stone ['flæg,stoun] *n.* **1** a large, flat stone, used for paving walks, patios, etc. **2** such stones collectively or the rock from which they are cut or split.

flag•wav•ing ['flæg,weivɪŋ] *n., adj. —n.* **1** behaviour, such as speeches or tracts, designed to provoke intense patriotic or nationalist feelings. **2** any display of patriotism.
—adj. indulging in such behaviour **—'flag,wav•er,** *n.*

flail [fleil] *n., v. —n.* an instrument for threshing grain by hand. A flail consists of a wooden handle with a short, heavy stick fastened at one end by a thong.
—v. **1** strike with a flail. **2** beat; thrash: *to flail one's arms about.* ⟨OE *fligel.* Related to FLY[2], v.⟩

flair [flɛr] *n.* **1** a keen perception: *That trader had a flair for bargains.* **2** a natural talent: *The poet had a flair for making clever rhymes.* **3** discriminating taste: *She dresses with flair.* **4** bold creativity; verve. ⟨< F *flair* scent < *flairer* smell < L *flagrare*⟩
☛ *Hom.* FLARE.

flak [flæk] *n.* **1** gunfire from the ground, directed against aircraft. **2** anti-aircraft guns. **3** *Informal.* continuing, insistent criticism, complaints, etc.: *She got a lot of flak for what she said on television.* ⟨< G, an acronym for the initials of *Fliegerabwehrkanone* anti-aircraft gun⟩

flake[1] [fleik] *n., v.* **flaked, flak•ing.** *—n.* **1** a small, light mass; a soft, loose bit: *a flake of snow.* **2** a thin, flat piece or layer: *flakes of rust, flakes of ice floating on the pond, corn flakes.* **3** *Informal.* a strange, eccentric person.
—v. **1** come off in flakes; take off, chip, or peel in flakes: *Dirty spots showed where the paint had flaked off.* **2** break or separate into flakes. **3** cover or mark with flakes; make spotted. **4** form into flakes.
flake out, *Slang.* drop with exhaustion; lose consciousness. ⟨ME ? < Scand.; cf. ON *flaki*⟩ **—'flake,like,** *adj.* **—'flak•er,** *n.*

flake[2] [fleik] *n.* a slatted platform used for drying fish; fish flake. ⟨ME < ON *flake, fleke* a hurdle, wicker shield⟩

flak•y ['fleiki] *adj.* **flak•i•er, flak•i•est. 1** consisting of flakes: *Mica is a flaky substance.* **2** easily broken or separated into flakes. **3** *Informal.* odd; eccentric. **—'flak•i•ly,** *adv.* **—'flak•i•ness,** *n.*

flam [flæm] *n.* a drumbeat in which the drumsticks strike in such quick succession as to be almost simultaneous. ⟨probably echoic⟩

flambé [flɑm'bei]; *French,* [flɑ̃'be] *adj., v.* **-béd** or **-béed, -bé•ing.** *—adj.* of food, served with alcoholic liquor that has been poured over it and set alight (*used after a noun*): *peach flambé.*
—v. pour liquor over and set aflame. ⟨< F⟩

flam•beau ['flæmbou] *or* [flæm'bou]; *French,* [flɑ̃'bo] *n., pl.* **-beaux** [-bouz] or **-beaus. 1** a flaming torch. **2** a large, decorated candlestick. ⟨< F < OF *flambe* flame, ult. < L *flamma*⟩

flam•boy•ant [flæm'bɔɪənt] *adj., n. —adj.* **1** gorgeously brilliant; flaming: *flamboyant colours.* **2** very ornate; excessively decorated: *flamboyant architecture.* **3** given to display; ostentatious; showy: *a flamboyant person.* **4** having wavy lines or flamelike curves: *flamboyant designs.* **5** lively; high-spirited.
—n. ROYAL POINCIANA. Also called **flamboyant tree.** ⟨< F *flamboyant,* ppr. of *flamboyer* flame⟩ **—flam'boy•ance,** *n.* **—flam'boy•ant•ly,** *adv.*

flame [fleim] *n., v.* **flamed, flam•ing;** *adj. —n.* **1** one of the glowing red or yellow tongues of light that shoot out from a blazing fire. **2** burning gas or vapour. **3** a burning with flames; blaze. **4** a thing or condition, such as love or anger, that suggests flame. **5** a bright light. **6** a patch or streak of light colour. **7** a burning feeling; ardour; zeal. **8** *Informal.* sweetheart. **9** a bright reddish yellow or reddish orange.
—v. **1** burn with flames; blaze. **2** grow hot, red, etc.: *Her cheeks flamed.* **3** shine brightly; give out a bright light. **4** have or show a burning feeling. **5** burst out quickly and hotly; be or act like a flame. **6** treat with or subject to flame.
flame out, of jet engines, fail to function.
flame up, out, or **forth,** burst out quickly and hotly; flare up.
—adj. bright reddish yellow or reddish orange. ⟨ME < OF < L *flamma*⟩ **—'flame•less,** *adj.* **—'flame,like,** *adj.*
☛ *Syn. n.* **1, 3. Flame,** BLAZE[1] = a bright burning or fire. **Flame** applies to either a single glowing tongue of fire, such as from a candle, or to a fire burning brightly and quickly, and is often used in the plural to suggest a fire with many bright tongues darting or shooting up: *She turned up the flame of the kerosene lamp. The house burst into flames.* **Blaze** applies to a hotter, brighter, and steadier fire: *The whole room was lighted by the blaze in the fireplace.*

fla•men ['fleimən] *or* ['fleimɛn] *n., pl.* **fla•mens** or **flam•i•nes** ['flæmə,niz]. a Roman priest devoted to one particular god: *a flamen of Jupiter.* ⟨< L⟩

fla•men•co [flə'mɛŋkou] *n.* **1** a style of Spanish Gypsy dance performed with castanets, stamping and clapping to fast, fiery, vigorous rhythms. **2** a song or piece of music in this style, or for such a dance. ⟨< Sp. *flamenco* Flemish (applied to the Gypsies' dance celebrating their 19c. departure from Germany, later confused with Flanders)⟩

flame•out ['fleim,ʌut] *n.* the sudden failure of a jet engine to function, especially while the aircraft containing it is in flight.

flame•proof ['fleim,pruf] *adj.* **1** not liable to combustion. **2** not liable to burn when in contact with flames: *flameproof curtains.*

flame–re•sist•ant ['fleim rɪ,zɪstənt] *adj.* resistant to flame; not easily burned.

flame thrower 1 a weapon or device that directs a jet of burning gasoline mixture, napalm, etc. through the air. **2** a person who operates such a weapon or device. Also, **flamethrower.** ⟨translation of G *Flammenwerfer*⟩

flame tree any of various trees with bright red flowers, such as the bottletree (*Brachychiton acerifolium*).

flam•ing ['fleimɪŋ] *adj., v. —adj.* **1** burning with flames. **2** like a flame; very bright; brilliant. **3** showing or arousing strong feeling; violent; vehement.
—v. ppr. of FLAME.

fla•min•go [flə'mɪŋgou] *n., pl.* **-gos** or **-goes.** any of a family (Phoenicopteridae) of large, mostly tropical, wading birds having a very long neck and legs, a large, broad, downward-curving bill, and plumage ranging from pale pink to scarlet, with black wing tips. ⟨< Pg. < Sp. *flamenco* < Provençal *flamenc* < *flama* < L *flamma* flame⟩

Flamingos

Fla•min•i•an Way [flə'mɪniən] an old Roman road leading north from Rome to a port on the Adriatic Sea, built in 220 B.C.

flam•ma•ble ['flæməbəl] *adj.* easily set on fire; inflammable. **—,flam•ma'bil•i•ty,** *n.*
☛ *Usage.* **Flammable** and INFLAMMABLE mean the same, easily set on fire. Both words are borrowed from Latin; **flammable** is from the Latin verb *flammare,* and **inflammable** is from the Latin adjective *inflammabilis.* **Inflammable** is preferred for figurative use (*an inflammable temper*), while **flammable** is used in industry, on warning labels, etc. to avoid all possibility of misinterpretation. The negative is **non-flammable.**

flan [flæn] *n.* **1** a tart or open pastry filled or to be filled with fruit, custard, gelatin, etc. **2** a blank piece of metal, ready to be stamped and made into a coin. ⟨< MF *flaon* tart < Gmc.⟩

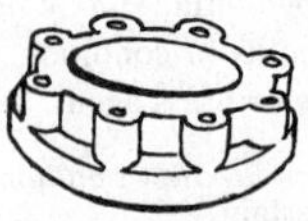
A flange for attaching a pipe to a surface

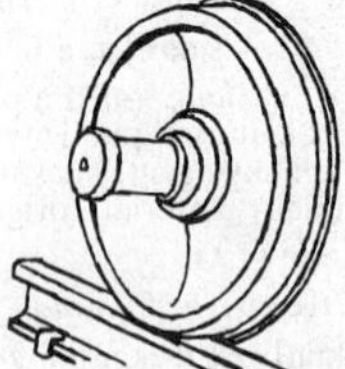
The wheel of a railway car, having a flange on the inner edge

flange [flændʒ] *n., v.* **flanged, flang•ing.** *—n.* a projecting edge, rim, collar, etc. on an object for keeping it in place, attaching it to another object, strengthening it, etc. Railway cars and locomotives have wheels with flanges to keep them on the track.
—v. provide with a flange. ⟨var. of *flanch,* n., < *flanch,* v., < OF *flanchir* bend⟩

flank [flæŋk] *n., v. —n.* **1** the fleshy part of the side between the ribs and the hip, especially on a four-footed animal. **2** a cut of beef from the flank. See BEEF, LAMB, and VEAL for pictures. **3** the side of a mountain, building, etc. **4** the far right or left side of an army, fleet, etc.
—v. **1** be at the side or both sides of: *High buildings flanked the dark, narrow alley.* **2** get around the far right or the far left side of. **3** attack from or on the side. **4** guard or protect the flank of. **5** occupy a position on the flank or side of (*used with* **on**). **6** present the flank or side. ⟨ME < OF *flanc* < Gmc.⟩ **—'flank•er,** *n.*

flan•nel ['flænəl] *n., adj. —n.* **1** a soft, warm woollen cloth. **2** flannelette. **3** *Brit.* a facecloth. **4 flannels,** *pl.* **a** clothes, especially pants, made of flannel. **b** woollen underwear.
—adj. made of flannel. ⟨< ME akin to *flanen* < Welsh *gwlanen* < *gwlan* wool⟩

flan•nel•board ['flænəl,bɔrd] *n.* a board with flannel stretched across it, to which cloth or specially backed paper cut-outs will cling on contact, used primarily in nursery and elementary schools as a teaching aid.

flan•nel•ette [,flænə'lɛt] *n.* a soft, warm cotton cloth with a fuzzy nap, that looks like flannel.

flap [flæp] *v.* **flapped, flap•ping;** *n. —v.* **1** swing or sway about loosely: *The curtains flapped in the open windows.* **2** cause to swing or sway loosely: *The breeze noisily flapped the sheets on the clothesline.* **3** move (wings, arms, etc.) up and down. **4** fly by moving wings up and down: *The large bird flapped away.* **5** strike noisily with something broad and flat. **6** *Slang.* become excited, confused, or alarmed. **7** *Phonetics.* pronounce (a consonant) as a flap.
—n. **1** a flapping motion. **2** a noise caused by flapping. **3** a blow from something broad and flat. **4** a broad, flat piece, usually hanging or fastened at one edge only: *His coat had flaps on the pockets.* **5** a small, movable section of an airplane wing near the fuselage that is lowered to increase lift at low air speeds. **6** *Slang.* a state of excitement or anger; commotion. **7** *Surgery.* a piece of flesh partially detached from adjacent tissue as for later use in grafting. **8** *Phonetics.* a type of trill in which the vibrating organ gives only a single tap, as in some British pronunciations of *merry, very,* etc. *T* and *d* between vowels are often pronounced as flaps in North American English, especially in fast speech as in *put it away.*
in a flap, *Informal.* upset; confused. ⟨ME; probably imitative⟩ **—'flap,like,** *adj.* **—'flap•py,** *adj.*

flap•doo•dle ['flæp,dudəl] *n. Slang.* nonsense; rubbish; humbug. ⟨a coined word⟩

flap•jack ['flæp,dʒæk] *n.* a pancake; griddlecake.

flap•per ['flæpər] *n.* **1** something broad and flat to strike with. **2** a broad, flat, hanging piece; flap. **3** a young bird just able to fly. **4** *Informal.* in the 1920s, a young woman, especially a rather forward and unconventional one.

flare [flɛr] *v.* **flared, flar•ing;** *n. —v.* **1** flame up briefly or unsteadily, sometimes with smoke: *A gust of wind made the torches flare.* **2** signal by flares: *The rockets flared a warning.*

3 spread or cause to spread outward from a narrower part, somewhat like a bell: *a flared skirt. The sides of a ship flare from the keel to the deck.* **4** blaze suddenly (*often used with* **up**): *The dying fire flared up briefly.* **5** break out suddenly (*usually used with* **up** *or sometimes* **out**): *The fighting has flared up again in spite of the peace talks. His temper flared up and he struck out with his fist.*
—*n.* **1** a bright, unsteady light or blaze that lasts only a short time: *The flare of a match showed us his face.* **2** a dazzling light that burns for a short time, used for signalling, lighting up a battlefield, etc. **3** a sudden brightening of part of the surface of the sun. **4** a sudden outburst. **5** a spreading out into a bell shape. **6** a part that spreads out: *the flare of a skirt.* ⟨cf. Norwegian *flara* blaze⟩
☛ *Hom.* FLAIR.

flare•pot ['flɛr,pɒt] *n.* a metal sphere, usually containing kerosene, that may be lit as a warning signal.

flare–up ['flɛr ,ʌp] *n.* **1** an outburst of flame. **2** *Informal.* a sudden outburst of anger, violence, etc. or resurgence of a disease.

flar•ing ['flɛrɪŋ] *adj., v.* —*adj.* **1** flaming. **2** gaudy. **3** spreading gradually outward in form or shape.
—*v.* ppr. of FLARE.

flash [flæʃ] *n., v., adj.* —*n.* **1** a sudden, brief light or flame or appearance of some bright colour, etc.: *a flash of lightning, a flash of yellow.* **2** a sudden, brief feeling, outburst, or display: *a flash of hope, a flash of temper, a flash of wit.* **3** a very brief time; instant. **4** a brief news report, usually received by teletype, or given over the radio or television: *a news flash.* **5** showy display. **6** a small piece of coloured ribbon, etc., worn on clothing as an insignia or emblem. **7 a** a rush of water, as produced by a dam or sluiceway, used to float a boat over shoals or for other purposes. **b** the device, as a lock or sluice, used for this purpose.
flash in the pan, a sudden, showy attempt or effort, often one that fails or is not followed by further efforts.
in a flash, in a very short time: *It all happened in a flash.*
—*v.* **1** give out a sudden, brief or intermittent light or flame. **2** come suddenly; pass quickly. **3** cause to flash. **4** give out or send out like a flash. **5** communicate (with) by flashes; send by telegraph, radio, etc. **6** *Informal.* briefly expose the genitals publicly (to). **7** *Informal.* show off; flaunt briefly: *to flash a diamond ring.* **8** cover with FLASHING (def. 1).
flash back, of a film or book plot, return to an earlier time.
—*adj.* **1** flashy. **2** using a flash: *a flash camera.* **3** happening or done in a flash; instantaneous or sudden. ⟨< ME *flasshe*(n), apparently imitative⟩
☛ *Syn. n.* **1. Flash,** GLITTER, SPARKLE = a sudden or unsteady light. **Flash** = a sudden, bright light that disappears immediately: *We saw a single flash of light from the signal tower.* **Glitter** = a bright and wavering light that off and on sends out brilliant flashes as light is reflected from a shining, hard surface: *We saw the glitter of swords in the moonlight.* **Sparkle** = light shooting out in many tiny, brief, brilliant flashes like sparks: *We looked at the sparkle of the little dancing waves in the sunlight.*

flash•back ['flæʃ,bæk] *n.* **1** in a novel, play, movie, etc., the introduction of some event or scene that took place or is supposed to have taken place at an earlier time. **2** the scene thus introduced.

flash•board ['flæʃ,bɔrd] *n.* a board or series of boards mounted on a dam to increase the depth of the water.

flash bulb a bulb, often containing magnesium, used to give a bright light for taking photographs indoors, in shadow, or at night. Also, **flashbulb.**

flash burn a severe burn caused by instantaneous thermal radiation, such as that from an atomic bomb.

flash card one of a set of cards displaying letters, words, figures, pictures, etc., intended to be shown briefly to elicit a desired response, used for drills in reading, arithmetic, and other school subjects, or for various other purposes.

flash cube a cube-shaped device containing four flash bulbs, that can be attached to certain kinds of cameras so that four flash pictures can be taken without having to change bulbs. Also, **flashcube.**

flash•er ['flæʃər] *n.* **1** *Informal. Cdn.* a bright piece of metal used to attract fish to a lure or bait. **2** *Informal.* a person who exposes his or her genitals in public.

flash fire a sudden fire that spreads rapidly.

flash flood **1** a very sudden, violent flooding of a river, stream, etc. **2** an abrupt onslaught of water down a ravine or over an inclined surface, due to heavy rainfall.

flash–for•ward ['flæʃ 'fɔrwərd] *n.* **1** in a novel, play, movie, etc., the introduction of some event or scene supposed to take place at a later time. **2** the scene thus introduced.

flash gun *Photography.* an apparatus for holding and setting off a flash bulb.

flash•ing ['flæʃɪŋ] *n., v.* —*n.* **1** the pieces of sheet metal used to cover and protect the joints and angles of a building to make them watertight. **2** the process of suddenly letting in a rush of water so as to produce an artificial flood, as for cleaning a sewer.
—*v.* ppr. of FLASH.

flash•light ['flæʃ,ləit] *n.* **1** a portable electric light, usually operated by batteries. **2** a light that flashes, used in a lighthouse or for signalling. **3** FLASH BULB.

flash•o•ver ['flæʃ,ouvər] *n. Electricity.* a discharge of electricity over an insulator.

flash paper chemically treated paper that vanishes when ignited.

flash•point ['flæʃ,pɔɪnt] *n.* **1** *Physical chemistry.* the lowest temperature at which vapour from a combustible substance such as gasoline will ignite if exposed to flame. **2** the point at which anger, indignation, etc. in a given individual bursts out into action or violence.

flash tube a tubular FLASH BULB.

flash•y ['flæʃi] *adj.* **flash•i•er, flash•i•est. 1** very bright for a short time; flashing. **2** showy; gaudy. —**'flash•i•ly,** *adv.* —**'flash•i•ness,** *n.*

flask [flæsk] *n.* **1** any bottle-shaped container, especially one having a narrow neck: *Flasks of thin glass are used in chemical laboratories for heating liquids.* **2** a small, flat or slightly convex, rectangular glass, plastic, or metal bottle made to be carried in the pocket. **3** a box or frame for holding the sand, etc. used as a mould in a foundry. ⟨OE *flasce;* cf. LL *flasca* < Gmc.⟩

flat[1] [flæt] *adj.* **flat•ter, flat•test;** *n., adv., v.* **flat•ted, flat•ting.** —*adj.* **1** smooth and level; even: *flat land.* **2** spread out horizontally; at full length: *The storm left the trees flat.* **3** not very deep or thick; not spherical, cylindrical, convex, or concave: *a flat bottle. A plate is flat.* **4** touching all over: *He put his chest flat against the X-ray machine.* **5** of a shoe, having little or no heel. **6** with little air in it: *a flat tire.* **7** not to be changed; positive: *A flat refusal is final. A flat rate does not vary according to scale.* **8** without much life, interest, flavour, etc.; dull: *flat food, a flat voice, flat beer.* **9** not shiny or glossy: *a flat yellow.* **10** having no relief or foreshortening: *a flat painting.* **11** not clear or sharp in sound. **12** *Music.* **a** below the true pitch. **b** one half step or half note below natural pitch. **c** marked with or having flats. **13** of feet, having the arches fallen.
that's flat, that's final.
—*n.* **1** something flat. **2** flatboat. **3** a shallow box or basket. **4** flatcar. **5** a piece of theatrical scenery made of a wooden frame covered with painted canvas. **6** *Informal.* a tire with little air in it. **7** a flat part: *The front of an open hand is the flat.* **8 flats,** flat-heeled shoes. **9** flat land. **10** land covered with shallow water; marsh; swamp. **11** *Music.* **a** a tone or note that is one half step or half note below natural pitch. **b** the sign ♭ that shows such a tone or note. **12** *Horse racing.* **a** a race on a flat course in contrast to a steeplechase or other jumping race. **b** the sport of racing on a track without jumps or obstacles.
—*adv.* **1** *Music.* below the true pitch. **2** in a flat manner; flatly. **3** in or into a flat position; horizontally: *Bill fell flat on the floor.* **4** directly; exactly. **5** *Informal.* completely: *I'm flat broke.*
fall flat, fail completely; have no effect or interest.
flat out, a at maximum speed or effort. **b** bluntly; without pretence: *She refused flat out.*
—*v.* **1** make or become flat. **2** *Music.* make or sound flat. ⟨ME < ON *flatr*⟩ —**'flat•ly,** *adv.* —**'flat•ness,** *n.*

flat[2] [flæt] *n.* an apartment or set of rooms on the same floor and generally not self-contained. ⟨alteration of *flet,* OE *flett*⟩

flat•bed ['flæt,bɛd] *n.* **1** a truck or trailer without top or sides, used for carrying heavy machinery. **2** (*adjl.*) being or designating such a vehicle: *a flatbed truck.*

flat•boat ['flæt,bout] *n., v.* —*n.* a large boat with a flat bottom, often used for carrying goods on a river or canal.
—*v.* transport in a flatboat.

flat•bot•tomed ['flæt,bɒtəmd] *adj.* of a boat, having a flat bottom.

flat•bread ['flæt,brɛd] *n.* a thin, dry cracker usually made from rye flour.

flat•car ['flæt,kɑr] *n.* a railway freight car without a roof or sides.

flat•fish ['flæt,fɪʃ] *n., pl.* **-fish** or **-fish•es.** any of an order (Heterosomata; also called Pleuronectiformes) of spiny-finned marine fishes having a very compressed (flattened) body and both eyes on one side, which is kept uppermost as the fish swim along the bottom of the sea.

flat•foot ['flæt,fʊt] *n., pl.* **-feet. 1** a foot with a flattened arch. **2** a condition in which the feet have flattened arches. **3** *Slang.* police officer.

flat–foot•ed ['flæt ,fʊtɪd] *adj.* **1** having feet with flattened arches. **2** *Informal.* **a** not to be changed or influenced; firm; uncompromising. **b** downright, plain, blunt, or straightforward. **3** *Informal.* clumsy; graceless.
catch (someone) **flat-footed,** catch (someone) off guard.
—'flat-'foot•ed•ly, *adv.* **—'flat-'foot•ed•ness,** *n.*

Flat•head ['flæt,hɛd] *n.* a member of an American Indian people living in W Montana. ⟨from their supposed practice of flattening the heads of their children⟩

flat•i•ron ['flæt,aɪərn] *n.* an early form of IRON (def. 4), heated on a stove.

flat•land ['flæt,lænd] *n.* sometimes, **flatlands,** *pl.,* level ground with no hills or valleys.

flat–out ['flæt 'ʌut] *adj., adv.* —*adj. Informal.* absolute: *a flat-out insult.*
—*adv. Informal.* absolutely: *You are flat-out mistaken.*

flat•ten ['flætən] *v.* **1** make or become flat. **2** raze to the ground.
flatten out, a spread out flat. **b** return to a level position from a dive or climb; level off. **—'flat•ten•er,** *n.*

flat•ter¹ ['flætər] *v.* **1** praise too much or beyond what is true; praise insincerely. **2** show to be better looking than is actually the case: *This picture flatters her.* **3** try to please or win over by flattering. **4** cause to be pleased or feel honoured. **5** falsely encourage the attentions of. **6** use flattery.
flatter oneself, a be gratified to know or think. **b** overestimate oneself. ⟨? extended use of ME *flateren* float. Related to FLUTTER.⟩ **—'flat•ter•er,** *n.* **—'flat•ter•ing•ly,** *adv.*

flat•ter² ['flætər] *n.* an appliance used by a blacksmith to forge flat surfaces. ⟨< *flat¹*⟩

flat•ter•y ['flætəri] *n., pl.* **-ter•ies. 1** the act of flattering. **2** words of praise, usually untrue or overstated.

flat•tish ['flætɪʃ] *adj.* somewhat flat.

flat•top ['flæt,tɒp] *n.* **1** *Esp. U.S. Informal.* AIRCRAFT CARRIER. **2** a haircut similar to a crew cut but completely flat across the top.

flat•u•lent ['flætʃələnt] *adj.* **1** having gas in the stomach or intestines. **2** causing gas in the stomach or intestines. **3** pompous in speech or behaviour; vain; empty. ⟨< F < L *flatus* a blowing < *flare* blow⟩ **—'flat•u•lence,** *n.* **—'flat•u•lent•ly,** *adv.*

fla•tus ['fleitəs] *n., pl.* **-tus•es.** gas in the stomach, intestines, etc. or expelled from the intestines. ⟨< L⟩

flat•ware ['flæt,wɛr] *n.* **1** knives, forks, and spoons. **2** plates, platters, saucers, etc.

flat•ways ['flæt,weiz] *adv.* with the flat side forward, upward, or touching. Also, **flatwise** ['flæt,waɪz].

flat•work ['flæt,wɜrk] *n.* laundered articles that need no ironing.

flat•worm ['flæt,wɜrm] *n.* any of a phylum (Platyhelminthes) of invertebrates having an unsegmented, usually flat body, including some, such as tapeworms and flukes, that are parasites in humans and animals.

flaunt ['flɒnt] *v., n.* —*v.* **1** show off. **2** wave proudly: *banners flaunting in the breeze.*
—*n.* a flaunting. ⟨? < Scand.; cf. Norwegian *flanta* gad about⟩
—'flaunt•er, *n.* **—'flaunt•ing•ly,** *adv.*
☛ *Usage.* **Flaunt,** FLOUT. Because of their form and the common ingredient of 'brazenness' or 'pride' in their meanings these words are often confused. One *flaunts* something one feels to be superior or prestigious, but *flouts* something for which one feels contempt.

flau•tist ['flʌutɪst] *or* ['flɒtɪst] *n.* flutist.

fla•vin ['fleivɪn] *n. Chemistry.* a yellow colouring matter derived from a ketone and occurring naturally (in plants and animals) or synthetically. Also, **flavine.** *Formula:* $C_{10}H_6N_4O_2$ ⟨< L *flavus* yellow + E *-in*⟩

fla•vone ['fleivoun] *n. Chemistry.* a colourless ketone used as a base for yellow dyes, obtained from plants or synthetically. *Formula:* $C_{15}H_{10}O_2$ ⟨< G *flavon* < L *flavus* yellow⟩

fla•vo•nol ['fleivə,nɒl] *n. Chemistry.* a yellow colouring matter found in plants and derived from flavone. *Formula:* $C_{15}H_{10}O_3$

fla•vo•pro•tein [,fleivou'proutin] *n. Chemistry.* an enzyme consisting of a protein and a flavin group, concerned in respiration.

fla•vo•pur•pu•rin [,fleivou'pɜrpərɪn] *n. Chemistry.* a yellow compound used to make dye. *Formula:* $C_{14}H_8O_5$ ⟨< L *flavus* yellow + *purpura* purple + *-in*⟩

fla•vour or **fla•vor** ['fleivər] *n., v.* —*n.* **1** a taste, especially a characteristic taste: *Chocolate and vanilla have different flavours.* **2** anything used to give a certain taste to food or drink; flavouring. **3** a characteristic quality: *Many stories by Joseph Conrad have a flavour of the sea.* **4** an interesting quality: *His many fascinating anecdotes added flavour to the lecture.* **5** an aroma; odour. **6** *Physics.* any of the six fundamental kinds of quarks or leptons.
—*v.* **1** give an added taste to; season: *We use salt, pepper, and spices to flavour food.* **2** give a characteristic or interesting quality to: *Many exciting adventures flavour an explorer's life.* ⟨ME < OF *flaur,* ult. < L *fragrare* emit odour⟩ **—'fla•vour•er** or **'fla•vor•er,** *n.* **—'fla•vour•less** or **'fla•vor•less,** *adj.*
—'fla•vour•ful or **'fla•vor•ful,** *adj.*
☛ *Syn. n.* **1.** See note at TASTE.

fla•vour•ing or **fla•vor•ing** ['fleivərɪŋ] *n.* something used to give a certain taste to food or drink: *vanilla flavouring, chocolate flavouring.*

fla•vox•ate [flə'vɒkseit] *n.* a muscle relaxant drug used to treat certain urinary problems.

flaw¹ [flɒ] *n., v.* —*n.* **1** a defective place; crack: *A flaw in the dish caused it to break.* **2** a fault; defect.
—*v.* make or become defective; crack. ⟨ME < Scand.; cf. Swedish *flaga*⟩
☛ *Syn. n.* See note at DEFECT.

flaw² [flɒ] *n.* a gust of wind; sudden squall. ⟨< Scand.; cf. Norwegian *flaga* gust⟩

flaw•less ['flɒlɪs] *adj.* perfect; without a flaw. **—'flaw•less•ly,** *adv.* **—'flaw•less•ness,** *n.*

flax [flæks] *n.* **1** any of a genus (*Linum*) of annual herbs, especially *L. usitatissimum,* which has been cultivated in several varieties since ancient times for its seeds and fibre. The seeds (flaxseed) yield linseed oil and the fibre of the stems is processed to make linen thread, which is woven into linen cloth. **2** the stem fibre of flax, especially when prepared for spinning into thread. ⟨OE *fleax*⟩

flax•en ['flæksən] *adj.* **1** made of flax. **2** like the colour of flax; pale yellow: *flaxen hair.*

flax•seed ['flæks,sid] *n.* the seed of flax; linseed: *Flaxseed is used to make linseed oil and some medicines.*

flay [flei] *v.* **1** strip the skin or outer covering from by whipping or lashing: *The tyrant had his enemies flayed alive.* **2** scold severely; criticize without pity or mercy: *The angry man flayed his servant with his tongue.* **3** rob; cheat. ⟨OE *flēan*⟩ **—'flay•er,** *n.*

F layer F REGION.

fld. field.

fl. dr. FLUID DRAM.

flea [fli] *n.* any of a large order (Siphonaptera) of small, wingless, jumping insects with mouthparts adapted for sucking blood. Fleas are parasitic on mammals and birds.
flea in one's ear, a a severe scolding; rebuff. **b** a sharp hint. ⟨OE *flēah*⟩
☛ *Hom.* FLEE.

flea•bane ['fli,bein] *n.* **1** any of a genus (*Erigeron*) of plants of the composite family found throughout the world, traditionally believed to ward off fleas. Several fleabanes are common Canadian weeds; other species are cultivated as garden flowers. **2** any of various other similar composite plants.

flea•bite ['fli,bəit] *n.* **1** the bite of a flea or the itchy red spot left by such a bite. **2** a small pain or annoyance.

flea–bit•ten ['fli ,bɪtən] *adj.* **1** bitten or infested by fleas. **2** having reddish brown spots on a light-coloured hide: *a flea-bitten horse.* **3** *Informal.* wretched; shabby.

flea collar a collar permeated with insecticides, used on cats and dogs.

fleam [flim] *n.* a surgical lancet. ⟨< ME *fleme* < OF *flieme* < VL **fleutomum* for LL *phlebotomus* phlebotomy⟩

flea market a market selling a mixture of cheap or odd items, junk, antiques, etc.

flea•pit ['fli,pɪt] *n.* an apartment, cinema, etc. that is shabby and squalid.

flea•wort ['fli,wɜrt] *n.* fleabane.

fle•cai•nide [flə'kaınaıd] *n.* a drug used to treat certain heart conditions.

flèche [flɛʃ] *or* [fleiʃ] *n.* a thin spire such as found in Gothic churches over the join of the nave and transept. ⟨< F, arrow⟩
☛ *Hom.* FLESH [flɛʃ].

fleck [flɛk] *n., v.* —*n.* **1** a spot or patch of colour, light, etc.: *Freckles are brown flecks on the skin.* **2** a small particle; flake.
—*v.* sprinkle with small particles or with spots or patches of colour, light, etc.; speckle: *Sunlight coming through the branches flecked the shadow cast by the tree.* ⟨ME < ON *flekkr*⟩

flec•tion ['flɛkʃən] *n.* **1** a bending: *Every flection of his arm caused the muscles to bulge.* **2** a bent part; bend. **3** *Grammar.* inflection. **4** *Physiology.* flexion. ⟨< L *flexio, -onis* < *flectere* bend⟩

fled [flɛd] *v.* pt. and pp. of FLEE.

fledge [flɛdʒ] *v.* **fledged, fledg•ing. 1** grow the feathers needed for flying. **2** bring up (a young bird) until it is able to fly. **3** provide or cover with feathers. ⟨cf. OE *unfligge* unfledged, unfit to fly⟩

fledg•ling or **fledge•ling** ['flɛdʒlıŋ] *n.* **1** a young bird just able to fly. **2** a young, inexperienced person. **3** (*adjl.*) new and untried: *a fledgling organization.*

flee [fli] *v.* **fled, flee•ing. 1** run away; try to get away by running. **2** run away from; try to get away from by running. **3** go quickly; move swiftly: *The clouds are fleeing before the wind.* **4** pass away; cease; vanish: *The shadows flee as day breaks.* ⟨OE *flēon*⟩ —**'fle•er,** *n.*
☛ *Hom.* FLEA.

fleece [flis] *n., v.* **fleeced, fleec•ing.** —*n.* **1** the wool that covers a sheep or similar animal. **2** the quantity of wool cut from a sheep at one time. **3** something like a fleece: *a fleece of hair, the fleece of new-fallen snow.* **4** a fabric with a soft, silky pile, used to make sweat tops and sweat pants, to line outer garments, etc. **5** the pile of such a fabric: *She likes to wear her sweat shirts with the fleece out.*
—*v.* **1** cut the fleece from. **2** strip of money or belongings; rob; cheat: *The gamblers fleeced him of a large sum.* **3** cover with fleecy stuff. ⟨OE *flēos*⟩ —**'fleec•er,** *n.* —**'fleece,like,** *adj.*

fleec•y ['flisi] *adj.* **fleec•i•er, fleec•i•est. 1** like a fleece; soft and white: *Fleecy clouds floated in the blue sky.* **2** covered with fleece. **3** made of fleece. —**'fleec•i•ly,** *adv.* —**'fleec•i•ness,** *n.*

fleet[1] [flit] *n.* **1** a group of warships under one command; navy: *the Canadian fleet.* **2** a group of boats, aircraft, automobiles, etc. moving or working together: *a fleet of trucks.* ⟨OE *flēot* ship, vessel < *flēotan* float⟩

fleet[2] [flit] *adj., v.* —*adj.* swift; rapid.
—*v.* pass swiftly; move rapidly. ⟨OE *flēotan*, v.; adj. < ON *fljótr.* Akin to FLOAT.⟩ —**'fleet•ly,** *adv.* —**'fleet•ness,** *n.*

fleet•ing ['flitıŋ] *adj., v.* —*adj.* passing swiftly; moving rapidly; soon gone.
—*v.* ppr. of FLEET. —**fleet•ing•ly,** *adv.*

Fleet Street in London, England: **1** a very old street, now the location of many newspaper offices. **2** the newspaper industry.

Flem•ing ['flɛmıŋ] *n.* **1** a native of Flanders, a region on the North Sea extending from NW France to the SW Netherlands. **2** a Belgian whose native language is Flemish. ⟨< ME < MDu. *Vlaming*⟩

Flem•ish ['flɛmıʃ] *n., adj.* —*n.* **1** the language of the Flemings, a Germanic language very similar to Dutch. It is one of the two official languages of Belgium. **2 the Flemish,** *pl.* Flemish-speaking people collectively; the Flemings.
—*adj.* of or having to do with Flanders, the Flemings, or their language.

flense [flɛns] *v.* **flensed, flens•ing.** strip skin or blubber from (a seal or whale). ⟨< Du. *flensen* or Danish and Norwegian *flense*⟩ —**'flens•er,** *n.*

flesh [flɛʃ] *n., v.* —*n.* **1** the soft substance of a human or animal body that covers the bones and is covered by skin. Flesh consists mostly of muscles and fat. **2** the tissue or muscles of animals. **3** fatness. **4** meat, especially of a sort not usually eaten by human beings. **5** the body, not the soul or spirit. **6** the physical side of human nature, as distinguished from the spiritual or moral side. **7** the human race; people as a group. **8** all living creatures. **9** one's family or relatives by birth. **10** the soft or edible part of fruits or vegetables: *The McIntosh apple has crisp, juicy, white flesh.* **11** the colour of a white person's skin; pinkish white with a little yellow. **12** *Christianity.* unregenerate human nature; human nature unchanged and unaided by God.
in the flesh, a alive. **b** in person.
press the flesh, *Informal.* shake hands, especially as a political campaigner.
—*v.* **1** plunge (a weapon) into the flesh. **2** feed (a hound or hawk) with flesh. **3** excite to passion, bloodshed, etc. by a foretaste. **4** remove flesh, tissue, etc. from (hides). **5** make or become fleshy (*often used with* **out**): *Sam was always skinny, but he has fleshed out lately.* **6** fill up or out as if with flesh; give body or substance to (*usually used with* **out**): *to flesh out a bare plot outline.* ⟨OE *flæsc*⟩ —**'flesh•less,** *adj.*

flesh and blood 1 the body; the material composing a human being's physical frame. **2** an individual person or persons. **3** human nature: *The temptation was more than flesh and blood could resist.* **4** one's family or relatives by birth; a child or relative by birth.

flesh–and–blood ['flɛʃ ən 'blʌd] *adj.* having human existence; real: *a flesh-and-blood heroine.*

flesh–col•oured or **–col•ored** ['flɛʃ ˌkʌlərd] *adj.* pinkish white with a tinge of yellow.

flesh–eating ['flɛʃ ˌitıŋ] *adj.* meat-eating; carnivorous.

–fleshed *combining form.* having ——flesh: *solid-fleshed = having solid flesh.*

flesh•er ['flɛʃər] *n.* an implement for scraping flesh from hides.

flesh fly any of a family (Sarcophagidae) of two-winged flies resembling houseflies, including many species that are scavengers and others that are parasites in living animals.

flesh•ings ['flɛʃıŋz] *n.* **1** the flesh-coloured tights worn by actors, acrobats, dancers, etc. **2** bits of flesh scraped from a hide.

flesh•ly ['flɛʃli] *adj.* **-li•er, -li•est. 1** of the flesh; bodily. **2** sensual. **3** of or having to do with human nature; mortal; human. **4** worldly. —**'flesh•li•ness,** *n.*

flesh•pot ['flɛʃˌpɒt] *n.* **1** a container for meat. **2 fleshpots,** *pl.* good food and bodily comfort; luxury. **3** Usually, **fleshpots,** *pl.* places or establishments offering luxurious, sensual living or entertainment: *visiting the fleshpots of the city.*

flesh wound a wound that merely injures the flesh; slight wound.

flesh•y ['flɛʃi] *adj.* **flesh•i•er, flesh•i•est. 1** having much flesh: *The calf is the fleshy part of the lower leg.* **2** plump; fat. **3** of flesh; like flesh. **4** pulpy. —**'flesh•i•ly,** *adv.* —**'flesh•i•ness,** *n.*

fletch [flɛtʃ] *v.* put a feather or feathers on (an arrow). ⟨altered (after *fletcher*) < *fledge*⟩ —**'fletch•er,** *n.*

Two styles of fleur-de-lis. The one on the left is from the Canadian coat of arms.

fleur–de–lis [ˌflɜr də 'li] *or* [ˌflɜr də 'lis]; *French,* [flœʀd'li] *n., pl.* **fleurs-de-lis** [ˌflɜr də 'liz] *or* [ˌflɜr də 'li]; *French,* [flœʀd'li]. **1** *Heraldry.* a design or device representing a lily. **2** the former royal coat of arms of France. **3** the emblem of the province of Québec. **4** iris. ⟨< F *fleur-de-lis* lily flower⟩

flew [flu] *v.* pt. of FLY[2].
☛ *Hom.* FLU, FLUE.

flews [fluz] *n.pl.* the overhanging part of the lip of certain dogs, especially hounds. ⟨origin uncertain⟩

flex [flɛks] *v., n.* —*v.* **1** bend: *He slowly flexed his stiff arm.* **2** of muscles, tighten and relax alternately.
—*n.* **1** flexibility. **2** a bend or contraction of a muscle. **3** flexible insulated wire used to connect electric appliances or lamps; cord. ⟨< L *flexus,* pp. of *flectere* bend⟩

flex•i•ble ['flɛksəbəl] *adj.* **1** easily bent; not stiff; bending without breaking: *Leather, rubber, and wire are flexible materials.* **2** easily adapted to fit various uses, purposes, etc.: *flexible plans. The actor's flexible voice accommodated itself to every emotion.* **3** willing and able to adapt to a variety of situations or to accommodate the needs and ideas of others. ⟨< F < L *flexibilis* < *flexus.* See FLEX.⟩ —ˌ**flex•i'bil•i•ty,** *n.* —**'flex•i•bly,** *adv.*
☛ *Syn.* **Flexible,** PLIANT, LIMBER[1] = easily bent. **Flexible** = capable of being bent or twisted easily and without breaking, or, used figuratively of people and their minds, etc., capable of being turned or managed with little trouble if handled skilfully: *Great thinkers have flexible minds.* **Pliant,** literally and figuratively, emphasizes having the quality of bending or adapting itself easily rather than of being easily affected by outside force:

English is a pliant language. **Limber,** used chiefly of the body, means 'having flexible muscles and joints': *A jumper has limber legs.*

flex•ile ['flɛksaɪl] *or* ['flɛksəl] *adj.* flexible.

flex•ion ['flɛkʃən] *n. Physiology.* **a** a bending of some part of the body by the action of flexors. **b** a being bent in this way. ⟨var. of *flection*⟩

flex•or ['flɛksər] *n. Physiology.* any muscle that bends some part of the body. ⟨< NL⟩

flex•time ['flɛks,taɪm] *n.* a flexible system of working hours, whereby employees can choose their starting and finishing times, provided that they put in the required hours of work.

flex•ure ['flɛkʃər] *n.* **1** bending; curving. **2** a bend; curve. ⟨< L *flexura* < *flexus.* See FLEX.⟩ **—'flex•ur•al,** *adj.*

flib•ber•ti•gib•bet ['flɪbərti,dʒɪbɪt] *n.* **1** a frivolous, flighty person. **2** chatterbox. ⟨extended < ME *flypergebet* < ?⟩ **—'flib•ber•ti'gib•bet•y,** *adj.*

flic [flik] *n. French. Informal.* a police officer; cop.

flick [flɪk] *n., v.* *—n.* **1** a quick, light blow; sudden, snapping stroke: *By a flick of his whip, he drove the fly from the horse's head.* **2** the light, snapping sound of such a blow or stroke. **3** a sudden jerk; a short, quick movement: *The fisher made a short cast with a flick of her wrist.* **4** a streak; splash; fleck. **5** *Slang.* movie.
—v. **1** strike lightly with a quick, snapping blow: *He flicked the dust from his shoes with a handkerchief.* **2** make a sudden, snapping stroke with: *The boys flicked wet towels at each other.* **3** flutter; move quickly and lightly. ⟨probably imitative⟩

flick•er[1] ['flɪkər] *v., n.* *—v.* **1** shine with a wavering light; burn with an unsteady flame: *A dying fire flickered on the hearth.* **2** move quickly and lightly in and out or back and forth: *The tongue of a snake flickers.* **3** cause to flicker: *There was just enough breeze to flicker the candle.*
—n. **1** a wavering, unsteady light or flame. **2** a brief flame; spark. **3** a quick, light movement. **4** a dying spurt of energy, emotion, etc.: *a flicker of enthusiasm.* **5** a change in brightness on a video screen or in clarity of the picture on a movie screen. ⟨OE *flicorian*⟩

flick•er[2] ['flɪkər] *n.* any of several North American woodpeckers (genus *Colaptes*) having a brown back barred with black, a conspicuous white rump, and pale, black-spotted underparts. The **yellow-shafted flicker** (*Colaptes auratus*), common in many parts of Canada, has yellow on the underside of wings and tail. ⟨? imitative of its note⟩

flied [flaɪd] *v.* pt. and pp. of FLY[2] (def. 14).

fli•er ['flaɪər] See FLYER.

flight[1] [fləit] *n.* **1** the act or manner or power of flying. **2** the distance flown by a bird, bullet, aircraft, etc. **3** a group of things flying through the air together: *a flight of six birds.* **4** an air force unit of either planes or personnel. **5** a trip in an aircraft. **6** a swift movement. **7** a soaring above or beyond what is ordinary. **8** a set of stairs or steps between landings or storeys of a building. **9** a group of swallows.
take flight, fly away. ⟨OE *flyht.* Related to FLY[2].⟩

flight[2] [fləit] *n.* **1** the act of fleeing or running away: *The defeated army was in flight.* **2** escape: *The flight of the prisoners was soon discovered.*
put to flight, force to flee.
take to flight, flee. ⟨ME *fliht* < OE *flēon* flee⟩

flight attendant a person employed by an airline to look after passengers during a flight.

flight bag a small, lightweight bag of vinyl, canvas, etc., having a zippered closing and designed to be carried as hand luggage on an airplane, etc.

flight deck **1** a separate compartment in some aircraft for the pilot and crew. **2** the uppermost deck on an aircraft carrier, which functions as a takeoff and landing area.

flight engineer *Aeronautics.* in an aircraft, the member of the crew who maintains the mechanical systems. **—flight engineering.**

flight feather a particularly strong feather in a bird's wing which enables it to fly.

flight•less ['fləitlɪs] *adj.* unable to fly.

flight lieutenant an air force officer ranking next above a flying officer and below a squadron leader. See chart of ranks in the Appendix. *Abbrev.:* F/L, F.L., or Flt.Lt.

flight lock a lock in a canal which is in levels to allow simultaneous two-way traffic.

flight•path ['fləit,pæθ] *n.* **1** the course taken by an aircraft, missile, etc. **2** a course indicated by an electronic beam as a navigation aid. Also, **flight path.**

flight sergeant an air force non-commissioned officer ranking next above a sergeant and below a warrant officer. *Abbrev.:* Flt.Sgt.

flight test the testing of an aircraft's flight performance. **—'flight-,test,** *v.*

flight•y ['fləiti] *adj.* **flight•i•er, flight•i•est. 1** likely to have sudden fancies; full of whims; frivolous. **2** slightly crazy; light-headed. **—'flight•i•ly,** *adv.* **—'flight•i•ness,** *n.*

flim•flam ['flɪm,flæm] *n., v.* **-flammed, -flam•ming.** *Informal.*
—n. **1** nonsense; rubbish. **2** deception; a low trick.
—v. cheat (a person) out of money; trick. ⟨? reduplication < *flam* deceptive trick⟩ **—'flim,flam•mer,** *n.*

flim•sy ['flɪmzi] *adj.* **-si•er, -si•est;** *n., pl.* **-sies.** *—adj.* **1** light and thin or poorly constructed; frail: *Muslin is too flimsy to be used for sails.* **2** not serious or convincing; inadequate: *a flimsy excuse.*
—n. **1** a thin paper used by reporters. **2** a newspaper report on this paper. **3** a sheet of very thin paper for typing or writing. **4** material typed or written on such paper. ⟨? < alteration of *film* + *-sy,* adj. suffix⟩ **—'flim•si•ly,** *adv.* **—'flim•si•ness,** *n.*

flinch [flɪntʃ] *v., n.* *—v.* **1** draw back from difficulty, danger, or pain; shrink. **2** wince.
—n. **1** a drawing back: *He took his punishment without a flinch.* **2** a game played with cards bearing numbers from 1 to 14. ⟨probably < OF *flenchir* < Frankish **hlankjan* bend; cf. G *lenken*⟩ **—'flinch•ing•ly,** *adv.*
☛ *Syn. v.* See note at SHRINK.

flin•ders ['flɪndərz] *n.pl.* small pieces; fragments; splinters: *The box was smashed into flinders.* ⟨cf. Norwegian *flindra*⟩

fling [flɪŋ] *v.* **flung, fling•ing;** *n.* *—v.* **1** throw forcefully; hurl violently: *The angry man flung his hat on the floor.* **2** move rapidly; rush; flounce: *She flung angrily out of the room.* **3** put suddenly or violently: *Fling her into jail.* **4** move (a part of the body) in an impulsive, unrestrained way: *The girl happily flung her arms around her mother's neck.* **5** embark upon a project with animation (*used reflexively*): *She flung herself into her course work.*
—n. **1** a violent throw. **2** a plunge; kick. **3** a time of doing as one pleases: *He had his fling when he was young; now he must work.* **4** a lively Scottish dance: *the Highland fling.* **5** *Informal.* a shortlived and casual love affair.
have or **take a fling at,** *Informal.* **a** try; attempt. **b** make scornful remarks about. ⟨? akin to ON *flengja* flog⟩

flint [flɪnt] *n.* **1** a very hard grey or brown stone, a kind of quartz, that makes a spark when struck against steel. **2** a piece of this stone used with steel to light fires, explode gunpowder, etc. **3** anything very hard or unyielding: *He had a heart of flint.* **4** a small piece of metal used to produce the spark in a cigarette lighter. ⟨OE⟩

flint glass a brilliant glass containing lead, potassium or sodium, and silicon. It is used for lenses, dishes, etc.

flint•lock ['flɪnt,lɒk] *n.* **1** a gunlock in which a flint striking against steel makes sparks that explode the gunpowder. Flintlocks were used on guns from the 1600s to the 1800s. **2** a gun with such a gunlock. See FIREARM for picture.

flint•y ['flɪnti] *adj.* **flint•i•er, flint•i•est. 1** containing flint: *a flinty rock formation.* **2** hard like flint: *The girls were tired after walking over the flinty asphalt.* **3** hard; unyielding: *The sergeant had flinty eyes.* **—'flint•i•ly,** *adv.* **—'flint•i•ness,** *n.*

flip[1] [flɪp] *v.* **flipped, flip•ping;** *n.* *—v.* **1** toss or move with a snap of a finger and thumb: *She flipped a coin on the counter.* **2** flip a coin in the air to decide something by chance: *They flipped to see who would pay for the coffee.* **3** jerk; turn or move with a jerk; flick: *She flipped her fan shut. The branch flipped back. The driver flipped his whip at a fly.* **4** turn over quickly: *He flipped the pages of the magazine. She flipped the eggs before serving them. The swimmer flipped onto her back.*
flip (one's) **lid,** *Informal.* lose control of oneself; go crazy.
flip out, *Informal.* lose one's composure in anger, astonishment, excitement, etc.: *He flipped out when he heard the news.*
flip through, read quickly and randomly.
—n. **1** a smart tap; snap; a sudden jerk: *The cat gave the kitten a flip on the ear.* **2** a quick overturning: *The airplane did a flip just before it crashed.* ⟨probably imitative⟩

flip[2] [flɪp] *n.* a hot drink containing beer, ale, cider, or the like, with sugar and spice. ⟨nominal use of *flip*[1], *v.*⟩

flip[3] [flɪp] *adj.* **flip•per, flip•pest.** *Informal.* flippant; cheeky.

flip•chart ['flɪp,tʃɑrt] *n.* a display technique consisting of a large pad of paper on an easel. The teacher or workshop leader writes on the top sheet with a large pen, as on a chalkboard, and then turns the top sheet over the back of the easel, leaving the next sheet available for writing.

flip–flop ['flɪp ˌflɒp] *n., v.* **-flopped, -flop•ping.** *Informal.* *—n.* **1** a sudden change of opinion. **2 flip-flops,** *pl.* rubber thongs worn at the beach or pool.
—v. abruptly change opinion: *She flip-flopped on the issue of free trade.*

flip•pan•cy ['flɪpənsi] *n., pl.* **-cies. 1** a being flippant. **2** a flippant remark or act.

flip•pant ['flɪpənt] *adj.* smart or pert in speech; not respectful: *a flippant answer.* ⟨? < *flip*[1] + *-ant*⟩ **—'flip•pant•ly,** *adv.*

flip•per ['flɪpər] *n.* **1** a broad, flat fin specially adapted for swimming: *Seal flippers are a popular food in Newfoundland.* **2** a piece of rubber or plastic that fits onto the foot and has a broad, flat blade extending from the toe, used by swimmers to give extra power, especially when swimming underwater: *A pair of flippers is part of every skindiver's equipment.* **3** a person or thing that flips: *a pancake flipper.* **4** a stabilizing fin on an ocean liner. **5** *Slang.* the hand.

flip side **1** the reverse side of a phonograph record, especially the less well-known or less popular side. **2** *Informal.* the opposite or complementary side of anything.

flirt [flərt] *v., n. —v.* **1** try to win the attention and affection of someone by amorous behaviour of a playful or frivolous kind. **2** trifle; toy: *He flirted with the idea of going to Europe, though he couldn't afford it.* **3** move quickly to and fro; flutter: *She flirted her fan impatiently.* **4** toss; jerk.
—n. **1** a person who flirts. **2** a quick movement or flutter: *With a flirt of its tail, the bird flew away.* **3** a toss; jerk. ⟨ult. imitative (see v. def. 4)⟩ **—'flirt•er,** *n.*

flir•ta•tion [flər'teiʃən] *n.* **1** a pretending to be in love with someone. **2** a love affair that is not serious. **3** a flirting or toying.

flir•ta•tious [flər'teiʃəs] *adj.* **1** inclined to flirt. **2** having to do with flirtation. **—flir'ta•tious•ly,** *adv.* **—flir'ta•tious•ness,** *n.*

flit [flɪt] *v.* **flit•ted, flit•ting;** *n. —v.* **1** fly lightly and quickly; flutter: *Birds flitted from tree to tree.* **2** pass lightly and quickly: *Many idle thoughts flitted through his mind as he lay in the sun.*
—n. a light, quick movement. ⟨ME < ON *flytja.* Akin to FLEET[2].⟩ **—flit•ter,** *n.*

flitch [flɪtʃ] *n., v. —n.* **1** a side of a pig salted and cured; side of bacon. **2** a strip of wood cut from the length of a tree trunk. **3** either of the two boards that form a **flitch beam,** attached by a steel bolt.
—v. cut into flitches. ⟨OE *flicce*⟩

flit•ter ['flɪtər] *v. or n.* flutter. ⟨< *flit*⟩

fliv•ver ['flɪvər] *n. Slang.* a small, cheap automobile. ⟨origin unknown⟩

float [flout] *v., n. —v.* **1** stay on top of or be held up by air, water, or other liquid. **2** move with a moving liquid; drift: *The boat floated out to sea.* **3** rest or move in a liquid, the air, etc. **4** cause to float. **5** cover with liquid; flood. **6** sell (securities): *to float an issue of stock.* **7** launch or set up (a company, etc.), especially by issuing and selling securities. **8** launch or initiate (a plan, idea, etc.). **9** move about aimlessly or effortlessly: *She floats from job to job.* **10** of currency, interest rates, etc., be allowed to find a level on the market based on supply and demand, without restrictions or artificial support. **11** even or flatten (cement, plaster, etc.)
—n. **1** anything that stays up or holds up something else in water, such as a raft or life preserver. **2** a cork, bob, etc. on a fishing line. **3** an air-filled organ that supports a fish. **4** an air-filled, watertight part on an aircraft for landing or floating on water; pontoon. **5** a hollow, metal ball that regulates the level, supply, or outlet of a liquid. **6** a flat board of a water wheel or paddle wheel. **7 a** a low, flat car that carries something to be shown in a parade. **b** the thing on it. **8** a drink consisting of ginger ale or a similar beverage with ice cream in it. **9** *Geology.* **a** fragments of rock, mineral, or ore loosened from their source and deposited elsewhere: *iron ore float.* **b** (*adjl.*) consisting of fine mineral particles floating in water: *They have located the source of the float coal.* **10** a sum of money put in a cash register or till so that change can be made. **11 floats,** in the theatre, footlights. **12** a tool used to even or flatten cement, plaster, etc. **13** any of the floating positions used in swimming: *starfish float.* **14** *Banking.* the value of cheques or drafts in circulation that have not yet been collected. ⟨OE *flotian* < *flēotan.* Related to FLEET[2].⟩ **—'float•a•ble,** *adj.*

float•er ['floutər] *n.* **1** a person or thing that floats. **2** *Informal.* a person who often changes his or her place of living, working, etc. **3** *Sports.* a ball thrown or hit so as to travel slowly and appear to hang in the air, usually on a slightly arched course. **4** an insurance policy covering a category of goods, as household furnishings, rather than specific items, as a particular gem. **5** a person who can fill in for anyone absent from work.

float•house ['flout,hʌus] *n. Cdn.* scow-house.

float•ing ['floutɪŋ] *adj., v. —adj.* **1** that floats. **2** not fixed; not staying in one place; moving around. **3** in use or circulation; not permanently invested. **4** not funded; changing: *The floating debt of a business consists of notes, drafts, etc. payable within a short time.* **5** *Medicine.* not in the normal position; displaced: *a floating kidney.* **6** of or having to do with a machine part, such as a connecting rod or coupler, that is connected or hung in such a way that it functions without causing vibration.
—v. ppr. of FLOAT. **—'float•ing•ly,** *adv.*

floating (dry) dock a dock that can be lowered to allow a ship to enter or raised to be used as a dry dock.

floating–point representation ['floutiŋ 'pɔɪnt] the use of scientific notation to express numbers, rather than a fixed decimal, as 2500 written as 2.5×10^3. Compare FIXED-POINT REPRESENTATION.

floating ribs *Anatomy.* the ribs not attached to the breastbone; last two pairs of ribs.

float plane a seaplane equipped with two floats, or pontoons, on which it lands, rests, and takes off.

float•stone ['flout,stoun] *n.* **1** a stone used to smooth the surface of bricks used in curved work. **2** a whitish grey spongy variety of opal, light enough to float.

floc•cu•lant ['flɒkjələnt] *n.* a chemical agent causing flocculation, used especially in the treatment of waste water.
☛ *Hom.* FLOCCULENT.

floc•cu•late ['flɒkjə,leit] *v.* **-lat•ed, -lat•ing.** form small particles, as in a suspended liquid. ⟨< NL *flocculus,* dim. of *floccus,* + *-ate*⟩ **—,floc•cu'la•tion,** *n.*

floc•cule ['flɒkjul] *n.* a bit of matter in a form like wool.

floc•cu•lent ['flɒkjələnt] *adj.* **1** like bits of wool. **2** made up of soft, woolly masses. **3** covered with a soft, woolly substance. ⟨< L *floccus* tuft of wool⟩ **—'floc•cu•lence,** *n.*
☛ *Hom.* FLOCCULANT.

floc•cus ['flɒkəs] *n.* a woolly tuft of hairs or hairy particles. ⟨< L, flock of wool⟩

flock[1] [flɒk] *n., v. —n.* **1** animals of one kind that feed and move about in a group, especially sheep, goats, or birds. **2** a large group; crowd. **3** people of a church regarded as the charges of their pastor.
—v. go or gather in a flock; come crowding: *The children flocked around the Christmas tree.* ⟨OE *flocc*⟩

flock[2] [flɒk] *n., v. —n.* **1** a tuft of wool. **2** waste wool or cotton used to stuff mattresses and cushions. **3** finely powdered or very short fibres of wool, etc. used to form a velvety, raised pattern on wallpaper or fabric.
—v. **1** stuff with flock. **2** cover or coat with flock. ⟨ME < OF *floc* < L *floccus*⟩ **—'flock•ing,** *n.*

floe [flou] *n.* **1** a field or sheet of floating ice. **2** a floating piece broken off from such a field or sheet. ⟨? < Norwegian *flo*⟩
☛ *Hom.* FLOW.

flog [flɒg] *v.* **flogged, flog•ging. 1** whip very hard; beat with a whip, stick, etc. **2** *Slang.* sell or try to sell.
flog a dead horse, pursue a futile argument or a lost cause.
flog to death, be too persistent in trying to persuade or convince someone of (something), causing the person to lose interest: *It wasn't a bad idea, but he flogged it to death.* ⟨? English school slang for L *flagellare* whip⟩ **—'flog•ger,** *n.*

flo•ka•ti [flou'kɑti] *n.* **1** originally, a heavy, coarse, white wool Greek rug in various sizes. **2** a similar rug now made of synthetic fibres in other colours.

flood [flʌd] *n., v. —n.* **1** a flow of water over what is usually dry land. **2** *Poetic.* a large amount of water; ocean; sea; lake; river. **3** a great outpouring of anything: *a flood of light, a flood of words.* **4** a flowing of the tide toward the shore; rise of the tide. **5** *Informal.* floodlight. **6 the Flood,** in the Bible, the water that deluged the earth in the time of Noah.
in flood, filled to overflowing with an unusual amount of water: *The river was in flood.*
—v. **1** flow over or into: *When the snows melted last spring, the river rose and flooded our fields.* **2** fill much fuller than usual. **3** become covered or filled with water: *During the thunderstorm, our cellar flooded.* **4** cover the surface of something with water: *The attendants flooded the ice before every hockey game.* **5** pour

out or stream like a flood: *Sunlight flooded into the room.* **6** fill, cover or overcome like a flood: *Flood the front of the stage with light. The rich woman was flooded with requests for money.* **7** flow like a flood. **8** cause or allow too much fuel into the carburetor of (an engine) so that it fails to start; receive too much fuel into the carburetor. ⟨OE *flōd*⟩ **—'flood•er,** *n.*

☛ *Syn. n.* **1. Flood,** DELUGE, INUNDATION = a great flow of water. **Flood** applies particularly to a great flow of water over land, usually dry, caused by the rising and overflowing of a river or other body of water: *Floods followed the melting of mountain snow.* **Deluge** applies to a great flood that washes away everything in its path, or, sometimes, to a heavy, continuous rain that causes a flood: *Livestock drowned in the deluge.* **Inundation,** formal, means an overflow covering everything around: *Crops were destroyed by the inundation of the fields.*

flood control the control of floods and the prevention of damage caused by them, by means of dams, levees, dikes, extra outlets, reforestation, etc.

flood•gate ['flʌd,geit] *n.* **1** a gate in a canal, river, stream, etc. to control the flow of water. **2** something that controls any flow or passage.

flood•light ['flʌd,lɔit] *n., v.* **-light•ed** or **-lit, -light•ing.** *—n.* **1** a lamp that gives a broad beam of light: *Several floodlights were used to illuminate the stage.* **2** the broad beam of light it gives. *—v.* illuminate with floodlights.

flood plain a plain bordering a river and made of soil deposited by floods.

flood tide the flowing of the tide toward the shore; the rise of the tide.

flood•way ['flʌd,wei] *n.* a giant ditch dug around a city to divert spring flood waters away from the city: *There is a floodway around Winnipeg.*

floor [flɔr] *n., v.* *—n.* **1** the inside bottom covering of a room. **2** a storey of a building. **3** a flat inside surface at the bottom of anything. **4** the part of a room or hall where members of an assembly or a lawmaking body, etc. sit and from which they speak: *the floor of the House of Commons.* **5** the right or privilege to speak in a lawmaking body, assembly, etc.: *The chairperson decides who has the floor.* **6** the main part of an exchange, where buying and selling of stocks, bonds, etc. is done. **7** *Informal.* of prices, amounts, etc., the lowest level. **8** *Mining.* an underlying stratum on which a seam of coal, etc. lies.
—v. **1** put a floor in or over. **2** knock down. **3** *Informal.* defeat. **4** *Informal.* confuse or puzzle completely: *The last question on the exam floored us all.* **5** place upon a floor; base.
floor it, *Informal.* bear down on the accelerator of an automobile so that the pedal is down to the floor. ⟨OE *flōr*⟩ **—'floor•er,** *n.*

floor•board ['flɔr,bɔrd] *n.* **1** one of the strips of wood used in a wooden floor. **2** Usually, **floorboards,** *pl.* the floor of an automobile.

floor exercises *Gymnastics.* a set of tumbling and other acrobatic movements, performed on mats without apparatus.

floor hockey an indoor game derived from hockey, in which the players use a long stick to carry and pass a plastic puck or a ring resembling a quoit of rope or felt.

floor•ing ['flɔrɪŋ] *n., v.* *—n.* **1** a floor. **2** floors collectively. **3** material for making floors.
—v. ppr. of FLOOR.

floor plan a scale map of one floor of a building, showing rooms, windows, etc.

floor price a minimum price set by the government on a commodity to protect the producer against sudden declines in price.

floor show an entertainment consisting of music, singing, dancing, etc. presented at a night club, hotel, etc.

floor•walk•er ['flɔr,wɒkər] *n.* a person employed in a large store to oversee sales, direct customers, etc.

flop [flɒp] *v.* **flopped, flop•ping;** *n.* *—v.* **1** move loosely or heavily; flap around clumsily: *The fish flopped helplessly on the deck.* **2** fall, drop, throw, or move heavily or clumsily: *She flopped down into a chair.* **3** change or turn suddenly. **4** *Informal.* fail. **5** *Slang.* sleep; spend the night: *Can I flop on this couch?*
—n. **1** flopping. **2** the sound made by flopping. **3** *Informal.* a failure: *The new play was a flop.* ⟨imitative var. of *flap*⟩ **—'flop•per,** *n.*

flop•house ['flɒp,hʌus] *n.* a cheap, run-down hotel or rooming house, especially one used by down-and-outs, etc.

flop•py ['flɒpi] *adj.* **-pi•er, -pi•est.** *Informal.* flopping; tending to flop: *She bought a sunhat with a floppy brim.* **—'flop•pi•ly,** *adv.* **—'flop•pi•ness,** *n.*

floppy disk *Computer technology.* a thin, round, magnetized flexible plate used for storing data for a computer; diskette.

flo•ra ['flɔrə] *n.* **1** the plants of a particular region or time: *the flora of the West Indies.* **2** a work that systematically describes such plants. ⟨< L *flos, floris* flower⟩

Flo•ra ['flɔrə] *n. Roman mythology.* the goddess of flowers and spring.

flo•ral ['flɔrəl] *adj.* **1** of or having to do with flowers: *floral decorations.* **2** resembling flowers: *a floral design.* **—'flo•ral•ly,** *adv.*

floral envelope *Botany.* the floral leaves (petals or sepals, or both) of a flower, collectively.

Flor•ence flask ['flɔrəns] **1** a thin glass bottle with a long neck, usually covered with straw or something similar, for holding olive oil or wine. **2** a bottle of this shape used in a laboratory for heating chemicals.

Flor•en•tine ['flɔrən,tin] *adj., n.* *—adj.* **1** of or having to do with Florence, a city in Italy. **2** cooked with spinach.
—n. **1** a native or inhabitant of Florence. **2 florentine,** a twilled silk cloth, used for clothing.

flo•res•cence [flɔ'rɛsəns] *n.* **1** the act of blossoming. **2** the condition of blossoming. **3** the period of blossoming. **4** a time of success. ⟨< NL *florescentia,* ult. < L *florere* flourish⟩

flo•res•cent [flɔ'rɛsənt] *adj.* blossoming.

flo•ret ['flɔrɪt] *n.* **1** a small flower. **2** *Botany.* one of the small flowers in the flower head of a composite plant, such as an aster. ⟨< OF *florete,* dim. of *flor* flower < L *flos, floris*⟩

flo•ri•ate ['flɔri,eit] *v.* **-at•ed, -at•ing.** ornament with floral designs. **—,flo•ri'a•tion,** *n.* ⟨< L *flos, floris* flower + *-ate*⟩

flor•i•bun•da [,flɔrə'bʌndə] *n.* a variety of hybrid cultivated rose producing a number of flowers on a single stem, each flower often as large as a tea rose. ⟨< NL *floribunda* < L *flos, floris* flower⟩

flo•ri•cul•ture ['flɔrə,kʌltʃər] *n.* the cultivation of flowering plants. **—,flo•ri'cul•tur•al,** *adj.* **—,flo•ri'cul•tur•ist,** *n.*

flor•id ['flɔrɪd] *adj.* **1** highly coloured; ruddy: *a florid complexion.* **2** elaborately ornamented; flowery; showy; ornate. ⟨< L *floridus* < *flos, floris* flower⟩ **—'flor•id•ly,** *adv.* **—flo'rid•i•ty** or **'flor•id•ness,** *n.*

Flo•ri•da ['flɔrɪdə] *n.* the most south-easterly state of the United States. See HAITI for map.

flor•i•gen ['flɔrədʒən] *n. Botany.* the hormone responsible for flowering in plants. ⟨< L *flos, floris* flower + E *-gen*⟩

flor•in ['flɔrɪn] *n.* **1** a former British coin worth two shillings. **2** a gold coin issued at Florence in 1252. **3** gulden. **4** any of various gold or silver coins used at different times in European countries. ⟨< F < Ital. *fiorino* a Florentine coin marked with a lily < *fiore* flower < L *flos, floris*⟩

flo•rist ['flɔrɪst] *n.* a person who raises or sells flowers.

flo•ris•tics [flɔ'rɪstɪks] *n.* the area of botany concerning plant geography and the distribution of plant species.

floss [flɒs] *n., v.* *—n.* **1** short, loose silk fibres. **2** a soft, shiny, untwisted silk or cotton thread used for embroidery. **3** DENTAL FLOSS. **4** soft, silky fluff or fibres, such as the fibres inside milkweed pods or a silkworm's cocoon.
—v. use dental floss to clean (teeth). ⟨apparently related to FLEECE⟩

floss•y ['flɒsi] *adj.* **floss•i•er, floss•i•est.** **1** of floss. **2** like floss. **3** *Informal.* fancy; glamorous; highly decorated. **—'floss•i•ness,** *n.*

flo•ta•tion [flou'teiʃən] *n.* **1** floating or launching. **2** a getting started or established. **3** the act of selling or putting on sale. **4** the ability of automobile tires to remain on the surface of snow or sand. **5** *Mining.* a technique to separate ores in which fine-grained ore is put into a solution containing oils. Certain minerals will float to the top, while others will sink. ⟨var. of *floatation* < *float,* v.⟩

flo•til•la [flou'tɪlə] *or* [flə'tɪlə] *n.* **1** a small fleet. **2** a fleet of small ships. ⟨< Sp., dim. of *flota* fleet < F < ON *floti* fleet⟩

flot•sam ['flɒtsəm] *n.* the wreckage of a ship or its cargo found floating on the sea. Compare JETSAM.
flotsam and jetsam, a wreckage or cargo found floating on the sea or washed ashore. **b** odds and ends; useless things. **c** people without steady work or permanent homes. ⟨< AF *floteson* < *floter* float. Akin to FLOAT.⟩

flounce[1] [flaʊns] *v.* **flounced, flounc•ing;** *n.* *—v.* **1** go with an

angry or impatient movement of the body: *She flounced out of the room in a rage.* **2** twist; turn; jerk.
—*n.* **1** an angry or impatient fling or turn of the body. **2** a twist; turn; jerk. ⟨? < Scand.; cf. Swedish *flunsa* plunge⟩ **—'floun•cy,** *adj.*

flounce[2] [flaʊns] *n., v.* **flounced, flounc•ing.** —*n.* a wide strip of cloth, gathered along the top edge and sewed to a dress, skirt, etc. as trimming; a wide ruffle.
—*v.* trim with a flounce or flounces. ⟨var. of *frounce* < OF *fronce* wrinkle < Gmc.⟩

flounc•ing ['flaʊnsɪŋ] *n., v.* —*n.* **1** fabric for flounces. **2** a flounce or flounces.
—*v.* ppr. of FLOUNCE.

floun•der[1] ['flaʊndər] *v., n.* —*v.* **1** struggle awkwardly without making much progress; plunge about: *Men and horses were floundering in the deep snowdrifts.* **2** be clumsy or confused and make mistakes: *The frightened girl could only flounder through her song.*
—*n.* a floundering. ⟨? blend of *founder*[1] and *blunder*⟩

floun•der[2] ['flaʊndər] *n., pl.* **-der** or **-ders.** any of numerous flatfishes constituting two families (Pleuronectidae and Bothidae), including some very important food fishes, such as plaice, halibut, and turbot. ⟨< AF *floundre* < Scand.; cf. Swedish *flundra*⟩

flour [flaʊr] *or* ['flaʊər] *n., v.* —*n.* **1** a fine, powdery substance made by grinding and sifting wheat or other grain. **2** any fine, soft powder.
—*v.* **1** cover with flour. **2** grind and sift (grain) into flour. ⟨special use of *flower*; i.e., the flower (best) of the meal⟩
☛ *Hom.* FLOWER ['flaʊər].

flour•ish ['flɜrɪʃ] *v., n.* —*v.* **1** grow or develop with vigour; thrive; do well. **2** be in the best time of life or activity. **3** wave (a sword, stick, arm, etc.) in the air. **4** make a showy display.
—*n.* **1** a waving in the air. **2** a showy decoration in handwriting. **3** *Music.* a showy trill or passage: *a flourish of trumpets.* **4** a showy display of enthusiasm, heartiness, etc. **5** an expression used for effect in speech or writing. **6** the state of being in the best time of life: *in full flourish.* ⟨ME < OF *floriss-*, a stem of *florir* < L *florere* bloom < *flos, floris* flower⟩ **—'flour•ish•ing•ly,** *adv.*

flour mill **1** a machine for grinding wheat or other grain into flour. **2** a place or establishment where there is such a machine or machines.

flour•y ['flaʊri] *adj.* **1** of or like flour. **2** covered or white with flour.
☛ *Hom.* FLOWERY.

flout [flʌut] *v., n.* —*v.* **1** treat with contempt or scorn; mock; scoff at: *The disobedient boy flouted his mother's advice.* **2** show contempt or scorn; scoff.
—*n.* a contemptuous speech or act; insult; mockery; scoffing. ⟨var. of *flute,* v.⟩ **—'flout•er,** *n.* **—'flout•ing•ly,** *adv.*
☛ *Usage.* See note at FLAUNT.

flow [flou] *v., n.* —*v.* **1** run like water; move in a current or stream. **2** pour out; pour along. **3** move easily or smoothly; glide. **4** of hair, etc., hang loosely and waving. **5** be plentiful; be full and overflowing: *a land flowing with milk and honey.* **6** of the tide, flow in; rise. **7** have continuous smoothness: *the flowing lines of her skirt.* **8** *Geology.* alter in shape due to pressure, without breaking or splitting off.
flow from, originate in.
—*n.* **1** the act or way of flowing. **2** any continuous movement like that of water in a river: *a rapid flow of speech.* **3** the rate of flowing. **4** something that flows; current; stream. **5** the flowing of the tide toward the shore; rise of the tide. **6** *Physics.* the directional movement in a current or stream that is a characteristic of all fluids as air or electricity.
go with the flow, *Informal.* let things be. ⟨OE *flōwan*⟩
☛ *Hom.* FLOE.
☛ *Syn. v.* **Flow,** GUSH, STREAM = run or pour out or along. **Flow** emphasizes the continuous forward movement of running or pouring water, whether fast or slow, in great or small quantity: *Water flowed in the streets.* **Gush** = rush out or flow forth suddenly in considerable quantity from an opening: *Oil gushed from the new well.* **Stream** = pour forth steadily from a source or flow steadily, always in the same direction: *Rain streamed down the gullies.*

flow•age ['flouɪdʒ] *n.* **1** a flowing or flooding. **2** the state of being flooded. **3** the liquid that flows or floods. **4** the rate at which a liquid flows or floods. **5** *Physics.* the gradual structural alteration of a solid, such as asphalt, by intermolecular movement.

flowchart or **flow chart** ['flou,tʃɑrt] a diagram showing sequence of operations and the relationship between different elements of a complex system or process, as in manufacturing or data processing.

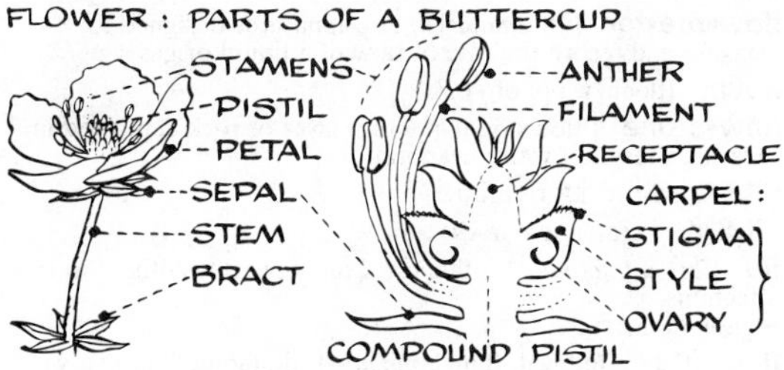

Flower: the parts of a buttercup

flow•er ['flaʊər] *n., v.* —*n.* **1** the often showy and brightly coloured part of an angiosperm plant that appears before the fruit and includes the reproductive organs and surrounding structures, such as petals and sepals and the receptacle on which they are borne. **2** a showy part of such a plant made up of a group of flowers, or of flowers and surrounding, petal-like bracts. The flower of a daisy is composed of central disk flowers surrounded by petal-like ray flowers. The flower of the dogwood and poinsettia consists of tiny, inconspicuous flowers surrounded by coloured, petal-like bracts. **3** a plant that bears flowers, especially a herbaceous plant: *The rose is a common garden flower.* **4** a flowerlike reproductive structure on a flowerless plant, such as a moss. **5** the finest part: *The flower of the country's youth was killed in the war.* **6** the time of being at one's best: *a man in the flower of life.* **7** an embellishment or decoration: *flowers of speech.* **8 flowers,** *pl. Chemistry.* a fine powder produced by sublimation or condensation: *flowers of sulphur.*
in flower, flowering: *Our apple tree is in flower.*
in full flower, a flowering all over; with all the blossoms open. **b** at the peak of attainment: *At 19 his creative ability was in full flower.*
in the full flower of, at the peak of attainment of: *in the full flower of her career.*
—*v.* **1** have or produce flowers: *Our lilac didn't flower this year.* **2** reach or be at one's best. **3** cause to blossom or bloom. **4** decorate with flowers or a floral design. ⟨ME < OF *flour* < L *flos, floris*⟩ **—'flow•er•er,** *n.* **—'flow•er•less,** *adj.* **—'flow•er,like,** *adj.*
☛ *Hom.* FLOUR.

flower bed a border or area of earth in a garden in which flowers are grown. Also, **flowerbed.**

flower child hippie.

flow•ered ['flaʊərd] *adj., v.* —*adj.* **1** having flowers. **2** covered or decorated with flowers.
—*v.* pt. and pp. of FLOWER.

flow•er•et ['flaʊərɪt] *n.* **1** a small flower. **2** floret.

flower girl **1** a girl who sells flowers. **2** a girl who carries the flowers for a bride at her wedding.

flower head a bloom, or blossom, composed of many tiny flowers grouped together so that they appear to be a single flower; compound flower: *Composite plants, such as the daisy and dandelion, have flower heads.* See COMPOSITE for picture.

flow•er•ing ['flaʊərɪŋ] *adj., v.* —*adj.* having flowers.
—*v.* ppr. of FLOWER.

flowering almond a tree (*Prunus triloba*) naturalized in Canada, grown for its blossom as an ornamental.

flowering crab any of various kinds of apple trees bearing small fruit, and blossoms ranging in colour from white to reddish purple.

flowering quince any of a genus (*Chaenomeles*) of Asian shrubs and small trees of the rose family, widely cultivated for their showy, usually red, flowers.

flow•er•pot ['flaʊər,pɒt] *n.* **1** a pot to hold earth for a plant to grow in. **2** *Geology.* a pillar of rock which has been left behind as the escarpment of which it formed a part has eroded.

flow•er•y ['flaʊəri] *or* ['flaʊri] *adj.* **-er•i•er, -er•i•est. 1** having many flowers. **2** containing many fine words and fanciful expressions. **—'flow•er•i•ly,** *adv.* **—'flow•er•i•ness,** *n.*
☛ *Hom.* FLOURY ['flaʊri].

flow•ing ['flouɪŋ] *adj., v.* —*adj.* **1** moving in a current or stream: *flowing water.* **2** moving easily or smoothly: *flowing words.* **3** hanging loosely: *flowing robes.*
—*v.* ppr. of FLOW. **—'flow•ing•ly,** *adv.* **—'flow•ing•ness,** *n.*

flow•me•ter ['flou,mitər] *n.* any apparatus designed to measure and record the rate of flow of a liquid or gas.

flown [floun] *v.* pp. of FLY².

flow•stone ['flou,stoun] *n.* a thin layer of rock deposited in caves as a result of water evaporation.

Flt.Lt. FLIGHT LIEUTENANT.

Flt.Sgt. FLIGHT SERGEANT.

flu [flu] *n. Informal.* **1** influenza. **2** any of various other viral infections.
☛ *Hom.* FLEW, FLUE.

flub [flʌb] *v.* **flubbed, flub•bing;** *n.* —*v.* do (something) very clumsily; make a mess of.
—*n.* a failure in performance; botch; mistake; error.

fluc•tu•ate ['flʌktʃu,eit] *v.* **-at•ed, -at•ing. 1** rise and fall; change continually; vary irregularly: *The temperature fluctuates from day to day.* **2** move in waves. ⟨< L *fluctuare* < *fluctus* wave⟩

fluc•tu•a•tion [,flʌktʃu'eiʃən] *n.* **1** a rising and falling; continual change; irregular variation. **2** a wavelike motion.

flu•dro•cor•ti•sone [,fludrou'kɔrtə,soun] or [,fludrou'kɔrtə,zoun] *n.* a drug used to treat Addison's disease.

flue [flu] *n.* **1** a tube, pipe, or other enclosed passage for conveying smoke, hot air, etc.: *Our chimney has several flues.* **2** FLUE PIPE. **3** the air passage in such a pipe. ⟨origin uncertain⟩
☛ *Hom.* FLEW, FLU.

flue–cured ['flu ,kjɔrd] *adj.* of tobacco, cured by being hung for several days in a place heated through flues, without smoke.

flu•en•cy ['fluənsi] *n.* **1** a flowing quality: *The orator had great fluency of speech.* **2** easy, rapid speaking or writing.

flu•ent ['fluənt] *adj.* **1** flowing smoothly or easily: *Long practice had enabled the traveller to speak fluent French.* **2** speaking or writing easily and rapidly. **3** not fixed or stable; fluid. ⟨< L *fluens, -entis,* ppr. of *fluere* flow⟩ **—'flu•ent•ly,** *adv.*
☛ *Syn.* **2. Fluent,** GLIB, VOLUBLE = speaking easily. **Fluent** suggests being knowledgeable or well prepared and speaking or writing easily and rapidly: *He is a fluent lecturer.* **Glib** = speaking too easily and smoothly, suggesting a lack of sincerity behind the words or superficial talk: *He is a glib liar.* **Voluble** = speaking fluently and continuously, often suggesting an uncheckable flood of words: *Detained by my voluble friend, I was late.*

flue pipe *Music.* in an organ, a pipe in which the sound is made by a current of air striking its mouth or opening.

fluff [flʌf] *n., v.* —*n.* **1** soft, light, downy particles: *Woollen blankets often have fluff on them.* **2** a soft, light, downy mass: *The little kitten looked like a ball of fluff.* **3** *Informal.* a mistake in reading, speaking, etc. on the stage or on radio or television. **4** light or inconsequential conversation, writing, etc.
—*v.* **1** shake up into a soft, light, downy mass: *I fluffed the pillows when I made the bed.* **2** become fluffy. **3** move or float softly like fluff. **4** *Informal.* make a mistake in reading (one's lines, etc.).
fluff off, *Informal.* take no notice of.
fluff up, *Informal.* aggrandize (oneself). ⟨apparently var. of *flue* downy matter (? OE *flug-* in *flugol* fleeting, related to *flēogan* to fly); influenced by *puff*⟩

fluff•y ['flʌfi] *adj.* **fluff•i•er, fluff•i•est. 1** soft and light like fluff: *Whipped cream is fluffy.* **2** covered with fluff; downy: *fluffy baby chicks.* **—'fluff•i•ly,** *adv.* **—'fluff•i•ness,** *n.*

flü•gel•horn or **flu•gel•horn** ['flugəl,hɔrn] *n.* one of several brass wind instruments similar in design to a cornet but having a more mellow tone. ⟨< G *Flügelhorn* < *Flügel* wing + *Horn* horn⟩

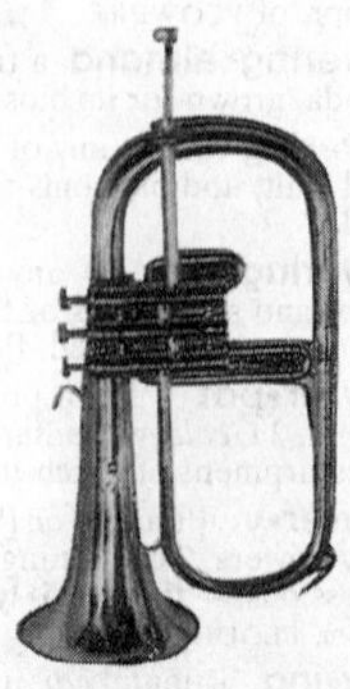

A flügelhorn

flu•id ['fluɪd] *n., adj.* —*n.* **1** any liquid or gas; any substance that flows: *Water, mercury, air, and oxygen are fluids.* **2** liquid to drink: *Due to a severe digestive disorder, she is restricted to fluids.*
—*adj.* **1** in the state of a fluid; like a fluid; flowing. **2** of or having to do with fluids. **3** changing easily; not fixed. **4** ready to be converted into cash or other investments: *fluid assets.* ⟨< L *fluidus* < *fluere* flow⟩ **—flu'id•i•ty,** *n.* **—'flu•id•ly,** *adv.* **—'flu•id•ness,** *n.*
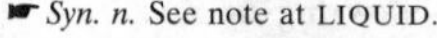
☛ *Syn. n.* See note at LIQUID.

fluid dram one-eighth of a fluid ounce (about 3.6 cm³).

flu•id•ic [flu'ɪdɪk] *adj.* of or having to do with fluidics.

flu•id•ics [flu'ɪdɪks] *n.* (*used with a singular verb*) the technology and use of systems or devices that depend for their operation on the flow and pressure of a fluid or a gas in small jets, instead of electronic or mechanical elements.

flu•id•ize ['fluə,daɪz] *v.* **-ized, -iz•ing.** make fluid; especially, make (a solid) like a fluid by pulverizing it and suspending the particles in a stream of gas so that the whole can be transported as a fluid.

fluid ounce a unit for measuring liquids, equal to one-twentieth of a pint, or about 28.4 cm³.

fluke¹ [fluk] *n.* **1** the pointed part of an anchor that catches in the ground. See ANCHOR for picture. **2** the barbed head or barb of an arrow, harpoon, etc. **3** either half of a whale's tail. ⟨? special use of *fluke³*⟩

fluke² [fluk] *n., v.* **fluked, fluk•ing.** *Informal.* —*n.* **1** *Billiards or pool.* a lucky shot. **2** a lucky chance; fortunate accident.
—*v.* **1** *Billiards or pool.* make or hit by a lucky shot. **2** get by chance or accident. ⟨origin uncertain⟩

fluke³ [fluk] *n.* **1** any of numerous parasitic flatworms constituting two classes (Monogenea and Digenea, formerly placed in the single class Trematoda). Some flukes have very complex life cycles, requiring three different types of host. **2** a flatfish, especially any of various flounders. ⟨OE *flōc*⟩

fluk•ey or **fluk•y** ['fluki] *adj.* **fluk•i•er, fluk•i•est.** *Informal.* **1** obtained by chance rather than by skill. **2** uncertain: *flukey weather.* **—'flu•ki•ness,** *n.*

flume [flum] *n.* **1** a deep, narrow valley with a stream running through it. **2** a large, inclined trough or chute for carrying water. Flumes are used to transport logs and to furnish water for power or irrigation. ⟨ME < OF *flum* < L *flumen* river < *fluere* flow⟩

flu•meth•a•sone [flu'mɛθə,soun] *n.* a drug used in a cream form to treat certain infected skin conditions.

flum•mer•y ['flʌməri] *n., pl.* **-mer•ies. 1** pudding made of milk, eggs, flour, sugar, etc; blancmange thickened with cornflour. **2** an empty compliment; empty trifling; nonsense. ⟨< Welsh *llymru*⟩

flum•mox ['flʌməks] *v. Informal.* confuse; bewilder; confound. ⟨? < dial. *flummocks* to maul, mangle⟩ **—'flum•mox•er,** *n.*

flu•na•ri•zine [flu'nɛrə,zin] *n.* a drug used to treat migraine headaches.

flung [flʌŋ] *v.* pt. and pp. of FLING.

flu•nis•o•lide [flu'nɪsə,laɪd] *n.* a drug used to treat allergic rhinitis.

flunk [flʌŋk] *v., n. Informal.* —*v.* **1** fail (school work): *He flunked his chemistry examination but passed all the others.* **2** cause to fail. **3** mark or grade as having failed.
flunk out, a dismiss or be dismissed from school, college, etc. because of inferior work. **b** give up; back out.
—*n.* **1** a failure. **2** a failing grade. ⟨origin uncertain⟩

flunk•ey ['flʌŋki] *n., pl.* **-eys. 1** a manservant who wears livery; footman. **2** a flattering, fawning person. **3** *Dialect.* a farm hand; cook's assistant. Also, **flunky.** ⟨? alteration of *flanker* one posted on the flank of a person or group < *flank,* v. < *flank,* n. < OF *flanc* < Gmc.⟩

flu•o•cin•a•lone [,fluə'sɪnə,loun] *n.* an antibiotic drug used to treat certain skin conditions.

flu•o•cin•o•nide [,fluə'sɪnə,naɪd] *n.* a drug used in a cream form to treat certain skin conditions.

flu•or ['fluɔr] *n.* fluorite. ⟨< L *fluor* a flowing < *fluere* flow⟩

fluo•resce [flʊ'rɛs], [flɔ'rɛs], *or* [,fluə'rɛs] *v.* **-resced, -resc•ing.** give off light by fluorescence. ⟨< *fluorescence*⟩

flu•o•res•cein [,fluə'rɛsein] *n.* a drug used to diagnose certain eye conditions.

fluo•res•cence [flʊ'rɛsəns], [flɔ'rɛsəns], *or* [,fluə'rɛsəns] *n. Physics, chemistry.* **1** a giving off of light from a substance exposed to certain rays (X-rays and ultraviolet rays). **2** the property of a substance that causes this. Fluorescence is an ability to transform light so as to emit rays of a different wavelength or colour. **3** the light given off in this way. ⟨< *fluor(spar)* + *-escence,* as in *phosphorescence*⟩

fluo•res•cent [flʊ'rɛsənt], [flɔ'rɛsənt], *or* [,fluə'rɛsənt] *adj.* that gives off light by fluorescence. Fluorescent substances glow in the dark when exposed to X-rays.

fluorescent lamp a type of electric lamp, usually a cathode-ray tube containing a gas or vapour that produces light (**fluorescent light**) when acted on by an electric current.

flu•or•ic [flu'ɔrɪk] *adj.* of, having to do with, or obtained from fluorite or fluorine.

fluor•i•date ['flʊrə,deit] *or* ['flɔrə,deit] *v.* **-dat•ed, -dat•ing.** add small amounts of fluoride to (drinking water), especially to prevent tooth decay in children. ⟨back formation < *fluoridation*⟩ **—,fluor•i'da•tion,** *n.*

fluor•ide ['flʊraɪd], ['flɔraɪd], *or* ['fluə,raɪd] *n.* a compound of fluorine and another element or radical.

fluor•ine ['flʊrin] *or* ['flʊrɪn], ['flɔrin] *or* ['flɔrɪn], ['fluə,rin] *or* ['fluərɪn] *n. Chemistry.* a poisonous, greenish yellow gaseous chemical element similar to chlorine. *Symbol*: F; *at.no.* 9; *at.mass* 19.00. ⟨< *fluor(ite)*; because found in *fluorite*⟩

fluor•ite ['flʊrəit], ['flɔrəit], *or* ['fluə,rəit] *n.* a transparent, crystalline mineral that occurs in many colours; calcium fluoride. It is used for fusing metals, making glass, etc. *Formula*: CaF_2 ⟨< *fluor*⟩

fluor•o•car•bon [,flʊrou'kɑrbən], [,flɔrou'kɑrbən], *or* [,fluərou'kɑrbən] *n. Chemistry.* any of a group of synthetic compounds derived from hydrocarbons, in which some or all of the hydrogen atoms have been replaced by fluorine atoms. Fluorocarbons are usually nonflammable, non-toxic, and resilient to chemical change; they are used for making resins and plastics and as refrigerants and solvents.

flu•o•rom•e•ter [,fluə'rɒmətər] *n.* an instrument used to calculate the wavelength and degree of fluorescence. **—,fluo•ro'met•ric,** *adj.* **—,flu•o'rom•e•try,** *n.*

fluor•o•meth•o•lone [,flʊrou'mɛθə,loun] *or* [,flɔrou'mɛθə,loun] *n.* a drug used to treat certain eye conditions.

fluor•o•scope ['flʊrə,skoup] *or* ['flɔrə,skoup] *n.* a device containing a fluorescent screen for examining objects exposed to X-rays or other radiations. The parts of the object not penetrated by the rays cast shadows on the screen. ⟨< *fluor(escence)* + *-scope*⟩

fluor•o•scop•ic [,flʊrə'skɒpɪk] *or* [,flɔrə'skɒpɪk] *adj.* of or having to do with the fluoroscope or with fluoroscopy. **—,fluor•o'scop•i•cal•ly,** *adv.*

fluo•ros•co•py [flʊ'rɒskəpi] *or* [flɔ'rɒskəpi] *n.* an examination with a fluoroscope.

fluor•o•sis [flʊ'rousɪs], [flɔ'rousɪs], *or* [,fluə'rousɪs] *n. Pathology.* poisoning by the excessive use of fluorides.

fluor•o•ur•a•cil [,flʊrou'jʊrəsɪl] *or* [,flɔrou'jʊrəsil] *n.* a drug used to treat certain forms of cancer.

fluor•spar ['flʊr,spɑr], ['flɔr,spɑr], *or* ['fluər,spɑr] *n.* fluorite.

flu•ox•e•tine [flu'ɒksə,tin] *n.* a drug used to treat depression. *Formula*: $C_{17}H_{18}F_3NO$

flu•phen•a•zine [flu'fɛnə,zin] *n.* a drug used to treat schizophrenia.

flu•raz•e•pam [flʊ'ræzə,pæm] *n.* a drug used to treat insomnia.

flur•bi•pro•fen [,flɜrbaɪ'proufən] *n.* a drug used to relieve pain, especially that of rheumatoid arthritis.

flur•ry ['flɜri] *n., pl.* **-ries;** *v.* **-ried, -ry•ing.** *—n.* **1** a sudden gust of wind: *A flurry upset the small sailboat.* **2** a light fall of snow or, less usually, rain: *snow flurries.* **3** a sudden excitement, confusion, or disturbance. **4** a sudden rush: *a flurry of activity.* **5** a sudden fluctuation or increase in the stock market.
—v. excite; confuse; disturb: *Noise in the audience flurried the actor so that he forgot his lines.* ⟨? blend of *flutter* and *hurry*⟩

flush¹ [flʌʃ] *v., n.* *—v.* **1** blush; glow. **2** cause to blush or glow: *Exercise flushed his face.* **3** rush suddenly; flow rapidly: *Embarrassment caused the blood to flush to her cheeks.* **4** wash or cleanse with a rapid flow of water: *The city streets were flushed every night.* **5** empty out; drain: *flush water from flooded land.* **6** of a toilet, empty itself with a rapid flow of water; cause (a toilet) to empty itself out: *Did you remember to flush the toilet? This toilet won't flush.* **7** make joyful and proud; excite: *The team was flushed with its first victory.* **8** of a plant, send out shoots.
—n. **1** a blush; glow. **2** a sudden rush; rapid flow. **3** an act or instance of flushing a toilet. **4** an excited condition or feeling; sudden rush of joyous pride, etc. **5** a sudden, fresh growth: *April brought the first flush of grass.* **6** glowing vigour; freshness: *the first flush of youth.* **7** a fit of feeling very hot. ⟨? blend of *flash* and *blush*⟩

flush² [flʌʃ] *adj., adv., v.* *—adj.* **1** even; level: *The edge of the new shelf must be flush with the old one.* **2** well supplied; having plenty: *The rich man was always flush with money.* **3** abundant; plentiful: *Money is flush when times are good.* **4** liberal; lavish. **5** prosperous. **6** direct; square.
—adv. **1** so as to be level; evenly: *The rest of the paragraph should be flush left.* **2** directly; squarely: *The fighter hit him flush on the nose.*
—v. make even; level. ⟨? extended use of *flush¹*⟩

flush³ [flʌʃ] *v.* **1** fly or start up suddenly. **2** cause to fly or start up suddenly: *The hunter's dog flushed a partridge in the woods.* ⟨origin uncertain⟩ **—'flush•er,** *n.*

flush⁴ [flʌʃ] *n. Card games.* a hand all of one suit. ⟨< OF *flus,* *flux* < L *fluxus* flow⟩

flu•sol ['flusɒl] *n.* artificial blood for emergency use.

flu•spir•i•lene [flu'spirə,lin] *n.* a drug used to treat schizophrenia.

flus•ter ['flʌstər] *v., n.* *—v.* make or become nervous and excited; confuse.
—n. nervous excitement; confusion. ⟨< Scand.; cf. Icelandic *flaustr* bustle and *flaustra* be flustered⟩

flu•ta•mide ['flutə,maɪd] *n.* a drug used to treat certain forms of cancer.

A flute

flute [flut] *n., v.* **flut•ed, flut•ing.** *—n.* **1** a reedless woodwind instrument consisting of a long, slender tube of metal or wood, with holes stopped by fingers or keys for producing the different tones, and a mouth hole in the side near one end. A flute has a range of three octaves upward from middle C. **2** an organ stop which produces the timbre of a flute. **3** a long, rounded groove, as in the shaft of a column, etc. **4** any of several instruments similar to the flute, such as the recorder or fipple flute. **5** a tall, narrow wine glass, used to serve champagne.
—v. **1** play on a flute. **2** make high-pitched, melodious sounds similar to those of a flute; sing, speak like a flute. **3** make long, rounded grooves in. ⟨ME < OF *fleüte, flaüte* < Provençal *flauta,* ult. < L *flatus* pp. of *flare* blow⟩ **—'flute,like,** *adj.*

flut•ed ['flutɪd] *adj., v.* *—adj.* **1** having long, rounded grooves: *a fluted column.* **2** sounding like a flute: *speaking in fluted tones.* *—v.* pt. and pp. of FLUTE.

flut•ing ['flutɪŋ] *n., v.* *—n.* a type of decoration consisting of long, rounded grooves.
—v. ppr. of FLUTE.

flut•ist ['flutɪst] *n.* a person who plays a flute, especially a skilled player. Also, **flautist.**

flut•ter ['flʌtər] *v., n.* *—v.* **1** wave back and forth quickly and lightly. **2** flap the wings; flap. **3** come or go with a fluttering motion. **4** move about restlessly; flit. **5** be in a state of excitement: *The crowd fluttered with expectation.* **6** beat feebly and irregularly: *Her pulse fluttered.* **7** confuse; excite.
—n. **1** the action of fluttering. **2** a confused or excited condition: *The appearance of the Queen caused a great flutter in the crowd.* **3** unstable vibration of some part of an aircraft: *wing flutter.* **4** a heart condition with rapid beating. **5** in high-fidelity sound reproduction, a change in pitch caused by variations in the speed of a record turntable or reel of tape. **6** *Music.* a method of tonguing on a flute or similar instrument, in which the tongue moves rapidly and repetitively. Also, **flitter.** ⟨ME *floteren* < OE *flotorian* < *flēotan* float. Related to FLEET¹.⟩ **—'flut•ter•er,** *n.* **—'flut•ter•ing•ly,** *adv.*

flutter kick a swimming kick in which the legs beat the water rapidly and in quick succession.

flu•vi•al ['fluviəl] *adj.* of, found in, or produced by a river: *A delta is a fluvial deposit.* ⟨< L *fluvialis* < *fluvius* river⟩

flu•vox•a•mine [flu'vɒksə,min] *n.* a drug used to treat depression.

flux [flʌks] *n., v.* *—n.* **1** a flow; flowing. **2** a flowing in of the tide. **3** continuous change: *New words and meanings keep the English language in a state of flux.* **4** an unnatural discharge of blood or liquid matter from the body. **5** a substance used to help metals or minerals fuse together: *Rosin is used as a flux in soldering.* **6** the rate of flow of a fluid, heat, etc. across a certain surface or area.
—v. **1** cause an unnatural discharge of blood or liquid matter in; purge. **2** fuse together. **3** heat with a substance that helps metals or minerals fuse together. **4** make liquid or fluid. ⟨< L *fluxus* < *fluere* flow⟩

flux•ion ['flʌkʃən] *n.* **1** a flowing; flow. **2** a discharge.

3 *Mathematics. Now rare.* the rate of change of a continuously varying quantity; first derivative.

fly[1] [flaɪ] *n., pl.* **flies. 1** any of a large order (Diptera) of two-winged insects, especially the housefly and related, stout-bodied insects. **2** any of various other winged insects (*usually used in compounds*): *dragonfly, firefly, caddis fly.* **3** a fishing lure consisting of a fish-hook with feathers, silk, tinsel, etc. attached to make it resemble an insect.
fly in the ointment, a small thing that spoils something else or lessens its value.
no flies on (someone), *Informal.* someone is clearthinking and alert. ⟨OE *flēoge* < *flēogan* fly[2]⟩

fly[2] [flaɪ] *v.* **flew, flown, fly•ing** *for 1-15*; **flied, fly•ing** *for 16*; *n., pl.* **flies.** *—v.* **1** move through the air with wings. **2** float or wave in the air. **3** cause to float or wave in the air: *to fly a kite.* **4** travel through the air in an aircraft. **5** operate (an aircraft): *The pilot has to fly long hours.* **6** travel over in an aircraft. **7** carry in an aircraft. **8** move through the air in bits or shreds: *The bottle flew into a thousand pieces.* **9 a** hunt with (a falcon). **b** attack by flying, as a hawk does. **10** *Theatre.* lift and hang (scenery, lights, etc.) in the flies. **11** move swiftly; go rapidly. **12** run away; flee; flee from; shun. **13** *Informal.* of a project, idea, proposal, etc., be a success; make headway: *That new design won't fly!* **14** use a particular airline: *We flew KLM to Holland.* **15** *Theatre.* hang lights and scenery in the space above and behind the proscenium arch. **16** *Baseball.* hit a ball high into the air with the bat.
fly at, attack violently.
fly in the face of. See FACE.
fly off, leave suddenly; break away.
fly off the handle. See HANDLE.
fly up, be promoted from Brownie to Girl Guide.
let fly, a aim; shoot; throw: *The hunter let fly an arrow.* **b** say violently.
—n. **1** Also, (*esp. Brit.*), **flies,** *pl.* a flap or opening in a garment, especially in the front of pants. **2** a piece of canvas that serves as an outer flap or roof for a tent. **3** the length of an extended flag from the staff to the outer edge. **4** the outer edge of a flag. **5** *Baseball.* a ball hit high into the air with a bat. **6 flies,** *pl.* in a theatre, the space above the stage. **7** *Cdn.* a sheet of canvas or hide erected for protection against the weather. **8** a regulating mechanism, usually found in a timepiece, composed of vanes around a rotating shaft.
on the fly, a while still in the air; before touching the ground. **b** without stopping or interrupting what one is doing: *We worked all day, eating snacks on the fly.* ⟨OE *flēogan*⟩

fly•a•ble ['flaɪəbəl] *adj.* suitable for flying: *flyable weather, a flyable old aircraft.*

fly agaric a very poisonous mushroom (*Amanita muscaria*) having a conspicuous orange or yellow cap and white gills.

fly ash a troublesome pollutant that goes up the stacks of coal-burning thermal power plants; unburnable ash.

fly•a•way ['flaɪə,wei] *adj.* **1** fluttering; streaming. **2** frivolous; flighty. **3** produced and packaged for shipment by air: *flyaway supplies.* **4** of hair, **a** charged with static electricity. **b** so fine and dry that individual strands tend to float up at the ends.

fly–beer ['flaɪ ,bir] *n. Cdn. Maritimes.* a kind of beer brewed from potatoes and hop yeast mixed with molasses or sugar and water.

fly•blow ['flaɪ,blou] *v.,* **-blew, -blown,** *n. —v.* **1** of a fly, place eggs or larvae in (food, etc.) **2** taint; spoil.
—n. the eggs or larvae of a fly.

fly•blown ['flaɪ,bloun] *adj., v. —adj.* **1** tainted by the eggs or larvae of flies. **2** spoiled. **3** covered with FLY SPECKS.
—v. pp. of FLYBLOW.

fly book a container shaped like a book, for a fisher to keep artificial flies in.

fly•by ['flaɪ,baɪ] *n.* a flight past a designated point by a spacecraft.

fly–by–night ['flaɪ baɪ 'nəit] *adj., n. —adj.* not reliable; not to be trusted.
—n. Informal. **1** a person who avoids paying his or her debts by leaving secretly at night. **2** an unreliable or irresponsible person.

fly–camp ['flaɪ ,kæmp] *n. Cdn.* FLY-IN CAMP.

fly•cast•ing ['flaɪ,kæstɪŋ] *n.* the act of fishing with a rod and line, using artificial flies. **—'fly,cast,** *v.*

fly•catch•er ['flaɪ,kætʃər] *n.* **1** any of an Old World subfamily (Muscicapinae, of the family Muscicapidae) of small songbirds characterized by the habit of darting out from a perch to catch flying insects. **2** any of a New World family (Tyrannidae) of songbirds, such as the kingbirds or phoebes, having similar habits.

fly–dope ['flaɪ ,doup] *n. Cdn. Informal.* any insect repellant.

fly•er or **fli•er** ['flaɪər] *n.* **1** a person who or thing that flies. **2** pilot. **3** a very fast train, ship, bus, etc. **4** *Slang.* a reckless financial venture. **5** *Informal.* a try; an experimental venture into something. **6** a small handbill, used for advertising. **7** one step of a straight flight of stairs.

fly–fish•ing ['flaɪ ,fɪʃɪŋ] *n.* fishing with natural or artificial flies as bait. **—'fly-,fish,** *v.*

fly–in ['flaɪ 'ɪn] *adj. Cdn.* **1** designed for flying into; having landing facilities: *a fly-in fishing camp.* **2** arriving by plane: *a fly-in delegate.*

fly–in camp *Cdn.* a fishing or hunting camp that is accessible only by airplane.

fly•ing ['flaɪɪŋ] *adj., v. —adj.* **1** that flies; moving through the air. **2** floating or waving in the air. **3** swift; like flight: *a flying leap.* **4** short and quick; hasty: *Aunt Mary paid us a flying visit last week.* **5** organized for swift work: *the flying squad.* **6** of cattle brands, wavy.
—v. ppr. of FLY
with flying colours or **colors,** successfully; triumphantly: *He passed the examination with flying colours.*

flying boat a type of seaplane having a boatlike hull.

flying boxcar *Cdn. Slang.* a freight plane.

flying bridge on a ship, a duplicate pilot house, usually not enclosed.

flying buttress an arched support or brace built between the wall of a building and a supporting column to bear some of the weight of the roof. See BUTTRESS for picture.

Flying Dutchman 1 a legendary Dutch sea captain condemned to sail the seas until the day of judgment. **2** his ghostlike ship, supposed to appear at sea and to be a bad omen.

flying field an airport for small aircraft.

flying fish any of a family (Exocoetidae) of marine fishes found in warm and tropical seas, having large, winglike pectoral fins by means of which they can glide some distance through the air after leaping from the water.

flying fox any of several fruit-eating bats with a head like a fox.

flying jib a small, triangular sail set in front of the regular jib.

flying officer an air-force officer ranking next above a pilot officer and below a flight lieutenant. *Abbrev.*: F.O. or F/O

flying saucer a disklike object that some people claim to have seen flying in the sky at great speed over various parts of the world; UFO.

flying spot *Television.* a moving beam of light that produces a succession of thin lines against a surface containing an image. The areas of lightness and darkness are electronically picked up and transmitted to receiving sets where the image is reproduced.

flying squirrel any of a subfamily (Petauristinae) of nocturnal squirrels of North America, Asia, and Europe, having a fold of fur-covered skin along each side joining the front and hind legs, which is stretched taut when the animals spread out their legs, permitting them to glide through the air.

flying start 1 the start of a race in which the contestants have already started moving from a line farther back. **2** any advantage: *Knowing how to read will give you a flying start in school.*

flying wing 1 *Cdn. Football.* a player whose position is variable behind the line of scrimmage: *There is no flying wing on American football teams.* **2** a type of aircraft in which the motors, fuselage, etc. are inside the wing structure.

fly•leaf [flaɪ,lif] *n., pl.* **-leaves.** a blank sheet of paper at the beginning or end of a book, pamphlet, etc.

fly•man ['flaɪmən] *n., pl.* **-men.** *Theatre.* a stagehand who works in the flies above the stage.

fly•o•ver ['flaɪ,ouvər] *n.* **1** flypast. **2** *Brit.* a highway overpass.

fly•pa•per ['flaɪ,peipər] *n.* a paper coated with a sticky substance to catch flies.

fly•past ['flaɪ,pæst] *n.* a display in which aircraft in formation fly over a reviewing stand located on the ground: *We enjoyed the flypast at the air show.*

fly•sheet ['flaɪ,ʃit] *n.* **1** a flyer; pamphlet. **2** a sheet of canvas, nylon, etc. that one drapes over a pitched tent.

fly specks the tiny, dark spots left by flies on windows, light bulbs, etc.; fly dung.

fly swatter a device for killing flies, usually consisting of a long wooden or wire handle to which is attached a broad, flat, flexible piece of perforated rubber, plastic, etc.

fly•trap ['flaɪ,træp] *n.* **1** a plant that traps insects. **2** a trap to catch flies.

fly–up ['flaɪ ,ʌp] *n.* a ceremony at which Brownies are promoted to Girl Guides.

fly•way ['flaɪ,weɪ] *n.* an established route followed by migrating birds.

fly•weight ['flaɪ,weit] *n.* a boxer who weighs between 49 kg and 51 kg.

fly•wheel ['flaɪ,wil] *n.* a heavy wheel attached to machinery to keep the speed even. See STEAM ENGINE for picture.

fm. fathom.

Fm fermium.

FM or **F.M.** FREQUENCY MODULATION.

F.M. FIELD MARSHAL.

fn footnote.

f number *Photography.* the number obtained by dividing the focal length of a lens by its effective diameter.

foal [foul] *n., v.* —*n.* a young horse, donkey, etc.; colt or filly.
in or **with foal,** of a mare, pregnant.
—*v.* give birth to (a foal). ⟨OE *fola*⟩

foam [foum] *n., v.* —*n.* **1** a mass of very small bubbles. **2** a frothy mass formed in the mouth as saliva or on the skin of animals as sweat: *The dog with foam around its mouth is suffering from rabies.* **3** a spongy, flexible material made from plastics, rubber, etc. **4** *Poetic.* the sea.
—*v.* **1** form or gather foam. **2** cause to foam. **3** break into foam: *The stream foams over the rocks.* **4** cover with foam. **5** cause to have a foamy structure by trapping air bubbles inside.
foam at the mouth, be greatly enraged. ⟨OE *fām*⟩ —**'foam•less,** *adj.* —**'foam,like,** *adj.*

foam•flow•er ['foum,flaʊər] *n.* a plant (*Tiarella cordifolia*) native to eastern North America, bearing white blossoms that flower in spring.

foam rubber a firm, spongy foam of natural or synthetic rubber, used especially for mattresses and upholstery.

foam•y ['foumi] *adj.* **foam•i•er, foam•i•est;** *n.* —*adj.* **1** covered with foam; foaming. **2** made of foam. **3** like foam.
—*n.* a foam rubber mattress. —**'foam•i•ly,** *adv.* —**'foam•i•ness,** *n.*

fob[1] [fɒb] *n.* **1** a small pocket in trousers to hold a watch, etc. **2** a short watch chain, ribbon, etc. that hangs out of a watch pocket. **3** an ornament worn at the end of such a chain, ribbon, etc. ⟨cf. dial. HG *fuppe* pocket⟩

fob[2] [fɒb] *v.* **fobbed, fob•bing;** *n.* —*v.* trick; deceive; cheat.
fob off, a put off or deceive by a trick. **b** palm off or get rid of by a trick.
—*n.* a trick. ⟨? extended use of *fob*[1]⟩

f.o.b. or **F.O.B.** FREE ON BOARD.

fo•cal ['foukəl] *adj.* of, having to do with, or situated at a focus. —**'fo•cal•ly,** *adv.*

focal infection *Pathology, dentistry.* a localized bacterial infection.

fo•cal•ize ['foukə,laɪz] *v.* **-ized, -iz•ing. 1** focus. **2** bring or come into focus. —**,fo•cal•i'za•tion,** *n.*

focal length *Optics.* the distance of a focus from the optical centre of a lens or concave mirror. Also, **focal distance.**

fo•ci ['fousaɪ] *or* ['fousi] *n.* a pl. of FOCUS.

fo'c'sle ['fouksəl] *n. Nautical.* forecastle.

fo•cus ['foukəs] *n., pl.* **-cus•es** or **-ci** [-saɪ] *or* [-si]; *v.* **-cus•ses** or **-cus•es, -cussed** or **-cused, -cus•sing** or **-cus•ing.** —*n.* **1** a point at which rays of light, heat, etc. meet or from which they diverge or seem to diverge after being reflected by a mirror or refracted by a lens. **2** FOCAL LENGTH. **3** the correct adjustment of a lens, the eye, etc. to make a clear image: *to bring a telescope into focus.* **4** the central point of attention, activity, disturbance, etc.: *The focus of a disease is the part of the body where it is most active.* **5** *Geometry.* **a** either of two fixed points used in determining an ellipse. **b** a point used in determining some other curve.
in focus, a clear; distinct. **b** at the centre of attention.
out of focus, blurred; indistinct.
—*v.* **1** bring (rays of light, heat, etc.) to a point. **2** adjust (a lens, the eye, etc.) to make a clear image: *A near-sighted person cannot focus accurately on distant objects.* **3** make (an image, etc.) clear by adjusting a lens, the eye, etc. **4** converge; meet at a focus. **5** concentrate: *When studying, he focussed his mind on his lessons.* ⟨< L *focus* hearth⟩ —**'fo•cus•ser** or **'fo•cus•er,** *n.*

fod•der ['fɒdər] *n., v.* —*n.* coarse food for horses, cattle, etc.: *Hay and cornstalks are fodder.*
—*v.* give fodder to (horses, cattle, etc.). ⟨OE *fōdor* < *fōda* food⟩
☛ *Syn. n.* See note at FEED.

foe [fou] *n.* an enemy. ⟨OE *fāh* hostile⟩
☛ *Hom.* FAUX.
☛ *Syn.* See note at ENEMY.

foehn [fein]; *German,* [fœn] *n. Meteorology.* a warm, dry wind that blows down the slopes of a mountain and across a valley, especially in the Alps. Also, **föhn.** ⟨< dial. G *föhn,* ult. < L *Favonius* the west wind⟩

foe•man ['foumən] *n., pl.* **-men.** *Archaic.* enemy.

foe•tal ['fitəl] See FETAL.

foet•id ['fɛtɪd] *or* ['fitɪd] *adj.* See FETID.

foe•tor ['fitər] *n.* See FETOR.

foe•tus ['fitəs] See FETUS.

fog[1] [fɒg] *n., v.* **fogged, fog•ging.** —*n.* **1 a** a cloud of fine drops of water that forms just above the earth's surface; thick mist. **b** a layer of such mist condensed on glass or clear plastic, making it cloudy. **2** a darkened condition; dim, blurred state. **3** a confused or puzzled condition: *His mind was in a fog during most of the examination.* **4** *Photography.* a greyish area obscuring part of a photograph. **5** any vaporized liquid, such as insecticide.
—*v.* **1** cover with fog. **2** darken; dim; blur. **3** become covered or filled with fog. **4** confuse; puzzle. **5** spray with insecticide: *We'll have to fog the whole house.* **6** *Photography.* add greyish areas to (a photograph, negative, etc.). ⟨< Scand. *fog* spray⟩

fog[2] [fɒg] *n.* **1** a second growth of grass. **2** tall grass. ⟨< ME *fogge* tall grass⟩

fog bank a dense mass of fog.

fog•bound ['fɒg,baʊnd] *adj.* **1** kept from travelling, especially from sailing, by fog. **2** of an airport or port, unable to operate because of fog.

fog•bow ['fɒg,bou] *n.* a white or yellow rainbow seen against a bank of fog.

fog•dog ['fɒg,dɒg] *n.* a bright spot seen in a fogbank.

fo•gey ['fougi] *n., pl.* **-geys.** one who is behind the times or lacks enterprise. Also, **fogy.** ⟨origin uncertain⟩ —**'fo•gey•ish,** *adj.* —**'fo•gey,ism,** *n.*

fog•gy ['fɒgi] *adj.* **-gi•er, -gi•est. 1** having much fog; misty. **2** not clear; dim; blurred: *Her understanding of geography was rather foggy.* **3** confused; puzzled. —**'fog•gi•ly,** *adv.* —**'fog•gi•ness,** *n.*

fog•horn ['fɒg,hɔrn] *n.* **1** a horn or siren used in foggy weather to warn ships of danger from rocks, collision, etc. **2** a loud, harsh voice.

fo•gy ['fougi] *n., pl.* **-gies.** See FOGEY.

föhn [fein]; *German,* [fœn] *n.* See FOEHN.

foi•ble ['fɔɪbəl] *n.* a weak point; a weakness in character: *Talking too much is one of her foibles.* ⟨< F *foible,* older form of modern *faible* feeble⟩

foie gras [fwɒ 'grɑ]; *French,* [fwa'gʀa] See PÂTÉ DE FOIE GRAS.

foil[1] [fɔɪl] *v.* **1** prevent (someone) from carrying out plans, attempts, etc.; get the better of; turn aside or hinder: *The hero foiled the villain.* **2** prevent (a scheme, plan, etc.) from being carried out or from succeeding. **3** spoil (a trace or scent) by crossing it. ⟨< OF *fouler* trample, full (cloth) < VL *fullare* < L *fullo* a fuller; with reference to spoiling a trace or scent by crossing it⟩

foil[2] [fɔɪl] *n., v.* —*n.* **1** metal beaten, hammered, or rolled into a very thin sheet: *tin foil, aluminum foil.* **2** a person who or thing that makes another look or seem better by contrast. **3** a very thin layer of polished metal, placed under a gem to give it more colour or sparkle. **4** a backing on glass to form a mirror. **5** *Architecture.* a leaflike ornament; arc or rounded space between cusps.
—*v.* **1** coat or back with foil. **2** set off by contrast. ⟨ME < OF < L *folia* leaves⟩

foil[3] [fɔɪl] *n.* **1** a long, narrow sword with a knob or button on the point to prevent injury, used in fencing. **2 foils,** *pl.* fencing. ⟨origin uncertain⟩

foils•man [ˈfɔɪlzmən] *n., pl.* **-men.** one who uses a foil in fencing.

foist [fɔɪst] *v.* **1** palm off as genuine; impose slyly: *The dishonest shopkeeper foisted inferior goods on his customers.* **2** put in secretly or slyly: *The author discovered that the translator had foisted several passages into her book.* **3** compel (someone) to accept (something): *My aunt is one of those well-meaning but irritating hostesses who always foist more food on you than you want to eat.* ⟨probably < dial. Du. *vuisten* take in hand < *vuist* fist⟩

fol. **1** folio. **2** following.

fo•la•cin [ˈfouləsɪn] *n.* FOLIC ACID.

fold[1] [fould] *v., n.* —*v.* **1** bend or double over on itself. **2** bring together with the parts in or around one another. **3** bring close to the body. **4** place one over and under the other: *to fold the arms.* **5** put the arms around and hold tenderly. **6** wrap; enclose. **7** *Informal.* close on account of failure or bankruptcy; terminate: *They folded the business after only two months and with great loss.* **8** *Informal.* break down under physical or mental exhaustion; collapse: *The student folded under the pressure of exams.*
fold in, in cooking, add to a mixture by gently turning one part over another with strokes of a spoon: *Fold in beaten egg whites.*
fold out, unfold, open out.
fold up, a make or become smaller by folding. **b** break down; collapse. **c** *Informal.* fail.
—*n.* **1** a layer of something folded. **2** a hollow or mark made by folding: *Fold up the map along the original folds.* **3** something that is or can be folded. **4** the act or process of folding. **5** *Geology.* a bend in a layer of rock. ⟨OE *fealdan*⟩

fold[2] [fould] *n., v.* —*n.* **1** a pen to keep sheep in. **2** sheep kept in a pen. **3** a faith or other community.
return to the fold, a return to active membership in one's faith community. **b** return to the place or group of people to which one naturally belongs.
—*v.* put or keep (sheep) in a pen. ⟨OE *falod*⟩

-fold *suffix.* **1** times as many; times as great: *tenfold.* **2** composed of or divided into——parts: *manifold.* ⟨OE *-feald.* Related to FOLD[1].⟩

fold•a•way [ˈfouldə,wei] *adj.* usually of a piece of furniture, made so as to fold up into a smaller space: *a foldaway cot.*

fold•er [ˈfouldər] *n.* **1** a person who or thing that folds. **2** a holder for papers, made by folding a piece of cardboard. **3** a pamphlet made of one or more folded sheets.

fol•de•rol [ˈfɒldə,rɒl] See FALDERAL.

folding door one of a pair of doors having one part hinged to another so that they can open and close by folding and unfolding.

folding money *Informal.* paper money, as opposed to coins.

fold•out [ˈfould,ʌut] *n.* an extra wide page inserted into a magazine or book, which the reader unfolds to read: *A foldout is usually a picture or map.*

fo•li•a•ceous [,fouliˈeiʃəs] *adj.* **1** leaflike; leafy. **2** made of leaflike plates or thin layers. ⟨< L *foliaceus* < *folia* leaves⟩

fol•i•age [ˈfouliɪdʒ] *n.* **1** the leaves of a plant, especially of a tree. **2** a decoration made of carved or painted leaves, flowers, etc. ⟨alteration of F *feuillage* < *feuille* leaf < L *folia* leaves⟩

fo•li•ate *adj.* [ˈfoulɪɪt] *or* [ˈfouli,eit]; *v.* [ˈfouli,eɪt] *adj., v.* **-at•ed, -at•ing.** —*adj.* **1** having leaves; covered with leaves. **2** resembling a leaf; leaflike.
—*v.* **1** put forth leaves. **2** split into leaflike plates or thin layers. **3** shape like a leaf. **4** decorate with leaflike ornaments. **5** beat (metal) until it is thin like foil. **6** number the leaves of (a book). **7** apply metal foil to the back of (a glass sheet) to make a mirror. ⟨< L *foliatus* < *folia* leaves⟩

fo•li•a•tion [,fouliˈeiʃən] *n.* **1** a growing of leaves; putting forth of leaves: *foliation of trees in the spring.* **2** being in leaf. **3** the arrangement of leaves within a bud. **4** the beating of metal into foil. **5** a decoration with leaflike ornaments or foils. **6** *Geology.* **a** the property of splitting up into leaflike layers. **b** any of the leaflike plates or layers into which crystalline rocks are divided.

fo•lic acid [ˈfoulɪk] *or* [ˈfɒlɪk] *Biochemistry.* a crystalline compound of the vitamin B complex, found in green leaves, mushrooms, and some animal tissue and used in the treatment of anemia. *Formula*: $C_{19}H_{19}N_7O_6$ ⟨< L *folium* leaf + E *-ic*⟩

fo•li•ic•o•lous [,fouliˈɪkələs] *adj.* growing on leaves. ⟨< *folii* (< L *folium* leaf) + *-colous*, base of L *colere* to cultivate⟩

fo•li•o [ˈfouli,ou] *n., pl.* **-li•os;** *v.* —*n.* **1** a large sheet of paper folded once to make two leaves, or four pages, of a book, etc. **2 a** a book of the largest size, having pages made by folding large sheets of paper once; large volume. A folio is usually any book more than 28 cm in height. **b** the size of a folio book. **3** (*adjl.*) of the largest size; made of large sheets of paper folded once: *The encyclopedia was in twenty volumes folio.* **4** *Printing.* a page number of a book, etc. **5** a leaf of a book, manuscript, etc., numbered on the front side only. **6** a case for loose papers, etc. **7** a unit for computing the length of a document. **8** *Bookkeeping.* left- and right-hand ledger pages with the same number.
in folio, of folio size or form.
—*v.* number the pages or folios of (a book, etc.); page. ⟨< L *folio*, ablative of *folium* leaf⟩

fo•li•o•late [ˈfouliəlɪt] *or* [ˈfouliə,leit] *adj.* having leaflets; having to do with leaflets.

fo•li•ose [ˈfouli,ous] *adj.* FOLIATE (def. 1).

folio verso [ˈfoulɪ,ou ˈvɜrsou] *Latin.* on the back of the page.

fo•li•um [ˈfouliəm] *n.* **1** *Geology.* a thin layer. **2** *Geometry.* a loop.

folk [fouk] *n., pl.* **folk** or **folks;** *adj.* —*n.* **1** people as a group: *Most city folk know very little about farming.* **2** a tribe; nation. **3 folks,** *pl.* **a** people. **b** *Informal.* the members of one's own family; one's relatives, esp. one's parents. **4** FOLK MUSIC (def. 2).
—*adj.* **1** of or having to do with people, their beliefs, legends, customs, etc. **2** of or having to do with folk songs or folk music: *a folk festival.* ⟨OE *folc*⟩

folk•a•thon [ˈfoukə,θɒn] *n. Informal.* a gathering for the singing of folk songs for a long period of time. ⟨< *folk* songs + (*mar*)*athon*⟩

folk ballad an anonymous long poem in verse, usually a narrative, that is passed on orally from generation to generation.

folk dance **1** a dance originating and handed down among the common people. **2** the music for such a dance.

Fol•ke•ting [ˈfoulkə,tɪŋ] *n.* the Danish legislature. ⟨< Danish *folke* people + *ting* assembly⟩

folk etymology popular misconception of the origin of a word that often results in a modification of its sound or spelling. Thus, ME *crevice* became E *crayfish*, influenced by *fish.*

folk hero a popular hero, often mythological: *James Bond is a folk hero.*

folk•ie [ˈfouki] *n.* folknik.

folk•lore [ˈfouk,lɔr] *n.* **1** the beliefs, legends, customs, etc. of a people, etc. **2** the study of folklore.

folk•lor•ic [ˈfouk,lɔrɪk] *adj.* of, having to do with, or characteristic of folklore.

folk•lor•ist [ˈfouk,lɔrɪst] *n.* a person who studies or knows much about folklore. **—,folk•lor'is•tic,** *adj.*

folk medicine popular remedies, often herbal, passed down the generations.

folk music **1** music originating among the common people and passed on from generation to generation, especially by oral tradition. **2** any of many kinds of modern popular music, usually similar in style to traditional folk music.

folk•nik [ˈfouknɪk] *n. Slang.* a person keen on singing or listening to folk songs. Also, **folkie.** ⟨< *folk* songs + (*beat*)*nik*⟩

folk–rock [ˈfouk ,rɒk] *n.* light rock music with folk-song themes or lyrics.

folk singer a person who sings folk songs.

folk song **1** a song originating, as a rule, among the common people and handed down from generation to generation: *"Alouette" is a well-known French-Canadian folk song.* **2** a modern song imitating or similar to a traditional folk song.

folk•sy [ˈfouksi] *adj.* **-si•er, -si•est.** *Informal.* **1** friendly; social: *It was just a nice, folksy evening.* **2** plain and unpretentious. **3** artificially or affectedly simple or familiar: *The movie was full of folksy stupidity.* **—ˈfolk•si•ness,** *n.* **—ˈfolk•si•ly,** *adv.*

folk tale a story or legend originating among the common people and handed down from generation to generation.

folk•way [ˈfouk,wei] *n.* a traditional custom of a people or a social group.

fol•li•cle [ˈfɒləkəl] *n.* **1** a small cavity, sac, or gland. Hair grows from follicles. See EPIDERMIS for picture. **2** a one-celled seed vessel. It is a dry fruit that splits open along one seam only. Milkweed pods are follicles. See FRUIT for picture. ⟨< L *folliculus*, dim. of *follis* bellows⟩ **—fol'li•cu•late** [fəˈlɪkjəlɪt], *adj.*

fol•li•cle–stim•u•lat•ing hormone [ˈfɒləkəl ,stɪmjə,leitɪŋ] a hormone produced by the pituitary gland, responsible for the maturing of ova in the female and of testicles in the male. *Abbrev.*: FSH

fol•lic•u•lar [fə'lɪkjələr] *adj.* **1** of or resembling a follicle or follicles. **2** *Medicine.* affecting the follicles: *follicular tonsillitis.*

fol•low ['fɒlou] *v., n.* —*v.* **1** go or come after: *Night follows day. You lead; we follow.* **2** result from; result: *Misery follows war. If you eat too much candy, a stomach ache will follow.* **3** succeed (*with*); cause to come after: *The maple tree follows blossom with leaves.* **4** be next in a position after: *Lester Pearson followed John Diefenbaker as prime minister.* **5** go along: *Follow this road to the corner.* **6** go along with; accompany: *My dog followed me to school.* **7** pursue: *The hounds followed the fox.* **8** act according to; take as a guide; use; obey: *Follow her advice.* **9** accept (a person) as a guide or leader; accept the authority or example of. **10** keep the eyes or attention on: *I could not follow that bird's flight.* **11** keep the mind on; keep up with and understand: *She found it hard to follow the conversation.* **12** take as one's work or profession; be concerned with: *She expects to follow law.* **13** take an interest in; keep informed about: *I have followed tennis for many years.*
as follows, a the following: *The duties of the various officers are as follows.* **b** in the following way: *Assemble frame as follows.*
follow out, carry out to the end.
follow through, a continue a stroke or motion through to the end: *Most golfers follow through after hitting the ball.* **b** carry out fully; complete: *When one begins a job, one should try to follow it through.*
follow up, a follow closely and steadily. **b** increase the effect of by further action: *He followed up his first request by asking again a week later.* **c** carry out to the end.
—*n.* **1** the act of following. **2** *Billiards.* a stroke that causes the player's ball to roll on after the ball struck by it. ⟨OE *folgian*⟩

☛ *Syn. v.* **1, 2. Follow,** SUCCEED, ENSUE = come after. **Follow** is the general word meaning 'come or go after': *He has come to take up his new position, but his wife will follow later.* **Succeed** = come next in order of time, and usually suggests taking the place of someone or something: *He succeeded his father as president of the company.* **Ensue,** formal, means 'follow as a result or conclusion': *A lasting friendship ensued from our working together during the war.*

fol•low•er ['fɒlouər] *n.* **1** a person who follows the ideas or beliefs of another; adherent: *a follower of Socrates.* **2** an attendant or supporter. **3** a person or thing that follows, or comes after. **4** a part of a machine that takes its motion from another part.

☛ *Syn.* **1. Follower,** ADHERENT, DISCIPLE = someone who follows another, his or her beliefs, a cause, etc. **Follower** is the general word: *Those who promise security always find followers among unthinking people.* **Adherent** means a faithful follower who gives active and loyal support to a belief, cause, party, or leader: *Socialized medicine has many adherents.* **Disciple** emphasizes both devotion to a person as leader and teacher and firm belief in his or her teachings: *He is a disciple of Einstein.*

fol•low•ing ['fɒlouɪŋ] *n., adj., prep., v.* —*n.* **1** a group of followers; attendants. **2 the following,** the persons, things, items, etc. now to be named, related, described, etc.
—*adj.* **1** that follows; next. **2** to be mentioned next: *The following people will form the committee.* **3** of the tide or wind, flowing in the same direction as a ship or aircraft: *We arrived early because we had a following wind.*
—*prep.* immediately after: *Following lunch he took a nap.*
—*v.* ppr. of FOLLOW.

follow–through ['fɒlou ,θru] *n.* **1** *Sports.* the smooth completion of a movement, especially of a stroke in golf or tennis after the ball has been hit. **2** any logical continuation and completion.

fol•low–up ['fɒlou ,ʌp] *n., adj.* —*n.* **1** the act of following up. **2** any action or thing, such as a second or third visit, appeal, letter, etc., designed to be a further effort in achieving some goal.
—*adj.* sent or used as a follow-up: *a follow-up circular.*

fol•ly ['fɒli] *n., pl.* **-lies. 1** a being foolish; lack of sense; unwise conduct. **2** a foolish act, practice, or idea; something silly. **3** a costly but foolish undertaking. ⟨ME < OF *folie* < *fol* foolish. See FOOL.⟩

Fol•som ['fɒlsəm] *adj.* of a prehistoric people in North America known for their use of flint blades. ⟨< *Folsom,* village in New Mexico where artifacts were found⟩

Fo•mal•haut ['foumәl,hɒt] *or* ['foumә,lou] *n. Astronomy.* the brightest star in the constellation Piscis Austrinus. ⟨< F < Arabic *fum al-hut* fish's mouth⟩

fo•ment [fou'mɛnt] *v.* **1** promote; foster (trouble, rebellion, etc.). **2** apply warm water, hot cloths, etc. to (a hurt or pain). ⟨< LL *fomentare* < *fomentum* a warm application < L *fovere* warm⟩ **—fo'ment•er,** *n.*

☛ *Usage.* See note at FERMENT.

fo•men•ta•tion [,foumɛn'teiʃən] *n.* **1** a stirring up; instigation; incitement. **2** the application of moist heat. **3** a hot, moist substance applied.

fond¹ [fɒnd] *adj.* **1** expressing affection: *a fond look.* **2** loving foolishly or too much. **3** cherished: *fond hopes.* **4** *Archaic.* foolish; foolishly ready to believe or hope.
be fond of, a have a liking for: *My uncle is fond of children.* **b** like to eat: *Most cats are fond of fish.* ⟨ME *fonned,* pp. of *fonne(n)* be foolish; origin uncertain⟩ **—'fond•ly,** *adv.* **—'fond•ness,** *n.*

fond² [fɒnd] *n.* a background or groundwork, especially of lace. ⟨< F < L *fundus* bottom, land, estate⟩

fon•dant ['fɒndənt] *n.* **1** a creamy sugar candy used as a filling or coating for other candies. **2** a candy consisting mainly of fondant. ⟨< F *fondant,* literally, melting, ppr. of *fondre* melt. See FOUND³.⟩

fon•dle ['fɒndəl] *v.* **-dled, -dling.** pet; caress lovingly: *The mother fondled her baby's hands.* ⟨< *fond,* v., special use of *fond,* adj.⟩ **—'fon•dler,** *n.*

fon•due [fɒn'du] *or* ['fɒndu] *n.* **1** a dish usually consisting of melted Swiss cheese, white wine, seasonings, and, often, brandy, into which cubes of bread are dipped and then eaten. **2** any of various similar dishes consisting of small pieces of food cooked in a hot liquid at the table. ⟨< F *fondue,* fem. pp. of *fondre* melt. See FOUND³.⟩

font¹ [fɒnt] *n.* **1** a basin holding water for baptism. **2** a basin for holy water. **3** *Poetic or archaic.* fountain or source: *the font of truth.* ⟨ML *fons, fontis* spring⟩

font² [fɒnt] *n. Printing.* a complete set of type of one size and style. Also, **fount.** ⟨< F *fonte* < *fondre* melt. See FOUND³.⟩

fon•ta•nel [,fɒntə'nɛl] *n. Anatomy.* a membrane-covered gap between the bones of the growing skull of an infant or fetus. ⟨< F *fontanelle,* dim. of *fontaine.* See FOUNTAIN.⟩

Fon•ti•na [fɒn'tinə] *n.* an Italian cheese made from sheep's milk.

food [fud] *n.* **1** what an animal or plant takes in to enable it to live and grow. **2** what is eaten as opposed to drunk; solid nourishment: *Give her food and drink.* **3** a particular kind or article of food. **4** what helps anything to live and grow. **5** what sustains or serves for consumption in any way: *food for thought.* ⟨OE *fōda*⟩

☛ *Syn.* **1. Food,** PROVISION, RATION = what human beings and animals eat. **Food** is the general word for what is taken in by people, animals, or plants to keep them alive and help them grow: *Milk is a valuable food.* **Provisions** = a supply of food, either for immediate use or stored away: *I must buy provisions for the holidays.* **Rations** = fixed allowances of food set for one day's use or allowed under some system of rationing: *The survivors lived for three days on small rations of water and chocolate.*

food bank an organization which collects and sorts donations of food, to be given free to the unemployed, the homeless, or those with low incomes.

foo•die ['fudi] *n. Informal.* one with great interest in the preparation and eating of culinary delicacies.

food•land ['fud,lænd] *n.* land used to grow edible crops: *the Ontario foodland.*

food poisoning sickness from eating contaminated or poisonous food, usually characterized by vomiting, diarrhea, etc.; also, in certain acute types of poisoning, by prostration, respiratory paralysis, etc.

food processor a kitchen appliance having a number of interchangeable blades and other attachments for performing a variety of functions in the preparation of food, such as slicing, grating, dicing, chopping, mixing, and blending.

food•stuff ['fud,stʌf] *n.* **1** any material for food: *Grain and meat are foodstuffs.* **2** any nutritionally valuable element in food, as protein or carbohydrate.

food web the inter-related feeding patterns of a community of living things.

foo•fa•raw or **foo•fe•raw** ['fufə,rɒ] *n.* **1** unnecessary ornamentation, as frills, fringes, bows, etc. **2** *Slang.* a loud disturbance caused by something of no importance. ⟨origin uncertain⟩

fool [ful] *n., v., adj.* —*n.* **1** a person without sense; unwise or silly person. **2** formerly, a clown kept by a king, queen, or lord to amuse people; jester. **3** a person who has been deceived or tricked; dupe.
be nobody's fool, be clever and sharp-witted.
play the fool, clown around; act silly.

—*v.* **1** act like a fool for fun; play; joke: *The teacher told him not to fool during class.* **2** make a fool of; deceive; trick.
fool around, *Informal.* **a** waste time foolishly. **b** engage in illicit sex.
fool (around) with, *Informal.* meddle foolishly with.
fool away, *Informal.* waste (time, resources, etc.) foolishly.
—*adj. Informal.* of a resistant or frustrating object: *Tell me how to open that fool door!* ⟨ME < OF *fol* madman, probably < LL *follis* empty-headed < L *follis* bag, bellows⟩

☛ *Syn. n.* **1. Fool,** IDIOT, IMBECILE, in non-technical use, mean 'a foolish person'. **Fool** suggests absence of wisdom, and expresses contempt for someone who acts without good sense or judgment: *She is a fool to leave school when her grades are so high.* **Idiot** is used of someone acting as if he or she were totally feeble-minded: *She was such an idiot that she walked in the deep snow without her boots.* **Imbecile** is used of someone the speaker considers half-witted: *Look at that imbecile grinning at nothing.*

fool•er•y ['fuləri] *n., pl.* **-er•ies.** foolish action.

fool•har•dy ['ful,hɑrdi] *adj.* **-di•er, -di•est.** foolishly bold; rash. —**'fool,har•di•ness,** *n.* —**'fool,har•di•ly,** *adv.*

fool hen *Cdn.* any of various grouse, especially the spruce grouse, which has never learned to fear humans and therefore can be easily captured or killed. Fool hens have often been killed with a stick or stone.

fool•ish ['fulɪʃ] *adj.* **1** like a fool; without sense; unwise; silly. **2** ridiculous. **3** embarrassed; ashamed: *She made him feel foolish.* —**'fool•ish•ly,** *adv.* —**'fool•ish•ness,** *n.*

☛ *Syn.* **1. Foolish,** SILLY, FATUOUS = without sense. **Foolish** = like a fool, showing lack of common sense and judgment: *The foolish girl insists on having her own way.* **Silly** = seeming weakminded, doing and saying things without sense or point, often making oneself ridiculous: *It is silly to giggle at everything.* More contemptuous, **fatuous** = silly, empty-headed, and stupid, but also self-satisfied: *After his boring speech, the fatuous speaker waited for applause.*

fool•proof ['ful,pruf] *adj.* so safe or simple that even a fool can use or do it: *The car had a foolproof safety catch on the door.*

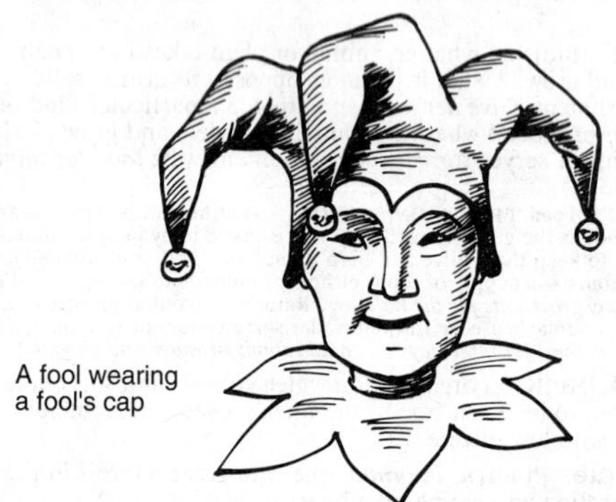
A fool wearing a fool's cap

fool's cap **1** a cap or hood worn by a fool or jester. **2** a dunce cap.

fools•cap ['fʊl,skæp] *n.* writing paper in sheets usually about 21 cm wide by 35 cm long. ⟨from the watermark⟩

fool's errand a foolish or useless undertaking.

fool's gold a mineral that looks like gold; iron pyrites or copper pyrites.

fool's paradise a condition of happiness based on false beliefs or hopes.

foot [fʊt] *n., pl.* **feet;** *v.* —*n.* **1** the end part of a leg; the part that a person, animal, or thing stands on. **2** the part near the feet; the end toward which the feet are put: *the foot of the bed.* **3** the lowest part; bottom; base. **4** the end opposite the head: *the foot of the table.* **5** the part of a stocking, etc. that covers the foot. **6** soldiers that go on foot; infantry. **7** a unit for measuring length, equal to 12 inches (30.48 cm). *Symbol:* ′ **8** *Prosody.* one of the metrical parts into which a line of verse is divided. *Example:* The boy | stood on | the burn | ing deck. This line has four feet. **9** the last of a list or series. **10** the part on a sewing machine that keeps the cloth in place. **11** the dregs in a liquid.
get or **have one's foot in the door,** *Informal.* be in a propitious position for success.
my foot! *Informal.* an interjection denoting strong scepticism: *Sick, my foot! He ran the marathon this morning.*
on foot, a standing or walking. **b** going on; in progress.
put (one's) **best foot forward,** *Informal.* **a** do one's best. **b** try to make a good impression.
put (one's) **foot down,** *Informal.* make up one's mind and act firmly.
put one's foot in one's mouth, say something unintentionally rude, tactless, or embarrassing.
put (one's) **foot in it,** *Informal.* get into trouble by meddling; blunder.
set foot on or **in,** enter; be in a particular location (*usually in the conditional or negative*): *I've never set foot in her apartment.*
under foot, a in the way. **b** in one's power; in subjection.
with one foot in the grave, almost dead; dying.
—*v.* **1** make or renew the foot of (a stocking, etc.). **2** walk. **3** dance. **4** add (*often with* **up**). **5** *Informal.* pay (a bill, etc.).
foot it, *Informal.* **a** travel on foot. **b** run. **c** dance. ⟨OE *fōt*⟩

foot•age ['fʊtɪdʒ] *n.* **1** the length in feet. **2** quantity of lumber expressed in board feet. **3** a quantity of film: *We shot some good footage today.* **4** film that has been processed: *some footage on the war.*

foot–and–mouth disease ['fʊt ən 'mʌuθ] a dangerous, contagious virus disease of cattle and some other animals, causing blisters in the mouth and around the hoofs.

foot•ball ['fʊt,bɒl] *n.* **1** an outdoor game played by two teams, in which each side tries to kick, pass, or carry a ball across the opposing team's goal line. Canadian and American football have different regulations with regard to size of field, number of players, number of downs, rules of play, etc. **2** the oval, air-filled, usually leather ball used in playing this game. **3** *Brit.* **a** soccer. **b** the round, air-filled, usually leather ball used in soccer; a soccer ball. **4** *Informal.* any subject of discussion that is passed around: *a political football.* —**'foot,ball•er,** *n.*

foot•board ['fʊt,bɔrd] *n.* **1** a board or small platform to be used as a support for the feet. **2** an upright piece across the foot of a bed.

foot brake a brake in a motor vehicle, operated by foot pressure.

foot•bridge ['fʊt,brɪdʒ] *n.* a bridge for pedestrians only.

foot–can•dle ['fʊt ,kændəl] *n. Optics.* a unit for measuring illumination, equal to about 10.8 lux. It is the amount of light produced by a standard candle at a distance of one foot (30.48 cm).

foot–dragging ['fʊt ,drægɪŋ] *n.* stalling; delay.

foot•ed ['fʊtɪd] *adj., v.* —*adj.* **1** having a foot or feet: *a footed wine glass.* **2** having a foot or feet of a specific kind, number, etc. (*used in compounds*): *swift-footed, flat-footed, a four-footed animal.*
—*v.* pt. and pp. of FOOT.

foot•er ['fʊtər] *n.* RUNNING FOOT. Compare HEADER (def. 7).

-footer *combining form.* a person or thing——feet in height or length: *six-footer = a person or thing six feet in height or length.*

foot•fall ['fʊt,fɒl] *n.* **1** the sound of steps coming or going. **2** footstep.

foot fault *Tennis.* a failure to keep both feet behind the base line when serving, or to keep one foot on the ground.

foot•gear ['fʊt,gir] *n.* shoes, boots, etc.

foot•hill ['fʊt,hɪl] *n.* a low hill at the base of a mountain or mountain range: *We visited a cattle ranch in the foothills of the Rockies.*

foot•hold ['fʊt,hould] *n.* **1** a place to put a foot; support for the feet; surface to stand on: *He climbed the steep cliff by finding footholds in cracks in the rock.* **2** a firm footing or position: *It is hard to break a habit that has gained a foothold.*

foot•ing ['fʊtɪŋ] *n., v.* —*n.* **1** a firm placing or position of the feet: *He lost his footing and fell down on the ice.* **2** the position of the feet: *When he changed his footing, he lost his balance.* **3** a place to put a foot; a support for the feet; surface to stand on: *The steep cliff gave us no footing.* **4** a firm place or position: *The newly rich family struggled for a footing in society.* **5** a basis of understanding; relationship: *Canada and the United States are on a friendly footing.* **6** an adding up. **7** the amount found by adding; sum; total. **8** the act of moving on the feet; walking, dancing, etc. **9** the manner of placing or using the feet; footwork. **10 footings,** *pl.* the concrete foundations of a building, wall, etc.
—*v.* ppr. of FOOT.

foot•less ['fʊtlɪs] *adj.* **1** without a foot or feet. **2** without support; not substantial. **3** *Informal.* awkward; helpless; inefficient. —**'foot•less•ly,** *adv.* —**'foot•less•ness,** *n.*

foot•let ['fʊtlɪt] *n.* a very short sock sometimes worn by women.

foot•lights ['fʊt,ləits] *n.pl.* **1** a row of lights on the floor at the front of a stage, now rarely used. **2** the profession of acting; the stage; theatre.

foot•lock•er ['fʊt,lɒkər] *n.* a small chest in which a soldier's personal belongings are kept, often at the foot of the bed.

foot•loose ['fʊt,lus] *adj. Informal.* free to go anywhere or do anything.

foot•man ['fʊtmən] *n., pl.* **-men. 1** a male servant who answers the bell, waits on table, goes with an automobile or carriage to open the door, etc. Footmen, who usually wear special uniforms, are now found mainly in royal palaces or great houses. **2** *Archaic.* FOOT SOLDIER.

foot•mark ['fʊt,mɑrk] *n.* footprint.

foot•note ['fʊt,nout] *n., v.* **-not•ed, -not•ing.** *–n.* **1** a note at the bottom of a page about something in the text. **2** *Informal.* a similar reference note placed at the end of a chapter or book. **3** a subsidiary comment or event: *He added as a footnote that his parents were in town. That battle was a mere footnote to World War I.*
–v. provide such an explanatory note: *Have you footnoted all references?*

foot•pace ['fʊt,peis] *n.* walking pace; speed of ordinary walking.

foot•pad ['fʊt,pæd] *n. Archaic.* a highway robber who goes on foot only.

foot•path ['fʊt,pæθ] *n.* a path for pedestrians only.

foot–pound ['fʊt ,paʊnd] *n.* in a non-metric system, a unit for measuring energy, equal to the energy needed to raise a weight of one pound to a height of one foot; about 1.36 J. *Abbrev.*: F.P., f.p., or fp

foot–pound–second ['fʊt 'paʊnd 'sɛkənd] *adj.* of or designating the non-metric measurement system. Length, mass, and time are expressed respectively in feet, pounds, and seconds.

foot•print ['fʊt,prɪnt] *n.* **1** the mark made by a foot. **2** a specification of something in terms of the area affected or occupied by it, as the space used by a computer system or the area covered by the downblast of a hovercraft.

foot•race ['fʊt,reis] *n.* a race run on foot, as distinguished from one on horseback, etc.

foot•rest ['fʊt,rɛst] *n.* a support on which to rest the feet.

foot rule a wooden or metal ruler one foot long.

foot•sie ['fʊtsi] *n. Informal.* foot (*especially a child's term*).
play footsie, *Informal.* **a** touch feet, knees, etc. in a flirtatious way, especially secretly while sitting at a table. **b** toy or flirt with, especially in a secretive or ambiguous way: *Some government MPs were playing footsie with the opposition.*

foot•slog ['fʊt,slɒg] *v.* **-slogged, -slog•ging.** march or plod, especially a long distance, or through or as through difficult terrain. **–'foot,slog•ger,** *n.*

foot soldier a soldier who fights on foot; member of the infantry.

foot•sore ['fʊt,sɔr] *adj.* having sore feet, especially from much walking.

foot•stalk ['fʊt,stɒk] *n.* **1** *Botany.* the stem of a leaf, flower, or flower cluster. **2** *Zoology.* a stemlike part of an animal, by which it is supported or attached to something; pedicel.

foot•step ['fʊt,stɛp] *n.* **1** a person's step. **2** the distance covered in one step. **3** the sound of steps coming or going. **4** the mark made by a foot; footprint. **5** a step on which to go up or down.
follow in someone's footsteps, do as another has done.

foot•stool ['fʊt,stul] *n.* a low stool on which to rest the feet when one is sitting in a chair, etc.

foot•way ['fʊt,wei] *n.* a path for pedestrians only; sidewalk.

foot•wear ['fʊt,wɛr] *n.* shoes, slippers, stockings, etc.

foot•work ['fʊt,wɜrk] *n.* the way of using the feet: *Footwork is important in boxing and dancing.*

foot•worn ['fʊt,wɔrn] *adj.* **1** worn by feet: *a footworn path.* **2** having tired feet.

foo•zle ['fuzəl] *v.* **-zled, -zling;** *n.*
–v. do clumsily; bungle (a golf stroke, etc.).
–n. a clumsy failure, especially a badly played stroke in golf. ⟨cf. dial. G *fuseln* work badly or slowly⟩

fop [fɒp] *n.* a vain man who is very fond of fine clothes and has affected manners; empty-headed dandy. ⟨< ME *foppe*⟩

fop•per•y ['fɒpəri] *n., pl.* **-per•ies.** foppish behaviour; fine clothes, affected manners, etc.

fop•pish ['fɒpɪʃ] *adj.* **1** of a fop; suitable for a fop. **2** vain; empty-headed; affected. **–'fop•pish•ly,** *adv.* **–'fop•pish•ness,** *n.*

for [fɔr]; *unstressed,* [fər] *prep., conj. –prep.* **1** as: *We used boxes for chairs. They know it for a fact. The navy trains people for sailors.* **2** in support of; in favour of: *She voted for Laurier.* **3** representing; in the interest of: *A lawyer acts for her client.* **4** in return for; in consideration of: *These apples are five for a dollar. We thanked him for his kindness.* **5** with the object or purpose of taking, achieving, keeping, or obtaining: *He went for a walk. She is looking for a job. He ran for his life.* **6** in order to get to: *She has just left for Toronto.* **7** meant to belong to or with, or to be used by or with; suited to: *a box for gloves, books for children, paper for drawing.* **8** because of; by reason of: *to shout for joy. He was punished for stealing.* **9** in honour of: *A party was given for her.* **10** with a feeling toward: *She has an eye for beauty. We longed for home.* **11** with respect or regard to: *Eating too much is bad for one's health.* **12** as far or as long as; throughout; during: *We walked for four kilometres. She worked for an hour.* **13** in spite of: *For all his faults, we like him still.* **14** in proportion to: *For every poisonous snake there are many harmless ones.* **15** in the amount of: *His father gave him a cheque for $20.* **16** considering what is typical of: *It is warm for April. She is tall for a ballet dancer.* **17** scheduled at or on: *I have a booking for the 5th. His appointment is for 2:30.*
for (one) **to,** that (one) will, should, must, etc.: *It is time for me to leave. For Ludmilla to keep going over there is a waste of time.*
Oh! for, I wish that I might have: *Oh! for the wings of a bird!*
–conj. because: *We can't go, for it is raining.* ⟨OE⟩
☛ *Hom.* FORE, FOUR.
☛ *Usage.* **For.** A comma is usually needed between two co-ordinate clauses joined by **for;** without it the **for** might be read as a preposition: *He was glad to go, for Mrs. Crane had been especially good to him.* (not: *He was glad to go for Mrs. Crane....*)
☛ *Syn.* See another note at BECAUSE.

for– *prefix.* away; opposite; completely: *forbid, forswear.* ⟨OE⟩

for. **1** foreign. **2** forestry.

for•age ['fɔrɪdʒ] *n., v.* **-aged, -ag•ing.** *–n.* **1** food for horses, cattle, etc. **2** the act of hunting or searching for anything, especially food: *We went on a forage for supplies.*
–v. **1** supply with food; feed. **2** hunt or search for anything, especially food: *The girls foraged in the kitchen till they found some cookies. The man made a living by foraging for old metal.* **3** get by hunting or searching about. **4** get or take food from. **5** plunder: *The soldiers foraged the villages near their camp.* ⟨ME < OF *fourrager* < *fuerre* fodder < Gmc.⟩ **–'for•ag•er,** *n.*

fo•ra•men [fɔ'reimən] *n., pl.* **-ra•mens** [-'reimənz], **-ram•i•na** [-'ræmənə]. *Biology.* a small hole or hollow, especially a natural cavity in a bone. ⟨< L⟩ **–fo'ram•i•nal,** *adj.*

foramen magnum the large opening at the base of the skull to allow space for the spinal cord to pass through. ⟨< NL; literally, great hole⟩

for•a•min•i•fer [,fɔrə'mɪnəfər] *n.* any of an order (Foraminifera) of protozoans having a calcareous shell that in many species has many tiny holes through which slender processes protrude for locomotion and feeding. ⟨< NL < L *foramen* a small opening + *ferre* bear⟩ **–fo,ram•i'nif•er•al** [fɔ,ræmə'nɪfərəl] or **fo,ram•i'nif•er•ous,** *adj.*

for•as•much as [,fɔrəz'mʌtʃ] in view of the fact that; because; since.

for•ay ['fɔrei] *n., v. –n.* a raid for plunder.
–v. plunder; lay waste; pillage. ⟨ME < OF *fourrier* < *fuerre* fodder. See FORAGE.⟩

forb [fɔrb] *n.* any herb that is not grass. ⟨< Gk. *phorbe* fodder +*pherbein* to feed, graze⟩

for•bade [fər'bæd] *or* [fər'beid] *v.* pt. of FORBID. Also, **forbad.**

for•bear¹ [fɔr'bɛr] *v.* **-bore, -borne, -bear•ing. 1** hold back; keep from (doing, saying, using, etc.); refrain from: *The boy forbore to hit back because the other boy was smaller. She forbore comment. He forbore lecturing her on her behaviour.* **2** be patient; control oneself. ⟨OE *forberan*⟩ **–for'bear•er,** *n.* **–for'bear•ing•ly,** *adv.*
☛ *Usage.* **Forbear** (def. 1) may be followed by an infinitive, by a gerund, or by a noun denoting an action. When used in the sense of def. 2, it usually takes the form of a participial adjective: *He was a gentle, forbearing old man.*

for•bear² ['fɔr,bɛr] See FOREBEAR.

for•bear•ance [fɔr'bɛrəns] *n.* **1** the act of forbearing. **2** patience; self-control.
☛ *Syn.* **2.** See note at PATIENCE.

for•bid [fər'bɪd] *v.* **-bade** or **-bad, -bid•den** or **-bid, -bid•ding. 1** order (someone) not to do something. **2** make a rule against (something); prohibit. **3** keep from happening; prevent: *God forbid!* **4** command to keep away from; exclude from: *I forbid you the house.* ⟨OE *forbēodan*⟩

☛ *Syn.* **1, 2. Forbid,** PROHIBIT = order not to do something. **Forbid** = give an order, often directly or personally, or make a rule that something must not be done, and suggests that obedience is expected: *His mother forbade him to smoke.* **Prohibit** is formal, and means 'to make a formal regulation against something', usually by law or official action, and suggests power to enforce it: *Smoking is often prohibited in theatres.*

for•bid•den [fər'bɪdən] *adj., v.* *—adj.* not allowed; against the law or rules.
—v. pp. of FORBID.

forbidden fruit any pleasure that is prohibited.

for•bid•ding [fər'bɪdɪŋ] *adj., v.* *—adj.* **1** causing fear or dislike; hostile; grim: *The enemy soldier's look was forbidding.* **2** looking dangerous or unpleasant; threatening: *The coast was rocky and forbidding.*
—v. ppr. of FORBID. **—for'bid•ding•ly,** *adv.*
—for'bid•ding•ness, *n.*

for•bore [fɔr'bɔr] *v.* pt. of FORBEAR¹.

for•borne [fɔr'bɔrn] *v.* pp. of FORBEAR¹.

force [fɔrs] *n., v.* **forced, forc•ing.** *—n.* **1** active power or strength; energy: *the force of running water.* **2** strength used against a person or thing; violence or constraint: *to rule by force. The rebels took the village by force.* **3** the power to control, influence, persuade, convince, etc.; effectiveness; vividness: *force of character. She writes with force.* **4** a group of people working or acting together: *our office force.* **5** a body of persons organized for or assigned to a military or policing function. **6 forces,** *pl.* the whole military strength of a nation or state; armed forces. **7** *Physics.* any cause that produces, changes, or stops the motion of a body. **8** an agency, influence, or source of power likened to a physical force: *social forces.* **9** the precise meaning or import (of a word, etc.): *What is the force of that question?* **10** binding power; validity, as of a law or contract: *The force of some laws has to be tested in court.*
by force of, by means of: *by force of argument.*
in force, a in effect or operation; binding; valid. **b** with full strength or in great numbers: *The press turned out in force to the news conference.*
—v. **1** use force on. **2** make or drive (someone) to do something by force. **3** get or take by force. **4** put by force. **5** impose or impress by force: *to force one's views on another.* **6** break open or through by force. **7** overpower by force. **8** urge to violent effort. **9** make by an unusual or unnatural effort; strain. **10** hurry the growth or development of, by unnatural or artificial means: *He forced his rhubarb by growing it in a dark, warm place.* **11** *Baseball.* compel (a player) to leave one base and try in vain to reach the next.
force in, *Baseball.* of a pitcher, cause (a run) to be scored by issuing a walk when the bases are loaded: *He forced in a run in the bottom of the ninth.* ⟨< F, ult. < L *fortis* strong⟩ **—'force•less,** *adj.* **—'forc•er,** *n.*

☛ *Syn. n.* **1.** See note at POWER.

forced [fɔrst] *adj., v.* *—adj.* **1** made, compelled, or driven by force: *The work of slaves is forced labour.* **2** made by an unusual or unnatural effort: *She hid her dislike for him with a forced smile.* **3** brought about by emergency: *a forced landing.*
—v. pt. and pp. of FORCE. **—for•ced•ly** ['fɔrsədli], *adv.*

forced march an unusually long, fast march.

force–feed ['fɔrs ˌfid] *v.* **-fed, -feed•ing. 1** feed (an animal or person) by forcible means, as by passing a tube through the mouth into the stomach: *Geese were formerly often fattened by force-feeding.* **2** force (someone) to accept or take in (ideas, etc.).

force•ful ['fɔrsfəl] *adj.* full of force; strong; powerful; vigorous; effective: *a forceful manner.* **—'force•ful•ly,** *adv.* **—'force•ful•ness,** *n.*

☛ *Syn.* **Forceful,** FORCIBLE. Both terms mean 'showing force, powerful', but only **forcible** (def. 1) means 'done with force, or violence': *a forceful style* but *a forcible entry.*

force majeure ['fɔrs ma'ʒɜr] *Law.* any event that may allow a party to break a contract. ⟨< F; literally, superior force⟩

force•meat ['fɔrs,mit] *n.* chopped and seasoned meat, used for stuffing, etc. ⟨< *force,* var. of obs. *farce* stuffing + *meat*⟩

force–out ['fɔrs ˌʌut] *n. Baseball.* a means of getting a batter out when he or she has been forced to leave the previous base, and does not get to the next base before the ball does.

force play *Baseball.* a rule which forces a base runner to run to the next base when the batter hits the ball and is not caught out.

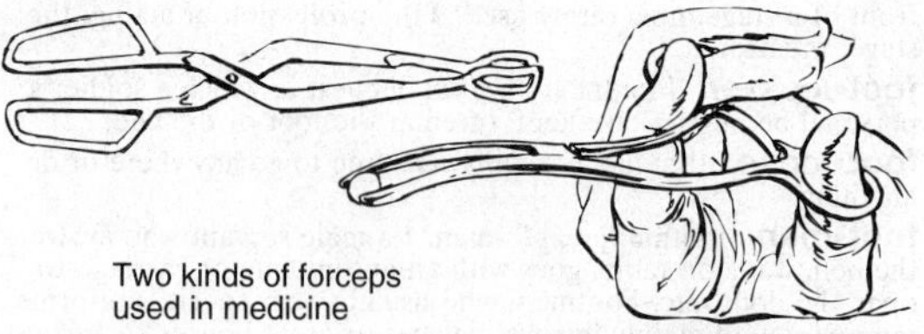

Two kinds of forceps used in medicine

for•ceps ['fɔrsɛps] *or* ['fɔrsəps] *n., pl.* **-ceps.** a pair of small pincers or tongs used by surgeons, dentists, etc. for seizing, holding, and pulling. ⟨< L *forceps* < *formus* hot + *capere* take⟩

force pump a pump with a valveless piston whose action forces liquid through a pipe; any pump which delivers liquid under pressure.

for•ci•ble ['fɔrsəbəl] *adj.* **1** made or done by force; using force: *a forcible entry into a house.* **2** having or showing force; strong; powerful; effective; convincing: *a forcible speaker.* **—'for•ci•ble•ness,** *n.* **—'for•ci•bly,** *adv.*

☛ *Syn.* See note at FORCEFUL.

ford [fɔrd] *n., v.* *—n.* a place where a river or stream is shallow enough to be crossed by walking or driving through the water.
—v. cross (a river, etc.) by walking or driving through the water: *They spent an hour looking for a place to ford the river.* ⟨OE⟩
—'ford•a•ble, *adj.*

for•done [fɔr'dʌn] *adj. Archaic.* worn out; exhausted. Also, **foredone.**

fore¹ [fɔr] *adj., adv., n.* *—adj. or adv.* at the front; toward the beginning or front; forward.
—n. the forward part; front, especially of a ship or boat.
to the fore, a in or into full view; in or into a conspicuous place or position. **b** at hand; ready. **c** alive. ⟨adj. < *fore-*; adv. < OE⟩

☛ *Hom.* FOR, FOUR.

fore² [fɔr] *interj. Golf.* a shout of warning to persons ahead on the fairway who are liable to be struck by the ball. ⟨? for *before*⟩

☛ *Hom.* FOR, FOUR.

fore– *prefix.* **1** front; in front; at or near the front, as in *forecastle, foremast.* **2** before; beforehand, as in *foreknow, foresee.* ⟨OE *fore* before⟩

fore–and–aft ['fɔr ənd 'æft] *or* ['fɔr ən 'æft] *adj., adv. Nautical.* lengthwise on a ship; from bow to stern; placed lengthwise. A ship rigged fore-and-aft has the sails set lengthwise.

fore•arm¹ ['fɔr,ɑrm] *n.* the part of the arm between the elbow and wrist.

fore•arm² [fɔr'ɑrm] *v.* prepare for trouble ahead of time; arm beforehand.

fore•bear ['fɔr,bɛr] *n.* an ancestor; forefather. Also, **forbear.** ⟨< *fore-* + *be* + *-er¹*⟩

fore•bode [fɔr'boud] *v.* **-bod•ed, -bod•ing. 1** give warning of; predict: *Black clouds forebode a storm.* **2** have a feeling that something bad is going to happen. **—fore'bod•er,** *n.*

fore•bod•ing [fɔr'boudɪŋ] *n., adj., v.* *—n.* **1** a prediction; warning. **2** a feeling that something bad is going to happen: *As the lights went out, we were filled with foreboding.*
—adj. warning; threatening: *The big dog gave a foreboding growl.*
—v. ppr. of FOREBODE. **—for'bod•ing•ly,** *adv.*

fore•brain ['fɔr,brein] *n. Anatomy.* the front section of the brain, consisting of the cerebrum, the pituitary gland, and the pineal body.

fore•cast ['fɔr,kæst] *v.* **-cast** or **-cast•ed, -cast•ing;** *n.* *—v.* **1** prophesy; predict: *Cooler weather is forecast for tomorrow.* **2** be a prophecy or prediction of. **3** foresee; plan ahead. **4** make a forecast.
—n. **1** a prophecy; prediction. **2** a planning ahead; foresight.
—'fore,cast•er, *n.*

fore•cas•tle ['fouksəl] *or* ['fɔr,kæsəl] *n. Nautical.* **1** the upper deck in front of the foremast of a ship or boat. **2** the sailors' quarters in a merchant ship, formerly in the forward part of the ship.

fore•check ['fɔr,tʃɛk] *v. Cdn. Hockey.* check an opposing player in his or her own defensive zone, to prevent the opposing team from organizing an attack. **—'fore,check•er,** *n.*

fore•check•ing ['fɔr,tʃɛkɪŋ] *n. Cdn. Hockey.* the practice or skill of one who forechecks.

fore•close [fɔr'klouz] *v.* **-closed, -clos•ing. 1** shut out; prevent; exclude. **2** *Law.* **a** take away the right to redeem (a mortgage): *When the conditions of a mortgage are not met, the* *holder can foreclose and have the property sold to satisfy his claim.* **b** take away the right of (a mortgager) to redeem his or her property. **c** establish an exclusive claim to. ⟨ME < OF *forclos*, pp. of *forclore* exclude < *for-* out (< L *foris*) + *clore* shut < L *claudere*⟩ **—fore'clos•a•ble,** *adj.*

fore•clo•sure [fɔr'klouʒər] *n.* the foreclosing of a mortgage.

fore•court ['fɔr,kɔrt] *n.* **1** an enclosed space in front of a building. **2** *Tennis, badminton, basketball, etc.* the area at the front of the court, especially the area near the net.

fore•deck ['fɔr,dɛk] *n. Nautical.* the forepart of a weather deck; the bow end of the main deck.

fore•done [fɔr'dʌn] *adj. or v. Archaic.* See FORDONE.

fore•doom [fɔr'dum] *v.* doom beforehand.

fore•fa•ther ['fɔr,fɒðər] *n.* ancestor.

fore•feel [fɔr,fil] *v.,* **-felt, -feel•ing.** perceive beforehand; experience a foreboding.

fore•fend [fɔr'fɛnd] *v.* See FORFEND.

fore•fin•ger ['fɔr,fɪŋgər] *n.* the finger next to the thumb; first finger; index finger. See ARM for picture.

fore•foot ['fɔr,fʊt] *n., pl.* **-feet. 1** one of the front feet of an animal. **2** *Nautical.* the forward end of a ship's keel, where the stem of the hull joins the keel.

fore•front ['fɔr,frʌnt] *n.* **1** the place of greatest importance, activity, etc. **2** foremost part.

fore•gath•er [fɔr'gæðər] See FORGATHER.

fore•go[1] [fɔr'gou] *v.* **-went, -gone, -go•ing.** See FORGO. **—fore'go•er,** *n.*

fore•go[2] [fɔr'gou] *v.* **-went, -gone, -go•ing.** precede; go before. ⟨OE *foregān*⟩ **—fore'go•er,** *n.*

fore•go•ing ['fɔr,gouɪŋ] *adj., n., v. —adj.* preceding; previous.
—n. **the foregoing,** that which has already been referred to.
—v. ppr. of FOREGO.

fore•gone [fɔr'gɒn] *adj., v. —adj.* that has gone before; previous.
—v. pp. of FOREGO.

foregone conclusion a fact or result that was expected with certainty; inevitable result: *It was a foregone conclusion that there would be traffic jams while the road was being repaired.*

fore•ground ['fɔr,graʊnd] *n.* the part of a picture or scene nearest the observer; part toward the front.
in the foreground, conspicuous; the focus of attention.

fore•hand ['fɔr,hænd] *adj., n., adv. —adj.* made with the palm of the hand turned forward.
—n. **1** *Tennis, etc.* a stroke made with the palm of the hand turned forward. **2** a position in front or above; advantage. **3** the half of a horse in front of a rider astride.
—adv. **1** in a forehand motion: *She threw me the ball forehand.* **2** at the forefront: *He kept that thought forehand in his thinking.*

fore•hand•ed ['fɔr'hændɪd] *adj.* **1** providing for the future; prudent; thrifty. **2** done beforehand; early; timely. **3** forehand. **—'fore'hand•ed•ness,** *n.*

fore•head ['fɔr,hɛd] *or* ['fɔrɪd] *n.* **1** the part of the face above the eyes. **2** a front part. ⟨OE *forhēafod*⟩

for•eign ['fɔrɪn] *adj.* **1** outside one's own country: *She has travelled much in foreign countries.* **2** of, characteristic of, or coming from outside one's own country: *a foreign ship, a foreign language, foreign money.* **3** having to do with other countries; carried on or dealing with other countries: *foreign trade.* **4** not belonging; not related: *Sitting still all day is foreign to a healthy girl's nature.* **5** not related to the matter that is being discussed or considered. **6** *Law.* falling outside the jurisdiction of a particular country. **7** not belonging naturally to the place where found: *a foreign object in the eye, a foreign substance in the blood.* ⟨ME < OF *forain,* ult. < L *foras* outside⟩ **—'for•eign•ness,** *n.*

foreign affairs a country's relations with other countries.

for•eign–born ['fɔrɪn 'bɔrn] *adj.* born in another country.

foreign correspondent a journalist or radio or television reporter who sends news from the foreign country where he or she is based.

for•eign•er ['fɔrənər] *n.* **1** a person from another country; alien. **2** *Informal.* a person strange to one's own customs, ideas, etc. **3** a foreign ship.

foreign exchange 1 the settling of debts between residents of different countries. **2** the foreign currency, bills of exchange, etc., used to settle such debts. **3** a place, such as in an airport, where one can change one's money into a foreign currency: *Could you please direct me to the foreign exchange?*

Foreign Office *Brit.* the government department in charge of foreign affairs.

fore•judge [fɔr'dʒʌdʒ] *v.* **-judged, -judg•ing.** judge beforehand.

fore•knew [fɔr'nju] *or* [fɔr'nu] *v.* pt. of FOREKNOW.

fore•know [fɔr'nou] *v.* **-knew, -known, -know•ing.** know beforehand.

fore•knowl•edge [fɔr'nɒlɪdʒ] *or* ['fɔr,nɒlɪdʒ] *n.* knowledge of a thing before it happens.

fore•known [fɔr'noun] *v.* pp. of FOREKNOW.

fore•land ['fɔr,lænd] *or* ['fɔrlənd] *n.* a cape; headland; promontory.

fore•leg ['fɔr,lɛg] *n.* one of the front legs of an animal.

fore•lock ['fɔr,lɒk] *n.* a lock of hair that grows just above the forehead.
take time by the forelock, act promptly.

fore•man ['fɔrmən] *n., pl.* **-men. 1** the person in charge of a group of workers or of some part of a factory. **2** the chair of a jury.

fore•mast ['fɔr,mæst] *or* ['fɔrməst] *n. Nautical.* the mast nearest the bow. See MAST and SCHOONER for pictures.

fore•men•tioned ['fɔr,mɛnʃənd] *or* [fɔr'mɛnʃənd] *adj.* mentioned previously; aforementioned.

fore•most ['fɔr,moust] *adj., adv. —adj.* **1** first. **2** chief; leading; most notable.
—adv. **1** first: *He stumbled and fell head foremost.* **2** in the first place; firstly: *First and foremost, we must protect the population from this hazard.* ⟨OE *formest*; double superlative of *forma* first, superlative of *fore* before⟩

fore•name ['fɔr,neim] *n.* a person's first name.

fore•named ['fɔr,neimd] *adj.* aforementioned.

fore•noon ['fɔr,nun] *n., adj. —n.* the time between early morning and noon.
—adj. between early morning and noon.

fo•ren•sic [fə'rɛnsɪk] *adj., n. —adj.* **1** of or suitable for a law court or public debate. **2** of or having to do with the application of medical and other science to police work.
—n. a spoken or written exercise in argumentation, as in a college or high-school class in speech or rhetoric. ⟨< L *forensis* < *forum* forum⟩

forensic medicine the application of medical science to problems of law; medical jurisprudence.

fore•or•dain [,fɔrɔr'dein] *v.* ordain beforehand; predestine.

fore•or•di•na•tion [,fɔrɔrdə'neiʃən] *n.* an ordaining beforehand; predestination.

fore•part ['fɔr,pɑrt] *n.* the front part.

fore•paw ['fɔr,pɒ] *n.* a front paw.

fore•peak ['fɔr,pik] *n. Nautical.* the forward part of a ship's hull.

fore•piece ['fɔr,pis] *n.* the front or first piece of something.

fore•play ['fɔr,plei] *n.* the period of mutual sexual activity preceding intercourse.

fore•quar•ter ['fɔr,kwɔrtər] *n.* **1** a front leg, shoulder, and nearby ribs of beef, lamb, pork, etc.; front quarter. **2** FORECASTLE (def. 1). **3** FORECASTLE (def. 2). **4 forequarters,** *pl.* the front part of a horse, etc., including the front legs.

fore•ran [fɔr'ræn] *v.* pt. of FORERUN.

fore•reach [fɔr'ritʃ] *v.* **1** move ahead quickly, as a ship does after coming into the wind. **2** move ahead of; pass. **3** get the better of.

fore•run [fɔr'rʌn] *v.* **-ran, -run, -run•ning. 1** precede. **2** be a sign or warning of (something to come). **3** forestall.

fore•run•ner ['fɔr,rʌnər] *n.* **1** a person going before or sent before to show that someone or something else is coming; herald. **2** a sign or warning of something to come: *Black clouds are often the forerunners of a storm.* **3** a predecessor; ancestor.

fore•sail ['fɔr,seil] *or* ['fɔrsəl] *n. Nautical.* **1** the principal sail on the foremast of a schooner. **2** the lowest sail on the foremast of a square-rigged ship. **3** JIB[1].

fore•saw [fɔr'sɒ] *v.* pt. of FORESEE.

fore•see [fɔr'si] *v.* **-saw, -seen, -see•ing.** see or know beforehand: *Mother put up a big picnic lunch, because she foresaw* *how hungry we would be.* ⟨OE *foresēon*⟩ **—fore'see•a•ble,** *adj.* **—fore'see•a•bly,** *adv.* **—for'se•er,** *n.*

fore•seen [fɔr'sin] *v.* pp. of FORESEE.

fore•shad•ow [fɔr'ʃædou] *v.* **1** indicate beforehand; be or give a warning of: *Black clouds foreshadow a storm. The author carefully foreshadows the tragic end.* **2** PREFIGURE (def. 1). **—fore'shad•ow•ing,** *n.*

fore•shank ['fɔr,ʃæŋk] *n.* the upper part of the foreleg of an animal, or a cut of meat from this part.

fore•sheet ['fɔr,ʃit] *n. Nautical.* **1** one of the ropes used to hold a foresail in place. **2 foresheets,** *pl.* the space in the forward part of an open boat.

fore•shore ['fɔr,ʃɔr] *n.* **1** the part of the shore between the high-water mark and low-water mark. **2** the part of the shore nearest the water.

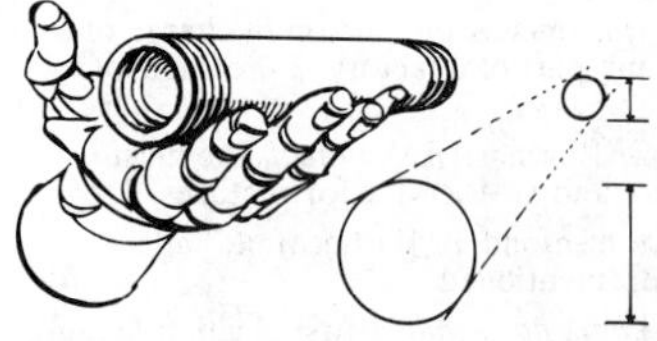

In perspective drawing, the shortening and converging of lines as they appear to recede from the viewer to give the illusion of distance

fore•short•en [fɔr'ʃɔrtən] *v.* **1** in a drawing or painting, represent (lines, etc.) as of less than true length in order to give the proper impression to the eye. **2** abridge; condense. **—fore'short•en•ing,** *n.*

fore•show [fɔr'ʃou] *v.* **-showed, -shown, -show•ing.** show beforehand; foretell; foreshadow. ⟨OE *forescēawian*⟩

fore•shown [fɔr'ʃoun] *v.* pp. of FORESHOW.

fore•side ['fɔr,saɪd] *n.* **1** the front. **2** the upper side.

fore•sight ['fɔr,səit] *n.* **1** the power to see or realize beforehand what is likely to happen. **2** careful thought for the future; prudence. **3** a looking ahead; a view into the future.
☛ *Syn.* **2.** See note at PRUDENCE.

fore•sight•ed ['fɔr,səitɪd] *adj.* having or showing foresight. **—'fore,sight•ed•ness,** *n.* **—'fore,sight•ed•ly,** *adv.*

fore•skin ['fɔr,skɪn] *n.* the fold of skin that covers the end of the penis; prepuce.

for•est ['fɔrɪst] *n., v.* *—n.* **1** a large area of land covered with trees; thick woods; woodland. **2** the trees themselves. **3** (*adjl.*) of or in a forest: *forest fires.*
—v. plant with many trees; make into a forest. ⟨ME < OF *forest,* ult. < L *foris* out of doors⟩ **—'for•est•less,** *adj.*

fore•stage ['fɔr,steidʒ] *n.* that part of a proscenium stage which is in front of the curtain.

fore•stall [fɔr'stɒl] *v.* **1** prevent by acting first: *The mayor forestalled a riot by having the police ready.* **2** deal with (a thing) in advance; anticipate; be ahead of. **3** buy up goods, etc. in (a market) in advance in order to increase the price. ⟨ME *forstalle(n)* < OE *foresteall* prevention⟩ **—fore'stall•er,** *n.*

for•est•a•tion [,fɔrə'steiʃən] *n.* the planting or taking care of forests.

fore•stay ['fɔr,stei] *n. Nautical.* the rope or cable reaching from the top of a ship's foremast to the bowsprit. The forestay helps to support the foremast.

for•est•ed ['fɔrəstɪd] *adj., v.* *—adj.* covered with trees.
—v. pt. and pp. of FOREST.

for•est•er ['fɔrəstər] *n.* **1** a person trained in forestry, especially one whose work it is. **2** FOREST RANGER. **3** a person, bird, or animal that lives in a forest. **4** a green or black moth of the family Agaristidae.

forest goat a goat (*Pseudoryx mgetinhensis*) found in Vietnam. Also called **spindle horn.** ⟨loan translation from Vietnamese⟩

forest preserve a forest protected by the government from wasteful cutting, fires, etc.

forest ranger a government official in charge of patrolling and guarding a public forest or section of forest and its wildlife.

for•est•ry ['fɔrəstri] *n.* the science and art of cultivating, caring for, managing, and utilizing forests.

fore•taste *n.* ['fɔr,teist]; *v.* [fɔr'teist] *n., v.* **-tast•ed, -tast•ing.** *—n.* a preliminary taste; anticipation: *The boy got a foretaste of business life by working during his vacation.*
—v. have a foretaste of.

fore•tell [fɔr'tɛl] *v.* **-told, -tell•ing.** tell or show beforehand; predict; prophesy: *Who can foretell what a baby will do next?* **—fore'tell•er,** *n.*

fore•thought ['fɔr,θɒt] *n.* **1** previous thought or consideration; planning. **2** careful thought for the future; prudence; foresight: *A little forethought will often prevent mistakes.*

fore•to•ken *v.* [fɔr'toukən]; *n.* ['fɔr,toukən] *—v.* indicate beforehand; be an omen of.
—n. an indication of something to come; omen. ⟨OE *foretācn*⟩

fore•told [fɔr'tould] *v.* pt. and pp. of FORETELL.

fore•top ['fɔr,tɒp] *or* ['fɔrtəp] *n. Nautical.* a platform at the top of the foremast.

fore–top•gal•lant [,fɔr tɒp'gælənt] *or* [,fɔr tə'gælənt] *adj. Nautical.* of or being the mast, sail, yard, etc. next above the fore-topmast.

fore–top•mast [,fɔr 'tɒp,mæst] *or* [,fɔr 'tɒpməst] *n. Nautical.* the mast next above the foremast.

fore–top•sail [,fɔr 'tɒp,seil] *or* [,fɔr 'tɒpsəl] *n. Nautical.* the sail set on the fore-topmast and next above the foresail.

for•ev•er [fə'rɛvər] *or* [fɔr'ɛvər] *adv., n.* *—adv.* **1** for always; without ever coming to an end. **2** *Informal.* all the time; always: *That person is forever talking.*
—n. Informal. an excessively long time; an eternity: *She is taking forever to write that book.*

for•ev•er•more [fə,rɛvər'mɔr] *or* [fɔr,ɛvər'mɔr] *adv.* forever.

fore•warn [fɔr'wɔrn] *v.* warn beforehand: *The dark clouds forewarned us of a thunderstorm.*

fore•went [fɔr'wɛnt] *v.* pt. of FOREGO.

fore•wing ['fɔr,wɪŋ] *n.* the front wing of an insect.

fore•wom•an ['fɔr,wʊmən] *n., pl.* **-wom•en. 1** a woman who supervises a group of workers, as in a factory, etc. **2** a chairwoman of a jury.

fore•word ['fɔr,wərd] *n.* a short preface to a book or other writing, especially an introductory note on the work of the author by a distinguished writer, scholar, public figure, etc.
☛ *Syn.* See note at INTRODUCTION.

for•feit ['fɔrfɪt] *v., n., adj.* *—v.* lose or have to give up as a penalty for some act, neglect, fault, etc.: *He forfeited his deposit when he lost the library book.*
—n. **1** something lost or given up because of some act, neglect, or fault; penalty; fine: *A headache was the forfeit she paid for staying up late.* **2** the loss or giving up of something as a penalty. **3 forfeits,** a children's game in which the loser forfeits something.
—adj. lost or given up as a penalty; forfeited. ⟨ME < OF *forfait* < *forfaire* transgress < *for-* wrongly (< L *foris* outside) + *faire* do < L *facere*⟩ **—'for•feit•a•ble,** *adj.* **—'for•feit•er,** *n.*

for•fei•ture ['fɔrfətʃər] *n.* **1** the loss or giving up of something as a penalty; a forfeiting. **2** the thing forfeited; penalty; fine.

for•fend [fɔr'fɛnd] *v. Archaic.* ward off; avert; prevent: *Heaven forfend!* Also, **forefend.**

for•fi•cate ['fɔrfəkɪt] *or* ['fɔrfɪ,keit] *adj.* of the tails of certain birds, jagged or forked. ⟨< L *forfex, forficis* pair of shears + *-ate*⟩

for•gath•er [fɔr'gæðər] *v.* **1** gather together; assemble; meet. **2** meet by accident. **3** be friendly; associate (*with*). Also, **foregather.**

for•gave [fər'geiv] *v.* pt. of FORGIVE.

forge¹ [fɔrdʒ] *n., v.* **forged, forg•ing.** *—n.* **1** a furnace or open fireplace where metal is heated to a high temperature before being hammered into shape: *The blacksmith took the white-hot horseshoe out of the forge.* **2** a blacksmith's shop; smithy. **3** a place where iron or other metal is melted and refined.
—v. **1** heat (metal) to a high temperature and then hammer it into shape. **2** make; shape or form: *They forged a strong and lasting friendship.* **3** make or write a fraudulent or counterfeit imitation of: *to forge a signature. The supposed will of the dead woman had been forged.* **4** make a fraudulent imitation of another person's signature on (a cheque, etc.): *He was sent to jail for forging cheques.* **5** commit forgery. ⟨ME < OF *forge,* ult. < L *fabrica* workshop. Doublet of FABRIC.⟩ **—'forg•er,** *n.*

forge² [fɔrdʒ] *v.* **forged, forg•ing.** move forward slowly but steadily: *to forge ahead.* ⟨origin uncertain⟩

for•ger•y ['fɔrdʒəri] *n., pl.* **-ger•ies. 1** the act of forging a signature, etc. **2** something made or written falsely to deceive: *The painting was a forgery. The signature on the cheque was not mine but a forgery.*

for•get [fər'gɛt] *v.* **-got, -got•ten** or **-got, -get•ting. 1** let go out of the mind; fail to remember; be unable to remember: *I couldn't introduce her because I had forgotten her name.* **2** omit or neglect without meaning to: *She said she would not forget to send him a postcard.* **3** leave behind unintentionally: *She had to return home because she had forgotten her purse.* **4** put aside: *Let's forget our quarrel.*
forget it, *Informal.* **a** don't concern yourself about this. **b** absolutely not.
forget oneself, a not think of oneself and one's interests; be unselfish. **b** fail to consider what one should do or be; say or do something improper: *He forgot himself and blurted out the name.* ⟨OE *forgietan* < *for-* (opposite) + ON *geta* get⟩ **—for'get•ta•ble,** *adj.* **—for'get•ter,** *n.*

for•get•ful [fər'gɛtfəl] *adj.* **1** apt to forget; having a poor memory. **2** heedless: *forgetful of danger.* **3** *Poetic.* causing to forget: *forgetful slumbers.* **—for'get•ful•ly,** *adv.* **—for'get•ful•ness,** *n.*

for•get–me–not [fər'gɛt mi ˌnɒt] *n.* **1** any of a genus (*Myosotis*) of low-growing herbs of the borage family having blue or white flowers. Some species are cultivated as garden flowers. **2** the flower of this plant.

forg•ing ['fɔrdʒɪŋ] *n., v.* *—n.* something forged; a piece of metal that has been forged.
—v. ppr. of FORGE.

for•give [fər'gɪv] *v.* **-gave, -giv•en, -giv•ing. 1** give up the wish to punish or get even with; pardon; excuse; not have hard feelings about or toward. **2** give up all claim to; not demand payment for: *to forgive a debt.* ⟨OE *forgiefan* < *for-* away + *giefan* give⟩ **—for'giv•a•ble,** *adj.* **—for'giv•a•bly,** *adv.*
☛ *Syn.* **1.** See note at EXCUSE.

for•giv•en [fər'gɪvən] *v.* pp. of FORGIVE.

for•give•ness [fər'gɪvnɪs] *n.* **1** the act of forgiving; pardon. **2** willingness to forgive.

for•giv•ing [fər'gɪvɪŋ] *adj., v.* *—adj.* that forgives; willing to forgive.
—v. ppr. of FORGIVE. **—for'giv•ing•ly,** *adv.* **—for'giv•ing•ness,** *n.*

for•go [fɔr'gou] *v.* **-went, -gone, -go•ing.** do without; give up: *She decided to forgo the movies and do her essay.*

for•gone [fɔr'gɒn] *v.* pp. of FORGO.

for•got [fər'gɒt] *v.* a pt. and a pp. of FORGET.

for•got•ten [fər'gɒtən] *v.* a pp. of FORGET.

for•int ['fɔrɪnt] *n.* **1** the basic unit of money in Hungary, divided into 100 fillér. See money table in the Appendix. **2** a coin worth one forint. ⟨< Hungarian *forint,* prob. < Ital. *fiorino* florin⟩

fork [fɔrk] *n., v.* *—n.* **1** an instrument having a handle and two or more long, pointed prongs, or tines, at one end: *a table fork, a garden fork.* **2** anything shaped like a fork, such as a tuning fork or a divining rod. **3** the place where a tree, road, or stream divides into two branches: *They parted at the fork of the road.* **4** one of the branches into which any such thing is divided.
—v. **1** lift, throw, or dig with a fork. **2** make in the shape or form of a fork. **3** have a fork or forks; divide into branches. **4** *Chess.* threaten (two chess pieces) with one move.
fork up, out or **over,** *Slang.* hand over; pay out. ⟨OE *forca* < L *furca*⟩ **—'fork•less,** *adj.* **—'forkˌlike,** *adj.*

forked [fɔrkt]; *archaic or poetic,* ['fɔrkɪd] *adj., v.* *—adj.* **1** having a fork or forks; divided into branches. **2** zigzag: *forked lightning.*
speak with a forked tongue, speak untruths; tell lies.
—v. pt. and pp. of FORK.

fork•lift ['fɔrkˌlɪft] *n., v.* *—n.* a self-propelled vehicle having a power-operated horizontal forklike device that can be raised and lowered for lifting and moving heavy objects.
—v. lift with a forklift.

for•lorn [fɔr'lɔrn] *adj.* **1** left alone; neglected; deserted: *The lost kitten, a forlorn little animal, was wet and dirty.* **2** wretched in feeling or looks; unhappy. **3** hopeless; desperate. **4** bereft (*of*): *forlorn of hope.* ⟨OE *forloren* lost, pp. of *forlēosan*⟩ **—for'lorn•ly,** *adv.* **—for'lorn•ness,** *n.*

forlorn hope 1 a desperate enterprise. **2** an undertaking almost sure to fail. **3** a party of soldiers engaged in a very dangerous job. **4** a slim or futile chance: *She waited an hour in the forlorn hope that the train would still arrive.* ⟨alteration of Du. *verloren hoop* lost troop⟩

form [fɔrm] *n., v.* *—n.* **1** appearance apart from colour or materials; shape. **2** a shape of body; body of a person or animal. **3** something that gives shape to something else: *A mould is a form.* **4** a model of the human torso, used in dressmaking and tailoring. **5** an orderly arrangement of parts: *The effect of a work of literature, art, or music comes from its form as well as its content.* **6** a way of doing something; manner; method: *He is a fast runner, but his form in running is bad.* **7** a record of previous behaviour or achievement: *According to form, this horse should win the race. The child is behaving true to form.* **8** a set way of doing something; behaviour according to custom or rule; formality; ceremony: *Shaking hands is a form. Many forms have little or no real meaning.* **9** a set order of words; formula: *A written agreement to buy, sell, or do something follows a certain form.* **10** a document with printing or writing on it and blank spaces to be filled in: *To get a licence, you must fill out a form.* **11** the way in which a thing exists, takes shape, or shows itself; condition; character; manifestation: *Water appears also in the forms of ice, snow, and steam.* **12** kind; sort; variety: *Heat, light, and electricity are forms of energy.* **13** a good condition of body or mind: *Athletes exercise to keep in form.* **14** *Grammar.* any of the ways in which a word is spelled or pronounced to express different ideas and relationships. *Boys* is the plural form of *boy. Saw* is the past form of *see. My* and *mine* are the possessive forms of *I.* **15** *Brit.* a grade in school, especially in high school. **16** a long seat; bench. **17** *Printing.* type fastened in a frame ready for printing or making plates. **18** *Philosophy.* the essence or quality in a thing that makes it what it is. **19** the home of a hare. **20** *Linguistics.* any speech unit bearing meaning. Sentences, phrases, words, and morphemes are all forms.
bad form, behaviour contrary to accepted customs.
good form, behaviour in accord with accepted customs.
—v. **1** give shape to; make: *The cook formed the dough into loaves.* **2** be formed; take shape: *Clouds form in the sky.* **3** become: *Water forms ice when it freezes.* **4** make up; compose: *Parents and children form a family.* **5** organize; establish: *We formed a club.* **6** develop: *Form good habits while you are young.* **7** arrange in some order: *The soldiers formed themselves into lines.* **8** put together (opinions, images, etc.), in one's mind; conceive. ⟨ME < OF < L *forma* form, mould⟩ **—'form•a•ble,** *adj.*
☛ *Syn. n.* **1. Form,** SHAPE, FIGURE = the appearance of something apart from the colour or the material of which it is made. **Form** particularly suggests that there is substance or structure under the surface, giving rise to the special appearance seen: *There have been many improvements in the form of airplanes.* **Shape,** more informal, emphasizes definiteness of form and solidness of body or substance, and means the whole outline or mould of the person or thing: *Her head has a strange shape.* **Figure** applies only to the outline of a form: *She drew figures of animals.*

-form *suffix.* **1** having the form of ——: *cruciform.* **2** having —— form or forms: *multiform.* ⟨< L *-formis* < *forma* form⟩

for•mal ['fɔrməl] *adj., n.* *—adj.* **1** with strict attention to outward forms and ceremonies; not familiar and homelike; stiff: *The judge always had a formal manner in court.* **2** according to set customs or rules. **3** done with the proper forms; clear and definite: *A written contract is a formal agreement to do something.* **4** requiring correct, elegant dress: *a formal dance, a formal wedding.* **5** suitable for a formal occasion: *formal dress.* **6** very regular; symmetrical; orderly. **7** having to do with the form, not the content. **8** of language, conforming to a studied style in vocabulary, syntax, and pronunciation, as accepted for dignified use. **9** of or having to do with institutions: *a formal education.* **10** *Philosophy.* of or having to do with the inherent nature of something.
—n. **1** a social gathering at which formal dress is worn. **2** a gown worn to formal social gatherings: *She was dressed in her first formal.* ⟨< L *formalis* < *forma* form⟩ **—'for•mal•ly,** *adv.*
☛ *Syn.* **1, 2. Formal,** CONVENTIONAL = according to outward forms and rules. **Formal** = showing strict attention to rules and set ways of doing things, and implies correctness, stiffness, and lack of warmth and naturalness: *The formal way in which she greeted me suggested she had not yet forgiven me.* **Conventional** = showing attention to generally accepted forms and customs, especially in social behaviour, and emphasizes lack of originality: *She wrote a conventional note of sympathy.*
☛ *Usage.* See note at INFORMAL.

form•al•de•hyde [fɔr'mældəˌhaɪd] *n. Chemistry.* a colourless gas with a sharp, irritating odour, used in solution as a disinfectant and preservative. *Formula:* CH_2O ⟨< *form(ic acid)* + *aldehyde*⟩

For•ma•lin ['fɔrməlɪn] *n. Trademark. Chemistry.* a solution of formaldehyde in water.

for•mal•ism ['fɔrməˌlɪzəm] *n.* strict attention to outward forms and ceremonies. **—'for•mal•ist,** *n.* **—ˌfor•mal'is•tic,** *adj.*

for•mal•i•ty [fɔr'mæləti] *n., pl.* **-ties. 1** a procedure required by custom or rule; outward form; ceremony. **2** attention to forms and customs: *Visitors at the court of a king are received with formality.* **3** stiffness of manner, behaviour, or arrangement.

for•mal•ize ['fɔrməˌlaɪz] *v.* **-ized, -iz•ing. 1** make formal or official. **2** give a definite form to. **—ˌfor•mal•i'za•tion,** *n.* **—'for•malˌiz•er,** *n.*

formal logic the branch of logic that deals with the structure or form of propositions (apart from their content) and the process of deductive reasoning by which conclusions are drawn.

for•mant ['fɔrmənt] *n. Phonetics.* on a sound spectrogram, any of the dark bands of frequencies that indicate the distinctive quality of a vowel or sonorant consonant. ⟨< G < L *formans, formantis* ppr. of *formare* form⟩

for•mat ['fɔrmæt] *n., v.* —*n.* **1** the shape, size, and general arrangement of a book, magazine, etc. **2** the design, plan, or arrangement of anything: *the format of a legislative program, television show, etc.* **3** a particular method of dealing with computer data. **4** a specific type of video or audio recording, as VHS or Beta.
—*v.* **1** determine the characteristics and layout of (a book, document, etc.). **2** *Computer technology.* prepare (a computer disk) for use by having the operating system write certain essential data on it: *He had to format the diskette before he could save his spreadsheet on it.* Also called **initialize.** ⟨< F < L *(liber) formatus* (book) formed (in a special way)⟩

for•ma•tion [fɔr'meiʃən] *n.* **1** a forming or being formed: *Heat causes the formation of steam from water. The formation of words is a fascinating study.* **2** the way in which a thing is arranged; arrangement; order: *troops in battle formation. There was an interesting formation of ice crystals on the window.* **3** the thing formed: *Clouds are formations of tiny drops of water in the sky.* **4** *Geology.* a series of layers or deposits of the same kind of rock or mineral. **5** *Ecology.* the most populous plant community in a particular region, as tundra, prairie, etc.

form•a•tive ['fɔrmətɪv] *adj.* **1** having to do with formation or development; forming; moulding: *Home and school are the chief formative influences in a child's life.* **2** *Grammar.* used to form words. Words may be made from other words by adding formative endings, such as *-ly* and *-ness.* **3** *Biology.* that can produce new cells or tissues: *formative tissue, formative yolk.* **—'for•ma•tive•ly,** *adv.* **—'for•ma•tive•ness,** *n.*

form class *Linguistics.* a set of words which share certain grammatical characteristics, such as abstract nouns.

forme fruste ['fɔrm 'frʊst] *Genetics.* an extremely mild expression of a trait. ⟨< F⟩

for•mer[1] ['fɔrmər] *adj.* **1** designating the first of two: *the former case.* **2** earlier or previous: *former times, a former classmate.* **3** (*noml.*) **the former,** the first of two: *When Sue is offered ice cream or pie, she always chooses the former.* Compare LATTER. ⟨ME *formere*, comparative back-formation from *formest.* See FOREMOST.⟩

for•mer[2] ['fɔrmər] *n.* a person or thing that forms. ⟨< *form*⟩

for•mer•ly ['fɔrmərli] *adv.* in the past; some time ago: *Mrs. Smith was formerly known as Miss Snell.*

form•fit•ting ['fɔrm,fɪtɪŋ] *adj.* closely following the shape of the body.

form genus a genus of species that appear similar but do not have the same evolutionary history.

for•mic ['fɔrmɪk] *adj.* **1** of ants. **2** *Chemistry.* of or having to do with FORMIC ACID.

For•mi•ca [fɔr'məikə] *n. Trademark.* a laminated plastic material with a hard, smooth, shiny, heat-resistant surface, used mainly for counter and table tops.

formic acid *Chemistry.* a colourless liquid that is irritating to the skin. It occurs in ants, spiders, nettles, etc. and is used in dyeing, finishing textiles, etc. *Formula*: CH_2O_2 ⟨< L *formica* ant⟩

for•mi•da•ble ['fɔrmədəbəl] *or* [fər'mɪdəbəl] *adj.* **1** hard to overcome; hard to deal with; to be dreaded. **2** *Informal.* impressive, awesome. ⟨< L *formidabilis* < *formidare* dread⟩ **—'for•mi•da•ble•ness** or **,for•mi•da'bil•i•ty,** *n.* **—'for•mi•da•bly,** *adv.*

form•less ['fɔrmlɪs] *adj.* without definite or regular form; shapeless. **—'form•less•ly,** *adv.* **—'form•less•ness,** *n.*

form letter a letter so phrased that it may be sent to many different people; a letter copied from a pattern.

form sheet 1 a detailed information sheet having the names of the horses and jockeys in the day's races, records of past performances, weights carried, etc. **2** a list giving the records of participants in any match, contest, etc.

for•mu•la ['fɔrmjələ] *n., pl.* **-las** or **-lae** [-,li] *or* [-,laɪ]. **1** a set form of words, especially one that by much use has partly lost its meaning: *"How do you do?" is a formula of greeting.* **2** a statement of religious belief or doctrine: *The Apostles' Creed is a formula of the Christian faith.* **3** a rule for doing something, especially as used by those who do not know the reason on which it is based. **4** a recipe; prescription: *a formula for making soup.* **5** a mixture, especially one for feeding a baby, made according to a recipe or prescription. **6** *Chemistry.* an expression showing by symbols and figures the composition of a compound: *The formula for water is H_2O.* **7** *Mathematics.* an expression showing by algebraic symbols a rule, principle, etc. $(a + b)^2 = a^2 + 2ab + b^2$ is an algebraic formula. **8** a ranking of racing car, usually by the power of the engine. ⟨< L *formula*, dim. of *forma* form⟩

for•mu•la•ic [,fɔrmjə'leiɪk] *adj.* based on or consisting of formulas.

for•mu•lar•y ['fɔrmjə,lɛri] *n., pl.* **-lar•ies;** *adj.* —*n.* **1** a collection of formulas. **2** a set form of words; formula. **3** *Pharmacy.* a book of formulas for standard preparations used in medicines.
—*adj.* having to do with formulas.

for•mu•late ['fɔrmjə,leit] *v.* **-lat•ed, -lat•ing. 1** state definitely; express in systematic form: *Our ideas of fair treatment for all Canadians are formulated in a Bill of Rights.* **2** express in a formula; reduce to a formula. **3** invent; create by thinking. **—'for•mu,la•tor,** *n.*

for•mu•la•tion [,fɔrmjə'leiʃən] *n.* **1** a definite statement; an expression in systematic form. **2** expression in a formula.

for•mu•lism ['fɔrmjə,lɪzəm] *n.* **1** reliance on, or adherence to, formulas. **2** a group or set of formulas. **—'for•mu•list,** *n.* **—,for•mu'lis•tic,** *adj.*

for•myl ['fɔrmɪl] *n. Chemistry.* the radical HCO.

For•nax ['fɔrnæks] *n. Astronomy.* a southern constellation between Cetus and Eridanus.

for•ni•cate ['fɔrnə,keit] *v.* **-cat•ed, -cat•ing.** commit fornication. ⟨< Ecclesiastical L *fornicari* < *fornix* brothel⟩ **—'for•ni,ca•tor,** *n.*

for•ni•ca•tion [,fɔrnə'keiʃən] *n.* voluntary sexual intercourse other than between a married couple, especially where either person or both persons are unmarried.

for•sake [fər'seik] *v.* **-sook, -sak•en, -sak•ing.** give up; leave alone; abandon. ⟨OE *forsacan* < *for-* away + *sacan* dispute, deny⟩
☛ *Syn.* See note at DESERT[2].

for•sak•en [fər'seikən] *v., adj.* —*v.* pp. of FORSAKE.
—*adj.* deserted; abandoned: *a forsaken house.* **—for'sak•en•ly,** *adv.*

for•sook [fər'sʊk] *v.* pt. of FORSAKE.

for•sooth [fər'suθ] *adv. Archaic.* in truth; indeed. ⟨OE *forsōth* < *for* for + *sōth* sooth, truth⟩

for•swear [fɔr'swɛr] *v.* **-swore, -sworn, -swear•ing. 1** renounce on oath; swear or promise solemnly to give up. **2** deny solemnly or on oath. **3** be untrue to one's sworn word or promise; perjure (oneself). ⟨OE *forswerian*⟩

for•swore [fɔr'swɔr] *v.* pt. of FORSWEAR.

for•sworn [fɔr'swɔrn] *adj., v.* —*adj.* untrue to one's sworn word or promise; perjured.
—*v.* pp. of FORSWEAR.

for•syth•i•a [fɔr'sɪθjə], [fɔr'sɪθiə], *or* [fɔr'səiθiə], *n.* **1** any of a genus (*Forsythia*) of European and Asian shrubs of the olive family having yellow flowers that appear early in spring, before the leaves. Forsythias are widely cultivated. **2** the flower of any of these plants. ⟨< NL; after William *Forsyth* (1737-1804), an English horticulturist⟩

El Morro, a Spanish type of fort commanding the harbour of San Juan, Puerto Rico. The fort was built in 1584.

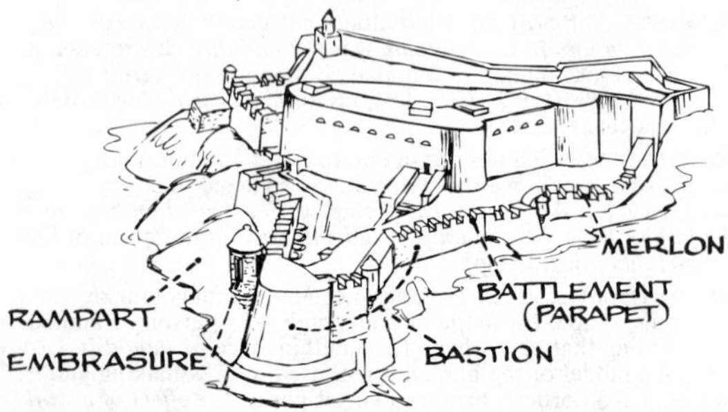

fort [fɔrt] *n.* **1** a strong building or place that can be defended

against an enemy. **2** formerly, a trading post. In the early days of the fur trade, these posts were usually fortified: *Winnipeg is built on the site of Fort Garry, an old Hudson's Bay Company post.*
hold the fort, **a** make a defence. **b** *Informal.* keep things functioning; stay on duty. ⟨< F < L *fortis* strong⟩

forte[1] ['fɔrtei] *or* [fɔrt] *n.* something a person does very well; strong point: *Cooking is her forte.* ⟨< F *forte,* fem. of *fort* strong < L *fortis*⟩

for•te[2] ['fɔrtei] *adj., adv., n. Music. —adj. or adv.* loud.
—n. a loud passage or tone. ⟨< Ital. *forte* strong < L *fortis*⟩

for•te•pia•no [ˌfɔrtei'pjɑnou] *adj., adv., n. —adj., adv. Music.* loud and then soft.
—n. an early instrument, the predecessor of the modern pianoforte. ⟨< Ital.⟩

forth [fɔrθ] *adv.* **1** forward; onward. **2** into view or consideration; out. **3** away.
and so forth, and so on; and the like: *We ate cake, candy, nuts, and so forth.* ⟨OE⟩

forth•com•ing ['fɔrθˌkʌmɪŋ] *or* [ˌfɔrθ'kʌmɪŋ] *adj., n. —adj.* **1** about to appear; approaching: *The forthcoming week will be busy.* **2** ready when wanted: *She needed help, but none was forthcoming.* **3** ready to meet or make advances; accommodating.
—n. an appearance; approach.

forth•right *adj.* ['fɔrθˌrəit]; *adv.* [ˌfɔrθ'rəit] *or* ['fɔrθˌrəit] *adj., adv. —adj.* frank and outspoken; straightforward; direct.
—adv. **1** straight ahead; directly forward. **2** at once; immediately.
—'forth,right•ly, *adv.* **—'forth,right•ness,** *n.*

fort hunter *Cdn.* formerly, a hunter, usually a member of a First Nations people, employed by a fur company to provide meat for a trading post or fort.

forth•with [ˌfɔrθ'wɪθ] *or* [ˌfɔrθ'wɪð] *adv.* at once; immediately: *She said she would be there forthwith.*

for•ti•eth ['fɔrtiɪθ] *adj. or n.* **1** next after the 39th; last in a series of forty; 40th. **2** one, or being one, of 40 equal parts.

for•ti•fi•ca•tion [ˌfɔrtəfə'keiʃən] *n.* **1** a fortifying: *Soldiers were busy with the fortification of the village.* **2** anything used in fortifying; a fort, wall, ditch, etc. **3** a fortified place. **4** the enriching of foods with vitamins and minerals.

for•ti•fy ['fɔrtəˌfaɪ] *v.* **-fied, -fy•ing. 1** build forts, walls, etc.; strengthen against attack; provide with forts, walls, etc. **2** give support to; strengthen. **3** add something to (food or drink) that strengthens or enriches: *Brandy is used to fortify port wine. Refined foods are often fortified with vitamins and minerals.* ⟨ME < OF *fortifier* < LL *fortificare,* ult. < L *fortis* strong + *facere* make⟩ **—'for•ti,fi•er,** *n.*

for•tis ['fɔrtɪs] *n. Phonetics.* a speech sound made with aspiration and comparatively tense articulators, such as [p], [t], [k], [s], [ʃ], [f], [θ], and [h]. Compare LENIS.

for•tis•si•mo [fɔr'tɪsəˌmou] *adj., adv., n. Music. —adj. or adv.* very loud.
—n. a very loud passage or tone. *Abbrev.*: ff ⟨< Ital. *fortissimo,* superlative of *forte* strong⟩

for•ti•tude ['fɔrtəˌtjud] *or* ['fɔrtəˌtud] *n.* courage in facing pain, danger, or trouble; firmness of spirit. ⟨< L *fortitudo* < *fortis* strong⟩
☛ *Syn.* See note at PATIENCE.

for•ti•tu•di•nous [ˌfɔrtə'tjudənəs] *or* [ˌfɔrtə'tudənəs] *adj.* having or characterized by fortitude: *a fortitudinous display of character.*

fort•night ['fɔrtˌnəit] *n.* two weeks. ⟨ME *fourtenight,* contraction of OE *fēowertēne niht* fourteen nights⟩

fort•night•ly ['fɔrtˌnəitli] *adv., adj., n. —adv.* once every two weeks.
—adj. appearing or happening once in every two weeks.
—n. a periodical published every two weeks.

FOR•TRAN ['fɔrtræn] *n. Computer technology.* a high-level computer programming language used especially in scientific and mathematical fields. ⟨< *for(mula) tran(slation).* 20c.⟩

for•tress ['fɔrtrɪs] *n.* a fortified place; a large and well-protected fort. ⟨ME < OF *forteresse* < *fort* strong < L *fortis*⟩

for•tu•i•tous [fɔr'tjuətəs] *or* [fɔr'tuətəs] *adj.* **1** happening by chance; accidental: *a fortuitous meeting, a fortuitous acquaintance.* **2** happening by lucky chance: *a fortuitous discovery such as penicillin.* ⟨< L *fortuitus,* ult. < *fors, fortis* chance⟩
—for'tu•i•tous•ly, *adv.* **—for'tu•i•tous•ness,** *n.*
☛ *Syn.* **Fortuitous** is sometimes used to refer to events that, besides being accidental and unintentioned, happen to be providential or fortunate. **Fortuitous** and FORTUNATE have a common origin: L *fors, fortis* luck. However, not every **fortunate** happening may be correctly referred to as **fortuitous,** but only those that are accidentally so.

for•tu•i•ty [fɔr'tjuəti] *or* [fɔr'tuəti] *n., pl.* **-ties. 1** chance; accident. **2** fortuitous quality.

for•tu•nate ['fɔrtʃənɪt] *adj.* **1** having good luck; lucky. **2** bringing good luck; having favourable results. ⟨< L *fortunatus,* pp. of *fortunare* assign fortune to < *fortuna* fortune⟩
—'for•tu•nate•ly, *adv.*
☛ *Syn.* **1, 2. Fortunate,** LUCKY = having or bringing good luck. **Fortunate** suggests being favoured by circumstances strongly to one's advantage or helpful in bringing about success that could not have been counted on or in bringing something wholly unexpected: *He made a fortunate decision when he went into advertising.* **Lucky** is less formal and emphasizes the idea of accident or pure chance: *It was lucky that he missed his train the day it was wrecked.*

for•tune ['fɔrtʃən] *n.* **1** a great deal of money or property; riches; wealth. **2** what is going to happen to a person; fate: *Gypsies often claim that they can tell people's fortunes.* **3** good luck; prosperity; success. **4** what happens; luck; chance: *Fortune was against us; we lost.*
a small fortune, a large sum of money: *That can of caviar cost a small fortune.* ⟨ME < OF < L *fortuna*⟩

fortune cookie a small, sweet cookie served at the end of a Chinese meal, containing a slip of paper bearing advice, a motto, etc.

fortune hunter **1** a person who tries to get a fortune by marrying someone rich. **2** anybody who seeks wealth.

for•tune•tell•er ['fɔrtʃənˌtɛlər] *n.* a person who claims to be able to tell what is going to happen to other people.

for•ty ['fɔrti] *n., pl.* **-ties;** *adj. —n.* **1** four times ten; 40. **2 forties,** *pl.* the years from forty through forty-nine, especially of a century or of a person's life: *She achieved success as a playwright in her forties.*
—adj. four times ten; 40. ⟨OE *fēowertig*⟩

For•ty–Nin•er ['fɔrti 'naɪnər] *n.* **1** a person who went to California to seek gold in 1849. It had been discovered there in 1848. **2** *Cdn.* a person in power in Newfoundland when it joined Confederation in 1949.

forty winks *Informal.* a short nap.

fo•rum ['fɔrəm] *n.* **1** the public square or marketplace in ancient Rome. The forum in Rome was used for public assemblies and business. **2** an assembly for discussing questions of public interest. **3** a law court; tribunal. **4** an occasion or place for public discussion: *The* Opinions *page is a forum for readers' comments.* ⟨< L⟩

for•ward ['fɔrwərd] *adv., adj., v., n. —adv.* **1** ahead; onward: *The men marched forward.* **2** toward the front. **3** out; into view or consideration: *In his talk he brought forward several new ideas.* **4** later in time: *We put the clocks forward in April.* **5** earlier in time: *to move a meeting forward.*
—adj. **1** toward the front: *the forward part of a ship.* **2** far ahead; advanced: *She was forward for her age.* **3** pert; bold. **4** ready; eager: *He knew his lesson and was forward with his answers.*
—v. **1** send on further: *Please forward my mail to my new address.* **2** help along: *He did all he could to forward his friend's plan.*
—n. Sports. a player whose position is in the front line. ⟨OE *forweard*⟩ **—'for•ward•er,** *n.* **—'for•ward•ly,** *adv.*
☛ *Syn. adj.* **3.** See note at BOLD.

forward–looking ['fɔrwərd ˌlʊkɪŋ] *adj.* taking care to anticipate the future.

for•ward•ness ['fɔrdwərdnɪs] *n.* **1** pertness; boldness. **2** readiness; eagerness.

forward pass *Football.* the throwing of a football to a player on the same team in the direction of the opponent's goal.

for•wards ['fɔrwərdz] *adv.* forward.

for•went [fɔr'wɛnt] *v.* pt. of FORGO.

fos•sa ['fɒsə] *n., pl.* **fos•sae** ['fɒsi] *or* ['fɒsaɪ]. *Anatomy.* a shallow depression or cavity in a bone, etc. ⟨< L *fossa* ditch⟩

fosse [fɒs] *n.* a ditch; trench; canal; moat. Also, **foss.** ⟨ME < OF < L *fossa* ditch⟩

fos•sil ['fɒsəl] *n.* **1** the remains of prehistoric animals or plants preserved in rocks where they have become petrified: *Bone fossils of dinosaurs have been discovered in Alberta. Fossils of ferns are often found in coal.* **2** traces of animal life preserved in ancient rocks: *fossils of footprints.* **3** (*adjl.*) forming or having the characteristics of a fossil: *fossil remains.* **4** (*adjl.*) derived from the remains of living things: *fossil resins. Coal, oil, and natural gas are fossil fuels.* **5** *Informal.* a very old-fashioned person, set in his or her ways. **6** (*adjl.*) belonging to the outworn past: *fossil ideas.* ⟨< F < L *fossilis* dug up < *fodere* dig⟩ **—'fos•sil-ˌlike,** *adj.*

fossil fuels fuels obtained from within the earth, such as coal, petroleum, and natural gas.

fos•sil•if•er•ous [ˌfɒsəˈlɪfərəs] *adj.* containing fossils.

fos•sil•ize [ˈfɒsəˌlaiz] *v.* **-ized, -iz•ing. 1** make into a fossil; change into a fossil; turn into stone. **2** make or become antiquated, set, stiff, or rigid. **—ˌfos•sil•iˈza•tion,** *n.*

fos•so•ri•al [fɒˈsɔriəl] *adj.* burrowing or adapted for burrowing. ⟨< LL *fossorius* < L *fossor* digger < *fossus* pp. of *fodere* to dig up⟩

fos•ter [ˈfɒstər] *v., adj. —v.* **1** help the growth or development of; encourage: *Ignorance fosters superstition.* **2** care for fondly; cherish. **3** bring up; rear.
—adj. **1** of or involved in a relationship like that between parent and child or between siblings, although not closely related by birth or bound by legal adoption: *a foster child, a foster mother.* **2** designating or of a home where one or more children of other parents are given parental care, often temporary: *The baby was in a foster home for a year before being adopted.* ⟨OE *fōstrian* nourish, *fōster* nourishment. Related to FOOD.⟩
☛ *Syn. v.* **2.** See note at CHERISH.

fou•droy•ant [fuˈdrɔɪənt]; *French,* [fudʀwaˈjɑ̃] *adj.* **1** striking like lightning; suddenly overwhelming. **2** *Medicine.* starting suddenly and severely: *a foudroyant TB case.* ⟨< F *foudroyant* < *foudroyer* strike like lightning < OF *fouldre* lightning < LL *fulgere* < L *fulgur* lightning⟩

fouet•té [fwɛˈtei] *n., v.* **-téd, -té•ing.** *Ballet. —n.* a quick turn in which one leg acts as a pivot as the other leg is thrown sideways and then bent in with the toes pointing toward the other knee.
—v. perform a fouetté. ⟨< F *fouetté,* literally, a whipped step, pp. of *fouetter* whip, beat⟩

fought [fɒt] *v.* pt. and pp. of FIGHT.

foul [faʊl] *adj., v., n., adv. —adj.* **1** very dirty; impure; nasty; smelly; containing or covered with filth: *Open the windows and let out the foul air.* **2** very wicked; vile: *Murder is a foul crime.* **3** obscene; indecent: *foul language.* **4** against the rules; unfair. **5** hitting against (*used with* **of**): *One boat was foul of the other.* **6** tangled up; caught: *The sailor cut the foul rope.* **7** clogged up: *The fire will not burn because the chimney is foul.* **8** *Nautical.* of a ship, having the bottom covered with seaweed, barnacles, etc. **9** unfavourable; stormy: *Foul weather delayed the ship.* **10** contrary: *a foul wind.* **11** *Informal.* very unpleasant or objectionable. **12** *Baseball.* of or having to do with FOUL BALLS or FOUL LINES.
—v. **1** make dirty or impure; pollute; soil; defile: *Exhaust fumes fouled the air.* **2** become dirty or impure: *Spark plugs foul if not cared for properly.* **3** dishonour; disgrace: *a name fouled by misdeeds.* **4** make a foul; make a foul against. **5** *Baseball.* hit a ball so that it falls outside the foul lines. **6** hit against: *One boat fouled the other.* **7** get tangled up with; catch: *The rope fouled the anchor chain.* **8** clog up: *Grease fouled the drain.* **9** *Nautical.* cover (a ship's bottom) with seaweed, barnacles, etc.
foul out, a *Baseball.* be put out by hitting a ball that is caught outside the foul lines. **b** *Basketball.* be put out of a game for having committed too many fouls.
foul up, *Informal.* make a mess of; bungle.
—n. **1** something done contrary to the rules; unfair play. **2** *Baseball.* FOUL BALL. **3** an entanglement or crash, especially between boats.
—adv. in a foul way.
go, fall, or **run foul of, a** hit against and get tangled up with. **b** get into trouble or difficulties with: *to run foul of the law.* ⟨OE *fūl*⟩ **—ˈfoul•ly,** *adv.* **—ˈfoul•ness,** *n.*
☛ *Hom.* FOWL.
☛ *Syn. adj.* **1.** See note at DIRTY.

fou•lard [fuˈlɑrd] *n.* **1** a soft, thin fabric made of silk, rayon, or cotton, usually with a printed pattern. It is used for neckties, dresses, etc. **2** a necktie or handkerchief made from this material. ⟨< F < Swiss F *foulat* cloth that has been cleansed and thickened⟩

foul ball *Baseball.* a ball hit so that it falls outside the foul lines.

foul line 1 *Baseball.* either the line from home to first base, or from home to third base, with their marked or unmarked continuations. **2** *Basketball.* a line within the circle in front of each basket from which foul shots are made. **3** a line or mark which may not be stepped on or over in making a broad jump, throwing the javelin, etc.

foul–mouthed [ˈfaʊl ˌmʌuθt] *or* [ˈfaʊl ˌmaʊðd] *adj.* habitually using vile, offensive language.

foul play 1 unfair play; a thing or things done against the rules. **2** treachery; violence.

foul shot *Basketball.* **1** a free shot awarded to one team for a foul by the opponent's team. **2** a score of one point for putting such a shot into the basket.

foul tip *Baseball.* a ball deflected by the bat back to the catcher.

foul–up [ˈfaʊl ˌʌp] *n. Slang.* a disorder or muddle that interferes with a project or operation: *There was a last-minute foul-up in the sports program.*

found[1] [faʊnd] *adj., v., —adj.* of a work of art made from material or words found by chance and considered to be artistic: *found poetry, found art.*
—v. pt. and pp. of FIND.
and found, *Informal.* including room and board.

found[2] [faʊnd] *v.* **1** establish; set up: *Champlain founded Québec in 1608.* **2** rest for support; base: *He founded his claim on facts.* ⟨ME < OF *fonder* < L *fundare* < *fundus* bottom⟩

found[3] [faʊnd] *v.* melt and mould (metal); make of molten metal; cast. ⟨< F *fondre* < L *fundere* pour⟩

foun•da•tion [faʊnˈdeiʃən] *n.* **1** the part on which the other parts rest for support; base: *the foundation of a house.* **2** the basis of a belief, idea, argument, etc.: *The report has no foundation in fact.* **3** a founding or being founded. **4** an institution founded and endowed: *a charitable foundation.* **5** a fund given to support an institution. **6** a part over which something is laid: *Her full skirt swirled over a foundation of starched cotton petticoats.* **7** FOUNDATION GARMENT. **8** a cream or liquid cosmetic applied on the face as a base for rouge, powder, etc. **9** (*adjl.*) of, having to do with, for, or serving as a foundation: *a foundation plan, foundation planting.* **—founˈda•tion•al,** *adj.* **—founˈda•tion•al•ly,** *adv.*
☛ *Syn.* **1, 2.** See note at BASE[1].

foundation garment a woman's corset, girdle, etc., usually having a brassiere attached.

foun•der[1] [ˈfaʊndər] *v.* **1** fill or cause to fill with water and sink: *The ship foundered in the storm.* **2** bog down in soft ground; mire. **3** break down; go lame or stumble, or cause to do so: *Her horse foundered.* **4** become worn out; fail. **5** *Golf.* hit (the ball) into the ground. **6** of animals, fall ill through overeating. ⟨ME < OF *fondrer,* ult. < L *fundus* bottom⟩

found•er[2] [ˈfaʊndər] *n.* a person or thing that founds or establishes something. ⟨< *found*[2]⟩

found•er[3] [ˈfaʊndər] *n.* a person who casts metals. ⟨< *found*[3]⟩

founder effect *Genetics.* a change in gene frequencies, often to abnormal genes, that occurs when the frequencies in the founders of a new population are not representative of the parent population.

Founder's Day *Buddhism.* the festival celebrated in October, commemorating the introduction of Buddhism to Canada in 1905, and the assembly of Buddhists in Toronto in 1930, which led to the formation of the Buddhist Council of Canada.

found–in [ˈfaʊnd ˌɪn] *n. Cdn.* a person arrested for being present in a brothel, in an illegal drinking or gambling establishment, etc.

founding father 1 a man involved in the founding of some institution. **2 Founding Father,** *Cdn.* one of the FATHERS OF CONFEDERATION.

found•ling [ˈfaʊndlɪŋ] *n.* a baby or child found abandoned. ⟨ME *fundeling.* Related to FIND.⟩

found•ry [ˈfaʊndri] *n., pl.* **-ries. 1** a place where metal is melted and moulded; place where things are made of molten metal. **2** the melting and moulding of metal; process of making things of molten metal. **3** things made of molten metal; castings. ⟨< F *fonderie* < *fondre* found[3]⟩

fount[1] [faʊnt] *n.* **1** fountain. **2** an abundant source: *She is a fount of knowledge.* ⟨< L *fons, fontis* spring⟩

fount[2] [faʊnt] *n.* FONT[2].

foun•tain [ˈfaʊntən] *n.* **1** a stream or spray of water rising into the air. **2** a decorative structure through which water is forced into the air in a stream or spray. **3** a spring of water. **4** a device by which a jet of water is forced upward so that people may get a drink: *a drinking fountain.* **5** SODA FOUNTAIN. **6** an abundant source; origin: *Solomon was a fountain of wisdom.* **7** a container to hold a steady supply of ink, oil, etc. ⟨ME < OF *fontaine* < LL *fontana,* originally fem. of *fontanus* of a spring < L *fons, fontis* spring⟩

foun•tain•head [ˈfaʊntənˌhɛd] *n.* **1** the source of a stream. **2** an original source. **3** a chief source of anything.

Fountain of Youth a legendary spring whose waters were supposed to cure any sickness and restore youth.

fountain pen a pen for writing that automatically supplies liquid ink to the nib from a rubber or plastic tube inside.

four [fɔr] *n., adj. —n.* **1** one more than three; 4: *There are four left in the box.* **2** the numeral 4: *She crossed the 3 out and put a 4 in its place.* **3** the fourth in a set or series, especially a playing card or side of a die having four spots: *He threw a four.* **4** *Rowing.* **a** a crew of four rowers. **b** the boat they use. **5** *Cricket.* a hit for which four runs are scored. **6** any set or series of four persons or things: *They set up a four to play cards.*
on all fours, a on all four feet. **b** on hands and knees.
—adj. **1** being one more than three. **2** being fourth in a set or series (*used mainly after the noun*): *I don't understand Section Four of the manual.* ⟨OE *fēower*⟩
☛ *Hom.* FOR, FORE.

four–colour or **four–color** ['fɔr 'kʌlər] *adj. Printing.* of a printing process which can reproduce any colour by the judicious mixing of red, yellow, blue, and black.

four flush **1** *Poker.* a four-card suit (instead of the five needed for a flush). **2** *Informal.* false pretence; bluff.

four–flush•er ['fɔr ˌflʌʃər] *n. Informal.* a person who pretends to be more or other than he or she really is; bluffer.

four–flushing ['fɔr ˌflʌʃɪŋ] *adj. Informal.* treacherous.

four•fold ['fɔrˌfould] *adj., adv. —adj.* **1** four times as much or as many: *a fourfold increase in profits.* **2** having four parts.
—adv. by four times as much or as many: *We increased our profits fourfold.*

four–foot•ed ['fɔr 'fʊtɪd] *adj.* having four feet.

four–four ['fɔr 'fɔr] *adj. Music.* indicating or having four quarter notes in a bar or measure, the first and third of which are accented.

four freedoms freedom of speech, freedom of worship, freedom from want, and freedom from fear, set forth in 1941 by President Franklin D. Roosevelt of the United States.

four–hand•ed ['fɔr 'hændɪd] *adj.* **1** having four hands. **2** *Music.* for two players.

Four–H clubs or **4–H clubs** a national system of clubs to teach rural children agriculture and home economics. Their purpose is the improvement of head, heart, hands, and health.

Four Horsemen of the Apocalypse in the Bible, the riders of four different coloured horses, seen in a prophetic vision, the red horse representing War, the black horse, Famine, the pale horse, Death and Pestilence, the white horse, Christ or Victory.

Fou•ri•er series ['fɔriˌei] *or* ['fɔriər] *Mathematics.* an infinite trigonometric series of the form
$\frac{1}{2}a_0 + (a_1 \cos x + b_1 \sin x) + (a_2 \cos 2x + b_2 \sin 2_x) + \ldots$ It is used to represent single-valued periodic functions. ⟨< Jean Baptiste Joseph *Fourier*, French mathematician (1768–1830) who formulated it⟩

four–in–hand ['fɔr ɪn ˌhænd] *n.* **1** a necktie tied in a slip knot with the ends left hanging. **2** a carriage pulled by four horses driven by one person. **3** a team of four horses.

four–letter word ['fɔr 'lɛtər] any of a group of one-syllable words referring to sexual organs or acts or to excretory functions, often used as expletives and generally thought of as obscene or vulgar.

four–o'clock ['fɔr əˌklɒk] *n.* a small plant (*Mirabilis jalapa*) having red, white, or yellow trumpet-shaped flowers that open late in the afternoon and close in the morning.

four of a kind *Poker.* a hand having four cards of the same value.

four•plex ['fɔrˌplɛks] *n. Cdn.* a building containing four dwelling units. ⟨by analogy with *duplex*⟩

four–poster ['fɔr ˌpoustər] *n.* a bed having a column at each corner, supporting a canopy.

four•score ['fɔr'skɔr] *adj. or n.* four times twenty; 80. ⟨ME⟩

four•some ['fɔrsəm] *n.* **1** a group of four people. **2** a game played by four people, two on each side. **3** the players.

four•spine stickleback ['fɔrˌspaɪn] an eastern Canadian fish (*Apeltes quadracus*) found in fresh, brackish or salt water, and growing to a length of 6 cm.

four•square ['fɔr'skwɛr] *adj., adv., n. —adj.* **1** square. **2** frank; outspoken. **3** not yielding; firm.
—adv. **1** in a square form. **2** without yielding; firmly.
—n. a square. **—'four'square•ly,** *adv.*

four–stroke ['fɔr ˌstrouk] *adj. Machinery.* of or having to do with an engine requiring four piston strokes to complete a fuel cycle.

four•teen ['fɔrt'tin] *n., adj. —n.* **1** four more than ten; 14. **2** the numeral 14: *That should be a 14, not a 15.* **3** the fourteenth in a set or series. **4** a set or series of fourteen persons or things.
—adj. **1** being four more than ten; 14. **2** being fourteenth in a set or series (*used after the noun*): *Lesson Fourteen.* ⟨OE *fēowertēne*⟩

four•teenth ['fɔrt'tinθ] *adj. or n.* **1** next after the 13th; last in a series of fourteen; 14th. **2** one, or being one, of 14 equal parts.

fourth [fɔrθ] *adj., n. —adj.* **1** next after the third; last in a series of four; 4th. **2** being one of four equal parts.
—n. **1** the next after the third; last in a series of four; 4th. **2** one of four equal parts. **3** in automobiles and similar machines, the forward gear next above third; high gear in a four-gear system. **4** *Music.* **a** the fourth tone from the keynote of a scale. **b** the interval between such tones. **c** a combination of such tones.

fourth dimension a dimension in addition to length, breadth, and depth: *Time has been thought of as a fourth dimension.*

fourth estate the press; newspapers and those who work for them. See ESTATE (def.4).

fourth•ly ['fɔrθli] *adv.* in the fourth place.

Fourth of July in the United States, a holiday in memory of the adoption of the Declaration of Independence on July 4, 1776.

Fourth World the poorest nations of the Third World, without resources such as oil.

four–wheel drive ['fɔr 'wil] describing a vehicle in which power is transmitted to all four wheels at once. *Abbrev.*: 4WD

four–wheeled ['fɔr 'wild] *adj.* having four wheels; running on four wheels.

fo•vea cen•tra•lis ['fouviə sɛn'trælɪs] *pl.* **foviae** ['foviˌi] *or* ['foviˌaɪ] *Anatomy.* a small depression on the retina, where vision is best. See EYE for picture. ⟨< NL⟩

fowl [faʊl] *n., pl.* **fowls** or (*esp. collectively*) **fowl;** *v. —n.* **1** a chicken or domestic turkey. **2** any of various other birds of the same order (Galliformes), especially those hunted as game. **3** the flesh of a fowl used for food. **4** *Archaic.* (*except in compounds*) any bird: *waterfowl.*
—v. hunt, shoot, catch, or trap wildfowl. ⟨OE *fugol*⟩
☛ *Hom.* FOUL.

fowl•er ['faʊlər] *n.* a person who hunts, shoots, catches, or traps wild birds.

fowling piece a light gun for shooting wild birds.

fox [fɒks] *n., v. —n.* **1** any of various carnivorous mammals (genera *Vulpes, Alopex,* etc.) of the dog family that do not hunt in packs and that have large, pointed ears, a slender, pointed muzzle, and a bushy tail. Foxes are famous for their cunning, especially in escaping hunters. **2** the fur of a fox. **3** a sly, cunning person.
—v. **1** *Informal.* trick in a sly and crafty way. **2** of beer, turn sour. **3** make (beer) sour. **4** discolour; stain (the pages of a book). **5** become discoloured or stained. **6 a** make or repair (a boot, shoe, etc.) by covering with or adding upper leather. **b** trim (the upper of a shoe) with leather. **7** hunt the fox. **8** confuse; puzzle. ⟨OE⟩ **—'fox,like,** *adj.*

Fox [fɒks] *n., pl.* **Fox•es** or **Fox. 1** a member of an American Indian people formerly living in the Fox River valley in Wisconsin. **2** the Algonquian language of the Fox and Sauk peoples.

fox•ber•ry ['fɒksˌbɛri] *n. Cdn.* MOUNTAIN CRANBERRY.

fox•fire ['fɒksˌfaɪr] *n.* the luminescence emitted by decaying wood, caused by fungi.

fox•glove ['fɒksˌglʌv] *n.* **1** any of a genus (*Digitalis*) of biennial and perennial herbs of the figwort family native to Europe and Asia, especially *D. purpurea,* cultivated for its showy spikes of tubular purple or white flowers or for its leaves, which are a source of the drug digitalis. **2** the flower of any of these plants. ⟨OE *foxes glōfa*⟩

fox grape a wild grape (*Vitis labrusca*) of eastern North America, parent to many domestic wine grapes, as the Concord and Catawba.

fox•hole ['fɒksˌhoul] *n.* a hole in the ground for protection against enemy fire.

fox•hound ['fɒksˌhaʊnd] *n.* either of two breeds of large, short-haired hound (the **American foxhound** and the **English foxhound**) trained especially for hunting foxes.

fox hunt an event in which hunters on horseback follow dogs that find and chase a fox.

fox–hunt ['fɒks ˌhʌnt] *v.* pursue or hunt foxes with hounds. **—'fox,hunt•er,** *n.* **—'fox-,hunt•ing,** *n., adj.*

fox•ing ['fɒksɪŋ] *n., v. —n.* **1** the discoloration caused by age on books, papers, etc. **2** a piece of leather used to fox a shoe or boot.
—v. ppr. of FOX.

fox squirrel a North American squirrel (*Sciurus niger*) of several different colours.

fox•tail ['fɒks,teil] *n.* **1** any grass of two genera (*Setaria* and *Alopecurus*) having soft, round, bushlike spikes of flowers. **2** a wild barley (*Hordeum jubatum*) having a bushy, tasslelike flower spike. Often called **foxtail barley. 3** the tail of a fox.

fox terrier either of two breeds of terrier (**wire-haired fox terrier** and **smooth fox terrier**) having a white and black or white and brown coat, originally bred in England for driving foxes from their holes.

fox trot 1 a dance in 2/4 or 4/4 time with short, quick steps. **2** the music for this dance. **3** a gait of a horse intermediate between a trot and a walk. The forelegs move in a trot, while the hind legs move in a long stride.

fox–trot ['fɒks ˌtrɒt] *v.* **-trot•ted, -trot•ting.** dance the fox trot.

fox•y ['fɒksi] *adj.* **fox•i•er, fox•i•est. 1** like a fox; sly; crafty. **2** discoloured; stained. **3** of certain wines, tasting of FOX GRAPES. **4** *Slang.* sexy; seductive. **—'fox•i•ly,** *adv.* **—'fox•i•ness,** *n.*

foy•er ['fɔiei] *or* ['fɔiər] *n.* **1** an entrance hall used as a lounging room in a theatre or hotel; lobby. **2** an entrance hall. ⟨< F, ult. < L *focus* hearth⟩

F.P., f.p., or **fp 1** FOOT-POUND. **2** FREEZING POINT.

fpm or **f.p.m.** feet per minute.

fps or **f.p.s.** feet per second.

fr. 1 franc. **2** from. **3** fragment.

Fr francium.

Fr. 1 France; French. **2** Father. **3** Friday. **4** Friar.

Fra [frɑ] *n.* Brother. It is used as the title of an Italian monk or friar. ⟨< Ital. *fra,* abbreviation of *frate* brother < L *frater*⟩

fra•cas ['frækəs] *or* ['freikəs]; *French,* [fʀa'ka] *n.* a noisy quarrel or fight; disturbance; uproar; brawl. ⟨< F < Ital. *fracasso* < *fracassare* smash⟩

frac•tal ['fræktəl] *n. Mathematics.* an irregular or fragmented shape or surface not normally represented in geometry. ⟨< L *fractus* pp. of *frangere* break + *-al*⟩

frac•tar ['fræktɑr] *n.* a medicinal shampoo used to treat certain scalp conditions.

frac•tion ['frækʃən] *n.* **1** *Mathematics.* **a** one or more of the equal parts of a whole. ½, ⅔, ¾, ⅚, and ⅞ are fractions. **b** a division of one mathematical expression by another, indicated by a line with one quantity above it and another below it. **2** a very small part, amount, etc.; fragment. **3** a breaking. **4** *Chemistry.* any of the components of a substance separated by distillation, crystallization, etc. ⟨< LL *fractio, -onis* < L *frangere* break⟩

frac•tion•al ['frækʃənəl] *adj.* **1** having to do with fractions. **2** forming a fraction: *440 metres is a fractional part of a kilometre.* **3** very small; insignificant. **4** *Chemistry.* of or designating a method for separating a mixture into its component parts based on certain differences in boiling points, solubility, etc. of these parts: *fractional crystallization, fractional oxidation.* **5** in stock exchanges, being less than the amount used as a standard unit of measurement, as less than 100 shares of stock, or $10 000 of bonds. **—'frac•tion•al•ly,** *adv.*

frac•tion•al•ize ['frækʃənə,laɪz] *v.,* **-ized, -iz•ing.** divide into fractions; split up. Also, **fractionize. —,frac•tion•al•i'za•tion,** *n.*

frac•tion•ate ['frækʃə,neit] *v.* **-at•ed, -at•ing. 1** *Chemistry.* separate (a mixture) into components or properties by distillation, crystallization, etc. **2** acquire or obtain by this process. **—,frac•tion'a•tion,** *n.*

frac•tious ['frækʃəs] *adj.* **1** cross; fretful; peevish. **2** hard to manage; unruly. ⟨< *fraction* (in obs. sense of discord, brawling), on the model of *captious,* etc.⟩ **—'frac•tious•ly,** *adv.* **—'frac•tious•ness,** *n.*

frac•ture ['fræktʃər] *v.* **-tured, -tur•ing;** *n. —v.* **1** break; crack: *The boy fell from a tree and fractured his arm.* **2** cause (a person's life, relationships, etc.) to be disrupted.
—n. **1** a break; crack. **2** a breaking or being broken. **3** a breaking of a bone or cartilage. **4** the surface of a freshly broken mineral. ⟨< F < L *fractura* < *frangere* break⟩

frag•ile ['frædʒaɪl] *or* ['frædʒəl] *adj.* **1** easily broken, damaged, or destroyed; delicate; frail. **2** slight; ineffectual: *a fragile hope.* **3** *Informal.* nervous; hypersensitive; easily upset: *I feel fragile this morning.* ⟨< L *fragilis* (related to *frangere* break). Doublet of FRAIL.⟩ **—'frag•ile•ly,** *adv.* **—fra'gil•i•ty** [frə'dʒɪləti], *n.* **—'frag•ile•ness,** *n.*

fragile X syndrome *Genetics.* a syndrome characterized by the presence of a constriction near the end of the long arm of the X chromosome in affected males, associated with mental retardation and characteristic physical abnormalities.

frag•ment *n.* ['frægmənt]; *v.* [fræg'mɛnt] *n., v. —n.* **1** a broken piece; part broken off. **2** an incomplete or disconnected part: *He could hear only fragments of the conversation.* **3** a part of an incomplete or unfinished work.
—v. break or divide into fragments. ⟨< L *fragmentum* < *frangere* break⟩

frag•men•tal [fræg'mɛntəl] *adj.* **1** fragmentary. **2** *Geology.* formed from parts of older rocks. **—frag'men•tal•ly,** *adv.*

frag•men•tar•y ['frægmən,tɛri] *or* [fræg'mɛntəri] *adj.* **1** made up of fragments; incomplete; disconnected: *fragmentary remains of a temple, fragmentary evidence, a fragmentary account.* **2** *Geology.* fragmental. **—'frag•men,tar•i•ly,** *adv.* **—'frag•men,tar•i•ness,** *n.*

frag•men•ta•tion [,frægmən'teiʃən] *n.* the process of breaking into many pieces.

fragmentation bomb a bomb, grenade, etc. that throws bits of metal in all directions as it bursts.

frag•ment•ed [fræg'mɛntɪd] *or* ['frægmɛntɪd] *adj., v. —adj.* broken into pieces; separated.
—v. pt. and pp. of FRAGMENT.

frag•ment•ize ['frægmən,taɪz] *v.* **-ized, -iz•ing.** break into fragments. **—,frag•ment•i'za•tion,** *n.*

fra•grance ['freigrəns] *n.* **1** a sweet smell; pleasing odour. **2** a prepared perfume; scent.

fra•grant ['freigrənt] *adj.* having or giving off a pleasing odour; sweet-smelling. ⟨< L *fragrans, -antis,* ppr. of *fragrare* emit odour⟩ **—'fra•grant•ly,** *adv.*

fragrant white water lily a North American wildflower (*Nymphaea adorata*), growing in ponds and having large white flowers and flat leaves that float on the water.

frail[1] [freil] *adj.* **1** not very strong; weak; physically delicate: *a frail child.* **2** easily broken, damaged, or destroyed; fragile: *Be careful, those branches are a very frail support.* **3** morally weak; liable to yield to temptation. ⟨ME < OF *fraile* < L *fragilis* fragile. Doublet of FRAGILE.⟩ **—'frail•ly,** *adv.* **—'frail•ness,** *n.*

frail[2] [freil] *n.* a basket made of rushes, used for gathering fruit, etc. ⟨< ME *fraiel* < OF *frael* rush basket < Med.L *fraellum* < L *flagellum* young branch, whip⟩

frail•ty ['freilti] *n., pl.* **-ties. 1** the fact or quality of being frail: *human frailty.* **2** a fault or sin caused by moral weakness.

fram•be•sia [fræm'biʒə] *or* [fræm'biziə] *n.* yaws. ⟨< NL < F *framboise* raspberry, altered (after *fraise* strawberry) < Frankish⟩

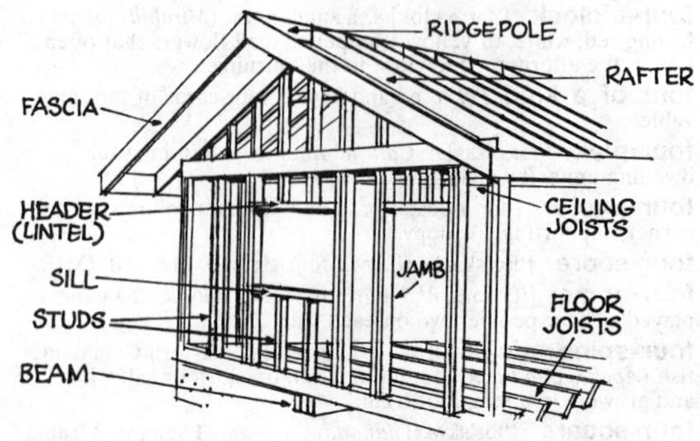

Part of the frame of a house

frame [freim] *n., v.* **framed, fram•ing.** *—n.* **1** a supporting structure over which something is stretched or built: *the frame of*

a house. **2** anything made of parts fitted and joined together; structure. **3** the body; bodily structure: *a man of heavy frame.* **4** skeleton. **5** the way in which a thing is put together. **6** an established order; plan; system. **7** a shape; form. **8** the border in which a thing is set: *a window frame, a picture frame.* **9** one of a series of pictures on a strip of film. **10** one image transmitted by television. **11** one turn at bowling. **12** *Informal. Baseball.* an inning. **13** in programmed learning, a single item or statement presented at one time. **14** *Pool, snooker.* **a** the triangular form used to arrange the balls at the start of a game. **b** the triangle of balls thus placed. **c** the period of play between two placings of the balls. **15** a glass box protecting young plants out of doors. **16 frames,** *pl.* eyeglasses minus the lenses.
—v. **1** build frames of houses or other buildings. **2** shape; form: *to frame one's life according to a noble pattern.* **3** put together; plan; make: *Laws are framed in Parliament.* **4** put a border around; enclose with a frame. **5** *Informal.* prearrange falsely; make seem guilty. **6** compose in speech; devise: *She framed her excuses timidly.* **7** accommodate to a particular intent; adjust: *They framed the proposal so as to include everyone.* ⟨OE *framian* to profit < *fram* forth⟩ **—'fram•er,** *n.*

frame house a house made of a wooden framework covered with boards.

frame of mind a way of thinking or feeling; disposition; mood.

frame of reference **1** *Mathematics.* any set of lines, curves, or planes by means of which the position of a point in space may be uniquely described. **2** the criteria used to make a judgment. **3** a point of view; the entire circumstances within which something exists.

frame•shift mutation ['freim,ʃɪft] *Genetics.* a permanent heritable change in the sequence of genomic DNA, in which there is a deletion or insertion that is not an exact multiple of three base pairs, and thus changes the reading frame of the gene and leads to the formation of a shortened or elongated protein product.

frame–up ['freim ,ʌp] *n. Informal.* **1** a secret and dishonest arrangement made beforehand. **2** a prearranged scheme made to have a person falsely accused.

frame•work ['freim,wɜrk] *n.* **1** an open frame or skeletal structure over which something is stretched or built or in which something is encased. **2** the way in which a thing is put together; structure; system. **3** the larger branches of a tree. **4** FRAME OF REFERENCE (def. 3).

fram•ing ['freimɪŋ] *n., v. —n.* **1** the work of someone who frames houses. **2** the manner in which something is framed: *There's a fault in the framing of this picture.* **3** frames collectively. *—v.* ppr. of FRAME.

franc [fræŋk] *n.* **1** the basic unit of money in Belgium, Benin, Burkina Faso, Burundi, Cameroon, Central African Republic, Chad, Congo Republic, Djibouti, Equatorial Guinea, France, Gabon, Ivory Coast, Liechtenstein, Luxembourg, Madagascar, Mali, Monaco, Niger, Rwanda, Senegal, Switzerland and Togo, divided into 100 centimes. See money table in the Appendix. **2** a coin worth one franc. ⟨ME < OF *franc* < *Francorum Rex* king of the Franks, on an early gold coin first struck in 1360⟩
☛ *Hom.* FRANK.

France [fræns] *n.* a large country in W Europe.

fran•chise ['fræntʃaɪz] *n., v.* **-chised, -chis•ing.** *—n.* **1** a privilege or right granted by a government: *The city granted the company a franchise to operate buses on the city streets.* **2** the right to vote: *A Canadian citizen receives the federal franchise at the age of 18.* **3** the privilege, often exclusive, of selling the products of a manufacturer or providing a company's service in a given area. **4** a business given such a privilege. **5** the territory granted to such a business. **6** authorization to own a member team, granted by a professional sports league.
—v. **1** give (a person, company, etc.) a franchise. **2** make (a product, service, etc.) available as a franchise. ⟨ME < OF *franchise* a freeing < *franc* free. See FRANK.⟩

fran•chi•see [,fræntʃaɪ'zi] *n.* a person or business that holds a franchise.

fran•chis•er ['fræntʃaɪzər] *n.* a company that grants a franchise. Also, **franchisor.**

Fran•cis•can [fræn'sɪskən] *n., adj. —n.* a member of a religious order founded by Saint Francis of Assisi (1182-1226) in 1209.
—adj. of or having to do with this religious order.

fran•cis•ca•na [,frænsə'skanə] *n.* a dolphin (*Pontoporia blainvillei*) of E South American waters. It is an endangered species.

fran•ci•um ['frænsiəm] *n. Chemistry.* a rare radioactive chemical element. *Symbol:* Fr; *at.no.* 87; *at.mass* (223); *half-life* 22 minutes. ⟨< NL; after *France*⟩

fran•ci•za•tion or **fran•ci•sa•tion** [,frænsə'zeiʃən] *or* [,frænsaɪ'zeiʃən] *n. Cdn.* the act or process of making or becoming French or French-speaking: *the francization of industry in Québec.*

fran•cize or **fran•cise** ['frænsaɪz] *v.* **-cized, -ciz•ing; -cised, -cis•ing.** *Cdn.* make or become French or French-speaking.

Fran•co– *combining form.* **1** French or French-speaking: *Francophile.* **2** French and ——: *the Franco-Prussian war.* **3** French-Canadian: *Franco-Albertan.*

fran•co•lin ['fræŋkəlɪn] *n.* any one of the European family of gallinaceous birds. ⟨< F < Ital. *francolino*⟩

Fran•co•phile ['fræŋkə,faɪl] *n.* **1** a person who greatly admires France, its people, and its culture. **2** *Cdn.* a non-French-Canadian who shows particular sympathy with the policies and culture of French-speaking Canada.

Fran•co•phobe ['fræŋkə,foub] *n.* **1** a person who hates or fears French people or French influences. **2** *Cdn.* a person who is hostile to the policies, language, culture, etc. of French-speaking Canada.

Fran•co•phone ['fræŋkə,foun] *n. Cdn.* **1** a person in a bilingual or multilingual country whose native or principal language is French. **2** (*adjl.*) of, having to do with, or made up of people whose native or principal language is French: *a Francophone riding, Francophone Africa.*

franc–ti•reur [fʀɑ̃ti'ʀœʀ] *n., pl.* **francs-ti•reurs** [fʀɑ̃ti'ʀœʀ] *French.* **1** a member of an irregular light infantry corps. **2** a guerrilla fighter or sniper. ⟨literally, freeshooter < *franc* free + *tireur* shooter⟩

fran•gi•ble ['frændʒəbəl] *adj.* breakable. ⟨< F < L *frangere* break⟩

fran•gi•pan•i [,frændʒə'pæni] *n., pl.* **-pan•is** or **-pan•i.** **1** any of various tropical American shrubs or small trees (genus *Plumeria*) of the dogbane family having large, very fragrant flowers. **2** a perfume made from the flowers of a frangipani or imitating their odour. **3** a custardy dessert sometimes used as a cake or pie filling and flavoured with ground almonds. ⟨< Muzio *Frangipani,* a 16c. Italian marquis, supposed inventor of the perfume⟩

Fran•glais [frɑŋ'glei]; *French,* [fʀɑ̃glɛ] *n. Cdn. Informal.* French spoken with many English words and expressions. Also, **Franglish.** ⟨< F *français* French + *anglais* English⟩

frank[1] [fræŋk] *adj., v., n. —adj.* **1** free in expressing one's real thoughts, opinions, and feelings; not hiding what is in one's mind; not afraid to say what one thinks. **2** clearly manifest; undisguised; plain; downright: *frank mutiny.*
—v. **1** send (a letter, package, etc.) without charge. **2** mark (a letter, package, etc.) for free mailing. **3** put a postmark on: *Have all the letters been franked?*
—n. **1** a mark to show that a letter, package, etc. is to be sent without charge. **2** the right to send letters, packages, etc. without charge. **3** a letter, package, etc. sent without charge. ⟨< OF *franc* free, sincere (originally, a Frank, freedom in early France being confined to the Franks, the dominant tribe) < Gmc.⟩ **—'frank•ly,** *adv.* **—'frank•ness,** *n.*
☛ *Hom.* FRANC.
☛ *Syn. adj.* **1. Frank,** OUTSPOKEN, CANDID = not afraid to say what one thinks or feels. **Frank** = free in expressing or showing, by manner or looks or actions, one's real thoughts and feelings: *Her eyes are frank and honest.* **Outspoken** = speaking out frankly and openly, hiding or keeping back nothing even when it involves giving offence: *He was outspoken in his criticism.* **Candid** = frank and sincere and, above all, completely truthful and impartial: *His candid account of his best friend's dishonesty surprised some people.*

frank[2] [fræŋk] *n. Informal.* frankfurter.
☛ *Hom.* FRANC.

Frank [fræŋk] *n.* a member of a group of West Germanic peoples who crossed the Rhine and invaded the Roman Empire in the 4th century A.D., gradually conquering most of Gaul and Germany. The Frankish empire was at its height under Charlemagne. ⟨? named for their national weapon; cf. OE *franca* spear⟩
☛ *Hom.* FRANC.

Frank•en•stein ['fræŋkɪn,staɪn] *n.* **1** in a novel by Mary Shelley (1797-1851), a man who creates a monster that he cannot control. **2** Also, **Frankenstein's monster,** a thing that causes the ruin of its creator. **3** monster. **4** any person brought down by his or her invention.

frank•furt•er ['fræŋk,fɜrtər] *n.* wiener. Also, **frankfurt.** ⟨< G *Frankfurter* of Frankfurt⟩

frank•in•cense ['fræŋkɪn,sɛns] *n.* a fragrant resin from certain Asiatic or African trees that gives off a sweet, spicy odour when burned. ⟨ME < OF *franc encens* pure incense⟩

Frank•ish ['fræŋkɪʃ] *adj., n. —adj.* of or having to do with the Franks.
—n. the language of the Franks.

frank•lin ['fræŋklɪn] *n.* formerly, a landowner of free but not noble birth in 14th and 15th century England. ⟨ME *francoleyn*, ult. < Med.L *francus* free < Gmc.⟩

frank•lin•ite ['fræŋklənəit] *n. Chemistry.* an oxide containing iron, manganese, and zinc. ⟨< after *Franklin*, New Jersey, where this mineral is found⟩

Franklin stove an iron stove for heating a room, looking like a fireplace. ⟨< Benjamin *Franklin* (1706-1790), who invented it⟩

frank•ly ['fræŋkli] *adv.* speaking bluntly; to be honest: *Frankly, that class is a drag.*

fran•tic ['fræntɪk] *adj.* **1** wild with fright, pain, rage, or frustration. **2** marked by wild, uncontrolled action or activity: *She made a frantic effort to stop the car.* **3** *Archaic.* insane. ⟨ME < OF *frénétique* < L < Gk. Doublet of FRENETIC.⟩ **—'fran•ti•cal•ly,** *adv.*

frap•pé [fræ'pei] *adj., n. —adj.* iced; cooled.
—n. **1** fruit juice sweetened and frozen. **2** any frozen or iced food or drink. ⟨< F *frappé*, pp. of *frapper* chill, beat⟩

fra•ter•nal [frə'tɜrnəl] *adj.* **1** brotherly. **2** of, having to do with, or being a fraternity, society, or guild. **3** of twins, developing from two separately fertilized egg cells. Compare IDENTICAL (def. 3). ⟨< L *fraternus* brotherly < *frater* brother⟩ **—fra'ter•nal•ly,** *adv.* **—fra'ter•nal,ism,** *n.*

fra•ter•ni•ty [frə'tɜrnəti] *n., pl.* **-ties. 1** a male students' society in a university or college, basically a social club, usually having secret rites and a name made up of Greek letters. Compare SORORITY. **2** a society, guild, or order of people, especially men, with common interests or a common goal. **3** people having similar interests, work, etc.: *the publishing fraternity.* **4** fraternal feeling; brotherhood. ⟨< L *fraternitas* brotherhood⟩

frat•er•nize ['frætər,naɪz] *v.* **-nized, -niz•ing. 1** associate in a brotherly way; be friendly. **2** associate in a friendly way with citizens of a hostile nation during occupation of their territory. **—,frat•er•ni'za•tion,** *n.* **—'frat•er,niz•er,** *n.*

frat•ri•cide ['frætrə,saɪd] *n.* **1** the act of killing one's brother or sister. **2** the act of killing a relative or compatriot, as in a civil war. **3** a person who commits fratricide. ⟨< L *fratricidium* the murder of one's brother < *frater* brother + *-cidium* act of killing (for def. 1); < L *fratricida* one who murders his brother < *frater* + *-cida* killer (for def. 3)⟩ **—,frat•ri'cid•al,** *adj.*

fraud [frɒd] *n.* **1** deceit; cheating; dishonesty: *Any intent to deceive is considered fraud.* **2** a dishonest act, statement, etc.; something done to deceive or cheat; trick. **3** *Informal.* a person who is not what he or she pretends to be. **4** *Law.* deliberate deception used to induce an individual to give up property or money. ⟨ME < OF *fraude* < L *fraus, fraudis* cheating⟩

fraud•u•lence ['frɒdʒələns] *or* ['frɒdjələns] *n.* **1** the fact of being fraudulent. **2** an instance of fraud. Also, **fraudulency.**

fraud•u•lent ['frɒdʒələnt] *or* ['frɒdjələnt] *adj.* **1** deceitful; cheating; dishonest. **2** intended to deceive. **3** done by fraud; obtained by trickery. ⟨ME < OF < L *fraudulentus*⟩ **—'fraud•u•lent•ly,** *adv.*

fraught [frɒt] *adj.* loaded; filled: *A battlefield is fraught with horror.* ⟨pp. of obs. *fraught* load, verbal use of noun < MDu. or MLG *vracht* freight⟩

Fraun•ho•fer lines ['fraʊn,houfər] dark lines in the solar spectrum caused by the absorption of some of the light by gaseous elements. ⟨< Joseph von *Fraunhofer* (1787-1826), German optician and physicist⟩

fray[1] [frei] *n.* a noisy quarrel; fight. ⟨var. of *affray*⟩

fray[2] [frei] *v.* **1** separate into threads; make or become ragged or worn along the edge. **2** wear away; rub. **3** become weakened or stretched beyond its strength. **4** cause strain on (something); upset: *The constant tension in the office frayed their nerves.* ⟨< F *frayer* < L *fricare* rub⟩

frazil ['fræzəl] *or* [frə'zil] *n. Cdn. Geology.* ice crystals or flakes formed in the turbulent waters of rivers, rapids, etc. and often accumulating as icebanks along the shore. Also, **frazil ice.** ⟨< Cdn.F < F *fraisil* coal cinders, ult. < L *fax, facis,* torch⟩
☛ *Hom.* FRAZZLE ['fræzəl].

fraz•zle ['fræzəl] *v.* **-zled, -zling;** *n. Informal. —v.* **1** tear to shreds; fray; wear out. **2** tire out; weary.
—n. a frazzled condition. ⟨blend of *fray*[2] and obs. *fazle,* ME *faselyn* unravel < OE *fæs* a fringe⟩
☛ *Hom.* FRAZIL.

freak [frik] *n., v. —n.* **1** an event, object, etc. that is very strange or unusual: *a freak of nature.* **2** (*adjl.*) very strange or unusual: *a freak storm.* **3** a person or animal having some extreme abnormality or deformity; monstrosity. **4** *Slang.* enthusiast; buff: *a hockey freak.* **5** a sudden change or turn of mind without reason; an odd notion or fancy; caprice.
—v.
freak out, *Slang.* **a** experience or cause to experience the disorientation, altered perception, hallucinations, etc. brought on by psychedelic drugs. **b** react or cause to react strongly to any experience; make or become extremely excited, afraid, angry, etc.: *The new roller coaster ride really freaked her out.* ⟨Cf. OE *frīcian* dance⟩

freak•ish ['frikɪʃ] *adj.* like, characteristic of, or full of freaks; strange, unusual, or capricious. **—'freak•ish•ly,** *adv.* **—'freak•ish•ness,** *n.*

freak•out ['frik,ʌut] *n. Slang.* the act or an instance of freaking out.

freak•y ['friki] *adj.* **1** freakish. **2** *Slang.* very odd or unconventional; bizarre; outlandish: *freaky clothes, a freaky rock group.* **—'freak•i•ness,** *n.*

freck•le ['frɛkəl] *n., v.* **-led, -ling.** *—n.* a small, light brown spot on the skin.
—v. **1** make freckles on; cover with freckles: *The sun freckles the skin of some people.* **2** become marked or spotted with freckles. ⟨probably alteration of *frecken* < ON *freknur*, pl.⟩

freck•le–faced ['frɛkəl ,feist] *adj.* having many freckles on the face.

freck•ly ['frɛkli] *adj.* covered with freckles.

free [fri] *adj.* **fre•er, fre•est;** *adv., v.* **freed, free•ing.** *—adj.* **1** not under another's control; having liberty; able to do, act, or think as one pleases. **2** showing liberty; caused by liberty. **3** not held back, fastened, or shut up; released; loose. **4** unhindered. **5** clear (*of* or *from*); exempt from; not marred or bothered by: *free of error, free from taxes. The whole community was free of disease.* **6** allowed; permitted (*to*): *You are free to speak.* **7** clear; open. **8** open to all: *a free port.* **9** without cost or payment. **10** without payment (*of*) a tax or duty. **11** generous: *I appreciated his free offer to carry my suitcase.* **12** giving or using much. **13** abundant. **14** not following rules, forms, or words exactly; not strict: *free verse.* **15** saying what one thinks; frank. **16** not restrained enough by manners or morals. **17** *Chemistry.* not combined with something else: *Oxygen exists free in the atmosphere.* **18** unconstrained; at ease; easy; *a free walk.* **19** *Linguistics.* of a morpheme, that may appear as a single word. *Cheer* is a free morpheme, but *-ful* in *cheerful* is not. Compare BOUND.
for free, *Informal.* without costing anything.
free and easy, paying little attention to rules or customs; unrestrained.
free from or **of,** without; lacking (something undesirable).
free with, giving or using freely.
make free (with), a use as if one owned or had complete rights; act uninhibitedly. **b** take liberties (with).
set free, make free; let loose; release.
with a free hand, generously.
—adv. **1** without cost or payment. **2** in a free manner.
—v. **1** relieve from any kind of burden, bondage, or slavery; make free: *The prisoner was freed early for good behaviour.* **2** let loose; release: *to free a boat from weeds.* **3** clear: *He will have to free himself of this charge of stealing.* ⟨OE *frēo, frīo*⟩ **—'free•ly,** *adv.* **—'free•ness,** *n.*
☛ *Syn. v.* **1, 2.** See note at RELEASE.

-free *combining form.* without; not containing: *sugar-free, fat-free.*

free agency in professional sports, the condition of being a free agent.

free agent a professional athlete who is free to sign with any team.

free association **1** *Psychology.* a technique of letting the patient's mind wander at will, inadvertently focussing on subconsciously important matters. **2** any instance of spontaneous mental association of things not obviously related. **3** the ability to join in groups without restriction. **—,free-as'so•ci,ate,** *v.*

free•base ['fri,beis] *n., v.* **-based, -bas•ing.** *—n. Informal.* a form of cocaine specially prepared for smoking.
—v. Informal. smoke this form of cocaine.

free•bie ['fribi] *n. Slang.* something free, especially a gift offered as a perquisite or a promotional gimmick. Also, **freebee, freeby.**

free•board ['fri,bɔrd] *n.* **1** *Nautical.* that part of a ship's side between the water line and the deck or gunwale. **2** the distance between the ground and the under part of the frame of an automobile.

free•boot ['fri,but] *v.* act as a freebooter; plunder. ⟨back formation < *freebooter*⟩ **—'free,boot•ing,** *n.*

free•boot•er ['fri,butər] *n.* a pirate; buccaneer. ⟨< Du. *vrijbuiter* < *vrij* free + *buit* booty⟩

free•born ['fri,bɔrn] *adj.* **1** born free, not in slavery. **2** of or suitable for people born free.

free•by ['fribi] *n.* See FREEBIE.

Free Church a Presbyterian church, known as the 'Free Church of Scotland' that seceded from the established Presbyterian Church in 1843.

free city a city forming an independent state.

freed•man ['fridmən] *n., pl.* **-men.** a man freed from slavery.

free•dom ['fridəm] *n.* **1** the state or condition of being free. **2** the condition of not being under another's control; power to do, say, or think as one pleases; liberty. **3** free use: *We give all guests the freedom of our home.* **4** lack of restraint; frankness. **5** ease of movement or action.
freedom of the press, freedom to publish anything without restriction except for the laws of libel, copyright, etc.
freedom of the seas, the right of ships to come and go on the high seas, no state having any jurisdiction over foreign vessels except within its own territorial waters. ⟨OE *frēodōm*⟩

☛ *Syn.* **2. Freedom,** LIBERTY, INDEPENDENCE = not being under the rule or control of another. **Freedom** emphasizes the power to make one's own laws, impose one's own restraints, control one's own life. **Liberty** emphasizes the right or power to do as one pleases, without restraint: *Freedom of speech does not mean liberty to gossip or tell lies.* **Independence** emphasizes the power to stand alone, not subject to or dependent on someone or something else: *Parents generally try to teach their children independence.*

Free•dom•ite ['fridə,məit] *n. Cdn.* a member of the Sons of Freedom, a Doukhobour sect.

freed•wom•an ['frid,wʊmən] *n., pl.* **-wom•en.** a woman freed from slavery.

free enterprise an economic system based on the right of a private individual to run a business for profit, with a minimum of government control.

free fall **1** the fall of a body when it is unrestrained by anything except gravity. **2** the period in a parachute jump between jumping off and the opening of a parachute.

free flight the flight of a spaceship after the power is shut down.

free–floating ['fri 'floutɪŋ] *adj. Informal.* widespread but lacking a clear cause: *free-floating anxiety.*

free–for–all ['fri fər ,ɒl] *adj., n. —adj.* open to all.
—n. a fight, race, etc. open to all or in which everybody participates, usually resulting in confusion.

free–form ['fri ,fɔrm] *adj.* free from convention: *free-form sculpture.*

Free French the French people who continued resistance to the Nazis during World War II after the Franco-German armistice of 1940.

free•hand ['fri,hænd] *adj., adv. —adj.* done by hand without using instruments, measurements, etc.: *freehand drawing.*
—adv. in a freehand way: *She drew it freehand.*

free hand the authority to act as one sees fit; carte blanche: *The committee was given a free hand, with no questions asked about how they spent the money.*

free•hand•ed ['fri,hændɪd] *adj.* generous; liberal.

free•hold ['fri,hould] *n. Law.* **1** a piece of land held for life or with the right to transfer it to one's heirs. **2** the holding of land in this way.

free•hold•er ['fri,houldər] *n.* a person who has a freehold.

free•lance ['fri,læns] *n., adj., v.* **-lanced, -lanc•ing.** *—n.* **1** a writer, artist, etc. who works independently and sells his or her work to anyone who will buy it. **2 free lance, a** in the Middle Ages, a soldier who fought for any person, group, or state that would pay him. **b** a person who fights or works for any cause that he or she chooses.
—adj. working as a freelance: *a freelance photographer.*
—v. work as a freelance. **—'free,lanc•er,** *n.*

free list a list of duty-free items.

free–living ['fri 'lɪvɪŋ] *adj.* **1** eating and drinking freely, sometimes to excess, according to one's desires; loose. **2** of an organism, existing independently of any other.

free•load or **free–load** ['fri,loud] *v. Slang.* **1** attend a party, convention, etc. chiefly for the free food and drink. **2** take liberally, without contributing anything of one's own.
—'free,load•er, *n.*

free love freedom to engage in sex outside of marriage.

free•man ['frimən] *n., pl.* **-men. 1** a person who is not a slave or a serf. **2** a person who has civil or political freedom; citizen.

free market an economic system in which prices are determined by supply and demand, and are not subject to government controls.

free•mar•tin ['fri,mɑrtən] *n.* a sterile female calf born as a twin to a male calf. ⟨origin unknown; 17c.⟩

free•ma•son ['fri,meisən] *n.* **1** formerly, a member of a guild of itinerant skilled stoneworkers in the Middle Ages, who had passwords and secret signs by which they recognized each other. **2 Freemason,** a member of the Ancient Free and Accepted Masons, a worldwide fraternal society pledged to brotherliness, mutual aid, and charity; Mason.

free•ma•son•ry ['fri,meisənri] *n.* **1 Freemasonry,** the principles, doctrines, etc. of the society of Freemasons; Masonry. **2** the members of this society; Freemasons collectively. **3** natural or instinctive understanding and sympathy.

free on board delivered free of charge on a train, ship, etc. *Abbrev.*: f.o.b. or F.O.B.

free port **1** a port open to traders of all countries on the same conditions. **2** a port where no taxes or duties have to be paid.

free press a press not censored or controlled by the government of the country where it operates.

free radical *Chemistry.* an atom or molecule having one unpaired electron, formed by destruction of a larger molecule. Free radicals are often temporary and unstable.

free–range ['fri ,reindʒ] *adj.* of or coming from fowl that are allowed to roam freely rather than being shut up in a small space: *Have you any free-range eggs?*

free ride or **lunch** *Informal.* any service or enjoyment acquired without the usual payment.

free•sia ['friʒə] *n.* any of a genus (*Freesia*) of S African plants of the iris family having fragrant red, yellow, white, or pink flowers. Freesias are widely cultivated as greenhouse plants. ⟨< NL; after F.H.T. *Freese* (1795?-1876), a German botanist⟩

Freesia

free–spo•ken ['fri 'spoukən] *adj.* speaking freely; saying what one thinks; frank.

free–standing ['fri ,stændɪŋ] *adj.* standing alone; not attached to any other structure, or supported with wires: *The CN Tower in Toronto is the tallest free-standing structure in the world.*

free•stone ['fri,stoun] *n.* **1** any stone, such as limestone or sandstone, that can easily be cut without splitting. **2** a fruit stone, or pit, that can be easily separated from the pulp. **3** a fruit having such a stone. **4** (*adjl.*) having such a stone: *freestone peaches.*

free•style ['fri,stail] *adj., n. —adj.* of or designating a performance, event, etc., as in a sports competition, in which the performer or contestant is not confined to a specific style or bound by the usual rules of execution.
—n. a freestyle performance, event, etc.

free–swim•ming ['fri ,swɪmɪŋ] *adj.* of a small organism, able to swim about without restriction.

free•think•er ['fri'θɪŋkər] *n.* a person who forms his or her religious or other opinions independently of authority or tradition.

free thought religious or other opinions formed independently of authority or tradition.

free throw *Basketball.* an unchallenged throw of the ball at the net from a special point (the **free-throw line**) as a penalty against the opposing team.

free trade 1 international trade free from protective duties and subject only to tariffs for revenue. 2 the system, principles, or practice of maintaining such trade. 3 trade unrestricted by taxes, customs, duties, or differences of treatment.

free•trad•er ['fri,treidər] *n.* 1 a person who favours the system of free trade. 2 *Cdn.* formerly, someone who traded in furs independently of such companies as the Hudson's Bay Company.

free verse poetry not restricted by the usual conventions of metre, rhyme, etc.

free•way ['fri,wei] *n. Esp. U.S.* a high-speed highway on which no tolls are charged.

free•wheel ['fri,wil] *n., v. —n.* 1 in the transmission of an automobile, etc., a device that permits the drive shaft to run freely when it is turning faster than the engine shaft. 2 on a bicycle, a device that enables the wheels to continue turning while the pedals are held still.
—v. coast.

free•wheel•ing ['fri'wilıŋ] *adj.* 1 using or having a freewheel. 2 independent or unhampered: *a freewheeling lifestyle.*

free•will ['fri'wıl] *adj.* voluntary: *a freewill offering.*

free will 1 voluntary choice; freedom of decision. 2 **a** the freedom of will to choose a particular course according to the desires, ideals, and viewpoint of the individual, not subject to outside pressure. **b** the belief that human beings have such freedom.

free world the non-communist nations. **—'free-,world,** *adj.*

freeze ['friz] *v.* **froze, fro•zen, freez•ing;** *n. —v.* 1 turn into ice; harden by cold: *to freeze ice cream. The water in the pond has frozen.* 2 cause something to become hard and stiff by lowering the temperature to below the FREEZING POINT (0°C): *By freezing meat we can keep it from spoiling.* 3 feel or be very cold: *You'll freeze if you don't have a good sleeping bag.* 4 be of the degree of cold at which water becomes ice: *It is freezing tonight.* 5 kill or damage by frost. 6 be killed or damaged by frost. 7 form ice on the surface: *Does the lake freeze in winter?* 8 become clogged by pieces of ice: *The car stalled because the gas line froze.* 9 fix or become fixed to something by freezing. 10 make or become stiff and unfriendly. 11 chill or be chilled with fear, etc. 12 become suddenly motionless: *The cat froze as soon as it saw the bird. He heard a step behind him and froze with fear.* 13 fix (prices, wages, etc.) at a definite amount, usually by governmental decree. 14 make (funds, bank balances, etc.) unusable and inaccessible. 15 prohibit the further use of (a raw material) in any way: *Cobalt was frozen during the war.* 16 make numb by injecting or applying an anesthetic: *to freeze the gum before extracting a tooth.* 17 interrupt or postpone (something, especially the production of something), in mid-process: *to freeze the production of fighter planes.*
freeze onto, *Informal.* hold on tightly to.
freeze out, *Informal.* force out or exclude socially: *The clique's unfriendliness froze out all newcomers.*
freeze over, form ice on the surface.
—n. 1 a state of extreme coldness; frost; freezing: *The freeze last night damaged the apple trees.* 2 a period during which there is freezing weather. ⟨OE *frēosan*⟩
☛ *Hom.* FRIEZE.

freeze–dried ['friz ,draıd] *adj., v. —adj.* preserved by freeze-drying.
—v. pt. and pp. of FREEZE-DRY.

freeze–dry ['friz ,draı] *v.* **-dried, -dry•ing.** preserve (food, vaccine, etc.) by quick-freezing and then evaporating the frozen moisture content in a high vacuum. Freeze-dried substances keep for a long period without refrigeration.

freeze–dry•ing ['friz ,draııŋ] *n., v. —n.* 1 the act of one who freeze-dries. 2 the process by which food, vaccine, etc. is freeze-dried.
—v. ppr. of FREEZE-DRY.

freeze–frame ['friz ,freim] *n.* a picture held still in a movie or television program.

freez•er ['frizər] *n.* 1 an insulated cabinet, compartment, or room maintained at a temperature at least several degrees below the freezing point, for freezing perishable foods and storing them in the frozen state. 2 a device for making ice cream. 3 anything that freezes.

freeze–up ['friz ,ʌp] *n. Cdn.* the time of year when rivers and lakes freeze over; onset of winter: *Freeze-up came late last year.*

freez•ing ['frizıŋ] *n., adj., v. —n.* FREEZING POINT, especially that of water: *It's below freezing outside.*
—adj. Informal. very cold: *It's freezing in here.*
—v. ppr. of FREEZE.

freezing point the temperature at which a liquid freezes. The freezing point of water at sea level is 0°C. *Abbrev.:* F.P., f.p., or fp

F region the part of the ionosphere comprising the two layers above the E layer. The two sections, both of which reflect radio waves, are known as the **F1 layer** and **F2 layer**. Compare E REGION.

freight [freit] *n., v. —n.* 1 the load of goods carried on a train, ship, etc.: *It took a whole day to unload the freight.* 2 the carrying of goods on a train, ship, etc. 3 the charge for this. 4 anything carried for pay by land, water, or air; goods in transit. 5 a train for carrying goods. 6 a load; burden.
—v. 1 load with freight. 2 carry as freight. 3 send as freight. 4 load; burden. ⟨ME < MDu. or MLG *vrecht*⟩

freight•age ['freitıdʒ] *n.* 1 the carrying of goods on a train, ship, etc. 2 a charge for this. 3 freight; cargo.

freight car a railway car for carrying freight.

freight•er ['freitər] *n.* 1 a ship or aircraft for carrying freight. 2 a person or agent who ships goods by freight.

freight train a railway train made up exclusively of freight cars.

French [frɛntʃ] *adj., n. —adj.* 1 of or having to do with France, its people, or their language. 2 French Canadian; of or having to do with French Canada, French Canadians, or their language.
—n. **1 the French,** *pl.* **a** the people of France. **b** *Cdn.* the people of French Canada. 2 the French language. The kind of French spoken in Canada is called Canadian French. ⟨OE *Francisc* < *Franca* Frank⟩

French and Indian War the part of the Seven Years' War fought in North America between Britain and France, with Indian allies (1754-1763).

French braid a woman's or girl's hairstyle in which braiding is begun at the top of the head, with more hair being added bit by bit as the braid descends, ending in a conventional braid of the loose hair.

French bread white bread baked in a long, slim loaf with a crisp crust.

French Canada 1 French Canadians as a group; all French Canadians. 2 the part of Canada inhabited mainly or entirely by French Canadians, especially the province of Québec.

French Canadian 1 a Canadian whose ancestors came from France or whose first language is French. 2 of or having to do with French Canada or French Canadians. 3 the language of the French Canadians; Canadian French.

French chalk talc used for marking lines on cloth or removing grease.

French Community an association formed in 1958 of France and its dependent territories, and many of its former colonies.

French cuff a sleeve cuff that is folded back at the wrist and fastened with a cuff link instead of a button.

French curve a template used by drafters to draw various curves.

French doors a pair of doors hinged at the sides and opening in the middle. They have panes of glass all the way down like a window, and often open onto a patio.

French dressing a salad dressing made of olive oil, vinegar, salt, spices, etc.

French Fact *Cdn.* the existence of French Canada as a distinct cultural entity.

French fry a strip of potato that has been French-fried, that is, fried in deep fat until brown and crisp on the outside; CHIP (def. 4). Also, **french fry.**

French–fry ['frɛntʃ ,fraı] *v.,* **-fried, -fry•ing.** cook in deep fat. Also, **french-fry. —'French-,fried,** *adj.*

A French horn

French horn a brass wind instrument that has a mellow tone.

French knot an embroidery stitch in which the needle is pushed through the fabric from below, then the thread is wrapped several times around the needle, which is pushed back through the fabric very near the original hole. Pulling the thread tight secures the knot: *A French knot is often used to form the raised centre of a flower design.*

French leave 1 the act of leaving without ceremony, permission, or notice; secret or hurried departure. 2 originally, the custom of going away from a reception, etc., without taking leave of the host or hostess.

French•man ['frɛntʃmən] *n., pl.* **-men.** 1 a native or inhabitant of France. 2 a citizen of France. 3 a French Canadian. 4 a French ship.

French marigold a small marigold (*Tagetes patula*) having red marks on its yellow petals.

French pastry 1 small, individual, rich cakes, tarts, eclairs, etc. 2 one of these cakes.

French polish a highly glossy finish, based on shellac, applied to quality furniture by hand in several coats.

French Provincial 1 of, like, or having to do with a style of furniture, architecture, or fabric design that originated in the 17th and 18th century French provinces. 2 this style of furniture.

French Revolution the revolution in France from 1789 to 1799, which ousted the monarchy and set up a republic.

French seam a seam stitched first on the right side of the material, then on the wrong side, to cover the raw edges.

French Shore *Cdn.* 1 the west coast of Newfoundland, where the French held fishing and other rights from 1713 till 1904. 2 an area originally settled by the Acadian French, located on the southwest coast of Nova Scotia.

French toast slices of bread dipped in a mixture of egg and milk and then fried in a small quantity of oil.

French windows a pair of long windows like doors, hinged at the sides and opening in the middle.

French•wom•an ['frɛntʃ,wʊmən] *n., pl.* **-wom•en.** 1 a woman who is a native or inhabitant of France. 2 a woman who is a citizen of France. 3 a French-Canadian woman.

fre•net•ic [frə'nɛtɪk] *adj.* frenzied; frantic. ⟨var. of *phrenetic*⟩ **—fre'net•i•cal•ly,** *adv.*

fre•num ['frinəm] *n., pl.* **-na** [-nə] or **-nums.** *Anatomy, zoology.* a fold of mucous membrane serving to support and restrain the movement of a movable organ or part, such as the membrane under the tongue.

fren•zied ['frɛnzid] *adj.* greatly excited; frantic. **—'fren•zied•ly,** *adv.*

fren•zy ['frɛnzi] *n., pl.* **-zies.** 1 a state of near madness: *She was in a frenzy of grief when she heard of her son's death.* 2 a state of very great excitement: *The spectators were in a frenzy after the home team scored the winning goal.* ⟨ME < OF *frenesie* < L *phrenesis,* ult. < Gk. *phrēn* mind⟩

Fre•on ['friɒn] *n. Chemistry. Trademark.* any of a class of fluorated hydrocarbons formerly used especially as refrigerants and as propellants for aerosol sprays.

fre•quen•cy ['frikwənsi] *n., pl.* **-cies.** 1 frequent occurrence. 2 the rate of occurrence. 3 *Physics.* the number of times that any regularly repeated event, as a vibration, occurs in a given unit of time. 4 the number of complete cycles per second of an alternating current or any type of wave motion: *Different radio stations broadcast at different frequencies so that their signals can be heard distinctly.* 5 *Mathematics.* the ratio of the number of times an event actually occurs to the number of times it might occur in a given period. 6 *Statistics.* for a collection of data, the number of items in a given category. The ratio of this number to the total number of items gives the relative frequency.

frequency band *Television, radio, etc.* a certain range of wavelengths; channel.

frequency distribution *Statistics.* a set of categories of a variable, classified according to the frequencies associated with each category.

frequency modulation *Radio.* 1 a method of transmitting the sound signals of a broadcast by changing the frequency of the carrier waves to match the sound signals. 2 a broadcasting system that uses this method. Compare AMPLITUDE MODULATION. *Abbrev.*: FM or F.M.

fre•quent *adj.* ['frikwənt]; *v.* [frɪ'kwɛnt] *or* ['frikwənt] *adj., v.* *—adj.* 1 occurring often, near together, or every little while. 2 regular; habitual: *She is a frequent caller at our house.*
—v. go often to; be often in: *Frogs frequent ponds, streams, and marshes.* ⟨< L *frequens, -entis* crowded⟩

fre•quen•ta•tive [frɪ'kwɛntətɪv] *adj., n. Grammar. —adj.* expressing frequent repetition of an action. *Wrestle* is a frequentative verb from *wrest.*
—n. a frequentative verb or morpheme.

fre•quent•er [frɪ'kwɛntər] *n.* a habitual visitor.

fre•quent•ly ['frikwəntli] *adv.* often, repeatedly; every little while.

fres•co ['frɛskou] *n., pl.* **-coes** or **-cos;** *v.* **-coed, -co•ing.** *—n.* 1 the act or art of painting with water colours on damp, fresh plaster. 2 a picture or design so painted.
—v. paint in fresco. ⟨< Ital. *fresco* cool, fresh⟩

fresh [frɛʃ] *adj.* 1 newly made, arrived, or obtained: *fresh footprints.* 2 not known, seen, or used before; new; recent. 3 additional; further; another: *After her failure she made a fresh start.* 4 not salty: *There is fresh water in the Great Lakes.* 5 not spoiled; newly grown, produced, or gathered; not stale. 6 not artificially preserved. 7 not wearied; vigorous; lively. 8 innovative; creative or original: *We need a fresh approach to our problem.* 9 not faded or worn; bright. 10 looking healthy or young. 11 clean; newly washed: *a fresh shirt.* 12 pure; cool; refreshing: *a fresh breeze.* 13 fairly strong; brisk: *a fresh wind.* 14 not experienced. 15 *Informal.* too bold; impudent.
fresh out of, *Informal.* having just used or sold the last of; having none left of. ⟨OE *fersc;* but influenced in form by OF *fresche,* fem. of *freis* < Gmc.⟩ **—'fresh•ly,** *adv.* **—'fresh•ness,** *n.*

fresh breeze *Meteorology.* in the Beaufort scale of wind speeds (see Appendix), a moderate wind of between 29 and 38 km/h.

fresh•en ['frɛʃən] *v.* make or become fresh or fresher: *She thought it would be a good idea to freshen the paint on the house. The wind freshened at sunset.*
freshen up, do something to make, or feel, fresh: *He freshened up by taking a bath and changing his clothes.*

fresh•et ['frɛʃɪt] *n.* 1 a flood caused by heavy rains or melted snow. 2 a rush of fresh water flowing into the sea. ⟨< *fresh* flood, stream, or pool of fresh water + diminutive *-et*⟩

fresh gale *Meteorology.* in the Beaufort scale of wind speeds (See Appendix), a strong wind of between 62 and 74 km/h.

fresh•man ['frɛʃmən] *n., pl.* **-men.** *—n.* 1 a student in the first year of a university course. 2 beginner. 3 (*adjl.*) of or having to do with freshmen.

fresh•wa•ter ['frɛʃ,wɒtər] *adj.* 1 of, having to do with, or living in water that is not salty: *The catfish is a freshwater fish.* 2 not used to sailing on the sea: *a freshwater sailor.*

freshwater dogfish a fish of the family Amiidae, of the upper St. Lawrence River and Great Lakes.

freshwater eel an eel of the family Anguillidae, that lives in rivers, lakes, etc. and only goes out to sea to spawn.

freshwater herring a fish (*Leucichthys artedi*) which prefers deep water and is valued as a tasty food fish.

freshwater stickleback a fish (*Eucalia inconstans*) native to most parts of Canada west of New Brunswick. It grows to a length of 6 cm.

Fres•nel lens [frei'nɛl] a lens with a grooved surface of concentric rings, used in cameras, headlights, spotlights, etc. ⟨after Augustin Jean *Fresnel* (1788-1827), French physicist⟩

fret[1] [frɛt] *v.* **fret•ted, fret•ting;** *n. —v.* 1 be peevish, unhappy, discontented, or worried: *A baby sometimes frets in hot weather. Don't fret about your mistake.* 2 make peevish, unhappy, discontented, or worried. 3 eat away; wear; rub. 4 roughen; disturb.
—n. 1 a peevish complaining; worry; a discontented condition. 2 a hole worn through by fretting. ⟨OE *fretan* eat⟩ **—'fret•ter,** *n.*

fret[2] [frɛt] *n., v.* **fret•ted, fret•ting.** *—n.* an ornamental pattern made of straight lines bent or combined at angles.
—v. decorate with fretwork or with a fret or frets. ⟨ME < OF *frete* trellis work⟩

fret[3] [frɛt] *n., v.* **fret•ted, fret•ting.** *—n.* one of a series of ridges of wood, ivory, or metal on a guitar, banjo, etc. to show where to put the fingers to produce particular tones.
—v. **1** provide with frets. **2** push down the strings of (an instrument) to touch the frets. ⟨origin uncertain⟩

fret•ful ['frɛtfəl] *adj.* **1** inclined to fret; peevish; unhappy; discontented. **2** agitated; seething: *the fretful sea.* **3** gusty: *the fretful wind.* **—'fret•ful•ly,** *adv.* **—'fret•ful•ness,** *n.*

fret saw a saw with a very narrow, fine blade set in a U-shaped frame, used for cutting open designs in thin wood. Fret saws usually have between seven and fourteen teeth per centimetre. Compare COPING SAW.

fret•ted ['frɛtɪd] *adj., v. —adj.* having frets.
—v. pt. and pp. of FRET.

fret•work ['frɛt,wɜrk] *n.* ornamental openwork or carving.

Freud•i•an ['frɔɪdiən] *adj., n. —adj.* of or having to do with Sigmund Freud (1856-1939), an Austrian physician, who developed a theory and technique of psychoanalysis, or with his teachings.
—n. a person who believes in Freud's teachings or follows his technique of psychoanalysis.

Freud•i•an•ism ['frɔɪdiə,nɪzəm] *n.* **1** the teachings of Freud. **2** a Freudian quality or character.

Freudian slip a slip of the tongue which seems to reveal what one is really thinking.

Frey [frei] *n. Norse mythology.* the god of plenty, fruitfulness, peace, and love, brother of Freya.

Frey•a ['freiə] *n. Norse mythology.* the goddess of beauty and love, sister of Frey.

Fri. Friday.

fri•a•ble ['fraɪəbəl] *adj.* easily crumbled: *Dry soil is friable.* ⟨< L *friabilis* < *friare* crumble⟩ **—,fri•a'bil•i•ty,** *n.*

fri•ar ['fraɪər] *n.* a member of certain religious orders, especially the Roman Catholic mendicant orders, the Franciscans, Dominicans, Carmelites, and Augustinians. ⟨ME < OF *frere* < L *frater* brother⟩
☛ *Hom.* FRYER.

Friar's balsam an aromatic preparation for the treatment of colds, sinus problems, etc.

friar's lantern IGNIS FATUUS.

fri•ar•y ['fraɪəri] *n., pl.* **-ar•ies. 1** a building or buildings where friars live; monastery. **2** a brotherhood of friars.

fric•an•deau [,frɪkən'dou] *or* ['frɪkən,dou] *n., pl.* **-deaus** or **-deaux** [-'dou] *or* [-,dou]. veal or other meat larded, braised, or fried, and served with a sauce. ⟨< F *fricandeau,* related to *fricassée.* See FRICASSEE.⟩

fric•as•see [,frɪkə'si] *n., v.* **-seed, -see•ing.** *—n.* meat cut up, stewed, and served in a sauce made with its own gravy.
—v. prepare (meat) in this way. ⟨< F *fricassée* < *fricasser* mince and cook in sauce⟩

fric•a•tive ['frɪkətɪv] *adj., n. —adj. Phonetics.* of consonants, pronounced by forcing the breath through a narrow opening. The English fricative consonants are [f], [v], [θ], [ð], [s], [z], [ʃ], [ʒ], and [h].
—n. a fricative consonant. ⟨< NL < L *fricare* to rub⟩

fric•tion ['frɪkʃən] *n.* **1** a rubbing of one object against another; rubbing: *Matches are lighted by friction.* **2** *Physics.* the resistance to motion of surfaces that touch; resistance of a moving body to water, air, etc. through which it travels or to the surface on which it moves: *A sled moves more easily on smooth ice than on rough ground because there is less friction.* **3** conflict of differing ideas, opinions, etc.; disagreement: *Political differences caused friction between the two countries.* ⟨< L *frictio, -onis* < *fricare* rub⟩

fric•tion•al ['frɪkʃənəl] *adj.* having to do with friction; caused by friction. **—'fric•tion•al•ly,** *adv.*

Fri•day ['fraɪdei] *or* ['fraɪdi] *n.* **1** the sixth day of the week, following Thursday. **2** the servant of Robinson Crusoe. **3** any faithful servant or devoted follower.
man Friday or **girl Friday,** a reliable and devoted assistant, so called after Robinson Crusoe's servant. ⟨OE *Frīgedæg* Frigg's day < gen. of *Frīg* + *dæg* day; based on L *dies Veneris* Venus' day⟩

Fri•days ['fraɪdeiz] *adv.* every Friday; happening on a Friday regularly.

fridge [frɪdʒ] *n. Informal.* refrigerator. Also, **frig.** ⟨shortening of *refrigerator* or *Frigidaire* (a trademark)⟩

fried [fraɪd] *adj., v. —adj.* cooked in fat.
—v. pt. and pp. of FRY[1].

fried cake a small cake fried in deep fat; doughnut or cruller.

friend [frɛnd] *n.* **1** a person who knows and likes another. **2** a person who favours and supports. **3** a person who belongs to the same side or group: *Are you friend or foe?* **4 Friend,** a member of the Society of Friends; Quaker: *The Friends favour simplicity in clothes and manners.* **5** an object that provides reliable assistance; anything helpful: *A flashlight is a good friend in the wilderness.*
be friends with, be a friend of.
make friends with, become a friend of. ⟨OE *frēond,* originally ppr. of *frēogan* love⟩

friend at court a person who can help one to influence others; influential friend.

friend•less ['frɛndlɪs] *adj.* without friends.
—'friend•less•ness, *n.*

friend•ly ['frɛndli] *adj.* **-li•er, -li•est;** *adv. —adj.* **1** of a friend; having the attitude of a friend; kind: *a friendly greeting.* **2** like a friend; like a friend's. **3** on good terms; not hostile: *friendly relations between countries.* **4** wanting to be a friend: *a friendly dog.* **5** favouring and supporting; favourable: *a friendly breeze.*
—adv. in a friendly manner; as a friend. ⟨OE *frēondlīc*⟩
—'friend•li•ness, *n.*

friend•ship ['frɛndʃɪp] *n.* **1** the state of being friends. **2** a liking between friends. **3** friendly feeling; friendly behaviour: *His smile radiated friendship.*

fries [fraɪz] *n.pl.* FRENCH FRIES.

frieze[1] [friz] *n.* **1** a horizontal band of decoration around a room, building, mantel, etc. **2** *Architecture.* a horizontal band forming part of the upper section of a wall, often ornamented with sculpture. The frieze is the part of an entablature between the cornice and architrave. See COLUMN for picture. ⟨< F *frise* < Med.L *frisium* < L *Phrygium* of Phrygia⟩
☛ *Hom.* FREEZE.

frieze[2] [friz] *n., v. —n.* a thick woollen cloth with a shaggy nap on one side.
—v. raise a nap on (cloth). ⟨ME < OF *(drap de) frise* Frisian (cloth)⟩
☛ *Hom.* FREEZE.

frig [frɪdʒ] *n.* See FRIDGE.

frig•ate ['frɪgɪt] *n.* **1** a modern warship larger than a corvette and smaller than a destroyer, used especially as an escort vessel. **2** formerly, a three-masted sailing warship of medium size. ⟨< F *frégate* < Ital. *fregata*⟩

frigate bird any of a genus (*Fregata,* constituting the family Fregatidae) of tropical and subtropical sea birds having mainly black plumage, long, slender, strong wings, a long forked tail, and a long bill that curves downward at the tip. Frigate birds are noted for robbing other birds of their fish.

Frigg [frɪg] *n. Norse mythology.* the wife of Odin and goddess of the sky. Also, **Frigga.**

fright [frəit] *n., v. —n.* **1** sudden fear; sudden terror. **2** *Informal.* a person or thing that is ugly, shocking, or ridiculous: *She looked a fright in that hat.*
take fright, become alarmed; panic.
—v. Poetic. frighten. ⟨OE *fryhto*⟩

fright•en ['frəitən] *v.* **1** fill with fright; make afraid; scare. **2** become afraid. **3** cause (someone or an animal) to move in a certain direction or persuade (someone or an animal) into something or doing something, through fear: *Keep still, or you'll frighten the deer off. Ringing the doorbell frightens our cat into hiding in the closet. The gunshot frightened the crowd into silence.*
—'fright•en•er, *n.*
☛ *Syn.* **1. Frighten,** SCARE, ALARM = fill with fear. **Frighten** is the general word: *The rattlesnake frightened me.* **Scare** particularly suggests suddenly giving sharp fear or terror to a timid person or animal: *The firecrackers scared the puppy.* **Alarm** = fill with intense fear and anxiety: *Her failure to come home at midnight alarmed us.*

fright•ened ['frəitənd] *adj., v. —adj.* filled with fright; afraid.
—v. pt. and pp. of FRIGHTEN.
☛ *Syn.* See note at AFRAID.

fright•en•ing ['frəitənɪŋ] *adj., v. —adj.* causing fright or fear: *a frightening experience.*
—v. ppr. of FRIGHTEN. **—'fright•en•ing•ly,** *adv.*

fright•ful ['frəitfəl] *adj.* **1** causing fright or horror; dreadful; terrible: *a frightful thunderstorm.* **2** ugly; shocking. **3** *Informal.*

very great. **4** *Informal.* disagreeable; irritating: *What a frightful cough he has.* **—'fright•ful•ly,** *adv.* **—'fright•ful•ness,** *n.*

frig•id ['frɪdʒɪd] *adj.* **1** very cold: *a frigid climate.* **2** cold in feeling or manner; stiff; unfriendly: *a frigid reception.* **3** of a woman, sexually unresponsive. ⟨< L *frigidus* < *frigere* be cold < *frigus* cold⟩ **—fri'gid•i•ty,** *n.* **—'frig•id•ly,** *adv.* **—'frig•id•ness,** *n.*

Frigid Zone formerly, either of two regions comprising the high latitudes, north of the Arctic Circle in the northern hemisphere and south of the Antarctic Circle in the southern hemisphere, forming part of a now obsolete classification system for world climate zones. See also TEMPERATE ZONE, TORRID ZONE.

fri•jol ['fri,houl] *or* [fri'houl] *n., pl.* **fri•jo•les** [fri'houliz] *or* [fri'houleis]. **1** a kidney bean used as food, common in Mexican and SW American cooking. Also, **frijole. 2 frijoles,** *pl.* a Mexican dish consisting of pinto beans boiled until tender and then fried, often misleadingly called **refried beans**. ⟨< Sp. *frijol, frejol* < L *faseolus*, earlier *phaselus* < Gk. *phaselos* kind of bean⟩

frill [frɪl] *n., v.* —*n.* **1** a RUFFLE[1] (def. 2). **2** *Informal.* anything added merely for show; useless ornament; affectation of dress, manner, speech, etc. **3** anything desirable but inessential: *Curriculum planners are often guilty of treating music as a frill.* **4** a fringe of feathers, hair, etc. around the neck of a bird or animal.
—*v.* **1** decorate with a frill; adorn with frills. **2** form into a frill. ⟨origin uncertain⟩

fril•ly [frɪli] *adj.* **1** having ruffles or frills. **2** like a frill.

fringe [frɪndʒ] *n., v.* **fringed, fring•ing.** —*n.* **1** a border or trimming made of threads, cords, etc., either loose or tied together in small bunches: *The chesterfield had a fringe along the bottom edge.* **2** anything like this; border: *a fringe of hair over her forehead.* **3** (*adjl.*) of the border or outside. **4** anything thought of as marginal rather than central: *He belongs to the radical fringe of the labour movement.* **5** (*adjl.*) marginal; not central: *They didn't want to spend too much time on fringe issues.* **6** *Optics.* the dark or light bands due to diffraction of light or interference.
—*v.* **1** put a border on. **2** be a border for; border: *Bushes fringed the road.* ⟨ME < OF *frenge* < L *fimbria*⟩

fringe area an area on the edge of something, such as a field or city.

fringe benefit any employment benefit given to an employee over and above his or her regular wages: *Pensions and medical insurance are fringe benefits.*

fringed gentian a North American gentian (*Gentiana crinita*), having blue petals divided like a fringe.

fringed po•lyg•a•la [pə'lɪgələ] a North American wildflower (*Polygala paucifolia*), having showy purple flowers.

fringe land *Cdn.* in the North, land that is relatively far from a railway.

fringe tree any member of genus *Chionanthus* of the olive family, having white flowers.

fringing reef a coral reef attached at one end to the shore.

frip•per•y ['frɪpəri] *n., pl.* **-per•ies. 1** cheap, showy clothes; gaudy ornaments. **2** a cheap, showy article of clothing; gaudy ornament. **3** a showing off; foolish display; pretended refinement: *Affectations of manner and speech are mere frippery.* ⟨< F *friperie*, ult. < *frepe* rag⟩

Fris•bee ['frɪzbi] *n. Trademark.* a light disk, usually of plastic, that is shaped like an upside-down saucer with a flange turned inward at the bottom to facilitate throwing and catching. It is spun through the air in various ways. ⟨Named after Mother *Frisbie's* Pie Company in Bridgeport, Connecticut, whose pie plates were formerly used in a similar way⟩

Fri•sian ['friʒən] *n., adj.* —*n.* **1** a native or inhabitant of Friesland, a district in N Netherlands, or certain nearby islands. **2** the language spoken in Friesland and certain nearby islands. Frisian is a West Germanic dialect, closely akin to English. **3** any member of an ancient Germanic people living in N Holland.
—*adj.* of or having to do with Friesland, its people, or their language.

frisk [frɪsk] *v.* **1** run and jump about playfully; skip and dance joyously; frolic. **2** *Informal.* search (a person) for concealed weapons, stolen goods, etc. by running a hand quickly over the person's clothes. **3** *Slang.* steal from (a person) in this way. ⟨originally adj., < OF *frisque* < Gmc.; cf. G *frisch*⟩

frisk•y ['frɪski] *adj.* **frisk•i•er, frisk•i•est.** playful; lively. **—'frisk•i•ly,** *adv.* **—'frisk•i•ness,** *n.*

fris•son [fʀi'sɔ̃] *n. French.* a shiver, as of pleasure or fear; thrill.

frit [frɪt] *n., v.* **frit•ted, frit•ting** —*n.* a partly melted mixture of sand and other materials from which glass, glazes, and enamels are made.
—*v.* make (substances) into frit. ⟨< F *fritte* < Ital. *fritta* fried pp. of *friggere* < L *frigere* fry⟩

frit fly any of various tiny flies (family Chloropidae) whose larvae destroy grain by feeding on it.

frith [frɪθ] *n.* firth. ⟨var. of *firth*⟩

frit•il•lar•y ['frɪtə,lɛri] *n., pl.* **-lar•ies. 1** any of a genus (*Fritillaria*) of plants of the lily family of north temperate regions, having drooping, bell-shaped flowers often spotted or checkered with green or purple. **2** any of various butterflies (family Nymphalidae, especially of genera *Speyeria* and *Boloria*) having orange or brownish wings spotted with black and sometimes silver. ⟨< NL *fritillaria* < L *fritillus* dice box; with reference to the checkered markings on the petals⟩

frit•ta•ta [fri'tatə] *n.* a Mexican dish consisting of an omelette cooked with pieces of meat and vegetables.

frit•ter[1] ['frɪtər] *v., n.* —*v.* **1** waste little by little (*used with* **away**) **2** cut or tear into small pieces; break into fragments.
—*n.* a small piece; fragment. ⟨< OF *freture, fraiture* < L *fractura.* See FRACTURE.⟩ **—'frit•ter•er,** *n.*

frit•ter[2] ['frɪtər] *n.* a small cake of batter, sometimes containing fruit or other food, fried in fat: *corn fritters.* ⟨ME < OF *friture*, ult. < L *frigere* fry⟩

fritz [frɪts] *n.*
on the fritz, *Slang.* out of order; not working or functioning: *The TV is on the fritz again.*

fri•vol [,frɪvəl] *v.* **fri•volled, fri•vol•ling.** fritter away (time or money) on foolish things. ⟨back formation < *frivolous*⟩

fri•vol•i•ty [frə'vɒləti] *n., pl.* **-ties. 1** a being frivolous. **2** a frivolous act or thing.

friv•o•lous ['frɪvələs] *adj.* **1** lacking in seriousness or sense; silly: *Frivolous behaviour is out of place in church.* **2** of little worth or importance; trivial: *He wasted his time on frivolous matters.* ⟨< L *frivolus*⟩ **—'friv•o•lous•ly,** *adv.* **—'friv•o•lous•ness,** *n.*

frizz or **friz** [frɪz] *v.* **frizzed, friz•zing;** *n., pl.* **friz•zes.** —*v.* form into small, crisp curls; curl.
—*n.* hair curled in small, crisp curls or a very close crimp. ⟨apparently < F *friser*⟩

friz•zle[1] ['frɪzəl] *v.* **-zled, -zling;** *n.* —*v.* form into small, crisp curls; curl.
—*n.* **1** being frizzled. **2** a small, crisp curl. ⟨? related to OE *frīs* curly⟩ **—'friz•zler,** *n.*

friz•zle[2] ['frɪzəl] *v.* **-zled, -zling;** *n.* —*v.* **1** make a hissing, sputtering noise when cooking; sizzle. **2** fry or broil until crisp.
—*n.* a sizzle. ⟨? < *fry* and *sizzle*⟩

friz•zly ['frɪzli] *adj.* **-zli•er, -zli•est.** full of small, crisp curls; curly.

friz•zy ['frɪzi] *adj.* **-zi•er, -zi•est.** frizzly. **—'friz•zi•ly,** *adv.* **—'friz•zi•ness,** *n.*

fro [frou] *adv.*
to and fro, first one way and then back again; back and forth. ⟨< ON *frá.* Akin to FROM.⟩

frock [frɒk] *n., v.* —*n.* **1** a gown; dress. **2** a loose outer garment. **3** a robe worn by a member of the clergy.
—*v.* **1** clothe in a frock. **2** invest with clerical authority. ⟨ME < OF *froc*⟩

frock coat a man's coat with a full skirt reaching approximately to the knees, and equally long in front and at the back. It was worn in the 19th century.

frog[1] [frɒg] *n.* **1** any of a family (Ranidae) of small, squat, tailless amphibians having smooth, usually green or brown skin, and long, strong hind legs adapted for leaping. Compare TOAD. **2** any of various other amphibians of the same order (Anura; also called Salientia), such as the tree frogs. **3** a device on a rail where a railway track crosses or branches from another. **4** a pad of horny substance in the middle of the bottom of a foot of a horse, donkey, etc. **5** a small, perforated or spiked device for holding flowers upright in a vase, bowl, etc. **6** the part by which the bow of a stringed instrument is held.
frog in (one's) **throat,** *Informal.* a slight hoarseness caused by soreness or swelling in the throat. ⟨OE *frogga*⟩

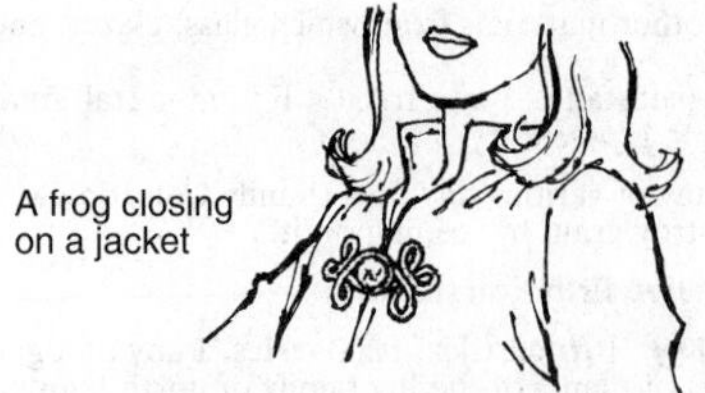
A frog closing on a jacket

frog² [frɒg] *n.* **1** an ornamental fastening for a coat or dress. **2** an attachment or loop on a belt, for carrying a sword, bayonet, etc. ⟨? < Pg. *froco* < L *floccus* flock²⟩

frog kick *Swimming.* a movement of the legs in which the swimmer draws his or her knees forward and then kicks out to the sides and brings both legs together again. The frog kick is done in the breast stroke.

frog•man ['frɒg,mæn] *or* ['frɒgmən] *n., pl.* **-men.** a skindiver, especially one in or working for the armed forces. Most of the world's navies now have frogmen.

frog run *Cdn.* in sugaring-off operations, the second run of sap in the maple trees, inferior to the first, or ROBIN RUN, for making syrup or sugar. Compare with BUD RUN and ROBIN RUN.

frol•ic ['frɒlɪk] *n., v.* **-icked, -ick•ing.** *—n.* **1** a merry prank; fun. **2** a merry game or party. **3** formerly, a gathering for work, such as a husking bee or a barn raising.
—v. play; have fun; make merry. ⟨< Du. *vrolijk* < MDu. *vrō* glad + *-lijk* -ly⟩ **—'frol•ick•er,** *n.*

frol•ic•some ['frɒlɪksəm] *adj.* full of fun; merry.

from [frʌm] *or* [frɒm]; *unstressed,* [frəm] *prep.* **1** out of; of: *Bricks are made from clay.* **2** starting out at; beginning with: *the train from Montréal. Study the lesson from page 10 to page 15.* **3** originating in; having a source in or at: *The river flows from the mountain. Much of our clothing is from Québec.* **4** caused by; because of; by reason of: *to act from a sense of duty.* **5** as being unlike: *Anyone can tell apples from oranges.* **6** off; out of: *She took a book from the table. He took a shirt from the drawer.* **7** out of the control or possession of: *He took the knife from the baby.* **8** out of proximity to: *Keep the baby away from the barbecue.* **9** as part of; less than; subtract: *Take three from six.* **10** so as not to be: *stop from sleeping, refrain from chattering.* **11** given or sent by: *a gift from my father.*
keep from. See KEEP. ⟨OE *fram, from*⟩

frond [frɒnd] *n.* **1** a divided leaf of a fern, palm, etc. **2** a leaflike part of a seaweed, lichen, etc. ⟨< L *frons, frondis* leaf⟩

front [frʌnt] *n., adj., v., adv.* *—n.* **1** the first part; foremost part: *the front of a car.* **2** the part that faces forward: *the front of a dress.* **3** something fastened or worn on the front. **4** *Military.* the area where active fighting is going on between opposing armies. **5** a sphere of activity combining different groups in a political or economic battle: *the labour front.* **6** the forces fighting for some political or social aim. **7** the land facing a street, river, lake, etc. **8** a manner of looking or behaving. **9** *Informal.* an outward appearance of wealth, importance, etc. **10** *Informal.* a person appointed to add respectability or prestige to an enterprise. **11** *Informal.* a person or thing that serves as a cover for illegal activities. **12** forehead. **13** the face. **14** *Cdn.* **a** the settled, civilized part of the country at the edge of the frontier. **b** in Newfoundland and Nova Scotia, the area where the spring seal hunt took place, at the edge of the Arctic ice fields. **15** the dividing surface between two dissimilar air masses: *The weather report says there is a cold front approaching from the northwest.* **16** impertinence; nerve. **17** a position in the vanguard. **18** an avenue by the water's edge.
in front of, in a place or position before (a person or thing): *She stood in front of me.*
—adj. **1** of, on, in, or at the front. **2** *Phonetics.* pronounced by raising the tongue against or near the forward part of the hard palate. The *e* [i] in *she* is a front vowel.
—v. **1** have the front toward; face (*often used with* **on**). **2** be in front of. **3** furnish with a front. **4** meet face to face; defy; oppose. **5** *Informal.* serve as a cover for a pressure group, an illegal activity, or the like: *Some claimed that the dockers' union fronted for the smuggling ring.*
—adv.
eyes front! look forward! direct the eyes ahead! ⟨< L *frons, frontis,* literally, forehead⟩

front•age ['frʌntɪdʒ] *n.* **1** the front of a building or of a lot. **2** the length of this front. **3** the direction that the front of a building or lot faces. **4** the land facing a street, river, etc. **5** the land between a building and a street, river, etc.

frontage road a road parallelling an expressway or freeway to provide access for local traffic.

fron•tal ['frʌntəl] *adj., n.* *—adj.* **1** of, on, in, for, or at the front. **2** of the forehead.
—n. a bone of the forehead. ⟨< NL *frontalis* < L *frons, frontis,* literally, forehead⟩ **—'front•al•ly,** *adv.*

frontal lobe *Anatomy.* the front part of each hemisphere of the brain.

frontal zone *Meteorology.* a zone where different air masses meet.

front bench **1** in a legislative chamber, the front seats on either side, reserved for the party leaders. **2** the party leaders.

frontbencher in a legislative body, one of the leading members of a political party: *Cabinet ministers are the government frontbenchers.*

front court *Basketball.* **1** the half of the playing area which contains the basket. **2** a team's forward line.

front–end loader ['frʌnt 'ɛnd] a tracked vehicle having a hydraulically operated scoop at the front, used for picking up a load of dirt, rocks, etc. from the ground and transferring it to a truck or dumping place.

front ice *Cdn.* ice near the shore, especially that east of Labrador.

fron•tier [frɒn'tir] *or* [frʌn'tir] *n.* **1** the farthest part of a settled country, where the wilds begin: *The Yukon is part of Canada's present-day frontier.* **2** a part of one country that touches on the border of another; boundary line or border between two countries. **3** an uncertain or undeveloped region: *the frontiers of science.* **4** (*adjl.*) of, on, or like a frontier: *frontier life, the frontier spirit.* ⟨ME < OF *frontiere* < *front* front < L *frons, frontis,* literally, forehead⟩

Frontier College a famous Canadian educational body serving isolated mining and logging camps.

fron•tiers•man [frɒn'tirzmən] *or* [frʌn'tirzmən] *n., pl.* **-men.** someone who lives on the frontier.

fron•tis•piece ['frʌntɪs,pis] *or* ['frɒntɪs,pis] *n.* **1** a picture facing the title page of a book or of a division of a book. **2** *Architecture.* **a** the main part or the decorated entrance of a building. **b** a pediment over a door, gate, etc. ⟨< F *frontispice* < LL *frontispicium,* literally, looking at the forehead < L *frons, frontis* forehead + *specere* look⟩

front•let ['frʌntlɪt] *n.* **1** a band or ornament worn on the forehead. **2** the forehead of an animal or bird.

front line *Military.* the part of the front nearest to enemy positions in battle.

front man **1** one who officially represents a group or organization. **2** one who fronts for another: *The pleasant storekeeper was front man for a gang of jewel smugglers.*

front matter *Printing.* the pages of a book that precede the actual text. The preface and table of contents belong to the front matter.

fron•to•gen•e•sis [,frʌntou'dʒɛnəsɪs] *n. Meteorology.* the formation of a front as air masses move and meet.

fron•tol•y•sis [frʌn'tɒləsɪs] *n. Meteorology.* the dissipation of a frontal zone.

front–page ['frʌnt 'peidʒ] *adj., v.* **-paged, -pag•ing.** *—adj.* suitable for the front page of a newspaper; important: *front-page news.*
—v. put on the front page; play up; emphasize.

front–run•ner ['frʌnt ,rʌnər] *n.* the leader in any contest.

front–wheel drive ['frʌnt 'wil] describing a type of automobile or truck in which power from the engine is transmitted to the front wheels instead of the rear wheels: *Front-wheel drive gives a better grip on ice.*

frosh [frɒʃ] *n. Slang.* a first-year student in high school or university. ⟨altered < *freshman*⟩

frost [frɒst] *n., v.* *—n.* **1** a freezing condition; very cold weather; temperature below the point at which water freezes: *There was frost last night.* **2** the moisture frozen on or in a surface; feathery crystals of ice that are formed when water vapour in the air condenses at a temperature below freezing: *frost on the grass, frost on windows.* **3** a coldness of manner or feeling. **4** *Slang.* failure.
—v. **1** cover or become covered with frost. **2** cover with something that suggests frost; especially, cover with icing: *to frost a cake.*

3 kill or injure by frost. 4 impart an opaque surface to: *to frost glass.* 5 bleach (selected strands of hair). ⟨OE⟩ —**'frost·less,** *adj.* —**'frost,like,** *adj.*

frost•bite ['frɒst,bəit] *n., v.* **-bit, -bit·ten, -bit·ing.** —*n.* an injury to a part of the body caused by severe cold.
—*v.* injure (a part of the body) by severe cold.

frost•bit•ten ['frɒst,bɪtən] *adj., v.* —*adj.* injured by severe cold.
—*v.* pp. of FROSTBITE.

frost boil a defective place in a paved road where the pavement has heaved as a result of the expansion of trapped moisture frozen during the cold weather; a frost heave.

frost•ed ['frɒstɪd] *adj., v.* —*adj.* **1** covered with frost: *a frosted window.* **2** finished or decorated with a surface suggesting frost: *frosted glass.* **3** covered with icing: *a frosted cake.* **4** frozen.
—*v.* pt. and pp. of FROST.

frost•fish ['frɒst,fɪʃ] *n.* an Atlantic fish (*Microgadus tomcod*), also known as Atlantic tomcod.

frost•flow•er ['frɒst,flaʊər] *n.* an aster (*Milla biflora*) of the amaryllis family, native to Mexico and SW U.S.

frost heave FROST BOIL.

frost•ing ['frɒstɪŋ] *n., v.* —*n.* **1** a mixture of sugar and some liquid, with flavouring, etc., used to cover and decorate a cake; icing. **2** a dull finish on glass, metal, etc.
—*v.* ppr. of FROST.

frost•line ['frɒst,laɪn] *n. Geology.* the depth to which frost penetrates into the ground.

frost•work ['frɒst,wɜrk] *n.* the delicate designs formed on glass by the action of frost.

frost•y ['frɒsti] *adj.* **frost·i·er, frost·i·est. 1** cold enough for frost; freezing: *a frosty morning.* **2** covered with frost: *The glass is frosty.* **3** covered with anything like frost. **4** cold in manner or feeling; unfriendly: *a frosty greeting.* **5** hoary or grey, as if covered with frost. —**'frost·i·ly,** *adv.* —**'frost·i·ness,** *n.*

froth *n.* [frɒθ]; *v.* [frɒθ] *or* [frɒð] *n., v.* —*n.* **1** a mass of very small bubbles; foam: *The bottle of pop had been shaken so much that it was half froth.* **2** foaming saliva caused by disease, exertion, etc. **3** something light and trifling; trivial notions, talk, etc.
—*v.* **1** give out froth; foam. **2** cover with foam. **3** cause to foam by beating, pouring, etc. ⟨ME < ON *frotha*⟩

froth•y ['frɒθi] *or* ['frɒði] *adj.* **froth·i·er, froth·i·est. 1** of or like froth; foamy. **2** light; trifling; shallow; unimportant. —**'froth·i·ly,** *adv.* —**'froth·i·ness,** *n.*

frou–frou ['fru ,fru] *n.* **1** a swishing sound; rustling, especially of a woman's clothes. **2** *Informal.* fancy or fussy trimmings; frills. ⟨< F⟩

fro•ward ['frouwərd] *or* ['frouərd] *adj.* not easily managed; willful; contrary. ⟨< *fro* + *-ward*⟩ —**'fro·ward·ly,** *adv.* —**'fro·ward·ness,** *n.*

frown [fraʊn] *n., v.* —*n.* **1** a drawing together of the brows, usually in deep thought or disapproval. **2** any expression or show of disapproval.
—*v.* **1** draw the brows together, as in deep thought or disapproval: *She frowned, trying to remember the name.* **2** show displeasure or anger. **3** express by frowning: *He frowned his annoyance.*
frown on, disapprove of: *They frown on gambling.* ⟨ME < OF *froignier* < Celtic⟩ —**'frown·ing·ly,** *adv.*
☛ *Syn. v.* **1, 2. Frown,** SCOWL = draw the eyebrows together, usually to express feeling or attitude. **Frown** = draw the eyebrows tightly together, sometimes in looking closely at something or concentrating, but usually to express irritation or displeasure: *The teacher frowned when the boy came in late.* **Scowl** = look sullen or sour out of discontent or ill temper: *He is a disagreeable person, always scowling.*

frowz•y ['fraʊzi] *adj.* **frowz·i·er, frowz·i·est. 1** slovenly; dirty; untidy. **2** smelling bad or stale; musty. Also, **frowsy.** ⟨Cf. obs. *frowze* frizz, ruffle, rumple, and dial. Brit. *frowsty* musty⟩ —**'frowz·i·ly,** *adv.* —**'frowz·i·ness,** *n.*

froze [frouz] *v.* pt. of FREEZE.

fro•zen ['frouzən] *adj., v.* —*adj.* **1** turned into ice; hardened by cold: *a frozen dessert. The water in the pail was frozen.* **2** very cold: *the frozen north.* **3** kept at a temperature below freezing to prevent spoiling: *frozen foods.* **4** killed or injured by frost. **5** covered or clogged with ice: *a frozen lake, a frozen water main.* **6** too frightened or stiff to move; made motionless as if turned to ice: *frozen to the spot in horror.* **7** without affection or feeling: *a frozen heart.* **8** temporarily forbidden to be sold or exchanged: *frozen assets.* **9** of prices, wages, etc., fixed at a particular amount or level.
—*v.* pp. of FREEZE.

F.R.S.C. Fellow of the Royal Society of Canada.

frt. freight.

fruc•tif•er•ous [frʌk'tɪfərəs] *adj.* bearing fruit. ⟨< L *fructifer* < *fructus* fruit + *ferre* to bear⟩

fruc•ti•fi•ca•tion [,frʌktəfə'keiʃən] *n.* **1** a forming or bearing of fruit. **2** a fertilizing or making fruitful. **3** fruit. **4** the spore-bearing structure in a fern, moss, etc.

fruc•ti•fy ['frʌktə,faɪ] *v.* **-fied, -fy·ing. 1** bear fruit. **2** make fruitful; fertilize. ⟨< F < L *fructificare* < *fructus* fruit + *facere* make⟩

fruc•tose ['frʌktous] *or* ['frʊktous] *n.* a sugar occurring in three different forms, especially the sweet form found in fruit juices, honey, etc. *Formula*: $C_6H_{12}O_6$ ⟨< L *fructus* fruit⟩

frug [frʌg] *n., v.,* **frugged, frug·ging.** —*n.* a dance, a variety of the twist.
—*v.* perform this dance.

fru•gal ['frugəl] *adj.* **1** avoiding waste; saving; tending to avoid unnecessary spending: *A frugal housekeeper buys and uses food carefully.* **2** costing little; barely sufficient: *She ate a frugal supper of bread and milk.* ⟨< L *frugalis,* ult. < *frux, frugis* fruit⟩ —**fru'gal·i·ty** [fru'gæləti], *n.* —**'fru·gal·ly,** *adv.*
☛ *Syn.* **1.** See note at ECONOMICAL.

fru•gi•vor•ous [fru'dʒɪvərəs] *adj.* fruit-eating, as certain bats. ⟨< L *frux, frugis* fruit + *-vorus* < *vorare* devour⟩

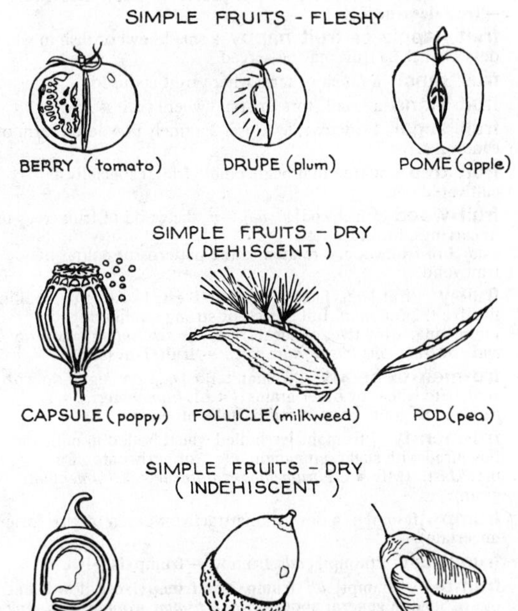

Some types of simple fruit. Compound fruits include aggregate fruits (e.g. raspberry) and multiple fruits (e.g. pineapple).

fruit [frut] *n., v.* —*n.* **1** the sweet or tart, fleshy, edible, usually seed-bearing product of a flowering tree, shrub, or vine, usually eaten raw and as a dessert. Apples, oranges, raspberries, and saskatoons are fruits. **2** *Botany.* the part of a plant that contains the seeds. It is the ripened ovary of a flower and the tissues connected with the ovary. Pea pods, acorns, grains of wheat, cucumbers, tomatoes, etc. are fruits. **3** the useful product of plants: *the fruits of the earth.* **4** a product; result: *Her invention was the fruit of much effort.*
—*v.* produce or cause to produce fruit. ⟨ME < OF < L *fructus* < *frui* enjoy⟩ —**'fruit·er,** *n.* —**'fruit,like,** *adj.*

fruit•age ['frutɪdʒ] *n.* **1** the bearing of fruit. **2** fruit; crop of fruit. **3** a product; result.

fruit bat any species of bat that lives on fruit, especially in tropical or subtropical regions.

fruit•cake ['frut,keik] *n.* **1** a rich cake containing preserved fruits, nuts, raisins, spices, etc. **2** *Slang.* a weird or eccentric person.

fruit cup mixed fruits served in a cup or glass as an appetizer or a dessert.

fruit•er•er ['frutərər] *n.* a dealer in fruit.

fruit fly **1** any of a family (Trypetidae) of small, two-winged flies whose larvae feed on plant tissues. Many species are serious orchard pests because their larvae feed on fruits. **2** drosophila.

fruit•ful ['frutfəl] *adj.* **1** producing or bearing much fruit; productive or fertile: *a fruitful tree, a fruitful garden, fruitful soil.* **2** producing much of anything; especially, producing good results: *a fruitful discussion. The trade mission proved to be fruitful.* **3** favourable to the growth of fruit or useful vegetation in general: *fruitful showers.* **—'fruit•ful•ly,** *adv.* **—'fruit•ful•ness,** *n.*

fruiting body *Botany.* an organ that produces spores; fructification.

fru•i•tion [fru'ɪʃən] *n.* **1** the state of having results; fulfilment; realization: *Her plans have at last come to fruition.* **2** *Archaic.* the pleasure that comes from possession or use. **3** the bearing of fruit. ⟨< LL *fruitio, -onis* < *frui* enjoy⟩

fruit•land ['frut,lænd] *n.* a fruit-growing region: *The Niagara peninsula is often called Ontario's fruitland.*

fruit•less ['frutlɪs] *adj.* **1** having no results; useless; unsuccessful. **2** producing no fruit; barren. **—'fruit•less•ly,** *adv.* **—'fruit•less•ness,** *n.*

fruit nappie or **fruit nappy** a small bowl or dish in which dessert such as fruit may be served.

fruit ranch a ranch or farm where fruit is raised.

fruit stand a small store or stand where fruit is sold.

fruit sugar **1** fructose; levulose. **2** a finely powdered form of cane sugar.

fruit tree any tree that bears edible fruit, especially a cultivated one.

fruit•wood ['frut,wʊd] *n., adj.* *—n.* the wood of fruit trees used in carvings, furniture, etc.
—adj **1** of fruitwood. **2** related to the patterns or colour of fruitwood.

fruit•y ['fruti] *adj.* **fruit•i•er, fruit•i•est. 1** tasting or smelling like fruit. **2** *Informal.* full of rich or strong quality; highly interesting, attractive, or suggestive: *His description was fruity but embarrassing. She has a fruity voice.* **—'fruit•i•ness,** *n.*

fru•men•ta•ceous [,frumən'teiʃəs] *adj.* having to do with or similar to wheat or other grains. ⟨< LL *frumentaceus* < L *frumentum* grain, base of *frui* partake of, enjoy⟩

fru•men•ty ['frumənti] *n.* hulled wheat boiled in milk and flavoured with sugar, cinnamon, etc., formerly eaten for breakfast. ⟨ME < OF *frumentee* < *frument* < L *frumentum* grain⟩

frump [frʌmp] *n.* a dowdy, unattractive woman or girl. ⟨origin uncertain⟩

frump•ish ['frʌmpɪʃ] *adj.* frumpy. **—'frump•ish•ly,** *adv.*

frump•y ['frʌmpi] *adj.* **frump•i•er, frump•i•est.** dowdy and out of style in general appearance: *a frumpy woman, a frumpy old coat.* **—'frump•i•ly,** *adv.* **—'frump•i•ness,** *n.*

frus•trate ['frʌstreit] *v.* **-trat•ed, -trat•ing. 1** bring to nothing; make useless or worthless: *Heavy rain frustrated our plan for a picnic.* **2** prevent from succeeding; oppose successfully; defeat: *to frustrate an opponent.* **3** make discouraged or discontented by preventing the realization of a purpose or desire: *It's very frustrating to stand in line for an hour to get into a movie and then not get seats.* ⟨< L *frustrari* < *frustra* in vain⟩ **—'frus•trat•er,** *n.*

☛ *Syn.* **1, 2. Frustrate,** THWART, BAFFLE = keep from doing something. **Frustrate** emphasizes making all efforts and plans useless and vain, and thus keeping a person from achieving his or her aim: *The boy's waywardness frustrated his father's plans for his future.* **Thwart** = block someone's effort by some contrary action: *The sudden storm thwarted the men who were trying to reach the wrecked plane.* **Baffle** suggests causing confusion or bewilderment: *The absence of clues baffled the police.*

frus•trat•ed ['frʌstreitɪd] *adj., v.* *—adj.* **1** foiled or defeated in one's purpose or desire: *He makes a good living as an accountant, but he's actually a frustrated painter.* **2** filled with frustration; feeling discontented or discouraged because of not being able to fulfil one's desires or purposes: *Everything had gone wrong that day, and by evening she was so frustrated, she couldn't enjoy the show. He's just a frustrated old busybody.*
—v. pt. and pp. of FRUSTRATE.

frus•tra•tion [frʌ'streiʃən] *n.* **1** the act of frustrating. **2** the state or condition of being frustrated: *After spending two hours trying to find the place, she gave up in frustration.* **3** a feeling of discontent or discouragement, because of not being able to achieve one's desires: *He takes out his frustration on unsuspecting customers.* **4** something that frustrates: *the frustrations of city driving.*

frus•tum ['frʌstəm] *n.* **-tums, -ta** [-tə]. **1** *Geometry.* the part of a cone-shaped solid or pyramid left after the top has been cut off by a plane parallel to the base. See CONE for picture. **2** the part of a solid between two cutting planes, especially two parallel planes. ⟨< L *frustum* piece⟩

fru•ti•cose ['frutɪ,kous] *adj.* of or like a fruit.

fry[1] [fraɪ] *v.* **fried, fry•ing;** *n., pl.* **fries.** *—v.* **1** cook in a pan or on a griddle over direct heat, usually in hot fat or oil. **2** undergo this type of cooking: *While the hamburgers were frying, he set the table.* **3** *Slang.* burn out; wreck: *You'll fry your brains if you try to write the essay in one night.* **4** *Slang.* electrocute; be electrocuted.
—n. **1** fried food; a dish of fried meat, fish, etc. **2** a social gathering at which food is fried and eaten: *a fish fry.* ⟨ME < OF *frire* < L *frigere*⟩

fry[2] [fraɪ] *n., pl.* **fry. 1** a young fish, from the time that it is hatched and free-swimming. **2** small adult fish, such as sardines, that live together in large schools. **3** the young of any of various other animals. **4** *Informal.* child. **5** See SMALL FRY. ⟨ME < ON *frjó* seed⟩

fry•er ['fraɪər] *n.* **1** a chicken young and tender enough for frying. A fryer usually weighs less than 1.5 kg. **2** a deep utensil for deep-frying food.
☛ *Hom.* FRIAR.

frying pan a shallow pan with a long handle, used for frying food.
out of the frying pan into the fire, straight from one danger or difficulty into a worse one.

fry pan or **fry•pan** ['fraɪ,pæn] *n.* FRYING PAN.

FSH FOLLICLE STIMULATING HORMONE.

f–stop ['ɛf ,stɒp] *n. Photography.* a setting for a camera which determines how much light will fall on the film. ⟨< *f*(*ocal length*) *stop*⟩

ft. **1** foot; feet. **2** fort.

fth. or **fthm.** fathom.

fuch•sia ['fjuʃə] *n., adj.* *—n.* **1** any of a genus (*Fuchsia*) of mostly tropical shrubs of the evening-primrose family having showy, hanging flowers of pink, purple, or red. Fuchsias are widely cultivated as pot plants. **2** an intense purplish red or purplish pink. ⟨< NL; after Leonard *Fuchs* (1501-1566), a German botanist⟩

fuch•sin ['fʊksɪn] *n.* a green substance obtained from coal tar, which turns red in solution and is used as a dye. ⟨< *fuchs*(*ia*)⟩

fud•dle ['fʌdəl] *v.* **-dled, -dling;** *n.* *—v.* **1** make stupid with alcohol; intoxicate. **2** confuse; muddle.
—n. Informal. a confused state: *She was all in a fuddle when I called.* ⟨origin uncertain⟩

fud•dy–dud•dy ['fʌdi ,dʌdi] *n., pl.* **-dies;** *adj. Informal.* *—n.* a fussy or stuffy old-fashioned person.
—adj. old-fashioned. ⟨origin uncertain⟩

fudge[1] [fʌdʒ] *n.* a soft candy made of sugar, milk, butter, and a flavouring such as chocolate or caramel. ⟨origin unknown⟩

fudge[2] [fʌdʒ] *n., interj., v.* **-fudged, fudg•ing.** *—n.* **1** an item of last-minute news or other material added to the type page or printing plate of a newspaper page. **2** nonsense; empty talk: *That's a lot of fudge.*
—interj. a word used to express annoyance.
—v. **1** insert (an item of last-minute news, etc.) into a type page or printing plate. **2** avoid committing oneself on an issue or coming to grips with a problem; hedge; waffle: *Don't let her fudge on the issue.* **3** put together in a makeshift or dishonest way; fake. **4** cheat or welsh: *to fudge on a promise.* ⟨? < obs. *fadge* make fit, adjust⟩

Fu•eg•i•an [fju'idʒiən] *or* ['fweidʒiən] *n., adj.* *—n.* any member of a South American Indian people living in Tierra del Fuego.
—adj. of Tierra del Fuego, these people, or their culture.

Fueh•rer ['fjʊrər]; *German,* ['fyʀəʀ] See FÜHRER.

fu•el ['fjuəl] *n., v.* **-elled** or **-eled, -el•ling** or **-el•ing.** *—n.* **1** something burned to provide heat or power: *Coal, wood, gas, and oil are fuels.* **2** a material from which atomic energy can be obtained, as in a reactor. **3** material that supplies nutrients for a living organism: *Your body needs fuel to live and grow.* **4** anything

that keeps up or increases a feeling, thought, or action: *His insults were fuel to her hatred.*
—v. **1** supply with fuel. **2** get fuel. **3** be an impetus for: *The ongoing indignation of students fuelled a program of administrative reform.* ⟨ME < OF *fouaille*, ult. < L *focus* hearth⟩

fuel cell an electric cell that produces electrical energy directly from the oxidation of a fuel that is continuously added to the cell.

fu•el–ef•fi•cient ['fjuəl ə'fɪʃənt] *adj.* economical; obtaining high results from a relatively small expenditure of energy; of a vehicle, achieving good mileage. **—fuel efficiency.**

fuel injection a system of distributing gasoline under pressure to the cylinders of a vehicle to improve fuel efficiency.

fuel oil oil used for fuel, especially in diesel engines.

fuel rod a group of long tubes containing nuclear fuel and used in nuclear reactors.

fug [fʌg] *n.* stuffy air in a room.

fu•gal ['fjugəl] *adj.* of, having to do with, or in the style of a fugue.

–fuge *combining form.* something that draws out or repels: *febrifuge, centrifuge.* ⟨< L *-fugia, fugāre* to put to flight⟩

fu•gi•tive ['fjudʒətɪv] *n., adj. —n.* **1** a person who is fleeing or who has fled: *The murderer became a fugitive from justice.*
2 something short-lived or hard to grasp.
—adj. **1** fleeing; having fled; runaway. **2** lasting only a very short time; passing swiftly: *fugitive thoughts, the fugitive hours.* **3** of literary works, being of passing interest. **4** moving about; shifting or roving. ⟨ME < OF < L *fugitivus* < *fugere* flee⟩ **—'fu•gi•tive•ly,** *adv.* **—'fu•gi•tive•ness,** *n.*

fu•gu ['fugu] *n.* the liver of a particular Japanese fish, which is considered a great delicacy in Japan, but is highly poisonous unless properly prepared. ⟨< Japanese⟩

fugue ['fjug] *n.* **1** *Music.* a contrapuntal composition based on one or more short themes in which different voices or instruments repeat the same melody with slight variations.
2 *Psychiatry.* a mental condition in which the sufferer does not remember actions he or she has performed, especially a journey. ⟨< F < Ital. < L *fuga* flight⟩ **—'fu•guist,** *n.*

Füh•rer ['fjʊrər]; *German,* ['fyʀəʀ] *n.* **1** leader. **2 der Führer,** the title given to Adolf Hitler (1889-1945), the German dictator. Also, **Fuehrer.**

–ful *suffix.* **1** full of——: *cheerful.* **2** characterized by or having the qualities of——: *careful, masterful.* **3** having a tendency or the ability to——: *forgetful, harmful, mournful.* **4** enough to fill: *cupful, handful.* ⟨OE; representing *full,* adj.⟩

Fu•la•ni ['fulɑni] *or* [fu'lɑni] *n., adj. —n.* **1** any member of a people living in W Africa. **2** their Niger-Congo language.
—adj. of or having to do with these people or their language.

ful•crum ['fʌlkrəm] *or* ['fʊlkrəm] *n., pl.* **-crums, -cra** [-krə]. **1** a support on which a lever turns or rests in moving or lifting something. See LEVER for picture. **2** anything on which something else depends; support. **3** any position, circumstance, etc. by which power or influence may be brought to bear. ⟨< L *fulcrum* bedpost < *fulcire* support⟩

ful•fil or **ful•fill** [fʊl'fɪl] *v.* **-filled, -fill•ing. 1** carry out (a promise, prophecy, etc.); cause to happen or take place. **2** do or perform (a duty); obey (a command, law, etc.). **3** satisfy (a requirement, condition, etc.); serve (a purpose): *to fulfil a need.*
4 finish; complete: *to fulfil a contract.*
fulfil oneself, make the best of one's potential; achieve satisfaction. ⟨OE *fullfyllan*⟩ **—ful'fill•er,** *n.*

ful•fil•ment or **ful•fill•ment** [fʊl'fɪlmənt] *n.* a fulfilling or being fulfilled; completion; accomplishment: *Winning the race brought her a feeling of fulfilment.*

ful•gent ['fʌldʒənt] *adj. Poetic.* bright; shining; gleaming. ⟨< ME < L *fulgens* shining⟩ **—'ful•gent•ly,** *adv.*

ful•gur•a•tion [,fʌlgjə'reiʃən] *n. Medicine.* the destruction of abnormal tissue, especially tumours, by electricity. ⟨< L *fulguratus* pp. of *fulgere* to shine, flash + *-ation*⟩

ful•gur•ite ['fʌlgjə,rəit] *n.* a glasslike substance formed by the fusion of sand or rock when struck by lightning. ⟨< L *fulgur* lightning + *-ite*⟩

full[1] [fʊl] *adj., adv., n., v. —adj.* **1** able to hold no more; with no empty space; filled: *a full cup.* **2** complete; entire: *a full supply, a full treatment. I waited a full hour.* **3** of the greatest size, amount, extent, development, etc.: *She was running at full speed. The rose is in full bloom.* **4** more than enough to satisfy: *She ate a full meal.* **5** having had enough food: *a full stomach. He was full after the first course.* **6** plump; round; well filled out: *a full face.*
7 having a large amount or number (*used with* **of**): *Her room was full of toys. The lake is full of fish.* **8** made with a large amount of material, in gathers, folds, pleats, etc.: *a full skirt, full sleeves.* **9** of the highest grade or rank: *a full professor.* **10** of sound, strong and deep; sonorous: *a full alto voice.* **11** completely taken up with; absorbed (*used with* **of**): *He's full of his latest project.*
12 thorough; detailed: *a full description.* **13** sharing the same mother and father: *full sisters.* **14** overflowing with emotion.
—adv. **1** completely; entirely. **2** squarely; directly: *The blow hit him full in the face.* **3** very: *He knew full well that he would have to go back.*
—n.
in full, a to or for the complete amount: *The account has been paid in full.* **b** written or said with all the words; not shortened: *Write your name in full.*
the full, the greatest size, amount, extent, etc.: *The moon is past the full.*
to the full, completely; entirely: *He satisfied his ambition to the full.*
—v. make or become full, as a garment or the moon. ⟨OE⟩

full[2] [fʊl] *v.* clean and thicken (cloth). ⟨< *fuller*⟩

full•back ['fʊl,bæk] *n. Football, etc.* a player whose position is farthest behind the front line.

full blast *Informal.* in full operation; at highest speed or largest capacity.

full–blood•ed ['fʊl 'blʌdɪd] *adj.* **1** of pure race, breed, or strain; thoroughbred. **2** vigorous; hearty. **3** real; bona fide; genuine.

full–blown ['fʊl 'bloun] *adj.* **1** in full bloom. **2** completely developed or matured.

full–bod•ied ['fʊl 'bɒdid] *adj.* having considerable strength, flavour, etc.: *a full-bodied wine.*

full dress the formal clothes worn for important social or ceremonial occasions.

full–dress ['fʊl 'drɛs] *adj.* **1** having to do with or requiring full dress; formal: *a full-dress reception.* **2** utilizing all resources; all-out; exhaustive: *a full-dress report, a full-dress debate.*

full•er[1] ['fʊlər] *n.* a person whose work is cleaning and thickening cloth. ⟨OE *fullere* < L *fullo* fuller⟩

full•er[2] ['fʊlər] *n.* **1** a blacksmith's tool used to create grooves in metal. **2** a groove made in this way. ⟨< ? obsolete *full* to make full, complete⟩

fuller's earth a soft, claylike mixture used for removing grease from cloth and for purifying oil.

full–fash•ioned ['fʊl 'fæʃənd] *adj.* knitted to fit the shape of the foot, leg, or body.

full•fledged ['fʊl'flɛdʒd] *adj.* **1** of a bird, having a complete set of feathers and therefore able to fly. **2** fully developed. **3** of full rank or standing.

full–grown ['fʊl 'groun] *adj.* fully grown; mature.

full house 1 *Theatre, etc.* the fact or state of every seat being occupied. **2** *Poker.* a hand made up of three cards of one kind and two of another, such as three sixes and two kings.

full–length ['fʊl 'lɛŋθ] *or* ['lɛŋkθ] *adj.* **1** showing or for the full length of the human figure: *a full-length portrait, a full-length mirror.* **2** reaching almost to the floor: *full-length drapes, a full-length dress.* **3** of traditional or standard size, length, duration, etc.: *a full-length novel, a full-length chesterfield.*

full moon 1 the moon seen with the whole disk illuminated.
2 the period when this occurs. See MOON for picture.

full nelson *Wrestling.* a hold applied by hooking both arms under the opponent's with the hands gripped behind the opponent's neck.

full•ness ['fʊlnɪs] *n.* **1** the state or condition of being full. **2** of drapes, the ratio of the width of the cloth to the width of the window: *Good drapes should have a fullness of at least $1^1/_2$, preferably 2.* Also, **fulness.**
in the fullness of time, in due course.

full–rigged ['fʊl 'rɪgd] *adj.* **1** of a sailing ship, completely equipped with masts and sails. **2** completely equipped.

full sail 1 with all sails set. **2** with all possible power and energy.

full–scale ['fʊl 'skeil] *adj.* **1** made in the original or actual size: *a full-scale drawing, a full-scale working model.* **2** using or involving all available resources; total or all-out: *a full-scale investigation, full-scale fighting.*

full stop *Punctuation.* period.

come to a full stop, end abruptly.

full swing 1 full operation; vigorous activity or movement: *The party was in full swing.* 2 with vigour: *She ran full swing.*

full–throat•ed ['fʊl 'θroutɪd] *adj.* 1 clamorous and loud; vociferous. 2 rich and full in sound; sonorous.

full–time ['fʊl 'taɪm] *adj.* for the usual or normal number of hours per week: *Full-time clerk wanted.*

full time for the usual or normal number of hours per week: *The plant employs workers full time only.*

ful•ly ['fʊli] *adv.* 1 in a full manner or degree; completely: *She was now fully awake. He could not fully describe what he had seen.* 2 abundantly; plentifully: *fully covered by insurance.* 3 at least; quite: *It was fully three hours before they could reach her.*

ful•mar ['fʊlmər] *n.* any of various heavily built, gull-like sea birds (family Procellariidae) of polar regions, especially an arctic bird (*Fulmarus glacialis*) having two colour phases: a mainly white phase with grey back and wings and a smoky grey phase. Fulmars belong to the same family as the shearwaters. ⟨< ON *fúll* foul + *már* gull; from the foul-smelling liquid it ejects in self-defence⟩

ful•mi•nant ['fʌlmənənt] *adj.* exploding suddenly.

ful•mi•nate ['fʌlmə,neit] *or* ['fʊlmə,neit] *v.* **-nat•ed, -nat•ing;** *n.* —*v.* 1 thunder forth censure, threats, decrees, etc.: *The churches and the newspapers fulminated against the crime wave.* 2 denounce violently; censure strongly. 3 explode violently; cause to explode. 4 of a disease, develop suddenly and severely. 5 thunder and lighten.
—*n.* 1 a violent explosive. 2 *Chemistry.* a salt of fulminic acid. The fulminates, chiefly mercury and silver, are very unstable compounds, exploding with great violence by percussion or heating. ⟨< L *fulminare* < *fulmen* lightning⟩ **—'ful•mi,na•tor,** *n.*

ful•mi•na•tion [,fʌlmə'neiʃən] *or* [,fʊlmə'neiʃən] *n.* 1 a violent denunciation; strong censure. 2 a violent explosion.

ful•min•ic acid [fʌl'mɪnɪk] *Chemistry.* an acid encountered only in its salts, the fulminates, which are highly explosive. *Formula*: CNOH

ful•ness ['fʊlnɪs] See FULLNESS.

ful•some ['fʊlsəm] *adj.* 1 offensive or distasteful because of excessiveness, insincerity, etc.: *fulsome praise.* 2 abundant; profuse: *a fulsome harvest, fulsome detail.* 3 *Archaic.* loathsome. ⟨< *full* + *-some*[1]; influenced in meaning by *foul*⟩ **—'ful•some•ly,** *adv.* **—'ful•some•ness,** *n.*

ful•vous ['fʌlvəs] *adj.* of a red-yellow or brown-yellow colour.

fu•ma•ric acid [fju'mærɪk] *or* [fju'mɛrɪk] *Chemistry.* a colourless organic acid derived from plants or made synthetically, used in making resins and processing foods. *Formula*: $C_4H_4O_4$
⟨< NL *fumaria* fumitory (< L *fumanium* chimney) + *-ic*⟩

fu•ma•role ['fjumə,roul] *n.* in volcanic areas, an opening in the earth's crust from which steam and gases issue: *There are many fumaroles near Katmai volcano in Alaska.* ⟨< F *fumarolle* < Ital. *fumaruolo* < LL *fumariolum* smoke hole, ult. < L *fumus* smoke⟩ **—,fu•ma'rol•ic** [,fjumə'rɒlɪk], *adj.*

fum•ble ['fʌmbəl] *v.* **-bled, -bling;** *n.* —*v.* 1 feel or grope about clumsily; search awkwardly: *He fumbled about in his pockets for the ticket. Jane fumbled for words to express her thanks.* 2 handle awkwardly: *She fumbled the introduction.* 3 *Sports.* fail to catch and hold (a ball).
—*n.* 1 an awkward groping or handling. 2 *Sports.* a failure to catch and hold a ball. ⟨Cf. LG *fummeln*⟩ **—'fum•bler,** *n.* **—'fum•bling•ly,** *adv.*

fume [fjum] *n., v.* **fumed, fum•ing.** —*n.* 1 Usually, **fumes,** *pl.* a vapour, gas, or smoke, especially if harmful, strong, or odorous: *The strong fumes of the acid nearly choked him.* 2 an angry or irritable mood: *She was obviously in a fume.*
—*v.* 1 give off fumes. 2 pass off in fumes. 3 be in a state of anger or great irritation: *By the time we got there she was fuming.* 4 treat with fumes. ⟨ME < OF *fum* < L *fumus* smoke⟩ **—'fum•er,** *n.*

fumed oak oak darkened and coloured by exposure to ammonia fumes.

fu•mi•gant ['fjumɪgənt] *n.* a substance used for fumigating.

fu•mi•gate ['fjumə,geit] *v.* **-gat•ed, -gat•ing.** expose to fumes in order to kill vermin or to disinfect: *The whole apartment building needs to be fumigated.* ⟨< L *fumigare* to smoke < *fumus* smoke, fume⟩ **—,fumi'ga•tion,** *n.*

fu•mi•ga•tor ['fjumə,geitər] *n.* 1 a person who fumigates. 2 an apparatus for fumigating.

fun [fʌn] *n., v.* **funned, fun•ning.** —*n.* 1 lively play or playfulness; amusement: *an evening full of fun.* 2 a source of amusement: *That game is fun.* 3 (*adjl.*) *Informal.* amusing or entertaining: *It was a fun evening.* 4 ridicule: *He became a figure of fun.*
for fun or **in fun,** not seriously; as a joke; playfully: *The trick was meant in fun.*
like fun, *Informal.* by no means; not at all.
make fun of or **poke fun at,** laugh at; ridicule.
—*v. Informal.* act or speak in fun. ⟨? originally v., var. of obs. *fon* befool⟩

fu•nam•bu•list [fju'næmbjəlɪst] *n.* one who walks a tightrope. ⟨< L *funambulus* < *funis* a rope + *ambulare* walk⟩

func•tion ['fʌŋkʃən] *n., v.* —*n.* 1 the proper work of something; normal action or use; purpose: *The function of the stomach is to digest food.* 2 a formal public or social gathering for some purpose: *All the local dignitaries attended the great function to welcome the Queen.* 3 occupation; job. 4 *Mathematics.* an association between two sets where exactly one object from one set (the range) is paired with one object from the other set (the domain): *The volume of a sphere is a function of the radius.* 5 anything likened to a mathematical function in that two variables are in consistent relation to each other: *Success is a function of attitude.* 6 *Grammar.* the position or positions in which a linguistic form occurs in an utterance.
—*v.* 1 work; be used; act: *My new pen does not function very well.* 2 have a function; serve (*as*): *That heavy old china ornament functions as a doorstop now.* ⟨< L *functio, -onis* < *fungi* perform⟩ **—'func•tion•less,** *adj.*

func•tion•al ['fʌŋkʃənəl] *adj.* 1 of or having to do with a function or functions. 2 having a function; working; acting. 3 stressing usefulness instead of beauty: *a functional approach to furniture design.* 4 designed or developed mainly from the point of view of usefulness: *functional clothing.* 5 *Medicine.* affecting the function of an organ or part of the body, but not its structure: *functional heart disease.* **—'func•tion•al•ly,** *adv.*

functional illiterate a person whose ability to read is too poor for practical purposes. **—functional illiteracy. —functionally illiterate.**

func•tion•al•ism ['fʌŋkʃənə,lɪzəm] *n. Architecture and design.* the principle that the design of a structure should be determined primarily by its purpose or function. **—'func•tion•al•ist,** *n.* **—,func•tion•al'ist•ic,** *adj.*

functional shift *Linguistics.* the process by which the usage of a word is extended to include another part of speech. The extension of the noun *butter* to include the verb *butter* is the result of a functional shift.

func•tion•ar•y ['fʌŋkʃə,nɛri] *n., pl.* **-ar•ies;** *adj.* official.

function key *Computer technology.* a keyboard key that causes some specialized operation to take place (save, exit, etc.). The operations assigned to function keys vary depending on the software being used.

function word *Grammar.* a word having little or no meaning of its own, used to show relationships between other words. Words like *of* and *but* are function words.

fund [fʌnd] *n., v.* —*n.* 1 a sum of money set aside for a special purpose: *The school has a fund of $1000 to buy books with.* 2 an organization which administers such money; foundation. 3 a stock or store ready for use; supply: *There is a fund of information in a dictionary.* 4 **funds,** *pl.* money available for use: *He had to cancel his trip because he ran out of funds.*
—*v.* 1 provide funds for: *A summer recreation program is being funded by the community association.* 2 set aside a sum of money to pay the interest on (a debt). 3 change (a debt) from a short term to a long term. 4 put into a fund or store; collect; store up. ⟨< L *fundus* bottom, a piece of land⟩

fun•da•men•tal [,fʌndə'mɛntəl] *adj., n.* —*adj.* 1 of or forming a foundation or basis; essential; basic: *the fundamental principles of design.* 2 involving or affecting a basic structure, function, etc.; radical: *a fundamental change of attitude.* 3 principal; main: *The fundamental purpose of her campaign is to block the legislation.* 4 *Music.* **a** having to do with the lowest note of a chord. **b** having to do with the primary tone of a harmonic series.
—*n.* 1 a principle, rule, law, etc. that forms a foundation or basis; essential part: *the fundamentals of grammar.* 2 *Music.* the lowest note of a chord. 3 *Physics.* the component of a wave that has the greatest wavelength. ⟨< NL *fundamentalis* < L *fundamentum* foundation, ult. < *fundus* bottom⟩ **—,fun•da'men•tal•ly,** *adv.*

fun•da•men•tal•ism [,fʌndə'mɛntə,lɪzəm] *n.* 1 in Christianity, the belief that all the actual words of the Bible were directly inspired by God and should be believed and followed literally. 2 Often, **Fundamentalism,** a movement in certain churches upholding this belief. **3** a parallel belief or movement, often militant, in any faith.

fun•da•men•tal•ist [ˌfʌndəˈmɛntəlɪst] *n.* a person who believes in fundamentalism.

fund•ing [ˈfʌndɪŋ] *n., v.* —*n.* money for a special purpose: *He contacted several corporations, trying to get funding for his new project.*
—*v.* ppr. of FUND.

fund–rais•ing [ˈfʌnd ˌreizɪŋ] *n.* the act or process of raising donations of money for a special purpose or organization. —**ˈfund-ˌrais•er,** *n.*

fun•dus [ˈfʌndəs] *n. Anatomy.* in a hollow organ, the base or the area farthest from the opening. ⟨< NL < L bottom⟩

fu•ner•al [ˈfjunərəl] *n.* **1** the ceremonies that accompany the burial or burning of the dead, which usually include holding a religious or memorial service and taking the body to the place of burial. **2** the procession taking a dead person's body to the place where it is to be buried or burned. **3** (*adjl.*) of or suitable for a funeral: *A funeral march is very slow.*
be (one's) **funeral,** *Informal.* be (one's) responsibility, especially in the case of disagreeable consequences. ⟨< LL *funeralis* of a funeral < L *funus, funeris* funeral, death⟩

funeral director a person who manages a FUNERAL HOME; undertaker.

funeral home a business establishment that makes arrangements for or conducts funeral services and has facilities for preparing the bodies of the dead for burial or cremation.

funeral parlour or **parlor** FUNERAL HOME.

fu•ner•ar•y [ˈfjunəˌrɛri] *adj.* of a funeral or burial: *A funerary urn holds the ashes of a dead person's body.*

fu•ne•re•al [fjuˈniriəl] *adj.* **1** of or suitable for a funeral. **2** sad; gloomy; dismal. ⟨< L *funereus* < *funus, -neris* funeral⟩ —**fuˈne•re•al•ly,** *adv.*

fun fair 1 a local fund-raising bazaar offering many attractions for children. **2** *Brit.* AMUSEMENT PARK.

fun•gal [ˈfʌŋgəl] *adj., n.* —*adj.* fungous.
—*n.* fungus.

fun•gi [ˈfʌŋgaɪ] *or* [ˈfʌŋgi], [ˈfʌndʒaɪ] *or* [ˈfʌndʒi] *n.* pl. of FUNGUS.

fun•gi•cid•al [ˌfʌndʒəˈsaɪdəl] *or* [ˌfʌŋgəˈsaɪdəl] *adj.* that destroys fungi.

fun•gi•cide [ˈfʌndʒəˌsaɪd] *or* [ˈfʌŋgəˌsaɪd] *n.* any substance that destroys fungi. ⟨< L *fungus* + E *-cide²*⟩

fun•gi•form [ˈfʌndʒəˌfɔrm] *or* [ˈfʌŋgəˌfɔrm] *adj.* having the shape and structure of a fungus.

fun•gi•stat [ˈfʌndʒɪˌstæt] *or* [ˈfʌŋgɪˌstæt] *n.* a substance that prevents the development of fungus. ⟨< *fungi* + Gk. *-states* < *histanai* (cause to) stand⟩

fun•goid [ˈfʌŋgɔɪd] *adj., n.* —*adj.* resembling a fungus; having spongy, unhealthful growths.
—*n.* a fungus.

fun•gous [ˈfʌŋgəs] *adj.* **1** of a fungus or of fungi; like a fungus; spongy. **2** growing or springing up suddenly, but not lasting. **3** caused by a fungus. ⟨< L *fungosos* < *fungus* fungus⟩
☛ *Hom.* FUNGUS.

fun•gus [ˈfʌŋgəs] *n., pl.* **fun•gi** or **fun•gus•es. 1** any of a major group (Fungi) of plantlike organisms that lack chlorophyl and also lack the characteristic plant structures such as stems, leaves, and roots. They are parasitic, and reproduce by means of spores. The group includes yeasts, moulds, rusts, mildews, mushrooms, etc. It is usually classified as a division of the plant kingdom, but some taxonomists place the group in the kingdom Protista, along with the bacteria, protozoans, etc., while others propose classifying it as a separate kingdom. **2** something that grows or springs up rapidly like a mushroom. **3** a diseased, spongy growth on the skin. **4** (*adjl.*) fungous. ⟨< L; probably akin to Gk. *sphongos* sponge⟩ —**ˈfun•gus,like,** *adj.*
☛ *Hom.* FUNGOUS.

fun house a carnival or amusement park attraction, consisting of a passageway of rooms with crooked floors, distorting mirrors, etc.

fu•nic•u•lar [fjuˈnɪkjələr] *adj.* of, hanging from, or operated by a rope or cable. A **funicular railway** is a railway system in which the cars are moved by cables. ⟨< L *funiculus,* dim. of *funis* rope⟩

funk¹ [fʌŋk] *n., v. Informal.* —*n.* **1** a state of extreme fear; panic. **2** often, **blue funk,** a depressed mood: *He's been in a funk since he and his girlfriend broke up.* **3** coward.
—*v.* **1** be afraid; shrink back or flinch. **2** frighten. ⟨origin uncertain⟩

funk² [fʌŋk] *n.* a type of popular music developed from and succeeding rock.

funk•y¹ [ˈfʌŋki] *adj.* **funk•i•er, funk•i•est.** *Informal.* being in a state of panic or mental depression.

funk•y² [ˈfʌŋki] *adj.* **funk•i•er, funk•i•est.** *Informal.* **1** *Music.* of or having an earthy, emotional blues style. **2** offbeat, especially in a campy or earthy way: *funky clothes, a funky restaurant.* ⟨originally black slang, literally smelly, hence musty, earthy < obs. *funk* smell, smoke, probably < F dial. *funkier* to smoke < VL **fumicare,* for L *fumigare* to smoke⟩

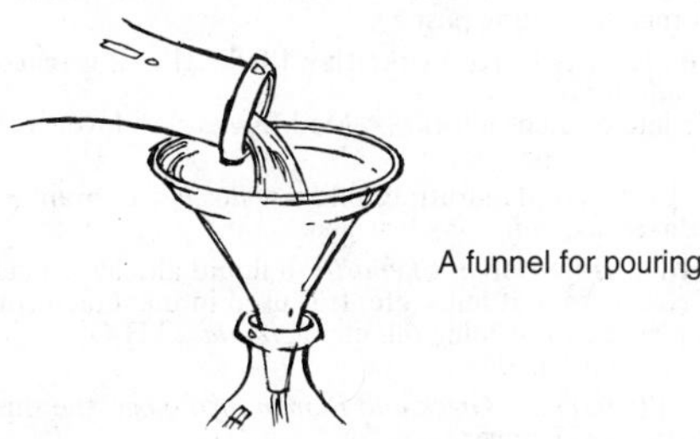
A funnel for pouring

fun•nel [ˈfʌnəl] *n., v.* **-nelled** or **-neled, -nel•ling** or **-nel•ing.** —*n.* **1** a tapering tube with a wide, cone-shaped mouth, used for pouring a liquid or powder into a container with a small opening: *She used a funnel to pour the gas into the tank.* **2** anything shaped like a funnel: *the funnel of a tornado.* **3** a cylindrical metal chimney; smokestack: *The steamship had two funnels.* **4** flue.
—*v.* **1** pass or feed through or as if through a funnel. **2** make into the shape of a funnel. ⟨ME < OF *fonel* < LL *fundibulum* < L *infundibulum* < *in-* in + *fundere* pour⟩

fun•ny [ˈfʌni] *adj.* **-ni•er, -ni•est;** *n., pl.* **-nies.** —*adj.* **1** causing laughter; amusing or comical: *a funny story, a funny accident. My little brother was very funny the first time he tried to skate.* **2** trying or intended to amuse: *She was just being funny.* **3** *Informal.* strange; peculiar; odd: *That's funny; I thought I left my wallet right here. He said he went home because his stomach was feeling funny.* **4** deceptive or tricky: *Don't try anything funny or you might get hurt.*
—*n.* **1 funnies,** *pl. Informal.* **a** comic strips. **b** a section of a newspaper devoted to comic strips: *Who's got the funnies?* **2** a joke; an amusing story: *Jean told a funny.*
get funny with, *Informal.* be fresh with. ⟨< *fun*⟩ —**ˈfun•ni•ly,** *adv.* —**ˈfun•ni•ness,** *n.*
☛ *Syn. adj.* **1. Funny,** LAUGHABLE = such as to cause laughter or amusement. **Funny** particularly suggests being unusual or extraordinary in a way that causes amusement or laughter: *The funny little man and his funny little children keep our neighbourhood smiling.* **Laughable** is the general word meaning 'ridiculous, fit to cause or causing laughter': *Her fine airs are laughable.*

funny bone 1 the part of the elbow over which a nerve passes. When the funny bone is struck, a sharp, tingling sensation is felt in the arm and hand. **2** sense of humour: *The comment struck her funny bone and she burst out laughing.* ⟨< a pun on *humerus,* the bone of the upper arm⟩

funny money *Informal.* counterfeit bills.

funny paper or **papers** the section of a newspaper containing the comic strips.

fur [fɜr] *n., v.* **furred, fur•ring.** —*n.* **1** the thick covering of hair on the skin of certain animals. **2** skin with such hair on it: *Fur is used to make, cover, trim, or line clothing.* **3** (*adjl.*) made of fur. **4** Usually, **furs,** *pl.* a garment made of fur. **5** a furlike coating, such as the whitish matter on the tongue during illness.
make the fur fly, *Informal.* **a** cause trouble; quarrel; fight. **b** achieve a great deal swiftly.
—*v.* **1** make, cover, trim, or line with fur. **2** coat or become coated with a furlike matter, such as on the tongue during illness. **3** fasten thin strips of wood to (beams, walls, etc.) to make a support for laths, etc. or to provide air spaces. ⟨ME < OF *forrer* line, encase < *forre* sheath < Gmc.⟩ —**ˈfur•less,** *adj.*
☛ *Hom.* FIR.

fur. 1 furlong. **2** furnished.

fur•be•low ['fɜrbə,lou] *n., v.* *—n.* a bit of elaborate trimming: *a dress with many frills and furbelows.*
—v. trim in an elaborate way. ⟨var., by folk etymology, of F dial. *ferbalaw, farbala,* var. of F *falbala*⟩

fur•bish ['fɜrbɪʃ] *v.* **1** brighten by rubbing or scouring; polish: *He furbished up the rusty sword.* **2** restore to good condition; make usable again (*usually used with* **up**): *Before going to France, he furbished up his half-forgotten French.* ⟨ME < OF *forbiss-,* a stem of *forbir* polish < Gmc.⟩ **—'fur•bish•er,** *n.*

Furbish lousewort a rare type of lousewort (*Pedicularis furbishiae*), bearing yellowish green flowers and found in Canada and Maine.

fur brigade *Cdn.* formerly, a convoy of freight canoes, dogsleds, York boats, etc. that carried furs and other goods to and from remote trading posts.

fur•cate *adj.* ['fɜrkɪt] *or* ['fɜrkeit]; *v.* ['fɜrkeit] *adj., v.* **-cat•ed, -cat•ing.** *adj.* forked.
—v. divide into branches; fork. ⟨< Med.L *furcatus* cloven < L *furca* fork⟩

fur•fur ['fɜrfər] *n.* dandruff; branlike scales. ⟨< L, bran⟩ **—,fur•fur'a•ceous,** *adj.*

fur•fur•al ['fɜrfjə,ræl] *n. Chemistry.* a liquid aldehyde made by distilling corn cobs, oat hulls, etc. It is used in manufacturing dyes and plastics, in refining oil, etc. *Formula*: $C_5H_4O_2$ ⟨< *furfur*ane + *al*dehyde⟩

Fu•ries ['fjʊriz] *n.pl. Greek and Roman mythology.* the three spirits of revenge; Erinyes.

fu•ri•ous ['fjʊriəs] *adj.* **1** intensely violent; raging: *a furious storm.* **2** full of wild, fierce anger. **3** of unrestrained energy, speed, etc.: *furious activity.* ⟨< L *furiosus* < *furia* fury⟩ **—'fu•ri•ous•ly,** *adv.*

furl [fɜrl] *v., n.* *—v.* roll up; fold up; curl: *to furl a sail, furl a flag.* *—n.* **1** the act of furling. **2** the manner in which a sail, flag, etc. is furled. **3** a roll, coil, or curl of anything furled. ⟨< F *ferler* < OF *ferlir* < *fer* firm (< L *firmus*) + *lier* bind < L *ligare*⟩ **—'furl•er,** *n.*

fur•long ['fɜrlɒŋ] *n.* a unit for measuring distance, equal to 0.2 km. *Abbrev.*: fur. ⟨OE *furlang* < *furh* furrow + *lang* long⟩

fur•lough ['fɜrlou] *n., v.* *—n.* a leave of absence, especially for a soldier or missionary.
—v. give leave of absence to. ⟨< Du. *verlof*⟩

fur•nace ['fɜrnɪs] *n.* **1** an enclosed structure for providing heat for buildings by warming water or air that circulates through pipes and radiators, hot-air registers, etc. **2** an enclosed structure for providing intense heat for use in separating metal from ore, in treating metal, in producing coke, etc. **3** a very hot place: *The room was a furnace when the windows were closed.* **4** a severe test. ⟨ME < OF *fornais, fornaise* < L *fornax, -acis* < *fornus* oven⟩

fur•nish [,fɜrnɪʃ] *v.* **1** supply; provide: *The sun furnishes heat.* **2** supply (a room, house, etc.) with furniture, equipment, etc. ⟨< OF *furniss-,* a stem of *furnir* accomplish < Gmc.⟩
—'fur•nish•er, *n.*

☛ *Syn.* **1, 2. Furnish,** EQUIP = provide or supply. **Furnish** = provide things or services necessary for existence or wanted for use or comfort: *We furnished the living room. The caterer furnished both food and waiters. Furnish one good reason.* **Equip** = fit out with what is needed to do work or to work with: *We equipped the kitchen. He is not equipped to translate Latin.*

fur•nish•ings ['fɜrnəʃɪŋz] *n.pl.* **1** the furniture or equipment for a room, house, etc. **2** accessories of dress; articles of clothing: *That store sells men's furnishings.*

fur•ni•ture ['fɜrnətʃər] *n.* **1** the movable articles needed in a room, house, etc.: *Beds, chairs, tables, and desks are furniture.* **2** *Archaic.* articles needed; equipment, especially the harness and ornamental coverings for a horse. **3** apparatus, appliances, or instruments for work, now especially the tools, utensils, rigging, stores, and tackle of a ship. **4** *Printing.* strips or blocks of wood or metal, lower than type-high, set in and about pages of type to fill out large white areas such as margins. ⟨< F *fourniture*⟩

fu•ror ['fjʊrɔr] *or* ['fjʊrər] *n.* **1** an outburst of wild enthusiasm or excitement among a group; uproar: *There was a great furor in the crowd when the announcement was made.* **2** an inspired or excited mood: *He wrote the poem in a furor.* **3** fury; rage. ⟨< F *fureur* < L *furor* < *furere* rage⟩

fu•rore ['fjʊrɔr] *or* [fjʊ'rɔr] *n. Brit.* furor. ⟨< Ital. *furore* < L *furor*⟩

fu•ros•e•mide [fjʊ'rɒsə,maɪd] *n.* a diuretic drug.

furred [fɜrd] *adj., v.* *—adj.* **1** having fur. **2** made, covered, trimmed, or lined with fur. **3** wearing fur. **4** coated with matter suggesting fur: *A furred tongue is a sign of illness.* **5** provided with furring strips: *a furred wall.*
—v. pt. and pp. of FUR.

fur•ri•er ['fɜriər] *n.* **1** a dealer in furs. **2** a person whose work is preparing furs or making and repairing fur garments.

fur•ri•er•y ['fɜriəri] *n., pl.* **-er•ies. 1** furs. **2** the business or work of a furrier.

fur•ring ['fɜrɪŋ] *n., v.* *—n.* **1** fur used to make, cover, trim, or line clothing. **2** a coating of matter suggesting fur. **3** the application of thin strips of wood to beams, walls, etc. to make a level support for laths, etc. or to provide air spaces. **4** the strips used for this, also called **furring strips.**
—v. ppr. of FUR.

fur•row ['fɜrou] *n., v.* *—n.* **1** a long, narrow groove or track cut in the ground by a plough. **2** any long, narrow groove or track: *Heavy trucks made deep furrows in the muddy road.* **3** a deep wrinkle.
—v. **1** make furrows in. **2** wrinkle: *Her face was furrowed with age.* **3** plough. ⟨OE *furh*⟩

fur•ry ['fɜri] *adj.* **-ri•er, -ri•est. 1** consisting of fur. **2** covered with or wearing fur: *a furry animal.* **3** looking or feeling like fur. **4** coated or covered as if with fur: *a furry tongue.*
—'fur•ri•ness, *n.*

fur seal any of various eared seals, highly valued as a source of sealskin because of their thick coats with fine underfur. The **northern fur seal** (*Callorhinus ursinus*) of the N Pacific Ocean is one of the most important for the fur trade.

fur•ther ['fɜrðər] *adj., adv.* (*a comparative of* FAR); *v.*
—adj. **1** more; additional: *Have you any further need of me?* **2** farther; more distant: *on the further side.*
—adv. **1** to a greater extent. **2** at or to a greater distance. **3** moreover; furthermore; besides: *He said further that he would support us in any way he could.*
—v. help forward; promote. ⟨OE *furthra,* adj., *furthor,* adv. < *forth* forth⟩
☛ *Syn. v.* See note at PROMOTE.
☛ *Usage.* See note at FARTHER.

fur•ther•ance ['fɜrðərəns] *n.* an act of furthering; helping forward; advancement; promotion.

fur•ther•more ['fɜrðər,mɔr] *adv.* moreover; also; besides.

fur•ther•most ['fɜrðər,moust] *adj.* furthest.

fur•thest ['fɜrðɪst] *adv. or adj.* (a superlative of FAR). **1** to or at the greatest degree or extent. **2** to or at the greatest distance in space or time. ⟨ME⟩

fur•tive ['fɜrtɪv] *adj.* **1** done stealthily; secret: *He made a furtive attempt to read his sister's letter.* **2** sly; stealthy; shifty: *The thief had a furtive manner.* ⟨< L *furtivus* < *fur* thief⟩ **—'fur•tive•ly,** *adv.* **—'fur•tive•ness,** *n.*

fu•run•cle ['fjʊrʌŋkəl] *n. Pathology.* a boil; inflammatory sore. ⟨< L *furunculus,* dim. of *fur* thief⟩

fu•run•cu•lo•sis [fjə,rʌnkjə'lousɪs] *n. Pathology.* a condition characterized by the presence of multiple boils. ⟨< L *furunculus* petty thief, boil. See FURUNCLE.⟩

fu•ry ['fjʊri] *n., pl.* **-ries. 1** wild, fierce anger; a rage. **2** violence; fierceness. **3** a raging or violent person. **4** unrestrained energy, speed, etc.: *work with fury.* **5 Fury,** *Greek and Roman mythology.* any one of the three spirits of revenge.
like fury, *Informal.* violently; very rapidly. ⟨< L *furia*⟩
☛ *Syn.* **1.** See note at RAGE.

furze [fɜrz] *n.* **1** a low, prickly, European evergreen shrub (*Ulex europaeus*) of the pea family having yellow flowers, common on wastelands; gorse. **2** any of several related plants. **3** the flower of any of these plants. ⟨OE *fyrs*⟩

fu•sain [fju'zein] *or* ['fjuzein] *n.* **1** a charcoal pencil made from spindle tree wood. **2** a drawing made with such a pencil. **3** a component of coal similar to charcoal. ⟨< F, originally, spindle tree < VL **fusago, *fusaginis* < L *fusus* a spindle⟩

fus•cous ['fʌskəs] *adj.* of a greyish brown or deep grey tone. ⟨< L *fuscus*⟩

fuse¹ [fjuz] *n., v.* **fused, fus•ing.** *—n.* **1** a wick or a long, narrow sheath filled with combustible powder used to ignite an explosive charge from a safe distance. **2** any of various mechanical or electrical devices for detonating a bomb, shell, etc.
have a short fuse, anger easily.
—v. fit or provide with a fuse. ⟨< Ital. *fuso* < L *fusus* spindle⟩

fuse² [fjuz] *n., v.* **fused, fus•ing.** *—n. Electricity.* a safety device in an electric circuit consisting of or containing a metal strip or wire that melts when the current exceeds a specific amperage, thus breaking the circuit.

blow a fuse, **a** cause the safety device to trip, through overloading or a short circuit. **b** burst out in anger.
—*v.* **1** melt or melt together, especially by the action of heat. **2** blend or unite as if by melting together. **3** cease or cause to cease functioning because of the melting of a fuse: *The lights fused when we turned on the heater.* ⟨< L *fusus*, pp. of *fundere* pour, melt⟩

fuse box a compartment in which electric fuses are stored.

fu•see [fju'zi] *or* ['fjuzi] *n.* **1** a large-headed match that will burn in a wind. **2** a flare used by railways as a signal: *A fusee burns with a red or green light.* Also, **fuzee. 3** formerly, part of the machinery of a clock or watch. **4** a fuse on an explosive. ⟨< F *fusée* spindleful < OF **fus* spindle < L *fusus*⟩

fu•se•lage ['fjuzə,lɑʒ] *or* ['fjuzəlɪdʒ], ['fjusə,lɑʒ] *or* ['fjusəlɪdʒ] *n.* the body of an aircraft that holds passengers, cargo, etc. The wings and tail are attached to the fuselage. ⟨< F *fuselage* < *fuselé* spindle-shaped⟩

fu•sel oil or **fu•sel** ['fjuzəl] *or* ['fjusəl] a sharp or bitter, poisonous, oily liquid that occurs in alcoholic liquors when they are not distilled enough. ⟨*fusel* < G *Fusel* bad liquor⟩
☛ *Hom.* FUSIL.

fu•si•ble ['fjuzəbəl] *adj.* that can be fused or melted. **—'fu•si•ble•ness, ,fu•si'bil•i•ty,** *n.* **—'fu•si•bly,** *adv.*

fu•sid•ic acid [fu'sɪdɪk] an antibiotic drug.

fu•si•form ['fjuzə,fɔrm] *adj.* rounded and tapering from the middle toward each end; spindle-shaped: *A milkweed pod is somewhat fusiform.* ⟨< L *fusus* spindle + E *-form*⟩

fu•sil ['fjuzəl] *or* ['fjusəl] *n.* a light flintlock musket. ⟨< F *fusil* steel for tinder box, ult. < L *focus* hearth⟩
☛ *Hom.* FUSEL.

fu•si•lier [,fjuzə'lir] *n.* **1** formerly, a soldier armed with a light flintlock musket called a fusil. **2** a private soldier in a regiment that used to be armed with fusils. Also, **fusileer.** ⟨< F *fusilier* < *fusil* musket⟩

fu•sil•lade [,fjuzə'lɑd] *or* [,fjuzə'leid], ['fjusə'lɑd] *or* ['fjusə'leid] *n., v.* **-lad•ed, -lad•ing.** —*n.* **1** a discharge of many firearms at the same time or in rapid succession. **2** something that resembles a fusillade: *The reporters greeted the mayor with a fusillade of questions.*
—*v.* attack or shoot down by a fusillade. ⟨< F *fusillade* < *fusiller* shoot < *fusil* musket⟩

fu•sion ['fjuʒən] *n.* **1** a melting; melting together; fusing: *Bronze is made by the fusion of copper and tin.* **2** a blending; union: *A new party was formed by the fusion of two political groups.* **3** the product of fusing. **4** *Nuclear physics.* the combining of two nuclei to create a nucleus of greater mass. The fusion of atomic nuclei releases tremendous amounts of energy, which can be used in such things as the hydrogen or fusion bomb. **5** *Music.* a type of popular music dating from the 1970s in which elements of jazz, funk, rock, and sometimes other forms are blended. ⟨< L *fusio, -onis* < *fundere* pour, melt⟩

fusion bomb a nuclear bomb using the principle of fusion, rather than fission, to produce an explosion. The hydrogen bomb is a fusion bomb.

fu•sion•ist ['fjuʒənɪst] *n.* a person taking part in a union of political parties or factions. **—'fu•sion,ism,** *n.*

fuss [fʌs] *n., v.* —*n.* **1** too much bother about small matters; useless talk and worry; attention given to something not worth it. **2** a person who fusses too much. **3** a state of great nervousness. **4** a dispute or quarrel. **5** elaborate and noisy enjoyment: *They all made such a fuss over the new baby.*
—*v.* **1** make a fuss: *Nervously she fussed about her work.* **2** make nervous or worried; bother. **3** of a baby, make fretful noises; whine.
fuss around, *Informal.* engage in a pointless, irritating or tiresome activity; mess around: *I can't be bothered fussing around with that broken alarm clock.* ⟨origin uncertain⟩ **—'fuss•er,** *n.*

fuss•budg•et ['fʌs,bʌdʒɪt] *n. Informal.* a fussy person.

fuss•y ['fʌsi] *adj.* **fuss•i•er, fuss•i•est. 1** inclined to fuss; hard to please; very particular: *When he is sick he is fussy about his food. The baby is being fussy again.* **2** with much trimming; elaborately made: *fussy clothes.* **3** full of details; requiring much care: *a fussy job.* **—'fuss•i•ly,** *adv.* **—'fuss•i•ness,** *n.*

fus•tian ['fʌstʃən] *n., adj.* —*n.* **1** a coarse, heavy cloth made of cotton and flax: *Fustian was used for clothing in Europe throughout the Middle Ages.* **2** a thick cotton cloth like corduroy. **3** pompous and high-sounding language; would-be eloquence.
—*adj.* **1** made of fustian. **2** pompous and high-sounding, but cheap. ⟨ME < OF *fustaigne* < LL *fustaneum* < L *fustis* stick of wood⟩

fus•tic ['fʌstɪk] *n.* **1** a tropical American tree of the mulberry family. **2** the wood of this tree. **3** the dye extracted from this wood. **4** any of various other trees (especially *Rhus cotinus*) yielding a similar dye. ⟨< F *fustoc* < Sp. < Arabic *fustuq.* Akin to PISTACHIO.⟩

fus•ti•gate ['fʌstɪ,geit] *v.,* **-gat•ed, -gat•ing. 1** beat. **2** criticize. ⟨< L *fustigatus* pp. of *fustigare* < *fustis* a stick + *agere* to do⟩ **—,fus•ti'ga•tion,** *n.* **—'fus•ti,ga•tor,** *n.*

fust•y ['fʌsti] *adj.* **fust•i•er, fust•i•est. 1** having a stale smell; musty; mouldy; stuffy. **2** old-fashioned; out-of-date. ⟨< *fust,* obs. n., < OF *fust* wine cask < L *fustis* staff⟩ **—'fust•i•ly,** *adv.* **—'fust•i•ness,** *n.*

fut. future.

fu•thork or **fu•thark** ['fuθɔrk] *or* ['fjuθɑrk] *n.* the runic alphabet, so called from its first six letters. See RUNE for picture.

fu•tile ['fjutaɪl] *or* ['fjutəl] *adj.* **1** not successful; useless. **2** not important; trifling. **3** occupied with things of no value or importance; lacking in purpose: *a futile life.* ⟨< L *futilis* pouring easily, worthless < *fundere* pour⟩ **—'fu•tile•ly,** *adv.* **—'fu•tile•ness,** *n.*
☛ *Syn.* **1.** See note at VAIN.

fu•til•i•ty [fju'tɪləti] *n., pl.* **-ties. 1** uselessness. **2** unimportance. **3** a useless or unimportant action, event, etc.

fu•ton ['futɒn] *or* ['fjutɒn] **1** a Japanese quilted pad or mattress that can be placed on the floor to sleep on: *Futons have become popular in Canada.* **2** a piece of furniture consisting of a wooden frame covered by a quilted pad and typically used as a bed at night and a couch by day. ⟨< Sino-Japanese, originally, round cushions filled with cattail flower spikes < Chinese *fu* cattail + *ton* round⟩

fut•tock ['fʌtək] *n. Nautical.* one of the curved timbers that form the middle of a rib in a ship. ⟨? for *foot hook*⟩

fu•ture ['fjutʃər] *n., adj.* —*n.* **1** the time to come; the days, years, etc. ahead: *She has not done very well so far but hopes to do better in the future.* **2** what is to come; what will be: *She claims she can foretell the future.* **3** a chance or expectation of success and prosperity: *a young woman with a future.* **4** *Grammar.* **a** a future tense. **b** a verb form in this tense. **5 futures,** *pl.* commodities or stocks bought or sold to be received or delivered at a future date.
—*adj.* **1** that is to come; that will be; coming. **2** *Grammar.* of, having to do with, or being a verb tense that indicates time to come. *Will go* is the future tense of *go.* ⟨< L *futurus,* future participle of *esse* be⟩ **—'fu•ture•less,** *adj.*

future perfect *Grammar.* **1** in English, a verb tense formed by adding *will have* or *shall have* to the past participle, to express action to be completed in the future: *By next week, he will have gone.* **2** designating this tense. **3** a verb form or verb phrase in this tense. **4** a similar tense in certain other languages.

future shock inability of people to adjust to rapid change, especially technological change. ⟨coined by Alvin Toffler in his book *Future Shock,* after *culture shock*⟩

fu•tur•ism ['fjutʃə,rɪzəm] *n.* **1** a movement in art, literature, and music that began in Italy in the early 20th century, and that rejected traditional forms and methods in an attempt to express the violence, speed, and noise of contemporary civilization. **2** the practice or policy of concentrating on predictions of what will happen in the future as the basis for present-day decisions and actions. **3** the quality of being futuristic. **—'fu•tur•ist,** *n., adj.*

fu•tur•is•tic [,fjutʃə'rɪstɪk] *adj.* **1** of or having to do with the future or what is thought of as characteristic of the future: *a futuristic movie, set in the year 2050. The display featured futuristic designs in furnishings.* **2** of or having to do with futurism. **—,fu•tur'is•ti•cal•ly,** *adv.*

fu•tu•ri•ty [fju'tʃʊrəti] *or* [fju'tjʊrəti] *n., pl.* **-ties. 1** the time to come; future. **2** a future state or event. **3** the quality of being future.

fu•tur•ol•o•gist [,fjutʃə'rɒlədʒɪst] *n.* a person who practises or studies futurology; futurist.

fu•tur•ol•o•gy [,fjutʃə'rɒlədʒi] *n.* the profession or policy of using forecasts of the future as a basis for present-day decisions and actions; FUTURISM (def. 2). **—,fu•tur•o'log•i•cal,** *adj.*

fu•zee [fju'zi] See FUSEE.

fuzz [fʌz] *n., v.* —*n.* **1** loose, fine, light fibres or hairs; fluff or down: *Peaches and some caterpillars are covered with fuzz.* **2** an audio blur or distortion produced by deliberately overloading an

amplification circuit. Also, **fuzz tone.** 3 *Slang.* Usually, **the fuzz,** the police or a police officer.
—*v.* make or become fuzzy: *The blanket is fuzzing.* ⟨< Du. *voos* spray⟩

fuzz•y ['fʌzi] *adj.* **fuzz•i•er, fuzz•i•est.** 1 of fuzz: *The baby's hair was just a fuzzy halo.* 2 like fuzz: *My hair gets fuzzy when it's humid outside.* 3 covered with fuzz: *a fuzzy caterpillar.* 4 not clear or distinct; blurred or imprecise: *Everything looks fuzzy when I don't have my glasses on. That argument is an example of fuzzy thinking.* —**'fuzz•i•ly,** *adv.* —**'fuzz•i•ness,** *n.*

fv FOLIO VERSO.

fwd. forward.

–fy *suffix.* 1 make or make into; cause to be: *simplify, intensify, pacify, horrify.* 2 become: *solidify, putrify.* 3 make like: *citify.* ⟨< F *-fier* < *-ficare* < L *facere* do, make⟩

FY FISCAL YEAR.

FYI for your information.

fyl•fot ['fɪlfɒt] *n.* swastika. ⟨? < *fill foot,* a design for filling the foot of a painted window⟩

G g *G g*

g or **G** [dʒi] *n., pl.* **g's** or **G's. 1** the seventh letter of the English alphabet. **2** any speech sound represented by this letter. **3** a person or thing identified as *g,* especially the seventh in a series. **4** *Music.* **a** the fifth tone of the scale of C major. **b** a symbol representing this tone. **c** a key string, etc. of a musical instrument that produces this tone. **d** the scale or key that has G as its keynote. **5 g,** *Physics.* a unit of acceleration equal to the force of gravity upon a body at rest, used to measure the force exerted on an accelerating body. **6** something shaped like the letter G. **7 G,** force equal to the gravitational pull of the earth. **8** something, such as a printer's type, a lever, or a key on a keyboard, that produces a g or G. **9** *(adjl.)* of or being a G or g.

g 1 gram(s). **2** gravity.

g. or **g 1** gravity. **2** guinea. **3** gauge. **4** genitive. **5** gender. **6** goalkeeper. **7** *Electricity.* conductance. **8** specific gravity.

G 1 German. **2** giga- (an SI prefix). **3** *Slang.* a grand; one thousand dollars.

G. Gulf.

Ga gallium.

G.A. 1 in the United Nations, General Assembly. **2** General Agent.

gab [gæb] *n., v.* **gabbed, gab•bing.** *Informal.* —*n.* chatter; gabble; idle talk.
gift of (the) gab, fluency of speech; glibness.
—*v.* talk too much; chatter; gabble. ⟨probably imitative⟩

gab•ar•dine [ˌgæbər'din] *or* ['gæbərˌdin] *n.* **1** a closely woven, woollen, cotton, or rayon cloth having small, diagonal ribs on its surface, used for raincoats, suits, etc. **2** a garment of gabardine. ⟨var. of *gaberdine*⟩

gab•ble ['gæbəl] *v.* **-bled, -bling;** *n.* —*v.* **1** make unintelligible or animal sounds: *They heard the geese gabbling in the yard.* **2** talk rapidly, without making much sense: *She was gabbling on excitedly about a fire she had seen.* **3** utter rapidly and unintelligibly.
—*n.* rapid, nonsensical talk or unintelligible sounds: *the gabble of geese.* ⟨< *gab,* var. of *gob* < Gaelic *gob* mouth⟩ —**'gab•bler,** *n.*

gab•bro ['gæbrou] *n.* a dark, granular igneous rock, mostly feldspar and pyroxine. ⟨< Ital. < L *glaber* bare⟩

gab•by ['gæbi] *adj.* **-bi•er, -bi•est.** *Informal.* very talkative. —**'gab•bi•ness,** *n.*

gab•er•dine [ˌgæbər'din] *or* ['gæbərˌdin] *n.* **1** a man's long, loose coat or cloak worn in the Middle Ages, especially by Jews. **2** See GABARDINE. ⟨< Sp. *gabardina*⟩

gab•fest ['gæbˌfɛst] *n. Informal.* **1** a long conversation. **2** an informal gathering for conversation and discussion.

ga•bi•on ['geibiən] *n.* **1** *Military.* a cylinder of wicker filled with earth, formerly used as a defence. In modern warfare sandbags are used in place of gabions. **2** a similar cylinder made of metal, etc. and filled with stones, used in building dams, supporting bridge foundations, etc. ⟨< F < Ital. *gabbione,* ult. < L *cavea* cage⟩

ga•ble ['geibəl] *n.* **1** the end of a ridged roof, with the triangular upper part of the wall that it covers. **2** an end wall topped by a gable. **3** a triangular ornament or canopy over a door, window, etc. ⟨ME < OF *gable* < ON *gafl*⟩ —**'ga•ble,like,** *adj.*

ga•bled ['geibəld] *adj.* built with a gable or gables; having or forming gables.

gable roof a roof that slopes down on either side from a single ridgepole, forming a gable at either end. See ROOF for picture.

gable window 1 a window in a GABLE (def. 1). **2** a window with an ornamental GABLE (def. 3) over it.

Ga•bon [gæ'boun] *or* [gə'boun]; *French,* [ga'bɔ̃] a country in W Africa, properly called the **Gabonese Republic.**

ga•by ['geibi] *n., pl.* **-bies.** *Informal.* a fool; simpleton. ⟨origin uncertain⟩

gad[1] [gæd] *v.* **gad•ded, gad•ding;** *n.* —*v.* **1** go about looking for pleasure or excitement: *She was always gadding about town.* **2** move about restlessly.
—*n.* **1** the act of gadding. **2** gadabout: *He is a born gad.* ⟨? back formation < obs. *gadling* companion < OE *gædeling* < *gæd* fellowship + *-ling*⟩ —**'gad•der,** *n.*

gad[2] [gæd] *n., v.* **gad•ded, gad•ding.** —*n.* **1** a goad. **2** a pointed mining tool for breaking up rock, coal, ore, etc.
—*v.* **1** goad. **2** break up (rock or ore) with a gad. ⟨< Scand.; cf. Icelandic *gaddr*⟩

gad•a•bout ['gædəˌbʌut] *n. Informal.* a person who goes about looking for pleasure or excitement; person fond of going from place to place. ⟨< *gad[1]*⟩

gad•fly ['gædˌflaɪ] *n., pl.* **-flies. 1** any of several large flies that sting cattle, horses, etc. The horsefly and botfly are gadflies. **2** a person who irritates others or rouses them from a state of self-satisfaction by calling attention to their faults, etc. ⟨< *gad[2]* + *fly[1]*⟩

gadg•et ['gædʒɪt] *n. Informal.* a small mechanical, electrical, or electronic device or contrivance; any ingenious device: *She's always buying gadgets for her car; the latest one is a coffee maker that plugs into the lighter.* ⟨origin uncertain⟩

gadg•et•eer [ˌgædʒə'tir] *n.* one who invents or likes gadgets.

gadg•et•ry ['gædʒətri] *n.* **1** gadgets collectively: *electronic gadgetry.* **2** the inventing, making, and using of gadgets. **3** great interest in gadgets.

ga•did ['geidɪd] *adj., n.* —*adj.* of the cod family (Gadidae).
—*n.* a gadid fish.

ga•doid ['geidɔɪd] *n.* any of various bony fishes (family Gadidae, order Gadiformes) such as cod, hake, or burbot. ⟨< NL *gadus* cod < Gk. *gados* kind of fish⟩

gad•o•lin•ite ['gædələˌnəit] *n.* a black or brown mineral containing iron and some rare-earth metals. ⟨< G *Gadolinit* after Johann *Gadolin* (1760-1852), a Finnish chemist⟩

gad•o•lin•i•um [ˌgædə'lɪniəm] *n.* a rare magnetic metallic chemical element. *Symbol:* Gd; *at.no.* 64; *at.mass* 157.25. ⟨See GADOLINITE⟩

ga•droon [gə'drun] *n.* a moulding of decorative flutings on silverwork. ⟨< F *godron* probably < *godet* a small cup without a handle < Middle Du. *kodde* wooden cylinder, rounded object⟩

gad•wall ['gædˌwɒl] *n.* a medium-sized duck (*Anas strepera*) found mainly around sloughs and shallow lake margins in W North America, Europe, and Asia, the male having mainly grey plumage, the female brownish. ⟨origin unknown. 17c.⟩

Gae•a ['dʒiə] *n. Greek mythology.* the goddess of the earth and mother of the Titans. Also, **Gaia.**

Gael [geil] *n.* **1** a Scottish Highlander. **2** a Celt who is a native or inhabitant of Scotland, Ireland, or the Isle of Man. ⟨< Scots Gaelic *Gaidheal* < OIrish *Goidhel*⟩
☛ *Hom.* GALE.

Gael•ic ['geilɪk]; *also, esp. Scottish,* ['gɑlɪk] *adj., n.* —*adj.* of or having to do with the Gaels, especially the Scottish Highlanders, or their language.
—*n.* the language of the Gaels. Gaelic is a Celtic language, related to Welsh.

gaff [gæf] *n., v.* —*n.* **1** a strong hook or barbed spear for pulling large fish out of the water. **2** a sharp metal spur fastened to the leg of a gamecock. **3** a spar or pole extending along the upper edge of a fore-and-aft sail. See SLOOP for picture. **4** something uncomfortable or hard to take. **5** *Slang.* a hoax, fraud, or trick. **6** a steel point on a climber's iron.
blow the gaff, *Slang.* give away a secret.
stand the gaff, *Slang.* hold up well under strain or punishment of any kind.
—*v.* **1** hook or pull (a fish) out of the water with a gaff. **2** *Slang.* **a** deceive or trick. **b** fix for the purpose of cheating; rig: *to gaff the dice.* ⟨< F *gaffe* < Celtic; cf. Irish Gaelic *gaf, gafa*⟩
☛ *Hom.* GAFFE.

gaffe [gæf] *n.* a tactless or indiscreet remark, action, etc.; faux pas. ⟨< F⟩
☛ *Hom.* GAFF.

gaf•fer ['gæfər] *n.* **1** *Informal.* an old man. **2** the chief electrician on the set of a television program or film. **3** a master glassblower. **4** a foreperson. ⟨alteration of *godfather*⟩
☛ *Usage.* **Gaffer** (def. 1) is now normally used in a humorous or unfavourable sense; it is the masculine counterpart of **gammer,** an old gossip.

gaff•top•sail [ˌgæf'tɒpˌseil] *or* [ˌgæf'tɒpsəl] *n.* a topsail set above a gaff.

gag [gæg] *n., v.* **gagged, gag•ging.** —*n.* **1** something thrust into

a person's mouth to keep him or her from talking, crying out, etc. **2** anything used to silence a person; a restraint or hindrance to free speech. **3** *Informal.* an amusing remark or trick; something said or done to cause a laugh; a joke: *The comedian's gags made the audience laugh.* **4** CLOSURE (def. 4). **5** a device used by dentists to keep the patient's mouth open.
—*v.* **1** keep from talking, crying out, etc. by means of a gag: *The bandits tied the watchman's arms and gagged him.* **2** force to keep silent; restrain or hinder from free speech. **3** say something to cause a laugh. **4** choke or strain or cause to choke or strain in an effort to vomit. ⟨probably imitative⟩ **—'gag•ger,** *n.*

ga•ga ['gɑ,gɑ] *adj. Slang.* **1** crazy or mentally confused. **2** wildly or foolishly enthusiastic: *They went gaga over the show.* ⟨< F *gaga* old fool⟩

gage[1] [geidʒ] *n., v.* **gaged, gag•ing.** *—n.* **1** a pledge to fight; challenge: *The knight threw down his gauntlet as a gage of battle.* **2** something deposited as security; a pledge.
—*v. Archaic.* offer as a pledge or security; wager. ⟨ME < OF *gage* < Frankish *wadja-. Doublet of WAGE.⟩
☛ *Hom.* GAUGE.

gage[2] [geidʒ] *n., v.* **gaged, gag•ing.** See GAUGE. **—'gage•a•ble,** *adj.* **—'gag•er,** *n.*

gage[3] [geidʒ] *n. Informal.* greengage.
☛ *Hom.* GAUGE.

ga•ger ['geidʒər] See GAUGER.

gag•gle ['gægəl] *n., v.* **-gled, -gling.** *—n.* **1** a flock of geese on water or land. **2** *Informal.* a group or cluster of people or things: *A gaggle of autograph hunters waited outside the door.* **3** a gabbling or cackling sound, as that made by geese.
—*v.* make gabbling or cackling sounds. ⟨< ME *gagel* < *gagelen* to cackle⟩

gag•man ['gæg,mæn] *n., pl.* **-men.** a person who invents comic lines and situations for comedians.

gag rule a prohibition on publication or broadcast.

gahn•ite ['gɑnəit] *n.* zinc aluminate. ⟨< G *Gahnit* after J.G. *Gahn* (1745-1818), a Swedish chemist⟩

Gai•a ['geiə], ['gaɪə] *or* ['dʒiə] *n.* Gaea.

gai•e•ty ['geiəti] *n., pl.* **-ties.** **1** cheerful liveliness; merriment: *Her gaiety enlivened the party.* **2** lively entertainment. **3** bright appearance; showiness; finery: *gaiety of dress.* Also, **gayety.** ⟨< F *gaieté*⟩

gail•lar•di•a [gə'lɑrdiə] *or* [gei'lɑrdiə] *n.* any of a genus (*Gaillardia*) of North American plants of the composite family having large, showy flower heads with yellow or reddish ray florets and brownish purple disk florets.

gai•ly ['geili] *adv.* **1** in a gay manner; happily; merrily: *She ran gaily to meet them. The children chattered gaily.* **2** brightly, showily: *The room was gaily decorated.* Also, **gayly.**

gain[1] [gein] *v., n.* *—v.* **1** get; obtain; secure: *The king gained possession of more lands.* **2** get as an increase, addition, advantage, or profit. **3** make progress; advance; improve: *The sick child is gaining and will soon be well.* **4** win; be the victor in: *to gain the prize, to gain the battle.* **5** get to; arrive at; reach: *The swimmer gained the shore.* **6** of a timepiece, run too fast (by): *My watch gains about six minutes a week.* **7** come closer; begin to catch up or catch up *(on)*: *He saw that the second runner was gaining. The pirate ship was slowly gaining on them.* **8** put on (weight): *The baby gained five pounds in a week. I've been dieting, but I can't seem to stop gaining.*
—*n.* **1** an increase in profit or advantage: *He has made a substantial gain over his opponent in this competition.* **2** the act of getting wealth: *Greed is love of gain.* **3** an increase in amount or degree: *a gain in speed, a gain of ten percent.* **4** *Electronics.* amplification of a radio signal, etc. **5 gains,** *pl.* profits; earnings; winnings. ⟨< F *gagner* < Gmc.⟩

gain[2] [gein] *n.* rabbet.

gain•er ['geinər] *n.* **1** one who gains. **2** *Swimming.* a fancy dive in which the diver turns a back somersault in the air.

gain•ful ['geinfəl] *adj.* bringing in money or advantage; profitable: *gainful employment.* **—'gain•ful•ly,** *adv.*

gain•said ['gein,sɛd] *v.* a pt. and a pp. of GAINSAY.

gain•say ['gein,sei] *or* [,gein'sei] *v.* **-said** or **-sayed, -saying.** *Archaic or poetic.* **1** deny; dispute: *The facts cannot be gainsaid.* **2** contradict; speak against: *to gainsay an opponent.* ⟨< obs. *gain-* against + *say*⟩ **—'gain,say•er,** *n.*

gainst or **'gainst** [gɛnst] *or* [geinst] *prep. or conj. Poetic.* against.

gait [geit] *n., v.* *—n.* **1** the kind of step used in walking or running. A gallop is one of the gaits of a horse. **2** a way of walking or running; carriage or bearing of the body in moving: *He has a lame gait because of an injured foot.*
—*v.* teach (a horse) a gait. ⟨ME < ON *gata* way⟩
☛ *Hom.* GATE.

gait•ed ['geitɪd] *adj.* having a certain gait: *heavy-gaited oxen.*

gai•ter ['geitər] *n.* **1** a cloth or leather covering for the lower leg, buttoned or buckled on one side and extending from the instep up to the ankle, the calf, or the knee. **2** a similar covering extending only up to the ankle; a spat (see SPAT[3]). **3** an ankle-high shoe with an elastic insert in each side and no laces. Also called **gaiter shoe.** ⟨< F *guêtre*⟩

gal[1] [gæl] *n. Informal.* girl.

gal[2] [gæl] a unit used in geodesy and geophysics for measuring acceleration due to gravity. It is equal to one centimetre per second per second (1 cm/s^2). ⟨after *Galileo* (1564-1642), Italian mathematician, astronomer, and physicist; 20c.⟩

gal. gallon(s).

ga•la ['gælə], ['geilə], *or* ['gɑlə] *n.* **1** a festive occasion; festival. **2** (*adjl.*) of, for, or involving festivity: *a gala occasion.* ⟨< F < Ital.; cf. OF *gale* merriment⟩

ga•la•bia or **ga•la•bi•ya** [dʒə'lɑbiə] *or* [gə'lɑbiə] *n.* See DJELLABA.

ga•lac•ta•gogue [gə'læktə,gɒg] *n.* an agent increasing the amount of milk collected from an animal. ⟨< Gk. *gala, galaktos* milk + *agogos* leading < *agein* lead⟩

ga•lac•tic [gə'læktik] *adj.* **1** *Astronomy.* of or having to do with a galaxy of stars, especially the Milky Way. **2** milky. ⟨< Gk. *galaktikos* < *gala, galaktos* milk⟩

galactic circle *Astronomy.* the great circle whose plane passes almost centrally along the Milky Way.

galactic cluster *Astronomy.* any diffuse group of stars, usually numbering over a hundred, such as the Pleiades.

galactic noise *Astronomy.* a broad range of signals originating in the Milky Way.

ga•lac•tose [gə'læktous] *n.* a levulose sugar found in milk. *Formula*: $C_6H_{12}O_6$ ⟨< Gk. *gala, galaktos* milk + E *-ose*[2]⟩

ga•lac•to•se•mia [gə,læktə'simiə] *n.* a genetic disorder resulting from the absence of an enzyme needed to convert galactose into glucose. Galactosemia can cause retardation, cataracts, and liver problems. ⟨< *galactose* + *-emia*⟩

ga•lah [gə'lɑ] *n.* a cockatoo (*Cacatua roseicapilla*) with pink and grey plumage, found mainly in inland Australia and kept as a domestic bird. ⟨< Australian aboriginal language⟩

Gal•a•had ['gælə,hæd] *n.* **1** *Arthurian legend.* the noblest and purest knight of the Round Table. Sir Galahad was the only knight who succeeded in the quest for the Holy Grail. **2** any man considered to be very noble and pure.

gal•an•tine ['gælən,tin] *n.* veal, chicken, or other white meat boned, boiled, and seasoned, and then served cold in its own jelly. ⟨< OF⟩

gal•a•te•a [,gælə'tiə] *n.* a durable cotton twill, used to make uniforms, play clothes, children's sailor suits, etc. ⟨after a 19c. English warship H.M.S. *Galatea*⟩

Gal•a•te•a [,gælə'tiə] *n. mythology.* an ivory statue of a maiden, carved by Pygmalion. When he fell in love with the statue, Aphrodite gave it life.

Ga•la•tian [gə'leiʃən] *n., adj.* *—n.* a native or inhabitant of Galatia, an ancient country in central Asia Minor that later became a Roman province.
—*adj.* of or having to do with Galatia or its people.

ga•lax ['geilæks] *n.* an evergreen plant (*Galax aphylla*) native to the southeastern United States, bearing glossy leaves and small, white flowers. ⟨< NL probably < Gk. *gala* milk, from its white flower⟩

gal•ax•y ['gæləksi] *n., pl.* **-ax•ies.** **1** *Astronomy.* any of the many systems or groupings of stars making up the universe. A galaxy may contain millions or billions of stars. **2 Galaxy,** the Milky Way, the faintly luminous band of countless stars that stretches across the sky. **3** a brilliant or splendid group: *The queen was followed by a galaxy of brave knights and fair ladies.* ⟨< OF < LL < Gk. *galaxias* < *gala, -aktos* milk⟩

gal•ba•num ['gælbənəm] *n.* an aromatic gum resin obtained from some Asian plants. ⟨< ME < L < Gk. *chalbane* < Hebrew *chelbenah*⟩

gale[1] [geil] *n.* **1** a very strong wind. **2** *Meteorology.* a wind with a velocity of 50-88 km/h (28-47 knots). Winds of gale force are represented by numbers 7 to 9 on the Beaufort scale. See chart

of Beaufort scale in the Appendix. **3** *Archaic or poetic.* breeze. **4** a noisy outburst: *gales of laughter.* ⟨origin uncertain⟩
☛ *Hom.* GAEL.

gale² [geil] *n.* SWEET GALE. ⟨OE *gagel*⟩
☛ *Hom.* GAEL.

gal•ea ['geiliə] *or* ['gæliə] *n., pl.* **gal•e•ae** [-li,i] *or* [-li,aɪ]. *Botany.* part of the calyx in the shape of a helmet. ⟨< NL < L a helmet, probably < Gk. *galee* a weasel, marten⟩

gal•e•ate ['gælint] *or* ['geili,eit] *adj.* having a galea.

ga•le•na [gə'linə] *n.* a grey metallic ore consisting of lead sulphide. It is the most important source of lead. Also called **galenite.** *Formula:* PbS ⟨< L⟩

ga•len•i•cal [gə'lɛnɪkəl] *n.* a herbal or vegetable medicine made according to a recipe. ⟨after *Galen* (c. A.D. 130-200), Greek physician and philosopher⟩

ga•le•nite [gə'linəit] *n.* galena.

ga•lette [gə'lɛt] *n. Cdn.* a flat, unleavened cake made by baking in a frying pan or covering with hot ashes in a fireplace. ⟨< F⟩

Ga•li•bi [gə'libi] *n.* a Guyanan Indian. ⟨< Carib⟩

Ga•li•cian [gə'lɪʃən] *n., adj.* —*n.* **1** a native or inhabitant of Galicia, a region in central Europe. **2** a native or inhabitant of Galicia, a region and former kingdom in NW Spain. **3** the language spoken by the Spanish Galicians, related to Portuguese.
—*adj.* of or having to do with either Galicia.

Gal•i•le•an¹ [,gælə'liən] *n., adj.* —*n.* **1** a native or inhabitant of Galilee, a region in N Palestine that was a Roman province in the time of Jesus. **2** a Christian. **3 the Galilean,** Jesus.
—*adj.* of or having to do with Galilee or its people.

Gal•i•le•an² [,gælə'leiən] *or* [,gælə'liən] *adj.* of or having to do with Galileo (1564-1642), the Italian mathematician, astronomer, and physicist who is regarded as the founder of modern experimental science.

gal•i•lee ['gælə,li] *n.* the porch of some English churches.

gal•i•ot or **gal•li•ot** ['gæliət] *n.* **1** a small, fast galley equipped with both oars and sails that was used until the end of the 18th century. **2** a heavy, single-masted, Dutch cargo vessel or fishing boat. ⟨ME < OF *galiote,* dim. of *galie* ult. < Med.Gk. *galea*⟩

gal•i•pot ['gælə,pɒt] *n.* a type of turpentine. Also, **gallipot.** ⟨< F earlier *garipot,* probably altered < Middle Du. *harpois* boiled resin⟩

gall¹ [gɒl] *n.* **1** bile, especially animal bile used in medicine, etc. **2** *Archaic.* GALL BLADDER. **3** anything very bitter or harsh. **4** bitterness; hate: *His heart was filled with gall.* **5** *Informal.* excessive boldness; impudence: *He had a lot of gall to talk to his employer in such a nasty way.* ⟨OE *gealla*⟩

gall² [gɒl] *v., n.* —*v.* **1** make or become sore by rubbing: *The rough strap galled the horse's skin.* **2** annoy; irritate.
—*n.* **1** a sore spot on the skin caused by rubbing. **2** a cause of annoyance or irritation. ⟨extended use of *gall¹*⟩

gall³ [gɒl] *n.* a growth, or tumour, on the leaves, stems, or roots of plants, caused by insects, fungi, bacteria, etc. The galls of oak trees contain tannic acid used in making ink, medicine, etc. ⟨< F *galle* < L *galla*⟩

gal•la•mine ['gælə,min] *n.* a muscle relaxant drug.

gal•lant *adj. 1-3* ['gælənt], *adj. 4,5 & n.* [gə'lænt], [gə'lɒnt], *or* ['gælənt] *adj., n.* —*adj.* **1** noble; brave; daring: *King Arthur was a gallant knight. They made a gallant effort to save the building.* **2** grand; fine; stately: *a gallant ship.* **3** showy in dress or appearance. **4** very polite and attentive to women. **5** amorous.
—*n.* **1** *Archaic.* a man who wears showy clothes; man of fashion. **2** a man who is very polite and attentive to women. **3** lover. ⟨ME < OF *galant,* ppr. of *galer* make merry < *gale.* See GALA.⟩
—**'gal•lant•ly,** *adv.* —**'gal•lant•ness,** *n.*

gal•lant•ry ['gæləntri] *n., pl.* **-ries. 1** noble spirit or conduct; bravery; dashing courage. **2** great politeness and chivalrous attention to women. **3** a gallant act or speech. **4** *Archaic.* a gay appearance; showy display.

gall bladder or **gall•blad•der** ['gɒl ,blædər] *n.* a sac attached to the liver, in which excess bile is stored until needed. See LIVER for picture.

gal•le•ass ['gæli,æs] *n.* formerly, a heavy, low-built warship larger than a galley and equipped with both oars and sails. It was used in the 16th and 17th centuries. ⟨< MF *galeasse* < Ital. *galeazza* < *galea* < Med.Gk.⟩

gal•le•on ['gæliən] *or* ['gæljən] *n.* a large, heavy sailing ship, usually having three or four decks, used in Europe as a warship and armed trading ship, especially from the 15th to the end of the 16th century. The Spaniards used many galleons in the fleet of the Armada. ⟨< Sp. *galeón* < *galea* < Med.Gk.⟩

gal•ler•y ['gæləri] *n., pl.* **-ler•ies. 1** a long, narrow platform or passage projecting from the wall of a building. **2** a projecting upper floor in a church, theatre, or hall, with seats or room for part of the audience; balcony. **3** the highest floor of this kind in a theatre. **4** the least expensive seats in a theatre. **5** the people who sit in the highest balcony of a theatre. **6** a group of people watching or listening; audience. **7** a long, narrow room or passage; hall. **8** a covered walk or porch. **9** an underground passage. **10** a room or building where works of art are shown. **11** a collection of works of art. **12** a room or building for use as a shooting range, etc. **13** any room in a museum in which objects are displayed.
play to the gallery, *Informal.* try to get the praise or favour of the common people by doing or saying what will please them, in the manner of actors who used to style their performance to suit the tastes of the people watching from the gallery. ⟨< Ital. *galleria*⟩

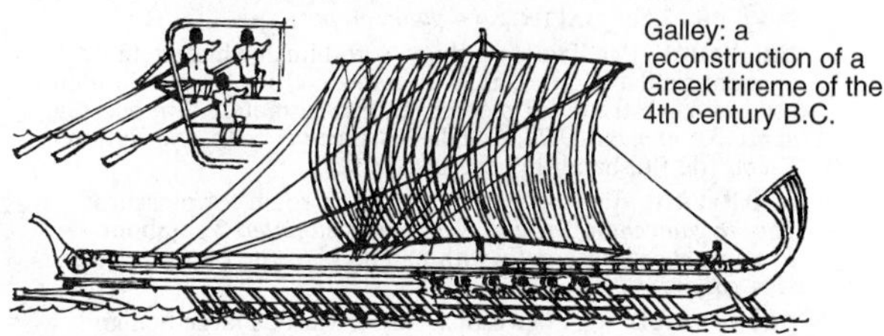
Galley: a reconstruction of a Greek trireme of the 4th century B.C.

gal•ley ['gæli] *n., pl.* **-leys. 1** a long, low ship propelled mainly by one or more banks of oars, used in ancient and medieval times as a warship and a trading ship. Ancient galleys sometimes carried a square sail. The medieval Mediterranean galleys had a large lateen sail. **2** a large rowboat. **3** the kitchen of a ship or aircraft. **4** a long, narrow kitchen. **5** *Printing.* **a** a shallow, oblong tray for holding type that has been set. **b** a proof taken from the type in a galley, used to make corrections before the type is made up into pages. ⟨ME < OF *galee,* ult. < Med.Gk. *galea*⟩

galley proof *Printing.* GALLEY (def. 5b).

galley slave 1 a person compelled or condemned to row a galley. **2** a drudge, especially in a kitchen.

gall•fly ['gɒl,flaɪ] *n., pl.* **-flies.** any of various small insects that deposit their eggs on plants and cause galls that the larvae feed on.

gal•liard ['gæljərd] *n.* **1** a lively dance in triple time, popular in the 16th and 17th centuries. **2** the music for this dance. **3** *Archaic.* a strong, valiant, or gallant man. ⟨< ME *gaillard* < OF brave < Med.L **galia* strength⟩

gal•lic ['gælɪk] *adj. Chemistry.* **1** of gallium. **2** containing gallium, especially with a valence of three.

Gal•lic ['gælɪk] *adj.* **1** of or having to do with Gaul or its people. **2** French. ⟨< L *Gallicus* < *Gallus* a Gaul⟩

gal•lic acid an acid obtained especially from galls on plants, used in making ink, dyes, etc. *Formula:* $C_7H_6O_5H_2O$

Gal•li•cism or **gal•li•cism** ['gælə,sɪzəm] *n.* **1** a French idiom or expression. **2** such an idiom or expression literally translated into another language. *Example: that leaps to the eyes,* from French *ça saute aux yeux,* meaning 'that is obvious'. **3** a French trait or characteristic.

Gal•li•cize or **gal•li•cize** ['gælə,saɪz] *v.* **-cized, -ciz•ing.** make or become French in character, habits, language, etc.
—**,Gal•li•ci'za•tion** *or* **,gal•li•ci'za•tion,** *n.*

gal•li•gas•kins [,gælə'gæskɪnz] *n.pl.* **1** loose breeches. **2** leggings. ⟨formerly *garragascoynes* < MF *garguesque,* var. of *(à la) greguesque* < Ital. *alla grechesca* in the Greek fashion < *greco* Greek < L *Graecus;* influenced by earlier *Gascoyne* Gascon⟩

gal•li•mauf•rey [,gælə'mɒfri] *n.* a hash made of leftovers. ⟨< F *galimafrée* probably < OF *galer* + Picardy dial. *mafrer* to eat much < M.Du. *maffelen*⟩

gal•li•na•ceous [,gælə'neiʃəs] *adj.* of or having to do with an order (Galliformes) of heavy-bodied birds that nest on the ground and fly only short distances, including chickens, turkeys, pheasants, and grouse. ⟨< L *gallinaceus* < *gallina* hen⟩

gall•ing ['gɒlıŋ] *adj., v.* —*adj.* bitterly disappointing; very annoying or irritating: *a galling defeat at the hands of an inferior opponent.*
—*v.* ppr. of GALL.

gal•li•nip•per ['gælə,nıpər] *n. Informal.* any mosquito, fly, bee, etc., with a painful sting. ⟨probably altered < gurnipper < ?⟩

gal•li•nule ['gælə,njul] *or* ['gælə,nul] *n.* any of several marsh birds of the rail family found throughout the world, having long thin toes and a fleshy shield on the forehead. The common gallinule (*Gallinula chloropus*), found in many parts of the world, occurs in Canada only in southern Ontario. ⟨< NL *gallinula* < L *gallina* hen, ult. < *gallus* cock⟩

Gal•li•o ['gæli,ou] *n.* any person, especially an official, who avoids becoming involved in matters which are not his immediate concern; an easygoing, indifferent person. ⟨in the Bible, a Roman proconsul who, when the Jews accused St. Paul, refused to take action against him⟩

gal•li•pot ['gælə,pɒt] *n.* **1** a small pot or jar of glazed earthenware. Gallipots were used by druggists to hold medicine, salve, etc. **2** See GALIPOT. ⟨< *galley* + *pot*⟩

gal•li•um ['gæliəm] *n.* a shiny, soft, bluish white metallic element similar to mercury, with a low melting point. Gallium is used as a substitute for mercury in thermometers. *Symbol*: Ga; *at.no.* 31; *at.mass* 69.74. ⟨< NL ? < L *gallus* cock, translation of *Lecoq* (de Boisbaudran), the discoverer⟩

gal•li•vant ['gælə,vænt] *v.* **1** travel or roam for pleasure: *They're gallivanting around Europe this summer.* **2** go about frivolously or indiscreetly with members of the opposite sex. ⟨? < *gallant*⟩

gal•li•wasp ['gælə,wɒsp] *n.* any of various large benign lizards (genus *Diploglossus*, family Anguidae) living in swamps in the West Indies and Central America. ⟨origin uncertain⟩

gall midge any of several tiny midges (family Cecidomyiidae) that create galls on plants.

gall mite any of several four-legged mites (family Eriophyidae) that create galls on plants.

gall•nut ['gɒl,nʌt] *n.* a nutlike gall on plants.

gal•lon ['gælən] *n.* a unit for measuring liquids, equal to 4 quarts. The traditional Canadian gallon is equal to about 4.55 dm^3; the United States gallon is equal to about 3.79 dm^3. *Abbrev.*: gal. ⟨ME < ONF *galon*⟩

gal•lon•age ['gælənıdʒ] *n.* the number of gallons.

gal•loon [gə'lun] *n.* a narrow braid of gold, silver, or silk thread used in trimming uniforms, furniture, etc. ⟨< F *galon* < *galonner* dress the hair with ribbons < OF *gale* merriment. See GALA.⟩

gal•lop ['gæləp] *n., v.* —*n.* **1** the fastest gait of horses and other four-footed animals. In a gallop, all four feet are off the ground together once in each stride. **2** a ride taken at this gait. **3** a fast pace or progression: *doing the chores at a gallop.*
—*v.* **1** ride at a gallop: *The cowboy galloped along the trail.* **2** go at a gallop: *The pony galloped up to the fence.* **3** cause to gallop: *John galloped his horse down the road.* **4** go very fast; hurry: *She came galloping downstairs to tell us the news.* ⟨< F *galoper* < Gmc.⟩ —**'gal•lop•er,** *n.*
☛ *Hom.* GALOP *['gæləp].*

gal•lous ['gæləs] *adj. Chemistry.* containing gallium, especially with a valence of two.

Gal•lo•way ['gælə,wei] *n.* a Scottish breed of beef cattle. ⟨< *Galloway*, a region in SW Scotland, where these cattle are common⟩

gal•lows ['gælouz] *n., pl.* **-lows** or **-lows•es. 1** a wooden structure usually consisting of a crossbar on two upright posts, used for hanging criminals. **2** a structure like this, used for supporting or suspending something. **3 the gallows,** punishment by hanging: *Many people are against the gallows.*
cheat the gallows, escape the death penalty for a crime. ⟨OE *galga*⟩

gallows bird *Informal.* a person who deserves to be hanged.

gallows humour BLACK HUMOUR.

gall•stone ['gɒl,stoun] *n.* a pebblelike mass that sometimes forms in the gall bladder or its duct. When one or more gallstones stop the flow of bile, a painful illness results.

Gal•lup poll ['gæləp] a poll or opinion on social and political issues, etc., taken from a selected group of people and intended to reflect the opinion of the general public. ⟨< George *Gallup*, an American statistician, born 1901⟩

gal•lus•es ['gæləsəz] *n.pl. Informal.* suspenders. ⟨< *gallus*, dial. variant of *gallows*⟩

gal•op ['gæləp]; *French* [ga'lo] *n., v.* —*n.* **1** a lively dance in two-four time. **2** the music for this dance.
—*v.* dance a galop. ⟨< F⟩
☛ *Hom.* GALLOP ['gæləp].

ga•lore [gə'lɔr] *adj.* in abundance (*used after the noun*): *Over Christmas we had parties galore.* ⟨< Irish *go leōr* to sufficiency⟩

ga•losh [gə'lɒʃ] *n.* a high overshoe having a rubber or plastic sole and a rubber, plastic, or fabric top, worn in wet or snowy weather (*usually used in the plural*): *I hate wearing galoshes.* Also, **golosh**. ⟨< F *galoche*⟩

ga•lumph [gə'lʌmf] *v.* **1** move or run heavily or clumsily: *He went galumphing up the stairs in his great boots.* **2** gallop triumphantly. ⟨blend of *gallop* and *triumph*; coined by Lewis Carroll⟩

gal•van•ic [gæl'vænık] *adj.* **1** producing a direct current of electricity, especially by chemical action. **2** of or caused by an electric current. **3** affecting as if by galvanism; startling or stimulating: *a galvanic personality.* **4** produced as if by an electric shock: *a galvanic reaction.* ⟨< *galvanism*⟩ **—gal'van•i•cal•ly,** *adv.*

gal•va•nism ['gælvə,nızəm] *n.* **1** a direct electric current, especially one produced by chemical action. **2** *Medicine.* the therapeutic use of such electricity to stimulate muscles and nerves. **3** any power or quality that arouses a sudden or forceful reaction: *We were overwhelmed by the galvanism of the actor's performance.* ⟨< F *galvanisme*, after Luigi *Galvani* (1737-1798), an Italian physicist⟩

gal•va•nize ['gælvə,naız] *v.* **-nized, -niz•ing. 1** apply an electric current to. **2** arouse suddenly; startle. **3** cover (iron or steel) with a thin coating of zinc to prevent rust, formerly by a galvanic process. **—,gal•va•ni'za•tion,** *n.* **—'gal•va,niz•er,** *n.*

galvanized iron iron covered with a thin coating of zinc, to resist rust.

gal•va•nom•e•ter [,gælvə'nɒmətər] *n.* an instrument for detecting and measuring a small electric current. ⟨< *galvano-*, combining form of *galvanic* + *-meter*⟩

gal•va•no•met•ric [,gælvənə'mɛtrık] *or* [gæl,vænə'mɛtrık] *adj.* **1** having to do with a galvanometer. **2** measured by a galvanometer. **3** having to do with galvanometry.

gal•va•nom•e•try [,gælvə'nɒmətri] *n.* the detection, measurement, and determination of the direction of electric currents by a galvanometer.

gal•va•no•scope ['gælvənə,skoup] *or* [gæl'vænə,skoup] *n.* an instrument for detecting very small electric currents and showing their direction. ⟨< *galvano-*, combining form of *galvanic* + *-scope*⟩

gal•yak or **gal•yac** ['gæljæk] *n.* fur made from lambskin. ⟨< Russian *golyc* naked⟩

gam¹ [gæm] *n. Slang.* a leg, especially a woman's leg. ⟨prob. < F dial. *gambe* < ONF; ult. < LL *gamba* leg⟩

gam² [gæm] *n.* a group of whales.

ga•ma grass ['gɑmə] any of various tall grasses (genus *Tripsacum*), native to the United States, used for forage. ⟨altered < *grama* grass⟩

gam•ba•do [gæm'beidou] *n.* a long gaiter or legging. ⟨< Ital. < *gamba* leg⟩

gam•be•son ['gæmbəsən] *n.* a leather or quilted jacket, worn as armour in the Middle Ages. ⟨< ME < OF < Med.L *wambasium* < L.Gk. *bambax* cotton⟩

Gam•bia ['gæmbiə] *n.* a country in W Africa, properly called Republic of the Gambia. See SENEGAL for map.

gam•bit ['gæmbıt] *n.* **1** *Chess.* a way of opening a game by purposely risking a pawn or a piece to gain some advantage. **2** any rather risky move or stratagem intended to gain an advantage: *His opening gambit was to call for an investigation.* **3** a way of starting anything, such as a conversation. ⟨< F < Provençal *cambi* an exchange < Ital. *cambio* < LL *cambiare* to change ? < Celtic⟩

gam•ble ['gæmbəl] *v.* **-bled, -bling;** *n.* —*v.* **1** play games of chance for money or some other prize or stake. **2** take a risk in order to gain some advantage: *She decided to gamble by refusing the job offer and hoping for a better one.* **3** bet; wager. **4** lose or squander by gambling (used with **away**): *He gambled away his inheritance.*
gamble on, count on in making one's plans: *You can't gamble on getting that job.*
—*n. Informal.* **1** a risky venture or undertaking. **2** an act of gambling. ⟨probably related to GAME, *v.*⟩
☛ *Hom.* GAMBOL.

gam•bler ['gæmblər] *n.* a person who gambles a great deal, especially one who lives on money won in games of chance.

gam•bling ['gæmblɪŋ] *n., v.* —*n.* **1** the playing of games of chance for money or some other prize or stake. **2** the taking of risks in order to gain some advantage.
—*v.* ppr. of GAMBLE.

gambling stick *Cdn.* formerly, a small stick used by First Nations people to keep score when gambling. Those of the Pacific Coast were beautifully made and decorated.

gambling stone *Cdn.* formerly , a small stone, often having a carved design, used by First Nations people in gambling games.

gam•boge [gæm'boudʒ] *or* [gæm'buʒ] *n.* a gum resin from certain tropical trees, used as a yellow pigment and as a cathartic. ⟨< NL *gambogium* < *Cambodia*⟩

gam•bol ['gæmbəl] *n., v.* **-bolled** or **-boled, -bol•ling** or **-bol•ing.** —*n.* a playful running and jumping about; caper; frolic.
—*v.* frisk about; run and jump about in play: *Lambs gambolled in the meadow.* ⟨< F *gambade* < Ital. *gambata* < *gamba* leg⟩
☛ *Hom.* GAMBLE.

gam•brel ['gæmbrəl] *n.* **1** the hock of a horse or other animal. **2** GAMBREL ROOF. **3** a metal or wooden frame used by butchers for hanging carcasses. ⟨< ONF *gamberel* < *gambe* leg < LL *gamba, camba* < Gk. *kampē* bend⟩

gambrel roof a two-sided roof having two slopes on each side, with the lower slope steeper than the upper one. See ROOF for picture.

gam•bu•sia [gæm'bjuʒə] *or* [gæm'bjuziə] *n.* any fish of the genus *Gambusia,* which eats mosquitoes.

game¹ [geim] *n., adj.* **gam•er, gam•est;** *v.* **gamed, gam•ing.** —*n.* **1** an activity done for entertainment or amusement; a way of playing: *Football, solitaire, and chess are games.* **2** the equipment, etc. necessary to play a particular game, especially any of various table games: *We got several games for Christmas.* **3** a physical or mental exercise with certain rules, played either alone or with another person or group, and often involving competition: *a game of tag. Are you going to the game tonight?* **4** any one of a number of contests making up a set or series: *The tennis champion won four games out of six.* **5** the condition of the score in a game: *At the end of the first period the game was 6 to 3 in our favour.* **6** the number of points required to win. **7** a victory in a game. **8** a particular manner of playing: *He plays a good game.* **9** any activity or undertaking that is carried on as if under set rules and that tests one's skill or endurance: *the game of life, the game of diplomacy.* **10** *Informal.* any business venture, profession, etc.: *the acting game.* **11** a plan; scheme: *He tried to trick us, but we saw through his game.* **12** what is hunted or pursued. **13** wild animals, birds, or fish hunted or caught for sport or for food. **14** flesh of wild animals or birds used for food.
ahead of the game, winning rather than losing.
be off (one's) **game,** play badly.
be on (one's) **game,** play well.
make game of, make fun of; laugh at; ridicule.
play the game, *Informal.* follow the rules; be a good sport.
the game is up, *Informal.* the plan or scheme has failed.
—*adj.* **1** having to do with game, hunting, or fishing: *Game laws protect wildlife.* **2** brave; plucky: *The losing team put up a game fight.* **3** having enough spirit or will: *The explorer was game for any adventure.*
die game, die fighting; die bravely.
—*v.* gamble. ⟨OE *gamen* joy⟩ —**'game•ly,** *adv.* —**'game•ness,** *n.*
☛ *Syn. n.* **1.** See note at PLAY.

game² [geim] *adj. Informal.* lame; crippled; injured: *a game leg.* ⟨origin uncertain⟩

game bag **1** a bag for carrying game that has been killed. **2** the amount of game killed.

game bird a bird hunted for sport or food.

game•cock ['geim,kɒk] *n.* a rooster bred and trained for cockfighting.

game fish a fish caught for sport.

game fowl any of several breeds or strains of domestic fowl from which gamecocks are produced.

game•keep•er ['geim,kipər] *n.* a person employed to breed and look after game animals and birds on an estate and to prevent anyone from stealing them or killing them without permission.

gam•e•lan or **gam•e•lin** ['gæmələn] *n.* a Balinese or Javanese, orchestra comprising bowed, stringed instruments, flutes, and a variety of percussion instruments. ⟨< Javanese, a bamboo xylophone⟩

game law a law made to restrict and regulate hunting and fishing in order to preserve or protect game animals, birds, and fish.

game manager GAME WARDEN.

game misconduct *Hockey.* a penalty banishing a player from the ice for the remainder of the game, awarded for gross misconduct or after the player has received three major penalties in the same game.

game of chance any game depending on luck, not skill.

game plan a course of action for achieving an aim.

game point a final point needed to win a game, especially of tennis.

game preserve or **reserve** *Cdn.* a large tract of land set aside by the government for the protection of wildlife.

game show a radio or especially a television program in which contestants can win prizes.

games•man•ship ['geimzmən,ʃɪp] *n.* the art or practice of defeating an opponent, as in a game, by skilful but somewhat underhanded manoeuvres and ploys: *learning the fine points of political gamesmanship.*

game•some ['geimsəm] *adj.* full of play; sportive; ready to play. —**'game•some•ly,** *adv.*

game•ster ['geimstər] *n.* gambler.

gam•e•tan•gi•um [,gæmə'tændʒiəm] *n. Botany.* a structure that produces gametes. ⟨< *gamete* + Gk. *angeion* case⟩

gam•ete ['gæmit] *or* [gə'mit] *n. Biology.* a mature reproductive cell capable of uniting with another to form a fertilized cell that can develop into a new plant or animal. Gametes are produced by a special type of cell division called meiosis; each gamete has only half the number of chromosomes of other body cells. ⟨< NL *gameta* < Gk. *gametē* wife, *gametēs* husband, ult. < *gamos* marriage⟩ —**ga'met•ic** [gə'mɛtɪk], *adj.*

game theory *Mathematics.* a theory that uses a method of mathematical analysis to arrive at the optimum choice of strategy in situations involving a conflict of interest.

ga•me•to•cyte [gə'mitə,səit] *n. Biology.* a cell which produces gametes.

ga•me•to•gen•e•sis [gə,mitou'dʒɛnəsɪs] *or* [,gæmətou'dʒɛnəsɪs] *n. Biology.* the development of gametes. —**ga,me•to'gen•ic** or **,gam•e'tog•e•nous,** *adj.*

ga•me•to•phyte [gə'mitə,fəit] *n.* the gamete-producing form or generation of a plant that reproduces by alternation of generations. In lower plants, such as mosses, the gametophyte is the dominant form. Compare SPOROPHYTE. ⟨< *gamete* + *-phyte*⟩ —**ga,me•to'phyt•ic** [-fɪtɪk], *adj.*

game warden *Cdn.* an official whose duty it is to enforce the game laws in a certain district.

gam•ey ['geimi] See GAMY.

gam•ic ['gæmɪk] *adj. Biology.* of reproduction, sexual.

gam•in ['gæmən] *n.* **1** a neglected boy left to roam about the streets; urchin. **2** any small, lively person. **3** (*adjl.*) like an urchin; impudent. ⟨< F⟩
☛ *Hom.* GAMMON.

gam•ine [gæ'min]; *French,* [ga'min] *n.* **1** a young girl, abandoned and living on the streets; a waif. **2** an impish or tomboyish girl. ⟨< F⟩

gam•ing ['geimɪŋ] *n., v.* —*n.* the playing of games of chance for money; gambling.
—*v.* ppr. of GAME¹.

gam•ma ['gæmə] *n.* **1** the third letter of the Greek alphabet (Γ, γ = English G, g). **2** the third in any series or group.

gamma decay radioactive decay giving off gamma rays; DECAY (def. *n.* 3).

gam•ma•di•on [gə'meidiən] *n.* an ornamental cross consisting of repetitions of the Greek letter gamma to form a swastika. ⟨< Med.Gk., dim. of *gamma*⟩

gamma globulin the constituent of blood plasma that contains the most antibodies and is often used for temporary immunization against infectious diseases such as measles and hepatitis.

gamma rays electromagnetic radiation similar to X rays but shorter in wavelength, of very high frequency and great penetrating power, given off by radioactive substances.

gam•mer ['gæmər] *n.* **1** *Archaic.* an old woman. **2** a gossip. ⟨alteration of *godmother*⟩
☛ *Usage.* See note at GAFFER.

gam•mon[1] ['gæmən] *n., v. —n. Brit. Informal.* nonsense; humbug.
—v. **1** talk nonsense, especially with intent to deceive. **2** deceive; hoax: *We were gammoned into sounding the fire alarm.* ⟨cf. ME *gamen* game[1]⟩ **—'gam•mon•er,** *n.*
☛ *Hom.* GAMIN.

gam•mon[2] ['gæmən] *n.* **1** the lower end of a side of bacon. **2** a smoked or cured ham. ⟨< ONF *gambon* < *gambe* leg < LL *gamba.* See GAMBREL.⟩
☛ *Hom.* GAMIN.

ga•mo•gen•e•sis [,gæmə'dʒɛnəsɪs] *n. Biology.* sexual reproduction. ⟨< Gk. *gamos* marriage + *genesis*⟩

gam•o•pet•al•ous [,gæmə'pɛtələs] *adj. Botany.* having the petals joined to form a tube-shaped corolla. ⟨< Gk. *gamos* marriage + E *petal* + *-ous*⟩

gam•o•phyl•lous [,gæmə'fɪləs] *adj. Botany.* having leaves joined by their edges. ⟨< Gk. *gamos* marriage + *phyllon* a leaf⟩

gam•o•sep•al•ous [,gæmə'sɛpələs] *adj. Botany.* having the sepals joined together. ⟨< Gk. *gamos* marriage + E *sepal* + *-ous*⟩

–gamous *combining form.* characterized by marriage or sexual union, as in *bigamous.* ⟨< Gk. *-gamos* < *gamos* marriage + *-ous*⟩

gam•ut ['gæmət] *n.* **1** *Music.* **a** the whole series of recognized notes. **b** the complete scale of any key, especially the major scale. **2** the entire range of anything: *In one minute I ran the gamut of feeling from hope to despair.* ⟨contraction of Med.L *gamma ut,* the notes of the medieval scale⟩

gam•y ['geimi] *adj.,* **gam•i•er, gam•i•est. 1** having a taste or smell characteristic of the meat of wild animals or birds when it is too strong, as when the meat is tainted or improperly cooked. **2** brave or plucky. **3** scandalous or racy. Also, **gamey. —'gam•i•ly,** *adv.* **—'gam•i•ness,** *n.*

–gamy *combining form.* marriage or sexual union, as in *bigamy.* ⟨< Gk. *-gamia* < *gamos* marriage⟩

gan or **'gan** [gæn] *v. Archaic or poetic.* began, pt. of GIN[4].

gan•cic•lo•vir [gæn'sɪklə,vir] *n.* an antiviral drug.

gan•der ['gændər] *n.* **1** an adult male goose. **2** a fool; simpleton.
take a gander, *Informal.* look: *Take a gander at that outfit.* ⟨OE *gandra*⟩

gan•dy dancer ['gændi] a member of a railway section gang, especially a seasonal or itinerant labourer. ⟨? < former *Gandy* Manufacturing Company of Chicago, Ill. that made tools used by railway labourers⟩

Ga•ne•sha [gə'neiʃə] *n.* in Hinduism, the god of wisdom.

gang [gæŋ] *n., v. —n.* **1** a group of people acting or going around together, especially for criminal or other purposes generally considered antisocial. **2** a group of people working together under one supervisor: *Two gangs of workers were repairing the road.* **3** a group of people closely associated for social purposes: *Let's have the gang over for coffee after the show.* **4** a set of tools, machines, or components arranged to work together. **5** (*adjl.*) consisting of such a set: *a gang saw.* **6** a group of elk.
—v. Informal. **a** form a gang. **b** attack in a gang.
gang up, come together into a group for some purpose: *We ganged up to give a party for our coach.*
gang up on, oppose as a group: *Let's gang up on that bully.* ⟨OE *gang* a going⟩
☛ *Hom.* GANGUE.

gang•er ['gæŋər] *n.* the supervisor of a group of labourers.

Gan•ges river dolphin ['gændʒiz] a dolphin (*Platanista gangetica*) native to the River Ganges in India and Bangladesh. It is an endangered species.

gang•land ['gæŋ,lænd] *n.* **1** the world of organized criminal gangs. **2** (*adjl.*) of or having to do with this world: *a gangland slaying.*

gan•gle ['gæŋgəl] *v.* **-gled, -gling.** move in an awkward manner.

gan•gli•a ['gæŋgliə] *n.* a pl. of GANGLION.

gan•gling ['gæŋglɪŋ] *adj.* awkwardly tall and slender; lank and loosely built. ⟨apparently ult. < *gang,* v.⟩

gan•gli•on ['gæŋgliən] *n., pl.* **-gli•a** or **-gli•ons. 1** a mass of nerve cells forming a nerve centre outside of the brain or spinal cord. **2** a cyst on the sheath of a tendon or on the outer membrane of a joint. **3** a centre or concentration of force or energy. ⟨< LL *ganglion* a type of swelling < Gk.⟩ **—,gang•li'on•ic,** *adj.*

gan•gli•o•side ['gæŋgliə,saɪd] *n.* any of various complex lipids located in the liver, kidneys, and spleen, and on nerve tissue membranes.

gan•gly ['gæŋgli] *adj.* gangling.

gang•plank ['gæŋ,plæŋk] *n.* a movable bridge used by persons or animals in getting on and off a ship, etc.

gang plough or **plow** a plough consisting of several shares for turning several furrows at a time.

gan•grene ['gæŋgrin] *or* [gæŋ'grin] *n., v.* **-grened, -gren•ing.** *—n.* the decay of tissue in a part of a living person or animal when the blood supply is interfered with by injury, infection, freezing, etc.
—v. affect or become affected with gangrene: *The wounded leg gangrened and had to be amputated.* ⟨< L *gangraena* < Gk. *gangraina*⟩

gan•gre•nous ['gæŋgrənəs] *adj.* of or having gangrene; decaying.

gang•ster ['gæŋstər] *n.* a member of an organized gang of criminals.

gang•ster•ism ['gæŋstə,rɪzəm] *n.* **1** the committing of crimes by members of an organized gang. **2** gangsters or their crimes: *The fight against gangsterism never stops.*

gangue [gæŋ] *n.* the earthy materials found with metallic ore in a vein or lode. ⟨< F < G *Gang* metallic vein passage⟩
☛ *Hom.* GANG.

gang•way ['gæŋ,wei] *n., interj. —n.* **1** passageway. **2** a passageway on a ship. **3** gangplank. **4** an aisle, especially one in the House of Commons that keeps the frontbenchers and backbenchers apart.
—interj. Informal. get out of the way! stand aside! make room!

gan•net ['gænɪt] *n.* any of several large, white, fish-eating sea birds (family Sulidae), especially *Morus bassanus,* having long, black-tipped wings, a pointed bill and tail, and webbed feet. Gannets nest in colonies on cliffs in eastern Canada. ⟨OE *ganot*⟩

gan•oid ['gænɔɪd] *adj., n. —adj.* **1** designating a type of fish scale that has a bright, enamel-like outer layer. **2** designating a fish or group of fishes having such scales: *The bowfin is a ganoid fish.*
—n. a ganoid fish. ⟨< Gk. *ganos* brightness⟩

gant•let ['gɒntlɪt] *n., v.* **-let•led, -let•ting.** *—n.* See GAUNTLET[2].
—v. join (railroad tracks) so as to form a section where two lines of track overlap.

gant•line ['gænt,laɪn] *n.* a rope through a block, used to hoist flags or people up to the top of a ship's mast.

gan•try ['gæntri] *n., pl.* **-tries. 1** a towerlike, movable framework with platforms at different levels, used for servicing a rocket on its launching pad. **2** a movable, bridgelike structure for carrying a travelling crane, consisting of side towers on parallel tracks that support a horizontal framework along which the crane moves. **3** a similar structure spanning several railway tracks, used to carry block signals. **4** a similar structure spanning a road, used to carry directions, especially one showing which lane to use. **5** a frame for supporting a barrel or cask on its side. ⟨< ONF *gantier* < L *canterius* beast of burden, rafter, framework < Gk. *kanthēlios* pack ass⟩

Gan•y•mede ['gænə,mid] *n.* **1** *Greek and Roman mythology.* a handsome youth, cupbearer to the gods of Olympus. **2** a satellite of Jupiter.

gap [gæp] *n., v.* **gapped, gap•ping.** *—n.* **1** a broken place; hole or opening, as in a fence, hedge, or wall. **2** an empty part; unfilled space; blank: *My diary is not complete; there are several gaps in it. Why is there this gap in your employment history?* **3** a wide difference of opinion, character, etc; disparity: *the generation gap.* **4** a narrow way or route through or between something, as a mountain pass or as a channel between islands or an island and the mainland. **5** the space crossed by an electric spark.
bridge, close, fill, or **stop a gap,** make up a deficiency.
—v. make a gap in. ⟨ME < ON. Related to GAPE.⟩

gape [geip] *v.* **gaped, gap•ing;** *n. —v.* **1** open wide; be wide open: *A deep crevasse gaped before us.* **2** open the mouth wide, as when hungry or yawning. **3** stare with the mouth open: *The children gaped when they saw the huge birthday cake.*
—n. **1** a wide opening. **2** the act of opening the mouth wide. **3** an open-mouthed stare. **4 the gapes, a** a fit of yawning. **b** a disease of birds and poultry characterized by gasping. ⟨ME < ON *gapa*⟩ **—'gap•er,** *n.*

gape•worm ['geip,wɜrm] *n.* a nematode worm that causes the GAPES (**b**).

gap•toothed ['gæp,tuθt] *or* ['gæp,tuðd] *adj.* having a gap between two teeth.

gar [gɑr] *n., pl.* **gar** or **gars. 1** any of a genus (*Lepisosteus*) making up a small family (Lepisosteidae) of mainly freshwater fishes of North and Central America having a long, slender, round body covered with an armour of very hard scales and a long, narrow, alligatorlike snout with many needlelike teeth. **2** needlefish. ⟨shortened form of *garfish*⟩

ga•rage [gə'rɑʒ], [gə'rædʒ], *or* [gə'ræʒ] *n., v.* **-raged, -rag•ing.** *—n.* **1** a shelter for automobiles, trucks, etc.: *Their new house has a two-car garage.* **2** a commercial establishment for repairing and servicing automobiles, trucks, etc.
—v. put or keep in a garage. ⟨< F *garage* < *garer* put in shelter⟩

garage sale an informal sale of personal possessions, furniture, etc., usually held in a private garage or driveway and patronized mostly by neighbours and passers-by. See also YARD SALE.

garb [gɑrb] *n., v. —n.* **1** the way one is dressed; a characteristic style of clothing: *a doctor's garb, a painter's garb.* **2** the outward covering, form, or appearance.
—v. clothe: *The doctor was garbed in white.* ⟨< F *garbe* < Ital. *garbo* grace⟩

gar•bage ['gɑrbɪdʒ] *n.* **1** waste matter; trash, rubbish to be thrown away or any worthless material: *We threw out several boxes of garbage when we cleaned out the attic.* **2** *Informal.* inferior, worthless, or offensive speech, writings, etc.: *That argument is a lot of garbage and shouldn't be taken seriously.* ⟨ME, animal entrails; origin uncertain⟩

garbage dump *Cdn.* a place where garbage and other refuse are disposed of.

garbage fish *Cdn.* fish of no commercial value, such as coarse fish or lampreys.

garbage in, garbage out *Computer technology.* an aphorism expressing the principle that if inaccurate or unreliable data is provided to a computer then the output produced will also be inaccurate or unreliable. *Abbrev.:* GIGO

gar•ban•zo [gɑr'bænzou] *or* [gɑr'bɑnzou] *n.* CHICK PEA. ⟨< Sp. < Gk. *erebinthos* < *orobos* chick pea⟩

gar•ble ['gɑrbəl] *v.* **-bled, -bling. 1** make unfair or misleading selections from (facts, statements, writings, etc.); omit parts of, often in order to misrepresent: *Foreign newspapers gave a garbled account of the ambassador's speech.* **2** confuse or mix up (statements, words, etc.) unintentionally. ⟨< Ital. *garbellare* < Arabic *gharbala* sift, probably < LL *cribellare*, ult. < *cribrum* sieve⟩ **—'gar•bler,** *n.*

gar•çon [gaʀ'sɔ̃] *n., pl.* **-çons** [-sɔ̃] *French.* **1** a young man or boy. **2** a male servant. **3** waiter.

gar•den ['gɑrdən] *n., v. —n.* **1** a piece of ground used for growing vegetables, herbs, flowers, or fruits. **2** (*adjl.*) **a** growing or grown in a garden: *garden flowers.* **b** in or for a garden: *garden tools, a garden walk.* **3** a park or other place where plants or animals may be viewed by the public: *The city has a fine botanical garden.* **4** a fertile and delightful region or place. **5** (*adjl.*) common or ordinary: *His jokes were all the garden variety.*
lead up (or **down**) **the garden path,** *Informal.* mislead or entice.
—v. make, take care of, or work in a garden: *He loves to garden.* ⟨ME < ONF *gardin* < Gmc.⟩ **—'gar•den,like,** *adj.*

garden apartment a street-level apartment, especially one with gardens or grounds around it.

garden balm BALSAM (def. 5).

garden cress an annual plant (*Lepidium sativum*) of the mustard family, native to Asia, but widely cultivated as a salad plant.

gar•den•er ['gɑrdənər] *n.* **1** a person whose occupation is taking care of a garden, lawn, etc. **2** a person who makes a garden, loves gardening, or works in a garden.

garden heliotrope 1 the common heliotrope (*Heliotropium arborescens*), a garden plant having wrinkled leaves and clusters of lilac or blue flowers with a fragrance like vanilla. **2** the common valerian (*Valeriana officinalis*), a garden plant having clusters of tiny, very fragrant, white or reddish flowers.

gar•de•nia [gɑr'dinjə] *or* [gɑr'diniə] *n.* **1** any of a large genus (*Gardenia*) of tropical and subtropical trees and shrubs of the madder family, having fragrant, roselike, white or yellow flowers with waxy petals. **2** a flower of any of these trees or shrubs, often worn as a corsage. ⟨< NL; after Alexander *Garden* (1730-1791), an American botanist⟩

A gardenia

garden sage SAGE (def. 2).

gar•den–var•i•e•ty ['gɑrdən və,raɪəti] *adj.* common; undistinguished; ordinary: *a garden-variety poet.*

gar•fish ['gɑr,fɪʃ] *n.* gar. ⟨< OE *gār* spear + *fisc* fish⟩

gar•ga•ney ['gɑrgəni] *n.* a European duck (*Anas querquedula*), the male having a striped white head. ⟨< Ital.⟩

gar•gan•tu•an [gɑr'gæntʃuən] *adj.* Sometimes, **Gargantuan,** enormous; gigantic: *a gargantuan meal, a gargantuan undertaking.* ⟨< *Gargantua*, a good-natured giant of enormous appetite in a satire by Rabelais⟩

gar•get ['gɑrgɪt] *n.* **1** in cattle and pigs, an inflamed condition of the head or throat. **2** in cows, ewes, etc., an inflammation of the udder. ⟨< OF *gargate*⟩

gar•gle ['gɑrgəl] *v.* **-gled, -gling;** *n. —v.* **1** wash or rinse (the inside of the throat) with liquid kept in motion in the throat by the air that is slowly expelled from the lungs. **2** utter with a sound like gargling.
—n. **1** a liquid used for gargling. **2** a sound like that produced by gargling. ⟨probably imitative and influenced by OF *gargouiller* < *gargoule* throat < L *gurgulio* windpipe⟩

Gargoyles on the Peace Tower of the Houses of Parliament, Ottawa

gar•goyle ['gɑrgɔɪl] *n.* **1** a spout for carrying off rainwater, projecting from the gutter of a building and usually having the form of a grotesque head or creature. Gargoyles are characteristic of Gothic architecture. **2** a projection or ornament on a building resembling a gargoyle. **3** a person having an extremely ugly face. ⟨ME < OF *gargole* water spout⟩

gar•i•bal•di [,gærə,bɒldi] *or* [,gɛrə,bɒldi] *n.* a woman's blouse with a high neck and flowing sleeves. ⟨after the red shirts worn by disciples of *Garibaldi*, 19c. Italian patriot⟩

gar•ish ['gærɪʃ] *or* ['gɛrɪʃ] *adj.* **1** unpleasantly bright; glaring. **2** showy; gaudy. ⟨ult. < obs. *gaure* stare⟩ **—'gar•ish•ly,** *adv.* **—'gar•ish•ness,** *n.*

gar•land ['gɑrlənd] *n., v. —n.* **1** a wreath of flowers, leaves, etc. worn on the head or hung as a decoration. Garlands are often used as symbols of peace, victory, etc. **2** something like a garland. **3** a collection of short poems, ballads, etc.; anthology. **4** a collar or loop of rope on a ship's mast, used to hoist spars, etc. or to prevent chafing or fraying.
—v. decorate with or form into a garland or garlands. ⟨ME < OF *garlande*⟩

gar•lic ['gɑrlɪk] *n.* **1** a perennial plant (*Allium sativum*) of the lily family, widely grown for its strong-smelling and strong-tasting bulb. The bulb of garlic is made up of small sections called cloves. **2** a bulb or clove of this plant, used to season meats, salads, etc. ⟨OE *gārlēac* < *gār* spear + *lēac* leek⟩

gar•lick•y ['gɑrlɪki] *adj.* smelling or tasting of garlic.

gar•ment ['gɑrmənt] *n., v. —n.* **1** any article of clothing. **2** an outer covering of anything.

—*v.* clothe. ⟨ME < OF *garnement* < *garnir* fit out. See GARNISH.⟩ **—'gar•ment•less,** *adj.*

gar•ner ['garnər] *v., n.* —*v.* **1** gather and store away: *Wheat is cut and garnered at harvest time. Squirrels garner nuts in the fall.* **2** earn; get as deserved: *to garner respect.*
—*n.* **1** a storehouse for grain; granary. **2** a store of anything. ⟨ME < OF *gernier, grenier* < L *granarium* < *granum* grain⟩

gar•net[1] ['garnɪt] *n., adj.* —*n.* **1** a brittle silicate mineral occurring mainly in red crystals. The transparent, deep-red variety of garnet is used as a semiprecious gemstone; other varieties are used as abrasives. **2** a gem cut from this mineral. **3** a synthetic form of this mineral, having a single crystal, used in laser technology and in electronics. **4** a deep red.
—*adj.* deep red. ⟨ME *gernet* < OF *grenat* grained (stone) < LL *granatum* < L *granum* grain, seed. See GRENADE.⟩ **—'gar•net,like,** *adj.*

gar•net[2] ['garnɪt] *n.* a special kind of block and tackle used to hoist cargo onto a ship. ⟨? > MDu. *garnaat*⟩

garnet paper a fine sandpaper made of garnets crushed in glue, used for polishing.

gar•ni•er•ite ['garniə,rəit] *n.* hydrous nickel magnesium silicate, a source of nickel. ⟨< J. *Garnier*, 19c. French geologist⟩

gar•nish ['garnɪʃ] *n., v.* —*n.* **1** something laid on or around food as a decoration: *a garnish of parsley.* **2** a decoration; trimming.
—*v.* **1** decorate (food). **2** decorate; trim. **3** *Law.* warn or notify by a garnishment.
garnish with, embellish with: *writing garnished with anecdotes.* ⟨ME < OF *garniss-*, a stem of *garnir* provide, defend < Gmc.⟩ **—'gar•nish•er,** *n.*

gar•nish•ee [,garnə'ʃi] *v.* **-nish•eed, -nish•ee•ing;** *n. Law.* —*v.* **1** take (money or property) from a person, by the authority of a court, to pay a debt. If a creditor garnishees a debtor's salary, a certain portion of the salary is withheld and paid to the creditor. **2** notify (a person) not to hand over money or property belonging to the defendant in a lawsuit until the plaintiff's claims have been settled: *The debtor's employer was garnisheed.*
—*n.* a person notified to hold the defendant's money or property as a trustee until the lawsuit is settled.

gar•nish•ment ['garnɪʃmənt] *n.* **1** decoration; trimming. **2** *Law.* **a** a legal notice warning a person to hold in his or her possession property that belongs to the defendant in a lawsuit until the plaintiff's claims have been settled. **b** a summons to a third person to appear in court while a lawsuit between others is being heard.

gar•ni•ture ['garnətʃər] *n.* decoration; trimming; garnish, especially of food. ⟨< F⟩

ga•rotte [gə'rɒt] *or* [gə'rout] *n., v.* **-rot•ted, -rot•ting.** See GARROTE. **—ga'rot•ter,** *n.*

gar•pike ['gar,pəik] *n.* gar, especially a species *(Lepisosteus osseus)* found in eastern North America from southern Ontario and Québec to the Gulf of Mexico, also called **longnose gar.** ⟨formed after *garfish*⟩

gar•ret ['gærɪt] *or* ['gɛrɪt] *n.* **1** a space in a house just below a sloping roof; attic. **2** a room or apartment in such a place. ⟨ME < OF *garite* watchtower < *garir* defend < Gmc.⟩

gar•ri•son ['gærəsən] *or* ['gɛrəsən] *n., v.* —*n.* **1** the soldiers stationed in a fort, town, etc., usually for the purpose of defending it. **2** a place where such troops are stationed. **3** (*adjl.*) of, associated with, or having a garrison: *Kingston is a garrison town.*
—*v.* **1** station troops in (a fort, town, etc.) to defend it. **2** take over or occupy (a fort, town, etc.) as a garrison. ⟨ME < OF *garison* < *garir.* See GARRET.⟩

gar•rote [gə'rɒt] *or* [gə'rout] *n., v.* **-rot•ed, -rot•ing.** —*n.* **1** a method of execution formerly used in Spain, in which the person was strangled with an iron collar. **2** the iron collar used for this type of execution. **3** a cord, wire, etc. used for strangling in a robbery, a surprise attack on an enemy, etc. **4** strangulation by this method.
—*v.* **1** execute by garroting. **2** attack or kill with a garrote. Also, **garotte, garrotte.** ⟨< Sp. *garrote* stick for twisting cord⟩ **—gar'rot•er,** *n.*

gar•rotte [gə'rɒt] *ot* [gə'rout] *n., v.* **-rot•ted, -rot•ting.** See GARROTE. **—gar'rot•ter,** *n.*

gar•ru•li•ty [gə'rulәti] *n.* the quality or state of being garrulous.

gar•ru•lous ['gærələs] *or* ['gærjələs], ['gɛrələs] *or* ['gɛrjələs] *adj.* **1** talking too much about trifles. **2** using too many words. ⟨< L *garrulus* < *garrire* chatter⟩ **—'gar•ru•lous•ly,** *adv.* **—'gar•ru•lous•ness,** *n.*

Garry oak *Cdn.* a British Columbian oak tree (*Quercus garryana*), of little commercial value, having hairy twigs, buds and acorns, and twisted branches.

gar•ter ['gartər] *n., v.* —*n.* **1** a band or strap, usually of elastic, used to hold up a stocking or sock. **2** an elastic band worn around the arm to keep the sleeve pushed up. **3 Garter, a** See ORDER OF THE GARTER. **b** the badge of this order. **c** membership in this order.
—*v.* support or fasten with or as if with a garter. ⟨ME < OF *gartier* < *garet* bend of the knee < Celtic⟩

garter belt a broad elastic belt, with garters attached to it, worn by women for keeping up stockings.

garter snake any of various small, harmless, brownish or greenish snakes (genus *Thamnophis*) of North America having yellow or red stripes along the body.

gas[1] [gæs] *n., pl.* **gas•es;** *v.* **gassed, gas•sing.** —*n.* **1** any fluid substance that can expand without limit; not a solid or liquid. Oxygen and nitrogen are gases. **2** any gas or mixture of gases except air. **3** any mixture of gases that can be burned, usually obtained from coal but occasionally from other substances. Gas was once much used for lighting, but is now used chiefly for cooking and heating. **4** any gas used as an anesthetic, such as nitrous oxide (laughing gas). **5** *Mining.* an explosive mixture of methane with air. **6** a substance that vaporizes and then poisons, suffocates, or stupefies: *The police used tear gas to dispel the mob.* **7** gas accumulated in or released from the stomach, usually as a result of indigestion or some other stomach disorder. **8** *Slang.* empty or boasting talk. **9** *Slang.* a person or thing that is very amusing, appealing, exciting, etc.: *The party was a gas.*
—*v.* **1** supply with gas. **2** treat with gas; use gas on. Some kinds of seeds are gassed to hasten sprouting. **3** give off gas. **4** attack with gas; use gas on: *The police were forced to gas the violent criminals who refused to leave the building.* **5** *Slang.* talk idly, emptily, or boastfully. **6** *Slang.* excite, amuse, or appeal to greatly. ⟨alteration of Gk. *chaos* chaos; coined by Jean B. van Helmont (1577-1644), a Flemish physicist⟩ **—'gas•less,** *adj.* **—'gas•like,** *adj.*

gas[2] [gæs] *n., v.* **gassed, gas•sing.** *Informal.* —*n.* **1** gasoline. **2** (*adjl.*) powered by gas: *a gas lawn mower.*
step on the gas, a push down the accelerator of a motor vehicle. **b** go or act faster; hurry: *We'd better step on the gas and get these dishes done.*
—*v.* fill the tank of a motor vehicle with gasoline (*usually used with* **up**): *We gassed up before we left the city.*

gas•bag ['gæs,bæg] *n.* **1** a container to hold gas. **2** an inflatable bag used to plug a gas pipe during repairs. **3** *Slang.* a person who talks too much; windbag.

gas black CARBON BLACK.

gas boat *Cdn.* a boat powered by a gasoline engine.

gas burner the small nozzle of a gas fixture from which gas comes out and is burned.

gas chamber a room for the execution of people by means of poisonous gas.

gas chromatography chromatography in which a vaporized substance is mixed with a known gas and passed in this form through an absorbing material.

gas coal BITUMINOUS COAL.

Gas•con ['gæskən] *n., adj.* —*n.* **1** a native of Gascony, a region in SW France. Gascons were formerly noted for their boastfulness. **2 gascon,** a boastful, swaggering person.
—*adj.* **1** of or having to do with Gascony or its people. **2 gascon,** boastful. ⟨< F⟩

gas•con•ade [,gæskə'neid] *n., v.* **-ad•ed, -ad•ing.** —*n.* extravagant boasting.
—*v.* boast extravagantly. ⟨< F *gasconnade* < *gascon* Gascon⟩

gas•e•li•er [,gæsə'lir] *n.* See GASOLIER.

gas engine See GASOLINE ENGINE.

gas•e•ous ['gæsiəs], ['geisiəs], *or* ['gæʃəs] *adj.* in the form of gas; of or like a gas. Steam is water in a gaseous condition.

gas–fired ['gæs ,faird] *adj.* using gas as a fuel.

gas fitter a person whose work is putting in and repairing pipes and fixtures for the use of gas in buildings.

gas fixture a fixture for holding a gaslight.

gas giant a planet that is a huge ball of gas and that appears to have no solid surface.

gas guzzler *Informal.* a vehicle such as a car or snowmobile that uses a lot of fuel.

gash [gæʃ] *n., v.* —*n.* a long, deep cut or wound.
—*v.* make a long, deep cut or wound in. ⟨earlier *garsh* < ONF *garser* scarify⟩

gas•i•fy ['gæsə,faɪ] *v.* **-fied, -fy•ing.** change into a gas. —,**gas•i•fi'ca•tion,** *n.* —'**gas•i,fi•er,** *n.*

gas jet **1** a small nozzle or burner at the end of a gas fixture where the gas comes out. **2** a flame of gas.

gas•ket ['gæskɪt] *n.* **1** a ring or strip of rubber, metal, plaited hemp, etc. packed around a piston, pipe joint, etc. to make it leakproof. **2** a cord used to secure a furled sail on a yard.
blow a gasket, *Slang.* get very angry; lose one's temper. ⟨probably altered < F *garcette* < OF *garcete* small cord, originally little girl, dim. of *garce* fem. of *gars* boy < Med.L **warkjone* < Frankish **wrakje* mercenary soldier⟩

gas•kin ['gæskɪn] *n.* part of the hind leg of any hoofed quadruped between the joint and the hock. ⟨contraction of *galligaskins*⟩

gas•light ['gæs,ləit] *n.* **1** light made by burning gas. **2** a gas burner or gas jet. **3** of or suggesting a period when gaslight was used: *a gaslight melodrama.*

gas log a gas burner in a fireplace, made to look like a log.

gas main a large underground pipe to carry gas.

gas•man ['gæs,mæn] *n., pl.* **-men. 1** a person whose work is to read consumers' gas meters and report the amount of gas used. **2** a person who manufactures or supplies gas. **3** GAS FITTER. **4** a person who inspects coal mines for firedamp.

gas mantle a lacelike tube of non-flammable material around a gas flame that glows and gives off light when heated.

gas mask a helmet or mask that covers the mouth and nose and is supplied with a filter containing chemicals to neutralize poisons. The wearer breathes only filtered air.

gas meter a device for recording the amount of gas used in a building such as a dwelling.

gas•o•hol ['gæsə,hɒl] *n.* a mixture of gasoline and alcohol used as a fuel for motor vehicles. A mixture of about nine parts gasoline to one part alcohol can be used in a conventional vehicle without engine modification.

gas•o•lene [,gæsə'lin] *or* ['gæsə,lin] *n.* See GASOLINE.

gas•o•li•er [,gæsə'liər] *n.* a chandelier with gaslights. ⟨< *gas*+*o*+(*chande*)*lier*⟩

gas•o•line [,gæsə'lin] *or* ['gæsə,lin] *n.* a colourless liquid consisting of a mixture of hydrocarbons, which evaporates and burns very easily and is made by distilling petroleum. Gasoline is used mainly as a fuel in internal-combustion engines. Also, **gasolene.** ⟨< *gas* + *-ol,* suffix meaning 'oil' (< L *oleum*) + *-ine²*⟩

gasoline engine an internal-combustion engine which uses gasoline as fuel.

gas•om•e•ter [gæs'ɒmətər] *n.* **1** a container for holding and measuring gas. **2** a gas tank. ⟨< F *gazomètre* < *gaz* gas + *mètre* measure < Gk. *metron*; influenced by *gas*⟩

gasp [gæsp] *n., v.* —*n.* **1** a sudden, short intake of breath through the mouth. A gasp often indicates suspense, shock, or fear. **2** one of a series of short breaths caused by having difficulty in breathing: *After her hard run, her breath came in gasps.*
at the last gasp, a about to die. **b** at the final moment.
—*v.* **1** catch the breath with difficulty. **2** breathe with gasps. **3** utter with gasps. **4** wish (*for*); long (*for*); yearn (*for*): *I was gasping for a cigarette.* ⟨ME < ON *geispa* yawn⟩

Gaspé Peninsula a large peninsula in the province of Québec.

gasp•er ['gæspər] *n. Slang.* cigarette.

gas•pe•reau [,gæspə'rou] *n., pl.* **gas•pe•reaux.** *Cdn.* the alewife, an Atlantic food fish. ⟨< Cdn.F⟩

Gas•pe•sian [gæ'speiʒən] *or* [gæ'spiʒən] *n., adj. Cdn.* —*n.* a native or inhabitant of the Gaspé Peninsula in E Québec. ⟨< Cdn.F *Gaspésien*⟩
—*adj.* of or having to do with the Gaspé or its inhabitants.

gas plant a flowering plant (*Euonymus atropurpureus*) that gives off a flammable vapour at night.

gas•ser ['gæsər] *n.* **1** a person who or thing that gasses. **2** a natural gas well. **3** *Slang.* **a** something of more than usual merit; a huge success. **b** something or someone funny. **c** someone talkative or boastful.

gas station a place for supplying motor vehicles with gasoline, motor oil, water, etc.

gas•sy ['gæsi] *adj.* **-si•er, -si•est. 1** full of gas; containing gas. **2** like gas: *a gassy smell.* **3** *Informal.* full of boastful talk.

gas•trec•to•my [gæ'strɛktəmi] *n.* partial or complete removal of the stomach.

gas•tric ['gæstrɪk] *adj.* of, in, or near the stomach. ⟨< Gk. *gastēr, gastros* stomach⟩

gastric juice the thin, nearly clear digestive fluid secreted by glands in the mucous membrane that lines the stomach. It contains pepsin and other enzymes and hydrochloric acid.

gastric ulcer an ulcer in the stomach lining.

gas•trin ['gæstrɪn] *n.* a hormone secreted by the mucous lining of the stomach that stimulates the secretion of gastric juice. ⟨< *gastr-* + *-in*⟩

gas•tri•tis [gæ'strəitɪs] *n. Medicine.* an inflammation of the stomach, especially of its mucous membrane. ⟨< Gk. *gastēr, gastros* stomach + E *-itis*⟩

gastro– *combining form.* **1** the stomach: *gastrotomy = surgical incision into the stomach.* **2** the stomach and ——: *gastrohepatic = of or having to do with the stomach and liver.* Also, **gastr-** before vowels. ⟨< Gk. *gastēr, gastros*⟩

gas•troc•ne•mi•us [,gæstrouk'nimiəs] *or* [,gæstrə'nimiəs] *n.* the largest muscle in the lower leg, used to extend the foot, lift the heel, and bend the knee. ⟨< NL < Gk. *gastroknemia* calf of the leg + L *-ius* nominal suffix⟩

gas•tro•en•ter•i•tis [,gæstrou,ɛntə'rəitɪs] *n. Medicine.* inflammation of the membranes of the stomach and intestines.

gas•tro–en•ter•ol•ogy [,gæstrou ,ɛntə'rɒlədʒi] *n.* the study and treatment of diseases of the stomach and intestines. —'**gas•tro-,en•ter'ol•o•gist,** *n.*

gas•tro–in•tes•tin•al [,gæstrou in'tɛstənəl] *adj.* having to do with the stomach and intestines.

gas•tro•lith ['gæstrə,lɪθ] *n.* a stony mass found in the stomach.

gas•tro•nome ['gæstrə,noum] *n.* a person who is expert in gastronomy; epicure. Also, **gastronomer, gastronomist.** ⟨< F *gastronome,* back formation < *gastronomie.* See GASTRONOMY.⟩

gas•tro•nom•ic [,gæstrə'nɒmɪk] *adj.* of or having to do with gastronomy. Also, **gastronomical.** —,**gas•tro'nom•i•cal•ly,** *adv.*

gas•tron•o•my [gæ'strɒnəmi] *n.* the art or science of good eating. ⟨< F < Gk. *gastronomia* < *gastēr, gastros* stomach + *nomos* law⟩

gas•tro•plas•ty ['gæstrə,plæsti] *n.* a surgical procedure to reduce the size of the stomach.

gas•tro•pod ['gæstrə,pɒd] *n.* **1** any of a large class (Gastropoda) of molluscs having one-piece shells or no shells, and most of which move by means of a single, broad, disklike foot attached to the undersurface of their bodies. Snails, limpets, and slugs are gastropods. **2** (*adjl.*) of, having to do with, or designating this class of molluscs. ⟨< NL *Gastropoda,* pl. < Gk. *gastēr, gastros* stomach + *-podos* footed < *pous, podos* foot⟩

gas•tro•scope ['gæstrə,skoup] *n.* a medical instrument for inspecting the inside of the stomach.

gas•trot•o•my [gæ'strɒtəmi] *n.* the surgical procedure of cutting into the stomach.

gas•tro•trich ['gæstrə,trɪk] *n.* a microscopic and multicellular animal of the phylum Gastrotricha, which lives in salt water or fresh water. ⟨< *gastro-* + NL *tricha* ciliate organism < Gk. *trichos* < *thrix* hair⟩

gas•tro•vas•cu•lar [,gæstrou'væskjələr] *adj.* **1** used for digestion. **2** used for circulation.

gas•tru•la ['gæstrələ] *n., pl.* **-lae** [-,li] *or* [-,laɪ]. *Biology.* the stage in the development of all many-celled animals when the embryo is usually saclike and composed of two layers of cells. ⟨< NL *gastrula,* dim. of Gk. *gastēr, gastros* stomach⟩

gas•tru•late ['gæstrə,leit] *v.* **-at•ed, -at•ing.** undergo gastrulation.

gas•tru•la•tion [,gæstrə'leiʃən] *n.* the formation of a gastrula.

gas turbine an internal-combustion engine using as power the gas from burning fuel.

gas•works ['gæs,wɜrks] *n.* an industrial plant that manufactures gas for heating, cooking, and illumination.

gat¹ [gæt] *v. Archaic.* a pt. of GET.

gat² [gæt] *n.* a narrow channel of water extending inland (used only in geographical names such as Kattegat).

gate [geit] *n.* **1** a movable part or frame for closing an opening in a wall or fence. It turns on hinges or slides open and shut. **2** an opening in a wall, usually fitted with a door, turnstile, or some other barrier; gateway. **3** the part of a building containing the gate or gates, with the adjoining towers, walls, etc. **4** a way to go in or out; a way to get to something. **5** a barrier intended to prevent entrance, stop traffic, etc.: *Level crossings are often equipped with gates to keep cars off the track when a train is passing.* **6** a door, valve, etc. to stop or control the flow of water in a pipe, dam, lock, etc. **7** the number of people who pay to see a contest, exhibition, performance, etc. **8** the total amount of money received from these people: *The two teams divided a gate of $3250.* **9** *Skiing.* **a** an obstacle in a slalom course, consisting of two upright poles anchored in the snow a certain distance apart. **b** the opening between these poles, through which a slalom racer must ski. **10** a pipe through which molten metal is poured into a mould. **11** spillage of molten metal from such a pipe, outside the mould. **12** a mountain pass.
get the gate, *Slang.* be dismissed.
give the gate to, *Informal.* **a** dismiss or turn away. **b** *Hockey.* award a player a penalty, thus putting him or her off the ice.
⟨OE *gatu,* pl. of *geat*⟩ —**'gate•less,** *adj.* —**'gate,like,** *adj.*
☛ *Hom.* GAIT.

ga•teau [gæ'tou]; *French* [ga'to] *n.* a rich layer cake.

gate–crash ['geit ˌkræʃ] *v. Informal.* attend a party, social function, or entertainment without being invited or without a ticket.

gate–crash•er ['geit ˌkræʃər] *n. Informal.* a person who attends parties, gatherings, etc. without an invitation; an uninvited guest.

gate•fold ['geit,fould] *n.* an outsize sheet in a book that is folded over to bring it into line with the pages.

gate•house ['geit,hʌus] *n.* **1** a house at or over a gate, used as the gatekeeper's quarters. See CASTLE for picture. **2** a structure at the gate of a reservoir, dam, etc., with machinery for regulating the flow of water.

gate•keep•er ['geit,kipər] *n.* a person employed to guard a gate and control passage through it.

gate•leg ['geit,lɛg] *n.* a folding leg that supports a drop leaf of a table.

gateleg table a table having drop leaves supported by gatelegs. Also, **gatelegged table.**

gate•post ['geit,poust] *n.* one of the posts on either side of a gate. A swinging gate is fastened to one gatepost and closes against the other.

gate•way ['geit,wei] *n.* **1** an opening in a wall, fence, etc., fitted with a gate or some other barrier. **2** a way to go in or out; way to get to or attain something: *a gateway to success. Winnipeg was known as the Gateway to the West.* **3** the frame of a gate or a structure built over it.

Gath•as ['gɑtəz] *n.pl. Zoroastrianism.* that portion of the Avesta containing the hymns written by Zoroaster.

gath•er ['gæðər] *v., n.* —*v.* **1** bring into one place or group: *He gathered his books and papers and started off to school.* **2** come together; assemble: *A crowd gathered at the scene of the accident.* **3** get together gradually or from various places or sources: *to gather sticks for a fire.* **4** form a mass; collect: *Tears gathered in her eyes.* **5** pick and collect; take: *Farmers gather their crops.* **6** get or gain little by little: *The train gathered speed as it left the station.* **7** collect (oneself, one's strength, energies, thoughts, etc.) for an effort. **8** put together in the mind; conclude; infer: *I gathered from his words that he was really much upset.* **9** pull together in folds; wrinkle: *She gathered her brow in a frown.* **10** pull together in little folds and stitch: *The skirt is gathered at the waist.* **11** draw together or closer: *Gather your robe around you.* **12** come to a head and form pus: *A boil is a painful swelling that gathers under the skin.* **13** *Bookbinding.* collect and place in order (the printed, folded sheets of a book).
gathered to (one's) **fathers,** dead and buried.
gather (oneself) **together,** prepare oneself mentally.
gather up, a pick up and put together. **b** pull together; bring into a smaller space.
gather up the threads, begin again after an interruption.
—*n.* **1** one of the little folds between the stitches when cloth is pulled together in folds. **2** a contraction; drawing together. **3** *Glassmaking.* a blob of glass collected on the end of a blowpipe. ⟨OE *gaderian* < *geador* (to)gether⟩ —**'gath•er•er,** *n.*
☛ *Syn. v.* **Gather,** COLLECT, ASSEMBLE = bring or come together. **Gather,** the general word, is interchangeable with **collect,** though the former is the more colloquial and idiomatic. **Collect** is of Latin origin and sometimes has a more professional air: *collect stamps, collect taxes*; but *gather wealth, gather honey.* **Assemble,** more formal, has the special sense of 'bringing or coming together according to a definite plan or purpose': *assemble a watch. Parliament assembles.*

gath•er•ing ['gæðərɪŋ] *n.* **1** the act of one that gathers. **2** that which is gathered. **3** a meeting; assembly; party; crowd. **4** a swelling that comes to a head and forms pus.
☛ *Syn.* **3.** See note at MEETING.

Gat•ling gun ['gætlɪŋ] an early type of machine gun consisting of a revolving cluster of barrels around a central axis. ⟨after Richard J. *Gatling* (1818-1903), an American inventor⟩

GATT GENERAL AGREEMENT ON TARIFFS AND TRADE.

gauche [gouʃ] *adj.* awkward or clumsy in social situations; tactless. ⟨< F *gauche* left-handed⟩ —**'gauche•ly,** *adv.* —**'gauche•ness,** *n.*

gau•che•rie ['gouʃəri] *or* [ˌgouʃə'ri]; *French* [go'ʃʀi] *n.* **1** awkwardness in social situations; tactlessness. **2** an awkward or tactless movement, act, etc. ⟨< F⟩

gau•cho ['gʌutʃou] *n., pl.* **-chos.** a cowboy or herdsman of the southern plains of South America. ⟨< Sp.⟩

gaud [gɒd] *n.* a cheap, showy ornament; trinket: *beads, mirrors, and such gauds.* ⟨apparently < AF *gaude* < *gaudir* rejoice < L *gaudere*⟩
☛ *Hom.* GOD.

gaud•ery ['gɒdəri] *n.* ostentatious but useless things.

gaud•y[1] [gɒdi] *adj.* **gaud•i•er, gaud•i•est.** bright or ornate in a cheap and tasteless way: *gaudy jewellery.* ⟨< *gaud* + *-y*⟩ —**'gaud•i•ly,** *adv.* —**gaud•i•ness,** *n.*

gaud•y[2] ['gɒdi] *n.* an annual dinner given mainly for former students at certain British universities. ⟨< L *gaudium* joy < *gaudere* rejoice⟩

gauge [geidʒ] *n., v.* **gauged, gaug•ing.** —*n.* **1** a standard measure or scale of measurement to which something must conform. There are gauges of the capacity of a barrel, the thickness of sheet iron, the diameter of wire, etc. **2** an instrument for measuring. A steam gauge measures the pressure of steam. **3** a means of estimating or judging. **4** size, capacity, or extent. **5** the diameter of the bore of a firearm, especially a shotgun. **6** the distance between rails of a railway track or between the right and left wheels of a wagon, automobile, etc. Standard gauge between rails is 143.5 cm. Compare BROAD-GAUGE and NARROW-GAUGE. **7** the position of one sailing ship with reference to another and to the wind. A ship having the weather gauge of another is to the windward of it. **8** the length of the exposed part of shingles, tiles, etc. when laid in rows. **9** a measure of the fineness of knitted fabric, expressed as the number of loops made per unit of width; the higher the number, the finer the texture.
—*v.* **1** measure accurately with a measuring device: *She had a special instrument to gauge the width of the metal strip.* **2** estimate; judge: *It is difficult to gauge the character of a stranger.* Also, **gage.** ⟨ME < ONF⟩ —**'gauge•a•ble,** *adj.*
☛ *Hom.* GAGE.

gaug•er ['geidʒər] *n.* **1** a person who or thing that gauges. **2** an official who measures the contents of barrels of taxable liquor. **3** a collector of excise taxes. Also, **gager.**

Gaul [gɒl] *n.* **1** part of the Roman Empire that included modern N Italy, France, Belgium, and Switzerland. **2** one of the Celtic inhabitants of Gaul. **3** a French citizen. ⟨< F *Gaule* < L *Gallia* < *Gallus* a Gaul; (def. 2) < L *Gallus*⟩

Gau•lei•ter ['gaʊ,ləitər]; *German,* ['gaʊ,laɪtəʀ] *n.* **1** a high official in the Nazi party who acted as governor of a district in Germany or German-occupied territory. **2 gauleiter,** any subordinate who carries out harsh or criminal orders. ⟨< G < *Gau* district + *Leiter* leader⟩

Gaul•ish ['gɒlɪʃ] *n., adj.* —*n.* the extinct Celtic language of ancient Gaul.
—*adj.* having to do with ancient Gaul.

gaul•the•ria [gɒl'θiriə] *n.* any evergreen aromatic shrub of the genus *Gaultheria,* such as the wintergreen. ⟨< J-F. *Gaulthier,* 18c. Canadian physician and botanist⟩

gaunt [gɒnt] *adj.* **1** very thin and bony; with hollow eyes and a starved look: *A gaunt stranger came to my door.* **2** looking bare and gloomy; desolate, forbidding or grim: *a gaunt landscape.* ⟨origin uncertain⟩ —**'gaunt•ly,** *adv.* —**'gaunt•ness,** *n.*
☛ *Syn.* **1.** See note at THIN.

gaunt•let[1] ['gɒntlɪt] *n.* **1** a stout, heavy glove, usually of leather covered with plates of iron or steel, that was part of a knight's armour. See ARMOUR for picture. **2** a stout, heavy glove

with a wide, flaring cuff, used for protection in industry, etc. **3** the wide, flaring cuff of such a glove.
take up the gauntlet, a accept a challenge. **b** take up the defence of a person, opinion, etc.
throw down the gauntlet, issue a challenge. ⟨ME < OF *gantelet*, dim. of *gant* glove < Gmc.⟩

gaunt•let² ['gɒntlɪt] *n.* formerly, a military punishment in which the offender had to run between two rows of men who struck him with clubs or other weapons as he passed.
run the gauntlet, a pass between two rows of men, each of whom strikes the runner as he passes. **b** carry out an action in spite of danger threatening on all sides: *During the war, convoys ran the gauntlet of enemy submarines.* **c** be exposed to unfriendly attacks, criticism, etc.
Also, **gantlet.** ⟨< Swedish *gatlopp* < *gata* lane + *lopp* course⟩

gaunt•let•ed ['gɒntlɪtɪd] *adj.* wearing a heavy glove.

gaur [gaʊr] *n.* a large wild ox *(Bibos frontalis gaurus)* of SE Asia and the Malay archipelago. ⟨< Hind. < Skt. *gaura*, akin to *gáuh* cow⟩

gauss [gʌus] *n.* a unit of magnetic induction. ⟨after K.F. *Gauss* (1777-1855), German mathematician and astronomer⟩

Gaus•sian curve ['gʌusiən] *Statistics.* a normal curve.

Gau•ta•ma ['gɒtəmə] *or* ['gʌutəmə] *n.* Buddha. Also, **Gotama.**

gauze [gɒz] *n.* **1** a very thin, light cloth of cotton, silk, etc., easily seen through. Cotton gauze is often used for bandages. **2** any material with an open weave. **3** a thin haze. ⟨< F *gaze*; after *Gaza*, the capital of the Gaza Strip, SW of Israel⟩
—'gauze,like, *adj.*

gauz•y ['gɒzi] *adj.* **gauz•i•er, gauz•iest.** like gauze; thin and light as gauze. **—'gauz•i•ly,** *adv.* **—'gauz•i•ness,** *n.*

gav•age ['gævɪdʒ] *or* [gə'vɑʒ]; *French,* [ga'vaʒ] *n.* forced feeding of animals or people by means of a tube. ⟨< F *gaver* to stuff⟩

gave [geiv] *v.* pt. of GIVE.

gav•el ['gævəl] *n.* a small mallet used by a presiding officer to signal for attention and order or by an auctioneer to announce that the bidding is over. ⟨origin uncertain⟩

gav•el•kind ['gævəl,kaɪnd] *n.* formerly, **a** a system whereby the heirs of a holder of land received equal shares of it. **b** land tenure on payment of rent rather than rendering service. **c** a piece of land held under either system. ⟨< OE *gafol* tribute + *kynd* kind⟩

ga•vi•al ['geiviəl] *n.* **1** a crocodilian reptile (*Gavialis gangeticus*) of India, the only species in the family Gavialidae, resembling crocodiles and alligators but having a very long, slender snout. **2** a reptile of the order Crocodilia, which includes alligators and crocodiles. ⟨< F < Hind, *ghariyāl*⟩

ga•votte [gə'vɒt] *n.* **1** a dance like a minuet but much more lively. **2** the music for this dance. ⟨< F < Provençal *gavoto* < *Gavots*, Alpine people⟩

gawk [gɒk] *n., v.* *—n.* an awkward person; clumsy fool.
—v. Informal. stare rudely or stupidly. ⟨origin uncertain⟩
—'gawk•er, *n.*

gawk•y ['gɒki] *adj.* **gawk•i•er, gawk•i•est.** awkward; clumsy.
—'gawk•i•ly, *adv.* **—gawk•i•ness,** *n.*

gawp [gɒp] *v. Slang.* gape; stare (*at*). ⟨dial. altered < ME *galpen* to yawn, gape⟩

gay [gei] *adj.* **gay•er, gay•est;** *n.* *—adj.* **1** happy and full of fun: *gay laughter.* **2** bright-coloured; showy: *gay decorations.* **3** fond of pleasures: *They had led a gay and wild life.* **4** dissolute or licentious: *a gay old bachelor.* **5** *Informal.* homosexual. **6** *Informal.* of or for homosexuals: *gay literature.*
—n. Informal. homosexual. ⟨< F *gai*⟩ **—'gay•ness,** *n.*
☛ *Syn. adj.* **1. Gay,** MERRY = lively and light-hearted. **Gay** emphasizes being free from care and full of life, joy, and high spirits; **merry** emphasizes being full of laughter and lively pleasure and fun: *The gay young people were merry as they danced.*
☛ *Usage.* Many people now avoid the uses in defs. 1–4 of **gay** because of the widespread use of the word (def. 5) to mean 'homosexual'.

gay•e•ty ['geiəti] *n., pl.* **-ties.** See GAIETY.

Gay–Lus•sac's law [,gei lu'sæks] *Physics.* the statement that the volume of a contained gas varies inversely with the temperature of the gas. ⟨after J.L. *Gay-Lussac* (1778-1850), French chemist and physicist⟩

gay•ly ['geili] See GAILY.

gay•wings ['gei,wɪŋz] *n.* a herb or shrub of the genus *Polygala;* milkwort, having showy rose-purple flowers.

gaz. gazette; gazetteer.

gaze [geiz] *v.* **gazed, gaz•ing;** *n.* *—v.* look long and steadily.
—n. a long, steady look. ⟨cf. Norwegian and Swedish dial. *gasa*⟩
—'gaz•er, *n.* **—'gaz•ing•ly,** *adv.*
☛ *Syn. v.* **Gaze,** STARE = look long and steadily at someone or something. **Gaze** emphasizes looking steadily and intently, chiefly in wonder, delight, or interest: *For hours he sat gazing at the stars.* **Stare** emphasizes looking with wide-open eyes steadily and directly at someone or something or off into space, chiefly in curiosity, rudeness, surprise, or stupidity: *The little girl stared at the stranger briefly before answering his question.*

ga•ze•bo [gə'zibou] *n., pl.* **-bos** or **-boes.** a summerhouse, balcony, etc. that commands a wide view. ⟨supposedly < *gaze*, on the pattern of Latin future tenses in *-bo*⟩

ga•zelle [gə'zɛl] *n.* any of a genus (*Gazella*) of small to medium-sized antelope of Africa and Asia, having a slender, graceful body, long, thin legs, and lustrous eyes. ⟨< F < Arabic *ghazāl*⟩ **—ga'zelle,like,** *adj.*

ga•zette [gə'zɛt] *n., v.* **-zet•ted, -zet•ting.** *—n.* **1** newspaper. **2** an official government journal containing lists of appointments, promotions, etc.
—v. publish, list, or announce in a gazette. ⟨< F < Ital. *gazzetta*, originally, coin; from the price of a paper⟩

gaz•et•teer [,gæzə'tir] *n.* **1** a dictionary or index of geographical names. **2** a writer for a gazette. **3** an official appointed to publish a gazette. ⟨< F *gazettier*⟩

gaz•pa•cho [gə'spɑtʃou]; *Spanish,* [gaθ'patʃo] *n.* a vegetable soup served cold, made with tomatoes, cucumbers, onions, peppers, olive oil, etc. ⟨< Sp.⟩

GB *Computer technology.* gigabyte.

GB or **G.B.** GREAT BRITAIN.

G.C. GEORGE CROSS.

g–cal GRAM CALORIE.

GCD, G.C.D., or **g.c.d.** greatest common divisor.

GCF, G.C.F., or **g.c.f.** greatest common factor.

G clef *Music.* the treble clef.

GCM, G.C.M., or **g.c.m.** greatest common measure.

Gd gadolinium.

Ge germanium.

ge•an•ti•clin•al [dʒi,æntɪ'klaɪnəl] *n., adj. Geology.* *—n.* geanticline.
—adj. of or having to do with a geanticline: *a geanticlinal fold.*

ge•an•ti•cline [dʒi'æntɪ,klaɪn] *n. Geology.* an anticlinal fold over a large area of the earth.

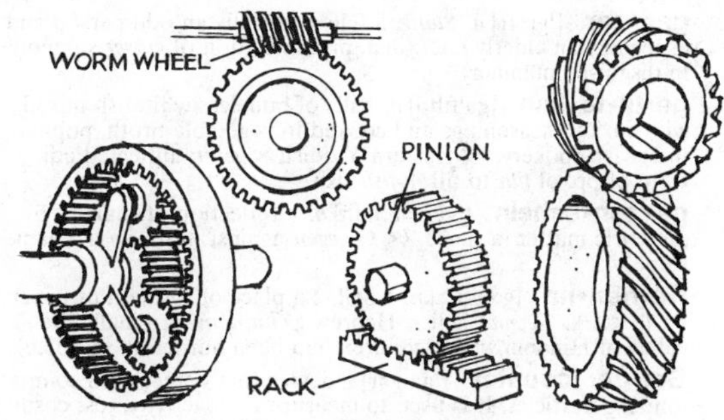

Four types of gear assembly: from left to right, a planetary gear train, worm gear, rack and pinion, and helical gears.

gear [gir] *n., v.* *—n.* **1** a wheel having teeth that fit between the teeth of another wheel or moving part of the same kind. If the wheels are of different sizes, they will turn at different speeds. **2** an arrangement of fixed and moving parts for transmitting or changing motion; mechanism; machinery: *The car ran off the road when the steering gear broke.* **3** working order; adjustment: *Her watch got out of gear and would not run.* **4** the equipment needed for some purpose. Harness, clothes, household goods, tools, tackle, and rigging are various kinds of gear.
in gear, a connected to the motor, etc. **b** in working order.
in or **into high gear,** in or into a state of speed or efficiency: *Three weeks before the election the campaign moved into high gear.*
out of gear, a disconnected from the motor, etc. **b** out of working order.

shift gears, a change from one gear to another; connect a motor, etc. to a different set of gears. **b** change topic, mood, point of view, etc.
–v. **1** connect by gears. An automobile moves when the motor is geared to the driving wheels. **2** fit or work together; mesh: *The cogs gear smoothly.* **3** provide with gear; equip; harness. **4** put into gear. **5** make subordinate (*to*) in order to serve: *The steel industry was geared to the needs of war.*
gear up (or **down**), **a** shift to a higher (or lower) gear in a vehicle. **b** increase (or decrease) speed or activity. ⟨ME < ON *gervi*⟩ **–'gear•less,** *adj.*

gear•box ['gir,bɒks] *n. Esp. Brit.* the transmission in an automobile or other vehicle.

gear•ing ['giriŋ] *n., v. –n.* **1** a set of gears, chains, etc. for transmitting motion or power; gears. **2** the act of fitting a machine with gears. **3** the way in which a machine is fitted with gears.
–v. ppr. of GEAR.

gear•shift ['gir,ʃift] *n.* a device for connecting a motor, etc. to any of several sets of gears.

gear•wheel ['gir,wil] *n.* a wheel having teeth that fit between the teeth of another wheel or moving part of the same kind.

geck•o ['gɛkou] *n., pl.* **geck•os** or **geck•oes.** any of several small, soft-skinned, insect-eating lizards (family Gekkonidae) found in the tropics, having suction pads on its toes for climbing. ⟨< Malay *gekok*; imitative of its cry⟩

gee¹ [dʒi] *interj., n., v.* **geed, gee•ing.** *–interj. or n.* a command to horses, oxen, etc. directing them to turn to the right. *Haw* is used for 'left'.
gee up, a command to turn right or to go ahead.
–v. turn to the right. ⟨origin uncertain⟩

gee² [dʒi] *interj.* an exclamation or mild oath. ⟨a shortened form of *Jesus*⟩

geek [gik] *n. Slang.* **1** a circus performer whose act consists of eating or biting the heads off live animals, such as chickens or snakes. **2** an odd or weird person. ⟨< dial. *geck* fool < Du. *gek* madman, fool < MLG *geck* originally echoic of unintelligible cries⟩

geese [gis] *n.* pl. of GOOSE.

geese•wark ['gis,wɑrk] *n. Cdn.* formerly, a calendar used by First Nations people. ⟨< Algonquian⟩

Geez [gi'ɛz] *n.* Ethiopic, an extinct language now used only in liturgy.

gee•zer ['gizər] *n. Slang.* a fellow, usually an odd person and especially an elderly one. ⟨dial. pronunciation of *guiser* someone in disguise, mummer⟩

ge•fil•te fish [gə'fɪltə] *n.* balls of boneless whitefish mixed with various seasonings and cooked in vegetable broth, popular in Jewish cookery. ⟨< Eastern Yiddish < *gefilte* inflected adj. form of pp. of *filn* to fill + *fish* fish⟩

ge•gen•schein ['geigən,ʃaɪn] *n.* a reflection of sunlight by meteoric matter in space. ⟨< G *gegen* against + *schein* a gleam, shine⟩

Ge•hen•na [gə'hɛnə] *n.* **1** hell. **2** a place of torment or misery. ⟨< L < Gk. *Geenna* hell < Hebrew *gê'hinnōm*, originally the valley of Hinnom where children had been burned in sacrifice⟩

Gei•ger counter ['gaɪgər] a device that detects and counts ionizing particles. It is used to measure radioactivity, test cosmic ray particles, etc. ⟨after Hans *Geiger* (1882-1945), a German physicist⟩

Geiger–Mül•ler counter ['mjulər] *or* ['mʌlər]; *German,* ['mylər] an improved, more sensitive form of the Geiger counter.

gei•sha ['geiʃə] *or* ['giʃə] *n., pl.* **-sha** or **-shas.** a Japanese girl specially trained in singing, dancing, the art of conversation, etc., in order to act as a hostess or companion for men. ⟨< Japanese⟩

Geiss•ler tube ['gəislər] a glass tube used to examine incandescent gases with a spectroscope. ⟨after H. *Geissler* (1814-1879), German inventor⟩

gel [dʒɛl] *n., v.* **gelled, gel•ling.** *–n.* a jellylike or solid material formed from a colloidal solution. When glue sets, it forms a gel.
–v. form a gel. Egg white gels when it is cooked. ⟨shortened form of *gelatin*⟩
☛ *Hom.* JELL.

gel•a•da ['dʒɛlədə], [dʒə'lɑdə], *or* [dʒə'lædə] *n.* a baboon of Ethiopia (*Theropithecus gelada*) with a mane covering its shoulders, and a red patch on the chest. ⟨< Arabic *qiladah* a mane⟩

Ge•län•de•sprung [gə'lɛndə,ʃprʊŋ] *n. Skiing.* a jump over an obstacle, using ski poles. ⟨< G *Gelände* terrain + *sprung* jump⟩

gel•a•tin ['dʒɛlətən] *n.* **1** an odourless, tasteless substance obtained by boiling animal tissues, bones, hoofs, etc. Gelatin dissolves easily in hot water and becomes jellylike when cool; it is used in making jellied desserts, camera film, glue, etc. **2** any of various vegetable substances having similar properties. **3** a preparation or product in which gelatin is the basic constituent. **4** a transparent material, usually in the form of a framed sheet (**gelatin slide**), in any of several colours, put over stage lights to produce a certain effect. ⟨< F < Ital. *gelatina* < *gelata* jelly < L *gelare* freeze⟩

gel•a•tine ['dʒɛlətən] *or* ['dʒɛlə,tin] *n. Esp. Brit.* gelatin.

ge•lat•i•nize [dʒə'lætə,naɪz] *or* ['dʒɛlətə,naɪz] *v.* **-ized, -iz•ing, 1** coat with gelatine. **2** become gelatinous.

ge•lat•i•noid [dʒə'lætə,nɔɪd] *adj., n. –adj.* like gelatin.
–n. a gelatinous substance.

ge•lat•i•nous [dʒə'lætənəs] *adj.* **1** jellylike; of the consistency of jelly. **2** of or containing gelatin.

ge•la•tion¹ [dʒi'leiʃən] *or* [dʒə'leiʃən] *n.* solidification by freezing. ⟨< L *gelatio* < *gelare* freeze⟩

gel•a•tion² [dʒɛ'leiʃən] *or* [dʒə'leiʃən] *n. Chemistry.* the process of gelling.

geld [gɛld] *v.* **geld•ed** or **gelt, geld•ing.** remove the testicles of (an animal), especially a horse; castrate. ⟨ME < ON *gelda* castrate < *geldr* barren⟩

geld•ing ['gɛldiŋ] *n., v. –n.* a gelded horse or other animal.
–v. ppr. of GELD.

gel•id ['dʒɛlɪd] *adj.* cold as ice; frosty. ⟨< L *gelidus* < *gelum* cold⟩ **–ge'lid•i•ty,** *n.*

gel•ig•nite ['dʒɛlɪg,nəit] *or* [dʒə'lɪgnəit] *n.* a type of dynamite in which the absorbent base for the nitroglycerin consists mainly of wood pulp and a nitrate such as potassium nitrate. ⟨< *gel(atin)* + L *lign(um)* wood + *-ite*⟩

gel•se•mi•um [dʒɛl'simiəm] *n.* any of various vinelike bushes (genus *Gelsemium*) having sweet-smelling yellow blossoms. ⟨< NL < Ital. *gelsomino* jessamine < Arabic *yasamin* jasmine⟩

gelt¹ [gɛlt] *v.* a pt. and a pp. of GELD.

gelt² [gɛlt] *n. Slang.* money. ⟨< Yiddish *geld* < MHG < G or Du *geld*⟩

gem [dʒɛm] *n., v.* **gemmed, gem•ming.** *–n.* **1** a precious stone; jewel. Diamonds and rubies are gems. **2** a person or thing that is very precious, beautiful, etc.: *The gem of his collection was a rare Iranian stamp.* **3** a kind of muffin made of coarse flour.
–v. set or adorn with gems, or set as if with gems: *Stars gem the sky.* ⟨< F < L *gemma* gem, bud⟩ **–'gem,like,** *adj.*

Ge•ma•ra [gə'mɑrə] *or* [gə'mɔrə] *n.* the second main part of the Talmud, consisting of a commentary on the first part, called the Mishnah. ⟨< Aramaic *gemara* completion⟩

ge•mein•schaft [gə'maɪnʃaft] *n. Sociology.* social organization characterized chiefly by a shared feeling of belonging or a sense of community. Compare GESELLSCHAFT. ⟨< G, literally, community⟩

gem•i•nate *v.* ['dʒɛmə,neit]; *adj.* ['dʒɛmənɪt] *or* ['dʒɛmə,neit] *v.* **-nat•ed, -nat•ing;** *adj. –v.* make or become double; combine in pairs.
–adj. combined in a pair or pairs; coupled. ⟨< L *geminare* < *geminus* twin⟩ **–,gem•i'na•tion,** *n.*

Gem•i•ni ['dʒɛmə,naɪ] *or* ['dʒɛmə,ni] *n.pl.* (*used with a singular verb*) **1** *Astronomy.* a northern constellation containing the two bright stars, Castor and Pollux. **2** *Astrology.* **a** the third sign of the zodiac. The sun enters Gemini about May 21. See ZODIAC for picture. **b** a person born under this sign. **3** any of a series of two-person spacecraft launched by the U.S. on various missions. ⟨< L *gemini* twins⟩

gem•ma ['dʒɛmə] *n., pl.* **gem•mae** ['dʒɛmi] *or* ['dʒɛmaɪ] **1** *Botany.* a bud. **2** *Biology.* a budlike growth that can develop into a new plant or animal. ⟨< L *gemma* bud⟩ **–gem'ma•tion,** *n.* **–gem'ma•ceous,** *adj.*

gem•mate ['dʒɛmeit] *adj., v.* **-mat•ed, -mat•ing.** *–adj.* having buds.
–v. put out buds.

gem•mi•par•ous [dʒɛ'mɪpərəs] *adj.* reproducing by means of buds.

gem•mol•o•gist or **gem•ol•o•gist** [dʒɛ'mɒlədʒɪst] *n.* an expert in gemmology.

gem•mol•o•gy or **gem•ol•o•gy** [dʒɛ'mɒlədʒi] *n.* the study of gems, their origins, uses, etc.

gem•mule ['dʒɛmjul] *n.* **1** a small gemma. **2** *Biology.* one of Darwin's hypothetical hereditary units. ⟨< L *gemmula,* dim. of *gemma* bud⟩

gem•my ['dʒɛmi] *adj.* **1** set with gems. **2** sparkling like a gem.

gems•bok ['gɛmz,bɒk] *n.* a large oryx (*Oryx gazella*) of S Africa. ⟨< Afrikaans < G *Gemsbock* < *Gemse* chamois + *Bock* buck⟩

gem•stone ['dʒɛm,stoun] *n.* a precious or semiprecious stone, capable of being cut and polished to make a gem.

gen [dʒɛn] *n., v.* **genned, gen•ning.** *Slang. —n.* authentic, detailed information.
—v. give authentic, detailed information to. ⟨originally Royal Air Force slang, perhaps < *gen(uine information)*⟩

-gen *suffix.* producing or produced: *antigen, nitrogen.* ⟨< F < Gk. *-genēs,* ult. < *gignesthai* be born⟩

gen. 1 gender. **2** general. **3** genitive. **4** genus. **5** generator.

Gen. or **Gen** general.

gen•darme [ʒɒn'dɑrm]; *French,* [ʒɑ̃'daʀm] *n., pl.* **-darmes** [-dɑrmz]; *French,* [-daʀm]. **1** especially in France, one of a body of soldiers employed as armed police officers. **2** any police officer. ⟨< F *gendarme* < *gens d'armes* men of arms⟩

gen•der ['dʒɛndər] *n.* **1** *Grammar.* **a** a system of grouping nouns and their modifiers into two or more classes, either arbitrarily or according to certain features of structure or meaning, such as sex, social rank, shape, size, or kind of existence (living things as opposed to non-living). **b** any such category. **c** a form or inflection used to indicate such a category. **2** sex (def. 2) viewed as a sociological category. ⟨ME < OF *gendre* < L *genus, -neris* kind, sort⟩
☛ *Usage.* **Grammatical gender.** Many languages have special endings for masculine, feminine, and neuter nouns and for adjectives modifying them, but English lost such formal distinctions several hundred years ago. Now, except in pronouns and a few nouns borrowed from other languages (*mistress, alumnus, alumna, blonde, masseur, masseuse*), gender is indicated only by the meaning of the word: *man—woman, nephew—niece, rooster—hen.*

gen•der–neu•tral ['dʒɛndər 'njutrəl] *or* ['nutrəl] *adj.* taking care to apply equally to men and women: *gender-neutral language, a gender-neutral law.*

gene [dʒin] *n. Genetics.* a part of a germ cell that occupies a fixed place on a chromosome and determines the nature and development of an inherited characteristic. The genes inherited from its parents determine what kind of plant or animal will develop from a fertilized egg cell. There are about 100 000 human genes. ⟨< Gk. *genea* breed, kind⟩
☛ *Hom.* JEAN.

ge•ne•a•log•i•cal [,dʒiniə'lɒdʒəkəl] *or* [,dʒɛniə'lɒdʒəkəl] *adj.* having to do with genealogy. A genealogical table or chart shows the descent of a person or family from an ancestor. **—,ge•ne•a'log•i•cal•ly,** *adv.*

ge•ne•al•o•gist [,dʒini'ɒlədʒɪst] *or* [,dʒini'ælədʒɪst], [,dʒɛni'ɒlədʒɪst] *or* [,dʒɛni'ælədʒɪst] *n.* a person who traces genealogies; person who makes a study of genealogies.

ge•ne•al•o•gy [,dʒini'ɒlədʒi] *or* [,dʒini'ælədʒi], [,dʒɛni'ɒlədʒi] *or* [,dʒɛni'ælədʒi] *n., pl.* **-gies. 1** an account or record of the descent of a person or family from an ancestor or ancestors. **2** the descent of a person or family from an ancestor; pedigree; lineage. **3** the study or investigation of lines of descent; study of pedigrees. ⟨< L < Gk. *genealogia,* ult. < *genea* generation + *-logos* treating of⟩

gene expansion *Genetics.* the property of some genes of lengthening by repetition of certain triplet base sequences within the gene, leading to variability in phenotypic expression.

gene flow *Genetics.* gradual spread of genes between populations by migrating and mating.

gene frequency *Genetics.* the frequency of a particular allele of a gene in a given population.

gene map *Genetics.* a map of the set of chromosomes characteristic of a given species, indicating the exact position of each gene that has been located.

gene mapping *Genetics.* the process of finding the location of specific genes on the chromosomes.

gene pool *Genetics.* the full set of genes in a population.

gene product *Genetics.* the protein product encoded in a gene.

gen•er•a ['dʒɛnərə] *n.* pl. of GENUS.

gen•er•a•ble ['dʒɛnərəbəl] *adj.* capable of being produced.

gen•er•al ['dʒɛnərəl] *adj., n. —adj.* **1** of all; for all; from all: *A government takes care of the general welfare.* **2** common to many or most; not limited to a few; widespread: *There is a general interest in sports.* **3** not specialized; not limited to one kind, class, department, or use: *A general reader reads different kinds of books.* **4** not detailed; sufficient for practical purposes: *general instructions.* **5** indefinite; vague: *She referred to her trip in a general way.* **6** of or for all those forming a group: *The word* cat *can be used as a general term for cats, lions, and tigers.* **7** of highest rank; in chief: *a general manager, the solicitor general.*
—n. **1** *Canadian Forces.* the highest-ranking officer, next above a lieutenant-general. *Abbrev.:* Gen. or Gen **2** an officer of similar rank in the armed forces of other countries. **3** any officer ranking above a colonel and entitled to command a force larger than a regiment, such as a lieutenant-general. **4** any officer in command of many soldiers: *Sir Arthur Currie was a famous Canadian general.* **5** a general fact, idea, principle, or statement. **6** the head of a religious order. **7** *Archaic.* people as a group; the public.
in general, a referring to all or most of those in a given class. **b** usually; for the most part: *In general, people get along fairly well together.* ⟨< L *generalis* of a whole class < *genus, -neris* class, race⟩ **—'gen•er•al•ness,** *n.*
☛ *Syn. adj.* **1, 2. General,** COMMON, POPULAR = belonging or relating to all. **General** = belonging to or existing among all, or almost all, of a group or class of people or things thought of as a whole: *Laws are made for the general good.* **Common** = shared by all the members of a group or class: *English is the common language in the United States.* **Popular** = belonging to, existing among, or representing the general public: *Various polls are devised to find out popular opinions.*

General Agreement on Tariffs and Trade an international organization dating from 1949, whose goal is to promote free trade and set up guidelines concerning tariffs. *Abbrev.:* GATT

General Assembly the legislative body of the United Nations.

gen•er•al•cy ['dʒɛnərəlsi] *n.* the office of a general.

general delivery 1 a department of a post office that handles mail which is not addressed to a street number or box number. **2** such mail.

general election 1 an election involving all the voters of a country. **2** *Cdn.* an election in which a new federal Parliament is elected.

gen•er•al•is•si•mo [,dʒɛnərə'lɪsə,mou] *n., pl.* **-mos.** in certain countries **1** the commander-in-chief of all the military forces of a country. **2** the commander-in-chief of several armies in the field. ⟨< Ital. *generalissimo,* superlative of *generale* general⟩

gen•er•al•ist ['dʒɛnərəlɪst] *n.* a person who does not specialize in any one field of study but has a wide general knowledge. **—'gen•er•al,ism,** *n.*

gen•er•al•i•ty [,dʒɛnə'ræləti] *n., pl.* **-ties. 1** a general statement; a word or phrase not definite enough to have much meaning or value: *The candidate spoke only in generalities; not once did he mention definite laws that he and his party would try to pass.* **2** a general principle or rule: *"Nothing happens without a cause" is a generality.* **3** the greater part; main body; mass: *The generality of people must work for a living.* **4** general quality or condition: *A rule of great generality has very few exceptions.*

gen•er•al•iz•able [,dʒɛnərə'laɪzəbəl] *adj.* that can be generalized.

gen•er•al•i•za•tion [,dʒɛnərəlaɪ'zeiʃən] *or* [,dʒɛnərələ'zeiʃən] *n.* **1** the act or process of generalizing. **2** a general idea, statement, principle, or rule: *Her argument was weakened by too many generalizations.*

gen•er•al•ize ['dʒɛnərə,laɪz] *v.* **-ized, -iz•ing. 1** refer to in one general statement; bring under a common heading, class, or law: *All men, women, and children can be generalized under the term 'human being'.* **2** infer (a general rule) from particular facts: *If you have seen cats, lions, leopards, and tigers eat meat, you can generalize that the cat family eats meat.* **3** state in a more general form; extend in application. The statement that 5 + 3 = 8 and 50 + 30 = 80 can be generalized to the form $5a + 3a = 8a$. **4** talk indefinitely or vaguely; use generalities. **5** make or become general; bring or come into general use or knowledge. **6** make general inferences. **—'gen•er•al,iz•er,** *n.*

gen•er•al•ly ['dʒɛnərəli] *adv.* **1** as a rule; in most cases; usually: *He is generally on time.* **2** by or to most people; commonly; widely: *It was once generally believed that the earth is flat.* **3** in a general way; without giving details; not specially: *Generally speaking, our coldest weather comes in January.*

General of the Army *U.S.* the highest-ranking officer in the army.

general practitioner a medical doctor who does not specialize in one area.

gen•er•al–pur•pose ['dʒənərəl 'pɜrpəs] *adj.* suitable for use for a number of different purposes; having a number of different uses.

General Radio Service *Cdn.* a range of radio frequencies officially reserved for use by the general public for short-range, private communication. The U.S. name, widely used in Canada, is Citizens' Band. *Abbrev.*: GRS

general semantics a theory of language and other symbols that emphasizes their arbitrariness and their effects on people in relation to each other and their environment, first propounded by Alfred Korzybski in 1921.

gen•er•al•ship ['dʒɛnərəl,ʃɪp] *n.* **1** ability as a general; skill in commanding an army. **2** skilful management; leadership. **3** the rank, commission, authority, or term of office of a general.

general staff *Military.* a group of high army officers who make plans of war or national defence. *Abbrev.*: G.S.

general store a small store that carries a wide variety of goods for sale but is not divided into departments. General stores are usually located in small communities and rural areas.

general strike a stopping of work in many or all industries and trades in a country or region.

gen•er•ate ['dʒɛnə,reit] *v.* **-at•ed, -at•ing. 1** produce; cause to be: *Rubbing generates heat. Steam can be used to generate power or electricity.* **2** produce (offspring). **3** *Mathematics.* form (a line, surface, figure, or solid) by moving a point, line, or plane. ⟨< L *generare* < *genus, -neris* race⟩

gen•er•a•tion [,dʒɛnə'reiʃən] *n.* **1** all the people born about the same time. Your parents and their friends belong to one generation; you and your friends belong to the following generation. **2** the average time from the birth of one generation to the birth of the next generation; about 30 years. **3** one step, or stage, in the history of a family: *The picture showed four generations—great-grandmother, grandmother, mother, and baby.* **4** the production of offspring. **5** production; a causing to be; act of generating: *Steam and water power are used for the generation of electricity.* **6** *Biology.* a form or stage of a plant or animal, with reference to its method of reproduction; process of reproduction: *the asexual generation of a fern.* **7** one step, or stage, or the individuals representing it, in the history or development of something: *an earlier generation of computers.* **8** *Mathematics.* the formation of a line, surface, figure, or solid by moving a point, line, or plane. **—,gen•er'a•tion•al,** *adj.*

generation gap a wide difference in attitudes between young and older people.

gen•er•a•tive ['dʒɛnərətɪv] *or* ['dʒɛnə,reitɪv] *adj.* **1** having to do with the production of offspring. **2** having the power of producing. **—'gen•er•a•tive•ly,** *adv.* **—'gen•er•a•tive•ness,** *n.*

generative grammar a theory of human grammars proposed in the late 1950s by Noam Chomsky. It seeks to account for the ability of human beings to produce an infinite variety and number of sentences, by positing a small set of rules that allow the speaker to generate any sentence from a limited number of basic structures.

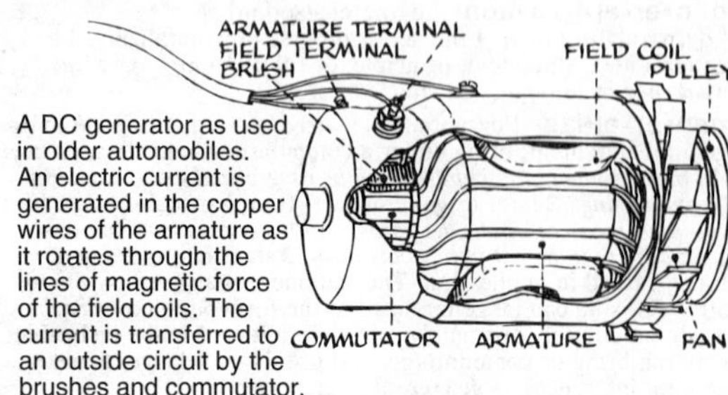

A DC generator as used in older automobiles. An electric current is generated in the copper wires of the armature as it rotates through the lines of magnetic force of the field coils. The current is transferred to an outside circuit by the brushes and commutator.

gen•er•a•tor ['dʒɛnə,reitər] *n.* **1** a machine that changes mechanical energy into electrical energy. **2** an apparatus for producing gas or steam. **3** any person or thing that generates; originator. ⟨< L⟩

gen•er•a•trix [,dʒɛnə'reitrɪks] *n., pl.* **gen•er•a•tri•ces** [,dʒɛnərə'trəisiz] *or* [,dʒɛnə'reitrɪsiz] *Mathematics.* a point, line, etc. whose motion produces a line, surface, figure, or solid. ⟨< L⟩

ge•ner•ic [dʒə'nɛrɪk] *adj.* **1** having to do with or characteristic of a genus of plants or animals: *Cats and lions show generic differences.* **2** having to do with a class or group of similar things; inclusive; not specific: *Liquid is a generic term.* **3** applied to, or referring to, a group or class; general; not special. **4** of or having to do with a group or class as distinct from a brand name: *Most drugs have a generic name as well as one or more brand names.* ⟨< L *genus, generis* kind⟩ **—ge'ner•i•cal•ly,** *adv.*

gen•er•os•i•ty [,dʒɛnə'rɒsəti] *n., pl.* **-ties. 1** a being generous; willingness to share with others; unselfishness. **2** nobleness of mind; absence of mean-spiritedness. **3** a generous act.

gen•er•ous ['dʒɛnərəs] *adj.* **1** willing to share with others; unselfish. **2** having or showing a noble mind; willing to forgive; not mean-spirited: *a generous mind.* **3** large; plentiful: *A quarter of a pie is a generous serving.* **4** of wine, rich and full of flavour. **5** fertile; yielding much. ⟨< L *generosus* of noble birth < *genus, -neris* race, stock⟩ **—'gen•er•ous•ly,** *adv.* **—'gen•er•ous•ness,** *n.*

genes in common *Genetics.* the proportion of their genes two people share by their descent from common ancestors.

gen•e•sis ['dʒɛnəsɪs] *n., pl.* **-ses** [-,siz]. origin; creation; coming into being. ⟨< L < Gk.⟩

gen•et[1] ['dʒɛnɪt] See JENNET.

gen•et[2] ['dʒɛnɪt] *or* [dʒə'nɛt] *n.* an Old World carnivore related to the civet cat. ⟨< ME; ult. < Arabic *jarnayt*⟩

gene targeting *Genetics.* the procedure of altering a gene by substituting one of its DNA sequences for another, so as to activate it and to allow the introduction of a new or corrected gene in its place.

gene therapy *Genetics.* the treatment of a genetic disorder by insertion of copies of the normal gene into the cells of an individual who has a mutant form of the gene.

ge•net•ic [dʒə'nɛtɪk] *adj.* **1** having to do with origin and natural growth. **2** of or having to do with genetics. **3** determined by genes. ⟨< Gk. *genētikos* < *genesis* origin, creation⟩

ge•net•i•cal•ly [dʒə'nɛtɪkli] *adv.* **1** with respect to genesis or origin. **2** according to the laws of genetics.

genetic code *Genetics.* the triplets of bases in DNA or RNA that code for the 20 amino acids, and for termination of a growing chain of amino acids, so determining the synthesis of proteins by a cell.

genetic counselling *Genetics.* the process of explaining to a patient or family affected by or at risk of a genetic disorder the genetic facts about the disorder, their implications, and the options for dealing with it.

genetic disorder a disease or disorder caused at least in part by abnormal genes.

genetic drift *Genetics.* random variation in the frequency of allelic genes from generation to generation, especially in small populations.

genetic engineering *Genetics.* the ways in which genetic material can be altered by recombinant DNA to change hereditary characteristics.

genetic equilibrium *Genetics.* in a population, the state in which the gene frequencies remain unaltered from one generation to the next.

genetic heterogeneity *Genetics.* the production of the same or similar phenotypes by different genetic mechanisms.

genetic information *Genetics.* the instructions for protein synthesis carried in the genes.

ge•net•i•cist [dʒə'nɛtəsɪst] *n.* a person trained in genetics, especially one whose work it is.

genetic load *Genetics.* the sum total of death and defect caused by mutant genes.

genetic marker *Genetics.* a segment of DNA within a chromosome that can be used as a reference point for mapping other places.

genetic material *Genetics.* DNA in almost all organisms. Some viruses have their genetic material in the form of RNA.

genetic polymorphism *Genetics.* the occurence of two or more relatively common forms of a trait, determined by different alleles, in a population.

ge•net•ics [dʒə'nɛtɪks] *n.* **1** the branch of biology dealing with the principles of heredity and variation in animals and plants of the same or related kinds. **2** the genetic make-up of an individual organism or a type or group. **3** the genetic aspects of a condition: *the genetics of cystic fibrosis.*

ge•ne•va [dʒə'nivə] *n.* a Dutch gin in which the flavourings are distilled at the start instead of being put in after distillation; Hollands. ⟨< Du. *genever* < OF *genevre* juniper berry < L *juniperus* juniper⟩

Ge•ne•va Convention [dʒə'nivə] an agreement between nations providing for the neutrality of the members and buildings of the medical departments on battlefields. It was first formulated at Geneva, Switzerland, in 1864.

Geneva cross a red Greek cross on a white background, used to mark ambulances, hospitals, and the Red Cross Society.

Ge•ne•van [dʒə'nivən] *n., adj.* *—n.* a native or inhabitant of Geneva, a city in SW Switzerland.
—adj. of or having to do with Geneva or its people.

gen•ial[1] ['dʒinjəl] *or* ['dʒiniəl] *adj.* **1** smiling and pleasant; cheerful and friendly; kindly: *a genial welcome.* **2** helping growth; pleasantly warming; comforting: *genial sunshine.* ⟨< L *genialis,* literally, belonging to the genius < *genius.* See GENIUS.⟩
—'gen•ial•ly, *adv.* **—'gen•ial•ness,** *n.*

ge•ni•al[2] [dʒə'niəl] *or* [dʒə'naɪəl] *adj.* of or having to do with the chin. ⟨< Gk. *geneion* chin⟩

ge•ni•al•i•ty [,dʒini'æləti] *n.* a genial quality.

gen•ic ['dʒɛnɪk] *adj. Biology.* of, relating to, or like a gene; genetic.

–genic *combining form.* **1** producing; having to do with production: *carcinogenic = producing cancer.* **2** suitable for; suitable for production or reproduction by: *photogenic = suitable for photography.*

gen•ic•u•late [dʒə'nɪkjəlɪt] *or* [dʒə'nɪkjə,leit] *adj.* **1** having joints like knees.
2 bent like a knee or joint. ⟨< L *geniculatus* < *geniculum,* dim. of *genu* knee⟩

gen•ic•u•la•tion [dʒə,nɪkjə'leiʃən] *n.* a geniculate formation.

ge•nie ['dʒini,aɪ] *n.* a spirit; jinni: *When Aladdin rubbed his lamp, the genie came and did whatever Aladdin asked.* ⟨< F *génie*⟩

ge•ni•i ['dʒini,aɪ] *n.* a pl. of GENIUS.

gen•i•pap ['dʒɛnɪ,pæp] *n.* **1** an American tropical tree (*Genipa americana*) of the madder family. **2** the round, brown fruit of this tree, eaten as food. ⟨< Pg. *genipapo* < the West Indian (Tupi) name⟩

gen•i•tal ['dʒɛnətəl] *adj.* of or having to do with sexual reproduction or the sex organs. ⟨< L *genitalis,* ult. < *gignere* beget⟩

gen•i•ta•lia [,dʒɛnɪ'teiliə] *n.* genitals.

gen•i•tals ['dʒɛnətəlz] *n.pl.* the external sex organs.

gen•i•ti•val [,dʒɛnə'taɪvəl] *adj.* of or in the genitive case.

gen•i•tive ['dʒɛnətɪv] *adj., n.* *—adj.* of, having to do with, or being the grammatical case that shows that a noun, pronoun, or adjective refers to the possessor or source of something: *her coat, Shakespeare's plays.*
—n. **1** the genitive case. **2** a word or construction in the genitive case. ⟨< L *genitivus* of origin⟩

gen•i•to–ur•i•na•ry ['dʒənɪtou 'jʊrə,nɛri] *adj.* of the genital and urinary organs.

gen•ius ['dʒinjəs] *or* ['dʒiniəs] *n., pl.* **gen•ius•es** *for 1-4, 8,* **ge•ni•i** *for 5, 6, 7, 9, 10* **1** very great natural power of mind. Genius is shown by extraordinary ability to think, invent, or create. **2** a person having such power: *Shakespeare was a genius.* **3** a great natural ability of a specified kind: *Mozart played the piano well, but he had a genius for composing.* **4** the special character or spirit of a person, nation, age, language, etc.: *Shakespeare gave expression to the genius of Elizabethan England.* **5** a guardian spirit of a person, place, institution, etc.: *the genius of the hill.* **6** a personification of a quality. **7** either of two spirits, one good and one evil, supposed to influence a person's fate. **8** a person who powerfully influences another. **9** inclination; disposition. **10** a spirit; genie; jinni. ⟨< L *genius* god presiding over birth, ult. < *genere* beget⟩

genius lo•ci ['lousaɪ] **1** in Greek and Roman mythology, the guardian of a place. **2** the impression a place makes on the mind.

gen•o•cid•al [,dʒɛnə'saɪdəl] *adj.* of or having to do with genocide.

gen•o•cide ['dʒɛnə,saɪd] *n.* systematic measures for the extermination of a national, cultural, religious, or racial group. ⟨< Gk. *genos* race + *-cide*[1]; coined by R. Lemkin in 1944⟩

Gen•o•ese [,dʒɛnou'iz] *n., pl.* **-ese;** *adj.* *—n.* a native or inhabitant of Genoa, a seaport in NW Italy.
—adj. of or having to do with Genoa or its people.

ge•nome ['dʒinoum] *n. Genetics.* the full DNA sequence, containing the entire genetic information. It may refer to a gamete, an individual, a population, or a species. ⟨< *gene* + (*chromos*)*ome*⟩

ge•nom•ic DNA [dʒə'nɒmɪk] *or* [dʒə'noumɪk] *Genetics.* the entire DNA contained in the genome, including exons, introns, and controlling sequences.

gen•o•type ['dʒɛnə,təip] *or* ['dʒinə,təip] *n. Biology.* **1** the arrangement or combination of genes in an organism. **2** the total genetic make-up of the individual. **3** a group of organisms each having the same combinations of hereditary characteristics. ⟨< Gk. *genos* race + E *type*⟩

–genous *combining form.* producing: *erogenous.*

gen•re ['ʒɒnrə]; *French* [ʒɑ̃ʀ] *n.* kind; sort; style, especially of works of literature, art, etc.: *The novel and the drama are two literary genres.* ⟨< F < L *genus* kind⟩

genre painting a style of painting that shows scenes from ordinary life.

gens[1] [dʒɛnz] *n., pl.* **gen•tes** ['dʒɛntiz]. **1** in ancient Rome, a group of families that claimed the same ancestor and were united by a common name and common religious ceremonies: *Julius Caesar was a member of the Julian gens.* **2** a tribe; clan. **3** *Ethnology.* a group of people descended through their fathers from a common ancestor. ⟨< L⟩

gens[2] [ʒɑ̃] *n.pl. French.* any group of people following the same occupation, engaged in the same business, or inhabiting the same region. **Gens de chantier** are loggers.

gent [dʒɛnt] *n. Informal.* gentleman.

gen•ta•mi•cin [,dʒɛntə'məisɪn] *n.* an antibiotic drug in the form of drops for the eyes.

gen•teel [dʒɛn'til] *adj.* **1** belonging or suited to polite society. **2** polite; well-bred; fashionable; elegant. **3** trying to be aristocratic, but not really being so. ⟨< F *gentil* < L *gentilis.* Doublet of GENTILE, GENTLE, JAUNTY.⟩ **—gen'teel•ly,** *adv.* **—gen'teel•ness,** *n.*

gen•tian ['dʒɛnʃən] *n.* **1** any of a genus (*Gentiana*) of mostly perennial plants having blue, white, red, or yellow funnel-shaped flowers and stemless leaves. **2** the dried rhizome and root of a yellow-flowered European gentian (*G. lutea*), which is used as a tonic. **3** (*adjl.*) designating the family of plants (Gentianaceae) that includes the gentians. ⟨< L *gentiana;* said to be named for *Gentius,* king of Illyria (ancient country on the Adriatic)⟩

gentian violet a crystalline derivative of aniline that forms a violet solution in water, used as a dye, chemical indicator, and antiseptic.

gen•tile or **Gen•tile** ['dʒɛntaɪl] *n., adj.* *—n.* **1** a person who is not a Jew. **2** a heathen; pagan.
—adj. **1** not Jewish. **2** heathen; pagan. ⟨ME < LL *gentilis* foreign < L *gentilis* of a people, national. Doublet of GENTEEL, GENTLE, JAUNTY.⟩

gen•til•i•ty [dʒɛn'tɪləti] *n., pl.* **-ties. 1** membership in the aristocracy or upper class. **2** good manners; refinement: *The lady had an air of gentility.* **3** pretended refinement. **4** members of the upper class as a group.

gen•tle ['dʒɛntəl] *adj.* **-tler, -tlest;** *v.* *—adj.* **1** not severe, rough, or violent; mild: *a gentle tap.* **2** soft; low: *a gentle sound.* **3** moderate: *gentle heat, a gentle slope.* **4** kindly; friendly: *a gentle disposition.* **5** easily handled or managed: *a gentle dog.* **6** of good family and social position; well-born. **7** honourable; good; superior. **8** *Archaic.* noble; gallant: *a gentle knight.* **9** refined; polite.
—v. treat in a soothing way; make quiet or gentle: *The rider gentled her excited horse.* ⟨ME < OF *gentil* < L *gentilis* of the (same) family, national < *gens, gentis* family, nation. Doublet of GENTEEL, GENTILE, JAUNTY.⟩ **—'gen•tle•ness,** *n.*

➨ *Syn. adj.* **1. Gentle,** MILD, MEEK = agreeable, not harsh, rough, or violent. **Gentle** emphasizes control of strength or force, and suggests being pleasant or pleasing or being soft, tender, calm, or kindly: *My nurse is gentle in touch, manner, and voice.* **Mild** emphasizes being by nature not disagreeable, lacking in harshness, severity, etc.: *He is a mild man and seldom gets angry.* **Meek,** applying only to people, and meaning mild or gentle in disposition, emphasizes being patient and humble: *The meek boy, instead of returning the insults of the school bully, picked up his books for him with a friendly smile.*

gentle breeze a wind of force 3 on the Beaufort scale, with a speed of 12-19 km/h. See chart of Beaufort scale in the Appendix.

gen•tle•folk ['dʒɛntəl,fouk] *n.pl.* people of good family and social position.

gen•tle•man ['dʒɛntəlmən] *n., pl.* **-men. 1** a man of good family and social position. **2** a man who is honourable, polite,

and considerate of others. **3** a man of independent means, who does not work at any occupation or profession. **4** a personal servant of a gentleman, used especially in the phrase *gentleman's gentleman.* **5** a polite term for any man, also used (in the plural) as a form of address: *Ask the gentleman to come in, please. Ladies and gentlemen, please take your seats.* **—'gen•tle•man,like,** *adj.*
☛ *Usage.* See note at MAN.

gen•tle•man–at–arms ['dʒɛntəlmən ət 'ɑrmz] one of a guard of 40 gentlemen with their officers who attend the British Sovereign on state occasions.

gentleman farmer a man who farms as a hobby and not for a livelihood.

gen•tle•man–in–wait•ing ['dʒɛntəlmən ɪn 'weitɪŋ] *n.* a man of good family who attends a king or prince.

gen•tle•man•ly ['dʒɛntəlmənli] *adj.* of, characteristic of, or suitable for a gentleman: *a gentlemanly bow, a gentlemanly sport.* **—'gen•tle•man•li•ness,** *n.*

gentleman's agreement or **gentlemen's agreement** an unwritten agreement that is not legally binding but depends only on the honour of the people or countries that participate in it.

gen•tle•wom•an ['dʒɛntəl,wʊmən] *n., pl.* **-wom•en. 1** a woman of good family and social position. **2** a woman who is courteous and cultured. **3** a woman attendant of a lady of rank. **—'gen•tle,wom•an•ly,** *adj.*

gen•tly ['dʒɛntli] *adv.* **1** in a gentle way; tenderly; softly. **2** gradually: *a gently sloping hillside.*

gen•tri•fi•ca•tion [,dʒɛntrəfə'keiʃən] *n.* the renovation of old houses in urban areas by wealthy newcomers.

gen•tri•fy ['dʒɛntrə,faɪ] *v.,* **gen•tri•fi•ed, gen•tri•fy•ing.** upgrade something such as a city area.

gen•try ['dʒɛntri] *n.* **1** people of good family and social position; formerly, in the British Isles, members of the class of wealthy landowners ranking just below the nobility. **2** a group of professional people considered as rather superior by others: *the legal gentry, the medical gentry.* ⟨alteration of *gentrice* < OF *genterise,* ult. < *gentil.* See GENTLE.⟩

ge•nu ['dʒɛnju] *or* ['dʒinu] *n., pl.* **ge•nu•a.** *Anatomy.* the knee. ⟨< L⟩

gen•u•flect ['dʒɛnjə,flɛkt] *v.* bend the knee as an act of reverence or worship. ⟨< Med.L *genuflectere* < L *genu* knee + *flectere* bend⟩

gen•u•flec•tion [,dʒɛnjə'flɛkʃən] *n.* a bending of the knee as an act of reverence or worship.

gen•u•ine ['dʒɛnjuən] *or* ['dʒɛnju,aɪn] *adj.* **1** actually being what it seems or is claimed to be; real; true: *genuine leather, a genuine diamond.* **2** without pretence; sincere; frank: *genuine sorrow.* ⟨< L *genuinus* native, natural, ult. < *gignere* beget⟩ **—'gen•u•ine•ly,** *adv.* **—'gen•u•ine•ness,** *n.*
☛ *Syn.* **1. Genuine,** AUTHENTIC = what it is claimed to be. **Genuine** refers to something that is real, pure, actually having the nature or quality it is supposed to have: *The table is genuine mahogany, not wood stained to look like mahogany.* **Authentic** = of genuine origin or authorship: *That is her authentic signature, not a forgery.*

ge•nus ['dʒinəs] *or* ['dʒɛnəs] *n., pl.* **gen•er•a** or **ge•nus•es. 1** *Biology.* a major category in the classification of plants and animals, more specific than the family and more general than the species. The prairie crocus (*Anemone patens*) and the Canada anemone (*Anemone canadensis*) belong to the same genus. The scientific name of every species of animal or plant is made up of the genus name (capitalized) followed by the species name (not capitalized). See classification chart in the Appendix. **2** any kind or sort. **3** *Logic.* a class or group of individuals divided into subordinate groups called species. ⟨< L⟩

–geny *combining form.* origin, as in *phylogeny.* ⟨< Gk. *-geneia*⟩

geo– *combining form.* earth; land, as in *geocentric.* ⟨< Gk. *geō* < *gē* earth⟩

ge•o•cen•tric [,dʒiou'sɛntrɪk] *adj.* **1** as viewed or measured from the earth's centre. **2** having or representing the earth as a centre: *The people of medieval times had a geocentric view of the universe.* Compare HELIOCENTRIC. Also, **geocentrical.** ⟨< *geo-* + Gk. *kentron* centre⟩ **—,ge•o'cen•tri•cal•ly,** *adv.*

ge•o•chem•ist [,dʒiou'kɛmɪst] *n.* a person trained in geochemistry, especially one whose work it is.

ge•o•chem•is•try [,dʒiou'kɛməstri] *n.* the science dealing with the chemistry of the earth.

ge•o•chro•nol•o•gy [,dʒioukrə'nɒlədʒi] *n.* the history of the earth determined by geology.

ge•ode ['dʒioud] *n.* **1** a rock having a cavity lined with crystals. **2** the cavity itself. ⟨< F *géode* < L < Gk. *geōdēs* earthy < *gē* earth + *eidos* form⟩

ge•o•des•ic [,dʒiə'dɛsɪk] *or* [,dʒiə'dizɪk] *n., adj.* —*n.* the shortest possible distance between two points along a surface, especially a curved surface.
—*adj.* **1** of or having to do with geodesy or the geometry of curved lines. **2** *Architecture.* built with short, straight, lightweight struts forming a spherical grid of polygons: *A geodesic dome uses the minimum amount of material to produce a given volume.*

geodesic dome a dome made of light materials forming polygons that interlock.

ge•od•e•sy [dʒi'ɒdəsi] *n.* the branch of applied mathematics dealing with the shape and dimensions of the earth or large areas on its surface, determining the exact position of points on the surface, and variations in the earth's gravity and magnetism. Geodesy is based on the notion of measuring a sphere by dividing its surface area into triangles. ⟨< NL < Gk. *geodaisia* < *gē* earth + *daiein* divide⟩ **—ge'od•e•sist,** *n.*

ge•o•det•ic [,dʒiə'dɛtɪk] *adj.* of, having to do with, or involving geodesy: *geodetic measurements, a geodetic project.* **—,ge•o'det•i•cal•ly,** *adv.*

ge•o•duck ['dʒiou,dʌk], ['goui,dʌk], *or* ['gui,dʌk] *n.* a large, edible, burrowing clam (*Panope generosa*) of the Pacific coast. ⟨< Chinook jargon⟩

ge•o•dy•nam•ics [,dʒioudaɪ'næmɪks] *n.* the science of dynamic forces in the earth. **—,ge•o•dy'nam•ic,** *adj.*

ge•og•no•sy [dʒi'ɒgnəsi] *n.* the branch of geology that deals with the structure of the earth, the distribution of its rocks and minerals, and the water and air surrounding it. ⟨< F < Gk. *gē* earth + *gnōsis* knowledge⟩

ge•og•ra•pher [dʒi'ɒgrəfər] *n.* a person trained in geography, especially one whose work it is.

ge•o•graph•i•cal [,dʒiə'græfəkəl] *adj.* of or having to do with geography. Also, **geographic. —,ge•o'graph•i•cal•ly,** *adv.*

geographical mile NAUTICAL MILE.

ge•og•ra•phy [dʒi'ɒgrəfi] *n., pl.* **-phies. 1** the science that deals with the earth's surface and its division into continents and countries, and the climate, animal and plant life, peoples, resources, industries, and products of these divisions. **2** the surface features of a place or region. **3** a book about geography. ⟨< L < Gk. *geōgraphia* < *gē* earth + *graphein* describe⟩

ge•oid ['dʒiɔɪd] *n.* the surface of the earth that is hypothetically at sea level everywhere.

geol. geology; geological; geologist.

ge•o•log•i•cal [,dʒiə'lɒdʒəkəl] *adj.* of or having to do with geology. Also, **geological. —,ge•o'log•i•cal•ly,** *adv.*

ge•ol•o•gist [dʒi'ɒlədʒɪst] *n.* a person trained in geology, especially one whose work it is.

ge•ol•o•gize [dʒi'ɒlə,dʒaɪz] *v.* **-gized, -gizing. 1** study geology **2** examine something geologically.

ge•ol•o•gy [dʒi'ɒlədʒi] *n., pl.* **-gies. 1** the science that deals with the earth's crust, the layers of which it is composed, and their history. **2** the features of the earth's crust in a place or region; rocks, rock formation, etc. of a particular area. **3** a book about geology. ⟨< NL *geologia* < Gk. *gē* earth + *-logos* treating of⟩

geom. geometry; geometric.

ge•o•mag•net•ic [,dʒioumæg'nɛtɪk] *adj.* of or having to do with this.

geo•mag•net•ism [,dʒiou'mægnə,tɪzəm] *n.* **1** the magnetism of the earth. **2** the science concerned with this.

ge•om•e•ter [dʒi'ɒmətər] *n.* geometrician. ⟨< L < Gk. *geōmetrēs* < *gē* earth + *metrēs* measurer⟩

ge•o•met•ric [,dʒiə'mɛtrɪk] *adj.* **1** of geometry or according to its principles: *geometric proof.* **2** consisting of or characterized by straight lines, circles, triangles, etc.; regular and symmetrical: *a geometric design.* Also, **geometrical. —,ge•o'met•ri•cal•ly,** *adv.*

ge•om•e•tri•cian [dʒi,ɒmə'trɪʃən] *or* [,dʒiəmə'trɪʃən] *n.* a person trained in geometry, especially one whose work it is.

geometric mean the mean of *n* positive numbers obtained by taking the *n*th root of the product of the numbers. The geometric mean of 6 and 24 is 12.

geometric progression a sequence or ordered set of numbers in which the ratio of each term to its predecessor is constant. *Examples*: 2, 4, 8, 16, 32; 125, 25, 5, 1, 1/5, 1/25; 1, –3, 9, –27, 81. Compare ARITHMETIC PROGRESSION.

ge•om•e•trid [dʒi'ɒmətrɪd] *n.* any of a family (Geometridae) of medium-sized, grey or greenish moths whose larvae are called measuring worms or inchworms. ⟨< NL *Geometridae*, pl. < L < Gk. *geōmetrēs.* See GEOMETER.⟩

A geometrid

ge•om•e•trize [dʒi'ɒmə,traɪz] *v.* **-rized, -riz•ing. 1** put into geometric form. **2** work out by geometry.

ge•om•e•try [dʒi'ɒmətri] *n., pl.* **-tries. 1** the branch of mathematics that deals with lines, angles, surfaces, and solids. Geometry includes the definition, comparison, and measurement of squares, triangles, circles, cubes, cones, spheres, etc. **2** a book about geometry. **3** any specific system of geometry that operates like Euclidean geometry. ⟨< L < Gk. *geōmetria* < *gē* earth + *-metria* measuring⟩

ge•o•mor•phic [,dʒiə'mɔrfɪk] *adj.* of or having to do with the shape or the surface features of the earth or a heavenly body such as the moon.

ge•o•mor•pho•log•i•cal [,dʒiou,mɔrfə'lɒdʒəkəl] *adj.* of or having to do with geomorphology.

ge•o•mor•phol•o•gist [,dʒioumɔr'fɒlədʒɪst] *n.* a person trained in geomorphology, especially one whose work it is.

ge•o•mor•phol•o•gy [,dʒioumɔr'fɒlədʒi] *n.* the science that deals with the surface features of the earth or a heavenly body such as the moon, and with the origin and development of these features and their relationship with geological structures.

ge•oph•a•gy [dʒi'ɒfədʒi] *n.* the practice of eating earth, either as a symptom of psychotic disturbance or as a substitute for food, as during a famine. ⟨< *geo-* + *-phage*⟩

ge•o•phone ['dʒiə,foun] *n.* a microphone which records vibrations in the earth, such as shock waves, to give a seismic picture; used in oil exploration.

ge•o•phys•i•cal [,dʒiou'fɪzəkəl] *adj.* of or having to do with geophysics.

ge•o•phys•i•cist [,dʒiou'fɪzə,sɪst] *n.* a person trained in geophysics, especially one whose work it is.

ge•o•phys•ics [,dʒiou'fɪzɪks] *n.* the science that deals with the relations between the features of the earth and the forces that produce them; the physics of the earth (*used with a singular verb*). Geophysics includes magnetism, meteorology, oceanography, seismology, etc.

ge•o•phyte ['dʒiə,fəit] *n.* a plant with buds that grow underground.

ge•o•po•lit•i•cal [,dʒioupə'lɪtəkəl] *adj.* of, having to do with, or involved in geopolitics. **—,ge•o•po'lit•i•cal•ly,** *adv.*

ge•o•pol•i•ti•cian [,dʒiou,pɒlə'tɪʃən] *n.* a person who has special skill in, or knowledge of, geopolitics.

ge•o•pol•i•tics [,dʒiou'pɒlətɪks] *n.* the study of government and its policies as affected by physical geography.

ge•o•pon•ic [,dʒiou'pɒnɪk] *adj.* having to do with agriculture or farmers.

ge•o•pon•ics [,dʒiou'pɒnɪks] *n.* the art or science of agriculture (*used with a singular verb*).

George [dʒɔrdʒ] *n.* **1** a part of the insignia of the Order of the Garter, representing Saint George slaying the dragon. It may be a piece set with jewels or a single carved gem. **2** *Brit. Slang.* the automatic pilot of an aircraft.

George Cross in the Commonwealth of Nations, the highest award for civilian courage, established by King George VI. See MEDAL for picture. *Abbrev.*: G.C.

geor•gette [dʒɔr'dʒɛt] *n.* a light, fine, sheer crepe fabric having a dull pebbled or crinkly surface. ⟨from the name of a French modiste⟩

Geor•gia ['dʒɔrdʒə] *n.* **1** a republic in the former Soviet Union. **2** a southeastern state of the U.S.

Geor•gian ['dʒɔrdʒən] *adj., n.* —*adj.* **1** of, having to do with, or characteristic of the reigns of the four Georges, Kings of Great Britain and Ireland from 1714 to 1830: *Georgian architecture, Georgian furniture.* **2** of, having to do with, or characteristic of the reigns of King George V (1910-1936) and King George VI (1936-1952), especially of George V: *the Georgian poets.* **3** of or having to do with Georgia, its people, or their language. **4** of or having to do with the state of Georgia in the United States.
—*n.* **1** a British person, such as a writer, belonging to either of the Georgian periods. **2** a native or inhabitant of Georgia. **3** the Caucasian language of the people of Georgia. **4** a native or inhabitant of the state of Georgia in the United States.

geor•gic ['dʒɔrdʒɪk] *n., adj.* —*n.* a poem about agriculture. —*adj.* having to do with agriculture; bucolic. ⟨< L *georgicus* < Gk. *georgikos* agricultural < *georgos* husbandman, farmer⟩

ge•o•sci•ence [,dʒiou'saɪəns] *n.* any physical science dealing with the earth, such as geology or geochemistry.

ge•o•sphere ['dʒiə,sfir] *n.* the earth.

ge•o•sta•tion•ary [,dʒiou'steiʃə,nɛri] *adj.* moving at the same speed as the earth, therefore apparently stationary.

ge•o•stroph•ic [,dʒiou'strɒfɪk] *or* [,dʒiou'stroufɪk] *adj.* of or having to do with a force causing deflection due to the rotation of the earth. ⟨< *geo-* + Gk. *strophe* a turning, twist⟩

ge•o•syn•cline [,dʒiou'sɪnklaɪn] *n. Geology.* a sediment-filled trough that surrounds continents.

ge•o•tax•is [,dʒiou'tæksɪs] *n.* the response of a mobile object to or against the pull of gravity. ⟨< *geo-* + Gk. *taxis* arrangement, division⟩

ge•o•tec•ton•ic [,dʒioutɛk'tɒnɪk] *adj.* of or having to do with the structure, geography, etc., of rock bodies and the forces and shiftings of the earth's crust that formed them.

ge•o•ther•mal [,dʒiou'θɜrməl] *adj.* of or having to do with heat energy produced deep inside the earth.

ge•o•trop•ic [,dʒiə'trɒpɪk] *adj. Biology.* affected by geotropism; responding to gravity. ⟨< *geo-* + Gk. *tropikos* < *tropē* turning⟩

ge•ot•ro•pism (dʒi'ɒtrə,pɪzəm] *n. Biology.* a response to gravity. **Positive geotropism** is a tendency to move down into the earth, as roots do. **Negative geotropism** is a tendency to move upward.

ger. gerund.

Ger. 1 German. **2** Germany. **3** Germanic.

ge•rah ['girə] *n.* an ancient Hebrew weight and coin, equal to 1/20 of a shekel. ⟨< Hebrew, literally, bean⟩

ge•ra•ni•ol [dʒə'reini,ɒl] *n.* oil of geranium, used in flavouring and perfumes. *Formula*: $C_{10}H_{12}O$

ge•ra•ni•um [dʒə'reiniəm] *or* [dʒə'reinjəm] *n., adj.* —*n.* **1** any of various cultivated plants (genus *Pelargonium*) native to S Africa, having showy clusters of pink, red, or white flowers. Geraniums are very popular house and garden plants. **2** any of a genus (*Geranium*) of plants found mainly in temperate regions, having divided leaves, pink or purple flowers, and long, pointed pods. **3** (*adjl.*) designating the family (Geraniaceae) of plants that includes the genera *Pelargonium* and *Geranium.*
—*adj.* scarlet. ⟨< L < Gk. *geranion* < *geranos* crane; from the resemblance of the pod to a crane's bill⟩

ger•be•ra ['dʒɜrbərə] *or* [dʒər'birə], ['gɜrbərə] *or* [gər'birə] *n.* an African perennial plant *(Gerbera jamesonii)* of the composite family, having strong stems and large daisylike flowers in red, yellow, white, crimson, rose, or salmon pink.

ger•bil ['dʒɜrbəl] *n.* any of a subfamily (Gerbillinae, of the family Cricetidae) of small burrowing rodents native to the Old World, having large eyes and ears, soft, brown or greyish fur, and a long, hairy tail. Gerbils have been popular as cage pets in North America since the 1960s. ⟨< F *gerbille* < NL *gerbillus*, dim. of *gerbo* jerboa⟩

A gerbil

ger•fal•con ['dʒɜr,fɒlkən], ['dʒɜr,fælkən], *or* ['dʒɜr,fɒkən] *n.* See GYRFALCON. ⟨ME < OF *gerfaucon* < Gmc.⟩

ger•i•a•tric•ian [,dʒɛriə'trɪʃən] *n.* one trained in geriatrics, especially one whose work it is.

ger•i•at•rics [,dʒɛri'ætrɪks] *n.* the branch of medicine that deals with the study of old age and its diseases. Compare GERONTOLOGY. ⟨< Gk. *gēras* old age + *iatreia* healing⟩ **—,ger•i'at•ric,** *adj.*

germ [dʒɜrm] *n.* **1** a micro-organism, especially one that causes disease. **2** the earliest form of a living thing; seed; bud. **3** the beginning of anything; origin. ⟨< F < L *germen* sprout⟩ **—'germ•less,** *adj.* **—'germ,like,** *adj.*

☛ *Usage.* **Germ** is a non-scientific word used of a virus, bacterium, or bacillus.

ger•man¹ ['dʒɜrmən] *adj.* (*usually in compounds*) **1** having the same parents. Children of the same father and mother are **brothers-german** or **sisters-german. 2** being a child of one's uncle or aunt. A **cousin-german** is a first cousin. ⟨ME < OF *germain* < L *germanus,* related to *germen* sprout⟩

ger•man² ['dʒɜrmən] *n.* **1** a dance with complicated steps and frequent changing of partners; cotillion. **2** a party at which it is danced. ⟨short for *German cotillion*⟩

Ger•man ['dʒɜrmən] *n., adj. —n.* **1** a native or inhabitant of Germany. **2** a person of German descent. **3** the Germanic language of Germany and Austria and parts of Switzerland; especially, the standard form used in literature, on radio, television, and the stage, etc.
—adj. of or having to do with Germany, Germans, or German. ⟨< L *Germanus*⟩

ger•man•der [dʒər'mændər] *n.* any of a genus (*Teucrium*) of plants of the mint family found in all parts of the world, typically having spikes of small, two-lipped flowers with the lower lip more prominent than the upper. ⟨< LL *germandra* < Gk. *chamaidryas*, alteration of *chamaidrys* ground oak⟩

ger•mane [dʒər'mein] *adj.* closely connected; to the point; pertinent: *Your statement is not germane to the discussion.* ⟨var. of *german¹*⟩

ger•man•ic [dʒər'mænɪk] *n.* of or containing germanium.

Ger•man•ic [dʒər'mænɪk] *n., adj. —n.* a main branch of the Indo-European family of languages, including English, German, Dutch, Frisian, Flemish, Danish, Norwegian, Swedish, Icelandic, and Gothic, that have developed from a common language spoken in Europe up to about 2500 years ago.
—adj. **1** of, having to do with, or designating this group of languages or the language they descended from. **2** of, having to do with, or designating any of the peoples speaking these languages. **3** German.

ger•ma•ni•um [dʒər'meiniəm] *n.* a rare, greyish white, brittle, metallic element. Germanium is used in making transistors. *Symbol*: Ge; *at.no.* 32; *at.mass* 72.59. ⟨< NL < L *Germania* Germany⟩

German measles a contagious viral disease resembling measles, but milder. It can cause congenital defects in a child whose mother catches it during the early months of pregnancy.

Ger•ma•no– *combining form.* German: *Germanophile*.

Ger•man•o•phile [dʒər'mænou,faɪl] *n.* a lover of Germany and things German.

Ger•man•o•phobe [dʒər'mænə,foub] *n.* one who detests Germany and all things German.

German shepherd a breed of large, intelligent dog developed in Germany, often trained to work with soldiers and police, to guide the blind, etc.; Alsatian.

German shorthaired pointer a lean hunting dog with a large frame and a short, thick, red-brown or red-brown-and-white coat.

German silver NICKEL SILVER.

Ger•man•y ['dʒɜrməni] *n.* a large country in central Europe. See NETHERLANDS for map.

germ cell 1 in the embryo, a primordial cell of the type that evenually gives rise to reproductive cells. **2** one of the reproductive cells in a sexually reproducing animal or plant which undergo meiosis to produce gametes (egg or sperm cells). Compare SOMATIC CELL.

ger•mi•cid•al [,dʒɜrmə'saɪdəl] *adj.* capable of killing germs.

ger•mi•cide ['dʒɜrmə,saɪd] *n.* any substance that kills germs, especially disease germs. ⟨< *germ* + *-cide²*⟩

ger•mi•nal ['dʒɜrmənəl] *adj.* **1** of, like, or characteristic of germs or germ cells. **2** in the earliest stage of development; embryonic.

germinal disk *Embryology.* blastodisk.

germinal mosaicism [mou'zeiɪ,sɪzəm] *Genetics.* GERM-LINE MOSAICISM.

germinal vesicle *Embryology.* the vesicular nucleus of an ovum.

ger•mi•nant ['dʒɜrmənənt] *adj.* germinating.

ger•mi•nate ['dʒɜrmə,neit] *v.* **-nat•ed, -nat•ing. 1** grow or sprout, or cause to grow or sprout: *Seeds germinate in the spring. Warmth and moisture germinate seeds.* **2** start growing or developing: *An idea was germinating in his head.* ⟨< L *germinare* < *germen* sprout⟩ **—,ger•mi'na•tion,** *n.* **—'ger•mi,na•tor,** *n.*

ger•mi•na•tive ['dʒɜrmənətɪv] *adj.* capable of germinating.

germ layer *Genetics.* one of the three layers of the early embryo, ectoderm, mesoderm, and endoderm, from which all body tissues develop.

germ line *Genetics.* cells derived from the primordial germ cells of the early embryo, from which gametes are eventually formed.

germ–line mosaicism *Genetics.* the presence in an individual of two or more genetically different types of gametes, resulting from mutation during germ-line development.

germ plasm a substance in germ cells that transmits hereditary characteristics to the offspring.

germ theory the theory that diseases are transmitted by micro-organisms.

germ warfare the spreading of germs to produce disease among the enemy in time of war.

ger•on•toc•ra•cy [,dʒɛrən'tɒkrəsi] *n.* government by a council of elders. ⟨< F *gérontocratie* < Gk. *geronto-* (< *geron* old man) + *-kratia* rule < *kratos* rule, strength⟩

ger•on•tol•o•gist [,dʒɛrən'tɒlədʒɪst] *n.* one trained in gerontology, especially one whose work it is.

ger•on•tol•o•gy [,dʒɛrən'tɒlədʒi] *n.* the branch of science that studies the aging process and the problems of old people. Compare GERIATRICS. ⟨< Gk. *geronto-* (< *geron* old man) + *-logy*⟩ **—,ger•on•to'log•ic•al,** *adj.*

ger•ry•man•der ['dʒɛri,mændər] *v., n. —v.* **1** arrange the boundaries of (the political constituencies of a region) so as to give the party in power an undue advantage in an election. **2** manipulate unfairly.
—n. such an arrangement of political boundaries. ⟨< *Gerry* + *(sala)mander*; Governor Gerry's party rearranged the districts of Massachusetts in 1812, and Essex County was divided so that one district became roughly salamander-shaped⟩

ger•und ['dʒɛrənd] *n. Grammar.* a verb form used as a noun. *Abbrev.*: ger. ⟨< LL *gerundium*, ult. < L *gerere* bear⟩

☛ *Usage.* The English **gerund** ends in *-ing.* It has the same form as the present participle but differs in use. Gerund: *Running a hotel appealed to her.* Participle: *Running around the corner, he bumped into his father.* A gerund may take an object (*running a hotel*) or a complement (*being a hero*), and it may serve in any of the functions of a noun: Subject: *Kayaking always fascinated her.* Object: *He taught dancing.* Predicate noun: *Seeing is believing.* Adjectival use: *a fishing boat* (a boat for fishing, not a boat that fishes). Object of a preposition: *a great day for hiking.*

ge•run•di•al [dʒə'rʌndiəl] *adj.* **1** of a gerund. **2** used as a gerund.

ge•run•dive [dʒə'rʌndɪv] *n.* a Latin verb form used as an adjective, frequently expressing the idea of necessity.

ge•sell•schaft [gə'zɛlʃɑft] *n. Sociology.* social organization in which impersonal relationships, institutionalism, and orderly structure predominate. Compare GEMEINSCHAFT. ⟨< G, literally, society⟩

ges•ne•ri•ad [dʒɛs'niri,æd] *n.* any of a family (Gesneriaceae) of plants with showy tubelike flowers. ⟨< K.V. *Gesner,* 16c. Swiss naturalist⟩

ges•so ['dʒɛsou] *n.* a plastic or liquid coating used to give surfaces the correct finish for painting. Gesso usually contains plaster of Paris. ⟨< Ital., gypsum, chalk < L *gypsum* gypsum⟩

gest or **geste** [dʒɛst] *n. Archaic.* **1** a story or romance in verse. **2** a story; tale. **3** a deed; exploit. ⟨ME < OF < L *gesta* deeds < *gerere* carry on, accomplish⟩

Ges•talt [gə'ʃtɑlt] *or* [gə'stɒlt] *n., pl.* **-s** *or* **-en.** [-ən]. *Psychology.* the total structure or pattern of various acts, experiences, and elements, so integrated as to constitute a whole that is greater than the sum of its parts. ⟨< G *Gestalt* form, configuration⟩

Gestalt psychology the theory that explains human behaviour as the configuration of Gestalts.

ges•tate ['dʒɛsteit] *v.* **-at•ed, -at•ing, 1** carry (young) during pregnancy. **2** develop slowly.

ges•ta•tion [dʒɛ'steiʃən] *n.* **1** the act or period of carrying young in the uterus from conception to birth; pregnancy. **2** the formation and development of a project, etc. in the mind. ⟨< L *gestatio, -onis* < *gestare* carry⟩

ges•tic ['dʒɛstɪk] *adj.* having to do with bodily movements, as in dancing. ⟨< F *geste* gesture < L *gestus*⟩

ges•tic•u•late [dʒə'stɪkjə,leit] *v.* **-lat•ed, -lat•ing. 1** make or use gestures, especially vehement gestures. **2** express (meaning) by gestures. ⟨< L *gesticulari,* ult. < *gestus* gesture⟩ **—ges'tic•u,la•tor,** *n.* **—ges'tic•u•la,to•ry,** *adj.*

ges•tic•u•la•tion [dʒə,stɪkjə'leiʃən] *n.* **1** the act of gesticulating. **2** gesture.
☛ *Syn.* **2.** See note at GESTURE.

ges•tic•u•la•tive [dʒɛ'stɪkjələtɪv] *or* [dʒə'stɪkjə,leitɪv] *adj.* making or using gestures.

ges•ture ['dʒɛstʃər] *n., v.* **-tured, -turing.** *—n.* **1** a movement of the hands, arms, or any part of the body, used instead of words or with words to help express an idea or feeling: *a gesture of dismissal. His speech was accompanied by many gestures.* **2** any action made for effect or to impress others: *Her refusal was merely a gesture; she really wanted to go.*
—v. make or use gestures: *She gestured sharply to silence him.* ⟨< Med.L *gestura* < L *gerere* to bear, conduct⟩ **—'ges•tur•al,** *adj.* **—'ges•tur•er,** *n.*
☛ *Syn. n.* **1. Gesture,** GESTICULATION = movement of the head, shoulders, hands, or arms to express thought or feeling. **Gesture** applies to any such movement or motion used to take the place of words or add to the meaning expressed by the words: *He did not speak, but with a gesture indicated that I should follow him.* **Gesticulation** applies only to wild, excited, or clumsy gestures: *Her gesticulations suggested she was losing her temper rapidly.*

Ge•sund•heit [gə'zʊnthəit] *interj.* a wish for good health to a person who has just sneezed. ⟨< G, health⟩

get [gɛt] *v.* **got, got** or **got•ten, get•ting. 1** come to have; obtain; receive; gain: *I got a new coat yesterday. She got first prize in the spelling contest.* **2** arrive (at) or come (*to*); reach: *I got home early last night. Your letter got here yesterday.* **3** go and bring; fetch: *Get the ball!* **4** cause; cause to be: *I can't get this thing to work. They got the fire under control.* **5** *Informal.* be obliged (*used with some form of* **have**): *We have got to win.* **6** become: *to get sick, to get old.* **7** be: *Don't get nervous when you have to take the test.* **8** learn by heart: *to get a poem.* **9** persuade; influence: *We got her to speak.* **10** prepare: *Will you help me get dinner?* **11** begin; start: *We soon got talking about our days at camp.* **12** possess; have (*used with some form of* **have**): *She has got black hair.* **13** usually of animals, beget. **14** *Informal.* hit; strike: *The bullet got the soldier in the arm.* **15** *Informal.* kill. **16** *Informal.* puzzle; annoy. **17** *Informal.* understand: *I don't get what you mean.* **18** *Informal.* receive as a prison sentence: *She got two years for tax evasion.* **19** *get* is also used informally with the past participle to form a passive: *to get beaten. She got converted.*
get about, a go from place to place. **b** spread; become widely known. **c** go to many social events.
get across, make an impression: *How did her speech get across?*
get across (to), *Informal.* **a** make understand; communicate: *You can't get anything across to her when she's in that mood.* **b** become clear (*to*) or understood: *It finally got across to him that he wasn't welcome.*
get after, a scold. **b** urge. **c** chase.
get ahead, advance one's position, career, etc.; be successful.
get along, a go away. **b** advance. **c** manage. **d** make an impression; prosper. **e** be on good terms: *He doesn't get along with his neighbours.*
get around, a go from place to place. **b** become widely known; spread. **c** overcome opposition by charm, flattery, etc.; win over: *Her winning smile often helped her to get around her father.* **d** deceive; trick.
get around to, finally deal with: *I'll get around to that letter tomorrow.*
get at, a reach. **b** find out: *Try to get at the truth.* **c** *Informal.* tamper with; influence with money or threats. **d** imply: *What are you getting at?*
get away, a leave: *I won't be able to get away from here until after lunch.* **b** escape: *She got away through the window. The dog got away from her.* **c** set out; start: *The last car got away at 10 o'clock.*
get away with, *Informal.* succeed in taking or doing (something) and escaping safely: *He thought he could get away with being late but he was caught.*
get back, a return. **b** recover.
get back at, *Informal.* get revenge on.
get behind, a support; endorse. **b** fail to keep up to schedule.
get by, *Informal.* **a** go past. **b** not be noticed or caught. **c** do well enough; manage all right: *They got by on his small salary.*
get down to, a begin: *It took her a long time to get down to work.* **b** reach by removing what stands in the way: *After much questioning of the witness, the lawyer got down to the truth.*
get even, a pay back for a wrong done; obtain revenge (*used with* **with**): *He promised to get even with his sister for twisting his arm.* **b** win back what was lost: *After she had lost twenty marbles, she played all afternoon trying to get even.*
get in, a go in. **b** put in. **c** arrive: *I just got in.* **d** *Informal.* become friendly or familiar (*with*).
get into, a find out about. **b** get access to. **c** come to be in; end up in: *get into trouble.* **d** *Informal.* become interested in: *She got into music at an early age.* **e** put on (clothes).
get it, *Informal.* **a** be reprimanded or punished: *I'll get it if I'm late again.* **b** understand.
get off, a come down from or out of. **b** take off. **c** escape the full punishment deserved: *The naughty boy got off with a scolding.* **d** help to escape. **e** start. **f** put out; issue; send: *I must get this letter off today.* **g** say or express (a joke or funny remark). **h** deliver (a speech).
get on, a go up on or into. **b** put on. **c** advance. **d** manage. **e** succeed. **f** agree. **g** grow older.
get (one's) **own back,** be revenged.
get on for, approach (a time).
get on to, a learn; grasp. **b** communicate with.
get out, a go out. **b** take out. **c** go away. **d** escape. **e** help to escape. **f** become known. **g** publish. **h** find out.
get over, a recover from: *He was a long time getting over his illness.* **b** overcome. **c** *Informal.* make clear or convincing. **d** *Informal.* succeed.
get (something) **over with,** come to grips with and dispose of (something unpleasant).
get set, get ready; prepare.
get (someone) **down,** make downhearted; discourage; depress: *The hot weather was getting him down.*
get there, succeed.
get through, a get to the end of; finish: *She always gets through her homework quickly.* **b** complete or cause to complete successfully: *She got through the test. His friend's help got him through.* **c** make or get a telephone connection: *I tried to phone you but I couldn't get through.* **d** make oneself understood; succeed in communicating: *No one can get through to her when she's angry.*
get to, a manage to talk or communicate with: *I finally got to her last night at midnight.* **b** *Informal.* affect: *Her grief really gets to you, doesn't it?*
get together, *Informal.* **a** bring or come together; meet; assemble. **b** come to an agreement: *The workers and their employer couldn't get together about wages.*
get up, a get out of bed, etc. **b** stand up. **c** prepare; arrange: *She spent all evening getting up the next day's lesson.* **d** dress (someone) up. **e** (*used to command a horse to advance*); giddy up. ⟨ME *gete*(n) < ON *geta*⟩
☛ *Syn.* **1. Get,** OBTAIN, ACQUIRE = come to have something. **Get** = come to have something in some way or by some means, whether or not one wants or tries to gain it: *I got a new car. She got a bad reputation.* **Obtain** usually suggests working hard or trying to get something one wants: *I obtained permission to go.* **Acquire** emphasizes getting possession of something, usually by one's own efforts or actions: *I acquired a reading knowledge of German.*
☛ *Usage.* **Get up (a, b).** See note at RISE.

get•a•way ['gɛtə,wei] *n. Informal.* **1** the act of getting away; escape. **2** the start of a race. **3** (*adjl.*) used for an escape: *a getaway car.*

geth•sem•a•ne [gɛθ'sɛməni] *n.* a place of suffering. ⟨< *Gethsemane,* in the Bible, a garden near Jerusalem, the scene of Jesus' agony, betrayal, and arrest⟩

get–out ['gɛt ,ʌut] *or* [gɛt 'ʌut] *n. Informal.* a way of avoiding a problem.
as all get-out, *Informal.* to an extreme extent: *cold as all get-out.*

get•ter ['gɛtər] *n.* **1** one who or that which gets. **2** a chemically active substance such as magnesium, used in vacuum tubes to clear gases. **3** a sire, especially a begetter of superior offspring. **4** *Cdn.* poisoned bait used in exterminating wolves, gophers, etc.

get–to•geth•er ['gɛt tə,gɛðər] *n. Informal.* an informal social gathering or party.

get–up ['gɛt ,ʌp] *n. Informal.* **1** the way a thing is put together; arrangement; style. **2** dress; costume.

get–up–and–go ['gɛt ʌp ən 'gou] *Informal. n., adj.*
—n. energy; initiative.
—adj. full of energy and initiative; enterprising.

ge•um ['dʒiəm] *n.* any plant of the genus *Geum,* such as the avens. ⟨< L⟩

GeV gigaelectronvolt; one billion electronvolts.

ge•va ['dʒivə] *n.* a plant (*Exocoecaria agallocha*) yielding wood for pulp as newsprint. ⟨origin uncertain⟩

gew•gaw ['gjugɒ] *n., adj. —n.* a showy trifle; gaudy, useless ornament or toy; bauble.

—adj. showy but trifling. ⟨< ME *giuegoue, gugaw*, reduplicated < ?⟩

gey•ser ['gaɪzər] *or* ['gəisər] *n., v. —n.* **1** a spring that sends a column of hot water and steam into the air at intervals. **2** anything that spurts or gushes like a geyser.
—v. spurt or cause to spurt like a geyser. ⟨< Icel. *geysir* a gusher⟩

gey•ser•ite ['gaɪzə,rəit] *or* ['gəisə,rəit] *n.* a type of silica deposited around a geyser.

Gha•na ['gɑnə] *or* ['gænə] *n.* a country in W Africa, since 1957 a member of the Commonwealth. See SENEGAL for map.

Gha•na•ian or **Gha•ni•an** ['gɑniən] *or* [gɑ'neiən] *adj., n.* *—adj.* of or having to do with Ghana or its people.
—n. a native or inhabitant of Ghana.

ghast•ly ['gæstli] *adj.* **-li•er, -li•est;** *adv. —adj.* **1** horrible: *Murder is a ghastly crime.* **2** like a dead person or ghost; deathly pale: *The sick man's face was ghastly.* **3** *Informal.* shocking: *a ghastly failure.*
—adv. in a ghastly manner. ⟨OE *gāstlic* < *gāst* ghost + *-lic* -ly⟩ **—'ghast•li•ness,** *n.*

☛ *Syn. adj.* **1. Ghastly,** GRISLY, HORRIBLE refer to something that causes terror or horror. **Ghastly** suggests a connection or association with death, and emphasizes the frightening or horrifying appearance or nature of what is described: *We saw a ghastly accident.* **Grisly** emphasizes being so ghastly or horrible, and sometimes unearthly or weird, as to cause a person to shudder with horror or dread: *Robbing graves is a grisly occupation.* **Horrible** emphasizes the feeling of horror or abhorrence caused by what is described: *It was a horrible murder.*

ghat or **ghaut** [gɑt] *or* [gɒt] *n.* in India: **1** steps or a stairway leading down to a river; landing place. **2** a mountain pass or range. ⟨< Hind.⟩
☛ *Hom.* GOT [gɒt].

Ghe•ber or **Ghe•bre** ['geibər] *or* ['gibər] *n.* the Muslim word for Zoroastrian.

ghee [gi] *n.* a semiliquid butter clarified by boiling; it is made especially in India, with butter from the milk of cows or buffaloes. ⟨< Hind.⟩

gher•kin ['gɜrkən] *n.* **1** the small, prickly, cucumberlike fruit of an annual vine (*Cucumis anguria*) of the gourd family, used for pickles. **2** the vine itself. **3** the small, immature fruit of a cucumber when pickled. ⟨< earlier Du. *agurkje*, dim. of *agurk* < G < Slavic < Med.Gk., ult. < Iranian *angorah* watermelon⟩

ghet•to ['gɛtou] *n., pl.* **-tos. 1** a part of a city inhabited mainly or entirely by a minority group that is obliged to live there for reasons of poverty, prejudice, or government policy. **2** formerly, a part of a European city where Jews were obliged to live. **3** a part of a city given over to one purpose: *the industrial ghetto.* ⟨< Ital.⟩

ghet•to•ize ['gɛtou,aɪz] *v.* **-ized, -iz•ing.** separate as if in a ghetto.

ghost [goust] *n., v. —n.* **1** the spirit of a dead person. It is supposed to live in another world and appear to living people as a pale, dim, shadowy form. **2** anything pale, dim, or shadowy like a ghost; a faint image; the slightest suggestion: *the ghost of a smile, not a ghost of a chance.* **3** *Informal.* GHOST WRITER. **4** *Television.* a secondary or multiple image resulting from the reflection of a transmitted signal.
give up the ghost, die.
—v. **1** *Informal.* write (a book, etc.) or work as a ghost writer: *Her autobiography was ghosted by a journalist. The journalist had ghosted for several other public figures.* **2** haunt as a ghost does. ⟨OE *gāst*⟩ **—'ghost,like,** *adj.*

☛ *Syn. n.* **1. Ghost,** SPECTRE, APPARITION = an appearance or visible form of someone or something not really present. **Ghost** applies chiefly to the spirit of a dead person: *Hamlet saw his father's ghost.* **Spectre** applies to a ghostly, mysterious, usually frightening shape, something appearing as if by magic: *A spectre flitted through the graveyard.* **Apparition** applies especially to an appearance, often of someone dead or about to die, seeming very real to the person seeing it and impossible to explain or understand: *The apparition of her mother startled her.*

ghost car *Cdn.* an unmarked automobile used by police officers in plain clothes to apprehend persons who are speeding or breaking the law in other ways.

ghost•ly ['goustli] *adj.* **-li•er, -li•est. 1** like a ghost; pale, dim, and shadowy: *In the darkness she seemed to see ghostly forms.* **2** of or having to do with a ghost. **3** *Archaic.* spiritual; religious. **—'ghost•li•ness,** *n.*

ghost town a town that has become empty and lifeless: *When the gold rush was over, the once-flourishing community became a ghost town.*

ghost–write ['goust ,rəit] *v.* **-wrote, -writ•ten, -writ•ing.** write (something) for another who is nominally the author.

ghost writer a person who writes something for another who is nominally the author. Also, **ghost-writer, ghostwriter.**

ghoul [gul] *n.* **1** in Oriental stories, a horrible demon, believed to feed on corpses. **2** a person who robs graves or corpses. **3** a person who enjoys what is revolting, brutal, and horrible. ⟨< Arabic *ghūl* ogre, monster⟩

ghoul•ish ['gulɪʃ] *adj.* like a ghoul; revolting, brutal, and horrible. **—'ghoul•ish•ly,** *adv.* **—'ghoul•ish•ness,** *n.*

GHQ General Headquarters.

GHz gigahertz.

G.I. or **GI** ['dʒi 'aɪ] *adj., n., pl.* **G.I.'s, GI's,** or **GIs** ['dʒi 'aɪz] *U.S. —adj.* **1** government issue: *G.I. shoes, G.I. socks.* **2** *Informal.* conforming to regulations; standard: *G.I. uniform.*
—n. Informal. soldier. ⟨abbreviation of *G*overnment *I*ssue⟩

Gi gilbert, a unit of magnetomotive force. ⟨after William *Gilbert* (c. 1540-1603), English physician⟩

gi•ant ['dʒaɪənt] *n., adj. —n.* **1** a legendary being having human form, but superhuman size and strength. **2** a person or thing of unusual size, strength, importance, etc. **3** an unusually large star.
—adj. like a giant; unusually big and strong; huge. ⟨ME < OF *geant* < L *gigas, gigantis* < Gk.⟩

giant anteater ANT BEAR.

giant arborvitae or **giant cedar** WESTERN RED CEDAR.

gi•ant•ess ['dʒaɪəntɪs] *n.* a female giant.

gi•ant•ism ['dʒaɪən,tɪzəm] *n.* gigantism.

giant panda PANDA (def. 1).

giant powder an explosive resembling dynamite, used in blasting.

giant sequoia a tall evergreen tree (*Sequoia gigantea*) found in mountain areas of S California.

giant star any of a class of very bright and unusually large stars.

giaour [dʒaʊr] *n. Islam.* a person who does not believe in the Muslim religion. ⟨< Turkish *giaur* < Iranian *gaur*⟩

gi•ar•di•a•sis [,dʒiɑr'daɪəsɪs] *or* [dʒɑr'daɪəsɪs] *n.* a parasitic intestinal infection caused by a protozoan (*Giardia lamblia*). It causes severe pain and diarrhea. ⟨< NL *giardia* genus name (after A.M. *Giard* (d. 1908), French biologist) + L *-asis* suffix, a condition resembling or characterized by⟩

gib¹ [gɪb] *n.* a piece of wood or metal used to hold part of a structure in place. ⟨< ME *gibbe* a swelling < L *gibba* a hump < *gibbus* bent⟩

gib² [gɪb] *n.* a male cat. ⟨< ME *gibbe*⟩

gib•ber ['dʒɪbər] *or* ['gɪbər] *v., n. —v.* chatter senselessly; talk rapidly and indistinctly: *The monkeys gibbered angrily at each other.*
—n. senseless chattering; rapid, indistinct talking. ⟨imitative⟩

gib•be•rel•lic acid [,dʒɪbə'rɛlɪk] a substance obtained from fungi, used to promote the rapid growth of seedlings.

gib•be•rel•lin [,dʒɪbə'rɛlɪn] *n.* a form of gibberellic acid obtained from plants other than fungi. ⟨< NL *gibberella* (dim. of L *gibber* hump on the back < *gibbus* bent) + *-in*⟩

gib•ber•ish ['dʒɪbərɪʃ] *or* ['gɪbərɪʃ] *n.* meaningless chatter or unintelligible language: *the gibberish of monkeys.* ⟨imitative⟩

gib•bet ['dʒɪbɪt] *n., v.* **-bet•ed, -bet•ing.** *—n.* **1** an upright post with a projecting arm at the top, from which the bodies of criminals were hung after execution. **2** gallows.
—v. **1** hang on a gibbet. **2** hold up to public scorn or ridicule. **3** put to death by hanging. ⟨ME < OF *gibet*, dim. of *gibe* club⟩

gib•bon ['gɪbən] *n.* any of a genus (*Hylobates*) of small, long-armed, humanlike apes found in the forests of S and SE Asia. Gibbons live mainly in trees but on the ground they walk upright. ⟨< F⟩

A gibbon

gib•bo•si•ty [gɪ'bɒsəti] *n.* **1** a swelling. **2** gibbous condition.

gib•bous ['gɪbəs] *adj.* **1** curved out; bulging. **2** referring to the moon or a planet in the phase during which more than half but less than the whole disk is illuminated. **3** humpbacked. ⟨< L *gibbosus* < *gibbus* hump⟩ **—'gib•bous•ly,** *adv.* **—'gib•bous•ness,** *n.*

gibe or **jibe** [dʒaɪb] *v.* **gibed, gib•ing;** *n.* jeer; scoff; sneer. ⟨? < OF *giber* handle roughly < *gibe* staff⟩ **—'gib•er,** *n.* **—'gib•ing•ly,** *adv.*

gib•let ['dʒɪblɪt] *n.* **1 giblets,** *pl.* the heart, liver, and gizzard of a fowl. **2** (*adjl.*) made from giblets: *giblet gravy.* ⟨< OF *gibelet* stew of game⟩

Gi•bral•tar [dʒə'brɒltər] *n.* a strongly fortified place; impregnable stronghold. ⟨< *Gibraltar,* a British fortress built on the Rock of Gibraltar, a huge hill of rock at the southern tip of Spain.⟩

G.I.C. or **GIC** guaranteed investment certificate.

gid [gɪd] *n.* a sheep disease caused by the presence of tapeworm larvae in the brain or spinal cord. ⟨< ME *gidie* < OE *gydig* insane, possessed by a god⟩

gid•dee ['gɪdi] *n. Cdn.* a breed of dog used by certain Athabascan First Nations people as a draft animal. ⟨< Athabascan⟩
☛ *Hom.* GIDDY.

gid•dy ['gɪdi] *adj.* **-di•er, -di•est. 1** having a confused, whirling feeling in one's head; dizzy. **2** likely to make dizzy; causing dizziness: *a giddy height.* **3** rarely or never serious; flighty; heedless: *Nobody can tell what that giddy youth will do next.* ⟨OE *gydig* mad, possessed (by an evil spirit) < *god* a god⟩ **—'gid•di•ly,** *adv.* **—'gid•di•ness,** *n.*
☛ *Hom.* GIDDEE.

gift [gɪft] *n.* **1** something given; a present: *a birthday gift.* **2** the act of giving: *The house came to her by gift from an uncle.* **3** the power or right of giving: *The job is within her gift.* **4** a natural ability; special talent: *a gift for painting.* **5** (*adjl.*) that is a gift or suitable for giving: *gift books.*
look a gift horse in the mouth, question the value of a gift. ⟨ME < ON *gipt.* Akin to GIVE.⟩

gift•ed ['gɪftɪd] *adj.* having natural ability or special talent: *a gifted musician.*

gift–wrap ['gɪft ,ræp] *v.* **-wrapped, -wrap•ping;** *n.* *—v.* wrap for presentation as a gift, using decorative paper, ribbon, etc.
—n. decorative paper, etc. suitable for wrapping gifts.

gig[1] [gɪg] *n., v.* **gigged, gig•ging.** *—n.* **1** a light, open, two-wheeled carriage drawn by one horse. **2** a light, narrow ship's boat moved by oars or sails, often for the use of the captain in going to and from shore. **3** a long, light rowboat used especially for racing. **4** a machine for raising the nap on cloth.
—v. **1** travel in a gig. **2** raise the nap of (cloth) with a gig. ⟨origin uncertain⟩

gig[2] [gɪg] *n., v.* **gigged, gig•ging.** *—n.* a fish spear; harpoon.
—v. spear (fish) with a gig. ⟨short for *fishgig,* ult. < Sp. *fisga* harpoon⟩

gig[3] [gɪg] *n. Slang.* an engagement for a band, singer, etc. to perform, especially for one night only.

giga– *SI prefix.* one billion. A gigametre is one billion metres. Compare KILO-, MEGA-. *Symbol:* G ⟨< Gk. *gigas* giant⟩

gi•ga•byte ['gɪgə,bəit] *or* ['dʒɪgə,bəit] *n. Computer technology.* A measure of the storage capacity of a computer system, roughly equal to one billion bytes. *Abbrev.:* GB

gi•ga•hertz ['gɪgə,hɜrts] *or* ['dʒɪgə,hɜrts] *n.* one billion hertz.

gi•gan•tesque [,dʒaɪgæn'tɛsk] *adj.* suitable for a giant; huge.

gi•gan•tic [dʒaɪ'gæntɪk] *adj.* **1** like a giant: *Paul Bunyan was a gigantic logger.* **2** huge; enormous: *a gigantic building project.* ⟨< L *gigas, gigantis* giant. See GIANT.⟩ **—gi'gan•ti•cal•ly,** *adv.*

gi•gan•tism [dʒaɪ'gæntɪzəm] *n.* **1** abnormal growth or size. **2** *Medicine.* pathological overdevelopment caused by malfunction of the pituitary gland; acromegaly. Also, **giantism.**

gi•ga•volt ['gɪgə,voult] *or* ['dʒɪgə,voult] *n.* one billion volts.

gig•gle ['gɪgəl] *v.* **-gled, -gling;** *n.* *—v.* laugh in a silly or nervous way.
—n. a silly or nervous laugh. ⟨imitative⟩ **—'gig•gler,** *n.* **—'gig•gling•ly,** *adv.*

gig•gly ['gɪgli] *adj.* having a tendency to giggle.

GIGO *Computer technology.* garbage in, garbage out.

gig•o•lo ['dʒɪgəlou] *or* ['ʒɪgəlou] *n., pl.* **-los. 1** a man who is paid for being a dancing partner or escort for a woman. **2** a man who is supported by a woman. ⟨< F⟩

gig•ot ['dʒɪgət] *or* ['ʒɪgou] *n.* **1** a leg-of-mutton sleeve. **2** a leg of mutton, veal, etc. ⟨< F⟩

gigue [ʒig] JIG (def. 1).

Gi•la monster ['hilə] a large, poisonous lizard (*Heloderma suspectum*) found in the SW United States and N Mexico, having a stout body with black and pink, or black and orange, beadlike scales. It grows to about 50 cm long. ⟨after *Gila* River, Arizona⟩

gil•bert ['gɪlbərt] *n.* an electromagnetic unit of magnetomotive force. *Abbrev.:* Gi ⟨after William *Gilbert* (1540-1603), English physician⟩

gild[1] [gɪld] *v.* **1** cover with a thin layer of gold or gold-coloured material; make golden. **2** make (something) shine as if with gold: *The light from the setting sun gilded the windows.* **3** make (something) seem better than it is.
gild the lily, a adorn something that is beautiful enough not to need adornment; adorn unnecessarily. **b** praise something fine or beautiful excessively or unnecessarily. ⟨OE *gyldan* < *gold* gold⟩
☛ *Hom.* GUILD.

gild[2] [gɪld] See GUILD.

gild•ed ['gɪldɪd] *adj., v.* *—adj.* golden. Also, **gilt.**
—v. pt. and pp. of GILD.

gild•ing ['gɪldɪŋ] *n., v.* *—n.* **1** a thin layer of gold or gold-coloured material with which a thing is gilded. **2** an attractive outer appearance hiding an unattractive or unpleasant reality or fact. **3** the art or process of gilding.
—v. ppr. of GILD.

gil•guy ['gɪlgaɪ] *n.* **1** a temporary rope or rigging on a ship. **2** a gaudy, useless trinket; gimcrack. ⟨? < *guy*[1]⟩

gil•ia ['dʒɪliə] *n.* a wildflower of arid regions from Saskatchewan to British Columbia and south to Chile, having tubular red flowers that attract hummingbirds, and an unpleasant smell; skunk flower.

gill[1] [gɪl] *n., v.* *—n.* **1** an organ of aquatic animals such as fish, tadpoles, or crabs, that enables them to obtain oxygen from the water. **2** any of the thin, leaflike, radiating structures on the underside of the cap of a mushroom. **3 gills,** *pl.* **a** the red, hanging flesh under the throat of a fowl; wattle. **b** the flesh below a person's jaws.
green about the gills, of a person, looking sick.
—v. **1** catch (fish) by the gills in a gill net. **2** clean (fish). **3** cut away the gills of (a mushroom). ⟨ME < ON; cf. Swedish *gäl*⟩

gill[2] [dʒɪl] *n.* a unit for measuring liquids, equal to 142 mL. ⟨ME < OF *gille* wine measure⟩

gill fungus [gɪl] any fleshy fungus with gills under its cap.

gil•lie ['gɪli] *n.* **1** in the Scottish Highlands, a man who acts as an attendant or guide for a hunter or fisher. **2** formerly, a male servant or attendant to a Highland chief. Also, **gilly.** ⟨< Scots Gaelic *gille* lad⟩

gill net [gɪl] a net suspended upright in the water, for catching fish by entangling their gills in its meshes.

gill•net ['gɪl,nɛt] *v.* **-net•ted, -net•ting.** catch fish by using a gill net.

gill•net•ter ['gɪl,nɛtər] *n.* **1** a person who fishes with a gill net. **2** a boat used for gillnetting.

gill slit [gɪl] an opening connecting with the pharynx, found in the embryonic stage of vertebrates.

gil•ly ['gɪli] *n., pl.* **-lies.** See GILLIE.

gil•ly•flow•er ['dʒɪli,flaʊər] *n.* any of various clove-scented flowers, especially the clove pink, stock, or wallflower. Also, **gilliflower.** ⟨ME < OF *gilofre* < L < Gk. *karyophyllon* clove tree < *karyon* clove + *phyllon* leaf⟩

Gil•son•ite ['gɪlsə,nəit] *n. Trademark.* a black bitumen found in Utah, used for waterproof coatings. ⟨after S.H. *Gilson* of Salt Lake City, Utah⟩

gilt[1] [gɪlt] *adj., n.* *—adj.* gilded.
—n. a thin layer of gold or gold-coloured material with which a thing is gilded; gilding.
gilt on the gingerbread, an additional adornment to something that is already sufficiently attractive.
☛ *Hom.* GUILT.

gilt[2] [gɪlt] *n.* a young sow that has not farrowed. ⟨< ME *gilte* < ON *gyltr*⟩
☛ *Hom.* GUILT.

gilt–edged ['gɪlt ,ɛdʒd] *adj.* **1** having gilded edges. **2** of the very best quality: *gilt-edged stocks and securities.*

gilt•head ['gɪlt,hɛd] *n.* any of several saltwater fishes, as the European porgy (*Sparus aurata*), having gold marks on the head.

gim•bals ['dʒɪmbəlz] *or* ['gɪmbəlz] *n.pl.* an arrangement for keeping an object horizontal. A ship's compass is supported on gimbals made of a pair of rings pivoted to swing, one within the other, on axes at right angles to each other. ⟨ult. < OF *gemel* twin < L *gemellus*⟩

gim•crack ['dʒɪm,kræk] *n., adj.* *—n.* a showy, useless trifle.
—adj. showy but useless. ⟨origin uncertain⟩

gim•el ['gɪməl] *n.* the fourth letter of the Hebrew alphabet. See table of alphabets in the Appendix.

gim•let¹ ['gɪmlɪt] *n., v.* —*n.* a small hand tool for boring small holes in wood, consisting of a shaft having a screw point and attached to a crosswise handle.
—*v.* make a hole in, with or as if with a gimlet. ⟨ME < OF *guimbelet*⟩

gim•let² ['gɪmlɪt] *n.* a cocktail made with vodka or gin, lime juice, and sugar. ⟨< *gimlet¹*, coined on model of *screwdriver*, another cocktail⟩

gim•let–eyed ['gɪmlɪt ,aɪd] *adj.* having sharp and piercing eyes.

gim•mal ['gɪməl] *or* ['dʒɪməl] *n.* a ring made of two interlocking rings. ⟨< ME *gemelles* twins < L *gemellus*, dim. of *geminus* twin⟩

gim•mick ['gɪmɪk] *n., v.* —*n.* **1** *Informal.* any small device, especially one used secretly or in a tricky manner. **2** a deceptive thing or quality; trick. **3** something to attract attention; stunt. **4** a secret method of controlling a gambling mechanism such as a roulette wheel.
—*v.* furnish with gimmicks or gadgets to make more enticing. ⟨origin uncertain⟩ —**'gim•mick•y,** *adj.*

gim•mic•kry ['gɪmɪkri] *n.* **1** gimmicks collectively. **2** the use of gimmicks.

gimp¹ [gɪmp] *n.* a braidlike trimming made of silk, worsted, or cotton, sometimes stiffened with wire, used on garments, curtains, furniture, etc. ⟨< F *guimpe* < OF < Gmc. Doublet of GUIMPE.⟩
☛ *Hom.* GUIMPE.

gimp² [gɪmp] *n. Slang.* pep.
☛ *Hom.* GUIMPE.

gin¹ [dʒɪn] *n.* **1** a strong, colourless alcoholic drink, made from grain and usually flavoured with juniper berries. **2** a similar liquor flavoured with aniseed. ⟨shortened form of *geneva* liquor⟩
☛ *Hom.* DJINN.

gin² [dʒɪn] *n., v.* **ginned, gin•ning.** —*n.* **1** a machine for separating cotton from its seeds. **2** a trap; snare. **3** a machine used to raise heavy things.
—*v.* **1** separate (cotton) from its seeds. **2** trap; snare. ⟨ME < OF (*en*)*gin* engine⟩ —**'gin•ner,** *n.*
☛ *Hom.* DJINN.

gin³ [dʒɪn] *n.* GIN RUMMY.
☛ *Hom.* DJINN.

gin⁴ [gɪn] *v.* **gan, gun, gin•ning.** *Archaic or poetic.* begin. ⟨OE *ginnan*, short for *aginnan*, var. of *onginnan*⟩

gin•ger ['dʒɪndʒər] *n., adj., v.* —*n.* **1** the aromatic, hot-tasting underground stem of an East Indian plant (*Zingiber officinale*) used as a spice, sweetmeat (preserved with sugar or syrup), or flavouring for beverages, and also used in medicine. **2** the perennial, reedlike plant which produces this underground stem, cultivated throughout the tropics. **3** any of several related plants. **4** (*adjl.*) designating the family (Zingiberaceae) of plants that includes ginger and cardamom. **5** *Informal.* liveliness; energy: *That horse has plenty of ginger.* **6** a light, reddish brown colour.
—*adj.* having the colour ginger: *ginger hair.*
—*v.* **1** treat or flavour with ginger. **2** *Informal.* make spirited or enliven: *The new manager soon gingered up the company.* ⟨OE *gingiber* < LL < L *zingiber* < Gk. *zingiberis* < Prakrit *singabēra* ? < Malayalam *inchi-ver*⟩

ginger ale a non-alcoholic, sweetened, carbonated drink flavoured with ginger.

ginger beer a drink similar to ginger ale, but made with fermenting ginger and having a stronger taste.

gin•ger•bread ['dʒɪndʒər,brɛd] *n.* **1** a cake flavoured with molasses and ginger. **2** a kind of cookie made of similar ingredients, usually cut into various shapes and often decorated with icing. **3** intricate wooden decoration, such as fretwork or carving on the gables of houses, etc. Many old houses, especially in central and eastern Canada, are trimmed with gingerbread. **4** (*adjl.*) of or designating such decoration. **5** (*adjl.*) of ornamentation on furniture, etc.; tasteless and gaudy.

gingerbread palm an African palm tree (*Hyphaene thebaica*) having fruit tasting like gingerbread.

Ginger Group *Cdn.* formerly, a number of progressives (six, later ten) in the House of Commons from 1924-1932, so called because of their spirited questioning of government policy and their energetic championing of the interests of the farmer and of labour.

gin•ger•ly ['dʒɪndʒərli] *adv. or adj.* with extreme care or caution. —**'gin•ger•li•ness,** *n.*

gin•ger•snap ['dʒɪndʒər,snæp] *n.* a thin, crisp cookie flavoured with ginger and molasses.

gin•ger•y ['dʒɪndʒəri] *adj.* **1** like ginger; hot and sharp; spicy. **2** light reddish or brownish yellow. **3** alert; full of vigour.

ging•ham ['gɪŋəm] *n.* **1** a plain-woven fabric usually of cotton or a cotton blend and usually having a woven two-colour pattern of checks or stripes. **2** (*adjl.*) made of gingham: *a gingham dress.* ⟨< F *guingan* < Malay *ginggang*, originally, striped⟩

gin•gi•val ['dʒɪndʒəvəl] *or* [dʒɪn'dʒaɪvəl] *adj.* **1** of or having to do with the gums. **2** *Phonetics.* referring to the ridge behind and above the upper front teeth; alveolar. ⟨< NL *gingivalis* < L *gingiva* gum⟩

gin•gi•vi•tis [,dʒɪndʒə'vəitɪs] *n.* inflammation of the gums.

gink•go ['gɪŋkou] *or* ['dʒɪŋkou] *n., pl.* **-goes.** a large deciduous tree (*Ginkgo biloba*) native to China and Japan but widely cultivated in temperate regions as an ornamental tree, having fan-shaped leaves and yellow fruit. The ginkgo, the only living species of the order Ginkgoales, is often called a 'living fossil' because it does not exist in the wild; it has apparently escaped extinction because since ancient times it has been cultivated in Chinese temple gardens. ⟨< Japanese⟩

gin mill [dʒɪn] *Slang.* saloon; lounge.

gin rummy [dʒɪn] a kind of rummy in which players form sequences and matching combinations, laying down their hands when having ten or fewer points. ⟨origin uncertain⟩

gin•seng ['dʒɪnsɛŋ] *n.* **1** either of two herbs (*Panax schinseng* of China and *P. quinquefolius* of North America) having leaves with five lobes, scarlet berries, and a thick, forked, aromatic root used in medicine, especially in China. **2** the root of this plant. **3** (*adjl.*) designating the family (Araliaceae) of plants that includes the ginsengs and ivy. ⟨< Chinese *jên shên* (*jên* man, from a frequent shape of the root)⟩

Gio•con•da [dʒou'kɒndə] *or* [,dʒiə'kɒndə] *n.* **La Gioconda,** a famous portrait usually called the *Mona Lisa*, painted by Leonardo da Vinci (1452-1519), Italian painter and scientist. It hangs in the Louvre in Paris, France.

La Gioconda (the Mona Lisa)

gio•co•so [dʒou'kousou] *adv. Music.* in a playful, lively manner. ⟨< Ital. < L *jocosus* < *jocus* a jest, joke⟩

Gip•sy or **gip•sy** ['dʒɪpsi] *n., pl.* **-sies;** *adj.* See GYPSY.

gipsy moth See GYPSY MOTH.

gi•raffe [dʒə'ræf] *n.* a large, hoofed, cud-chewing, African mammal (*Giraffa camelopardalis*) having a very long neck and legs and a beige coat with reddish brown spots. It is the tallest of all living mammals, reaching a height of 5.5 m or more. ⟨< F < Arabic *zarāfah*⟩

Gi•raffe [dʒə'ræf] *n.* the northern constellation Camelopardis.

gir•an•dole ['dʒirən,doul] *n.* **1** a decorative branched candleholder attached to a wall. **2** a rotating jet of water. **3** a rotating firework. **4** an earring consisting of a large precious stone surrounded by smaller ones. ⟨< F *girandole* < Ital. *girandola* fireworks circle, dim. of *giranda* fire circle < *girare* turn in a circle < LL *gyrare* turn < Gk. *gyros* ring⟩

gi•ra•sol ['dʒirə,sɒl] *n.* **1** an opal. **2** JERUSALEM ARTICHOKE. ⟨< F < Ital. *girasole* < *girare* to turn + *sole* sun⟩

gird [gɜrd] *v.* **girt** or **gird•ed, gird•ing. 1** put a belt or band around. **2** fasten with a belt or band. **3** surround; enclose. **4** get ready for action: *They girded themselves for battle.* **5** clothe; furnish; equip, etc. **6** endow with some quality: *girded with honesty.* ⟨OE *gyrdan*⟩

gird•er ['gɜrdər] *n.* a main supporting beam, usually horizontal. Steel girders are often used to make the framework of bridges and tall buildings. ⟨< *gird*⟩

gir•dle ['gɜrdəl] *n., v.* **-dled, -dling.** —*n.* **1** a belt, sash, cord, etc. worn around the waist. **2** anything that surrounds or encloses: *a girdle of trees around the pond.* **3** a support like a corset worn about the hips or waist. **4** a ring made around a tree trunk, etc.

by cutting the bark. **5** the edge of a gem held by the setting. **6** the pelvic arch.
—*v.* **1** form a girdle around; encircle: *Wide roads girdle the city.* **2** *Cdn.* cut away the bark so as to make a ring around (a tree, branch, etc.). **3** put a girdle on or around. ⟨OE *gyrdel* < *gyrdan* gird⟩

gird•ler ['gɜrdlər] *n.* **1** a maker of girdles. **2** a person who or thing that encircles or cuts away bark. **3** any insect that chews rings around the stems of plants.

girl [gɜrl] *n.* **1** a female child. **2** *Informal.* a young, unmarried woman. **3** a female servant. **4** *Informal.* sweetheart. ⟨ME *gurle, girle* child, young person; origin uncertain⟩

girl Friday a female assistant or aid with miscellaneous duties.

girl•friend ['gɜrl,frɛnd] *n.* **1** a female companion of a boy or man; sweetheart or lover: *Does he have a girlfriend?* **2** a girl who is one's friend.

Girl Guides **1** a non-political, non-denominational organization for girls and young women whose aim is to help them to learn co-operation, leadership, self-reliance, and consideration for others, and to develop physical fitness and spiritual values, in order to become responsible, resourceful, and happy members of society. The Girl Guides of Canada has five programs for different ages: Sparks, Brownies, Guides, Pathfinders, and Cadets and Rangers. **2 Girl Guide**, a member, aged nine to twelve, of the Girl Guides.

girl•hood ['gɜrl,hʊd] *n.* **1** the time or condition of being a girl: *The old woman recalled her girlhood with pleasure.* **2** girls as a class.

girl•ish ['gɜrlɪʃ] *adj.* **1** of a girl. **2** like that of a girl. **3** proper or suitable for girls: *She thought she was too old now for such girlish games.* **—'girl•ish•ly,** *adv.* **—'girl•ish•ness,** *n.*

girt[1] [gɜrt] *v.* a pt. and a pp. of GIRD.

girt[2] [gɜrt] *v.* **1** put a belt, girdle, or girth around; gird. **2** fasten with a belt, girdle, or girth. **3** measure around something or someone. ⟨See GIRD⟩

girth [gɜrθ] *n., v.* —*n.* **1** the measure around anything: *a man of large girth, the girth of a tree.* **2** a girth that keeps a saddle, pack, etc. in place on a horse's back. See HARNESS and SADDLE for pictures.
—*v.* **1** measure in girth. **2** fasten with a girth. **3** ring; encircle: *The belt girthed her waist.* ⟨ME < ON *gjörth* girdle. Akin to GIRD.⟩

GIS *Computer technology.* geographical information system.

gist [dʒɪst] *n.* **1** the essential part; real point or main idea; the substance of an argument. **2** *Law.* grounds for legal action. ⟨< OF *gist* (it) consists (in), depends (on) < L *jacet* it lies⟩

Git•chi Man•i•tou ['gɪtʃi 'mænɪ,tu] *Cdn.* the supreme deity of the Crees, Ojibwas, and related peoples, identified by some whites and Christian First Nations people with God. ⟨< Algonkian 'Great Spirit'⟩

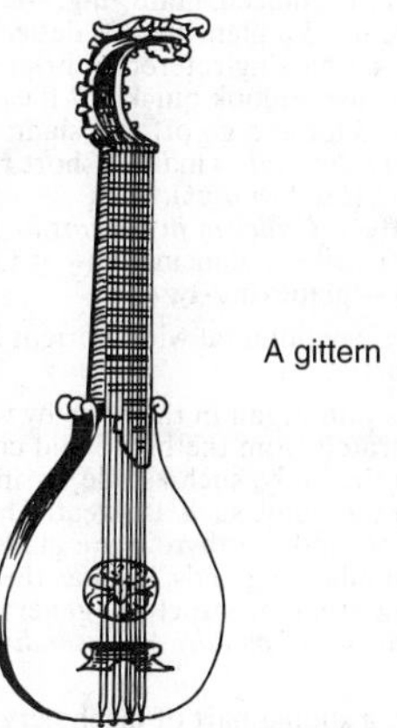

A gittern

git•tern ['gɪtərn] *n.* an old musical instrument with wire strings, resembling a guitar. ⟨ME < OF *guiterne*⟩

give [gɪv] *v.* **gave, giv•en, giv•ing;** *n.* —*v.* **1** hand over as a present; make a present of: *My brother gave me his watch.* **2** hand over; deliver: *to give a person into custody, to give one's word.* **3** hand over in return for something: *I gave it to her for $5.* **4** let have; cause to have: *Give me permission to leave. Please give me a drink.* **5** deal; administer (to): *She gives hard blows even in play. She gave the ball a kick.* **6** offer; present: *This newspaper gives a full story of the game. She gave a lecture.* **7** put forth; make; do; utter: *He gave a cry of pain.* **8** furnish; supply: *to give aid to the enemy.* **9** produce; yield; deliver: *The garden gives enough tomatoes for us and all our friends.* **10** cause; create: *Don't give the teacher any trouble.* **11** relinquish; surrender: *to give ground.* **12** yield to pressure or force: *The lock gave when she battered the door.* **13** provide a view or passage; open; lead: *This window gives onto the courtyard.* **14** make a donation: *Please give to this cause.* **15** host (a party, social function, etc.): *They gave a party for their daughter's birthday.*
give and take, exchange evenly or fairly.
give away, a give as a present. **b** give as a bride: *The bride's father gave her away.* **c** cause to become known; reveal; betray: *The spy gave away secrets to the enemy.*
give back, return: *Give back the book you borrowed.*
give in, a stop fighting and admit defeat; yield. **b** hand in: *He gave in his history project when it was due.*
give it to, *Informal.* **a** beat; punish. **b** scold.
give off, send out; put forth.
give or take, add or subtract (a few): *The distance is two kilometres, give or take a few metres.*
give out, a send out; put forth: *The roses gave out a sweet smell.* **b** distribute: *The boys gave out the handbills.* **c** make known: *The news was given out at midnight.* **d** become used up: *The food gave out during the famine.* **e** become worn out or exhausted: *The old man's strength gave out during the long walk. The engine finally gave out.*
give over, a hand over; deliver. **b** stop.
give rise to, cause.
give up, a hand over; deliver; surrender. **b** stop having or doing. **c** stop trying: *Don't give up now; we're almost there.* **d** have no more hope for: *They've given her up for dead.* **e** devote entirely: *He gave himself up to his studies.*
what gives? *Informal.* what's going on?
—*n.* a yielding to force or pressure; elasticity: *You need a fabric with give for this pattern.* ⟨ME *give(n)* < *yive(n)*; initial *g* in ME form influenced by ON *gefa* give⟩ **—'giv•er,** *n.*

➡ *Syn. v.* **Give,** PRESENT, CONFER = hand over or bestow something as a gift. **Give** is the general word: *He gave me these books.* **Present** = give in a formal way, often with ceremony: *The Board of trade presented a trophy to the football team.* **Confer** = give in a kindly or courteous way, as to an inferior, or as an honour or favour: *She conferred her smiles on the admiring crowd.*

give–and–take ['gɪv ən 'teik] *n.* **1** an even or fair exchange; mutual concession. **2** good-natured banter; exchange of talk.

give•a•way ['gɪvə,wei] *n. Informal.* **1** an unintentional revelation; exposure; betrayal. **2** a radio or television show in which contestants participate and receive prizes. **3** anything given away or sold at a cheap price to promote business, good relations, etc.

giveaway show or **program** GIVEAWAY (def. 2).

give•back ['gɪv,bæk] *n.* in labour relations, a voluntary reduction in wages in exchange for other benefits.

giv•en ['gɪvən] *adj., v., n.—adj.* **1** stated; fixed; specified: *You must finish the test in a given time.* **2** assigned as a basis of calculating, reasoning, etc.: *Given that the radius is 19 cm, find the circumference.*
—*v.* pp. of GIVE.
given to, inclined or disposed toward: *The old soldier was given to boasting.*
—*n.* **1** something taken for granted: *The minimum wage is a given.* **2** any fact assumed to be correct or accepted as a commonplace: *It is a given that children must eventually leave their parents.*

given name a personal name given to a person as a child, and used especially by the person's friends and family: Gordon *and* Charles *are the given names of Gordon Charles McRae*; McRae *is his surname, or last name.*

giz•mo ['gɪzmou] *n.* a word used for the name of an object that one cannot recall.

giz•zard ['gɪzərd] *n.* **1** a bird's second stomach, where the food from the first stomach is ground up. **2** a muscular organ in insects and earthworms that is posterior to the crop and serves to grind the food. ⟨ME < OF *gister,* ult. < L *gigeria* cooked entrails of a fowl⟩

Gk. Greek.

gla•bel•la [glə'bɛlə] *n., pl.* **gla•bel•lae** [-i] *or* [-aɪ] the area between the eyebrows, usually hairless, above the nose. ⟨< NL < L fem. of *glabellus* without hair < *glaber* smooth, bald⟩

gla•brous ['gleibrəs] *adj.* without hair or down; smooth: *Nasturtiums have glabrous stems.* ⟨< L *glaber* smooth⟩

gla•cé [glæ'sei] *adj., v.* **-céed, -céing.** *—adj.* **1** coated with a glaze of sugar. **2** frozen. **3** finished with a glossy surface: *glacé silk.*
—v. glaze with sugar. ⟨< F *glacé,* pp. of *glacer* impart a gloss to⟩

gla•cial ['gleiʃəl] *adj.* **1** of ice or glaciers; having much ice or many glaciers. **2** relating to a glacial epoch or period. **3** made by the pressure and movement of ice or glaciers: *a glacial plain.* **4** like ice; very cold; icy: *She gave him a glacial stare.* **5** moving as slowly as a glacier: *She crept along at glacial speed.* **6** *Chemistry.* resembling ice in its appearance, especially of acids, such as pure acetic acid, that form crystals a little below room temperature. ⟨< L *glacialis* < *glacies* ice⟩ **—'gla•cial•ly,** *adv.*

gla•cial•ist ['gleiʃəlɪst] *n.* glaciologist.

gla•ci•ate ['gleiʃi,eit] *or* ['gleisi,eit] *v.* **-at•ed, -at•ing. 1** cover with ice or glaciers. **2** expose to or change by the action of glaciers. **3** freeze. **—,gla•ci'a•tion,** *n.*

gla•cier ['gleiʃər] *or* ['gleisjər] *n.* a large mass of ice formed from snow on high ground wherever winter snowfalls exceed summer melting. It moves very slowly down a mountain or along a valley. ⟨< F *glacier* < *glace* ice < L *glacies*⟩

glacier lily a plant (*Erythronium grandiflorum*) of the lily family found in the mountains of W North America, having yellow flowers that appear in May and June, often before the snow has disappeared; snow lily.

gla•ci•o•log•i•cal [,gleiʃiə'lɒdʒəkəl] *or* [,gleisiə'lɒdʒəkəl] *adj.* of or having to do with glaciers or glaciology.

gla•ci•ol•o•gist [,gleiʃi'ɒlədʒɪst] *or* [,gleisi'ɒlədʒɪst] *n.* a person trained in glaciology, especially one whose work it is.

gla•ci•ol•o•gy [,gleiʃi'ɒlədʒi] *or* [,gleisi'ɒlədʒi] *n.* the science that deals with glaciers and glaciation. ⟨< F < L *glacies* + E *-logy*⟩

gla•cis ['gleisɪs], ['glæsɪs], *or* ['glæsi] *n., pl.* **glacis** [-siz] *or* **glacises** [-sɪsɪz]. **1** a gentle slope. **2** in fortification, a bank of earth in front of a counterscarp, having a gradual slope toward the field or open country. ⟨< F *glacis,* originally, slippery place < *glacer* freeze, make icy < *glace* ice⟩

glad¹ [glæd] *adj.* **glad•der, glad•dest. 1** happy; feeling joy: *I'm glad you could come. I'll be glad when exams are over.* **2** bringing joy; very pleasant: *glad news.* **3** caused by or expressing happiness: *We heard her glad shout when she saw us.* **4** very willing: *I'd be glad to help out.* **5** bright and cheerful. ⟨OE *glæd* bright, shining⟩ **—'glad•ly,** *adv.* **—'glad•ness,** *n.*
☛ *Syn.* **1. Glad,** HAPPY = feeling pleasure or joy. **Glad,** which is seldom used before the noun when describing people (as distinct from their looks, etc.), particularly suggests feeling contented and filled with pleasure or delight: *She was glad to see him.* **Happy** particularly suggests feeling deeply and fully contented or satisfied and at peace, or filled with joy: *He will never be happy until he has paid all his debts.*

glad² [glæd] *n. Informal.* gladiolus.

glad•den ['glædən] *v.* make or become glad: *Her heart was gladdened by the good news.* **—'glad•den•er,** *n.*
☛ *Syn.* See note at CHEER.

glade [gleid] *n.* an open space in a wood or forest. ⟨probably related to GLAD¹⟩

glad hand a very warm welcome.

glad–hand ['glæd ,hænd] *v.* give a very warm welcome to.

glad•i•ate ['gleidiɪt] *or* ['gleidi,eit] *adj. Botany.* shaped like a sword.

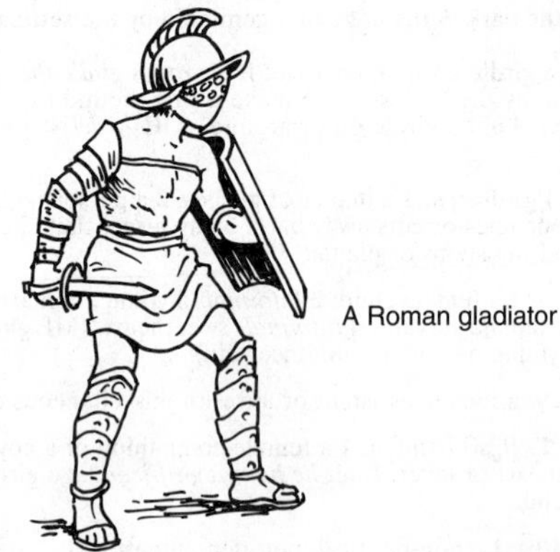
A Roman gladiator

glad•i•a•tor ['glædi,eitər] *n.* **1** in ancient Rome, a slave, captive, or paid fighter who fought at the public shows. **2** a person who argues, fights, wrestles, etc. with great skill. ⟨< L *gladiator* < *gladius* sword⟩

glad•i•a•to•ri•al [,glædiə'tɔriəl] *adj.* of or having to do with gladiators.

glad•i•o•la [,glædi'oulə] *n., pl.* **-la** *or* **-las.** gladiolus.

glad•i•o•lus [,glædi'ouləs] *n., pl.* **-li** [-lai] *or* [-li]. **1** any of a genus (*Gladiolus*) of plant of the iris family that grow from bulblike underground stems, having stiff, sword-shaped leaves and spikes of large, showy flowers all growing on one side of the stem. Gladioli are widely grown for their flowers. **2** *Anatomy.* the middle of the sternum. ⟨< L *gladiolus,* dim. of *gladius* sword⟩

glad rags *Slang.* one's best clothes.

glad•some ['glædsəm] *adj. Poetic or archaic.* **1** glad; joyful; cheerful. **2** causing gladness; pleasant; delightful.
—'glad•some•ly, *adv.* **—'glad•some•ness,** *n.*

glair [glɛr] *n., v.* *—n.* **1** the raw white of an egg or any similar viscous substance. **2** a glaze or size made from it.
—v. apply glair to. ⟨ME < OF *glaire,* ult. < L *clarus* clear⟩
☛ *Hom.* GLARE.

glaive [gleiv] *n. Archaic.* a sword; broadsword. ⟨ME < OF < L *gladius* sword⟩

glam•or ['glæmər] See GLAMOUR.

glam•or•ize ['glæmə,raɪz] *v.* **-ized, -iz•ing.** make someone or something glamorous. **—,glam•or•i'za•tion,** *n.*

glam•or•ous ['glæmərəs] *adj.* full of glamour; fascinating; charming. **—'glam•or•ous•ly,** *adv.*

glam•our ['glæmər] *n.* **1** a romantic or exciting fascination; alluring charm: *the glamour of show business. The mysterious stranger had a glamour about him.* **2** a magic spell or influence. Sometimes, **glamor.** ⟨alteration of *grammar* or its var. *gramarye* occult learning; originally, a spell⟩
☛ *Spelling.* See note at -OR.

glance¹ [glæns] *n., v.* **glanced, glanc•ing.** *—n.* **1** a quick look. **2** a flash of light; gleam. **3** a glancing off; deflected motion; swift, oblique movement. **4** a passing reference; brief allusion.
—v. **1** look quickly; cause to look quickly. **2** flash with light; gleam: *eyes glancing.* **3** hit and go off at a slant: *The spear glanced off his armour and hit the wall.* **4** make a short reference and go on to something else (*used with* **at**).
glance off, fail to affect: *Criticism just seems to glance off her.*
⟨var. of ME *glace(n)* strike a glancing blow < OF *glacier* to slip, ult. < L *glacies* ice⟩ **—'glanc•ing•ly,** *adv.*

glance² [glæns] *n.* any mineral with a bright lustre. ⟨< G *Glanz* brightness, lustre⟩

gland¹ [glænd] *n.* **1** an organ in the body by which certain substances are separated from the blood and changed into some secretion for use in the body, such as bile, or into a product to be discharged from the body, such as sweat. The liver, the kidneys, the pancreas, and the thyroid are glands. **2** any of various structures similar to glands, such as the lymph nodes. **3** *Botany.* a secreting organ or structure, generally on or near a surface. ⟨< F *glande* < OF *glandre* < L *glandula,* dim. of *glans, glandis* acorn⟩

gland² [glænd] *n.* a sliding part of machinery made to hold another part in place. ⟨origin unknown⟩

glan•ders ['glændərz] *n.* a serious contagious disease of horses, mules, etc., accompanied by swellings beneath the lower jaw and a profuse discharge from the nostrils. ⟨< OF *glandre* gland < L *glandula.* See GLAND.⟩

glan•du•lar ['glændʒələr] *or* ['glændjələr] *adj.* of or like a gland; having glands; made up of glands. **—'glan•du•lar•ly,** *adv.*

glandular fever infectious mononucleosis.

glan•du•lous ['glændʒələs] *or* ['glændjələs] *adj.* glandular.

glans clitoris [glænz] erectile tissue in the clitoris.

glans penis [glænz] the cone-shaped tip of the penis.

glare[1] [glɛr] *n., v.* **glared, glar•ing.** *—n.* **1** a strong, bright light; light that shines so brightly that it hurts the eyes: *The glare from the ice made her eyes sore.* **2** a fierce, angry stare. **3** excessive brightness and showiness.
—v. **1** give off a strong, bright light; shine so brightly as to hurt the eyes. **2** stare fiercely and angrily: *The angry man glared at his defiant son.* **3** express by a fierce, angry stare. **4** be too bright and showy. ⟨ME *glaren;* cf. OE *glæren* glassy⟩
☛ *Hom.* GLAIR.

glare[2] [glɛr] *n., adj. —n.* a bright, smooth surface.
—adj. bright and smooth. ⟨extended use of *glare[1]*⟩
☛ *Hom.* GLAIR.

glare ice *Cdn.* ice that has a smooth, glassy surface.

glar•ing ['glɛrɪŋ] *adj., v. —adj.* **1** very bright; shining so brightly as to hurt the eyes; dazzling: *glaring headlights.* **2** too bright and showy: *glaring colours.* **3** very easily seen; conspicuous: *a glaring error in spelling.* **4** fixing angrily with the eyes: *a glaring look.*
—v. ppr. of GLARE. **—'glar•ing•ly,** *adv.* **—'glar•ing•ness,** *n.*

glar•y ['glɛri] *adj.* glaring.

Glas•phalt ['glæsfɒlt] *n. Trademark.* crushed waste glass mixed with asphalt, used for paving roads.

glass [glæs] *n., v. —n.* **1** a hard, brittle substance that is usually transparent, made by fusing sand with soda, potash, lime, or other substances: *Windows are made of glass.* **2** a tumbler or similar drinking vessel made of glass, plastic, etc.: *He knocked a glass off the table.* **3** the amount that a glass can hold: *to drink a glass of water.* **4 glasses,** *pl.* **a** a pair of glass or plastic lenses together with the frame that holds them in place, worn to correct defective vision or to protect the eyes; eyeglasses; spectacles. **b** binoculars. **5** a piece of glass used for a particular purpose, such as a windowpane or a plate of glass covering a picture. **6** mirror. **7** barometer. **8** an optical lens or instrument, such as a telescope, magnifying glass, or monocle. **9** (*adjl.*) made of glass: *a glass dish.* **10** (*adjl.*) having to do with glass or the manufacture of glass: *the glass industry.*
see through rose-coloured glasses, be very, often unduly, optimistic about something.
—v. **1** enclose or protect with glass (*often used with* **in**): *to glass in a porch.* **2** fit or provide with glass. **3** reflect; mirror. **4** make or become glassy. ⟨OE *glæs*⟩ **—'glass•less,** *adj.* **—'glass,like,** *adj.*

glass blower a person who shapes glass by blowing it while it is still hot and soft.

glass blowing the art or process of shaping glass by blowing it while it is still hot and soft.

glass cutter **1** one who cuts sheets of glass into various shapes and sizes. **2** one who etches designs on such sheets. **3** the tool used to cut these sheets and etch these designs.

glass eel an eel in the young adult stage, when it is flat and transparent.

glass•ful ['glæsfʊl] *n., pl.* **-fuls.** as much as a drinking glass holds.

glass harmonica a musical instrument consisting of glasses of various sizes that give out notes when rubbed with a moistened finger.

glass•house ['glæs,hʌus] *n.* a greenhouse; hothouse.

glass•ine [glæ'sin] *n.* a thin, tough, glazed, almost transparent paper, used in packaging and in envelope windows.

glass•mak•er ['glæs,meikər] *n.* one who makes glass. **—'glass,mak•ing,** *n.*

glass snake a lizard of the genus *Ophisaurus,* having no legs and an easily broken tail.

glass•ware ['glæs,wɛr] *n.* articles made of glass.

glass wool glass spun in very fine threads, with a texture resembling loose fibres of wool, used for insulation, etc.

glass•work ['glæs,wɜrk] *n.* **1** the manufacture of glass or glassware. **2** objects or articles made of glass; glassware. **3** the fitting of window glass; glazing.

glass•wort ['glæs,wɜrt] *n.* any of a genus (*Salicornia*) of annual plants of the goosefoot family native to European saltwater marshes, having fleshy stems with leaves reduced to

scalelike sheaths. Glasswort ashes were formerly used as a source of soda for glassmaking.

glass•y ['glæsi] *adj.* **glass•i•er, glass•i•est,** *n. —adj.* **1** like glass; smooth or easily seen through: *glassy water.* **2** having a fixed, expressionless stare: *The dazed man's eyes were glassy.*
—n. a type of marble made of coloured glass. **—'glass•i•ly,** *adv.* **—'glass•i•ness,** *n.*

Glau•ber's salt ['glaʊbərz] *or* ['glɒbərz] sodium sulphate, used as a cathartic, etc. ⟨after Johann R. *Glauber* (1604-1668), a German chemist⟩

glau•co•ma [glɒ'koumə] *or* [glʌu'koumə] *n.* a disease of the eye, characterized by increased pressure in the eyeball causing gradual loss of sight. ⟨< Gk. *glaukoma* < *glaukos* grey⟩ **—glau'com•a•tous,** *adj.*

glau•con•ite ['glɒkə,nəit] *n.* a water softener, a hydrous silicate of potassium, iron, aluminum, etc., also used as a fertilizer.

glau•cous ['glɒkəs] *adj.* **1** light bluish green. **2** covered with a bloom as plums and grapes are. ⟨< L *glaucus* < Gk. *glaukos* grey⟩

glaucous gull a large, grey-blue and white gull (*Larus hyperboreus*) native to the Arctic and feeding on smaller birds.

glaze [gleiz] *v.* **glazed, glaz•ing;** *n. —v.* **1** put glass in; cover with glass. Pieces of glass cut to the right size are used to glaze windows and picture frames. **2** make a smooth, glassy surface or glossy coating on (china, food, etc.). **3** become smooth, glassy, or glossy (*often with* **over**). **4** coat with a thin sheet of ice: *The frost glazed the windows of the car.*
—n. **1** a smooth, glassy surface or glossy coating: *the glaze on a china cup, a glaze of ice.* **2** a substance used to make such a surface or coating on things. ⟨ME *glase(n)* < *glas* glass, OE *glæs*⟩ **—'glaz•er,** *n.*

gla•zier ['gleiʒər] *or* ['gleiziər] *n.* a person whose work is putting glass in windows, picture frames, etc. ⟨ME *glasier* < *glas* glass, OE *glæs*⟩

glaz•ing ['gleizɪŋ] *n., v. —n.* **1** the work of a glazier. **2** glass set or to be set in frames. **3** a substance used to make a smooth, glassy surface or glossy coating on things. **4** such a surface or coating.
—v. ppr. of GLAZE.

gleam [glim] *n., v. —n.* **1** a flash or beam of light. **2** a short or faint light. **3** a short appearance; faint show: *After one gleam of hope, they all became discouraged.*
—v. **1** flash or beam with light: *A cat's eyes gleam in the dark.* **2** shine with a short or faint light. **3** appear suddenly; be shown briefly. ⟨OE *glǣm*⟩
☛ *Syn. n.* **2. Gleam,** GLIMMER (def. 1) = a brief or not bright light. **Gleam** applies to a steady light that comes out of the darkness and disappears soon, or is softened or toned down: *We saw the gleam of headlights through the rain.* **Glimmer** applies to a faint gleam, a light shining feebly or with varying intensity: *We saw the glimmer of a distant light through the trees.*

glean [glin] *v.* **1** gather (grain) left on a field by reapers. **2** gather little by little or slowly: *The spy gleaned information from the soldier's talk.* ⟨ME < OF *glener* < LL *glennare* < Celtic⟩ **—'glean•er,** *n.*

glean•ings ['glinɪŋz] *n.pl.* something that is gleaned.

glebe [glib] *n.* **1** *Poetic.* soil; earth; field. **2** a portion of land assigned to a member of the clergy as part of his or her living. ⟨< L *gleba*⟩

glede [glid] *n.* a red kite (*Milvus milvus*) common in Europe. ⟨< ME < OE *glida* akin to glide < ON *gletha*⟩

glee [gli] *n.* **1** joy; delight; mirth. **2** a song for three or more usually male voices each singing a different part. A glee is usually sung without accompaniment. ⟨OE *glēo*⟩

glee club a society or group organized for singing glees or other part songs.

glee•ful ['glifəl] *adj.* filled with glee; merry; joyous. **—'glee•ful•ly,** *adv.* **—'glee•ful•ness,** *n.*

glee•man ['glimən] *n., pl.* **-men.** *Archaic.* a singer; minstrel.

glee•some ['glisəm] *adj. Archaic or poetic.* gleeful.

glen [glɛn] *n.* a small, narrow valley. ⟨< Scots Gaelic *gleann*⟩

glen•gar•ry [glɛn'gæri] *or* [glɛn'gɛri] *n., pl.* **-ries.** a Scottish cap with straight sides and a lengthwise crease in the top, often having short ribbons at the back. See CAP for picture. Also called **glengarry bonnet.** ⟨after *Glengarry,* a valley in Scotland⟩

gley [glei] *n.* a bluish grey clay soil, resulting from excess moisture. ⟨< earlier *glei* < Ukrainian⟩

gli•a•din ['glaɪədɪn] *n.* a protein derived from gluten.

glib [glɪb] *adj.* **glib•ber, glib•best. 1** speaking or spoken too smoothly and easily to be sincere: *a glib sales talk. No one believed her glib excuses.* **2** without depth; not thought out; superficial: *a glib solution.* ⟨short for *glibbery* slippery; cf. Du. *glibberig*⟩ **—'glib•ly,** *adv.* **—'glib•ness,** *n.*
☛ *Syn.* **1.** See note at FLUENT.

glic•la•zide ['glɪklə,zaɪd] *n.* a drug used to treat certain forms of diabetes.

glide [glaɪd] *v.* **glid•ed, glid•ing;** *n.* *—v.* **1** move along smoothly, evenly, and easily. Birds, ships, dancers, and skaters glide. **2** pass gradually, quietly, or imperceptibly: *The years glided past.* **3** of an aircraft, come or cause to come down slowly at a slant without using a motor. Under favourable circumstances, an airplane can glide about 1.5 km for every 300 m that it is above the ground. **4** fly by means of a glider. **5** *Music.* pass from one tone to another without a break; slur. **6** *Phonetics.* produce a glide.
—n. **1** a smooth, even, easy movement. **2** of an aircraft, a coming down slowly at a slant without using a motor. **3** *Music.* a slur. **4** *Phonetics.* **a** a vowel or semivowel made in passing from one speech sound to another, such as the [j] often heard between the *i* and *r* in *hire.* **b** any semivowel. **5** *Dancing.* **a** a step made by sliding rather than raising the foot. **b** a waltz or other dance using such steps. **6** a metal or plastic attachment under a piece of furniture to make it easy to move. ⟨OE *glīdan*⟩
☛ *Syn. v.* **1.** See note at SLIDE.

glid•er ['glaɪdər] *n.* **1** a person who or thing that glides, especially an aircraft resembling an airplane but without a motor. A glider has very long wings in proportion to the body, and is kept up in the air by rising air currents. **2** a type of chair with a sliding base.

glim [glɪm] *n. Slang.* a light; lamp; candle. ⟨related to GLEAM, GLIMMER⟩

glim•mer ['glɪmər] *n., v.* *—n.* **1** a faint or unsteady light. **2** a vague idea or feeling; a faint glimpse: *The doctor's report gave us only a glimmer of hope.*
—v. **1** shine with a faint or unsteady light: *The candle glimmered and went out.* **2** appear faintly or dimly. ⟨ME. Related to GLEAM.⟩
☛ *Syn. n.* **1.** See note at GLEAM.

glim•mer•ing ['glɪmərɪŋ] *n., v.* *—n.* glimmer.
—v. ppr. of GLIMMER.

glimpse [glɪmps] *n., v.* **glimpsed, glimps•ing.** *—n.* **1** a short, quick view: *I caught a glimpse of the falls as our train went by.* **2** a short, faint appearance.
—v. **1** catch a short quick view of. **2** look quickly at; glance at. ⟨ME. Related to GLIM, GLIMMER.⟩

glint [glɪnt] *v. or n.* gleam; flash: *Her eyes glinted fiercely in the light. (v.) There was a glint of steel as the man swung his axe. (n.)* ⟨Cf. dial. Swedish *glinta*⟩

gli•o•ma [gli'oumə] *or* [glaɪ'oumə] *n.* a brain tumour composed of neuroglia, the tissue of nerve structures. ⟨< NL < Med.Gk. *glia* glue + Gk. *oma* mass⟩

glis•sade [glɪ'sæd], [glɪ'sɑd], *or* [glɪ'seid] *n., v.* **-sad•ed, -sad•ing.**
—n. **1** *Ballet.* a gliding step, often ending in a leap. **2** a sliding down any smooth, sloping surface.
—v. perform a glissade; slide. ⟨< F *glissade* < *glisser* slide⟩

glis•san•do [glɪ'sɑndou] *adj., n., pl.* **-di** [-di]. *Music.*
—adj. performed with a gliding effect. A pianist plays a glissando passage by sliding the back of the finger tips rapidly over the keys.
—n. **1** a gliding effect. **2** a glissando passage. ⟨in imitation of Italian, < F *glissant*, ppr. of *glisser* slide⟩

glis•ten ['glɪsən] *v. or n.* sparkle; shine. ⟨OE *glisnian*⟩

glis•ter ['glɪstər] *v. or n. Archaic.* glisten; glitter; sparkle. ⟨< *glisten*; cf. MDu. *glisteren*⟩

glitch [glɪtʃ] *n.* **1** *Slang.* a sudden malfunction. **2** a brief, sudden irregularity in the frequency of the radiation of a pulsar. ⟨< Yiddish⟩

glit•ter ['glɪtər] *v., n.* *—v.* **1** glisten, sparkle; shine with a bright, sparkling light: *Jewels and new coins glitter.* **2** be bright and showy. **3** *Cdn.* become covered with ice after a freezing rain.
—n. **1** a bright, sparkling light. **2** brightness; showiness; a bright display. **3** *Cdn.* the bright, sparkling ice that forms on everything outdoors after a rain that freezes. Also called **glitter ice.** ⟨ME < ON *glitra*⟩ **—'glit•ter•er,** *n.*
☛ *Syn. n.* **1.** See note at FLASH.

glit•ter•y ['glɪtəri] *adj.* glittering.

glitz [glɪts] *n. Informal.* GLITTER (def. 2).

glit•zy ['glɪtsi] *adj.* **-zi•er, zi•est.** *Informal.* showy; tastelessly ornate; gaudy.

gloam•ing ['gloumɪŋ] *n.* evening twilight; dusk. ⟨OE *glōmung* < *glōm* twilight; influenced by *glow*⟩

gloat [glout] *v.* **1** gaze intently. **2** ponder with self-indulgent pleasure: *The miser gloated over his gold.* **3** show malicious pleasure: *They gloated over her failure.* ⟨Cf. ON *glotta* smile scornfully⟩ **—'gloat•er,** *n.* **—'gloat•ing•ly,** *adv.*

glob [glɒb] *n.* a less technical word for GLOBULE.

glob•al ['gloubəl] *adj.* **1** of the earth as a whole; worldwide: *the threat of global war.* **2** comprehensive; sweeping: *global dysfunction.* **3** shaped like a globe. **—'glob•al•ly,** *adv.*

global village the world considered as being a small community. ⟨coined by H. Marshall McLuhan (1911-1980), Canadian writer⟩

glo•bate ['gloubeit] *adj.* shaped like a globe.

globe [gloub] *n., v.* **globed, glob•ing.** *—n.* **1** anything round like a ball; a sphere. **2** the earth; world. **3** a sphere with a map of the earth or sky on it. **4** anything rounded like a globe. An electric light bulb may be covered by a globe.
—v. gather or form into a globe. ⟨< F < L *globus*⟩ **—'globe,like,** *adj.*
☛ *Syn. n.* **2.** See note at EARTH.

globe•fish ['gloub,fɪʃ] *n., pl.* **-fish** or **-fish•es.** puffer.

globe•flow•er ['gloub,flaʊər] *n.* any of a genus (*Trollius*) of plants of the buttercup family having globe-shaped, usually yellow, flowers.

globe•trot•ter ['gloub,trɒtər] *n.* a person who travels widely over the world, especially for pleasure.

globe•trot•ting ['gloub,trɒtɪŋ] *n. or adj.* travelling widely throughout the world, especially as a tourist.

glo•bin ['gloubɪn] *n.* a simple protein obtained from hemaglobin.

glo•boid ['gloubɔɪd] *n.* spheroid.

glo•bose ['gloubous] *or* [glou'bous] *adj.* globular. ⟨< L *globosus* < *globus* globe⟩

glob•u•lar ['glɒbjələr] *adj.* **1** shaped like a globe or globule; round; spherical. **2** consisting of globules. **—'glob•u•lar•ly,** *adv.*

glob•ule ['glɒbjul] *n.* a very small ball; tiny drop: *globules of sweat.* Also, **glob.** ⟨< F < L *globulus*, dim. of *globus* globe⟩

glob•u•lin ['glɒbjəlɪn] *n.* any of a group of proteins, found in plant and animal tissues, that are soluble in weak salt solutions but insoluble in water.

glo•chid•i•um [glou'kɪdiəm] *n.* **1** *Botany.* a thorny tuft or bristle found on various cacti and on certain ferns. **2** *Zoology.* a stage in the development of larval freshwater mussels in which the larvae live parasitically in the gills of many fishes. ⟨< NL < Gk. *glochis* point + NL *-idium* suffix < Gk. *-idion*⟩

glock•en•spiel *n.* ['glɒkən,spil] *or* ['glɒkən,ʃpil] a musical instrument consisting of a graduated series of small, tuned bells, metal bars, or tubes mounted in a frame and struck by two little hammers. ⟨< G *Glockenspiel* < *Glocke* bell + *Spiel* play⟩

glom [glɒm] *v.* **glommed, glom•ming.** *Informal.*
glom onto, seize; grab; acquire. ⟨< earlier *glaum* < Scottish dial. probably < Gaelic *glaim* to snatch⟩

glom•er•ate ['glɒmərɪt] *adj.* clustered together; collected into a rounded mass. ⟨< L *glomeratus*, pp. of *glomerare* < *glomus*, *-meris* ball⟩

glom•er•ule ['glɒmə,rul] *n.* **1** any compact cluster. **2** a compact cluster of flowers. ⟨< NL *glomerulus*, dim. of L *glomus* ball⟩ **—glo'mer•u•late** [glou'mɛrjəlɪt], *adj.*

glom•er•u•lo•ne•phri•tis [glou,mɛrjəlounə'fraɪtɪs] *n.* a kind of nephritis whose symptoms are inflamed glomeruli. It is most likely caused by antibody-antigen complexes passing through the kidney.

glom•er•ul•us [glou'mɛrjələs] *n., pl.* **-li** [-,laɪ] *or* [-,li]. any compact cluster of blood vessels or nerves, especially those in the kidney, that form urine. **—glo'mer•u•lar,** *adj.*

gloom [glum] *n., v.* *—n.* **1** deep shadow; darkness; dimness. **2** low spirits; sadness. **3** a dejected or sad look.
—v. **1** be or become dark, dim, or dismal. **2** be in low spirits; feel miserable. **3** look sad or dismal. ⟨ME *gloume(n)* look sullen, lower[2]; origin uncertain⟩
☛ *Hom.* GLUME.

gloom•y ['glumi] *adj.* **gloom•i•er, gloom•i•est. 1** dark; dim: *a gloomy winter day.* **2** in low spirits; sad; melancholy: *a gloomy mood.* **3** causing low spirits; discouraging; dismal: *a gloomy book.* **4** morose; sullen. ⟨< *gloom,* v.⟩ **—'gloom•i•ly,** *adv.* **—'gloom•i•ness,** *n.*

Gloos•cap ['gluskæp] *n. Cdn.* a legendary demigod of the Micmacs, Malecites, and kindred First Nations peoples, revered as a mighty warrior and magician. ⟨< Algonkian⟩

glo•ri•a ['glɔriə] *n.* **1** a Christian song of praise to God, or its musical setting. **2 Gloria,** one of three Christian songs of praise to God, beginning "Glory be to God on high," "Glory be to the Father," and "Glory be to Thee, O Lord." **3** halo. **4** a fabric made of silk and some other material, used for umbrellas. ⟨< L⟩

glo•ri•fi•ca•tion [,glɔrəfə'keiʃən] *n.* **1** a glorifying or being glorified. **2** an embellished version of something. **3** *Brit. Informal.* celebration.

glo•ri•fy ['glɔrə,faɪ] *v.* **-fied, -fy•ing. 1** give glory to; make glorious. **2** praise; honour; worship. **3** exalt to the glory of heaven. **4** cause to seem more splendid, important, etc. than is actually the case: *I'm just a glorified handyman around the place. She glorified the essay by calling it a monograph.* ⟨ME < OF *glorifier* < L *glorificare* < *gloria* glory + *facere* make⟩ **—'glo•ri,fi•er,** *n.*

glo•ri•ole ['glɔri,oul] *n.* **1** halo. **2** GLORIA (def. 4).

glo•ri•ous ['glɔriəs] *adj.* **1** having or deserving glory; illustrious. **2** giving glory; worthy of high praise: *a glorious victory.* **3** magnificent; splendid: *a glorious pageant.* **4** *Informal.* admirable; delightful; fine: *have a glorious time. Isn't it a glorious day?* ⟨ME < AF < L *gloriosus* < *gloria* glory⟩ **—'glo•ri•ous•ly,** *adv.* **—'glo•ri•ous•ness,** *n.*

glo•ry ['glɔri] *n., pl.* **-ries;** *v.* **-ried, -ry•ing.** *—n.* **1** great praise and honour; fame; renown. **2** that which brings praise and honour; a source of pride and joy: *Her real glory was not her beauty but her success as a doctor.* **3** adoring praise and thanksgiving. **4** radiant beauty; brightness; magnificence; splendour. **5** a condition of magnificence, splendour, or greatest prosperity. **6** the splendour and bliss of heaven; heaven. **7** halo.
go to glory, die.
in (one's) **glory,** *Informal.* in a state of greatest satisfaction or enjoyment: *He's in his glory with a dish of ice cream.*
—v. be proud; rejoice.
glory in, take great pride or delight in: *Her father gloried in her success as a pianist.* ⟨ME < OF *glorie* < L *gloria*⟩

gloss[1] [glɒs] *n., v. —n.* **1** a smooth, shiny surface; lustre: *Varnished furniture has a gloss.* **2** an outward appearance or surface that covers faults underneath.
—v. **1** put a smooth, shiny surface on. **2** become glossy.
gloss over, smooth over or explain away (a fault, error, etc.): *He tried to gloss over his negligence.* ⟨Cf. ON *glossi* flame⟩

gloss[2] [glɒs] *n., v. —n.* **1** an explanation; comment. **2** glossary. **3** an interlinear or other rough translation. **4** a deliberately misleading explanation.
—v. **1** comment on; explain. **2** translate. **3** give a false interpretation of. ⟨< L < Gk. *glōssa,* literally, tongue⟩ **—'gloss•er,** *n.*

glos•sa ['glɒsə] *or* ['glousə] *n.* the tongue or tonguelike structure of any animal, as the middle lobe of the labium of a moth or butterfly. ⟨< NL < Gk. tongue⟩

glos•sal ['glɒsəl] *or* ['glousəl] *adj.* of or having to do with the tongue.

glos•sar•i•al [glɒ'sɛriəl] *adj.* having to do with a glossary; like a glossary.

glos•sa•ry ['glɒsəri] *n., pl.* **-ries.** a list of special, technical, or difficult words with explanations or comments: *a glossary to Shakespeare's plays, a glossary of terms used in chemistry. Textbooks sometimes have glossaries at the end.* ⟨< L *glossarium* < *glossa.* See GLOSS[2].⟩

glos•si•tis [glɒ'saitɪs] *n.* inflammation of the tongue.

glos•sog•ra•phy [glɒ'sɒgrəfi] *n.* a compilation of glossaries. **—glos'sog•ra•ph•er,** *n.*

glos•so•la•lia [,glɒsou'leiliə] *n.* SPEAKING IN TONGUES; speaking in languages unknown to the speaker, regarded as a manifestation of the Holy Spirit. ⟨< NL *glosso* < Gk. *glossa* tongue + *lalia* a speaking < *lalein* speak⟩

glos•sy ['glɒsi] *adj.* **gloss•i•er, gloss•i•est;** *n. —adj.* smooth and shiny.
—n. **1** *Informal.* a photograph printed on glossy paper. **2** a magazine printed on glossy paper. **—'gloss•i•ly,** *adv.* **—'gloss•i•ness,** *n.*

glot•tal ['glɒtəl] *adj.* **1** of the glottis. **2** *Phonetics.* produced in the glottis. *H* in *hope* is a glottal sound.

glottal stop *Phonetics.* a speech sound formed by opening and closing the glottis. In German, words beginning with a vowel start with a glottal stop.

glot•tis ['glɒtɪs] *n.* the opening in the upper part of the windpipe, between the vocal cords. See WINDPIPE for picture. ⟨< NL < Gk. *glōttis,* ult. < *glōtta* tongue⟩

glot•to•chro•nol•o•gy [,glɒtoukrə'nɒlədʒi] *n.* the study of the vocabularies of related languages to determine the time of their separation.

glove [glʌv] *n., v.* **gloved, glov•ing.** *—n.* **1** a covering for the hand, having separate sections for each of the four fingers and the thumb. **2** a padded covering to protect the hand: *a hockey glove, a baseball glove.*
fit like a glove, fit perfectly or tightly.
hand in glove, in intimate relationship.
handle with (kid) gloves, treat gently or carefully.
—v. **1** cover or provide with a glove or gloves. **2** *Baseball.* catch (a ball) with a glove. ⟨OE *glōf*⟩ **—'glove•less,** *adj.* **—'glove,like,** *adj.*

glove compartment a small compartment in the dashboard of a vehicle for holding small articles. Some glove compartments are fitted with a lock.

glov•er ['glʌvər] *n.* a person who makes or sells gloves.

glow [glou] *n., v. —n.* **1** the shine from something that is red-hot or white-hot. **2** any similar shine: *The firefly's glow was fascinating.* **3** brightness: *the glow of sunset.* **4** a warm feeling or colour of the body: *the glow of health on her cheeks.* **5** an eager look on the face: *a glow of interest or excitement.*
—v. **1** shine as if red-hot or white-hot. **2** show a warm colour; look warm; be red or bright: *Her cheeks glowed as she danced.* **3** be hot; burn. **4** be eager or animated. ⟨OE *glōwan*⟩

glow•er ['glaʊər] *v., n. —v.* stare angrily; scowl: *The fighters glowered at each other.*
—n. an angry or sullen look. ⟨? < obs. *glow,* v., stare⟩ **—'glow•er•ing•ly,** *adv.*

glow•ing ['glouɪŋ] *adj., v. —adj.* **1** shining with heat. **2** bright: *glowing colours.* **3** showing a warm colour: *glowing cheeks.* **4** eager; animated: *a glowing description.*
—v. ppr. of GLOW. **—'glow•ing•ly,** *adv.*

glow–worm ['glou ,wɜrm] *n.* any of various insect larvae or wingless adult insects that emit a glow from the abdomen, either continuously or for prolonged periods; especially, a larva or wingless adult female of any of the fireflies.

glox•in•i•a [glɒk'sɪniə] *n.* any of several plants (genus *Sinningia*) native to tropical South America, especially *S. speciosa,* widely cultivated as a pot plant, having large, bell-shaped, velvety flowers that are usually mainly red or purple. ⟨< NL; after Benjamin P. *Gloxin,* 18c. German botanist⟩

Gloxinias

gloze [glouz] *v.* **glozed, gloz•ing.** *Rare.* smooth or gloss (over): *His friends glozed over his faults.* ⟨ME < OF *gloser* < *glose* < L *glossa.* See GLOSS[2].⟩

glu•ca•gon ['glukə,gɒn] *n.* a pancreatic hormone that raises the concentration of blood sugar and acts against insulin. ⟨< G *Glukagon* < *Glukose* (< F *glucose* glucose) + Gk. *agon* struggle⟩

glu•co•ne•o•gen•e•sis [,glukou,niou'dʒɛnəsɪs] *n.* the conversion of proteins or fats into glucose.

glu•con•ic acid [glu'kɒnɪk] a crystalline material formed by the oxidation of glucose, used in industry for cleaning metals, and in pharmaceuticals. *Formula*: $CH_2OH(CHOH)_4COOH$

glu•cose ['glukous] *n.* **1** a kind of sugar occurring naturally in fruits. It is about half as sweet as cane sugar. *Formula*: $C_6H_{12}O_6$ **2** a syrup containing this and other sugars, made from starch. ⟨< F < Gk. *glykys* sweet⟩

glu•co•side ['glukə,saɪd] *n. Chemistry.* any compound that yields glucose and some other substance or substances when treated with a dilute acid. Glucoside is a glycoside containing glucose.

glu•co•sin•o•late [,glukou'sɪnə,leit] *n.* a salt found in rapeseed (canola) that breaks down by hydrolysis into harmful sulphur-bearing products if improperly heated.

glue [glu] *n., v.* **glued, glu•ing.** *—n.* **1** a substance used to stick things together, often made by boiling the hoofs, skins, and

bones of animals in water. **2** any similar sticky substance made of casein, rubber, etc.; adhesive. Glues are stronger than pastes.
—v. **1** stick together with glue. **2** fasten tightly; attach firmly: *During the ride down the mountain her hands were glued to the steering wheel.* **3** regard or look at fixedly: *He walked on, his eyes glued to the road.* ⟨ME < OF *glu* < LL *glus, glutis*⟩ **—'glu•er,** *n.*

glue•pot ['glu,pɒt] *n.* a pot in the form of a double boiler, for melting glue.

glue•y ['glui] *adj.* **glu•i•er, glu•i•est. 1** like glue; sticky. **2** full of glue; smeared with glue. **—'glu•ey•ness,** *n.*

glug [glʌg] *v.* **glugged, glug•ging,** *n. —v.* **1** drink in gulps. **2** make a gurgling noise like a liquid being poured into a bottle. *—n.* a gulp. ⟨imitative⟩

glum [glʌm] *adj.* **glum•mer, glum•mest.** gloomy; dismal; sullen: *a glum look.* ⟨cf. LG *glum* turbid, muddy. Akin to GLOOM.⟩ **—'glum•ly,** *adv.* **—'glum•ness,** *n.*
☛ *Syn.* See note at SULLEN.

glu•ma•ceous [glu'meiʃəs] *adj.* like a glume or having glumes.

glume [glum] *n.* either of two dry bracts at the base of a spikelet on the head of a grass such as wheat. ⟨< L *gluma* husk, related to L *glubere* to peel, remove the husk from. 18c.⟩
☛ *Hom.* GLOOM.

glu•on ['gluɒn] *n.* a particle supposed to hold quarks together. ⟨< *glue* + *-on,* suffix forming nouns⟩

glut [glʌt] *v.* **glut•ted, glut•ting;** *n. —v.* **1** fill full; feed or satisfy fully: *Years of war had glutted his appetite for adventure.* **2** fill too full; supply too much for: *The prices for wheat dropped when the market was glutted with it.* **3** eat too much.
—n. **1** a full supply; great quantity. **2** too great a supply. ⟨< obs. *glut,* n., glutton < OF⟩

glu•tam•ic acid [glu'tæmɪk] a white, crystalline amino acid obtained from proteins, used to treat certain stomach problems. *Formula*: $C_5H_9NO_4$ ⟨*glut(en)* + *am(ide)* + *-ic*⟩

glu•ta•mine ['glutə,min] *or* ['glutəmɪn] *n.* a crystalline amine derived from glutamic acid. *Formula*: $C_5H_{10}N_2O_3$ ⟨< *glutam(ic acid)* + *ine*[2]⟩

glu•te•al ['glutiəl] *or* [glu'tiəl] *adj.* having to do with the buttocks or their muscles. ⟨< *gluteus*⟩

glu•ten ['glutən] *n.* a tough, sticky substance that remains in flour when the starch is taken out. ⟨< L *gluten* glue⟩

gluten bread bread made from flour that is high in gluten and low in starch.

glu•te•nous ['glutənəs] *adj.* **1** like gluten. **2** containing much gluten.
☛ *Hom.* GLUTINOUS.

glu•te•us ['glutiəs] *or* [glu'tiəs] *n.* any of the three muscles that make up the buttock and control the movement of the thigh. ⟨< NL < Gk. *gloutos* rump, buttock⟩

glu•ti•nous ['glutənəs] *adj.* sticky. **—'glu•ti•nous•ly,** *adv.* **—'glu•ti•nous•ness,** *n.*
☛ *Hom.* GLUTENOUS.

glut•ton[1] ['glʌtən] *n.* **1** a greedy eater; a person who eats too much. **2** a person who never seems to have enough of something: *That boxer is a glutton for punishment.* ⟨ME < OF *glouton* < L *glutto*⟩

glut•ton[2] ['glʌtən] *n.* wolverine. ⟨translation of G *Vielfrass,* literally, great eater, derived by popular etymology from Swedish *fjällfräs* mountain cat⟩

glut•ton•ous ['glʌtənəs] *adj.* **1** greedy for food; having the habit of eating too much. **2** greedy. **—'glut•ton•ous•ly,** *adv.* **—'glut•ton•ous•ness,** *n.*

glut•ton•y ['glʌtəni] *n., pl.* **-ton•ies.** greediness for food; the habit of eating too much.

gly•bur•ide ['glaɪbə,raɪd] *n.* a drug used to treat certain forms of diabetes.

glyc•er•al•de•hyde ['glɪsə'rældə,haɪd] *n. Biochemistry.* a white crystalline solid, yielding glycerol on reduction and formed in the body by the oxidation of sugar. *Formula*: $C_3H_6O_3$ ⟨< *glycer(in)* + *aldehyde*⟩

gly•cer•ide ['glɪsə,raɪd] *n.* an ester of fatty acids.

glyc•er•in ['glɪsərɪn] *n.* glycerol. Also, **glycerine** ['glɪsərɪn] *or* ['glɪsə,rin]. ⟨< F *glycérine* < Gk. *glykeros* sweet⟩

gly•cer•in•ate ['glɪsərɪ,neit] *v.* **-at•ed, -at•ing.** treat with glycerin.

glyc•er•ol ['glɪsə,rɒl] *or* ['glɪsə,roul] *n.* a colourless, syrupy, sweet liquid obtained from fats and oils, used in ointments, lotions, antifreeze solutions, explosives, etc. *Formula*: $C_3H_8O_3$

glyc•er•yl group or **radical** ['glɪsərɪl] the trivalent group derived from glycerol.

gly•cine ['gləisin] *or* [gləi'sin] *n.* the simplest amino acid, used in medicine.

gly•co•gen ['gləikədʒən] *n.* a starchlike substance in the liver and other animal tissues that is changed into glucose when needed. ⟨< Gk. *glykys* sweet + E *-gen*⟩ **—,gly•co'gen•ic,** *adj.*

gly•co•gen•e•sis [,gləikou'dʒɛnəsɪs] *n.* **1** the formation of glycogen. **2** the formation of sugar from glycogen. ⟨< Gk. *glykys* sweet + E *genesis*⟩

gly•col ['gləikɒl] *or* ['gləikoul] *n. Chemistry.* **1** a colourless liquid obtained from certain ethylene compounds and used as an antifreeze, solvent, etc. *Formula*: $C_2H_6O_2$ **2** any of a similar group of alcohols. ⟨< *glyc(erin)* + *-ol*⟩

gly•col•ic acid [gləi'kɒlɪk] a colourless compound found in cane sugar and sugar beets, used in a number of pesticides and adhesives.

gly•co•pro•tein [,gləikou'proutin] *n.* any of a group of proteins consisting of a carbohydrate combined with a protein. ⟨< Gk. *glykys* sweet + E *protein*⟩

gly•co•side ['gləikə,saɪd] *n.* any of various derivatives of sugar, widespread in plants, and yielding sugar and other substances on hydrolysis. ⟨< F < *glycose* (altered after G *Glykos*) for *glucose* + *-ide*⟩

gly•co•su•ria [,gləikou'sʊriə] *or* [,gləikou'sjʊriə], [,gləikousə'riə] *or* [,gləikəsjə'riə] *n.* sugar in the urine, often used as a test for diabetes. ⟨< NL < Gk. *glykys* sweet + *ouron* urine⟩

glyph [glɪf] *n.* a pictograph or other symbol, especially one etched in a surface. ⟨< Gk. *glyphe* a carving < *glyphein* to carve, cut⟩

glyp•tic ['glɪptɪk] *adj., n. —adj.* having to do with carving on precious stones.
—n. the process of carving on gems. ⟨< F < Gk. *glyptikos* < *glyptos* < *glyphein* carve⟩

glyp•to•dont ['glɪptə,dɒnt] *n.* an extinct South American mammal (family Glyptodontidae), similar to a large armadillo. ⟨< NL < Gk. *glyptos* carved + *odon, odontos* tooth⟩

glyp•to•graph ['glɪptə,græf] *n.* an engraving on a gem. ⟨< Gk. *glyptos* carved + *-graph* < Gk. *graphein* to write⟩

glyp•tog•ra•phy [glɪp'tɒgrəfi] *n.* the art of engraving on gems.

gm gram.

G.M. George Medal.

G–man ['dʒi ,mæn] *n., pl.* **-men.** *U.S. Informal.* a special agent of the United States Department of Justice; an agent of the FBI. ⟨for *G*overnment *man*⟩

Gmc. Germanic.

G.M.T. GREENWICH MEAN TIME.

gnarl [narl] *n., v. —n.* **1** a knot in wood; hard, rough lump. Wood with gnarls is hard to cut.
—v. **1** make knotted and rugged like an old tree; contort; twist. **2** form gnarls. ⟨< *gnarled*⟩

gnarled [narld] *adj., v. —adj.* **1** having many knots or hard, rough lumps; knotty and twisted: *a gnarled old cypress.* **2** rough and hard; rugged and sinewy, as the hands of a person who has done much hard, rough manual work.
—v. pt. and pp. of GNARL. ⟨var. of *knurled*⟩

gnash [næʃ] *v.* **1** grind (the teeth) together. **2** bite by gnashing the teeth. ⟨var. of ME *gnast,* apparently < ON *gnastan* a gnashing⟩

gnat [næt] *n.* any of various small two-winged flies that bite, such as black flies.
strain at a gnat, a be indecisive. **b** worry about trivialities. ⟨OE *gnætt*⟩ **—'gnat,like,** *adj.*

gnat•catch•er ['næt,kætʃər] *n.* a small Ontario bird *(Polioptila caerulea),* having black, grey, and white plumage.

gnath•ic ['næθɪk] *adj.* having to do with the jaw. ⟨< Gk. *gnathos* jaw⟩

gnath•ite ['næθəit] *or* ['neiθəit] *n.* that part of an insect that serves as a jaw. ⟨See GNATHIC⟩

gnaw [nɒ] *v.* **gnawed, gnawed** or **gnawn, gnaw•ing. 1** wear away by biting: *to gnaw a bone. The mouse has gnawed right through the oatmeal box.* **2** make by biting: *A rat gnaws a hole.* **3** wear away; consume or corrode. **4** torment: *A feeling of guilt gnawed my conscience.* ⟨OE *gnagan*⟩ **—'gnaw•er,** *n.* **—'gnaw•ing•ly,** *adv.*

gnawn [nɒn] *v.* a pp. of GNAW.

gneiss [nəis] *n.* a metamorphic rock composed of quartz, feldspar, and mica or hornblende. It is distinguished from granite by its layered structure. ⟨< G⟩
☛ *Hom.* NICE.

gnoc•chi ['nɒki] *or* ['nouki]; *Italian,* ['njɔkki] *n.pl.* an Italian dish of boiled dumplings served with Parmesan cheese.

gnome[1] [noum] *n.* **1** *Folklore.* a dwarf that lives underground and guards treasures of precious metals and stones. **2** an odd-looking, dwarfish person: *a little gnome of a man.* ⟨< F < NL *gnomus;* invented by Paracelsus (16c.)⟩

gnome[2] [noum] *or* ['noumi] *n.* aphorism. ⟨< Gk. *gnome* judgment, opinion⟩

gno•mic ['noumɪk] *or* ['nɒmɪk] *adj.* **1** full of maxims or instructive sayings; aphoristic. **2** having to do with one of the Greek poets who used aphorisms.

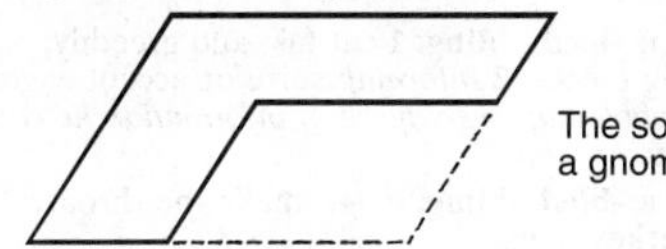
The solid outline is a gnomon (def. 2).

gno•mon ['noumɒn] *n.* **1** a rod, pointer, or triangular piece on a sundial, etc. that shows the time of day by casting its shadow on a marked surface. See SUNDIAL for picture. **2** *Geometry.* what is left of a parallelogram after a similar parallelogram has been taken away at one corner. ⟨< Gk. *gnōmōn* indicator < *gignōskein* know⟩

gno•mon•ic [nou'mɒnɪk] *adj.* **1** of or having to do with a gnomon or sundial. **2** having to do with the measuring of time, etc. by a sundial.

–gnomy *combining form.* knowledge: *physiognomy.* ⟨< LL *-gnomia* < Gk. *-gnōmia*⟩

gno•sis ['nousɪs] *n.* mystical knowledge. ⟨< Gk., knowledge⟩

gnos•tic ['nɒstɪk] *adj.* of, having to do with, or possessing knowledge, especially of spiritual things. ⟨< *Gnostic*⟩

Gnos•tic ['nɒstɪk] *n., adj.* —*n.* a believer in Gnosticism.
—*adj.* of Gnosticism or Gnostics. ⟨< Gk. *gnōstikos* of knowledge < *gignōskein* know⟩

Gnos•ti•cism ['nɒstə,sɪzəm] *n.* a mystical religious and philosophical doctrine of pre-Christian and early Christian times. It regarded matter as evil and mystical knowledge as the key to salvation, and was rejected by the Apostles as heretical.

G.N.P. GROSS NATIONAL PRODUCT.

gnu [nju] or [nu] *n., pl.* **gnu** or **gnus.** either of two large African antelopes (*Connochaetes taurinus* and *C. gnou*) having an oxlike head, curved horns, and a long, tufted tail; wildebeest. ⟨< Hottentot⟩
☛ *Hom.* KNEW, NEW.

go[1] [gou] *v.* **went, gone, go•ing;** *n., pl.* **goes;** *adj.* —*v.* **1** proceed; advance; move along: *to go to Edmonton. Go straight home.* **2** move away; leave: *It is time for us to go.* **3** be in motion; act; work; run: *Does your watch go well?* **4** get to be; become: *to go mad.* **5** be habitually; be: *to go hungry.* **6** attend on a regular basis: *He goes to the vocational school.* **7** be current: *A rumour went through the town.* **8** be known: *She went under a false name.* **9** put oneself: *Don't go to any trouble for me.* **10** extend; reach: *His memory does not go back that far.* **11** pass: *The summer holidays go quickly.* **12** be given or sold: *First prize goes to the winner. The painting goes to the highest bidder.* **13** tend; lead: *This goes to show that you must work harder.* **14** turn out; have a certain result: *How did the game go?* **15** have its place; belong: *This book goes on the top shelf.* **16** make a certain sound: *The cork went "Pop!"* **17** have certain words, melody, rules, etc.: *How does that poem go?* **18** refer; appeal: *to go to court.* **19** deteriorate, break down or be used up: *His eyesight is going. The engine in the old car finally went.* **20** die: *His wife went first.* **21** *Informal.* put up with; stand: *I can't go tea.* **22** continue: *to go unpunished.* **23** *Informal.* urinate or defecate. **24** travel over a scheduled route: *Does this bus go to Winnipeg?* **25** be able to be divided (*into*): *6 goes into 18 three times.* **26** *Informal.* say (used when reporting dialogue): *"No!" she goes. "Never!"* **27** provide (bail) for one who has been arrested.

as people (or **things**) **go,** considering how other people (or things) are.

from the word 'go', from the very beginning.

go about, a be busy at; work on. **b** move from place to place. **c** turn around; change direction.

go ahead, a proceed without hesitating; carry on: *He went ahead with his plan in spite of their objections.* **b** advance or improve one's position.

go all out, strive to the utmost extent.

go along, agree; co-operate.

go around, a move from place to place or person to person. **b** be enough to give some to all.

go at, a attack: *With a snarl, the dog went at the intruder.* **b** *Informal.* make a start on: *The boys went at the dinner as if they were starving.*

go back on. See BACK.

go by, a pass. **b** be guided by; follow: *He promised to go by the rules.* **c** be controlled by. **d** be known by: *She goes by the nickname of "Slim."*

go down, a descend; decline; sink. **b** be defeated; lose. **c** lose violence; subside: *The wind went down in the evening.* **d** be accepted by: *Her motion did not go down with the assembly.* **e** in contract bridge, fail to fulfill one's contract. **f** be swallowed: *The jello went down easily, despite the sore throat.* **g** *Slang.* happen.

go down the road, *Informal.* move to another place, usually a city.

go for, *Informal.* **a** try to get. **b** favour; support. **c** be attracted to. **d** attack.

go in for, *Informal.* **a** try to do; take part in; spend time and energy at: *She used to go in for basketball.* **b** favour; support.

go into, a *Arithmetic.* be contained in: *3 goes into 9 three times.* **b** investigate. **c** become involved with: *to go into music.*

go in with, join; share with.

go it, *Informal.* go fast (*used in imperative only).*

go it alone, act without assistance; act independently or solely.

go off, a leave; depart. **b** be fired; explode: *The gun went off accidentally.* **c** stop functioning; cease working: *The hydro went off during the storm.* **d** of food, become tainted or sour; lose quality; deteriorate. **e** take place; happen.

go on, a go ahead; go forward. **b** continue; last: *The noise went on for another two hours.* **c** start functioning: *The radio goes on when you turn this switch.* **d** manage. **e** behave: *If you go on that way, you'll get into trouble.* **f** happen: *What's going on here?* **g** talk a lot.

go out, a leave a room, one's home, etc.: *She went out at eight o'clock.* **b** stop burning or shining: *Don't let the candle go out. The lights went out during the storm.* **c** go to parties, movies, about town, etc.: *They don't go out much.* **d** date; keep company: *Are she and Rocco still going out?* **e** of the heart, feelings, etc., feel sympathy (for a person or persons): *His heart went out to them.* **f** go on strike. **g** cease to be fashionable. **h** *Golf.* play the first nine holes of a course. **i** *Cdn.* of ice, break up in spring and move with the current until melted.

go over, *Informal.* **a** look at carefully. **b** do again. **c** read again. **d** succeed. **e** change sides, political party, etc.: *go over to the opposition.* **f** *Slang.* beat up.

go (someone) **one better, a** outdo or excel to some extent in quality or fitness of action. **b** accept a bet and offer to increase it by a unit in kind.

go through, a go to the end of; do all of; finish: *I went through two books over the weekend.* **b** undergo; experience: *She went through some hard times.* **c** search: *He went through his pockets to find a nickel.* **d** use up; spend; exhaust: *She went through all her money.* **e** be accepted or approved: *The new schedule did not go through.*

go through with, complete; carry out to the end: *He disliked the job so much that he refused to go through with it.*

go together, a match; harmonize: *Pink and orange don't go together.* **b** keep steady company.

go under, a be overwhelmed; sink. **b** be ruined; fail.

go up, a ascend; rise. **b** increase: *The price went up.* **c** be built; be raised: *New houses are going up quickly. The curtain goes up at 7 p.m.*

go with, a accompany. **b** keep company with: *He's been going with Peg for a long time.* **c** be in harmony with: *That tie goes with your suit.* **d** belong with.

go without, do without the thing stated or implied.

let go, a allow to escape. **b** give up one's hold (*of*). **c** give up. **d** fail to keep in good condition. **e** fire from a job.

let (oneself) **go, a** give way to one's feelings or desires. **b** fail to keep oneself in good condition.

to go, of prepared food, for taking away from the place where it was bought, to be eaten elsewhere: *She ordered two hamburgers to go.*

—*n.* **1** the act of going. **2** *Informal.* spirit; energy. **3** *Informal.* the state of affairs; way things are. **4** *Informal.* a fashion; style; rage. **5** *Informal.* a try; attempt; chance: *Let's have another go at this problem.* **6** something successful; a success: *He seems to be making a go of his new store.* **7** *Informal.* a bargain; anything agreed on: *It's a go.*

no go, *Informal.* not to be done or had; impossible; useless; worthless.
on the go, *Informal.* always moving or acting: *He is so busy that he's on the go from morning till night.*
—adj. Slang. in the launching of space capsules, missiles, etc., in perfect order and ready to proceed; A-one: *All systems are go.* ⟨OE *gān*⟩ **—'go•er,** *n.*

☛ *Syn. v.* **2. Go,** LEAVE = move away from a point or place. **Go,** the opposite of *come,* emphasizes the movement involved: *He comes and goes as he pleases.* **Leave** emphasizes the departure from the place where one is (or has been): *He has left home. The boat left yesterday.*

☛ *Usage.* **Go and** is used informally to introduce or emphasize a verb: *Go and try it yourself* (no actual movement meant). *She went and shot the bear herself.* Sometimes the phrase suggests criticism of the action referred to: *He went and bought that rusty old car.* Though **go and** is appropriate in writing dialogue and in some narration, it should be omitted in exposition and in all formal writing.

go² [gou] *n.* a Japanese game for two people, played on a gridded board with white and black pieces. The object is to surround one's opponent's pieces. ⟨< Sino-Japanese⟩

goa ['gouə] *n.* a small Tibetan antelope (*Procapra picticaudata*) with long hair and a grey-brown coat. ⟨< Tibetan *dgoba*⟩

goad [goud] *n., v. —n.* **1** a sharp-pointed stick for driving cattle, etc.; gad. **2** anything that drives or urges one on.
—v. drive or urge on; act as a goad to: *Hunger goaded him to steal a loaf of bread.* ⟨OE *gād*⟩

go–a•head ['gou ə,hɛd] *Informal. n.* **1** the act of going forward; ambition; spirit. **2** authority to proceed. **3** (*adjl.*) disposed to push ahead; ambitious. **4** (*adjl.*) giving authority to proceed: *a go-ahead signal.*

goal [goul] *n.* **1** *Sports.* **a** the space between two posts into which a player tries to shoot a puck, kick a ball, etc. in order to score. **b** the act of scoring in such a manner. **c** the point or points counted for scoring a goal; a score: *Our team won, four goals to three.* **d** the position of goalkeeper. **2** the finish line of a race. **3** something for which an effort is made; something wanted; one's aim or object in doing something: *Her goal was to be a great doctor.* ⟨ME *gol*; origin uncertain⟩ **—'goal-less,** *adj.*

goal•ie ['gouli] *n. Sports.* the player who guards the goal to prevent scoring; goalkeeper. Also, **goaler, goalkeeper.**

goal•keep•ing ['goul,kipɪŋ] *n. Sports.* guarding the goal.

goal line the line marking the goal in a game.

goal–mouth ['goul ,mʌuθ] *n. Sports.* the area just in front of the goal. See CREASE (def. 2).

goal post *Sports.* one of a pair of posts with a bar across them, forming a goal.

goal•tender goalie.

go•an•na [gou'ænə] *n.* a large flesh-eating lizard of Australia. ⟨aphetic form of *iguana*⟩

Go•a powder ['gouə] a yellowish crystalline powder obtained from the wood of *Andira araroba,* a tropical tree native to Brazil. ⟨< *Goa,* an administrative district of India, formerly Portuguese⟩

goat [gout] *n., pl.* **goat** or **goats. 1** any of a genus (*Capra*) of bovid mammals with backward-curving horns, native to stony and mountainous regions of Europe, Asia, and N Africa, and including numerous domestic breeds and varieties raised for milk, meat, and wool. Goats are most closely related to sheep, but are lighter in build, stronger, and more agile. **2** *Informal.* scapegoat. **3 Goat,** *Astronomy or astrology.* Capricorn.
get (someone's) **goat,** *Informal.* make someone annoyed or angry. ⟨OE *gāt*⟩ **—'goat,like,** *adj.*

goat antelope any of various bovid ruminants, sharing characteristics of both goats and antelopes. The serow, goral, and chamois are all goat antelopes.

goat•ee [gou'ti] *n.* a small, pointed beard on a man's chin. See BEARD for picture.

goat•fish ['gout,fɪʃ] *n.* any of various brightly coloured tropical fishes (family Mullidae), living in reefs and having large scales and barbels hanging from their lower jaw.

goat•herd ['gout,hɜrd] *n.* a person who tends goats.

goats•beard ['gouts,bird] *n.* **1** a composite plant (*Tragopogon pratensis*) having yellow flowers. **2** a plant (*Aruncus dioicus*) of the rose family, having clusters of white flowers.

goat•skin ['gout,skɪn] *n.* **1** the hide of a goat. **2** leather made from the hide of goats. **3** something made of goatskin, such as a container for wine or water.

goat's–rue ['gouts ,ru] *n.* **1** a plant (*Tephrosia virginiana*) bearing yellow and purple blossoms and belonging to the pea family. **2** a large plant (*Galega officinalis*) native to Europe, Asia, and Africa, having bushy white and blue blossoms and belonging to the pea family.

goat•suck•er ['gout,sʌkər] *n.* any of a family (Caprimulgidae) of nocturnal, insect-eating birds having long, slender wings, a very short bill, an enormous mouth, and soft, mottled plumage resembling that of owls. Two goatsuckers found in Canada are the whippoorwill and the nighthawk. ⟨so called from an ancient belief that these birds with their enormous mouths sucked milk from goats in pastures; the birds often fly around grazing animals at night, catching insects on the wing⟩

gob [gɒb] *n. Informal.* a lump; mass: *She put a big gob of honey on her bread.* ⟨apparently < OF *gobe*⟩

gob•bet ['gɒbɪt] *n.* a lump; mass. ⟨ME < OF *gobet,* dim. of *gobe*⟩

gob•ble¹ ['gɒbəl] *v.* **-bled, -bling. 1** eat fast and greedily; swallow quickly in big pieces. **2** *Informal.* seize or accept eagerly (*used with* **up**): *He gobbled up every piece of information he could find on the rock group.* ⟨< *gob*⟩

gob•ble² ['gɒbəl] *v.* **-bled, -bling;** *n. —v.* make the throaty sound that a male turkey does.
—n. the throaty sound that a male turkey makes. ⟨imitative⟩

gob•ble•dy•gook or **gob•ble•de•gook** ['gɒbəldi,guk] *n. Informal.* speech or writing that is unnecessarily complicated or involved: *Official documents are often full of gobbledygook.* ⟨coined by Maury Maverick, U.S. Congressman, in 1944⟩

gob•bler ['gɒblər] *n.* a male turkey.

Gob•e•lin ['gɒbəlɪn] *or* ['goubəlɪn]; *French,* [gɔ'blɛ̃] *adj., n.*
—adj. **1** made at the factory of the Gobelins in Paris: *Gobelin tapestry or upholstery.* **2** of or having to do with such tapestry or upholstery.
—n. a Gobelin tapestry.

go–be•tween ['gou bɪ,twin] *n.* a person who goes back and forth between others with messages, proposals, suggestions, etc.; intermediary: *She acted as a go-between in the settlement of the strike.*

gob•let ['gɒblɪt] *n.* **1** a drinking glass with a base and stem. **2** *Archaic.* a hollow dish to drink from, usually without a handle. ⟨ME < OF *gobelet,* dim. of *gobel* cup⟩

gob•lin ['gɒblɪn] *n. Folklore.* an ugly sprite that is mischievous or evil. ⟨ME < MF *gobelin* ? < MHG *kobold* sprite⟩

go•by ['goubi] *n., pl.* **-by** or **-bies.** any of a large family (Gobiidae) of small, mainly marine fishes having a large head and two spiny dorsal fins, and with the pelvic fins united to form a kind of suction cup which permits the fishes to cling to rocks, etc. ⟨< L *gobius, cobius,* a kind of fish < Gk. *kōbios*⟩

go–by ['gou ,baɪ] *n. Informal.* a going by or casting off; a slight; intentional neglect: *He gave her the go-by.*

god [gɒd] *n., interj. —n.* **1 God,** in the Christian, Jewish, Muslim, and certain other religions, the creator and ruler of the universe; the Supreme Being, perfect in goodness, knowledge, and power. **2** a being thought of as superior to nature and to human beings and considered worthy of worship. **3** a male god. **4** an image of a god; idol. **5** a person or thing intensely admired and respected: *His father was a god to him.*
—interj. Often, **God,** *Slang.* an exclamation or oath, often regarded as blasphemous or improper, expressing surprise, admiration, dismay, irritation, etc.; often used in expressions such as **My God!** or **God in Heaven!** ⟨OE⟩
☛ *Hom.* GAUD.

god•child ['gɒd,tʃaɪld] *n., pl.* **-chil•dren.** a child for whom an adult takes vows at its baptism.

god•damned ['gɒd'dæmd] *adj.* cursed by God (*used as an expletive*).

god•daugh•ter ['gɒd,dɒtər] *n.* a female godchild.

god•dess ['gɒdɪs] *n.* **1** a female god. **2** a very beautiful or charming woman. **3** a woman who is intensely admired and respected.

go–dev•il ['gou ,dɛvəl] *n.* **1** *Cdn. Mining and lumbering.* a type of sleigh used, especially formerly, to move ore, logs, etc.; stoneboat or drag. **2** a device flushed through a pipeline to clean the inside of the pipe. **3** a handcar or handcart.

god•fa•ther ['gɒd,fɒðər] *n.* a man who takes vows for a child when it is baptized.

god•for•sak•en ['gɒdfər,seikən] *adj.* **1** Often, **Godforsaken,** apparently forsaken by God. **2** completely given over to evil; totally depraved. **3** desolate; wretched.

God–giv•en ['gɒd 'gɪvən] *adj.* **1** given by God. **2** very welcome and suitable.

God•head ['gɒd,hɛd] *n.* **1** God. **2 godhead,** divine nature; divinity.

god•hood ['gɒd,hʊd] *n.* divine character; divinity.

god•less ['gɒdlɪs] *adj.* **1** not believing in God; not religious. **2** wicked; evil. **—'god•less•ly,** *adv.* **—'god•less•ness,** *n.*

god•like ['gɒd,ləik] *adj.* **1** like God or a god; divine. **2** suitable for God or a god.

god•ling ['gɒdlɪŋ] *n.* in Greek and Roman mythology, a minor god, especially one associated with a place.

god•ly ['gɒdli] *adj.* **-li•er, -li•est. 1** obeying God's laws; religious; pious; devout. **2** *Archaic.* of or from God; divine. **—'god•li•ness,** *n.*

god•moth•er ['gɒd,mʌðər] *n.* a woman who takes vows for a child when it is baptized.

god•par•ent ['gɒd,pɛrənt] *n.* a godfather or godmother.

God's acre a churchyard with graves in it; a burial ground; cemetery.

god•send ['gɒd,sɛnd] *n.* something unexpected and very welcome, as if sent from God.

god•son ['gɒd,sʌn] *n.* a male godchild.

God•speed ['gɒd,spid] *n.* a wish of success to a person starting on a journey or undertaking.

god•wit ['gɒdwɪt] *n.* any of a genus (*Limosa*) of large shore birds having a long, upturned bill and long legs. Godwits belong to the same family (Scolopacidae) as snipes and sandpipers. ⟨origin uncertain⟩

go•e•lette [,gouə'lɛt] *n. Cdn.* a flat-bottomed, motor-driven vessel for carrying freight. ⟨< Cdn.F < F *goellette* fishing boat⟩

goers and comers *Cdn.* formerly, voyageurs plying between Québec and the fur country.

goe•thite or **go•thite** ['goutəit] *or* ['gœtəit] *n.* a mineral consisting of a hydrous oxide of iron. ⟨< Johann W. von *Goethe* (1749-1832), German writer, noted also for studies in mineralogy⟩

go•fer ['goufər] *n. Informal.* a person who runs errands. ⟨< *go for* fetch⟩
☛ *Hom.* GOPHER.

gof•fer ['gɒfər] *v., n.* —*v.* crimp or pleat (cloth or paper).
—*n.* **1** a crimp in cloth or paper. **2** an iron used for pleating cloth. ⟨< F *gaufrer* to crimp < *gaufre* waffle < Du. *wafel* waffle⟩

go–get•ter ['gou ,gɛtər] *n. Informal.* an aggressive person who tries hard for, and usually gets, what he or she wants.

gog•gle ['gɒgəl] *v.* **-gled, -gling;** *n.* —*v.* **1** stare with wide-open or bulging eyes: *We all goggled at the huge dog.* **2** of the eyes, bulge or open very wide: *The children's eyes goggled as the magician pulled a rabbit out of the empty hat.* **3** of eyes, roll. **4** be goggle-eyed with surprise, wonder, or disbelief.
—*n.* **1** Usually, **goggles,** *pl.* a pair of large, close-fitting spectacles to protect the eyes from light, dust, etc.: *She wore goggles while welding the broken steel rod.* **2** (*adjl.*) bulging: *the goggle eyes of a frog.* ⟨ME *gogel(en)*; origin uncertain⟩

goggle–eye ['gɒgəl ,aɪ] *n.* any of several fishes with large, globular eyes. The rock bass is a goggle-eye.

gog•gle–eyed ['gɒgəl ,aɪd] *adj.* having rolling, bulging, or staring eyes.

gog•let ['gɒglɪt] *n.* a water jug used in India. ⟨< Pg. *gorgoleta,* dim. of *gorja* throat; from its long neck⟩

go–go ['gou ,gou] *adj.* **1** of, having to do with, or designating a type of dance characterized by rapid, rhythmic body movements and performed either alone or without body contact between partners. **2** performing such a dance, especially in a discothèque: *a go-go dancer.*

Goi•del ['gɔɪdəl] *n.* **1** any member of the Gaelic branch of the Celts. **2** a speaker of a Goidelic language. ⟨< Irish *Góidil* Gael⟩

Goi•del•ic [gɔɪ'dɛlɪk] *adj., n.* —*adj.* **1** of or having to do with the Goidels. **2** of, having to do with, or denoting the Celtic language group to which Scots Gaelic, Irish, and Manx belong.
—*n.* one of the two main divisions of the Celtic language (the other being *Brythonic*), including Scots Gaelic, Irish, and Manx.

go•ing ['gouɪŋ] *n., adj. v.* —*n.* **1** a going away; leaving: *His going was sudden.* **2** the condition of the ground or road for walking, riding, etc.: *The going is bad on a muddy road.*
—*adj.* **1** moving; acting; working; running. **2** that goes; that can or will go. **3** in existence; existing; current: *the going price for gold.*
be going to, will; be about to: *It is going to rain soon.*
going on, almost; nearly: *It is going on four o'clock.*
—*v.* ppr. of GO.

going concern a company, person, etc. that is busy and doing well.

go•ing–o•ver ['gouɪŋ ,ouvər] *n.* **1** *Informal.* a thorough study; intense and critical examination. **2** *Slang.* **a** a scolding. **b** a beating.

go•ings–on ['gouɪŋz 'ɒn] *n.pl.* actions or behaviour, especially when viewed with disapproval or suspicion: *Her parents were unhappy about the goings-on at the party.*

goi•tre ['gɔɪtər] *n.* chronic enlargement of the thyroid gland, usually producing a large swelling in the throat. Also, **goiter.** ⟨< F *goitre,* ult. < L *guttur* throat⟩ **—'goi•trous,** *adj.*

Gol•con•da [gɒl'kɒndə] *n.* a mine or source of wealth. ⟨after an ancient city in S India, famed for its wealth and for its diamond cutting⟩

gold [gould] *n., adj.* —*n.* **1** a shiny, yellow, non-rusting, metallic chemical element that is a precious metal used especially for making jewellery and coins. *Symbol*: Au (for L *aurum*); *at.no.* 79; *at.mass* 196.97. **2** coins made of gold. **3** money in large sums; wealth; riches. **4** a gold medal: *She won gold in the Olympics.* **5** a bright, beautiful, or precious thing or material: *He has a heart of gold.* **6** a deep, slightly brownish yellow.
—*adj.* **1** made of gold: *gold coins, a gold bracelet.* **2** resembling gold; having the metallic colour of gold: *a book bound in dark blue, with gold lettering.* **3** of a record, tape, etc., selling a large number of copies. **4** deep, slightly brownish yellow: *a gold carpet.* ⟨OE⟩

gold•beat•er ['gould,bitər] *n.* a person whose work is beating gold into very thin sheets or gold leaf.

gold•beat•ing ['gould,bitɪŋ] *n.* the process of beating gold sheets into gold leaf.

gold brick 1 gilded metal passed off as gold. **2** *Informal.* anything that looks good at first, but turns out to be worthless.

gold•brick ['gould,brɪk] *v., n. Slang.* —*v.* **1** swindle, as by means of a gold brick. **2** pretend illness to avoid duties.
—*n.* a person, especially in the armed forces, who avoids duty or shirks work. **—'gold,brick•er,** *n.*

gold digger 1 a person who digs for or mines gold. **2** *Slang.* a person whose primary motive for associating with another person (often a member of the opposite sex) is one of material gain.

gold dust very tiny bits of gold; gold in a fine powder.

gold•en ['gouldən] *adj.* **1** made or consisting of gold: *golden earrings.* **2** resembling gold; having the metallic colour of gold: *a golden buckle.* **3** shining or lustrous like gold: *The windows were golden from the light of the setting sun.* **4** deep, slightly brownish yellow: *golden velvet upholstery.* **5** blond: *golden hair.* **6** most excellent or precious; extremely valuable, important, etc.: *golden deeds.* **7** extremely favourable or advantageous: *a golden opportunity.* **8** very happy and prosperous; flourishing: *the golden days of youth, a golden age.* **9** having to do with the fiftieth year or event in a series: *a golden wedding anniversary.* **10** of a voice, rich and mellow.

Golden Age 1 *Greek and Roman mythology.* the first age of humankind, an era of perfect prosperity, happiness, and innocence. **2** a legendary and imaginary age, long past, of perfect human happiness and innocence. **3 golden age,** a period of great progress, cultural achievement, etc.

golden ager ['eidʒər] a senior citizen, especially a retired one.

golden aster any North American plant of the genus *Chrysopsis,* having golden flowers.

golden calf wealth too highly esteemed. ⟨in the Bible, an idol made of gold, set up by the Israelites in the wilderness⟩

golden carp goldfish.

golden eagle a large, mainly dark brown eagle (*Aquila chrysaetos*) of the northern hemisphere having golden brown feathers on the back of the head and neck, legs that are feathered to the toes, and a large bill.

gold•en•eye ['gouldə,naɪ] *n., pl.* **-eye** or **-eyes.** either of two northern diving ducks having black and white plumage and yellow eyes: the **common goldeneye** (*Bucephala clangula*) and **Barrow's goldeneye** (*B. islandica*).

Golden Fleece *Greek mythology.* a fleece of gold that hung in a sacred grove, where it was guarded by a dragon until Jason and the Argonauts carried it away with the help of Medea.

golden handshake *Informal.* an early pension or a lump sum of money given at early retirement.

golden mean the avoidance of extremes; a safe, sensible way of doing things; moderation.

golden nematode a nematode that lives as a parasite on the roots of tomato and potato plants.

golden oldie ['ouldi] *Informal.* a piece of popular music, etc. that has withstood the test of time.

golden pheasant a pheasant (*Chrysolophus pictus*) with colourful plumage and an orange crest, native to China and Tibet.

gold•en•rain tree ['gouldən,rein] a deciduous tree (*Koelreuteria paniculata*) native to Asia, bearing small yellow blossoms and paperlike fruit pods, and belonging to the soapberry family.

golden retriever a breed of medium-sized retriever having a golden, water-resistant coat, and often trained to retrieve game, especially waterfowl.

gold•en•rod ['gouldən,rɒd] *n.* any of a genus (*Solidago*) of mostly perennial plants of the composite family having toothed leaves and spikes or panicles of tiny flower heads that are composed of both disk and ray flowers. **Canada goldenrod** (*S. canadensis*) is a common Canadian weed.

golden rule a rule of conduct that people should treat others as they themselves would want to be treated.

gol•den•seal ['gouldən,sil] *n.* a North American plant of the buttercup family (*Hydrastis canadensis),* once used as a medicine.

golden wedding the 50th anniversary of a wedding.

Golden West *Cdn.* formerly, the Prairie Provinces.

gold•eye ['goul,daɪ] *n., pl.* **-eye** or **-eyes.** *Cdn.* an edible freshwater fish (*Hiodon alosoides*) native to rivers and lakes from Ontario to the Northwest Territories and south to Oklahoma and Mississippi. Goldeye is smoked and dyed for marketing as a table delicacy.

gold–filled ['gould 'fɪld] *adj.* made of cheap metal covered with a layer of gold.

gold•finch ['gould,fɪntʃ] *n.* **1** any of several small North American songbirds (genus *Spinus*), especially *S. tristis*, the male of which has bright yellow and black plumage in breeding season. **2** a small European songbird (*Carduelis carduelis*) often kept as a cage bird, the male of which has a red and white head, mainly black body, and gold patches on the wings. ⟨OE *goldfinc*⟩

gold•fish ['gould,fɪʃ] *n., pl.* **-fish** or **-fish•es.** a thick-bodied freshwater fish (*Carassius auratus*) of the same family as minnows and carps, native to E Asia but widely raised in many different breeds as an ornamental fish for aquariums and ponds. In the wild, goldfish are usually olive green but as ornamental fish they are selectively bred for a golden or orange colour. Also called **golden carp**.

gold•i•locks ['gouldi,lɒks] *n.* **1** a person, especially a girl, with blond hair. **2** a yellow-flowered Eurasian plant (*Aster linosyris*) of the composite family.

gold leaf gold beaten into very thin sheets.

gold medal **1** the highest award for an event in the Olympic games. **2** the highest award in other contests.

gold mine **1** a mine where ore yielding gold is obtained. **2** the source of something of great value: *His wide reading made him a gold mine of information. Her real estate business is a gold mine.*

gold plate cutlery or crockery plated with gold.

gold–plate ['gould 'pleit] *v.* **-plat•ed, -plat•ing.** coat (another metal or a metal object) with gold, especially by electroplating.

gold reserve the gold at the disposal of the government of a nation, used to pay debts to other governments, sustain credit expansion, etc.

gold rush a sudden and large-scale movement of people to a place where gold has just been found.

gold•smith ['gould,smɪθ] *n.* a person whose work is making articles of gold. ⟨OE⟩

goldsmith beetle **1** a large American scarab (*Cotalpa lanigera*), bright lemon in colour, whose diet consists of tree foliage. **2** a glossy European scarab (*Cetonia aurata*), golden in colour.

gold standard the use of gold as the standard of value for the money of a country. The nation's unit of money value is declared by the government to be equal to and exchangeable for a certain amount of gold.

gold•thread ['gould,θrɛd] *n.* any one of a number of North American plants of the buttercup family, especially one with white flowers.

go•lem ['gouləm] *n. Jewish legend.* a being created artificially and given life supernaturally. ⟨< Hebrew, monster⟩

golf [gɒlf] *n., v. —n.* an outdoor game played with a small, hard ball and a set of long-handled clubs having wooden or iron heads. The player tries to drive the ball into a series of holes, usually 9 or 18, with as few strokes as possible.
—v. play the game of golf: *He golfs every Saturday.* ⟨origin uncertain⟩ **—'golf•er,** *n.*

golf club **1** a long-handled club having a wooden or iron head, used in playing golf. **2** a group of people joined together for the purpose of playing golf. **3** the buildings, land, etc. used by such a group.

golf course or **links** a place where golf is played, having tees, greens, and a fairway.

Gol•go•tha ['gɒlgəθə] *or* [gɒl'gɒθə] *n.* **1** the place of Christ's crucifixion; Calvary. **2** a place of burial. **3** a place of suffering or sacrifice. ⟨< Gk. < Aramaic *gūlgūlthā* place of skulls < Hebrew⟩

Go•li•ath [gə'laɪəθ] *n.* any huge, extremely strong man. ⟨in the Bible, a Philistine giant whom David killed with a stone from a sling⟩

gol•li•wog ['gɒli,wɒg] *n.* a black-faced rag doll. ⟨< the name of a doll in children's books by the American sisters Bertha and Florence Upton in the early 20c., perhaps a blend of *golly* and *polliwog*⟩

gol•ly ['gɒli] *interj.* a word used to express surprise, etc. ⟨euphemism for *God*⟩

go•losh [gə'lɒʃ] See GALOSH.

gom•broon [gɒm'brun] *n.* a type of Persian pottery from the Persian Gulf. ⟨after *Gombroon* (Bandar Abbas), town on the Persian Gulf⟩

Go•mor•rah or **Go•mor•rha** [gə'mɔrə] *n.* any extremely wicked place. ⟨in the Bible, a wicked city destroyed, together with Sodom, by fire from heaven⟩

go•mu•ti [gou'muti] *n.* a palm tree (*Arenga pinnata*) native to the Malay Peninsula, bearing featherlike leaves. A crude sugar is made from its sap as an alcoholic beverage called arrack. ⟨< Malay *gemuti*⟩

–gon *combining form.* a figure having —— angles: *octagon.* ⟨< Gk. *gonon* having angles⟩

go•nad ['gounæd] *or* ['gɒnæd] *n.* an organ in which reproductive cells develop. Ovaries and testes are gonads. ⟨< NL < Gk. *gonē* seed < *gignesthai* be produced⟩ **—go'nad•al,** *adj.*

gonadal dys•gen•e•sis [dɪs'dʒɛnəsɪs] Turner syndrome and its variants, in which the development of the gonads is defective. See TURNER SYNDROME.

go•na•dor•e•lin [,gounə'dɔrəlɪn] *n.* a drug used as a diagnostic test for disorders of the pituitary gland.

go•nad•o•trop•ic [gou,nædou'trɒpɪk] *adj.* stimulating the gonads. Also, **gonadotrophic.**

go•nad•o•trop•in [gou,nædou'troupɪn] *n.* a gonadotropic substance. Also, **gonadotrophin.**

Gond [gɒnd] *n.* a member of a Dravidian people living in central India.

Gon•di ['gɒndi] *n.* the Dravidian language of the Gonds.

gon•do•la ['gɒndələ] *or* [gɒn'doulə] *n.* **1** a long, narrow, flat-bottomed boat with a high peak at each end, used on the canals of Venice. **2** a large, flat-bottomed river boat with pointed ends. **3** a freight car that has low sides and no top. **4** a car that hangs under a dirigible and holds the motors, passengers, etc. **5** *Cdn.* a broadcasting booth up near the roof of a hockey arena. **6** a car that hangs from and moves along a cable: *We went up the mountain in the gondola.* ⟨< dial. Ital. *gondola* < *gondolare* to rock⟩

gon•do•lier [,gɒndə'lir] *n.* one who rows or poles a gondola. ⟨< F < Ital. *gondoliere* < *gondola* gondola⟩

Gond•wa•na•land [gɒn'dwɑnə,lænd] *n.* a hypothetical continent of the Mesozoic era that linked what are now Africa, India, and Australia. ⟨< *Gondwana* region in India, where tillite deposits were found⟩

gone [gɒn] *adj., v. —adj.* **1** moved away; left. **2** lost; hopeless: *a gone case.* **3** dead. **4** used up. **5** failed; ruined. **6** weak; faint: *a gone feeling.* **7** pregnant: *She's six months gone.* **8** *Slang.* **a** very good; great: *the gone blues sung by Bessie Smith.* **b** that carries

strong feeling; transported; inspired: *a gone look on his face, gone music.*
far gone, a much advanced; deeply involved. **b** near death or ruin.
gone on, *Informal.* in love with: *She's completely gone on Fred.*
—v. pp. of GO.

gon•er ['gɒnər] *n. Informal.* a person or thing that is dead, ruined, past help, etc.

gon•fa•lon ['gɒnfələn] *n.* a flag or banner hung from a crossbar instead of a pole, often having several streamers. Gonfalons were used by medieval Italian republics. ⟨< Ital. *gonfalone*, ult. < OHG *gundfano,* literally, war banner⟩

gong [gɒŋ] *n.* **1** a percussion instrument consisting of a platelike metal disk with a turned-up rim that is struck with a usually soft-headed hammer, producing a hollow, bell-like sound of indefinite pitch. **2** a similar metal disk or hemisphere producing a tone when struck with a hammer, used as a signalling device, alarm, etc. ⟨< Malay⟩

go•nid•i•um [gou'nɪdiəm] *n. Botany.* a reproductive cell, as a tetraspore or a zoospore, created through asexual reproduction in various algae. ⟨< NL dim. < Gk. *gonos, gone* procreation⟩

gonio– *combining form.* angle: *goniometer.* Compare -GON. ⟨< Gk. combining form of *gōnía* angle⟩

go•ni•om•e•ter [ˌgouni'ɒmətər] *n.* an instrument for measuring the angles of solids such as crystals.

go•ni•om•et•ry [ˌgouni'ɒmətri] *n.* the science of measuring angles.

–go•ni•um ['gouniəm] *combining form.* a structure in which reproductive cells develop. ⟨< NL < Gk. *gonos* procreation⟩

gono– *combining form.* reproductive. ⟨< Gk. *gonos, gone* procreation⟩

gon•o•coc•cus [ˌgɒnə'kɒkəs] *n.* the bacterium causing gonorrhea. ⟨< NL < Gk. *gonos, gone* procreation + Gk. *kokkos* seed⟩

gon•o•phore ['gɒnəˌfɔr] *n. Botany.* the end of the axis of a flower, raising the pistil and stamens out of the floral envelope. ⟨< Gk. *gonos, gone* procreation + *-phore*⟩

gon•o•pore ['gɒnə'pɔr] *n. Zoology.* an outer opening in insects and earthworms through which reproductive cells are released. ⟨< Gk. *gonos, gone* procreation + *poros* a passage⟩

gon•or•rhe•a or **gon•or•rhoe•a** [ˌgɒnə'riə] *n.* a contagious venereal disease that causes inflammation of the genital, urinary, and certain other organs. ⟨< LL < Gk. *gonorrhoia* < *gonos* seed + *rhoia* flow⟩

–gony *combining form.* genesis: *cosmogony.* ⟨< L *-gonia* < Gk. *-goneia,* equiv. to *gon(os)*⟩

goo [gu] *n. Slang.* **1** any thick, sticky substance. **2** sentimentalism; gush. ⟨origin uncertain⟩ **—'goo•ey,** *adj.*

good [gʊd] *adj.* **bet•ter, best;** *n., interj. —adj.* **1** true; upright; moral. **2** having the right qualities; admirable; desirable: *a good book, a good game.* **3** as it ought to be; right; proper: *Do what seems good to you.* **4** well-behaved: *a good boy.* **5** kind; friendly: *Say a good word for me.* **6** benevolent; gracious: *a good queen.* **7** honourable; worthy: *my good friend.* **8** reliable; dependable: *good judgment.* **9** real; genuine: *It is hard to tell counterfeit money from good money.* **10** agreeable; pleasant: *Have a good time.* **11** beneficial; advantageous; useful: *drugs good for a fever.* **12** well-suited to its purpose: *An artisan insists on good tools.* **13** satisfying; sufficient in size and quality: *a good meal.* **14** not spoiled; sound: *a good apple.* **15** thorough; complete: *to do a good job.* **16** skilful; clever: *a good manager, to be good at arithmetic.* **17** fairly great; more than a little: *a good while.* **18** best: *her good china.* **19** at least: *a good 20 minutes.*
as good as, almost the same as; almost; practically: *The day is as good as over.*
feel good, *Informal.* feel well or elated.
good and, *Informal.* very; extremely: *She was good and angry.*
good for, a able to last for. **b** able to pay. **c** worth: *a coupon good for a free ride.* **d** resulting in: *good for a laugh.* **e** a term of praise: *Good for you!*
make good, a make up for; give or do in place of; pay for: *She made good the damage done by her car.* **b** fulfil; carry out: *to make good a promise.* **c** succeed in doing. **d** succeed; prosper: *His parents expected him to make good.* **e** prove.
—n. **1** benefit; advantage; use: *work for the common good.* **2** that which is good: *He always looked for the good in people.* **3** a good thing. **4** good people.
come to no good, end badly.
for good or **for good and all,** forever; finally and permanently: *He has left Canada for good.*
to the good, on the side of profit or advantage; in one's favour.
up to no good, making mischief; misbehaving.
—interj. that is good! ⟨OE *gōd*⟩
☛ *Usage.* **good,** WELL. Careful speakers maintain the distinction between **good** and **well**, using the former as adjective only: *Her playing is good (adj.) She plays well (adv.).* Both terms are used as adjectives to mean 'fit, in good health': *I feel good. I feel well.* While both these sentences are acceptable, many people prefer *I feel well* to be used in writing. *I feel good* can have an emotional meaning.

good afternoon a salutation of leave-taking or greeting spoken in the afternoon.

good•bye or **good–bye** [ˌgʊd'baɪ] *interj. or n., pl.* **-byes.** an expression of good wishes on parting or ending a telephone conversation; farewell. Sometimes, **good-by.** ⟨contraction of *God be with ye*⟩

good cheer 1 feasting and merrymaking. **2** good food and drink. **3** a spirit of optimism and courage: *Be of good cheer.*

good day a form of greeting or farewell used in the daytime.

good deal 1 much; many: *It cost a good deal more than I expected.* **2** *Informal.* a favourable business transaction; bargain: *It was a good deal all around.*

good evening a form of greeting or farewell used in the evening.

good–for–noth•ing ['gʊd fər 'nʌθɪŋ] *adj., n. —adj.* worthless; useless.
—n. a person considered worthless or useless.

Good Friday the Friday before Easter, observed by Christians in commemoration of Christ's crucifixion.

good–heart•ed ['gʊd 'hɑrtɪd] *adj.* kind and generous. **—'good-'heart•ed•ly,** *adv.* **—'good-'heart•ed•ness,** *n.*

good humour or **humor** a cheerful, pleasant disposition or mood.

good–hu•moured or **good–hu•mored** ['gʊd 'hjumərd] *adj.* cheerful; pleasant. **—'good-'hu•moured•ly** or **'good-'hu•mored•ly,** *adv.* **—'good-'hu•moured•ness** or **'good-'hu•mored•ness,** *n.*

good•ish ['gʊdɪʃ] *adj. Informal.* **1** pretty good. **2** fairly great; considerable: *There was a goodish amount of work involved.*

good–look•er ['gʊd 'lʊkər] *adj. Informal.* a person or animal of good or attractive appearance.

good–look•ing ['gʊd 'lʊkɪŋ] *adj.* having a pleasing appearance; handsome; attractive: *a good-looking woman.*

good looks a handsome or pleasing personal appearance.

good•ly ['gʊdli] *adj.* **-li•er, -li•est. 1** considerable: *a goodly quantity.* **2** *Archaic.* **a** excellent; fine: *a goodly land.* **b** good-looking: *a goodly youth.* **—'good•li•ness,** *n.*

good morning a form of greeting or farewell used in the morning.

good nature pleasant or kindly disposition; amiability.

good–na•tured ['gʊd 'neitʃərd] *adj.* pleasant; kindly; cheerful; agreeable. **—'good-'na•tured•ly,** *adv.* **—'good-'na•tured•ness,** *n.*

good•ness ['gʊdnɪs] *n., interj. —n.* **1** the quality or state of being good. **2** excellence; virtue. **3** kindness; friendliness. **4** the valuable quality; best part.
—interj., often, **my goodness,** an exclamation of surprise.
☛ *Syn. n.* **2. Goodness,** VIRTUE = excellence in character. **Goodness** applies to the inner quality in a person that makes him or her kind, generous, fair, sympathetic, and otherwise acceptable in character and conduct: *His goodness is shown by the many kind deeds he does.* **Virtue** applies to moral excellence that is acquired by consciously developing particular qualities of character, such as moral courage, justice, wise judgment, etc., or by consciously following the principles of right and wrong: *She is a woman of the highest virtue.*

good night 1 a form of farewell used at night. **2** *Informal.* an exclamation of surprise.

goods [gʊdz] *n.pl.* **1** personal property; belongings. **2** things for sale; wares. **3** material for clothing; cloth. **4** *Slang.* what is needed to do something. **5** *Brit.* freight (*often adjectival*).
catch with the goods, a catch with stolen goods. **b** catch in the act of committing a crime.
deliver the goods, *Slang.* do what is expected or wanted.
get or **have the goods on,** *Slang.* find out or know something bad about.
☛ *Syn.* **1.** See note at PROPERTY.

Good Samaritan any person who is unselfish in helping others. ⟨in the Bible, a traveller who rescued and cared for another traveller who had been beaten and robbed by thieves⟩

good–sized ['gʊd 'saɪzd] *adj.* large or somewhat large; ample: *a good-sized helping.*

good speed a farewell expressing a wish for success or good luck, or safety in travel.

good–tem•pered ['gʊd 'tɛmpərd] *adj.* easy to get along with; cheerful; agreeable. **—'good-'tem•pered•ly,** *adv.*

good turn a kind or friendly act; favour.

good will **1** a kindly or friendly feeling. **2** cheerful consent; willingness. **3** the reputation and steady trade that a business has with its customers.
☛ *Syn.* **1.** See note at FAVOUR.

good•y¹ ['gʊdi] *n., pl.* **good•ies;** *interj., adj. Informal.* *—n.* **1** something very good to eat; a piece of candy or cake: *There were lots of goodies at the party.* **2** anything desirable, pleasurable, or attractive: *a list of election goodies.*
—interj. a child's exclamation of pleasure.
—adj. making too much of being good; goody-goody. ⟨< *good*⟩

good•y² ['gʊdi] *n., pl.* **good•ies.** *Archaic.* an old woman of humble station. ⟨var. of *goodwife*⟩

good•y–good•y ['gʊdi ˌgʊdi] *adj., n., pl.* **-good•ies.** *—adj.* self-righteously virtuous; good in an affected, prim, or weak way. *—n.* a person who makes too much of being good.

goof [guf] *n., v. Slang.* *—n.* **1** a stupid or foolish person. **2** a blunder; an obvious or careless error.
—v. **1** make a mistake; blunder. **2** make a complete hash of (something undertaken); bungle (*used with* **up**): *Don't ask him to do it, because he's sure to goof it up.*
goof off or **around,** waste time; loaf; shirk work or duty. ⟨apparently < dial. var. of earlier *goff* dunce < F *goffe* awkward, stupid⟩

goof•ball ['guf,bɒl] *n. Slang.* **1** a barbiturate pill, especially one taken with alcohol. **2** an odd, peculiar, or crazy person. **3** (*adjl.*) stupid: *What a goofball way to do it!*

goo•gly ['gugli] *n. Cricket.* a tricky manner of delivering the ball; an off-break disguised as a leg-break.

goo•gly–eyed ['gugli ˌaɪd] *adj.* GOGGLE-EYED.

goo•gol ['gugəl] *n.* a number represented by one followed by a hundred zeros; 10^{100}. ⟨coined by Dr. Edward Kasner (1878-1955), an American mathematician, on the basis of a child's word for a very large number⟩

goo•gol•plex ['gugəl,plɛks] *n.* a number represented by one followed by a googol zeros; $10^{10^{100}}$

goon [gun] *n. Slang.* **1** a ruffian hired to disrupt labour strikes. **2** a stupid person. ⟨< dialect *gooney* an idiot⟩

goo•ney bird ['guni] albatross. ⟨< *gooney,* sailor's name for the albatross, originally simpleton, probably < or akin to ME *gonen* to gape < OE *ganian* to gape⟩

goos•an•der [gu'sændər] *n.* the merganser duck. ⟨probably < goose + *bergander* sheldrake⟩

goose [gus] *n., pl.* **geese** *for 1 & 2,* **goos•es** *for 4-6; v.* **goosed, goos•ing.** *—n.* **1** any of various large, long-necked, web-footed waterfowl belonging to the same family (Anatidae) as ducks and swans. Geese are intermediate in size between ducks and swans and are less aquatic than either of these groups. **2** a female goose as distinguished from the male (gander). **3** the flesh of a goose. **4** a silly person: *What a goose you are!* **5** a tailor's smoothing iron with a long, curved handle like a goose's neck. **6** a playful prod in the behind.

Geese and goslings

cook (someone's) **goose,** *Informal.* ruin someone's chances, plans, etc.
kill the goose that lays the golden eggs, sacrifice future good or profit to satisfy present needs or greed.
—v. **1** feed gasoline suddenly to (an engine). **2** prod playfully in the behind. ⟨OE *gōs*⟩ **—'goose,like,** *adj.*

goose barnacle *Zoology.* any of various barnacles (genera *Lepas* and *Mitella*) that cling to rocks, ship bottoms, etc., by a thin, fleshy stem.

goose•ber•ry ['gus,bɛri] *or* ['guz,bɛri] *n., pl.* **-ries. 1** any of various shrubs (genus *Ribes*) of the northern hemisphere bearing yellowish green or reddish purple acid berries, some of which have prickly skins. **2** the fruit of any of these shrubs, used especially in pies, jellies, and preserves. ⟨? alteration of F *groseille* + E *berry*⟩

goose flesh or **bumps** or **pimples** skin that has become rough like that of a plucked goose, from cold or fright.

goose•foot ['gus,fʊt] *n., pl.* **-foots. 1** any of a genus (*Chenopodium*) of weedy plants having small, greenish flowers, dry, seedlike fruits, and, in some species, leaves shaped like the foot of a goose. **2** (*adjl.*) designating the family of herbs, shrubs, and small trees that includes the goosefoots and also the common vegetables beets and spinach.

goose•herd ['gus,hɜrd] *n.* a person who tends geese.

goose•neck ['gus,nɛk] *n.* anything long and curved like a goose's neck, such as an iron hook, a flexible support for a lamp, or a curved connecting pipe.

gooseneck lamp an electric light supported by a flexible tube like a goose's neck.

goose pimples GOOSE FLESH.

goose step a marching step in which the leg is swung high with straight, stiff knee.

goose–step ['gus ˌstɛp] *v.* **-stepped, -step•ping.** march with a goose step.

go•pher ['goufər] *n.* **1** a buff-coloured, burrowing ground squirrel (*Spermophilus richardsonii*) found in the central plains of North America, having short legs, short, rounded ears, small pouches inside the cheeks, and a slightly bushy tail about one third as long as the body. The gopher is one of the commonest mammals of the Canadian Prairies. **2** any of various other ground squirrels. **3** POCKET GOPHER. ⟨< Cdn.F *gaufre* < F *gaufre* honeycomb, from the structure of the animal's burrow⟩
☛ *Hom.* GOFER.

gopher snake **1** any of various large, harmless colubrine snakes (genus *Pituophis*) native to North America, whose diet consists of rodents; bullsnake. **2** a large, non-poisonous colubrine snake (*Drymarchon corais*) living in the lowlands from South Carolina to Texas.

go•ral ['gɔrəl] *n.* a goat antelope (genus *Naemorhedus*) of mountainous regions in Asia from Siberia to the Himalayas.

Gor•di•an knot ['gɔrdiən] **1** a knot tied by Gordius, King of Phrygia, to be undone only by the person who should rule Asia. Alexander the Great cut the knot with his sword after failing to untie it. **2** an intricate or baffling problem.
cut the Gordian knot, solve an intricate or vexing problem by some quick and drastic means.

Gor•don setter ['gɔrdən] a breed of setter developed in Scotland, having a black coat with tan markings. ⟨after 4th Duke of *Gordon* (1743-1827), Scottish nobleman and sportsman. 19c.⟩

gore¹ [gɔr] *n.* blood that is shed; thick blood; clotted blood: *Her injured arm was covered with gore.* ⟨OE *gor* dirt, dung⟩

gore² [gɔr] *v.* **gored, gor•ing.** wound with a horn or tusk: *The savage bull gored the farmer to death.* ⟨ME *gorre(n)*; origin uncertain⟩

gore³ [gɔr] *n., v.* **gored, gor•ing.** *—n.* **1** a tapering or triangular piece of cloth put in a skirt, sail, etc. to give greater width or change the shape. **2** *Cdn.* an unassigned tract of land remaining after the surveying and marking out of a township into lots.
—v. put or make a gore in. ⟨OE *gāra* point < *gār* spear⟩

gorge [gɔrdʒ] *n., v.* **gorged, gorg•ing.** *—n.* **1** a deep, narrow valley, usually steep and rocky. **2** a gorging; gluttonous meal. **3** the contents of a stomach. **4** a feeling of disgust, indignation, resentment, etc. **5** a narrow rear entrance from a fort into an outwork or outer part. **6** a mass stopping up a narrow passage: *An ice gorge blocked the river.* **7** *Archaic.* the throat; gullet.
stick in one's gorge, be hard to accept.
—v. **1** eat greedily until full; stuff (oneself) with food. **2** fill full; stuff. ⟨ME < OF *gorge* throat, ult. < LL *gurges* throat, jaws < L *gurges* abyss, whirlpool⟩ **—'gorg•er,** *n.*

gor•geous ['gɔrdʒəs] *adj.* **1** richly coloured; splendid: *a gorgeous sunset.* **2** very beautiful. ⟨< OF *gorgias* fashionable, with reference to the ruff for the throat < *gorge* throat. See GORGE.⟩ **—'gor•geous•ly,** *adv.* **—'gor•geous•ness,** *n.*

gor•ge•rin ['gɔrdʒərɪn] *n. Architecture.* the neck of a column. ⟨< F *gorgère* < OF *gorgiere* ruff for the neck⟩

gor•get ['gɔrdʒɪt] *n.* **1** formerly, a piece of armour for the throat. See ARMOUR for picture. **2** a covering for the neck and breast, formerly worn by women. **3** an ornamental collar. **4** a patch of colour on a bird's throat. ⟨< OF *gorgete,* dim. of *gorge.* See GORGE.⟩

Gor•gon ['gɔrgən] *n. Greek mythology.* any of three horrible sisters who had snakes for hair and whose look turned the beholder to stone. Medusa is the best-known of the three Gorgons. ⟨< L *Gorgo, -onis* < Gk. *Gorgō* < *gorgos* terrible⟩

gor•go•ni•an [gɔr'gouniən] any coral of the order Gorgonacea, having a skeleton divided into whiplike branches. ⟨< *Gorgon*⟩

gor•gon•ize ['gɔrgə,naiz] *v.* **-ized, -iz•ing.** paralyse with fear, especially by a look.

Gor•gon•zo•la [,gɔrgən'zoulə] *n.* a strong, white Italian cheese that looks and tastes much like Roquefort cheese. ⟨< *Gorgonzola*, a town in Italy⟩

go•ril•la [gə'rɪlə] *n.* **1** the largest and most powerful anthropoid ape (*Gorilla gorilla*), found in the forests of central Africa. **2** *Slang.* a strong and brutal man. ⟨< NL < Gk. < W African word, according to a traveller in 5c. B.C.⟩
☛ *Hom.* GUERRILLA.

gor•mand ['gɔrmənd] *n.* gourmand.

gor•mand•ize ['gɔrmən,daiz] *v.* **-ized, -iz•ing.** stuff oneself with food; eat very greedily; gorge. ⟨originally n., < F *gourmandise* gluttony⟩ **—'gor•mand,iz•er,** *n.*

gorp [gɔrp] *n.* a trail mix of nuts, raisins, etc. ⟨origin unknown⟩

gorse [gɔrs] *n.* furze. ⟨OE *gorst*⟩ **—'gors•y,** *adj.*

gor•y ['gɔri] *adj.* **gor•i•er, gor•i•est. 1** very bloody. **2** characterized by violence, bloodshed, etc. **—'gor•i•ly,** *adv.* **—'gor•i•ness,** *n.*

go•ser•e•lin [gə'sɛrəlɪn] *n.* a drug used to treat certain forms of prostate cancer.

gosh [gɒʃ] *interj.* an exclamation or mild oath.
by gosh, by God. ⟨euphemism for *God*⟩

gos•hawk ['gɒs,hɒk] *n.* any of several short-winged hawks (genus *Accipiter*), especially *A. gentilis*, a large, mainly grey hawk of the northern hemisphere, formerly used in falconry. ⟨OE *gōshafoc* < *gōs* goose + *hafoc* hawk⟩

Go•shen ['gouʃən] *n.* a land of plenty and comfort. ⟨in the Bible, a fertile part of Egypt where the Israelites were permitted to live before the Exodus⟩

gos•ling ['gɒzlɪŋ] *n.* a young goose. ⟨ME⟩

go–slow ['gou ,slou] *n. Informal.* **1** a change, development, etc., that progresses at a slow pace. **2** a deliberate slowing down of the rate of work, production, etc.; slowdown.

gos•pel ['gɒspəl] *n.* **1** the teachings of Jesus and the Apostles. **2** Usually, **Gospel, a** any one of the first four books of the New Testament, by Matthew, Mark, Luke, and John. **b** a part of one of these books read during a religious service. **3** *Informal.* anything earnestly believed or taken as a guide for action. **4** the absolute truth. **5** a type of music originating in black churches of the southern U.S., characterized by highly devotional or evangelistic lyrics, and vocals with much improvised embellishment. ⟨OE *gōdspel* good tidings (i.e., of the Nativity) < *gōd* good + *spel* spell[2]⟩

gos•sa•mer ['gɒsəmər] *or* ['gɒzəmər] *n., adj.* *—n.* **1** a film or thread of cobweb. **2** a very thin, light cloth. **3** a thin, light, waterproof cloth or coat. **4** anything very light and thin.
—adj. like gossamer; very light and thin; filmy. ⟨ME, prob. < *gossomer* goose summer, a name for Indian summer, referring to a time of year when goose was eaten and cobwebs were plentiful⟩

gos•san ['gɒsən] *or* ['gɒzən] *n. Mining.* decomposed rock that often indicates an ore-bearing vein, because of its rusty-red colour resulting from oxidized iron pyrites. ⟨< Cornish *gossen* < *gōs* blood⟩

gos•sip ['gɒsɪp] *n., v.* **-siped, -sip•ing.** *—n.* **1** idle talk, not always truthful, about people and their affairs. **2** a person who gossips a good deal. **3** *Archaic.* friend. **4** *Archaic.* godparent.
—v. repeat what one knows, or the idle talk that one hears, about people and their affairs. ⟨OE *godsibb*, originally, godparent < *god* God + *sibb* relative⟩ **—'gos•sip•er,** *n.*

gos•sip•mon•ger ['gɒsɪp,mʌŋgər] *or* [-,mɒŋgər] *n.* a person who spreads gossip.

gos•sip•y ['gɒsɪpi] *adj.* **1** fond of gossip. **2** full of gossip.

gos•soon [gɒ'sun] *n. Irish.* a boy, especially one who is a servant. ⟨an Irish alteration of F *garçon*⟩

gos•sy•pol ['gɒsi,pɒl] *or* ['gɒsi,poul] *n.* a toxic pigment present in cotton plants. It suppresses the production of sperm and is being tested as a male contraceptive. *Formula*: $C_{30}H_{30}O_8$ ⟨< G < NL *Gossypium* genus name of cotton⟩

got [gɒt] *v.* pt. and a pp. of GET.
☛ *Hom.* GHAT.
☛ *Usage.* **Gotten,** the older past participle of the verb **get,** has largely been replaced by **got.** Nevertheless, depending on the meaning of the sentence, the form **gotten** (instead of **got**) is still considered acceptable by some people. However, only **got** should be used as a way of intensifying 'have' in the sense of 'possess' (*Have you got a pencil?*) or 'be obligated' (*I've got to study now.*).

Go•ta•ma ['gɒtəmə] *n.* Gautama or Buddha.

Goth [gɒθ] *n.* **1** a member of a Germanic people that overran the Roman Empire in the 3rd, 4th, and 5th centuries A.D. The Goths settled in S and E Europe. **2** an uncivilized person; barbarian. ⟨ME < LL *Gothi*, pl.⟩

Goth•ic ['gɒθɪk] *n., adj.* *—n.* **1** *Architecture.* a style characterized by pointed arches and high, steep roofs, developed in W Europe during the Middle Ages. **2** the East Germanic language of the Goths. **3** Often, **gothic,** *Printing.* **a** a family of heavy, angular typefaces or lettering styles based on medieval scripts and used especially by the earliest European printers, characterized by thick-and-thin lines and thin serifs; black letter. Gothic was used in Germany until about the 1930s. **b** sans-serif.
—adj. **1** of or having to do with the Goths or their language. **2** of or designating the style of architecture called Gothic. **3** crude or barbarous. **4** medieval. **5** of or designating a style of literature that emphasizes the supernatural and the grotesque, usually having a medieval setting. ⟨< LL *Gothicus*⟩ **—'Goth•i•cal•ly,** *adv.*

got•ten ['gɒtən] *v.* a pp. of GET.
☛ *Usage.* See note at GOT.

Göt•ter•däm•mer•ung [,gœtəʀ'dɛməʀʊŋ] *n. German.* in Germanic mythology, the destruction of everything in a final battle with evil. ⟨literally, the twilight of the gods⟩

gouache [gwɑʃ] *n.* **1** a method of painting with opaque water colours obtained by mixing pigments with water and gum. **2** a colour made in this way. **3** a painting using this medium. ⟨< F *gouache* < Ital. *guazzo* water colours, mire; earlier, watering place < L *aquatio* watering place⟩

Gou•da ['gaʊdə] *or* ['gudə] *n.* a mild, yellow cheese made in Holland. ⟨< *Gouda*, a city in the Netherlands⟩

gouge [gaʊdʒ] *n., v.* **gouged, goug•ing.** *—n.* **1** a chisel with a concave blade used for cutting round grooves or holes in wood, stone, etc. **2** a groove, trench, or hole made by gouging: *There was a long gouge in the desktop.* **3** *Informal.* a cutting with or as if with a gouge. **4** *Informal.* a trick; cheat; swindle.
—v. **1** cut with a gouge or something like it: *to gouge a piece of wood.* **2** make by gouging: *to gouge a channel.* **3** dig or tear (*out*): *to gouge out dirt.* **4** force out (someone's eye). **5** *Informal.* overcharge or swindle. ⟨< F < LL *gulbia*⟩ **—'goug•er,** *n.*

gou•lash ['gulɑʃ] *or* ['gulæʃ] *n.* a highly seasoned stew made of beef or veal and vegetables. It is usually seasoned with paprika. ⟨< Hungarian *gulyás (hús)* herdsman's (meat)⟩

gou•ra•mi ['gʊrəmi] *or* [gʊ'rɑmi] *n., pl.* **-mis.** any of various tropical freshwater fishes (family Anabantidae) of SE Asia, including some brightly coloured species that are popular for home aquariums. ⟨< Malay *gurami*⟩

gourd [gurd] *or* [gɔrd] *n.* **1** the hard-shelled, inedible fruit of any of various vines (genera *Cucurbita* and *Lagenaria*), often dried and used for ornament or for making bowls, cups, etc. **2** any of the plants that bear such fruit. **3** (*adj.*) designating the family (Cucurbitaceae) of climbing or trailing plants that includes the gourds as well as cucumbers, pumpkins, muskmelons, and squashes. **4** the hard-shelled fruit of any of various other plants, such as calabash, which is dried and used for utensils, etc. **5** a bowl, bottle, etc. made from the dried shell of a gourd. ⟨ME < F *gourde* < OF *cohorde* < L *cucurbita*⟩ **—'gourd,like,** *adj.*

gourde [gurd] *n.* **1** the basic unit of money in Haiti, divided into 100 centimes. See money table in the Appendix. **2** a note worth one gourde. ⟨< F⟩

gour•mand [gʊr'mɑnd], ['gʊrmænd], *or* ['gʊrmənd] *n.* **1** a person who is fond of good eating. **2** a person who is greedy; glutton. Also, **gormand.** ⟨< F *gourmand* gluttonous < *gourmet* gourmet⟩

gour•mand•ise [,gʊrmən'diz]; *French,* [guʀmɑ̃'diz] *n.* a taste for good food.

gour•met [gʊr'mei] *or* ['gʊrmei]; *French,* [guʀ'mɛ] *n.* a person who is expert in judging and choosing fine foods, wines, etc.; epicure. ⟨< F < OF *gourmet, groumet* wine taster < *gromet* servant⟩

gout [gʌut] *n.* **1** a painful disease of the joints, often characterized by a painful swelling of the big toe, caused by an excess of uric acid. It is a form of arthritis. **2** a drop; splash; clot: *gouts of blood.* ⟨ME < OF *goute* < L *gutta* a drop, with reference to the medieval theory of the flow of body humours⟩

goût [gu] *n. French.* taste.

gout•y ['gʌuti] *adj.* **gout•i•er, gout•i•est. 1** swollen with gout: *a gouty toe.* **2** of or like gout. **3** causing or caused by gout. **4** having or tending to have gout. **—'gout•i•ly,** *adv.* **'gout•i•ness,** *n.*

Gov. or **gov. 1** governor. **2** government.

gov•ern ['gʌvərn] *n.* **1** rule; control; manage: *to govern a country, to govern one's temper.* **2** exercise a directing or restraining influence over; determine: *the motives governing a person's decision.* **3** hold back; restrain; check. **4** be a rule or law for: *the principles governing a case.* **5** *Grammar.* require (a word) to be in a certain case, number, or mood; require (a certain case, number, or mood). **6** regulate the speed of (a vehicle) using a GOVERNOR (def. 5). ⟨ME < OF *governer* < L *gubernare* < Gk. *kybernaein* steer⟩ **—'gov•ern•a•ble,** *adj.*

☛ *Syn.* **1.** See note at RULE.

gov•ern•ance ['gʌvərnəns] *n.* the act, manner or right of government; rule; control.

gov•ern•ess ['gʌvərnɪs] *n.* a woman who teaches children in a private house.

gov•ern•ment ['gʌvərmənt] *or* ['gʌvərnmənt] *n.* **1** the rule or authority over a country, province, district, etc.; direction of the affairs of state. **2** the person or persons ruling a country, state, district, etc.; administration. **3** a system of ruling: *Canada has a democratic government.* **4** the country, province, district, etc. ruled. **5** rule; control. **6** *Grammar.* the relationship by which one word determines the case, number, or person of another depending on it.

gov•ern•men•tal [,gʌvər'mɛntəl] *or* [,gʌvərn'mɛntəl] *adj.* of or having to do with government. **—,gov•ern'men•tal•ly,** *adv.*

Government House *Cdn.* **1** the official residence of the Governor General in Ottawa, also known as Rideau Hall. **2** in some provinces, the official residence of the Lieutenant-Governor.

gov•er•nor ['gʌvərnər] *n.* **1** the appointed ruler of a colony; the representative of a monarch in a colony. **2** an official appointed to govern a province, city, fort, etc. **3** in the United States, an official elected as the executive head of a state. **4** one of a group of people who manage or direct a club, society, institution, etc. A club often has a board of governors. **5** an automatic device that controls the supply of steam, gas, etc. and keeps a machine going at a certain speed. ⟨ME < OF *governeor* < L *gubernator* steersman⟩ **—'gov•er•nor•ship,** *n.*

governor general *pl.* **governors general. 1** a governor who has subordinate or deputy governors under him or her. **2 Governor General, a** in Canada, the representative of the Crown, appointed on the advice of the prime minister for a term of five years. **b** the representative of the Crown in certain other independent countries of the British Commonwealth of Nations.

Govt. or **govt.** government.

gow•an ['gaʊən] *n. Scottish.* any of various white or yellow wildflowers, especially a daisy. ⟨< dial. *gowlan,* var. of *golding* gold coloured⟩

gown [gaʊn] *n., v.* *—n.* **1** a woman's dress, especially a formal or evening dress. **2** a loose outer garment with very wide sleeves, such as those worn by judges, clergy, members of a university, and students graduating from university to show their position, profession, etc. **3** a nightgown or dressing gown. **4** a loose garment worn in hospital **a** by patients, **b** by doctors and nurses. **5** the members of a university: *arguments between town and gown.* *—v.* put a gown on; dress in a gown. ⟨ME < OF *goune* < LL *gunna*⟩ **—'gown•less,** *adj.*

gowns•man ['gaʊnzmən] *n., pl.* **-men. 1** a person such as a judge or member of the clergy who wears a gown as a mark of his or her profession. **2** a member of a university; wearer of an academic gown.

gp. group(s).

G.P. *Medicine.* GENERAL PRACTITIONER.

GPM, gpm, or **g.p.m.** gallons per minute.

G.P.O. General Post Office.

gr. 1 grain(s). **2** gross. **3** grade. **4** grammar. **5** group. **6** great.

Gr. Greek; Greece.

G.R. King George (for L *Georgius Rex).*

Graaf•i•an follicle ['grɑfiən] any of the follicles in the ovary of a mammal that contains a maturing ovum. ⟨< R. de *Graaf,* 17c. Dutch anatomist⟩

grab [græb] *v.* **grabbed, grab•bing;** *n.* *—v.* **1** seize suddenly; snatch: *The dog grabbed the meat and ran.* **2** take possession of in an unscrupulous manner: *to grab land.* **3** *Informal.* capture; arrest: *The police grabbed the robbers after a long chase.* **4** get or take in a hurry: *to grab a sandwich.* **5** of brakes, clutch, or other mechanical part, engage suddenly or jerkily. **6** *Slang.* strike the attention of; impress: *Does that idea grab you?*
—n. **1** the act of snatching; a sudden seizing: *She made a grab for the apple.* **2** that which is grabbed. **3** a mechanical device for firmly holding something that is to be lifted or raised.
up for grabs, *Informal.* available. ⟨Cf. MDu. *grabben*⟩ **—'grab•ber,** *n.*

grab bag 1 a bag or other receptacle filled with an assortment of articles, one of which may be selected, sight unseen, by a person paying a certain price. **2** *Informal.* any varied assortment.

grab•ble ['græbəl] *v.* **-bled, -bling. 1** grope. **2** sprawl. ⟨< Du. *grabbelen,* frequentative of MDu. *grabben* grab⟩

grab•by ['græbi] *adj.* avaricious.

gra•ben ['grɑbən] *n. Geology.* a depression of the earth's crust between two faults that run parallel. ⟨< G, a ditch < OHG *grabo* < *graban* to dig⟩

grace [greis] *n., v.* **graced, grac•ing.** *—n.* **1** beauty of form, movement, or manner; a pleasing or agreeable quality. **2** mercy; pardon. **3** *Christian theology.* **a** God's free and undeserved favour to and love for humankind; the influence of God operating in humans to improve or strengthen them. **b** the condition of being influenced and favoured by God. **4** a short prayer of thanks said before or after a meal. **5** the favour shown by granting the postponement of a deadline. **6** an allowance of time: *The bank gave her three days' grace.* **7** virtue; merit; excellence. **8** decency; thoughtfulness. **9** Usually, **Grace,** a title used in speaking to or of a duke, duchess, or archbishop: *He spoke a few words to his Grace the Duke of Bedford.* **10** *Music.* GRACE NOTE. **11 Graces,** *pl. Greek mythology.* three sister goddesses controlling beauty and charm in people and in nature.
have the grace, have the goodness or courtesy: *He had the grace to say he was sorry.*
in (someone's) **bad graces,** out of favour with or disliked by (someone): *She was in the teacher's bad graces for a week after that episode.*
in (someone's) **good graces,** favoured or liked by (someone).
with bad grace, unpleasantly; unwillingly.
with good grace, pleasantly; willingly.
—v. **1** give or add grace to; set off with grace. **2** do a favour or honour to: *The Queen graced the ball with her presence.* **3** *Music.* add grace notes to. ⟨< F < L *gratia* < *gratus* pleasing⟩

grace cup 1 the final toast at a banquet. **2** the cup used for this toast.

grace•ful ['greisfəl] *adj.* having or showing grace; beautiful in form, movement, or manner; pleasing; agreeable: *A good dancer must be graceful. She thanked him with a graceful speech.* **—'grace•ful•ly,** *adv.* **—'grace•ful•ness,** *n.*

grace•less ['greislɪs] *adj.* **1** without grace. **2** not caring for what is right and proper: *That boy is a graceless rascal.* **—'grace•less•ly,** *adv.* **—'grace•less•ness,** *n.*

grace note *Music.* a note or group of notes added for ornament and not essential to the harmony or melody. It is written in as a small note, with a slur leading to the following note.

grac•ile ['græsaɪl] *or* ['græsɪl] *adj.* gracefully slender. **—gra'cil•i•ty** [grə'sɪləti], *n.*

gra•cious ['greiʃəs] *adj., interj.* *—adj.* **1** pleasant; kindly; courteous: *The bride's gracious manner pleased everyone.* **2** pleasant, kindly, and courteous to people of lower social position: *The Queen greeted the crowd with a gracious smile.* **3** characterized by sophisticated taste and social urbanity, coming from affluence and education: *gracious living.* **4** of God, merciful; kind.
—interj. an exclamation of surprise. ⟨ME < OF < L *gratiosus*⟩ **—'gra•cious•ly,** *adv.* **—'gra•cious•ness,** *n.*

grack•le ['grækəl] *n.* any of several large American blackbirds having dark, iridescent plumage. The common grackle (*Quiscalus quiscula*) is found throughout Canada east of the Rockies. ⟨< L *graculus* jackdaw⟩

grad. graduate; graduated.

gra•date [grei'deit] *or* ['greideit] *v.* **-at•ed, -at•ing. 1** pass from one degree of colour or tone to another. **2** arrange according to grades.

gra•da•tion [grei'deiʃən] *or* [grə'deiʃən] *n.* **1** a change by steps or stages; gradual change: *Human behaviour shows gradation between right and wrong.* **2** a step, stage, or degree in a

series: *There are many gradations between poverty and wealth. The rainbow shows gradations of colour.* **3** the act or process of grading. ⟨< L *gradatio, -onis* < *gradus* step, degree⟩
—gra'da•tion•al, *adj.* **—gra'da•tion•al•ly,** *adv.*

grade [greid] *n., v.* **grad•ed, grad•ing.** *—n.* **1** in schools: **a** any one division, or class, arranged according to the pupil's progress. Its curriculum generally spans one school year. **b** the pupils in any such division. **2** a step or stage in a course or process. **3** a degree in a scale of rank, quality, value, etc.: *grade A milk.* **4** a group of people or things having the same rank, quality, value, etc. **5** a number or letter that shows how well one has done: *Her grade in English is B.* **6** the slope of a road, railway track, etc. **7** the amount of slope. **8** *Stock breeding.* an animal having one purebred parent.
at grade, on the same level.
make the grade, a ascend a steep slope. **b** overcome difficulties. **c** perform up to standard.
—v. **1** arrange in classes; arrange according to size, value, etc; sort: *These apples are graded by size.* **2** be of a particular grade or quality. **3** give a grade to: *The teacher graded the papers.* **4** *Stock breeding.* improve (stock) by breeding with purebred stock (*often used with* **up**). **5** make more nearly level: *The workers graded the land around the new house.* **6** change gradually; go through a series of steps, stages, or degrees: *Red and yellow grade into orange.* ⟨< F < L *gradus* step, degree⟩

–grade *combining form.* moving: *plantigrade.*

grade crossing LEVEL CROSSING.

grad•er ['greidər] *n.* **1** a person who or thing that grades, especially a machine for levelling earth. **2** *Esp. U.S.* a person who is in a certain grade in elementary or secondary school (*used only in compounds*): *a sixth-grader.*

grade school ELEMENTARY SCHOOL.

gra•di•ent ['greidiənt] *n., adj.* *—n.* **1** the rate at which a road, railway track, etc. rises. **2** the sloping part of a road, etc. **3** *Physics.* the rate at which temperature or pressure changes. **4** a curve or graph representing such a rate.
—adj. **1** going up or down gradually. **2** moving by taking steps; walking. ⟨< L *gradiens, -entis,* ppr. of *gradi* walk, go < *gradus* step, degree⟩

gra•din ['greidın] *or* [grei'din] *n.* **1** one of a series of steps or rows of seats. **2** a shelf behind an altar. Also, **gradine.**

grad•u•al ['grædʒuəl] *or* ['grædjuəl] *adj.* occurring, developing, etc. by degrees too small to be separately noticed; little by little: *a gradual increase in sound. The hill had a gradual slope.* ⟨< Med.L *gradualis* < L *gradus* step, degree⟩
—'grad•u•al•ly, *adv.* **—'grad•u•al•ness,** *n.*

grad•u•al•ism ['grædʒuə,lızəm] *or* ['grædjuə,lızəm] *n.* the principle of making progress in easy stages.

grad•u•and ['grædʒu,ænd] *or* ['grædju,ænd] *n. Esp. Cdn.* a student who is about to graduate. ⟨< Med.L *graduandus* < *graduare.* See GRADUATE.⟩

grad•u•ate *v.* ['grædʒu,eit] *or* ['grædju,eit]; *n.* ['grædʒuıt], ['grædjuıt], *or* ['grædʒu,eit] *v.* **-at•ed, -at•ing;** *n.* *—v.* **1** finish a course of study at a school, college, or university and receive a diploma or paper saying one has done so: *Mary's brother graduated from university last year.* **2** give a diploma to for finishing a course of study. **3** mark with degrees for measuring: *A thermometer is graduated.* **4** arrange in regular steps, stages, or degrees: *An income tax is graduated so that the people who make the most money pay the highest rate of taxes.* **5** change gradually.
—n. **1** a person who has graduated. **2** a container marked with degrees for measuring. **3** (*adjl.*) of, having to do with, or for graduates: *a graduate dinner.* **4** (*adjl.*) **a** being a person who has received a first degree from a university: *A graduate student is one who is studying for an advanced degree.* **b** of or for such persons: *graduate school.* ⟨< Med.L *graduare* < L *gradus* step, degree⟩ **—'grad•u,a•tor,** *n.*

grad•u•a•tion [,grædʒu'eiʃən] *or* [,grædju'eiʃən] *n.* **1** a graduating or being graduated from a school, college, or university. **2** the ceremony of graduating; graduating exercises. **3** a marking with degrees for measuring. **4** a mark or set of marks to show degrees for measuring. **5** an arrangement in regular steps, stages, or degrees.

Grae•ae ['grii] *n. Greek mythology.* the three old women guarding the Gorgons, and sharing among them a single tooth and a single eye.

Graf [grɑf] *n.* a German, Austrian, or Swedish title equivalent to an English earl.

graf•fi•ti [grə'fiti] *n.* pl. of **graffito.** verses, sayings, or pictures drawn, scribbled, or scratched on a public surface such as a wall or fence. Graffiti are usually anonymous and are often cleverly done. ⟨< Ital. *graffito* scribbling < *graffio* a scratch, scribble < Gk. *graphein* draw, write⟩

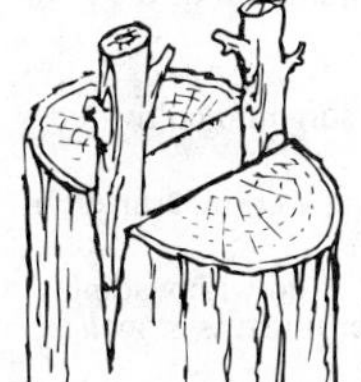

Three kinds of plant graft. The pieces are tied or taped together and kept moist until the graft begins to grow.

graft[1] [græft] *v., n.* *—v.* **1** insert (a shoot, bud, etc.) from one tree or plant into a slit in another so that it will grow there permanently. **2** produce or improve (a fruit, flower, etc.) by grafting. **3** do grafting on. **4** transfer (a piece of skin, bone, etc.) from one part of the body to another so that it will grow there permanently. **5** insert or fix as if by grafting. **6** become grafted.
—n. **1** the shoot, bud, etc. used in grafting. **2** the place on a tree or plant where the shoot, bud, etc. is inserted. **3** the tree or plant that has had a shoot, bud, etc. grafted on it. **4** the act of grafting. **5** a piece of skin, bone, etc. transferred in grafting. ⟨earlier *graff* < OF *grafe* < L *graphium* < Gk. *grapheion* stylus (< *graphein* write); from similarity of shape⟩ **—'graft•er,** *n.*

graft[2] [græft] *n., v.* *—n.* **1** the taking of money dishonestly, especially in connection with government business; political dishonesty, corruption, etc. **2** a method of getting money dishonestly. **3** money dishonestly taken or obtained.
—v. Informal. make (money) dishonestly through one's job, especially in political positions. ⟨origin uncertain⟩ **—'graft•er,** *n.*

gra•ham ['greiəm] *n.* (*adjl.*) designating or made from a finely ground, unsifted, whole-wheat flour: *graham crackers.* ⟨after Sylvester *Graham* (1794-1851), an American reformer of dietetics⟩

Grail [greil] *n.* the cup or dish supposed to have been used by Christ at the Last Supper, in which one of His followers received the last drops of blood from Christ's body on the cross; Holy Grail. ⟨ME < OF *graal* < Med.L *gradale* plate, or VL *cratale* < *crater* bowl < Gk. *kratēr*⟩

grain [grein] *n., v.* *—n.* **1** a single seed or seedlike fruit of wheat, oats, and similar cereal grasses. **2** the seeds or seedlike fruits of such plants in the mass. **3** the plants that these seeds or seedlike fruits grow on. **4** a tiny, hard particle of sand, salt, sugar, etc. **5** a unit for measuring mass, equal to about 0.065 g. The grain is the smallest unit in avoirdupois, troy, and apothecaries' weight. *Abbrev.*: gr **6** the smallest possible amount; tiniest bit: *a grain of truth.* **7** the arrangement or direction of fibres in wood, layers in stone, etc. Wood and stone split along the grain. **8** paint or other artificial finish made to look like natural grain. **9** the little lines and other markings in wood, marble, etc. **10** the rough surface of leather, originally the hairy side of the skin. **11 a** the plane of cleavage in anything crystalline. **b** the directions in which cleavage occurs in diamond polishing. **12** the quality of a substance due to the size, character, or arrangement of its constituent particles; texture: *a stone or salt of coarse grain.* **13** *Photography.* any of the small, separate particles of light-sensitive material emulsified and deposited on photographic film. The size of the particle limits the possible enlargement of the image and affects the speed of exposure.
go against the grain, be contrary to one's natural disposition: *Laziness went against the grain for her.*
—v. **1** form into grains. **2** paint in imitation of the grain in wood, marble, etc. **3** remove the hair from (a skin or skins). **4** soften and raise the grain of (leather). ⟨ME < OF < L *granum* grain, seed⟩ **—'grain•less,** *adj.*

grain alcohol ethyl alcohol, often made from grain.

grained [greind] *adj., v.* *—adj.* **1** having little lines and markings. **2** painted in imitation of the grain in wood, marble, etc. **3** with the hair removed; roughened on the surface.
—v. pt. and pp. of GRAIN.

grain elevator a building for storing grain.

grain fair *Cdn.* a fair where wheat, barley, oats, etc. are exhibited and judged.

grain•field ['grein,fild] *n.* a field in which grain grows.

grain•ing ['greinɪŋ] *n., v.* —*n.* painting in imitation of the grain in wood, marble, etc.
—*v.* ppr. of GRAIN.

grain sorghum any of several strains of sorghum cultivated mainly for grain.

grain•y ['greini] *adj.* **1** of wood, etc., having a grain. **2** made of grains; granular.

gral•la•tor•ial [,grælə'tɔriəl] *adj.* having to do with wading birds. ⟨< NL *grallatorius* < L *grallator* walker on stilts < *grallae* stilts⟩

gram¹ [græm] *n.* an SI unit for measuring mass, equal to one one-thousandth of a kilogram: *A nickel has a mass of about five grams.* Also, **gramme**. Symbol: g ⟨< F *gramme* < LL < Gk. *gramma* small marked weight < *graphein* mark, write⟩

gram² [græm] *n.* any of a number of leguminous plants used to feed farm animals. The chick pea is a gram. ⟨< Pg. *grao* < L *granum* grain⟩

–gram¹ *combining form.* something written; message: *cablegram, telegram, monogram.* ⟨< Gk. *-gramma* something written, ult. < *graphein* write⟩

–gram² *combining form.* grams; of a gram: *kilogram, milligram.* ⟨See GRAM⟩

gra•ma ['græmə] *or* ['grɒmə] *n.* any of various grasses (genus *Bouteloua*) growing in the ranges of the western United States. ⟨< Sp. < L *gramen* grass⟩

gram atom the mass in grams of an element numerically equal to the atomic mass.

gram calorie the amount of heat required to raise the temperature of one gram of water by one degree Celsius.

gra•mer•cy [grə'mɜrsi] *or* ['græmərsi] *interj. Archaic.* **1** many thanks; thank you. **2** an exclamation of surprise. ⟨ME < OF *grant merci* (God give you) great reward⟩

gra•mi•ci•din [,græmə'saɪdən] *n.* an antibiotic produced by a bacterium (*Bacillus brevis).*

gram•mar ['græmər] *n.* **1** the scientific study and classification of a language with reference to the sounds and forms of words and the structure of sentences. **2** a systematic study comparing the forms and constructions of two or more languages. **3** a systematic study comparing present with past forms and usage of a language. **4** a treatise or book on any of these subjects. **5** the system of the forms and uses of words in a particular language. Grammar is often thought of as a set of rules. **6** the use of words according to this system. **7** the elements of any subject: *the grammar of painting.* **8** a book about the elements of a field of study. ⟨ME < OF *grammaire* < L *grammatica* < Gk. *grammatikē (technē)* (art) of letters, ult. < *graphein* write⟩

gram•mar•i•an [grə'mɛriən] *n.* a person knowledgable about or studying grammar.

grammar school **1** formerly, a public school having the grades between primary school and high school. **2** in the United Kingdom, a secondary school that prepares students for university.

gram•mat•i•cal [grə'mætəkəl] *adj.* **1** according to the GRAMMAR (def. 5) of a particular language: *Our French teacher speaks grammatical English but has a French accent.* **2** of or having to do with grammar: *a grammatical error.*

gram•mat•i•cal•ly [grə'mætɪkli] *adv.* according to the principles and rules of grammar; as regards grammar.

gramme [græm] See GRAM¹.

gram–mo•lec•u•lar ['græm mə'lɛkjələr] *adj.* of or having to do with GRAM-MOLECULAR MASS.

gram–molecular mass the mass of one molecule of an element or compound, expressed in grams. Also, **gram molecule.**

gram–neg•a•tive or **Gram–neg•a•tive** ['græm 'nɛgətɪv] *adj.* designating bacteria that do not retain the violet colour when stained by GRAM'S METHOD.

gram•o•phone ['græmə,foun] *n.* record player; phonograph. ⟨inversion of *phonogram* < Gk. *phōnē* sound + *-gram¹*⟩

gram–pos•i•tive ['græm 'pɒzətɪv] *adj.* designating bacteria that retain the violet colour when stained by GRAM'S METHOD.

gram•pus ['græmpəs] *n.* **1** a large grey dolphin (*Grampus griseus*) found in the Atlantic and Pacific Oceans. **2** any of various other relatively small cetaceans, such as the killer whale. ⟨*graundepose* < earlier *grapeys* < OF *graspeis* < L *crassus piscis* fat fish⟩

Gram's method [græmz] *Bacteriology.* a technique for classifying bacteria, by which they are stained with gentian violet and then treated with a decolourizing agent. Certain species (called **gram-positive** bacteria) retain the violet stain after this treatment, while others (**gram-negative** bacteria) lose it. ⟨after H.C.J. *Gram* (1853-1938), Danish physician⟩

gra•na•dil•la [,grænə'dɪlə] *n.* the fruit of a tropical passionflower. ⟨< Sp. dim of *granada* pomegranate < L *granatus* containing seeds < *granum* seed⟩

gran•a•ry ['grænəri] *or* ['greinəri] *n., pl.* **-ries. 1** a place or building where grain is stored. **2** a region in which much grain is grown. ⟨< L *granarium* < *granum* grain⟩

grand [grænd] *adj., n.* —*adj.* **1** large and of fine appearance: *grand mountains.* **2** fine; noble; dignified; stately; splendid: *grand music, a grand old man.* **3** highest or very high in rank; chief: *a grand duke, a grand master in chess.* **4** great; important; main: *the grand staircase.* **5** complete; comprehensive: *grand total.* **6** *Informal.* very pleasing: *a grand time.* **7** in terms of kinship, in the second degree of ascent or descent: *grandmother, grandson.* —*n.* **1** *Slang.* a thousand dollars. **2** GRAND PIANO. ⟨< MF *grant, grand* < L *grandis* big⟩ —**'grand•ly,** *adv.* —**'grand•ness,** *n.*

☛ *Syn. adj.* **2. Grand,** STATELY, NOBLE = great, dignified, fine, and impressive. **Grand** emphasizes greatness that makes the person or thing described stand out, and suggests impressive dignity or splendour: *Under the leadership of that grand old man, the nation withstood its peril.* **Stately** emphasizes impressive dignity, sometimes also appearance: *She was moved by the stately rhythm of processional music.* **Noble** emphasizes an imposing greatness, splendour, or stateliness in appearance: *The Rocky Mountains are a noble sight.*

gran•dad or **grand•dad** ['græn,dæd] *n. Informal.* GRANDFATHER (def. 1).

gran•dam ['græn,dæm] *n. Archaic.* **1** grandmother. **2** an old woman. Also, **grandame.** ⟨ME < AF *graund dame*⟩

grand•aunt ['grænd,ænt] *n.* an aunt of one's father or mother; great-aunt.

Grand Banks or **Grand Bank** a shallow region, or shoal, of the ocean lying southeast of Newfoundland. The Grand Banks are famous as a fishing ground for cod.

grand•child ['græn,tʃaɪld] *or* ['grænd,tʃaɪld] *n., pl.* **-chil•dren.** a child of one's son or daughter.

grand•dad•dy ['græn,dædi] *n. Informal.* **1** grandfather. **2** the largest one of its kind: *the granddaddy of all the fish.*

grand•daugh•ter ['græn,dɒtər] *n.* a daughter of one's son or daughter.

grand duchess **1** the wife or widow of a grand duke. **2** a lady equal in rank to a grand duke. **3** in Russia before 1917, a princess of the ruling house. **4** the female ruler of a small country, known as a grand duchy.

grand duchy the territory under the rule of a grand duke or grand duchess.

grand duke **1** a prince who rules a small state or country called a grand duchy. A grand duke ranks just below a king. **2** in Russia before 1917, a prince of the ruling house.

gran•dee [græn'di] *n.* **1** in Spain or Portugal, a nobleman of the highest rank. **2** a person of high rank or great importance. ⟨< Sp., Pg. *grande*⟩

gran•deur ['grændʒər] *or* ['grændjər] *n.* greatness; majesty; nobility; dignity; splendour. ⟨< F *grandeur* < *grand* grand⟩

grand•fa•ther ['græn,fɒðər] *or* ['grænd,fɒðər] *n.* **1** the father of one's father or mother. **2** forefather.

grandfather clock or **grandfather's clock** a pendulum clock in a tall, wooden case that stands on the floor.

grand•fa•ther•ly ['græn,fɒðərli] *or* ['grænd,fɒðərli] *adj.* **1** of a grandfather. **2** like or characteristic of a grandfather.

grand fir LOWLAND FIR.

Grand Guignol ['gʀɑ̃ gi'njɔl] *French.* a type of drama which emphasizes the grisly and horrible. ⟨< the name of a former theatre in Paris, which specialized in such dramas⟩

gran•di•flo•ra [,grændə'flɔrə] *n., adj.* —*n.* a variety of hybrid cultivated rose developed from crosses of floribunda and tea roses, and combining attributes of both.
—*adj.* bearing large flowers (*used especially in specific names of plants*). ⟨< NL *Grandiflora* < L *grandis* grand + *flos, floris* flower⟩

gran•dil•o•quence [græn'dɪləkwəns] *n.* the use of lofty or pompous words.

gran•dil•o•quent [græn'dɪləkwənt] *adj.* using lofty or pompous words. ⟨< L *grandiloquus* < *grandis* grand + *loqui* speak; influenced by the form of E *eloquent*⟩
—gran'dil•o•quent•ly, *adv.*

gran•di•ose [,grændi'ous] *or* ['grændi,ous] *adj.* **1** grand in an imposing or impressive way; magnificent. **2** grand in an affected or pompous way; trying to seem magnificent. ⟨< F < Ital. *grandioso*⟩ **—,gran•di'ose•ly,** *adv.* **—,gran•di'os•i•ty,** *n.*

gran•di•o•so [,grændi'ousou] *adv. Music.* in a noble style.

grand jury a special jury called to examine a charge against a person to determine if there is sufficient evidence to warrant bringing the accused to trial on that charge. Grand juries have been abolished in most of the Canadian provinces that had them. Compare PETIT JURY.

Grand Lama DALAI LAMA.

grand•ma ['græmə], ['græn,mɑ], ['græm,mɑ], ['græmɑ], *or* ['grænd,mɑ] *n. Informal.* GRANDMOTHER (def. 1).

grand mal ['grænd 'mæl] a type of epilepsy characterized by seizures and loss of consciousness. Compare PETIT MAL.

grand march a ceremony at a ball in which the guests march around the ballroom in couples.

grand master **1** the head of a military order of knighthood, of a lodge, etc. **2** an expert chess player who has consistently done well in international championships.

grand•moth•er ['græn,mʌðər] *or* ['grænd,mʌðər] *n.* **1** the mother of one's father or mother. **2** a female ancestor.

grand•moth•er•ly ['græn,mʌðərli] *or* ['grænd,mʌðərli] *adj.* **1** of a grandmother. **2** like or characteristic of a grandmother.

grand•neph•ew ['græn,nɛfju] *or* ['grænd,nɛfju] *n.* the son of one's nephew or niece.

grand•niece ['græn,nis] *or* ['grænd,nis] *n.* the daughter of one's nephew or niece.

Grand Old Party *Cdn.* formerly, the Conservative Party, especially under the leadership of Sir John A. Macdonald.

grand opera a musical drama, having a serious and often tragic theme, in which all the speeches are sung or recited to the accompaniment of an orchestra.

grand•pa ['græmpə], ['græn,pɑ], ['græm,pɑ], *or* ['grænd,pɑ] *n. Informal.* GRANDFATHER (def. 1).

grand•par•ent ['græn,pɛrənt] *or* ['grænd,pɛrənt] *n.* a grandfather or grandmother.

grand piano a large, harp-shaped piano with horizontal frame and strings. Compare UPRIGHT PIANO.

Grand Portage *Cdn.* formerly, a rendezvous point for fur traders at the Lake Superior end of the long portage to the Rainy River waterway, used by the North West Company as the main entrepôt between Montréal and the inland posts of the Northwest.

Grand Prix ['grɑn 'pri] any one of several road races for sports cars with a specified size of engine.

grand•sire ['græn,saɪr] *or* ['grænd,saɪr] *n. Archaic.* **1** grandfather. **2** forefather. **3** an old man.

grand slam **1** *Bridge.* the winning of all the tricks in a hand. **2** *Tennis, golf, etc.* the winning of several major tournaments in one season. **3** *Baseball.* a home run with three runners on base. **4** a multiple victory in any series: *She had a grand slam in all her final examinations.*

grand•son ['græn,sʌn] *or* ['grænd,sʌn] *n.* a son of one's son or daughter.

grand•stand ['græn,stænd] *or* ['grænd,stænd] *n., v.* *—n.* the main seating place for people at an athletic field, racetrack, parade, etc., usually having a roof.
—v. act or speak ostentatiously to impress an audience.
—'grand,stand•er, *n.*

grand•un•cle ['grænd,ʌŋkəl] *n.* great-uncle.

grange [greindʒ] *n.* **1** a farm with its buildings; farmstead. **2 the Grange,** *U.S.* **a** an organization of farmers to promote agricultural interests, founded in 1867. **b** a local branch of this organization. ⟨ME < OF < VL *granica* < L *granum* grain⟩

grang•er ['greindʒər] *n.* **1** farmer. **2 Granger,** a member of the Grange.

grang•er•ize ['greindʒə,raɪz] *v.* **-ized, -iz•ing.** plagiarize by illustrating (a book) with material from other books. ⟨after J. *Granger*, author of *A Biographical History of England* (1769), which included blank pages for such illustrations⟩

gra•nif•er•ous [grə'nɪfərəs] *adj.* bearing grain. ⟨< L *granifer* bearing grain⟩

gran•ite ['grænɪt] *n.* a hard igneous rock consisting chiefly of quartz and feldspar. Granite is much used for buildings and monuments. ⟨< Ital. *granito* grained, pp. of *granire* < *grano* grain < L *granum*⟩

gran•ite•ware ['grænɪt,wɛr] *n.* ironware covered with grey enamel to look like granite.

gra•nit•ic [grə'nɪtɪk] *adj.* of or like granite.

gra•niv•o•rous [grə'nɪvərəs] *adj.* eating grain and other seeds: *Finches are granivorous birds.* ⟨< L *granum* grain + *-vorus* < *vorare* to devour⟩

gran•nie or **gran•ny** ['græni] *n., pl.* **-nies.** *Informal.* **1** grandmother. **2** an old woman. **3** a fussy person. **4** (*adjl.*) suitable for a grandmother: *grannie glasses.*

grannie knot or **granny knot** a knot differing from a square knot in having the ends crossed the wrong way. A grannie knot is not as secure as a square knot. See KNOT for picture.

Granny Smith a tart, green apple, good for eating and cooking.

gra•no•la [grə'noulə] *n.* a breakfast cereal consisting of rolled oats, wheat germ, chopped nuts, and seeds, etc. ⟨coined circa 1870 < ? L *granum* grain + *-ola* Ital. dim. suffix⟩

gran•o•phyre ['grænə,faɪr] *n.* a granite porphyry. ⟨< G *Granophyr*, arbitrary blend < *Granit* granite + *Porphyr* porphyry⟩

grant [grænt] *v., n.* *—v.* **1** give what is asked; allow: *to grant a request, to grant permission.* **2** admit to be true; accept without proof; concede: *I grant that you are right.* **3** bestow or confer (a right, etc.) by formal act; transfer or convey (the ownership of property), especially by deed or writing.
take for granted, a assume to be true; accept as proved or as agreed to. **b** assume the presence and support of (someone).
—n. **1** something granted, such as a privilege, right, sum of money, or tract of land: *The companies that built the railways received large grants of land from the government.* **2** the act of granting. ⟨ME < OF *graanter*, var. of *creanter*, promise, authorize, ult. < L *credens*, ppr. of *credere* trust⟩ **—'grant•a•ble,** *adj.* **—'grant•er,** *n.*

grant•ee [græn'ti] *n.* a person to whom a grant is made.

Granth [grænθ] *or* [grɑnθ] *n.* the Sikh holy book.

grant•or ['græntər] *or* ['græntɔr] *n.* a person who makes a grant.

gran•u•lar ['grænjələr] *adj.* **1** consisting of or containing grains or granules. **2** resembling grains or granules. **3** having a coarsely textured surface. **—'gran•u•lar•ly,** *adv.*

gran•u•late ['grænjə,leit] *v.* **-lat•ed, -lat•ing.** **1** form into grains or granules. **2** roughen on the surface. **3** become granular; develop granulations. Wounds granulate in healing.
—'gran•u,la•tor, *n.* **—'gran•u•la•tive,** *adj.*

gran•u•lat•ed ['grænjə,leitɪd] *adj., v.* *—adj.* **1** formed into grains or granules: *granulated sugar.* **2** roughened on the surface. **3** having granulations.
—v. pt. and pp. of GRANULATE.

gran•u•la•tion [,grænjə'leiʃən] *n.* **1** a formation into grains or granules. **2** a roughening on the surface. **3** a granule on a roughened surface. **4** the formation of small, grainlike bodies, especially in the process of healing. **5** a small, grainlike body or elevation, especially one of those that form on the surface of wounds during healing.

gran•ule ['grænjul] *n.* **1** a small grain. **2** a small bit or spot like a grain. **3** any of the small brilliant marks in the sun's photosphere. ⟨< LL *granulum*, dim. of *granum* grain⟩

gran•u•lite ['grænjə,ləit] *n.* a rock made of feldspar, garnet, and quartz.

gran•u•lo•cyte ['grænjələ,səit] *n. Anatomy.* a leucocyte with a cytoplasm containing granules.

gran•u•lo•ma [,grænjə'loumə] *n., pl.* **-mas** or **-ma•ta** [-mətə]. *Pathology.* a growth composed of granular tissue.

gran•u•lose ['grænjə,lous] *n., adj.* *—n.* that part of a starch granule on which diastase and saliva act.
—adj. granular.

grape [greip] *n.* **1** a small, round, juicy, thin-skinned fruit that grows in bunches on grapevines and is eaten as a fruit, either fresh or dried, used for making jellies, or fermented to make wine. Grapes may be greenish white, red, or purple. **2** grapevine. **3** (*adjl.*) designating the family (Vitaceae) of mainly tropical, climbing shrubs that includes grapes and the Virginia creeper. **4 a** a bluish purple colour. **b** violet or dark purplish red. **5 the**

grape, wine. **6** grapeshot. ⟨ME < OF *grape* bunch of grapes < *graper* pick grapes < *grape* hook < Gmc.⟩ **—'grape,like,** *adj.*

grape•fruit ['greip,frut] *n., pl.* **-fruit** or **-fruits. 1** a large, edible citrus fruit with a thick yellow rind and juicy, acid, white or pink pulp. **2** the tropical and subtropical evergreen tree (*Citrus paradisi*) of the rue family that bears such fruit.

grape hyacinth a plant of the genus *Muscari,* having narrow leaves and blue flowers clustered like grapes.

grape ivy an evergreen climbing plant (*Cissus incisa*) kept as a house plant and belonging to the grape family.

grape•shot ['greip,ʃɒt] *n.* a cluster of small iron balls formerly used as a charge for cannon.

grape sugar a sugar formed in all green plants, but especially in grapes; dextrose.

grape•vine ['greip,vaɪn] *n.* **1** any of numerous vines (genus *Vitis*) of the grape family native to north temperate regions, especially an E Asian species, *V. Vinifera,* which has been cultivated in many varieties since ancient times for its fruit, called grapes. **2** *Informal.* a means of circulating information, etc. unofficially or secretly from person to person.

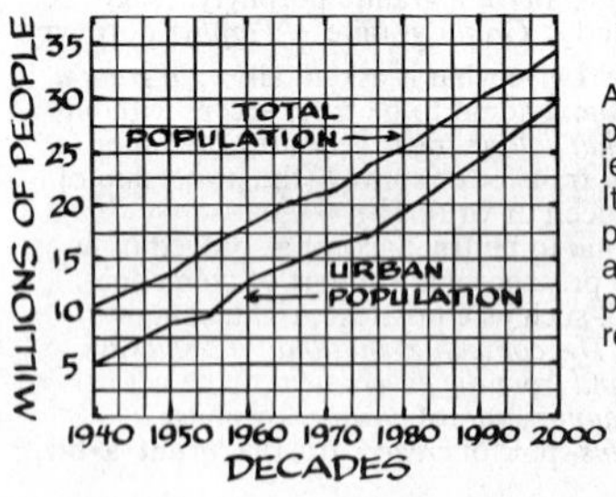

A graph of Canadian population trends projected to the year 2000. It shows that the total population is increasing, and also that the urban population is increasing relative to the rural.

graph [græf] *n., v.* *—n.* **1** a line or diagram showing how one quantity depends on or changes with another. **2** *Mathematics.* any line or lines representing an equation or function. **3** any of the most basic symbols in a writing system; letter.
—v. show (a change, equation, or function) by drawing a line or diagram; draw (a line) representing some change, equation, or function. ⟨for *graphic formula.* See GRAPHIC.⟩

–graph *combining form.* **1** make a picture, draw, or write: *photograph.* **2** a machine that makes a picture, draws, or writes: *seismograph.* **3** drawn or written: *autograph.* **4** something drawn or written: *lithograph.* ⟨< Gk. *-graphos* < *graphein* write⟩

graph•eme ['græfim] *n.* **1** a letter of an alphabet. **2** the set of allographs that represent one phoneme, such as *ph* and *f* which represent [f].

graph•em•ics [græ'fimɪks] *n.* *(used with a singular verb)* the study of writing systems and their relationship with speech.

graph•ic ['græfɪk] *adj.* **1** lifelike; vivid: *a graphic account of the battle.* **2** of or about diagrams and their use. **3** shown by a graph: *a graphic record of school attendance for a month.* **4** of or about drawing, painting, engraving, or etching: *the graphic arts.* **5** of or used in handwriting: *graphic symbols.* **6** written; inscribed. Also, **graphical**. ⟨< L *graphicus* < Gk. *graphikos* < *graphein* write⟩

graph•i•cal•ly ['græfɪkli] *adv.* **1** by a diagram or pictures. **2** vividly.

graphic arts drawing, painting, engraving, etching, etc.

graph•ics ['græfɪks] *n.* *(used with a singular verb)* **1** the art of drawing. **2** the art or science of making architectural plans in accordance with strict principles. **3** the science of calculating by using diagrams.

graph•ite ['græfəit] *n.* a soft, black form of carbon found in nature, having a metallic lustre, used for pencil leads, electrodes, and crucibles, as a lubricant for machinery, and as a moderator in nuclear reactors. ⟨< G *Graphit* < Gk. *graphein* write⟩ **—gra'phit•ic** [gra'fɪtɪk], *adj.*

graph•i•tize ['græfɪ,taɪz] *v.* **-tized, -tiz•ing. 1** coat with graphite. **2** heat so as to convert to graphite.

grapho– *combining form.* writing: *graphology.* ⟨< Gk. *graphe*⟩

graph•o•log•i•cal [,græfə'lɒdʒəkəl] *adj.* of or having to do with graphology: *graphological analysis.*

graph•ol•o•gist [græ'fɒlədʒɪst] *n.* a person trained in graphology, especially one whose work it is.

graph•ol•o•gy [græ'fɒlədʒi] *n.* the study of handwriting, especially as a means of analysing a person's character. ⟨< Gk. *graphē* writing + E *-logy*⟩

graph•o•phon•ic [,græfə'fɒnɪk] *adj.* having to do with letters and their sounds, as in learning to read.

graph paper paper with small ruled squares for the drawing of diagrams, graphs, etc. Graph paper has squares measured in centimetres to allow accuracy in producing diagrams.

–graphy *combining form.* **1** a writing, describing, or recording: *telegraphy.* **2** a descriptive science: *geography.* ⟨< Gk. *-graphia* < *graphein* write⟩

grap•nel ['græpnəl] *n.* **1** an instrument with one or more hooks for seizing and holding something. **2** a small anchor with three or more hooks. See ANCHOR for picture. ⟨ME *grapenel,* dim. of OF *grapin* hook, dim. of *grape* hook < Gmc. Related to GRAPE.⟩

grap•pa ['græpə]; *Italian,* ['grappa] *n.* Italian brandy made from what is left of the grapes after pressing to make wine. ⟨< Ital. < Gmc. **krappa,* akin to Frankish **krappo*⟩

grap•ple ['græpəl] *v.* **-pled, -pling;** *n.* *—v.* **1** seize and hold fast; grip or hold firmly. **2** struggle; fight: *The wrestlers grappled in the centre of the ring.* **3** use a grappling iron; search with a grappling iron. **4** try to deal (*with*): *She grappled with the problem for an hour before she solved it.*
—n. **1** a seizing and holding fast; a firm grip or hold. **2** an iron bar with hooks at one end for seizing and holding fast an object; grappling iron; grapnel. ⟨< OF *grapil* hook < Gmc. Related to GRAPE.⟩ **—'grap•pler,** *n.*

grappling iron grapnel.

grasp [græsp] *v., n.* *—v.* **1** seize and hold fast by closing the fingers around. **2** seize eagerly: *to grasp an opportunity.* **3** understand.
grasp at, a try to grasp; try to take hold of. **b** accept eagerly: *Joan grasped at the opportunity.*
grasp at a straw, seize even the slightest opportunity.
—n. **1** a seizing and holding tightly; clasp of the hand. **2** the power of seizing and holding; reach: *He has a strong grasp. Success is within his grasp.* **3** control; possession. **4** understanding: *She has a good grasp of mathematics.* ⟨ME *graspe(n).* Related to GROPE.⟩ **—'grasp•a•ble,** *adj.* **—'grasp•er,** *n.*
☛ *Syn. v.* **1.** See note at SEIZE.

grasp•ing ['græspɪŋ] *adj., v.* *—adj.* eager to get all that one can; greedy.
—v. ppr. of GRASP. **—'grasp•ing•ly,** *adv.* **—'grasp•ing•ness,** *n.*

grass [græs] *n., v.* *—n.* **1** non-woody green plants that grow in pastures and meadows and are suitable for food for grazing animals: *Horses, cows, and sheep eat grass.* **2** any of a large family (Gramineae) of plants having jointed, non-woody stems, long, narrow leaves, and flowers in spikelets. Wheat, corn, sugar cane, and bamboo are grasses. **3** land covered with grass: *There was a sign saying "Keep off the grass."* **4** pasture. **5** *Slang.* marijuana.
at grass, a out to pasture. **b** out of work; at leisure.
go to grass, a graze; go to pasture. **b** take a rest.
let the grass grow under (one's) **feet,** waste time; lose chances.
put, send, or **turn out to grass, a** turn (an animal) out to pasture. **b** *Informal.* force (a person) into retirement.
—v. **1** seed to grass; grow grass over or on. **2** feed on grass: *to grass livestock.* ⟨OE *gærs, græs.* Related to GREEN, GROW.⟩ **—'grass•less,** *adj.* **—'grass,like** *adj.*

grass cloth a fabric made from the fibres of plants such as jute, often used as an expensive wallpaper.

grass hockey *Cdn.* FIELD HOCKEY.

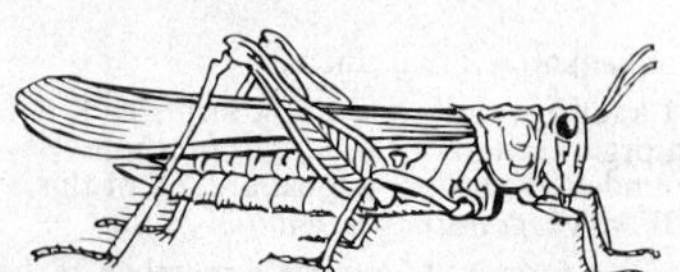

A common North American grasshopper—about 3 cm long

grass•hop•per ['græs,hɒpər] *n.* **1** any insect belonging to the orthopteran families Acrididae and Tettigoniidae, having biting mouthparts, two pairs of wings, and long, strong hind legs adapted for jumping. Grasshoppers eat plants and are often serious pests in grainfields. **2** a cocktail made of crème de menthe, crème de cacao, and cream.

grass•land ['græs,lænd] *n.* **1** land with grass on it, used for pasture. **2** prairie.

grass pink a Canadian orchid (*Calopogon pulchellus)* with no scent, having vivid pink flowers.

grass roots **1** *Politics.* people and party organizations at the local level. **2** soil near or at the surface. **3** the beginning or source. **—'grass-'roots,** *adj.*

grass snake any of various harmless snakes (family Colubridae), such as garter snakes or water snakes.

grass tree any of various Australian plants (genus *Xanthorrhea*) having short, stumpy trunks, and leaves like grass.

grass widow **1** a woman whose husband is often temporarily away. **2** a woman who is divorced or separated from her husband. ⟨originally, an unmarried woman who had lived with a man, prob. from the idea of a bed of grass or straw typifying such a relationship⟩

grass widower **1** a man whose wife is often temporarily away. **2** a man who is divorced or separated from his wife.

grass widows a western wildflower (*Sisyrinchium douglasii)* having rose-red blooms on 30 cm stems, and grasslike leaves.

grass•y ['græsi] *adj.* **grass•i•er, grass•i•est. 1** covered with grass: *a grassy meadow.* **2** of or like grass in colour or odour. **—'grass•i•ness,** *n.*

grate¹ [greit] *n., v.* **grat•ed, grat•ing.** *—n.* **1** a framework of iron bars to hold a fire. A coal furnace has a grate. See FIREPLACE for picture. **2** fireplace. **3** a framework of bars over a window or opening; grating. **4** *Mining.* a screen used for separating or grading ore.
—v. furnish with a grate or grating. ⟨< Med.L *grata* < L *cratis* hurdle⟩ **—'grate,like,** *adj.*
☛ *Hom.* GREAT.

grate² [greit] *v.* **grat•ed, grat•ing. 1** have an annoying or unpleasant effect; annoy: *His rude manners grate on other people.* **2** rub harshly together: *to grate the teeth.* **3** make a grinding sound; sound harshly. **4** move with a harsh sound: *The door grated on its old, rusty hinges.* **5** wear down or grind off in small pieces: *to grate cheese.* **6** *Archaic.* wear away by rubbing. ⟨< OF *grater* < Gmc.⟩
☛ *Hom.* GREAT.

grate•ful ['greitfəl] *adj.* **1** feeling gratitude; thankful. **2** pleasing; welcome; causing thankfulness: *a grateful breeze.* ⟨< obs. *grate* agreeable (< L *gratus*) + *-ful*⟩ **—'grate•ful•ly,** *adv.* **—'grate•ful•ness,** *n.*
☛ *Syn.* **1. Grateful,** THANKFUL = feeling or expressing gratitude. **Grateful** emphasizes recognizing and gladly acknowledging favours or kindness shown to one by others: *I am grateful to the friends who have helped me.* **Thankful,** often used as if it were a less formal substitute for **grateful,** emphasizes giving or feeling thanks for one's good fortune: *I am thankful that I have good friends.*

grat•er ['greitər] *n.* a device with a rough surface for wearing vegetables, cheese, etc. down into shreds or particles.

grat•i•fi•ca•tion [,grætəfə'keiʃən] *n.* **1** gratifying or being gratified: *The gratification of every wish of every person is not possible.* **2** something that satisfies or pleases.

grat•i•fy ['grætə,faɪ] *v.* **-fied, -fy•ing. 1** give pleasure or satisfaction to; please: *Flattery gratifies a vain person.* **2** satisfy; indulge: *to gratify a craving for chocolate.* ⟨< F < L *gratificari* < *gratus* pleasing + *facere* make, do⟩ **—'grat•i,fi•er,** *n.* **—'grat•i,fy•ing•ly,** *adv.*
☛ *Syn.* **2.** See note at HUMOUR.

grat•ing¹ ['greitɪŋ] *n., v.* *—n.* **1** a framework of bars over a window or opening. **2** *Physics.* a band of parallel lines on glass or polished metal to diffract light into optimal spectra.
—v. ppr. of GRATE¹. ⟨< *grate¹*⟩

grat•ing² ['greitɪŋ] *adj., v.* *—adj.* **1** unpleasant; annoying; irritating. **2** harsh or jarring in sound: *a grating voice.*
—v. ppr. of GRATE². ⟨< *grate²*⟩

grat•is ['grætɪs] *or* ['greitɪs] *adv. or adj.* for nothing; free of charge. ⟨< L *gratis,* ult. < *gratia* favour⟩

grat•i•tude ['grætə,tjud] *or* ['grætə,tud] *n.* a kindly feeling because of a favour received; desire to do a favour in return; thankfulness. ⟨< LL *gratitudo* < *gratus* thankful⟩

gra•tu•i•tous [grə'tjuətəs] *or* [grə'tuətəs] *adj.* **1** freely given or obtained; free. **2** without reason or cause; unnecessary; uncalled for: *a gratuitous remark.* **—gra'tu•i•tous•ly,** *adv.* **—gra'tu•i•tous•ness,** *n.*

gratuitous contract *Law.* a contract given without any value in return.

gra•tu•i•ty [grə'tjuəti] *or* [grə'tuəti] *n., pl.* **-ties. 1** a present, usually of money, given in place of or in addition to a fee, in return for a service; tip. Gratuities are given to waiters, porters, servants, etc.; they are voluntary but usually expected. **2** a payment given to members of the armed forces on being discharged or at retirement. ⟨< Med.L *gratuitas* gift, apparently < L *gratuitus* free⟩

grat•u•late ['grætʃə,leit] *v.* **-lat•ed, -lat•ing.** *Archaic.* **1** congratulate. **2** greet with joy. ⟨< L *gratulatus,* ult. < *gratus* pleasing, thankful. 16c.⟩ **—,grat•u'la•tion,** *n.*

grat•u•la•to•ry ['grætʃələ,tɔri] *adj. Archaic.* congratulatory.

grau•pel ['grʌupəl] *n.* soft hail. ⟨< G *graupeln* to sleet < *Graupelein* dim. of *Graupe* hulled barley, granule of ice⟩

gra•va•men [grə'veimən] *n., pl.* **-vam•i•na** [-'væmənə] **1** grievance. **2** *Law.* the part of an accusation that weighs most heavily against the accused. ⟨< L *gravamen* < *gravare* load < *gravis* heavy⟩

grave¹ [greiv] *n.* **1** a hole dug in the ground in which a dead body is to be buried. **2** a mound or monument over it. **3** any place that becomes the receptacle of what is dead: *a watery grave.* **4** death.
have one foot in the grave, be near death.
make (someone) **turn over in his or her grave,** say or do something that someone who is dead would have objected to strongly while alive.
secret as the grave, kept as a close secret. ⟨OE *græf.* Related to GRAVE³.⟩ **—'grave,like,** *adj.*

grave² [greiv] *for adj. 1-4;* [grɑv], [greiv], *or* [græv] *for adj. 5, n. adj.* **grav•er, grav•est;** *n. —adj.* **1** important; weighty; momentous: *It was a grave decision to make.* **2** serious; threatening: *grave questions, doubts, symptoms, news.* **3** dignified; sober; solemn: *a grave face, a grave ceremony.* **4** sombre: *grave colours.* **5** *Phonetics.* **a** LOW (def. 23); not acute. **b** having a grave accent.
—n. a grave accent. ⟨< F < L *gravis* serious⟩ **—'grave•ly,** *adv.* **—'grave•ness,** *n.*
☛ *Syn. adj.* **3. Grave,** SERIOUS, SOBER = thoughtful and free from frivolity or gaiety in mood, looks, behaviour, etc. **Grave** emphasizes dignity and lack of gaiety, especially in looks, behaviour, and attitude, and suggests having a great problem on one's mind: *His expression was grave.* **Serious** emphasizes being thoughtful, concerned with important things, and free from frivolity or giddiness, especially in disposition and manner: *He became serious when he spoke of finding a job.* **Sober** suggests a settled or self-restrained seriousness or gravity, especially in looks, behaviour, and speech: *Her words were sober and wise.*

grave³ [greiv] *v.* **graved, graved** or **grav•en, grav•ing. 1** *Archaic.* engrave; carve; sculpture. **2** impress deeply; fix firmly. ⟨OE *grafan*⟩ **—'grav•er,** *n.*

grave⁴ [greiv] *v.* **graved, grav•ing.** clean (the bottom of a wooden ship) and cover with tar. ⟨origin uncertain⟩

gra•ve⁵ ['grɑvei] *adj., adv. Music. —adj.* slow and solemn in tempo.
—adv. slowly and solemnly. ⟨< Ital. *grave,* learned borrowing from L *gravis* serious, heavy⟩

grave accent [grɑv] a mark (`) placed over a vowel to indicate stress, pitch, quality of sound (as in French *père*), or syllabic value (as in *belovèd*).

grave•dig•ger ['greiv,dɪgər] *n.* a person whose work is digging graves.

grav•el ['grævəl] *n., v.* **-elled** or **-eled, -el•ling** or **-el•ing.** *—n.* **1** pebbles and pieces of rock coarser than sand. Gravel is much used for roads and walks. **2** a road surfaced with gravel. **3** small concretions formed in the kidneys or bladder.
—v. **1** cover with gravel: *to gravel a road.* **2** puzzle; perplex. ⟨ME < OF *gravele,* dim. of *grave* sand, seashore < Celtic⟩

gravel–blind ['grævəl ,blaɪnd] purblind.

grav•el•ly ['grævəli] *adj.* **1** having much gravel. **2** consisting of or like gravel. **3** rough; rasping; grating: *a gravelly voice.*

gra•ven ['greivən] *adj., v.* *—adj.* **1** engraved; carved; sculptured. **2** deeply impressed; firmly fixed.
—v. a pp. of GRAVE³.

graven image idol.

grav•er ['greivər] *n.* **1** a tool for cutting, engraving, etc. **2** engraver.

Graves [grɑv]; *French,* [gʀav] *n.* a red or white wine of the Graves region of Bordeaux.

Graves's disease [greivz] a disease of unknown origin whose symptoms are a prominent thyroid gland, overactivity of the thyroid hormone, and slightly bulging eyeballs. ⟨after R.J. *Graves* (1797-1853), Irish physician⟩

grave•stone ['greiv,stoun] *n.* a stone that marks a grave.

Gra•vet•ti•an [grə'vɛtiən] *adj.* characteristic of an Upper Paleolithic culture in Europe. ⟨< La *Gravette*, France⟩

grave•yard ['greiv,jɑrd] *n.* **1** a place for burying the dead; cemetery; burial ground. **2** a lot, yard, etc. in which old or useless objects are discarded. **3** *Slang.* GRAVEYARD SHIFT: *She has been working on graveyard for a month now.*

graveyard shift *Slang.* the working hours between midnight and the morning shift; **night shift**.

grav•id ['grævɪd] *adj.* pregnant. ⟨< L *gravidus* < *gravis* heavy⟩

gra•vim•e•ter [grə'vɪmətər] *n.* **1** a device used to measure gravity at the earth's surface; a gravity meter. **2** any instrument used to measure specific gravity. ⟨< F *gravimètre* < L *gravis* heavy + F *mètre* measure⟩

grav•i•met•ric [,grævə'mɛtrɪk] *adj.* **1** of or having to do with gravimetry. **2** *Chemistry.* of or having to do with measurement by weight. **3** of or having to do with the use of gravity measurements to calculate distances and draw maps.

gra•vim•et•rist [grə'vɪmətrɪst] *n.* one skilled in gravimetry, especially one whose work it is.

gra•vim•e•try [grə'vɪmətri] *n.* the measurement of weight, specific gravity, or density.

graving dock ['greivɪŋ] a dry dock where ships are repaired or have their hulls cleaned.

grav•i•tate ['grævə,teit] *v.* **-tat•ed, -tat•ing. 1** move or cause to move by gravitation. **2** settle down; sink; fall: *The sand and dirt in the water gravitated to the bottom of the bottle.* **3** tend to go; be strongly attracted. ⟨< NL *gravitare*, ult. < L *gravis* heavy⟩

grav•i•ta•tion [,grævə'teiʃən] *n.* **1** *Physics.* the fact that the earth pulls any object toward it and that the sun, moon, stars, and other such bodies in the universe do the same; the force or pull that makes bodies in the universe tend to move toward one another. **2** a moving or tendency to move caused by this force. **3** a settling down; sinking; falling. **4** a natural tendency toward some point or object of influence: *the gravitation of population to the cities.* **—'grav•i,ta•tive,** *adj.*

grav•i•ta•tion•al [,grævə'teiʃənəl] *adj.* of gravitation; having to do with gravitation. **—,gra•vi'ta•tion•al•ly,** *adv.*

grav•i•ty ['grævəti] *n., pl.* **-ties. 1 a** the natural force that causes objects to move or tend to move toward the centre of the earth, the moon, or a planet. Gravity is slightly less at the top of a high mountain than at sea level. **b** the natural force that makes objects move or tend to move toward each other; gravitation. **2** (*adjl.*) of or having to do with gravity or gravitation or the effect of either. **3** heaviness; weight (*used especially in* **centre of gravity**): *The toy was hard to tip over because it had a low centre of gravity.* **4** a serious or solemn manner or behaviour: *a look of gravity.* **5** a serious or critical character: *When she had explained the gravity of the situation, they were all willing to help.* **6** lowness of pitch. ⟨< L *gravitas* < *gravis* heavy⟩

gra•vure [grə'vjʊr] *or* ['greivjər] *n.* **1** photogravure. **2** a plate or print produced by photogravure. ⟨< F *gravure* < *graver* engrave < Gmc.⟩

gra•vy ['greivi] *n., pl.* **-vies. 1** a sauce for meat, potatoes, etc., made from the juice that comes out of meat in cooking. **2** the juice itself. **3** *Slang.* easy gain or profit over and above what would normally be expected: *We've covered all our expenses; the rest is gravy.* **4** *Slang.* easy money illegally gained. ⟨ME *grave*, a misreading of OF *grané* sauce, originally, properly grained, seasoned, ult. < L *granum* grain⟩

gravy boat a jug shaped like a boat, used at the table for serving gravy.

gravy train *Slang.* a situation in which sizable profits can be realized with little effort.
ride a gravy train, a realize easy profits. **b** enjoy an easy life.

gray [grei] See GREY.

gray•beard ['grei,bird] See GREYBEARD.

gray•fish ['grei,fɪʃ] *n. Cdn.* on the Pacific coast, the dogfish (*Squalus suckleyi*).

gray–head•ed ['grei 'hɛdɪd] See GREY-HEADED.

gray•ish ['greiɪʃ] See GREYISH.

gray•lag ['grei,læg] See GREYLAG.

gray•ling ['greilɪŋ] *n.* **1** any of a genus (*Thymallus*) making up a subfamily (Thymallinae) of freshwater fishes found in the cold, clear streams of northern North America, Europe, and Asia, famous as a food and game fish and also for their beautiful colouring and the smell of wild thyme that freshly caught specimens have. Some authorities place the graylings in a distinct family (Thymallidae). **2** any of various greyish or brownish butterflies (family Satyridae), especially a European species, *Hipparchia semele.*

gray matter See GREY MATTER.

graze[1] [greiz] *v.* **grazed, graz•ing;** *n.* *—v.* **1** feed on growing grass. Cattle and sheep graze. **2** put (cattle, sheep, etc.) to feed on growing grass or a pasture. **3** tend or look after (cattle, sheep, etc.) while they are grazing. **4** *Informal.* nibble all day instead of eating meals. **5** *Informal.* sample a lot of different foods in small portions at one sitting.
—n. a grazing or feeding on grass. ⟨OE *grasian* < *græs* grass⟩ **—'graz•er,** *n.*

graze[2] [greiz] *v.* **grazed, graz•ing;** *n.* *—v.* **1** touch lightly in passing; rub lightly (against). **2** scrape the skin from: *The bullet grazed his shoulder.*
—n. **1** a slight wound made by grazing. **2** the act of grazing. ⟨origin uncertain⟩

gra•zier ['greiʒər] *n.* a person who grazes cattle for market.

gra•zing ['greizɪŋ] *n., v.* *—n.* the growing grass that cattle, sheep, etc. feed on; pasture.
—v. ppr. of GRAZE.

gra•zi•o•so [,grɑtsi'ousou]; *Italian,* [gra'tsjozo] *adv., adj. Music* *—adv.* gracefully.
—adj. in a graceful style. ⟨< Ital. < L *gratiosus* in favour, popular⟩

Gr.Brit. or **Gr.Br.** GREAT BRITAIN.

grease [gris] *n., v.* **greased, greas•ing.** *—n.* **1** animal fat that has been melted and then allowed to cool to a soft solid. **2** any thick, oily substance, especially one used as a lubricant. **3** shorn, uncleaned wool. **4** the natural oil in raw wool. **5** *Hunting.* the fat or fatness of deer, etc. Animals fat enough for killing are said to be **in grease** or **in pride** (or **prime**) **of grease.**
—v. **1** smear with grease; put grease on or in: *Long-distance swimmers grease their bodies for protection against the cold water.* **2** lubricate with grease: *He took his car to have it greased.* **3** *Slang.* give money to as a bribe or tip. ⟨ME < OF *graisse* < L *crassus* fat⟩ **—'grease•less,** *adj.*

grease cup a small cup to hold oil or grease, fastened on machinery to supply grease to parts that need it.

grease gun a device, usually consisting of a grease-filled cylinder with a plunger at one end and a nozzle at the other, for lubricating bearings, etc.

grease monkey *Slang.* a motor vehicle mechanic.

grease•paint ['gris,peint] *n.* make-up used in the theatre.

grease pencil a writing device of compressed and coloured grease for writing on smooth surfaces.

greas•er ['grisər] *n.* one who or that which greases.

grease trail *Cdn.* formerly, any of a number of ancient trails leading from the Pacific coast into the interior of British Columbia, used by First Nations people for the trade in oolichan oil and other items.

grease•wood ['gris,wʊd] *n.* **1** a low, spiny shrub (*Sarcobatus vermiculatus*) of the goosefoot family found in alkaline regions in the western parts of Canada and the United States. **2** any of various similar or related shrubs.

greas•y ['grisi] *adj.* **greas•i•er, greas•i•est. 1** smeared with grease; having grease on it. **2** containing much grease: *greasy food.* **3** like grease; smooth; slippery: *The roads were greasy after the snowfall.* **4** disagreeably unctuous; oily in manner, expression, etc. **—'greas•i•ly,** *adv.* **—'greas•i•ness,** *n.*

greasy spoon *Slang.* a small, cheap restaurant having an unsanitary appearance, especially one that specializes in short-order fried foods.

great [greit] *adj., adv., n.* *—adj.* **1** big; large: *a great house, a great crowd.* **2** more than usual; much: *great ignorance.* **3** important; remarkable; famous: *a great composer.* **4** most important; main; chief: *the great seal.* **5** noble; generous: *a great heart.* **6** much in use; favourite: *That is a great habit of hers.* **7** very much of a: *a great talker.* **8** *Informal.* very good; fine: *We had a great time at the party.* **9** *Informal.* skilful; expert: *He's great at skiing.* **10** in kinship terms, of the next generation before or after: *great-grandmother, great-grandson.*
go great guns, *Slang.* move vigorously ahead; advance at full speed.
—adv. Informal. very well: *Things are going great.*
—n. Usually, **greats,** *pl. Informal.* a great or outstanding person; celebrity: *All the greats of show business have appeared at the Palace.* ⟨OE *grēat*⟩ **—'great•ness,** *n.*
☛ *Hom.* GRATE.

☛ *Syn.* **1, 2. Great,** LARGE, BIG = above average in size or measure. **Great** chiefly means 'more than usual' (in degree), but sometimes is used to describe physical size that is impressive in some way: *We saw the great redwoods* (size). *They are trees of great age* (degree). **Large** = of great size, amount, etc. but never degree: *We saw many large trees.* **Big** particularly emphasizes weight and bulk: *A redwood is a big tree, very heavy and thick.*

great ape any of various primates (family Pongidae) such as the gorilla, chimpanzee, and orangutan.

great auk a flightless seabird (*Pinguinus impennis*) which is now extinct.

great–aunt ['greit ˌænt] *n.* an aunt of one's father or mother; grandaunt.

Great Bear *Astronomy.* URSA MAJOR.

great blue heron the largest heron common in southern Canada, having a bill about 12.7 cm long and greyish blue plumage.

Great Britain the principal island of the United Kingdom, including England, Scotland, and Wales.

great circle **1** any circle on the surface of a sphere having its plane passing through the centre of the sphere. The equator is one of the great circles of the earth. **2** an arc of such a circle; the line of shortest distance between two points on the earth's surface.

great•coat ['greitˌkout] *n.* a heavy overcoat, especially one worn by members of the armed forces.

Great Dane a breed of large, rangy, powerful dog with a smooth, short coat.

Great Danes

Great Divide in Canada, the height or crest of land extending northwest along the Rocky mountain range, from which rivers flow west to the Pacific Ocean or east and north to Hudson Bay and the Arctic Ocean; the Continental Divide.

Great Dog *Astronomy.* CANIS MAJOR.

Great•er ['greitər] *adj.* denoting a large city with its adjacent suburbs and towns: *Greater Victoria.*

great–grand•child [ˌgreit 'grænˌtʃaɪld] *or* [ˌgreit 'grændˌtʃaɪld] *n., pl.* **-chil•dren.** a grandchild of one's son or daughter.

great–grand•daugh•ter [ˌgreit 'grænˌdɒtər] *n.* a granddaughter of one's son or daughter.

great–grand•fa•ther [ˌgreit 'grænˌfɒðər] *or* [ˌgreit 'grændˌfɒðər] *n.* a grandfather of one's father or mother.

great–grand•moth•er [ˌgreit 'grænˌmʌðər] *or* [ˌgreit 'grændˌmʌðər] *n.* a grandmother of one's father or mother.

great–grand•par•ent [ˌgreit 'grænˌpɛrənt] *or* [ˌgreit 'grændˌpɛrənt] *n.* a grandfather or grandmother of one's mother or father.

great–grand•son [ˌgreit 'grænˌsʌn] *or* [ˌgreit 'grændˌsʌn] *n.* a grandson of one's son or daughter.

great grey owl a very large owl (*Strix nebulosa*) of coniferous forests of the northern hemisphere, having a round head with a very large face, yellow eyes, a long tail, and grey plumage. It is the largest North American owl.

great–heart•ed ['greit ˌhartɪd] *adj.* **1** noble; generous. **2** brave; fearless. **—'great-'heart•ed•ness,** *n.*

great horned owl a large owl (*Bubo virginianus*) of the New World having mottled brown and white plumage and large, hornlike tufts of feathers on the head.

Great Lakes the five large bodies of fresh water that are included in the St. Lawrence Seaway; Lakes Superior, Michigan, Huron, Erie, and Ontario.

great laurel a large eastern American bush (*Rhododendron maximum*) bearing long, forest green leaves and fragile pink-and-white blossoms, and belonging to the heath family.

great•ly ['greitli] *adv.* to a great degree; very much.

Great Mogul **1** the emperor of Delhi, of the Mogul dynasty that ruled over a large part of India from 1526 to 1857. **2 great mogul,** a great or important person, especially a tycoon.

great–neph•ew ['greit ˌnɛfju] *n.* a son of one's nephew or niece; grandnephew.

great–niece ['greit ˌnis] *n.* a daughter of one's nephew or niece; grandniece.

Great Pyr•e•nees ['pirəˌniz] a big dog with a thick white coat.

Great Russians a Slavic people living in central northern and NE Russia.

great seal the most important seal of a country, province, etc., stamped on official documents as proof of their approval by the government.

Great Spirit a deity worshipped by certain First Nations peoples; a translation of GITCHI MANITOU.

great–un•cle ['greit ˌʌŋkəl] *n.* an uncle of one's father or mother; granduncle.

Great Vowel Shift *Linguistics*. the change in English vowels, often from monophthong to diphthong, that took place in medieval times.

Great Wall of China a huge stone wall on the boundary between northern and northwestern China and Mongolia, about 2400 km long. It was begun in the 3rd century B.C. for the defence of China against attack by nomads from the north.

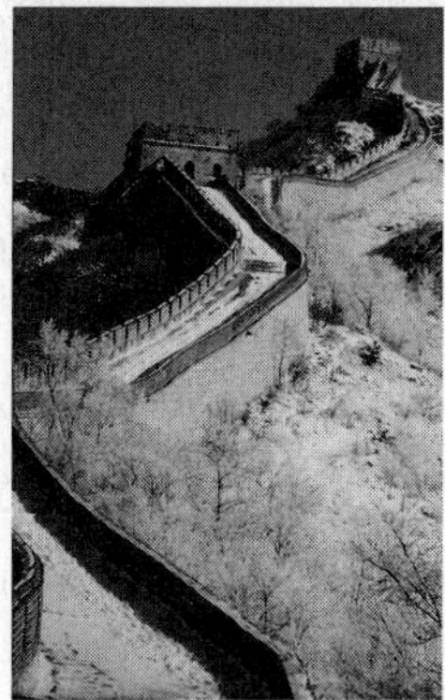
The Great Wall of China

Great War the First World War, from 1914 to 1918.

great white trillium a North American wildflower (*Trillium grandiflorum*), the largest of the trilliums. It is the provincial flower of Ontario, and is protected by law from picking.

Great White Way the brightly lighted theatre district along Broadway, a very well-known street in New York City.

great willow herb a North American wildflower (*Epilobium angustifolium*) which blooms after forest fires, having spikes of pink flowers as tall as 2 m; fireweed.

greave [griv] *n.* a piece of armour for the front of the leg below the knee (*usually used in the plural*). ⟨ME < OF *greves*, pl.; origin uncertain⟩
☛ *Hom.* GRIEVE.

grebe [grib] *n.* any of a family (Podicipitidae) of swimming and diving birds resembling loons, having lobed toes and a pointed bill. Most grebes have crests or ruffs during the nesting season. ⟨< F *grèbe*⟩

Gre•cian ['griʃən] *adj., n. —adj.* **1** of architecture, art, facial features, etc., conforming to the styles or forms of ancient Greece: *a Grecian profile, a façade of Grecian elegance.* **2** Greek. *—n.* **1** a Greek. **2** a person skilled in the Greek language or literature.

Grecian nose a straight nose; a nose that does not dip at the forehead.

Greco– *combining form.* **1** Greece; Greek things: *Grecophile.* **2** Greek and ——: *Greco-Roman.* ⟨< L *Graeco-* < Gk. *Graikos* a Greek⟩

Gre•co•phile ['grikəˌfaɪl], ['grikəfɪl], *or* ['grɛkəˌfaɪl] *n.* a person who loves Greece and Greek things.

Gre•co–Ro•man ['grikou 'roumən] *adj.* Greek and Roman.

Greece [gris] *n.* a kingdom in E Europe, in the S Balkan peninsula. See CRETE for map.

greed [grid] *n.* the wanting of more than one's share; extreme or excessive desire: *a miser's greed for money.* ⟨< *greedy*⟩

greed•y ['gridi] *adj.* **greed•i•er, greed•i•est. 1** wanting to get more than one's share; having a very great desire to possess something. **2** wanting to eat or drink a great deal in a hurry; piggish. **3** eager; keen: *greedy for new experiences.* ⟨OE *grǣdig*⟩ **—'greed•i•ly,** *adv.* **—'greed•i•ness,** *n.*

Greek [grik] *n., adj. —n.* **1** a native or inhabitant of Greece. **2** a person of Greek descent. **3** the Indo-European language of the Greeks. **Ancient Greek** is the language used from prehistoric times until about A.D. 200; **late Greek,** the language from about A.D. 200 until about 700; **medieval Greek,** the language during the Middle Ages until about A.D. 1500; **modern Greek,** the language from about 1500 on. **4** a member of the Greek Orthodox Church.

it's Greek to me, I can't understand it.
—adj. **1** of or having to do with Greece, its people, or their language. **2** *Architecture.* of or having to do with a style developed by the ancient Greeks, characterized by symmetry and graceful proportion, plain or fluted pillars, and pediments. **3** of or having to do with the Greek Orthodox Church. **4** of or having to do with the Eastern Orthodox Church. ⟨OE *grēcas* (earlier *Crēcas*), pl. < L *Graeci*, pl. of *Graecus* a Greek < Gk. *Graikos*⟩

Greek Catholic **1** a member of a small Eastern rite church within the Catholic Church, originating in SE Europe and now active especially in Greece and Turkey. **2** a member of the Greek Orthodox Church. **3** of or having to do with Greek Catholics or their churches.

Greek cross a cross whose four arms are of the same length and form right angles. See CROSS for picture.

Greek fire a substance used in warfare by the Byzantine Greeks, probably a petroleum-based mixture that apparently burst into flame spontaneously when wet and that could not be put out with water.

Greek gift a gift offered to conceal treachery or as part of a treacherous plan. ⟨< the story of the Trojan horse⟩

Greek Orthodox Church **1** the established church of Greece, a member of the Eastern Orthodox Church. **2** EASTERN ORTHODOX CHURCH.

green [grin] *n., adj., v.* *—n.* **1** the colour of most growing plants, grass, and leaves; the colour in the spectrum between yellow and blue. **2** green colouring matter, dye, paint, etc. **3** green cloth or clothing. **4** grassy land or a plot of grassy ground. **5** putting green. **6 greens,** *pl.* **a** green leaves and branches used for decoration, wreaths, garlands, etc. **b** leaves and stems of plants used as food: *salad greens.* **7 the Green,** the national colour of the Irish Republic.
—adj. **1** having the colour green. **2** covered with growing plants, grass, leaves, etc.: *green fields.* **3** composed of leafy, green vegetables such as spinach or lettuce: *green salad.* **4** characterized by growing grass, etc.: *a green Christmas.* **5** vigorous: *a garden still green.* **6** not dried, cured, seasoned, or otherwise prepared for use: *green tobacco.* **7** not ripe; not fully grown: *green peaches.* **8** not trained or experienced; not mature in age, judgment, etc.: *a green employee.* **9** easily fooled; easy to trick or cheat. **10** recent; fresh; new: *a green wound.* **11** having a pale, sickly colour because of fear, jealousy, or sickness. **12** helping to maintain a healthy natural environment: *green products.*
—v. make or become green. ⟨OE *grēne.* Related to GRASS, GROW.⟩ **—'green•ness,** *n.*

green algae any of the algae Chlorophyta.

green bean any of various cultivated varieties of bean whose green pods with the seeds inside are used as a vegetable when still young and tender.

green belt a circle of parks and other undeveloped land around a city.

green•bri•er ['grin,braɪər] *n.* any of several climbing plants (genus *Smilax*) of the lily family having prickly stems and greenish flowers.

Green Chamber a name given to the Canadian House of Commons because of the colour of the rugs, draperies, etc. in the room in which the House meets.

green corn ears of sweet corn in the young, tender, milky stage, suitable for eating roasted or boiled.

green dragon an American perennial flower (*Arisaema dracontium*) having a long spadix in a green spathe, and belonging to the arum family.

green earth any of various clays or earths used by watercolourists as a green-grey pigment.

green•er•y ['grinəri] *n., pl.* **-er•ies.** **1** green plants, grass, or leaves; verdure. **2** a place where green plants are grown or kept.

green–eyed ['grin ,aɪd] *adj.* **1** having green eyes. **2** jealous.

green•finch ['grin,fɪntʃ] *n.* a European finch (*Carduelis chloris*), the male having olive green and yellow plumage.

green•gage ['grin,geidʒ] *n.* a large plum having a light green skin and pulp. ⟨after Sir William *Gage*, who introduced it into England c. 1725⟩

green gland *Zoology.* one of two excretory organs in either side of the head in certain crustaceans.

green•gro•cer ['grin,grousər] *n. Esp. Brit.* a person who sells fresh vegetables and fruit.

green•gro•cer•y ['grin,grousəri] *n., pl.* **-cer•ies.** *Esp. Brit.* a store that sells fresh vegetables and fruit.

green•heart ['grin,hɑrt] *n.* **1** a large, tropical American tree (*Ocotea rodioei*, also classified as *Nectandra rodioei*) of the laurel family valued especially for its timber and also for the quinine-like alkaloid obtained from its bark. **2** the strong, dense, durable, greenish wood of this tree. **3** any of various similar trees or their wood.

green•horn ['grin,hɔrn] *n. Cdn. Informal.* **1** a person without experience. **2** a person easy to trick or cheat. ⟨with reference to the green horns of young oxen⟩

green•house ['grin,hʌus] *n.* a building with transparent or translucent glass or plastic roof and sides, used for growing and displaying plants in a controlled atmosphere.

greenhouse effect *Ecology.* the result of the emission of carbon dioxide (CO_2) into the atmosphere, leading to the trapping of heat on the planet by the layer of CO_2: *The greenhouse effect is raising the world's temperature.*

green•ing ['grinɪŋ] *n.* an apple having a yellowish green skin when ripe.

green•ish ['grinɪʃ] *adj.* somewhat green.

Green•land ['grinlənd] a large island in the N Atlantic off the NE coast of Canada, and part of the kingdom of Denmark.

Green•land•ic [grin'lændɪk] *n.* a language of the Inuit people of Greenland.

Green•land whale ['grinlənd] bowhead.

green light *Informal.* permission to proceed on a particular task or undertaking.

green•ling ['grinlɪŋ] *n.* any fish of the family Hexagrammidae, used for food.

green manure **1** green, leafy plants ploughed under to enrich the soil. **2** manure that has not decayed.

green monkey a small West African monkey (*Cercopithecus sabaeus*) with a greenish coat, living on the ground.

green mould any of various kinds of fungi (especially *Penicillium*) that leave blue-green spots on food.

green•ock•ite ['grinə,kəit] *n.* a mineral, a cadmium ore, red to brown in colour. *Symbol*: CdS ⟨< Lord C.C. *Greenock*, 19c. English general who discovered it⟩

green onion a young onion pulled before it is mature. Its thin, tender green leaves and small, undeveloped bulb are eaten raw, as in salads, or cooked.

green paper *Cdn.* a government document.

green pepper the unripe fruit of various peppers, especially capsicum, used as a vegetable.

green•room ['grin,rum] *or* ['grin,rʊm] *n. Theatre.* a room for the use of actors when not on the stage.

green•sand ['grin,sænd] *n.* a sediment made green by the presence of grains of glauconite.

green•shank ['grin,ʃæŋk] *n.* a European wading bird (*Tringa nebularia*) having green legs.

green snake any of various small, non-poisonous North American colubrine snakes.

green•stick fracture ['grin,stɪk] a breaking of part of a bone, leaving the rest intact. It is particularly common in children.

green•stone ['grin,stoun] *n.* **1** *Geology.* any of various igneous rocks having a greenish colour. **2** a variety of jade. **3** a piece of this stone.

green•sward ['grin,swɔrd] *n. Archaic or poetic.* growing grass; turf.

green tea tea made from leaves that have been steamed and then crushed and dried in ovens without fermenting.

green thumb a remarkable ability to grow flowers, vegetables, etc., especially as a hobby: *When Aunt Mary saw our garden, she said Mother must certainly have a green thumb.*

green turtle a large, edible sea turtle (*Chelonia mydas*) found in warm coastal waters throughout the world, having greenish flesh that is especially valued for turtle soup.

green vitriol FERROUS SULPHATE.

Green•wich mean time ['grɛnɪtʃ], ['grɪnɪdʒ], *or* ['grɪnɪtʃ] the basis for setting standard time worldwide, reckoned from the prime meridian passing through Greenwich, England, from which all longitudes are given. Greenwich mean time is the basic time used in navigation. Also, **Greenwich Time.** *Abbrev.*: G.M.T.

Greenwich Village ['grɛnɪtʃ] a section of New York City, famous as a district where artists, writers, etc. live.

green•wood ['grin,wʊd] *n.* the forest in spring and summer when the trees are green with leaves.

greet [grit] *v.* **1** speak or write to in a friendly, polite way; address in welcome. **2** address; salute: *She greeted him sternly.* **3** receive: *His speech was greeted with cheers.* **4** present itself to; meet: *A strange sight greeted her eyes.* ⟨OE *grētan*⟩ **—'greet•er,** *n.*

greet•ing ['gritɪŋ] *n.* **1** the act or words of a person who greets another; welcome. **2 greetings,** *pl.* friendly wishes on a special occasion: *birthday greetings.*

greeting card a rectangular card of usually folded stiff paper, illustrated and often bearing some printed message or greeting.

gre•ga•rine ['grɛgə,rin] *n.* a parasite of the subclass Gregarinia. ⟨ult. < L *gregarius.* See GREGARIOUS.⟩

gre•gar•i•ous [grə'gɛriəs] *adj.* **1** living in flocks, herds, or other groups: *Sheep and cattle are gregarious.* **2** fond of being with others; sociable. **3** of or having to do with a flock or crowd. **4** of flowers, growing in groups. ⟨< L *gregarius* < *grex, gregis* flock⟩ **—gre'gar•i•ous•ly,** *adv.* **—gre'gar•i•ous•ness,** *n.*

Gre•go•ri•an [grə'gɔriən] *adj.* **1** of or having to do with Pope Gregory I, pope from A.D. 590 to 604: *Gregorian music.* **2** of or introduced by Pope Gregory XIII, pope from 1572 to 1585.

Gregorian calendar the calendar now in use in most countries, introduced by Pope Gregory XIII in 1582 as an improvement on the Julian calendar.

Gregorian chant vocal music having free rhythm and a limited scale, introduced by Pope Gregory I, 540?-604, and still used in the Roman Catholic Church. It is usually sung without an accompaniment. Also called **plainsong.**

grei•sen ['graɪzən] *n.* a rock compound of quartz and mica. ⟨< dial. G *greissen* split⟩

grem•lin ['grɛmlɪn] *n.* an imaginary mischievous spirit or goblin, especially one supposed to trouble airplane pilots. ⟨origin uncertain⟩

Gre•na•da [grə'neidə] *or* [grə'nɑdə] *n.* a country in Central America.

gre•nade [grə'neid] *n.* **1** a small bomb, usually thrown by hand: *The soldiers threw grenades into the enemy's trenches.* **2** a round, glass bottle filled with chemicals that scatter as the glass breaks. Fire grenades are thrown on fires to extinguish them. ⟨< F < OF *(pome) grenate* pomegranate, fruit full of seeds; ult. < L *granum* seed, grain⟩

gren•a•dier [,grɛnə'dir] *n.* **1** originally, a soldier who threw grenades. **2** today, a soldier in any one of several infantry regiments. **3** a fish of the family Macrouridae. ⟨< F *grenadier* < *grenade.* See GRENADE.⟩

gren•a•dine[1] ['grɛnə,din] *or* [,grɛnə'din] *n.* a thin, openwork fabric used for women's dresses. ⟨< F, ? after *Granada,* Spain⟩

gren•a•dine[2] ['grɛnə,din] *or* [,grɛnə'din] *n.* a syrup made from pomegranate or currant juice. ⟨< F *grenadin* < *grenade.* See GRENADE.⟩

Gresham's Law in monetary policy, the tendency of an inferior currency to circulate because people hoard the superior version. ⟨after Sir Thomas *Gresham* (1519-1579), English financier, formerly thought to have formulated the law⟩

gres•sor•ial [grɛ'sɔriəl] *adj.* adapted for movement by legs. ⟨< L *gressus* pp. of *gradi* to step, walk⟩

Gret•na Green ['grɛtnə] a village in S Scotland in which many runaway couples from England used to be married because the age of consent was lower in Scotland.

grew [gru] *v.* pt. of GROW.

grew•some ['grusəm] *adj.* See GRUESOME. **—'grew•some•ly,** *adv.* **—'grew•some•ness,** *n.*

grey [grei] *n., adj., v.* —*n.* **1** the colour made by mixing black and white. **2** something having this colour, as: **a** grey cloth or clothing. **b** a grey horse.
—*adj.* **1** having a colour between black and white: *Ashes are grey.* **2** having grey hair: *She's very grey.* **3** old; ancient. **4** dark; gloomy; dismal: *a grey day.* **5** being intermediate or indeterminate in character, condition, or situation: *There are too many grey areas in our club's constitution.*
—*v.* make or become grey. Also, **gray.** ⟨OE *græg*⟩ **—'grey•ly,** *adv.* **—'grey•ness,** *n.*

grey•beard ['grei,bird] *n.* an old man. Also, **graybeard.**

Grey Cup *Cdn.* **1** a trophy awarded to the champion professional football team each year in Canada. It is competed for annually in a single game by the winning teams of the Eastern Football Conference and the Western Football Conference. **2** the game played to decide the winner of this trophy. ⟨< Earl *Grey,* Governor General of Canada, 1904-1911, who first presented the cup in 1909⟩

grey eminence ÉMINENCE GRISE.

Grey Friar a Franciscan friar.

grey–head•ed ['grei ,hɛdɪd] *adj.* having grey hair. Also, **gray-headed.**

grey hen the female of the black grouse.

grey•hound ['grei,haʊnd] *n.* a breed of tall, slender, swift dog having a smooth coat and sharp sight. ⟨OE *grīghund;* not connected with *grey;* cf. ON *greyhunda* < *grey* bitch⟩

grey•ish ['greiɪʃ] *adj.* somewhat grey. Also, **grayish.**

grey jay CANADA JAY.

grey•lag ['grei,læg] *n.* a large, grey goose (*Anser anser*) common in Europe and Asia.

grey matter **1** the greyish tissue in the brain and spinal cord that contains nerve cells and some nerve fibres. **2** *Informal.* intelligence; brains.

grey mullet MULLET (def. 1).

Grey Nun *Cdn.* a member of a congregation of nuns founded in 1747 in Montréal, devoted to social service. Also, **Grey Sister.**

grey power the power of elderly people, organized politically.

grey seal a large, silvery to dusky grey or brownish hair seal (*Halichoerus grypus*) found along the temperate coasts of the Atlantic Ocean.

grey squirrel a common arboreal squirrel (*Sciurus carolinensis*) native to E North America from the Gulf of Mexico north to the Great Lakes region, and now also found in Europe. The typical colour of this squirrel is grizzled grey, but there is a common black phase, especially in the northern part of its range.

grey•wacke ['greiwæk] *n.* a dark sandstone containing various dark minerals. ⟨partial translation of G *Grauwacke* grey basalt⟩

grey whale a black whalebone whale (*Eschrichtius robustus*) found in the N Pacific. The grey whale is the only member of the Eschrichtidae family.

grey wolf TIMBER WOLF.

grib•ble ['grɪbəl] *n.* a crustacean (*Limnoria lignorum*) which burrows into wood under water. ⟨probably dim. < base of *grub*⟩

grid [grɪd] *n.* **1** a framework of parallel iron bars; grating; gridiron. **2** the numbered squares drawn on maps and used for map references. **3** *Surveying.* **a** the system of survey lines running parallel to lines of latitude and longitude, used in the division of an area into counties, sections, lots, etc. **b** one of these lines. **4** an arrangement of evenly-spaced horizontal and vertical lines for any purpose. **5** the lead plate in a storage battery. **6** an electrode in a vacuum tube that controls the flow of current between the filament and the plate. **7** a network of electric lines and connections. **8** *Theatre.* a framework above the stage, from which scenery, lights, etc. are hung and manipulated. ⟨shortened form of *gridiron*⟩

grid bias the difference in potential applied between a grid and the cathode of a vacuum tube.

grid current the current that moves from the grid to the cathode of a vacuum tube.

grid•dle ['grɪdəl] *n., v.* **-dled, -dling.** —*n.* a heavy flat plate of metal or soapstone, used for cooking bacon, pancakes, etc.
—*v.* cook on a griddle. ⟨ME < OF **gredil* (cf. OF *grediller* singe) < L *craticulum.* See GRILL.⟩

grid•dle•cake ['grɪdəl,keik] *n.* a thin, flat cake of batter cooked on a griddle; pancake; flapjack.

gride [graɪd] *v.* **grid•ed, grid•ing,** *n.* —*v.* make a grating noise. —*n.* a grinding sound. ⟨ME *girde* pierce⟩

grid•i•ron ['grɪd,aɪərn] *n.* **1** GRILL (def. 1). **2** a framework or network resembling a grill. **3** a football field. **4** *Theatre.* grid. ⟨ME *gredire* griddle, var. of *gredile* < OF **gredil* (see GRIDDLE); final element assimilated to *iron*⟩

grid leak a very high resistance placed in a vacuum tube to permit the escape of excess electrons.

grid•lock ['grɪd,lɒk] *n.* **1** a cessation of activity due to overloading. **2** a total paralysis of traffic because key intersections are blocked by traffic.

grid road *Cdn.* a municipal road that follows a grid line established by survey.

grief [grif] *n.* **1** deep sadness caused by trouble or loss; heavy

sorrow. **2** a cause of sadness or sorrow: *Her son's incurable illness was a great grief to her.*
come to grief, have trouble; fail: *Although he worked hard, his plan came to grief.* ⟨ME < OF *grief* < *grever.* See GRIEVE.⟩
☛ *Syn.* **1.** See note at SORROW.

grief–stricken ['grif ˌstrɪkən] *adj.* consumed with sorrow.

griev•ance ['grivəns] *n.* **1** a real or imagined wrong; reason for being angry or annoyed; cause for complaint. **2** *Labour.* an objection to the breaking of a union agreement or policy.

griev•ant ['grivənt] *n. Labour.* one who submits a complaint for arbitration.

grieve [griv] *v.* **grieved, griev•ing. 1** feel grief; be very sad: *She grieved over her kitten's death.* **2** cause to feel grief; make very sad; afflict. **3** in labour relations, raise an objection. ⟨ME < OF *grever,* ult. < L *gravis* heavy⟩ **—'griev•er,** *n.* **—'griev•ing•ly,** *adv.*
☛ *Hom.* GREAVE.

griev•ous ['grivəs] *adj.* **1** hard to bear; causing great pain or suffering: *grievous cruelty.* **2** flagrant; atrocious: *Wasting food when people are starving is a grievous wrong.* **3** causing grief: *a grievous loss.* **4** full of grief; showing grief: *a grievous cry.* **—'griev•ous•ly,** *adv.* **—'griev•ous•ness,** *n.*

griffe [grɪf] *n. Architecture.* a projecting decoration at the base of a column. ⟨< F, claw < Frankish **grif,* akin to OHG *grif*⟩

grif•fin ['grɪfən] *n.* a mythical creature with the head, wings, and forelegs of an eagle, and the body, hind legs, and tail of a lion. Also, **griffon, gryphon.** ⟨ME < OF *grifon* < L *gryphus,* var. of *gryps* < Gk.⟩
☛ *Hom.* GRIFFON.

A wirehaired pointing griffon. Height at shoulder: 60 cm

grif•fon[1] ['grɪfən] *n.* either of two breeds of dog: the **Brussels griffon,** a terrierlike toy dog with a smooth or wiry coat, originally from Belgium; and the **wire-haired pointing griffon,** a medium-sized sporting dog with a wiry, grey and chestnut coat, originally from the Netherlands. ⟨< F *griffon,* an English breed of dog < OF *grifon.* See GRIFFIN.⟩
☛ *Hom.* GRIFFIN.

grif•fon[2] ['grɪfən] See GRIFFIN.

grift [grɪft] *v.* obtain money by fraud. ⟨probably altered < *graft*⟩

grift•er ['grɪftər] *n. Slang.* a swindler, especially one who operates a dishonest game of chance at a fair, circus, etc. ⟨perhaps var. of *grafter*⟩

grig [grɪg] *n. Dialect.* **1** a small or young eel. **2** a cricket or grasshopper. **3** a cheerful, lively person. ⟨ME *grege,* originally, dwarf; origin uncertain. 14c.⟩

grill [grɪl] *n., v.* *—n.* **1** a cooking utensil consisting of a framework of thin metal bars on which meat, fish, etc. is placed to be cooked by a fire or electric heating element. **2** food that is cooked in this way. **3** a restaurant or dining room specializing in broiled meat, fish, etc.
—v. **1** cook by direct heat, as on a grill; broil. **2** torture or torment with heat: *grilled by the hot desert sun.* **3** question severely and persistently: *The detectives grilled the prisoner until he confessed.* ⟨< F *gril* < OF *greil,* earlier *grail* < L *craticulum,* var. of *craticula* gridiron, dim. of *cratis* latticework. Doublet of GRIDDLE.⟩

gril•lage ['grɪlɪdʒ] *n.* a framework used as a foundation.

grille [grɪl] *n.* **1** an ornamental metal grating used as a barrier or screen. The grille on the front of a car protects the radiator. **2** a square opening at the back of a tennis court. Also called **grillwork.** ⟨< F < L *cracticula* < *cratis* hurdle⟩

grilled [grɪld] *adj., v.* *—adj.* cooked on an open framework over heat.
—v. pt. and pp. of GRILL.

grill•room ['grɪlˌrum] *or* ['grɪlˌrʊm] *n.* GRILL (def. 3).

grill•work ['grɪlˌwɜrk] *n.* grille.

grilse [grɪls] *n., pl.* **grilse** or **gril•ses.** a salmon that is returning from the sea to fresh water for the first time. ⟨ME; ? var. of *grisle* greyish⟩

grim [grɪm] *adj.* **grim•mer, grim•mest. 1** without mercy; stern; harsh; fierce. **2** not yielding; not relenting. **3** looking stern, fierce, or harsh. **4** horrible; ghastly: *She made grim jokes about death and ghosts.* **5** not appealing or attractive: *a grim task.* ⟨OE *grimm* fierce⟩ **—'grim•ly,** *adv.* **—'grim•ness,** *n.*

gri•mace ['grɪmɪs] *or* [grə'meis] *n., v.* **-maced, -mac•ing.** *—n.* a twisting of the face; an ugly or funny smile.
—v. make grimaces. ⟨< F < Sp. *grimazo* panic⟩ **—'gri•mac•er,** *n.* **—'gri•mac•ing•ly,** *adv.*

gri•mal•kin [grə'mælkən] *n.* **1** cat. **2** an old female cat. **3** a spiteful old woman. ⟨probably < *grey* + *Malkin,* dim. of *Maud,* proper name⟩

grime [graɪm] *n., v.* **grimed, grim•ing.** *—n.* dirt rubbed deeply and firmly into a surface: *the grime on a coal miner's hands.*
—v. cover with grime; make very dirty. ⟨? OE *grīma* mask⟩

Grimm's Law *Linguistics.* the statement of the development of stops and fricatives in the Germanic branch of languages. ⟨after Jakob *Grimm* (1785-1863), German philologist⟩

grim•y ['graɪmi] *adj.* **grim•i•er, grim•i•est.** covered with grime; very dirty. **—'grim•i•ly,** *adv.* **—'grim•i•ness,** *n.*

grin [grɪn] *v.* **grinned, grin•ning;** *n.* *—v.* **1** smile broadly. **2** show, make or express by smiling broadly: *He grinned approval.* **3** draw back the lips and show the teeth in anger, pain, scorn, etc.: *A snarling dog grins.*
grin and bear it, put up with life's trials.
—n. **1** a broad smile. **2** the act of showing the teeth in anger, pain, scorn, etc. ⟨OE *grennian*⟩ **—'grin•ner,** *n.* **—'grin•ning•ly,** *adv.*

grind [graɪnd] *v.* **ground** or *(rare)* **grind•ed, grind•ing;** *n.*
—v. **1** crush into bits or into powder: *Our back teeth grind food. Wheat is ground into flour in a mill.* **2** produce or make by grinding: *to grind flour.* **3** crush by harshness or cruelty: *The slaves were ground down by their masters.* **4** sharpen, smooth, or wear by rubbing on something rough: *An axe is ground on a grindstone.* **5** rub harshly (on, into, against, or together): *to grind one's heel into the earth, to grind one's teeth in anger.* **6** work by turning a crank: *to grind a coffee mill.* **7** produce by turning a crank: *to grind out music on a hand organ.* **8** *Informal.* work or study long and hard. **9** *Slang.* rotate the hips in dancing.
—n. **1** the act of grinding. **2** a grinding sound. **3** *Informal.* long, hard work or study. **4** a dull and laborious task. **5** *Informal.* a person who works long and hard at his or her studies. ⟨OE *grindan*⟩ **—'grind•a•ble,** *adj.* **—'grind•ing•ly,** *adv.*

grin•de•lia [grɪn'diljə] *or* [grɪn'diliə] *n.* a herb of the genus *Grindelia,* of the composite family, having yellow flowers.

grind•er ['graɪndər] *n.* **1** a person or thing that grinds: *a coffee grinder.* **2** a person or machine that sharpens tools. **3** a back tooth for grinding food; molar.

grind•stone ['graɪnˌstoun] *or* ['graɪndˌstoun] *n.* a flat, round stone set in a frame and turned by a crank, treadle, etc. It is used to sharpen tools, such as axes and knives, or to smooth and polish things.
have, keep or **put** (one's) **nose to the grindstone,** work long and hard.

grip [grɪp] *n., v.* **gripped, grip•ping.** *—n.* **1** a firm hold; a seizing and holding tight; tight grasp. **2** the power of gripping: *He has a healthy grip.* **3** the manner or style of holding something, such as a golf club or tennis racket. **4** a tool or device for grasping and holding something. **5** a part to take hold of; handle: *the grip of a suitcase.* **6** a special way of shaking hands, as used by members of a secret society to identify each other. **7** a small suitcase; travelling bag. **8** firm control or mastery: *in the grip of fear, to get a grip on oneself. The country is in the grip of winter.* **9** mental grasp: *She has a good grip on the problem.* **10** a sudden, sharp pain. **11** a stagehand or a member of a film production crew who adjusts sets or scenery and props.
come to grips with, a attempt to deal or cope with (a problem, situation, etc.). **b** engage in combat with (an enemy).

—*v.* **1** take a firm hold on; seize and hold tight. **2** get and keep the interest and attention of: *An exciting story grips the reader.* ⟨OE *gripe* < *grīpan* grasp⟩ **—'grip•less,** *adj.* **—grip•per,** *n.*
☛ *Hom.* GRIPPE.

gripe [grəip] *v.* **griped, grip•ing;** *n.* —*v.* **1** *Informal.* complain, especially continually and in an ill-tempered manner: *What's he griping about now?* **2** cause a sudden, sharp pain in the bowels of (a person). **3** experience such pain. **4** *Archaic.* clutch; grip. **5** *Archaic.* oppress or distress.
—*n.* **1** *Informal.* a grievance or complaint. **2 a** Usually, **gripes,** *pl.* colic. **b** (*adjl.*) for the relief of colic: *gripe water.* **3** *Archaic.* the act of clutching or gripping. **4** *Archaic.* grasp; control: *The empire held many small nations in its gripe.* ⟨OE *grīpan*⟩ **—'grip•er,** *n.* **—'grip•ing•ly,** *adv.*

grippe [grɪp] *n.* a contagious disease like a very severe cold with fever; influenza. ⟨< F < Russian *khrip* hoarseness⟩
☛ *Hom.* GRIP.

grip•ping ['grɪpɪŋ] *adj., v.* —*adj.* that grips; especially, that holds the attention or interest: *a gripping story.*
—*v.* ppr. of GRIP. **—'grip•ping•ly,** *adv.*

gri•saille [grɪ'zeil] *or* [grɪ'zaɪl]; *French,* [gʀi'zaj] *n.* a style of painting in shades of grey. ⟨< F⟩

Gri•sel•da [grə'zɛldə] *n.* a very meek, patient woman. ⟨< *Griselda,* the heroine of several medieval romances, including Chaucer's *Clerk's Tale,* famed for her meekness and patience when cruelly treated by her husband⟩

gri•se•ous ['grɪsiəs] *or* ['grɪziəs] *adj.* rather grey. ⟨< Med.L *griseus* < Gmc.⟩

gris•ly ['grɪzli] *adj.* **-li•er, -li•est.** frightful; horrible; ghastly. ⟨OE *grislic*⟩ **—'gris•li•ness,** *n.*
☛ *Hom.* GRIZZLY.
☛ *Syn.* See note at GHASTLY.

grist [grɪst] *n.* **1** grain to be ground. **2** grain that has been ground; meal or flour.
grist to or **for** (someone's) **mill,** source of profit to someone. ⟨OE *grīst* < *grindan* grind⟩

gris•tle ['grɪsəl] *n.* cartilage; firm, tough, elastic tissue. Babies have gristle instead of bone in some parts of the skull. ⟨OE⟩

gris•tly ['grɪsli] *adj.* **-tli•er, -tli•est.** of, containing, or like gristle. **—'grist•li•ness,** *n.*

grist mill a mill for grinding grain.

grit [grɪt] *n., v.* **grit•ted, grit•ting.** —*n.* **1** very fine bits of gravel or sand: *There was grit in the spinach.* **2** a coarse sandstone. **3** the grain or texture of a stone with respect to fineness, coarseness, etc. **4** the abrasive quality of a sanding disk, cloth, paper, etc. **5** *Informal.* courage; pluck: *The fighter showed plenty of grit.* **6 Grit,** *Cdn. Informal.* **a** a member of the Liberal party in Canada. **b** (*adjl.*) of or associated with the Liberals.
—*v.* **1** grate; grind; clench: *He gritted his teeth and plunged into the cold water.* **2** cover or spread with grit. **3** make or cause to make a grating or gritty sound. ⟨OE *grēot*⟩

grits [grɪts] *n.pl.* **1** coarsely ground corn, oats, etc., with the husks removed. **2** *U.S.* coarse hominy. ⟨OE *grytte*⟩

grit•ty ['grɪti] *adj.* **-ti•er, -ti•est. 1** of or containing grit; like grit; sandy. **2** *Informal.* courageous; plucky. **—'grit•ti•ly,** *adv.* **—'grit•ti•ness,** *n.*

griv•et ['grɪvɪt] *n.* an East African monkey (*Cercopithecus aethiops*) living on the ground and having long white hairs on either side of its face. ⟨< F⟩

griz•zle ['grɪzəl] *n., adj., v.* **-zled, -zling.** —*n.* **1** greying hair. **2** a wig. **3** the colour grey. **4** a grey animal, especially a horse.
—*adj.* grey; grizzled.
—*v.* make or become grey. ⟨ME < MF *grisel,* dim. of *gris* grey < Gmc.⟩

griz•zled ['grɪzəld] *adj., v.* —*adj.* **1** grey; greyish. **2** grey-haired.
—*v.* pt. and pp. of GRIZZLE.

griz•zly ['grɪzli] *adj.* **-zli•er, -zli•est;** *n., pl.* **-zlies.**
—*adj.* grizzled.
—*n.* **1** GRIZZLY BEAR. **2** *Mining.* a screening device made of iron bars or rails and used to separate ore from gravel.
☛ *Hom.* GRISLY.

grizzly bear a large bear (*Ursus horribilis*), a subspecies of the brown bear found in the alpine and arctic tundra and subalpine forests of W North America. Most of the grizzlies in the Rocky Mountains are dark brown with long, white-tipped hairs on the shoulders and back; in the arctic tundra, however, many have a cream-coloured back with reddish brown underparts and legs.

A grizzly bear

groan [groun] *n., v.* —*n.* a deep-throated sound expressing grief, pain, or disapproval; deep, short moan.
—*v.* **1** give a groan or groans. **2** be loaded or overburdened: *The table groaned with food.* **3** express by groaning. **4** suffer greatly. ⟨OE *grānian*⟩ **—'groan•er,** *n.*
☛ *Syn. n.* **Groan,** MOAN = a low sound expressing painful feelings. **Groan** suggests a heavier sound than **moan** and implies suffering too hard to bear and, often, rebelliousness: *the groans of people caught in the wreckage, the groans of slaves under a yoke.* **Moan** implies a more continuous and involuntary cry of pain or some similar sound: *the moan of the wind.*

groat [grout] *n.* **1** an old English silver coin worth about six cents. **2** a very small sum. ⟨< MDu. *groot,* literally, thick (coin)⟩

groats [grouts] *n.pl.* hulled grain; hulled and crushed grain. ⟨OE *grotan,* pl.⟩

gro•cer ['grousər] *n.* a merchant who sells food and household supplies. ⟨ME < OF *grossier,* originally, one who sells in bulk; ult. < L *grossus* thick⟩

gro•cer•y ['grousəri] *n., pl.* **-cer•ies. 1** a store that sells food and household supplies. **2 groceries,** *pl.* commodities sold by a grocer, especially food. **3** the business or trade of a grocer.

gro•ce•te•ri•a [ˌgrousə'tiriə] *n. Cdn.* a self-service grocery store. ⟨*groce(ry)* + *(cafe)teria*⟩

grog [grɒg] *n.* **1** a drink made of rum or any other strong alcoholic liquor diluted with water. **2** any strong alcoholic liquor. ⟨short for *grogram,* nickname of British Admiral Vernon, who had sailors' rum diluted; from his *grogram* cloak⟩

grog•gy ['grɒgi] *adj.* **-gi•er, -gi•est.** *Informal.* **1** shaky; unsteady. **2** drunk; intoxicated. **3** sluggish from tiredness or anesthetic, etc. **—'grog•gi•ly,** *adv.* **—'grog•gi•ness,** *n.*

grog•ram ['grɒgrəm] *n.* a coarse cloth made of silk, wool, or combinations of these with mohair. ⟨< F *gros grain* coarse grain⟩

grog•shop ['grɒgˌʃɒp] *n. Esp. Brit.* saloon.

groin [grɔɪn] *n.* **1** the hollow on either side of the body where the thigh joins the abdomen. **2** *Architecture.* a curved edge or line where two vaults of a roof intersect. **3** a small jetty to prevent sea erosion. ⟨ME *grynde,* influenced by *loin*⟩

grom•met ['grɒmɪt] *or* ['grʌmɪt] *n.* **1** a metal eyelet. **2** a ring of rope, used as an oarlock, to hold a sail on its stays, etc. Also, **grummet.** ⟨< obs. F *gromette* curb of bridle < *gourmer* curb⟩

grom•well ['grɒmwɛl] *or* ['grɒmwəl] *n.* any of various plants (genus *Lithospermum*) bearing yellow or orange blossoms and small, hard nuts, belonging to the borage family. ⟨altered < ME *gromil* < OF < Med.L *gruinum milium* kind of millet < *gruinus* of a crane (< L *grus* crane) + L *milium* millet⟩

groom [grum] *n., v.* —*n.* **1** a man or boy who has charge of horses. **2** a man just married or about to be married; bridegroom. **3** in England, any of several officers of the royal household. **4** *Archaic.* manservant.
—*v.* **1** feed and take care of (horses); rub down and brush (a domestic animal). **2** take care of the appearance of; make neat and tidy. **3** prepare (a person) to run for a political office or to fill some other superior social niche. ⟨ME *grom(e)* boy; origin uncertain; cf. OF *gromet* servant⟩ **—'groom•er,** *n.*

grooms•man ['grumzmən] *n., pl.* **-men.** a man who attends the bridegroom at a wedding.

groove [gruv] *n., v.* **grooved, groov•ing.** —*n.* **1** a long, narrow channel or furrow, especially one cut by a tool: *The plate rests in a groove on the rack.* **2** any similar channel; rut: *Wheels leave grooves in a dirt road.* **3** a fixed way of doing things: *It is hard to get out of a groove.*
in the groove, *Slang.* **a** smoothly and with great skill. **b** excellent or excellently. **c** in fashion; up-to-date.
—*v.* **1** make a groove or grooves in. **2** *Slang.* feel enjoyment or excitement, especially as a result of being in tune with the surrounding atmosphere or stimuli (*often used with* **on**): *He*

grooves on classical jazz. ⟨< MDu. *groeve* furrow, ditch⟩ **—'groov•er,** *n.* **—'groove•less,** *adj.* **—'groove,like,** *adj.*

groov•y ['gruvi] *adj. Slang.* **1** fashionable and exciting: *a groovy new singer. They thought it would be groovy to live in a van.* **2** wonderful; marvellous.

grope [group] *v.* **groped, grop•ing;** *n.* *—v.* **1** feel about with the hands: *He groped for a flashlight when the lights went out.* **2** search blindly and uncertainly: *The detectives groped for some clue to the murder.* **3** find by feeling about with the hands; feel (one's way) slowly: *The blind man groped his way to the door.* **4** *Slang.* touch (someone) sexually, especially when unwanted.
—n. the act of groping. ⟨OE *grāpian.* Related to GRASP, GRIP, GRIPE.⟩ **—'grop•er,** *n.* **—'grop•ing•ly,** *adv.*

A grosbeak. Length: 20 cm

gros•beak ['grous,bik] *n.* any of various North American or European finches having a large, strong, cone-shaped bill. Common Canadian grosbeaks are the **rose-breasted grosbeak** (*Pheucticus ludovicianus*), **evening grosbeak** (*Hesperiphona vespertina*), and **pine grosbeak** (*Pinicola enucleator*). ⟨< F *grosbec* < *gros* large + *bec* beak⟩

gro•schen ['grouʃən] *n.* a unit of money in Austria, equal to 1/100 of a schilling. ⟨< G < ML *(denarius) grossus* thick denarius⟩

gros•grain ['grou,grein] *n., adj.* *—n.* a closely woven silk or rayon cloth with heavy cross threads and a dull finish.
—adj. having heavy cross threads and a dull finish. ⟨var. of *grogram*⟩

gros point ['grous,pɔint]; *French,* [gʀo'pwɛ] *n.* a coarse cross-stitch used for needlepoint embroidery. ⟨< F *gros* large + *point* stitch⟩

gross [grous] *adj., n., pl.* **gross•es** *for 1,* **gross** *for 2; v.*
—adj. **1** with nothing taken out; whole; entire. The gross receipts are all the money taken in before costs are deducted. **2** obviously bad; glaring: *gross misconduct. She makes gross errors in pronunciation.* **3** coarse; vulgar: *Her manners are too gross for a lady.* **4** too big and fat; overfed. **5** thick; heavy; dense: *the gross growth of a jungle.* **6** concerned with large masses or outlines; general. **7** *Informal.* disgusting.
—n. **1** the whole sum; total amount. **2** a unit consisting of twelve dozen; 144.
in the gross, a as a whole; in bulk. **b** wholesale.
—v. make a gross profit of; earn a total of: *She grosses $60 000 per year.* ⟨ME < OF *gros* < L *grossus* thick⟩ **—'gross•er,** *n.* **—'gross•ly,** *adv.* **—'gross•ness,** *n.*

gross national product the total market value of a nation's goods and services, before allowances or deductions. *Abbrev.:* GNP or G.N.P.

gross profit the difference between the cost and the selling price of goods, before deductions.

gross ton LONG TON.

gros•su•lar•ite ['grɒsjələ,rəit] *or* ['grɒsələ,rəit] *n.* a type of garnet, found in several different colours. *Formula:* $Ca_3Al_2(SiO_4)_3$ ⟨< G *Grossularit* < NL *grossularia* originally, gooseberry genus (in reference to the colour of certain varieties) < F *groseille* gooseberry⟩

gross weight the total weight, including wastage, packaging, etc.

grosz [grɒʃ] *n., pl.* **gro•szy** ['grɒʃi] a unit of money in Poland, equal to 1/100 of a zloty. ⟨< Polish⟩

grot [grɒt] *n. Poetic.* GROTTO[1].

gro•tesque [grou'tɛsk] *adj., n.* *—adj.* **1** odd or unnatural in shape, appearance, manner, etc.; fantastic; queer: *The book had pictures of hideous dragons and other grotesque monsters.* **2** ridiculous; absurd: *The monkey's grotesque antics made the children laugh.* **3** of painting, etc., combining designs, ornaments, figures, etc. in a fantastic or unnatural way.
—n. **1** a painting, etc. combining designs, ornaments, figures, etc. in a fantastic or unnatural way. **2** a fantastic character in a play or film. **3** a grotesque quality or object. ⟨< F < Ital. *grottesco* < *grotta.* See GROTTO.⟩ **—gro'tesque•ly,** *adv.* **—gro'tesque•ness,** *n.*

gro•tes•que•ry [grou'tɛskəri] *n.* **1** something grotesque. **2** grotesqueness. Also, **grotesquerie.**

grot•to ['grɒtou] *n., pl.* **-toes** or **-tos. 1** a cave. **2** an artificial cave made for coolness or pleasure. **3** a shrine in or like a cave. ⟨< Ital. *grotta* < L *crypta* < Gk. *kryptē* vault. Doublet of CRYPT.⟩

grot•ty ['grɒti] *adj.* **-ti•er, -ti•est.** *Slang.* unpleasant, seedy, or nasty. ⟨< *grotesque.* 20c.⟩ **—'grot•ti•ness,** *n.*

grouch [grʌutʃ] *v., n. Informal.* *—v.* be sulky or ill-tempered; complain.
—n. **1** a sulky person. **2** a sulky, discontented feeling. ⟨var. of obs. *grutch* < OF *groucher* murmur, grumble. Doublet of GROUSE[2], GRUDGE.⟩

grouch•y ['grʌutʃi] *adj.* **grouch•i•er, grouch•i•est.** *Informal.* sulky; sullen; discontented. **—'grouch•i•ly,** *adv.* **—'grouch•i•ness,** *n.*

ground[1] [graʊnd] *n., adj., v.* *—n.* **1** the solid part of the earth's surface: *Snow covered the ground.* **2** earth; soil; dirt: *The ground was hard.* **3** a particular piece of land; land for some special purpose: *The Cariboo was her favourite hunting ground.* **4** Often, **grounds,** the foundation for what is said, thought, claimed, or done; basis; reason; justification: *no grounds for complaint.* **5** underlying surface; background: *The cloth has a blue pattern on a white ground.* **6 grounds,** *pl.* **a** land or area for some purpose or special use. **b** the land, lawns, and gardens around a house, school, etc. **7 grounds,** *pl.* the small bits that sink to the bottom of a drink such as coffee or tea; dregs; sediment. **8** the connection of an electrical conductor with the earth. **9** in a radio, television set, etc., the connection for the conductor that leads to the ground. **10** the bottom of an ocean, lake, pond, etc.
above ground, alive.
break ground, a dig; plough. **b** begin building.
break new ground, a do something for the first time. **b** do something in a new and original manner.
cover ground, a go over a certain distance or area. **b** travel. **c** do a certain amount of work, etc.
cut the ground from under (someone's) **feet,** spoil a person's defence or argument by meeting it in advance.
down to the ground, *Informal.* completely; through and through.
fall to the ground, fail; be given up.
from the ground up, completely; entirely; thoroughly; from the humblest level: *She learned her father's business from the ground up.*
gain ground, a go forward; advance; progress: *During the second day of fighting, the army began to gain ground.* **b** become more common or widespread.
get off the ground, make a successful beginning.
give ground, retreat; yield: *Under our attack the enemy was forced to give ground.*
hold (one's) **ground,** keep one's position; not retreat or yield.
lose ground, a retreat; yield. **b** fall back; give up what has been gained: *As soon as the runner became tired, he began to lose ground.* **c** become less common or widespread.
on (one's) **own ground,** in a context, etc., one finds comfortable or familiar.
on the grounds of, because of; by reason of.
run into the ground, *Informal.* **a** overdo; repeat to excess: *You've run that topic into the ground.* **b** use (a motor vehicle) until it breaks down.
shift (one's) **ground,** change one's position; use a different defence or argument.
stand (one's) **ground,** keep one's position; refuse to retreat or yield: *Even though the boxer was hurt, she stood her ground.*
—adj. of, on, at, or near the ground; living or growing in, on, or close to the ground.
—v. **1** put on the ground; cause to touch the ground. **2** run aground; hit the bottom or shore: *The boat grounded in shallow water.* **3** put on a firm foundation or basis; establish firmly. **4** instruct in the first principles or elements: *The class is well grounded in grammar.* **5** furnish with a background. **6** connect (an electric wire or other conductor) with the earth. **7** prohibit (an aviator or an aircraft) from flying. **8** restrict (a child or teenager) from participating in certain social activities, usually evening

ones, as a punishment. 9 *Baseball.* hit a grounder. ⟨OE *grund* bottom⟩

ground² [graʊnd] *v.* pt. and pp. of GRIND.

ground bass *Music.* repeated notes in the bass, giving harmony for the upper notes.

ground–cherry ['graʊnd ˌtʃɛri] *n.* any of various plants belonging to the nightshade family, bearing small red berries in a paperlike calyx.

ground control the personnel and equipment needed to control an aircraft or spacecraft before, during, and after its flight.

ground cover any low-growing and spreading plant used to control weeds and provide interest between plants, shrubs, etc.

ground crew 1 the non-flying personnel responsible for the conditioning and maintenance of airplanes. 2 any group of people responsible for maintaining a baseball field or other playing field.

ground–drift ['graʊnd ˌdrɪft] *n. Cdn.* snow driven along the surface by wind.

ground•er ['graʊndər] *n. Baseball.* a ball hit or thrown so as to bound or roll along the ground.

ground•fire ['graʊnd,faɪr] *n.* anti-aircraft fire from the ground.

ground•fish ['graʊnd,fɪʃ] *n.* any fish that lives at or near the bottom of the sea, such as cod or haddock.

ground floor 1 the floor of a building at street level. 2 the beginning of a venture: *to get in on the ground floor.* 3 *Informal.* the best position in relation to a business deal, etc.

ground glass 1 glass with the surface roughened so that it is not transparent. 2 glass that has been ground to powder.

ground hemlock a common low-growing shrub (*Taxus canadensis*), a species of yew found in forests from Newfoundland to Manitoba and the NE United States.

ground•hog ['graʊnd,hɒg] *n.* a marmot (*Marmota monax*) found across most of Canada south of the Barren Lands and in the NE United States, having a thickset body, a flat head on a very short neck, and short, rounded ears. Also called **woodchuck.**

A groundhog

Groundhog Day February 2, when the groundhog is supposed to come out of its burrow to see whether the sun is shining. If the sun is shining and it sees its shadow, it returns to its burrow for six more weeks of winter; if the sky is overcast, it expects an early spring.

ground ice 1 ice formed below the surface of a body of water, either at the bed or attached to submerged objects. Also called **anchor ice.** 2 ice spread throughout the soil in permafrost.

ground ivy a trailing aromatic plant (*Glechoma hederacea*).

ground•less ['graʊndlɪs] *adj.* without foundation, basis, or reason. **—'ground•less•ly,** *adv.* **—'ground•less•ness,** *n.*

ground•ling ['graʊndlɪŋ] *n.* 1 a plant or animal that lives close to the ground. 2 a fish that lives at the bottom of the water. 3 a spectator or reader who has poor taste. 4 formerly, a spectator of a play who sat or stood in the pit.

ground•mass ['graʊnd,mæs] *n. Geology.* the crystalline base of porphyrytic rock.

ground mer•i•stem ['mɛrɪ,stɛm] *Botany.* the primary part of the growing end of a root from which the cortex, rays, and pith develop.

ground•nut ['graʊnd,nʌt] *n.* 1 any of various plants having edible tubers or nutlike underground seeds, such as the peanut. 2 the edible tuber, pod, etc. of such a plant.

ground pine 1 any of several North American club mosses, (genus *Lycopodium*) having creeping stems and erect branches with needlelike leaves. 2 a European and N African plant (*Ajuga chamaepitys*) of the mint family having a pinelike smell when crushed.

ground plan 1 the plan of a floor of a building. 2 the first or fundamental plan.

ground plum a wild, leafy plant (*Astragalus crassicarpus*) having thick-skinned, edible pods.

ground rule one of a set of basic rules or principles for action or procedure.

ground•sel ['graʊndsəl] *or* ['graʊnsəl] *n.* any of several plants (genus *Senecio*) of the composite family having chiefly yellow flower heads, especially *S. vulgaris*, a common weed of Europe and Asia. ⟨OE *g(r)undeswelge* < *grund* ground or *gund* pus + *swelgan* swallow¹; variously explained as meaning 'ground-swallower' because it spreads rapidly, or 'pus absorber' because it was used to reduce abcesses⟩

ground•sheet ['graʊnd,ʃit] *n.* a waterproof sheet, as of rubber or plastic, used under a tent, sleeping bag, etc. to protect against damp from the ground.

ground•sill ['graʊnd,sɪl] *n.* a horizontal timber used as a foundation; lowest part of a wooden framework; sill. ⟨ME *gronsel* < OE *grund* ground + *syll(e)* sill; the modern form has been influenced by its components *ground* and *sill*⟩

ground•speed ['graʊnd,spid] *n.* the speed of an airborne aircraft in relation to the ground it flies over.

ground squirrel 1 *Cdn.* any of a genus (*Spermophilus*, also classified as genus *Citellus*) of small, burrowing rodents of North America, Europe, and Asia belonging to the same family as squirrels, including some, such as the prairie gopher, that are pests in grainfields. 2 any of various other rodents of the same family (Sciuridae), such as chipmunks.

ground stroke *Tennis.* a forehand or backhand made on the half-volley.

ground swell 1 the broad, deep waves caused by a distant storm, earthquake, etc. 2 a great rise or increase in the amount, degree, or force of anything, such as popular opinion.

ground water water that flows or seeps through the ground into springs and wells.

ground wave a radio wave travelling across the earth's surface.

ground wire a wire connecting electric wiring, a radio, etc. with the ground.

ground•work ['graʊnd,wɜrk] *n.* a foundation or first part.

ground zero the exact point where a bomb strikes the ground or, in an atomic explosion, the area directly beneath the core of radiation.

group [grup] *n., v.* —*n.* 1 a number of persons or things together: *A group of children were playing tag.* 2 a number of persons or things belonging or classed together: *Wheat, rye, and oats belong to the grain group.* 3 an air force unit larger than a squadron, and smaller than a wing. 4 a number of musicians playing or singing together. 5 *Chemistry.* **a** a radical. **b** a set of elements sharing similar properties, constituting a vertical column in the periodic table. **c** a set of elements involved in similar chemical reactions. 6 *Geology.* a rock arrangement composed of two or more formations.
—*v.* 1 form a group. 2 bring together; put in a group. 3 arrange in groups. ⟨< F < Ital. *gruppo* < Gmc.⟩

group captain an air-force officer ranking next above a wing commander and below an air commodore. *Abbrev.*: G.C. or G/C

group•er ['grupər] *n., pl.* **-er** or **-ers.** any of numerous large-mouthed food fishes (family Serranidae, especially genera *Epinephelus* and *Mycteroperca*) found in warm seas, including some very large species that reach a length of 2 m and a mass of 225 kg. Groupers belong to the same family as the sea basses. ⟨< Pg. *garupa*⟩

group home a home where several people live who need a sheltered environment, such as those with mental disabilities, or ex-prisoners.

group•ie ['grupi] *n. Slang.* 1 a fan who follows members of touring musical groups, sports teams, etc., especially one who seeks sexual intimacy with them. 2 any avid fan or follower; hanger-on.

group•ing ['grupɪŋ] *n., v.* —*n.* 1 a placing or manner of being placed in a group or groups. 2 the resulting group.
—*v.* ppr. of GROUP.

group insurance health or life insurance available at a reduced rate to members of a group, especially employees of a company.

Group of Seven *Cdn.* a group of seven painters who organized themselves in 1920 to promote a movement in Canadian landscape painting different from European traditions.

group therapy psychotherapy in which a group of people sharing similar emotional problems and disturbances discuss their experiences under the supervision of a therapist.

A ruffed grouse—about 45 cm long with the tail

grouse[1] [grʌus] *n., pl.* **grouse.** any of numerous birds (family Tetraonidae) hunted as game, having a plump body and feathered legs and mainly brownish plumage. Some Canadian grouse are the ruffed grouse, spruce grouse, and prairie chicken; the largest grouse is the Old World capercaillie. ⟨origin uncertain⟩

grouse[2] [grʌus] *v.* **groused, grous•ing;** *n. Informal.* —*v.* grumble; complain.
—*n.* **1** complaint. **2** a person who complains; grumbler. ⟨apparently < OF *groucer*, var. of *groucher* murmur, grumble. Doublet of GROUCH, GRUDGE.⟩

grous•er[1] ['grʌusər] *n. Informal.* a grouch or complainer.

grous•er[2] ['grʌusər] *n.* **1** a pole driven into a river bottom, etc. to keep a boat or other floating object in place. **2** on a tractor, one of a set of cleats attached to a wheel or track to prevent slipping. ⟨origin unknown⟩

grout [grʌut] *n., v.* —*n.* thin mortar used to fill cracks, etc.
—*v.* fill up or finish with this mortar. ⟨OE *grūt*⟩

grove [grouv] *n.* a group of trees standing together. An orange grove is an orchard of orange trees. ⟨OE *grāf*⟩

grov•el ['grɒvəl] *or* ['grʌvəl] *v.* **-elled** or **-eled, -el•ling** or **-el•ing. 1** lie or crawl face downward at someone's feet; humble oneself: *The frightened slaves grovelled before their cruel master.* **2** enjoy low, mean, or contemptible things. ⟨back formation from ME *grovelinge* (adv.) on the face < *on grufe* prone < ON *á grúfu*⟩ **—'grov•el•ler** or **'grov•el•er,** *n.* **—'grov•el•ling•ly** or **'grov•el•ing•ly,** *adv.*

grow [grou] *v.* **grew, grown, grow•ing. 1** become bigger by taking in food, as plants and animals do. **2** exist; sprout; spring; arise: *a tree growing only in the tropics.* **3** become greater; increase: *Her fame grew.* **4** get into a certain state or condition by growth: *The vine has grown fast to the wall.* **5** become: *to grow cold, to grow rich.* **6** cause to grow; produce; raise: *to grow corn.* **7** allow to grow: *to grow a beard.* **8** develop.
grow on or **upon,** have an increasing effect or influence on: *The habit grew on me.*
grow out of, a grow too big for. **b** grow too old for.
grow up, a advance to or arrive at full growth and maturity. **b** come into being; be produced; develop. **c** begin to behave maturely. ⟨OE *grōwan.* Related to GRASS, GREEN.⟩

grow•er ['grouər] *n.* **1** a person who grows something: *a fruit grower.* **2** a plant that grows in a certain way: *a quick grower.*

growing pains 1 pains during childhood and youth, supposed to be caused by growing. **2** troubles that arise when something new is just developing.

growing point *Botany.* the tip of a stem or root where dividing and elongating cells are found.

growl [graʊl] *v., n.* —*v.* **1** make a deep, low, angry sound: *The dog growled at the tramp.* **2** express by growling: *He growled his thanks.* **3** complain angrily: *The soldiers growled about the poor food.* **4** rumble.
—*n.* **1** a deep, low, angry sound; deep, warning snarl. **2** an angry complaint. **3** a rumble. ⟨probably imitative⟩

growl•er ['graʊlər] *n.* **1** a person who or animal that growls. **2** a floating piece of ice resembling a small iceberg, broken off from a glacier or larger iceberg. **3** an electromagnetic device with two poles, used for magnetizing and demagnetizing.

grown [groun] *adj., v.* —*adj.* **1** arrived at full growth. **2** covered with a growth.
—*v.* pp. of GROW.

grown–up *adj.* ['groun 'ʌp]; *n.* ['groun ,ʌp] *adj., n.* —*adj.* **1** adult. **2** characteristic of or suitable for adults.
—*n.* an adult: *The boy went to the theatre with the grown-ups.*

growth [grouθ] *n.* **1** the process of growing; development. **2** the amount of growing or developing; increase: *one year's growth.* **3** what has grown or is growing: *A thick growth of bushes covered the ground.* **4** an abnormal mass of tissue formed in or on the body. Cancer causes a growth. **5** (*adjl.*) of or having to do with stocks, or an industry, whose value or earnings multiply at a higher than average rate.

growth hormone 1 a hormone from the front of the pituitary gland, which regulates growth in humans. **2** a similar hormone governing the growth of plants and animals.

GRS *Cdn.* GENERAL RADIO SERVICE.

grub [grʌb] *n., v.* **grubbed, grub•bing.** —*n.* **1** a wormlike form or larva of an insect. A grub is usually the smooth, thick larva of a beetle. **2** a drudge. **3** *Informal.* food.
—*v.* **1** dig: *Pigs grub for roots.* **2** root out of the ground; dig up: *It took the farmer weeks to grub the stumps on his land.* **3** rid (ground) of roots, etc. **4** drudge; toil. **5** search or rummage. **6** *Slang.* eat. ⟨ME *grubbe(n); related to OE grafan,* OHG *grubilōn* to dig⟩ **—'grub•ber,** *n.*

grub•by ['grʌbi] *adj.* **-bi•er, -bi•est. 1** dirty; grimy: *grubby hands.* **2** mean or contemptible: *a grubby little con artist.* **3** infested with grubs. **—'grub•bi•ness,** *n.*

grub•stake ['grʌb,steik] *n., v.* **-staked, -stak•ing.** —*n.* **1** the food, outfit, money, etc. supplied to a prospector on the condition of sharing in whatever he or she finds. **2** the arrangement by which this is done. **3** *Cdn.* the money or the means to buy food and other provisions for a certain period. **4** *Cdn.* a store of food or provisions.
—*v.* provide with a grubstake. **—'grub,stak•er,** *n.*

Grub Street 1 a former street in London where poor, struggling writers lived. **2** writers of little ability who write merely to earn money; hack writers.

grub•street ['grʌb,strit] *adj.* written by a hack; of poor quality: *grubstreet fiction.*

grudge [grʌdʒ] *n., v.* **grudged, grudg•ing.** —*n.* ill will; a sullen feeling against; dislike of long standing.
bear a grudge, have and keep a grudge.
—*v.* **1** feel anger or dislike toward (a person) because of (something); envy the possession of: *He grudged me my little prize even though he had won a bigger one.* **2** give or let have unwillingly: *The mean man grudged his horse the food that it ate.* ⟨earlier meaning, grumble, complain; var. of obs. *grutch* < OF *groucher* murmur, grumble. Doublet of GROUCH, GROUSE[2].⟩
☛ *Syn. n.* **1.** See note at SPITE.

grudg•ing•ly ['grʌdʒɪŋli] *adv.* unwillingly.

gru•el ['gruəl] *n., v.* **-elled** or **-eled, -el•ling** or **-el•ing.** —*n.* a thin, almost liquid food made by boiling oatmeal, etc. in water or milk. Gruel is often given to those who are sick or old.
—*v. Informal.* tire out completely; exhaust. ⟨ME < OF *gruel,* ult. < Gmc.⟩

gru•el•ling ['gruəlɪŋ] *adj., n., v. Informal.* —*adj.* exhausting; very tiring: *a gruelling contest.*
—*n.* an exhausting or very tiring experience.
—*v.* ppr. of GRUEL. Also, **grueling.**

grue•some ['grusəm] *adj.* horrible; frightful; revolting. Also, **grewsome.** ⟨< *grue* shudder; cf. MDu., MLG *gruwen*⟩ **—'grue•some•ly,** *adv.* **—'grue•some•ness,** *n.*

gruff [grʌf] *adj.* **1** deep and harsh; hoarse. **2** rough; rude; unfriendly; bad-tempered: *a gruff manner.* ⟨< MDu. *grof*⟩ **—'gruff•ly,** *adv.* **—'gruff•ness,** *n.*

gru•gru ['grugru] *n.* **1** a palm tree (*Acrocomia sclerocarpa*) of the West Indies, with a thorny trunk and leaves, and nuts eaten as food. **2** the larva of various weevils (genus *Rhynchophorus*) that feeds on this tree. ⟨< Sp. *grugru,* probably < Carib name⟩

gru•i•form ['gruə,fɔrm] *adj.* of or having to do with various swampland or grassland birds, such as rails, cranes, and bustards, belonging to the order Gruiformes.

grum•ble ['grʌmbəl] *v.* **-bled, -bling;** *n.* —*v.* **1** mutter in discontent; complain in a bad-tempered way. **2** express by grumbling. **3** rumble: *Her stomach was grumbling from hunger.*
—*n.* **1** a mutter of discontent; bad-tempered complaint. **2** a rumble. ⟨related to OE *grymettan* roar, and *grim*⟩ **—'grum•bler,** *n.* **—'grum•bling•ly,** *adv.*
☛ *Syn. v.* **1, 2.** See note at COMPLAIN.

grum•met ['grʌmət] *n.* See GROMMET.

grump [grʌmp] *n., v.* —*n.* an ill-tempered person.
—*v.* complain; grumble.

grump•y ['grʌmpi] *adj.* **grump•i•er, grump•i•est.** surly; ill-humoured; gruff: *The grumpy old woman found fault with everything.* ⟨origin uncertain⟩ **—'grump•i•ly,** *adv.* **—'grump•i•ness,** *n.*

Grun•dy ['grʌndi] *n.* **Mrs. Grundy,** a character who personifies prudish or narrow-minded disapproval of manners, actions, etc.: *What would Mrs. Grundy say to such brief swimsuits?* ⟨from a person often referred to by the characters in Thomas Morton's play *Speed the Plough* (1798)⟩

grunge [grʌndʒ] *n.* **1** dirt. **2** a fashion movement featuring a studied slobby appearance. ⟨< *grungy*⟩

grun•gy ['grʌndʒi] *adj. Slang.* unkempt, unattractive, dirty, etc.: *a grungy hotel in the old part of town.* ⟨a blend of *grimy, dirty,* and *grunt* childish euphemism for defecate⟩

gru•ni•on ['grʌnjən] *n.* a small fish (*Leuresthes tenuis*) of the coastal waters of Mexico and California.

grunt [grʌnt] *n., v.* —*n.* **1** the deep, hoarse sound that a pig makes. **2** a sound like this: *The old man got out of his chair with a grunt.* **3** any of various marine fishes (family Pomadasyidae) found mostly in tropical coastal waters, that can produce a grunting sound with their teeth. Some authorities classify the grunts with the drumfishes in the family Sciaenidae. **4** any of various saltwater fishes that grunt when taken from the water, belonging to the family Haemulidae.
—*v.* **1** make the deep, hoarse sound of a pig. **2** say with a sound like this: *The sullen boy grunted his apology.* ⟨OE *grunnettan* < *grunian* grunt⟩

grunt•er ['grʌntər] *n.* **1** one who or that which grunts. **2** GRUNT (def. 3).

Grus [grus] *n.* a southern constellation between Indus and Phoenix.

Gru•yère [gru'jɛr] *or* [gri'jɛr] *n.* a variety of firm, light yellow cheese made from whole milk. ⟨< *Gruyère*, a district in Switzerland⟩

gryph•on ['grɪfən] See GRIFFIN.

G.S. GENERAL STAFF.

G string **1** on a musical instrument, a string tuned to G. **2** a narrow loincloth held up by a cord around the waist. **3** a similar covering worn by striptease artists. **4** a single-wire method of television transmission.

G–suit ['dʒi ,sut] *n.* ANTI-G SUIT.

gt. **1** great. **2** *Pharmacy.* drop (for L *gutta*).

Gt.Br. or **Gt.Brit.** GREAT BRITAIN.

gtd. guaranteed.

gua•ca•mo•le [,gwɑkɑ'mouli]; *Spanish,* [,gwaka'mole] *n.* a dip or sauce made from seasoned avocado pulp. ⟨< Am.Sp. < Nahuatl *a:wakamo:lli* < *a:waka* avocado + *mo:lli* a sauce⟩

gua•cha•ro ['gwɑtʃə,rou] *n.* a nocturnal goat-sucker (*Steatornis caripensis*) of South America; oilbird. The fat of the young birds is melted and used as fuel. ⟨< Sp. *guácharo* sickly, whining, probably so called from its cry⟩

gua•co ['gwɑkou] *n.* any of several tropical plants of the genus *Mikania,* used against snakebite. ⟨< Am.Sp. < Mayan⟩

guai•a•col ['gwaɪə,kɒl] *n.* an expectorant or local anesthetic. *Formula:* $C_7H_8O_2$ ⟨< *guaiacum* + *-ol*⟩

guai•a•cum ['gwaɪəkəm] *n.* **1** any of a genus (*Guaiacum*) of tropical American evergreen trees, such as the lignum vitaes, having bluish flowers, capsular fruit, and pinnate leaves. **2** the hard, heavy, greenish brown wood of any of these trees, especially a lignum vitae. **3** a resin obtained from a lignum vitae, used in making varnishes and formerly also used in medicine. ⟨< NL *Guaiacum* the genus name < Sp. *guayacán* < Arawak (West Indies) *guayacan*⟩

Guam [gwɑm] *n.* an island in the N Pacific.

guan [gwɑn] *n.* any of various fruit-eating birds (family Cracidae) native to Central and South America. ⟨< Am.Sp. < the Carib name⟩

gua•na•co [gwɑ'nɑkou] *n., pl.* **-cos.** a South American wild mammal (*Lama guanicoe*) belonging to the same family as the camel, having a thick, soft, pale brown coat. The guanaco is closely related to the vicuña, llama, and alpaca. ⟨< Sp. < Quechua (Indian lang. of Peru) *huancau*⟩

gua•nay [gwɑ'naɪ] *n.* a Peruvian or Chilean cormorant (*Phalacrocorax bougainvillii*) with a crest and a white breast. Guano is obtained from the guanay. ⟨< Sp. < the Quechua name⟩

gua•neth•i•dine [gwɑ'nɛθə,din] *n.* a drug used to lower blood pressure.

gua•nine ['gwɒnin] *n.* a constituent of ribonucleic and deoxyribonucleic acids. *Formula:* $C_5H_5N_5O$

gua•no ['gwɑnou] *n., pl.* **-nos. 1** the manure of sea birds or bats, found especially on islands near Peru. Guano is an excellent fertilizer. **2** an artificial fertilizer made from fish. ⟨< Sp. < Quechua (Indian lang. of Peru) *huanu*⟩

guar [gwɑr] *n.* an annual plant (*Cyamopsis tetragonoloba*) of the legume family, originally from India but cultivated in the southwestern United States for forage and for its seeds, which yield a gum used in industry. ⟨< Hind. *guar*⟩

gua•ra•ni [,gwɑrɑ'ni] *or* ['gwɑrəni] *n.* **1** the basic unit of money in Paraguay, divided into 100 centimos. See money table in the Appendix. **2** a coin worth one guarani. **3 Guarani, a** a South American Indian people living between the Paraguay River and the Atlantic. **b** their language. ⟨< Sp.⟩

guar•an•tee [,gærən'ti], [,gɛrən'ti], *or* [,gɑrən'ti] *n., v.* **-teed, -tee•ing.** —*n.* **1** a promise to pay or do something if another fails; a pledge to replace goods if they are not as represented; backing. **2** a person who so promises. **3** one to whom such a pledge is made. **4** something given or taken as security; guaranty. **5** an assurance; promise: *Wealth is not a guarantee of happiness.*
—*v.* **1** stand behind; give a guarantee for; assure genuineness or permanence of; answer for fulfilment of (a contract, etc.): *This company guarantees its clocks for a year. The father guaranteed his son's future behaviour.* **2** undertake to secure for another: *She will guarantee us possession of the house by May.* **3** secure (*used with* **against** *or* **from**): *Her insurance guaranteed her against money loss in case of fire.* **4** promise (to do something): *I will guarantee to prove every statement I made.* **5** pledge that (something) has been or will be: *The advance payment of money guarantees the good faith of the purchaser.* **6** make sure or certain: *Wealth does not guarantee happiness.* ⟨probably var. of *guaranty*⟩

guar•an•tor ['gærən,tɔr], ['gɛrən,tɔr], *or* ['gɑrən,tɔr] *n.* a person who makes or gives a guarantee.

guar•an•ty ['gærənti], ['gɛrənti], *or* ['gɑrənti] *n., pl.* **-ties;** *v.* **-tied, -ty•ing.** —*n.* **1** the act or fact of giving security. **2** a pledge or promise given as security; security.
—*v.* guarantee. ⟨< OF *guarantie* < *guarantir* to warrant < *guarant* a warrant < Gmc. Doublet of WARRANTY.⟩

guard [gɑrd] *v., n.* —*v.* **1** keep safe; watch over carefully; take care of: *The dog guards the house.* **2** defend; protect: *The goalie guards the goal.* **3** keep from escaping: *The soldiers guarded the prisoners day and night.* **4** keep in check; hold back; keep under control: *Guard your tongue.*
guard against, avoid or prevent by being careful: *His mother told him to guard against getting his feet wet.*
—*n.* **1** a person or group that guards. A soldier or group of soldiers guarding a person or place is a guard. **2** anything that gives protection; contrivance or appliance to protect against injury, loss, etc.: *A guard was placed in front of the fire.* **3** a careful watch: *A soldier kept guard over the prisoners.* **4** a picked body of soldiers: *a guard of honour.* **5** defence; protection. **6** *Boxing, fencing, or cricket.* a position of defence. **7** arms or weapons held in a position of defence. **8** *Football.* a player on either side of the centre. **9** *Basketball.* either of the two players serving as defence. **10** *Brit.* a person in charge of a railway train; brakes operator. **11** formerly, the person in charge of a stagecoach. **12 the Guards, a** certain British regiments whose duties include guarding the sovereign. **b** certain Canadian regiments: *the Governor General's Horse Guards.*
off (one's) **guard,** unready; unprepared: *She caught the goalie off guard and scored.*
on guard, ready to defend or protect; watchful: *A dog stood on guard near the door.*
stand guard, do sentry duty: *The soldier stood guard at the gate of the fort.* ⟨< F *garder* (earlier *guarder*), v., *garde* (earlier *guarde*), n. < Gmc. Doublet of WARD.⟩ **—'guard•er,** *n.*

☛ *Syn. v.* **1, 2. Guard,** DEFEND, PROTECT = keep safe. **Guard** = keep safe by watching over carefully: *The dog guarded the child night and day.* **Defend** = guard from harm by keeping away, turning aside, or resisting danger or attack: *He defended the child against the big boys.* **Protect** = keep safe by means of something that serves as a shield and keeps away danger or harm: *Proper food protects a person's health.*

guard•ant ['gɑrdənt] *adj. Heraldry.* of an animal, with its face toward the viewer.

guard cell *Botany.* one of the epidermal cells controlling the stomata.

guard•ed ['gɑrdɪd] *adj., v.* —*adj.* **1** kept safe; carefully watched over; protected. **2** careful; cautious: *"Maybe" is a guarded answer to a question.*
—*v.* pt. and pp. of GUARD. **—'guard•ed•ly,** *adv.* **—'guard•ed•ness,** *n.*

guard hair *Cdn.* the coarse, glossy hair protecting the soft underfur on a fur-bearing animal.

guard•house ['gɑrd,hʌus] *n.* **1** a building used as a jail for soldiers. **2** a building used by soldiers on guard.

guard•i•an ['gɑrdiən] *or* ['gɑrdjən] *n., adj.* —*n.* **1** a person who takes care of another or of some special thing. **2** a person appointed by law to take care of the affairs of someone who is young or cannot take care of them himself or herself.
—*adj.* protecting: *a guardian angel.* ⟨ME < AF *gardein*, var. of OF *g(u)arden* < *guarde* < Gmc. Doublet of WARDEN.⟩

guard•i•an•ship ['gɑrdiən,ʃɪp] *n.* the position or care of a guardian.

guard•rail ['gɑrd,reil] *n.* a rail or railing for protection.

guard•room ['gɑrd,rum] *or* ['gɑrd,rʊm] *n.* **1** a room used by soldiers on guard. **2** a room used as a jail for soldiers.

guards•man ['gɑrdzmən] *n., pl.* **-men. 1** GUARD (def. 1). **2** a private in any one of the Guards regiments. **3** any man serving in such a regiment.

Guar•ner•i•us [gwɑr'nɛriəs] *n.* a violin made by one of the Guarneri family of Cremona, Italy, in the 17th and 18th centuries.

Gua•te•ma•la [,gwɒtə'mɑlə] *n.* a republic in N Central America, bordered by the Pacific Ocean and Caribbean Sea.

gua•va ['gwɑvə] *n.* **1** any of several tropical American trees and shrubs (genus *Psidium*) of the myrtle family, especially *P. guajava*, widely cultivated in tropical regions for its sweet, edible, pear-shaped fruit. **2** the fruit of a guava, used especially for jams, jellies, and preserves. ⟨< Sp. *guayaba* < native name⟩

gua•yule [gwɑ'juli], [gwaɪ'juli], *or* [waɪ'juli] *n.* a small bush (*Parthenium argentatum*) cultivated in the southwestern United States for the rubber it yields. ⟨< Am.Sp. < Nahuatl *kʷawolli* < *kʷawil* tree + *olli* rubber⟩

gu•ber•na•to•ri•al [,gjubərnə'tɔriəl] *or* [,gubərnə'tɔriəl] *adj. Esp. U.S.* of a governor; having to do with a governor. ⟨< L *gubernator*, originally, pilot < *gubernare.* See GOVERN.⟩

guck [gʌk] *n. Informal.* anything oozy, slimy, or similarly distasteful. ⟨? < *goo* + *muck*⟩

gudg•eon ['gʌdʒən] *n.* **1** a small freshwater fish (*Gobio gobio*) of the minnow and carp family found in Europe and N Asia, having a barbel on each side of the mouth. Gudgeons are used for food and also for fishing bait. **2** any of various other small fishes. **3** a person easily fooled or cheated. ⟨ME < OF *goujon*, ult. < L *gobius* a kind of fish < Gk.⟩

guel•der•rose ['gɛldə,rouz] *n.* the European cranberry tree (*Viburnum opulus*). ⟨after *Guelderland* or *Gelderland* a province of the eastern Netherlands⟩

gue•non [gə'nɒn] *n.* any African monkey of the genus *Cercopithecus,* including the green monkey. ⟨< F⟩

guer•don ['gɜrdən] *n. or v. Poetic.* reward. ⟨ME < OF *guerdon*, var. of *werdon* < Med.L *widerdonum* < OHG *widarlōn* repayment, influenced by L *donum* gift⟩

gue•ril•la [gə'rɪlə] See GUERRILLA.

Guern•sey ['gɜrnzi] *n., pl.* **-seys. 1** a breed of dairy cattle originally from the island of Guernsey, resembling Jersey cattle, but somewhat larger. **2 guernsey,** a close-fitting, woollen sweater worn especially by sailors, originating on the island of Guernsey.

guer•ril•la [gə'rɪlə] *n., adj.* —*n.* **1** a member of a small independent band of fighters who harass the enemy by sudden raids, ambushes, etc. **2** warfare carried on by such fighters.
—*adj.* of or by guerrillas: *a guerrilla attack.* Also, **guerilla.** ⟨< Sp. *guerrilla*, dim. of *guerra* war⟩
☛ *Hom.* GORILLA.

guess [gɛs] *v., n.* —*v.* **1** form an opinion (of) without really knowing: *to guess the height of a tree.* **2** get right or find out by guessing: *to guess a riddle.* **3** think; believe; suppose.
—*n.* **1** an opinion formed without really knowing. **2** an act of guessing. ⟨n. < v., ME; cf. Swedish *gissa*⟩ **—'guess•er,** *n.*
☛ *Syn. v.* **1. Guess,** CONJECTURE, SURMISE = form an opinion without knowing enough. **Guess,** the least formal word, suggests forming an opinion on the basis of what one thinks likely, without really knowing for certain: *She guessed the distance to the nearest town.* **Conjecture** suggests having some evidence, but not enough for proof: *Scientists conjecture the value of a new drug.* **Surmise** = form a conjecture more on what one suspects might be true than on facts one knows: *She surmised his thoughts.*

guess•ti•mate *n.* ['gɛstəmət]; *v.* ['gɛstə,meit] *n., v.* **-mat•ed, -mat•ing.** *Informal.* —*n.* an informal estimate based mainly on guesswork.
—*v.* make a guesstimate of. ⟨< *guess* + *estimate*⟩

guess•work ['gɛs,wɜrk] *n.* work, action, or result based on guessing; guessing: *There is a lot of guesswork involved in buying a used car.*

guest [gɛst] *n., adj., v.* —*n.* **1** a person who is received and entertained at another's home, club, restaurant, etc. **2** a person who is not a regular member; visitor. **3** a person staying at a hotel, motel, boarding house, etc. **4** a person appearing on a show by invitation.
be my guest, *Informal.* you are welcome to do as you wish; help yourself: *"May I use your phone?" "Certainly; be my guest."*
—*adj.* **1** of or for guests: *a guest room, guest towels.* **2** being a guest: *a guest conductor, a guest lecturer.*
—*v.* be or appear as a guest: *He guested on the new talk show last night.* ⟨OE *giest* stranger (friend or foe)? < ON *gestr.* Akin to HOST².⟩
☛ *Syn. n.* See note at VISITOR.

guest of honour the most important guest at a social function; the guest in honour of whom the function is held.

guff [gʌf] *n. Informal.* foolish talk, especially when used in an attempt to hide the real facts. ⟨probably imitative⟩

guf•faw [gʌ'fɒ] *n., v.* —*n.* a loud, coarse burst of laughter.
—*v.* laugh loudly and coarsely. ⟨imitative⟩

guid•ance ['gaɪdəns] *n.* **1** a guiding; leadership; direction: *Under her mother's guidance Nan learned to cook.* **2** something that guides. **3** *Education.* studies and counselling intended to help students understand their school environment, make the most of their opportunities, and plan for the future.
4 *Aeronautics.* the regulation of the path of rockets, missiles, etc. in flight.

guide [gaɪd] *v.* **guid•ed, guid•ing;** *n.* —*v.* **1** show (someone) the way; lead; conduct; direct. **2** manage; control; regulate.
—*n.* **1** a person who or thing that shows the way, leads, conducts, or directs: *Tourists and hunters sometimes hire guides.* **2** a part of a machine for directing or regulating motion or action. **3** guidebook. **4 Guide,** GIRL GUIDE. **5** a handbook giving instructions or assistance on some subject: *an income tax guide.* ⟨ME < OF *guider* < Gmc.⟩
—'guid•er, *n.* **—'guide•less,** *adj.*
☛ *Syn. v.* **1. Guide,** LEAD, CONDUCT = show the way. **Guide** emphasizes knowing the way and all the points of interest or danger along it, and means to go along to point these out: *The warden guided the hikers.* **Lead** emphasizes going ahead to show the way, expecting the person or thing to follow: *The dog led his master to the injured man.* **Conduct** emphasizes going with the person or thing to guide or assist him or her: *She conducted a party of tourists to Europe.*

A Girl Guide

guide•board ['gaɪd,bɔrd] *n.* a board or sign with directions for travellers, often attached to a guidepost.

guide•book ['gaɪd,bʊk] *n.* a book of directions and information, especially one for travellers, tourists, etc.

guide dog a dog specially trained to guide a blind person; seeing-eye dog.

guided missile a missile whose course may be controlled during flight, usually by means of radio signals.

guide•line ['gaɪd,laɪn] *n.* a principle or instruction set forth as a guide.

guide•post ['gaɪd,poust] *n.* a post with signs and directions on it for travellers. A guidepost where roads meet tells travellers what places each road goes to and how far it is to each place.

Guid•er ['gaɪdər] *n.* an adult who is associated in some way with the Girl Guides or Brownies.

guide rope 1 a rope that is used to steady and guide something. **2** a long rope hanging from a dirigible or balloon for regulating its speed and altitude.

guide word in dictionaries and similar reference works, either of two words appearing at the top of a page, one indicating the first entry word on the page and the other showing the last entry word on the page.

gui•don ['gaɪdən] *or* ['gaɪdɒn] *n.* **1** a small flag or streamer carried as a guide by soldiers, or used for signalling. **2** a soldier who carries the guidon. ⟨< F < Ital. *guidone*⟩

guild [gɪld] *n.* **1** a society for mutual aid or for some common purpose: *the Canadian Guild of Potters.* **2** in the Middle Ages, a union of those in trade, formed to keep standards high and

to protect their common interests: *the guild of silversmiths.* ⟨ME < ON *gildi*⟩
☛ *Hom.* GILD.

guil•der ['gɪldər] *n.* gulden. ⟨alteration of *gulden*⟩

guild•hall ['gɪld,hɒl] *n.* **1** the hall in which a guild meets. **2** a town hall; city hall.

guilds•man ['gɪldzmən] *n., pl.* **-men.** a member of a guild.

guile [gaɪl] *n.* crafty deceit; craftiness; sly tricks: *A swindler uses guile; a robber uses force.* ⟨ME < OF < Gmc. Akin to WILE.⟩
☛ *Syn.* See note at DECEIT.

guile•ful ['gaɪlfəl] *adj.* crafty and deceitful; sly and tricky. **—'guile•ful•ly,** *adv.* **—'guile•ful•ness,** *n.*

guile•less ['gaɪllɪs] *adj.* without guile; honest; frank; sincere. **—'guile•less•ly,** *adv.* **—'guile•less•ness,** *n.*

Guil•lain–Bar•ré syndrome [gɪ'læn bɑ'rei] a neurological disorder of unknown origin, characterized by partial paralysis of certain muscles or decreased muscle strength, and occurring after viral illnesses or vaccinations. ⟨after G. *Guillain* and J. *Barré*, 20c. French neurologists⟩

guil•le•mot ['gɪlə,mɒt] *n.* **1** any of a genus (*Cepphus*) of black-and-white northern sea birds of the auk family having a straight, pointed, black bill. **2** *Esp. Brit.* MURRE (def. 1). ⟨< F *guillemot*, probably < *Guillaume* William⟩

guil•loche [gɪ'louʃ] *or* [gɪ'lɒʃ] *n. Architecture.* a border consisting of more than two bands interlaced to repeat a design. ⟨< F *guillochis* < *guillocher* to ornament with lines < OItal. *ghiocciare* to drop, drip⟩

guil•lo•tine *n.* ['gɪlə,tin]; *v.* [,gɪlə'tin] *n., v.* **-tined, -tin•ing.**
—n. **1** a machine for beheading persons by means of a heavy blade that slides down between two grooved posts. The guillotine was much used during the French Revolution. **2** a machine for cutting paper.
—v. **1** behead with a guillotine. **2** cut with a guillotine. ⟨< F, after Joseph I. *Guillotin* (1738-1814), a French physician and advocate of its use⟩ **—,guil•lo'tin•er,** *n.*

guilt [gɪlt] *n.* **1** the fact or state of having done wrong; a being guilty; being blameworthy. **2** guilty action or conduct; a crime; offence. ⟨OE *gylt* offence⟩
☛ *Hom.* GILT.

guilt•less ['gɪltlɪs] *adj.* not guilty; free from guilt; innocent.
☛ *Syn.* See note at INNOCENT.

guilt•y ['gɪlti] *adj.* **guilt•i•er, guilt•i•est. 1** having done wrong; deserving to be blamed and punished: *The jury pronounced the prisoner guilty of murder.* **2** knowing or showing that one has done wrong: *The one who did the crime had a guilty conscience and a guilty look.* ⟨OE *gyltig*⟩ **—'guilt•i•ly,** *adv.* **—'guilt•i•ness,** *n.*

guimpe [gɪmp] *or* [gæmp] *n.* a blouse worn under a dress and showing at the neck or at the neck and arms. ⟨< F < Gmc. Doublet of GIMP.⟩
☛ *Hom.* GIMP [gɪmp].

guin•ea ['gɪni] *n.* **1** an amount equal to 21 shillings (£1.05), formerly used in the British Isles in stating prices, fees, etc. **2** a former British gold coin worth 21 shillings. ⟨< *Guinea* (Pg. *Guiné*, F *Guinée*) in W Africa, since the coin was originally made of gold from there; 17c.⟩

Gui•nea ['gɪni] *n.* a country in W Africa, formerly French. See SENEGAL for map.

Guinea–Bis•sau ['gɪni bɪ'sou] *n.* a country in W Africa, formerly Portuguese. See SENEGAL for map.

guinea fowl a domestic fowl (*Numida meleagris*) resembling a pheasant, having dark grey plumage with small white spots, and a naked head and neck. It is native to Africa, but raised for food in many parts of the world. ⟨< Guinea. See GUINEA.⟩

guinea hen 1 GUINEA FOWL. **2** a female guinea fowl.

guinea pepper 1 any of various plants (genus *Xylopia*) native to Africa and belonging to the custard-apple family. **2** the fruit of any of these plants, used in spices and folk medicine.

guinea pig 1 a plump-bodied, short-eared, short-tailed rodent (*Cavia cobaya*) often kept as a cage pet and extensively used in scientific research. **2** any person or thing serving as a subject for experiment or testing. ⟨< *Guinea*, in the sense of coming from a distant country; the animal actually came from South America. See GUINEA.⟩

guinea worm a tropical African or South Asian parasite (*Dranunculus medinensis*) that lives in the subcutaneous tissue of humans and animals. The female guinea worm has been known to reach a length of 90 cm.

Guin•e•vere ['gwɪnə,vir] *n. Arthurian legend.* Arthur's wife, who became the mistress of Lancelot. Also, **Guinever** ['gwɪnəvər].

gui•pure [gi'pjʊr] *n.* a coarse kind of lace. ⟨< F *guiper* to cover with silk < Frankish **wipan* to wind⟩

gui•ro ['gwirou] *or* ['gwɪrou] *n.* a Latin American musical instrument made from a long-necked gourd. It is played by dragging a stick across raised cuts made on the surface of the gourd. ⟨< Am.Sp. *guiro* gourd⟩

guise [gaɪz] *n.* **1** a style of dress; garb, especially when used as a disguise. *The soldier went into the village in the guise of a monk so that he would not be recognized.* **2** external appearance; aspect; semblance: *Her theory is nothing but an old idea in a new guise.* **3** an assumed appearance; pretence: *Under the guise of friendship she plotted treachery.* ⟨ME < OF < Gmc. Akin to WISE².⟩

Guitars: a Spanish guitar and an electric guitar

gui•tar [gə'tɑr] *n.* a musical instrument having usually six strings that are plucked or strummed with the fingers or a pick, a flat face and back, and a long neck with frets, serving as a fingerboard. ⟨< Sp. *guitarra* < Gk. *kithara* cithara. Doublet of CITHARA and ZITHER.⟩

gui•tar•fish [gə'tɑr,fɪʃ] *n.* any of various cartilaginous fishes belonging to the order Rhinobatiformes and having a long, thin tail and a broad body.

gui•tar•ist [gə'tɑrɪst] *n.* one who plays the guitar, especially a skilled player.

Gu•ja•ra•ti [,gudʒə'rɑti] *n., adj. —n.* **1** an Indic language, the official language of the Indian state of Gujarat. **2** an inhabitant of Gujarat or speaker of Gujarati.
—adj. of or relating to Gujarat, its people, or their language.

gu•lag ['gulæg] *n.* in the former Soviet Union, a forced labour camp notorious for bad conditions. ⟨< Russian acronym for *G*lavnoe *u*pravlenie ispravitel' no trudovykh *lag*erei, Chief Administration of Corrective Labour Camps⟩

gu•lar ['gjulər] *or* ['gulər] *adj. Anatomy.* having to do with the throat. ⟨< L *gula* throat⟩

gulch [gʌltʃ] *n.* a deep, narrow ravine with steep sides, especially one marking the course of a stream or torrent. ⟨origin unknown⟩

gul•den ['gʊldən] *n., pl.* **-dens** or **-den. 1** the basic unit of money in the Netherlands and Surinam, divided into 100 cents. See table of money in the Appendix. **2** a coin or note worth one gulden. Also called **guilder.** ⟨< Du., literally, golden⟩

gules [gjulz] *n. or adj. Heraldry.* red. ⟨ME < OF *goules* red fur neck-piece (originally, pieces of neck fur) < *goule* throat < L *gula*⟩

gulf [gʌlf] *n.* **1** a large bay; an arm of an ocean or sea extending into the land. **2** a very deep break or cut in the earth. **3** any wide separation: *The quarrel left a gulf between the two friends.* **4** something that swallows up; whirlpool. ⟨ME < OF *golfe* < Ital. *golfo*, ult. < Gk. *kolpos*, originally, bosom⟩ **—'gulf,like,** *adj.*

Gulf States 1 those states of the U.S. bordering the Gulf of Mexico. **2** PERSIAN GULF STATES.

gulf•weed ['gʌlf,wid] *n.* any of a genus (*Sargassum*) of brown seaweeds, especially a tropical American species (*S. bacciferum*) having many berrylike sacs that keep it afloat.

gull¹ [gʌl] *n.* any of numerous aquatic birds (family Laridae, especially genus *Larus*) having long wings, webbed feet, a strong, slightly hooked bill, and mainly white plumage with some grey and black, especially on the wings and back. ⟨ME ? < Welsh *gwylan*⟩

gull² [gʌl] *v., n. —v.* deceive; cheat.

—n. a person who is easily deceived or cheated. ⟨origin uncertain⟩

Gul•lah ['gʌlə] *n.* **1** a member of a group of black people living along the coast of South Carolina and Georgia and on the islands off the coast. **2** the dialect of English spoken by the Gullahs, characterized by elements of various African languages.

gull•er•y ['gʌləri] *n.* a breeding place of gulls.

gul•let ['gʌlɪt] *n.* **1** a passage for food from the mouth to the stomach; esophagus. **2** the throat. ⟨ME < OF *goulet*, ult. < L *gula* throat⟩

gul•li•bil•i•ty [,gʌlə'bɪləti] *n.* a being gullible; tendency to be easily deceived or cheated.

gul•li•ble ['gʌləbəl] *adj.* easily deceived or cheated. ⟨< *gull*[2]⟩ **—'gul•li•bly,** *adv.*

gul•ly ['gʌli] *n., pl.* **-lies;** *v.* **-lied, -ly•ing.** *—n.* **1** a narrow gorge; a small ravine. **2** a channel or ditch made by heavy rains or running water: *After the storm, the newly-seeded lawn was full of gullies.* **3** *Cricket.* **a** the part of the playing field behind the slip. **b** a fielder stationed in the gully.
—v. make gullies in. ⟨? var. of *gullet*⟩

gulp [gʌlp] *v., n. —v.* **1** swallow eagerly or greedily. **2** keep in; choke back; repress: *The disappointed boy gulped down a sob.* **3** gasp; choke.
—n. **1** the act of swallowing. **2** the amount swallowed at one time; mouthful. ⟨imitative⟩ **—'gulp•er,** *n.*

gum[1] [gʌm] *n., v.* **gummed, gum•ming.** *—n.* **1** a sticky juice, obtained from or given off by certain trees and plants, that hardens in the air and dissolves in water. Gum is used to make glue, drugs, candy, etc. **2** any similar secretion, such as resin, gum resin, etc. **3** a preparation of such a substance for use in industry or the arts. **4** CHEWING GUM. **5** the substance on the back of a stamp, the flap of an envelope, etc.; mucilage; glue. **6** rubber. **7** GUM TREE.
—v. **1** smear, stick, stick together, or stiffen with gum. **2** give off gum; form gum. **3** make or become sticky; clog or become clogged with something sticky.
gum up, *Slang.* mess up; put out of order. ⟨ME < OF *gomme* < L *gummi* < Gk. *kommi*⟩

gum[2] [gʌm] *n.* Often, **gums,** *pl.* the flesh around the teeth. ⟨OE *gōma* palate⟩

gum ammoniac a natural mixture of gum and resin, used in medicine; ammoniac.

gum arabic the gum obtained from acacia trees, used in making candy, medicine, mucilage, etc.

gum•bo ['gʌmbou] *n., pl.* **-bos. 1** the pods of the okra plant. **2** the plant itself. **3** soup thickened with okra pods: *chicken gumbo soup.* **4** soil that contains much silt and becomes very sticky when wet, especially that found on the western prairies. ⟨of African origin⟩

gum•boil ['gʌm,bɔɪl] *n.* a small abscess on the gum.

gum•boot ['gʌm,but] *n.* a high rubber boot.

gum•drop ['gʌm,drɒp] *n.* a stiff, jellylike piece of candy made of gum arabic, gelatin, etc., sweetened and flavoured.

gum•ma ['gʌmə] *n.* a tumour with a soft, rubbery consistency, arising in various organs and tissues, especially during the later stages of syphilis. ⟨< NL < L *gummi* gum⟩

gum•mite ['gʌməit] *n.* a red-brown or yellowish mineral whose components are uranium and pitchblende, appearing in greasy, gumlike lumps. ⟨named in 1868 by J.D. Dana < L *gummi* gum + *-ite*[1]⟩

gum•my ['gʌmi] *adj.* **-mi•er, -mi•est. 1** sticky; like gum. **2** covered with gum. **3** giving off gum. **—'gum•mi•ness,** *n.*

gump•tion ['gʌmpʃən] *n. Informal.* **1** initiative; energy; resourcefulness. **2** common sense; good judgment. ⟨< Scots dial.; origin uncertain⟩

gum resin a natural mixture of gum and resin, obtained from certain plants.

gum•shoe ['gʌm,ʃu] *n., v.* **-shoed, shoe•ing.** *—n.* **1** a rubber overshoe. **2 gumshoes,** *pl.* running shoes. **3** *Slang.* detective.
—v. Slang. go around quietly and secretly.

gum tragacanth tragacanth.

gum tree any of various trees, such as the sweet gum and eucalyptus, that yield gum.

gum•weed ['gʌm,wid] a W North American wildflower (*Grindelia integrifolia*), having large yellow flowers on a 60 cm stem, used by the First Nations people as an antidote to poison ivy.

gum•wood ['gʌm,wʊd] *n.* the wood of a gum tree, especially the sweet gum.

gun[1] [gʌn] *n., v.* **gunned, gun•ning.** *—n.* **1** a weapon with a long metal tube for shooting shells, bullets, shot, etc. An artillery piece or a cannon is properly a gun; rifles, pistols, and revolvers are commonly called guns. **2** (*adjl.*) of or involving a gun or guns: *a gun barrel, a gun battle.* **3** the firing of a gun as a signal or salute. **4** *Slang.* gunman: *a hired gun.* **5** a hunter or member of a shooting party. **6** a device for ejecting or discharging something: *a spray gun, an electron gun, a grease gun.* **7** See BIG GUN.
give it the gun, *Informal.* speed up greatly; suddenly go, act, etc. much faster.
jump or **beat the gun, a** of a competitor in a race, etc., start before the signal is given. **b** act prematurely or before the expected or permitted time.
spike (someone's) **guns.** See SPIKE[1].
stick to (one's) **guns,** keep one's position under opposition or attack; refuse to retreat or yield.
under the gun, *Informal.* in a difficult position; having to defend one's position, actions, etc.
—v. **1** hunt or hunt (*for*) with a gun. **2** shoot (someone) with a gun (*usually used with* **down**): *He was gunned down as he left his car.* **3** go after, with intent to hurt, destroy, etc. (*used with* **for**): *They'll be gunning for you when they read the report.* **4** try hard (*used with* **for**): *gunning for a victory.* **5** cause to accelerate suddenly and fast: *She gunned the engine to pass.* ⟨ME ? < ON *Gunna*, shortened form of *Gunnhilda*, a woman's name applied to engines of war⟩

gun[2] [gʌn] *v. Archaic or poetic.* pp. of GIN[4].

gun barrel the metal tube of a gun.

gun•boat ['gʌn,bout] *n.* a small warship, often one that can be used in shallow water.

gun carriage a structure on which a gun is mounted or moved and on which it is fired.

gun•cot•ton ['gʌn,kɒtən] *n.* cellulose nitrate, especially when highly nitrated for use as an explosive.

gun•dog ['gʌn,dɒg] *n.* a dog trained to locate, flush, or retrieve game for hunters who use guns. Pointers, setters, and retrievers are breeds commonly trained as gundogs.

gun•fight ['gʌn,fəit] *n.* a fight in which guns are used. **—'gun,fight•er,** *n.*

gun•fire ['gʌn,faɪr] *n.* **1** the shooting of a gun or guns. **2** the sound of shooting.

gung–ho ['gʌŋ 'hou] *adj. Slang.* full of unrestrained energy and enthusiasm; eager to begin, carry on, take part, etc.: *He's just starting out in business and is very gung-ho.* ⟨< Chinese *kung-ho* work together⟩

Gun•ite ['gʌnəit] *n. Trademark.* a cement mixture sprayed under pressure over a structure as reinforcement. It is used in making swimming pools.

gunk [gʌŋk] *n. Informal.* any unpleasant, heavy, oily or sticky matter; guck.

gunk hole [gʌŋk] *Cdn.* a tiny, rocky-sided cove with deep water, making an excellent fishing spot.

gun•lock ['gʌn,lɒk] *n.* the part of a gun by which the charge is fired.

gun•man ['gʌnmən] *n., pl.* **-men. 1** a man who uses a gun to rob or kill. **2** a man noted for his skill in using a gun.

gun•met•al ['gʌn,mɛtəl] **1** any of various dark grey alloys used for chains, buckles, handles, etc. **2** a dark, somewhat bluish grey. **3** a kind of bronze formerly used for making guns. **4** (*adjl.*) of, having to do with, or resembling gunmetal.

gun•nel[1] ['gʌnəl] See GUNWALE.

gun•nel[2] ['gʌnəl] *n.* any of a family (Pholidae) of eel-like marine fishes of northern coastal regions. ⟨origin uncertain⟩

gun•ner ['gʌnər] *n.* **1** a person trained to fire artillery pieces; a soldier, flyer, etc. who handles and fires guns. **2** a naval officer in charge of a ship's guns. **3** a person, especially a private, serving in the artillery. **4** a person who hunts with a gun.

gun•ner•y ['gʌnəri] *n.* **1** the art and science of constructing and managing big guns. **2** the use of guns; the shooting of guns. **3** guns collectively.

gun•ning ['gʌnɪŋ] *n., v.* —*n.* the act of shooting with a gun; hunting with a gun.
—*v.* ppr. of GUN[1].

gun•ny ['gʌni] *n., pl.* **-nies. 1** a strong, coarse fabric used for sacks, bags, etc. **2** GUNNY SACK. ⟨< Hind. *goni*⟩

gunny sack a sack or bag made of gunny.

gun pit an excavation where artillery is placed.

gun•point ['gʌn,pɔɪnt] *n.* the tip or point of a gun barrel. **at gunpoint,** being threatened by a gun; having a gun pointed at one.

gun•pow•der ['gʌn,paʊdər] *n.* **1** a powder that explodes with force when brought into contact with fire. Gunpowder is used in guns, fireworks, and blasting. One kind of gunpowder is made of saltpetre, sulphur, and charcoal. **2** a kind of green Chinese tea.

gun room 1 a room where guns are kept. **2** a room for junior officers of a warship.

gun•run•ning ['gʌn,rʌnɪŋ] *n.* the bringing of guns and ammunition into a country illegally. **—'gun,run•ner,** *n.*

gun•shot ['gʌn,ʃɒt] *n.* **1** a shot fired from a gun. **2** the shooting of a gun. **3** the distance that a gun will shoot.

gun•sight ['gʌn,səit] *n.* a device on a gun to help in taking aim.

gun•sling•er ['gʌn,slɪŋər] *n. Slang.* gunman.

gun•smith ['gʌn,smɪθ] *n.* a person whose work is making or repairing small guns.

gun•stock ['gʌn,stɒk] *n.* the wooden support or handle to which the barrel of a gun is fastened.

Gun•ter's chain ['gʌntərz] *Surveying.* a measuring chain 20 m long. ⟨named after Edmund *Gunter* (1581-1626), an English mathematician⟩

gun•wale ['gʌnəl] *n.* the reinforced top edge of the side of a boat, designed to add strength and rigidity and to provide support for a rowlock or tholepins. Also, **gunnel**[1]. ⟨< *gun*[1] + *wale* a plank; because formerly used to support guns⟩

gup•py ['gʌpi] *n., pl.* **-pies.** a small, brightly coloured, freshwater fish (*Lebistes reticulatus*) native to NE South America and the West Indies, that bears live young instead of laying eggs as most fish do. Guppies are popular for home aquariums. ⟨after Robert J.L. *Guppy,* 19c., of Trinidad, who supplied the first specimens⟩

gur•dwa•ra [gər'dwɑrə] *n.* a Sikh temple in which services of worship are held on Sundays. It also serves as a Sikh community centre. ⟨< Skt. *guru* teacher + *dwara* door⟩

gur•gi•ta•tion [,gɜrdʒə'teiʃən] *n.* a whirling motion. ⟨< L *gurgitare* flood < *gurges* whirlpool, abyss⟩

gur•gle ['gɜrgəl] *v.* **-gled, -gling;** *n.* —*v.* **1** flow or run with a bubbling sound: *Water gurgles when it is poured out of a bottle or when it flows over stones.* **2** make a bubbling sound: *The baby gurgled happily.* **3** express with a gurgle.
—*n.* a bubbling sound. ⟨? imitative⟩

Gurk•ha ['gɜrkə] *n.* a member of a Nepalese Hindu people famous for its soldiers.

gur•nard ['gɜrnərd] *n.* sea robin; especially, any of several European species. ⟨ME < OF *gornart* grunter < *grognier* to grunt < L *grunnire*⟩

gur•ney ['gɜrni] *n.* a stretcher or cot on wheels, used in a hospital to move sick people.

gu•ru ['guru] *or* ['gʊru] *n.* **1** *Hinduism.* a personal religious adviser or teacher. **2** a person who guides others, especially in a spiritual way. **3** an honorary title for any popular leader: *The young activist was hailed as a guru of pop culture.* ⟨< Hind. *gurū*⟩

Gu•ru ['guru] in Sikhism: **1** any of the ten founding teachers of Sikhism. **2** the honorific title given to the Granth, the Sikh holy book.

Gu•ru Granth Sa•hib *Sikhism.* the sacred scriptures containing the teachings of the ten founding Gurus.

gush [gʌʃ] *v., n.* —*v.* **1** rush out suddenly; pour out. **2** *Informal.* talk in a silly way about one's affections or enthusiasms. **3** give forth suddenly or very freely. **4** have an abundant flow of blood, tears, etc.
—*n.* **1** a rush of water or other liquid from an enclosed place: *If you get a deep cut, there is usually a gush of blood.* **2** *Informal.* silly, emotional talk. **3** a sudden and violent outbreak; burst: *a gush of anger.* ⟨probably imitative⟩
☛ *Syn. v.* **1.** See note at FLOW.

gush•er ['gʌʃər] *n.* **1** an oil well that flows copiously without being pumped. **2** *Informal.* a gushy person.

gush•ing ['gʌʃɪŋ] *adj., v.* —*adj.* **1** that gushes. **2** effusive.
—*v.* ppr. of GUSH. **—'gush•ing•ly,** *adv.*

gush•y ['gʌʃi] *adj.* **gush•i•er, gush•i•est.** showing one's feelings in a silly way; effusive; sentimental. **—'gush•i•ly,** *adv.* **—'gush•i•ness,** *n.*

gus•set ['gʌsɪt] *n.* **1** a triangular piece of material inserted in a dress, etc. to give greater strength or more room. **2** a bracket or plate used to reinforce the joints of a structure. ⟨ME < OF *gousset* < *gousse* husk⟩

gus•sy ['gʌsi] *v. Slang.* make seemly or attractive; spruce (*up*): *The girls gussied themselves up for the party.* ⟨origin uncertain⟩

gust [gʌst] *n., v.* —*n.* **1** a sudden, violent rush of wind: *A gust upset the small sailboat.* **2** a sudden burst of rain, smoke, sound, etc. **3** an outburst of anger, enthusiasm, etc.
—*v.* to blow or rush in gusts. ⟨< ON *gustr*⟩

gus•ta•tion [gʌ'steiʃən] *n.* taste.

gus•ta•to•ry ['gʌstə,tɔri] *adj.* of the sense of taste; having to do with tasting: *Eating fine foods gives gustatory pleasure.* ⟨< L *gustatus*, pp. of *gustare* taste⟩

gus•to ['gʌstou] *n., pl.* **-tos. 1** keen relish; hearty enjoyment: *The hungry boy ate his dinner with gusto.* **2** a liking or taste. **3** spirited activity. ⟨< Ital. *gusto*, originally, taste < L *gustus*⟩

gust•y ['gʌsti] *adj.* **gust•i•er, gust•i•est. 1** coming in gusts; windy; stormy. **2** marked by outbursts: *gusty laughter.* **—'gust•i•ly,** *adv.* **—'gust•i•ness,** *n.*

gut [gʌt] *n., v.* **gut•ted, gut•ting;** *adj.* —*n.* **1** intestine. **2 guts,** *pl.* entrails; bowels. **3** catgut. **4** a narrow channel or gully. **5 guts,** *pl. Informal.* **a** courage or forcefulness. **b** the inner or essential part: *the guts of a car, the guts of the problem.*
—*v.* **1** remove the entrails of; disembowel. **2** plunder or destroy the inside of: *Fire gutted the building and left only the brick walls standing.*
—*adj.* **1** *Slang.* vital; basic: *The gut issue is the demand for higher wages.* **2** *Informal.* arising from deep, basic feelings; instinctive: *a gut reaction.* ⟨OE *guttas*, pl.⟩

gut•buc•ket ['gʌt,bʌkɪt] *adj.* of jazz, played in a noisy, vigorous style as in the bars of New Orleans.

gut•less ['gʌtlɪs] *adj.* cowardly; lacking force or persistence.

gut•sy ['gʌtsi] *adj.* **-si•er, -si•est.** *Slang.* courageous or forceful; having guts: *a gutsy political leader.*

gut•ta ['gʌtə] *n., pl.* **gut•tae** [-i] *or* [-aɪ] **1** *Pharmacy:* one drop. **2** *Architecture.* in Doric architecture, a group of ornaments like drops.

gut•ta–per•cha ['gʌtə 'pɜrtʃə] *n.* a substance resembling rubber, obtained from the thick milky juice (latex) of any of several Malaysian trees of the sapodilla family, used in dentistry, for insulating electric wires, etc. ⟨< Malay⟩

gut•tate ['gʌteit] *adj.* **1** in the form of drops. **2** spotted.

gut•ter ['gʌtər] *n., v.* —*n.* **1** a channel or ditch along the side of a street or road to carry off water; the low part of a street beside the sidewalk. **2** eavestrough. **3** any channel or groove, such as the channel along each side of a bowling lane. **4 the gutter,** a wretched, poverty-stricken, or deprived environment: *a child of the gutter.* **5** (*adjl.*) having to do with, characteristic of, or associated with a depraved environment: *gutter language, gutter journalism.* **6** *Printing.* the white space formed by the inner margins of two facing pages of a book.
—*v.* **1** form gutters in. **2** flow or melt in streams: *A candle gutters when the melted wax runs down its sides.* **3** become channelled. ⟨ME < AF *gotere*, ult. < L *gutta* drop⟩

gut•ter•snipe ['gʌtər,snəip] *n. Informal.* **1** an urchin who lives in the streets. **2** any ill-bred person.

gut•tur•al ['gʌtərəl] *adj.* **1** of the throat. **2** formed in the throat; harsh: *The man spoke in a guttural voice.* ⟨< NL *gutturalis* < L *guttur* throat⟩ **—'gut•tur•al•ly,** *adv.* **—'gut•tur•al•ness,** *n.*

guy[1] [gaɪ] *n., v.* **guyed, guy•ing.** —*n.* a rope, chain, wire, etc. attached to something to steady or secure it.
—*v.* steady or secure with a guy or guys. ⟨< OF *guie* < *guier* to guide, ult. < Gmc.⟩

guy[2] [gaɪ] *n., v.* **guyed, guy•ing.** —*n.* **1** *Informal.* fellow; chap. **2** *Informal.* any person of either sex and any age. **3** *Esp.Brit.* a queer-looking or oddly dressed person.
—*v. Informal.* make fun of; tease. ⟨< *Guy* Fawkes, a leader of the Gunpowder Plot (1605) to blow up the British King and Parliament⟩

Guy•a•na [gaɪ'ænə] *or* [gaɪ'ɑnə] *n.* a country in South America, formerly British Guiana.

Guy•a•nese [ˌgaɪəˈniz] *n., pl.* **-ese;** *adj.* *—n.* a native or inhabitant of Guyana.
—adj. of or having to do with Guyana.

guy rope one of several ropes attached to a tent, marquee, etc. for pegging it to the ground as a means of support.

guz•zle [ˈgʌzəl] *v.* **-zled, -zling.** drink greedily; drink too much. ⟨probably < OF *gosiller* vomit (? originally, pass through the throat); cf. F *gosier* throat⟩ **—ˈguz•zler,** *n.*

GVW gross vehicle weight.

gybe [dʒaɪb] *v.* **gybed, gyb•ing,** of a yacht, turn so that the mainsail crosses its centre line, with the wind from behind.
☛ *Hom.* JIBE.

gym [dʒɪm] *n.* gymnasium.

gym•kha•na [dʒɪmˈkɑnə] *n.* an exhibition of athletic contests or of equestrian skills. ⟨< Anglo-Indian, altered (by analogy with *gymnasium*) < Hind. *gend-khana* racket court < *gend* ball + *khana* court, place⟩

gym•na•si•a [dʒɪmˈneiziə] *n.* a pl. of GYMNASIUM.

gym•na•si•um [dʒɪmˈneiziəm] *n., pl.* **-si•ums** or **si•a** [-ziə]. a room, building, etc. fitted up for physical exercise or training and for indoor athletic sports. ⟨< L < Gk. *gymnasion* < *gymnazein* exercise (naked) < *gymnos* naked⟩

Gym•na•si•um [dʒɪmˈneiziəm]; *German,* [gymˈnaziʊm] *n.* in Germany, etc., a secondary school that prepares students for the university.

gym•nast [ˈdʒɪmnəst] *or* [ˈdʒɪmnæst] *n.* an expert in gymnastics. ⟨< Gk. *gymnastēs* < *gymnazein* exercise. See GYMNASIUM.⟩

gym•nas•tic [dʒɪmˈnæstɪk] *adj.* having to do with bodily exercise or activities. **—gymˈnas•ti•cal•ly,** *adv.*

gym•nas•tics [dʒɪmˈnæstɪks] *n.pl.* **1** physical exercises for developing the muscles, such as are performed in a gymnasium. **2** the sport of doing exercises in agility and balance.

gym•no•pho•bia [ˌdʒɪmnəˈfoubiə] *n.* abnormal fear of nakedness. ⟨< Gk. *gymnos* naked + E *-phobia*⟩

gym•no•sperm [ˈdʒɪmnəˌspɜrm] *n.* any of a division (Gymnospermae; also called Pinophyta) of plants producing seeds that are exposed, not enclosed in an ovary. Many gymnosperms, such as pines, spruces, firs, junipers, and cedars, bear their seeds on cones. ⟨< NL < Gk. *gymnospermos* < *gymnos* naked + *sperma* seed⟩

gym•no•sper•mous [ˌdʒɪmnəˈspɜrməs] *adj.* belonging to the gymnosperms; having the seeds exposed.

gy•nae•col•o•gist [ˌgaɪnəˈkɒlədʒɪst], [ˌdʒaɪnəˈkɒlədʒɪst], *or* [ˌdʒɪnəˈkɒlədʒɪst] *n.* See GYNECOLOGIST.

gy•nae•col•o•gy [ˌgaɪnəˈkɒlədʒi], [ˌdʒaɪnəˈkɒlədʒi], *or* [ˌdʒɪnəˈkɒlədʒi] *n.* See GYNECOLOGY.

gy•nan•dro•morph [dʒɪˈnændrouˌmɔrf] *or* [dʒaɪˈnændrouˌmɔrf] *n.* an individual having male and female characteristics; hermaphrodite.

gy•nan•drous [dʒɪˈnændrəs] *or* [dʒaɪˈnændrəs] *adj.* **1** *Botany.* having stamens and pistil joined as one, as in an orchid. **2** hermaphroditic. ⟨< Gk. *gynandros* of doubtful sex < *gynē* woman + *anēr, andros* man⟩

gyn•ar•chy [ˈdʒɪnɑrki] *or* [ˈdʒaɪnɑrki] *n.* government by women.

gyneco– *combining form.* woman: *gynecology.* ⟨< Gk. *gyne*⟩

gy•ne•coid [ˈdʒɪnəˌkɔɪd] *or* [ˈdʒaɪnəˌkɔɪd] *adj.* of or like a woman.

gy•ne•co•log•i•cal [ˌgaɪnəkəˈlɒdʒɪkəl], [ˌdʒaɪnəkəˈlɒdʒɪkəl], *or* [ˌdʒɪnəkəˈlɒdʒɪkəl] *adj.* of or having to do with gynecology. **—ˌgy•ne•coˈlog•i•cal•ly,** *adv.*

gy•ne•col•o•gist [ˌgaɪnəˈkɒlədʒɪst], [ˌdʒaɪnəˈkɒlədʒɪst], *or* [ˌdʒɪnəˈkɒlədʒɪst] *n.* a physician who specializes in gynecology. Also, **gynaecologist.**

gy•ne•col•o•gy [ˌgaɪnəˈkɒlədʒi], [ˌdʒaɪnəˈkɒlədʒi], *or* [ˌdʒɪnəˈkɒlədʒi] *n.* the branch of medicine dealing with the diseases and reproductive functions specific to women. Also, **gynaecology.** ⟨< Gk. *gynē, gynaikos* woman + E *-logy*⟩

gy•ne•pho•bia [ˌgaɪnəˈfoubiə], [ˌdʒaɪnəˈfoubiə], *or* [ˌdʒɪnəˈfoubiə] *n.* fear of women. **—ˌgy•neˈpho•bic,** *adj., n.*

gyno– *combining form.* female; woman. ⟨< Gk. *gyne*⟩

gy•noe•ci•um [dʒaɪˈnisiəm] *or* [dʒəˈnisiəm] *n., pl.* **-ci•a** [-siə]. *Botany.* the pistil or pistils of a flower. ⟨< NL < Gk. *gynē* woman + *oikion* house⟩

gy•no•phore [ˈdʒɪnəˌfɔr] *or* [ˈdʒaɪnəˌfɔr] *n. Botany.* the elongated stalk carrying the pistil in certain flowers.

–gynous *combining form.* female; woman; female organs: *misogynous.* ⟨< Gk. *-gynos* < *gynē* woman⟩

–gyny *combining form.* femaleness: *androgyny.* ⟨< Gk. *gyno-* + *-y*[3] or *-gynous* + *-y*[3]⟩

gyp [dʒɪp] *v.* **gypped, gyp•ping;** *n. Slang.* *—v.* cheat; swindle: *She gypped me out of three dollars.*
—n. **1** a swindle; fraud: *That show was a big gyp; it wasn't anything like the ad.* **2** a cheat; swindler. ⟨shortened form of *gypsy*⟩
—ˈgyp•per, *n.*

gyp•se•ous [ˈdʒɪpsiəs] *adj.* having to do with gypsum.

gyp•sif•er•ous [dʒɪpˈsɪfərəs] *adj.* having or yielding gypsum.

gyp•soph•i•la [dʒɪpˈsɒfələ] *n.* any of a genus (*Gypsophila*) of Old World plants of the pink family, such as baby's breath, having many small, white or pink flowers on delicate branching stems with few leaves. ⟨< NL < Gk. *gypsos* gypsum + *philos* fond of⟩

gyp•sum [ˈdʒɪpsəm] *n.* a mineral used for making plaster of Paris, fertilizer, etc.; hydrated calcium sulphate. Alabaster is one form of gypsum. *Formula*: $CaSO_4 \cdot 2H_2O$ ⟨< L < Gk. *gypsos* chalk, plaster⟩

gypsum board plasterboard.

Gyp•sy [ˈdʒɪpsi] *n., pl.* **-sies;** *adj.* *—n.* **1** Sometimes, **gypsy,** a member of a wandering people having dark skin and black hair who originally migrated to Europe from N India in the 15th and 16th centuries. They have continued to live a nomadic life in Europe and North America. **2** Romany, the language of the Gypsies. **3 gypsy,** a person who looks like a Gypsy or leads a wandering life.
—adj. **gypsy,** of, having to do with, or like a Gypsy or the Gypsies: *a gypsy girl, gypsy music.* Also, **Gipsy, gipsy.** ⟨< *Egyptian,* since the Gypsies were thought to have originated in Egypt; 16c.⟩

gypsy moth a European moth (*Porthetria dispar*), a kind of tussock moth introduced into North America in the 19th century. Its hairy, greyish brown larvae eat the leaves of trees and have become a serious pest in North America.

gy•ral [ˈdʒaɪrəl] *adj.* gyratory.

gy•rate [ˈdʒaɪreit] *or* [dʒaɪˈreit] *v.* **-rat•ed, -rat•ing.** move in a circle or spiral; whirl; rotate: *A top gyrates.* ⟨< L *gyrare* < *gyrus* circle < Gk. *gyros*⟩ **—ˈgy•ra•tor,** *n.*

gy•ra•tion [dʒaɪˈreiʃən] *n.* a circular or spiral motion; whirling; rotation. **—gyˈra•tion•al,** *adj.*

gy•ra•to•ry [ˈdʒaɪrəˌtɔri] *adj.* gyrating.

gyre [dʒaɪr] *n. Poetic.* a circle. ⟨< L *gyrus circle*⟩

gyr•fal•con [ˈdʒɜrˌfɒlkən], [ˈdʒɜrˌfælkən], *or* [ˈdʒɜrˌfɒkən] *n.* the largest falcon (*Falco rusticolus*), found mainly in arctic and subarctic regions, varying in colour from almost pure white with black streaks and speckles to dark greyish brown. ⟨< ME *gerfaucoun* < OF *girfaucon* < Frankish **gerfalko* < **ger* < OHG *gir* hawk⟩.

gyro– *combining form.* circle; spiral: *gyroscope.* ⟨< Gk. *gyro-* < *gyros*⟩

gy•ro•com•pass [ˈdʒaɪrouˌkʌmpəs] *n.* a compass using a motor-driven gyroscope instead of a magnetic needle to point to the north. It points to the geographic North Pole instead of to the magnetic pole.

gy•ro horizon [ˈdʒaɪrou] **1** an artificial horizon in the form of a level reflector, used for calculating the altitude of a star. **2** a gyroscopic device that shows the degree of banking of an aircraft.

gy•ro•mag•net•ic [ˌdʒaɪroumægˈnɛtɪk] *adj.* having to do with the magnetic forces of a rotating and charged particle.

gy•ro•pi•lot [ˈdʒaɪrouˌpaɪlət] *n. Aeronautics.* a device that automatically keeps an aircraft on course; automatic pilot.

gy•ro•plane [ˈdʒaɪrəˌplein] *n.* an aircraft that is kept in the air by means of horizontal blades rapidly rotating around a vertical axis.

gy•ros [ˈjirɒs] *or* [ˈdʒirɒs] *n.* a Greek dish comprising various meats mixed and cooked on a vertical skewer.

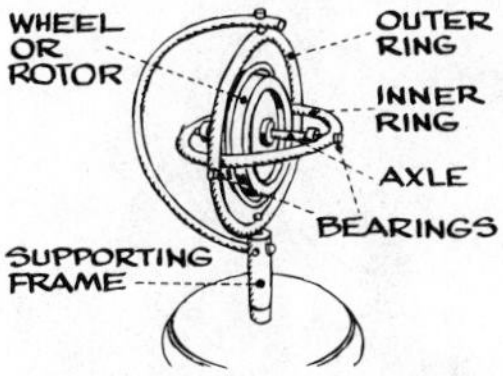

WHEEL OR ROTOR
OUTER RING
INNER RING
AXLE
BEARINGS
SUPPORTING FRAME

A gyroscope. Once it is set spinning rapidly, it will continue to rotate in the same plane regardless of magnetic forces and no matter which way the supporting frame is turned.

gy•ro•scope ['dʒaɪrə,skoup] *n.* a heavy wheel or disk mounted so that its axis can turn freely in one or more directions. A spinning gyroscope tends to resist change in the direction of its axis, and is used to keep ships and aircraft balanced.

gy•ro•scop•ic [,dʒaɪrə'skɒpɪk] *adj.* having to do with a gyroscope. **—,gy•ro'scop•i•cal•ly,** *adv.*

gy•rose ['dʒaɪrous] *adj. Botany.* marked with wavy lines.

gy•ro•sta•bi•liz•er [,dʒaɪrə'steibə,laɪzər] *n.* a gyroscopic device for stabilizing a seagoing vessel by counteracting its rolling motion.

gy•ro•stat•ics [,dʒaɪrə'stætɪks] *n.* the branch of physics that deals with the laws governing the rotation of solid bodies.

gy•rus ['dʒaɪrəs] *n.* a convolution, especially of the brain. ⟨< L, circle⟩

gyve [dʒaɪv] *n., v.* **gyved, gyv•ing.** *—n.* a fetter; shackle, especially for the leg.
—v. put fetters or shackles on. ⟨ME; origin uncertain⟩
☛ *Hom.* JIVE.

H h *H h*

h or **H** [eitʃ] *n., pl.* **h's** or **H's. 1** the eighth letter of the English alphabet. **2** any speech sound represented by this letter. **3** a person or thing identified as *h*, especially the eighth in a series. **4 H,** a symbol used on pencils to indicate the degree of hardness of the lead. A 2H pencil is hard; 4H is very hard. Compare **B** and **HB. 5** something shaped like the letter H. **6** any device, such as a printer's type, a lever, or a key on a keyboard, that produces an h or H. **7** *(adjl.)* of or being an H or h.

h 1 hour. **2** hecto- (an SI prefix).

h. or **h** *Baseball.* hit(s).

h. or **H 1** harbour. **2** hard; hardness. **3** high; height. **4** hundred. **5** husband.

H 1 hydrogen. **2** *Physics.* **a** intensity of magnetic field. **b** the horizontal component of Earth's magnetic field. **3** *Electricity.* henry. **4** *Slang.* heroin.

ha [hɑ], [hɒ], *or* [hæ] *interj.* **1** an exclamation of surprise, joy, triumph, etc.: *"Ha! I've caught you!" cried the farmer to the boys stealing her apples.* **2** in writing, a way of indicating laughter: *"Ha! ha! ha!" laughed the boys.* Also, **hah.**

ha hectare.

h.a. this year (for L *hoc anno*).

Ha hahnium.

ha•ba•ne•ra [ˌhɑbəˈnɛrə] *n.* **1** a slow Cuban dance. **2** the music for this dance, in double time. ⟨< Sp., of Havana⟩

ha•be•as cor•pus [ˈheibiəs ˈkɔrpəs] *Law.* a writ or order requiring that a prisoner be brought before a judge or into court to decide whether he or she is being held lawfully. The right of habeas corpus is a protection against unjust imprisonment. ⟨< L *habeas corpus* you may have the person⟩

hab•er•dash•er [ˈhæbərˌdæʃər] *n.* **1** a dealer in men's furnishings, such as hats, ties, shirts, socks, etc. **2** a dealer in small articles, such as buttons, needles, and trimmings. ⟨? < AF *hapertas*, a kind of cloth⟩

hab•er•dash•er•y [ˈhæbərˌdæʃəri] *n., pl.* **-er•ies. 1** the articles sold by a haberdasher. **2** the shop of a haberdasher.

hab•er•geon [ˈhæbərdʒən] *n. Armour.* **1** a short coat of mail without sleeves. **2** a hauberk. Also (def. 1), **haubergeon.** ⟨ME < OF *haubergeon*, dim. of *hauberc.* See HAUBERK.⟩

ha•bil•i•ment [həˈbɪləmənt] *n.* **1 habiliments,** *pl.* articles of clothing. **2** dress; attire. ⟨ME < OF *(h)abillement* < *abiller* prepare, fit out; originally, reduce (a tree) to a trunk by stripping off branches < *bille* long stock, log < Celtic⟩

hab•it [ˈhæbɪt] *n., v.* —*n.* **1** a tendency to act in a certain way or do certain things: *His habit is to do the hardest job first.* **2** disposition or character: *a man of morose habit.* **3** a pattern of behaviour acquired by repetition and that is regularly followed in certain circumstances or situations; often one that has become automatic: *the habit of brushing one's teeth. It is her habit to check all the doors and windows before going to bed.* **4** addiction. **5** the distinctive dress or costume worn by members of some religious orders: *The Grey Nuns traditionally wore a grey habit.* **6** a costume worn for riding; riding habit. **7** the characteristic form, mode of growth, etc., of an animal or plant: *The honeysuckle is of a twining habit.* **8** *Archaic.* clothing.
take the habit, become a nun.
—*v.* clothe. ⟨ME < OF < L *habitus* < *habere* hold, live in, stay⟩

☛ *Syn.* **Habit** and CUSTOM both refer to an established practice. **Habit** refers more to a personal practice, something one does without thinking about it: *Biting one's fingernails is a bad habit.* **Custom** refers especially to practice consciously adopted by a group of people or an individual and continued over a long period of time: *It was a custom in her family to play euchre every Friday evening.*

hab•it•a•ble [ˈhæbətəbəl] *adj.* fit to live in.
—**ˈhab•it•a•ble•ness,** *n.* —**ˈhab•it•a•bly,** *adv.*

hab•it•ant *n. 1* [ˈhæbətənt]; *n. 2, adj.* [ˈhæbəˌtɒnt]; *French,* [abiˈtɑ̃] *n., adj.* —*n.* **1** inhabitant. **2** *Cdn.* a French-Canadian farmer.
—*adj. Cdn.* of or having to do with French Canadians or French Canada, especially with regard to country life. ⟨< Cdn.F < F < L *habitans, -antis,* ppr. of *habitare* live in < *habere*⟩

hab•i•tat [ˈhæbəˌtæt] *n.* **1** the place where an animal or plant naturally lives or grows: *The jungle is the habitat of tigers.* **2** a place of living; a dwelling place. ⟨< L *habitat* it inhabits⟩

hab•i•ta•tion [ˌhæbəˈteiʃən] *n.* **1** a place to live in; home; dwelling. **2** an inhabiting.

ha•bit•u•al [həˈbɪtʃuəl] *adj.* **1** done by habit; caused by habit: *a habitual smile, habitual courtesy.* **2** being or doing something by habit: *A habitual reader reads a great deal.* **3** often done, seen, or used; usual; customary: *Ice and snow are a habitual sight in arctic regions.* —**haˈbit•u•al•ly,** *adv.* —**haˈbit•u•al•ness,** *n.*

ha•bit•u•ate [həˈbɪtʃuˌeit] *v.* **-at•ed, -at•ing. 1** make used *(to)*; accustom: *Loggers are habituated to hard work.* **2** go to (a place) frequently. ⟨< LL *habituari* be in a state of, be characterized by (? passive of **habituare* bring into a state) < L *habitus* condition (See HABIT); influenced in meaning by E *habit*⟩ —**haˌbit•uˈa•tion,** *n.*

hab•i•tude [ˈhæbəˌtjud] *or* [ˈhæbəˌtud] *n.* **1** a characteristic condition of body or mind. **2** a habit; custom; practice. ⟨< F < L *habitudo* condition⟩

ha•bit•u•é [həˌbɪtʃuˈei] *or* [həˈbɪtʃuˌei] *n.* a person who has the habit of going to a place frequently: *a habitué of the theatre.* ⟨< F *habitué,* pp. of *habituer* accustom⟩

ha•bi•tus [ˈhæbɪtəs] *n., pl.* **habitus.** the physical characteristics that render one susceptible to disease; CONSTITUTION (def. 1).

Habs•burg [ˈhæpsbərg]; *German,* [ˈhapsbʊʀk] See HAPSBURG.

ha•chure *n.* [ˈhæʃʊr] *or* [ˈhæʃjʊr]; *v.* [hæˈʃʊr]; *French,* [aˈʃyʀ] *n., v.* **ha•chured, ha•chur•ing.** —*n.* any of a series of parallel lines used in mapmaking to indicate a slope.
—*v.* show by such lines.

ha•ci•en•da [ˌhɑsiˈɛndə] *or* [ˌhæsiˈɛndə] *n. Spanish American.* a large ranch; landed estate; country house. ⟨< Sp. < L *facienda* (things) to be done < *facere* do⟩

hack[1] [hæk] *v., n.* —*v.* **1** cut with repeated rough or uneven blows: *She hacked the crate apart with an old axe. He hacked away at the tree.* **2** make (one's way) by cutting away vegetation: *hacking our way through the underbrush.* **3** *Slang.* handle (something) successfully; cope or tolerate (*often used with* **it**): *She couldn't hack the long hours. It takes a special kind of person to hack it in this business.* **4** cough in short, dry bursts. **5** *Basketball.* commit the foul of hitting the arm of (an opponent who has the ball).
—*n.* **1** a rough cut. **2** a tool or instrument for hacking or cutting, such as an axe, pick, hoe, etc. **3** *Curling.* a notch cut in the ice at one end of a rink, used as a foothold when a player throws a rock. **4** a short, dry cough. **5** *Basketball.* a personal foul committed by striking the arm of a player who has the ball. ⟨OE *haccian*⟩

☛ *Syn. v.* **1.** See note at CUT.

hack[2] [hæk] *n., v., adj.* —*n.* **1** a carriage for hire. **2** *Informal.* taxi. **3** an old or worn-out horse. **4** a horse for ordinary riding. **5** a person hired to do routine literary work; drudge. **6** a plodding, faithful, but undistinguished worker in an organization, as a political party: *an old party hack.*
—*v.* **1** ride on horseback over roads. **2** *Informal.* drive a taxi. **3** write or act as a hack.
—*adj.* working or done merely for money; hired; drudging. ⟨short for *hackney*⟩

hack[3] [hæk] *n., v.* —*n.* a rack for drying fish or produce, or holding feed for animals.
—*v.* place in such a rack. ⟨var. of HATCH[2]⟩

hack•a•more [ˈhækəˌmɔr] *n.* **1** HALTER[1] (def. 1). **2** a simple looped bridle, whereby a horse is controlled by means of pressure exerted on its nose. ⟨< Sp. *jáquima*⟩

hack•ber•ry [ˈhækˌbɛri] *n., pl.* **-ries. 1** any of a genus (*Celtis*) of trees and shrubs of the elm family found mainly in temperate and tropical regions, having small, edible, cherrylike fruits. **2** the fruit of any of these trees. **3** the soft wood of any of these trees. ⟨var. of *hagberry* < Scand.; cf. Danish *hæggebær*⟩

hack•er [ˈhækər] *n.* **1** one who hacks. **2** a person skilled in the use of computers, especially one who uses this skill to gain access illegally to government or business data.

hack•le[1] [ˈhækəl] *n., v.* **-led, -ling.** —*n.* **1** a comb used in dressing flax, hemp, etc. **2** one of the long, slender feathers on the neck of certain male birds. **3** the neck plumage of certain birds. **4** *Fishing.* **a** the part of an artificial fly corresponding to the legs of an insect, made from feathers from the neck of a rooster. **b** HACKLE FLY. **5 hackles,** *pl.* the erectile hairs on the back of a dog's neck.

raise the hackles of, *Informal.* arouse the suspicion or anger of.
—v. comb (flax, hemp, etc.) with a hackle. ⟨ME *hakell.* Related to HECKLE.⟩

hack•le[2] ['hækəl] *v.* **-led, -ling.** cut roughly; hack; mangle. ⟨< *hack[1]*⟩

hackle fly a wingless artificial fly used in fishing.

hack•man ['hækmən] *n., pl.* **-men.** the driver of a hack or carriage for hire.

hack•ma•tack ['hækmə,tæk] *n. Cdn.* **1** any of various evergreens, especially the tamarack. **2** the wood of this tree. ⟨< Algonquian⟩

hack•ney ['hækni] *n., pl.* **-neys;** *adj., v.* **-neyed, -ney•ing.**
—n. **1** a horse for ordinary riding. **2** a carriage for hire.
—adj. hired; let out, employed, or done for hire.
—v. use too often; make commonplace. ⟨ME *hakeney* < *Hackney,* a borough of London, England⟩

hack•neyed ['hæknid] *adj.* used too often; commonplace: *"White as snow" is a hackneyed comparison.*

hack•saw ['hæk,sɒ] *n.* a saw for cutting metal, having a narrow, fine-toothed blade fixed under tension in a frame. See SAW[1] for picture.

hack•work ['hæk,wɜrk] *n.* **1** routine literary work done by a hack. **2** any similar work of a routine or unstimulating nature.

had [hæd]; *unstressed,* [həd] *or* [əd] *v.* pt. and pp. of HAVE.
☛ *Usage.* **Had better, had rather. Had better** is the usual idiom for giving advice or making an indirect command: *You had better take cover before she sees you.* Informally, a shorter form without *had* is common, but this should not be used in formal writing: *If she asks you to do it, you better do it.*

had•dock ['hædək] *n., pl.* **-dock** or **-docks.** an important food fish (*Melanogrammus aeglefinus*) of the northern Atlantic, related to and resembling the cod, but smaller. ⟨ME *haddok;* origin uncertain⟩

hade [heid] *n., v.* **had•ed, had•ing.** *Geology.* *—n.* the angle between the plane of a fault and the vertical.
—v. incline from a vertical position; lean. ⟨origin uncertain⟩

Ha•des ['heidiz] *n.* **1** *Greek mythology.* **a** the home of the dead, below the earth. **b** the god of the lower world, also called Pluto. **2** often, **hades,** *Informal.* hell. ⟨< Gk. *Haidēs*⟩

had•ith [hɑ'diθ] *or* [hæ'diθ] *n. Islam.* a compilation of the teachings, sayings, and actions of the prophet Mohammed, collected by his followers.

had•n't ['hædənt] had not.

had•ron ['hædrɒn] *n. Physics.* any of a class of particles, including protons and neutrons, that are capable of taking part in strong nuclear reactions and whose constituent particles are quarks. **—ha'dron•ic,** *adj.*

hadst [hædst] *v. Archaic.* 2nd pers. sing., past tense, of HAVE. *Thou hadst* means *you* (sing.) *had.*

haem– *combining form.* HEM-.

haema– *combining form.* HEMA-. Also, **haemo-.**
☛ *Spelling.* Words beginning with **haem-** or **haema-** are entered under their **hem-** and **hema-** forms.

ha•fiz ['hɑfɪz] *n. Islam.* a title of respect for a Muslim who can recite the entire Koran from memory. ⟨< Arabic⟩

haf•ni•um ['hæfniəm] *n. Chemistry.* a rare metallic chemical element somewhat like zirconium. *Symbol*: Hf; *at.no.* 72; *at.mass* 178.49. ⟨< *Hafnia,* L name for Copenhagen⟩

haft [hæft] *n., v.* *—n.* the handle of a knife, sword, dagger, etc.
—v. furnish with a handle or hilt; set in a haft. ⟨OE *hæft*⟩

hag [hæg] *n.* **1** a very ugly old woman, especially one who is vicious or malicious. **2** witch. ⟨ME *hagge,* related to OE *hægtesse* witch, fury⟩ **—'hag,like,** *adj.*

Ha•gen ['hɑgən] *n.* in the *Nibelungenlied,* the murderer of Siegfried. ⟨< G⟩

hag•fish ['hæg,fɪʃ] *n., pl.* **-fish** or **-fish•es.** any of about 20 species of primitive, eel-like, marine vertebrates constituting the family Myxinidae, having a round sucking mouth surrounded by thick barbels, and horny teeth which they use to bore into the bodies of fish they feed on, eating them from inside.

Hag•ga•dah or **Hag•ga•da** [hə'gɑdə] *n., pl.* **-doth** [-douθ] *or* **-dot** [-dout]. *Judaism.* **1** in the Talmud: **a** a story or legend that explains or illustrates the Jewish law. **b** the section containing such stories and legends. **2 a** the text of the Seder service on the first, or the first two, evenings of Passover. **b** a book containing this text. ⟨< Hebrew *haggadah* story < *higgid* relate⟩

hag•ga•dist [hə'gɑdɪst] *n.* a writer of the Haggadah. **—hag'ga•dic,** *adj.*

hag•gard ['hægərd] *adj.* wild-looking from pain, fatigue, worry, hunger, etc.; gaunt; careworn. ⟨< MF *hagard* of the hedges, untamed (hawk) ? < MHG *hag* hedge⟩ **—'hag•gard•ly,** *adv.* **—'hag•gard•ness,** *n.*

hag•gis ['hægɪs] *n. Scottish.* the heart, lungs, and liver of a sheep mixed with suet and oatmeal and boiled in the stomach of the animal. ⟨ME ? < Scottish *hag* chop; cf. ON *höggva.* Akin to HEW.⟩

hag•gish ['hægɪʃ] *adj.* of or like a hag. **—'hag•gish•ly,** *adv.* **—'hag•gish•ness,** *n.*

hag•gle ['hægəl] *v.* **-gled, -gling;** *n.* *—v.* **1** dispute about a price or the terms of a bargain; wrangle. **2** mangle in cutting; hack.
—n. the act of haggling; a wrangle or dispute about terms. ⟨< Scottish *hag* chop, hack < ON *höggva*⟩ **—'hag•gler,** *n.*

hag•i•ar•chy ['hægi,ɑrki] *or* ['heidʒi,ɑrki] *n.* government by holy people.

hagio– *combining form.* **1** saint. **2** a holy place. ⟨< Gk. *hagios* holy, sacred⟩

hag•i•og•ra•pher [,hægi'ɒgrəfər] *or* [,heidʒi'ɒgrəfər] *n.* **1** a writer of the lives of the saints. **2** any writer on sacred subjects.

hag•i•o•graph•ic [,hægiə'græfɪk] *or* [,heidʒiə'græfɪk] *adj.* of or having to do with hagiography.

hag•i•og•ra•phy [,hægi'ɒgrəfi] *or* [,heidʒi'ɒgrəfi] *n.* the writing of the lives of the saints. ⟨< LL < Gk. *hagios* holy + *graphos* thing written⟩

hag•i•o•log•i•cal [,hægiə'lɒdʒɪkəl] *or* [,heidʒiə'lɒdʒɪkəl] *adj.* of or having to do with hagiology. Also, **hagiologic.**

hag•i•ol•o•gy [,hægi'ɒlədʒi] *or* [,heidʒi'ɒlədʒi] *n., pl.* **-gies.** **1** literature that deals with the lives and legends of saints. **2** a book on this subject. **3** a list of saints. ⟨< Gk. *hagios* holy + E *-logy*⟩

hag•rid•den ['hæg,rɪdən] *adj.* worried or tormented, as if by witches; harassed.

Hague Tribunal [heig] the permanent body, founded in 1899, for judging cases in international law and proposing nominees to the International Court of Justice.

hah [hɑ] *interj.* See HA.

ha–ha ['hɑ ,hɑ] *n.* a park fence set in a trench or ditch.

hahn•i•um ['hɑniəm] a very unstable, artificially created element. *Symbol*: Ha; *at.no.* 105; *at.mass* (262) or (260). ⟨after Otto *Hahn* (1879-1968), a German physicist⟩

Hai•da ['haɪdə] *n., pl.* **Hai•da;** *adj.* *—n.* **1** a member of a First Nations people of western British Columbia and Alaska. **2** the language of the Haida.
—adj. of or having to do with the Haida or their language.

hai•den [haɪ'dɛn] *n.* the small outer shrine of a Shinto temple which worshippers may enter for their devotions. ⟨< Japanese⟩

haik [həik] *or* [heik] *n.* an Arabian garment worn over the head and body. ⟨< Arabic *hayk* < *haka* weave⟩
☛ *Hom.* HAKE [heik].

hai•ku ['haɪku] *n., pl.* **hai•ku.** **1** a Japanese verse form consisting of three lines of five, seven, and five syllables respectively. **2** a poem in this form. ⟨< Japanese⟩

hail[1] [heil] *v., n., interj.* *—v.* **1** shout in welcome to; greet; cheer; congratulate: *The crowd hailed the winner.* **2** greet as; call: *They hailed her a leader.* **3** call loudly to; shout to: *The captain hailed the passing ship. Please hail a cab for me.*
hail from, come from.
—n. **1** a greeting; cheer; shout of welcome. **2** a loud call; shout.
within hail, near enough to hear a call or shout.
—interj. Poetic. greetings! welcome! congratulations!: *Hail to the winner!*
hail fellow well met, very friendly. ⟨earlier *be hail!* < ON *heill* healthy⟩ **—'hail•er,** *n.*
☛ *Hom.* HALE.

hail[2] [heil] *n., v.* *—n.* **1** rounded lumps of ice, usually not much bigger than large raindrops, that fall instead of rain from cumulus clouds under certain meteorological conditions involving rising air currents (*used with a singular verb*): *The hail was coming down hard. Our garden was destroyed by hail.* **2** a fall or shower of such lumps of ice: *It was the first hail of the season.* **3** a penetrating or forceful rush or shower of something, having the effect of hail: *a hail of abuse. They were met by a hail of bullets.*
—v. **1** be the case that hail is falling (*used with the subject* **it**): *It hailed yesterday.* **2** pour down like hail: *The critics hailed scorn on his inept performance.*

hailed out, destroyed by hail: *Their crop was hailed out.* ⟨OE *hægel*⟩
☛ *Hom.* HALE.

hail•stone ['heil,stoun] *n.* a piece of hail: *There were large hailstones all over the lawn.*

hail•storm ['heil,stɔrm] *n.* a storm with hail.

hair [hɛr] *n., adj.* —*n.* **1** a fine, threadlike outgrowth from the skin of human beings and animals. **2** a mass of such growths. **3** the hair of the human head: *I must get my hair cut.* **4** a fine, threadlike growth from the outer layer of plants. **5** a very narrow space; something very small; least degree: *She won the race by a hair.*
get in (someone's) **hair,** annoy; be a nuisance to.
have by the short hairs, be in a position to coerce (someone) to do something.
let (one's) **hair down,** be informal or unconventional in behaviour; relax.
not turn a hair, not show any sign of being disturbed or embarrassed.
split hairs, make excessively fine distinctions.
to a hair, exactly; just right.
—*adj.* **1** made of or with hair. **2** for care of the hair: *hair conditioner*. ⟨OE *ǣr*⟩
☛ *Hom.* HARE, HERR.

hair•breadth ['hɛr,brɛdθ] *or* ['hɛr,brɛtθ] *n. or adj.* hair's-breadth.

hair•brush ['hɛr,brʌʃ] *n.* a brush for the hair.

hair•cloth ['hɛr,klɒθ] *n.* a cloth made of horsehair or camel's hair, used to cover furniture, stiffen garments, etc.

hair•cut ['hɛr,kʌt] *n.* **1** the act or an instance of cutting the hair of the head: *I need a haircut.* **2** the result of cutting the hair; hairstyle.

hair•do ['hɛr,du] *n., pl.* **-dos.** the way in which the hair, especially of a woman, is arranged.

hair•dress•er ['hɛr,drɛsər] *n.* a person whose work is cutting and taking care of people's hair.

hair•dress•ing ['hɛr,drɛsɪŋ] *n.* **1** the act or process of cutting and arranging someone's hair. **2** the business or occupation of a hairdresser.

haired [hɛrd] *adj.* having hair, especially of a specified kind (*usually used in compounds*): *dark-haired, curly-haired.*

hair•less ['hɛrlɪs] *adj.* without hair.

hair•line ['hɛr,laɪn] *n.* **1** the natural irregular margin where hair growth ends on the head, especially the forehead. **2** a very thin line. **3** (*adjl.*) very thin or narrow: *a hairline crack in a wall.* **4** *Printing.* a very fine line, especially a stroke or part of a letter thinner than other parts. **5** a very small margin of difference.

hair net a net worn to keep one's hair in place.

hair•piece ['hɛr,pis] *n.* **1** a wig or section of real or artificial hair worn to cover baldness; toupee. **2** an extra length or section of real or artificial hair worn as part of a coiffure, to add bulk or length.

hair•pin ['hɛr,pɪn] *n., adj.* —*n.* **1** a pin, usually a U-shaped piece of wire, shell, or plastic, used to keep the hair in place. **2** a sharp bend in a road, river, etc., likened to a hairpin in shape.
—*adj.* shaped like a hairpin; U-shaped: *a hairpin bend.*

hair–rais•ing ['hɛr ,reizɪŋ] *adj. Informal.* making the hair seem to stand on end; terrifying.

hair's–breadth or **hairs•breadth** ['hɛrz ,brɛdθ] *or* ['hɛrz ,brɛtθ] *adj., n.* —*adj.* very narrow; extremely close: *a hairbreadth escape.*
—*n.* a very narrow space; a very small distance.

hair seal any of a family (Phocidae) of seals highly specialized for an aquatic life, having hind limbs reduced to flippers that cannot be rotated forward, a broad head with large eyes and no external ears, and a coat consisting of stiff hair with only a thin undercoat. The harbour seal, ringed seal, and harp seal are hair seals.

hair shirt a rough shirt or girdle made of horsehair, worn as a penance.

hair•split•ting ['hɛr,splɪtɪŋ] *n., adj.* —*n.* the making of excessively fine distinctions.
—*adj.* excessively subtle.

hair•spring ['hɛr,sprɪŋ] *n.* a very fine spiral spring that regulates the motion of the balance wheel in a watch or clock. See ESCAPEMENT for picture.

hair•streak ['hɛr,strik] *n.* a butterfly of the subfamily Theclinae, having transverse streaks under the wings.

hair stroke serif.

hair•style ['hɛr,staɪl] *n.* a way of arranging or wearing the hair: *Her new hairstyle is very attractive.*

hair•styl•ing ['hɛr,staɪlɪŋ] *n.* the act or work of arranging the hair, usually done by a hairstylist.

hair•styl•ist ['hɛr,staɪlɪst] *n.* a hairdresser, especially one who creates hairstyles to suit individual customers.

hair trig•ger a trigger that operates by very slight pressure.

hair–trig•ger ['hɛr ,trɪgər] *adj.* **1** having a hair trigger. **2** set off by the slightest pressure: *a hair-trigger temper.*

hair•y ['hɛri] *adj.* **hair•i•er, hair•i•est. 1** covered with hair; having much hair. **2** of or like hair. **3** *Slang.* difficult; disturbing; dismaying; frightening: *a hairy situation.* —**'hair•i•ly,** *adv.* —**'hair•i•ness,** *n.*

Hai•sla ['həislə] *n., pl.* **Hai•sla** or **Hai•slas.** a member of the northern branch of the Kwakiutl people of British Columbia.

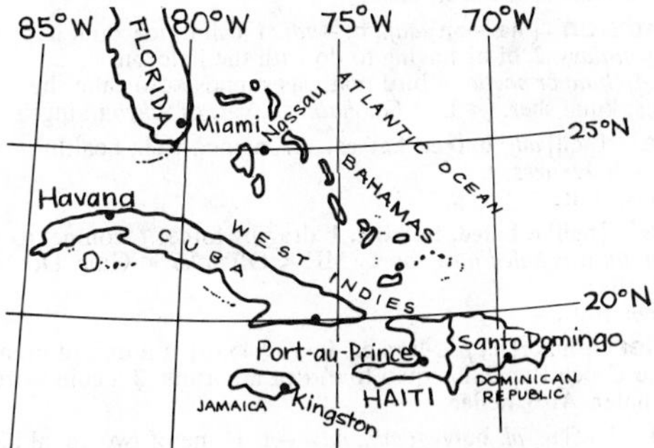

Haïti, showing its position in the Caribbean

Haï•ti ['heiti] *or* [hɑ'iti] a country in the Caribbean, being the western portion of the island of Hispaniola.

Hai•ti•an ['heiʃən], ['heitiən], *or* [haɪ'iʃən] *n., adj.* —*n.* **1** a native or inhabitant of Haïti. **2** HAITIAN CREOLE.
—*adj.* of or having to do with Haiti, its people, or their language.

Haitian Creole the language of the majority of Haitians, based on French, but incorporating features of various West African languages.

haj [hædʒ] *n. Islam.* a pilgrimage to the sacred shrine at Mecca, to be undertaken at least once in the lifetime of all devout Muslims. ⟨< Arabic⟩

ha•ji ['hædʒi] *n., pl.* **ha•jis.** *Islam.* one who has performed the HAJ.

hak•a•pik ['hɑkə,pɪk] *or* ['hækə,pɪk] *n.* a long pole having a hammer head and a spike at one end, used in killing seals. ⟨< Norwegian⟩

hake [heik] *n., pl.* **hake** or **hakes.** any of several marine food fishes (genera *Merluccius* and *Urophycis*) of the cod family, having an elongated body and large head. Some authorities classify hakes as a separate family, Merlucciidae. ⟨dial. var. of *hook*; from the hooklike growth under the lower jaw; cf. Norwegian *hakefisk*⟩
☛ *Hom.* HAIK [heik].

ha•kim[1] [hə'kim] *n.* in Muslim countries, a physician. ⟨< Arabic *hakīm* wise man⟩

ha•kim[2] ['hɑkɪm] *n.* in Muslim countries, a ruler; judge or governor. ⟨< Arabic *hākim* ruler⟩

ha•la•la [hə'lɑlə] *n.* a unit of money in Saudi Arabia, equal to 1/100 of a rial. ⟨< Arabic⟩

ha•la•tion [hə'leiʃən] *n.* a halolike spreading of light around an object on a photographic print or television image.

A halberd

hal•berd ['hælbərd] *n.* a weapon that was both a spear and a battle-axe, used in warfare in the 15th and 16th centuries. ⟨< F *hallebarde* < Ital. *alabarda* < Gmc.⟩

hal•berd•ier [,hælbər'dir] *n.* formerly, a soldier armed with a halberd.

hal•bert ['hælbərt] *n.* halberd.

hal•cin•o•nide [hæl'sɪnə,naɪd] *n.* a drug used as a cream to treat certain skin conditions.

hal•cy•on ['hælsiən] *adj., n. —adj.* **1** calm; peaceful; happy: *halcyon days.* **2** of or having to do with the halcyon.
—n. Archaic or poetic. a bird that was supposed to calm the waves; kingfisher. ⟨< L < Gk. *halkyon*, var. of *alkyon* kingfisher⟩

hale[1] [heil] *adj.* **hal•er, hal•est.** strong and well; healthy. ⟨OE *hāl*⟩ **—'hale•ness,** *n.*
☛ *Hom.* HAIL.

hale[2] [heil] *v.* **haled, hal•ing. 1** drag by force. **2** compel to go: *The man was haled into court.* ⟨ME < OF *haler* < Gmc. Doublet of HAUL.⟩
☛ *Hom.* HAIL.

ha•ler ['hɑlər] *n., pl.* **-lers** or **-le•ru** [-lə,ru]. **1** a unit of money in the Czech Republic equal to 1/100 of a koruna. **2** a coin worth one haler. Also, **heller.**

half [hæf] *n., pl.* **halves;** *adj., adv. —n.* **1** one of two equal parts. **2** in certain games, one of two equal periods. **3** *Golf.* a score equal to that of one's opponent, on any hole or on a round. **4** one of two nearly equal parts: *Which is the bigger half?* **5** *Football.* a halfback.
by half, by far.
—adj. **1** forming a half; being or making half of. **2** not complete; being only part of: *A half-truth is often no better than a lie.*
—adv. **1** to half of the full amount or degree: *a glass half full of milk.* **2** partly: *half understood.* **3** almost: *The beggar was half dead from hunger.*
half past, thirty minutes after a specified hour: *It's half past four.*
not half, a to a very slight extent. **b** *Informal.* not at all; the reverse of: *not half bad.* ⟨OE *healf*⟩

half–and–half ['hæf ən 'hæf] *adj., adv., n. —adj.* **1** half one thing and half another. **2** not clearly one thing or the other.
—adv. in two equal parts.
—n. **1** a mixture of milk and cream. **2** *Brit.* a beverage consisting of two drinks, especially ale and porter, mixed together.

half•back ['hæf,bæk] *n. Sports.* in football or soccer, a player whose position is behind the forward line.

half–baked ['hæf 'beikt] *adj.* **1** not cooked enough. **2** *Informal.* not fully worked out; incomplete. **3** *Informal.* not experienced; showing poor judgment.

half•beak ['hæf,bik] a fish of the family Hemirhamphidae, found in salt water or fresh water, having a long lower jaw like a beak.

half binding a method of binding a book in which the covers may have different materials at the corners from the rest of the covers.

half blood the relationship between persons who are related through one parent only.

half–blood•ed ['hæf ,blʌdɪd] *adj.* **1** having parents of different races. **2** related through only one parent.

half boot a boot reaching about halfway to the knee.

half brother a brother related through one parent only.

half–caste ['hæf ,kæst] *n., adj. —n.* a person whose parents belong to different races, especially an offspring of a European father and an Asiatic mother.
—adj. being such a person.

half cock the position of the hammer of a gun when it is pulled back halfway. At half cock the trigger is locked and the gun cannot be fired.
go off at half cock, a fire too soon. **b** act or speak without sufficient thought or preparation.

half–cocked ['hæf 'kɒkt] *adj.* **1** of a gun, in the position of half cock. **2** not well conceived.

half crown formerly, a British silver coin worth two shillings and sixpence.

half dollar a coin of Canada and the U.S., worth 50 cents.

half eagle a former gold coin of the United States, worth $5.

half–heart•ed ['hæf 'hɑrtɪd] *adj.* lacking interest or enthusiasm; not earnest: *a half-hearted attempt.*
—'half-'heart•ed•ly, *adv.* **—'half-'heart•ed•ness,** *n.*

half hitch a knot formed by passing the end of a rope under and over its standing part and then inside the loop. See KNOT for picture.

half–hour ['hæf 'aʊr] *n.* **1** thirty minutes; half an hour: *It took us a half-hour to get there.* **2** the halfway point in one of the 24 hours of the day: *The bus goes every 30 minutes, on the hour and the half-hour.* **3** (*adjl.*) of, having to do with, or lasting a half-hour: *a half-hour wait, the half-hour chime of a clock.*
—'half-'hour•ly, *adv., adj.*

half–length ['hæf ,lɛŋθ] *adj.* **1** of a portrait, showing head and shoulders only. **2** of half the full length.

half–life ['hæf ,ləif] *n.* **1** *Nuclear physics.* the time in which half of the original radiant energy of a radioactive substance is given off, used to distinguish one such substance from another and as a measurement of radioactivity. **2** of any substance, usually harmful, the time it takes for the amount of the substance in the environment to be reduced by half by decay.

half–light ['hæf ,ləit] *n.* a dim light, as of early evening.

half–mast ['hæf 'mæst] *n., v. —n.* a position halfway or part way down from the top of a mast, staff, etc.: *When the Governor General died, flags were lowered to half-mast as a mark of respect.*
—v. put (a flag) at half-mast: *They have half-masted the flag.*

half moon 1 the moon when only half of its surface appears bright. See MOON for picture. **2** something shaped like a half moon or crescent.

half nelson *Wrestling.* a hold applied by hooking one arm under an opponent's armpit and putting a hand on the back of the opponent's neck.

half note *Music.* a note held half as long as a whole note; MINIM (def. 4). See NOTE for picture.

half•pence ['heipəns] *n.pl.* a pl. of HALFPENNY.

half•pen•ny ['heipəni] *or* ['heipni] *n., pl.* **half•pen•nies** ['heipəniz] *or* ['heipniz] or **half•pence. 1** a small British coin worth half a penny, or one two-hundredths of a pound. **2** a former British coin in use before 1972, worth half an old penny, or one twenty-fourth of a shilling. **3** (*adjl.*) worth a halfpenny. **4** (*adjl.*) having little value.

half pint 1 a non-metric, usually liquid measure equal to 0.2 L. **2** *Informal.* a small person.

half rest *Music.* a rest lasting as long as a half note. See REST for picture.

half–section ['hæf ,sɛkʃən] *n. Cdn.* an area of land covering 130 ha.

half sibling or **sib** a brother or sister who shares one but not both parents.

half sister a sister related through one parent only.

half size any of a series of sizes in women's clothing, 12½ through 24½, denoting a short bodice.

half slip a woman's undergarment like a skirt.

half•sole ['hæf,soul] *v.* **-soled, -sol•ing.** put a new half sole or half soles on (shoes, etc.).

half sole the sole of a shoe or boot from the toe to the instep.

half sovereign formerly, a British gold coin worth ten shillings.

half–staff ['hæf 'stæf] *n. or v. Esp. U.S.* half-mast.

half step 1 *Music.* the difference in pitch between two adjacent keys on a piano; a semitone. **2** in military marching, a step of 38.1 cm in quick time or 46 cm in double time.

half–tim•bered ['hæf ,tɪmbərd] *adj.* having walls of wooden framework with the spaces filled by plaster, stone, or brick.

half–time ['hæf 'taɪm] *n.* **1** *Sports.* the interval between two halves of a game. **2** (*adj.*) having to do with this period: *the half-time score.* **3** *Music.* a tempo half as fast as the previous tempo.

half tone *Music.* an interval equal to half a tone on the scale; half step.

half–tone ['hæf ˌtoun] *n.* **1** *Photo-engraving.* **a** a process used in making pictures for books and magazines, in which the subject is photographed through a fine screen, breaking the image into tiny dots. **b** a picture made by this process. **2** a tone in a painting, etc., halfway between the highlights and deep shades.

half–track or **half•track** ['hæf ˌtræk] *n.* an army motor vehicle that has wheels in front and short tracks in the rear for driving, used to carry personnel and weapons.

half–truth ['hæf ˌtruθ] *n.* an assertion or statement that is only partly true.

half–volley ['hæf 'vɒli] *n. Tennis.* the striking of the ball on its first bounce after hitting the court.

half•way ['hæf'wei] *adv., adj. —adv.* half the way; half the required distance: *The rope reached only halfway to the boat.*
go or **meet halfway,** do one's share toward reaching an agreement or toward patching up a quarrel.
—adj. **1** midway: *The inn served as a halfway house between the two towns.* **2** not going far enough; incomplete; inadequate: *Halfway measures are never satisfactory.*

halfway house **1** an inn or other resting place at a midway point on a route or journey. **2** a place or hostel offering a somewhat structured and sheltered environment designed to help recently released convicts, mental patients, etc. become gradually adjusted to society.

half–wit ['hæf ˌwɪt] *n.* **1** a feeble-minded person. **2** a stupid, foolish person.

half–wit•ted ['hæf 'wɪtɪd] *adj.* **1** feeble-minded. **2** stupid; foolish. **—'half-'wit•ted•ly,** *adv.* **—'half-'wit•ted•ness,** *n.*

hal•i•but ['hæləbət] *n., pl.* **-but** or **-buts. 1** a North Atlantic flatfish (*Hippoglossus hippoglossus*) highly valued as a commercial food fish. It is the largest flatfish, sometimes reaching a length of 2 m and a mass of over 300 kg. **2** any of various similar and related flatfishes, such as the **Pacific halibut** (*H. stenolepsis*) or the **Greenland halibut** (*Reinhardtius hippoglossoides*). ⟨ME *halybutte* < *haly* holy + *butte* flatfish; eaten on holy days⟩

hal•ide ['hælaɪd] *or* ['hælɪd], ['heilaɪd] *or* ['heilɪd] *n., adj. Chemistry. —n.* any compound of a halogen with another element or radical. Sodium chloride is a halide.
—adj. haloid. ⟨< *hal(ogen)* + *-ide*⟩

ha•li•er ['hɑliˌɛr] *n., pl.* **ha•li•er•ov** [-ɒv]. a unit of money in the Slovak Republic, equal to 1/100 of a koruna. See table of money in the Appendix.

Hal•i•go•ni•an [ˌhælɪ'gouniən] *n., adj. —n.* **1** native or inhabitant of Halifax, Nova Scotia. **2** a native or inhabitant of Halifax, a city in Yorkshire, England.
—adj. of or having to do with either Halifax.

hal•ite ['hælɔit] *or* ['heilɔit] *n.* native rock salt. ⟨< NL *halites* < Gk. *hals* salt⟩

hal•i•to•sis [ˌhælə'tousɪs] *n.* a disorder characterized by persistent bad or offensive breath. ⟨< NL < L *halitus* breath⟩

hall [hɒl] *n.* **1** a way to go through a building; passageway; corridor. **2** a passageway or room at the entrance of a building. **3** a large room for holding meetings, parties, banquets, etc. **4** a building for public business: *The mayor's office is in the town hall.* **5** a building of a school, college, or university. **6** a mansion, especially the manor of an estate. ⟨OE *heall*⟩
☛ *Hom.* HAUL.

hal•le•lu•jah or **hal•le•lu•iah** [ˌhælə'lujə] *interj., n.*
—interj. praise the Lord!
—n. a song of praise to God. Also, **alleluia.** ⟨< Hebrew *halleluyah* praise ye Yah (Jehovah)⟩

Halley's comet ['hæliz] *or* ['heiliz] the comet that Halley predicted could be seen about every 75 years, last seen in 1986. ⟨after Edmund *Halley* (1656–1742), an English astronomer⟩

hal•liard ['hæljərd] *n.* See HALYARD.

hall•mark ['hɒlˌmɑrk] *n., v. —n.* **1** an official mark indicating standard of purity, put on gold and silver articles. **2** a mark or sign of genuineness or good quality: *Courtesy and self-control are the hallmarks of a gentleman.*
—v. put a hallmark on. ⟨from Goldsmiths' *Hall* in London, the seat of the Goldsmiths' Company, by whom the stamping was legally regulated in Britain⟩

hal•lo or **hal•loa** [hə'lou] See HELLO.

Hall of Fame a society into which famous professional sports players are inducted.

hal•loo [hə'lu] *interj., n., pl.* **-loos;** *v.* **-looed, -loo•ing.** *—interj.* **1** *Hunting.* a shout to make hounds run faster. **2** a call or shout to attract attention.
—n. **1** *Hunting.* a shout to make hounds run faster. **2** a call or shout to attract attention. **3** a shout; call.
—v. shout; call to attract attention. Also, **hallow.** ⟨ME < OF *halloer* chase with shouts, var. of *haler* < *hale, hare* (the shout). Cf. HARASS.⟩

hal•low[1] ['hælou] *v.* **1** make holy; make sacred. **2** honour as holy or sacred. ⟨OE *hālgian* < *hālig* holy⟩

hal•low[2] [hə'lou] *interj., n., or v.* halloo.

hal•lowed ['hæloud]; *in church use, often* ['hælouɪd] *adj., v.*
—adj. **1** made holy; sacred; consecrated: *A churchyard is hallowed ground.* **2** honoured or observed as holy.
—v. pt. and pp. of HALLOW.

Hal•low•een or **Hal•low•e'en** [ˌhælə'win] or [ˌhɒlou'in] *n.* the evening of October 31. The next day is Allhallows or All Saints's Day. ⟨for *Allhallow-even* < *all* + obs. *hallow* (ME *halwe* < OE *hālga* saint) + *even*[2]. See HALLOW[1].⟩

Hal•low•mas ['hæloumǝs] *or* ['hælouˌmæs] *n.* a former name of the Christian church feast of Allhallows or All Saints's Day, observed on November 1.

Hall•statt ['hɑlstɑt] *or* ['hɒlstɑt] *adj.* having to do with an Iron Age culture of western and central Europe from the 9th to the 5th century B.C. ⟨< *Hallstatt,* Austria, where remains were found⟩

hal•lu•ci•nate [hə'lusəˌneit] *v.* **-nat•ed, -nat•ing.** experience hallucinations.

hal•lu•ci•na•tion [həˌlusə'neiʃən] *n.* **1** the perception of an external object that is not in fact present. Hallucination is characteristic of some mental illnesses and can be induced by hypnosis, fever, or drugs. **2** the object of such perception. **3** any false impression or notion; delusion. ⟨< L *hallucinatio, -onis* < *hallucinari* wander (of the mind), ult. < Gk. *haluein* be beside oneself; form influenced by L *vaticinari* rave⟩ **—hal'lu•ci•na•tive,** *adj.* **—hal'lu•ci•naˌto•ry,** *adj.*

hal•lu•cin•o•gen [hə'lusənədʒən] *n.* a drug or substance that produces hallucinations.

hal•lu•cin•o•gen•ic [həˌlusənə'dʒɛnɪk] *adj.* of, producing, or tending to produce, hallucinations: *hallucinogenic drugs.*

hal•lu•cin•o•sis [həˌlusə'nousɪs] *n. Psychiatry.* an abnormal state characterized by hallucinations.

hal•lux ['hæləks] *n., pl.* **hal•lu•ces** ['hæljəˌsiz] **1** in humans, the big toe. **2** the first digit of an animal's hind foot. ⟨< NL⟩

hall•way ['hɒlˌwei] *n.* **1** a way to go through a building; passageway; corridor. **2** a passageway or room at the entrance of a building.

ha•lo ['heilou] *n., pl.* **-los** or **-loes;** *v.* **-loed, -lo•ing.** *—n.* **1** a series of coloured rings appearing around the sun or moon when it is seen through a cloud or ice crystals suspended in the atmosphere. The colours of the halo range from a red inner ring to a blue outer ring. Compare CORONA (def. 2), PARHELIC CIRCLE. **2** a ring or circle of light shown around the head of a saint or divine being in a painting, etc. to symbolize saintliness; nimbus. **3** a kind of splendour, glory, or glamour that surrounds an idealized person or thing: *A halo of romance surrounds King Arthur and his knights.*
—v. surround with a halo. ⟨< L *halo* < Gk. *halōs* disk, threshing floor (with reference to circular path of the oxen)⟩

halo– *combining form.* sea salt: *halophyte.* ⟨< Gk. *hals, halos* salt⟩

hal•o•bi•ont [ˌhælou'baɪɒnt] *n.* any organism that grows in a salty environment. ⟨< *halo-* + Gk. *bios* life⟩

hal•o•gen ['hælədʒən] *or* ['heilədʒən] *n. Chemistry.* any one of the chemical elements, iodine, bromine, chlorine, fluorine, and astatine, that combine directly with metals to form salts. The halogens are the most active elements. ⟨< Gk. *hals, halos* salt + E *-gen*⟩

hal•o•gen•ate ['hælədʒəˌneit], ['heilədʒəˌneit], *or* [hə'lɒdʒəˌneit] *v.* **-at•ed, -at•ing.** *Chemistry.* **1** treat with a halogen. **2** combine with a halogen.

hal•oid ['hælɔɪd] *or* ['heilɔɪd] *adj., n. Chemistry. —adj.* **1** of or like a salt. **2** formed from a halogen.
—n. halide. ⟨< Gk. *hals, halos* salt + E *-oid*⟩

hal•o•pe•ri•dol [ˌhælə'pɛrɪˌdɒl] *n.* a drug used to treat schizophrenia.

hal•o•phyte ['hæləˌfɔit] *n.* a plant growing in salty soil.

hal•o•pro•gin [ˌhælə'proudʒɪn] *n.* a drug used as a cream to treat certain fungal skin conditions.

hal•o•thane ['hælə,θein] *n.* a non-explosive, volatile liquid, the vapour of which is inhaled to produce general anesthesia. *Formula:* $C_2HBrClF_3$ ⟨< *halo-* + *(e)th(er)* + *-ane*⟩

halt[1] [hɒlt] *v., n., interj.* —*v.* **1** stop for a time. **2** cause to stop for a time.
—*n.* a stop for a time; stopping.
call a halt (to), **a** order a stop. **b** cause something to stop.
—*interj.* a command to stop or come to a halt. ⟨< F *halte* < G *halt* < *halten* stop, hold⟩

halt[2] [hɒlt] *v., adj., n.* —*v.* **1** be in doubt; hesitate; waver: *Shyness made her halt as she talked.* **2** be faulty or imperfect: *A poor argument halts.* **3** *Archaic.* be lame or crippled; limp.
—*adj. Archaic.* lame; crippled; limping.
—*n.* **1** *Archaic.* lameness; crippled condition; limping walk. **2 the halt,** persons who halt, limp, or hesitate. ⟨OE *healt,* adj., *haltian,* v.⟩ —**'halt•ing•ly,** *adv.*

hal•ter[1] ['hɒltər] *n., v.* —*n.* **1** a headstall with an attached strap or rope for leading a horse, cow, etc. **2** a rope for hanging a convicted criminal; noose. **3** death by hanging. **4** a woman's top, consisting of a front bodice fastened behind at the neck and at the back or waist, leaving the arms, shoulders, most of the back, and, sometimes, the midriff bare. **5** *(adjl.)* designating a dress neckline or bodice like this.
—*v.* put a halter on (an animal) or tie (an animal) with a halter. ⟨OE *hælftre*⟩

hal•ter[2] ['hɒltər] *n., pl.* **hal•te•res** [hæl'tiriz] the rudimentary hind wing of a dipterous insect such as a mosquito or fly.

hal•vah or **hal•va** ['hɑlvə] *or* [hɑl'vɑ] *n.* a confection of ground sesame seeds and honey, etc. ⟨ult. < Arabic *halwa*⟩

halve [hæv] *v.* **halved, halv•ing. 1** divide into two equal parts; share equally: *The two girls agreed to halve expenses on their trip.* **2** reduce to half: *The new machine halves the time of doing the work by hand.* ⟨< *half*⟩
☛ *Hom.* HAVE.

halves [hævz] *n.* pl. of HALF.
by halves, a not completely; partly. **b** in a half-hearted way.
go halves, share equally.

hal•yard ['hæljərd] *n.* on a ship, a rope or tackle used to raise or lower a sail, yard, flag, etc. Also, **halliard.** ⟨ME *hallyer* < *hale*[2]; form influenced by *yard*[2]⟩

ham [hæm] *n., v.* **hammed, ham•ming.** —*n.* **1** salted and smoked meat from the upper part of a pig's hind leg. **2** the upper part of an animal's hind leg, used for food: *a whole ham.* See PORK for picture. **3** Often, **hams,** *pl.* the back of the thigh; thigh and buttock. **4** the part of the leg behind the knee.
5 *Informal.* **a** an actor who exaggerates his or her speeches, gestures, etc. in a play or film; one who overacts. **b** clumsy or exaggerated acting. **c** any person who behaves or poses in an exaggerated way before an audience, photographer, etc.
6 *Informal.* an amateur radio operator.
—*v. Informal.* exaggerate (a dramatic part) or behave in an exaggerated manner; overact. ⟨OE *hamm* bend of the knee⟩

ham•a•dry•ad [ˌhæmə'draɪəd] *or* [ˌhæmə'draɪæd] *n.* **1** *Greek and Roman mythology.* one of a class of wood nymphs, each inhabiting a tree of which she was the spirit, and dying when the tree died. **2** KING COBRA. **3** hamadryas. ⟨< L < Gk. *Hamadryas, -adis* < *hama* together (with) + *drys* tree⟩

ham•a•dry•as [ˌhæmə'draɪəs] *n.* a baboon (*Papio hamadryas*) of the savanna regions of S Arabia and NE Africa, the adult male having a grey coat with a long mane extending from the head to the middle of the back. The hamadryas, also called **sacred baboon,** was regarded as sacred by the ancient Egyptians.

ha•ma•te bone ['heimeit] a wedge-shaped bone of the carpus.

Ha•mat•sa [hə'mætsə] *n. Cdn.* a member of the Cannibal Society of the Kwakiutl people, who pretend to eat human flesh.

ham•burg•er ['hæm,bɜrgər] *n.* **1** ground beef. **2** this meat shaped into flat cakes and fried or broiled, especially when served in a split roll. Also, **hamburg.** ⟨< G *Hamburger* pertaining to Hamburg⟩

Hamburg steak or **hamburg steak** HAMBURGER (def. 1).

hame [heim] *n.* either of two curved pieces on either side of the collar in a horse's harness. The traces are fastened to the hames. See HARNESS for picture. ⟨OE *hama* covering⟩

Ham•ite ['hæməit] *n.* a member of various peoples in N and E Africa. ⟨< *Ham,* in the Bible, a son of Noah⟩

Ham•it•ic [hæ'mɪtɪk] *or* [hə'mɪtɪk] *adj.* **1** of or having to do with the Hamites. **2** of or having to do with a group of languages in N and E Africa, including ancient Egyptian, Berber, Ethiopian, etc.

ham•let ['hæmlɪt] *n.* a small group of houses together with a few businesses and services such as stores and a post office, situated in the country and having no fixed boundaries. A hamlet is usually smaller than a village and has no local government of its own. ⟨< OF *hamelet,* dim. of *hamel* village < Gmc. Akin to HOME.⟩

ham•mer ['hæmər] *n., v.* —*n.* **1** a tool with a metal head and a handle, used to drive nails and beat metal into shape. See CLAW HAMMER for picture. **2** a machine in which a heavy block of metal is used for beating, striking, etc.: *a steam hammer, trip hammer.* **3** a small mallet used by auctioneers to indicate by a rap the sale of an article. **4** one of the padded mallets for striking the string of a piano. **5** a lever with a hard head for striking a bell, as in a clock. **6** the part of the firing mechanism of a gun that is released by the tripper so that it strikes the percussion cap of a cartridge or pushes the firing pin and explodes the charge. **7** the malleus of the ear. See EAR[1] for picture. **8** *Track and field.* a metal ball attached to a length of steel wire with a handle on the other end by which it is twirled around in a circle and thrown for distance. **9** anything shaped or used like a hammer.
come or **go under the hammer,** be sold at auction.
hammer and tongs, with all one's force and strength: *The two girls fought hammer and tongs.*
under the hammer, for sale at an auction.
—*v.* **1** drive, hit, or work with a hammer. **2** beat into shape with a hammer. **3** fasten by using a hammer. **4** beat again and again: *He hammered on the door with his fist.* **5** force by many efforts.
6 work (something) out with much effort.
hammer away, a work hard; keep working: *She hammered away at her homework. He hammered away till the job was done.* **b** keep nagging; badger: *He hammered away at his mother till he got what he wanted.*
hammer out, a beat into shape with a hammer. **b** flatten or spread with a hammer. **c** remove with a hammer. **d** work (something) out with much effort. **e** make clear by much thinking or talking: *The girls finally hammered out the plans for their clubhouse.* ⟨OE *hamor*⟩ —**'ham•mer•er,** *n.* —**'ham•mer,like,** *adj.*

hammer and sickle the former Soviet emblem of a crossed hammer and sickle, standing for the labourer and the farmer, that symbolized Russian communism.

ham•mer•head ['hæmər,hɛd] *n.* any of a genus (*Sphyrna*) of sharks found in warm and temperate seas throughout the world, having a broad, flattened head resembling a double-headed hammer or a broad shovel. The hammerheads constitute the family Sphyrnidae.

ham•mer•less ['hæmərlɪs] *adj.* **1** having no hammer. **2** of firearms, having no visible hammer. A hammerless pistol has its hammer covered.

hammer lock *Wrestling.* a hold in which an opponent's arm is twisted and held behind the opponent's back.

ham•mer•toe ['hæmər,tou] *n.* **1** a toe with a deformity that causes the joints to be permanently bent. **2** the deformity itself.

ham•mock ['hæmək] *n.* a swinging bed or couch made of canvas, netted cord, etc. that is suspended at both ends. ⟨< Sp. *hamaca* < Carib⟩

ham•per[1] ['hæmpər] *v.* hold back; hinder: *The unwieldy bundle severely hampered his progress.* ⟨ME *hampre(n)*; origin uncertain⟩

ham•per[2] ['hæmpər] *n.* a large container, often a wicker basket, usually having a cover: *a picnic hamper, a clothes hamper.* ⟨var. of *hanaper*⟩

ham•ster ['hæmstər] *n.* any of various Old World rodents (family Cricetidae) having a short tail, stocky body, and large cheek pouches. Hamsters are often kept as cage pets. ⟨< G⟩

ham•string ['hæm,strɪŋ] *n., v.* **-strung** or *(rare)* **-stringed, -string•ing.** —*n.* **1** in a human being, one of the tendons at the back of the knee. **2** in a four-footed animal, the great tendon at the back of the hock.
—*v.* **1** cripple by cutting the hamstring. **2** cripple; disable; destroy the activity, efficiency, etc. of.

ham•strung ['hæm,strʌŋ] *v.* pt. and pp. of HAMSTRING.

ham•u•lus ['hæmjələs] *n., pl.* **-li** [-,li] *or* [-,laɪ]. *Biology.* a small hooklike formation. ⟨< L dim. of *hamus* hook⟩

han•a•per ['hænəpər] *n.* a basket for documents. ⟨< OF *hanapier* < *hanap* cup < Gmc.⟩

hand [hænd] *n., v., adj.* —*n.* **1** the end part of the arm; part that a person grasps and holds things with. **2** the end of any limb that grasps, holds, or clings. We call a monkey's feet hands. **3** something resembling a hand in shape, appearance, or use: *The hands of a clock or watch show the time.* **4** a hired worker who uses his or her hands: *a factory hand, a farm hand.* **5** a member of a ship's crew; sailor. **6** Usually, **hands,** *pl.*
a possession; control: *The property is no longer in my hands.*
b care or charge: *The baby-sitter was glad when the sick child was taken off his hands.* **7** a part or share in doing something: *She had no hand in the matter.* **8** side: *At her left hand stood two men.* **9** one's style of handwriting: *He writes in a clear hand.* **10** a person's signature. **11** skill; ability: *The artist's work showed a master's hand.* **12** a person, with reference to action, skill, or ability: *She is a great hand at thinking up new games.* **13** a round of applause or clapping: *The crowd gave the winner a big hand.* **14** a promise of marriage. **15** a measure used in giving the height of horses, etc.; the breadth of a hand, about 10 cm: *This big horse is 18 hands high.* **16** *Card games.* **a** the cards held by a player in one round of a card game. **b** one round of a card game. **c** a player in a card game.
all hands, a all sailors of a ship's crew. **b** *Informal.* all members of a group.
at first hand, from direct knowledge or experience.
at hand, a within reach; near; close. **b** ready.
at second hand, from a source other than the original source: *The story she had heard at second hand proved to be an exaggeration.*
at the hand (or **hands**) **of,** from (a person, as giver, doer, etc.): *We have received many favours at her hands.*
bear a hand, help.
by hand, by using the hands, not machinery.
change hands, pass from one person to another: *During the sale a lot of money changed hands.*
clean hands, freedom from crime or dishonesty.
eat out of (someone's) **hand,** follow one's ideas, leadership, etc.; submit to someone's authority.
force (someone's) **hand, a** make a person do something. **b** make a person show what he or she is going to do.
from hand to mouth, without being able to put something aside for the future: *During the long strike, many families lived from hand to mouth.*
give a hand, assist; help: *Please give me a hand with this trunk.*
hand in (or **and**) **glove (with),** intimate; in close relations.
hand in hand, a holding hands. **b** together.
hands down, easily: *She won the contest hands down.*
hand to hand, close together; at close quarters: *to fight hand to hand.*
have (one's) **hands full,** be very busy; be able to do no more; have as much to do as one can manage.
in hand, a under control. **b** in possession. **c** in progress; being done.
join hands, a become partners. **b** marry.
keep (one's) **hand in,** keep up one's skill; keep in practice.
lay hands on, a seize; take; get. **b** arrest. **c** attack; harm. **d** bless by touching with the hands.
lend a hand, help or assist: *He asked his brother to lend a hand with the chores.*
on hand, a within reach; near; close. **b** ready; in stock: *The supermarket has lots of oranges on hand.* **c** present: *I will be on hand again tomorrow.*
on the one hand, considering this side; from this point of view: *On the one hand, I feel that to buy this house would be a good investment in the long run.*
on the other hand, considering the other side of the question or argument; from the opposite point of view: *I want the bicycle very much; on the other hand, I can't afford to buy it.*
out of hand, a out of control: *The angry crowd soon got out of hand.* **b** at once; without hesitation: *The boy was expelled out of hand.* **c** finished; done with.
show (one's) **hand,** reveal one's real intentions.
sit on (one's) **hands,** *Informal.* **a** applaud feebly; show little enthusiasm for a play, performance, etc. **b** do nothing.
take a hand (at), take part or make an attempt: *It looked so interesting that he was tempted to take a hand himself.*
take in hand, a bring under control: *That child should be taken in hand by someone.* **b** start to deal with: *The supervisor promised to take the matter in hand.*
tie (someone's) **hands,** make someone unable to do something.
to hand, a within reach; near; close. **b** in one's possession.
try (one's) **hand at,** try to do; test one's ability at: *After trying his hand at politics, he soon went back into business.*
turn (one's) **hand to,** work at.
wait on (someone) **hand and foot,** serve diligently; do everything for.
wash (one's) **hands of,** have no more to do with; refuse to be responsible for.
—*v.* **1** give with the hand; pass; pass along: *Please hand me the butter.* **2** help with the hand: *The hotel doorman handed the lady into her car.*
hand down, a pass along. **b** *Law.* announce (a decision, opinion, etc.).
hand in, give or pass to a person in authority: *The tests were handed in to the teacher.*
hand it to, *Informal.* acknowledge as commendable or superior: *You've got to hand it to him; he's quite a salesman.*
hand on, pass along: *She read the note and handed it on to the person next to her.*
hand out, give out; distribute: *The storekeeper handed out free suckers.*
hand over, give to another; deliver: *When John asked for his book, I handed it over.*
—*adj.* of, for, by, or in the hand. ⟨OE⟩ —**'hand,like,** *adj.*

hand axe a stone axe of paleolithic times.

hand•bag ['hænd,bæg] *n.* **1** a small bag for money, keys, cosmetics, etc.; purse. **2** a small travelling bag to hold clothes, etc.

hand•ball ['hænd,bɒl] *n.* **1** a game in which two or four players use their hands, usually gloved, to hit a small, hard, rubber ball against a wall or board or against the walls of a court. **2** the ball used in this game.

hand•bar•row ['hænd,bærou] *or* ['hænd,bɛrou] *n.* **1** a frame with two handles at each end by which it is carried. **2** handcart.

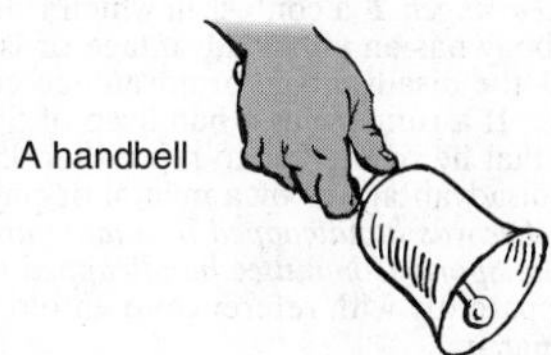
A handbell

hand•bell ['hænd,bɛl] *n.* a bell with a handle, to be rung by hand, especially one of a tuned set used for musical performances.

hand•bill ['hænd,bɪl] *n.* a printed notice, announcement, advertisement, etc. to be handed out to people.

hand•blown ['hænd,bloun] *adj.* of glassware, created as separate pieces by a glassblower.

hand•book ['hænd,bʊk] *n.* **1** a small book of directions or reference, especially in some field of study; manual: *a handbook of engineering.* **2** a guidebook for tourists. **3** a book for recording bets.

hand brake a brake operated by a manual lever. The emergency brake on some automobiles is a hand brake.

hand•breadth ['hænd,brɛdθ] *or* ['hænd,brɛtθ] *n.* the breadth of a hand, used as a measure. It varies from about 6 to 10 cm.

hand•car ['hænd,kɑr] *n. Cdn.* a small car used on railway tracks by maintenance people and driven by a hand lever that is pumped up and down.

hand•cart ['hænd,kɑrt] *n.* a small cart pulled or pushed by hand.

hand•clap ['hænd,klæp] *n.* a striking together of the hands to signal, mark rhythm, applaud, etc.

hand•craft ['hænd,kræft] *n., v.* —*n.* handicraft.
—*v.* make by hand or handicraft: *She handcrafted the furniture.*

A pair of handcuffs

hand•cuff ['hænd,kʌf] *n., v.* —*n.* Usually, **handcuffs,** *pl.* a device to secure a prisoner, usually consisting of a pair of metal

rings or clasps joined by a short chain, that are fastened and locked about the wrists.
—*v.* put handcuffs on: *They handcuffed him to a post.*

-handed *combining form.* **1** having a hand or hands. **2** having or using a certain kind or number of hands: *left-handed, a two-handed stroke.*

hand•ed•ness ['hændɪdnɪs] *n.* preference for using the right or left hand.

hand•ful ['hænd,fʊl] *n., pl.* **-fuls. 1** as much or as many as the hand can hold. **2** a small number or quantity. **3** *Informal.* a person or thing that is hard to handle or control: *That girl is quite a handful.*

hand glass 1 a magnifying glass. **2** a mirror with a handle.

hand grenade a small bomb designed to be thrown by hand.

hand•grip ['hænd,grɪp] *n.* **1** a grip or grasping of the hand, used in greeting. **2** a handle.
come to handgrips, get into a hand-to-hand fight.

hand•gun ['hænd,gʌn] *n.* a firearm that is held and fired with one hand. A revolver is a handgun.

hand–held ['hænd 'hɛld] *adj.* of an appliance, machine, etc., designed to be operated while being held in the hand: *a hand-held electric mixer.*

hand•hold ['hænd,hould] *n.* a place to put the hands for holding on, such as in a climb.

hand•i•cap ['hændi,kæp] *or* ['hændə,kæp] *n., v.* **-capped, -cap•ping.** —*n.* **1** something that puts a person at a disadvantage; hindrance; mental or physical defect: *A sore throat is a handicap to a singer.* **2** a contest in which rules are applied to ensure that nobody has an unfair advantage or is at an unfair disadvantage. **3** the disadvantage or advantage given in such a contest or game. If a runner has a handicap of 5 m in a 100 m dash, it means that he or she has to run either 95 m or 105 m.
—*v.* **1** put at a disadvantage as by a mental or physical defect; hinder: *The pitcher was handicapped by a lame arm.* **2** give a handicap to: *The Sports Committee handicapped me 5 m.* ⟨for *hand in cap*; apparently with reference to an old game⟩
—'hand•i,cap•per, *n.*

hand•i•capped ['hændi,kæpt] *or* ['hændə,kæpt] *adj., v.* —*adj.* having a handicap.
—*v.* pt. and pp. of HANDICAP.

hand•i•craft ['hændi,kræft] *or* ['hændə,kræft] *n.* **1** skilful use of the hands: *The design on the leather purse showed fine handicraft.* **2** a trade or art requiring skill with the hands: *Basket weaving is a handicraft.* **3** an article made by hand, especially one requiring skill or imagination to make: *The display of handicrafts included wooden ware, pottery, and children's clothes.* ⟨alteration of *handcraft*, patterned after *handiwork*⟩

hand•i•crafts•man ['hændi,kræftsmən] *or* ['hændə,kræftsmən] *n., pl.* **-men.** a person skilled with the hands in a trade or art; craftsman.

hand•i•work ['hændi,wɜrk] *or* ['hændə,wɜrk] *n.* **1** work done with the hands. **2** work that a person has done himself or herself. **3** the result of a person's action. ⟨OE *handgeweorc* handwork⟩

hand•ker•chief ['hæŋkərtʃɪf] *or* ['hæŋkər,tʃif] *n., pl.* **-chiefs. 1** a piece of fine cotton, linen, silk, etc., generally square, used especially for wiping the nose. **2** kerchief. ⟨< *hand* + *kerchief*⟩

hand–knit ['hænd 'nɪt] *adj.* knitted by hand.

han•dle ['hændəl] *n., v.* **-dled, -dling.** —*n.* **1** the part of a thing made to be held or grasped by the hand. **2** a chance; opportunity; occasion: *Don't let your conduct give any handle for gossip.* **3** *Slang.* a name or title.
fly off the handle, *Slang.* get angry or excited; lose one's temper or self-control.
handle to (one's) **name,** *Slang.* a title of nobility, etc.
—*v.* **1** touch, feel, hold, or move with the hand; use the hands on: *Don't handle the ornaments; they're very delicate.* **2** manage; direct; control: *The captain handles the soldiers well.* **3** behave or perform in a certain way when driven, managed, directed, etc.: *This car handles easily.* **4** deal with; treat: *The boy handled his kitten roughly.* **5** deal in; trade in: *The store handles meat and groceries.* ⟨OE *handle* < *hand* hand⟩

han•dle•bars ['hændəl,bɑrz] *n.pl.* the bars, usually curved, in front of the rider, by which a bicycle, etc. is guided.

-handled *combining form.* having a —— handle: *a black-handled pot = a pot having a black handle.*

han•dler ['hændlər] *n.* **1** a person who or thing that handles. **2** a person who helps to train a boxer, or who acts as that boxer's second during a boxing match. **3** a person who guides a politician, etc. **4** a person who shows dogs or cats, etc. in a contest.

hand•line ['hænd,laɪn] *n.* a fishing line held by hand without a rod or pole.

hand•lin•er ['hænd,laɪnər] *n. Cdn.* a fisher who uses a handline.

hand•lin•ing ['hænd,laɪnɪŋ] *n. Cdn.* fishing with handlines.

hand•log ['hænd,lɒg] *v.* **-logged, -log•ging.** *Cdn.* engage in logging using hand tools only, such as axes, peaveys, and jacks.

hand•made ['hænd'meid] *adj.* made by hand, not machinery; not machine-made.

hand•maid ['hænd,meid] *n.* **1** a female servant. **2** a female attendant. Also, **handmaiden.**

hand–me–down ['hænd mi ,daʊn] *n., adj. Informal.* —*n.* **1** a second-hand article, especially a garment, passed from one person to another. **2** any cheap, badly tailored coat, suit, etc.
—*adj.* having been passed on or handed down.

hand•off ['hænd,ɒf] *n. U.S. football.* a play in which a player, usually a back, hands the ball to a teammate.

hand organ a large music box that is made to play tunes by turning a crank.

hand•out ['hænd,ʌut] *n.* **1** food or money handed out: *The beggar was given a handout.* **2** a news story or piece of publicity issued to the press by a business organization, government agency, etc. **3** a set of duplicated notes issued to students in connection with their courses, to people attending a public lecture, etc.

hand–picked ['hænd 'pɪkt] *adj.* **1** picked by hand. **2** carefully selected: *a hand-picked successor.*

hand•rail ['hænd,reil] *n.* a railing used as a guard or support on a stairway, platform, etc.

hand•saw ['hænd,sɒ] *n.* a saw used with one hand and not motorized.

hand•sel ['hænsəl] *n., v.* **-selled** or **-seled, -sel•ling** or **-sel•ing.** —*n.* **1** a gift given in token of good wishes, as at New Year's, to one entering a new job or house, etc. **2** a first payment; the first money taken in by a dealer in the morning, or on opening a new store. **3** a first experience of anything; foretaste.
—*v.* **1** give a handsel to. **2** inaugurate. **3** be the first to use, try, taste, etc. Also, **hansel.** ⟨OE *handselen* giving of the hand (i.e., to confirm a bargain)⟩

hand•set ['hænd,sɛt] *n.* a telephone that has the receiver, dial or keypad, and mouthpiece in the same unit.

hand•shake ['hænd,ʃeik] *n.* a clasping and shaking of hands by two people as a sign of friendship when meeting or parting, or to seal a bargain.

hand•some ['hænsəm] *adj.* **-som•er, -som•est. 1** good-looking; pleasing in appearance. **2** fairly large; considerable: *Ten thousand dollars is a handsome amount of money.* **3** generous: *a handsome gift.* **4** gracious; well-mannered. ⟨ME *handsom* easy to handle, ready at hand < *hand* + *-some*[1]⟩ **—'hand•some•ly,** *adv.* **—'hand•some•ness,** *n.*
☛ *Syn.* **1.** See note at BEAUTIFUL.
☛ *Hom.* HANSOM.

hands–on ['hænz 'ɒn] *adj.* making use of personal, especially physical, involvement: *A hands-on learning process is better than theory.*

hand•spike ['hænd,spəik] *n.* a bar used as a lever, especially on a ship.

hand•spring ['hænd,sprɪŋ] *n.* a somersault made from a standing position, in which the person comes down first on the hands, turning the body forward or backward in a full circle, and landing again on the feet.

hand–stand ['hænd ,stænd] *n.* an act or feat of supporting the body on the hands alone, while the trunk and legs are stretched in the air.

hand–to–hand ['hænd tə 'hænd] *adj. or adv.* close together; at close quarters: *a hand-to-hand fight.*

hand–to–mouth ['hænd tə 'mʌuθ] *adj.* having nothing to spare; being unable to save or provide for the future; not thrifty.

hand–tooled ['hænd 'tuld] *adj.* ornamented by handwork, not by machinery.

hand•work ['hænd,wɜrk] *n.* work done by hand, not by machinery.

hand•wov•en ['hænd'wouvən] *adj.* **1** woven on a loom operated by hand. **2** of basketwork, etc., woven by hand.

hand•writ•ing ['hænd,rəitɪŋ] *n.* **1** writing done by hand; writing done with pen, pencil, etc. **2** a manner or style of writing: *He recognized his mother's handwriting on the envelope.*
handwriting on the wall, a in the Bible, a cryptic handwriting seen by Belshazzar, King of Babylon, on the wall of his palace, which Daniel interpreted as a prophecy of the fall of Babylon. **b** a portent of doom.
see or **read the handwriting on the wall, a** perceive that an institution, order, way of life, etc. is coming to an end. **b** see things as they really are.

hand•writ•ten ['hænd,rɪtən] *adj.* written by hand, not typed or printed.

hand•y ['hændi] *adj.* **hand•i•er, hand•i•est. 1** easy to reach or use; saving work; useful; convenient: *handy shelves, a handy tool.* **2** skilful with the hands: *She's handy with tools.* **3** easy to handle or manage.
come in handy, be useful. **—'hand•i•ly,** *adv.* **—'hand•i•ness,** *n.*

hand•y•man ['hændi,mæn] *n., pl.* **-men. 1** someone who does odd jobs. **2** someone who is good at fixing things.

hang [hæŋ] *v.* **hung** or (for defs. 3, 4) **hanged, hang•ing;** *n.* *—v.* **1** fasten or be fastened to something above. **2** fasten or be fastened so as to swing or turn freely: *to hang a door on its hinges.* **3** put or be put to death by hanging with a rope around the neck: *He was hanged several weeks after being sentenced.* **4** die by hanging. **5** cover or decorate with things that hang: *to hang a window with curtains. The walls were hung with pictures.* **6** bend down; let droop: *He hung his head in shame.* **7** *Computer technology.* of a computer system, program, etc., stop working suddenly and inexplicably. **8** attach (wallpaper, pictures, etc.) to walls. **9** depend. **10** be wearisome or tedious: *Time hangs on her hands.* **11** hold fast; cling. **12** be doubtful or undecided; hesitate; waver. **13** keep (a jury) from making a decision or reaching a verdict. One member can hang a jury by refusing to agree with the others. **14** loiter; linger: *Don't hang about!* **15** hover.
hang around or **about, a** loiter in a particular place, or in the company of a particular person, but with no definite purpose in mind. **b** wait near: *There's a small crowd hanging around the door.*
hang back, be unwilling to go forward; be hesitant.
hang in, *Informal.* be persistent; not give up.
hang in the balance, be undecided.
hang it (all)! an expression of annoyance.
hang on, a hold tight. **b** be unwilling to let go, stop, or leave. **c** depend on. **d** consider or listen to very carefully: *She hung on the teacher's every word.* **e** wait, especially on the telephone.
hang one's head, be ashamed.
hang onto, a try to keep control or possession of: *The dying woman hung onto life for several days.* **b** depend for comfort or support on: *Hang onto this thought, it may help you.*
hang out, a show by hanging outside. **b** lean out. **c** *Slang.* live; stay. **d** *Slang.* loiter habitually (*at* or *in* a place).
hang over, a be about to happen to; threaten: *The possibility of being punished hung over her for days.* **b** *Informal.* remain from an earlier time or condition.
hang together, a remain united. **b** be coherent or consistent: *The story does not hang together.*
hang up, a put on a hook, peg, etc. **b** put (a telephone receiver) back in place. **c** hold back; delay; detain. **d** *Cdn. Lumbering.* **a** (*usually as p.p.*) of the movement of logs, slow down or stop en route from forest to deck, water, or mill. **b** of a tree or log, become caught on a snag while being felled or yarded.
—n. the way that something hangs: *I don't like the hang of the skirt.*
get the hang of, *Informal.* **a** get the knack of; discover how to operate, do, etc.: *She had never used a calculator before, but it didn't take her long to get the hang of it.* **b** understand the meaning or significance of: *I didn't quite get the hang of what he said.*
give or **care a hang,** *Informal.* care or be concerned about (*usually used with a negative*): *He doesn't give a hang about anybody.* ⟨OE *hōn* (with past *hēng*) suspend, and OE *hangian* be suspended, blended with ON *hengja* suspend⟩ **—'hang•a•ble,** *adj.*
☛ *Usage.* **Hanged, hung.** In formal English, the preferred form of the past tense and past participle for defs. 3 and 4 only is **hanged**: *The murderer was hanged.* In informal English, however, **hung** is often used: *He was hung for his crimes.*

hang•ar ['hæŋər] *n.* **1** a shed for aircraft. **2** a shed. ⟨< F < Med.L *angarium* shed for shoeing horses, ? < Gmc.⟩
☛ *Hom.* HANGER.

hang•bird ['hæŋ,bɜrd] *n.* any of various birds that build a hanging nest, especially the Baltimore oriole.

hang•dog ['hæŋ,dɒg] *adj.* ashamed; sneaking; degraded: *a hangdog look.*

hang•er ['hæŋər] *n.* **1** a person who hangs things. A paperhanger puts on wallpaper. **2** a tool or machine that hangs things. **3** anything on which something else is hung: *a coat hanger.* **4** a loop, ring, etc. attached to something to hang it up by. **5** a kind of short, light sword formerly worn by sailors on their belts.
☛ *Hom.* HANGAR.

hang•er–on ['hæŋər 'ɒn] *n., pl.* **hang•ers-on. 1** a follower; dependent. **2** an undesirable follower. **3** a person who often goes to a place.

hang–glide ['hæŋ ,glaɪd] *v.* **-id•ed, -id•ing.** take part in the sport of hang-gliding.

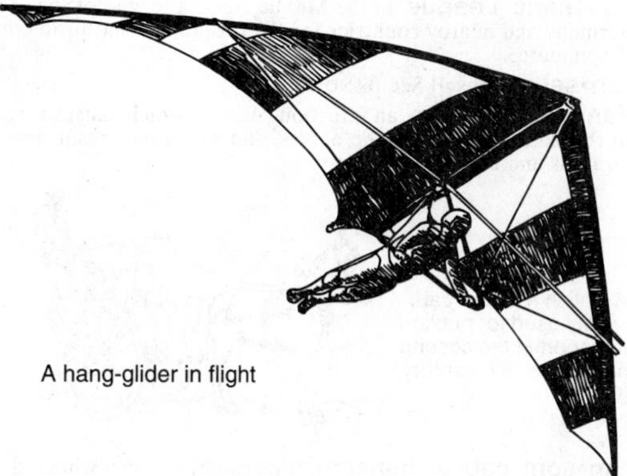

A hang-glider in flight

hang–glid•er ['hæŋ ,glaɪdər] *n.* **1** a large, flat, usually delta-shaped motorless aircraft with an attached harness or seat, designed to carry a person or two people through the air for a short while. The pilot runs into the wind toward the edge of a cliff and soars down to earth, suspended from the kite. Various controls are possible. **2** a person who engages in hang-gliding.

hang–glid•ing ['hæŋ ,glaɪdɪŋ] *n.* the sport of gliding through the air while suspended from a hang-glider.

hang•ing ['hæŋɪŋ] *n., adj.,v.* *—n.* **1** death by hanging with a rope around the neck. **2** Often, **hangings,** *pl.* something that hangs from a wall, bed, etc: *Curtains and valances are hangings.* *—adj.* **1** deserving to be punished by hanging: *a hanging crime.* **2** fastened to something above. **3** leaning over or down. **4** located on a height or steep slope.
—v. ppr. of HANG.

hang•man ['hæŋmən] *or* ['hæŋ,mæn] *n., pl.* **-men.** a man who hangs criminals who have been sentenced to death by hanging.

hang•nail ['hæŋ,neil] *n.* a bit of skin that hangs partly loose near a fingernail. ⟨alteration of *agnail*, OE *angnægl* (< *ang-* compressed, painful + *nægl* nail, corn), under the influence of *hang*⟩

hang•out ['hæŋ,ʌut] *n. Slang.* **1** a place one lives in or goes to often. **2** a rendezvous, especially for criminals.

hang•o•ver ['hæŋ,ouvər] *n.* **1** *Informal.* something that remains from an earlier time or condition. **2** *Slang.* a condition characterized by headache and nausea resulting from consumption of too much alcohol the previous night.

hang–up ['hæŋ ,ʌp] *n.* **1** *Slang.* a personal or emotional difficulty; an obsession or inhibition. **2** *Cdn. Lumbering.* a log caught on a snag or obstruction when being transported.

hank [hæŋk] *n.* **1** a coil; loop. **2** a loop or coil of yarn, especially one containing a definite length. ⟨< ON *hönk*⟩

han•ker ['hæŋkər] *v.* wish; crave (*used with* **for** *or* **after**). ⟨origin uncertain⟩

han•ker•ing ['hæŋkərɪŋ] *n., v.* *—n.* a longing; craving: *I have a hankering for a large, juicy steak.*
—v. ppr. of HANKER.

hank•y ['hæŋki] *n., pl.* **hank•ies.** *Informal.* handkerchief. Also, **hankie.**

hank•y–pank•y ['hæŋki 'pæŋki] *n. Slang.* underhand or questionable dealings or behaviour; dishonest or illicit goings-on: *He denied that there was any hanky-panky involved in his getting the contract.*

Han•o•ve•ri•an [ˌhænəˈvirjən] *adj., n. —adj.* **1** of or having to do with Hanover, Germany. **2** of or having to do with Hanover, the English royal house from 1714 to 1901.
—n. **1** a native or inhabitant of Hanover. **2** a supporter of the House of Hanover.

Han•sard [ˈhænsərd] *n.* the printed record of the proceedings of the Canadian or British Parliaments. ⟨after Luke *Hansard* (1752-1828), first compiler⟩

hanse [hæns] *n.* in the Middle Ages, a merchant guild of a town. ⟨ME < OF < MHG *hanse* merchants' guild < OHG *hansa* band⟩

Han•se•at•ic [ˌhænziˈætɪk] *adj.* of or having to do with the Hanseatic League.

Hanseatic League in the Middle Ages, a league of towns in Germany and nearby countries for the promotion and protection of commerce.

han•sel [ˈhænsəl] See HANDSEL.

Hansen's disease an infectious disease which causes sores on the skin and injury to the nerves, and which may result in paralysis and deformity; leprosy.

A British hansom cab, widely used for public transport in the second half of the 19th century

han•som cab or **hansom** [ˈhænsəm] *n.* a two-wheeled cab for two passengers drawn by one horse. ⟨after Joseph *Hansom*, an early designer of such cabs⟩
☛ *Hom.* HANDSOME.

han•ta•vi•rus [ˈhæntəˌvaɪrəs] *n.* a family of viruses responsible for Korean hemorrhagic fever (kidney failure).

Ha•nuk•kah or **Ha•nuk•ka** [ˈhɑnəkə] *or* [ˈhɑnʊˌkɑ]; *Hebrew,* [ˈxɑnʊˌkɑ] *n.* the Feast of Dedication or the Feast of Lights, an eight-day Jewish festival falling in December. Also, **Chanukah** or **Chanukkah.** ⟨< Hebrew *hannukah* dedication⟩

hao [haʊ] *n.* a unit of currency in Vietnam, equal to 1/10 of a dong.
☛ *Hom.* HOW.

hap [hæp] *n., v.* **happed, hap•ping.** *Archaic. —n.* chance; luck.
—v. happen. ⟨ME < ON *happ*⟩

hap•haz•ard [ˌhæpˈhæzərd] *n., adj., adv. —n.* chance: *Events seemed to happen at haphazard.*
—adj. random; casual; not planned: *Haphazard answers are usually wrong.*
—adv. by chance; at random; casually: *She took a card haphazard from the deck.* **—ˌhapˈhaz•ard•ly,** *adv.* **—ˌhapˈhaz•ard•ness,** *n.*
☛ *Syn. adj.* See note at RANDOM.

hap•less [ˈhæplɪs] *adj.* unlucky; unfortunate. **—ˈhap•less•ly,** *adv.* **—ˈhap•less•ness,** *n.*

haplo– *combining form.* single; simple: *haplotype.* ⟨< Gk. *haplous* single, simple⟩

hap•loid [ˈhæplɔɪd] *adj., n. Biology. —adj.* designating a nucleus, cell, or organism possessing a single set of unpaired chromosomes. When a diploid germ cell undergoes meiosis, it becomes a haploid cell, or gamete.
—n. a haploid nucleus, cell, or organism. Compare DIPLOID. ⟨< Gk. *haploeidēs* single-formed < *haplous* single + *eidos* form.⟩

hap•lol•o•gy [hæpˈlɒlədʒi] *n.* the contraction of a word in pronunciation by leaving out a syllable that repeats a following or preceding sound. *Example*: preventive *from* preventative.

hap•lo•sis [hæpˈlousɪs] *n. Biology.* the production of a haploid chromosome group.

hap•lo•type [ˈhæpləˌtaip] *n. Genetics.* **1** a set of alleles at different gene places that are so closely linked that the alleles are usually inherited as a unit. **2** the genetic constitution of an individual with respect to the alleles present in a set of closely linked genes. ⟨< Gk. *haplous* single + *typos* figure < *typtein* to strike⟩

hap•ly [ˈhæpli] *adv. Archaic.* perhaps; by chance.

hap•pen [ˈhæpən] *v.* **1** take place; occur: *Nothing interesting happens here.* **2** be or take place by chance: *Accidents will happen.* **3** have the fortune *(to)*; chance *(to)*: *I happened to sit next to a famous hockey player.* **4** be done *(to)*; go wrong with: *Something has happened to this lock; the key won't turn.*
as it happens, by chance; as it turns out: *As it happens, I have no money with me.*
happen on or **upon, a** meet by chance. **b** find by chance: *She happened on a dime while looking for her ball.*
happen to, be the fate of; become of: *Nobody knew what happened to the last explorer.* ⟨ME *happene(n)* < *hap*⟩

hap•pen•ing [ˈhæpənɪŋ] *n., v. —n.* **1** anything that happens; event; occurrence. **2** a theatre form based on improvisation.
—v. ppr. of HAPPEN.

hap•pen•stance [ˈhæpənˌstæns] *n. Informal.* a situation or circumstance that is the result of chance: *The success of the deal was more happenstance than shrewd bargaining.*

hap•pi•ly [ˈhæpəli] *adv.* **1** in a happy manner; with pleasure, joy, and gladness: *She lives happily.* **2** luckily; fortunately: *Happily, he saved her from falling.* **3** aptly; appropriately.

hap•pi•ness [ˈhæpinɪs] *n.* **1** a being happy; gladness. **2** good luck; good fortune. **3** aptness.
☛ *Syn.* **1. Happiness,** FELICITY, BLISS = a feeling of satisfaction and pleasure. **Happiness** is the general word, applying to a feeling of contentment coming from being and doing well or of satisfaction at having got what one wanted: *His promotion brought him happiness.* **Felicity,** formal, means great or joyous happiness: *May the couple live their lives together in health and felicity.* **Bliss** suggests feeling lifted to the heights of happiness or joy: *They are in a state of bliss now that they are engaged.*

hap•py [ˈhæpi] *adj.* **-pi•er, -pi•est. 1** feeling or showing pleasure and joy; glad; pleased; contented. **2** lucky, fortunate: *By a happy chance, I found the lost money.* **3** clever and fitting; apt; successful and suitable: *a happy way of expressing an idea.* **4** much given to using —— *(used in compounds)*: *trigger-happy.* ⟨ME *happy* < *hap*⟩
☛ *Syn.* **1.** See note at GLAD.

hap•py–go–luck•y [ˈhæpi gou ˈlʌki] *adj.* taking things easily; trusting to luck.

happy hunting ground 1 paradise. **2** any pleasant place with which one is particularly associated: *He returns every summer to his happy hunting ground in California.*

Haps•burg [ˈhæpsbərg]; *German,* [ˈhapsbʊrk] *n.* a German ruling family, prominent since about 1100. The Hapsburgs were rulers of the Holy Roman Empire from 1438 to 1806, of Austria from 1804 to 1918, of Hungary from 1526 to 1918, and of Spain from 1516 to 1700. Also, **Habsburg.** ⟨< *Habsburg*, shortening of *Habichtsburg* (meaning hawk's castle), name of a castle in Aargau, Switzerland⟩

hap•ten [ˈhæptɛn] *n. Immunology.* an incomplete antigen. Also, **haptene.** ⟨< G < Gk. *haptein* fasten, touch⟩

hap•tic [ˈhæptɪk] *adj.* having to do with the sense of touch.

har•a–ki•ri [ˈhærə ˈkiri], [ˈhɛrə ˈkiri], *or* [ˈhɑrə ˈkiri] *n.* suicide committed by ripping open the abdomen with a knife, the national form of honourable suicide in Japan. Also, **hara-kari** or **hari-kari.** ⟨< Japanese < *hara* belly + *kiri* cutting⟩

ha•rangue [həˈræŋ] *n., v.* **-rangued, -rangu•ing.** *—n.* **1** a noisy speech. **2** a long, pompous speech.
—v. **1** address in a harangue. **2** deliver a harangue. ⟨ME < OF *arenge* < Gmc.⟩ **—haˈrangu•er,** *n.*

har•ass [ˈhærəs], [ˈhɛrəs], *or* [həˈræs] *v.* **1** trouble by repeated attacks; harry: *Pirates harassed the villages along the coast.* **2** disturb; worry; torment. ⟨< F *harasser* < OF *harer* set dogs on⟩
☛ *Syn.* **2.** See note at WORRY.

har•ass•ment [ˈhærəsmənt], [ˈhɛrəsmənt], *or* [həˈræsmənt] *n.* **1** harassing. **2** being harassed; worry. **3** something that harasses.

har•bin•ger [ˈhɑrbɪndʒər] *n., v. —n.* one that goes ahead to announce another's coming; forerunner: *The robin is a harbinger of spring.*
—v. announce beforehand; announce. ⟨ME < OF *herbergere* provider of shelter (hence, one who goes ahead), ult. < *herberge* lodging < Gmc. Akin to HARBOUR.⟩

har•bour or **har•bor** [ˈhɑrbər] *n., v. —n.* **1** a naturally or artificially sheltered area of deep water where ships may dock or anchor. A harbour may have loading and unloading facilities for passengers and cargo. **2** any place of shelter.
—v. **1** give shelter to; give a place to hide: *It is an offence to harbour a criminal.* **2** take shelter or refuge. **3** keep or nourish in the mind: *Don't harbour unkind thoughts.* **4** be the habitat of: *This forest harbours deer and skunks.* ⟨OE *herebeorg* lodgings < *here* army + *beorg* shelter⟩ **—ˈhar•bour•er** *or* **ˈhar•bor•er,** *n.* **—ˈhar•bour•less** *or* **ˈhar•bor•less,** *adj.*
☛ *Syn. n.* **1. Harbour,** PORT[1] = place of shelter for ships. **Harbour** emphasizes shelter, and applies to a protected part of the sea, or other

large body of water, where land or breakwaters shield against wind and heavy waves: *Many yachts are lying at anchor in the harbour.* **Port** emphasizes the idea of a place to put in to land or unload at the end of a voyage, and applies particularly to a harbour where commercial ships dock for loading and unloading: *The ship arrived in port. v.* **3.** See note at CHERISH.

har•bour•age or **har•bor•age** ['hɑrbərɪdʒ] *n.* **1** a shelter for ships and boats. **2** any shelter.

harbour master or **harbor master** an officer who has charge of a harbour or port and enforces its regulations.

harbour seal or **harbor seal** a hair seal (*Phoca vitulina*) found along the northern coasts of North America, Europe, and Asia in salt waters and inland waters, having a usually light or medium brown coat with irregular, dark brown spots or streaks.

hard [hɑrd] *adj., adv. —adj.* **1** solid and firm to the touch; not soft: *Rocks are hard.* **2** firmly formed; tight: *Her muscles were hard.* **3** needing much ability, effort, or time; difficult: *a hard problem.* **4** causing much pain, trouble, care, etc.; severe: *a hard illness.* **5** stern; unfeeling: *a hard master.* **6** not pleasant; harsh: *a hard face, a hard laugh.* **7** acting or done with energy, persistence, etc.: *a hard worker.* **8** vigorous; violent: *a hard storm, a hard run.* **9** containing mineral salts that interfere with the action of soap: *hard water.* **10** containing much alcohol: *hard liquor.* **11** of wheat, having a hard kernel and high gluten content. **12** *Informal.* real and significant: *hard facts, hard news.* **13** *Phonics.* of the pronunciation of *c* and *g* as [k] (*corn*) and [g] (*get*) and not as in *city* and *gem.* Compare SOFT (def. 11). **14** of a drug, seriously addictive and harmful to health: *hard drugs such as heroin and cocaine.* Compare SOFT (def. 14). **15** of currency, fully backed by gold or silver and therefore stable and high in exchange value. Compare SOFT (def. 15).
hard put (to it), in much difficulty or trouble; hard pressed.
hard up, *Informal.* needing money or anything very badly: *He is always hard up the day before he is paid. It rained throughout our holiday, and we were hard up for things to do.*
—adv. **1** so as to be hard, solid, or firm: *frozen hard.* **2** firmly; tightly: *Don't hold hard.* **3** with difficulty: *to breathe hard.* **4** so as to cause trouble, pain, care, etc.: harshly; severely: *taxes that bear hard upon us.* **5** with steady effort or much energy: *Try hard.* **6** with vigour or violence: *She hit hard.* **7** earnestly; intently: *look hard at a person.* **8** to the extreme limit; fully.
go hard with, cause severe trouble or pain to: *It will go hard with the murderer when she is caught.*
hard by, near; close to: *The house stands hard by the bridge.* ⟨OE heard⟩ **—'hard•ness,** *n.*
☛ *Syn.* See note at FIRM.

hard and fast ['hɑrd ən fæst] *adj.* that cannot be changed or broken; strict (**hard-and-fast** *before a noun): hard-and-fast rules.*

hard•back ['hɑrd,bæk] *adj. or n.* hardbound.

hard–bit•ten ['hɑrd 'bɪtən] *adj.* stubborn; unyielding.

hard•board ['hɑrd,bɔrd] *n.* a thin, strong building board made in large sheets by compressing wood fibres and sawdust with a resinous or plastic binder under heat. Hardboard with a decorative surface finish, such as imitation wood grain or brick, is often used for interior panelling.

hard–boiled ['hɑrd 'bɔɪld] *adj.* **1** boiled until hard: *hard-boiled eggs.* **2** *Informal.* not very emotional; tough; rough.

hard•bound ['hɑrd,baʊnd] *adj., n. —adj.* of a book or edition, having relatively rigid covers of cardboard, cloth, leather, etc.; hardcover; hardback.
—n. a book or edition bound in such a way.

hard cash **1** coins. **2** cash.

hard cider fermented cider, containing alcohol.

hard coal anthracite.

hard copy information that can be read without special equipment, such as a computer printout on paper.
—'hard-,cop•y, *adj.*

hard core the permanent or most lasting part of any thing or any group; the central or vital part.

hard–core ['hɑrd 'kɔr] *adj.* **1** showing or describing explicit sex, often involving sadism or masochism: *hard-core pornography, hard-core movies.* **2** solidly or permanently established or committed: *hard-core disco fans.*

hard•cov•er ['hɑrd,kʌvər] *adj. or n.* hardbound.

hard disk *Computer technology.* a large capacity storage device used to retain computer programs and data.

hard edge a style of painting or photography in which the edges of the objects are sharply defined.

hard•en ['hɑrdən] *v.* **1** make or become hard. **2** make or become capable of endurance. **3** make or become unfeeling or pitiless. **4** temper or make (metals and alloys, especially steel) hard by raising to a high temperature and then cooling in oil, water, or air. **5** of prices of stocks, commodities, etc., become higher; rise. **—'hard•en•er,** *n.*

hard–fea•tured ['hɑrd 'fitʃərd] *adj.* having stern or cruel features.

hard•hack ['hɑrd,hæk] *n.* a North American spirea (*Spiraea tomentosa*) having tapering clusters of small pink or white flowers and woolly leaves and branches.

hard hat *n.* **1** a rigid helmet, as of metal or fibreglass, worn by construction workers, miners, etc. for protection against falling objects. **2** *Informal.* a construction worker or miner, etc. or a person thought of as typical of such people.

hard–hat ['hɑrd ,hæt] *adj. Informal.* of or having to do with construction workers or miners, etc. or the conservative attitudes considered to be typical of them.

hard•head ['hɑrd,hɛd] *n.* **1** a person not easily moved; a shrewd, unemotional person. **2** any of various fishes, such as the lake trout or alewife.

hard–head•ed ['hɑrd 'hɛdɪd] *adj.* **1** not easily excited or deceived; practical; shrewd. **2** stubborn; obstinate.
—'hard-'head•ed•ly, *adv.* **—'hard-'head•ed•ness,** *n.*

hard–heart•ed ['hɑrd 'hɑrtɪd] *adj.* without pity; cruel; unfeeling. **—'hard-'heart•ed•ly,** *adv.* **—'hard-'heart•ed•ness,** *n.*

har•di•hood ['hɑrdi,hʊd] *n.* boldness; daring.

har•di•ness ['hɑrdinɪs] *n.* **1** endurance; strength. **2** hardihood.

hard labour or **labor** **1** hard work in addition to imprisonment. **2** the end of the first stage of childbirth, when uterine contractions are too painful to talk or walk through. Opposed to EARLY LABOUR.

hard line a stern, aggressive, or uncompromising attitude or policy: *taking a hard line against minority language rights.*
—'hard-'line, *adj.* **—'hard-,lin•er,** *n.*

hard•ly ['hɑrdli] *adv.* **1** only just; barely: *We hardly had time for breakfast.* **2** not quite; not altogether: *hardly strong enough.* **3** most probably not: *She will hardly come now.* **4** with trouble or effort: *money hardly earned.* **5** in a hard manner; harshly; severely: *to deal hardly with a person.*
☛ *Syn.* **1. Hardly,** BARELY, SCARCELY = only just or almost not what is named or stated, and are often used interchangeably. But **hardly** = near or close to the minimum limit, with little to spare: *I had hardly reached there when it began to rain.* **Barely** = just enough, with nothing to spare: *He eats barely enough.* **Scarcely** = almost not at all: *He has scarcely anything to eat.*
☛ *Usage.* **Hardly** and **scarcely** are treated as negatives and so should not have another negative with them: *The film showed hardly anything that was new to them* (not *hardly nothing*). *I scarcely had enough money* (not *I didn't scarcely have*).
☛ *Usage.* Both **hardly** and **scarcely,** when used at the beginning of a sentence, are followed by inverted word order: *Hardly had she left when it started to rain. Scarcely had she asked when the reply arrived.*

hard maple *Cdn.* **1** the sugar maple (*Acer saccharum*). **2** the black maple (*Acer nigrum*). **3** the wood of either of these trees.

hard–nosed ['hɑrd ,nouzd] *adj. Informal.* practical and unsentimental, often to the point of ruthlessness: *a hard-nosed executive.*

hard of hearing somewhat deaf.

hard palate the front, bony part of the roof of the mouth.

hard•pan ['hɑrd,pæn] *n.* **1** hard, firm, underlying earth. **2** the fundamental or basic aspect of anything.

hard pressed confronted with the necessity to act or react quickly or to work intensively; subject to severe pressure, attack, etc.: *She was hard pressed to get the manuscript ready for the publisher.*

hard put having one's resources heavily taxed; barely able: *He was hard put to think of an excuse.*

hard return *Computer technology.* a RETURN (def. 8) inserted by the user. Compare SOFT RETURN.

hard•rock ['hɑrd,rɒk] *n., adj. Cdn. —n.* **1** *Mining.* rock, such as quartz, that can be removed only by drilling or blasting. **2** *Slang.* a strong, rough person.
—adj. Often, **hard-rock. 1** of or having to do with hardrock: *hardrock miners.* **2** *Slang.* characterized by hardness and strength: *That hockey player was feared for her hardrock checking.*

hard rock *Music.* very loud, fast rock with simple rhythm and melody.

hard rubber vulcanized rubber.

hard sauce a sauce made by creaming sugar, butter, and flavouring together, used on cakes, puddings, etc.

hard–scrab•ble ['hɑrd ˌskræbəl] *adj.* giving a small return for hard work: *a hard-scrabble farm.*

hard sell *Informal.* a forceful and direct method of advertising; aggressive, high-pressure approach to selling: *The company is using the hard sell to promote its new products.* Compare SOFT SELL. **—'hard-ˌsell,** *adj.*

hard–set ['hɑrd 'sɛt] *adj.* **1** firmly set. **2** obstinate. **3** in a difficult situation.

hard–shell ['hɑrd 'ʃɛl] *adj.* **1** having a hard shell. **2** *Informal.* strict; uncompromising.

hard•ship ['hɑrdʃɪp] *n.* something hard to bear; hard condition of living: *Hunger, cold, and sickness are hardships.*

hard sledding difficult going; unfavourable conditions. ⟨from the difficulty of pulling a sled through deep snow⟩

hard•tack ['hɑrd,tæk] *n.* a very hard, dry biscuit which keeps well and is used on ships.

hard•top ['hɑrd,tɒp] *n., adj. —n. Informal.* an automobile having a body design similar to that of a convertible except that the top is rigid.
—adj. having to do with such an automobile.

hard•ware ['hɑrd,wɛr] *n.* **1** articles made from metal. Locks, hinges, nails, and tools are hardware. **2** *Military.* manufactured equipment such as guns, tanks, aircraft, or missiles. **3** *Computer technology.* the mechanical, electronic, or structural parts of a computer, teaching machine, etc. Compare SOFTWARE.

hard water water containing minerals that hinder the action of soap.

hard wheat wheat having a hard kernel and high gluten content, used in making bread, macaroni, etc.

hard–wired ['hɑrd ˌwaɪrd] *adj.* of an electric circuit, made to perform only one task in a computer.

hard•wood ['hɑrd,wʊd] *n., adj. —n.* **1** any hard, compact wood. **2** *Forestry.* any tree that has broad leaves or does not have needles. **3** the wood of such a tree. Oak, cherry, maple, etc. are hardwoods; pine and fir are softwoods.
—adj. **1** made of hardwood: *a hardwood floor.* **2** composed of hardwood trees: *a hardwood forest.*

hard•work•ing ['hɑrd'wɜrkɪŋ] *adj.* usually working hard; diligent: *She is a hardworking student.*

har•dy[1] ['hɑrdi] *adj.* **-di•er, -di•est. 1** able to bear hard treatment, fatigue, etc.; strong; robust. **2** able to withstand the cold of winter in the open air: *hardy plants.* **3** bold; daring. **4** too bold; rash. ⟨ME < OF *hardi,* pp. of *hardir* harden < Gmc.⟩ **—'har•di•ly,** *adv.*

har•dy[2] ['hɑrdi] *n.* a chisel with a square shank. ⟨< probably < *hard*⟩

hare [hɛr] *n., pl.* **hare** or **hares;** *v.* **hared, har•ing.** *—n.* any of several small mammals (family Leporidae, especially genus *Lepus*) resembling and related to rabbits, but generally larger and having longer ears and legs and whose young are born fully furred, with open eyes.
—v. hurry; run: *They hared off after the thief.* ⟨OE *hara*⟩ **—'hare,like,** *adj.*
☛ *Hom.* HAIR, HERR.

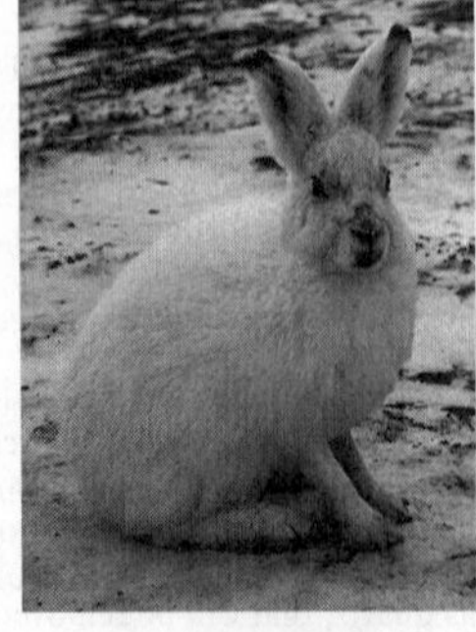
A hare

Hare [hɛr] *n.* **1** a member of a First Nations people, a branch of the Athapascans, now living in Canada in the Mackenzie Valley. **2** the Athapascan language of these people.
☛ *Hom.* HAIR, HERR.

hare•bell ['hɛr,bɛl] *n.* BLUEBELL (def. 1).

hare•brained ['hɛr,breind] *adj.* giddy; heedless; reckless.

Hare Krishna ['hɑri 'krɪʃnə] *or* ['hɛri] *n.* a Hindu religion based on Vedic writings.

hare•lip ['hɛr,lɪp] *n.* **1** a deformity caused when parts of the lip fail to grow together before birth. **2** a lip that is deformed in this way. **—'hare,lipped,** *adj.*

har•em ['hɛrəm] *n.* **1** the part of a Muslim house where the women live. **2** its occupants; the wives, female relatives, female servants, etc. of a Muslim household. **3** of fur seals, wild horses, and certain other animals, a number of females controlled by one male. ⟨< Arabic *haram, harim* forbidden⟩

harem pants wide-cut decorative pants gathered at the waist and ankles, worn by women.

hare's tail a Canadian wildflower (*Eriphorum spissum*) growing in sphagnum bogs in the north and having tufts of silky bristles on the end of long stems; cotton grass.

har•i•cot ['hærə,kou] *or* ['hɛrəkou] *n.* **1** a string bean. **2** a kidney bean. ⟨< F⟩

har•i–kar•i ['hæri 'kæri], ['hɛri 'kɛri], *or* ['hɑri 'kɑri] *n.* HARA-KIRI.

Ha•ri Ra•ya ['hɑri 'rɑjɑ] *Islam.* a festival celebrating the family, held after Ramadan.

hark [hɑrk] *v.* listen.
hark back, a go back; turn back: *His ideas hark back twenty years.* **b** return to a previous point or subject; revert: *Whenever we chat together, he is always harking back to his time in the army.* ⟨ME *herkien*⟩

hark•en ['hɑrkən] See HEARKEN.

Har•le•quin ['hɑrlə,kwɪn] *or* ['hɑrlə,kɪn] *n.* **1** in traditional Italian comedy and in pantomime, the lover of Columbine. He is usually masked, wears a costume of varied colours, and carries a wooden sword. **2 harlequin,** a mischievous person; buffoon. **3** (*adjl.*) varied in colour; many-coloured. ⟨< F < OF var. of *Herlequin* < ME *Herle King* King Herla (mythical figure); modern meaning in French is from Ital. *arlecchino* < OF *Harlequin*⟩

har•le•quin•ade [ˌhɑrləkwɪ'neid] *or* [ˌhɑrləkɪ'neid] *n.* **1** a pantomime or play in which the harlequin and the clown are the leading players. **2** buffoonery; clownish antics.

harlequin bug a brightly coloured North American bug (*Murgantia histrionica*) that is a pest of vegetable crops such as cabbage.

harlequin duck a small diving duck (*Histrionicus histrionicus*) native to North America, Iceland, and Siberia, the male being mainly bluish grey marked with black, white, and chestnut. It is an endangered species. Also called **lord and lady duck.**

har•lot ['hɑrlət] *n.* prostitute. ⟨ME < OF *harlot* vagabond⟩

har•lot•ry ['hɑrlətri] *n.* **1** prostitution. **2** prostitutes as a group.

harm [hɑrm] *n., v. —n.* **1** hurt; damage: *The accident did a lot of harm to the car.* **2** evil; wrong: *What harm is there in "borrowing" a friend's bicycle?*
—v. damage; injure; hurt. ⟨OE *hearm*⟩ **—'harm•er,** *n.*
☛ *Syn. v.* **Harm,** DAMAGE = hurt or injure a person or thing. **Harm** = injure, but is a more informal word, and especially suggests injuring a person or his or her mind, health, rights, business, etc. so as to cause pain, loss, or suffering of some kind: *Unfounded and malicious rumours harmed his reputation.* **Damage** = hurt or harm so as to lessen the value, usefulness, or appearance of a person or thing: *The furniture was damaged in the fire.*

har•mat•tan [ˌhɑrmə'tæn] *n.* a dry wind that blows from the Sahara. ⟨< Sp. < Twi *haramata*⟩

harm•ful ['hɑrmfəl] *adj.* causing harm; injurious; hurtful. **—'harm•ful•ly,** *adv.* **—'harm•ful•ness,** *n.*

harm•less ['hɑrmlɪs] *adj.* **1** causing no harm; that would not harm anyone or anything. **2** inoffensive. **—'harm•less•ly,** *adv.* **—'harm•less•ness,** *n.*

har•mon•ic [hɑr'mɒnɪk] *adj., n. —adj.* **1** *Music.* **a** of or having to do with harmony as distinguished from melody and rhythm. **b** of or having to do with overtones that are heard along with the main tone. **c** musical. **2** having to do with or marked by harmony, agreement, or concord; concordant; consonant. **3** *Physics.* of or having to do with any of the frequencies making up a wave or alternating current, that are integral multiples of the fundamental frequency. **4** *Mathematics.* having relations similar to the frequencies of tones that are consonant. 1, ½, ⅓, ¼, etc. are in harmonic progression.

—*n.* **1** *Music.* **a** a tone produced on a stringed instrument by a light pressure at a point on a string. **b** an overtone whose rate of vibration is an integral multiple of the main tone. Harmonics have a higher pitch and lower volume than main tones. **2** a fainter and higher tone heard along with the main tone; overtone. ⟨< L *harmonicus* < Gk. *harmonikos* harmonic, musical < *harmonia.* See HARMONY.⟩ **—har'mon•i•cal•ly,** *adv.*

har•mon•i•ca [hɑr'mɒnəkə] *n.* a small, oblong musical instrument having several metal reeds which are caused to vibrate by air from the player's mouth controlled by the tongue and lips; mouth organ. ⟨< L *harmonica* fem. of *harmonicus.* See HARMONIC.⟩

A harmonica

harmonic progression **1** *Mathematics.* a series of numbers with reciprocals in arithmetic progression. **2** *Music.* the sequence of chords providing harmony for a melody.

har•mon•ics [hɑr'mɒnɪks] *n.* the science of musical sounds.

har•mo•ni•ous [hɑr'mouniəs] *adj.* **1** agreeing in feelings, ideas, or actions; getting along well together: *The children played together in a harmonious group.* **2** arranged so that the parts are orderly or pleasing; going well together: *This picture is remarkable for its harmonious colours.* **3** sweet-sounding; musical. **—har'mo•ni•ous•ly,** *adv.* **—har'mo•ni•ous•ness,** *n.*

har•mon•ist ['hɑrmənɪst] *n.* **1** one skilled in harmony. **2** one who makes a harmony of writings as a basis of comparison.

har•mo•ni•um [hɑr'mouniəm] *n.* a small musical organ with metal reeds. ⟨< F *harmonium* < *harmonie.* See HARMONY.⟩

har•mo•nize ['hɑrmə,naɪz] *v.* **-nized, -niz•ing. 1** bring into harmony or agreement: *to harmonize several different points of view.* **2** go or put together in a pleasing way: *The colours in the room harmonized.* **3** *Music.* add tones to (a melody) to make successive chords. **—,har•mo•ni'za•tion,** *n.* **—'har•mo,niz•er,** *n.*

har•mo•ny ['hɑrməni] *n., pl.* **-nies. 1** an agreement of feeling, ideas, or actions; getting along well together: *The two brothers lived and worked in perfect harmony.* **2** an orderly or pleasing arrangement of parts; going well together: *a harmony of design and colour.* **3** *Music.* **a** a sounding together of tones in a chord. **b** the study of chords and of relating them to successive chords. **4** a sweet or musical sound; music. **5** the act of harmonizing, especially of singing voices: *The quartet achieved excellent harmony.* **6** a grouping of passages on the same subject from different stories or accounts, showing their points of agreement: *a harmony of the Gospels.* ⟨< F *harmonie* < L < Gk. *harmonia* concord, a joining < *harmos* joint⟩

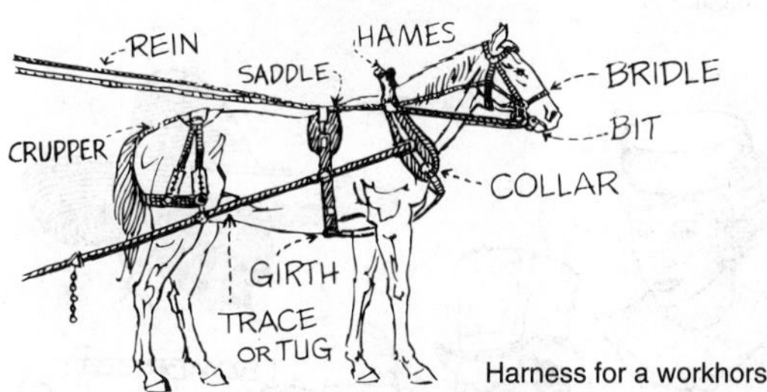

Harness for a workhorse

har•ness ['hɑrnɪs] *n., v.* —*n.* **1** the leather straps, bands, and pieces of various other shapes used to hitch a horse or other animal to a carriage, wagon, plough, etc. **2** an arrangement of straps to fasten or hold: *a parachute harness, a shoulder harness. We need a harness for the baby's stroller.* **3** *Archaic.* the armour for a knight, soldier, or horse.
in harness, at one's regular work: *She was content to be back in harness after a good holiday.*
—*v.* **1** put harness on. **2** attach (a horse) with harness to a wagon, etc. **3** control so as to use the power of. Water in a stream is harnessed by allowing it to accumulate behind a dam and installing turbines that it can drive. **4** *Archaic.* put armour on.
harness to, use for: *If only we could find a way of harnessing children's energy to their school work.* ⟨ME < OF *harneis,* ? < Scand.⟩

A harp

harp [hɑrp] *n., v.* —*n.* **1** a musical instrument with strings set in a triangular frame, played by plucking the strings with the fingers. **2** HARP SEAL.
—*v.* play on a harp.
harp on, keep on tiresomely talking or writing about; refer continually to. ⟨OE *hearpe*⟩ **—'harp•er,** *n.*

harp•ist ['hɑrpɪst] *n.* a person who plays the harp, especially a skilled player.

har•poon [hɑr'pun] *n., v.* —*n.* a barbed spear with a rope tied to it, used for catching whales and other sea animals. It is either hurled by the hand or fired from a gun.
—*v.* strike, catch, or kill with a harpoon. ⟨< F *harpon* < MF *harper* grip < Gmc.⟩ **—har'poon•er** *or* **,har•poon'eer,** *n.*

harp seal *Cdn.* a hair seal (*Pagophilus groenlandicus*) found in the arctic and subarctic waters of the Atlantic Ocean, mainly pale grey in colour, with a dark brown or black head and a large, irregular, horseshoe-shaped marking on its back.

harp•si•chord ['hɑrpsə,kɔrd] *n.* a stringed musical instrument resembling a piano, still played but used especially from about 1550 to 1750. It sounds somewhat like a harp because the strings are plucked by leather or quill points instead of being struck by hammers. ⟨< obs. F *harpechorde* < *harpe* harp (< Gmc.) + *chorde* string of a musical instrument < L < Gk.⟩ **—'harp•si,chord•ist,** *n.*

Har•py ['hɑrpi] *n., pl.* **-pies. 1** *Greek mythology.* any of several repulsive, filthy, greedy monsters having a woman's head and torso and a bird's wings, tail, and claws. **2 harpy,** a very greedy person who preys upon others. ⟨< L *Harpyia* < Gk., probably related to *harpazein* snatch⟩

harpy eagle an eagle of tropical America (*Harpia harpyja*) having black-and-white plumage, short wings, and a double crest.

har•que•bus ['hɑrkwəbəs] *n.* a form of portable firearm used before muskets were invented. Also, **arquebus.** ⟨< F *(h)arquebus* < Ital. *archibuso* < Du. *haakbus,* literally, hook gun⟩

har•ri•dan ['hærədən] *or* ['hɛrədən] *n.* a bad-tempered, disreputable old woman. ⟨probably < F *haridelle* a worn-out horse⟩

har•ri•er[1] ['hæriər] *or* ['hɛriər] *n.* **1** a breed of small hound resembling the English foxhound, used to hunt hares. **2** a cross-country runner. ⟨apparently < *hare*⟩

har•ri•er[2] ['hæriər] *or* ['hɛriər] *n.* **1** a person who harries. **2** a hawk that preys on small animals. ⟨< *harry*⟩

Har•ris Tweed ['hærɪs] *or* ['hɛrɪs] *Trademark.* hand-woven tweed of very high quality, originally made on the Island of Harris in the Hebrides.

har•row ['hærou] *or* ['hɛrou] *n., v.* —*n. Agriculture.* a heavy frame with iron teeth or upright disks. Harrows are drawn over ploughed land to break up clods, cover seeds, etc.
—*v.* **1** *Agriculture.* draw a harrow over (land, etc.). **2** hurt; wound. **3** arouse uncomfortable feelings in; distress; torment. ⟨ME *harwe*⟩ **—'har•row•er,** *n.*

har•row•ing ['hærouɪŋ] *or* ['hɛrouɪŋ] *adj., v.* —*adj.* painful; moving to pity: *She gave a harrowing account of her ordeal.*
—*v.* ppr. of HARROW.

har•ry ['hæri] *or* ['hɛri] *v.* **-ried, -ry•ing. 1** raid and rob with violence: *The pirates harried the towns along the coast.* **2** keep troubling; worry; torment: *He was harried by fear of losing his job.* ⟨OE *hergian* < *here* army⟩

harsh [hɑrʃ] *adj.* **1** rough to the touch, taste, eye, or ear; sharp and unpleasant: *a harsh voice.* **2** without pity; cruel; severe: *a harsh man.* **3** stern; grim; forbidding: *a harsh expression.*

4 rugged; bleak: *a harsh landscape.* ⟨var. of ME *harsk*; cf. Danish *harsk* rancid⟩ **—'harsh•ly,** *adv.* **—'harsh•ness,** *n.*

hart [hɑrt] *n., pl.* **hart** or **harts.** an adult male deer, especially the male of the European red deer after its fifth year. ⟨OE *heorot*⟩
☛ *Hom.* HEART.

har•te•beest ['hɑrtə,bist] *or* ['hɑrt,bist] *n., pl.* **-beest** or **-beests. 1** either of two large African antelopes (*Alcelaphus buselaphus* and *A. lichtensteini*) having a fawn-coloured coat, a long, thin muzzle, and ringed, lyre-shaped horns. **2** any of several similar antelopes, such as *Damaliscus hunteri.* ⟨< Afrikaans *hartebeest* hart beast⟩

harts•horn ['hɑrts,hɔrn] *n.* **1** ammonia dissolved in water. **2** smelling salts; sal volatile.

hart's–tongue or **harts–tongue** ['hɑrts ,tʌŋ] *n.* a fern (*Phyllitis scolopen*) found in NE North America, Asia, and Europe, having narrow fronds. ⟨from the shape of the fronds⟩

har•um–scar•um ['hɛrəm 'skɛrəm] *adj., adv., n. —adj.* reckless; rash; thoughtless: *What a harum-scarum child you are!* *—adv.* recklessly; wildly: *She rushed harum-scarum down the main street.*
—n. a reckless person. ⟨apparently < *hare* frighten + *scare*⟩

ha•rus•pex [hə'rʌspɛks], ['hærə,spɛks], *or* ['hɛrə,spɛks] *n., pl.* **ha•rus•pi•ces** [hə'rʌspə,siz] in ancient Rome, a member of a class of minor priests or soothsayers who made predictions by examining the entrails of animals killed in sacrifice, by observing lightning, etc. ⟨< L *haruspex* < **haru-* entrails + *specere* inspect⟩

har•vest ['hɑrvɪst] *n., v. —n.* **1** a reaping and gathering in of grain and other food crops, usually in the late summer or early autumn. **2** the time or season when grain, fruit, etc. are gathered in. **3** one season's yield of any natural product; a crop: *The oyster harvest was small this year.* **4** the result; consequences: *He is reaping the harvest of his mistakes.*
—v. **1** gather in for use: *to harvest wheat.* **2** gather a crop from (a field). **3** win or undergo as a result or consequence. ⟨OE *hærfest*⟩
☛ *Syn. n.* **3.** See note at CROP.

har•vest•a•ble ['hɑrvəstəbəl] *adj.* suitable or ready for harvesting.

har•vest•er ['hɑrvəstər] *n.* **1** a person who works in a harvest field; reaper. **2** a machine for harvesting crops, especially grain.

harvest excursion formerly, a low-fare railway trip for fieldworkers travelling to the West to harvest grain.

harvest home 1 the end of harvesting. **2** a festival to celebrate the end of harvesting. **3** a harvest song.

har•vest•man ['hɑrvɪstmən] *n.* **1** HARVESTER (def. 1). **2** daddy-longlegs.

harvest mite chigger.

harvest moon the full moon at harvest time, or about September 23.

harvest mouse 1 any of a genus (*Reithrodontomys*) of small, greyish, New World mice found in open, grassy areas from Canada south to N South America. **2** a very small Old World mouse (*Micromys minutus*) having reddish brown fur, found in grain fields, etc.

harvest special *Cdn.* formerly, a train taking part in a HARVEST EXCURSION.

has [hæz]; *before 'to' in def. 6 of* HAVE, [hæs]; *unstressed,* [həz] *or* [əz] *v.* 3rd pers. sing. present tense of HAVE.

has–been ['hæz ,bɪn] *or* ['hæz ,bin] *n. Informal.* a person or thing whose best days are past.

has•en•pfef•fer ['hɑzən,fɛfər] *or* ['hɑzən,pfɛfər] *n.* a German dish consisting of rabbit stewed in vinegar. ⟨< G *Hase* rabbit + *Pfeffer* pepper⟩

hash[1] [hæʃ] *n., v. —n.* **1** a mixture of cooked meat, potatoes, etc. chopped into small pieces and fried or baked. **2** a mixture; jumble. **3** a mess; muddle.
make a hash of, make a mess of: *She made a hash of mounting stamps in her album.*
settle (someone's) **hash,** *Informal.* subdue or silence someone completely; get even with someone.
—v. **1** chop into small pieces. **2** make a mess or muddle of. **3** *Informal.* talk about in detail; discuss or review thoroughly (*often used with* **over, through,** *etc.*): *The two leaders spent hours hashing over their problems.* ⟨< F *hacher* < *hache* hatchet⟩

hash[2] [hæʃ] *n. Slang.* hashish.

hash browns a dish consisting of potatoes boiled and then cut up and sautéed.

hash•eesh ['hæʃiʃ] *or* [hə'ʃiʃ] *n.* hashish.

hash•ish ['hæʃiʃ], ['hæʃɪʃ], *or* [hə'ʃiʃ] *n.* an extract from the dried flowers of the female hemp plant, that is smoked, chewed, or drunk for its intoxicating effect. Compare CANNABIS, MARIJUANA. ⟨< Arabic *hashish* dried hemp leaves⟩

Hasid ['hæsɪd] *or* [hɑ'sid] *n., pl.* **Hasidim** ['hæsədɪm] *or* [hɑ'sidim] a member of a mystical Jewish sect emphasizing joy and personal devotion. Also, **Chasid. —Ha'sid•ic** [hə'sɪdɪk], *adj.*

has•let ['hæzlət] *or* ['hæslət] *n.* the edible viscera of any animal used as food, served as a seasoned meat loaf. ⟨< ME *hastelet* < OF, meat roasted on a spit < Gmc.⟩

has•n't ['hæzənt] *v.* has not.

hasp [hæsp] *n.* a clasp or fastening for a door, window, trunk, box, etc., especially a hinged metal clasp that fits over a staple or into a hole and is fastened by a peg, padlock, etc. ⟨var. of OE *hæpse*⟩

has•sle ['hæsəl] *n., v.* **hassled, has•sling.** *Informal. —n.* **1** a struggle; argument: *There was a hassle about who was going to ride in the front seat of the car.* **2** trouble; annoyance; bother: *Driving in city traffic is too much hassle.*
—v. **1** struggle; argue. **2** annoy; bother: *The film star was being hassled by newspaper reporters.* ⟨origin uncertain⟩

has•sock ['hæsək] *n.* **1** a padded footstool or thick cushion to rest the feet on, sit on, or kneel on. **2** a tuft or bunch of coarse grass. ⟨OE *hassuc* coarse grass⟩

hast [hæst] *v. Archaic.* 2nd pers. sing. present tense of HAVE. *Thou hast* means *you* (sing.) *have.*

has•tate ['hæsteit] *adj.* shaped like the head of a spear. ⟨< L *hastatus* < *hasta* spear⟩

haste [heist] *n., v.* **hast•ed, hast•ing.** *—n.* **1** a trying to be quick; hurrying: *The king's business required haste.* **2** quickness without thought or care: *Haste makes waste.*
in haste, a in a hurry; quickly. **b** without careful thought; rashly.
make haste, hurry; be quick.
—v. Poetic. hasten. ⟨ME < OF < Gmc.; cf. OE *hǣst* violence⟩
☛ *Syn. n.* **1.** See note at HURRY.

has•ten ['heisən] *v.* **1** cause to be quick; speed; hurry: *She hastened the children off to bed.* **2** be quick; act or go fast: *Let me hasten to explain.*

has•ten•er ['heisənər] *n.* **1** one who hastens. **2** a follow-up note to hurry delivery of an order, payment of a bill, etc.

hast•y ['heisti] *adj.* **hast•i•er, hast•i•est. 1** hurried; quick: *a hasty visit.* **2** not well thought out; rash: *His hasty decisions caused many mistakes.* **3** easily angered; quick-tempered: *She should not be so hasty.* **4** irritable; snappish. **—'hast•i•ly,** *adv.* **—'hast•i•ness,** *n.*

hasty pudding 1 a mush of meal or flour made with boiling water (or milk) and seasoning. **2** *U.S.* a mush made with cornmeal.

hat [hæt] *n., v.* **hat•ted, hat•ting.** *—n.* **1** a covering for the head, usually with a crown and brim and usually worn outdoors. **2** *Roman Catholic Church.* **a** a red head covering worn by a

cardinal. **b** the dignity or office of a cardinal. **3** any of a person's roles, positions, etc.: *She's wearing her director's hat today.*
hat in hand, a with the head uncovered in respect.
b obsequiously; servilely.
old hat, out-of-date or fashion; commonplace.
pass the hat, take up a collection.
take off (one's) **hat to,** salute or honour by or as if by removing one's hat: *I take my hat off to anybody who can make that jump.*
talk through (one's) **hat,** talk without knowing what one is talking about; talk foolishly.
throw (one's) **hat into the ring,** *Informal.* enter a contest, especially for election to a public office.
under (one's) **hat,** *Informal.* as a secret; to oneself: *Keep it under your hat.*
—v. cover or furnish with a hat. ⟨OE *hætt*⟩ **—'hat•less,** *adj.*
—'hat,like, *adj.*

hat•band ['hæt,bænd] *n.* a band around the crown of a hat, just above the brim.

hat•box ['hæt,bɒks] *n.* a box, usually round and deep, for carrying a hat.

hatch[1] [hætʃ] *v., n.* *—v.* **1** bring forth (young) from an egg or eggs: *A hen hatches chickens.* **2** keep (an egg or eggs) warm until the young come out: *The heat of the sun hatches turtles' eggs.* **3** come out from the egg: *Three chickens hatched today.* **4** of an egg, produce living young: *Not all eggs hatch properly.* **5** of a bird, brood: *Don't annoy the hen while she's hatching.* **6** arrange; plan, especially in secret; plot: *The robbers were hatching an evil scheme.*
—n. **1** the act of hatching. **2** the brood hatched. **3** something that is hatched. ⟨ME *hæche(n)*⟩ **—'hatch•a•ble,** *adj.*
—'hatch•er, *n.*

hatch[2] [hætʃ] *n.* **1** an opening in a ship's deck through which the cargo is loaded. See CAPSTAN for picture. **2** the trap door covering such an opening. **3** an opening in the floor or roof of a building, etc.: *an escape hatch.* **4** the lower half of a divided door. **5** floodgate. **6 a** HATCHBACK (def. 1). **b** the cargo area in a hatchback automobile. ⟨OE *hæcc*⟩

hatch[3] [hætʃ] *v., n.* *—v.* draw, cut, or engrave fine parallel lines on: *With a sharp pencil the artist hatched certain parts of the picture to darken and shade them.*
—n. one of such a set of lines. ⟨< F *hacher* chop, hatch. See HASH.⟩

hatch•back ['hætʃ,bæk] *n.* **1** a sloping back on a two-door or four-door automobile, the whole of which swings up like a hatch, giving access to the interior of the car. **2** an automobile having a hatchback.

hatch•el ['hætʃəl] *n., v.* **-elled** or **-eled, -el•ling** or **-el•ing.**
—n. a comb used in cleaning flax, hemp, etc.
—v. **1** comb (flax, hemp, etc.) with a hatchel. **2** annoy; torment; heckle. ⟨var. of *hackle*[1]⟩ **—'hatch•el•ler** *or* **'hatch•el•er,** *n.*

hatch•er•y ['hætʃəri] *n., pl.* **-er•ies.** a place for hatching eggs of fish, hens, etc.

hatch•et ['hætʃɪt] *n.* **1** a small axe with a short handle, for use with one hand. **2** tomahawk.
bury the hatchet, make peace.
dig up the hatchet, make war. ⟨ME < OF *hachette*, dim. of *hache* axe⟩

hatchet job *Informal.* a vicious or malicious attack in speech or writing.

hatchet man *Informal.* **1** a person who makes vicious or malicious attacks, especially one hired to do so. **2** a hired murderer. **3** a person hired to get rid of employees.

hatch•ing ['hætʃɪŋ] *n., v.* *—n.* fine, parallel lines drawn, cut, or engraved close together.
—v. ppr. of HATCH[1] or HATCH[3].

hatch•ment ['hætʃmənt] *n. Heraldry.* a square panel set diagonally, bearing the coat of arms of a recently deceased person, for temporary display of the noble house to which he or she belonged. ⟨earlier *atcheament*, *achement*, contraction of *achievement*⟩

hatch•way ['hætʃ,wei] *n.* **1** an opening in the deck of a ship to the lower part. **2** a similar opening in a floor, roof, etc.

hate [heit] *v.* **hat•ed, hat•ing;** *n.* *—v.* **1** dislike very strongly; feel extreme hostility or aversion to: *Many people hate snakes.* **2** dislike: *I hate that shade of blue.* **3** be unwilling; hesitate: *I hate to disturb you this late at night.*
—n. **1** a very strong dislike; hatred: *There was hate in his voice.* **2** an object of hatred. **3** *(adjl.)* characterized by hate: *hate literature.* ⟨OE *hatian*⟩ **—'hat•er,** *n.*

☛ *Syn. v.* **1. Hate,** DETEST, ABHOR = dislike someone or something very much. **Hate,** the general word, suggests very strong dislike and a feeling of hostility, often a desire to hurt or harm: *The prisoners hated the wicked guards.* **Detest** suggests strong or deep fixed dislike mixed with scorn for something or someone disagreeable or disgusting: *I detest a coward.* **Abhor** suggests a dislike that makes one shudder or shrink away from someone or something extremely disagreeable, disgusting, or shocking: *I abhor filth of any kind.*

hate•ful ['heitfəl] *adj.* **1** causing hate; to be hated. **2** feeling hate; showing hate. **—'hate•ful•ly,** *adv.* **—'hate•ful•ness,** *n.*
☛ *Syn.* **1. Hateful,** ODIOUS, OBNOXIOUS = causing strong dislike or hate. **Hateful** emphasizes the hatred caused, a feeling of strong dislike and hostility combined with anger, fear, spite, a feeling of injury, etc.: *A bully does hateful things.* **Odious,** formal, emphasizes having qualities that cause hatred or strong dislike, and suggests being disagreeable, irritating, or disgusting: *Conditions in the slums are odious.* **Obnoxious** = being so disagreeable or annoying to a person that he or she cannot stand the sight or thought of what is described: *His disgusting table manners made him obnoxious to us.*

hate•mong•er ['heit,mʌŋgər] *n.* one who tries to stir up hatred, especially against a certain group.

hat•ful ['hætfʊl] *n.* **1** the amount a hat can hold. **2** a great deal; considerable amount.

hath [hæθ] *v. Archaic.* 3rd pers. sing. present tense of HAVE. *He hath* means *he has.*

Hatha Yoga ['hɑθə 'jougə] *or* ['hæθə 'jougə] *n.* a system of physical exercises which twist and stretch the muscles and tone the body, combined with meditation, leading to physical and spiritual improvement.

hat•pin ['hæt,pɪn] *n.* a long pin used by women to fasten a hat to the hair.

hat•rack ['hæt,ræk] *n.* a rack, shelf, or arrangement of hooks or pegs to put hats on.

ha•tred ['heitrɪd] *n.* very strong dislike; hate. ⟨ME *hatred, hatereden* < *hate* hate + *-reden,* OE *ræden* condition, state⟩

hat•ter ['hætər] *n.* a person who makes or sells hats.

hat trick **1** *Cdn. Hockey and soccer.* three goals scored in a single game by the same player. **2** *Cricket.* the taking of three wickets with three successive balls. **3** *Informal.* any feat consisting of three or more victories in a row. ⟨< the fact of a *hat* formerly being the prize for this feat in cricket⟩

hau•ber•geon ['hɒbərdʒən] *n.* HABERGEON (def. 1).

hau•berk ['hɒbərk] *n.* a long coat of mail. ⟨ME < OF *hauberc* < Gmc.; cf. OE *healsbeorg*, literally, neck cover⟩

haugh•ty ['hɒti] *adj.* **-ti•er, -ti•est. 1** too proud of oneself and too scornful of others. **2** showing too great pride in oneself and scorn for others: *a haughty smile.* ⟨< *haut* or *haught* < OF *haut* < L *altus* high; French form influenced by OHG *hoh* high⟩
—'haugh•ti•ly, *adv.* **—'haugh•ti•ness,** *n.*
☛ *Syn.* **1. Haughty,** ARROGANT = too proud. **Haughty** = feeling oneself superior to others and showing it by treating them with cold indifference and scorn: *A haughty girl is always unpopular at school.* **Arrogant** = thinking oneself more important than one is and showing it by treating others in a domineering and slighting manner: *He was so arrogant that he lost his job.*

haul [hɒl] *v., n.* *—v.* **1** pull or drag with force: *The logs were hauled to the mill by horses.* **2** change direction; shift: *The wind hauled around to the east.* **3** transport by truck or railway: *Those trains haul coal to Vancouver.* **4** of seals, come up out of the water onto land (*used with* **out**): *Harbour seals haul out at low tide to rest and sleep.*
haul off, a turn a ship away from an object. **b** draw away; withdraw. **c** *Informal.* draw back one's arm to give a blow.
haul on or **to the wind,** sail nearer to the direction of the wind.
haul up, a turn a ship nearer to the direction of the wind.
b change the course of (a ship).
—n. **1** the act of hauling; hard pull. **2** the load hauled: *Powerful trucks are used for heavy hauls.* **3** the distance that a load is hauled. **4** the amount won, taken, etc. at one time; catch: *a good haul of fish.* ⟨< F *haler* < Gmc. Doublet of HALE[2].⟩ **—'haul•er,** *n.*
☛ *Hom.* HALL.
☛ *Syn. v.* **1.** See note at DRAW.

haul•age ['hɒlɪdʒ] *n.* **1** the act of hauling. **2** the force used in hauling. **3** a charge made for hauling.

haulm [hɒm] *n.* material used for thatching. ⟨< ME *halm* < OE *healm* straw⟩

haunch [hɒntʃ] *n.* **1** the part of the body around the hip; the hip. **2** the hind quarter of an animal. A dog sits on its haunches. **3** a cut of meat consisting of the leg and loin of a deer, sheep, etc. **4** *Architecture.* the side of an arch curving downwards. ⟨ME < OF *hanche* < Gmc.⟩

haunt [hɒnt] *v., n.* —*v.* **1** of a ghost, appear frequently to (a person) or in (a place); be continually present at (a place): *People say ghosts haunt that old house.* **2** go often to; visit frequently: *They haunt the new bowling alley. Teenagers haunt the shopping malls.* **3** be often with; come often to: *Memories of his youth haunted the old man.*
—*n.* **1** a place frequently gone to or often visited: *returning to their old haunts. The swimming pool was our favourite haunt in the summer.* **2** a place where wild animals habitually come to drink or feed. **3** *Dialect.* a ghost. ⟨ME < OF *hanter* < Gmc.; related to OE *hāmettan* shelter (cf. HOME)⟩ —**'haunt•er,** *n.* —**'haunt•ing•ly,** *adv.*

haunt•ed ['hɒntɪd] *adj., v.* —*adj.* **1** visited by ghosts. **2** harried or harassed, as if by ghosts; troubled; worried.
—*v.* pt. and pp. of HAUNT.

Hau•sa ['hʌusə] *or* ['haʊzə] *n.* **1** an African people of the Sudan and northern Nigeria. **2** a member of this people. **3** the Chad language of this people.

haus•tel•lum [hɒ'stɛləm] *n.* that part of the proboscis of an insect used for sucking blood. ⟨< NL, dim. of L *haustrum* < *haurire* draw water. Related to EXHAUST.⟩

haut•boy ['houbɔi] *or* ['oubɔɪ] *n.* an early name for the oboe. ⟨< F *hautbois* < *haut* high + *bois* wood; with reference to its high notes⟩

haute cou•ture [otku'tyʀ] *French.* **1** the best-known fashion houses and designers. **2** the clothes made by leading designers and dressmakers.

haute cui•sine [otkwi'zin] *French.* **1** cooking as a fine art, especially as practised by acknowledged master chefs. **2** food that is prepared in this way.

hau•teur [hou'tɜr] *or* [ou'tɜr] *n.* haughtiness; a haughty manner or spirit. ⟨< F *hauteur* < *haut* high⟩

Ha•van•a [hə'vænə] *n.* a cigar made from Cuban tobacco. ⟨< *Havana,* the capital of Cuba⟩

ha•var•ti [hə'vɑrti] *n.* a soft Danish cheese having small holes.

have [hæv]; *unstressed,* [həv] *or* [əv]; *before 'to' in def. 6, usually* [hæf] *v. pres. 1* **have,** *2* **have,** *3* **has,** *pl.* **have;** *pt. and pp.* **had;** *ppr.* **hav•ing. 1** hold: *I have a book in my hand.* **2** possess; own: *She has a big house and farm.* **3** have as a part, quality, etc.: *The house has many windows. He has a pleasant face.* **4** cause to: *Have them send an extra copy.* **5** cause to be: *I'm having the dress made by a local dressmaker. He had his hair cut yesterday.* **6** be compelled or obliged: *We all have to eat. I had to explain it three times before he understood.* **7** take; obtain or receive: *Have a seat. She always has good marks in French.* **8** show by action: *to have the courage to.* **9** experience: *to have a pain, to have fear.* **10** be infected or afflicted with: *I have a bad cold.* **11** engage in; carry on; perform: *Have a talk with her.* **12** allow; permit (*used with a negative*): *They won't have any liquor in the house.* **13** maintain; assert: *They will have it so.* **14** keep; retain: *He has the directions in his mind.* **15** know; understand: *She has no Latin.* **16** hold in the mind: *to have an idea.* **17** be in a certain relation to: *She has three brothers.* **18** *Informal.* hold an advantage over: *You have him there.* **19** *Slang.* fool or cheat: *I think I've been had.* **20** become the parent of; bear or beget: *They plan to have children. She had her baby yesterday.* **21 have** is also used as an auxiliary for compound tenses expressing completed action: *They have arrived. She has already had four pieces of cake.*
have at, attack; hit.
have done, stop; be through.
have had it, *Slang.* **a** become disgusted; become fed up. **b** reach an end; lose effectiveness, popularity, etc.
have it, a will; make happen: *As luck would have it, we missed the train.* **b** gain a victory or advantage. **c** discover or hit upon an answer, solution, etc.: *Eureka! I have it!* **d** *Informal.* find oneself in certain (good or bad) circumstances: *You never had it so good.*
have it in for, *Informal.* have a grudge against; try to get revenge on.
have it out, fight or argue until a question is settled.
have nothing on, have no advantage of or superiority over.
have on, a be wearing. **b** have scheduled.
have to, must: *All animals have to sleep. We will have to go now.*
have to be, be undeniably: *That has to be the stupidest excuse I've ever heard.*
have to do with, a be connected with; be related to. **b** be a companion, partner, or friend of; associate with.
let (someone) **have it,** scold or punish someone severely.
to have and to hold, to keep and possess. ⟨OE *habban*⟩
☛ *Hom.* HALVE.
☛ *Syn.* **1. Have,** HOLD, OWN = possess or be in possession of something. **Have** is the general word: *He has many friends.* **Hold** emphasizes having control over or keeping: *She holds the office of treasurer. He cannot hold a friend long.* **Own** suggests having a right, especially a legal right, to hold a thing as property: *He owns a farm.*

have•lock ['hævlɒk] *n.* a white cloth covering for a cap. It falls over the back of the neck and gives protection against the sun. ⟨after Henry *Havelock,* a British general⟩

ha•ven ['heivən] *n., v.* —*n.* **1** a harbour, especially one providing shelter from a storm. **2** a place of shelter and safety.
—*v.* shelter in a haven. ⟨OE *hæfen*⟩

have–not ['hæv ,nɒt] *n., adj. Informal.* —*n.* a person, province, or country that has little or no property or wealth.
—*adj.* of a person, province, or country that has little or no property or wealth: *a have-not province.*

have•n't ['hævənt] *v.* have not.

hav•er•sack ['hævər,sæk] *n.* a canvas bag with straps for wearing on the back or over one shoulder, used by soldiers, hikers, etc., for carrying food and equipment. ⟨< F *havresac* < LG *Habersack* oat sack⟩

hav•oc ['hævək] *n.* very great destruction or injury: *Tornadoes, severe earthquakes, and plagues create widespread havoc.*
play havoc with, damage severely; ruin; destroy. ⟨< AF var. of OF *havot* plundering, devastation (especially in phrase *crier havot* cry havoc) < Gmc.⟩

haw¹ [hɒ] *n.* **1** the red berry of the hawthorn. **2** the hawthorn. ⟨OE *haga*⟩

haw² [hɒ] *interj., n., v.* —*interj. or n.* a stammering sound between words.
—*v.* make this sound; stammer. ⟨imitative⟩

haw³ [hɒ] *interj., n., v.* —*interj. or n.* a command to horses, oxen, etc., directing them to turn to the left. *Gee* is used for 'right'.
—*v.* turn to the left. ⟨origin uncertain⟩

haw⁴ [hɒ] *n.* the third eyelid of many animals, especially of a domesticated animal.

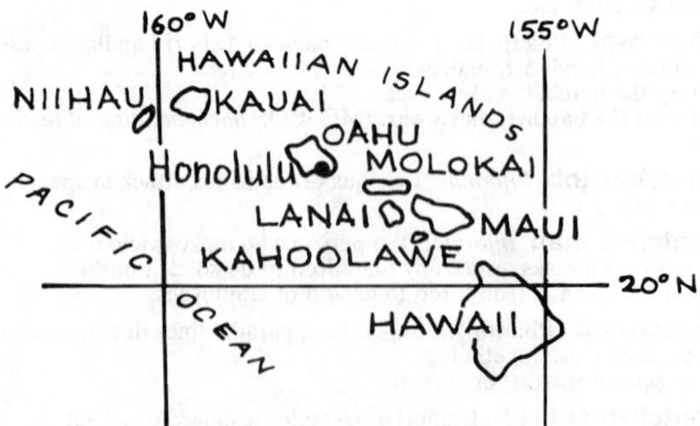

Hawaii, showing the different islands

Ha•waii [hə'waii] *n.* a group of islands in the Pacific Ocean, now a state of the United States.

Ha•wai•ian [hə'waijən] *n., adj.* —*n.* **1** a native or inhabitant of Hawaii, especially a person of Polynesian descent. **2** the Polynesian language of the Hawaiians.
—*adj.* of or having to do with Hawaii, its people, or their language.

haw•finch ['hɒ,fɪntʃ] *n.* an Old World bird (*Coccothraustes coccothraustes*) of the finch family.

hawk[1] [hɒk] *n., v.* —*n.* **1** any of a genus (*Accipiter*) of small or medium-sized birds of prey that are active during the day, such as the goshawk and sparrow hawk. Hawks typically have short, rounded wings and a long tail. **2** any of various other related and similar birds of the family Accipitridae (kites, buzzards, etc.) or the family Falconidae (falcons). **3** a person who tends to take an aggressive or militant stand in controversial issues, especially one who favours war or a policy of military strength. Compare DOVE[1] (def. 3). **4** a rapacious or grasping person.
—*v.* **1** hunt with trained hawks. **2** hunt or pursue like a hawk. ⟨OE *hafoc*⟩ —**'hawk,like,** *adj.*
☛ *Hom.* HOCK.

A hawk

hawk[2] [hɒk] *v.* **1** carry (goods) about for sale as a street peddler does. **2** advertise by shouting that goods are for sale. **3** spread (a report) around. ⟨< *hawker[1]*⟩
☛ *Hom.* HOCK.

hawk[3] [hɒk] *v., n.* —*v.* clear the throat noisily.
—*n.* **1** a noisy effort to clear the throat. **2** the noise made in such an effort. ⟨probably imitative⟩
☛ *Hom.* HOCK.

hawk•er[1] ['hɒkər] *n.* a person who carries his or her wares around and offers them for sale by shouting; peddler. ⟨probably < MLG *hoker.* Akin to HUCKSTER.⟩

hawk•er[2] ['hɒkər] *n.* a person who hunts with a hawk. ⟨< *hawk[1]*⟩

hawk–eyed ['hɒk ,aɪd] *adj.* having sharp eyes like a hawk.

hawk•ing ['hɒkɪŋ] *n., v.* —*n.* the act of hunting with hawks; falconry.
—*v.* ppr. of HAWK.

hawk•ish ['hɒkɪʃ] *adj.* **1** of or like a hawk or like that of a hawk. **2** militant or aggressive; like or characteristic of a HAWK[1] (def. 3): *a hawkish policy, a hawkish atmosphere.*

hawk moth any of numerous large moths (family Sphingidae) having long, narrow forewings and short hindwings and a long, stout body.

hawk's–beard ['hɒks ,bird] *n.* any plant of the dandelion family, of the genus *Crepis.*

hawk's–bill turtle ['hɒks ,bɪl] a small, tropical sea turtle (*Eretmochelys imbricata*) having hooked jaws resembling the bill of a hawk. Tortoise-shell is made from the overlapping plates of its upper shell.

hawk•weed ['hɒk,wid] *n.* any of a large genus (*Hieracium*) of hairy plants of the composite family found in temperate regions of the world, having small, orange or yellow flower heads.

hawse [hɒz] *or* [hɒs] *n.* **1** the part of a ship's bow where the hawseholes are located. See CAPSTAN for picture. **2** hawsepipe. **3** the distance between the bow of a moored ship and its anchor or anchors. ⟨< ON *hals*⟩
☛ *Hom.* HOSS [hɒs].

hawse•hole ['hɒz,houl] *or* ['hɒs,houl] *n.* a hole in the bow of a ship for a hawser or anchor chain to pass through. See CAPSTAN for picture.

hawse•pipe ['hɒz,pɔip] *or* ['hɒs,pɔip] *n.* a heavy iron or steel pipe lining a hawsehole. A hawsepipe has a curved rim that fits tightly against the edge of the hawsehole. See CAPSTAN for picture.

haw•ser ['hɒzər] *or* ['hɒsər] *n.* a large, stout rope or a thin steel cable, used for mooring or towing ships. ⟨ME < OF *haucier* hoist, ult. < L *altus* high⟩

haw•thorn ['hɒ,θɔrn] *n.* any of a genus (*Crataegus*) of thorny shrubs and small trees of the rose family, having simple, usually toothed or lobed leaves, white or pink flowers, and small, usually red fruits called haws. Many hawthorns are cultivated as ornamental shrubs and trees. ⟨OE *hagathorn* < *haga* hedge + *thorn* thorn⟩

hay [hei] *n., v.* —*n.* **1** grass, alfalfa, clover, etc. that has been cut and dried for use as food for cattle, horses, etc. **2** grass ready for mowing.
hit the hay, *Slang.* go to bed.
make hay, a cut and dry grass, alfalfa, clover, etc. for hay. **b** *Informal.* take advantage of some opportunity.
make hay while the sun shines, make hay (def. b).
—*v.* **1** cut and dry grass, alfalfa, clover, etc. for hay: *The workers are haying in the east field.* **2** supply with hay. ⟨OE *hēg.* Related to HEW.⟩
☛ *Hom.* HE[2], HEIGH, HEY.

hay•cock ['hei,kɒk] *n.* a small, cone-shaped pile of hay in a field.

hay•coil ['hei,kɔɪl] *n.* haycock.

hay fever an allergy affecting the respiratory tract and the eyes as a severe cold does, caused by the pollen of ragweed and other plants.

hay•field ['hei,fild] *n.* a field where crops such as grass, alfalfa, or clover are grown or cut for hay.

hay•fork ['hei,fɔrk] *n.* **1** a pitchfork. **2** a mechanically operated device for loading hay into or out of a hayloft.

hay•loft ['hei,lɒft] *n.* the upper storey of a stable or barn, where hay is stored.

hay•mak•er ['hei,meikər] *n.* **1** a person who tosses and spreads hay to dry after it is cut. **2** an apparatus for shaking up and drying hay. **3** *Slang. Boxing.* a hard, swinging, upward blow with the fist.

hay•mow ['hei,mou] *or* ['hei,maʊ] *n.* **1** a place in a barn where hay is stored; hayloft. **2** a heap of hay stored in a barn.

hay•rack ['hei,ræk] *n.* **1** a rack or frame used for holding hay to be eaten by cattle, horses, etc. **2** a framework on a wagon used in hauling hay, straw, etc. **3** the wagon and framework together.

hay•rick ['hei,rɪk] *n.* haystack.

hay•ride ['hei,raɪd] *n.* a ride for fun on a wagon filled with hay, usually horse-drawn.

hay•seed ['hei,sid] *n.* **1** grass seed, especially that shaken out of hay. **2** the chaff that falls from hay. **3** *Cdn. Slang.* an unsophisticated person from the country; rustic.

hay•stack ['hei,stæk] *n.* a large pile of hay outdoors.

hay•wire ['hei,waɪr] *n., adj.* —*n.* wire used to tie up bales of hay.
—*adj.* **1** out of order; tangled up. **2** emotionally disturbed or upset. **3** *Slang.* shoddy; stop-gap; flimsy: *a haywire repair job.* **4** *Cdn. Lumbering slang.* poorly organized and equipped; less than efficient; second-rate.
go haywire, get out of order; act in an excited or confused manner.

haz•ard ['hæzərd] *n., v.* —*n.* **1** risk; danger; peril: *The life of an explorer is full of hazards.* **2** chance. **3** *Golf.* any obstruction on a course that can trap a ball. **4** *Billiards.* a stroke by which the player sends the object ball or his or her own ball (after it hits another) into a pocket. **5** an old and complicated dice game from which craps developed.
at all hazards, whatever the risk; in spite of great danger or peril.
—*v.* take a chance with; risk; venture: *I would hazard my life on her honesty.* ⟨ME < OF *hasard* < Arabic *al-zahr* the die[2]⟩

haz•ard•ous ['hæzərdəs] *adj.* dangerous; risky; perilous. —**'haz•ard•ous•ly,** *adv.* —**'haz•ard•ous•ness,** *n.*

haze[1] [heiz] *n., v.* **hazed, haz•ing.** —*n.* **1** a small amount of mist, smoke, dust, etc. in the air: *A thin haze veiled the hills.* **2** vagueness of the mind during which one sees things indistinctly: *After he was hit on the head, everything was in a haze for him.*
—*v.* make or become hazy (*used with* **over**). ⟨origin uncertain; cf. E dial. *haze* drizzle, be foggy⟩

haze[2] [heiz] *v.* **hazed, haz•ing. 1** force to do unnecessary or ridiculous tasks as part of an initiation process: *The new student resented being hazed by the older students.* **2** in western Canada and the United States, drive (cattle, horses, etc.) from horseback. ⟨? < OF *haser* irritate, harass⟩ —**'haz•er,** *n.*

ha•zel ['heizəl] *n., adj.* —*n.* **1** any of a genus (*Corylus*) of shrubs and small trees of the birch family bearing round, brown, edible nuts. **2** the wood of any of these trees. **3** hazelnut. **4** a greenish brown colour.
—*adj.* having the colour hazel: *hazel eyes.* ⟨OE *hæsel*⟩

ha•zel•nut ['heizəl,nʌt] *n.* the round, brown, edible nut of a hazel; filbert.

ha•zy ['heizi] *adj.* **-zi•er, -zi•est. 1** full of haze; misty; smoky:

hazy air. **2** rather confused; vague; obscure: *hazy ideas.*
—'ha•zi•ly, *adv.* **—'ha•zi•ness,** *n.*

HB a symbol used on pencils to indicate a medium degree of hardness of the lead. Compare B (def. 8) and H (def. 4).

H.B.C. HUDSON'S BAY COMPANY.

H–bomb ['eitʃ ,bɒm] *n.* HYDROGEN BOMB.

H.C. HOUSE OF COMMONS.

H.C.F., h.c.f., or **hcf** highest common factor.

h.c.l. *Informal.* high cost of living.

hd. head(s).

hdbk. handbook(s).

hdkf. handkerchief(s).

HDL high-density lipoprotein, a lipoprotein that helps rid the bloodstream of cholesterol.

HDN HEMOLYTIC DISEASE OF THE NEWBORN.

hdqrs. headquarters.

HDTV high-definition television.

he[1] [hi]; *unstressed and non-initial,* [i] *pron., subj.* **he,** *obj.* **him,** *poss.* **his,** *pl. subj.* **they,** *pl. obj.* **them,** *pl. poss.* **theirs;** *n., pl.* **he's.**
—pron. **1** a boy, man, or male animal that has just been referred to: *Miso has to work hard, but he likes his job and it pays him well.* **2** anyone; a person: *He who hesitates is lost.*
—n. a male human being or animal: *There were three he's and two she's in the litter of kittens.* ⟨OE *hē*⟩

he[2] [hei] *n.* the sixth letter of the Hebrew alphabet. See table of alphabets in the Appendix.
☛ *Hom.* HAY, HEIGH, HEY.

He helium.

HE or **H.E.** HIGH EXPLOSIVE.

H.E. **1** His Eminence. **2** His Excellency; Her Excellency.

head [hɛd] *n., pl.* **heads** (for 1-9, 11-32) or **head** (for 10); *adj., v., adv.* *—n.* **1** the top part of the human body where the eyes, ears, and mouth are. **2** the corresponding part of an animal's or insect's body. **3** the top part of anything: *the head of a pin, the head of a page.* **4** the foremost part or end of anything; the front: *the head of a procession.* **5** a likeness of a head, especially as a work of art: *A marble head of the emperor was in the museum.* **6** the side of a coin bearing the likeness of a head, especially that of a king, queen, president, etc.: *The head of a Canadian coin carries a portrait of Queen Elizabeth II.* **7** the chief person; leader; commander; director. **8** the position of head; chief authority; leadership; command; direction. **9** a person; an individual: *Kings and queens are crowned heads.* **10** a unit, used in counting animals: *She sold fifty head of cattle and ten head of horses.* **11** anything rounded like a head: *a head of cabbage or lettuce.* **12** *Botany.* a cluster of small flowers growing closely together, as in composite plants or clover. **13** the part of a boil or pimple where pus is about to break through the skin. **14** the striking part of a tool or implement: *the head of a hammer.* **15** a piece of skin stretched tightly over the end of a drum, tambourine, etc. **16** either end of a barrel or cask. **17** the end of a bed, couch, etc. at which a person's head is placed. **18** mind; understanding; intelligence; intellect: *The old woman has a wise head.* **19** a particular mental ability: *a good head for figures.* **20** a topic; point: *He arranged his speech under four main heads.* **21** headline. **22** headland. **23** *Music.* the round part of a note, as distinct from the stem. **24** *Slang.* one who uses drugs: *an acid head.* **25** a decisive point; crisis; conclusion: *Her sudden refusal brought matters to a head.* **26** strength or force gained little by little: *As more people joined, the movement gathered head.* **27** pressure of water, steam, etc. **28** the source of a river or stream. **29** foam; froth, as on beer. **30** *Nautical.* **a** the forward part of a ship. **b** a toilet. **31** the device in a tape-recorder that records or deletes information on a magnetic tape or disk. **32** *Computer technology.* the component of a computer peripheral (disk drive, tape drive, etc.) that contacts or is situated very close to the recording surface for purposes of reading or writing data. Also called **read/write head.**
come to a head, a of boils, pimples, etc., reach the stage where they are about to break through the skin. **b** reach a decisive stage: *The international crisis came to a head and war was declared.*
give (someone) **his** or **her head,** let someone go as he or she pleases.
go to (one's) **head, a** affect one's mind. **b** make one dizzy or intoxicated. **c** make one conceited.
hang or **hide** (one's) **head,** be ashamed and show that one is so.
head over heels, a in a somersault. **b** hastily; rashly. **c** completely; thoroughly.
heads up, be careful; watch out: *Heads up! The principal's coming.*
keep (one's) **head,** not get excited; stay calm.
keep (one's) **head above water, a** stay afloat. **b** keep out of trouble or difficulty, especially financial difficulty: *He's finding it hard to keep his head above water these days.*
lay or **put heads together, a** confer; consult. **b** plot; conspire.
lose (one's) **head,** get excited; lose one's self-control.
make head, move forward; make progress; advance.
make head or tail of, understand.
on or **upon** (one's) **head,** on one's responsibility.
(one's) **head off,** (do something) very much: *to laugh one's head off, to work one's head off.*
out of or **off** (one's) **head,** *Informal.* crazy; insane.
over (someone's) **head, a** beyond one's power to understand or manage. **b** bypassing a person of lesser authority: *She threatened to go to the manager over the crew supervisor's head.* **c** so as to slight or ignore a person who has a prior claim, or a better right: *An outsider has now been promoted over their heads.*
take it into (one's) **head, a** get the idea. **b** plan; intend.
talk (someone's) **head off,** talk endlessly.
turn (someone's) **head,** make someone conceited: *Her early success has not turned her head.*
—adj. **1** at the head, top, or front: *the head division of a parade.* **2** coming from in front: *a head wind.* **3** chief; leading; commanding, directing. **4** of, having to do with, or for the head.
—v. **1** be or go at the head, top, or front of: *to head a parade.* **2** cause to move or face in a certain direction: *to head a boat toward shore.* **3** move or go in a certain direction: *It's getting late; we'd better head for home.* **4** be the head or chief of; lead; command; direct: *to head a business.* **5** put a head on; furnish with a head. **6** form a head; come to a head. **7** cut off the head of. **8** *Soccer.* direct the movement of (the ball) with one's head: *He headed the ball away from his opponent.*
head off, a get in front of and turn back or aside: *The cow hands tried to head off the stampeding herd.* **b** prevent; forestall: *She tried to head off possible trouble for herself by taking great care.*
—adv. **heads,** of a coin, with the head side uppermost: *The coin came up heads.* ⟨OE *hēafod*⟩ **—'head,like,** *adj.*

head•ache ['hɛd,eik] *n.* **1** pain in the head. **2** *Informal.* any thing, situation, etc. that is the cause of great bother, annoyance, etc.

head•ach•y ['hɛd,eiki] *adj.* liable to have headaches.

head•band ['hɛd,bænd] *n.* **1** a band of cloth, ribbon, leather, etc. worn around the head to hold the hair in place or for ornament, for warmth, or to prevent sweat from running down the face. **2** a flexible metal or plastic band that holds an earphone or earphones or earmuffs in place over the ear. **3** a decorative strip of material at the top and sometimes at the bottom of the spine of a book. **4** a decorative printed strip at the head of a page or chapter in a book.

head•board ['hɛd,bɔrd] *n.* a board or frame that forms the head of a bed.

head•cheese ['hɛd,tʃiz] *n.* a jellied loaf formed of parts of the head and feet of pigs cut up, cooked, and seasoned.

head cold the common cold when it affects mostly the sinus passages.

head crash *Computer technology.* the destructive contact of a read/write head with a computer disk's recording surface. A head crash renders the disk unusable and usually results in lost data.

head•dress ['hɛd,drɛs] *n.* **1** a covering or decoration for the head. **2** a way of wearing or arranging the hair.

head•ed ['hɛdɪd] *adj., v.* *—adj.* **1** having a head or heads. **2** having a head or heads of a specified kind or number (*used in compounds*): *pig-headed, bald-headed, light-headed.* **3** having a (specified) heading.
—v. pt. and pp. of HEAD.

head•er ['hɛdər] *n.* **1** a person, tool, or machine that puts on or takes off heads of grain, barrels, pins, etc. **2** *Informal.* a plunge or dive headfirst: *She took a header into the water.* **3** *Masonry.* a brick or stone laid with its length across the thickness of a wall and its end facing the outer surface of the wall. Compare STRETCHER (def. 3). **4** *Carpentry.* **a** a beam set across and supporting the ends of joists, studs, or rafters to form one side of an opening in a wall, floor, or roof. See FRAME for picture. **b** lintel. **5** a pipe that is a central connection for other pipes. **6** *Soccer.* the act of hitting the ball with the head. **7** a running title appearing at the top of each page of a chapter, section, etc. Compare FOOTER.

head•first ['hɛd'fɜrst] *adv., adj.* *—adv.* **1** with the head first.

2 rashly.
—*adj.* done or going with the head first: *a headfirst dive.*

head•fore•most ['hɛd'fɔr,moust] *adv.* headfirst.

head•frame ['hɛd,freim] *n. Mining.* the structure over a shaft to support the hoisting equipment.

head gate 1 an upstream gate of a lock in a canal or river. 2 the floodgate of a race, sluice, etc.

head•gear ['hɛd,gir] *n.* 1 a covering for the head; hat, cap, etc. 2 the harness for an animal's head.

head–hunt•er ['hɛd ,hʌntər] *n.* 1 a person who practises head-hunting. 2 *Slang.* a person or agency that tries to find highly skilled people to work for a particular company, often luring away those already employed elsewhere.

head–hunt•ing ['hɛd ,hʌntɪŋ] *n., adj.* —*n.* 1 the practice, among certain primitive people, of trying to get the heads of enemies as a sign of victory, adulthood, etc. 2 the search for skilled employees by a professional head-hunter.
—*adj.* of or having to do with head-hunters.

head•ing ['hɛdɪŋ] *n., v.* —*n.* 1 the part forming the head, top, or front. 2 something written or printed at the top of a page. 3 the title of a page, chapter, etc.; topic. 4 the direction of a ship or aircraft as indicated by a compass.
—*v.* ppr. of HEAD.

head•lamp ['hɛd,læmp] *n.* 1 a small lamp worn on the cap or the forehead. 2 a headlight on a train, automobile, etc.

head•land ['hɛdlənd] *or* ['hɛd,lænd] *n.* a point of land jutting out into water; cape.

head•less ['hɛdlɪs] *adj.* 1 having no head. 2 without a leader. 3 without brains; stupid.

head lettuce a variety of lettuce whose leaves form a solid head.

head•light ['hɛd,ləit] *n.* 1 of vehicles such as automobiles, one of two large lights at the front. 2 a large single light at the front of a locomotive, streetcar, etc. 3 on a ship, a light at a masthead.

head•line ['hɛd,laɪn] *n., v.* **-lined, -lin•ing.** —*n.* 1 the words printed at the top of an article in a newspaper or magazine to indicate the topic dealt with. 2 a line printed at the top of a page giving the running title, page number, etc. 3 a summary of radio or television news, read before giving details. 3 **headlines,** publicity: *He's the kind of man who gets plenty of headlines.* **make headlines,** receive publicity: *The new discovery made headlines everywhere.*
—*v.* furnish with a headline.

head•lin•er ['hɛd,laɪnər] *n.* one who makes headlines; a star.

head•lock ['hɛd,lɒk] *n. Wrestling.* a hold in which a person's head is held between the body and arm of the opponent.

head•long ['hɛd,lɒŋ] *adv. or adj.* 1 headfirst. 2 moving with great speed and force. 3 without stopping to think; in too great a rush; rash or rashly: *rushing headlong into trouble.* ⟨ME *hedlong,* alteration of earlier *hedlyng* < *hed* head + *-ling,* adv. suffix expressing direction, OE *-ling*⟩

head•man ['hɛd,mæn] *or* ['hɛdmən] *n., pl.* **-men.** a chief; leader.

head•mas•ter ['hɛd,mæstər] *n.* a man in charge of a school, especially of a private school; principal. —**'head,mas•ter,ship,** *n.*

head•mis•tress ['hɛd,mɪstrəs] *n.* a woman in charge of a school, especially of a private school; principal.

head•most ['hɛd,moust] *adj.* first; most advanced.

head of steel *Cdn.* END OF STEEL.

Head of the Lake *Cdn.* formerly, the western end of Lake Ontario; the vicinity of Burlington, Hamilton, and Niagara-on-the-Lake.

head–on ['hɛd 'ɒn] *adj., adv.* —*adj.* with the head or front first: *a head-on collision.*
—*adv.* in a direct way: *to tackle the issue head-on.*

head•phone ['hɛd,foun] *n.* a telephone or radio receiver held on the head, against the ears.

head•piece ['hɛd,pis] *n.* 1 a piece of armour for the head; helmet. 2 a hat, cap, or other covering for the head. 3 headphone. 4 *Informal.* the head; mind; intellect. 5 *Printing.* a decoration at the head of a page, chapter, etc.

head pin *Bowling.* the front pin of the triangle of pins.

head•quar•ters ['hɛd,kwɔrtərz] *n.pl. or sing.* 1 the place from which the chief or commanding officer of an army, police force, etc. sends out orders. 2 the centre from which any organization is controlled and directed; main office: *The headquarters of the Canadian Red Cross Society is in Ottawa.*

head•race ['hɛd,reis] *n.* a channel leading water into any machinery operated by it, such as a mill wheel.

head register *Music.* the upper range of a voice.

head•rest ['hɛd,rɛst] *n.* a support for the head: *The dentist's chair has a headrest.*

head•room ['hɛd,rum] *or* ['hɛd,rʊm] *n.* a clear space above; clearance; headway: *Some bridges do not have enough headroom to allow high trucks to pass underneath.*

head•sail ['hɛd,seil] *or* ['hɛdsəl] *n.* any sail set before the foremast.

head•set ['hɛd,sɛt] *n.* a pair of earphones, often with a small microphone attached.

head•ship ['hɛdʃɪp] *n.* the position of head; chief authority.

head•shrink•er ['hɛd,ʃrɪŋkər] *n.* 1 *Slang.* psychiatrist. 2 a head-hunter who cuts off and shrinks the heads of enemies.

heads•man ['hɛdzmən] *n., pl.* **-men.** a man who puts condemned persons to death by cutting off their heads.

head•spring ['hɛd,sprɪŋ] *n.* a source.

head•stall ['hɛd,stɒl] *n.* an arrangement of leather straps or rope that fits over the head of an animal, especially one that forms part of the bridle or halter of a horse.

head•stand ['hɛd,stænd] *n.* a position in which the head is on the floor while the rest of the body, supported by the hands, is upright.

head start 1 an advantage or lead allowed someone at the beginning of a race: *The smaller boy was given a head start.* 2 an advantage gained by beginning something before somebody else or by making a better beginning than others: *That team is playing better hockey than we are because they had a head start in practising. Breastfeeding gives your baby a head start in life.*

head•stock ['hɛd,stɒk] *n.* 1 the part of a machine that contains the revolving or working parts. 2 the part of a lathe that holds the spindle.

head•stone ['hɛd,stoun] *n.* 1 a stone set at the head of a grave; tombstone. 2 the principal stone in a foundation; cornerstone.

head•stream ['hɛd,strim] *n.* a stream that is the source of a larger stream.

head•strong ['hɛd,strɒŋ] *adj.* 1 rashly or foolishly determined to have one's own way; hard to control or manage; obstinate: *a headstrong youth.* 2 showing rash or foolish determination to have one's own way: *a headstrong action.*

heads–up ['hɛdz 'ʌp] *adj.* alert for possible opportunities.

head–to–head ['hɛd tə 'hɛd] *adj.* directly opposed.

head tone a note produced in the second or third register of the voice, causing vibration in the cavities of the head.

head•wait•er ['hɛd'weitər] *n.* one in charge of the waiters in a restaurant, hotel, etc.

head•wa•ters ['hɛd,wɒtərz] *n.pl.* the sources or upper parts of a river.

head•way ['hɛd,wei] *n.* 1 forward motion: *The ship could make no headway against the strong wind and tide.* 2 progress with work, etc. 3 a clear space overhead in a doorway or under an arch, bridge, etc; clearance. 4 the interval of time between two trains, streetcars, ships, etc. going in the same direction over the same route.

head wind a wind blowing straight against the front of a ship, plane, etc.

head•word ['hɛd,wɜrd] *n.* 1 a word that is modified by another word or words; the main word of a phrase. 2 ENTRY WORD.

head•work ['hɛd,wɜrk] *n.* mental work; effort with the mind.

head•y ['hɛdi] *adj.* **head•i•er, head•i•est.** 1 hasty; rash. 2 apt to affect the head and make one dizzy; intoxicating. ⟨ME *hevedi* headlong⟩ —**'head•i•ly,** *adv.* —**'head•i•ness,** *n.*

heal [hil] *v.* 1 make whole, sound, or well; bring back to health; cure (a disease or wound). 2 become whole or sound; get well; return to health; be cured: *His cut finger healed in a few days.* 3 make free from anything bad, such as a quarrel. 4 get rid of (anything bad). ⟨OE *hǣlan* < *hāl* well, whole⟩ —**'heal•er,** *n.*
☛ *Hom.* HEEL, HE'LL.
☛ *Syn.* 1. See note at CURE.

health [hɛlθ] *n., interj.* —*n.* 1 a being well; freedom from sickness. 2 a condition of body or mind: *She is in poor health.* 3 a toast drunk in honour of a person with a wish that she or he

may be healthy and happy: *We all drank a health to the bride.* **4** moral soundness.
—*interj.* **your health,** a phrase used in drinking a person's health. ⟨OE *hǣlth* < *hāl* well, whole⟩

health club an organization providing exercise facilities and sometimes healthy food for its members.

health food natural foodstuffs chosen for their healthy effect on the body, such as grains and nuts. **—'health-,food,** *adj.*

health•ful ['hɛlθfəl] *adj.* giving health; good for the health: *healthful exercise, a healthful diet.* **—'health•ful•ly,** *adv.* **—'health•ful•ness,** *n.*

☛ *Usage.* **Healthful,** HEALTHY. Formal usage tends to distinguish between these words, using **healthful** to mean 'giving health', and **healthy** to mean 'having good health'. Places and food are *healthful;* persons and animals are *healthy.*

health spa a place where people can go to benefit from exercise, steam baths, etc.

healthy ['hɛlθi] *adj.* **health•i•er, health•i•est. 1** having good health: *a healthy baby.* **2** showing good health: *a healthy appearance.* **3** *Informal.* healthful. **—'health•i•ly,** *adv.* **—'health•i•ness,** *n.*

☛ *Syn.* **1, 2. Healthy,** WHOLESOME = having or showing health. **Healthy** emphasizes energy, strength, and freedom from sickness (physical or mental) both when used literally of people and when used figuratively of ideas, society, etc.: *He has a healthy appearance.* **Wholesome** emphasizes soundness and freedom from weakness, decay, or harmfulness physically or, particularly, emotionally or morally: *Our uncle gave us some wholesome advice.*

☛ *Usage.* See note at HEALTHFUL.

heap [hip] *n., v.* —*n.* **1** a pile of many things thrown or lying together: *a heap of stones, a sand heap.* **2** *Informal.* a large amount.
—*v.* **1** form into a heap; gather in heaps: *She heaped the dirty clothes beside the washing machine.* **2** give generously or in large amounts: *His mother heaped potatoes on his plate. His friends heaped praise on him after his victory.* **3** fill to the point of overflowing; load: *a plate heaped with potatoes.* ⟨OE *hēap*⟩

hear [hir] *v.* **heard, hear•ing;** *interj.* —*v.* **1** perceive by the ear: *to hear sounds, to hear voices.* **2** be able to perceive things by the ear: *She does not hear well.* **3** listen to: *to hear a person's explanation.* **4** listen. **5** give a chance to be heard; give a formal hearing to, as a king, a judge, a teacher, or an assembly does. **6** find out by hearing: *to hear news.* **7** be told; receive news or information: *I don't know the plans for the meeting; I haven't heard yet.* **8** listen to with favour: *Lord, hear my prayer.*
hear from, a receive news or information from: *Have you heard from your friend?* **b** receive a reprimand from.
hear of, have some knowledge of: *I've never heard of her.*
hear out, listen to till the end.
will not hear of it, will not listen to, think of, agree to, or allow it.
—*interj.* **hear! hear!** shouts of approval; cheering. ⟨OE *hēran*⟩ **—'hear•er,** *n.*

☛ *Hom.* HERE.

☛ *Syn. v.* **1. Hear,** LISTEN = perceive by the ear. **Hear** applies to the physical act of receiving sound through the ear: *Do you hear a noise?* **Listen** = pay attention to a sound and try to hear or understand it: *I heard him talking, but did not listen to what he said.*

heard [hɜrd] *v.* pt. and pp. of HEAR.

hear•ing ['hiriŋ] *n., v.* —*n.* **1** the sense by which sound is perceived: *The old man's hearing is poor.* **2** the act or process of perceiving sound: *Hearing the good news made her happy.* **3** a formal or official listening: *The Royal Commission has set a date for its next hearing.* **4** the trial of an action: *The judge gave both sides a hearing in court.* **5** a chance to be heard: *Give us a hearing.* **6** the distance that a sound can be heard: *to be within hearing of the baby, to talk freely in the hearing of others.*
—*v.* ppr. of HEAR.

hearing aid a device used to improve hearing. Most modern hearing aids are operated by batteries, which provide power for making sounds louder.

hear•ing–im•paired ['hiriŋ ɪm'pɛrd] *adj.* deaf or somewhat deaf.

heark•en ['hɑrkən] *v. Archaic.* listen; listen attentively. Also, **harken.** ⟨OE *hercnian, heorcnian*⟩

hear•say ['hir,sei] *n.* common talk; gossip.

hearsay evidence *Law.* evidence based on the testimony of another person, rather than on the first-hand knowledge of the witness. Such evidence is usually not admissible.

hearse [hɜrs] *n.* an automobile, carriage, etc. used in funerals to carry a dead person to his or her grave. ⟨ME < OF *herce* < L *hirpex, -picis,* harrow; originally, a frame like a harrow⟩

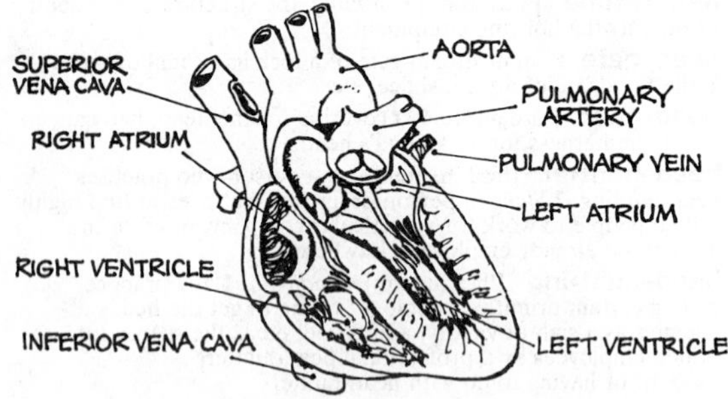

The human heart

heart [hɑrt] *n.* **1** a hollow, muscular organ that pumps the blood throughout the body by contracting and dilating. **2** the region of the heart; breast; bosom: *She clasped her hands to her heart.* **3** the feelings; mind; soul: *She has a kind heart.* **4** the source of the emotions, especially of love: *to give one's heart.* **5** a person, especially one who is loved or praised: *a group of stout hearts.* **6** kindness; sympathy: *to have no heart.* **7** spirit; courage; enthusiasm: *The losing team showed plenty of heart.* **8** the innermost part; middle; centre: *in the heart of the forest.* **9** the main part; vital or most important part: *the very heart of the matter.* **10** a conventional figure shaped somewhat like a heart: *There was a big red heart on the front of the valentine.* **11 a** a playing card with one or more red heart-shaped figures. **b hearts,** *pl.* a suit of playing cards with red heart-shaped designs on them. **c hearts,** a game in which the players try to get rid of cards of this suit (*used with a singular verb*).
after (one's) **own heart,** just as one likes it; pleasing one perfectly.
at heart, in one's deepest thoughts or feelings; really.
break the heart of, crush with envy or grief.
by heart, a by memory. **b** from memory.
change of heart, a complete reversal of opinion.
eat (one's) **heart out,** feel great envy, grief, or worry.
from (one's) **heart,** with deepest feeling; sincerely.
get to the heart of, find out the fundamental nature or significance of.
have a heart, *Informal.* be kind, merciful, or sympathetic.
have (one's) **heart in** (one's) **boots** or **mouth,** be very frightened.
have (one's) **heart in the right place,** mean well; have good intentions.
have the heart, a be courageous or spirited enough (to do something). **b** be hard-hearted enough: *He hadn't the heart to refuse his son's request.*
heart and soul, with all one's affections and energies.
heart of gold, an extremely kind, generous, and sympathetic nature.
in (one's) **heart of hearts,** in one's deepest thoughts or feelings.
lay to heart, a keep in mind; remember. **b** think seriously about.
lose (one's) **heart to,** fall in love with; become devoted to.
near (one's) **heart,** of great value or interest to one.
set (one's) **heart at rest,** comfort or reassure one.
set (one's) **heart on,** be determined to have or do.
steal (one's) **heart,** cause one to love.
take heart, be encouraged.
take to heart, think seriously about or be deeply affected by.
to (one's) **heart's content,** as much as one wants.
wear (one's) **heart on** (one's) **sleeve,** show one's feelings too plainly.
with all (one's) **heart, a** sincerely. **b** gladly. ⟨OE *heorte*⟩

☛ *Hom.* HART.

heart•ache ['hɑrt,eik] *n.* sorrow; grief.

heart attack a sudden instance of heart disease, especially a coronary thrombosis resulting in the destruction of an area of heart muscle.

heart•beat ['hɑrt,bit] *n.* a pulsation of the heart, including one complete contraction and dilation.

heart block a defect in co-ordination of the beat of the heart.

heart•break ['hɑrt,breik] *n.* a crushing sorrow or grief.

heart•break•ing ['hɑrt,breikiŋ] *adj.* crushing with sorrow or grief. **—'heart,break•ing•ly,** *adv.*

heart•brok•en ['hɑrt,broukən] *adj.* crushed with sorrow or grief. **—'heart,brok•en•ly,** *adv.* **—'heart,brok•en•ness,** *n.*

heart•burn ['hɑrt,bɜrn] *n.* a burning sensation in the lower chest and the stomach, generally caused by digestive juices escaping from the stomach up into the esophagus.

heart•burn•ing ['hɑrt,bɜrnɪŋ] *n.* a feeling of envy or jealousy.

–hearted *combining form.* having a heart of a specified kind: *good-hearted, light-hearted.*

heart•en ['hɑrtən] *v.* encourage; cheer up: *Good news heartens you.* **—'heart•en•er,** *n.*

heart failure **1** a condition in which one or both sides of the heart are unable to pump enough blood to meet the needs of the body. **2** a sudden stopping of the heartbeat, resulting in death.

heart•felt ['hɑrt,fɛlt] *adj.* sincere; genuine.

hearth [hɑrθ] *n.* **1** the floor of a fireplace. **2** the home; fireside: *The soldier longed for his own hearth.* **3** the lowest part of a blast furnace. ⟨OE *heorth*⟩

hearth•side ['hɑrθ,saɪd] *n.* **1** the side of a hearth. **2** the home.

hearth•stone ['hɑrθ,stoun] *n.* **1** a stone forming a hearth. **2** the home; fireside. **3** a type of soft sandstone used for cleaning a hearth or stone steps.

heart•i•ly ['hɑrtəli] *adv.* **1** sincerely; genuinely; in a warm, friendly way: *to express good wishes very heartily.* **2** with enthusiasm; with a good will; vigorously: *to set to work heartily.* **3** with a good appetite. **4** very; completely; thoroughly.

heart•i•ness ['hɑrtinɪs] *n.* **1** sincerity. **2** warmth: *The heartiness of her laugh was pleasant.*

heart•land ['hɑrt,lænd] *n.* any area or region that is the centre of, or vital to, an institution, industry, country, etc.

heart•less ['hɑrtlɪs] *adj.* **1** without kindness or sympathy; unfeeling; cruel. **2** *Archaic.* without courage, spirit, or enthusiasm. **—'heart•less•ly,** *adv.* **—'heart•less•ness,** *n.*

heart–lung machine or **pump** ['hɑrt 'lʌŋ] *Medicine.* a device used during heart surgery to pump blood through the body, thus temporarily taking the place of the heart.

heart•nut ['hɑrt,nʌt] *n.* a tree (*Juglans cordiformis ailanthifolia)* bearing heart-shaped nuts resembling walnuts.

heart–rend•ing ['hɑrt ,rɛndɪŋ] *adj.* causing mental anguish; very distressing. **—'heart-,rend•ing•ly,** *adv.*

hearts•ease or **heart's–ease** ['hɑrts ,iz] *n.* **1** WILD PANSY. **2** peace of mind.

heart•sick ['hɑrt,sɪk] *adj.* sick at heart; very much depressed; very unhappy.

heart•sore ['hɑrt,sɔr] *adj.* feeling or showing grief; grieved.

heart–strick•en ['hɑrt ,strɪkən] *adj.* struck to the heart with grief; shocked with fear; dismayed.

heart•strings ['hɑrt,strɪŋz] *n.pl.* deepest feelings; strongest affections: *The new baby tugs at my heartstrings.*

heart–throb ['hɑrt ,θrɒb] *n.* **1** heartbeat. **2** *Informal.* a person with whom one is infatuated.

heart–to–heart ['hɑrt tə 'hɑrt] *adj.* without reserve; frank; sincere: *a heart-to-heart talk.*

heart•warm•ing ['hɑrt,wɔrmɪŋ] *adj.* able to stir up warm, sympathetic, or happy feelings.

heart–whole ['hɑrt ,houl] *adj.* **1** not in love. **2** hearty; sincere.

heart•wood ['hɑrt,wʊd] *n.* the hard, central wood of a tree.

heart•worm ['hɑrt,wɜrm] *n.* a nematode worm (*Dirofilaria immitis)* parasitic on dogs and cats.

heart•y ['hɑrti] *adj.* **heart•i•er, heart•i•est;** *n., pl.* **heart•ies.**
—adj. **1** warm and friendly; genuine; sincere: *a hearty welcome.* **2** strong and well; vigorous: *The old man was still hale and hearty.* **3** full of energy and enthusiasm; not restrained: *He burst out in a loud, hearty laugh.* **4** with plenty to eat; nourishing: *A hearty meal satisfied her hunger.* **5** requiring or using much food: *a hearty eater.*
—n. **1** a fellow sailor; a brave and good comrade. **2** an excessively hearty and effusive person; backslapper. ⟨< *heart*⟩

heat [hit] *n., v.* *—n.* **1** the quality or state of being hot; hotness; high temperature. **2** the degree of hotness; temperature. **3** the sensation or perception of hotness or warmth. **4** *Physics.* a form of energy that consists in the motion of the molecules of a substance. The rate at which the molecules move determines the temperature. **5** hot weather. **6** the artificial warming of a house or apartment: *Does the rent include heat?* **7** warmth or intensity of feeling; anger; violence; excitement; eagerness; ardour. **8** the hottest point; most violent or active state: *In the heat of the fight he lost his temper.* **9** *Slang.* pressure; coercion; torture. **10** one trial in a race: *She won the first heat, but lost the final race.* **11** one operation of heating in a furnace or a forge. **12** the amount processed in one such operation. **13** a periodically recurring condition of sexual excitement in female mammals; estrus. **14** the time during which this excitement lasts.
in heat, in such a condition of excitement, and so able to be mated.
—v. **1** make hot or warm; become hot or warm (*often with* **up).** **2** fill with strong feeling; inflame; excite; become excited. ⟨OE *hǣtu.* Related to HOT.⟩

heat barrier See THERMAL BARRIER.

heat•ed ['hitɪd] *adj., v.* *—adj.* angry or excited: *a heated debate, a heated reply.*
—v. pt and pp. of HEAT. **—'heat•ed•ly,** *adv.*

heat engine a machine that converts heat to mechanical energy.

heat•er ['hitər] *n.* **1** a device that gives heat or warmth, especially one that is not part of a central heating system: *an electric baseboard heater. They have a block heater for their car.* **2** *Electronics.* an element in a vacuum tube that carries current to heat the cathode.

heat exchanger a device by means of which heat is transferred from one medium to another in order that it may be utilized as a source of power, as in an atomic power plant, certain gas turbine engines, etc.

heat exhaustion a condition due to prolonged exposure to heat, characterized by excessive sweating, faintness, dizziness, and, often, nausea. Compare HEATSTROKE.

heath [hiθ] *n.* **1** *Brit.* open wasteland, usually having sandy, acid soil and scrubby vegetation; moor. **2** any of a genus (*Erica*) of evergreen shrubs or trees having whorls of small, needlelike leaves and clusters of small, bell-shaped or tubular flowers. Heaths are common in much of Europe and Africa, especially on open wasteland with acid soil. **3** any of various other shrubs of similar habit and appearance, especially of the same family. **4** (*adjl.*) designating the family (Ericaceae) of shrubs and trees that includes the heaths, heathers, rhododendrons, and blueberries.
(one's) **native heath,** the place where one was born or brought up. ⟨OE *hǣth*⟩

heath•bird ['hiθ,bɜrd] *n. Brit.* BLACK GROUSE.

heath•cock ['hiθ,kɒk] *n. Brit.* a male black grouse.

hea•then ['hiðən] *n., pl.* **-thens** or (*esp. collectively*) **-then;** *adj.*
—n. **1** a polytheist, pantheist, or animist. **2** a person thought to have no religion or culture; barbarian.
—adj. of or being a heathen or heathens. ⟨OE *hǣthen,* probably originally, heath dweller < *hǣth* heath⟩
☛ *Usage.* See note at PAGAN.

hea•then•dom ['hiðəndəm] *n.* **1** heathen ways. **2** heathen lands or people.

hea•then•ish ['hiðənɪʃ] *adj.* resembling or characteristic of the heathen; barbarous. **—'hea•then•ish•ly,** *adv.* **—'hea•then•ish•ness,** *n.*

hea•then•ism ['hiðə,nɪzəm] *n.* **1** heathen ways. **2** the lack of religion or culture; barbarism.

heath•er ['hɛðər] *n.* any of several species of heath, especially a plant (*Calluna vulgaris*) native to northern and alpine regions of Europe and Asia and common in the British Isles, having clusters of tiny, bell-shaped, usually purplish pink flowers. ⟨? < *heath*⟩

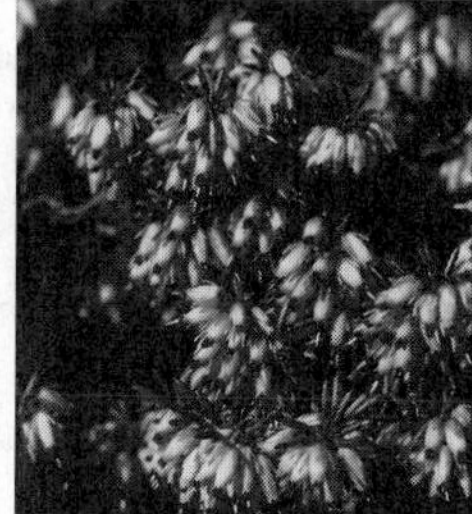
Heather

heath•er•y ['hɛðəri] *adj.* **1** of or like heather. **2** covered with heather.

heath•hen ['hiθ,hɛn] *n. Brit.* a female black grouse.

heating element the part of an electrical heating device that gets hot.

heating pad a pad of cloth covering a heating element powered by electricity, used to soothe a part of the body that aches.

heat lightning flashes of light seen near the horizon,

especially on hot summer evenings, thought to be a reflection of more distant lightning.

heat of fusion the heat needed to melt a solid into a liquid.

heat of vaporization the heat needed to convert a liquid into a gas.

heat pump a device using mechanical energy to transfer heat from one place or space to another one that is at a higher temperature. A heat pump can be used to heat a house in winter when the air is warmer inside, and to cool it in summer when the air is warmer outside.

heat shield a coating or covering of special material on the nose cone of a missile or spacecraft to protect it from the heat produced when it re-enters the earth's atmosphere.

heat sink a device for storing heat absorbed by a cooling system.

heat•stroke ['hit,strouk] *n.* a serious illness produced by long exposure to extreme heat and humidity, in which the body temperature rises dangerously high because sweating can no longer function to cool the body. Compare HEAT EXHAUSTION.

heat wave a long period of very hot weather.

heave [hiv] *v.* **heaved** or *(esp. def. 9 and idioms)* **hove, heav•ing;** *n., interj.* *—v.* **1** lift with force or effort: *He heaved the heavy box into the wagon.* **2** lift and throw: *The sailors heaved the anchor overboard.* **3** pull with force or effort; haul: *They heaved on the rope.* **4** utter with effort: *He heaved a sigh of relief.* **5** rise and fall rhythmically: *the heaving sea.* **6** rise; swell or bulge: *The ground heaved during the earthquake.* **7** pant: *She was heaving from the exertion.* **8** try to vomit; retch. **9** of a ship, train, etc., move in a certain direction: *The ship hove northward.* **10** *Geology.* thrust (a vein, etc.) out of place horizontally.
heave in sight, come into view.
heave to, a stop (a ship) as by trimming the sails, etc. **b** of a ship, stop.
—n. **1** the act or fact of heaving: *With a great heave, they got the dresser onto the truck.* **2** *Geology.* a horizontal displacement or dislocation of a vein or stratum at a fault. **3 heaves,** a disease of horses characterized by difficult breathing, coughing, and heaving of the flanks (*used with a singular verb*).
—interj. **heave ho!** a sailor's cry when pulling up the anchor, or pulling on any rope or cable. ⟨OE *hebban*⟩ **—'heav•er,** *n.*

heave–ho ['hiv 'hou] *n. Informal.* rejection: *She gave him the old heave-ho.*

heav•en ['hɛvən] *n.* **1 a** in various belief systems, the place where God or the gods, angels, heroes, etc. live and where the blessed go after death, traditionally thought of as beyond the sky. Compare HELL (def. 1). **b Heaven,** God; Providence: *They felt it was the will of Heaven.* **2** a place or condition of greatest happiness: *It was heaven just to be able to relax after the uproar.* **3** Usually, **heavens,** *pl.* the space that appears to be a dome over the earth, in which the sun, moon, and stars are seen; sky: *Millions of stars were shining in the heavens.*
for heaven's sake or **good heavens!** an exclamation of surprise or protest.
move heaven and earth, do everything possible. ⟨OE *heofon*⟩

heav•en•ly ['hɛvənli] *adj.* **1** of or in heaven; divine; holy: *the heavenly Father, heavenly choirs.* **2** like or suitable for heaven; of more than human excellence: *heavenly peace.* **3** *Informal.* delightful; excellent: *a heavenly spot for a picnic, heavenly weather.* **4** of or in the heavens; in the sky: *The sun, moon, stars, planets, and comets are heavenly bodies.* **—'heav•en•li•ness,** *n.*

heav•en•ward ['hɛvənwərd] *adv. or adj.* toward heaven. Also (*adv.*), **heavenwards.**

heav•i•ly ['hɛvəli] *adv.* in a heavy way or manner: *He fell heavily to the floor.*

heav•i•ness ['hɛvinɪs] *n.* **1** the state or condition of being heavy; great mass. **2** sadness: *The loss filled them with heaviness.*

Heav•i•side layer ['hɛvi,saɪd] **1** the second, or middle, layer of the ionosphere, which reflects radio waves of frequencies produced in short-wave broadcasting. **2** the ionosphere. ⟨after Oliver *Heaviside* (1850-1925), an English physicist⟩

heav•y ['hɛvi] *adj.* **heav•i•er, heav•i•est;** *n., pl.* **heav•ies;** *adv.* *—adj.* **1** hard to lift or carry; of great weight: *a heavy load.* **2** having much mass for its size; of great density: *heavy metal.* **3** of more than usual mass for its kind: *heavy silk.* **4** of great amount, force, or intensity; greater than usual; large; violent: *a heavy vote, heavy strain, heavy sea, heavy sleep, heavy rain, a heavy meal, a heavy crop.* **5** able to carry big loads: *a heavy truck.* **6** being such to an unusual degree or extent: *a heavy buyer, a heavy smoker.* **7** hard to bear or endure: *heavy taxes.* **8** hard to deal with; requiring much physical effort: *a heavy road, a heavy slope, heavy food, heavy soil.* **9** weighted down; laden: *air heavy with moisture, eyes heavy with sleep.* **10** causing sorrow; sorrowful; gloomy: *heavy news.* **11** grave; serious; sober; sombre: *a heavy part in a play.* **12** cloudy: *a heavy sky.* **13** broad; thick; coarse: *a heavy line, heavy features.* **14** clumsy; sluggish; slow: *a heavy walk.* **15** ponderous; dull: *heavy reading.* **16** loud and deep: *the heavy roar of cannon.* **17** *Military.* **a** heavily armed or equipped: *heavy tanks.* **b** of large size: *heavy artillery.* **18** having risen very little: *heavy bread.* **19** *Chemistry.* designating an isotope possessing a greater atomic mass than the most abundant isotope of the same element: *heavy water.* **20** *Informal.* emotionally involving.
heavy with child, pregnant, especially in the last months of pregnancy.
—n. **1** a heavy person or thing. **2** *Informal. Theatre.* **a** the villain in a play. **b** an actor who plays villains or takes similar parts. **3** *Informal.* any person who tries to accomplish matters by force or manipulation. **4** a HEAVYWEIGHT (def. 3).
—adv. in a heavy manner; heavily.
hang heavy, of time, pass slowly and boringly: *He had nothing to do, and time was hanging heavy on his hands.* ⟨OE *hefig* < *hebban* heave⟩

☛ *Syn. adj.* **1, 7, 11. Heavy,** WEIGHTY, BURDENSOME = of great weight. **Heavy** emphasizes being hard to lift or carry, and used figuratively suggests something pressing down on or weighing down the mind or feelings: *He has heavy responsibilities.* **Weighty** = having great weight, but is used chiefly figuratively, applying to something of great importance: *He made a weighty announcement.* **Burdensome** suggests something very heavy or oppressive that interferes with freedom of movement and puts a strain on the person or thing carrying it: *The extra load was burdensome.*

heav•y–armed ['hɛvi 'ɑrmd] *adj.* equipped with heavy weapons or armour.

heavy–duty ['hɛvi 'djuti] *or* ['hɛvi 'duti] *adj.* durably built to withstand unusual strain or very hard use: *a heavy-duty vacuum cleaner.*

heavy–footed ['hɛvi 'fʊtɪd] *adj.* having an awkward gait; noisy in movement.

heav•y–hand•ed ['hɛvi 'hændɪd] *adj.* **1** clumsy; awkward: *Her heavy-handed attempts at humour were embarrassing.* **2** harsh; cruel. **—'heav•y-'hand•ed•ly,** *adv.* **—'heav•y-'hand•ed•ness,** *n.*

heav•y–heart•ed ['hɛvi 'hɑrtɪd] *adj.* sad; gloomy; in low spirits. **—'heav•y-'heart•ed•ly,** *adv.* **—'heav•y-'heart•ed•ness,** *n.*

heavy hydrogen *Chemistry.* an isotope of hydrogen having a mass number of 2; deuterium. Heavy hydrogen has one proton and one neutron in its nucleus, while ordinary hydrogen has no neutrons. *Symbol*: D or ${}^{2}_{1}H$

heavy industry the manufacture of large objects for use by other industries.

heav•y•set ['hɛvi,sɛt] *adj.* of a sturdy, compact, and often stout build: *a heavyset man.*

heavy spar barite.

heavy water *Chemistry.* water composed of oxygen and heavy hydrogen, represented by the formula D_2O, present in very small quantities in ordinary water. If ordinary water is electrolyzed, the percentage of heavy water in it is increased. Heavy water is used in nuclear power plants to moderate and control nuclear reactions. *Formula*: D_2O

heav•y•weight ['hɛvi,weit] *n.* **1** a person or thing of much more than average mass. **2** a boxer weighing more than 81 kg. **3** *Informal.* a person of great importance or influence: *a heavyweight in the political field.*

heb•do•mad ['hɛbdə,mæd] *n.* **1** a group of seven. **2** a week. **—heb'dom•a•dal,** *adj.*

He•be ['hibi] *n. Greek mythology.* the goddess of youth, the daughter of Zeus and Hera. Hebe was the cupbearer to the gods before Ganymede was given that duty.

he•be•phre•nia [,hibə'friniə] *n.* a form of schizophrenia occurring in adolescents, accompanied by hallucinations and juvenile behaviour. ⟨< NL < Gk. *hebe* youth + *phren* mind⟩

heb•e•tate ['hɛbi,teit] *v.* **-at•ed, -at•ing.** make blunt. ⟨< L *hebetare* < *hebes* dull⟩

he•bet•ic [hə'bɛtɪk] *adj.* having to do with puberty. ⟨< Gk. *hebe* youth⟩

heb•e•tude ['hɛbə,tjud] *or* ['hɛbə,tud] *n.* lethargy. ⟨< LL *hebetudo* < L *hebes* dull⟩

He•bra•ic [hɪ'breiɪk] *or* [hi'breiɪk] *adj.* of or having to do with the Hebrews or their language or culture; Hebrew. ⟨< LL *Hebraicus* < Gk. *Hebraikos*⟩ **—he'bra•i•cal•ly,** *adv.*

He•bra•ism ['hibrei,ɪzəm] *n.* **1** a linguistic structure or idiom peculiar to Hebrew. **2** such a structure or idiom translated literally into another language. **3** Hebrew character, spirit, thought, or practice.

He•bra•ist ['hibreiɪst] *n.* **1** a scholar skilled in the Hebrew language and literature. **2** a person imbued with the Hebraic spirit.

He•bra•is•tic [,hibrei'ɪstɪk] *adj.* of or having to do with Hebraism or Hebraists; Hebraic.

He•bra•ize ['hibrei,aɪz] *v.* **-ized, -iz•ing.** make conform with Hebrew practices.

He•brew ['hibru] *n., adj.* *—n.* **1** a member of any of a group of Semitic peoples of ancient Palestine, especially an Israelite. **2** a descendant of any of these peoples, especially the Israelites. **3** the Semitic language of the ancient Hebrews. **4** the modern form of this language, one of the official languages of present-day Israel.
—adj. of or having to do with the Hebrews or their language. ⟨ME < OF *Ebreu* < L *Hebraeus* < Gk. *Hebraios* < Aramaic *'ebrai* < Hebrew *'ibri*, literally, one from beyond (the river)⟩

Heb•ri•des ['hɛbrɪ,diz] *n.pl.* a group of islands in the Atlantic off the west coast of Scotland. **—,Heb•ri'de•an,** *adj.*

Hec•a•te ['hɛkəti] *or, formerly,* ['hɛkɪt] *n. Greek mythology.* the goddess of the moon, earth, and realm of the dead. Hecate later came to be regarded as the goddess of witchcraft. Also, **Hekate.**

hec•a•tomb ['hɛkə,toum], ['hɛkə,tum], *or* ['hɛkə,tɒm] *n.* **1** in ancient Greece and Rome, the sacrifice of 100 oxen at one time. **2** any great slaughter. ⟨< L < Gk. *hekatombē* sacrifice of 100 oxen < *hekaton* hundred + *bous* ox⟩

heck [hɛk] *interj., n. Informal.* a mild form of the word **hell**, used to express anger, annoyance, surprise, etc.: *Heck! I forgot the book. That's a heck of a thing to say.*

heck•le ['hɛkəl] *v.* **-led, -ling.** harass, taunt, and annoy (a speaker, etc.) by asking bothersome questions, etc. ⟨< *heckle* comb for flax or hemp, ME *hekele.* Related to HACKLE[1].⟩ **—'heck•ler,** *n.*

hect– *SI prefix.* a form of **hecto-** used before a vowel.

hec•tare ['hɛktɛr] *or* ['hɛktɑr] *n.* a unit used with the SI for measuring land area, equal to 10 000 m^2. *Symbol*: ha ⟨< F *hectare* < Gk. *hekaton* hundred + F *are* are[2]⟩

hec•tic ['hɛktɪk] *adj., n.* *—adj.* **1** filled with or characterized by great excitement or confusion: *a hectic life. We spent three hectic days packing for the move.* **2** showing signs of a fever: *a hectic flush, hectic cheeks.* **3** of or designating the fever characteristic of such diseases as tuberculosis: *hectic fever, a hectic cough.* **4** consumptive.
—n. a flush or fever. ⟨ME < OF *etique* < LL < Gk. *hektikos* habitual, consumptive < *hexis* habit⟩ **—'hec•ti•cal•ly,** *adv.*

hecto– *SI prefix.* hundred: *hectometre. Symbol*: h ⟨< F < Gk. *hekaton*⟩

hec•to•cot•y•lus [,hɛktə'kɒtələs] *n., pl.* **-li** [-,laɪ]. *Zoology.* a modified arm of certain male cephalopods serving as a reproductive organ.

hec•to•gram ['hɛktə,græm] *n.* one hundred grams.

hec•to•graph ['hɛktə,græf] *n., v.* *—n.* a machine for making many copies of a page of writing, a drawing, etc. The original writing is transferred to a surface coated with gelatin, and the copies are made from this.
—v. make copies of with a hectograph. **—,hec•to'graph•ic,** *adj.* **—,hec•to'graph•i•cal•ly,** *adv.*

hec•to•li•tre ['hɛktə,litər] *n.* one hundred litres.

hec•to•met•re [,hɛk'tɒmətər] *or* ['hɛktə,mitər] *n.* a measure of length equal to one hundred metres.

hec•tor ['hɛktər] *n., v.* *—n.* a bragging, bullying fellow.
—v. bluster; bully; tease. ⟨< *Hector*, a Trojan hero⟩

Hector's dolphin a dolphin *(Cephalorhynchus hectori)* native to the waters off New Zealand. It is an endangered species.

he'd [hid]; *unstressed,* [id], [ɪd], *or* [hɪd] **1** he had. **2** he would.
☛ *Hom.* HEED.

hed•dle ['hɛdəl] *n.* that part of a loom that guides the warp. ⟨< ME *helde* < OE *hefeld* thread, chain⟩

he•der ['heidər] *n., pl.* **ha•da•rim** [,hɑdɑ'rim] a Jewish school for teaching Hebrew and prayers. Also, **cheder.** ⟨< Hebrew, literally room⟩

hedge [hɛdʒ] *n., v.* **hedged, hedg•ing.** *—n.* **1** a thick row of bushes or small trees, planted as a fence or boundary. **2** any barrier or boundary. **3** a means of protection or defence. **4** the act of hedging.
—v. **1** enclose or separate with a hedge; put a hedge around or along: *to hedge a garden.* **2** avoid giving a direct answer; evade questions; avoid taking a definite stand: *Stop hedging and tell us what you want to do.* **3** protect oneself from losing money on (a bet, investment, etc.) by making other bets.
hedge in, a hem in; surround on all sides: *The town was hedged in by mountains and a forest.* **b** keep from getting away or moving freely. ⟨OE *hecg*⟩ **—'hedg•er,** *n.*

hedge bindweed a Canadian wildflower (*Convolvulus sepium),* growing over walls and fences across Canada and south to Florida, having large pink or white flowers.

hedge•hog ['hɛdʒ,hɒg] *n.* **1** any of a subfamily (Erinaceinae) of small mammals of Europe, Asia, and Africa, having a short tail, long nose, and short, thick, sharp spines on the back. When attacked or frightened, hedgehogs roll up into a bristling ball. **2** *Esp. U.S.* the porcupine of North America. **3** *Military.* **a** an X-shaped portable obstacle, usually laced with barbed wire. **b** an area defended by pillboxes, mines, and lanes for machine gun fire.

hedge–hop ['hɛdʒ ,hɒp] *v.* **-hopped, -hop•ping.** fly an aircraft very low. **—'hedge-,hop•per,** *n.* **—'hedge-,hop•ping,** *n.*

hedge hyssop any herb of the genus *Gratiola,* growing in damp places.

hedge•row ['hɛdʒ,rou] *n.* a thick row of bushes or small trees forming a hedge.

hedge sparrow a small, sparrowlike, European songbird (*Prunella modularis*) that nests in hedges and other shrubbery.

he•don•ic [hi'dɒnɪk] *adj.* marked by pleasure.

he•don•ics [hi'dɒnɪks] *n.pl. (used with a singular verb)* the study of the psychology and physiology of pleasure.

he•don•ism ['hidə,nɪzəm] *n.* **1** *Philosophy.* the doctrine that pleasure or happiness is the highest good. **2** *Psychology.* the theory that human behaviour always aims to achieve pleasure and avoid pain. **3** the pursuit of sensual pleasure as a lifestyle. ⟨< Gk. *hēdonē* pleasure⟩

he•don•ist ['hidənɪst] *n.* a person who believes in or practises hedonism.

-hedral *combining form.* It is used to form adjectives corresponding to nouns with stems in **-hedron**: *polyhedral.*

-hedron *combining form.* face; a geometric figure with —— faces: *polyhedron.* ⟨< Gk. *hedra* seat, side⟩

heed [hid] *v., n.* *—v.* give careful attention (to); take notice (of): *Now heed what I say.*
—n. careful attention; notice: *She went on as before, paying no heed to the warning signal.* ⟨OE *hēdan*⟩ **—'heed•er,** *n.*
☛ *Hom.* HE'D.

heed•ful ['hidfəl] *adj.* careful; attentive. **—'heed•ful•ly,** *adv.* **—'heed•ful•ness,** *n.*

heed•less ['hidlɪs] *adj.* careless; thoughtless. **—'heed•less•ly,** *adv.* **—'heed•less•ness,** *n.*

hee•haw ['hi,hɒ] *n., v.* *—n.* **1** the braying sound made by a donkey. **2** a loud, coarse laugh.
—v. **1** make the braying sound of a donkey. **2** laugh loudly and coarsely.

heel[1] [hil] *n., v.* *—n.* **1** the back part of a person's foot, below the ankle. **2** the part of a stocking or shoe that covers the heel. **3** the part of a shoe or boot that is under the heel or raises the heel. **4** the part of an animal's hind leg that corresponds to a person's heel. **5** anything shaped, used, or placed at an end like a heel. The end crust of a loaf of bread is sometimes called a heel. **6** *Informal.* an untrustworthy or contemptible person.
at heel, near the heels; close behind.
cool (one's) **heels,** *Informal.* be kept waiting a long time: *She was left cooling her heels for an hour in the waiting room.*
down at (the) heel or **heels, a** of a shoe or shoes, with the heels worn down. **b** in a shabby or run-down condition: *The whole place looked very down at the heel.*
drag (one's) **heels, a** hold back or slow up on purpose. **b** agree reluctantly; work without interest or enthusiasm.
kick up (one's) **heels,** behave in a merry and exuberant way; have fun: *He really kicked up his heels at the party.*
lay by the heels, put in prison or in stocks.
out at the heels, a with the heel of the stocking or shoe worn through. **b** shabby and run-down.
show a clean pair of heels, run away.
take to (one's) **heels,** run away.
to heel, a near a person's heels; close behind: *The dog walked to heel.* **b** under control: *He soon brought the mutineers to heel.*
—v. **1** follow closely behind (someone): *I'm teaching my dog to heel.* **2** put a heel or heels on. **3** touch or drive forward with the heel or as if with the heel: *She heeled the horse.* **4** perform (a

dance) with the heels. **5** *Golf.* strike (the ball) with the heel of the club. ⟨OE *hēla*⟩ **—'heel•less,** *adj.*
☛ *Hom.* HEAL, HE'LL.

heel² [hil] *v., n.* *—v.* lean over to one side; tilt; tip: *The ship heeled as it turned.*
—n. the act or degree of heeling. ⟨alteration of earlier *heeld* < OE *h(i)eldan* < *heald* inclined⟩
☛ *Hom.* HEAL, HE'LL.

heel–and–toe ['hil ən 'tou] *adj.* of a pace in which the heel touches the ground before the toes do.

heeled [hild] *adj., v.* *—adj.* **1** having a heel or heel-like projection. **2** *Slang.* **a** provided with money. **b** armed with a revolver or other weapon.
—v. pt. and pp. of HEEL.

heel•er ['hilər] *n.* **1** a person who puts heels on shoes. **2** *Esp. U.S. Slang.* a follower or hanger-on of a political boss. **3** *Cdn. Slang.* a subservient party worker who comes to heel readily when ordered: *a ward heeler.*

heel•tap ['hil,tæp] *n.* **1** a layer of leather, etc. in the heel of a shoe. **2** a small amount of liquor left in a glass after drinking.

heft [hɛft] *Informal. n., v.* *—n.* **1** mass or heaviness. **2** *Archaic.* the greater part; bulk.
—v. **1** judge the mass or heaviness of by lifting: *She hefted the baseball bat to get the feel of it.* **2** lift; heave. ⟨< *heave*⟩

heft•y ['hɛfti] *adj.* **heft•i•er, heft•i•est.** *Informal.* **1** weighty; heavy: *a hefty load.* **2** large; considerable: *They got a hefty bill for repairs.* **3** big and strong. ⟨< *heft*⟩ **—'heft•i•ly,** *adv.* **—'heft•i•ness,** *n.*

he•ga•ri [hɪ'gɛri] *or* ['hɛgəri] *n.* a grain with chalky white seeds. ⟨< Arabic *hajari* stony⟩

He•ge•li•an [hə'geiliən] *adj., n.* *—adj.* of, having to do with, or characteristic of Georg W.F. Hegel (1770-1831), a German philosopher, or his philosophy.
—n. a follower of Hegel.

He•ge•li•an•ism [hə'geiliə,nɪzəm] *n. Philosophy.* the Hegelian philosophy, which maintains that facts and ideas merge in a total reality (the Absolute), and which incorporates a dialectic method of analysis by which a higher level of truth (synthesis) is arrived at through the resolution of logical opposites (thesis and antithesis).

he•gem•o•ny [hɪ'dʒɛməni] *or* ['hɛdʒə,mouni] *n., pl.* **-nies.** political domination, especially, leadership or domination by one state over others in a group. ⟨< Gk. *hēgemonia* < *hēgemōn* leader < *hēgeesthai* lead⟩ **—,heg•e'mon•ic** or **,heg•e'mon•i•cal,** *adj.*

He•gi•ra [hɪ'dʒaɪrə] *or* ['hɛdʒərə] *n.* **1** the flight of Mohammed from Mecca to Medina in A.D. 622. The Muslims use a calendar reckoned from this date. **2** the Muslim era. **3 hegira,** a journey, especially to escape; flight. Also, **Hejira.** ⟨< Med.L < Arabic *hijrah* flight, departure⟩

Hei•del•berg man ['haɪdəl,bɔrg] a prehistoric human being, so called from the lower jaw which was found near Heidelberg, Germany, in 1907.

heif•er ['hɛfər] *n.* a young cow that has not yet had a calf. ⟨OE *hēahfore*⟩

heigh [haɪ] *or* [hei] *interj.* a sound used to attract attention, give encouragement, express surprise, etc.
☛ *Hom.* HIGH, HI, HIE [haɪ]; HE², HEY, HAY [hei].

heigh–ho ['haɪ 'hou] *or* ['hei 'hou] *interj.* an exclamation to express surprise, boredom, weariness, etc.

height [həit] *n.* **1** the measurement from top to bottom; the tallness of anyone or anything; the point to which anything rises above ground: *My father's height is 187 cm.* **2** the distance above sea level. **3** a fairly great distance up: *rising at a height above the valley.* **4** a high point or place; hill: *the height overlooking the river, on the mountain heights.* **5** the highest part; top: *She had reached the height of her career by the age of forty.* **6** the highest point; greatest degree: *the height of folly.* **7** high rank; high degree. ⟨OE *hīehthu* < *hēah* high⟩
☛ *Pronun.* The pronunciation [həitθ] is heard in some dialects, but the standard form is [həit].
☛ *Hom.* HIGHT.

height•en ['həitən] *v.* **1** make or become higher. **2** make or become stronger, greater, more intense, etc.: *The background music heightened the feeling of suspense.* **—'height•en•er,** *n.*

height of land **1** a region higher than its surroundings. **2** *Cdn.* a watershed; divide: *A height of land marks the boundary between Labrador and Québec.*

Heimlich manoeuvre ['haɪmlɪk] an emergency procedure used to dislodge food from a person's airway by pressing one's fist into the victim's abdomen and giving upward thrusts. ⟨after H.J. *Heimlich*, American physician who invented it⟩

hei•nous ['heinəs] *or* ['hinəs] *adj.* very wicked; atrocious; abominable: *a heinous murder.* ⟨ME < OF *haïnos*, ult. < *haïr* to hate < Gmc.⟩ **—'hei•nous•ly,** *adv.* **—'hei•nous•ness,** *n.*

heir [ɛr] *n.* **1** a person who receives, or has the right to receive, someone's property or title after the death of its owner; a person who inherits property. **2** a person to whom some trait, ideal, task, etc. passes from someone who lived before him or her. ⟨ME < OF < L *heres* heir⟩
☛ *Hom.* AIR, E'ER, ERE, ERR, EYRE.

heir apparent *pl.* **heirs apparent.** a person who will be the first to succeed to a property or title. The Queen's eldest son, Prince Charles, is heir apparent to the throne.

heir–at–law ['ɛr ət 'lɒ] *n.* a person who has the right to inherit from an intestate person.

heir•ess ['ɛrɪs] *n.* **1** a female heir. **2** a female heir to great wealth.

heir•loom ['ɛr,lum] *n.* **1** a possession handed down from generation to generation. **2** *Law.* a piece of personal property that an heir inherits along with the estate. ⟨< *heir* + *loom*, originally, implement⟩

heir presumptive *pl.* **heirs presumptive.** a person who will be heir unless someone with a stronger claim is born.

heir•ship ['ɛrʃɪp] *n.* the position or rights of an heir; right of inheritance; inheritance.
☛ *Hom.* AIRSHIP.

heist [həist] *v., n. Slang.* *—v.* rob or steal.
—n. a theft or robbery. ⟨alteration of *hoist*⟩

He•ji•ra [hɪ'dʒaɪrə] *or* ['hɛdʒərə] See HEGIRA.

Hek•a•te ['hɛkəti] *or, formerly,* ['hɛkɪt] See HECATE.

Hel [hɛl] *n. Norse mythology.* **1** the goddess of death and of the lower world. **2** the lower world, inhabited by those who did not die in battle.
☛ *Hom.* HELL.

held [hɛld] *v.* pt. and pp. of HOLD¹.

hel•den•ten•or ['hɛldən,tɛnər]; *German,* ['hɛldəntɛ,noʀ] *n. Music.* a tenor singer with a high range, as required in the operas of Richard Wagner. ⟨literally, hero tenor⟩

Hel•en of Troy ['hɛlən] *Greek mythology.* a very beautiful Greek woman, the wife of King Menelaus of Sparta. Helen's abduction by Paris started the Trojan War.

heli– *combining form.* the form of *helio-* used before vowels, as in *heliac.*

he•li•an•thus [,hili'ænθəs] *n.* any of a genus (*Helianthus*) of plants of the composite family, including the sunflower and Jerusalem artichoke. ⟨< NL < Gk. *hēlios* sun + *anthos* flower⟩

hel•i•cal ['hɛləkəl] *adj.* having to do with, or having the form of, a helix; spiral. **—'hel•i•cal•ly,** *adv.*

hel•i•ces ['hɛlə,siz] *n.* a pl. of HELIX.

helico– *combining form.* of or shaped like a helix; spiral: *helicon.* ⟨< Gk. *helix, -ikos* spiral⟩

hel•i•coid ['hɛlə,kɔɪd] *n., adj.* *—n. Geometry.* a surface generated by a straight line moving along a fixed helix and maintaining a constant angle with its axis.
—adj. like a helix; spiral, as in certain univalve shells.
—,hel•i'coid•al, *adj.*

hel•i•con ['hɛlə,kɒn] *or* ['hɛləkən] *n.* a large bass tuba shaped into a large coil that passes round the player and over one shoulder. ⟨< *helico-*, influenced by *Helicon*⟩

Hel•i•con ['hɛlə,kɒn] *n. Greek mythology.* the mountain home of the Muses. ⟨< Gk., the name of a mountain in Boeotia⟩

A helicopter

hel•i•cop•ter ['hɛlə,kɒptər] *n., v.* *—n.* an aircraft having one

or more horizontal propellers, or rotors, by means of which it can hover, take off and land vertically, and move forward, backward, or sideways in the air.
—v. travel or carry by helicopter. ⟨< F *hélicoptère* < Gk. *helix, -ikos* spiral + *pteron* wing⟩

helio– *combining form.* the sun: *heliograph.* ⟨< Gk. *hēlios* sun⟩

he•li•o•cen•tric [ˌhiliouˈsɛntrɪk] *adj.* **1** viewed or measured from the centre of the sun. **2** having or representing the sun as a centre: *The Copernican system of astronomy is heliocentric.* Compare GEOCENTRIC. ⟨< *helio-* + Gk. *kentron* centre⟩

He•li•o•chrome [ˈhiliəˌkroum] *n. Trademark.* a photograph that reproduces natural colour.

he•li•o•gram [ˈhiliəˌgræm] *n.* a message transmitted by heliograph.

he•li•o•graph [ˈhiliəˌgræf] *n., v.* *—n.* **1** a device for signalling by means of a movable mirror that flashes beams of light to a distance. The flashes of the mirror represent the dots and dashes of the Morse code. **2** an apparatus for taking photographs of the sun.
—v. communicate or signal by heliograph.

he•li•ol•at•ry [ˌhiliˈɒlətri] *n.* sun worship.

He•li•os [ˈhiliˌɒs] *n. Greek mythology.* the god of the sun, corresponding to the Roman god Sol. Helios is represented as driving his chariot across the heavens every day. He was later seen as equivalent to Apollo.

he•li•o•scope [ˈhiliəˌskoup] *n.* **1** a device for looking at the sun without injury to the eye. **2** a telescope having such a device.

he•li•o•stat [ˈhiliəˌstæt] *n.* an instrument that reflects the sun's rays. ⟨< *helio-* + E *-stat* < Gk. *-states* < *histanai* stand⟩

he•li•o•tax•is [ˌhiliouˈtæksɪs] *n. Biology.* movement toward or away from sunlight.

he•li•o•ther•a•py [ˌhiliouˈθɛrəpi] *n.* the treatment of disease by means of sunlight.

he•li•o•trope [ˈhiliəˌtroup] *or* [ˈhiljəˌtroup] *n., adj.* *—n.* **1** any of a genus (*Heliotropium*) of herbs or shrubs of the borage family having spikes or clusters of small white, lilac, or blue flowers that always turn to face the sun. The common heliotrope is a popular garden plant having oval, wrinkled leaves and clusters of lilac or blue flowers with a fragrance like vanilla. **2** the common valerian, also called **garden heliotrope**. **3** a reddish purple. **4** a bloodstone, a semiprecious stone.
—adj. reddish purple. ⟨< L < Gk. *hēliotropion* < *hēlios* sun + *-tropos* turning⟩

he•li•ot•ro•pism [ˌhiliˈɒtrəˌpɪzəm] *n.* of certain plants and other organisms, a tendency to respond to sunlight by turning or bending toward it or away from it. Sunflowers exhibit positive heliotropism; that is, the flowers turn toward the sunlight. ⟨< *heliotrope* any plant that turns toward the sun⟩
—ˌhe•li•o'trop•ic, *adj.* **—ˌhe•li•o'trop•i•cal•ly,** *adv.*

he•li•o•type [ˈhiliəˌtəip] *n.* **1** a picture or print produced by a photomechanical process in which the impression in ink is taken directly from a prepared gelatin film that has been exposed under a negative. **2** this process. **—'he•li•oˌty•py,** *n.*

hel•i•pad [ˈhɛləˌpæd] *n.* a small piece of level surface for helicopters to land or take off.

hel•i•port [ˈhɛlɪˌpɔrt] *n.* a place for helicopters to land or take off. Heliports are sometimes built on rooftops.

he•li•um [ˈhiliəm] *n.* a rare, gaseous chemical element, first discovered in the sun's atmosphere. It is a very light, colourless, inert gas that will not burn, much used in balloons and dirigibles. *Symbol:* He; *at.no.* 2; *at.mass* 4.00. ⟨< NL < Gk. *hēlios* sun⟩

he•lix [ˈhilɪks] *n., pl.* **hel•i•ces** [ˈhɛləˌsiz] or **he•lix•es. 1** a spiral shape or form. A screw thread and a watch spring are helices. **2** *Architecture.* an ornamental spiral, as on the capital of a Corinthian or Ionic column; volute. **3** *Anatomy.* the inward-curving cartilaginous rim of the outer ear. **4** *Geometry.* the curve traced by a straight line on a plane that is wrapped around a cylinder, as the thread of a screw. ⟨< L < Gk. *helix* a spiral⟩

hell [hɛl] *n., interj.* *—n.* **1** in various belief systems: **a** the home of the Devil, where wicked persons suffer punishment after death, traditionally thought of as below or within the earth. Compare HEAVEN (def. 1). **b** the powers of evil. **c** the abode of the dead; Hades. **2** a place or state of wickedness, torment, or misery: *War is hell.* **3** *Informal.* a severe scolding, punishment, etc.: *Her mother gave her hell for being so rude.* **4** *Informal.* wild, mischievous spirits: *The kids were full of hell that day.*
come hell or high water, *Informal.* whatever difficulties or problems arise: *I'm going, come hell or high water.*
hell and high water, *Informal.* extreme difficulties or problems, whatever they may be: *He will keep his word through hell and high water.*
like hell, a *Informal.* very hard, fast, etc.: *I worked like hell.* **b** *Slang.* an exclamation expressing strong disagreement with a statement, proposal, etc.: *Like hell is she going to use my car!*
raise hell, *Informal.* cause trouble; make a disturbance: *The disgruntled prisoners started raising hell.*
—interj. Slang. an exclamation of annoyance, irritation, anger, or surprise: *Hell! There goes another fuse.* ⟨OE⟩
☛ *Hom.* HEL.

he'll [hil]; *unstressed,* [hɪl] he will.
☛ *Hom.* HEAL, HEEL.

Hel•lad•ic [həˈlædɪk] *adj.* having to do with the BRONZE AGE in Greece.

hell•bend•er [ˈhɛlˌbɛndər] *n.* an aquatic salamander (*Cryptobranchus alleganiensis).*

hell•bent [ˈhɛlˈbɛnt] *adj., adv. Slang.* *—adj.* recklessly or stubbornly determined (*usually used with* **for** *or* **on**): *He was hellbent on spending all his money as soon as he got it.*
—adv. recklessly or wildly: *She came tearing hellbent around the corner.*

hell•box [ˈhɛlˌbɒks] *n. Printing.* a box for broken or discarded type.

hell•cat [ˈhɛlˌkæt] *n.* **1** a mean, spiteful woman. **2** witch.

hell•div•er [ˈhɛlˌdaɪvər] *n.* an American grebe (*Podilymbus podiceps)* having a black band around its beak; pied-billed grebe.

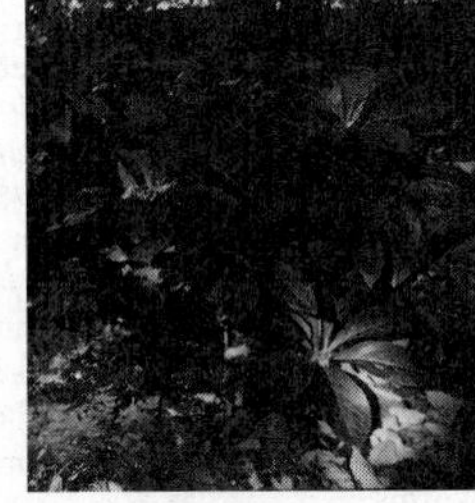
Hellebore

hel•le•bore [ˈhɛləˌbɔr] *n.* **1** any of a genus (*Helleborus*) of poisonous plants of the buttercup family, especially the **black hellebore** (*H. niger*), an evergreen plant having showy white or pinkish flowers. **2** the dried underground stem of the black hellebore, or an extract from it, formerly used in medicine. **3** any of various poisonous, north temperate plants (genus *Veratrum*) of the lily family, especially *V. album*, having underground stems that yield alkaloids used to treat heart disease and also as an insecticide. **4** the dried underground stem of *V. album* or an extract from it. ⟨< L < Gk. *helleboros*⟩

Hel•lene [ˈhɛlin] *n.* Greek. ⟨back-formation singular of Gk. *Hellēnes*, literally, descendants of Hellēn, mythical father of the Greeks⟩

Hel•len•ic [həˈlɛnɪk] *or* [həˈlinɪk] *adj., n.* *—adj.* **1** Greek. **2** of Greek history, language, or culture from about 776 B.C. to the death of Alexander the Great in 323 B.C.
—n. **1** the Greek language. **2** the branch of the Indo-European languages that includes the various dialects of Greek.

Hel•len•ism [ˈhɛləˌnɪzəm] *n.* **1** the ancient Greek culture or ideals. **2** the adoption or imitation of Greek speech, ideals, etc. **3** an idiom or expression peculiar to the Greek language. **4** such an idiom or expression translated literally into another language.

Hel•len•ist [ˈhɛlənɪst] *n.* **1** a scholar skilled in the ancient Greek language, literature, and culture. **2** a person who uses or imitates Greek language, ideals, or customs.

Hel•len•is•tic [ˌhɛləˈnɪstɪk] *adj.* **1** of or having to do with Hellenists. **2** of or having to do with Greek history, language, and culture after the death of Alexander the Great in 323 B.C.

Hel•len•ize [ˈhɛləˌnaɪz] *v.* **-ized, -iz•ing. 1** make Greek in character. **2** use or imitate the Greek language, ideals, or customs. **—ˌHel•len•i'za•tion,** *n.* **—'Hel•lenˌiz•er,** *n.*

hel•ler[1] [ˈhɛlər] *n., pl.* **haleru** [ˌhæləˈru]. haler.

hel•ler[2] [ˈhɛlər] *n. Slang.* a very mischievous or troublesome person; hellion: *She was a real heller as a child.*

hel•ler•y [ˈhɛləri] *n. Slang.* mischief; wild behaviour.

Hel•les•pont [ˈhɛləˌspɒnt] *n.* the ancient name of the Dardanelles, a strait between Europe and Turkey.

hell•fire [ˈhɛlˌfaɪr] *n.* the fire of hell; punishment in hell.

hell•gram•mite [ˈhɛlgrəˌməit] *n.* the larva of a dobsonfly, often used for fish bait. ⟨origin uncertain⟩

hell•hole [ˈhɛlˌhoul] *n. Informal.* a dreadful place; a place of great discomfort, filth, squalor, etc.

hell•hound ['hɛl,haʊnd] *n.* **1** *Mythology.* Cerberus, the watchdog of Hades. **2** a dog or hound of hell. **3** a cruel, fiendish person.

hel•lion ['hɛljən] *n. Informal.* a very mischievous or troublesome person. ⟨origin uncertain⟩

hell•ish ['hɛlɪʃ] *adj.* **1** fit to have come from hell; devilish; fiendish. **2** of hell. **3** *Informal.* very unpleasant. **—'hell•ish•ly,** *adv.* **—'hell•ish•ness,** *n.*

hel•lo [hɛ'lou] *or* [hə'lou] *interj., n., pl.* **-los;** *v.* **-loed, -lo•ing.** *—interj.* an exclamation to attract attention or to express a greeting or surprise.
—n. a call of greeting or surprise, or to attract attention: *The girl gave a loud hello to tell us where she was.*
—v. **1** shout; call. **2** say hello (to). Also, **hallo, hullo.**

hell•rais•er ['hɛl,reizər] *n.* HELLER[2].

Hel•lu•land ['hɛlu,lænd] *n.* the Viking name for a region on the NE coast of North America, possibly Baffin Island.

helm[1] [hɛlm] *n.* **1** the handle or wheel by which a ship is steered. **2** a position of control or guidance: *The situation began to improve soon after the new director took over the helm.* ⟨OE *helma*⟩ **—'helm•less,** *adj.*

helm[2] [hɛlm] *n., v. Archaic. —n.* helmet.
—v. put a helmet on. ⟨OE. Akin to HELMET.⟩

hel•met ['hɛlmɪt] *n.* **1** a covering to protect the head, usually made of a thick or rigid material, such as metal, fibreglass, or leather. Helmets are worn by soldiers, firefighters, football players, motorcyclists, cyclists, etc. **2** the headpiece of ancient or medieval armour. See ARMOUR for picture. **3** something like a helmet, such as a hood-shaped part of the calyx or corolla of some flowers. ⟨ME < OF *helmet,* dim. of *helme* helm[2]. Gmc.⟩

hel•met•ed ['hɛlmətid] *adj.* equipped with or wearing a helmet: *a helmeted motorcyclist.*

hel•minth ['hɛlmɪnθ] *n.* an intestinal worm, especially a roundworm or fluke. ⟨< Gk. *helmins, -inthos*⟩

hel•min•thi•a•sis [,hɛlmɪn'θaɪəsɪs] *n. Pathology.* a disease in which intestinal worms infect the body.

hel•min•thic [hɛl'mɪnθɪk] *adj.* having worms in the intestines.

hel•min•thol•o•gy [,hɛlmɪn'θɒlədʒi] *n.* the study of parasitic worms.

helms•man ['hɛlmzmən] *n., pl.* **-men.** the person at the helm of a ship.

hel•ot ['hɛlət] *or* ['hilət] *n.* **1 Helot,** a member of a class of serfs of ancient Sparta. **2** any slave or serf. ⟨< L *Helotes,* pl. < Gk. *Heilōs,* probably related to Gk. *haliskesthai* be captured⟩

hel•ot•ism ['hɛlə,tɪzəm] *or* ['hilə,tɪzəm] *n.* **1** serfdom like that of ancient Sparta. **2** *Biology.* a form of symbiosis among ants, in which one species is forced by another to do the work of the colony.

hel•ot•ry ['hɛlətri] *or* ['hilətri] *n.* **1** helots; slaves. **2** serfdom; slavery.

help [hɛlp] *v., n. —v.* **1** provide with what is needed or useful: *to help a person with one's money.* **2** aid; assist: *to help someone with her work.* **3** give aid or assistance (*often used with* **out**): *We could finish the job faster if he would help.* **4** wait on or serve in a store, etc.: *"May I help you?" asked the clerk.* **5** make better; relieve: *This medicine should help your cough.* **6** prevent; stop: *It can't be helped.* **7** avoid; keep from: *He can't help yawning.* **8** serve with food (*usually used with a reflexive pronoun*): *The host told them to help themselves to some sandwiches.*
cannot help but, *Informal.* cannot avoid; cannot fail to: *I cannot help but admire her endurance.*
help oneself, a take what one wishes, etc.: *Help yourself to a drink while you wait.* **b** control oneself: *She couldn't help herself.*
help out, give temporary help.
so help me or **so help me God,** a mild oath meaning: I solemnly promise; I speak the truth.
—n. **1** anything done or given in helping: *Your advice is a great help.* **2** aid; assistance: *I need some help with my work.* **3** a person or thing that helps; helper. **4** a hired helper or group of hired helpers: *The storekeeper treats her help well.* **5** a means of making better; remedy: *The medicine was a help.* **6** a means of preventing or stopping: *There's no help for it; we've got to spend the night here.* ⟨OE *helpan*⟩

☛ *Syn. v.* **1, 2. Help,** AID, ASSIST = give support to someone or something by providing something needed or useful. **Help** emphasizes actively providing whatever physical, moral, or material support another needs for any purpose: *She helps her mother at home.* **Aid** particularly suggests helping in a less personal way or working together with another to do or get something: *She aids the children's hospital.* **Assist** suggests standing by to help or serve in any way needed or useful, especially in doing something: *A nurse assists a doctor.*

help•er ['hɛlpər] *n.* a person or thing that helps, especially a person who assists or supports another.

help•ful ['hɛlpfəl] *adj.* giving help; useful. **—'help•ful•ly,** *adv.* **—'help•ful•ness,** *n.*

help•ing ['hɛlpɪŋ] *n., v. —n.* **1** the portion of food served to a person at one time. **2** a portion: *The program included a generous helping of contemporary music.*
—v. ppr. of HELP.

help•less ['hɛlplɪs] *adj.* **1** not able to help oneself; weak. **2** without help, protection, etc. **—'help•less•ly,** *adv.* **—'help•less•ness,** *n.*

help•mate ['hɛlp,meit] *n.* a companion and helper, especially a spouse.

help•meet ['hɛlp,mit] *n.* helpmate. ⟨from a misinterpretation of biblical 'an *help meet* for him' in which *meet* = suitable⟩

hel•ter–skel•ter ['hɛltər 'skɛltər] *adv., n., adj. —adv.* with headlong, disorderly haste: *The children ran helter-skelter when the dog rushed at them.*
—n. noisy and disorderly haste, confusion, etc.
—adj. carelessly hurried; disorderly; confused.

helve [hɛlv] *n., v.* **helved, helv•ing.** *—n.* the handle of an axe, hammer, etc.
—v. put a handle on. ⟨OE *hielfe*⟩

Hel•ve•tia [hɛl'viʃə] *n.* the Latin name for Switzerland.

Hel•ve•tian [hɛl'viʃən] *adj., n. —adj.* Swiss.
—n. a Swiss person.

Hel•ve•tii [hɛl'viʃi,aɪ] *n.* a Celtic people who lived in Helvetia during the time of Julius Caesar.

hem[1] [hɛm] *n., v.* **hemmed, hem•ming.** *—n.* **1** a finished border or edge on an article of cloth; especially, an edge made by folding the cloth under and sewing it down. **2** any rim or margin.
—v. **1** fold under and sew down the edge of (cloth). **2** border; edge.
hem in, around, or **about, a** surround on all sides. **b** keep from getting away or moving freely. ⟨OE *hemm*⟩

hem[2] [hɛm] *n., interj., v.* **hemmed, hem•ming.** *—n. or interj.* a word written to represent the sound of clearing the throat to attract attention or to show doubt or hesitation.
—v. make a sound like that of clearing the throat: *"Uh...," she hemmed, and then kept quiet.*
hem and haw, hesitate in order to avoid committing oneself; stall: *The committee hemmed and hawed for several weeks and then turned the problem over to a subcommittee.* ⟨imitative⟩

hem– *combining form.* the form of **hemo-** occurring before a vowel: *hemal.* Also, **haem-.**

hema– *combining form.* variation of **hemo-**: *hemacytometer.* Also, **haema-.** ⟨< Gk. *haima, -atos* blood⟩

hem•a•cy•tom•e•ter [,himəsai'tɒmətər] *or* [,hɛməsai'tɒmətər] *n. Medicine.* an instrument used to estimate the number of blood cells. Also, **haemacytometer.**

hem•ag•glu•tin•ate [,himə'glutə,neit] *or* [,hɛmə'glutə,neit] *v.* **-at•ed, -at•ing.** cause the agglutination of red blood cells. Also, **haemagglutinate.** **—,hem•ag,glu•ti'na•tion,** *n.*

hem•ag•glu•ti•nin [,himə'glutənɪn] *or* [,hɛmə'glutənɪn] *n. Immunology.* an antibody causing hemagglutination. Also, **haemagglutinin.**

he•mal ['himəl] *adj.* **1** of the blood. **2** on the side of the body containing the heart. Also, **haemal.**

he–man ['hi ,mæn] *Informal. n., adj. —n.* a virile, rugged man. *—adj.* tough; masculine; rugged.

he•man•gi•o•ma [hi,mændʒi'oumə] *n., pl.* **-mas** or **-ma•ta** [-mətə] *Pathology.* angioma.

he•ma•te•in [,himə'tiɪn] *or* ['hɛmə,tin] *n. Chemistry. a reddish brown, crystalline, slightly water-soluble solid obtained from logwood and used chiefly as a stain in microscopy. Formula*: $C_{16}H_{12}O_6$

he•mat•ic [hɪ'mætɪk] *adj.* having to do with blood. Also, **haematic.**

hem•a•tite ['hɛmə,tɔit] *or* ['himə,tɔit] *n.* a naturally occurring mineral that is a valuable ore of iron, consisting of ferric oxide in a red earthy form or blackish crystalline form. *Formula*: Fe_2O_3 Also, **haematite.** ⟨< L *haematites* < Gk. *haimatitēs* bloodlike < *haima, -matos* blood⟩

hemato– *combining form.* blood: *hematogenesis = the formation of blood.* Also, **haemato-.** ⟨< Gk. *haima, -atos* blood⟩

hem•a•to•blast ['hɛmətə,blæst] *or* ['himətə,blæst] *n.* **1** a blood platelet. **2** an undeveloped blood cell. Also, **haematoblast.**

hem•a•to•gen•e•sis [,hɛmətə'dʒɛnəsɪs] *or* [,himətə'dʒɛnəsɪs] *n.* the formation of blood in the body. Also, **haematogenesis.**

he•ma•tog•en•ous [,himə'tɒdʒənəs] *or* [,hɛmə'tɒdʒənəs] *adj.* **1** producing blood. **2** originating in the blood. Also, **haematogenous.**

he•ma•tol•o•gist [,himə'tɒlədʒɪst] *or* [,hɛmə'tɒlədʒɪst] *n.* a person who studies blood, or an expert in the diseases of the blood. Also, **haematologist.**

he•ma•tol•o•gy [,himə'tɒlədʒi] *or* [,hɛmə'tɒlədʒi] *n.* the branch of physiology that deals with the structure, function, and diseases of the blood. Also, **haematology.**

he•ma•to•ma [,himə'toumə] *or* [,hɛmə'toumə] *Pathology. n., pl.* **-mas** or **-ma•ta** [-mətə]. a swelling filled with blood. Also **haematoma.**

hem•a•to•zo•on [,hɛmətə'zouən] *or* [,himətə'zouən] *n.* an animal parasite in the blood, often a protozoan. Also, **haematozoon.**

he•ma•tu•ria [,himə'tjʊriə] *or* [,himə'tʊriə] *n. Pathology.* the presence of blood in the urine.

heme [him] *n. Biochemistry.* a component of hemoglobin, without protein but containing ferrous iron. *Formula*: $C_{34}H_{32}N_4O_4Fe$

hemi– *prefix.* half, as in *hemisphere.* ⟨< Gk.⟩

he•mic ['himɪk] *or* ['hɛmɪk] *adj.* of the blood. Also, **haemic.**

hem•i•cy•cle ['hɛmə,saikəl] *n.* a semi-circle.

hem•i•he•dral [,hɛmə'hidrəl] *adj.* of a crystal, having only half the normal surfaces.

hem•i•hy•drate [,hɛmə'haɪdreit] *n. Chemistry.* a compound having two molecules of substance to one of water.

hem•i•me•tab•o•lous [,hɛmɪmə'tæbələs] *adj.* not undergoing complete metamorphosis.

hem•i•mor•phite [,hɛmə'mɔrfəit] *n.* a white, crystalline mineral, hydrated zinc silicate, that is a common zinc ore. *Formula*: $Zn_4Si_2O_7(OH)_2•H_2O$

hem•i•par•a•site [,hɛmə'pærə,səit] *or* [,hɛmə'pɛrə,səit] *n.* an organism that is only partially parasitic.

hem•i•ple•gia [,hɛmə'plidʒiə] *n. Pathology.* paralysis of one side of the body. ⟨< Gk. *hēmi-* half + *plēgē* stroke⟩

hem•i•ple•gic [,hɛmə'plidʒɪk] *or* [,hɛmə'plɛdʒɪk] *adj., n.*
—adj. **1** suffering from hemiplegia. **2** having to do with hemiplegia.
—n. a person suffering from hemiplegia.

he•mip•ter•an [hə'mɪptərən] *n., adj. —n.* a hemipterous insect.
—adj. of or designating the order (Hemiptera) comprising these insects.
☛ *Usage.* See note at HETEROPTEROUS.

he•mip•ter•ous [hə'mɪptərəs] *adj.* of or having to do with the insect order Hemiptera (usually called Heteroptera) that comprises the 'true bugs'. ⟨< *hemi-* + Gk. *pteron* wing⟩
☛ *Usage.* See note at HETEROPTEROUS.

hem•i•sphere ['hɛmɪ,sfir] *n.* **1** a half of a sphere or globe. **2** a half of the earth's surface. North America and South America are in the western hemisphere. Europe, Asia, Africa, and Australia are in the eastern hemisphere. All countries north of the equator are in the northern hemisphere. **3** a half of the celestial sphere, as divided by the celestial equator, the ecliptic, or the horizon. **4** *Anatomy.* CEREBRAL HEMISPHERE. ⟨< F < L < Gk. *hēmisphairion* < *hēmi-* half + *sphaira* sphere⟩ **—,hem•i'spher•ic,** *adj.*

hem•i•spher•i•cal [,hɛmɪ'sfɛrəkəl] *adj.* **1** shaped like a hemisphere. **2** of a hemisphere.

hem•i•spher•oid [,hɛmɪ'sfirɔɪd] *n.* half a spheroid.

hem•i•stich ['hɛmə,stɪk] *n.* half a line of verse, especially one separated from the rest of the line by a CAESURA. ⟨< L < Gk. *hēmistichion* < *hēmi-* half + *stichos* line of verse⟩

hem•i•trope ['hɛmə,troup] *n.* a twin crystal.

hem•i•zy•gos•i•ty [,hɛməzaɪ'gɒsəti] *n. Genetics.* the state of being hemizygous. ⟨< *hemi-* + Gk. *zygon* yoke⟩

hem•i•zy•gote [,hɛmə'zaɪgout] *n. Genetics.* an individual who is hemizygous with respect to a particular gene.

hem•i•zy•gous [,hɛmə'zaɪgəs] *adj. Genetics.* having only a single representative of a particular gene rather than the usual pair.

hem•line ['hɛm,laɪn] *n.* the relative length of a skirt or dress.

hem•lock ['hɛmlɒk] *n.* **1** any of a genus (*Tsuga*) of evergreen trees of the pine family found in North America and E Asia, having hanging cones, needlelike leaves growing spirally along the stem, and bark that is rich in tannin. The three species of hemlock native to Canada are the western hemlock, mountain hemlock, and eastern hemlock. **2** the relatively hard wood of any of these trees. **3** a poisonous European plant (*Conium maculatum*) of the parsley family having spotted stems, finely divided leaves, and small, white flowers. **4** a poison made from this plant. ⟨OE *hymlice*⟩

hem•mer ['hɛmər] *n.* **1** a person who or thing that hems. **2** an attachment to a sewing machine for hemming.

hemo– *combining form.* blood: *hemoglobin.* ⟨< Gk. *haima* blood⟩

he•mo•cyte ['himə,səit] *or* ['hɛmə,səit] *n.* a blood cell. Also, **haemocyte.**

he•mo•glo•bin ['himə,gloubən], ['hɛmə,gloubən], [,himə'gloubən], *or* [,hɛmə'gloubən] *n. Biochemistry.* **1** the protein matter in the red corpuscles of the blood, which carries oxygen from the lungs to the tissues and carbon dioxide from the tissues to the lungs. **2** a substance serving a similar function in some invertebrates and plants. Also, **haemoglobin.** See GLOBIN. ⟨for *hematoglobulin*, ult. < Gk. *haima* blood + L *globulus*, dim. of *globus* globe⟩

he•mo•lyt•ic disease of the newborn [,himə'lɪtɪk] anemia caused by destruction of fetal red blood cells by maternal antibodies such as Rh antibody. *Abbrev.*: HDN ⟨< *hemo-* + Gk. *lytikos* able to loose⟩

he•mo•phil•i•a [,himə'fɪliə] *or* [,hɛmə'fɪliə] *n. Pathology.* an inherited condition in which the blood does not clot normally. Excessive bleeding results from the slightest cut. Also, **haemophilia.** ⟨< NL *haemophilia* < Gk. *haima* blood + *philia* affection, tendency⟩

he•mo•phil•i•ac [,himə'fɪli,æk] *or* [,hɛmə'fɪli,æk] *n.* a person suffering from hemophilia. Also, **haemophiliac.**

he•mop•ty•sis [hɪ'mɒptəsɪs] *n. Medicine.* the spitting of blood from the lungs or bronchi. ⟨< *hemo-* +Gk. *ptysis* < ptyein spit⟩

hem•or•rhage ['hɛmərɪdʒ] *n., v.* **-rhaged, -rhag•ing.** *—n.* **1** a discharge of blood from the blood vessels, especially a heavy discharge. **2** a steady loss of other vital supplies, such as money.
—v. **1** suffer from a heavy or uncontrollable bleeding. **2** suffer a steady loss of money or other vital supplies. Also, **haemorrhage.** ⟨< L *haemorrhagia* < Gk. *haimorrhagia*, ult. < *haima* blood + *rhēgnynai* break, burst⟩ **—,hem•or'rhag•ic** [-'rædʒɪk], *adj.*

hem•or•rhoi•dal [,hɛmə'rɔɪdəl] *adj.* **1** of or having to do with hemorrhoids. **2** suffering from hemorrhoids. Also, **haemorrhoidal.**

hem•or•rhoids ['hɛmə,rɔɪdz] *n.pl.* swollen veins near the anus caused by the dilation of blood vessels, often painful. Also, **haemorrhoids.** ⟨< L *haemorrhoida* < Gk. *haimorrhois*, ult. < *haima* blood + *-rhoos* flowing⟩

hem•or•roid•ec•to•my [,hɛmərɔɪ'dɛktəmi] *n.* the surgical removal of hemorrhoids.

he•mo•sta•sis [,himou'steisɪs] *or* [,hɛmou'steisɪs] *n.* the stopping of the flow of blood. Also, **haemostasis.** ⟨< *hemo-* + Gk. *stasis* < *histanai* stand⟩

he•mo•stat ['himə,stæt] *or* ['hɛmə,stæt] *n.* anything that stops bleeding, including a surgical clamp. **—,he•mo'stat•ic,** *adj.*

hemp [hɛmp] *n.* **1** a tall annual plant (*Cannabis sativa*) of the mulberry family, native to Asia, whose tough fibres are made into heavy string, rope, coarse cloth, etc. **2** hashish, marijuana, or some other drug obtained from the female hemp plant. **3** any of various other strong plant fibres or the plants yielding them, such as sisal hemp or Manila hemp. ⟨OE *henep*⟩

hemp•en ['hɛmpən] *adj.* of, made of, or resembling hemp.

hemp nettle any of various plants (genus *Galeopsis*) of the mint family, especially a hairy, weedy plant (*G. tetrahit*) having toothed leaves and helmet-shaped flowers.

hem•stitch ['hɛm,stɪtʃ] *n., v. —n.* **1** an ornamental stitch made by pulling out several parallel threads at or near a hem and gathering the remaining cross threads into small bunches. See EMBROIDERY for picture. **2** ornamental needlework made in this way.
—v. hem or decorate with hemstitch.

hen [hɛn] *n.* **1** the adult female of the domestic fowl. **2** the adult female of certain other birds and a few animals: *a hen sparrow, a hen lobster.*
like a hen with one chicken, *Informal.* very fussy.
scarce as hen's teeth, *Informal.* very scarce. ⟨OE *henn*⟩
—'hen,like, *adj.*

hen–and–chick•ens ['hɛn ən 'tʃɪkənz] *n.* (*used with a singular or plural verb*) any of various low-growing plants that spread by means of runners, especially the houseleek.

hen•bane ['hɛn,bein] *n.* a poisonous plant (*Hyoscyamus niger*) of the nightshade family native to Europe and Asia but now growing in North America, having large, sticky, hairy leaves and funnel-shaped yellowish flowers and a strong, unpleasant smell. Henbane yields several powerful drugs used in medicine.

hence [hɛns] *adv., interj. —adv.* **1** as a result of this; therefore: *The attempts to raise money have failed; hence the project will have to be abandoned.* **2** from now; from this time onward: *A year hence, the incident will have been forgotten.* **3** *Archaic.* from here; away: *She went hence many years ago.* **4** *Archaic.* from this world or life. **5** from this source or origin: *Hence came several problems.*
—interj. Archaic. go away! begone!
hence with, *Archaic.* away with; take away. ⟨ME *hennes* < OE *heonan* + *-s,* adv. ending⟩
☛ *Usage adv. 1.* **Hence** is a formal word for the less formal **consequently** or **therefore** and the general **so:** *She has not answered our last letter; hence it would seem she is not interested.*

hence•forth [,hɛns'fɔrθ] *adv.* from this time on; from now on.

hence•for•ward [,hɛns'fɔrwərd] *adv.* henceforth.

hench•man ['hɛntʃmən] *n., pl.* **-men. 1** a follower or aide who obeys orders without scruple: *He had one of his henchmen collect the blackmail money.* **2** a trusted attendant or follower. ⟨ME *henxtman* < OE *hengest* horse + *man* man; originally, a groom and, later, a page or squire. The derogatory sense of def. 1 seems to have developed in the 19c.⟩

hen•coop ['hɛn,kup] *n.* a coop for poultry.

hen•dec•a•gon [hɛn'dɛkə,gɒn] *n.* a polygon having 11 angles. ⟨< Gk. *hendeka* eleven + *gōnia* angle⟩ **—,hen•de'cag•o•nal,** *adj.*

hen•dec•a•he•dron [,hɛndɛkə'hidrən] *n.* a polyhedron having 11 faces.

hen•e•quen or **hen•e•quin** ['hɛnəkɪn] *n.* **1** an agave (*Agave fourcroydes*) native to Mexico. **2** a strong, yellowish fibre obtained from the leaves of this plant, used for making binder twine and rope and also coarse fabrics used for sacks, hammocks, etc. ⟨< Sp. < native Yucatán word⟩

hen•house ['hɛn,hʌus] *n.* a shelter for poultry.

hen•na ['hɛnə] *n., adj., v.* **-naed, -na•ing.** *—n.* **1** a small shrub (*Lawsonia inermis*) of the loosestrife family native to N Africa, the Mediterranean, Asia, and Australia, having small, fragrant white flowers and lance-shaped leaves which yield a dark orange-red dye. Henna is often grown as an ornamental. **2** the dye made from the leaves of this shrub. Henna has been used in different periods since ancient times to colour fingernails, hair, beards, parts of the hands and feet, the manes and hoofs of horses, and also leather, wool, and silk. **3** a reddish brown.
—adj. reddish brown.
—v. colour with henna: *to henna one's hair.* ⟨< Arabic *henna'*⟩

hen•ner•y ['hɛnəri] *n., pl.* **-ner•ies.** a place where poultry is kept.

hen•o•the•ism ['hɛnəθi,ɪzəm] *or* ['hɛnə,θiɪzəm] *n.* belief in and worship of one god while accepting the existence of others. ⟨< Gk. *hen* one + *theos* god⟩

hen party *Informal.* a social gathering of women.

hen•pecked ['hɛn,pɛkt] *adj. Informal.* domineered over by one's wife: *He's a tyrant at work, but henpecked at home.*

hen•ry ['hɛnri] *n., pl.* **-ries** or **-rys.** *Electricity.* an SI unit for measuring inductance. When a current varying at the rate of one ampere per second induces an electromotive force of one volt, the circuit has inductance of one henry. *Symbol:* H ⟨after Joseph *Henry* (1797-1878), an American physicist⟩

hep [hɛp] *adj. Slang.* HIP[3]. ⟨origin uncertain⟩

hep•a•rin ['hɛpərɪn] *n.* a blood thinner found naturally in the liver and lungs, used as a drug to treat phlebitis.

he•pat•ic [hə'pætɪk] *adj., n. —adj.* **1** of, having to do with, or affecting the liver. **2** resembling the liver, especially in colour. **3** *Botany.* of or designating the liverworts.
—n. **1** a medicine used in treating the liver. **2** liverwort. ⟨< L < Gk. *hēpatikos* < *hēpar* liver⟩

he•pat•i•ca [hə'pætəkə] *n.* any of a genus (*Hepatica*) of small, stemless plants of the buttercup family found in wooded areas of the temperate regions of the northern hemisphere, having lobed leaves and purple, blue, pink, or white flowers that bloom in early spring. ⟨< NL, ult. < Gk. *hēpar* liver; the leaf is thought to resemble the liver in shape⟩

hep•a•ti•tis [,hɛpə'təitɪs] *n. Pathology.* inflammation of the liver. ⟨< Gk. *hēpar, hēpatos* liver + E *-itis*⟩

He•phaes•tus [hɪ'fɛstəs] *n. Greek mythology.* the god of fire and metalworking, corresponding to the Roman god Vulcan.

Hep•ple•white ['hɛpəl,wəit] *adj., n. —adj.* of, like, or having to do with a style of furniture having graceful curves and slender lines.
—n. **1** this style of furniture. **2** a piece of furniture in this style. ⟨after George *Hepplewhite* ?-1786), an English furniture designer⟩

hept– the form of **hepta-** before vowels, as in *heptarchy.*

hepta– *combining form.* seven: *heptagon.* ⟨< Gk. *hepta*⟩

hep•tad ['hɛptæd] *n.* a group of seven.

hep•ta•gon ['hɛptə,gɒn] *n.* a polygon having seven sides. ⟨< LL < Gk. *heptagonon* < *hepta* seven + *gōnia* angle⟩

hep•tag•o•nal [hɛp'tægənəl] *adj.* having the form of a heptagon.

hep•ta•he•dron [,hɛptə'hidrən] *n.* a polyhedron having seven faces.

hep•tam•er•ous [hɛp'tæmərəs] *adj.* having seven parts. ⟨< *hepta-* + Gk. *meros* part⟩

hep•tam•e•ter [hɛp'tæmətər] *n.* a line of verse having seven feet. *Example:*

And thríce | he róut | ed áll | his foés, |
and thríce | he sléw | the sláin.

⟨< LL < Gk. *heptametron* < *hepta* seven + *mētron* measure⟩

hep•tane ['hɛptein] *n. Chemistry.* a liquid hydrocarbon or solvent. *Formula:* C_7H_{16}

hep•tar•chy ['hɛptɑrki] *n., pl.* **-chies. 1** a government by seven persons. **2** a group of seven states, each under its own ruler. **3 the Heptarchy,** the seven principal Anglo-Saxon kingdoms between A.D. 449 and A.D. 838. ⟨< *hept-* + Gk. *-archia* rule < *archos* ruler⟩

hep•ta•stich ['hɛptə,stɪk] *n.* a group of seven lines forming a strophe, stanza, or poem. ⟨< *hepta-* + Gk. *stichos* line of verse⟩

Hep•ta•teuch ['hɛptə,tjuk] *or* ['hɛptə,tuk] *n.* the first seven books of the Bible. ⟨< Gk. *heptateuchos* < *hepta-* seven + *teuchos* book⟩

her [hɜr]; *unstressed,* [hər] *or* [ər] *pron., adj. —pron.* the objective form of SHE: *I like her.*
—adj. **1** the possessive form of **she:** of, belonging to, or made or done by her or herself: *She raised her hand. Her graduation is next week. That's one of her paintings.* **2 Her,** a word used as part of any of certain formal titles when using the title to refer to the woman holding it: *Her Majesty the Queen.* ⟨OE *hire*⟩
☛ *Usage.* **Her** and **hers** are possessive forms of **she. Her** is a determiner and is always followed by a noun: *This is her bicycle.* **Hers** is a pronoun and stands alone: *This bicycle is hers.*

her. heraldry; heraldic.

He•ra ['hirə] *or* ['hɛrə] *n. Greek mythology.* the queen of the gods, the wife and sister of Zeus, who was also the special goddess of women and marriage. Hera corresponds to the Roman goddess Juno. Also, **Here.**

Her•a•cles ['hɛrə,kliz] *n.* Hercules.

her•ald ['hɛrəld] *n., v. —n.* **1** in the Middle Ages, in western Europe, an officer who carried messages, made announcements, arranged and supervised tournaments and other public ceremonies, and regulated the use of armorial bearings. **2** a person who carries official messages, or makes important announcements. The word *Herald* is often used as the name of a newspaper. **3** a forerunner; harbinger: *Dawn is the herald of day.* **4** in the United Kingdom, an officer in charge of granting arms and recording arms and pedigrees, who also has important duties in various royal ceremonies.
—v. **1** give news of; announce or usher in: *The robins heralded the arrival of spring.* **2** greet enthusiastically; hail: *Her election was heralded by the newspapers.* ⟨ME < OF < W.Gmc. *heriwald* army chief⟩

he•ral•dic [hə'rældɪk] *adj.* of or having to do with heraldry or heralds.

her•ald•ry ['hɛrəldri] *n., pl.* **-ries. 1** the science or art dealing with coats of arms. Heraldry deals with a person's right to use a coat of arms, the tracing of family descent, the creating of a coat of arms for a new country, etc. **2** a heraldic device or coat of arms; collection of such devices. **3** the ceremony or pomp connected with the life of noble families; pageantry.

herb [hɜrb] *or* [ɜrb] *n.* **1** any flowering plant whose stalk or stem lives only one season. Herbs do not form woody tissue as shrubs and trees do, though their roots may live many years. Peonies, buttercups, corn, wheat, cabbage, lettuce, etc. are herbs. **2** any of many herbaceous plants having aromatic leaves, roots, etc. that are used for flavouring food or in medicines or perfumes. Sage, mint, and lavender are herbs. ⟨ME < OF < L *herba*⟩ **—'herb,like,** *adj.*

her•ba•ceous [hər'beiʃəs] *adj.* **1** of or like a herb; having stems that are soft and not woody. **2** *Botany.* having the colour, texture, etc. of leaves: *a flower with herbaceous sepals; a herbaceous border.* ⟨< L *herbaceus*⟩

herb•age ['hɜrbɪdʒ] *or* ['ɜrbɪdʒ] *n.* **1** herbs collectively, especially grass used for grazing. **2** the green leaves and soft stems of plants.

herb•al ['hɜrbəl] *or* ['ɜrbəl] *adj., n. —adj.* of, having to do with, or made of herbs: *herbal tea.*
—n. a book about herbs, especially one that describes their uses as medicine.

herb•al•ist ['hɜrbəlɪst] *or* ['ɜrbəlɪst] *n.* a person who gathers herbs or deals in them.

her•bar•i•um [hər'bɛriəm] *n., pl.* **-bar•i•ums, -bar•i•a** [-'bɛriə]. **1** a collection of dried plants systematically arranged. **2** a room or building where such a collection is kept. ⟨< LL *herbarium* < L *herba* herb. Doublet of ARBOUR[2].⟩

her•bi•cide ['hɜrbə,saɪd] *n.* any chemical substance used to destroy plants or stop their growth. ⟨< L *herba* herb + *-cida* killer⟩

her•bi•vore ['hɜrbə,vɔr] *n.* any animal that feeds on plants, especially a hoofed animal such as a cow, horse, or deer.

her•biv•o•rous [hər'bɪvərəs] *adj.* feeding on grass or other plants. Cattle are herbivorous animals. ⟨< NL *herbivorus* < L *herba* herb + *vorare* devour⟩

herb Rob•ert ['rɒbərt] a wild geranium (*Geranium robertianum*) having aromatic leaves and pink or purple flowers.

herb•y ['hɜrbi] *or* ['ɜrbi] *adj.* **1** having many herbs; grassy. **2** of or like herbs.

her•cu•le•an [,hɜrkjə'liən] *or* [hər'kjuliən] *adj.* **1 Herculean,** of or having to do with Hercules or his labours. **2** having great strength or courage. **3** requiring or showing great strength or courage; very hard to do: *a herculean task, a herculean effort.*

Her•cu•les ['hɜrkjə,liz] *n.* **1** *Greek and Roman mythology.* a hero of immense strength who performed twelve extraordinary tasks or labours imposed on him by the goddess Hera. **2** *Astronomy.* a northern constellation. **3 hercules,** any man of great strength. ⟨< L < Gk. *Hēraklēs*, literally, the glory of Hera < *Hēra* + *kleos* glory⟩

herd [hɜrd] *n., v. —n.* **1** a number of animals of one kind together: *a herd of cows, a herd of horses, a herd of elephants.* **2** people as a mass or mob; rabble: *the common herd.* **3** the keeper of a herd (*usually used in compounds*): *cowherd, goatherd.*
—v. **1** bring or come together in a herd or as if in a herd: *The cattle were herded into the corral. Many animals herd for protection.* **2** drive or take care of cattle, sheep, etc.: *Her job is herding sheep.* ⟨OE *heord*⟩

herd•er ['hɜrdər] *n.* herdsman.

herds•man ['hɜrdzmən] *n., pl.* **-men. 1** a manager or keeper of a herd or herds of animals. **2 Herdsman,** the northern constellation Boötes.

here [hir] *adv., n., interj. —adv.* **1** in or at this place: *Put it down here. We have lived here for two years.* **2** to this place: *Come here.* **3** at this point in argument, conversation, etc.: *Here the speaker paused.* **4** a word used to call attention to the presence of a person or thing mentioned: *Here, take your scarf. Al here could probably tell you where they are.* **5** on earth; in this life.
here! present! (in answer to a roll call)
here and there, in various places; at scattered intervals: *Here and there we saw an early crocus blooming.*
here below, on earth; in this life.
here goes! *Informal.* announcement of something bold about to be done.
here's to, a wish for health, happiness, or success to.
here, there, and everywhere, in many different places: *There were toys here, there, and everywhere throughout the house.*
here you are, *Informal.* here is what you want.
neither here nor there, not to the point; off the subject; unimportant: *Why she took it is neither here nor there; what we want to know is what she did with it.*
—n. this place: *Here is a good place to stop. Fill the bottle up to here.*
the here and now, the present time and place.
—interj. **1** an exclamation expressing indignation, rebuke, etc.: *Here, give me that! Here, that's not the way to talk!* **2** an answer showing that one is present when roll is called. ⟨OE *hēr*⟩
☛ *Hom.* HEAR.

He•re ['hirə] *n.* Hera.

here•a•bout [,hirə'bʌut] *or* ['hirə,bʌut] *adv.* around here; about this place; near here. Also, **hereabouts.**

here•af•ter [,hir'æftər] *adv.* **1** after this; in the future. **2** in life after death. **3** (*noml.*) **the hereafter, a** the future. **b** life after death.

here•at [,hir'æt] *adv. Archaic.* **1** when this happened; at this time. **2** because of this.

here•by [,hir'baɪ] *or* ['hir,baɪ] *adv.* by this means; in this way: *I hereby certify that I am over 21 years of age.*

he•red•i•ta•ble [hə'rɛdətəbəl] *adj.* that can be inherited.

her•e•dit•a•ment [,hɛrə'dɪtəmənt] *n. Law.* any property that can be inherited.

he•red•i•tar•y [hə'rɛdə,tɛri] *adj.* **1** coming by inheritance: Prince *is a hereditary title.* **2** holding a position by inheritance: *The Queen is a hereditary ruler.* **3** *Biology.* transmitted or caused by heredity: *Colour blindness is hereditary.* Compare CONGENITAL. **4** derived from one's parents or ancestors; established by tradition: *hereditary beliefs, a hereditary enemy.* **5** of or having to do with inheritance or heredity. ⟨< L *hereditarius* < *hereditas.* See HEREDITY.⟩

he•red•i•ty [hə'rɛdəti] *n., pl.* **-ties. 1** *Biology.* the transmission of physical or mental characteristics or qualities from parent to offspring through elements called genes in the chromosomes of the germ cells that produce the offspring. **2** the qualities that have come to offspring from parents. **3** the tendency of offspring to be like the parents. **4** the transmission from one generation to another of property, titles, customs, etc. by inheritance or tradition. ⟨< MF *heredite* < L *hereditat* inheritance⟩

Here•ford ['hɜrfərd] *or* ['hɛrəfərd] *n.* a breed of beef cattle having a red body, white face, and white markings under the body. ⟨< *Herefordshire*, England⟩

here•in [,hir'ɪn] *adv.* **1** in this place, book, document, etc. **2** in this: *It is herein that the difference lies.*

here•in•af•ter [,hirɪn'æftər] *adv.* afterward in this document, statement, etc.

here•in•be•fore [,hirɪnbɪ'fɔr] *adv.* before in this document, statement, etc.

here•in•to [,hir'ɪntu] *or* [,hirɪn'tu] *adv.* **1** into this place. **2** into this matter.

here•of [,hir'ʌv] *or* [,hir'ɒv] *adv.* of or about this.

here•on [,hir'ɒn] *adv.* **1** on this. **2** immediately after this.

here's [hirz] here is.

he•re•si•arch [hə'rizi,ɑrk] *n.* the founder of a heresy.

her•e•sy ['hɛrəsi] *n., pl.* **-sies. 1** a belief different from the accepted belief of a church, school, profession, etc. **2** the holding of such a belief. ⟨ME < OF < LGk. *hairesis* a taking, choosing < *haireein* take⟩

her•e•tic ['hɛrətɪk] *n., adj. —n.* a person who holds a belief that is different from the accepted belief of his or her church, school, profession, etc.
—adj. holding such a belief. ⟨< F *hérétique* < LL *haereticus* < Gk. *hairetikos* able to choose⟩

he•ret•i•cal [hə'rɛtəkəl] *adj.* **1** of or having to do with heresy or heretics. **2** containing heresy; characterized by heresy. **—he'ret•i•cal•ly,** *adv.*

here•to [,hir'tu] *adv. Formal.* to this place, thing, etc.

here•to•fore [,hirtə'fɔr] *or* ['hirtə,fɔr] *adv. Formal.* before this time; until now.

here•un•der [,hir'ʌndər] *or* ['hir,ʌndər] *adv. Formal.* **1** in a book, document, etc., below: *according to the terms specified hereunder.* **2** in accordance with or under the authority of this.

here•un•to [,hirʌn'tu] *or* [hi'rʌntu] *adv. Archaic.* to this.

here•up•on [,hirə'pɒn] *or* ['hirə,pɒn] *adv.* **1** upon this. **2** immediately after this.

here•with [ˌhir'wɪθ] *or* [ˌhir'wɪð] *adv. Formal.* **1** with this. **2** by this means; in this way.

her•it•a•bil•i•ty [ˌhɛrətə'bɪləti] *n.* a statistical measure of the proportion of variation in a trait in a population, that is caused by genetics rather than environment or chance.

her•it•a•ble ['hɛrətəbəl] *adj.* **1** capable of being inherited. **2** capable of inheriting.

her•it•age ['hɛrətɪdʒ] *n.* **1** what is or may be handed on to a person from his or her ancestors; inheritance. **2** something that a person has as a result of having been born in a certain time, place, condition, etc.: *a heritage of violence. Their heritage was freedom.* ⟨ME < OF *heritage* < *heriter* inherit < LL *hereditare*, ult. < L *heres, -redis* heir⟩

he•ri•tor ['hɛrɪtər] *n.* an inheritor; heir.

her•maph•ro•dite [hər'mæfrəˌdəit] *n., adj.* —*n.* **1** *Biology.* an animal or plant having the reproductive organs of both sexes. **2** a person or thing that combines opposite qualities.
3 HERMAPHRODITE BRIG.
—*adj.* of or like a hermaphrodite. ⟨< L < Gk. *Hermaphroditos* Hermaphroditus, a son of Hermes and Aphrodite, who became united in body with a nymph⟩

A hermaphrodite brig, showing the types of sail

hermaphrodite brig a sailing ship with two masts, square-rigged forward and schooner-rigged aft.

her•maph•ro•dit•ic [hərˌmæfrə'dɪtɪk] *adj.* of or like a hermaphrodite. **—herˌmaph•ro'dit•i•cal•ly,** *adv.*

her•me•neu•tic [ˌhɜrmə'njutɪk] *or* [ˌhɜrmə'nutɪk] *adj.* of or having to do with hermeneutics. Also, **hermeneutical**. **—ˌher•me'neu•ti•cal•ly,** *adv.*

her•me•neu•tics [ˌhɜrmə'njutɪks] *or* [ˌhɜrmə'nutɪks] *n.* (*used with a singular verb*) the study of the principles of interpretation of literary works. ⟨< Gk. *hermēneutikos* expert in interpretation < *hermēneus* interpreter, translator⟩

Her•mes ['hɜrmiz] *n. Greek mythology.* a god who was the messenger of Zeus and the other gods, corresponding to the Roman god Mercury. Hermes was the god of boundaries and roads, of science and invention, of eloquence, luck, and cunning, and he was the patron of thieves.

her•met•ic [hər'mɛtɪk] *adj.* **1** closed tightly so that air cannot get in; airtight. **2** of a poem, having a meaning that is difficult to decipher; obscure. **3** magical; alchemical. Also, **hermetical**. ⟨< Med.L *hermeticus* < *Hermes* Trismegistus, supposed author of a work on magic and alchemy⟩ **—her'met•i•cal•ly,** *adv.*

her•mit ['hɜrmɪt] *n.* **1** a person who goes away from other people and lives alone in some lonely or out-of-the-way place, often for religious reasons. **2** a kind of spiced cookie made with molasses or brown sugar and usually containing raisins and nuts. ⟨ME < OF < LL < Gk. *erēmitēs* < *erēmia* desert < *erēmos* uninhabited. Doublet of EREMITE.⟩ **—'her•mitˌlike,** *adj.*

her•mit•age ['hɜrmətɪdʒ] *n.* **1** the home of a hermit. **2** a place to live away from other people; retreat.

hermit crab any of various small, soft-bodied, decapod crustaceans resembling lobsters or crabs, that live in and carry around the empty shells of snails or other molluscs; especially, any of the genus *Pagurus* (family Paguridae), such as the common *P. bernhardus* of the coastal waters of North America and Europe.

hermit thrush a North American thrush (*Hylocichla guttata*) having a brownish back, reddish brown tail, and spotted breast, and noted for its beautiful, varied evening song.

her•ni•a ['hɜrniə] *n., pl.* **-ni•as, -ni•ae** [-niˌi] *or* [-niˌaɪ]. *Pathology.* the protrusion of a part of the intestine or some other organ through a break in its surrounding walls; a rupture. ⟨< L⟩

her•ni•al ['hɜrniəl] *adj.* of or having to do with a hernia.

he•ro ['hirou] *n., pl.* **-roes. 1** a person who does great and brave deeds and is admired for them: *the heroes of old.* **2** a person admired for contributing to a particular field: *a football hero, heroes of science.* **3** the most important male person in a story, play, motion picture, etc. **4** *Mythology and legend.* a man of more than human qualities, such as Hercules and Achilles. ⟨ult. < L *heros* < Gk.⟩

He•ro ['hirou] *n. Greek mythology.* a priestess of Aphrodite, whose lover Leander swam the Hellespont every night to visit her. One night he drowned, and, on learning of his death, Hero killed herself.

he•ro•ic [hɪ'rouɪk] *adj., n.* —*adj.* **1** like a hero or heroine in deeds or in qualities; brave; noble: *the heroic deeds of our firefighters.* **2** of or about heroes and their deeds: The Iliad *and the* Odyssey *are heroic poems.* **3** resembling the language or style of heroic poetry: *heroic prose.* **4** unusually daring or bold: *Only heroic measures could save the town from the flood.* **5** unusually large; larger than life size. Also, **heroical.**
—*n.* **1** a heroic poem. **2 heroics,** *pl.* **a** high-sounding language. **b** words, feelings, or actions that seem grand or noble but are only for effect. **c** heroic verse. **—he'ro•i•cal•ly,** *adv.*

heroic age the period of the legendary heroes of a nation or folk: *the heroic age of Greece.*

he•ro•i•cal [hɪ'rouəkəl] *adj.* heroic.

heroic couplet two successive and rhyming lines of verse in iambic pentameter:

Let such teach others who themselves excel,
And censure freely who have written well.

heroic verse a poetic form used in heroic and other long poems. In English, German, and Italian, it is iambic pentameter. In French it is the Alexandrine. In Greek and Latin, it is dactylic hexameter.

her•o•in ['hɛrouɪn] *n.* a very powerful, habit-forming sedative drug made from morphine. *Formula*: $C_2H_{23}NO_5$ ⟨< G, formerly a trademark ? < *hero*⟩
☛ *Hom.* HEROINE.

her•o•ine ['hɛrouɪn] *n.* **1** a woman or girl admired for her bravery or great deeds: *Laura Secord and Madeleine de Verchères are Canadian heroines.* **2** a woman or girl admired for contributing to a particular field: *Roberta Bondar is a space heroine.* **3** the most important female person in a story, play, motion picture, etc. **4** *Mythology and legend.* a woman or girl having more than human qualities, such as Medea. ⟨< L < Gk. *hērōinē*, fem. of *hērōs* hero⟩
☛ *Hom.* HEROIN.

her•o•ism ['hɛrouˌɪzəm] *n.* **1** the actions and qualities of a hero or heroine; great bravery; daring courage. **2** a very brave act or quality.

her•on ['hɛrən] *n.* any of various wading birds (family Ardeidae) having a long neck that is doubled back in flight, a long bill, long legs, and a short tail. The great blue heron (*Ardea herodias*) is the largest Canadian heron. ⟨ME < OF *hairon* < Gmc.⟩

her•on•ry ['hɛrənri] *n., pl.* **-ries.** a place where many herons come in the breeding season.

hero sandwich a long roll filled with meat, cheese, lettuce, etc.

he•ro–wor•ship ['hirou ˌwɜrʃɪp] *v.* **-shipped** or **-shiped, -ship•ping** or **-ship•ing;** *n.* —*v.* idolize; worship as a hero.
—*n.* Also, **hero worship, 1** in ancient Greece and Rome, the worship of ancient heroes as gods. **2** the idolizing of great persons, or of persons thought of as heroes.
—'he•ro-ˌwor•ship•per or **-ˌwor•ship•er,** *n.*

her•pes ['hɜrpiz] *n.* any of several virus diseases of the skin or mucous membranes, characterized by clusters of blisters. **Herpes simplex** is a type of herpes marked by watery blisters especially on the mouth, lips, or genitals. ⟨< L < Gk. *herpēs* shingles < *herpein* creep⟩

her•pe•tol•o•gist [ˌhɜrpə'tɒlədʒɪst] a person trained in herpetology, especially one whose work it is.

her•pe•tol•o•gy [ˌhɜrpə'tɒlədʒi] *n.* the branch of zoology dealing with reptiles and amphibians. ⟨< Gk. *herpeton* reptile (< *herpein* creep) + E *-logy*⟩ **—ˌher•pe•to'log•i•cal,** *adj.*

Herr [hɛr] *n., pl.* **Her•ren** ['hɛrən]. a courtesy title in Germany, equivalent to English *Mr.*
☛ *Hom.* HAIR, HARE.

her•ring ['hɛrɪŋ] *n., pl.* **-ring** or **-rings. 1** a small, silvery fish (*Clupea harengus*) of the North Atlantic and Pacific Oceans that is one of the most important food fishes in the world. Herring are caught in huge quantities and sold fresh, salted, smoked, dried, or pickled, and are also canned, in which case they are called sardines. **2** any of a number of related fishes. **3** (*adjl.*) designating a family (Clupeidae) of seawater and freshwater fishes that includes the herring as well as the alewife, pilchard, and shad. **4** any of various other unrelated fishes, such as the lake herring (cisco) or the yellow herring (goldeye). ⟨OE *hǣring*⟩

her•ring•bone ['hɛrɪŋ,boun] *n., v.* **-boned, -bon•ing.** *—n.* **1** a zigzag pattern, resembling the spine of a herring. **2** cloth in a twill weave with a small, woven zigzag pattern: *He chose a herringbone for his suit.* **3** a zigzag arrangement of bricks, tiles, etc. **4** (*adjl.*) of or designating a herringbone: *a herringbone tweed, a herringbone pattern.* **5** *Skiing.* a method of going up a slope by pointing the front of the skis outward and putting the weight on the inner side.
—v. **1** produce a herringbone pattern. **2** *Skiing.* go up (a slope) by pointing the skis outward and putting one's weight on the inner side.

herringbone stitch *Embroidery.* a stitch consisting of crosses in a herringbone design.

herring choker *Cdn. Slang.* a person from the Maritime Provinces, especially one from New Brunswick.

herring gull a large gull (*Larus argentatus*) widely distributed throughout the northern hemisphere, the adults having white plumage with pearl-grey back and black wing tips. The herring gull is common in most of Canada, including the interior regions.

hers [hɜrz] *pron.* a possessive form of SHE: that which belongs to her: *This money is hers. My answers were wrong, but hers were right.*
of hers, belonging to or associated with her: *He's a friend of hers.*
☛ *Usage.* See note at HER.

her•self [hər'sɛlf]; *unstressed,* [ər'sɛlf] *pron.* **1** a reflexive pronoun, the form of **she** used as an object when it refers to the same person or thing as the subject: *She asked herself if it was really worth all the trouble.* **2** a form of **she** or **her** added for emphasis: *She did it herself. She herself brought the book.* **3** her usual self: *In those fits she is not herself.*

hertz [hɜrts] *n., pl.* **hertz.** an SI unit for measuring the frequency, or rate of occurrence, of waves and vibrations, equal to one cycle per second. The musical tone A above middle C has a frequency of 440 vibrations per second, or 440 hertz. *Symbol*: Hz ⟨See HERTZIAN WAVES⟩

Hertz•i•an waves ['hɜrtsiən] electromagnetic radiation, such as the waves used in communicating by radio. Hertzian waves are produced by irregular fluctuations of electricity in a conductor. ⟨first investigated by Heinrich Rudolph *Hertz* (1857-1894), a German physicist⟩

he's [hiz]; *unstressed,* [iz] **1** he is. **2** he has: *He's broken his hockey stick.*

Hesh•van ['hɛʃvæn] *n.* in the Hebrew calendar, the eighth month of the ecclesiastical year, and the second month of the civil year. Also, **Heshwan, Hesvan.**

hes•i•tan•cy ['hɛzətənsi] *n., pl.* **-cies.** hesitation; doubt; indecision. Also, **hesitance.**

hes•i•tant ['hɛzətənt] *adj.* hesitating; doubtful; undecided. **—'hes•i•tant•ly,** *adv.*

hes•i•tate ['hɛzə,teit] *v.* **-tat•ed, -tat•ing. 1** hold back because one feels doubtful; be undecided or uncertain: *She hesitated, wondering which road to take.* **2** be unwilling or reluctant because of scruples: *I hesitated to ask you because you were so busy.* **3** stop for an instant; pause: *He hesitated before asking the question.* **4** speak with stops or pauses; stammer. ⟨< L *haesitare* < *haerere* stick fast⟩
☛ *Syn.* **1. Hesitate,** FALTER, WAVER = show doubt or lack of firmness in deciding or acting. **Hesitate** emphasizes holding back, unable to make up one's mind firmly or to act promptly: *I hesitated about taking the position.* **Falter** suggests losing courage and hesitating or giving way after starting to act: *I went to apologize, but faltered at the door.* **Waver** suggests being unable to stick firmly to a decision and giving way or drawing back: *My confidence in him wavers.*

hes•i•tat•ing•ly ['hɛzə,teitɪŋli] *adv.* with hesitation.

hes•i•ta•tion [,hɛzə'teiʃən] *n.* **1** the act or an instance of hesitating: *After some hesitation she decided to come with us.* **2** the state of being hesitant.

Hes•pe•ria [hɛ'spiriə] *n.* **1** the ancient Greek name for Italy. **2** the Roman name for Spain.

Hes•pe•ri•an [hɛ'spiriən] *adj.* **1** having to do with either Hesperia. **2** of or having to do with the Hesperides.

Hes•per•i•des [hɛ'spɛrə,diz] *n.pl. Greek mythology.* **a** the four nymphs who guarded the golden apples of Hera. **b** the garden where these apples grew.

hes•pe•ri•din [hə'spɛrɪdɪn] *n.* a substance found in citrus fruits. *Formula*: $C_{28}H_{34}O_{15}$

Hes•per•us ['hɛspərəs] *n.* an evening star, especially the planet Venus. ⟨< L < Gk. *Hesperos*, originally adj., pertaining to the evening, western⟩

hes•sian ['hɛʃən] *n.* a coarse fabric of jute and hemp, used in making bags, etc. ⟨< *Hessian*⟩

Hes•sian ['hɛʃən] *n., adj. —n.* **1** a native or inhabitant of Hesse, a district in Germany. **2** any of the German mercenary soldiers in the British army that fought against the Americans during the American Revolution. **3** a mercenary.
—adj. of Hesse or its people. ⟨< *Hesse*, a state in Germany⟩

Hessian boots high boots with tassels, popular in England during the 19th century.

Hessian fly a small, two-winged fly (*Mayetiola destructor*) whose larvae are destructive to wheat.

hest [hɛst] *n. Archaic.* behest; command. ⟨alteration of OE *hǣs*⟩

Hes•ti•a ['hɛstiə] *n. Greek mythology.* the goddess of the hearth, corresponding to the Roman goddess Vesta.

Hes•van ['hɛsvæn] *n.* Heshvan.

het [xɛt] *n.* the ninth letter of the Hebrew alphabet. See table of alphabets in the Appendix.

he•tae•ra [hə'tirə] *n., pl.* **-tae•rae** [-'tiri] *or* [-'tiraɪ]. in ancient Greece, a courtesan. Also, **hetaira.** ⟨< Gk. *hetaira*, fem., companion⟩

he•tae•rism [hə'tirɪzəm] *n.* concubinage.

he•tai•ra [hə'taɪrə] *n., pl.* **-rai** [-raɪ]. See HETAERA.

hetero– *combining form.* other; different: *heterogeneous.* ⟨< Gk. *hetero-* < *heteros*⟩

het•er•o•chro•ma•tin [,hɛtərə'kroumətɪn] *n. Genetics.* highly condensed chromatin that contains few genes, and stains deeply in interphase cells. ⟨< *hetero-* different + Gk. *chroma* colour⟩

het•er•o•cy•clic [,hɛtərə'səiklɪk] *adj. Chemistry.* having atoms of carbon and any other element(s) joined in a ring.

het•er•o•dox ['hɛtərə,dɒks] *adj.* **1** contrary to or differing from an acknowledged standard; not orthodox: *a heterodox belief.* **2** rejecting the regularly accepted beliefs or doctrines: *a heterodox priest.* ⟨< LL < Gk. *heterodoxos* < *heteros* other + *doxa* opinion⟩

het•er•o•dox•y ['hɛtərə,dɒksi] *n., pl.* **-dox•ies. 1** the quality or state of being heterodox. **2** a heterodox belief, doctrine, or opinion.

het•er•o•dyne ['hɛtərə,daɪn] *adj., v. —adj.* of or designating a strong, stable radio frequency called a beat, produced by combining the high, unstable incoming frequency with another slightly different one given out by an oscillator in the receiver itself. The heterodyne frequency is the difference between the original two frequencies.
—v. combine (two similar radio frequencies) to produce a beat.

het•er•og•a•mous [,hɛtə'rɒgəməs] *adj. Biology.* **1** of reproduction in which uniting gametes are unlike in function, size, or structure. **2** of reproduction in which asexual generation alternates with sexual. **—,het•er'og•a•my,** *n.*

het•er•o•ge•ne•i•ty [,hɛtərədʒə'niəti] *n., pl.* **-ties.** the quality or state of being heterogeneous; dissimilarity.

het•er•o•ge•ne•ous [,hɛtərə'dʒiniəs] *adj.* **1** different in kind; unlike; varied. **2** made up of unlike elements or parts; miscellaneous. Compare HOMOGENEOUS. **3** *Mathematics.* of different kinds and having no common integral division except 1. **4** of different degrees or dimensions. ⟨< Med.L *heterogeneus*, ult. < Gk. *heteros* other + *genos* kind⟩ **—,het•er•o'ge•ne•ous•ly,** *adv.* **—,het•er•o'ge•ne•ous•ness,** *n.*

het•er•o•gen•e•sis [,hɛtərə'dʒɛnəsɪs] *n.* ALTERNATION OF GENERATIONS. **—,het•er•o•ge'net•ic,** *adj.*

het•er•og•y•nous [,hɛtə'rɒdʒənəs] *adj. Zoology.* having one sterile female and one reproductive, like ants.

het•er•ol•o•gy [,hɛtə'rɒlədʒi] *n.* lack of normal correspondence in bodily parts, resulting from different origins. **—,het•er'ol•og•ous,** *adj.*

het•er•ol•y•sis [ˌhɛtəˈrɒləsɪs] *n. Biochemistry.* the destruction of protein by lytic agents.

het•er•om•er•ous [ˌhɛtəˈrɒmərəs] *adj.* having different parts in the same structure. ⟨< *hetero-* + Gk. *meros* part⟩

het•er•o•mor•phic [ˌhɛtərəˈmɔrfɪk] *adj.* unlike in any way.

het•er•on•o•mous [ˌhɛtəˈrɒnəməs] *adj. Biology.* controlled by different laws of growth. ⟨< *hetero-* + Gk. *nomos* law⟩

het•er•o•nym [ˈhɛtərəˌnɪm] *n.* a word spelled the same as another but having a different sound and meaning. *Example*: *lead*, to conduct, and *lead*, a metal. ⟨< *hetero-* + Gk. dial. *onyma* name; formed on the pattern of *homonym*⟩ **—ˌhet•er'on•y•mous,** *adj.*

het•er•o•plas•ty [ˈhɛtərəˌplæsti] *n.* surgical repair by a tissue transplant.

het•er•o•ploid [ˈhɛtərəˌplɔɪd] *n. Genetics.* any chromosome number in an individual different from the standard number for the species. Compare EUPLOID. ⟨< *hetero-* different + Gk. *-ploos* -fold⟩

het•er•op•ter•an [ˌhɛtəˈrɒptərən] *n., adj. —n.* a heteropterous insect.
—adj. of or designating the order (Heteroptera) comprising these insects. ⟨< *hetero-* + Gk. *pteran* wing⟩
☛ *Usage.* See note at HETEROPTEROUS.

het•er•op•ter•ous [ˌhɛtəˈrɒptərəs] *adj.* of or having to do with an insect order (Heteroptera) that comprises 'true bugs' and includes the bedbug. Heteropterous insects usually have two pairs of wings, with the front pair thickened at the base; the wings are folded flat on the back when at rest.
☛ *Usage.* Some authorities classify all sucking insects as belonging to two separate orders: Heteroptera (also called Hemiptera), the 'true bugs', including the bedbug, and Homoptera, including aphids, scale insects, etc.

het•er•o•sex•u•al [ˌhɛtərəˈsɛkʃuəl] *adj., n. —adj.* **1** *Biology.* of or having to do with the different sexes. **2** of, having to do with, or characterized by sexual feeling for a person of the opposite sex. Compare HOMOSEXUAL.
—n. a heterosexual person. **—ˌhet•er•o'sex•u•al•ly,** *adv.*

het•er•o•sex•u•al•i•ty [ˌhɛtərəˌsɛkʃuˈæləti] *n.* the quality or fact of being heterosexual.

het•er•o•sis [ˌhɛtəˈrousɪs] *n.* HYBRID VIGOUR.

het•er•os•po•ry [ˌhɛtəˈrɒspəri] *n. Botany.* the production of microspores as well as megaspores. **—ˌhet•er'os•po•rous,** *adj.*

het•er•o•tax•is [ˌhɛtərəˈtæksɪs] *n.* abnormality in the structure of the body, organs, rock strata, etc. **—ˌhet•er•o'tac•tic,** *adj.*

het•er•o•thal•lic [ˌhɛtərəˈθælɪk] *adj.* of algae or fungi, producing male and female in two different bodies. ⟨< *hetero-* + Gk. *thallos* shoot, twig⟩

het•er•o•to•pia [ˌhɛtərəˈtoupiə] *n. Pathology.* formation of abnormal tissue. ⟨< *hetero-* + Gk. *topos* place⟩

het•er•ot•rich•ous [ˌhɛtəˈrɒtrəkəs] *adj.* of or having to do with the suborder Heterotricha, having uniformly short cilia all over the body.

het•er•o•troph [ˈhɛtərəˌtrɒf] *n.* an organism using only complex organic compounds as sources of food. ⟨< *hetero-* + Gk. *trophe* food⟩

het•er•o•typ•ic [ˌhɛtərəˈtɪpɪk] *adj. Biology.* in meiosis, having to do with the first division.

het•er•o•zy•gos•i•ty [ˌhɛtərəzaɪˈgɒsəti] *n.* the state of being heterozygous.

het•er•o•zy•gote [ˌhɛtərəˈzaɪgout] *n. Genetics.* an individual having different alleles at a given place on a pair of homologous chromosomes, one normal and one abnormal. ⟨< *hetero-* different + Gk. *zygon* yoke⟩

heterozygote advantage the situation in which, in a population, the heterozygote is more fit than either the normal or the abnormal homozygote. For example, in parts of the world where malaria is common, heterozygotes for sickle cell disease do not have the disease, and are more fit than normal homozygotes because they are resistant to malaria.

het•er•o•zy•gous [ˌhɛtərəˈzaɪgəs] *adj.* **1** being a heterozygote. **2** of a genotype in which the two alleles at a given place are different.

het•man [ˈhɛtmən] *n., pl.* **-mans.** a Cossack leader or chief. ⟨< Polish < G *Hauptmann* chief < *Haupt* head + *Mann* man⟩

heu•lan•dite [ˈhjulənˌdəit] *n.* a white, red, or yellow mineral. *Formula*: $CaAl_2Si_6O_{16}•5H_2O$ ⟨after H. *Heuland*, 19c. English mineralogist⟩

heu•ris•tic [hjʊˈrɪstɪk] *adj., n. —adj.* **1** guiding or helping one to discover: *heuristic reasoning.* **2** *Education.* having to do with a method that encourages students to use personal investigation, observation, etc. so that they may find things out for themselves.
—n. Computer technology. a technique or procedure used to solve a particular problem in a way that imitates human intelligence. ⟨< Gk. *heuristein* to find + E *-ist* + *-ic*⟩ **—heu'ris•ti•cal•ly,** *adv.*

hew [hju] *v.* **hewed, hewed** or **hewn, hew•ing. 1** cut with an axe, sword, etc.: *She hewed down the tree.* **2** cut into shape; form by cutting with an axe, adze, etc.: *to hew stone for building, to hew logs into beams.* **3** make or produce with cutting blows: *The knight hewed his way through the enemy.* **4** conform (*to*): *The newspaper hews strictly to the party line.* ⟨OE *hēawan*⟩
☛ *Hom.* HUE.

hewn [hjun] *adj., v. —adj.* felled and cut to shape.
—v. a pp. of HEW.

hex [hɛks] *Informal. v., n. —v.* practise witchcraft on; bewitch.
—n. **1** a witch. **2** a magic spell. ⟨< Pennsylvania G < G *Hexe* witch⟩

hex– the form of **hexa-** before vowels.

hexa– *combining form.* six: *hexagon.* ⟨< Gk. *hex* six⟩

hex•a•chlor•o•eth•ane [ˌhɛksəˌklɔrouˈɛθein] *n.* a substitute for camphor, with many uses. *Formula*: $Cl_3C_2Cl_3$

hex•a•chlor•o•phene [ˌhɛksəˈklɔrəˌfin] *n.* a white powder used in soaps and deodorants against bacteria. *Formula*: $(C_6HCl_3OH)_2CH_2$

hex•ad [ˈhɛksæd] *n.* a group of six.

hex•a•gon [ˈhɛksəˌgɒn] *n.* a polygon having six sides. See POLYGON for picture. ⟨< L < Gk. *hexagōnon*, neut. of *hexagōnos* hexagonal, ult. < *hex* six + *gōnia* angle⟩

hex•ag•o•nal [hɛkˈsægənəl] *adj.* **1** of or having the form of a hexagon. **2** having a hexagon as base or cross section. **—hex'ag•o•nal•ly,** *adv.*

hex•a•gram [ˈhɛksəˌgræm] *n.* a six-pointed star formed of two equilateral triangles: ✡

hex•a•he•dral [ˌhɛksəˈhidrəl] *adj.* having six faces.

hex•a•he•dron [ˌhɛksəˈhidrən] *n., pl.* **-drons, -dra** [-drə]. a polyhedron having six faces. ⟨< Gk. *hexaedron*, neut. of *hexaedros* < *hex* six + *hedra* base, surface⟩

hex•am•er•ous [hɛkˈsæmərəs] *adj.* of a flower, having six parts. ⟨< *hexa-* + Gk. *meros* part⟩

hex•am•e•ter [hɛkˈsæmətər] *n.* **1** a line of poetry consisting of six metrical feet. *Example*:
Thiś is the | foŕest pri | méval. The | muŕmuring | pineś and the | heḿlocks.
2 poetry consisting of hexameters. **3** (*adjl.*) of, having to do with, or consisting of hexameters. ⟨< L < Gk. *hexametros* < *hex* six + *metron* measure⟩ **—ˌhex•a'met•ric,** *adj.*

hex•a•meth•yl•mel•a•mine [ˌhɛksəˌmɛθəlˈmɛləˌmin] *n.* a drug used to treat certain forms of cancer; altretamine.

hex•a•mine [ˈhɛksəˌmin] *n.* an antibacterial drug used as a cream to treat sweaty feet; methenamine.

hex•ane [ˈhɛksein] *n.* a colourless liquid used in low-temperature thermometers.

hex•an•gu•lar [hɛkˈsæŋgjələr] *adj.* having six angles.

hex•a•pod [ˈhɛksəˌpɒd] *n.* an INSECT (def. 1); a member of the class Insecta. ⟨< Gk. *hexapous, -podos* < *hex* six + *pous, podos* foot⟩ **—hex'ap•o•dous,** *adj.*

hex•a•stich [ˈhɛksəˌstɪk] *n.* a group of six lines forming a strophe, stanza, or a poem. ⟨< *hexa-* + Gk. *stichos* line of verse⟩

hex•et•i•dine [hɛkˈsɛtɪˌdin] *n.* a drug used as a mouthwash to treat certain throat conditions.

hex•o•san [ˈhɛksəˌsæn] *n.* a substance, such as starch, that forms a simple sugar by hydrolysis.

hex•ose [ˈhɛksous] *n.* a sugar having six carbon atoms in each molecule.

hex•yl [ˈhɛksɪl] *n.* a hydrocarbon radical with a valence of one.

hex•yl•re•sor•ci•nol [ˌhɛksɪlrəˈzɔrsəˌnɒl] *n.* a kind of phenol used in medicine. *Formula*: $C_{12}H_{18}O_2$

hey [hei] *interj.* a sound made to attract attention, to express surprise or other feeling, or to ask a question.
☛ *Hom.* HE[2], HAY, HEIGH (hei).

hey•day [ˈheiˌdei] *n.* the period of greatest strength, vigour, spirits, prosperity, etc. ⟨origin uncertain⟩

hf. half.

Hf hafnium.

HF, H.F., or **h.f.** high frequency.

hg hectogram.

Hg mercury (for L *hydrargyrum).*

HG High German.

H.G. His Grace; Her Grace.

H.H. **1** His Highness; Her Highness. **2** His Holiness.

hhd. hogshead(s).

hi [haɪ] *interj.* a call of greeting; hello.
☛ *Hom.* HEIGH, HIE, HIGH.

hi•a•tus [haɪ'eitəs] *n., pl.* **-tus•es** or **-tus. 1** an empty space; gap; a space that needs to be filled. **2** a slight pause between two vowels that come together in successive syllables or words. There is a hiatus between the *e*'s in *pre-eminent.* ⟨< L *hiatus* gap < *hiare* gape⟩

hi•ba•chi [hɪ'bɑtʃi] *n.* a cast-iron or similar container in which charcoal is burned for cooking, heating, etc. ⟨< Japanese *hibachi* < *hi* fire + *bachi* bowl⟩

hi•ber•nac•u•lum [ˌhaɪbər'nækjələm] *n., pl.* **-la** [-lə]. a structure in which dormant animals hibernate.

hi•ber•nal [haɪ'bɜrnəl] *adj.* of or having to do with winter; wintry. ⟨< L *hibernus* wintry⟩

hi•ber•nate ['haɪbərˌneit] *v.* **-nat•ed, -nat•ing. 1** spend the winter in sleep or in an inactive condition, as bears, groundhogs, and some other wild animals do. Compare ESTIVATE. **2** be or become inactive: *I think I'll just hibernate for the first week of my holidays.* ⟨< L *hibernare* < *hibernus* wintry⟩ **—ˌhi•ber'na•tion,** *n.*

Hi•ber•ni•a [haɪ'bɜrniə] *n.* **1** *Poetic.* Ireland. **2** an oil field off the coast of Newfoundland. ⟨< L⟩

Hi•ber•ni•an [haɪ'bɜrniən] *adj., n. —adj.* Irish.
—n. a native of Ireland.

hi•bis•cus [hə'bɪskəs] *or* [haɪ'bɪskəs] *n.* any of a genus (*Hibiscus*) of herbs, shrubs, and small trees of the mallow family found in temperate and tropical regions around the world, often cultivated for their large, usually bell-shaped white, pink, red, blue, or yellow flowers. ⟨< L⟩

hic•cough ['hɪkʌp] *n. or v.* hiccup.

hic•cup ['hɪkʌp] *or* ['hɪkəp] *n., v.* **hic•cupped, hic•cup•ping.** *—n.* **1** a sudden, involuntary contraction of the diaphragm that causes the glottis to close just when one is inhaling, producing a characteristic short clicking sound. **2 the hiccups,** *pl.* the state of having one hiccup after another: *I've got the hiccups.*
—v. **1** make a hiccup or hiccups: *He hiccupped.* **2** say with a hiccup or hiccups: *She hiccupped her apologies.* ⟨probably imitative⟩

hic ja•cet ['hɪk 'dʒeisɪt] **1** *Latin.* here lies (inscription on a tombstone). **2** epitaph.

hick [hɪk] *n., adj. Slang. —n.* **1** a farmer or farm worker. **2** an unsophisticated person.
—adj. of or like hicks. ⟨< *Hick*, a form of *Richard*, a man's name⟩

hick•ey ['hɪki] *n. Informal.* **1** a pimple or other blemish. **2** a gadget; dingus. **3** a device for bending a pipe. **4** a lovebite.

hick•o•ry ['hɪkəri] *n., pl.* **-ries.** *—n.* **1** any of a genus (*Carya*) of North American and Asian trees of the walnut family bearing egg-shaped nuts which in some species, such as the pecan, are edible. **2** the tough, hard wood of any of these trees. **3** the nut of any of these trees, also called **hickory nut. 4** a rod or switch made of this wood. **5** (*adjl.*) made of this wood. ⟨< Algonquian⟩

hid [hɪd] *v.* pt. and a pp. of HIDE.

hi•dal•go [hɪ'dælgou] *n., pl.* **-gos.** a Spanish nobleman of the second class, not as high in rank as a grandee. ⟨< Sp. < OSp. *hijo de algo* son of someone (important)⟩

Hi•dat•sa [hɪ'dɑtsə] *n.* **1** a member of a Native American people now living in North Dakota. **2** the Siouan language of these people.

hid•den ['hɪdən] *adj., v. —adj.* **1** concealed or secret: *a hidden staircase.* **2** mysterious or obscure: *a statement full of hidden meanings.*
—v. a pp. of HIDE[1].

hid•den•ite ['hɪdəˌnəit] *n.* a mineral varying from yellow to green in colour, a type of spodumene and a semi-precious stone. ⟨after W.E. *Hidden*, 19c. U.S. mineralogist⟩

hide[1] [haɪd] *v.* **hid, hid•den** or **hid, hid•ing,** *n. —v.* **1** put out of sight; conceal: *She hid the presents in the attic. He hid his face in the pillow.* **2** shut off from sight; screen or obscure: *Clouds hid the moon.* **3** keep secret: *She hid her anxiety.* **4** conceal oneself: *The shy little boy hid behind his mother's skirt.*
hide out or **up,** remain concealed: *The bandits hid out for several weeks in a mountain shack.*
—n. a shelter for hiding from birds or animals; blind. ⟨OE *hȳdan*⟩ **—'hid•er,** *n.*
☛ *Syn.* **1. Hide,** CONCEAL = put or keep out of sight. **Hide** is the general word: *I hid the present in my closet.* **Conceal** is more formal and usually suggests hiding with intent to deceive, or keeping under cover: *She concealed the note in her dress.*

hide[2] [haɪd] *n., v.* **hid•ed, hid•ing.** *—n.* **1** the skin of an animal, either raw or tanned. **2** a person's skin.
neither hide nor hair, nothing at all.
—v. Informal. beat; thrash. ⟨OE *hȳd*⟩
☛ *Syn. n.* **1.** See note at SKIN.

hide[3] [haɪd] *n.* formerly, an old English measure of land area varying from 24 to 49 hectares. ⟨OE *hīgid*⟩

hide–and–seek ['haɪd ən 'sik] *n.* a children's game in which one player has to find all the others, who are hidden in different places. The player who has to find the others is called 'it'. Also, **hide-and-go-seek.**

hide•a•way ['haɪdəˌwei] *n.* **1** a place of concealment or hiding. **2** a quiet, restful place, especially one in an isolated area, for a person or small group of people to be alone.

hide•bound ['haɪdˌbaʊnd] *adj.* **1** of cattle, etc., with the skin sticking close to the bones. **2** narrow-minded and stubborn.

hid•e•ous ['hɪdiəs] *adj.* **1** very ugly; frightful; horrible: *a hideous monster.* **2** terrible; revolting; abominable: *a hideous crime.* ⟨ME < OF *hide* fear, horror⟩ **—'hid•e•ous•ly,** *adv.* **—'hid•e•ous•ness,** *n.*

hide–out or **hide•out** ['haɪd ˌʌut] *n.* a place for hiding or being alone.

hid•ey–hole or **hid•y–hole** ['haɪdi ˌhoul] *n. Informal.* hideaway.

hid•ing[1] ['haɪdɪŋ] *n., v. —n.* **1** the condition of being hidden; concealment: *The bandits are still in hiding in the mountains. They went into hiding right after the robbery.* **2** the act of one who hides. **3** a place in which to hide.
—v. ppr. of HIDE[1]. ⟨< *hide[1]*⟩

hid•ing[2] ['haɪdɪŋ] *n., v. —n. Informal.* beating.
—v. ppr. of HIDE[2]. ⟨< *hide[2]*⟩

hid•ing place *n.* a place to hide: *We found a good hiding place in the hedge.*

hi•dro•sis [haɪ'drousɪs] *n.* sweating. ⟨< NL < Gk. < *hidroun* to sweat⟩ **—hi'drot•ic** [-'drɒtɪk], *adj.*

hie [haɪ] *v.* **hied, hie•ing** or **hy•ing.** *Archaic or poetic.* hasten; go quickly (*usually reflexive*): *He hied him to the rescue.* ⟨OE *hīgian*⟩
☛ *Hom.* HEIGH, HI, HIGH.

hi•e•mal ['haɪəməl] *adj.* having to do with winter. ⟨< L *hiemalis* of winter < *hiems* winter⟩

hier– *combining form.* the form of **hiero-** occurring before a vowel: *hierarchy*.

hi•er•arch ['haɪəˌrɑrk] *or* ['haɪrɑrk] *n.* **1** a chief priest. **2** any person in a high position.

hi•er•ar•chi•cal [ˌhaɪə'rɑrkəkəl] *or* [haɪ'rɑrkəkəl] *adj.* of, having to do with, or belonging to a hierarchy. Also, **hierarchic. —ˌhi•er'ar•chi•cal•ly,** *adv.*

hi•er•ar•chy ['haɪəˌrɑrki] *or* ['haɪˌrɑrki] *n., pl.* **-chies. 1** the order of higher and lower ranks in an organization or system. **2** church government by a body of clergy according to rank. **3** a body of clergy organized in orders or ranks, especially members of the highest orders. ⟨< Med.L < Gk. *hierarchia* < *hieros* sacred + *archos* ruler⟩

hi•er•at•ic [ˌhaɪə'rætɪk] *or* [haɪ'rætɪk] *adj.* **1** having to do with the priestly caste; used by the priestly class; priestly. **2** designating or having to do with a form of Egyptian writing used by the early priests in their records. Hieratic writing is a simplified form of hieroglyphics. **3** of or having to do with certain styles in art, such as the Egyptian or Greek, in which earlier types or methods, fixed by religious tradition, are conventionally followed. Also, **hieratical.** ⟨< *hieraticus* < Gk. *hieratikos*, ult. < *hieros* sacred⟩ **—ˌhi•er'at•i•cal•ly,** *adv.*

hiero– *combining form*. sacred: *hierology*. ⟨< Gk. *hiero(s)* holy, sacred⟩

hi•er•o•glyph ['haɪrəˌglɪf] *n.* hieroglyphic.

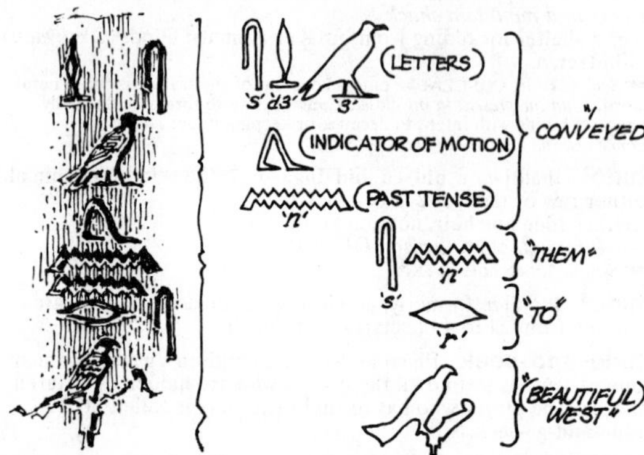

A section of a hieroglyphic inscription in the tomb of an official of the Egyptian Fifth Dynasty, c. 2350 B.C. The inscription describes the official's piety and devotion toward his parents, and his filial act in providing them with a proper burial. The part shown means 'I conveyed them [his dead parents] to the [beautiful] West'

hi•er•o•glyph•ic [,haırə'glıfık] *n., adj.* *—n.* **1** a character, symbol, or picture of an object standing for a word, idea, or sound. The ancient Egyptians used hieroglyphics instead of an alphabet like ours. **2** a secret symbol. **3** a letter or word that is hard to read. **4 hieroglyphics,** *pl.* **a** any system of writing that uses hieroglyphics. **b** *Informal.* writing that is hard to read.
—adj. **1** of or written in hieroglyphics. **2** symbolic. **3** hard to read. Also, **hieroglyphical.** ⟨< LL < Gk. *hieroglyphikos* < *hieros* sacred + *glyphē* carving⟩ **—,hi•er•o'glyph•i•cal•ly,** *adv.*

hi•er•ol•o•gy [,haıə'rɒlədʒi] *or* [haı'rɒlədʒi] *n.* the holy writings of a people.

hi•er•o•phant ['haıərə,fænt], ['haırə,fænt], *or* [haı'ɛrə,fænt] *n.* **1** in ancient Greece, a demonstrator of sacred mysteries or religious knowledge. **2** any interpreter of sacred knowledge. ⟨< L < Gk. *hierophantes* < *hieros* sacred + *phainein* show⟩

hi–fi ['haı 'faı] *adj., n. Informal.* *—adj.* high-fidelity.
—n. high-fidelity reproduction of music, etc. or the equipment for such reproduction.

hig•gle ['hıgəl] *v.* **-gled, -gling.** haggle. ⟨? akin to HAGGLE.⟩

hig•gle•dy–pig•gle•dy ['hıgəldi 'pıgəldi] *adv., adj., n.* *—adv.* in jumbled confusion.
—adj. jumbled; confused.
—n. a jumble; confusion.

high [haı] *adj., adv., n.* *—adj.* **1** of more than usual height; tall: *a high building.* **2** being a specified distance or extent from top to bottom (*used following a noun*): *The mountain is 6100 m high.* **3** far above the ground or some base: *an airplane high in the air.* **4** extending to or down from a height: *a high leap, a high dive.* **5** senior to others in rank or position: *a high official.* **6** superior; noble; honourable: *a person of high character.* **7** great; strong; intense: *high temperature.* **8** most important; chief; main: *the high altar.* **9** extreme of its kind: *high crimes.* **10** costly: *Strawberries are high in winter.* **11** above the normal pitch; shrill; sharp: *a high voice.* **12** advanced to its peak: *high summer.* **13** smelling bad as a result of decay; tainted: *Some people prefer to eat game after it has become high.* **14** haughty: *a high manner.* **15** *Slang.* excited by or as if by alcohol or drugs. **16** of a system of gears, having a driving gear larger than the driven gear, so as to cause the driven gear to revolve more rapidly than the other: *the high gear of an automobile.* **17** having extreme or rigid political or religious opinions, usually ultraconservative: *a high ritualist, a high Tory.* **18** *Biology.* highly developed; more advanced in structure, intelligence, etc.: *the higher algae, the higher apes.*
—adv. at or to a high point, place, rank, amount, degree, price, pitch, etc.: *The eagle flies high.*
fly high, have big ideas, plans, hopes, ambitions, etc.
high and dry, a out of the water; out of reach of the current or tide: *The fish was high and dry on the beach.* **b** all alone; without help: *She has left me high and dry with all this work to do.*
high and low, everywhere: *We looked high and low but couldn't find the letter.*
run high, a be strong or rough: *The tide runs high.* **b** become heated; reach a high pitch: *Tempers ran high at election time.*
—n. **1** something that is high. **2** in automobiles and similar machines, an arrangement of gears to give the greatest speed. **3** a high point, level, position, etc.: *Food prices reached a new high last month.* **4** *Meteorology.* an area of relatively high barometric pressure; anticyclone: *The meteorologist reports that a high is approaching.* **5** *Slang.* a state of euphoria produced by or as if by drugs.
from on high, a from a high place or position. **b** from heaven.
on high, a in or to a high place or position; up in the air. **b** in or to heaven. ⟨OE *hēah*⟩
☛ *Hom.* HEIGH, HI, HIE.
☛ *Syn. adj.* **1. High,** TALL, LOFTY = of more than usual height. **High,** the general word, describes things, not people, that rise to more than usual height: *High hills surround the valley.* **Tall** = higher than the average of its kind, and is used to describe people or something that is or grows both high and narrow or slender: *He is a tall man. The corn grows tall here.* **Lofty,** more literary, means 'very high, rising to an impressive height': *We saw the lofty Mount Robson, snow-capped and rising almost 4000 m.*

High Arctic *Cdn.* the arctic islands and the northeastern part of the arctic mainland of Canada.

high•ball ['haı,bɒl] *n., v.* *—n.* **1** whisky, brandy, etc. mixed with soda water or ginger ale and served with ice in a tall glass. **2** a railway signal to proceed.
—v. **1** *Slang.* **a** move or drive at high speed. **b** run on an accelerated schedule. **2** signal to (the engineer of a train) to proceed.

high blood pressure elevation of the arterial blood pressure.

high•born ['haı,bɔrn] *adj.* of noble birth.

high•boy ['haı,bɔı] *n.* a tall chest of drawers on legs.

high•bred ['haı,brɛd] *adj.* **1** of superior breeding or stock. **2** well-mannered; very refined.

high•brow ['haı,braʊ] *n., adj. Informal.* *—n.* a person who has strong intellectual and cultural interests, especially one thought to have a feeling of superiority because of this.
—adj. of, appealing to, or suitable for highbrows: *highbrow music, a highbrow discussion.*

high•chair ['haı,tʃɛr] *n.* a baby's tall chair for feeding, with a detachable feeding tray.

High Church a branch of the Anglican Communion laying great emphasis on church authority, ceremonial observances, etc. Compare LOW CHURCH.

high–class ['haı 'klæs] *adj.* of or for a high social class; superior in quality, etc.

high–col•oured or **high–col•ored** ['haı 'kʌlərd] *adj.* **1** having a deep or vivid colour. **2** florid; red.

high comedy comedy dealing with polite society and depending more on witty dialogue and well-drawn characters than on comic situations.

High Commission the embassy of one Commonwealth country in another.

High Commissioner the chief representative of one Commonwealth country in another. A High Commissioner has the status of an ambassador.

high day a holy day.

high–energy physics ['haı 'ɛnərdʒi] the branch of physics that studies matter and energy in their most elementary forms, especially the study of particles that appear only at high speeds.

higher education education beyond the level of secondary school, especially university education.

higher mathematics mathematics that is more advanced and abstract than what is normally taught in secondary school.

high•er–up ['haıər 'ʌp] *n. Informal.* a person occupying a superior position.

high explosive a fast and powerful explosive.

high•fa•lu•tin or **high•fa•lu•ting** ['haıfə'lutən] *or* ['haıfə'lutıŋ] *adj. Informal.* pompous; pretentious.

high–fi•del•i•ty ['haı fə'dɛləti] *adj.* **1** *Electronics.* indicating reproduction of the full audio range of a transmitted signal with a minimum of distortion. **2** of or having to do with high-fidelity reproduction, equipment, recordings, etc.

high•fli•er ['haı'flaıər] *n.* **1** a person who or thing that flies high. **2** a person who is extravagant or has pretentious ideas, ambitions, etc. Also, **highflyer.**

high–flown ['haı 'floun] *adj.* **1** aspiring; extravagant. **2** attempting to be elegant or eloquent: *high-flown compliments.*

high•fly•er ['haı'flaıər] See HIGHFLIER.

high frequency the range of radio frequencies between 3 MHz and 30 MHz. High frequency is the range directly above

medium frequency. *Abbrev.:* HF, H.F., or h.f.
—'high-'fre•quen•cy, *adj.*

High German the literary and official language of Germany and Austria and one of the official languages of Switzerland. It developed from the dialects of the highlands in central and southern Germany. Compare LOW GERMAN.

high–grade *adj.* ['haɪ 'greid]; *n., v.* ['haɪ ˌgreid] *adj., n., v.* **-grad•ed, -grad•ing.**
—adj. **1** of fine quality; superior: *high-grade bonds, a high-grade performance.* **2** *Mining.* designating or containing gold-bearing ore of a high assay value: *high-grade gold ore, high-grade dirt.* **3** of or having to do with high-grading.
—n. **1** gold nuggets or rich ore. **2** gold nuggets or rich ore stolen in small quantities from a mine.
—v. Cdn. **1** steal small quantities of gold or ore from a mine. **2** *Logging.* take only the best timber from a stand.
—'high-ˌgrad•er, *n.*

high–grad•ing ['haɪ ˌgreidɪŋ] *n., v. —n. Cdn.* the theft of gold or ore from mines in small quantities.
—v. ppr. of HIGH-GRADE.

high–hand•ed ['haɪ 'hændɪd] *adj.* arbitrary or overbearing; disregarding the feelings of others: *a high-handed way of running things.* **—'high-'hand•ed•ly,** *adv.* **—'high-'hand•ed•ness,** *n.*

high hat a tall black silk hat; top hat.

high–hat ['haɪ 'hæt] *v.* **-hat•ted, -hat•ting;** *adj. Slang. —v.* treat as inferior; snub.
—adj. putting on a superior, contemptuous air; snobbish.

high•jack ['haɪˌdʒæk] See HIJACK. **—'highˌjack•er,** *n.*

high jinks [dʒɪŋks] boisterous merrymaking; lively fun and sport.

high jump **1** an athletic contest or event in which the contestants try to jump as high as possible over a bar. **2** a jump of this kind.

high–keyed ['hai 'kid] *adj.* **1** shrill in tone. **2** nervous. **3** bright in colour.

high•land ['haɪlənd] *n.* **1** a country or region that is higher and hillier than the neighbouring country. **2** *(adjl.)* of, having to do with, or in such country: *a highland meadow.* **3 the Highlands,** a hilly region in northern and western Scotland. **4** *(adjl.)* **Highland,** of, having to do with, or in the Highlands.

Highland cattle a breed of small cattle from the Scottish Highlands, having shaggy fur and long, curved, widely set horns.

High•land•er ['haɪləndər] *n.* **1** a native or inhabitant of the Highlands of Scotland. **2** a soldier of a regiment from the Highlands of Scotland. **3** a soldier in an allied British or Canadian regiment.

Highland fling a lively dance originating in the Highlands of Scotland.

high–lev•el language ['haɪ 'lɛvəl] *Computer technology.* a computer language that uses a number of everyday words such as *enter, add.*

high life a fashionable lifestyle.

high•light ['haɪˌləit] *n., v.* **-light•ed, -light•ing.** *—n.* **1** the representation or effect of light falling on a particular part of something: *Rembrandt is famous for his use of dramatic highlights in his paintings. The photographer caught the highlight in the child's hair.* **2** the most interesting or most striking part, event, scene, etc.: *The highlight of our trip was the drive along the Cabot Trail.*
—v. **1** emphasize (a part of a painting, photograph, etc.) with lighting, light or bright colour, etc. **2** make prominent: *The new product was highlighted in all the company's brochures.* **3** be the highlight of: *A spectacular acrobatic act highlighted the grandstand show.*

high•line ['haɪˌlaɪn] *n.* highliner.

high•lin•er ['haɪˌlaɪnər] *n.* in a Maritime fishing fleet: **1** the boat making the largest catch within a specified time. **2** the captain of such a boat.

high•ly ['haɪli] *adv.* **1** in a high degree; very; very much. **2** favourably; with much approval; with great praise or honour. **3** at a high price.

High Mass a complete ritual of the Mass sung by the priest, with instrumental and choral accompaniment. Compare LOW MASS.

high–mind•ed ['haɪ 'maɪndɪd] *adj.* **1** having or showing high principles and feelings: *a high-minded person, a high-minded act of charity.* **2** *Archaic.* proud. **—'high'mind•ed•ly,** *adv.*
—'high'mind•ed•ness, *n.*

high muck•a•muck ['mʌkəˌmʌk] *Cdn. Slang.* a leading person in a group; big-shot. ⟨< Chinook jargon *hyiu muckamuck* a good big meal⟩

high•ness ['haɪnɪs] *n.* **1** the quality of being high; height. **2 Highness,** a title of honour given to members of royal families. The Prince of Wales is addressed as "Your Highness" and spoken of as "His Royal Highness."

high noon fully noon; exactly midday.

high north *Cdn.* the far north, especially the Arctic.

high–oc•tane ['haɪ 'ɒktein] *adj.* of gasoline, having a high percentage of octane or a high octane number.

high–pitched ['haɪ 'pɪtʃt] *adj.* **1** of high tone or sound; shrill: *a high-pitched whistle.* **2** of a roof, having a steep slope. **3** marked by or showing intense feeling; agitated: *the high-pitched excitement of the chase.*

high–pow•ered ['haɪ 'paʊərd] *adj.* having much power or energy: *a high-powered car or rifle, a high-powered sales talk.*

high–pres•sure ['haɪ 'prɛʃər] *adj., v.* **-sured, -sur•ing.**
—adj. **1** having, involving, or requiring the use of a relatively high pressure: *a high-pressure cylinder, a high-pressure laminate.* **2** having or showing a high barometric pressure: *There is a high-pressure area just to the south.* **3** *Informal.* using or involving a strong, insistent approach or argument, especially in selling: *a high-pressure sales pitch.* **4** involving a lot of emotional tension or strain: *She has a high-pressure job.*
—v. persuade or influence by using a strong, insistent approach or argument: *He was high-pressured into buying the more expensive rug.*

high–priced ['haɪ 'prəist] *adj.* expensive.

high priest **1** a chief priest. **2** the head of the ancient Jewish priesthood.

high–proof ['haɪ 'pruf] *adj.* high in alcohol content.

high relief a relief sculpture in which the modelled forms project well out from the background and parts may be undercut. See RELIEF for picture.

high•rise ['haɪˌraɪz] *adj., n. —adj.* having many storeys: *highrise apartment buildings.*
—n. a building having many storeys: *She lives in a highrise downtown.*

high•road ['haɪˌroud] *n.* **1** a main road; highway. **2** a direct and easy way: *There is no highroad to success.*

high school a school attended after elementary school. Some provinces have junior high schools intermediate between elementary and high school. **—'high-ˌschool,** *adjl.*
☛ *Usage.* **High school.** Capitalize only when referring to a particular school: *She graduated from high school at seventeen. I graduated from Collins Bay High School in 1992.*

high seas the open ocean. The high seas are outside the jurisdiction of any country.

high sign *Informal.* a gesture used as a signal.

high–sound•ing ['haɪ 'saʊndɪŋ] *adj.* having an imposing or pretentious sound: *high-sounding words.*

high–spir•it•ed ['haɪ 'spirətɪd] *adj.* **1** having or showing a bold, proud, or energetic spirit: *a high-spirited horse. The team put up a high-spirited defence, even though they knew they were losing.* **2** happy. **—'high-'spir•it•ed•ly,** *adv.*
—'high-'spir•it•ed•ness, *n.*

high spirits happiness; cheerfulness; gaiety.

high spot **1** the main part; the climax. **2** an attraction or place of interest for sightseers.

high•stick ['haɪˌstɪk] *v.* **high•sticked, high•sticking.** *Hockey and lacrosse.* illegally strike or hinder (an opposing player) with one's stick raised above shoulder level.

high•stick•ing ['haɪˌstɪkɪŋ] *n., v. —n. Hockey and lacrosse.* the act or practice of illegally striking or hindering an opposing player with one's stick carried above shoulder level: *She received a penalty for highsticking.*
—v. ppr. of HIGHSTICK.

high–strung ['haɪ 'strʌŋ] *adj.* very sensitive; easily excited; nervous.

hight [həit] *v. pt. and pp. Archaic.* named; called: *The knight was hight Gawain.* ⟨OE *heht,* pt. of *hātan* be called⟩
☛ *Hom.* HEIGHT.

high–tail ['haɪ ˌteil] *v. Slang.* run away at full speed; hurry.
high-tail it, hurry or run fast.

high tea *Brit.* a substantial meal served in late afternoon.

high tech [tɛk] *Informal.* **1** a style of interior design that exploits the materials and structural features of industrial design. **2** HIGH TECHNOLOGY. **—'high-'tech,** *adj.*

high technology advanced modern technology involving electronics, especially micro-electronics.

high–ten•sion ['haɪ 'tɛnʃən] *adj.* having or accommodating a high voltage: *high-tension wiring.*

high–test ['haɪ ˌtɛst] *adj.* **1** passing very difficult requirements and tests. **2** of gasoline, vaporizing at a low temperature.

high tide 1 the highest level of the tide. **2** the time when the tide is highest. **3** the highest point; a culminating point.

high time 1 the time just before it is too late: *It is high time that we got ready to go.* **2** *Informal.* a lively, jolly time at a party, etc.

high–toned ['haɪ 'tound] *adj.* **1** having a high character or high principles; dignified. **2** *Informal.* fashionable; stylish. **3** high in tone or pitch.

high treason treason against one's ruler, state, or government.

high water ['haɪ 'wɒtər] **1** the highest level of water. **2** HIGH TIDE.

high–water mark ['haɪ 'wɒtər] **1** the highest level of water in a river or lake. **2** any highest point.

high•way ['haɪˌwei] *n.* **1** a main road or route connecting cities or towns. **2** *Cdn.* a high-speed, controlled-access expressway. **3** a direct line or way to some end.

high•way•man ['haɪweimən] *n., pl.* **-men.** formerly, a man, usually on horseback, who robbed travellers on a public road.

H.I.H. 1 His Imperial Highness. **2** Her Imperial Highness.

hi•jack ['haɪˌdʒæk] *v.* **1** stop (a vehicle) in transit by force or threat in order to steal it or its cargo: *The truck was hijacked about 70 km out of the city.* **2** steal (goods, etc.) by force or threat while they are being transported: *Several shipments have been hijacked.* **3** seize control of (an aircraft) in flight by force or threat in order to obtain money or some other concession.
—'hiˌjack•er, *n.* ⟨origin uncertain⟩

hi•jack•ing ['haɪˌdʒækɪŋ] *n.* the forcible seizure of a vehicle or airplane to gain some end.

hi–jinks ['haɪ ˌdʒɪŋks] *n.* HIGH JINKS.

hike [həik] *v.* **hiked, hik•ing;** *n. Informal. —v.* **1** take a long walk; tramp; march. **2** move, draw, or raise with a jerk: *He hiked himself up onto the platform.* **3** raise; increase: *The company is going to hike wages.*
—n. **1** a long walk; a march or tramp. **2** an increase: *a hike in prices.* ⟨? related to HITCH⟩ **—'hik•er,** *n.*

hi•lar•i•ous [hə'lɛriəs] *adj.* **1** very merry; noisily cheerful: *It was a hilarious party.* **2** very funny: *The joke was hilarious.* ⟨< L *hilaris.* See HILARITY.⟩ **—hi'lar•i•ous•ly,** *adv.*
—hi'lar•i•ous•ness, *n.*

hi•lar•i•ty [hə'lærəti] *or* [hə'lɛrəti] *n.* great mirth; noisy gaiety. ⟨< L *hilaritas* < *hilaris, hilarus* gay < Gk. *hilaros*⟩

hill [hɪl] *n., v. —n.* **1** a raised part on the earth's surface, smaller than a mountain. **2** a heap, pile, or mound of earth, sand, etc.: *Moles had made hills all over the lawn. The potatoes were planted in hills.* **3** a plant or plants growing in a mound of earth: *a hill of corn.* **4 the Hill,** *Cdn. Informal.* **a** Parliament Hill. **b** Parliament.
over the hill, *Informal.* past one's prime.
—v. **1** put a little heap of soil over and around. **2** form into a little heap. ⟨OE *hyll*⟩ **—'hill•er,** *n.*

hill•bil•ly ['hɪlˌbɪli] *n., pl.* **-lies;** *adj. Informal. —n.* a person who lives in the backwoods or a mountain region, especially in the S United States.
—adj. of, having to do with, or characteristic of a hillbilly: *hillbilly music.*

hill•ock ['hɪlək] *n.* a little hill. **—'hil•lock•y,** *adj.*

hill•side [hɪlˌsaɪd] *n.* the side of a hill.

hill•top ['hɪlˌtɒp] *n.* the top of a hill.

hill•y ['hɪli] *adj.* **hill•i•er, hill•i•est. 1** having many hills. **2** like a hill; steep. **—'hill•i•ness,** *n.*

hilt [hɪlt] *n., v. —n.* the handle of a sword, dagger, etc. See SWORD for picture.
to the hilt, thoroughly; completely.
—v. provide with a hilt. ⟨OE⟩

hi•lum ['haɪləm] *n., pl.* **-la** [-lə]. **1** *Botany.* the mark or scar on a seed at the point of attachment to the seed vessel. The eye of a bean is a hilum. **2** *Anatomy.* a small opening for ducts or nerves. **3** the centre of a grain of starch. ⟨< L *hilum* trifle⟩

him [hɪm]; *unstressed,* [ɪm] *or* [əm] *pron.* the objective case of **he:** *Take him home.* ⟨OE *him,* dative of *hē* he⟩
☛ *Hom.* HYMN.

H.I.M. His (or Her) Imperial Majesty.

Him•a•la•yan [ˌhɪmə'leiən] *or* [hə'mɑliən] *adj.* **1** of or having to do with the Himalayas, a mountain range along the border between India and Tibet. **2** a breed of domestic cat, a cross between Persian and Siamese, having blue eyes and a pale coat shading to darker on the points.

him•self [hɪm'sɛlf]; *unstressed,* [ɪm'sɛlf] *pron.* **1** a reflexive pronoun, the form of **he** used as an object when it refers to the same person or thing as the subject: *He cut himself. He asked himself what he really wanted. He kept the toy for himself.* **2** a form of **he** or **him** added for emphasis: *Did you see Roy himself?* **3** his usual self: *He feels himself again.*

Hi•na•ya•na [ˌhinə'jɑnə] *n.* a branch of Buddhism that follows the Pali scriptures and stresses meditation.

hind[1] [haɪnd] *adj.* **hind•er, hind•most** or **hind•er•most.** back; rear: *The mule kicked up its hind legs.* ⟨See HINDER[2]⟩

hind[2] [haɪnd] *n., pl.* **hind** or **hinds.** a female deer, especially the female of the European red deer after its third year. ⟨OE⟩

Hind. 1 Hindustan. **2** Hindustani. **3** Hindu. **4** Hindi.

hind•brain ['haɪndˌbrein] *n.* the back of the brain, especially the part including the cerebellum and the medulla oblongata.

hin•der[1] ['hɪndər] *v.* keep or hold back; get in the way of or make difficult: *recurring problems that hinder completion of a project. We were hindered by deep snow.* ⟨OE *hindrian*⟩
—'hin•der•er, *n.*
☛ *Syn.* See note at PREVENT.

hind•er[2] ['haɪndər] *adj.* hind; back; rear. ⟨Cf. OE *hinder* and *hindan* in back, behind⟩

hind•er•most ['haɪndərˌmoust] *adj.* hindmost.

hind•gut ['haɪndˌgʌt] *n. Zoology.* the posterior portion of the embryonic alimentary canal.

Hin•di ['hɪndi] *n.* the most widely spoken language of India, an Indo-European language that exists in several very different dialects as well as a standard literary form that is one of the official languages of India. ⟨< Hind. *Hindī* < *Hind* India < Persian *Hind.* See HINDU.⟩

hind•most ['haɪndˌmoust] *adj.* farthest back; nearest the rear; last.

Hin•doo ['hɪndu] *n., pl.* **-doos;** *adj. Archaic.* See HINDU.

hind•quar•ter ['haɪndˌkwɔrtər] *n.* **1** the hind leg and loin of a carcass of beef, lamb, etc. **2 hindquarters,** the hind part of any four-legged animal.

hin•drance ['hɪndrəns] *n.* **1** a person or thing that hinders; obstacle. **2** the act of hindering.
☛ *Syn.* **1.** See note at OBSTACLE.

hind•sight ['haɪndˌsəit] *n.* **1** *Informal.* the ability to see, after the event is over, what should have been done. **2** the sight nearest the breech in a firearm.

Hin•du ['hɪndu] *n., pl.* **-dus;** *adj. —n.* **1** a person who believes in Hinduism. **2** formerly, a native or inhabitant of India.
—adj. **1** of or having to do with Hinduism or Hindus. **2** formerly, of or having to do with India. ⟨< Persian *Hindū* < *Hind* India < OPersian *Hindu*⟩

Hin•du•ism ['hɪnduˌɪzəm] *n.* a religion and way of life that is practised mainly in India, having an ancient tradition characterized by the doctrine of transmigration of souls, the worship of many gods who are all thought of as aspects of the one god, and, formerly, the support of a system of hereditary social classes generally called castes. The three great divinities of classical Hinduism are Vishnu, Shiva, and Shakti. A fourth divinity, Brahma, was widely worshipped for a time as the highest god.

Hin•du•sta•ni [ˌhɪndu'stɑni] *or* [ˌhɪndu'stæni] *n., adj. —n.* a dialect of N India that was used as a common language of trade throughout India for a century and a half until 1947, when India was divided into India, Pakistan, and Bangladesh. Literary Hindi and Urdu both developed from Hindustani.
—adj. of or having to do with Hindustan (India or N India), its people, or the language Hindustani. ⟨< Hind., Persian *Hindūstānī* Indian < *Hindūstān* India < *Hindū* Hindu + *stan* place, country⟩

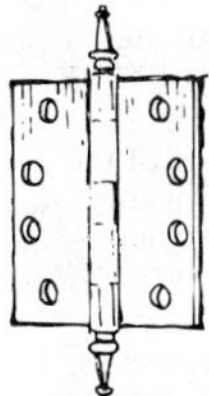
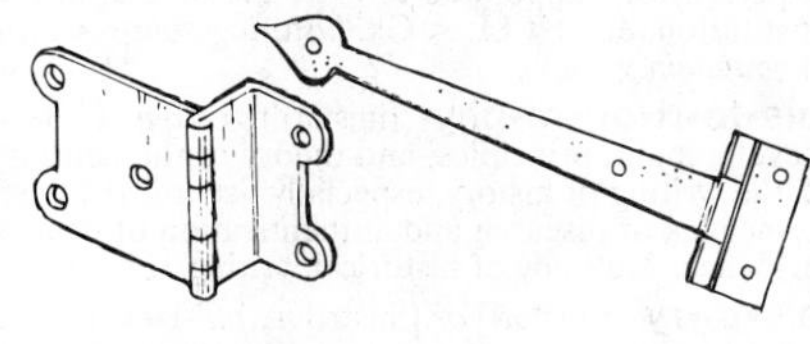

Three types of hinge

hinge [hɪndʒ] *n., v.* **hinged, hing•ing.** *—n.* **1** a movable joint or mechanism by which a door, gate, cover, lid, etc. moves back and forth or up and down on its post, base, etc. **2** a natural joint that has a similar function: *the hinge of a clam shell.* **3** that on which something turns or depends; central principle or determining factor. **4** STAMP HINGE.
—v. **1** furnish with or attach by a hinge or hinges. **2** depend (*used with* **on** *or* **upon**): *The success of the enterprise will hinge on the dedication of the people involved.* **3** hang or turn on a hinge. ⟨ME *heng.* Related to HANG.⟩ **—hinged,** *adj.*

hin•ny ['hɪni] *n., pl.* **-nies.** the sterile offspring of a male horse and a female donkey. Compare MULE¹. ⟨< L *hinnus* (influenced by *hinnire* neigh) < Gk. *innos*⟩

hint [hɪnt] *n., v. —n.* **1** a slight indication; clue: *A small black cloud gave a hint of the coming storm.* **2** a statement or action implying something that the person prefers not to say directly; an indirect suggestion: *When she stood up, he took it as a hint that the interview was over.* **3** a very small amount or suggestion: *The soup has just a hint of garlic.* **4** a piece of practical information: *helpful hints for the traveller.*
—v. give a hint (often used with **at**): *The unsettled weather hinted at a storm.* ⟨apparently < *hent*, v., seize, OE *hentan*⟩ **—'hint•er,** *n.* **—'hint•ing•ly,** *adv.*
☛ *Syn. v.* **1. Hint,** INSINUATE = suggest indirectly. **Hint** = say something in a roundabout way, not openly, directly, or frankly: *She hinted that it was time to go to bed by saying, "Do you often stay up this late?"* **Insinuate** = suggest or hint something unkind or nasty in a sly or underhand way: *Are you insinuating that I am a liar?*

hin•ter•land ['hɪntər,lænd] *n.* **1** the country or region behind a coast; the inland region. **2** a region remote from and outside the influence of major urban centres; backwater. ⟨< G⟩

hip¹ [hɪp] *n., v.* **hipped, hip•ping,** *—n.* **1** hipbone: *He broke his right hip when he fell.* **2** Usually, **hips,** *pl.* the part of the body between the waist and the thighs: *The skirt fits well over the hips.* **3** pelvis. **4** HIP JOINT. **5** a similar part in animals, where the hind leg joins the body. **6** *Architecture.* the ridge formed by two sloping sides of a roof or by a sloping side meeting a sloping end.
on the hip, at a disadvantage.
—v. in architecture, form with a hip or hips. ⟨OE *hype*⟩
—'hip•less, *adj.* **—'hip,like,** *adj.*

hip² [hɪp] *n.* a pod containing the ripe seed of a rosebush. ⟨OE *hēope*⟩

hip³ [hɪp] *adj. Slang.* showing interest in and knowledge about the latest trends in fashion, music, etc.; aware; sophisticated: *She's hip to the music.* ⟨var. of HEP⟩

hip⁴ [hɪp] *interj.* used as a signal for a cheer: *Hip, hip, hooray!*

hip•bone ['hɪp,boun] *n.* **1** either of the large, irregular bones that form the main part of the pelvis in mammals. The hipbone is composed of the ilium, ischium, and pubis, which are fused into one bone in adults. See SOCKET for picture. **2** the rear, upper portion of either of these bones; ilium. See PELVIS for picture.

hip joint the ball-and-socket joint formed by the top of the thighbone and the hipbone; the joint that connects the upper leg with the trunk.

hipped¹ [hɪpt] *adj.* **1** having a hip or hips. **2** having a hip or hips of a specified kind (*used in compounds*): *a narrow-hipped torso.* **3** of an animal, having a dislocated hip joint. ⟨< *hip¹*⟩

hipped² [hɪpt] *adj. Slang.* obsessed. ⟨var. of *hypt* < *hyp*, n., for *hypochondria*⟩

hip•pie ['hɪpi] *n., adj. Slang. —n.* **1** a person who rejects many of the customs and beliefs of conventional modern society and believes in simplicity, freedom of expression, and in love and fellowship; especially, any of the many young people of the 1960s who attempted to express such ideas through communal living, mysticism, the use of drugs, etc. **2** any radical person who defies convention by affecting an unkempt appearance, discourteous behaviour, etc.
—adj. having to do with a hippie: *a hippie costume.* ⟨< *hip³* + *-ie*⟩

☛ *Usage.* Definition 2 is often used loosely as a term of disapproval, without regard for the full range of meaning involved in definition 1.

hip•po ['hɪpou] *n. Informal.* hippopotamus.

hip•po•cam•pus [,hɪpou'kæmpəs] *n., pl.* **hip•po•cam•pi** [-paɪ] *or* [-pi]. **1** *Greek mythology.* a seahorse. **2** *Anatomy.* one of two ridges in each lateral ventricle of the brain. ⟨< Gk. *hippokampos* < *hippos* horse + *kampos* sea monster⟩

Hip•po•crat•ic [,hɪpə'krætɪk] *adj.* of or having to do with Hippocrates (460?-377? B.C.), the ancient Greek physician who is called the father of medicine.

Hippocratic oath an oath describing the duties and obligations of a physician, usually taken by those about to become physicians.

Hip•po•crene ['hɪpə,krin] *or* [,hɪpə'krini] *n.* a fountain on Mt. Helicon, sacred to the Muses and regarded as a source of poetic inspiration. ⟨< L < Gk. *Hippokrēnē* < *hippos* horse + *krēnē* fountain⟩

hip•po•drome ['hɪpə,droum] *n.* **1** in ancient Greece and Rome, an oval track for horse races and chariot races, surrounded by tiers of seats for spectators. **2** an arena or building for a circus, rodeo, etc. ⟨< L < Gk. *hippodromos* < *hippos* horse + *dromos* course⟩

hip•po•griff ['hɪpə,grɪf] *n.* a mythical monster, part griffin and part horse. ⟨< F *hippogriffe* < Gk. *hippos* horse + L *gryphus* griffin⟩

Hip•pol•y•tus [hɪ'pɒlətəs] *n. Greek mythology.* the son of Theseus. Falsely accused by his stepmother Phaedra, he was cursed by his father, and killed when his chariot overturned.

hip•po•pot•a•mus [,hɪpə'pɒtəməs] *n., pl.* **-mus•es** or **-mi** [-,maɪ] *or* [-,mi]. **1** a very large, plant-eating, hoofed mammal (*Hippopotamus amphibius*) found in and near lakes and rivers in tropical Africa, having thick, almost hairless skin, short legs, and a large head with an enormous mouth. Hippopotamuses may reach a length of 4.5 metres and a mass of over 2 tonnes. **2** a smaller animal (*Choeropsis liberiensis*) of the same family (Hippopotamidae) of W Africa that reaches a length of about 1.5 m. It is usually called the **pygmy hippopotamus.** ⟨< L < Gk. *hippopotamus* < *hippos* horse + *potamos* river⟩

hip roof a roof with sloping ends and sides. See ROOF for picture.

hip•shot ['hɪp,ʃɒt] *adj.* **1** lame. **2** having a dislocated hip.

hip wader a long rubber boot reaching to the hip, used when fishing, etc.

hir•cine ['hɜrsaɪn] *or* ['hɜrsɪn] *adj.* **1** *Archaic.* of or having to do with goats; resembling a goat, especially in having a strong, unpleasant odour. **2** lustful. ⟨< L *hircinus* < *hircus* he-goat⟩

hire [haɪr] *v.* **hired, hir•ing;** *n. —v.* **1** take on as an employee; engage: *The manager hired two more clerks last week.* **2** agree to pay for the temporary use of (a thing) or the work or services of (a person): *He hired a car and a woman to drive it.* **3** give the use of (a thing) or the work or services of (a person), or one's own services, in return for payment (*usually with* **out**): *She hired out as a carpenter.*
—n. **1** payment for the use of a thing or the work or services of a person. **2** the act of hiring.
for or **on hire,** available for use or work in exchange for payment: *They have boats for hire.* ⟨OE *hȳr* (*n.*), *hȳrian* (*v.*)⟩
☛ *Syn. v.* **1.** See note at EMPLOY.

hire•ling ['haɪrlɪŋ] *n.* **1** a person available for hire, especially one who will follow anyone's orders and is interested only in the pay. **2** (*adj.*) mercenary.

hir•sute ['hɜrsut] *or* [hər'sut] *adj.* hairy. **—'hir•sute•ness,** *n.* ⟨< L *hirsutus*⟩

hi•ru•din ['hirjədɪn] *or* ['hirədɪn] *n.* an anticoagulant.

his [hɪz]; *unstressed,* [ɪz] *adj., pron. —adj.* **1** the possessive form of **he;** of, belonging to, or made or done by him or himself: *He shook his head. They attended his graduation. His novels are very good.* **2 His,** a word used as part of any of certain formal titles when using the title to refer to the man holding it: *His Majesty the King.*
—pron. the possessive form of **he;** that which belongs to him: *The writing is his. Those tapes are his.*
of his, belonging to or associated with him: *She's just a friend of his.* ⟨OE *his,* genitive of *hē* he⟩

His•pa•ni•a [hɪ'speiniə] *or* [hɪ'spɒniə], [hɪ'speinjə] *or* [hɪ'spɒnjə] *n. Poetic.* Spain.

his•pid ['hɪspɪd] *adj.* covered with bristles. ⟨< L *hispidus*⟩

hiss [hɪs] *v., n.* —*v.* **1** make a sound like that of the *s* in *see: The snake hissed as we approached.* **2** make this sound as a sign of disapproval. **3** force or drive by hissing: *They hissed him off the stage.* **4** utter by hissing or as if by hissing: *"Sit down and be quiet!" he hissed.*
—*n.* **1** the sound of hissing: *There was a loud hiss as the water boiled over onto the hot stove.* **2** the sound or act of hissing to express disapproval: *The actor was upset by the hisses of the crowd.* ⟨imitative⟩ —**'hiss•er,** *n.*

hist [hɪst] *interj.* be still! listen!

hist– *combining form.* the form of HISTO- used before a vowel: *histamine.*

hist. 1 history; historian. **2** histology.

his•ta•meth•i•zine [ˌhɪstə'mɛθəˌzin] *n.* a drug used to treat motion sickness; meclizine hydrochloride.

his•tam•i•nase [hɪ'stæməˌneis] *n. Biochemistry.* an enzyme in the digestive system.

his•ta•mine ['hɪstəˌmin] *or* ['hɪstəmɪn] *n. Biochemistry.* an amine released by the body in allergic reactions. It lowers the blood pressure and is used in the diagnosis and treatment of various allergies. *Formula:* $C_5H_9N_3$ ⟨< *hist(idine),* an amino acid (< Gk. *histion* tissue) + *amine*⟩

his•ti•dine ['hɪstəˌdin] *or* ['hɪstədɪn] *n. Biochemistry.* a basic amino acid found in many proteins. It is important in diet control. *Formula:* $C_6H_9N_3O_2$ ⟨< Gk. *histion* tissue, web + *-ide* + *-ine*[2]⟩

his•ti•o•cyte ['hɪstiouˌsəit] *n. Anatomy.* a body cell that fights infection.

histo– *combining form.* tissue: *histology.* ⟨< Gk. *histos* web (of a loom), tissue⟩

his•to•chem•is•try [ˌhɪstou'kɛmɪstri] *n.* the branch of science dealing with the chemistry of tissues and cells.

his•to•com•pat•i•bil•i•ty [ˌhɪstoukəmˌpætə'bɪləti] *n.* compatibility between the tissues of a donated organ, such as kidney, and the tissues of the recipient, usually a prerequisite for successful organ transplantation.

his•to•gen•e•sis [ˌhɪstə'dʒɛnəsɪs] *n. Biology.* the formation of bodily tissues.

his•to•log•i•cal [ˌhɪstə'lɒdʒəkəl] *adj.* of or having to do with histology. Also, **histologic.** —ˌ**his•to'log•i•cal•ly,** *adv.*

his•tol•o•gist [hɪ'stɒlədʒɪst] *n.* a person trained in histology, especially one whose work it is.

his•tol•o•gy [hɪ'stɒlədʒi] *n.* **1** the branch of biology dealing with the structures of animal and plant tissues as seen through a microscope. **2** the tissue structure of an animal or plant. ⟨< Gk. *histos* web + E *-logy*⟩

his•tol•y•sis [hɪ'stɒləsɪs] *n. Biology.* the disintegration of tissue. —ˌ**his•to'lyt•ic** [-'lɪtɪk], *adj.* —ˌ**his•to'lyt•i•cal•ly,** *adv.*

his•tone ['hɪstoun] *n. Biochemistry.* a protein in glandular tissue.

his•to•path•ol•o•gy [ˌhɪstoupə'θɒlədʒi] *n.* the pathology of diseased tissue.

his•to•ri•an [hɪ'stɔriən] *n.* **1** a person who has much knowledge of history, especially one who writes or lectures about history. **2** a person who records events; chronicler.

his•tor•ic [hɪ'stɔrɪk] *adj.* **1** famous or important in history: *Halifax and Kingston are historic cities.* **2** HISTORICAL (defs. 1-3).

his•tor•i•cal [hɪ'stɔrəkəl] *adj.* **1** of or having to do with history: *a historical term.* **2** according to history; based on history. **3** known to be real or true; in history, not in legend. **4** HISTORIC (def. 1). ⟨< L < Gk. *historikos* < *historia.* See HISTORY.⟩ —**his'tor•i•cal•ly,** *adv.*

historical linguistics the study of changes in a language or group of languages over a period of time.

historical present the present tense used in describing past events to make them seem more vivid.

historical school a theory that stresses the influence of history on social sciences such as law and economics.

his•tor•i•cism [hɪ'stɔrɪˌsɪzəm] *n.* the belief that we can do nothing to alter processes shaping our future.
—**his'tor•i•cist,** *n., adj.*

his•to•ric•i•ty [ˌhɪstə'rɪsəti] *n.* authenticity proved by history.

his•to•ri•og•ra•pher [hɪˌstɔri'ɒgrəfər] *n.* **1** a person specializing in historiography; one who studies the development, theory, and principles of historical writing. **2** a historian, especially one appointed to write the official history of an institution, etc. ⟨< LL < Gk. *historiographos* < *historia* history + *graphein* write⟩

his•to•ri•og•ra•phy [hɪˌstɔri'ɒgrəfi] *n.* **1** the study of the development, principles, and theory of the writing of history. **2** the writing of history, especially according to established principles of research and authentication of documentary evidence. **3** a body of historical writing.

his•to•ry ['hɪstəri] *or* ['hɪstri] *n., pl.* **-ries. 1** a statement of what has happened. **2** a systematic written account of a person, nation, movement, etc.: *a history of the fur trade.* **3** a known past: *This ship has an interesting history.* **4** all past events considered together; the course of human affairs: *one of the greatest achievements in history.* **5** the branch of knowledge or study that deals with the record and interpretation of past events: *a course in history.* **6** *Informal.* something that is over and done with; something past: *That whole affair is history now.* **7** a statement or record of all the facts or events having to do with a person being treated by a doctor, social worker, etc.; CASE HISTORY. **8** a textbook on history. **9** something worth remembering: *It's history when someone as great as she is visits our humble town.* **10** a historical play.
make history, a influence or guide the course of history. **b** do something spectacular or worthy of remembrance. ⟨< L *historia* < Gk. *historia* inquiry, record, history. Doublet of STORY[1].⟩

his•tri•on•ic [ˌhɪstri'ɒnɪk] *adj., n.* —*adj.* **1** theatrical and insincere; deliberately affected. **2** having to do with actors or acting; dramatic.
—*n.* **histrionics,** *pl.* **1** a deliberately dramatic show of emotions, etc. for effect. **2** *Rare.* DRAMATICS (defs. 1 & 2) (*used with a singular verb*). ⟨< L *histrionicus* < *histrio, -onis* actor⟩
—ˌ**his•tri'on•i•cal•ly,** *adv.*

hit [hɪt] *v.* **hit, hit•ting;** *n.* —*v.* **1** give a blow (to); strike; knock: *She hit the ball with the bat. He hit out against his opponents.* **2** get to (what is aimed at): *Her second arrow hit the bull's-eye.* **3** cause to knock, bump, etc. accidentally: *I hit my head on the desk as I fell.* **4** make a sudden attack: *We were all sleeping peacefully when the enemy hit.* **5** have a painful or distressing effect on: *The death of his sister hit him hard. The province was hard hit by the drought.* **6** occur suddenly (to): *when the tornado hit. As he lifted the heavy box, a sharp pain hit him hard in the back. An idea just hit me.* **7** reach (a certain point or place): *Prices hit a new high. The temperature hit an all-time low yesterday.* **8** attack or criticize sharply (*often used with* **at**): *The reviews hit the new play.* **9** please; appeal to: *This hits my fancy.* **10** *Baseball.* make (a base hit): *She hit a double.*
hard hit, affected deeply or painfully: *She was hard hit by the news of her mother's death.*
hit back, retaliate.
hit below the belt, be unfair to (an opponent).
hit it off, *Informal.* agree or get along well with someone: *Ron hit it off with his new neighbour right away.*
hit off, mimic or represent cleverly or accurately.
hit on or **upon, a** discover by chance: *They've hit on a new idea for advertising the contest.* **b** *Slang.* make sexual advances to.
hit or miss, whether one succeeds or fails; regardless of results; by chance; at random.
hit the books, *Informal.* begin to study, especially very hard: *She decided it was time to hit the books.*
hit the nail on the head. See NAIL.
hit the roof or **ceiling,** *Informal.* react with a burst of anger or shock: *When their father saw the condition of his car, he hit the roof.*
—*n.* **1** a blow; stroke. **2** violent contact. **3** the act of reaching a target. **4** a sharp attack or criticism. **5** a very successful or popular person or thing: *My brother was a big hit at my party. That new play is sure to be a hit.* **6** a stroke of luck. **7** *Baseball.* a successful hitting of the ball by a batter so that he or she can get at least to first base without the help of an error; base hit. ⟨OE *hittan* < ON *hitta* meet with⟩ —**'hit•less,** *adj.* —**'hit•ta•ble,** *adj.*
☛ *Syn. v.* **1.** See note at BEAT.

hit–and–run ['hɪt ən 'rʌn] *adj., n.* —*adj.* **1** of or caused by a driver who runs into another person or vehicle and drives away without stopping. **2** of or suggesting any similar act: *a hit-and-run attack.*
—*n.* **1** such an attack or accident. **2** *Baseball.* a play in which the batter tries to hit the ball to protect a runner who has already left base.

hitch [hɪtʃ] *v., n.* —*v.* **1** fasten with a hook, ring, rope, strap, etc.: *She hitched her horse to a post.* **2** harness to a wagon, carriage, etc. (*used with* **up**): *She hitched up the team and drove to town.* **3** become fastened or caught; fasten; catch. **4** move or pull with a jerk; move jerkily: *He hitched his chair nearer the fire.* **5** limp; hobble. **6** tie a hitch (def. 5 *n.*) in: *He hitched a rope*

around the spar. **7** *Informal.* obtain by hitchhiking: *She hitched a ride home.*
be or **get hitched,** *Slang.* be or get married.
—n. **1** a fastening; catch: *The hitch joining the plough to the tractor is broken.* **2** a short, sudden pull or jerk; jerky movement: *The sailor gave his pants a hitch.* **3** a limp; hobble. **4** an obstacle; hindrance; a going wrong: *A hitch in their plans made them miss the train.* **5** a kind of knot used for temporary fastening: *She put a hitch in the rope.* **6** *Informal.* a free ride from a passing automobile. **7** *Slang.* a period of time, especially a period of service in the armed forces.
without a hitch, smoothly; successfully. ⟨ME *hyche(n)*; origin uncertain⟩ **—'hitch•er,** *n.*

hitch•hike ['hɪtʃ,haik] *v.* **-hiked, -hik•ing;** *n. Informal.*
—v. **1** travel by asking for free rides from passing motorists: *They hitchhiked across the country last summer.* **2** ask for (a ride).
—n. a journey made in this way. **—'hitch,hik•er,** *n.*

hitching post ['hɪtʃɪŋ] a stand or post for hitching horses, etc.

hith•er ['hɪðər] *adv., adj. —adv.* to or toward this place; here.
hither and thither or **hither and yon,** in all directions; this way and that: *The frightened chickens ran hither and thither.*
—adj. on this side; nearer. ⟨OE *hider.* Related to HERE.⟩

hith•er•most ['hɪðər,moust] *adj.* nearest.

hith•er•to ['hɪðər,tu] *or* [,hɪðər'tu] *adv.* up to this time; until now.

hith•er•ward ['hɪðərwərd] *adv.* toward this place; hither. Also, **hitherwards.**

Hit•ler•ism ['hɪtlə,rɪzəm] *n.* the totalitarian and nationalistic policies and beliefs of Adolf Hitler and the Nazi party in Germany (1933 to 1945). See NAZISM.

hit list *Slang.* a list of people designated to be eliminated by a particular person or group.

hit man *Slang.* a hired murderer.

hit–or–miss ['hɪt ər 'mɪs] *adj.* showing a lack of care or planning; careless or haphazard: *He has always done his accounts in a hit-or-miss fashion.*

hit•ter ['hɪtər] *n.* especially in sports, a person who hits: *She's a good hitter, but not much of a catcher.*

Hit•tite ['hɪtəit] *n., adj. —n.* **1** a member of an ancient people of Asia Minor and Syria. Their civilization existed from about 2000 B.C. until about 1200 B.C. **2** the Indo-European language of the Hittites.
—adj. of or having to do with the Hittites or their language.
⟨< Hebrew *Hittim*⟩

HIV human immunovirus, a virus that destroys the body's capacity for immunity, and so causes AIDS.

hive [haɪv] *n., v.* **hived, hiv•ing.** *—n.* **1** a house or box for bees to live in. **2** a large number of bees living together. **3** a busy place full of people: *On Saturdays the department store is a hive.* **4** a swarming crowd.
—v. **1** put (bees) in a hive. **2** of bees, enter a hive. **3** store up (honey) in a hive. **4** lay up for future use. **5** live close together like bees. ⟨OE *hȳf*⟩

hives [haɪvz] *n.* a condition characterized by small, very itchy, fluid-filled swellings on the skin, usually caused by an allergic reaction; urticaria. ⟨Scottish; origin unknown⟩

H.J. HIC JACET.

hkf. handkerchief(s).

hL hectolitre(s).

H.L. HOUSE OF LORDS.

HLA human leukocyte antigen.

h'm [həm] hem; hum.

hm hectometre(s).

H.M. His Majesty; Her Majesty.

H.M.C.S. **1** Her (or His) Majesty's Canadian Ship: *H.M.C.S.* St. Laurent. **2** Her (or His) Majesty's Canadian Service.

Hmong [hə'mɒŋ] *n.* Miao.

H.M.S. **1** Her (or His) Majesty's Ship. **2** Her (or His) Majesty's Service.

ho [hou] *interj.* **1** an exclamation of surprise, joy, or scorn. **2** an exclamation used to attract attention: *Land ho!*
☛ *Hom.* HOE.

ho. house.

Ho holmium.

hoagie or **hoagy** ['hougi] *n. Esp. U.S.* HERO SANDWICH. ⟨origin unknown⟩

hoar [hɔr] *adj., n. —adj.* hoary.
—n. **1** hoariness. **2** hoarfrost. ⟨OE *hār*⟩
☛ *Hom.* WHORE.

hoard [hɔrd] *n., v. —n.* what is saved and stored away; things stored.
—v. **1** save and store away: *A squirrel hoards nuts for the winter.* **2** obtain and save (money or goods). ⟨OE *hord*⟩ **—'hoard•er,** *n.*
☛ *Hom.* HORDE.

hoard•ing ['hɔrdɪŋ] *n.* **1** a temporary board fence put up around a construction site or a building that is being repaired. **2** *Brit.* billboard. ⟨< *hoard* fence, apparently < AF *hurdis,* ult. < Gmc.⟩

hoar•frost ['hɔr,frɒst] *n.* a film of tiny ice crystals that sometimes forms on a cold surface.

hoar•hound See HOREHOUND.

hoarse [hɔrs] *adj.* **hoars•er, hoars•est. 1** rough and deep in sound; husky: *Her voice was hoarse from shouting at the game.* **2** having a rough voice: *He's hoarse because of a cold.* ⟨OE *hās*; influenced by ON **hárs*⟩ **—'hoarse•ly,** *adv.* **—'hoarse•ness,** *n.*
☛ *Hom.* HORSE.

hoarsen ['hɔrsən] *v.* make or become hoarse.

hoar•y ['hɔri] *adj.* **hoar•i•er, hoar•i•est. 1** of hair, grey or white. **2** having such hair; white or grey with age: *a hoary old man.* **3** very old; ancient. **—'hoar•i•ly,** *adv.* **—'hoar•i•ness,** *n.*

hoar•y–head•ed ['hɔri ,hɛdɪd] *adj.* having white or grey hair.

hoary marmot *Cdn.* a large grey marmot (*Marmota caligata*) found in the mountains of western Canada. The hoary marmot is the largest North American marmot. Also, **whistler.**

hoax [houks] *n., v. —n.* a mischievous trick, especially one based on a fabricated story: *The report of an attack from Mars was a hoax.*
—v. play a mischievous trick on; deceive. ⟨probably an alteration of *hocus*⟩ **—'hoax•er,** *n.*

hob[1] [hɒb] *n.* **1** a shelf at the back or side of a fireplace, used for keeping things warm. **2** a peg at which quoits, etc. are thrown. **3** a rotating device with a spiral cutting edge, used for cutting the teeth of worm gears, etc. ⟨var. of HUB⟩

hob[2] [hɒb] *n.* a hobgoblin; elf.
play or **raise hob (with),** cause trouble; disrupt: *She played hob with my presentation.* ⟨ME for *Rob* (*Robert* or *Robin*)⟩

hob•bit ['hɒbɪt] *n.* a member of an imaginary race of small, good-natured people about half as tall as human beings, having beardless faces, curly hair, and woolly, leathery-soled feet. ⟨created by J.R.R. Tolkien (1892-1973) in his books *The Hobbit* and *The Lord of the Rings*⟩

hob•ble ['hɒbəl] *v.* **-bled, -bling;** *n. —v.* **1** walk or move awkwardly or unsteadily; limp: *She managed to hobble to the phone without using the crutches.* **2** cause to walk awkwardly or limp. **3** put a strap, rope, etc. around the legs of (an animal, especially a horse) so that it can move a little but not run away. **4** hinder.
—n. **1** an awkward walk; limp. **2** a rope or strap used to hobble a horse, etc. ⟨ME *hobelen*; cf. Du. *hobbelen* rock⟩ **—'hob•bler,** *n.*

hob•ble•bush ['hɒbəl,bʊʃ] *n.* a shrub (*Viburnum alnifolium*) having white flowers and red berries.

hob•ble•de•hoy ['hɒbəldi,hɔɪ] *n.* a youth between boyhood and adulthood, especially one who is clumsy or awkward. ⟨origin uncertain⟩

hobble skirt a woman's skirt that is very narrow below the knees, especially a style popular from 1910-1914.

hob•by[1] ['hɒbi] *n., pl.* **-bies.** something a person especially likes to work at or study apart from his or her main business or occupation; any favourite pastime, topic of conversation, etc.
ride a hobby, give too much time or attention to one's hobby. ⟨ME *hobyn, hoby,* prob. from proper name *Robin.* See DOBBIN.⟩ **—'hob•by•ist,** *n.*

hob•by[2] ['hɒbi] *n., pl.* **-bies.** any bird of the genus *Falco*; falcon.

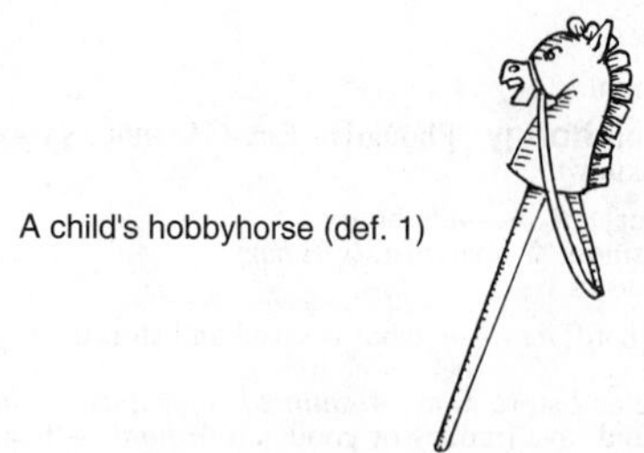
A child's hobbyhorse (def. 1)

hob•by•horse ['hɒbi,hɔrs] *n.* **1** a stick with a horse's head, used as a toy by children. **2** a rocking horse. **3** an imitation horse attached to the waist of a dancer. **4** a dancer wearing such a horse, pretending to be riding it. **5** a favourite idea or topic: *Father is again on his hobbyhorse of cutting costs.* ⟨< *hobby*; orig. a small horse or figure of a horse. 16c.⟩

hob•gob•lin ['hɒb,gɒblən] *n.* **1** a mischievous elf; goblin. **2** something imaginary that gives rise to fear. ⟨< *hob*[2] + *goblin*⟩

hob•nail ['hɒb,neil] *n., v.* —*n.* a short nail with a large head, used to protect the soles of heavy shoes or boots.
—*v.* put hobnails on. ⟨< *hob* peg + *nail*⟩

hob•nailed ['hɒb,neild] *adj., v.* —*adj.* having hobnails: *hobnailed boots.*
—*v.* pt. and pp. of HOBNAIL.

hob•nob ['hɒb,nɒb] *v.* **-nobbed, -nob•bing.** *Informal.* **1** associate intimately; talk together on familiar terms. **2** drink together. ⟨from drinking phrase *hob or nob* give or take, ult. < OE *hæbbe* have + *næbbe* not have⟩

ho•bo ['houbou] *n., pl.* **-bos** or **-boes;** *v.* —*n.* an itinerant worker.
—*v.* travel like a hobo. ⟨origin uncertain⟩

Hob•son's choice ['hɒbsənz] the choice of taking the thing offered or nothing. ⟨< Thomas *Hobson* (?-1631), an English stablekeeper, who would rent only the horse nearest his stable door or none⟩

hock[1] [hɒk] *n., v.* —*n.* **1** the joint in the hind leg of a horse, cow, etc. above the fetlock joint. See HORSE for picture. **2** the corresponding joint in the leg of a fowl.
—*v.* cripple by cutting the tendons of the hock; hamstring. Also, **hough.** ⟨OE *hōh*⟩
☛ *Hom.* HAWK.

hock[2] [hɒk] *n. Esp. Brit.* a kind of white Rhine wine. ⟨for *Hockamore*, alteration of *Hochheimer* (from *Hochheim*, Germany)⟩
☛ *Hom.* HAWK.

hock[3] [hɒk] *v. Informal.* PAWN[1]: *He hocked his watch to buy a ticket.*
in hock, a in another's possession as security; in pawn. **b** in debt: *She is in hock to her mother for the down payment on the house.*
out of hock, a no longer in another's possession as security. **b** no longer in debt. ⟨originally, *n.*; cf. Du. *hok* pen, jail⟩
☛ *Hom.* HAWK.

hock[4] [hɒk] *v. Slang.* steal: *Who hocked my pen?* ⟨origin uncertain⟩
☛ *Hom.* HAWK.

hock•ey ['hɒki] *n.* **1** a game played on ice by two teams of six players wearing skates, in which the members of each team use hooked sticks to try to shoot a small, thick, black rubber disk (the puck) into the opposing team's goal; ice hockey. **2** FIELD HOCKEY. ⟨< *hock* hooked stick, var. of *hook*⟩

hockey stick a hooked or curved stick used in playing hockey.

hock•shop ['hɒk,ʃɒp] *n. Informal.* a store where goods may be pawned.

ho•cus ['houkəs] *v.* **-cussed** or **-cused, -cus•sing** or **-cus•ing.** **1** play a trick on; hoax; cheat. **2** stupefy with drugs. **3** put drugs in (alcoholic drink). ⟨short for HOCUS-POCUS⟩

ho•cus–po•cus ['houkəs 'poukəs] *n.* **1** sleight of hand; magic. **2** any meaningless or insincere talk or action designed to cover up a deception: *All his talk about our beautiful house and garden was just hocus-pocus.* **3** a typical formula for conjuring. ⟨sham Latin used by jugglers, etc.; probably alteration of *hoc est corpus* (this is the Body) from the Eucharist⟩

hod [hɒd] *n.* **1** a trough or tray on a long handle, used for carrying bricks, mortar, etc. on the shoulder. **2** COAL SCUTTLE. ⟨< MDu. *hodde*⟩

hod carrier a labourer who carries bricks, mortar, etc. in a hod.

hodge•podge ['hɒdʒ,pɒdʒ] *n.* **1** a disorderly mixture; a mess or jumble. **2** a type of stew. ⟨var. of HOTCHPOTCH, var. of HOTCHPOT < OF *hochepot* ragout < *hocher* shake (< Gmc.) + *pot* pot⟩

Hodg•kin's disease ['hɒdʒkənz] a cancer characterized by chronic enlargement of the lymph nodes, spleen, and, often, the liver. It often produces anemia and continuous or recurring fever. ⟨after Thomas *Hodgkin* (1798-1866), the English physician who described it⟩

hoe [hou] *n., v.* **hoed, hoe•ing.** —*n.* an implement with a small blade set across the end of a long handle, used to loosen soil and cut weeds.
—*v.* **1** loosen, dig, or cut with a hoe: *There are a lot of weeds to hoe again.* **2** work with a hoe: *She spent all morning hoeing.* ⟨ME < OF *houe* < Gmc.⟩ —**'ho•er,** *n.*
☛ *Hom.* HO.

hoe•down ['hou,daʊn] *n.* **1** a lively dance, especially a square dance. **2** the music for such a dance. **3** a party featuring hoedowns: *There's a hoedown Saturday night.*

hog [hɒg] *n., v.* **hogged, hog•ging.** —*n.* **1** a domestic pig, especially a full-grown, castrated male raised for meat. **2** *Informal.* a selfish, greedy person.
go (the) whole hog, go to the limit; do something thoroughly.
live or **eat high off the hog,** *Informal.* live well.
—*v.* **1** *Informal.* take more than one's share of: *Don't hog the blanket.* **2** arch the back upward like a hog. **3** be arched, with a high centre and low ends, like a hog's back. ⟨OE *hogg*⟩
—**'hog,like,** *adj.*

ho•gan ['hougən] *n.* a round dwelling of certain Native American peoples such as the Navaho, having timber supports and adobe walls. ⟨< Navaho, house⟩

hog•back ['hɒg,bæk] *n.* **1** *Geology.* a low, sharp ridge with steep sides. **2** an arching back like that of a hog.

hog•fish ['hɒg,fɪʃ] *n.* any of several fishes, especially *Lachnolaimus maximus*, that look like a hog.

hog•gish ['hɒgɪʃ] *adj.* very selfish, greedy, or filthy.
—**'hog•gish•ly,** *adv.* —**'hog•gish•ness,** *n.*

hog line *Curling.* a line marked across the ice 6.4 m in front of each tee, the minimum distance for a rock to remain in play.

hog•ma•nay [,hɒgmə'nei] *n.* in Scotland, New Year's Eve, when children knock on doors for presents, cakes, etc. Adults also celebrate. ⟨origin uncertain⟩

hogs•head ['hɒgz,hɛd] *n.* **1** a large barrel or cask, especially one having a capacity of from 455 L to 635 L. **2** a unit for measuring liquids, equal to 245 L. ⟨? from shape of cask⟩

hog•suck•er ['hɒg,sʌkər] *n.* a fish of the family Catostomidae, about 15 cm long, common in Ontario and in the eastern U.S.

hog•tie ['hɒg,taɪ] *v.* **-tied, -ty•ing.** **1** tie the legs of. **2** obstruct the motion of.

Hog•town ['hɒg,taʊn] *n. Cdn.* an old name for Toronto.

hog•wash ['hɒg,wɒʃ] *n.* **1** refuse given to hogs; swill. **2** *Slang.* worthless stuff; nonsense.

hog•weed ['hɒg,wid] *n.* any coarse weed.

hog–wild ['hɒg ,waɪld] *adj. Slang.* frenzied; wildly aroused; berserk.

Hoh•en•stau•fen ['hoən,stʌufən]; *German*, ['hoən,ʃtaʊfən] *n.* a German princely family to which some of the German kings and Holy Roman emperors between 1138 and 1254 belonged.

Hoh•en•zol•lern ['houən,zɒlərn]; *German*, ['hoən,tsoləʀn] *n.* the German princely family that included the kings of Prussia from 1701 to 1918, and the emperors of Germany from 1871 to 1918.

hoi•den ['hɔɪdən] See HOYDEN.

hoi•den•ish ['hɔɪdənɪʃ] See HOYDENISH.

hoi pol•loi [,hɔɪ pə'lɔɪ] ordinary people; the general populace. ⟨< Gk. *hoi polloi* the many⟩

hoist [hɔɪst] *v., n.* —*v.* **1** raise on high; lift up, often with ropes and pulleys: *hoist sails, hoist blocks of stone.* **2** *Slang.* drink (liquor).
hoist with (one's) **own petard.** See PETARD.
—*n.* **1** a hoisting; lift. **2** an elevator or other apparatus for hoisting heavy loads. See CAISSON for picture. **3** the perpendicular height of a sail or flag on a ship. **4** a signal or

message sent by means of flags hoisted. ⟨earlier *hoise* < Du. *hijschen*⟩ —'**hoist•er,** *n.*

hoi•ty–toi•ty ['hɔɪti 'tɔɪti] *adj., n., interj.* —*adj.* **1** inclined to put on airs; haughty or pompous. **2** flighty or silly.
—*n.* hoity-toity behaviour.
—*interj.* an exclamation of indignant surprise.

hok•ey ['houki] *adj. Slang.* exaggerated or contrived. ⟨< *hokum*⟩

ho•key–po•key ['houki 'pouki] *n.* **1** trickery; hocus-pocus. **2** a cheap kind of ice cream sold by street vendors. **3** a singing and dancing game performed usually by children.

ho•kum ['houkəm] *n. Informal.* **1** pretentious nonsense; humbug; BUNK[2]. **2** elements such as crude comedy or maudlin sentiment introduced into a play, show, etc. merely for their immediate effect on the audience. ⟨? < *hocus*⟩

ho•lan•dric [hə'lændrɪk] *adj. Genetics.* of or having to do with a pattern of inheritance in which males transmit a trait to all of their sons but none of their daughters. ⟨< *holo-* + Gk. *aner, andros* man⟩

Hol•arc•tic [hɒ'lɑrktɪk] *or* [hɒ'lɑrtɪk] *adj.* of the region that includes all the northern areas of the earth, considered as an ecosystem. ⟨< *holo-* + *arctic*⟩

hold[1] [hould] *v.* **held, held, hold•ing;** *n.* —*v.* **1** take in the hands or arms and be or stay; not let go; keep from getting away: *Please hold my hat. Hold my watch while I play this game.* **2** keep in some position or condition; force to be or stay: *She will hold the paper steady while you draw.* **3** keep from falling; support: *He held his head in his hands.* **4** not break, loosen, or give way: *The dike held during the flood.* **5** keep from acting; keep back: *Hold your breath.* **6** keep; retain: *This package will be held until called for. The hijackers held three people hostage.* **7** oblige (a person) to adhere (*to* a promise), etc.: *They held him to his promise.* **8** keep from lapsing: *In your speech, be sure to hold the attention of the audience.* **9** keep by force against an enemy; defend: *Hold the fort.* **10** keep or have within itself; contain: *This theatre holds 500 people.* **11** reserve: *Please hold the room for me till eight o'clock.* **12** have and keep as one's own; possess; occupy: *to hold an office. She holds a valid driver's licence.* **13** have and take part in; carry on together: *Shall we hold a meeting of the club?* **14** not get drunk on: *Can he hold his liquor?* **15** keep or have in mind: *to hold a belief.* **16** retain a grip: *Hold tight!* **17** think; consider: *People once held that the earth was flat.* **18** remain faithful or firm: *He held to his promise.* **19** stay on a telephone: *Please hold while I put you through.* **20** be true; be in force or effect: *The rule holds in all cases.* **21** keep on; continue: *The weather held warm.* **22** judge legally: *The court holds him guilty.* **23** *Music.* keep on singing or playing (a note). **24** *Informal.* leave out; omit (from a food order): *Hold the anchovies.*
hold against, a blame for: *Don't hold it against me; it's not my fault.* **b** continue to resent (someone) for.
hold back, a keep back; keep from acting. **b** avoid disclosing: *to hold back the truth.* **c** withhold (money, wages, etc.)
hold down, a keep down; keep under control. **b** *Informal.* have and keep: *to hold down a job.*
hold forth, a talk; preach (often used disparagingly). **b** offer.
hold in, a keep in; keep back. **b** restrain; control: *He was so angry he couldn't hold in his temper.*
hold it! stop! wait!
hold off, a keep at a distance. **b** keep from acting or attacking. **c** delay acting.
hold on, *Informal.* **a** keep one's hold: *I held on to the capsized boat till help came.* **b** keep on; continue. **c** stop! wait a minute!
hold (one's) **own,** maintain one's strength or position in the face of opposition or difficulty.
hold out, a continue; last: *The water would not hold out much longer.* **b** stretch forth; extend: *Hold out your hand.* **c** keep resisting; not give in: *The company of soldiers held out for six days until help arrived.* **d** offer. **e** *Slang.* keep back something expected or due (*on* someone): *Don't hold out on me, Sue; tell the truth.*
hold out for, continue action to get: *The strikers held out for more pay.*
hold over, a keep longer than originally scheduled: *The movie was so popular that it was held over for another week.* **b** postpone: *The game has been held over until next week.* **c** *Music.* hold (a tone) from one bar to the next.
hold the fort, be in charge to see that nothing goes wrong.
hold up, a keep from falling; support. **b** show; display. **c** continue; last; endure. **d** stop: *The police officer held up the traffic.* **e** *Informal.* stop by force and rob. **f** delay; prevent from proceeding: *We were held up by an accident on the highway.*
hold with, a side with. **b** agree with. **c** approve of.
—*n.* **1** the act of holding (on): *to release one's hold.* **2** the manner of grasping or holding: *You must take a better hold if you are to pull your weight.* **3** something to hold by: *She looked for a hold on the smooth rock but couldn't find any.* **4** something to hold something else with. **5** a holding back; delay: *a hold in the launching of a missile.* **6** an order to delay or temporarily halt something. **7** a controlling force or influence: *A habit has a hold on you. Keep a hold over the situation.* **8** *Wrestling.* a way of holding one's opponent. **9** *Music.* a sign for a continued note. **10** a prison cell. **11** *Archaic.* a fort; stronghold.
get hold of, a grasp. **b** get in touch with (someone).
lay or **take hold of, a** seize; grasp. **b** get control or possession of.
no holds barred, any method is acceptable.
on hold, waiting on the telephone: *She put me on hold while she looked for the file.* ⟨OE *healdan*⟩
☛ *Syn. v.* **10.** See note at CONTAIN. **12.** See note at HAVE.

hold[2] [hould] *n.* **1** the interior of a ship below the deck. A ship's cargo is carried in its hold. **2** a similar cargo compartment in an aircraft. ⟨var. of HOLE⟩

hold•back ['hould,bæk] *n.* **1** something that holds back; restraint; hindrance. **2** an iron or strap on the shaft of a wagon or carriage to which the harness is attached, enabling a horse to stop or back the vehicle. **3** the act of holding back. **4** something held back.

hold•en ['houldən] *v. Archaic.* a pp. of HOLD[1].

hold•er ['houldər] *n.* **1** a person who holds a bill, note, cheque, etc. and is legally entitled to receive payment on it. **2** a person who owns or occupies property. **3** a device for holding something (*usually used in compounds*): *a cigarette holder, a potholder.* **4** any person who or thing that holds.

hold•fast ['hould,fæst] *n.* anything used to hold something else in place. A catch, hook, or clamp is a holdfast.

hold•ing ['houldɪŋ] *n., v.* —*n.* **1** land, especially a piece of land rented from someone else. **2** Usually, **holdings,** *pl.* property, especially in the form of stocks or bonds. **3** *Sports.* the illegal hindering of an opponent's movements.
—*v.* ppr. of HOLD[1].

holding company a company that owns stocks or bonds of other companies and thus often controls them.

holding pattern the usually circular pattern of movement of a plane waiting in the air for landing instructions.

hold•out ['hould,ʌut] *n. Informal.* **1** a person or group that refuses to submit or give in or accept an agreement. **2** refusal to settle or comply; continued resistance.

hold•o•ver ['hould,ouvər] *n.* **1** a person or thing that is held over from another time or place: *She was a holdover from last year's team.* **2** a person who remains in office beyond the regular time.

hold•up ['hould,ʌp] *n.* **1** the act or an instance of forcibly stopping and robbing. **2** delay or hindrance: *She got out of her car to see what the holdup was.*

hole [houl] *n., v.* **holed, hol•ing.** —*n.* **1** an opening in or through something, often a break or tear: *a hole in a stocking, a hole in a window. The calendar has a hole at the top to hang it up by.* **2** a hollow place; pit; a place that is lower than the parts around it: *a hole in the road. There's a hole in the lawn where the ground caved in.* **3** burrow: *Rabbits live in holes.* **4** a small, dark, dreary, or dirty place: *I wouldn't want to live in that hole.* **5** *Informal.* a flaw or defect: *That argument has several holes.* **6** *Informal.* an embarrassing, awkward, or difficult position: *He got himself into a hole, financially.* **7** *Golf.* **a** a small, round hollow to hit a ball into. **b** the part of a golf course leading from a tee to such a place. A regular golf course has 18 holes. **8** a small, narrow indentation in a coastline, especially in a bay or harbour (*often used in place names*). **9** a pool or part of a river: *a swimming hole.*
burn a hole in (one's) **pocket,** of money, make one want badly to spend; be easily spent: *His birthday gift is burning a hole in his pocket.*
hole in one, *Golf.* a hit made from the tee so that the ball goes straight into the hole on the green.
in the hole, in debt or financial difficulties.
make a hole in, use up a large amount of: *The new radio made quite a hole in my savings.*
pick holes in, find fault with; criticize.
the hole, solitary confinement in a prison.
—*v.* **1** make a hole or holes in: *The side of the ship was holed by an iceberg.* **2** hit or drive into a hole.
hole out, hit a golf ball into a hole.
hole up, a of animals, go into a hole. **b** *Slang.* go into hiding for a time: *The robbers holed up in an old cabin.* ⟨OE *hol*⟩

☛ *Hom.* WHOLE.
☛ *Syn. n.* **1, 2. Hole,** CAVITY = an open or hollow place in something. **Hole** is the common word applying to an opening in or through anything, or to a hollow space in something solid: *Fire burned a hole in the roof. She bored a hole in the tree.* **Cavity** is chiefly scientific or technical, and applies only to a hollow space inside a solid mass or body, often with an opening at the surface: *The dentist filled several cavities in my teeth.*

hole–and–corner or **hole–in–corner** ['houl ən 'kɔrnər] *or* ['houl ɪn 'kɔrnər] *adj. Informal.* furtive; underhand.

hole–in–the–wall ['houl ɪn ðə ˌwɒl] *adj. Informal.* insignificant; shabby; grubby.

hol•ey ['houli] *adj.* having holes.
☛ *Hom.* HOLI, HOLY, WHOLLY.

Ho•li ['houli] *n. Hinduism.* a popular spring festival generally dedicated to Krishna.
Hom. HOLEY, HOLY, WHOLLY.

hol•i•day ['hɒlə,dei] *n., v.* —*n.* **1** a day free of work; a day for pleasure and enjoyment. **2** a day on which, either by law or custom, general business is suspended: *Labour Day and July 1st are both holidays as specified by law.* **3** Often, **holidays,** *pl.* vacation; period of rest or recreation: *the summer holidays. My mother gets three weeks of holidays a year.* **4** (*adjl.*) suited to a holiday; festive: *in holiday spirits.* **5** a holy day; religious festival.
on holiday, taking a vacation.
—*v.* take or have a holiday: *They are holidaying in the tropics.* ⟨OE *hāligdæg* holy day⟩

holiday–maker ['hɒlə,dei ˌmeikər] *n.* someone taking a vacation: *The beach was crowded with holiday-makers.*

ho•li•er–than–thou ['houliər ðən 'ðaʊ] *adj., n. Informal.*
—*adj.* self-righteous.
—*n.* a self-righteous person.

ho•li•ness ['houlinɪs] *n.* **1** a being holy. **2 Holiness,** a title used in speaking to or of the Pope. ⟨OE *hālignes*⟩

ho•lism ['houlɪzəm] *n. Philosophy.* the theory that living nature consists of wholes that are more than just the sum of their parts. Also, **wholism.** ⟨< Gk. *hólos* whole + *ism*⟩
—'ho•list, *n.*

ho•lis•tic [hou'lɪstɪk] *adj.* **1** emphasizing the importance of the relationship between parts or elements and wholes: *holistic medicine.* **2** of or having to do with holism. Also, **wholistic.**
—ho'lis•ti•cal•ly, *adv.*

hol•land ['hɒlənd] *n.* a linen or linen and cotton cloth used for window shades, upholstery, etc. It is usually light brown and sometimes glazed. ⟨first made in *Holland*⟩

Hol•land ['hɒlənd] *n.* **1** the part of the Netherlands consisting of the two provinces North and South Holland, corresponding to a county of the former Holy Roman Emperor. **2** another name for the Netherlands.

hol•lan•daise sauce [ˌhɒlən'deiz] a creamy sauce made from egg yolks, butter, lemon juice, and seasoning, served with fish, vegetables, etc. ⟨< F *hollandaise,* fem. of *hollandais* Dutch⟩

Hol•land•er ['hɒləndər] *n.* a native or inhabitant of the Netherlands; Dutch citizen.

Holland gin ['hɒlənd] Hollands.

Hol•lands ['hɒləndz] *n.* a strong gin made in the Netherlands. ⟨< Du. *hollandsch* < *hollandsche genever* Dutch gin. 18c.⟩

hol•ler ['hɒlər] *v., n. Informal.* —*v.* shout.
—*n.* a loud cry or shout.

hol•low ['hɒlou] *adj., n., v., adv.* —*adj.* **1** having a hole or cavity inside; not solid: *A tube or pipe is hollow. Some plants have hollow stems.* **2** shaped like a bowl or cup; having an inward curve; concave or sunken: *hollow cheeks. There is a large hollow place in the lawn where the earth has settled.* **3** sounding as if coming from something hollow; deep-toned and muffled: *a hollow voice, a hollow groan.* **4** lacking real worth, truth, or significance; worthless or false: *hollow promises, hollow joys, a hollow victory.* **5** empty or hungry: *a hollow stomach.*
—*n.* **1** a hollow place; a wide, shallow hole: *a hollow in the road.* **2** a small valley: *They built their house in a hollow.*
—*v.* **1** make or become hollow. **2** make or form by hollowing (*usually used with* **out**): *She hollowed out a canoe from a log.*
—*adv.*
beat (all) hollow, *Informal.* defeat soundly in a competition. ⟨OE *holh,* n.; influenced in use by *hol,* adj.⟩ **—'hol•low•ly,** *adv.*
—'hol•low•ness, *n.*

hol•low–eyed ['hɒlou ˌaɪd] *adj.* **1** having eyes set deep in the head. **2** having dark shadows under the eyes: *hollow-eyed from lack of sleep.*

hol•low•ware ['hɒlou,wɛr] *n.* bowls and pitchers of silver.

hol•ly ['hɒli] *n., pl.* **-lies. 1** any of a genus (*Ilex*) of trees and shrubs having thick, shiny leaves with spiny points along the edges, and clusters of bright red berries. **2** the leaves and berries of a holly, used as Christmas decorations: *a wreath of holly.* **3** (*adjl.*) designating the family (Aquifoliaceae) of trees and shrubs that includes the hollies. ⟨OE *holegn*⟩

A hollyhock

hol•ly•hock ['hɒli,hɒk] *n.* **1** a tall perennial plant (*Althaea rosea*) of the mallow family native to China, but widely grown for its spikes of large, showy flowers. Hollyhock flowers are usually white, pink, red, or yellow. **2** the flower of this plant. ⟨ME *holihoc* < *holi* holy (OE *hālig*) + *hoc* mallow (OE *hocc*)⟩

Hol•ly•wood ['hɒli,wʊd] *n.* the American film industry. ⟨< *Hollywood,* a section of Los Angeles, California, centre of the United States film industry⟩

holm¹ [houm] *n. Esp. Brit.* **1** low, flat land by a stream. **2** a small island in a river or lake near a large island or the mainland. ⟨OE⟩
☛ *Hom.* HOME.

holm² [houm] *n.* HOLM OAK.
☛ *Hom.* HOME.

hol•mi•um ['houlmiəm] *n. Chemistry.* a rare metallic chemical element belonging to the yttrium group. *Symbol:* Ho; *at.no.* 67; *at.mass* 164.93. ⟨< NL; < Stock*holm*⟩

holm oak [houm] **1** an evergreen oak (*Quercus ilex*) of S Europe having leaves that look like holly. **2** the wood of this tree. ⟨OE *holegn* holly + *āc* oak⟩

holo– *combining form.* whole; entire: *holograph.* ⟨< Gk. *holos* whole⟩

hol•o•caust ['hɒlə,kɒst] *or* ['houlə,kɒst] *n.* **1** a sacrificial offering, all of which is burned. **2** great or total destruction of life, especially by fire. **3 the Holocaust,** the systematic killing of over six million Jews by the Nazi regime in Germany before and during World War II. ⟨< L < Gk. *holokauston,* neut. of *holokaustos* < *holos* whole + *kaustos* burned⟩

Hol•o•cene ['hɒlə,sin] *or* ['houlə,sin] *adj., n. Geology.* RECENT (def. 4). ⟨< *holo-* + Gk. *kainos* recent⟩

hol•o•gram ['hɒlə,græm] *or* ['houlə,græm] *n. Optics.* a three-dimensional photograph obtained by holography.

hol•o•graph ['hɒlə,græf] *or* ['houlə,græf] *adj., n.* —*adj.* wholly written in the handwriting of the person in whose name it appears: *a holograph will.*
—*n.* a holograph manuscript, letter, document, etc. ⟨< LL < Gk. *holographos* < *holos* whole + *graphē* writing⟩ **—ˌhol•o'graph•ic,** *adj.*

ho•log•ra•phy [hə'lɒgrəfi] *n.* a photographic process for making three-dimensional pictures without the use of lenses, in which a split beam of laser light causes a diffraction pattern that is reconstructed in visible light.

ho•lo•he•dral [ˌhɒlə'hidrəl] *or* [ˌhoulə'hidrəl] *adj.* of a crystal, having faces completely symmetrical.

ho•lo•me•ta•bol•ism [ˌhɒləmə'tæbə,lɪzəm] *or* [ˌhouləmə'tæbə,lɪzəm] *n.* complete metamorphosis.
—ˌho•lo•me'ta•bo•lous, *adj.*

ho•lo•morph•ic [ˌhɒlə'mɔrfɪk] *or* [ˌhoulə'mɔrfɪk] *adj. Mathematics.* of a curve, showing parametric equations.

ho•lo•phyt•ic [ˌhɒlə'fɪtɪk] *or* [ˌhoulə'fɪtɪk] *adj.* of plants, obtaining food by synthesis of inorganic material.

ho•lo•thur•ian [ˌhɒlə'θjʊriən] *or* [ˌhɒlə'θʊriən] *n.* a class of echinoderms including the sea cucumbers.

ho•lo•type ['hɒlə,taip] *or* ['houlə,taip] *n.* the specimen used as a basis for the description of a species.

ho•lo•zo•ic [ˌhɒlə'zouɪk] *or* [ˌhoulə'zouɪk] *adj.* eating complex organic material such as other plants and animals, as most mammals do.

holp [houlp] *v. Archaic.* a pt. of HELP.

hol•pen ['houlpən] *v. Archaic.* a pp. of HELP.

Hol•stein ['houlstaɪn] *or* ['houlstin] *n.* a breed of large, black-and-white dairy cattle, originating in Schleswig-Holstein, a state in Germany.

Hol•stein–Frie•sian ['houlstaın 'friʒən] *or* ['houlstin-] *n.* Holstein.

hol•ster ['houlstər] *n.* a leather case for a pistol, usually attached to a belt. ⟨< Du. *holster*⟩

ho•lus–bo•lus ['houləs 'bouləs] *adv. Informal.* all at once; altogether. ⟨humorous Latinization of E *whole bolus*⟩

ho•ly ['houli] *adj.* **-li•er, -li•est;** *n., pl.* **-lies.** *—adj.* **1** belonging to or coming from God or a god; set apart for the service of God or a god; sacred: *the Holy Bible.* **2** perfect in nature; sinless and abhorring sin: *God is holy.* **3** pure in heart; godly: *a holy man.* **4** declared sacred by religious use and authority: *a holy day.* **5** worthy of deep respect and love: *the holy Cross.*
—n. a holy place. ⟨OE *hālig*⟩ **—'hol•i•ly,** *adv.*
☛ *Hom.* HOLEY, HOLI, WHOLLY.

Holy Alliance a league formed by the rulers of Russia, Austria, and Prussia in 1815, supposedly uniting their governments in a Christian brotherhood.

Holy City **1** a city considered sacred by the adherents of a religion. Jerusalem, Rome, and Mecca are Holy Cities. **2** heaven.

Holy Communion *Christianity.* the commemoration of Christ's Last Supper, in which bread and wine are consecrated and taken as the body and blood of Christ or as symbols of them; the Eucharist.

holy day **1** a Christian religious festival, especially one not occurring on a Sunday. Ash Wednesday and Good Friday are holy days. **2** a religious festival of any other religion.

Holy Father *Roman Catholic Church.* a title of the Pope.

Holy Ghost See HOLY SPIRIT.

Holy Grail Grail.

Holy Land Israel.

Holy Office **1** *Roman Catholic Church.* the papal Congregation of the Holy Office, charged with the supervision and protection of Catholic faith and morals. **2** formerly, the Inquisition.

holy of holies **1** the inner shrine of the Jewish tabernacle and temple. **2** any place that is most sacred.

holy orders *Christianity.* **1** the rite or sacrament of ordination. **2** the rank or position of an ordained Christian minister or priest. **3** *Roman Catholic and Anglican Churches.* the three higher ranks or positions of the clergy. Bishops, priests, and deacons are members of holy orders.
take holy orders, become a Christian minister or priest.

Holy Roman Empire an empire in western and central Europe regarded both as the continuation of the Roman Empire and as the temporal form of a universal dominion whose spiritual head was the Pope. It began in A.D. 962, or, according to some, in A.D. 800, and ended in 1806.

Holy Rood **1** the cross on which Jesus died. **2** a representation of it.

Holy Saturday *Christianity.* the Saturday before Easter.

Holy Scripture **1** the Bible. **2** the sacred writings of any religion.

Holy See *Roman Catholic Church.* **1** the position or authority of the Pope. **2** the Pope's court.

Holy Spirit *Christian theology.* **1** the spirit of God. **2** the third person in the Trinity. Also, **Holy Ghost.**

ho•ly•stone ['houlə,stoun] *n., v.* **-stoned, -ston•ing.** *—n.* a piece of soft sandstone used for scrubbing the wooden decks of ships.
—v. scrub with a holystone.

Holy Synod the church council that governs an Eastern Orthodox Church.

Holy Thursday *Christianity.* **1** the Thursday before Easter. **2** the fortieth day after Easter; Ascension Day.

holy water water blessed by a priest.

Holy Week *Christianity.* the week before Easter.

Holy Writ the Bible; the Scriptures.

hom. homonym.

hom•age ['hɒmıdʒ] *or* ['ɒmıdʒ] *n.* **1** respect; reverence; honour: *Everyone paid homage to the great leader.* **2** in feudal times: **a** a formal acknowledgment by a vassal that he owed loyalty and service to his lord. **b** anything done or given to show such acknowledgment. **3** a formal statement, or oath, of loyalty and service owed to one's sovereign. ⟨ME < OF *homage* < *hom* man, vassal < L *homo*⟩
☛ *Syn.* **1.** See note at HONOUR.

hom•bre ['ɒmbrei] *or* ['ɒmbri]; *Spanish,* ['ombre] *n.* man. ⟨< Sp.⟩

Hom•burg ['hɒmbərg] *n.* a man's felt hat having a slightly rolled brim and a crown creased lengthwise. Also, **homburg.** ⟨< *Homburg,* a German resort where it was first worn⟩

home [houm] *n., v.* **homed, hom•ing.** *—n.* **1** the place where a person or family lives; one's own house. **2** the place where a person was born or brought up or now lives; one's own town or country. **3** (*advl.*) at, to, or toward one's own home: *She's not home. I want to go home.* **4** the social unit formed by a family, etc. living together in one house or apartment: *He comes from a broken home.* **5** a house built for occupation by one family: *luxury homes for sale.* **6** the natural habitat of an animal or plant: *The beaver makes its home in the water. The Canadian tundra is the home of the musk-ox.* **7** any place where a person can rest and be safe. **8** a place where people who are homeless, poor, old, sick, blind, etc. may live. **9** the place of origin or development of something. **10** (*adjl.*) of one's own country: *the home office.* **11** *Games.* the objective or goal; especially, in baseball, home plate. **12** (*adjl.*) *Games.* **a** having to do with or situated at or near home. **b** reaching or enabling a player to reach home. **13** (*advl.*) **a** to the thing aimed at: *to drive a nail home.* **b** to the heart or core; deep in: *Her accusing words struck home and they were ashamed.* **c** successfully or effectively: *to speak home.* **14** (*adjl.*) of, having to do with, or coming from home: *one's home country, home remedies, a home game.*
at home, a in one's own home or country. **b** in a friendly place or familiar condition; at ease; comfortable. **c** ready to receive visitors. **d** a reception.
bring home to, make clear, emphatic, or realistic to.
close to or **near home,** affecting one deeply.
come home to, be understood or realized by.
drive home, a make secure with a hammer: *With the second blow, she drove the peg home.* **b** make someone understand or realize: *He thumped the table to drive home his argument.*
home free, *Informal.* sure of success or victory: *One more game and then we're home free.*
see (someone) **home,** escort a person to that person's home: *He offered to see her home.*
to write home about, remarkable: *That's nothing to write home about.*
—v. **1** go home. **2** bring, carry, or send home. **3** of birds, return home. **4** have a home. **5** furnish with a home.
home (in) on, be guided toward (a goal or target) by or as if by radar. ⟨OE *hām*⟩
☛ *Hom.* HOLM.

home•bo•dy ['houm,bɒdi] *n.* one whose activities and interests centre around the house or apartment.

home•bound ['houm,baʊnd] *adj.* **1** headed for home. **2** restricted to the house or apartment.

home•bred ['houm'brɛd] *adj., n. —adj.* **1** bred or reared at home; native; domestic. **2** not polished or refined; crude; unsophisticated.
—n. Slang. Sports. homebrew.

home•brew ['houm'bru] *n.* **1** an alcoholic liquor made at home, especially beer. **2** *Cdn. Slang.* **a** in Canadian professional football, a native-born player. **b** a local player in any sport; a player trained by the team for which he or she plays. **c** any person or thing of native origin.

home•com•ing ['houm,kʌmıŋ] *n.* **1** a coming home. **2** an annual celebration held at many universities and colleges for alumni.

home economics the science and art that deals with the management of a household.

home fries slices of boiled potato cut and fried.

home front in war, civilians and their activities.

home–grown ['houm 'groun] *adj.* of produce, grown locally.

home•land ['houm,lænd] *or* ['houmlənd] *n.* one's own or native land.

home•less ['houmlıs] *adj.* **1** having no home. **2** (*noml.*) **the homeless,** people without homes. **—'home•less•ness,** *n.*

home•like ['houm,ləik] *adj.* like home; friendly; familiar; comfortable. **—'home,like•ness,** *n.*

home•ly ['houmli] *adj.* **-li•er, -li•est. 1** not good-looking; plain: *His homely face lit up in a smile.* **2** suited to home life; simple; everyday: *homely pleasures, homely food.*
—'home•li•ness, *n.*
☛ *Syn.* **1.** See note at UGLY.

home•made ['houm'meid] *adj.* **1** made at home. **2** not elegant; amateurish. **3** made or prepared locally: *homemade preserves.*

home•mak•er ['houm,meikər] *n.* a person who manages a home, especially one who is a spouse and parent.

home•mak•ing ['houm,meikɪŋ] *n.* the art or practice of managing a home and looking after a family.

homeo– *combining form.* similar: *homeostasis.* ⟨< Gk. *homoios* similar, like⟩

ho•me•o•path ['houmiə,pæθ] *or* ['hɒmiə,pæθ] *n.* a person who practises homeopathy.

ho•me•o•path•ic [,houmiə'pæθɪk] *or* [,hɒmiə'pæθɪk] *adj.* of or having to do with homeopathy or homeopaths. **—,ho•me•o'path•i•cal•ly,** *adv.*

ho•me•op•a•thist [,houmi'ɒpəθɪst] *or* [,hɒmi'ɒpəθɪst] *n.* homeopath.

ho•me•op•a•thy [,houmi'ɒpəθi] *or* [,hɒmi'ɒpəθi] *n.* a system of treating disease by giving very small doses of a drug that in large quantities would produce symptoms of the disease in healthy persons. It is based on the theory that making the symptoms more intense will stimulate the body to do what it does in fighting disease. Compare ALLOPATHY. ⟨< Gk. *homoios* similar + E *-pathy*⟩

ho•me•o•sta•sis [,houmiə'steisɪs] *or* [,houmiə'stæsɪs] *n.* **1** the state of equilibrium between the different body activities of an organism, or the tendency to return to or compensate for loss of equilibrium. **2** the maintenance of or return to equilibrium between interdependent elements of a group, society, etc.

ho•me•o•stat•ic [,houmiə'stætɪk] *adj.* of, having to do with, or showing homeostasis.

ho•me•o•typ•ic [,houmiə'tɪpɪk] *adj. Biology.* having to do with the second division in meiosis.

home–own•er ['houm ,ounər] *n.* a person who owns his or her own home.

home page *Computer technology.* the first file reached at an address on the WORLD WIDE WEB, from which others can be entered by a hypertext link.

home plate *Baseball.* the block or slab beside which a player stands to hit the ball, and to which he or she must return, after hitting the ball and rounding the bases, in order to score.

hom•er ['houmər] *n., v. Informal. —n.* **1** *Baseball. Informal.* HOME RUN. **2** *Slang.* a referee, umpire, etc. who favours, or is said to favour, the home team. **3** *Slang.* a supporter of the hometown team. **4** *Slang.* a player or team that plays well in home games. **5** HOMING PIGEON.
—v. Baseball. Informal. hit a home run.

home range the area in which a creature normally lives.

Ho•mer•ic [hou'mɛrɪk] *adj.* **1** by Homer, the epic poet of Ancient Greece. **2** of or having to do with Homer or his poems. **3** in the style of Homer; having some characteristics of Homer's poems. **4** of or having to do with Greek life from about 1200 to about 800 B.C. **5** on a large scale.

Homeric laughter loud, hearty laughter.

home•room ['houm'rum] *or* ['houm'rʊm] *n.* **1** the classroom in a school where a given class meets first every day to be checked for attendance, hear announcements, etc. **2** the classroom in a school, especially an elementary school, where a given class is taught most subjects, usually by the same teacher. **3** the period during which a class meets in the homeroom. **4** the students of a given homeroom. **5** (*adjl.*) of or having to do with a homeroom or homerooms: *a homeroom plan. My homeroom teacher taught French.* Also, **home room.**

home rule the management of the affairs of a country, district, or city by its own people; local self-government.

home run *Baseball.* a run made by a player on a hit that enables him or her, without aid from fielding errors of the opponents, to make the entire circuit of the bases without a stop.

home•sick ['houm,sɪk] *adj.* ill or depressed because one is away from home; longing for home. **—'home-,sick•ness,** *n.*

home•spun ['houm,spʌn] *adj., n. —adj.* **1** spun or made at home. **2** made of homespun cloth. **3** not polished; plain; simple: *homespun manners.*
—n. **1** cloth made of yarn spun at home. **2** a strong, loosely woven cloth similar to homespun.

home•stand ['houm,stænd] *n.* a series of games played in the home stadium or ground.

home•stead ['houm,stɛd] *n., v. —n.* **1** a house with its land and other buildings; a farm with its buildings. **2** *Cdn.* in the West, a parcel of public land, usually consisting of a quarter section, 65 ha, granted to a settler under certain conditions by the federal government.
—v. **1** settle on such land: *His grandfather homesteaded in Saskatchewan.* **2** settle and work (land, etc.): *They homesteaded a quarter section west of the river.*

Homestead Act the Act of 1872 under which settlers became homesteaders in the Canadian West, under certain conditions.

home•stead•er ['houm,stɛdər] *n.* **1** a person who has a homestead. **2** a settler granted a homestead by the federal government.

home stretch **1** the part of a track over which the last part of a race is run. **2** the last part of any undertaking.

home town **1** the town or city where one grew up or spent most of one's early life. **2** the town or city of one's principal residence. **—'home,town,** *adj.*

home•ward ['houmwərd] *adv. or adj.* toward home. Also (adv.), **homewards.**

home•work ['houm,wɜrk] *n.* **1** a lesson or lessons to be studied or prepared outside the classroom. **2** any work done at home. **3** work done in preparation for something; background reading or research: *The interviewer's searching questions showed that she had done her homework.*

home•y ['houmi] *adj.* **hom•i•er, hom•i•est.** *Informal.* like home; cosy and comfortable: *The old inn had a very homey atmosphere.*

hom•i•cid•al [,hɒmə'saɪdəl] *or* [,houmə'saɪdəl] *adj.* **1** of or having to do with homicide. **2** murderous. **—,hom•i'cid•al•ly,** *adv.*

hom•i•cide ['hɒmə,saɪd] *or* ['houmə,saɪd] *n.* **1** the killing of one human being by another. Intentional homicide is murder. **2** a person who kills a human being. ⟨ME < OF < L *homicidium* a killing, *-cida* killer < *homo* man + *-cidium, -cida*⟩

hom•i•let•ic [,hɒmə'lɛtɪk] *adj.* having to do with sermons or the art of preaching. ⟨< LL < Gk. *homilētikos* affable, ult. < *homileein* associate with < *homilos.* See HOMILY.⟩

hom•i•let•ics [,hɒmə'lɛtɪks] *n.* the art of composing and preaching sermons.

hom•i•ly ['hɒməli] *n., pl.* **-lies. 1** a sermon, usually based on some part of the Bible. **2** a serious moral talk or writing. ⟨ME < OF *omelie* < LL < Gk. *homilia* < *homilos* throng < *homou* together + *ilē* crowd⟩ **—'hom•i•list,** *n.*

hom•i•nes ['hɒmə,niz] *Latin. n.pl.* of HOMO.

hom•ing ['houmɪŋ] *adj.* **1** able to return home. **2** assisting in guiding home.

homing pigeon a pigeon trained to fly home from great distances. Homing pigeons are often used in racing or for carrying written messages.

hom•i•nid ['hɒmənɪd] *n.* **1** any of a family (Hominidae) of primate mammals, including modern humans (*Homo sapiens*), the only surviving member of the group. **2** (*adjl.*) of, having to do with, or belonging to the family Hominidae. ⟨< NL *Hominidae*, the family name⟩

hom•i•noid ['hɒmə,nɔɪd] *adj., n. —adj.* like a man; of the form of a man.
—n. a hominoid animal; a member of the Hominoidea superfamily that includes humans and the great apes. ⟨< L *homo, -inis* man + E *-oid*⟩

hom•i•ny ['hɒməni] *n.* dried, hulled corn. **Hominy grits** is coarsely ground hominy that is boiled in water or milk for food. ⟨< short for *rockahominy* < Algonquian⟩

ho•mo[1] ['houmou] *n., pl.* **hom•i•nes** ['hɒmə,niz] any member of the genus *Homo*, which includes present and extinct peoples. ⟨< L⟩

ho•mo[2] ['houmou] *n. Cdn. Informal.* homogenized whole milk.

homo– *combining form.* the same: *homopterous.* ⟨< Gk. *homo-* < *homos* same⟩

ho•mo•cer•cal [,houmə'sɜrkəl] *or* [,hɒmə'sɜrkəl] *adj.* of a fish, having a tail divided equally. ⟨< *homo-* + Gk. *kerkos* tail⟩

ho•mog•a•mous [hə'mɒgəməs] *adj.* having flowers that are sexually alike. **—ho'mog•a•my,** *n.*

ho•mo•ge•ne•i•ty [,houmədʒə'niəti] *or* [,hɒmədʒə'niəti] *n.* the state of being homogeneous.

ho•mo•ge•ne•ous [,houmə'dʒiniəs] *or* [,hɒmə'dʒiniəs],

[ˌhoumə'dʒinjəs] *or* [ˌhɒmə'dʒinjəs] *adj.* **1** of the same kind; similar: *homogeneous interests.* **2** composed of similar elements or parts; of uniform nature or character throughout: *a homogeneous rock, a homogeneous community.* Compare HETEROGENEOUS (defs. 1,2) **3** *Mathematics.* **a** of the same kind and commensurable. **b** of the same degree or dimensions. Also (defs. 1, 2), **homogenous** [hə'mɒdʒənəs]. ⟨< Med.L < Gk. *homogenēs* < *homos* same + *genos* kind⟩
—ˌho•mo'ge•ne•ous•ly, *adv.*

ho•mog•e•nize [hə'mɒdʒəˌnaɪz] *v.* **-nized, -niz•ing. 1** make homogeneous. **2** break up the fat globules of (whole milk) into extremely small particles so that the fat remains emulsified and does not rise to the top to form cream. **—hoˌmog•e•ni'za•tion,** *n.*

ho•mog•e•nous [hə'mɒdʒənəs] See HOMOGENEOUS (defs. 1, 2).

ho•mo•graft ['houməˌgræft] *or* ['hɒməˌgræft] *n.* the surgical transplant of tissue of one individual to another of the same species.

hom•o•graph ['hɒməˌgræf] *or* ['houməˌgræf] *n.* one of two or more words having the same spelling but different meanings, origins, or pronunciations. *Mail,* meaning 'letters', and *mail,* meaning 'armour', are homographs. ⟨< Gk. *homographos* < *homos* same + *graphē* writing⟩ **—ˌho•mo'graph•ic,** *adj.*

ho•moi•o•therm•al [houˌmɔɪə'θɜrməl] *or* [ˌhoumɔɪə'θɜrməl] *adj. Zoology.* warm-blooded.

ho•mo•lo•gize [hə'mɒləˌdʒaɪz] *or* [hou'mɒləˌdʒaɪz] *v.* **-gized, -giz•ing.** make homologous.

ho•mol•o•gous [hə'mɒləgəs] *adj.* **1** corresponding in position, proportion, value, structure, etc. **2** *Biology.* corresponding in type of structure and in origin but not necessarily in function. The wing of a bird and the foreleg of a horse are homologous. **3** *Chemistry.* differing in composition successively by a constant amount of certain constituents, and showing a gradation of chemical and physical properties. **4** *Genetics.* referring to a pair of matching chromosomes. One member of the pair is received from each parent at conception, and one member of the pair is transmitted to each offspring. ⟨< Gk. *homologos* agreeing < *homos* same + *logos* reasoning, relation⟩

hom•o•lo•graph•ic [ˌhɒmələ'græfɪk] *adj.* maintaining the ratio of parts.

hom•o•logue ['hɒməˌlɒg] *n.* **1** a homologous thing, organ, or part. **2** *Genetics.* one of a pair of matching chromosomes.

ho•mol•o•gy [hə'mɒlədʒi] *n., pl.* **-gies. 1** a correspondence or similarity in position, proportion, value, structure, etc. **2** *Biology.* correspondence in type of structure and in origin. **3** *Chemistry.* the relation among compounds forming a homologous series. ⟨< Gk. *homologia* agreement < *homologos.* See HOMOLOGOUS.⟩

ho•mo•morph•ism [ˌhoumə'mɔrˌfɪzəm] *n.* near identity in outward form. **—ˌho•mo'mor•phic** or **ˌho•mo'mor•phous,** *adj.*

hom•o•nym ['hɒməˌnɪm] *n.* **1** HOMOPHONE (def. 1). **2** one of two or more words having the same pronunciation and spelling but different meanings and origins. *Rose,* past tense of the verb *rise,* and *rose,* meaning the flower, are homonyms; homograph. ⟨< L < Gk. *homonymos* < *homos* same + dial. *onyma* name⟩

ho•mon•y•mous [hə'mɒnəməs] *adj.* **1** being homonyms; alike in spelling and/or sound but not in meaning. **2** having, or being called by, the same name.

ho•mo•phile ['houməˌfaɪl] *or* ['hɒməˌfaɪl] *n. or adj.* homosexual.

ho•mo•pho•bia [ˌhoumə'foubiə] *n.* prejudice against homosexuals.

hom•o•phone ['hɒməˌfoun] *or* ['houməˌfoun] *n.* **1** one of two or more words having the same pronunciation but different meanings, origins, and, usually, spellings. *Pear, pair,* and *pare* are homophones. **2** one of two or more letters or symbols having the same sound. The letters *c* and *k* are homophones in the word *cork.* ⟨< Gk. *homophonos* < *homos* same < *phōnē* sound⟩

hom•o•phon•ic [ˌhɒmə'fɒnɪk] *or* [ˌhoumə'fɒnɪk] *adj.* **1** having the same sound. **2** *Music.* **a** in unison. **b** having one part or melody predominating.

ho•moph•o•nous [hə'mɒfənəs] *adj.* homophonic.

ho•moph•o•ny [hə'mɒfəni] *n.* **1** sameness of sound. **2** homophonic music.

ho•mo•pla•sy ['houməˌpleisi] *or* ['houməˌplæsi] *n.* a structural similarity that is purely superficial or due to environment. ⟨< *homo-* + Gk. *plasis* moulding < *plassein* mould⟩

ho•mop•ter•an [hə'mɒptərən] *n., adj.* *—n.* a homopterous insect.
—adj. of or designating the order (Homoptera) comprising these insects.
☛ *Usage.* See note at HETEROPTEROUS.

ho•mop•ter•ous [hə'mɒptərəs] *adj.* of or having to do with an order (Homoptera) of sucking insects that feed on plants, including aphids, cicadas, and scale insects. Most homopterous insects have two pairs of wings, with the front pair of the same thickness throughout, either all leathery or all thin and membranous; the wings at rest are usually sloped upward in a tentlike position over the body. ⟨< *homo-* + Gk. *pteron* wing⟩
☛ *Usage.* See note at HETEROPTEROUS.

Ho•mo sa•pi•ens ['houmou 'seipiənz] *or* ['sæpiənz] the specific name given to modern humans, including all existing races, in the standard biological taxonomy. The species includes extinct types of humans as well, such as Cro-Magnon. ⟨< L *homo sapiens,* literally, man having wisdom⟩

ho•mo•sex•u•al [ˌhoumə'sɛkʃuəl] *or* [ˌhɒmə'sɛkʃuəl] *adj., n.* *—adj.* of, having to do with, or showing sexual desire for one of the same sex. Compare HETEROSEXUAL.
—n. a homosexual person. **—ˌho•mo'sex•u•al•ly,** *adv.*

ho•mo•sex•u•al•i•ty [ˌhouməˌsɛkʃu'æləti] *or* [ˌhɒməˌsɛkʃu'æləti] *n.* the fact or quality of being homosexual.

ho•mos•po•rous [hə'mɒspərəs] *or* [ˌhoumə'spɔrəs] *adj. Botany.* producing one type of spore.

ho•mo•thal•lic [ˌhoumə'θælɪk] *adj. Botany.* in some algae, having male and female reproductive systems.

ho•mo•zy•gote [ˌhoumə'zaɪgout] *n. Genetics.* an individual or genotype having identical alleles at a given place on a pair of homologous chromosomes. ⟨< *homo-* same + Gk. *zygon* yoke⟩

ho•mo•zy•gous [ˌhoumə'zaɪgəs] *adj. Genetics.* of or referring to a homozygote. **—ˌho•mo•zy'gos•i•ty** [ˌhoumouzaɪ'gɒsəti], *n.*

ho•mun•cu•lus [hə'mʌŋkjələs] *n., pl.* **-li** [-ˌlaɪ] *or* [-ˌli] **1** a little person; dwarf. **2** a model of a little person used for demonstrating anatomy, etc. ⟨< L *homunculus,* dim. of *homo* man⟩

hon. 1 honorary. **2** honourable or honorable.

Hon. 1 Honourable. **2** Honorary. **3** Honours.

ho•nan ['hounæn] *or* ['hounɑn] *n.* a fabric made originally from the silk of wild silkworms in Henan, formerly called Honan, a province of China.

hon•don [hɒn'dɒn] *n. Shintoism.* the inner shrine of a temple which worshippers may not enter, and in which the chief treasure of the shrine is housed.

Hon•du•ran [hon'djʊrən] *or* [hɒn'dʊrən] *adj., n.* *—adj.* of or having to do with Honduras.
—n. a native or inhabitant of Honduras.

Hon•du•ras [hɒn'djʊrəs] *or* [hɒn'dʊrəs] *n.* a country in central America, with Pacific and Caribbean coasts.

hone [houn] *n., v.* **honed, hon•ing.** *—n.* a fine-grained whetstone on which to sharpen cutting tools, especially razors.
—v. **1** sharpen on a hone. **2** make more precise, effective, etc. ⟨OE *hān* a stone⟩

hon•est ['ɒnɪst] *adj.* **1** not lying, cheating, or stealing; fair and upright; truthful: *an honest person.* **2** obtained by fair and upright means; without lying, cheating, or stealing: *honest profits.* **3** not hiding one's real nature; frank; open: *honest opposition. I would like your honest opinion.* **4** not mixed with something of less value; genuine; pure: *honest goods.* **5** *Archaic.* chaste; virtuous. ⟨ME < OF < L *honestus* < *honos* honour⟩
—'hon•est•ly, *adv.*

hon•est–to–good•ness ['ɒnɪst tə 'gʊdnɪs] *adj. Informal.* sincere; genuine.

hon•es•ty ['ɒnəsti] *n.* **1** fairness and uprightness. **2** truthfulness. **3** candour, frankness. **4** *Botany.* a garden herb of the mustard family, with large, purple flowers and flat, round, semitransparent, satiny pods, which can be dried as an ornament. **5** *Archaic.* chastity.
☛ *Syn.* **1-3. Honesty,** INTEGRITY = the quality of being honourable and upright in character and actions. **Honesty** emphasizes fairness and uprightness in relations with others, and refusal to steal, lie, cheat, or misrepresent: *He shows honesty in all his business affairs.* **Integrity** applies more directly to character than to actions, and means soundness of character, having very high standards of right and wrong, and refusing to do anything that does not measure up to them: *A woman of integrity can be trusted.*

hon•ey ['hʌni] *n., pl.* **hon•eys;** *v.* **hon•eyed** or **hon•ied, hon•ey•ing.** *—n.* **1** a thick, sweet, liquid that bees make out of the nectar they collect from flowers. **2** any of various substances similar in taste, texture, etc., especially the nectar of flowers. **3** (*adjl.*) of, having to do with, or like honey. **4** sweetness. **5** darling; sweetheart. **6** (*adjl.*) lovable; dear. **7** *Informal.* a person or thing that is very attractive, pleasing, etc.: *He's a honey. That's a honey of a boat.*
—v. **1** sweeten with or as if with honey. **2** talk sweetly (to); flatter. ⟨OE *hunig*⟩ **—'hon•ey,like,** *adj.*

honey badger ratel.

honey bag *Cdn. Slang.* a heavy plastic bag used in an outdoor toilet as a receptacle for human waste.

honey bear kinkajou.

hon•ey•bee ['hʌni,bi] *n.* any of various social bees that produce honey, especially the common hive bee (*Apis mellifera*), widely kept for its honey and wax.

honey bucket *Cdn. Slang.* a bucket or pail used in an outdoor toilet as a receptacle for human waste.

hon•ey•comb ['hʌni,koum] *n., v. —n.* **1** a structure of wax containing rows of six-sided cells made by bees, in which they store honey, pollen, and their eggs. **2** anything like this. **3** (*adjl.*) like a honeycomb: *a honeycomb weave of cloth, a honeycomb pattern in knitting.*
—v. **1** make or decorate in a pattern like a honeycomb. **2** pierce with many holes or tunnels: *The rock was honeycombed with passages.* **3** weaken or harm by spreading through: *That city is honeycombed with crime.* ⟨OE *hunigcamb*⟩

hon•ey•dew ['hʌni,dju] *or* ['hʌni,du] *n.* **1** a sweet substance that oozes from the leaves of certain plants in hot weather. **2** a sweet, sticky substance excreted especially by aphids or scale insects, found as a deposit on the leaves and stems of plants. **3** HONEYDEW MELON.

honeydew melon a variety of muskmelon having sweet, green flesh and a smooth, whitish skin.

hon•eyed or **hon•ied** ['hʌnid] *adj., v. —adj.* **1** sweetened with honey. **2** laden with honey. **3** sweet as honey. **4** smooth; flattering: *honeyed words.*
—v. pt. and pp. of HONEY.

honey locust a tall, thorny North American tree (*Gleditsia triacanthos*) of the pea family having long compound leaves, small, greenish white flowers, and large, flat, reddish brown pods containing a sweet pulp.

hon•ey•moon ['hʌni,mun] *n., v. —n.* **1** the holiday spent together by a newly married couple. **2** the initial period of marriage. **3** the initial period of any new agreement, arrangement, etc., when things are harmonious and peaceful.
—v. spend or have a honeymoon. **—'hon•ey,moon•er,** *n.*

hon•ey•suck•le ['hʌni,sʌkəl] *n.* **1** any of a genus (*Lonicera*) of shrubs or vines found in temperate regions, many of which are cultivated for their showy, often fragrant, tubular flowers. **2** (*adjl.*) designating a family (Caprifoliaceae) of plants, mostly shrubs and vines, found in many parts of the world, but especially in north temperate regions, and including the honeysuckles, elders, and viburnums. **3** any of various plants similar to the honeysuckles, having flowers rich in nectar. ⟨ME *hunisuccle*, dim. of OE *hunisūce* privet, literally, honey-suck < *hunig* honey + *sūcan* suck⟩

hon•ied ['hʌnid] See HONEYED.

honk [hɒŋk] *n., v. —n.* **1** the cry of the wild goose. **2** any similar sound: *the honk of a car horn.*
—v. **1** make the cry of a wild goose or a similar sound. **2** cause to make a sound similar to that of a goose: *to honk a horn.* ⟨imitative⟩

honk•er ['hɒŋkər] *n.* **1** *Cdn. Informal.* CANADA GOOSE. **2** *Slang.* a large nose. **3** any person who or thing that honks.

hon•ky–tonk ['hɒŋki ,tɒŋk] *Slang. n., adj. —n.* **1** a cheap bar or drinking place, especially one playing lowbrow music. **2** a low-class dance hall, night club, etc. **3** the kind of music played there.
—adj. of or having to do with the entertainment or music in a low-class dance hall, etc.: *a honky-tonk piano.* ⟨? imitative of the music typically found there⟩

hon•or ['ɒnər] *n., v.* See HONOUR.

hon•o•rar•i•um [,ɒnə'rɛriəm] *n., pl.* **-rar•i•ums, -rar•i•a** [-'rɛriə] an honorary fee for professional services on which no fixed price is set: *The guest speaker received an honorarium.* ⟨< L *honorarium*, originally neut. of *honorarius* honorary⟩

hon•or•ar•y ['ɒnə,rɛri] *adj.* **1** given or done as an honour: *an honorary degree.* **2** as an honour only; without pay or regular duties. Some associations have honorary secretaries, etc., as well as those who are regularly employed. **3** of an obligation, depending on one's honour for fulfillment, but not enforceable otherwise. ⟨< L *honorarius* < *honos, honour* honour⟩

hon•or•ee [,ɒnə'ri] *n.* the recipient of an honour.

hon•or•if•ic [,ɒnə'rɪfɪk] *adj., n. —adj.* doing or giving honour; showing respect or deference.
—n. **1** a title of respect. *Sir* is an honorific. **2** in some languages, a special form of a word to show respect.

hon•our or **hon•or** ['ɒnər] *n.* **1** glory; fame; renown. **2** credit for acting well; good name: *It was greatly to his honour that he refused the reward.* **3 honours** or **honors,** *pl.* **a** special favours or courtesies. **b** a special mention, grade, or credit given to a student for unusually excellent work. **c** an honours course or degree. **d** *Bridge.* the ace, king, queen, jack, and ten of trumps, or the four aces in no-trump. **4** a source of credit; cause of honour. **5** a clear sense of what is right or proper; sticking to action that is right or that is usual and expected. **6** great respect; high regard: *Our Queen is held in honour. We pay honour to heroes.* **7** an act of respect: *funeral honours.* **8** rank; dignity; distinction: *Knighthood is an honour.* **9 Honour** or **Honor,** a title used in speaking to or of a judge, mayor, etc. **10** chastity; virtue. **11** *Golf.* the privilege of teeing off first, awarded to the player or side winning the previous hole.
do honour or **honor to, a** show honour to; treat with great respect. **b** cause honour to; bring honour to.
do the honours or **honors,** act as host or hostess.
on or **upon** (one's) **honour,** pledged to do what is expected; on the pledge of one's word: *He was on his honour not to divulge the secret.*
—v. **1** respect greatly; regard highly. **2** show respect to. **3** confer dignity upon; be an honour to; favour: *to be honoured by a royal visit.* **4** accept and pay (a bill, draft, note, etc.) when due. ⟨ME < OF < L *honos, honor*⟩ **—'hon•our•er** or **'hon•or•er,** *n.*
☛ *Syn. n.* **5. Honour,** DEFERENCE, HOMAGE = respect shown to someone. **Honour** = respect felt or shown in acknowledgment or appreciation of a person's high character or position or something he or she has done with high courage or ability: *We pay honour to heroes.* **Deference** = respect shown a person, or his or her age or position, by putting his or her wishes or opinions before one's own: *In deference to his mother's wishes, he stopped smoking at the table.* **Homage** applies to honour paid with reverence: *He bowed in homage to the Unknown Soldier.*

hon•our•a•ble or **hon•or•a•ble** ['ɒnərəbəl] *adj.* **1** having or showing a sense of what is right and proper; honest; upright. **2** causing honour; bringing honour to the one that has it; suffered under creditable circumstances. **3** accompanied by honour or honours: *an honourable burial, an honourable discharge.* **4** worthy of honour; to be respected; noble. **5** showing honour or respect. **6** having a title, rank, or position of honour.
—'hon•our•a•ble•ness or **'hon•or•a•ble•ness,** *n.*
—'hon•our•a•bly or **'hon•or•a•bly,** *adv.*

Hon•our•a•ble or **Hon•or•a•ble** ['ɒnərəbəl] *adj.* **1** in Canada, a title given to members of the Privy Council (which includes the Federal Cabinet), to the Speakers of both the House of Commons and the provincial legislative assemblies, and to certain senior judges. **2** in the United Kingdom and elsewhere, a title of respect used under various conditions.

honourable or **honorable mention** a citation given to a competitor who has done well, but not enough for a prize.

honours course or **honors course** **1** a university program of study, usually taking a year or more longer than a general course, offered to superior scholars for specialization in certain major subjects. **2** a school course of advanced studies for certain students.

honours degree or **honors degree** the university degree awarded to candidates successful in an honours course.

honours list or **honors list** **1** a list of persons receiving special honours or recognition. **2** *Esp. Brit.* a list of persons honoured by the sovereign with titles or other distinctions.

honours of war or **honors of war** special favours or courtesies shown to a brave but defeated enemy.

honour system or **honor system** a system of trusting people to obey the rules, pay their fare, etc. without being watched or forced.

hooch [hutʃ] See HOOTCH.

Two types of hood

hood[1] [hʊd] *n., v.* *—n.* **1** a soft, loose covering for the head and neck, either separate or as part of a coat or cloak. **2** anything like a hood in shape or use. **3** a metal covering over the engine of an automobile. **4** *Falconry.* a cover for the head of a hawk, used to blind the hawk when not pursuing game. **5** a fold of cloth worn over an academic gown, having a band or bands of colour to indicate the degree held and the university or college of the wearer. **6** a crest or other part on a bird's or animal's head that suggests a hood in shape, colour, etc. **7** HOOD SEAL.
—v. cover or furnish with a hood. ⟨OE *hōd*⟩ **—'hood•less,** *adj.* **—'hood,like,** *adj.*

hood[2] [hʊd] *n. Slang.* HOODLUM.

-hood *noun-forming suffix.* **1** the state or condition of being: *boyhood, likelihood.* **2** the character or nature of: *adulthood, sainthood.* **3** a group or body of: *priesthood, a sisterhood of noble women.* ⟨OE *-hād* < *hād* state⟩

hood•ed ['hʊdɪd] *adj., v.* *—adj.* **1** having a hood. **2** shaped like a hood. **3** covered with or wearing a hood: *a hooded figure.* **4** of a bird, having a distinctly coloured or crested head.
—v. pt. and pp. of HOOD.

hooded seal a large, grey hair seal (*Cystophora cristata*) of the North Atlantic and Arctic Oceans, the adult males having a large nasal cavity that can be inflated to form a 'hood' on top of the snout. Also (*Cdn.*), **hood seal.**

A hooded seal

hood•lum ['hʊdləm] *n.* *Informal.* **1** a young rowdy; street ruffian. **2** a criminal, especially one who uses force; gangster. ⟨probably < G (Bavarian dial.) *Hodalum, Huddellump*⟩ **—'hood•lum,ism,** *n.*

hoo•doo ['hudu] *n., pl.* **-doos;** *v.* **-dooed, -doo•ing.** *—n.* **1** voodoo. **2** *Cdn. Informal.* a person or thing that brings bad luck. **3** a natural pillar of rock, cemented gravel, or clay caused by erosion and often having a fantastic shape, found in western North America. Hoodoos are common in the Alberta badlands. **4** *Informal.* bad luck.
—v. Informal. bring or cause bad luck to. ⟨? < var. of VOODOO⟩ **—'hoo•doo,ism,** *n.*

hood seal *Cdn.* HOODED SEAL.

hood•wink ['hʊd,wɪŋk] *v.* **1** mislead by a trick; deceive. **2** *Archaic.* blindfold. ⟨< *hood* + *wink,* make one wink (close the eyes) by covering with a hood⟩ **—'hood,wink•er,** *n.*

hoof [huf] *or* [hʊf] *n., pl.* **hoofs** or **hooves;** *v.* *—n.* **1** a hard, horny covering on the feet of horses, cattle, sheep, pigs, and some other animals. See HORSE for picture. **2** the whole foot of such animals. **3** *Slang.* the human foot.
on the hoof, of beef cattle, etc. alive; not killed and butchered.
—v. **1** *Informal.* walk (*often with* **it**). **2** *Slang.* dance (*often with* **it**). **3** strike with the hoof. ⟨OE *hōf*⟩ **—'hoof•less,** *adj.* **—'hoof,like,** *adj.*

hoof•beat ['huf,bit] *or* ['hʊf,bit] *n.* the sound made by an animal's hoofs.

hoof•bound ['huf,baʊnd] *or* ['hʊf,baʊnd] *adj.* of a horse, having a contraction of the hoof because of drying out.

hoofed [huft] *or* [hʊft] *adj., v.* *—adj.* having hoofs.
—v. pt. and pp. of HOOF.

hoof•er ['hufər] *or* ['hʊfər] *n. Slang.* a professional dancer.

hook [hʊk] *n., v.* *—n.* **1** a piece of metal, wood, or other stiff material, curved or having a sharp angle for catching, holding, or fastening something or for hanging things on: *a clothes hook.* **2** a curved piece of wire, usually with a barb at the end, for catching fish: *a fish-hook.* **3** a snare; trap. **4** anything curved or bent like a hook. **5** a large, curved knife for cutting down grass or grain. **6** a sharp bend. **7** a point of land. **8** the act of hooking. **9** *Sports.* the flight of a ball curving across the body of the person propelling it. Compare SLICE (def. 4). **10** *Boxing.* a short, swinging blow. **11** *Hockey.* an instance of hooking. **12** *Music.* a line on the stem of certain notes, indicating time value.
by hook or by crook, in any way at all; by fair means or foul.
get one's hooks into, *Informal.* seize; influence (a person).
get the hook, *Slang.* be dismissed; lose one's job.
hook, line, and sinker, *Informal.* **a** the whole lot. **b** completely.
off the hook, a *Informal.* free of responsibility; out of a predicament. **b** of a telephone, in active use.
on (one's) **own hook,** *Informal.* independently.
—v. **1** attach or fasten with a hook or hooks. **2** catch or take hold of with a hook. **3** catch (fish) with a hook. **4** give the form of a hook to. **5** be curved or bent like a hook. **6** catch by a trick. **7** *Cdn. Informal.* steal. **8** make (rugs, etc.) by pulling loops of yarn or strips of cloth through canvas, burlap, etc. with a hook. **9** *Sports.* hit or throw (a ball) so that it curves across the body of the person propelling it. Compare SLICE (def. 7). **10** *Boxing.* hit with a short, swinging blow. **11** *Hockey.* impede the progress of (a puck-carrier) illegally by catching at his or her body from the side or rear with one's hockey stick.
hook up, a attach or fasten with a hook or hooks. **b** connect (an electric light or appliance), or arrange and connect the parts of (a radio set, telephone, etc.) ⟨OE *hōc*⟩ **—'hook,like,** *adj.*

hook•a ['hʊkə] *or* ['hukɑ] See HOOKAH.

hook•ah ['hʊkə] *or* ['hukɑ] *n.* a tobacco pipe with a long tube by which the smoke is drawn through water for cooling; water pipe. Hookahs are used in Asia. ⟨< Arabic *huqqah* vase, pipe⟩

hook and eye a fastener for a garment, etc., consisting of a loop or bar and a hook that catches on it.

hooked [hʊkt] *adj., v.* *—adj.* **1** curved or bent like a hook. **2** having hooks: *a hooked fastening on a dress.* **3** made with a hook; made by hooking: *A hooked rug is made by pulling yarn or strips of cloth through canvas, etc. with a hook.* **4** *Informal.* addicted, especially to drugs. **5** *Informal.* attached; dating someone, engaged, or married.
—v. pt. and pp. of HOOK.

hook•er[1] ['hʊkər] *n.* **1** a person who or thing that hooks. **2** *Informal.* thief; pilferer. **3** *Cdn.* a drink of straight liquor: *a hooker of whisky.* **4** *Slang.* prostitute.

hook•er[2] ['hʊkər] *n.* **1** a small fishing boat. **2** an old-fashioned or clumsy ship. ⟨apparently < Du. *hoeker, hoekerschip* < *hoek* hook, angle; allusion uncertain⟩

hook•nose ['hʊk,noʊz] *n.* a large nose which curves downwards. **—'hook,nosed,** *adj.*

hook shot *Basketball.* a shot at the basket made from behind the head.

hook•up ['hʊk,ʌp] *n.* **1** the arrangement and connection of the parts of a radio or television set, telephone, broadcasting facilities, etc. **2** facilities for connecting a camper or trailer to water, electricity, etc.

hook•worm ['hʊk,wɜrm] *n.* **1** any of various parasitic roundworms (family Ancylostomatidae) having hooked mouthparts by means of which they attach themselves to the intestinal lining to feed on blood and body fluids. The two species most commonly infesting humans are *Necator americanus* of the S United States and Africa and *Ancylostoma duodenale* of Europe and Asia. **2** infestation with hookworms, producing anemia, fatigue and dullness, malnutrition, etc; **hookworm disease.**

hook•y [hʊki] *n. Cdn.*
play hooky, *Informal.* stay away from school without permission; play truant. ⟨? < Du. *hoekje* hide-and-seek < *hoek* corner⟩

hoo•li•gan ['huləgən] *n. Informal.* one of a gang of street ruffians; hoodlum. ⟨? < an Irish surname⟩

hoo•li•gan•ism ['huləgə,nɪzəm] *n. Informal.* rough, noisy behaviour; lawless fun.

hoop [hup] *n., v.* *—n.* **1** a ring or flat band in the form of a circle: *A hoop holds together the staves of a barrel.* **2** a large wooden, metal, or plastic ring used as a toy: *The boy rolled his hoop along the sidewalk.* **3** a circular frame formerly worn to spread out a woman's skirt. **4** *Croquet.* one of the metal arches through which players try to hit the balls. **5** anything shaped like a hoop.

—*v.* bind or fasten together with a hoop or hoops. ⟨OE *hōp*⟩
—'hoop,like, *adj.*
☛ *Hom.* WHOOP.

hoop•er ['hupər] *n.* a person who makes or repairs hoops on casks, barrels, etc.; cooper.

hoop game *Cdn.* a First Nations game in which a hoop is rolled in such a way as to fall on an arrow slid along the ground just behind it.

hoop•la ['huplɑ] *n. Slang.* **1** uproar; hullabaloo. **2** sensational advertising; ballyhoo. ⟨originally, a coach driver's exclamation⟩

hoo•poe ['hupu] *n.* a bird (*Upupa epops*) of S Europe, Africa, and Asia having pinkish brown plumage with black-and-white wings, a fanlike crest, and a long, downward curving bill. It is the only member of its family (Upupidae). ⟨earlier *hoop* < F *huppe* < L *upupa* (imitative of its cry)⟩

hoop skirt formerly, a woman's skirt worn over a framework of connected flexible hoops making it stand out from the body.

hoo•ray [hə'rei] *interj., n., or v.* hurrah.

hoose•gow ['husgaʊ] *n. Slang.* jail. ⟨< Mexican Sp. *juzgado* tribunal < pp. of *juzgar* to judge⟩

hoot [hut] *n., v.* —*n.* **1** the sound that an owl makes. **2** a sound like that made by an owl: *the hoot of an automobile horn.* **3** a sound to show disapproval or scorn. **4** *Informal.* a tiny amount; a bit (*used only in the negative*): *He doesn't give a hoot what happens. That show wasn't worth a hoot.* **5** *Informal.* something causing laughter: *Her clown costume was a hoot.*
—*v.* **1** make the sound that an owl makes or one like it. **2** show disapproval, scorn, or enjoyment (of) by hooting: *The audience hooted the speaker's words. We hooted with laughter.* **3** force or drive by hooting: *They hooted her off the platform.* **4** say or show by hooting: *They hooted their scorn.* ⟨ME *hute(n)*; ? imitative⟩
—'hoot•er, *n.*

hootch [hutʃ] *n. Cdn.* **1** hootchinoo. **2** *Slang.* any alcoholic liquor, especially cheap whisky. ⟨shortening of HOOTCHINOO⟩

hoo•tchi•noo ['hutʃə,nu] *n. Cdn.* in the Yukon and Alaska, a potent alcoholic liquor distilled illegally. ⟨< *Hootchinoo*, a Native American people of S Alaska < Tlingit *khutsnuwu* (literally, grizzly bear fort)⟩

Hoo•tchi•noo ['hutʃə,nu] *n.* a Tlingit people living on Admiralty Island, in the Arctic.

hoot•chy–koot•chy ['hutʃi 'kutʃi] *n. Slang.* a belly dance.

hoo•te•nan•ny ['hutə,næni] *n., pl.* **-nies.** an informal party or jamboree featuring folk singing. ⟨developed from *hoot*⟩

hooves [huvz] *or* [hʊvz] *n.* a pl. of HOOF.

hop¹ [hɒp] *v.* **hopped, hop•ping;** *n.* —*v.* **1** spring, or move by springing, on one foot. **2** spring, or move by springing, with both or all feet at once: *Many birds hop.* **3** jump over: *to hop a ditch.* **4** *Informal.* get on or in (a train, plane, etc.): *I can just hop a bus and be there in 20 minutes.* **5** move or jump quickly (onto, out of, etc.): *He hopped onto his bicycle and rode off. She hopped off the bus.* **6** *Informal.* fly across in an aircraft.
hop it, *Slang.* depart; go away.
hop to it, *Informal.* be quick; hurry up.
—*n.* **1** a hopping; a spring. **2** *Informal.* a flight in an airplane. **3** *Informal.* a dancing party: *the annual spring hop.* **4** a short trip. ⟨OE *hoppian*⟩

hop² [hɒp] *n., v.* **hopped, hop•ping.** —*n.* **1** a vine (*Humulus lupulus*) of the mulberry family having flower clusters that look like small pine-cones. **2 hops,** *pl.* the dried, ripe flower clusters of the hop vine, used to flavour beer and other malt drinks.
—*v.* **1** pick hops. **2** flavour with hops. ⟨< MDu. *hoppe*⟩

hope [houp] *n., v.* **hoped, hop•ing.** —*n.* **1** an expectation that what one desires will happen. **2** a desire that something believed possible might be the case. **3** a generalized attitude of optimism or confidence about the future. **4** a person or thing in which one places hope: *She is the hope of the family.* **5** something hoped for. **6** *Archaic.* trust; reliance.
—*v.* **1** wish and expect. *She hopes to pass her entrance examination. We have been hoping for fine weather for a week. I hope (that) you like your present.* **2** *Archaic.* trust; rely.
hope against hope, keep on hoping even though there is no good reason to have hope. ⟨OE *hopa*⟩

hope chest a chest in which a young woman collects articles that will be useful after she marries.

hope•ful ['houpfəl] *adj., n.* —*adj.* **1** feeling or showing hope: *a hopeful smile. They were all in a hopeful frame of mind by morning.* **2** giving or inspiring hope: *The lessening of the fever was a hopeful sign.*
—*n.* a person who expects or is likely to achieve something: *The room was filled with young hopefuls waiting for auditions.*
—'hope•ful•ness, *n.*

hope•ful•ly ['houpfəli] *adv.* **1** in a hopeful manner: *I went hopefully to my father.* **2** *Informal.* it is to be hoped: *Hopefully the weather will improve.*
☛ *Usage.* The use of **hopefully** (def. 2) to modify a sentence rather than the actual verb should be avoided in formal writing.

hope•less ['houplıs] *adj.* **1** feeling no hope. **2** giving no hope: *a hopeless illness.* **—'hope•less•ly,** *adv.* **—'hope•less•ness,** *n.*
☛ *Syn.* **1. Hopeless** (def. 1), DESPERATE, DESPAIRING = without hope. **Hopeless** suggests giving up completely: *She had been disappointed so often that she felt hopeless.* **Desperate** suggests a rash hopelessness, being without real hope but willing to run any risk to improve the situation: *The desperate gunman tried to shoot his way out of the trap.* **Despairing** = completely hopeless because unable to think of anything else to do or anywhere else to look for help: *Despairing of saving his business, he shot himself.*

hop•head ['hɒp,hɛd] *n. Slang.* a drug addict.

Ho•pi ['houpi] *n., pl.* **-pis. 1** a member of a Native American Pueblo people living mainly in stone-built towns in N Arizona. **2** the language of this people.

hop•lite ['hɒplɔit] *n.* in ancient Greece, a heavily armed foot soldier. ⟨< Gk. *hoplitēs* < *hopla* arms⟩

hopped–up ['hɒpt 'ʌp] *adj. Slang.* **1** exhilarated; excited. **2** stimulated by drugs; high. **3** of engines, supercharged.

hop•per ['hɒpər] *n.* **1** a person or thing that hops. **2** a grasshopper or other hopping insect. **3** a container, usually funnel-shaped, into which grain, corn, etc. is poured in order to be fed evenly into another container or a machine for grinding, mixing, etc.: *Some cement mixers are equipped with hoppers.* **4** Also, **hopper car,** a freight car used for transporting grain.

hop•scotch ['hɒp,skɒtʃ] *n.* a children's game in which the players hop over the lines of a figure drawn on the ground. ⟨< *hop¹* + *scotch* a scratch, line⟩

ho•ra ['hɔrə] *n.* **1** a Romanian and Israeli folk dance with a lively, syncopated rhythm. **2** the music for such a dance. ⟨< Mod. Hebrew *horah*, ult. < Turkish⟩

ho•ra•ry ['hɔrəri] *adj.* **1** indicating an hour. **2** lasting an hour. **3** occurring every hour. ⟨< Med.L *horarius* < L *hora* hour⟩

Ho•ra•tian [hə'reiʃən] *adj.* of, like, or having to do with the Roman poet and satirist Horace (65-8 B.C.) or his poetry.

Ho•ra•tius [hə'reiʃəs] *n. Roman legend.* a Roman hero who held back an invading Etruscan army until a bridge behind him was destroyed.

horde [hɔrd] *n., v.* —*n.* **1** a crowd; swarm. **2** a wandering group or troop: *Hordes of Mongols and Turks invaded Europe during the Middle Ages.*
—*v.* gather in a horde; live in a horde. ⟨< F < G < Polish < Turkish *ordu* camp⟩
☛ *Hom.* HOARD.

hore•hound ['hɔr,haʊnd] *n.* **1** a tall, Eurasian perennial herb (*Marrubium vulgare*) of the mint family having small white flowers and downy leaves. Also called **white horehound. 2** an extract from the leaves or flowers of this plant, used as a flavouring and also formerly in medicine. **3** candy or cough medicine flavoured with this extract. **4** a Eurasian perennial herb (*Ballota nigra*), also of the mint family, having purple flowers and hairy leaves and an unpleasant smell. Also called **black horehound.** Also, **hoarhound.** ⟨OE *hārhūne* < *hār* hoar + *hūne*, the name of a plant⟩

ho•ri•zon [hə'raızən] *n.* **1** the line where the earth and sky seem to meet. You cannot see beyond the horizon. **2** Usually, **horizons,** *pl.* the limit of one's thinking, experience, interest, or outlook. **3** the actual or imaginary horizontal line in perspective drawing, etc., toward which receding parallel lines converge. It represents the eye level of the observer. See VANISHING POINT for picture. **4** *Geology.* a distinct layer or group of layers of rock or soil. ⟨ME < OF *orizonte* < L < Gk. *horizōn (kyklos)* bounding (circle), ult. < *horos* limit⟩ **—ho'ri•zon•less,** *adj.*

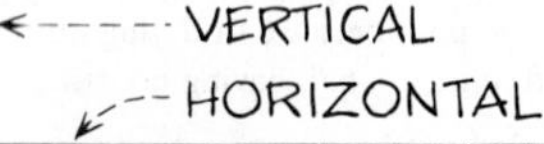

hor•i•zon•tal [,hɔrə'zɒntəl] *adj., n.* —*adj.* **1** parallel to the horizon; at right angles to a vertical line. **2** flat; level: *You need a horizontal surface to work on.* **3** placed, acting, or working wholly or mainly in a horizontal direction: *A helicopter has horizontal*

rotors. **4** of or having to do with the horizon; on, at, or near the horizon. **5** so organized as to include only one stage in production or one group of people or trades: *a horizontal union, horizontal trusts.*
—*n.* something that is horizontal, such as a line, plane, direction, or position. **—,hor•i'zon•tal•ly,** *adv.*

horizontal bar *Gymnastics.* a bar hung horizontally at some distance above the floor for chinning and other exercises.

horizontal union a labour union including people from one specific trade or craft.

hor•mone ['hɔrmoun] *n.* **1** *Physiology.* a substance formed in certain parts of the body, which enters the bloodstream and influences the activity of some organ. Adrenalin and insulin are hormones. **2** *Botany.* a substance carried in the sap of plants that acts similarly. **3** a synthetic substance that has the effect of a hormone. ⟨< Gk. *hormōn* setting in motion, ult. < *hormē* impulse⟩ **—hor'mo•nal,** *adj.*

horn [hɔrn] *n., v.* —*n.* **1** a hard growth, usually curved and pointed, on the heads of cattle, sheep, goats, and certain other animals. **2** one of a pair of branching growths on the head of a deer, which fall off and grow afresh each year. **3** the tough fibrous material that horns are made of. A person's fingernails, the beaks of birds, the hoofs of horses, and tortoise shells are all made of horn. **4** anything that sticks up on the head of an animal: *a snail's horns, an insect's horns.* **5** something made, or formerly made, of horn. **6** a container made by hollowing out a horn: *a drinking horn, a powder horn.* **7** (*adjl.*) made of horn. **8** a musical instrument shaped like a horn and formerly made of horn, sounded by blowing into the smaller end: *The brass section of an orchestra includes several kinds of horn.* **9** *Jazz.* any wind instrument. **10** a device sounded as a warning signal: *a foghorn, an automobile horn.* **11** *Informal.* the telephone: *He's been on the horn all morning.* **12** anything that projects like a horn or is shaped like a horn: *a saddle horn, the horn of a bay.* See SADDLE for picture. **13** either pointed tip of a new or old moon, or of some other crescent.
blow (one's) **own horn,** speak in praise of oneself.
draw or **pull in** (one's) **horns, a** restrain oneself. **b** back down; withdraw.
lock horns, engage in conflict (*with*).
on the horns of a dilemma, having two unpleasant choices, one of which must be taken.
—*v.* **1** hit or wound with horns; gore. **2** furnish with horns.
horn in, *Slang.* meddle or intrude: *She kept trying to horn in on our conversation.* ⟨OE⟩ **—'horn•less,** *adj.* **—'horn,like,** *adj.*

horn•beam ['hɔrn,bim] *n.* **1** any of various trees of the genus (*Carpinus*) of the birch family found in north temperate regions, having smooth, grey bark and very hard white wood. **2** the wood of any of these trees.

horn•bill ['hɔrn,bɪl] *n.* any of a tropical Old World family (Bucerotidae) of birds having a large bill which in some species has a bony lump, or casque, on the top of it.

horn•blende ['hɔrn,blɛnd] *n.* a common black, dark green, or brown mineral found in granite and other rocks. ⟨< F⟩

horn•book ['hɔrn,bʊk] *n.* **1** a page with the alphabet, etc. on it, covered with a sheet of transparent horn and fastened in a frame with a handle, formerly used in teaching children to read. **2** an elementary treatise.

horned [hɔrnd] *adj., v.* —*adj.* having a horn or horns.
—*v.* pt. and pp. of HORN.

horned lark a brown-and-white lark (*Eremophila alpestris*) found throughout much of the northern hemisphere, having a black head and throat patches and small black tufts of feathers on either side of the head, resembling horns. The horned lark is found in open terrain throughout Canada, from the Arctic tundra south.

horned toad any of several small, insect-eating lizards (genus *Phrynosoma*) of North America, having a broad, flat body, short tail, and many spines on the back and tail.

hor•net ['hɔrnɪt] *n.* any of several large wasps (family Vespidae), mostly dark-coloured with white or yellow markings, that live in colonies above ground, in large roundish nests made of a papery material. Hornets often build their nests under the eaves of buildings. ⟨OE *hyrnet(u)*; form influenced by E *horn*⟩

hornet's nest trouble in store; a situation likely to be troublesome.
stir up a hornet's nest, cause an outburst or angry reaction.

horn–mad ['hɔrn'mæd] *adj.* furious.

horn of plenty CORNUCOPIA (def. 2).

horn•pipe ['hɔrn,pəip] *n.* **1** a lively dance done by one person, formerly popular among sailors. **2** the music for it. **3** a musical wind instrument consisting of a wooden pipe with a bell-shaped end, used to accompany this dance.

horn silver SILVER CHLORIDE.

horn•swog•gle ['hɔrn,swɒgəl] *v.* **-gled, -gling.** swindle; cheat.

horn•tail ['hɔrn,teil] *n.* a female insect of the family Siricidae, having an extended ovipositor.

horn•worm ['hɔrn,wɜrm] *n.* the caterpillar of a hawk moth, having a smooth body and a hornlike projection at the back end.

horn•y ['hɔrni] *adj.* **horn•i•er, horn•i•est. 1** made of horn or a substance like it. **2** hard like horn: *The farmer's hands were horny from work.* **3** having a horn or horns. **4** *Slang.* sexually eager or excited; randy. **—'horn•i•ness,** *n.*

hor•o•loge ['hɔrə,loudʒ] *or* ['hɔrə,lɒdʒ] *n.* a timepiece; clock, sundial, hourglass, etc. ⟨ME < OF *orloge* < L < Gk. *hōrologion* < *hōra* hour + *-logos* -telling⟩

ho•rol•o•gist [hɔ'rɒlədʒɪst] *n.* a person skilled in horology, especially one whose work it is. Also, **horologer.**

Ho•ro•lo•gi•um [,hɔrə'loudʒiəm] *n.* a constellation in the southern hemisphere, near Eridanus.

ho•rol•o•gy [hɔ'rɒlədʒi] *n.* **1** the science of measuring time. **2** the art of making timepieces. ⟨< Gk. *hōra* time + E *-logy*⟩ **—,ho•ro'log•i•cal,** *adj.*

hor•o•scope ['hɔrə,skoup] *n. Astrology.* **1** the position of the planets and stars relative to each other at the hour of a person's birth, regarded as influencing his or her life. **2** a diagram of the heavens at given times, used in telling fortunes by the planets and the stars. **3** a fortune told by this means.
cast a horoscope, discover the influence that the stars and planets are supposed to have upon a person's life. ⟨< L < Gk. *hōroskopos* < *hōra* time + *skopos* watcher⟩ **—,ho•ro'scop•ic** [-'skɒpɪk], *adj.*

ho•ros•co•py [hɔ'rɒskəpi] *n.* **1** the practice of casting horoscopes. **2** the position of the planets, especially at a person's birth.

hor•ren•dous [hə'rɛndəs] *adj.* horrible; terrible; frightful. ⟨< L *horrendus*⟩ **—hor'ren•dous•ly,** *adv.*

hor•ri•ble ['hɔrəbəl] *adj.* **1** causing horror; terrible; dreadful; frightful; shocking: *a horrible crime, a horrible disease.* **2** *Informal.* extremely unpleasant or annoying: *a horrible noise.* ⟨ME < OF < L *horribilis* < *horrere* bristle⟩ **—'hor•ri•ble•ness,** *n.* **—'hor•ri•bly,** *adv.*
☛ *Syn.* **1.** See note at GHASTLY.

hor•rid ['hɔrɪd] *adj.* **1** terrible; frightful. **2** *Informal.* very unpleasant: *a horrid little boy, a horrid day.* ⟨< L *horridus*⟩ **—'hor•rid•ly,** *adv.* **—'hor•rid•ness,** *n.*

hor•rif•ic [hɔ'rɪfɪk] *adj.* producing horror; horrifying.

hor•ri•fy ['hɔrə,faɪ] *v.* **-fied, -fy•ing. 1** cause to feel horror. **2** *Informal.* shock very much. ⟨< L *horrificare*⟩ **—,hor•ri•fi'ca•tion,** *n.*

hor•rip•i•late [hɔ'rɪpə,leit] *v.* **-lat•ed, -lat•ing.** experience or cause to experience horripilation. ⟨< L *horripilare* < *horrere* bristle + *pilus* hair⟩

hor•rip•i•la•tion [hɔ,rɪpə'leiʃən] *n.* GOOSE FLESH.

hor•ror ['hɔrər] *n.* **1** a shivering, shaking fear and dislike; terror and disgust caused by something frightful or shocking. **2** a very strong dislike; very great disgust. **3** the quality of causing horror. **4** a cause of horror. **5** *Informal.* something very bad or unpleasant. **6 the horrors,** *Informal.* **a** a fit of horror, as in delirium tremens. **b** extreme depression; the blues. ⟨ME < OF < L *horror* < *horrere* bristle⟩

hor•ror–struck ['hɔrər ,strʌk] *adj.* affected by horror; horrified. Also, **horror-stricken.**

hors concours [ɔr kən'kur]; *French,* [ɔʀkɔ̃'kuʀ] in a class by itself. ⟨literally, out (of the) contest⟩

hors de com•bat [ɔʀdəkɔ̃'ba] *French.* out of the fight; disabled.

hors d'oeu•vre [,ɔr 'dɜrv]; *French,* [ɔʀ'dœvʀ] *pl.* **hors d'oeu•vres** [,dɜrvz]; *French,* ['dœvʀ] a relish or light food served before the regular courses of a meal: *Olives, celery, anchovies, etc. are often served as hors d'oeuvres.* ⟨< F *hors d'œuvre*, literally, apart from (the main) work⟩

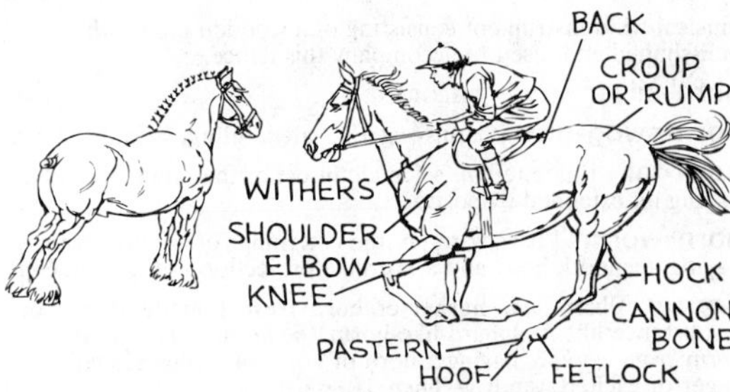

Horses: a draft horse and a racehorse

horse [hɔrs] *n., pl.* **hors•es** or *(esp. collectively)* **horse;** *v.* **horsed, hors•ing.** *—n.* **1** a large, four-legged animal (*Equus caballus*) with solid hoofs and a mane and tail of long, coarse hair. Horses have been used from very early times for riding and for carrying and pulling loads. **2** a full-grown male horse. **3** (*adjl.*) designating a family (Equidae) of hoofed mammals, including the living and extinct horses, the ass, onager, and zebras. **4** *Zoology.* any member of the horse family. **5** (*adjl.*) of or having to do with horses. **6** soldiers on horses; cavalry: *a troop of horse.* **7** (*adjl.*) on horses. **8** *Gymnastics.* a piece of gymnasium apparatus to jump or vault over. **9** a frame with legs to support something; trestle.
a horse of a different colour, something different.
back the wrong horse, forecast inaccurately.
hold (one's) **horses,** *Informal.* restrain oneself: *Hold your horses till we get there.*
look a gift horse in the mouth, be ungrateful.
on (one's) **high horse,** *Informal.* behaving in an arrogant or pretentious way: *He got up on his high horse and said he wasn't used to being treated that way.*
the horse's mouth, the original source; a well-informed source: *news straight from the horse's mouth.*
to horse! mount horses! get on horseback!
—v. **1** provide with a horse or horses. **2** put, carry, or go on horseback. **3** *Slang.* perform boisterously, as a part or a scene in a play.
horse around, *Slang.* **a** fool around; get into mischief. **b** engage in horseplay. ⟨OE *hors*⟩
☛ *Hom.* HOARSE.

horse–and–bug•gy ['hɔrs ən 'bʌgi] *adj.* outdated; old-fashioned: *horse-and-buggy ideas.*

horse•back ['hɔrs,bæk] *n., adv. —n.* **1** the back of a horse. **2** a ridge; hogback.
—adv. on the back of a horse.

horse•boat ['hɔrs,bout] *n.* formerly, a kind of ferry boat propelled by a paddle wheel that was turned by horses walking a treadmill on the boat. Horseboats were used in Canada in the 19th century.

horse•car ['hɔrs,kɑr] *n.* **1** a streetcar pulled by a horse or horses. **2** a car used for transporting horses.

horse chestnut **1** a large tree (*Aesculus hippocastanium*) native to Europe and Asia, widely used in North America for ornament and shade, having showy spikes of white flowers and leaves made up of leaflets radiating out from the tip of the leaf stalk. The shiny brown seeds of the horse chestnut resemble chestnuts, but they are bitter and poisonous. **2** the nut of this tree. **3** (*adjl.*) designating the family (Hippocastanaceae) of trees and shrubs that includes the horse chestnut and the buckeyes.

horse•draw•ing ['hɔrs,drɒɪŋ] *n.* a contest in which horses or teams of horses draw increasingly heavier loads on a stoneboat until all but the strongest are eliminated. Also, **horsehauling.**

horse–drawn ['hɔrs ,drɒn] *adj.* pulled by a horse or horses.

horse•flesh ['hɔrs,flɛʃ] *n.* **1** horses for riding, driving, and racing. **2** meat from horses.

horse•fly ['hɔrs,flaɪ] *n., pl.* **-flies.** any of a family (Tabanidae) of large, two-winged flies that suck the blood of horses, cattle, etc.

horse gentian feverwort.

horse•hair ['hɔrs,hɛr] *n.* **1** the hair from the mane or tail of a horse. **2** a stiff fabric made of this hair. **3** (*adjl.*) made of or stuffed with horsehair: *a horsehair sofa.*

horse•haul•ing ['hɔrs,hɒlɪŋ] *n.* horsedrawing.

horse•hide ['hɔrs,haɪd] *n.* **1** the hide of a horse. **2** leather made from this hide.

horse latitudes two regions where there is often very calm weather and that extend around the world at about 30° north and 30° south of the equator.

horse laugh *Informal.* a loud, boisterous laugh; guffaw.

horse•leech ['hɔrs,litʃ] *n.* **1** any of several large leeches (genus *Haemopis*) formerly thought to attach themselves to the mouths of horses as they drank. **2** *Archaic.* veterinarian.

horse•less ['hɔrslɪs] *adj.* **1** without a horse. **2** not requiring a horse; self-propelled: *Automobiles used to be called horseless carriages.*

horse•man ['hɔrsmən] *n., pl.* **-men. 1** a man who rides on horseback. **2** a man skilled in riding or managing horses. **3** *Cdn. Slang.* a member of the Royal Canadian Mounted Police. **4** *Cdn. West.* a rancher who raises horses.

horse•man•ship ['hɔrsmən,ʃɪp] *n.* the art of riding on horseback; skill in riding or managing horses.

horse•meat ['hɔrs,mit] *n.* the meat or flesh of a horse, especially when used for food.

horse opera *Slang.* a motion picture, radio or television drama, etc. about cowboys, horses, etc.; a western.

horse pistol a large pistol formerly carried by horsemen.

horse•play ['hɔrs,pleɪ] *n.* rough, boisterous play.

horse•pow•er ['hɔrs,paʊər] *n.* a unit of power equal to 746 W, used for measuring the power of engines, motors, etc. One horsepower is about three-quarters of a kilowatt; therefore, a 40 hp outboard motor would be about equal to a 30 kW outboard motor. *Symbol*: hp

horse•pow•er–hour ['hɔrs,paʊər ,aʊr] a unit of energy or work performed in one hour by a device producing one horsepower.

horse•rad•ish ['hɔrs,rædɪʃ] *n.* **1** a tall perennial herb (*Armoracia rusticana*) of the mustard family native to Europe and Asia, but widely cultivated for its pungent, thick, white root. **2** the root of this plant or a condiment made from it, used especially with beef.

horse sense *Informal.* common sense; plain, practical good sense.

horse•shoe ['hɔrs,ʃu] *or* ['hɔrʃ,u] *n., v.* **-shoed, -shoe•ing.** *—n.* **1** a U-shaped metal plate nailed to a horse's hoof to protect it. **2** anything shaped like a horseshoe: *a horseshoe of flowers.* **3 horseshoes,** a game in which the players try to throw horseshoes over or near a stake 12 m away (*used with a singular verb*).
—v. put a horseshoe or horseshoes on.

horseshoe crab **1** any of a genus (*Limulus*) of marine arthropods (order Xiphosura) found in shallow water along the east coasts of North America and Asia, having a body covered by a broad, rounded, domed carapace, and a long, slender spinelike tail. **2** any of various other living or extinct arthropods of the same order.

horse's neck a non-alcoholic drink containing ginger ale and ice, with fruit garnishes.

horse•tail ['hɔrs,teil] *n.* **1** any of a genus (*Equisetum*) of rushlike, perennial, flowerless plants having hollow, jointed stems surrounded by whorls of scalelike leaves. Horsetails are the only living members of the class Sphenopsida and belong to the same plant division as ferns and club mosses. **2** a horse's tail. **3** formerly, a stylized horsetail used as the emblem of a pasha in the Ottoman Empire.

horse trade **1** dealing in horses. **2** a transaction with vigorous bargaining.

horse trader **1** a buyer or seller of horses. **2** a shrewd negotiator.

horse•weed ['hɔrs,wid] *n.* a North American weed (*Erigeron canadensis*) of the composite family, having clusters of greenish white flowers.

horse•whip ['hɔrs,wɪp] *n., v.* **-whipped, -whip•ping.** *—n.* a whip for driving or controlling horses.
—v. beat with a horsewhip.

horse•wom•an ['hɔrs,wʊmən] *n., pl.* **-wom•en. 1** a woman who rides on horseback. **2** a woman skilled in riding or managing horses.

horst [hɔrst] *n. Geology.* a block of the earth's crust between two faults. ⟨< G, literally, thicket⟩

hors•y ['hɔrsi] *adj.* **hors•i•er, hors•i•est. 1** of, like, or having to do with horses. **2** fond of horses or horse racing. **3** dressing or talking like people who spend much time with horses. **4** *Slang.* large and awkward in appearance. Also, **horsey. —'hors•i•ly,** *adv.* **—'hors•i•ness,** *n.*

hort. horticulture; horticultural.

hor•ta•tive ['hɔrtətɪv] *adj., n. —adj.* tending to exhort or encourage; hortatory.
—n. an exhortation. **—'hor•ta•tive•ly,** *adv.*

hor•ta•to•ry ['hɔrtə,tɔri] *adj.* serving to urge or encourage; giving advice; exhorting. ⟨< LL *hortatorius* < L *hortari* exhort⟩

hor•ti•cul•tur•al [,hɔrtə'kʌltʃərəl] *adj.* of or having to do with horticulture. **—,hor•ti'cul•tur•al•ly,** *adv.*

hor•ti•cul•ture ['hɔrtə,kʌltʃər] *n.* the cultivation of flowers, fruits, vegetables, etc. ⟨< L *hortus* garden + E *culture*⟩

hor•ti•cul•tur•ist [,hɔrtə'kʌltʃərɪst] *n.* a person trained in horticulture, especially one whose work it is.

Ho•rus ['hɔrəs] *n.* a sun god of ancient Egypt, son of Osiris and Isis. Horus was represented as having the head of a hawk.

ho•san•na [hou'zænə] *interj. or n.* **1** a shout of praise to the Lord. **2** a shout of praise, adoration, etc. ⟨< LL < Gk. < Hebrew *hoshi'ahnna* save now, we pray⟩

hose [houz] *n.pl.* (defs. 1 and 2), *n.sing., pl.* **hos•es** (def. 3); *v.* **hosed, hos•ing.** *—n.* **1** stockings or socks. **2** an outer garment formerly worn by men, extending from the waist to the knees or to the toes and covering each leg separately. Hose were attached to the doublet by laces or ribbons called points. **3** a tube made of rubber, plastic, canvas, or other material that will bend, used to carry water or other liquids for short distances.
—v. **1** put water on with a hose (*often used with* **down**): *She hosed down the lawn furniture.* **2** *Slang.* get the better of, especially by unfair means; cheat: *He said the team was tired of being hosed by the officials in the league.* ⟨OE *hosa*⟩

ho•sen ['houzən] *n.* archaic pl. of HOSE (defs. 1 and 2).

ho•ser ['houzər] *Cdn. Slang.* a Canadian.

ho•sier ['houʒər] *n.* a person who makes or sells hosiery.

ho•sier•y ['houʒəri] *n.* **1** hose; stockings. **2** the business of a hosier.

hos•pice ['hɒspɪs] *n.* **1** a house where travellers can lodge, especially such a house kept by monks. **2** an institution providing homelike care for the terminally ill. ⟨< F < L *hospitium* < *hospes, -pitis* guest, host[1]⟩

hos•pi•ta•ble ['hɒspətəbəl] *or* [hə'spɪtəbəl] *adj.* **1** giving or liking to give a welcome, food and shelter, and friendly treatment to guests or strangers: *a hospitable family, etc.* **2** willing and ready to consider; favourably receptive or open: *a person hospitable to new ideas.* **3** showing hospitality: *a hospitable reception.* ⟨ME < L *hospitari* stay as a guest < *hospes, -pitis* guest, host[1]⟩ **—'hos•pi•ta•ble•ness,** *n.* **—'hos•pi•ta•bly,** *adv.*

hos•pi•tal ['hɒspətəl] *n.* **1** a place where sick or injured people are treated and cared for. **2** a similar place for sick or injured animals.
in the hospital or (*esp. Brit*) **in hospital,** in a hospital as a patient: *Two of the accident victims are in the hospital with serious injuries.* ⟨ME < OF < Med.L *hospitale* inn, sing. of L *hospitalia* guest rooms, *ult.* < *hospes, -pitis* guest, host[1]. Doublet of HOSTEL, HOTEL.⟩

Hos•pi•tal•er ['hɒspətələr] See HOSPITALLER.

hos•pi•tal•i•ty [,hɒspə'tæləti] *n., pl.* **-ties. 1** friendly, generous reception and treatment of guests or strangers. **2** (*adjl.*) of the hotel business: *the hospitality industry.* ⟨< L *hospitalitas* < *hospes* guest, host[1]⟩

hospitality suite *Cdn.* at a convention, conference, etc., a room or suite where free refreshments are offered, especially alcoholic drinks.

hos•pi•tal•ize ['hɒspɪtə,laɪz] *v.* **-ized, -iz•ing.** put in a hospital to be treated or cared for. **—,hos•pi•tal•i'za•tion,** *n.*

Hos•pi•tal•ler or **Hos•pi•tal•er** ['hɒspətələr] *n.* **1** a member of a military religious order, the Knights of the Hospital of St. John of Jerusalem (also called Knights Hospitallers), founded by crusaders in the 11th century to care for the sick. **2** a member of any religious order founded to take care of the sick, or for other charitable purposes.

hoss [hɒs] *n. Dialect.* horse.
☛ *Hom.* HAWSE.

host[1] [houst] *n., v. —n.* **1** a person who receives another at his or her house or entertains another as his or her guest. **2** the keeper of an inn or hotel. **3** a country or city staging an event such as the Olympic Games. **4** one who conducts a talk show on radio or television. **5** *Biology.* a plant or animal in or on which a parasite lives: *The oak tree is the host of the mistletoe that grows on it.*
reckon without (one's) **host, a** overlook the chances of one's plans going wrong. **b** calculate one's bill or score without consulting the host or landlord.
—v. act as host (to or at). ⟨ME < OF < L *hospes, -pitis* guest, host⟩ **—'host•less,** *adj.*

host[2] [houst] *n.* **1** a large number; multitude: *A host of stars glittered in the sky.* **2** *Archaic.* army. ⟨ME < OF < LL *hostis* army < L *hostis* enemy (originally, stranger)⟩

Host [houst] *n. Roman Catholic Church.* the bread or wafer used in the Mass. ⟨ME < OF *oiste* < L *hostia* animal sacrificed; form influenced by *host[1]*⟩

hos•tage ['hɒstɪdʒ] *n.* **1** a person given up to another or held by an enemy as a pledge that certain promises, agreements, etc. will be carried out. **2** the state or condition of such a person. **3** a pledge; security.
give hostages to fortune, have persons or things that one may lose, such as children. ⟨ME < OF *hostage, ostage* status of guest, status of hostage, *hostage* < *oste* guest < L *hospes, -pitis*⟩

hos•tel ['hɒstəl] *n.* **1** a lodging place, especially a supervised lodging place for young travellers, students, or the homeless. **2** an inn; hotel. **3** *Cdn.* especially formerly, a residential boarding school for Inuit or First Nations children attending school away from home. ⟨ME < OF *hostel, ostel* < Med.L *hospitale* inn. Doublet of HOSPITAL, HOTEL.⟩
☛ *Hom.* HOSTILE.

hos•tel•ry ['hɒstəlri] *n., pl.* **-ries.** an inn; hotel.

hostel school *Cdn. North.* RESIDENTIAL SCHOOL.

hos•tile ['hɒstaɪl] *or* ['hɒstəl] *adj.* **1** of or having to do with an enemy or enemies: *the hostile army.* **2** opposed; unfriendly: *a hostile look.* **3** unfavourable; harsh: *a hostile climate.* ⟨< L *hostilis* < *hostis* enemy⟩ **—'hos•tile•ly,** *adv.*
☛ *Syn.* **2. Hostile,** UNFRIENDLY, INIMICAL = not friendly or favourable. **Hostile,** describing people or things, emphasizes being opposed, either actively unfriendly in purpose or spirit or openly acting against a person or thing: *Their hostile looks showed that he was unwelcome.* **Unfriendly** places less emphasis on active ill will, and suggests being unwilling to be agreeable, kindly, helpful, or encouraging in any way: *A cold, damp climate is unfriendly to tuberculosis.* **Inimical,** a formal word meaning 'hostile', particularly suggests having harmful effects: *Jealousy is inimical to friendship.*
☛ *Hom.* HOSTEL ['hɒstəl].

hos•til•i•ty [hɒ'stɪləti] *n., pl.* **-ties. 1** the feeling that an enemy has; the state of being an enemy; unfriendliness. **2** the state of being at war. **3** opposition; resistance. **4** a hostile act. **5 hostilities,** *pl.* acts of war; warfare; fighting.

hos•tler ['hɒslər] *or* ['ɒslər] *n.* a person who takes care of horses at an inn or stable. Also, **ostler.** ⟨var. of *ostler* < OF *hostelier* < *hostel.* See HOSTEL.⟩

hot [hɒt] *adj.* **hot•ter, hot•test;** *adv., v.* **hot•ted, hot•ting.**
—adj. **1** much warmer than the body; having much heat: *That fire is hot.* **2** having a relatively high temperature: *This food is too hot to eat.* **3** giving or capable of giving a feeling of bodily heat: *a hot flush. This coat is too hot for summer wear.* **4** feeling uncomfortable due to heat: *I'm too hot to sit in the sun.* **5** spicy: *This chili is too hot for me.* **6** full of any strong feeling; passionate, violent, angry, etc.: *hot with rage.* **7** full of great interest or enthusiasm; very eager. **8** intense; violent: *a hot fight.* **9** of a colour, bright and glowing: *hot red.* **10** new; fresh: *a hot scent or trail.* **11** near or approaching an object or answer sought. **12** following closely: *in hot pursuit.* **13** radioactive: *hot debris left by a nuclear explosion.* **14** electrically charged. **15** of jazz, played with exciting variations from the score. **16** *Slang.* obtained illegally; stolen: *hot diamonds.* **17** *Slang.* wanted by the police. **18** *Informal.* likely to win or succeed; difficult to beat, stop, or hinder: *a hot favourite, a hot team.* **19** *Slang.* **a** very fashionable. **b** excellent. **20** *Cdn. Mining slang.* characterized by rich ore finds; potentially rich in minerals: *a hot mineral area.*
hot under the collar, very angry.
make it hot for, *Informal.* make trouble for; make things unpleasant or uncomfortable for.
—adv. in a hot manner: *The sun beats hot upon the sand.*
blow hot and cold, waver in mind or opinion; vacillate.
—v.
hot up, a become intense: *as the situation hots up.* **b** make intense: *hot up the dramatic force of the play.* ⟨OE *hāt*⟩ **—'hot•ly,** *adv.* **—'hot•ness,** *n.*

hot air *Slang.* empty, pompous talk or writing.

hot•bed ['hɒt,bɛd] *n.* **1** a bed of earth covered with glass and kept warm for the growing of plants. **2** any place favourable to rapid growth: *These slums are a hotbed of crime.*

hot•blood•ed ['hɒt'blʌdɪd] *adj.* **1** easily excited or angered. **2** rash; reckless. **3** passionate.

hot•box ['hɒt,bɒks] *n.* an overheated bearing on a shaft or axle.

hot cake a flapjack or pancake.
go or **sell like hot cakes, a** be sold quickly. **b** be in great demand.

hotch•pot ['hɒtʃ,pɒt] *n. Law.* the collection and assessment of all property to make sure that the heirs get an equal distribution. ⟨See HODGEPODGE⟩

hotch•potch ['hɒtʃ,pɒtʃ] *n.* hodgepodge.

hot cross bun a bun marked with a cross, eaten during Lent, especially on Good Friday.

hot dog 1 a sandwich made of a hot wiener enclosed in a long roll and usually served with mustard, relish, etc. **2** wiener.

hot–dog ['hɒt ,dɒg] *v.* **-dogged, -dog•ging.** do stunts while skiing or surfing. **—'hot-,dog•ger,** *n.*

ho•tel [hou'tɛl] *n.* **1** a building where rooms may be rented and meals bought on a day-to-day basis. **2** *Cdn. Informal.* a place where beer and wine are sold for drinking on the premises; beer parlour. ⟨< F *hôtel* < OF *hostel* < Med.L *hospitale* inn. Doublet of HOSPITAL, HOSTEL.⟩

hô•tel de ville [otɛldə'vil] *French.* city hall; town hall.

ho•tel•ier [hou'tɛljei], [hou'tɛljər], *or* [,houtə'lir]; *French,* [otəl'je] *n.* the owner or manager of a hotel.

hot•foot ['hɒt,fʊt] *adv., v. Informal. —adv.* in great haste: *She went hotfoot up the stairs with me after her.*
—v. go in great haste; hurry (*usually used with* **it**): *We hotfooted it out to the airport.*

hot•head ['hɒt,hɛd] *n.* a hot-headed person.

hot–head•ed ['hɒt ,hɛdɪd] *adj.* **1** having a fiery temper; easily angered. **2** impetuous; rash. **—'hot-,head•ed•ly,** *adv.* **—'hot-,head•ed•ness,** *n.*

hot•house ['hɒt,hʌus] *n.* **1** a greenhouse that is heated for growing plants out of season or for growing tropical plants in a colder climate. **2** (*adjl.*) grown in a hothouse: *hothouse tomatoes.* **3** any overly sheltered environment. **4** (*adjl.*) needing nurturing or careful handling, as if in a hothouse; delicate or sensitive: *She's no hothouse creature.*

hot–line or **hot•line** ['hɒt ,laɪn] *n.* **1** a direct means of communication for use in emergencies, especially between heads of state of different countries. **2** (*adjl.*) of, having to do with, or being a radio or television show which broadcasts the comments of members of the public who phone in to express their views, especially on a controversial subject. **3** a hot-line radio or television show.

hot–lin•er or **hot•lin•er** ['hɒt,laɪnər] *n.* a person who conducts, or hosts, a hot-line show on radio or television.

hot pants very brief, tight shorts for women.

hot pepper 1 any of various strong peppers, especially chili. **2** a plant producing hot peppers.

hot plate 1 a small, portable, gas or electric stove for cooking. **2** a heated metal plate for cooking food or keeping it hot.

hot pot 1 an English dish consisting of meat or fish cooked with vegetables in a pot with a lid. **2** a Chinese dish consisting of meat, vegetables, and spices, cooked in a pot with a lid.

hot potato *Slang.* something too controversial or too complex to handle.

hot•press ['hɒt,prɛs] *n.* a machine in which heat and pressure are applied together.

hot–press ['hɒt ,prɛs] *v.* extract oil from cloth by heat and pressure.

hot rod *Slang.* a rebuilt or modified automobile with a supercharged engine.

hot rod•der ['rɒdər] *Slang.* a person who drives a hot rod.

hot seat 1 *Slang.* ELECTRIC CHAIR. **2** an embarrassing predicament. **3** the chair occupied by the victim of an aggressive type of interview.
in the hot seat, in a situation in which one is subject to aggressive and searching questioning.

hot•shot ['hɒt,ʃɒt] *n. Slang.* **1** a person who is skilful or competent in a flashy and often aggressive way. **2** (*adjl.*) of or characteristic of a hotshot: *a hotshot young politician.*

hot spot 1 an exciting and fashionable nightclub, resort, etc. **2** a local place or region of potential or actual unrest or violence. **3** a local area showing significant radioactivity. **4** a point in the earth's crust, above a plume, where a volcano is likely to form. **5** the hottest place on a particular day.

hot spring Usually, **hot springs,** *pl.* a natural spring whose water has a higher temperature than the average temperature of its locality, especially one having water above 37°C.

hot•spur ['hɒt,spɜr] *n.* an impetuous or reckless person. ⟨< *Hotspur,* the nickname of Sir Henry Percy (1364-1403), portrayed as an impetuous character in Shakespeare's *Henry IV, Part 1*⟩

hot–stove league ['hɒt ,stouv] *Cdn.* a group that gathers to discuss sports, especially and originally hockey, usually between periods of play.

hot–tem•pered ['hɒt 'tɛmpərd] *adj.* having a quick temper; easily angered.

Hot•ten•tot ['hɒtən,tɒt] *n., adj. —n.* **1** formerly, a member of a people of southern Africa. **2** the language of the Hottentots. *—adj.* of or having to do with the Hottentots or their language. ⟨native word⟩

hot tub a large, circular, often wooden tub filled with hot water, in which several people can soak at the same time.

hot war a war involving actual fighting. Compare COLD WAR.

hot water *Informal.* trouble.

hot–wire ['hɒt ,waɪr] *v.* **-wired, -wir•ing.** *Informal.* start (a vehicle) without a key by connecting a wire bearing current, bypassing the ignition lock.

hou•dah ['haʊdə] See HOWDAH.

Hou•dan ['hudæn] *n.* a breed of chicken developed in France, having black-and-white plumage, a V-shaped comb, and five toes on each foot. ⟨after the town in France where it was bred⟩

hough [hɒk] See HOCK[1].

hound[1] [haʊnd] *n., v. —n.* **1** any of various breeds of hunting dog, most of which hunt by scent and have large, drooping ears and short hair. **2** any dog. **3** *Slang.* a person who is very keen about pursuing or getting something: *an autograph hound, a news hound.* **4** a contemptible person.
follow the hounds or **ride to hounds,** go hunting on horseback with hounds.
—v. **1** keep on chasing or driving: *The police hounded the thief until they caught her.* **2** urge (on) continually or repeatedly; keep urging or pestering: *His parents hounded him to do his homework.* ⟨OE *hund*⟩

hound[2] [haʊnd] *n.* one of a pair of braces used to reinforce a vehicle. ⟨< ME *houn* < ON *hunn* knob⟩

hound's tongue or **hound's–tongue** ['haʊndz ,tʌŋ] *n.* a plant (*Cynoglossum officinale*) of the borage family having tongue-shaped leaves and red, white, or blue flowers.

A hound's-tooth check

hound's tooth a pattern of broken checks. **—'hound's-,tooth,** *adj.*

hour [aʊr] *n.* **1** a unit used with the SI for measuring time, equal to 3600 seconds or 60 minutes: *There are 24 hours in a day. Symbol*: h **2** one of the 12 points, separated by hour-long intervals, that measure time from noon to midnight and from midnight to noon: *Some clocks strike the hours and the half-hours.* **3** the time of day: *The hour is 7:30.* **4** a particular or fixed time for something: *Our breakfast hour is at seven o'clock.* **5** the distance travelled in an hour. **6** a short or limited space of time: *After his hour of glory, he was soon forgotten.* **7** a period in a classroom, often more or less than a full hour. **8** the present time: *questions of the hour, the man of the hour.* **9** 15 degrees of longitude. **10 hours,** *pl.* **a** the time for work, study, etc.: *Our school hours are 9 to 12 and 1 to 4.* **b** the usual times for going to bed and getting up. **c** seven special times of the day set aside for Christian prayer and worship. **d** the Christian prayers or services for these times. **e Hours,** the Greek goddesses of the seasons, orderliness, justice, and peace.
in an evil hour, at a bad or unlucky time. ⟨ME < OF *hure* < L < Gk. *hōra* season, time, hour⟩ **—'hour•less,** *adj.*
☛ *Hom.* OUR.

☛ *Usage.* **Hours.** In very formal writing, hours are written in words: *four o'clock.* In most informal writing, figures are used with the abbreviations 'a.m.' and 'p.m.', especially if several times are mentioned.

hour angle *Astronomy.* the hour that is measured westwards along the celestial equator from the celestial meridian of the observer to the hour circle.

hour circle *Astronomy.* a great circle passing through the poles of the celestial sphere to intersect the celestial equator at right angles.

hour•glass ['aʊr,glæs] *n.* **1** a device for measuring time, consisting of two glass bulbs joined by a very narrow neck and containing a quantity of fine sand or other material that takes one hour to run from the upper bulb through the neck to the lower one. When the contents have run through, the hourglass can be reversed. **2** (*adjl.*) resembling an hourglass in shape, with a very narrow central section: *an hourglass figure.*

hour hand the short hand on a clock or watch, which moves around the whole dial once in twelve hours.

hou•ri ['huri] *or* ['haʊri] *n., pl.* **-ris. 1** *Islam.* one of the young, eternally beautiful maidens promised in the Koran to the faithful in paradise. **2** a beautiful and alluring woman. ⟨< F < Persian *huri* < Arabic *haura (hawira* with eyes like a gazelle's)⟩

hour•ly ['aʊrli] *adj., adv. —adj.* **1** done, happening, or counted every hour: *hourly news reports, an hourly wage.* **2** coming very often; frequent. **3** occurring in the course of an hour.
—adv. **1** every hour; hour by hour. **2** very often; frequently.

house *n.* [hʌus]; *v.* [haʊz] *n., pl.* **hous•es** ['haʊzɪz]; *v.* **housed, hous•ing,** *adj. —n.* **1** a building designed for people to live in, especially one for a single family. **2** the people living in a house; household: *The whole house was awake by 7 o'clock.* **3** an abode; habitation. **4** a building designed to shelter animals: *the ape house in the zoo.* **5** a house of worship; a church, temple, synagogue, etc. **6** a building to hold anything: *an engine house.* **7 House, a** an assembly for making laws and considering questions of government; lawmaking body: *the House of Commons.* **b** the building in which such an assembly meets. **8** a place of business. **9** a business firm. **10** a place of entertainment; theatre. **11** an audience; attendance: *A large house heard the singer.* **12** *Astrology.* **a** a twelfth part of the heavens as divided by great circles through the north and south points of the horizon. **b** a sign of the zodiac considered as the seat of the greatest influence of a particular planet. **13** a family regarded as consisting of ancestors, descendants, and kindred, especially a noble or royal family: *He was a prince of the house of Hanover.* **14** a religious order. **15** *Curling.* the goal or target. **16** (*adjl.*) prepared by a particular restaurant: *the house dressing.*
bring down the house, *Informal.* be loudly and vigorously applauded.
clean house, a set a house in order. **b** get rid of bad conditions; set a business, institution, etc. in order.
keep house, manage a home and its affairs.
like a house on fire or **afire, a** very well. **b** very rapidly.
on the house, free; paid for by the owner of the business: *After visiting the candy factory, we were each given a box of chocolates on the house.*
put or **set** (one's) **house in order,** arrange one's affairs in good order.
—v. **1** put or receive into a house; provide with a house: *Where can we house all these children?* **2** place in a secure or protected position, as mechanical parts in a case or housing. **3** take shelter. ⟨OE *hūs*⟩

house arrest confinement to one's house by order of a court.

house•boat ['hʌus,bout] *n.* a boat that can be used as a place to live in.

A houseboat

house•bound ['hʌus,baʊnd] *adj.* confined to the house; not able to leave one's house: *He is housebound because of his arthritis.*

house•break•er ['hʌus,breikər] *n.* a person who breaks into a house to steal or commit some other crime.

house•break•ing ['hʌus,breikɪŋ] *n. Law.* the crime of breaking and entering a dwelling for an unlawful purpose.

house•bro•ken ['hʌus,broukən] *adj.* **1** of a pet such as a dog or cat, trained to urinate and defecate only outdoors or in a special place indoors. **2** made docile and easy to manage.

house call a visit to a home to give medical care: *Do you know a doctor who makes house calls?*

house•clean ['hʌus,klin] *v.* clean the house or apartment. **—'house,clean•ing,** *n.*

house•coat ['hʌus,kout] *n.* a woman's loose, informal garment, usually long, for wearing at home.

house•fly ['hʌus,flaɪ] *n., pl.* **-flies.** a two-winged fly (*Musca domestica*) that lives around and in houses, feeding on food and garbage. Its larvae (maggots) develop in decaying organic matter.

house•ful ['hʌusfəl] *n.* as many as a house will hold: *a houseful of guests for the wedding.*

house•hold ['hʌus,hould] *n.* **1** all the people living in a house; family; family and servants. **2** a home and its affairs. **3** (*adjl.*) of or having to do with a household; domestic: *household expenses, household cares.* **4** (*adjl.*) common or familiar: *a household word.*

house•hold•er ['hʌus,houldər] *n.* **1** a person who owns or lives in a house. **2** the head of a family.

house•hus•band ['hʌus,hʌzbənd] *n.* a man who stays at home to look after the house and, usually, children, while the woman goes out to work.

house•keep•er ['hʌus,kipər] *n.* a person who manages a home and its affairs and does the housework, especially one hired to do so.

house•keep•ing ['hʌus,kipɪŋ] *n.* **1** the managing of a home and its affairs. **2** the internal operations and management of an organization or business.

housekeeping genes *Genetics.* genes expressed in most or all cells of the body because their products are required for basic functions.

house•leek ['hʌus,lik] *n.* any of a genus (*Sempervivum*) of Old World plants having thick, fleshy leaves growing in rosettes around the stems, especially a pink-flowered species (*S. tectorum*) often grown as a garden plant. Houseleeks spread by means of runners.

house•lights ['hʌus,ləits] *n.* the lighting in the audience part of a theatre or cinema.

house•maid ['hʌus,meid] *n.* a female servant who does housework.

housemaid's knee an inflammation near the knee, usually caused by much kneeling.

house•mas•ter ['hʌus,mæstər] *n.* a male teacher in charge of a residence hall in a boarding school.

house•mate ['hʌus,meit] *n.* one who shares a house, apartment, etc. with another person or persons.

house•mis•tress ['hʌus,mɪstrɪs] *n.* a female teacher in charge of a residence hall in a boarding school.

house•moth•er ['hʌus,mʌðər] *n.* a woman who supervises and takes care of a group of people living together as a family.

House of Assembly *Cdn.* in Newfoundland, the provincial legislature, consisting of 36 elected members.

house of cards anything that can be easily knocked down; flimsy structure.

House of Commons 1 in Canada, the elected representatives who meet in Ottawa to make laws and debate questions of government. There are 282 members of the House of Commons. **2** the chamber in which the representatives, or members, meet. **3** in the United Kingdom, the elected members of Parliament. **4** the buildings in which these members meet.

house of correction any of various institutions for the confinement of juvenile offenders or other persons who have committed minor offences, such as a training school or reformatory.

house of God a place of worship; church; temple.

House of Lords in the United Kingdom, the upper, non-elective branch of the lawmaking body, composed of nobles and clergy of high rank.

House of Parliament *Cdn.* **1** the legislative body in a province, usually the lower of two bodies. **2** the chamber or building in which such an assembly meets.

House of Representatives 1 in the United States: **a** the lower branch of the federal lawmaking body or of the lawmaking body of certain states. **b** the chamber in which the representatives meet. **2** the lower branch of the Parliament of Australia, or of the General Assembly of New Zealand.

house organ a newsletter or magazine printed for internal distribution in a company.

house•par•ent ['hʌus,pɛrənt] *n.* one of a married couple in charge of a residence at a school, college, or other institution.

house party 1 the entertainment of guests in a home, especially for a few days. 2 a group of guests thus entertained.

house physician a resident physician of a hotel, hospital, etc.

house plant a plant grown indoors in a pot or planter. Tropical plants, such as African violets and philodendrons, are popular as house plants in colder climates.

house–post ['hʌus ,poust] *n. Cdn.* one of several posts supporting the framework of a First Nations building, often carved and decorated to symbolize identification with a certain clan or family. Also, **house-pole.**

house–proud ['hʌus ,praʊd] *adj.* proud of the appearance of one's house, especially to the point of being too fussy or fastidious.

house–rais•ing ['hʌus ,reizɪŋ] *n. Cdn.* the construction of a house by a group of neighbours.

house•room ['hʌus,rum] *or* ['hʌus,rʊm] *n.* room or space in a house.

house–sit ['hʌus ,sɪt] *v.* **house-sat, house-sit•ting.** live in a house to look after it while the owners are away.

house sparrow ENGLISH SPARROW.

house–to–house ['hʌus tə 'hʌus] *adv., adj.* from one house to the next, stopping at each in turn: *a house-to-house campaign.*

house•top ['hʌus,tɒp] *n.* the top of a house; roof.
shout from the housetops, make public.

house•wares ['hʌus,wɛrz] *n.pl.* equipment, etc. for a household, especially dishes, kitchen utensils and tools, small appliances, etc.

house•warm•ing ['hʌus,wɔrmɪŋ] *n.* a party given when a person or family moves into a new residence.

house•wife ['hʌus,wəif] *for 1;* ['hʌzɪf] *for 2. n., pl.* **-wives** ['hʌzɪfs] *for 2.* **1** a woman who manages a home and its affairs for her husband, children, etc.; homemaker. **2** a small case for needles, thread, etc.

house•wife•ly ['hʌus,wəifli] *adj.* of or like a housewife; thrifty or skilled in household affairs.

house•wif•er•y ['hʌus,wəifəri] *or* ['hʌus,wɪfəri] *n.* the work of a housewife; housekeeping.

house•work ['hʌus,wɜrk] *n.* the work to be done in housekeeping, such as washing, ironing, cleaning, and cooking.

hous•ing¹ ['haʊzɪŋ] *n., v.* —*n.* **1** the act of sheltering; provision of houses as homes. **2** houses. **3** a shelter; covering. **4** a frame or plate for holding together and protecting the parts of a machine. **5** *Carpentry.* a groove in a piece of wood ready to take another piece. **6** *Nautical.* the part of a mast below the deck.
—*v.* ppr. of HOUSE.

hous•ing² ['haʊzɪŋ] *n.* **1** an ornamental or protective covering for the back and flanks of a horse: *Under the saddle was a housing of red velvet.* **2** Usually, **housings**, *pl.* TRAPPINGS. ⟨< *house* covering < OF *houce* < Gmc.⟩

housing start the building of new houses, seen as an economic indicator: *Housing starts are up this quarter.*

hove [houv] *v.* a pt. and a pp. of HEAVE.

hov•el ['hʌvəl] *or* ['hɒvəl] *n.* **1** a house that is small, crude, and unpleasant to live in. **2** an open shed for sheltering cattle, storing tools, etc. ⟨ME; origin uncertain⟩

hov•er ['hʌvər] *or* ['hɒvər] *v.* **1** stay in or near one place in the air: *The hummingbird hovered in front of the flower.* **2** stay in or near one place; wait nearby: *The dogs hovered around the kitchen door at mealtime.* **3** be in an uncertain condition; waver: *The sick woman hovered between life and death.*
hover over, threaten: *The fear of failure hovered over the young executive.* ⟨ME *hover(en)* < *hoven* hover; origin uncertain⟩

Hov•er•craft ['hʌvər,kræft] *or* ['hɒvər,kræft] *n. Trademark.* a motorized vehicle capable of travelling just above the surface of water or land on a cushion of air created by powerful fans blowing downward from the chassis.

how [haʊ] *adv., n.* —*adv.* **1** in what way; by what means: *Tell her how to do it.* **2** to what degree, extent, etc.: *How long will it take you to do this?* **3** at what price: *How do you sell these apples?* **4** in what state or condition: *Tell me how Mrs. Akisi is.* **5** for what reason; why: *How is it you are late?* **6** to what effect; with what meaning; by what name: *How do you mean?*
here's how! a toast to one's health.
how come? *Informal.* what is the reason or cause? why?: *How come you didn't call last night?*
how now? what does this mean?
how so? why is it so?
how's that? what did you say?
how then? what does this mean?
—*n.* a way or manner of doing: *She considered all the hows and wherefores.* ⟨OE *hū*⟩
☛ *Hom.* HAO.

how•be•it [haʊ'biɪt] *adv. Archaic.* however it may be; nevertheless; however.

how•dah ['haʊdə] *n.* a seat for riding on an elephant's back, usually having a canopy and seating two or more persons. Also, **houdah.** ⟨< Hind. *haudah* < Arabic *haudaj*⟩

how•e'er [haʊ'ɛr] *conj. or adv. Poetic.* however.

how•ev•er [haʊ'ɛvər] *conj., adv.* —*conj.* nevertheless; yet; in spite of that: *It is his; however, you may borrow it.*
—*adv.* **1** to whatever extent, degree, or amount; no matter how: *However you do it, the effect will be the same.* **2** in whatever way; by whatever means: *However did you manage to get here?*
☛ *Syn. conj.* See note at BUT.

how•itz•er ['haʊɪtsər] *n.* a short artillery piece for firing shells in a high curve. ⟨earlier *howitz* < Du. < G *Haubitze* < Czech *houfnice* catapult⟩

howl [haʊl] *v., n.* —*v.* **1** give a long, loud, mournful cry: *Dogs and wolves howl.* **2** make a sound like this: *Listen to the wind howling in the trees.* **3** give a long, loud cry of pain, rage, distress, etc. **4** yell; shout: *It was so funny that we howled with laughter.* **5** force or drive by howling: *The angry mob howled the speaker off the platform.*
howl down, drown out the words of by howling.
—*n.* **1** a long, loud, mournful cry. **2** a loud cry of pain, rage, etc. **3** a yell of scorn, amusement, etc. **4** a yell; shout. **5** *Informal.* something causing laughter: *The skit by the teachers was a howl.* ⟨ME *houle(n)*⟩

howl•er ['haʊlər] *n.* **1** a person or thing that howls. **2** *Informal.* a ridiculous mistake; stupid blunder.

how•so•ev•er [,haʊsou'ɛvər] *adv.* **1** to whatever extent, degree, or amount; however. **2** in whatever way; by whatever means; however.

how–to ['hʌu ,tu] *adj.* giving basic instructions for making or doing something.

hoy ['hɔɪ] *n.* a heavy freight barge. ⟨ME *hoye* < MDu. *hoei*⟩

ho•ya ['hɔɪə] *n.* a small vine *(Hoya carnosa)* grown as a house plant, having waxy flowers. ⟨after Thomas *Hoy*, English gardener⟩

hoy•den ['hɔɪdən] *n.* a boisterous, romping girl; tomboy. Also, **hoiden.** ⟨< Du. *heiden* a rustic person⟩

hoy•den•ish ['hɔɪdənɪʃ] *adj.* of or like a hoyden; boisterous; romping. Also, **hoidenish.**

Hoyle [hɔɪl] *n.* a book of rules and instructions for playing card games.
according to Hoyle, according to the rules or customs; fair; correct. ⟨< Edmond *Hoyle* (1672-1769), an English writer on card games⟩

hp horsepower.

HP, H.P., or **h.p.** **1** high pressure. **2** horsepower. **3** *Electricity.* high power.

HQ or **hq** headquarters.

hr. hour.

HR or **h.r.** *Baseball.* home run.

H.R.H. His Royal Highness; Her Royal Highness.

hrs. hours.

H.S. or **HS** High School.

ht. **1** height. **2** heat.

Hts. Heights.

hu•a•ra•che [wɑ'rɑtʃi] *n.* a flat Mexican sandal with leather straps to cover the upper foot. ⟨< Mexican Sp.⟩

Hu•as•tec ['wɑstɛk] *or* [wɑs'tɛk] *n.* **1** a member of a Native American people living in Mexico. **2** the Mayan language of these people.

hub [hʌb] *n.* **1** the central part of a wheel. **2** any centre of interest, importance, activity, etc.: *London is the hub of the Commonwealth.* ⟨origin uncertain⟩

Hub•bard squash ['hʌbərd] **1** a winter squash with a yellow skin and yellow edible flesh. **2** the edible flesh of this squash.

hub•ble ['hʌbəl] *n.* a small hump. ⟨< *hubbly* rough, uneven, var. of E dial. *hobbly* < *hobble*, in the meaning 'move unsteadily up and down'⟩

hub•ble–bub•ble ['hʌbəl 'bʌbəl] *n.* **1** a bubbling sound. **2** hookah.

Hubble's constant *Astronomy.* the ratio of the speed at which a distant galaxy is receding from the earth to its distance from the earth. It is one hundred kilometres per second per million parsecs. ⟨< E.P. *Hubble,* U.S. astronomer (1889-1953)⟩

hub•bub ['hʌbʌb] *n.* a noisy tumult; uproar. ⟨imitative⟩

hub•cap ['hʌb,kæp] *n.* the cap that fits over the hub of an automobile wheel.

hu•bris ['hjubrɪs] *or* ['hubrɪs] *n.* insolence; arrogance; wanton or contemptuous pride. ⟨< Gk. *hybris*⟩ **—hu'bris•tic,** *adj.*

huck•a•back ['hʌkə,bæk] *n.* a heavy, coarse linen or cotton cloth with a rough surface, used for towels. Also, **huck.** ⟨origin uncertain⟩

huck•le•ber•ry ['hʌkəl,bɛri] *n., pl.* **-ries. 1** any of a genus (*Gaylussacia*) of New World shrubs of the heath family, bearing sweet, edible, dark blue berries resembling blueberries. **2** the berry of any of these shrubs. ⟨apparently alteration of *hurtleberry* < **hurtle* (dim. of E dial. *hurt,* OE *horte* whortleberry) + *berry*⟩

huck•ster ['hʌkstər] *n., v.* *—n.* **1** peddler. **2** a person who sells small articles. **3** *Esp. U.S. Informal.* a person who is in the advertising business. **4** a mean and unfair trader.
—v. **1** sell; peddle; haggle. **2** advertise aggressively. ⟨Cf. MDu. *hokester,* originally fem. Akin to HAWKER[1].⟩

hud•dle ['hʌdəl] *v.* **-dled, -dling;** *n.* *—v.* **1** crowd close: *The sheep huddled in a corner of the pen.* **2** crowd or put close together: *She huddled all four boys into one bed.* **3** curl oneself up: *The rescued swimmer sat huddled in a blanket by the fire. The cat huddled in a sunny spot.* **4** of football players, group together behind the line of scrimmage to receive signals. **5** *Informal.* hold a secret, casual conference. **6** make or do hurriedly.
—n. **1** a confused heap or mass of people or things crowded together. **2** *Football.* a grouping of players behind the line of scrimmage to receive signals, plan the next play, etc. **3** *Informal.* a secret conference: *The management has gone into a huddle about a new pricing policy.* **4** confusion. ⟨Cf. ME *hodre(n)*⟩

Hudson Bay ['hʌdsən] an inland sea in N Canada. ⟨< Henry *Hudson,* English explorer, died 1611⟩

Hudson's Bay Company *Cdn.* a trading company chartered by Charles II in 1670, as the Company of Adventurers of England trading into Hudson's Bay, to carry on the fur trade with the Native peoples of North America. The Hudson's Bay Company played a great part in the exploration and development of Canada's Northwest.

Hudson seal *Cdn.* muskrat fur that is dyed and processed to look like seal.

hue[1] [hju] *n.* **1** that property of colour by which it can be distinguished from grey of equal brightness; colour; shade; tint: *all the hues of the rainbow.* **2** a variety of a colour; a particular colour. **3** aspect or type: *politicians of every hue.* ⟨OE *hīw*⟩
☛ *Hom.* HEW.
☛ *Syn.* See note at COLOUR.

hue[2] [hju] *n. Archaic* (*except in* **hue and cry**). shouting.
hue and cry, a shouts of alarm or protest. **b** an outcry or alarm formerly raised to call people to pursue a criminal, in which they were obliged by law to join. **c** the pursuit of a criminal in this way. ⟨< F *hu* < *huer* shout⟩
☛ *Hom.* HEW.

hue•vos ran•che•ros ['weivous ræn'tʃɛrous] a Mexican dish consisting of eggs fried with a spicy sauce. ⟨< Mexican Sp., literally, rancher eggs⟩

huff [hʌf] *n., v.* *—n.* a fit of anger or peevishness.
—v. **1** make angry; offend. **2** *Dialect.* puff; blow. ⟨imitative⟩

huff•y ['hʌfi] *adj.* **huff•i•er, huff•i•est. 1** offended. **2** tending to be easily offended; touchy. **—'huff•i•ly,** *adv.* **—'huff•i•ness,** *n.*

hug [hʌg] *v.* **hugged, hug•ging;** *n.* *—v.* **1** put the arms around and hold close, especially in affection; embrace: *She hugged her sister and wished her good luck.* **2** squeeze tightly between the forelegs, as a bear does. **3** cling firmly or fondly to: *They still hug their belief in her story.* **4** keep close to: *The boat hugged the shore.*
—n. **1** a tight clasp with the arms. **2** a tight squeeze with the arms especially as a grip in wrestling. ⟨apparently < ON *hugga* to comfort⟩ **—'hug•ga•ble,** *adj.*

huge [hjudʒ] *adj.* **hug•er, hug•est. 1** extremely large in size, quantity, etc.: *A whale or an elephant is a huge animal.*
2 unusually great in extent, scope, degree, or capacity: *a huge undertaking.* ⟨ME < OF *ahuge*⟩ **—'huge•ly,** *adv.* **—'huge•ness,** *n.*
☛ *Syn.* **Huge,** ENORMOUS, IMMENSE. **Huge** is the most general word: *A St. Bernard is a huge dog.* **Enormous** implies 'abnormally or excessively large or great': *enormous dimensions.* **Immense** often carries the original sense of being so large or great as to be impossible to measure by ordinary standards: *an immense body of water.*

hug•ger–mug•ger ['hʌgər ,mʌgər] *n., adj., adv. Informal.*
—n. confusion; disorder.
—adj. confused, disorderly.
—adv. in a confused, disorderly manner. ⟨origin uncertain⟩

Hu•gue•not ['hjugə,nɒt] *or* ['hjugə,nou] *n.* **1** a Calvinistic French Protestant of the 16th and 17th centuries. **2** any member of a church founded by John Calvin. ⟨< F *huguenot,* earlier *eigenot* (< Swiss G *Eidgenoss* confederate < *Eid* oath + *Genoss* comrade), influenced by the name of *Hugues* Besançon, a party leader; originally applied to Genevans who were partisans against the Duke of Savoy⟩

hu•la ['hulə] *n.* **1** a native Hawaiian dance characterized by rhythmic movement of the hips and hand gestures that tell a story. **2** the music for this dance. ⟨< Hawaiian⟩

Hula Hoop *Trademark.* a plastic hoop designed to be rotated around the body by swinging the hips.

hu•la–hu•la ['hulə 'hulə] *n.* hula.

hulk [hʌlk] *n., v.* *—n.* **1** the body of an old or worn-out ship. **2** a ship used as a prison. **3** a big, clumsy ship. **4** a big, clumsy person or thing. **5** a forsaken ruin or wreck.
—v. **1** be bulky or unwieldy; loom bulkily. **2** lounge or slouch clumsily or boorishly. **3** rise in an impressive way. ⟨OE *hulc,* a fast ship⟩

hulk•ing ['hʌlkɪŋ] *adj., v.* *—adj.* big and clumsy. Also, **hulky.**
—v. ppr. of HULK.

hull[1] [hʌl] *n., v.* *—n.* **1** the outer covering of a seed. **2** the calyx of some fruits. The green leaves at the stem of a strawberry are called its hull. **3** any outer covering.
—v. remove the hull or hulls from: *to hull strawberries, to hull grain.* ⟨OE *hulu*⟩ **—'hull•er,** *n.*

hull[2] [hʌl] *n., v.* *—n.* **1** the body or frame of a ship. Masts, sails, and rigging are not part of the hull. **2** the main body or frame of a seaplane, airship, etc.
hull down, of ships, so far away that the hull is below the horizon.
—v. strike or pierce the hull of (a ship) with a shell, torpedo, etc. ⟨? extended use of *hull*[1]⟩

hul•la•ba•loo [,hʌləbə'lu] *or* ['hʌləbə,lu] *n.* a loud noise or disturbance; uproar. ⟨imitative, probably < reduplication of *hullo*⟩

hul•lo [hə'lou] *interj., n., pl.* **-los;** *v.* **-loed, -lo•ing.** hello.

hum [hʌm] *v.* **hummed, hum•ming;** *n., interj.* *—v.* **1** make a continuous murmuring sound like that of a bee or of a spinning top: *The sewing machine hums busily.* **2** make a low sound like that symbolized by the letter *m,* in hesitation, embarrassment, dissatisfaction, etc. **3** sing with closed lips, not sounding words. **4** business; bustle. **4** put or bring by humming: *The mother hummed her baby to sleep.* **5** *Informal.* be busy and active: *The new president made things hum.*
—n. **1** a continuous murmuring sound: *the hum of the bees, the hum of the city street.* **2** a low sound like that symbolized by the letter *m,* used to express hesitation, disagreement, etc. **3** a singing with closed lips, not sounding words. **4** busyness; bustle.
—interj. a low sound like that symbolized by the letter *m,* used to express hesitation, disagreement, etc. ⟨imitative⟩ **—'hum•mer,** *n.*

hu•man ['hjumən] *adj., n.* *—adj.* **1** of, having to do with, or belonging to people: *human nature, human affairs. To know the future is beyond human power.* **2** consisting of people: *the human race.* **3** having or showing qualities, good or bad, natural to people, as opposed to machines, animals, or divine beings: *human error. After all, she's only human.* **4** warm, open, responsive, etc.: *She's becoming more human as she gets to know us.*
—n. a human being; person. ⟨ME < OF *humain* < L *humanus*⟩
☛ *Usage.* Do not confuse **human** (*adj.* 3, 4) and HUMANE (def. 1). **Human** describes or suggests any quality, good or bad, belonging specially to people as distinct from animals or God, but particularly suggests their feelings or faults: *He is a very human person, warm and understanding and not too perfect.* **Humane** chiefly suggests a person's tender and compassionate feelings and actions toward animals or people who are helpless, troubled, or suffering: *A humane person will not condone the torture of prisoners.*

human being a man, woman, or child; person.

hu•mane [hju'mein] *adj.* **1** kind; merciful; not cruel or brutal. **2** tending to humanize and refine: *humane studies.* ⟨var. of *human*⟩ **—hu'mane•ly,** *adv.* **—hu'mane•ness,** *n.*
☛ *Usage.* See note at HUMAN.

human genetics the science concerned with the description and analysis of heredity and variation in human beings.

Human Genome Project a current international project that aims to map and sequence the entire human DNA.

human immunovirus HIV.

hu•man•ism ['hjumə,nɪzəm] *n.* **1** a non-theistic, rationalistic philosophy of life based on the principle that human beings alone are responsible for giving meaning and purpose to their lives, relying upon their human capacities of reason and responsibility. **2 Humanism,** the study of the humanities; literary culture. Humanism spread throughout Europe in the Middle Ages when scholars began to study Latin and Greek culture. As a result there was the great revival of art and learning that is called the Renaissance.

hu•man•ist ['hjumənɪst] *n.* **1** a proponent of humanism. **2** a student of the humanities or of Latin and Greek culture.

hu•man•is•tic [,hjumə'nɪstɪk] *adj.* of humanism or humanists. **—,hu•man'is•ti•cal•ly,** *adv.*

hu•man•i•tar•i•an [hju,mænə'tɛriən] *adj., n.* *—adj.* **1** helpful to humanity; philanthropic. **2** of or having to do with humanitarianism, especially in theology.
—n. **1** a person who is devoted to the welfare of all human beings. **2** a believer in theological or ethical humanitarianism. ⟨< *humanity*; patterned after *unitarian*, etc.⟩

hu•man•i•tar•i•an•ism [hju,mænə'tɛriə,nɪzəm] *n.* **1** humanitarian principles or practices. **2** *Theology.* the doctrine that Jesus Christ was only human, not divine. **3** the ethical doctrine that people's obligations are concerned wholly with human relations and the welfare of the human race.

hu•man•i•ty [hju'mænəti] *n., pl.* **-ties. 1** human beings taken as a group; people: *Advances in medical science help all humanity.* **2** the fact of being human; good human character or quality. **3** the fact of being humane; humane treatment; kindness; mercy: *Treat animals with humanity.* **4 the humanities, a** the Latin and Greek languages and literatures. **b** languages, literatures, philosophies, art, etc. **c** the branches of learning concerned with human ideas and their values, as opposed to the sciences. ⟨< F *humanité* < L *humanitas*⟩

hu•man•ize ['hjumə,naɪz] *v.* **-ized, -iz•ing. 1** make human; give a human character or quality to. **2** make humane; cause to be kind or merciful. **—,hu•man•i'za•tion,** *n.* **—'hu•man,iz•er,** *n.*

hu•man•kind ['hjumən'kaɪnd] *n.* the human race; people.

human leukocyte antigen complex *Genetics.* an array of closely linked gene loci on chromosome 6, also known as the **major histocompatibility complex**, that initiates and controls the body's response to foreign tissue.

hu•man•ly ['hjumənli] *adj.* **1** in a human manner. **2** by human means or powers: *The task is humanly impossible.* **3** according to human knowledge, experience, or viewpoint.

human nature 1 the qualities that are characteristic of people. **2** human behaviour resulting from living in groups.

hu•man•oid ['hjumə,nɔɪd] *adj., n.* *—adj.* having human characteristics; resembling a human being: *humanoid robots.*
—n. **1** one of the earliest ancestors of humankind. **2** any creature closely resembling a human being: *Science fiction often deals with humanoids from other planets.*

human resources 1 the personnel department in a company. **2** resources in the form of human energy, employable people, etc.

human rights the rights of an individual in any democratic society, such as the right to justice, equality of opportunity, and religious freedom, that are considered basic to life in any human society.

hum•ble ['hʌmbəl] *adj.* **-bler, -blest;** *v.* **-bled, -bling.** *—adj.* **1** low in position or condition; not important or grand: *A one-room cabin is a humble place in which to live.* **2 a** having or showing a feeling that one is unimportant, weak, poor, etc. **b** modest in spirit; not proud. **3** deeply or courteously respectful: *in my humble opinion.*
—v. **1** make humble; bring down. **2** make lower in position, condition, or pride. ⟨ME < OF < L *humilis* low < *humus* ground⟩ **—'hum•ble•ness,** *n.* **—'hum•bler,** *n.* **—'hum•bly,** *adv.*

hum•ble•bee ['hʌmbəl,bi] *n.* bumblebee. ⟨ME *humbylbee*, ult. < *hum*⟩

humble pie an inferior pie made of the inward parts of an animal, formerly served to the hunters and servants after a hunt. **eat humble pie, a** be forced to do something very disagreeable and humiliating. **b** admit one's mistakes and apologize. ⟨var. of *umble pie* < *umbles*, var. of *numbles* entrails < OF, pl. < L *lumbulus*, dim. of *lumbus* loin⟩

Hum•boldt current ['hʌmboult] *or* ['hʊmboult] a cold current of the Pacific Ocean, flowing north along the coasts of Chile and Peru. ⟨after Baron von *Humboldt*. 19c. German scientist⟩

hum•bug ['hʌm,bʌg] *n., v.* **-bugged, -bug•ging.** *—n.* **1** a person who pretends to be what he or she is not; fraud. **2** a cheat. **3** pretence; sham. **4** nonsense; foolishness: *Dad says our argument is humbug.* **5** a hard candy, usually brown with light stripes.
—v. deceive with a sham; cheat. ⟨origin unknown⟩
—'hum,bug•ger, *n.*

hum•ding•er ['hʌm,dɪŋər] *n. Slang.* a person or thing that is first-rate, extraordinary, or striking: *a humdinger of a car. Her retort was a humdinger.*

hum•drum ['hʌm,drʌm] *adj., n.* *—adj.* without variety; commonplace; dull.
—n. **1** a humdrum routine. **2** anything that is dull or tiresome. **3** a dull person. ⟨varied reduplicaton of *hum*, v.⟩

hu•mec•tant [hju'mɛktənt] *n., adj.* *—n.* a substance that increases the ability to retain moisture.
—adj. moistening. ⟨< L *umectare* moisten < *umere* be moist⟩

hu•mer•al ['hjumərəl] *adj.* **1** of or near the humerus. **2** of or near the shoulder.

hu•mer•us ['hjumərəs] *n., pl.* **-mer•i** [-mə,raɪ] *or* [-mə,ri]. the long bone in the upper part of the forelimb or arm, reaching from the shoulder to the elbow. See ARM and COLLARBONE for pictures. ⟨< L *umerus*⟩
☛ *Hom.* HUMOROUS.

hu•mic ['hjumɪk] *adj.* having to do with humus.

hu•mid ['hjumɪd] *adj.* moist; damp: *The air is very humid here.* ⟨< L *umidus* < *umere* be moist⟩ **—'hu•mid•ly,** *adv.*
—'hu•mid•ness, *n.*
☛ *Syn.* See note at DAMP.

hu•mi•dex ['hjumɪ,dɛks] *n. Cdn.* an index of discomfort resulting from a combination of humidity and heat. The humidex is calculated by adding a given value based on the dew point level to the temperature of the atmosphere (1 for a dew point of 10°C, 6 for a dew point of 18°C, etc.). Thus, at a temperature of 25°C, the humidex is 26 when the dew point is 10°C and 31 when the dew point is 18°C.

Humidex	*Level of discomfort*
20-29	comfortable
30-39	varying degrees of discomfort
40-45	almost everyone feels uncomfortable
46 and over	many types of work must be discontinued

⟨< *humid(ity)* + *(ind)ex*; first used by the Toronto Weather Office in 1965⟩

hu•mid•i•fi•ca•tion [hju,mɪdəfə'keiʃən] *n.* a humidifying.

hu•mid•i•fi•er [hju'mɪdə,faɪər] *n.* a device for keeping air moist.

hu•mid•i•fy [hju'mɪdə,faɪ] *v.* **-fied, -fy•ing.** make humid or more humid.

hu•mid•i•stat [hju'mɪdə,stæt] *n.* a device to regulate the humidity of the air.

hu•mid•i•ty [hju'mɪdəti] *n.* **1** the state of the atmosphere with respect to the amount of water vapour present in it. See RELATIVE HUMIDITY and ABSOLUTE HUMIDITY. **2** moistness, especially of the atmosphere: *The humidity today is worse than the heat.*

hu•mi•dor ['hjumə,dɔr] *n.* **1** a box, jar, etc. for keeping tobacco moist. **2** any similar device. **3** the device in the box which keeps the humidity constant.

hu•mil•i•ate [hju'mɪli,eit] *v.* **-at•ed, -at•ing.** lower the pride, dignity, or self-respect of; make ashamed. ⟨< L *humiliare* < *humilis.* See HUMBLE.⟩ **—hu'mil•i,at•ing•ly,** *adv.*
—hu'mil•i,a•tor, *n.*

hu•mil•i•at•ed [hju'mɪli,eitɪd] *adj., v.* *—adj.* made to feel ashamed.
—v. pt. and pp. of HUMILIATE.
☛ *Syn.* See note at ASHAMED.

hu•mil•i•a•tion [hju,mɪli'eiʃən] *n.* a lowering of pride, dignity, or self-respect; a making or being made ashamed.

hu•mil•i•ty [hju'mɪləti] *n., pl.* **-ties.** humbleness of mind; lack of pride; meekness. ⟨< F *humilité* < *humilitas*⟩

hum•ma•ble ['hʌməbəl] *adj.* able to be hummed: *a hummable tune.*

hum•ming•bird ['hʌmɪŋ,bɜrd] *n.* any of a family (Trochilidae) of tiny New World birds having brightly coloured, iridescent plumage, a long, slender bill, and long, narrow wings, and noted for their ability to hover in the air as they feed on the nectar of flowers and also for the characteristic humming sound made by their rapidly beating wings. The commonest Canadian species is the ruby-throated hummingbird (*Archilochus colubris*).

A hummingbird

hum•mock ['hʌmək] *n.* **1** a very small, rounded hill; knoll; hillock. **2** a bump or ridge in a field of ice. **3** fertile woodland above the level of a surrounding marsh. ⟨origin unknown⟩

hum•mock•y ['hʌməki] *adj.* **1** full of hummocks. **2** like a hummock.

hum•mus ['hʌməs] *or* ['hʊməs] *n.* a Middle Eastern dish consisting of ground chick peas and spices, eaten as an appetizer. ⟨< Turkish *humus*⟩

hu•mong•ous [hju'mʌŋgəs] *or* [hju'mɒŋgəs] *adj. Informal.* very large.

hu•mor ['hjumər] See HUMOUR.

hu•mor•esque [,hjumə'rɛsk] *n.* a light, playful, or humorous piece of music. ⟨< G *Humoreske*⟩

hu•mor•ist ['hjumərɪst] *n.* **1** a person with a strong sense of humour. **2** a humorous talker or writer; a person who tells or writes jokes and funny stories.

hu•mor•ous ['hjumərəs] *adj.* full of humour; funny; amusing. **—'hu•mor•ous•ly,** *adv.* **—'hu•mor•ous•ness,** *n.*

☛ *Hom.* HUMERUS.

hu•mour or **hu•mor** ['hjumər] *n., v.* *—n.* **1** a funny or amusing quality: *I see no humour in your tricks.* **2** the ability to see or show the funny or amusing side of things. **3** speech, writing, etc. showing this ability. **4** a state of mind; mood; disposition: *Success puts you in good humour.* **5** a fancy; whim. **6** any of various body fluids formerly supposed to determine a person's health and disposition. They were blood, phlegm, choler (yellow bile), and melancholy (black bile). **7** any clear body fluid such as the AQUEOUS HUMOUR.

out of humour or **humor,** angry; displeased; in a bad mood.

sense of humour or **humor,** the ability to see the amusing side of things.

—v. **1** give in to the fancies or whims of (a person); indulge. **2** adapt oneself to; act so as to agree with. ⟨ME < AF < L *umor* fluid⟩ **—'hu•mor•less** or **'hu•mor•less,** *adj.*

☛ *Syn. n.* **2.** See note at WIT[1]. *—v.* **1. Humour,** INDULGE, GRATIFY = give someone what he or she wants. **Humour** = give in to someone's whims, changing moods, unreasonable demands, or purely imaginary desires, in order to quiet or comfort him or her: *Unless the little boy is humoured, he has tantrums.* **Indulge** = give way, often too easily, to someone's wishes, especially ones that should not be granted, in order to please: *Many parents indulge their children by giving them too much candy and ice cream.* **Gratify** = make someone happy by providing what he or she likes or longs for: *Praise gratifies most people.*

hump [hʌmp] *n., v.* *—n.* **1** a rounded lump that sticks out: *Some camels have two humps on their backs.* **2** a mound; a hill. **3** a long, gradual hill in a railway yard where cars are uncoupled and allowed to roll down into the classification yard, where switches sort them out onto different tracks.

over the hump, past a difficult period or crucial test.

—v. **1** rise or cause to rise or bend up into a hump: *The cat humped its back when it saw the dog.* **2** move (a railway car) over the hump for sorting in the classification yard. **3** *Slang.* exert oneself; make an effort. ⟨Cf. Du. *homp* lump⟩

hump•back ['hʌmp,bæk] *n.* **1** hunchback. **2** a large baleen whale (*Megaptera novaeangliae*) found in all oceans, belonging to the same family (Balaenopteridae) as the rorquals but having a shorter and stouter body and a rounded back that shows as a hump above the water just before the whale sounds. Also called **humpback whale. 3** PINK SALMON. Also called **humpback salmon.**

hump•backed ['hʌmp,bækt] *adj.* hunchbacked.

humph [hʌmpf] *interj. or n.* an exclamation expressing doubt, disgust, contempt, etc.

hump•y ['hʌmpi] *adj.* **hump•i•er, hump•i•est. 1** full of humps. **2** humplike.

hu•mus ['hjuməs] *n.* the dark brown or black part of soil formed from decayed leaves and other vegetable matter. Humus contains valuable plant foods. ⟨< L *humus* earth⟩

Hun [hʌn] *n.* **1** a member of an Asiatic people who, mostly under the leadership of Attila, overran much of eastern and central Europe between about A.D. 375 and 450. **2** Often, **hun,** a barbarous, destructive person. **3** *Cdn.* HUNGARIAN PARTRIDGE. ⟨OE (pl.) *Hūne, Hūnas*; probably < the native name of the people⟩

hunch [hʌntʃ] *v., n.* *—v.* **1** hump. **2** draw, bend, or form into a hump: *He sat hunched up with his chin on his knees.* **3** move, push, or shove by jerks.

—n. **1** a hump. **2** *Informal.* a vague feeling or suspicion: *I had a hunch we would win the game.* **3** a thick slice or piece; chunk. ⟨origin unknown⟩

hunch•back ['hʌntʃ,bæk] *n.* **1** a person with a crooked back that forms a hump at the level of the shoulders. **2** a crooked back that has a hump at the shoulders.

hunch•backed ['hʌntʃ,bækt] *adj.* having a HUNCHBACK (def. 2).

hun•dred ['hʌndrəd] *n., pl.* **-dreds** or (after a number, etc.) **-dred;** *adj.* *—n.* **1** ten times ten; 100: *five hundred.* **2** a 100-dollar bill. **3 hundreds,** *pl.* the numbers between 100 and 999. **4** formerly, a division of a British county.

—adj. being ten times ten: *a hundred men.* ⟨OE *hund* 100 + *red* reckoning⟩

Hundred Days the period of Napoleon's return to power in France in 1815, between his escape from Elba and his defeat, abdication, and final exile.

hun•dred•fold ['hʌndrəd,fould] *adj., adv. or n.* a hundred times as much or as many.

hun•dredth ['hʌndrədθ] *adj. or n.* **1** next after the 99th; last in a series of 100; 100th. **2** one, or being one, of 100 equal parts.

hun•dred•weight ['hʌndrəd,weit] *n., pl.* **-weights** or (after a number, etc.) **-weight.** a unit for measuring mass equal to 100 pounds (about 45 kg) in Canada and 112 pounds (about 50 kg) in the British Isles.

Hundred Years' War a series of wars between England and France from 1337 to 1453.

hung [hʌŋ] *v.* a pt. and a pp. of HANG.

hung over, having a hangover.

hung up, *Informal.* unable to get away; delayed: *to be hung up in traffic.*

hung up on, *Informal.* **a** disturbed or troubled by: *to be hung up on one's anxieties.* **b** very enthusiastic about: *to be hung up on rock music.*

☛ *Usage.* See note at HANG.

Hun•gar•i•an [hʌŋ'gɛriən] *n., adj.* *—n.* **1** a native or inhabitant of Hungary. **2** a person of Hungarian descent. **3** the Finno-Ugric language of Hungary; Magyar.

—adj. of or having to do with Hungary, its people, or their language.

Hungarian partridge *Cdn.* a partridge (*Perdix perdix*) introduced to North America from Europe as a game bird. Many of the first such birds to be brought over came from Hungary.

Hun•ga•ry ['hʌŋgəri] *n.* a country in central Europe.

hun•ger ['hʌŋgər] *n., v.* *—n.* **1** an uncomfortable or painful feeling or a weak condition caused by lack of food. **2** a desire or need for food. **3** a strong desire; longing: *a hunger for kindness.* *—v.* **1** feel hunger; be hungry (*for*). **2** *Archaic.* starve. **3** have a strong desire (*for*). ⟨OE *hungor*⟩ **—'hun•ger•er,** *n.* **—'hun•ger•less,** *adj.*

hunger strike a refusal to eat until certain demands are met.

hung jury a jury that cannot agree on a verdict.

hun•gry ['hʌŋgri] *adj.* **-gri•er, -gri•est. 1** feeling a desire or need for food: *I'm hungry.* **2** showing hunger: *a hungry look.* **3** causing hunger: *This is hungry work.* **4** having a strong desire or craving; eager: *hungry for knowledge.* **5** not rich or fertile: *hungry soil.* ⟨OE *hungrig*⟩ **—'hun•gri•ly,** *adv.* **—'hun•gri•ness,** *n.*

☛ *Syn.* **1. Hungry,** FAMISHED = needing food. **Hungry** is the general word: *Boys are always hungry.* **Famished** = brought to a serious state of physical exhaustion, sometimes even to the point of dying, by lack of food: *We try to feed and save famished war orphans.* But in informal use, it often means no more than 'very hungry'.

Hungry Thir•ties ['θɜrtiz] *Cdn.* the period 1930-1939, when many people were unemployed and on relief; the Great Depression of the 1930s.

hunk [hʌŋk] *n.* **1** *Informal.* a big lump, piece, or roughly cut slice. **2** *Slang.* a good-looking man. ⟨cf. Flemish *hunke* hunk⟩

hun•ker ['hʌŋkər] *v.* squat on one's haunches (*used with* **down**). ⟨origin uncertain⟩

hun•kers ['hʌŋkərz] *n.pl.* haunches.

hunk•y–do•ry ['hʌŋki 'dɔri] *adj. Slang.* fine; just right; satisfactory.

hunt [hʌnt] *v., n.* —*v.* **1** go after (wild animals, game birds, etc.) to catch or kill them for food or sport. **2** search through (a region) in pursuit of game. **3** use (horses or dogs) in the chase. **4** drive (out, away, etc.); pursue; harry; persecute. **5** try to find: *to hunt a clue.* **6** look thoroughly; search carefully: *to hunt through drawers.*
hunt down, a hunt for until caught or killed. **b** look for until found.
hunt out, seek and find.
hunt up, a look carefully for. **b** find by search.
—*n.* **1** the act of hunting: *Our gear for the duck hunt is all ready.* **2** a group of persons hunting together. **3** an attempt to find something; thorough look; careful search. ⟨OE *huntian*⟩

hunt•er ['hʌntər] *n.* **1** a person who hunts. **2** a horse or dog trained for hunting. **3** a pocket watch with a hinged cover, often gold, to protect the crystal. Also, **hunting watch**.

hunter's moon the full moon after the harvest moon.

hunt•ing ['hʌntɪŋ] *n., v.* —*n.* **1** the act of a person who or animal that hunts, especially the pursuit of game: *They went hunting last weekend.* **2** oscillation.
—*v.* ppr. of HUNT.

hunting case a watchcase with a hinged cover to protect the crystal.

hunting ground 1 a place or region for hunting. **2** See HAPPY HUNTING GROUND.

hunting horn a horn used in a hunt.

Hun•ting•ton's chorea ['hʌntɪŋtənz] a hereditary chorea of middle age, characterized by involuntary twitching of the face and extremities, followed by mental deterioration. ⟨after G. *Huntington* (1851-1916), American physician⟩

hunts•man ['hʌntsmən] *n., pl.* **-men. 1** hunter. **2** the manager of a hunt.

Hu•pa ['hupə] *n.* **1** a member of a Native American people living in NW California. **2** the Athapascan language of these people.

hur•dle ['hɜrdəl] *n., v.* **-dled, -dling.** —*n.* **1** in a race, a barrier for people or horses to jump over. **2 hurdles,** *pl.* a race in which the runners jump over hurdles. **3** an obstacle, difficulty, etc. **4** a frame made of sticks used as a temporary fence. **5** *Brit.* a portable frame resembling a stoneboat or sled, formerly used for dragging traitors to a place of execution.
—*v.* **1** jump over: *The horse hurdled both the fence and the ditch.* **2** overcome (an obstacle, difficulty, etc.). **3** enclose with a frame of sticks. ⟨OE *hyrdel*⟩ —**'hur•dler,** *n.*

hur•dy ['hɜrdi] *n. Cdn.* HURDY-GURDY GIRL.

Two types of hurdy-gurdy: left, def. 1; right, def.2: the drawing is from an 18th century French painting.

hur•dy–gur•dy ['hɜrdi 'gɜrdi] *n., pl.* **-dies. 1** a hand organ played by turning a handle. **2** formerly, an instrument shaped like a guitar, played by turning a wheel. **3** *Cdn.* HURDY-GURDY GIRL. ⟨probably imitative⟩

hurdy–gurdy girl *Cdn. Informal.* formerly, a dancing girl, especially one of a number of young women imported into British Columbia mining communities as dancing partners.

hurl [hɜrl] *v., n.* —*v.* **1** throw with much force: *The man hurled his spear at one bear; the dogs hurled themselves at the other.* **2** speak with strong feeling; utter violently: *He hurled insults at me.*
—*n.* a forcible or violent throw. ⟨cf. LG *hurreln*⟩ —**'hurl•er,** *n.*

hurl•ing ['hɜrlɪŋ] *n.* an Irish game similar to lacrosse in that the ball is kept in the air all the time, but played with a stick having a broad blade.

hurl•y–burl•y ['hɜrli 'bɜrli] *n., pl.* **-burl•ies.** disorder and noise; tumult. ⟨< earlier *hurling and burling*, varied reduplication of *hurling* in obs. sense of 'commotion' < *hurl*⟩

Hu•ron ['hjurɒn] *or* ['hjurən] *n., adj.* —*n.* **1** a member of a First Nations people formerly living in the region between Lake Huron and Lake Ontario. The Hurons were organized in a confederacy of four separate peoples. **2** the Iroquoian language of the Hurons.
—*adj.* of or having to do with the Hurons or their language. ⟨< F *huron* unkempt person, ruffian < *hure* dishevelled head of hair; a name applied to these people from about 1600⟩

Hu•ro•nia [hju'rouniə] *n.* a tract of land in Ontario on the shore of Lake Huron, around Georgian Bay.

Hu•ro•ni•an [hju'rouniən] *adj., n. Geology.* —*adj.* **1** of or having to do with a rock system north of Lake Huron. **2** of or having to do with the period of the Proterozoic era in which these rocks originated. See geological time chart in the Appendix.
—*n.* **1** a geological period of the Proterozoic era. **2** the rocks formed during this period.

hur•rah [hə'rɑ] *interj., n., v.* —*interj. or n.* a shout of joy, approval, etc.
—*v.* shout hurrahs; cheer. Also, **hooray, hurray**.

hur•ray [hə'rei] *interj., n., v.* hurrah. Also, **hooray**.

hur•ri•cane ['hɜrə,kein] *or* ['hɜrəkən] *n.* **1** a tropical cyclone that forms over the Atlantic Ocean, with winds of more than 120 km/h and, usually, very heavy rain. Hurricanes sometimes move into temperate regions. **2** any wind with a speed of more than 117 km/h. See chart of Beaufort scale in the Appendix. **3** a sudden, violent outburst or commotion: *a hurricane of cheers.* ⟨< Sp. *huracán* < Carib⟩

hurricane deck the upper deck on a river boat, etc.

hurricane lamp an oil lamp with a chimney to protect the flame from wind.

hur•ried ['hɜrid] *adj., v.* —*adj.* **1** done or made in a hurry; hasty: *a hurried reply.* **2** forced to hurry.
—*v.* pt. and pp. of HURRY. —**'hur•ried•ly,** *adv.*

hur•ry ['hɜri] *v.* **-ried, -ry•ing.** *n., pl.* **-ries.** —*v.* **1** drive, carry, send, or move quickly. **2** move or act with more than an easy or natural speed. **3** urge to act or move quickly; hasten; urge to great speed: *Don't hurry the driver.* **4** cause to happen or occur more quickly; hasten.
—*n.* **1** hurried movement or action. **2** an eagerness to have or do quickly. **3** need of haste: *There is no hurry for this.* ⟨origin uncertain⟩

☛ *Syn. n.* **1. Hurry,** HASTE, RUSH[1] = quickness or swiftness in action or movement. **Hurry** = action that is quicker than is easy or natural, sometimes quicker than necessary, and often suggests bustling or rushing: *In her hurry she dropped the eggs.* **Haste** emphasizes trying to save time, and often suggests hurried or rushed action, sometimes too rushed to get the desired results: *All this haste was of no use.* **Rush** = swift or rapid movement of people or things: *They did the work in a rush.*

hur•ry–scur•ry or **hur•ry–skur•ry** ['hɜri 'skɜri] *n., pl.* **-ries;** *adj., adv., v.* **-scur•ried, -scur•ry•ing.** *Informal.*
—*n.* a hurrying and confusion.
—*adj.* hurried and confused.
—*adv.* with hurrying and confusion.
—*v.* act or move with speed and confusion.

hurt [hɜrt] *v.* **hurt, hurt•ing;** *n.* —*v.* **1** cause pain, harm, distress, or damage: *Falling on concrete hurts. My new shoes hurt.* **2** cause pain to; give a wound to; injure: *I hurt my arm when I fell.* **3** feel pain; suffer: *He said he hurt all over after his fall. My sprained ankle hurts terribly.* **4** have a bad effect on; do damage or harm to: *Will it hurt this hat if it gets wet? The scandal has hurt his chances of getting elected.* **5** grieve; distress with inconsiderate behaviour: *He hurt his mother's feelings.*
be hurting for, *Informal.* lack; need very much: *We're hurting for time, folks.*
—*n.* **1** a wound or injury: *It was just a small hurt.* **2** a bad effect; damage, distress, or harm, or a cause of this: *The failure was a great hurt to her pride.* ⟨apparently < OF *hurter* strike < Gmc.⟩
—**'hurt•er,** *n.*

☛ *Syn. v.* **2, 4.** See note at INJURE.

hurt•ful ['hɜrtfəl] *adj.* causing pain, harm, distress, or damage;

injurious: *a mean and hurtful remark.* —'**hurt•ful•ly,** *adv.* —'**hurt•ful•ness,** *n.*

hur•tle ['hɜrtəl] *v.* **-tled, -tling;** *n.* —*v.* **1** dash or drive violently; come or fling suddenly: *The car hurtled across the road into a fence. The impact of the crash hurtled the driver against the windshield of the car.* **2** move with a clatter; rush noisily or violently: *The express train hurtled past.*
—*n.* the act or fact of hurtling; clash; clatter. ⟨ME, frequentative of *hurten* strike < OF < Gmc.; cf. ON *hrutr* a ram⟩

hur•tle•ber•ry ['hɜrtəl,bɛri] *n.* huckleberry.

hus•band ['hʌzbənd] *n., v.* —*n.* **1** a married man, especially when considered with reference to the woman he is married to. **2** *Archaic.* manager.
—*v.* **1** manage carefully; be saving of: *A sick person must husband his or her strength.* **2** *Archaic.* of a woman, marry. **3** *Archaic.* till (soil); cultivate (plants). ⟨OE *hūsbonda* < *hūs* house + *bonda* head of family (< ON *bóndi*)⟩ —'**hus•band•er,** *n.* —'**hus•band•less,** *adj.*

hus•band•ly ['hʌzbəndli] *adj.* of, like, or befitting a husband.

hus•band•man ['hʌzbəndmən] *n., pl.* **-men.** *Archaic.* farmer.

hus•band•ry ['hʌzbəndri] *n.* **1** careful management; thrift. **2** *Rare.* the management of one's affairs or resources. **3** farming, especially as a science or art.

hush [hʌʃ] *v., n., interj.* —*v.* **1** stop making a noise; make or become silent or quiet. **2** soothe; calm.
hush up, a keep from being told; stop discussion of. **b** *Informal.* be silent.
—*n.* a stopping of noise; silence; quiet.
—*interj.* stop the noise! be silent! keep quiet! ⟨ME *hussht* silent, originally interj., silence!⟩

hush–hush ['hʌʃ 'hʌʃ] *adj. Informal.* secret; confidential: *hush-hush plans.*

hush money *Informal.* money paid to keep a person from telling something.

husk[1] [hʌsk] *n., v.* —*n.* **1** the dry outer covering of certain seeds or fruits. The husk surrounding an ear of corn is made up of modified leaves. **2** the dry or worthless outer covering of anything.
—*v.* remove the husk from. ⟨ME *huske;* origin uncertain; cf. MDu. *huyskijn,* dim. of *huus* house⟩ —'**husk•er,** *n.* —'**husk,like,** *adj.*

husk[2] [hʌsk] *n.* a husky condition or quality of the voice. ⟨back formation from *husky*[1]⟩

husking bee *Cdn.* formerly, a community gathering where neighbours husked corn and had a party.

husk•y[1] ['hʌski] *adj.* **husk•i•er, husk•i•est. 1** dry in the throat; hoarse; rough of voice: *A cold sometimes causes a husky cough.* **2** of, like, or having husks. **3** *Cdn.* big and strong: *a husky young man.* ⟨< *husk*[1], n.⟩ —'**husk•i•ly,** *adv.* —'**husk•i•ness,** *n.*

husk•y[2] ['hʌski] *n., pl.* **-ies. 1** SIBERIAN HUSKY. **2** *Cdn.* any northern working dog. ⟨abbrev. of an early variant of *Eskimo.* 19c.⟩

husky mouse *Cdn. North.* one of several voles of the tundra.

hus•sar [hə'zɑr] *n.* **1** a light-armed cavalry soldier. **2** a member of certain armoured regiments. ⟨< Hungarian *huszár,* originally, freebooter < Old Serbian *husar,* var. of *kursar* < Ital. *corsaro* runner < VL *cursarius* < L *cursus* a run. Doublet of CORSAIR.⟩

Huss•ite ['hʌsəit] *n., adj.* —*n.* a follower of John Huss (1369?-1415), a Bohemian religious reformer and martyr.
—*adj.* of or having to do with John Huss or his teachings.

hus•sy ['hʌsi] *or* ['hʌzi] *n., pl.* **-sies. 1** a bold or bad-mannered girl. **2** a promiscuous woman or one who disregards moral conventions. ⟨< E *huswif* housewife⟩

hus•tings ['hʌstɪŋz] *n.pl. or sing.* **1** in England, a platform from which candidates for Parliament were formerly nominated and from which they addressed the voters. **2** a platform from which speeches are made in a political campaign. **3** the campaign route taken by a political candidate. **4** the proceedings at an election. ⟨OE < ON *hústhing* council < *hús* house + *thing* assembly⟩

hus•tle ['hʌsəl] *v.* **-tled, -tling;** *n.* —*v.* **1** hurry. **2** force hurriedly or roughly: *The police hustled the tramps out of town.* **3** push or shove roughly; jostle rudely: *The other boys hustled him along the street.* **4** *Informal.* go or work quickly or with tireless energy: *He had to hustle to earn enough money to support his family.* **5** *Slang.* sell or solicit, especially in an aggressive or deceitful way.
—*n.* **1** a hurry. **2** a rough pushing or shoving; rude jostling. **3** *Informal.* tireless energy. ⟨< MDu. *hutselen* shake⟩ —'**hus•tler,** *n.*

hut [hʌt] *n.* **1** a small, roughly built house; a small cabin. **2** a temporary wooden or metal structure for quartering troops. ⟨< F *hutte* < MHG *hütte*⟩ —'**hut,like,** *adj.*

hutch [hʌtʃ] *n., v.* —*n.* **1** a pen for rabbits, etc. **2** a hut. **3** a box, chest, or bin. **4** a cupboard, open or with glass doors, having shelves for dishes, etc. and set on a buffet. **5** a high cupboard with usually open shelves on the upper part; china cabinet.
—*v.* put or keep in a hutch. ⟨ME < OF *huche* < Med.L *hutica* chest⟩

Hut•ter•ite ['hʌtə,rəit] *n., adj. Cdn.* —*n.* a member of an originally Austrian religious and ethnic group of frugal farmers living mainly in Alberta and Manitoba. They are Anabaptist and emphasize simplicity and pacifism.
—*adj.* of or having to do with these people: *Hutterite communities, a Hutterite colony.* ⟨< Jacob *Hutter* (? -1535), who founded the group in 1528 + *-ite*[1]⟩

hutz•pah ['hutspɑ] *or* ['hʊtspɑ] *n.* See CHUTZPAH.

huz•za [hə'zɑ] *interj., n., pl.* **-zas;** *v.* **-zaed, -za•ing.** —*interj. or n.* a loud shout of joy, encouragement, or applause; hurrah.
—*v.* shout huzzas; cheer.

H.V., h.v., or **hv** high voltage.

h.w. HIGH WATER.

hwy. highway.

Hyacinths

hy•a•cinth ['haɪə,sɪnθ] *n.* **1** any of a genus (*Hyacinthus*) of plants of the lily family, especially *H. orientalis,* cultivated in many varieties for its spikes of small, fragrant, bell-shaped flowers. **2** the flower or flower spike of a hyacinth. Hyacinths are usually blue, pink, or white. **3** a reddish orange gem; a variety of zircon. **4** in antiquity, the aquamarine. **5** a purplish blue. ⟨< L *hyacinthus* < Gk. *hyakinthos,* a kind of flower. Doublet of JACINTH.⟩

hy•a•cin•thine [,haɪə'sɪnθən] *or* [,haɪə'sɪnθaɪn] *adj.* **1** of or like the hyacinth. **2** adorned with hyacinths.

Hy•a•des ['haɪə,diz] *n.pl.* **1** *Astronomy.* a group of stars in the constellation Taurus. In ancient times, they were supposed to be a sign of rain when they rose with the sun. **2** *Greek mythology.* the daughters of Atlas, nymphs who supplied the earth with moisture and who were placed in the sky by Zeus.

hy•ae•na [haɪ'inə] See HYENA.

hy•a•line ['haɪəlɪn] *or* ['haɪə,laɪn] *adj., n.* —*adj.* glassy; transparent. A hyaline cartilage contains little fibre.
—*n.* something glassy or transparent. ⟨< LL *hyalinus* < Gk. *hyalinos* < *hyalos* glass⟩

hyaline membrane disease a disease of newborn babies, especially if premature, in which a membrane forms in the lungs, restricting respiration.

hy•a•lite ['haɪə,ləit] *n.* a colourless variety of opal, sometimes transparent like glass and sometimes whitish and translucent. ⟨< Gk. *hyalos* glass + E *-ite*⟩

hy•a•loid ['haɪə,lɔɪd] *adj.* glassy; transparent; crystalline; hyaline.

hy•a•lu•ron•i•dase [,haɪəlʊ'rɒnɪ,deis] *n.* a drug used to aid injection by breaking down the viscosity of tissues, etc.

hy•brid ['haɪbrɪd] *n., adj.* —*n.* **1** the offspring of two animals or plants of different species, varieties, etc. **2** anything of mixed origin. **3** a word formed of parts from different languages. *Example: starvation,* from English *starve* and Latin *-ation.*
—*adj.* **1** bred from two different species, varieties, etc.: *A mule is a hybrid animal.* **2** of mixed origin. ⟨< L *hybrida,* var. of *ibrida* mongrel, hybrid⟩

hy•brid•ism ['haıbrı,dızəm] *n.* **1** the production of hybrids; crossbreeding. **2** a hybrid character, nature, or condition.

hy•brid•i•za•tion [,haıbrıdə'zeiʃən] *or* [,haıbrıdaı'zeiʃən] *n.* the production of hybrids; crossing of different species.

hy•brid•ize ['haıbrı,daız] *v.* **-ized, -iz•ing. 1** cause to produce hybrids; crossbreed. Botanists hybridize different kinds of plants to get new varieties. **2** produce hybrids. **—'hy•brid,iz•er,** *n.*

hybrid tea rose any of numerous relatively hardy varieties of bush rose developed from crosses of tea roses with other hybrids and valued for their large, profuse blooms, which occur in a wide range of colours and scents and also include many scentless varieties.

hybrid vigour a phenomenon of crossbreeding, in which the offspring are stronger and healthier than either parent; heterosis.

hy•da•tid ['haıdə,tıd] *n., adj. Pathology. —n.* a cyst produced by a tapeworm, containing the larvae and fluid.
—adj. of or being such a cyst. ⟨< Gk. *hydatis* watery blister < *hydor* water⟩

Hyde [haıd] *n.* **Mr.** See JEKYLL.

hydr– *combining form.* the form of HYDRO- before vowels, as in *hydraulic.*

hy•dra ['haıdrə] *n., pl.* **-dras, -drae** [-dri] *or* [-draı]. **1 Hydra, a** *Greek mythology.* a monstrous serpent having nine heads, each of which, after being cut off, was replaced by two heads unless the wound was cauterized. The Hydra was slain by Hercules. **b** *Astronomy.* a southern constellation represented as a serpent. **2** any persistent evil. **3** a kind of freshwater polyp, so called because when the tubelike body is cut into pieces, each piece forms a new individual. ⟨< L < Gk. *hydra* water serpent < *hydōr* water⟩

hy•dral•a•zine [haı'drælə,zin] *n.* a drug used to lower blood pressure.

hy•dran•gea [haı'dreindʒə] *or* [haı'dreindʒiə] *n.* **1** any of a genus (*Hydrangea*) of shrubs or woody vines of the saxifrage family, several of which are cultivated in gardens and greenhouses for their large, showy clusters of small white, pink, or blue flowers. **2** the flower of this plant. ⟨< NL < Gk. *hydōr* water + *angeion* vessel, capsule; with reference to its cup-shaped seed capsule⟩

hy•drant ['haıdrənt] *n.* a large, upright pipe with a valve for drawing water directly from a water main. Hydrants are used to get water to put out fires, to wash the streets, etc. ⟨< Gk. *hydōr* water⟩

hy•dranth ['haıdrænθ] *n. Zoology.* the mouth and tentacles of a polyp. ⟨< *hydr-* + Gk. *anthos* flower⟩

hy•drast•ine [haı'dræstin] *n.* a poisonous white alkaloid obtained from goldenseal. *Formula:* $C_{21}H_{21}NO_6$ ⟨< *Hydrastis* genus name (< Gk. *hydor* water) + *-inc*⟩

hy•drate ['haıdreit] *n., v.* **-drat•ed, -drat•ing.** *Chemistry. —n.* a compound produced when any of certain other substances unite with water, represented in formulas as containing molecules of water. Washing soda ($Na_2CO_3 \cdot 10H_2O$) is a hydrate.
—v. become or cause to become a hydrate; combine with water to form a hydrate. Blue vitriol is hydrated copper sulphate. ⟨< Gk. *hydōr* water⟩

hy•dra•tion [haı'dreiʃən] *n.* the act or process of combining with water, especially to form a hydrate.

hy•drau•lic [haı'drɒlık] *adj.* **1** having to do with water or other liquid in motion. **2** operated by the pressure of water or other liquid: *a hydraulic press, hydraulic brakes.* **3** hardening under water: *hydraulic cement.* **4** of or having to do with hydraulics: *a hydraulic engineer.* ⟨< L *hydraulicus* < Gk. *hydraulikos*, ult. < *hydōr* water + *aulos* pipe⟩ **—hy'drau•li•cal•ly,** *adv.*

hydraulic ram a water pump that forces water upwards.

hy•drau•lics [haı'drɒlıks] *n.* the branch of science dealing with water and other liquids in motion, their uses in engineering, the laws of their action, etc. (*used with a singular verb*).
☛ *Syn.* See note at HYDRODYNAMICS.

hy•dra•zine ['haıdrə,zin] *or* ['haıdrəzın] *n.* **1** *Chemistry.* a colourless, fuming, toxic liquid used in organic synthesis and as rocket fuel. *Formula:* N_2H_4 **2** any of various compounds obtained from this liquid by replacing one or more hydrogen atoms with an organic radical.

hy•dric ['haıdrık] *adj.* of or containing hydrogen.

hy•dride ['haıdraıd] *or* ['haıdrıd] *n. Chemistry.* a compound of hydrogen with another element or radical.

hy•dri•od•ic [,haıdri'ɒdık] *adj. Chemistry.* containing hydrogen and iodine. Hydriodic acid (HI) is a colourless gas with a suffocating odour.

hy•dro ['haıdrou] *n. Cdn.* **1** hydro-electric power: *Niagara Falls provides hydro for many factories.* **2** electricity as a utility distributed by a power company or commission: *The hydro was off for two hours during the storm.* **3 Hydro,** a company or commission producing and distributing electricity as a utility.

hydro– *combining form.* **1** of or having to do with water: *hydrometer, hydrostatics.* **2** combined with hydrogen, as in *hydrochloric, hydrosulphide.* Also, **hydr-,** before vowels. ⟨< Gk. *hydro-* < *hydōr* water⟩

hy•dro•bro•mic acid [,haıdrou'broumık] *Chemistry.* an aqueous solution of hydrogen bromide.

hy•dro•car•bon [,haıdrou'karbən] *n. Chemistry.* any of a class of compounds containing only hydrogen and carbon. Methane, benzene, and acetylene are hydrocarbons. Gasoline is a mixture of hydrocarbons.

hy•dro•cele ['haıdrə,sil] *n. Pathology.* an abnormal accumulation of fluid in a body cavity, especially the testes. ⟨< Gk. *hydrokēlē* < *hydor* water + *kēlē* tumour, swelling⟩

hy•dro•ce•phal•ic [,haıdrousə'fælık] *adj.* affected with or having to do with hydrocephalus.

hy•dro•ceph•a•lous [,haıdrə'sɛfələs] *adj.* hydrocephalic.
☛ *Hom.* HYDROCEPHALUS.

hy•dro•ceph•a•lus [,haıdrə'sɛfələs] *n. Pathology.* an accumulation of fluid within the cranium, especially in infancy, often causing great enlargement of the head. ⟨< *hydro-* + Gk. *kephalē* head⟩
☛ *Hom.* HYDROCEPHALOUS.

hy•dro•chlo•ric [,haıdrə'klɔrık] *adj. Chemistry.* containing hydrogen and chlorine.

hydrochloric acid *Chemistry.* a clear, colourless solution of hydrogen chloride, that has a strong, sharp odour and is highly corrosive. Hydrochloric acid is present in a dilute form in gastric juice and is used in various industrial processes, in dyeing, and in medicine. *Formula:* HCl

hy•dro•chlor•ide [,haıdrə'klɔraıd] *n. Chemistry.* a compound resulting from the action of hydrochloric acid on an organic base.

hy•dro•co•done ['haıdroukə,doun] *n. Pharmacy.* a drug used to treat a bad cough.

hy•dro•cor•ti•sone [,haıdrou'kɔrtə,zoun] *n. Pharmacy.* an adrenal hormone similar to cortisone, used in treating arthritis. *Formula:* $C_{21}H_{30}O_5$

hy•dro•cy•an•ic [,haıdrousaı'ænık] *adj. Chemistry.* containing hydrogen and cyanogen.

hydrocyanic acid *Chemistry.* a colourless, volatile solution of hydrogen cyanide, that has an odour like that of bitter almonds and is highly poisonous; prussic acid. It is used as a fumigant and in the manufacture of dyes, plastics, etc. *Formula:* HCN

hy•dro•dy•nam•ic [,haıdroudaı'næmık] *adj.* of or having to do with the force or motion of fluids, or with hydrodynamics. **—,hy•dro•dy'nam•i•cal•ly,** *adv.*

hy•dro•dy•nam•ics [,haıdroudaı'næmıks] *n.* the branch of physics dealing with the forces that water and other liquids exert.
☛ *Syn.* Although **hydrodynamics,** HYDROKINETICS, HYDROMECHANICS and HYDRAULICS all deal with the study of liquids in motion, only **hydraulics** deals with their use as a source of energy.

hy•dro–e•lec•tric ['haıdrou ı'lɛktrık] *adj.* of or having to do with the generation of elecricity by water power, or by the friction of water or steam: *There is a large hydro-electric power plant on the St. Lawrence Seaway.*

hy•dro–e•lec•tric•i•ty [,haıdrou ılɛk'trısəti] *n.* electricity produced from water power, etc.

hy•dro•flu•or•ic [,haıdrou'flɔrık] *adj. Chemistry.* containing hydrogen and fluorine.

hydrofluoric acid *Chemistry.* a colourless, corrosive, volatile solution of hydrogen fluoride, used for etching glass. *Formula:* HF

hy•dro•foil ['haıdrə,fɔıl] *n.* **1** one of a set of blades or fins attached to the hull of a boat at an angle so that the boat, when moving, is lifted just clear of the water. Hydrofoils reduce friction and thus increase speed. **2** a boat equipped with hydrofoils.

hy•dro•gen ['haıdrədʒən] *n. Chemistry.* a colourless, odourless, gaseous chemical element that burns easily and weighs less than any other known element. Hydrogen combines chemically with oxygen to form water. *Symbol*: H; *at.no.* 1; *at.mass* 1.01. ⟨< F *hydrogène*, ult. < Gk. *hydōr* water + *-genēs* born⟩

hy•drog•e•nate [haɪ'drɒdʒə,neit] *or* ['haɪdrədʒə,neit] *v.* **-nat•ed, -nat•ing.** *Chemistry*. combine or treat with hydrogen; especially, combine an unsaturated organic compound with hydrogen. Vegetable oils are hydrogenated to produce solid fats.

hy•dro•gen•a•tion [,haɪdrədʒə'neiʃən] *n. Chemistry*. the process of combining with hydrogen.

hydrogen bomb a bomb that uses the fusion of atoms to cause an explosion of tremendous force. It is many times more powerful than an atomic bomb.

hydrogen bromide *Chemistry*. a colourless gas used in the manufacture of barbiturates. *Formula*: HBr

hydrogen chloride *Chemistry*. a colourless, strong-smelling, poisonous gas, a compound of hydrogen and chlorine. It is soluble in water, forming hydrochloric acid. *Formula*: HCl

hydrogen cyanide *Chemistry*. a colourless, highly poisonous gas, a compound of hydrogen and cyanogen. It has an odour of bitter almonds and dissolves in water to form hydrocyanic acid. *Formula*: HCN

hydrogen fluoride *Chemistry*. a colourless, corrosive, poisonous liquid or gas, a compound of hydrogen and fluorine. It is soluble in water, forming hydrofluoric acid. *Formula*: HF

hydrogen iodide *Chemistry*. a colourless gas used to make hydriodic acid. *Formula*: HI

hydrogen ion *Chemistry*. the positively charged ion of hydrogen.

hy•drog•e•nize [haɪ'drɒdʒə,naɪz] *or* ['haɪdrədʒə,naɪz] *v.* **-nized, -niz•ing.** hydrogenate.

hy•drog•e•nous [haɪ'drɒdʒənəs] *adj.* of or containing hydrogen.

hydrogen peroxide a colourless, unstable liquid often used in dilute solution as an antiseptic, a bleaching agent, etc. *Formula*: H_2O_2

hydrogen sulphide or **sulfide** *Chemistry*. a flammable, poisonous gas having a strong, offensive odour, found especially in mineral waters and decaying matter. *Formula*: H_2S

hy•dro•graph ['haɪdrə,græf] *n.* a hydrographic diagram, chart, or record.

hy•drog•ra•pher [haɪ'drɒgrəfər] *n.* a person trained in hydrography, especially one whose work it is.

hy•dro•graph•ic [,haɪdrə'græfɪk] *adj.* of or having to do with hydrography. **—,hy•dro'graph•i•cal•ly,** *adv.*

hy•drog•ra•phy [haɪ'drɒgrəfi] *n.* **1** the study, measurement, and description of oceans, lakes, rivers, etc., especially with reference to their use for navigation and commerce. **2** oceans, lakes, rivers, etc., especially as dealt with on a map of a certain region, or in treatises or surveys: *the hydrography of northern Saskatchewan.*

hy•droid ['haɪdrɔɪd] *n.* **1** a very simple form of hydrozoan that grows into branching colonies by budding; polyp. **2** any hydrozoan. ⟨< *hydra* + *-oid*⟩

hy•dro•ki•net•ic [,haɪdroukɪ'nɛtɪk] *adj.* of or having to do with hydrokinetics. **—,hy•dro•ki'net•i•cal•ly,** *adv.*

hy•dro•ki•net•ics [,haɪdroukɪ'nɛtɪks] *n.* the branch of physics dealing with the motion, or kinetics, of fluids.
☛ *Syn.* See note at HYDRODYNAMICS.

hy•dro•log•i•cal [,haɪdrə'lɒdʒɪkəl] *adj.* of or having to do with hydrology. Also, **hydrologic**.

hydrologic cycle the circular process in which water evaporates from the ocean, falling to earth as rain or snow, to return to the ocean from rivers fed by rain or melting snow.

hy•drol•o•gist [haɪ'drɒlədʒɪst] *n.* a person trained in hydrology, especially one whose work it is.

hy•drol•o•gy [haɪ'drɒlədʒi] *n.* the branch of physical geography that deals with the laws, properties, distribution, etc. of water.

hy•drol•y•sate [haɪ'drɒlə,seit] *n. Chemistry*. any chemical compound formed by hydrolysis.

hy•drol•y•sis [haɪ'drɒləsɪs] *n., pl.* **-ses** [-,siz]. *Chemistry*. a chemical decomposition that changes a compound into other compounds by taking up the elements of water. ⟨< *hydro-* + Gk. *lysis* a loosening⟩

hy•dro•lyte ['haɪdrə,ləit] *n. Chemistry*. any substance subjected to hydrolysis.

hy•dro•lyt•ic [,haɪdrə'lɪtɪk] *adj.* producing, noting, or resulting in hydrolysis.

hy•dro•lyze ['haɪdrə,laɪz] *v.* **-lyzed, -lyz•ing. 1** decompose by hydrolysis. **2** undergo hydrolysis. **—,hy•dro•ly'za•tion,** *n.*

hy•dro•man•cy ['haɪdrə,mænsi] *n.* the use of signs observed in water to tell the future. ⟨< OF *ydromancie* < L < Gk. *hydromanteia* < *hydor* water + *manteia* divination < *mantis* prophet⟩

hy•dro•me•chan•ics [,haɪdroumə'kænɪks] *n.* the branch of physics dealing with the mechanics of fluids, or of their laws of equilibrium or motion. **—,hy•dro•me'chan•i•cal,** *adj.*
☛ *Syn.* See note at HYDRODYNAMICS.

hy•dro•met•al•lur•gy [,haɪdrə'mɛtə,lɜrdʒi] *n.* the process of extracting metals from bodies of ore by the use of liquids.

hy•drom•e•ter [haɪ'drɒmətər] *n.* a graduated instrument for finding the specific gravities of liquids.

hy•dro•met•ric [,haɪdrə'mɛtrɪk] *adj.* **1** of or having to do with hydrometry. **2** of or having to do with a hydrometer. Also, **hydrometrical**.

hy•drom•e•try [haɪ'drɒmətri] *n.* the determination of specific gravity, purity, etc. by means of a hydrometer.

hy•dro•mor•phone [,haɪdrə'mɔrfoun] *n. Pharmacy*. an analgesic drug.

hy•dro•ni•um [haɪ'drouniəm] *n. Chemistry*. a hydrated hydrogen ion. ⟨< *hydro(gen)* + *(ammo)nium*⟩

hy•dro•path•ic [,haɪdrə'pæθɪk] *adj., n. —adj.* of or using hydropathy.
—n. a sanitarium that specializes in hydropathy.

hy•drop•a•thy [haɪ'drɒpəθi] *n.* the treatment of disease by drinking mineral water and by hydrotherapy.

hy•dro•phane ['haɪdrə,fein] *n.* an opal that changes from opaque to transparent when wet. ⟨< Gk. *hydor* water + *phanein* appear⟩

hy•dro•phil•ic [,haɪdrə'fɪlɪk] *adj. Chemistry*. capable of combining with water.

hy•droph•i•lous [haɪ'drɒfələs] *adj. Botany.* growing in water.

hy•dro•pho•bi•a [,haɪdrə'foubiə] *n.* **1** a morbid dread of water. **2** rabies, especially in human beings. Rabies in people is called hydrophobia because one of the symptoms is a dislike and fear of water and other liquids.

hy•dro•pho•bic [,haɪdrə'foubɪk] *adj.* **1** of or having to do with hydrophobia. **2** suffering from hydrophobia. **3** *Chemistry*. not easily mixed with or made wet by water.

hy•dro•phone ['haɪdrə,foun] *n.* **1** an instrument for detecting the position and source of sounds under water. **2** an instrument detecting water flowing in a pipe, used in finding leaks. **3** *Medicine.* a listening instrument for detecting sounds through a column of water.

hy•dro•phyte ['haɪdrə,fəit] *n.* any plant that can grow only in water or very wet soil. Most algae are hydrophytes.
—,hy•dro'phyt•ic [-'fɪtɪk] *adj.*

hy•dro•plane ['haɪdrə,plein] *n.* **1** a light speedboat with hydrofoils or a bottom shaped so that the hull will rise out of the water at high speeds. **2** hydrofoil. **3** seaplane. **4** a horizontal rudder on a submarine for making it go up and down.

hy•dro•pon•ic [,haɪdrə'pɒnɪk] *adj.* of, produced, or grown by hydroponics. **—,hy•dro'pon•i•cal•ly,** *adv.*

hy•dro•pon•ics [,haɪdrə'pɒnɪks] *n.* the growing of plants in water containing the necessary nutrients instead of in soil. ⟨< *hydro-* + L *ponere* to place⟩

hy•drops ['haɪdrɒps] *n.* the abnormal accumulation of fluid in the body cavity or in tissues. ⟨< Gk. *hydrops* dropsy⟩
—hy'drop•ic, *adj.*

hydrops fe•tal•is [fi'tælɪs] hydrops occurring prenatally.

hy•dro•qui•none [,haɪdroukwɪ'noun] *or* [,haɪdrou'kwɪnoun] *n. Chemistry*. a white, sweetish, crystalline compound, used in photographic developers and in medicine. *Formula*: $C_6H_4(OH)_2$

hy•dro•scope ['haɪdrə,skoup] *n.* a device for looking at objects deep in water.

hy•dro•sol ['haɪdrə,sɒl] *or* ['haɪdrə,soul] *n. Chemistry.* a colloid in a water solution.

hy•dro•sphere ['haɪdrə,sfir] *n.* **1** the water on the surface of the globe. **2** the water vapour in the atmosphere.

hy•dro•stat ['haɪdrə,stæt] *n.* **1** any of various devices for preventing damage to a steam boiler as a result of lack of water.

2 an electrical device for detecting the presence of water from overflow, leakage, etc. ⟨< *hydro-* + Gk. *-statos* that stands⟩

hy•dro•stat•ic [ˌhaɪdrəˈstætɪk] *adj.* of or having to do with hydrostatics. **—ˌhy•droˈstat•i•cal•ly,** *adv.*

hy•dro•stat•ics [ˌhaɪdrəˈstætɪks] *n.* the branch of physics that deals with the equilibrium and pressure of water and other liquids.

hy•dro•sul•phide [ˌhaɪdrəˈsʌlfaɪd] *n. Chemistry.* a chemical compound derived from hydrogen sulphide by replacing one of its hydrogen atoms with a base radical.

hy•dro•tax•is [ˌhaɪdrəˈtæksɪs] *n. Biology.* the movement of an organism toward or away from water.

hy•dro•ther•a•peu•tics [ˌhaɪdrouˌθɛrəˈpjutɪks] *n.* hydropathy. **—ˌhy•droˌther•aˈpeu•tic,** *adj.*

hy•dro•ther•a•py [ˌhaɪdrəˈθɛrəpi] *n.* the treatment of various diseases by means of water, especially bathing or doing exercises in warm water.

hy•dro•therm•al [ˌhaɪdrəˈθɜrməl] *adj.* having to do with hot water. **—ˌhy•droˈther•mal•ly,** *adv.*

hy•dro•thor•ax [ˌhaɪdrəˈθɔræks] *n. Pathology.* fluid in the lungs.

hy•dro•trop•ic [ˌhaɪdrəˈtrɒpɪk] *adj. Biology.* having the tendency to turn or move toward, or away from, moisture.

hy•drot•ro•pism [haɪˈdrɒtrəˌpɪzəm] *n. Biology.* a tendency to turn or move toward or away from water. Hydrotropism causes roots to grow toward water.

hy•drous [ˈhaɪdrəs] *adj.* containing water, usually in combination. A hydrous salt is a crystalline compound. ⟨< Gk. *hydōr* water⟩

hy•drox•ide [haɪˈdrɒksaɪd] *or* [haɪˈdrɒksɪd] *n. Chemistry.* any compound consisting of an element or radical combined with one or more hydroxyl radicals. Hydroxides of metals are bases; those of non-metals are acids.

hy•drox•o•co•bal•a•min [ˌhaɪdrɒkˌsoukouˈbæləmin] *n.* Vitamin B_{12a}.

hy•dro•xy [haɪˈdrɒksi] *adj. Chemistry.* containing the hydroxyl group.

hy•dro•xy•chlo•ro•quine [ˌhaɪdrɒksiˈklɔrəˌkwin] *or* [ˌhaɪdrɒksiˈklɔrəkwɪn] *n.* a drug used to treat malaria and certain forms of arthritis.

hy•drox•yl [haɪˈdrɒksəl] *n. Chemistry.* a univalent radical found in all hydroxides. *Formula*: OH

hy•drox•y•prop•yl [ˌhaɪdrɒksiˈprɒpɪl] *n.* an opthalmic insert to treat a dry eye.

hy•drox•y•ur•ea [ˌhaɪdrɒksiˈjʊriə] *n.* a drug used to treat certain forms of cancer.

hy•dro•zo•an [ˌhaɪdrəˈzouən] *n., adj. —n.* any of a class (Hydrozoa) of invertebrate water animals having a simple body consisting of two layers of cells and a mouth that opens into the body, including hydras, polyps, many jellyfishes, etc.
—adj. belonging to the class Hydrozoa. ⟨< NL *Hydrozoa*, the genus name < Gk. *hydōr* water + *zōon* animal⟩

Hy•drus [ˈhaɪdrəs] *n.* a constellation near the south celestial pole.

A spotted hyena—about 90 cm high at the shoulder

hy•e•na [haɪˈinə] *n.* any of a very small family (Hyaenidae) of wolflike carnivorous animals of Africa and Asia that live mainly as scavengers, having short hind legs and a large head with very powerful jaws and teeth. The spotted, or laughing, hyena is noted for a kind of howl that sounds like demented laughter. Also, **hyaena.** ⟨< L *hyaena* < Gk. *hyaina* < *hys* pig⟩

hyeto– *combining form.* rain: *hyetography.* ⟨< Gk. *hyetos* rain⟩

hy•et•o•graph [haɪˈɛtəˌgræf] *or* [ˈhaɪətəˌgræf] *n.* a map of the rainfall in the localities presented.

hy•e•tog•ra•phy [ˌhaɪəˈtɒgrəfi] *n.* the study of rainfall.

Hy•ge•ia [haɪˈdʒiə] *n. Greek mythology.* the goddess of health.

hy•giene [ˈhaɪdʒin] *n.* **1** the principles of keeping well and preventing disease; the science of health. **2** practices such as cleanliness that help to preserve health: *personal hygiene.* ⟨< F < NL *(ars) hygieina* the healthful art < Gk. *hygieinē* < *hygiēs* healthy⟩

hy•gien•ic [haɪˈdʒinɪk] *or* [haɪˈdʒɛnɪk] *adj.* **1** healthful; sanitary. **2** having to do with health or hygiene. **—hyˈgien•i•cal•ly,** *adv.*

hy•gien•ist [haɪˈdʒinɪst], [haɪˈdʒɛnɪst], *or* [ˈhaɪdʒinɪst] *n.* a person trained in hygiene, especially one whose work it is, such as a dental hygienist.

hygro– *combining form.* wet; moist; moisture: *hygrometer.* ⟨< Gk. *hygro-* < *hygros* wet⟩

hy•gro•graph [ˈhaɪgrəˌgræf] *n.* a hygrometer that is self-recording.

hy•grom•e•ter [haɪˈgrɒmətər] *n.* any instrument for determining the amount of moisture in the air.

hy•gro•met•ric [ˌhaɪgrəˈmɛtrɪk] *adj.* of or having to do with the measurement of moisture in the air.

hy•grom•e•try [haɪˈgrɒmətri] *n.* the measurement of the amount of moisture in the air.

hy•gro•scope [ˈhaɪgrəˌskoup] *n.* an instrument that shows the changes in the humidity of the air.

hy•gro•scop•ic [ˌhaɪgrəˈskɒpɪk] *adj.* **1** having to do with or perceptible by the hygroscope. **2** absorbing or attracting moisture from the air.

hy•ing [ˈhaɪɪŋ] *v.* ppr. of HIE.

Hyk•sos [ˈhɪksɒs] *or* [ˈhɪksous] *n.pl.* Shepherd Kings, the foreign rulers of Egypt from about 1750 B.C. to about 1600 B.C. ⟨< Egyptian, leader⟩

hy•la [ˈhaɪlə] *n.* any of a genus (*Hyla*) of tree frogs. ⟨< NL < Gk. *hylē* wood⟩

hylo– *combining form.* wood; matter: *hylophagous.* ⟨< Gk. *hyle* wood, matter⟩

hy•loph•a•gous [haɪˈlɒfəgəs] *adj.* feeding on wood.

Hy•men [ˈhaɪmən] *n. Greek mythology.* the god of marriage.

hy•men [ˈhaɪmən] *n. Anatomy.* a fold of mucous membrane extending partly across the opening of the vagina and usually ruptured the first time sexual intercourse takes place. **—ˈhy•men•al,** *adj.* ⟨< LL < Gk. *hymēn* membrane. 17c.⟩

hy•me•ne•al [ˌhaɪməˈniəl] *adj., n. —adj.* having to do with marriage.
—n. a wedding song.

hy•me•nop•ter•an [ˌhaɪməˈnɒptərən] *n., adj. —n.* a hymenopterous insect.
—adj. hymenopterous.

hy•me•nop•ter•ous [ˌhaɪməˈnɒptərəs] *adj.* of or belonging to an order (Hymenoptera) of insects that includes ants, bees, and wasps. Winged hymenopterous insects have four membranous wings. ⟨< Gk. *hymenopteros* < *hymēn* membrane + *pteron* wing⟩

hymn [hɪm] *n., v. —n.* **1** a song of praise to God, sung as part of a religious service. A hymn generally has more than one stanza, uses strict metre and rhyme, and is set to relatively sedate music. Compare CHORUS. **2** any song of praise.
—v. praise or honour with a hymn. ⟨< L < Gk. *hymnos*⟩
—ˈhymnˌlike, *adj.*
☛ *Hom.* HIM.

hym•nal [ˈhɪmnəl] *n., adj. —n.* a book of hymns.
—adj. having to do with hymns.

hym•nar•y [ˈhɪmnəri] *n., pl.* **-ies.** hymnal.

hymn•ist [ˈhɪmnɪst] *n.* a composer of hymns.

hym•no•dy [ˈhɪmnədi] *n.* the singing, study, composing or history of hymns.

hym•nol•o•gist [hɪmˈnɒlədʒɪst] *n.* **1** a person knowledgeable in or studying hymnology. **2** a composer of hymns.

hym•nol•o•gy [hɪmˈnɒlədʒi] *n.* **1** the study of hymns, their history, classification, etc. **2** hymns collectively. **3** the composing of hymns.

hy•oid [ˈhaɪɔɪd] *n.* **1** *Anatomy.* a U-shaped bone that supports the tongue in human beings, lying at the base of the tongue above the thyroid cartilage. **2** *Zoology.* a corresponding bone or group of bones in other vertebrates. ⟨< F < NL < Gk. *hyoeidēs* U-shaped < *hy* (υ, upsilon) + *eidos* form⟩

hy•o•scine ['haɪə,sin] *or* ['haɪəsɪn] *n.* scopolamine. ⟨< L *hyosc(yamus)* henbane + E *-ine*⟩

hy•os•cy•a•mine [,haɪə'saɪə,min] *n.* a drug used to treat peptic ulcer. It is extracted from henbane. ⟨< L *hyoscyamus* henbane + E *-ine*⟩

hyp. 1 hypothesis. 2 hypotenuse.

hyp•a•bys•sal [,hɪpə'bɪsəl] *adj. Geology.* of rocks, solidifying before reaching the earth's surface.

hy•pa•eth•ral [hɪ'piθrəl] *adj.* without a roof. ⟨< Gk. *hypo* under + *aither* clear sky⟩

hy•pan•thi•um [hɪ'pænθiəm] *n.* a cuplike ring of tissue around the stem, supporting the flower of certain plants. ⟨< Gk. *hypo-* under + *anthos* flower⟩

Hy•pa•tia [həi'peiʃə] *or* [həi'pætiə] *n.* a Greek philosopher (c. A.D. 370-415) noted for her beauty.

hype[1] [həip] *n., v.* **hyped, hyp•ing.** *Slang. —n.* a drug addict. *—v.* excite with drugs or as if with drugs. ⟨< *hypodermic*⟩

hype[2] [həip] *n., v.* **hyped, hyp•ing.** *Informal. —n.* sensational or exaggerated advertising.
—v. advertise extravagantly. ⟨< Gk. *hyper* exceedingly⟩

hyp•er ['həipər] *adj. Slang.* overwrought or overexcited: *We were all pretty hyper after winning the third straight game.*

hyper– *prefix.* over; above; beyond; exceedingly; to excess: *hyperacidity, hypersensitive.* ⟨< Gk. *hyper-* < *hyper*⟩

hy•per•a•cid•i•ty [,həipərə'sɪdəti] *n.* more than the normal amount of acid, especially in the stomach juices. **—,hy•per'ac•id,** *adj.*

hy•per•ac•tive [,həipər'æktɪv] *adj.* of, having to do with, or characterized by hyperactivity: *a hyperactive child.*

hy•per•ac•tiv•i•ty [,həipəræk'tɪvəti] *n.* excessive or exaggerated activity or extreme restlessness, associated with physical or psychological disorders, especially in children.

hy•per•bar•ic [,həipər'bærɪk] *or* [,həipər'bɛrɪk] *adj.* having to do with abnormally high atmospheric pressure.

hyperbaric chamber DECOMPRESSION CHAMBER.

hy•per•bo•la [həi'pɜrbələ] *n., pl.* **-las.** *Geometry.* a curve formed when a cone is cut by a plane making a larger angle with the base than the side of the cone makes. See CONE for picture. ⟨< NL < Gk. *hyperbolē*, ult. < *hyper-* beyond + *ballein* throw⟩

hy•per•bo•le [həi'pɜrbəli] *n.* exaggeration for effect. *Example*: *Waves high as mountains broke over the reef.* Compare LITOTES. ⟨< L < Gk. *hyperbolē.* See HYBERBOLA.⟩

hy•per•bol•ic [,həipər'bɒlɪk] *adj.* **1** of, like, or using hyperbole; exaggerated; exaggerating. **2** of or having to do with hyperbolas. **3** *Mathematics.* having the form of a hyperbola. **—,hy•per'bol•i•cal•ly,** *adv.*

hy•per•bol•ism [həi'pɜrbə,lɪzəm] *n.* the use of hyperbole.

hy•per•bol•ize [həi'pɜrbə,laɪz] *v.* **-ized, -iz•ing.** exaggerate.

Hy•per•bo•re•an [,həipər'bɔriən] *or* [,həipərbə'riən] *n., adj.* *—n.* **1** *Greek legend.* one of a group of people described as living in a land of perpetual sunshine and plenty beyond the north wind. **2 hyperborean,** an inhabitant of the far north.
—adj. **hyperborean,** of the far north; arctic; frigid. ⟨< LL *Hyperboreanus* < L *Hyperboreus* < Gk. *Hyperboreos* beyond the north < *hyper-* beyond + *boreios* northern < *boreas* the north wind⟩

hy•per•cor•rec•tion [,həipərkə'rɛkʃən] a speech change made on the basis of a faulty understanding of some grammatical rule. 'Between you and I' is a hypercorrection.

hy•per•crit•ic [,həipər'krɪtɪk] *n.* an excessively critical person.

hy•per•crit•i•cal [,həipər'krɪtəkəl] *adj.* excessively critical. **—,hy•per'crit•i•cal•ly,** *adv.* **—,hy•per'crit•i,cism,** *n.*

hy•per•es•the•sia [,həipərɛs'θiʒə] *or* [,həipərɛs'θɪziə] *n.* abnormal sensitivity. Also, **hyperaesthesia. —,hy•per•es'thet•ic** [-'θɛtɪk], *adj.*

hy•per•gly•ce•mi•a [,həipərgləi'simiə] *n.* an abnormally high concentration of sugar in the blood. Also, **hyperglycaemia.** ⟨< *hyper-* + Gk. *glyko-* sweet + E *-emia*⟩
—,hy•per•gly'ce•mic, *adj.*

hy•per•gol•ic [,həipər'gɒlɪk] *adj.* lighting spontaneously when its components are brought together: *hypergolic rocket fuel.* ⟨< *hyp(er-)* + Gk. *erg(on)* work + E *-ol* + *-ic*⟩

Hy•pe•ri•on [həi'piriən] *n.* **1** *Greek mythology.* **a** a Titan, father of the sun god Helios. **b** Helios. **c** Apollo. **2** a satellite of Saturn.

hy•per•ki•ne•sis [,həipərkə'nisɪs] *n.* excessive motion.

hy•per•o•pi•a [,həipər'oupiə] *n.* far-sightedness. ⟨< NL < Gk. *hyper-* beyond + *ōps* eye⟩

hy•per•op•ic [,həipər'ɒpɪk] *adj.* FAR-SIGHTED (def. 1).

hy•per•os•to•sis [,həipərɒs'tousɪs] *n.* abnormal bone thickening. ⟨< *hyper-* + *ost(eo-)* + *-osis*⟩

hy•per•phys•i•cal [,həipər'fɪzɪkəl] *adj.* supernatural. **—,hy•per'phys•i•cal•ly,** *adv.*

hy•per•pla•sia [,həipər'pleiʒə] *or* [,həipər'pleiziə] *n.* *Pathology.* overgrowth of a tissue, with abnormal increase in the number of cells of normal size and arrangement. Compare HYPERTROPHY. ⟨< NL < *hyper-* + *plasis* a moulding⟩

hy•perp•nea [,həipərp'niə] *or* [,həipər'niə] *n.* abnormally rapid and deep breathing. ⟨< *hyper-* + Gk. *pnoē* breathing < *pnein* breathe⟩

hy•per•py•rex•ia [,həipərpaɪ'rɛksiə] *n.* a high fever.

hy•per•sen•si•tive [,həipər'sɛnsətɪv] *adj.* excessively sensitive. **—,hy•per'sen•si•tive•ness,** *n.*

hy•per•sen•si•tiv•i•ty [,həipər,sɛnsə'tɪvəti] *n.* excessive sensitiveness.

hy•per•son•ic [,həipər'sɒnɪk] *adj.* **1** of or denoting speed five or more times faster than that of sound. **2** able to travel at this speed.

hy•per•sthene ['həipərs,θin] *n.* iron magnesium silicate. ⟨< *hyper-* + Gk. *sthenos* strength⟩

hy•per•ten•sion [,həipər'tɛnʃən] *n.* abnormally high blood pressure.

hy•per•text ['həipər,tɛkst] *n. Computer technology.* **1** in a piece of software, document, Web page, etc., a feature whereby supplementary textual information, linked to a text or image but not displayed on the screen, can be accessed and displayed by selecting a specially marked word on the screen (**hyperlink text**) or, sometimes, an icon. **2** the text so accessed. **3** loosely, **a** a document or documents using this feature. **b** the specially marked word embodying the link.

hy•per•ther•mia [,həipər'θɜrmiə] *n.* hyperpyrexia. Also, **hyperthermy** ['həipər,θɜrmi].

hy•per•thy•roid [,həipər'θaɪrɔɪd] *n., adj. —n.* **1** an overactive thyroid gland. **2** a person having such a gland.
—adj. relating to an overactive thyroid gland.

hy•per•thy•roid•ism [,həipər'θaɪrɔɪ,dɪzəm] *n.* excessive activity of the thyroid gland. Compare HYPOTHYROIDISM.

hy•per•ton•ic [,həipər'tɒnɪk] *adj. Chemistry.* of a solution, having a higher concentration of solute than another solution has. A hypertonic solution in a cell has a higher concentration of solute than that of the cytoplasm, so that a cell loses water and volume by osmosis. Compare with HYPOTONIC and ISOTONIC.

hy•per•tro•phy [həi'pɜrtrəfi] *n., pl.* **-phies;** *v.* **-phied, -phy•ing.** *—n.* the enlargement of a part or organ due to an increase in the size of its cells; growing too big.
—v. grow too big. ⟨< NL *hypertrophia* < Gk. *hyper-* over + *trophē* nourishment⟩ **—,hy•per'troph•ic** [-'trɒfɪk] *or* [-'troufɪk], *adj.*

hy•per•ven•til•a•tion [,həipər,vɛntə'leiʃən] *n.* hyperpnea. **—,hy•per'ven•til•ate,** *v.*

hy•per•vi•ta•mi•no•sis [,həipər,vəitəmɪ'nousɪs] *n.* an abnormal condition caused by the intake of too many vitamins, especially Vitamin A.

hy•pha ['həifə] *n., pl.* **-phae** [-fi] any of the fibrous structures that make up fungi. ⟨< L < Gk., web⟩

hy•phen ['həifən] *n., v. —n.* a mark (-) used to connect words to form certain compounds (*double-dealer*, *light-hearted*, *door-to-door*); to separate certain affixes to indicate special meaning (*re-creation* vs. *recreation*) or facilitate recognition of word elements for purposes of pronunciation, etc. (*re-enter*); to indicate a break in a word at the end of a line of printing or writing.
—v. hyphenate. ⟨< LL < Gk. *hyphen* in one, hyphen < *hypo-* under + *hen* one⟩

hy•phen•ate ['həifə,neit] *v.* **-at•ed, -at•ing.** connect by a hyphen; write or print with a hyphen.

hy•phen•at•ed ['həifə,neitɪd] *adj., v. —adj.* **1** joined with a hyphen. **2** of foreign or mixed birth: *a hyphenated Canadian.*
—v. pt. and pp. of HYPHENATE.

hy•phen•a•tion [,həifə'neiʃən] *n.* the act of connecting by or writing with a hyphen.

hy•phen•ize ['həifə,naɪz] *v.* **-ized, -iz•ing.** hyphenate.

hyp•na•gog•ic [ˌhɪpnə'gɒdʒɪk] *adj.* having to do with the period immediately before falling asleep. Compare HYPNOPOMPIC. ⟨< *hypno-* + Gk. *agogos* leading⟩

hypno– *combining form.* **1** sleep: *hypnology.* **2** hypnosis: *hypnotherapy.* ⟨< Gk. *hypno(s)* sleep⟩

hyp•no•an•a•ly•sis [ˌhɪpnouə'næləsɪs] *n. Psychoanalysis.* the use of hypnotism to elicit subconscious material from a person.

hyp•no•gen•e•sis [ˌhɪpnou'dʒɛnəsɪs] *n.* the inducing of a hypnotic state.

hyp•nol•o•gy [hɪp'nɒlədʒi] *n.* the branch of science dealing with the phenomena of sleep.

hyp•no•pomp•ic [ˌhɪpnou'pɒmpɪk] *adj.* having to do with the period immediately preceding awakening. Compare HYPNAGOGIC. ⟨< *hypno-* + Gk. *pompē* a sending forth or out⟩

hyp•no•sis [hɪp'nousɪs] *n., pl.* **-ses** [-siz]. a state resembling deep sleep, but more active, in which a person has little will of his or her own and little feeling, and acts according to the suggestions of the person who induced the hypnosis. ⟨< NL⟩

hyp•no•ther•a•pist [ˌhɪpnou'θɛrəpɪst] *n.* a person trained in hypnotherapy, especially one whose work it is.

hyp•no•ther•a•py [ˌhɪpnou'θɛrəpi] *n.* the use of hypnotism to treat disorders, especially emotional, behavioural, or psychiatric disorders.

hyp•not•ic [hɪp'nɒtɪk] *adj., n. —adj.* **1** of, having to do with, or producing hypnosis. **2** easily hypnotized. **3** causing or tending to cause sleep: *the hypnotic monotone of his voice.*
—n. **1** a person under hypnosis or one who is easily hypnotized. **2** a drug or other means of causing sleep. ⟨< LL *hypnoticus* < Gk. *hypnotikos* putting to sleep < *hypnoein* put to sleep < *hypnos* sleep⟩ **—hyp'not•i•cal•ly,** *adv.*

hyp•no•tism ['hɪpnəˌtɪzəm] *n.* **1** the inducing of hypnosis; act of hypnotizing. **2** the study of hypnosis.

hyp•no•tist ['hɪpnətɪst] *n.* a person who hypnotizes.

hyp•no•tize ['hɪpnəˌtaɪz] *v.* **-tized, -tiz•ing. 1** put into a hypnotic state; cause hypnosis in. **2** *Informal.* dominate or control the will of by suggestion. **—'hyp•no,tiz•a•ble,** *adj.* **—ˌhyp•no•ti'za•tion,** *n.* **—'hyp•no,tiz•er,** *n.*

hy•po[1] ['həipou] *n.* a colourless crystalline salt used as a fixing agent in photography; sodium thiosulphate or sodium hyposulphite. *Formula*: $Na_2S_2O_3•5H_2O$ ⟨short for *hyposulphite*⟩

hy•po[2] ['həipou] *n., pl.* **-pos.** *Informal.* hypodermic.

hypo– *prefix.* **1** under; beneath; below: *hypodermic.* **2** less than; less than normal: *hypothyroid.* ⟨< Gk. *hypo-* < *hypo* under, below⟩

hy•po•blast ['həipəˌblæst] *n.* endoblast.

hy•po•caust ['həipəˌkɒst] *or* ['hɪpəˌkɒst] *n.* in ancient Rome, the space below a floor in which hot air was circulated to warm the room. ⟨< L *hypocaustum* < Gk. *hypokauston* < *hypokaiein* heat with fire from below < *hypo-* below + *kaiein* burn⟩

hy•po•cen•tre ['həipəˌsɛntər] *n.* the area immediately below the centre of a nuclear explosion.

hy•po•chlo•rite [ˌhəipə'klɔrəit] *n. Chemistry.* a salt of hypochlorous acid.

hy•po•chlo•rous acid [ˌhəipə'klɔrəs] a yellow solution with an irritating odour, used as a bleach, disinfectant, etc. *Formula*: HClO

hy•po•chon•dri•a [ˌhəipə'kɒndriə] *n.* **1** unnatural anxiety about one's health; imaginary illness. **2** low spirits without any real reason. Also, **hypochondriasis** [ˌhəipəkɒn'draɪəsɪs]. ⟨< LL *hypochondria* abdomen < Gk. *hypochondria,* neut. pl. < *hypo-* under + *chondros* cartilage (of the breastbone); from the supposed seat of melancholy⟩

hy•po•chon•dri•ac [ˌhəipə'kɒndriˌæk] *n., adj. —n.* a person with hypochondria.
—adj. having hypochondria.

hy•po•chon•dri•um [ˌhəipə'kɒndriəm] *n.* that part of the abdomen laterally below the ribs.

hy•po•co•rist•ic [ˌhəipəkə'rɪstɪk] *adj.* **1** being or forming a pet name. **2** euphemistic. **—hy'poc•o,rism** [həi'pɒkəˌrɪzəm], *n.*

hy•po•cot•yl [ˌhəipə'kɒtəl] *n.* the part of a plant embryo stem below the cotyledons. It produces the main root (radicle) at its lower end. See EMBRYO for picture. ⟨< *hypo-* + *cotyl(edon)*⟩

hy•poc•ri•sy [hɪ'pɒkrəsi] *n., pl.* **-sies.** the act or fact of putting on a false appearance, especially of goodness or religion; a pretending to be what one is not; pretence. ⟨ME < OF *ypocrisie* < LL < Gk. *hypokrisis* acting, dissimulation, ult. < *hypo-* under + *krinein* judge⟩

hyp•o•crite ['hɪpəˌkrɪt] *n.* a person who pretends to be what he or she is not, especially one who puts on an appearance of goodness or religion. ⟨ME < OF *ypocrite* < L < Gk. *hypokritēs* actor. Related to HYPOCRISY.⟩

hyp•o•crit•i•cal [ˌhɪpə'krɪtəkəl] *adj.* of or like a hypocrite; insincere. **—ˌhyp•o'crit•i•cal•ly,** *adv.*

hy•po•cy•cloid [ˌhəipə'səiklɔid] *n. Geometry.* the curve traced by a point on the circumference of a circle rolling around the inner circumference of a larger circle in the same plane.

hy•po•der•mal [ˌhəipə'dɜrməl] *adj.* below the epidermis.

hy•po•der•mic [ˌhəipə'dɜrmɪk] *adj., n. —adj.* **1** under the skin. **2** injected or for injecting under the skin: *The doctor used a hypodermic needle.*
—n. **1** a dose of medicine injected under the skin: *The doctor gave her a hypodermic to make her sleep.* **2** a syringe used to inject medicine under the skin. ⟨< NL *hypoderma* < Gk. *hypo-* under + *derma* skin⟩ **—ˌhy•po'der•mi•cal•ly,** *adv.*

hy•po•derm•is [ˌhəipə'dɜrmɪs] *n.* in plants, a layer of epidermal cells.

hy•po•gas•tri•um [ˌhəipə'gæstriəm] *n.* the lowest of the three regions of the abdomen. **—ˌhy•po'gas•tric,** *adj.*

hy•po•ge•al [ˌhəipə'dʒiəl] *or* [ˌhɪpə'dʒiəl] *adj.* underground.

hy•po•gene ['həipəˌdʒin] *adj.* hypogeal.

hy•po•gen•ous [həi'pɒdʒənəs] *or* [hɪ'pɒdʒənəs] *adj.* growing, as some fungi do, below the surface of a leaf.

hy•po•ge•um [ˌhəipə'dʒiəm] *n.* a catacomb.

hy•po•glos•sal [ˌhəipə'glɒsəl] *adj.* **1** under the tongue. **2** having to do with the **hypoglossal nerve**, which moves the tongue muscles.

hy•po•gly•ce•mi•a [ˌhəipəgləi'simiə] *n.* an abnormally low concentration of sugar in the blood. Also, **hypoglycaemia.** ⟨< *hypo-* + Gk. *glyko-* sweet + E *-emia*⟩

hy•po•gly•ce•mic [ˌhəipəgləi'simɪk] *adj.* **1** causing or caused by a decrease or lack of sugar in the blood. **2** suffering from hypoglycemia.

hy•po•ma•nia [ˌhəipə'meiniə] *n.* a mania of low intensity. **—ˌhy•po'man•ic** [-'mænɪk], *adj.*

hy•po•ni•trous acid [ˌhəipə'nəitrəs] *Chemistry.* an unstable crystalline acid. *Formula*: $H_2N_2O_2$

hy•po•phos•phate [ˌhəipə'fɒsfeit] *n. Chemistry.* a salt of hypophosphoric acid.

hy•po•phos•phite [ˌhəipə'fɒsfəit] *n. Chemistry.* a salt of hypophosphorous acid, used in medicine as a tonic.

hy•po•phos•phor•ic [ˌhəipəfɒs'fɔrɪk] *adj. Chemistry.* of or having to do with an acid ($H_4P_2O_6$) produced by the slow oxidation of phosphorus in moist air.

hy•po•phos•pho•rous [ˌhəipə'fɒsfərəs] *adj. Chemistry.* of or having to do with an acid of phosphorus (H_3PO_2) having salts which are used in medicine.

hy•poph•y•sis [həi'pɒfəsɪs] *n., pl.* **-ses** [-ˌsiz]. *Anatomy.* the pituitary gland. ⟨< Gk. *hypophysis* attachment underneath < *hypo-* under + *physis* a growing < *phyein* cause to grow⟩

hy•po•pla•sia [ˌhəipə'pleiʒə] *or* [ˌhəipə'pleiziə] *n. Pathology.* underdevelopment of a tissue or organ. ⟨< NL < Gk. *hypo-* + *plasis* a moulding⟩

hy•po•sul•phite or **hy•po•sul•fite** [ˌhəipə'sʌlfəit] *n. Chemistry.* a salt of hyposulphurous acid.

hy•po•sul•phur•ous acid or **hy•po•sul•fur•ous acid** [ˌhəipou'sʌlfərəs], [-'sʌlfjʊrəs], *or* [-sʌl'fjurəs] *Chemistry.* an unstable acid used as a reducing and bleaching agent. *Formula*: $H_2S_2O_4$

hy•pot•e•nuse [həi'pɒtəˌnjus] *or* [həi'pɒtəˌnus], [haɪ'pɒtəˌnjuz] *or* [haɪ'pɒtəˌnuz] *n. Geometry.* the side of a right-angled triangle opposite the right angle. See TRIANGLE for picture. Also, **hypothenuse.** ⟨< LL *hypotenusa* < Gk. *hypoteinousa* subtending, ppr. of *hypoteinein* < *hypo-* under + *teinein* stretch⟩

hy•po•tha•lam•ic [ˌhəipəθə'læmɪk] *or* [ˌhɪpəθə'læmɪk] *adj. Anatomy.* of or having to do with the hypothalamus.

hy•po•thal•a•mus [ˌhəipə'θæləməs] *or* [ˌhɪpə'θæləməs] *n. Anatomy.* the part of the brain beneath the thalamus. It controls hunger, thirst, temperature, and growth.

hy•poth•e•cate [həi'pɒθəˌkeit] *v.* **-cat•ed, -cat•ing.** pledge (property, stock, etc.) to a creditor as security for a loan or debt; mortgage. ⟨< Med.L *hypothecare* < L < Gk. *hypothēkē* pledge < *hypo-* under + *tithenai* place⟩ **—hy'poth•e,ca•tor,** *n.*

hy•poth•e•ca•tion [həi,pɒθə'keiʃən] *n.* **1** the act or fact of depositing as security. **2** a claim against property deposited as security.

hy•poth•e•nuse [həi'pɒθə,njus] *or* [həi'pɒθə,nus], [haɪ'pɒθənjuz] *or* [haɪ'pɒθə,nuz] *n.* hypotenuse.

hy•po•ther•mi•a [,həipə'θɜrmiə] *n.* abnormally low body temperature. Hypothermia can be produced by exposure to cold air or water, leading to death in a matter of hours. Hypothermia is sometimes induced in medicine to slow a patient's metabolism, thus reducing the need for oxygen, especially during heart or brain surgery.

hy•poth•e•sis [həi'pɒθəsɪs] *n., pl.* **-ses** [-,siz]. **1** something assumed because it seems likely to be a true explanation; theory. **2** a proposition assumed as a basis for reasoning. ⟨< NL < Gk. *hypothesis* < *hypo-* under + *thesis* a placing⟩
☛ *Syn.* **1.** See note at THEORY.

hy•poth•e•size [həi'pɒθə,saɪz] *v.* **-sized, -siz•ing. 1** make a hypothesis. **2** assume; suppose.

hy•po•thet•i•cal [,həipə'θɛtəkəl] *adj.* **1** of or based on a hypothesis; assumed; supposed. **2** *Logic.* **a** of a proposition, involving a hypothesis or condition; conditional. **b** of a syllogism, having a hypothetical proposition for one of its premises. **3** fond of making hypotheses: *a hypothetical scientist.* Also, **hypothetic.** ⟨< L < Gk. *hypothetikos*⟩ **—,hy•po'thet•i•cal•ly,** *adv.*

hy•po•thy•roid [,həipə'θaɪrɔɪd] *n., adj.* *—n.* **1** an underactive thyroid gland. **2** a person having such a gland.
—adj. relating to an underactive thyroid gland.

hy•po•thy•roid•ism [,həipə'θaɪrɔɪ,dɪzəm] *n. Pathology.* insufficient activity of the thyroid gland. Compare HYPERTHYROIDISM.

hy•po•ton•ic [,həipə'tɒnɪk] *adj. Chemistry.* of a solution, having a lower concentration of solute than another solution. A hypotonic solution in a cell has a lower concentration of solute than that of the cytoplasm, so that a cell gains water and volume by osmosis.

hy•pox•ia [həi'pɒksiə] *n.* lack of oxygen reaching body tissues.

hypso– *combining form.* height; altitude: *hypsometer*. ⟨< Gk. *hypsos* height⟩

hyp•sog•ra•phy [hɪp'sɒgrəfi] *n.* the study of elevations.

hyp•som•e•ter [hɪp'sɒmətər] *n.* an instrument to determine land elevations.

hy•qua ['həikwə] *n.* dentalium shells used as currency by Pacific Northwest Native peoples. ⟨< Chinook jargon⟩

hy•ra•coid ['haɪrə,kɔɪd] *n., adj.* *—n.* a member of the order Hyracoidea; hyrax.
—adj. having to do with the order Hyracoidea.

hy•rax ['haɪræks] *n.* any of an order (Hyracoidea) of small, agile, rodentlike mammals native to Africa and extreme SW Asia, having a plump body, short ears, tail, and neck, short, slender legs, and feet with pads on the soles and hooflike toes. ⟨< NL *Hyrax* the generic name < Gk. *hyrax* shrew-mouse⟩

hy•son ['həisən] *n.* a Chinese green tea. ⟨< Chinese *hsi-ch'un* blooming spring⟩

hys•sop ['hɪsəp] *n.* **1** a sweet-scented, perennial herb (*Hyssopus officinalis*) of the mint family native to Europe and Asia but widely cultivated as a garden herb, having evergreen leaves and spikes of small flowers used as flavouring for food and beverages and, formerly, as a medicine. **2** any of several related or similar plants. **3** a plant used in purification rites by the ancient Hebrews. ⟨ME < OF < L < Gk. *hyssōpos* < Semitic⟩

hys•ter•ec•to•my [,hɪstə'rɛktəmi] *n.* the surgical removal of the uterus. ⟨< Gk. *hystera* uterus + E *-ectomy*⟩

hys•te•ri•a [hɪ'stiriə] *or* [hɪ'stɛriə] *n.* **1** a nervous disorder that causes violent fits of laughing and crying, imaginary or real illnesses, lack of self-control, etc. **2** a state of uncontrolled excitement, especially involving laughing or crying. ⟨< NL < Gk. *hystera* uterus; because it was formerly thought that women are more often affected than men⟩

hys•ter•ic [hɪ'stɛrɪk] *adj., n.* *—adj.* hysterical.
—n. a hysterical person.

hys•ter•i•cal [hɪ'stɛrəkəl] *adj.* **1** unnaturally excited. **2** showing an extreme lack of control; unable to stop laughing, crying, etc.; suffering from hysteria: *He was hysterical with grief.* ⟨< L < Gk. *hysterikos* < *hystera* uterus⟩ **—hys'ter•i•cal•ly,** *adv.*

hys•ter•ics [hɪ'stɛrɪks] *n.pl.* HYSTERIA (def. 2).

hys•ter•o•gen•ic [,hɪstərə'dʒɛnɪk] *adj.* causing hysteria.

hys•ter•oid ['hɪstə,rɔɪd] *adj.* like hysteria.

hys•ter•on pro•te•ron ['hɪstə,rɒn 'prɒtə,rɒn] **1** an expression in which the expected elements are reversed. *Example*: *raised and born* instead of *born and raised*. **2** *Logic.* the error of taking as a premise something that is not proved. ⟨< LL < Gk., the latter (as) the former⟩

Hz hertz.

I i *I i*

i or **I** [aɪ] *n., pl.* **i's** or **I's. 1** the ninth letter of the English alphabet. **2** any speech sound represented by this letter. **3** a person or thing identified as *i*, especially the ninth in a series. **4** the Roman numeral for 1. **5** something shaped like the letter I. **6** (*adjl.*) of or being an I or i. **7** something, such as a printer's type, a lever, or a key on a keyboard, that produces an i or I.

I [aɪ] *pron., subj.* **I,** *obj.* **me,** *poss.* **mine,** *pl. subj.* **we,** *pl. obj.* **us,** *pl. poss.* **ours;** *n., pl.* **I's. 1** the person who is speaking or writing. **2** the ego or individual self. ⟨OE *ic*⟩

☛ *Hom.* AYE², EYE.

☛ *Usage.* The pronoun *I* is written with a capital simply because in the old handwritten manuscripts a small *i* was likely to be lost or to get attached to a neighbouring word, and a capital helped keep it a distinct word.

i– *prefix.* not; the form of IN-¹ before *gn*, as in *ignore.*

i. 1 intransitive. **2** island. **3** interest. **4** incisor. **5** imperator (emperor).

i 1 *Mathematics.* the symbol for the imaginary square root of minus one (-1). **2** *Astronomy.* the inclination of a planet in orbit to a plane of reference.

I 1 iodine. **2** *Physics.* electric current.

I. 1 Island(s). **2** Isle(s). **3** *Politics.* Independent.

–ia *suffix.* used in English to form: **1** names of diseases: *malaria.* **2** names of places: *Romania.* **3** names of plants: *begonia.* **4** names of alkaloids: *morphia.* **5** other nouns: *insignia, militia.* ⟨< L⟩

IAEA International Atomic Energy Agency (of the United Nations).

–ial *suffix.* a form of **-al,** used in *adverbial, facial,* etc.

i•amb ['aɪæm] *or* ['aɪæmb] *n.* an iambic foot or measure. ⟨< F < L < Gk. *iambos*⟩

i•am•bic [aɪ'æmbɪk] *adj., n. Prosody. —adj.* **1** of or designating a metrical foot consisting basically of two syllables, the first one having a weak stress and the second a strong stress. It has been by far the commonest metrical measure in English-language verse since the Middle Ages. *Example*:
The sún | that bríef | Decém | ber dáy
Rose chéer | less ó | ver hílls | of gréy.
2 in classical Latin and Greek verse, of or designating a metrical measure, or foot, consisting of two syllables, the first one short and the second one long.
—n. **1** iamb. **2** Usually, **iambics,** *pl.* iambic verse.

iambic pentameter a poetic metre based on five iambic feet in a line of verse. Iambic pentameter was the standard metre for English verse from about the 15th century to the 19th.

i•am•bus [aɪ'æmbəs] *n., pl.* **-bi** [-baɪ] *or* [-bi] or **bus•es.** iamb.

–ian *suffix.* a form of -AN, used in certain words, such as *mammalian, Canadian,* etc.

–iana *suffix.* a form of -ANA, as in *Canadiana.*

I•ap•e•tus [aɪ'æpətəs] *or* [i'æpətəs] *n.* one of the nine satellites of Saturn. ⟨< the name of a giant in Greek mythology⟩

–iasis *suffix.* used in Greek words to indicate a pathological condition: *psoriasis.* ⟨< NL < Gk.⟩

IATA International Air Transport Association.

–iatric *suffix.* used to indicate a specific kind of medical treatment: *geriatric.* ⟨< Gk. *iatrik(os)* of healing⟩

iatro– *combining form.* healer: *iatrogenic.* ⟨< Gk. *iatros* healer⟩

i•at•ro•gen•ic [aɪ,ætrə'dʒɛnɪk] *adj.* of a disease or symptoms, caused or induced by medical treatment. ⟨< Gk. *iatros* doctor + *genic*⟩

ib. ibid.

I–beam ['aɪ ,bim] *n.* a steel girder in the shape of the letter I.

I•be•ri•an [aɪ'biriən] *n., adj. —n.* **1** a member of a group of peoples of European race, probably related to the peoples of N Africa, who inhabited the Iberian Peninsula (present-day Spain and Portugal) in ancient times. **2** any of the languages of the ancient Iberians. **3** a native or inhabitant of Spain or Portugal. **4** a native or inhabitant of an ancient region in W Asia, south of the Caucasus, called Iberia.
—adj. **1** of or having to do with the ancient Iberian Peninsula or ancient Iberia in Asia, or their peoples. **2** of or having to do with present-day Spain or Portugal or their inhabitants or languages.

i•bex ['aɪbɛks] *n., pl.* **i•bex•es, ib•i•ces** ['ɪbə,siz] *or* ['aɪbə,siz], or (*esp. collectively*) **i•bex.** any of several wild goats (genus *Capra*) of Europe, Asia, and NE Africa having large horns that curve back in a semicircle and have broad ridges across the front surfaces. ⟨< L⟩

Ib•i•bi•o [,ɪbi'biou] *n.* **1** a people living in SE Nigeria. **2** the Niger-Congo language of these people.

ibid. in the same place (for L *ibidem*).

☛ *Usage.* **Ibid.** is used in a footnote to refer to the book, article, etc. mentioned in the immediately preceding footnote.

i•bis ['aɪbɪs] *n., pl.* **i•bis•es** or (*esp. collectively*) **i•bis.** any of various medium-sized wading birds (family Threskiornithidae) of warm regions having a long, slender, downward-curved bill. The sacred ibis (*Threskiornis aethiopica*) of ancient Egypt, a black-and-white bird, is now found only south of the Sahara in Africa. The scarlet ibis (*Eudocimus ruber*) is found in tropical America. ⟨< L < Gk. < Egyptian⟩

–ible *adjective-forming suffix.* that can be ——ed: *impressible, perfectible, reducible.* ⟨< OF < L *-ibilis*⟩

☛ *Usage.* See note at -ABLE.

ibn– an Arabic prefix meaning 'son of', used in personal names.

I•bo ['ibou] *n.* **1** a member of various peoples of Nigeria. **2** the Sudanese language of these people.

i•bu•pro•fen [,aɪbju'proufən] *n. Pharmacy.* an analgesic drug. *Formula*: $C_{13}H_{18}O_2$

IC *Computer technology.* INTEGRATED CIRCUIT.

–ic *suffix.* **1** of or having to do with: *atmospheric, Icelandic.* **2** having the nature of: *artistic, heroic.* **3** constituting or being: *bombastic, monolithic.* **4** characterized by; containing; made up of: *alcoholic, iambic.* **5** made by; caused by: *phonographic.* **6** like; like that of; characteristic of: *meteoric, antagonistic, idyllic, sophomoric.* Many words ending in *-ic* have two or more of these meanings (1 to 6). **7** *Chemistry.* implying a smaller proportion of the element that *-ous* implies, as in *boric, chloric, ferric, sulphuric.* ⟨< F *-ique* or L *-icus* or Gk. *-ikos*⟩

–ical *suffix.* **1** -IC, as in *geometrical, parasitical, hysterical.* **2** -IC, specialized or differentiated in meaning, as in *economical.* **3** *-ical* sometimes arises from the addition of -AL to nouns ending in -IC, as in *critical, musical.* ⟨< L *-icalis*⟩

–ically *suffix.* used to form adverbs from adjectives ending in **-ic.** Instead of *artistic-ly* we write *artistically*; instead of *alphabetic-ly* we write *alphabetically.* The only exception is *publicly.* In speaking, the suffix is ordinarily pronounced in two syllables [-ɪkli].

ICAO International Civil Aviation Organization (of the United Nations).

I•car•i•an [ɪ'kɛriən] *or* [əi'kɛriən] *adj.* **1** having to do with Icarus. **2** rash; carelessly bold. ⟨< *Icarus*⟩

Ic•a•rus ['ɪkərəs] *or* ['əikərəs] *n. Greek mythology.* the son of Daedalus. When he and his father were escaping from Crete, using wings that Daedalus had made, Icarus flew so high that the sun melted the wax which held the wings on, and he fell to his death in the sea.

ICBM intercontinental ballistic missile.

ice [əis] *n., adj., v.* **iced, ic•ing.** *—n.* **1** water made solid by freezing; frozen water. **2** a layer or surface of ice. **3** a frozen area of sea or land: *Icebreakers cut through ice. Baby seals are found on the ice.* **4** a frozen surface for skating, curling, hockey, etc. **5 the ice,** *Cdn.* especially in Newfoundland, the edge of the Arctic ice fields where seal hunting takes place. **6** something that looks or feels like ice: *camphor ice.* **7** a frozen dessert, usually made of sweetened fruit juice. **8** icing. **9** *Slang.* diamonds. **10** coldness of manner.
break the ice, *Informal.* **a** make a beginning; start something dangerous or difficult. **b** overcome first difficulties in talking or getting acquainted.
cut no ice, *Informal.* have little or no effect.
on ice, ready and waiting.
on thin ice, in a dangerous or difficult position.
—adj. **1** of ice; having to do with ice. **2** made or consisting of ice.
—v. **1** cool with ice; put ice in or around. **2** cover with ice. **3** turn to ice; freeze (*used with* **over**): *The lake usually ices over in January.* **4** cover with icing. **5** *Hockey.* **a** shoot (a puck) from the defensive zone past the red line at the opposite end of the rink: *No player may ice the puck when his or her team is at full strength.*

b put (a team) into play: *Our town iced a good hockey team.* **6** *Slang.* kill. ⟨OE *īs*⟩ **—'ice•less,** *adj.*

ice age **1** any of the times in geological history when much of the earth was covered with glaciers. **2** Often, **Ice Age,** the most recent such time, the Pleistocene epoch, when most of the northern hemisphere was covered by glaciers.

ice–ang•ling ['əis ,æŋglıŋ] *n. Cdn.* ICE FISHING.

ice axe *Cdn.* a tool for cutting ice.

ice bag a small waterproof bag containing ice to apply to a swollen part of the body.

ice–ball ['əis ,bɒl] *n. Cdn.* a ball-like bit of ice that forms on the paws of sled dogs, under the hooves of horses, etc.

ice–bank ['əis ,bæŋk] *n. Cdn.* a perpendicular ridge of ice along a river.

ice•berg ['əıs,bɜrg] *n.* a large mass of ice floating in the sea. **tip of the iceberg,** a small part of something much larger. ⟨? < Du. *ijsberg,* literally, ice mountain⟩

iceberg lettuce a variety of lettuce with a head like a small cabbage, and crisp leaves.

ice–blind[1] ['əis ,blaınd] *n. Cdn.* a place of concealment for a hunter, built of blocks of ice.

ice–blind[2] ['əis ,blaınd] *adj. Cdn.* temporarily blind from exposure to the glare from expanses of ice. Compare SNOW-BLIND.

ice•blink ['əis,blıŋk] *n.* a yellowish white glare in the sky over an ice field, caused by reflection.

ice•boat ['əis,bout] *n.* **1** a light frame, often triangular, set on runners and fitted with sails or a propeller for skimming along the frozen surface of a lake, river, etc. **2** icebreaker. **—'ice,boat•ing,** *n.*

ice boom a boom of logs placed in a river to halt the flow of ice.

ice•bound ['əıs,baʊnd] *adj.* **1** held fast by ice; frozen in: *The ship was icebound for several weeks.* **2** shut in or obstructed by ice: *The port at Churchill is icebound for about 10 months of the year.*

ice–box or **ice•box** ['əıs ,bɒks] *n.* **1** an insulated chest or box in which food is kept cool by ice. **2** *Archaic.* a refrigerator.

ice•break•er ['əis,breikər] *n.* **1** a ship designed for breaking a passage through ice. **2** a dock used as a protection against floating ice. **3** something, such as a joke, which helps to put people at their ease at gatherings or parties.

ice bridge **1** a winter road over a frozen river, lake, etc. **2** *Cdn.* a bridge of ice formed by the jamming of ice in a river or other channel.

ice–cake ['əis ,keik] *n. Cdn.* a piece or slab of ice.

ice canoe *n. Cdn.* a small, sturdy boat long used in crossing the St. Lawrence River in winter.

ice•cap ['əis,kæp] *n.* a permanent covering of ice over an area, sloping down on all sides from an elevated centre.

ice carnival *Cdn.* an organized winter social activity featuring winter sports, ice sculpture, etc.

ice–chisel ['əis ,tʃızəl] *n. Cdn.* an ice-cutting tool.

ice–cold ['əis 'kould] *adj.* as cold as ice.

ice cream a frozen dessert made of cream sweetened and flavoured.

ice–cream parlour or **parlor** ['əıs ,krim] *Cdn.* a small cafe that sells ice cream to be eaten on the premises.

ice cube a small chunk of ice, usually having six sides, used for chilling drinks or food.

iced [əıst] *adj.* **1** cooled with ice. **2** covered with ice. **3** covered with icing.

ice field **1** a large sheet of ice floating in the sea, larger than a floe. **2** a large sheet of ice on land.

ice fisher *Cdn.* a person who goes ice fishing.

ice fishing *Cdn.* the act or practice of fishing through a hole or holes cut through ice.

ice floe floe.

ice fog a dense fog of ice particles suspended in the air.

ice foot *Cdn.* a ledge of ice formed on the shoreline in the Arctic. ⟨translation of Danish *eis-fod*⟩

ice hockey HOCKEY (def. 1).

ice•house ['əıs,hʌus] *n.* **1** *Cdn.* a building where ice is stored and kept from melting. **2** a structure or pit having insulated walls and roof and used as a cold storage for meat and other perishables which are stored with blocks of ice or snow. **3** *Cdn.* a snow house. **4** an ice-making plant.

ice–hunting ['əis ,hʌntıŋ] *n. Cdn.* the chasing of seals on the coast of Newfoundland. **—'ice-,hunter,** *n.*

ice hut a small building towed onto the ice in winter and used by ice fishers as a shelter while angling through holes cut in the ice; bobbing shack.

ice island a very large iceberg, often several kilometres across, having a flattish top.

ice–jam ['əis ,dʒæm] *n., v.* **-jammed, -jam•ming.** *—n.* Also, **ice jam,** the damming up of a river or other watercourse with masses of ice that cannot float down owing to some obstruction. *—v.* block by an ice-jam.

Ice•land ['əislənd] *n.* an island country in the N Atlantic.

Ice•land•er ['əis,lændər] *or* ['əisləndər] *n.* a native or inhabitant of Iceland.

Ice•lan•dic [əis'lændık] *n., adj. —n.* the North Germanic language of Iceland. *—adj.* of or having to do with Iceland, its people, or their language.

Iceland moss a brownish or greyish lichen (*Cetraria islandica*) of arctic and northern alpine regions, an important food for caribou, muskoxen, etc. and also used in human food.

Iceland poppy **1** a garden plant (*Papaver nudicaule*) having fragrant, cup-shaped flowers on long stems. **2** the flower of this plant, red, cream, or white.

Iceland spar a transparent calcite obtained from Iceland and used in optical instruments.

ice lens *Cdn.* a layer of ice in permafrost.

ice•man ['əis,mæn] *or* ['əismən] *n., pl.* **-men** [-,mɛn] *or* [-mən]. **1** a person who sells, delivers, or handles ice. **2** *Cdn.* a sailor or sealer experienced at moving about on the ice or in the ice fields.

ice milk a smooth, cold, sweet food made of frozen skim milk.

ice needle a long, thin crystal of ice floating high in the atmosphere in cold weather.

I•ce•ni [əı'sinaı] *n. sing. or pl.* an ancient Celtic tribe of Southern England whose queen was Boadicea.

ice pack **1** *Cdn.* a large expanse of floating ice, consisting of many small floes packed together. **2** a bag containing ice for application to the body to relieve pain, swelling, itch, etc.

ice palace *Cdn.* **1** a building made of blocks of clear ice. **2** *Slang.* an ice ARENA (def. 1).

ice pan *Cdn.* a fairly substantial slab of ice broken off from a large expanse of ice; ice floe. Also called **pan ice.**

ice pick a sharp-pointed tool for breaking up ice.

ice plant a plant (*Mesembryanthemum crystallinum*) having fleshy leaves and pink or white flowers.

ice pool *Cdn.* a sweepstake, the winner being the person who makes the closest guess as to the date of the BREAK-UP (def. 1) in spring, as marked by the actual movement of the ice.

ice road ICE BRIDGE (def. 1).

ice sheet a broad, thick sheet of ice covering a very large area for a long time.

ice•shelf ['əis,ʃɛlf] *n.* **1** a shelf of ice anchored to the bank of a river. **2** sea ice that extends from the shore as a huge shelf.

ice skate SKATE[1] (defs. 1 and 2).

ice–skate ['əis ,skeit] *v.* **-skat•ed, -skat•ing.** skate on ice. **—'ice-,skat•er,** *n.*

ice storm a freezing rain that covers exposed surfaces with a layer of glistening ice; SILVER THAW (def. 1).

ice time **1** *Hockey.* the time actually spent on the ice by a player or players during a game. **2** the time during which the ice at a rink is available to a team, group, or individuals.

ice–trap ['əis ,træp] *n. Cdn.* an engineering technique for slowing down the flow of a river during break-up, involving the dredging of holes into the river bottom so that ice will build up, forming a barrier.

ice water **1** water cooled with ice. **2** melted ice.

ice worm **1** *Cdn.* in the North: **a** a fictional creature, thought up as a joke. **b ice-worm cocktail,** a cocktail having bits of spaghetti in it. **2** a worm (*Mesenchytraeus solifugus*) found on mountain snow and ice fields. ⟨coined during the Klondike gold rush⟩

I Ching an ancient Chinese book of divination; the Book of Changes.

ich•neu•mon [ɪk'njumən] *or* [ɪk'numən] *n.* **1** a mongoose (*Herpestes ichneumon*) of Africa and S Europe. **2** ICHNEUMON WASP. ⟨< L < Gk. *ichneumōn*, literally, searcher (supposedly of crocodile's eggs), ult. < *ichnos* track⟩

ichneumon wasp or **ich•neumonid** [ɪk'njumənɪd] *or* [ɪk'numənɪd] *n.* any of a very large family of wasps of the order Hymenoptera, found in many parts of the world, including North America, whose larvae are parasites of many other insect larvae, especially caterpillars. Ichneumon wasps are considered generally beneficial because they destroy insect pests.

An ichneumon wasp

ich•nite ['ɪknəit] *n.* a fossilized footprint. ⟨< Gk *ichnos* footprint + E *-ite*⟩

ichno– *combining form.* footprint: *ichnite.* ⟨< Gk. *ichnos* footprint⟩

ich•nol•o•gy [ɪk'nɒlədʒi] *n.* the branch of paleontology dealing with fossilized footprints. ⟨< Gk. *ichnos* footprint + *ology*⟩

i•chor[1] ['əikɔr] *or* ['əikər] *n. Greek mythology.* the fluid supposed to flow in the veins of the gods. ⟨< Gk.⟩

i•chor[2] ['əikɔr] *or* ['əikər] *n.* an acrid, watery discharge from ulcers, wounds, etc. ⟨< NL < Gk.⟩

ich•thy•ic ['ɪkθiɪk] *adj.* having to do with fishes.

ichthyo– *combining form.* fishes: *ichthyology.* ⟨< Gk. *ichthys* fish⟩

ich•thy•oid ['ɪkθi,ɔɪd] *adj., n. —adj.* like a fish. *—n.* a fish or a vertebrate like a fish.

ich•thy•o•lite ['ɪkθiə,ləit] *n.* a fossilized fish.

ich•thy•ol•o•gist [,ɪkθi'ɒlədʒist] *n.* a person trained in ichthyology, especially one whose work it is.

ich•thy•ol•o•gy [,ɪkθi'ɒlədʒi] *n.* the branch of zoology dealing with fishes. ⟨< Gk. *ichthys* fish + E *-logy*⟩ **—,ich•thy•o'log•i•cal,** *adj.*

ich•thy•oph•a•gy [,ɪkθi'ɒfədʒi] *n.* the practice of subsisting on fish. **—,ich•thy'oph•a•gous,** *adj.*

ich•thy•or•nis [,ɪkθi'ɔrnɪs] *n.* an extinct genus of birds having teeth set in sockets resembling those of fish vertebrae. ⟨< *ichthyo-* + Gk. *ornis* bird⟩

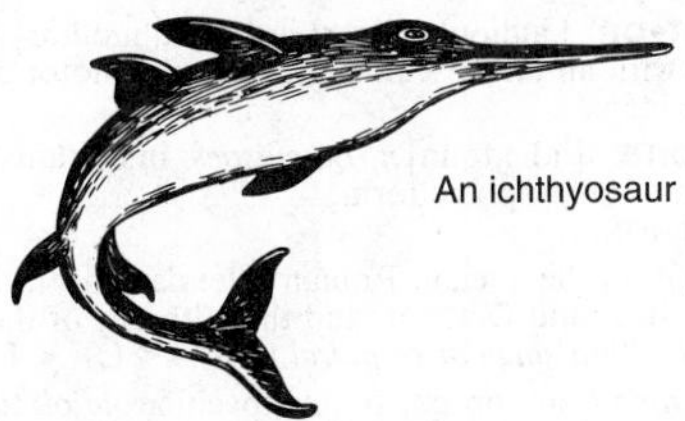
An ichthyosaur

ich•thy•o•saur ['ɪkθiə,sɔr] *n.* any of an order (Ichthyosauria) of extinct sea reptiles having a fishlike body, four flippers, and a long snout. ⟨< NL *ichthyosaurus* < Gk. *ichthys* fish + *sauros* lizard⟩ **—,ich•thy•o'sau•ri•an,** *adj.*

ich•thy•o•sau•rus [,ɪkθiə'sɔrəs] *n., pl.* **-sau•ri** [-'sɔraɪ] *or* [-'sɔri]. any of an order (Ichthyosauria) of extinct, porpoiselike marine reptiles of the Mesozoic Era.

ich•thy•o•sis [,ɪkθi'ousɪs] *n.* a congenital skin disease in which the epidermis continually flakes off; fishskin disease.

i•ci•cle ['əisəkəl] *n.* **1** a pointed, hanging stick of ice formed by the freezing of dripping water. **2** anything resembling this, such as tinsel for trimming a Christmas tree. **3** *Informal.* a cold or unemotional person. ⟨ME *isykle* < OE *īs* ice + *gicel* icicle⟩ **—'i•ci•cled,** *adj.*

ic•ing ['əisɪŋ] *n., v. —n.* **1** a sweet, creamy mixture used to cover cakes, etc., made of sugar and some liquid, flavouring, sometimes the beaten whites of eggs, etc. **2** in hockey, the shooting of the puck from within one's own defensive zone across the opponent's goal line.
—v. ppr. of ICE.

icing sugar powdered sugar, usually containing a small amount of cornstarch. It is used in making icing, candy, etc.

ICJ International Court of Justice, the principal judicial body of the United Nations, established in 1945, originally the World Court.

ick•y ['ɪki] *adj.* **ick•i•er, ick•i•est.** *Slang.* **1** repulsive. **2** sticky. ⟨origin uncertain⟩

i•con or **i•kon** ['əikɒn] *n., pl.* **i•cons,** *sometimes,* **i•co•nes** ['əikə,niz]. **1** a sacred picture or image of Christ, an angel, a saint, etc. **2** any picture or image. **3** *Computer technology.* on a computer screen, a symbol that represents an object (file, document, etc.) or an operation (delete, print, etc.). Also (defs. 1, 2), **eikon.** ⟨< L < Gk. *eikōn*⟩

i•con•ic [əi'kɒnɪk] *adj.* **1** of or having to do with icons or resembling an icon. **2** of memorial sculptures, etc., conventional in style.

icono– *combining form.* image; likeness: *iconoclast.* ⟨< Gk. *eikon* image⟩

i•con•o•clasm [əi'kɒnə,klæzəm] *n.* the belief or practice of iconoclasts.

i•con•o•clast [əi'kɒnə,klæst] *n.* **1** a person who attacks cherished beliefs or institutions. **2** a person opposed to the use of images in religious worship. ⟨< Med.L *ikonoklastes* < Med.Gk. *eikonoklastēs* < Gk. *eikōn* image + *klaein* break⟩

i•con•o•clas•tic [əi,kɒnə'klæstɪk] *adj.* of or having to do with iconoclasts. **—i,con•o'clas•ti•cal•ly,** *adv.*

i•co•nog•ra•phy [,əikə'nɒgrəfi] *n., pl.* **-phies. 1** the art or study of illustrating by means of icons, symbols, etc. **2** the representation of an individual in portraits, statues, etc. **3** all the icons of a particular artist, group, religion, etc. ⟨< Med.L < Gk. *eikonographia.* See ICON, -GRAPHY.⟩

i•co•nol•at•ry [,əikə'nɒlətri] *n.* the worship of images or icons.

i•co•nol•o•gy [,əikə'nɒlədʒi] *n.* the historical study of icons.

i•con•o•scope [əi'kɒnə,skoup] *n.* a camera tube used in television for rapid scanning of images.

i•co•nos•ta•sis [,əikə'nɒstəsɪs] *n., pl.* **-ses** [-,siz]. a screen in front of the sanctuary in an Eastern Orthodox church.

i•co•sa•he•dron [,əikousə'hidrən] *n.* a solid figure with 20 faces. ⟨< Gk. *eikosi* twenty⟩

–ics *suffix.* **1** facts; principles; science: *physics.* **2** methods; system; activities: *tactics.* **3** qualities; properties. ⟨originally pl. of *-ic* < L *-ica* < Gk. *-ika,* neut. pl. of *-ikos*⟩

ic•tas ['ɪktɑs] *n.pl.* See IKTAS.

ic•ter•ic [ɪk'tɛrɪk] *n., adj. —n.* **1** a remedy for jaundice. **2** one who is affected with jaundice.
—adj. of or having to do with icterus.

ic•ter•us ['ɪktərəs] *n.* **1** jaundice. **2** *Botany.* the yellowing of certain plants, caused by too much cold or moisture. ⟨< L *icterus* jaundice < Gk. *ikteros* a yellow bird believed to cure jaundice⟩

ic•tus ['ɪktəs] *n., pl.* **-tus•es** or **-tus. 1** rhythmical or metrical stress. **2** *Music.* the moment of attack in a performance. **3** *Medicine.* a stroke or attack. ⟨< L *ictus* a blow < *icere* to hit⟩

ICU intensive care unit.

i•cy ['əisi] *adj.* **i•ci•er, i•ci•est. 1** like ice; very cold: *an icy blast of wind.* **2** having much ice; covered with ice: *an icy road.* **3** slippery because frozen. **4** of ice. **5** without warm feeling; cold and unfriendly: *an icy stare.* **—'i•ci•ly,** *adv.* **—'i•ci•ness,** *n.*

id [ɪd] *n. Psychoanalysis.* that part of the self which is subconscious and instinctive. ⟨special use of L *id* it, as a trans. of G *Es* primal urge⟩

I'd [aɪd] **1** I would: *I'd leave tomorrow if I could.* **2** I had: *I'd better get back to work.*

–id *suffix.* indicating: **1** *Astronomy.* a comet originating in a particular constellation: *Geminid.* **2** *Zoology.* a member of a family: *hominid.* **3** *Chemistry.* a variant of -IDE.

id. idem.

–idae *Zoology. suffix.* indicating the taxonomic name of a family: *Hominidae.* ⟨< NL, L < Gk. *-idai, -ides* offspring of⟩

I•da•ho ['aɪdə,hou] *n.* a northern state of the U.S.

ID card identification card, an official card or other document such as a driver's licence, birth certificate, or credit card that helps to establish one's identity.

-ide or **-id** *suffix. Chemistry.* compound of ——: *chloride, sulphide.* ⟨< *oxide*⟩

i•de•a [aɪ'diə] *n.* **1** a mental concept or abstraction: *the idea of immortality.* **2** an opinion: *to force one's ideas on others.* **3** a plan, scheme, or design: *She told them her idea for the publicity campaign.* **4 ideas,** *pl.* resourcefulness; creative thinking: *a man of ideas, full of ideas.* **5** the point or purpose: *The idea of a vacation is to relax.* **6** a fancy or notion: *I had an idea you would be here for dinner.* **7** *Music.* a theme. **8 a** in Hegelian philosophy, the absolute truth. **b** in Platonism, the eternal archetype of a class of objects; FORM (def. 18).

get ideas into (one's) **head,** expect too much.

the very idea, it is outrageous or ridiculous, etc.: *Crash the party? The very idea!* ⟨< L < Gk. *idea* form, kind < base *id-* see⟩

☛ *Syn.* **Idea,** NOTION, THOUGHT = something understood or formed in the mind. **Idea** is the general word applying to something existing in the mind as the result of understanding, thinking, reasoning, imagining, etc.: *Learn to express your ideas clearly.* **Notion** applies to an idea not fully, clearly, plainly, or completely formed or understood: *I have only a notion of what you mean.* **Thought** applies to an idea formed by reflection or reasoning, rather than by the imagination: *Tell me your thoughts on this proposal.*

i•de•al [aɪ'diəl] *n., adj.* —*n.* a perfect type; model to be imitated; what one would wish to be: *Her mother is her ideal.* —*adj.* **1** just as one would wish; perfect: *A warm, sunny day is ideal for a picnic.* **2** existing only in thought: *A point without length, breadth, or thickness is an ideal object.* **3** not practical; visionary. **4** having to do with ideas; representing an idea. **5** existing as an archetypal model. **6** imaginary. ⟨< LL *idealis* < L *idea.* See IDEA.⟩ —**i'de•al•less,** *adj.*

i•de•al•ism [aɪ'diə,lɪzəm] *n.* **1** the practice of living or acting according to one's ideals or what ought to be, regardless of circumstances or of the approval or disapproval of others. **2** a cherishing of fine ideals. **3** the imaginative or idealized treatment of things in art or literature as opposed to a faithful rendering of nature. **4** *Philosophy.* the belief that all our knowledge is a knowledge of ideas and that it is impossible to know whether there really is a world of objects on which our ideas are based. Idealism is opposed to materialism, which holds that objects not only really exist apart from our ideas about them, but are also the ultimate reality.

i•de•al•ist [aɪ'diəlɪst] *n.* **1** a person who has high ideals and strives to act according to them. **2** a person who neglects practical matters in following ideals. **3** one who follows or practises idealism in art, literature, or philosophy.

i•de•al•is•tic [,aɪdiə'lɪstɪk] *or* [aɪ,diə'lɪstɪk] *adj.* **1** having high ideals and acting according to them. **2** forgetting or neglecting practical matters in trying to follow one's ideals; not practical. **3** of or having to do with idealism or idealists. —**,i•de•al'is•ti•cal•ly,** *adv.*

i•de•al•i•ty [,aɪdi'æləti] *n., pl.* **-ties. 1** an ideal quality or character. **2** something ideal or imaginary.

i•de•al•i•za•tion [aɪ,diəlaɪ'zeiʃən] *or* [aɪ,diələ'zeiʃən] *n.* **1** an idealizing or being idealized. **2** the result of idealizing.

i•de•al•ize [aɪ'diə,laɪz] *v.* **-ized, -iz•ing.** make ideal; think of or represent as perfect rather than as is actually the case: *Douglas idealized his older sister and thought that everything she did was right.* —**i'de•al,iz•er,** *n.*

i•de•al•ly [aɪ'diəli] *adv.* **1** according to an ideal; perfectly. **2** in idea or theory.

i•de•ate ['aɪdi,eit] *or* [aɪ'di,eit] *v.* **-at•ed, -at•ing. 1** imagine. **2** think.

i•de•a•tion [,aɪdi'eiʃən] *n.* the formation of ideas.

i•de•a•tion•al [,aɪdi'eiʃənəl] *adj.* having to do with the process of forming ideas.

i•dée fixe [idei'fiks] *French.* a fixed idea; obsession.

idem ['aɪdəm] *or* ['ɪdəm] *pron. or adj. Latin.* the same as previously given or mentioned.

i•den•ti•cal [aɪ'dɛntəkəl] *adj.* **1** the same: *Both events happened on the identical day.* **2** exactly alike: *The lengths 15 cm and 1.5 dm are identical.* **3** of twins, developing from a single fertilized egg cell that split in two. Identical twins are always the same sex and usually resemble each other very closely. Compare FRATERNAL (def. 3). ⟨< Med.L *identicus* < L *idem* same⟩ —**i'den•ti•cal•ly,** *adv.* —**i'den•ti•cal•ness,** *n.*

☛ *Syn.* **1, 2.** See note at SAME.

i•den•ti•fi•ca•tion [aɪ,dɛntəfə'keiʃən] *n.* **1** an identifying or being identified. **2** something used to identify a person or thing: *She showed her driver's licence as identification.* **3** a person's awareness of a group identity.

identification card ID.

identification tag either of two rectangular metal tags issued to military personnel, bearing the wearer's name, rank, serial number, blood type, etc., and worn on a chain around the neck at all times.

i•den•ti•fy [aɪ'dɛntə,faɪ] *v.* **-fied, -fy•ing. 1** recognize as being, or show to be, a certain person or thing; prove to be the same: *Fred identified the bag as his by what it contained.* **2** make the same; treat as the same: *The good king identified his people's welfare with his own.* **3** connect closely; link; associate: *He identified himself with the revolutionary movement.* —**i'den•ti,fi•able,** *adj.* —**i'den•ti,fi•er,** *n.*

i•den•ti•ty [aɪ'dɛntəti] *n., pl.* **-ties. 1** being oneself or itself and not another; who or what one is: *The writer concealed her identity under an assumed name.* **2** exact likeness; sameness: *an identity of interests.* **3** the state or fact of being the same one or ones as described, mentioned, etc.: *They have established identity of these pearls with the ones reported missing.* ⟨< LL *identitas,* ult. < L *idem* same⟩

identity element *Mathematics.* a member of a set which can operate on *x,* another member of the set, to produce *x.* The identity element for the operation addition of numbers is zero, since $x + 0 = x$.

ideo– *combining form.* idea: *ideogram.* ⟨< Gk. *ide-* idea⟩

id•e•o•gram ['ɪdiə,græm] *or* ['aɪdiə,græm] *n.* a graphic symbol that represents a thing or an idea directly, without representing the sounds of the word for the thing or idea. Most Egyptian hieroglyphics and some Chinese characters are ideograms, as are numerals. Also, **ideograph.**

☛ *Hom.* IDIOGRAM.

id•e•og•ra•phy [,ɪdi'ɒgrəfi] *or* [,aɪdi'ɒgrəfi] *n.* the representation of ideas by symbols; the use of ideograms for ideas. —**,id•e•o'graph•ic,** *adj.*

i•de•o•log•i•cal [,aɪdiə'lɒdʒəkəl] *or* [,ɪdiə'lɒdʒəkəl] *adj.* of or having to do with ideology. —**,i•de•o'log•i•cal•ly,** *adv.*

i•de•ol•o•gist [,aɪdi'ɒlədʒɪst] *or* [,ɪdi'ɒlədʒɪst] *n.* **1** a person who supports or expounds a particular ideology. **2** a person who studies ideologies or ideology. **3** a theorist, especially as opposed to a practical person.

i•de•o•logue ['aɪdiə,lɒg] *or* ['ɪdiə,lɒg] *n.* an ideologist, especially a person who supports or expounds a particular social or political ideology.

i•de•ol•o•gy [,aɪdi'ɒlədʒi] *or* [,ɪdi'ɒlədʒi] *n., pl.* **-gies. 1** a body of doctrines or concepts, especially about social, political, or economic systems. **2** the combined doctrines, assertions, and intentions of a social or political movement. **3** abstract speculation, especially theorizing or speculation of a visionary or unpractical nature. **4** the study of ideas, their nature and origin.

id•e•o•mot•or [,aɪdiou'moutər] *or* [,ɪdiou'moutər] *adj.* having to do with an unconscious or automatic motor activity caused by an idea.

id•e•o•phone ['ɪdiə,foun] *n. Linguistics.* in certain African languages, an onomatopoeic form.

☛ *Hom.* IDIOPHONE.

ides [aɪdz] *n.* in the ancient Roman calendar, the 15th day of March, May, July, and October, and the 13th day of the other months (*used with a singular or plural verb*). ⟨< OF < L *idus*⟩

idio– *combining form.* proper to one; peculiar: *idiolect.* ⟨< Gk. *idios* own, personal, separate, distinct⟩

id•i•o•blast ['ɪdiə,blæst] *n.* a cell that is completely different from surrounding tissue.

id•i•o•cy ['ɪdiəsi] *n., pl.* **-cies. 1** the state of being an idiot. **2** an acting like an idiot. **3** very great stupidity or folly. **4** a stupid act or remark.

id•i•o•gram ['ɪdɪə,græm] *n. Genetics.* a diagrammatic representation of a typical set of chromosomes.

☛ *Hom.* IDEOGRAM.

id•i•o•lect ['ɪdiə,lɛkt] *n.* the dialect of a person; the form of speech, including the sounds, grammar, usage, and vocabulary, used by an individual. ⟨< *idio-* + (*dia*)*lect*⟩

☛ *Syn.* See note at LANGUAGE.

id•i•om ['ɪdiəm] *n.* **1** an expression whose meaning is not predictable from the usual meanings of its constituent elements. *Example*: chew the fat *means* talk casually *or* chat. **2** dialect: *He speaks in the idiom of the Ottawa Valley.* **3** a people's way of expressing themselves: *In the Hopi idiom, time is not an important*

category. **4** *Music, arts, etc.* an individual manner of expression. ⟨< LL < Gk. *idioma,* ult. < *idios* one's own⟩
☛ *Syn.* **2, 3.** See note at LANGUAGE.

id•i•o•mat•ic [ˌɪdiəˈmætɪk] *adj.* **1** using an idiom or idioms. **2** of, being, or concerning idioms. **3** showing the individual character of a language; characteristic of a particular language. **—ˌid•i•o'mat•i•cal•ly,** *adv.*

id•i•o•morph•ic [ˌɪdiəˈmɔrfɪk] *adj.* **1** having its own characteristic form. **2** *Mineralogy.* of a crystal in rock, having the shape associated with a particular mineral. **—ˌid•i•o'mor•phi•cal•ly,** *adv.* **—ˌid•i•o'mor•phism,** *n.*

id•i•op•a•thy [ˌɪdiˈɒpəθi] *n.* **1** a disease of unknown origin. **2** a disease for which no cure exists. **—ˌid•i•o'path•ic,** *adj.* **—ˌid•i•o'path•i•cal•ly,** *adv.*

id•i•o•phone [ˈɪdiəˌfoun] *n.* a musical instrument, such as a gong, made from a solid, naturally sonorous material.
☛ *Hom.* IDEOPHONE.

id•i•o•plasm [ˈɪdiəˌplæzəm] *n. Biology.* a hypothetical unit in the stucture of a germ plasm. **—ˌid•i•o'plas•mic,** *adj.* **—ˌid•i•o•plas'mat•ic,** *adj.*

id•i•o•syn•cra•sy [ˌɪdiəˈsɪŋkrəsi] *n., pl.* **-sies. 1** a personal peculiarity of taste, behaviour, opinion, etc.: *He was an eccentric person with many idiosyncrasies.* **2** an individual reaction to a food or drug that differs from the norm. ⟨< Gk. *idiosynkrasia* < *idios* one's own + *synkrasis* temperament < *syn* together + *kerannynai* mix⟩

id•i•o•syn•crat•ic [ˌɪdiəsɪŋˈkrætɪk] *adj.* having to do with or due to idiosyncrasy. **—ˌid•i•o•syn'crat•ic•al•ly,** *adv.*

id•i•ot [ˈɪdiət] *n. Psychology.* **1** a person born with little ability to learn; a person who does not develop mentally beyond the age of three or four years. **2** a very stupid or foolish person: *He was an idiot to refuse that offer.* ⟨< L < Gk. *idiōtēs,* originally, private person < *idios* one's own⟩
☛ *Syn.* See note at FOOL.

idiot board or **card** *Slang.* a prompt card used in television work.

idiot box *Slang.* television.

id•i•ot•ic [ˌɪdiˈɒtɪk] *adj.* of or like an idiot; very stupid or foolish. **—ˌid•i'ot•i•cal•ly,** *adv.*

idiot savant [ˈɪdiət səˈvɑnt]; *French,* [idjosavɑ̃] person with a mental handicap but with one extraordinary mental gift, as, in mathematics.

idiot stick *Cdn. Slang.* a low-priced souvenir totem pole.

i•dle [ˈaɪdəl] *adj.* **i•dler, i•dlest;** *v.* **i•dled, i•dling.** *—adj.* **1** doing nothing; not busy; not working: *idle hands.* **2** not willing to do things; lazy. **3** useless; worthless: *He wasted his time in idle pleasures.* **4** without any good reason, cause, or foundation: *idle fears, idle rumours.* **5** of a gear, serving only to transmit power.
—v. **1** be idle; waste time; do nothing: *Are you going to spend your whole vacation just idling?* **2** run slowly without transmitting power: *The motor of a car idles when it is out of gear.* **3** cause (a motor) to idle: *Don't idle the motor too long.* **4** spend (time) wastefully (*used with* **away**): *She idled away the hours.* **5** cause (a person or thing) to be idle; take out of work or use.
idle away, spend wastefully: *She idled away many hours lying in the hammock.* ⟨OE *īdel*⟩ **—'i•dle•ness,** *n.*
☛ *Hom.* IDOL, IDYLL.
☛ *Syn. adj.* **1, 2. Idle,** LAZY, INDOLENT = not active or working. **Idle** = not busy or working at the moment, and does not always suggest cause for blame: *The long drought made many farm workers idle.* **Lazy,** usually suggesting cause for blame, means 'not liking to work', and 'not industrious when at work': *Lazy people are seldom successful.* **Indolent** = by nature or habit fond of ease and opposed to work or activity: *Too much idleness sometimes makes one indolent.*

i•dler [ˈaɪdlər] *n.* **1** a lazy person. **2** a device allowing a motor to idle. **3** an IDLE WHEEL.

idle wheel *Machinery.* **1** a gear wheel placed between two others to transfer motion from one axis to another without change in direction or speed. **2** a pulley for taking up slack in a belt; idle pulley.

i•dly [ˈaɪdli] *adv.* in an idle manner; doing nothing.

I•do [ˈidou] *n.* an artificial language based on Esperanto. ⟨< Esperanto *ido* child, offspring < Gk. *id-* + *-o*⟩

i•do•crase [ˈaɪdouˌkreis] *n.* a green, brown, or yellow mineral, also called Vesuvian because of its origin in the volcano Vesuvius. ⟨< F < Gk. *eidos* form + *krasis* mixture⟩

i•dol [ˈaɪdəl] *n.* **1** an image or other object worshipped as a god. **2** in the Bible, a false god. **3** a person or thing worshipped or loved too much; object of extreme devotion. ⟨ME < OF < L *idolum* < Gk. *eidōlon* image < *eidos* form⟩
☛ *Hom.* IDLE, IDYLL.

i•dol•a•ter [aɪˈdɒlətər] *n.* **1** a person who worships idols. **2** an admirer; adorer; devotee.

i•dol•a•trize [aɪˈdɒləˌtraɪz] *v.* **-ized, -iz•ing.** idolize.

i•dol•a•trous [aɪˈdɒlətrəs] *adj.* **1** worshipping idols. **2** having to do with idolatry. **3** blindly adoring. **—i'dol•a•trous•ly,** *adv.* **—i'dol•a•trous•ness,** *n.*

i•dol•a•try [aɪˈdɒlətri] *n., pl.* **-tries. 1** the worship of idols. **2** worship of a human person or thing; too great love or admiration; extreme devotion. ⟨< OF < L < Gk. *eidōlolatreia* < *eidōlon* image + *latreia* service⟩

i•dol•ism [ˈaɪdəˌlɪzəm] *n.* **1** idolatry. **2** *Archaic.* a fallacy.

i•dol•ize [ˈaɪdəˌlaɪz] *v.* **-ized, -iz•ing. 1** worship as an idol; make an idol of: *The boys idolized the hockey star.* **2** love or admire very much; be extremely devoted to: *The boy idolizes his mother.* **—ˌi•dol•i'za•tion,** *n.*

i•dox•ur•i•dine [ˌaɪdɒksˈjʊrəˌdin] *n.* a drug used to treat certain viral infections. *Formula:* $C_9H_{11}IN_2O_5$

I•dun [ˈiðun] *n. Norse mythology.* the goddess of spring and youth. ⟨variant of *Ithunn*⟩

i•dyll or **i•dyl** [ˈaɪdəl] *or* [ˈɪdəl] *n.* **1** in poetry or prose, a short description of a simple and charming scene or event, especially one connected with country life. **2** a simple and charming scene, event, or experience suitable for such a description. **3** a short musical composition in a pastoral or sentimental mood. **4** a long narrative poem on a major theme; epic: *Idylls of the King.* ⟨< L *idyllium* < Gk. *eidyllion,* dim. of *eidos* form⟩
☛ *Hom.* IDLE, IDOL (ˈaɪdəl).

i•dyl•lic [aɪˈdɪlɪk] *or* [ɪˈdɪlɪk] *adj.* suitable for an idyll; simple and charming. **—i'dyl•li•cal•ly,** *adv.*

i•dyl•list [ˈaɪdəˌlɪst] *n.* a writer of idylls.

-ie *suffix.* little; darling: *dearie, lassie.* ⟨var. of *-y*⟩

i.e. that is. ⟨< L *id est*⟩

IE Indo-European.

-ier *suffix.* a person occupied or concerned with ——: *financier, clothier.* ⟨< F < L *-arius*⟩

if [ɪf] *conj., n. —conj.* **1** supposing that; on condition that; in case that: *If you are going, leave now. I'll go if you will.* **2** whether: *I wonder if he will go.* **3** although; even though: *If he is little, he is strong.*
as if, as it would be if.
—n. a condition or supposition. ⟨OE *gif*⟩

I.F., IF, or **i.f.** INTERMEDIATE FREQUENCY.

if•fy [ˈɪfi] *adj. Informal.* uncertain, undecided, or risky: *an iffy proposition.*

I–formation [ˈaɪ fɔrˌmeiʃən] *n. Football.* a play in which three players form a line behind the centre.

i•fos•fa•mide [əiˈfɒsfəˌmaɪd] *n.* a drug used to treat certain forms of cancer.

IFR INSTRUMENT FLIGHT RULES.

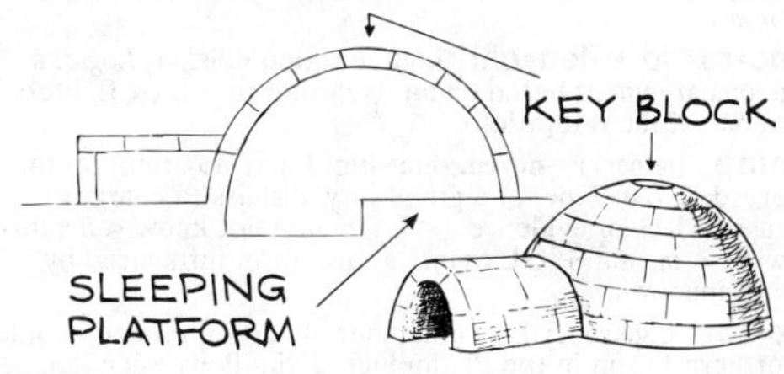

An igloo

i•gloo [ˈɪglu] *n., pl.* **-loos.** *Cdn.* **1** an Inuit dwelling, especially a domed structure built of blocks of snow. **2** any structure resembling this in shape. ⟨< Inuktitut *iglu, igdlu* abode, dwelling (irrespective of material and style of structure)⟩

ign. 1 ignition. **2** unknown. ⟨< L *ignatus* unknown⟩

ig•ne•ous [ˈɪgniəs] *adj.* **1** of or having to do with fire.

2 *Geology.* designating rock formed by the solidification of molten matter: *Granite is igneous rock.* ⟨< L *igneus* < *ignis* fire⟩

ig•nes•cent [ɪg'nɛsənt] *adj.* **1** bursting into flames. **2** giving off sparks, as flint does when struck with steel. ⟨< L *ignescens* < *ignescere* ignite, burn < *ignis* fire⟩

ig•nis fat•u•us ['ɪgnɪs 'fætʃuəs] *pl.* **ig•nes fat•u•i** ['ɪgniz 'fætʃu,aɪ] *or* ['fætʃu,i] **1** a flitting phosphorescent light seen at night chiefly over marshy ground; will-o'-the-wisp. **2** something deluding or misleading. ⟨< NL *ignis fatuus,* literally, foolish fire⟩

ig•nite [ɪg'nəit] *v.* **-nit•ed, -nit•ing. 1** set on fire. **2** make intensely hot; cause to glow with heat. **3** take fire; begin to burn. **4** *Chemistry.* heat to the point of combustion or chemical change. **5** make excited; inflame the feelings of. ⟨< L *ignire* < *ignis* fire⟩ **—ig'nit•er** or **ig'nit•or,** *n.* **—ig'nit•a•ble** or **ig'nit•i•ble,** *adj.*
☛ *Syn.* **1.** See note at KINDLE.

ig•ni•tion [ɪg'nɪʃən] *n.* **1** a setting on fire. **2** a catching fire. **3** a means of igniting or setting on fire. **4** the apparatus for igniting the explosive vapour in the cylinders of an internal-combustion engine. **5** the switch for controlling this explosion. **6** any chemical or mechanical device used to ignite a rocket propellant or a fuel mixture in a jet engine. **7** the heating of a substance to produce a complete chemical change.

ig•ni•tron [ɪg'nəitrɒn] *n. Electronics.* a heavy-duty rectifier, such as a diode, to convert current from alternating to direct.

ig•no•ble [ɪg'noubəl] *adj.* **1** mean; base; without honour: *To betray a friend is ignoble.* **2** not of noble birth or position; humble: *Thomas Beckett came from an ignoble family.* ⟨< L *ignobilis* < *in-* not + OL *gnobilis* noble⟩ **—,ig•no'bil•i•ty** [-nə'bɪləti] or **ig'no•ble•ness,** *n.* **—ig'no•bly,** *adv.*

ig•no•min•i•ous [,ɪgnə'mɪniəs] *adj.* **1** shameful; disgraceful; dishonourable; humiliating. **2** contemptible. ⟨< L *ignominiosus* < *ignominia.* See IGNOMINY.⟩ **—,ig•no'min•i•ous•ly,** *adv.* **—,ig•no'min•i•ous•ness,** *n.*

ig•no•min•y ['ɪgnə,mɪni] *n., pl.* **-min•ies. 1** loss of one's good name; public shame and disgrace; dishonour. **2** shameful action or conduct. ⟨< L *ignominia* < *in-* not + *nomen* name; form influenced by OL *gnoscere* come to know⟩
☛ *Syn.* **1.** See note at DISGRACE.

ig•no•ra•mus [,ɪgnə'reiməs] *or* [,ɪgnə'ræməs] *n., pl.* **-mus•es.** an ignorant person. ⟨< the name of a lawyer in a play by 17c. English dramatist G. Ruggle < L *ignoramus* we do not know⟩

ig•no•rance ['ɪgnərəns] *n.* **1** a lack of knowledge; the quality or condition of being ignorant. **2** lack of awareness.

ig•no•rant ['ɪgnərənt] *adj.* **1** knowing little or nothing; without knowledge: *A person who has not had much opportunity to learn may be ignorant without being stupid.* **2** caused by or showing lack of knowledge: *an ignorant remark.* **3** uninformed; unaware: *He was ignorant of the fact that his house had been burned.* ⟨< L *ignorans, -antis,* ppr. of *ignorare* not know. See IGNORE.⟩ **—'ig•no•rant•ly,** *adv.*
☛ *Syn.* **1. Ignorant,** ILLITERATE, UNEDUCATED = without knowledge. **Ignorant** = without general knowledge, sometimes without knowledge of some particular subject: *People who live in the city are often ignorant of farm life.* **Illiterate** = unable to read or write: *It is a disadvantage to be illiterate.* **Uneducated** = without systematic training or learning, in schools or from books: *Because of the shortage of schools many people in early Canada were uneducated.*

ig•no•ra•tio e•len•chi [,ɪgnou'rɑtiou ei'lɛŋki] *Logic.* a fallacious argument based on an irrelevant proof. ⟨< L, literally, ignorance of the refutation⟩

ig•nore [ɪg'nɔr] *v.* **-nored, -nor•ing. 1** pay no attention to; disregard. **2** *U.S. Law.* of a grand jury, dismiss (a charge) because of lack of evidence. ⟨< L *ignorare* not know < *ignarus* unaware < *in-* not + OL *gnarus* aware; form influenced by *ignotus* unknown⟩

I•go•rot ['ɪgə,rout] *n.* **1** a member of certain related peoples in northern Luzon in the Philippines. **2** the Polynesian language of these people.

i•gua•na [ɪ'gwɑnə] *n.* any of the larger lizards of the chiefly tropical American lizard family Iguanidae. The bright green, common iguana (*Iguana iguana*), found from Mexico south to N South America, often grows to a length of over 150 cm. ⟨< Sp. < Carib⟩

i•gua•na•don [ɪ'gwɑnə,dɒn] *n.* one of the large dinosaurs of the Jurassic and Cretaceous periods. ⟨< *iguana* + Gk. *odon. odontos* tooth⟩

ih•ram [i'rɑm] *n.* **1** the sacred white cotton clothing of Muslim pilgrims. **2** the holy state given to pilgrims wearing this clothing. ⟨< Arabic, a prohibiting⟩

IHS Jesus (*a Christian emblem or monogram*). ⟨ME < LL, a misinterpretation of Gk. I H Σ, the first three letters of the name Jesus⟩

i•ke•ba•na [,ɪkə'bɑnə] *or* [,ikə'bɑnə] *n.* the Japanese art of flower arranging, which emphasizes a symmetrical balance and simplicity of design. ⟨< Japanese⟩

i•kon ['əikɒn] See ICON.

ik•tas ['ɪktɑs] *n.pl. Cdn.* on the West Coast, goods or belongings; things: *We've got food and all the iktas we need for now.* Also, **ictas.** ⟨< Chinook Jargon⟩

il–[1] *prefix.* a form of IN-[1] occurring before *l,* as in *illegal.*

il–[2] *prefix.* a form of IN-[2] occurring before *l,* as in *illuminate.*

i•lang–i•lang ['ilæŋ 'ilæŋ] *n.* **1** a perfumed tree (*Cananga odorata*) of the Philippines. **2** the essence obtained from this tree, used in perfumery. Also, **ylang-ylang.**

–ile *suffix.* used in adjectives to show capability: *agile.* ⟨< L *-ilis*⟩

il•e•ac ['ɪli,æk] *adj.* of or having to do with the ileum.
☛ *Hom.* ILIAC.

il•e•i•tis [,ɪli'əitɪs] *n.* an inflammation of the ileum, due to infection, a tumour, etc. and involving partial or complete blocking of the passage of food through the small intestine.

ileo– *combining form.* ileum: *ileostomy.*

il•e•os•to•my [,ɪli'ɒstəmi] *n. Surgical.* the formation of an artificial opening into the ileum.

il•e•um ['ɪliəm] *n. Anatomy.* the lowest part of the small intestine. See ALIMENTARY CANAL for picture. ⟨< LL *ileum,* var. of *ilium,* sing. of L *ilia* loins, entrails⟩
☛ *Hom.* ILIUM.

il•e•us ['ɪliəs] *n.* an obstruction in the intestines.

i•lex ['aɪlɛks] *n.* **1** HOLM OAK. **2** holly. ⟨< L⟩

il•i•ac ['ɪli,æk] *adj.* of, having to do with, or near the ilium.
☛ *Hom.* ILEAC.

Il•i•ad ['ɪliəd] *n.* a Greek epic poem, by Homer, about the siege of Ilium (Troy). ⟨< L < Gk. *Ilias, -iados* < *Ilion* Ilium⟩

Il•i•on ['ɪliən] *n. Poetic.* Ilium.

il•i•um ['ɪliəm] *n., pl.* **il•i•a** ['ɪliə]. the broad, flat, upper portion of the hipbone. See PELVIS for picture. ⟨< NL < LL *ilium,* sing. L *ilia* loins, entrails⟩
☛ *Hom.* ILEUM.

Il•i•um ['ɪliəm] *n. Poetic.* ancient Troy.

ilk [ɪlk] *adj., n.* —*adj. Archaic.* same.
—*n. Informal.* kind; sort.
of that ilk, *Informal.* **a** of the same place or name. **b** of that kind or sort. ⟨OE *ilca* same⟩

ill [ɪl] *adj., adv.* **worse, worst;** *n.* —*adj.* **1** having some disease; not well; sick. **2** bad; evil; harmful: *an ill deed.* **3** unfavourable; unfortunate: *an ill wind.* **4** unkind; harsh; cruel. **5** not up to recognized standards.
ill at ease, uncomfortable.
—*adv.* **1** badly; harmfully. **2** unfavourably; unfortunately: *to fare ill.* **3** in an unkind manner; harshly; cruelly: *He speaks ill of his former friends.* **4** with trouble or difficulty; scarcely: *You can ill afford to waste your money.*
go ill with, affect badly.
take ill, fall sick; become ill.
take (something) **ill,** take offence at or be offended by (something).
—*n.* **1** a sickness; disease. **2** an evil; a harm; a trouble: *Poverty is an ill.* ⟨ME < ON *illr*⟩
☛ *Syn.* **1.** See note at SICK.

I'll [aɪl] **1** I will. **2** I shall.
☛ *Hom.* AISLE, ISLE.

ill. illustration; illustrated.

ill–ad•vised ['ɪl əd'vaɪzd] *adj.* acting or done without enough consideration; unwise. **—ill-ad'vis•ed•ly** [,ɪl əd'vaɪzɪdli], *adv.*

il•la•tion [ɪ'leiʃən] *n.* **1** the drawing of conclusions. **2** whatever is deduced. ⟨< LL *illation-* (stem of *illatio*) a carrying in < L *illat(us)* brought in, pp. of *inferre* bring in⟩
☛ *Hom.* ELATION.

il•la•tive ['ɪlətɪv] *adj.* **1** having to do with an illation. **2** of a word, such as *so* or *hence,* used to introduce an inference. **—'il•la•tive•ly,** *adv.*

ill–be•ing ['ɪl 'biɪŋ] **1** the condition of lacking what is desirable, such as health, solvency, etc.

ill–bod•ing ['ɪl 'boudɪŋ] *adj.* inauspicious; unlucky.

ill–bred [ˈɪl ˈbrɛd] *adj.* badly brought up; impolite; rude.

ill breeding bad manners; lack of a good upbringing; impoliteness; rudeness.

ill–con•ceived [ˈɪl kənˈsivd] *adj.* ILL-CONSIDERED.

ill–con•sid•ered [ˈɪl kənˈsɪdərd] *adj.* not well considered; unwise; unsuitable.

ill–de•fined [ˈɪl dɪˈfaɪnd] *adj.* not clear; not clearly indicated or explained; hazy.

ill–dis•posed [ˈɪl dɪˈspouzd] *adj.* unfriendly; unfavourable.

il•le•gal [ɪˈligəl] *adj.* **1** prohibited by law: *illegal parking.* **2** prohibited by an accepted set of rules, especially in sports: *an illegal punch in boxing.* **—il'le•gal•ly,** *adv.*

il•le•gal•i•ty [ˌɪliˈgæləti] *n., pl.* **-ties. 1** unlawfulness. **2** an illegal act; act contrary to law.

il•le•gal•ize [ɪˈligəˌlaɪz] *v.* **-ized, -iz•ing.** make illegal.

il•leg•i•ble [ɪˈlɛdʒəbəl] *adj.* very hard or impossible to read. **—il,leg•i'bil•i•ty** or **il'leg•i•ble•ness,** *n.* **—il'leg•i•bly,** *adv.*

il•le•git•i•ma•cy [ˌɪləˈdʒɪtəməsi] *n., pl.* **-cies.** the fact or condition of being illegitimate.

il•le•git•i•mate [ˌɪləˈdʒɪtəmɪt] *adj.* **1** born of parents who are not married to each other. **2** not according to the law or the rules. **3** not logical; not properly deduced. **4** incorrect in grammatical usage. **—,il•le'git•i•mate•ly,** *adv.*

ill–equipped [ˈɪl ɪˈkwɪpt] *adj.* poorly equipped or prepared.

ill fame a bad reputation.

ill–fat•ed [ˈɪl ˈfeitɪd] *adj.* **1** sure to have a bad fate or end. **2** bringing bad luck; unlucky.

ill–fa•voured or **ill–fa•vored** [ˈɪl ˈfeivərd] *adj.* **1** not beautiful to look at; ugly. **2** unpleasant; offensive. **—'ill-'fa•voured•ly,** or **'ill-'fa•vored•ly,** *adv.* **—'ill-'fa•voured•ness** or **'ill-'fa•vored•ness,** *n.*

ill feeling dislike; mistrust: *There has been ill feeling between them since they quarrelled.*

ill–fit•ting [ˈɪl ˈfɪtɪŋ] *adj.* fitting badly: *ill-fitting trousers.*

ill–found•ed [ˈɪl ˈfaʊndɪd] *adj.* without a good reason or sound basis.

ill–got•ten [ˈɪl ˈgɒtən] *adj.* acquired by unfair, dishonest, or evil means.

ill health poor health.

ill humour or **humor** a cross, unpleasant temper or mood.

ill–hu•moured or **ill–hu•mored** [ˈɪl ˈhjumərd] *adj.* cross; unpleasant. **—'ill-'hu•moured•ly** or **'ill-'hu•mored•ly,** *adv.* **—'ill-'hu•moured•ness** or **'ill-'hu•mored•ness,** *n.*

il•lib•er•al [ɪˈlɪbərəl] *adj.* **1** not liberal; narrow-minded; prejudiced. **2** stingy; miserly. **3** without liberal culture; unscholarly; ill-bred. **—il,lib•er'al•i•ty,** *n.* **—il'lib•er•al•ly,** *adv.*

il•lic•it [ɪˈlɪsɪt] *adj.* **1** not permitted or condoned by common custom: *an illicit love affair.* **2** ILLEGAL (def. 1): *illicit gambling.* **—il'lic•it•ly,** *adv.* **—il'lic•it•ness,** *n.*

☛ *Hom.* ELICIT.

il•lim•it•a•ble [ɪˈlɪmətəbəl] *adj.* limitless; boundless; infinite. **—il'lim•it•a•ble•ness,** *n.* **—il,lim•it•a'bil•i•ty,** *n.* **—il'lim•it•a•bly,** *adv.*

Il•li•nois [ˌɪləˈnɔɪ] *n.* a midwestern state of the U.S.

il•li•quid [ɪˈlɪkwɪd] *adj.* not easily converted into money. **—,il•li'quid•i•ty,** *n.*

il•lit•er•a•cy [ɪˈlɪtərəsi] *n., pl.* **-cies. 1** the quality or state of being illiterate, especially the inability to read or write. **2** an error in speaking or writing, suggesting a lack of education or knowledge.

il•lit•er•ate [ɪˈlɪtərɪt] *adj., n.* *—adj.* **1** unable to read or write. **2** unable to read or write as well as expected or required: *a newspaper editorial about illiterate university students.* **3** showing a lack of education or knowledge; not cultured: *He writes in a very illiterate way.* **4** violating accepted standards of writing.
—n. a person who is illiterate, often in a particular field: *a computer illiterate*. **—il'lit•er•ate•ly,** *adv.* **—il'lit•er•ate•ness,** *n.*

☛ *Syn. adj.* **1.** See note at IGNORANT.

ill–judged [ˈɪl ˈdʒʌdʒd] *adj.* unwise; rash.

ill–looking [ˈɪl ˈlʊkɪŋ] *adj.* ILL-FAVOURED.

ill–man•nered [ˈɪl ˈmænərd] *adj.* having or showing bad manners; impolite; rude. **—'ill-'man•nered•ly,** *adv.* **—'ill-'man•nered•ness,** *n.*

ill nature crossness; disagreeableness; spite.

ill–na•tured [ˈɪl ˈneitʃərd] *adj.* cross; disagreeable; spiteful. **—'ill-'na•tured•ly,** *adv.*

ill•ness [ˈɪlnɪs] *n.* **1** a sickness; disease. **2** poor health; a sickly condition: *She suffered from long periods of illness.*

il•lo•cu•tion [ˌɪləˈkjuʃən] *n.* the performing of an act by speaking certain words, as in betting, promising, threatening, etc. **—,il•lo'cu•tion,ary,** *adj.*

il•log•ic [ɪlˈlɒdʒɪk] *n.* a lack of logic.

il•log•i•cal [ɪˈlɒdʒəkəl] *adj.* **1** not according to the rules of logic. **2** not reasonable; foolish: *an illogical fear of the dark.* **—il'log•i•cal•ly,** *adv.* **—il'log•i•cal•ness,** *n.* **—il,log•i'cal•i•ty,** *n.*

ill–omened [ˈɪl ˈoumənd] *adj.* marked by bad omens.

ill–sorted [ˈɪl ˈsɔrtɪd] *adj.* not matched very well.

ill–spent [ˈɪl ˈspɛnt] *adj.* spent badly; wasted; misspent.

ill–starred [ˈɪl ˈstɑrd] *adj.* unlucky; unfortunate; disastrous.

ill–suit•ed [ˈɪl ˈsutɪd] *adj.* poorly suited; unsuitable.

ill temper bad temper or disposition; crossness.

ill–tem•pered [ˈɪl ˈtɛmpərd] *adj.* having or showing a bad temper; cross. **—'ill-'tem•pered•ly,** *adv.* **—'ill-'tem•pered•ness,** *n.*

ill–timed [ˈɪl ˈtaɪmd] *adj.* done or happening at a bad time; inappropriate.

ill–treat [ˈɪl ˈtrit] *v.* treat badly or cruelly; do harm to; abuse. **—'ill-'treat•ment,** *n.*

ill turn **1** an action that is unkind, unfriendly, or spiteful. **2** a change for the worse.

il•lume [ɪˈlum] *v.* **-lumed, -lum•ing.** *Poetic.* illuminate.

il•lu•mi•nance [ɪˈlumɪnəns] *n. Physics.* ILLUMINATION (def. 7).

il•lu•mi•nant [iˈlumənənt] *n., adj., —n.* something that gives light. Electricity and oil are illuminants.
—adj. giving light.

il•lu•mi•nate [ɪˈluməˌneit] *v.* **-nat•ed, -nat•ing. 1** light up; make bright: *The room was illuminated by four large lamps.* **2** make clear; explain: *Our teacher could illuminate almost any subject we studied.* **3** decorate with lights: *The streets were illuminated for the celebration.* **4** decorate with gold, colours, pictures, and designs. In former times books and manuscripts were often illuminated. **5** enlighten; inform; instruct. **6** make illustrious. ⟨< L *illuminare* < *in-* in + *lumen* light⟩ **—il'lu•mi•na•ble,** *adj.*

il•lu•mi•na•ti [ɪˌluməˈnɑti] *n.pl.* **1** people claiming special intellectual or spiritual knowledge. **2 Illuminati,** a name given to certain religious sects and secret societies, especially in the 18th century.

An illuminated initial letter from a Flemish manuscript of the Bible in Latin, dated A.D. 1148

il•lu•mi•na•tion [ɪˌluməˈneiʃən] *n.* **1** an illuminating; a lighting up; a making bright. **2** the amount of light; light. **3** a making clear; explanation. **4** a decoration with lights. **5** the decoration of books and letters with gold, colours, pictures, and designs. **6** enlightenment. **7** *Physics.* the intensity of light falling at a given place on a lighted surface.

il•lu•mi•na•tive [ɪˈlumənətɪv] *or* [ɪˈluməˌneitɪv] *adj.* illuminating; tending to illuminate.

il•lu•mi•na•tor [ɪˈluməˌneitər] *n.* **1** a person who or thing that illuminates. **2** any instrument for illuminating, such as a lens for concentrating light or a mirror for reflecting light. **3** one who decorates manuscripts, books, etc. with colour, gold, etc.

il•lu•mine [ɪˈlumɪn] *v.* **-mined, -min•ing.** make or become bright; illuminate; light up: *A smile can often illumine a homely face.* ⟨< F *illuminer*⟩

il•lu•mi•nism [ɪˈluməˌnɪzəm] *n.* **1** belief in personal enlightenment. **2** the doctrines of any of the Illuminati. **—il'lu•mi•nist,** *n.*

illus. illustration; illustrated.

ill–us•age ['ɪl 'jusɪdʒ] *n.* bad, cruel, or unfair treatment.

ill–use *v.* ['ɪl 'juz]; *n.* ['ɪl 'jus] *v.* **-used, -us•ing;** *n.* —*v.* treat badly, cruelly, or unfairly.
—*n.* bad, cruel, or unfair treatment.

Horizontal lines A and B are the same length but A appears shorter. The three figures are the same size, but the lines suggesting perspective make the ones on the right appear larger.

il•lu•sion [ɪ'luʒən] *n.* **1** an appearance or feeling that misleads because it is not real; something that deceives by giving a false idea: *an illusion of reality.* **2** a false impression or perception: *an optical illusion.* **3** a false idea, notion, or belief: *Many people have the illusion that wealth is the chief cause of happiness.* **4** a fine, delicate net fabric used especially for veils and trimmings. ⟨< L *illusio, -onis* < *illudere* mock < *in-* at + *ludere* play⟩
—il'lu•sion•al or **il'lu•sion•ary,** *adj.*

☛ *Syn.* **1-3. Illusion,** DELUSION = something mistakenly or falsely believed to be true or real. **Illusion** applies to something appearing to be real or true, but actually not existing or being quite different from what it seems: *Good motion pictures create an illusion of reality.* **Delusion** applies to a false and often harmful belief about something that does exist: *The old woman had the delusion that the butcher was always trying to cheat her.*

☛ *Usage.* Do not confuse **illusion** and ALLUSION. An **illusion** is a misleading appearance: *an illusion of wealth.* An **allusion** is an indirect reference or slight mention: *He made several allusions to recent novels.*

☛ *Hom.* ELUSION.

il•lu•sion•ism [ɪ'luʒə,nɪzəm] *n.* the use of illusionary techniques in art.

il•lu•sion•ist [ɪ'luʒənɪst] *n.* **1** a person who produces illusions; conjurer. **2** a person who has illusions; dreamer. **3** an artist who uses illusionary techniques.

il•lu•sive [ɪ'lusɪv] *adj.* illusory. **—il'lu•sive•ly,** *adv.*
—il'lu•sive•ness, *n.*

☛ *Hom.* ELUSIVE.

il•lu•so•ry [ɪ'lusəri] *or* [ɪ'luzəri] *adj.* due to or resulting in an illusion; unreal or misleading. **—il'lu•so•ri•ly,** *adv.*
—il'lu•so•ri•ness, *n.*

☛ *Hom.* ELUSORY [ɪ'lusəri].

illust. illustration; illustrated.

il•lus•trate ['ɪlə,streit] *or* [ɪ'lʌstreit] *v.* **-trat•ed, -trat•ing.**
1 make clear or explain by pictures, charts, stories, examples, comparisons, etc.: *The way that a pump works was used to illustrate the action of the heart in circulating blood through the body.* **2** provide with pictures, diagrams, maps, etc. that explain or decorate: *This book is well illustrated.* **3** work as an illustrator. **4** give an illustration: *Let me illustrate.* ⟨< L *illustrare* light up, ult. < *in-* in + *lustrum,* originally, lighting⟩

il•lus•tra•tion [,ɪlə'streiʃən] *n.* **1** a picture, diagram, map, etc. used to explain or decorate something. **2** a story, example, comparison, etc. used to make clear or explain something: *The teacher cut an apple into four equal pieces as an illustration of what 'quarter' means.* **3** the act or process of illustrating.
—,il•lus'tra•tion•al, *adj.*

il•lus•tra•tive [ɪ'lʌstrətɪv] *or* ['ɪlə,streitɪv] *adj.* illustrating; used to illustrate; helping to explain: *A good teacher uses illustrative examples to explain difficult ideas.* **—il'lus•tra•tive•ly,** *adv.*

il•lus•tra•tor ['ɪlə,streitər] *n.* a person or thing that illustrates, especially an artist who makes illustrations for books, magazines, etc.

il•lus•tri•ous [ɪ'lʌstriəs] *adj.* very famous; great; outstanding; eminent: *an illustrious statesman, an illustrious deed.* ⟨< L *illustris* lighted up, bright⟩ **—il'lus•tri•ous•ly,** *adv.*
—il'lus•tri•ous•ness, *n.*

il•lu•vi•al [ɪ'luviəl] *adj.* having to do with illuviation.

il•lu•vi•ate [ɪ'luvi,eit] *v.* **-at•ed, -at•ing. 1** undergo illuviation. **2** produce illuviation of or in.

il•lu•vi•a•tion [ɪ,luvi'eiʃən] *n.* the leaching of minerals, etc. from one layer of soil into another layer beneath it.

il•lu•vi•um [ɪ'luviəm] *n., pl.* **illuviums** or **illuvia** [-viə]. the material accumulated through illuviation. ⟨< L *illuvi(es)* mud, flood (literally, what washes or is washed in)⟩

ill will unkind or unfriendly feeling; hostility; hate.

ill–wisher ['ɪl 'wɪʃər] *n.* a person who wishes bad fortune on another.

Il•lyr•i•a [ɪ'liriə] *n.* an ancient country in the region east of the Adriatic. **—Il'lyr•i•an,** *adj., n.*

il•men•ite ['ɪlmə,nəit] *n.* a luminous black mineral consisting of iron, titanium, and oxygen. *Formula*: $FeTiO_3$ ⟨< *Ilmen* Mountains in the Urals, where it was first discovered + *-ite*[1]⟩

ILO International Labour Organization.

Il•o•ca•no [,ilou'kɑnou] *n.* **1** a member of a people living in the Philippines. **2** the Austronesian language of these people.

ILS Instrument Landing System.

I'm [aɪm] I am.

im–[1] *prefix.* a form of IN-[1] occurring before *b, m, p,* as in *imbalance, immoral, impatient.*

im–[2] *prefix.* a form of IN-[2] occurring before *b, m, p,* as in *imbibe, immure, impart.*

im•age ['ɪmɪdʒ] *n., v.* **-aged, -ag•ing.** —*n.* **1** an artificial likeness or representation of a person or thing, especially a statue: *an image of a god.* **2** a person or thing resembling another; counterpart: *She is the very image of her mother.* **3** a picture in the mind; idea. **4** a description or figure of speech that helps the mind to form forceful or beautiful pictures. Poetry often contains images. **5** public personality; the way a person, group, nation, etc. is regarded by the world at large or by clients, customers, etc.: *Canada's foreign image. He drives a conservative car because he feels it is good for his image.* **6** a symbol; type. **7** the impression of something produced optically, as by a lens or mirror. A **real image** is projected by a lens (by refraction) and a **virtual image** is reflected in a mirror. **8** the optical impression of something produced by an electronic device: *an image on a television screen.*
—*v.* **1** make or form an image of; be an image of. **2** reflect as a mirror does. **3** picture in one's mind; imagine. **4** describe with images. ⟨ME < OF < L *imago*⟩

image converter a device which converts an optical image into an electronic one.

image or•thi•con ['ɔrθɪ,kɒn] a television camera pickup tube, a kind of iconoscope that scans by focussing electrons from a photo-emissive surface onto the target, which reflects them, sending the charge containing the signal to an output electrode. ⟨< *ortho-* + *icon(oscope)*⟩

im•age•ry ['ɪmɪdʒri] *n., pl.* **-ries. 1** pictures in the mind; things imagined. **2** descriptions and figures of speech that help the mind to form forceful or beautiful pictures. **3** images; statues.

i•mag•i•na•ble [ɪ'mædʒənəbəl] *adj.* that can be imagined; possible. **—i'mag•i•na•bly,** *adv.*

im•ag•in•al[1] [ɪ'mædʒənəl] *adj.* imaginary.

im•ag•in•al[2] [ɪ'mædʒənəl] *adj.* of an insect in the final adult stage (imago).

i•mag•i•nar•y [ɪ'mædʒə,nɛri] *adj.* **1** existing only in the imagination; not real: *Elves are imaginary. The equator is an imaginary line circling the earth midway between the North and South Poles.* **2** *Mathematics.* having to do with an imaginary number. **—i'mag•i,nar•i•ly,** *adv.* **—i'mag•i,nar•i•ness,** *n.*

imaginary number *Mathematics.* **1** a COMPLEX NUMBER in which the coefficient *b* is not zero. **2 pure imaginary number,** a complex number whose real part equals zero.

imaginary part *Mathematics.* the coefficient *b* in a COMPLEX NUMBER.

imaginary unit *Mathematics.* the positive square root of minus 1 (–1), represented by *i.*

i•mag•i•na•tion [ɪ,mædʒə'neiʃən] *n.* **1** an imagining. **2** the power of forming in the mind pictures of things not present to the senses. **3** the ability to create new things or ideas or to combine old ones in new forms. **4** a creation of the mind; fancy. **5** the ability to deal with new situations. **6** the ability to appreciate the creations of others, as in art or music.

☛ *Syn.* **2-4. Imagination,** FANCY, FANTASY = the creative power of forming ideas or pictures in the mind. **Imagination** emphasizes the power to combine and shape ideas in new ways: *Poets, artists, and inventors make use of their imagination.* **Fancy** applies especially to the ability to develop original, often light-hearted ideas: *The playwright's comic fancy leads her to invent outrageous situations.* **Fantasy** emphasizes the unreality or incredibility of the ideas: *Her short stories owed more to fantasy than to the observation of reality.*

i•mag•i•na•tive [ɪ'mædʒənətɪv] *or* [ɪ'mædʒə,neitɪv] *adj.* **1** showing imagination: *Her imaginative solution to the difficult problem saved them weeks of work.* **2** having a good imagination; able to imagine well; fond of imagining: *The imaginative child made up fairy stories.* **3** of imagination. **—i'mag•i•na•tive•ly,** *adv.* **—i'mag•i•na•tive•ness,** *n.*

i•mag•ine [ɪ'mædʒɪn] *v.* **-ined, -in•ing. 1** picture in one's mind; form an image or idea of: *We can hardly imagine life without electricity.* **2** suppose; guess: *I cannot imagine what you mean.* **3** think; believe falsely; have the delusion that: *She imagined someone was watching her.* ⟨ME < OF < L *imaginari* < *imago, -ginis* image⟩

☛ *Syn.* **1. Imagine,** CONCEIVE = form in the mind. **Imagine** = form a clear and definite picture of something in the mind: *I like to imagine myself flying a plane.* **Conceive** = bring (an idea) into existence and give it an outline or pattern or shape in the mind: *The Wright brothers conceived the first successful motor-powered airplane.*

im•ag•ism ['ɪmə,dʒɪzəm] *n.* an early 20th-century movement in poetry that advocates the use of clear and precise imagery and opposes symbolism and conventional metrical rhythm.

im•ag•ist ['ɪmədʒɪst] *n.* a poet who practises imagism. Most imagists use free verse.

im•ag•is•tic [,ɪmə'dʒɪstɪk] *adj.* of, having to do with, or characteristic of imagism: *imagistic verse.* **—,im•ag'is•ti•cal•ly,** *adv.*

i•ma•go [ɪ'meigou] *or* [ɪ'mɑgou] *n., pl.* **i•ma•gos, i•mag•i•nes** [ɪ'mædʒə,niz] **1** an insect in the final adult, especially winged, stage. **2** *Psychoanalysis.* an unconscious childhood concept of a parent or other person, carried over unchanged into adulthood. ⟨< L *imago* image⟩

i•mam [ɪ'mɑm] *n. Islam.* **1** in the Sunni tradition, a leader of worship in a mosque. **2** in the Shiite tradition, a spiritual leader whose authority derives directly from the prophet Mohammed. ⟨< Arabic *imam* < *amma* go before⟩

i•mam•ate [ɪ'mɑmeit] *n.* **1** the rank or office of an imam. **2** the territory governed by an imam.

im•ar•et [ɪ'mɑrɛt] *n.* an inn for Muslim pilgrims in Turkey. ⟨< Turkish < Arabic *imarah* building⟩

im•bal•ance [ɪm'bæləns] *n.* **1** the state or condition of lacking balance or of being out of balance. **2** *Medicine.* a lack or defect of co-ordination in glands, muscles, etc.

im•balm [ɪm'bɒm] *or* [ɪm'bɑm] *v.* embalm. **—im'balm•er,** *n.* **—im'balm•ment,** *n.*

im•be•cile ['ɪmbə,saɪl] *or* ['ɪmbəsəl] *n., adj.* *—n.* a very stupid or foolish person: *Don't be an imbecile.*
—adj. very stupid or foolish: *an imbecile question.* ⟨< F < L *imbecillus* weak, ult. < *in-* without + *baculum* staff⟩
—im•be'cil•ic [-'sɪlɪk], *adj.*

☛ *Syn.* See note at FOOL.

im•be•cil•i•ty [,ɪmbə'sɪləti] *n., pl.* **-ties. 1** the state or condition of being an imbecile. **2** great stupidity or dullness. **3** a very stupid or foolish action, remark, etc.

im•bed [ɪm'bɛd] *v.* **-bed•ded, -bed•ding.** embed.

im•bibe [ɪm'baɪb] *v.* **-bibed, -bib•ing. 1** drink; drink in. **2** absorb: *The roots of a plant imbibe moisture from the earth.* **3** take into one's mind: *Children often imbibe superstitions that last all their lives.* ⟨< L *imbibere* < *in-* in + *bibere* drink⟩ **—im'bib•er,** *n.* **—,im•bi'bi•tion,** *n.*

☛ *Syn.* **1.** See note at DRINK.

im•bit•ter [ɪm'bɪtər] *v.* embitter.

im•bo•som [ɪm'bʊzəm] *v.* embosom.

im•bow•er [ɪm'baʊər] *v.* embower.

im•bri•cate *v.* ['ɪmbrə,keit]; *adj.* ['ɪmbrəkɪt] *or* ['ɪmbrə,keit] *v.* **-cat•ed, -cat•ing;** *adj.* *—v.* **1** overlap as tiles or shingles do. **2** arrange (tiles) in an overlapping pattern.
—adj. **1** like roof tiles in shape, composition, etc. **2** like the pattern of overlapping tiles. **3** having decorative overlapping tiles. ⟨< L *imbricare* cover with tiles < *imbrex, -ricis* hollow tile⟩ **—'im•bri,ca•tive,** *adj.*

im•bri•cat•ed ['ɪmbrə,keitɪd] *adj., v.* *—adj.* overlapping. *—v.* pt. and pp. of IMBRICATE.

im•bri•ca•tion [,ɪmbrə'keiʃən] *n.* **1** an overlapping like that of tiles, shingles, etc. **2** a decorative pattern in imitation of this.

im•bro•glio [ɪm'brouljou] *n., pl.* **-glios. 1** a complicated or difficult situation. **2** a complicated misunderstanding or disagreement. ⟨< Ital.⟩

im•brown [ɪm'braʊn] *v.* embrown.

im•brue [ɪm'bru] *v.* **-brued, -bru•ing.** wet; stain: *His sword was*

imbrued with blood. ⟨ME < OF *embreuver* give to drink, ult. < L *bibere* drink⟩

im•brute [ɪm'brut] *v.* **-brut•ed, -brut•ing.** make brutal.

im•bue [ɪm'bju] *v.* **-bued, -bu•ing. 1** fill; inspire: *He imbued his son's mind with the ambition to succeed.* **2** fill with moisture or colour. ⟨< L *imbuere* soak⟩ **—im'bue•ment,** *n.*

IMF INTERNATIONAL MONETARY FUND.

im•id•az•ole [,ɪmɪ'dæzoul] *or* [,ɪmɪdə'zoul] *n. Chemistry.* a colourless, crystalline, water-soluble, heterocyclic compound used chiefly in organic synthesis. *Formula*: $C_3H_4N_2$

im•ide ['ɪmaɪd] *n. Chemistry.* a compound derived from ammonia, containing the imido group. ⟨altered < *amide*⟩

imido group ['ɪmɪ,dou] *Chemistry.* the bivalent group NH, linked to one or two acid groups.

im•ine [ɪ'min] *or* ['ɪmɪn] *n.* a compound containing the imido group plus a non-acid group.

i•mip•e•nem [aɪ'mɪpənəm] *n. Pharmacy.* an antibiotic drug.

im•ip•ra•mine [ɪ'mɪprə,min] *n. Pharmacy.* a drug used to treat depression. *Formula*: $C_{19}H_{24}N_2$

im•i•ta•ble ['ɪmətəbəl] *adj.* that can be imitated. **—,im•i•ta'bil•i•ty,** *n.* **—'im•i•ta•ble•ness,** *n.*

im•i•tate ['ɪmə,teit] *v.* **-tat•ed, -tat•ing. 1** try to be or act like; follow the example of: *The little boy imitated his father.* **2** make or do something like; copy: *A parrot imitates the sounds it hears.* **3** act like, especially for amusement: *He made us laugh by imitating a bear.* **4** be or look like; resemble: *Plastic is often made to imitate wood.* ⟨< L *imitari*⟩

☛ *Syn.* **2.** See note at COPY.

im•i•ta•tion [,ɪmə'teiʃən] *n.* **1** the act or an instance of imitating: *We learn many things by imitation.* **2** something produced in this way; a copy or counterfeit: *He gave an imitation of a rooster crowing. This is an imitation of an 18th-century chair.* **3** (*adjl.*) made to look like something else, especially something better, rarer, etc.: *imitation pearls, imitation leather.* **4** *Philosophy.* the representation of something as it might be, or as it is in essence rather than in appearance. **5** *Music.* the repetition of a melodic phrase or theme in a different pitch or key from the original, or in a different voice part, or with modifications of rhythm or intervals that do not destroy the resemblance.
in imitation of, imitating; in order to be like or look like.
—,im•i'ta•tion•al, *adj.*

im•i•ta•tive ['ɪmə,teitɪv] *adj.* **1** fond of imitating; likely or inclined to imitate others. Monkeys are imitative. **2** imitating; showing imitation. *Bang* and *whizz* are imitative words. **3** reproducing an original. **4** not real. **—'im•i,ta•tive•ly,** *adv.* **—'im•i,ta•tive•ness,** *n.*

im•i•ta•tor ['ɪmə,teitər] *n.* a person who or animal that imitates.

im•mac•u•late [ɪ'mækjəlɪt] *adj.* **1** without spot or stain; absolutely clean: *The newly laundered shirts were immaculate.* **2** without fault; in perfect order: *His appearance was immaculate.* **3** without sin; pure. **4** *Biology.* without coloured marks or spots; unspotted. ⟨< L *immaculatus* < *in-* not + *macula* spot⟩ **—im'mac•u•late•ly,** *adv.* **—im'mac•u•late•ness,** *n.* **—im'mac•u•la•cy,** *n.*

Immaculate Conception *Roman Catholic Church.* **1** the doctrine that the Virgin Mary was conceived free from original sin. **2** a festival observed on December 8 commemorating the Immaculate Conception.

im•ma•nence ['ɪmənəns] *n.* the state of being immanent. Also, **immanency.**

☛ *Hom.* IMMINENCE.

im•ma•nent ['ɪmənənt] *adj.* **1** remaining within; inherent. **2** of God, pervading the universe and time. ⟨< L *immanens, -entis,* ppr. of *immanere* < *in-* in + *manere* stay⟩ **—'im•ma•nent•ly,** *adv.*

☛ *Hom.* IMMINENT.

im•ma•nent•ism ['ɪmənən,tɪzəm] *n.* the belief that God pervades the universe and time.

Im•man•u•el [ɪ'mænjuəl] *or* [ɪ'mænju,ɛl] *n.* Christ. Also, **Emmanuel.** ⟨< Hebrew *'Immānū'ēl*, literally, God with us⟩

im•ma•ter•i•al [,ɪmə'tiriəl] *adj.* **1** not important; insignificant. **2** not material; spiritual rather than physical. **—,im•ma'te•ri•al•ly,** *adv.* **—,im•ma'te•ri•al•ness,** *n.*

im•ma•ter•i•al•ism [,ɪmə'tiriə,lɪzəm] *n.* a metaphysical doctrine that denies corporeal reality. **—,im•ma'te•ri•al•ist,** *n.*

im•ma•ter•i•al•i•ty [ˌɪmə,tiri'æləti] *n.* **1** the state of not being material. **2** inconsequentiality.

im•ma•ter•i•al•ize [ˌɪmə'tiriə,laɪz] *v.* **-ized, -iz•ing.** render immaterial.

im•ma•ture [ˌɪmə'tʃʊr] *or* [ˌɪmə'tjʊr] *adj.* **1** not mature; not ripe; not full-grown; not fully developed. **2** of an adult, behaving irresponsibly. **3** *Geology.* very recent. ⟨< L *immatur(us)* unripe, untimely⟩ **—,im•ma'ture•ly,** *adv.*

im•ma•tu•ri•ty [ˌɪmə'tʃʊrəti] *or* [ˌɪmə'tjʊrəti] *n.* the state of being immature.

im•meas•ur•a•ble [ɪ'mɛʒərəbəl] *adj.* too vast to be measured; boundless; without limits. **—im'meas•ur•a•bly,** *adv.* **—im,meas•ur•a'bil•i•ty** or **im'meas•ur•a•ble•ness,** *n.*

im•me•di•a•cy [ɪ'midiəsi] *n.* **1** the state or condition of being immediate. **2** topical significance; immediate importance.

im•me•di•ate [ɪ'midiɪt] *adj.* **1** coming at once; without delay: *an immediate reply.* **2** with nothing between: *in immediate contact.* **3** direct: *the immediate result.* **4** closest; nearest: *my immediate neighbour.* **5** close; near: *the immediate neighbourhood.* **6** having to do with the very near future: *our immediate plans.* **7** closely related: *my immediate family.* **8** *Philosophy.* directly or intuitively perceived or known: *an immediate inference.* ⟨< LL *immediatus*, ult. < L *in-* not + *medius* middle⟩ **—im'me•di•ate•ness,** *n.*

☛ *Syn.* **3.** See note at DIRECT.

immediate constituent *Grammar.* one of the parts of a grammatical construction at the first level of analysis, before subdivision. *Example*: *The immediate constituents of* Anju liked her editor *are* Anju *and* liked her editor.

im•me•di•ate•ly [ɪ'midiɪtli] *adv., conj.* *—adv.* **1** at once; without delay: *I need an answer immediately because I have to leave.* **2** with nothing between; next. **3** directly.
—conj. as soon as.

☛ *Syn.* **1. Immediately,** INSTANTLY, PRESENTLY = with little or no delay. **Immediately** = without delay, with no noticeable time in between: *Please close your books immediately and answer these questions.* **Instantly** = right now, without a second's delay: *The driver was killed instantly.* **Presently,** less common, means 'soon, before very long': *I will do the dishes presently, but I want to finish this story first.*

im•med•i•ca•ble [ɪ'mɛdəkəbəl] *adj.* incapable of being healed; incurable: *immedicable wounds, immedicable wrongs.*

Im•mel•mann turn ['ɪməlmən] in flying, the directing of an aircraft through a half loop and then a half roll, to gain altitude.

im•me•mo•ri•al [ˌɪmə'mɔriəl] *adj.* extending back beyond the bounds of memory; extremely old: *time immemorial.* **—,im•me'mo•ri•al•ly,** *adv.*

im•mense [ɪ'mɛns] *adj.* very big; huge; vast: *The Pacific Ocean is an immense body of water.* ⟨< L *immensus* < *in-* not + *mensus* pp. of *metiri* measure⟩ **—im'mense•ly,** *adv.* **—im'mense•ness,** *n.*

☛ *Syn.* See note at HUGE.

im•men•si•ty [ɪ'mɛnsəti] *n., pl.* **-ties. 1** a very great or boundless extent; vastness. **2** an infinite space or existence.

im•men•sur•a•ble [ɪ'mɛnʃərəbəl] *or* [ɪ'mɛnsərəbəl] *adj.* limitless; immeasurable. **—im,men•su•ra'bil•i•ty,** *n.*

im•merge [ɪ'mɜrdʒ] *v.* **-merged, -merg•ing.** immerse. ⟨< L *immergere.* See IMMERSE.⟩ **—im'mer•gence,** *n.*

☛ *Hom.* EMERGE.

im•merse [ɪ'mɜrs] *v.* **-mersed, -mers•ing. 1** dip or lower into a liquid until covered by it. **2** baptize by dipping under water. **3** involve deeply; absorb: *immersed in business affairs, immersed in debts.* ⟨< L *immersus*, pp. of *immergere* < *in-* in + *mergere* plunge⟩

☛ *Syn.* **1.** See note at DIP.

im•mersed [ɪ'mɜrst] *adj., v.* *—adj.* **1** put under a liquid. **2** *Biology.* embedded in the surrounding parts, as an organ may be. **3** *Botany.* growing under water.
—v. pt. and pp. of IMMERSE.

im•mers•i•ble [ɪ'mɜrsəbəl] *adj.* that can be immersed without damage; especially of an electric appliance, that can be immersed in water without damage to the electric element: *an immersible frying pan.*

im•mer•sion [ɪ'mɜrʒən] *or* [ɪ'mɜrʃən] *n.* **1** an immersing or being immersed. **2** a baptism by dipping a person under water. **3** *Cdn.* a method of teaching a second or additional language to a person by means of intensive exposure to and practice in the language. **4** *Cdn.* (*adjl.*) designating a course, school, etc. incorporating or employing such a method: *immersion French.* **5** *Astronomy.* the entrance of a celestial body into an eclipse by another body.

☛ *Hom.* EMERSION.

immersion heater an electric coil to heat the liquid in which it is placed.

im•mi•grant ['ɪməgrənt] *n., adj.* *—n.* **1** a person who comes into a country or region to live: *Canada has many immigrants from Europe.* Compare EMIGRANT. **2** a new plant or animal in an area.
—adj. **1** immigrating or recently immigrated: *an immigrant family.* **2** of or having to do with immigrants or immigration: *an immigrant visa.*

immigrant runner *Cdn.* formerly, a person acting on behalf of a steamboat company, railway company, hotel, etc. to solicit the patronage of immigrants.

immigrant shed, house, or **station** *Cdn.* formerly, any place at which immigrants or passengers were examined, inspected, treated, or detained.

im•mi•grate ['ɪmə,greit] *v.* **-grat•ed, -grat•ing.** come into a country or region to live. Compare EMIGRATE. ⟨< L *immigrare* < *in-* into + *migrare* move⟩ **—'im•mi,gra•tor,** *n.*

im•mi•gra•tion [ˌɪmə'greiʃən] *n.* **1** a coming into a country or region to live: *There has been immigration to Canada from most of the countries of the world.* Compare EMIGRATION. **2** immigrants: *The immigration of 1956 included many people from Hungary.*

immigration officer *Cdn.* a government official appointed to assist immigrants to find land or employment on their arrival in Canada.

immigration shed *Cdn.* formerly, a building equipped to shelter immigrants newly arrived in the country.

im•mi•nence ['ɪmənəns] *n.* **1** the state or fact of being imminent. **2** something that is imminent, especially something dangerous or evil. Also, **imminency.**

☛ *Hom.* IMMANENCY.

im•mi•nent ['ɪmənənt] *adj.* likely to happen soon; about to occur: *The rapidly approaching black clouds show that a storm is imminent.* ⟨< L *imminens, -entis*, ppr. of *imminere* overhang⟩ **—'im•mi•nent•ly,** *adv.*

☛ *Syn.* **Imminent,** IMPENDING =likely to happen soon. **Imminent,** chiefly describing danger, death, etc., suggests 'hanging threateningly over a person' and means 'likely to happen any minute without further warning': *Swept along by the swift current, he was in imminent danger of going over the falls.* **Impending** suggests hanging over one, often indefinitely, and keeping one in suspense, and means 'near and about to take place': *impending disaster.*

☛ *Hom.* IMMANENT.

im•min•gle [ɪ'mɪŋgəl] *v.* **-gled, -gling.** intermingle.

im•mis•ci•ble [ɪ'mɪsəbəl] *adj.* incapable of being mixed: *Water and oil are immiscible.* **—im'mis•ci•bly,** *adv.*

im•mit•i•ga•ble [ɪ'mɪtəgəbəl] *adj.* incapable of being mitigated. ⟨< LL *immitigabil(is)* that cannot be softened⟩ **—im,mit•i•ga'bil•i•ty,** *n.* **—im'mit•i•ga•bly,** *adv.*

im•mix [ɪ'mɪks] *v.* blend. **—im'mix•ture,** *n.*

im•mo•bile [ɪ'moubaɪl] *or* [ɪ'moubəl] *adj.* **1** not movable; firmly fixed. **2** not moving; not changing; motionless. ⟨ME *inmobile* < L *immobil(is)*⟩ **—,im•mo'bil•i•ty,** *n.*

im•mo•bi•lize [ɪ'moubə,laɪz] *v.* **-lized, -liz•ing.** make immobile or almost immobile: *an immobilized truck. She has been immobilized by a severe back injury.* **—im,mo•bi•li'za•tion,** *n.*

im•mod•er•ate [ɪ'mɒdərɪt] *adj.* not moderate; too much; going too far; extreme; more than is right or proper. ⟨< L *immoderat(us)*⟩ **—im'mod•er•ate•ly,** *adv.* **—im'mod•er•ate•ness,** *n.* **—im'mod•er•a•cy,** *n.* **—im,mod•er'a•tion,** *n.*

im•mod•est [ɪ'mɒdɪst] *adj.* **1** bold or rude. **2** indecent or improper. ⟨< L *immodest(us)* unrestrained, immoderate⟩ **—im'mod•est•ly,** *adv.*

im•mod•es•ty [ɪ'mɒdɪsti] *n.* lack of modesty; boldness, impudence, or impropriety.

im•mo•late ['ɪmə,leit] *v.* **-lat•ed, -lat•ing. 1** kill as a sacrifice. **2** sacrifice. **3** destroy. ⟨< L *immolare* sacrifice; originally, sprinkle with sacrificial meal < *in-* on + *mola* sacrificial meal⟩

im•mo•la•tion [ˌɪmə'leiʃən] *n.* a sacrifice.

im•mo•la•tor ['ɪmə,leitər] *n.* a person who offers sacrifice.

im•mor•al [ɪ'mɔrəl] *adj.* **1** morally wrong; wicked: *Lying and stealing are immoral.* **2** lewd; unchaste. **—im'mor•al•ly,** *adv.*

im•mo•ral•i•ty [ˌɪmə'ræləti] *n., pl.* **-ties. 1** wickedness; wrongdoing; vice. **2** lewdness; unchastity. **3** an immoral act.

im•mor•tal [ɪ'mɔrtəl] *adj., n.* *—adj.* **1** living forever; never dying; everlasting. **2** of or having to do with immortal beings or immortality; divine. **3** likely to be remembered or famous forever.
—n. **1** a person living forever. **2 immortals,** *pl.* the gods of ancient Greek and Roman mythology. **3** a person likely to be remembered or famous forever: *Shakespeare is one of the immortals.* ⟨ME < L *immortal(is)*⟩ **—im'mor•tal•ly,** *adv.*

im•mor•tal•ity [,ɪmɔr'tæləti] *n.* **-ties. 1** endless life; the fact or condition of living forever. **2** fame that is likely to last forever.

im•mor•tal•ize [ɪ'mɔrtə,laɪz] *v.* **-ized, iz•ing. 1** make immortal. **2** give everlasting fame to. **—im,mor•tal•i'za•tion,** *n.* **—im'mor•tal,iz•er,** *n.*

im•mor•telle [,ɪmɔr'tɛl] *n.* any of various everlasting plants, especially those species grown by florists, such as *Xeranthemum annuum* and species of *Anaphilis.* Their flowers are often dyed in different colours when they are dry. ⟨< F *immortelle* immortal⟩

im•mo•tile [ɪ'moutaɪl] *or* [ɪ'moutəl] *adj.* not able to move; not motile.

im•mov•a•ble [ɪ'muvəbəl] *adj., n.* *—adj.* **1** that cannot be moved; firmly fixed. **2** not moving; not changing position; motionless. **3** firm; steadfast; unyielding. **4** unfeeling; impassive. **5** *Law.* not to be moved: *immovable goods.*
—n. **immovables,** *pl. Law.* land, buildings, and other property that cannot be carried from one place to another. **—im'mov•a•bly,** *adv.* **—im,mov•a'bil•i•ty,** *n.*

im•mune [ɪ'mjun] *adj.* **1** protected from or resistant to disease, poison, etc.; not susceptible; having immunity (*used with* **to**): *Some people are immune to poison ivy; they can touch it without getting a rash.* **2** free from some duty or obligation, or from something unpleasant; exempt (*used with* **from**): *immune from taxes. Nobody is immune from criticism.* ⟨< L *immunis,* originally, free from obligation⟩

immune body antibody.

immune response the protective biological mechanisms by which the body responds to challenge by foreign antigens.

im•mu•ni•ty [ɪ'mjunəti] *n., pl.* **-ties. 1** resistance to disease, poison, etc.: *One attack of measles often gives a person immunity to that disease for a number of years.* **2** freedom; protection: *The law gives schools and churches immunity from taxation.* ⟨< L *immunitas* < *immunis.* See IMMUNE.⟩
☛ *Syn.* **2.** See note at EXEMPTION.

im•mu•nize ['ɪmjə,naɪz] *v.* **-nized, -niz•ing.** give immunity to; make immune: *Vaccination immunizes people against smallpox.* **—,im•mu•ni'za•tion,** *n.*

immuno– *combining form.* immune or immunity: *immunology.*

im•mu•no•chem•is•try [,ɪmjənou'kɛmɪstri] *n.* the chemistry of antigens.

im•mu•no•flu•or•es•cence [,ɪmjənouflɔ'rɛsəns] *or* [,ɪmjənou,fluə'rɛsəns] *n.* the use of a microscope with ultraviolet light to show antigens by means of dyes.
—,im•mu•no,flu•or'es•cent, *adj.*

im•mu•no•ge•net•ics [,ɪmjənoudʒə'nɛtɪks] *n., sing.* the study of the relationship between immunity to disease and a person's genetic make-up.

im•mu•no•gen•ic [,ɪmjənou'dʒɛnɪk] *adj.* producing immunity. **—,im•mu•no'gen•i•cal•ly,** *adv.*

im•mu•no•glob•u•lin [,ɪmjənou'glɒbjəlɪn] *n.* a protein that is an antibody.

im•mu•nol•o•gist [,ɪmjə'nɒlədʒɪst] *n.* a person trained in immunology, especially one whose work it is.

im•mu•nol•o•gy [,ɪmjə'nɒlədʒi] *n.* **1** the branch of biological science dealing with the study of the structure and function of the immune system. **2** the study of immunogenetics.
—im,mu•no'log•i•cal, *adj.*

im•mu•no•re•ac•tion [,ɪmjənouri'ækʃən] *n.* the interaction between an antigen and the antibody.

im•mu•no•sup•pres•sion [,ɪmjənousə'prɛʃən] *n.* the suppression of natural immunity, especially as a treatment to prevent rejection of a transplant. **—,im•mu•no•sup'pres•sant** or **,im•mu•no•sup'pres•sive,** *adj.*

im•mu•no•the•ra•py [,ɪmjənou'θɛrəpi] *n.* the use of vaccines to boost a flagging immune system.

im•mure [ɪ'mjɔr] *v.* **-mured, -mur•ing. 1** imprison. **2** confine closely. ⟨< Med.L *immurare* < L *in-* in + *murus* wall⟩
—im'mure•ment, *n.*

im•mu•ta•ble [ɪ'mjutəbəl] *adj.* never changing; unchangeable. **—im'mu•ta•ble•ness,** *n.* **—im,mu•ta'bil•i•ty,** *n.* **—im'mu•ta•bly,** *adv.*

imp [ɪmp] *n.* **1** a young or small devil or demon. **2** a mischievous child. ⟨OE *impe* a shoot, graft, ult. < VL *imputus* < Gk. *emphytos* engrafted⟩

imp. 1 imperative. **2** import; imported. **3** imperfect. **4** imprimatur. **5** imperial. **6** imprimis.

im•pact *n.* and *v. 2* ['ɪmpækt]; *v. 1* [ɪm'pækt] *n., v.* *—n.* **1** a striking (of one thing against another); collision: *The impact of the two swords broke both of them.* **2** *Physics.* the single instantaneous blow of a moving body when it meets another body. **3** a forceful effect; dramatic effect: *the impact of automation on society.*
—v. **1** drive or press closely or firmly into something; pack in. **2** to have impact or make contact forcefully (*usually used with* **on, upon, against,** *etc.*): *The bat impacted against the ball with a crack.* **3** *Informal.* affect. ⟨< L *impactus* struck against, pp. of *impingere.* See IMPINGE.⟩

im•pact•ed [ɪm'pæktɪd] *adj.* **1** firmly wedged in place. **2** of a tooth, pressed between the jawbone and another tooth. **3** closely packed; driven or pressed tightly together.

impact printer *Computer technology.* a printer that prints characters by pressing a physical image of the character against an inked ribbon in front of the paper.

im•pair [ɪm'pɛr] *v.* make worse; damage; weaken: *Poor food impaired his health.* ⟨ME < OF *empeirer,* ult. < L *in-* + *pejor* worse⟩ **—im'pair•a•ble,** *adj.*
☛ *Syn.* See note at INJURE.

im•paired [ɪm'pɛrd] *adj., v.* *—adj. Cdn. Law.* of a driver of a motor vehicle, under the influence of alcohol or any narcotic or hallucinogenic drug: *an impaired driver. She was charged with driving while impaired.*
—v. pt. and pp. of IMPAIR.

impaired driving *Cdn. Law.* the illegal act of being in control of a motor vehicle while the ability to drive is weakened by alcohol or narcotics.

im•pair•ment [ɪm'pɛrmənt] *n.* **1** an impairing or being impaired. **2** an injury; damage.

An impala

im•pa•la [ɪm'pælə] *or* [ɪm'pɑlə] *n., pl.* **-las** or (*esp. collectively*) **-la.** a medium-sized, slender, reddish brown antelope (*Aepycerosmelampus*) of the savannah and bush country of S and E Africa, the adult males having long, slender horns that curve in an S, so that from the front the two horns form the outline of a lyre. ⟨< Zulu⟩

im•pale [ɪm'peil] *v.* **-paled, -pal•ing. 1** pierce through with something pointed; fasten upon something pointed: *The butterflies were impaled on small pins stuck in a sheet of cork.* **2** torture or punish by thrusting upon a pointed stake. **3** make helpless as if by piercing: *The teacher impaled the cheeky student with a look of ice.* ⟨< F *empaler,* ult. < L *in-* on + *palus* stake⟩ **—im'pale•ment,** *n.*

im•pal•pa•ble [ɪm'pælpəbəl] *adj.* **1** that cannot be perceived by the sense of touch: *Sunbeams are impalpable. A thread of a spider's web is so thin as to be almost impalpable.* **2** so fine as to be very hard for the mind to grasp: *impalpable distinctions.*
—im'pal•pa•bly, *adv.* **—im,pal•pa'bil•i•ty,** *n.*

im•pan•a•tion [,ɪmpə'neiʃən] *n. Christian theology.* the doctrine that after consecration, the blood and body of Christ become part of the wine and bread. Compare TRANSUBSTANTIATION. ⟨< ML *impanat(us)* embodied in bread < L *im-* + *pan(is)* bread + *-atus*⟩

im•pan•el [ɪm'pænəl] *v.* **-elled** or **-eled, -el•ling** or **-el•ing. 1** put on a list for duty on a jury. **2** select (a jury) from the list. Also, **empanel.** ⟨ME *empanel* < AF *empanell(er)*⟩
—im'pan•el•ment, *n.*

im•par•a•dise [ɪm'pærə,dəis] *or* [ɪm'pɛrə,dəis] *v.* **-dised, -dis•ing. 1** put in paradise; make supremely happy. **2** make a paradise of.

im•par•i•ty [ɪm'pærəti] *or* [ɪm'pɛrəti] *n.* **1** inequality. **2** disparity.

im•part [ɪm'pɑrt] *v.* **1** give a part or share of; give: *The furnishings imparted an air of elegance to the room.*
2 communicate; tell: *The interviewer asked her to impart the secret of her success.* ⟨< L *impartire* < *in-* in + *pars, partis* part⟩
–,im•par'ta•tion, *n.*
☛ *Syn.* See note at COMMUNICATE.

im•par•tial [ɪm'pɑrʃəl] *adj.* showing no more favour to one side of any contest or conflict than to the other; fair; just. **–im'par•tial•ly,** *adv.*
☛ *Syn.* See note at FAIR[1].

im•par•ti•al•i•ty [ɪm,pɑrʃi'æləti] *n.* fairness; justice.

im•part•i•ble [ɪm'pɑrtəbəl] *adj.* indivisible. ⟨ME < LL *impartibil(is)*⟩

im•pass•a•ble [ɪm'pæsəbəl] *adj.* not passable; so that one cannot go through or across: *Deep mud made the road impassable.* **–im'pass•a•ble•ness,** *n.* **–im,pass•a'bil•i•ty,** *n.* **–im'pass•a•bly,** *adv.*
☛ *Hom.* IMPASSIBLE.

im•passe ['ɪmpæs] *or* [ɪm'pæs] *n.* **1** a position from which there is no escape; a problem with no apparent solution; deadlock. **2** a road or way closed at one end; blind alley. ⟨< F⟩

im•pas•si•ble [ɪm'pæsəbəl] *adj.* **1** unable to suffer or feel pain. **2** that cannot be harmed. **3** without feeling; impassive. ⟨ME < L *impassibilis,* ult. < *in-* not + *pati* suffer⟩
–im,pas•si'bil•i•ty, *n.* **–im'pas•si•bly,** *adv.*
☛ *Hom.* IMPASSABLE.

im•pas•sion [ɪm'pæʃən] *v.* arouse the passions. ⟨< Ital. *impassion(are)*⟩

im•pas•sioned [ɪm'pæʃənd] *adj., v.* *–adj.* full of strong feeling; ardent; rousing: *an impassioned speech.*
–v. pt. and pp. of IMPASSION. **–im'pas•sion•ed•ly,** *adv.*

im•pas•sive [ɪm'pæsɪv] *adj.* **1** not showing any feeling or emotion; expressionless: *He listened with an impassive face.* **2** not feeling any emotion; placid or apathetic. **3** not feeling pain or injury; insensible. **–im'pas•sive•ly,** *adv.* **–im'pas•sive•ness,** *n.* **–,im•pas'siv•i•ty,** *n.*

im•paste [ɪm'peist] *v.* **-past•ed, -past•ing. 1** make into a paste. **2** apply thickly, as with pigments. ⟨< Ital. *impast(are)*⟩

im•pas•to [ɪm'pɑstou] *n.* **1** a painting technique in which the oil paint is thickly applied, often with a palette knife. **2** the paint thus applied. ⟨< Ital. *impasto* < *impastare* impaste⟩

im•pa•tience [ɪm'peiʃəns] *n.* the quality or state of being impatient. ⟨ME *impacience* < L *impatientia*⟩
☛ *Hom.* IMPATIENS.

im•pa•tiens [ɪm'peiʃəns] *n.* any of a genus (*Impatiens*) of annual and biennial plants having spurred or pouch-shaped flowers and seed pods that burst open when ripe; especially, a common garden plant (*I. petersiana*) cultivated in many varieties for its bright red, pink, white, or variegated flowers. ⟨< NL, L *impatiens* not enduring, not bearing⟩
☛ *Hom.* IMPATIENCE.

im•pa•tient [ɪm'peiʃənt] *adj.* **1** not patient; not willing to bear delay, opposition, pain, bother, etc.: *His work is never done properly because he is too impatient to attend to details.* **2** restless; anxious: *They were impatient to see the new puppy.* **3** caused by or showing lack of patience: *an impatient answer.*
impatient of, unwilling to endure; not liking or wanting. ⟨ME *impacient* < L *impatient-* (stem of *impatiens*) not putting up with⟩ **–im'pa•tient•ly,** *adv.*

im•peach [ɪm'pitʃ] *v.* **1** call in question; cast doubt on: *to impeach a person's honour, to impeach the testimony of a witness.* **2** charge with wrongdoing; accuse. **3** bring a (public official) to trial before a special court or tribunal for wrong conduct during office: *The judge was impeached for taking a bribe.* ⟨ME < OF *empeechier* hinder < LL *impedicare* < L *in-* on + *pedica* shackle⟩

im•peach•a•ble [ɪm'pitʃəbəl] *adj.* **1** liable to be impeached. **2** likely to cause impeachment: *an impeachable offence.* **–im,peach•a'bil•i•ty,** *n.*

im•peach•ment [ɪm'pitʃmənt] *n.* an impeaching or being impeached.

im•pearl [ɪm'pɜrl] *v.* **1** form into pearl-like drops. **2** adorn with pearls or pearl-like drops.

im•pec•ca•ble [ɪm'pɛkəbəl] *adj.* **1** faultless. **2** sinless. ⟨< LL *impeccabilis* < *in-* not + *peccare* sin⟩ **–im'pec•ca•bly,** *adv.* **–im,pec•ca'bil•i•ty,** *n.*

im•pec•cant [ɪm'pɛkənt] *adj.* without sin.

im•pe•cu•ni•ous [,ɪmpə'kjuniəs] *adj.* having little or no money; penniless; poor. ⟨< *in-* not + L *pecuniosus* rich < *pecunia* money < *pecu* head of cattle⟩ **–,im•pe'cu•ni•ous•ly,** *adv.* **–,im•pe,cu•ni'os•i•ty** or **,im•pe'cu•ni•ous•ness,** *n.*

im•ped•ance [ɪm'pidəns] *n.* **1** *Electricity.* the apparent resistance in an alternating-current circuit, made up of two components, reactance and true or ohmic resistance. **2** *Physics.* the ratio of pressure in a sound wave to the product of the particle velocity and the area of a cross section of the wave at a given point.

im•pede [ɪm'pid] *v.* **-ped•ed, -ped•ing.** hinder; obstruct. ⟨< L *impedire* < *in-* on + *pes, pedis* foot⟩ **–im'ped•er,** *n.*
☛ *Syn.* See note at PREVENT.

im•ped•i•ment [ɪm'pɛdəmənt] *n.* **1** a hindrance; obstruction. **2** a defect in speech: *Stuttering is an impediment.* **3** *Law.* a bar to the making of a valid marriage contract. ⟨< L *impedimentum*⟩

im•ped•i•men•ta [ɪm,pɛdə'mɛntə] *n.pl.* **1** travelling equipment or baggage, especially the military supplies carried along with an army. **2** any equipment, belongings, etc. that one carries and that obstruct one or hinder progress. **3** *Law.* obstacles; hindrances. ⟨< L⟩

im•pel [ɪm'pɛl] *v.* **-pelled, -pel•ling. 1** drive; force; cause: *Hunger impelled the lazy man to work.* **2** cause to move; drive forward; push along: *The wind impelled the boat to shore.* ⟨< L *impellere* < *in-* on + *pellere* push⟩
☛ *Syn.* **1.** See note at COMPEL.

im•pel•lent [ɪm'pɛlənt] *adj., n.* *–adj.* tending to impel; impelling.
–n. a person who or a force or thing that impels.

im•pel•ler [ɪm'pɛlər] *n.* **1** a person who or thing that impels. **2** the rotating blades of a centrifugal pump or blower.

im•pend [ɪm'pɛnd] *v.* **1** be likely to happen soon; be ready to occur; be near: *When war impends, wise people try to prevent it.* **2** hang; hang threateningly. **3** threaten. ⟨< L *impendere* < *in-* over + *pendere* hang⟩

im•pend•ent [ɪm'pɛndənt] *adj.* impending **–im'pen•dence** or **im'pen•den•cy,** *n.*

im•pend•ing [ɪm'pɛndɪŋ] *adj., v.* *–adj.* **1** likely to happen soon; about to occur (*used especially of something unpleasant*): *She dreaded the impending exams.* **2** overhanging: *Above him were impending cliffs.*
–v. ppr. of IMPEND.
☛ *Syn.* **1.** See note at IMMINENT.

im•pen•e•tra•bil•i•ty [ɪm,pɛnətrə'bɪləti] *n.* **1** the state or quality of being impenetrable. **2** *Physics.* that property of matter by virtue of which two bodies cannot occupy the same space simultaneously.

im•pen•e•tra•ble [ɪm'pɛnətrəbəl] *adj.* **1** that cannot be entered, pierced, or passed: *A thick sheet of steel is impenetrable by an ordinary bullet.* **2** not open to ideas, influences, etc. **3** impossible to explain or understand; inscrutable: *an impenetrable mystery.* **4** *Physics.* of a body, excluding all other bodies from the space it occupies. **–im'pen•e•tra•bly,** *adv.*

im•pen•i•tence [ɪm'pɛnətəns] *n.* a lack of any sorrow or regret for doing wrong.

im•pen•i•tent [ɪm'pɛnətənt] *adj.* not penitent; feeling no sorrow or regret for having done wrong. ⟨< LL *impaenitent-* (stem of impaenitens)⟩ **–im'pen•i•tent•ly,** *adv.*

imper. imperative.

im•per•a•tive [ɪm'pɛrətɪv] *adj., n.* *–adj.* **1** not to be avoided; urgent; necessary: *It is imperative that a very sick child stay in bed.* **2** expressing a command; commanding. **3** *Grammar.* denoting the mood of a verb that expresses a command, request, or advice. "Go!" and "Stop, look, listen!" are in the imperative mood.
–n. **1** a command: *The great imperative is "Love thy neighbour as thyself."* **2** a necessary or required thing. **3** *Grammar.* **a** the imperative mood. **b** a verb form in this mood. *Abbrev.:* imp. *or* imper. Compare INDICATIVE, SUBJUNCTIVE. ⟨< L *imperativus* < *imperare* command⟩ **–im'per•a•tive•ly,** *adv.* **–im'per•a•tive•ness,** *n.*

im•pe•ra•tor [,ɪmpə'reitər] *or* [,ɪmpə'rɑtɔr] *n.* **1** an absolute or supreme ruler. **2** in ancient Rome: **a** a victorious military commander. **b** the emperor. ⟨< L *imperator* < *imperare* command⟩ **–im,per•a'tor•i•al,** *adj.* **–im,per•a'to•ri•al•ly,** *adv.*

im•per•cep•ti•ble [,ɪmpər'sɛptəbəl] *adj.* **1** very slight; gradual. **2** that cannot be perceived or felt. ⟨< ML *imperceptibil(is)*⟩ **–,im•per'cep•ti•ble•ness** or **,im•per,cep•ti'bil•i•ty,** *n.* **–,im•per'cep•ti•bly,** *adv.*

imperf. imperfect.

im•per•fect [ɪm'pɜrfɪkt] *adj., n.* *—adj.* **1** not perfect; having some defect or fault. **2** not complete; lacking some part. **3** *Grammar.* expressing continued or customary action or state in the past. **4** *Music.* **a** denoting any interval other than a fourth, fifth, or octave. **b** of a cadence, ending on the dominant rather than the tonic.
—n. Grammar. **1** the imperfect tense. English has no imperfect, but such forms as *was studying* and *used to study* are similar to the imperfect in other languages. **2** a verb form in this tense. *Abbrev.*: imp., imperf. ⟨< L *imperfect(us)*⟩ **—im'per•fect•ly,** *adv.* **—im'per•fect•ness,** *n.*

im•per•fec•tion [,ɪmpər'fɛkʃən] *n.* **1** a lack of perfection; imperfect condition or character. **2** a fault; defect: *an emerald with imperfections.*

im•per•fo•rate [ɪm'pɜrfərɪt] *or* [ɪm'pɜrfə,reit] *adj.* **1** not pierced through with holes. **2** of stamps, not separated from other stamps by perforations; having the margins whole. **—im,per•fo'ra•tion,** *n.*

im•pe•ri•al [ɪm'piriəl] *adj., n.* *—adj.* **1** of or having to do with an empire or its ruler. **2** of or having to do with the rule or authority of one country over other countries and colonies. **3** having the rank of an emperor. **4** supreme; majestic; magnificent. **5** of larger size or better quality. **6** designating a system of weights and measures traditionally used in the U.K. Many units of the traditional systems of Canada and other countries are equivalent or nearly equivalent to those of the imperial system. See table of measurements in the Appendix.
—n. **1** a small, pointed beard growing beneath the lower lip. See BEARD for picture. **2** a size of paper, 58.4 × 78.7 cm (in the U.K., 55.9 × 76.2 cm). **3** the top of a horse-drawn coach. ⟨< L *imperialis* < *imperium* empire⟩ **—im'pe•ri•al•ly,** *adv.*

imperial gallon the traditional British gallon, equal to 160 fluid ounces (about 4.55 dm^3). It is almost identical with the traditional Canadian gallon; both the imperial and Canadian gallons are about 20 percent bigger than the U.S. gallon.

im•pe•ri•al•ism [ɪm'piriə,lɪzəm] *n.* **1** the policy of extending the rule or authority of one country over other countries and territories. **2** an imperial system of government. **3** the dominating of another nation's economic, political, and even military structure without actually taking governmental control.

im•pe•ri•al•ist [ɪm'piriəlɪst] *n., adj.* *—n.* a person who favours imperialism.
—adj. imperialistic.

im•pe•ri•al•is•tic [ɪm,piriə'lɪstɪk] *adj.* **1** of imperialism or imperialists. **2** favouring imperialism. **—im,pe•ri•al'is•ti•cal•ly,** *adv.*

imperial moth a large moth (*Eacles imperialis*) having yellow wings and brown or purple markings in the form of spots or a diagonal stripe.

Imperial Order Daughters of the Empire *Cdn.* an organization of women founded in 1900, whose purpose is to stimulate patriotism and promote good citizenship.

im•per•il [ɪm'pɛrəl] *v.* **-illed** or **-iled, -il•ling** or **-il•ing.** put in danger. **—im'per•il•ment,** *n.*

im•pe•ri•ous [ɪm'piriəs] *adj.* **1** haughty; arrogant; domineering; overbearing. **2** imperative; necessary; urgent. ⟨< L *imperiosus* commanding⟩ **—im'pe•ri•ous•ly,** *adv.* **—im'pe•ri•ous•ness,** *n.*

im•per•ish•a•bil•i•ty [ɪm,pɛrɪʃə'bɪləti] *n.* the quality or state of being imperishable; enduring quality.

im•per•ish•a•ble [ɪm'pɛrɪʃəbəl] *adj.* everlasting; not perishable; indestructible. **—im'per•ish•a•bly,** *adv.*

im•pe•ri•um [ɪm'piriəm] *n., pl.* **-pe•ri•a** [-'piriə]. **1** command; supreme power; empire. **2** *Law.* the right to use the force of the state in order to enforce the law. ⟨< L⟩

im•per•ma•nence [ɪm'pɜrmənəns] *n.* the state or condition of being impermanent.

im•per•ma•nent [ɪm'pɜrmənənt] *adj.* not lasting; temporary. **—im'per•ma•nent•ly,** *adv.*

im•per•me•a•ble [ɪm'pɜrmiəbəl] *adj.* **1** that cannot be passed through; impassable. **2** not permitting the passage of fluid through the pores, interstices, etc. **—im,per•me•a'bil•i•ty,** *n.* **—im'per•me•a•bly,** *adv.*

im•per•mis•si•ble [,ɪmpər'mɪsəbəl] *adj.* not allowed. **—,im•per,mis•si'bil•i•ty,** *n.*

impers. impersonal.

im•per•son•al [ɪm'pɜrsənəl] *adj.* **1** referring to all or any persons, not to any special one: *"First come, first served" is an impersonal remark.* In the expression *One must do one's best,* the word *one* is impersonal. **2** not affected by personal feelings; objective: *an impersonal approach to the case.* **3** having no existence as a person: *Electricity is an impersonal force.* **4** *Grammar.* of a verb, having nothing but an indefinite *it* for a subject. *Example*: *rained* in *It rained yesterday.* ⟨< LL *impersonal(is)*⟩ **—im'per•son•al•ly,** *adv.*

im•per•son•al•i•ty [ɪm,pɜrsə'næləti] *n., pl.* **-ties. 1** the quality or state of being impersonal; absence of personal quality. **2** an impersonal thing, force, etc.

im•per•son•al•ize [ɪm'pɜrsənə,laɪz] *v.* **-ized, -iz•ing.** make impersonal. **—im,per•son•al•i'za•tion,** *n.*

impersonal pronoun a pronoun that is used to refer to a person or thing not named or identified. In English, *it, one, they,* and *you* can function as impersonal pronouns: *It is cold today. One must do one's best. They say that life begins at forty. You should be careful when crossing the street.*

im•per•son•ate [ɪm'pɜrsə,neit] *v.* **-at•ed, -at•ing. 1** pretend to be; do an impression of; mimic the voice, appearance, and manners of, especially in trying to deceive: *The thief impersonated a police officer.* **2** act the part of: *to impersonate Hamlet.* **3** *Archaic.* represent in personal form; personify; typify: *To many people Henry Hudson impersonates the spirit of adventure.* **—im,per•son'a•tion,** *n.*

im•per•son•a•tor [ɪm'pɜrsə,neitər] *n.* one who impersonates, especially an actor who impersonates particular persons or types; professional mimic.

im•per•ti•nence [ɪm'pɜrtənəns] *n.* **1** impudence; insolence. **2** a lack of pertinence; irrelevance. **3** an impertinent act or remark. Also, **impertinency.**

im•per•ti•nent [ɪm'pɜrtənənt] *adj.* **1** saucy; impudent; insolent; rude. **2** not pertinent; not to the point; out of place; not relevant. ⟨ME < LL *impertinent-* (stem of *impertinens* not belonging)⟩ **—im'per•ti•nent•ly,** *adv.*

☛ *Syn.* **1. Impertinent,** IMPUDENT, SAUCY = showing lack of proper respect. **Impertinent** = showing lack of respect: *Talking back to older people is impertinent.* **Impudent** adds the idea of shamelessness and defiance: *The impudent boy made faces at the teacher.* **Saucy** suggests a disrespectful attitude shown by a light and flippant manner or speech: *The saucy girl tossed her head when her father scolded her.*

im•per•turb•a•ble [,ɪmpər'tɜrbəbəl] *adj.* characterized by great calmness and steadiness; not readily perturbed. ⟨< LL *imperturbabil(is)*⟩ **—,im•per,turb•a'bil•i•ty,** *n.* **—,im•per'turb•a•bly,** *adv.*

im•per•turb•a•tion [,ɪmpərtər'beiʃən] *n.* tranquillity; calmness.

im•per•vi•ous [ɪm'pɜrviəs] *adj.* **1** not letting anything pass through; not allowing passage: *Rubber cloth is impervious to moisture.* **2** not open to or affected by argument, suggestions, etc.: *She is impervious to all the gossip about her.* **—im'per•vi•ous•ly,** *adv.* **—im'per•vi•ous•ness,** *n.*

im•pe•ti•go [,ɪmpə'taɪgou] *or* [,ɪmpə'tigou] *n.* an infectious skin disease causing pimples filled with pus. ⟨< L *impetigo* < *impetere* attack < *in-* + *petere* aim for⟩ **—im•pe'ti•gi•nous** [,ɪmpə'tidʒənəs], *adj.*

im•pe•trate ['ɪmpə,treit] *v.* **-trat•ed, -trat•ing.** entreat. ⟨< L *impetrat(us)* got by asking⟩ **—,im•pe'tra•tion,** *n.* **—'im•pe,tra•tive,** *adj.* **—'im•pe,tra•tor,** *n.*

im•pet•u•os•i•ty [ɪm,pɛtʃu'ɒsəti] *n., pl.* **-ties. 1** sudden or rash energy; violence; ardour: *The impetuosity of the speaker stirred the audience.* **2** an impetuous action or impulse.

im•pet•u•ous [ɪm'pɛtʃuəs] *adj.* **1** acting hastily, rashly, or with sudden feeling: *Children are usually more impetuous than adults.* **2** moving with great force or speed: *the impetuous rush of water over Niagara Falls.* ⟨< LL *impetuosus* < L *impetus* attack⟩ **—im'pet•u•ous•ly,** *adv.* **—im'pet•u•ous•ness,** *n.*

im•pe•tus ['ɪmpətəs] *n.* **1** the force with which a moving body tends to maintain its velocity and overcome resistance: *the impetus of a moving automobile.* **2** a driving force; incentive: *Ambition is an impetus that impels some people toward success.* ⟨< L *impetus* attack < *impetere* attack < *in-* + *petere* aim for⟩

imp. gal. IMPERIAL GALLON.

im•pi•e•ty [ɪm'paɪəti] *n., pl.* **-ties. 1** lack of piety or reverence for God; wickedness. **2** lack of dutifulness or respect. **3** an impious act. ⟨ME *impietie* < L *impietas, impius*⟩

im•pinge [ɪm'pɪndʒ] *v.* **-pinged -ping•ing. 1** hit; strike (*used with* **on**): *Rays of light impinge on the eye.* **2** encroach; infringe. ⟨< L *impingere* + *in-* on + *pangere* strike⟩

im•pinge•ment [ɪm'pɪndʒmənt] *n.* an impinging.

im•pi•ous [ˈɪmpiəs] *or* [ɪmˈpaɪəs] *adj.* **1** not pious; not having or not showing reverence for God; wicked; profane. **2** not showing proper dutifulness or respect. ⟨< L *impius*⟩ **—ˈim•pi•ous•ly,** *adv.* **—ˈim•pi•ous•ness,** *n.*

imp•ish [ˈɪmpɪʃ] *adj.* of or like an imp; especially, mischievous: *an impish grin, an impish trick.* **—ˈimp•ish•ly,** *adv.* **—ˈimp•ish•ness,** *n.*

im•plac•a•ble [ɪmˈplækəbəl] *or* [ɪmˈpleikəbəl] *adj.* that cannot be placated, pacified, or appeased; relentless. **—imˈplac•a•bly,** *adv.* **—im,plac•aˈbil•i•ty,** *n.*

im•pla•cen•tal [,ɪmpləˈsɛntəl] *adj., n. —adj. Zoology.* having no placenta, as a monotreme or marsupial.
—n. an implacental animal.

im•plant *v.* [ɪmˈplænt]; *n.* [ˈɪmplænt] *v., n. —v.* **1** instil; fix deeply: *A good teacher implants high ideals in children.* **2** insert; set in a base: *A steel tube is then implanted in the socket.* **3** set in the ground; plant. **4** graft or set (a piece of skin, bone, etc.) into the body.
—n. **1** tissue or other substance grafted into the body. **2** a small radioactive tube or needle inserted into the body, especially to treat cancer. **,im•planˈta•tion,** *n.*

im•plau•si•bil•i•ty [ɪm,plɒzəˈbɪləti] *n., pl.* **-ties. 1** the quality or condition of being implausible. **2** that which is implausible.

im•plau•si•ble [ɪmˈplɒzəbəl] *adj.* not plausible; lacking the appearance of truth or trustworthiness. **—imˈplau•si•bly,** *adv.*

im•plead [ɪmˈplid] *v. Law.* sue in a court of law. ⟨ME *emplede(n)* < AF *empled(er)*⟩ **—imˈplead•a•ble,** *adj.*

im•plead•er [ɪmˈplidər] *n. Law.* a legal procedure that allows a plaintiff to add a second person to the one originally sued.

im•ple•ment *n.* [ˈɪmpləmənt]; *v.* [ˈɪmpləmɛnt] *n., v. —n.* **1** a useful piece of equipment; tool; instrument; utensil. Ploughs, axes, shovels, can openers, and brooms are all implements. **2** an agent or means.
—v. **1** provide with implements or other means to carry out a task. **2** put (something) into effect: *to implement an order.* **3** carry out; get done: *Do not undertake a project unless you can implement it.* ⟨< LL *implementum*, literally, that which fills a need < L *implere* < *in-* in + *-plere* fill⟩ **—,im•ple•menˈta•tion,** *n.* **—,im•pleˈment•al,** *adj.* **—ˈim•ple,ment•or** or **ˈim•ple,ment•er,** *n.*
☛ *Syn. n.* See note at TOOL.

im•pli•cate [ˈɪmplə,keit] *v.* **-cat•ed, -cat•ing. 1** show to have a part in or to be connected with a crime, fault, etc.; involve: *The thief's confession implicated two other people.* **2** involve as a consequence; imply. **3** *Archaic.* entangle; fold or twist together. ⟨< L *implicare* < *in-* in + *plicare* fold. Doublet of EMPLOY, IMPLY.⟩
☛ *Syn.* **1.** See note at INVOLVE.

im•pli•ca•tion [,ɪmpləˈkeiʃən] *n.* **1** an implying or being implied. **2** something implied; an indirect suggestion; hint: *There was no implication of dishonesty in his failure in business.* **3** *Logic.* the relationship between two propositions that makes one an outcome of the other. **4** an implicating or being implicated.

im•plic•a•tive [ɪmˈplɪkətɪv] *adj.* **1** tending to implicate. **2** involving implication. **—imˈplic•a•tive•ly,** *adv.*

im•plic•it [ɪmˈplɪsɪt] *adj.* **1** without doubting, hesitating, or asking questions; absolute: *implicit trust, implicit obedience.* **2** meant, but not clearly expressed or distinctly stated; implied: *His silence gave implicit consent.* Compare EXPLICIT. **3** involved as a necessary part or condition. ⟨< L *implicitus*, pp. of *implicare.* See IMPLICATE.⟩ **—imˈplic•it•ness,** *n.*

im•plic•it•ly [ɪmˈplɪsɪtli] *adv.* **1** unquestioningly. **2** by implication.

im•plied [ɪmˈplaɪd] *adj., v. —adj.* involved, indicated, suggested, or understood without a clear statement: *an implied contract, an implied rebuke.*
—v. pt. and pp. of IMPLY.

im•pli•ed•ly [ɪmˈplaɪədli] *adv.* by implication.

im•plode [ɪmˈploud] *v.* **-plod•ed, -plod•ing. 1** burst or cause to burst inward: *External pressure can cause a vacuum tube to implode.* **2** *Phonetics.* pronounce (a consonant) by implosion. ⟨*im-*[1] + *explode*⟩

im•plore [ɪmˈplɔr] *v.* **-plored, -plor•ing. 1** beg earnestly for. **2** beg (a person to do something). ⟨< L *implorare*, originally, invoke with weeping < *in-* toward + *plorare* cry⟩ **—imˈplor•er,** *n.* **—imˈplor•ing•ly,** *adv.*
☛ *Syn.* See note at BEG.

im•plo•sion [ɪmˈplouʒən] *n.* **1** the action of imploding. **2** *Phonetics.* the sudden release of air into the pharynx in pronouncing an ingressive stop, as in some African languages.

im•plo•sive [ɪmˈplousɪv] *adj., n. Phonetics. —adj.* pronounced by implosion.
—n. a consonant pronounced by implosion.

im•ply [ɪmˈplaɪ] *v.* **-plied, -ply•ing. 1** indicate without saying outright; express indirectly; suggest: *Silence often implies consent. Her smile implied that she had forgiven us.* **2** involve as a necessary part or condition: *Speech implies the existence of a speaker.* ⟨ME < OF *emplier* involve, put (in) < L *implicare.* Doublet of EMPLOY, IMPLICATE.⟩
☛ *Usage.* See note at INFER.

im•po•li•cy [ɪmˈpɒləsi] *n., pl.* **-cies. 1** inexpediency. **2** an injudicious act.

im•po•lite [,ɪmpəˈlait] *adj.* not polite; having or showing bad manners; rude. **—,im•poˈlite•ly,** *adv.* **—,im•poˈlite•ness,** *n.*

im•pol•i•tic [ɪmˈpɒlə,tɪk] *adj.* not politic; not expedient; unwise: *It is impolitic to offend people who could be of help to you.* **—imˈpol•i•tic•ly,** *adv.*

im•pon•der•a•ble [ɪmˈpɒndərəbəl] *adj., n. —adj.* that cannot be explained, or measured exactly: *Faith and love are imponderable forces.*
—n. something imponderable. **—imˈpon•der•a•bly,** *adv.* **—im,pon•der•aˈbil•i•ty,** *n.*

im•port *v.* [ɪmˈpɔrt] *or* [ˈɪmpɔrt]; *n.* [ˈɪmpɔrt] *v., n. —v.* **1** bring in from a foreign country for sale or use: *Canada imports coffee from Brazil.* **2** mean; signify: *Tell me what your remark imports.* **3** be of importance or consequence.
—n. **1** anything imported: *Rubber is a useful import.* **2** an importing; importation: *The import of diseased animals is forbidden.* **3** meaning; significance: *What is the import of your remark?* **4** importance: *It is a matter of great import.* **5** *Cdn.* **a** in professional football, a non-Canadian player who has played less than five years in Canada. **b** in other sports, a player who is not a native of the country or area in which he or she is playing. **6** (*adjl.*) of or for importing: *an import store.* ⟨< L *importare* < *in-* in + *portare* carry⟩ **—im,port•aˈbil•i•ty,** *n.* **—imˈport•a•ble,** *adj.*

im•por•tance [ɪmˈpɔrtəns] *n.* being important; consequence; significance; value.
☛ *Syn.* **Importance,** CONSEQUENCE = the quality of having much value, meaning, influence, etc. **Importance,** the general word, emphasizes being of great value, meaning, etc. in itself: *Anybody can see the importance of good health.* **Consequence** emphasizes having, or being likely to have, important or far-reaching results or effects: *The discovery of insulin was an event of great consequence for diabetics.*

im•por•tant [ɪmˈpɔrtənt] *adj.* **1** meaning much; worth noticing or considering; having value or significance. **2** having social position or influence. **3** acting as if important; seeming to be important; self-important: *He rushed around in an important manner, giving orders.* ⟨< F < Med.L *importans, -antis,* ppr. of *importare* be significant < L *importare* bring on or in. See IMPORT.⟩ **—imˈpor•tant•ly,** *adv.*

im•por•ta•tion [,ɪmpɔrˈteiʃən] *n.* **1** the act of importing. **2** something imported.

im•port•er [ɪmˈpɔrtər] *or* [ˈɪmpɔrtər] *n.* a person or company whose business is importing goods.

im•por•tu•nate [ɪmˈpɔrtʃənɪt] *adj.* asking repeatedly; annoyingly persistent; urgent. **—imˈpor•tu•nate•ly,** *adv.* **—imˈpor•tu•nate•ness,** *n.*

im•por•tune [,ɪmpɔrˈtjun], [,ɪmpɔrˈtʃun], *or* [,ɪmpɔrˈtun] *v.* **-tuned, -tun•ing.** ask urgently or repeatedly; trouble with demands. ⟨< MF < L *importunus* inconvenient⟩ **—,im•porˈtune•ly,** *adv.* **—,im•porˈtun•er,** *n.*

im•por•tu•ni•ty [,ɪmpɔrˈtjunəti], [,ɪmpɔrˈtʃunəti], *or* [,ɪmpɔrˈtunəti] *n., pl.* **-ties.** persistence in asking; the act of demanding again and again.

im•pose [ɪmˈpouz] *v.* **-posed, -pos•ing. 1** put (a burden, tax, punishment, etc.) (*on*): *The judge imposed a fine of $500 on the convicted man.* **2** force or thrust one's authority or influence (*on* another or others). **3** force or thrust (oneself or one's company) (*on* another or others); obtrude; presume. **4** pass off (a thing upon a person) to deceive. **5** *Printing.* arrange (pages of type) in the correct order.
impose on or **upon, a** take advantage of; use in a selfish way: *to impose on the good nature of others.* **b** deceive; cheat; trick. ⟨< F *imposer* < *in-* on + *poser* put, place⟩ **—imˈpos•a•ble,** *adj.* **—imˈpos•er,** *n.*

im•pos•ing [ɪmˈpouzɪŋ] *adj., v. —adj.* impressive because of size, appearance, or dignity; commanding attention: *The Peace*

Tower of the Parliament Buildings is an imposing landmark. —*v.* ppr. of IMPOSE. **—im'pos•ing•ly,** *adv.*

im•po•si•tion [ˌɪmpəˈzɪʃən] *n.* **1** the act or fact of imposing. **2** a tax, duty, task, burden, etc. **3** an unfair tax, etc. **4** an imposing upon a person by taking advantage of his or her good nature: *Would it be an imposition to ask you to mail this parcel?* **5** a deception; fraud; trick. **6** a ceremonial laying on of hands in confirmation or ordination. **7** *Printing.* the act or process of arranging pages of type.

im•pos•si•bil•i•ty [ɪmˌpɒsəˈbɪləti] *n., pl.* **-ties. 1** the condition or quality of being impossible. **2** something impossible.

im•pos•si•ble [ɪmˈpɒsəbəl] *adj., n.* —*adj.* **1** that cannot be reached, done, or fulfilled; hopeless: *an impossible task, an impossible plan.* **2** that cannot be or happen: *It is impossible for two and two to be six.* **3** that cannot be true: *an impossible story.* **4** not able to be tolerated; very objectionable: *an impossible person.*
—*n.* **1** something that is or seems impossible: *The sergeant always demanded the impossible of his men.* **2** an impossibility: *His statement is in the nature of an impossible.* ⟨ME < L *impossibil(is)*⟩ **—im'pos•si•bly,** *adv.* **—im'pos•si•ble•ness,** *n.*

im•post[1] [ˈɪmpoust] *n.* **1** a tax on goods brought into a country; customs duty. **2** a tax; tribute. **3** *Racing.* the weight that a horse must carry in a handicap, assigned on the basis of age. ⟨< OF, ult. < L *in-* on + *ponere* place, put⟩

im•post[2] [ˈɪmpoust] *n. Architecture.* the uppermost part of a column, etc. on which the end of an arch rests. See ARCH for picture. ⟨< F < Ital. *imposta,* ult. < L *in-* on + *ponere* place, put⟩

im•pos•tor [ɪmˈpɒstər] *n.* **1** a person who assumes a false name or character. **2** a deceiver; cheat. ⟨< F *imposteur* < LL *impostor* < L *imponere* impose < *in* on + *ponere* place, put⟩

im•pos•ture [ɪmˈpɒstʃər] *n.* the act or practice of deceiving by assuming a false character or name. ⟨< F < LL *impostura* < L *imponere* impose⟩

im•po•tence [ˈɪmpətəns] *n.* **1** a lack of power; helplessness; the condition or quality of being impotent. **2** a lack of ability to have sexual intercourse. Also, **impotency.** ⟨ME, var. of *impotencie* < L *impotentia* want of self-control⟩

im•po•tent [ˈɪmpətənt] *adj.* **1** not having power or strength; helpless: *an impotent rage, a law against strikes that rendered the trade unions impotent.* **2** lacking bodily strength. **3** incapable of having sexual intercourse, especially, in a male, because of an inability to have an erection. ⟨ME < L *impotent-* (stem of *impotens*) without power over oneself or others⟩ **—'im•po•tent•ly,** *adv.*

im•pound [ɪmˈpaʊnd] *v.* **1** shut up in or as if in a pen or pound: *to impound stray animals.* **2** take and hold in the custody of the law: *to impound documents for use as evidence in court.* **3** collect and confine (water) in a reservoir or behind a dam, as for irrigation. **—im'pound•er,** *n.* **—im'pound•ment,** *n.*

im•pov•er•ish [ɪmˈpɒvərɪʃ] *v.* **1** make very poor. **2** exhaust the strength, richness, or resources of: *to impoverish the soil.* ⟨ME < OF *empoveriss-,* a stem of *empoverir,* ult. < L *in-* + *pauper* poor⟩ **—im'pov•er•ish•er,** *n.* **—im'pov•er•ish•ment,** *n.*

im•pov•er•ished [ɪmˈpɒvərɪʃt] *adj., v.* —*adj.* **1** very poor. **2** deprived of strength, vitality, creativity, etc.
—*v.* pt. and pp. of IMPOVERISH.
☛ *Syn.* See note at POOR.

im•pow•er [ɪmˈpaʊər] *v.* empower. **—im'pow•er•ment,** *n.*

im•prac•ti•ca•bil•i•ty [ɪmˌpræktəkəˈbɪləti] *n., pl.* **-ties. 1** the condition or quality of being impracticable. **2** something impracticable.

im•prac•ti•ca•ble [ɪmˈpræktəkəbəl] *adj.* **1** impossible to be done or put into practice: *His suggestions were impracticable.* **2** that cannot be used: *an impracticable road.* **3** *Archaic.* very hard to manage; intractable. **—im'prac•ti•ca•bly,** *adv.*
☛ *Usage.* See note at IMPRACTICAL.

im•prac•ti•cal [ɪmˈpræktəkəl] *adj.* **1** not practical; unrealistic: *To build a bridge across the Atlantic Ocean is an impractical scheme.* **2** unusable: *This pen with a broken nib is impractical.* **3** idealistic. **—im'prac•ti•cal•ly,** *adv.*
☛ *Usage.* **Impractical,** IMPRACTICABLE. **Impractical** describes things that are useless or people who have a very unrealistic view of life or show little judgment or common sense in what they do: *Buying useless things because they are on sale is impractical.* **Impracticable** describes things that have been proved unusable in actual practice or that would be impossible to put into practice: *Most schemes to abolish poverty are impracticable.*

im•pre•cate [ˈɪmprəˌkeit] *v.* **-cat•ed, -cat•ing.** call down (curses, evil, etc.): *The witch doctor imprecated ruin on his people's enemies.* ⟨< L *imprecare* < *in -* on + *prex, precis* prayer⟩ **—'im•preˌca•tor,** *n.* **—'im•pre•caˌto•ry** [ˈɪmprəkəˌtɔri], *adj.*

im•pre•ca•tion [ˌɪmprəˈkeiʃən] *n.* **1** the act of calling down curses, evil, etc. **2** a curse.

im•pre•cise [ˌɪmprɪˈsəis] *adj.* lacking precision; inexact. **—ˌim•pre'ci•sion** [-ˈsɪʒən], *n.* **—ˌim•pre'cise•ly,** *adv.*

im•preg•na•ble[1] [ɪmˈprɛgnəbəl] *adj.* able to resist attack; not yielding to force, persuasion, etc.: *an impregnable fortress, an impregnable argument.* ⟨ME < OF *imprenable* < *in-* not + *prenable* pregnable < *prendre* take; influenced by *pregnant*⟩ **—imˌpreg•na'bil•i•ty,** *n.* **—im'preg•na•bly,** *adv.*

im•preg•na•ble[2] [ɪmˈprɛgnəbəl] *adj.* of an egg, able to be impregnated. ⟨< LL *impraegnare* + E *-able.* See IMPREGNATE.⟩

im•preg•nate [ɪmˈprɛgneit] *v.* **-nat•ed, -nat•ing;** *adj.* —*v.* **1** make pregnant. **2** *Biology.* fertilize: *to impregnate an egg cell.* **3** fill (with); saturate: *Sea water is impregnated with salt.* **4** fertilize. **5** instil into (the mind); inspire; imbue: *A great book impregnates the mind with new ideas.*
—*adj.* impregnated. ⟨< LL *impraegnare* make pregnant < *in-* + *praegnans* pregnant⟩ **—im'preg•na•tor,** *n.*

im•preg•na•tion [ˌɪmprɛgˈneiʃən] *n.* **1** an impregnating or being impregnated. **2** the thing, influence, etc. with which anything is impregnated.

im•pre•sa•ri•o [ˌɪmprəˈsɛriˌou] *or* [ˌɪmprəˈsariˌou] *n., pl.* **-sa•ri•os.** a person who presents or manages a concert tour, an opera or ballet company, or other, especially musical, entertainment. ⟨< Ital. *impresario* < *impresa* undertaking, ult. < L *in-* + *prehendere* take⟩

im•pre•scrip•ti•ble [ˌɪmprɪˈskrɪptəbəl] *adj.* **1** existing independently of law or custom; that cannot justly be taken away or violated: *imprescriptible rights.* **2** *Law.* not subject to prescription.

im•press[1] *v.* [ɪmˈprɛs]; *n.* [ˈɪmprɛs] *v., n.* —*v.* **1** have a strong effect on the mind or feelings of: *A hero impresses us with his courage.* **2** fix in the mind: *She repeated the words to impress them on her memory.* **3** make marks on by pressing or stamping: *to impress wax with a seal.* **4** imprint or stamp (a mark, seal, etc.).
—*n.* an impression; a special mark or quality; stamp: *The author left the impress of his personality on his work.* ⟨ME < OF < L *impressus,* pp. of *imprimere* < *in-* in + *premere* press⟩ **—im'press•er,** *n.*

im•press[2] [ɪmˈprɛs] *v.* **1** seize by force for public use: *The police impressed our car in order to pursue the escaping robbers.* **2** force into military service: *He was impressed into the navy as a young man.* **3** bring in and use. ⟨< *in-*[2] + *press*[2]⟩

im•press•i•ble [ɪmˈprɛsəbəl] *adj.* impressionable. **—im'pres•si•bly,** *adv.* **—ˌim•pres•si'bil•i•ty,** *n.*

im•pres•sion [ɪmˈprɛʃən] *n.* **1** an effect produced on a person: *Punishment seemed to make little impression on the child.* **2** an idea; notion: *I have a vague impression that I left the house unlocked.* **3** something produced by pressure as a mark, stamp, print, etc.: *The thief left an impression of his feet in the garden.* **4** an impressing or being impressed. **5** a result produced by work: *Scrubbing the floor made little impression on the dirt.* **6** *Dentistry.* a mould of the teeth and the surrounding gums. **7** any mould, such as that used to make an inlay. **8** *Printing.* **a** the total number of copies of a book made at one time. **b** a printed copy. **9** an impersonation or mimicking of someone. ⟨ME *impressio(u)n* < L *impression-* (stem of *impressio*), *impress(us)*⟩

im•pres•sion•a•ble [ɪmˈprɛʃənəbəl] *adj.* sensitive to impressions; easily impressed or influenced. **—imˌpres•sion•a'bil•i•ty,** *n.*

im•pres•sion•ism [ɪmˈprɛʃəˌnɪzəm] *n.* **1** Often, **Impressionism,** a school of painting developed by French painters of the late 19th century and characterized by the use of strong, bright, unmixed colours applied in small dabs to suggest natural reflected light. **2** a style in literature characterized by subjective impressions of reality presented in vivid, colourful scenes. **3** a style in music characterized by the use of unusual and rich harmonies, tonal qualities, etc. to suggest the composer's impressions of nature, emotion, etc.

im•pres•sion•ist [ɪmˈprɛʃənɪst] *n.* **1** Usually, **Impressionist,** a painter of the 19th-century French school of Impressionism. **2** Often, **Impressionist,** a painter, writer, or composer who follows a style that presents subjective, often emotional, impressions of reality. **3** an entertainer who does impersonations or impressions, especially of famous persons.

im•pres•sion•is•tic [ɪmˌprɛʃəˈnɪstɪk] *adj.* **1** of or characteristic of impressionism or impressionists. **2** giving only a general or hasty impression. **—im,pres•sion'ist•i•cal•ly,** *adv.*

im•pres•sive [ɪm'prɛsɪv] *adj.* making an impression on the mind, feelings, conscience, etc.: *an impressive lecture, an impressive storm, an impressive ceremony.* **—im'pres•sive•ly,** *adv.* **—im'pres•sive•ness,** *n.*

im•press•ment [ɪm'prɛsmənt] *n.* the act or practice of impressing men or property for public service or use, such as in the navy.

im•pri•ma•tur [,ɪmprɪ'meitər] *or* [,ɪmprɪ'mɑtər] *n.* **1** an official licence to print or publish a book, etc., now generally used of works sanctioned by the Roman Catholic Church. **2** sanction; approval. ⟨< NL *imprimatur* let it be printed⟩

im•pri•mis [ɪm'primɪs] *or* [ɪm'praɪmɪs] *adv. Latin.* in the first place; first.

im•print *n.* ['ɪmprɪnt]; *v.* [ɪm'prɪnt] *n., v. —n.* **1** a mark made by pressure; print: *the imprint of a foot in the sand.* **2** an impression; mark: *Suffering left its imprint on her face.* **3** a publisher's name, with the place and date of publication, on the title page or at the end of a book; a printer's name and address as printed on his or her work.
—v. **1** mark by pressing or stamping; print: *to imprint a postmark on an envelope, to imprint a letter with a postmark.* **2** press or impress: *to imprint a kiss on someone's cheek, a scene imprinted on the memory.* **—im'print•er,** *n.*

im•print•ing [ɪm'prɪntɪŋ] *n.* **1** the process by which certain characteristics are transferred from one person or animal to another. **2** the process by which a young animal regards and treats the first creature seen as its mother. **3** *Genetics.* the phenomenon by which an allele of a gene pair is altered or inactivated depending on whether it has been inherited from the mother or from the father.

im•pris•on [ɪm'prɪzən] *v.* **1** put in prison. **2** confine closely; restrain. ⟨ME *enprisone(n)* < OF *enprison(er)*⟩ **—im'pris•on•er,** *n.*

im•pris•on•ment [ɪm'prɪzənmənt] *n.* **1** a putting or keeping in prison. **2** a being put or kept in prison. **3** close confinement; restraint.

im•prob•a•bil•i•ty [ɪm,prɒbə'bɪləti] *n., pl.* **-ties. 1** the fact of being improbable; unlikelihood. **2** something improbable.

im•prob•a•ble [ɪm'prɒbəbəl] *adj.* **1** not probable; not likely to happen. **2** not likely to be true: *an improbable story.* ⟨< L *improbabil(is)*⟩

im•prob•a•bly [ɪm'prɒbəbli] *adv.* with little or no probability.

im•pro•bi•ty [ɪm'proubəti] *n.* dishonesty. ⟨ME *improbite* < L *improbitas*⟩

im•promp•tu [ɪm'prɒmptju] *or* [ɪm'prɒmptu] *adj., adv., n.* *—adj. or adv.* without previous thought or preparation; offhand: *an impromptu speech, a speech made impromptu.*
—n. an impromptu speech, performance, etc.; improvisation. ⟨< L *in promptu* in readiness⟩

im•prop•er [ɪm'prɒpər] *adj.* **1** not according to rules of conduct; not decent or polite: *improper language.* **2** not suitable for the purpose or in the circumstances; inappropriate: *improper clothing for a hike.* **3** incorrect: *an improper conclusion.* **4** not properly so called: *an improper fraction.* ⟨< L *impropr(ius)*⟩ **—im'prop•er•ly,** *adv.*

☛ *Syn.* **1, 2. Improper,** INDECENT = not right or fitting according to accepted standards. **Improper** describes something that goes against or fails to observe standards of manners, morals, health, etc. set by those who know what is right or fitting: *Talking in church is improper.* **Indecent** = contrary to standards of good taste in behaviour, modesty, and morals: *That girl looks indecent in those tight clothes.*

improper fraction a fraction greater than 1. *Examples:* $^3/_2$, $^4/_3$, $^{27}/_4$.

im•pro•pri•ate [ɪm'proupri,eit] *v.* **-at•ed, -at•ing.** place (church property) into the control of laity. ⟨< ML *impropriat(us)* made one's own⟩ **—im,pro•pri'a•tion,** *n.* **—im'pro•pri,a•tor,** *n.*

im•pro•pri•e•ty [,ɪmprə'praɪəti] *n., pl.* **-ties. 1** a lack of propriety; the quality of being improper. **2** improper conduct. **3** an improper act, expression, use of a word, etc. Using *learn* in speech or writing to mean *teach* is an impropriety.

im•prov ['ɪmprɒv] *n., adj., v. Informal. —n.* improvisation.
—adj. improvisatorial: *our improv group.*
—v. improvise: *Let's improv the story first.*

im•prove [ɪm'pruv] *v.* **-proved, -prov•ing. 1** make better: *You could improve your handwriting if you tried.* **2** become better: *Her health is improving.* **3** increase the value of (land or property). **4** formerly, in Upper Canada, clear (virgin land) of trees, underbrush, etc. in preparation for seeding. **5** *Archaic.* use well; make good use of: *Improve your time by studying.*
improve on, a make better; **b** do better than. ⟨< AF *emprouer* < OF *en-* in + *prou* profit⟩ **—im'prov•a•ble,** *adj.* **—im'prov•er,** *n.*

im•prove•ment [ɪm'pruvmənt] *n.* **1** a making better or becoming better. **2** an increase in value. **3** a change or addition that increases value: *An old house can be made to look modern by judicious improvements.* **4** a better condition; anything that is better than another; advance. **5** formerly, in Upper Canada: **a** the condition of land cleared of trees and underbrush in preparation for seeding. **b** a piece of land in this condition: *an improvement of fifty hectares.* **6 improvements,** *pl.* buildings, fences, etc. added to land.

im•prov•i•dence [ɪm'prɒvədəns] *n.* a lack of foresight or thrift; failure to look ahead; carelessness in providing for the future.

im•prov•i•dent [ɪm'prɒvədənt] *adj.* lacking foresight or thrift; not looking ahead; not careful in providing for the future. **—im'prov•i•dent•ly,** *adv.*

im•pro•vi•sa•tion [,ɪmprəvaɪ'zeiʃən] *or* [ɪm,prɒvə'zeiʃən] *n.* **1** the act or art of improvising. **2** something improvised. **—,im•pro•vi'sa•tion•al,** *adj.*

im•prov•i•sa•tor•ial [ɪm,prɒvɪzə'tɔriəl] *adj.* having to do with an improvisation.

im•pro•vise ['ɪmprə,vaɪz] *v.* **-vised, -vis•ing. 1** compose or sing, speak, perform, etc. without preparation. **2** engage in role-playing without preparation or script: *Come and watch the children improvising.* **3** make or provide offhand, using whatever resources happen to be available: *The girls improvised a tent out of two blankets and some long poles.* ⟨< F < Ital. *improvvisare,* ult. < L *in-* not + *pro-* beforehand + *videre* see⟩ **—'im•pro,vis•er,** *n.*

im•pru•dence [ɪm'prudəns] *n.* a lack of prudence; imprudent behaviour.

im•pru•dent [ɪm'prudənt] *adj.* not prudent; rash; unwise: *an imprudent decision.* ⟨ME < L *imprudent-* (stem of *imprudens*) unforeseeing, rash⟩ **—im'pru•dent•ly,** *adv.*

im•pu•dence ['ɪmpjədəns] *n.* **1** the quality or state of being impudent; insolence. **2** impudent conduct or language. ⟨ME < L *impudentia* shamelessness⟩

im•pu•dent ['ɪmpjədənt] *adj.* rudely bold; insolent; forward. ⟨< L *impudens, -entis,* ult. < *in-* not + *pudere* be modest⟩ **—'im•pu•dent•ly,** *adv.*

☛ *Syn.* See note at IMPERTINENT.

im•pu•di•ci•ty [,ɪmpju'dɪsəti] *n.* immodesty.

im•pugn [ɪm'pjun] *v.* call in question; attack by words or arguments; challenge as false. ⟨ME < OF < L *impugnare* assault < *in-* against + *pugnare* fight⟩ **—im'pugn•a•ble,** *adj.* **—,im•pug'na•tion** [,ɪmpʌg'neiʃən], *n.*

im•puis•sance [ɪm'pwɪsəns] *or* [ɪm'pjuɪsəns] *n.* lack of power. **—im'puis•sant,** *adj.*

im•pulse ['ɪmpʌls] *n.* **1** a sudden, driving force or influence; thrust; push: *the impulse of a wave, the impulse of hunger.* **2** the effect of a sudden, driving force or influence. **3** an impelling action. **4** a sudden inclination or tendency to act: *A mob is influenced more by impulse than by reasoning.* **5** the stimulating force of desire or emotion: *The murderer acted on impulse.* **6** *Physiology.* a stimulus that is transmitted, especially by nerve cells, and influences action in the muscle, gland, or other nerve cells that it reaches. **7** *Mechanics.* the product obtained by multiplying the value of a force by the time during which it acts. **8** *Electricity.* PULSE[1] (def. 5). ⟨< L *impulsus* < *impellere.* See IMPEL.⟩

im•pul•sion [ɪm'pʌlʃən] *n.* **1** an impelling; driving force. **2** impulse. **3** impetus.

im•pul•sive [ɪm'pʌlsɪv] *adj.* **1** acting upon impulse; easily moved: *The impulsive child gave all his money to the beggar.* **2** coming from a sudden impulse: *an impulsive sneer.* **3** driving with sudden force; able to impel: *an impulsive force.* **4** of a force, acting at brief intervals. **—im'pul•sive•ly,** *adv.* **—im'pul•sive•ness,** *n.*

im•pu•ni•ty [ɪm'pjunəti] *n.* freedom from punishment, injury, or other unpleasant consequences: *If laws are not enforced, crimes are committed with impunity.* ⟨< L *impunitas,* ult. < *in-* without + *poena* punishment⟩

im•pure [ɪm'pjur] *adj.* **1** not pure; dirty; unclean. **2** mixed with something, especially a substance of lower value; adulterated. **3** not of one colour, style, etc.; mixed. **4** forbidden by religion as unclean. **5** bad; corrupt; immoral: *impure thoughts.* **6** marked and spoiled by elements of speech or writing that are not appropriate: *an impure text.* ⟨< L *impur(us)*⟩ **—im'pure•ly,** *adv.* **—im'pure•ness,** *n.*

im•pu•ri•ty [ɪm'pjʊrəti] *n., pl.* **-ties. 1** a lack of purity; the state of being impure. **2** Often, **impurities,** *pl.* an impure thing or element; anything that makes something else impure: *Unfiltered water has impurities.*

im•pu•ta•tion [,ɪmpjə'teiʃən] *n.* **1** the act of imputing. **2** a charge or hint of wrongdoing: *No imputation has ever been made against his good name.*

im•pute [ɪm'pjut] *v.* **-put•ed, -put•ing.** consider as belonging; attribute; charge (a fault, etc.) to a person; blame: *I impute his failure to laziness.* ⟨< L *imputare* < *in-* in + *putare* reckon⟩ **—im'put•a•ble,** *adj.* **—im'put•a•tive,** *adj.* **—im'put•a•bly,** *adv.* **—im,put•a'bil•i•ty,** *n.*

in [ɪn] *prep., adv., adj., n.* **In** expresses inclusion, situation, presence, existence, position, and action within limits of space, time, state, circumstances, etc. *—prep.* **1** inside; within: *in an hour, in the box.* **2** into: *Put it in the fire.* **3** with; having: *to wrap in paper, dressed in blue, to be in trouble.* **4** of; made of; using: *a table in mahogany.* **5** surrounded by; in the midst of: *in the dust, in cold water.* **6** from among; out of: *one in a hundred.* **7** because of; for: *to act in self-defence.* **8** about; concerning: *a course in Canadian history.* **9** at; during; after: *in the present time.* **10** while; when: *in crossing the street.* **11** by; through: *It is in giving that we receive.*

in that, because.

—adv. **1** in or into some place, position, condition, etc.: *to come in. A sheepskin coat has the woolly side in.* **2** present, especially in one's home or office: *The doctor is not in today.* **3** *Informal.* in fashion: *Cocktail parties are in again.*

in for, unable to avoid; sure to get or have: *We are in for a storm.*

in on, taking part in; involved in: *A lot of people were in on the planning.*

in with, a friendly with. **b** partners with.

—adj. **1** that is in; being in. **2** coming or going in. **3** *Informal.* fashionable: *Pistachio is the in colour this fall.*

—n. **1** *Informal.* **a** a way of approach: *an in to a career in business.* **b** a position of familiarity or influence: *an in with the company president.* **2 ins,** *pl.* the group in office or in power.

ins and outs, a the turns and twists; nooks and corners: *the ins and outs of the road.* **b** the different parts; details: *The manager knows the ins and outs of the business better than the owner.* ⟨OE⟩

☛ *Hom.* INN.

☛ *Usage.* **In,** INTO. **In** generally shows location (literal or figurative); **into** generally shows direction: *He was in the house. She came into the house. He was in a stupor. She fell into a deep sleep.* Informally, **in** is often used for **into:** *He fell in the creek.*

☛ *Usage.* See AT[1] for another usage note.

in–[1] *prefix.* not; the opposite of, or the absence of: *inexpensive, inattention, inconvenient.* Also: **i-** (before *gn*), **il-** (before *l*), **im-** (before *b, m, p*), **ir-** (before *r*). ⟨< L⟩

☛ *Usage.* **In-** or **un-** prefixed to many words gives them a negative meaning, as in *inconsiderate, incapable, uneven, unloved.* Some words take both prefixes and one of them may be more current. Thus *indistinguishable* is preferred to *undistinguishable.*

in–[2] *prefix.* **1** in, into, on, or upon: *inhale, inscribe.* **2 in-** is also used to strengthen a meaning or change an intransitive verb to a transitive, usually with little change in meaning. Also, **il-** (before *l*), **im-** (before *b, m, p*), **ir-** (before *r*). ⟨< L *in-* < *in,* prep.⟩

–in *suffix.* a variant of -INE[2], sometimes used in chemical terms to denote neutral substance, as in *albumin, stearin.* ⟨< NL < L *-ina,* fem. suffix to abstract nouns⟩

in. inch(es).

In indium.

in•a•bil•i•ty [,ɪnə'bɪləti] *n.* a lack of ability, power, or means; condition of being unable. ⟨ME *inabilite* < ML *inhabilitas*⟩

in ab•sen•tia [ɪn æb'sɛnʃə] *Latin.* while absent.

in•ac•ces•si•ble [,ɪnək'sɛsəbəl] *adj.* **1** not accessible; that cannot be reached or entered. **2** hard to get at; hard to reach or enter: *The fort on top of the steep hill is inaccessible.* **3** that cannot be obtained; hard to obtain. **4** hard to understand or appreciate. ⟨< LL *inaccessibil(is)*⟩ **—,in•ac,ces•si'bil•i•ty,** *n.* **—,in•ac'ces•si•bly,** *adv.*

in•ac•cu•ra•cy [ɪn'ækjərəsi] *n., pl.* **-cies. 1** the quality or state of being inaccurate; a lack of accuracy: *The inaccuracy of the report was not hard to prove.* **2** an error or mistake: *There are several inaccuracies in the statistics.*

in•ac•cu•rate [ɪn'ækjərɪt] *adj.* not accurate; faulty; containing mistakes: *an inaccurate report. His aim was inaccurate and he missed the target.* **—in'ac•cu•rate•ly,** *adv.*

in•ac•tion [ɪn'ækʃən] *n.* an absence of action; idleness.

in•ac•tiv•ate [ɪn'æktə,veit] *v.* **-at•ed, -at•ing. 1** render inactive. **2** *Immunology.* end the activity of (some biological substances). **3** *Chemistry.* prevent from participating in chemical reactions.

in•ac•tive [ɪn'æktɪv] *adj.* **1** not active. **2** idle; sluggish. **—in'ac•tive•ly,** *adv.*

☛ *Syn.* **Inactive,** INERT, DORMANT = not in action or showing activity. **Inactive** = not acting or working, and suggests nothing more: *He is an inactive member of the club.* **Inert** = having by nature, condition, or habit no power or desire to move or act, and suggests being hard or impossible to set in motion or moving slowly: *He dragged the inert, unconscious body from the water.* **Dormant** suggests being asleep, and means 'temporarily inactive': *Some animals and plants are dormant during the winter.*

inactive X chromosome *Genetics.* the inactivated X chromosome in somatic cells of female mammals. See SEX CHROMATIN.

in•ac•tiv•i•ty [,ɪnæk'tɪvəti] *n.* **1** the state of being inactive. **2** idleness; sluggishness.

in•ad•e•qua•cy [ɪn'ædəkwəsi] *n., pl.* **-cies. 1** a being inadequate. **2** something that makes one inadequate: *Though conscious of her many inadequacies, she assumed the mayoralty with confidence.*

in•ad•e•quate [ɪn'ædəkwɪt] *adj.* not adequate; not enough; not as much as is needed: *inadequate preparation for an examination.* **—in'ad•e•quate•ly,** *adv.*

in•ad•mis•si•ble [,ɪnəd'mɪsəbəl] *adj.* **1** not allowable. **2** not to be admitted. **—,in•ad,mis•si'bil•i•ty,** *n.* **—,in•ad'mis•si•bly,** *adv.*

in•ad•vert•ence [,ɪnəd'vɜrtəns] *n.* **1** a lack of attention; carelessness. **2** an oversight; mistake. Also, **inadvertency.** ⟨< ML *inadvertentia*⟩

in•ad•vert•ent [,ɪnəd'vɜrtənt] *adj.* **1** not attentive; heedless; negligent. **2** not done on purpose; caused by oversight. **—,in•ad'vert•ent•ly,** *adv.*

in•ad•vis•a•ble [,ɪnəd'vaɪzəbəl] *adj.* not advisable; unwise; not prudent. **—,in•ad,vis•a'bil•i•ty,** *n.* **—,in•ad'vis•a•bly,** *adv.*

in•al•ien•a•ble [ɪn'eiliənəbəl] *or* [ɪn'eiljənəbəl] *adj.* that cannot be given away or taken away: *Every person has the inalienable right of equality before the law.* **—in,al•ien•a'bil•i•ty,** *n.* **—in'al•ien•a•bly,** *adv.*

in•al•ter•a•ble [ɪn'ɒltərəbəl] *adj.* not changeable. **—in'al•ter•a•bly,** *adv.* **—in,al•ter•a'bil•i•ty,** *n.*

in•am•o•ra•ta [ɪ,næmə'rɑtə] *or* [,ɪnæmə'rɑtə] *n., pl.* **-tas.** the girl or woman with whom one is in love; sweetheart. ⟨< Ital. *innamorata* < L, pp. of *inamorare* fall in love *in-* in + *amor* love⟩

in–and–in ['ɪn ənd 'ɪn] *adv., adj. —adv.* of breeding, repeatedly within the same stocks: *to breed dogs in-and-in.*

—adj. of such breeding methods: *in-and-in breeding.*

in•ane [ɪ'nein] *adj., n. —adj.* **1** silly or foolish; empty of meaning; senseless: *an inane thing to do, inane remarks.* **2** *Archaic.* empty; void.

—n. Archaic. something empty or without substance, especially the void of space. ⟨< L *inanis* empty⟩ **—in'ane•ly,** *adv.*

in•an•i•mate [ɪn'ænəmɪt] *adj.* **1** not having life; not animate; lifeless: *the inanimate desert. Stones are inanimate.* **2** not animated; dull: *an inanimate face.* **3** appearing lifeless. ⟨< LL *inanimat(us)*⟩ **—in'an•i•mate•ly,** *adv.* **—in'an•i•mate•ness** or **in,an•i'ma•tion,** *n.*

in•a•ni•tion [,ɪnə'nɪʃən] *n.* **1** emptiness. **2** weakness from lack of food. **3** exhaustion. ⟨< LL *inanitio, -onis* < L *inanire* to empty < *inanis* empty⟩

in•an•i•ty [ɪ'nænəti] *n., pl.* **-ties. 1** silliness; lack of sense. **2** a silly or senseless act, practice, remark, etc. **3** emptiness. ⟨< L *inanitas*⟩

in•ap•peas•a•ble [,ɪnə'pizəbəl] *adj.* not able to be appeased.

in•ap•pe•tence [ɪn'æpətəns] *n.* lack of appetite. Also, **inappetency. —in'ap•pe•tent,** *adj.*

in•ap•pli•ca•ble [ɪn'æpləkəbəl] *or* [,ɪnə'plɪkəbəl] *adj.* not applicable; not appropriate; not suitable. **—in,ap•pli•ca'bil•i•ty,** *n.* **—in'ap•pli•ca•bly,** *adv.*

in•ap•po•site [ɪn'æpəzɪt] *adj.* not pertinent; not suitable; inappropriate. **—in'ap•po•site•ly,** *adv.*

in•ap•pre•ci•a•ble [,ɪnə'priʃiəbəl] *or* [,ɪnə'priʃəbəl] *adj.* too small to be noticed or felt; very slight. **—,in•ap'pre•ci•a•bly,** *adv.*

in•ap•pre•ci•a•tive [,ɪnə'priʃətɪv] *or* [,ɪnə'priʃi,eitɪv] *adj.* not showing appreciation. **—in•ap'pre•ci•a•tive•ly,** *adv.* **—,in•ap'pre•ci•a•tive•ness,** *n.*

in•ap•pre•hen•si•ble [ˌɪnæprɪˈhɛnsəbəl] *adj.* not to be understood by the mind or feelings.

in•ap•pre•hen•sive [ˌɪnæprɪˈhɛnsɪv] *adj.* **1** not understanding (*used with* **of**). **2** without apprehension. **—ˌin•ap•preˈhen•sive•ly,** *adv.* **—ˌin•ap•preˈhen•sive•ness,** *n.*

in•ap•proach•a•ble [ˌɪnəˈproutʃəbəl] *adj.* **1** not to be approached. **2** without a rival.

in•ap•pro•pri•ate [ˌɪnəˈproupriɪt] *adj.* not appropriate; not suitable; not fitting: *Jokes are inappropriate at a funeral.* **—ˌin•apˈpro•pri•ate•ly,** *adv.* **—ˌin•apˈpro•pri•ate•ness,** *n.*

in•apt [ɪnˈæpt] *adj.* **1** not apt; not suitable. **2** unskilful; inept. **—inˈapt•ly,** *adv.* **—inˈapt•ness,** *n.*
☛ *Syn.* See note at INEPT.

in•ap•ti•tude [ɪnˈæptəˌtjud] *or* [ɪnˈæptəˌtud] *n.* **1** unfitness. **2** lack of skill.

in•arch [ɪnˈɑrk] *v. Horticulture.* graft a branch of a tree to (another tree) without cutting off the first graft.

in•ar•tic•u•late [ˌɪnɑrˈtɪkjəlɪt] *adj.* **1** not distinct; not like regular speech: *an inarticulate mutter or groan.* **2** unable to speak in words; unable to say what one thinks; dumb: *Cats and dogs are inarticulate.* **3** unable to talk comprehensibly. **4** not expressed: *inarticulate grief.* **5** *Zoology.* not jointed: *A jellyfish's body is inarticulate.* ⟨< LL *inarticulatus*⟩ **—ˌin•arˈtic•u•late•ly,** *adv.* **—ˌin•arˈtic•u•late•ness,** *n.*

in•ar•tis•tic [ˌɪnɑrˈtɪstɪk] *adj.* **1** not following the principles of art. **2** lacking talent in or appreciation of art. **—ˌin•arˈtis•ti•cal•ly,** *adv.*

in•as•much as [ˌɪnəzˈmʌtʃ] **1** because; since; in view of the fact that: *Inasmuch as he was smaller than the other boys, he was given a head start in the race.* **2** to such a degree as.

in•at•ten•tion [ˌɪnəˈtɛnʃən] *n.* a lack of attention; heedlessness; negligence.

in•at•ten•tive [ˌɪnəˈtɛntɪv] *adj.* not attentive; careless; heedless; negligent. **—ˌin•atˈten•tive•ly,** *adv.* **—ˌin•atˈten•tive•ness,** *n.*

in•au•di•ble [ɪnˈɒdəbəl] *adj.* that cannot be heard. **—inˈau•di•bly,** *adv.* **—inˈau•di•ble•ness** or **inˌau•diˈbil•i•ty,** *n.*

in•au•gu•ral [ɪnˈɒgjərəl] *or* [ɪnˈɒgərəl] *adj., n.* *—adj.* of or for an inauguration: *an inaugural address.*
—n. an inaugural address or speech. ⟨< F *inaugural* < *inaugurer* inaugurate⟩

in•au•gu•rate [ɪnˈɒgjəˌreit] *or* [ɪnˈɒgəˌreit] *v.* **-rat•ed, -rat•ing. 1** install in office with a ceremony: *The new mayor will be inaugurated at noon tomorrow.* **2** make a formal beginning of; begin: *The development of the airplane inaugurated a new era in transportation.* **3** open for public use with a ceremony or celebration. ⟨< L *inaugurare* < *in-* for + *augur* taker of omens⟩ **—inˈau•guˌra•tor,** *n.*

in•au•gu•ra•tion [ɪnˌɒgjəˈreiʃən] *or* [ɪnˌɒgəˈreiʃən] *n.* **1** the act or ceremony of installing a person in office. **2** a beginning, especially a formal one. **3** the opening or bringing into use of public buildings, etc. with a ceremony or celebration: *We were present at the inauguration of the new City Hall.*

in•aus•pi•cious [ˌɪnɒˈspɪʃəs] *adj.* showing signs of probable failure; unfavourable; unlucky. **—ˌin•ausˈpi•cious•ly,** *adv.* **—ˌin•ausˈpi•cious•ness,** *n.*

in•au•then•ti•ci•ty [ˌɪnɒθənˈtɪsəti] *n.* lack of authenticity.

inbd. inboard.

in•be•ing [ˈɪnˌbiɪŋ] *n.* **1** inward nature. **2** inherence.

in–be•tween [ˈɪn bɪˈtwin] *adj., n.* *—adj.* **1** coming or belonging in the middle; relating to the space or time separating two things: *He is at that in-between age, neither boy nor man.* **2** being neither one thing nor another; neutral; indifferent.
—n. a person or thing that is in-between.

in•board [ˈɪnˌbɔrd] *adv., adj., n.* *—adv. or adj.* **1** inside the hull of a ship; in or toward the middle of a ship. **2** close to the fuselage of an aircraft. **3** toward the centre of a machine.
—n. **1** a motorboat having its motor inside the hull. **2** the motor itself. Compare OUTBOARD.

in•born [ˈɪnˌbɔrn] *adj.* **1** born in a person; instinctive; natural: *an inborn sense of rhythm.* **2** inherited. ⟨OE *inboren* native⟩

inborn error of metabolism a genetically caused, metabolic disorder in which a genetic defect leads to a block in a normal metabolic process, with pathological consequences such as PHENYLKETONURIA.

in•bound [ˈɪnˌbaʊnd] *adj.* inward bound.

in•bounds line [ˈɪnˌbaʊndz] *Football.* one of the lines that form a boundary to the field.

in•breathe [ˈɪnˌbrið] *v.* **-breathed, -breath•ing.** infuse; inspire: *to inbreathe new ideas.*

in•bred [ˈɪnˌbrɛd] *adj.,v.* *—adj.* **1** inborn; natural: *an inbred courtesy.* **2** bred for generations from ancestors closely related.
—v. pt. and pp. of INBREED.

in•breed [ˈɪnˌbrid] *or* [ɪnˈbrid] *v.* **-bred, -breed•ing. 1** breed from closely related persons, animals, or plants. **2** engender.

in•breed•ing [ˈɪnˌbridɪŋ] *n., v.* *—n.* the practice of breeding from closely related stock in order to develop or preserve desirable characteristics. Compare OUTBREEDING.
—v. ppr. of INBREED.

inc. 1 incorporated. **2** inclosure. **3** including; included; inclusive. **4** increase. **5** income.

In•ca [ˈɪŋkə] *n.* **1** a member of an Indian people of South America that held power in Peru before the Spanish conquest. **2** a ruler of the Incas. ⟨< Sp. < Quechua (SAm.Ind.) *ynca* prince of the ruling family⟩ **—ˈIn•can,** *n., adj.*

in•cal•cu•la•ble [ɪnˈkælkjələbəl] *adj.* **1** too great in number to be counted; innumerable: *The sands of the beach are incalculable.* **2** not able to be reckoned beforehand: *A flood in the valley would cause incalculable losses.* **3** not to be relied on; uncertain. **—inˈcal•cu•la•bly,** *adv.* **—inˈcal•cu•la•ble•ness** or **inˌcal•cu•laˈbil•i•ty,** *n.*

in•cal•es•cent [ˌɪnkəˈlɛsənt] *adj.* **1** increasing in heat. **2** increasing in feeling. ⟨< L *incalescent-* (stem of *incalescens*) glowing⟩ **—ˌin•calˈes•cence,** *n.*

in cam•e•ra [ɪn ˈkæmərə] **1** *Law.* in the privacy of a judge's chambers, rather than in open court. **2** in a closed session, as of a committee. ⟨< L *in camera* in a room, chamber⟩

in•can•desce [ˌɪnkənˈdɛs] *v.* **-desced, -des•cing. 1** glow with heat. **2** cause to glow with heat. ⟨< L *incandescere* begin to glow⟩

in•can•des•cence [ˌɪnkənˈdɛsəns] *n.* the quality or state of being incandescent.

in•can•des•cent [ˌɪnkənˈdɛsənt] *adj.* **1** glowing with heat; red-hot or white-hot. **2** intensely bright; brilliant. **3** having to do with or containing a material that gives light by incandescence. An **incandescent lamp** is an electric lamp with a filament of very fine wire that becomes white-hot when current flows through it. ⟨< L *incandescens, -entis,* ppr. of *incandescere* begin to glow < *in-* in + *candere* be gleaming white⟩ **—ˌin•canˈdes•cent•ly,** *adv.*

incandescent lamp LIGHT BULB.

in•can•ta•tion [ˌɪnkænˈteiʃən] *n.* **1** a set of words spoken as a magic charm or to cast a magic spell. *Double, double, toil and trouble, Fire burn and cauldron bubble* is an incantation. **2** the use of such words. **3** magical ceremonies; magic; sorcery. ⟨< L *incantatio, -onis* < *incantare* chant a magic formula against < *in-* against + *cantare* chant⟩ **—ˌin•canˈta•tion•al** or **inˈcan•ta,to•ry,** *adj.*

in•ca•pa•ble [ɪnˈkeipəbəl] *adj.* without ordinary ability; not efficient; not competent: *An employer cannot afford to hire incapable workers.*
incapable of, a without the ability, power, or fitness for: *His honesty made him incapable of lying.* **b** not legally qualified for: *Certain beliefs make a person incapable of serving on a jury.* **c** not susceptible to; not capable of receiving or admitting: *incapable of exact measurement.* ⟨< LL *incapabilis*⟩ **—inˌca•paˈbil•i•ty,** *n.* **—inˈca•pa•bly,** *adv.*

in•ca•pac•i•tate [ˌɪnkəˈpæsəˌteit] *v.* **-tat•ed, -tat•ing. 1** deprive of ability, power, or fitness; disable: *The man's injury incapacitated him for working.* **2** legally disqualify. **—ˌin•caˌpac•iˈta•tion,** *n.*

in•ca•pac•i•ty [ˌɪnkəˈpæsəti] *n., pl.* **-ties. 1** a lack of ability, power, or fitness; disability. **2** a legal disqualification. ⟨< ML *incapacitas*⟩

in•cap•su•late [ɪnˈkæpsjəˌleit] *or* [ɪnˈkæpsəˌleit] *v.,* **-lat•ed, -lat•ing.** encapsulate.

in•car•cer•ate [ɪnˈkɑrsəˌreit] *v.* **-at•ed, -at•ing. 1** imprison. **2** confine; shut in. ⟨< LL *incarcerare* < L *in-* in + *carcer* jail⟩ **—inˈcar•cerˌa•tor,** *n.*

in•car•cer•a•tion [ɪnˌkɑrsəˈreiʃən] *n.* imprisonment.

in•car•na•dine [ɪnˈkɑrnəˌdaɪn], [ɪnˈkɑrnəˌdin], *or* [ɪnˈkɑrnədɪn] *adj., v.* **-dined, -din•ing,** *n.* *—adj.* **1** blood-red. **2** flesh-coloured.
—v. make blood-red or flesh-coloured.
—n. a blood-red colour. ⟨< F < Ital. *incarnadino,* ult. < L *in-* in + *caro, carnis* flesh⟩

in•car•nate *adj.* [ɪn'kɑrnɪt] *or* [ɪn'kɑrneit]; *v.* [ɪn'kɑrneit] *adj., v.* **-nat•ed, -nat•ing.** *—adj.* **1** embodied in flesh, especially in human form: *The villain was an incarnate fiend.* **2** personified or typified (*follows the noun*): *evil incarnate.* **3** *Botany.* flesh-coloured or crimson.
—v. **1** make incarnate; embody: *She incarnates all womanly virtues in her own person.* **2** put into an actual form; realize: *The sculptor incarnated his vision in a beautiful statue.* ⟨< L *incarnatus*, pp. of *incarnare* < *in-* in + *caro, carnis* flesh⟩

in•car•na•tion [,ɪnkɑr'neiʃən] *n.* **1** the taking on of human form by a spiritual being. **2** embodiment. **3** a person or thing that represents some quality or idea: *A miser is an incarnation of greed.* **4 the Incarnation,** the Christian doctrine of the union of divine nature and human nature in the person of Jesus Christ; assumption of human form by the Son of God.

in•case [ɪn'keis] *v.* **-cased, -cas•ing.** encase. **—in'case•ment,** *n.*

in•cau•tion [ɪn'kɒʃən] *n.* carelessness.

in•cau•tious [ɪn'kɒʃəs] *adj.* not cautious; heedless; reckless; rash. **—in'cau•tious•ly,** *adv.* **—in'cau•tious•ness,** *n.*

in•cen•di•a•rism [ɪn'sɛndiə,rɪzəm] *n.* **1** the crime of maliciously setting fire to property. **2** the deliberate stirring up of strife or rebellion.

in•cen•di•ar•y [ɪn'sɛndi,ɛri] *adj., n., pl.* **-ar•ies.** *—adj.* **1** having to do with the malicious setting on fire of property. **2** causing fires; used to start a fire: *The enemy town was set on fire with incendiary shells and bombs.* **3** deliberately stirring up strife or rebellion: *The agitator was arrested for making incendiary speeches.*
—n. **1** a person who maliciously sets fire to property. **2** a person who deliberately stirs up strife or rebellion. **3** a shell or bomb containing chemical agents that cause fire. ⟨< L *incendiarius* < *incendium* fire⟩

in•cense[1] ['ɪnsɛns] *n., v.* **-censed, -cens•ing.** *—n.* **1** a substance giving off a sweet smell when burned. **2** the perfume or smoke from it. **3** something sweet, such as the perfume of flowers, or the pleasure given by flattery or praise.
—v. perfume with incense. ⟨ME < OF < LL *incensus* < L *incendere* burn⟩

in•cense[2] [ɪn'sɛns] *v.* **-censed, -cens•ing.** make very angry; fill with rage: *Cruelty incenses kind people.* ⟨< L *incensus*, pp. of *incendere* kindle⟩

in•cen•tive [ɪn'sɛntɪv] *n., adj.* *—n.* something that urges a person on; the cause of action or effort; a motive; stimulus.
—adj. motivating. ⟨< L *incentivus* < *incinere* sound, cause to sound < *in-* in + *canere* sing⟩

in•cept [ɪn'sɛpt] *v.* **1** take in. **2** begin. **3** *Brit.* formerly, complete a degree at Cambridge University.

in•cep•tion [ɪn'sɛpʃən] *n.* a beginning; commencement. ⟨ME < L *inceptio, -onis* < *incipere* begin < *in-* on + *capere* take⟩

in•cep•tive [ɪn'sɛptɪv] *adj., n.* *—adj.* **1** beginning; initial. **2** *Grammar.* expressing the beginning of an action or state. *Phosphoresce* is an inceptive verb. All verbs ending in *-esce* and adjectives ending in *-escent* are inceptives.
—n. Grammar. an inceptive word or structure.
—in'cep•tive•ly, *adv.*

in•cer•ti•tude [ɪn'sɜrtə,tjud] *or* [ɪn'sɜrtə,tud] *n.* **1** uncertainty; doubt. **2** insecurity. ⟨< LL *incertitudo*⟩

in•ces•sant [ɪn'sɛsənt] *adj.* never stopping; continued or repeated without interruption: *The roar of Niagara Falls is incessant. The incessant noise of traffic kept her awake all night.* ⟨< LL *incessans, -antis* < L *in-* not + *cessare* cease⟩
—in'ces•sant•ly, *adv.*

in•cest ['ɪnsɛst] *n.* the crime of sexual intercourse between persons so closely related that their marriage is prohibited by law. ⟨< L *incestum* < *incestus* unchaste < *in-* not + *castus* chaste⟩

in•ces•tu•ous [ɪn'sɛstʃuəs] *adj.* **1** involving incest. **2** guilty of incest. **3** of a relationship, abnormally involved or intimate.
—in'ces•tu•ous•ly, *adv.* **—in'ces•tu•ous•ness,** *n.*

inch [ɪntʃ] *n., v.* *—n.* **1** a unit for measuring length, equal to 1/12 of a foot (2.54 cm). *Symbol:* ″ **2** the smallest part, amount, or degree; very little bit: *He would not yield an inch. If only he'd back down just an inch, I know she'd come around.*
by inches or **inch by inch,** by degrees; gradually.
every inch, in every way; completely.
within an inch of, very near; very close to: *The man was within an inch of death.*
—v. move slowly or little by little: *The worm inched along.* ⟨OE *ynce* < L *uncia*, originally, a twelfth. Doublet of OUNCE[1].⟩

inch•meal ['ɪntʃ,mil] *adv., adj., n.* *—adv.* little by little; slowly.
—adj. very slow.
—n.
by inchmeal, little by little; slowly. ⟨ME *inch* + *-mele* < OE *mælum* by measures < *mæl* measure⟩

in•cho•ate [ɪn'kouɪt] *adj.* **1** incomplete; undeveloped. **2** just begun; in an early stage; incipient. ⟨< L *inchoatus*, var. of *incohatus*, pp. of *incohare* begin, originally, harness < *in-* on + *cohum* yoke fastener⟩ **—in'cho•ate•ly,** *adv.* **—in'cho•ate•ness,** *n.*

in•cho•a•tion [,ɪnkou'eiʃən] *n.* origin.

in•cho•a•tive [ɪn'kouətɪv] *adj., n.* *—adj.* **1** inchoate. **2** *Grammar.* inceptive.
—n. Grammar. an inceptive word or structure.

inch•worm ['ɪntʃ,wɜrm] *n.* MEASURING WORM.

in•ci•dence ['ɪnsədəns] *n.* **1** the act or fact of coming in contact with, occurring, or influencing. **2** the manner, extent, or rate of occurrence or effect: *a high incidence of traffic accidents during the holiday weekend. In an epidemic, the incidence of a disease is widespread.* **3 a** *Physics.* the falling of a line, or of something moving in a line, on a surface. **b** the direction such a line, etc. takes in falling on a surface. The angle of incidence of a ray of light falling on a surface is the angle between the ray and a line perpendicular to that surface. See ANGLE OF INCIDENCE for picture. **4** *Geometry.* the partial coincidence of two figures.

in•ci•dent ['ɪnsədənt] *n., adj.* *—n.* **1** a happening; event. **2** an event that helps or adds to something else. **3** a distinct piece of action in a story, play, or poem. **4** a minor event that causes a public crisis.
—adj. **1** liable to happen; belonging: *Hardships are incident to the life of an explorer.* **2** falling or striking (*upon*): *rays of light incident on a mirror.* ⟨< L *incidens, -entis*, pp. of *incidere* happen < *in-* on + *cadere* to fall⟩
☛ *Syn. n.* **1.** See note at EVENT.

in•ci•den•tal [,ɪnsə'dɛntəl] *adj., n.* *—adj.* **1** happening or likely to happen along with something else more important: *Certain discomforts are incidental to camping out.* **2** occurring by chance.
—n. Often, **incidentals,** *pl.* something incidental: *On our trip we spent $350 for meals, room, and bus fare, and $28 for incidentals, such as candy, magazines, and stamps.*
☛ *Syn. adj.* **1.** See note at ACCIDENTAL.

in•ci•den•tal•ly [,ɪnsə'dɛntəli] *adv.* **1** in an incidental manner; as an incident along with something else (*also used as a sentence adverb*): *She mentioned incidentally that she had had no dinner. Incidentally, I found another of those plates.* **2** accidentally; by chance.

incidental music music played as accompaniment to a film, play, etc. to help evoke the appropriate mood.

in•cin•er•ate [ɪn'sɪnə,reit] *v.* **-at•ed, -at•ing.** burn or be burned to ashes. ⟨< Med.L *incinerare* < L *in-* into + *cinis, -neris* ashes⟩ **—in,cin•er'a•tion,** *n.*

in•cin•er•a•tor [ɪn'sɪnə,reitər] *n.* a furnace or other arrangement for burning garbage, trash, etc. to ashes.

in•cip•i•ence [ɪn'sɪpiəns] *n.* the very beginning; the earliest stage.

in•cip•i•ent [ɪn'sɪpiənt] *adj.* just beginning; in an early stage. ⟨< L *incipiens, -entis*, ppr. of *incipere* begin < *in-* on + *capere* take⟩ **—in'cip•i•ent•ly,** *adv.*

in•ci•pit ['ɪnsɪpɪt] *n.* **1** the opening words of a book. **2** the opening notes of a musical composition.

in•cise [ɪn'saɪz] *v.* **-cised, -cis•ing. 1** cut into with a sharp tool. **2** carve; engrave. ⟨< F *inciser* < L *incidere* < *in-* into + *caedere* cut⟩

in•cised [ɪn'saɪzd] *adj., v.* *—adj.* **1** that is cut into with a sharp tool. **2** carved; engraved. **3** having notches around the edge: *an incised leaf.*
—v. pt. and pp. of INCISE.

in•ci•sion [ɪn'sɪʒən] *n.* **1** a cut made in something; gash: *The doctor made a small incision to remove all the glass from her foot.* **2** a notch. **3** the act of incising. **4** an incisive quality.

in•ci•sive [ɪn'saisɪv] *adj.* **1** sharp; penetrating; piercing; keen: *an incisive criticism.* **2** of the incisors. ⟨< Med.L *incisivus* < L *incidere.* See INCISE.⟩ **—in'ci•sive•ly,** *adv.* **—in'ci•sive•ness,** *n.*

in•ci•sor [ɪn'saɪzər] *n.* a tooth having a sharp edge for cutting; one of the front teeth between the canine teeth in either jaw: *Humans have eight incisors in all.* See TEETH for diagram. ⟨< NL⟩

in•ci•ta•tion [,ɪnsəi'teiʃən] *or* [,ɪnsə'teiʃən] *n.* an inciting.

in•cite [ɪn'səit] *v.* **-cit•ed, -cit•ing.** urge on; stir up; rouse. ⟨< L *incitare*, ult. < *in-* on + *ciere* cause to move⟩ **—in'cit•er,** *n.* **—in'cit•ing•ly,** *adv.*

☛ *Syn.* **Incite,** INSTIGATE = stir up or urge on to action. **Incite** = stir someone up or urge him or her on to do something good or bad: *Their captain's example incited the men to fight bravely.* **Instigate** = bring about something bad, such as a plot or rebellion, by inciting others to act: *The police never discovered who instigated the looting.*

in•cite•ment [ɪn'səitmənt] *n.* **1** something that urges on, stirs up, or rouses: *Extreme poverty was their incitement to rebellion.* **2** the act of urging on, stirring up, or rousing.

in•ci•vil•i•ty [,ɪnsə'vɪləti] *n., pl.* **-ties. 1** the quality or condition of being uncivil. **2** rudeness; lack of courtesy; impoliteness. **3** a rude or impolite act. ⟨< LL *incivilitas*⟩

incl. **1** inclosure. **2** including; inclusive.

in•clem•en•cy [ɪn'klɛmənsi] *n.* severity; harshness: *The inclemency of the weather kept us at home.*

in•clem•ent [ɪn'klɛmənt] *adj.* **1** rainy; rough and stormy: *inclement weather.* **2** severe; harsh: *an inclement ruler.* ⟨< L *inclemens, -entis*⟩ **—in'clem•ent•ly,** *adv.*

in•clin•a•ble [ɪn'klaɪnəbəl] *adj.* **1** having a certain tendency. **2** favourable. **3** able to be inclined.

in•cli•na•tion [,ɪnklə'neiʃən] *n.* **1** a preference; liking: *a strong inclination for sports.* **2** tendency: *Many middle-aged people have an inclination to become fat.* **3** a leaning; bending; bowing: *A nod is an inclination of the head.* **4** a slope; slant: *the inclination of a roof.* **5** *Geometry.* the difference of direction of two lines, especially as measured by the angle between them. ⟨< L *inclinatio, -onis* < *inclinare.* See INCLINE.⟩ **—,in•cli'na•tion•al,** *adj.*

in•cline *v.* [ɪn'klaɪn]; *n.* ['ɪnklaɪn] *or* [ɪn'klaɪn] *v.* **-clined, -clin•ing;** *n.* *—v.* **1** be favourable or willing; tend: *Dogs incline to meat as a food.* **2** make favourable or willing; influence. **3** slope; slant: *That roof inclines steeply.* **4** lean; bend; bow.
incline one's ear, listen favourably.
—n. **1** a slope; slant: *There is quite an incline to that roof.* **2** a sloping surface. *The side of a hill is an incline.* ⟨ME < OF < L *inclinare* < *in-* in + *clinare* bend⟩

in•clined [ɪn'klaɪnd] *adj., v.* *—adj.* **1** willing; tending: *I am inclined to agree with you.* **2** sloping; slanting.
—v. pt. and pp. of INCLINE.

inclined plane a plane surface set at an oblique angle to a horizontal surface.

in•cli•nom•e•ter [,ɪnklə'nɒmətər] *n.* **1** an instrument for measuring the slope of anything. **2** an instrument for measuring the angle that an aircraft makes with the horizontal. **3** an instrument for measuring the inclination of the earth's magnetic field. ⟨< *incline* + *-meter*⟩

in•close [ɪn'klouz] *v.* **-closed, -clos•ing.** enclose.

in•clo•sure [ɪn'klouʒər] *n.* enclosure.

in•clude [ɪn'klud] *v.* **-clud•ed, -clud•ing. 1** contain; comprise: *The farm includes about 65 ha.* **2** put in a total, a class, or the like; reckon in a count: *The number of people lost included the captain of the ship.* **3** allow to participate: *He tried to include her in all his activities.* ⟨ME < L *includere* < *in-* in + *claudere* shut⟩ **—in'clud•a•ble,** *adj.*

☛ *Syn.* **2. Include,** COMPRISE, COMPREHEND = contain or take in as a part or parts. **Include** emphasizes containing or taking in as an element or part of the whole: *The list includes my name.* **Comprise** emphasizes being made up of parts going together to make up the whole: *The list comprises the names of those who passed.* **Comprehend,** formal and applying to ideas, statements, outlines, etc., emphasizes holding or taking within the limits or scope of the whole: *The examination comprehended the whole course.*

in•clud•ed [ɪn'kludɪd] *adj., v.* *—adj.* **1** counted in a total. **2** formed by and between two intersecting lines: *an included angle.*
—v. pt. and pp. of INCLUDE.

in•clud•ing [ɪn'kludɪŋ] *prep., v.* *—prep.* counting as a part of a total: *He took my purse, including all my money.*
—v. ppr. of INCLUDE.

in•clu•sion [ɪn'kluʒən] *n.* **1** an including or being included. **2** the thing included. **3** *Mineralogy.* any foreign body enclosed in a rock. **4** *Biology.* any non-living part in a cytoplasm. ⟨< Med.L *inclusio, -onis* < *includere.* See INCLUDE.⟩

inclusion body *Pathology.* that part of a cell nucleus or protoplasm that is not normal.

in•clu•sive [ɪn'klusɪv] *adj.* **1** including in consideration the extremes mentioned. *Read pages 10 to 20 inclusive* means *Read pages 10 and 20 and all those in between.* **2** including much; including everything concerned; comprehensive: *Make an inclusive list of your expenses.* **3** *Grammar.* of a first-person plural pronoun, including the person spoken to: *The inclusive* we *includes* you. Compare EXCLUSIVE.
inclusive of, including; taking in; counting on.
—in'clu•sive•ly, *adv.* **—in'clu•sive•ness,** *n.*

in•co•erc•i•ble [,ɪnkou'ɜrsəbəl] *adj.* not able to be coerced.

in•cog [ɪn'kɒg] *adj., adv., n. Informal.* incognito.

incog. incognito.

in•cog•i•tant [ɪn'kɒdʒətənt] *adj.* **1** thoughtless. **2** unable to think.

in•cog•ni•to [,ɪnkɒg'nitou] *or* [ɪn'kɒgnə,tou] *adj., adv., n., pl.* **-tos.** *—adj. or adv.* with one's name, character, rank, etc. concealed: *The prince travelled incognito to avoid crowds and ceremonies.*
—n. **1** a person who is incognito. Also, for female, **incognita. 2** a disguised state or condition: *His incognito was not successful and he was recognized almost immediately.* ⟨< Ital. < L *incognitus* unknown < *in-* not + *cognitus,* pp. of *cognoscere* come to know⟩

in•cog•ni•zant [ɪn'kɒgnəzənt] *adj.* not aware.

in•co•her•ence [,ɪnkou'hirəns] *n.* **1** a failure to stick together; looseness. **2** a lack of logical connection. **3** disconnected thought or speech: *the incoherence of a drunken person.* Also, **incoherency.**

in•co•her•ent [,ɪnkou'hirənt] *adj.* **1** not sticking together. **2** disconnected; confused: *incoherent speech.*
—,in•co'her•ent•ly, *adv.*

in•com•bus•ti•bil•i•ty [,ɪnkəm,bʌstə'bɪləti] *n.* the quality of being incombustible.

in•com•bus•ti•ble [,ɪnkəm'bʌstəbəl] *adj., n.* *—adj.* that cannot be burned; fireproof.
—n. an incombustible substance. ⟨late ME < ML *incombustibil(is)*⟩

in•come ['ɪnkʌm] *n.* what comes in from property, business, work, etc.; receipts; returns. A person's yearly income is all the money that he or she gets in a year. ⟨ME, literally, that which has come in, n. use of *incomen* (pp. of *income* to come in), OE *incumen*⟩

income account or **statement** **1** an account kept for one item of income. **2** a statement of income and expenditures at the end of the fiscal year.

income tax a government tax on a person's income.

in•com•ing ['ɪn,kʌmɪŋ] *adj., n.* *—adj.* coming in: *The incoming tenant will pay a higher rent.*
—n. **1** a coming in: *the incoming of the tide.* **2 incomings,** *pl.* revenue.

in•com•men•su•ra•bil•i•ty [,ɪnkə,mɛnʃərə'bɪləti] *or* [,ɪnkə,mɛnsərə'bɪləti] *n.* the quality of being incommensurable; absence of a common measure or standard of comparison.

in•com•men•su•ra•ble [,ɪnkə'mɛnʃərəbəl] or [,ɪnkə'mɛnsərəbəl] *adj.* **1** that cannot be compared because not measurable in the same units or by the same scale: *Money and human life are incommensurable.* **2** *Mathematics.* having no common integral divisor except 1. *Example*: 8, 17, and 11.
—,in•com'men•su•ra•bly, *adv.*

in•com•men•su•rate [,ɪnkə'mɛnʃərɪt] *or* [,ɪnkə'mɛnsərɪt] *adj.* **1** not in proportion; not adequate: *strength incommensurate to a task.* **2** having no common measure; incommensurable.
—,in•com'men•su•rate•ly, *adv.*

in•com•mode [,ɪnkə'moud] *v.* **-mod•ed, -mod•ing. 1** inconvenience; trouble. **2** impede; hinder. ⟨< L *incommodare* < *incommodus* < *in-* not + *commodus* convenient⟩

in•com•mo•di•ous [,ɪnkə'moudiəs] *adj.* **1** not roomy enough. **2** inconvenient; uncomfortable. **—,in•com'mo•di•ous•ly,** *adv.* **—,in•com'mo•di•ous•ness,** *n.*

in•com•mu•ni•ca•ble [,ɪnkə'mjunəkəbəl] *adj.* not capable of being communicated or told. **—,in•com'mu•ni•ca•bly,** *adv.* **—,in•com,mu•ni•ca'bil•i•ty,** *n.*

in•com•mu•ni•ca•do [,ɪnkə,mjunə'kɑdou] *adj.* deprived of or refusing communication with others: *The prisoner was being held incommunicado.* ⟨< Sp. *incomunicado*⟩

in•com•mu•ni•ca•tive [,ɪnkə'mjunəkətɪv] *adj.* **1** reserved in behaviour. **2** uncommunicative.

in•com•mu•ta•ble [,ɪnkə'mjutəbəl] *adj.* **1** not able to be exchanged. **2** not able to be altered.

in•com•pact [,ɪnkəm'pækt] *adj.* not compact.

in•com•pa•ra•ble [ɪn'kɒmpərəbəl] *or* [,ɪnkəm'pɛrəbəl] *adj.* **1** without equal; matchless: *Helen of Troy had incomparable beauty.* **2** not to be compared; unsuitable for comparison. ⟨ME

< L *incomparibil(is)*⟩ **—in'com•pa•ra•bly,** *adv.* **—in,com•pa•ra'bil•i•ty** or **in'com•par•a•ble•ness,** *n.*
☛ *Pronun.* See note at COMPARABLE.

in•com•pat•i•bil•i•ty [,ɪnkəm,pætə'bɪləti] *n., pl.* **-ties. 1** the quality of being incompatible; a lack of harmony. **2** an incompatible thing, quality, etc. **3** *Medicine.* an antigenic difference between individuals that leads to an immune response to transfused cells or grafted tissue.

in•com•pat•i•ble [,ɪnkəm'pætəbəl] *adj., n. —adj.* **1** not able to live or act together peaceably; opposed in character: *My cat and my dog are incompatible.* **2** inconsistent: *Late hours are incompatible with health.* **3** of or denoting drugs, blood types, etc. that cannot be combined or used together because of undesirable chemical or physiological reactions. **4** of positions or ranks, unable to be held simultaneously by one person. **5** of two propositions, unable to be true simultaneously.
—n. an incompatible person or thing. **—,in•com'pat•i•bly,** *adv.*

in•com•pe•tence [ɪn'kɒmpətəns] *n.* **1** a lack of ability, power, or fitness. **2** a lack of legal qualification. Also, **incompetency.**

in•com•pe•tent [ɪn'kɒmpətənt] *adj., n. —adj.* **1** not competent; lacking ability, power, or fitness. **2** not legally qualified.
—n. an incompetent person. ⟨< LL *incompetent-, incompetens* unequal to⟩ **—in'com•pe•tent•ly,** *adv.*

in•com•plete [,ɪnkəm'plit] *adj., n. —adj.* not complete; lacking some part; unfinished.
—n. something incomplete, as an unfinished course of studies: *I took an incomplete in English.* ⟨< LL *incompletus*⟩ **—,in•com'plete•ness** or **,in•com'ple•tion,** *n.*

in•com•plete•ly [,ɪnkəm'plitli] *adv.* not fully; imperfectly.

in•com•pli•ant [,ɪnkəm'plaɪənt] *adj.* unyielding; not compliant. **—,in•com'pli•ant•ly,** *adv.* **—,in•com'pli•ance,** *n.*

in•com•pre•hen•si•ble [,ɪnkɒmprɪ'hɛnsəbəl] *adj.* impossible to understand. ⟨ME < L *incomprehensibil(is)*⟩ **—,in•com•pre,hen•si'bil•i•ty,** *n.* **—,in•com•pre'hen•si•bly,** *adv.*

in•com•pre•hen•sion [,ɪnkɒmprɪ'hɛnʃən] *n.* lack of comprehension.

in•com•pre•hen•sive [,ɪnkɒmprɪ'hɛnsɪv] *adj.* limited in scope. **—,in•com•pre'hen•sive•ly,** *adv.*

in•com•press•i•ble [,ɪnkəm'prɛsəbəl] *adj.* not capable of being squeezed into a smaller size. **—,in•com,press•i'bil•i•ty,** *n.*

in•com•put•a•ble [,ɪnkəm'pjutəbəl] *adj.* not able to be calculated.

in•con•ceiv•a•ble [,ɪnkən'sivəbəl] *adj.* **1** impossible to imagine: *A circle without a centre is inconceivable.* **2** hard to believe; incredible: *The new jet can travel at an inconceivable speed.* **—,in•con,ceiv•a'bil•i•ty,** *n.* **—,in•con'ceiv•a•ble•ness,** *n.*

in•con•ceiv•a•bly [,ɪnkən'sivəbli] *adv.* **1** in an inconceivable manner. **2** to an inconceivable degree.

in•con•clu•sive [,ɪnkən'klusɪv] *adj.* not convincing; not settling or deciding something doubtful: *The jury found the evidence against the prisoner inconclusive and acquitted her.* **—,in•con'clu•sive•ly,** *adv.* **—,in•con'clu•sive•ness,** *n.*

in•con•dens•a•ble [,ɪnkən'dɛnsəbəl] *adj.* not able to be condensed. **—,in•con,dens•a'bil•i•ty,** *n.*

in•con•form•i•ty [,ɪnkən'fɔrməti] *n.* non-conformity.

in•con•gru•ent [ɪn'kɒŋgruənt] *adj.* **1** not congruent. **2** incongruous. **—in'con•gru•ent•ly,** *adv.* **—in'con•gru•ence,** *n.*

in•con•gru•i•ty [,ɪnkən'gruəti] *n., pl.* **-ties. 1** unfitness; inappropriateness; a being out of place. **2** a lack of agreement or harmony; inconsistency. **3** something that is incongruous.

in•con•gru•ous [ɪn'kɒŋgruəs] *adj.* **1** out of keeping; not appropriate; out of place: *Heavy walking shoes would be incongruous with evening dress.* **2** lacking in agreement or harmony; not consistent. **3** made up of disparate parts. ⟨< L *incongruus*⟩ **—in'con•gru•ous•ly,** *adv.* **—in'con•gru•ous•ness,** *n.*

in•con•nu ['ɪnkə,nju] *or* ['ɪnkə,nu] *n., pl.* **-nu** or **-nus.** *Cdn.* a whitefish (*Stenodus leucichthys*) of northwestern North America and parts of northern Asia, generally valued as a food fish. ⟨< F *inconnu* unknown, because little known to anglers⟩

in•con•se•quence [ɪn'kɒnsə,kwɛns] *or* [ɪn'kɒnsəkwəns] *n.* a lack of logic or logical sequence; irrelevance; quality of being inconsequent.

in•con•se•quent [ɪn'kɒnsə,kwɛnt] or [ɪn'kɒnsəkwənt] *adj.* **1** not logical; not logically connected: *an inconsequent argument.* **2** not to the point; off the subject: *an inconsequent remark.* **3** not being a result. **4** apt to think or talk without logical connection. ⟨< LL *inconsequent-* (stem of *inconsequens*) not following⟩ **—in'con•se,quent•ly,** *adv.*

in•con•se•quen•tial [,ɪnkɒnsə'kwɛnʃəl] *or* [ɪn,kɒnsə'kwɛnʃəl] *adj., n. —adj.* **1** unimportant; trifling. **2** inconsequent.
—n. something trivial. **—,in•con•se'quen•tial•ly,** *adv.* **—in,con•se,quen•ti'al•i•ty,** *n.*

in•con•sid•er•a•ble [,ɪnkən'sɪdərəbəl] *adj.* not worthy of consideration; not important. **—,in•con'sid•er•a•ble•ness,** *n.* **—,in•con'sid•er•a•bly,** *adv.*

in•con•sid•er•ate [,ɪnkən'sɪdərɪt] *adj.* **1** not thoughtful of the rights and feelings of others. **2** thoughtless; heedless. ⟨late ME < L *inconsiderat(us)*⟩ **—,in•con'sid•er•ate•ly,** *adv.* **—,in•con'sid•er•ate•ness,** *n.*

in•con•sist•en•cy [,ɪnkən'sɪstənsi] *n., pl.* **-cies. 1** a lack of agreement or harmony; variance. **2** a failure to keep to the same principles, course of action, etc.; changeableness. **3** the thing, act, etc. that is inconsistent. Also, **inconsistence.**

in•con•sist•ent [,ɪnkən'sɪstənt] *adj.* **1** lacking in agreement or harmony; at variance: *The police officer's accepting the bribe was inconsistent with her reputation for honesty.* **2** lacking harmony between its different parts; not uniform. **3** failing to keep to the same principles, course of action, etc.; changeable: *An inconsistent person's opinions change frequently without reason.* **—,in•con'sist•ent•ly,** *adv.*

inconsistent equations *Mathematics.* two or more equations not satisfied by any one set of values of the variables.

in•con•sol•a•ble [,ɪnkən'souləbəl] *adj.* not to be comforted; broken-hearted. ⟨< L *inconsolabil(is)*⟩ **—,in•con'sol•a•bly,** *adv.* **—,in•con,sol•a'bil•i•ty** or **,in•con'sol•a•ble•ness,** *n.*

in•con•so•nant [ɪn'kɒnsənənt] *adj.* not harmonious; not in agreement or accord. **—in'con•so•nant•ly,** *adv.* **—in'con•so•nance,** *n.*

in•con•spic•u•ous [,ɪnkən'spɪkjuəs] *adj.* not conspicuous; attracting little or no attention. ⟨< LL *inconspicuus*⟩ **—,in•con'spic•u•ous•ly,** *adv.* **—,in•con'spic•u•ous•ness,** *n.*

in•con•stant [ɪn'kɒnstənt] *adj.* **1** not constant; changeable; fickle. **2** variable. ⟨ME < L *inconstant-* (stem of *inconstans*) changeable⟩ **—in'con•stan•cy,** *n.* **—in'con•stant•ly,** *adv.*

in•con•su•ma•ble [,ɪnkən'sjuməbəl] *or* [,ɪnkən'suməbəl] *adj.* not able to be consumed.

in•con•test•a•ble [ɪnkən'tɛstəbəl] *adj.* not to be disputed; unquestionable. **—,in•con'test•a•bly,** *adv.* **—,in•con,test•a'bil•i•ty,** *n.*

in•con•ti•nent [ɪn'kɒntənənt] *adj.* **1** *Medicine.* unable to control natural discharges or evacuations. **2** without self-restraint. **3** not chaste; licentious. **4** incapable of holding back (*used with* **of**): *incontinent of tears.* ⟨< L *incontinens, -entis*⟩ **—in'con•ti•nence,** *n.* **—in'con•ti•nent•ly,** *adv.*

in•con•trol•la•ble [,ɪnkən'trouləbəl] *adj.* uncontrollable.

in•con•tro•vert•i•ble [,ɪnkɒntrə'vɜrtəbəl] *adj.* that cannot be disputed; too clear or certain to be argued about; unquestionable. **—,in•con•tro'vert•i•bly,** *adv.* **—in,con•tro,vert•i'bil•i•ty,** *n.*

in•con•ven•ience *n.* [,ɪnkən'vinjəns] *n., v.* **-ienced, -ienc•ing.** *—n.* **1** lack of convenience or ease; trouble; bother. **2** a cause of trouble, difficulty, or bother.
—v. cause trouble, difficulty, etc. to: *Would it inconvenience you to carry this package for me?*

in•con•ven•ient [,ɪnkən'vinjənt] *adj.* not convenient; causing trouble, difficulty, or bother; troublesome. ⟨< L *inconveniens, -entis*⟩ **—,in•con'ven•ient•ly,** *adv.*

in•con•vert•i•ble [,ɪnkən'vɜrtəbəl] *adj.* not convertible; incapable of being converted or exchanged: *Paper money is inconvertible when it cannot be exchanged for gold or silver.* ⟨< LL *inconvertibil(is)* not alterable⟩ **—,in•con,vert•i'bil•i•ty,** *n.*

in•con•vinc•i•ble [,ɪnkən'vɪnsəbəl] *adj.* not able to be convinced.

in•co–or•di•nate [,ɪnkou 'ɔrdənɪt] *adj.* **1** not of the same order. **2** not co-ordinate.

in•co–or•din•a•tion [,ɪnkou ,ɔrdə'neiʃən] *n.* lack of co-ordination.

in•cor•por•a•ble [ɪn'kɔrpərəbəl] *adj.* able to be incorporated.

in•cor•po•rate *v.* [ɪn'kɔrpə,reit]; *adj.* [ɪn'kɔrpərɪt] *v.* **-rat•ed, -rat•ing;** *adj. —v.* **1** make (something) a part of something else; join or combine (something) with something else: *We shall*

incorporate your suggestion into this new plan. **2** form into a corporation: *When the business became large, the owners incorporated it.* **3** form a corporation: *Let's incorporate with them for a better capital base.* **4** unite or combine so as to form one body. **5** embody; give material form to: *to incorporate one's thoughts in an article.*
—adj. united; combined; incorporated. ⟨< L *incorporare* < *in-* into + *corpus, -poris* body⟩

in•cor•po•rat•ed [ɪn'kɔrpə,reitɪd] *adj., v. —adj.* being a corporation.
—v. pt. and pp. of INCORPORATE.

in•cor•po•ra•tion [ɪn,kɔrpə'reiʃən] *n.* **1** the act of incorporating: *The incorporation of air bubbles in the glass spoiled it.* **2** the state of being incorporated. Incorporation gives a company the power to act as one person.

in•cor•po•ra•tor [ɪn'kɔrpə,reitər] *n.* **1** a person who incorporates. **2** one of the original members of a corporation.

in•cor•po•re•al [,ɪnkɔr'pɔriəl] *adj.* **1** not made of any material substance; spiritual. **2** *Law.* not tangible but existing as a right. ⟨< LL *incorpore(us)* + E *-al*[1]⟩ **—,in•cor'po•re•al•ly,** *adv.* **—in,cor•po're•i•ty** [ɪn,kɔrpə'riiti] or **,in•cor,po•re'al•i•ty,** *n.*

in•cor•rect [,ɪnkə'rɛkt] *adj.* **1** containing errors or mistakes; wrong; faulty. **2** not proper. ⟨ME < L *incorrect(us)* not corrected⟩ **—,in•cor'rect•ly,** *adv.* **—,in•cor'rect•ness,** *n.*

in•cor•ri•gi•ble [ɪn'kɔrədʒəbəl] *adj., n. —adj.* **1** so firmly fixed (in bad ways, a bad habit, etc.) that nothing else can be expected: *an incorrigible liar.* **2** of such a habit, so fixed that it cannot be changed or cured: *an incorrigible habit of wrinkling one's nose.*
—n. an incorrigible person. ⟨ME < LL *incorrigibil(is)*⟩
—in,cor•ri•gi'bil•i•ty, *n.* **—in'cor•ri•gi•bly,** *adv.*
—in'cor•ri•gi•ble•ness, *n.*

in•cor•rupt [,ɪnkə'rʌpt] *adj.* **1** not corruptible; honest. **2** free from decay; sound. **3** not marred by errors, alterations, etc.: *The manuscript appeared to be an incorrupt text of Chaucer's original poem.* **4** not immoral. ⟨ME < L *incorrupt(us)* unspoiled⟩

in•cor•rupt•i•ble [,ɪnkə'rʌptəbəl] *adj.* **1** not to be corrupted; honest: *The incorruptible judge could not be bribed.* **2** not capable of decay: *Diamonds are incorruptible.* **—,in•cor•'rupt•i•bly,** *adv.*
—,in•cor,rup•ti'bil•i•ty, *n.*

in•cras•sate [ɪn'kræseit] *v.* **-at•ed, -at•ing.** *Pharmacology.* thicken (a liquid). ⟨< LL *incrassat(us)* made thick or stout, pp. of *incrassare*⟩ **—,in•cras'sa•tion,** *n.* **—in'cras•sa•tive,** *adj.*

in•crease *v.* [ɪn'kris]; *n.* ['ɪnkris] *v.* **-creased, -creas•ing;** *n. —v.* **1** make or become greater in size, number, degree, etc.: *to increase the speed of a car. The world leader sought to increase her power through tactical manoeuvres and diplomacy.* **2** multiply by propagation: *The flowers will increase every year if you don't thin them out.*
—n. **1** a gain in size, numbers, etc.; growth; multiplication by propagation. **2** an addition; the amount of increasing. **3** the production of offspring. **4** offspring.
on the increase, increasing: *The movement of people to the cities is on the increase.* ⟨ME < AF *encress-*, var. of OF *encreiss-*, a stem of *encreistre* < L *increscere* < *in-* in + *crescere* grow⟩
—in'creas•er, *n.*

☛ *Syn. v.* **1, 2. Increase,** ENLARGE, AUGMENT = make or become greater. **Increase** = make or grow greater in amount, number, wealth, power, etc.: *His weight has increased by 10 kg.* **Enlarge** = make or become larger, chiefly in size, extent, or capacity: *They enlarged the school auditorium.* **Augment,** more formal, means 'increase by adding amounts or sums to what there is': *Many teachers do outside work to augment their salaries.*

in•creas•ing•ly [ɪn'krisɪŋli] *adv.* more and more.
☛ *Usage.* Careful writers avoid using **increasingly** with a comparative. Write 'increasingly active', not 'increasingly more active'.

in•cre•ate [,ɪnkri'eit] *or* ['ɪnkri,eit] *adj.* of a divinity, existing without creation. ⟨ME *increat* < LL *increat(us)* not made⟩

in•cred•i•ble [ɪn'krɛdəbəl] *adj.* **1** unbelievable: *If the story had not been so well documented, it would have been incredible.* **2** *Informal.* extraordinary; so unusual as to seem impossible: *Her last race was incredible; I've never seen anything like it.* ⟨ME < L *incredibil(is)*⟩ **—in,cred•i'bil•i•ty,** *n.* **—in'cred•i•ble•ness,** *n.*
—in'cred•i•bly, *adv.*
☛ *Usage.* Do not confuse **incredible** and INCREDULOUS. **Incredible** = unbelievable; **incredulous** = not ready to believe or showing a lack or belief: *Her story of having seen a ghost seemed incredible to her family. If they are incredulous, show them the evidence.*

in•cre•du•li•ty [,ɪnkrə'djuləti] *or* [,ɪnkrə'duləti] *n.* lack of belief; doubt. ⟨< L *incredulitas*⟩

in•cred•u•lous [ɪn'krɛdʒələs] *or* [ɪn'krɛdjələs] *adj.* **1** not willing, able, or likely to believe; not credulous; doubting: *Most people are incredulous about ghosts and witches.* **2** showing a lack of belief: *an incredulous smile.* ⟨< L *incredulus*⟩
—in'cred•u•lous•ly, *adv.* **—in'cred•u•lous•ness,** *n.*
☛ *Usage.* See note at INCREDIBLE.

in•cre•ment *n.* ['ɪnkrəmənt] *or* ['ɪŋkrəmənt]; *v.* ['ɪnkrə,mɛnt] *or* ['ɪŋkrə,mɛnt] *n., v. —n.* **1** an increase; growth. **2** the amount by which something increases. **3** one of a series of usually small increases: *an annual increment in pay.* **4** *Mathematics.* **a** the amount, positive or negative, by which the value of an independent variable changes. **b** the amount by which the dependent function changes as a result. Compare DECREMENT.
—v. increase by small stages. ⟨< L *incrementum* < *increscere.* See INCREASE.⟩ **—,in•cre'ment•al,** *adj.*

in•cres•cent [ɪn'krɛsənt] *adj.* increasing or waxing, as the moon. ⟨< L *increscent-* (stem of *increscens* growing, ppr. of *increscere*) < *in-* in + *cresc-* grow + *-ent*⟩ **—in'cres•cence,** *n.*

in•crim•i•nate [ɪn'krɪmə,neit] *v.* **-nat•ed, -nat•ing. 1** accuse of a crime; show to be guilty. **2** implicate: *In her confession the thief incriminated two of her accomplices.* ⟨< LL *incriminare* < L *in-* against + *crimen, -minis* charge⟩ **—in,crim•i'na•tion,** *n.*
—in'crim•i,na•tor, *n.*

in•crim•i•na•to•ry [ɪn'krɪmənə,tɔri] *adj.* tending to incriminate.

in•crust [ɪn'krʌst] *v.* encrust. **—,in•crus'ta•tion,** *n.*

in•cu•bate ['ɪnkjə,beit] *or* ['ɪŋkjə,beit] *v.* **-bat•ed, -bat•ing. 1** sit on (eggs, etc.) in order to hatch them; brood. **2** keep (an egg, embryo, etc.) under conditions that will enable it to hatch, develop, etc. **3** go through incubation: *The eggs are incubating.* **4** of a disease, go through INCUBATION (def. 2). **5** gradually develop or cause to develop or take form: *The writer's last great novel was incubating in her mind for several years.* ⟨< L *incubare* < *in-* on + *cubare* lie⟩ **—'in•cu,ba•tive,** *adj.*

in•cu•ba•tion [,ɪnkjə'beiʃən] *or* [,ɪŋkjə'beiʃən] *n.* **1** an incubating or being incubated. **2** the stage of a disease from the time of infection until the appearance of the first symptoms.
—,in•cu'ba•tion•al, *adj.*

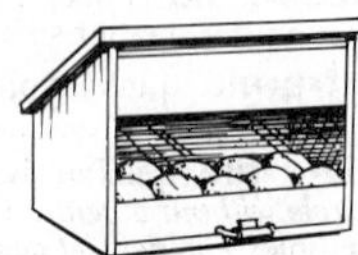

Two types of incubator: left, an incubator for a baby in a hospital; right, an incubator for chicken eggs

in•cu•ba•tor ['ɪnkjə,beitər] *or* ['ɪŋkjə,beitər] *n.* **1** an apparatus for keeping eggs warm so that they will hatch. It has a box or chamber that can be kept at a certain temperature. **2** a similar apparatus for protecting babies born very small or prematurely. **3** an apparatus in which bacterial cultures are developed. **4** any person who or thing that incubates: *the incubator of separatism.* ⟨< L⟩

in•cu•bus ['ɪnkjəbəs] *or* ['ɪŋkjəbəs] *n., pl.* **-bi** [-,bai] or [-,bi] or **-bus•es. 1** an evil spirit supposed, in medieval times, to descend upon sleeping persons, especially women. Compare SUCCUBUS. **2** nightmare. **3** an oppressive or burdensome thing: *This debt will be an incubus until I have paid it.* ⟨< Med.L (def. 1), LL (def. 2) < L *incubare* < *in-* on + *cubare* lie⟩

in•cu•des [ɪn'kjudiz] *n.* pl. of INCUS.

in•cul•cate [ɪn'kʌlkeit] *or* ['ɪnkʌl,keit] *v.* **-cat•ed, -cat•ing.** impress by repetition; teach persistently. ⟨< L *inculcare,* originally, trample in, ult. < *in-* in + *calx, calcis* heel⟩
—in'cul•ca•tor, *n.*

in•cul•ca•tion [,ɪnkʌl'keiʃən] *n.* the act or process of impressing principles, etc. on the mind by persistent urging or teaching.

in•culp•a•ble [ɪn'kʌlpəbəl] *adj.* blameless; guiltless; not culpable. ⟨late ME < LL *inculpabil(is)*⟩ **—in,cul•pa'bil•i•ty,** *n.*
—in'cul•pa•bly, *adv.*

in•cul•pate [ɪn'kʌlpeit] *or* ['ɪnkʌl,peit] *v.* **-pat•ed, -pat•ing. 1** blame; accuse. **2** involve in responsibility for wrongdoing;

incriminate. ⟨< LL *inculpare* < L *in-* in + *culpa* blame⟩
—in'cul•pa,to•ry, *adj.* **—,in•cul'pa•tion,** *n.*

in•cult [ɪn'kʌlt] *adj. Archaic.* **1** uncultivated; untilled. **2** wild; unrefined. ⟨< L *incult(us)* < *in-* + *cultus* tilled (pp. of *colere*)⟩

in•cum•ben•cy [ɪn'kʌmbənsi] *n., pl.* **-cies. 1** the holding of an office, position, etc. and performance of its duties; term of office: *During my aunt's incumbency as mayor, the city prospered.* **2** an obligation.

in•cum•bent [ɪn'kʌmbənt] *adj., n. —adj.* **1** lying, leaning, or pressing *(on).* **2** resting (on a person) as a duty: *She felt it incumbent upon her to answer the letter at once.* **3** currently holding office: *the incumbent minister.* **4** *Poetic.* overhanging.
—n. a person holding an office, position, church living, etc. ⟨< L *incumbens, -entis*, ppr. of *incumbere* lie down on⟩

in•cum•ber [ɪn'kʌmbər] *v.* encumber.

in•cum•brance [ɪn'kʌmbrəns] *n.* encumbrance.

in•cu•nab•u•lum [,ɪnkjə'næbjələm] *n., pl.* **-la** [-lə]. **1** the earliest stages or first traces of anything; beginnings. **2** a book printed before the year 1500. ⟨< L *incunabula* swaddling clothes < *cunae* cradle⟩ **—,in•cu'nab•u•lar,** *adj.*

in•cur [ɪn'kɜr] *v.* **-curred, -cur•ring. 1** run into or meet with (something unpleasant): *to incur many expenses. The explorers incurred great danger when they tried to cross the rapids.* **2** bring on oneself: *to incur someone's anger.* ⟨< L *incurrere* < *in-* upon + *currere* run⟩

in•cur•a•ble [ɪn'kjʊrəbəl] *adj., n. —adj.* not capable of being cured or remedied: *an incurable invalid.*
—n. a person having an incurable disease. ⟨ME < LL *incurabil(is)*⟩ **—in,cur•a'bil•i•ty,** *n.* **—in'cur•a•bly,** *adv.*

in•cu•ri•ous [ɪn'kjʊriəs] *adj.* **1** not curious; inattentive; unobservant; indifferent. **2** deficient in interest or novelty. ⟨< L *incurios(us)*⟩ **—in'cu•ri•ous•ly,** *adv.* **—,in•cu•ri'os•i•ty** or **in'cu•ri•ous•ness,** *n.*

in•cur•rence [ɪn'kɜrəns] *n.* the act of incurring, bringing on, or subjecting oneself to something.

in•cur•rent [ɪn'kɜrənt] *adj.* carrying on or relating to an inward flow. ⟨< L *incurrent-* stem of *incurrens*), ppr. of *incurrere*⟩

in•cur•sion [ɪn'kɜrʒən] *or* [ɪn'kɜrʃən] *n.* **1** an invasion; raid; sudden attack: *The pirates made incursions along the coast.* **2** a running or flowing in: *Dikes protected the lowland from incursions of the sea.* ⟨ME < L *incursio, -onis* < *incurrere.* See INCUR.⟩

in•cur•sive [ɪn'kɜrsɪv] *adj.* making incursions.

in•curv•ate *adj.* [ɪn'kɜr,veit] *or* [ɪn'kɜrvɪt]; *v.* [ɪn'kɜr,veit] *adj., v.* **-at•ed, -at•ing.** *—adj.* curved, especially inward.
—v. curve inward. ⟨< L *incurvatus*, pp. of *incurvare*⟩
—,in•curv'a•tion, *n.* **—in'curv•a•ture,** *n.*

in•curve *n.* ['ɪn,kɜrv]; *v.* [ɪn'kɜrv] *n., v.* **-curved, -curv•ing.**
—n. Baseball. a pitch that curves toward the batter.
—v. curve in. ⟨< L *incurvare* to bend in⟩

in•cus ['ɪŋkəs] *n., pl.* **in•cu•des** [ɪn'kjudiz]. *Anatomy.* the middle one of a chain of three small bones in the middle ear. The incus is shaped somewhat like an anvil. See EAR[1] for picture. ⟨< L *incus, -udis* anvil⟩

in•cuse [ɪn'kjuz] *or* [ɪn'kjus] *v.* **-cused, -cus•ing;** *adj., n. —v.* hammer (a design) on (metal).
—adj. hammered in.
—n. a stamped or hammered figure. ⟨< L *incusus* forged with a hammer (pp. of *incudere*) < *in-* + *cud-* beat + *-tus*⟩

ind. 1 independent. **2** indicative. **3** industrial. **4** index. **5** indirect. **6** indigo.

Ind [ɪnd] *n. Poetic.* **1** India. **2** Indies.

Ind. 1 India; Indian. **2** *Politics.* Independent.

in•da•ba [ɪn'dɑbɑ] *n.* a conference with or between South African native peoples. ⟨< Zulu⟩

in•da•mine ['ɪndə,min] *n. Chemistry.* any of a series of basic organic compounds used as dyes. ⟨< *ind(igo)* + *amine*⟩

in•dap•a•mide [ɪn'dæpə,maɪd] *n.* a drug used to lower blood pressure.

in•debt•ed [ɪn'dɛtɪd] *adj.* in debt; obliged; owing money or gratitude: *We are indebted to scientists for many of our comforts.*

in•debt•ed•ness [ɪn'dɛtɪdnɪs] *n.* **1** the condition of being in debt. **2** the amount owed; debts.

in•de•cen•cy [ɪn'disənsi] *n., pl.* **-cies. 1** lack of decency; the quality of being indecent. **2** an indecent act or word. ⟨< L *indecentia*⟩

in•de•cent [ɪn'disənt] *adj.* not decent; unseemly, improper, or morally offensive: *an indecent lack of gratitude, an indecent haste to sell off his father's belongings.* ⟨ME < L *indecent-* (stem of *indecens*) unseemly⟩ **—in'de•cent•ly,** *adv.*
☛ *Syn.* See note at IMPROPER.

in•de•cid•u•ous [,ɪndɪ'sɪdʒuəs] *adj.* **1** of trees, evergreen. **2** of leaves, not deciduous.

in•de•ci•pher•a•ble [,ɪndɪ'səifərəbəl] *adj.* incapable of being deciphered; illegible. **—,in•de,ci•pher•a'bil•i•ty,** *n.* **—,in•de'ci•pher•a•bly,** *adv.*

in•de•ci•sion [,ɪndɪ'sɪʒən] *n.* lack of decision; delay or hesitation; a tendency to put off deciding or to change one's mind.

in•de•ci•sive [,ɪndɪ'səisɪv] *adj.* **1** having the habit of hesitating and putting off decisions. **2** not deciding or settling the matter: *an indecisive battle, an indecisive answer.*
—,in•de'ci•sive•ly, *adv.* **—,in•de'ci•sive•ness,** *n.*

in•de•clin•a•ble [,ɪndɪ'klaɪnəbəl] *adj. Grammar.* of nouns, adjectives, pronouns, and articles, having the same form in all grammatical constructions. *None* is an indeclinable pronoun. ⟨ME < L *indeclinabilis* unchangeable⟩
—,in•de'clin•a•ble•ness, *n.*

in•de•com•pos•a•ble [,ɪndikəm'pouzəbəl] *adj.* not able to be split into components; incapable of being decomposed.

in•dec•o•rous [ɪn'dɛkərəs] *adj.* not suitable; improper; unseemly. ⟨< L *indecorus*⟩ **—in'dec•o•rous•ly,** *adv.*
—in'dec•o•rous•ness, *n.*

in•de•co•rum [,ɪndɪ'kɔrəm] *n.* **1** lack of decorum. **2** improper behaviour, speech, dress, etc. ⟨< L *indecorum*, originally neut. of *indecorus* indecorous⟩

in•deed [ɪn'did] *adv., interj. —adv.* in fact; really; truly; surely: *War is indeed terrible.*
—interj. an expression of surprise, doubt, contempt, sarcasm, etc.: *Indeed! I would not have done it.*

indef. indefinite.

in•de•fat•i•ga•ble [,ɪndɪ'fætəgəbəl] *adj.* never getting tired or giving up; tireless. ⟨< L *indefatigabilis* < *in-* not + *defatigare* tire out < *de-* completely + *fatigare* tire⟩
—,in•de,fat•i•ga'bil•i•ty, *n.* **—,in•de'fat•i•ga•bly,** *adv.*

in•de•fea•si•ble [,ɪndɪ'fizəbəl] *adj.* not to be annulled or made void: *Kings were once believed to have an indefeasible right to rule.* ⟨< *in-*[1] + *defeasible* that may be annulled < AF *defeasible* < OF *desfaire* undo < *des-* apart + *faire* < L *facere* do⟩
—,in•de,fea•si'bil•i•ty, *n.* **—,in•de'fea•si•bly,** *adv.*

in•de•fect•i•ble [,ɪndɪ'fɛktəbəl] *adj.* **1** that does not decay or deteriorate. **2** flawless. **—,in•de'fect•i•bly,** *adv.*
—,in•de,fect•i'bil•i•ty, *n.*

in•de•fen•si•ble [,ɪndɪ'fɛnsəbəl] *adj.* **1** that cannot be defended: *an indefensible island.* **2** not justifiable: *an indefensible lie.* **—,in•de'fen•si•ble•ness,** *n.* **—,in•de'fen•si•bly,** *adv.*
—,in•de,fen•si'bil•i•ty, *n.*

in•de•fin•a•ble [,ɪndɪ'faɪnəbəl] *adj.* that cannot be defined.
—,in•de'fin•a•ble•ness, *n.* **—,in•de'fin•a•bly,** *adv.*
—,in•de,fin•a'bil•i•ty, *n.*

in•def•i•nite [ɪn'dɛfənɪt] *adj.* **1** not clearly defined; not precise; vague: *"Maybe" is a very indefinite answer.* **2** not limited: *We have an indefinite time to finish this work.* **3** *Grammar.* not specifying precisely. An indefinite adjective, pronoun, etc. does not determine the person, thing, time, etc. to which it refers. *Some, any, many,* and *few* are indefinite pronouns. **4** *Botany.* of stamens, numerous. ⟨< L *indefinitus*⟩ **—in'def•i•nite•ly,** *adv.*
—in'def•i•nite•ness, *n.*

indefinite article *Grammar.* in English, either of the articles A or AN.
☛ *Usage.* **A, an.** *A dog* or *an animal* means *any dog* or *any animal*; *the dog* means *a certain or particular dog.*

indefinite integral *Mathematics.* the set of all functions of which a given function is the derivative.

in•de•his•cent [,ɪndɪ'hɪsənt] *adj. Botany.* not dehiscent; not opening at maturity: *Acorns are indehiscent fruits.* See FRUIT for picture. **—,in•de'his•cence,** *n.*

in•del•i•ble [ɪn'dɛləbəl] *adj.* **1** that cannot be erased or removed; permanent: *indelible ink. He left an indelible impression of greatness.* **2** capable of making an indelible mark: *an indelible pencil.* ⟨< L *indelebilis* < *in-* not + *delebilis* able to be destroyed < *delere* destroy⟩ **—in,del•i'bil•i•ty,** *n.* **—in'del•i•bly,** *adv.*

in•del•i•ca•cy [ɪn'dɛləkəsi] *n., pl.* **-cies. 1** lack of delicacy; a being indelicate. **2** an instance of vulgar language.

in•del•i•cate [ɪn'dɛləkɪt] *adj.* **1** not delicate; coarse; crude. **2** improper; immodest. **–in'del•i•cate•ly,** *adv.* **–in'del•i•cate•ness,** *n.*

in•dem•ni•fi•ca•tion [ɪn,dɛmnəfə'keiʃən] *n.* **1** an indemnifying or being indemnified. **2** a compensation; recompense.

in•dem•ni•fy [ɪn'dɛmnə,faɪ] *v.* **-fied, -fy•ing. 1** repay; make good; compensate for damage, loss, or expense incurred: *She promised to indemnify me for my losses.* **2** secure against damage or loss; insure. ⟨< L *indemnis* without loss (< *in-* not + *damnum* damage) + E *-fy*⟩ **–in'dem•ni,fi•er,** *n.*

in•dem•ni•ty [ɪn'dɛmnəti] *n., pl.* **-ties. 1** the payment for damage, loss, or expense incurred. Money demanded by a victorious nation at the end of a war as a condition of peace is an indemnity. **2** a security against damage or loss; insurance. **3** in Canada, the remuneration paid to an M.P. or M.L.A. ⟨< LL *indemnitas* < L *indemnis* without loss < *in-* not + *damnum* damage⟩

in•de•mon•stra•ble [,ɪndə'mɒnstrəbəl] *or* [ɪn'dɛmənstrəbəl] *adj.* not able to be proved or demonstrated. **–,in•de,mon•stra'bil•i•ty,** *n.* **–,in•de'mon•stra•bly,** *adv.*

in•dene ['ɪndin] *n. Chemistry.* a colourless liquid derived from coal tar. *Formula*: C_9H_8

in•dent[1] *v.* [ɪn'dɛnt]; *n.* ['ɪndɛnt] *or* [ɪn'dɛnt] *v., n.* *–v.* **1** make or form notches or jags in (an edge, line, border, etc.): *an indented coastline. The rim of the plate was indented.* **2** begin (a line) farther from the edge of a page than the other lines: *Some poets indent an opening line.* **3** order (goods, etc.) by an indent. **4** draw an order upon (a source of supply). **5** mortise. **6** cut (an agreement such as a contract) with a notched line so that each part can be identified as part of the whole.
–n. **1** a notch; indentation. **2** an official requisition for supplies. **3** an order for goods. ⟨ME < OF *endenter*, ult. < L *in-* in + *dens, dentis* tooth⟩

in•dent[2] [ɪn'dɛnt] *v.* **1** make a dent in; mark with a dent. **2** press in; stamp. ⟨< *in-*[2] + *dent*⟩

in•den•ta•tion [,ɪndɛn'teiʃən] *n.* **1** an indenting or being indented. **2** a dent; notch; cut. **3** indention.

in•den•tion [ɪn'dɛnʃən] *n.* **1** a beginning of a line farther from the edge of a page than the other lines. **2** the blank space left by doing this. **3** indentation.

in•den•ture [ɪn'dɛntʃər] *n., v.* **-tured, -tur•ing.** *–n.* **1** a written agreement. **2** Usually, **indentures,** *pl.* a contract by which a person is bound to serve someone else, especially as an apprentice. **3** indentation. **4** an inventory or list. **5** an agreement between the holders of bonds and the sellers.
–v. bind (a person) by indentures. ⟨ME < MF *endenteüre* indentation < OF *endenter.* See INDENT[1].⟩

in•de•pend•ence [,ɪndɪ'pɛndəns] *n.* **1** the quality or state of being independent; freedom from dependence on or control by another: *independence from one's parents. Jamaica and Trinidad and Tobago achieved independence within the Commonwealth in 1962.* **2** *Archaic.* enough income to live on; competence: *an independence from her rich uncle.*
☛ *Syn.* **1.** See note at FREEDOM.

Independence Day *U.S.* the Fourth of July, commemorating the anniversary of the U.S. Declaration of Independence in 1776.

in•de•pend•en•cy [,ɪndɪ'pɛndənsi] *n., pl.* **-cies. 1** independence. **2** an independent country, territory, etc.

in•de•pend•ent [,ɪndɪ'pɛndənt] *adj., n.* *–adj.* **1** done without help or input from others; not connected with others: *independent work, independent thinking.* **2** not needing, wanting, or getting help from others; not influenced by others; thinking or acting for oneself: *An independent person votes as she pleases.* **3** guiding, ruling, or governing oneself; not under another's rule: *Canada is an independent country within the British Commonwealth of Nations.* **4** not depending on others: *Miss Jones has an independent fortune.* **5** not resulting from another thing; not controlled or influenced by something else; separate; distinct. **6** objective; disinterested. **7** *Mathematics.* of a variable, that can be assigned any value.
independent of, apart from; without regard to: *independent of the feelings of others.*
–n. **1** a person who is independent in thought or behaviour, especially one who votes without regard to party. **2 Independent,** a person who stands for election to, or is an elected member of, a legislature without being a representative of any political party. **3** a business that operates without any outside management or control by another company or companies.

independent assortment See MENDEL'S LAWS.

independent clause *Grammar.* a grammatical construction consisting of a subject and predicate that can function alone as a sentence.

in•de•pend•ent•ly [,ɪndɪ'pɛndəntli] *adv.* in an independent manner.
independently of, apart from; without regard to.

independent variable *Mathematics.* in a statement, a variable whose value determines the value of the dependent variable. In $y = f(x)$, x is the independent variable.

in–depth ['ɪn 'dɛpθ] *adj.* going below the surface; deep; detailed: *an in-depth study.*

in•de•scrib•a•ble [,ɪndɪ'skraɪbəbəl] *adj.* that cannot be described; beyond description. **–,in•de'scrib•a•bly,** *adv.* **–,in•de'scrib•a•ble•ness,** *n.*

in•de•struct•i•ble [,ɪndɪ'strʌktəbəl] *adj.* that cannot be destroyed. **–,in•de,struct•i'bil•i•ty,** *n.* **–,in•de'struct•i•bly,** *adv.*

in•de•ter•mi•na•ble [,ɪndɪ'tɜrmənəbəl] *adj.* **1** not capable of being settled or decided. **2** not capable of being found out exactly. ⟨< LL *indeterminabilis*⟩ **–,in•de'ter•mi•na•bly,** *adv.*

in•de•ter•mi•na•cy [,ɪndɪ'tɜrmənəsi] *n.* the state or quality of being indeterminate.

indeterminacy principle *Physics.* the principle of quantum mechanics, formulated by Heisenberg, that the accurate measurement of one quantity produces inaccuracy in the other. Also, **uncertainty principle**.

in•de•ter•mi•nate [,ɪndɪ'tɜrmənɪt] *adj.* **1** not determined; not fixed; indefinite; vague. **2** *Botany.* not terminating in a flower. ⟨ME < LL *indeterminatus*⟩ **–,in•de'ter•mi•nate•ly,** *adv.*

in•de•ter•mi•na•tion [,ɪndɪ,tɜrmə'neiʃən] *n.* **1** a lack of determination. **2** an unsettled state.

in•de•ter•min•ism [,ɪndɪ'tɜrmə,nɪzəm] *n.* a philosophical doctrine that human actions are based on free will.

in•dex ['ɪndɛks] *n., pl.* **in•dex•es** or **in•di•ces** ['ɪndə,siz]; *v.* *–n.* **1** a list of the contents of a book, giving page, paragraph, or section references for each of the subjects discussed. The index is usually put at the end of a book and is arranged in alphabetical order. **2** something that points out or shows; a sign: *A person's face is often an index of his or her mood.* **3** INDEX FINGER. **4** a pointer: *A dial or scale usually has an index.* **5** *Printing.* a sign (☛) used to point out a particular note, paragraph, etc. **6** a number or formula expressing some property, ratio, etc. **7** *Mathematics.* **a** an exponent. **b** the number indicating the root. In $\sqrt[3]{764}$ the index is 3. **c** a number used to indicate a specific characteristic. **8** a number that indicates the relative amount, intensity, value, etc. of something: *the cost-of-living index, a pollution index.*
–v. **1** provide with an index. **2** enter in an index. **3** prepare an index. **4** serve to indicate. **5** make provision for (income, income tax, etc.) to be adjusted automatically according to changes in the cost of living: *an indexed pension.* ⟨< L *index*, originally, that which points out < *indicare.* See INDICATE.⟩ **–'in•dex•er,** *n.* **–in'dex•i•cal,** *adj.* **–in'dex•i•cal•ly,** *adv.* **–'in•dex•less,** *adj.*

in•dex•a•tion [,ɪndɛk'seiʃən] *n.* the act or policy of indexing income, taxes, etc.

Index Ex•pur•ga•to•ri•us [ɛks,pɜrgə'tɔriəs] formerly, a list of books that the Roman Catholic Church forbade its members to read until objectionable parts had been taken out or changed.

index finger the finger next to the thumb; forefinger.

index fossil a fossil used as an indication of the age of the area where it is found.

Index Li•bro•rum Pro•hib•i•to•rum [lɪ'brɔrəm prou,hɪbə'tɔrəm] formerly, a list of books that the Roman Catholic Church forbade its members to read.

In•dia ['ɪndiə] *n.* a large country in S Asia, forming, with other smaller, adjacent countries, a subcontinent.

India ink 1 a black pigment consisting of lampblack mixed with a binding material and moulded into sticks or cakes. India ink is made chiefly in China and Japan. **2** a liquid ink prepared from this pigment. Also, **Indian ink.**

In•di•a•man ['ɪndiəmən] *n., pl.* **-men.** formerly, a ship in the trade with India, especially a large one belonging to the East India Company.

In•di•an ['ɪndiən] *n., adj.* *–n.* **1** formerly, a member of any of the peoples who are the original inhabitants of the western hemisphere south of the Arctic coast region. The accepted name for original inhabitants of Canada on the North American continent is now First Nations peoples. **2** a member of any of the peoples who are the original inhabitants of: **a** the U.S.;

American Indian; Native American. **b** South or Central America. **3** *Informal.* any of the languages spoken by any of these peoples. **4** a native or inhabitant of the Republic of India. **5** a native or inhabitant of the Indian subcontinent.
—adj. **1** of or having to do with the original inhabitants of the U.S. or South or Central America or, formerly, Canada, or their languages. **2** of or having to do with the inhabitants of India or the Indian subcontinent. **3** made of corn or cornmeal: *Indian meal, Indian pudding.*

In•di•an•a [ˌɪndiˈænə] *n.* a northern state of the U.S.

Indian bread *Cdn.* **1** a strip of fat from the backbone of a buffalo, eaten fried and smoked. **2** a food prepared from tree moss by certain British Columbia First Nations people.

Indian club a bottle-shaped wooden club that is swung for exercise.

Indian corn *Cdn.* CORN[1] (defs. *n.* 1, 2).

Indian cu•cum•ber–root [ˈkjukʌmbər ˌrut] a Canadian wildflower of the lily family (*Medeola virginiana*), having pale yellow flowers.

Indian currant coralberry.

Indian Days *Cdn.* an exhibition during which First Nations people revive their customs, as traditional dress and dances, often in conjunction with a stampede or rodeo.

Indian devil *Cdn.* **1** the carcajou or wolverine. **2** the cougar. **3** a malevolent spirit; werewolf.

Indian dog *Cdn.* any of various breeds of dog found among the First Nations peoples.

Indian fig another name for the PRICKLY PEAR (*Opuntia polyacantha*), growing in arid regions of British Columbia.

Indian file SINGLE FILE.

Indian hall *Cdn.* formerly, a building or room where First Nations people bringing fur and other goods for sale were received.

Indian hemp **1** a North American dogbane (*Apocynum cannabinum*) having tough stem fibres that were used by First Nations and American Indian peoples to make cordage. **2** hemp.

Indian horse or **pony** *Cdn.* a smallish type of horse bred by the western First Nations and American Indian peoples; cayuse.

Indian ice cream *Cdn., B.C.* a pinkish, frothy substance having a somewhat bitter taste, made from beating soapberries.

Indian ink INDIA INK.

Indian licorice a vine of tropical Asia (*Abrus precatorius*), having poisonous seeds used as beads.

Indian mallow a plant (*Abutilon theophrasti*) with yellow flowers, native to S Asia.

Indian meal meal made from Indian corn; cornmeal.

Indian paintbrush *Cdn.* any of various plants (genus *Castilleja*) of the figwort family having spikes of flowers and showy, bright scarlet or orange leaves just below the flowers.

An Indian paintbrush

Indian pipe *Cdn.* a whitish or pinkish North American and Asian woodland plant (*Monotropa uniflora*) that lacks chlorophyl, getting its nourishment from the remains of dead plants, and that has scalelike leaves and a single drooping flower at the top of the stem, giving the plant the appearance of a pipe.

Indian pudding a baked pudding of cornmeal, molasses, and milk.

Indian red **1** an earth found in the Persian Gulf, used as a pigment. **2** iron oxide used as a pigment.

Indian reserve *Cdn.* a tract of land set aside by the government for the exclusive use of a First Nations band, usually by treaty.

Indian summer *Cdn.* **1** a time of mild, dry, hazy weather that sometimes occurs in October or early November, after the first frosts of autumn. **2** a period or time of flourishing.

Indian thistle an edible west coast wildflower (*Cirsium edule*), having purple flowers and growing to a height of 1 m to 2 m.

Indian tobacco *Cdn.* a North American wild lobelia (*Lobelia inflata*) having small, pale blue flowers and toothed leaves, formerly used in medicine but now regarded as poisonous.

Indian turnip *Cdn.* jack-in-the-pulpit.

Indian wrestling *Cdn.* a form of wrestling in which each contestant tries to overcome his or her opponent by the pressure of his or her hands against the opponent's hands.

India paper **1** a thin, tough paper, used for Bibles, prayer books, etc. **2** a thin, soft paper, used for the first or finest impressions of engravings, etc.

India rubber or **india rubber** a substance of great elasticity obtained from the coagulated, milky juice of various tropical plants; rubber. **—ˈIn•di•a–ˌrub•ber,** *adj.*

indic. **1** indicative. **2** indicator.

in•dic•an [ˈɪndəkən] *n. Chemistry.* **1** a glucoside that yields indigo. *Formula*: $C_{14}H_{17}NO_6$ **2** indoxyl potassium sulphate. *Formula*: $C_8H_6NOSO_2OH$ ⟨< L *indicum* indigo + E *-an*⟩

in•di•cate [ˈɪndəˌkeit] *v.* **-cat•ed, -cat•ing. 1** point out; point to: *The arrow on the sign indicates the right way to go.* **2** show; make known: *A thermometer indicates temperature.* **3** be a sign or hint of: *The haze indicated heat.* **4** give a sign or hint of: *A dog indicates its feelings by growling, whining, barking, or wagging its tail.* **5** *Medicine.* **a** show to be needed as a remedy or treatment: *The examination indicated surgery.* **b** show the presence of (a disease). **6** need; require: *an old book for which leather binding is indicated.* **7** state in general terms: *The government has indicated its intention to lower taxes.* ⟨< L *indicare* < *in-* towards + *dicare* proclaim⟩ **—ˈin•diˌcat•a•ble,** *adj.*

in•di•ca•tion [ˌɪndəˈkeiʃən] *n.* **1** an indicating. **2** something that indicates; a sign: *There was no indication that the house was occupied.* **3** the amount or degree indicated: *The speedometer indication was 80 km/h.* **4** something indicated as expedient.

in•dic•a•tive [ɪnˈdɪkətɪv] *adj., n. —adj.* **1** pointing out; showing; being a sign (*of*); suggestive: *A headache is sometimes indicative of eye strain.* **2** *Grammar.* expressing or denoting a state, act, or happening as actual; asking a question of simple fact. In *I am going, Did you go?* and *He isn't here* the verbs are in the indicative mood.
—n. Grammar. **a** the INDICATIVE MOOD. **b** a verb form in this mood. Compare IMPERATIVE, SUBJUNCTIVE. **—inˈdic•a•tive•ly,** *adv.*

indicative mood *Grammar.* the form of the verb used to show that something is a fact. *Example*: *Close the door* is in the imperative mood. *You closed the door* is in the indicative mood.

in•di•ca•tor [ˈɪndəˌkeitər] *n.* **1** a person who or thing that indicates. **2** the pointer, etc. on an instrument that measures something. **3** a measuring or recording instrument. **4** *Chemistry.* a substance used to indicate chemical conditions or changes. **5** *Ecology.* a plant whose existence shows that its environment is of a certain kind.

in•di•ces [ˈɪndəˌsiz] *n.* a pl. of INDEX.

in•di•cia [ɪnˈdɪʃə] *n.pl., sing.* **in•di•ci•um** [ɪnˈdɪʃəm]. **1** distinctive markings. **2** a mark or code printed directly on mail indicating prepayment of postage. ⟨< L, notice < *index.* See INDEX.⟩

in•dict [ɪnˈdəit] *v.* **1** charge with an offence or crime; accuse. **2** of a grand jury, find enough evidence against (an accused person) to justify a trial. ⟨ME < AF *enditer* < OF. See INDITE.⟩ **—inˈdict•er** or **inˈdict•or,** *n.*
☛ *Hom.* INDITE.

in•dict•a•ble [ɪnˈdəitəbəl] *adj.* **1** making a person liable to be indicted: *an indictable offence.* **2** liable to be indicted. **—inˈdict•a•bly,** *adv.*

indictable offence *Law.* a crime, such as armed robbery or murder, that is more serious than a summary offence. A person charged with an indictable offence in Canada may be arrested without a warrant and may be fingerprinted and photographed for police records. Compare SUMMARY OFFENCE.

in•dict•ment [ɪnˈdəitmənt] *n.* **1** the formal, written charge made against a person accused of a serious criminal offence. In Canada, an indictment is issued for any offence not punishable by summary conviction. **2** accusation.

indie rock [ˈɪndi] *Music. Informal.* a type of rock music promoted by small, independent record companies, selling through small, private stores. ⟨< *independent*⟩

in•dif•fer•ence [ɪnˈdɪfrəns] *or* [ɪnˈdɪfərəns] *n.* **1** a lack of interest or attention. **2** little or no importance: *Where we ate was a matter of indifference to us.*

☛ *Syn.* **1. Indifference,** UNCONCERN, APATHY = lack of interest. **Indifference** emphasizes not caring one way or the other, showing no interest: *A lazy, careless person treats his or her work with indifference.* **Unconcern** emphasizes not caring enough to take a natural or proper interest, and suggests being unaware of any cause for anxiety or need for personal attention: *Nobody understands the unconcern of her parents.* **Apathy** suggests indifference to everything except one's own troubles, sorrow, or pain: *We have been worried about her apathy since her husband died.*

in•dif•fer•ent [ɪn'dɪfrənt] *or* [ɪn'dɪfərənt] *adj.* **1** having no feeling for or against; having or showing no interest: *an indifferent attitude toward the environment.* **2** impartial; neutral; without preference: *an indifferent decision.* **3** unimportant; not mattering much: *an indifferent success.* **4** not bad, but less than good; just fair: *an indifferent ballplayer.* **5** rather bad. **6** neutral in chemical, electrical, or magnetic quality. **7** *Biology.* of a cell, undifferentiated. ⟨ME < L *indifferent-* (stem of *indifferens*)⟩

in•dif•fer•ent•ism [ɪn'dɪfrən,tɪzəm] *n.* the belief that all religions are equally valid. **—in'dif•fer•ent•ist,** *n.*

in•dif•fer•ent•ly [ɪn'dɪfrəntli] *or* [ɪn'dɪfərəntli] *adv.* **1** with indifference. **2** without distinction; equally. **3** moderately; tolerably; passably. **4** poorly; badly; in an inferior manner: *He did his work indifferently.*

in•di•gen ['ɪndədʒən] *n.* a person, animal, or plant native to an area. Also, **indigene** ['ɪndə,dʒin]. ⟨< MF < L *indigena* a native⟩

in•di•gence ['ɪndədʒəns] *n.* poverty.

in•dig•e•nous [ɪn'dɪdʒənəs] *adj.* **1** originating or produced in a particular country; growing or living naturally in a certain region, soil, climate, etc.; native: *Musk-oxen are indigenous to Canada.* **2** innate; inherent. ⟨< LL *indigenus* native < L *indigena* a native⟩ **—in'dig•e•nous•ly,** *adv.* **—in'dig•e•nous•ness,** *n.*

in•di•gent ['ɪndɪdʒənt] *adj., n.* —*adj.* very poor and needy.
—*n.* an indigent person. ⟨< L *indigens, -entis,* ppr. of *indigere* need⟩ **—'in•di•gent•ly,** *adv.*

in•di•gest•ed [,ɪndə'dʒɛstɪd] *or* [,ɪndaɪ'dʒɛstɪd] *adj. Archaic.* **1** not digested. **2** chaotic. **3** poorly planned.

in•di•gest•i•ble [,ɪndə'dʒɛstəbəl] *or* [,ɪndaɪ'dʒɛstəbəl] *adj.* that cannot be properly digested; hard to digest. ⟨< L *indigestibilis*⟩ **—,in•di,gest•i'bil•i•ty,** *n.* **—,in•di'gest•i•bly,** *adv.*

in•di•ges•tion [,ɪndə'dʒɛstʃən] *or* [,ɪndaɪ'dʒɛstʃən] *n.* **1** inability to digest food properly; difficulty in digesting food. **2** the pain arising from this condition. ⟨late ME < LL *indigestion-* (stem of *indigestio*)⟩

in•dign [ɪn'daɪn] *adj. Poetic.* not deserved. ⟨late ME *indigne* < MF < L *indignus* < *in-* not + *dignus* worthy⟩

in•dig•nant [ɪn'dɪgnənt] *adj.* angry at something unworthy, unjust, or mean. ⟨< L *indignans, -antis,* ppr. of *indignari* be indignant (at), regard as unworthy < *indignus* unworthy < *in-* not + *dignus* worthy⟩ **—in'dig•nant•ly,** *adv.*

in•dig•na•tion [,ɪndɪg'neɪʃən] *n.* anger at something unworthy, unjust, or mean; anger mixed with scorn; righteous anger: *Cruelty to animals arouses our indignation.*

☛ *Syn.* See note at ANGER.

in•dig•ni•ty [ɪn'dɪgnəti] *n., pl.* **-ties. 1** an injury to dignity; lack of respect or proper treatment; insult. **2** a state of humiliation. ⟨< L *indignitas*⟩

☛ *Syn.* See note at INSULT.

in•di•go ['ɪndə,gou] *n., pl.* **-gos** or **-goes;** *adj.* —*n.* **1** a blue dyestuff that can be obtained from certain plants, but is now usually made artificially. **2** any of a genus (*Indigofera*) of plants of the pea family from which indigo is obtained. **3** a deep violet-blue, the extreme end of the spectrum before violet.
—*adj.* deep violet-blue. ⟨< Sp. < L < Gk. *indikon,* originally *adj.,* Indian (dye)⟩

indigo bunting a bunting (*Passerina cyanea*) of central and E North America, the adult male having violet-blue plumage during the breeding season and brownish plumage, similar to that of the female, the rest of the year.

in•di•goid ['ɪndɪ,gɔɪd] *adj., n.* —*adj.* of dyes that colour indigo blue.
—*n.* one of those dyes.

indigo snake a dark blue snake (*Drymarchon corais*) that preys on small mammals, found in S U.S.

in•di•go•tin [ɪn'dɪgətɪn] *or* [,ɪndə'goutɪn] *n.* a dark blue powder, the base of indigo.

in•di•rect [,ɪndə'rɛkt] *or* [,ɪndaɪ'rɛkt] *adj.* **1** not direct; not straight: *an indirect route.* **2** not directly connected; secondary: *Happiness is an indirect consequence of doing one's work well.* **3** not straightforward and to the point: *The witness gave an indirect answer to the lawyer's question instead of a frank "Yes" or "No."* **4** dishonest; deceitful: *indirect methods.* ⟨ME < Med.L *indirectus*⟩ **—,in•di'rect•ly,** *adv.* **—,in•di'rect•ness,** *n.*

indirect discourse discourse in which a speaker's words are reported indirectly. *He replied that he would think it over* is an example of indirect discourse. Compare DIRECT DISCOURSE.

in•di•rec•tion [,ɪndə'rɛkʃən] *or* [,ɪndaɪ'rɛkʃən] *n.* **1** a roundabout act, means, or method. **2** dishonesty; deceit. **3** a lack of direction; aimlessness.

indirect lighting illumination by reflected or diffused light.

indirect object *Grammar.* with verbs of saying, giving, or showing, the person or thing to which something is said, given, or shown. The indirect object usually comes before the direct object and shows to whom or for whom something is done. *Example*: In *I gave John a book, John* is the indirect object, and *book* is the direct object. Compare DIRECT OBJECT.

indirect question a question reported indirectly. *Example*: *She asked when they had arrived* is an example of an indirect question. Compare DIRECT QUESTION.

indirect tax a tax paid indirectly by the consumer and included in the price of an article or service.

in•dis•cern•i•ble [,ɪndɪ'sɜrnəbəl] *or* [,ɪndɪ'zɜrnəbəl] *adj.* not discernible; imperceptible. **—,in•dis,cern•i'bil•i•ty,** *n.* **—in•dis'cern•i•bly,** *adv.*

in•dis•ci•pline [ɪn'dɪsəplɪn] *n.* **1** a lack of discipline. **2** an example of this lack.

in•dis•creet [,ɪndɪ'skrit] *adj.* not discreet; not wise and judicious; imprudent: *The boy's indiscreet remark made the stranger feel insulted.* **—,in•dis'creet•ly,** *adv.* **—,in•dis'creet•ness,** *n.*

☛ *Hom.* INDISCRETE.

in•dis•crete [,ɪndɪ'skrit] *adj.* not divided into parts. ⟨< L *indiscretus* undivided⟩

☛ *Hom.* INDISCREET.

in•dis•cre•tion [,ɪndɪ'skrɛʃən] *n.* **1** a being indiscreet; lack of good judgment; imprudence. **2** an indiscreet act. **—,in•dis'cre•tion,ar•y,** *adj.*

in•dis•crim•i•nate [,ɪndɪ'skrɪmənɪt] *adj.* **1** confused: *She tipped everything out of her suitcase in an indiscriminate mass.* **2** done, made, etc. without discriminating and with no feeling for differences: *Indiscriminate reading.* **—,in•dis'crim•i•nate•ly,** *adv.* **—,in•dis,crim•i'na•tion,** *n.* **—,in•dis'crim•i•na•tive,** *adj.*

☛ *Syn.* **2.** See note at MISCELLANEOUS.

in•dis•crim•i•nat•ing [,ɪndɪ'skrɪmə,neitɪŋ] *adj.* not discriminating. **—,in•dis'crim•i,nat•ing•ly,** *adv.*

in•dis•pen•sa•ble [,ɪndɪ'spɛnsəbəl] *adj., n.* —*adj.* absolutely necessary: *Air is indispensable to life.*
—*n.* an indispensable person or thing. ⟨< Med.L *indispensabilis*⟩ **—,in•dis,pen•sa'bil•i•ty,** *n.*

☛ *Syn.* See note at NECESSARY.

in•dis•pen•sa•bly [,ɪndɪ'spɛnsəbli] *adv.* so as to be indispensable; necessarily.

in•dis•pose [,ɪndɪ'spouz] *v.* **-posed, -pos•ing. 1** make unwilling; make averse: *Hot weather indisposes a person to work hard.* **2** make slightly ill. **3** make unfit or unable. ⟨back formation from INDISPOSED⟩

in•dis•posed [,ɪndɪ'spouzd] *adj., v.* —*adj.* **1** slightly ill. **2** unwilling; without inclination; averse: *The men were indisposed to work nights.*
—*v.* pt. and pp. of INDISPOSE. ⟨ME *indisposid* out of order, not suitable < L *indispositus*⟩

in•dis•po•si•tion [,ɪndɪspə'zɪʃən] *n.* **1** a disturbance of health; slight illness. **2** an unwillingness; disinclination; aversion.

in•dis•put•a•ble [,ɪndɪ'spjutəbəl] *or* [ɪn'dɪspjətəbəl] *adj.* not to be disputed; undoubtedly true; unquestionable. ⟨< LL *indisputabilis*⟩ **—,in•dis,put•a'bil•i•ty,** *n.* **—,in•dis'put•a•bly,** *adv.*

in•dis•sol•u•bil•i•ty [,ɪndɪ,sɒljə'bɪləti] *n.* a being indissoluble; stability.

in•dis•sol•u•ble [,ɪndɪ'sɒljəbəl] *adj.* not capable of being dissolved, undone, or destroyed; lasting; firm. ⟨< L *indissolubilis*⟩ **—,in•dis'sol•u•bly,** *adv.*

in•dis•tinct [,ɪndɪ'stɪŋkt] *adj.* not distinct; not clear to the eye, ear, or mind; confused. ⟨< L *indistinctus*⟩ **—,in•dis'tinct•ly,** *adv.* **—,in•dis'tinct•ness,** *n.*

in•dis•tinct•ive [ˌɪndɪ'stɪŋktɪv] *adj.* **1** not distinctive. **2** not distinguishing. **—ˌin•dis'tinct•ive•ness,** *n.*

in•dis•tin•guish•a•ble [ˌɪndɪ'stɪŋgwɪʃəbəl] *adj.* **1** that cannot be distinguished; virtually identical. **2** not easily perceptible. **—ˌin•dis'tin•guish•a•bly,** *adv.*

in•dite [ɪn'dəit] *v.* **-dit•ed, -dit•ing.** put in words or writing; compose. ⟨ME < OF *enditer* make known < L *in-* in + *dictare* dictate, express in writing. Cf. INDICT.⟩ **—in'dite•ment,** *n.*
☛ *Hom.* INDICT.

in•di•um ['ɪndiəm] *n. Chemistry.* a rare, metallic chemical element that is soft, white, malleable, and easily fusible. *Symbol*: In; *at.no.* 49; *at.mass* 114.82. ⟨< NL < L *indicum.* See INDIGO.⟩

in•di•vert•i•ble [ˌɪndə'vɜrtəbəl] *adj.* not to be turned aside. **—ˌin•di'vert•i•bly,** *adv.*

in•di•vid•u•al [ˌɪndə'vɪdʒuəl] *or* [ˌɪndə'vɪdjuəl] *n., adj. —n.* **1** person: *She is a clever individual.* **2** a single or distinct person, animal, or thing: *She tries to remain an individual. The herd of giraffes consisted of thirty individuals.*
—adj. **1** single; particular; separate: *an individual question.* **2** for one only: *We use individual salt-cellars.* **3** having to do with or peculiar to one person or thing: *individual tastes.* **4** distinctive; unique: *Each girl has an individual style of arranging her hair.* ⟨< Med.L *individualis* < L *individuus* < *in-* not + *dividuus* divisible⟩
☛ *Syn.* See note at PERSON.

in•di•vid•u•al•ism [ˌɪndə'vɪdʒuəˌlɪzəm] *n.* **1** a theory that individual freedom is as important as the welfare of the community or group as a whole. **2** any ethical, economic, or political theory that emphasizes the importance of individuals. **3** *Philosophy.* the doctrine that all actions are selfish. **4** a striving of each for himself or herself; the absence of co-operation; wanting a separate existence for oneself. **5** individuality.

in•di•vid•u•al•ist [ˌɪndə'vɪdʒuəlɪst] *n.* **1** one who goes his or her own way, independent of the views or interests of others. **2** a supporter of individualism.

in•di•vid•u•al•is•tic [ˌɪndəˌvɪdʒuə'lɪstɪk] *adj.* of individualism or individualists. **—ˌin•diˌvid•u•al'is•ti•cal•ly,** *adv.*

in•di•vid•u•al•i•ty [ˌɪndəˌvɪdʒu'æləti] *n., pl.* **-ties.** **1** individual character; the sum of the qualities that make one person or thing different from another. **2** the condition of being individual; existence as an individual. **3** an individual person or thing.
☛ *Syn.* **1.** See note at CHARACTER.

in•di•vid•u•al•ize [ˌɪndə'vɪdʒuəˌlaɪz] *v.* **-ized, -iz•ing. 1** make individual; cause to be different from others; give a distinctive character to. **2** consider as individuals; list one by one; specify. **—ˌin•diˌvid•u•al•i'za•tion,** *n.*

in•di•vid•u•al•ly [ˌɪndə'vɪdʒuəli] *adv.* **1** personally; one at a time; as individuals: *The teacher helps us individually.* **2** each from the others: *People differ individually.*

in•di•vid•u•ate [ˌɪndə'vɪdʒuˌeit] *v.* **-at•ed, -at•ing.** form into a distinct entity. ⟨< Med.L *individuatus* made individual, pp. of *individuare*⟩

in•di•vid•u•a•tion [ˌɪndəˌvɪdʒu'eiʃən] *n.* **1** an individuating or being individuated. **2** *Philosophy.* the development of the specific from the general.

in•di•vis•i•ble [ˌɪndə'vɪzəbəl] *adj., n. —adj.* **1** not capable of being divided. **2** not capable of being divided without leaving a remainder.
—n. something indivisible. ⟨ME < LL *indivisibilis*⟩ **—ˌin•diˌvis•i'bil•i•ty,** *n.* **—ˌin•di'vis•i•bly,** *adv.*

Indo– *combining form.* **1** Indian; of India or the East Indies: *Indo-Aryan = of or having to do with the Aryans of India.* **2** Indian and: *Indo-European = of India and Europe.*

In•do–Ar•yan ['ɪndou 'ɛrjən] *or* ['ɑrjən] *adj. or n.* an old term for Indo-European.

In•do–Chi•nese ['ɪndou tʃaɪ'niz] *n., adj. —n.* **1** a native or inhabitant of Indochina, a historical name for either the peninsula south of China that includes Burma, Thailand, Laos, Kampuchea, and Vietnam, or the eastern part of this peninsula, formerly under French control, including Vietnam, Laos, and Kampuchea. **2** Sino-Tibetan.
—adj. of or having to do with Indochina or the Indo-Chinese.

in•doc•ile [ɪn'dɒsaɪl] *or* [ɪn'dɒsɪl] *adj.* not docile; not able to be taught or trained. ⟨< L *indocilis*⟩

in•doc•tri•nate [ɪn'dɒktrəˌneit] *v.* **-nat•ed, -nat•ing. 1** teach a doctrine, belief, or principle to, often by unacceptable methods. **2** instruct. ⟨probably < Med.L *indoctrinare* < *in-* in + *doctrinare* teach < L *doctrina* doctrine⟩ **—inˌdoc•tri'na•tion,** *n.* **—in'doc•triˌna•tor,** *n.*

In•do–Eu•ro•pe•an ['ɪndou ˌjʊrə'piən] *adj., n. —adj.* **1** of India and Europe. **2** of or having to do with a group of related languages spoken in India, W Asia, and Europe. English, German, Latin, Greek, Persian, and Sanskrit are Indo-European languages.
—n. **1** this group of languages. **2** the reconstructed prehistoric language from which they are derived; Aryan. **3** a member of a people that speaks an Indo-European language.

In•do–Ger•man•ic ['ɪndou dʒər'mænɪk] *adj. or n.* an old term for Indo-European.

In•do–Hit•tite ['ɪndou 'hɪtəit] *n.* a hypothetical language including Hittite and Indo-European.

In•do–I•ra•ni•an ['ɪndou ɪ'reiniən] *adj., n. —adj.* of or having to do with a division of the Indo-European family of languages that comprises the Indic and Iranian branches.
—n. this division.

in•dole ['ɪndoul] *n. Chemistry.* a crystalline compound obtained from coal tar and used in making perfumes. *Formula*: C_8H_7N ⟨< *indigo* + (*phen*)*ol*⟩

in•dole•a•cet•ic acid [ˌɪndoulə'sitɪk] a hormone used in stimulating the root growth of plants and cuttings. *Formula*: $C_{10}H_9NO_2$

in•dole•bu•tyr•ic acid [ˌɪndoulbju'tirɪk] a hormone used in stimulating the root growth of plants and cuttings. *Formula*: $C_{12}H_{13}NO_2$

in•do•lence ['ɪndələns] *n.* laziness; dislike of work; idleness. ⟨< L *indolentia* painlessness⟩

in•do•lent ['ɪndələnt] *adj.* **1** lazy; disliking work. **2** *Pathology.* causing little or no pain. ⟨< LL *indolens, -entis* < L *in-* not + *dolens,* ppr. of *dolere* be in pain⟩ **—'in•do•lent•ly,** *adv.*
☛ *Syn.* **1.** See note at IDLE.

in•do•meth•a•cin [ˌɪndou'mɛθəsɪn] *n.* a drug used to relieve the pain of arthritis and other inflammatory conditions, and in certain eye conditions.

in•dom•i•ta•bil•i•ty [ɪnˌdɒmətə'bɪləti] *n.* the quality or state of being indomitable.

in•dom•i•ta•ble [ɪn'dɒmətəbəl] *adj.* unconquerable; unyielding: *indomitable courage.* ⟨< LL *indomitabilis,* ult. < L *in-* not + *domare* tame⟩ **—in'dom•i•ta•bly,** *adv.* **—in'dom•i•ta•ble•ness,** *n.*

In•do•ne•sia [ˌɪndə'niʒə] *or* [ˌɪndə'niʃə] *n.* a country in SE Asia.

In•do•ne•sian [ˌɪndə'niʒən] *or* [ˌɪndə'niʃən] *n., adj. —n.* **1** a native or inhabitant of the Republic of Indonesia, formerly the East Indies. **2** Bahasa Indonesia, the official language of Indonesia. **3** a member of a people believed to have been dominant on the Malay Archipelago before the Malays.
—adj. of or having to do with Indonesia, its people, or their language. ⟨< Gk. *Indos* Indian + *nēsos* island⟩

in•door ['ɪn'dɔr] *adj.* **1** done, played, used, etc. in a house or building: *indoor tennis, indoor skating.* **2** that is indoors: *an indoor rink.*

in•doors ['ɪn'dɔrz] *adv.* in or into a house or building: *go indoors.*

In•do–Pa•cif•ic hump–backed dolphin ['ɪndou pə'sɪfɪk 'hʌmp ˌbækt] a dolphin (*Sousa chinensis*) of the coasts of India, Pakistan, E Africa, Indonesia, China, and Australia. It is an endangered species.

in•do•phe•nol [ˌɪndou'finɒl] *n.* the basis of blue and green dyes.

in•dorse [ɪn'dɔrs] *v.* **-dorsed, -dors•ing.** endorse.

in•dor•see [ˌɪndɔr'si] *n.* endorsee.

in•dorse•ment [ɪn'dɔrsmənt] *n.* endorsement.

in•dox•yl [ɪn'dɒksɪl] *n. Chemistry.* a crystalline compound forming indigo when oxidized. *Formula*: C_8H_7NO

In•dra ['ɪndrə] *n. Hinduism.* the principal deity of the Rig-Veda, god of war and storm.

in•draft ['ɪnˌdræft] *n.* **1** a drawing in. **2** an inward flow or current of water, air, etc.

in•drawn ['ɪnˌdrɒn] *adj.* **1** drawn in. **2** preoccupied; introspective.

in•dri ['ɪndri] *n.* a short-tailed lemur (*Indri indri*) of Madagascar. Also called **indrid lemur.** ⟨< F < Malagasy *indry!* behold!⟩

in•du•bi•ta•ble [ɪn'djubətəbəl] *or* [ɪn'dubətəbəl] *adj.* not to be doubted; certain. ⟨< L *indubitabilis*⟩ **—in'du•bi•ta•ble•ness,** *n.* **—in'du•bi•ta•bly,** *adv.* **—in,du•bi•ta'bil•i•ty,** *n.*

in•duce [ɪn'djus] *or* [ɪn'dus] *v.* **-duced, -duc•ing. 1** lead on; influence; persuade: *Advertising induces people to buy.* **2** cause; bring about: *Some drugs induce sleep. Her labour was induced.* **3** *Electricity.* produce (an electric current, electric charge, or magnetic charge) without direct contact. **4** *Logic.* infer by reasoning from particular facts to a general rule or principle. ⟨< L *inducere* < *in-* in + *ducere* lead or bring in, introduce⟩ **—in'duc•er,** *n.* **—in'duc•i•ble,** *adj.*

in•duce•ment [ɪn'djusmənt] *or* [ɪn'dusmənt] *n.* **1** something that influences or persuades; incentive: *Prizes are inducements to try hard to win.* **2** *Law.* an introductory statement to explain a plea.

in•duct [ɪn'dʌkt] *v.* **1** bring in; introduce (into a place, seat, position, office, etc.). **2** put formally into a position, office, etc.: *They proposed to induct him as secretary.* **3** *U.S.* take into or enroll in military service. **4** initiate. ⟨< L *inductus,* pp. of *inducere.* See INDUCE.⟩

in•duct•ance [ɪn'dʌktəns] *n. Electricity.* **1** the property of an electrical conductor or circuit that makes induction possible. **2** a circuit or a device having this property. **3** the lag in an electric circuit when the current goes on or off. **4** a conducting coil that generates electromotive force by electromagnetic induction.

in•duc•tee [,ɪndʌk'ti] *n.* a person who is soon to be inducted, especially, in the United States, into military service.

in•duc•tile [ɪn'dʌktaɪl] *or* [ɪn'dʌktəl] *adj.* not ductile; not pliable or yielding. **—,in•duc'til•i•ty** [,ɪndʌk'tɪləti], *n.*

in•duc•tion [ɪn'dʌkʃən] *n.* **1** *Electricity.* the process by which electrical or magnetic properties are transferred from one circuit or object to another, without direct contact between the two. **2** *Logic.* the act of reasoning from particular facts to a general rule or principle. **3** *Logic.* the conclusion reached in this way. **4** the act of inducting; act or ceremony of installing a person in office. **5** the act of bringing into existence or operation; the act of producing, causing, or inducing: *induction of a hypnotic state.* **6** the drawing of the fuel mixture into the cylinder or cylinders of an internal-combustion engine.
☛ *Usage* (def. 2). See note at DEDUCTION.

induction coil *Electricity.* a device for producing a high, pulsating voltage from a current of low, steady voltage, such as that from a battery.

in•duc•tive [ɪn'dʌktɪv] *adj.* **1** of or using induction; reasoning by induction. **2** having to do with or produced by electrical or magnetic induction. **3** producing a response in an organism. **4** introductory. **—in'duc•tive•ly,** *adv.*

in•duc•tiv•i•ty [,ɪndʌk'tɪvəti] *n., pl.* **-ties.** an inductive property; capacity for induction.

in•duc•tor [ɪn'dʌktər] *n.* **1** *Electricity.* a part of an electrical apparatus that works or is worked by induction. **2** a person who inducts another into office.

in•due [ɪn'dju] *or* [ɪn'du] *v.* **-dued, -du•ing.** endue. ⟨< L *induere* put on⟩

in•dulge [ɪn'dʌldʒ] *v.* **-dulged, -dulg•ing. 1** yield to the wishes of; humour: *We often indulge a sick person.* **2** give in to one's pleasures; let oneself have, use, or do what one wants (*often used with* **in**): *He indulges in tobacco.* **3** give in to: *She indulged her fondness for candy by eating a whole box.* **4** let (oneself) have, use, or do (*usually used with* **in**): *to indulge oneself in dreaming.* ⟨< L *indulgere*⟩ **—in'dulg•ing•ly,** *adv.*
☛ *Syn.* **1.** See note at HUMOUR.

in•dul•gence [ɪn'dʌldʒəns] *n.* **1** the act of yielding to the wishes of another or allowing oneself one's own desires. **2** something indulged in. **3** a favour; privilege. **4** *Roman Catholic Church.* **a** a remission of the punishment still due for a sin, after the guilt has been forgiven. **b** dispensation. **5** permission to extend the time of payment.

in•dul•gent [ɪn'dʌldʒənt] *adj.* indulging or showing indulgence; lenient and agreeable, often excessively so: *an indulgent parent, an indulgent smile.* **—in'dul•gent•ly,** *adv.*

in•du•line ['ɪndjə,lin] *or* ['ɪndə,lin] *n.* any one of a large class of dyes that produce colours resembling indigo. ⟨< *indigo* + *-ule* + *-ine*⟩

in•du•pli•cate [ɪn'djuplɪkɪt] *or* [ɪn'duplɪkɪt] *adj. Botany.* of a flower bud, curled inward. **—in,du•pli'ca•tion,** *n.*

in•du•rate *v.* ['ɪndjə,reit] *or* ['ɪndə,reit]; *adj.* ['ɪndjərɪt] *or* ['ɪndərɪt] *v.* **-rat•ed, -rat•ing;** *adj.* *—v.* **1** harden. **2** make or become unfeeling. **3** confirm.
—adj. **1** hardened. **2** unfeeling. ⟨< L *indurare* < *in-* + *durus* hard⟩ **—,in•du'ra•tion,** *n.*

In•dus ['ɪndəs] *n. Astronomy.* a southern constellation between Grus and Pavo.

in•du•si•um [ɪn'djuziəm] *or* [ɪn'duziəm] *n., pl.* **-sia** [-ziə]. *Biology.* an enclosing membrane. ⟨< NL < L, a kind of tunic⟩

Indus River dolphin a dolphin (*Platanista minor*) found only in the Indus River in Pakistan. It is an endangered species.

in•dus•tri•al [ɪn'dʌstriəl] *adj., n.* *—adj.* **1** of or resulting from industry or productive labour: *industrial products.* **2** having to do with or connected with an industry or industries: *an industrial exhibition, industrial workers.* **3** for use in industry. **4** of or having to do with the workers in industries: *industrial insurance.*
—n. a stock, bond, etc. of an industrial enterprise. ⟨earlier < Med.L *industrialis* < L *industria* diligence; later < F *industriel* < L *industria*⟩ **—in'dus•tri•al•ly,** *adv.*

industrial arts a course in various manual skills such as welding, woodworking, etc. offered by some schools.

in•dus•tri•al•ism [ɪn'dʌstriə,lɪzəm] *n.* a system of social and economic organization in which large industries are very important and industrial activities or interests prevail.

in•dus•tri•al•ist [ɪn'dʌstriəlɪst] *n.* **1** a person who conducts or owns an industrial enterprise. **2** an industrial worker.

in•dus•tri•al•i•za•tion [ɪn,dʌstriəlaɪ'zeiʃən] *or* [ɪn,dʌstriələ'zeiʃən] *n.* the development of large industries as an important feature in a country or a social or economic system.

in•dus•tri•al•ize [ɪn'dʌstriə,laɪz] *v.* **-ized, -iz•ing. 1** make or become industrial; develop industry (in). **2** organize as an industry.

industrial park a small area of low-rise buildings housing offices and light industry.

Industrial Revolution the change from an agricultural to an industrial civilization, especially that which took place in England from about the middle of the 18th century to the middle of the 19th century.

industrial union a labour union which looks after all workers in a given industry regardless of their trade.

in•dus•tri•ous [ɪn'dʌstriəs] *adj.* working hard and steadily: *an industrious student.* ⟨< L *industriosus*⟩ **—in'dus•tri•ous•ly,** *adv.* **—in'dus•tri•ous•ness,** *n.*
☛ *Syn.* See note at BUSY.

in•dus•try ['ɪndəstri] *n., pl.* **-tries. 1** any branch of business, trade, or manufacture: *the steel industry, the automobile industry.* **2** all such enterprises taken collectively: *Canadian industry is expanding.* **3** the production of goods; manufacturing in general: *She would rather be a professor than work in industry.* **4** the people in charge of industry. **5** systematic work or labour. **6** steady effort; close attention to work: *Industry and thrift favour success.* ⟨< L *industria*⟩

in•dwell [ɪn'dwɛl] *v.* abide within, as a divine spirit or force. ⟨ME indwellen < *in-* + *dwell*⟩ **—in'dwell•er,** *n.*

in•dwell•ing [ɪn'dwɛlɪŋ] *adj., v.* *—adj.* dwelling within.
—v. ppr. of INDWELL.

-ine[1] *suffix.* of; like; like that of; characteristic of; having the nature of; being: *crystalline, elephantine.* ⟨< L *-inus,* sometimes < Gk. *-inos*⟩

-ine[2] *suffix.* used especially in the names of some chemicals, as in *chlorine, aniline.* ⟨< F (< L *-ina*) or directly < L *-ina*⟩

in•e•bri•ant [ɪ'nibriənt] *adj., n.* *—adj.* intoxicating.
—n. an intoxicant.

in•e•bri•ate *v.* [ɪ'nibri,eit]; *n., adj.* [ɪ'nibriɪt] *v.* **-at•ed, -at•ing;** *n., adj.* *—v.* make drunk; intoxicate.
—n. a habitual drunkard; intoxicated person.
—adj. intoxicated; drunk. ⟨< L *inebriare* < *in-* + *ebrius* drunk⟩ **—in,e•bri'a•tion,** *n.*

in•e•bri•e•ty [,ɪnɪ'braɪəti] *n.* drunkenness.

in•ed•i•ble [ɪn'ɛdəbəl] *adj.* not fit to eat: *Some toadstools are inedible.* **—in,ed•i'bil•i•ty,** *n.*

in•ed•it•ed [ɪn'ɛdɪtəd] *adj.* **1** unpublished. **2** not edited; published without corrections, etc.

in•ed•u•ca•ble [ɪn'ɛdʒəkəbəl] *adj.* incapable of being educated.

in•ef•fa•ble [ɪn'ɛfəbəl] *adj.* **1** not to be expressed in words; too great to be described in words. **2** that must not be spoken, because too sacred. ⟨< L *ineffabilis,* ult. < *in-* not + *ex-* out + *fari* speak⟩ **—in'ef•fa•ble•ness** or **in,ef•fa'bil•i•ty,** *n.* **—in'ef•fa•bly,** *adv.*

in•ef•face•a•ble [ˌɪnɪ'feisəbəl] *adj.* that cannot be rubbed out or wiped out. **—ˌin•efˌface•a'bil•i•ty,** *n.* **—ˌin•ef'face•a•bly,** *adv.*

in•ef•fec•tive [ˌɪnɪ'fɛktɪv] *adj.* **1** not effective; of little or no use: *An ineffective medicine fails to cure a disease or relieve pain.* **2** unfit for work; incapable. **—ˌin•ef'fec•tive•ly,** *adv.* **—ˌin•ef'fec•tive•ness,** *n.*

in•ef•fec•tu•al [ˌɪnɪ'fɛktʃuəl] *adj.* failing or unable to have the effect wanted; useless. **—ˌin•ef'fec•tu•al•ly,** *adv.* **—ˌin•efˌfec•tu'al•i•ty,** *n.*

in•ef•fi•ca•cious [ˌɪnɛfə'keiʃəs] *adj.* not efficacious; not able to produce the effect wanted. **—ˌin•ef•fi'ca•cious•ly,** *adv.*

in•ef•fi•ca•cy [ɪn'ɛfəkəsi] *n.* a lack of efficacy; inability to produce the effect wanted.

in•ef•fi•cien•cy [ˌɪnɪ'fɪʃənsi] *n.* a lack of efficiency; inability to get things done; failure to make maximum use of time, energy, etc.

in•ef•fi•cient [ˌɪnɪ'fɪʃənt] *adj.* **1** not efficient; not able to produce an effect without waste of time, energy, etc.; wasteful: *A machine that uses too much power is inefficient.* **2** incapable; not able to get things done: *an inefficient housekeeper.* **—ˌin•ef'fi•cient•ly,** *adv.*

in•e•las•tic [ˌɪnɪ'læstɪk] *adj.* not elastic; stiff; inflexible; unyielding.

in•e•las•tic•i•ty [ˌɪnɪlæ'stɪsəti] *n.* a lack of elasticity.

in•el•e•gance [ɪn'ɛləgəns] *n.* **1** a lack of elegance; lack of good taste. **2** something that is not elegant or graceful. Also, **inelegancy.**

in•el•e•gant [ɪn'ɛləgənt] *adj.* not elegant; not in good taste; crude; not graceful or fine. ⟨< *inelegant-* (stem of *inelegans*)⟩ **—in'el•e•gant•ly,** *adv.*

in•el•i•gi•ble [ɪn'ɛlədʒəbəl] *adj., n.* —*adj.* not suitable; not qualified: *His youth makes him ineligible for the post.*
—*n.* a person who is not suitable or not qualified. **—inˌel•i•gi'bil•i•ty,** *n.* **—in'el•i•gi•bly,** *adv.*

in•el•o•quent [ɪn'ɛləkwənt] *adj.* not eloquent. **—in'el•o•quence,** *n.* **—in'el•o•quent•ly,** *adv.*

in•e•luc•ta•ble [ˌɪnɪ'lʌktəbəl] *adj.* unable to be avoided; inescapable; inevitable. ⟨< L *ineluctabilis* < *eluctari* < *ex-* out + *luctari* struggle⟩ **—in•eˌluc•ta'bil•i•ty,** *n.* **—ˌin•e'luc•ta•bly,** *adv.*

in•e•lud•a•ble [ɪnɪ'ludəbəl] *adj.* not able to be escaped.

in•ept [ɪn'ɛpt] *adj.* **1** not suitable; out of place: *He would be an inept choice as captain.* **2** awkward; clumsy; incompetent: *That was an inept performance.* **3** absurd; foolish: *inept ideas.* ⟨< L *ineptus* < *in-* not + *aptus* apt⟩ **—in'ept•ly,** *adv.* **—in'ept•ness,** *n.*
☛ *Syn.* **1, 2.** INAPT and **inept** have similar meanings, but only **inept** (def. 3) = foolish, absurd.

in•ept•i•tude [ɪn'ɛptəˌtjud] *or* [ɪn'ɛptəˌtud] *n.* **1** unfitness; foolishness. **2** a silly or inappropriate act or remark. **3** awkwardness; incompetence.

in•e•qual•i•ty [ˌɪnɪ'kwɒləti] *n., pl.* **-ties. 1** lack of equality; the state or condition of being unequal in amount, size, value, rank, etc. **2** a lack of evenness, regularity, or uniformity. **3** *Mathematics.* an expression showing that two quantities are not equal, such as $a < b$ (a is less than b), $a > b$ (a is greater than b), *or* $a \neq b$ (a is not equal to b). ⟨late ME < L *inaequalitas*⟩

in•e•qua•tion [ˌɪnɪ'kweɪʒən] *n.* INEQUALITY (def. 3).

in•eq•ui•ta•ble [ɪn'ɛkwətəbəl] *adj.* unfair; unjust. **—in'eq•ui•ta•bly,** *adv.*

in•eq•ui•ty [ɪn'ɛkwəti] *n., pl.* **-ties. 1** unfairness; injustice. **2** an unfair or unjust act or situation.

in•e•rad•i•ca•ble [ˌɪnɪ'rædəkəbəl] *adj.* that cannot be rooted out or got rid of. **—ˌin•eˌrad•i•ca'bil•i•ty,** *n.* **—ˌin•e'rad•i•ca•bly,** *adv.*

in•er•ra•ble [ɪn'ɛrəbəl] *adj.* incapable of erring; infallible. ⟨< LL *inerrabilis* unerring⟩ **—inˌer•ra'bil•i•ty,** *n.* **—in'er•ra•bly,** *adv.*

in•ert [ɪn'ɜrt] *adj.* **1** having no inherent power to move or act; lifeless: *A stone is an inert mass of matter.* **2** inactive; slow; sluggish. **3** *Chemistry.* with few or no active properties: *Helium and neon are inert gases.* ⟨< L *iners, inertis* idle, unskilled < *in-* without + *ars, artis* art, skill⟩ **—in'ert•ly,** *adv.* **—in'ert•ness,** *n.*
☛ *Syn.* **2.** See note at INACTIVE.

in•er•tia [ɪn'ɜrʃə] *n.* **1** a tendency to remain in the state one is in and not start changes. **2** *Physics.* the tendency of all objects and matter in the universe to stay still if still, or if moving, to go on moving in the same direction unless acted on by some outside force. ⟨< L *inertia* < *iners.* See INERT.⟩

in•er•tial [ɪn'ɜrʃəl] *adj.* that uses the principle of inertia: *Inertial navigation is made possible by gyroscopic control.*

inertial guidance or **navigation** in rocketry, the guiding of a missile by flight instruments that are within it.

in•es•cap•a•ble [ˌɪnɪ'skeipəbəl] *adj.* that cannot be escaped or avoided. **—ˌin•es'cap•a•bly,** *adv.*

in•es•sen•tial [ˌɪnɪ'sɛnʃəl] *adj.* **1** not essential. **2** without essence or being.

in•es•ti•ma•ble [ɪn'ɛstəməbəl] *adj.* too good, great, valuable, etc. to be measured or estimated: *Freedom is an inestimable privilege.* **—inˌes•ti•ma'bil•i•ty,** *n.* **—in'es•ti•ma•bly,** *adv.*

in•ev•i•ta•ble [ɪn'ɛvətəbəl] *adj., n.* —*adj.* not avoidable; sure to happen; certain to come.
—*n.*
the inevitable, that which is bound to happen. ⟨< L *inevitabilis* < *in-* not + *evitabilis* avoidable < *evitare* avoid < *ex-* + *vitare* avoid⟩ **—inˌev•i•ta'bil•i•ty,** *n.* **—in'ev•i•ta•bly,** *adv.*

in•ex•act [ˌɪnɪg'zækt] *adj.* not exact; with errors or mistakes; not just right. **—ˌin•ex'act•ly,** *adv.* **—ˌin•ex'act•ness,** *n.*

in•ex•act•i•tude [ˌɪnɪg'zæktəˌtjud] *or* [ˌɪnɪg'zæktəˌtud] *n.* **1** the condition of being inexact or inaccurate. **2** an instance of inexactness or inaccuracy.

in•ex•cus•a•ble [ˌɪnɪk'skjuzəbəl] *adj.* that ought not to be excused; that cannot be justified. ⟨ME < L *inexcusabilis*⟩ **—ˌin•ex'cus•a•bly,** *adv.* **—ˌin•ex'cus•a•ble•ness,** *n.*

in•ex•er•tion [ˌɪnɪg'zɜrʃən] *n.* inaction.

in•ex•haust•i•bil•i•ty [ˌɪnɪgˌzɒstə'bɪləti] *n.* an inexhaustible nature or quality.

in•ex•haust•i•ble [ˌɪnɪg'zɒstəbəl] *adj.* **1** that cannot be exhausted; very abundant. **2** tireless. ⟨< *inexhaustus* not exhausted⟩ **—ˌin•ex'haust•i•bly,** *adv.*

in•ex•ist•ent [ˌɪnɪg'zɪstənt] *adj.* having no existence. ⟨< LL *inexistent-* (stem of *inexistens*) not existing⟩ **—ˌin•ex'ist•ence,** *n.*

in•ex•o•ra•ble [ɪn'ɛgzərəbəl] *or* [ɪn'ɛksərəbəl] *adj.* **1** relentless; unyielding; not influenced by prayers or entreaties: *The forces of nature are inexorable.* **2** unalterable. ⟨< L *inexorabilis* < *in-* not + *ex-* (intensive) + *orare* entreat⟩ **—inˌex•o•ra'bil•i•ty,** *n.* **—in'ex•o•ra•bly,** *adv.*
☛ *Syn.* See note at INFLEXIBLE.

in•ex•pe•di•en•cy [ˌɪnɪk'spidiənsi] *n.* lack of expediency; being inexpedient. Also, **inexpedience.**

in•ex•pe•di•ent [ˌɪnɪk'spidiənt] *adj.* not expedient; not practicable, suitable, or wise. **—ˌin•ex'pe•di•ent•ly,** *adv.*

in•ex•pen•sive [ˌɪnɪk'spɛnsɪv] *adj.* not expensive; cheap; low-priced. **—ˌin•ex'pen•sive•ly,** *adv.* **—ˌin•ex'pen•sive•ness,** *n.*
☛ *Syn.* See note at CHEAP.

in•ex•pe•ri•ence [ˌɪnɪk'spiriəns] *n.* lack of experience or practice; lack of skill or wisdom gained from experience. ⟨< LL *inexperientia*⟩ **—ˌin•ex'pe•ri•enced,** *adj.*

in•ex•pert [ɪn'ɛkspərt] *or* [ˌɪnɪk'spɜrt] *adj.* not expert; unskilled. ⟨late ME < L *inexpertus*⟩ **—in'ex•pert•ly,** *adv.* **—in'ex•pert•ness,** *n.*

in•ex•pi•a•ble [ɪn'ɛkspiəbəl] *adj.* that cannot be atoned for: *Murder is an inexpiable crime.* ⟨< L *inexpiabilis*⟩ **—in'ex•pi•a•bly,** *adv.*

in•ex•plain•a•ble [ˌɪnɪk'spleinəbəl] *adj.* inexplicable.

in•ex•pli•ca•ble [ˌɪnɪk'splɪkəbəl] *or* [ɪn'ɛkspləkəbəl] *adj.* impossible to explain or understand; mysterious. ⟨< L *inexplicabilis*⟩ **—in•exˌpli•ca'bil•i•ty,** *n.* **—in•ex'pli•ca•bly,** *adv.*

in•ex•plic•it [ˌɪnɪk'splɪsɪt] *adj.* not explicit or clear; not clearly stated. ⟨< L *inexplicitus* not straightforward⟩ **—ˌin•ex'plic•it•ly,** *adv.* **—ˌin•ex'plic•it•ness,** *n.*

in•ex•press•i•ble [ˌɪnɪk'sprɛsəbəl] *adj.* that cannot be expressed; beyond expression. **—ˌin•ex'press•i•bly,** *adv.* **—ˌin•exˌpress•i'bil•i•ty** or **ˌin•ex'press•i•ble•ness,** *n.*

in•ex•pres•sive [ˌɪnɪk'sprɛsɪv] *adj.* not expressive; lacking in expression. **—ˌin•ex'pres•sive•ly,** *adv.* **—ˌin•ex'pres•sive•ness,** *n.*

in•ex•pug•na•ble [ˌɪnɪk'spʌgnəbəl] *adj.* incapable of being taken by force; impregnable. ⟨< L *inexpugnabilis* < *in-* in + *expugnabilis, expugnare* to take by storm⟩ **—ˌin•exˌpug•na'bil•i•ty,** *n.* **—ˌin•ex'pug•na•bly,** *adv.*

in•ex•ten•si•ble [ˌɪnɪk'stɛnsɪbəl] *adj.* not extensible. **—ˌin•exˌten•si'bil•i•ty,** *n.*

in ex•ten•so [ɪn ɛk'stɛnsou] *Latin.* at full length; in full. ⟨< L *in extenso*, literally, in an extended (state)⟩

in•ex•tin•guish•a•ble [ˌɪnɪk'stɪŋgwɪʃəbəl] *adj.* that cannot be put out or stopped: *An inextinguishable fire keeps on burning.* **—ˌin•ex'tin•guish•a•bly,** *adv.*

in•ex•tir•pa•ble [ˌɪnɪk'stɜrpəbəl] *adj.* impossible to exterminate; not removable or eradicable.

in ex•tre•mis [ɪn ɛkstrɛmɪs] *Latin.* at the point of death. ⟨< L *in extremis*, literally, amid the final things⟩

in•ex•tri•ca•ble [ɪn'ɛkstrəkəbəl] *or* [ˌɪnɪk'strɪkəbəl] *adj.* **1** that one cannot get out of. **2** that cannot be disentangled or solved. ⟨ME < L *inextricabilis*⟩ **—inˌex•tri•ca'bil•i•ty,** *n.* **—in'ex•tri•ca•bly,** *adv.* **—ˌin•ex'tri•ca•ble•ness,** *n.*

inf. **1** infantry. **2** infinitive. **3** inferior. **4** below (for L *infra).* **5** information.

Inf. infantry.

in•fal•li•bil•i•ty [ɪnˌfælə'bɪləti] *n.* absolute freedom from error: *The infallibility of the Pope when speaking officially on matters of faith and morals was proclaimed by the Vatican Council in 1870.*

in•fal•li•ble [ɪn'fæləbəl] *adj.* **1** free from error; that cannot be mistaken: *an infallible rule.* **2** absolutely reliable; sure: *infallible obedience.* **3** *Roman Catholic Church.* incapable of error in the exposition of doctrine on faith and morals (said of the Pope as head of the Church). ⟨ME < Med.L *infallibilis*⟩ **—in'fal•li•bly,** *adv.*

in•fa•mous ['ɪnfəməs] *adj.* **1** deserving or causing a very bad reputation; shamefully bad; extremely wicked. **2** having a very bad reputation; in public disgrace: *an infamous traitor.* **3** *Law.* having to do with a crime of moral turpitude, leading to a loss of civil rights on conviction. ⟨< Med.L *infamosus* < L *infamis*⟩ **—'in•fa•mous•ly,** *adv.* **—'in•fa•mous•ness,** *n.*

in•fa•my ['ɪnfəmi] *n., pl.* **-mies. 1** a very bad reputation; public disgrace: *His act brought infamy to his family and himself.* **2** shameful badness; extreme wickedness. **3** a shamefully bad or extremely wicked act. **4** the loss of civil rights because of conviction of an infamous offence. ⟨late ME *infamye* < L *infamia* < *in-* without + *fama* (good) reputation⟩

in•fan•cy ['ɪnfənsi] *n., pl.* **-cies. 1** the condition or time of being an infant; babyhood; early childhood. **2** an early stage; beginning of development: *Space travel is in its infancy.* **3** the condition of being under the legal age of responsibility (in common law, under 18). ⟨< L *infantia*⟩

in•fant ['ɪnfənt] *n., adj.* *—n.* **1** a baby; very young child. **2** a person under the legal age of responsibility; minor.
—adj. **1** of or for an infant. **2** in an early stage; just beginning to develop. ⟨< L *infans, infantis*, originally, not speaking < *in-* not + *fari* speak⟩ **—'in•fantˌhood,** *n.* **—'in•fantˌlike,** *adj.*

in•fan•ta [ɪn'fɑntə] *n.* **1** a daughter of a king of Spain or Portugal. **2** the wife of an infante. ⟨< Sp., Pg. *infanta*, fem.⟩

in•fan•te [ɪn'fɑntei] *n.* a son of a king of Spain or Portugal, but not the heir to the throne. ⟨< Sp., Pg.⟩

in•fan•ti•cide [ɪn'fæntəˌsaɪd] *n.* **1** the act of killing a baby under a year old. **2** a person who kills a baby under a year old. ⟨< L *infanticidium* the killing of a baby < *infans, -antis* infant + *-cidium* act of killing (for def. 1) or *-cida* killer (for def. 2)⟩

in•fan•tile ['ɪnfənˌtaɪl] *or* ['ɪnfəntəl] *adj.* **1** of an infant or infants; having to do with infants: *infantile diseases.* **2** like an infant; babyish; childish: *infantile behaviour.* **3** in an early stage; just beginning to develop. ⟨< LL *infantilis*⟩

infantile paralysis poliomyelitis; polio.

in•fan•ti•lism [ɪn'fæntəˌlɪzəm] *or* ['ɪnfəntəˌlɪzəm] *n.* an abnormal persistence or appearance of childish traits in adults.

in•fan•tine ['ɪnfənˌtaɪn] *or* ['ɪnfəntɪn] *adj.* infantile; babyish; childish.

in•fan•try ['ɪnfəntri] *n., pl.* **-tries. 1** soldiers trained, equipped, and organized to fight on foot. **2** the branch of an army made up of such soldiers. ⟨< F *infanterie* < Ital. *infanteria* < *infante, fante* foot soldier; originally, a youth < L *infans, -fantis.* See INFANT.⟩

in•fan•try•man ['ɪnfəntrimən] *n., pl.* **-men.** a soldier who fights on foot.

in•farct [ɪn'fɑrkt] *n. Pathology.* an area of dead tissue resulting from obstruction of the blood supply to that area by a blood clot, air bubble, or other material. ⟨< NL *infarctus* < L, stuffed in⟩ **—in'farct•ed,** *adj.*

in•farc•tion [ɪn'fɑrkʃən] *n. Pathology.* **1** a stoppage or sudden insufficiency of the blood supply due to a blood clot, air bubble, etc. in a vein or artery that results in the death of a portion of a tissue or an organ. **2** an infarct.

in•fat•u•ate *v.* [ɪn'fætʃuˌeit]; *adj.* [ɪn'fætʃuɪt] *or* [ɪn'fætʃuˌeit] *v.* **-at•ed, -at•ing;** *adj.* *—v.* **1** make foolish. **2** inspire with a foolish or unreasoning passion.
—adj. infatuated. ⟨< L *infatuare* < *in-* in + *fatuus* foolish⟩ **—in'fat•uˌa•tor,** *n.*

in•fat•u•at•ed [ɪn'fætʃuˌeitɪd] *adj., v.* *—adj.* extremely adoring; foolishly in love: *He is infatuated with the girl.*
—v. pt. and pp. of INFATUATE. **—in'fat•uˌat•ed•ly,** *adv.*

in•fat•u•a•tion [ɪnˌfætʃu'eiʃən] *n.* **1** infatuating or being infatuated. **2** a foolish love; unreasoning fondness.

in•fea•si•ble [ɪn'fizəbəl] *adj.* not feasible. **—inˌfea•si'bil•i•ty** or **in'fea•si•ble•ness,** *n.*

in•fect [ɪn'fɛkt] *v.* **1** cause illness in (a person, animal, etc.) by the action of disease-producing organisms: *A person who has influenza may infect other people.* **2** contaminate (the air, etc.) with such organisms. **3** produce infection in: *Dirt may infect an open wound.* **4** influence in a bad way; corrupt. **5** affect with a particular character, mood, belief, etc., as if by contagion: *The soldiers were infected with their captain's courage.* **6** *Computer technology.* introduce a computer virus or similar, potentially damaging software into (a computer system, disk, etc.). ⟨< L *infectus*, pp. of *inficere* dye, originally, put in < *in-* in + *facere* make⟩ **—in'fec•tor,** *n.*

in•fec•tion [ɪn'fɛkʃən] *n.* **1** the multiplication of harmful micro-organisms within the body: *The wound was cleaned to avoid infection.* **2** the condition produced by the establishment of such organisms in the body: *The pain was caused by a gum infection.* **3** an agent responsible for infection. **4** an infectious disease. **5** the communication of ideas, feelings, etc. by persuasion, example, etc.

in•fec•tious [ɪn'fɛkʃəs] *adj.* **1** of a disease, communicable by infection, with or without direct contact. Compare CONTAGIOUS. **2** capable of producing an infection: *infectious agents such as viruses.* **3** designating a disease caused by a micro-organism: *infectious hepatitis.* **4** capable of readily affecting others; spreading easily or rapidly; catching: *She has an infectious laugh. Their enthusiasm was infectious.* **—in'fec•tious•ly,** *adv.* **—in'fec•tious•ness,** *n.*

infectious mononucleosis an acute form of mononucleosis marked by fever and swelling of the lymph nodes.

in•fec•tive [ɪn'fɛktɪv] *adj.* infectious. ⟨ME < Med.L *infectivus*⟩

in•fe•cund [ɪn'fɛkənd] *or* [ɪn'fikənd] *adj.* barren; unfruitful. ⟨ME *infecounde* < L *infecundus*⟩ **—ˌin•fe'cun•di•ty** [ˌɪnfɪ'kʌndəti] *n.*

in•fe•lic•i•tous [ˌɪnfə'lɪsətəs] *adj.* **1** unsuitable; not appropriate. **2** unfortunate; unhappy. **—ˌin•fe'lic•i•tous•ly,** *adv.*

in•fe•lic•i•ty [ˌɪnfə'lɪsəti] *n., pl.* **-ties. 1** unsuitability; inappropriateness. **2** a misfortune; unhappiness. **3** something unsuitable; an inappropriate word, remark, etc. ⟨ME *infelicite* < L *infelicitas*⟩

in•fer [ɪn'fɜr] *v.* **-ferred, -fer•ring. 1** find out by reasoning; conclude: *Seeing the frown on my face, the boy inferred that I was displeased.* **2** *Informal.* indicate; imply: *Ragged clothing infers poverty.* **3** draw inferences. ⟨< L *inferre* < *in-* in + *ferre* bring⟩ **—in'fer•a•ble,** *adj.* **—in'fer•a•bly,** *adv.* **—in'fer•rer,** *n.*

☛ *Usage.* **Infer,** IMPLY. Though **infer** (def. 2) sometimes means **imply** in informal usage, careful writers do not confuse the two words. A writer or speaker **implies** something in his or her words or manner; a reader or listener **infers** something from what he or she reads, sees, or hears: *She implied by the look in her eyes that she did not intend to keep the appointment. We inferred from the principal's announcement that she already knew who had broken the window.*

in•fer•ence ['ɪnfərəns] *n.* **1** the process of inferring: *What happened is only a matter of inference; no one saw the accident.* **2** that which is inferred; conclusion: *What inference do you draw from smelling smoke?*

in•fer•en•tial [ˌɪnfə'rɛnʃəl] *adj.* having to do with or depending on inference. **—ˌin•fer'en•tial•ly,** *adv.*

in•fe•ri•or [ɪn'firiər] *adj., n.* *—adj.* **1** low in quality; below average: *an inferior grade of coffee.* **2** lower in importance, quality, merit, etc.: *This fabric is inferior to silk in strength. He has always felt inferior to his brothers.* **3** lower in position or rank: *an inferior officer. A lieutenant is inferior to a captain.* **4** *Botany.* **a** growing below some other organ. **b** belonging to the part of the flower that is farthest from the main stem. **c** of an ovary, below the calyx. **5** *Zoology.* below or posterior to others of the same kind, or to the usual or normal position: *the inferior vena cava.*

6 *Printing.* set below the main line of type, as letters or numerals in chemical formulas: *In* H_2O, *the 2 is inferior.*
7 *Astronomy.* of a planet, having an orbit within the earth's orbit.
—n. **1** a person who is lower in rank or station. **2** an inferior thing. ⟨< L *inferior,* comparative of *inferus,* adj., situated below⟩

in•fe•ri•or•i•ty [ɪn,firi'ɔrəti] *n.* an inferior condition or quality.

inferiority complex **1** *Psychology.* an abnormal or morbid feeling of being inferior to other people, resulting in timidity in certain cases and aggressiveness in others. **2** any lack of self-confidence.

in•fer•nal [ɪn'fɜrnəl] *adj.* **1** of hell; having to do with the lower world. **2** hellish; diabolical: *infernal heat.* **3** *Informal.* abominable; outrageous. ⟨< LL *infernalis,* ult. < L *inferus* below⟩ **—in'fer•nal•ly,** *adv.*

infernal machine *Archaic.* a disguised bomb or other explosive apparatus intended for the malicious destruction of life and property.

in•fer•no [ɪn'fɜrnou] *n., pl.* **-nos. 1** hell. **2** a place or thing that seems to be like hell: *Within half an hour of the start of the fire, the whole building was a raging inferno.* ⟨< Ital.⟩

in•fer•tile [ɪn'fɜrtaɪl] *or* [ɪn'fɜrtəl] *adj.* not fertile; not fruitful; sterile. ⟨< *infertilis*⟩ **—in'fer•tile•ly,** *adv.* **—in'fer•tile•ness,** *n.*

in•fer•til•i•ty [,ɪnfər'tɪləti] *n.* a lack of fertility; infertile state.

in•fest [ɪn'fɛst] *v.* trouble or disturb frequently or in large numbers (*used with* **by** *or* **with**): *Swamps are often infested with mosquitoes.* ⟨< L *infestare* attack < *infestus* hostile⟩

in•fes•ta•tion [,ɪnfɛ'steiʃən] *or* [,ɪnfə'steiʃən] *n.* **1** infesting. **2** the condition of being infested.

in•feu•da•tion [,ɪnfju'deiʃən] *n.* **1** the granting of an estate in fee. **2** the relation of lord and vassal established by such a grant. ⟨< Med.L *infeudation-* (stem of *infeudatio*)⟩

in•fi•del ['ɪnfədəl] *n., adj.* *—n.* **1** a person who does not believe in religion. **2** a person who rejects or opposes a particular faith, especially Christianity or Islam.
—adj. **1** being an infidel. **2** of, having to do with, or characteristic of infidels. ⟨< L *infidelis* < *in-* not + *fidelis* faithful < *fides* faith⟩

in•fi•del•i•ty [,ɪnfə'dɛləti] *n., pl.* **-ties. 1** lack of religious faith. **2** lack of belief in Christianity or Islam, etc. **3** unfaithfulness, especially of husband or wife; disloyalty. **4** an unfaithful or disloyal act. ⟨ME < L *infidelitas, infidelis*⟩

in•field ['ɪn,fild] *n.* **1** *Baseball.* **a** the part of the field within the base lines; DIAMOND (def. 7). **b** the first, second, and third base players and shortstop of a team: *That team has a good infield.* **2** *Horse Racing.* the land within a racetrack, used for field events. **3** *Agriculture.* **a** the part of farm lands nearest the buildings. **b** land regularly tilled. Compare OUTFIELD.

in•field•er ['ɪn,fildər] *n. Baseball.* a player of the infield.

in•fight•ing ['ɪn,fəitɪŋ] *n.* **1** *Informal.* internal dissension or conflict: *Infighting among staff lost their company the contract.* **2** *Boxing.* fighting at close quarters. **—'in,fight•er,** *n.*

in•fil•trate ['ɪnfɪl,treit] *or* [ɪn'fɪltreit] *v.* **-trat•ed, -trat•ing.** **1** *Military.* pass into or through by, or as by, filtering: *Enemy troops infiltrated the front lines.* **2** filter into or through; permeate or cause to permeate. **3** enter secretly or by deception. **—'in•fil,tra•tive,** *adj.* **—'in•fil,tra•tor,** *n.*

in•fil•tra•tion [,ɪnfɪl'treiʃən] *n.* **1** an infiltrating or the condition of being infiltrated. **2** something that infiltrates. **3** *Military.* a method of attack in which small groups of soldiers penetrate the enemy's lines at various weak points.

infin. infinitive.

in•fi•nite ['ɪnfənɪt] *adj., n.* *—adj.* **1** without limits or bounds; endless: *the infinite extent of space.* **2** extremely great: *Teaching little children takes infinite patience.* **3** *Mathematics.* **a** greater than any assignable quantity or magnitude of the sort in question. **b** beyond any finite magnitude, extending to infinity.
—n. **1** that which is infinite. **2** *Mathematics.* an infinite quantity or magnitude. **3 the Infinite,** God. ⟨< L *infinitus* < *in-* not + *finis* boundary⟩ **—'in•fi•nite•ness,** *n.*

in•fi•nite•ly ['ɪnfənɪtli] *adv.* **1** to an infinite degree. **2** *Informal.* very or very much: *I'm infinitely obliged to you.*

in•fi•ni•tes•i•mal [,ɪnfənə'tɛsəməl] *adj., n.* *—adj.* **1** so small as to be almost nothing: *A millionth of a centimetre is an infinitesimal length.* **2** *Mathematics.* less than any assignable quantity or magnitude of the sort in question.
—n. **1** an infinitesimal amount. **2** *Mathematics.* a variable continually approaching zero as a limit. ⟨< NL *infinitesimus* the 'nth' < L *infinitus.* See INFINITE.⟩ **—,in•fin•i,tes•i'mal•i•ty,** *n.* **—,in•fi•ni'tes•i•mal•ly,** *adv.*

in•fin•i•tive [ɪn'fɪnətɪv] *n. Grammar.* a form of a verb not limited by person, number, tense, voice, or mood. In *We want to go now, to go* is the infinitive. *Abbrev.:* infin. ⟨< LL *infinitivus* < L *infinitus* unrestricted. See INFINITE.⟩ **—in,fin•i'tiv•al** [,ɪnfənə'taɪvəl], *adj.*

☛ *Usage.* **infinitive.** The infinitive is the simple form of the verb, often preceded by *to: I want* to buy *a hat. Let him* leave *if he wants* to leave. Infinitives are used as: **a** nouns: To swim *across the English Channel is her ambition.* **b** adjectives: *She had money* to burn. **c** adverbs: *He went home* to rest. **d** part of verb phrases: *Henry is going* to do *most of the work.*

☛ *Usage.* See also note at SPLIT INFINITIVE.

in•fin•i•tude [ɪn'fɪnə,tjud] *or* [ɪn'fɪnə,tud] *n.* **1** the state or quality of being infinite. **2** an infinite extent, amount, or number.

in•fin•i•ty [ɪn'fɪnəti] *n., pl.* **-ties. 1** the state of being infinite: *the infinity of space.* **2** an infinite distance, space, or time. **3** an infinite extent, amount, or number: *the infinity of God's mercy.* **5** *Mathematics.* **a** an infinite quantity or magnitude. **b** the limit that a function is said to approach in certain conditions. **6** *Photography.* the setting for distant objects. ⟨< L *infinitas*⟩
to infinity, without limits or bounds; endlessly.

in•firm [ɪn'fɜrm] *adj.* **1** weak; feeble. **2** weak in will or character; not steadfast. **3** not firm; not stable. ⟨ME *infirme* < L *infirmus*⟩ **—in'firm•ly,** *adv.* **—in'firm•ness,** *n.*

in•fir•ma•ry [ɪn'fɜrməri] *n., pl.* **-ries.** a place for the care of the sick or injured, especially a small hospital or dispensary in a school or other institution. ⟨late ME < Med.L *infirmaria*⟩

in•fir•mi•ty [ɪn'fɜrməti] *n., pl.* **-ties. 1** weakness; feebleness. **2** a sickness; illness. **3** a moral weakness or failing. ⟨ME *infirmite* < L *infirmitas*⟩

in•fix *n.* ['ɪnfɪks]; *v.* [ɪn'fɪks] *or* ['ɪnfɪks] *n., v. Grammar.* *—n.* an inflectional or derivational morpheme in the body of a word.
—v. **1** fix firmly into something. **2** insert a morphological element as an infix.

in•flame [ɪn'fleim] *v.* **-flamed, -flam•ing. 1** become or cause to become on fire. **2** arouse to violent emotion or action: *Her impassioned accusations inflamed the crowd.* **3** make more violent or intense: *to inflame a hatred.* **4** become aroused to violent emotion or action. **5** produce inflammation in: *The smoke had inflamed the firefighter's eyes.* **6** of an organ or tissue in the body, become inflamed. ⟨ME < OF *enflamer* < L *inflammare* < *in-* in + *flamma* flame⟩ **—in'flam•er,** *n.*

in•flam•ma•ble [ɪn'flæməbəl] *adj., n.* *—adj.* **1** easily set on fire: *Paper and gasoline are inflammable.* **2** easily excited or aroused.
—n. something inflammable. ⟨< Med.L *inflammabilis* < L *inflammare*⟩ **—in'flam•ma•bly,** *adv.* **—in,flam•ma'bil•i•ty,** *n.* **—in'flam•ma•ble•ness,** *n.*

☛ *Usage.* See note at FLAMMABLE.

in•flam•ma•tion [,ɪnflə'meiʃən] *n.* **1** a diseased condition of some part of the body, marked by heat, redness, swelling, and pain. **2** the act of inflaming. **3** the condition of being inflamed.

in•flam•ma•to•ry [ɪn'flæmə,tɔri] *adj.* **1** tending to excite or arouse: *The leader of the opposition made an inflammatory speech attacking the government.* **2** of, causing, or accompanied by inflammation: *an inflammatory condition of the tonsils.* ⟨< L *inflammatus*⟩

in•flat•a•ble [ɪn'fleitəbəl] *adj., n.* *—adj.* that can be inflated.
—n. an inflatable boat, raft, etc.

in•flate [ɪn'fleit] *v.* **-flat•ed, -flat•ing. 1** blow out or swell with air or gas: *to inflate a balloon.* **2** swell or puff out: *to inflate with pride.* **3** increase (prices or currency or any figure) beyond a reasonable or normal amount. ⟨< L *inflatus,* pp. of *inflare* < *in-* into + *flare* blow⟩ **—in'flat•er** or **in'fla•tor,** *n.*

in•flat•ed [ɪn'fleitɪd] *adj., v.* *—adj.* **1** filled with air or gas. **2** bombastic. **3** filled with pride. **4** of currency or prices or other figures, unreasonably raised.
—v. pt. and pp. of INFLATE.

in•fla•tion [ɪn'fleiʃən] *n.* **1** a swelling (with air, gas, pride, etc.) **2** a swollen state; excessive expansion. **3** an increase of the currency of a country by issuing much paper money. **4** a sharp and sudden rise of prices resulting from too great an increase in the supply of paper money or bank credit. Compare DEFLATION. ⟨ME *inflacioun* < L *inflation-* (stem of *inflatio*)⟩

in•fla•tion•ar•y [ɪn'fleiʃə,nɛri] *adj.* of or having to do with inflation; tending to inflate.

inflationary spiral spiralling prices resulting from increasing costs of labour and services.

in•fla•tion•ism [ɪn'fləiʃə,nɪzəm] *n.* the policy or practice of inflation through expansion of currency or bank deposits.

in•fla•tion•ist [ɪn'fleiʃənɪst] *n.* a person who advocates inflation.

in•flect [ɪn'flɛkt] *v.* **1** change the tone or pitch of (the voice). **2** *Grammar.* vary the form of (a word) to show case, number, gender, person, tense, mood, comparison, etc. By inflecting *who,* we have *whose* and *whom.* **3** undergo such variations: *Latin nouns inflect for case and number.* **4** bend; curve. ⟨ME *inflecten* < L *inflectere* < *in-* in + *flectere* bend⟩ **—in'flect•ed•ness,** *n.* **—in'flec•tive,** *adj.* **—in'flec•tor,** *n.*

in•flec•tion [ɪn'flɛkʃən] *n.* **1** a change in the tone or pitch of the voice: *We end certain questions with a rising inflection.* **2** *Grammar.* **a** a variation in the form of a word to show case, number, gender, person, tense, mood, or comparison. **b** a suffix or other element used to indicate such a variation. **c** an inflected form. **3** a bending; curving. **4** a bend; curve. ⟨var. spelling of *inflexion* < L *inflexion-* (stem of *inflexio*) a bending⟩ **—in'flec•tion•less,** *adj.*

in•flec•tion•al [ɪn'flɛkʃənəl] *adj.* of, having to do with, or showing grammatical inflection. **—in'flec•tion•al•ly,** *adv.*

in•flexed [ɪn'flɛkst] *adj. Biology.* bent or folded downward or inward. ⟨< L *inflexus* bent in (pp. of *inflectere*)⟩

in•flex•i•ble [ɪn'flɛksəbəl] *adj.* **1** firm; unyielding; steadfast: *inflexible determination.* **2** that cannot be changed; unalterable. **3** not easily bent; stiff; rigid: *an inflexible steel rod.* ⟨< L *inflexibilis* that cannot be bent⟩ **—in,flex•i'bil•i•ty,** *n.* **—in'flex•i•ble•ness,** *n.* **—in'flex•i•bly,** *adv.*

☛ *Syn.* **1. Inflexible,** INEXORABLE, UNRELENTING = unyielding in character or purpose. **Inflexible** = unbending, holding fast or doggedly to what one has made up one's mind to do, think, or believe: *It is a waste of time to argue with someone whose attitude is inflexible.* **Inexorable** = not to be influenced or affected by begging or pleading, but firm and pitiless: *The principal was inexorable in her decision.* **Unrelenting** = not softening in force, harshness, or cruelty: *He was unrelenting in his hatred.*

in•flict [ɪn'flɪkt] *v.* **1** cause someone to have or suffer; give (a blow, wound, pain, etc.) **2** impose (a burden, suffering, anything unwelcome, etc.): *to inflict a penalty. Mrs. Jones inflicted herself upon her relatives for a long visit.* ⟨< L *inflictus,* pp. of *infligere* < *in-* on + *fligere* dash⟩ **—in'flict•or** or **in'flict•er,** *n.* **—in'flict•ive,** *adj.*

in•flic•tion [ɪn'flɪkʃən] *n.* **1** the act of inflicting. **2** something inflicted; pain; suffering; burden; punishment.

in–flight ['ɪn 'fləit] *adj.* served or shown during a flight: *an in-flight movie.*

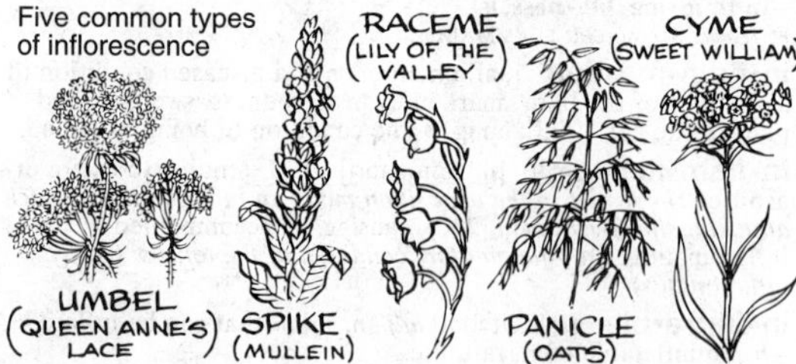

in•flo•res•cence [,ɪnflɔ'rɛsəns] *or* [,ɪnflə'rɛsəns] *n.* **1** the flowering stage. **2** *Botany.* **a** the arrangement of flowers on the stem or axis. **b** a flower cluster. **3** the state of being in flower; flowering. ⟨< NL *inflorescentia* < L *in-* in + *flos, floris* flower⟩

in•flo•res•cent [,ɪnflɔ'rɛsənt] *or* [,ɪnflə'rɛsənt] *adj.* showing inflorescence; flowering.

in•flow ['ɪn,flou] *n.* **1** a flowing in or into. **2** that which flows in; influx.

in•flu•ence ['ɪnfluəns] *n., v.* **-enced, -enc•ing.** *—n.* **1** the power of persons or things to act on others, seen only in its effects: *the influence of the moon on the tides.* **2** the power to produce an effect without using force: *A person may have influence by his or her ability, personality, position, or wealth.* **3** a person who or thing that has such power. **4** *Electricity.* induction, especially electrostatic induction. **5** *Astrology.* the supposed power of the stars over the characters and destinies of human beings.
—v. have power over; change the nature or behaviour of: *The moon influences the tides.* ⟨ME < OF < Med.L *influentia,* originally, a flowing in < L *in-* in + *fluere* flow⟩ **—'in•flu•ence•a•ble,** *adj.* **—'in•flu•enc•er,** *n.*

☛ *Syn. n.* **2.** See note at AUTHORITY.

in•flu•ent ['ɪnfluənt] *n., adj. —n.* a tributary.
—adj. flowing in. ⟨ME < L *influent-* (stem of *influens*) inflowing⟩

in•flu•en•tial [,ɪnflu'ɛnʃəl] *adj.* **1** having much influence; having influence: *Influential friends helped him to get a job.* **2** using influence. **3** producing results. ⟨< Med.L *influentia*⟩ **—,in•flu'en•tial•ly,** *adv.*

in•flu•en•za [,ɪnflu'ɛnzə] *n.* **1** an acute, contagious viral disease, occasionally resembling a severe cold in some of its symptoms, but much more dangerous and exhausting; flu. **2** a similar contagious disease of cats, horses, and pigs. ⟨< Ital. *influenza* < Med.L *influentia* influence⟩ **—in•flu'en•zal,** *adj.* **—,in•flu'en•za,like,** *adj.*

in•flux ['ɪnflʌks] *n.* **1** a flowing in; steady flow: *the influx of immigrants into a country.* **2** the point where a river or stream flows into another river, a lake, or the sea; mouth. **3** that which flows in. ⟨< LL *influxus,* ult. < L *in-* in + *fluere* flow⟩

in•fo ['ɪnfou] *n. Slang.* information.

In•fo•Can ['ɪnfou,kæn] *n. Cdn.* Information Canada, a supervisory and co-ordinating body.

in•fold [ɪn'fould] *v.* enfold. **—in'fold•er,** *n.* **—in'fold•ment,** *n.*

in•fo•ma•ni•ac or **in•for•ma•ni•ac** [,ɪnfou'meiniæk] *or* [,ɪnfər'meiniæk] *n.* a person who collects facts for their own sake.

in•fo•mer•cial or **in•for•mer•cial** ['ɪnfou,mɜrʃəl] *or* ['ɪnfər,mɜrʃəl] *n.* a television program which consists entirely of long advertisements.

in•form [ɪn'fɔrm] *v.* **1** give knowledge, facts, or news to: *The club secretary sent out letters informing members of a special meeting.* **2** give information about an offender or illegal or criminal activity to the police or some other authority; act as an informer (*usually used with* **against** *or* **on**). **3** inspire; animate. **4** give (something) its essential form or character. ⟨< L *informare* < *in-* in + *forma* form⟩

☛ *Syn.* **1. Inform,** ACQUAINT, NOTIFY = tell or let someone know something. **Inform** emphasizes telling or passing along directly to a person facts or knowledge of any kind: *Her letter informed us how and when she expected to arrive.* **Acquaint** emphasizes introducing someone to facts or knowledge that he or she has not known before: *He acquainted us with his plans.* **Notify** = inform someone, by an official announcement or formal notice, of something he or she ought to or needs to know: *The university notified him that he was awarded a scholarship.*

in•for•mal [ɪn'fɔrməl] *adj.* **1** not formal; not in the regular or prescribed manner: *informal proceedings.* **2** without ceremony; casual: *an informal party, informal clothes.* **3** used in general, everyday English, but not used in formal speech or writing. *Kids* is an informal term for *children.* Compare COLLOQUIAL. **—in'for•mal•ly,** *adv.*

☛ *Usage.* **Informal** English is the kind of English used by people in everyday speaking and writing; it ranges in style from the familiar, or casual, to the careful and precise. **Formal** English is used in lectures, speeches, learned articles, legal documents, and so on. As a usage label in this dictionary, **Informal** is used to mean 'acceptable in everyday use, but not appropriate in situations requiring more precise or formal language'.

in•for•mal•i•ty [,ɪnfɔr'mæləti] *n., pl.* **-ties. 1** the quality of being informal; lack of ceremony. **2** an informal act.

in•form•ant [ɪn'fɔrmənt] *n.* **1** a person who gives information to another; informer: *My informant saw the accident happen.* **2** *Linguistics.* a native speaker of a language, who supplies utterances and forms for one analysing or learning the language.

in•for•ma•tion [,ɪnfər'meiʃən] *n.* **1** knowledge; facts; news: *A dictionary gives information about words. The general sent information of his victory to headquarters.* **2** the act of informing: *A guidebook is for the information of travellers.* **3** a person or office whose duty is to answer questions. **4** an accusation or complaint against a person. **5** any message or part of a message in coded form assembled by or fed to a computer.

☛ *Syn.* **1.** See note at KNOWLEDGE.

in•for•ma•tion•al [,ɪnfər'meiʃənəl] *adj.* for the purpose of or having to do with giving information or instruction.

information highway *Computer technology.* all electronic media and communication systems.

information theory the study of the efficiency of any communication system.

in•form•a•tive [ɪn'fɔrmətɪv] *adj.* giving information; instructive. ⟨< L *informatus* (pp. of *informare*) + *-ive*⟩ **—in'form•a•tive•ly,** *adv.* **—in'form•a•tive•ness,** *n.*

in•form•er [ɪn'fɔrmər] *n.* **1** a person who gives information about an offender or illegal or criminal activity to the police or some other authority, especially one who does so for money or some other reward; an informant. **2** any person who provides information: *a financial informer.*

in•fra ['ɪnfrə] *adv. or prep. Latin.* beneath; below.

infra– *prefix.* below; beneath: *infrared.* ⟨< L *infra*, adv., prep.⟩

in•fract [ɪn'frækt] *v.* violate; break; infringe. ⟨< L *infractus* broken, bent, weakened (pp. of *infringere*)⟩ **—in'fract•or,** *n.*

in•frac•tion [ɪn'frækʃən] *n.* a breaking of a law or obligation; violation: *Reckless driving is an infraction of the law.* ⟨< L *infractio, -onis* < *infringere.* See INFRINGE.⟩

infra dig ['ɪnfrə 'dɪg] *Informal.* beneath one's dignity. ⟨< L *infra dignitatem,* beneath one's dignity⟩

in•fran•gi•ble [ɪn'frændʒəbəl] *adj.* **1** unable to be broken; unbreakable: *the infrangible laws of nature.* **2** inviolable: *an infrangible rule.* ⟨< L *infrangibilis*⟩ **—in,fran•gi'bil•i•ty,** *n.* **—in'fran•gi•bly,** *adv.*

in•frared ['ɪnfrə'rɛd] *adj.* of or having to do with the long, invisible light waves just beyond the red end of the colour spectrum. Most of the heat from sunlight, incandescent lamps, carbon arcs, resistance wires, etc. is from infrared rays.

in•fra•struc•ture ['ɪnfrə,strʌkʃər] *n.* the essential or foundational elements of a system or structure: *Roads, sewers, and water and power supply are the infrastructure of a city.*

in•fre•quen•cy [ɪn'frikwənsi] *n.* scarcity; rarity. Also, **infrequence.** ⟨< L *infrequentia*⟩

in•fre•quent [ɪn'frikwənt] *adj.* not frequent; occurring seldom or far apart; scarce; rare. ⟨< L *infrequens, -entis*⟩ **—in'fre•quent•ly,** *adv.*

in•fringe [ɪn'frɪndʒ] *v.* **-fringed, -fring•ing. 1** act contrary to or violate (a law, obligation, right, etc.): *A false label infringes the laws relating to food and drugs.* **2** trespass; encroach (*used with* **on** *or* **upon**): *to infringe on the rights of another.* ⟨< L *infringere* < *in-* in + *frangere* break⟩ **—in'fring•er,** *n.*

in•fringe•ment [ɪn'frɪndʒmənt] *n.* a breach or infraction, as of a law, obligation, or right; violation.

in•fun•dib•u•li•form [,ɪnfən'dɪbjələ,fɔrm] *adj. Biology.* shaped like a funnel.

in•fun•dib•u•lum [,ɪnfən'dɪbjələm] *n. Anatomy.* a funnel-shaped part of the cerebrum connecting to the thyroid at the base of the brain. ⟨< NL < L, funnel⟩ **—,in•fun'dib•u•lar** or **,in•fun'dib•u•late,** *adj.*

in•fu•ri•ate [ɪn'fjʊri,eit] *v.* **-at•ed, -at•ing.** fill with extreme anger; make furious; enrage. ⟨< Med.L *infuriare* < L *in-* into + *furia* fury⟩ **—in'fu•ri•at•ing•ly,** *adv.* **—in,fu•ri'a•tion,** *n.*

in•fuse [ɪn'fjuz] *v.* **-fused, -fus•ing. 1** permeate or fill someone with (a principle, quality, idea, etc.); impart (*used with* **into**): *The captain infused his own courage into his soldiers.* **2** inspire (*used with* **with**): *He infused the soldiers with his courage.* **3** steep or soak in a liquid to draw out flavour, minerals, etc. or to make a drink, drug, or other preparation: *We infuse tea leaves in hot water to make tea.* ⟨< L *infusus*, pp. of *infundere* < *in-* in + *fundere* pour⟩ **—in'fus•er,** *n.*

in•fu•si•ble¹ [ɪn'fjuzəbəl] *adj.* that cannot be fused or melted.

in•fu•si•ble² [ɪn'fjuzəbəl] *adj.* capable of being infused.

in•fu•sion [ɪn'fjuʒən] *n.* **1** the act or process of infusing. **2** something poured in or mingled; an infused element. **3** a liquid extract obtained by steeping or soaking, as tea.

in•fu•sive [ɪn'fjusɪv] *adj.* **1** capable of infusing. **2** inspiring.

in•fu•so•rial [,ɪnfjə'sɔriəl] *adj.* having to do with an infusorian or infusorians.

in•fu•so•ri•an [,ɪnfjə'sɔriən] *n., adj.* —*n.* any of a group of one-celled animals of the phylum Protozoa or the order Rotifera, that move by vibrating filaments.
—*adj.* of or belonging to this group. ⟨< NL *Infusoria*, genus name < L *infusus*, pp. of *infundere* pour in. See INFUSE.⟩

-ing¹ *suffix forming nouns.* the performance, result, product, material, etc. of some activity or thing, as in *hard thinking, the art of painting, a beautiful drawing, fine sewing, a blue lining, rich trimming, a metre of cotton shirting.* ⟨ME *-ing*, OE *-ing, -ung*⟩

-ing² *suffix.* **1** an element forming the present participle of verbs, as in *raining, staying, talking.* **2** that ——s: *lasting happiness.* ⟨ME *ing*(*e*), var. of *-ind*(*e*), *-end*(*e*), OE *-ende*⟩

in•gath•er ['ɪngæðər] *or* [ɪn'gæðər] *v.* gather in, as at harvest.

in•gem•i•nate [ɪn'dʒɛmə,neit] *v.* **-nat•ed, -nat•ing.** repeat. ⟨< *ingeminatus* redoubled, repeated (pp. of *ingeminare*)⟩ **—in,gem•i'na•tion,** *n.*

in•gen•er•ate [ɪn'dʒɛnə,rɪt] *adj.* not generated; self-existent. ⟨< LL *ingeneratus* not begotten⟩

in•gen•ious [ɪn'dʒinjəs] *adj.* **1** clever; skilful in planning or making: *The ingenious girl made a radio set.* **2** cleverly planned or made: *This mousetrap is an ingenious device.* ⟨< L *ingeniosus* < *ingenium* natural talent⟩ **—in'ge•ni•ous•ly,** *adv.* **—in'ge•ni•ous•ness,** *n.*

☛ *Syn.* **1.** See note at CLEVER.

☛ *Usage.* Do not confuse **ingenious** and INGENUOUS. **Ingenious** = clever; skilful; **ingenuous** = frank; sincere; simple: *Fay is so ingenious that she is sure to think of some way of doing this work more easily. The ingenuous child had never thought of being suspicious of what others told her.*

in•gé•nue [,ænʒə'nu] *or* ['ɒnʒə,nu]; *French, sing. and pl.* [ɛ̃ʒe'ny] *n., pl.* **-nues. 1** a simple, innocent girl or young woman, especially as represented on the stage, in films, etc. **2** an actress who plays such a part. ⟨< F *ingénue*, originally fem. adj., ingenuous⟩

in•ge•nu•ity [,ɪndʒə'njuəti] *or* [,ɪndʒə'nuəti] *n., pl.* **-ties. 1** skill in planning, inventing, etc.; cleverness. **2** a cleverly planned act, device, etc. ⟨< L *ingenuitas* frankness < *ingenuus* ingenuous; influenced by association with *ingenious*⟩

in•gen•u•ous [ɪn'dʒɛnjuəs] *adj.* **1** frank; open; sincere. **2** simple; natural; innocent. ⟨< L *ingenuus*, originally, native, free born⟩ **—in'gen•u•ous•ly,** *adv.* **—in'gen•u•ous•ness,** *n.*

☛ *Usage.* See note at INGENIOUS.

in•gest [ɪn'dʒɛst] *v.* **1** take (food, etc.) into the body for digestion. **2** take in: *He ingested the new idea slowly.* ⟨< L *ingestus*, pp. of *ingerere* < *in-* in + *gerere* carry⟩ **—in'gest•i•ble,** *adj.* **—in'gest•ion,** *n.* **—in'gest•ive,** *adj.*

in•ges•ta [ɪn'dʒɛstə] *n.pl.* whatever is ingested. ⟨< L⟩

in•gle ['ɪŋgəl] *n.* **1** fireplace. **2** a fire burning on the hearth. ⟨? < Scots Gaelic *aingeal* fire⟩

in•gle•nook ['ɪŋgəl,nʊk] *n.* a corner by the fire.

in•glo•ri•ous [ɪn'glɔriəs] *adj.* **1** bringing no glory; shameful; disgraceful. **2** *Archaic.* having no glory; not famous. ⟨< L *inglorius*⟩ **—in'glo•ri•ous•ness,** *n.* **—in'glo•ri•ous•ly,** *adv.*

in•go•ing ['ɪn,gouɪŋ] *adj.* going in; entering.

in•got ['ɪŋgət] *n.* a mass of metal, such as gold, silver, or steel, cast into a block or bar. ⟨OE *in-* in + *goten*, pp. of *gēotan* pour⟩

in•graft [ɪn'græft] *v.* engraft.

in•grain *v.* [ɪn'grein]; *adj., n.* ['ɪn,grein] *v., adj., n.* —*v.* **1** fix deeply and firmly; make an integral part of: *Certain habits are ingrained in one's nature.* **2** dye (fibre) before it is spun or woven.
—*adj.* **1** dyed before manufacture. **2** made of yarn dyed before weaving: *an ingrain rug.*
—*n.* yarn, wool, etc. dyed before manufacture. ⟨original phrase (*dyed*) *in grain*⟩

in•grained *adj.* [ɪn'greind] *or* ['ɪn,greind]; *v.* [ɪn'greind] *adj., v.* —*adj.* deeply fixed; integrated: *ingrained characteristics.*
—*v.* pt. and pp. of INGRAIN.

in•grate ['ɪngreit] *n., adj.* —*n.* an ungrateful person.
—*adj. Archaic.* ungrateful. ⟨< L *ingratus* < *in-* not + *gratus* thankful⟩

in•gra•ti•ate [ɪn'greiʃi,eit] *v.* **-at•ed, -at•ing.** bring (oneself or someone) into favour (*usually followed by* **with**): *He tried to ingratiate himself with the teacher by giving her presents.* ⟨apparently < Ital. *ingraziare*, ult. < L *in gratiam* into favour⟩ **—in,gra•ti'a•tion,** *n.*

in•gra•ti•at•ing [ɪn'greiʃi,eitɪŋ] *adj.* **1** charming; agreeable; pleasing. **2** meant to gain favour: *an ingratiating smile.* **—in'gra•ti,at•ing•ly,** *adv.*

in•grat•i•tude [ɪn'grætə,tjud] *or* [ɪn'grætə,tud] *n.* a lack of gratitude or thankfulness; ungratefulness. ⟨ME < Med.L *ingratitudo*⟩

in•gre•di•ent [ɪn'gridiənt] *n.* one of the parts of a mixture: *the ingredients of a cake.* ⟨< L *ingrediens, -entis*, ppr. of *ingredi* < *in-* in + *gradi* go⟩

in•gress ['ɪngrɛs] *n.* **1** a going in: *A high fence prevented ingress to the field.* **2** a way in; entrance. **3** a right to go in. ⟨< L *ingressus* < *ingredi.* See INGREDIENT.⟩ **—in•gres•sion** [ɪn'grɛʃən], *n.*

in•gres•sive [ɪn'grɛsiv] *adj.* **1** having to do with a way in. **2** having a right to enter. **3** *Phonetics.* involving the suction of air into the pharynx. **—in'gres•sive•ness,** *n.*

in–group ['ɪn ,grup] *n. Sociology.* a group of people sharing interests, aims, and a sense of being exclusive, especially such a group having power or prestige.

in•grow•ing ['ɪn,grouɪŋ] *adj.* **1** growing within; growing inward. **2** growing into the flesh: *an ingrowing toenail.*

in•grown [ˈɪn,groun] *adj.* **1** grown within; grown inward. **2** grown into the flesh.

in•gui•nal [ˈɪŋgwənəl] *adj.* of the groin; in or near the groin. ⟨< L *inguinalis* < *inguen* groin⟩

in•gulf [ɪnˈgʌlf] *v.* engulf.

in•gur•gi•tate [ɪnˈgɜrdʒɪ,teit] *v.* **-tat•ed, -tat•ing. 1** swallow in great amounts, as food. **2** engulf; swallow up.
—in,gur•gi'ta•tion, *n.*

in•hab•it [ɪnˈhæbɪt] *v.* **1** live in (a place, region, house, cave, tree, etc.) *Fish inhabit the sea.* **2** exist or be situated within: *Thoughts inhabit the mind.* **3** live; dwell. ⟨< L *inhabitare* < *in-* in + *habitare* dwell < *habere* have, dwell⟩ **—in,hab•i'ta•tion,** *n.*

in•hab•it•a•ble [ɪnˈhæbɪtəbəl] *adj.* **1** capable of being inhabited. **2** fit to live in; habitable. **—in,hab•it•a'bil•i•ty,** *n.*

in•hab•it•an•cy [ɪnˈhæbɪtənsi] *n., pl.* **-cies. 1** the act of dwelling. **2** a dwelling place.

in•hab•it•ant [ɪnˈhæbɪtənt] *n.* a person or animal that lives in a place. ⟨< L *inhabitans, -antis,* ppr. of *inhabitare.* See INHABIT.⟩

in•hal•ant [ɪnˈheilənt] *n., adj. —n.* **1** a medicine to be inhaled. **2** an apparatus for inhaling it.
—adj. used for inhaling.

in•ha•la•tion [,ɪnhəˈleiʃən] *n.* **1** the act of inhaling. **2** a medicine to be inhaled.

in•ha•la•tor [ˈɪnhə,leitər] *n.* an apparatus for inhaling anesthetics, medicine, etc.

in•hale [ɪnˈheil] *v.* **-haled, -hal•ing.** draw into the lungs; breathe in (air, gas, fragrance, tobacco smoke, etc.). ⟨< L *inhalare* < *in-* in + *halare* breathe⟩

in•hal•er [ɪnˈheilər] *n.* **1** an apparatus used in inhaling medicine, a gas, etc. **2** an apparatus for filtering dust, gases, etc. from air. **3** one who inhales.

in•har•mon•ic [,ɪnhɑrˈmɒnɪk] *adj.* not harmonic; not musical.

in•har•mo•ni•ous [,ɪnhɑrˈmouniəs] *adj.* **1** not harmonious; discordant. **2** not congenial; disagreeable.
—,in•har'mo•ni•ous•ly, *adv.* **—,in•har'mo•ni•ous•ness,** *n.*

in•haul [ˈɪn,hɒl] *n.* any of the lines used to haul in a sail for storage. Also, **inhauler.**

in•here [ɪnˈhir] *v.* **-hered, -her•ing.** exist; belong to as a basic, essential, or natural quality or attribute: *Greed inheres in human nature. Power inheres in that ruler.* ⟨< L *inhaerere* < *in-* in + *haerere* stick⟩

in•her•ence [ɪnˈhirəns] *or* [ɪnˈhɛrəns] *n.* the quality of being inherent.

in•her•en•cy [ɪnˈhirənsi] *or* [ɪnˈhɛrənsi] *n., pl.* **-cies.**
1 inherence. **2** something inherent. ⟨< Med.L *inhaerentia*⟩

in•her•ent [ɪnˈhirənt] *or* [ɪnˈhɛrənt] *adj.* existing as a natural or basic quality of a person or thing: *inherent honesty, the inherent sweetness of sugar.* ⟨< L *inhaerens, -entis,* ppr. of *inhaerere.* See INHERE.⟩

in•her•ent•ly [ɪnˈhirəntli] *or* [ɪnˈhɛrəntli] *adv.* by its own nature; essentially.

in•her•it [ɪnˈhɛrɪt] *v.* **1** get or have after another person dies; receive as an heir: *Mrs. Chan's niece inherited the farm.* **2** succeed as an heir to property, a right, title, privilege, etc.: *When the old bachelor dies, his nephew will inherit.* **3** get or possess from one's ancestors; have as a trait by heredity: *Mary has inherited her father's blue eyes.* **4** receive (anything) as by succession from predecessors: *When we took the house, we inherited the previous owner's carpets. The new government inherited a financial crisis.* ⟨ME < OF *enheriter* < LL *inhereditare* < L *in-* in, + *heres, -redis* heir⟩

in•her•it•a•ble [ɪnˈhɛrɪtəbəl] *adj.* **1** capable of being inherited. **2** capable of inheriting; qualified to inherit. ⟨late ME < AF⟩ **—in,her•it•a'bil•i•ty** or **in'her•it•a•ble•ness,** *n.*

in•her•it•ance [ɪnˈhɛrɪtəns] *n.* **1** the act of inheriting: *He obtained his house by inheritance from an aunt.* **2** the right of inheriting. **3** anything inherited: *Good health is a fine inheritance.* **4** *Genetics.* the pattern by which a genetically determined trait is transmitted in a family.

inheritance tax SUCCESSION DUTY.

in•her•i•tor [ɪnˈhɛrətər] *n.* one who inherits; heir. ⟨ME *enheritour, -er*⟩

in•he•sion [ɪnˈhiʒən] *n.* inherence. ⟨< L *inhaesio* < *inhaerere.* See INHERE.⟩

in•hib•it [ɪnˈhɪbɪt] *v.* **1** check; hold back; hinder or restrain: *The soldier's sense of duty inhibited his impulse to desert.* **2** prohibit; forbid. **3** *Chemistry.* decrease the rate of action of or stop (a chemical reaction). ⟨< L *inhibitus,* pp. of *inhibere* < *in-* in + *habere* hold⟩ **—in'hib•it•a•ble,** *adj.*

in•hi•bi•tion [,ɪnəˈbɪʃən] *or* [,ɪnhəˈbɪʃən] *n.* **1** the act of inhibiting. **2** the state of being inhibited. **3** an idea, emotion, attitude, habit, or other inner force that restrains natural impulses.

in•hib•i•tive [ɪnˈhɪbɪtɪv] *adj.* inhibitory.

in•hib•i•tor [ɪnˈhɪbətər] *n.* **1** a person or thing that inhibits. **2** *Chemistry.* anything that checks or interferes with a chemical reaction: *Antifreeze is an inhibitor.* Also, **inhibiter.**

in•hib•i•to•ry [ɪnˈhɪbɪ,tɔri] *adj.* inhibiting; tending to inhibit.

in•hom•o•ge•ne•ous [,ɪnhouməˈdʒiniəs] *or* [,ɪnhɒməˈdʒiniəs] *adj.* not homogeneous.

in•hos•pi•ta•ble [,ɪnhɒˈspɪtəbəl] *or* [ɪnˈhɒspɪtəbəl] *adj.* **1** not hospitable. **2** providing no shelter; barren: *The colonists encountered a rocky, inhospitable shore.* ⟨< Med.L *inhospitabilis*⟩ **—in•hos'pi•ta•ble•ness,** *n.* **—in•hos'pi•ta•bly,** *adv.*

in•hos•pi•tal•i•ty [,ɪnhɒspɪˈtæləti] *n.* a lack of hospitality; inhospitable behaviour. ⟨< L *inhospitalitas*⟩

in–house [ˈɪn ˈhʌus] *adj., adv.* using an organization's own resources: *an in-house magazine. We can check that in-house.*

in•hu•man [ɪnˈhjumən] *or* [ɪnˈjumən] *adj.* **1** without kindness; brutal; cruel. **2** not human; having or showing qualities not considered natural to a human being: *almost inhuman powers of endurance, an inhuman coldness of manner.* **3** not up to normal standards for human beings: *inhuman living conditions.* ⟨ME < MF *inhumain* < L *inhumanus* < *in-* not + *humanus* human; later influenced in spelling by L *inhumanus*⟩ **—in'hu•man•ly,** *adv.*

in•hu•mane [,ɪnhjuˈmein] *or* [,ɪnjuˈmein] *adj.* not humane; lacking in compassion, humanity, or kindness. ⟨var. of INHUMAN⟩ **—,in•hu'mane•ly,** *adv.*

in•hu•man•i•ty [,ɪnhjuˈmænəti] *or* [ɪnjuˈmænəti] *n., pl.* **-ties. 1** an inhuman quality; lack of feeling; cruelty; brutality. **2** an inhuman, cruel, or brutal act.

in•hume [ɪnˈhjum] *v.* **-humed, -hum•ing.** bury. ⟨< F *inhumer* < L *inhumare* < *in-* in + *humus* ground⟩ **—,in•hu'ma•tion,** *n.*

in•im•i•cal [ɪˈnɪməkəl] *adj.* **1** unfriendly; hostile. **2** adverse; unfavourable; harmful: *Lack of ambition is inimical to success.* ⟨< LL *inimicalis* < L *inimicus* < *in-* not + *amicus* friendly⟩ **—i'nim•i•cal•ly,** *adv.* **—in,im•i'cal•i•ty,** *n.*
☛ *Syn.* **1.** See note at HOSTILE.

in•im•i•ta•ble [ɪˈnɪmətəbəl] *adj.* that cannot be imitated or copied; matchless. ⟨< L *inimitabilis*⟩ **—i'nim•i•ta•bly,** *adv.* **—i'nim•i•ta•ble•ness** or **i,nim•i•ta'bil•i•ty,** *n.*

in•iq•ui•tous [ɪˈnɪkwətəs] *adj.* very unjust; wicked. **—i'niq•ui•tous•ly,** *adv.* **—i'niq•ui•tous•ness,** *n.*

in•iq•ui•ty [ɪˈnɪkwəti] *n., pl.* **-ties. 1** very great injustice; wickedness. **2** a wicked or unjust act. ⟨< L *iniquitas* < *iniquus* < *in-* not + *aequus* just⟩

in•i•tial [ɪˈnɪʃəl] *adj., n., v.* **-tialled** or **-tialed, -tial•ling** or **-tial•ing.** *—adj.* occurring at the beginning; first; earliest.
—n. **1** the first letter of a word or name. **2** an extra large letter, often decorated, at the beginning of a chapter or other division of a book or illuminated manuscript. **3 initials,** the first letters of one's surname and one or more given names used instead of one's signature.
—v. mark or sign with initials: *John Allen Smith initialled the note J.A.S.* ⟨< L *initialis* < *initium* beginning < *inire* begin < *in* -in + *ire* go⟩

in•i•tial•ize [ɪˈnɪʃə,laɪz] *v.* **-ized, -iz•ing.** *Computer technology.* **1** FORMAT (def. *v.* 2). **2** set to an intitial value or state: *The year-to-date total was initialized to zero on January 1st.*

in•i•tial•ly [ɪˈnɪʃəli] *adv.* at the beginning.

Initial Teaching Alphabet an alphabet of 44 letters, supposed to represent basic English sounds, used in teaching beginners to read.

in•i•ti•ate *v.* [ɪˈnɪʃi,eit]; *n., adj.* [ɪˈnɪʃiɪt] *or* [ɪˈnɪʃi,eit] *v.* **-at•ed, -at•ing;** *n., adj. —v.* **1** be the first one to start; begin. **2** admit (a person) by special forms or ceremonies (into mysteries, secret knowledge, or a society). **3** help to get a first understanding; introduce into the knowledge of some art or subject: *to initiate a person into business methods.*
—n. a person who is initiated.
—adj. initiated. ⟨< L *initiare* < *initium* beginning < *inire* begin. See INITIAL.⟩ **—in'i•ti,a•tor,** *n.*

in•i•ti•a•tion [ɪ,nɪʃiˈeiʃən] *n.* **1** the act or process of initiating;

beginning: *the initiation of Senate reform.* **2** a being initiated. **3** a formal admission into a group or society. **4** the ceremonies by which one is admitted to a group or society.

in•i•ti•a•tive [ɪ'nɪʃətɪv] *n.* **1** the active part in taking the first steps in any undertaking; the lead: *She is shy and does not take the initiative in making acquaintances.* **2** the readiness and ability to be the one to start something; enterprise: *A good leader must have initiative.* **3** the right to be the first to act, legislate, etc.

in•i•ti•a•to•ry [ɪ'nɪʃə,tɔri] *adj.* **1** first; beginning; introductory. **2** of initiation.

in•ject [ɪn'dʒɛkt] *v.* **1** force (liquid) into a passage, cavity, or tissue: *to inject cortisone into a muscle, to inject fuel into an engine.* **2** fill (a cavity, etc.) with fluid forced in. **3** throw in; introduce: *The stranger injected a remark into their conversation.* ⟨< L *injectus*, pp. of *inicere* < *in-* in + *jacere* throw⟩ **—in'jec•tor,** *n.* **—in'ject•a•ble,** *adj.*

in•jec•tion [ɪn'dʒɛkʃən] *n.* **1** the act or process of injecting: *Drugs are given by injection as well as through the mouth.* **2** something injected.

in•ju•di•cious [,ɪndʒə'dɪʃəs] *adj.* showing lack of judgment; unwise; not prudent. **—,in•ju'di•cious•ly,** *adv.* **—,in•ju'di•cious•ness,** *n.*

in•junc•tion [ɪn'dʒʌŋkʃən] *n.* **1** a command; order: *Injunctions of secrecy did not prevent the news from leaking out.* **2** *Law.* a formal order issued by a court or judge ordering a person or group to refrain from doing something; a prohibition. **3** the act of commanding or authoritatively directing. ⟨< LL *injunctio, -onis* < L *injungere* enjoin < *in-* in + *jungere* join. Related to ENJOIN.⟩ **—in'junct•ive,** *adj.*

in•jure ['ɪndʒər] *v.* **-jured, -jur•ing. 1** cause damage to; wound, hurt, or harm: *She injured her arm when she fell. The fruit trees were injured by the frost. Her pride has been injured.* **2** do wrong to: *You injure him when you doubt his ability.* ⟨< *injury*⟩

☛ *Syn.* **1. Injure,** HURT, IMPAIR = do harm or damage to someone or something. **Injure** is a general word meaning 'to do something that harms, reduces, or takes away strength, health, perfection, rights, value, usefulness, etc.': *Dishonesty injures a business.* **Hurt,** a less formal substitute for **injure,** particularly means 'to cause physical injury to a person, or bodily or mental pain': *He hurt my hand by twisting it.* **Impair** = injure (a process, faculty, or other abstraction) by weakening, diminishing, or decreasing strength or value: *Poor eating habits impair health.*

in•ju•ri•ous [ɪn'dʒʊriəs] *adj.* **1** causing injury; harmful: *Hail is injurious to crops.* **2** unfair; unjust; wrongful. **3** slanderous: *injurious remarks.* **—in'ju•ri•ous•ly,** *adv.* **—in'ju•ri•ous•ness,** *n.*

in•ju•ry ['ɪndʒəri] *n., pl.* **-ju•ries. 1** hurt or loss caused to or endured by a person or thing; damage; harm: *She escaped from the train wreck without injury.* **2** a wound; hurt; an act that harms or damages: *He received a serious injury in the accident. The accident will certainly be an injury to the reputation of the airline.* **3** unfairness; injustice; wrong: *You did me an injury when you said I lied.* ⟨< L *injuria* < *in-* not + *jus, juris* right⟩

in•jus•tice [ɪn'dʒʌstɪs] *n.* **1** a lack of justice; being unjust. **2** an unjust act: *To send an innocent man to jail is an injustice.* ⟨ME < MF < L *injustitia*⟩

ink [ɪŋk] *n., v.* *—n.* **1** a coloured substance, usually a liquid, used for writing, printing, or drawing. **2** a dark liquid squirted out for protection by cuttlefish, squids, etc.
—v. **1** put ink on; mark, colour, or stain with ink. **2** put (an agreement, contract, etc.) in writing.
ink in, fill in (an outline) with ink. ⟨ME < OF *enque* < LL < Gk. *enkauston* < *en* in + *kaiein* burn⟩ **—'ink•er,** *n.* **—'ink,like,** *adj.*

ink•ber•ry ['ɪŋk,bɛri] *n., pl.* **-ries. 1** a shrub (*Ilex glabra*) having evergreen leaves and black berries. **2** one of these berries. **3** pokeweed.

ink•horn ['ɪŋk,hɔrn] *n.* a small container formerly used to hold ink, often made of horn.

ink–jet printer ['ɪŋk ,dʒɛt] *Computer technology.* a non-impact printer that prints characters by spraying ink onto the paper in the appropriate pattern.

in•kle ['ɪŋkəl] *n.* a linen tape used for trimming. ⟨origin uncertain⟩

ink•ling ['ɪŋklɪŋ] *n.* a slight suggestion; vague notion; hint. ⟨ME *inclen* whisper, hint < OE *inca* doubt⟩

ink•stand ['ɪŋk,stænd] *n.* **1** a stand to hold ink and pens. **2** a container used to hold ink.

ink•well ['ɪŋk,wɛl] *n.* a container used to hold ink on a desk or table.

ink•y ['ɪŋki] *adj.* **ink•i•er, ink•i•est. 1** dark or black, like ink: *inky shadows.* **2** covered with ink; marked or stained with ink. **3** of ink. **—'ink•i•ly,** *adv.* **—'ink•i•ness,** *n.*

inky cap any of various mushrooms of the genus *Coprinus*, with gills that become like ink, dark and liquid, at maturity.

in•laid ['ɪn,leid] *or* [ɪn'leid] *adj., v.* *—adj.* **1** set in the surface as a decoration or design: *The desk had an inlaid design of light wood in dark.* **2** decorated with a design or material set in the surface: *The box had an inlaid cover.*
—v. pt. and pp. of INLAY.

in•land *adj.* ['ɪnlənd]; *n., adv.* ['ɪn,lænd] *or* ['ɪnlənd] *adj., n., adv.* *—adj.* **1** away from the coast or the border; having to do with or situated in the interior: *an inland sea.* **2** domestic; not foreign: *inland trade.*
—n. the interior of a country; land away from the border or the coast.
—adv. in or toward the interior.

inland boat *Cdn.* formerly, a YORK BOAT.

in•land•er ['ɪnləndər] *or* ['ɪnlændər] *n.* one who lives inland.

in–law ['ɪn ,lɒ] *n. Informal.* a relative by marriage. ⟨ME *inlawen*, OE *inlagian*⟩

in•lay *v.* ['ɪn,lei] *or* [ɪn'lei]; *n.* ['ɪn,lei] *v.* **-laid, -lay•ing;** *n.* *—v.* **1** set as a decoration or design into a shallow recess in a surface: *to inlay strips of gold.* **2** decorate with something set into the surface: *to inlay a wooden box with silver.*
—n. **1** an inlaid decoration, design, or material. **2** a shaped piece of gold, porcelain, etc. cemented in a tooth as a filling. **3** a graft made by inlaying. **—'in,lay•er,** *n.*

in•let ['ɪn,lɛt] *or* ['ɪnlət] *n.* **1** a narrow strip of water extending from a larger body of water into the land or between islands. **2** entrance. ⟨ME⟩

in•li•er ['ɪn,laɪər] *n. Geology.* an old rock formation surrounded by new strata.

inline skates ['ɪn,laɪn] roller skates having four wheels in a single row, one behind the other. **—inline skating.**

in loc. cit. in the place cited. ⟨< L *in loco citato*⟩

in lo•co pa•ren•tis [ɪn 'loukou pɑ'rɛntiz] *or* [pə'rɛntɪs] *Latin.* in the place of a parent; as a parent.

in•ly ['ɪnli] *adv. Poetic.* **1** inwardly; within. **2** thoroughly; deeply. ⟨OE *inlīce*⟩

in•mate ['ɪn,meit] *n.* a person who lives with others in the same building, especially one confined in a prison, hospital, etc. ⟨< *in-*[2] + *mate*[1]⟩

in me•di•as res [ɪn 'meidiɑs 'reis] *or* [ɪn 'midiəs 'riz] *Latin.* in the midst of things.

in me•mo•ri•am ['ɪn mə'mɔriəm] *Latin.* in memory (of); to the memory (of).

in•most ['ɪn,moust] *adj.* **1** farthest in; deepest within: *We went to the inmost depths of the mine.* **2** most private or personal: *Her inmost desire was to be an astronaut.* ⟨OE *innemest*, double superlative of *inne* within; influenced by *most*⟩

inn [ɪn] *n.* **1** a public house for lodging and caring for travellers: *Many old inns in England are still flourishing.* **2** hotel. **3** tavern. ⟨OE *inn* lodging⟩
☛ *Hom.* IN.

in•nards ['ɪnərdz] *n.pl. Informal.* **1** the internal organs of the body; insides; viscera. **2** the internal workings or parts of any complex mechanism, structure, etc. ⟨var. of *inward*⟩

in•nate [ɪ'neit] *or* ['ɪneit] *adj.* **1** natural; inborn: *an innate talent for drawing.* **2** existing as a natural characteristic: *the innate complexity of the problem.* ⟨< L *innatus* < *in-* in + *nasci* be born⟩ **—in'nate•ly,** *adv.* **—in'nate•ness,** *n.*

in•ner ['ɪnər] *adj.* **1** farther in; inside: *the inner bark of a tree, an inner room.* **2** intimate or private; close to the central or most important part: *the inner circle of government. She kept her inner thoughts to herself.* **3** spiritual: *her inner grace.* ⟨OE *innera*, comparative of *inne* within⟩

inner cabinet *Cdn.* a small number of members of the Cabinet, who have the most power.

inner city the older, central part of a large city, especially when it is densely populated and less affluent than the rest of the city. **—'in•ner-'cit•y,** *adj.*

in•ner–di•rect•ed ['ɪnər daɪ'rɛktɪd] *or* [dɪ'rɛktɪd] *adj.* guided by one's internal values, not by external pressure.

inner ear the cavity behind the three bones of the middle ear. In human beings it contains the semicircular canals, the cochlea, and part of the auditory nerve. See EAR[1] for picture.

inner man 1 one's spiritual being. **2** *Informal.* the appetite.

in•ner•most [ˈɪnər,moust] *adj.* **1** farthest in; inmost: *the innermost parts.* **2** most secret.

inner planet TERRESTRIAL PLANET.

in•ner–spring mat•tress [ˈɪnər ˈsprɪŋ] a mattress with springs usually coiled inside it.

inner tube a separate rubber tube that fits inside some tires and is inflated with air.

in•ner•vate [ɪˈnɜrveit] *v.* **-vat•ed, -vat•ing.** communicate nervous energy to; stimulate through nerves.

in•nerve [ɪˈnɜrv] *v.* **-nerved, -nerv•ing.** stimulate; invigorate.

in•ning [ˈɪnɪŋ] *n.* **1** *Baseball.* the period of play in which each team has a turn at bat. **2 innings,** *Cricket.* the period of a game when one team is batting (*used with a singular verb*). **3** Usually, **innings**, the time when a person or group has a chance for action or accomplishment (*usually used with a singular verb*): *The Tories are finally going to have their innings.* ⟨OE *innung* a getting in⟩

inn•keep•er [ˈɪn,kipər] *n.* a person who owns, manages, or keeps an inn.

in•no•cence [ˈɪnəsəns] *n.* **1** the state or quality of being free from sin or moral guilt, or from legal guilt for a particular offence: *The trial established his innocence.* **2** the state or quality of being free from guile or cunning; simplicity: *the innocence of a child.* **3** lack of worldly experience; naïvete: *In his innocence, he believed everything the stranger told him.* **4** a bluet. ⟨ME < L *innocentia*⟩

in•no•cen•cy [ˈɪnəsənsi] *n. Archaic.* INNOCENCE (defs. 1-3).

in•no•cent [ˈɪnəsənt] *adj., n.* —*adj.* **1** free from wrongdoing: *An innocent bystander was hit in the shootout between police and the bank robbers.* **2** not legally guilty of a particular offence: *The trial proved that the accused was innocent.* **3** not wrong or bad; harmless: *innocent amusements.* **4** without knowledge of evil, and therefore free from sin or wrong: *as innocent as a baby.* **5** free from cunning or guile; simple and open; artless: *an innocent question.* **6** free from responsibility with regard to a specified evil. **7** naïve. **8** lacking (*usually used with* **of**): *a bare, bleak room innocent of all adornment.*

—*n.* **1** a person who has no knowledge of evil or who is artless or naïve. **2** *Archaic.* a foolish or simple-minded person. ⟨< L *innocens, -entis* < *in-* not + *nocere* harm⟩ **—ˈin•no•cent•ly,** *adv.*

☛ *Syn. adj.* **1, 2. Innocent,** BLAMELESS, GUILTLESS = free from fault or wrong. **Innocent** emphasizes having intended or consciously done no wrong, having broken no moral, social, or statute law: *The truck driver was proved innocent of manslaughter.* **Blameless** = not to blame, not to be held responsible or punished, whether or not wrong has actually been done: *He was held blameless, although the child was killed.* **Guiltless** = without guilt in thought, intention, or act: *The other driver was not guiltless.*

in•noc•u•ous [ɪˈnɒkjuəs] *adj.* **1** harmless; not capable of causing damage or injury: *an innocuous medicine.* **2** not likely to arouse hostility or strong feelings; not offensive or provocative: *innocuous remarks.* ⟨< L *innocuus* < *in-* not + *nocuus* hurtful < *nocere* to harm⟩ **—inˈnoc•u•ous•ly,** *adv.* **—inˈnoc•u•ous•ness,** *n.*

in•nom•in•ate [ɪnˈnɒmɪnət] *or* [ɪˈnɒmɪnət] *adj.* **1** with no specific name. **2** anonymous.

innominate bone hipbone.

in•no•vate [ˈɪnə,veit] *v.* **-vat•ed, -vat•ing.** make changes; bring in something new or do something in a new way. ⟨< L *innovare* < *in-* in + *novus* new⟩

in•no•va•tion [,ɪnəˈveiʃən] *n.* **1** a change made in the established way of doing things. **2** the making of changes; act of bringing in new things or new ways of doing things: *He is strongly opposed to innovation of any kind.* **—,in•noˈva•tion•al,** *adj.*

in•no•va•tive [ˈɪnə,veitɪv] *adj.* characterized by or bringing in innovation.

in•no•va•tor [ˈɪnə,veitər] *n.* a person who makes changes or introduces new methods.

in•nox•ious [ɪˈnɒkʃəs] *adj.* harmless. ⟨< L *innoxius*⟩ **—inˈnox•ious•ly,** *adv.* **—inˈnox•ious•ness,** *n.*

In•nu [ˈɪnu] *n. Cdn.* **1** a member of a First Nations people living in northern Québec. **2** the Cree dialect of these people; Montagnais; Naskapi.

in•nu•en•do [,ɪnjuˈɛndou] *n., pl.* **-does. 1** an indirect hint or reference, especially an indirect suggestion against someone's character or reputation; insinuation. **2** *Law.* in a lawsuit, the interpretation by the plaintiff of what he or she considers to be slander. ⟨< L *innuendo*, literally, by giving a nod to, ablative gerund of *innuere* < *in-* in + *-nuere* nod⟩

In•nu•it [ˈɪnuɪt] *or* [ˈɪnjuɪt] *Cdn.* See INUIT.

in•nu•mer•a•ble [ɪˈnjumərəbəl] *or* [ɪˈnumərəbəl] *adj.* too many to count; countless: *innumerable stars.* Also, **innumerous.** ⟨ME < L *innumerabilis* < *in-* not + *numerabilis* that can be counted or numbered (*numerus* a number + *-a-* + *-bilis*)⟩ **—inˈnu•mer•a•ble•ness** or **in,nu•mer•aˈbil•i•ty,** *n.*

in•nu•mer•a•bly [ɪˈnjumərəbli] *or* [ɪˈnumərəbli] *adv.* countlessly; in very great numbers.

in•nu•mer•a•cy [ɪˈnjumərəsi] *or* [ɪˈnumərəsi] *n.* lack of ability to do simple calculations; the mathematical equivalent of illiteracy.

in•nu•mer•ate [ɪˈnjumərɪt] *or* [ɪˈnumərɪt] *adj.* unable to do simple calculations; the mathematical equivalent of **illiterate**.

in•nu•tri•tion [,ɪnnjuˈtrɪʃən] *or* [,ɪnnuˈtrɪʃən] *n.* lack of nutrition. **—,in•nuˈtri•tious,** *adj.*

in•ob•ser•vance [,ɪnəbˈzɜrvəns] *n.* inattention.

in•oc•u•la•ble [ɪˈnɒkjələbəl] *adj.* capable of being inoculated. **—in,oc•u•laˈbil•i•ty,** *n.*

in•oc•u•late [ɪˈnɒkjə,leit] *v.* **-lat•ed, -lat•ing. 1** infect (a person or animal) with organisms that will cause a very mild form of a disease, thus reducing the individual's chances of contracting the disease thereafter. **2** use disease-producing organisms to prevent or cure diseases. **3** put bacteria, serums, etc. into. Farmers inoculate the soil with bacteria that will take nitrogen from the air and change it so that it can be used by plants. **4** fill (a person's mind) with ideas, opinions, etc. ⟨ME < L *inoculatus* implanted (pp. of *inoculare*) < *in-* in + *oculus* bud, eye⟩ **—inˈoc•u,la•tor,** *n.*

in•oc•u•la•tion [ɪ,nɒkjəˈleiʃən] *n.* the act or process of inoculating, especially in order to immunize against disease.

in•oc•u•lum [ɪˈnɒkjələm] *n., pl.* **-la** [-lə]. a substance used in an inoculation.

in•o•dor•ous [ɪnˈoudərəs] *adj.* having no scent. ⟨< L *inodorus*⟩

in•of•fen•sive [,ɪnəˈfɛnsɪv] *adj.* not offensive; harmless; not arousing objections. **—,in•ofˈfen•sive•ly,** *adv.* **—,in•ofˈfen•sive•ness,** *n.*

in•of•fi•cious [,ɪnəˈfɪʃəs] *adj. Law.* contrary to moral duty, such as disinheriting one's heirs. ⟨< L *inofficiosus*⟩

in•op•er•a•ble [ɪnˈɒpərəbəl] *adj.* **1** not practicable; unworkable: *an inoperable plan.* **2** unable to be cured by surgery: *an inoperable cancer.* **—in,op•er•aˈbil•i•ty,** *n.*

in•op•er•a•tive [ɪnˈɒpərətɪv] *or* [ɪnˈɒpə,reitɪv] *adj.* not operative; not working; without effect. **—inˈop•er•a•tive•ness,** *n.*

in•op•por•tune [ɪn,ɒpərˈtjun] *or* [ɪn,ɒpərˈtun] *adj.* not opportune; coming at a bad time; inconvenient: *An inopportune call delayed us.* **—in,op•porˈtune•ly,** *adv.* **—in,op•porˈtune•ness,** *n.* **—in,op•porˈtu•ni•ty,** *n.*

in•or•di•nate [ɪnˈɔrdənɪt] *adj.* **1** much too great; excessive; immoderate: *He spends an inordinate amount of time tinkering with those old radios.* **2** irregular: *She works inordinate hours.* ⟨< L *inordinatus* < *in-* not + *ordo, -dinis* order⟩ **—inˈor•di•nate•ly,** *adv.*

☛ *Syn.* **1.** See note at EXCESSIVE.

in•or•gan•ic [,ɪnɔrˈgænɪk] *adj.* **1** composed of or referring to matter that is not animal or vegetable, fungus, protist or moneran; not having the organized structure of animals or plants: *Minerals are inorganic.* **2** *Chemistry.* of or referring to any chemical compound not classified as organic. **3** of or referring to the branch of chemistry that deals with inorganic compounds and elements. **4** lacking structure or system. **5** not resulting from natural growth; extraneous or artificial. **—,in•orˈgan•i•cal•ly,** *adv.*

inorganic chemistry the branch of chemistry dealing with inorganic compounds and elements, primarily compounds not containing carbon.

in•os•cu•late [ɪˈnɒskjə,leit] *v.* **-lat•ed, -lat•ing. 1** join (veins or ducts) by means of small openings. **2** blend. **3** open into each other.

i•nos•i•plex [aɪˈnɒsɪ,plɛks] *n.* a drug used to treat one form of encephalitis.

in•o•si•tol [ɪˈnousə,tɒl] *n. Biochemistry.* any of nine isomeric alcohols regarded as members of the Vitamin B complex.

in–patient [ˈɪn,peiʃənt] *n.* a patient who lives in a hospital while being treated. Compare OUT-PATIENT.

in per•pet•u•um [,ɪn pərˈpɛtʃuəm] *or* [,ɪn pərˈpɛtjuəm] *Latin.* for all time.

in per•so•nam [,ɪn pərˈsounəm] *Latin. Law.* of legal action, against a person.

in•phase ['ɪn,feiz] *adj. Electricity.* having the same phase.

in•put ['ɪn,pʊt] *n., v.* **in•put, in•put•ting.** *—n.* **1** the act or process of putting in or contributing: *She felt there was too little opportunity for input as an ordinary member of the club.* **2** the amount of material, energy, resources, etc. put in: *hoping for an increased input of funds.* **3** energy, electric current, etc. supplied for the purpose of producing an output of some kind. **4** data fed into a computer or data-processing system. **5** (*adjl.*) having to do with input.
—v. feed (data) into a computer or data-processing system.

in•quest ['ɪnkwɛst] *n.* **1** a legal inquiry led by a coroner, usually with a jury to determine the cause of a sudden death when there is a possibility that the death was the result of a crime or of a situation that could be dangerous to others. **2** a jury appointed to hold such an inquiry: *The inquest was told that one of the witnesses had been delayed.* **3** any other investigation into the cause of an event, situation, etc. ⟨ME < OF *enqueste,* ult. < L *inquirere.* See INQUIRE.⟩

in•qui•e•tude [ɪn'kwaɪə,tjud] *or* [ɪn'kwaɪə,tud] *n.* restlessness; uneasiness. ⟨late ME < L *inquietudo*⟩

in•qui•line ['ɪnkwə,laɪn] *or* ['ɪnkwəlɪn] *n., adj. —n.* an animal that lives in the home of another animal.
—adj. like or being an inquiline. ⟨< L *inquilinus* tenant⟩ **—,in•qui'lin•i•ty** [,ɪnkwə'lɪnəti], *n.* **—,in•qui'li•nous** [,ɪnkwə'laɪnəs], *adj.*

in•quire [ɪn'kwaɪr] *v.* **-quired, -quir•ing. 1** try to find out by questions; ask. **2** make an investigation or examination, especially by asking questions; search (*into*): *to inquire into someone's past.* Also, **enquire.** ⟨< L *inquirere* < *in-* into + *quaerere* ask⟩ **—in'quir•er,** *n.* **—in'quir•ing•ly,** *adv.*
☛ *Syn.* **1.** See note at ASK.

in•quir•y [ɪn'kwaɪri] *or* ['ɪnkwəri] *n., pl.* **-quir•ies. 1** the act of inquiring. **2** a question. **3** an investigation or examination: *The authorities are conducting an inquiry into the cause of the explosion.* Also, **enquiry.**
☛ *Syn.* **3.** See note at INVESTIGATION.

in•qui•si•tion [,ɪnkwə'zɪʃən] *n.* **1** an official investigation; a judicial inquiry. **2** an inquest. **3 the Inquisition, a** a court established by the Roman Catholic Church in 1229 to discover and suppress heresy and to punish heretics. During the 15th and 16th centuries, the powers of the Inquisition were tremendously enlarged, especially in Spain, Portugal, and parts of Italy. It was abolished in 1834. **b** the activities of this court. **4** any very severe or intensive questioning. ⟨< L *inquisitio, -onis* < *inquirere.* See INQUIRE.⟩ **—,in•qui'si•tion•al,** *adj.*

in•quis•i•tive [ɪn'kwɪzətɪv] *adj.* **1** curious; asking many questions. **2** too curious; prying into other people's affairs. ⟨< LL *inquisitivus,* L *inquisitus* sought for⟩ **—in'quis•i•tive•ly,** *adv.* **—in'quis•i•tive•ness,** *n.*
☛ *Syn.* **1.** See note at CURIOUS.

in•quis•i•tor [ɪn'kwɪzətər] *n.* **1** a person who makes an inquisition; official investigator; judicial inquirer. **2 Inquisitor,** a member of the Inquisition. **3** a person who conducts an inquiry in a very harsh or hostile manner.

in•quis•i•to•ri•al [ɪn,kwɪzə'tɔriəl] *adj.* **1** of or like an inquisitor or inquisition. **2** making searching inquiry; thorough. **3** unduly curious. ⟨< Med.L *inquisitorius,* L *inquisitor-* + *-ius*⟩ **—in,quis•i'to•ri•al•ly,** *adv.*

in re [ɪn 'ri] *or* [ɪn 'rei] *Latin.* concerning; in the matter of.

I.N.R.I. Jesus of Nazareth, King of the Jews. ⟨< L *Iesus Nazarenus Rex Iudaeorum*⟩

in•road ['ɪn,roud] *n.* **1** an attack or raid; entry by force. **2** Usually, **inroads,** *pl.* an advance or penetration that destroys, injures, or lessens something: *The unusual expenses made serious inroads on her savings.*

in•rush ['ɪn,rʌʃ] *n.* a rushing in; inflow. **—'in,rush•ing,** *n., adj.*

ins. 1 inches. **2** insurance. **3** insulated. **4** inspected.

in•sal•i•vate [ɪn'sælə,veit] *v.* **-at•ed, -at•ing.** mix (food) with saliva.

in•sa•lu•bri•ous [,ɪnsə'lubriəs] *adj.* unfavourable to health. **—,in•sa'lu•bri•ous•ly,** *adv.* **—,in•sa'lu•bri•ty,** *n.* ⟨< L *insalubris* + *-ous*⟩

in•sane [ɪn'sein] *adj.* **1** not sane; mentally deranged; crazy. **2** *Law.* mentally unsound, temporarily or permanently, so as to be considered not competent or not responsible for one's actions. **3** (*noml.*) **the insane,** *pl.* those who are insane: *an institution for the criminally insane.* **4** characteristic of one who is insane: *an insane laugh.* **5** extremely foolish; completely lacking in common sense: *an insane plot to overthrow the government.* ⟨< L *insanus*⟩ **—in'sane•ly,** *adv.* **—in'sane•ness,** *n.*
☛ *Syn.* **1.** See note at MAD.

in•san•i•tar•y [ɪn'sænə,tɛri] *adj.* not sanitary; not clean; unhealthy. **—in'san•i,tar•i•ness,** *n.*

in•san•i•ty [ɪn'sænəti] *n., pl.* **-ties. 1** the state of being insane; mental illness; madness. **2** *Law.* any state of mental unsoundness, temporary or permanent, in which a person is not considered competent or held responsible for his or her actions. **3** extreme folly. ⟨< L *insanitas*⟩

in•sa•tia•ble [ɪn'seiʃəbəl] *or* [ɪn'seiʃiəbəl] *adj.* that cannot be satisfied; always wanting more: *an insatiable appetite for sweets.* ⟨ME *insaciable* < L *insatiabilis*⟩ **—in'sa•tia•bly,** *adv.* **—in,sa•tia'bil•i•ty** or **in'sa•tia•ble•ness,** *n.*

in•sa•ti•ate [ɪn'seiʃiɪt] *adj.* insatiable. ⟨< L *insatiatus* not filled full⟩ **—in'sa•ti•ate•ly,** *adv.* **—in'sa•ti•ate•ness,** *n.*

in•sa•ti•e•ty [,ɪnsə'taɪɪti], [ɪn'seiʃiti], *or* [ɪn'seiʃɪɪti] *n.* the quality of not being satisfied.

in•scribe [ɪn'skraɪb] *v.* **-scribed, -scrib•ing. 1** write or engrave on a surface: *Her initials were inscribed on the bracelet.* **2** write on or engrave with words, letters, etc.: *How shall we inscribe the ring?* **3** write a message in or informally dedicate (a book, etc.): *The book was inscribed, "To Paula, with love from Dad."* **4** impress deeply: *His father's words are inscribed on his memory.* **5** put in a list; enrol. **6** *Geometry.* draw (a figure) inside another figure so that their boundaries touch in as many places as possible. To inscribe a triangle in a circle, you must make all the points of the triangle touch the circle. ⟨< L *inscribere* < *in-* on + *scribere* write⟩ **—in'scrib•a•ble,** *adj.* **—in'scrib•er,** *n.*

in•scrip•tion [ɪn'skrɪpʃən] *n.* **1** something inscribed; words, letters, etc. written or engraved on stone, metal, paper, etc. A monument or a coin has an inscription on it. **2** the act of inscribing. ⟨< L *inscriptio, -onis* < *inscribere.* See INSCRIBE.⟩

in•scru•ta•bil•i•ty [ɪn,skrutə'bɪləti] *n., pl.* **-ties. 1** the quality of being inscrutable. **2** something inscrutable.

in•scru•ta•ble [ɪn'skrutəbəl] *adj.* that cannot be understood; so mysterious or obscure that one cannot make out its meaning; incomprehensible: *an inscrutable look.* ⟨< LL *inscrutabilis* < L *in-* not + *scrutari* examine, ransack < *scruta* trash⟩ **—in'scru•ta•ble•ness,** *n.* **—in'scru•ta•bly,** *adv.*
☛ *Syn.* See note at MYSTERIOUS.

in•sect ['ɪnsɛkt] *n.* **1** any of a large class (Insecta) of small invertebrate animals having the body divided into three well-defined parts (head, thorax, and abdomen), and having three pairs of legs and, usually, one or two pairs of wings. Flies, mosquitoes, grasshoppers, bees, and beetles are insects. **2** loosely, any similar small animal with its body divided into several parts, having several pairs of legs. Spiders, centipedes, mites, and ticks are often called insects. **3** *Informal.* an insignificant or contemptible person. ⟨< L *insectum,* literally, divided, neut. pp. of *insecare* < *in-* into + *secare* cut⟩ **—in'sect•ile,** *adj.* **—'in•sect,like,** *adj.*

in•sect•ar•i•um [,ɪnsɛk'tɛriəm] *n., pl.* **-tar•i•ums, -tar•i•a** [-'tɛriə]. a place for keeping living insects. ⟨< NL⟩

in•sec•ti•cide [ɪn'sɛktə,saɪd] *n.* a substance for killing insects. ⟨< L *insectum* + E *-cide*[2]⟩ **—in,sec•ti'ci•dal,** *adj.*

in•sec•ti•vore [ɪn'sɛktə,vɔr] *n.* **1** any of an order (Insectivora) of mainly small mammals, most of which are active at night and feed largely on insects. Moles, hedgehogs, and shrews are insectivores. **2** any insect-eating animal or plant. ⟨< F < NL *insectivorus.* See INSECTIVOROUS.⟩

in•sec•tiv•o•rous [,ɪnsɛk'tɪvərəs] *adj.* **1** insect-eating; feeding mainly on insects. **2** of or belonging to the insectivores. ⟨< NL *insectivorus* < L *insectum* insect + *vorare* devour; formed on the pattern of L *carnivorus* meat-eating⟩

in•se•cure [,ɪnsɪ'kjur] *adj.* **1** not properly guarded or maintained; not safe from danger, failure, etc.: *insecure investments, an insecure position, an insecure marriage.* **2** liable to give way; not firm: *an insecure lock.* **3** lacking confidence; not sure of oneself; filled with fear and anxiety: *an insecure person.* ⟨< Med.L *insecurus*⟩ **—,in•se'cure•ly,** *adv.*
☛ *Syn.* **1.** See note at UNCERTAIN.

in•se•cu•ri•ty [,ɪnsɪ'kjʊrəti] *n., pl.* **-ties. 1** a lack of security; being insecure. **2** something insecure. ⟨< Med.L *insecuritas*⟩

in•sem•i•nate [ɪn'sɛmə,neit] *v.* **-nat•ed, -nat•ing. 1** inject semen into; fertilize; impregnate. **2** sow with seed; implant seeds into. **3** instil (ideas or opinions). ⟨< L *inseminare* (with E *-ate*[1]) < *in-* not + *seminare* to sow < *semen, -inis* seed⟩ **—in,sem•i'na•tion,** *n.* **—in'sem•i,na•tor,** *n.*

in•sen•sate [ɪn'sɛnsɪt] *or* [ɪn'sɛnseit] *adj.* **1** without sensation; inanimate: *the insensate stones.* **2** insensitive; unfeeling: *insensate* *cruelty.* **3** senseless; stupid: *insensate folly.* ⟨< Med.L *insensatus* irrational⟩ **—in'sen•sate•ly,** *adv.* **—in'sen•sate•ness,** *n.*

in•sen•si•bil•i•ty [ɪn,sɛnsə'bɪləti] *n., pl.* **-ties. 1** lack of physical sensibility; lack of feeling or sensation. **2** lack of moral sensibility.

in•sen•si•ble [ɪn'sɛnsəbəl] *adj.* **1** not having the power to perceive with the senses: *A blind person is insensible to colours.* **2** not able to respond emotionally: *We were thrilled by the view but Irene was insensible to it.* **3** not able to feel anything; unconscious: *The man hit by the truck was insensible for four hours.* **4** not easily felt or realized: *The room grew cold by insensible degrees.* **5** not aware: *The girls in the boat were insensible of the danger.* ⟨ME < L *insensibilis*⟩ **—in'sen•si•bly,** *adv.*

in•sen•si•tive [ɪn'sɛnsətɪv] *adj.* **1** not responsive or susceptible to beauty, the thoughts or feelings of others, etc.; lacking feeling: *an insensitive nature.* **2** not able to be affected by touch, light, etc. Dentists often give an injection to make a tooth insensitive so that the drilling does not hurt. **—in'sen•si•tive•ly,** *adv.* **—in'sen•si•tive•ness,** *n.* **—in,sen•si'tiv•i•ty,** *n.*

in•sen•ti•ent [ɪn'sɛnʃiənt] *or* [ɪn'sɛnʃənt] *adj.* unable to feel; lifeless. **—in'sen•ti•ence,** *n.*

in•sep•a•ra•ble [ɪn'sɛpərəbəl] *adj.* that cannot be separated or parted: *inseparable pals.*
—n. usually, **inseparables,** *pl.* inseparable persons or things. **—in'sep•a•ra•bly,** *adv.* **—in'sep•a•ra•ble•ness,** *n.* **—in,sep•a•ra'bil•i•ty,** *n.*

in•sert *v.* [ɪn'sɜrt]; *n* ['ɪnsɜrt] *v., n.* *—v.* **1** thrust, fit, or set in, into, between something else, etc.: *to insert elastic into the waistband of a skirt, to insert a lining. He inserted the key in the lock and turned it quietly.* **2** set or introduce something into written material, a newspaper, etc.: *to insert a missing letter into a word, to insert an advertisement in a newspaper.*
—n. something set in or introduced: *Some magazines have a local insert for certain regions. The dress has lace inserts in the sleeves.* ⟨< L *insertus,* pp. of *inserere* < *in-* in + *serere* entwine⟩ **—in'sert•a•ble,** *adj.* **—in'sert•er,** *n.*

in•sert•ed [ɪn'sɜrtɪd] *adj., v.* *—adj.* **1** *Botany.* of parts of a flower, growing from another part. **2** *Anatomy.* having an insertion such as a ligament.
—v. pt. and pp. of INSERT.

in•ser•tion [ɪn'sɜrʃən] *n.* **1** the act or process of inserting. **2** a single appearance of an advertisement in a newspaper, etc. **3** a band of lace, embroidery, etc. set into a cloth article for decoration; an insert: *The dress had a lace insertion near the neckline.* **4** *Anatomy.* the attachment of an organ or part of it.

in–serv•ice ['ɪn ,sɜrvɪs] *or* [ɪn 'sɜrvɪs] *adj.* of or having to do with a program for the training of employees: *in-service courses for civil servants.*

in•set *n.* ['ɪn,sɛt]; *v.* [ɪn'sɛt] *or* ['ɪn,sɛt] *n., v.* **-set, -set•ting.** *—n.* **1** a small map, photograph, etc. set within the border of a larger one, to show some part in detail or to give extra information, etc. **2** a piece of lace or other material set into a dress, etc. for decoration; insert.
—v. set or put in as an inset. **—'in,set•ter,** *n.*

in•shore ['ɪn'ʃɔr] *adj., adv.* *—adj.* **1** near the shore: *inshore shoals.* **2** done or working near the shore: *the inshore fishery of Newfoundland, inshore fishers.*
inshore of, nearer the shore than (another boat).
—adv. in toward the shore.

in•side *n., prep.* ['ɪn'saɪd]; *adj.* ['ɪn,saɪd] *or* [,ɪn'saɪd]; *adv.* [,ɪn'saɪd] *n., adj., prep., adv.* *—n.* **1** the side or surface that is within; inner part; contents: *the inside of a house.* **2** Often, **insides,** *pl. Informal.* the parts inside the body, especially the stomach and bowels. **3** *Informal.* those who are in a position to know about something or who are in a position of authority.
—adj. **1** being on the inside: *an inside seat.* **2** of or used for the inside: *an inside paint.* **3** *Informal.* done or known by those within an organization or group or inside a building: *inside information. The police suspected that the theft was an inside job.* **4** *Informal.* working within an organization or group, as an emissary or spy: *an inside man.* **5** indoor. **6** that is nearer the centre of a curve: *the inside skate.* **7** *Baseball.* **a** of a pitch, close to the batter and missing the strike zone. **b** of a part of the home plate, on the same side as the batter.
—adv. on, at, or to the inside of a place or thing; within: *Please go inside, into the living room. We had to clean the box inside before we could use it.*
inside out, a so that what should be inside is outside; with the inside showing: *He turned his pockets inside out.* **b** completely: *He learned his lessons inside out.*
—prep. on, at, or to the inside of: *We left the blankets inside the trunk. The nut is inside the shell.*
inside of, *Informal.* in a period of time less than; within the limits of: *We should be back inside of a week.*
☛ *Usage.* **Inside of** is a doubling of prepositions common in informal expressions of time: *She'll be back inside of an hour.* The more formal idiom is **within**: *She will return within an hour.*

inside job a crime committed by a person or persons closely associated with the victim, as, robbery by employees.

inside money a fee paid to get one's product displayed on a supermarket shelf.

in•sid•er [,ɪn'saɪdər] *or* ['ɪn,saɪdər] *n. Informal.* **1** a person who is recognized as being established within an organization, etc., especially someone who has power or access to important or confidential information: *an insider's report on the workings of Parliament.* **2** a person who has some special advantage.

insider trading the crime of using private information about stocks to trade on the stock market.

inside track 1 on a race track, the lane nearest the inside of the curve, and so the shortest way round. **2** *Informal.* an advantageous position or situation.

in•sid•i•ous [ɪn'sɪdiəs] *adj.* **1** wily; sly; crafty; tricky; treacherous: *an insidious plot.* **2** working secretly or subtly; developing gradually without attracting attention: *an insidious disease.* ⟨< L *insidiosus* < *insidiae* ambush < *insidere* < *in-* in + *sedere* sit⟩ **—in'sid•i•ous•ly,** *adv.* **—in'sid•i•ous•ness,** *n.*

in•sight ['ɪn,səit] *n.* **1** an understanding or awareness based on a seeing of the inside or inner nature of something. **2** wisdom and understanding in dealing with people or with facts. **3** *Psychology.* **a** the relatively sudden awareness of a solution to a problem. **b** understanding of oneself. ⟨ME⟩
☛ *Syn.* **2. Insight,** DISCERNMENT, PENETRATION = ability to understand people or things. **Insight** suggests both the power to see deeply into the inner workings of things and of people's minds and feelings and the ability to understand them: *Good teachers have insight into the problems of their students.* **Discernment** = the ability to see below the surface clearly and sharply and to judge accurately: *In selecting employees he shows discernment.* **Penetration** emphasizes going deeply into things and seeing fine distinctions and relations: *Solving the mystery required penetration.*

in•sight•ful [ɪn'səitfəl] *or* ['ɪn,səitfəl] *adj.* discerning.

in•sig•ni•a [ɪn'sɪgniə] *n.pl.* of **insigne. 1** the emblems, badges, or other distinguishing marks of a high position, honour, military order, etc.: *The crown, orb, and sceptre are the insignia of monarchs.* **2** the distinguishing badges, crests, etc. of a unit or branch of the armed forces. ⟨< L *insignia,* pl. of *insigne* badge < *in-* on + *signum* mark. Doublet of ENSIGN.⟩

in•sig•nif•i•cance [,ɪnsɪg'nɪfəkəns] *n.* **1** unimportance. **2** meaninglessness.

in•sig•nif•i•cant [,ɪnsɪg'nɪfəkənt] *adj.* **1** having little importance; trivial or trifling: *an insignificant error, insignificant losses.* **2** having little weight or influence: *The once thriving town had become an insignificant backwater. He has an insignificant position in a large company.* **3** having little or no meaning: *insignificant chatter.* **—,in•sig'nif•i•cant•ly,** *adv.*

in•sin•cere [,ɪnsɪn'sir] *adj.* not sincere; not honest or candid; deceitful. **—,in•sin'cere•ly,** *adv.*

in•sin•cer•i•ty [,ɪnsɪn'sɛrəti] *n., pl.* **-ties. 1** a lack of sincerity; hypocrisy. **2** an insincere comment or behaviour.

in•sin•u•ate [ɪn'sɪnju,eit] *v.* **-at•ed, -at•ing. 1** suggest or hint (something) indirectly, especially in an artful or scheming way: *She made no charge, but insinuated that the mayor had accepted bribes.* **2** get in or introduce by gradual, subtle, and stealthy means: *to insinuate doubt into a person's mind. The spy insinuated himself into the confidence of important army officers.* **3** make indirect suggestions. ⟨< L *insinuare* < *in-* in + *sinus* a curve, winding⟩ **—in'sin•u•a•tive,** *adj.* **—in'sin•u,a•tor,** *n.*
☛ *Syn.* **1.** See note at HINT.

in•sin•u•a•ting [ɪn'sɪnju,eitɪŋ] *adj., v.* *—adj.* **1** tending to cause doubt. **2** winning favour artfully.
—v. ppr. of INSINUATE. **—in'sin•u,a•ting•ly,** *adv.*

in•sin•u•a•tion [ɪn,sɪnju'eiʃən] *n.* **1** the act or process of insinuating. **2** a hint or indirect suggestion, especially a sly, subtle, unpleasant one.

in•sip•id [ɪn'sɪpɪd] *adj.* **1** without much taste: *A mixture of milk and water is an insipid drink.* **2** colourless and uninteresting; dull; lifeless: *insipid writing.* ⟨< LL *insipidus* < L *in-* not + *sapidus* tasty⟩ **—in'sip•id•ly,** *adv.* **—in'sip•id•ness,** *n.*

in•si•pid•i•ty [,ɪnsɪ'pɪdəti] *n., pl.* **-ties. 1** a lack of flavour; lack of interesting quality. **2** something insipid.

in•sist [ɪn'sɪst] *v.* keep firmly to some demand, statement, or position; take a stand and refuse to give in: *to insist that something should be done, to insist on one's innocence.* ⟨< L *insistere* < *in-* on + *sistere* take a stand⟩ **—in'sist•er,** *n.* **—in'sist•ing•ly,** *adv.*

in•sist•ence [ɪn'sɪstəns] *n.* **1** the act of insisting. **2** the quality of being insistent. Also, **insistency.**

in•sist•ent [ɪn'sɪstənt] *adj.* **1** insisting; continuing to make a strong, firm demand or statement: *Although it was raining, he was insistent about going for a walk.* **2** compelling attention or notice; pressing; urgent: *an insistent knocking at the door.* **—in'sist•ent•ly,** *adv.*

in si•tu ['sɪtu], ['situ], *or* ['sitju] *Latin.* in its original place; in position.

in•snare [ɪn'snɛr] *v.* **-snared, -snar•ing.** ensnare. **—in'snare•ment,** *n.* **—in'snar•er,** *n.*

in•so•bri•e•ty [,ɪnsə'braɪəti] *n.* intemperance; drunkenness.

in•so•far [,ɪnsou'fɑr] *or* [,ɪnsə'fɑr] *adv.* to such a degree or extent (*usually used with* **as**): *He should be told the facts insofar as they concern him.*

in•so•late ['ɪnsou,leit] *v.* **-lat•ed, -lat•ing. 1** expose to the sun's rays. **2** treat by exposure to sunlight. ⟨< L *insolatus* placed in the sun, pp. of *insolare*⟩

in•so•la•tion [,ɪnsou'leiʃən] *n.* **1** exposure to the sun's rays. **2** sunstroke. **3** solar radiation for therapy.

in•sole ['ɪn,soul] *n.* **1** the inner sole of a shoe or boot. **2** a shaped piece of warm, cushioning, or waterproof material laid on the sole inside a shoe or boot.

in•so•lence ['ɪnsələns] *n.* **1** bold rudeness; insulting behaviour or speech. **2** the quality or condition of being insolent. ⟨ME < L *insolentia*⟩

in•so•lent ['ɪnsələnt] *adj.* boldly rude; insulting. ⟨< L *insolens, -entis* departing from custom < *in-* not + *solere* be accustomed⟩ **—'in•so•lent•ly,** *adv.*

in•sol•u•ble [ɪn'sɒljəbəl] *adj.* **1** that cannot be dissolved: *Diamonds are insoluble.* **2** that cannot be solved or explained: *an insoluble mystery.* ⟨< L *insolubilis*⟩ **—in'sol•u•bly,** *adv.* **—in'sol•u•ble•ness** or **in,sol•u'bil•i•ty,** *n.*

in•solv•a•ble [ɪn'sɒlvəbəl] *adj.* that cannot be solved; insoluble.

in•sol•ven•cy [ɪn'sɒlvənsi] *n., pl.* **-cies.** the condition or an instance of not being able to pay one's debts; bankruptcy.

in•sol•vent [ɪn'sɒlvənt] *adj., n.* *—adj.* **1** not able to pay one's debts; bankrupt. **2** of or having to do with bankrupt persons or bankruptcy. **3** of a fund, inadequate to meet all debts.
—n. an insolvent person.

in•som•ni•a [ɪn'sɒmniə] *n.* the inability to sleep, especially when chronic; sleeplessness. ⟨< L *insomnia* < *in-* not + *somnus* sleep⟩ **—in'som•ni•ous,** *adj.*

in•som•ni•ac [ɪn'sɒmni,æk] *n., adj.* *—n.* a person who is unable to sleep, especially one who habitually has trouble getting enough sleep.
—adj. of, having to do with, or affected with insomnia.

in•so•much [,ɪnsou'mʌtʃ] *adv.* **1** to such an extent or degree; so (*usually used with* **that**). **2** inasmuch (*usually used with* **as**).

in•sou•ci•ance [ɪn'susiəns] *n.* lack of concern; carelessness; indifference: *He seemed to go through the whole trial with a smiling insouciance.*

in•sou•ci•ant [ɪn'susiənt] *adj.* carefree; unconcerned: *an insouciant disposition.* ⟨< F *insouciant* < *in-* not (< L *in-*) + *souciant*, ppr. of *soucier* care, ult. < L *sollicitus* solicitous⟩ **—in'sou•ci•ant•ly,** *adv.*

in•soul [ɪn'soul] *v.* endow with a soul.

insp. inspected; inspector.

in•spect [ɪn'spɛkt] *v.* **1** look over carefully; examine: *A dentist inspects the children's teeth twice a year.* **2** examine officially: *The factory was inspected annually by a government official.* ⟨< L *inspectus*, pp. of *inspicere* < *in-* upon + *specere* look⟩ **—in,spect•a'bil•i•ty,** *n.* **—in'spect•a•ble,** *adj.* **—in'spect•ing•ly,** *adv.*

in•spec•tion [ɪn'spɛkʃən] *n.* **1** inspecting: *An inspection of the roof showed no leaks.* **2** a formal or official examination: *The soldiers lined up for their daily inspection by their officers.*

in•spect•ive [ɪn'spɛktɪv] *adj.* of or pertaining to inspection.

in•spec•tor [ɪn'spɛktər] *n.* **1** a person who inspects. **2** an officer or official appointed to inspect. **3** a police officer, usually ranking next below a superintendent. ⟨< L⟩ **—in'spec•to•ral** or **,in•spec'tor•i•al,** *adj.* **—in'spec•tor,ship,** *n.*

in•spec•tor•ate [ɪn'spɛktərɪt] *n.* **1** the office of an inspector. **2** a staff of inspectors. **3** whatever is controlled by an inspector.

in•sphere [ɪn'sfir] *v.* **-sphered, -spher•ing.** ensphere.

in•spi•ra•tion [,ɪnspə'reiʃən] *n.* **1** the influence of thought and strong feelings on actions, especially a good or creative influence: *Some people get inspiration from sermons; some from poetry.* **2** a person or thing that arouses effort to do well: *The captain was an inspiration to his men.* **3** an idea that is inspired: *a sudden inspiration.* **4** a suggestion to another; the act of causing something to be told or written by another. **5** *Theology.* a divine influence directly and immediately exerted upon the mind or soul of a human. **6** a breathing in; the drawing of air into the lungs.

in•spi•ra•tion•al [,ɪnspə'reiʃənəl] *adj.* **1** inspiring. **2** inspired. **3** of or having to do with inspiration. **—,in•spi'ra•tion•al•ly,** *adv.*

in•spir•a•to•ry [ɪn'spaɪrə,tɔri] *adj.* having to do with inhalation. ⟨< L *inspiratus* breathed upon or into, pp. of *inspirare*⟩

in•spire [ɪn'spaɪr] *v.* **-spired, -spir•ing. 1** put thought, feeling, life, force, etc. into: *The speaker inspired the crowd.* **2** cause (thought or feeling): *The leader's courage inspired confidence in others.* **3** affect; influence; fill (one) with a thought or feeling: *His sly ways inspire me with distrust.* **4** arouse or influence by a divine force. **5** suggest; cause to be told or written: *His enemies inspired false stories about him.* **6** breathe in; breathe in air. ⟨< L *inspirare* < *in-* in + *spirare* breathe⟩ **—in'spir•a•ble,** *adj.* **—in'spir•er,** *n.* **—in'spir•ing•ly,** *adv.*

in•spir•it [ɪn'spɪrɪt] *v.* put spirit into; encourage; hearten. Also, **enspirit.**

in•spis•sate [ɪn'spɪseit] *v.* **-sat•ed, -sat•ing.** thicken, as by evaporation; condense. ⟨< LL *inspissare* < L *in-* in + *spissus* thick⟩ **—,in•spis'sa•tion,** *n.* **—'in•spis,sa•tor,** *n.*

inst.[1] *Archaic.* instant. 'The 10th inst.' means 'the tenth day of the present month'.

☛ *Usage.* **inst.** Abbreviations such as **inst.** (of the current month) and **ult.** (of last month) are no longer considered good form in business correspondence.

inst.[2] **1** instantaneous. **2** instructor. **3** instrument. **4** instrumental.

Inst. **1** institute. **2** institution.

in•sta•bil•i•ty [,ɪnstə'bɪləti] *n.* **1** the quality or state of being unstable: *the instability of the dollar. His emotional instability made him a poor risk as an employee.* **2** *Chemistry.* a change of form: *A radioactive element shows instability if it becomes an isotope.* ⟨ME *instabilite* < L *instabilitas*⟩

in•stall [ɪn'stɒl] *v.* **1** place formally in a position, office, etc.: *to install a new judge.* **2** put in a place or position; settle: *The cat installed itself in an easy chair.* **3** put in position for use: *to install a telephone.* ⟨< Med.L *installare* < *in-* in (< L) + *stallum* stall[1] (< Gmc.)⟩ **—in'stall•er,** *n.*

in•stal•la•tion [,ɪnstə'leiʃən] *n.* **1** an installing or being installed. **2** the thing installed; machinery placed in position for use: *They have requested new lighting installations.* **3** a military organization including personnel, equipment, buildings, etc.

☛ *Hom.* INSTILLATION.

in•stal•ment[1] or **in•stall•ment**[1] [ɪn'stɒlmənt] *n.* **1** a part of a sum of money or of a debt to be paid at certain regular times with interest: *The furniture cost $500; we paid for it in instalments of $52 a month for ten months.* **2** any of several parts furnished or issued at successive times as part of a series: *The magazine has a serial story in six instalments.* ⟨alteration of earlier *(e)stallment* < *stall* agree to the payment of (a debt) by instalments < OF *estaler* fix, place < *estal* position < Gmc.⟩

in•stal•ment[2] or **in•stall•ment**[2] [ɪn'stɒlmənt] *n.* an installing or being installed.

instalment plan or **installment plan** a system of paying for goods in instalments.

in•stance ['ɪnstəns] *n., v.* **-stanced, -stanc•ing.** *—n.* **1** a person or thing serving as an example; case: *Her rude question was an instance of bad manners.* **2** a stage or step in an action; occasion: *He said he preferred, in this instance, to remain where he was.*
at the instance of, on the suggestion of.
for instance, as an example: *Her many hobbies include, for instance, skating and stamp collecting.*
—v. **1** refer to as an example. **2** exemplify. ⟨ME < OF < L *instantia* insistence < *instans* insistent. See INSTANT.⟩

☛ *Syn. n.* **1.** See note at CASE[1].

in•stan•cy ['ɪnstənsi] *n.* **1** urgency. **2** immediateness.

in•stant ['ɪnstənt] *n., adj.* —*n.* **1** a particular point in time: *Stop talking this instant!* **2** a very short time: *He paused for an instant.*
the instant, just as soon as: *The instant she came in the door, everyone stopped talking.*
—*adj.* **1** immediate; without delay: *The medicine gave instant relief from pain.* **2** pressing; urgent: *When there is a fire, there is an instant need for action.* **3** prepared beforehand and requiring little or no cooking, mixing, or additional ingredients: *instant pudding, instant coffee.* **4** able, or seemingly able, to be done, acquired, or used immediately and effortlessly: *instant knowledge.* ⟨< L *instans, -antis,* ppr. of *instare* insist, stand near < *in-* in + *stare* stand⟩
☛ *Syn. n.* See note at MINUTE.

in•stan•ta•ne•ous [,ɪnstən'teiniəs] *adj.* **1** done, happening, or acting in an instant or without delay: *instantaneous applause. Her reaction was instantaneous.* **2** having to do with a particular instant. **—,in•stan'ta•ne•ous•ly,** *adv.*
—,in•stan'ta•ne•ous•ness, *n.*

in•stan•ter [ɪn'stæntər] *adv. Formal.* at once; immediately. ⟨< L *instanter* insistently < *instans.* See INSTANT.⟩

in•stan•ti•ate [ɪn'stænʃi,eit] *v.* **-at•ed, -at•ing.** provide or be concrete evidence in support of (a claim or theory).

in•stant•ly ['ɪnstəntli] *adv.* in an instant; at once; immediately.
☛ *Syn.* See note at IMMEDIATELY.

instant replay an immediate retelecast of an event or situation taken from a complete telecast, especially of professional sports. It is often in slow motion.

in•star ['ɪnstɑr] *n.* any arthropod during metamorphosis and between its moulting periods. ⟨< NL, L, image, likeness (literally, a stand-in)⟩

in•state [ɪn'steɪt] *v.* **-stat•ed, -stat•ing.** put into a certain state, position, or office; install. **—in'state•ment,** *n.*

in sta•tu quo [ɪn 'steitʃu 'kwou], [ɪn 'stætʃu 'kwou], *or* [ɪn 'stɑtu kwou] *Latin.* in the same situation, condition, or state.

in•stau•ra•tion [,ɪnstɔ'reiʃən] *n.* **1** restoration. **2** an establishing. **—'in•stau,ra•tor,** *n.*

in•stead [ɪn'stɛd] *adv.* in place of someone or something; as a substitute or equivalent: *If you cannot go, let her go instead.*
instead of, rather than; in place of; as a substitute for: *Instead of studying, she read a story.* ⟨earlier *in stead* in place⟩

in•step ['ɪn,stɛp] *n.* **1** the upper surface of the human foot between the toes and the ankle. See LEG for picture. **2** the part of a shoe, stocking, etc. over the instep. **3** the front part of the hind leg of a horse between the hock and the pastern joint.

in•sti•gate ['ɪnstə,geit] *v.* **-gat•ed, -gat•ing.** stir up; set in motion, especially something undesirable: *Foreign agents instigated a rebellion.* **—'in•sti,gat•ing•ly,** *adv.* **—'in•sti,ga•tive,** *adj.* **—'in•sti,ga•tor,** *n.* ⟨< L *instigare*⟩
☛ *Syn.* See note at INCITE.

in•sti•ga•tion [,ɪnstə'geiʃən] *n.* the act of instigating.
at the instigation of, instigated by.

in•stil or **in•still** [ɪn'stɪl] *v.* **-stilled, -still•ing. 1** put in little by little; impart gradually: *Reading good books instils a love for really fine literature.* **2** put in drop by drop. ⟨< L *instillare* < *in-* in + *stilla* a drop⟩ **—in'stil•ler,** *n.* **—in'stil•ment** or **in'still•ment,** *n.*

in•stil•la•tion [,ɪnstə'leiʃən] *n.* **1** an instilling. **2** something instilled.
☛ *Hom.* INSTALLATION.

in•stinct[1] ['ɪnstɪŋkt] *n.* **1** a natural feeling, knowledge, or power, such as guides animals; an inborn tendency to act in a certain way: *Birds do not learn to fly; they fly by instinct.* **2** a natural tendency or ability; talent: *Even as a child, the artist had an instinct for colour.* **3** an inborn pattern of behaviour in a species. ⟨< L *instinctus,* n. < *instinctus,* pp. of *instinguere* impel⟩

in•stinct[2] [ɪn'stɪŋkt] *adj.* charged or filled with something: *The picture is instinct with life and beauty.* ⟨< L *instinctus,* pp. of *instinguere* impel⟩

in•stinc•tive [ɪn'stɪŋktɪv] *adj.* **1** of or having to do with instinct. **2** caused or done by instinct; independent of thought, will, or training: *He felt an instinctive distrust of the stranger. Climbing is instinctive in monkeys.* Also, **instinctual.**
—in'stinc•tive•ly or **in'stinc•tu•al•ly,** *adv.*

in•sti•tute ['ɪnstɪ,tjut] *or* ['ɪnstɪ,tut] *n., v.* **-tut•ed, -tut•ing.**
—*n.* **1** an organization or society for the support or promotion of a particular cause: *an art institute, the Canadian National Institute for the Blind.* **2** the building used by such an organization: *We spent the afternoon at the Art Institute.* **3** an educational institution; school: *a collegiate institute.* **4** a college or university specializing in some field: *the Southern Alberta Institute of Technology, the Ontario Institute for Studies in Education.* **5** an established principle, law, or custom. **6 institutes,** *pl. Esp. Law.* a collection or digest of established principles. **7** a short program of instruction for a particular group.
—*v.* originate or set going; establish or begin: *The police instituted an inquiry into the causes of the accident.* ⟨< L *institutus,* pp. of *instituere* < *in-* in + *statuere* establish < *status* position⟩

in•sti•tu•tion [,ɪnstə'tjuʃən] *or* [,ɪnstə'tuʃən] *n.* **1** an organization or society established for some public or social purpose: *A church, school, college, hospital, or prison is an institution.* **2** a building used by such an organization or society. **3** an established law, custom, or system: *Giving presents on birthdays is an institution.* **4** a setting up; establishing; beginning: *Many people favour the institution of more clubs for young people.* **5** *Informal.* a very familiar person or thing: *He's an institution around here.*

in•sti•tu•tion•al [,ɪnstə'tjuʃənəl] *or* [,ɪnstə'tuʃənəl] *adj.* **1** of, having to do with, like, or characteristic of institutions; impersonal, regimented, etc.: *She hated the institutional life of the boarding school. Institutional food is sometimes bland and boring.* **2** intended or designed for institutions: *Their main business is in institutional sales rather than retail trade.* **3** especially of advertising, designed to promote reputation and establish good will for a business rather than to help immediate sales.
—,in•sti'tu•tion•al•ly, *adv.*

in•sti•tu•tion•al•ism [,ɪnstə'tjuʃənə,lɪzəm] *or* [,ɪnstə'tuʃənə,lɪzəm] *n.* **1** belief in the importance of established organizations, especially religious institutions. **2** the practice of committing to institutions the care and maintenance of people unable to care for themselves. **3** emphasis on the formal, impersonal aspects of the operation or maintenance of institutions: *She reacted against the institutionalism of education.*

in•sti•tu•tion•al•ize [,ɪnstɪ'tjuʃənə,laɪz] *or* [,ɪnstɪ'tuʃənə,laɪz] *v.* **-ized, -iz•ing. 1** make into or treat as an acceptable and established principle or custom: *to institutionalize gambling in the form of lotteries.* **2** make into or treat as an institution; make impersonal and formal: *He argued that charity had become too institutionalized.* **3** commit to a public institution for care or detention: *They decided not to institutionalize their mentally retarded son.* **4** make accustomed to an institution: *After three years in the hospital, she had become institutionalized and had difficulty relating to normal life.*
—,in•sti,tu•tion•al•i'za•tion, *n.*

in•struct [ɪn'strʌkt] *v.* **1** teach formally. **2** give directions or orders to; order: *The owner instructed her agent to sell the property.* **3** inform; tell: *My lawyer instructs me that your last payment is due March first.* **4** *Law.* of a judge, give (the jury) a final explanation of the points of law in a case. **5** *Brit.* of a solicitor, engage the services of (a barrister) on behalf of his or her client. ⟨< L *instructus,* pp. of *instruere* arrange, furnish, instruct < *in-* on + *struere* to pile⟩ **—in'struct•i•ble,** *adj.*
☛ *Syn.* **1.** See note at TEACH.

in•struc•tion [ɪn'strʌkʃən] *n.* **1** teaching or lessons: *instruction in boat building.* **2** Usually, **instructions,** *pl.* orders: *Their instructions were to be there at 7 o'clock.* **3 instructions,** *pl.* an outline of procedure, etc.; directions: *The kit includes complete instructions for assembling the airplane.*

in•struc•tion•al [ɪn'strʌkʃənəl] *adj.* of or for instruction; educational. **—in'struc•tion•al•ly,** *adv.*

in•struc•tive [ɪn'strʌktɪv] *adj.* useful for instruction; instructing; giving knowledge or information: *A trip around the world is an instructive experience.* **—in'struc•tive•ly,** *adv.*
—in'struc•tive•ness, *n.*

in•struc•tor [ɪn'strʌktər] *n.* **1** teacher. **2** in some colleges and universities, a teacher ranking below an assistant professor. ⟨< Med.L *instructor* teacher < L *instructor* preparer⟩
—in'struc•tor,ship, *n.*

in•stru•ment *n.* ['ɪnstrəmənt]; *v.* ['ɪnstrə,mɛnt] *n., v.* —*n.* **1** a precision tool or mechanical device: *surgical instruments.* **2** a device for producing musical sounds: *wind instruments, stringed instruments.* **3** a device for measuring, recording, or controlling: *A thermometer is an instrument for measuring temperature.* **4** a person or thing by means of or through which something is done; agent or means. **5** a formal legal document, such as a contract, deed, or grant. **6** a test. **7** (*adjl.*) relying on instruments for navigation: *instrument flying, an instrument landing.*
—*v.* **1** equip with instruments, especially with scientific recording devices: *a fully instrumented missile.* **2** score or arrange (music)

for instruments; orchestrate. ⟨< L *instrumentum* < *instruere* arrange, furnish, instruct < *in-* on + *struere* pile⟩

in•stru•men•tal [ˌɪnstrəˈmɛntəl] *adj., n.* *—adj.* **1** acting or serving as a means; useful; helpful: *His aunt was instrumental in getting him a job.* **2** performed on or written for a musical instrument: *an instrumental arrangement. She prefers instrumental music to choral music.* **3** of, having to do with, or done by a device or tool.
—n. a piece of music composed for or played on a musical instrument or instruments, without vocal accompaniment.
—ˌin•stru'men•tal•ly, *adv.*

in•stru•men•tal•ism [ˌɪnstrəˈmɛntəˌlɪzəm] *n. Philosophy.* a philosophy advocating that the value of an idea is determined by its function in human experience or progress.

in•stru•men•tal•ist [ˌɪnstrəˈmɛntəlɪst] *n.* **1** a person who plays a musical instrument. **2** an adherent of instrumentalism.

in•stru•men•tal•i•ty [ˌɪnstrəmənˈtæləti] *n., pl.* **-ties. 1** the quality or state of being instrumental; usefulness or helpfulness. **2** agency; means.

in•stru•men•ta•tion [ˌɪnstrəmənˈteiʃən] *n.* **1** the arrangement or composition of music for instruments. **2** the use of instruments; work done with instruments. **3** the mechanized use of instruments, especially for scientific or technical purposes. **4** the act of fitting out with instruments.

instrument board INSTRUMENT PANEL.

instrument flight rules the rules of instrument flying.

instrument flying the directing of an aircraft by instruments only, without being able to observe points or objects on the ground. Compare CONTACT FLYING.

instrument landing the landing of an aircraft by the use of its instruments alone.

instrument panel on an aircraft, motor vehicle, or other machine, a panel displaying gauges, indicator lights, switches, etc., permitting the operator to check on and control specific functions of the machine.

in•sub•or•di•nate [ˌɪnsəˈbɔrdənɪt] *adj., n.* *—adj.* resisting authority; disobedient; unruly.
—n. an insubordinate person. **—ˌin•sub'or•di•nate•ly,** *adv.*

in•sub•or•di•na•tion [ˌɪnsəˌbɔrdəˈneiʃən] *n.* resistance to authority; active disobedience: *The private was charged with insubordination.*

in•sub•stan•tial [ˌɪnsəbˈstænʃəl] *adj.* **1** frail; flimsy; weak: *A cobweb is very insubstantial.* **2** unreal; not actual; imaginary: *Dreams and ghosts are insubstantial.* ⟨< LL *insubstantialis*⟩
—ˌin•sub'stan•tial•ly, *adv.* **—ˌin•subˌstan•ti'al•i•ty,** *n.*

in•suf•fer•a•ble [ɪnˈsʌfərəbəl] *adj.* intolerable; unbearable: *insufferable insolence.* **—in'suf•fer•a•ble•ness,** *n.*
—in'suf•fer•a•bly, *adv.*

in•suf•fi•cien•cy [ˌɪnsəˈfɪʃənsi] *n.* too small an amount; lack; deficiency.

in•suf•fi•cient [ˌɪnsəˈfɪʃənt] *adj.* not enough; less than is needed: *insufficient sleep.* ⟨ME < *insufficientis, insuffiens*⟩
—ˌin•suf'fi•cient•ly, *adv.*

in•suf•flate [ɪnˈsʌfleit] *or* [ˈɪnsəˌfleit] *v.* **-flat•ed, -flat•ing. 1** breathe into or on. **2** give medical treatment by blowing a powder into a body cavity. **—'in•sufˌfla•tor,** *n.*

in•suf•fla•tion [ˌɪnsəˈfleiʃən] *n.* **1** a ritual breathing on one being baptized. **2** the act of insufflating.

in•su•lar [ˈɪnsələr] *or* [ˈɪnsjələr] *adj.* **1** of or having to do with islands or islanders: *a moderate, insular climate.* **2** living or situated on an island: *an insular people.* **3** forming an island; standing alone like an island. **4** like or characteristic of people who live in isolation, especially when thought of as narrow-minded or ignorant: *an insular point of view, insular intolerance.* **5** *Anatomy.* designating isolated tissue, especially an island of it. ⟨< LL *insularis* < L *insula* island⟩ **—'in•su•larˌism,** *n.*
—'in•su•lar•ly, *adv.*

in•su•lar•i•ty [ˌɪnsəˈlærəti] *or* [ˌɪnsəˈlɛrəti] *n.* **1** the fact or condition of being an island or of living on an island. **2** narrow-mindedness or ignorance.

in•su•late [ˈɪnsəˌleit] *or* [ˈɪnsjəˌleit] *v.* **-lat•ed, -lat•ing. 1** keep from losing or transferring electricity, heat, sound, etc. by covering or surrounding with a non-conducting material. Wires are often insulated by a covering of rubber: *Our heating bills are lower now that our house is better insulated.* **2** pack with material that will not burn, so as to prevent the spread of fire. **3** set apart; separate from others; isolate. ⟨< L *insula* island⟩

in•su•la•tion [ˌɪnsəˈleiʃən] *or* [ˌɪnsjəˈleiʃən] *n.* **1** insulating or being insulated. **2** the material used in insulating.

in•su•la•tor [ˈɪnsəˌleitər] *or* [ˈɪnsjəˌleitər] *n.* **1** something that insulates, especially a material that prevents the passage of electricity or heat; a non-conductor. Glass is an effective insulator. **2** one who or something that insulates.

in•su•lin [ˈɪnsəlɪn] *n.* **1** a hormone secreted by the pancreas that enables the body to use sugar and other carbohydrates. **2** a preparation containing this hormone, used especially in the treatment of diabetes. Human insulin is obtained by recombinant DNA techniques. ⟨< L *insula* island (i.e., of the pancreas)⟩

insulin shock a state of collapse caused by excessive use of insulin, creating a decrease in blood sugar.

in•sult *v.* [ɪnˈsʌlt]; *n.* [ˈɪnsʌlt] *v., n.* *—v.* treat with scorn, abuse, or great rudeness: *The rebels insulted the flag by throwing mud on it.*
—n. **1** an insulting speech or action. **2** *Medicine.* an injury. **3** the agent that causes it. ⟨< L *insultare*, frequentative of *insilire* leap at or upon < *in-* on, at + *salire* leap⟩ **—in'sult•er,** *n.*
—in'sult•a•ble, *adj.* **—in'sult•ing•ly,** *adv.*

☛ *Syn. n.* **Insult,** AFFRONT, INDIGNITY = something said or done to offend by showing disrespect or contempt. **Insult** emphasizes insolence and abuse, and intention to hurt or shame: *Stamping on the flag is an insult.* **Affront** applies to a deliberate and open show of disrespect: *Leaving during her song was an affront to my sister.* **Indignity** applies to an act that hurts a person's dignity, suggests lack of respect, but emphasizes the feelings of the victim: *Being treated like a child is an indignity to a teenager.*

in•su•per•a•ble [ɪnˈsupərəbəl] *adj.* that cannot be passed over or overcome: *an insuperable barrier.* ⟨ME < L *insuperabilis*⟩
—in'su•per•a•ble•ness, *n.* **—in'su•per•a•bly,** *adv.*
—inˌsu•per•a'bil•i•ty, *n.*

in•sup•port•a•ble [ˌɪnsəˈpɔrtəbəl] *adj.* **1** unbearable; unendurable; intolerable. **2** that cannot be upheld or justified: *insupportable rudeness.* **—ˌin•sup'port•a•ble•ness,** *n.*
—ˌin•sup'port•a•bly, *adv.*

in•sur•a•ble [ɪnˈʃʊrəbəl] *adj.* capable of being insured; fit to be insured. **—inˌsur•a'bil•i•ty,** *n.*

in•sur•ance [ɪnˈʃʊrəns] *n.* **1** an insuring of property, person, or life: *fire insurance, burglary insurance, accident insurance, life insurance, health insurance.* **2** the business of insuring property, life, etc.: *My aunt works in insurance.* **3** the amount of money for which a person or thing is insured: *He has $100 000 insurance.* **4** the amount of money paid for insurance; premium: *She pays her insurance in two instalments.* **5** the written contract made between insurer and insured.

in•sure [ɪnˈʃʊr] *v.* **-sured, -sur•ing. 1** arrange for money payment in case of loss of (property, income, etc.) or in case of accident, sickness, or death; take out or give insurance on or for: *They neglected to insure their house. She insured her art collection against theft, damage, and fire.* **2** give or buy insurance. **3** make safe or certain; ensure. ⟨ME; var. of *ensure* < AF *enseurer* < *en-* in + OF *seür* sure < L *securus.* Related to SURE.⟩

☛ *Usage.* See note at ENSURE.

in•sured [ɪnˈʃʊrd] *n., v.* *—n.* a person whose life or property is insured.
—v. pt. and pp. of INSURE.

in•sur•er [ɪnˈʃʊrər] *n.* a person or company, etc. that insures; one that sells insurance.

in•sur•gence [ɪnˈsɜrdʒəns] *n.* a rising in revolt; rebellion. Also, **insurgency.**

in•sur•gent [ɪnˈsɜrdʒənt] *n., adj.* *—n.* **1** a person who rises in revolt; a rebel. **2** a member of a political group who rebels.
—adj. **1** rising in revolt; rebellious. **2** rushing in. ⟨< L *insurgens, -entis,* ppr. of *insurgere* < *in-* against + *surgere* rise⟩

in•sur•mount•a•ble [ˌɪnsərˈmaʊntəbəl] *adj.* that cannot be overcome. **—ˌin•sur'mount•a•bly,** *adv.*
—ˌin•surˌmount•a'bil•i•ty, *n.*

in•sur•rec•tion [ˌɪnsəˈrɛkʃən] *n.* a rising against established authority; revolt. ⟨ME < OF < LL *insurrectio, -onis* < L *insurgere.* See INSURGENT.⟩ **—ˌin•sur'rec•tion•al,** *adj.*

☛ *Syn.* See note at REVOLT.

in•sur•rec•tion•ar•y [ˌɪnsəˈrɛkʃəˌnɛri] *adj.* **1** having a tendency to revolt. **2** having to do with revolt.

in•sur•rec•tion•ist [ˌɪnsəˈrɛkʃənɪst] *n.* a person who takes part in or favours an insurrection; a rebel.

in•sus•cep•ti•ble [ˌɪnsəˈsɛptəbəl] *adj.* not susceptible; not easily influenced. **—ˌin•susˌcep•ti'bil•i•ty,** *n.* **—ˌin•sus'cep•ti•bly,** *adv.*

int. 1 interest. **2** international. **3** internal. **4** interior. **5** intransitive. **6** interval.

in•tact [ɪn'tækt] *adj.* with no part missing or damaged; whole: *I checked the dishes when we unpacked them and found that they were all intact.* ⟨< L *intactus* < *in-* not + *tactus*, pp. of *tangere* touch⟩ **—in'tact•ly,** *adv.* **—in'tact•ness,** *n.*

The process of making an intaglio print: first, the design is cut into the block; then the whole block is inked; next, the ink is wiped off the top surface of the block; last, a print is taken of the design.

in•tagl•io [ɪn'tæljou] *or* [ɪn'tɑljou] *n., pl.* **in•tagl•ios. 1** a design incised beneath the surface of metal or stone. **2** the process of carving such a design. **3** a die incised to produce a design in relief. ⟨< Ital. *intaglio* < *intagliare* engrave < *in-* into + *tagliare* cut⟩

in•take ['ɪn,teik] *n.* **1** a place where water, air, gas, etc. enters a channel, pipe, or other narrow opening. **2** a taking in. **3** the amount or thing taken in. **4** a narrowing or contraction in a tube, stocking, etc., or the point at which this begins.

in•tan•gi•ble [ɪn'tændʒəbəl] *adj., n. —adj.* **1** not capable of being touched or felt: *Sound and light are intangible.* **2** not easily grasped by the mind; vague: *She had that intangible quality called charm.*
—n. something intangible. ⟨< Med.L *intangibilis*⟩
—in,tan•gi'bil•i•ty, *n.* **—in'tan•gi•ble•ness,** *n.* **—in'tan•gi•bly,** *adv.*

intangible asset something that is not tangible, especially an asset that cannot be felt or seen.

in•tar•si•a *n.* [ɪn'tɑrsiə] the art or technique of decorating a surface with or as if with inlaid wood: *Sweaters can be made in a pattern resembling intarsia.* ⟨< Arabic *tarsi* an inlay⟩
—in'tar•si•ate, *adj.*

in•te•ger ['ɪntədʒər] *n.* **1** any positive or negative whole number or zero: *The numbers* 4, –37, –8, 106, *etc. are integers.* **2** a thing complete in itself; something whole. ⟨< L *integer* whole. Doublet of ENTIRE.⟩

in•teg•ra•ble ['ɪntəgrəbəl] *adj.* able to be integrated.

in•te•gral ['ɪntəgrəl] *or* [ɪn'tɛgrəl] *adj., n. —adj.* **1** necessary to the completeness of the whole; essential: *Steel is an integral part of a modern skyscraper.* **2** entire; complete. **3** *Mathematics.* having to do with whole numbers; not fractional. **4** expressed in terms of integrals.
—n. a whole; a whole number. ⟨< LL *integralis* < L *integer* whole⟩

integral calculus the branch of mathematics dealing with the finding of integrals and their application to the finding of areas, lengths, volumes, etc. and to the solution of differential equations. Compare DIFFERENTIAL CALCULUS.

in•teg•rand ['ɪntə,grænd] *n. Mathematics.* the expression to be integrated.

in•te•grate ['ɪntə,greit] *v.* **-grat•ed, -grat•ing. 1** make more unified or harmonious: *The government should integrate its approach to unemployment.* **2** bring together (parts) into a whole; unify. **3** bring in (individuals or groups) as part of a larger group: *to integrate immigrants into Canadian society.* **4** make (facilities, institutions, etc.) available to all people regardless of race, nationality, religion, etc.; desegregate: *to integrate a school.* **5** become unified, brought together, or desegregated: *The three neighbouring cities have decided to integrate.* **6** *Mathematics.* calculate the integral of. **7** bring all aspects of (personality) into a harmonious whole. ⟨< L *integrare* < *integer* whole⟩
—'in•te,gra•tor, *n.*

integrated circuit *Electronics.* a miniature electronic circuit that is a complete system made up of many inseparable components incorporated into or on a single chip of semiconducting material, usually crystalline silicon.

integrated visual resource a form of book for schools in which pictures, graphs, and maps play an important role.

in•te•gra•tion [,ɪntə'greiʃən] *n.* **1** the act or process of integrating. **2** the state of being integrated.

in•te•gra•tion•ist [,ɪntə'greiʃənɪst] *n.* a person who believes in, or practises, integration.

in•te•gra•tive ['ɪntə,greitɪv] *adj.* directed toward or fostering integration: *an integrative approach to the study of Inuit art, involving persons trained in art and anthropology.*

in•te•gra•tor ['ɪntə,greitər] *n.* an instrument for calculating numerical integrals.

in•teg•ri•ty [ɪn'tɛgrəti] *n.* **1** firm attachment to moral or artistic principle; honesty and sincerity; uprightness: *People realized that he was a victim of circumstances, and did not question his integrity. Her poetry is too slick and commercial to have integrity.* **2** wholeness; completeness. **3** the condition of being unmarred or uncorrupted; the original, perfect condition: *Several scholars have questioned the integrity of the text of this poem.* ⟨< L *integritas* < *integer* whole⟩
☛ *Syn.* **1.** See note at HONESTY.

in•teg•u•ment [ɪn'tɛgjəmənt] *n.* a natural outer covering of an animal or plant or of one of its parts. The skin or shell of an animal and the husk of a seed or fruit are integuments. ⟨< L *integumentum* < *integere* cover < *in-* on + *tegere* cover⟩
—in,teg•u'men•ta•ry, *adj.*

in•tel•lect ['ɪntə,lɛkt] *n.* **1** the power of knowing and understanding as distinguished from will and feeling. **2** great intelligence; high mental ability: *Isaac Newton was a man of intellect.* **3** a person having high mental ability: *Newton was one of the greatest intellects of all time.* **4** the intellectual members of a group. ⟨< L *intellectus* < *intelligere.* See INTELLIGENT.⟩
☛ *Syn.* **1.** See note at MIND.

in•tel•lec•tion [,ɪntə'lɛkʃən] *n.* **1** the use of the intellect; reasoning or thought. **2** an idea or perception.

in•tel•lec•tu•al [,ɪntə'lɛktʃuəl] *adj., n. —adj.* **1** of or having to do with the intellect: *Thinking is an intellectual process.* **2** needing or involving the intellect: *an intellectual puzzle. Mathematics is an intellectual discipline.* **3** inclined toward or favouring things that involve the intellect: *intellectual tastes, an intellectual person.* **4** having superior intelligence.
—n. a person who is interested in intellectual things; an intellectual person: *a magazine designed for intellectuals.*

in•tel•lec•tu•al•ism [,ɪntə'lɛktʃuə,lɪzəm] *n.* **1** the exercise of the intellect; a devotion to intellectual pursuits. **2** *Philosophy.* the doctrine that knowledge is wholly or chiefly derived from pure reason. **—,in•tel'lec•tu•a•list,** *n.* **—,in•tel,lec•tu•al'ist•ic,** *adj.* **—,in•tel,lec•tu•al'is•ti•cal•ly,** *adv.*

in•tel•lec•tu•al•i•ty [,ɪntə,lɛktʃu'æləti] *n., pl.* **-ties.** a being intellectual; intellectual nature or power.

in•tel•lec•tu•al•ize [,ɪntə'lɛktʃuə,laɪz] *v.* **-ized, -iz•ing. 1** interpret or express (feelings, attitudes, etc.) in intellectual or rational terms, especially in a narrow or formalized way: *The explanation is intellectual without being intellectualized.* **2** undertake an intellectual analysis (of).
—,in•tel,lec•tu•al•i'za•tion, *n.* **—,in•tel'lec•tu•al,iz•er,** *n.*

in•tel•lec•tu•al•ly [,ɪntə'lɛktʃuəli] *adv.* **1** in an intellectual way. **2** so far as intellect is concerned.

in•tel•li•gence [ɪn'tɛlədʒəns] *n.* **1** the ability to learn and know; the ability to use the reason or intellect in dealing with a new situation, solving a problem, etc. **2** knowledge or information: *The government received secret intelligence of the plans of the enemy.* **3** the getting or distributing of information, especially secret information: *She worked in intelligence during the war.* **4** a group or agency engaged in obtaining secret information: *military intelligence; Intelligence had informed them of the planned attack.* **5** Often, **Intelligence,** an intelligent being or spirit.

intelligence quotient a number used to describe a person's relative intelligence in terms of certain thinking skills. It is computed by dividing his or her apparent mental age, as shown by a standardized test, by his or her actual age and multiplying by 100. *Abbrev.:* IQ or I.Q.

intelligence test a standardized test designed to measure a person's relative intelligence.

in•tel•li•gent [ɪn'tɛlədʒənt] *adj.* **1** having intelligence; rational: *Is there intelligent life on other planets?* **2** having or showing a high degree of intelligence; clever, perceptive, or bright: *an intelligent student, an intelligent remark.* **3** of a computer, having ARTIFICIAL INTELLIGENCE. ⟨< L *intelligens, -entis,* ppr. of *intelligere* understand < *inter-* between + *legere* choose⟩ **—in'tel•li•gent•ly,** *adv.*

in•tel•li•gent•si•a [ɪn,tɛlə'dʒɛntsiə] *or* [ɪn,tɛlə'gɛntsiə] *n. sing. or pl.* the persons representing, or claiming to represent, the superior intelligence or enlightened opinion of a society; the intellectuals. ⟨< Russian *intelligentsiya* < L *intelligentia* < *intelligens.* See INTELLIGENT.⟩

in•tel•li•gi•ble [ɪn'tɛlədʒəbəl] *adj.* capable of being understood; clear; comprehensible: *He was so upset that his account of the accident was hardly intelligible.* ⟨< L *intelligibilis* < *intelligere.* See INTELLIGENT.⟩ **—in,tel•li•gi'bil•i•ty,** *n.* **—in'tel•li•gi•bly,** *adv.*

in•tem•per•ance [ɪn'tɛmpərəns] *n.* **1** a lack of moderation or self-control; excess. **2** the excessive drinking of intoxicating liquor, especially habitually. ⟨ME < L *intemperantia*⟩

in•tem•per•ate [ɪn'tɛmpərɪt] *adj.* **1** not moderate; lacking in self-control; excessive: *an intemperate appetite, an intemperate anger.* **2** drinking too much intoxicating liquor. **3** not temperate; extreme in temperature; severe: *an intemperate climate.* **—in'tem•per•ate•ly,** *adv.*

in•tend [ɪn'tɛnd] *v.* **1** have in mind as a purpose; plan: *We intend to go home soon. He apologized and said he had intended no insult.* **2** mean for a particular purpose or use; design or destine: *That gift was intended for you.* **3** *Archaic.* direct: *to intend one's course.* ⟨ME < OF < L *intendere* < *in-* toward + *tendere* stretch⟩ **—in'tend•er,** *n.*

☛ *Syn.* **1. Intend,** MEAN = have in mind as a purpose. **Intend** = have some definite purpose or plan and be determined to carry it out: *I intend to finish this work before I go to bed.* **Mean** is sometimes used interchangeably with **intend,** but puts greater emphasis on having something in mind to do or get and less emphasis on the determination to carry it out or gain it: *I meant to get up early, but forgot to set the alarm.*

in•tend•an•cy [ɪn'tɛndənsi] *n., pl.* **-cies. 1** the position or work of an intendant. **2** intendants collectively. **3** a district under an intendant.

in•tend•ant [ɪn'tɛndənt] *n.* **1** a person in charge; superintendent; manager; director. **2** formerly, **a** the most important administrative office in New France, eventually responsible for the administration of finance, justice, and police in the colony. **b** an official who held this office: *Jean Talon was the first and greatest intendant of New France.* **c Intendant,** the title of such an official. ⟨< F, ult. < L *intendere* attend to. See INTEND.⟩

in•tend•ed [ɪn'tɛndɪd] *adj., n., v. —adj.* **1** meant; planned. **2** prospective: *a woman's intended husband.*
—n. Informal. a prospective husband or wife.
—v. pt. and pp. of INTEND.

in•tend•ment [ɪn'tɛndmənt] *n. Law.* the true meaning or intention as established legally.

in•tense [ɪn'tɛns] *adj.* **1** existing in or being of a very high degree; very strong; extreme: *intense pain, an intense colour, an intense light.* **2** of action, activity, etc., strenuous, eager, or ardent: *intense thought. She lived an intense life.* **3** having or showing strong feeling, purpose, etc.: *an intense face. He is an intense person.* ⟨< L *intensus,* pp. of *intendere* strain. See INTEND.⟩ **—in'tense•ly,** *adv.* **—in'tense•ness,** *n.*

in•ten•si•fi•er [ɪn'tɛnsə,faɪər] *n.* **1** *Photography.* a chemical used to increase contrast in a negative. **2** *Grammar.* an intensive.

in•ten•si•fy [ɪn'tɛnsə,faɪ] *v.* **-fied, -fy•ing. 1** make or become intense or more intense; strengthen; increase: *Blowing on a fire intensifies the heat. Her first failure only intensified her desire to succeed.* **2** *Photography.* make (parts of a negative) more dense or opaque by treating with chemicals. **—in,ten•si•fi'ca•tion,** *n.*

in•ten•sion [ɪn'tɛnʃən] *n.* **1** *Logic.* the set of attributes belonging to any thing to which a given term is correctly applied; connotation. **2** determination; exertion of the mind.
☛ *Hom.* INTENTION.

in•ten•si•ty [ɪn'tɛnsəti] *n., pl.* **-ties. 1** the quality or state of being intense; very great strength, force, etc. **2** the strength of a colour based on the degree of difference from the grey of the same brightness; saturation. **3** *Physics.* the amount or degree of strength of heat, light, sound, etc. per unit of area, volume, etc. **4** *Photography.* of parts of a negative, density; opaqueness.

in•ten•sive [ɪn'tɛnsɪv] *adj., n. —adj.* **1** deep and thorough: *An intensive study of a few books is more valuable than a superficial reading of many.* **2** having to do with a system of farming in which more money and work is spent on a small area to produce larger crops. **3** *Grammar.* **a** serving as an intensive: *an intensive prefix.* **b** of or being an INTENSIVE PRONOUN.
—n. Grammar. a word element, word, phrase, etc. that adds force or emphasis but has little meaning of its own in the context. The prefix *super* in *superstar* is an intensive. **—in'ten•sive•ly,** *adv.*

intensive pronoun a pronoun ending in *self* or *selves* used to emphasize the noun or pronoun it follows: *The explorer herself talked to our class. They themselves caused the problem.*

in•tent¹ [ɪn'tɛnt] *n.* **1** that which is intended; purpose; intention: *The thief shot with intent to kill.* **2** meaning; significance: *What is the intent of that sentence?* **3** *Law.* a person's attitude toward an action.

to all intents and purposes, in almost every way; practically. ⟨ME < OF *entent, entente* < L *intendere.* See INTEND.⟩

in•tent² [ɪn'tɛnt] *adj.* **1** very attentive; having the eyes or thoughts earnestly fixed on something; earnest: *an intent look.* **2** earnestly engaged; much interested; determined (*used with* **on**): *He is intent on making money.* ⟨< L *intentus,* pp. of *intendere* strain. See INTEND.⟩ **—in'tent•ly,** *adv.* **—in'tent•ness,** *n.*

in•ten•tion [ɪn'tɛnʃən] *n.* **1** the act or fact of having in mind as a purpose; determination to act in a certain way: *I'm sure he had no intention of hurting your feelings.* **2** what is intended; an object or purpose: *It wasn't my intention to start an argument.* **3 intentions,** *pl. Informal.* purpose with respect to marrying. **4** *Logic.* INTENSION (def. 1). **5** the healing of a wound by granulation. **—in'ten•tion•less,** *adj.*

☛ *Syn.* **1. Intention,** PURPOSE, DESIGN = what a person intends or plans to get or do. **Intention** = what one has in mind to do, but does not always suggest determination or definite planning: *My intention was to arrive early.* **Purpose** = a definite thing a person intends to do or get and toward which he strives with determination: *My purpose was to avoid the crowd.* **Design** suggests deliberate intention, with definite planning or preparations, often underhand, for carrying out one's purpose: *I arrived early by design. He had designs on her fortune.*
☛ *Hom.* INTENSION.

in•ten•tion•al [ɪn'tɛnʃənəl] *adj.* done on purpose; meant; planned; intended; deliberate: *His insult was intentional; he wanted to hurt your feelings.* **—in'ten•tion•al•ly,** *adv.*

in•ten•tioned [ɪn'tɛnʃənd] *adj.* having a specific intention.

in•ter [ɪn'tɜr] *v.* **-terred, -ter•ring.** put (a dead body) into a grave or tomb; bury. ⟨ME < OF *enterrer* + L *interrare* < *in-* in + *terra* earth⟩

☛ *Usage.* Do not confuse **inter** 'bury' with INTERN¹ 'confine in a certain place'. One **inters** a dead body; one **interns** a live person who might cause trouble.

inter– *prefix.* **1** together; one with the other: *intercommunicate = communicate with each other.* **2** between: *interpose = put between.* **3** between or among members of a group: *interscholastic = between or among schools.* ⟨< L *inter-* < *inter,* prep. adv., among, between, during⟩

in•ter•act [,ɪntər'ækt] *v.* act on another.

in•ter•ac•tion [,ɪntər'ækʃən] *n.* reciprocal action or influence.

in•ter•act•ive [,ɪntər'æktɪv] *adj. Computer technology.* involving direct communication between a computer system and a user.

in•ter a•li•a [,ɪntər 'ɑliə] *or* ['eiliə] *Latin.* among other things.

in•ter–A•mer•i•can [,ɪntər ə'mɛrəkən] *adj.* between or among countries of North, South, or Central America.

in•ter•bor•ough [,ɪntər'bɜrou] *adj.* between boroughs.

in•ter•brain ['ɪntər,brein] *n.* the back section of the forebrain; diencephalon.

in•ter•breed [,ɪntər'brid] *v.* **-bred, -breed•ing.** breed by the mating of different kinds; breed by using different varieties or species of animals or plants.

in•ter•ca•lar•y [ɪn'tɜrkə,lɛri] *or* [,ɪntər'kæləri] *adj.* **1** inserted in the calendar to make the calendar year agree with the solar year. February 29 is an intercalary day. **2** having an added day, month, etc. as a particular year. **3** put in between; interposed; intervening. ⟨< L *intercalaris, intercalarius* < *intercalare.* See INTERCALATE.⟩

in•ter•ca•late [ɪn'tɜrkə,leit] *v.* **-lat•ed, -lat•ing. 1** add into the calendar. **2** put in between; interpolate. ⟨< L *intercalare* < *inter-* between + *calare* proclaim⟩

in•ter•ca•la•tion [ɪn,tɜrkə'leiʃən] *n.* **1** an intercalating. **2** something intercalated.

in•ter•cede [,ɪntər'sid] *v.* **-ced•ed, -ced•ing. 1** plead or ask a favour in another's behalf: *Friends of the condemned man interceded with the authorities for a pardon.* **2** intervene in order to bring about an agreement; mediate. ⟨< L *intercedere* < *inter-* between + *cedere* go⟩

in•ter•cel•lu•lar [,ɪntər'sɛljələr] *adj.* situated between or among cells.

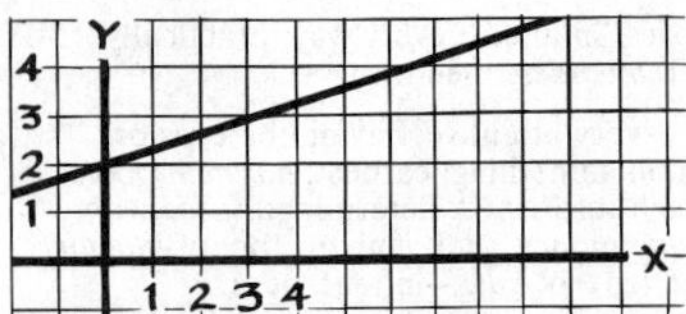

Intercept (def. 3). In the diagram the y-intercept is 2.

in•ter•cept *v.* [ˌɪntər'sɛpt]; *n.* ['ɪntərˌsɛpt] *v., n.* —*v.* **1** take, seize, or stop (a person, vehicle, etc.) on the way from one place to another: *to intercept a messenger or a letter, to intercept an enemy aircraft, to intercept a pass in football.* **2** interrupt or stop (motion, passage, progress, etc.): *to intercept the flight of a criminal.* **3** intersect. **4** *Mathematics.* cut off or give a boundary to (part of a line or plane).
—*n. Mathematics.* the distance from the origin to the point where a line crosses an axis on a graph. ⟨< L *interceptus,* pp. of *intercipere* < *inter-* between + *capere* catch⟩ —ˌ**in•ter'cep•tion,** *n.* —ˌ**in•ter'cept•ive,** *adj.*

in•ter•cep•tor [ˌɪntər'sɛptər] *n.* a person or thing that intercepts, especially a fighter aircraft or missile designed to stop enemy aircraft or missiles. Also, **intercepter.**

in•ter•ces•sion [ˌɪntər'sɛʃən] *n.* **1** the act or fact of interceding. **2** a prayer or petition in behalf of another person or persons. ⟨< L *intercessio, -onis* < *intercedere.* See INTERCEDE.⟩ —ˌ**in•ter'ces•sion•al,** *adj.*

in•ter•ces•sor [ˌɪntər'sɛsər] *or* ['ɪntərˌsɛsər] *n.* a person who intercedes.

in•ter•ces•so•ry [ˌɪntər'sɛsəri] *adj.* making or relating to intercession; interceding.

in•ter•change *v.* [ˌɪntər'tʃeindʒ]; *n.* ['ɪntərˌtʃeindʒ] *v.* **-changed, -chang•ing;** *n.* —*v.* **1** put each of (two or more persons or things) in the other's place. **2** give and take; exchange: *to interchange gifts.* **3** cause to follow one another alternately: *to interchange severity with indulgence.*
—*n.* **1** the putting of each of two or more persons or things in the other's place: *The word* team *may be turned into* meat *by the interchange of the end letters.* **2** a road that permits traffic from one highway to change to another without crossing in front of other traffic; cloverleaf. **3** a giving and taking; exchanging. **4** an alternate succession; alternation: *an interchange of hard work with rest.* ⟨ME *entrechange(n)* < OF *entrechangier* < *entre-* (< L *inter-*) + *changier* (< L *cambiare* exchange); later influenced by *inter-*⟩
☛ *Syn. v.* **2.** See note at EXCHANGE.

in•ter•change•a•ble [ˌɪntər'tʃeindʒəbəl] *adj.* capable of being used in place of each other: *This saw has several interchangeable blades.* —ˌ**in•terˌchange•a'bil•i•ty,** *n.* —ˌ**in•ter'change•a•bly,** *adv.*

in•ter•class [ˌɪntər'klæs] *adj.* between classes: *interclass swimming meets.*

in•ter•col•le•giate [ˌɪntərkə'lidʒɪt] *or* [ˌɪntərkə'lidʒiɪt] *adj.* between colleges, universities, or high schools: *intercollegiate football games.*
☛ *Usage.* See note at INTRAMURAL.

in•ter•co•lo•ni•al [ˌɪntərkə'louniəl] *adj.* between colonies; *intercolonial trade.*

in•ter•col•um•ni•a•tion [ˌɪntərkəˌlʌmni'eiʃən] *n. Architecture.* **1** the space between two adjacent columns. **2** the system of spacing columns. ⟨< L *intercolumnium* space between columns⟩

in•ter•com ['ɪntərˌkɒm] *n. Informal.* a system of radio or telephone communication between rooms of a building, parts of a ship or aircraft, etc. ⟨a shortened form of *intercommunication system*⟩

in•ter•com•mu•ni•cate [ˌɪntərkə'mjunəˌkeit] *v.* **-cat•ed, -cat•ing.** communicate with each other. ⟨< Med.L *intercommunicatus*⟩ —ˌ**in•ter•comˌmu•ni•ca'bil•i•ty,** *n.* —ˌ**in•ter•com'mu•ni•ca•ble,** *adj.* —ˌ**in•ter•comˌmu•ni'ca•tion,** *n.* —ˌ**in•ter•com'mu•ni•ca•tive,** *adj.* —ˌ**in•ter•com'mu•niˌca•tor,** *n.*

in•ter•con•nect [ˌɪntərkə'nɛkt] *v.* connect with each other. —ˌ**in•ter•con'nec•tion,** *n.*

in•ter•con•ti•nen•tal [ˌɪntərˌkɒntə'nɛntəl] *adj.* **1** extending or carried on between or among continents: *intercontinental travel.* **2** capable of travelling between continents: *intercontinental ballistic missiles.*

in•ter•cos•tal [ˌɪntər'kɒstəl] *adj., n.* —*adj.* between the ribs. —*n. Anatomy.* a muscle or part situated between the ribs. ⟨< NL *intercostalis* < L *inter-* between + *costa* rib⟩ —ˌ**in•ter'cos•tal•ly,** *adv.*

in•ter•course ['ɪntərˌkɔrs] *n.* **1** communication; dealings between people; exchange of thoughts, services, feelings, etc.: *Airplanes, good roads, and telephones make intercourse between different parts of the country far easier than it was fifty years ago.* **2** SEXUAL INTERCOURSE. ⟨ME *entercourse* < OF *entrecours* < L *intercursus* a running between, ult. < *inter-* between + *currere* run; later influenced by *inter-*⟩

in•ter•crop [ˌɪntər'krɒp] *v.* **-cropped, -crop•ping.** grow a crop between rows of another crop.

in•ter•cross [ˌɪntər'krɒs] *v.* **1** cross things with each other. **2** interbreed. **3** intersect.

in•ter•cur•rent [ˌɪntər'kʌrənt] *adj.* **1** happening as an interruption. **2** of a disease, occurring while another disease is in progress.

in•ter•cut [ˌɪntər'kʌt] *v.* **-cut -cut•ting.** interpose (a camera shot or scene) in a movie sequence.

in•ter•de•nom•i•na•tion•al [ˌɪntərdɪˌnɒmə'neiʃənəl] *adj.* between or involving different religious denominations.

in•ter•dent•al [ˌɪntər'dɛntəl] *adj., n.* —*adj.* **1** situated between the teeth. **2** *Phonetics.* pronounced with the tip of the tongue between the teeth, as [θ] in *thin,* [ð] in *then.*
—*n. Phonetics.* such a speech sound.

in•ter•de•part•men•tal [ˌɪntərˌdipɑrt'mɛntəl] *adj.* between departments. —ˌ**in•terˌde•part'men•tal•ly,** *adv.*

in•ter•de•pend•ence [ˌɪntərdɪ'pɛndəns] *n.* dependence on each other; mutual dependence. Also, **interdependency.**

in•ter•de•pend•ent [ˌɪntərdɪ'pɛndənt] *adj.* dependent each upon the other. —ˌ**in•ter•de'pend•ent•ly,** *adv.*

in•ter•dict *n.* ['ɪntərˌdɪkt]; *v.* [ˌɪntər'dɪkt] *n., v.* —*n.* **1** an official prohibition; a formal, authoritative order forbidding something. **2** *Roman Catholic Church.* a censure excluding a place or person from certain sacraments and privileges. **3** *Cdn.* especially in British Columbia, a person forbidden to buy alcoholic liquor.
—*v.* **1** place under an interdict: *to interdict a parish.* **2** prohibit or forbid by authority: *to interdict trade with other countries.* **3** restrain by authority: *interdicted from buying alcoholic liquor.* ⟨ME < OF < L *interdictus,* pp. of *interdicere* prohibit < *inter-* between + *dicere* speak⟩ —ˌ**in•ter'dic•tor,** *n.*

in•ter•dic•tion [ˌɪntər'dɪkʃən] *n.* an interdicting or being interdicted.

in•ter•dig•i•tate [ˌɪntər'dɪdʒəˌteit] *v.* **-tat•ed, -tat•ing.** interlock like the fingers of both hands.

in•ter•dis•ci•plin•a•ry [ˌɪntər'dɪsəpləˌnɛri] *adj.* involving two or more academic disciplines.

in•ter•est ['ɪntrɪst] *or* ['ɪntərɪst] *n., v.* —*n.* **1** a feeling of wanting to know, see, do, own, share in, or take part in: *He has no interest in sports.* **2** the power of arousing such a feeling: *A dull book lacks interest.* **3** something that stirs up such feelings. Any activity, pastime, or hobby can be an interest. **4** a share or part in property and actions: *She bought a half interest in the farm.* **5** something in which a person has a share or part. **6** a group of people financially interested in the same business, activity, etc.: *mining interests.* **7** advantage; benefit: *Each person should look after his or her own interest.* **8** money paid for the use of money, usually a percentage of the amount invested, borrowed, or loaned: *The annual interest on the loan was 15 percent.*
in the interest of, a in behalf of. **b** with a view to; with the objective of.
with interest, with something extra given in return: *She returned our favour with interest.*
—*v.* **1** make curious and hold the attention of: *An exciting story interests you.* **2** cause (a person) to take a share or part in something: *The agent tried to interest us in buying a car.* ⟨ME < AF < L *interest* it is of importance, it makes a difference, 3rd person sing. present of *interesse* < *inter-* between + *esse* be⟩

in•ter•est•ed ['ɪntrɪstɪd], ['ɪntərɪstəd], *or* ['ɪntəˌrɛstɪd] *adj., v.* —*adj.* **1** feeling or showing interest: *He gave a demonstration before a crowd of interested spectators. Are you interested in running for class president?* **2** involved or concerned; having an interest or share: *A meeting will be held tonight for all interested parties.* **3** influenced by personal considerations; prejudiced: *interested motives.*
—*v.* pt. and pp. of INTEREST. —**'in•ter•est•ed•ly,** *adv.* —**'in•ter•est•ed•ness,** *n.*
☛ *Usage.* **Interested.** The adjective **interested** has two opposites: UNINTERESTED, which is merely its negative, and DISINTERESTED, which

means 'free from selfish motives; impartial; fair': *He was uninterested in the outcome of the game. A disinterested spectator offered to referee.* See also DISINTERESTED.

in•ter•est•ing ['ɪntrɪstɪŋ], ['ɪntərɪstɪŋ], *or* ['ɪntə,rɛstɪŋ] *adj., v.* —*adj.* arousing interest; holding one's attention.
—*v.* ppr. of INTEREST. **—'in•ter•est•ing•ly,** *adv.*

in•ter•face ['ɪntər,feis] *n., v.* —*n.* **1** a surface that forms a common boundary between two regions, bodies, spaces, etc.: *the interface of air and water.* **2** an area or place where different systems, processes, etc. act on or influence each other: *Taxation is the most critical interface between government and business.* **3** the means by which different systems, processes, modes of thought, etc. interact: *serving as an interface between the two groups.* **4** *Computer technology.* the program necessary to connect computers to each other or to other machines.
—*v.* **1** serve as or form an interface: *There are problems where the two groups interface.* **2** bring into contact or interaction: *Can one interface programs in* BASIC *and* FORTRAN? **3** add interfacing to: *to interface a collar.*

in•ter•fa•cing ['ɪntər,feisɪŋ] *n., v.* —*n.* a relatively stiff material placed between two layers of fabric in a collar, cuff, etc. to give shape or body to it. The interfacing is sewn or fused between the outside layer and the facing.
—*v.* ppr. of INTERFACE.

in•ter•fere [,ɪntər'fir] *v.* **-fered, -fer•ing. 1** come into opposition; come between in a way that obstructs or hinders: *I will come on Saturday if nothing interferes.* **2** disturb the affairs of others; meddle: *This has nothing to do with you, so don't interfere.* **3** intervene for a particular purpose: *The police interfered to stop the riot.* **4** *Sports.* obstruct or hinder the action of an opposing player in an illegal way. **5** *Physics.* of waves, act upon one another in such a way as to increase, lessen, neutralize, etc. each other.
interfere with, a prevent or obstruct: *The rain interfered with our plans.* **b** distort by interfering. ⟨< OF *entreferir* strike each other < *entre-* between (< L *inter-*) + *ferir* strike < L *ferire*⟩
☛ *Syn.* **2.** See note at MEDDLE.

in•ter•fer•ence [,ɪntər'firəns] *n.* **1** an interfering. **2** something that interferes; obstruction. **3** *Physics.* the effect that light or sound waves have on each other when their paths meet or cross, to intensify or neutralize each other, produce beats, etc. **4** *Radio and television.* **a** confusion of radio signals, producing static, distortion of sound, etc. **b** something that produces such confusion. **5** *Football.* **a** the legal blocking of an opposing player to clear the way for the ball carrier. **b** the players protecting or blocking for the ball carrier. **6** *Sports.* **a** the illegal obstructing or hindering of an opposing player. **b** the penalty for this.
run interference (for), a *Football.* clear the way for the ball carrier. **b** act as a go-between or screen: *She never has to deal directly with the public because her secretary runs interference for her.* **—,in•ter•fer'en•tial** [-fə'rɛnʃəl], *adj.*

in•ter•fer•om•e•ter [,ɪntərfə'rɒmətər] *n. Optics.* an instrument for measuring wavelengths of light, testing the refraction of prisms and lenses, measuring very small distances, etc. by means of light interference patterns produced when parts of a ray of light that have travelled different distances overlap again. **—,in•ter,fer•o'met•ric** [-,firə'mɛtrɪk], *adj.* **—,in•ter•fer'om•et•ry,** *n.*

in•ter•fer•on [,ɪntər'firɒn] *n. Biochemistry.* a protein produced in virus-infected cells to counteract the infection.

in•ter•fer•tile [,ɪntər'fɜrtaɪl] *adj. Botany, zoology.* able to interbreed.

in•ter•file [,ɪntər'faɪl] *v.* **-filed, -fil•ing.** combine two or more similarly arranged sets of (items, as cards or documents) into one.

in•ter•fold [,ɪntər'fould] *v.* fold, one within another; fold together.

in•ter•fuse [,ɪntər'fjuz] *v.* **-fused, -fus•ing. 1** intersperse or permeate with something. **2** fuse together; blend. **3** infuse. ⟨< L *interfusus,* pp. of *interfundere* < *inter-* between + *fundere* pour⟩ **—,in•ter'fu•sion,** *n.*

in•ter•ga•lac•tic [,ɪntərgə'læktɪk] *adj.* occurring or situated between galaxies: *intergalactic travel.*

in•ter•gen•er•a•tion•al [,ɪntər,dʒɛnə'reiʃənəl] *adj.* taking place between two different generations: *intergenerational conflict.*

in•ter•gla•cial [,ɪntər'gleiʃəl] *adj., n.* —*adj. Geology.* of or occurring in the period between two glacial epochs.
—*n.* the period between two glacial epochs.

in•ter•gov•ern•men•tal [,ɪntər,gʌvərn'mɛntəl] *or* [,ɪntər,gʌvər'mɛntəl] *adj.* **1** taking place between two or more governments. **2** taking place between two or more levels of government: an *intergovernmental conference.*

in•ter•grade *v.* [,ɪntər'greid]; *n.* ['ɪntər,greid] *v.* **-grad•ed, -grad•ing,** *n.*
—*v.* merge gradually.
—*n.* an intermediate grade. **—,in•ter•gra'da•tion** [-grə'deiʃən], *n.* **—,in•ter•gra'da•tion•al,** *adj.* **—,in•ter•gra'da•tion•al•ly,** *adv.*

in•ter•group [,ɪntər'grup] *adj. Sociology.* taking place between two groups or among several groups.

in•ter•im ['ɪntərɪm] *n., adj.* —*n.* meantime; time between.
—*adj.* for the meantime; temporary: *an interim report.* ⟨< L *interim* in the meantime < *inter* between⟩

in•te•ri•or [ɪn'tiriər] *n., adj.* —*n.* **1** the inside; inner surface or part: *The interior of the house was beautifully decorated.* **2** the part of a region or country away from the coast or border. **3** a picture or stage setting of the inside of a room, house, etc. **4** one's mental or spiritual being. **5 Interior,** the inland area of British Columbia, such as the Okanagan.
—*adj.* **1** on the inside; inner. **2** away from the coast or border. **3** having to do with affairs within a country; domestic. **4** private; secret. ⟨< L *interior* inner⟩

interior angle 1 any of the four angles formed on the inner sides of two lines by a straight line cutting through the lines. **2** the angle formed on the inside of a polygon between two adjacent sides. Compare EXTERIOR ANGLE. See ANGLE and TRIANGLE for pictures.

interior decoration 1 the colours, materials, furnishings, etc. used in a room, house, etc. and their arrangement. **2** interior design.

interior decorator 1 a person whose work is painting or wallpapering the interiors of houses and other buildings. **2** a person whose work is helping to plan furnishings, decor, etc. for the interior of a home, office, or other building.

interior design the art or practice of planning furnishings, decorations, etc. for the interiors of homes, offices, and other buildings.

interior designer a person trained in interior design, especially one whose work it is.

interior monologue *Literature.* a form of writing that gives the innermost thoughts of a character.

interj. interjection.

in•ter•ject [,ɪntər'dʒɛkt] *v.* throw in between other things; insert abruptly: *Every now and then the speaker interjected some witty remark.* ⟨< L *interjectus,* pp. of *interjicere* < *inter-* between + *jacere* throw⟩ **—,in•ter'jec•tor,** *n.*

in•ter•jec•tion [,ɪntər'dʒɛkʃən] *n.* **1** the act of interjecting. **2** something interjected, such as a word or remark. **3** *Grammar.* an exclamation of surprise, sorrow, delight, etc., that has no grammatical connection with what precedes or follows it. *Oh! Ah! Ouch!* and *Whoops!* are interjections.

in•ter•jec•tion•al [,ɪntər'dʒɛkʃənəl] *adj.* **1** of an interjection; used as an interjection. **2** containing an interjection. **3** interjected. Also, **interjectory. —,in•ter'jec•tion•al•ly,** *adv.*

in•ter•knit [,ɪntər'nɪt] *v.* **-knit•ted, -knit•ting.** knit together; intertwine.

in•ter•lace [,ɪntər'leis] *v.* **-laced, -lac•ing. 1** arrange or cross (threads, strips, branches, etc.) so that they go over and under each other; weave together; intertwine: *Baskets are made by interlacing reeds or fibres.* **2** give variety to; intersperse: *a speech interlaced with silly jokes.* **—,in•ter'lace•ment,** *n.*

in•ter•lam•i•nate [,ɪntər'læmə,neit] *v.* **-nat•ed, -nat•ing.** lay between; interpose; interlay.

in•ter•lard [,ɪntər'lɑrd] *v.* **1** give variety to; mix so as to give variety to; intersperse: *The speaker interlarded his long speech with amusing stories.* **2** of things, become intermixed. ⟨< F *entrelarder* < *entre-* between (< L *inter-*) + *larder* lard < L *lardum* fat⟩

in•ter•lay [,ɪntər'lei] *v.* **-laid, -lay•ing.** interpose.

in•ter•leaf ['ɪntər,lif] *n., pl.* **-leaves.** a leaf of paper, usually blank, put between others, as in a book, for notes, to protect colour plates, etc.

in•ter•leave [,ɪntər'liv] *v.* **-leaved, -leav•ing.** insert a leaf or leaves of paper between the pages of (a book, album, etc.).

in•ter•line [,ɪntər'laɪn] *v.* **-lined, -lin•ing. 1** insert words, etc. between the lines of: *The document had been interlined in several places.* **2** write, print, or mark between the lines: *The teacher* *interlined corrections on the students' themes.* **3** provide with an interlining. ⟨ME *interlynen* < Med.L *interlineare*⟩

in•ter•lin•e•ar [ˌɪntərˈlɪniər] *adj.* **1** inserted between the lines: *an interlinear translation.* **2** containing two different languages or versions in alternate lines. **—ˌin•terˈlin•e•ar•ly,** *adv.*

in•ter•lin•e•a•tion [ˌɪntərˌlɪniˈeiʃən] *n.* **1** interlining; the insertion of matter between the lines of writing or print. **2** the matter thus inserted.

In•ter•lin•gua [ˌɪntərˈlɪŋgwə] *n.* an artificial language based on the Romance languages and intended for use internationally by scientists. ⟨< Ital.⟩

in•ter•lin•ing [ˈɪntərˌlaɪnɪŋ] *n.* **1** an extra lining between the outer fabric of a garment and the lining: *The coat has a warm woollen interlining.* **2** a fabric used to interline.

in•ter•link [ˌɪntərˈlɪŋk] *v.* link together.

in•ter•lock *v.* [ˌɪntərˈlɒk]; *n.* [ˈɪntərˌlɒk] *v., n.* *—v.* **1** join or fit tightly together; lock together: *The antlers of the two stags were interlocked.* **2** be connected so that all action is synchronized.
—n. a device to ensure that parts of a machine will operate in the proper sequence.

in•ter•lo•cu•tion [ˌɪntərləˈkjuʃən] *n.* conversation; dialogue.

in•ter•loc•u•tor [ˌɪntərˈlɒkjətər] *n.* **1** a person who takes part in a conversation or dialogue. **2** in a minstrel show, the person who asks the end person questions. ⟨< L *interlocutus*, pp. of *interloqui* converse[1] < *inter-* between + *loqui* speak⟩

in•ter•loc•u•to•ry [ˌɪntərˈlɒkjəˌtɔri] *adj.* **1** of or in conversation or dialogue. **2** *Law.* **a** made during a lawsuit or other action; not final: *The judge granted an interlocutory decree after the hearing.* **b** of or having to do with a decision made in this way. **3** inserted into a conversation, speech, etc: *interlocutory anecdotes.*

in•ter•lope [ˌɪntərˈloup] *or* [ˈɪntərˌloup] *v.* **-loped, -lop•ing.**
1 intrude without permission. **2** interfere in the affairs of others.

in•ter•lop•er [ˈɪntərˌloupər] *n.* a person who intrudes on or meddles in others' affairs. ⟨probably < Du. *enterloper* < *entre-* between (< L *inter-*) + *loper* runner < *lopen* run⟩

in•ter•lude [ˈɪntərˌlud] *n.* **1** anything thought of as filling the time between two things; interval: *There were only a few interludes of fair weather during the rainy season.* **2** *Music.* a composition played between the parts of a song, church service, play, etc.
3 an entertainment between the acts of a play. **4** in early English drama: **a** a short, humorous play, commonly introduced between the parts of the long mystery plays or given as part of other entertainment. **b** a stage play of a popular nature; comedy; farce. ⟨< Med.L *interludium* < L *inter-* between + *ludus* play⟩

in•ter•lu•nar [ˌɪntərˈlunər] *adj.* having to do with the period each month, between the old moon and the new moon, when the moon is not visible.

in•ter•mar•riage [ˌɪntərˈmærɪdʒ] *or* [ˌɪntərˈmɛrɪdʒ] *n.*
1 marriage between members of different religious, social, or ethnic groups. **2** marriage between close blood relations.

in•ter•mar•ry [ˌɪntərˈmæri] *or* [ˌɪntərˈmɛri] *v.* **-ried, -ry•ing.**
1 of families, peoples, etc., become connected by marriage.
2 marry within the family or with close relations.

in•ter•med•dle [ˌɪntərˈmɛdəl] *v.* **-dled, -dling.** interfere; meddle.

in•ter•me•di•ar•y [ˌɪntərˈmidiˌɛri] *n., adj.* *—n.* **1** a person who deals with each side in settling a dispute, negotiating a business arrangement, etc.; go-between: *She acted as intermediary in the land deal between the city and the developer.* **2** a medium; means. **3** an intermediate form or stage.
—adj. **1** acting between two persons or groups as an intermediary: *an intermediary agent.* **2** being between; intermediate: *A chrysalis is an intermediary stage between caterpillar and butterfly.* ⟨< L *intermedius* intermediate < *inter-* between + *medius* in the middle⟩

in•ter•me•di•ate *adj., n.* [ˌɪntərˈmidiɪt]; *v.* [ˌɪntərˈmidiˌeit] *adj., n., v.* **-at•ed, -at•ing.** *—adj.* **1** being or occurring between extremes or in a middle stage, place, or degree: *The language school offers only beginning and intermediate courses in French.*
2 of a car, larger than a compact but not full-sized.
—n. **1** the second largest of the four basic sizes of automobile, larger than a compact and smaller than a standard. Compare COMPACT[1], SUBCOMPACT, and STANDARD. **2** anything intermediate. **3** intermediary; go-between. **4** a compound formed between the initial and final stages in a chemical process.
—v. act as intermediary; mediate. ⟨< Med.L *intermediatus* < L *intermedius* < *inter-* between + *medius* in the middle⟩

intermediate frequency *Radio.* the middle frequency in a superheterodyne receiver, at which most of the amplification occurs.

in•ter•ment [ɪnˈtɜrmənt] *n.* the act of putting a dead body into a grave or tomb; burial.

in•ter•mez•zo [ˌɪntərˈmɛtsou] *or* [ˌɪntərˈmɛdzou] *n., pl.* **-mez•zos, -mez•zi** [-ˈmɛtsi] *or* [-ˈmɛdzi] **1** a short, dramatic, musical or other entertainment of a light character between the acts of a drama or opera. **2** *Music.* **a** a short composition between the main divisions of an extended musical work. **b** an independent composition of similar character. ⟨< Ital.⟩

in•ter•mi•na•ble [ɪnˈtɜrmənəbəl] *adj.* endless or so long as to seem endless; very long and tiring: *an interminable speech.* ⟨ME < LL *interminabilis*, ult. < L *in-* not + *terminare* to end⟩ **—inˈter•mi•na•ble•ness,** *n.* **—inˈter•mi•na•bly,** *adv.*

in•ter•min•gle [ˌɪntərˈmɪŋgəl] *v.* **-gled, -gling.** mix together; mingle.

in•ter•mis•sion [ˌɪntərˈmɪʃən] *n.* **1** a time between periods of activity; a pause, especially between acts of a play, parts of a musical performance, etc.: *There were two fifteen-minute intermissions in the performance.* **2** a stopping for a time; interruption: *The rain continued all day without intermission.* ⟨< L *intermissio, -onis* < *intermittere.* See INTERMIT.⟩

in•ter•mis•sive [ˌɪntərˈmɪsɪv] *adj.* **1** intermittent.
2 characterized by intermission.

in•ter•mit [ˌɪntərˈmɪt] *v.* **-mit•ted, -mit•ting.** stop for a time. ⟨< L *intermittere* < *inter-* between + *mittere* leave⟩ **—ˌin•terˈmit•ter,** *n.*

in•ter•mit•tent [ˌɪntərˈmɪtənt] *adj.* stopping and beginning again; pausing at intervals. **—ˌin•terˈmit•tent•ly,** *adv.* **—ˌin•terˈmit•tence** or **ˌin•terˈmit•ten•cy,** *n.*

intermittent current a unidirectional electric current that is periodically interrupted.

intermittent fever a fever that is recurrent.

in•ter•mix [ˌɪntərˈmɪks] *v.* mix or become mixed together; blend: *Oil and water do not intermix.*

in•ter•mix•ture [ˌɪntərˈmɪkstʃər] *n.* **1** a mixing together. **2** a mass of ingredients mixed together.

in•ter•mod•al [ˌɪntərˈmoudəl] *adj.* of a system of transport that uses surface, sea, and air transportation for one shipment.

in•ter•mon•tane [ˌɪntərmɒnˈtein] *adj.* situated between or among mountains. Also, **inter-mountain.**

in•ter•mus•cu•lar [ˌɪntərˈmʌskjələr] *adj.* found or set between muscles or muscle fibres.

in•tern[1] *v.* [ɪnˈtɜrn]; *n.* [ˈɪntɜrn] *v., n.* *—v.* confine within a country or place; force to stay in a certain place, especially during a war: *Aliens are sometimes interned in wartime.*
—n. one who is interned; internee. ⟨< F *interner* < *interne* inner, internal < L *internus* < *in* in⟩
☛ *Usage.* See note at INTER.

in•tern[2] [ˈɪntɜrn] *n., v.* *—n.* **1** a medical doctor working as an assistant in a hospital. A doctor has to serve at least one year as an intern before he or she can practise medicine on his or her own. **2** a recent graduate, etc. in any of various other fields undergoing supervised practical training.
—v. act as an intern. Also, **interne.** ⟨< F *interne* < *interne*, adj. See INTERN[1].⟩ **—inˈtern•ship,** *n.*

in•ter•nal [ɪnˈtɜrnəl] *adj.* **1** inner; on the inside: *internal injuries.* **2** to be taken inside the body: *internal remedies.*
3 entirely inside; coming from within: *The date of the author's death is unknown, but events in the poem provide internal evidence that she was still alive in 1920.* **4** having to do with affairs within a country; domestic: *internal disturbances.* **5** of the mind; subjective: *Thoughts are internal.* **6** *Anatomy.* not superficial; away from the surface of the body. ⟨< Med.L *internalis* < L *internus* within < *in* in⟩ **—inˈter•nal•ly,** *adv.* **—ˌin•terˈnal•i•ty** or **inˈter•nal•ness,** *n.*

internal–combustion engine **1** an engine in which the power comes from each piston being moved by explosions within its cylinder. **2** a gas-turbine engine that uses for its power the gas formed by burning or exploding fuel.

internal ear INNER EAR.

in•ter•na•lize [ɪnˈtɜrnəˌlaɪz] *v.* **-lized, -liz•ing. 1** give a subjective character to. **2** adopt (the values of another person or group). **—inˌter•na•liˈza•tion,** *n.*

internal medicine the branch of medicine dealing with the diagnosis and non-surgical treatment of diseases.

internal revenue government income from taxes.

internal rhyme a rhyme in which a rhyming syllable is in the middle of the line rather than at the end.

internal secretion a secretion from an endocrine gland, which enters the blood directly.

in•ter•na•tion•al [ˌɪntərˈnæʃənəl] *adj., n.* —*adj.* **1** between or among nations: *international trade.* **2** accepted by or agreed on by many or all nations: *an international driver's licence, an international unit of measure, international law.* **3** for the use of all nations: *international waters.*
—*n.* **1 International,** any of several international socialist or communist organizations. **2** a person who is at home in several countries. **—ˌin•terˌna•tion'al•i•ty,** *n.* **—ˌin•ter'na•tion•al•ly,** *adv.*

international candle *Optics.* candela.

International Court of Justice the official name of the WORLD COURT.

International Date Line DATE LINE (def. 1).

In•ter•na•tio•nale [ˌɪntərˌnæʃəˈnæl] *or* [ˌɪntərˈnæʃənəl]; *French,* [ɛ̃tɛʀnasjɔˈnal] *n.* formerly, the anthem of the international socialist and communist organizations of the late 19th and early 20th centuries and the national anthem of the Soviet Union until 1944. ⟨< F⟩

in•ter•na•tion•al•ism [ˌɪntərˈnæʃənəˌlɪzəm] *n.* **1** the principle of international co-operation for the good of all nations. **2** international quality, character, interests, etc.

in•ter•na•tion•al•ist [ˌɪntərˈnæʃənəlɪst] *n.* **1** a person who favours internationalism. **2** a person familiar with international law and relations.

in•ter•na•tion•al•ize [ˌɪntərˈnæʃənəˌlaɪz] *v.* **-ized, -iz•ing.** make international; bring (territory) under the control of several nations. **—ˌin•terˌna•tion•al•i'za•tion,** *n.*

International Joint Commission a committee set up by Canada and the United States to settle possible disputes between the two countries concerning boundary waters.

international law the body of rules that most nations recognize as binding in international relations.

International Monetary Fund an agency of the United Nations which is intended to stabilize the currencies of the world and which lends money to member nations.

International Phonetic Alphabet a system of symbols designed to represent the speech sounds of any language. The International Phonetic Alphabet is used to show the pronunciation of words in this book.

international pitch *Music.* the standard pitch of musical instruments, in which the A above middle C is at 440 hertz.

International Style a style of architecture developed between 1920 and 1930, characterized by geometric forms with large areas of glass.

in•terne [ˈɪntərn] See INTERN².

in•ter•ne•cine [ˌɪntərˈnisən], [ˌɪntərˈnisaɪn], *or* [ˌɪntərˈnɛsin] *adj.* **1** destructive to both sides. **2** deadly; destructive. **3** of a dispute within a group: *internecine conflict.* ⟨< L *internecinus* < *internecere* kill < *inter-* between + *nex, necis* slaughter⟩

in•tern•ee [ˌɪntərˈni] *n.* a person who is interned.

In•ter•net [ˈɪntərˌnɛt] *n. Computer technology.* **1** an international computer network giving access to a broad range of information and providing electronic communication services such as e-mail. The Internet is accessible to the general public via modem through various user networks known as providers, usually for a fee. **2** loosely, the ensemble of networks consisting of Internet and all the user networks linked to it. Also called **the Net.**

in•ter•neu•ron [ˌɪntərˈnjurɒn] *or* [ˌɪntərˈnurɒn] *n.* INTERNUNCIAL NEURON.

in•ter•nist [ɪnˈtɜrnɪst] *or* [ˈɪntɜrnɪst] *n.* a specialist in internal medicine, as distinguished from a surgeon, obstetrician, etc.

in•tern•ment [ɪnˈtɜrnmənt] *n.* an interning or being interned.

in•ter•node [ˈɪntərˌnoud] *n. Botany.* a portion between two nodes or joints, as the portion of a plant stem between two nodes. **—ˌin•ter'nod•al,** *adj.*

in•ter•nun•ci•al neuron [ˌɪntərˈnʌnʃəl] *Anatomy.* a neuron or chain of neurons that links ingoing and outgoing fibres of the nervous system.

in•ter•nun•cio [ˌɪntərˈnʌnʃiou] *or* [ˌɪntərˈnʌnsiou] *n.* **1** a papal envoy ranking below a nuncio. **2** any messenger. ⟨< Ital. < L *internuntius.* See INTER-, NUNCIO.⟩

in•ter•o•ce•an•ic [ˌɪntərˌouʃiˈænɪk] *adj.* between oceans.

in•ter•o•cep•tor [ˌɪntərouˈsɛptər] *n. Physiology.* a sensory receptor that responds to stimuli from within the body. ⟨< NL < L *intero-* inside + *-ceptor* receiver⟩

in•ter•of•fice [ˌɪntərˈɒfɪs] *adj.* operating between the offices of an organization: *an interoffice memo.*

in•ter•os•cu•late [ˌɪntərˈɒskjəˌleit] *v.* **-lat•ed, -lat•ing.** **1** interpenetrate. **2** serve as a connection. **—ˌin•terˌos•cu'la•tion,** *n.*

in•ter•pel•late [ˌɪntərˈpɛleit] *or* [ɪnˈtɜrpəˌleit] *v.* **-lat•ed, -lat•ing.** make an interpellation. ⟨< L *interpellare* interrupt⟩ **—ˌin•ter'pel•lant,** *adj.*
☛ *Hom.* INTERPOLATE [ɪnˈtɜrpəˌleit].

in•ter•pel•la•tion [ˌɪntərpəˈleiʃən] *or* [ɪnˌtɜrpəˈleiʃən] *n.* a formal request in a legislature for an explanation of official action or government policy.
☛ *Hom.* INTERPOLATION [ɪnˌtɜrpəˈleiʃən].

in•ter•pen•e•trate [ˌɪntərˈpɛnəˌtreit] *v.* **-trat•ed, trat•ing.** penetrate thoroughly; permeate. **—ˌin•terˌpen•e'tra•tion,** *n.*

in•ter•per•son•al [ˌɪntərˈpɜrsənəl] *adj.* **1** happening between two persons. **2** describing relations between two persons. **—ˌin•ter'per•son•al•ly,** *adv.*

in•ter•phase [ˈɪntərˌfeiz] *n.* the stage of a cell between periods of mitosis. See CELL CYCLE.

in•ter•phone [ˈɪntərˌfoun] *n.* intercom.

in•ter•plan•e•tar•y [ˌɪntərˈplænəˌtɛri] *adj.* **1** existing or taking place between the planets; within the solar system, but outside the atmosphere of any of the planets or the sun: *interplanetary space.* **2** carried on between planets: *interplanetary travel.*

in•ter•play *n.* [ˈɪntərˌplei]; *v.* [ˌɪntərˈplei] *n., v.* —*n.* the action or influence of things on each other; interaction: *the interplay of light and shadow.*
—*v.* exert mutual influence; have reciprocal action: *Their opposing views interplayed successfully.*

in•ter•plead [ˌɪntərˈplid] *v. Law.* determine, by an interpleader, which of two plaintiffs has the right to make claims on a defendant.

in•ter•plead•er [ˌɪntərˈplidər] *n.* a legal process whereby two or more parties having a claim on a defendant can be required to settle it in a lawsuit between themselves without involving the defendant.

In•ter•pol [ˈɪntərˌpoul] *or* [ˈɪntərˌpɒl] *n.* an international organization of the criminal police forces of more than 100 countries, whose aim is to provide the greatest possible mutual assistance among the members, within the limits of the law in each country, for the prevention and suppression of crime. Its headquarters is in Paris. ⟨*Inter*national Criminal *Pol*ice Organization⟩

in•ter•po•late [ɪnˈtɜrpəˌleit] *v.* **-lat•ed, -lat•ing.** **1** alter (a book, passage, etc.) by putting in new words or groups of words. **2** put in (new words, passages, etc.). **3** *Mathematics.* insert (intermediate terms) in a series. **4** insert or introduce (something additional or different) between other things, or in a series; interpose. ⟨< L *interpolare* freshen up⟩ **—in'ter•poˌlat•er** or **in'ter•poˌla•tor,** *n.* **—in'ter•poˌla•tive,** *adj.* **—in'ter•poˌla•tive•ly,** *adv.*
☛ *Hom.* INTERPELLATE.

in•ter•po•la•tion [ɪnˌtɜrpəˈleiʃən] *n.* **1** the act of interpolating. **2** something interpolated.
☛ *Hom.* INTERPELLATION.

in•ter•pose [ˌɪntərˈpouz] *v.* **-posed, -pos•ing.** **1** put between; insert. **2** put forward; break in with; introduce as an interruption: *She interposed an objection.* **3** intervene in a dispute; mediate: *He quickly interposed between the angry children.* ⟨< F *interposer* < *inter-* between (< L *inter-*) + *poser* place (See POSE¹)⟩ **—ˌin•ter'pos•er,** *n.* **—ˌin•ter'pos•al,** *n.* **—ˌin•ter'pos•a•ble,** *adj.* **—ˌin•ter'pos•ing•ly,** *adv.*

in•ter•po•si•tion [ˌɪntərpəˈzɪʃən] *n.* **1** the act of interposing. **2** the thing interposed.

in•ter•pret [ɪnˈtɜrprɪt] *v.* **1** explain the meaning of: *to interpret a difficult passage in a book, to interpret a dream.* **2** bring out the meaning of (a dramatic part, a character, music, etc.) in performing it. **3** understand according to one's own judgment: *We interpreted your silence as consent.* **4** serve as an interpreter; translate orally for speakers of different languages. **5** explain to visitors the purpose and importance of national and provincial park systems and the influence of park visitors on the ecology of

a park. ⟨< L *interpretari* < *interpres*, *-pretis* negotiator⟩ **—in,ter•pret•a'bil•i•ty,** *n.* **—in'ter•pret•a•ble,** *adj.*
☛ *Syn.* **1.** See note at EXPLAIN.

in•ter•pre•ta•tion [ɪn,tɜrprə'teiʃən] *n.* **1** an interpreting; explanation: *different interpretations of the same facts.* **2** a bringing out of the meaning of a dramatic part, a piece of music, etc. by performance. **3** the explanation to visitors of the purpose and importance of national and provincial park systems and the influence of park visitors on the ecology of a park. **4** oral translation. **—in,ter•pre'ta•tion•al,** *adj.*

in•ter•pre•ta•tive [ɪn'tɜrprətətɪv] *or* [ɪn'tɜrprə,teitɪv] *adj.* interpretive. **—in'ter•pre•ta•tive•ly,** *adv.*

in•ter•pret•er [ɪn'tɜrprətər] *n.* a person who interprets, especially one whose work is translating a language orally, as in a conversation between people who do not understand each other's language.

in•ter•pre•tive [ɪn'tɜrprətɪv] *adj.* **1** used for interpreting; explanatory. **2** of, having to do with, or referring to the interpretation of parks and park systems. All Canada's national parks have interpretive programs. **—in'ter•pre•tive•ly,** *adv.*

in•ter•pro•vin•cial [,ɪntərprə'vɪnʃəl] *adj.* **1** between or among provinces. **2** connecting two or more provinces: *an interprovincial highway.* **—,in•ter•pro'vin•cial•ly,** *adv.*

in•ter•ra•cial [,ɪntər'reiʃəl] *adj.* between or involving different races. **—,in•ter'ra•cial•ly,** *adv.*

in•ter•ra•di•al [,ɪntər'reidiəl] *adj.* situated between the radii or rays. **—,in•ter'ra•di•al•ly,** *adv.*

in•ter•reg•num [,ɪntər'rɛgnəm] *n., pl.* **-nums, -na** [-nə]. **1** the time between the end of one ruler's reign and the beginning of the next one. **2** any time during which a nation is without its usual ruler or government. **3** a period of inactivity; pause. ⟨< L < *inter-* between + *regnum* reign⟩ **—,in•ter'reg•nal,** *adj.*

in•ter•re•late [,ɪntərrɪ'leit] *v.* **-lat•ed, -lat•ing.** relate to one another; connect: *The two proposals are interrelated.* **—,in•ter•re'la•tion** or **,in•ter•re'la•tion•ship,** *n.*

in•ter•rex ['ɪntər,rɛks] *n., pl.* **in•ter•reg•es** [,ɪntər'ridʒiz]. one who rules during an interregnum. ⟨< L *inter-* between + *rex* king, ruler⟩

in•ter•ro•gate [ɪn'tɛrə,geit] *v.* **-gat•ed, -gat•ing. 1** ask questions of, especially formally and systematically; examine by asking questions: *The lawyer took two hours to interrogate the witness.* **2** ask a series of questions. ⟨< L *interrogare* < *inter-* between + *rogare* ask⟩ **—in'ter•ro•ga•ble,** *adj.* **—in'ter•ro,gat•ing•ly,** *adv.*
☛ *Syn.* **1, 2.** See note at QUESTION.

in•ter•ro•ga•tion [ɪn,tɛrə'geiʃən] *n.* **1** a questioning. The formal examination of a witness by asking questions is an interrogation. **2** a question. ⟨ME *interrogacioun* < L *interrogation-* (stem of *interrogatio*)⟩ **—in,ter•ro'ga•tion•al,** *adj.*

interrogation mark QUESTION MARK.

in•ter•rog•a•tive [,ɪntə'rɒgətɪv] *adj., n.* *—adj.* **1** of or having the form of a question: *an interrogative look or tone of voice.* **2** *Grammar.* used in asking questions: *an interrogative pronoun.* *—n. Grammar.* an interrogative word: *Who, why,* and *what* are interrogatives. ⟨< LL *interrogativus*⟩ **—,in•ter'rog•a•tive•ly,** *adv.*

in•ter•ro•ga•tor [ɪn'tɛrə,geitər] *n.* **1** questioner. **2** in radar systems, a transmitter to activate a transponder.

in•ter•rog•a•to•ry [,ɪntə'rɒgə,tɔri] *adj., n., pl.* **-to•ries.** *—adj.* questioning.
—n. a question; inquiry. **—,in•ter,rog•a'to•ri•ly,** *adv.*

in•ter•rupt [,ɪntə'rʌpt] *v.* **1** break in upon (talk, work, rest, a person speaking, etc.); hinder; stop. **2** break the continuity of; obstruct: *A building interrupts the view from our window.* **3** cause a break; break in: *It is not polite to interrupt when someone is talking.* ⟨ME < L *interruptus*, pp. of *interrumpere* < *inter-* between + *rumpere* break⟩ **—,in•ter'rupt•er,** *n.* **—,in•ter'rup•tive,** *adj.*

in•ter•rup•ted [,ɪntə'rʌptɪd] *adj., v.* *—adj. Botany.* of leaves on a stem, not evenly arranged.
—v. pt. and pp. of INTERRUPT.

in•ter•rupt•er [,ɪntə'rʌptər] *n.* **1** one who interrupts. **2** *Electricity.* a device for opening and closing an electric circuit.

in•ter•rup•tion [,ɪntə'rʌpʃən] *n.* **1** an interrupting or being interrupted. **2** something that interrupts. **3** an intermission.

in•ter•scho•las•tic [,ɪntərskə'læstɪk] *adj.* between schools: *interscholastic competition.*
☛ *Usage.* See note at INTRAMURAL.

in•ter•sect [,ɪntər'sɛkt] *v.* **1** cut or divide by passing through or crossing: *Draw a line to intersect two parallel lines at an angle of 45°.* **2** cross each other: *Streets usually intersect at right angles.* ⟨< L *intersectus*, pp. of *intersecare* < *inter-* between + *secare* cut⟩

in•ter•sec•tion [,ɪntər'sɛkʃən] *or* ['ɪntər,sɛkʃən] *n.* **1** the act or process of intersecting: *the intersection of two lines. Bridges and overpasses are used to avoid the intersection of a railway and a highway.* **2** a point, line, or place where two or more things cross each other: *The light changed just before we got to the intersection.* **3** *Mathematics.* the set of points or other elements common to two or more given sets. **—,in•ter'sec•tion•al,** *adj.*

in•ter•ses•sion ['ɪntər,sɛʃən] *n.* a university session between regular sessions, similar to summer school, at which a student may take one full course in a three-, four-, five-, or six-week period.

in•ter•sex ['ɪntər,sɛks] *n. Biology.* an individual with sexual characteristics which are neither fully male nor fully female. ⟨back formation from INTERSEXUAL⟩

in•ter•sex•ual [,ɪntər'sɛkʃuəl] *adj.* **1** existing between the sexes. **2** *Biology.* having the characteristics of an intersex.

in•ter•space *n.* ['ɪntər,speis]; *v.* [,ɪntər'speis] *n., v.* **-spaced, -spac•ing.** *—n.* **1** a space between things. **2** an intervening period of time; interval.
—v. **1** put a space between. **2** occupy or fill the space between.

in•ter•sperse [,ɪntər'spɜrs] *v.* **-spersed, -spers•ing. 1** decorate or vary with other things put here and there: *The lawn was interspersed with beds of flowers.* **2** scatter or place here and there: *He interspersed amusing anecdotes throughout his talk.* ⟨< L *interspersus* scattered < *inter-* between + *spargere* scatter⟩

in•ter•sper•sion [,ɪntər'spɜrʒən] *or* [,ɪntər'spɜrʃən] *n.* an interspersing or being interspersed.

in•ter•state ['ɪntər,steit] *adj.* between states: *an interstate highway.*

in•ter•stel•lar [,ɪntər'stɛlər] *adj.* **1** existing between or among the stars: *interstellar space.* **2** carried on between stars or star systems: *dreams of interstellar travel.*

in•ter•stice [ɪn'tɜrstɪs] *n., pl.* **-sti•ces** [-stə,siz]. a small or narrow space between things or parts; CHINK[1]. ⟨< LL *interstitium* < L *inter-* between < *stare* to stand⟩ **—in'ter•sticed,** *adj.*

in•ter•sti•tial [,ɪntər'stɪʃəl] *adj.* **1** of, in, or forming interstices. **2** *Anatomy.* situated between the cellular elements. **—,in•ter'sti•tial•ly,** *adv.*

in•ter•tex•ture [,ɪntər'tɛkstʃər] *n.* **1** the process of interweaving. **2** something created by interweaving.

in•ter•tid•al [,ɪntər'taɪdəl] *adj.* of, having to do with, or being the zone of a shore between the high-water and low-water marks.

in•ter•trop•ic•al [,ɪntər'trɒpəkəl] *adj.* situated or occurring between the two tropics, of Cancer and Capricorn.

in•ter•twine [,ɪntər'twaɪn] *v.* **-twined, -twin•ing.** twine around each other; twist or become twisted together: *Two vines intertwined on the wall.*

in•ter•twist [,ɪntər'twɪst] *v.* twist together; intertwine.

in•ter•ur•ban [,ɪntər'ɜrbən] *adj., n.* *—adj.* **1** between cities or towns. **2** having to do with two or more cities.
—n. **1** a transportation system between two cities. **2** a train, bus, or plane so operating.

in•ter•val ['ɪntərvəl] *n.* **1** an intervening period of time: *an interval of several weeks.* **2** the time or space between: *intervals of freedom from pain.* **3** *Music.* the difference in pitch between two tones. **4** *Mathematics.* a set of all the numbers between two given numbers. An **open interval** contains neither of its end parts; a **closed interval** contains both of its end parts. **5** intervale.
at intervals, a now and then: *Stir the pudding at intervals.* **b** here and there: *We saw many lakes at intervals along the way.* ⟨< L *intervallum*, originally, space between palisades < *inter-* between + *vallum* wall⟩

in•ter•vale ['ɪntər,veil] *n.* **1** a low-lying area of rich land between hills or by a river. **2** *Cdn., esp. Atlantic Provinces.* the low-lying land adjacent to a river, usually of rich soil because of alluvial deposits left by spring freshets. Also, **interval.** ⟨< *interval*, influenced by *vale[1]*⟩

in•ter•vene [,ɪntər'vin] *v.* **-vened, -ven•ing. 1** come or be (between): *A week intervenes between Christmas and New Year's.* **2** come in to help settle a dispute: *The prime minister was asked to intervene in the railway strike.* **3** *Law.* enter into a suit as protecting some supposed interest. ⟨< L *intervenire* < *inter-* between + *venire* come⟩ **—,in•ter'ven•er** or **,in•ter've•nor,** *n.* **—,in•ter'ven•i•ent,** *adj.*

in•ter•ven•tion [ˌɪntər'vɛnʃən] *n.* **1** the act of intervening. **2** interference, especially by one nation in the affairs of another. **3** *Medicine.* taking medical action rather than letting a disease take its course.

in•ter•ven•tion•ist [ˌɪntər'vɛnʃənɪst] *n., adj.* —*n.* **1** a person who supports interference in the affairs of another country. **2** *Medicine.* a person who prefers medical action rather than letting a disease take its course.
—*adj.* **1** of or having to do with intervention or interventionists. **2** approving intervention. **—ˌin•ter'ven•tion•ism,** *n.*

in•ter•ver•te•bral disk [ˌɪntər'vɜrtəbrəl] *Anatomy.* the plate of cartilage between the bones of the spine.

in•ter•view ['ɪntərˌvju] *n., v.* —*n.* **1** a meeting of people face to face, to talk over something special: *John applied for the job and had an interview with the manager.* **2** a meeting between a reporter, writer, radio or television commentator, etc. and a person from whom information is sought. **3** a printed report or broadcast of such a meeting.
—*v.* **1** meet and talk with, especially to obtain information: *Reporters interviewed the returning explorers.* **2** conduct an interview or interviews: *She's been interviewing all morning.* ⟨< F *entrevue* < *entrevoir* glimpse < L *inter-* between + *videre* see⟩ **—'in•terˌview•er,** *n.* **—ˌin•ter•view'ee** [ˌɪntərvju'i], *n.*

in•ter vi•vos ['ɪntər 'vaɪvous] *or* ['vivous] *Law.* a gift or trust for the benefit of the parties during their lives. ⟨< L, literally, among (the) living⟩

in•ter•voc•al•ic [ˌɪntərvə'kælɪk] *adj.* between two vowels: *An intervocalic consonant is often voiced.*

in•ter•volve [ˌɪntər'vɒlv] *v.* **-volved, -volv•ing.** wind one thing within another.

in•ter•weave [ˌɪntər'wiv] *v.* **-wove** or **-weaved, -wo•ven** or **-wove** or **-weaved, -weav•ing. 1** weave together. **2** intermingle; blend; connect closely: *In his book he has interwoven the stories of two families.*

in•ter•wove [ˌɪntər'wouv] *v.* a pt. and a pp. of INTERWEAVE.

in•ter•wo•ven [ˌɪntər'wouvən] *adj., v.* —*adj.* **1** woven together. **2** intermingled.
—*v.* a pp. of INTERWEAVE.

in•tes•ta•cy [ɪn'tɛstəsi] *n.* the condition of being intestate at death.

in•tes•tate [ɪn'tɛsteit] *or* [ɪn'tɛstɪt] *adj., n.* —*adj.* **1** having made no will. **2** not disposed of by a will.
—*n.* a person who has died without making a will. ⟨< L *intestatus* < *in-* not + *testari* make a will < *testis* witness⟩

in•tes•ti•nal [ɪn'tɛstənəl] *adj.* of or in the intestines. **—in'tes•ti•nal•ly,** *adv.*

intestinal fortitude *Informal.* courage; guts.

in•tes•tine [ɪn'tɛstən] *n., adj.* —*n. Anatomy.* **1** either of the two parts of the alimentary canal extending from the stomach to the anus. Partially digested food passes from the stomach into the small intestine for further digestion and for absorption of nutrients by the blood, and into the large intestine for elimination. In adults, the **small intestine** is about 640 cm long; the **large intestine** is about 165 cm long. See ALIMENTARY CANAL for picture. **2 intestines,** *pl.* the intestine; the bowels.
—*adj.* within the country; internal. Intestine strife is civil war. ⟨< L *intestina,* neut. pl., internal < *intus* within < *in* in⟩

in•thral or **in•thrall** [ɪn'θrɒl] *v.* **-thralled, -thral•ling.** enthral. **—in'thral•ment** or **in'thrall•ment,** *n.*

in•throne [ɪn'θroun] *v.* **-throned, -thron•ing.** enthrone.

in•ti ['ɪnti] *n.* a unit of currency of Peru, divided into 100 centavos. See table of money in the Appendix.

in•ti•ma ['ɪntəmə] *n., pl.* **-mae** [-ˌmi] or **-mas.** *Anatomy.* a membrane, especially of an artery. ⟨< NL, fem. of *intimus.* See INTIMATE.⟩ **—'in•ti•mal,** *adj.*

in•ti•ma•cy ['ɪntəməsi] *n., pl.* **-cies. 1** deep friendship; close association; being intimate. **2** a familiar or intimate act. **3** sexual intercourse.

in•ti•mate[1] ['ɪntəmɪt] *adj., n.* —*adj.* **1** very familiar; known very well: *an intimate friend.* **2** resulting from close familiarity; close: *an intimate knowledge.* **3** personal; private: *A diary is a very intimate book.* **4** far within; inmost: *the intimate recesses of the heart.* **5** engaged in or characterized by sexual relations.
—*n.* a close friend. ⟨earlier *intime* < L *intimus* inmost (and, as a noun, close friend), superlative of *in* in; later altered under the influence of L *intimatus,* pp. of *intimare.* See INTIMATE².⟩ **—'in•ti•mate•ly,** *adv.* **—'in•ti•mate•ness,** *n.*
☛ *Syn.* **1.** See note at FAMILIAR.

in•ti•mate[2] ['ɪntəˌmeit] *v.* **-mat•ed, -mat•ing. 1** suggest indirectly; hint: *In her statement to the press, she intimated that an arrest would be made soon.* **2** *Archaic.* announce; notify. ⟨< L *intimare,* originally, press in < L *intimus* inmost. See INTIMATE¹.⟩ **—'in•tiˌmat•er,** *n.*

in•ti•ma•tion [ˌɪntə'meiʃən] *n.* **1** an indirect suggestion; hint: *She said nothing, but her frown was an intimation of disapproval.* **2** *Archaic.* an announcement; notice.

in•tim•i•date [ɪn'tɪməˌdeit] *v.* **-dat•ed, -dat•ing. 1** frighten, especially in order to influence or force: *The banker told police that the men had tried to intimidate him by telling him they were holding his wife as hostage.* **2** overcome with awe: *Her great expertise intimidates some people.* ⟨< Med.L *intimidare* < L *in-* + *timidus* fearful⟩ **—inˌtim•i'da•tion,** *n.* **—in'tim•iˌda•tor,** *n.*

in•tim•ist ['ɪntəmɪst] *adj.* of literature, art, etc., dealing with personal feelings.

in•ti•tle [ɪn'tɔitəl] *v.* **-tled, -tling.** entitle.

in•to ['ɪntu]; *before consonants, often* ['ɪntə] *prep.* **1** to the inside of; toward the inside; within: *to go into the house.* **2** to the condition of; to the form of: *to get into mischief, a house divided into ten rooms. Cold weather turns water into ice.* **3** to a further time or place in: *He worked on into the night.* **4** against: *He wasn't watching and ran into the wall.* **5** *Mathematics.* going into (implying or expressing division): 5 *into* 30 *is* 6. **6** *Informal.* involved or concerned with: *He's really into philosophy these days.* ⟨ME, OE. See IN, TO.⟩
☛ *Usage.* See note at IN.

in•tol•er•a•ble [ɪn'tɒlərəbəl] *adj.* unbearable; too much, too painful, etc. to be endured. ⟨< L *intolerabilis*⟩ **—inˌtol•er•a'bil•i•ty,** *n.* **—in'tol•er•a•ble•ness,** *n.* **—in'tol•er•a•bly,** *adv.*

in•tol•er•ance [ɪn'tɒlərəns] *n.* **1** lack of tolerance; unwillingness to let others do and think as they choose. **2** inability or unwillingness to endure: *intolerance of popular music.* **3** a sensitivity or allergy to a food, drug, etc.: *intolerance to penicillin.*

in•tol•er•ant [ɪn'tɒlərənt] *adj.* **1** not tolerant; unwilling to let others do and think as they choose. **2** unwilling to accept persons of different races, backgrounds, etc. as equals. **3** unable or unwilling to endure (*used with* **of**): *intolerant of criticism.* ⟨< L *intolerant-* (stem of *intolerans*) impatient⟩ **—in'tol•er•ant•ly,** *adv.*

in•tomb [ɪn'tum] *v.* entomb. **—in'tomb•ment,** *n.*

in•to•nate ['ɪntəˌneit] *v.* **-nat•ed, -nat•ing. 1** intone. **2** speak with a particular tone.

in•to•na•tion [ˌɪntə'neiʃən] *n.* **1** the manner of uttering or sounding words: *She has a monotonous intonation.* **2** *Linguistics.* the sound pattern of speech produced by differences in stress and pitch: *British intonation is different from standard Canadian intonation. The English sentence* She's gone *is a question if spoken with a rising intonation and a statement if spoken with a falling intonation.* **3** the production of musical tones; singing or playing in tune: *Intonation is a major problem for cellists.* **4** the act of intoning: *the intonation of a psalm.* **5** the opening phrase of a Gregorian chant.

in•tone [ɪn'toun] *v.* **-toned, -ton•ing. 1** read or recite in a singing voice; chant. **2** utter with a particular tone. **3** make musical sounds, especially in a slow, drawn-out manner. ⟨ME < Med.L *intonare,* ult. < L *in-* in + *tonus* tone⟩

in to•to [ɪn 'toutou] *Latin.* as a whole; completely.

in•tox•i•cant [ɪn'tɒksəkənt] *n., adj.* —*n.* something that intoxicates, especially alcoholic liquor.
—*adj.* intoxicating: *an intoxicant drug.*

in•tox•i•cate [ɪn'tɒksəˌkeit] *v.* **-cat•ed, -cat•ing. 1** make drunk: *Too much wine intoxicates people.* **2** of a drug, affect the nervous system in such a way as to make (the person) lose control; poison the system of. **3** excite greatly; exhilarate: *The early election returns intoxicated her supporters with thoughts of victory.* ⟨< Med.L *intoxicare,* ult. < L *in-* in + *toxicum* poison < Gk. *toxicon (pharmakon)* (poison) for shooting arrows < *toxon* bow. Related to TOXIC.⟩

in•tox•i•cat•ed [ɪn'tɒksəˌkeitɪd] *adj., v.* —*adj.* **1** drunk. **2** greatly excited.
—*v.* pt. and ppr. of INTOXICATE. **—in'tox•iˌcat•ed•ly,** *adv.*

in•tox•i•cat•ing [ɪn'tɒksəˌkeitɪŋ] *adj., v.* —*adj.* that intoxicates: *intoxicating drinks, intoxicating beauty.*
—*v.* ppr. of INTOXICATE. **—in'tox•iˌcat•ing•ly,** *adv.*

in•tox•i•ca•tion [ɪnˌtɒksə'keiʃən] *n.* **1** drunkenness. **2** great excitement. **3** *Medicine.* poisoning.

intr. intransitive.

intra– *prefix.* within; inside: *intravenous.* ⟨< L *intra-* < *intra*, prep., adv.⟩

in•tra•cel•lu•lar [ˌɪntrəˈsɛljələr] *adj.* within a cell or cells.

in•tra•ci•ty [ˌɪntrəˈsɪti] *adj., n.* —*adj.* within a city.
—*n.* **1** a transportation system within a city. **2** a bus or train operating within a city.

in•trac•ta•ble [ɪnˈtræktəbəl] *adj.* **1** hard to manage; stubborn. **2** difficult to remedy. **3** difficult to mould or otherwise manipulate. ⟨< L *intractabilis*⟩ **—inˈtrac•ta•bly,** *adv.* **—inˈtrac•ta•ble•ness** or **inˌtrac•taˈbil•i•ty,** *n.*

in•tra•cu•ta•ne•ous [ˌɪntrəkjuˈteiniəs] *adj. Anatomy.* within the skin. ⟨See INTRA- + CUTANEOUS⟩

in•tra•derm•al [ˌɪntrəˈdɜrməl] *adj.* **1** intracutaneous. **2** of an injection, made between layers of skin. Also, **intradermic.** **—ˌin•traˈder•mal•ly** or **ˌin•traˈder•mi•cal•ly,** *adv.*

in•tra•dos [ˈɪntrəˌdɒs], [ˈɪntrəˌdous], [ɪnˈtreidɒs], *or* [ɪnˈtreidous] *n. Architecture.* the interior curve or surface of an arch or vault. ⟨< F < L *intra-* within + F *dos* back⟩

in•tra•mo•le•cu•lar [ˌɪntrəməˈlɛkjələr] *adj.* existing within a molecule.

in•tra•mu•ral [ˌɪntrəˈmjʊrəl] *adj.* **1** within the walls of some institution; inside. In intramural games, all the players belong to the same school. Compare EXTRAMURAL. **2** *Anatomy.* within the wall of an organ or cavity.

☛ *Usage.* **Intramural** is written without a hyphen. It is applied specifically to school activities carried on by groups belonging to the same school, as contrasted with INTERCOLLEGIATE or INTERSCHOLASTIC, which are applied to activities of groups belonging to different schools.

in•tra•mus•cu•lar [ˌɪntrəˈmʌskjələr] *adj.* within a muscle: *an intramuscular injection.* **—ˌin•traˈmus•cu•lar•ly,** *adv.*

intrans. intransitive.

in trans. in transit; en route. ⟨< L *in transitu*⟩

in•tran•si•gence [ɪnˈtrænzədʒəns] *n.* the quality of being intransigent; uncompromising unwillingness to agree. Also, **intransigency.**

in•tran•si•gent [ɪnˈtrænzədʒənt] *adj., n.* —*adj.* unwilling to agree or compromise.
—*n.* a person who is unwilling to agree or compromise. ⟨< F < Sp. *los intransigentes*, name for various extreme political parties, ult. < L *in-* not + *transigere* come to an agreement < *trans-* through + *agere* drive⟩ **—inˈtran•si•gent•ly,** *adv.*

in•tran•si•tive [ɪnˈtrænzətɪv] *adj., n.* —*adj. Grammar.* not taking a direct object. The verbs *belong, go,* and *seem* are intransitive.
—*n.* an intransitive verb. *Abbrev.:* intr., intrans. ⟨< L *intransitivus*⟩ **—inˈtran•si•tive•ly,** *adv.* **—inˈtran•si•tive•ness,** *n.*

☛ *Usage.* See note at VERB.

in•tra•pre•neur [ˌɪntrəprəˈnɜr] *n.* an employee of a large corporation, who is allowed to introduce new products. **—ˌin•tra•preˈneur•ial** [-ˈnɜriəl], [-ˈnjʊriəl], *or* [-ˈnʊriəl], *adj.*

in•tra•tel•lur•ic [ˌɪntrətəˈlʊrɪk] *adj. Geology.* **1** resulting from action below the lithosphere. **2** having to do with the crystallization of rock before it comes to the surface.

in•tra•u•ter•ine [ˌɪntrəˈjutərɪn] *or* [ˌɪntrəˈjutəˌraɪn] *adj.* within the uterus.

intrauterine device a contraceptive device usually in the form of a metal or plastic loop, coil, or ring that is inserted and left in the uterus. *Abbrev.:* IUD

in•trav•a•sa•tion [ɪnˌtrævəˈseiʃən] *n. Pathology.* the entrance of foreign matter into a blood vessel. ⟨< *intra-* + *(extra)vasation*⟩

in•tra•ve•nous [ˌɪntrəˈvinəs] *adj.* **1** within a vein or the veins. **2** into a vein: *an intravenous injection.* ⟨< *intra-* + L *vena* vein⟩ **—ˌin•traˈve•nous•ly,** *adv.*

in•treat [ɪnˈtrit] *v.* entreat.

in•trench [ɪnˈtrɛntʃ] *v.* entrench. **—inˈtrench•er,** *n.* **—inˈtrench•ment,** *n.*

in•trep•id [ɪnˈtrɛpɪd] *adj.* fearless; dauntless; courageous; very brave. ⟨< L *intrepidus* < *in-* not + *trepidus* alarmed⟩ **—inˈtrep•id•ly,** *adv.* **—inˈtrep•id•ness,** *n.*

in•tre•pid•i•ty [ˌɪntrəˈpɪdəti] *n.* fearlessness; dauntless courage; great bravery.

in•tri•ca•cy [ˈɪntrəkəsi] *n., pl.* **-cies. 1** the state or quality of being intricate; complexity: *They admired the delicacy and intricacy of the design.* **2** something intricate: *the intricacies of international diplomacy.*

in•tri•cate [ˈɪntrəkɪt] *adj.* **1** with many twists and turns; entangled or complicated: *an intricate knot, an intricate maze, an intricate plot.* **2** complex; hard to understand; obscure or puzzling: *an intricate problem.* **3** detailed. ⟨< L *intricatus* < *intricare* entangle, ult. < *in-* in + *tricae* hindrances⟩ **—ˈin•tri•cate•ly,** *adv.* **—ˈin•tri•cate•ness,** *n.*

in•trig•ant [ˈɪntrɪgənt]; *French,* [ɛ̃tʀiˈgɑ̃] *n.* one who engages in intrigue. Also, **intrigante** [ˌɪntrəˈgɑnt], fem. ⟨< F < Ital. *intrigante*, pp. of *intrigare*. See INTRIGUE.⟩

in•trigue *n.* [ɪnˈtrig] *or* [ˈɪntrig]; *v.* [ɪnˈtrig] *n., v.* **-trigued, -tri•guing.** —*n.* **1** underhand planning; secret scheming; plotting: *The royal palace was filled with intrigue.* **2** a crafty plot; a secret scheme. **3** a secret love affair. **4** the plot of a play, dramatic poem, etc., especially the development of a complex or involved situation.
—*v.* **1** carry on an underhand plan; scheme secretly; plot. **2** excite the curiosity and interest of: *The book's unusual title intrigued me.* **3** have a secret love affair. ⟨< F < Ital. *intrigo* < *intrigare* < L *intricare* entangle. See INTRICATE.⟩ **—inˈtri•guer,** *n.* **—inˈtri•guing•ly,** *adv.*

in•trin•sic [ɪnˈtrɪnzɪk] *adj.* **1** belonging to a thing by its very nature; essential; inherent: *The intrinsic value of a five-dollar bill is only that of the paper it is printed on.* **2** *Anatomy.* originating or being inside the part on which it acts: *the intrinsic muscles of the larynx.* Also, **intrinsical.** Compare EXTRINSIC. ⟨< F < Med.L *intrinsecus* internal < L *intrinsecus* inwardly⟩

in•trin•si•cal•ly [ɪnˈtrɪnzɪkli] *adv.* by its very nature; essentially; inherently.

intro– *prefix.* **1** in; into: *introduce.* **2** inward; within: *introvert.* Compare EXTRO-. ⟨< L *intro-* < *intro*, adv., inwardly, within⟩

intro. or **introd.** introduction; introductory.

in•tro•duce [ˌɪntrəˈdjus] *or* [ˌɪntrəˈdus] *v.* **-duced, -duc•ing. 1** bring in: *to introduce a new subject into the conversation.* **2** put in; insert: *The doctor introduced a long tube into the woman's throat.* **3** bring into use, notice, knowledge, etc.: *to introduce a reform, to introduce a new word.* **4** make known: *The hostess introduced the speaker to the audience.* **5** bring (a person) to acquaintance with something: *I introduced my country cousin to the city by showing her the sights.* **6** bring forward: *to introduce a question for debate.* **7** begin; start: *He introduced his speech with a joke.* ⟨< L introducere < *intro-* in + *ducere* lead⟩ **—ˌin•troˈduc•er,** *n.* **—ˌin•troˈduc•i•ble,** *adj.*

☛ *Syn.* **4. Introduce,** PRESENT² = make someone known to another or others. **Introduce** = make a person known, in a more or less formal way, to another or to a group, or to make two people acquainted with each other: *Mrs. Brown, may I introduce Mr. Smith?* **Present,** always suggesting formality, means 'introduce, with more or less ceremony, a person or group to one regarded or treated as superior': *The new ambassador was presented to the governor general.*

in•tro•duc•tion [ˌɪntrəˈdʌkʃən] *n.* **1** an introducing or being introduced: *The introduction of steel revolutionized the construction industry. They were waiting for an introduction to him.* **2** a preliminary part of a book, speech, musical composition, etc. that leads into the main part or gives information necessary for understanding the main part. **3** a first book, course, etc. for beginners in a given field of study: *an introduction to biology.* **4** something introduced; a thing brought into use: *Radios are a later introduction than telephones.* ⟨ME < L *introductio, -onis* < *introducere.* See INTRODUCE.⟩

☛ *Syn.* **2. Introduction,** PREFACE, FOREWORD = a section at the beginning of a book, etc. **Introduction** applies to an actual part of the book, article, play, etc. that leads into or gives what is necessary for understanding the main part: *School editions of literary works usually have introductions.* **Preface** applies to a separate section coming before the actual book, explaining something, such as the purpose, method, importance, etc. **Foreword** may mean a short, simple preface but applies especially to an introductory note on the book or the author by a distinguished writer, scholar, or public figure: *A foreword by the president of the university came before the author's preface.*

in•tro•duc•to•ry [ˌɪntrəˈdʌktəri] *or* [ˌɪntrəˈdʌktri] *adj.* used to introduce; serving as an introduction; preliminary. Also, **introductive.** **—ˌin•troˈduc•to•ri•ly,** *adv.*

in•tro•it [ɪnˈtrouɪt] *or* [ˈɪntrɔɪt] *n.* **1** *Roman Catholic Church.* a hymn or responsive anthem recited by the priest at the beginning of Mass or sung by the choir at High Mass. **2** *Anglican Church.* a psalm, hymn, etc. at the beginning of the communion service. ⟨ME < L *introitus* entrance < *introire* enter < *intro-* in + *ire* go⟩

in•tro•jec•tion [ˌɪntrəˈdʒɛkʃən] *n. Psychoanalysis.* the act of directing energy and emotion inward onto a mental image of some person or thing rather than onto the actual person or thing.

in•tro•mit [ˈɪntrəˌmɪt] *v.* **-mit•ted, -mit•ting.** admit. **—ˌin•troˈmis•sion,** *n.* **—ˌin•troˈmit•tent,** *adj.*

in•tron [ˈɪntrɒn] *n. Genetics.* a DNA segment between two successive exons of a gene, initially transcribed into RNA but excised during the formation of mature messenger RNA. Compare EXON. ⟨< *intra* because inside the gene⟩

in•trorse [ɪn'trɔrs] *adj. Botany.* turned or facing inward. A violet has introrse stamens. ⟨< L *introrsus*, ult. < *intro-* inward + *versus* turned⟩

in•tro•spect [ˌɪntrə'spɛkt] *v.* examine one's inner feelings. **—ˌin•tro'spec•tor,** *n.*

in•tro•spec•tion [ˌɪntrə'spɛkʃən] *n.* examination and analysis of one's own thoughts and feelings. ⟨< L *introspectus*, pp. of *introspicere* < *intro-* into + *specere* look⟩

in•tro•spec•tive [ˌɪntrə'spɛktɪv] *adj.* **1** inclined to examine one's own thoughts and feelings. **2** contemplative. **3** concerning introspection. **—ˌin•tro'spec•tive•ly,** *adv.* **—ˌin•tro'spec•tive•ness,** *n.*

in•tro•ver•sion [ˌɪntrə'vɜrʒən] *or* [ˌɪntrə'vɜrʃən], *n.* **1** a tendency toward reflection and introspection rather than activity or social interaction. Compare EXTROVERSION. **2** the act or fact of turning inward. ⟨< *intro-* + *version*, as in *reversion*, etc.⟩ **—ˌin•tro'ver•sive,** *adj.* **—ˌin•tro'ver•tive,** *adj.*

in•tro•vert *n.* ['ɪntrəˌvɜrt]; *v.* [ˌɪntrə'vɜrt] *n., v.* *—n.* a person more interested in his or her own thoughts and feelings than in other persons or in what is going on around him or her; a person who is thoughtful rather than active or expressive. Compare EXTROVERT.
—v. **1** introspect. **2** *Zoology.* pull (a tubular part or organ) inward by invagination. **3** fold (something) inward. ⟨< *intro-* within + L *vertere* turn⟩

in•trude [ɪn'trud] *v.* **-trud•ed, -trud•ing. 1** thrust oneself in; come unasked and unwanted: *If you are busy, I will not intrude.* **2** give when not wanted; force in: *Do not intrude your opinions upon others.* **3** *Geology.* thrust (molten rock) into a stratum. ⟨< L *intrudere* < *in-* in + *trudere* thrust⟩ **—in'trud•er,** *n.* **—in'trud•ing•ly,** *adv.*

☛ *Syn.* **1. Intrude,** TRESPASS, ENCROACH = thrust oneself into or upon the presence, possessions, territory, or rights of others. **Intrude** = thrust in, without permission, where uninvited, unwanted, or having no right to go: *He intrudes upon their hospitality.* **Trespass** = intrude unlawfully or by overstepping the limits of what is proper or right: *Joe trespassed on another boy's paper route.* **Encroach** adds the idea of gradually or secretly taking the property or rights of another: *Our neighbour's irrigation system is encroaching on our land.*

in•tru•sion [ɪn'truʒən] *n.* **1** the act of intruding; coming unasked and unwanted. **2** *Law.* an unlawful entry or seizure of land or rights belonging to another. **3** *Geology.* **a** the forcing of molten rock into fissures or between strata. **b** the molten rock forced in and solidified in place. ⟨ME < Med.L *intrusio, -onis* < L *intrusus*, pp. of *intrudere.* See INTRUDE.⟩ **—in'tru•sion•al,** *adj.*

in•tru•sive [ɪn'trusɪv] *adj.* **1** intruding; coming unasked and unwanted. **2** *Geology.* forced into fissures or between strata while molten. Compare EXTRUSIVE. **3** *Phonetics.* inserted purely for phonetic reasons, without any etymological or historical basis. The [p] sometimes heard in *warmth* [wɔrmpθ] is intrusive. **—in'tru•sive•ly,** *adv.* **—in'tru•sive•ness,** *n.*

in•trust [ɪn'trʌst] *v.* entrust.

in•tu•bate ['ɪntjəˌbeit] *or* ['ɪntəˌbeit] *v.* **-bat•ed, -bat•ing.** *Medicine.* insert a tube into. **—ˌin•tu'ba•tion,** *n.*

in•tu•it [ɪn'tjuɪt] *or* [ɪn'tuɪt] *v.* know or learn by intuition. ⟨back formation from INTUITON⟩ **—in'tu•it•a•ble,** *adj.*

in•tu•i•tion [ˌɪntju'ɪʃən] *or* [ˌɪntu'ɪʃən] *n.* **1** immediate perception or understanding of truths, facts, etc. without reasoning: *Her intuition told her that the strangers were not what they appeared to be.* **2** something known or understood in this way. ⟨< LL *intuitio, -onis* a gazing at < L *intueri* < *in-* at + *tueri* look⟩ **—ˌin•tu'i•tion•less,** *adj.*

in•tu•i•tion•al [ˌɪntju'ɪʃənəl] *or* [ˌɪntu'ɪʃənəl] *adj.* of, having to do with, or characterized by intuition; based on intuition. **—ˌin•tu'i•tion•al•ly,** *adv.*

in•tu•i•tion•ism [ˌɪntju'ɪʃəˌnɪzəm] *or* [ˌɪntu'ɪʃəˌnɪzəm] *n.* **1** the theory that truth is known by intuition. **2** the theory that ethical behaviour is intuitive and not learned. Also, **intuitionalism.** **—ˌin•tu'i•tion•ist,** *n.*

in•tu•i•tive [ɪn'tjuətɪv] *or* [ɪn'tuətɪv] *adj.* **1** perceiving by intuition: *an intuitive person.* **2** acquired by intuition: *intuitive knowledge.* **3** of the nature of an intuition: *an intuitive guess.* **4** of or relating to intuition: *intuitive power.* **—in'tu•i•tive•ly,** *adv.*

in•tu•mesce [ˌɪntjʊ'mɛs] *or* [ˌɪntʊ'mɛs] *v.* **-mesced, -mes•cing.** swell. ⟨< L *intumescere* to swell up⟩

in•tum•es•cence [ˌɪntjʊ'mɛsəns] *or* [ˌɪntʊ'mɛsəns] *n.* **1** the process of swelling. **2** a swollen part. **—ˌin•tu'mes•cent,** *adj.*

in•tus•sus•cept [ˌɪntəsə'sɛpt] *v.* invaginate. ⟨back formation from INTUSSUSCEPTION⟩ **—ˌin•tus•sus'cep•tive,** *adj.*

in•tus•sus•cep•tion [ˌɪntəsə'sɛpʃən] *n.* **1** invagination. **2** *Biology.* cell growth by the interposition of tiny new particles between those already forming part of the cell wall. ⟨< L *intus* within + *susception-, susceptus* taken up⟩

I•nu•it ['ɪnjuɪt], ['ɪnuɪt] *n.pl., adj.* *—n.* a people living mainly in northern Canada, Greenland, Alaska, and eastern Siberia, who are the original inhabitants of the Arctic; formerly, the Eskimo people.
—adj. of or having to do with the Inuit. ⟨< Inuktitut *inuit*, pl. of *inuk* man, person⟩

I•nuk ['ɪnʊk] *n., pl.* **I•nu•it.** *Cdn.* a member of the Inuit.

i•nuk•shuk [ɪ'nʊkʃʊk] *n., pl.* **i•nuk•shuks** or **i•nuk•shu•it** [-ʃuɪt]. *Cdn.* a stone cairn having the rough outline of a human figure. Inukshuks were traditionally built by the Inuit to serve as landmarks or, in some parts of the Arctic, in long rows to drive caribou toward waiting hunters. Also, **inukshook.** ⟨< Inuktitut *inukshuk* something in the shape of a man⟩

An inukshuk

I•nuk•ti•tuk [ɪ'nʊktəˌtʊk] *n. Cdn.* Inuktitut.

I•nuk•ti•tut [ɪ'nʊktəˌtʊt] *n. Cdn.* the language of the Inuit. There are many dialects of Inuktitut. ⟨< Inuktitut *inuk* man, person + *titut* speech⟩

in•u•lin ['ɪnjəlɪn] *n.* a carbohydrate in the roots of some plants, used to make fructose. ⟨< NL *Inula* a genus of plants⟩

in•unc•tion [ɪn'ʌŋkʃən] *n.* **1** *Medicine.* the application of a salve. **2** an ointment or lubricant. **3** in some religious ceremonies, an anointing. ⟨late ME < L *inunction-* (stem of *inunctio*), *inunctus* anointed⟩

in•un•dant [ɪ'nʌndənt] *adj.* flooding; overflowing. ⟨L *inundans, inundare*⟩

in•un•date ['ɪnənˌdeit] *or* [ɪ'nʌndeit] *v.* **-dat•ed, -dat•ing. 1** overflow; flood. **2** overwhelm, as if by a flood: *The radio station was inundated with requests for the pamphlet.* ⟨< L *inundare* < *in-* onto + *undare* flow < *unda* wave⟩ **—ˌin•un'da•tion,** *n.* **—'in•unˌda•tor,** *n.*

in•un•da•tion [ˌɪnən'deiʃən] *n.* an overflowing; flood.

☛ *Syn.* See note at FLOOD.

in•ur•bane [ˌɪnər'bein] *adj.* lacking in refinement. **—ˌin•ur'bane•ly,** *adv.* **—ˌin•ur'ban•i•ty** [ˌɪnər'bænəti], *n.*

in•ure [ɪ'njʊr] *v.* **-ured, -ur•ing. 1** toughen or harden; accustom; habituate: *Many years in the wilderness had inured them to hardship.* **2** especially of a law or agreement, take or have effect; be operative: *The agreement inures to the benefit of the employees.* Also, **enure.** ⟨< *in* + obs. *ure* use, n. < AF *ure* < L *opera* work⟩ **—in'ure•ment,** *n.*

in•urn [ɪn'ɜrn] *v.* **1** put in a funeral urn. **2** bury. **—in'urn•ment,** *n.*

inv. 1 invoice. **2** inventor; invented. **3** inventory. **4** investment.

in va•cu•o [ɪn 'vækjuˌou] *Latin.* in a vacuum.

in•vade [ɪn'veid] *v.* **-vad•ed, -vad•ing. 1** enter with force or as an enemy: *Soldiers invaded the country. Diseases invade the body.* **2** enter as if to take possession: *Tourists invaded the city. Night invades the sky.* **3** interfere with; break in on; violate: *The law punishes people who invade the rights of others.* ⟨< L *invadere* < *in-* in + *vadere* go, walk⟩ **—in'vad•a•ble,** *adj.* **—in'vad•er,** *n.*

in•vag•i•nate [ɪn'vædʒəˌneit] *v.* **-nat•ed, -nat•ing. 1** enclose in or as in a sheath. **2** introvert. **3** become introverted. ⟨< Med.L *invaginatus* sheathed in, pp. of *invaginare*⟩

in•vag•i•na•tion [ɪnˌvædʒə'neiʃən] *n.* **1** an invaginating or being invaginated. **2** *Embryology.* the infolding of the blastula to form the gastrula.

in•va•lid[1] ['ɪnvəlɪd] *n., adj., v.* *—n.* a person who is weak because of sickness or injury: *An invalid cannot get about and do things.*
—adj. **1** not well; disabled. **2** of or for an invalid or invalids.

—v. **1** make weak or sick; disable. **2** release or retire from active service because of sickness or injury: *He was invalided out of the army.* ⟨< L *invalidus* not strong. 17c. See INVALID².⟩

in•val•id² [ɪn'vælɪd] *adj.* not valid; without force or effect; worthless: *If a will is not signed, it is invalid.* ⟨< L *invalidus* < *in-* not + *validus* strong < *valere* be strong. 16c.⟩ **—in'val•id•ly,** *adv.* **—in'val•id•ness,** *n.*

in•val•i•date [ɪn'vælɪ,deit] *v.* **-dat•ed, -dat•ing.** make valueless; deprive of force or effect: *A contract is invalidated if only one party signs it.* **—in,val•i'da•tion,** *n.* **—in'val•i,da•tor,** *n.*

in•va•lid•ism ['ɪnvəlɪ,dɪzəm] *n.* the condition of being an invalid; prolonged ill health.

in•va•lid•i•ty [,ɪnvə'lɪdəti] *n.* a lack of validity, force, or effect; worthlessness.

in•val•u•a•ble [ɪn'væljəbəl] *or* [ɪn'væljuəbəl] *adj.* priceless; very precious; valuable beyond measure. **—in'val•u•a•bly,** *adv.* **—in'val•u•a•ble•ness,** *n.*

in•var•i•a•ble [ɪn'vɛriəbəl] *adj., n.* *—adj.* always the same; unchangeable; unchanging.
—n. a constant; something that never changes. **—in'var•i•a•bly,** *adv.* **—in'var•i•a•ble•ness** or **in,var•i•a'bil•i•ty,** *n.*

in•var•i•ant [ɪn'vɛriənt] *adj., n.* *—adj.* never changing.
—n. Mathematics. a property not altered by a particular transformation. **—in'var•i•ant•ly,** *adv.*

in•va•sion [ɪn'veiʒən] *n.* **1** the act of invading. **2** interference; encroachment; infringement: *She objected to the invasion of her privacy.* ⟨< LL *invasio, -onis* < *invadere.* See INVADE.⟩ **—in'va•sive** [-'veisɪv], *adj.*

in•vec•tive [ɪn'vɛktɪv] *n., adj.* *—n.* a violent attack in words; abusive language.
—adj. characterized by abusive language. ⟨ME < LL *invectivus* abusive < L *invehi.* See INVEIGH.⟩ **—in'vec•tive•ness,** *n.* **—in'vec•tive•ly,** *adv.*

in•veigh [ɪn'vei] *v.* make a violent attack in words; complain bitterly (*used with* **against**): *He inveighed against the poor working conditions in the factory.* ⟨< L *invehi* launch an attack < *in-* against + *vehere* carry⟩

in•vei•gle [ɪn'veigəl] *or* [ɪn'vigəl] *v.* **-gled, -gling.** win over by trickery; entice; lure: *The saleswoman inveigled the poor girl into buying four hats.* ⟨apparently alteration of earlier **avegle* < F *aveugler* make blind < *aveugle* blind < VL *aboculus* < L *ab-* without + *oculus* eye⟩ **—in'vei•gle•ment,** *n.* **—in'vei•gler,** *n.*

in•vent [ɪn'vɛnt] *v.* **1** make for the first time; think out (something new): *Alexander Graham Bell invented the telephone.* **2** make up; think up; fabricate: *to invent an excuse.* ⟨< L *inventus,* pp. of *invenire* < *in-* in + *venire* come⟩

in•ven•tion [ɪn'vɛnʃən] *n.* **1** the act or process of inventing: *The Chinese are credited with the invention of gunpowder.* **2** the thing invented: *Radio was a wonderful invention.* **3** the power of inventing; inventiveness: *To be a good novelist, a person needs invention.* **4** a made-up story, especially a falsehood: *His account of the robbery was pure invention.* **5** *Music.* a short instrumental composition consisting of one or two simple melodies developed in two- or three-part harmony. **—in'ven•tion•al,** *adj.* **—in'ven•tion•less,** *adj.*

in•ven•tive [ɪn'vɛntɪv] *adj.* **1** good at inventing: *An inventive person thinks up ways to save time, money, and work.* **2** of invention. **3** showing power of inventing. **—in'ven•tive•ly,** *adv.* **—in'ven•tive•ness,** *n.*

in•ven•tor [ɪn'vɛntər] *n.* a person who invents: *Alexander Graham Bell was a great inventor.*

in•ven•to•ry ['ɪnvən,tɔri] *n., pl.* **-to•ries;** *v.* **-to•ried, -to•ry•ing.** *—n.* **1** a detailed list of articles with their estimated value. **2** a collection of articles that are or may be so listed; stock: *A storekeeper had a sale to reduce his inventory.* **3** the act of making a detailed list.
take inventory, make such a list.
—v. make a detailed list of; enter in a list: *Some stores inventory their stock once a month.* ⟨< Med.L *inventorium* < LL < *inventus,* pp. of *invenire.* See INVENT.⟩ **—,in•ven'to•ri•al,** *adj.*

in•ve•rac•i•ty [,ɪnvə'ræsɪti] *n.* **1** untruthfulness. **2** an untruth; falsehood.

in•ver•ness [,ɪnvər'nɛs] *n.* **1** a man's overcoat, often sleeveless, with a waist-length, removable cape. **2** the cape itself. ⟨< *Inverness,* Scotland⟩

in•verse [ɪn'vɜrs] *or* ['ɪnvɜrs] *adj., n.* *—adj.* **1** reversed in position, direction, or tendency; inverted: *DCBA is the inverse order of ABCD.* **2** *Meteorology.* showing an inversion.
—n. **1** something reversed: *The inverse of* 3/4 *is* 4/3. **2** direct opposite: *Evil is the inverse of good.* **3** *Mathematics.* the reciprocal of a designated quantity, also called **multiplicative inversion**.
4 *Mathematics.* the negation of a designated quantity, also called **additive inverse**. ⟨< L *inversus,* pp. of *invertere.* See INVERT.⟩ **—in'verse•ly,** *adv.*

inverse function *Mathematics.* the function that results when dependent and independent variables are interchanged. If $y = f(x)$ and $x = g(y)$, then f and g are inverses of each other.

in•ver•sion [ɪn'vɜrʒən] *or* [ɪn'vɜrʃən] *n.* **1** inverting or being inverted. **2** something inverted. **3** *Chemistry.* the hydrolysis of certain carbohydrates which produces a solution with reverse rotation. **4** *Grammar.* any change from the usual word order. **5** *Music.* the transposition from bass to tenor or treble. ⟨< L *inversus* turned in, pp. of *invertere*⟩

inversion layer *Meteorology.* a layer of air warmer than the air beneath it.

in•vert [ɪn'vɜrt] *v.* **1** turn upside down: *to invert a glass.* **2** turn the other way; reverse in position, direction, order, etc.: *If you invert* I can, *you have* Can I? **3** *Music.* change by making the lower or lowest note an octave higher or the higher or highest note an octave lower. ⟨< L *invertere* < *in-* over, around + *vertere* turn⟩ **—in'vert•er,** *n.* **—in,vert•i'bil•i•ty,** *n.* **—in'vert•i•ble,** *adj.*
☛ *Syn.* **1.** See note at REVERSE.

in•vert•ase [ɪn'vɜrteis] *n. Biochemistry.* an enzyme that produces invert sugar from cane sugar.

in•ver•te•brate [ɪn'vɜrtəbrɪt] *or* [ɪn'vɜrtə,breit] *n., adj.*
—n. Zoology. any animal lacking a backbone; any animal that is not a vertebrate, including annelids, molluscs, arthropods, and echinoderms (starfishes, etc.).
—adj. **1** *Zoology.* of, having to do with, or designating the invertebrates. **2** *Informal.* lacking character, conviction, or purpose. ⟨< NL *invertebratus*⟩

inverted mordent ['mɔrdənt] *Music.* a melodic ornamentation using the tone above the principal tone.

in•vert•er [ɪn'vɜrtər] *n. Electricity.* a converter.

invert sugar ['ɪnvɜrt] a mixture of glucose and fructose using their dextrorotatory forms.

in•vest [ɪn'vɛst] *v.* **1** use (money) to buy something that is expected to produce a profit, or income, or both: *She invested her money in stocks, bonds, and land.* **2** invest money: *Learn to invest wisely.* **3** spend or put in (time, energy, etc.) for later benefit: *The volunteer group invested its energies in developing new playgrounds.* **4** give power, authority, or right to: *He invested his lawyer with complete power to act for him.* **5** install in office with a ceremony: *A monarch is invested by being crowned.* **6** clothe; cover; surround: *Darkness invests the earth by night.* **7** surround with soldiers or ships; besiege: *The enemy invested the city and cut it off from our army.* ⟨< L *investire* < *in-* in + *vestis* clothing⟩ **—in'vest•a•ble** or **in'vest•i•ble,** *adj.*

in•ves•ti•gate [ɪn'vɛstə,geit] *v.* **-gat•ed, -gat•ing. 1** search into carefully; examine closely: *to investigate a complaint. Detectives investigate crimes.* **2** make an examination. ⟨< L *investigare* < *in-* in + *vestigare* track, trace⟩ **—in'ves•ti•ga•ble,** *adj.*

in•ves•ti•ga•tion [ɪn,vɛstə'geiʃən] *n.* a careful search; detailed or careful examination.
☛ *Syn.* **Investigation,** EXAMINATION, INQUIRY = a search for information or truth. **Investigation** emphasizes carefully tracking down everything that can be found out, in order to bring out hidden facts and learn the truth: *An investigation of the accident by the police put the blame on the drivers of both cars.* **Examination** emphasizes looking something or someone over closely or testing carefully in order to learn the facts about it, its condition, value, etc.: *The doctor gave him a physical examination.* **Inquiry** especially suggests a search made by asking questions: *Counsellors began an inquiry into the industrial needs of the region.*

in•ves•ti•ga•tive [ɪn'vɛstə,geitɪv] *adj.* of, having to do with, involving, or involved in investigation: *investigative news reporting, superior investigative powers.*

in•ves•ti•ga•tor [ɪn'vɛstə,geitər] *n.* a person who investigates.

in•ves•ti•ga•to•ry [ɪn'vɛstəgə,tɔri] *adj.* investigative.

in•ves•ti•tive [ɪn'vɛstətɪv] *adj.* **1** having the power to invest authority or rank. **2** of or pertaining to investiture.

in•ves•ti•ture [ɪn'vɛstətʃər] *n.* **1** a formal investing of a person with an office, dignity, power, right, etc. **2** clothing; apparel; covering. **3** in ecclesiastical law, the giving of a right such as possession of a benefice. ⟨ME< Med.L *investitura, investitus* installed⟩

in•vest•ment [ɪn'vɛstmənt] *n.* **1** an investing; a laying out of energy, time, or money: *Getting an education is a wise investment of time and money.* **2** the amount of money invested: *Her investments amount to thousands of dollars.* **3** something that is expected to yield a profitable return: *Canada Savings Bonds are a safe investment. Children are an investment in the future.* **4** the act of surrounding with soldiers or ships; siege. **5** investiture.

investment bank or **banker** a financial institution that deals in securities.

investment company or **trust** a company that issues its own securities based on its holdings.

in•ves•tor [ɪn'vɛstər] *n.* a person who invests money.

in•vet•er•a•cy [ɪn'vɛtərəsi] *n.* a settled, fixed condition; the nature of a fixed habit.

in•vet•er•ate [ɪn'vɛtərɪt] *adj.* **1** confirmed in a habit, practice, feeling, etc.; habitual: *an inveterate liar.* **2** long and firmly established: *Cats have an inveterate dislike of dogs.* ⟨< L *inveteratus*, pp. of *inveterascere* make old < *in-* in + *veterascere* grow old < *vetus, -teris* old⟩ **—in'vet•er•ate•ly,** *adv.* **—in'vet•er•ate•ness,** *n.*

in•vid•i•ous [ɪn'vɪdiəs] *adj.* likely to arouse ill will or resentment; giving offence because unfair or unjust: *invidious comparisons.* ⟨< L *invidiosus* < *invidia* envy. Related to ENVY.⟩ **—in'vid•i•ous•ly,** *adv.* **—in'vid•i•ous•ness,** *n.*

in•vig•i•late [ɪn'vɪdʒə,leit] *v.* **-lat•ed, -lat•ing.** supervise students, etc. writing an examination. ⟨*invigilatus* watched over⟩ **—in,vig•i'la•tion,** *n.* **—in'vig•i,la•tor,** *n.*

in•vig•or•ate [ɪn'vɪgə,reit] *v.* **-at•ed, -at•ing.** give vigour to; fill with life and energy. ⟨< L *in-* in + *vigor*⟩ **—in'vig•or,at•ing•ly,** *adv.* **—in'vig•or•a•tive,** *adj.*

in•vig•or•a•tion [ɪn,vɪgə'reiʃən] *n.* an invigorating or being invigorated.

in•vin•ci•ble [ɪn'vɪnsəbəl] *adj.* impossible to overcome; unconquerable: *an invincible opponent.* ⟨ME < OF < L *invincibilis* < *in-* not + *vincere* conquer⟩ **—in,vin•ci'bil•i•ty,** *n.* **—in'vin•ci•ble•ness,** *n.* **—in'vin•ci•bly,** *adv.*

in vi•no ve•ri•tas [ɪn 'vinou 'vɛrɪtɑs] *or* ['vɛrɪtæs] *Latin.* intoxication makes people reveal their true thoughts; literally, in wine (there is) truth.

in•vi•o•la•ble [ɪn'vaɪələbəl] *adj.* **1** that must not be violated or injured; sacred: *an inviolable vow, an inviolable sanctuary.* **2** that cannot be violated or injured: *The gods are inviolable.* ⟨L *inviolabilis*⟩ **—in,vi•o•la'bil•i•ty,** *n.* **—in'vi•o•la•bly,** *adv.*

in•vi•o•late [ɪn'vaɪəlɪt] *or* [ɪn'vaɪə,leit] *adj.* not violated; uninjured; unbroken; not profaned. **—in'vi•o•late•ly,** *adv.* **—in'vi•o•late•ness** or **in'vi•o•la•cy** [ɪn'vaɪələsi], *n.*

in•vis•i•ble [ɪn'vɪzəbəl] *adj., n. —adj.* **1** not visible; not capable of being seen: *Thought is invisible.* **2** not in sight; hidden: *The queen kept herself invisible in her palace.* **3** too small to be seen: *Bacteria are invisible.* **4** not easily seen; inconspicuous: *invisible mending.* **5** *Business.* **a** not listed in the regular financial statements: *an invisible asset.* **b** not appearing in returns of exports and imports, but for which payment is accepted from or made to a foreign country.
—n. **1** an invisible being or thing. **2 invisibles,** *pl. Business.* invisible exports or imports: *Insurance, freight, royalties, investment earnings, etc. are invisibles.* **3 the Invisible,** God. ⟨ME < L *invisibilis*⟩ **—in'vis•i•ble•ness** or **in,vis•i'bil•i•ty,** *n.*

invisible ink ink that is colourless and thus invisible until treated by a chemical, heat, or light.

in•vis•i•bly [ɪn'vɪzəbli] *adv.* without being seen; so as not to be seen.

in•vi•ta•tion [,ɪnvə'teiʃən] *n.* **1** a request to come to some place or to do something: *Formal invitations are written or printed.* **2** the act of inviting. **3** attraction; enticement; temptation: *Leaving the keys in the car was an open invitation to theft.* ⟨< L *invitation-* (stem of *invitatio*), *invitatus* invited (pp. of *invitare*)⟩

in•vi•ta•tion•al [,ɪnvə'teiʃənəl] *adj., n. —adj.* restricted to invited persons.
—n. Sports. a tournament by invitation.

in•vite *v.* [ɪn'vəit]; *n.* ['ɪnvəit] *v.* **-vit•ed, -vit•ing;** *n. —v.* **1** ask (someone) politely to come to some place or to do something: *We invited her to join our club.* **2** make a polite request for: *The author invited our opinion of her story.* **3** give grounds for; tend to cause: *The letter invites some questions.* **4** attract; tempt: *The calm water invited us to swim.*
—n. Slang. invitation. ⟨< L *invitare*⟩ **—in'vit•er,** *n.*
☛ *Syn. v.* **1.** See note at CALL.

in•vit•ing [ɪn'vəitɪŋ] *adj., v. —adj.* attractive; tempting.
—v. ppr. of INVITE. **—in'vit•ing•ly,** *adv.*

in vit•ro [ɪn 'vitrou] *Biology.* within an artificial environment of glass, such as a test tube: *The baby was born as a result of in vitro fertilization.* ⟨< L⟩

in vitro fertilization the process of fertilizing ova with sperm in the laboratory, outside the body.

in vi•vo [ɪn 'vivou] *Biology.* within a living body. ⟨< L⟩

in•vo•ca•tion [,ɪnvə'keiʃən] *n.* **1** the act of calling upon in prayer; appeal for help or protection: *A church service often begins with an invocation to God.* **2** the form of words used in this. **3 a** a calling forth of spirits by magic. **b** a set of magic words used to call forth spirits; incantation. **4** a formal appeal at or near the beginning of a long poem, in which the poet asks a Muse to give him or her inspiration. **5** *Law.* a call for evidence, papers, etc. from another case. ⟨< L *invocatus, invocare* < *in-* in + *vocare* to call⟩ **—,in•vo'ca•tion•al** or **in'vo•ca,to•ry** [ɪn'vɒkə,tɔri], *adj.*

in•voice ['ɪnvɔɪs] *n., v.* **-voiced, -voic•ing.** *—n.* **1** a list of goods or services sent to a purchaser showing prices, amounts, shipping charges, etc. **2** a shipment of such goods or services. **3** the form used for listing such goods or services.
—v. **1** make an invoice of; enter on an invoice. **2** submit an invoice to. ⟨earlier *invoyes*, pl. of *invoy*, var. of *envoy* < OF *envoy* < *envoier* send < VL < L *in via* on the way⟩

in•voke [ɪn'vouk] *v.* **-voked, -vok•ing. 1** call on in prayer; appeal to for help, protection, blessing, etc.: *The tribe invoked their rain gods when the drought became severe.* **2** appeal to for confirmation or judgment: *to invoke an authority.* **3** ask earnestly for; beg for: *The condemned criminal invoked the judge's mercy.* **4** call forth by magic: *Aladdin invoked the genie of the magic lamp.* **5** resort to; use or apply: *The governor general invoked her power of veto.* ⟨< L *invocare* < *in-* on + *vocare* call⟩ **—in'vo•ca•ble,** *adj.* **—in'vok•er,** *n.*

in•vo•lu•cel [ɪn'vɒljə,sɛl] *n. Botany.* a secondary involucre, as in a compound cluster of flowers. ⟨< NL *involucellum, involucrum*⟩

in•vo•lu•crate [,ɪnvə'lukrɪt] *or* [,ɪnvə'lukreit] *adj. Botany.* having an involucre.

in•vo•lu•cre ['ɪnvə,lukər] *or* [,ɪnvə'lukər] *n.* **1** *Botany.* one or more circles of small leaves, called bracts, around the base of a flower, flower cluster, or fruit. **2** *Anatomy.* a membranous sheath or cover. Also, **involucrum.** ⟨< F < L *involucrum* a cover < *involvere.* See INVOLVE.⟩ **—,invo'lu•cral,** *adj.*

in•vol•un•tar•y [ɪn'vɒlən,tɛri] *adj.* **1** not voluntary; not done of one's own free will; unwilling. **2** not done on purpose; not intended: *An accident is involuntary.* **3** not controlled by the will: *Breathing is mainly involuntary.* **4** done without a person's consent; forced: *involuntary commitment to a psychiatric hospital.* **—in'vol•un,tar•i•ly,** *adv.* **—in'vol•un,tar•i•ness,** *n.*

in•vo•lute *adj., n.* ['ɪnvə,lut]; *v* [,ɪnvə'lut] *or* ['ɪnvə,lut] *adj., n., v.* **-lut•ed, -lut•ing.** *—adj.* **1** involved; intricate. **2** rolled up on itself; curved spirally. **3** *Botany.* of a leaf or petal, having the margins rolled inward toward the centre. **4** *Zoology.* of a shell, having closely coiled whorls.
—n. Geometry. the curve formed by a given point on a taut thread as it is unwound from or wound onto another curve in the same plane. Compare EVOLUTE.
—v. become involute. ⟨< L *involutus*, pp. of *involvere.* See INVOLVE.⟩

in•vo•lu•tion [,ɪnvə'luʃən] *n.* **1** an involving. **2** a being involved; entanglement; complexity. **3** something involved; a complication. **4** *Mathematics.* the raising of a quantity to any power. **5** *Biology.* degeneration; retrograde change. **6** *Botany.* **a** a rolling inward from the edge. **b** a part thus formed. **7** *Grammar.* a complex construction in which the subject is separated from its verb by one or more intervening phrases or clauses.
8 *Medicine.* **a** regressive changes in the body due to old age. **b** the shrinking of an organ, as the uterus after childbirth.

in•volve [ɪn'vɒlv] *v.* **-volved, -volv•ing. 1** have as a necessary part, condition, or result; take in; include: *Housekeeping involves cooking, washing dishes, sweeping, and cleaning.* **2** have an effect on; affect: *These changes in the business involve the interests of all the owners.* **3** cause to be unpleasantly concerned; bring (into difficulty, danger, etc.): *One foolish mistake can involve you in a good deal of trouble.* **4** entangle; complicate: *A sentence that is involved is generally hard to understand.* **5** take up the attention of; occupy: *She was involved in working out a puzzle.* **6** wrap; enfold; envelop: *The outcome of the war is involved in doubt.* **7** *Mathematics.* raise to a given power. ⟨ME < L *involvere* < *in-* in + *volvere* roll⟩ **—in'volve•ment,** *n.* **—in'volv•er,** *n.*

☛ *Syn.* **3. Involve,** IMPLICATE = draw someone or something into a situation hard to get out of. **Involve** = get someone or something caught in a situation that is unpleasantly embarrassing, mixed up, or complex and hard to solve or settle: *Buying an expensive car involved him in debt. Telling one lie usually involves you in many more.* **Implicate** = show that someone is involved in or closely connected with something, usually disgraceful or bad: *Having the stolen goods in his possession implicated him in the robbery.*

in•volved [ɪn'vɒlvd] *adj., v. —adj.* **1** intricate. **2** affected or implicated. **3** *Informal.* having a relationship (with someone). *—v.* pt. and pp. of INVOLVE.

in•vul•ner•a•ble [ɪn'vʌlnərəbəl] *adj.* **1** that cannot be wounded or injured: *Achilles was invulnerable except for his heel.* **2** proof against attack; not easily assailable: *an invulnerable argument.* ⟨< L *invulnerabilis*⟩ **—in,vul•ner•a'bil•i•ty,** *n.* **—in'vul•ner•a•bly,** *adv.*

in•ward ['ɪnwərd] *adv., adj. —adv.* **1** toward the inside: *a passage leading inward.* **2** into the mind or soul: *Turn your thoughts inward.*
—adj. **1** placed within; internal: *the inward parts of the body.* **2** directed toward the inside: *an inward slant of the eyes.* **3** in mind or soul: *inward peace.* **4** intrinsic; inherent; essential: *the inward nature of something.* ⟨OE *inweard*⟩

in•ward•ly ['ɪnwərdli] *adv.* **1** on the inside; within. **2** toward the inside or centre. **3** in the mind or soul. **4** not openly; secretly: *He was inwardly pleased but said nothing.*

in•ward•ness ['ɪnwərdnɪs] *n.* **1** inner nature or meaning. **2** spirituality. **3** earnestness.

in•wards *adv.* ['ɪnwərdz]; *n.* ['ɪnərdz] *adv., n.pl. —adv.* inward. *—n. Informal.* parts inside the body; stomach and intestines; innards.

in•weave [ɪn'wiv] *v.* **-wove** or **-weaved, -wo•ven** or **-wove** or **-weaved, -weav•ing.** weave in; weave together; interweave.

in•wove [ɪn'wouv] *v.* a pt. and a pp. of INWEAVE.

in•wo•ven [ɪn'wouvən] *v.* a pp. of INWEAVE.

in•wrap [ɪn'ræp] *v.* **-wrapped, -wrap•ping.** enwrap.

in•wreathe [ɪn'rið] *v.* **-wreathed, -wreath•ing.** enwreathe.

in•wrought [ɪn'rɒt] *adj.* **1** having a decoration worked in. **2** worked in. **3** mixed together; closely blended.

I•o ['aiou] *n.* **1** *Greek mythology.* a maiden loved by Zeus, who changed her into a white heifer to save her from the jealousy of Hera. Hera, however, sent a gadfly to torment Io and caused her to wander through many lands until she reached Egypt, where Zeus restored her to her natural form. **2** IO MOTH. **3** *Astronomy.* the third largest satellite of Jupiter.

Io ionium.

I/O *Computer technology.* input/output.

i•o•date ['aiə,deit] *n., v.* **-dat•ed, -dat•ing.** *—n. Chemistry.* a salt of iodic acid.
—v. iodize. **—,i•o'da•tion,** *n.*

IODE or **I.O.D.E.** IMPERIAL ORDER DAUGHTERS OF THE EMPIRE.

i•od•ic [ai'ɒdɪk] *adj. Chemistry.* containing iodine.

iodic acid *Chemistry.* a crystalline solid used as a reagent in analytical chemistry.

i•o•dide ['aiə,daid] *or* ['aiədɪd] *n. Chemistry.* a compound of iodine with another element or radical.

i•o•dine ['aiə,dain] *or* ['aiədɪn]; *in chemistry,* ['aiə,din] *n.* **1** *Chemistry.* a chemical element of the halogen group usually obtained in the form of greyish black crystals that give off a dense, violet-coloured vapour with an irritating odour. Iodine is used in medicine, in making dyes, in photography, etc. *Symbol:* I; *at.no.* 53; *at.mass* 126.90. **2** a brown liquid, **tincture of iodine,** used as an antiseptic. ⟨< F *iode* iodine < Gk. *ioeidēs* violet-coloured < *ion* violet⟩

i•o•dip•a•mide [,aiə'dɪpə,maid] *n.* a drug used to diagnose certain conditions of the gall bladder.

i•o•dism ['aiə,dɪzəm] *n. Pathology.* iodine poisoning.

i•o•dize ['aiə,daiz] *v.* **-dized, -diz•ing.** combine, treat, or impregnate with iodine or an iodide: *iodized salt.* **—'i•o,diz•er,** *n.* **—,i•o•di'za•tion,** *n.*

i•o•do•form [ai'oudə,fɔrm] *or* [ai'ɒdə,fɔrm] *n. Chemistry.* a crystalline compound of iodine, used as an antiseptic. *Formula:* CHI_3 ⟨< *iodo-* iodine (< NL *iodum*) + *form(yl)* (< *formic acid*)⟩

i•o•dom•et•ry [,aiə'dɒmətri] *n. Chemistry.* a volumetric analytical procedure to detect iodine or iodine-producing agents. **—,i•o•do'met•ric** [,aiədə'mɛtrɪk], *adj.* **—,i•o•do'met•ri•cal•ly,** *adv.*

i•o•dop•sin [,aiə'dɒpsɪn] *n.* a photosensitive pigment in the retina that aids daytime vision.

i•o•doq•ui•nol [,aiə'dɒkwɪ,nɒl] *n.* a drug used to treat certain intestinal conditions.

i•o•dous [ai'oudəs] *or* ['aiədəs] *adj.* **1** like iodine. **2** containing trivalent iodine.

IOF or **I.O.F.** Independent Order of Foresters.

i•o•lite ['aiə,ləit] *n.* a blue mineral containing a silicate of iron, aluminum, and magnesium; cordierite. ⟨< Gk. *ion* violet + E *-lite*⟩

Io moth ['aiou] a large North American moth (*Automeris io*) having yellow wings with a large, bluish, eyelike spot on each hind wing. ⟨named after *Io,* who was tormented by a gadfly, because of the larva's stinging spines; 19c.⟩

i•on ['aiən] *or* ['aiɒn] *n. Physics, chemistry.* **1** an atom or group of atoms having a negative or positive electric charge as a result of having lost or gained one or more electrons. **Positive ions** (cations) are formed in electrolysis by the loss of electrons. **Negative ions** (anions) are formed by the gain of electrons. **2** an electrically charged particle formed in a gas. ⟨< Gk. *ion,* neut. ppr. of *ienai* go⟩

-ion *suffix.* **1** the act of ——ing: *attraction, calculation.* **2** the condition or state of being ——ed: *elation, fascination.* **3** the result of ——: *abbreviation, collection, connection.* ⟨< F < L *-io, -ionis,* or directly < L⟩

ion engine a rocket engine using ions instead of gases for propulsion.

ion exchange reciprocal transfer of ions between a solution and a solid.

I•o•ni•an [ai'ouniən] *n., adj. —n.* a member of an ancient Hellenic people that occupied Attica, the Ionian Islands, and the eastern coast of the Aegean Sea.
—adj. of or having to do with the Ionians or Ionia, the region occupied by them.

i•on•ic [ai'ɒnɪk] *adj.* having to do with ions.

I•on•ic [ai'ɒnɪk] *n., adj. —n.* the dialect of ancient Greek spoken by the Ionians, including Homeric and Attic Greek.
—adj. **1** of or having to do with Ionia, the Ionians, or their dialect. **2** *Architecture.* of, having to do with, or designating the second of the three orders of ancient Greek architecture. The characteristic Ionic column is in height nine times the diameter of the base, with an ornate base, a slender, deeply fluted shaft, and a capital with scrolls, called volutes, projecting on either side of its front and rear faces. See ORDER for picture. ⟨< L *Ionicus* < Gk. *Iōnikos*⟩

ionic bond *Chemistry.* a chemical bond in salts formed by the transfer of electrons.

i•o•ni•um [ai'ouniəm] *n. Chemistry.* a naturally occurring radioactive isotope of thorium having a mass number of 230. *Symbol:* Io; *half-life* 80 000 years. ⟨< *ion* + *(uran)ium;* for its ionizing action⟩

i•on•i•za•tion [,aiənə'zeiʃən] *or* [,aiənai'zeiʃən] *n.* a separation into ions; dissociation; formation of ions.

ionization chamber *Physics.* an apparatus for analysing ionizing radiation.

i•on•ize ['aiə,naiz] *v.* **-ized, -iz•ing.** separate into ions; produce ions in. Acids, bases, and salts ionize in solution. The gas in a neon light must be ionized before it can conduct an electric current. **—'i•on,iz•er,** *n.*

i•on•o•sphere [ai'ɒnə,sfir] *n.* a region of ionized layers of air above the stratosphere. Low pressure and solar radiation in the ionosphere help to reflect radio waves so that they travel over long distances. **—i,on•o'spher•ic** [-'sfɛrɪk], *adj.*

IOOF or **I.O.O.F.** Independent Order of Odd Fellows.

i•o•pam•i•dol [,aiou'pæmɪ,dɒl] *n.* a drug used to diagnose certain conditions of the spinal cord.

i•o•pa•no•ic acid [,aioupə'nouɪk] a drug used to help diagnose certain conditions of the gall bladder.

i•o•ta [ai'outə] *n.* **1** the ninth letter of the Greek alphabet (Ι, ι). **2** a very small quantity: *There is not an iota of truth in the prisoner's story.* ⟨< L < Gk. *iōta.* Doublet of JOT.⟩

i•o•thal•a•mate [,aiou'θælə,meit] *n.* a medium used to aid diagnosis of certain conditions of the urinary tract and of the brain.

IOU or **I.O.U.** an informal note acknowledging a debt: *Write me an IOU for ten dollars.* ⟨for the phrase *I owe you*⟩

i•o•ver•sol [ˌaɪouˈvɜrsɒl] *n.* a medium used to aid diagnosis of certain conditions of the brain and the urinary tract.

I•o•wa [ˈaɪəwə] *n.* a midwestern state of the U.S.

Iowa darter a common Canadian fish (*Poecilichthys exilis*) of the perch family, about 10 cm long.

i•ox•a•glate [aɪˈɒksəˌgleit] *n.* a medium used to aid diagnosis of certain conditions of the brain and body. One form is used to aid COMPUTERIZED AXIAL TOMOGRAPHY.

IPA or **I.P.A.** **1** INTERNATIONAL PHONETIC ALPHABET. **2** International Phonetic Association.

ip•e•cac [ˈɪpəˌkæk] *n.* **1** a South American creeping plant (*Cephaelis ipecacuanha*) of the madder family. **2** the dried roots of this plant. **3** a medicine made from the dried roots, used as an emetic or purgative. ⟨< Pg. < Tupi-Guarani *ipe-kaa-guéne* creeping plant causing nausea⟩

ip•e•cac•u•an•ha [ˌɪpəˌkækjuˈænə] *or* [ˌɪpəˌkækuˈænjə] *n.* ipecac.

Iph•i•ge•ni•a [ˌɪfədʒəˈnaɪə] *or* [ˌɪfədʒəˈniə] *n. Greek mythology.* the daughter of Agamemnon. He intended to sacrifice her to Artemis to obtain favourable winds for the Greek ships sailing to Troy, but Artemis put a hart in her place and carried Iphigenia off to Tauris to become her priestess.

Ip•i•u•tak [ˌɪpiˈutæk] *n., adj. —n.* a member of a prehistoric Inuit people around the Bering Strait, whose culture flourished from about 400 B.C. to 400 A.D.
—adj. of or having to do with the culture of this people: *Ipiutak art.* ⟨after site where cultural relics were found⟩

i•po•date [ˈəipəˌdeit] *n.* a medium used to aid diagnosis of certain conditions of the intestinal tract.

ip•o•moe•a [ˌɪpəˈmiə] *or* [ˌəipəˈmiə] *n.* any plant of the genus *Ipomoea*, having showy flowers. ⟨< Gk. *ips, ipos* worm + *homoios* same⟩

ip•se dix•it [ˈɪpsei ˈdɪksɪt] an assertion without proof. ⟨< L *ipse dixit* he himself said (it)⟩
☛ *Usage.* **Ipse dixit.** The Latin phrase, when used in English as a noun, takes the regular plural ending: *His argument was merely a succession of ipse dixits.*

i•pra•tro•pi•um [ˌəiprəˈtroupiəm] *n.* a drug used to keep the airway open, as in bronchitis.

ip•so fac•to [ˈɪpsou ˈfæktou] *Latin.* by that very fact; by the fact itself.

IQ or **I.Q.** *Psychology.* INTELLIGENCE QUOTIENT.

ir–¹ *prefix.* the form of IN-¹ occurring before *r*, as in *irrational, irresolute.*

ir–² *prefix.* the form of IN-² occurring before *r,* as in *irrigate, irradiate.*

Ir iridium.

Ir. Ireland; Irish.

IRA or **I.R.A.** **1** Irish Republican Army. **2** International Reading Association.

I•ran [ɪˈræn] *or* [iˈrɑn] *n.* a republic in SW Asia, east of Iraq, north of the Persian Gulf, and west of Afghanistan and Pakistan; until 1935 called Persia.

I•ra•ni•an [ɪˈreiniən], [aɪˈreiniən], *or* [iˈrɑniən] *n., adj. —n.* **1** a native or inhabitant of Iran. **2** a branch of the Indo-European family of languages that includes Persian and Kurdish.
—adj. of or having to do with Iran or its people.

I•raq [ɪˈræk] *or* [iˈrɑk] *n.* a republic in SW Asia, north of Saudi Arabia and west of Iran. See LEBANON for map.

I•ra•qi [ɪˈræki] *or* [iˈrɑki] *n., adj. —n.* a native or inhabitant of Iraq.
—adj. of or having to do with Iraq or its people.

i•ras•ci•ble [ɪˈræsəbəl] *or* [aɪˌræsəbəl] *adj.* **1** easily made angry; irritable. **2** showing anger. ⟨< LL *irascibilis* < L *irasci* grow angry < *ira* anger⟩ **—iˌras•ciˈbil•i•ty,** *n.* **—iˈras•ci•bly,** *adv.* **—iˈras•ci•ble•ness,** *n.*
☛ *Syn.* **1.** See note at IRRITABLE.

i•rate [aɪˈreit] *or* [ˈaɪreit] *adj.* angry. ⟨< L *iratus* < *ira* anger⟩ **—iˈrate•ly,** *adv.*

IRBM intermediate range ballistic missile.

ire [aɪr] *n.* anger; wrath. ⟨ME < OF < L *ira*⟩

ire•ful [ˈaɪrfəl] *adj.* **1** angry; wrathful. **2** easily made angry; irascible. **—ˈire•ful•ly,** *adv.* **—ˈire•ful•ness,** *n.*

Ire•land [ˈaɪrlənd] *n.* **1** an island of the British Isles, comprising the countries Northern Ireland and Ireland. **2** a republic in the southern part of this island.

i•ren•ic [aɪˈrɛnɪk] *or* [aɪˈrinɪk] *adj.* conciliatory. ⟨< Gk. *eirenikos* < *eirene* peace⟩ **—iˈren•i•cal•ly,** *adv.*

ir•i•dec•to•my [ˌɪrɪˈdɛktəmi] *n., pl.* **-mies.** *Surgical.* the excision of part of the iris.

ir•i•des [ˈɪrɪˌdiz] *or* [ˈaɪrɪˌdiz] *n.* a plural of IRIS.

ir•i•des•cence [ˌɪrɪˈdɛsəns] *n.* a changing or play of colours, as in mother-of-pearl, opals, or a peacock's feathers.

ir•i•des•cent [ˌɪrɪˈdɛsənt] *adj.* **1** displaying colours like those of the rainbow. **2** changing colours according to position. ⟨< L *iris, iridis* rainbow < Gk.⟩ **—ˌir•iˈdes•cent•ly,** *adv.*

i•rid•ic [ɪˈrɪdɪk] *or* [aɪˈrɪdɪk] *adj. Chemistry.* containing iridium.

i•rid•i•um [ɪˈrɪdiəm] *or* [aɪˈrɪdiəm] *n. Chemistry.* a white, rare, metallic chemical element that resembles platinum and is twice as heavy as lead, used for the points of pen nibs. *Symbol*: Ir; *at.no.* 77; *at.mass* 192.22. ⟨< NL < L *iris, -idis* rainbow; with reference to its iridescence in solution⟩

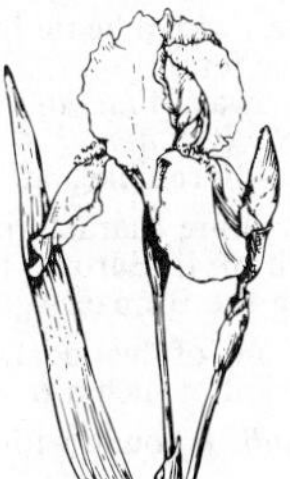
An iris

i•ris [ˈaɪrɪs] *n., pl.* **i•ris•es** or **i•ri•des** [ˈɪrɪˌdɪz] *or* [ˈaɪrɪˌdɪz]. **1** *Botany.* any of a large genus (*Iris*) of perennial plants found in temperate regions of the northern hemisphere, having sword-shaped leaves and large, showy flowers. There are many cultivated varieties of iris. **2** the flower of an iris. **3** (*adjl.*) designating a family (Iridaceae) of plants found in tropical and temperate regions, growing from an underground stem or a bulb. Irises, crocuses, and gladiola belong to the iris family. **4** *Anatomy.* the coloured part of the eye, having a round opening, called the pupil, in its centre. The iris is a kind of diaphragm that controls the amount of light entering the eye. See EYE for picture. **5** **Iris,** *Greek mythology.* the goddess of the rainbow and messenger of the gods. **6** *Poetic.* rainbow. ⟨< L *iris* rainbow < Gk.⟩

iris diaphragm a DIAPHRAGM (def. 4) that controls the aperture of a camera lens or of a microscope. Its central opening can be increased or decreased at need.

I•rish [ˈaɪrɪʃ] *n., adj. —n.* **1 the Irish,** *pl.* the people of Ireland, a large island west of Great Britain. **2** the Celtic language spoken in parts of Ireland; Irish Gaelic.
—adj. of or having to do with Ireland, its people, or their language. ⟨ME *Irisc, Irish* < OE *Iras*, pl., the people of Ireland⟩

Irish coffee coffee with Irish whisky and cream.

Irish Gaelic the Celtic language of ancient and modern Ireland.

I•rish•ism [ˈaɪrɪˌʃɪzəm] *n.* anything characteristic of the Irish.

I•rish•man [ˈaɪrɪʃmən] *n., pl.* **-men.** **1** a man who is a native or inhabitant of Ireland. **2** a man of Irish descent.

Irish moss carrageen.

Irish potato potato.

Irish setter a breed of large hunting dog having long, silky, reddish brown hair.

Irish stew a stew made of meat, potatoes, and onions.

Irish terrier a breed of small dog having wiry brown or reddish hair.

Irish wolfhound a breed of very large, powerful dog, formerly used in hunting wolves.

I•rish•wom•an [ˈaɪrɪʃˌwʊmən] *n., pl.* **-wom•en.** **1** a woman who is a native or inhabitant of Ireland. **2** a woman of Irish descent.

ir•i•tis [aɪˈrəitɪs] *n. Ophthalmology.* inflammation of the iris. **—iˈrit•ik** [aɪˈrɪtɪk] *adj.*

irk [ɜrk] *v.* weary; disgust; annoy; bore: *It irks us to wait for people who are always late.* ⟨ME *irke(n)* (to) grow tired, tire < Scand.⟩

irk•some [ˈɜrksəm] *adj.* tiresome; tedious. **—ˈirk•some•ly,** *adv.* **—ˈirk•some•ness,** *n.*

IRO or **I.R.O.** International Refugee Organization.

i•ron ['aɪərn] *n., adj., v.* —*n.* **1** *Chemistry.* a heavy, hard, strong, malleable, silver-white metallic element. It is the commonest and most useful metal, used for tools, machinery, etc. *Symbol*: Fe; *at.no.* 26; *at.mass* 55.85. **2** a tool, instrument, or weapon made from this metal. **3** great hardness and strength; firmness: *women of iron.* **4** an appliance with a flat surface for smoothing cloth or pressing clothes. **5** a golf club with an iron or steel head. **6** *Slang.* a pistol. **7** a branding iron. **8** a harpoon. **9** *Medicine.* a preparation of or containing iron, used as a tonic. **10 irons,** *pl.* chains or bands of iron; handcuffs; shackles.
have too many irons in the fire, try to do too many things at once.
strike while the iron is hot, act while conditions are favourable.
—*adj.* **1** made of iron; having to do with iron. **2** like iron; hard or strong; unyielding: *an iron will.* **3** harsh or cruel: *the iron hand of fate.*
—*v.* **1** smooth or press (cloth, etc.) with a heated iron. **2** furnish or cover with iron. **3** put in irons; fetter.
iron out, straighten out; smooth away: *A tactful person can iron out many problems between people.* ⟨OE *īren*, ? < Celtic⟩
—**'i•ron•er,** *n.* —**'i•ron•less,** *adj.* —**'i•ron,like,** *adj.*

Iron Age a period of human culture characterized by the use of tools, weapons, etc. made of iron. In Europe, the Iron Age began about 1000 B.C., following the Bronze Age.

i•ron•bark ['aɪərn,bɑrk] *n.* **1** any of the eucalyptus trees having hard, solid bark. **2** the wood of such a tree.

i•ron•bound ['aɪərn,baʊnd] *adj.* **1** bound with iron. **2** hard; rigid; unyielding. **3** rocky.

i•ron•clad ['aɪərn'klæd] *or* ['aɪərn,klæd] *adj., n.* —*adj.* **1** protected with iron plates. **2** very hard to change or get out of: *an ironclad agreement.*
—*n.* formerly, a warship protected with iron plates.

i•ron•fist•ed ['aɪərn'fɪstɪd] *adj.* unyielding; cruel; despotic.

i•ron–grey or **i•ron–gray** ['aɪərn 'greɪ] *adj.* having the colour of freshly broken cast iron: *iron-grey hair.*

iron hand strict or harsh control.

i•ron–hand•ed ['aɪərn 'hændɪd] *adj.* exercising stern discipline or tight control. —**'i•ron'hand•ed•ness,** *n.*

i•ron•ic [aɪ'rɒnɪk] *adj.* **1** expressing one thing and meaning the opposite. *Example*: Speedy *would be an ironic name for a snail.* **2** contrary to what would naturally be expected: *It was ironic that the man was run over by his own car.* **3** using or having a habit of using irony: *an ironic person.* **4** showing irony: *an ironic statement.* Also, **ironical.** ⟨< LL *ironicus* < Gk. *eironikos.* See IRONY.⟩ —**i'ron•i•cal•ly,** *adv.*

ironing board a board covered with a smooth cloth, used for ironing clothes on.

i•ro•nist ['aɪrənɪst] *n.* a person who takes an ironical view of life and things, especially as a writer.

iron lung a device that gives artificial respiration by rhythmically alternating the air pressure in a chamber enclosing the patient's chest.

i•ron•mon•ger ['aɪərn,mʌŋgər] *or* ['aɪərn,mɒŋgər] *n. Brit.* a dealer in ironware or hardware. —**'i•ron,mon•ge•ry,** *n.*

iron–on ['aɪərn ,ɒn] *adj.* made of or coated on the reverse side with a substance that, when heated, as with an iron, will form a permanent bond with fabric: *iron-on interfacing.*

iron pyrites pyrite; FOOL'S GOLD.

i•ron•sides ['aɪərn,saɪdz] *n.* **1** a man of great strength or endurance. **2** an armour-plated warship. **3 Ironsides, a** Oliver Cromwell, 17th century English revolutionary. **b** the regiment led by Oliver Cromwell. **c** his army.

i•ron•stone ['aɪərn,stoun] *n.* **1** any iron ore with clay or other impurities in it. **2** a hard variety of white ceramic ware; iron stoneware.

i•ron•ware ['aɪərn,wɛr] *n.* articles made of iron, such as pots, kettles, tools, etc.; hardware.

i•ron•weed ['aɪərn,wid] *n.* any of several perennial plants (genus *Vernonia*) of the composite family found in many parts of the world, having lance-shaped, toothed leaves and clusters of tubular flowers, usually purple or red.

i•ron–willed ['aɪərn 'wɪld] *adj.* having an exceptionally firm will.

i•ron•wood ['aɪərn,wʊd] *n.* **1** any of various trees such as some species of hornbeam, having very hard, heavy wood. **2** the wood itself.

i•ron•work ['aɪərn,wɜrk] *n.* **1** works of iron. **2 ironworks,** a place where iron or steel is smelted or fashioned into heavy products (*often used with a singular verb*).

i•ron•work•er ['aɪərn,wɜrkər] *n.* **1** a person who makes things of iron. **2** a person whose work is building the framework of bridges, skyscrapers, etc.

i•ro•ny[1] ['aɪrəni] *or* ['aɪərni] *n., pl.* **-nies. 1** a method of expression in which the intended meaning is the opposite of, or different from, that expressed: *Calling their small bungalow a mansion is irony.* **2** an event or outcome contrary to what would naturally be expected: *It was an amusing irony when a fake diamond was stolen instead of the real one. It was the irony of fate that the great cancer doctor herself died of cancer.* **3** an instance of irony. **4 dramatic irony,** a situation in which the audience knows something which a character does not. **5** feigned ignorance in an argument, sometimes called **Socratic irony.** ⟨< L *ironia* < Gk. *eirōneia* dissimulation < *eirōn* dissembler⟩

☛ *Usage.* **Irony,** SARCASM, SATIRE are often confused. **Irony,** applying to a kind of humour or way of expressing wit, emphasizes deliberately saying the opposite of what one means, depending on tone of voice or writing to show the real meaning. **Sarcasm** applies only to cruel, biting, contemptuous remarks that may be stated ironically or directly but are always intended to hurt and ridicule: *When children call a boy 'Four Eyes' because he wears glasses, they are using sarcasm.* **Satire** is the formal use of irony, sarcasm, and other kinds of humour to expose, criticize, or attack follies or vices.

i•ro•ny[2] ['aɪərni] *adj.* of or having to do with iron; containing iron.

Ir•o•quoi•an [,ɪrə'kwɔɪən] *n., adj.* —*n.* **1** a family of North American First Nations and American Indian languages, including Huron, Mohawk, Oneida, Onondaga, Cayuga, Seneca, Tuscarora, and Cherokee. **2** a First Nations person or American Indian belonging to an Iroquoian tribe; an Iroquois.
—*adj.* **1** of or having to do with Iroquoian languages. **2** of or having to do with Iroquois First Nations people and American Indians or their languages.

Ir•o•quois ['ɪrə,kwɒ] *n.sing. or pl.* a member of any of a powerful group of North American First Nations peoples and American Indians called the FIVE NATIONS (later, the SIX NATIONS) living mostly in Québec, Ontario, and New York State.

ir•ra•di•ance [ɪ'reidiəns] *n.* radiance; shine. Also, **irradiancy.**

ir•ra•di•ant [ɪ'reidiənt] *adj.* irradiating; radiant; shining.

ir•ra•di•ate [ɪ'reidi,eit] *v.* **-at•ed, -at•ing. 1** shine upon; make bright; illuminate. **2** shine. **3** radiate; give out. **4** treat with ultraviolet rays. **5** expose to radiation. ⟨< L *irradiare* < *in-* + *radius* ray⟩ —**ir'ra•di,a•tor,** *n.* —**ir'ra•di,a•tive,** *adj.*
☛ *Hom.* ERADIATE.

ir•ra•di•a•tion [ɪ,reidi'eiʃən] *n.* **1** the act or process of irradiating. **2** the state or condition of being irradiated. **3** a stream of light; ray. **4** enlightenment of the mind or spirit. **5** *Optics.* the apparent enlargement of an object seen against a dark background.

ir•ra•tion•al [ɪ'ræʃənəl] *adj.* **1** not rational; unreasonable: *It is irrational to be afraid of the number 13.* **2** unable to think and reason clearly. **3** *Mathematics.* **a** that cannot be expressed by a whole number or a common fraction. $\sqrt{3}$ is an irrational number. **b** of functions, that cannot be expressed as the ratio of two algebraic polynomials in its variables. ⟨< L *irrationalis*⟩
—**ir'ra•tion•al•ly,** *adv.*

ir•ra•tion•al•ism [ɪ'ræʃənə,lɪzəm] *n.* thought or behaviour that is not rational.

ir•ra•tion•al•i•ty [ɪ,ræʃə'næləti] *n., pl.* **-ties. 1** the fact of being irrational. **2** something irrational; an absurdity.

irrational number *Mathematics.* a number which cannot be expressed as a whole number or fraction. Its decimal expansion neither terminates nor repeats. *Examples:* π, $\sqrt{2}$

ir•re•claim•a•ble [,ɪrɪ'kleiməbəl] *adj.* that cannot be reclaimed. —**,ir•re'claim•a•bly,** *adv.*

ir•rec•on•cil•a•ble [ɪ'rɛkən,saɪləbəl] *or* [ɪ,rɛkən'saɪləbəl] *adj., n.* —*adj.* that cannot be reconciled; that cannot be made to agree; opposed.
—*n.* **1** a person who refuses to compromise or collaborate: *The irreconcilables in the party made discussion of the proposal very difficult.* **2 irreconcilables,** *pl.* conflicting ideas.
—**ir'rec•on,cil•a•bly,** *adv.* —**ir,rec•on,cil•a'bil•i•ty** or **ir'rec•on,cil•a•ble•ness,** *n.*

ir•re•cov•er•a•ble [,ɪrɪ'kʌvərəbəl] *adj.* **1** that cannot be regained or got back: *Wasted time is irrecoverable.* **2** that cannot be remedied: *irrecoverable sorrow.* —**,ir•re'cov•er•a•bly,** *adv.*

ir•re•cu•sa•ble [,ɪrɪ'kjuzəbəl] *adj.* undeniable.

ir•re•deem•a•ble [ˌɪrɪ'diməbəl] *adj.* **1** that cannot be bought back. **2** that cannot be exchanged for coin: *irredeemable paper money.* **3** beyond remedy; hopeless. **—ˌir•re,deem•a'bil•i•ty,** *n.* **—ˌir•re'deem•a•bly,** *adv.*

Ir•re•den•tist [ˌɪrɪ'dɛntɪst] *n.* **1** a member of an Italian political party that became important in 1878. The Irredentists advocated that Italy should gain control of neighbouring regions with Italian populations that were under foreign rule. **2 irredentist,** one who advocates the recovery of lands of which his or her nation has been deprived. ⟨< Ital. *irredentista* < *(Italia) irredenta* unredeemed (Italy), ult. < L *in-* not + *redemptus,* pp. of *redimere* redeem⟩ **—ˌir•re'dent•ism,** *n.*

ir•re•duc•i•ble [ˌɪrɪ'djusəbəl] *or* [ˌɪrɪ'dusəbəl] *adj.* that cannot be reduced. **—ˌir•re'duc•i•bly,** *adv.* **—ˌir•re,duc•i'bil•i•ty** or **ˌir•re'duc•i•ble•ness,** *n.*

ir•ref•ra•ga•ble [ɪ'rɛfrəgəbəl] *adj.* that cannot be refuted; unanswerable; undeniable. ⟨< LL *irrefragabilis* < L *in-* not + *refragari* oppose⟩ **—ir'ref•ra•ga•bly,** *adv.* **—ir,ref•ra•ga'bil•i•ty,** *n.*

ir•ref•u•ta•ble [ɪ'rɛfjətəbəl] *or* [ˌɪrɪ'fjutəbəl] *adj.* that cannot be refuted or disproved. **—ir'ref•u•ta•bly,** *adv.* **—ir,ref•u•ta'bil•i•ty** or **ˌir•re'fu•ta•ble•ness,** *n.*

ir•reg•u•lar [ɪ'rɛgjələr] *adj., n.* *—adj.* **1** not regular; erratic: *irregular breathing; an irregular heartbeat.* **2** not even; not smooth; not straight; without symmetry: *irregular features, an irregular coastline.* **3** not according to law or morals: *irregular behaviour.* **4** *Military.* not in the regular army. **5** *Grammar.* not inflected in the usual way. *Be* is an irregular verb. **6** of merchandise, falling below the usual specifications. **7** *Botany.* having varying floral parts.
—n. Military. a soldier not in the regular army. **—ir'reg•u•lar•ly,** *adv.*

☛ *Syn. adj.* **1. Irregular,** ABNORMAL = out of the usual or natural order or way. **Irregular** = not according to rule or the accepted standard, pattern, way, etc. for the kind of thing or person described: *He has irregular habits.* **Abnormal** = departing from what is regarded as normal, average, or typical, and may describe people or things either above or below normal or showing little relation to the normal: *Two hundred centimetres is an abnormal height for a man.*

ir•reg•u•lar•i•ty [ɪˌrɛgjə'lærəti] *or* [ɪˌrɛgjə'lɛrəti] *n., pl.* **-ties.** **1** a lack of regularity; the condition of being irregular. **2** something irregular. **3** lack of regularity of bowel movements: *Do you suffer from irregularity?*

ir•rel•a•tive [ɪ'rɛlətɪv] *adj.* not relevant (*usually used with* **to**).

ir•rel•e•vance [ɪ'rɛləvəns] *n.* **1** the condition of being irrelevant. **2** something irrelevant. Also, **irrelevancy.**

ir•rel•e•vant [ɪ'rɛləvənt] *adj.* not to the point; off the subject: *A question about economics is irrelevant in a music lesson.* **—ir'rel•e•vant•ly,** *adv.*

ir•re•liev•a•ble [ˌɪrɪ'livəbəl] *adj.* not able to be relieved.

ir•re•li•gion [ˌɪrɪ'lɪdʒən] *n.* **1** lack of religion. **2** hostility to or disregard of religion. **—ˌir•re'li•gion•ist,** *n.*

ir•re•li•gious [ˌɪrɪ'lɪdʒəs] *adj.* **1** not religious; indifferent to religion. **2** contrary to religious principles; impious. ⟨< L *irreligiosus*⟩ **—ˌir•re'li•gious•ly,** *adv.* **—ˌir•re'li•gious•ness,** *n.*

ir•re•me•di•a•ble [ˌɪrɪ'midiəbəl] *adj.* that cannot be remedied; incurable. ⟨< L *irremidiabilis*⟩ **—ˌir•re,me•di•a'bil•i•ty,** *n.* **—ˌir•re'me•di•a•bly,** *adv.*

ir•re•mis•si•ble [ˌɪrɪ'mɪsəbəl] *adj.* not pardonable. ⟨ME < LL *irremissibilis*⟩ **—ˌir•re'mis•si•bly,** *adj.* **—ˌir•re,mis•si'bil•i•ty** or **ˌir•re'mis•si•ble•ness,** *n.*

ir•re•mov•a•ble [ˌɪrɪ'muvəbəl] *adj.* that cannot be removed. **—ˌir•re'mov•a•bly,** *adv.* **—ˌir•re,mov•a'bil•i•ty** or **ˌir•re'mov•a•ble•ness,** *n.*

ir•rep•a•ra•ble [ɪ'rɛpərəbəl] *adj.* that cannot be repaired or made good. ⟨ME < L *irreparabilis*⟩ **—ir'rep•a•ra•bly,** *adv.* **—ir,rep•a•ra'bil•i•ty** or **ir'rep•a•ra•ble•ness,** *n.*

ir•re•peal•a•ble [ˌɪrɪ'piləbəl] *adj.* not able to be revoked. **—ˌir•re,peal•a'bil•i•ty,** *n.* **—ˌir•re'peal•a•bly,** *adv.*

ir•re•place•a•ble [ˌɪrɪ'pleisəbəl] *adj.* not replaceable; impossible to replace with another. **—ˌir•re'place•a•bly,** *adv.*

ir•re•press•i•ble [ˌɪrɪ'prɛsəbəl] *adj.* that cannot be repressed or restrained. **—ˌir•re,press•i'bil•i•ty,** *n.* **—ˌir•re'press•i•bly,** *adv.*

ir•re•proach•a•ble [ˌɪrɪ'proutʃəbəl] *adj.* free from blame; faultless: *He had led an irreproachable life.* **—ˌir•re'proach•a•bly,** *adv.* **—ˌir•re'proach•a•ble•ness,** *n.* **—ˌir•re,proach•a'bil•i•ty,** *n.*

ir•re•sist•i•ble [ˌɪrɪ'zɪstəbəl] *adj.* that cannot be resisted; too great to be withstood; overwhelming: *an irresistible desire to laugh.* ⟨< LL *irresistibilis*⟩ **—ˌir•re'sist•i•bly,** *adv.* **—ˌir•re,sist•i'bil•i•ty** or **ˌir•re'sist•i•ble•ness,** *n.*

ir•res•o•lu•ble [ɪ'rɛzəljəbəl] *or* [ˌɪrɪ'zɒljəbəl] *adj.* not able to be explained or solved. ⟨< L *irresolubilis*⟩ **—ir,res•o•lu'bil•i•ty,** *n.*

ir•res•o•lute [ɪ'rɛzəˌlut] *adj.* **1** unable to make up one's mind; not sure of what one wants; hesitating: *He stood there irresolute, not knowing which path to try.* **2** lacking in resoluteness: *An irresolute person makes a poor leader.* **—ir'res•o,lute•ly,** *adv.* **—ir'res•o,lute•ness,** *n.*

ir•res•o•lu•tion [ɪˌrɛzə'luʃən] *n.* a being irresolute; hesitation or a lack of resolution.

ir•re•spec•tive [ˌɪrɪ'spɛktɪv] *adj.* regardless: *Any person, irrespective of age, may join the club.* **—ˌir•re'spec•tive•ly,** *adv.*

ir•res•pir•a•ble [ɪ'rɛspərəbəl] *or* [ˌɪrɪ'spaɪrəbəl] *adj.* not fit for breathing. ⟨< LL *irrespirabilis*⟩

ir•re•spon•si•ble [ˌɪrɪ'spɒnsəbəl] *adj., n.* *—adj.* **1** not having or not showing a proper sense of responsibility: *It was irresponsible to leave the broken glass on the sidewalk.* **2** not responsible to any authority; that cannot be called to account: *A dictator is an irresponsible ruler.*
—n. a person who is irresponsible. **—ˌir•re,spon•si'bil•i•ty,** *n.* **—ˌir•re'spon•si•bly,** *adv.* **—ˌir•re'spon•si•ble•ness,** *n.*

ir•re•spon•sive [ˌɪrɪ'spɒnsɪv] *adj.* **1** not responding. **2** *Medicine.* not responding to treatment. **—ˌir•re'spon•sive•ly,** *adv.* **—ˌir•re'spon•sive•ness,** *n.*

ir•re•trace•a•ble [ˌɪrɪ'treisəbəl] *adj.* that cannot be retraced. **—ˌir•re'trace•a•bly,** *adv.*

ir•re•triev•a•ble [ˌɪrɪ'trivəbəl] *adj.* that cannot be retrieved or recovered; that cannot be recalled or restored to its former condition. **—ˌir•re,triev•a'bil•i•ty** or **ˌir•re'triev•a•ble•ness,** *n.* **—ˌir•re'triev•a•bly,** *adv.*

ir•rev•er•ence [ɪ'rɛvərəns] *n.* **1** lack of reverence; disrespect. **2** an act showing irreverence. ⟨ME < L *irreverentia*⟩

ir•rev•er•ent [ɪ'rɛvərənt] *adj.* not reverent; disrespectful. ⟨< L *irreverens, -entis*⟩ **—ir'rev•er•ent•ly,** *adv.*

ir•re•vers•i•ble [ˌɪrɪ'vɜrsəbəl] *adj.* not capable of being reversed. **—ˌir•re,vers•i'bil•i•ty, ˌir•re'vers•i•ble•ness,** *n.* **—ˌir•re'vers•i•bly,** *adv.*

ir•rev•o•ca•ble [ɪ'rɛvəkəbəl] *adj.* not to be recalled, withdrawn, or annulled: *an irrevocable decision.* ⟨ME < L *irrevocabilis*⟩ **—ir'rev•o•ca•bly,** *adv.* **—ir'rev•o•ca•ble•ness** or **ir,rev•o•ca'bil•i•ty,** *n.*

ir•ri•ga•ble ['ɪrəgəbəl] *adj.* that can be irrigated. **—'ir•ri•ga•bly,** *adv.*

ir•ri•gate ['ɪrəˌgeit] *v.* **-gat•ed, -gat•ing.** **1** supply (land) with water by means of ditches, sprinklers, etc. **2** *Medicine.* wash out or flush (a wound, cavity) in the body, etc. with a flow of some liquid: *to irrigate the nose and throat with warm water.* ⟨< L *irrigatus* watered (pp. of *irrigare* L) < *in-* in + *rigare* to lead water⟩ **—'ir•ri,ga•tor,** *n.*

ir•ri•ga•tion [ˌɪrə'geiʃən] *n.* an irrigating or being irrigated: *Irrigation is needed to make crops grow in dry regions.* **—ˌir•ri'ga•tion•al,** *adj.*

ir•ri•ta•bil•i•ty [ˌɪrɪtə'bɪləti] *n., pl.* **-ties.** **1** the quality or state of being irritable: *irritability of temper, irritability of skin.* **2** *Physiology, biology.* the ability to respond to a stimulus; the capacity of living things to react to changes in their environment. ⟨< L *irritabilitas*⟩

ir•ri•ta•ble ['ɪrətəbəl] *adj.* **1** easily made angry; impatient. **2** of an organ or part of the body, unusually sensitive or sore: *A baby's skin is often quite irritable.* **3** *Biology.* able to respond to stimuli. ⟨< L *irritabilis*⟩ **—'ir•ri•ta•ble•ness,** *n.* **—'ir•ri•ta•bly,** *adv.*

☛ *Syn.* **1. Irritable,** IRASCIBLE = easily made angry. **Irritable** = easily annoyed or angered, especially by little things, and suggests being in a nervous or overstressed condition rather than having an impatient or excitable temperament: *She has been so irritable lately that I think she must be ill.* **Irascible** = having a quick temper, being by nature or disposition liable to become angry at the slightest excuse: *Irascible people should not have positions which require them to meet the public.*

ir•ri•tant ['ɪrɪtənt] *n., adj.* *—n.* a thing that causes irritation: *A mustard plaster is an irritant.*
—adj. causing irritation. ⟨< L *irritans, -antis,* ppr. of *irritare* enrage, provoke⟩ **—'ir•ri•tan•cy,** *n.*

ir•ri•tate ['ɪrɪˌteit] *v.* **-tat•ed, -tat•ing.** **1** make impatient or angry; annoy; provoke; vex: *The boy's foolish questions irritated his father. Flies irritate horses.* **2** make unnaturally sensitive or sore: *Too much sun irritates the skin.* **3** *Pathology.* bring (an organ or part) to an excessively sensitive condition. **4** *Biology.* stimulate (an organ, muscle, tissue, etc.) to perform some characteristic action or function: *A muscle contracts when it is irritated by an electric shock.* ⟨< L *irritare* enrage, provoke⟩ **—'ir•ri,tat•ed•ly,** *adv.* **—'ir•ri,tat•ing•ly,** *adv.* **—'ir•ri,ta•tor,** *n.*

☛ *Syn.* **1. Irritate,** EXASPERATE, PROVOKE = excite to impatience or anger. **Irritate** suggests annoying a person until he or she loses patience or flares up in anger: *Her untidiness irritates me.* **Exasperate** = make extremely annoyed or angry by irritating beyond endurance: *Her constant cheating exasperates me.* **Provoke** = do, or keep doing, something displeasing or disturbing to make a person lose patience and become very much annoyed, vexed, or angry: *Her constant interruptions provoke me.*

ir•ri•ta•tion [,ɪrɪ'teiʃən] *n.* **1** the act or process of irritating; annoyance; vexation. **2** an irritated condition.

ir•ri•ta•tive ['ɪrɪ,teitɪv] *adj.* **1** producing or causing irritation; irritating. **2** accompanying or caused by irritation: *an irritative fever.* **—'ir•ri,ta•tive•ness,** *n.*

ir•rupt [ɪ'rʌpt] *v.* **1** rush in suddenly or violently. **2** of an animal population, increase suddenly in numbers, as when the natural ecological balance has been disturbed. ⟨< L *irruptis*, pp. of *irrumpere* invade⟩

☛ *Hom.* ERUPT.

ir•rup•tion [ɪ'rʌpʃən] *n.* **1** a breaking or bursting in; violent invasion. **2** a sudden increase in an animal population. ⟨< L *irruptio, -onis* < *irrumpere* < *in-* in + *rumpere* break⟩

☛ *Hom.* ERUPTION.

ir•rup•tive [ɪ'rʌptɪv] *adj.* **1** bursting in; rushing in or upon anything. **2** having to to with irruption. **—ir'rup•tive•ly,** *adv.*

☛ *Hom.* ERUPTIVE.

is [ɪz] *v.* 3rd pers. sing., present indicative of BE.
as is, as it is now; in its present condition. ⟨OE⟩

i•sa•go•ge ['əisə,goudʒi] *n.* an introduction to a field of study. ⟨< L < Gk. *eisagoge, eisagein* to introduce (*eis* into + *agein* to lead)⟩ **—,i•sa'gog•ic** [,əisə'gɒdʒɪk], *adj.*

i•sa•gog•ics [,əisə'gɒdʒɪks] *n.* **1** introductory studies. **2** the branch of theology that deals with the history of the Bible.

is•al•lo•bar [əi'sælə,bɑr] *n. Meteorology.* a line on a weather map used to connect points of equal pressure changes.

ISBN International Standard Book Number.

Is•car•i•ot [ɪ'skæriət] *or* [ɪ'skɛriət] *n.* **1** the surname of Judas, the disciple who betrayed Jesus for thirty pieces of silver. **2** any traitor.

is•che•mia [ɪ'skimiə] *n. Pathology.* local anemia caused by obstruction of the blood supply. ⟨< Gk. *ischein* hold + *haima* blood⟩ **—is'che•mic,** *adj.*

is•chi•um ['ɪskiəm] *n., pl.* **-chi•a** [-kiə]. *Anatomy.* the lower back and side portion of the hipbone. See PELVIS for picture. ⟨< NL < Gk. *ischion*⟩

–ise *suffix.* variant of -IZE.

☛ *Usage.* See note at -IZE.

I•seult [ɪ'sult] *n. Medieval legend.* **1** an Irish princess, wife of King Mark of Cornwall. She was loved by Tristram. **2** the daughter of the king of Brittany, whom Tristram married after his love for the Irish Iseult was discovered. Also, **Isolde, Isolt.**

–ish *suffix.* **1** somewhat: *oldish, sweetish.* **2** resembling; like: *a childish person.* **3** like that of; having the characteristics of: *a childish idea.* **4** of or having to do with; belonging to: *British, Spanish, Turkish.* **5** tending to; inclined to: *bookish, thievish.* **6** near, but usually somewhat past: *fortyish.* ⟨OE *-isc*⟩

Ish•ma•el ['ɪʃmiəl] *or* ['ɪʃmeiəl] *n.* **1** in the Bible, a son of Abraham. Because of Sarah's jealousy, he was driven out into the wilderness. **2** any outcast; someone who is at odds with society.

Ish•ma•el•ite ['ɪʃmeiə,ləit] *n.* **1** a descendant of Ishmael. **2** an outcast.

i•sin•glass ['aɪzən,glæs] *or* ['aɪzɪŋ,glæs] *n.* **1** a kind of gelatin obtained from the air bladders of sturgeon, cod, and similar fishes, used for making glue, clarifying liquors, etc. **2** mica, especially when split into thin, semi-transparent sheets. ⟨alteration of MDu. *huysenblas* sturgeon bladder; influenced by *glass*⟩

I•sis ['əisɪs] *n. Egyptian mythology.* the goddess of fertility, represented as wearing on her head cow's horns enclosing a solar disk.

Is•lam [ɪs'lɑm], [ɪz'lɑm], *or* ['ɪsləm] *n.* **1** the religion of Muslims, including belief in Allah as the one God and following the teachings of Mohammed as the prophet of Allah. **2** Muslims as a group. **3** the civilization of Muslim peoples. **4** all the countries in which Islam is the main religion. ⟨Arabic *islām* submission (to God) < *aslama* he surrendered himself⟩

Is•lam•ic [ɪs'lɑmɪk], [ɪz'lɑmɪk], *or* [ɪs'læmɪk] *adj.* of or having to do with Islam; Muslim. **—Is'lam•ic•al•ly,** *adv.*

Is•lam•ism ['ɪslə,mɪzəm] *or* ['ɪzlə,mɪzəm] *n.* the faith or cause of Islam.

Is•lam•ite ['ɪslə,məit] *or* ['ɪzlə,məit] *n. or adj.* Muslim.

Is•lam•ize ['ɪslə,maɪz] *or* ['ɪzlə,maɪz] *v.* **-ized, -iz•ing.** bring under the influence of Islam. **—,Is•lam•i'za•tion,** *n.*

is•land ['aɪlənd] *n., v.* —*n.* **1** a body of land smaller than a continent and completely surrounded by water: *Cuba is a very large island.* **2** something resembling this. **3** a superstructure, especially of a battleship or aircraft carrier. **4 a** a piece of woodland surrounded by prairie. **b** an elevated piece of land surrounded by marshes, etc. **5** *Anatomy.* a group of cells different in structure or function from those around it.
—*v.* make into an island. ⟨OE *īgland* < *īg* island + *land* land; spelling influenced by *isle*⟩ **—'is•land,like,** *adj.*

is•land•er ['aɪləndər] *n.* a native or inhabitant of an island.

isle [aɪl] *n.* **1** a small island. **2** island. ⟨ME < OF < L *insula*⟩

☛ *Hom.* AISLE, I'LL.

is•let ['aɪlɪt] *n.* a little island. ⟨< earlier F *islette*, dim. of *isle* isle⟩

☛ *Hom.* EYELET.

islet of Langerhans *Anatomy.* any of several masses of endocrine cells in the pancreas that secrete insulin.

ism ['ɪzəm] *n. Informal.* a distinctive doctrine, theory, system, or practice. *Capitalism, socialism, communism,* and *fascism* are well-known isms. ⟨See -ISM⟩

–ism *suffix.* **1** an action; practice: *baptism, criticism.* **2** a doctrine; system; principle: *communism, socialism.* **3** a quality; characteristic; state; condition: *heroism, paganism.* **4** an illustration; case; instance: *colloquialism, witticism.* **5** an unhealthy condition caused by——: *alcoholism, morphinism.* ⟨< Gk. *-ismos, -isma*⟩

I.S.M. Imperial Service Medal.

Is•mae•li [ɪs'meili] *or* [ɪz'meili] *n.* a Muslim of the Shia sect. Also, **Ismaelian.**

is•n't ['ɪzənt] is not.

iso– *combining form.* **1** equal; alike: *isosceles, isometric, isothermal, isotope.* **2** *Chemistry.* isomeric. ⟨< Gk. *iso-* < *isos* equal⟩

ISO *Computer technology.* International Standards Organization.

I.S.O. Imperial Service Order.

i•so•ag•glu•ti•nin [,əisouə'glutənɪn] *n.* an isoantibody that causes red blood cells to clump together.
—,i•so•ag,glu•ti'na•tion, *n.*

i•so•an•ti•bo•dy [,əisou'æntɪ,bɒdi] *n. Biochemistry.* a rare antibody that reacts with isoantigens in certain individuals.

i•so•an•ti•gen [,əisou'æntɪdʒən] *n. Biochemistry.* a rare antigen found in only some members of a species.

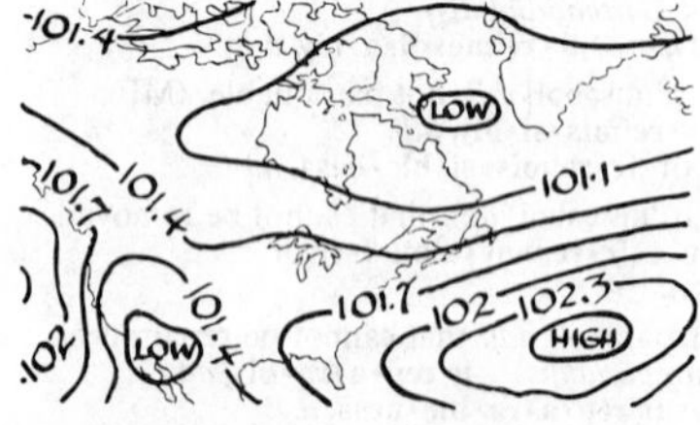

Isobars showing atmospheric pressures for an average July. The pressures are given in kilopascals.

i•so•bar ['əisə,bɑr] *n.* **1** *Meteorology.* a line on a weather map connecting places having the same average atmospheric pressure (after allowance for height above sea level). **2** *Physics, chemistry.* one of two or more kinds of atoms that have the same atomic weight, but in most cases different atomic numbers. ⟨< Gk. *isobarēs* < *isos* equal + *baros* weight⟩

i•so•bar•ic [,əisə'bærɪk] *or* [,əisə'bɛrɪk] *adj. Meteorology.* **1** of or pertaining to isobars. **2** having or indicating equal atmospheric pressure.

i•so•bath ['əisə,bæθ] *n.* a line on a map which connects points of equal depth below a body of water. ⟨< Gk. *isobathes* < *isos* equal + *bathes* depth⟩ **—,i•so'bath•ic,** *adj.*

i•so•bu•ty•lene [,əisou'bjutə,lin] *n. Chemistry.* a colourless liquid used in making butyl rubber in liquid or gaseous form. *Formula*: $(CH_3)_2C{:}CH_2$

i•so•car•box•a•zid [ˌəisoukɑrˈbɒksəzɪd] *n.* a drug used to relieve depression.

i•so•cheim [ˈəisəˌkaɪm] *n. Climatology.* a line on a map connecting areas of equal winter temperature. ⟨< *iso-* + Gk. *cheima* winter⟩

i•so•chro•mat•ic [ˌəisəkrouˈmætɪk] *adj.* **1** having the same colour. **2** uniform in colour.

i•so•chro•mo•some [ˌəisəˈkrouməˌsoum] *n. Genetics.* an abnormal chromosome in which one arm has been deleted and the other arm duplicated.

i•soch•ro•nal [əɪˈsɒkrənəl] *adj.* **1** equal or uniform in time. **2** characterized by motions or vibrations of equal duration. ⟨< Gk. *isochronos* < *isos* equal + *chronos* time⟩ **—iˈsoch•ro•nal•ly,** *adv.* **—iˈsoch•roˌnism,** *n.*

i•soch•ro•nous [əiˈsɒkrənəs] *adj.* isochronal. **—iˈsoch•ro•nous•ly,** *adv.*

i•soch•ro•ous [əiˈsɒkrouəs] *adj.* of uniform colour. ⟨< *iso-* + Gk. *chroos* colour⟩

i•so•cli•nal [ˌəisouˈklaɪnəl] *adj.* with the same inclines. ⟨*iso-* + *clinal* < Gk. *klinein* to slope + E *-al*[1]⟩

i•so•cline [ˈəisəˌklaɪn] *n. Geology.* a compressed fold of strata with parts on each side having the same incline. ⟨back formation from ISOCLINAL⟩

i•so•cy•a•nine [ˌəisouˈsaɪəˌnaɪn] *n. Chemistry.* one of a group of cyanine dyes.

i•so•di•a•met•ric [ˌəisəˌdaɪəˈmɛtrɪk] *adj.* having equal axes or diameters.

i•so•di•morph•ism [ˌəisoudaɪˈmɔrfɪzəm] *n.* isomorphism between crystalline forms of two dimorphic substances.

i•so•dy•nam•ic [ˌəisoudaɪˈnæmɪk] *adj.* of equal force.

i•so•el•ec•tron•ic [ˌəisouɪlɛkˈtrɒnɪk] *or* [ˌəɪsouˌilɛkˈtrɒnɪk] *adj.* of atoms, radicals, and ions, having the same number of electrons.

i•so•flu•rane [ˌəisouˈflurein] *n.* an anesthetic drug.

i•so•gam•ete [ˌəisəˈgæmit] *or* [ˌəisougəˈmit] *n. Biology.* a gamete that has the same morphology as the one it joins.

i•sog•a•my [əiˈsɒgəmi] *n. Biology.* the fusion of two gametes of similar morphology. **—iˈsog•a•mous,** *adj.*

i•sog•en•ous [əiˈsɒdʒənəs] *adj. Biology.* of the same or similar origin. **—iˈsog•e•ny,** *n.*

i•so•ge•o•therm [ˌəisəˈdʒiəˌθɜrm] *n.* a hypothetical line on the earth's surface, connecting areas with the same temperature.

i•so•gloss [ˈəisəˌglɒs] *n. Linguistic geography.* a line on a map to separate two adjacent areas in each of which different variants of a pronunciation, grammatical form, or word are current. **—ˌi•soˈglos•sal,** *adj.*

i•so•gon•ic [ˌəisəˈgɒnɪk] *adj.* **1** having equal angles; having to do with equal angles. **2** connecting points on the surface of the earth having the same magnetic deviation. ⟨< Gk. *isogōnios* < *isos* equal + *gōnia* angle⟩

i•so•gram [ˈəisəˌgræm] *n.* isoline.

i•so•hel [ˈəisəˌhɛl] *n. Meteorology.* a line on a map connecting areas of equal sunlight. ⟨*iso-* + Gk. *helios sun*⟩

i•so•hy•et [ˌəisəˈhaɪət] *n.* a line on a map or chart connecting places having the same average precipitation. ⟨*iso-* + Gk. *hyetos* rain⟩

i•so•hy•et•al [ˌəisouˈhaɪətəl] *adj.* of, having to do with, or being an isohyet.

i•so•late *v.* [ˈəisəˌleit]; *n.* [ˈəɪsəlɪt] *v.* **-lat•ed, -lat•ing;** *n.* *—v.* **1** place apart; separate from others; keep alone: *People with contagious diseases should be isolated.* **2** *Chemistry.* obtain (a substance) in a pure or uncombined form: *A chemist can isolate the oxygen from the hydrogen in water.*
—n. a person, thing, or group that is isolated or is the product of isolation. ⟨< *isolated* < F *isolé* < Ital. *isolato*, pp. of *isolare* < L *insulare* < *insula* island⟩

i•so•la•tion [ˌəisəˈleiʃən] *n.* **1** the act or process of isolating. **2** the condition or state of being isolated: *living in isolation.*
in isolation, without reference to related matter: *Considered in isolation, the whole thing assumes a less significant aspect.*
☛ *Syn.* **2.** See note at SOLITUDE.

i•so•la•tion•ism [ˌəisəˈleiʃəˌnɪzəm] *or, esp. U.S.,* [ˌɪsəˈleiʃəˌnɪzəm] *n.* the principles or practice of isolationists.

i•so•la•tion•ist [ˌəisəˈleiʃənɪst] *or, esp. U.S.,* [ˌɪsəˈleiʃənɪst] *n.* **1** one who objects to his or her country's participation in international affairs. **2** in Canada and the United States, a person who favours keeping his or her country out of European affairs, wars, etc.

I•sol•de [ɪˈsouldə] *or* [ɪˈsould]; *German,* [iˈzɔldə] *n.* Iseult.

i•so•line [ˈəisəˈlaɪn] *n. Meteorology, geology.* a line on a map or chart connecting places sharing some geographical or meteorological feature or phenomenon, such as degree of atmospheric pressure, amount of precipitation, etc.

i•sol•o•gous [əiˈsɒləgəs] *adj. Chemistry.* of organic compounds, not identical. ⟨< *iso-* + (*homo*)*logous*⟩

i•so•logue [ˈəisəˌlɒg] *n. Chemistry.* an isologous compound.

I•solt [ɪˈsoult] *n.* Iseult.

i•so•mag•net•ic [ˌəisoumægˈnɛtɪk] *adj.* of a line on a map, connecting areas with the same magnetic elements.

i•so•mer [ˈəisəmər] *n.* **1** *Chemistry.* an isomeric compound. **2** *Physics.* a nucleus of an atom which can be measured in an excited state. ⟨back formation from *isomeric*⟩

i•so•mer•ic [ˌəisəˈmɛrɪk] *adj.* **1** *Chemistry.* composed of the same elements in the same proportions by weight, and (in the usual, restricted sense of the term) having the same molecular weight, but differing in one or more properties because of the difference in arrangement of atoms. **2** *Physics.* of the nuclei of atoms, differing in energy and behaviour, but having the same atomic number and mass number. ⟨< Gk. *isomerēs* < *isos* equal + *meros* part⟩ **—ˌi•soˈmer•i•cal•ly,** *adv.*

i•som•er•ism [əiˈsɒməˌrɪzəm] *n.* **1** the existence of isomers. **2** the chemical and physical attributes of an isomer.

i•som•er•ous [əɪˈsɒmərəs] *adj.* **1** having an equal number of parts, markings, etc. **2** *Botany.* of a flower, having the same number of members in each whorl.

i•so•met•ric [ˌəɪsəˈmɛtrɪk] *adj.* having to do with equality of measure; having equality of measure. A crystal is isometric if it has three equal axes at right angles to one another. Also, **isometrical.** ⟨< Gk. *isometros* < *isos* equal + *metron* measure⟩ **—ˌi•soˈmet•ri•cal•ly,** *adv.*

isometric exercise exercise which involves alternate tensing and relaxing of chosen muscles. Isometric exercises are done without perceptible movement of body parts.

i•so•me•tro•pia [ˌəɪsouməˈtroupiə] *n. Ophthalmology.* a condition in which refraction is the same in both eyes.

i•som•et•ry [əiˈsɒmətri] *n.* **1** equality of measurement. **2** *Geography.* equality of elevation above sea level.

i•so•morph [ˈəisəˌmɔrf] *n.* **1** an isomorphic organism or substance. **2** *Linguistic geography.* an isogloss setting off different morphological features. ⟨back formation from *isomorphous*⟩

i•so•mor•phic [ˌəisəˈmɔrfɪk] *adj.* **1** *Biology.* having similar appearance or structure, but different ancestry. **2** isomorphous. ⟨*iso-* + Gk. *morphē* form⟩

i•so•morph•ism [ˌəisəˈmɔrfɪzəm] *n.* similarity in morphology.

i•so•mor•phous [ˌəisəˈmɔrfəs] *adj.* **1** *Chemistry.* crystallizing in the same form or related forms. The term *isomorphous* is used especially of substances of analogous chemical composition. **2** *Biology.* showing similarity of form in different organisms. ⟨*iso-* + Gk. *-morphos*, *morphe* form⟩

i•so•ni•a•zid [ˌəisouˈnaɪəzɪd] *n.* a drug chemically related to nicotinic acid, used in the treatment of tuberculosis. ⟨< *isoni(cotinic acid hydr)azid(e)*. See ISO-.⟩

i•son•o•my [əiˈsɒnəmi] *n.* equality of political rights. ⟨< Gk. *isonomia* < *isos* equal + *nomia* law⟩ **—i•soˈnom•ic** [ˌəisəˈnɒmɪk], *adj.* **—iˈson•o•mous,** *adj.*

i•so–oc•tane [ˌəisou ˈɒktein] *n. Chemistry.* a liquid used to measure the octane value of fuels.

i•so•pi•es•tic [ˌəisoupaɪˈɛstɪk] *adj.* isobaric. ⟨< *iso-* + Gk. *piestos* compressible < *piezein* press⟩

i•so•pleth [ˈəisəˌplɛθ] *n.* isoline. ⟨< *iso-* + Gk. *plethos* multitude, quantity⟩

i•so•pod [ˈəisəˌpɒd] *n.* any of an order (Isopoda) of crustaceans having a long, somewhat flat body made up of seven segments, each of which has a pair of legs. The sow bug is an isopod. ⟨< NL *Isopoda*, pl. < Gk. *isos* equal + *pous, podos* foot⟩ **—iˈsop•o•dan** [əiˈsɒpədən], *adj.* **—iˈsop•o•dous,** *adj.*

i•so•prene [ˈəisəˌprin] *n. Chemistry.* a volatile liquid hydrocarbon used in synthetic rubber and turpentine. *Formula*: C_5H_8 ⟨< *iso-* + *pr*(*opyl*) + *-ene*, as in *benzene,* etc.⟩

i•so•prop•a•mide [ˌəisou'prɒpəˌmaɪd] *n.* a drug used to treat peptic ulcer and anxiety.

i•so•pro•pa•nol [ˌəisə'proupəˌnɒl] *n.* a drug used to treat itching.

i•so•pro•pyl alcohol [ˌəisə'proupɪl] an antifreeze, also used in medicine as a cleanser. *Formula*: C_3H_7

i•so•pro•pyl me•prob•a•mate ['əisouˌproupɪl mə'prɒbəˌmeit] carisoprodol.

i•so•pro•ter•e•nol [ˌəɪsouprə'tɛrəˌnɒl] *n.* a drug used to treat bronchial asthma.

i•sos•ce•les [əi'sɒsəˌliz] *adj.* of a triangle, having two sides equal. See TRIANGLE for picture. ⟨< LL < Gk. *isoskelēs* < *isos* equal + *skelos* leg⟩

i•so•seis•mic [ˌəɪsə'saɪzmɪk] *adj.* having equal seismic intensities.

i•so•sor•bide di•ni•trate [ˌəisou'sɔrbaɪd daɪ'nəitreit] *n.* a drug used to treat certain heart conditions.

i•sos•ta•sy [əi'sɒstəsi] *n.* **1** a state in which each side bears equal pressure. **2** *Geology.* a state of balance in the earth's crust as it floats on the mantle. ⟨*iso-* + *-stasy* < Gk. *-stasia*. See STASIS.⟩ **—,i•so'stat•ic** [ˌəisə'stætɪk], *adj.*

i•so•sul•phan blue [ˌəisou'sʌlfən] a drug used as a diagnostic agent.

i•so•there ['əisəˌθir] *n. Climatology.* a line on a map connecting areas with the same summer temperature. ⟨*iso-* + Gk. *there-*, *theros* summer⟩

i•so•therm ['əɪsəˌθɜrm] *n. Meteorology.* a line on a weather map connecting places having the same average temperature. ⟨back formation from *isothermal*⟩

i•so•ther•mal [ˌəisə'θɜrməl] *adj.* **1** indicating equality of temperatures. **2** having to do with isotherms. **3** indicating change of pressure and volume at a constant temperature. ⟨*iso-* + Gk. *therme* heat⟩

i•so•tone ['əisəˌtoun] *n. Physics.* an atom sharing with another atom the same number of neutrons, but having a different atomic number.

i•so•ton•ic [ˌəisə'tɒnɪk] *adj.* **1** *Physical chemistry.* having the same osmotic pressure. Compare HYPERTONIC and HYPOTONIC. **2** *Physiology.* having to do with muscle contractions caused by minor, but constant, tension. **3** *Music.* characterized by equal tones. ⟨< Gk.⟩ **—,i•so'ton•i•cal•ly,** *adv.* **—,i•so•to'nic•i•ty,** *n.*

i•so•tope ['əisəˌtoup] *n. Chemistry.* any of two or more kinds of atom of a chemical element having the same number of protons and almost the same chemical properties, but having a different number of neutrons and different physical properties. Most elements have naturally occurring isotopes; the known isotopes of hydrogen are ordinary hydrogen (sometimes called light hydrogen), deuterium, and tritium. ⟨*iso-* + Gk. *topos* place⟩ **—,i•so'top•ic** [-'tɒpɪk], *adj.* **—i'sot•o•py** [əi'sɒtəpi], *n.*

i•so•tre•tin•oin [ˌəisoutrɛ'tɪnouɪn] *or* [-ˌnɔɪn] *n.* a drug used to treat acne.

i•so•trop•ic [ˌəisə'trɒpɪk] *adj. Physics.* having the same properties, such as elasticity or conduction, in all directions. ⟨*iso-* + Gk. *tropos* turn, way⟩ **—i'sot•ro•py** [əi'sɒtrəpi], *n.*

i•sot•ro•pous [əi'sɒtrəpəs] *adj.* isotropic.

i•sox•su•prine [ˌəi'sɒksəˌprin] *n.* a drug used to manage premature childbirth.

Is•ra•el ['ɪzriəl] *or* ['ɪzreiəl] *n.* **1** in the Bible, a name given to Jacob after he had wrestled with the angel. **2** the name given to his descendants; the Jews; the Hebrews. **3** the modern nation of Israel, a country in SW Asia. See LEBANON for map.

Is•rae•li [ɪz'reili] *n., pl.* **-lis;** *adj.* *—n.* a native or inhabitant of modern Israel.
—adj. of or having to do with modern Israel or its people.

Is•ra•el•ite ['ɪzriəˌləit] *or* ['ɪzreiəˌləit] *n., adj.* *—n.* a descendant of Jacob, especially a native or inhabitant of the ancient kingdom of Israel; a Jew; Hebrew.
—adj. of or having to do with ancient Israel or the Israelites.

Is•ra•el•it•ish ['ɪzriəˌləitɪʃ] *or* ['ɪzreiəˌləitɪʃ] *adj.* Jewish.

Is•sei ['ɪsˌsei] *or* ['isei] *n., pl.* **-sei.** a first-generation Japanese living in Canada or the United States. A second-generation Japanese living in Canada or the United States is a Nisei. ⟨< Japanese *is-sei* first generation < *ichi* one + *sei* generation⟩

ISSN International Standard Serial Number.

is•su•ance ['ɪʃuəns] *n.* an issuing; issue.

is•su•ant ['ɪʃuənt] *adj. Heraldry.* of a beast, in an erect position facing frontward.

is•sue ['ɪʃu] *v.* **-sued, -su•ing;** *n.* *—v.* **1** send out; put forth: *The government issues money and stamps.* **2** come out; go out; proceed: *Smoke issues from the chimney.* **3** be published. **4** put into public circulation; publish. **5** distribute; give out to a person or persons: *Heavy boots were issued to all the troops.* **6** send forth; discharge; emit: *The chimney issues smoke from the fireplace.* **7** emerge. **8** result or end (*in*): *The game issued in a tie.* **9** result (*from*). **10** be born; be descended; be derived.
—n. **1** something sent out; quantity (of bonds, stamps, copies of a magazine, etc.) sent out at one time. **2** a sending out; putting forth: *The next issue of new stamps will be on June 11.* **3** a coming forth; a flowing out; a discharge: *A nosebleed is an issue of blood from the nose.* **4** a way out; outlet; exit. **5** that which comes out. **6** a profit; proceeds. **7** the result; outcome: *The issue of the game remained uncertain until the last moment.* **8** a point to be debated; problem: *political issues.* **9** a child or children; offspring: *She died without issue.*
at issue, in question; to be considered or decided.
burning issue, a matter of great or topical importance.
face the issue, admit the facts and do what must be done.
join issue, take opposite sides in an argument.
make an issue, cause to become a point of debate or argument: *He made an issue of every minor point of procedure at the meeting.*
take issue, disagree: *I take issue with you on that point.* ⟨ME < OF *issue* < *eissir* go out < L *exire* < *ex-* out + *ire* go⟩
—'is•su•a•ble, *adj.* **—'is•su•er,** *n.*

☛ *Syn. v.* **2, 7. Issue,** EMERGE, EMANATE = come out. **Issue** = go or come out, usually through an opening, from a source or place where it has been confined, and often suggests flowing out in a moving mass like water: *Pus issued from the wound.* **Emerge** emphasizes coming into sight from a place where it has been hidden or covered up: *The train emerged from the tunnel.* **Emanate,** used only of things without physical body, means 'flow out from a source': *Heat emanates from fire.*

-ist *suffix.* **1** a person who does or makes: *theorist, tourist.* **2** one who knows about or has skill with: *biologist, flutist.* **3** one engaged in or busy with: *horticulturist, machinist.* **4** one who believes in; an adherent of: *abolitionist, idealist.* ⟨ME *-iste* < L *-ista* < Gk. *-istēs*⟩

isth•mi•an ['ɪsmiən] *adj., n.* *—adj.* **1** of or having to do with an isthmus. **2 Isthmian, a** of or having to do with the Isthmus of Panama. **b** of or having to do with the Isthmus of Corinth in Greece. The **Isthmian games** were national festivals of ancient Greece.
—n. a native or inhabitant of an isthmus.

isth•mus ['ɪsməs] *n., pl.* **-mus•es, -mi** [-maɪ] *or* [-mi]. **1** a narrow strip of land, having water on either side, connecting two large bodies of land: *The Isthmus of Panama joins North and South America.* **2** *Anatomy.* **a** a narrow structure connecting two larger structures. **b** a narrow cavity connecting two larger cavities. ⟨< L < Gk. *isthmos* neck of land⟩

is•tle ['ɪstli] *n.* a fibre of certain tropical American plants, used in making bags, carpets, cordage, nets, etc. ⟨< Mexican Sp. *ixtle* < Nahuatl *ixtli*⟩

it [ɪt] *pron., subj., or obj.* **it,** *poss.* **its,** *pl. subj.* **they,** *pl. obj.* **them,** *pl. poss.* **theirs;** *n., pl.* **it's.** *—pron.* **1** this or that one; a thing, idea, part, animal, or person already mentioned: *The plan is basically sound, but it is too complicated. The dog was whimpering; I think it was hurt. There's somebody at the door, but I don't know who it is.* **2** the subject of an impersonal verb, that does not refer to an agent: *It is snowing.* **3** a subject of a clause that anticipates the real, or logical, subject that comes later (often used to shift emphasis from the logical subject to another part of a sentence): *It is hard to believe that he is dead. It was here that the fossils were found.* **4** a direct object without specific force of meaning: *He lorded it over us. She beat it back to town as soon as she heard. I've had it, I'm leaving!* **5** *Informal.* predicatively, the final or ultimate thing: *That's it, I quit. She's it in country music.*
—n. **1** in certain children's games, the player who must catch, find, guess, etc. **2** something neither male nor female: *If it's not a he or a she, it must be an it.* ⟨OE *hit*⟩

it. italic(s).

ITA INITIAL TEACHING ALPHABET.

it•a•col•u•mite [ˌɪtə'kɒljəˌməit] *n.* a sandstone noted for its flexibility when in thin slabs. ⟨< *Itacolumi*, a mountain in Brazil where it is found⟩

ital. italic(s).

I•tal•ian [ɪ'tæljən] *n., adj.* *—n.* **1** a native or inhabitant of Italy. **2** a person of Italian descent. **3** the Romance language of Italy.
—adj. of or having to do with Italy, its people, or their language.
—I,tal•ian'esque, *adj.*

I•tal•ian•ate *adj.* [ɪ'tæljənɪt] *or* [ɪ'tæljə,neit]; *v.* [ɪ'tæljə,neit] *adj., v.* **-at•ed, -at•ing.** *—adj.* of Italian style, manner, or form. *—v.* Italianize. **—I,tal•ian'a•tion,** *n.*

I•tal•ian•ism [ɪ'tæljə,nɪzəm] *n.* **1** an Italian custom. **2** something regarded as Italian.

I•tal•ian•ize [ɪ'tæljə,naɪz] *v.* **-ized, -iz•ing.** make Italian. **—I,tal•ian•i'za•tion,** *n.*

Italian sonnet PETRARCHAN SONNET.

i•tal•ic [ɪ'tælɪk] *or* [əi'tælɪk] *adj., n. —adj.* **1** of or designating a style of type in which the letters and numerals slant to the right. It is usually used in printing foreign words, book titles, etc., or to indicate emphasis. *This sentence is in italic.* Compare ROMAN. **2 Italic,** of ancient Italy, its people, or their languages. **3 Italic,** a style of handwriting or calligraphy. **4 Italic,** of or having to do with a branch of the Indo-European language family that includes French, Italian, Portuguese, Romanian, Spanish, Latin, etc.
—n. **1** an italic type, letter, or number. **2** Usually, **italics,** *pl.* italic type or print. Example sentences in this dictionary are in italics. **3 Italic,** the Italic branch of languages. ⟨< L *Italicus* < *Italia* Italy < Gk.⟩
☛ *Usage.* **Italics.** In manuscript, both longhand and typewritten, italics are shown by single underlining.

i•tal•i•cize [ɪ'tælə,saɪz] *or* [əi'tælə,saɪz] *v.* **-cized, -ciz•ing. 1** print in type in which the letters slant to the right. *This sentence is italicized.* **2** underline with a single line to indicate italics. **3** use italics. **—i,tal•i•ci'za•tion,** *n.*

Italo– *combining form.* **1** Italian: *Italo-Canadian.* **2** Italian and ——: *the Italo-German alliance in World War II.*

It•al•y ['ɪtəli] *n.* a country in S Europe.

itch [ɪtʃ] *n., v. —n.* **1** a tickly, prickling feeling in the skin that makes one want to scratch. **2 the itch,** a contagious disease of the skin caused by a tiny mite, and accompanied by an itchy feeling. **3** a restless, uneasy feeling, longing, or desire for anything: *an itch to get away and explore.*
—v. **1** cause an itching feeling: *Mosquito bites itch.* **2** have an itching feeling. **3** have an uneasy desire: *He itched to know our secret.* ⟨ME *yicchen,* OE *gyccan*⟩

itch•y ['ɪtʃi] *adj.* **itch•i•er, itch•i•est.** itching; like the itch. **—'itch•i•ness,** *n.*

–ite[1] *suffix.* **1** a native or inhabitant of ——: *Israelite.* **2** a person associated with ——: *labourite.* **3** a mineral, a fossil, or a rock substance: *hematite.* **4** especially in the names of commercially manufactured products, resembling; derived from; having the property of ——: *dynamite, ebonite.* **5** a part of the body: *somite.* ⟨< F *-ite* (< L *-ita, ites*) or < L (< Gk. *-itēs*) or directly < Gk. *-itēs*⟩

–ite[2] *suffix.* a salt of ——: *phosphite, sulphite, nitrite.* ⟨< F *-ite,* arbitrarily created var. of *-ate*[2]⟩

i•tem ['əitəm] *n., adv. —n.* **1** a separate thing or article: *This list contains twelve items.* **2** a piece of news; a bit of information: *There were several interesting items in today's paper.*
—adv. also; likewise (in introducing each item of an enumeration). ⟨< L *item,* adv., likewise⟩
☛ *Syn. n.* **1. Item,** DETAIL, PARTICULAR = a separate thing that is part of a whole. **Item** applies to a separate thing included in a list, account, or total, or to an article listed: *An itemized account should list every item.* **Detail,** usually of information, applies to a separate thing that is part of something larger put together or done: *His report gave all the details.* **Particular,** never a concrete object, emphasizes the individuality of a detail, item, point, circumstance, etc.: *She carefully examined each particular in the report.*

i•tem•ize ['əitə,maɪz] *v.* **-ized, -iz•ing.** give each item of; list by items: *to itemize the cost of a trip.* **—,i•tem•i'za•tion,** *n.*

it•er•ate ['ɪtə,reit] *v.* **-at•ed, -at•ing.** repeat. ⟨< L *iterare* < *iterum* again⟩ **—,it•er'a•tion,** *n.*

it•er•a•tive ['ɪtərətɪv] *or* ['ɪtə,reitɪv] *adj.* **1** repeating; full of repetitions. **2** *Grammar.* frequentative.

Ithunn or **Ithun** ['iðun] *n. Norse mythology.* Idun, the wife of Bragi, and the goddess of youth and spring.

ith•y•phal•lic [,ɪθə'fælɪk] *adj.* **1** of or having to do with any of the prosodic metres used in hymns to Bacchus: *ithyphallic verse.* **2** obscene; lewd. ⟨< Gk. *ithyphallikos* < *ithyphallos* erect phallus < *ithys* straight + *phallos* phallus⟩

i•tin•er•an•cy [əɪ'tɪnərənsi] *or* [ɪ'tɪnərənsi] *n.* **1** a travelling from place to place. **2** a body of itinerant preachers or judges. **3** official work requiring much travel from place to place, or frequent changes of residence. Also, **itineracy.**

i•tin•er•ant [əi'tɪnərənt] *or* [ɪ'tɪnərənt] *adj., n. —adj.* travelling from place to place, especially on a regular route: *an itinerant sales rep.*
—n. a person who travels from place to place. ⟨< LL *itinerans, -antis,* ppr. of *itinerari* travel < L *iter, itineris* journey < *ire* go⟩ **—i'tin•er•ant•ly,** *adv.*

i•tin•er•ar•y [əi'tɪnə,rɛri] *or* [ɪ'tɪnə,rɛri] *n., pl.* **-ar•ies;** *adj. —n.* **1** the route or plan of a journey. **2** a travel diary. **3** a guidebook for travellers.
—adj. of travelling or routes of travel.

i•tin•er•ate [əi'tɪnə,reit] *or* [ɪ'tɪnə,reit] *v.* **-at•ed, -at•ing.** travel from place to place. ⟨< L *itinerari.* See ITINERANT.⟩

–itious *suffix.* of or having the nature of ——. *Example:* Fictitious *means* having the nature of fiction. ⟨< L *icius; itiosus*⟩

–itis *suffix.* **1** inflammation of or inflammatory disease of: *appendicitis, tonsillitis.* **2** *Informal.* an abnormal use or state: *telephonitis.* ⟨< Gk. *-itis,* fem. of *-itēs.* Cf. -ITE[1].⟩

–itol *Chemistry.* a suffix used in the names of alcohols having more than one hydroxyl: *inositol.* ⟨< *-ite*[2] + *-ol*⟩

it'll ['ɪtəl] it will.

ITO International Trade Organization.

its [ɪts] *adj., pron.* (*possessive form of* **it**). *—adj.* of, belonging to, or made or done by it or itself: *The dog hurt its paw. The report is important, and its delay now could cause problems.*
—pron. that which belongs to it: *A dog's kennel is its and its alone.*
☛ *Hom.* IT'S.
☛ *Usage.* See note at IT'S.

it's [ɪts] **1** it is: *It's my turn.* **2** it has: *It's been a beautiful day.*
☛ *Hom.* ITS.
☛ *Usage.* It's, ITS. The 's in it's means that something has been left out: *it* is or *it has.* Nothing is left out of *its.*

it•self [ɪt'sɛlf] *pron.* **1** a reflexive pronoun, the form of *it* used as an object when it refers to the same animal or thing as the subject: *The horse tripped and hurt itself.* **2** a form of *it* added for emphasis: *The land itself is worth more than they paid for the house.* **3** its usual self: *After repairs, the car is itself again.*

–ity *noun-forming suffix.* condition or quality of ——: *absurdity, activity, hostility, sincerity.* ⟨< F *-ité* < L *itas, -itatis*⟩

IU or **I.U.** international unit; international units.

IUD INTRAUTERINE DEVICE.

–ium *Chemistry.* a suffix used to form the name of an element or of a chemical group: *barium, ammonium.* ⟨< NL, L, neut. suffix⟩

IV intravenous.

I've [aɪv] I have.

–ive *suffix.* **1** of or having to do with ——: *interrogative, inductive.* **2** tending to; likely to ——: *active, appreciative, imitative.* ⟨< F *-ive* (fem. of *-if* < L *-ivus*) or directly < L *-ivus*⟩

i•vied ['aɪvid] *adj.* covered or overgrown with ivy.

i•vo•ry ['aɪvəri] *n., pl.* **-ries;** *adj. —n.* **1** a hard, white substance, a form of dentine, composing the tusks of elephants: *The trafficking of ivory is illegal.* **2** a similar substance forming teeth or tusks of certain other animals, such as the walrus. **3** a creamy white. **4 ivories,** *pl. Slang.* **a** piano keys. **b** dice. **c** billiard balls. **d** teeth.
—adj. **1** made of ivory. **2** of or like ivory. **3** creamy white. ⟨ME < AF *ivorie* < L *eboreus* of ivory < *ebur* ivory < Egyptian⟩ **—'i•vo•ry,like,** *adj.*

ivory black a fine-quality, deep black pigment made from ivory that has been burned.

Ivory Coast a republic in W Africa, formerly part of French West Africa. See SENEGAL for map.

ivory nut the hard, white, nutlike seed of the ivory palm (*Phytelephas macrocarpa*), formerly much used as a substitute for ivory.

ivory palm a short South American palm (*Phytelephas macrocarpa*) having featherlike leaves and fragrant flowers, whose seeds are called ivory nuts.

ivory tower a condition or attitude of withdrawal from the world of practical affairs into a world of ideas and dreams.

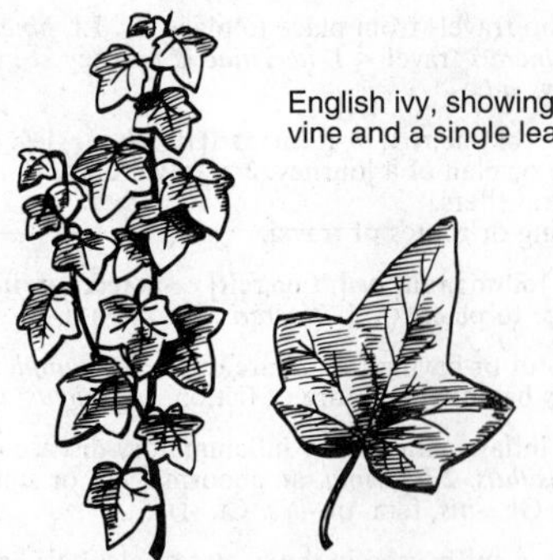
English ivy, showing the vine and a single leaf

i•vy ['aɪvi] *n., pl.* **i•vies. 1** any of a genus (*Hedera*) of Old World climbing or trailing plants of the ginseng family having woody stems and evergreen leaves, especially *H. helix*, a commonly grown climber. **2** any of various other climbing or creeping plants. ⟨OE *īfig*⟩ **–'i•vy,like,** *adj.*

i•vy–league ['aɪvi ,lig] *adj.* characteristic of or having to do with the Ivy League, the colleges belonging to it, their faculties, or their students.

Ivy League 1 a group of eight old and prestigious universities of eastern U.S., including Harvard, Yale, and Princeton. **2** the behaviour, customs, etc. associated with the students of these colleges. ⟨originally, an athletic association composed of the eight colleges, so named because many of the buildings were ivy-covered⟩

i•wis [ɪ'wɪs] *adv. Obsolete.* certainly; indeed. ⟨OE *gewis*⟩

Ix•i•on [ɪk'saɪən] *or* ['ɪksi,ɒn] *n. Greek legend.* the father of the Centaurs, who made love to Hera and was punished in Hades by being bound to a fiery wheel.

ix•tle ['ɪkstli] *or* ['ɪstli] *n.* istle.

I•yar or **Iy•yar** ['ijɑr] *or* [i'jɑr] *n.* in the Hebrew calendar, the second month of the ecclesiastical year and the eighth month of the civil year. ⟨< Hebrew⟩

–ize *suffix.* **1** make ——: *legalize, centralize.* **2** become ——: *crystallize, materialize.* **3** engage in; be busy with; use ——: *apologize, theorize.* **4** treat or combine with ——: *macadamize, oxidize.* Also, **-ise.** ⟨< F *iser* (< L *-izare*) or < L (< Gk. *-izein*) or directly < Gk. *-izein*⟩

☛ *Usage.* Many English verbs ending in the sound [aɪz] can be spelled with **-ize** or **-ise.** In Canadian usage **-ize** is preferred for words containing the Greek suffix, such as *apologize, civilize, visualize.* But **-ise** is usual in differently formed words derived from Old French, such as *advertise, exercise, supervise.* The spelling **-ize** is used in forming new words, such as *customize, slenderize.*

iz•zard ['ɪzərd] *n. Archaic or dialect.* the letter Z.
from A to izzard, from beginning to end; completely. ⟨< *ezed*, variant of *zed*, ? < F *et zed* and Z⟩

J j *J j*

j or **J** [dʒei] *n., pl.* **j's** or **J's. 1** the tenth letter of the English alphabet. **2** any speech sound represented by this letter. **3** a person or thing identified as *j*, especially the tenth in a series. **4** something shaped like the letter J. **5** anything, such as a printer's type, a lever, or a key on a keyboard, that produces a j or J. **6** *(adj.)* of or being a J or j.
☛ *Hom.* JAY.

J 1 January. **2** joule.

J or **J. 1** judge. **2** justice. **3** journal.

Ja. January.

JA or **J.A.** JUDGE ADVOCATE.

jab [dʒæb] *v.* **jabbed, jab•bing;** *n.* *—v.* **1** thrust (something pointed); poke roughly: *He jabbed his fork into the potato.* **2** pierce; stab: *I just jabbed myself with a pin.* **3** punch with a short, straight blow; especially, in boxing, hit with the arm extended straight from the shoulder.
—n. **1** a thrust with a pointed thing, a fist, etc.: *She gave him a jab with her elbow.* **2** *Boxing.* a blow in which the arm is extended straight from the shoulder. ⟨var. of *job.* v., ME *jobbe(n)*; probably imitative⟩

jab•ber ['dʒæbər] *v., n.* *—v.* talk very fast in a confused, senseless way; chatter.
—n. very fast, confused, or senseless talk; chatter. ⟨probably imitative⟩ **—'jab•ber•er,** *n.* **—'jab•ber•ing•ly,** *adv.*

ja•bi•ru ['dʒæbə,ru] *or* [,dʒæbə'ru] *n.* a large stork (*Jabiru mycteria*). ⟨< Pg. < Tupi-Guarani⟩

ja•bo•ran•di [,dʒæbə'rændi] *n.* **1** any shrub of the genus *Pilocarpus.* **2** the leaves of one species (*Pilocarpus jaborandi*), dried and used as a medication. ⟨< Pg. < Tupi-Guarani⟩

ja•bot [ʒæ'bou], ['ʒæbou], *or* ['dʒæbou] *n.* a ruffle or frill of lace or cloth, worn at the throat or down the front of a blouse, shirt, etc. ⟨< F *jabot*, originally, maw of a bird; akin to OF *gave* throat⟩

ja•ca•na [,ʒɑsə'nɑ] *or* ['ʒɑsə,nɑ] *n.* any of several tropical birds of the family Jacanidae, living in marshes. ⟨< Pg. *jaçaña* < Tupi-Guarani *jasaná*⟩

jac•a•ran•da [,dʒækə'rændə] *n.* **1** any of a genus (*Jacaranda*) of tropical American trees of the bignonia family, having showy blue or violet flowers and compound leaves. **2** the hard, fragrant wood of any of these trees. **3** any of several similar trees or their wood, such as several trees (genus *Machaerium*) of the pea family. ⟨< Pg. < Tupi-Guarani *yacarandá*⟩

ja•cinth ['dʒeisɪnθ] *or* ['dʒæsɪnθ] *n.* a reddish orange gem, a kind of zircon. ⟨ME < OF *jacinte* < L *hyacinthus* hyacinth < Gk. *hyakinthos*, a kind of flower. Doublet of HYACINTH.⟩

jack [dʒæk] *n., v.* *—n.* **1** any of various mechanical devices for raising a heavy object a short distance. **2** a man or boy; fellow. **3** Also, **Jack,** a sailor. **4** a playing card with a picture of a court page on it; knave. **5 jacks,** a game in which stone or metal pieces are tossed up and caught or picked up in various groupings between bounces of a small rubber ball (*used with a singular verb*). **6** one of the pieces used in this game. **7** *Lawn bowling.* a small ball for players to aim at. **8** a small flag used on a ship to show nationality or to serve as a signal. **9** a device to turn roasting meat. **10** a male donkey. **11** jack-rabbit. **12** an electrical device to receive a plug, as, a telephone or radio jack. **13** *Cdn.* jacklight. **14** *Cdn.* jackfish. **15** *Slang.* money: *Have you got any jack?*
every man jack, everyone.
—v. **1** raise by means of a jack (*often used with* **up**): *to jack up a car in order to change a tire.* **2** *Informal.* raise or increase the level or quality of (*usually used with* **up**): *to jack up prices.* **3** remind (someone) of his or her duty (*usually used with* **up**). **4** hunt or fish (*for*) using a jacklight, especially when it is illegal. ⟨ME *Jakke* < OF *Jaques*, a popular name for the French peasant < LL *Jacobus* Jacob⟩

jack•al ['dʒækəl] *n.* **1** any of several wild animals (genus *Canis*) of Asia, Africa, and SW Europe, closely related to the dog. Jackals hunt in packs at night and feed on small animals and carrion left by large animals. **2** a person who does drudgery for another. ⟨< Turkish *chakal* < Persian *shagal*⟩

jack•a•napes ['dʒækə,neips] *n.* **1** an insolent, conceited fellow. **2** a saucy or mischievous child. ⟨var. of ME *Jack Napes*, a name applied to William, Duke of Suffolk, whose badge was a clog and chain, such as was used for tame apes; probably originally the name for a tame ape⟩

jack•ass ['dʒæk,æs] *n.* **1** a male donkey. **2** a very stupid person; fool. **3** See LAUGHING JACKASS.

jack•boot ['dʒæk,but] *n.* a heavy, leather, military boot reaching up to or above the knee. **—'jack,boot•ed,** *adj.*

jack•daw ['dʒæk,dɒ] *n.* a common black bird (*Corvus monedula*) of Europe and Asia closely related to the common crow, but smaller.

jack•et ['dʒækɪt] *n., v.* *—n.* **1** an outer garment for the upper part of the body, having a front opening, sleeves, and, usually, a collar with lapels. **2** any of various kinds of outer covering such as the skin of a potato or the casing around a steampipe. **3** DUST JACKET. **4** a thin envelope for a phonograph record. **5** LIFE JACKET.
—v. put a jacket on; cover with a jacket. ⟨ME < OF *jaquette*, dim. of *jaque* peasant's tunic < *Jaques.* See JACK.⟩ **—'jack•et•ed,** *adj.* **—'jack•et•less,** *adj.* **—'jack•et,like,** *adj.*

jack•fish ['dʒæk,fɪʃ] *n., pl.* **-fish** or **-fish•es.** *Cdn.* a common game fish (*Esox lucius*) of the pike family having a long, slender body and large head, found throughout most of Canada; northern pike.

Jack Frost frost or freezing cold weather personified.

jack•fruit ['dʒæk,frut] *n.* **1** a tree (*Artocarpus heterophyllus*) native to tropical America. **2** the large, edible fruit of this tree.

jack•ham•mer ['dʒæk,hæmər] *n.* a hand-held tool for drilling or breaking up rock, concrete, etc., driven by compressed air.

jack herring *Cdn., B.C.* a small male herring used as bait in angling.

jack–in–the–box ['dʒæk ɪn ðə ,bɒks] *n., pl.* **-box•es. 1** a toy consisting of a box containing a figure that springs up when the lid is unfastened. **2** the figure in this box. Also, **jack-in-a-box.**

jack–in–the–pul•pit ['dʒæk ɪn ðə 'pʊlpɪt] *n.* any of several woodland plants (genus *Arisaema*) of the arum family, especially either of two North American species (*A. triphyllum* or *A. atrorubens*) found from Manitoba eastward and south to the Gulf of Mexico, having a greenish, leaflike spathe arching over a clublike spadix.

Jack Ketch [kɛtʃ] *Brit.* a public executioner; hangman. ⟨< John *Ketch*, an English executioner, died 1686⟩

jack–knife or **jack•knife** ['dʒæk ,nəif] *n., pl.* **-knives;** *v.* **-knifed, -knif•ing.** *—n.* **1** a large, strong pocketknife. **2** a kind of headfirst dive in which the diver touches the feet with the hands while keeping the legs straight, and then straightens out again before touching the water.
—v. **1** double up like a jack-knife. **2** perform a jack-knife dive. **3** of a tractor-trailer, a connected pair of railway cars, etc., double up at the connecting hitch when the brakes are applied suddenly or the vehicle is thrown off course.

jack•lad•der ['dʒæk,lædər] *n.* **1** *Nautical.* JACOB'S LADDER (def. 2). **2** *Cdn. Logging.* a slanting trough having an endless chain by means of which logs are moved from the water to the mill.

jack•light ['dʒæk,ləit] *n., v. Cdn.* *—n.* a light used for hunting or fishing at night. Fish or game are attracted by the jacklight so that they may be easily caught.
—v. hunt or fish *(for)* using a jacklight, especially when it is illegal; jack. **—'jack,light•er,** *n.*

jack•light•ing ['dʒæk,ləitɪŋ] *n. Cdn.* the act or practice, often illegal, of hunting or fishing with a jacklight.

jack mackerel a food fish (*Trachurus symmetricus*) resembling a mackerel, found off the Pacific coast of the U.S.

jack of all trades a person who can do many different kinds of work fairly well.

jack–o'–lan•tern [,dʒæk ə'læntərn] *or* ['dʒæk ə ,læntərn] *n.* **1** a pumpkin hollowed out and cut to look like a face, used as a lantern at Halloween. **2** WILL-O'-THE-WISP (def. 1).

jack pine 1 *Cdn.* a medium-tall pine (*Pinus banksiana*) found in central and E North America, having stiff, sharp, light green needles and cones that are often curved. The wood of the jack pine is used in general construction and for pulp. 2 any of several other species of pine, such as the lodgepole or ponderosa pine.

Jack pines

jack•pot ['dʒæk,pɒt] *n.* 1 a large fund or pool of money that is competed for regularly and that increases as contestants fail to win it. 2 any large gain. 3 *Poker.* the stakes that accumulate until some player wins with a pair of jacks or something better.
hit the jackpot, a win a jackpot. **b** have a stroke of very good luck.

jack–rab•bit ['dʒæk ,ræbɪt] *n. Cdn.* any of several large hares (genus *Lepus*) of W North America, having very long ears and long back legs. ⟨shortened from *jackass rabbit*, so called because of its long ears; 19c.⟩

jack•screw ['dʒæk,skru] *n. Cdn.* a kind of jack for lifting heavy masses, such as furs, short distances, operated by turning a screw.

jack•snipe ['dʒæk,snəip] *n.* a snipe (*Lymnocryptes minimus*) with a short bill, native to Europe and Asia.

jack•stay ['dʒæk,stei] *n. Nautical.* 1 a batten along a boom holding one edge of a sail. 2 a brace on racing vessels to strengthen the mast.

jack•stone ['dʒæk,stoun] *n.* 1 **jackstones,** the game of jacks (*used with a singular verb*). 2 one of the pieces used in this game.

jack•straw ['dʒæk,strɒ] *n.* 1 a straw, strip of wood, bone, etc. used in a game. 2 **jackstraws,** a game played with a set of these thrown down in a confused pile and picked up one at a time without moving any of the rest of the pile (*used with a singular verb*).

Jack Tar or **jack tar** a sailor.

Jac•o•be•an [,dʒækə'biən] *adj.* 1 of King James I of England (1566-1625). 2 of the early 17th century, especially the period of his reign, from 1603 to 1625. Jacobean architecture is late English Gothic with a large admixture of Italian forms. 3 any important person of this period. ⟨< NL *Jacobaeus* < LL *Jacobus* James⟩

Jac•o•bin ['dʒækəbɪn] *n.* 1 in France, a member of a radical political organization formed at Versailles in 1789, later spreading throughout France, and abolished in 1796. 2 an extreme radical in politics. 3 a Dominican friar. ⟨< F < Med.L *Jacobinus* of James < LL *Jacobus* James, from the Dominican convent near the Church of St. James of Compostella, where the Paris organization held its meetings⟩ **—,Jac•o'bin•ic,** *adj.* **—'Jac•o•bin,ize,** *v.* **—,Jac•o•bin•i'za•tion,** *n.*

Jac•o•bin•ism ['dʒækəbɪ,nɪzəm] *n.* 1 the principles of the French Jacobins. 2 extreme radicalism in politics.

Jac•o•bite ['dʒækə,bəit] *n.* in England, a supporter of James II (1633-1701) and his descendants in their claims to the throne after the Revolution in 1688. ⟨< LL *Jacobus* James⟩ **—,Jac•o'bit•ic** [,dʒækə'bɪtik], *adj.*

Jacob's ladder 1 any of a genus (*Polemonium*) of herbs of the phlox family found in most parts of the world, especially a widely cultivated European perennial (*P. caeruleum*) having blue or white flowers and pinnately compound leaves. 2 *Nautical.* a ladder with wooden or iron rungs supported by ropes or chains; jackladder. 3 *Cdn.* a wicker and pole swing to serve as a bridge across a chasm. ⟨from the ladder to heaven in the Bible, seen by Jacob in a dream⟩

ja•co•net ['dʒækə,nɛt] *n.* a light cotton cloth used for clothing and bandages. ⟨< Urdu *jagannathi,* after *Jagannath,* a town in India (now called Puri) where it was made⟩

jac•quard or **Jac•quard** [dʒə'kɑrd] *or* ['dʒækɑrd] *adj.* of or indicating a pattern or a fabric woven on a Jacquard loom.

Jacquard loom a loom that can produce a figured pattern in more elaborate designs in woven fabrics than the limited patterns obtainable from a standard loom. ⟨< Joseph *Jacquard* (1752-1834), the French weaver who invented it⟩

Jacque•rie [ʒɑk'ri] *n.* 1 a revolt of the peasants of N France against the nobles in 1358. 2 Also, **jacquerie,** any revolt of peasants. ⟨< F *Jacquerie* peasants < *Jacques.* See JACK.⟩

jac•ta•tion [dʒæk'teiʃən] *n.* boasting. ⟨< L *jactatio* bragging < *jactare* frequentative of *jacere* throw⟩

jac•ti•ta•tion [,dʒæktɪ'teiʃən] *n.* 1 jactation. 2 *Law.* a false claim that causes injury to another person. 3 restlessness in bed. ⟨< LL *jactitatio* < *jactitare* utter publicly⟩

jade¹ [dʒeid] *n., adj. —n.* 1 either of two hard minerals, nephrite or jadeite, occurring in a wide variety of colours, especially green and white. 2 a gem or ornament made from this mineral. 3 a medium green.
—adj. 1 made of jade: *a jade bracelet.* 2 medium green. ⟨< F < Sp. *(piedra de) ijada* (stone of) colic (jade being supposed to cure this), ult. < L *ilia* flanks⟩

jade² [dʒeid] *n., v.* **jad•ed, jad•ing.** *—n.* an inferior or worn-out horse.
—v. 1 wear out; tire; weary. 2 dull by continual use; surfeit; satiate. ⟨origin uncertain; cf. ON *jalda* mare⟩

jad•ed ['dʒeidɪd] *adj., v. —adj.* 1 worn out; tired; weary: *a jaded horse, a jaded appearance.* 2 dulled from continual use; surfeited; satiated: *a jaded appetite.*
—v. pt. and pp. of JADE². **—'jad•ed•ly,** *adv.* **—'jad•ed•ness,** *n.*

jade•ite ['dʒeid,əit] *n.* a mineral, a silicate of sodium-aluminum that is harder and more valuable than nephrite, the other variety of jade.

jae•ger ['jeigər] *n.* any of three species of gull-like sea birds (genus *Stercorarius*) of northern seas, having mainly dark brown plumage and elongated central tail feathers, and noted for their aggressiveness against smaller birds, such as terns, which they frighten into dropping or disgorging their food. The jaegers and the skua make up the family Stercorariidae. ⟨< G *Jäger,* literally, hunter⟩

Jaf•fa ['dʒæfə] *n.* a type of orange from Jaffa, a seaport of Israel.

jag¹ [dʒæg] *n., v.* **jagged, jag•ging.** *—n.* a sharp point sticking out; pointed projection.
—v. 1 make notches or indentations in. 2 cut or tear unevenly. ⟨< late ME *jagge* a cut⟩

jag² [dʒæg] *n.* 1 *Dialect.* a small load: *a jag of fish.* 2 *Slang.* a state of intoxication. 3 *Slang.* a period of uncontrolled indulgence or behaviour: *a crying jag.* ⟨origin uncertain⟩

jag•ged ['dʒægɪd] *adj.* with sharp points sticking out; unevenly cut or torn: *jagged rocks.* **—'jag•ged•ly,** *adv.* **—'jag•ged•ness,** *n.*

jag•gy ['dʒægi] *adj.* jagged.

jag•uar ['dʒægwɑr] *or* ['dʒægju,ɑr] *n.* a large wild animal (*Panthera onca*) of the cat family resembling the leopard but generally somewhat larger and having a typically tawny coat with black spots arranged in large rosettes with a spot in the centre. The jaguar was formerly common from Mexico south to central South America but is now greatly reduced in numbers and protected by law in most of the countries where it still exists. ⟨< Pg. < Tupi *jaguara*⟩

jag•ua•run•di [,dʒægwə'rʌndi] *n.* a small wild animal of the cat family (*Herpailurus yagouaroundi*), native to South America. ⟨< Pg. < Tupi⟩

Jah•veh or **Jah•ve** ['jɑvɛ] *or* [jɑ'vɛ] *n.* See YAHWEH.

jai a•lai ['haɪ 'laɪ], ['haɪ ə,laɪ], *or* [,haɪ ə'laɪ] a court game that is a variation of pelota, played by two or four players. ⟨< Sp. < Basque < *jai* celebration, game + *alai* merry⟩

jail [dʒeil] *n., v. —n.* 1 a prison, especially one for people awaiting trial or being punished for minor offences. 2 imprisonment.
break jail, escape from jail.
—v. put in jail; keep in jail. ⟨ME < OF *jaiole,* ult. < L *cavea* cage⟩ **—'jail•less,** *adj.* **—'jail-,like,** *adj.*

jail•bird ['dʒeil,bɜrd] *n. Slang.* 1 a prisoner in jail. 2 a person who has been in jail many times.

jail•break ['dʒeil,breik] *n. Informal.* an escape from prison.

jail•er or **jail•or** ['dʒeilər] *n.* 1 a keeper of a jail. 2 a person who keeps someone or something confined.

Jain [dʒaɪn] *or* [dʒein] *n., adj. —n.* a member or adherent of Jainism.
—adj. of or having to do with the Jains or their religion. ⟨< Hind. *Jaina* < *Jina* victorious⟩

Jain•ism ['dʒaɪnɪzəm] *or* ['dʒeinɪzəm] *n.* a religion of India founded about 500 B.C. and having Hindu and Buddhist elements. Its beliefs include non-violence, asceticism, and the transmigration of souls.

jal•ap ['dʒæləp] *n.* 1 a Mexican vine (*Exogonium purga*) of the morning-glory family having a turnip-shaped root that yields a resinous substance used as a laxative. **2** the dried root of this plant or the resinous powder prepared from it. **3** any of several similar or related plants or a resin obtained from them. ⟨< Sp. *jalapa* < *Jalapa*, a city in Mexico⟩

ja•la•pe•ño [,hɑlə'peinjou] *n.* a Mexican hot pepper. ⟨< Mexican Sp.⟩

ja•lop•y [dʒə'lɒpi] *n., pl.* **-lop•ies.** *Informal.* an old automobile in a poor state of repair: *Is she still driving that old jalopy?* ⟨origin uncertain⟩

jal•ou•sie ['ʒælʊ,zi] *or* ['dʒælə,si] *n.* a window blind or shutter made of horizontal slats of wood, metal, or glass, that can be adjusted to regulate the light or air entering a room. ⟨< F *jalousie*, literally, jealousy < *jaloux* jealous, from enabling one to see through the shutter without being seen⟩

jam[1] [dʒæm] *v.* **jammed, jam•ming;** *n.* —*v.* **1** press; squeeze; hold; stick: *The ship was jammed between two rocks.* **2** crush; bruise: *Her fingers were jammed in the door.* **3** push or thrust (something) hard into a place; shove: *to jam one more book into the bookcase.* **4** fill up; block up: *The river was jammed with logs.* **5** stick or cause to stick fast or get caught so as not to work properly: *The window has jammed.* **6** make unworkable: *The key broke off and jammed the lock.* **7** make (radio signals, etc.) unintelligible by sending out others of approximately the same frequency. **8** have a JAM SESSION.
jam on, *Informal.* apply hastily: *jam on the brakes.*
—*n.* **1** a mass of people or things crowded together so that they cannot move freely: *a traffic jam.* **2** jamming or being jammed. **3** *Informal.* a difficult or tight spot. ⟨? imitative⟩
☛ *Hom.* JAMB.

jam[2] [dʒæm] *n.* a preserve made by boiling fruit with sugar until thick. ⟨? special use of *jam[1]*⟩ **—'jam,like,** *adj.* **—'jam•my,** *adj.*
☛ *Hom.* JAMB.

Ja•mai•ca [dʒə'meikə] *n.* an island country in the West Indies. See HAITI for map.

Jamaica mignonette henna.

Ja•mai•can [dʒə'meikən] *n., adj.* —*n.* a native or inhabitant of Jamaica.
—*adj.* of or having to do with Jamaica.

Ja•mai•ca rum a dark, full-bodied rum made in Jamaica.

jamb [dʒæm] *n.* the upright piece forming the side of a doorway, window, fireplace, etc. See FRAME for picture. ⟨ME < OF *jambe*, originally, leg < LL *gamba* hock < Gk. *kampē* a bending⟩
☛ *Hom.* JAM.

jam•ba•la•ya [,dʒʌmbe'laɪə] *n.* a Creole dish consisting of rice, tomatoes, shrimps, and herbs. ⟨< Am.F (Louisiana) < Provençal *jambalaia*⟩

jam•beau ['dʒæmbou] *n., pl.* **-beaux** [-bouz]. a piece of armour for the leg below the knee; greave. ⟨< ME *jambe* leg⟩

jam•bo•ree [,dʒæmbə'ri] *n.* **1** *Informal.* a noisy party; lively entertainment. **2** a large rally or gathering of Scouts. ⟨coined from *jam[1]* after *corroboree, shivaree*⟩

jam–packed ['dʒæm 'pækt] *adj. Informal.* filled to capacity; packed tightly.

jam session an informal gathering of musicians, especially jazz musicians, at which they play improvisations.

Jan. January.

jan•gle ['dʒæŋgəl] *v.* **-gled, -gling;** *n.* —*v.* **1** sound harshly; make a loud, clashing noise. **2** cause to make a hard, clashing sound: *He jangled the bell.* **3** quarrel; dispute. **4** speak angrily. **5** make tense or strained; upset: *Their continual complaints jangled her nerves.*
—*n.* **1** a harsh sound; clashing noise or ring: *The jangle of the telephone woke him up.* **2** a quarrel; dispute. ⟨ME < OF *jangler*⟩ **—'jan•gler,** *n.* **—'jan•gly,** *adj.*

Jan•is•sar•y or **jan•is•sar•y** ['dʒænə,sɛri] *or* ['dʒænə,zɛri] *n., pl.* **-sar•ies.** See JANIZARY.

jan•i•tor ['dʒænətər] *n.* a person hired to take care of and clean a building, offices, etc.; caretaker. ⟨< L *janitor* doorkeeper < *janus* arched passageway⟩ **—jan•i'tor•ial,** *adj.* **—'jan•i•tor,ship,** *n.*

Jan•i•zar•y or **jan•i•zar•y** ['dʒænə,zɛri] *n., pl.* **-zar•ies.** **1** in Turkey, a soldier in the Sultan's guard. Janizaries formed the crack fighting force of the Turkish army from the 14th century until 1826. **2** any Turkish soldier. Also, **Janissary** or **janissary.** ⟨< F *janissaire* < Ital. *giannizzero* < Turkish *yeñicheri* < *yeñi* new + *cheri* soldiery⟩

jan•na ['dʒɑnə] *n. Islam.* heaven or paradise. ⟨< Arabic⟩

jan•na•nam ['dʒɑnə,næm] *n. Islam.* hell. ⟨< Arabic⟩

Jan•sen•ism ['dʒænsə,nɪzəm] *n.* the doctrine of a Dutch theologian, Cornelis Jansen (1585-1638), who held that the human will is not free to do good and that salvation is limited to God's chosen few.

Jan•sen•ist ['dʒænsənɪst] *n.* a believer in, or follower of, Jansenism.

Jan•u•ar•y ['dʒænju,ɛri] *n., pl.* **-ar•ies.** the first month of the year. It has 31 days. ⟨< L *Januarius* < *Janus* Janus⟩

January thaw *Cdn.* a spell of mild weather occurring annually in January and causing the snow to melt.

Ja•nus ['dʒeinəs] *n.* **1** *Roman mythology.* the god of gates and doors, and of beginnings and endings, represented as having two faces, one looking forward and the other looking backward. **2** a satellite of Saturn. ⟨< L, special use of *janus* doorway, archway⟩

Ja•nus–faced ['dʒeinəs ,feist] *adj.* two-faced; double-dealing; deceitful.

ja•pan [dʒə'pæn] *n., v.* **-panned, -pan•ning.** —*n.* **1** a hard, glossy varnish. Black japan is used on wood or metal. **2** articles varnished and decorated in the Japanese manner. **3** a liquid used to make paint dry faster.
—*v.* put japan on. ⟨< *Japan*⟩ **—ja'pan•ner,** *n.*

Ja•pan [dʒə'pæn] *n.* an island country off the east coast of Asia.

Japan clover a perennial bush clover (*Lespedeza striata*) used for pasture and fodder.

Japan current or **Japanese current** a current of warm water in the Pacific Ocean, flowing north from the Philippine Sea, past SE Japan, and then into the N Pacific Ocean, thought to affect the weather on the Pacific coast.

Jap•a•nese [,dʒæpə'niz] *n., pl.* **-nese;** *adj.* —*n.* **1** a native or inhabitant of Japan. **2** a person of Japanese descent. **3** the language of the Japanese.
—*adj.* of or having to do with Japan, its people, or their language.

Japanese andromeda a flowering evergreen shrub (*Pieris japonica*) native to Japan.

Japanese beetle a small, green and brown beetle (*Popillia japonica*) that eats fruits, leaves, and grasses. It was accidentally brought from Japan to North America, where it has done much damage to crops.

Japanese iris a variety of iris (*Iris kaempferi*) native to Japan but widely grown for its showy flowers.

Japanese ivy BOSTON IVY.

Japanese lamprey a fish (*Entosphenus japonicus*) found in the Yukon and Mackenzie Rivers.

Japanese persimmon **1** an Asian tree (*Diospyros kaki*) having orange-coloured fruit. **2** the large, edible fruit of this tree.

Japanese quince japonica.

Japanese spurge any plant of the genus *Pachysandra*, used as a ground cover in the U.S.

Jap•a•nesque [,dʒæpə'nɛsk] *adj.* in the Japanese style.

Japan wax a solid wax obtained from the berries of plants of the genus *Rhus*, used in soaps and candles.

jape [dʒeip] *n., v.* **japed, jap•ing.** —*n. or v.* joke or jest. ⟨ME; origin uncertain⟩ **—'jap•er,** *n.* **—'jap•er•y,** *n.* **—'jap•ing•ly,** *adv.*

ja•pon•i•ca [dʒə'pɒnəkə] *n.* **1** any of several flowering quinces, especially *Chaenomeles japonica* or *C. speciosa.* Also called **Japanese quince. 2** camellia (*Camellia japonica*). ⟨< NL *japonica*, originally fem. adj., Japanese⟩

jar[1] [dʒɑr] *n.* **1** a deep container made of glass, earthenware, etc. with a wide mouth and a removable lid. **2** the amount that it holds. **3** a jar and its contents. ⟨< F *jarre*, ult. < Arabic *jarrah*⟩

jar[2] [dʒɑr] *v.* **jarred, jar•ring;** *n.* —*v.* **1** cause to shake or rattle; vibrate: *The aftershock jarred my desk so that I had trouble writing.* **2** make a harsh, discordant noise. **3** have a harsh, unpleasant effect on; shock: *The children's playful screams jarred his nerves.* **4** clash; be in conflict: *Our opinions jar.*
—*n.* **1** a shake; rattle. **2** a harsh, discordant noise. **3** a harsh, unpleasant effect; shock. **4** a clash; quarrel. ⟨probably imitative⟩ **—'jar•ring•ly,** *adv.*

jar[3] [dʒɑr] *n. Archaic.* a turn; a turning.
on the jar, ajar; slightly open. ⟨OE *cierr*⟩

jar•di•niere [,dʒɑrdə'nir]; *French,* [ʒaʀdi'njɛʀ] *n.* **1** an ornamental pot or stand for flowers or plants. **2** various cooked vegetables as a garnish for a main dish. ⟨< F *jardinière* < *jardin* garden⟩

jar•gon¹ ['dʒɑrgən] *n.* **1** language that fails to communicate because it is full of long or fancy words, uses more words than necessary, and contains lengthy, awkward sentences. **2** a form of speech made up of features from two or more languages, used for communication between peoples whose native languages differ: *the Chinook jargon. Pidgin English is a jargon.* **3** the language of a particular group, profession, etc.: *the jargon of sailors.* **4** *Archaic.* any speech or language that is strange to one and therefore seems meaningless. **5** meaningless talk or chatter; gibberish. ⟨ME < OF; probably ult. imitative⟩

☛ *Usage.* Definitions 2 and 3 carry no slur or criticism but are technical senses of **jargon** as used by linguists. They should not be confused with definition 1, which does suggest poor expression and muddled thinking.

jar•gon² ['dʒɑrgɒn] *or* ['dʒɑrgən] *n.* a variety of zircon with a smoky colour or no colour at all. Also, **jargoon** [dʒɑr'gun]. ⟨< F < Ital. *giargone* < Persian *zargūn* gold-coloured⟩

jarl [jɑrl] *n.* in ancient Scandinavia, a chief or nobleman. ⟨< ON. Related to EARL.⟩ **—'jarl•dom,** *n.*

Jarls•berg ['jɑrlz,bɜrg] *n.* a mild Norwegian cheese with holes in it.

ja•ro•vize ['jɑrə,vaɪz] *v.* **-vized, -viz•ing.** vernalize. ⟨< Russian *yarovoe* spring grain (< *yara* spring) + -IZE⟩

jas•mine ['dʒæzmɪn] *or* ['dʒæsmɪn] *n.* **1** any of a large genus (*Jasminum*) of tropical and subtropical shrubs and vines of the olive family, especially any of a number of species cultivated for their highly fragrant flowers, such as *J. officinalis*, whose usually white or yellow flowers are used in perfumery. **2** any of various other plants having fragrant flowers, such as the frangipani, often called **red jasmine,** or **yellow jasmine** (*Gelsemium sempervirens*). **3** a brilliant yellow. ⟨< F *jasmin* < Arabic < Persian *yasmin*⟩

Ja•son ['dʒeisən] *n. Greek mythology.* the Greek hero who led the expedition of the Argonauts and won the Golden Fleece.

jas•per ['dʒæspər] *n.* **1** an opaque variety of quartz, usually red, yellow, or brown. **2** a gem made from this stone. ⟨ME < OF *jaspre* < L < Gk. *iaspis* < Semitic⟩

jasper ware a white stoneware.

Jat [dʒɑt] *n.* a member of an Indo-European people living mainly in NW India.

ja•to ['dʒeitou] *n. Aeronautics.* a unit consisting of one or more jet engines, used to provide auxiliary propulsion for speeding up the takeoff of an aircraft. ⟨acronym of < *j*et-*a*ssisted *t*ake*o*ff⟩

jaun•dice ['dʒɒndɪs] *n., v.* **-diced, -dic•ing.** *—n.* **1** *Pathology.* a disease of the liver, characterized by yellowness of the skin, eyes, and body fluids, and disturbed vision. **2** an increase of bile pigments in the blood, characteristic of several diseases. **3** a cynical or sour mental outlook, due to envy, jealousy, etc.
—v. **1** cause jaundice in. **2** prejudice the mind and judgment of by envy, discontent, etc.; sour the temper of. ⟨ME < OF *jaunisse* < *jaune* yellow < L *galbinus* greenish yellow⟩

jaunt [dʒɒnt] *n., v. —n.* a short pleasure trip or excursion.
—v. take a short pleasure trip or excursion. ⟨origin uncertain⟩

jaunting car a light, two-wheeled, one-horse cart having two seats back to back, formerly used in Ireland.

jaun•ty ['dʒɒnti] *adj.* **-ti•er, -ti•est. 1** easy and lively; sprightly; carefree: *The happy boy walked with jaunty steps.* **2** smart; stylish: *She wore a jaunty little hat.* ⟨formerly *janty* < F *gentil* noble, gentle < L *gentilis.* Doublet of GENTEEL, GENTILE, GENTLE.⟩ **—'jaun•ti•ly,** *adv.* **—'jaun•ti•ness,** *n.*

Ja•va ['dʒɑvə] *or* ['dʒævə] *n.* **1** an island of Indonesia, in SE Asia. **2** a kind of coffee obtained from Java. **3** *Slang.* coffee.

Java man a very early form of human being inferred from fossil remains found in Java.

Jav•a•nese [,dʒævə'niz] *n., pl.* **-nese;** *adj. —n.* **1** a native or inhabitant of Java. **2** the Austronesian language of the Javanese. *—adj.* of or having to do with Java, its people, or their language.

Java sparrow a small grey bird (*Padda orzivora*) native to Asia.

jave•lin ['dʒævlɪn] *n.* **1** a light spear thrown by hand. **2** a wooden or metal spear, thrown for distance in track and field contests. **3** a field event in which such a spear is thrown. ⟨< F *javeline*⟩

Ja•vel water [dʒə'vɛl] *or* [ʒə'vɛl] a solution of sodium or potassium hypochlorite, used as a bleach and disinfectant. ⟨*Javel* < F *Javelle,* a former town now included in Paris⟩

jaw [dʒɒ] *n., v. —n.* **1** either of the two bones or sets of bones that hold the teeth and together form the framework of the mouth in most vertebrates. The lower jaw is usually movable; the upper jaw is usually fixed. **2** the lower part of the face, especially the lower jaw: *She has a square jaw.* **3 jaws,** *pl.* **a** the mouth with its jawbones and teeth. **b** a narrow entrance to a valley, mountain pass, channel, etc. **c** the parts in a tool or machine that grip and hold: *the jaws of a vise.* **4** *Slang.* talk; gossip.
—v. Slang. **1** talk; gossip. **2** find fault with; scold. ⟨? related to CHEW; influenced by F *joue* cheek⟩ **—'jaw•less,** *adj.*

jaw•bone ['dʒɒ,boun] *n., v.* **-boned, -bon•ing.** *—n.* **1** the bone of the lower jaw. **2** the bone of the upper jaw.
—v. talk vehemently or manipulatively to.

jaw•break•er ['dʒɒ,breikər] *n.* **1** *Informal.* a big, hard piece of candy. **2** *Informal.* a word that is hard to pronounce. **3** a machine for crushing ore. **—'jaw,break•ing,** *adj.* **—'jaw,break•ing•ly,** *adv.*

Jaws of Life *Trademark.* a large pneumatic tool used to pry accident victims out of wrecked vehicles.

jay [dʒei] *n.* **1** any of various birds of the same family as the crows, noted for being noisy and aggressive, many species being brightly coloured and having a crest. The bluejay and Canada jay are common Canadian birds. The common Eurasian jay (*Garrulus glandarius*) has mainly pinkish brown plumage with mainly blue and black wings and a black-and-white crest. **2** *Informal.* an impertinent or foolish chatterer. **3** *Informal.* a simple-minded or gullible person. ⟨ME < OF < LL *gaius gaia,* special use of L *Gaius,* a man's name⟩

☛ *Hom.* J.

jay•bird ['dʒei,bɜrd] *n.* JAY (def. 1).

Jay•cee ['dʒei'si] *n.* a member of a Junior Chamber of Commerce. ⟨from *j*unior *c*hamber⟩

jay•walk ['dʒei,wɒk] *v.* walk across a street at a place other than a regular crossing or without paying attention to traffic. ⟨< *jay* a stupid person + *walk*⟩ **—'jay,walk•er,** *n.*

jazz [dʒæz] *n., v. —n.* **1** a style of music characterized by strong, often complex rhythms, improvisation of a basic melody, and unusual features of musical tone, such as long-drawn wavering or wailing sounds. Jazz originated among black musicians in New Orleans in the rhythmic traditions of African music. **2** (*adj.*) of, having to do with, or playing jazz: *a jazz band.* **3** any popular dance music having a pronounced rhythm. **4** *Slang.* anything considered tiresome, affected, trite, etc.: *I'm tired of all that jazz about how hard he works.*
—v. **1** play or arrange (music) as jazz. **2** *Slang.* make more exciting, lively, or decorative (*usually used with* **up**): *to jazz up a dull colour scheme.* ⟨origin uncertain⟩ **—'jazz•er,** *n.*

jazz•man ['dʒæz,mæn] *n.* a musician who plays jazz.

jaz•zy ['dʒæzi] *adj.* **jazz•i•er, jazz•i•est. 1** having the qualities of jazz. **2** *Informal.* loud, flashy, or unrestrained: *jazzy clothes.* **—'jazz•i•ly,** *adv.* **—'jazz•i•ness,** *n.*

J.C. 1 Jesus Christ. **2** Julius Caesar.

J.C.C. Junior Chamber of Commerce.

jct. or **jctn.** junction.

Je. June.

jeal•ous ['dʒɛləs] *adj.* **1** fearful that a person one loves may love or prefer someone else. One may be jealous of the person loved or of the rival. **2** full of envy; envious (*often used with* **of**): *He is jealous of John or of John's marks.* **3** requiring complete loyalty or faithfulness. **4** watchful in keeping or guarding something; careful: *A democracy is jealous of its freedom. The dog was a jealous guardian of the child.* ⟨ME < OF *gelos* < LL *zelosus* < L *zelus* zeal < Gk. *zēlos.* Related to ZEAL.⟩ **—'jeal•ous•ly,** *adv.* **—'jeal•ous•ness,** *n.*

jeal•ous•y ['dʒɛləsi] *n., pl.* **-ous•ies.** a jealous condition or feeling.

jean [dʒin] *n.* **1 jeans,** *pl.* pants made of denim, usually blue, or a similar strong cloth. **2** a strong, twilled cotton cloth used for work clothes, etc. ⟨probably < F *Gênes* Genoa, Italy⟩

☛ *Hom.* GENE.

Jean Baptiste [ʒɑ̃ba'tist] *Cdn. Informal.* a French Canadian. ⟨< Saint *Jean Baptiste* St. John the Baptist, regarded as the patron saint of French Canada⟩

Jeep [dʒip] *n. Trademark.* a small four-wheel drive vehicle able to travel over relatively rugged terrain, similar to an all-purpose military vehicle.

jeep•ers ['dʒipərz] *interj.* an exclamation of surprise. ⟨< *Jesus*⟩

jeep•ney ['dʒipni] *n.* a public vehicle in the Philippines built like a Jeep. ⟨< *Jeep* + (*jit*)*ney*⟩

jeer [dʒir] *v., n.* —*v.* make fun rudely or unkindly; mock; scoff (*at*).
—*n.* a jeering remark; rude, sarcastic comment. ⟨origin uncertain⟩ **—'jeer•er,** *n.* **—'jeer•ing•ly,** *adv.*
☛ *Syn. v.* See note at SCOFF[1].

Je•ho•vah [dʒɪ'houvə] *n.* God. ⟨modern vocalized representation of Hebrew *Yahweh* (originally written without vowels as JHVH), meaning 'I am', 'the self-existent'⟩

Jehovah's Witnesses a Christian sect founded by Charles T. Russell in Pennsylvania in the 1870s. Some of their tenets are that personal religious conviction is beyond civil authority and that the end of the world is near.

je•hu ['dʒihu] *or* ['dʒeihu] *n. Informal.* a fast driver. ⟨< *Jehu* (842-815 B.C.), King of Israel, with reference to his furious driving⟩

je•june [dʒɪ'dʒun] *adj.* **1** lacking nourishing qualities. **2** flat and uninteresting. **3** naïve; unsophisticated. ⟨< L *jejunus,* originally, hungry⟩ **—je'june•ly,** *adv.* **—je'june•ness,** *n.* **—je'ju•ni•ty,** *n.*

je•ju•num [dʒɪ'dʒunəm] *n. Anatomy.* the middle portion of the small intestine, between the duodenum and the ileum. See ALIMENTARY CANAL for picture. ⟨< NL < L *jejunum,* neut., empty⟩ **—je'ju•nal,** *adj.*

Jek•yll ['dʒɛkəl] *n.* **1 Dr. Jekyll,** the chief character in R.L. Stevenson's story *Dr. Jekyll and Mr. Hyde.* He discovered a drug that changed him into a brutal person (Mr. Hyde) and another that changed him back to himself. **2 Jekyll and Hyde,** a dual personality, part good or pleasant and part evil or unpleasant.

jell [dʒɛl] *v.* **1** set; make or become jelly. **2** *Informal.* take definite form; become fixed: *Our plans have jelled.* ⟨< *jelly*⟩

jel•lied ['dʒɛlid] *adj., v.* —*adj.* **1** turned into jelly; having the consistency of jelly. **2** spread with jelly. **3** prepared in or covered with jelly: *jellied eels.*
—*v.* pt. and pp. of JELLY.

jel•li•fy ['dʒɛlɪ,faɪ] *v.* **-fied, -fy•ing.** make into a jelly. **—,jel•li•fi'ca•tion,** *n.*

jel•ly ['dʒɛli] *n., pl.* **-lies;** *v.* **-lied, -ly•ing.** —*n.* **1** a food that is liquid when hot but rather firm when cold. Jelly can be made by boiling fruit juice and sugar together, or by cooking bones and meat in water, or by using some stiffening preparation like gelatin. **2** a jellylike substance: *petroleum jelly.*
—*v.* **1** become jelly; turn into jelly. **2** prepare in or cover with jelly. ⟨ME < OF *gelée,* originally, frost < L *gelata,* originally fem. pp. of *gelare* congeal⟩ **—'jel•ly,like,** *adj.*

jel•ly•bean ['dʒɛli,bin] *n.* a small, bean-shaped candy, made of jellied sugar coated in different colours.

jel•ly•fish ['dʒɛli,fɪʃ] *n., pl.* **-fish** or **-fishes. 1** any of a class (Scyphozoa) of invertebrate marine animals having a jellylike, translucent, umbrella-shaped body with a tube-shaped mouth hanging from the bottom and tentacles around the margin of the body that are armed with stinging cells. **2** a free-swimming hydrozoan. **3** *Informal.* a person of weak will or character.

jel•ly•roll ['dʒɛli,roul] *n.* a thin layer of sponge cake spread with jelly and rolled up while still warm.

je ne sais quoi [ʒənsɛ'kwa] *French.* an indefinable something (literally, *I don't know what*).

jen•net ['dʒɛnɪt] *n.* **1** a breed of small Spanish horses. **2** a horse of this breed. **3** a female donkey. Also, **genet.** ⟨< F *genet* < Sp. *jinete* mounted soldier < Arabic *Zenāta,* a Berber tribe noted for its cavalry⟩

jen•ny ['dʒɛni] *n., pl.* **-nies. 1** SPINNING JENNY. **2** the female of certain animals and birds. ⟨originally a proper name, dim. of *Jane,* fem. of *John*⟩

jeop•ard ['dʒɛpərd] *v. Rare.* jeopardize.

jeop•ard•ize ['dʒɛpər,daɪz] *v.* **-ized, -iz•ing.** put in danger; risk; imperil: *Soldiers jeopardize their lives in war.*

jeop•ard•y ['dʒɛpərdi] *n., pl.* **-dies. 1** risk; danger; peril: *The firefighters put their lives in jeopardy when they entered the burning building.* **2** *Law.* the peril of the defendant when put on trial for a crime. ⟨ME < OF *jeu parti* an even or divided game, ult. < L *jocus* play + *pars, partis* part⟩

je•qui•ri•ty [dʒə'kwirəti] *n., pl.* **-ties.** a vine (*Abrus precatorius*) of tropical Asia, having poisonous seeds used as beads. ⟨< Pg. *jequiriti* < Tupi-Guarani *jekiriti*⟩

jer•bo•a [dʒər'bouə] *n.* any of several small, nocturnal, mouselike, jumping rodents (family Dipodidae) of Asia and N Africa having very long hind legs, a long tail, and large ears. ⟨< NL < Arabic *yarbu'*⟩

jer•e•mi•ad [,dʒɛrə'maɪəd] *n.* a mournful complaint; lamentation. ⟨< F *jérémiade* < *Jérémie* Jeremiah, the reputed author of *Lamentations* in the Bible⟩

Jer•e•mi•ah [,dʒɛrə'maɪə] *n.* a Hebrew prophet of the 7th and 6th centuries B.C. who denounced and lamented the evils of his time, as recorded in the Book of Jeremiah in the Bible. **2** a pessimistic person who sees mainly evil around him and predicts a terrible future. Also called **Jeremias.**

jerk[1] [dʒɜrk] *n., v.* —*n.* **1** a sudden, sharp pull, twist, or start. **2** an involuntary pull or twist of the muscles; twitch. **3** *Slang.* an unpleasant or stupid person.
—*v.* **1** pull or twist suddenly. **2** throw with a movement that stops suddenly. **3** move with jerks: *The old wagon jerked along.* **4** speak or say abruptly. **5** twitch. ⟨probably imitative⟩
☛ *Syn. v.* **1.** See note at PULL.

jerk[2] [dʒɜrk] *v.* preserve (meat) by cutting it into long thin slices and drying it in the sun. The First Nations people and American Indians taught the early settlers in North America how to jerk beef. ⟨< Sp. *charquear* < *charquí* jerked meat < Quechua⟩

jer•kin ['dʒɜrkɪn] *n.* a short, close-fitting, open outer vest. Leather jerkins were worn by men in the 16th and 17th centuries. ⟨origin uncertain⟩

jerk•wa•ter ['dʒɜrk,wɒtər] *adj., n. Informal.* —*adj.* **1** remote and rustic: *a jerkwater town.* **2** trifling or insignificant.
—*n. Informal.* a train on a branch railway. ⟨from the fact that trains on branch lines had to get their water supply by 'jerking' it in buckets from streams, etc. 19c.⟩

jerk•y[1] ['dʒɜrki] *adj.* **jerk•i•er, jerk•i•est.** making or causing jerks; stopping and starting suddenly. **—'jerk•i•ly,** *adv.* **—'jerk•i•ness,** *n.*

jerk•y[2] ['dʒɜrki] *n. Cdn.* strips of dried beef. ⟨< Sp. *charquí.* See JERK[2].⟩

jer•o•bo•am [,dʒɛrə'bouəm] *n.* **1** a wine bottle holding 3.64 L. **2** this amount. **3** any large container or bottle for alcoholic beverages. **4** its contents. ⟨< *Jeroboam,* a king of ancient Israel⟩

jer•ry–build ['dʒɛri ,bɪld] *v.* **-built, -building.** build cheaply. **—'jer•ry,build•er,** *n.*

jer•ry–can ['dʒɛri ,kæn] *n. Slang.* an 18 L gasoline container of rectangular shape. It was devised by the Germans during World War II. ⟨< *jerry,* short for *jeroboam,* + *can*[2]⟩

jer•sey ['dʒɜrzi] *n., pl.* **-seys. 1** a soft, somewhat elastic, machine-knitted fabric made with a plain stitch like that used in hand knitting. It may be of wool, cotton, silk, or synthetics and is used for undergarments and for dresses, blouses, etc. **2** a close-fitting, knitted garment for the upper body. **3 Jersey,** a breed of small, fawn-coloured dairy cattle that give very rich milk. ⟨< *Jersey,* one of the Channel Islands. The knitted fabric and garments are named for the woollen sweaters traditionally worn by the fishers of Jersey. Jersey cattle originally came from this island.⟩ **—'jer•seyed,** *adj.*

Jerusalem artichoke [dʒə'rusələm] **1** a perennial North American herb (*Helianthus tuberosus*) of the composite family closely related to the sunflower and widely cultivated for its edible tubers. **2** the tuber of this plant, which is cooked and eaten as a vegetable, especially in Europe. ⟨< *Jerusalem,* as an alteration of Ital. *girasole* sunflower⟩

Jerusalem cherry a shrub (*Solanum pseudo-capsicum*) with ornamental red berries, native to South America.

Jerusalem oak a plant (*Chenopodium botrys*) of North America, having leaves that smell like turpentine.

Jerusalem thorn a tropical American tree (*Parkinsonia aculeata*) with yellow flowers.

jess [dʒɛs] *n., v.* —*n.* a short strap fastened around a falcon's leg and attached to the leash.
—*v.* put the jesses on (a falcon). ⟨ME < OF *ges,* ult. < L *jacere* to throw⟩

jes•sa•mine ['dʒɛsəmɪn] *n.* jasmine.

jest [dʒɛst] *v., n.* —*v.* **1** act or speak playfully, teasingly, or amusingly; joke. **2** make fun of; laugh at.
—*n.* **1** a joke. **2** the act of making fun or teasing; mockery. **3** something intended to be mocked or laughed at.
in jest, in fun; not seriously. ⟨< OF *geste,* originally, story, exploit < L *gesta,* neut. pl., exploits < *gestus,* pp. of *gerere* accomplish⟩ **—'jest•ful,** *adj.* **—'jest•ing•ly,** *adv.*
☛ *Syn. v.* **1.** See note at JOKE.

jest•er [ˈdʒɛstər] *n.* a person who jests. In the Middle Ages kings often had jesters to amuse them.

Je•su [ˈdʒeizu] *or* [ˈdʒizu], [ˈdʒeisu], [ˈdʒisu], *or* [ˈjeizu] *n. Poetic.* Jesus.

Jes•u•it [ˈdʒɛzjuɪt] *or* [ˈdʒɛʒuɪt] *n. Roman Catholic Church.* a member of a religious order called the Society of Jesus, founded by Saint Ignatius Loyola in 1534. Some of the first explorers of America were Jesuits. ⟨< NL *Jesuita* < LL *Jesus* Jesus⟩

Jes•u•it•ic [ˌdʒɛzjuˈɪtɪk] *or* [ˌdʒɛʒuˈɪtɪk] *adj.* of or having to do with the Jesuits.

Jes•u•it•ism [ˈdʒɛzjuəˌtɪzəm] *or* [ˈdʒɛʒuəˌtɪzəm] *n.* **1** the religious order of the Jesuits, or their principles and practices.

Je•sus [ˈdʒizəs] *or* [ˈdʒizəz] *n.* Jesus of Nazareth (? 4 B.C. - A.D. ?29), who is regarded by Christians as the incarnate Son of God and the true Messiah. Brought up as a Jew and trained as a carpenter, he became a teacher of note, whose teachings incurred the wrath of the Roman and Jewish authorities and ultimately led to his death by crucifixion. His disciples' account of his birth, life, teachings, death, and resurrection constitute the four Gospels of the New Testament.

Jesus Christ Jesus, especially when regarded as the Messiah. ⟨See CHRIST⟩

jet[1] [dʒɛt] *n., v.* **-jet•ted, -jet•ting.** *—n.* **1** a stream of gas or liquid, sent with force, especially from a small opening: *A fountain sends up a jet of water.* **2** a spout or nozzle for sending out a jet. **3** a jet-propelled aircraft. **4** JET ENGINE. **5** (*adj.*) of, having to do with, or involving the use of jet-propelled aircraft or jet propulsion: *the jet age, jet travel.*
—v. **1** gush out; shoot forth in a jet or forceful stream. **2** travel or carry by jet aircraft. ⟨< F *jet* < *jeter* throw⟩

jet[2] [dʒɛt] *n.* **1** a hard, black variety of lignite that can be carved and polished to a high sheen. Jet is used for making buttons, beads, etc. **2** deep, glossy black: *Her hair is the colour of jet.* ⟨ME < OF *jaiet* < L < Gk. *gagatēs* < *Gagas*, a town in Lycia, Asia Minor⟩

jet–black [ˈdʒɛt ˈblæk] *adj.* deep black.

je•té [ʒəˈtei] *n., pl.* **-tés** [-ˈteiz] *Ballet.* a leap from one foot to the other in a forward or backward direction. ⟨F, literally, thrown, pp. of *jeter* to throw⟩

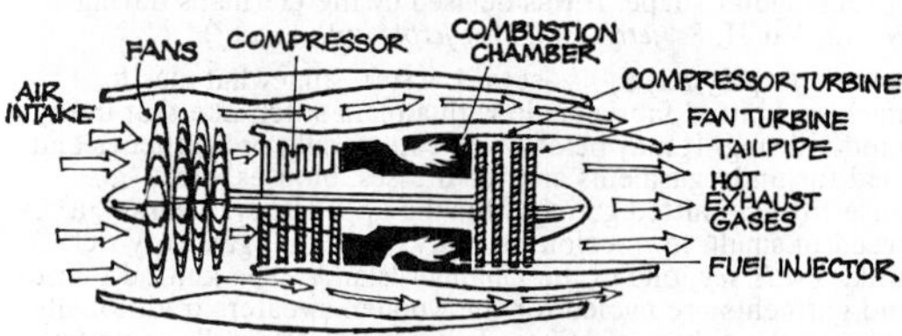

Jet engine: a turbofan

jet engine an engine that produces motion by jet propulsion, especially an aircraft engine that moves the aircraft forward by the reaction to the discharge of heated gases from the combustion chamber through one or more exhaust nozzles at the rear. Two types of jet engine are the turbojet and the ramjet.

jet lag *n.* a delayed effect of fatigue and sleepiness after a long flight in an aircraft, especially when several time zones have been crossed.

jet•lin•er [ˈdʒɛtˌlaɪnər] *n.* a large jet aircraft used for carrying passengers on commercial flights.

jet plane an aircraft that is driven by one or more jet engines.

jet•port [ˈdʒɛtˌpɔrt] *n.* an airport for jet planes.

jet–prop [ˈdʒɛt ˈprɒp] *adj., n. —adj.* equipped with turboprop engines.
—n. an aircraft thus equipped.

jet–pro•pelled [ˈdʒɛt prəˈpɛld] *adj.* **1** driven by jet propulsion. **2** moving very fast and energetically.

jet propulsion propulsion in a given direction by a jet of air, gas, etc. forced in the opposite direction.

jet•sam [ˈdʒɛtsəm] *n.* **1** goods thrown overboard to lighten a ship in distress. **2** such goods washed ashore. **3** anything tossed aside as useless. Compare FLOTSAM. ⟨var. of *jetson*, a var. of *jettison.* Doublet of JETTISON.⟩

jet set an international social set composed of wealthy people who frequent fashionable cities and resorts in various countries, travelling by jet plane. **—ˈjet,set•ter,** *n.*

jet–ski [ˈdʒɛt ˌski] *n., v.* **-skied, -ski•ing.** *—n.* a motorized craft for a driver and one, two, or sometimes three persons, with a seat, handlebars, and a ski on the bottom, for skimming over water.
—v. ride on such a craft. **—ˈjet-ˌski•er,** *n.*

jet stream **1** a current of air travelling at very high speed (often more than 350 km/h) from west to east at high altitudes (13 km to 20 km). Jet streams are often used by airplane pilots to gain extra speed when travelling in an easterly direction. **2** the stream of exhaust from a rocket engine.

jet•ti•son [ˈdʒɛtəsən] *or* [ˈdʒɛtəzən] *v., n. —v.* **1** throw (goods) overboard to lighten a ship, aircraft, etc. in distress. **2** throw away; discard.
—n. **1** the act of throwing goods overboard to lighten a ship, aircraft, etc. in distress. **2** the goods thrown overboard; jetsam. ⟨< OF *getaison* < L *jactatio, -onis* < *jactare* toss < *jacere* throw. Doublet of JETSAM.⟩

jet•ty[1] [ˈdʒɛti] *n., pl.* **-ties. 1** a structure built out into the water to protect a harbour or to control the current or tide; breakwater. **2** a landing place; pier or dock. ⟨< OF *jetée* (something) thrown out < *jeter* throw, ult. < L *jacere*⟩

jet•ty[2] [ˈdʒɛti] *adj.* **1** made of jet. **2** jet-coloured. **—ˈjet•ti•ness,** *n.*

Jew [dʒu] *n.* **1** a person descended from the ancient Israelites, who originally settled in Palestine and who now live in Israel and many other countries; Hebrew. **2** a person whose religion is Judaism. ⟨ME < OF *giu, jueu* < L *Judaeus* < Gk. *Ioudaios* < Hebrew *y'hudi* belonging to the tribe of Judah⟩

jew•el [ˈdʒuəl] *n., v.* **-elled** or **-eled, -el•ling** or **-el•ing.** *—n.* **1** a precious stone; gem. **2** a valuable ornament to be worn, set with precious stones. **3** a person or thing that is very precious. **4** a gem or other piece of hard material used as a bearing in a watch.
—v. set or adorn with jewels or with things like jewels: *to jewel a bracelet.* ⟨ME < AF *juel* trinket, plaything < Med.L *jocalis* < L *jocus* joke, game⟩ **—ˈjew•el-ˌlike,** *adj.*

jew•el•ler [ˈdʒuələr] *n.* a person who makes, sells, or repairs jewels, jewelled ornaments, watches, etc. Also, **jeweler.**

jew•el•ler•y or **jew•el•ry** [ˈdʒuəlri] *n.* jewels and ornaments set with gems.

jew•el•weed [ˈdʒuəlˌwid] *n.* any of several species of wild impatiens having yellow or orange flowers; touch-me-not.

jew•fish [ˈdʒuˌfɪʃ] *n., pl.* **-fish** or **-fish•es.** any of various large, dark-coloured fishes (family Serranidae) of warm seas, such as *Epinephelus itajara*, of the Atlantic coast of tropical America. ⟨origin uncertain⟩

Jew•ish [ˈdʒuɪʃ] *adj., n. —adj.* **1** of, belonging to, or characteristic of the Jews: *Jewish customs.* **2** *Informal.* Yiddish.
—n. Informal. Yiddish. **—ˈJew•ish•ness,** *n.*

Jewish calendar the Hebrew calendar, which dates the Creation at 3761 B.C. and divides the year into 12 months of 29 or 30 days each, allowing for an extra month of 29 days every second or third year. The ecclesiastical year begins in March or April, and the civil year in September or October.

Jew•ry [ˈdʒuri] *n., pl.* **-ries.** Jews as a group; the Jewish people.

jews'–harp or **jew's–harp** [ˈdʒuz ˌhɑrp] *n.* a simple musical instrument, held between the teeth and played by striking with a finger the free end of a piece of metal. ⟨< *jaws'-harp*⟩

Jez•e•bel [ˈdʒɛzəˌbɛl] *or* [ˈdʒɛzəbəl] *n.* any shameless, immoral woman. Also, **jezebel.** ⟨in the Bible, the depraved and wicked wife of Ahab, King of Israel⟩

J.H.S. JUNIOR HIGH SCHOOL.

jib[1] [dʒɪb] *n. Nautical.* on a ship or boat, a triangular sail in front of the foremast. See SCHOONER for picture.
cut of (one's) jib, *Informal.* one's outward appearance. ⟨origin uncertain⟩

jib[2] [dʒɪb] *v.* **jibbed, jib•bing.** JIBE[1].

jib[3] [dʒɪb] *v.* **jibbed, jib•bing;** *n. —v.* move sideways or backward instead of forward; refuse to go ahead.
jib at, *Informal.* refuse to face or deal with: *The horse jibbed at the high fence. Management have jibbed at the strikers' latest proposals.*
—n. a horse or other animal that jibs. ⟨origin uncertain⟩ **—ˈjib•ber,** *n.*

jib[4] [dʒɪb] *n.* the projecting arm of a crane or derrick. ⟨probably < *gibbet*⟩

jib boom *Nautical.* a spar extending out from a ship's bowsprit.

jibe[1] [dʒaɪb] *v.* **jibed, jib•ing.** *Nautical.* **1** of a sail, shift from one side of a ship to the other when sailing before the wind. **2** change the course of (a ship) so that the sails shift in this way. Also, **jib.** ⟨< Du. *gijben*, var. of *gijpen*⟩
☛ *Hom.* GYBE.

jibe[2] [dʒaɪb] *v.* **jibed, jib•ing;** *n.* See GIBE. **—'jib•er,** *n.* **—'jib•ing•ly,** *adv.*
☛ *Hom.* GYBE.

jibe[3] [dʒaɪb] *v.* **jibed, jib•ing.** *Informal.* be in harmony; agree. Also, **jive.** ⟨origin uncertain⟩
☛ *Hom.* GYBE.

jif•fy ['dʒɪfi] *n., pl.* **jif•fies.** *Informal.* a very short time; moment: *I'll be there in a jiffy.* ⟨origin uncertain⟩

jig[1] [dʒɪg] *n., v.* **jigged, jig•ging.** *—n.* **1** any of several lively dances, often in 3/4 time. **2** the music for a jig.
the jig is up, *Slang.* it's all over; there's no more chance: *She knew the jig was up the moment she heard the wail of police sirens.*
in jig time, quickly; rapidly: *I'll do it in jig time.*
—v. **1** dance a jig. **2** move jerkily; jerk up and down or back and forth. **3** sing or play (music) as a jig or in the style of a jig. Also, **gigue.** ⟨< OF *giguer* dance < *gigue* fiddle < Gmc.⟩ **—'jig,like,** *adj.*

jig[2] [dʒɪg] *n., v.* **jigged, jig•ging.** *—n.* **1** a fishing lure made of one or more fish-hooks, weighted with a bright metal or having a spoon-shaped piece of bone attached, for bobbing or drawing through the water. **2** any of various mechanical contrivances or devices; especially, a guide in using a drill, file, etc.
—v. fish with a jig. ⟨origin uncertain⟩

jig•ger[1] ['dʒɪgər] *n.* **1** *Nautical.* **a** a small set of ropes and pulleys used on a ship. **b** a small sail. **c** JIGGER MAST. **2** any of various machines that operate with a jerky, up-and-down or back-and-forth motion. **3** *Informal.* some device, article, or part that one cannot name more precisely; gadget; contraption. **4** a jig used in fishing. **5** *Cdn.* a device used for setting a gill net under the ice on lakes and rivers. **6 a** a small glass used for measuring liquor in preparing drinks, usually holding about 43 mL. **b** the amount that a jigger can hold. **c** a jigger and its contents. **7** *Cdn.* a small, flat car used by work crews, etc. on a railway, driven by a handle that is pumped up and down or by a gas motor. ⟨< *jig*[2]⟩

jig•ger[2] ['dʒɪgər] *n.* **1** a small flea; chigoe. **2** chigger. ⟨alteration of *chigoe*⟩

jigger mast *Nautical.* a mast in the stern of a ship.

jig•ger•y–pok•er•y ['dʒɪgəri 'poukəri] *n., pl.* **-ies.** *Slang.* humbug; fraud; bunk.

jig•gle ['dʒɪgəl] *v.* **-gled, -gling;** *n.* *—v.* shake or jerk slightly. *—n.* a slight shake; light jerk. ⟨< *jig*[1]⟩ **—'jig•gly,** *adj.*

jig•saw ['dʒɪg,sɒ] *n.* a saw with a narrow blade mounted in a frame and worked with an up-and-down motion, used to cut curves or irregular lines.

jigsaw puzzle a picture cut into irregular pieces that can be fitted together again.

ji•had [dʒɪ'hɑd] *n. Islam.* **1** the duty to strive against the enemies of Islam. **2** holy war; any crusade against rival beliefs. ⟨< Arabic *jihād* struggle, strife⟩

jil•lion ['dʒɪljən] *n., pl.* **-dies.** *Informal.* a non-existent number meaning a large quantity.

jilt [dʒɪlt] *v., n.* *—v.* cast off (a lover or sweetheart) after giving encouragement.
—n. a person who jilts a lover. ⟨origin uncertain⟩ **—'jilt•er,** *n.*

jim–dan•dy ['dʒɪm 'dændi] *adj., n., pl.* **-dies.** *Informal. —adj.* excellent; great: *Everything is jim-dandy.*
—n. an excellent person or thing.

jim•jams ['dʒɪm,dʒæmz] *n.pl. Slang.* **1** DELIRIUM TREMENS. **2** jitters; a creepy, uneasy feeling. ⟨coined word⟩

jim•my ['dʒɪmi] *n., pl.* **-mies;** *v.* **-mied, -my•ing.** *—n.* a short crowbar used especially by burglars to force windows, doors, etc. *—v.* force (open) with or as if with a jimmy: *to jimmy a lock.* ⟨apparently a special use of *Jimmy*, familiar form of *James*⟩

jim•son•weed ['dʒɪmsən,wid] *n.* a tall, coarse, poisonous annual plant (*Datura stramonium*) of the nightshade family having white or purplish, trumpet-shaped flowers and bad-smelling leaves. It is found throughout much of the northern hemisphere. ⟨*jimson*, alteration of *Jamestown*, Va.⟩

ji•na ['dʒɪnə] *n. Jainism.* one who has attained an eternal state of bliss.

jin•gle ['dʒɪŋgəl] *n., v.* **-gled, -gling.** *—n.* **1** a sound like that of little bells, or of coins or keys striking together. **2** a verse or song that repeats sounds or has a catchy rhythm: *She writes advertising jingles for radio and television.*
—v. **1** make a jingling sound: *The sleigh bells jingle as we ride.* **2** cause to jingle: *He jingled the coins in his pocket.* **3** contain many simple rhymes and repetitions: *jingling Mother Goose rhymes.* ⟨imitative⟩ **—'jing•ler,** *n.*

jin•gly ['dʒɪŋgli] *adj.* like a jingle.

jin•go ['dʒɪŋgou] *n., pl.* **-goes. 1** a person who favours an aggressive foreign policy that might lead to war with other nations; chauvinist. **2** (*adjl.*) of jingoes or characterized by jingoism. ⟨< *by Jingo*, a phrase in the refrain of a music-hall song, which became the 'theme song' of Disraeli's supporters in 1878 < *jingo*, a magician's term; origin uncertain⟩

jin•go•ism ['dʒɪŋgou,ɪzəm] *n.* the attitude, policy, or practices of jingoes; chauvinism. **—'jin•go•ist,** *n., adj.*

jin•go•is•tic ['dʒɪŋgou'ɪstɪk] *adj.* of jingoes or like that of jingoes. **—jin•go'is•ti•cal•ly,** *adv.*

jin•ker [,dʒɪŋkər] *n. Cdn. Newfoundland.* **1** an imaginary creature to whom bad luck is attributed; gremlin. **2** a person blamed for bad luck; Jonah. ⟨origin uncertain⟩

jinn [dʒɪn] *n.* pl. of JINNI (*often used as a singular*). Also, **djinn.** ⟨< Arabic *jinn*, pl. of *jinni*⟩

jin•ni or **jin•nee** [dʒɪ'ni] *or* ['dʒɪni] *n., pl.* **jinn.** *Muslim mythology.* a spirit that can appear in human or animal form and do good or harm to people. Also, **djinni.** ⟨< Arabic *jinnī* demon⟩

jin•rik•i•sha or **jin•rick•sha** [dʒɪn'rɪkʃɒ] *or* [dʒɪn'rɪkʃə] *n.* rickshaw. ⟨< Japanese *jinrikisha* < *jin* man + *riki* power + *sha* vehicle⟩

jinx [dʒɪŋks] *n., v. Slang. —n.* a person or thing that is believed to bring bad luck: *He must be a jinx; we've lost every game since he joined the team.*
—v. bring bad luck to. ⟨< L *iynx*, bird used in magic < Gk.⟩

jit•ney ['dʒɪtni] *n., pl.* **-neys.** *Slang.* **1** an automobile or horse-drawn trap that carries passengers for a small fare. It usually travels along a regular route but will take passengers wherever they want to go. **2** *Rare.* a five-cent piece; nickel. ⟨origin uncertain⟩

jit•ter ['dʒɪtər] *v. Informal.* be nervous; act or speak nervously. ⟨< ? var. of E dial. *chitter* shiver, tremble, var. of *chatter*⟩

jit•ter•bug ['dʒɪtər,bʌg] *n., v.* **-bugged, -bug•ging.** *Informal.* *—n.* **1** a person who is enthusiastic about swing music and excited by it to lively dance movements and gestures. **2** a frenzied dance with lively movement.
—v. dance in such a way. ⟨< *jitter*, v. (See JITTERS) + *bug*⟩

jit•ters ['dʒɪtərz] *n.pl.* **the jitters.** *Slang.* extreme nervousness.

jit•ter•y ['dʒɪtəri] *adj. Informal.* nervous. **—'jit•ter•i•ness,** *n.*

jiu•jit•su or **jiu•jut•su** [dʒu'dʒɪtsu] See JUJITSU.

ji•va ['dʒivə] *n. Jainism.* **1** the individual and eternal soul of every living thing. **2** the vital energy of life; the opposite of AJIVA. ⟨< Skt. *jiva* living⟩

jive[1] [jīv] *n., v.* **jived, jiv•ing.** *Slang. —n.* **1** a kind of lively jazz; swing music. **2** dancing to jive music. **3** the talk of swing enthusiasts. **4** the latest slang.
—v. **1** dance to music, especially jive. **2** play jive music. ⟨origin uncertain⟩
☛ *Hom.* GYVE.

jive[2] [dʒaɪv] *v.* **jived, jiv•ing.** JIBE[3].

job [dʒɒb] *n., v.* **jobbed, job•bing.** *—n.* **1** a piece of work: *Dick did the job of painting the boat.* **2** a definite piece of work undertaken for a fixed price: *If you want your house painted, Mr. Huebert will do the job for $5000.* **3** (*adjl.*) done by the job; hired for a particular piece of work. **4** work; employment: *Mary's brother is hunting for a job.* **5** anything a person has to do: *I'm not going to wash the dishes; that's your job.* **6** *Informal.* an affair; matter. **7** a piece of public or official business managed dishonestly for private gain.
a good job, good work: *You did a good job on that garden.*
on the job, a at the workplace. **b** attending to one's work or duty.
—v. **1** buy (goods) from manufacturers in large quantities and sell to retailers in smaller lots. **2** let out (work) to different contractors, workers, etc. **3** manage (a public matter) for private gain in a dishonest way. **4** work at odd jobs. ⟨origin uncertain⟩
☛ *Syn. n.* **4.** See note at POSITION.

Job [dʒoub] *n.* any patient, enduring person.
Job's comforter, a person who increases the misery of the person he or she pretends to comfort.

patience of Job, great self-control despite trouble or irritation. ⟨in the Bible, a very patient man who kept his faith in God in spite of many troubles⟩

job•ber ['dʒɒbər] *n.* **1** a person who buys goods from manufacturers in small quantities and sells to retailers in smaller quantities. **2** a person who manages public business dishonestly for private gain. **3** a person who works by the job; pieceworker. **4** *Cdn. Logging.* an independent operator who undertakes to log a certain area for a specified price per thousand board feet or per cord. Under such an arrangement, the jobber may undertake to build camps and roads, provide horses, equipment, and supplies, and find the necessary workers.

job•hold•er ['dʒɒb,houldər] *n.* a person regularly employed.

job•less ['dʒɒblɪs] *adj.* **1** not having regular work; unemployed. **2** (*noml.*) **the jobless,** *pl.* all the people who are unemployed. **—'job•less•ness,** *n.*

job lot a quantity of goods bought or sold together, usually containing several different kinds of things.

jock¹ [dʒɒk] *n. Informal.* jockey.

jock² [dʒɒk] *n.* **1** *Slang.* a male athlete or sports enthusiast, or a person who adopts a lifestyle or values considered typical of athletes. **2** *Informal.* jockstrap. ⟨< *jock*, formerly, the genitals⟩

jock•ey ['dʒɒki] *n., pl.* **-eys;** *v.* **-eyed, -ey•ing.** *—n.* a person whose occupation is riding horses in races.
—v. **1** ride (a horse) in a race. **2** trick; cheat: *Swindlers jockeyed Mr. Smith into buying some worthless land.* **3** manoeuvre to get advantage: *The crews were jockeying their boats to get into the best position for the race.*
jockey for, try to win by taking advantage: *Several entrants were jockeying for first place in the music competition.* ⟨originally a proper name, dim. of *Jock*, Scottish var. of *Jack*⟩

jockey shorts underpants for boys or men which fit tightly at the crotch, giving support to the genitals.

jock•strap ['dʒɒk,stræp] *n. Informal.* an elastic supporter for the genitals, used by men when participating in sports. ⟨< *jock* formerly, the genitals + *strap*⟩

jo•cose [dʒə'kous] *adj.* jesting; humorous; playful: *He was fond of making jocose remarks about their old car.* ⟨< L *jocosus* < *jocus* jest⟩ **—jo'cose•ly,** *adv.* **—jo'cose•ness,** *n.*

jo•cos•i•ty [dʒə'kɒsɪti] *n., pl.* **-ties. 1** the quality or state of being jocose. **2** a jocose remark, etc.

joc•u•lar ['dʒɒkjələr] *adj.* **1** full of fun; jolly and fond of joking. **2** playful; jesting: *a jocular remark.* ⟨< L *jocularis* < *joculus*, dim. of *jocus* jest⟩ **—'joc•u•lar•ly,** *adv.*

joc•u•lar•i•ty [,dʒɒkjə'kærəti] *or* [,dʒɒkjə'lɛrəti] *n., pl.* **-ties. 1** the quality of being jocular. **2** jocular talk, behaviour, etc. **3** a jocular remark or act.

joc•und ['dʒɒkənd] *or* ['dʒoukənd] *adj.* cheerful; merry; gay. ⟨< L *jocundus*, var. (influenced by *jocus* jest) of *jucundus* pleasant < *juvare* please⟩ **—'joc•und•ly,** *adv.*

jo•cun•di•ty [dʒou'kʌndəti] *n., pl.* **-ties. 1** cheerfulness; merriment; gaiety. **2** a jocund remark, act, etc.

jodh•purs ['dʒɒdpərz] *n.pl.* breeches for horseback riding, loose above the knees and fitting closely below. ⟨< *Jodhpur*, India⟩

joe or **Joe** [dʒou] *Slang. n.* fellow: *a good joe.*

joe–job ['dʒou ,dʒɒb] *n. Informal.* a dull, run-of-the mill job or task.

joe–pye weed ['dʒou 'paɪ] any of several tall North American plants (genus *Eupatorium*) of the composite family having clusters of purplish flowers. ⟨origin uncertain⟩

jog¹ [dʒɒg] *v.* **jogged, jog•ging;** *n.* *—v.* **1** shake with a push or jerk: *I jogged his elbow to get his attention.* **2** stir up with a hint or reminder: *to jog one's memory.* **3** move up and down with a jerking or shaking motion: *The old horse jogged me up and down on its back.* **4** carry on; go (on) in a steady or humdrum fashion: *He is not very enterprising but just jogs along.* **5** run at a slow, steady rate: *My mother goes jogging every day for exercise.*
—n. **1** a shake, push, or nudge. **2** a hint or reminder: *Give your memory a jog.* **3** a slow walk or trot: *The riders went at a jog along the path.* ⟨ME; origin uncertain⟩ **—'jog•ger,** *n.*

jog² [dʒɒg] *n., v.* *—n.* **1** a part that sticks out or in; the unevenness in a line or a surface: *a jog in a wall.* **2** an abrupt, temporary change in direction: *There's a jog in the road where it goes around the poplar bluff.*
—v. make or form a jog: *The road jogs to the left just before you get to our place* ⟨var. of *jag*⟩

jog•gle¹ ['dʒɒgəl] *v.* **-gled, -gling;** *n.* *—v.* shake or jolt slightly: *The milk spilled because you joggled my elbow.*
—n. a slight shake or jolt. ⟨< *jog¹*⟩

jog•gle² ['dʒɒgəl] *n., v.* **-gled, -gling.** *—n.* **1** a projection on one of two joining surfaces, or a notch on the other, to prevent slipping. **2** a joint made in this way.
—v. join or fasten with a joggle. ⟨? < *jog²*⟩

jog trot 1 a slow, regular trot. **2** a routine or humdrum way of doing things.

john [dʒɒn] *n.* **1** *Informal.* toilet. **2** any man, especially one who is vulnerable to a con game. **3** the male client of a prostitute.

John Bar•ley•corn ['bɑrli,kɔrn] a personification of alcoholic beverages, especially malt liquor.

John Bull 1 a supposedly typical Englishman, often represented as stout and red-faced, in top hat and high boots. **2** a personification of England and its people. ⟨named after the title character in *The History of John Bull* (1712) by John Arbuthnot, a Scottish writer⟩

John Doe 1 a fictitious name used in legal forms, documents, proceedings, etc. to represent an unspecified person. **2** an anonymous, average man.

John Do•ry ['dɔri] *pl.* **John Dories** or (sometimes) **Dorys.** a European marine food fish (*Zeus faber*) having a very deep, almost oval-shaped, compressed body, spiny dorsal fins, and a large, yellow-ringed black spot on each side. ⟨< *John* + *dory²*⟩

John Han•cock ['hænkɒk] *Esp. U.S. Informal.* a person's signature. ⟨< signature of *John Hancock*, first signer of the Declaration of Independence⟩

John Henry *pl.* **John Henries.** *Informal.* a person's signature: *Put your John Henry at the bottom of this form.*

john•ny•cake ['dʒɒni,keik] *n.* corn bread in the form of a flat cake. ⟨origin uncertain⟩

Johnny Canuck *Cdn.* **1** a Canadian, especially a member of the armed forces during the First or Second World War. **2** a personification of Canada: *Johnny Canuck can do a lot more than play hockey.*

John•ny–come–late•ly ['dʒɒni kʌm 'leitli] *n., pl.* **John•ny-come-late•lies, John•nies-come-lately.** *Informal.* a newcomer; late arrival or participant.

John•ny–jump–up ['dʒɒni 'dʒʌmp ,ʌp] *n.* **1** wild pansy. **2** any of various North American violets. ⟨so called because of its rapid rate of growth⟩

John•son•ese [,dʒɒnsə'niz] *n.* a learned, Latinate literary style, resembling that of Samuel Johnson (1709-1784), an English author, lexicographer, and literary leader.

John•son grass ['dʒɒnsən] a coarse grass (*Sorghum halepense*) of the Mediterranean, used as fodder. ⟨named after William *Johnson*, the American agriculturalist who first planted it in 1840⟩

John•so•ni•an [dʒɒn'souniən] *adj.* of, having to do with, or characteristic of English writer and lexicographer Samuel Johnson (1709-1784), his writings, or his literary style.

joie de vi•vre [ʒwad'vivʀ] *French.* joy of living; enjoyment of life.

join [dʒɔɪn] *v., n.* *—v.* **1** bring or put together; connect; fasten: *to join hands.* **2** come together; meet: *The two roads join here.* **3** meet and unite with: *The brook joins the river.* **4** *Geometry.* draw a connecting line between (two points). **5** make or become one; combine; unite: *to join in marriage.* **6** take part (in) with others: *to join in song.* **7** become a member (of): *to join a club.* **8** come into the company of: *I'll join you later.* **9** return to or take one's place in: *After a few days on shore the sailor joined his ship.* **10** adjoin: *Her farm joins mine.*
join battle, begin to fight.
join forces, give mutual support.
join hands, a shake or clasp hands. **b** agree; co-operate.
join in, take part.
join up, enlist in the armed forces.
—n. **1** a place or line of joining; seam. **2** a joining or being joined. ⟨ME < OF *joindre* < L *jungere*⟩

☛ *Syn. v.* **5. Join,** COMBINE, UNITE = put or come together so as to form one thing. **Join** emphasizes bringing or coming together, and does not suggest how firm or lasting the association may be: *The two clubs joined forces during the campaign.* **Combine** emphasizes mixing or blending into one, for a common purpose: *He combines business with pleasure.* **Unite** emphasizes the oneness of the result and the loss of separate or divided purposes, interests, etc.: *The members of her family united to help her.*

join•der ['dʒɔɪndər] *n.* **1** a joining. **2** *Law.* the combining of causes in a suit. ⟨< F *joindre*⟩

join•er ['dʒɔɪnər] *n.* **1** a person who or thing that joins. **2** a skilled woodworker and furniture maker. **3** *Informal.* a person who joins many clubs, societies, etc.

join•er•y ['dʒɔɪnəri] *n.* **1** the skill or trade of a joiner. **2** woodwork or furniture made by a joiner.

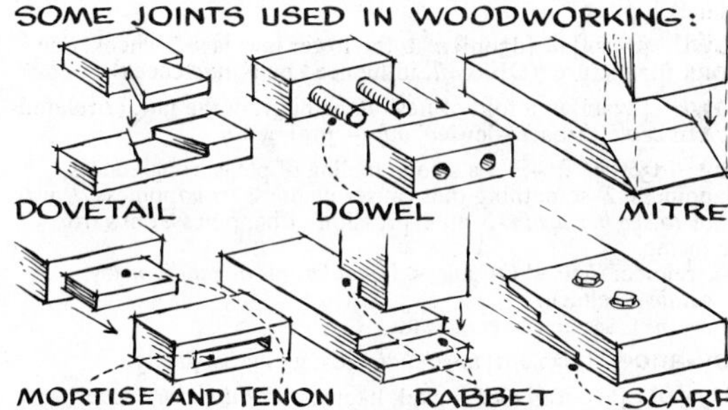

joint [dʒɔɪnt] *n., v., adj. —n.* **1** the place at which two things or parts are joined together. **2** the way parts are joined: *a perfect joint.* **3** *Anatomy.* the junction between two bones, usually formed of cartilage and connective tissue, that allows movement. **4** one of the parts of which a jointed thing is made up: *the middle joint of the finger.* **5** *Botany.* the part of the stem from which a leaf or branch grows. **6** a large piece of meat for roasting. **7** *Slang.* **a** a low-class place for cheap eating, drinking, or entertainment, formerly for the illegal sale of liquor. **b** any place, building, etc. **8** *Slang.* a marijuana cigarette. **9** *Geology.* a fracture in rocks.
out of joint, a out of place at the joint. **b** out of order; in bad condition.
—v. **1** connect by a joint or joints. **2** divide at the joints: *Please joint this chicken before wrapping it.*
—adj. **1** shared or done by two or more persons: *By our joint efforts we managed to push the car back on the road.* **2** joined together; sharing: *My sister and I are joint owners of the house.* ⟨ME < OF *joint* < *joindre.* See JOIN.⟩ **—'joint•er,** *n.*

joint account a bank account used by two or more persons jointly.

joint committee **1** in Canada, a parliamentary committee with members from the Commons and the Senate. **2** any committee with members from different groups.

joint•ed ['dʒɔɪntɪd] *adj., v. —adj.* **1** having joints. **2** formed with nodes.
—v. pt. and pp. of JOINT. **—'joint•ed•ly,** *adv.* **—'joint•ed•ness,** *n.*

joint•ly ['dʒɔɪntli] *adv.* together; in common: *The two girls owned the boat jointly.*

joint•ress ['dʒɔɪntrɪs] *n. Law.* a woman on whom a jointure is settled.

joint–stock company ['dʒɔɪnt 'stɒk] a company or firm whose capital is owned in shares by stockholders, any of whom can sell some or all of his or her shares without the consent of the others.

join•ture ['dʒɔɪntʃər] *n. Law.* property given to a wife by her husband, for her support in the event of his death. ⟨< F < L *junctura* a joining < *jungere* join. Doublet of JUNCTURE.⟩

joint•worm ['dʒɔɪnt,wɜrm] *n.* the larva of certain wasps, that damage wheat.

joist [dʒɔɪst] *n., v. —n.* one of the parallel horizontal pieces of timber extending from wall to wall across a building, to which the boards of a floor or ceiling are fastened. See FRAME for picture.
—v. provide with or lay across joists. ⟨ME < OF *giste,* ult. < L *jacere* lie⟩

joke [dʒouk] *n., v.* **joked, jok•ing.** *—n.* **1** something said or done to make somebody laugh; remark that is clever and amusing; something amusing; jest: *to tell jokes.* **2** a person or thing laughed at. **3** something that is not in earnest or actually meant.
crack a joke, tell a joke; say something funny.
no joke, a serious matter: *Poverty is no joke.*
—v. **1** make jokes; say or do something as a joke; jest. **2** laugh at; make fun of; tease. ⟨< L *jocus*⟩ **—'joke•less,** *adj.* **—'jok•ing•ly,** *adv.*

☛ *Syn. n.* **1. Joke,** JEST = something said or done to cause amusement or laughter. **Joke** applies to anything said or done in fun and intended to cause laughter. **Jest,** more formal, applies chiefly to language, and suggests playful and merry joking, teasing, or poking fun: *Many a truth has been spoken in jest.*

jok•er ['dʒoukər] *n.* **1** a person who tells funny stories or plays tricks on others. **2** *Slang.* any person; a fellow: *Who does that joker think he is?* **3** *Card games.* an extra card added in some games as a wild card or the highest-ranking card. **4** a trick for getting the better of someone. **5** *Informal.* an obscure phrase or sentence in a law, contract, etc. inserted to defeat the original purpose of the law, contract, etc.

jol•li•fi•ca•tion [,dʒɒləfə'keiʃən] *n.* festivity; merrymaking.

jol•li•fy ['dʒɒlɪ,faɪ] *v.* **-fied, -fy•ing.** cheer up.

jol•li•ty ['dʒɒlɪti] *n., pl.* **-ties.** fun; merriment; festivity; gaiety.

jol•ly ['dʒɒli] *adj.* **-li•er, -li•est;** *adv., v.* **-lied, -ly•ing;** *n., pl.* **-lies.** *—adj.* **1** full of fun; merry. **2** *Brit. Informal.* pleasant; agreeable; delightful.
—adv. Informal. **1** very: *You can jolly well wait like everyone else.* **2** *Esp. Brit.* extremely: *a jolly good film.*
—v. Informal. **1** flatter (a person) to make him or her feel good or agreeable. **2** tease playfully; banter.
—n. Usually, **jollies,** *pl. Slang.* good times, fun.
get (one's) **jollies,** *Slang.* obtain pleasure or excitement: *She gets her jollies by putting people down.* ⟨ME < OF *joli,* ? < Gmc.⟩ **—'jol•li•ly,** *adv.* **—'jol•li•ness,** *n.*

jolly boat *Nautical.* a small boat carried on a ship. ⟨< Danish *jolle* yawl⟩

Jolly Rog•er ['rɒdʒər] a traditional pirates' flag, with a white skull and crossbones on a black background.

jolt [dʒoult] *v., n. —v.* **1** jar; shake up: *The wagon jolted us when the wheels went over a rock.* **2** move with shocks or jerks: *The car jolted across the rough ground.* **3** shock; surprise: *She was jolted out of her complacency by news of the company's bankruptcy.*
—n. **1** a jar; jerk: *He put his brakes on suddenly and the car stopped with a jolt.* **2** a sudden surprise or shock: *The loss of so much money gave him a severe jolt.* ⟨origin uncertain⟩ **—'jolt•er,** *n.* **—'jolt•i•ness,** *n.* **—'jolt•ing•ly,** *adv.* **—'jolt•y,** *adj.*

Jo•nah ['dʒounə] *n.* any person whose presence is supposed to bring bad luck. Also called **Jonas.** ⟨in the Bible, a Hebrew prophet who caused a storm by trying to flee from God⟩

Jon•a•than ['dʒɒnəθən] *n.* **1** See DAVID. **2** a bright red apple that has a fine flavour and ripens in the late autumn.

jon•gleur ['dʒɒŋglər]; *French,* [ʒɔ̃'glœʀ] *n.* a wandering minstrel or entertainer in medieval France. ⟨< F < OF *jogleor* juggler; influenced by *jangleor* chatterer. Doublet of JUGGLER.⟩

jon•quil ['dʒɒŋkwɪl] *n.* **1** a perennial bulbous plant (*Narcissus jonquilla*) of the amaryllis family, native to the Mediterranean but widely cultivated as a garden and greenhouse plant, having clusters of fragrant, yellow or white, short-tubed flowers and long, rushlike leaves. **2** the flower or bulb of this plant. ⟨< F < Sp. *junquillo,* dim. of *junco* reed < L *juncus*⟩

Jor•dan ['dʒɔrdən] *n.* a kingdom in SW Asia. See LEBANON for map.

Jordan almond **1** a large almond of high quality. **2** an almond with a coating of hard, coloured sugar. ⟨alteration of ME *jardyne almaund* garden almond⟩

Jor•da•ni•an [dʒɔr'deiniən] *n., adj. —n.* a native or inhabitant of Jordan.
—adj. of or having to do with Jordan or its people.

jo•rum ['dʒɔrəm] *n.* **1** a large drinking bowl. **2** the amount that a jorum can hold. **3** a jorum and its contents. ⟨? < *Joram,* who brought David drinking vessels of silver⟩

joseph's coat a tropical plant (*Amaranthus tricolor*) grown as a houseplant because of its showy leaves. ⟨after Joseph (in the Bible) and his coat of many colours⟩

josh [dʒɒʃ] *v., n. Slang. —v.* make good-natured fun of; tease playfully.
—n. banter; raillery. ⟨origin uncertain⟩ **—'josh•er,** *n.*

joss [dʒɒs] *n.* an image of a Chinese god; a Chinese idol. ⟨pidgin English form of Pg. *deos* god < L *deus*⟩

joss house a Chinese temple.

joss stick a slender stick of dried, fragrant paste, burned by the Chinese as incense.

jos•tle ['dʒɒsəl] *v.* **-tled, -tling;** *n. —v.* **1** crowd, shove, or push against; elbow roughly: *We were jostled by the impatient crowd at the entrance to the circus.* **2** compete (*for* something): *to jostle for position.*
—n. a jostling; push; knock. Also, **justle.** ⟨< *joust*⟩ **—'jos•tler,** *n.*

jot [dʒɒt] *v.* **jot•ted, jot•ting;** *n.,* —*v.* write briefly or in haste: *The clerk jotted down the order.*
—*n.* a little bit; a very small amount: *I do not care a jot.* ⟨< L < Gk. *iōta* iota, the smallest letter in the Greek alphabet. Doublet of IOTA.⟩ —**'jot•ter,** *n.*

jo•ta ['houtə] *n.* **1** a Spanish dance for a couple, executed with the sound of castanets. **2** the music for this dance. ⟨< Sp. < OSp. *sota* < *sotare* to dance < L *saltare* to leap⟩

jot•ting ['dʒɒtɪŋ] *n., v.* —*n.* something jotted down; a short, informal note: *the published jottings of a noted wit.*
—*v.* ppr. of JOT.

Jo•tun, Jo•tunn, or **Jö•tunn** ['jɒtʊn] *n. Norse mythology.* a giant.

Jo•tun•heim, Jo•tunn•heim, or **Jö•tunn•heim** ['jɒtʊn,heim] *n. Norse mythology.* the home of the giants.

joual [ʒwɑl], [ʒu'ɑl], *or* [ʒu'æl] *n. Cdn.* uneducated or dialectal Canadian French. ⟨< Cdn.F < dial. pronunciation of F *cheval* horse⟩

joule [dʒul] *n. Physics.* an SI unit for measuring energy. One joule is the amount of work done in applying one newton of force to move a body one metre. *Symbol*: J ⟨< James Prescott *Joule* (1818-1889), an English physicist⟩

jounce [dʒaʊns] *v.* **jounced, jounc•ing;** *n.* —*v. or n.* bounce; bump; jolt. ⟨ME; origin uncertain⟩

jour•nal ['dʒɜrnəl] *n.* **1** a daily record, such as a diary, a ship's log, or written records of the meetings of a society. **2** a book for keeping such a record. **3** a newspaper or magazine.
4 *Bookkeeping.* **a** a book in which every item of business is written down so that the item can be entered under the proper account. **b** a daybook. **5** the part of a shaft or axle that turns on a bearing. ⟨ME < OF < LL *diurnalis* daily. Doublet of DIURNAL.⟩

journal box a housing for a JOURNAL (def. 5) and its bearings.

jour•nal•ese [,dʒɜrnə'liz] *n.* a careless or loose style of writing such as is sometimes used in newspapers, magazines, etc. Journalese is characterized by loose constructions, imprecise wording, and far-fetched or sensational expressions.

jour•nal•ism ['dʒɜrnə,lɪzəm] *n.* **1** the work of writing for, editing, managing, or publishing a newspaper or magazine.
2 newspapers and magazines as a group.

jour•nal•ist ['dʒɜrnəlɪst] *n.* a person engaged in journalism: *Editors and reporters are journalists.*

jour•nal•is•tic [,dʒɜrnə'lɪstɪk] *adj.* of or like journalism or journalists. —**jour•nal'is•ti•cal•ly,** *adv.*

jour•nal•ize ['dʒɜrnə,laɪz] *v.* **-ized, -iz•ing.** record in a journal. —**,jour•nal•i'za•tion,** *n.* —**'jour•nal,iz•er,** *n.*

jour•ney ['dʒɜrni] *n., pl.* **-neys;** *v.* **-neyed, -ney•ing.** —*n.* **1** a trip, especially a fairly long one: *a journey around the world.*
2 the distance covered in a journey: *two days' journey from here.*
3 a passage or course from one stage to another: *one's journey through life.*
—*v.* make a journey. ⟨ME < OF *journée*, originally, a day, ult. < L *diurnus* of one day < *dies* day⟩
☛ *Syn. n.* See note at TRIP.

jour•ney•man ['dʒɜrnimən] *n., pl.* **-men. 1** a worker who has completed an apprenticeship or is otherwise qualified to practise his or her trade, but who is not a master or employer. Originally, journeymen were hired and paid by the day. **2** a person who is a competent worker or performer but is not outstanding or brilliant.

jour•ney•work ['dʒɜrni,wɜrk] *n.* the work done by a journeyman.

joust [dʒʌust], [dʒʌst], *or* [dʒust] *n., v.* —*n.* **1** formerly, a combat, for sport or exercise, between two knights on horseback, in which they charged at each other, each trying to unseat the other with his lance. **2** Usually, **jousts,** *pl.* a tournament consisting of a series of such combats.
—*v.* engage in such a combat. Compare TILT. ⟨ME < OF *jouste* (*n.*), *jouster* (*v.*) < VL *juxtare* be next to < L *juxta* beside⟩
—**'joust•er,** *n.*

Jove [dʒouv] *n.* **1** *Roman mythology.* Jupiter. **2** *Poetic.* the planet Jupiter.
by Jove, an exclamation of surprise, pleasure, etc.

jo•vi•al ['dʒouviəl] *adj.* good-hearted and full of fun; good-humoured and merry. ⟨< L *Jovialis* pertaining to Jupiter (those born under the planet's sign being supposedly cheerful)⟩
—**'jo•vi•al•ly,** *adv.* —**'jo•vi•al•ness,** *n.*

jo•vi•al•i•ty [,dʒouvi'æləti] *n.* jollity; merriment.

Jo•vi•an ['dʒouviən] *adj.* **1** of or like the god Jove. **2** of the planet Jupiter.

jowl[1] [dʒaʊl] *or* [dʒoul] *n.* **1** the lower jaw; jaw. **2** cheek. See PORK for picture. ⟨OE *ceafl*, influenced by F *joue* cheek⟩

jowl[2] [dʒaʊl] *n.* a fold of flesh hanging from the jaw. ⟨? related to OE *ceole* throat⟩ —**jowled,** *adj.* —**'jowl•y,** *adj.*

joy [dʒɔɪ] *n., v.* —*n.* **1** a strong feeling of pleasure; gladness; happiness. **2** something that causes gladness or happiness: *It was a joy to see her again.* **3** an expression of happiness; outward rejoicing.
—*v.* rejoice. ⟨ME < OF *joie* < L *gaudia*, pl. of *gaudium* joy < *gaudere* rejoice⟩
☛ *Syn. n.* **1.** See note at PLEASURE.

joy•ance ['dʒɔɪəns] *n. Archaic.* joy; gladness; gaiety.

joy•ful ['dʒɔɪfəl] *adj.* **1** glad; happy: *a joyful heart.* **2** causing joy: *joyful news.* **2** showing joy: *a joyful look.* —**'joy•ful•ly,** *adv.* —**'joy•ful•ness,** *n.*

joy•less ['dʒɔɪlɪs] *adj.* **1** without joy; sad; dismal. **2** not causing joy: *a joyless prospect.* —**'joy•less•ly,** *adv.*
—**'joy•less•ness,** *n.*

joy•ous ['dʒɔɪəs] *adj.* joyful; glad: *a joyous song.* —**'joy•ous•ly,** *adv.* —**'joy•ous•ness,** *n.*

joy ride *Informal.* a ride in an automobile for pleasure, especially when the car is driven recklessly or is used without the owner's permission. —**'joy-,ride,** *v.* —**'joy-,rid•er,** *n.*

joy•stick ['dʒɔɪ,stɪk] *n. Computer technology.* a computer input device in which the movement of a small lever causes a corresponding movement of an object or cursor on the screen.

J.P. JUSTICE OF THE PEACE.

Jr. or **jr.** junior.

ju•bi•lance ['dʒubələns] *n.* a rejoicing; great joy.

ju•bi•lant ['dʒubələnt] *adj.* expressing or showing joy; rejoicing; exulting: *The people were jubilant when the war was over.* ⟨< L *jubilans, -antis*, ppr. of *jubilare* shout with joy < *jubilum* wild shout⟩ —**'ju•bi•lant•ly,** *adv.*

ju•bi•late ['dʒubə,leit] *v.* **-lat•ed, -lat•ing.** rejoice.
—**'ju•bi•la,to•ry** ['dʒubələ,tɔri], *adv.*

Ju•bi•la•te [,dʒubə'lɑtei], [,jubə'lɑtei], *or* [,dʒubə'leiti] *n.* the 100th Psalm in the Protestant Bible or the 99th Psalm in the Roman Catholic Bible. ⟨< L *jubilate* shout ye, the first word of the psalm < *jubilare* shout with joy. See JUBILANT.⟩

ju•bi•la•tion [,dʒubə'leiʃən] *n.* **1** rejoicing. **2** a joyful celebration.

ju•bi•lee [,dʒubə'li] *or* ['dʒubə,li] *n.* **1** an anniversary thought of as a time of rejoicing: *a fiftieth wedding jubilee.* **2** a time of rejoicing or great joy: *to have a jubilee in celebration of a victory.* **3** rejoicing; great joy. **4** *Roman Catholic Church.* a year in which punishment for sin is remitted, after repentance and the performance of certain acts. **5** in the Old Testament, a year of rest, release from debts, and redistribution of wealth every 50 years. ⟨ME < OF *jubile* < LL *jubilaeus*, adj. < Gk. *iōbēlaios* < Hebrew *yobel* trumpet; originally, a ram's horn, ram⟩

Ju•dae•o–Chris•tian [dʒu'deiou 'krɪstʃən] *or* [dʒu'diou 'krɪstʃən] *adj.* common to Christianity and Judaism; both Jewish and Christian: *the Judaeo-Christian heritage.* Also, **Judeo-Christian.** ⟨< L *Judaeus* < Gk. *Ioudaios* Jew + E *Christian*⟩

Ju•da•ic [dʒu'deiɪk] *adj.* of the Jews; Jewish. —**Ju'da•i•cal,** *adj.* —**Ju'da•i•cal•ly,** *adv.*

Ju•da•i•ca [dʒu'deiɪkə] *n.pl.* books about Jewish life and Judaism.

Ju•da•ism ['dʒudei,ɪzəm] *or* ['dʒudi,ɪzəm] *n.* **1** the religion of the Jews, based on the teachings of Moses and the prophets as found in the Bible and in the Talmud. **2** the following of Jewish rules and customs.

Ju•da•ist ['dʒudeiɪst] *or* ['dʒudiɪst] *n.* **1** a follower of Judaism. **2** in the early Christian church, a Jewish convert who advocated retaining Jewish rites and customs. —**,Ju'da'is•tic,** *adj.*

Ju•da•ize ['dʒudei,aɪz] *or* ['dʒudi,aɪz] *v.* **-ized, -iz•ing.** conform or cause to conform to Jewish usages or ideas.
—**,Ju•da•i'za•tion,** *n.* —**'Ju•da,iz•er,** *n.*

Ju•das ['dʒudəs] *n.* any treacherous betrayer of friendship; traitor. ⟨in the Bible, the disciple who betrayed Jesus Christ for thirty pieces of silver⟩

Judas tree a redbud, especially a Eurasian species (*Cercis siliquastrum*), the tree on which, according to legend, Judas Iscariot hanged himself.

Ju•de•an [dʒu'diən] *n., adj. —n.* a native or inhabitant of Judea, the southern part of Palestine when it was a province of the Roman Empire.
—adj. of or having to do with Judea. ⟨< L *Judaeus.* See JEW.⟩

judge [dʒʌdʒ] *n., v.* **judged, judg•ing.** *—n.* **1** a government official appointed or elected to hear and decide cases in a court of law. In Canada all judges are appointed. **2** a person chosen to settle a dispute or decide who wins. **3** a person who can decide how good a thing is: *a good judge of cattle, a poor judge of poetry.* **4** a ruler in ancient Israel before the time of the kings.
—v. **1** hear and decide in a court of law. **2** settle (a dispute); decide who wins (a race, contest, etc.). **3** make up one's mind about; form an opinion or estimate of: *to judge the merits of a book.* **4** criticize; condemn: *You had little cause to judge him so harshly.* **5** think; suppose; conclude: *I judged that you had forgotten to come.* ⟨ME < OF *juge* < L *judex* < *jus* law + root of *dicere* say⟩ **—'judg•er,** *n.* **—'judge•a•ble,** *adj.* **—'judge,like,** *adj.*

judge advocate *Military.* an officer appointed to superintend the proceedings of a court-martial, to advise the court on matters of law, and to elicit facts material to the defence. *Abbrev.:* JA or J.A.

Judge Advocate General the senior legal officer in the armed forces. *Abbrev.:* JAG or J.A.G.

judge•ment ['dʒʌdʒmənt] See JUDGMENT.

judge•ship ['dʒʌdʒ,ʃɪp] *n.* the position, duties, or term of office of a judge.

judg•ment or **judge•ment** ['dʒʌdʒmənt] *n.* **1** the act of judging. **2** *Law.* **a** a decision, decree, or sentence given by a judge or court of law. **b** a debt arising from a judge's decision. **c** the official certificate recording such a decision. **3** an opinion or estimate: *It was a bad plan in his judgment.* **4** the ability to form opinions; good sense. **5** a decision made by anybody who judges. **6** criticism; condemnation. **7** a misfortune considered as a punishment from God: *The neighbours considered his broken leg a judgment on him for his evil deeds.* **8 the Judgment,** JUDGMENT DAY.

judg•men•tal or **judge•men•tal** [dʒʌdʒ'mɛntəl] *adj.* **1** of, having to do with, or characterized by judgment. **2** too ready to criticize or condemn.

Judgment Day the day of God's final judgment of humankind at the end of the world.

ju•di•ca•ble ['dʒudəkəbəl] *adj.* able to be tried or judged.

ju•di•ca•tive ['dʒudəkətɪv] *adj.* able to judge.

ju•di•ca•tor ['dʒudə,keitər] *n.* a person who acts as judge or sits in judgment. **—ju•di•ca'to•ri•al,** *adj.*

ju•di•ca•to•ry ['dʒudəkə,tɔri] *adj., n., pl.* **-to•ries.** *—adj.* of or having to do with the administration of justice.
—n. **1** the administration of justice. **2** a court of law. ⟨< LL *judicatorius* < L *judex, -dicis* judge⟩

ju•di•ca•ture ['dʒudəkətʃər] *or* ['dʒudəkə,tʃʊr] *n.* **1** the administration of justice. **2** the position, duties, or authority of a judge. **3** the extent of jurisdiction of a judge or court of law. **4** a group of judges. **5** a court of law. ⟨< Med.L *judicatura,* ult. < L *judex, -dicis* judge⟩

ju•di•cial [dʒu'dɪʃəl] *adj.* **1** of or having to do with courts, judges, or the administration of justice. **2** ordered, permitted, or enforced by a judge or a court of law. **3** of or suitable for a judge; impartial; fair: *Before making a decision, a judicial mind considers fairly both sides of a dispute.* ⟨ME < L *judicialis* < *judicium* judgment < *judex, -dicis* judge⟩ **—ju'di•cial•ly,** *adv.*

ju•di•ci•ar•y [dʒu'dɪʃi,ɛri] *or* [dʒu'dɪʃəri] *n., pl.* **-ar•ies;** *adj.* *—n.* **1** the branch of government that administers justice; system of courts of law of a country. **2** judges as a group.
—adj. of or having to do with courts, judges, or the administration of justice. **—ju,di•ci'ar•i•ly,** *adv.*

ju•di•cious [dʒu'dɪʃəs] *adj.* having, using, or showing good judgment; wise; sensible: *a judicious use of money. A judicious historian selects and considers facts carefully and critically.* ⟨< F *judicieux* < L *judicium* judgment < *judex, -dicis* judge⟩ **—ju'di•cious•ly,** *adv.* **—ju'di•cious•ness,** *n.*

ju•do ['dʒudou] *n.* a form of jujitsu. ⟨< Japanese *ju* gentle + *do* art⟩ **—'ju•do•ist,** *n.*

ju•do•ka ['dʒudou,kɑ] *n., pl.* **-kas, -ka. 1** a judo expert. **2** a contestant in a judo match.

Ju•dy ['dʒudi] *n.* the wife of Punch in the puppet show *Punch and Judy.*

jug [dʒʌg] *n., v.* **jugged, jug•ging.** *—n.* **1** a container for liquids. A jug usually has a handle and either a spout or a narrow neck. **2** the amount that a jug can hold. **3** a jug and its contents. **4** *Slang.* jail.
—v. **1** *Slang.* jail. **2** put in a jug. **3** stew in an earthenware container: *to jug hare.* ⟨probably originally proper name, alteration of *Joan,* fem. of *John*⟩

ju•gal ['dʒugəl] *adj.* having to do with the cheek. ⟨< L *jugalis, jugum* yoke⟩

ju•gate ['dʒugeit] *adj. Botany.* having the leaflets in pairs, as a pinnate leaf. ⟨< L *jugatus* pp. of *jugare* < to yoke < *jugum* yoke⟩

Jug•ger•naut ['dʒʌgər,nɒt] *n.* **1** *Hinduism.* **a** Krishna. **b** an idol of Krishna in Puri, India, that is pulled through the streets on a huge chariot at an annual festival. Devotees are said to have formerly thrown themselves under the wheels to be crushed to death. **2** an idea, institution, etc. to which a person blindly devotes himself or herself, or is cruelly sacrificed. **3 juggernaut,** a huge, overpowering, inexorable force or object that destroys everything in its path. ⟨< Hind. *Jagannath* < Skt. *Jagannatha* < *jagat* world + *natha* lord⟩

jug•gle ['dʒʌgəl] *v.* **-gled, -gling;** *n.* *—v.* **1** keep (several objects) in motion in the air at the same time by rapidly tossing them up in turn and catching them as they fall: *The acrobat juggled three plates while balancing on a wire.* **2** do tricks that require great dexterity. **3** fumble; try awkwardly to catch. **4** manage to keep (several activities, etc.) going at the same time: *juggling two jobs and a night class.* **5** manipulate or change so as to deceive or cheat: *juggling accounts to hide a theft.* **6** deceive or cheat: *He juggled his brother out of his inheritance.*
—n. **1** the act or an instance of juggling. **2** deception or fraud. ⟨ME < OF *jogler* < L *joculari* joke < *joculus,* dim. of *jocus* jest⟩ **—'jug•gling•ly,** *adv.*

jug•gler ['dʒʌglər] *n.* **1** a person who can do juggling tricks. **2** a person who uses tricks, deception, or fraud. ⟨ME < OF *jogleor* < L *joculator* joker, ult. < *jocus* jest. Doublet of JONGLEUR.⟩

jug•gler•y ['dʒʌgləri] *n., pl.* **-gler•ies. 1** the skill or tricks of a juggler; sleight of hand. **2** trickery; deception; fraud.

jug milk outlet or **store** CONVENIENCE STORE.

jug•u•lar ['dʒʌgjələr] *or* ['dʒugjələr] *adj., n. —adj.* **1** of the neck or throat. **2** of the jugular vein.
—n. JUGULAR VEIN. ⟨< NL *jugularis* < L *jugulum* collarbone, dim. of *jugum* yoke⟩

jugular vein one of the two large veins on either side of the neck that return blood from the head to the heart.

ju•gu•late ['dʒʌgjə,leit] *or* ['dʒugjə,leit] *v.* **-lat•ed, -lat•ing.** take severe measures in suppressing (a disease). ⟨< L *jugulare* cut the throat of < *jugulum.* See JUGULAR.⟩ **—ju•gu'la•tion,** *n.*

ju•gum ['dʒugəm] *n. Zoology.* the lobe joining the bases of the wings of certain insects. ⟨< NL, L *jugum* yoke⟩

juice [dʒus] *n.* **1** the liquid in fruits, vegetables, and meats. **2** a natural liquid in the body. The gastric juices of the stomach help to digest food. **3** *Slang.* electricity. **4** *Slang.* gasoline. ⟨ME < OF < L *jus* broth⟩ **—'juice•less,** *adj.*

juic•er ['dʒusər] *n.* an apparatus for squeezing juice out of fruits or vegetables.

juic•y ['dʒusi] *adj.* **juic•i•er, juic•i•est. 1** full of juice; having much juice. **2** full of interest; lively. **—'juic•i•ly,** *adv.* **—'juic•i•ness,** *n.*

ju•jit•su [dʒu'dʒɪtsu] *n.* a traditional Japanese method of fighting without weapons, employing blows that can paralyse an opponent and holds and throws designed to use the opponent's own strength and weight against him or her. Also, **jujutsu, jiujitsu, jiujutsu.** ⟨< Japanese *jūjutsu* < *jū* soft + *jutsu* art⟩

ju•ju ['dʒudʒu] *n.* **1** a charm among some W African peoples. **2** the power of such a charm. **—'ju•ju,ism,** *n.* **—'ju•ju•ist,** *n.*

ju•jube ['dʒudʒub] *n.* **1** a chewy candy or lozenge made of fruit-flavoured gelatin. **2** the edible, datelike fruit of any of several Old World trees (genus *Ziziphus*) of the buckthorn family, especially an Asian species (*Z. jujuba*). **3** a tree producing such fruit. ⟨< F *jujube* or < Med.L *jujuba* < LL *zizyphum* < Gk. *zizyphon*⟩

ju•jut•su [dʒu'dʒʊtsu] See JUJITSU.

juke box [dʒuk] *Informal.* an automatic phonograph that plays a record when money is deposited in the slot. ⟨< Gullah *juke* disorderly, wicked, from the origin of juke boxes in cheap inns⟩

A juke box

Jul. July.

ju•lep ['dʒulɪp] *n.* **1** a drink made with water, sugar or syrup, and, sometimes, flavouring. **2 mint julep,** a drink made of whisky or brandy, sugar, crushed ice, and fresh mint. ⟨< F < Arabic < Pers. *gulab*, originally, rose water⟩

Jul•ian ['dʒuliən] *adj.* of Julius Caesar, Roman dictator (100-44 B.C.)

Julian calendar a calendar in which the average length of a year was 365¼ days. It was introduced by Julius Caesar in 46 B.C.

ju•li•enne [ˌdʒuli'ɛn] *adj., n. —adj.* of vegetables, cut in thin strips or small pieces (*used after the noun*): *potatoes julienne.*
—n. a clear soup containing vegetables cut into thin strips or small pieces. ⟨< F⟩

Ju•li•et cap ['dʒuliət] a bridal cap set with jewels. ⟨< Juliet, the heroine of Shakespeare's play *Romeo and Juliet*⟩

Ju•ly [dʒə'laɪ] *n., pl.* **-lies.** the seventh month of the year. It has 31 days. ⟨OE *Julius* < L *Julius*, after *Julius* Caesar⟩

jum•ble ['dʒʌmbəl] *v.* **-bled, -bling;** *n. —v.* mix; confuse: *He jumbled up everything in the drawer when he was hunting for his socks.*
—n. a confused mixture. ⟨? imitative⟩ **—'jum•ble•ment,** *n.* **—'jum•bler,** *n.* **—'jum•bling•ly,** *adv.*

jumble sale *Esp. Brit.* RUMMAGE SALE.

jum•bo ['dʒʌmbou] *n., pl.* **-bos;** *adj. Informal. —n.* a big, clumsy person, animal, or thing; something unusually large of its kind.
—adj. very big: *a jumbo jet.* ⟨< *Jumbo*, an elephant exhibited by P.T. Barnum (1810-1891), U.S. showman⟩

jumbo jet an airplane for several hundred passengers.

jump [dʒʌmp] *v., n. —v.* **1** spring into the air by the muscular action of the legs and feet; leap; bound: *to jump high, to jump over a fence.* **2** leap over: *to jump a stream.* **3** cause to jump: *to jump a horse over a fence.* **4** give a sudden start or jerk: *You made me jump.* **5** rise suddenly: *Prices jumped.* **6** *Checkers.* pass over and capture (an opponent's piece). **7** pounce upon; attack: *The robbers jumped the shopkeeper.* **8** *Slang.* evade (something) by running away: *to jump bail, jump ship.* **9** *Slang.* get aboard (a train, etc.) by jumping.
jump a claim, seize a piece of land claimed by another.
jump at, accept eagerly and quickly.
jump on, *Slang.* blame; scold; criticize.
jump the track, of a train, leave the rails suddenly.
jump to conclusions, make an unfair assessment (of a person or situation) based on little evidence.
jump to it! *Informal.* be quick!
—n. **1** the act or an instance of jumping. **2** something to be jumped over. **3** the distance jumped. **4** a contest in jumping. **5** a sudden nervous start or jerk. **6** a sudden rise. **7** *Checkers.* a move made to capture an opponent's piece. **8** a sudden and abrupt transition from one thing to another. **9 jumps,** *Informal.* a nervous condition characterized by sudden starts or jerks.
get or **have the jump on,** *Slang.* get or have an advantage over.
on the jump, *Informal.* rushing around; always busy. ⟨probably imitative⟩ **—'jump•a•ble,** *adj.* **—'jump•ing•ly,** *adv.*

☛ *Syn. v.* **1, 2. Jump,** LEAP = spring into or through the air. **Jump** emphasizes springing from the ground or other surface or point: *He jumped from the roof. She jumped across the puddle.* **Leap** emphasizes springing high into or through the air or to a point and suggests more grace, lightness, or liveliness than **jump**: *I love to watch a dancer leap. She leaped lightly to the opposite bank of the stream.*

jump area the locality assigned for the landing of parachute troops, usually behind enemy lines.

jump ball *Basketball.* the putting of the ball into play by the referee, who tosses it between two opposing players.

jump bid *Bridge.* the playing of a card higher than is necessary to cover the previous bid.

jump•er¹ ['dʒʌmpər] *n.* **1** a person who or thing that jumps. **2** a simply constructed sleigh on low wooden runners. **3** a short length of wire used to bypass part of an electric circuit or to make a temporary connection. ⟨< *jump*, v.⟩

jump•er² ['dʒʌmpər] *n.* **1** a sleeveless dress, usually worn over a blouse. **2** a loose jacket. Jumpers are worn by workers to protect their clothes and by sailors as part of their uniform. **3** a loose blouse reaching to the hips. **4 jumpers,** *pl.* rompers. ⟨< *jump* short coat, ? alteration of F *juppe*, ult. < Arabic *jubbah* long open coat⟩

jumper cables BOOSTER CABLES.

jump fire *Cdn.* a forest fire started by burning material that has been carried ahead by wind from another blaze.

jumping bean a seed of any of various Mexican shrubs (especially of genus *Sebastiana*) of the spurge family that contains a small moth caterpillar whose movements cause the seed to jump.

jumping jack **1** a toy man or animal that can be made to jump by pulling a string. **2** an exercise imitating the movement of such a toy.

jumping mouse any mouse of the family Zapodidae, having a long tail and long back legs suitable for jumping.

jump•ing–off place or **point** ['dʒʌmpɪŋ 'ɒf] **1** *Cdn., esp. North.* a place, usually a town, where one leaves the railway or other link with civilization to proceed into the wilderness. **2** *Cdn.* any starting place. **3** any place considered the ultimate in isolated, undeveloped wilderness.

jumping pound *Cdn.* BUFFALO JUMP.

jump•mas•ter ['dʒʌmpˌmæstər] *n.* a person in charge of the dropping of parachutists from an aircraft.

jump–off ['dʒʌmp ˌɒf] *n., adj. —n.* **1** the start of a race. **2** the beginning of an attack. **3** playoff.
—adj. beginning; starting: *a jump-off place for northern exploration parties.*

jump seat **1** a collapsible extra seat in an automobile, hinged to the floor between the front and back seats. **2** any similar seat in an airplane, elevator, etc.

jump shot or **pass** *Basketball.* a play in which a player throws the ball while at the height of his or her jump.

jump–start ['dʒʌmp ˌstɑrt] *v., n. —v.* start a vehicle by the use of booster cables.
—n. such a procedure.

jump•suit ['dʒʌmpˌsut] *n.* a one-piece garment consisting of a usually close-fitting top and long or short pants. ⟨< *jump* + *suit*, originally applied to a kind of suit worn by parachutists⟩

jump•y ['dʒʌmpi] *adj.* **jump•i•er, jump•i•est. 1** moving by jumps; making sudden, sharp jerks. **2** easily excited or frightened; nervous. **—'jump•i•ly,** *adv.* **—'jump•i•ness,** *n.*

Jun. **1** June. **2** Junior.

Junc. Junction.

jun•co ['dʒʌŋkou] *n., pl.* **-cos.** any of a genus (*Junco*) of small North American finches having mainly grey plumage with white outer tail feathers and white underparts. Juncos are common winter birds in many parts of Canada. ⟨< Sp. < L *juncus* reed⟩

junc•tion ['dʒʌŋkʃən] *n.* **1** a joining or being joined: *the junction of two rivers.* **2** a place where things join or meet. A railway junction is a place where railway lines meet or cross. **3** a connection between parts of a transmission line. ⟨< L *junctio, -onis* < *jungere* join⟩

junction box a panel for connecting or branching electric circuits without splicing the wires.

junc•ture ['dʒʌŋktʃər] *n.* **1** a point of time. **2** a state of affairs. **3** crisis. **4** joint. **5** a joining or being joined, or the place of joining. **6** *Linguistics.* a phonological feature that marks the boundaries of spoken words, as that distinguishing *syntax* and *sin tax.* ⟨< L *junctura* a joining < *jungere* join. Doublet of JOINTURE.⟩

June [dʒun] *n.* the sixth month of the year. It has 30 days. ⟨< L *Junius*, originally a Roman gens name⟩

June beetle *Cdn.* JUNE BUG.

June•ber•ry ['dʒunˌbɛri] *n.* serviceberry.

June bug any of various large, reddish brown beetles (family Scarabaeidae) of the northern hemisphere that fly about especially in late spring, feeding on flowers and foliage at night. Their larvae are white grubs that live in the soil, feeding mainly on plant roots.

Jung•i•an ['jʊŋiən] *adj., n. —adj.* of, having to do with, or

characteristic of Carl Gustav Jung (1875-1961), a Swiss psychologist, or his system of analytical psychology.
—n. a follower of the theories of Jung.

jun•gle ['dʒʌŋgəl] *n.* **1** wild land in the tropics thickly overgrown with bushes, vines, trees, etc. **2** a tangled mass. **3** a place characterized by vicious competition or struggle for survival: *She says the city is a jungle.* **4** *Slang.* a hobos' camp. ⟨< Hind. *jangal* < Skt. *jāngala* desert, forest⟩ **—'jun•gled,** *adj.* **—'jun•gly,** *adj.*

jungle fever a severe form of malaria.

jungle fowl any of several Asian wild birds (genus *Gallus*), the males of which have a fleshy comb and wattles and a long, high-arched tail. The **red jungle fowl** (*Gallus gallus*) is believed to be the ancestor of the common domestic fowl.

jungle gym a climbing apparatus for children's outdoor play, including ladders, climbing bars, etc.

jun•ior ['dʒunjər] *adj., n. —adj.* **1 Junior,** the younger: *John Parker, Junior, is the son of John Parker, Senior.* **2** of lower position, rank, or standing; of more recent appointment: *a junior officer, a junior partner.* **3** of or having to do with students in grades 4 to 6. **4** *Esp. U.S.* of, in, or having to do with the third year of a four-year program of high school or college. **5** of or for young people: *a junior tennis match, junior coats.* **6** of later date.
—n. **1** a younger person. **2** a person of lower rank or shorter service. **3** a student in grades 4 to 6. **4** *Esp. U.S.* in a high school or college, a student in the third year of a four-year course.
be (someone's) **junior,** be younger than someone. ⟨< L *junior*, comparative of *juvenis* young⟩

Junior Achievement a non-profit organization which gives young people practical experience in business.

junior college a college giving only the first year or the first two years of a university degree program.

junior high school a school consisting of grades 7, 8, and sometimes 9; any school intermediate between elementary school and high school.

jun•ior•i•ty [,dʒun'jɔrəti] *n.* the state of being junior in age or rank.

Junior League an organization of women who undertake such projects as community work, volunteer hospital work, etc.

ju•ni•per ['dʒunəpər] *n.* **1** any of a genus (*Juniperus*) of evergreen shrubs and trees of the northern hemisphere, belonging to the cypress family, having tiny, scalelike, overlapping leaves, small, blue, berrylike cones, and soft, fragrant wood that is used for lining closets and chests, etc. The four species of juniper native to Canada are the Rocky Mountain juniper, red juniper, dwarf or common juniper, and creeping juniper. **2** the wood of a juniper. ⟨< L *juniperus*⟩

junk[1] [dʒʌŋk] *n., v. —n.* **1** old metal, paper, rags, etc. **2** *Informal.* rubbish; trash. **3** a hard, salted meat eaten by sailors. **4** old rope used for making mats, oakum, etc. **5** *Slang.* a narcotic drug, such as heroin or morphine; dope.
—v. Informal. throw away or discard as junk: *We junked the old garden chairs last fall.* ⟨origin uncertain⟩

junk[2] [dʒʌŋk] *n.* a sailing ship traditionally used especially by the Chinese and Javanese, having a flat bottom, high stern, and two or three masts with lugsails stiffened by horizontal battens. ⟨< Pg. *junco*, probably ult. < Javanese *jong*⟩

junk bond any company bond that promises a yield that it cannot make.

junk•er ['dʒʌŋkər] *n.* a worn-out automobile, usually one sold for scrap.

Jun•ker ['jʊŋkər] *n.* a member of the aristocratic, formerly privileged class in Prussia. Also, **junker.** ⟨< G⟩

jun•ket ['dʒʌŋkɪt] *n., v. —n.* **1** curdled milk, sweetened and flavoured. **2** a feast; picnic. **3** a junket. **4** *Informal.* an unnecessary trip taken by an official at the expense of his or her government or the firm he or she works for.
—v. **1** feast; picnic. **2** go on a junket. ⟨< dial. OF *jonquette* basket < *jonc* reed < L *juncus*⟩ **—'jun•ket•er** or **jun•ke'teer,** *n.*

junk food food, especially prepackaged snack food, having a high carbohydrate content and little nutritive value.

junk•ie ['dʒʌŋki] *n. Slang.* **1** a drug addict. **2** a person who is addicted to anything. **3** a dealer in junk.

junk mail unsolicited mail consisting of advertisements and delivered in bulk.

junk•man ['dʒʌŋk,mæn] *n., pl.* **-men.** a man who buys and sells old metal, paper, rags, etc.

junk•y ['dʒʌŋki] *adj.* **-i•er, -i•est.** *Informal.* of or like junk; cheap or worthless: *junky magazines, junky furniture.*

junk•yard ['dʒʌŋk,jɑrd] *n.* a yard for the collection and resale of junk.

Ju•no ['dʒunou] *n., pl.* **-nos. 1** *Roman mythology.* the goddess of marriage and childbirth, wife of Jupiter and queen of the gods, corresponding to the Greek goddess Hera. **2** any stately, majestic woman.

Ju•no•esque [,dʒunou'ɛsk] *adj.* in the manner of Juno; stately and majestic.

jun•ta ['hʊntə], [dʒʊntə], or ['dʒʌntə]; *Spanish,* ['xʊnta] *n.* **1** a group of persons forming a government, especially as the result of a revolution: *The country was ruled by a military junta.* **2** a junto. **3** especially in Spanish or Latin American countries, a legislative or administrative council. ⟨< Sp. *junta*, ult. < L *jungere* join⟩

jun•to ['dʒʌntou] *n., pl.* **-tos.** a political faction; a group of plotters or partisans. ⟨alteration of *junta*⟩

Ju•pi•ter ['dʒupətər] *n.* **1** *Roman mythology.* the chief god, ruler of the gods and people, corresponding to the Greek god Zeus. **2** the largest planet, the fifth from the sun.

ju•pon ['dʒu,pɒn] *n.* TABARD (def. 2).

ju•ral ['dʒʊrəl] *adj.* **1** of law; legal. **2** having to do with rights and obligations. ⟨< L *jus, juris* law⟩ **—'jur•al•ly,** *adv.*

Ju•ras•sic [dʒə'ræsɪk] *n., adj. —n. Geology.* **1** the middle period of the Mesozoic era, beginning approximately 205 million years ago, when birds first appeared. **2** the rocks formed during this period. See geological time chart in the Appendix.
—adj. **1** of or having to do with the period when birds first appeared. **2** of or having to do with the rocks formed during this period. ⟨< F *jurassique*, after the *Jura* Mountains in France and Switzerland⟩

ju•rat ['dʒʊræt] *n.* **1** *Law.* an affidavit. **2** a magistrate. ⟨< F < ML *juratus*, literally, one sworn < L *juratus*, pp. of *jurare* to swear⟩

ju•ra•to•ry ['dʒʊrə,tɔri] *adj.* sworn on oath.

ju•rel [hu'rɛl] *n.* any fish of the genus *Caranx*, found in warm oceans. ⟨< Sp., ult. < Gk. *sauros* horse mackerel⟩

ju•rid•i•cal [dʒə'rɪdɪkəl] *adj.* **1** having to do with the administration of justice. **2** of law; legal. Also, **juridic.** ⟨< L *juridicus*, ult. < *jus, juris* law + *dicere* say⟩ **—ju'rid•i•cal•ly,** *adv.*

juridical day a day on which a court of law may sit.

ju•ris•con•sult [,dʒʊrɪskən'sʌlt] *or* [,dʒʊrɪs'kɒnsʌlt] *n.* jurist. ⟨< L *jurisconsultus*, ult. < *jus, juris* law + *consulere* consult⟩

ju•ris•dic•tion [,dʒʊrɪs'dɪkʃən] *n.* **1** the right or power of administering law or justice. **2** authority; power; control. **3** the extent of authority: *The judge ruled that the case was not within her jurisdiction.* **4** the territory over which authority extends. ⟨< L *jurisdictio, -onis*, ult. < *jus, juris* law + *dicere* say⟩ **—ju•ris'dic•tion•al,** *adj.* **—ju•ris'dic•tion•al•ly,** *adv.*

ju•ris•pru•dence [,dʒʊrɪs'prudəns] *n.* **1** the science or philosophy of law. **2** a system of laws. **3** a branch of law. Medical jurisprudence deals with the application of medical knowledge to certain questions of law. ⟨< L *jurisprudentia* < *jus, juris* law + *prudentia* prudence⟩ **—ju•ris•pru'den•tial,** *adj.* **—ju•ris•pru'den•tial•ly,** *adv.*

ju•ris•pru•dent [,dʒʊrɪs'prudənt] *n., adj. —n.* a person skilled in jurisprudence.
—adj. skilled in jurisprudence.

ju•rist ['dʒʊrɪst] *n.* **1** an expert in law. **2** a learned writer on law. **3** a civil lawyer. **4** a judge. ⟨< Med.L *jurista* < L *jus, juris* law⟩

ju•ris•tic [dʒə'rɪstɪk] *adj.* of or having to do with jurists or jurisprudence; relating to law. **—ju'ris•ti•cal•ly,** *adv.*

ju•ror ['dʒʊrər] *n.* **1** a member of a jury. **2** a person who has taken an oath, especially of allegiance. ⟨ME < AF *jurour* < L *jurator* a swearer < *jurare* swear⟩

ju•ry[1] ['dʒʊri] *n., pl.* **ju•ries. 1** a group of persons selected to hear evidence in a court of law and sworn to give a true verdict on questions of fact based on the evidence presented to it. See also TRIAL JURY, GRAND JURY. **2** a group of persons chosen to give a judgment or to decide who is the winner in a contest. ⟨ME < AF *jurie* < *jurer* swear < L *jurare*⟩

ju•ry[2] ['dʒʊri] *adj. Nautical.* for temporary use on a ship; makeshift. ⟨probably ult. < OF *ajurie, adjutorie* help < L *adjutare* < *ad-* to + *juvare* aid⟩

ju•ry•man ['dʒʊrimən] *n., pl.* **-men.** a member of a jury; juror.

ju•ry–rigged ['dʒʊri ˌrɪgd] *adj. Nautical.* rigged for temporary, usually emergency, use.

jus [dʒʌs] *or* [jus] *n., pl.* **ju•ra** ['dʒʊrə] *or* ['jʊrə]. *Law.* **1** a right. **2** the system of law.

jus ci•vi•le [jus sivilei] civil law as practised by the Romans. ⟨< L⟩

jus gen•ti•um [jus 'dʒɛnʃiəm] the law as applied internationally. ⟨< L⟩

jus na•tu•ra•le [jus ˌnætə'rɑlei] *or* [ˌnætʃə'rɑli] the law of nature. ⟨< L⟩

jus san•gui•nis [jus 'sæŋgwɪnɪs] *Law.* the principle that a child is a citizen of his or her parents' country. ⟨< L⟩

jus•sive ['dʒʌsɪv] *adj. Grammar.* **1** imperative. **2** in the imperative mood. ⟨< L *jussus* a command < *jubere* to command⟩

jus so•li [jus 'souli] *Law.* the principle that a child is a citizen of the country where he or she is born. ⟨< L⟩

just[1] [dʒʌst] *adj., adv. —adj.* **1** right; fair: *a just price.* **2** righteous: *a just life.* **3** deserved; merited: *a just reward.* **4** having good grounds; well-founded: *just anger.* **5** lawful: *a just claim.* **6** in accordance with standards or requirements; proper: *just proportions.* **7** true; correct: *a just description.* **8** exact: *just weights.*
—adv. **1** exactly: *just a metre.* **2** very close; immediately: *There was a picture just above the fireplace.* **3** a very short while ago: *She has just gone.* **4** barely: *I just managed to catch the train.* **5** only; merely: *He is just an ordinary man.* **6** *Informal.* quite; truly; positively: *The weather is just glorious.*
just now, a exactly at this moment; at present: *Just now we are trying to set a firm date for the meeting.* **b** only a very short time ago: *I saw her just now.* ⟨< L *justus* upright < *jus* right, law⟩ **—'just•ness,** *n.* **—'just•ly,** *adv.*
☛ *Syn. adj.* **1.** See note at FAIR[1].

just[2] [dʒʌst] *v. or n.* joust.

jus•tice ['dʒʌstɪs] *n.* **1** just conduct; fair dealing: *have a sense of justice.* **2** the fact of being just; fairness; rightness; correctness: *uphold the justice of our cause.* **3** rightfulness; lawfulness; well-founded reason: *He complained with justice of the bad treatment he had received.* **4** just treatment; deserved reward or punishment. **5** the exercise of power and authority to maintain what is just and right. **6** the administration of law; trial and judgment by process of law. **7** judge. **8 Justice,** *Cdn.* the title of a judge. JUSTICE OF THE PEACE.
bring (someone) **to justice,** do what is necessary in order that a person shall be legally punished for his or her crime or crimes.
do justice to, a treat fairly. **b** see the good points of. **c** show proper appreciation for: *She did justice to the dinner.*
do (oneself) **justice,** do as well as one really can do: *She did not do herself justice on the test.* ⟨ME < OF < L *justitia* < *justus* just, upright. See JUST[1].⟩

justice of the peace a provincial judicial officer who tries cases involving infractions of municipal by-laws, issues warrants for arrest, administers oaths, marries people, etc. *Abbrev.*: J.P.

jus•tice•ship ['dʒʌstɪsˌʃɪp] *n.* the position, duties, or term of office of a justice.

jus•ti•ci•a•ble [dʒʌ'stɪʃəbəl] *adj. Law.* negotiable in a legal sense; fit for the courts.

jus•ti•ci•a•ry [dʒʌ'stɪʃəri] *adj.* having to do with the administration of justice.

jus•ti•fi•a•ble ['dʒʌstəˌfaɪəbəl] *or* [ˌdʒʌstə'faɪəbəl] *adj.* capable of being justified; that can be shown to be just and right; defensible. **—jus•ti,fi•a'bil•i•ty,** *n.* **—'jus•ti,fi•a•bly,** *adv.*

jus•ti•fi•ca•tion [ˌdʒʌstəfə'keiʃən] *n.* **1** the act or process of justifying. **2** the state of being justified. **3** the fact or circumstance that justifies; a good reason or grounds for action, defence, complaint, etc. **4** *Printing.* adjustment of spacing to provide an even right-hand margin.

jus•tif•i•ca•to•ry [dʒʌs'tɪfəkəˌtɔri] *adj.* providing justification. Also, **justificative** ['dʒʌstəfəˌkeitɪv].

jus•ti•fy ['dʒʌstəˌfaɪ] *v.* **-fied, -fy•ing. 1** show to be just or right; give a good reason for: *The fine quality of the cloth justifies its high price.* **2** clear of blame or guilt. **3** *Printing.* adjust the space between the words of (a line of type) so that the line will conform to a given length and provide an even right-hand margin. **4** *Law.* show a satisfactory reason or excuse for (something done). **5** qualify as a surety. ⟨< MF *justifier* < LL *justificare* < L *justus* just + *facere* make⟩ **—'jus•ti,fi•er,** *n.*

jus•tle ['dʒʌsəl] *v.* **jus•tled, jus•tling.** See JOSTLE.

jut [dʒʌt] *v.* **jut•ted, jut•ting;** *n. —v.* stick out; project: *The pier juts out from the shore into the water.*
—n. the part that sticks out; projection. ⟨var. of *jet*[1]⟩

jute [dʒut] *n.* **1** a strong fibre used for making coarse sacks, burlap, rope, etc. **2** either of two tropical, Old World, herbaceous plants (*Corchorus olitorius* and *C. capsularis*) of the linden family yielding such fibre. ⟨< Bengali *jhoto* < Skt. *jata* mat of hair⟩

Jute [dʒut] *n.* a member of an early Germanic tribe. Some of the Jutes invaded and settled in SE England in the 5th century A.D. **—'Jut•ish,** *adj.*

ju•ve•nes•cence [ˌdʒuvə'nɛsəns] *n.* a renewal of youth; youthfulness.

ju•ve•nes•cent [ˌdʒuvə'nɛsənt] *adj.* growing young again; youthful. ⟨< L *juvenescens, -entis,* ppr. of *juvenescere* grow young again < *juvenis* young⟩

ju•ve•nile ['dʒuvəˌnaɪl] *or* ['dʒuvənəl] *adj., n. —adj.* **1** young; youthful. **2** of or for young people: *juvenile books, juvenile delinquency.* **3** behaving younger than one's years.
—n. **1** a young person. **2** a book for young people. **3** an actor who plays youthful parts. **4** a young bird, almost a fledgling. ⟨< L *juvenilis* < *juvenis* young⟩
☛ *Syn. adj.* **1.** See note at YOUNG.

juvenile court a law court where cases involving boys and girls are heard. In Canada, the maximum age at which offenders are tried in juvenile courts varies in the different provinces but is usually either sixteen or eighteen.

juvenile delinquency criminal behaviour by adolescents. **—juvenile delinquent.**

ju•ve•nil•i•a [ˌdʒuvə'nɪliə] *n.pl.* **1** early, immature works produced by an artist, author, or composer during childhood or adolescence. **2** literature or art produced for children.

ju•ve•nil•i•ty [ˌdʒuvə'nɪləti] *n.pl.* **-ties.** a juvenile quality, condition, manner, or act.

jux•ta•pose [ˌdʒʌkstə'pouz] *v.* **-posed, -posing.** put close together; place side by side. ⟨< F *juxtaposer* < L *juxta* beside + F *poser* place. See POSE[1].⟩

jux•ta•po•si•tion [ˌdʒʌkstəpə'zɪʃən] *n.* **1** a putting close together; a placing side by side. **2** a position close together or side by side.

K k *K k*

k or K [kei] *n., pl.* **k's** or **K's. 1** the eleventh letter of the English alphabet. **2** any speech sound represented by this letter. **3** a person or thing identified as *k*, especially the eleventh in a series. **4** something shaped like the letter K. **5** any device such as a printer's type, a lever or a key on a keyboard, that produces a k or K. **6** (*adjl.*) of or being a k or K. **7** *Slang.* kilometre: *It's 24 k's to the nearest town.*

k 1 kilo- (an SI prefix). **2** karat.

k. 1 kopek. **2** krona. **3** krone. **4** king. **5** knight.

K[1] 1 potassium (for L *Kalium*). **2** kelvin(s). **3** karat.

K[2] 1 one thousand. **2** a unit of computer memory. One K of computer memory is 1024 bytes: *This home computer has a storage capacity of 64 K.*

K. 1 king. **2** knight.

Ka [kɑ] *n.* in the religion of ancient Egypt, the soul said to dwell in a person's body, and, after death, in his or her tomb or statue. Sometimes, **ka.** ⟨< Egyptian⟩

Kaa•ba ['kɑbə] *n.* the most sacred Muslim shrine, a small structure within the Great Mosque at Mecca. It contains a black stone, believed to have been given to Abraham by the angel Gabriel, toward which Muslims face when praying. Also, **Caaba.** ⟨< Arabic *ka'bah*, literally, a square building⟩

Kab•loo•na or **kab•loo•na** [kæb'lunə] *n. Cdn.* a white person; European. Also, **Kadloona.** ⟨< Inuktitut *kabluna(k)* one having big eyebrows⟩

ka•bob [kə'bɒb] *n.* See KEBAB.

ka•bu•ki [kə'buki] *n.* in Japan, a popular type of drama in which both male and female parts are played by men. ⟨< Japanese *Kabu* music, dance + *ki* art⟩

Ka•byle [kə'baɪl] *or* [kə'bil] *n.* **1** a Berber people living in Tunisia and Algeria. **2** the language of these people. ⟨< F < Arabic *qaba'il*, pl. of *qabila* tribe⟩

ka•chi•na [kə'tʃinə] *n.* **1** among the Hopi Indians, any ancestral spirit. **2** a doll representing one of these spirits. ⟨< Hopi *kacina* < Keres⟩

kad•dish ['kɑdɪʃ] *or* [kɑ'diʃ] *n., pl.* **kad•dish•im** [-ɪm]. *Judaism.* a portion of the daily prayer said in the synagogue, also used as a public or official prayer of mourning for a dead relative. ⟨< Aramaic *qaddish* holy⟩

Kad•loo•na [kæd'lunə] *n.* Kabloona.

kaf [kɑf] *or* [kɒf] *n.* the twelfth letter of the Hebrew alphabet. See table of alphabets in the Appendix.

kaf•fee•klatsch ['kɑfei,klɑtʃ] *or* ['kɒfi,klætʃ] *n.* a gathering, often of women, to discuss matters over coffee. ⟨< G⟩

kaf•fir corn ['kæfər] an E African variety of sorghum grown in dry regions for grain and fodder. Also, **kafir corn.**

kaf•tan ['kæftən] *or* [kɑf'tɑn] See CAFTAN.

ka•fuf•fle [kə'fʌfəl] *n.* disorder; fuss. Also, **kerfuffle.**

ka•gu ['kɑgu] *n.* a large bird (*Rhynochetos jubatus*) found only in the forests of New Caledonia, and standing up to half a metre tall with a mass of one kilogram. It is mainly pale bluish grey. It is an endangered species.

Kah•na•wa•ke [,gɑnɑ'wɑgi] *n.* Caughnawaugha.

kai•ak ['kaɪæk] See KAYAK.

kail [keil] See KALE.

Kai•la ['kaɪlə] *n.* the supreme god of the Inuit. ⟨< Inuktitut⟩

kain•ite ['kaɪnəit] *or* ['keinəit] *n.* a mineral used as a fertilizer and consisting mainly of potassium. ⟨< G *Kainit* < Gk. *kainos* new⟩

kai•ser[1] ['kaɪzər] *n.* **1** the title of the emperors of Germany, 1871-1918. **2** the title of the emperors of Austria, 1804-1918. **3** the title of the emperors of the Holy Roman Empire from A.D. 962 to 1806. **4** emperor. ⟨< G < L *Caesar*⟩

kai•ser[2] ['kaɪzər] *n.* a large, round, crusty bun used especially for sliced meat sandwiches. Also called **kaiser bun, kaiser roll.** ⟨< G *kaisersemmel* kaiser bun, i.e., emperor's bun or roll. The kaisersemmel was invented by an anonymous Viennese baker for Emperor Frederick V in 1487.⟩

ka•ka ['kɑkə] *n.* any New Zealand parrot of the genus *Nestor.* ⟨< Maori; ? imitation of the bird's cry⟩

ka•ka•po [,kɑkə'pou] *n.* a New Zealand parrot (*Strigops habroptilus*) which cannot fly. ⟨< Maori, literally, night kaka⟩

ka•ki ['kɑki] *n.* **1** the Japanese persimmon tree. **2** the fruit of this tree. ⟨< Japanese⟩

kale [keil] *n.* **1** any of various kinds of cabbage that have loose leaves instead of a compact head. Kale resembles spinach in taste. **2** *Slang.* money; cash. ⟨var. of *cole*⟩

ka•lei•do•scope [kə'laɪdə,skoup] *n.* **1** a tube containing bits of coloured glass and two or more mirrors. As it is turned, it reflects continually changing patterns. **2** anything that changes continually; a continually changing pattern. ⟨< Gk. *kalos* pretty + *eidos* shape + E *-scope*⟩

ka•lei•do•scop•ic [kə,laɪdə'skɒpɪk] *adj.* of or like a kaleidoscope; continually changing. **—ka,lei•do'scop•i•cal•ly,** *adv.*

kal•ends ['kæləndz] See CALENDS.

Ka•le•va•la ['kɑlə,vɑlə] *or* [,kɑlə'vɑlə] *n.* the national epic poem of Finland, a collection of heroic songs and poems compiled from oral tradition. ⟨< Finnish *Kalevala*, literally, home of a hero⟩

Ka•li ['kɑli] *n. Hinduism.* goddess of life and death, the wife of Shiva.

kal•mi•a ['kælmiə] *n.* the mountain laurel, or any similar evergreen shrub, having clusters of cup-shaped flowers. ⟨< NL, after Peter *Kalm* (1715-1779), a Swedish botanist⟩

Kal•muck or **Kal•muk** ['kælmʌk] *or* [kæl'mʌk] *n., adj. —n.* **1** a member of any of the Mongol peoples, traditionally Buddhist, living in the area extending from W China to the Volga River. **2** the Mongolic language spoken by the Kalmuck. *—adj.* of or having to do with the Kalmuck or their language. ⟨< Turkic *kalmuk*, part of a Nomad Tartar tribe remaining at home⟩

ka•lo•tik ['kælətɪk] *n.* a special hook for towing home a seal. ⟨< Inuktitut⟩

kal•so•mine ['kælsə,maɪn] *or* ['kælsəmɪn] See CALCIMINE.

Ka•ma ['kɑmə] *n. Hinduism.* the god of love. ⟨< Skt. *kama* desire, love⟩

ka•ma•la [kə'mɑlə] *or* ['kæmələ] *n.* **1** a tree (*Mallotus philippinensis*) native to Asia. **2** a cathartic made from the seed capsules of this tree. ⟨< Skt. < Dravidian⟩

ka•mas ['kæməs] *n.* See CAMAS.

Ka•ma•su•tra [,kɑmə'sutrə] *n.* the Hindu manual of erotic love, written in Sanskrit. Also, **Kama sutra.** ⟨< Skt. *kama* love + *sutra* guide line, manual⟩

kame [keim] *n. Geology.* a small hill or ridge deposited by retreating glaciers. ⟨northern E dial. var. of *combe*⟩

ka•mi ['kɑmi] *n., pl.* **ka•mi.** *Shintoism.* any divine spirit. ⟨< Japanese⟩

ka•mik ['kɑmɪk] *n. Cdn.* a soft, knee-length boot of sealskin or caribou hide, worn in eastern arctic regions; mukluk. ⟨< Inuktitut⟩

ka•mi•ka•ze [,kɑmɪ'kɑzi] *or* [,kæmə'kæzi] *n.* **1** a member of a Japanese air corps in World War II that carried out suicide missions in which an aircraft loaded with explosives was deliberately crashed on a target by the pilot. **2** an aircraft used in such a mission. **3** (*adjl.*) of or having to do with such missions. **4** *Informal.* **a** a person who behaves in a self-destructive manner. **b** (*adjl.*) of or like such a person; suicidal: *a kamikaze taxi driver.* ⟨< Japanese *kamikaze*, literally, divine wind⟩

Kam•loops trout ['kæmlups] *Cdn.* a bright, silvery, medium-sized variety or stock of the rainbow trout found in British Columbia's small interior lakes, highly valued as a game and food fish. See also RAINBOW TROUT and STEELHEAD. ⟨< *Kamloops*, B.C.⟩

kam•pong ['kæmpɒŋ], [kæm'pɒŋ], *or* ['kɑmpɒŋ] *n.* a small village in Malay-speaking countries. ⟨< Malay⟩

Kam•pu•chea [,kæmpʊ'tʃiə] *n.* a country in SE Asia, formerly called Cambodia.

Kam•pu•che•an [,kæmpʊ'tʃiən] *n., adj. —n.* **1** a native or inhabitant of Kampuchea. **2** the language spoken in Kampuchea. *—adj.* of or having to do with Kampuchea.

ka•mu•tik [ˈkɒmətɪk] *n.* See KOMATIK.

ka•na [ˈkɑnə] *n.* Japanese syllabic writing with 71 symbols, used in two variations, **hiragana** and **katagana**.

Ka•nak•a [kəˈnækə], [kəˈnɑkə], *or* [ˈkænəkə] *n.* **1** a native Hawaiian. **2** a native or inhabitant of any of the S Pacific islands. ⟨< Hawaiian *kanaka* man⟩

Ka•na•rese [ˌkænəˈriz] *or* [ˌkɑnəˈriz] *adj., n. —adj.* of or having to do with the Kanara, a region in SW India.
—n. **1** a member of a Dravidian people living in the Kanara. **2** the language of these people.

kan•ga•roo [ˌkæŋgəˈru] *n., pl.* **-roos** or *(esp. collectively)* **-roo.** any of a family (Macropodidae) of marsupials of Australia, Tasmania, and New Guinea, typically having long, powerful hind legs adapted for leaping, a long, thick tail which is used for balancing, and small, short forelegs; especially, any of the genus *Macropus*, which includes the **red kangaroo** (*M. rufus*), the largest of all marsupials. See also WALLABY, WALLAROO. ⟨origin uncertain⟩ **—ˌkan•gaˈroo,like,** *adj.*

kangaroo court *Informal.* **1** an unauthorized or irregular court in which the law is deliberately disregarded or misinterpreted, especially one held by convicts in prison to settle disputes among themselves. **2** a mock court in which the judicial system, social conditions, etc. are satirized.

kangaroo rat any of a genus (*Dipodomys*) of small, mouselike, North American desert rodents having very long, strong hind legs adapted for leaping, a very long, tufted tail, and external fur-lined cheek pouches. Only one species (*D. ordii*) is found in Canada, in the sand hills of southern Saskatchewan and Alberta.

kan•ji [ˈkɑndʒi] *n., pl.* **-ji, -jis. 1** ideographic Japanese script using symbols from Chinese. **2** any of these symbols. ⟨< Japanese, *kan* Chinese + *ji* ideograph⟩

Kan•na•da [ˈkænədə] *or* [ˈkɑnədə] *n.* a Dravidian language used in Madras.

Kan•sas [ˈkænzəs] *n.* a midwestern state of the United States.

Kant•i•an [ˈkæntiən] *or* [ˈkɑntiən] *adj., n. —adj.* of or having to do with Immanuel Kant (1724-1804), a German philosopher, or his system of philosophy.
—n. a follower of Kant.

ka•o•lin or **ka•o•line** [ˈkeiəlɪn] *n.* a fine, white clay, used in making porcelain and in treating diarrhea. ⟨< F < Chinese *Kaoling*, a mountain in China which yielded the first kaolin sent to Europe (*kao* high + *ling* hill)⟩

ka•o•lin•ite [ˈkeiələˌnəit] *n.* a mineral which is the basis of kaolin.

ka•on [ˈkeiˌɒn] *n. Physics.* a K-meson, any of 4 mesons whose mass is almost a thousand times (964 or 996, depending on the charge) that of an electron. ⟨< *K- meson* < *K* symbol for one thousand + *meson*⟩

ka•peik [ˈkɑpeik] *n.* a unit of money in Belarus, equal to 1/100 of a ruble. See table of money in the Appendix.

Kap•ell•mei•ster [kəˈpɛlˌməistər] *n.* **1** a choirmaster. **2** the conductor of an orchestra. ⟨< G⟩

ka•pok [ˈkeipɒk] *n.* the silky fibres around the seeds of a tropical tree (*Ceiba pentandra*), used for stuffing pillows, life preservers, mattresses, etc. ⟨< Malay⟩

Ka•po•si's sar•co•ma [kəˈpouziz sɑrˈkoumə] a skin cancer due to a deficiency in the immune system. ⟨after M.K. *Kaposi* (1837-1902), Hungarian dermatologist⟩

kap•pa [ˈkæpə] *n.* the tenth letter (Κ, κ) of the Greek alphabet.

ka•put [kəˈpʊt] *adj. Informal.* ruined, broken, useless, etc. (*never used before a noun*): *All our plans are kaput.* ⟨< G *kaputt* < F *être capot* be without a score in piquet⟩

Ka•ra–Kal•pak [kəˌrɑ kəlˈpɑk] *or* [ˌkɑrə kəlˈpɑk] *n.* **1** a member of a Turkish people living in Uzbek. **2** the language of these people.

kar•a•kul [ˈkærəkəl *or* ˈkɛrəkəl] *n.* **1** a variety of Russian or Asiatic sheep, the young of which have a black fleece, the adults a brown or grey one. **2** fur with flat, loose curls; caracul. **3** a coat or other garment made of this fur. ⟨< *Kara Kul*, a lake in Turkestan (*kara* black + *kul* lake)⟩

ka•ra•o•ke [ˌkæriˈouki] *or* [ˌkɛriˈouki] *n.* a system allowing a person to sing, with amplification, to recorded music. ⟨< Japanese⟩

kar•at [ˈkærət] *or* [ˈkɛrət] *n.* a unit used to specify the proportion of gold in an alloy; one of 24 equal parts. An 18-karat gold ring is 18 parts pure gold and 6 parts alloy. *Symbol*: K or k Compare CARAT.
☛ *Hom.* CARAT, CARET, CARROT.

ka•ra•te [kəˈrɑti] *n.* a Japanese system of self-defence without weapons, using studied hand and foot strokes capable of crippling or killing. ⟨< Japanese, literally, empty-handed⟩

kar•bov•a•nets [kɑrˈbɒvəˌnɛts] *n., pl.* **kar•bo•van•ci** [ˌkɑrbəˈvæntʃi] the main unit of currency in Ukraine. See table of money in the Appendix.

Ka•rel•i•an [kəˈriliən] *or* [kəˈriljən] *n.* **1** a member of a people living in Karelia, a region along the E border of Finland. **2** the language of these people, a branch of Finnish.

Ka•ren [kəˈrɛn] *n.* **1** a group of people living in E and S Myanmar. **2** the Sino-Tibetan language of these people.

kar•ma [ˈkɑrmə] *n.* **1** *Buddhism and Hinduism.* the totality of a person's thoughts, actions, etc. that are supposed to affect or determine his or her fate in his or her next incarnation. **2** destiny; fate. ⟨< Skt. *karma* deed, action, fate⟩

kar•mic [ˈkɑrmɪk] *adj.* of, having to do with, or determined by karma.

ka•ross [kəˈrɒs] *n.* a cloak of animal skins worn by members of certain groups in S Africa. ⟨< Afrikaans *karos*; origin uncertain⟩

kar•roo or **ka•roo** [kəˈru] *n.* **1** **Karroo**, a plateau in the Cape of Good Hope, South Africa. **2** one of the arid areas of South Africa, having red soil. ⟨< Afrikaans *karo* < Hottentot *garo* desert⟩

karst [kɑrst] *n.* **1** an irregular limestone region marked by gullies, sinks, caverns, and underground streams. **2** (*adjl.*) of or designating such a region. ⟨< G *Karst*, from the name of a limestone plateau near Trieste⟩ **—ˈkarst•ic,** *adj.*

kart [kɑrt] *n., v. —n.* go-kart.
—v. take part in a go-kart race.
☛ *Hom.* CART, CARTE. **—ˈkart•er,** *n.*

karyo– *combining form.* the nucleus of a cell: *karyoplasm.* ⟨< Gk. *karyon* kernel, nut⟩

kar•y•o•ki•ne•sis [ˌkæriouкəˈnisɪs] *or* [ˌkɛriouкəˈnisɪs] *n. Biology.* **1** mitosis. **2** the series of changes that take place in a living cell in the process of division. **—ˌkar•y•o•kiˈnet•ic** [-kəˈnɛtɪk], *adj.*

kar•y•o•lymph [ˈkæriəˌlɪmf] *or* [ˈkɛriəˌlɪmf] *n. Botany.* the translucent fluid in a nucleus.

kar•y•o•plasm [ˈkæriəˌplæzəm] *or* [ˈkɛriəˌplæzəm] *n. Biology.* the substance of the nucleus of a cell. **—ˌkar•y•oˈplas•mic,** *adj.*

kar•y•o•some [ˈkæriəˌsoum] *or* [ˈkɛriəˌsoum] *n. Biology.* **1** a chromosome. **2** the nucleus of a cell.

kar•y•o•tin [ˈkæriətɪn] *or* [ˈkɛriətɪn] *n. Biology.* nuclear material; chromatin.

kar•y•o•type [ˈkæriəˌtəip] *or* [ˈkɛriəˌtəip] *n. Genetics.* **1** the chromosome constitution of an individual. **2** a photomicrograph of the chromosomes of an individual, set out in a standard pattern. The chromosomes of a karyotype are numbered in order of their size. **—ˌkar•y•oˈtyp•ic** [ˌkæriəˈtɪpɪk], *adj.* **—ˌkar•y•oˈtyp•i•cal,** *adj.*

kas•bah or **Kas•bah** [ˈkæzbə] *or* [ˈkɑzbə] *n.* See CASBAH.

ka•sha [ˈkɑʃə] *n.* a food prepared from cooked buckwheat. ⟨< Russian⟩

Kash•mir•i [kæʃˈmiri] *n., pl.* **-mir•is** or *(esp. collectively)* **-mir•i. 1** a native of Kashmir. **2** the Indo-European language of Kashmir. Also, **Kashmirian.**

kash•ruth [kɑʃˈrut] *or* [ˈkɑʃrut] *n.* dietary laws prescribed for Jews. ⟨< Hebrew, literally, fitness⟩

kat•a•bat•ic [ˌkætəˈbætɪk] *adj. Meteorology.* describing a wind moving in a downward direction. ⟨< Gk. *katabatikos* going down⟩

ka•tab•o•lism [kəˈtæbəˌlɪzəm] See CATABOLISM.

Ka•tar [kəˈtɑr] See QATAR.

ka•tha•rev•ou•sa [ˌkɑθəˈrɛvəˌsɑ] *n.* the Greek literary language, the closest to classical Greek. ⟨< Mod.Gk., literally, pure⟩

ka•ty•did [ˈkeitiˌdɪd] *n.* any of various large, green, long-horned grasshoppers. The male makes a shrill noise by rubbing its front wings together. ⟨imitative of the insect's sound⟩

kau•ri [ˈkaʊri] *n., pl.* **-ris. 1** a tall timber tree (*Agathis australis*) of the pine family found in New Zealand, having white, straight-grained wood. **2** the wood of this tree. **3** a resin that is obtained from it, used in varnish. Also, **kaury,** pl. **-ries.** ⟨< Maori⟩

ka•va ['kɑvə] *n.* **1** a Polynesian shrub (*Piper methysticum*). **2** a drink made from its roots. ⟨< Polynesian, literally, bitter⟩

kay•ak ['kaɪæk] *n. Cdn.* **1** a light, narrow boat with pointed ends, made of skins, etc. stretched over a frame of wood or bone, leaving only a small opening in the middle for the user. A kayak is propelled by a double-bladed paddle. Kayaks were traditionally used by the Inuit for hunting. **2** any similar craft. ⟨< Inuktitut⟩ **—'kay•ak•er,** *n.* **—'kay•ak•ing,** *n.*

Ka•zak [kə'zɑk] *or* [kə'zæk] *n.* a member of a Kirghiz people living in Kazakhstan in central Asia. See COSSACK.

Ka•zakh•stan [ˌkɑzək'stɑn] *or* ['kæzəkˌstæn] *n.* a country in central Asia.

ka•zoo [kə'zu] *n.* a toy musical instrument made of a tube sealed off at one end with a membrane or paper that produces a buzzing sound when one hums into the tube. ⟨imitative⟩

KB *Computer technology.* kilobyte.

K.B. **1** Knight of the (Order of the) Bath. **2** Knight Bachelor. **3** King's Bench.

K.B.E. Knight Commander of the (Order of the) British Empire.

kc kilocycle(s).

K.C. **1** KNIGHT(S) OF COLUMBUS. **2** KING'S COUNSEL.

K.C.B. Knight Commander of the (Order of the) Bath.

K.C.M.G. Knight or Dame Commander of (the Order of) St. Michael and St. George.

K.C.V.O. Knight Commander of the (Royal) Victorian Order.

ke•a ['keiə] *or* ['kiə] *n.* a large, greenish parrot (*Nestor notabilis*) of New Zealand that normally feeds on insects, but sometimes kills sheep to feed upon their fat. ⟨< Maori⟩

ke•bab [kə'bɒb] *n.* a dish comprising pieces of meat and vegetables cooked on a skewer and served with rice. Also, **kabob.** ⟨< Arabic *kabab*⟩

Kech•ua ['kɛtʃwɑ] *or* ['kɛtʃwə] See QUECHUA.

Kech•uan ['kɛtʃwən] See QUECHUAN.

kedge [kɛdʒ] *v.* **kedged, kedg•ing;** *n.* *—v.* move (a ship, etc.) by pulling on a rope attached to an anchor that has been dropped some distance away.
—n. a small anchor used in kedging a boat, etc. ⟨origin uncertain⟩

kedg•er•ee ['kɛdʒəˌri] *or* [ˌkɛdʒə'ri] *n.* **1** an Indian dish of rice, boiled with split peas, onions, eggs, butter, and spices. **2** a European dish made of fish, boiled rice, eggs, and spices, served hot. ⟨< Hind. *khichri*⟩

keek•wil•lie (house) ['kikwɪli] *n. Cdn. B.C.* a large subterranean winter dwelling formerly used by certain First Nations peoples, a typical example being 3-4 m deep and 8-12 m in diameter, covered with split logs and a layer of mud, and accommodating 12-15 persons. ⟨< Chinook Jargon, below < Chinook *gigwalix*⟩

keel¹ [kil] *n.* **1** *Nautical.* the main timber or steel piece that extends the whole length of the bottom of a ship or boat. **2** *Poetic.* a ship. **3** a part, as on an aircraft, that is like a ship's keel. **4** *Botany, zoology.* a ridge on a leaf or bone running longitudinally.
on an even keel, a horizontal. **b** steady; properly balanced: *His business affairs are on an even keel again.*
—v. turn upside down; upset.
keel over, a turn over or upside down; upset: *The sailboat keeled over in the storm.* **b** *Informal.* fall over suddenly. **c** *Informal.* faint. ⟨ME *kele* < ON *kjölr*⟩

keel² [kil] *n.* a red stain made of ochre, used for marking sheep, lumber, etc. ⟨late ME *keyle*; origin uncertain⟩

keel•haul ['kilˌhɒl] *v.* formerly, haul (a person) from side to side under the keel of a ship as a punishment. ⟨< Du. *kielhalen* < *kiel* keel + *halen* haul⟩

keel•son ['kɛlsən] *or* ['kilsən] *n. Nautical.* a beam or line of timbers or iron plates fastened along the top of a ship's keel to strengthen it. Also, **kelson.** ⟨< LG *kielswin*, literally, keel swine < Scand.; cf. Swedish *kölsvin*⟩

keen¹ [kin] *adj.* **1** sharp enough to cut well: *a keen blade.* **2** sharp; piercing; cutting: *a keen wind, keen hunger, keen wit, keen pain.* **3** strong; vigorous: *keen competition.* **4** able to do its work quickly and accurately: *a keen mind, a keen sense of smell.* **5** *Informal.* full of enthusiasm; eager (*often used with* **about, for,** *etc.*): *a keen player, keen about sailing.* ⟨ME *kene*, OE *cēne*⟩ **—'keen•ly,** *adv.* **—'keen•ness,** *n.*

☛ *Syn.* **2.** See note at SHARP. **5.** See note at EAGER.

keen² [kin] *n., v.* *—n.* a wailing lament for the dead.
—v. wail; lament. ⟨< Irish *caoine*⟩ **—'keen•er,** *n.*

keep [kip] *v.* **kept, keep•ing;** *n.* *—v.* **1** have permanently or forever: *You may keep this book.* **2** have and not let go; hold; detain: *They were kept in prison. He was kept in hospital for ten days.* **3** not reveal or divulge: *to keep a secret.* **4** have and take care of: *My uncle keeps chickens.* **5** take care of and protect: *May God keep you.* **6** have in one's service; employ: *to keep a servant.* **7** have; hold: *keep this in mind.* **8** hold back; prevent: *What is keeping her from accepting?* **9** restrain oneself (*from*); refrain: *The little boy couldn't keep from crying when he fell down.* **10** maintain in good or orderly condition: *to keep a house.* **11** be preserved; stay in good condition: *Butter will keep in a refrigerator.* **12** be postponable without ill effect: *This matter will keep.* **13** continue or cause to continue in some stated place, condition, etc.: *to keep awake, to keep a light burning, to keep students on their toes. Keep going along this road for 2 km.* **14** make regular entries or records in: *to keep books, to keep a diary.* **15** put in writing; make (a record, note, etc.): *No record of this conversation was kept.* **16** observe; celebrate: *to keep Thanksgiving as a holiday.* **17** be faithful (to): *to keep a promise.* **18** provide for; support: *He is not able to keep himself, much less a family.* **19** have habitually for sale: *That store keeps canned goods.* **20** set aside: *Keep the rest for later.*
keep in with, *Informal.* keep acquaintance or friendship with.
keep on, continue; go on: *The boys kept on swimming in spite of the rain.*
keep time, a of watches, clocks, etc., go correctly; move at the proper rate. **b** maintain a tempo: *The choir kept time well.*
keep to oneself, a not mix with others. **b** not reveal to others.
keep up, a continue; prevent from ending. **b** maintain in good condition. **c** not fall behind; remain close or alongside.
keep up with, a not fall behind; go or move as fast as. **b** live or do as well as: *She tried hard to keep up with her wealthy neighbours.* **c** stay up to date with: *He keeps up with the news. Try to keep up with your reading.*
—n. **1** food and a place to sleep; maintenance: *He earns his keep.* **2** the strongest part of a castle or fort. See CASTLE for picture.
for keeps, a for the winner to keep his or her winnings. **b** *Informal.* forever. ⟨OE *cēpan* observe⟩

☛ *Syn. v.* **2, 7. Keep,** RETAIN, WITHHOLD = hold in one's possession. **Keep** is the general word meaning 'have and not let go from one's possession, control, or care': *They were kept in prison.* **Retain,** more formal, emphasizes continuing to hold on to in spite of pressures or difficulties: *The patient retained her sense of humour.* **Withhold** means keep or hold back and suggests some check or obstacle to letting go: *Fear made him withhold the truth.*

keep•er ['kipər] *n.* **1** a person who or thing that keeps. **2** guard. **3** guardian; protector: *Am I my brother's keeper?* **4** *Brit.* gamekeeper. **5** a person who owns or carries on some establishment or business: *the keeper of an inn.* **6** any mechanical device for keeping something in its place, as a clasp, catch, or loop. **7** a link set across the poles of a magnet to preserve its magnetism when not in use. **8** a food or other produce that keeps (well or poorly). **9** *Informal.* a fish large enough to be legally caught and kept. **10** goalkeeper. **11** *Informal.* an unmarried mother who keeps her baby. **12** SLEEPER (def. 6).
—'keep•er•less, *adj.* **—'keep•er,ship,** *n.*

keep•ing ['kipɪŋ] *n., v.* *—n.* **1** care; charge: *She left the jewels in the keeping of a trustee.* **2** celebration; observance: *the keeping of Thanksgiving Day.* **3** agreement; harmony: *Don't trust him; his actions are not in keeping with his promises.* **4** the condition of being kept for future use; preservation.
—v. ppr. of KEEP.

keep•sake ['kipˌseik] *n.* something kept in memory of the giver: *My friend gave me his picture as a keepsake when he moved away.*

Kees•hond ['keisˌhɒnd] *or* ['kisˌhɒnd] *n., pl.* **-hon•den** or **-honds.** a breed of small dog developed in the Netherlands, having a thick, grey coat tipped with black. ⟨< Du. *keeshond* < *Kees* Cornelius + *hond* dog, hound⟩

keet [kit] *n.* the young of the guinea fowl. ⟨imitative⟩

Kee•wa•tin [ki'weitən] *or* [ki'wɑtən] *adj. Geology.* of or having to do with the earliest period of the Archaeozoic era. ⟨< *Keewatin*, a district of the Northwest Territories⟩

kef [kɛf] *n.* a preparation of hemp. ⟨< Arabic, var. of *kaif*⟩

keg [kɛg] *n.* **1** a small barrel or cask. **2** a keg and its contents. **3** as much as a keg can hold. **4** a unit by which to weigh nails, equivalent to 100 pounds (45.36 kg). ⟨ME < ON *kaggi*⟩

kelly green a strong yellowish green. ⟨< *Kelly,* an Irishman⟩

ke•loid ['kilɔɪd] *n. Pathology.* a tumour forming clawlike growths in the skin. ⟨< Gk. *kelis* stain, spot⟩

kelp [kɛlp] *n.* **1** any of the large, brown seaweeds, especially those of the order Laminariales, such as the giant Pacific kelps (genus *Macrocystis*) or the Atlantic kelps (genus *Laminaria*). **2** the ashes of such seaweeds, used especially as a source of iodine and potassium. ⟨earlier also *kilpe*, ME *culp(e)*; origin unknown⟩

kel•per ['kɛlpər] *n.* a native or inhabitant of the Falkland Islands. Also, **Kelper.**

kel•pie[1] or **kel•py**[1] ['kɛlpi] *n., pl.* **-pies.** in Scottish folklore, a water spirit, usually in the form of a horse, supposed to drown people or be an omen of death by drowning. ⟨origin uncertain⟩

kel•pie[2] or **kel•py**[2] ['kɛlpi] *n.* one of a breed of dog used in Australia for herding sheep. ⟨after the name of one of these dogs⟩

kel•son ['kɛlsən] *n.* keelson.

kelt [kɛlt] *n.* an Atlantic salmon or trout that has recently spawned. ⟨origin unknown. 14c.⟩

Kelt [kɛlt] *n.* See CELT.

Kelt•ic ['kɛltɪk] *adj. or n.* See CELTIC.

kel•vin ['kɛlvɪn] *n. Physics.* **1** (*adjl.*) **Kelvin,** of, based on, or according to a scale of thermodynamic temperature used in science, on which 0 represents absolute zero, theoretically the coldest possible state. Zero on the Kelvin scale is equal to –273.16°C. **2** an SI unit of temperature on this scale. One kelvin is equal to one degree Celsius. The kelvin is one of the seven base units in the SI. *Symbol*: K ⟨after William Thomson, Lord *Kelvin* (1824-1907), English physicist and mathematician⟩

ken [kɛn] *n., v.* **kenned** or **kent** [kɛnt], **ken•ning.** *–n.* **1** the range of sight. **2** the range of knowledge: *What happens on Mars is beyond our ken.*
–v. Scottish. know. ⟨OE *cennan* make declaration < *cann* know, can[1]⟩

ke•naf [kə'næf] *n.* **1** ambary (*Hibiscus cannabinus*), an East Indian plant. **2** its fibre, used in making canvas. ⟨< Persian, akin to *kanab* hemp⟩

Ken•dal green ['kɛndəl] **1** a coarse, green, woollen cloth. **2** the colour of this cloth. ⟨< *Kendal*, in Westmoreland, now part of Cumbria, England, where the cloth was originally made. 14c.⟩

ken•do [kɛn'dou] *or* ['kɛndou] *n.* a Japanese sport, fencing with wooden staves. ⟨< Japanese *ken* sword + *do* way⟩

ken•nel ['kɛnəl] *n., v.* **-nelled** or **-neled, -nel•ling** or **-nel•ing.** *–n.* **1** a house for a dog or dogs. **2** Often, **kennels,** *pl.* **a** a place where dogs are bred. **b** a place where dogs and cats may be lodged and cared for. **3** a pack of dogs.
–v. **1** put or keep in a kennel. **2** take shelter or lodge in a kennel. ⟨< AF, ult. < L *canis* dog⟩

kennel cough a disease of dogs.

Ken•ny method or **treatment** ['kɛni] a method of treating poliomyelitis with hot packs and exercises. ⟨after Elizabeth *Kenny* (1886-1952), an Australian nurse and researcher in poliomyelitis therapy⟩

ke•no ['kinou] *n.* a gambling game resembling lotto and bingo in which the players cover numbers on their cards. ⟨< F *quine* five winning numbers < L *quini* five each⟩

Kent•ish ['kɛntɪʃ] *adj., n. –adj.* of Kent, a county in SE England, or its people.
–n. an Old English dialect spoken in the early English kingdom of Kent.

kent•ledge ['kɛntlɪdʒ] *n. Nautical.* a permanent ballast of pig iron in a ship. ⟨< F *quintelage* ballast < *quintal* quintal⟩

Ken•tuck•y [kɛn'tʌki] *n.* a southeasterly state of the United States.

Kentucky coffee tree a tree (*Gymnocladus dioicus*), native to Ontario, whose seeds were formerly used as a substitute for coffee beans.

Ken•ya ['kɛnjə] *or* ['kinjə] *n.* a country in E Africa. See SUDAN for map.

Kenyan ['kɛnjən] *or* ['kinjən] *n., adj. –n.* a native or inhabitant of Kenya.
–adj. of or having to do with Kenya.

kep•i ['keipi] *or* ['kɛpi] *n., pl.* **kep•is.** a cap with a round, flat top, worn by French soldiers. See CAP for picture. ⟨< F *képi*, ult. < G *Kappe* cap⟩

kept [kɛpt] *v.* pt. and pp. of KEEP.

ker•a•tec•to•my [,kɛrə'tɛktəmi] *n., pl.* **-mies.** the removal of part or the whole of the cornea by surgery.

ker•a•tin ['kɛrətɪn] *n. Zoology.* a complex protein, the chief constituent of horn, nails, hair, feathers, etc. ⟨< Gk. *keras, -atos* horn⟩ **—ke'rat•i•nous** or **ke'rat•i•noid,** *adj.*

ker•a•tin•ize ['kɛrətə,naɪz] *or* [kə'rætə,naɪz] *v.* **-ized, -iz•ing.** make or become like keratin. **—,ker•a•tin•i'za•tion,** *n.*

ker•a•ti•tis [,kɛrə'taɪtɪs] *n. Pathology.* inflammation of the cornea.

kerato– *combining form.* **1** horn: *keratogenous*. **2** cornea: *keratectomy*. Also, before vowels, **kerat-.** ⟨< Gk. *keratos* horn⟩

ker•a•tog•e•nous [,kɛrə'tɒdʒənəs] *adj.* producing horn or a horny substance.

ker•a•toid ['kɛrə,tɔɪd] *adj.* like horn.

ker•a•to•plas•ty ['kɛrətou,plæsti] *n., pl.* **-ties.** plastic surgery on the cornea.

ker•a•to•sis [,kɛrə'tousɪs] *n., pl.* **-ses** [-siz]. *Pathology.* **1** a skin disease producing a horny growth. **2** any growth resembling horn. **—,ker•a'to•sic,** *adj.*

kerb [kɛrb] *n. Brit.* CURB (def. 1).

ker•chief ['kɜrtʃɪf] *n.* **1** a square piece of cloth worn over the head or around the neck. **2** handkerchief. ⟨ME < OF *couvrechief* < *couvrir* cover (< L *cooperire*) + *chief* head < L *caput*⟩ **—'ker•chiefed,** *adj.*

Ke•res ['keirɛs] *n.* **1** a member of an American Indian people now living in pueblos in New Mexico. **2** the language of these people.

kerf [kɜrf] *n.* **1** a cut made by an axe, saw, etc. **2** a piece cut off. ⟨OE *cyrf* < *ceorfan* carve⟩

ker•fuf•fle [kər'fʌfəl] *n.* See KAFUFFLE.

Ker•man [kər'mɑn] *n.* See KIRMAN.

ker•mes ['kɜrmiz] *n.* **1** a red dye made from scale insects of the genus *Kermes.* **2** the little oak (*Quercus coccifera*) which is host to these insects. ⟨earlier *chermez* < OItal. *chermes* < Arabic *qirmiz* < Persian⟩

ker•mis ['kɜrmɪs] *n.* **1** in the Netherlands, Belgium, etc., a fair with games and merrymaking. **2** any fair or entertainment, usually to raise money for charity. Also, **kermess, kirmess.** ⟨< Du. *kermis* < *kerk* church + *mis* Mass⟩

Ker•mode bear ['kɜrmoud] *Cdn.* **1** a subspecies of the black bear (*Ursus americanus kermodei*). **2** the white or creamy-white colour phase of this bear. ⟨after Francis *Kermode* (1874-1946), former director of the B.C. Provincial Museum⟩

kern[1] or **kerne** [kɜrn] *n.* **1** *Archaic.* **a** an Irish or Scottish foot soldier carrying light weapons. **b** a troop of such soldiers. **2** an Irish peasant. ⟨< Irish *ceithern* troop of soldiers⟩

kern[2] [kɜrn] *n., v. –n. Printing.* the part of a letter that projects beyond the body of the piece of type; serif.
–v. **1** furnish with a kern. **2** cause (letters) to be positioned, in print or on a computer screen, as closely together as their shapes will allow. ⟨< F *carne* edge < L *cardo, -dinis* hinge⟩

ker•nel ['kɜrnəl] *n.* **1** the softer part inside the hard shell of a nut or inside the stone of a fruit. **2** a grain or seed like wheat or corn. **3** the central or most important part: *the kernel of an argument.* ⟨OE *cyrnel* < *corn* seed, grain⟩
☛ *Hom.* COLONEL.

kern•ite ['kɜrnəit] *n.* a white, crystalline substance from which borax is obtained. *Formula*: $Na_2B_4O_7{\cdot}4H_2O$ ⟨after *Kern* county, California⟩

ker•o•sene ['kɛrə,sin] *or* [,kɛrə'sin] *n. Cdn.* a thin oil, a mixture of hydrocarbons, usually produced by distilling petroleum; coal oil. It is used as a fuel in lamps, stoves, some types of engines, etc. ⟨< Gk. *kēros* wax⟩

kerosene lamp *Cdn.* a lamp that burns kerosene.

Ker•ry ['kɛri] *n.* **-ries.** a breed of small, black dairy cattle. ⟨< *Kerry*, a county in SW Irish Republic, where this breed originated⟩

Kerry blue terrier one of an Irish breed of terrier with a soft bluish grey coat.

ker•sey ['kɜrzi] *n., pl.* **-seys. 1** a coarse, ribbed, woollen cloth with a cotton warp. **2 kerseys,** *pl.* trousers made of kersey. ⟨probably < *Kersey*, a village in Suffolk, England⟩

ker•sey•mere ['kɜrzi,mir] *n.* a fine woollen cloth, more compact than kersey. ⟨< *kersey* + (*cassi*)*mere*⟩

kes•trel ['kɛstrəl] *n.* any of several small falcons noted for their habit of hovering against the wind while hunting, just before diving for their prey; especially, a common European species (*Falco tinnunculus*). The North American sparrow hawk is sometimes called the **American kestrel** because of its close relationship with the Old World kestrels. ⟨probably < OF *cresserelle* < L *crista* crest⟩

A kestrel

ket•a ['kɛtə] *or* ['kitə] *n., pl.* **ket•a.** *Cdn.* a species of Pacific salmon, the chum. ⟨origin uncertain⟩

ket•a•mine ['kɛtə,min] *n.* an anesthetic drug.

ke•taz•o•lam [kɪ'tæzə,læm] *n.* a tranquillizing drug.

ketch [kɛtʃ] *n. Nautical.* **1** a fore-and-aft-rigged sailing ship with a large mainmast toward the bow and a smaller mast toward the stern. **2** formerly, a sturdy sailing vessel with two masts. ⟨? < *catch*⟩

ketch•up ['kɛtʃəp] *or* ['kætʃəp] *n.* a sauce for use with meat, fish, etc. Tomato ketchup is made of tomatoes, onions, salt, sugar, and spices. Also, **catsup.** ⟨< Malay *kechap* sauce, probably < Chinese *kôe-chiap* brine of pickled fish⟩

ke•tene ['kitin] *n.* a poisonous gas used as a welding agent. *Formula*: H_2C_2O

keto– a combining form of KETONE. Also, especially before a vowel, **ket-**.

ke•to•ac•i•do•sis [,kitou,æsɪ'dousɪs] *n. Pathology.* **1** a condition of the blood in which it becomes overloaded with acid, such as in alcoholism. **2** a diabetic coma.

ke•to•con•a•zole [,kitou'kɒnə,zoul] *n.* a drug used in a cream form to treat certain fungal conditions.

ke•tone ['kitoun] *n. Chemistry.* one of a group of organic compounds, such as acetone, containing aryl, alkyl, and carbonyl groups. ⟨< G⟩ **—ke'ton•ic** [ki'tɒnɪk], *adj.*

ketone body any substance, notably acetoacetic acid, that shows an increase in the blood in diabetes mellitus.

ke•to•nu•ria [,kitou'njʊriə] *or* [,kitou'nʊriə] *n. Medicine.* the presence of ketone bodies in the urine.

ke•to•pro•fen [,kitou'proufən] *n.* a pain-killing drug used to treat arthritis and other conditions.

ke•tose ['kitous] *n. Chemistry.* any carbohydrate with a ketone in each molecule.

ke•to•sis [ki'tousɪs] *n.* a condition of having too many ketones in the body, as in the condition diabetes acidosis.

ke•to•ti•fen [,kitou'təifən] *n.* a drug used to treat asthma in children.

ket•tle ['kɛtəl] *n.* **1** a metal container for boiling liquids, cooking fruit, etc. **2** teakettle. **3** *Geology.* a depression in glacial drift remaining after the melting of an isolated mass of buried ice.
kettle of fish, *Informal.* an awkward state of affairs; mess; muddle. ⟨OE *cetel* < L *catillus*, dim. of *catinus* vessel⟩

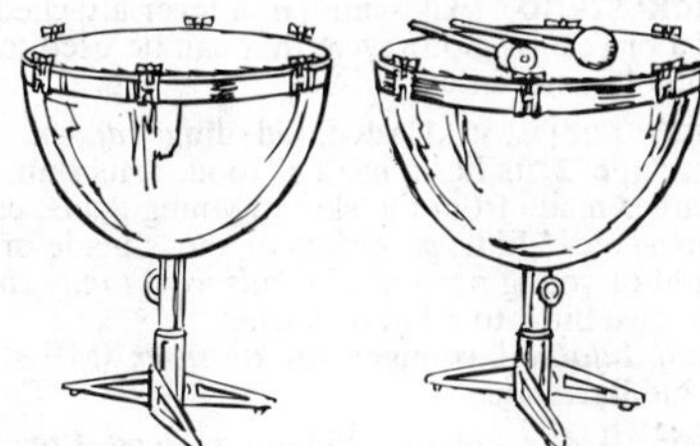
Kettledrums

ket•tle•drum ['kɛtəl,drʌm] *n.* a drum consisting of a hollow brass or copper hemisphere and a parchment top that can be tuned by adjusting the tension using screws around the circumference. See DRUM for picture.

ke•tu•bah or **Ke•tu•bah** [kə'tubə] *n., pl.* **ke•tu•both** [kə'tubous] *or* [kə'tubout] or **ke•tu•bahs.** *Judaism.* the marriage contract signed by a couple before the wedding, listing their obligations under Jewish law. ⟨< Hebrew *kethubhah* a writing, written document⟩

ke•vel ['kɛvəl] *n. Nautical.* a low metal post to which hawsers may be attached. ⟨< DNF *keville* < L *clavicula*, dim. of *clavis* key⟩

kew•pie doll ['kjupi] **1** a plastic or celluloid doll resembling a fat cherub with tiny wings and a curled topknot. **2 Kewpie Doll,** *Trademark.* a brand of such dolls. ⟨dim. of *Cupid*⟩

key[1] [ki] *n., pl.* **keys;** *adj., v.* **keyed, key•ing.** *—n.* **1** an instrument that locks and unlocks; something that turns the bolt in a lock: *I lost the key to the padlock on my bicycle.* **2** anything like this in shape or use: *a key to open a tin.* **3** something that explains or answers: *the key to a puzzle. The key to an arithmetic book gives the answers to all the problems.* **4** a place that commands or gives control of a sea, a district, etc. because of its position: *Gibraltar is the key to the Mediterranean.* **5** an important or essential person, thing, etc. **6** a pin, bolt, wedge, or other piece put in a hole or space to hold parts together. **7** a device to turn a bolt or nut, etc. Watches used to be wound with keys. **8** one of a set of parts pressed down by the fingers in playing a piano, a woodwind instrument, etc. and in keyboarding. **9** *Music.* a scale or system of related tones based on a particular tone: *a song written in the key of B flat.* **10** a tone of voice; style of thought or expression: *The poet wrote in a melancholy key.* **11** *Botany.* KEY FRUIT. **12** a systematic explanation of abbreviations or symbols used in a dictionary, map, etc.: *There is a pronunciation key at the beginning of the dictionary.* **13** *Electricity.* a device to open or close an electric circuit. **14** a means to achieve something: *the key to success.* **15** *Botany.* an indehiscent seed, often with winglike appendages.
—adj. controlling; very important: *the key industries of a nation.*
—v. **1** lock. **2** fasten or adjust with a key. **3** provide with a key or keys. **4** *Music.* regulate the pitch of; tune: *to key a piano in preparation for a concert.* **5** give a particular tone, style, etc. to: *a letter keyed in a tone of defiance. Her performance is keyed to a young audience.*
key in, enter data, etc. in a word processor, computer, etc. by means of a keyboard: *The computer operator keyed in the numbers.*
key up, a raise the courage or nerve of: *The coach keyed up the team for the big game.* **b** make or be excited or overexcited: *I was so keyed up I couldn't concentrate.* ⟨OE *cǣg*⟩ **—'key•less,** *adj.*
☛ *Hom.* CAY, QUAY.

key[2] [ki] *n., pl.* **keys.** a low island; reef. There are keys south of Florida. ⟨< Sp. *cayo* < Taino (an Arawakan language) *cayo*, or *caya* small island; influenced by *key[1]*⟩
☛ *Hom.* CAY, QUAY.

key block a large, conical block of snow, dropped into place at the centre of an igloo dome, serving to lock the structure firmly together. See IGLOO for picture.

key•board ['ki,bɔrd] *n., v. —n.* **1** the set of keys on a piano, typewriter, calculator, computer, etc. **2** any musical instrument having a keyboard, such as a synthesizer.
—v. **1** operate the keyboard of a typewriter, word processor, or computer: *She was learning to keyboard in school.* **2** set up type in printing by using a typesetting machine.

key•board•ing ['ki,bɔrdɪŋ] *n., v. —n.* skill in typing or word processing.
—v. ppr. of KEYBOARD.

key•chain ['ki,tʃein] *n.* a small chain to which keys may be attached.

keyed [kid] *adj., v. —adj.* **1** having keys: *a keyed flute or trombone.* **2** set or pitched in a particular key. **3** fastened or strengthened with a key. **4** reinforced by a keystone.
—v. pt. and pp. of KEY.
keyed up, excited or nervous.

key fruit *Botany.* a dry, winged fruit. The seeds of elm, ash, maple, etc. are contained in key fruits.

key•hole ['ki,houl] *n.* an opening in a lock through which a key is inserted to turn the lock.

keyhole saw a saw for cutting keyholes or small circles.

Key•nes•i•an economics ['keinziən] the theory of English economist J.M. Keynes (1883-1946) that in a depression a government should promote recovery by making projects to create employment and by adjusting interest rates to provide for business loans.

key•note ['ki,nout] *n., v.* **-not•ed, -not•ing.** *—n.* **1** *Music.* the note on which a scale or system of tones is based. **2** the main idea; guiding principle: *World peace was the keynote of his speech.*

—*v.* give the keynote speech of (a conference, political campaign, etc.)

keynote speech a speech, as at a political or educational gathering, that addresses the principal issues in which those present are interested. Also, **keynote address.**

key•pad ['ki,pæd] *n.* **1** that part of a computer keyboard that contains numbers and special keys. **2** the keyboard of a KEY PUNCH.

key punch an electronic machine operated by a keyboard, that punches holes in cards for use in a computer.

key seat the part of a machine able to receive a key.

key•seat ['ki,sit] *v.* furnish with a KEY SEAT.

key signature *Music.* one or more sharps or flats placed after the clef at the beginning of each staff to indicate the key.

key•stone ['ki,stoun] *n.* **1** *Architecture.* the middle stone at the top of an arch, holding the other stones or pieces in place. See ARCH for picture. **2** the part on which other associated parts depend; essential principle: *Freedom is the keystone of our policy.*

key•stroke ['ki,strouk] *n.* a stroke of a key on a keyboard.

key•way ['ki,wei] *n.* **1** a slot in a shaft or wheel hub for a key. **2** the hole in a cylinder lock in which the key fits.

kg **1** kilogram(s). **2** keg(s).

K.G. Knight (of the Order) of the Garter.

KGB formerly, the secret police of the Soviet Union. ⟨abbrev. of Russian *Komitet Gosudarstvennoi Bezopasnosti* State Security Committee⟩

khak•i ['kæki], ['kɑki], *or* ['kɑrki] *n., pl.* **khak•is;** *adj.* —*n.* **1** a dull, yellowish brown. **2** a stout, twilled cloth of this colour, used for soldiers' uniforms. **3** a uniform or uniforms made of this cloth: *Khakis will be worn for drill.*
—*adj.* **1** having the colour khaki. **2** made of khaki cloth. ⟨< Hind. *khaki*, originally, dust-coloured < Persian *khak* dust⟩

kha•lif ['keilɪf] *or* ['kælɪf] See CALIPH.

Khal•kha ['kælkə] *n.* **1** one of a group of people living in Mongolia. **2** the Altaic language of these people.

Khal•sa ['kɑlsə] *n. Sikhism.* the worldwide community of baptized members.

kham•sin [kæm'sɪn] *or* [kæm'sin] *n.* a hot, dry wind originating in the Sahara in the spring and lasting about 50 days. ⟨< Arabic, literally, fifty⟩

khan[1] [kɑn] *or* [kæn] *n.* **1** the title of a ruler among Tatar or Mongol tribes, or of the emperor of China during the Middle Ages. **2** a title of dignity in Iran, Afghanistan, India, etc. ⟨ME < MF < Turkish⟩

khan[2] [kɑn] *or* [kæn] *n.* in Turkey and nearby countries, an inn without furnishings. ⟨Arabic < Persian⟩

khan•ate ['kɑneit] *or* ['kæneit] *n.* **1** the territory ruled by a khan. **2** the position or authority of a khan.

kha•tib [kə'tib] *n. Islam.* the preacher—usually a mullah—who delivers the khutba in a mosque. ⟨< Arabic *khataba* to preach⟩

khe•dive [kə'div] *n.* the title of the Turkish viceroys who ruled Egypt between 1867 and 1914. ⟨< F < Persian *khidiv* ruler⟩

khet or **kheth** [xɛt] *n.* the eighth letter of the Hebrew alphabet. Also, **het.**

Khmer [kə'mɛr] *n.* **1** a member of a people in Kampuchea. **2** the Austro-asiatic language of these people.

Khoi•san ['kɔɪsɑn] *n.* a family of languages of SW Africa.

khoum [kum] *n.* a unit of currency in Mauritania, equal to ⅕ of an ougiya. See table of money in the Appendix.

khut•ba ['kʊtbɑ] *n. Islam.* a sermon given in a mosque.

kHz or **khz** kilohertz.

ki•ang [ki'æŋ] *n.* a wild ass (*Equus hemionus kiang*) of mountain regions of E Asia, including Tibet. ⟨< Tibetan *rkyan*⟩

kib•ble ['kɪbəl] *n., v.* **kib•bled, kib•bling.**
—*n.* a substance consisting of coarse particles, such as dogfood.
—*v.* grind up into coarse particles. ⟨origin uncertain⟩

kib•butz [kɪ'bʊts] *n., pl.* **kib•butz•im** [kɪbʊt'sim] *Hebrew.* a communal settlement or farm co-operative in Israel. ⟨literally, a gathering⟩

kib•butz•nik [kɪ'bʊtsnɪk] *n.* a member of a kibbutz.

kibe [kaɪb] *n.* a chapped or ulcerated sore, inflammation, or swelling on the heel caused by exposure to cold. ⟨ME; cf. Welsh *cibwst* chilblains, kibes⟩

kib•itz ['kɪbɪts] *v. Informal.* **1** look on as an outsider and offer unwanted advice, as in a card game. **2** joke or make wisecracks; chat in a joking or flippant manner. ⟨< *kibitzer*⟩

kib•itz•er ['kɪbɪtsər] *n. Informal.* **1** a person who watches a card game and insists on making suggestions to the players. **2** a person who gives unwanted advice; meddler. **3** a person who makes jokes or other distractions, especially while someone else is trying to work. ⟨< Yiddish⟩

kib•lah ['kɪb,lɑ] *n. Islam.* **1** the direction Muslims face when they pray. **2** in a mosque, a mark indicating this direction. ⟨< Arabic *qibla* something placed opposite < *qabala* to be opposite⟩

ki•bosh ['kaɪbɒʃ] *or* [kɪ'bɒʃ] *n. Informal.* humbug; nonsense. **put the kibosh on,** finish off; squelch: *The boss put the kibosh on long coffee breaks.* ⟨origin uncertain; probably < Yiddish⟩

kick[1] [kɪk] *v., n.* —*v.* **1** strike out with the foot: *That horse kicks when anyone comes near it.* **2** strike with the foot: *The horse kicked the boy.* **3** drive, force, or move by kicking: *to kick a ball.* **4** win by a kick: *to kick a goal in football.* **5** spring back when fired: *This shotgun kicks.* **6** *Informal.* complain; object; grumble. **7** *Slang.* overcome; break; make oneself free of (a habit).
kick around or **about,** *Informal.* **a** lie around. **b** go around aimlessly. **c** consider. **d** toy with: *You won't have me to kick around any more.*
kick back, *Informal.* **a** spring back suddenly and unexpectedly. **b** *Informal.* return (a portion of money received) as a kickback.
kick in, *Slang.* **a** die. **b** pay what is due or expected; contribute: *If everyone kicks in $3.00, we can order a large pizza.* **c** begin taking effect.
kick off, a *Football.* put a ball in play with a kick. **b** *Informal.* begin. **c** *Slang.* die.
kick out, *Informal.* expel or turn out in a humiliating or disgraceful way: *She should be kicked out of our club.*
kick the bucket. See BUCKET.
kick up, *Slang.* start; cause: *She kicks up a lot of trouble.*
—*n.* **1** the act of kicking. **2** the recoil of a gun when it is fired. **3** *Slang.* a complaint; cause for complaint; objection. **4** often, **kicks,** *pl. Slang.* excitement; thrill: *He gets a kick out of go-karting. We just did it for kicks.* **5** *Slang.* the power of a drink, drug, etc. to intoxicate. **6** *Slang.* a period of intense interest or activity (in something): *She is on a classical music kick.* ⟨origin uncertain⟩ **—'kick•a•ble,** *adj.* **—'kick•less,** *adj.*

kick[2] [kɪk] *n.* the solid base of a drinking glass. ⟨?< *kick*[1]⟩

Kick•a•poo ['kɪkə,pu] *n.* **1** a member of an American Indian people formerly living in Illinois and Wisconsin. **2** the Algonquian language of these people.

kick•back ['kɪk,bæk] *n.* **1** *Informal.* **a** payment, especially of part of a sum of money received, made by some illegal or otherwise secret agreement (such as for help in making profit) or by coercion. **b** money so paid. **2** a sudden violent or vigorous reaction, usually unexpected.

kick•er ['kɪkər] *n.* **1** a person who or animal or thing that kicks. **2** *Informal.* an outboard motor. **3** *Slang.* a surprising or tricky twist, condition, etc.; CATCH (def. *n.* 6): *The contract seemed generous; the kicker was that we would get no money until all the work was finished.*

kick•off ['kɪk,ɒf] *n.* **1** *Football, soccer, etc.* the start of a game, when the ball is kicked into play: *The kickoff is scheduled for 2:00 p.m.* **2** *Informal.* the start of any activity.

kick•shaw ['kɪk,ʃɒ] *n.* **1** a fancy article of food; delicacy. **2** trifle; trinket. ⟨alteration of F *quelque chose* something⟩

kick•stand ['kɪk,stænd] *n.* a lever attached to the rear wheel of a bicycle or motorcycle that can be used to support the vehicle when it is not in use.

kid[1] [kɪd] *n., v.* **kid•ded, kid•ding;** *adj.* —*n.* **1** a young goat or antelope. **2** its flesh, used as food. **3** its skin, used as fur. **4** the leather made from the skin of young goats, used for gloves, shoes, etc. **5 kids,** *pl.* gloves or shoes made of kid. **6** *Informal.* a child or young person: *The kids went to the circus.*
—*v.* give birth to a kid or kids.
—*adj. Informal.* younger: *my kid sister.* ⟨ME < ON *kith*⟩ **—'kid,like,** *adj.*

kid[2] [kɪd] *v.* **kid•ded, kid•ding.** *Slang.* **1** tease playfully; talk jokingly; banter. **2** deceive; fool.
kid around, joke.
no kidding! a an expression of incredulity. **b** I mean this; I am not joking. ⟨? < *kid*[1] in sense of 'treat as a child'⟩ **—'kid•der,** *n.* **—'kid•ding•ly,** *adv.*

Kid•der•min•ster ['kɪdər,mɪnstər] *n.* a reversible carpet having the pattern woven so as to appear on both sides. ⟨< *Kidderminster,* England, where these carpets were first made⟩

kid•die or **kid•dy** ['kɪdi] *n. Informal.* a child.

kid•do ['kɪdou] *n. Informal.* child (*a term of address*).

kid•dush [kɪ'duʃ] *or* ['kɪdəʃ] *n. Judaism.* the prayer or blessing recited over wine or bread on the Sabbath eve. ⟨< Hebrew *qiddūsh* sanctification⟩

kid–glove ['kɪd 'glʌv] *adj.* **1** wearing kid gloves. **2** *Informal.* careful; considerate; gentle: *This job requires a kid-glove approach.* Also, **kid-gloved.**

kid gloves smooth gloves made of soft kidskin.
handle with kid gloves, treat with special care or consideration.

kid•nap ['kɪdnæp] *v.* **-napped** or **-naped, -nap•ping** or **-nap•ing.** carry off and hold (a person) against his or her will by force or by fraud; abduct: *The banker's son was kidnapped and held for ransom.* ⟨< *kid*[1] child + *nap* snatch away⟩

kid•nap•per or **kid•nap•er** ['kɪdnæpər] *n.* a person who carries off and holds another by force: *The kidnappers demanded a ransom.*

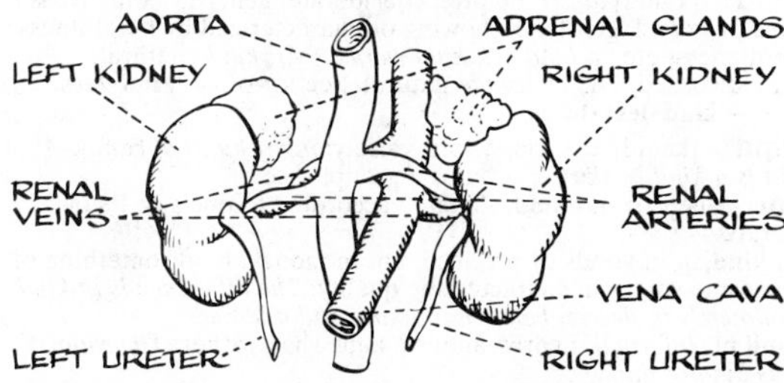

The kidneys of a human being, shown from the back

kid•ney ['kɪdni] *n., pl.* **-neys. 1** *Anatomy.* in vertebrates, one of the pair of organs in the body that separate waste matter and water from the blood and pass them off through the bladder as urine. **2** the kidney or kidneys of an animal, cooked for food. **3** nature; kind; sort: *We must guard our leaders against terrorists, assassins, and people of that kidney.* **4** temperament. ⟨ME < *kidenei* < *kiden-*, of uncertain meaning and origin + *ey* egg⟩
—'kid•ney,like, *adj.*

kidney bean 1 the kidney-shaped, usually dark red seed of any of several cultivated varieties of bean, dried for use in soups, casseroles, etc. **2** a plant that bears such seeds.

kidney stone *Pathology.* an abnormal stone found in the kidney.

kid•skin ['kɪd,skɪn] *n.* leather made from the skin of young goats, used for gloves and shoes.

kids' lit *Informal.* children's literature.

kier [kir] *n.* a vat in which fabrics are dyed. ⟨< Scand.; cf. Icel. *ker* tub⟩

kie•sel•guhr ['kizəl,gʊr] *n.* diatomite, used as an absorbent or insulator. ⟨< G *Kiesel* flint + *Guhr* earthy deposit⟩

kie•ser•ite ['kizə,rəit] *n.* a mineral, hydrous magnesium sulphate, white to yellow in colour, used as a fertilizer. ⟨< G *Kieserit*, named after D.G. *Kieser*, German physician⟩

Ki•ku•yu [kɪ'kuju] *n., pl.* **-yu** or **-yus;** *adj.* *—n.* **1** a member of a people living in the highlands of south central Kenya. **2** the Bantu language of the Kikuyu.
—adj. of or having to do with the Kikuyu or their language.

ki•lim [ki'lim] *n.* a woven oriental rug or other piece of textile. ⟨< Turkish < Persian⟩

kill [kɪl] *v., n.* *—v.* **1** put to death; cause the death of: *The blow from the axe killed him.* **2** cause death: *Thou shalt not kill.* **3** put an end to; get rid of; destroy: *to kill odours, to kill rumours, to kill faith.* **4** cancel (a word, paragraph, item, etc.). **5** defeat or veto (a legislative bill). **6** destroy or neutralize the active qualities of: *to kill land in farming.* **7** spoil the effect of: *One colour may kill another near it.* **8** *Informal.* use up (time): *We killed an hour at the zoo.* **9** *Cdn. Hockey.* overcome the disadvantage of (a penalty) by thwarting the opposing team's attempts to score while the penalized player is off the ice: *Toronto managed to kill the penalty and were then able to score the winning goal.* **10** stop; cut off the fuel supply or electrical current of: *He killed the engine.* **11** *Informal.* overcome completely: *My sore foot is killing me. His jokes really kill me.* **12** *Tennis, etc.* hit (a ball) so hard that it cannot be returned.
kill off, exterminate; wipe out.
—n. **1** the act or an instance of killing. **2** an animal or animals killed, especially in a hunt. **3** an enemy aircraft, ship, etc. destroyed in battle. **4** *Tennis, etc.* a ball hit so hard as to be unreturnable. ⟨ME *kyllen, cullen*; probably related to QUELL⟩
—'kill•a•ble, *adj.*
☛ *Hom.* KILN.
☛ *Syn. v.* **1. Kill,** MURDER, SLAY = cause the death of. **Kill** is the general word, meaning 'put to death or in any way cause the death of a person, animal, or plant': *Overwork killed him. Lack of water kills flowers.* **Murder** emphasizes wicked and cold-blooded killing, and means 'kill a person unlawfully, usually deliberately': *He murdered his rich uncle.* **Slay,** chiefly literary or journalistic, means 'kill with violence, in battle, or by murdering': *All the captives were slain.*

kill•deer ['kɪl,dir] *n., pl.* **-deers** or (*esp. collectively*) **-deer.** a common plover (*Charadrius vociferus*) of open uplands from southern Canada west of the Maritimes south to Peru, having mostly brown-and-white plumage with two broad bands across its white breast and noted for its loud, penetrating call. ⟨imitative of its call⟩

kill•er ['kɪlər] *n.* **1** a person, animal, or thing that kills. **2** *Slang.* a criminal who recklessly or wantonly kills others. **3** *Slang.* anything that is very difficult: *That climb is a killer.* **4** KILLER WHALE.

killer bee a honeybee (*Apis mellifera adansonii*) native to Africa, which attacks when provoked.

killer whale a black-and-white, migratory whale (*Orcinus orca*), the largest member of the dolphin family, found in all seas. It is noted for its boldness and rapaciousness, preying on fish, seals, sea lions, sea otters, narwhals, etc. and even larger baleen whales. Also called **orca.**

kil•lick ['kɪlɪk] *n.* an anchor made of wooden poles or sticks bound around a rock or rocks, used especially in the Maritimes and New England. Also, **killock.** ⟨origin uncertain⟩

kil•li•fish ['kɪlə,fɪʃ] *n.* any fish of the family Cyprinodontidae, found in warm waters. ⟨origin uncertain⟩

kill•ing ['kɪlɪŋ] *adj., n., v.* *—adj.* **1** deadly; destructive; fatal: *a killing frost.* **2** overpowering; exhausting: *They rode at a killing pace.* **3** *Informal.* extremely funny.
—n. **1** murder; slaughter. **2** *Informal.* a sudden great financial success: *He made a killing in stocks.*
—v. ppr. of KILL. **—'kill•ing•ly,** *adv.*

kill–joy ['kɪl ,dʒɔɪ] *n.* a person who spoils other people's fun; spoilsport. Also, **killjoy.**

kiln [kɪln] *or* [kɪl] *n., v.* *—n.* **1** a furnace or oven for burning, baking, or drying something. Limestone is burned in a kiln to make lime. Bricks are baked in a kiln. **2** a building containing a furnace for drying grain, hops, etc. or for making malt.
—v. burn, bake, or dry in a kiln. ⟨OE *cyln, cylen* < L *culina* kitchen⟩
☛ *Hom.* KILL [kɪl].

kiln–dry ['kɪln ,draɪ] *or* ['kɪl ,draɪ] *v.* **-dried, -dry•ing.** dry (a material such as wood) in a kiln instead of letting it weather naturally.

ki•lo ['kilou] *or* ['kɪlou] *n., pl.* **ki•los.** kilogram. ⟨< F⟩

kilo– *SI prefix.* thousand. One kilowatt is one thousand watts. Compare MEGA-, GIGA-. *Symbol*: k ⟨< F < Gk. *chilioi*⟩

kil•o•bar ['kɪlə,bɑr] *n.* a unit of pressure equal to 1000 bars.

kil•o•base ['kɪlə,beis] *n. Genetics.* a sequence of 1000 bases in DNA.

kil•o•byte ['kɪlə,bəit] *n. Computer technology.* A measure of the storage capacity of a computer system, roughly equal to one thousand bytes. *Symbol*: kB

kil•o•cal•or•ie ['kɪlə,kæləri] *n. Physics.* 1000 calories. *Symbol*: kcal

kil•o•cy•cle ['kɪlə,səikəl] *n.* 1000 cycles, especially 1000 cycles per second. Kilocycles have been replaced by kilohertz for expressing radio frequencies.

kil•o•el•ec•tron•volt ['kɪlouɪ'lɛktrən,voult] *n.* 1000 electronvolts. *Symbol*: keV

kil•o•gram ['kɪlə,græm] *n.* an SI unit for measuring mass. The kilogram is one of the seven base units in the SI. *Symbol*: kg Also, **kilogramme.** ⟨< F *kilogramme*⟩

kil•o•gram–me•tre ['kɪlə,græm 'mitər] *n. Physics.* a unit formerly used for measuring work, equal to 9.81 newton metres. Also, **kilogram-meter.**

kil•o•hertz ['kɪlə,hɜrts] *n., pl.* **kil•o•hertz.** *Physics.* an SI unit for measuring frequency of waves and vibrations, equal to 1000 hertz. *Symbol*: kHz

kil•o•joule ['kɪlə,dʒul] *n. Physics.* an SI unit for measuring energy, equal to 1000 joules. *Symbol*: kJ

kil•o•li•tre ['kɪlə,litər] *n.* a unit used with the SI for measuring volume or capacity, equal to 1000 L. *Symbol*: kL
Also, **kiloliter.** ⟨< F *kilolitre*⟩

ki•lo•me•tre [kə'lɒmətər] *or* ['kɪlə,mitər] *n.* an SI unit for measuring length or distance, equal to 1000 m. It takes about twelve minutes to walk one kilometre. *Symbol*: km
Also, **kilometer.** ⟨< F *kilomètre*⟩ **—,kil•o'met•ric,** *adj.*

kil•o•par•sec ['kɪlə,pɑr,sɛk] *n.* 1000 parsecs. *Symbol*: kpc

kil•o•pas•cal ['kɪlə,pæskəl] *n.* an SI unit for measuring pressure, equal to 1000 pascals. The kilopascal is used in recording air pressure; the standard pressure of the atmosphere is about 101 kPa. See ISOBAR for picture. *Symbol*: kPa

kil•o•ton ['kɪlə,tʌn] *n.* a unit for measuring explosive force, equal to 1000 tons of TNT (about 907 tonnes). ⟨< *kilo-* + *ton* (of explosive energy of TNT)⟩

kil•o•volt ['kɪlə,voult] *n. Electricity.* a unit equal to 1000 volts. *Symbol*: kV

kilovolt ampere *n.* a unit equal to 1000 volt amperes. *Symbol*: kVa

kil•o•watt ['kɪlə,wɒt] *n.* an SI unit for measuring power, equal to 1000 watts. *Symbol*: kW

kilowatt hour *Electricity.* a unit used with the SI for measuring electrical energy, defined as the number of kilowatts of electrical power used per hour. One kilowatt hour is equivalent to 3.6 megajoules. *Symbol*: kWh

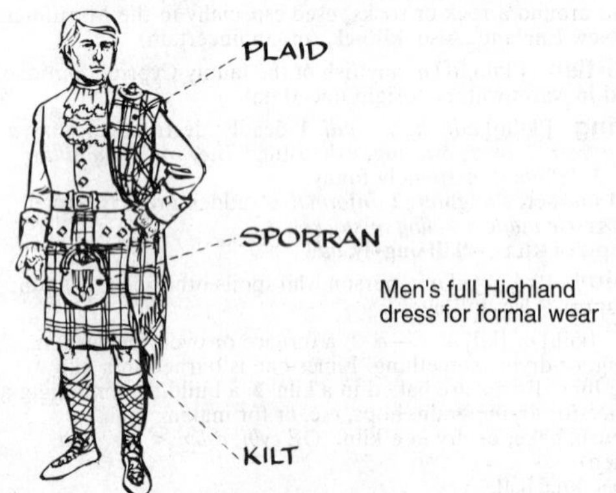

Men's full Highland dress for formal wear

kilt [kɪlt] *n., v.* *—n.* **1** a pleated, knee-length tartan skirt worn by men in the Scottish Highlands and by soldiers in Scottish and Irish regiments, including those in Canada. **2** a similar garment worn by women and girls.
—v. **1** *Scottish.* tuck up; fasten up. **2** provide with a kilt. ⟨probably < Scand.; cf. Danish *kilte* tuck (up)⟩ **—'kilt,like,** *adj.*

kil•ter ['kɪltər] *n. Informal.* good condition; order: *Our radio is out of kilter.* ⟨origin uncertain⟩

kim•chi ['kɪmtʃi] *n.* a Korean dish comprising spiced, fermented cabbage. ⟨< Korean⟩

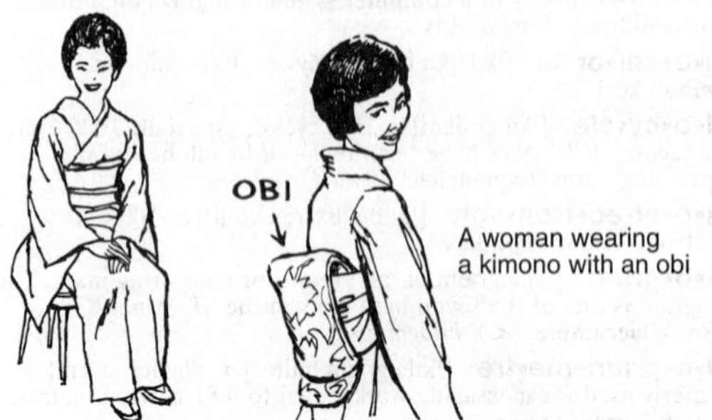

A woman wearing a kimono with an obi

ki•mo•no [kə'mounə] *or* [kə'mounou] *n., pl.* **-nos. 1** a loose outer garment held in place by a sash, worn by Japanese men and women. **2** a loose dressing gown. ⟨< Japanese⟩

kin [kɪn] *n., adj.* *—n.* **1** a person's family or relatives; kindred: *All our kin came to the family reunion.* **2** family relationship; connection by birth or marriage: *What kin is she to you?*
next of kin, nearest living relative: *His next of kin is his mother.*
of kin, of the same family; related: *They look alike, but they are not of kin.*
—adj. related. ⟨OE *cynn*; cf. *cennan* beget⟩ **—'kin•less,** *adj.*

-kin *suffix.* little: *lambkin.* ⟨ME; cf. MDu. *-kijn, -ken*⟩

ki•na ['kinə] *n.* the basic unit of money in Papua, New Guinea, divided into 100 toea. See table of money in the Appendix. ⟨< a Papuan language⟩

kin•aes•the•sia [,kɪnəs'θiʒə] *or* [,kɪnəs'θiziə] See KINESTHESIA. **—,kin•aes'thet•ic,** *adj.*

ki•nase ['kaɪneis] *or* ['kaɪneiz], ['kɪneis] *or* ['kɪneiz] *n. Biochemistry.* an enzyme able to activate the inactive form of another enzyme. ⟨< *kin(etic)* + *(diast)ase*⟩

kind¹ [kaɪnd] *adj.* **1** helpful, considerate, generous, etc.: *He is a kind person.* **2** gentle. **3** showing or characterized by helpfulness, gentleness, etc.: *a kind act, kind words.* ⟨ME *kinde* natural, well-disposed, OE *(ge)cynde* natural. See KIND².⟩ **—'kind•less,** *adj.* **—'kind•less•ly,** *adv.*

kind² [kaɪnd] *n.* **1** class; sort; variety: *many kinds of candy. A kilt is a kind of skirt.* **2** a natural group; race.
after (one's or its) **kind,** *Archaic.* according to one's or its own nature.
in kind, a in goods or produce, not in money. **b** in something of the same sort. **c** in characteristic quality: *The difference is in kind, not merely in degree, between a hound and a terrier.*
kind of, *Informal.* nearly; almost; somewhat; rather: *The room was kind of dark.*
of a kind, a of the same kind; alike: *She and her mother were two of a kind—tight-fisted.* **b** of a poor or mediocre quality: *Two boxes and a plank make a table of a kind.* ⟨OE *(ge)cynd* nature, origin⟩
☛ *Syn.* **1. Kind,** SORT = a group of people or things alike in some way. **Kind** applies particularly to a group of the same nature or character, having enough closely similar essential qualities in their make-up to put them together as a class or division in some system of classification: *What kind of cake do you like best?* **Sort,** often interchangeable with **kind,** is usually vaguer, and sometimes carries a suggestion of contempt: *a girl of that sort. That sort of action disgusts me.*
☛ *Usage.* **Kind,** SORT. **Kind** and **sort** can be singular or plural: *This kind of apple is likely to be wormy. These sorts of behaviour are out of place here.* Avoid using a plural determiner with a singular noun, as in *these kind of books* or *those sort of ideas.*

kin•der•gar•ten ['kɪndər,gɑrtən] *or* ['kɪndə,gɑrtən] *n.* **1** the year (or in some places two years) of school that comes before grade 1. **2** a school for younger children; nursery school. ⟨< G *Kindergarten* < *Kinder* children + *Garten* garden⟩
—'kin•der,gart•ner, *n.*
☛ *Pronun.* The pronunciation (as in German) with *t* in the final syllable is standard, though a *d* is often heard.

kind–heart•ed ['kaɪnd 'hɑrtɪd] *adj.* having or showing a kind heart; kindly; sympathetic. **—'kind-'heart•ed•ly,** *adv.* **—'kind-'heart•ed•ness,** *n.*

kin•dle¹ ['kɪndəl] *v.* **-dled, -dling. 1** set on fire; light. **2** catch fire; begin to burn: *This damp wood will never kindle.* **3** arouse; stir up: *His cruelty kindled our anger.* **4** become stirred up or aroused. **5** light up; brighten: *The boy's face kindled as he told about the circus.* ⟨ME < ON *kynda* kindle⟩ **—'kin•dler,** *n.*

kin•dle² ['kɪndəl] *v.* **-dled, -dling.** give birth to (a litter of kittens, rabbits, etc.) ⟨ME, v. use of *kindle* young, offspring; see KIND²⟩

kind•li•ness ['kaɪndlinɪs] *n.* **1** a kindly feeling or quality. **2** a kindly act; benevolence.

kin•dling ['kɪndlɪŋ] *n., v.* *—n.* small pieces of wood for starting a fire.
—v. ppr. of KINDLE¹. ⟨ME; see KINDLE¹⟩

kind•ly ['kaɪndli] *adj.* **-li•er, -li•est;** *adv.* *—adj.* **1** kind; friendly: *kindly faces.* **2** pleasant; agreeable: *a kindly shower.*
—adv. **1** in a kind or friendly way. **2** please (*used in formal or impersonal requests or to express impatience, etc.*): *Kindly return this portion of the bill with your payment. Will you kindly get your feet off the chair!*
take kindly to, like or accept: *He does not take kindly to criticism.* ⟨OE *(ge)cyndelīc* natural; see KIND¹⟩

kind•ness ['kaɪndnɪs] *n.* **1** a kind nature; a being kind: *We admire his kindness.* **2** kind treatment. **3** a kind act: *He showed me many kindnesses.* ⟨ME *kindeness*; see KIND¹⟩

kin•dred ['kɪndrɪd] *n., adj.* *—n.* **1** family relationship; connection by birth or marriage. **2** one's family or relatives. **3** a group of people who are related by blood or marriage.

—*adj.* **1** related: *kindred peoples.* **2** like; similar: *We are studying about dew, frost, and kindred facts of nature.* ⟨ME < *kyn* family (ON *cynn*) + *rede*, OE *rǣden* condition⟩

kine [kaın] *n.pl. Archaic or dialect.* cows; cattle. ⟨earlier *kyen*, double plural < OE *cȳ*, pl. of *cū* cow + plural suffix *-en*⟩

kin•e•mat•ic [,kınə'mætık] *adj.* having to do with pure motion or with kinematics.

kin•e•mat•ics [,kınə'mætıks] *n.* the branch of mechanics dealing with the different kinds of motion that are possible for a body or system of bodies, without reference to mass or to the force producing the motion. ⟨< Gk. *kinēma, -atos* motion < *kineein* move⟩

ki•ne•sic [kı'nisık], [kı'nizık], *or* [kaı'nisık] *adj.* of or having to do with kinesics.

ki•nes•ics [kı'nisıks], [kı'nizıks], *or* [kaı'nisıks] *n.* the study of communication by means of gestures, facial expressions, etc., especially as they accompany speech (*used with a singular verb*). ⟨< Gk. *kinēsis* motion + E *-ics*⟩

ki•ne•sis [kı'nisıs] *or* [kaı'nisıs] *n.* an involuntary reaction or movement resulting from an external stimulus. ⟨< Gk. *kinēsis* motion⟩

kin•es•the•sia [,kınəs'θiʒə] *or* [,kınəs'θiziə] *n.* **1** the sensation of movement in the muscles and joints. **2** the awareness of movement or position of the body created by the stimulation of sensory nerves. Also, **kinaesthesia.** ⟨< NL < Gk. *kineein* move + *-aisthesia* perception⟩

kin•es•thet•ic [,kınəs'θɛtık] *adj.* having to do with sensations from the muscles and joints. Also, **kinaesthetic.**

ki•net•ic [kı'nɛtık] *or* [kaı'nɛtık] *adj.* **1** of motion. **2** caused by motion. ⟨< Gk. *kinētikos* < *kineein* move⟩

kinetic energy *Physics.* the energy of a given body depending on its motion.

ki•net•ics [kı'nɛtıks] *or* [kaı'nɛtıks] *n.* the branch of mechanics dealing with the effects of forces in causing or changing the motion of bodies (*used with a singular verb*). Kinetics deals with the laws for predicting the motion that will occur in a particular situation.

kinetic theory *Physics.* the theory that the constituent particles of matter are in constant motion, and that the temperature of a substance is proportional to the velocity of the particles. Pressure, elasticity, diffusion, and other properties of gases are also explained in terms of molecular activity.

ki•net•o•chore [kı'nɛtə,kɔr] *n. Genetics.* a structure of the centromere of a chromosome to which the spindle fibres attach during cell division. ⟨Gk. *kinetos* movable + *choros* place⟩

kin•folk ['kın,fouk] *n.pl.* kinsfolk. Also, **kinfolks.**

king [kıŋ] *n.* **1** the male ruler of a nation; a male sovereign, with either absolute or limited power. **2** a person or animal or thing that is best or most important in a certain sphere or class: *The lion is called the king of the beasts. Babe Ruth was a king of baseball.* **3** *Chess.* the chief piece. **4** *Checkers.* a piece that has moved entirely across the board. **5** a playing card bearing a picture of a king. **6** KING SALMON. ⟨OE *cyning*⟩ **—'king•less,** *adj.* **—'king,like,** *adj.*

King Arthur the central figure in a group of legends about the knights of the Round Table.

king•bird ['kıŋ,bərd] *n.* any of several New World flycatchers (genus *Tyrannus*), such as the **eastern kingbird** (*T. tyrannus*), which is found throughout most of Canada.

king•bolt ['kıŋ,boult] *n.* a vertical bolt connecting the body of a wagon, etc. with the front axle, or the body of a railway car with a set of wheels.

King Charles spaniel a breed of black and tan toy spaniel. ⟨after *Charles* II of England who liked this breed⟩

king cobra a very large, poisonous snake (*Ophiophagus hannah*) of tropical Asia that feeds mainly on other snakes. The king cobra, often reaching a length of more than 3.5 m, is the largest poisonous snake in the world.

king crab HORSESHOE CRAB.

king•craft ['kıŋ,kræft] *n.* the art of ruling; royal statesmanship.

king•cup ['kıŋ,kʌp] *n.* MARSH MARIGOLD.

king•dom ['kıŋdəm] *n.* **1** a country that is governed by a king or a queen. **2** realm; domain; province: *The mind is the kingdom of thought.* **3 a** one of the broad divisions of the natural world as animals, plants, and minerals. **b** in present-day biology, one of the five major divisions of living things. Animals, plants, fungi, protists, and monerans are kingdoms. ⟨OE *cyningdōm*⟩

☛ *Usage.* This dictionary follows the five-kingdom classification of living things in preference to the classification of the natural world into three kingdoms: animal, vegetable, and mineral.

king duck *Cdn.* the king eider of the Arctic (*Somateria spectabilis*).

king•fish ['kıŋ,fıʃ] *n., pl.* **-fish** or **-fish•es.** any of various large marine food fishes of Atlantic or Pacific coastal waters, such as any of the genus *Menticirrhus* (family Sciaenidae) or any of certain mackerels.

king•fish•er ['kıŋ,fıʃər] *n.* any of a family (Alcedinidae) of birds having a large head, large, sharp bill, and short tail, with most species having brightly coloured plumage and a crest. The only Canadian species is the mainly blue-and-white **belted kingfisher** (*Megaceryle alcyon*), which has a tousled crest on its large head.

A kingfisher

King James Version an English translation of the Bible published in 1611, during the reign of James I; Authorized Version. *Abbrev.*: KJV

king•let ['kıŋlıt] *n.* **1** a king who is ruler over a small country. **2** either of two small birds (*Regulus satrapa* or *Regulus calendula*) having a small yellow or red patch on the crown of the head.

king•ly ['kıŋli] *adj.* **-li•er, -li•est;** *adv.* —*adj.* **1** of a king or kings; of royal rank. **2** fit for a king: *a kingly crown.* **3** like a king; regal or noble: *a kingly bearing, kingly pride.* —*adv.* as a king does; regally. **—'king•li•ness,** *n.*

☛ *Syn. adj.* See note at ROYAL.

king•mak•er ['kıŋ,meikər] *n.* **1** a person who makes or establishes a king. **2** a person of consequence who can influence or dictate the choice of candidates for political office. **—'king,mak•ing,** *n., adj.*

king•mik ['kıŋmık] *n.* the Inuit dog. ⟨< East Inuktitut *qimmiq* dog⟩

king–of–arms ['kıŋ əv 'ɑrmz] *n., pl.* **kings-of-arms.** *Heraldry. Brit.* an official responsible for the investigation of rights and titles, the granting of coats of arms, etc.

king•pin ['kıŋ,pın] *n.* **1** *Bowling.* the pin in front or in the centre. **2** *Informal.* the most important person or thing. **3** kingbolt.

king post *Building trades.* a vertical post between the apex of a triangular roof truss and a tie beam.

king salmon CHINOOK SALMON.

King's Bench See QUEEN'S BENCH.

King's Counsel See QUEEN'S COUNSEL. *Abbrev.*: K.C.

King's Domain *Cdn.* formerly, a vast tract of land lying north of the Lower St. Lawrence River and originally belonging to the French kings. ⟨< translation of F *Domaine du Roi*⟩

King's English See QUEEN'S ENGLISH.

King's evidence See QUEEN'S EVIDENCE.

king's evil scrofula, a disease that was supposed to be cured by the touch of a king.

King's girl *Cdn.* formerly, one of the women sent to New France by Louis XIV as wives for settlers.

king•ship ['kıŋʃıp] *n.* **1** the position, rank, or dignity of a king. **2** the rule of a king; government by a king.

king–size ['kıŋ ,saız] *adj.* **1** unusually large: *I made myself a king-size sandwich.* **2** longest or largest in a standard range of sizes: *king-size cigarettes. A king-size bed measures about 198 cm wide by 203 cm long.* **3** designed for use with a king-size bed: *king-size sheets.* Also, **'king-,sized.**

king snake any snake of the genus *Lampropeltis,* having red or yellow markings.

King's Post *Cdn.* formerly, one of a number of fur-trading and fishing posts in Québec, most of them in the region known as the KING'S DOMAIN.

king's ransom *Informal.* a very large amount of money: *They paid a king's ransom for that furniture.*

king truss *Building trades.* a truss framed with a KING POST.

king•wood ['kɪŋ,wʊd] *n.* **1** a South American tree (*Dalbergia cearensis*). **2** the hard purplish wood of this tree.

ki•nin ['kaɪnɪn] *or* ['kɪnɪn] *n. Biology.* **1** a hormone that causes cell division in plants. **2** a hormone that dilates the blood vessels of animals. ⟨< *kin(etic)* + *-in*⟩

kink [kɪŋk] *n., v.* —*n.* **1** a small, tight twist or curl in thread, rope, hair, etc. **2** a pain or stiffness in the muscles of the neck, back, etc.; crick. **3** a mental twist; eccentricity or quirk. **4** a hindrance or complication: *There are a few kinks in your plan.*
—*v.* make or form a kink or kinks: *The rope kinked when he stretched it out.* ⟨probably < Du. *kink* twist⟩

kin•ka•jou ['kɪŋkə,dʒu] *n.* a cat-sized, nocturnal mammal (*Potos flavus*) of the raccoon family found in the forests of Mexico and Central and South America, having soft, yellowish brown fur and a very long, prehensile tail. ⟨< F *quincajou* < Tupi-Guarani⟩

kink•y ['kɪŋki] *adj.* **kink•i•er, kink•i•est. 1** full of kinks; twisted; curly. **2** *Informal.* eccentric or bizarre; very unconventional, especially in sexual practices. —**'kink•i•ly,** *adv.* —**'kink•i•ness,** *n.*

kin•ni•kin•nick or **kin•ni•kin•ik** [,kɪnəkə'nɪk] *n. Cdn.* **1** a mixture of various ingredients, such as bearberry, sumac, or dogwood leaves, used by Canadian First Nations people for smoking. **2** a plant, especially the bearberry, from which this mixture is made. Also, **kinnikinnic.** ⟨< Algonquian *kinikinic* that which is mixed⟩

kins•folk ['kɪnz,fouk] *n.pl.* a person's family; relatives; kin.

kin•ship ['kɪnʃɪp] *n.* **1** a family relationship. **2** relationship. **3** resemblance.

kins•man ['kɪnzmən] *n., pl.* **-men.** a male relative.

Kins•men ['kɪnzmən] *n.pl. Cdn.* a national service-club organization of business and professional people, founded in 1920 in Hamilton, Ontario.

kins•wom•an ['kɪnz,wʊmən] *n., pl.* **-wom•en.** a female relative.

ki•osk ['kiɒsk] *or* [ki'ɒsk] *for 1;* [ki'ɒsk] *for 2; n.* **1** a small building, usually with one or more sides open, used as a newsstand, bus shelter, telephone booth, etc. **2** in Turkey, Persia, etc., a light, open summerhouse. ⟨< F < Turkish *kiushk* pavilion⟩

Ki•o•wa ['kaɪə,wɑ] *or* ['kaɪəwə] *n.* **1** a member of an American Indian people now living in Oklahoma. **2** the Tanoan language of these people.

kip[1] [kɪp] *n.* **1** the untanned hide of a young or undersized animal. **2** a bundle of such hides. ⟨ME *kipp* < MDu., MLG *kip* pack (of hides)⟩

kip[2] [kɪp] *n., v.* **kipped, kip•ping.** *Slang.* —*n.* **1** a sleeping place; bed. **2** sleep.
—*v.* go to bed. ⟨cf. Danish *kippe* low alehouse⟩

kip[3] [kɪp] *n.* **1** the basic unit of money in Laos, divided into 100 at. See table of money in the Appendix. **2** a coin worth one kip. ⟨< Thai⟩

kip[4] [kɪp] *n.* a unit of weight equal to 453.6 kg. ⟨< *ki(lo-)* + *p(ound)*⟩

kip•per ['kɪpər] *n., v.* —*n.* **1** a herring, salmon, etc. that has been salted and dried or smoked. **2** the male salmon or sea trout during or after the spawning season. **3** *Slang.* **a** a person, especially a child. **b** an English person.
—*v.* salt and dry or smoke (herring, salmon, etc.). ⟨OE *cypera* male salmon⟩

Kir•ghiz [kir'giz] *n., pl.* **-ghiz** or **-ghiz•es. 1** a member of a Mongolian people widely scattered over the western part of central Asia. **2** the Turkic language of the Kirghiz.

Kir•ghi•zia [kir'giʒə] *n.* a country in central Asia.

kirk [kɜrk] *n.* **1** *Scottish.* church. **2 the Kirk,** the national church of Scotland; the Presbyterian Church of Scotland. ⟨ME < ON *kirkja,* ult. < Gk. *kyriakon (doma).* See CHURCH.⟩

Kir•man [kər'mɑn] *n.* a type of Oriental rug having elaborate designs in soft, rich colours. Also, **Kerman.** ⟨< *Kerman,* in Persia, where the rugs are made⟩

kir•mess ['kɜrmɪs] See KERMIS.

kirsch [kirʃ] *n.* a clear, sweet brandy made from fermented wild black cherries, originally from Germany and Alsace. ⟨< F < G *Kirschwasser* cherry water⟩

Kirt•land's warbler ['kɜrtləndz] a bird (*Dendroica kirtlandii*), large for a warbler, the male having bluish grey upper plumage with black stripes and yellow below. It is noted for its habit of pumping the tail up and down. It nests in central Michigan and winters in the Bahamas. It is an endangered species.

kir•tle ['kɜrtəl] *n. Archaic.* **1** a skirt or dress. **2** a man's short coat. ⟨OE *cyrtel,* probably < L *curtus* short⟩

kish•ke ['kɪʃkə] *n.* in Jewish cookery, a type of sausage made of flour, onion, and suet. ⟨< Yiddish < Slavic; cf. Polish *kiszka* sausage⟩

Kis•lev or **Kis•lew** ['kɪslɛf] *or* [kis'lɛv] *n.* in the Hebrew calendar, the ninth month of the ecclesiastical year, and the third month of the civil year.

kis•met ['kɪzmɪt] *or* ['kɪsmɪt] *n.* fate; destiny. ⟨< Turkish < Arabic *qisma(t)* < *qasama* divide⟩

kiss [kɪs] *v., n.* —*v.* **1** touch with the lips as a sign of love, greeting, or respect. **2** touch gently: *A soft wind kissed the treetops.*
kiss away, put, bring, take, etc. by kissing: *He kissed away her tears.*
kiss off, *Slang.* reject; ignore.
—*n.* **1** a touch with the lips. **2** a gentle touch. **3** a piece of candy containing coconut, nuts, or the like and wrapped in a twist of paper. **4** a fancy cake made of egg white and powdered sugar. ⟨OE *cyssan*⟩ —**'kiss•a•ble,** *adj.* —**,kiss•a'bil•i•ty,** *n.*

kiss•er ['kɪsər] *n.* **1** a person who kisses. **2** *Slang.* the face or mouth.

kissing bug a small insect (*Melanolestes pipices*) that bites people, usually on the lips, while they are asleep.

kiss of death a fatal or destructive relationship or action; something that seems positive but is in reality very dangerous: *The yellow tabloid's story on the candidate was the kiss of death for his campaign.*

kiss–off ['kɪs ,ɒf] *n. Slang.* a rude dismissal.

kiss of life mouth-to-mouth resuscitation.

kit[1] [kɪt] *n.* **1** a set of materials, supplies, or tools required for a particular job or purpose: *a first-aid kit, a sewing kit, a shaving kit.* **2** a set of parts intended to be put together to make a particular thing: *a radio kit, a model airplane kit.* **3** a set of printed materials issued for instruction and information: *a selling kit, a visitor's kit.* **4** the uniform or other clothing and personal equipment required for a certain activity: *a soldier's kit, skiing kit.* **5** a bag, box, case, or other holder containing a set of materials or equipment. **6** such a container together with its contents.
the whole kit and caboodle, *Informal.* the complete group; the lot; everything or everybody: *They met the children and their friends at the theatre and took the whole kit and caboodle out to supper.* ⟨probably < MDu. *kitte* jug, tankard⟩

kit[2] [kɪt] *n., v.* **kit•ted, kit•ting.** —*n. Cdn.* **1** the young of certain fur-bearing wild animals such as the beaver. **2** kitten.
—*v.* give birth to kits.

Ki•tab–i–Aq•das [kɪ'tɑb i æk'dɑs] *n. Bahaism.* the laws and teachings of Baha-ullah, the most sacred portion of the Bahai scriptures.

Kit•a•mat ['kɪtə,mæt] *n., pl.* **-mat** or **-mats.** See KITIMAT.

kit–bag ['kɪt ,bæg] *n.* a bag, usually made of canvas and closed at the top by a drawstring, for carrying personal belongings.

kitch•en ['kɪtʃən] *n.* **1** a room with facilities for cooking food and otherwise preparing it for eating. **2** (*adjl.*) used in a kitchen: *a kitchen table.* **3** the people employed to cook and prepare food in a large household, restaurant, etc. ⟨OE *cycene* < L *coquina* < *coquus* a cook⟩

kitch•en•ette [,kɪtʃə'nɛt] *n.* **1** a very small, compactly arranged kitchen. **2** a part of a room fitted up as a kitchen. Also, **kitchenet.**

kitchen garden a garden where vegetables and fruit for a household are grown.

kitch•en•maid ['kɪtʃən,meid] *n.* a woman servant who helps in the kitchen.

kitchen midden a mound of shells, bones, and other refuse that accumulated at a site of prehistoric human habitation. ⟨translation of Danish *kjökken-mödding* < *kjökken* kitchen + *mödding* dunghill⟩

kitchen police *Esp. U.S.* **1** an army duty of helping the cook prepare and serve the food, wash the dishes, and clean up the kitchen. **2** soldiers assigned to this duty, often as punishment for slight offences. *Abbrev.:* K.P.

kitch•en•ware ['kɪtʃən,wɛr] *n.* kitchen utensils. Pots, kettles, and pans are kitchenware.

kite [kəit] *n., v.* **kit•ed, kit•ing.** *—n.* **1** a light frame covered with paper, cloth, or plastic, designed to be flown in the air on the end of a long string. **2** a hawk having long, pointed wings. **3** *Nautical.* any of the very high and light sails of a ship. **4** a type of aircraft pulled by a towline and supported by the force of air currents. **5** *Obsolete.* a person who preys upon others; rapacious person; sharper. **6** a fictitious cheque, bill of exchange, etc. representing no actual transaction, used to raise money or to sustain credit. **7** *Slang.* any airplane that was used in World War II.
—v. **1** *Informal.* fly like a kite; move rapidly and easily. **2** obtain money or credit through kites.
fly a kite, propose something simply to get a reaction.
go fly a kite, *Slang.* go away. ⟨OE *cȳta*⟩ **—'kite,like,** *adj.*

kit fox *Cdn.* SWIFT (def. *n.* 3).

kith [kɪθ] *n.* friends.
kith and kin, friends and relatives. ⟨OE *cȳththe* acquaintance < *cunnan* know⟩

Kit•i•mat ['kɪtə,mæt] *n., pl.* **-mat** or **-mats.** a member of a Kwakiutl First Nations people living near the Douglas Channel, B.C. Also, **Kitamat.**

kitsch [kɪtʃ] *n.* **1** mass-produced decorative articles, especially when gaudy, trite, or pretentious. **2** trite, uninspired art or literature. ⟨< G < *kitschen* to throw together a work of art < dial.⟩ **—'kitsch•y,** *adj.*

kit•ten ['kɪtən] *n., v.* *—n.* **1** a young cat. **2** the young of certain other small animals, such as rabbits.
have kittens, *Slang.* be extremely shocked and upset about something.
—v. bear kittens: *Our cat kittened yesterday.* ⟨ME < AF var. of OF *cheton* < LL *cattus* cat⟩

kit•ten•ish ['kɪtənɪʃ] *adj.* **1** like a kitten. **2** coquettish. **—'kit•ten•ish•ly,** *adv.* **—'kit•ten•ish•ness,** *n.*

kit•ti•wake ['kɪti,weik] *n.* a medium-sized oceanic gull (*Rissa tridactyla*) of North Atlantic coasts having mainly white plumage with black-tipped grey wings. Kittiwakes come ashore only to breed, at which time they nest in colonies on narrow cliff ledges. ⟨imitative of its call⟩

kit•ty[1] ['kɪti] *n., pl.* **-ties.** *Informal.* **1** kitten. **2** a pet name for a cat. ⟨ult. < *kitten*⟩

kit•ty[2] ['kɪti] *n., pl.* **-ties. 1** *Poker.* **a** the stakes. **b** a fund made up of contributions from each person's winnings, used to buy refreshments, etc. for the players. **2** a fund of money pooled by a group of people for a particular use: *a monthly contribution for the grocery kitty.* **3** *Card games.* a number of cards set aside that may be used by the player making the highest bid, etc. ⟨origin uncertain⟩

kit•ty–cor•ner ['kɪti ,kɔrnər] *adj., adv.* *—adj.* diagonally opposite; on a diagonal line: *There is a small drugstore kitty-corner from the garage.*
—adv. diagonally. Also, **kitty-cornered.** ⟨< *catty-corner*, var. of *cater-corner* < F *quatre* four + E *corner*⟩

ki•va ['kivə] *n.* an underground room used by the men of a Pueblo Indian village for ceremonies. ⟨< Hopi⟩

Ki•wa•ni•an [kɪ'wɑniən] *n., adj.* *—n.* a member of a Kiwanis Club.
—adj. of or having to do with Kiwanis Clubs.

Ki•wa•nis [kɪ'wɑnɪs] *n.* an international group of clubs of business and professional people, organized for civic service and higher ideals in business and professional life. The first Kiwanis Club was founded in Detroit in 1915.

ki•wi ['kiwi] *n., pl.* **-wis. 1** any of a small genus (*Apteryx*, constituting the order Apterygiformes) of flightless birds of New Zealand having shaggy, hairlike, greyish brown plumage and a long, slender bill. **2** KIWI FRUIT or the vine that bears it. **3 Kiwi,** *Informal.* a New Zealander. ⟨< Maori⟩

kiwi fruit or **ki•wi•fruit** ['kiwi,frut] *n.* the plum-sized, oval, edible fruit of a subtropical Asian vine (*Actinidia chinensis*), having a hairy, brownish skin and sweet, bright green pulp.

KJV KING JAMES VERSION.

KKK KU KLUX KLAN.

kL kilolitre(s).

kla•how•ya(h) [klə'haʊjə] *Cdn. B.C. interj.* Greetings! How are you? ⟨< Chinook jargon⟩

Kla•math ['klæməθ] *n.* **1** a member of an American Indian people now living in S Oregon. **2** the language of these people.

Klan [klæn] *n.* KU KLUX KLAN.

Klans•man ['klænzmən] *n., pl.* **-men.** a member of the Ku Klux Klan.

Klee•nex ['klinɛks] *n. Trademark.* a very soft, absorbent tissue, used as a handkerchief, for removing cosmetics, etc.

klep•to•ma•ni•a [,klɛptə'meiniə] *n.* an uncontrollable impulse to steal. ⟨< NL < Gk. *kleptēs* thief + E *mania* madness⟩

klep•to•ma•ni•ac [,klɛptə'meini,æk] *n.* a person who has uncontrollable impulses to steal.

klick [klɪk] *Slang.* kilometre: *It's 24 klicks to the next town.*

klieg light [klig] a bright, hot arc light used in shooting films. ⟨after Anton *Kliegl* (1872-1927) and his brother John (1869-1959), the inventors⟩

klip•spring•er ['klɪp,sprɪŋər] *n.* an African antelope (*Oreotragus oreotragus*). ⟨< Afrikaans < Du. *klip* a rock, cliff + *springer* springer⟩

Klon•dike ['klɒndəik] *n. Cdn.* **1** a region of the Yukon where gold was discovered in 1897. **2** Also, **klondike,** a variety of solitaire, or patience. ⟨< *Klondike*, Y.T.⟩

Klondike fever *Cdn.* formerly, the excitement and lust for gold generated by the Klondike gold rush.

Klon•dik•er ['klɒndəikər] *n. Cdn.* a person who took part in the Klondike gold rush to the Yukon, 1897-1899.

Klondike Trail *Cdn.* formerly, a route through the western prairies and B.C. leading to the Klondike.

kludge [klʌdʒ] *n. Informal.* a clumsy, improvised, patched-up adjustment made to a computer system or program, allowing it to function, at least temporarily.

klutz [klʌts] *n. Slang.* a person who is physically clumsy or socially inept. ⟨< Yiddish *klutz*, klutz < G. *klotz* wooden block, lout⟩ **—'klutz•y,** *adj.*

Klys•tron ['kləistrɒn] *n. Trademark. Electronics.* a vacuum tube for generating an ultrahigh-frequency current, using several resonators to bunch the electrons by advancing and retarding them. ⟨? Gk. *klystēr* pipe syringe + E (*elec*)*tron*⟩

km **1** kilometre(s). **2** kingdom.

K meson kaon.

km/h kilometres per hour: *The top speed of this car is 120 km/h.*

kn knot (unit of speed).

knack [næk] *n.* **1** a special skill. **2** the power to do something easily. **3** a trick; habit. ⟨origin uncertain⟩

knack•wurst ['nɑk,wɜrst] *n.* a highly seasoned sausage. ⟨< G, *knacken* to crack, break + *wurst* sausage⟩

knap•sack ['næp,sæk] *n.* a cloth or leather bag for provisions, having straps for carrying on the back. ⟨< LG *Knapsack* < *knappen* eat + *Sack* sack[1]⟩

knap•weed ['næp,wid] *n.* any of several Eurasian perennial plants (genus *Centaurea*) of the composite family having purplish or white thistlelike flowers. Knapweeds have become naturalized as common weeds in many temperate regions, including North America. ⟨OE *cnæp* knob + *weed*⟩

knar [nɑr] *n.* a knot on a tree or in a piece of wood. Also, **knur.** ⟨ME *knarre*⟩ **—knarred** or **'knar•ry,** *adj.*

knave [neiv] *n.* **1** a dishonest person; rogue; rascal. **2** the jack, a playing card with a picture of a servant or soldier on it. **3** *Archaic.* a male servant; a man of humble birth or position. ⟨OE *cnafa* boy⟩
☛ *Hom.* NAVE.

knav•er•y ['neivəri] *or* ['neivri] *n., pl.* **-er•ies. 1** behaviour characteristic of a knave. **2** a tricky, dishonest act.

knav•ish ['neivɪʃ] *adj.* tricky; dishonest. **—'knav•ish•ly,** *adv.* **—'knav•ish•ness,** *n.*

knead [nid] *v.* **1** work (dough, clay, etc.) by pressing, stretching, and squeezing with the hands until it has the proper consistency: *Most dough for homemade bread has to be kneaded before it is ready for baking.* **2** press and squeeze with the hands; massage: *Stiffness in the muscles may be taken away by kneading.* **3** make or shape by kneading. ⟨OE *cnedan*⟩ **—'knead•er,** *n.* **—,knead•a'bil•i•ty,** *n.* **—'knead•a•ble,** *adj.* **—'knead•ing•ly,** *adv.*
☛ *Hom.* NEED.

knee [ni] *n., v.* **kneed, knee•ing.** *—n.* **1** the joint between the thigh and the lower leg. See LEG for picture. **2** any joint corresponding to the human knee or elbow. **3** anything like a bent knee in shape or position. **4** the part of pants, stockings, etc. covering the knee. **5** LAP[1] (def. 1).
bring to (one's) **knees,** force to yield.
on (one's) **knees, a** pleading humbly: *I'm on my knees to you.* **b** in

a state of near collapse or defeat.
—*v.* strike with the knee. ⟨OE *cnēo*⟩

knee breeches breeches reaching to or just below the knees.

knee•cap ['ni,kæp] *n., v.* **-capped, -cap•ping.** —*n.* **1** the flat, movable bone at the front of the knee; patella. See LEG for picture. **2** a covering to protect the knee.
—*v.* shoot (a person) in the kneecaps, especially as an act of terrorism.

-kneed *combining form.* having a ——knee or knees: *knock-kneed = having knock-knees.*

knee–deep ['ni 'dip] *adj.* so deep as to reach the knees.

knee–high *adj.* ['ni 'haɪ]; *n.* ['ni ,haɪ] *adj., n.* —*adj.* so high as to reach the knees.
—*n.* a knee-high sock made of stocking material.

knee•hole ['ni,houl] *n.* a space for the knees, usually in a desk or dressing table.

knee jerk a reflex extension of the leg as a result of a tap on the patellar tendon.

knee–jerk ['ni,dʒɜrk] *adj. Informal.* responding in an unthinking way without question: *a knee-jerk reaction.*

kneel [nil] *v.* **knelt** or **kneeled, kneel•ing. 1** go down on one's knee or knees: *She knelt down to pull a weed from the flower bed.* **2** remain in this position: *They knelt in prayer for several minutes.* ⟨OE *cnēowlian* < *cnēo* knee⟩ —**'kneel•ing•ly,** *adv.*

kneel•er ['nilər] *n.* **1** one who kneels. **2** a stool, cushion, etc. to kneel on.

knee•pad ['ni,pæd] *n.* a pad worn around the knee for protection.

knee•pan ['ni,pæn] *n.* kneecap; patella.

knell [nɛl] *n., v.* —*n.* **1** the sound of a bell rung slowly after a death or at a funeral. **2** a sign or warning of death, failure, etc.: *Their refusal rang the knell of our hopes.* **3** a mournful sound.
—*v.* **1** ring slowly. **2** give a sign or warning of (death, failure, etc.) **3** make a mournful sound. ⟨ME *knell, knyll* < OE *cnyll* (*n.*); ME *knelle*(*n*), *knylle*(*n*) < OE *cnyllan* (*v.*); possibly influenced by *bell*⟩

knelt [nɛlt] *v.* a pt. and a pp. of KNEEL.

Knes•set ['knɛsət] *n.* the legislature of Israel, consisting of one chamber, or house. ⟨< Hebrew *Kneseth,* literally, assembly or gathering⟩

knew [nju] *or* [nu] *v.* pt. of KNOW.
☛ *Hom.* GNU, NEW.

Knick•er•bock•er ['nɪkər,bɒkər] *n. U.S.* **1** a person descended from the early Dutch settlers of New York. **2** a person living in New York. ⟨< Diedrich *Knickerbocker,* fictitious author of Washington Irving's *Knickerbocker's History of New York,* 1809⟩

knick•er•bock•ers ['nɪkər,bɒkərz] *n.pl.* KNICKERS (def. 1).

knick•ers ['nɪkərz] *n.pl.* **1** short, loose-fitting trousers gathered at, or just below, the knee. **2 a** a woman's undergarment for the lower part of the body; briefs with legs. **b** *Informal.* underpants. ⟨short for *knickerbockers* < *Knickerbocker* (said to be due to the costume shown in illustrations in Washington Irving's *Knickerbocker's History of New York*)⟩

knick–knack ['nɪk ,næk] *n.* a pleasing trifle; ornament; trinket. Also, **nick-nack.** ⟨varied reduplication of *knack*⟩

knife [nəif] *n., pl.* **knives;** *v.* **knifed, knif•ing.** —*n.* **1** a thin, flat blade, usually of metal, fastened in a handle so that it can be used to cut or spread. **2** any weapon having a short blade with a sharp edge and point, such as a dagger. **3** a cutting blade in a tool or machine. The knives of a lawn mower cut grass.
knife in the back, an act of betrayal: *Her gossiping about me was a knife in the back.*
under the knife, *Informal.* undergoing a surgical operation.
—*v.* **1** cut or stab with a knife. **2** pierce or cut as with a knife: *The wind knifed through his thin jacket.* **3** *Slang.* try to defeat in an underhand way. ⟨OE *cnīf*⟩ —**'knife,like,** *adj.* —**'knife•less.** *adj.* —**'knif•er,** *n.*

knife edge 1 the edge of a knife. **2** anything very sharp. **3** a wedge on the fine edge of which a scale, beam, pendulum, etc. is hung.

knight [nəit] *n., v.* —*n.* **1** in the Middle Ages, a man raised to an honourable military rank and pledged to do good deeds. After serving as a page and a squire, a man was made a knight by the king or a lord. **2** in modern times, a man raised to an honourable rank because of personal achievement or because he has won distinction in some way. A knight has the title *Sir* before his name. **3** a man devoted to the service or protection of a lady. **4** *Chess.* a piece usually shaped like a horse's head. **5 Knight,** a member or holder of a rank or degree in any order or society that bears the official title of *Knights*: *Knights of Columbus.*
—*v.* raise to the rank of knight. ⟨OE *cniht* boy⟩
☛ *Hom.* NIGHT.

knight bachelor *pl.* **knights bachelor.** BACHELOR (def. 5).

knight banneret *pl.* **knights banneret.** banneret.

knight errant ['nəit 'ɛrənt] *n., pl.* **knights errant. 1** formerly, a knight travelling in search of adventure. **2** a person of great chivalry. **3** an adventurous person, usually impractical.

knight errantry ['nəit 'ɛrəntri] *n., pl.* **knight errantries. 1** conduct or action characteristic of a knight errant. **2** quixotic conduct or action.

knight•hood ['nəit,hʊd] *n.* **1** the rank or dignity of a knight. **2** the profession or occupation of a knight. **3** the character, conduct, or qualities of a knight. **4** knights as a group or class: *All the knighthood of France came to the aid of the king.*

knight•ly ['nəitli] *adj., adv.* —*adj.* of, like, or having to do with a knight; brave; generous; courteous; chivalrous.
—*adv.* as a knight should do; bravely; generously; courteously.
—**'knight•li•ness,** *n.*
☛ *Hom.* NIGHTLY.

Knights Hospitallers or **Hospitalers** See HOSPITALLER.

Knights of Columbus a fraternal society of Roman Catholic men pledged to increase the religious and civic usefulness of its members and to encourage benevolence. It was founded in 1882.

Knight Templar *pl.* **Knights Templars** *for 1;* **Knights Templar** *for 2.* **1** TEMPLAR (def. 1). **2** a member of an order of Masons in the United States.

knish [knɪʃ] *or* [kə'nɪʃ] *n.* in Jewish cookery, dough stuffed with some filling and baked or fried. ⟨< Yiddish < Polish⟩

knit [nɪt] *v.* **knit•ted** or **knit, knit•ting,** *n.* —*v.* **1** make (an article or fabric) by looping yarn or thread together with long needles or by machinery. **2** join closely and firmly together. **3** grow together; be joined closely and firmly: *A broken bone knits.* **4** draw (the brows) together in wrinkles.
—*n.* **1** knitted fabric: *The tunic is in a soft cotton-polyester knit.* **2** a garment made from knitted fabric: *some new knits on sale.* ⟨OE *cnyttan* < *cnotta* knot[1]⟩ —**'knit•ta•ble,** *adj.* —**'knit•ter,** *n.*
☛ *Hom.* NIT.

knit•ting ['nɪtɪŋ] *n., v.* —*n.* **1** knitted work. **2** the action of a person who or machine that knits.
—*v.* ppr. of KNIT.

Knitting

knitting needle one of a pair of long needles used in knitting.

knit•wear ['nɪt,wɛr] *n.* knitted clothing, including hand-knitted or machine-knitted garments and also clothing made of machine-knitted fabric such as jersey.

knives [naɪvz] *n.* pl. of KNIFE.

knob [nɒb] *n.* **1** a rounded lump. **2** the handle of a door, drawer, etc. **3** a rounded hill or mountain. ⟨ME < MLG *knobbe*⟩ —**'knob,like,** *adj.*
☛ *Hom.* NOB.

knobbed [nɒbd] *adj.* having a knob or knobs.

knob•by ['nɒbi] *adj.* **-bi•er, -bi•est. 1** covered with knobs. **2** rounded like a knob. —**'knob•bi•ness,** *n.*

knob•ker•rie ['nɒb,kɛri] *n.* a short club used as a weapon. ⟨< Afrikaans *knopkirie* < Du. *knobbe* knob + Hottentot *kirri* a club⟩

knock [nɒk] *v., n.* —*v.* **1** hit; strike a blow with the fist, knuckles, or anything hard: *He knocked him on the head.* **2** hit and cause to fall: *Bill ran into the shelf and knocked all the books onto the floor.* **3** make a noise by hitting: *to knock on a door.* **4** make a noise, especially a rattling or pounding noise: *The engine is knocking.* **5** *Slang.* criticize; find fault with: *Don't knock the food; it's all we've got.*
knock around or **about,** *Informal.* **a** wander from place to place. **b** hit repeatedly.
knock down, a signify the sale of (an article) to the highest bidder at an auction by a blow of the mallet. **b** take apart: *We knocked down the bookcase and packed it in the car.* **c** strike down.
knock it off, *Slang.* stop it.

knock off, *Informal.* **a** take off; deduct: *to knock off 10 cents from the price.* **b** stop work: *We knock off at noon for lunch.* **c** accomplish hastily; do quickly: *He knocked off a new poem in just a few minutes.* **d** *Slang.* defeat or kill.
knock out, a hit so hard as to make helpless or unconscious. **b** drive out of the contest; defeat.
knock together, make or put together hastily.
knock up, a tire out; exhaust. **b** *Slang.* make pregnant. **c** *Esp. Brit.* get (someone) out of bed by knocking at the door or window.
—n. **1** a hit: *The hard knock made her cry.* **2** a hit with a noise. **3** the act of knocking. **4** the sound of knocking: *She did not hear the knock at the door.* **5** a pounding or rattling sound in an engine: *We learned that the knock was caused by loose parts.* **6** a criticism. ⟨OE *cnocian*⟩
☛ *Hom.* NOCK.

knock•a•bout ['nɒkə,bʌut] *n., adj. —n.* **1** *Nautical.* a small, easily handled sailboat equipped with one mast, a mainsail, and a jib, but no bowsprit. **2** *Brit.* slapstick; horseplay.
—adj. **1** noisy; boisterous: *a knockabout farce.* **2** suitable for rough use.

knock–down ['nɒk ,daʊn] *adj., n.—adj.* made to be taken apart or put together easily.
—n. anything quickly taken apart or assembled.

knock•er ['nɒkər] *n.* **1** a person or thing that knocks. **2** a knob, ring, etc. fastened on a door for use in knocking.

knock–knee ['nɒk ,ni] *n.* **1** an inward curving of the legs, so that the knees tend to knock together in walking. **2 knock-knees,** *pl.* knees that curve in this way.

knock–kneed ['nɒk ,nid] *adj.* having legs curved inward so that the knees tend to touch in walking.

knock•out ['nɒk,ʌut] *n., adj. —n.* **1** the act of rendering unconscious or helpless by a punch: *The boxer won the fight by a knockout.* **2** the condition of being knocked out. **3** a blow that knocks out. **4** *Slang.* a person or thing considered outstanding; a success: *The party was a knockout. She was a knockout at the fundraiser.*
—adj. Slang. that knocks out: *a knockout blow.*

knockout drops *Informal.* any drug, such as chloral hydrate, put in a drink to make a person unconscious.

knoll [noul] *n.* a small, rounded hill; mound. ⟨OE *cnoll*⟩

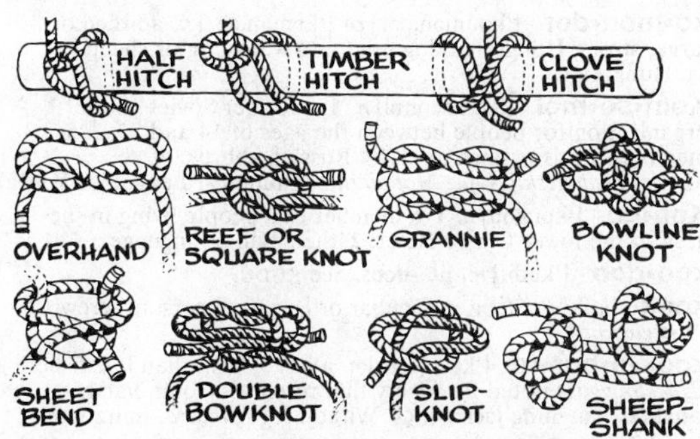

knot¹ [nɒt] *n., v.* **knot•ted, knot•ting.** *—n.* **1** a fastening made by tying or twining together pieces of rope, cord, string, etc. **2** an accidental tying or twisting of rope, cord, string, etc., usually drawn tight; tangle. **3** a bow of ribbon, etc. worn as an ornament. **4** a group; cluster: *A knot of people stood talking outside the door.* **5** a hard mass of wood formed where a branch grows out from a tree, which shows as a roundish, cross-grained piece in a board. **6** a hard lump. **7** *Botany.* a joint where leaves grow out on the stem of a plant. **8** a unit for measuring the speed of a ship or aircraft; one nautical mile per hour: *The ship averaged twelve knots.* **9** NAUTICAL MILE. **10** a difficulty; problem: *a knot in one's plans.* **11** something that unites closely or intricately. **12** a group of toads.
tie the knot, *Informal.* marry: *They tied the knot last spring.*
—v. **1** tie or twine together in a knot. **2** tangle in knots. **3** make knots for (a fringe). **4** make (a fringe) by tying knots. **5** form into a hard lump. **6** unite closely or intricately; bind. ⟨OE *cnotta*⟩ **—'knot•ter,** *n.* **—'knot•less,** *adj.* **—'knot,like,** *adj.*
☛ *Hom.* NAUGHT, NOT, NOUGHT.

knot² [nɒt] *n.* any of several small sandpipers (genus *Calidris*), especially *C. canutus,* having a short, straight bill and greyish plumage except in the breeding season when it has a brownish red throat and breast. Knots breed in the Arctic and winter in temperate or warm regions. ⟨origin uncertain⟩
☛ *Hom.* NAUGHT, NOT, NOUGHT.

knot garden a flower or herb garden having the plants and paths arranged in an intricate pattern.

knot•grass ['nɒt,græs] *n.* knotweed.

knot•hole ['nɒt,houl] *n.* a hole in a board where a knot has fallen out.

knot•ted ['nɒtɪd] *adj., v. —adj.* having a knot or knots; knotty.
—v. pt. and pp. of KNOT.

knot•ty ['nɒti] *adj.* **-ti•er, -ti•est. 1** full of knots: *knotty wood.* **2** difficult; puzzling: *a knotty problem.* **—'knot•ti•ly,** *adv.* **—'knot•ti•ness,** *n.*
☛ *Hom.* NAUGHTY.

knot•weed ['nɒt,wid] *n.* any of several weedy plants (genus *Polygonum*) of the buckwheat family having jointed stems and very small flowers. Also called **knotgrass.**

knout [nʌut] *n., v. —n.* a whip formerly used to inflict punishment.
—v. flog with a knout. ⟨< Russian *knut* < Scand.⟩

know [nou] *v.* **knew, known, know•ing;** *n. —v.* **1** be sure of; have correct information about: *He knows the facts of the case.* **2** have firmly in the mind or memory: *to know a lesson.* **3** be aware (of); have seen or heard: *to know a person's name.* **4** be sure or certain because of experience or knowledge: *He does not have to guess; he knows.* **5** be acquainted with; be familiar with: *I know her.* **6** have an understanding of; have experience with; be skilled in: *She knows Canadian literature.* **7** recognize; identify: *You would hardly know him since his illness.* **8** tell apart from others; distinguish: *You will know her house by the stone chimney.*
know what's what, *Informal.* be well-informed.
—n.
in the know, *Informal.* having inside information. ⟨OE *cnāwan*⟩
—'know•er, *n.*
☛ *Hom.* NO, NOH.
☛ *Syn. v.* **1. Know,** UNDERSTAND = be sure of the truth of something. **Know** emphasizes having a fact or idea firmly in mind or being well acquainted with a subject: *She knows more about Mexico than does anyone else in Canada.* **Understand** emphasizes having a thorough grasp of both facts and meaning, seeing clearly and fully not only the nature and all the implications of a fact or idea, but also its wider relationships: *She understands the workings of the stock market.*

know•a•ble ['nouəbəl] *adj.* capable of being known.

know–all ['nou ,ɒl] *n. Informal.* know-it-all.

know–how ['nou ,haʊ] *n. Informal.* the ability to do something; the knowledge required to get something done.
☛ *Hom.* NOHOW.

know•ing ['nouɪŋ] *adj., v. —adj.* **1** having knowledge; well-informed. **2** clever; shrewd. **3** suggesting shrewd or secret understanding of matters: *His only answer was a knowing look.* **4** deliberate; calculated: *I will not tolerate knowing disobedience.*
—v. ppr. of KNOW.

know•ing•ly ['nouɪŋli] *adv.* **1** in a knowing way. **2** with knowledge; on purpose: *He would not knowingly hurt anyone.*

know–it–all ['nou ɪt ,ɒl] *n. Slang.* a person having pretensions to knowing everything, and who thinks other people are wrong or ill-informed. Also, **know-all.**

knowl•edge ['nɒlɪdʒ] *n.* **1** what one knows: *His knowledge of the subject is limited.* **2** all that is known or can be learned. **3** the act or fact of knowing: *a knowledge of the surrounding countryside. The knowledge of our victory caused great joy.* ⟨ME *knawlechen* acknowledge, confess, ult. < OE *cnāwan* know⟩
☛ *Syn.* **1. Knowledge,** INFORMATION = what a person knows. **Knowledge** applies to all that one knows and understands of facts and general truths and principles, whether gained from books and teachers or by personal experience and observation: *His knowledge of the subject is limited.* **Information** applies to things one has learned through having been told by people or books or through observation, and often suggests isolated or unrelated facts: *She has acquired much information about trips to Europe.*

knowl•edge•a•ble ['nɒlədʒəbəl] *adj.* well-informed, especially about a particular subject. **—'knowl•edge•a•bly,** *adv.*

known [noun] *adj., v. —adj.* in the knowledge of everyone; widely recognized: *a known fact, a known artist.*
—v. pp. of KNOW.
☛ *Hom.* NONE².

know–noth•ing ['nou ,nʌθɪŋ] *n.* an ignorant person.

knuck•le ['nʌkəl] *n., v.* **-led, -ling.** *—n.* **1** a finger joint; especially the joint between a finger and the rest of the h
2 the rounded protuberance formed when such a joint

3 the knee or hock joint of an animal used as food: *boiled pigs' knuckles.* 4 **knuckles,** *pl.* knuckleduster. 5 the part of a hinge through which the pin passes.
—*v.* 1 press or rub with the knuckles. 2 put the knuckles on the ground in playing marbles.
knuckle down, *Informal.* **a** apply oneself earnestly; work hard: *Let's knuckle down and get the job done.* **b** knuckle under.
knuckle under, *Informal.* submit; yield: *He refused to knuckle under to his enemies.* ⟨ME < MDu., dim. of *knoke* bone⟩

knuckle ball *Baseball.* a pitch made by holding the ball with the thumb and the knuckles of the first two or three fingers.

knuck•le•bone ['nʌkəl,boun] *n.* 1 **a** a bone forming part of a knuckle. **b** the rounded end of such a bone. 2 **a** in quadrupeds, a bone corresponding to a wrist, ankle, or finger bone in humans. **b** the knobbed end of such a bone.

knuck•le•dust•er ['nʌkəl,dʌstər] *n. Informal.* a piece of metal worn over the knuckles as a weapon.

knuck•le•head ['nʌkəl,hɛd] *n. Slang.* a thoughtless or inept person.

knur [nɜr] *n.* knar.

knurl [nɜrl] *n., v.* —*n.* 1 a knot; knob. 2 a small ridge, such as on the edge of a coin or round nut.
—*v.* make knurls or ridges on. ⟨apparently dim. of *knur* knot, ME *knor(re)*; cf. MDu. *knorre*⟩

knurl•y ['nɜrli] *adj.* **knurl•i•er, knurl•i•est.** 1 gnarled. 2 ridged.

KO or **K.O.** ['kei'ou] *v.* **KO'd** or **K.O.'d, KO'ing** or **K.O.'ing;** *n., pl.* **K.O.'s.** *Slang.* —*v.* knock out: *He was KO'd in the fourth round.*
—*n.* knockout. ⟨*k*nock + *o*ut⟩

ko•a•la [kou'ɑlə] *n.* a furry, grey, arboreal marsupial (*Phascolarctos cinereus*) of Australia that lives in eucalyptus trees and feeds on the leaves and shoots of these trees.

A koala

ko•an ['kouɑn] *n., pl.* **-ans** or **-an.** *Zen Buddhism.* a seemingly meaningless puzzle designed to heighten awareness of truth. ⟨< Japanese, *kō* public + *an* proposal, design⟩

ko•bo ['koubou] *n.* 1 a unit of money in Nigeria, equal to 1/100 of a naira. See table of money in the Appendix. 2 a coin worth one kobo.

ko•bold ['koubɒld] *or* ['koubould] *n. German folklore.* 1 a sprite or goblin. 2 a gnome living in mines or caves. ⟨< G⟩

Ko•di•ak bear ['koudi,æk] *Cdn.* a subspecies of the brown bear, found on Kodiak Island off the southern coast of Alaska and adjacent coastal areas. It is the largest living carnivorous animal, averaging 2.7 m in length.

K. of C. KNIGHT(S) OF COLUMBUS.

Kog•mol•ik [kɒg'moulɪk] *n., pl.* **-ik** or **-iks.** *Cdn.* 1 a member of the Inuit peoples living to the east of Mackenzie Delta in the Coronation Gulf area. 2 the language of these people.

Koh•i•noor ['kouə,nʊr] *n.* a very large and famous diamond from India that has been one of the British crown jewels since 1849. ⟨< Persian *kohi nur,* literally, mountain of light⟩

kohl [koul] *n.* a dark grey or black powder, usually antimony sulphide, used for eye make-up, especially by women and girls in the Middle East and Asia. ⟨< Arabic *kohl,* var. of *Kuhl.* 18c. See ALCOHOL.⟩
☛ *Hom.* COAL, COLE.

kohl•ra•bi [koul'rɑbi] *or* ['koul,rɑbi] *n., pl.* **-bies.** a cultivated variety of cabbage (*Brassica oleracea caulorapa*) having a thickened, turnip-shaped stem that is eaten as a vegetable and also used as fodder. ⟨< G < Ital. *cavoli rape,* pl. See COLE, RAPE[2].⟩

Ko•hou•tek [kou'hutɛk] *n.* a comet, last seen in 1974. ⟨after L. *Kohoutek* (1935-), Czech astronomer, who discovered it⟩

koi [kɔɪ] *n.* a brightly coloured kind of carp, put into ornamental pools in temperate climates. ⟨< Japanese⟩

Koi•ne ['kɔinei] *or* [kɔɪ'nei] *n.* 1 the common language of the Greeks during the Hellenistic period, based on the dialect of Attica. It is the dialect used in the New Testament. 2 Often, **koine,** a dialect or language that has become the common tongue of several peoples over a wide area. ⟨< Gk. *koinē (dialektos)* common (language)⟩

ko•ji•ki [kou'dʒiki] *n. Shintoism.* one of the most highly revered of ancient texts, covering the history of Japan from the creation of the world to the middle of the 7th century.

ko•ka•nee ['koukə,ni] *n. Cdn.* a freshwater form of the sockeye salmon, common in British Columbia lakes and rivers. Compare OUANANICHE. ⟨? < *Kokanee* Creek, B.C.⟩

ko•la ['koulə] *n.* 1 either of two W African trees (*Cola acuminata* or *C. nitida*) of the same family as the cacao, cultivated extensively in tropical regions for their seeds, called kola nuts. Also called **kola tree.** 2 KOLA NUT. ⟨< native African⟩

ko•la•chi [kou'lɑtʃi] *n.* a type of Ukrainian bread served on Christmas Eve with a candle on top, as part of a twelve-course, meatless meal. ⟨< Czech *koláče, pl.* of *koláč* < *kolo* wheel, circle⟩

kola nut the caffeine-containing seed of the kola tree, chewed in tropical regions as a stimulant and exported to many parts of the world for use as a flavouring in soft drinks and medicines.

ko•lin•sky [kə'lɪnski] *n., pl.* **-skies.** 1 any of several Asian minks. 2 its tawny fur. 3 a coat or other garment made of this fur. ⟨< Russian *kolinski,* adj. < *Kola,* a region of the former Soviet Union⟩

Kol Nidre [koul 'nidrei], ['nɪdrə], *or* [ni'drei] *n. Judaism.* a prayer on the eve of Yom Kippur.

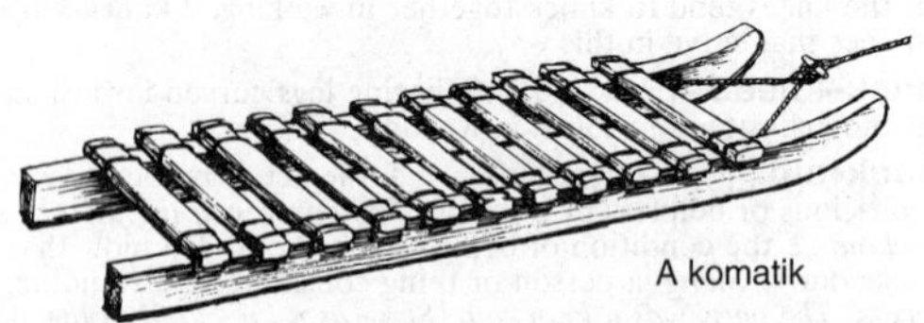
A komatik

ko•ma•tik ['koumə,tɪk] *n. Cdn. North.* a large, wooden dogsled made of closely spaced crossbars lashed to two broad runners. Also, **kamutik.** ⟨< eastern Inuktitut *qamutik,* dual form of *qamut* sled runner⟩

Ko•mo•do dragon [kə'moudou] the largest living lizard (*Varanus komodoensis*), found in southeast Asia.

ko•mon•dor ['koumən,dɔr] *or* ['kɒmən,dɔr] *n.* a breed of large, strong Hungarian dog used as a watchdog or sheepdog. ⟨< Hungarian⟩

Kom•so•mol ['kɒmsə,mɒl] *n.* 1 a former Soviet youth organization for people between the ages of 14 and 23. 2 a member of this organization. ⟨< Russian abbrev. of *Kommunisticheskij Sojuz Molodezhi* Communist League of Youth⟩

Kon•go ['kɒŋgou] *n.* 1 a member of a people living in the area of the lower Congo River. 2 their Bantu language.

koo•doo ['kudu] *n., pl.* **-doos.** See KUDU.

kook [kuk] *n. Slang.* a peculiar or eccentric person; screwball. ⟨? < *cuckoo*⟩

kook•a•bur•ra ['kʊkə,bɜrə] *n.* a large Australian kingfisher (*Dacelo gigas*) noted for its cry that resembles loud, harsh laughter; laughing jackass. ⟨< Wiradjuri *gugubarra,* imitative⟩

kook•y or **kook•ie** ['kuki] *adj. Slang.* peculiar or eccentric: *a kooky person, kooky clothes.* —**'kook•i•ness,** *n.*

koo•le•tah ['kulə,tɑ] *n. Cdn.* kuletuk.

koo•li•tak ['kulə,tæk] *n. Cdn.* kuletuk.

Koo•ten•ay ['kutə,nei] *n., pl.* **Koo•ten•ay** or **Koo•ten•ays.** 1 a member of a First Nations people living near Kootenay Lake in SE British Columbia. 2 the language of the Kootenay, constituting a separate language family. Also, **Kootenai.**

kop [kɒp] *n.* in S Africa, a hill. ⟨< Afrikaans < Du. *kop* head⟩

ko•pek or **ko•peck** ['koupɛk] *n.* 1 a unit of money in Russia, equal to 1/100 of a ruble. See table of money in the Appendix. 2 a coin worth one kopek. ⟨< Russian *kopejka,* orig. dim. of *kop'e* spear (kopeks minted from 1535-1719 bore a figure of Ivan IV with a lance)⟩

kop•je ['kɒpi] *n.* in S Africa, a small hill. ⟨< Afrikaans; dim. of *kop*⟩

Ko•ran [kə'rɑn] *or* [kə'ræn] *n.* the sacred book of Islam, consisting of the revelations made to the prophet Mohammed by Allah through the angel Gabriel. ⟨< Arabic *qurān* recitation < *qara'a* read⟩ —**Ko'ran•ic,** *adj.*

Kor•a•tron ['kɔrə,trɒn] *n. Trademark.* a resin finish that is heat-cured into a fabric after cutting and imparts permanent crease and shape to a garment.

Ko•rea [kə'riə] *n.* a peninsula in SE Asia, divided into North Korea and South Korea.

Ko•re•an [kə'riən] *n., adj.* —*n.* **1** a native or inhabitant of Korea. **2** the language of the Koreans.
—*adj.* of Korea, its people, or their language.

ko•ru•na ['kɔrunə] *n., pl.* **-ny** [-ni] *or* **-nas. 1** the basic unit of money in the Czech Republic, divided into 100 haleru. See table of money in the Appendix. **2** the basic unit of money in the Slovak Republic, divided into 100 halierov. **3** a coin worth one koruna. ⟨< Czech < L *corona* crown⟩

ko•sher ['kouʃər] *adj., v., n.* —*adj.* **1** right or clean according to Jewish ritual law: *kosher meat.* **2** dealing in products that meet the requirements of Jewish ritual law: *a kosher butcher.* **3** *Slang.* all right; legitimate: *It's not kosher to change the rules once the game has started.*
—*v.* prepare (food) according to the Jewish law.
—*n. Informal.* **1** food thus prepared. **2** a shop selling such food. ⟨< Hebrew *kasher* proper⟩

ko•to ['koutou] *n.* a Japanese musical instrument, having 13 strings stretched over an oblong box, and played with the thumb, index, and middle fingers. ⟨< Japanese⟩

ko•tow ['kou,taʊ] *v.* kowtow.

kou•mis or **kou•miss** or **kou•myss** ['kumɪs] See KUMISS.

kow•tow ['kaʊ,taʊ] *v., n.* —*v.* **1** kneel and touch the ground with the forehead to show deep respect, submission, or worship. **2** show slavish respect or obedience (*to*).
—*n.* the act of kowtowing. ⟨< Chinese *k'o-t'ou*, literally, knock (the) head⟩ —**'kow,tow•er,** *n.*

K.P. KITCHEN POLICE.

kPa kilopascal.

kr. 1 krona. **2** krone.

Kr krypton.

kraal [krɑl] *n., v.* —*n.* in South Africa: **1** a village protected by a fence. **2** a pen for cattle or sheep.
—*v.* enclose (cattle) in a kraal. ⟨< Afrikaans < Pg. *curral* corral⟩

kraft [kræft] *n.* a tough, brown wrapping paper made from chemically treated wood pulp. ⟨< G *Kraft* strength⟩

kra•ken ['krɑkən] *n.* a mythical monster supposed to live in Norwegian waters. ⟨< Norwegian⟩

kra•ter ['kreitər] *n.* See CRATER[1].

Krebs cycle [krɛbz] *Biochemistry.* the cycle of intracellular chemical reactions by means of which organisms convert food chemicals into physical energy. ⟨< Sir Hans A. *Krebs* (1900-1981), British biochemist who discovered it⟩

Krem•lin ['krɛmlɪn] *n.* **1** the citadel of Moscow. The chief offices of the Russian government are in the Kremlin. **2** the government of Russia. ⟨< F < Russian *kreml* citadel < Tartar⟩

Krem•lin•ol•o•gy [,krɛmlɪ'nɒlədʒi] *n.* the study and analysis of the domestic and foreign policies of the government of Russia. —**,Krem•lin'ol•o•gist,** *n.*

krep•lach ['krɛplɑx] *n.* a dish comprising dumplings of dough filled with meat or cheese and boiled in soup. ⟨< Yiddish *kreplech, pl.* of *krepel* < MHG dial. *kreppel*, dim. of *krapfe* fritter < OHG *krapfo* hook⟩

krill [krɪl] *n., pl.* **krill**, any of the tiny, shrimplike, planktonic crustaceans (making up the order Euphausiacea) that occur in periodic swarms, especially in polar seas. Krill constitutes the chief food of baleen whales. ⟨< Norwegian *kril* young fry (of fish)⟩

krim•mer ['krɪmər] *n.* a tightly curled, grey fur similar to Persian lamb, made from the pelts of Crimean lambs. ⟨< G *krimmer* < *Krim* Crimea. 20c.⟩

Kri•o ['kriou] *n.* a creole language based on English, spoken in Sierra Leone.

kris [kris] *n.* a Malayan or Indonesian dagger with a wavy blade. Also, **creese.** ⟨< Du. *kris* or Sp. or Pg. *cris* < Malay *kirīs*, krīs. 16c.⟩
☛ *Hom.* CREASE.

Krish•na ['krɪʃnə] *n.* an incarnation of the Hindu god Vishnu, occurring in many forms, but especially as the divine flute player, calling the human soul to God. ⟨< Sanskrit⟩ —**'Krish•na,ism,** *n.*

Kriss Krin•gle ['krɪs 'krɪŋgəl] Santa Claus. ⟨< G dial. *Christkindl* Christ child, Christmas gift⟩

kro•na[1] ['krounə] *n., pl.* **-nor** [-nɔr]. **1** the basic unit of money in Sweden, divided into 100 öre. See table of money in the Appendix. **2** a coin worth one krona. ⟨< Swedish, ult. < L *corona* crown⟩

kro•na[2] ['krounə] *n., pl.* **-nur** [-nər]. **1** the basic unit of money in Iceland, divided into 100 aurar. See table of money in the Appendix. **2** a coin worth one krona. ⟨< Icelandic, ult. < L *corona* crown⟩

kro•ne[1] ['krounə] *n., pl.* **-ner** [-nər]. **1** the basic unit of money in Denmark and Norway, divided into 100 öre. See table of money in the Appendix. **2** a coin worth one krone. ⟨< Danish, ult. < L *corona* crown⟩

kro•ne[2] ['krounə] *n., pl.* **-nen** [-nən]. **1** the basic unit of money in Austria between 1892 and 1925. **2** a silver coin worth one krone. **3** a former German gold coin. ⟨< G *Krone* < L *corona* crown⟩

kroon [krun] *n.* the main unit of money in Estonia. See table of money in the Appendix.

Kru•ger•rand ['krugər,rænd] *or* ['krugər,rɑnd] *n.* a South African gold coin, usually purchased for investment. Compare RAND.

krul•ler ['krʌlər] See CRULLER.

krumm•horn or **krum•horn** ['krʊm,hɔrn] *or* ['krʌm,hɔrn] *n.* See CRUMHORN.

kryp•ton ['krɪptɒn] *n. Chemistry.* a rare, inert, gaseous chemical element. *Symbol:* Kr *at.no.* 36; *at.mass* 83.80. ⟨< NL < Gk. *krypton*, neut. adj., hidden⟩

Kt. Knight.

K.T. 1 KNIGHT TEMPLAR. **2** Knight of the (Order of the) Thistle.

ku•chen ['kuxən] *or* ['kukən] *n.* a coffee cake containing fruit. ⟨< G, cake⟩

kud•lik ['kudlɪk] *n. Cdn.* a dishlike soapstone lamp that burns caribou or seal oil, traditionally used by Inuit. ⟨< Inuktitut *gudlik*⟩

ku•dos ['kjudɒs] *or* ['kudɒs], ['kjudouz] *or* ['kudouz] *n. Informal.* prestige; glory; fame; praise or credit. ⟨< Gk. *kydos*⟩

ku•du ['kudu] *n.* either of two large antelopes of the bush country of Africa, the **greater kudu** (*Tragelaphus strepsiceros*) and the **lesser kudu** (*T. imberbis*), both having spirally curved horns. Also, **koodoo.** ⟨< Hottentot⟩

Ku•fic ['kjufɪk] *or* ['kufɪk] *adj.* describing an early form of the Arabic alphabet, used to make copies of the Koran.

Ku Klux Klan ['ku 'klʌks 'klæn] *n. U.S.* **1** a secret society formed in the S United States after the Civil War to regain and maintain control by white people. **2** a secret society founded in the U.S. in 1915, opposed to Blacks, Jews, Catholics, and foreigners. *Abbrev.*: KKK ⟨probably < Gk. *kyklos* circle + E *clan*⟩ —**'Ku 'Klux 'Klan•ner,** *n.*

kuk•ri ['kʊkri] *n.* a knife with a curved, very sharp blade, used as a weapon by Gurkhas. ⟨< Nepali *kukri*⟩

ku•lak [ku'lɑk] *or* ['kulɑk] *n.* **1** in Russia, formerly, a well-to-do peasant, farmer, or trader who opposed collectivization. **2** a Russian peasant who owns and tills his or her land for his or her own profit. ⟨< Russian *kulak*, literally, fist; hence, tight-fisted⟩

ku•le•tuk ['kulə,tʌk] *n. Cdn.* a hooded, close-fitting jacket made of skin, often trimmed with fur; parka. Also, **kooletah, koolitak.**

ku•mik ['kumɪk] *n.* kamik.

ku•miss ['kumɪs] *n.* **1** fermented mare's or camel's milk used as a drink by Asiatic nomads. **2** a drink made from cow's milk, used in special diets. **3** an intoxicating liquor distilled from Asian KUMISS (def. 1). Also, **koumis, koumiss,** or **koumyss.** ⟨< Russian *kumys* < Tatar *kumiz*⟩

küm•mel ['kɪməl] *or* ['kʌməl]; *German,* ['kyməl] *n.* a liqueur flavoured with caraway seeds, anise, etc. ⟨< G⟩

kum•mer•bund ['kʌmər,bʌnd] See CUMMERBUND.

kum•quat ['kʌmkwɒt] *n.* **1** an orange yellow fruit resembling a small orange and having a sour pulp and a sweet rind, used especially for preserves and candy. **2** any of several trees or shrubs (genus *Fortunella*) of the rue family that produce this fruit. ⟨< Chinese (Cantonese dial.)⟩

kum•tux ['kʌmtʌks] *v. Cdn. Pacific coast.* understand; know; believe. ⟨< Chinook jargon⟩

ku•na ['kunə] *n.* the main unit of money of Croatia, divid into 100 lipa. See table of money in the Appendix.

kung fu ['kʊŋ 'fu] a Chinese art of fighting similar to karate, that dates back to ancient times. ⟨< Chinese *ch'uan-fa*, literally, boxing principles⟩

kunz•ite ['kʊntsəit] *n.* a transparent mineral used as a gem. ⟨after G.F. *Kunz*, U.S. gemmologist (1856–1932)⟩

Kuo•min•tang ['kwou'mɪn'tæŋ], ['kwou'mɪn'tɑŋ], *or* ['gwou'mɪn'dɑŋ] *n.* a Chinese nationalist party organized in 1912.

ku•pon ['kupɒn] *n.* the main unit of currency in the republic of Georgia. See table of money in the Appendix.

kur•cha•to•vi•um rutherfordium. ⟨after I.V. *Kurchatov* (1903–1960), Russian physicist⟩
☛ *Usage.* See RUTHERFORDIUM.

Kurd [kɜrd] *or* [kʊrd] *n.* a member of an Indo European people living chiefly in Kurdistan.

Kur•dish ['kɜrdɪʃ] *or* ['kʊrdɪʃ] *adj., n.* –*adj.* of or having to do with the Kurds or their language.
–*n.* the Iranian language of the Kurds.

Kur•dis•tan ['kɜrdɪ,stæn] *n.* a region in SW Asia, divided among Turkey, Iran, and Iraq.

kur•ra•jong ['kɜrə,dʒɒŋ] *n.* an Australian tree (*Brachychiton populneum*) having large red or yellow flowers. ⟨< from a native Australian language⟩

kur•to•sis [kər'tousɪs] *n. Statistics.* the quantity indicating a statistical frequency curve. ⟨< Gk. *kyrtosis* a curving < *kyrtos* curved⟩

ku•rus [kʊ'ruʃ] *n., pl.* **kurus.** a unit of money in Turkey, equal to 1/100 of a lira. Also called **piastre.** See table of money in the Appendix. ⟨< Turkish⟩

Kut•chin ['kʊtʃɪn] *n.* **1** a member of an American Indian people now living in the Yukon. **2** the Athapascan language of these people.

Ku•wait [ku'weit] *n.* a country in W Asia, between Iraq and Saudi Arabia.

Ku•wai•ti [ku'weiti] *n., adj.* –*n.* a native or inhabitant of Kuwait.
–*adj.* of Kuwait or its people.

kV kilovolt(s).

kvass or **kvas** [kə'vɑs] *or* [kvɑs] *n.* a drink made from fermented rye or barley, popular among Russians. ⟨< Russian⟩

kW kilowatt(s).

Kwa [kwɑ] *n.* a branch of the Niger-Congo family, spoken in W Africa.

kwa•cha ['kwɑtʃɑ] *n., pl.* **kwacha. 1** the basic unit of money in Zambia, divided into 100 ngwee. **2** the basic unit of money in Malawi, divided into 100 tambala. See table of money in the Appendix. **3** a note worth one kwacha. ⟨native term; literally, dawn⟩

Kwa•ki•u•tl [,kwɑki'utəl] *or* [kwɑ'kjutəl] *n.* **Kwa•ki•u•tl** or **Kwa•ki•u•tls. 1** a member of a First Nations people living on the shores of Queen Charlotte Sound and on N Vancouver Island. **2** the Wakashan language of the Kwakiutl.
☛ *Usage.* The people now call themselves Kwa Kwa Ka'wakw.

kwan•za ['kwɑnzə] *n.* the basic unit of money in Angola, divided into 100 lwei. See table of money in the Appendix. ⟨< a Bantu language⟩

kwa•shi•or•kor [,kwɑʃi'ɔrkɔr] *n. Pathology.* an often fatal condition, especially of infants and young children, caused by a protein deficiency in the diet. ⟨< Ashanti, literally, red boy, since it causes the hair to turn red⟩

kWh kilowatt hour(s).

kwun•u•se•la ['kwunusələ] *n. Cdn. Pacific coast.* thunderbird. ⟨< Kwakiutl⟩

kyat [kjɑt] *n.* **1** the basic unit of money in Myanmar, divided into 100 pyas. See table of money in the Appendix. **2** a coin or note worth one kyat. ⟨< Burmese⟩

ky•mo•graph ['kaɪmə,græf] *n.* an instrument for recording blood pressure or any other liquid pressure. **–,ky•mo'graph•ic,** *adj.*

ky•pho•sis [kəi'fousɪs] *n.* an abnormal curvature of the spine, producing a hunchback. ⟨< Gk. *kyphosis* a hunched state < *kyphos* hump⟩ **–ky'phot•ic** [kəi'fɒtɪk], *adj.*

Kyr•gyz Republic ['kirgɪz] See KIRGHIZIA.

L l *L l*

l or **L** [ɛl] *n., pl.* **l's** or **L's. 1** the twelfth letter of the English alphabet. **2** any speech sound represented by this letter. **3** a person or thing identified as *l*, especially the twelfth in a series. **4 L,** the Roman numeral for 50. **5** something shaped like the letter L, especially a wing of a building or a section of pipe; ell. **6** any device such as a printer's type, a lever, or a key on a keyboard that produces an l or an L. **7** (*adjl.*) of or being an L or l: *an L-shaped room.*

l or **l. 1** line. **2** league. **3** length. **4** lira; lire. **5** leaf. **6** left. **7** book (for L *liber).*

L 1 Latin. **2** litre(s). **3** *Physics.* length. **4** longitude. **5** pound (sterling). **6** Libra. **7** large.

L. 1 Latin. **2** low; lower. **3** licentiate. **4** lake. **5** law.

£ pound (or pounds) sterling.

la[1] [lɑ] *n. Music.* **1** the sixth tone of an eight-tone major scale. See DO[2] for picture. **2** the tone A. Also, **lah.** ⟨See GAMUT⟩

la[2] [lɑ] *interj. Archaic.* an exclamation of surprise.

La lanthanum.

L.A. LEGISLATIVE ASSEMBLY.

laa•ger ['lɑgər] *n., v. —n.* a camp surrounded by wagons. *—v.* set up such a camp. ⟨< Afrikaans < G *Lager*, Du. *leger* a camp⟩

laa•ri ['lɑri] See LARI.

lab [læb] *n. Informal.* laboratory.

Lab [læb] *n. Cdn. Informal.* LABRADOR RETRIEVER.

Lab. 1 Labrador. **2** *Brit.* **a** Labour (Party). **b** Labourite.

lab•ar•um ['læbərəm] *n., pl.* **-ara** [-ərə]. a banner carried in an ecclesiastical procession. ⟨< LL < LGk. *labaron*⟩

lab•da•num ['læbdənəm] *n.* a poisonous juice from flowers of the genus *Cistus*, used in making perfumes and fumigants. ⟨< ML, altered < L *ladanum* < Gk. *ladanon*⟩

la•bel ['leibəl] *n., v.* **-belled** or **-beled, -bel•ling** or **-bel•ing.** *—n.* **1** a slip of paper or other material attached to anything and marked to show what or whose it is, or where it is to go. **2** a short phrase used to describe some person, thing, or idea: *'Land of Opportunity' is a label often given to Canada.*
—v. **1** put or write a label on: *The bottle is labelled 'Poison'.* **2** describe as; call; name: *He labelled the boastful man a liar.* **3** infuse or treat (a substance) with a radioactive chemical or isotope so that its course or activity can be noted. ⟨ME < OF < Gmc.⟩ **—'la•bel•ler** or **'la•bel•er,** *n.*
☛ *Hom.* LABILE.

La Belle Province [labɛlpʀɔ'vɛ̃s] *Cdn. French.* Québec.

la•bel•lum [lə'bɛləm] *n., pl.* **-bel•la** [-'bɛlə]. *Botany.* the middle petal of an orchid, usually different in shape and colour from the other two and suggestive of a lip. ⟨< L *labellum*, dim. of *labium* lip⟩

la•be•ta•lol [lə'bitə,lɒl] *n.* a drug used to lower blood pressure.

la•bi•al ['leibiəl] *adj., n. —adj.* **1** of or having to do with a lip or lips. **2** *Phonetics.* articulated mainly with the lips: [v], [f], [b], [p], and [m] are labial consonants. **3** *Music.* producing tones by the action of an air current across a narrow, liplike opening, as in a flue pipe of an organ.
—n. **1** *Phonetics.* a sound articulated with the lips. **2** a flue pipe on an organ, as distinguished from a reed pipe. ⟨< Med.L *labialis* < L *labium* lip⟩ **—'la•bi•al•ly,** *adv.*

la•bi•al•ize ['leibiə,laɪz] *v.* **-ized, -iz•ing.** *Phonetics.* round (a vowel). **—,la•bi•al•i'za•tion,** *n.*

labia majora ['leibiə mə'dʒɔrə] folds of skin that are the outside boundaries of the vulva in human females. ⟨< Mod.L, literally, greater lips⟩

labia minora [mə'nɔrə] two thin folds of tissue within the labia majora, that form the margins of the vaginal and urinary openings in human females. ⟨< Mod.L, literally, lesser lips⟩

la•bi•ate ['leibiɪt] *or* ['leibi,eit] *adj., n. —adj.* having one or more liplike parts.
—n. a plant of the family Labiatae that includes the mints. ⟨< NL *labiatus* < L *labium* lip⟩

la•bile ['leibaɪl] *or* ['leibəl] *adj.* liable to change; unstable. ⟨< L *labilis* < *labi* fall⟩ **—la'bil•i•ty** [lə'bɪləti], *n.*
☛ *Hom.* LABEL ['leibəl].

labio– *combining form.* lips: *labiodental.* ⟨< L *labium* lip⟩

la•bi•o•den•tal [,leibiou'dɛntəl] *adj., n. Phonetics. —adj.* articulated with the lower lip and upper teeth.
—n. a sound articulated in this way. The sounds [f] and [v] are labiodentals.

la•bi•o•na•sal [,leibiou'neizəl] *adj., n. —adj.* being both labial and nasal.
—n. a speech sound of that kind, such as [m].

la•bi•o•ve•lar [,leibiou'vilər] *adj., n. —adj.* being both labial and velar.
—n. a speech sound of that kind, such as [w].

la•bi•um ['leibiəm] *n., pl.* **-bi•a** [-biə]. **1** a lip or liplike part. **2** *Botany.* a portion of the corolla of certain flowers, especially the lower part, shaped to suggest a lip. ⟨< L⟩

la•bor ['leibər] See LABOUR.

lab•o•ra•to•ry ['læbrə,tɔri] *or* [lə'bɔrə,tɔri] *n., pl.* **-ries. 1** a place where scientific work is done; a room or building fitted with apparatus for conducting scientific investigations, experiments, tests, etc. **2** a place fitted up for manufacturing chemicals, medicines, explosives, etc. **3** any place, not a classroom or library, equipped for systematic study: *a language laboratory.* ⟨< Med.L *laboratorium* < L *laborare* to work < *labor* work⟩

la•bo•ri•ous [lə'bɔriəs] *adj.* **1** requiring much work; requiring hard work: *Climbing a mountain is laborious.* **2** willing to work hard; hard-working; industrious. **3** showing signs of effort; not easy. ⟨< L *laboriosus* < *labor* labour⟩ **—la'bo•ri•ous•ly,** *adv.* **—la'bo•ri•ous•ness,** *n.*

la•bour or **la•bor** ['leibər] *n., v. —n.* **1** the effort in doing or making something; work; toil: *He was well paid for his labour.* **2** a piece of work; task: *The king gave Hercules twelve labours to perform.* **3** physical work or toil done for wages. **4** *Economics.* the work of human beings that produces goods or services. *Land, labour*, and *capital* are the three principal factors of production. **5** skilled and unskilled workers as a group: *Labour favours safe working conditions.* **6** the process of childbirth or the time during which it takes place: *in labour.* **7** (*adjl.*) of or having to do with this process: *labour pains.* **8** a group of moles.
—v. **1** do work; work hard; toil: *He laboured all day in the mill.* **2** elaborate with effort or in detail: *The speaker laboured the point so much that we lost interest.* **3** move slowly and heavily: *The ship laboured in the high waves.* **4** be burdened, troubled, or distressed. **5** act or function at a disadvantage (usually used with **under**): *to labour under a delusion.* **6** be in LABOUR (def. *n.* 6). ⟨ME < OF < L *labor*⟩
☛ *Syn. n.* **1.** See note at WORK.

Labour Day or **Labor Day 1** the first Monday in September, a legal holiday in Canada and the United States in honour of labour and workers. **2** for or occurring on Labour Day: *a Labour Day parade.*

la•boured or **la•bored** ['leibərd] *adj., v. —adj.* done with effort; forced; not easy or natural.
—v. pt. and pp. of LABOUR. **—'la•boured•ly** or **'la•bored•ly,** *adv.* **—'la•bour•ing•ly** or **'la•bor•ing•ly,** *adv.* **—'la•bour•less** or **'la•bor•less,** *adj.*
☛ *Syn.* See note at ELABORATE.

la•bour•er or **la•bor•er** ['leibərər] *n.* **1** a worker. **2** a person who does work requiring strength rather than skill or training.

la•bour–in•ten•sive or **la•bor–in•ten•sive** ['leibər ɪn'tɛnsɪv] requiring a huge labour force in relation to the amount of capital required. Compare CAPITAL-INTENSIVE.

la•bour•ite or **la•bor•ite** ['leibə,rəit] *n.* **1** a member of a labour party. **2 Labourite,** in the United Kingdom, a member of the Labour Party.

labour party or **labor party 1** any political party organized to protect and promote the interests of workers. **2 Labour Party,** in the United Kingdom, a political party that exists especially to protect and advance the interests of working people. It was founded by the trade unions.

Labour Progressive Party *Cdn.* the official name of the Communist Party of Canada from 1943-1959.

la•bour–sav•ing or **la•bor–sav•ing** ['leibər ,seivɪŋ] *adj.* that takes the place of or lessens labour.

labour union or **labor union** an association of workers organized to protect and promote the common interests of its members and to deal collectively with employers.

Lab•ra•dor ['læbrə,dɔr] *or* [,læbrə'dɔr] *for 1*, ['læbrə,dɔr] *for 2*. *n. Cdn.* **1** a region of eastern Canada, comprising the mainland part of Newfoundland. **2** *Cdn.* LABRADOR RETRIEVER.

Labrador Current the cold arctic current that flows southward past Labrador and Newfoundland, where it joins the Gulf Stream.

lab•ra•dor•ite ['læbrədɔ,rəit] *or* [,læbrə'dɔrəit] *n. Cdn.* **1** a kind of feldspar that gleams with brilliant colours. **2** a piece of this stone, or a gem made from it. ⟨< *Labrador*, where it is found + *-ite*⟩

Labrador retriever *Cdn.* a breed of medium-sized retriever originating in Newfoundland but developed mainly in England, having a thick, short coat that is black, chocolate brown, or yellow. ⟨< *Labrador*, where the breed was originated⟩

A Labrador retriever

Labrador tea *Cdn.* **1** any of several small evergreen shrubs (genus *Ledum*) of the heath family, especially a common bog plant (*L. groenlandicum*) of Greenland and N North America, having white flowers and leathery, oblong leaves with rolled-under margins and brownish, woolly undersides. **2** an infusion made from the leaves of *L. groenlandicum*, traditionally used as a tea substitute in the North.

la•bret ['leibrɛt] *n.* an ornament of bone, shell, wood, etc. stuck into or through the lower lip to stretch it, worn by various peoples, e.g., formerly, the Tlingit. ⟨< L *labrum* lip + *-et*⟩

lab•rid ['læbrɪd] *or* ['leibrɪd] *n.* any of various fishes of the family Labridae, including the tautog, the cunner, and the wrasses, being brightly coloured and having conspicuous teeth. ⟨< NL *Lābridae*, *lābrus*⟩

la•brum ['leibrəm] *or* ['læbrəm] *n., pl.* **la•bra** ['leibrə] *or* ['læbrə]. **1** a lip or liplike part. **2** *Anatomy.* a ring of cartilage surrounding a bony socket. ⟨< L, literally, lip⟩

la•bur•num [lə'bɜrnəm] *n.* any of a genus (*Laburnum*) of Eurasian trees and shrubs of the pea family having hanging clusters of yellow flowers. Some laburnums are cultivated as ornamental trees; others are valued for their hard, durable wood. The seeds are poisonous. ⟨< NL, special use of L *laburnum* golden chain⟩

lab•y•rinth ['læbə,rɪnθ] *n.* **1** a place through which it is hard to find one's way; maze. **2** a confusing, complicated arrangement. **3** a confusing, complicated state of affairs. **4 Labyrinth,** *Greek mythology.* the maze built by Daedalus for King Minos of Crete. The Minotaur was kept there. **5** *Anatomy.* the inner ear. ⟨< L < Gk. *labyrinthos*⟩

lab•y•rin•thine [,læbə'rɪnθin] *or* [,læbə'rɪnθɪn] *adj.* **1** of a labyrinth; forming a labyrinth. **2** intricate; confusing; complicated. Also, **labyrinthian, labyrinthic.**

lac [læk] *n.* a resinous substance secreted by certain homopterous insects of S Asia, especially *Laccifer lacca*, used especially for making shellac. ⟨< Hind. *lakh* < Skt. *laksha*⟩

L.A.C. LEADING AIRCRAFTMAN.

La Ca•di•a [læ 'kædiə] or **La Ca•die** [læ kə'di] *n. Cdn. Archaic.* Acadia.

l'Ac•a•die [laka'di] *n. Cdn. French.* Acadia.

lac•co•lith ['lækə,lɪθ] *n. Geology.* a bulge in strata such as on the outside of the crater of a volcano, formed by igneous rock which has not broken through to the surface. ⟨< Gk. *lákkos* pond + E *-lith*⟩ **—,lac•co'lith•ic, ,lac•co'lit•ic,** *adj.*

lace [leis] *n., v.* **laced, lac•ing.** *—n.* **1** a delicate, openwork or netlike fabric made by connecting base threads with ornamental stitches or by twisting, braiding, or knotting threads together in an ornamental pattern. **2** a cord, string, leather strip, etc. for pulling or holding together. **3** gold or silver braid used for trimming uniforms, etc.
—v. **1** put laces through; pull or hold together with a lace or laces. **2** be fastened or allow to be fastened with a lace or laces: *These shoes lace.* **3** trim with or as if with lace: *a uniform laced with gold.* **4** interlace; intertwine. **5** mark with streaks; streaked: *a white petunia laced with purple.* **6** *Informal.* lash; beat; thrash. **7** add a dash of brandy, whisky, etc. to (a beverage, especially coffee). **8** squeeze in the waist of (someone), by tightening the laces of a corset, etc.
lace into, *Informal.* **a** attack. **b** criticize severely: *to lace into someone for his or her incompetence.* ⟨ME < OF *laz* < L *laqueus* noose. Doublet of LASSO.⟩ **—'lace•less,** *adj.* **—'lace,like,** *adj.* **—'lac•er,** *n.*

Lace•dae•mo•ni•an [,læsədi'mouniən] *adj. or n.* Spartan.

lac•er•ate *v.* ['læsə,reit]; *adj.* ['læsərɪt] *or* ['læsə,reit] *v.* **-at•ed, -at•ing;** *adj. —v.* **1** tear roughly; mangle: *The bear's claws lacerated his flesh.* **2** cause pain or suffering to; distress: *The coach's sharp words lacerated her feelings.*
—adj. Also, **lacerated. 1** *Botany, zoology.* deeply or irregularly indented as if torn: *lacerate leaves.* **2** torn; jagged. ⟨< L *lacerare* < *lacer* mangled⟩ **—'lac•er•a•ble,** *adj.* **—'lac•er•a•tive,** *adj.*

lac•er•a•tion [,læsə'reiʃən] *n.* **1** the act of lacerating. **2** a rough or jagged tear or wound.

La•cer•ta [lə'sɜrtə] *n.* a constellation in the northern hemisphere, near Andromeda. ⟨< L lizard⟩

lac•er•til•ian [,læsər'tɪliən] *adj., n. —adj.* of the order Lacertilia, including the lizards.
—n. a reptile of that order. ⟨< NL *Lacertilia* < L *lacerta*⟩

lace•wing ['leis,wɪŋ] *n.* any of numerous insects (order Neuroptera) having two pairs of large wings with a lacelike network of veins, long, delicate antennae, and a slender body; especially, any member of the **green lacewing** family (Chrysopidae) or **brown lacewing** family (Hemerobiidae).

lace•work ['leis,wɜrk] *n.* **1** lace. **2** openwork like lace.

lach•es ['lætʃɪz] *n. Law.* failure to do a thing at the right time; inexcusable negligence. ⟨ME < OF *laschesse*, ult. < L *laxus* loose⟩

Lach•e•sis ['lækəsɪs] *or* ['lætʃəsɪs] *n. Greek mythology.* one of the three Fates. Lachesis measures off the thread of human life.

lach•ry•mal ['lækrəməl] *adj., n., pl.* **lachyrmals.** *—adj.* **1** of tears; producing tears. **2** for tears. **3** *Anatomy.* of, having to do with, or situated near the glands **(lachrymal glands)** that secrete tears, or the ducts leading from them.
—n. Anatomy. the gland that produces tears. Also, **lacrimal.** ⟨< Med.L *lachrymalis* < L *lacrima* tear⟩

lach•ry•ma•tor ['lækrɪ,meitər] *n.* any substance that produces tears. ⟨< L *lacrima* tear + E *-ator*⟩

lach•ry•ma•to•ry ['lækrəmə,tɔri] *adj., n., pl.* **-ries.** *—adj.* **1** of tears; producing tears. **2** for tears.
—n. a small vase with a narrow neck found in ancient Roman tombs and once believed to be used to hold the tears of mourning friends.

lach•ry•mose ['lækrə,mous] *adj.* tearful; mournful. ⟨< L *lacrimosus* < *lacrima* tear⟩ **—'lach•ry,mose•ly,** *adv.* **—,lach•ry'mos•i•ty** [,lækrə'mɒsəti], *n.*

lac•ing ['leisɪŋ] *n., v. —n.* **1** a cord, string, etc. for pulling or holding something together. **2** gold or silver braid used for trimming. **3** *Informal.* a lashing; beating; thrashing.
—v. ppr. of LACE.

la•cin•i•ate [lə'sɪnɪɪt] *or* [lə'sɪni,eit] *adj.* jagged.

lack [læk] *v., n. —v.* **1** have less than enough; need: *A desert lacks water.* **2** be without: *A homeless person lacks a home.* **3** be absent or missing.
—n. **1** a shortage; the fact of not having enough: *Lack of rest made her tired.* **2** the fact or condition of being without: *Lack of a fire made him cold.* **3** the thing needed: *The campers' main lack was fuel for a fire.*
supply the lack, supply what is needed. ⟨Cf. MDu. *lac*, MLG *lak*⟩
☛ *Syn. v.* **1, 2. Lack,** WANT, NEED = be without something. **Lack** = be completely without or without enough of something, good or bad: *A coward lacks courage.* **Want** (*Archaic*) = lack something worth having, desired, or, especially, necessary for completeness: *That dress wants a belt.* **Need** = lack something required for a purpose or that cannot be done without: *He does not have the tools he needs. She needs more sleep.*

lack•a•dai•si•cal [,lækə'deizəkəl] *adj.* languid; listless; dreamy; lazy. ⟨< *lackaday*⟩ **—,lack•a'dai•si•cal•ly,** *adv.* **—,lack•a'dai•si•cal•ness,** *n.*

lack•a•day ['lækə,dei] *interj. Archaic.* alas. ⟨var. of *alack a day!*⟩

lack•ey ['læki] *n., pl.* **-eys;** *v.* **-eyed, -ey•ing.** *—n.* **1** a male servant; footman. **2** a slavish follower.
—v. **1** wait on. **2** be slavish to. ⟨< F *laquais* < Sp. *lacayo* foot soldier⟩

lack•ing ['lækɪŋ] *adj., prep., v. —adj.* **1** not having enough; deficient: *A weak person is lacking in strength.* **2** absent; not present: *Water is lacking in a desert.*

—*prep.* without; in the absence of: *Lacking anything better, use what you have.*
—*v.* ppr. of LACK.

lack•lus•tre ['læk,lʌstər] *adj.* **1** not shining or bright; dull. **2** lacking vitality or interest: *a lacklustre production of a play.* Also, **lackluster.**

la•con•ic [lə'kɒnɪk] *adj.* using few words; brief in speech or expression; concise. ⟨< L < Gk. *lakōnikos* Spartan; Spartans were noted for the brevity, or terseness, of their speech⟩ **—la'con•i•cal•ly,** *adv.*

lac•o•nism ['lækə,nɪzəm] *n.* **1** laconic brevity. **2** a laconic speech or expression.

lac•quer ['lækər] *n., v.* —*n.* **1** a varnish consisting of shellac dissolved in a solvent, used to give a protective coating or a shiny appearance to metals, wood, paper, etc. **2** a varnish made from the resin of a sumac tree of SE Asia. It gives a very high polish on wood. **3** wooden articles coated with such varnish. **4** a dressing for the hair, made from gum or resin.
—*v.* coat with lacquer. ⟨< F < Pg. *laca* lac[1]⟩ **—'lac•quer•er,** *n.*

lac•ri•mal ['lækrəməl] See LACHRYMAL.

la•crosse [lə'krɒs] *n. Cdn.* a game played, either indoors (**box lacrosse**) or outdoors (**field lacrosse**) by two teams each of ten players equipped with lacrosse sticks, by means of which an India rubber ball is carried and passed from player to player in an attempt to score a goal. ⟨< Cdn.F *la crosse,* the racket used in the game⟩

lacrosse stick *Cdn.* an L-shaped stick strung with leather thongs that form a kind of pouch for carrying the ball in the game of lacrosse.

lac•ta•ry ['læktəri] *adj.* **1** milky. **2** having to do with milk.

lac•tase ['lækteis] *n. Biochemistry.* a digestive enzyme in the intestinal glands which helps to break down carbohydrates into glucose. It is used in medicine to help people digest milk and milk products.

lac•tate[1] ['lækteit] *n. Chemistry.* **1** any salt of lactic acid. **2** an ester of lactic acid. ⟨< *lact(ic acid)* + *-ate[2]*⟩

lac•tate[2] ['lækteit] *v.* **-tat•ed, -tat•ing. 1** secrete milk. **2** give suck. **3** convert into milk; cause to resemble milk. ⟨< L *lactare* suckle, with E *-ate[1]*⟩

lac•ta•tion [læk'teiʃən] *n.* **1** the secretion or formation of milk. **2** the time during which a mother gives milk. **3** the act of suckling a baby. **—lac'ta•tion•al,** *adj.* **—lac'ta•tion•al•ly,** *adv.*

lac•te•al ['læktiəl] *adj., n.* —*adj.* **1** of or like milk; milky. **2** of lymphatic vessels, carrying chyle.
—*n. Anatomy.* any of the lymphatic vessels in the wall of the intestine that carry chyle from the intestine to the thoracic duct, from which the chyle is taken into the bloodstream. ⟨< L *lacteus* < *lac* milk⟩ **—'lac•te•al•ly,** *adv.*

lac•te•ous ['læktiəs] *adj. Archaic.* milky.

lac•tes•cent [læk'tɛsənt] *adj.* **1** becoming milky. **2** exuding a milky substance, as certain plants do. **—lac'tes•cence, lac'tes•cen•cy,** *adj.*

lac•tic ['læktɪk] *adj.* of milk; from milk. ⟨< L *lac, lactis* milk⟩

lactic acid *Biochemistry.* a colourless, odourless organic acid occurring in several forms. One is produced by the action of bacteria on the lactose of milk in the process of souring; another form occurs in muscle tissue. Lactic acid is used in medicine and in industry. *Formula*: $C_3H_6O_3$

lac•tif•er•ous [læk'tɪfərəs] *adj.* **1** producing milk. **2** of some plants, yielding a milky liquid. **—lac'tif•er•ous•ness,** *n.*

lac•to– *combining form.* milk: *lactometer.* ⟨< L *lac, lactis* milk⟩

lac•to•fla•vin [,læktou'fleivɪn] *or* ['læktou,fleivɪn] *n. Biochemistry.* riboflavin.

lac•tom•e•ter [læk'tɒmətər] *n.* an instrument for testing the purity or richness of milk. ⟨< *lacto-* milk (< L *lac*) + *-meter*⟩

lac•tose ['læktous] *n. Biochemistry.* a white, odourless crystalline sugar present in milk; milk sugar. *Formula*: $C_{12}H_{22}O_{11}$ ⟨< L *lac, lactis* milk⟩

lac•tu•lose ['læktjə,lous] *n.* a drug used to treat certain forms of encephalopathy.

la•cu•na [lə'kjunə] *n., pl.* **-nas, -nae** [-ni *or* -nai]. **1** an empty space; gap; blank: *There were several lacunas in her letter where words had been erased.* **2** *Biology.* a tiny cavity in bones or tissues. ⟨< L *lacuna* hole < *lacus* cistern, lake. Doublet of LAGOON.⟩ **—la'cu•nal,** *adj.*

la•cus•trine [lə'kʌstrɪn] *adj.* **1** of lakes. **2** in or on lakes: *Some prehistoric peoples built lacustrine dwellings.* ⟨< L *lacustris,* adj. of *lacus* lake + E *-ine[1]*⟩

lac•y ['leisi] *adj.* **lac•i•er, lac•i•est. 1** of lace. **2** like lace; having an open pattern: *the lacy leaves of a fern.* **—'lac•i•ly,** *adv.* **—'lac•i•ness,** *n.*

lad [læd] *n.* **1** a boy; young man. **2** *Informal.* man. ⟨ME *ladde,* OE *Ladda* (a nickname)⟩ **—'lad•dish,** *adj.* **—'lad•hood,** *n.*

lad•der ['lædər] *n., v.* —*n.* **1** a set of rungs or steps fastened to two long sidepieces, for use in climbing. **2** a means of climbing higher. **3** an ascending series of little pools built to enable fish to swim upstream past a dam or falls; fishway. **4** anything resembling or suggesting a ladder: *This company has an elaborate promotion ladder.* **5** a run in a knitted garment such as a nylon stocking.
—*v.* of knitted garments, especially stockings, develop ladders as the result of the breaking of a thread. ⟨OE *hlǣder*⟩ **—'lad•der•less,** *adj.* **—'lad•der,like,** *adj.*

lad•der–back ['lædər ,bæk] *adj.* of a chair, having a tall back designed like the rungs of a ladder: *a ladder-back chair.*

lad•die ['lædi] *n. Scottish.* **1** a young lad. **2** boy.

lade [leid] *v.* **lad•ed, lad•en** or **lad•ed, lad•ing. 1** put a burden on; load. **2** dip; scoop; ladle. **3** take on cargo. ⟨OE *hladan*⟩
☛ *Hom.* LAID.

lad•en ['leidən] *adj., v.* —*adj.* loaded; burdened.
—*v.* a pp. of LADE.

la–di–da ['lɑ di 'dɑ] *adj. Informal.* affected in behaviour or pronunciation.

Ladies' Aid Society *Cdn.* an organization of women who raise funds and contribute other help in supporting the work of a church.

lad•ing ['leidɪŋ] *n., v.* —*n.* **1** the act of loading. **2** load; freight; cargo.
—*v.* ppr. of LADE.

la•dle ['leidəl] *n., v.* **-dled, -dling.** —*n.* a large, cup-shaped spoon with a long handle, for dipping out liquids.
—*v.* **1** dip out. **2** dip out and carry or serve in a ladle or other utensil: *The cook is ladling the soup.*
ladle out, *Informal.* give freely, usually something bad: *That teacher is too fond of ladling out punishments.* ⟨OE *hlædel* < *hladan* lade⟩ **—'la•dler,** *n.*

la•dy ['leidi] *n., pl.* **-dies. 1** a woman of refinement and courtesy. **2** a woman of high social position. **3** any woman: *She's a courageous lady. The lady who waited on us is from my home town.* **4** a woman who has the rights or authority of a lord; a mistress of a household. **5** noblewoman; a woman who has the title of Lady. **6 Lady,** in the United Kingdom, a title given to women of certain ranks of nobility, such as a marchioness, countess, etc., a daughter of a duke, earl, etc., or the wife or widow of a knight or baronet. **7** a woman whom a man loves or is devoted to. **8** *Informal.* wife. **9 Our Lady,** *Roman Catholic Church.* the Virgin Mary. ⟨OE *hlǣfdīge,* literally, loaf-kneader, < *hlāf* loaf + *-dīg-* to knead. Cf. LORD.⟩
☛ *Usage.* **Lady.** In formal English **lady** is used to mean a woman of refinement or high social position. Though **lady** is used in everyday speech to refer to any woman (*the lady selling tickets*), the term is often considered affected or patronizing. **Woman** is the preferred general term.

la•dy•bird ['leidi,bɜrd] *n.* ladybug.

la•dy•bug ['leidi,bʌg] *n.* any of numerous small beetles (family Coccinellidae) having a rounded back, usually red or orange with black spots. Both as larvae and adults, ladybugs feed on insects and insect eggs.

Lady chapel in a cathedral, a chapel dedicated to the Virgin Mary.

Lady Day *Christianity.* March 25, in some churches the day commemorating the visit of the angel to tell Mary that she would be the mother of Jesus; Annunciation Day.

la•dy•fin•ger ['leidi,fɪŋgər] *n.* a small sponge cake that resembles a finger in size and shape.

la•dy–in–wait•ing ['leidi in 'weitɪŋ] *n., pl.* **la•dies-in-wait•ing.** a lady who is an attendant of a queen or princess.

la•dy–kill•er ['leidi ,kɪlər] *n. Slang.* a man supposed to be dangerously fascinating to women.

la•dy•like ['leidi,ləik] *adj.* **1** having or showing the manners or appearance of a lady; well-bred or refined: *a ladylike cough.* **2** suitable for a lady: *a ladylike costume.*

la•dy•love ['leidi,lʌv] *n. Informal.* a woman who is loved by a man; sweetheart.

la•dy•ship ['leidi,ʃɪp] *n.* **1** the rank or position of a LADY (def. 5). **2** Often, **Ladyship,** in the United Kingdom, a title used in speaking to or of a woman having the rank of LADY (def. 6): *your Ladyship, her Ladyship.*

la•dy's–slip•per ['leidiz ˌslɪpər] *n.* any of several wild orchids (genus *Cypripedium*) found in temperate regions, having flowers whose shape suggests a slipper. The **pink lady's-slipper** (*C. acaule*) is the provincial flower of Prince Edward Island. Also, **lady-slipper.**

Lady's-slippers

lag¹ [læg] *v.* **lagged, lag•ging;** *n.* *—v.* **1** move too slowly; fall behind in movement, development, etc. (*often used with* **behind**): *The child lagged because she was tired.* **2** slacken or weaken; fall behind in strength, intensity, etc. *—n.* **1** the act or condition of lagging. **2** the amount by which a person or thing lags. **3** an interval of time, especially between related phenomena or events, such as an action and its effect. **4** the last or hindmost one (in a race, game, sequence of any kind). ⟨< Scand.; cf. Norwegian *lagga* to go slowly⟩ **—'lag•ger,** *n.*
☛ *Syn. v.* See note at LINGER.

lag² [læg] *n., v.* **lagged, lag•ging.** *—n.* **1** a strip of material used in encasing or insulating a drum, boiler, etc. **2** a barrel stave or slat. *—v.* cover with insulating material. ⟨? < Scand; cf. Old Icelandic *lögg* barrel rim. Related to Swedish *lagg* stave.⟩

la•gan ['lægən] *n.* jetsam with a marker for later retrieval. ⟨ME *laganum* right to own wreckage washed up from the sea, perhaps < Gmc.⟩

la•ger ['lɑgər] *or* ['lɒgər] *n.* a light beer which is slowly fermented at a low temperature and stored from six weeks to six months before being used. ⟨short for *lager beer,* half translation of G *Lagerbier* < *Lager* bed, storehouse + *Bier* beer⟩
☛ *Hom.* LOGGER ['lɒgər].

lag•gard ['lægərd] *n., adj. —n.* a person who moves too slowly or falls behind; backward person. *—adj.* slow; falling behind; backward. **—'lag•gard•ly,** *adv.* **—'lag•gard•ness,** *n.*

lagging¹ ['lægɪŋ] *n., adj., v. —n.* the act of lagging behind. *—adj.* lingering; dragging: *lagging footsteps.* *—v.* ppr. of LAG. **—'lag•ging•ly,** *adv.*

lag•ging² ['lægɪŋ] *n.* **1** the act of covering a drum, boiler, etc. with insulating material. **2** insulation for steam boilers and pipes. **3** planking or framing to prevent caveins of earthwork, or to support an arch in construction.

la•go•morph ['lægəˌmɔrf] *n.* any of an order (Lagomorpha) of mammals having two pairs of upper incisors, one behind the other, specialized for gnawing. The order comprises rabbits, hares, and pikas. ⟨< Gk. *lagos* hare + E *-morph*⟩ **—ˌlag•o'morph•ic, ˌlag•o'morph•ous,** *adj.*

la•goon [lə'gun] *n.* **1** a pond or small lake connected with a larger body of water. **2** shallow water separated from the sea by low sandbanks. **3** the water within a ring-shaped coral island. ⟨< Ital. *laguna* < L *lacuna* pond, hole. Doublet of LACUNA.⟩

lag screw a wooden screw with a square head.

lah [lɑ] See LA¹.

la•hal [lə'hɑl] *n. Cdn., esp. Pacific coast.* a First Nations gambling game taking various forms, the winner being the player to whom falls a marked object (as a disk) mixed with several similar but unmarked objects.

la•har ['lɑhɑr] *or* [lɑ'hɑr] *n.* **1** a landslide or river of mud formed by heavy rain mixed with volcanic ash. **2** the deposit left by such a landslide. ⟨< Javanese, lava⟩

la•ic ['leiɪk] *adj., n. —adj.* **1** lay; secular. **2** of the laity. *—n.* a lay person. ⟨< LL *laicus* < Gk. *laikos* < *laos* people. Doublet of LAY³.⟩ **—'la•i•cal•ly,** *adv.*

la•i•cize ['leiəˌsaɪz] *v.* **-cized, -ciz•ing.** remove from ecclesiastical control; secularize. **—ˌla•i•ci'za•tion,** *n.*

laid [leid] *v., adj. —v.* pt. and pp. of LAY¹. *—adj.* marked with close parallel lines or watermarks: *laid paper.* **laid up, a** stored up; put away for future use. **b** *Informal.* forced by illness or injury to stay indoors or in bed. **c** of ships, dismantled and put in dock.
☛ *Hom.* LADE.

laid–back ['leid 'bæk] *adj.* **1** placed in a backward position or direction: *The horse had laid-back ears.* **2** *Slang.* unexcited or unexcitable; relaxed and easygoing: *a laid-back entertainer. The whole evening was laid-back and low-key.*

lain [lein] *v.* pp. of LIE².

lair [lɛr] *n., v. —n.* **1** the den or resting place of a wild animal. **2** *Informal.* any refuge. *—v.* serve as a lair. ⟨OE *leger* < *licgan* lie²⟩

laird [lɛrd] *n. Scottish.* an owner of land, especially of a landed estate. ⟨Scottish var. of *lord*⟩

lais•sez faire or **lais•ser faire** ['lɛsei 'fɛr] **1** the principle of letting people do as they please. **2** *Economics.* the absence of governmental regulation and interference in trade, business, industry, etc. ⟨< F *laissez faire* allow to do⟩ **—'lais•sez-'faire,** *adj.*

la•i•ty ['leiəti] *n., pl.* **-ties.** lay people; the people as distinguished from the clergy or from a professional class: *Doctors use many words that the laity do not understand.* Compare CLERGY. ⟨< *lay³* + *-ity*⟩

lake¹ [leik] *n.* **1** a large body of fresh water usually surrounded by land. **2** a wide place in a river. ⟨< L *lacus*⟩

lake² [leik] *n.* **1** a deep red or purplish red colouring matter. **2** an insoluble coloured compound formed from animal, vegetable, or coal tar colouring materials and metallic oxides. **3** the colour of lake. ⟨< F *laque,* ult. < Persian *lak*⟩

lake boat *Cdn.* a vessel designed for service on the Great Lakes.

lake carrier *Cdn.* a freighter designed for service on the Great Lakes.

lake char *Cdn.* LAKE TROUT.

lake chub *Cdn.* a freshwater fish (*Couesius plumbeus*) found across Canada and north to Hudson Bay. It has a black back, silvery sides, and dark scales, and grows to about 10 cm long.

lake dwelling a prehistoric dwelling built on piles over a lake. **—lake dweller.**

lake•front ['leikˌfrʌnt] *n.* **1** land or land with buildings at the edge of a lake. **2** the part of a town or city next to a lake. **3** (*adjl.*) of or on a lakefront: *We have a lakefront cottage.*

Lake•head ['leikˌhɛd] *n. Cdn.* the city of Thunder Bay, Ontario, and the surrounding region, on the northwest shore of Lake Superior. Also, **lakehead.**

lake herring cisco.

Lake poets Coleridge, Southey, and Wordsworth, who spent time in the Lake District of England in the late 18th and early 19th centuries.

lak•er ['leikər] *n.* **1** a person living or working on a lake. **2** *Cdn.* a lake boat, especially one operating on the Great Lakes. **3** *Cdn.* a lake fish, especially a lake trout.

Lakes [leiks] *n. Cdn.* GREAT LAKES.

lake•side ['leikˌsaɪd] *n., adj. —n.* the land next to a lake. *—adj.* beside a lake: *a lakeside cottage.*

lake sturgeon a heavily armoured freshwater fish (*Acipenser fulvescens*), found in the Great Lakes and the St. Lawrence River.

lake trout *Cdn.* a large char (*Salvelinus namaycush*), typically dark greenish or greyish with light spots, native to the lakes of N North America but now introduced to many other parts of the world. It is highly prized as a game and food fish.

lake whitefish a freshwater food fish (*Coregonus clupeaformis*) found in the Great Lakes and other Canadian lakes.

lakh [læk] *n.* in the Indian subcontinent, 100 000, especially rupees. ⟨< Hind.⟩

Lak•shmi ['lʌkʃmi] *n. Hinduism.* the goddess of good fortune, to whom the Festival of Lights is dedicated.

Lal•lans ['lælənz] *n.* **1** the Lowlands of Scotland. **2** the form of English spoken there. ⟨< Scottish, lowlands⟩

lal•la•tion [læ'leiʃən] *n. Phonetics.* confusion of the sound [l] with another sound, usually [r], in pronunciation. Also, **lambdacism.**

lam [læm] *n. Slang.* a quick escape; flight. **on the lam, a** escaping. **b** in hiding. ⟨origin unknown⟩
☛ *Hom.* LAMB.

lam. laminated.

la•ma ['lɑmə] *or* ['læmə] *n.* in Tibet and Mongolia, a Buddhist priest or monk. ⟨< Tibetan *blama*⟩
☛ *Hom.* LLAMA.

La•ma•ism ['lɑmə,ɪzəm] *or* ['læmə,ɪzəm] *n.* the religious system of the lamas in Tibet and Mongolia, a form of Buddhism.

La•marck•i•an [lə'mɑrkiən] *adj., n.* —*adj.* of or having to do with Jean de Lamarck or Lamarckism.
—*n.* a person who supports Lamarckism.

La•marck•ism [lə'mɑrkɪzəm] *n.* the evolutionary theory of Jean de Lamarck (1744-1829), a French naturalist, who held that characteristics acquired by parents tend to be inherited by their descendants.

la•ma•ser•y ['lɑmə,sɛri] *or* ['læmə,sɛri] *n., pl.* **-ser•ies.** in Tibet and Mongolia, a building, or group of buildings, where lamas live, work, and worship.

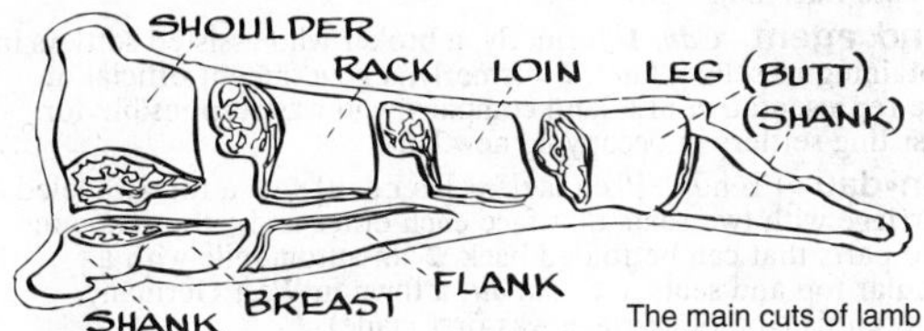

The main cuts of lamb

lamb [læm] *n., v.* —*n.* **1** a young sheep. **2** the meat from a lamb. **3** lambskin. **4 the Lamb,** or **Lamb of God,** *Christianity.* Jesus Christ. **5** a young, dear, or innocent person. **6** *Slang.* a person who is easily cheated. **7** *Slang.* an inexperienced speculator. **8** *Informal.* PERSIAN LAMB.
like a lamb, a meekly; timidly. **b** easily fooled.
—*v.* give birth to a lamb or lambs. ⟨OE⟩ **—'lamb,like,** *adj.*
☛ *Hom.* LAM.

lam•baste [læm'beist] *v.* **-bast•ed, -bast•ing.** *Slang.* **1** beat; thrash. **2** scold roughly; denounce. ⟨? < *lam* beat, thrash (cf. ON *lemja* and E *lame*) + *baste³*⟩

lamb•da ['læmdə] *n.* the eleventh letter of the Greek alphabet (Λ,λ).

lamb•da•cism ['læmdə,sɪzəm] *n.* lallation.

lam•ben•cy ['læmbənsi] *n.* a lambent quality or condition.

lam•bent ['læmbənt] *adj.* **1** moving lightly over a surface: *a lambent flame.* **2** playing lightly and brilliantly over a subject: *a lambent wit.* **3** softly bright: *Moonlight is lambent.* ⟨< L *lambens, -entis,* ppr. of *lambere* lick⟩

lam•bert ['læmbərt] *n. Optics.* an SI unit of brightness, equal to 0.32 candle/square centimetre. ⟨after J.H. *Lambert* (1728-1777), German physicist⟩

lambing pen *Cdn. West.* a pen or corral where ewes and lambs are protected.

lamb•kin ['læmkɪn] *n.* **1** a little lamb. **2** a young or dear person.

Lamb of God *Christianity.* Jesus Christ.

lam•bre•quin ['læmbrəkɪn] *or* ['læmbərkɪn] *n.* a drapery covering the top of a window or door, or hanging from a shelf. ⟨< F⟩

lamb•skin ['læm,skɪn] *n.* **1** the skin of a lamb, especially with the wool on it. **2** leather made from the skin of a lamb. **3** parchment.

lamb's•quar•ter ['læmz,kwɔrtər] *n.* an edible weed of the same family as spinach, used in salad or as a potherb.

lame¹ [leim] *adj.* **lam•er, lam•est;** *v.* **lamed, lam•ing.**
—*adj.* **1** not able to walk properly; having an injured leg or foot; crippled. **2** stiff and sore: *Her arm is lame from playing ball.* **3** *Informal.* poor; weak; unsatisfactory: *Sleeping too long is a lame excuse for being late.*
—*v.* **1** make lame; cripple: *The accident lamed her for life.* **2** become lame; go lame. ⟨OE *lama*⟩ **—'lame•ly,** *adv.* **—'lame•ness,** *n.*

lame² [leim] *n.* a thin plate in medieval armour. ⟨< MF < L *lāmina* a thin piece or plate⟩

la•mé [læ'mei] *or* [lɑ'mei] *n.* a rich fabric made wholly or partly of metal threads. ⟨< F *lamé,* literally, laminated < *lame* metal leaf⟩

la•med ['lɑmɪd] *n.* the thirteenth letter of the Hebrew alphabet. See table of alphabets in the Appendix.

lame duck **1** *Informal.* a helpless person or thing. **2** *Esp. U.S.* an elected representative or group, or any administrator, that is serving the last part of the current term.

la•mel•la [lə'mɛlə] *n., pl.* **-mel•las, -mel•lae** [-'mɛli] *or* [-'mɛlaɪ]. a thin plate, scale, or layer, especially of flesh or bone. ⟨< L *lamella,* dim. of *lamina* thin plate⟩

la•mel•lar [lə'mɛlər] *or* ['læmələr] *adj.* **1** having, consisting of, or arranged in lamellas. **2** resembling a lamella in shape; platelike. **—la'mel•lar•ly,** or **'la•mel•lar•ly,** *adv.*

lam•el•late ['læməlɪt] *or* ['læmə,leit], [lə'mɛlɪt] *or* [lə'mɛleit] [lə'mɛlɪt] *adj.* lamellar. **—'lam•el,late•ly,** *adv.*

la•mel•li– a combining form of **lamella**: *lamelliform.*

la•mel•li•branch [lə'mɛlɪ,bræŋk] *n.* any mollusc with a hinged shell.

la•mel•li•form [lə'mɛlɪ,fɔrm] *adj.* having the shape of a lamella.

la•ment [lə'mɛnt] *v., n.* —*v.* **1** feel or show grief for; mourn for: *to lament the dead.* **2** feel or show grief; weep: *Why does she lament?* **3** regret: *We lamented his absence.*
—*n.* **1** an expression of grief; wail. **2** a poem, song, or tune that expresses grief. **3** an expression of regret. ⟨< L *lamentari* < *lamentum* a wailing⟩ **—la'ment•er,** *n.* **—la'ment•ing•ly,** *adv.*

lam•en•ta•ble ['læməntəbəl] *or* [lə'mɛntəbəl] *adj.* **1** to be regretted or pitied; giving cause for sorrow: *a lamentable accident. It was a lamentable day when the old general store was torn down.* **2** not so good; inferior: *The singer gave a lamentable performance.* **—'lam•en•ta•bly,** *adv.*

lam•en•ta•tion [,læmən'teiʃən] *n.* the act or an instance of lamenting; grief or mourning.

la•mi•a ['leimiə] *n.* **1** *Greek mythology.* a fabulous monster that was part woman and part serpent. **2** a seductress. ⟨< L < Gk.⟩

lam•i•na ['læmənə] *n., pl.* **-nae** [-,ni] *or* [-,naɪ] or **-nas. 1** a thin plate, scale, or layer. **2** *Botany.* the flat, wide part of a leaf. ⟨< L; see LAME²⟩

lam•i•nar ['læmənər] *adj.* having, consisting of, or arranged in thin layers, plates, or scales.

laminar flow the flow of any oily fluid.

lam•i•nate *v.* ['læmə,neit]; *adj., n.* ['læmənɪt] *or* ['læmə,neit]; *v.* **-nat•ed, -nat•ing;** *adj., n.*
—*v.* **1** split into thin layers. **2** make by putting layer on layer. **3** beat or roll (metal) into a thin plate. **4** cover with thin plates.
—*adj.* laminated; laminar.
—*n.* **1** a laminated plastic. **2** any laminated product. ⟨< NL *lāminātus*⟩ **—'lam•i,na•tor,** *n.*

lam•i•nat•ed ['læmə,neitɪd] *adj., v.* —*adj.* made of layers joined one on another.
—*v.* pt. and pp. of LAMINATE.

lam•i•na•tion [,læmə'neiʃən] *n.* **1** the process of laminating. **2** the state of being laminated. **3** a laminated structure; an arrangement in thin layers. **4** a thin layer.

lam•i•ni•tis [,læmə'naitɪs] *n.* a disease of horses, inflammation of the laminae in a hoof.

Lam•mas ['læməs] *n.* **1** *Roman Catholic Church.* August 1, a religious feast commemorating the imprisonment and miraculous escape of Saint Peter. **2** August 1, the day of a harvest festival formerly held in England. Also, **Lammas Day.** ⟨OE *hlāfmæsse* < *hlāf* bread, loaf + *mæsse* mass (because of the consecration of loaves made from the year's first grain)⟩

lam•mer•gei•er ['læmər,gaɪər] *n.* a large, bearded Old World vulture (*Gypaetus barbatus*). ⟨< G *Lämmergeier* < *Lämmer,* pl. of *Lamm* lamb + *Geier* vulture⟩

lamp [læmp] *n.* **1** a device that provides artificial light: *a gas lamp, a street lamp, a floor lamp. An oil lamp holds oil and a wick by which the oil is burned.* **2** a similar device that gives heat: *a spirit lamp.* **3** a device producing radiation: *a sun lamp.* **4** an electric light bulb. ⟨ME < OF < L < Gk. *lampas* < *lampein* shine⟩ **—'lamp•less,** *adj.*

lamp•black ['læmp,blæk] *n.* a fine, black soot consisting of almost pure carbon that is deposited when oil, gas, etc. burn incompletely. Lampblack is used as a colouring agent in paint and ink.

lamper eel lamprey.

lamp•fish ['læmp,fɪʃ] *n.* oolichan.

lam•pi•on ['læmpiən] *n.* a lamp for use outdoors, usually burning oil. ⟨< F < Ital. *lampione* carriage or street light < *lampa* lamp⟩

lamp•light ['læmp,ləit] *n.* the light from a lamp.

lamp•light•er ['læmp,ləitər] *n.* **1** a person who lights street lamps. **2** a torch, twisted paper, etc. used to light lamps.

lam•poon [læm'pun] *n., v. —n.* a piece of writing that attacks and ridicules a person in a highly satirical way.
—v. attack in a lampoon. ⟨< F *lampon* drinking song < *lampons* let us drink⟩ **—lam'poon•er,** *n.*

lam•poon•ist [læm'punɪst] *n.* a person who writes lampoons.

lamp•post ['læmp,poust] *n.* a post used to support a street lamp.

lam•prey ['læmpri] *or* ['læmprei] *n., pl.* **-preys.** any of a family (Petromyzonidae) of primitive, freshwater and saltwater fishes, having an eel-like body and a round, sucking mouth with horny teeth. Most adult lampreys live as parasites, attaching themselves to fish with their mouths and feeding on the blood and tissues of their host. ⟨ME < OF *lampreie* < Med.L *lampreda* < LL *naupreda*; form influenced by L *lambere* lick. Doublet of LIMPET.⟩

lam•pri•cide ['læmprɪ,saɪd] *n.* a substance for destroying lampreys.

lamp•shade ['læmp,ʃeid] *n.* a cover fitted over a lamp to reflect and diffuse the light.

lamp•shell ['læmp,ʃɛl] *n.* any one of several brachiopods.

LAN [læn] *Computer technology.* LOCAL AREA NETWORK (def. 2).

Lan•cas•ter ['læŋkəstər] *n.* the English royal house from 1399 to 1461. Its emblem was a red rose.

Lan•cas•tri•an [læŋ'kæstriən] *adj., n. —adj.* **1** of the English royal house of Lancaster. **2** from or of Lancaster or Lancashire.
—n. **1** a supporter or member of the house of Lancaster. **2** a native or inhabitant of Lancaster or Lancashire.

lance [læns] *n., v.* **lanced, lanc•ing.** *—n.* **1** a long, wooden spear with a sharp iron or steel head. In the Middle Ages knights were often armed with lances. **2** a soldier armed with a lance. **3** any instrument like a soldier's lance. **4** lancet.
—v. **1** pierce with a lance. **2** cut open with a lancet: *The dentist lanced the gum so that the new tooth could come through.* ⟨< F < L *lancea* light Spanish spear⟩

lance–bom•bar•dier ['læns ,bɒmbə,dir] *n.* a non-commissioned artillery officer of the lowest rank, junior to a bombardier. *Abbrev.:* L/Bdr.

lance–corporal ['læns ,kɔrpərəl] *n.* a non-commissioned officer of the lowest rank in the armed forces of some countries.

lance–leaved white violet ['læns ,livd] a marsh wildflower (*viola lanceolata*) having long, narrow, lance-shaped leaves and white flowers on short stems, blooming in early spring across Canada and south to California and Florida.

lance•let ['lænslɪt] *n.* a member of the family Cephalochordata, of small, fishlike organisms.

Lan•ce•lot ['lænsə,lɒt] *n. Arthurian legend.* the bravest of the knights of the Round Table and the lover of Queen Guinevere.

lan•ce•o•late ['lænsiəlɪt] *or* ['lænsiə,leit] *adj.* shaped like the head of a lance: *a lanceolate leaf.* ⟨< L *lanceolatus* < *lanceola,* dim. of *lancea* lance⟩ **—'lan•ce•o,late•ly,** *adv.*

lanc•er ['lænsər] *n.* formerly, a mounted soldier armed with a lance. ⟨< F *lancier* < LL *lancearius*⟩

lanc•ers ['ləensərz] *n.pl.* **1** a form of square dance. **2** the music for this dance.

lance–sergeant ['læns ,sɑrdʒənt] *n.* a corporal appointed to act temporarily as sergeant. *Abbrev.:* L/Sgt.

lan•cet ['lænsɪt] *n.* **1** a small, sharp-pointed, surgical knife, usually having two sharp edges. Doctors use lancets for opening boils, abscesses, etc. **2** a narrow, sharply pointed arch or window. ⟨ME < OF *lancette*, dim. of *lance* lance < L *lancea*⟩

lancet arch an arch rising to a point.

lancet window a window with a LANCET ARCH.

lance•wood ['læns,wʊd] *n.* **1** a tough, straight-grained, springy wood, used for whip handles, fishing rods, cabinetwork, etc., and formerly much used for the shafts of carriages. **2** any of various tropical trees of the custard-apple family yielding this wood, especially *Oxandra lanceolata* of the West Indies and NE South America.

lan•ci•nate ['lænsə,neit] *v.* **-nat•ed, -nat•ing;** *adj. —v.* of pain, be stabbing or piercing.
—adj. of pain, stabbing or piercing. ⟨< L *lancinatus*, pp. of *lancinare* tear⟩

land [lænd] *n., v. —n.* **1** the solid part of the earth's surface: *dry land.* **2** ground; soil: *This is good land for a garden.* **3** ground used as property: *The farmer invested in land and machinery.* **4** *Economics.* anything furnished by nature without the help of humans, such as soil, mineral deposits, water, wildlife. *Land, labour,* and *capital* are the three principal factors of production. **5** country; region: *mountainous land.* **6** the people of a country; nation: *She collected folk songs from all the land.*
how the land lies, what the state of affairs is.
—v. **1** come to land; bring to land: *The ship landed at the pier. The pilot landed the airplane in a field.* **2** put on land; set ashore: *The ship landed its passengers.* **3** go ashore: *the passengers landed.* **4** *Cdn.* enter or be permitted to enter Canada as an immigrant. **5** come to a stop; arrive: *The thief landed in jail. The car landed in the ditch.* **6** cause to arrive: *This bus will land you in London.* **7** *Informal.* catch; get: *to land a job, to land a fish.* **8** *Slang.* get (a blow) home: *I landed one on his chin.* ⟨OE⟩ **—'land•er,** *n.* **—'land,like,** *adj.*

land agent *Cdn.* **1** formerly, a broker who assisted settlers in obtaining or selling land. **2** formerly, a government official or the representative of a land company who was responsible for assisting settlers in occupying new land.

lan•dau ['lændɒ], ['lændaʊ], *or* ['lændou] *n.* **1** a four-wheeled carriage with two seats that face each other and a top made in two parts that can be folded back. **2** an automobile with a similar top and seats. ⟨< *Landau*, a town in West Germany, where this type of carriage was first made⟩

lan•dau•let or **lan•dau•lette** [,lændə'lɛt] *n.* **1** a small landau. **2** an automobile with a folding top.

land bank an area or areas of land bought up and held for future development: *The corporation owns one of the largest land banks in the country.*

land–banking ['lænd ,bæŋkɪŋ] *n.* the practice or business of setting up land banks.

land breeze a breeze blowing from the land toward the sea.

land company *Cdn.* formerly, a company holding extensive blocks of land for sale to settlers.

land•ed ['lændɪd] *adj., v. —adj.* **1** owning land: *landed gentry.* **2** consisting of land. Landed property is real estate. **3** *Cdn.* formally admitted into Canada as an immigrant: *to apply for landed status. The officer asked him if he was landed.*
—v. pt. and pp. of LAND.

landed immigrant *Cdn.* a person admitted to Canada as a settler and potential Canadian citizen.

land•fall ['lænd,fɒl] *n.* **1** a sighting of land. **2** the land sighted or reached after a voyage or flight: *The explorer's landfall was near the mouth of the St. Lawrence.* **3** an approach to land from the sea or air; landing.

land fever *Cdn.* formerly, a strong desire to obtain title to public lands offered for settlement.

land•fill ['lænd,fɪl] *n.* **1** the disposal of waste by burying it under a shallow layer of ground. **2** a place where waste is disposed of in this way.

land•form ['lænd,fɔrm] *n. Geology.* a natural physical feature of the land.

land–grab•ber ['lænd ,græbər] *n. Cdn.* a person who buys up large amounts of land, usually intending to profit by speculation.

land grant *Cdn.* a grant of land; a gift of land by the government for a university, railway, etc.

land•grave ['lænd,greiv] *n.* **1** in the Middle Ages, a German count having authority over a considerable territory or over other counts. **2** in modern times, the title of certain German princes. ⟨< G *Landgraf* < *Land* land + *Graf* count⟩

land•gra•vi•ate ['lænd,greivɪt] *or* ['lænd,greivi,eit] *n.* the office of a landgrave.

land•gra•vine ['lændgrə,vin] *n.* the wife of a landgrave.

land•hold•er ['lænd,houldər] *n.* a person who owns or occupies land. **—'land,hold•ing,** *adj., n.*

land•ing ['lændɪŋ] *n., v. —n.* **1** a coming to land; a coming ashore: *The army made a landing in France.* **2** a bringing to land. **3** *Cdn.* formal admission into Canada as an immigrant. **4** a place where persons or goods are landed from a ship, helicopter, etc. A wharf, dock, or pier is a landing for boats. **5** a platform or floor area at the top of a flight of stairs. **6** *Logging.* a place where logs are gathered before being transported to a sawmill.
—v. ppr. of LAND.

landing craft any of various kinds of boats or ships used for landing troops or equipment on a shore, especially during an assault.

landing field a field large enough and smooth enough for aircraft to land on and take off from safely.

landing gear the wheels, pontoons, etc. of an aircraft, upon which it moves on the ground or on water.

landing net a net attached to a handle, for taking fish from the water after they are caught.

landing pad helipad.

landing stage a floating platform used for loading and unloading people and goods.

landing strip airstrip.

land•la•dy ['lænd,leidi] *n., pl.* **-dies. 1** a woman who owns buildings or land that she rents to others. **2** a woman who keeps a boarding house, lodging house, or inn.

☛ *Usage.* The legal term, regardless of gender, is **landlord**.

länd•ler ['lɛntlər] *n.* **1** an Austrian country dance. **2** the music for this dance. ⟨< G, literally, something connected with *Landl* (literally, little land), a popular name for Upper Austria, where the dance originated⟩

land•less ['lændlɪs] *adj.* without land; owning no land. **—'land•less•ness,** *n.*

land•line ['lænd,laɪn] *n.* a telegraph or similar cable running underground or on the ground.

land•locked [lænd,lɒkt] *adj.* **1** shut in, or nearly shut in, by land: *a landlocked harbour.* **2** of fish that are generally marine, living in waters shut off from the sea: *landlocked salmon.*

landlocked salmon ouananiche.

land•lord ['lænd,lɔrd] *n., v.* *—n.* **1** a person who owns buildings or land that he or she rents to others. **2** the keeper of a boarding house, lodging house, or inn.
—v. act as a landlord. **—'land,lord,ship,** *n.*

land•lord•ism ['lænd,lɔrdɪzəm] *n.* the practice of leasing land to tenants.

land•lub•ber ['lænd,lʌbər] *n.* a person not used to being on ships; a person clumsy on ships. **—'land,lub•ber•ish,** *adj.*

land•mark ['lænd,mɑrk] *n.* **1** something familiar or easily seen, used as a guide. **2** an important fact or event; a happening that stands out above others. The inventions of the printing press, telephone, telegraph, and radio are landmarks in the history of communications. **3** a stone or other object that marks the boundary of a piece of land.

land mass *Geology.* a vast, unbroken area of land.

land mine a container filled with explosives or chemicals, placed on the ground or lightly covered, and usually set off by the weight of vehicles or troops passing over it.

land office 1 *Cdn.* a government office that handles business relating to public lands. **2** *U.S.* a government office that takes care of the business connected with public lands, and that records sales, transfers, etc.

Land of Promise in the Bible, the country promised by God to Abraham and his descendants; Canaan.

Land of the Little Sticks *Cdn.* a region of stunted trees at the southern limits of the Barren Ground in northern Canada.

Land of the Midnight Sun *Cdn.* the Far North.

land otter *Cdn.* the Canadian otter (*Lutra canadensis*).

land•own•er ['lænd,ounər] *n.* a person who owns lands. **—'land,own•er,ship,** *n.* **—'land,own•ing,** *n., adj.*

land–poor ['lænd 'pur] *adj.* **1** owning much land but needing ready money. **2** poor because of taxes, etc. on one's land.

Land•sat ['lænd,sæt] *n.* any of a system of satellites collecting information about the earth.

land•scape ['lænd,skeip] *or* ['læn,skeip] *n., v.* **-scaped, -scap•ing.** *—n.* **1** a view of scenery on land. **2** a painting, etching, etc. showing such a view.
—v. make (land) more pleasant to look at by arranging trees, shrubs, flowers, etc.: *The builder agreed to landscape the lot around the new house.* ⟨< Du. *landschap* < *land* land + *-schap* -ship⟩ **—'land,scap•er,** *n.*

landscape gardening the arrangement of trees, shrubs, flowers, lawns, water, rocks, etc. to give a pleasing appearance to grounds, parks, etc. **—landscape gardener.**

land•shark ['lænd,ʃɑrk] *n.* a person who buys up land illegally or unfairly to make large profits on its resale.

land•side ['lænd,saɪd] *n.* the part of a plough opposite the mouldboard, used for guiding the plough and resisting the side pressure exerted by the furrow as it is turned up.

land•slide ['lænd,slaɪd] *n.* **1** a sliding down of a mass of soil or rock on a steep slope. **2** the mass that slides down. **3** an overwhelming majority of votes for one political party or candidate. **4** any overwhelming victory: *She won by a landslide.*

lands•man ['lændzmən] *n., pl.* **-men. 1** a person who lives or works on land. **2** an inexperienced sailor.

land•ward ['lændwərd] *adv. or adj.* toward the land.

land•wards ['lændwərdz] *adv.* landward.

land wind a wind blowing from the land toward the sea.

lane [lein] *n.* **1** a narrow road or path, especially one between hedges, walls, or fences. **2** any narrow way. A highway is often marked off in lanes for separate lines of traffic. **3** an alley between buildings. **4** a course or route used by ships or aircraft going in the same direction. **5** one of the narrow alleys on a track, marked by chalked lines, especially one in which a runner must stay during sprint or hurdle races. **6** BOWLING ALLEY (def. 1). **7** a narrow rural street. ⟨OE *lanu*⟩

lang. language.

lang syne ['læŋ 'zaɪn] *or* ['læŋ 'saɪn] *Scottish.* long since; long ago.

lan•guage ['læŋgwɪdʒ] *n.* **1** human speech, spoken or written. **2** the distinct form of speech common to a people, nation, or group of peoples: *the French language.* **3** a form or style of verbal expression: *bad language, Shakespeare's language.* **4** the special vocabulary, etc. of a particular group, field, etc.: *the language of chemistry.* **5** the wording or words (of a document, contract, etc.): *The lawyer explained the language of the contract to us.* **6** communication of meaning in any way: *the language of dance. A dog's language is made up of barks, looks, and actions.* **7** the study of language or languages; linguistics. **8** a set of assumptions or attitudes, often held by a group: *He just doesn't speak my language.* **9** *Computer technology.* a set of specifications that defines the form in which instructions for a computer are to be written. ⟨ME < OF *langage* < *langue* tongue < L *lingua*⟩

☛ *Syn.* **2. Language,** DIALECT, IDIOLECT, IDIOM = the forms and patterns of speech of a particular group of people. **Language** applies to the body of words, forms, and patterns of sounds and structures making up the speech of a people, nation, or group of peoples: *French Canadians speak the French language.* **Dialect** applies to a socially or regionally restricted variety of a language: *The dialect of the English language spoken in Newfoundland sounds strange to a westerner.* **Idiolect** applies to the sounds, usage, vocabulary, etc. used by an individual: *Her unusual idiolect is the result of her having lived in several different English-speaking countries.* **Idiom** applies to a particular language's characteristic manner of using words and putting them together in phrases and sentences: *Foreign students find the correct use of prepositions a difficult feature of English idiom.*

language arts the part of the elementary school curriculum directly concerned with the study of language, that is, the part devoted to reading, speaking, listening, and writing.

language death the cessation of existence of a language when its last few remaining native speakers die.

language laboratory in an educational institution, a room equipped with tape recorders, headphones, computers, monitors, etc. that enable students to practise hearing and speaking a language they are studying.

langue [lɑŋ] *n. French.* a linguistic system shared by members of a speech community. Compare PAROLE.

langue d'oc [lɑŋ'dɔk] *French.* of the group of dialects spoken in S France in the Middle Ages, the dialect that developed into modern Provençal. ⟨< OF; the two major OF dialect groups were named for the respective words for 'yes': *oc* and *oïl* (See next entry)⟩

langue d'o•ïl [lɑŋdɔ'il] *French.* of the group of dialects spoken in N France in the Middle Ages, the dialect that developed into modern standard French. ⟨See LANGUE D'OC⟩

lan•guet ['læŋgwɪt] *n.* anything shaped like a tongue. ⟨ME < MF, dim. of OF *langue* tongue < L *lingua*⟩

lan•guid ['læŋgwɪd] *adj.* **1** drooping; weak; weary; without energy: *A hot, sticky day makes a person feel languid.* **2** without interest or enthusiasm; indifferent. **3** sluggish; dull; not brisk or lively. ⟨< L *languidus* < *languere* be faint⟩ **—'lan•guid•ly,** *adv.* **—'lan•guid•ness,** *n.*

lan•guish ['læŋgwɪʃ] *v.* **1** become weak or weary; lose energy; droop: *The flowers languished from lack of water.* **2** suffer for a long period under unfavourable conditions: *to languish in poverty. Wild animals often languish in captivity.* **3** grow dull, slack, or less intense: *His vigilance never languished.* **4** long or pine (*for*): *She languished for home.* **5** assume a soft, tender look for effect. ⟨< F *languiss-*, a stem of *languir* < L *languere*⟩ **—'lan•guish•er,** *n.*

lan•guish•ing ['læŋgwɪʃɪŋ] *adj., v.* *—adj.* **1** drooping; pining;

longing. 2 affectedly tender; sentimental. 3 lasting; lingering: *the languishing effects of an illness.*
—*v.* ppr. of LANGUISH. **—lan•guish•ing•ly,** *adv.*

lan•guish•ment ['læŋgwɪʃmənt] *n. Archaic.* 1 a languishing; a drooping, pining condition. 2 a languishing look or manner.

lan•guor ['læŋgər] *n.* 1 a lack of energy; weakness; weariness: *A long illness causes languor.* 2 a lack of interest or enthusiasm; indifference. 3 sentimental tenderness of mood. 4 quietness; stillness: *the languor of a summer afternoon.* 5 lack of activity; sluggishness. ⟨< L⟩

lan•guor•ous ['læŋgərəs] *adj.* 1 languid. 2 causing languor. **—'lan•guor•ous•ly,** *adv.*

lan•gur [lʌŋ'gʊr] *n.* any of various large, slender, long-tailed Old World monkeys (as of genera *Presbytis* and *Rhinopithecus*) of S and SE Asia. ⟨< Hind.; akin to Skt. *lāngūlin* having a tail⟩

lan•iard ['lænjərd] *n.* See LANYARD.

la•nif•er•ous [lə'nɪfərəs] *adj.* wool-bearing. ⟨< L *lānifer*⟩

lank [læŋk] *adj.* 1 long and thin; slender; lean: *a lank boy.* 2 straight and flat; not curly or wavy: *lank hair.* ⟨OE *hlanc*⟩ **—'lank•ly,** *adv.* **—'lank•ness,** *n.*

lank•i•ly ['læŋkəli] *adv.* in a lanky condition or form.

lank•y ['læŋki] *adj.* **lank•i•er, lank•i•est.** awkwardly long and thin; tall and ungainly. **—'lank•i•ness,** *n.*

lan•ner ['lænər] *n.* a falcon (*Falco biarmicus*) of Africa. ⟨< ME *lanere* < MF *lanier* < L *laniarius*⟩

lan•o•lin ['lænəlɪn] *n.* fat or grease obtained from wool, used in cosmetics, ointments, etc. Also, **lanoline.** ⟨< L *lana* wool + *oleum* oil + E *-in*⟩

lan•o•line ['lænəlɪn] *or* ['lænə,lin] *n.* lanolin.

lan•ta•na [læn'tænə] *or* [læn'teinə] *n.* an aromatic shrub of the genus *Lantana*, native to tropical regions.

lan•tern ['læntərn] *n.* 1 a case to protect a light from wind, rain, etc. It has sides of glass or some other material through which the light can shine. 2 the room at the top of a lighthouse where the light is. 3 an upright structure on a roof or dome, for letting in light and air or for decoration. 4 MAGIC LANTERN. ⟨ME < OF < L *lanterna*⟩

lantern fish a deep-sea fish of the family Myctophidae, having phosphorescent organs.

lan•tern–jawed ['læntərn ,dʒɔd] *adj.* having hollow cheeks and long, thin jaws.

lantern slide a small, thin sheet of glass with a picture on it that is shown on a screen by a MAGIC LANTERN.

lantern wheel a small pinion of several disks, used in cheap clocks.

lan•tha•nide ['lænθə,naɪd] *n. Chemistry.* 1 any of a group or series of metallic elements closely related in their chemical and physical properties, beginning with lanthanum (atomic number 57) or, sometimes, with cerium (at.no. 58) and ending with lutetium (at.no. 71); a rare-earth element. See table of elements in the Appendix. 2 (*adjl.*) designating this group of elements: *the lanthanide series.*

lan•than•um ['lænθənəm] *n. Chemistry.* a soft, white, metallic rare-earth element that tarnishes easily. *Symbol*: La; *at.no.* 57; *at.mass* 138.91. ⟨< NL < Gk. *lanthanein* escape notice, lurk unseen⟩

la•nu•go [lə'njugou] *or* [lə'nugou] *n. Biology.* the downy hair covering the body of a newborn baby. ⟨< L, down < *lana* wool⟩

lan•yard ['lænjərd] *n.* 1 a short rope or cord used on ships to fasten rigging. Sailors sometimes use a lanyard to hang a knife around their necks. 2 a cord with a small hook at one end, used in firing certain kinds of cannon. Also, **laniard.** ⟨< *lanyer* (< F *lanière* thong) + *yard*[2]⟩

Lao [laʊ] the language of Laos.

La•oc•o•ön [lei'ɒkou,ɒn] *n. Greek mythology.* a priest of Apollo at Troy. He warned the Trojans against the wooden horse and was killed, together with his two sons, by two serpents sent by Athena.

La•od•i•ce•an [,leiədi'siən] *or* [lei,ɒdə'siən] *n.* 1 a lukewarm or indifferent Christian. 2 a lukewarm or indifferent person. ⟨with reference to the Christians of *Laodicea* in Asia Minor, mentioned in the Bible⟩

La•os ['lɑous] *or* ['leiɒs] *n.* a country in SE Asia.

La•o•tian [lei'ouʃən] *adj., n.* —*adj.* of or having to do with Laos.
—*n.* a native or inhabitant of Laos.

Lao•Tse, Lao•Tze, or **Lao Tzu** ['laʊ 'dzu] *n.* 604?-531? B.C., a Chinese philosopher and the founder of Taoism.

lap[1] [læp] *n.* 1 the front part from the hips to the knees of a person sitting down, with the clothing that covers it. 2 the place where anything rests or is cared for. 3 a loosely hanging edge of clothing; flap.
in the lap of luxury, in luxurious circumstances. ⟨OE *læppa*⟩
☛ *Hom.* LAPP.

lap[2] [læp] *v.* **lapped, lap•ping;** *n.* —*v.* 1 place or be placed together, one partly over or beside another; overlap: *We lapped shingles on the roof.* 2 extend beyond a limit: *The reign of Queen Elizabeth I lapped into the 17th century.* 3 wind or wrap *(around)*; fold *(over* or *about): He lapped the blanket around him.* 4 be wound or wrapped around something; be folded. 5 enwrap; wrap up (*in*): *He lapped himself in a warm blanket.* 6 surround; envelop. 7 in a race, get a lap or more ahead of (other racers).
—*n.* 1 a lapping over. 2 the amount of lapping over. 3 the part that laps over. 4 one time around a race-track. 5 a part of any course travelled: *The last lap of our all-day hike was the toughest.* ⟨ME *lappen* to fold, wrap; akin to LAP[1]⟩
☛ *Hom.* LAPP.

lap[3] [læp] *v.* **lapped, lap•ping;** *n.* —*v.* 1 drink by lifting up with the tongue: *Cats and dogs lap water.* 2 move or beat gently with a slight slapping sound; splash gently: *Little waves lapped against the boat.*
lap up, a drink by lapping. **b** *Informal.* consume or absorb eagerly: *The advanced students lapped up the new math course.*
—*n.* 1 the act of lapping. 2 the sound of lapping: *the lap of the waves against my boat.* ⟨OE *lapian*⟩ **—'lap•per,** *n.*
☛ *Hom.* LAPP.

lap•a•ro•scope ['læpərə,skoup] *n.* a small optical instrument which works like the periscope on a submarine, used in surgery. ⟨< Gk. *lapara-* flank (literally, soft part) + -SCOPE⟩

lap•a•ros•co•py [,læpə'rɒskəpi] *n.* examination by a doctor using a laparoscope.**–,lap•a•ro'scop•ic,** *adj.*

lap•a•rot•o•my [,læpə'rɒtəmi] *n.* a surgical cutting into the abdomen. ⟨< Gk. *lapara-* flank + E *-tomy*⟩

lap•board ['læp,bɔrd] *n.* a thin, flat board held on the lap and used as a table.

lap dog a small pet dog.

la•pel [lə'pɛl] *n.* the part of the front of a coat or jacket that is folded back just below the collar. ⟨*lap*[1] + dim. suffix *-el*⟩

lap•ful ['læpfʊl] *n., pl.* **-fuls.** as much as a LAP[1] can hold.

lap•i•dar•i•an [,læpə'dɛriən] *adj.* lapidary.

lap•i•dar•y ['læpə,dɛri] *n., pl.* **-dar•ies;** *adj.* —*n.* a person who cuts, polishes, or engraves precious stones.
—*adj.* 1 of or having to do with cutting or engraving precious stones. 2 engraved on stone. 3 characteristic of stone inscriptions; monumental; stately; grandiose: *lapidary language.* ⟨< L *lapidarius* < *lapis*, *-idis* stone⟩

la•pil•lus [lə'pɪləs] *n., pl.* **-li** [-laɪ] *or* [-li]. a solidified fragment of lava. ⟨< L, little stone, pebble; dim. of *lapis* stone⟩

lap•in ['læpɪn]; *French,* [la'pɛ̃] *n.* 1 rabbit. 2 rabbit fur. 3 a coat or other garment of this fur. ⟨< F⟩

lap•is laz•u•li ['læpɪs 'læzə,laɪ] *or* ['læzə,li], ['læzju,laɪ] *or* ['læzju,li] 1 a deep blue, opaque semiprecious stone containing sodium, aluminum, sulphur, and silicon in a mixture of minerals. 2 a piece of this stone or a gem made from it. 3 deep blue. ⟨< Med.L < L *lapis* stone + Med.L *lazuli*, gen. of *lazulum* lapis lazuli < Arabic < Persian *lajward.* Cf. AZURE.⟩

lap joint a joint with overlapping edges.

Lap•land•er ['læp,lændər] *n.* LAPP (def. 1).

Lap•land longspur ['læp,lænd] a finch (*Calcarius lapponicus*) that breeds in the Arctic and winters in temperate and subtropical regions. It is a familiar summer bird in Canada's low Arctic.

Lap•land rosebay an arctic wildflower (*Rhododendron lapponicum*) having bright pink to magenta flowers, blooming in spring in cold, northern or high locations across Canada.

Lapp [læp] *n.* 1 a member of a people living mainly in N Scandinavia and NW Russia. 2 the Finnic language of the Lapps, including several very different dialects. ⟨< Swedish⟩
☛ *Hom.* LAP.
☛ *Usage.* The preferred term for the language is **Saami.**

lap•pet ['læpɪt] *n.* **1** a small flap or fold. **2** a loose fold of flesh or membrane. **3** the lobe of the ear. ⟨< *lap*[1]⟩

lap robe a blanket, fur robe, etc. used to keep the lap and legs warm when riding in an automobile, carriage, etc.

lapse [læps] *n., v.* **lapsed, laps•ing.** *–n.* **1** a slight mistake or error. A slip of the tongue, pen, or memory is a lapse. **2** a slipping or falling away from what is right: *a moral lapse.* **3** a slipping back; sinking down; slipping into a lower condition: *a lapse into savage ways.* **4** a slipping by; a passing away: *A minute is a short lapse of time.* **5** the ending of a right or privilege because it was not renewed, not used, or otherwise neglected: *the lapse of a lease.*
–v. **1** make a slight mistake or error. **2** slip or fall away from what is right. **3** slip back; sink down: *The house lapsed into ruin.* **4** slip by; pass away: *The boy's interest in the story soon lapsed.* **5** of a right or privilege, end because it was not renewed, not used, etc. If a legal claim is not enforced, it lapses after a certain number of years. ⟨< L *lapsus* fall < *labi* to slip⟩

lapse rate *Meteorology.* the rate at which temperature goes down as altitude increases.

lap•strake ['læp,streik] *adj., n. –adj.* of boats, made of boards or metal plates that overlap one another; clinker-built.
–n. a boat that is clinker-built. Also, **lapstreak.**

lap•sus lin•guae ['læpsʊs 'lɪŋgwi] *or* ['lɪŋgwaɪ] *Latin.* a slip of the tongue.

lap•top computer ['læp,tɒp] a computer small enough to fit on a person's lap, usually powered by batteries. Also called a **laptop.**

lap•wing ['læp,wɪŋ] *n.* a crested plover (*Vanellus vanellus*) of Europe, Asia, and N Africa that has a slow, irregular flight and a peculiar wailing cry. ⟨OE *hlēapewince* < *hlēapan* leap + *-wince* (related to WINK)⟩

lar [lɑr] *n., pl.* **lares** ['lɛriz] or **lars.** a household god.

lar•board ['lɑrbərd] *or* ['lɑr,bɔrd] *n., adj. Nautical. –n.* the side of a ship to the left of a person looking from the stern toward the bow; port.
–adj. on this side of a ship. ⟨ME *ladeborde,* originally, the loading side; influenced by *starboard*⟩

lar•ce•nous ['lɑrsənəs] *adj.* **1** of or like larceny; characterized by larceny. **2** thievish; guilty of larceny. **–'lar•ce•nous•ly,** *adv.*

lar•ce•ny ['lɑrsəni] *n., pl.* **-nies.** *Legal.* theft. ⟨< AF *larcin* < L *latrocinium* < *latro* bandit⟩

A larch tree

larch [lɑrtʃ] *n.* **1** any of a small genus (*Larix*) of trees of the pine family found in the northern hemisphere, having small, upright cones and soft, flexible, needlelike leaves that are shed in the fall. The three species of larch native to Canada are the tamarack, alpine larch, and western larch. **2** the hard wood of any of these trees. ⟨< G *Lärche,* ult. < L *larix, -icis*⟩

lard [lɑrd] *n., v. –n.* the fat of pigs melted down into a clear liquid and hardening to a soft, white solid. It is used in cooking.
–v. **1** insert strips of bacon or salt pork in (meat or poultry) before cooking. **2** put lard on; grease. **3** give variety to; enrich: *to lard a long speech with stories.* ⟨ME < OF < L *lardum*⟩ **–'lard,like** *adj.*

lar•der ['lɑrdər] *n.* **1** a pantry; place where food is kept. **2** a supply of food. ⟨ME < OF *lardier* < *lard* lard < L *lardum*⟩

lar•don ['lɑrdən] *n.* fat for larding meat. ⟨late ME *lardun* < MF *lardon* piece of pork⟩

lard•y ['lɑrdi] *adj.,* **lard•i•er, lard•i•est.** like, tasting of, or consisting of lard: *lardy pastry.*

lar•es ['lɛriz] *n.pl.* in ancient Rome, the guardian spirits of the house. ⟨< L, pl. of *lar*⟩

lares and penates **1** in ancient Rome, the household gods, the lares protecting the home from outside damage, the penates protecting the interior. **2** the cherished possessions of a household. ⟨< L⟩

large [lɑrdʒ] *adj.* **larg•er, larg•est;** *n. –adj.* **1** of more than the usual size, amount, or number; big: *a large crowd, a large sum of money, a large animal. Canada is a large country.* **2** of great scope or range; extensive; broad: *a man of large experience.* **3** on a great scale: *a large employer of labour.*
–n.
at large, a at liberty; free: *Is the escaped prisoner still at large?* **b** fully; in detail. **c** as a whole; altogether: *The people at large want peace.* **d** representing a whole area, business, group, etc.: *the firm's representative at large.*
in large or **in the large,** on a big scale. ⟨ME < OF < L *largus* copious⟩ **–'large•ness,** *n.*
☛ *Syn. adj.* **1.** See note at GREAT.

large–flow•ered bellwort ['lɑrdʒ ,flaʊərd] a woodland wildflower (*Uvularia grandiflora*), having hanging yellow flowers, blooming in spring from Québec to North Dakota and south to Georgia and Oklahoma.

large–heart•ed ['lɑrdʒ 'hɑrtɪd] *adj.* generous; liberal.

large intestine the lower part of the intestines, between the small intestine and the anus. See ALIMENTARY CANAL for picture.

large•ly ['lɑrdʒli] *adv.* **1** to a great extent; mainly; for the most part: *This region consists largely of desert.* **2** in great quantity; much.

large•mouth bass ['lɑrdʒ,mʌuθ 'bæs] a freshwater food fish (*Micropterus salmoides*) having colouring that varies according to the water. It is native to southern Québec and Ontario, and has been planted in the Canadian West.

large–scale ['lɑrdʒ 'skeil] *adj.* **1** wide; extensive; involving many persons or things: *a large-scale disaster.* **2** made or drawn to a large scale.

lar•gesse or **lar•gess** [lɑr'dʒɛs] *or* ['lɑrdʒɪs]; *French,* [laʀ'ʒɛs] *n.* **1** generous giving. **2** a generous gift or gifts. ⟨ME < OF *largesse* < *large* < L *largus* copious⟩

lar•ghet•to [lɑr'gɛtou] *adj., adv., n., pl.* **-ghet•tos.** *Music.*
–adj. rather slow; not so slow as largo, but usually slower than andante.
–adv. rather slowly.
–n. a passage or composition in rather slow time. ⟨< Ital. *larghetto,* dim. of *largo*⟩

larg•ish ['lɑrdʒɪʃ] *adj. Informal.* rather large.

lar•go ['lɑrgou] *adj., adv., n., pl.* **-gos.** *Music. –adj.* slow and dignified; stately.
–adv. in largo tempo.
–n. a slow, stately passage or piece of music. ⟨< Ital. *largo* large, slow < L *largus* large⟩

la•ri ['lɑri] *n.* **1** a unit of currency of Maldives, equal to 1⁄100 of a rufiyaa. **2** a coin worth one lari. See table of money in the Appendix. Also, **laari.**

lar•i•at ['læriət] *or* ['lɛriət] *n.* **1** a long rope with a running noose at one end; lasso. **2** a rope for fastening horses, mules, etc. to a stake while they are grazing. ⟨< Sp. *la reata* the rope⟩

la•rine ['lærɪn] *or* ['lɛrɪn] *adj.* of or like a gull. ⟨< Mod.L *Larinae* name of the subfamily < LL *larus* a ravenous sea bird < Gk. *laros*⟩

lark[1] [lɑrk] *n.* **1** any of a family (Alaudidae) of mostly Old World songbirds that live mainly on the ground, having plain or streaked brownish plumage and noted for their song. The most well-known European lark is the skylark. The only lark native to the New World is the horned lark. **2** any of various other, usually ground-dwelling birds such as the meadowlark. ⟨OE *lāwerce*⟩

lark[2] [lɑrk] *n., v. Informal. –n.* a merry adventure or time; frolic or prank.
–v. have fun; sport, frolic, or play pranks: *They were larking about all afternoon.* ⟨origin uncertain⟩

lark bunting a finch (*Calamospiza melanocorys*) of the central plains of North America, the adult male in summer having black plumage with white wing patches.

lark•spur ['lɑrkspər] *n.* a delphinium, especially any of various wild species having blue or blue-and-white flowers. ⟨< *lark*[1] + *spur*⟩

lar•ri•gan ['lærəgən] *or* ['lɛrəgən] *n. Cdn.* an oiled leather moccasin, usually having a flexible sole. ⟨origin uncertain⟩

lar•rup ['lærəp] *v.* **-ruped, -rup•ing.** *Informal.* beat; thrash. ⟨origin uncertain⟩ **–'lar•rup•er,** *n.*

lar•va ['lɑrvə] *n., pl.* **-vae** [-vi] *or* [-vaɪ]. **1** the immature, wingless form of many insects from the time they leave the egg until they become a pupa. A caterpillar is the larva of a butterfly or moth. A grub is the larva of a beetle. Maggots are the larvae of flies. **2** an immature form of certain animals that is different in structure from the adult form. A tadpole is the larva of a frog or toad. ⟨< NL, special use of L *larva* ghost, spectre, skeleton⟩

lar•vae ['lɑrvi], ['lɑrvaɪ], *or* ['lɑrvə] *n.* pl. of LARVA.

lar•val ['lɑrvəl] *adj.* **1** of or having to do with a larva or larvae. **2** characteristic of larvae. **3** in the form of a larva. **4** of a disease, latent; undeveloped.

la•ryn•ge•al [lə'rɪndʒiəl] *or* [lə'rɪndʒəl] *adj., n. —adj.* **1** of or having to do with the larynx. **2** in or produced in the larynx. **3** used on the larynx.
—n. Phonetics. a laryngeal sound. ⟨< NL *laryngeus*⟩

lar•yn•gi•tis [,lærən'dʒəitɪs] *or* [,lɛrən'dʒəitɪs] *n.* inflammation of the larynx, often accompanied by a temporary loss of voice. ⟨< NL *laryngitis* < *laryng-* larynx (< Gk. *larynx, -yngos*) + *-itis*⟩

la•ryn•go•phar•ynx [lə,rɪŋgou'færɪŋks] *or* [-'fɛrɪŋks] *n., pl.* **-pha•ryn•ges** [-fə'rɪndʒiz] or **-phar•ynx•es.** the bottom section of the pharynx, just above the larynx.

la•ryn•go•scope [lə'rɪŋgə,skoup] *n.* an instrument equipped with mirrors for examining the larynx. ⟨< *laryngo-* larynx + *-scope*⟩ **–la,ryn•go'scop•ic** [-'skɒpɪk], *adj.*

lar•yn•gos•co•py [,lærɪŋ'gɒskəpi] *or* [,lɛrɪŋ'gɒskəpi] *n.* the examination of the larynx by means of a laryngoscope.

lar•ynx ['lærɪŋks] *or* ['lɛrɪŋks] *n., pl.* **la•ryn•ges** [lə'rɪndʒiz] or **lar•ynx•es. 1** *Anatomy.* the cavity at the upper end of the human windpipe, containing the vocal cords and acting as a speech organ. See WINDPIPE for picture. **2** *Zoology.* a similar organ or corresponding structure in other animals. ⟨< Gk.⟩

la•sa•gna [lə'zɑnjə] *or* [lə'sɑnjə] *n.* **1** a dish consisting of broad, flat, precooked noodles baked in layers with a sauce of tomatoes, cheese, and meat (usually ground beef). **2** the noodles used for lasagna; lasagne. ⟨< Ital.⟩

la•sa•gne [lə'zɑnjə] *or* [lə'sɑnjə], [lə'zɑnjei] *or* [lə'sɑnjei] *n.* pasta in the form of broad, flat noodles, used especially for making lasagna.

las•car ['læskər] *n.* an East Indian sailor. ⟨< Pg. *laschar*, probably < Persian *lashkar* army < Arabic *al'áskar*⟩

las•civ•i•ous [lə'sɪviəs] *adj.* **1** feeling lust. **2** showing lust. **3** causing lust. ⟨ME < LL *lasciviosus* < L *lascivia* wantonness < *lascivus* wanton⟩ **—las'civ•i•ous•ly,** *adv.* **—las'civ•i•ous•ness,** *n.*

la•ser ['leizər] *n.* **1** a device for amplifying and concentrating light waves, converting the different frequencies into a single, intense, narrow beam of coherent light. Lasers are used for cutting through metal, performing delicate surgery, as on the eye, in communications, etc. **2** (*adjl.*) of, having to do with, or utilizing such a device or the coherent light produced by such a device: *a laser knife.* ⟨*l*ight *a*mplification by *s*timulated *e*mission of *r*adiation⟩
☛ *Hom.* LAZAR.

laser beam a beam of intense radiation from a laser, used in surgery and industry.

laser disk a disk on which images and sounds are recorded, to be read by a special machine using a laser beam.

laser printer *Computer technology.* a non-impact printer that produces high-quality output using laser technology.

laser surgery surgery using laser beams, as in eye surgery.

lash[1] [læʃ] *n., v. —n.* **1** a whip, especially the rope, thong, etc. that is attached to the handle. **2** a stroke or blow with a whip, etc. **3** a sudden, swift movement. **4** anything that hurts like a blow from a whip. **5** eyelash.
—v. **1** beat or drive with a whip, etc. **2** wave or beat back and forth: *The lion lashed its tail. The wind lashes the sails.* **3** rush violently; pour: *The rain lashed against the windows.* **4** strike violently; hit: *The horse lashed at him with its hoofs.* **5** attack severely with words; scold sharply: *The editorial lashed the government for its indifference.*
lash out, strike at or attack sharply, with or as if with a whip: *In his autobiography he lashes out at those he feels have wronged him.* ⟨ME *lasche*, perhaps imitative⟩ **—'lash•er,** *n.* **—'lash•ing•ly,** *adv.* **—'lash•less,** *adj.*

lash[2] [læʃ] *v.* tie or fasten with a rope, cord, etc. ⟨late ME *lasschyn* < MDu. to patch, sew together, scarf (timber)⟩ **—'lash•er,** *n.* **—'lash•ing•ly,** *adv.*

lash•ing[1] ['læʃɪŋ] *n., v. —n.* **1** a whipping, especially as a punishment. **2** a severe attack in words; sharp scolding. **3 lashings,** *pl.* abundance; plentifulness.
—v. ppr. of LASH[1]. ⟨< *lash*[1]⟩

lash•ing[2] ['læʃɪŋ] *n., v. —n.* rope, cord, etc. used in tying or fastening.
—v. ppr. of LASH[2]. ⟨< *lash*[2]⟩

lass [læs] *n.* **1** a girl or young woman. **2** sweetheart. ⟨ME *lasse*; origin uncertain⟩

Las•sa fever ['lɑsə] a viral disease common in W Africa, characterized by fever and inflammation. ⟨after *Lassa*, a village in Nigeria, where it was first diagnosed⟩

las•sie ['læsi] *n. Esp. Scottish.* **1** a young girl. **2** sweetheart.

las•si•tude ['læsɪ,tjud] *or* ['læsɪ,tud] *n.* lack of energy; weakness; weariness. ⟨< L *lassitudo* < *lassus* tired⟩

las•so [læ'su], [lə'su], *or, esp. U.S.,* ['læsou] *n., pl.* **-sos** or **-soes;** *v.* **-soed, -so•ing.** *n., v. —n.* a long rope with a running noose at one end; lariat.
—v. catch with a lasso. ⟨< Sp. *lazo* < L *laqueus* noose. Doublet of LACE.⟩ **—las'so•er,** *n.*

last[1] [læst] *adj., adv., n. —adj.* **1** coming after all others; being at the end; final: *the last page of the book.* **2** next before a specified point of time: *last night, last week, last year.* **3** previous; the one before this one: *The last movie we saw was much better than this western.* **4** most unlikely; least suitable: *That is the last thing one would expect.* **5** being the only one that remains: *He spent his last dollar.* **6** very great; extreme; lasting: *a paper of last importance.* **7** single: *every last one of them.*
—adv. **1** after all others; at the end; finally: *He arrived last.* **2** on the latest or most recent occasion: *When did you last see her?*
—n. **1** a person or thing that comes after all others: *She was the last in the line.* **2** the end: *You have not heard the last of this.*
at last or **at long last,** at the end; after a long time; finally: *So you have come home at last!*
breathe (one's) **last,** die.
see the last of, not see again. ⟨OE *latost, lætest*, superlative of *læt* late⟩
☛ *Syn. adj.* **1. Last,** FINAL, ULTIMATE = coming after all others. **Last** = coming after all others in a series or succession of things, events, or people. **Final** emphasizes the idea of bringing to a definite end or completing a series of events or a set of actions: *The last day of school each year is the final one for the graduating class.* **Ultimate** = the last possible that can ever be reached either by going forward or by tracing backward: *The ultimate cause of some diseases is unknown.*
☛ *Usage.* See note at FIRST.

last[2] [læst] *v.* **1** go on; hold out; continue to be; endure: *The storm lasted three days.* **2** continue in good condition, force, etc.: *I hope these shoes last a year.* **3** be enough or enough for: *while our money lasts.* ⟨OE *lǣstan* < *lǣst* track. Related to LAST[3].⟩
☛ *Syn.* **1.** See note at CONTINUE.

last[3] [læst] *n., v. —n.* a block shaped like a person's foot, on which shoes and boots are formed or repaired.
stick to (one's) **last,** pay attention to one's own work; mind one's own business.
—v. form (shoes and boots) on a last. ⟨OE *lǣste* < *lǣst* track, follow (literally, go in the tracks of)⟩ **—'last•er,** *n.*

last–ditch ['læst 'dɪtʃ] *adj.* **1** serving as a last resort or line of defence: *a last-ditch move.* **2** resisting to the last extremity: *last-ditch survivors of the attack.*

last•ing ['læstɪŋ] *adj., v. —adj.* that lasts a long time; that lasts; that will last; permanent; durable.
—v. ppr. of LAST[2]. **—'last•ing•ly,** *adv.*
☛ *Syn.* **Lasting,** ENDURING, PERMANENT = existing or continuing for a long time or forever. **Lasting** emphasizes going on and on indefinitely, long past what would be normal or expected: *The experience had a lasting effect on him.* **Enduring** emphasizes the idea of being able to withstand the attacks of time and circumstance: *All the world hoped for enduring peace.* **Permanent** emphasizes staying in the same state or position, without changing or being likely to change: *At last he has a permanent job.*

Last Judgment *Christianity.* God's final judgment of all humankind at the end of the world.

last•ly ['læstli] *adv.* finally; in the last place; in conclusion.

last name surname; family name.

last offices prayers for a dead person.

last post in the armed forces, the bugle call that gives the hour of retiring. It is blown also at military funerals, Remembrance Day ceremonies, etc.

last quarter 1 the period between the second half moon and the new moon. **2** the phase of the moon represented by the half moon after full moon.

last rites religious rites performed for a dying person or at a funeral.

last sleep death.

last straw the last of a series of troublesome things resulting in a collapse, outburst, etc.

Last Supper the supper of Jesus and His disciples on the evening before He was crucified.

last word 1 the last thing said; the most conclusive thing said or written on a subject. **2** *Informal.* the latest thing; most up-to-date style: *the last word in casual wear.* **3** *Informal.* something that cannot be improved on.

lat [læt] *n.* the main unit of money in Latvia, divided into 100 santimi. See table of money in the Appendix.

lat. latitude.

Lat. Latin.

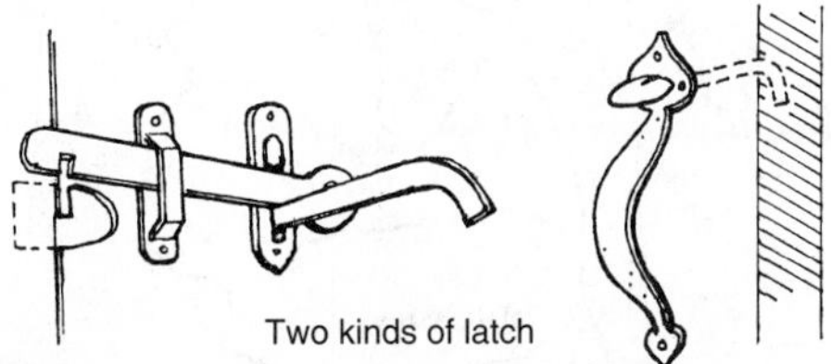

Two kinds of latch

latch [lætʃ] *n., v.* —*n.* a catch for fastening a door, gate, or window. It consists of a movable piece of metal or wood that fits into a notch, opening, etc.
on the latch, not locked; fastened only with a latch.
—*v.* fasten with a latch.
latch on, *Informal.* **a** understand. **b** of a nursing infant, get a proper grasp of the nipple.
latch onto, *Informal.* **a** seize. **b** get. **c** understand. **d** stick closely to (a person or group of people). ⟨OE *læccan* grasp⟩

latch•et [ˈlætʃɪt] *n. Archaic.* a strap or lace for fastening a shoe or sandal. ⟨< dial. OF *lachet,* ult. < *laz* lace. See LACE.⟩

latch•key [ˈlætʃˌki] *n.* a key used to draw back or unfasten the latch of a door.

latch•string [ˈlætʃˌstrɪŋ] *n.* a string used to unfasten the latch of a door.

late [leit] *adj.* **lat•er** or **lat•ter, lat•est** or **last;** *adv.* **lat•er, lat•est** or **last.** *adj., adv.* —*adj.* **1** happening, coming, etc. after the usual or proper time: *We had a late dinner last night.* **2** happening, coming, etc. at an advanced time: *success late in life.* **3** recent: *The late storm did much damage.* **4** recently dead: *The late Harvey Todd was a fine man.* **5** gone out of or retired from office: *The late prime minister is still working actively.*
of late, lately; recently: *I haven't seen him of late.*
—*adv.* **1** after the usual or proper time: *He worked late.* **2** at an advanced time: *It rained late in the afternoon.* **3** recently. **4** recently but no longer: *Yasmin Akasi, late of Victoria.* ⟨OE *læt*⟩ —**ˈlate•ness,** *n.*
☛ *Syn. adj.* **1. Late,** TARDY = happening or coming after the usual or proper time. **Late,** describing people or things, emphasizes the idea of being after the usual, right, proper, expected time: *He was late for school this morning.* **Tardy** = not prompt, not on time, and emphasizes delay and slowness in coming, getting somewhere, or doing something: *Please accept my tardy thanks.*
☛ *Usage.* **Latest.** See note at FIRST.

late•com•er [ˈleitˌkʌmər] *n.* a person who or thing that arrives, especially at an event, later than the expected or proper time: *Latecomers cannot be seated until the first intermission.*

la•teen–rigged [ləˈtin ˌrɪgd] *adj.* having a LATEEN SAIL.

lateen sail a triangular sail held up by a long yard on a short mast.

Late Greek the Greek language from about A.D. 300 to 700.

Late Latin the Latin language from about A.D. 300 to 700.

late Loyalist *Cdn.* formerly, an American settler who moved into Canada (1790-1800) after the influx of the true refugees, the motive usually being to take advantage of the Crown lands being opened for settlement.

late•ly [ˈleitli] *adv.* a short time ago; recently.

la•ten•cy [ˈleitənsi] *n.* a latent condition or quality.

La Tène [lɑ ˈtɛn] of a culture of the late Iron Age. ⟨after the name of a site, in Switzerland, where remains were found⟩

la•tent [ˈleitənt] *adj.* present or existing and capable of development, but not manifest, visible, or active: *a latent talent, a latent infection, a latent bud or spore.* ⟨< L *latens, -entis,* ppr. of *latere* lie hidden⟩ —**ˈla•tent•ly,** *adv.*
☛ *Syn.* **Latent,** POTENTIAL = existing as a possibility or fact, but not now showing itself plainly. **Latent** = actually existing as a fact, but lying hidden, not active or plainly to be seen at the present time: *The power of a grain of wheat to grow into a plant remains latent if it is not planted.* **Potential** = existing as a possibility and capable of coming into actual existence or activity if nothing happens to stop development: *That girl has great potential ability in science.*

latent heat *Physics.* the amount of heat absorbed or released when a substance changes its state.

lat•er•al [ˈlætərəl] *adj., n.* —*adj.* **1** of the side; at the side; from the side; toward the side. A lateral branch of a family is a branch not in the direct line of descent. **2** *Phonetics.* articulated so that the breath passes out on one or both sides of the tongue, as in pronouncing the English [l] in *law* or *all.* **3** of thinking, exploiting indirect or intuitive relationships. Compare LINEAR.
—*n.* **1** a lateral part or outgrowth. **2** *Phonetics.* a lateral sound, such as [l] in *law* or *all.* **3** *Mining.* **a** a drift other than the main drift. **b** a connecting tunnel between main haulage ways. **4** *Football.* LATERAL PASS. ⟨< L *lateralis* < *latus, -teris* side⟩ —**ˈlat•er•al•ly,** *adv.*

lateral line a line of sense organs on the side of a fish or amphibian.

lateral pass *Football.* a throwing of a ball from one player to another in a direction parallel with the goal line.

Lat•er•an [ˈlætərən] *n.* the church of St. John Lateran, the cathedral church of the pope as bishop of Rome.

lat•er•ite [ˈlætəˌrəit] *n. Geology.* a soil formed by the decomposition of rocks, red in colour because of its content of ferric hydroxide. ⟨< L *later* brick + E *-ite*⟩

la•tex [ˈleitɛks] *n., pl.* **lat•i•ces** [ˈlætɪˌsiz] or **la•tex•es. 1** a milky liquid present in certain plants, such as milkweed, poppies, and rubber plants, that is the basis of rubber, balata, gutta-percha, and chicle. **2** *Chemistry.* an emulsion of synthetic rubber or plastic in water, used in paints, adhesives, etc. **3** (*adjl.*) made with a base of synthetic latex: *latex paint.* ⟨< NL, special use of L *latex* something liquid⟩

lath [læθ] *n., pl.* **laths** [læðz] *or* [læθs] *v.* —*n.* **1** one of the thin, narrow strips of wood used to form a support for the plaster of a wall, ceiling, etc., or to make a lattice. **2** a wire cloth or sheet of metal with holes in it, used as a support for plaster. **3** a lining made of laths. The walls of a frame house are usually built with lath and plaster.
—*v.* cover or line with laths. ⟨ME *laththe*⟩ —**ˈlath,like,** *adj.*

lathe [leið] *n., v.* **lathed, lath•ing.** —*n.* a machine for holding pieces of wood, metal, etc. and turning them against a cutting tool that shapes them.
—*v.* cut or shape on a lathe. ⟨late ME *lath* stand < Scand.; cf. Danish *(dreje)lad* (turning) lathe⟩

lath•er[1] [ˈlæðər] *n., v.* —*n.* **1** the foam made from soap or detergent mixed in water. **2** foam formed in sweating: *the lather on a horse after a race.*
in (into) a lather (about something), *Informal.* in (or into) an overwrought or greatly excited state: *to work oneself into a lather about nothing. He's in a big lather about that phone call.*
—*v.* **1** put lather on. **2** form a lather. **3** become covered with the foam formed in sweating. **4** *Informal.* beat; flog. ⟨OE *lēathor*⟩

lath•er[2] [ˈlæθər] *n.* a worker who puts laths on walls, ceilings, etc. ⟨< *lath*⟩

lath•ing [ˈlæθɪŋ] *n.* **1** laths collectively. **2** the work of putting laths on walls, etc.

lath•work [ˈlæθˌwɜrk] *n.* lathing.

lath•y [ˈlæθi] *adj.* long and thin like a lath.

lath•y•rism [ˈlæθəˌrɪzəm] *n.* a condition caused by eating poisonous peas of the genus *Lathyrus,* and characterized by paralysis of the legs and pain.

lat•i•cif•er•ous [ˌlætɪˈsɪfərəs] *adj. Botany.* bearing or containing latex.

lat•i•go [ˈlætɪˌgou] *n.* in the West, a tough leather strap on a saddle for tightening and fastening the cinch. ⟨< Sp.⟩

Lat•in [ˈlætɪn] *n., adj.* —*n.* **1** the language of the ancient Romans, considered classical in the form it acquired during the 2nd and 1st centuries B.C. **2** a member of any of the peoples whose languages come from Latin. The Italians, French, Spanish, Portuguese, and Romanians are Latins. **3** a native or inhabitant of Latium, an ancient territory in W central Italy, or of ancient Rome.
—*adj.* **1** of or in Latin: *a Latin grammar, a Latin passage in a book.* **2** of or having to do with the peoples speaking Romance languages, or the languages themselves. **3** of or having to do with Latin America. **4** of or having to do with Latium or its people; ancient Roman. ⟨< L *Latinus* of Latium⟩
☛ *Hom.* LATTEN.

Latin America South America, Central America, Mexico, and much of the West Indies.

Lat•in–A•mer•i•can [ˈlætɪn əˈmɛrəkən] *n., adj.* —*n.* a native

or inhabitant of Latin America.
—adj. of or having to do with Latin America.

La•tin•ate ['lætə,neit] *adj.* **1** of, like, or pertaining to Latin. **2** having a large or excessive use of Latin words and constructions.

Latin Church that part of the Roman Catholic Church which uses Latin in its worship.

Latin cross a cross in which the upright is longer than the crossbeam. See CROSS for picture.

Lat•in•ism ['lætə,nɪzəm] *n.* **1** a Latin idiom or expression. **2** conformity to Latin models.

Lat•in•ist ['lætənɪst] *n.* a person with much knowledge of the Latin language; Latin scholar.

La•tin•i•ty [lə'tɪnəti] *n.* the knowledge or use of Latin language, style, or idiom. ⟨< L *latīnitās* Latin style⟩

Lat•in•ize ['lætə,naɪz] *v.* **-ized, -iz•ing. 1** translate into Latin. **2** make like Latin. **3** change into characters of the roman alphabet. **4** cause to conform to the ideas, customs, etc. of the Latins or the Latin Church. **—,Lat•in•i'za•tion,** *n.*

Latin Quarter a district in Paris, on the south bank of the Seine River, a traditional resort of artists. ⟨translation of F *Quartier Latin*⟩

Latin square *Statistics.* a series of items arranged in a square in which each item appears once in a row or in a column.

lat•ish ['leitɪʃ] *adj. or adv. Informal.* rather late.

la•tis•si•mus dor•si [lə'tɪsəməs 'dɔrsaɪ] *or* ['dɔrsi] *n., pl.* **la•tis•si•mi** [-,maɪ] or [-,mi] **dor•si.** *Anatomy.* a muscle on either side of the spine, in the middle of the back, that controls the movement of the arms.

lat•i•tude ['lætɪ,tjud] *or* ['lætɪ,tud] *n.* **1** *Geography.* the distance north or south of the equator, measured in degrees. On maps, lines parallel to the equator represent latitudes. See EQUATOR for picture. Compare LONGITUDE. **2** a place or region having a certain latitude: *Polar bears live in the cold latitudes.* **3** room to act or think; scope; freedom from narrow rules: *An artist is allowed more latitude than a bricklayer.* **4** *Photography.* the range between the shortest and the longest exposures that produce good negatives on a given film. **5** *Archaic.* transverse dimension; width. **6** CELESTIAL LATITUDE. ⟨< L *latitudo* < *latus* wide⟩ **–,lat•i'tu•di•nal,** *adj.*

lat•i•tu•di•nar•i•an [,lætɪ,tjudə'nɛriən] *or* [,lætɪ,tudə'nɛriən] *adj., n. —adj.* allowing others their own beliefs; not insisting on strict adherence to established principles, especially in religious views.
—n. a churchgoer who cares little about creeds, forms of worship, or methods of church government.

lat•i•tu•din•ous [,lætə'tjudənəs] *or* [,lætə'tudənəs] *adj.* broad in scope of ideas.

lat•ke ['lɑtkə] *n.* a Jewish potato pancake. ⟨< Yiddish < Russian *latka* patch⟩

la•tri•a [lə'traɪə] *n. Roman Catholic Church.* worship of a kind offered only to God. ⟨< LL < Gk. *latreia* service, worship; akin to *latris* hired servant⟩

la•trine [lə'trin] *n.* a toilet in a camp, factory, etc.; privy. ⟨< F < L *latrina*, originally, washroom < *lavare* wash⟩

-latry *suffix.* worship: *idolatry.* ⟨< Gk. *-latria.* See LATRIA.⟩

lat•ten ['lætən] *n.* any thin, metal sheet, formerly only brass. ⟨ME *latoun* < MF *laton* copper-zinc alloy < < Arabic *lātūn* < Turkic; cf. Turkic *altin* gold⟩
☛ *Hom.* LATIN.

lat•ter ['lætər] *adj.* **1** later; more recent; nearer the end: *Friday comes in the latter part of the week.* **2** (*noml.*) **the latter,** the second of two: *Canada and the United States are in North America; the former lies north of the latter.* Compare FORMER¹. ⟨OE *lætra* later⟩

lat•ter–day ['lætər 'dei] *adj.* of recent or modern times: *latter-day religions.*

Latter–day Saint a Mormon.

lat•ter•ly ['lætərli] *adv.* lately; recently.

lat•tice ['lætɪs] *n., v.* **-ticed, -tic•ing.** *—n.* **1** a structure of crossed wooden or metal strips with open spaces between them. **2** a window, gate, etc. having a lattice. **3** any pattern or decoration resembling a lattice. **4** *Physics.* the geometric structure of materials in a nuclear reactor.
—v. **1** form into a lattice; make like a lattice. **2** furnish with a lattice. ⟨ME < OF *lattis* < *latte* lath < Gmc.⟩ **—'lat•tice,like,** *adj.*

lat•tice•work ['lætɪs,wɜrk] *n.* a lattice or lattices.

Lat•vi•a ['lætviə] *n.* a country on the Baltic Sea.

Lat•vi•an ['lætviən] *adj., n. —adj.* of or having to do with Latvia, its people, or their language.
—n. **1** a native or inhabitant of Latvia. **2** the Baltic language of Latvia; Lettish.

laud [lɒd] *v., n. —v.* extol; praise.
—n. **1** praise. **2** a song or hymn of praise. **3 lauds** or **Lauds,** *pl.* **a** a morning Christian church service with psalms of praise to God. **b** *Roman Catholic Church.* a prescribed devotional service for priests and persons in religious orders, forming, with matins, the first of the seven canonical hours. ⟨ME < OF *laude* (*n.*) and L *laudare* (*v.*) < L *laus, laudis* praise⟩ **—'laud•er,** *n.*

laud•a•ble ['lɒdəbəl] *adj.* worthy of praise; commendable: *Selflessness is laudable.* **—'laud•a•bly,** *adv.* **—,laud•a'bil•i•ty,** *n.*

lau•da•num ['lɒdənəm] *n.* a solution of opium in alcohol used, especially formerly, for the relief of pain. ⟨< NL < Med.L *laudanum*, var. of L *ladanum* < Gk. *lādanon* mastic⟩

lau•da•tion [lɒ'deiʃən] *n.* praise.

laud•a•to•ry ['lɒdə,tɔri] *adj.* expressing praise.

laugh [læf] *v., n. —v.* **1** make the sounds and movements of the face and body that show amusement or pleasure at humour or nonsense, etc.: *We all laughed at the joke.* **2** express with laughter: *to laugh a reply.* **3** drive, put, bring, etc. by or with laughing: *to laugh one's tears away.* **4** suggest the feeling of joy; be lively.
laugh at, a make fun of; ridicule: *They laughed at.* **b** disregard or make light of: *at danger.*
laugh in or **up** (one's) **sleeve,** laugh secretly or to oneself.
laugh off, pass off or dismiss with a laugh: *She laughed off my warning and walked to the middle of the pond.*
laugh on the other or **wrong side of** (one's) **face** or **mouth,** be made to change from amusement or joy to sorrow or anger.
—n. the act or sound of laughing.
last laugh, a victory that defies the expectations of others: *When his old car won the race, Tim had the last laugh.* ⟨OE *hliehhan*⟩ **—'laugh•er,** *n.*

laugh•a•ble ['læfəbəl] *adj.* such as to cause laughter; amusing; ridiculous. **—'laugh•a•ble•ness,** *n.* **—'laugh•a•bly,** *adv.*
☛ *Syn.* See note at FUNNY.

laugh•ing ['læfɪŋ] *adj., n., v. —adj.* **1** that laughs or seems to laugh: *the laughing brook.* **2** accompanied by laughter.
no laughing matter, a matter that is serious: *The rise in juvenile crime is no laughing matter.*
—n. laughter.
—v. ppr. of LAUGH. **—'laugh•ing•ly,** *adv.*

laughing gas nitrous oxide, a colourless gas that makes one insensible to pain. This gas makes some people laugh and become excited. *Formula*: N_2O

laughing jackass kookaburra.

laugh•ing•stock ['læfɪŋ,stɒk] *n.* an object of ridicule; a person who or thing that is made fun of.

laugh•ter ['læftər] *n.* **1** the action of laughing. **2** the sound of laughing: *Laughter filled the room.* ⟨OE *hleahtor*⟩ **—'laugh•ter•less,** *adj.*

launch¹ [lɒntʃ] *v., n. —v.* **1** cause to slide into the water; set afloat: *A new ship is launched from the supports on which it has been built.* **2** push out or put forth on the water or into the air: *to launch a plane from an aircraft carrier.* **3** start; set going; set out: *to launch someone in business.* **4** throw or send out: *to launch a rocket or missile.*
launch out, begin; start.

—*n.* a launching or being launched: *We watched the rocket launch on TV.* ⟨ME < AF *launcher*, var. of *lancer* use a lance < *lance* lance < L *lancea*⟩ **—'launch•a•ble,** *adj.* **—'launch•er,** *n.*

launch² [lɒntʃ] *n.* **1** a motorboat used for pleasure trips. **2** the largest boat carried by a warship. ⟨< Sp., Pg. *lancha* < Malay *lanchāran* speedboat < *lanchar* speed⟩

launching pad a surface or platform from which a rocket or missile is launched into the air.

laun•der ['lɒndər] *v.* **1** wash and iron (clothes, linens, etc.). **2** be able to be washed; stand washing: *Cotton fabrics usually launder well.* **3** *Informal.* disguise the source of (money obtained illegally). ⟨ME *lander* one who washes linen < OF *lavandier* washer < VL *lavandarius* < L *lavanda* (things) to be washed < *lavare* wash⟩ **—,laun•der•a'bil•i•ty,** *n.* **—'laun•der•a•ble,** *adj.* **—'laun•der•er,** *n.*

laun•dress ['lɒndrɪs] *n.* a woman whose work is washing and ironing clothes, linens, etc.

Laun•dro•mat ['lɒndrə,mæt] *n. Trademark.* a self-service laundry having automatic washing machines and dryers, especially one having coin-operated machines.

laun•dry ['lɒndri] *n., pl.* **-dries. 1** a room or building or an establishment where clothes, linens, etc. are washed and ironed. **2** clothes, etc. washed or to be washed. **3** the washing and ironing of clothes, etc.

laun•dry•man ['lɒndrimən] *n.* **-men. 1** a man who works in a laundry. **2** a man who collects and delivers laundry.

laun•dry•wom•an ['lɒndri,wʊmən] *n., pl.* **-wom•en.** laundress.

lau•re•ate ['lɔriɪt] *adj., n.* —*adj.* **1** crowned with a laurel wreath as a mark of honour. **2** honoured; distinguished.
—*n.* POET LAUREATE. ⟨< L *laureatus* < *laurea* laurel wreath < *laurus* laurel⟩

lau•re•ate•ship ['lɔriɪt,ʃɪp] *n.* **1** the position of POET LAUREATE. **2** the time during which a poet is poet laureate.

lau•rel ['lɔrəl] *n.* **1** any of a genus (*Laurus*) of evergreen trees or shrubs; especially, *L. nobilis* (also called **bay** and **sweet bay**), a large shrub or small tree native to S Europe and N Africa, having stiff, glossy, dark green leaves, believed to be the leaves used by the ancient Greeks for wreaths to crown victors and heroes. **2** the foliage of the laurel: *wreaths of laurel.* **3 laurels,** *pl.* **a** a wreath of laurel for a crown. **b** honour, fame, or victory: *The laurels went to a young athlete who had not competed before.* **4** (*adjl.*) designating a family (Lauraceae) of evergreen shrubs and trees found mainly in tropical and subtropical regions, and including the laurel, cinnamon, avocado, etc. **5** any of various evergreen shrubs or trees not related to the true laurel. See MOUNTAIN LAUREL.
look to (one's) **laurels,** guard one's reputation or record from rival competitors.
rest on (one's) **laurels,** be satisfied with honours already won.
⟨ME < OF *lorier, laurier* < *lor* < L *laurus*⟩

lau•relled or **lau•reled** ['lɔrəld] *adj.* **1** crowned with a laurel wreath. **2** honoured.

Lau•ren•tia [lə'rɛnʃiə] *n. Cdn. Often poetic.* the region north of the St. Lawrence River, formerly New France and its hinterland. ⟨< fem. form of L *Laurentius* Lawrence⟩

Lau•ren•tian [lə'rɛnʃən] *adj., n.* —*adj.* **1** of or having to do with the St. Lawrence River and adjoining lands. **2** *Geology.* of or having to do with intrusive granites found in the oldest Precambrian rocks of the Canadian Shield. **3** of or having to do with the Laurentian Mountains; Laurentide. **4** of or having to do with the province of Québec.
—*n.* **Laurentians,** the region of the Laurentian Mountains. ⟨< *Laurentius,* L form of *Lawrence* + *-ian*⟩

Laurentian Mountains or **Highlands** a low range of mountains lying between Hudson Bay and the St. Lawrence River.

Laurentian Shield *Cdn.* CANADIAN SHIELD.

Lau•ren•tide ['lɔrən,taɪd] *adj. Cdn.* of or having to do with the Laurentians. ⟨< Cdn.F⟩

la•va ['lævə] *or* ['lɑvə] *n.* **1** the molten rock flowing from a volcano or fissure in the earth. **2** the rock formed by the cooling of this molten material. Some lavas are hard and glassy; others are light and porous. ⟨< dial. Ital. *lava* stream, ult. < L *lavare* wash⟩

lava bed a layer or surface of lava.

la•va•bo [lə'vɑbou] *or* [lə'veibou] *n., pl.* **-boes. 1** Also, **Lavabo.** *Roman Catholic Church.* **a** the ritual washing of the celebrant's hands during the Mass, before the consecration. **b** the portion of Psalm 25 said during this rite. **2** a washbasin and tank with a tap, hung on a wall. **3** an ornamental basin on a wall, used as a planter. ⟨< L *lavabo* I will wash, the first word of Ps. 25:6 in the Douay version⟩

lava field a large area of cooled lava.

la•vage [lə'vɑʒ] *or* ['lævɪdʒ] *n. Medicine.* the washing of some hollow body part such as the stomach or sinuses. ⟨< F *laver* < L *lavare* to wash⟩

lav•a•liere, lav•a•lier, or **lav•al•lière** [,lævə'lir]; *French,* [lava'ljɛʀ] *n.* an ornament hanging from a small chain, worn around the neck by women. ⟨< F *lavallière* < Louise, Duchesse de *La Vallière* (1644-1710), a mistress of Louis XIV of France⟩

lav•a•to•ry ['lævə,tɔri] *n., pl.* **-ries. 1** washroom; toilet. **2** a room for washing one's hands and face. **3** washbasin. ⟨ME < LL *lavatorium* < L *lavare* wash. Doublet of LAVER¹.⟩

lave [leiv] *v.* **laved, lav•ing.** *Poetic.* **1** wash; bathe. **2** wash or flow against: *The stream laves its banks.* ⟨OE *lafian* < L *lavare*⟩

lav•en•der ['lævəndər] *n., adj.* —*n.* **1** a pale purple. **2** any of a genus (*Lavandula*) of small, aromatic shrubs or perennial herbs of the mint family, especially a small, Mediterranean evergreen shrub (*L. officinalis,* also called *L. vera*) having greyish green, hoary leaves and spikes of light purple flowers which yield an essential oil used in perfumes. **3** the dried, fragrant flowers, leaves, and stalks of lavender, used in sachets.
—*adj.* pale purple. ⟨ME < AF < Med.L *lavendula*⟩

la•ver¹ ['leivər] *n. Archaic.* a bowl or basin to wash in. ⟨ME < OF *laveoir* < LL *lavatorium* a place for washing < L *lavare* wash. Doublet of LAVATORY.⟩

la•ver² ['leivər] *n.* an edible seaweed of the genus *Porhyra.* ⟨< L, water plant⟩

lav•ish ['lævɪʃ] *adj., v.* —*adj.* **1** very free or too free in giving or spending; prodigal: *A rich person can afford to be lavish with money.* **2** very abundant; more than enough; given or spent too freely: *many lavish gifts.*
—*v.* give or spend very freely or too freely: *to lavish kindness on one's guests.* ⟨ult. < OF *lavasse* flood < *laver* wash < L *lavare*⟩ **—'lav•ish•er,** *n.* **—'lav•ish•ly,** *adv.* **—'lav•ish•ness,** *n.*
☛ *Syn. adj.* **2.** See note at PROFUSE.

law [lɒ] *n.* **1** a body of rules recognized by a country, state, province, municipality, or community as binding on its members: *international law. British law is different from French law.* **2** one of these rules: *a law against slavery. Good citizens obey the laws.* **3** the controlling influence of these rules, or the condition of society brought about by their observance: *maintain law and order.* **4** law as a system: *courts of law.* **5** the department of knowledge or study concerned with these rules; jurisprudence: *the study of law.* **6** a body of such rules concerned with a particular subject or derived from a particular source: *commercial law, criminal law.* **7** the legal profession: *enter the law.* **8** legal action. **9** any statute passed by the legislative body of a province, state, or nation: *a Federal law.* **10** any rule or principle that must be obeyed: *the laws of hospitality, a law of grammar.* **11 a** legal authorities. **b** *Informal.* a police officer or detective. **12** (in philosophy, science, etc.) **a** a statement of a relation or sequence of phenomena invariable under the same conditions: *the law of gravitation, Mendel's law, Ohm's law.* **b** a mathematical rule on which the construction of a curve, a series, etc. depends. **13** a divine rule or commandment. **14 the Law,** *Judaism, Christianity.* **a** the books of the Bible that contain the Mosaic law; Pentateuch. **b** the commandments or will of God as set forth in the Bible.
go to law, appeal to law courts; take legal action.
lay down the law, a give orders that must be obeyed. **b** give a scolding.
read law, study to be a lawyer.
take the law into (one's) **own hands,** take steps to gain one's rights or avenge a wrong without going to court. ⟨OE *lagu* < Scand.; cf. ON *lög*⟩ **—'law,like,** *adj.*
☛ *Syn.* **2, 9. Law,** STATUTE = a rule or regulation recognized by a community as governing the action or procedure of its members. **Law** is the general word applying to any such rule or regulation, written or unwritten, laid down by the highest authority, passed by action of a lawmaking body such as Parliament, a provincial legislature, or a city council, or recognized as custom and enforced by the courts. **Statute** applies to a formally written law passed by a legislative body.

L.A.W. LEADING AIRCRAFTWOMAN.

law–a•bid•ing ['lɒ ə,baɪdɪŋ] *adj.* obedient to the law; peaceful and orderly. **—'law•a,bid•ing•ness,** *n.*

law•break•er ['lɒ,breikər] *n.* a person who breaks the law. **—'law,break•ing,** *n., adj.*

law court a place where justice is administered; a court of law.

law•ful ['lɒfəl] *adj.* **1** according to law; done as the law directs: *lawful arrest.* **2** allowed by law; rightful: *lawful demands.* **—'law•ful•ly,** *adv.* **—'law•ful•ness,** *n.*

☛ *Syn.* **1, 2. Lawful,** LEGAL, LEGITIMATE = according to law. **Lawful** = in agreement with or not against the laws of the community, the laws of a church, or moral law: *To some people gambling is not lawful.* **Legal** = authorized by or according to the actual terms of the laws of a community as enforced by the courts: *Lotteries are legal in most provinces.* **Legitimate** = rightful according to law, recognized authority, or established standards: *Sickness is a legitimate reason for a child's being absent from school.*

law•giv•er ['lɒ,gɪvər] *n.* a person who prepares and puts into effect a system of laws for a people; lawmaker.

law•less ['lɒlɪs] *adj.* **1** paying no attention to the law; breaking the law: *A thief leads a lawless life.* **2** hard to control; unruly: *a lawless mob.* **3** having no laws: *a lawless frontier town.* **—'law•less•ly,** *adv.* **—'law•less•ness,** *n.*

law•mak•er ['lɒ,meikər] *n.* a person who helps to make laws; a member of a parliament, legislature, or congress; legislator. **—'law,mak•ing,** *n., adj.*

law merchant the law of commercial transactions; commercial law.

lawn[1] [lɒn] *n.* land covered with grass kept closely cut, especially near or around a house. ⟨ME *launde* < MF *lande* glade < Celtic⟩ **—'lawn•y,** *adj.*

lawn[2] [lɒn] *n.* a fine, sheer cotton or linen cloth. ⟨? ult. < *Laon* a city in France⟩

lawn bowling a game played on a bowling green with a lopsided or unsymmetrically weighted wooden ball that is rolled toward a small, white stationary target ball (the jack); bowls.

lawn mower a machine with revolving blades for cutting the grass on a lawn.

lawn tennis an outdoor game in which a ball is hit back and forth over a low net.

law of averages **1** *Statistics.* the principle that the number of occurrences of an event is predictable from its number of random trials. **2** *Informal.* the principle that the greatest influence on any occurrence is probability.

law of Moses the first five books of the Old Testament: Genesis, Exodus, Leviticus, Numbers, and Deuteronomy.

law of the Medes and Persians a law that cannot be changed. ⟨so called because in ancient times these laws were thought to have come from the gods⟩

law•ren•ci•um [lɒ'rɛnsiəm] *n. Chemistry.* a short-lived, artificial, radioactive element produced from californium. *Symbol*: Lr; *at.no.* 103; *at.mass* (257); *half-life* 35 s. ⟨after Ernest O. *Lawrence* (1901-1958), an American physicist⟩

law•suit ['lɒ,sut] *n.* a case in a court of law; application to a court for justice: *Injustices are often remedied by lawsuits.*

law•yer ['lɔiər] *or* ['lɒjər] *n.* a person whose profession is giving advice about the laws or acting for others in a court of law. **—'law•yer,like,** *adj.* **—'law•yer•ly,** *adj.*

lax [læks] *adj.* **1** not firm or tight; loose or slack. **2** not strict; careless: *lax behaviour.* **3** loose in morals. **4** *Phonetics.* articulated with relatively relaxed jaw and tongue muscles. Compare TENSE. **5** not exact; vague. ⟨< L *laxus*⟩ **—'lax•ly,** *adv.* **—'lax•ness,** *n.*

lax•a•tive ['læksətɪv] *n., adj. —n.* a medicine that makes the bowels move.
—adj. making the bowels move. ⟨< L *laxativus* loosening, ult. < *laxus* loose⟩

lax•i•ty ['læksəti] *n.* the quality or state of being lax; looseness. ⟨< F *laxité* < L *laxitas* < *laxus* loose⟩

lay[1] [lei] *v.* **laid, lay•ing;** *n. —v.* **1** put down; place in a certain position: *Lay your hat on the table.* **2** place in a lying-down position or a position of rest: *Lay the baby down gently.* **3** place; put; set: *He lays great emphasis on good manners. The scene of the story is laid in Montréal. Lay aside the book for me. The horse laid its ears back.* **4** smooth down: *to lay the nap of cloth.* **5** bring down; beat down: *A storm laid the crops.* **6** place in proper position or in orderly fashion: *to lay bricks.* **7** devise; arrange: *to lay plans.* **8** put down as a bet; wager: *I lay five dollars that he will not come.* **9** make quiet or make disappear: *to lay a ghost.* **10** impose (a burden, penalty, etc.): *to lay a tax on property.* **11** present; bring forward: *to lay claim to an estate.* **12** impute; attribute: *The theft was laid to her.* **13** produce (an egg or eggs) from the body: *Birds, fish, and reptiles lay eggs. All the hens are laying well.* **14** apply oneself vigorously: *The women laid to their oars.* **15** *Nautical.* take up a specified position: *to lay aft.*

lay about, strike out on all sides.

lay a course, *Nautical.* lie or sail in a certain direction without being obliged to tack.

lay aside or **away, a** put away for future use; save: *I laid away ten dollars a week toward buying a bicycle.* **b** put away from one's person, from consideration, etc.; put on one side.

lay by, a put away for future use. **b** *Nautical.* of a ship, come to a standstill; lay to.

lay down, a declare; state. **b** give; sacrifice. **c** *Slang.* quit; resign from. **d** store away for future use. **e** bet. **f** survey; draw in on a chart or map.

lay for, *Informal.* lie in wait for.

lay in, get and save; put aside for future: *The trapper laid in enough supplies for the winter.*

lay into, a *Informal.* beat; thrash: *She laid into the vicious dog with a stick.* **b** *Slang.* scold: *My parents laid into me for not doing my homework.*

lay low, humble; bring down.

lay off, a put aside. **b** *Slang.* stop for a time; take a rest. **c** stop teasing or interfering with: *Let's lay off the new boy and give him a chance.* **d** put out of work: *Several workers were laid off because of a shortage of steel.* **e** mark off: *He laid off the boundaries of the tennis court.*

lay on, a apply. **b** supply. **c** strike. **d** inflict.

lay open, a expose (*to*): *He lays himself open to ridicule by his many boasts.* **b** make an opening in; wound.

lay (oneself) **out,** make a great effort; take pains (*to*): *He laid himself out to be agreeable.*

lay out, a spread out: *Supper was laid out on the table.* **b** prepare (a dead body) for burial. **c** arrange or plan: *to lay out a program.* **d** mark off: *They laid out a tennis court.* **e** *Slang.* spend: *They laid out two hundred dollars in repairs.* **f** *Slang.* knock unconscious; put out of the fight.

lay over, *Informal.* break a journey: *We'll lay over in Vancouver for a few days and then drive on to California.*

lay to, a blame on. **b** *Nautical.* of ships, head into the wind and stand still.

lay up, a put away for future use; save. **b** cause to stay in bed or indoors because of illness or injury: *He was laid up with flu for a week.* **c** *Nautical.* put (a ship) in dock.

—n. **1** the way or position in which a thing is laid or lies: *the lay of the ground.* **2** the amount and direction of the twist given to the strands or other components of a rope. **3** a share of the profits or of the catch of a whaling or fishing vessel. **4** *Cdn.* formerly, a lease to work a gold claim for a share of the proceeds. **5** terms of employment or sharing. ⟨OE *lecgan,* causative of *licgan* lie[2]⟩

☛ *Usage.* **Lay,** LIE. Although the past tenses of **lay**[1] and **lie**[2] are often confused, in standard English the two verbs are always kept distinct: **lie, lay, lain** and **lay, laid, laid. Lie** does not take an object: *I'm going to lie down for a rest. He lay down for a rest. The village lies in a valley.* **Lay** always takes an object: *We laid a new floor in the kitchen. Lay the book on the table.*
☛ *Hom.* LEI.

lay[2] [lei] *v.* pt. of LIE[2].
☛ *Hom.* LEI.

lay[3] [lei] *adj.* **1** of ordinary people; not of the clergy. A lay sermon is one preached by a person who is not of the clergy. **2** of ordinary people; not of lawyers, doctors, or those learned in the profession in question: *The lay mind understands little of the cause of the disease.* ⟨ME < OF *lai* < L *laicus.* Doublet of LAIC.⟩
☛ *Hom.* LEI.

lay[4] [lei] *n.* **1** a short poem to be sung; poem. **2** a song; tune. ⟨ME < OF *lai* < Gmc.; cf. OHG *leih* song⟩
☛ *Hom.* LEI.

lay•a•bout ['leiə,bʌut] *n.* a lazy, shiftless person; a loafer or bum.

lay•a•way ['leiə,wei] *n.* a system whereby goods are put away for a specific customer, who pays for them in instalments.

lay•er ['leiər] *n., v. —n.* **1** one that lays: *This hen is a good layer.* **2** one thickness or fold. A cake is often made of two or more layers put together. **3** a branch of a plant bent down and covered with earth so that it will take root and form a new plant.
—v. **1** lay down or arrange in layers. **2** form (new plants) by layers; spread by layers.

lay•ette [lei'ɛt] *n.* a set of clothes, bedding, etc. for a newborn baby. ⟨< F *layette* < *laie* chest⟩

lay figure **1** a jointed model of a human body. Lay figures are used by artists and for window displays. **2** an unimportant person; puppet. ⟨earlier *layman* < Du. *leeman* < *lee* limb + *man* man⟩

lay•man ['leimən] *n., pl.* **-men. 1** a male member of the church who is not a member of the clergy: *The priest and several* *laymen planned the church budget.* **2** a man who is not a member of a particular profession: *It is hard for most laymen to understand doctors' prescriptions.* ⟨< *lay*[3] + *man*⟩

lay•off ['lei,ɒf] *n.* **1** a temporary dismissal of workers: *Because of a shortage of steel, there was a layoff at the plant.* **2** the time during which such a dismissal lasts.

lay of the land **1** the nature of the place; the position of hills, water, woods, etc.: *Spies were sent out to find out the lay of the land.* **2** the existing situation; condition of things.

lay•out ['lei,ʌut] *n.* **1** the act of laying out. **2** an arrangement; plan: *This map shows the layout of the camp.* **3** a plan or design for an advertisement, book, etc. **4** the work or art of making such plans or designs. **5** a thing laid or spread out; display. **6** an outfit; supply; set.

lay•o•ver ['lei,ouvər] *n.* a stopping for a time in a place.

laz•ar ['læzər] *or* ['leizər] *n. Archaic.* **1** leper. **2** a poor, sick person. ⟨ME < Med.L *lazarus* < *Lazarus*, the beggar⟩
☛ *Hom.* LASER ['leizər].

laz•a•ret•to [,læzə'rɛtou] *n., pl.* **-tos.** **1** formerly, a hospital for people having contagious diseases, especially leprosy. **2** a building or ship used for quarantine purposes. **3** a place in some merchant ships, near the stern, in which supplies are kept. Also, **lazaret, lazarette** [,læzə'rɛt] ⟨< Ital. *lazzaretto*, blend of *lazzaro* lazar, and the name of a hospital, Santa Maria di *Nazaret*, Venice, Italy⟩

la•zar•oid ['læzə,rɔɪd] *n.* a drug used to treat Alzheimer's disease and heart disease. ⟨< *Lazarus*⟩

Laz•a•rus ['læzərəs] *n.* any diseased beggar, especially a leper. ⟨in the Bible, a beggar who suffered on earth but went to heaven⟩

laze [leiz] *v.* **lazed, laz•ing. 1** be lazy or idle. **2** pass (time) lazily. ⟨back formation from LAZY⟩

la•zu•lite ['læzə,ləit] *or* ['læzjə,ləit] *n.* LAPIS LAZULI. *Formula*: $(Fe\ Mg)Al_2P_2O_8(OH)_2$

la•zy ['leizi] *adj.* **la•zi•er, la•zi•est. 1** not willing to work or be active: *She was too lazy to get up and turn off the TV.* **2** characterized by, suggestive of, or conducive to idleness: *a lazy mood, a lazy summer day.* **3** moving slowly; not very active: *a lazy stream.* ⟨? < MLG *lasich* weak, feeble⟩ **—'la•zi•ly,** *adv.* **—'la•zi•ness,** *n.*
☛ *Syn.* **1.** See note at IDLE.

la•zy•bones ['leizi,bounz] *n.pl. or sing. Informal.* a lazy person.

lazy Su•san ['suzən] a revolving tray for holding different kinds of food, condiments, etc., placed on a table or used for storage in a cupboard.

lb. [paʊnd] pound (singular or collective plural). ⟨< L *libra*; pl. *librae*⟩

LB Labrador (*used esp. in computerized address systems*).

L/Bdr. LANCE-BOMBARDIER.

lbs. [paʊndz] pounds.

l.c. **1** LOWER CASE. **2** LOC. CIT. **3** LETTER OF CREDIT.

L.C. **1** LOWER CANADA. **2** Library of Congress.

LCD *Computer technology.* LIQUID-CRYSTAL DISPLAY.

LCD, L.C.D., or **l.c.d.** LEAST (or LOWEST) COMMON DENOMINATOR.

L.Cdr. or **LCdr** LIEUTENANT-COMMANDER.

LCM, L.C.M., or **l.c.m.** LEAST COMMON MULTIPLE.

L.Col. or **LCol** LIEUTENANT-COLONEL.

L/Cpl. LANCE-CORPORAL.

Ld. **1** Lord. **2** Limited.

L–do•pa ['ɛl 'doupə] *n.* levodopa.

lea[1] [li] *n.* a grassy field; meadow; pasture. ⟨OE *lēah*⟩
☛ *Hom.* LEE.

lea[2] [li] *n.* a measure of yarn: 80 yards (73.1 m) for wool; 120 yards (109.7 m) for silk; 300 yards (274.3 m) for linen. ⟨ME *lee* taken as sing. of *leese* < OF *lesse*⟩
☛ *Hom.* LEE.

leach [litʃ] *v., n.* —*v.* **1** run (water, etc.) through slowly; filter. **2** dissolve out by running water through slowly: *Potash is leached from wood ashes.* **3** dissolve out soluble parts from (ashes, etc.) by running water through slowly. **4** lose (soluble parts) when water passes through.
—*n.* a container for use in leaching. ⟨OE *leccan* wet⟩
—,leach•a'bil•i•ty, *n.* **—'leach•a•ble,** *adj.* **—'leach•er,** *n.*
☛ *Hom.* LEECH.

lead[1] [lid] *v.* **led, lead•ing;** *n.* —*v.* **1** show the way by going along with or in front of; guide: *The guide led the hunters through the forest.* **2** conduct by the hand, a rope, etc.: *to lead a horse.* **3** act as guide: *You lead, I will follow.* **4** be a means of proceeding to or effecting a certain result: *Hard work leads to success.* **5** conduct or bring (water, steam, a rope, etc.) in a particular channel or course. **6** pass or spend (life, time, etc.): *She leads a quiet life in the country.* **7** afford passage or way: *This road leads to the city.* **8** guide or direct in action, policy, opinion, etc.; influence; persuade: *Such actions led us to distrust him.* **9** be led; submit to being led: *This horse leads easily.* **10** *Archaic.* take or bring: *We led them away prisoners.* **11** go or be at the head of: *The elephants led the parade.* **12** go or be first; have first place (among): *In algebra he is low in the class, but in history he leads.* **13** be chief of; command; direct: *A general leads an army.* **14** be chief; direct; act as leader. **15** begin or open: *She led the dance.* **16** *Card games.* **a** begin with (the card or suit named). **b** make first play at cards. **17** *Boxing.* direct a blow at an opponent. **18** *Curling.* throw first on a team.
lead astray, a give false information to. **b** encourage to do wrong.
lead nowhere, have no effect; lead to a dead end.
lead off, begin; start.
lead on, a influence. **b** deceive. **c** take the lead.
lead up to, prepare the way for.
—*n.* **1** guidance or direction; example: *to follow someone's lead.* **2** the first or foremost place; a position in advance: *take the lead.* **3** the distance, number of points, etc. that one is ahead: *She had a lead of 3 m at the halfway mark.* **4** *Card games.* **a** the right of playing first. **b** the card or suit so played. **5** something that leads. **6** *Theatre or film.* **a** the principal role in a play, etc. **b** the person who plays such a part. **7** a string, strap, etc. for leading a dog or other animal; leash. **8** a guiding indication; clue: *He was not sure where to look for the information, but the librarian gave him some good leads.* **9** *Mining.* lode. **10** an open channel through an ice field. **11** *Electricity.* a conductor conveying electric current. **12** *Boxing.* a blow directed at an opponent. **13** the opening paragraph in a newspaper article. **14** the main front-page story in a magazine, newspaper, etc. **15** *Curling.* the person on a team who throws first in each end, usually the least experienced player. ⟨OE *lædan*⟩
☛ *Syn. v.* **1.** See note at GUIDE.
☛ *Spelling.* The past tense is spelled **led,** not **lead:** *We lead a quiet life right now (present tense). We led the horse home (past tense).*

lead[2] [lɛd] *n., adj., v.* —*n.* **1** *Chemistry.* a soft, heavy, easily melted, bluish grey, metallic chemical element. It is used in alloys, etc. *Symbol*: Pb; *at.no.* 82; *at.mass* 207.19. **2** something made of this metal or one of its alloys. **3** a weight on a line used to find the depth of water; plummet. **4** bullets; shot. **5** a long, thin piece of graphite or other substance in or for a pencil. **6** *Printing.* a metal strip for widening the space between lines. **7 leads,** *pl.* **a** strips of lead used to cover roofs. **b** the frames of lead in which panes of glass are set.
—*adj.* made of lead: *lead pipe.*
—*v.* **1** *Printing.* insert leads between the lines of (print). **2** cover, frame, or weight with lead. **3** glaze (pottery) with glaze containing lead. ⟨OE *lēad*⟩ **—'lead•less, 'lead-'free,** *adj.*

lead acetate [lɛd] *Chemistry.* a poisonous, crystalline salt used in making dyes, paints, and varnishes. *Formula*: $Pb(CH_3CO)_2$

lead article [lid] See LEADING ARTICLE.

lead chromate [lɛd] a poisonous yellow compound used industrially as a paint pigment. *Formula*: $PbCrO_4$

lead colic [lɛd] LEAD POISONING.

lead dog [lid] *Cdn.* in a dog team, the dog that leads the team, setting the pace and carrying out the driver's commands.

lead•en ['lɛdən] *adj.* **1** made of lead: *a leaden coffin.* **2** heavy; hard to lift or move: *The tired runner's legs felt leaden.* **3** oppressive: *leaden air.* **4** dull; gloomy. **5** bluish grey: *leaden clouds.* **—'lead•en•ly,** *adv.* **—'lead•en•ness,** *n.*

lead•er ['lidər] *n.* **1** a person or thing that leads: *a band leader.* **2** a person who is well fitted to lead. **3** the horse harnessed at the front of a team. **4** LEAD DOG. **5** LEADING ARTICLE. **6** a short length of nylon, wire, etc. used to attach the lure to a fishing line. **7** an article offered at a low price to attract customers. **8 leaders,** *pl.* a row of dots or dashes to guide the eye across a printed page. **—'lead•er•less,** *adj.*

leader board or **leaderboard** ['lidər,bɔrd] *n.* a notice posting the scores of golfers.

lead•er•ship ['lidər,ʃɪp] *n.* **1** the state or position of being a leader. **2** the act of leading. **3** leaders collectively. **4** the qualities of a leader; the ability to lead: *Leadership is a great asset to a politician.*

lead–in ['lid ,ɪn] *n.* **1** a wire that runs from an antenna to a radio or television receiver or transmitter. **2** introduction: *a lengthy lead-in.*

lead•ing[1] ['lidɪŋ] *adj., v. —adj.* **1** guiding; directing. **2** most important; chief; principal: *the leading lady in a play.* **3** the act of one who or that which leads; guidance; direction.
—v. ppr. of LEAD[1]. ⟨< *lead*[1]⟩

lead•ing[2] ['lɛdɪŋ] *n.* **1** a covering or frame of lead. **2** the metal strips for widening the space between lines of type. ⟨< *lead*[2]⟩

leading aircraftman an air-force serviceman ranking next above an aircraftman and below a corporal. *Abbrev.:* L.A.C.

leading aircraftwoman or **airwoman** an air-force servicewoman ranking next above an aircraftwoman and below a corporal. *Abbrev.:* L.A.W.

leading article ['lidɪŋ] an important editorial or article in a newspaper, magazine, etc. Also, **lead article, leader.**

leading lady an actor who plays the chief female part in a play or film.

leading man an actor who plays the chief male part in a play or film.

leading note ['lidɪŋ] *Music.* the seventh degree of the scale.

leading question ['lidɪŋ] a question so worded that it suggests the answer desired or makes the desired answer unavoidable.

leading seaman **1** *Canadian Forces.* in Maritime Command, the equivalent of a corporal. See chart of ranks in the Appendix. **2** a person of similar rank in the naval forces of other countries. *Abbrev.:* L.S. or LS

leading strings ['lidɪŋ] **1** strings for supporting a child when learning to walk. **2** a state of dependence or close guidance: *She was eighteen years old and still in leading strings.*

lead line [lɛd] PLUMB LINE.

lead–off ['lid ,ɒf] *n.* **1** the beginning of something. **2** *Baseball.* the opening hitter.

lead pencil [lɛd] an ordinary pencil having a graphite core for writing.

lead–pipe cinch ['lɛd 'pəip] *Slang.* **1** something absolutely certain: *It's a lead-pipe cinch that it'll rain; look at those black clouds.* **2** a very easy thing to do: *Making this soup is a lead-pipe cinch.*

lead poisoning [lɛd] poisoning caused by ingesting lead.

leads•man ['lɛdzmən] *n., pl.* **-men.** a seaman who takes soundings with a lead line.

lead time [lid] *Manufacturing.* the period needed to develop and manufacture a product.

lead•wort ['lɛd,wɜrt] *n.* any plant of the genus *Plumbago,* once thought to cause lead poisoning.

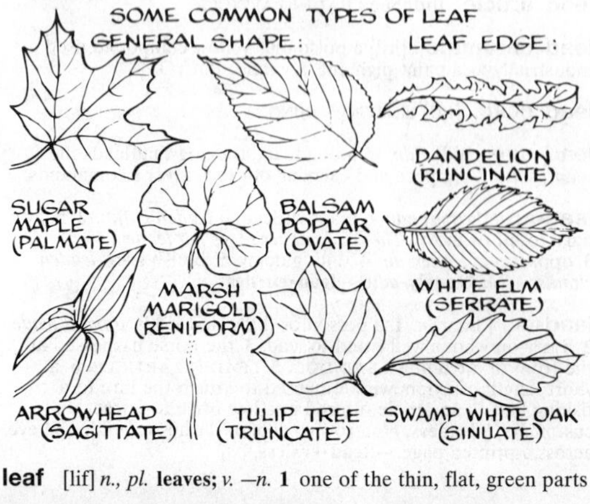

SOME COMMON TYPES OF LEAF
GENERAL SHAPE: LEAF EDGE:
SUGAR MAPLE (PALMATE)
MARSH MARIGOLD (RENIFORM)
BALSAM POPLAR (OVATE)
DANDELION (RUNCINATE)
WHITE ELM (SERRATE)
ARROWHEAD (SAGITTATE)
TULIP TREE (TRUNCATE)
SWAMP WHITE OAK (SINUATE)

leaf [lif] *n., pl.* **leaves;** *v. —n.* **1** one of the thin, flat, green parts that grow on the stem of a tree or other plant. **2** a petal of a flower: *a rose leaf.* **3** a sheet of paper. Each side of a leaf of a book is a page. **4** a very thin piece or sheet of metal, etc.: *gold leaf.* **5** a movable piece serving as an extension to a table. **6** the sliding, hinged, or movable part of a door, shutter, etc. **7** one of a number of curved metal strips that are clamped together to make up a LEAF SPRING.
in leaf, having completely developed foliage: *The trees were already in leaf when we came home.*
take a leaf from (someone's) **book,** *Informal.* follow someone's example; copy someone's conduct.
turn over a new leaf, start all over again; try to do or be better in the future: *I promised to turn over a new leaf and study harder.*
—v. **1** put forth leaves: *The trees along the river leaf earlier than those on the hill.* **2** turn pages. ⟨OE *lēaf*⟩ **—'leaf,like,** *adj.*
☛ *Hom.* LIEF.

leaf•age ['lifɪdʒ] *n.* leaves; foliage.

leaf bud a bud producing a stem having leaves only.

leaf fat a layer of fat protecting the kidneys.

leaf•hop•per ['lif,hɒpər] *n.* any of a family (Cicadellidae) of small, often brightly coloured, homopterous insects, many of which are agricultural pests because they suck the juices of plants.

leaf•less ['liflɪs] *adj.* having no leaves. **—'leaf•less•ness,** *n.*

leaf•let ['liflɪt] *n.* **1** a small, flat or folded sheet of printed matter: *advertising leaflets.* **2** a small or young leaf. **3** one of the separate blades or divisions of a compound leaf.

leaf miner a larva feeding on leaves.

leaf mould **1** compost made mainly of leaves. **2** a mould formed on leaves.

leaf peeper or **leaf–peeper** ['lif ,pipər] *n. Cdn.* a town dweller who visits the countryside to see autumn foliage. **—leaf peeping** or **leaf-peeping,** *n.*

leaf spring a spring made up of layers of metal strips in a single unit.

leaf•stalk ['lif,stɒk] *n.* the stalk by which a leaf is attached to a stem; petiole.

leaf•y ['lifi] *adj.* **leaf•i•er, leaf•i•est. 1** having many leaves; covered with leaves. **2** resembling a leaf: *We chose a fabric with a leafy design.* **—'leaf•i•ness,** *n.*

league[1] [lig] *n., v.* **leagued, leagu•ing.** *—n.* **1** an association of persons, parties, or countries formed to help one another. **2** a group of teams that play a schedule of games against each other: *a hockey league, a bowling league.* **3** *Informal.* a class or level: *The two contractors are just not in the same league.*
in league, united; in association: *They were in league against us. The suspected spies were thought to be in league with the enemy.*
—v. associate in a league; form a league. ⟨< F *ligue* < Ital. *liga,* var. of *lega* < *legare* bind⟩

league[2] [lig] *n.* an old unit for measuring distance, usually equal to about 5 km. ⟨ME < LL *leuga* < Celtic⟩

League of Nations an association of many countries, formed at the Treaty of Versailles in 1919 to promote peace and co-operation among nations. It was dissolved in April, 1946.

lea•guer[1] ['ligər] *v., n. Archaic. —v.* besiege.
—n. **1** a siege. **2** the camp of a besieging army. ⟨< Du. *leger* camp⟩

leagu•er[2] ['ligər] *n.* a member of a league. ⟨< *league*[1]⟩

leak [lik] *n., v. —n.* **1** a hole or crack, caused either by accident or by wear and tear, that lets something in or out: *a leak in a boat or a tire.* **2** leakage. **3** a means of escape, loss, etc. **4** the escape or loss itself: *a news leak.* **5** *Electricity.* **a** an escape of current from a conductor, especially as a result of poor insulation. **b** the point where such escape occurs.
—v. **1** go in or out through a hole or crack. **2** let something in that should be kept out; let something out that should be kept in: *Her boat leaks. The teakettle leaks.* **3** let (something) pass in or out: *That pipe leaks gas.* **4** make or become known: *The secret leaked out.* **5** come in or go out in a secret or stealthy way: *Spies somehow leaked into the city.* **6** pass (away) by gradual waste: *The natural resources of our country are leaking away through misuse.* ⟨ME *leken* < Scand.; cf. Icel. to drip, leak⟩ **—'leak•er,** *n.* **—'leak•less,** *adj.*
☛ *Hom.* LEEK.

leak•age ['likɪdʒ] *n.* **1** the act, process, or an instance of leaking: *a leakage in a pipeline, a leakage of news to the press.* **2** something that leaks in or out. **3** the amount or rate of leaking: *The leakage was estimated at 40 L an hour.*

leak•proof ['lik,pruf] *adj.* that will not allow anything to leak in or out.

leak•y ['liki] *adj.* **leak•i•er, leak•i•est.** leaking; having a leak or leaks. **—'leak•i•ness,** *n.*

lean[1] [lin] *v.* **leaned** or **leant, lean•ing;** *n.* *—v.* **1** stand slanting, not upright; bend: *A small tree leans over in the wind.* **2** rest in a sloping or slanting position: *Lean against me.* **3** set or put in a leaning position: *Lean the picture against the wall till I am ready for it.* **4** depend; rely: *to lean on a friend's advice.* **5** tend or incline; show a preference: *to lean toward mercy. Her favourite sport was tennis, but now she leans more to swimming.* **6** *Informal.* apply force or pressure to influence or persuade (*usually used with* **on**): *The school is starting to lean on students with poor attendance records.*
lean over backward, *Informal.* **a** do one's utmost. **b** go to extremes in one direction so as to more than balance a tendency in the opposite direction.
—n. the act or an instance of leaning; inclination: *The old barn has more of a lean this year.* ⟨OE *hlinian*⟩
☛ *Hom.* LIEN.

lean[2] [lin] *adj., n.* *—adj.* **1** with little or no fat: *a lean horse.* **2** producing little; scant: *a lean harvest, a lean diet.*
—n. meat having little fat. ⟨OE *hlǣne*⟩ **—'lean•ness,** *n.* **—'lean•ly,** *adv.*
☛ *Syn. adj.* **1.** See note at THIN.
☛ *Hom.* LIEN.

Le•an•der [li'ændər] *n. Greek legend.* a lover who swam the Hellespont to visit his sweetheart, Hero, every night until he was finally drowned. See also HERO.

lean•ing ['linɪŋ] *n., v.* *—n.* a tendency; inclination.
—v. ppr. of LEAN[1].

leaning fence *Cdn.* an old-fashioned rail fence having all the posts set at an angle of 40°.

leant [lɛnt] *v.* a pt. and a pp. of LEAN[1].
☛ *Hom.* LENT.

lean–to ['lin,tu] *n., pl.* **-tos. 1** a building attached to and partly supported by another, and having a sloping roof with its upper edge attached to the wall of the other building. **2** a crude shelter built or leaning against posts, trees, rock, etc.: *Hunters have a supply of wood in a lean-to here.* **3** (*adjl.*) having supports pitched against or leaning on an adjoining wall or building: *a lean-to roof.*

leap [lip] *n., v.* **leaped** or **leapt, leap•ing.** *—n.* **1** a jump or spring. **2** something to be jumped. **3** the distance covered by a jump. **4** a group of leopards.
by leaps and bounds, very fast and very much.
leap in the dark, an action taken without knowing what its results will be.
—v. **1** jump: *A frog leaps.* **2** pass, come, rise, etc. as if with a leap or bound: *An idea leaped to her mind. A sudden breeze made the leaves leap.* **3** jump over: *leap a fence.* **4** cause to leap.
leap at, *Informal.* take or accept with eagerness: *You should leap at such a chance.* ⟨OE *hlȳp,* n., *hlēapan,* v.⟩
☛ *Syn. v.* **1.** See note at JUMP.

leap•frog ['lip,frɒg] *n., v.* **-frogged, -frog•ging.** *—n.* a game in which one player jumps over the bent back of another.
—v. **1** leap or jump as in the game of leapfrog. **2** skip over; side-step; avoid.

leapt [lɛpt] *or* [lipt] *v.* a pt. and a pp. of LEAP.

leap year a year having 366 days, the extra day being February 29. A year is a leap year if its number can be divided exactly by four, except years at the end of a century, which must be exactly divisible by 400; thus 1960 and 2000 are leap years, whereas 1900 and 1961 are not.

learn [lɜrn] *v.* **learned** [lɜrnd] or **learnt, learn•ing. 1** gain knowledge of (a subject) or skill in (an art, trade, etc.) by study, instruction, or experience: *learn French.* **2** acquire knowledge, skill, etc.: *She learns easily.* **3** memorize: *He learned the poem in five minutes.* **4** find out; come to know: *She tried to learn the details of the train wreck.* **5** become informed; hear. **6** become able by study, discipline, or practice: *to learn to control one's temper.* ⟨OE *leornian*⟩ **—'learn•a•ble,** *adj.*
☛ *Usage.* Do not confuse **learn** with TEACH. Standard English keeps these two verbs completely distinct: *I learned how to play chess. She taught me how to play chess.*

learn•ed ['lɜrnɪd] *adj.* having, showing, or requiring much knowledge; scholarly: *a learned woman, a learned book.*
—'learn•ed•ly, *adv.* **—'learn•ed•ness,** *n.*

learned borrowing ['lɜrnɪd] a word or expression borrowed from a language at the scholarly, technical, or scientific level. *Flora* and *fauna* are learned borrowings from Latin.

learn•er ['lɜrnər] *n.* **1** a person who is learning. **2** beginner.

learn•ing ['lɜrnɪŋ] *n., v.* *—n.* **1** the gaining of knowledge or skill. **2** the possession of knowledge gained by study; scholarship. **3** knowledge.
—v. ppr. of LEARN.

learnt [lɜrnt] *v.* a pt. and a pp. of LEARN.

lear•y ['liri] See LEERY.

lease [lis] *n., v.* **leased, leas•ing.** *—n.* **1** a contract, usually in the form of a written agreement, giving the right to use property for a certain length of time, usually by paying rent. **2** the length of time for which such an agreement is made: *They have a one-year lease on the property.* **3** the property held by a lease.
new lease on life, the chance to live a longer, better, or happier life: *The successful surgery gave her a new lease on life.*
—v. **1** give a lease on. **2** take a lease on. **3** be leased. ⟨late ME *les* < AF, back formation from *lesser* to lease (literally, let go) < L *lazāre* to release, let go⟩ **—'leas•a•ble,** *adj.* **—'lease•less,** *adj.* **—'leas•er,** *n.*

lease•hold ['lis,hould] *n.* **1** a holding by a lease. **2** real estate held by a lease. **—'lease,hold•er,** *n.*

leash [liʃ] *n., v.* *—n.* **1** a strap, chain, etc. for restraining or leading a dog or other animal in check. **2** a group of three animals: *a leash of hounds.*
hold in leash, control; restrain: *She held her temper in leash with difficulty.*
strain at the leash, try to go ahead despite restraint.
—v. fasten or hold in with a leash; control. ⟨ME < OF *laisse* < L *laxa,* fem., loose⟩

least [list] *adj., n., adv.* *—adj.* less than any other; smallest; slightest: *The least bit of dirt in a watch may make it stop.*
—n. the least amount or degree: *That is the least you can do.*
at least or **at the least, a** at the lowest estimate: *The temperature was at least 35°C.* **b** at any rate; in any case: *He may have been late but at least he came.* **c** as a minimum requirement, offer, etc.: *You must be at least six years old to join.*
not in the least, not at all.
—adv. to the least extent, amount, or degree: *She liked that book least of all.* ⟨OE *lǣst*⟩

least common denominator *Mathematics.* the lowest common multiple of all the denominators of a group of fractions. The least common denominator of ½, ¾, ⅘ is 20. Also called **lowest common denominator.** *Abbrev.:* LCD, L.C.D. or l.c.d.

least common multiple the least quantity that contains two or more given quantities exactly. The least common multiple of 3 and 4 and 6 is 12. *Abbrev.:* LCM, L.C.M. or l.c.m.

least•wise ['list,waɪz] *adv. Informal.* at least; at any rate. Also, **leastways.**

leath•er ['lɛðər] *n., v.* *—n.* **1** animal skin that has been prepared for use by removing all the flesh and hair from the skin and then tanning it. **2** (*adjl.*) made of or covered with leather: *leather gloves, a leather chair.* **3** something made of leather.
—v. **1** furnish or cover with leather. **2** *Informal.* beat with a strap; thrash. ⟨OE *lether*⟩

leath•er•back turtle ['lɛðər,bæk] the largest living turtle (*Dermochelys coriacea*), having a leathery skin. It grows to over 2 m in length and can have a mass of 450 kg. It is an endangered species.

Leath•er•ette [,lɛðə'rɛt] *n. Trademark.* imitation leather.

leath•ern ['lɛðərn] *adj.* **1** made of leather. **2** like leather.

leath•er•neck ['lɛðər,nɛk] *n. U.S. Slang.* a United States marine.

leath•er•y ['lɛðəri] *adj.* like leather in appearance, texture, or toughness. **—'leath•er•i•ness,** *n.*

leave[1] [liv] *v.* **left, leav•ing. 1** go away: *We leave tonight.* **2** go away from: *She left the house.* **3** stop living in, belonging to, or working at or for: *leave the country, leave the club.* **4** go without taking; let remain: *I left a book on the table.* **5** go away and let remain in a particular condition: *leave a window open.* **6** let remain when one dies; bequeath: *She left a large fortune.* **7** give to be kept; deposit; give: *I left my suitcase in the station while I walked around the town.* **8** let (a person, etc.) alone to do something; let be: *Leave me to settle the matter.* **9** let remain for someone to do: *Leave the matter to me. I left the driving to my sister.* **10** let remain uneaten, unused, unremoved, etc.: *to leave one's dessert.* **11** not attend to: *I will leave my homework till tomorrow.*
leave off, stop: *Continue the story from where I left off.*
leave out, fail to do, say, or put in; omit: *She left out two words when she read the sentence.* ⟨OE lǣfan⟩ **—'leav•er,** *n.*
☛ *Hom.* LIEVE.
☛ *Syn.* **1.** See note at GO.

leave² [liv] *n.* **1** permission; consent: *They gave him leave to go.* **2** permission to be absent from duty; LEAVE OF ABSENCE. **3** the length of time that such permission lasts.
by your leave, with your consent; if you permit.
on leave, absent from duty with permission.
take leave (of), say goodbye (to): *We took leave of our hostess at the door.*
take (one's) **leave,** say goodbye and depart: *We took our leave soon after they did.* ⟨OE *lēaf*⟩
☛ *Hom.* LIEVE.

leave³ [liv] *v.* **leaved, leav•ing.** put forth leaves: *Trees begin to leave in the spring.* ⟨var. of *leaf*⟩
☛ *Hom.* LIEVE.

leav•en ['lɛvən] *n., v.* —*n.* **1** any substance, such as yeast, that will cause fermentation and make dough rise. **2** a small amount of fermenting dough kept for this purpose. **3** an influence that, spreading silently and strongly, changes conditions or opinions: *A leaven of hope brightened our despair.* **4** a tempering or modifying element; a tinge or admixture: *The solemn speech had a leaven of humour.*
—*v.* **1** cause to rise by means of a leaven; make (dough) light or lighter. **2** spread through or blend with some modifying element: *Hope leavened our despair.* ⟨ME < OF *levain* < L *levamen* a lifting < *levare* raise⟩

leav•en•ing ['lɛvənɪŋ] *n., v.* —*n.* something that leavens.
—*v.* ppr. of LEAVEN.

leave of absence **1** permission to be absent from duty. **2** the length of time that absence from duty is permitted.

leaves [livz] *n., v.* —*n.* **1** pl. of LEAF. **2** pl. of LEAVE².
—*v.* 3rd pers. sing., pres. indicative, of LEAVE¹.

leave–tak•ing ['liv ˌteikɪŋ] *n.* the act of taking leave; saying goodbye.

leav•ings ['livɪŋz] *n.pl.* leftovers; remnants.

Leb•a•nese [ˌlɛbə'niz] *adj., n.* —*adj.* of or having to do with Lebanon, or its people.
—*n.* a native or inhabitant of Lebanon.

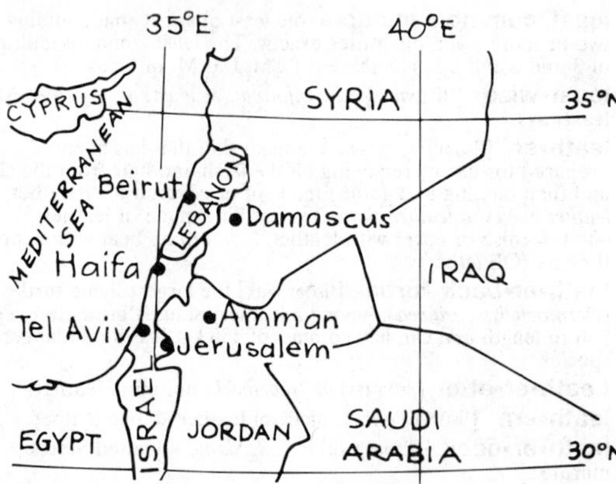

Leb•a•non ['lɛbəˌnɒn] *n.* a country at the eastern end of the Mediterranean.

Le•bens•raum or **le•bens•raum** ['leibənsˌraʊm]; *German,* ['lebənsʀaʊm] *n.* **1** the territory that a nation supposedly must possess in order to be economically self-sufficient. **2** the space, freedom, etc. required for existence, activity, or expansion. ⟨literally, living space⟩
☛ *Usage.* This word was used by the Nazis in World War II as an excuse for conquest.

lech•er ['lɛtʃər] *n.* a man who indulges in lechery. ⟨ME < OF *lecheor* licker < *lechier* lick < Gmc.⟩

lech•er•ous ['lɛtʃərəs] *adj.* lewd; lustful. —**'lech•er•ous•ly,** *adv.* —**'lech•er•ous•ness,** *n.*

lech•er•y ['lɛtʃəri] *n., pl.* **-er•ies. 1** lewdness; gross indulgence of lust. **2** a lecherous act. ⟨ME *lecherie* < OF *lecheor* glutton, libertine⟩

le•ci•thin ['lɛsəθɪn] *n. Biochemistry.* any fatty substance as found in egg yolks and in animal tissues. ⟨< Gk. *lekithos* yolk of an egg + E *-in*⟩

lec•tern ['lɛktərn] *n.* **1** a reading desk in a church, especially the stand with a sloping top from which the lessons are read at daily prayer. **2** any reading desk or stand with a sloping top. ⟨ME < OF *lettrun, leitrun* < Med.L *lectrum* < L *legere* read⟩

lec•tion ['lɛkʃən] *n.* **1** one version or rendition of a text. **2** a reading from the Scriptures in a service.

lec•ture ['lɛktʃər] *n., v.* **-tured, -tur•ing.** —*n.* **1 a** a speech or planned talk on a chosen subject, usually for the purpose of instruction. **b** such a speech or talk written down or printed. **2** a scolding.
—*v.* **1** give a lecture. **2** instruct or entertain by a lecture. **3** scold; reprove. ⟨ME < LL *lectura* < L *legere* read⟩

lec•tur•er ['lɛktʃərər] *n.* **1** a person who gives a lecture or lectures. **2** a teacher of junior rank at some universities.

led [lɛd] *v.* pt. and pp. of LEAD¹.
☛ *Hom.* LEAD².
☛ *Spelling.* See note at LEAD¹.

LED or **L.E.D.** LIGHT-EMITTING DIODE.

Le•da ['lidə] *n. Greek mythology.* a queen of Sparta. Leda was visited by Zeus in the form of a swan and by him became the mother of Castor and Pollux and of Helen of Troy.

ledge [lɛdʒ] *n.* **1** a narrow shelf: *a window ledge.* **2** a shelf or ridge of rock. **3** a layer or mass of metal-bearing rock. ⟨ME < *legge(n)*; akin to LAY¹⟩ —**'ledge,less,** *adj.*

ledg•er ['lɛdʒər] *n.* a book of accounts in which a business keeps a record of all money transactions. ⟨ME *legger* a book. See LEDGE.⟩

ledger board the top board of a fence.

ledger line *Music.* a line added above or below the staff for notes that are too high or too low to be put on the staff.

lee [li] *n., adj.* —*n.* **1** shelter. **2** the side or part sheltered or away from the wind: *the lee of the house.* **3** the direction toward which the wind is blowing.
—*adj.* **1** sheltered or away from the wind: *the lee side of a ship.* **2** on the side away from the wind. **3** in the direction toward which the wind is blowing. ⟨ME; OE *hlēow* shelter⟩
☛ *Hom.* LEA.

lee•board ['liˌbɔrd] *n. Nautical.* a large, flat board lowered into the water on the lee side of a sailboat to keep the boat from drifting sideways.

leech¹ [litʃ] *n., v.* —*n.* **1** any of a class (Hirudinea) of mostly freshwater annelid worms having a segmented body with a sucker at either end. Many leeches live by sucking the blood of other animals; one large European species (*Hirudo medicinalis*) was formerly much used for medical bloodletting. **2** *Informal.* a person who persistently tries to get what he or she can out of others. **3** *Archaic.* physician.
—*v.* **1** use leeches on (a person) for bloodletting. **2** *Informal.* live parasitically. **3** *Archaic.* cure or heal. ⟨OE *lǣce*⟩ —**'leech,like,** *adj.*
☛ *Hom.* LEACH.

leech² [litʃ] *n. Nautical.* the edge of a sail not fastened to a rope or spar. ⟨late ME *lek, leche, lyche*; akin to Du. *lijk* leech⟩
☛ *Hom.* LEACH.

leek [lik] *n.* a biennial plant (*Allium porrum*) of the lily family, closely related to the onion but having a somewhat milder flavour. It resembles a very large green onion, with a slender bulb and thick stalk. ⟨OE *lēac*⟩
☛ *Hom.* LEAK.

leer [lir] *n., v.* —*n.* a sly, sidelong look; evil or lewd glance.
—*v.* give a sly, sidelong look; glance evilly or lewdly. ⟨? OE *hlēor* cheek, from idea of looking over one's cheek, looking askance⟩ —**'leer•ing•ly,** *adv.*

leer•y ['liri] *adj. Informal.* **1** wary; suspicious. **2** afraid. **3** sly; cunning and knowing. —**'leer•i•ly,** *adv.* —**'leer•i•ness,** *n.*

lees [liz] *n.pl.* dregs; sediment. ⟨< F *lie* < Celtic⟩

lee•ward ['liwərd] *or, in nautical use,* ['luərd] *adj., adv., n.* —*adj. or adv.* **1** on the side away from the wind. **2** in the direction toward which the wind is blowing.
—*n.* the side away from the wind. —**'lee•ward•ly,** *adv.*

lee•way ['liˌwei] *n.* **1** *Nautical.* the side movement of a ship to leeward, out of its course. **2** extra space at the side; more time, money, etc. than is needed; a margin of safety: *She made it to work with five minutes' leeway.* **3** sufficient room or scope for action.

left¹ [lɛft] *adj., adv., n.* —*adj.* **1** of the side that is toward the west when the main side faces north: *the left wing of an army, a person's left hand.* **2** when looking to the front, situated nearer

the observer's or speaker's left hand than his or her right: *the left side of the room.* **3** toward this side or in this direction: *Make a left turn at the next light.* **4** Often, **Left,** *Politics.* of, having to do with, or belonging to the Left.
—adv. on or to the left side: *turn left.*
—n. **1** the left side or hand. **2 the Left** or **the left, a** a group or party advocating or favouring social, political, and economic policies aimed at more or less equal distribution of rights, obligations, and wealth within the community or state; a progressive, liberal, radical, or revolutionary group or party. **b** especially in some European legislatures, the members occupying the seats to the left of the presiding officer by virtue of their more liberal or radical views. **3** *Boxing.* a blow struck with the left hand. ⟨dial. OE *left* (for *lyft*) weak⟩

left[2] [lɛft] *v.* pt. and pp. of LEAVE[1].

left face a turn to the left.

left–hand ['lɛft 'hænd] *adj.* **1** on or to the left. **2** of, for, or with the left hand.

left–hand•ed ['lɛft 'hændɪd] *adj.* **1** using the left hand more easily and readily than the right. **2** done with the left hand. **3** made to be used with the left hand or by left-handed people. **4** turning from right to left: *a left-handed screw.* **5** clumsy; awkward. **6** doubtful; insincere: *a left-handed compliment.* **—'left-'hand•ed•ly,** *adv.* **—'left-'hand•ed•ness,** *n.*

left–hand•er ['lɛft 'hændər] *or* ['lɛft ,hændər] *n.* **1** a left-handed person. **2** a stroke or blow with the left hand.

left•ist ['lɛftɪst] *n., adj. Politics. —n.* a person who supports or favours the LEFT[1] (def. *n.* 2).
—adj. of, having to do with, or favouring or supporting the Left: *leftist ideas.* **—'left•ism,** *n.*

left•o•ver ['lɛft,ouvər] *n., pl.* **left•o•vers**; *adj. —n.* anything that is left. Scraps of food from a meal are leftovers.
—adj. that is left; remaining.

left wing **1** *Politics.* the more liberal or radical faction of an assembly, group, or party. **2** *Hockey, Lacrosse, etc.* the playing position to the left of centre of a forward line. **—'left-'wing,** *adj.* **—'left-'wing•er,** *n.*

left•y ['lɛfti] *n., pl.* **left•ies.** *Informal.* a left-handed person.

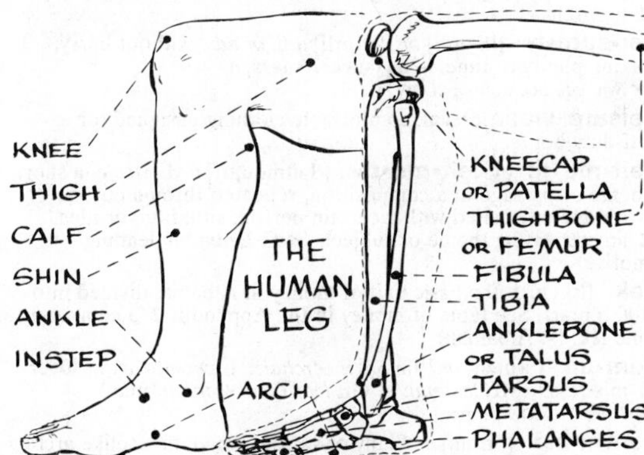

leg [lɛg] *n., v.* **legged, leg•ging.** *—n.* **1** one of the limbs on which human beings and animals support themselves and walk. **2** the part of a garment that covers a leg. **3** anything shaped or used like a leg: *a table leg.* **4** one of the distinct portions or stages of any course: *the last leg of a trip.* **5** the side of a triangle that is not the base or hypotenuse. **6** *Cricket.* **a** that part of the field to the left of and behind a right-handed player who is batting as he or she faces the bowler. Compare OFF. **b** the fielder placed there.
give (someone) **a leg up,** *Informal.* help (up).
have not a leg to stand on, *Informal.* have no defence or reason.
on (one's) **last legs,** *Informal.* about to fall, collapse, die, etc.: *I feel as if I am on my last legs but a swim should revive me.*
pull (someone's) **leg,** *Informal.* fool, trick, or make fun of one: *I didn't know she was pulling my leg until I heard you laugh.*
shake a leg, *Slang.* **a** hurry up: *We'd better shake a leg if we want to get there on time.* **b** dance.
stretch (one's) **legs,** *Informal.* take a walk.
—v. Informal. walk; run: *We could not get a ride, so we had to leg it.* ⟨ME < ON *leggr*⟩ **—'leg•less,** *adj.* **—'leg,like,** *adj.*

Leg. or **leg.** **1** legislature; legislative. **2** legal. **3** legate. **4** legato.

leg•a•cy ['lɛgəsi] *n., pl.* **-cies. 1** the money or other property left to a person by a will. **2** something that has been handed down from an ancestor or predecessor. ⟨ME < OF *legacie* < Med.L *legatia* < L *legatum* bequest, ult. < *lex, legis* covenant⟩

le•gal ['ligəl] *adj.* **1** of law: *legal knowledge.* **2** of lawyers. **3** according to law; lawful. ⟨< L *legalis* < *lex, legis* law. Doublet of LOYAL.⟩
☛ *Syn.* **3.** See note at LAWFUL.

legal aid *Law.* **1** the provision of legal assistance to needy people. **2** such assistance or the program or agency providing it.

le•gal•ese [,ligə'liz] *n.* the jargon of the legal profession commonly used in documents, legal submissions and forms, etc., especially when thought of as incomprehensible or excessively finicky.

legal holiday STATUTORY HOLIDAY.

le•gal•ism ['ligə,lɪzəm] *n.* overly strict adherence to law or prescription at the expense of deeper moral, aesthetic, spiritual, etc. values. **—'le•gal•ist,** *n.* **—,le•gal'ist•ic,** *adj.* **—,le•gal'is•ti•cal•ly,** *adv.*

le•gal•i•ty [lɪ'gæləti] *n., pl.* **-ties. 1** accordance with law; lawfulness. **2** a legal requirement or aspect.

le•gal•ize ['ligə,laɪz] *v.* **-ized, -iz•ing.** make legal; authorize by law; sanction. **—,le•gal•i'za•tion,** *n.*

le•gal•ly ['ligəli] *adv.* **1** in a legal manner. **2** according to law.

le•gal–size ['ligəl ,saɪz] *adj.* **1** of paper, measuring 22 cm × 36 cm. **2** of stationery, etc., made to fit legal-size paper: *a legal-size filing cabinet.* Compare LETTER-SIZE.

legal tender money that must, by law, be accepted in payment of debts.

leg•ate ['lɛgɪt] *n.* **1** a representative of the Pope. **2** an ambassador; representative; messenger. ⟨< L *legatus,* originally, provided with a contract < *lex, legis* contract⟩ **—'leg•ate,ship,** *n.*

leg•a•tee [,lɛgə'ti] *n.* a person to whom a legacy is left.

le•ga•tion [lɪ'geiʃən] *n.* **1** the diplomatic representative of a country and his or her staff of assistants. A legation ranks next below an embassy. **2** the official residence, offices, etc. of such a representative in a foreign country. **3** the office, position, or dignity of a legate. ⟨ME < L *legatio, -onis,* ult. < *legare* dispatch < *legatus.* See LEGATE.⟩ **—le'ga•tion,ar•y,** *adj.*

le•ga•to [lɪ'gatou] *adj., adv., n. Music. —adj.* smooth and connected; without breaks between successive tones. *Legato* is the opposite of *staccato.*
—adv. in a legato manner.
—n. a legato passage, style, or performance. ⟨< Ital. *legato* bound, *legare* < L *ligāre* to bind⟩

le•ga•tor [lɪ'geitər] *or* [,lɛgə'tɔr] *n.* a person who leaves a legacy. **—,leg•a'to•ri•al,** *adj.*

leg break *Cricket.* a ball directed by the bowler so as to deviate to the off side from the leg side.

leg bye *Cricket.* a run scored when the ball glances off the leg of the player who is batting.

leg•end ['lɛdʒənd] *n.* **1** a story coming down from the past, which has been widely accepted as true: *The stories about King Arthur and his Knights of the Round Table are legends, not history.* **2** such stories considered collectively. **3** the inscription on a coin or medal. **4** the words, etc. accompanying a picture, map, or diagram; caption. ⟨ME < OF *legende* < Med.L < L *legenda* (things) to be read < *legere* read⟩
☛ *Usage.* **Legend** and MYTH have somewhat different meanings. A **legend** is a story relating to a people's past and usually glorifies a hero, saint, great event, etc.; it may contain an element of fact, or it may be wholly untrue. A **myth** is a story relating to a people's religion or world view and is usually about a god, gods, or other superhuman beings or elemental principles; its aim is to explain a religious or philosophical belief or some aspect of life or nature.

leg•end•ar•y ['lɛdʒən,dɛri] *adj.* **1** of a legend or legends; like a legend; not historical. **2** famous. **—'leg•end,ar•i•ly,** *adv.*

leg•end•ry ['lɛdʒəndri] *n.* legends as a group.

leg•er•de•main [,lɛdʒərdə'mein] *n.* **1** sleight of hand; conjuring tricks; jugglery. A common trick of legerdemain is to take rabbits from an apparently empty hat. **2** trickery. ⟨< F *léger de main* quick of hand⟩ **—,leg•er•de'main•ist,** *n.*

legged ['lɛgɪd] *or* [lɛgd] **1** having a leg or legs. **2** having a leg or legs of a specified kind or number: *a three-legged stool, a long-legged bird.*

leg•gings ['lɛgɪŋz] *n.pl.* **1** extra outer coverings of cloth or leather for the legs, for use out-of-doors; gaiters. **2** tight, thin, very stretchy pants for women or girls.

leg•gy ['lɛgi] *adj.* **1** having long legs. **2** having awkwardly long legs. **—'leg•gi•ness,** *n.*

leg•horn ['lɛghɔrn] *or* ['lɛgərn] *n.* **1 Leghorn,** a breed of rather small chicken valued especially as a prolific egg layer. It produces white eggs. **2** a fine straw from an Italian wheat that is braided for making hats. **3** a hat made of this braided straw. ⟨< *Leghorn* (*Livorno*), a seaport in W Italy⟩

leg•i•bil•i•ty [,lɛdʒə'bɪləti] *n.* a legible condition or quality; clearness of print or writing.

leg•i•ble ['lɛdʒəbəl] *adj.* **1** that can be read. **2** easy to read; plain and clear: *legible handwriting.* ⟨< LL *legibilis* < L *legere* read⟩ **—'leg•i•ble•ness,** *n.* **—'leg•i•bly,** *adv.*

le•gion ['lidʒən] *n., adj.* *—n.* **1** a large body of soldiers; army. **2** in the ancient Roman army, a body of soldiers consisting of 3000 to 6000 foot soldiers and 300 to 700 cavalry. **3** a great many; a very large number. **4 Legion,** ROYAL CANADIAN LEGION.
—adj. very numerous: *The problems resulting from this are legion.* ⟨ME < OF < L *legio, -onis* < *legere* choose⟩

le•gion•ar•y ['lidʒə,nɛri] *adj., n., pl.* **-ar•ies.** *—adj.* of or belonging to a legion.
—n. a soldier of a legion.

legionary ant ARMY ANT.

Le•gion•naires' [,lidʒə'nɛr] *n.* **1** a member of the Royal Canadian Legion. **2** formerly, a member of the French Foreign Legion. **3** a soldier of a legion. ⟨< F⟩

Legionnaires' disease a pathological condition caused by the bacterium *Legionella pneumophila* and characterized by fever, cough, muscle aches, and chest pain. ⟨named after a convention of the American Legion in Philadelphia in 1976, where it was first reported⟩

Legion of Honour or **Honor** an honorary society founded by Napoleon in 1802, in which membership is given as a reward for great services to France.

leg•is•late ['lɛdʒə,sleit] *v.* **-lat•ed, -lat•ing. 1** make laws: *Parliament legislates for Canada.* **2** force by legislation: *The council legislated her out of office.* ⟨< *legislator*⟩

leg•is•la•tion [,lɛdʒə'sleiʃən] *n.* **1** the making of laws. **2** the laws made.

leg•is•la•tive ['lɛdʒə,sleitɪv] *adj.* **1** having to do with making laws: *legislative reforms.* **2** having the duty and power of making laws: *Parliament is a legislative body.* **3** ordered by law.
—'leg•is,la•tive•ly, *adv.*

Legislative Assembly *Cdn.* the group of representatives elected to the legislature of any of certain provinces or the Yukon Territory.

Legislative Council *Cdn.* formerly, the upper chamber of the Québec legislature, composed of 24 members appointed for life by the Lieutenant-Governor in Council. The Legislative Council in Québec was abolished in 1968.

leg•is•la•tor ['lɛdʒə,sleitər] *n.* a lawmaker; a member of a legislative body. ⟨< L *legis lator* proposer of a law⟩

leg•is•la•ture ['lɛdʒə,sleitʃər] *n.* **1** a group of persons having the duty and power to make laws for a country, province, or state. Each Canadian province has a legislature. **2** the place where the legislators meet.

le•gist ['lidʒɪst] *n.* a specialist in law.

le•git [lə'dʒɪt] *adj. Slang.* legitimate; truthful. ⟨shortened form⟩

le•git•i•ma•cy [lə'dʒɪtəməsi] *n.* the quality or state of being legitimate or lawful.

le•git•i•mate *adj.* [lə'dʒɪtəmɪt]; *v.* [lə'dʒɪtə,meit] *adj., v.* **-mat•ed, -mat•ing.** *—adj.* **1** rightful; lawful: *The Prince of Wales is the legitimate heir to the throne of England.* **2** allowed; acceptable: *Sickness is a legitimate reason for absence from school or work.* **3** conforming to accepted standards: *a legitimate work of art.* **4** born of parents who are married. **5** resting on, or ruling by, the principle of hereditary right: *the legitimate title to a throne, a legitimate sovereign.* **6** logical: *a legitimate conclusion.* **7** of, having to do with, or designating drama acted on stage, as opposed to film and other stage entertainment such as vaudeville or burlesque: *the legitimate theatre.*
—v. make or declare lawful. ⟨< Med.L *legitimatus* < L *legitimus* lawful < *lex, legis* law⟩ **—le'git•i•mate•ly,** *adv.*
—le'git•i•mate•ness, *n.* **—le,git•i'ma•tion,** *n.*
☛ *Syn. adj.* **1.** See note at LAWFUL.

le•git•i•mist [lə'dʒɪtəmɪst] *n.* a supporter of legitimate authority, especially of claims to rule based on direct descent.
—le'git•i,mism, *n.*

le•git•i•mize [lə'dʒɪtə,maɪz] *v.* **-mized, -miz•ing.** make or declare to be legitimate. **—le,git•i•mi'za•tion,** *n.*

leg•man ['lɛg,mæn] *or* ['lɛgmən] *n.* **-men. 1** a reporter who collects information at the scene of an event. **2** anyone who collects information, delivers messages, or does similar work.

leg–of–mut•ton ['lɛg əv 'mʌtən] *adj.* having the shape of a leg of mutton; wide at one end and narrow at the other: *a leg-of-mutton sleeve.*

leg•ume ['lɛgjum] *or* [lə'gjum] *n.* **1** the fruit or seed of any of various plants of the pea family used for food, especially beans or peas. **2** the plant bearing such fruit. **3** *Botany.* a long, dry, dehiscent fruit; pod. See FRUIT for picture. **4** any plant of the pea family. ⟨< F *légume* vegetable < L *legumen*⟩

le•gu•mi•nous [lə,gjumənəs] *adj.* **1** of or bearing legumes. **2** having to do with or belonging to the pea family of plants.

leg warmers coverings for the legs reaching from knee to ankle, used especially by dancers in preliminary or practice exercises.

lei [lei] *n., pl.* **leis.** a wreath of flowers, leaves, etc. ⟨< Hawaiian⟩
☛ *Hom.* LAY.

Leices•ter ['lɛstər] *n.* a breed of sheep having long wool. ⟨< *Leicester*, a county in England, where this breed originated⟩

leis•ter ['listər] *or* ['lɪstər] *n., v.* *—n.* a spear having two or more barbed prongs, used in fishing.
—v. spear with a leister. ⟨< ON *ljóstr* < *ljósta* strike⟩
☛ *Hom.* LISTER ['lɪstər].

lei•sure ['liʒər] *or* ['lɛʒər] *n.* **1** the time free from required work, in which a person may rest, be amused, and do the things he or she likes to do. **2** (*adjl.*) free; not busy: *leisure hours.* **3** (*adjl.*) having leisure.
at leisure, a free; not busy. **b** without hurry; taking plenty of time.
at (one's) **leisure,** when one has free time; at one's convenience. ⟨ME < OF *leisir* < L *licere* be allowed⟩ **—'lei•sure•less,** *adj.*

lei•sured ['liʒərd] *or* ['lɛʒərd] *adj.* **1** having leisure. **2** leisurely.

lei•sure•ly ['liʒərli] *or* ['lɛʒərli] *adj. or adv.* without hurry; taking plenty of time. **—'lei•sure•li•ness,** *n.*
☛ *Syn. adj.* See note at SLOW.

leisure wear casual, comfortable clothing designed for off-duty hours.

leit•mo•tif or **leit•mo•tiv** ['ləitmou,tif] *n.* **1** *Music.* a short theme or passage in a composition, repeated throughout the work and associated with a certain person, situation, or idea. **2** any repeating theme or subject. ⟨< G *Leitmotiv* leading motive⟩

lek [lɛk] *n.* **1** the basic unit of money in Albania, divided into 100 qintars. See table of money in the Appendix. **2** a coin worth one lek. ⟨< Albanian⟩

lem•an ['lɛmən] *or* ['limən] *n. Archaic.* **1** sweetheart or lover. **2** mistress. ⟨ME *leofman* < OE *lēof* dear + *mann* man⟩
☛ *Hom.* LEMON ['lɛmən].

lem•ming ['lɛmɪŋ] *n.* **1** any of various small, mouselike arctic rodents (genera *Lemmus* and *Dicrostonyx*) having greyish or brownish fur, a short tail, and furry feet. ⟨< Norwegian⟩

lem•nis•cus [lɛm'nɪskəs] *n., pl.* **-nis•ci** [-'nɪsaɪ] *or* [-'nɪski]. *Anatomy.* a group of nerve fibres in the brain. ⟨< Mod.L < L, hanging ribbon < Gk. *lemniskos* ribbon⟩

lem•on ['lɛmən] *n., adj.* *—n.* **1** an acid-tasting, light yellow citrus fruit growing in warm climates. **2** a thorny tree that bears this fruit. **3** a pale yellow. **4** *Slang.* a thing (usually a car) that or person who is considered inferior or disagreeable: *The last car I bought was a lemon.* **5** a soft drink flavoured with lemon juice.
—adj. pale yellow. ⟨ME < OF *limon* < Arabic *laimun* < Persian *limun*⟩
☛ *Hom.* LEMAN.

lem•on•ade [,lɛmə'neid] *or* ['lɛmə,neid] *n.* a soft drink made of lemon juice, sugar, and water. ⟨< F *limonade*⟩

lemon balm a plant (*Melissa officinalis*) of the mint family, whose lemon-scented leaves are used as seasoning.

lemon mint a plant (*Mentha piperita*) having pink or white flowers, and leaves that smell like lemon when crushed.

lemon oil an oil obtained from lemon rinds or manufactured synthetically, smelling of lemon, and used in perfumes, flavourings, and furniture polish.

lemon yellow a clear, light yellow, the colour of lemon rind.

lem•pi•ra [lɛm'pirə] *n.* **1** the basic unit of money in Honduras, divided into 100 centavos. See table of money in the Appendix. **2** a coin worth one lempira. ⟨< Am.Sp.⟩

le•mur ['limər] *n.* **1** any of a family (Lemuridae) of primates found mainly in the forests of Madagascar, having a foxlike face, large eyes, soft, woolly fur, and a long, bushy tail. **2** any of various similar or related animals, such as a loris. ⟨< L *lemures*, pl., spectres, ghosts; with reference to their nocturnal habits⟩

Le•na•pe ['lɛnə,pi] *n.* **1** a member of an American Indian people who lived in the Delaware River valley. **2** the Algonquian language of these people.

lend [lɛnd] *v.* **lent, lend•ing. 1** let another have or use for a time: *Will you lend me your bicycle for an hour?* **2** give the use of (money) for a fixed or specified amount of payment: *Banks lend money and charge interest.* **3** make a loan or loans. **4** give; contribute; add: *A lace curtain lends charm to a window. The Red Cross is quick to lend aid in time of disaster.*
lend a hand, help: *She lent a hand with the dishes.*
lend itself to, be suitable for: *The old engine lent itself to our purposes.*
lend (oneself) **to,** make oneself available for: *Don't lend yourself to foolish schemes.* ⟨OE *lǣnan* < *lǣn* loan⟩ **—'lend•er,** *n.*
☛ *Usage.* See note at LOAN.

lend–lease ['lɛnd 'lis] *n., v.* **-leased, -leas•ing.** *—n.* a system of making a loan of equipment in return for some service or material.
—v. lend under this system.

length [lɛŋθ], [lɛŋkθ], *or* [lɛnθ] *n.* **1** how long a thing is; a thing's measurement from end to end; the longest way a thing can be measured: *the length of your arm.* **2** the distance a thing extends: *The length of a race is the distance run.* **3** the extent in time; duration: *the length of a visit, the length of an hour.* **4** a long stretch or extent: *Quite a length of hair hung down in a braid.* **5** a piece or portion of cloth, pipe, rope, etc. of given length often either cut from a larger piece, or meant to be joined to another piece: *a length of rope, three lengths of pipe.* **6** the distance from end to end of a boat, horse, etc., considered as a unit of measurement in racing: *The grey horse finished the race two lengths ahead of the brown one.* **7** *Phonetics.* the quantity of a vowel, whether short or long.
at arm's length. See ARM[1].
at full length, with the body stretched out flat.
at length, a with all the details; fully: *She told of her adventures at length.* **b** at last; finally: *At length, after many delays, the meeting started.*
go to any length, do everything possible. ⟨OE *length* < *lang* long[1]⟩

length•en ['lɛŋθən], ['lɛŋkθən], *or* ['lɛnθən] *v.* **1** make longer. **2** become or grow longer.
☛ *Syn.* **1. Lengthen,** EXTEND, PROLONG = make longer. **Lengthen** = make longer in space or time: *There is no way to lengthen a day.* **Extend** suggests stretching out beyond the present point or limits: *We had to extend the time allowed for returning the questionnaires.* **Prolong** = lengthen in time beyond a normal, proper, or desirable limit: *She decided to prolong her visit.*

length•wise ['lɛŋθ,waɪz], ['lɛŋkθ,waɪz], *or* ['lɛnθ,waɪz] *adv. or adj.* in the direction of the length. Also, **lengthways.**

length•y ['lɛŋθi], ['lɛŋkθi], *or* ['lɛnθi] *adj.* **length•i•er, length•i•est.** long or too long: *Her directions were so lengthy that everybody got confused.* **—'length•i•ly,** *adv.* **—'length•i•ness,** *n.*

le•nien•cy ['linjənsi] *or* ['liniənsi] *n., pl.* **-cies.** mildness; gentleness; mercy, especially as regards justice. Also, **lenience.**

le•nient ['linjənt] *or* ['liniənt] *adj.* mild or gentle; merciful: *a lenient punishment.* ⟨< L *leniens, -entis,* ppr. of *lenire* soften < *lenis* mild⟩ **—'le•ni•ent•ly,** *adv.*

le•nis ['linɪs] *or* ['leinɪs] *n. Phonetics.* a speech sound with no aspiration, such as, in English, [b], [d], [g], [dʒ], [v], [ð], [z], [ʒ], [m], [n], [ŋ], [r], [l], [w], [j], and all vowels. Compare FORTIS. ⟨< L: soft, gentle, calm⟩

len•i•tive ['lɛnətɪv] *adj., n. —adj.* **1** softening; soothing; mitigating. **2** mildly laxative.
—n. **1** anything that soothes or softens; palliative. **2** a mild laxative. ⟨< Med.L *lenitivus* < L *lenitus,* pp. of *lenire* soften⟩

len•i•ty ['lɛnəti] *n., pl.* **-ties.** mildness; gentleness; mercifulness. ⟨< L *lenitas* < *lenis* mild⟩

lens [lɛnz] *n., pl.* **lens•es. 1** a piece of glass or similar transparent substance having two curved surfaces or one plane and one curved surface, used singly or in combination to focus rays of light passing through it. Lenses are used in cameras to form images and in telescopes, etc. to make things look larger and nearer. See CONCAVE and CONVEX for pictures. **2** a combination of two or more of these pieces, especially as used in a camera. **3** a clear, biconvex, lens-shaped, elastic structure in the eye directly behind the iris, that directs and focusses light rays upon the retina. The curvature of the lens changes to accommodate varying distances. See EYE for picture. **4** a device that focusses sound waves, streams of electrons, etc. **5** something shaped like an optical lens such as a round, convex formation of ice in permafrost or bitumen in sand or rock. ⟨< L *lens, lentis* lentil (which has a biconvex shape)⟩ **—'lens•less,** *adj.* **—'lens,like,** *adj.*

lent [lɛnt] *v.* pt. and pp. of LEND.
☛ *Hom.* LEANT.

Lent [lɛnt] *n.* the forty weekdays before Easter, observed in many Christian churches as a time for fasting and repenting of sins. ⟨OE *lencten* spring < W.Gmc. **lang* -long[1] (with reference to lengthening days)⟩

len•ta•men•te [,lɛntə'mɛntei] *adv. Music.* slowly. ⟨< Ital.⟩

len•tan•do [lɛn'tɑndou] *adj. Music.* slowing down. ⟨< Ital.⟩

Lent•en or **lent•en** ['lɛntən] *adj.* of Lent; during Lent; suitable for Lent. ⟨originally noun; OE *lencten.* See LENT.⟩

len•ti•cel ['lɛntə,sɛl] *n. Botany.* a ventilating pore in the bark of woody plants. ⟨< F *lenticelle,* dim. of L *lens, lentis* lentil, because of its shape⟩

len•ti•cle ['lɛntəkəl] *n.* the part of a clock case below the dial, with a window revealing the pendulum.

len•tic•u•lar [lɛn'tɪkjələr] *adj.* shaped like a lens.

len•ti•go [lɛn'taɪgou] *n., pl.* **-tig•i•nes** [-'tɪdʒə,niz]. *Medicine.* a freckle. ⟨< L *Lens* lentil⟩

len•til ['lɛntəl] *or* ['lɛntɪl] *n.* **1** a plant (*Lens culinaris*) of the pea family, having seeds shaped like biconvex lenses, native to S Europe and Asia but widely cultivated elsewhere. **2** the edible seed of this plant. ⟨< F *lentille* < L *lenticula,* dim. of *lens, lentis* lentil⟩

len•to ['lɛntou] *adj., adv., n. Music. —adj.* slow.
—adv. slowly.
—n. a slow movement or passage. ⟨< Ital.⟩

l'en•voi or **l'en•voy** ['lɛnvɔɪ] *or* [lɒn'vwɑ] *n.* **1** a short stanza ending a poem. **2** a postscript to a prose work, giving a moral, dedication, etc. ⟨< F *l'envoi,* literally, the sending. Cf. ENVOY[2].⟩

Le•o ['liou] *n., gen.* **Le•o•nis** [li,ounɪs] *for 1.* **1** *Astronomy.* a northern constellation thought of as having the shape of a lion. **2** *Astrology.* **a** the fifth sign of the zodiac. The sun enters Leo about July 22. See ZODIAC for picture. **b** a person born under this sign. ⟨< L⟩

Leo Minor a northern constellation near Leo.

le•one [li'oun] *or* [li'ouni] *n.* **1** the basic unit of money in Sierra Leone, divided into 100 cents. See table of money in the Appendix. **2** a note worth one leone.

Le•o•nid ['liənɪd] *n.* one of a shower of meteors, as if from the constellation Leo, occurring annually about November 14.

le•o•nine ['liə,naɪn] *adj.* of or like a lion. ⟨< L *leoninus* < *leo* lion⟩

leop•ard ['lɛpərd] *n.* **1** a large animal (*Panthera pardus*) of the cat family native to Africa and southern Asia, having usually buff or tawny fur with small, black spots arranged in rosettes. **2** any of several similar and related animals, such as the jaguar, cheetah, or ocelot. **3** the fur of the leopard. **4** *Heraldry.* a side-view representation of a lion with the face turned toward the viewer and one leg raised, as in the arms of England. ⟨ME < OF < L < Gk. *leopardos* < *leōn* lion + *pardos* leopard⟩

leop•ard•ess ['lɛpərdɪs] *n.* a female leopard.

leopard seal *Cdn.* HARBOUR SEAL.

le•o•tard ['liə,tɑrd] *n.* **1** a one-piece, close-fitting, knitted garment having long or short sleeves and usually extending just to the thighs, with holes for the legs. **2 leotards,** *pl.* tights. ⟨< Jules *Léotard,* 19c. French gymnast⟩

lep•er ['lɛpər] *n.* a person who has leprosy. ⟨ME < OF < L < Gk. *lepra* leprosy. See LEPROUS.⟩

lep•i•dop•ter•an [,lɛpə'dɒptərən] *n.* any of a large order (Lepidoptera) of insects comprising the butterflies, moths, and skippers, all having four broad, membranous wings covered with very tiny, often brightly coloured scales. The larvae of lepidopterans are called caterpillars and have chewing mouth parts for feeding on plants; the adults have sucking mouth parts. Also, **lepidopteron.** ⟨< NL *Lepidoptera,* pl. < Gk. *lepis, -idos* scale + *pteron* wing⟩

lep•i•dop•ter•ist [,lɛpɪ'dɒptərɪst] *n.* a person who studies the lepidopterans.

lep•i•dop•ter•ous [ˌlɛpɪ'dɒptərəs] *adj.* of or having to do with the lepidopterans.

lep•o•rine ['lɛpəˌraɪn] *or* ['lɛpərɪn] *adj.* having to do with rabbits and hares. ⟨< L *Leporinus* < *lepus* hare⟩

lep•re•chaun ['lɛprəˌkɒn] *n. Irish folklore.* a sprite or goblin resembling a little old man. ⟨< Irish *leipreachán, lupracán* < Old Irish *lúchorpán* < *lú* small + *corp* body < L *corpus* body; cf. *little people*, a term still used in Ireland for the fairies⟩

lep•ro•sy ['lɛprəsi] *n.* HANSEN'S DISEASE.

lep•rous ['lɛprəs] *adj.* **1** having leprosy. **2** of or like leprosy. **3** scaly or scurfy. **4** causing leprosy. ⟨< L *leprosus* < *lepra* leprosy < Gk. *lepra* < *lepein* to peel⟩ **—'lep•rous•ly,** *adv.* **—'lep•rous•ness,** *n.*

lep•ton[1] ['lɛptɒn] *n., pl.* **-ta** [-tə]. **1** a unit of money in Greece, equal to 1/100 of a drachma. See table of money in the Appendix. Also called **lepto** ['lɛptou]. **2** a coin worth one lepton. ⟨< Gk.⟩

lep•ton[2] ['lɛptɒn] *n. Physics.* any of a class of elementary particles that take part in weak interactions, have a spin of ½, and have less mass than mesons or baryons. The leptons include the electron, the muon, and the neutrino, and their antiparticles.

lep•to•spi•ro•sis [ˌlɛptouspaɪ'rousɪs] *n.* an infectious disease of humans and domestic animals, caused by spirochetes found in impure water, and affecting the liver, kidneys, and other organs. ⟨< NL *Leptospira* genus name (< Gk. *lepto-* thin + *speira* coil, spiral) + E *-osis*⟩

Lep•us ['lɛpəs] *or* ['lipəs] *n., gen.* **Lep•o•ris** ['lɛpərɪs]. *Astronomy.* a southern constellation near Orion. ⟨< L⟩

les•bi•an ['lɛzbiən] *n., adj.* *—n.* **1** a homosexual woman. **2 Lesbian,** a native or inhabitant of the Greek island of Lesbos.
—adj. **1** of or having to do with lesbians or lesbianism. **2 Lesbian,** of or having to do with Lesbos or its people. ⟨< *Lesbos*, the home of the supposedly homosexual Greek poetess *Sappho*, who lived about 600 B.C.⟩

les•bi•an•ism ['lɛzbiəˌnɪzəm] *n.* homosexuality in women.

lèse–ma•jes•té [lɛzmaʒɛs'te] *n. French.* lese-majesty.

lese–maj•es•ty ['liz 'mædʒɪsti] *n.* a crime or offence against the sovereign power in a state; treason. ⟨< F *lèse-majesté* < L *laesa majestas* injured majesty⟩

le•sion ['liʒən] *n.* **1** an injury; hurt. **2** *Medicine.* a diseased condition often causing a change in the structure of an organ or tissue. ⟨< L *laesio, -onis* injury < *laedere* to strike⟩

Le•so•tho [lə'soutou], [lə'souθou], *or* [lə'sutu] *n.* a country in SE Africa, formerly called Basutoland.

less [lɛs] *adj., n., adv., prep.* *—adj.* **1** smaller; not so much: *of less width, to eat less meat.* **2** fewer: *Five is less than seven.* **3** lower in age, rank, or importance: *no less a person than the Prince of Wales.*
more or less, a somewhat: *We are all more or less impatient.* **b** about, approximately: *The cost is fifty dollars, more or less.*
—n. a smaller amount or quantity: *She refused to take less than five dollars.*
—adv. to a smaller extent or degree: *less important.*
—prep. lacking; without; minus: *a year less two days.* ⟨OE *lǣs(sa)*⟩
☛ *Usage.* **Less,** LESSER. Both are used as comparative (of *little*), **less** more usually referring to size or quantity: *less time, less food*; **lesser** referring to value or importance: *a lesser writer.*
☛ *Usage.* See FEW for another note.

–less *suffix.* **1** without; that has no ——: *homeless = without a home.* **2** that does not ——: *ceaseless = that does not cease.* **3** that cannot be ——ed: *countless.* ⟨OE *-lēas*, suffixal use of *lēas* free from⟩
☛ *Usage.* **-less** is freely added to almost any noun and many verbs to form adjectives with the above meanings.

les•see [lɛ'si] *n.* a person to whom a lease is granted.

less•en ['lɛsən] *v.* **1** grow less. **2** make less; decrease. **3** represent as less; minimize; belittle.
☛ *Hom.* LESSON.

less•er ['lɛsər] *adj.* **1** less; smaller. **2** less important or of lower quality.
☛ *Usage.* See note at LESS.

les•son ['lɛsən] *n., v.* *—n.* **1** something learned or studied. **2** a unit of learning or teaching; what is to be studied or practised at one time: *Our math text is divided into twenty lessons.* **3** a meeting of a student or class with a teacher to study a given subject: *She has gone for a piano lesson. There will be no lesson today.* **4** an instructive experience, serving to encourage or warn: *The accident was a lesson to me.* **5** a selection from the Bible or other sacred writings, read as part of a religious service. **6** a rebuke; lecture.
—v. **1** give a lesson to. **2** rebuke; lecture. ⟨ME < OF *leçon* < L *lectio, -onis* reading < *legere* read⟩
☛ *Hom.* LESSEN.

les•sor ['lɛsɔr] *or* [lɛ'sɔr] *n.* a person who grants a lease.

lest [lɛst] *conj.* **1** for fear that: *Be careful lest you fall from that tree.* **2** that: *They were afraid lest he should come too late to save them.* ⟨ME *leste*, late OE *the lǣste*, earlier *thȳ lǣs the* by so much the less that⟩

let[1] [lɛt] *v.* **let, let•ting. 1** allow; permit: *Let the dog have a bone.* **2** allow to pass, go, or come: *Let all passengers board ship.* **3** allow to run out: *Doctors used to let blood from people to lessen a fever.* **4** rent; hire out: *to let a boat by the hour.* **5** be rented: *The house lets for $1450 a month.* **6** *Let* is used in giving suggestions or commands. *Let's go home* means *I suggest that we go home.* **7** suppose; assume: *Let the two lines be parallel.*
let down, a lower or let fall. **b** slow up: *As her interest in the work wore off, she began to let down.* **c** disappoint: *Don't let us down today; we're counting on you to help us.* **d** of mother's milk, begin to flow as a result of breast stimulation.
let go, a allow to escape; set at liberty; release one's hold of: *to let go a rope or an anchor. Let me go.* **b** give up; abandon; cease to regard or consider: *He let go all thought of winning a prize.* **c** dismiss from a job.
let in, admit; permit to enter.
let in for, expose to; cause (trouble, unpleasantness, etc.) for: *He let his friends in for a lot of questioning when he left town so suddenly.*
let in on, reveal (privileged information) to or allow to take part in.
let loose, allow to go free; liberate; release from restraint.
let off, a allow to go free; release: *let off poisonous gases. The drunk driver was let off with a small fine.* **b** free from; excuse from doing (a task): *The teacher would not let us off homework.* **c** fire; explode: *to let off a detonation.*
let off steam, give way to one's feelings: *She let off steam by shouting.*
let on, *Informal.* **a** allow to be known; reveal: *He didn't let on his surprise at the news.* **b** pretend; make believe: *She let on that she didn't see me.*
let (oneself) **go, a** cease to restrain oneself. **b** cease to take care of one's appearance.
let out, a permit to go out. **b** make (a garment) larger. **c** rent: *Has the room been let out yet?* **d** *Informal.* dismiss or be dismissed: *School lets out at 3:30.* **e** make known; disclose.
let up, *Informal.* **a** stop; pause: *They refused to let up in the fight.* **b** ease off; lessen. ⟨OE *lǣtan*⟩

let[2] [lɛt] *v.* **let•ted** or **let, let•ting;** *n.* *—v. Archaic.* prevent; hinder; obstruct.
—n. **1** *Archaic.* a prevention; hindrance; obstruction. **2** *Tennis, etc.* interference with the ball. When this fault occurs, the ball or point must be played over again.
without let or hindrance, with nothing to prevent, hinder, or obstruct. ⟨OE *lettan* < *læt* late⟩

–let *suffix.* **1** little ——: *booklet, streamlet, wavelet.* **2** a thing worn as a band on ——: *armlet, wristlet.* ⟨< OF *-elet* < *-el* (< L *-ellus*, dim. suffix or < L *-ale*, neut.) + *-et* < VL *-ittus*, dim. suffix, ? < Celtic⟩

let•down ['lɛtˌdaʊn] *n.* **1** a slowing up. **2** *Informal.* disappointment. **3** the reflex that causes mother's milk to begin flowing upon breast stimulation.

le•thal ['liθəl] *adj.* causing death; deadly: *lethal weapons, a lethal dose.* ⟨< L *let(h)alis* < *letum* death⟩ **—'le•thal•ly,** *adv.*
☛ *Syn.* See note at FATAL.

le•thar•gic [lə'θardʒɪk] *adj.* **1** unnaturally drowsy; sluggish; dull: *A hot, humid day often makes us feel lethargic.* **2** producing lethargy. **—le'thar•gi•cal•ly,** *adv.*

leth•ar•gy ['lɛθərdʒi] *n., pl.* **-gies. 1** drowsy dullness; lack of energy; sluggish inactivity. **2** a condition of unnatural drowsiness or prolonged sleep. ⟨< L < Gk. *lēthargia* < *lēthargos* forgetful < *lēthē* forgetfulness + *argos* lazy⟩

Le•the ['liθi] *n.* **1** *Greek mythology.* a river in Hades. By drinking its water, the dead could forget the past. **2** forgetfulness; oblivion. ⟨< L < Gk. *lēthē* oblivion⟩

Le•the•an [lɪ'θiən] *or* ['liθiən] *adj.* **1** having to do with Lethe or its water. **2** causing forgetfulness.

let's [lɛts] let us. See LET[1] (def. 6).

Lett [lɛt] *n.* **1** a member of a group of people living in Latvia, Lithuania, Estonia, and other Baltic regions. **2** their Baltic language; Lettish.

let•ter ['lɛtər] *n., v.* *—n.* **1** a symbol or sign, used alone or combined, that represents speech sounds; a character of an alphabet: *Both* must *and* mask *have four letters.* **2** a written or printed message, usually enclosed in an envelope and delivered by mail. **3** an official document granting some right or privilege. **4** the exact wording; actual terms: *He kept the letter of the law but not the spirit.* **5 letters,** *pl.* **a** literature. **b** a knowledge of literature; literary culture. **c** the profession of an author. **6** *Printing.* **a** a bit of metal type bearing a letter; typeface. **b** a particular style of type. **7** a badge representing the initial letter of a school or college, given as an award for achievement, especially in athletics.
to the letter, very exactly; just as one has been told: *I carried out your order to the letter.*
—v. **1** mark with letters. **2** inscribe (something) in letters. **3** make letters. ⟨ME < OF < L *littera*⟩ **—'let•ter•er,** *n.* **—'let•ter•less,** *adj.*

☛ *Syn. n.* **2.** Letter, EPISTLE = a written message. **Letter** is the general word applying to a written, typed, or printed message, either personal, business, or official: *Put a stamp on that letter before you mail it.* **Epistle,** chiefly literary, applies to a long letter written in formal or elegant language, especially one intended to teach or advise: *the epistles of famous poets.*

☛ *Usage.* Sometimes a single sound in English is represented in spelling by a combination of letters. Thus, the two letters *sh*, as in *wish*, represent one sound; in *match*, three letters, *tch*, represent one sound. On the other hand, one letter or combination of letters can stand for different sounds, as *ough* in *bough* and *though.*

letter bomb an explosive device contained in an envelope, designed to explode when the person to whom it is addressed opens the envelope.

letter carrier a person who collects or delivers mail: *My daughter was a letter carrier in Whitehorse.*

letter drop a slot in a door for delivery of mail.

let•tered ['lɛtərd] *adj., v.* *—adj.* **1** marked with letters. **2** able to read and write; educated. **3** knowing literature; having literary culture.
—v. pt. and pp. of LETTER.

let•ter•gram ['lɛtər,græm] *n.* a type of telegram in which up to 50 words are allowed at reduced rates, because it is transmitted outside regular business hours.

let•ter•head ['lɛtər,hɛd] *n.* **1** words printed at the top of a sheet of writing paper, usually the name and address of the person or company using it. **2** paper so printed.

let•ter•ing ['lɛtərɪŋ] *n., v.* *—n.* **1** letters drawn, painted, stamped, etc. **2** a marking with letters; the making of letters. **3** calligraphy.
—v. ppr. of LETTER.

letter of credit a document issued by a bank, allowing the person named in it to draw money up to a specified amount.

letter opener a long knife with two blunt edges, for opening sealed envelopes.

let•ter–per•fect ['lɛtər 'pərfɪkt] *adj.* **1** knowing one's part or lesson perfectly. **2** correct in every detail.

let•ter•press ['lɛtər,prɛs] *n.* printed words, as distinguished from illustrations, etc.

letter press **1** a machine for making copies of letters. **2** printing from type, or from relief plates, as distinguished from offset, lithography, photogravure, etc.

letter–quality ['lɛtər ,kwɒləti] *adj.* of computer printing, sufficiently clear and well-designed to be used in a formal letter. Compare NEAR-LETTER QUALITY.

letter rate the postage rate for first-class mail.

letters of marque or **letters of marque and reprisal** an official document giving a person permission from a government to capture the merchant ships of an enemy.

letter–size ['lɛtar,saɪz] *adj.* **1** of paper, measuring 22 cm × 28 cm. **2** of stationery, etc., made to fit letter-size paper: *a letter-size envelope.* Compare LEGAL-SIZE.

letters patent *Law.* an official document giving a person or a corporation authority from a government to do some act or to have some right, such as a patent.

Let•tish ['lɛtɪʃ] *adj., n.* *—adj.* of or having to do with the Letts or their language.
—n. the Baltic language of the Letts; Latvian.

let•tre de ca•chet ['lɛtʀdəka'ʃe] *French.* formerly, a letter under the seal of the King of France, especially one ordering someone to be sent to prison or exile.

let•tuce ['lɛtəs] *n.* **1** any of a genus (*Lactuca*) of annual plants of the composite family, especially a common garden vegetable (*L. sativa*) grown in several varieties, all having large, crisp, green leaves that grow out from a very short, central stalk. **2** the leaves of garden lettuce. Lettuce is usually eaten raw, in salads. ⟨ME < OF *laitues*, pl. < L *lactuca* lettuce < *lac, lactis* milk; with reference to the milky juice of the plant⟩

let•up ['lɛt,ʌp] *n. Informal.* a lessening or stopping: *After a slight letup, the rain started again, harder than ever.*

le•u ['lɛu] *n., pl.* **lei** [lei]. **1** the basic unit of money in Moldova and Romania, divided into 100 bani. See table of money in the Appendix. **2** a coin or note worth one leu. ⟨< Romanian⟩

leu•co•cyte or **leu•ko•cyte** ['lukə,səit] *n. Anatomy.* any of the white or colourless cells that occur in the blood and help the body fight infection; white blood cell. ⟨< Gk. *leukos* white + E *-cyte*⟩

leu•ke•mi•a [lu'kimjə] *or* [lu'kimiə] *n. Pathology.* a type of cancer occurring in several forms, characterized by the abnormal growth of white blood cells (leucocytes) in the bone marrow, lymphatic tissue, or spleen, usually resulting in an excess of these cells in the blood. ⟨< NL < Gk. *leukos* white + *-aimia* blood < *haima*⟩

leu•pro•lide ['luprə,laɪd] *n.* a drug used to treat prostate cancer in certain stages.

lev [lɛf] *n., pl.* **leva** ['lɛvə]. **1** the basic unit of money in Bulgaria, divided into 100 stotinki. See table of money in the Appendix. **2** a coin worth one lev. ⟨< Bulgarian⟩

Le•val•loi•si•an [,lɛvə'lɔɪziən] *or* [,lɛvə'lɔɪʒən] *adj.* of or having to do with a Middle Paleolithic culture, characterized by the production of sharp-edged flake tools. ⟨after *Levallois*-Perret, a city in N central France, where such tools were found⟩

le•vam•i•sole [lə'væmɪ,soul] *n.* a drug used to treat certain forms of cancer.

Le•van•tine ['lɛvən,taɪn], ['lɛvən,tin], *or* [lə'væntɪn] *n., adj.* *—n.* **1** formerly, an inhabitant or a ship of the Levant, a region that includes the countries on the Mediterranean Sea east of Italy. **2 levantine,** a strong, usually black, twilled silk cloth originally made in the Levant.
—adj. of or having to do with the Levant.

le•va•tor [lɪ'veitər] *n.* **1** a muscle used in lifting. Compare DEPRESSOR (def. 2). **2** a device for lifting the depressed part of a fractured skull. ⟨< NL, special use of Med.L *levātor* one who raises recruits (or levies taxes) < L *levātus* raised (pp. of levāre) + *-or*⟩

lev•ee[1] ['lɛvi] *n.* a bank built to keep a river from overflowing: *Many citizens guarded the levees during the flood.* ⟨< F *levée* < *lever* raise < L *levare*⟩
☛ *Hom.* LEVY.

lev•ee[2] or **lev•ée** ['lɛvi], [lə'vi], *or* [lə'vei] *n.* **1** *Cdn.* a usually formal reception, especially one held during the day: *The regiment holds a levee on New Year's Day. He received an invitation to the Governor General's levee.* **2** formerly, a reception held by a person of high rank on rising from bed. French kings used to hold levees in the morning while they were being dressed. ⟨< F *levé, lever* a rising < *lever* raise. See LEVEE[1].⟩
☛ *Hom.* LEVY ['lɛvi].

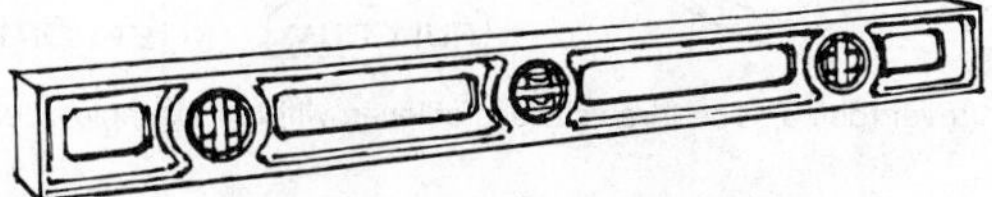

A level. It has vertical and horizontal glass tubes containing a liquid with an air bubble inside. If the surface on or against which the level is placed is perfectly horizontal (or vertical) the bubble stays in the centre.

lev•el ['lɛvəl] *adj., n., v.* **-elled** or **-eled, -el•ling** or **-el•ing.** *—adj.* **1** having the same height everywhere; completely flat and even, like the surface of still water: *level ground.* **2** not sloping; horizontal: *The floor is not quite level.* **3** of equal height or in the same plane: *The table is level with the window sill.* **4** *Informal.* steady, calm, or sensible: *She's got a level head. He answered in a level voice.* **5** equal or balanced in rank, degree, quality, etc.: *The two friends remained level in rank, but not in salary.* **6** of, suited to, or involving a particular rank, degree, etc. (*used only in compounds*): *High-level talks have begun between the major powers.*

(one's) **level best,** *Informal.* one's very best; as well or as much as one can do: *He tried his level best but couldn't persuade her.*
—n. **1** an instrument for showing whether a surface is horizontal. **2** a measuring of differences in height or altitude between two points by means of such an instrument: *to take a level.* **3** a level position or condition. **4** a place or surface that is level: *The climbers stopped for breath when they reached the level.* **5** height: *We hung the picture at eye level. By evening the flood waters had risen to a level of 3 m.* **6** degree, rate, or style: *The noise level in the library makes it hard to concentrate. He kept his remarks at a very informal level.* **7** a position or grade on a social, intellectual, or moral scale: *a professional level of work.*
find (one's) **level,** arrive at the most natural or most appropriate position, rank, etc.: *After failing as a painter, he found his level as a political cartoonist.*
on the level, *Informal.* **a** honest and straightforward: *Is that offer on the level?* **b** honestly and straightforwardly: *to work on the level.*
—v. **1** make level: *They used a bulldozer to level the ground.* **2** come to a level position or condition (*usually used with* **off** *or* **out**): *The path climbs for about 200 m and then levels off.* **3** demolish or lay low; raze: *The tornado levelled every house in the village.* **4** raise and hold level for shooting; aim: *The soldier levelled her rifle.* **5** aim or direct (words, intentions, etc.): *She levelled a stinging rebuke at the speaker.* **6** *Slang.* be honest and frank; tell the truth (*used with* **with**): *You can level with me; what really happened?* **7** bring to a common level or plane; remove or reduce differences: *Death levels all human ranks.* ⟨ME < OF *livel* < VL *libellum* < L *libella,* dim. of *libra* balance⟩ **—'lev•el•ler** or **'lev•el•er,** *n.* **—'lev•el•ly,** *adv.* **—'lev•el•ness,** *n.*

level crossing *Cdn.* a place where a railway track crosses a street or another railway track on the same level; railway crossing.

lev•el–head•ed ['lɛvəl 'hɛdɪd] *adj.* having good common sense or good judgment; sensible. **—'lev•el'head•ed•ness,** *n.* **—'lev•el-'head•ed•ly,** *adv.*

level rail crossing *Cdn.* LEVEL CROSSING.

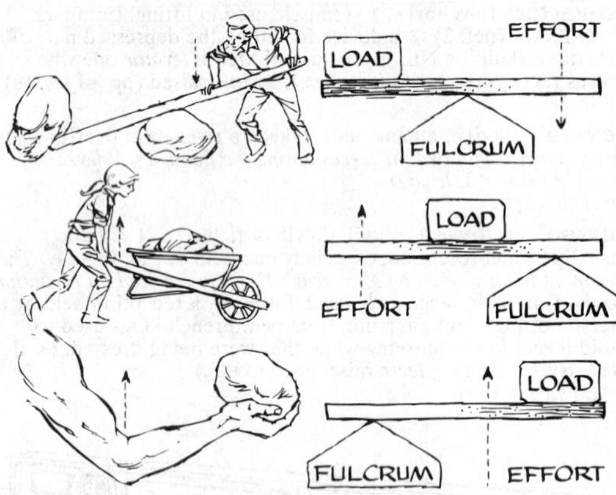

Lever (def. 3). The three classes of lever, with an example of each.

le•ver ['livər] *or (esp. for v.)* ['lɛvər] *n., v. —n.* **1** a bar used for moving or prying something: *A crowbar is a lever.* **2** anything used as a tool to influence or force: *He used his mother's name as a social lever.* **3** a simple machine consisting of a rigid bar supported and turning on a fixed point called the fulcrum, using force, or effort, at a second point to move or lift a mass situated at a third point: *A wheelbarrow is one kind of lever.* **4** a small handle, grip, etc. that one moves to operate a control on a machine, etc.: *To raise or lower the convertible's roof, just pull this little lever.*
—v. **1** pry, raise, or move with or as if with a lever: *She levered the rock out of the ground.* **2** use a lever or levers: *He levered for weeks and finally got the job.* ⟨ME < OF *leveor* < *lever* raise < L *levare*⟩
☛ *Hom.* LIVRE ['livər].

lev•er•age ['lɛvərɪdʒ] *or* ['livərɪdʒ] *n.* **1** the action of a lever. **2** the advantage or power gained by using a lever. **3** increased power of action.

leveraged buy–out *Business.* the purchase of a company using as collateral the assets of the company to be bought.

lev•er•et ['lɛvərɪt] *n.* a young hare. ⟨< AF *leveret,* dim. of OF *lievre* < L *lepus, -poris* hare⟩

le•vi•a•than [lə'vaɪəθən] *n.* **1** in the Bible, a huge sea animal. **2** a huge ship. **3** any great and powerful person or thing. ⟨< LL < Hebrew *livyathan* dragon⟩

lev•i•tate ['lɛvə,teit] *v.* **-tat•ed, -tat•ing. 1** rise or float in the air. **2** cause to rise or float in the air. ⟨< L *levitas* lightness (see LEVITY), modelled after *gravitate*⟩ **—'lev•i,ta•tor,** *n.*

lev•i•ta•tion [,lɛvə'teiʃən] *n.* **1** a levitating. **2** the act or process of rising, or raising (a body), from the ground by spiritualistic means. **—,lev•i'ta•tion•al,** *adj.* **—'lev•i,ta•tive,** *adj.*

Le•vite ['livəit] *n.* a member of the tribe of Levi, from which assistants to the Jewish priests were chosen.

lev•i•ty ['lɛvəti] *n., pl.* **-ties. 1** lack of seriousness; lightness of spirit or mind, especially when excessive or not appropriate; frivolity: *The issue is a serious one and should not be treated with levity.* **2** a light or flippant remark. ⟨< L *levitas* < *levis* light⟩

levo– *combining form.* toward the left: *levorotation.* ⟨< L *lævus* left, on the left⟩

le•vo•bu•no•lol [,lɛvou'bjunə,lɒl] *n.* a drug used to treat certain eye conditions, including glaucoma.

le•vo•do•pa [,lɛvou'doupə] *or* [,livou'doupə] *n.* a drug used to treat certain patients with Parkinson's disease. *Formula*: $C_9H_{11}NO_4$ *Abbrev.*: L-dopa

le•vo•gy•rate [,livə'dʒaɪreit] *adj.* levorotatory.

le•vo•nor•ges•trel [,lɛvounɔr'dʒɛstrəl] *n.* a drug used as an oral contraceptive.

le•vo•ro•ta•tion [,livourou'teiʃən] *n.* a rotation toward the left.

le•vo•ro•ta•to•ry [,livə'routə,tɔri] *adj.* turning to the left.

le•vor•pha•nol [lɛ'vɔrfə,nɒl] *n.* an analgesic drug. *Formula*: $C_{21}H_{29}NO_7$

lev•u•lose ['lɛvjə,lous] *n.* a form of sugar in honey, fruits, etc.; fruit sugar. *Formula*: $C_6H_{12}O_6$ ⟨< L *laevus* left; under polarized light its plane of polarization is turned to the left⟩

lev•y ['lɛvi] *v.* **lev•ied, lev•y•ing;** *n., pl.* **lev•ies.**
—v. **1** order to be paid: *The government levies taxes to pay its expenses.* **2** draft or enlist for an army: *to levy troops in time of war.* **3** seize by law for unpaid debts.
levy war on, make war on; start a war against.
—n. **1** an act of levying. **2** money collected by authority or force. **3** the troops drafted or enlisted for an army. ⟨< F *levée* < *lever* raise. See LEVEE[1].⟩
☛ *Hom.* LEVEE.

lewd [lud] *adj.* **1** showing or designed to arouse sexual desire, especially in a coarse or offensive way; obscene: *a lewd glance, lewd pictures.* **2** *Archaic.* uneducated; ignorant. ⟨OE *lǣwede* lay, unlearned⟩ **—'lewd•ly,** *adv.* **—'lewd•ness,** *n.*

lew•is•ite ['luɪ,səit] *n.* a colourless or brown oily liquid, developed for use in chemical warfare as a poison gas. It causes severe blistering of the skin and lungs. *Formula*: $C_2H_2AsCl_3$ ⟨after W. Lee *Lewis* (1878-1943), the American chemist who developed it⟩

lex [lɛks] *n., pl.* **le•ges** ['lɛgeis] *or* ['lɛdʒeis]. *Latin.* law.

lex•eme ['lɛksim] *n. Linguistics.* a word or stem; a meaningful vocabulary unit.

lex•i•cal ['lɛksəkəl] *adj.* **1** of or having to do with words as separate units, rather than as elements of phrases, sentences, etc. **2** of or having to do with lexicography or a lexicon. **—,lex•i'cal•i•ty,** *n.* **—'lex•i•cal•ly,** *adv.*

lex•i•cog•ra•pher [,lɛksə'kɒgrəfər] *n.* a person who compiles dictionaries; the author, editor, or compiler of a dictionary. ⟨< Gk. *lexikographos* < *lexikon* wordbook + *graphein* write⟩

lex•i•cog•ra•phy [,lɛksə'kɒgrəfi] *n.* the science or practice of compiling dictionaries. **—,lex•i•co'graph•ic** [,lɛksəkə'græfɪk] or **,lex•i•co'graph•i•cal,** *adj.* **—,lex•i•co'graph•i•cal•ly,** *adv.*

lex•i•col•o•gist [,lɛksə'kɒlədʒɪst] *n.* an expert in lexicology.

lex•i•col•o•gy [,lɛksə'kɒlədʒi] *n.* the study of the history, form, and meaning of words. ⟨< Gk. *lexikon* word + E *-logy*⟩ **—,lex•i•co'log•i•cal** [,lɛksəkə'lɒdʒɪkəl], *adj.*

lex•i•con ['lɛksə,kɒn] *or* ['lɛksəkən] *n.* **1** a dictionary, especially of Greek, Latin, or Hebrew. **2** the total vocabulary of a particular speaker or writer or of a particular subject. **3** *Linguistics.* the inventory, or total stock, of morphemes in a language. ⟨< Gk. *lexikon (biblion)* wordbook < *lexis* word < *legein* say⟩

lex•is ['lɛksɪs] *n.* the total vocabulary of a language, including idiomatic expressions. ⟨< Gk. *lexis* speech, word⟩

Ley•den jar ['laɪdən] a device for collecting and storing an electric charge, consisting of a glass jar coated inside and outside with metal foil almost to the top, and having a conducting rod connected to the inner coating and passing up through an insulating stopper. ⟨after *Leyden*, Netherlands, where it was invented⟩

LF, L.F., or **l.f.** LOW FREQUENCY.

lg. or **lge.** large.

l.g. left guard.

LG LOW GERMAN.

L.Gen. or **LGen** LIEUTENANT-GENERAL.

LGk. Late Greek.

l.h. or **L.H.** left hand.

Lha•sa ap•so ['lɑsə 'æpsou] *or* ['læsə] a Tibetan breed of small watchdog having a heavy, usually gold coat and much hair over the eyes. ⟨after *Lhasa*, the capital of Tibet + Tibetan *apso* watchdog⟩

A Lhasa apso

Li lithium.

li•a•bil•i•ty [,laɪə'bɪləti] *n., pl.* **-ties. 1** the state of being susceptible: *liability to disease.* **2** the state of being under obligation: *liability for a debt.* **3** Usually, **liabilities,** *pl.* debts: *The monthly statement shows the company's assets and liabilities.* **4** a person or thing that acts as a disadvantage: *Her short temper is a liability in dealing with people.*

li•a•ble ['laɪəbəl] *adj.* **1** likely, especially unpleasantly likely: *Glass is liable to break. One is liable to slip on ice.* **2** in danger of having, doing, etc.: *We are all liable to diseases.* **3** legally responsible or answerable: *The Post Office is not liable for damage to an uninsured parcel. The defendant in a civil action may be found liable and ordered to pay damages.* **4** under obligation; subject: *Citizens are liable to jury duty.* ⟨< F *lier* bind < L *ligare*⟩
☛ *Usage.* See note at LIKELY.

li•aise [li'eiz] *v.* **-aised, -ais•ing.** *Informal.* act as liaison officer; establish liaison *(with)*: *An envoy liaises with a foreign government.* ⟨back formation from *liaison*⟩

li•ai•son [li'eizɒn], [,liei'zɒn], *or* ['liə,zɒn]; *French,* [ljɛ'zɔ̃] *n.* **1** communication in order to co-ordinate activities between parts of a whole, such as parts of a military unit, schools in a system, or departments within a government. **2** any close bond or connection. **3** an illicit love affair. **4** *Phonetics.* in speaking French, the pronouncing of a usually silent final consonant when it occurs before a word beginning with a vowel sound. The consonant is spoken as though it belonged to the second word. *Example: Comment allez-vous?* [kɔmɑ̃tale'vu]. ⟨< F < L *ligatio, -onis* < *ligare* bind⟩

liaison officer a person, especially an officer in the armed forces, who acts as a go-between to ensure proper co-operation between departments, units, etc.

li•a•na [li'ɑnə] *or* [li'ænə] *n.* any of various woody vines found in tropical rain forests, that are rooted in the ground and twine around the trunks of trees, etc. for support. Some lianas may be 60 cm in diameter and reach a length of 100 m, climbing from tree to tree. Also, **liane.** ⟨< F *liane,* earlier *liorne*⟩ **—li'a,noid,** *adj.*

li•ar ['laɪər] *n.* a person who tells lies; a person who says what is not true. ⟨ME *lier* < OE *leogere*⟩

li•ard ['liərd], [li'ɑr], *or* [li'ɑrd] *n. Cdn.* especially in the North, the balsam poplar; tacamahac. ⟨< Cdn.F < OF *liard* gray⟩

lib [lɪb] *n. Informal.* liberation: *women's lib, kids' lib, men's lib.*

lib. 1 librarian; library. **2** book (for L *liber*).

Lib. Liberal.

li•ba•tion [laɪ'beiʃən] *n.* **1** a pouring out of wine, water, etc. as an offering to a god. **2** the wine, water, etc. offered in this way. ⟨< L *libatio, -onis* < *libare* pour out⟩

li•bel ['laɪbəl] *n., v.* **-belled** or **-beled, -bel•ling** or **-bel•ing.** *—n.* **1** *Law.* **a** a written or published statement, picture, etc. tending to damage a person's reputation. **b** the act or criminal offence of writing or publishing a libel. **2** any false or damaging written statement about a person. Compare SLANDER.
—v. **1** write or publish a libel about. **2** make false or damaging statements about. ⟨< L *libellus,* dim. of *liber* book⟩ **—'li•bel•ler** or **'li•bel•er,** *n.*

li•bel•lous or **li•bel•ous** ['laɪbələs] *adj.* **1** containing a libel. **2** spreading libels: *a libellous tongue.* **—'li•bel•lous•ly** or **'li•bel•ous•ly,** *adv.*

lib•er•al ['lɪbərəl] *adj., n. —adj.* **1** generous: *a liberal donation.* **2** plentiful; abundant: *He put in a liberal supply of wood for the winter.* **3** broad-minded; not narrow in one's ideas: *a liberal thinker.* **4** designed to broaden the mind in a general way; not professional or technical: *a liberal education.* **5** favouring or following the principles of liberalism. **6 Liberal,**
a of, having to do with, or belonging to a political party advocating or associated with moderate progress and reform.
b in Canada, of, having to do with, or belonging to the Liberal Party. **7** giving the general thought, not a word-for-word rendering: *a liberal interpretation of the speaker's ideas.*
—n. **1** a person who favours or follows principles of liberalism. **2 Liberal, a** a member of a political party advocating or associated with moderate progress and reform. **b** in Canada, a member of the Liberal Party. ⟨< L *liberalis* befitting free persons < *liber* free⟩ **—'lib•er•al•ly,** *adv.* **—'lib•er•al•ness,** *n.*

liberal arts subjects such as literature, languages, history, and philosophy as distinct from technical or professional subjects.

liberal education an education in the liberal arts, especially as distinct from a technical or professional education.

lib•er•al•ism ['lɪbərə,lɪzəm] *n.* **1** a political philosophy that emphasizes belief in progress, individual freedom, and a democratic form of government. **2** the quality or state of being liberal. **3 Liberalism.** the principles and practices of a Liberal political party.

lib•er•al•ist ['lɪbərəlɪst] *n.* a person who holds liberal principles and ideas; a believer in progress and reforms. **—,lib•er•al'is•tic,** *adj.*

lib•er•al•i•ty [,lɪbə'rælәti] *n., pl.* **-ties. 1** generosity; generous behaviour. **2** a gift. **3** broad-mindedness. **4** a tolerant and progressive nature: *The liberality of the class members helped them accept new pupils from many different backgrounds.*

lib•er•al•ize ['lɪbərə,laɪz] *v.* **-ized, -iz•ing.** make or become liberal. **—,lib•er•al•i'za•tion,** *n.* **—'lib•er•al,iz•er,** *n.*

liberal party 1 *Cdn.* **Liberal Party,** one of the principal political parties of Canada. **2** a political party in certain other countries, usually one having moderately progressive policies.

lib•er•ate ['lɪbə,reit] *v.* **-at•ed, -at•ing. 1** set free. **2** make free from injustice, constraints imposed by tradition or upbringing, etc. **3** *Chemistry.* set free from combination: *liberate a gas.* **3** *Slang.* steal. ⟨< L *liberare* < *liber* free⟩ **—'lib•er,a•tor,** *n.*

lib•er•a•tion [,lɪbə'reiʃən] *n.* **1** the act or process of liberating. **2** the state of being liberated. **3** a movement striving for equal social and economic status and rights: *women's liberation, gay liberation.*

Li•be•ria [laɪ'biriə] *n.* a country in W Africa. See SENEGAL for map.

Li•be•ri•an [laɪ'biriən] *n., adj. —n.* a native or inhabitant of Liberia.
—adj. of or having to do with Liberia or its people.

lib•er•tar•i•an [,lɪbər'tɛriən] *n., adj. —n.* **1** one who advocates full civil liberty in thought and action. **2** one who believes in freedom of the will. **3 Libertarian,** a member or supporter of a Canadian political party advocating maximum individual freedom and minimum governmental control.
—adj. **1** of, having to do with, or being a libertarian. **2 Libertarian,** of or having to do with the Libertarians or their party. **—,lib•er'tar•i•an,ism,** *n.*

lib•er•tine ['lɪbər,tin] *n.* **1** a person who lives without regard to convention or accepted moral standards, especially one who leads a dissolute, immoral life; rake. **2** *(adj.)* of, having to do with, or characteristic of such a person. **3** a freedman in ancient Rome. ⟨< L *libertinus* freedman < *libertus* made free < *liber* free⟩

lib•er•tin•ism ['lɪbərti,nɪzəm] *or* ['lɪbərtə,nɪzəm] *n.* the behaviour of a libertine.

lib•er•ty ['lɪbərti] *n., pl.* **-ties. 1** freedom; independence: *The prisoner yearned for liberty. The colony finally won its liberty.* **2** the right or power to do as one pleases; power or opportunity to do something: *liberty of speech or action.* **3** the leave granted to a

sailor to go ashore. **4** the right of being in, using, etc.: *We give our dog the liberty of the yard.* **5** a privilege or right granted by a government. **6** too great freedom in action or speech: *Her use of his first name and other liberties annoyed him greatly.*
at liberty, a free: *The escaped lion is still at liberty.* **b** allowed; permitted: *You are at liberty to make any choice you please.* **c** not busy: *The principal will see you as soon as she is at liberty.*
take liberties with, be too familiar with: *The soldiers soon gave up trying to take liberties with their new sergeant.* ⟨ME < OF < L *libertas* < *liber* free⟩
☛ *Syn.* **1.** See note at FREEDOM.

Liberty Ship a cargo ship carrying about 10 000 gross tonnes, built in large numbers by the United States during the Second World War.

li•bid•i•nous [lə'bɪdənəs] *adj.* lustful; lewd. ⟨< L *libidinosus* < *libido.* See LIBIDO.⟩ **—li'bid•i•nous•ly,** *adv.* **—li'bid•i•nous•ness,** *n.*

li•bi•do [lə'bidou] *or* [lə'baɪdou] *n.* **1** sexual desire or instinct. **2** emotional or mental drive or energy in general. ⟨< L *libido* desire < *libere* be pleasing⟩

Li•bra ['librə] *or* ['laɪbrə] *n.* **1** *Astronomy.* a southern constellation thought of as having the shape of a pair of scales. **2** *Astrology.* **a** the seventh sign of the zodiac. The sun enters Libra about September 23. See ZODIAC for picture. **b** a person born under this sign. ⟨< L *libra* a balance, pair of scales⟩

li•brar•i•an [laɪ'brɛriən] *n.* **1** a person trained in library science, especially one whose work it is. **2** a person in charge of a library. **—li'brar•i•an,ship,** *n.*

li•brar•y ['laɪbrɛri] *or* ['laɪbrəri] *n., pl.* **-brar•ies. 1** a room or building where a collection of books, periodicals, phonograph records, tapes, etc. is kept to be used, rented, or borrowed, but not sold. **2** a collection of books, periodicals, etc., especially a large collection that is systematically arranged: *They have an extensive library of rare books.* **3** a set of books having something in common: *a publisher's Library of Classics.* ⟨< L *librarium* bookcase < *liber* book⟩

library science the principles and practice of library organization and management.

li•bret•tist [lə'brɛtɪst] *n.* the writer of a libretto.

li•bret•to [lə'brɛtou] *n., pl.* **-tos. 1** the words of an opera, oratorio, operetta, etc. **2** a book containing these words. ⟨< Ital. *libretto,* dim. of *libro* book⟩

Lib•y•a ['lɪbiə] *or* ['lɪbjə] *n.* a country in N Africa. See SUDAN for map.

Lib•y•an ['lɪbiən] *or* ['lɪbjən] *n., adj. —n.* **1** a native or inhabitant of Libya. **2** the Berber language of ancient Libya. *—adj.* **1** of or having to do with Libya or its people. **2** of or having to do with ancient Libya, which consisted of N Africa west of Egypt.

lice [lɔɪs] *n.* pl. of LOUSE.

li•cence ['lɔɪsəns] *n.* **1** permission given by law to do something. **2** the paper, card, plate, etc. showing such permission: *The barber hung his licence on the wall.* **3** the fact or condition of being permitted to do something. **4** freedom of action, speech, thought, etc. that is permitted or conceded. Poetic licence is the freedom from rules that is permitted in poetry and art. **5** too much liberty; disregard of what is right and proper; abuse of liberty. Also, **license.** ⟨ME < OF *licence* < L *licentia* < *licere* be allowed⟩ **—'li•cence•less,** *adj.*
☛ *Spelling.* **Licence** is one of two words that in Canadian English are usually spelled differently as nouns and verbs. The preferred spelling for the noun is **licence** and for the verb **license.** For this reason the noun and verb are entered separately in this dictionary. The spellings of the other word are **practice** and **practise.**

licence plate one of a pair of metal plates bearing the registration number of a vehicle and an indication that the annual fee has been paid, affixed to the front and back of the vehicle.

li•cense ['lɔɪsəns] *v.* **-censed, -cens•ing;** *n. —v.* **1** give a licence to: *to license a new driver.* **2** permit or authorize, especially by law: *A doctor is licensed to practise medicine.*
—n. See LICENCE. **—'li•cens•er,** *n.*
☛ *Spelling.* See note at LICENCE.

li•censed ['lɔisənst] *adj.* **1** holding a government licence to sell alcoholic liquors for drinking on the premises: *a licensed restaurant. Beer parlours are licensed premises.* **2** holding any other kind of licence: *I am a licensed driver. She is a licensed hunter.*

li•cen•see [,lɔisən'si] *n.* a person to whom a licence is given.

li•cen•sor ['lɔisən,sɔr] *n.* one who grants a licence.

li•cen•ti•ate [lɔi'sɛnʃiɪt] *or* [lɔi'sɛnʃi,eit] *n.* **1** a person who has a licence or permit to practise an art or profession. **2** in some European and French-Canadian universities, an academic degree ranking below the doctorate. **—li'cen•ti•ate,ship,** *n.* **—li,cen•ti'a•tion,** *n.*

li•cen•tious [lɔi'sɛnʃəs] *adj.* **1** disregarding commonly accepted moral principles, especially in sexual behaviour; lewd. **2** *Archaic.* disregarding accepted rules or conventions; lawless. ⟨< L *licentiosus* < *licentia.* See LICENCE.⟩ **—li'cen•tious•ly,** *adv.* **—li'cen•tious•ness,** *n.*

li•chee ['litʃi] See LITCHI.

li•chen ['lɔikən] *n.* any of a large group of complex plants made up of an alga and a fungus in a permanent symbiotic relationship, with alga cells interwoven with filaments of the fungus to form a plant body that may be crusty, scaly, or bushy, often resembling mosses. Lichens are classified mainly according to the type of fungus involved. ⟨< L < Gk. *leichēn,* originally, what eats around itself < *leichein* lick⟩ **—'li•chen,like,** *adj.*
☛ *Hom.* LIKEN.

li•chen•ol•o•gy [,lɔikə'nɒlədʒi] *n.* the study of lichens. **—,li•chen•o'log•i•cal,** *adj.* **—,li•chen'ol•o•gist,** *n.*

li•chen•ous ['lɔikənəs] *adj.* of, like, or abounding in lichens.

lich–gate ['lɪtʃ ,geit] *n.* a roofed gateway at the entrance to a churchyard where a coffin can be set down to await the clergy's arrival. Also, **lych-gate.** ⟨*lich,* OE *līc* body, corpse⟩

lic•it ['lɪsɪt] *adj.* lawful; permitted. ⟨< L *licitus* < *licere* be allowed⟩ **—'lic•it•ly,** *adv.* **—'lic•it•ness,** *n.*

lick [lɪk] *v., n. —v.* **1** pass the tongue over. **2** lap up with the tongue. **3** make or bring by using the tongue: *The cat licked the plate clean.* **4** pass (about) or play (over) as a tongue would: *The flames were licking the roof.* **5** *Informal.* beat; thrash: *I could lick him with one hand tied behind my back.* **6** *Informal.* defeat or overcome; conquer: *So far we've licked every problem without help.*
lick into shape, *Informal.* make presentable or usable.
—n. **1** a stroke of the tongue over something. **2** a place where natural salt is found or a block of salt provided, and where animals go to lick it up. **3** *Informal.* a blow: *I lost the fight, but I got in a few good licks.* **4** a small quantity: *She didn't do a lick of work.* **5** *Informal.* a brief stroke of activity or effort: *a lick and a promise.* **6** *Informal.* **licks,** *pl.* opportunity; chance: *I'm sure you'll get your licks in later.* **7** *Informal.* speed; clip: *He came down the road at a great lick.* **8** *Informal.* a bold improvised musical embellishment, especially on the guitar. ⟨OE *liccian*⟩

lick•e•ty–split [,lɪkəti 'splɪt] *adv. Informal.* at a great speed; headlong: *She was off down the sidewalk lickety-split before they could stop her.*

lick•ing ['lɪkɪŋ] *n., v. —n. Informal.* **1** a thrashing or spanking. **2** a defeat or setback.
—v. ppr. of LICK.

lick•spit•tle ['lɪk,spɪtəl] *n.* a contemptible flatterer; parasite.

lic•o•rice ['lɪkərɪʃ] *or* ['lɪkərɪs] *n.* **1** a sweet, black, gummy substance obtained from the roots of a European plant (*Glycyrrhiza glabra*) of the pea family, used as a flavouring and as a laxative. **2** candy flavoured with this substance. **3** the plant that yields this substance. **4** the dried root of this plant. Also, **liquorice.** ⟨ME < AF *lycorys* < LL *liquiritia* < L *glycyrrhiza* < Gk. *glykyrrhiza* < *glykys* sweet + *rhiza* root⟩

lic•tor ['lɪktər] *n.* in ancient Rome, an attendant on a public official, who punished offenders at the official's orders. See FASCES for picture. ⟨< L *lictor,* related to *ligare* bind⟩

lid [lɪd] *n.* **1** a movable cover; top: *the lid of a box.* **2** the cover of skin that is moved in opening and shutting the eye; eyelid. **3** *Slang.* a hat; cap. **4** *Informal.* a restraint; check; curb: *put the lid on gambling.*
blow the lid off, *Slang.* expose to public view; reveal: *to blow the lid off a government's waste of public funds.*
flip (one's) **lid,** *Slang.* get very excited.
keep a lid on it! *Slang.* keep it quiet! ⟨OE *hlid*⟩

L.I.D. LOCAL IMPROVEMENT DISTRICT.

lid•ded ['lɪdəd] *adj.* having a lid.

lid•less ['lɪdlɪs] *adj.* **1** having no lid. **2** having no eyelids. **3** *Poetic.* watchful.

li•do•caine ['laɪdə,kein] *n.* a drug used as a local anesthetic. *Formula:* $C_{14}H_{22}N_2O$

lie[1] [laɪ] *n., v.* **lied, ly•ing.** *—n.* **1** a false statement, known to be false by the person who makes it. **2** something intended to give a false impression; falsehood.

give the lie to, a call a liar; accuse of lying. **b** show to be false: *Her dissertation gives the lie to rumours of her incompetence.*
—*v.* **1** tell lies. **2** get, bring, put, etc. by lying: *to lie oneself out of a difficulty.* **3** make a false statement. ⟨OE *lyge,* n., *lēogan,* v.⟩
☛ *Hom.* LYE.
☛ *Syn. n.* **1. Lie,** FALSEHOOD, FIB = an untruthful statement. **Lie** applies to an untruthful statement deliberately made with the purpose of deceiving, sometimes of hurting, others: *Saying that his friend had stolen the money was a lie.* **Falsehood** refers to any untruthful statement made for a purpose, but can apply to one made when the truth would be undesirable or impossible: *Not wishing to hurt his sister's feelings, he told a falsehood and said he didn't know.* **Fib** is informal and means a lie or excusable falsehood about something unimportant: *Many children tell fibs.*

lie² [laɪ] *v.* **lay, lain, ly•ing;** *n.* —*v.* **1** have one's body in a flat position along the ground or on some other horizontal surface: *to lie on the grass.* **2** assume such a position (*used with* **down**): *to lie down on the couch.* **3** be in a horizontal or flat position: *The book was lying on the table.* **4** be kept or stay in a given position, state, etc.: *to lie idle.* **5** be; be located: *The lake lies to the south of us.* **6** exist; be; be found; belong: *The cure lies in education.* **7** be in the grave; be buried: *Her body lies in Halifax.* **8** *Archaic.* spend the night; lodge.
lie around or **about, a** be lazy; do nothing. **b** be scattered around: *Please don't leave your clothes lying around.*
lie behind, cause; be the reason for.
lie down on the job, not give full time or attention to one's work or other obligations.
lie down under, suffer without complaint.
lie in, a be confined in childbirth. **b** stay in bed later than usual.
lie off, *Nautical.* of a ship, etc., stay not far from: *The ship lay off the coast of Norway.*
lie over, be left waiting until a later time.
lie to, *Nautical.* of a ship, etc., come almost to a stop, facing the wind: *During the storm, the ship lay to.*
take (a thing) **lying down,** yield to (something); not stand up to: *He won't take that insult lying down.*
—*n.* **1** the manner, position, or direction in which something lies. **2** the place where an animal is accustomed to lie or lurk. **3** *Golf.* the position of the ball after a drive, in regard to obstacles on the ground or accessibility to the green. ⟨OE *licgan*⟩
☛ *Hom.* LYE.
☛ *Usage.* See note at LAY¹.

Lieb•frau•milch [ˈlibfraʊ,mɪlk]; *German,* [ˈlipfʀaʊ,mɪlx] a German white wine. ⟨< G, literally, milk of our dear lady (the Virgin Mary)⟩

Liech•ten•stein [ˈlɪxtən,ʃtaɪn] *n.* a small country in west central Europe.

lied [ˈlaɪd] *v.* pt. and pp. of LIE¹.

Lie•der•kranz [ˈlidər,krants] *n.* **1** *Trademark.* a smooth, soft, creamy cheese with a strong odour. **2** a German singing club. ⟨< G *Liederkranz* garland of songs⟩

lief [lif] *adv. Archaic.* willingly: *I'd as lief stay here.* Also, **lieve.** ⟨OE *lēof* dear⟩
☛ *Hom.* LEAF.

liege [lidʒ] *or* [liʒ] *n., adj.* —*n.* formerly, in the Middle Ages: **1** a lord having a right to the homage and loyal service of his vassals. **2** a vassal obliged to give homage and loyal service to his lord.
—*adj.* **1** having a right to the homage and loyal service of vassals. **2** obliged to give homage and loyal service to a lord. ⟨ME < OF < LL *leticus* < *letus* freedman, ult. < Gmc.⟩

liege lord a feudal lord.

liege•man [ˈlidʒmən] *n., pl.* **-men. 1** vassal. **2** a faithful follower.

lien [lin] *or* [ˈliən] *n. Law.* a claim placed on the property of another as a safeguard for payment of a debt in connection with that property. ⟨< F < L *ligamen* bond < *ligare* bind⟩
—**ˈlien•a•ble,** *adj.*
☛ *Hom.* LEAN [lin].

lie of the land 1 the natural features of a landscape. **2** the condition in which things are.

lieu [lu] *n. Archaic* (*except in* **in lieu of**). place; stead.
in lieu of, in place of; instead of: *During the hard times they gave the landlord produce in lieu of money for rent.* ⟨< F < L *locus*⟩
☛ *Hom.* LOO.

Lieut. lieutenant.

lieu•ten•an•cy [lɛfˈtɛnənsi] *or, esp. U.S.,* [luˈtɛnənsi] *n., pl.* **-cies.** the rank, commission, or authority of a lieutenant.

lieu•ten•ant [lɛfˈtɛnənt] *or, esp. U.S.,* [luˈtɛnənt] *n.* **1** a person who acts for someone senior to him or her in authority: *She was one of the gang leader's lieutenants.* **2** *Canadian Forces.* **a** an officer ranking next above a second lieutenant and below a captain. *Abbrev.*: Lt. or Lt **b** in Maritime Command, the equivalent of a captain. *Abbrev.*: Lt.(N) or Lt(N) See chart of ranks in the Appendix. **3** an officer of similar rank in the armed forces of other countries. ⟨< F *lieutenant* < *lieu* a place (< L *locus*) + *tenant,* ppr. of *tenir* hold < L *tenere.* 16c.⟩

lieutenant–colonel [lɛfˈtɛnənt ˈkɜrnəl] *or, esp. U.S.,* [luˈtɛnənt] *n.* **1** *Canadian Forces.* an officer ranking next above a major and below a colonel. *Abbrev.*: L.Col., LCol, or Lt.Col. See chart of ranks in the Appendix. **2** an officer of similar rank in the armed forces of other countries.

lieutenant commander 1 *Canadian Forces.* in Maritime Command, the equivalent of a major. See chart of ranks in the Appendix. **2** a naval officer of similar rank in other countries. *Abbrev.*: L.Cdr., LCdr, or Lt.Cdr.

lieutenant–general [lɛfˈtɛnənt ˈdʒɛnərəl] *or, esp. U.S.,* [luˈtɛnənt] *n.* **1** *Canadian Forces.* an officer ranking next above a major-general and below a general. *Abbrev.*: L.Gen., LGen, or Lt.Gen. See chart of ranks in the Appendix. **2** an officer of similar rank in the armed forces of other countries.

lieutenant–governor [lɛfˈtɛnənt ˈgʌvərnər]; *esp. U.S., for 2,* [luˈtɛnənt] *n.* **1** in Canada, the official head of a provincial government, appointed by the Governor General in Council, for a term of five years; representative of the Crown in a province. *Abbrev.*: Lt.Gov. **2** Often, **lieutenant governor,** a deputy governor.

lieve [liv] *adv. Archaic.* lief.
☛ *Hom.* LEAVE.

life [ləif] *n., pl.* **lives. 1** the condition of living or being alive; the quality that people, animals, and plants have and that rocks, dirt, and metals lack. **2** the time of being alive: *a short life.* **3** the time of existence or action; a period of being in power, able to operate, etc.: *the short life of that government, the life of a battery, the life of a lease.* **4** a living being, especially a person: *Five lives were lost in the fire.* **5** living things considered together: *The desert island had almost no animal or vegetable life.* **6** a way of living: *a dull life.* **7** an account of a person's life; biography: *He's writing a life of Mackenzie King.* **8** spirit; vigour: *Put more life into your work.* **9** a source of activity or liveliness. **10** the living form or model, especially as represented in art: *The portrait was painted from life.* **11** a sentence of imprisonment for life: *He got life.* **12** a particular part of a person's life: *her love life.*
as large or **as big as life, a** as big as the living person or thing. **b** in person.
for dear life, to save or as if to save one's life: *He ran for dear life.*
for life, a during the rest of one's life. **b** to save one's life.
for the life of me (or **him, her,** etc.), *Informal.* even if my (or his, her, etc.) life depended on it (*used only in negative expressions*): *I can't for the life of me remember where I put my keys.*
see life, *Informal.* get experience, especially of the exciting features of human activity: *Most young people want to see life before they settle down.*
take life, kill.
take (one's) **own life,** kill oneself; commit suicide.
to the life, like the model; exactly; perfectly.
true to life, true to reality; as in real life. ⟨OE *līf*⟩

life and limb physical safety and survival: *The old bridge is a danger to life and limb.*

life belt a life preserver in the shape of a thick ring, worn around the chest and under the arms.

life•blood [ˈləif,blʌd] *n.* **1** blood necessary to life. **2** a source of strength and energy: *The young people became the lifeblood of the organization.*

life•boat [ˈləif,bout] *n.* **1** a strong boat specially built for saving lives at sea or along the coast. **2** a boat carried on davits on a ship for use by passengers or crew in an emergency.

life buoy LIFE PRESERVER (def. 1).

life cycle the various stages through which an organism goes in the course of its life, from fertilization to reproduction to death: *the life cycle of the frog.*

life expectancy the number of years one can reasonably expect to live: *The life expectancy of women is greater than that of men.* Compare LIFE SPAN.

life•guard [ˈləif,gard] *n.* a person who is trained in lifesaving and who is responsible for the safety of swimmers and bathers at a public pool or beach.

Life Guards two British cavalry regiments whose duty it is to guard the king and queen of England.

life history the history from birth to death of any organism.

life insurance insurance that provides for the payment of a specified amount of money to a beneficiary or beneficiaries on the death of the insured, or, sometimes, to the insured when he or she reaches a certain age.

life jacket or **vest** a life preserver in the form of a vest which is buoyant or inflatable.

life•less ['ləiflɪs] *adj.* **1** inanimate: *a lifeless statue.* **2** dead: *lifeless bodies on the battlefield.* **3** having no living things: *a lifeless planet.* **4** dull: *a lifeless performance.* **—'life•less•ly,** *adv.* **—'life•less•ness,** *n.*
☛ *Syn.* **2.** See note at DEAD.

life•like ['ləif,ləik] *adj.* like life; looking as if alive; like the real thing: *a lifelike portrait.* **—'life,like•ness,** *n.*

life•line ['ləif,laɪn] *n.* **1** a rope for saving life, such as one thrown to a ship from the shore. **2** a line across a deck or passageway of a ship to grab to prevent falling or being washed overboard. **3** a diver's line for signalling when he or she is ready to be brought to the surface. **4** anything that maintains or helps to maintain something that cannot exist by itself: *The bus service was a lifeline to the remote community.*

life•long ['ləif,lɒŋ] *adj.* lasting all one's life: *a lifelong friendship.*

life net a strong net or sheet of canvas, used especially to catch a person jumping from a burning building.

life of Ri•ley ['raɪli] an easy, luxurious life.

life peer *Brit.* a peer whose title is not hereditary.

life preserver 1 a device made of buoyant or inflatable material, designed to keep a person afloat in water to prevent drowning. It may be in the form of a vest, a wide belt, or a thick ring. **2** *Esp. Brit.* a short stick with a heavy head, used for self-defence.

lif•er ['ləifər] *n. Slang.* **1** a convict in prison for life. **2** someone who has a lifelong contract in an occupation such as the military.

life raft an inflatable or wooden raft for saving lives in a shipwreck or from the wreck of an aircraft at sea.

life•sav•er ['ləif,seivər] *n.* **1** a person who or thing that saves people from drowning, especially, a lifeguard. **2** *Informal.* a person who or thing that saves one from trouble, discomfort, embarrassment, etc.: *The interruption was a lifesaver, because I didn't know what to say to her any more.* **3 Lifesavers,** *Trademark.* a hard, round candy with a hole in it.

life•sav•ing ['ləif,seivɪŋ] *n., adj. —n.* the skill, act, or practice of saving people's lives, especially by preventing drowning.
—adj. designed for or having to do with saving people's lives: *lifesaving classes, lifesaving equipment.*

life sciences the sciences dealing with living organisms; zoology and botany.

life–size ['ləif ,saɪz] *adj.* of an artifact, having the same size as the living person, animal, etc.: *a life-size statue.* Also, **life-sized.**

life span the length of time that a person, animal, machine, institution, etc. continues or may be expected to continue to live or function. Compare LIFE EXPECTANCY.

life•style ['ləif,staɪl] *n.* a way of life; the typical habits, pastimes, attitudes, standard of living, etc. of a person or group: *a casual lifestyle. Their downtown apartment suits their lifestyle.*

life•time ['ləif,taɪm] *n.* **1** the length of time that someone is alive or that something exists or functions: *In his whole lifetime he had never been in an airplane.* **2** (*adjl.*) lasting for such a length of time: *a lifetime commitment.*

life vest LIFE JACKET.

life•work ['ləif,wɜrk] *n.* work that takes or lasts a whole lifetime; main work in life.

LIFO ['ləifou] *n. Computer technology.* a system of queuing in data storage, in which the last item input is the first one retrieved. ⟨< *l*ast *i*n, *f*irst *o*ut⟩

lift [lɪft] *v., n. —v.* **1** raise; take up; raise into a higher position: *lift a chair.* **2** hold up; display on high. **3** raise in rank, condition, estimation, etc.; elevate; exalt. **4** rise and go; be dissipated: *The fog lifted at dawn.* **5** go up; allow (itself, etc.) to be raised: *This window will not lift.* **6** pull or tug upward. **7** send up loudly: *to lift a voice in song.* **8** rise to view above the horizon. **9** tighten the skin and erase the wrinkles of (a person's face) through surgery. **10** take up out of the ground, as crops, treasure, etc. **11** *Slang.* pick or take up; steal: *lift things from a store.* **12** pay off: *lift a mortgage.* **13** plagiarize.
lift off, rise from the ground: *The spaceship will lift off in two hours.*
—n. **1** an elevating influence. **2** the act of lifting. **3** the distance through which a thing is lifted. **4** a helping hand: *I gave him a lift with the heavy box.* **5** a ride in a vehicle given to a pedestrian or hiker; free ride: *She often gave the neighbour's boy a lift to school.* **6** *Esp. Brit.* elevator. **7** one of the layers of leather in the heel of a shoe. **8** a rise in ground. **9** elevated carriage (of the head, neck, eyes, etc.): *a haughty lift of the chin.* **10** *Informal.* an improvement in spirits: *The promotion gave her a lift.* **11** *Skiing.* a cable or rope with seats or attachments for holding on to, to raise a skier to the top of a slope; ski lift. **12** *Aeronautics.* **a** the force exerted on an airfoil by a flow of air over and around it acting perpendicular to the direction of flight. **b** the upward tendency of an airship or balloon caused by the gas it contains. ⟨ME < ON *lypta* to raise; akin to *lopt* air. See LOFT.⟩ **—'lift•a•ble,** *adj.* **—'lift•er,** *n.*
☛ *Syn. v.* **1-3.** See note at RAISE.

lift lock a canal or river lock in which each water-filled compartment is itself hydraulically raised and lowered while the water level within the compartment remains the same.

lift•off ['lɪft,ɒf] *n. Aeronautics.* the vertical takeoff of an aircraft, rocket, etc.; the act or the moment of rising from the ground or launching pad.

lift pump a pump that lifts a liquid to a level at which it will run out, without forcing it out under pressure.

lig•a•ment ['lɪgəmənt] *n.* **1** a band of strong tissue that connects bones or holds organs in place. **2** a tie; bond. ⟨ME < L *ligamentum* < *ligare* bind⟩

lig•and ['lɪgənd] *n. Chemistry.* an atom, ion, or radical forming a complex with a central atom or ion in a CO-ORDINATION COMPOUND. ⟨< L *ligandum,* gerund of *ligare* bind⟩

li•gate ['laɪgeit] *v.* **-gat•ed, -gat•ing.** bind; tie up: *ligate a bleeding artery.* ⟨< L *ligare*⟩ **—li'ga•tion,** *n.*

lig•a•ture ['lɪgətʃər] *or* ['lɪgə,tʃʊr] *n., v.* **-tured, -tur•ing.**
—n. **1** something used to bind or tie up, especially a thread or filament used in surgery to tie up a blood vessel, etc.
2 something that unites or connects; a bond. **3** a binding or tying up. **4** *Music.* **a** a slur. **b** a group of notes connected by a slur. **5** *Printing.* two or three letters joined. Æ and Œ are ligatures. Compare DIGRAPH.
—v. bind or tie up with a ligature. ⟨ME < LL *ligatura* < L *ligare* bind⟩

light¹ [ləit] *n., adj., v.* **light•ed** or **lit, light•ing.** *—n.* **1** that by which we see; the form of radiant energy that acts on the retina of the eye. **2** anything that gives light. The sun, a lamp, or a lighthouse can be called a light. **3** a supply of light: *The tall building to the south of us cuts off our light.* **4** brightness; clearness; illumination: *a strong light, a dim light.* **5** a bright part: *light and shade.* **6** daytime. **7** dawn. **8** something by which to let light in, such as a window or a windowpane. **9** something with which to start something else burning; LIGHTER¹: *Give me a light so I can start the fire in the fireplace.* **10** knowledge; information; illumination of mind: *We need more light on this subject.*
11 public knowledge; open view. **12** the aspect in which a thing is viewed: *She put the matter in the right light.* **13** a shining figure; model; example: *The actor was a leading light in the theatre.*
14 favour; approval.
according to (one's) **lights,** following one's own ideas, intelligence, and conscience in the best way that one knows.
bring to light, reveal; expose: *Many facts were brought to light during the investigation.*
come to light, be revealed or exposed.
in the light of, a by considering. **b** from the standpoint of.
see the light, or **see the light of day, a** come into being. **b** be made public. **c** come to accept or understand something: *After struggling with the issue for a while, he finally saw the light.*
shed or **cast** or **throw light on,** explain; make clear.
strike a light, make a flame.
—adj. **1** having light or much light: *a light room.* **2** bright; clear: *It is as light as day.* **3** pale in colour; whitish: *light hair, light blue.*
—v. **1** cause to give light: *She lit the lamp.* **2** give light to; provide with light: *The room is lighted by six windows.* **3** make or become bright: *Her face was lighted by a smile.* **4** become light: *The sky lights up at sunset.* **5** show the way by giving light: *His flashlight lighted us through the tunnel.* **6** set fire to: *She lit the candles.*
7 take fire. ⟨OE *lēoht*⟩
☛ *Usage.* **Lighted,** LIT. Both forms are in good use as the past tense and past participle of *light. Lighted* is probably the form generally used as the adjective and past participle: *She carried a lighted lamp. Lit* is perhaps more common as the past tense: *He lit a cigarette.*

light² [ləit] *adj., adv. —adj.* **1** easy to carry; not heavy: *a light load.* **2** of little mass for its size or volume: *a light metal.* **3** of less than usual mass: *light clothing.* **4** less than usual in amount,

density, force, or strength: *a light meal, light fog, a light sleep, a light rain.* **5** easy to do or bear; not hard or severe: *light punishment, a light task.* **6** not looking heavy; graceful; delicate: *a light bridge, light carving.* **7** moving easily; nimble: *light on one's feet.* **8** cheerfully careless: *a light laugh, a light retort.* **9** not serious enough; fickle: *a light mind, light of purpose.* **10** aiming to entertain; not serious: *light reading.* **11** not important: *light losses.* **12** careless in morals. **13** porous; sandy: *a light soil.* **14** containing little alcohol: *a light wine.* **15** built small and without much weight; adapted for light loads and for swift movement: *a light truck.* **16** lightly armed or equipped: *light cavalry, in light marching order.* **17** not involving heavy machinery: *light industry.*
light in the head, **a** dizzy. **b** silly; foolish. **c** crazy; out of one's head.
make light of, treat as of little importance.
–adv. **1** lightly. **2** with as little luggage as possible: *I like to travel light.* ⟨OE *lēoht, līht*⟩

light³ [ləit] *v.* **light•ed** or (*esp. in idioms*) **lit, light•ing. 1** come down to the ground; alight: *He lighted from his horse.* **2** come down from flight: *A bird lighted on the branch.* **3** come by chance: *Her eye lighted upon a familiar face in the crowd.* **4** fall suddenly: *The blow lit on his head.*
light into, *Slang.* **a** attack. **b** scold.
light out, *Slang.* leave suddenly; go away quickly. ⟨ME *lihtan,* OE *līhtan* to make light, relieve of a weight; see LIGHT²⟩

light air *Meteorology.* a wind speed of 1-5 km/h. See Beaufort scale in the Appendix.

light–armed [ˈləit ˈɑrmd] *adj.* equipped with light weapons.

light breeze *Meteorology.* a wind speed of 6-11 km/h. See Beaufort scale in the Appendix.

light bulb a glass bulb containing a filament of very fine wire that becomes white-hot and glows when an electric current flows through it. Fluorescent light bulbs have no filament.

light cream thin cream with a butter fat content lower than that of heavy cream.

light–e•mit•ting diode [ˈləit iˌmɪtɪŋ] *Electronics.* a semiconductor diode that emits light when voltage is applied, used especially for low-voltage displays of numerals, etc. in calculators and digital clocks and watches. *Abbrev.*: LED or L.E.D.

light•en¹ [ˈləitən] *v.* **1** make or become bright or brighter: *Dawn lightens the sky. The sky gradually lightened. His face lightened when he saw her.* **2** make or become pale or paler in colour: *The summer sun lightened her hair.* **3** flash with lightning: *I just saw it lighten in the west.* ⟨ME; see LIGHT¹⟩
—'light•en•er, *n.*

light•en² [ˈləitən] *v.* **1** reduce the load of (a ship, etc.); have the load reduced. **2** make or become lighter in weight. **3** make or become less of a burden: *to lighten taxes.* **4** make or become more cheerful: *The good news lightened their hearts.* ⟨ME; see LIGHT²⟩

light•er¹ [ˈləitər] *n.* a thing that or person who starts something burning; especially, a device used to light a cigarette, cigar, or pipe. ⟨ME *lighter* < *light¹*, v.⟩

light•er² [ˈləitər] *n., v. –n.* a flat-bottomed barge used for loading and unloading ships.
–v. carry (goods) in such a barge. ⟨< *light²* or ? < Du. *lichter*⟩

light•er•age [ˈləitərɪdʒ] *n.* **1** the loading, unloading, or carrying of goods in a lighter. **2** the fee for this.

light•face [ˈləitˌfeis] *n. Printing.* the type normally used in the body of a work; opposed to **boldface.** The definitions and illustrative phrases and sentences in this dictionary are printed in lightface. **—'lightˌfaced,** *adj.*

light–fin•gered [ˈləit ˌfɪŋgərd] *adj.* **1** thievish; skilful at picking pockets. **2** having nimble fingers.

light–foot•ed [ˈləit ˌfʊtɪd] *adj.* stepping lightly.
—'light-'foot•ed•ly, *adv.* **—'light'foot•ed•ness,** *n.*

light–head•ed [ˈləit ˈhɛdɪd] *adj.* **1** dizzy or giddy: *The fever was gone, but she still felt a little light-headed.* **2** not sensible; silly; frivolous. **—'light-'head•ed•ly,** *adv.* **—'light-'head•ed•ness,** *n.*

light–heart•ed [ˈləit ˈhɑrtɪd] *adj.* carefree; cheerful; gay.
—'light-'heart•ed•ly, *adv.* **—'light-'heart•ed•ness,** *n.*

light heavyweight a boxer who weighs between 76 kg and 81 kg.

light horse cavalry that carries light weapons and equipment.

light–horse•man [ˈləit ˈhɔrsmən] *n., pl.* **-men.** a cavalryman who carries light weapons and equipment.

light•house [ˈləitˌhʌus] *n., pl.* **-hous•es** [-ˌhaʊzɪz] a tower or framework with a bright light that shines far over the water. Lighthouses are usually located at dangerous places along the coast to warn and guide ships.

light•ing [ˈləitɪŋ] *n., v. –n.* **1** the giving of light; providing with light. **2** the way in which lights are arranged, especially on the stage. **3** a starting to burn. **4** light, and lighting equipment.
–v. ppr. of LIGHT.

light•ly [ˈləitli] *adv.* **1** with little pressure, force, etc.; gently: *Her hand rested lightly on his arm. He held the bird lightly in his hand.* **2** to a small degree or extent: *lightly clad.* **3** quickly or easily; nimbly or gracefully: *She jumped lightly aside.* **4** cheerfully: *take bad news lightly.* **5** indifferently or carelessly: *The issue is too important to be passed over lightly.*

light meter a device for measuring the intensity of light, especially an exposure meter: *a built-in light meter on a camera.*

light–mind•ed [ˈləit ˌmaɪndɪd] *adj.* not serious; thoughtless and frivolous. **—'light-'mind•ed•ly,** *adv.*
—'light-'mind•ed•ness, *n.*

light•ness¹ [ˈləitnɪs] *n.* **1** the quality or state of being bright or clear: *The lightness of the sky showed that the rain was over.* **2** the quality or state of being pale or light in colour: *She has to be careful in the sun because of the lightness of her skin.* ⟨OE *līhtnes* < *lēoht* light¹⟩

light•ness² [ˈləitnɪs] *n.* **1** the quality or state of having little mass; not being heavy: *The lightness of the second load was a relief after the first one he had carried.* **2** lack of severity; leniency: *The lightness of the sentence surprised the defendant.* **3** a lack of pressure or force; delicacy: *the lightness of a touch.* **4** cheerfulness or gaiety: *lightness of spirits.* **5** gracefulness or nimbleness: *the lightness of a step.* **6** a lack of proper seriousness: *Such lightness of conduct is not to be permitted in a courtroom.* ⟨< *light²*⟩

light•ning [ˈləitnɪŋ] *n.* **1** a flash of light in the sky caused by a discharge of electricity between clouds, or between a cloud and the earth's surface. **2** (*adjl.*) like lightning; very fast or sudden: *a lightning decision, a lightning change of mood.* ⟨< *lighten¹*⟩

lightning bug firefly.

lightning rod a metal rod fixed on a building or ship to conduct lightning into the earth or water to prevent fire.

light pen *Computer technology.* an electronic device to allow the user to control data on a computer terminal by pointing to it.

light•proof [ˈləitˌpruf] that will not let light in; sealed so that no light can enter: *A camera must be lightproof.*

lights [ləits] *n.pl.* the lungs of sheep, pigs, etc. ⟨so called because of their light weight⟩

light•ship [ˈləitˌʃɪp] *n.* a ship with a bright light that shines far over the water, anchored at a dangerous place to warn and guide ships.

light show an entertainment in which lighting plays a prominent part. See also SON ET LUMIÈRE.

light•some [ˈləitsəm] *adj. Archaic or poetic.* **1** nimble and lively: *lightsome feet.* **2** carefree; cheerful: *a lightsome heart.* **3** frivolous. **—'light•some•ly,** *adv.* **—'light•some•ness,** *n.*

light•weight [ˈləitˌweit] *n., adj. –n.* **1** a person or thing of less than average mass. **2** a boxer weighing between 58 kg and 60 kg. **3** a person of little importance or influence: *He is regarded as a lightweight in the literary world.*
–adj. **1** having less than the average or usual mass: *a lightweight portable sewing machine.* **2** of, having to do with, or characteristic of lightweights: *the lightweight boxing championship.*

light–year [ˈləit ˌjir] *n. Astronomy.* a unit of distance equal to the distance that light travels in one year in a vacuum, about 9 460 500 000 000 km. The nearest star is more than four light-years away.

light–years [ˈləit ˌjirz] *adv. Informal.* a long way: *Our books are light-years ahead of those of our competitors.*

lig•ne•ous [ˈlɪgniəs] *adj.* of or like wood; woody. ⟨< L *ligneus* < *lignum* wood⟩

lig•nin [ˈlɪgnɪn] *n. Botany.* an organic substance which, together with cellulose, makes up the woody tissues of plants. ⟨< L *lignum* wood + E *-in*⟩

lig•nite [ˈlɪgnəit] *n.* a very soft, brownish black type of coal containing less carbon and more water than bituminous coal and often having a woody texture. Lignite is a poor quality, imperfectly formed coal, intermediate between peat and bituminous coal. ⟨< F < L *lignum* wood⟩ **—lig'nit•ic** [lɪgˈnɪtɪk], *adj.*

lig•num vi•tae ['lɪgnəm 'vəiti] *or* ['vitaɪ] **1** either of two tropical American trees (*Guaiacum officinale* or *G. sanctum*) having very heavy, hard, olive brown wood. **2** the wood of either of these trees, highly valued for making pulleys, bearings, casters, etc. Lignum vitae is very resinous and so dense that it will not float in water. ⟨< L *lignum vitae* wood of life; from its supposed medicinal value⟩

lig•ro•in ['lɪgrouən] *n.* benzine. ⟨origin uncertain⟩

li•gu•la ['lɪgjələ] *n.pl.* **-lae** [-,li] *or* [-,laɪ] or **-las.** *Zoology.* a tonguelike or strap-shaped part or organ. ⟨< NL, special use of L *ligula* spoon, shoe-strap⟩

li•gu•late ['lɪgjəlɪt] *or* ['lɪgjə,leit] *adj.* **1** having or forming a ligula. **2** having the shape of a strap.

li•gule ['lɪgjul] *n. Botany.* something that is like a strap or tongue in shape. ⟨See LIGULA⟩

li•gure ['lɪgjʊr] *n.* a precious stone of ancient Israel. ⟨ME *ligury* < LL *ligūrius* < LGk. *ligýrion* a kind of precious stone⟩

Li•gu•ri•an [lɪ'gjʊriən] *n., adj. —n.* **1** a native or inhabitant of Liguria, a district in NW Italy. **2** a language, apparently Indo-European, spoken by ancient peoples along the NW shore of the Ligurion Sea, around Genoa.
—adj. of Liguria or its people.

lik•a•ble ['ləikəbəl] *adj.* having qualities that win good will or friendship; popular: *a likable person.* Also, **likeable.**
—'lik•a•ble•ness, *n.* **—'lik•a•bly,** *adv.* **—,lik•a'bil•i•ty,** *n.*

like[1] [ləik] *prep., adj., conj., n., adv. —prep.* **1** having the characteristics of; resembling; similar to: *Mary is like her sister. I never saw anything like it.* **2** in the same way as; in the manner of; similarly to: *She can run like a deer. He acted like a tyrant.* **3** such as one would expect of; typical of: *Isn't that just like him?* **4** in the right state or frame of mind for doing or having: *He felt like working. I feel like a cup of coffee.* **5** indicative of or giving promise of: *It looks like rain.* **6** such as; as for example: *They offer technical courses like mechanics, drafting, and plumbing.*
like anything, crazy, mad, etc. *Informal.* very much; to a great degree; with great speed, effort, or intensity: *She works like crazy.*
nothing like, *Informal.* **a** not at all: *She is nothing like her brother.* **b** not nearly: *It's nothing like as cold as it was yesterday.*
something like, *Informal.* something approaching or approximating; something similar to: *The tune goes something like this.*
—adj. **1** of the same or nearly the same form, kind, appearance, amount, etc.; similar: *Suzanne's uncle promised her $20 if she could earn a like sum.* **2** *Archaic or dialect.* likely: *The king is sick and like to die.*
—conj. Informal. **1** the same as; as: *He reacted just like I did when I first saw it.* **2** as if: *It looks like we'll have to do it ourselves.*
—n. a person or thing like another; counterpart or equal; match: *We will not see her like again. They had never seen the like before.*
and the like, and similar things; and so forth: *He studied music, painting, and the like.*
the likes (or **like**) **of,** *Informal.* anyone or anything like.
—adv. **1** *Informal.* probably (*usually used with* **enough**): *Like enough it will rain.* **2** *Archaic.* in the same manner or to the same extent or degree. ⟨OE *(ge)līc*⟩
☛ *Usage.* In standard written English, a distinction is made between the use of **like** and **as. As** and **as if** are used as conjunctions to introduce clauses of comparison: *He still writes as he used to when he was a child. Act as if you were familiar with the place.* **Like** is used as a preposition in phrases of comparison: *She swims like a fish. He writes like a child.* In informal English, however, **like** is often used in place of **as** to introduce clauses: *He writes like he used to when he was a child.*

like[2] [ləik] *v.* **liked, lik•ing;** *n. —v.* **1** be pleased or satisfied with; enjoy: *Do you like milk? He likes the job but not the salary.* **2** have a friendly feeling toward; feel an attraction toward: *They like their new math teacher.* **3** wish for; want (*used with* **would**): *I would like a glass of milk, please. I would like to get my hands on whoever took my bike.* **4** be inclined; choose: *Come whenever you like.*
—n. **likes,** *pl.* likings; preferences: *My mother knows most of my likes and dislikes.* ⟨OE *līcian* to please⟩
☛ *Usage.* **Like,** LOVE are not interchangeable. *Like* = find pleasure or satisfaction in something or someone, or have friendly feelings for a person, but does not suggest strong feelings or emotion: *I like books. Girls like to play. Love* emphasizes strong feelings and deep attachment, and is used to express the emotion of love: *She loves her mother. He loves music.* But informally *love* is often used instead of *like* in an intensified sense: *I love peanut brittle.*

–like *suffix.* **1** like: *wolflike = like a wolf.* **2** like that of; characteristic of: *childlike = like that of a child.* **3** suited to; fit or proper for: *businesslike = suited to business.* ⟨< *like*[1], adj.⟩
☛ *Usage.* **-like** is a living suffix that can be freely added to nouns to form adjectives.

like•a•ble ['ləikəbəl] See LIKABLE.

like•li•hood ['ləikli,hʊd] *n.* probability: *Is there any likelihood of rain this afternoon?*

like•ly ['ləikli] *adj.* **-li•er, -li•est;** *adv. —adj.* **1** probable: *One likely result of the heavy rains is a flood.* **2** to be expected: *It is likely to be hot in August.* **3** suitable: *Is there a likely place to fish?* **4** promising: *a likely boy.* **5** plausible: *a likely story.*
—adv. probably: *I'll very likely be home all day.* ⟨< ON *líkligr*⟩
☛ *Usage.* **Likely,** APT, LIABLE. The principal meanings of these words are—**likely:** expected, probable; **liable:** possible (of an unpleasant event), responsible (as for damages); **apt:** tending toward, naturally fit. **Likely** is the most commonly used of the three, and informally both **apt** and (in some localities) **liable** are used in the ordinary sense of **likely:** *It's likely* (or *apt* or, locally, *liable) to rain when the wind is southwest.* In general, **liable** is best used when the reference is to something negative happening to someone or something: *He is liable to be blamed for the accident.*

like–mind•ed ['ləik 'maɪndɪd] *adj.* sharing the same tastes and ideas. **—'like-'mind•ed•ly,** *adv.* **—'like-'mind•ed•ness,** *n.*

lik•en ['ləikən] *v.* represent or describe as like; compare: *The poet likens life to a dream.*
☛ *Hom.* LICHEN.

like•ness ['ləiknɪs] *n.* **1** a resemblance; being alike: *There is a strong likeness between the boy and his mother.* **2** something that is like; a copy or representation, especially a painting, drawing, or photograph: *The portrait is a good likeness of her.* **3** the appearance or shape: *The wizard assumed the likeness of a very old man.*

like•wise ['ləik,waɪz] *adv.* **1** the same; in the same way: *See what I do. Now do likewise.* **2** also; moreover; too: *He was a painter, a sculptor, and likewise a writer.*

lik•ing ['ləikɪŋ] *n., v. —n.* **1** a preference or taste: *She had a liking for apples.* **2** a fondness or kindly feeling: *She had a liking for children.* **3** taste; pleasure: *food to your liking.*
—v. ppr. of LIKE. ⟨OE *līcung* < *līcian* to please⟩

li•ku•ta [li'kutɑ] *n., pl.* **ma•ku•ta** [mɑ'kutɑ]. **1** a unit of money in Zaire, equal to 1/100 of a zaire. **2** a coin worth one likuta. See table of money in the Appendix.

li•lac ['laɪlɑk], ['laɪlæk], *or* ['laɪlək] *n., adj. —n.* **1** any of various shrubs or small trees (genus *Syringa*) of the olive family, especially a European species (*S. vulgaris*) widely cultivated in temperate regions for its showy, erect clusters of fragrant, light to dark purple, pink, or white, spring-blooming flowers. **2** pale to medium purple.
—adj. having the colour lilac. ⟨< F < Sp. < Arabic < Persian *lilak* < *nil* indigo < Skt. *nila*⟩

li•lan•ge•ni ['lilaŋ,gɛni] *or* [lɪ'læŋgəni] *n., pl.* **e•ma•lan•ge•ni.** **1** a unit of currency of Swaziland, equal to 100 cents. **2** a coin or note worth one lilangeni. See table of money in the Appendix.

li•li•a•ceous [,lɪli'eiʃəs] *adj.* **1** of or like a lily. **2** belonging to the family Liliaceæ. ⟨< LL *liliaceus*⟩

Lil•ith ['lɪlɪθ] *or* ['laɪlɪθ] *n.* **1** *Semitic mythology.* a female spirit haunting lonely places. **2** *Jewish folklore.* the first wife of Adam, before Eve was created.

Lil•li•put ['lɪləpət] *or* ['lɪlə,pʌt] *n.* an imaginary island described in *Gulliver's Travels,* by Jonathan Swift (1667-1745). The island was inhabited by tiny people about 15 cm tall.

Lil•li•pu•tian [,lɪlə'pjuʃən] *adj., n. —adj.* **1** of or suitable for Lilliput. **2** very small; tiny; petty.
—n. **1** an inhabitant of Lilliput. **2** a very small person; dwarf.

lilt [lɪlt] *v., n. —v.* sing or play (a tune), speak, or move in a light, swinging manner.
—n. **1** a lively song or tune with a swing. **2** a way of speaking in which the pitch of the voice varies in a pleasing manner: *He talks with an Irish lilt.* **3** a lively, springy movement. ⟨ME *lulte,* ult. origin uncertain⟩

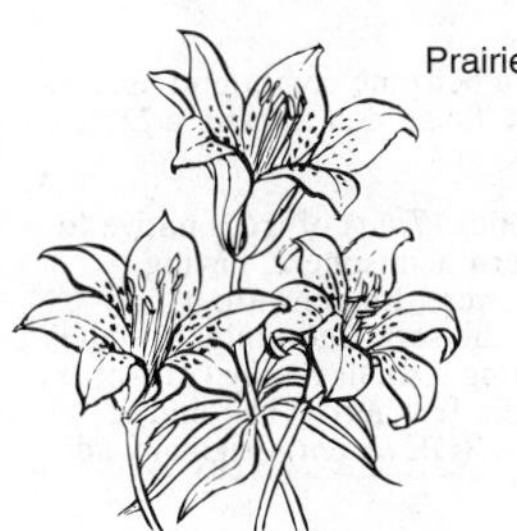

lil•y ['lɪli] *n., pl.* **lil•ies. 1** any of a genus (*Lilium*) of plants that grow from bulbs, having leafy stems and showy flowers. The prairie lily is the provincial flower of Saskatchewan. The Madonna lily is the provincial flower of Québec. **2** any of various other plants of the same family having similar flowers: *The glacier lily is a common wildflower of the Rockies.* **3** (*adjl.*) designating a family (Liliaceae) of plants that includes the lilies, as well as trilliums, hyacinths, tulips, onions, etc. **4** any of various other plants having showy flowers, such as the calla lily and water lily. **5** the flower of a lily. **6** the fleur-de-lis as a heraldic emblem. **7** (*adjl.*) like a lily in being white or pale, fragile, pure, etc.: *her lily hands.*
gild the lily. See GILD[1]. ⟨OE *lilie* < L *lilium* (akin to Gk. *leirion*)⟩ **—'lil•y,like,** *adj.*

lil•y–liv•ered ['lɪli ,lɪvərd] *adj.* cowardly.

lily of the valley *pl.* **lilies of the valley.** a low-growing, perennial plant (*Convallaria majalis*) of the lily family having small, bell-shaped, fragrant white flowers growing on short stems along a main stem.

lily pad one of the large, round, floating leaves of a water lily.

lil•y–white ['lɪli 'wəit] *adj., n.* —*adj.* **1** white as a lily: *lily-white sheets.* **2** pure; uncorrupted: *a lily-white politician.* **3** of or having to do with any group opposing the inclusion of Blacks, especially in political parties.
—*n.* a member of any lily-white group.

li•ma bean ['laɪmə] **1** any of several cultivated varieties of a tropical American bean (*Phaseolus lunatus*) having broad pods that contain broad, flat, light green seeds. **2** the seed of this plant, used as food. ⟨after *Lima*, Peru⟩

lim•a•cine ['lɪməsɪn] *or* ['lɪmə,saɪn], ['laɪməsɪn] *or* ['laɪmə,saɪn] *adj.* like a slug. ⟨< L *limus* slime⟩

limb [lɪm] *n.* **1** a leg, arm, or wing. **2** a large branch of a tree; bough: *They sawed off the dead limb.* **3** a part that projects: *the four limbs of a cross.* **4** a person or thing thought of as a part, member, representative, etc.
out on a limb, *Informal.* in or into a dangerous or exposed position: *The producer of the play was left out on a limb when her backers suddenly withdrew their support.*
tear limb from limb, 1 tear (a body) violently apart; dismember violently. **2** *Informal.* attack; criticize harshly. ⟨OE *lim*⟩
—'limb•less, *adj.*
☛ *Syn. n.* **2.** See note at BRANCH.
☛ *Hom.* LIMN.

lim•bate ['lɪmbeit] *adj. Botany.* having a border coloured differently from the leaf. ⟨< L *limbatus* bordered < *limbus* edge⟩

lim•ber[1] ['lɪmbər] *adj., v.* —*adj.* bending easily; flexible: *A pianist has to have limber fingers.*
—*v.* make or become supple or more easily flexed (*used with* **up**): *We did some exercises to limber up before the game.* ⟨? < *limp*[2] or *limb*⟩ **—'lim•ber•ness,** *n.*
☛ *Syn. adj.* See note at FLEXIBLE.

lim•ber[2] ['lɪmbər] *n.* the detachable front part of the carriage of a field gun. ⟨? < F *limonière* wagon with shafts < *limon* shaft⟩

limber pine the Rocky Mountain white pine (*Pinus flexilis*), having curved needles and cones bearing almost wingless seeds. It grows in the foothills of the Rockies.

lim•bic system ['lɪmbɪk] a primitive part of the brain below the cortex, thought to be responsible for emotions, the sense of smell, etc. ⟨< F *limbigue*, ult. < L *limbus* edge⟩

lim•bo[1] ['lɪmbou] *n.* **1** Often, **Limbo.** *Roman Catholic theology.* a place for those dead who have not received the grace of Christ while living, and yet have not deserved the punishment of willful and impenitent sinners. **2** a condition or place of neglect or disregard: *The belief that the earth is flat belongs to the limbo of outworn ideas.* **3** an indefinite or intermediate condition or place: *He was left in limbo for some time before he was told he definitely had the job.* **4** prison or confinement. ⟨< L *(in) limbo* on the edge⟩

lim•bo[2] ['lɪmbou] *n.* a dance originating in the West Indies, in which dancers bend over backward from the knees and pass under a low bar with only their feet touching the ground. The bar is brought lower for each pass a dancer makes. ⟨? < *limber*[1]⟩

Lim•burg•er ['lɪmbɜrgər] *n.* a soft cheese made from whole milk and having a strong odour. ⟨< *Limbourg*, a province of Belgium⟩

lime[1] [laɪm] *n., v.* **limed, lim•ing.** —*n.* **1** a white substance obtained by burning limestone, shells, bones, etc.; calcium oxide; quicklime. Lime is used to make mortar and on fields to improve soil. *Formula*: CaO **2** birdlime. **3** a deposit from hard water found on the inside of kettles, pipes, etc.
—*v.* **1** put lime on. **2** smear (branches, etc.) with birdlime. **3** catch (birds) with birdlime. ⟨OE *līm*⟩

lime[2] [laɪm] *n., adj.* —*n.* **1** a tropical and subtropical citrus tree (*Citrus aurantifolia*) bearing small, round or oval fruit with a green rind and yellowish green, fleshy, very acid pulp. **2** the fruit of this tree. Limes are used for flavouring food and drinks and as a source of vitamin C. **3** a drink flavoured with the juice of limes or a substitute. **4** a greenish yellow.
—*adj.* greenish yellow. ⟨< F < Sp. < Arabic *lima.* Akin to LEMON.⟩

lime[3] [laɪm] *n.* linden, especially the European linden. ⟨var. of earlier *line* < OE *lind*⟩

lime•ade ['laɪm,eid] *n.* a drink made of lime juice, sugar, and water.

lime•kiln ['laɪm,kɪln] *or* ['laɪm,kɪl] *n.* a furnace for making lime by burning limestone, shells, etc.

lime•light ['laɪm,ləit] *n.* **1** an intense white light produced by heating lime, formerly used as a stage spotlight in theatres. **2** the centre of public attention and interest: *Some politicians try to avoid the limelight.*

lim•er•ick ['lɪmərɪk] *n.* a kind of humorous poem consisting of five anapaestic lines, with the first two lines rhyming with the last, and the third and fourth shorter lines rhyming with each other. *Example*:

There was a young lady from Lynn
Who was so exceedingly thin
  That when she essayed
  To drink lemonade
She slid down the straw and fell in.

⟨apparently from a song about *Limerick*, Irish Republic⟩

lime•stone ['laɪm,stoun] *n.* rock formed mainly from organic remains, such as shells or coral, and consisting mostly of calcium carbonate, used for building and for making lime. Marble is a kind of limestone.

lime•wa•ter ['laɪm,wɒtər] *n.* a solution of slaked lime (calcium hydroxide) in water, used to counteract an acid condition.

lim•it ['lɪmɪt] *n., v.* —*n.* **1** the farthest point or edge; where something ends or must end: *the limit of one's vision. I have reached the limit of my patience.* **2** *Mathematics.* a value toward which terms of a sequence, values of a function, etc. approach indefinitely near. **3** in betting games, the agreed maximum amount of any bet or raise. **4** *Logging. Cdn.* a concession; timber limit. **5 limits,** *pl.* **a** boundary; bounds: *Keep within the limits of the school grounds.* **b** territories or regions. **c** constraints; limitations. **6** the maximum quantity of fish or game that the law allows one to take in a specified period. **7 the limit,** *Informal.* something very trying or very remarkable: *Isn't that just the limit? I couldn't believe my ears.*
—*v.* set a limit to; restrict: *We must limit our expenditure to $60.* ⟨ME < OF < L *limes, limitis* boundary⟩ **—'lim•it•a•ble,** *adj.* **—'lim•it•er,** *n.*

lim•i•ta•tion [,lɪmə'teiʃən] *n.* **1** a limiting. **2** a limited condition. **3** something that limits. **4** *Law.* a period of time after which a claim, suit, etc. cannot be brought in court. A **statute of limitations** is a statute that fixes such a period of time.

lim•i•ta•tive ['lɪmə,teitɪv] *adj.* limiting; restrictive.

lim•it•ed ['lɪmətɪd] *adj., n., v.* —*adj.* **1** kept or remaining within limits; restricted: *a limited edition, a limited number of seats. He's having only limited success in his new business.* **2** of business organizations, restricted as to the amount of debt that any individual member is liable for. **3** travelling rapidly and making only a few stops: *a limited train or bus.*

—*n.* a train, bus, etc. that travels rapidly and makes only a few stops.
—*v.* pt. and pp. of LIMIT.

lim•it•ed–ac•cess ['lɪmətɪd 'æksɛs] *adj.* of highways, having access roads at relatively few points.

limited company a corporation in which the liability of stockholders is limited to a specified amount.

limited edition **1** an edition of a book, etc. limited to a certain number of copies and often having a special format and binding. **2** any other collector's item, such as a doll or plate, of which few copies are made.

limited monarchy a monarchy in which the ruler's powers are limited by law.

lim•it•less ['lɪmɪtlɪs] *adj.* without limits; boundless; infinite. **—'lim•it•less•ly,** *adv.* **—'lim•it•less•ness,** *n.*

limn [lɪm] *v. Archaic.* **1** paint (a picture). **2** portray in words. ⟨ME *lymne(n)*, var. of *lumine(n)* < OF *luminer* < L *luminare* light up, make bright < *lumen* light⟩ **—'lim•ner** ['lɪmnər], *n.*
☛ *Hom.* LIMB.

lim•no•log•i•cal [,lɪmnə'lɒdʒɪkəl] *adj.* of or having to do with limnology. **—,lim•no'log•i•cal•ly,** *adv.*

lim•nol•o•gist [lɪm'nɒlədʒɪst] *n.* a person trained in limnology, especially one whose work it is.

lim•nol•o•gy [lɪm'nɒlədʒi] *n.* the study of the physical and chemical properties of bodies of fresh water and the conditions of their plant and animal life. ⟨< Gk. *limnē* lake + *-ology.* 20c.⟩

lim•o ['lɪmou] *n., pl.* **lim•os.** *Informal.* limousine.

Li•moges [lɪ'mouʒ]; *French,* [li'mɔʒ] *n.* a kind of fine porcelain made at Limoges, France.

li•mo•nite ['laɪmə,nəit] *n.* a kind of iron ore, varying in colour from dark brown to yellow. *Formula*: $2Fe_2O_3 \cdot 3H_2O$ ⟨< Gk. *leimōn* meadow⟩ **—,li•mo'nit•ic** [,laɪmə'nɪtɪk], *adj.*

li•mou•sin [limu'zæn]; *French* [limu'zɛ̃] *n. French.* a breed of sturdy beef cattle. ⟨< *Limousin,* a former province of France⟩

lim•ou•sine ['lɪmə,zin] *or* [,lɪmə'zin] *n.* **1** a large, luxurious automobile, especially one driven by a chauffeur. A limousine sometimes has a glass partition separating the passenger compartment from the driver's seat. **2** a large automobile or small bus used to carry passengers to and from an airport, etc. ⟨probably < early French dialect *limousine,* a coach⟩

limp[1] [lɪmp] *n., v.* —*n.* a lame step or walk.
—*v.* **1** walk with a limp: *After falling down the stairs, he limped for several days.* **2** proceed in a halting or laboured manner: *The new project limped along, for no one seemed very interested in it.* ⟨Cf. OE *lemphealt* lame⟩ **—'limp•er,** *n.* **—'limp•ing•ly,** *adv.*

limp[2] [lɪmp] *adj.* not stiff or firm; tending to bend or droop: *The lettuce had lost its crispness and was quite limp. I am so tired I feel as limp as a rag.* ⟨origin uncertain; cf. ON *limpa* weakness⟩ **—'limp•ly,** *adv.* **—'limp•ness,** *n.*
☛ *Syn.* **Limp,** FLABBY = lacking firmness, both literally and as used figuratively to describe character, principles, etc. **Limp** = lacking, or having lost, stiffness or firmness and strength, and suggests drooping or hanging loosely: *Hot weather always makes me feel limp. He has a limp handshake.* **Flabby** = lacking firmness and hardness or lacking forcefulness, energy, or strength, and suggests being soft and weak, flapping or shaking easily: *She is so fat her flesh is flabby.*

lim•pet ['lɪmpɪt] *n.* any of various small, marine gastropod molluscs having a single shell shaped like a squat cone and having a broad, fleshy foot by which they cling to rocks, etc. ⟨OE *lempedu* < Med.L *lampreda* lamprey. Doublet of LAMPREY.⟩

lim•pid ['lɪmpɪd] *adj.* clear; transparent: *limpid water, limpid eyes.* ⟨< L *limpidus* clear⟩ **—'lim•pid•ly,** *adv.* **—'lim•pid•ness,** *n.*

lim•pid•i•ty [lɪm'pɪdəti] *n.* a limpid quality or condition.

limp•kin ['lɪmpkɪn] *n.* a brown bird (*Aramus guarauna*) living in marshes.

lim•y ['laɪmi] *adj.* **lim•i•er, lim•i•est. 1** of, containing, or resembling lime. **2** smeared with birdlime. **—'lim•i•ness,** *n.*

lin•age ['laɪnɪdʒ] *n.* **1** the number of lines of printed or written matter on a page, or making up an article, advertisement, etc. **2** payment according to the number of lines. Also, **lineage.**

linch•pin ['lɪntʃ,pɪn] *n.* **1** a locking pin inserted through a hole in the end of an axle to keep the wheel on. **2** something or someone that is key to any endeavour. ⟨< *linch-*, OE *lynis* linchpin + *pin*⟩

Lin•coln ['lɪŋkən] *n.* a breed of English sheep having long wool. ⟨< *Lincolnshire*, a county in E England, where this breed originated⟩

lin•dane ['lɪndein] *n. Chemistry.* a benzene compound used as an insecticide. *Formula*: $C_6H_6Cl_6$ ⟨< T. van den *Linden,* a Dutch chemist + E *-ane.* 20c.⟩

lin•den ['lɪndən] *n.* **1** any of a genus (*Tilia*) of trees native to the temperate regions of the northern hemisphere, having heart-shaped leaves and fragrant flowers. Lindens are widely planted for ornament and shade. **2** the soft, fine-grained, white wood of a linden. **3** (*adjl.*) designating a small family (Tiliaceae) of mainly tropical trees, shrubs, and a few herbs. The linden family includes the lindens and jutes. ⟨OE *linden*, originally adj. < *lind* linden, lime[3]⟩

line[1] [laɪn] *n., v.* **lined, lin•ing.** —*n.* **1** a piece of rope, cord, or wire. **2** a cord for measuring, making level, etc. **3** a cord with a hook for catching fish. **4** a long, narrow mark: *Draw two lines along the margin.* **5** anything like such a mark. **6** a wrinkle or crease: *the lines in his face. The fortune teller studied the lines on the palm of my hand.* **7** a straight line: *The lower edges of the two pictures are about on a line.* **8** *Geometry.* the straight or curved path that a point may be imagined to make as it moves; CURVE (def. 5). **9** the way in which lines are used in drawing: *clearness of line.* **10 lines,** *pl.* **a** outline; contour: *a ship of fine lines.* **b** plan of construction: *The two books were written on the same lines.* **c** the words that an actor speaks in a play: *I forgot my lines and had to be prompted.* **d** reins. **e** one's fate or fortune: *His demotion was hard lines.* **f** *Informal.* a marriage certificate. **11** an edge; limit; boundary: *That hedge marks our property line.* **12** a row of persons or things: *a line of cars.* **13** a row of words on a page or in a column: *a column of 40 lines.* **14** a short letter; note: *Drop me a line.* **15** a connected series of persons or things following one another in time: *The Stuarts were a line of English kings.* **16** family or lineage: *of noble line.* **17** a course; track; direction: *the line of march of an army.* **18** a course of action, conduct, or thought: *a line of policy.* **19** *Military.* **a** the front. **b lines,** *pl.* a double row (front and rear rank) of soldiers. **c** troops or ships arranged abreast. **d** an arrangement of an army or fleet for battle. **20 the line, a** the equator. **b** the border between two countries, especially that between Canada and the United States: *south of the line.* **c** the regular armed forces; the soldiers, ships, or aircraft that do all the fighting. **21** in a telephone, telegraph, etc. system: **a** a wire or wires connecting points or stations. **b** the system itself. **22** any rope, wire, pipe, hose, etc. running from one point to another. **23** a single track of railway. **24 a** one branch of a system of transportation: *the main line of a railway.* **b** a whole system of transportation or conveyance: *the Cunard Line.* **25** a branch of business; kind of activity: *the dry-goods line.* **26** a kind or brand of goods: *a good line of hardware.* **27** *Slang.* an exaggerated story, intended to impress or deceive: *She gave me a line about why she was late, but I didn't believe it.* **28** a single row of words in poetry. **29** *Music.* one of the horizontal lines that make a staff. **30** a unit of length equivalent to 1/12 of an inch. **31** *Cdn.* in Ontario, CONCESSION ROAD.
all along the line, at every point; everywhere.
bring into line, cause to agree or conform: *She will bring the other members into line and the club will accept her plan.*
come into line, agree; conform.
draw the line. See DRAW.
get or **have a line on,** *Informal.* get or have information about.
hold the line, a wait on the phone. **b** withstand an attack.
in line, a in alignment. **b** in agreement. **c** ready. **d** in order; in succession: *next in line.*
in line with, according to; agreeing or conforming to.
in the line of duty, while pursuing one's career.
lay it on the line, state things firmly and clearly.
on a line, even; level.
on the line, a in between; neither one thing nor the other. **b** at risk: *A politician's job is on the line at election time.*
out of line, not in agreement; not suitable or proper: *Her last remark was out of line. He is always out of line with the rest of the club members.*
read between the lines. See READ[1].
string or **feed** (someone) **a line,** tell (someone) an untrue and exaggerated story to impress or deceive.
toe the line. See TOE.
—*v.* **1** mark (paper, etc.) with lines. **2** cover with lines: *Age had lined his face.* **3** form or arrange a line along: *Cars lined the road for a kilometre.* **4** form a line or form into a line (used with **up**): *People were lining up to get into the theatre.* **5** *Baseball.* hit a liner. **6** *Cdn.* float a canoe downstream by guiding it from the shore with ropes attached to the bow and stern (*often used with* **down**): *We often lined down rapids instead of portaging.*
line up, a make or wait in a queue. **b** plan; organize; assemble. **c** align; put in a line. ⟨fusion of OE *līne* line, rope and F *ligne* line, both < L *linea* line, linen thread < *linum* flax⟩ **—'lin•a•ble** or **'line•a•ble,** *adj.* **—'line•less,** *adj.* **—'line,like,** *adj.*

line² [laɪn] *v.* **lined, lin•ing. 1** put a lining inside (something). **2** fill: *to line one's pockets with money.* **3** serve as a lining for. ⟨OE *līn* flax⟩

lin•e•age¹ ['lɪniɪdʒ] *n.* **1** one's descent in a direct line from an ancestor. **2** one's family or race. ⟨ME < OF *lignage* < *ligne* line < L *linea*⟩

line•age² ['laɪnɪdʒ] *n.* See LINAGE.

lin•e•al ['lɪniəl] *adj.* **1** in the direct line of descent: *A granddaughter is a lineal descendant of her grandfather.* **2** having to do with or derived from ancestors; hereditary: *The lands were hers by lineal right.* **3** linear. ⟨ME < OF < LL *linealis* < L *linea* line¹⟩ **—'lin•e•al•ly,** *adv.*

lin•e•a•ment ['lɪniəmənt] *n.* **1** a part or feature; distinctive characteristic. **2** a part or feature of a face with attention to its outline. ⟨< L *lineamentum* < *linea* line¹⟩ **—,lin•e•a'men•tal,** *adj.* **—,lin•e•a•men'ta•tion,** *n.*

lin•e•ar ['lɪniər] *adj.* **1** of or having to do with a line or lines: *linear symmetry.* **2** made of lines; making use of lines: *a linear drawing.* **3** *Mathematics and physics.* involving measurement in one dimension only: *linear measure.* **4** long, narrow, and even in width: *Grass has linear leaves.* **5** of length: *the linear dimensions of the building.* **6** of thinking, using strictly logical reasoning and direct relationships. Compare LATERAL. ⟨< L *linearis* < *linea* line¹⟩ **—'lin•e•ar•ly,** *adv.*

Linear A a system of writing, not yet deciphered, found in Minos on Crete.

linear accelerator *Physics.* an accelerator in which charged particles are speeded up in a straight line by a series of electrical impulses along their path.

linear algebra *Mathematics.* the algebra that deals primarily with number sets and variables arranged in rows or columns (matrices) and with line segments representing physical quantities such as force or velocity (vectors).

Linear B a syllabic script used in Greek documents of Crete from the 14th to the 12th century B.C.

linear equation *Mathematics.* an equation whose graph is a straight line.

linear measure 1 a measure of length. **2** any unit or system of units for measuring length.

linear programming *Mathematics.* the minimization (or maximization) of a linear function subject to linear constraints expressed as qualities or inequalities.

li•ne•ate ['lɪniɪt] *or* ['lɪni,eit] *adj.* marked with lines; striated.

line•back•er ['laɪn,bækər] *n. Football.* a defensive player whose playing position is just behind the line of scrimmage.

line breeding selective breeding of animals to secure certain traits.

line dancing a popular form of dancing, often to country and western music, in which dancers of all ages and both sexes perform steps in rows, all facing the same way.

line drive *Baseball.* a ball hit in a straight line.

line judge LINESMAN (def. 2).

line•man ['laɪnmən] *n., pl.* **-men. 1** a person who sets up or repairs telegraph, telephone, or electric wires. **2** *Football.* a centre, guard, tackle, or end. **3** *Hockey.* any person playing in the forward line. **4** a person who inspects railway tracks. **5** *Surveying.* the person who carries the line or chain.

lin•en ['lɪnən] *n.* **1** thread or yarn spun from flax. **2** cloth made from flax thread or yarn: *Linen is very strong and is cool in summer.* **3** often **linens,** *pl.,* articles made of linen or of cotton, synthetics, or blends. Tablecloths and serviettes are called **table linen;** sheets, pillow cases, etc. are called **bed linen. 4** (*adjl.*) made of linen. **5** (*adjl.*) designed to hold or store linens: *a linen closet.* **6** *Archaic.* underwear.
wash (one's) **dirty linen in public.** See DIRTY LINEN. ⟨OE *līnen,* adj. < *līn* flax⟩

line of battle soldiers or ships in battle formation.

line of credit 1 credit advanced by a bank to a particular borrower up to a stated limit, with terms of repayment like those of a credit card rather than a regular loan. **2** the stated limit of such credit.

line of duty service or duty, especially military duty.
in the line of duty, in the course of doing one's duty, especially military duty.

line of fire 1 the path of a bullet, shell, etc. fired or about to be fired from a gun. **2** any very dangerous or vulnerable position.

line of force *Physics.* in a field of electrical or magnetic force, the line that indicates the direction in which the force is acting.

line of scrimmage SCRIMMAGE (def. 2).

line of sight 1 an imaginary line running straight through the sights of a firearm, theodolite, etc. **2** *Astronomy.* an imaginary line from a person to a star or planet.

line post *Cdn.* in the fur trade, a fur post close to a railway line.

line printer *Computer technology.* a high-speed, impact printer usually associated with mainframes and minicomputers.

lin•er¹ ['laɪnər] *n.* **1** a ship or airplane belonging to a transportation line or system. **2** a person who or thing that makes lines. **3** *Baseball.* a ball hit so that it travels not far above the ground.

lin•er² ['laɪnər] *n.* **1** something that serves as a lining: *a diaper liner, a hat liner.* **2** a paper envelope for a phonograph record inside the jacket, used as a protective covering.

liner notes information about a phonograph record, printed on the liner.

lines•man ['laɪnzmən] *n., pl.* **-men. 1** lineman. **2** *Sports.* a person who watches the lines that mark out the field, rink, court, etc. to assist the umpire or referee.

line spectrum *Physics.* a spectrum with narrow bands.

line–up or **line•up** ['laɪn ,ʌp] *n.* **1** a number of persons arranged in a line; especially, a group including a suspected offender, lined up for identification by police or the victim of an offence. **2** *Sports.* **a** the list of players on a team arranged according to position of play, etc. **b** the players on such a list. **3** a queue of people waiting for something: *There was a long line-up for tickets.* **4** any arrangement of persons or things in a line or as if in a line.

ling¹ [lɪŋ] *n., pl.* **ling** or **lings. 1** any of several edible fishes (genus *Molva*) of the cod family found along the coasts of N Europe and Greenland, especially *M. molva,* having a long, slender body. **2** burbot. ⟨ME *lenge* < OE *lang* long¹⟩

ling² [lɪŋ] *n.* heather. ⟨ME < ON *lying*⟩

–ling *suffix.* **1** little, young, or unimportant: *duckling, princeling.* **2** one that is ——: *underling.* **3** one belonging to or concerned with ——: *earthling, hireling.* ⟨OE⟩

ling. linguistics.

lin•ga ['lɪŋgə] *n.* **1** lingam. **2** *Sanskrit grammar.* the masculine gender.

Lin•ga•la [lɪŋ'gɑlə] *n.* a Bantu language used as a lingua franca in Zaire.

lin•gam ['lɪŋgəm] *n.* a phallus used as a symbol of the Hindu god Shiva. ⟨< Skt. *linga* penis⟩

ling•cod ['lɪŋ,kɒd] *n.* an important food fish (*Ophiodon elongatus*) of the Pacific coast of North America, related to the greenlings.

lin•ger ['lɪŋgər] *v.* **1** put off departure; stay on, especially because of reluctance to leave: *Several fans lingered at the stage door for some time after the actor had gone in.* **2** continue to stay or live, although gradually dying or becoming less: *Daylight lingers long in the summertime.* **3** go slowly; saunter; dally. **4** persist, especially in the mind: *The tune lingers in my mind.* ⟨frequentative of earlier *leng* delay, OE *lengan* < *lang* long¹⟩ **—'lin•ger•er,** *n.* **—'lin•ger•ing•ly,** *adv.*

☛ *Syn.* **Linger,** LOITER, LAG = delay in starting or along the way. **Linger** emphasizes delay in starting, and suggests slowness in going because of unwillingness to leave: *She lingered quite a while after the others had left.* **Loiter** emphasizes stopping along the way, and suggests moving slowly and aimlessly: *Mary loitered downtown, looking into all the shop windows.* **Lag** emphasizes falling behind others or in one's work, and suggests failing to keep up the necessary speed or pace: *The child lagged because he was tired.*

lin•ge•rie [,lɑ̃ʒə'rei], ['lɑ̃ʒə,rei], *or* ['lændʒəri]; *French,* [lɛ̃ʒ'ʀi] *n.* women's undergarments, nightgowns, etc. ⟨< F *lingerie* < *linge* linen⟩

lin•go ['lɪŋgou] *n., pl.* **-goes.** *Informal.* language, especially a dialect, jargon, etc. regarded as outlandish or incomprehensible: *the lingo of sports writers, the lingo of medical people.* ⟨blend of Provençal *lengo* and Ital. *lingua,* both < L *lingua* tongue⟩

lin•gon•ber•ry ['lɪŋgən,bɛri] *n.* **1** a small shrub (*Vaccinium vitis-idaea*) of the heath family, having white or pink flowers and dark red berries. **2** the berry of this plant. ⟨< Swedish *lingon* mountain cranberry + BERRY⟩

lin•gua fran•ca ['lɪŋgwə 'fræŋkə], *pl.* **lingua francas** or **linguae francae** ['lɪŋgwi 'frænsi] **1** a language or dialect used as a common means of communication between peoples having different native languages: *Swahili is the lingua franca of central Africa.* **2** a hybrid language developed for this purpose: *Chinook jargon was the lingua franca of Canada's Pacific coast.* **3 Lingua Franca,** a hybrid language based on Italian and using elements of Spanish, French, Greek, Arabic, and Turkish, used in Mediterranean ports. **4** any code or system used as a common means of communication between people having different languages, backgrounds, etc.: *Pop music is the new lingua franca.* ⟨< Ital. *lingua franca* Frankish language⟩

lin•gual ['lɪŋgwəl] *adj., n. —adj.* **1** of or having to do with the tongue: *a lingual defect.* **2** *Phonetics.* articulated with the aid of the tongue: *a lingual sound.* **3** of or having to do with speech or languages; linguistic.
—n. Phonetics. a sound articulated with the aid of the tongue. The sounds generally represented by *d* and *t* are linguals. ⟨< Med.L *lingualis* < L *lingua* tongue⟩

lin•gui•form ['lɪŋgwə,fɔrm] *adj.* tongue-shaped.

lin•gui•ne [lɪŋ'gwini] *n.* narrow strips of pasta, often served with seafood. ⟨< Ital. pl. of *linguino,* dim. of *lingua* tongue⟩

lin•guist ['lɪŋgwɪst] *n.* **1** a person trained in linguistics, especially one whose work it is. **2** a person skilled in a number of languages besides his or her own; polyglot. **3** philologist. ⟨< L *lingua* tongue + E *-ist*⟩

lin•guis•tic [lɪŋ'gwɪstɪk] *adj.* of or having to do with language or the study of language or languages. **—lin'guis•ti•cal•ly,** *adv.*

linguistic area a region in which several languages are spoken, having some features that are alike.

linguistic atlas a book or books containing maps showing the distribution of dialect words, pronunciations, etc.

linguistic form any part of language that has meaning such as a morpheme, word, phrase, or sentence.

linguistic geography the study of dialect in a region or regions.

lin•guis•tics [lɪŋ'gwɪstɪks] *n.* the study of human speech; the study of the structures, sounds, forms, functions, and varieties of language and languages (*used with a singular verb*). Compare PHILOLOGY.

linguistic universal a language feature common to, or potential in, all languages.

lin•gu•late ['lɪŋgjəlɪt] *or* ['lɪŋgjə,leit] *adj.* linguiform.

lin•i•ment ['lɪnəmənt] *n.* a liquid for rubbing on the skin to relieve soreness, sprains, bruises, etc. ⟨< LL *linimentum* < *linere* anoint⟩

lin•ing ['laɪnɪŋ] *n., v. —n.* **1** a layer of material covering the inner surface of something: *the lining of a coat, a copper kettle with a tin lining.* **2** the material used for lining: *I bought satin lining for the coat.*
—v. ppr. of LINE. ⟨< *line*[2]⟩

link[1] [lɪŋk] *n., v. —n.* **1** one ring or loop of a chain. **2** anything that joins as a link joins: *a cuff link.* **3** a fact or thought that connects others: *a link in a chain of evidence.* **4** a unit of length used in surveying; one one-hundredth of a chain (about 20 cm). **5** *Chemistry.* a bond. **6** *Computer technology.* connection; path: *telecommunications link.*
—v. join as a link does; unite or connect. ⟨ME < ON **hlenkr.* Akin to LANK.⟩

link[2] [lɪŋk] *n.* a torch formerly used for lighting people's way through the streets. ⟨origin uncertain⟩

link•age ['lɪŋkɪdʒ] *n.* **1** a linking or being linked. **2** an arrangement or system of links. **3** *Genetics.* the arrangement of non-allelic genes so close together on the same chromosome that they tend to be transmitted together rather than independently.

linkage disequilibrium *Genetics.* the state in which specific alleles at two or more linked gene loci occur together in a population more often than would be expected by chance, indicating that the loci are closely linked.

linkage group *Genetics.* a set of gene loci known to be closely linked.

linkage map *Genetics.* a chromosome map showing the relative positions of known genes, developed chiefly by linkage analysis.

linking verb a verb (such as **be, become,** or **seem**) that does not express action and is not followed by an object. It links a subject with an adjective that modifies the subject or with a noun that stands for the same person or thing as the subject; copula. *Examples*: I *am* sleepy. He *turned* pale. She *is* a doctor. They *became* friends.
☛ *Usage.* Many verbs with full meanings of their own (such as *taste, feel, act, look*) can also be used as linking verbs: *The butter tastes rancid. She felt sad. He acts old. This looks excellent.*

links [lɪŋks] *n.pl. Esp. Brit.* GOLF COURSE. ⟨OE *hlinc* rising ground⟩

Lin•ne•an or **Lin•nae•an** [lɪ'niən] *adj.* of Carolus Linnaeus (1707-1778), a Swedish botanist. The **Linnean system** of naming animals and plants uses two words, the first for the genus and the second for the species.

lin•net ['lɪnɪt] *n.* **1** a small, mainly brownish finch (*Acanthis cannabina;* also classified as *Carduelis cannabina*) found in dry, open regions of Europe and W Asia. The male has a red crown and breast and a beautiful song, which made it a popular cage bird in the 19th century. **2** any of various other finches of Europe or North America. ⟨< OF *linette* < *lin* flax < L *linum*; it feeds on flaxseed⟩

li•no•le•um [lə'nouliəm] *n.* **1** especially formerly, a durable, washable floor covering made by putting a hard surface of ground cork mixed with oxidized linseed oil on a canvas or burlap back. **2** a similar, more modern floor covering made of vinyl. ⟨coined from L *linum* flax + *oleum* oil⟩

Li•no•type ['laɪnə,təip] *n. Trademark.* a typesetting machine that is operated like a typewriter and that casts each line of type in one piece.

lin•seed ['lɪn,sid] *n.* the seed of flax. ⟨OE *līnsǣd* flaxseed⟩

linseed oil a yellowish oil pressed from linseed, used especially in making paints, printing inks, and varnishes.

lin•sey ['lɪnzi] *n., pl.* **-seys.** linsey-woolsey.

lin•sey–wool•sey ['lɪnzi 'wʊlzi] *n., pl.* **-wool•seys.** a strong, coarse fabric made of linen and wool or of cotton and wool. ⟨ME *linsey* a linen fabric (< *lin-,* OE *līn* linen) + E *wool,* with a rhyming ending⟩

lin•stock ['lɪn,stɒk] *n.* formerly, a stick used to hold a fuse or match in firing a cannon. ⟨< Du. *lontstok* < *lont* match + *stok* stock⟩

lint [lɪnt] *n.* **1** a soft down or fleecy material obtained by scraping linen. **2** fuzz or fluff consisting of tiny bits of fibre from yarn or cloth, often accumulating in clothes dryers. ⟨ME *linnet,* probably ult. < L *linum* or OE *līn* flax⟩ **—'lint•less,** *adj.*

lin•tel ['lɪntəl] *n.* a horizontal beam or stone over a door, window, etc., that carries the weight of the wall above it. See FRAME for picture. ⟨ME < OF *lintel,* ult. < L *limes, limitis* boundary⟩

li•on ['laɪən] *n.* **1** a large, wild animal (*Panthera leo*) of the cat family, having a dull yellow coat, a tufted tail, and, in the adult male, a heavy, shaggy, brown mane around the neck and shoulders. Lions are native to Africa and southwestern Asia. **2** a very brave or strong person. **3** a famous or important person: *a literary lion.* **4 a** the lion as a heraldic symbol, especially as the national emblem of Britain. **b** the British nation itself. **5 Lion,** *Astronomy or astrology.* Leo.
beard the lion in his den, defy a feared or powerful person in his or her own home, office, etc.
put (one's) **head in the lion's mouth,** put oneself in a dangerous position.
twist the lion's tail, intentionally provoke some government or other authority, especially the government or people of the U.K. ⟨ME < AF < L *leo* < Gk. *leōn*⟩ **—'li•on,like,** *adj.*

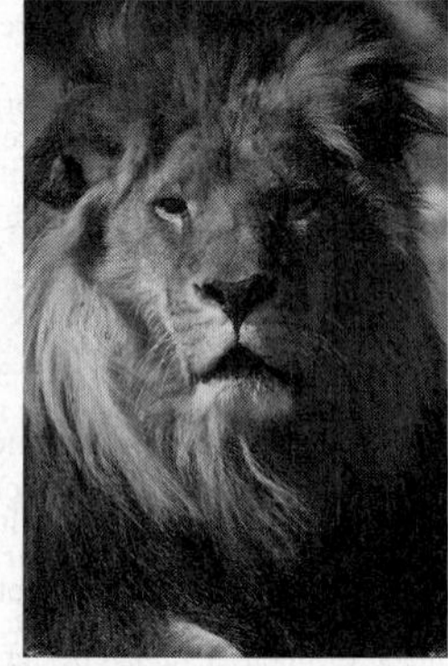
A lion

li•on•ess ['laɪənɪs] *n.* a female lion.

li•on•heart ['laɪən,hart] *n.* someone very brave.

li•on–heart•ed ['laɪən ,hartɪd] *adj.* brave.
—'li•on-,heart•ed•ly, *adv.* **—'li•on-,heart•ed•ness,** *n.*

li•on•ize ['laɪə,naɪz] *v.* **-ized, -iz•ing.** treat as very important: *The visiting artist was lionized by the press.* **—,li•on•i'za•tion,** *n.* **—'li•on,iz•er,** *n.*

Lions Club a society for community service.

lion's share the biggest or best part: *to get the lion's share of the publicity. She grabbed the lion's share of the dessert.*

li•o•thy•ro•nine [ˌlaɪouˈθaɪrəˌnin] *n.* a drug used to treat an inadequate thyroid gland and goitre.

lip [lɪp] *n., v.* **lipped, lip•ping.** —*n.* **1** either of the two fleshy, movable edges of the mouth. **2 lips,** *pl.* these parts as speech organs. **3** a folding or bent-out edge of any opening: *the lip of a pitcher.* **4** *Music.* **a** the mouthpiece of a musical instrument. **b** the shaping of the lips in order to play a wind instrument. **5** *Slang.* impudent talk: *Don't give me any lip.* **6** *Botany.* **a** either of the two parts of a labiate corolla or calyx, the upper lip being closest to the axis of the inflorescence and the lower lip farthest away from the axis. **b** in an orchid, the labellum.
bite one's lip, keep anger or other strong feeling under control.
button or **zip one's lip,** *Slang.* keep quiet, especially to keep a secret.
hang on the lips of, listen to with great attentiveness and admiration.
keep a stiff upper lip, be brave or firm; show no fear or discouragement.
smack one's lips, enjoy, especially food, in anticipation; anticipate something eagerly.
—*v.* **1** touch with the lips. **2** use the lips in playing a musical wind instrument. **3** murmur. **4** hit a golf ball so that it touches the hole but does not drop in. ⟨OE *lippa*⟩ **—ˈlip•less,** *adj.* **—ˈlipˌlike,** *adj.*

li•pase [ˈləipeis] *or* [ˈlɪpeis] *n. Biochemistry.* an enzyme occurring in the pancreatic juice, certain seeds, etc., capable of changing fats into fatty acids and glycerin. ⟨< Gk. *lipos* fat⟩

lip gloss a cosmetic applied to the lips to make them shiny, often containing some colour.

lip•id [ˈlɪpɪd] *or* [ˈləipɪd] *n. Biochemistry.* any of a large group of natural organic compounds, including fats, oils, waxes, and steroids, that are insoluble in water but soluble in certain organic solvents such as alcohol. Lipids, proteins, and carbohydrates are the main structural components of living organisms. Also, **lipide.**

lip•oid [ˈlɪpɔɪd] *or* [ˈləipɔɪd] *n.* any of a group of fats such as lecithin.

lip•o•suc•tion [ˈlɪpouˌsʌkʃən] *or* [ˈləipouˌsʌkʃən] *n.* surgical removal of fatty tissue by suction through a small hole.

lipped [lɪpt] *adj., v.* —*adj.* **1** having a lip or lips. **2** having a lip or lips of a specified kind (*used in compounds*): *thin-lipped, tight-lipped.*
—*v.* pt. and pp. of LIP.

lip•py [ˈlɪpi] *adj. Slang.* insolent or impudent; talking back: *Don't get lippy with me.*

lip–read [ˈlɪp ˌrid] *v.* **-read** [-ˌrɛd], **-read•ing.** understand (speech) by lip reading. **—lip reader,** *n.*

lip reading the act or process of interpreting speech without hearing it by watching the lip movements and facial expression of the speaker.

lip–serv•ice [ˈlɪp ˌsɜrvɪs] *n.* service expressed in words only; pretended loyalty or devotion; insincerity. **—ˈlip-ˌserv•er,** *n.*

lip•stick [ˈlɪpˌstɪk] *n.* **1** a smooth cosmetic paste for the lips, usually coloured and often in the form of a stick in a case. **2** a case containing this cosmetic.

lip–sync or **–synch** [ˈlɪp ˌsɪŋk] *v.* mouth the words of (a song) while it is played, to make it seem that one is singing. ⟨< *lip sync*(*hronization*)⟩

liq. 1 liquid. **2** liquor.

liq•ue•fac•tion [ˌlɪkwəˈfækʃən] *n.* **1** the process of changing into a liquid. **2** the state of being a liquid.

liq•ue•fy [ˈlɪkwəˌfaɪ] *v.* **-fied, -fy•ing.** change into a liquid; make or become liquid. ⟨< L *liquefacere* < *liquere* be fluid + *facere* make⟩ **—ˈliq•ueˌfi•a•ble,** *adj.* **—ˈliq•ueˌfier,** *n.*

li•ques•cent [lɪˈkwɛsənt] *adj.* becoming liquid; melting. ⟨< L *liquescens, -entis,* ppr. of *liquescere* become liquid⟩ **—liˈques•cence,** *n.*

li•queur [lɪˈkjʊr] *n.* a strong, sweet, highly flavoured alcoholic drink. ⟨< F < L *liquor.* Doublet of LIQUOR.⟩

liq•uid [ˈlɪkwɪd] *n., adj.* —*n.* **1** a substance that is neither a solid nor a gas; a substance that flows freely like water. **2** *Phonetics.* the sound of *l* or *r.*
—*adj.* **1** in the form of a liquid; melted: *liquid soap.* **2** clear and bright like water. **3** clear and smooth-flowing in sound: *the liquid notes of a bird.* **4** easily turned into cash: *Canada Savings Bonds are a liquid investment.* ⟨ME < L *liquidus* < *liquere* be fluid⟩ **—ˈliq•uid•ly,** *adv.* **—ˈliq•uid•ness,** *n.*

☛ *Syn. n.* **1. Liquid,** FLUID = a substance that flows. **Liquid** applies to a substance that is neither a solid nor a gas, but flows freely like water: *Milk and wine are liquids; oxygen is not.* **Fluid** applies to anything that flows in any way, either a liquid or a gas: *Milk, water, and oxygen are fluids.*

liquid air the intensely cold, transparent liquid formed when air is very greatly compressed and then cooled. Liquid air is used mainly as a refrigerant.

liquid assets things easily converted into cash: *Savings Bonds are liquid assets.*

liq•ui•date [ˈlɪkwəˌdeit] *v.* **-dat•ed, -dat•ing. 1** pay (a debt). **2** settle the accounts of (a business, etc.); clear up the affairs of (a bankruptcy). **3** convert into cash. **4** *Law.* determine and apportion by agreement or litigation the amount of (indebtedness or damages). **5** get rid of, especially by killing: *The Russian revolution liquidated the nobility.* ⟨< Med.L *liquidare* < L *liquidus.* See LIQUID.⟩ **—ˌliq•uiˈda•tion,** *n.* **—ˈliq•uiˌda•tor,** *n.*

liquid crystal display *Computer technology.* a means of displaying characters on a calculator, digital clock, etc., using a liquid with crystalline properties, especially certain optical properties in the presence of an electric field. *Abbrev.:* LCD

liquid fire flaming oil or a flaming chemical usually hurled from flame throwers, used against fortified emplacements, tanks, etc.

li•quid•i•ty [lɪˈkwɪdɪti] *n.* **1** the state of being a liquid. **2** the state of having liquid assets.

liquid measure 1 the measurement of liquids. **2** a unit or system of units for measuring liquids.

liquid oxygen oxygen at very low temperatures, at which it forms a liquid.

liq•uor [ˈlɪkər] *n.* **1** an alcoholic drink, such as brandy, gin, rum, or whisky. **2** any liquid, especially a liquid in which food is packaged, canned, or cooked: *Pickles are put up in salty liquor.* ⟨< L. Doublet of LIQUEUR.⟩

liquor control board *Cdn.* a government board regulating the distribution and sale of alcoholic beverages within a province, such as British Columbia.

liq•uo•rice [ˈlɪkərɪʃ] *or* [ˈlɪkərɪs] See LICORICE.

li•ra [ˈlɪrə] *n., pl.* **li•re** [ˈlirei] (def. 1), **li•ri** [ˈliri] (def. 3), or **li•ras. 1** the basic unit of money in Italy, divided into 100 centesimi. **2** the basic unit of money in Turkey, divided into 100 kurus. Also called **pound.** See table of money in the Appendix. **3** the basic unit of money in Malta, divided into 100 cents. **4** a coin worth one lira. ⟨< Ital. < L *libra,* a unit of weight⟩

li•sen•te [liˈsɛntei] *n.* pl. of SENTE.

lisle [laɪl] *n.* **1** a fine, strong, linen or cotton thread, used for making stockings, gloves, etc. **2** (*adjl.*) made of lisle. ⟨< F *Lisle,* the former name of *Lille,* a town in N France⟩

lisp [lɪsp] *v., n.* —*v.* **1** produce a *th* sound or something like it instead of the sound of *s* or *z* in speaking: *A person who lisps might say "thing a thong" for "sing a song."* **2** speak like a baby or child: *Babies are said to lisp.*
—*n.* the act, habit, or sound of lisping: *He speaks with a lisp.* ⟨ult. < OE *wlisp,* adj., lisping⟩ **—ˈlisp•er,** *n.* **—ˈlisp•ing•ly,** *adv.*

lis•some or **lis•som** [ˈlɪsəm] *adj.* **1** lithe; limber; supple. **2** nimble; active. ⟨var. of *lithesome*⟩ **—ˈlis•some•ly** or **ˈlis•som•ly,** *adv.* **—ˈlis•some•ness** or **ˈlis•som•ness,** *n.*

list[1] [lɪst] *n., v.* —*n.* **1** a series of names, numbers, words, or other items: *a shopping list.* **2** LIST PRICE.
—*v.* **1** make a list of; enter in a list. **2** *Archaic.* enlist. ⟨< F *liste* < Gmc.⟩

☛ *Syn. n.* **List,** CATALOGUE, ROLL = a series of names or items. **List** is the general word applying to a series of names, figures, etc.: *This is the list of the people who are going to the picnic.* **Catalogue** applies to a complete list arranged alphabetically or according to some other system, often with short descriptions of the items: *Has the new mail-order catalogue come?* **Roll** applies to a list of the names of all members of a group: *Her name is on the honour roll.*

list[2] [lɪst] *n., v.* —*n.* **1** the woven edge of cloth, where the material is a little different from the rest; selvage. **2** a cheap fabric made out of such edges.
—*v.* put a list around the edges of. ⟨OE *līste*⟩

list[3] [lɪst] *n., v.* —*n.* a tipping to one side; tilt: *the list of a ship.* —*v.* tip to one side; tilt: *The sinking ship was listing so that water lapped its decks.* ⟨extended use of *list* inclination, desire < *list*[4]⟩

list[4] [lɪst] *v. Archaic.* **1** be pleasing to; please: *It lists me not to speak.* **2** like; wish: *The wind bloweth where it listeth.* ⟨OE *lystan* < *lust* pleasure⟩

list[5] [lɪst] *v. Archaic and poetic.* **1** listen. **2** listen to. ⟨OE *hlystan* < *hlyst* hearing. Related to LISTEN.⟩

lis•tel [ˈlɪstəl] *n. Architecture.* a narrow moulding or border. ⟨< F < Ital. *listello,* dim. of *lista* band, LIST[2]⟩

lis•ten ['lɪsən] *v.* **1** try to hear; pay attention so as to hear: *She listened for the sound of the car. I like to listen to music.* **2** give heed (to advice, temptation, etc.); pay attention: *Politicians should listen to their constituents.*
listen in, **a** listen to others talking: *I listened in on the extension.* **b** listen to the radio: *Listen in next week for another drama.* ⟨OE *hlysna.* Related to LIST[5].⟩ **–lis•ten•er,** *n.*
☛ *Syn.* **1.** See note at HEAR.

list•er ['lɪstər] *n.* a plough with a double mouldboard that throws the dirt to both sides of the furrow. ⟨< *list*[2]⟩
☛ *Hom.* LEISTER.

list•ing ['lɪstɪŋ] *n., v. –n.* **1** a piece of real estate for sale: *three new listings today.* **2** *Computer technology.* a document produced by a computer, consisting of printed lines of information.
–v. ppr. of LIST.

list•less ['lɪstlɪs] *adj.* seeming too tired to care about anything; not interested in things; not caring to be active: *a dull and listless mood.* ⟨< *list*[4]⟩ **–'list•less•ly,** *adv.* **–'list•less•ness,** *n.*

list price the price given in a catalogue or list. Discounts are figured from it.

lists [lɪsts] *n.pl.* **1** in the Middle Ages: **a** a field where knights fought in tournaments. **b** the barriers enclosing such a field. **2** the tournament. **3** any place or scene of combat.
enter the lists, join in a contest; take part in a fight, argument, etc. ⟨blend of *list*[2] and OF *lice* place of combat < Gmc.⟩

lit [lɪt] *v.* a pt. and a pp. of LIGHT[1] and LIGHT[3].
☛ *Usage.* See note at LIGHT[1].

lit. **1** literature. **2** literal; literally.

li•ta ['litɑ] *n., pl.* **-tas** or **-tu** [-tu]. the main unit of money in Lithuania divided into 100 centas. See table of money in the Appendix.

lit•a•ny ['lɪtəni] *n., pl.* **-nies. 1** a form of prayer for use in church services, consisting of a series of petitions recited by the clergy, alternating with fixed responses from the congregation. **2** any recital or account involving much repetition: *a litany of complaints.* ⟨ME < OF < LL *litania* < Gk. *litaneia* litany, an entreating < *litesthai* entreat⟩

li•tchi ['litʃi] *n., pl.* **-tchis. 1** the small, round or oval fruit of a Chinese tree (*Litchi chinensis*) of the soapberry family having a brittle outer covering and white, very juicy pulp surrounding one seed. It is eaten fresh, canned, or dried. **2** the tree bearing this fruit. **3** See LITCHI NUT. Also, **lichee, lychee.** ⟨< Chinese *li chih*⟩

litchi nut the fruit of the litchi, especially when dried. ⟨< Chinese⟩

lit–crit ['lɪt 'krɪt] *n. Informal.* literary criticism.

–lite *combining form.* stone; stony: *Chrysolite = gold-coloured stone.* ⟨< F *-lite* < earlier *-lithe* < Gk. *lithos* stone⟩

li•ter ['litər] See LITRE.

lit•er•a•cy ['lɪtərəsi] *n.* **1** the ability to read and write. **2** minimal competence in any field: *computer literacy.*

lit•er•al ['lɪtərəl] *adj.* **1** following the exact words of the original: *a literal translation.* **2** taking words in their usual or basic meaning; actual: *a literal interpretation. When we say* He flew down the stairs to meet them, *we do not mean* fly *in the literal sense of the word.* **3** concerned mainly with facts; matter-of-fact: *a literal type of mind.* **4** true to fact; not exaggerated: *a literal account. The literal truth of the matter is that he was terrified.* **5** of, having to do with, or expressed by letters of the alphabet. ⟨ME < LL *lit(t)eralis* < L *lit(t)era* letter⟩ **–'lit•er•al•ness,** *n.*
☛ *Hom.* LITTORAL.

lit•er•al•ism ['lɪtərə,lɪzəm] *n.* **1** keeping to the literal meaning in translation or interpretation. **2** in visual art, utter realism.

lit•er•al•ist ['lɪtərəlɪst] *n.* **1** a person who adheres to the exact literal meaning. **2** a person who represents or portrays without idealizing. **–,lit•er•al'is•tic,** *adj.* **–,lit•er•al'is•ti•cal•ly,** *adv.*

lit•er•al•ize ['lɪtərə,laɪz] *v.,* **-ized, iz•ing.** make literal; interpret literally. **–,lit•er•al•i•'za•tion,** *n.* **–'lit•er•al,iz•er,** *n.*

lit•er•al•ly ['lɪtərəli] *adv.* **1** word for word; not figuratively or imaginatively: *to translate literally.* **2** actually; without exaggeration: *I was literally penniless; I couldn't even get a cup of coffee.* **3** *Informal.* virtually.
☛ *Usage.* **Literally** is sometimes used informally as a general intensifier: *The desk was literally buried in papers.* This usage gives **literally** the exact opposite of its real meaning of 'actually; without exaggeration', and should, therefore, be avoided in formal English.

lit•er•ar•y ['lɪtə,rɛri] *adj.* **1** having to do with literature or the humanities: *a literary treatise.* **2** of or having to do with books: *a literary agent.* **3** of or having to do with writers, scholars, etc., or writing as a profession: *a literary journal.* **4** knowing much about and enjoying literature; fond of books and reading: *They are a very literary family.* **–'lit•er,ar•i•ly,** *adv.* **–'lit•er,ar•i•ness,** *n.*

lit•er•ate ['lɪtərɪt] *adj., n. –adj.* **1** able to read and write. **2** acquainted with literature; educated. **3** minimally competent in any field.
–n. a literate person. ⟨ME < L *lit(t)eratus* < *lit(t)era* letter⟩ **–'lit•er•ate•ly,** *adv.* **–'lit•er•ate•ness,** *n.*

lit•e•ra•ti [,lɪtə'rɑti] *or* [,lɪtə'reitaɪ] *n.pl.* scholarly or literary people. ⟨< L *lit(t)erati,* pl., literally, lettered⟩

lit•e•ra•tim [,lɪtə'reitɪm] *adv.* letter for letter; exactly as written. ⟨< Med.L *lit(t)eratim* < L *lit(t)era* letter⟩

lit•er•a•ture ['lɪtərətʃər] *or* ['lɪtərə,tʃʊr] *n.* **1** the writings of a period or of a country, especially those kept alive by their excellence of style or thought: *Stephen Leacock is a famous name in Canadian literature.* **2** all the books and articles on a subject: *the literature of stamp collecting.* **3** the profession of a writer. **4** the study of literature: *I am going to take literature and mathematics this spring.* **5** *Informal.* printed matter of any kind: *Election campaign literature informs people about the candidates.* ⟨ME < L *lit(t)eratura* writing < *lit(t)era* letter⟩

–lith *combining form.* rock; stone: *megalith.* ⟨< Gk. *lithos*⟩

lith•arge ['lɪθɑrdʒ] *or* [lə'θɑrdʒ] *n.* a yellow oxide of lead, used in making glass, glazes for pottery, and dryers for paints and varnishes. *Formula:* PbO ⟨ME < OF *litarge* < L < Gk. *lithargyros* < *lithos* stone + *argyros* silver⟩

lithe [laɪð] *adj.,* **lith•er, lith•est.** bending easily; supple; flexible: *lithe of body, a lithe willow.* ⟨OE *līthe* mild⟩ **–'lithe•ly,** *adv.* **–'lithe•ness,** *n.*

lithe•some ['laɪðsəm] *adj.* lithe.

lith•i•a ['lɪθiə] *n.* a white, crystalline oxide of lithium. *Formula:* Li_2O ⟨< NL < Gk. *lithos* stone⟩

lith•ic ['lɪθɪk] *adj.* **1** consisting of stone or rock. **2** *Medicine.* of or having to do with stone or stony concretions formed within the body, especially in the bladder. ⟨< Gk. *lithikos* < *lithos* stone⟩

lith•i•um ['lɪθiəm] *n. Chemistry.* **1** a soft, silver-white, metallic chemical element similar to sodium. Lithium is the lightest of all the metals. *Symbol:* Li; *at.no.* 3; *at.mass* 6.94. **2** LITHIUM CARBONATE. ⟨< NL < Gk. *lithos* stone⟩

lithium carbonate ['kɑrbə,neit] a salt used in industry and also as a drug to treat manic-depressive illness.

litho– *combining form.* stone: *lithograph.* Also, **lith-** before vowels. ⟨< L < Gk. *lithos* stone⟩

lith•o•graph ['lɪθə,græf] *n., v. –n.* a picture, print, etc. made by lithography.
–v. produce or print by lithography. ⟨< *litho-* + *-graph*⟩

li•thog•ra•pher [lə'θɒgrəfər] *n.* a person trained in lithography, especially one whose work it is.

li•thog•ra•phy [lə'θɒgrəfi] *n.* the art or process of transferring an image onto paper from a flat surface such as a metal plate, by preparing the surface so that certain parts receive ink while other parts repel it. **–,lith•o'graph•ic** [,lɪθə'græfɪk], *adj.* **–,lith•o'graph•i•cal•ly,** *adv.*

li•thol•o•gy [lə'θɒlədʒi] *n.* the study of rocks.

lith•o•pone ['lɪθə,poun] *n.* a white pigment that is a mixture of zinc sulphide, zinc oxide, and barium sulphate, used in paints as a non-poisonous substitute for white lead. ⟨< *litho-* + Gk. *ponos* work. 20c.⟩

lith•o•sphere ['lɪθə,sfir] *n.* the solid outer shell of the earth, including the continental and oceanic crusts, thought to be about 100 km thick. Many scientists believe the lithosphere to consist of separate, rigid plates that move on the hot, thick asthenosphere. ⟨< *litho-* + *sphere*⟩

Lith•u•a•nia [,lɪθu'einjə] *or* [,lɪθju'eɪnjə] *n.* a country on the Baltic Sea. See LATVIA for map.

Lith•u•a•ni•an [,lɪθu'einjən] *or* [,lɪθju'einjən] *n., adj. –n.* **1** a native or inhabitant of Lithuania. **2** the Baltic language of the Lithuanians.
–adj. of or having to do with Lithuania, its people, or their language.

lit•i•ga•ble ['lɪtəgəbəl] *adj.* capable of being made the subject of a suit in a law court.

lit•i•gant ['lɪtəgənt] *n., adj. –n.* a person engaged in a lawsuit.
–adj. engaging in a lawsuit.

lit•i•gate ['lɪtə,geit] *v.* **-gat•ed, -gat•ing. 1** engage in a lawsuit.

2 contest in a lawsuit. ⟨< L *litigare* < *lis*, *litis* lawsuit + *agere* drive⟩ **—'lit•i,ga•tor,** *n.*

lit•i•ga•tion [,lɪtɪ'geiʃən] *n.* **1** the act of carrying on a lawsuit; going to law. **2** lawsuit.

li•ti•gious [lə'tɪdʒəs] *adj.* **1** having the habit of going to law. **2** offering material for a lawsuit; that can be disputed in a court of law. **3** of or pertaining to lawsuits. ⟨< L *litigiosus* < *litigium* dispute < *litigare.* See LITIGATE.⟩ **—li'ti•gious•ly,** *adv.* **—li'ti•gious•ness, li,ti•gi'os•i•ty** [lɪ,tɪdʒi'ɒsɪti], *n.*

lit•mus ['lɪtməs] *n.* a blue colouring matter obtained from lichens, that turns red in an acid solution and back to blue in an alkaline solution. It is used to indicate whether a particular chemical solution is an acid or a base. ⟨ME < ON *litmose* dyer's herb < *litr* colour + *mosi* moss⟩

litmus paper a strip of paper treated with litmus, used to indicate whether a solution is an acid or a base.

litmus test **1** *Chemistry.* a test using litmus paper to see whether a solution is acidic or alkaline. **2** any test dependent on one crucial factor.

li•to•tes ['ləitə,tiz], ['lɪtə,tiz], *or* [ləi'toutiz] *n., pl.* **-tes.** *Rhetoric.* a form of understatement in which something is said by denying its opposite. *Examples*: *The palace was no small bungalow. He had not a little to drink. Compare* HYPERBOLE. ⟨< Gk. *litotēs* < *litos* simple, plain⟩

li•tre ['litər] *n.* a unit used with the SI for measuring volume or capacity, equal to one cubic decimetre. One litre of water has a mass of one kilogram. The litre is used for measuring liquids and other products such as ice cream and fruit, and for measuring the capacity of containers such as gas tanks, cooking pots, jugs, and baskets. Also, **liter.** *Symbol*: L ⟨< F *litre* < *litron*, an obs. French measure of capacity < Med.L *litra* < Gk. *litra*, a unit of weight⟩

lit•ter ['lɪtər] *n., v.* *—n.* **1** scattered rubbish; things scattered about or left in disorder. **2** disorder; untidiness. **3** the young animals born at the same time from one mother: *a litter of puppies.* **4** straw, hay, etc. used as bedding for animals. **5** gravel or other material put in a cat's litter box. **6** a stretcher for carrying a sick or wounded person. **7** a framework to be carried on peoples' shoulders or by beasts of burden, consisting of a couch usually enclosed by curtains.
—v. **1** leave (odds and ends) lying around; scatter (things) about. **2** make disordered or untidy: *He littered the yard with bottles and cans.* **3** give birth to (young animals). **4** make a bed for (an animal) with straw, hay, etc. ⟨ME < AF *litere* < Med.L *lectaria* < L *lectus* bed⟩ **—'lit•ter•er,** *n.*

lit•téra•teur or **lit•te•ra•teur** [,lɪtərə'tɜr]; *French,* [liteʀa'tœʀ] *n.* a literary person; a writer or critic of literature. ⟨< F⟩

litter box a box containing gravel or other material, for use as a toilet by a cat.

lit•ter•bug ['lɪtər,bʌg] *n. Informal.* one who leaves litter lying about in public places.

lit•tle ['lɪtəl] *adj.* **less** or **less•er, least;** or **lit•tler, lit•tlest;** *adv.* **less, least;** *n.* *—adj.* **1** not great or big; small: *A grain of sand is little. The little dog barked loudly.* **2** not much; small in number, amount, degree, or importance: *little money, little hope, a little army.* **3** short, brief: *She took a little walk.* **4** mean and narrow in thought or feeling: *Only a little man would pinch a child. That little sneak stole my sweater.*
—adv. **1** in a small amount or degree; to a small extent; slightly: *He travels little.* **2** not at all: *He little knows what will happen.*
—n. **1** a small amount, quantity, or degree: *to add a little.* **2** a short time or distance: *to move a little to the left.*
in little, on a small scale.
little by little, by a small amount at a time; slowly; gradually: *She recovered her strength little by little.*
make little of, treat or represent as of little importance: *She made little of her troubles.*
not a little, much; very: *He was not a little upset by the accident.*
think little of, a not value much; consider as unimportant or worthless: *Criminals think little of their victims' rights.* **b** not hesitate about.
think nothing of, regard as trivial; do without hesitation: *He thinks nothing of driving 100 km to meet a friend for dinner.* ⟨OE *lȳtel*⟩ **—'lit•tle•ness,** *n.*

☛ *Syn. adj.* **1, 2. Little,** SMALL, DIMINUTIVE = not large or great. **Little** means not big or great in size, quantity, degree, importance, etc., and often carries positive or negative emotional overtones: *He is a funny little boy. You little tattletale.* **Small** suggests being below average in size, number, or measure: *He is small for his age.* **Diminutive** means very small in size: *Her feet are diminutive.*

Little Bear *Astronomy.* the northern constellation Ursa Minor.

Little Dipper *Astronomy.* the seven principal stars in the constellation Ursa Minor, arranged in a form that suggests a dipper. The star forming the end of the handle of the Little Dipper is the North Star. Compare BIG DIPPER.

Little Dog *Astronomy.* the constellation Canis Minor.

little finger the finger that is farthest from the thumb; the smallest finger: *She wears a ring on her little finger.*
twist or **wrap** (someone) **around one's little finger,** influence (someone) easily.

little magazine or **review** a small magazine devoted to printing new or experimental writing, criticism, etc.

lit•tle•neck ['lɪtəl,nɛk] *n.* a young quahog clam. Also called **littleneck clam.**

little people **1** in folklore, small imaginary beings, such as fairies, elves, leprechauns, etc. **2** the common people, especially the working class, small merchants, etc.

little theatre **1** a small, usually amateur theatre group. Some little theatres present experimental plays. **2** such groups collectively, or the drama produced by them.

lit•to•ral ['lɪtərəl] *adj., n.* *—adj.* **1** of or having to do with a shore, especially of the sea. **2** found or growing on or near the shore.
—n. the region along a shore, especially the zone between the marks of high and low tide. ⟨ult. < L *litoralis* < *litus*, *litoris* shore⟩
☛ *Hom.* LITERAL.

li•tu ['litu] *n.* a pl. of LITA.

li•tur•gi•cal [lə'tɜrdʒəkəl] *adj.* of or having to do with liturgy. Also, **liturgic. —li'tur•gi•cal•ly,** *adv.*

lit•ur•gy ['lɪtərdʒi] *n., pl.* **-gies. 1** a form or ritual for public worship: *Different churches use different liturgies.* **2** Often, **Liturgy,** the Eucharistic service, especially in the Eastern Orthodox Church. ⟨< LL *liturgia* < Gk. *leitourgia* public worship, ult. < *leitos* public + *ergon* work⟩

liv•a•ble ['lɪvəbəl] *adj.* **1** fit to live in: *livable surroundings.* **2** easy to live with. **3** worth living; endurable: *A good friendship often helps make life livable*. Also, *esp. U.S.* **liveable.** **—'liv•a•ble•ness,** *adj.* **—,liv•a'bil•i•ty** *n.*

live[1] [lɪv] *v.* **lived, liv•ing. 1** have life; be alive; exist: *All creatures have an equal right to live.* **2** remain alive; last; endure: *He managed to live through the war.* **3** support oneself: *live on one's income. She lives on government grants.* **4** subsist; feed: *They live on meat and potatoes. Rabbits live mainly on grass.* **5** pass (life): *to live well, to live a life of ease.* **6** dwell: *My aunt lives in Victoria.* **7** carry out or show in life: *to live one's ideals.* **8** have a rich and full life: *Those people know how to live*! **9** play (a part) effectively: *Good actors live the parts they play.*
live (something) **down,** live so worthily that (some fault or sin of the past) is overlooked or forgotten: *She is determined to live down that disgrace.*
live for, take great interest in; have a passion for: *She lives for dancing.*
live in, live at the place where one works.
live it up, *Slang.* enjoy life to the full.
live off, live on (defs. a-c).
live on, a support oneself by. **b** have as one's main diet. **c** use (someone) as a source of income or supplies. **d** continue to exist.
live out, a live away from where one works. **b** stay alive through; last through.
live up to, act according to; do (what is expected or promised): *The car has not lived up to the sales representative's description.*
live with, accept; tolerate; be reconciled to. ⟨OE *lifian, libban*⟩

live[2] [laɪv] *adj., adv.* *—adj.* **1** having life; alive: *a live dog.* **2** burning or glowing: *live coals.* **3** full of energy or activity: *She is a very live girl, always on the go.* **4** *Informal.* up-to-date: *live ideas.* **5** of present interest: *a live question.* **6** moving or imparting motion: *live wheels, a live axle.* **7** still in use or to be used: *live steam.* **8** *Electricity.* carrying an electric current; charged electrically: *a live wire.* **9** of telephones, microphones, etc., not shut off; operating or functioning. **10** charged with explosive: *a live cartridge.* **11** in the native state; not mined or quarried: *live metal.* **12** *Radio and television.* broadcast as performed and not from tape or film made beforehand: *a live television show.*
—adv. of recordings or broadcasts, made as performed before an audience: *The concert was recorded live.* ⟨var. of *alive*⟩
—'live•ness, *n.*

live•a•ble ['lɪvəbəl] *adj.* See LIVABLE.

live•bear•er ['laɪv,bɛrər] *n.* any fish that bears live young instead of laying eggs, such as the guppy.

–lived *combining form.* having a ——life or lives: *short-lived* = *having a short life.*

live–for•ev•er ['lɪv fər,ɛvər] *n.* sedum.

live–in ['lɪv 'ɪn] *adj., n.* —*adj.* **1** living at one's place of employment, usually a house. *a live-in nanny.* **2** cohabiting.
—*n.* **1** a live-in employee. **2** a cohabiting lover.

live•li•hood ['laɪvli,hʊd] *n.* a means of living, that is, of obtaining the money necessary to buy food, clothing, and shelter; a means of supporting oneself; LIVING (def. *n.* 3): *She writes for a livelihood. She earns her livelihood as a farmer.* ⟨OE *līf(ge)lād* (see LIFE, LOAD), influenced by obs. *livelihood* liveliness⟩
☛ *Syn.* See note at LIVING.

live load a variable weight that a structure carries in addition to its own weight, such as moving traffic on a bridge. Compare DEAD LOAD.

live•long ['lɪv,lɒŋ] *or* ['laɪv,lɒŋ] *adj.* the whole length of; whole; entire: *She is busy the livelong day.*

live•ly ['laɪvli] *adj.* **-li•er, -li•est;** *adv.* —*adj.* **1** full of life; active; vigorous; spirited. **2** exciting. **3** bright; vivid. **4** cheerful and spirited: *a lively conversation.* **5** bouncing well and quickly: *a lively tennis ball.*
—*adv.* in a lively manner. ⟨OE *līflīc* living⟩ —**'live•li•ness,** *n.*

liv•en ['laɪvən] *v.* make or become more lively or interesting (*often used with* **up**): *The show isn't bad, but they could liven it up a little.*

live oak [laɪv] any of various North American evergreen oaks valued as ornamental or timber trees, especially *Quercus virginiana* of SE North America and Cuba, having very hard, heavy, strong wood formerly much used in shipbuilding.

live off the country *Cdn., esp. North.* subsist on the food available in a region, as game, fish, berries, etc.

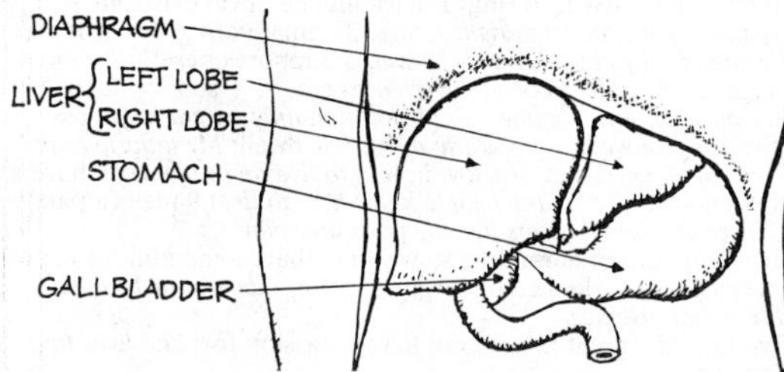

The human liver, seen from the front

liv•er[1] ['lɪvər] *n.* **1** *Anatomy.* in vertebrates, a large, reddish brown organ that secretes bile and helps in the absorption of food. The liver frees the blood of its waste matter and causes important changes in many of its substances. **2** an animal's liver used as food. ⟨OE *lifer*⟩ —**'liv•er•less,** *adj.*

liv•er[2] ['lɪvər] *n.* a person who lives in a certain way: *She is a fast liver.* ⟨< *live*[1]⟩

liv•ere ['lɪvjər] See LIVEYERE.

liv•er•ied ['lɪvərid] *adj.* clothed in a livery.

liv•er•ish ['lɪvərɪʃ] *adj. Informal.* having a sour or peevish disposition, one of the supposed symptoms of liver trouble; irritable. —**'liv•er•ish•ness,** *n.*

liv•er•wort ['lɪvər,wɜrt] *n.* **1** any of a class (Hepaticae) of creeping, flowerless plants that grow in wet soil or on damp rocks, fallen logs, etc. Liverworts resemble mosses and together with them make up the plant division Bryophyta. **2** hepatica.

liv•er•wurst ['lɪvər,wɜrst] *or* ['lɪvər,wʊrst] *n.* a sausage consisting largely of ground liver. Also called **liver sausage.** ⟨< G *Leberwurst* liver sausage⟩

liv•er•y ['lɪvəri] *n., pl.* **-er•ies. 1** any special uniform provided for the servants of a household, or adopted by any group or profession. **2** any characteristic dress, garb, or outward appearance. **3** the feeding, stabling, and care of horses for pay. **4** the hiring out of horses and carriages. **5** the keeping of cars, boats, bicycles, etc. for hire. **6** LIVERY STABLE. ⟨ME < AF *livere* < *livrer* dispense < L *liberare* liberate; originally, provisions dispensed to servants⟩

liv•er•y•man ['lɪvərimən] *n., pl.* **-men. 1** a person who owns or works in a livery stable. **2** a person who wears or is entitled to wear livery.

livery stable a place where horses and vehicles are kept for hire or where horses are fed and stabled for a fee.

lives [laɪvz] *n.* pl. of LIFE.

live•stock ['laɪv,stɒk] *n.* farm animals. Cows, horses, sheep, and pigs are livestock.

live wire 1 *Electricity.* a wire through which an electric current is flowing. **2** *Informal.* an energetic, wide-awake person: *Our new sales manager is a real live wire.*

live•yere ['lɪvjər] *n. Cdn.* **1** in Newfoundland, a permanent resident, as opposed to those who are on the island or in Labrador for the fishing or sealing season only. **2** a permanent resident of the north shore of the Gulf of St. Lawrence. Also, **livere, livier.** ⟨< *livier*, formerly, a type of manorial worker having certain property rights < AF *livere.* Cf. LIVERY.⟩

liv•id ['lɪvɪd] *adj.* **1** having a dull bluish or greyish colour, as from a bruise: *livid marks on an arm.* **2** very pale: *livid with shock.* **3** flushed; reddish: *livid with anger.* **4** *Informal.* very angry: *The insults made her livid.* ⟨< L *lividus* < *livere* be bluish⟩ —**'liv•id•ly,** *adv.* —**'liv•id•ness** or **li'vid•i•ty,** *n.*

liv•ier ['lɪvjər] See LIVEYERE.

liv•ing ['lɪvɪŋ] *adj., n., v.* —*adj.* **1** having life; being alive: *a living plant.* **2** full of life; vigorous; strong; active: *a living faith.* **3** in actual existence; still in use: *a living language.* **4** true to life; vivid; lifelike: *a living picture.* **5** of life; for living in: *living conditions.* **6** sufficient to live on: *a living wage.*
in living memory, within the lifetime of people still living.
—*n.* **1** the condition of being alive: *The old woman was filled with the joy of living.* **2 the living,** *pl.* all the people who are alive. **3** a means of obtaining what is needed to support life; livelihood. **4** a manner of life: *healthful living.* **5** a position in certain Christian churches, including the income attached to it; benefice.
—*v.* ppr. of LIVE.[1]
☛ *Syn. n.* **3. Living,** LIVELIHOOD, SUPPORT = a person's means of providing shelter, food, etc. for himself or herself. **Living** is the general word and suggests nothing more: *He always had to work hard for his living.* **Livelihood** often applies to the work a person does to earn enough to live on or to the pay he or she gets: *Mowing lawns is her only livelihood.* **Support** applies to the providing of a means of living: *They depend on his mother for their support.*

living quarters a place to live.

living room a room in a house or apartment, used for the general leisure activities of the occupants, for entertaining guests, etc.

living wage a wage sufficient to enable a person or family to live in reasonable comfort and security.

living will a document written by a person still healthy, stating his or her wishes for a future time when he or she may be dependent on life-support machines.

li•vre ['livər] *n.* **1** the main unit of money in Lebanon, divided into 100 piastres. See money table in the Appendix. **2** a former French silver coin. ⟨< F < L *libra*, a unit of weight⟩
☛ *Hom.* LEVER.

liz•ard ['lɪzərd] *n.* **1** any of a suborder (Lacertilia, also called Sauria) of reptiles belonging to the same order as snakes, having external ears, eyes with movable lids, dry, scaly skin, and, in most species, a long, slender body with a long tail and four short legs. Geckos, chameleons, and iguanas are lizards. **2** any of various animals having a relatively long body, short legs, and a tail, such as salamanders, alligators, or dinosaurs. ⟨ME < OF *lesard* < L *lacertus*⟩ —**'liz•ard,like,** *adj.*

ll. lines.

LL LATE LATIN.

A llama—
about 90 cm high
at the shoulder

lla•ma ['læmə] *or* ['lɑmə] *n., pl.* **-mas** or (*esp. collectively*) **-ma.** a domesticated South American hoofed mammal (*Lama glama*) closely related to the guanaco (from which it may be descended) and the alpaca, having a long neck, a small head with large, erect ears, and thick, shaggy wool. Llamas have long been raised for their wool, milk, and meat and are also used as beasts of burden. ⟨< Sp. < Quechua (Indian lang. of Peru)⟩
☛ *Hom.* LAMA.

lla•no ['lɑnou] *or* ['lænou]; *Sp.,* ['jɑno] *n., pl.* **-nos.** a broad, treeless plain. ⟨< Sp. < L *planus* level⟩

LNG liquefied natural gas.

lo [lou] *interj.* look! see! behold! ⟨OE *lā*⟩
☛ *Hom.* LOW.

loach [loutʃ] *n.* any of a family (Cobitidae) of small freshwater fishes of Asia and Europe with very small scales and having barbels around the mouth. ⟨ME < OF *loche*, ? < Celtic⟩

load [loud] *n., v.* —*n.* **1** whatever is being carried; a pack, cargo, burden, etc.: *The cart has a load of hay.* **2** the amount usually carried at one time; a more or less fixed quantity for a particular type of carrier (*often used in compounds*): *a planeload of tourists. Send us four loads of sand.* **3 loads,** *pl. Informal.* a great quantity or number: *Don't worry; we have loads of food.* **4** something that weighs down or oppresses: *That's a load off my mind!* **5** *Mechanics.* the weight supported by a structure or part. **6** the external resistance overcome by an engine, dynamo, or the like, under a given condition, measured by the power required. **7** one charge of powder and shot for a gun. **8** *Slang.* enough liquor to make one drunk.
—*v.* **1** place on or in a carrier of some kind: *The dockhands are loading grain.* **2** put a load in or on: *to load a ship, to load a basket with groceries.* **3** take on a load: *The ship is still loading.* **4** oppress or burden (*often used with* **down**): *loaded down with debt. They were loaded down with worries.* **5** supply amply or in excess: *They loaded her with compliments.* **6** add weight to: *load dice.* **7** put a charge in (a gun). **8** place (something needed to begin operation) into (a device): *to load a cassette into a videotape recorder, to load a camera.* **9** *Computer technology.* transfer (programs, data, etc.) from auxiliary storage into a computer's main memory. ⟨OE *lād* course, carrying; cf. *lode*⟩
—**'load•er,** *n.* —**'load•less,** *adj.*
☛ *Hom.* LODE.
☛ *Syn. n.* **1. Load,** BURDEN = what one is carrying. **Load,** the general word, applies literally to whatever is carried by a person or animal or in a vehicle, boat, or plane: *That is a heavy load of groceries.* It is also used figuratively to apply to something that weighs heavily on the mind or spirit: *His many responsibilities give him a heavy load.* **Burden** applies to something borne and is more often used figuratively, applying to sorrow, care, duty, or work: *She had too heavy a burden and became sick.*

load•ed ['loudɪd] *adj., v.* —*adj.* **1** carrying a load. **2** with a charge in it: *a loaded gun.* **3** weighted, especially with lead: *a loaded stick or whip.* **4** *Slang.* drunk. **5** *Slang.* having plenty of money; rich. **6** *Informal.* full of half-hidden and unexpected meanings and suggestions: *Loaded questions are often intended to trap a person into saying more than he or she wants to say.* **7** *Informal.* well equipped: *This new car is loaded with options.*
—*v.* pt. and pp. of LOAD.

load•star ['loud,stɑr] See LODESTAR.

load•stone ['loud,stoun] See LODESTONE.

loaf[1] [louf] *n., pl.* **loaves** [louvz]. **1** a quantity of bread baked as one piece in a more or less oblong or round shape: *Bread is usually sold by the loaf.* **2** any mass of food shaped like a loaf and baked: *a meat loaf, a salmon loaf.* **3** a cone-shaped mass of sugar. ⟨OE *hlāf*⟩

loaf[2] [louf] *v.* spend time idly; do nothing: *I can loaf all day Saturday.* ⟨origin uncertain; cf. G dial. *lofen* run about, idle⟩

loaf•er ['loufər] *n.* **1** a person who loafs; idler. **2** Usually **Loafers,** *pl. Trademark.* a shoe resembling a moccasin, but with sole and heel stitched to the upper.

loam [loum] *n., v.* —*n.* **1** rich, fertile earth in which decaying and decayed plant matter is mixed with clay and sand. **2** a mixture of clay, sand, and straw used to make moulds for large metal castings, and also to plaster walls, stop holes, etc.
—*v.* cover or fill with loam. ⟨OE *lām*⟩ —**'loam•i•ness,** *n.* —**'loam•less,** *adj.* —**'loam•y,** *adj.*

loan [loun] *n., v.* —*n.* **1** the act of lending; the granting of temporary use: *She asked for the loan of his pen.* **2** anything that is lent, especially money: *He asked his brother for a loan.*
—*v.* make a loan; lend.
on loan, lent or granted for temporary use or service: *Our department manager is on loan to another department for a week. The book was out on loan so I had to wait.* ⟨ME < ON *lān*⟩
—**'loan•a•ble,** *adj.* —**'loan•er,** *n.*
☛ *Hom.* LONE.
☛ *Usage.* **Loan,** LEND. Although some people object to the use of *loan* as a verb, its use as both a verb and a noun is standard current English: *I loaned* (or *lent*) *him my tuxedo. She asked me for a loan of five dollars.*

loan shark *Informal.* a person who lends money at an extremely high or unlawful rate of interest.

loan–shark•ing ['loun ,ʃɑrkɪŋ] *n.* the practice of lending money at extremely high or unlawful rates of interest.

loan translation calque.

loan•word ['loun,wɜrd] *n.* a word taken into a language from another language and adopted as part of that language, often being slightly changed in the process. *Degree* is a very old loanword that came into English from French about 700 years ago. More recent loanwords are *khaki*, from Hindi, and *intelligentsia*, from Russian.

loath [louθ] *or* [louð] *adj.* unwilling; reluctant: *The little girl was loath to leave her mother.*
nothing loath, willing; willingly.
Also, **loth.** ⟨OE *lāth* hostile⟩
☛ *Syn.* See note at RELUCTANT.

loathe ['louð] *v.* **loathed, loath•ing.** feel strong dislike and disgust for; abhor; hate. ⟨OE *lāthian* hate < *lāth* hostile⟩

loath•ing ['louðɪŋ] *n., v.* —*n.* strong dislike and disgust; intense aversion.
—*v.* ppr. of LOATHE.

loath•ly[1] ['louθli] *or* ['louðli] *adv.* unwillingly; reluctantly. ⟨OE *lāthlīce* < *lāth* hostile⟩

loath•ly[2] ['louðli] *adj. Archaic.* loathsome. ⟨OE *lāthlīc* < *lāth* hostile, odious⟩

loath•some ['louðsəm] *or* ['louθsəm] *adj.* disgusting; sickening; hateful; detestable; odious: *a loathsome odour.*
—**'loath•some•ly,** *adv.* —**'loath•some•ness,** *n.*

loaves [louvz] *n.* pl. of LOAF[1].

lob [lɒb] *n., v.* **lobbed, lob•bing.** —*n.* **1** *Tennis.* a ball hit high to the back of the opponent's court. **2** a slow, underarm throw.
—*v.* **1** *Tennis.* hit (a ball) high to the back of an opponent's court. **2** throw (a ball) with a slow, underarm movement. ⟨ME *lobbe(n)* move clumsily⟩ —**'lob•ber,** *n.*

lo•bar ['loubər] *or* ['loubɑr] *adj.* of or having to do with a lobe or lobes.

lo•bate ['loubeit] *adj.* having a lobe or lobes; having the form of a lobe. The liver is lobate. —**'lo•bate•ly,** *adv.*

lo•ba•tion [lou'beiʃən] *n.* **1** a lobate formation. **2** lobe.

lob•by ['lɒbi] *n., pl.* **-bies;** *v.* **-bied, -by•ing.** —*n.* **1** a large entrance hall or vestibule in an apartment building, theatre, hotel, etc.: *A lobby often has chairs or couches to sit on.* **2** a room or hall outside a legislative chamber: *the lobby of the House of Commons.* **3** a group of people that tries to influence legislators.
—*v.* try to influence legislators: *The textile manufacturers are lobbying for a tax on imported fabrics.* ⟨< Med.L *lobia* covered walk < Gmc. Doublet of LODGE.⟩

lob•by•ist ['lɒbiɪst] *n.* a person who tries to influence legislators.

lobe [loub] *n.* a rounded, projecting part. The lobe of the ear is the rounded, lower end. The leaves of the white oak have deeply cut, narrow lobes. ⟨< F < LL < Gk. *lobos*⟩

lobed [loubd] *adj.* having a lobe or lobes.

lo•be•lia [lou'biljə] *or* [lou'biliə] *n.* any of a genus (*Lobelia*) of plants having showy, usually blue, white, pink, or red two-lipped flowers. ⟨< NL; after Matthias de *Lobel* (1538-1616), a Flemish botanist⟩

lo•bot•o•mize [lə'bɒtə,maɪz] *v.* **-mized, -miz•ing.** treat with a lobotomy. **—lo,bot•o•mi'za•tion,** *n.*

lo•bot•o•my [lə'bɒtəmi] *n.* a surgical operation involving incision into a lobe of an organ; especially, the cutting of one or more nerve tracts in the frontal lobe of the brain, formerly used as a treatment for certain severe mental disorders thought to be otherwise incurable. ⟨< Gk. *lobos* lobe + *-tomy*⟩

lob•scouse ['lɒb,skʌus] *n.* scouse.

lob–shot ['lɒb ,ʃɒt] *n. Cdn. Hockey.* a deceptive, slow-moving shot on goal.

lob•ster ['lɒbstər] *n.* **1** any of a family (Homaridae) of edible sea crustaceans having eyes on stalks, a long body, and a pair of large pincers at the front with two pairs of much smaller pincers behind. Lobsters are found along the coasts on both sides of the Atlantic. **2** any of various similar crustaceans. **3** the flesh of a lobster used for food. ⟨OE *loppestre* < L *locusta* locust; influenced by OE < *loppe* spider⟩

lob•ster•man ['lɒbstərmən] *n., pl.* **-men.** a person who catches lobsters.

lobster pot a trap for lobsters.

lob•stick ['lɒb,stɪk] *n. Cdn.* in the North, a tall, prominently situated spruce or pine trimmed of all but its topmost branches, originally used by the First Nations people as a talisman and landmark. The voyageurs often trimmed a lobstick as a memorial to an honoured fellow traveller or a respected superior. Also, **lopstick.** ⟨< *lopped stick*⟩

lob•ule ['lɒbjul] *n.* **1** a small lobe. **2** a part of a lobe.

lob•worm ['lɒb,wɜrm] *n.* lugworm.

lo•cal ['loukəl] *adj., n. —adj.* **1** of or having to do with a certain place or places; limited to a certain place or places: *the local doctor, local politics, local news.* **2** restricted to one part of the body: *a local pain, local disease, local application of a remedy.* **3** making all, or almost all, stops: *a local train.*
—n. **1** a train, bus, etc. that stops at all of the stations on its route. **2** a local inhabitant. **3** a branch or chapter of a labour union, fraternity, etc. **4** a newspaper item of interest to a particular place. **5** a person, team, etc. from a given locality. **6** a telephone extension. **7** a local anesthetic. ⟨< L *localis* < *locus* place⟩ **—'lo•cal•ly,** *adv.* **—'lo•cal•ness,** *n.*

local area network **1** a group of centrally organized services in a locality. **2** *Computer technology.* a set of computers and peripherals connected by communications links to communicate or share resources. *Abbrev.:* LAN

local colour or **color** the customs, peculiarities, etc. of a certain place or period, used in writing by people who have visited the place, to make the story seem more real.

lo•cale [lou'kæl] *n.* location, site, or place, especially with reference to events or circumstances connected with it. ⟨< F *local* local⟩

local government **1** the system of administration of local affairs in a township, city, etc. by its own people through their elected representatives. **2** the group, or council, elected for this purpose.

local improvement district *Cdn.* in some provinces, a district administered by provincial officials because it is too thinly populated to have a municipal government of its own. Also called **local government district.**

lo•cal•ism ['loukə,lɪzəm] *n.* **1** a local practice, custom, etc. **2** a word or expression, etc. peculiar to a certain area. *Example:* Outport, *meaning* an outlying fishing village, *is a Newfoundland localism.* **3** provincialism. **4** attachment to a certain place. **—'lo•cal•ist,** *n.* **—,lo•cal'is•tic,** *adj.*

lo•cal•i•ty [lou'kæləti] *n., pl.* **-ties. 1** a particular place, location, neighbourhood, etc.: *Are there any stores in this locality?* **2** places and things considered as related to others in a region. A sense of locality enables one to find one's way.

lo•cal•ize ['loukə,laɪz] *v.* **-ized, -iz•ing.** make local; fix in, assign, or limit to a particular place or locality: *The infection seemed to be localized in the foot.* **—,lo•cal•i'za•tion,** *n.* **—'lo•cal,iz•er,** *n.*

local option the right of choice exercised by a minor political division, such as a county or city, especially as to whether the sale of liquor shall be permitted within its limits.

Lo•car•no Pact [lou'kɑrnou] a group of treaties and agreements made in 1925 in Locarno, Switzerland to guarantee boundaries and maintain peace in western and central Europe between Germany and Britain, France, Belgium, Italy, Czechoslovakia, and Poland.

lo•cate [lou'keit] *or* ['loukeit] *v.* **-cat•ed, -cat•ing. 1** establish in a place: *He located his new store in Yellowknife.* **2** establish oneself in a place: *Early settlers located where there was water.* **3** find out the exact position of: *The general tried to locate the enemy's camp.* **4** state or show the position of: *Locate Regina on the map.* **5** *Cdn.* formerly, establish (someone) legally as a settler on land under terms of settlement set by the government.
be located, be situated. ⟨< L *locare* < *locus* place⟩ **—lo'cat•a•ble,** *adj.* **—lo'cat•er,** *n.*

lo•ca•tion [lou'keiʃən] *n.* **1** locating or being located: *The scouts disputed about the location of the camp.* **2** a position or place: *The cottage was in a sheltered location.* **3** a plot of ground marked out by boundaries; lot: *a mining location.* **4** an area or place defined by lines of latitude and longitude: *Find the location of Toronto on the map.*
on location, at a place outside the studio for the purpose of filming a motion picture: *All the outdoor scenes were shot on location.*

location ticket *Cdn.* formerly, a certificate empowering its holder to take possession of the portion of land selected.

loc•a•tive ['lɒkətɪv] *adj., n. Grammar. —adj.* of, having to do with, or being the grammatical case, found in Latin and some other languages, that indicates place, as Latin *domī,* meaning 'at home'.
—n. **1** the locative case. **2** a word or construction in the locative case. ⟨< L *locatus,* pp. of *locate.* See LOCATE.⟩

loc. cit. in the place cited (for L *loco citato*).

loch [lɒk] *or* [lɒx] *n. Scottish.* **1** lake: *Loch Lomond.* **2** an arm of the sea partly shut in by land. ⟨< Scots Gaelic⟩
☛ *Hom.* LOCK [lɒk].

lo•chia ['loukiə] *n.* the uterine discharge that follows childbirth. ⟨< NL < Gk. *lochios* < *lochos* childbirth⟩

Loch•in•var ['lɒkɪn,vɑr] *or* [,lɒkɪn'vɑr] *n.* **1** the hero of a poem by Sir Walter Scott (1771-1832), who boldly carries off his sweetheart just as she is about to be married to another man. **2** any romantic suitor.

Loch Ness monster an aquatic serpent said to have been seen in Loch Ness, in NW Scotland.

lo•ci ['lousaɪ] *or* ['lousi], ['loukaɪ] *or* ['louki] *n.* pl. of LOCUS.

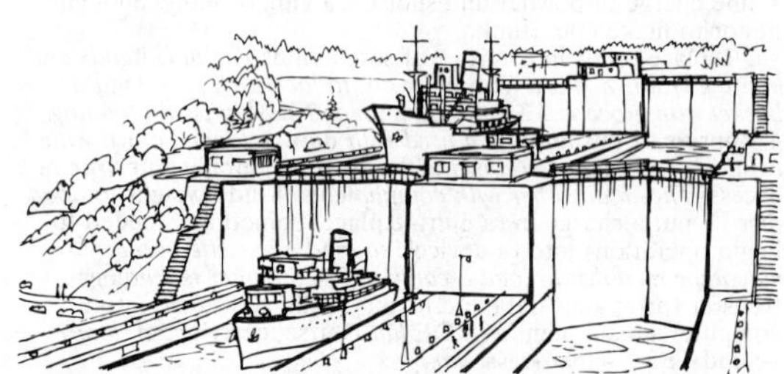

A set of locks in the Welland Canal, built to overcome the 99 m difference in levels between Lake Ontario and Lake Erie. When a ship enters from above, the gates are closed and water is let out until the level is equal to that below the lock. Then the lower gates are opened. When a ship enters from below, the opposite process takes place.

lock[1] [lɒk] *n., v. —n.* **1** a means of fastening doors, boxes, etc., usually needing a key of special shape to open it. **2** an enclosed section in a canal, dock, etc. which permits vessels to be raised or lowered to different water levels outside this compartment, either by letting water in or out of the compartment or, in a lift lock, by raising or lowering the water-filled compartment itself. **3** the part of a gun by which the charge is fired; gunlock. **4** a device to keep something from moving. A lock is used to prevent a parked vehicle from going downhill. **5** an airtight chamber providing entrance to a compartment in which there is compressed air. **6** *Wrestling.* a kind of hold. **7** the complete turning circle of a vehicle: *This car has a wide lock.*
lock, stock, and barrel, *Informal.* completely; entirely.
under lock and key, locked up; in a place that is locked.
—v. **1** fasten with a lock: *I forgot to lock the door.* **2** fasten the door, lid, etc. of with a lock: *to lock a box. Is the garage locked?* **3** shut (a person or thing) in; make (a person or thing) secure or inaccessible by locking something: *to lock old letters away in a*

trunk, to lock up one's private papers. We always lock the cat in the basement for the night. **4** keep (a person or thing) from entering or gaining access (*used with* **out**): *She was so angry she locked her sister out. They locked out of their minds all thought of returning.* **5** hold fast: *The ship was locked in ice. The secret was locked in her heart.* **6** join, fit, jam, or link together: *The girls locked arms.* **7** become locked: *Two cars locked together in passing.* **8** fasten (a wheel) to keep from turning. **9** *Printing.* fasten (type, blocks, etc. in a CHASE³) for printing or plating (*often used with* **up**). **10** make certain to accomplish or get (*used with* **up**): *We've got the championship locked up.* **11** go or pass by means of a lock (*n.* def. 2); move (a ship) by means of a lock.
lock in, invest (money) so that it cannot be taken out before a specified time.
lock out, refuse to give work to (workers) until they accept the employer's terms.
lock up, a lock a building for the night: *Be sure to lock up as you leave.* **b** have (a page of a newspaper) ready to print. **c** keep (money) in a savings account that cannot be used until a certain date: *Our savings are locked up in G.I.C.s.* ⟨OE *loc* fastening, bar⟩ **—'lock•a•ble,** *adj.* **—'lock•less,** *adj.*
☛ *Hom.* LOCH.

lock² [lɒk] *n.* **1** a curl or ringlet of hair. **2 locks,** *pl.* the hair of the head: *The child has curly locks.* **3** a tuft of wool, cotton, etc. ⟨OE *locc* lock of hair⟩
☛ *Hom.* LOCH.

lock•age ['lɒkɪdʒ] *n.* **1** the construction, use, or operation of locks (see LOCK¹, def. 2) in canals or streams. **2** the passing of ships through a lock. **3** the walls, gates, etc. forming a lock. **4** the amount of elevation and descent affected by a lock or locks. **5** the toll paid for passage through a lock.

lock box a box containing a key to a building, so that real estate agents may show it to possible buyers.

lock•er ['lɒkər] *n.* **1** a chest, drawer, closet, or cupboard that can be locked. **2** a large, refrigerated compartment, as at a cold-storage plant, for storing frozen food for a long time. **3** any person or thing that locks or locks something.

locker room a room in a sports facility where players can shower, keep their clothes in a locker, etc.

lock•et ['lɒkɪt] *n.* a small ornamental case of gold, silver, etc. for holding a picture of someone or a lock of hair. It is usually worn around the neck on a necklace. ⟨< F *loquet* latch, dim. of OF *loc* < Gmc.⟩

lock•jaw ['lɒk,dʒɒ] *n.* tetanus. A characteristic symptom of the disease is a stiffness or spasm of the jaw muscles, which may become so severe that the jaws remain clamped shut.

lock•out ['lɒk,ʌut] *n.* the closure of a factory, office, etc. or the refusal of work by an employer in order to make his or her employees agree to terms.

lock•smith ['lɒk,smɪθ] *n.* a person who makes or repairs locks and keys.

lock step a way of marching in step very close together.

lock stitch a sewing-machine stitch in which two threads are fastened together at short intervals.

lock•up ['lɒk,ʌp] *n.* **1** the act or time of locking up. **2** *Informal.* jail.

lo•co ['loukou] *n., pl.* **-cos;** *v.* **-coed, -co•ing;** *adj.*
—n. **1** locoweed. **2** the disease caused by eating this weed.
—v. poison with this weed.
—adj. Slang. crazy. ⟨< Sp. *loco* insane⟩

lo•co•mo•tion [,loukə'mouʃən] *n.* the act or power of moving from place to place. Walking and flying are common forms of locomotion. ⟨< L *loco* from a place + E *motion*⟩

lo•co•mo•tive [,loukə'moutɪv] *n., adj. —n.* an engine that runs on rails on its own power, used to move railway cars.
—adj. **1** moving from place to place: *locomotive bacteria.* **2** of or having to do with the power to move from place to place.

lo•co•mo•tor [,loukə'moutər] *adj.* of or having to do with locomotion.

locomotor ataxia a degenerative disease of the spinal cord, marked by loss of control over walking and certain other movements.

lo•co•weed ['loukou,wid] *n.* any of various plants (genera *Astragalus* and *Oxytropis*) of the pea family found in arid regions of W North America, that are poisonous to livestock, producing frenzied behaviour followed by impairment of vision, paralysis, and, sometimes, death.

lo•cum te•nens ['loukəm 'tinənz] a person temporarily holding the place or office of another, such as a doctor; deputy; substitute. Also, **locum.** ⟨< Med.L < L *locum*, accus. of *locus* place < *tenens*, ppr. of *tenere* hold⟩

lo•cus ['loukəs] *n., pl.* **lo•ci. 1** place or locality. **2** *Mathematics.* the set or system of all points whose location satisfies given conditions. The locus of points equidistant from two parallel lines is a line halfway between the two lines and parallel to them. **3** *Genetics.* **a** the position of a particular gene on a chromosome. **b** the gene itself rather than its position. ⟨< L⟩

lo•cust ['loukəst] *n.* **1** any of a family (Acrididae) of grasshoppers having short antennae, especially any of several species that migrate in great swarms, often destroying all vegetation in the areas they pass through. **2** *Esp. U.S.* cicada. **3** any of various hardwood trees of the pea family, such as the **black locust** (*Robinia pseudoacacia*) or the **honey locust** (*Gleditsia triacanthos*), both tall North American trees often planted for ornament. **4** the hard, decay-resistant wood of a locust tree. **5** carob. ⟨< L *locusta*⟩

lo•cu•tion [lou'kjuʃən] *n.* **1** a particular form of expression or phrasing, especially a word or expression characteristic of a particular region, group of people, etc. **2** style of speech: *He has no sense of formal locution.* ⟨< L *locutio, -onis* < *loqui* speak⟩

lode [loud] *n.* **1** a vein of metal ore: *The miners struck a rich lode of copper.* **2** a plentiful source of anything. ⟨OE *lād* course, carrying. Cf. LOAD.⟩
☛ *Hom.* LOAD.

lode mining hardrock mining.

lo•den ['loudən] *n.* **1** a waterproof, woollen fabric, often used to make coats. **2** an olive green, often the colour of this cloth. Also, **loden green.** ⟨< G⟩

lode•star ['loud,stɑr] *n.* **1** a star that shows the way, especially the North Star. **2** a guiding principle. Also, **loadstar.** ⟨< *load* + *star*⟩

lode•stone ['loud,stoun] *n.* **1** iron oxide (magnetite) that is naturally magnetic. **2** a person or thing that attracts strongly: *Gold was the lodestone that drew adventurers to the Yukon.* Also, **loadstone.** ⟨< *load* + *stone*⟩

lodge [lɒdʒ] *v.* **lodged, lodg•ing;** *n. —v.* **1** live in a place for a time. **2** provide with a place to live in or sleep in for a time: *Can you lodge us for the weekend?* **3** live in a rented room or rooms: *We are merely lodging at present.* **4** rent a room or rooms to. **5** get caught or stay in a place: *My kite lodged in the top of a tree.* **6** put or send into a place: *The hunter lodged a bullet in the lion's heart.* **7** put for safekeeping: *lodge money in a bank.* **8** put before some authority: *We lodged a complaint with the police.* **9** put (power, authority, etc.) in a person or thing. **10** of wind or rain, beat down (crops); lay flat.
—n. **1** an inn or resort hotel, etc. **2** a small or temporary house; house: *My uncle rents a lodge in the mountains every summer.* **3 a** a branch of a fraternal organization. **b** the place where such a group meets. **4** the den of an animal such as a beaver or otter. **5** a First Nations dwelling. **6** a First Nations household. ⟨ME < OF *loge* arbour, covered walk < OHG **laubja.* Doublet of LOBBY, LOGE, LOGGIA.⟩ **—'lodge•a•ble,** *adj.*
☛ *Hom.* LOGE.

lodge•ment ['lɒdʒmənt] See LODGMENT.

lodge•pole pine ['lɒdʒ,poul] *Cdn.* **1** a pine (*Pinus contorta*) found throughout British Columbia and western Alberta, occurring in two quite distinct forms: a short, often crooked tree growing along the coast and a tall, straight, slender tree growing inland. The inland form is an important timber-producing tree. The coastal form is often called the **shore pine. 2** its wood.

lodg•er ['lɒdʒər] *n.* a person who lives in a rented room or rooms.

lodg•ing ['lɒdʒɪŋ] *n., v. —n.* **1** a place to live in for a time. **2 lodgings,** *pl.* a rented room or rooms in a house, not in a hotel.
—v. ppr. of LODGE

lodging house a house in which rooms are rented.

lodg•ment or **lodge•ment** ['lɒdʒmənt] *n.* **1** a lodging or being lodged: *the lodgment of a complaint.* **2** something lodged or deposited: *a lodgment of earth on a ledge or rock.* **3** *Military.* **a** a position gained; foothold. **b** an entrenchment built temporarily on a position gained from the enemy.

lo•ess ['louɪs], [lɛs], *or* [lus]; *German,* [lœs] *n.* a deposit of fine, yellowish brown loam found in river valleys in North America, Europe, and Asia, believed to have been deposited by the wind. Loess is very fertile when irrigated. ⟨< G *Löss*⟩

loft [lɒft] *n., v. —n.* **1** attic. **2** a room under the roof of a barn or stable; hayloft. **3** a gallery in a church or hall: *a choir loft.*

4 the partly open or unpartitioned upper floor of a business or apartment building or warehouse: *a studio loft.* **5** *Golf.* **a** the backward slope of the face of a club to give elevation to a struck ball. **b** a stroke that drives a ball upward. **6** the natural resiliency of wool, down, or other material, enabling it to act as insulation by holding air.
—*v.* **1** *Golf.* hit (a ball) high up into the air. **2** propel or lift high in the air. ⟨OE < ON *lopt* air, sky, loft⟩

loft•y ['lɒfti] *adj.* **loft•i•er, loft•i•est. 1** very high: *lofty mountains.* **2** high in character or spirit; exalted; noble: *lofty aims, lofty ideals.* **3** proud; haughty: *He had a lofty contempt for others.* **—'loft•i•ly,** *adv.* **—'loft•i•ness,** *n.*
☛ *Syn.* **1.** See note at HIGH.

log[1] [lɒg] *n., v.* **logged, log•ging.** —*n.* **1** a length of wood just as it comes from the tree. **2** any piece of cut firewood. **3** *Nautical.* the daily record of a ship's voyage. **4** the record of an airplane trip, performance of an engine, etc. **5** a personal diary of a journey. **6** *Nautical.* a float for measuring the speed of a ship.
—*v.* **1** cut down trees, cut them into logs, and get them out of the forest. **2** cut (trees) into logs. **3** cut down trees on (land). **4** enter in a logbook or log. **5** enter the name and offence of (a sailor) in a ship's log. **6** travel (a particular distance) or reach (a particular speed): *We logged 800 km the first day.*
log in, mark one's arrival in a book.
log in or **on,** begin a session of work on a computer by entering a password or other identification.
log off or **out,** end a session of work on a computer by signing off.
log out, mark one's departure in a book. ⟨ME *logge;* origin uncertain⟩ **—'log,like,** *adj.*

log[2] [lɒg] *n.* logarithm.

lo•gan ['lougən] *n. Cdn.* pokelogan.

lo•gan•ber•ry ['lougən,bɛri] *n., pl.* **-ries. 1** a dark red berry closely resembling a blackberry, that is the fruit of a trailing, prickly plant (*Rubus loganobaccus*) of the rose family thought to be a cross between the wild blackberry of the Pacific coast and the red raspberry. **2** the plant that bears these berries, cultivated along the Pacific coast of North America. ⟨< J.H. *Logan* (1841-1928), a U.S. jurist and horticulturist, its first grower⟩

log•a•rithm ['lɒgə,rɪðəm] *n. Mathematics.* **1** an exponent of the power to which a fixed number (usually 10) must be raised in order to produce a given number. If the fixed number is 10, the logarithm of 1000 is 3; the logarithm of 10 000 is 4; the logarithm of 100 000 is 5. **2** one of a system of such exponents used to shorten calculations in mathematics. ⟨< NL *logarithmus* < Gk. *logos* proportion + *arithmos* number⟩ **—,log•a'rith•mic, ,log•a'rith•mi•cal,** *adj.* **—,log•a'rith•mi•cal•ly,** *adv.*

log–birl•ing ['lɒg ,bɜrlɪŋ] *n.* birling.

log•book ['lɒg,bʊk] *n.* **1** a book containing a permanent record of all the details of the voyage of a ship or aircraft. **2** a traveller's diary. **3** any book containing a record of progress or performance over a period of time.

log cabin a small house built entirely of logs, squared off and caulked with clay.

log drive *Cdn.* the transportation of logs by means of water. **—log driver.**

loge [louʒ] *or* [lɒʒ] *n.* **1** a box in a theatre or opera house. **2** a balcony or mezzanine in a theatre, especially the front part of such a balcony. ⟨< F. Doublet of LODGE.⟩
☛ *Hom.* LODGE [lɒdʒ].

logged–off ['lɒgd 'ɒf] *adj. Cdn. Lumbering.* cleared of timber through logging operations. Also, **logged-out.**

log•ger ['lɒgər] *n.* **1** *Cdn.* a person whose work is felling trees and getting the logs to the mill. **2** a machine for loading or hauling logs.
☛ *Hom.* LAGER.

log•ger•head ['lɒgər,hɛd] *n.* **1** *Archaic or dialect.* a stupid person; blockhead. **2** any of various very large, large-headed marine turtles (genus *Caretta*) of the warmer waters of the western Atlantic, especially a carnivorous species (*C. caretta*). **3** an iron instrument consisting of a long handle with a ball at the end that is heated for melting pitch, etc.
at loggerheads, disputing; in disagreement: *The council members are still at loggerheads over the housing issue.* ⟨< *logger*, var. of *log*[1] + *head*⟩

loggerhead shrike a bird (*Lanius ludoricianus*) smaller than the robin or northern shrike, native to southern Canada, the U.S., and Mexico, and having dark grey upper plumage with a black bar on the eye. It is an endangered species.

log•gia ['lɒdʒə] *or* ['lɒdʒiə]; *Italian,* ['lɔddʒa] *n., pl.* **log•gias** ['loudʒəz] *or* ['lɒdʒiəz]; *Italian,* **log•gie** ['lɔddʒe]. a gallery or arcade open to the air on at least one side. ⟨< Ital. < F *loge.* Doublet of LODGE.⟩

log•ging ['lɒgɪŋ] *n., v.* —*n. Cdn.* the work of cutting down trees, cutting them into logs, and removing them from the forest.
—*v.* ppr. of LOG.

logging bee *Cdn.* formerly, a gathering of neighbours to clear land by logging.

log•ic ['lɒdʒɪk] *n.* **1** the science of getting new and valid information by reasoning from facts that one already knows. **2** a book on logic. **3** reasoning; the use of argument: *The lawyer won her case because her logic was sound.* **4** reason; sound sense: *There is much logic in what you say.* ⟨ME < OF *logique* < LL < Gk. *logikē (technē)* reasoning (art) < *logos* word⟩
—'log•ic•less, *adj.*

log•i•cal ['lɒdʒəkəl] *adj.* **1** having to do with or according to the principles of logic: *logical reasoning.* **2** reasonable; reasonably expected. **3** reasoning correctly: *a clear and logical mind.*
—'log•i•cal•ly, *adv.* **—,log•i'cal•i•ty** or **'log•i•cal•ness,** *n.*

logic bomb *Computer technology.* a set of instructions in a computer program that can cause a program to fail in certain circumstances, especially when these instructions have been created intentionally.

lo•gi•cian [lə'dʒɪʃən] *n.* a person trained or skilled in logic.

lo•gis•tic [lə'dʒɪstɪk] *adj.* of or having to do with logistics. Also, **logistical. —lo'gis•ti•cal•ly,** *adv.*

lo•gis•tics [lə'dʒɪstɪks] *n.* **1** the art of planning and carrying out military movement, evacuation, and supply. **2** the planning and handling of any complex operation. ⟨< F *logistique*, ult. < *loger* lodge⟩

log•jam ['lɒg,dʒæm] *n., v.* **-jammed, -jam•ming.** —*n. Cdn.* **1** an accumulation of floating logs jammed together in the water. **2** any deadlock or blockage, often figurative, as a backlog of paperwork.
—*v.* delay, block, or obstruct.

lo•go ['lougou] *or* ['lɒgou] *n.* an identifying symbol used as a trademark, in advertising, etc.

LOGO a computer language devised specially for children. ⟨< Gk. *logos* word⟩

log•o•gram ['lɒgə,græm] *n.* a character or symbol used to represent a whole word, such as ¢ for *cent.*

lo•gom•a•chy [lə'gɒməki] *n., pl.* **-chies. 1** an argument about words. **2** a meaningless battle of words. ⟨< Gk. *logomachía* < *logos* word + *machia, machē* battle⟩

log•o•phile ['lɒgə,faɪl] *n.* a lover of words. ⟨< Gk. *logos* word⟩

log•or•rhea [,lɒgə'riə] *n.* excessive, especially compulsive, wordiness or talkativeness. ⟨< NL *logorrhoea* < Gk. *logos* word + *rhoia* (< rheîn to flow)⟩ **—,log•or'rhe•ic,** *adj.*

log•o•type ['lɒgə,təip] *n.* **1** *Printing.* a word or several frequently used letters cast in one piece but not connected, such as *Ltd., etc.* **2** logo.

log•roll ['lɒg,roul] *v. Informal.* **1** take part in logrolling. **2** *Esp. U.S.* get (a bill) passed by logrolling. **—'log,roll•er,** *n.*

log•roll•ing ['lɒg,roulɪŋ] *n., v.* —*n.* **1** the act of rolling logs, especially by walking on them. **2** the giving of political aid in return for a like favour.
—*v.* ppr. of LOGROLL.

log–trough roof ['lɒg ,trɒf] SCOOP ROOF.

log•wood ['lɒg,wʊd] *n.* **1** a tropical American tree (*Haematoxylon campechianum*) of the pea family. **2** its heavy, hard, brownish red wood, from which a dye is obtained that is used especially in biological stains. **3** the dye.

lo•gy ['lougi] *adj.* **-gi•er, -gi•est.** *Informal.* heavy; sluggish; dull. ⟨?< Du. *log* heavy, dull⟩

-logy *combining form.* **1** an account, doctrine, or science of ——: *biology, theology.* **2** writing; discourse; discussion: *eulogy, trilogy, anthology.* ⟨< Gk. *-logia*, in a few cases < *logos* word, discourse, but usually < *-logos* treating of < *legein* speak (of), mention⟩

loin [lɔɪn] *n.* **1** Usually, **loins,** *pl.* the part of the body between the ribs and the hips. The loins are on both sides of the backbone. **2** a piece of meat from this part: *a loin of pork.* See PORK, BEEF, LAMB, and VEAL for pictures.
gird up (one's) **loins,** get ready for action. ⟨ME < OF *loigne*, ult. < L *lumbus*⟩

loin•cloth [ˈlɔɪn,klɒθ] *n.* a piece of cloth fastened around the waist and covering the thighs. The loincloth is worn by people in certain warm countries.

loi•ter [ˈlɔɪtər] *v.* **1** linger or stand around idly. **2** dawdle. **3** spend (time) idly. ⟨ME < MDu. *loteren* be loose⟩
—ˈloi•ter•er, *n.*
☛ *Syn.* **1.** See note at LINGER.

Lo•ki [ˈlouki] *n. Norse mythology.* the god who constantly created trouble and evil, especially among his fellow gods. He caused the death of Balder.

L.O.L. LOYAL ORANGE ASSOCIATION (OR LODGE).

loll [lɒl] *v., n.* *—v.* **1** recline or lean in a lazy manner: *to loll on a chesterfield.* **2** hang out loosely or droop: *A dog's tongue lolls out in hot weather.* **3** allow to hang out or droop: *A dog lolls out its tongue.*
loll about, sit or rest comfortably and lazily.
—n. a lolling. ⟨ME *lolle(n)*⟩

Lol•lard [ˈlɒlərd] *n.* a follower of John Wycliffe (1320?-1384), an English religious reformer. The Lollards advocated certain religious, political, and economic reforms, and were persecuted as heretics. ⟨< MDu. *lollaerd* mumbler < *lollen* mumble⟩
—ˈLol•lard•ry or **ˈLol•lard,ism,** *n.*

lol•li•pop or **lol•ly•pop** [ˈlɒli,pɒp] *n.* a piece of hard candy on the end of a small stick; sucker. ⟨< dial. *lolly* tongue + *pop*⟩

Lom•bard [ˈlɒmbɑrd] *or* [ˈlɒmbərd], [ˈlʌmbɑrd] *or* [ˈlʌmbərd] *n.* **1** a member of a Germanic group that in the 6th century A.D. conquered the part of N Italy since known as Lombardy. **2** a native or inhabitant of Lombardy. **3** one that lends money or acts as a bank. ⟨< Ital. *Lombardo* < LL *Langobardus* < Gmc.; original meaning, long beard⟩

Lombard Street **1** a London street famous as a financial centre. **2** the London money market or financiers as a group.

Lom•bard•y poplar [ˈlɒmbərdi] *or* [ˈlʌmbərdi] a variety of European poplar (*Populus nigra italica*) having a narrow, spirelike crown and almost vertical branches, commonly grown in parts of Canada as an ornamental tree.

lo•mus•tine [ˈloumə,stin] *n.* a drug used to treat certain forms of cancer.

lon. longitude.

London plane a variety of sycamore tree (*Platanus acerifolia*) commonly planted, especially in Ontario and B.C., as a shade tree, having a leaf wider than it is long, and bearing hairy fruit.

lone [loun] *adj.* **1** having no company or companion; alone; solitary: *We met a lone traveller on our way.* **2** lonesome; lonely: *a lone life.* **3** standing apart; isolated: *a lone house on a hill.* **4** *Rare.* single or widowed. ⟨var. of *alone*⟩
☛ *Hom.* LOAN.

lone•li•ness [ˈlounlinɪs] *n.* a being lonely; solitude.

lone•ly [ˈlounli] *adj.* **-li•er, -li•est. 1** feeling oneself alone and longing for company: *He was lonely while his brother was away.* **2** without many people: *a lonely road.* **3** alone: *a lonely tree.*

lon•er [ˈlounər] *n. Informal.* a person who prefers to live or be alone.

lone•some [ˈlounsəm] *adj.* **-som•er, -som•est. 1** feeling lonely. **2** making one feel lonely. **3** unfrequented; desolate: *a lonesome road.* **4** solitary: *One lonesome pine stood there.*
—ˈlone•some•ly, *adv.* **—ˈlone•some•ness,** *n.*

lone wolf *Informal.* a person who prefers to work or live alone; loner.

long[1] [lɒŋ] *adj., adv.* **long•er** [ˈlɒŋgər], **long•est** [ˈlɒŋgɪst]; *n.* *—adj.* **1** measuring much, or more than usual, from end to end in space or time: *a long distance, a long speech.* **2** continuing too long; lengthy; tedious: *long hours of waiting.* **3** of a unit of measure, beyond the normal extension in space, duration, quantity, etc.: *a long dozen, a long ton.* **4** having a specified length in space or time: *five metres long, two hours long.* **5** thin and narrow: *a long pole.* **6** far-reaching; extending to a great distance in space or time: *a long memory, a long look into the future.* **7** *Phonetics.* **a** of vowels or syllables, taking a slightly longer time to pronounce than those classified as short. The vowel in *beet* is long in comparison to the vowel in *bit.*
b popularly, designating any of the English vowels in *bait, beet, bite, boat,* and *boot.* **8** involving considerable risk, liability to error, etc.: *a long chance.* **9** *Finance.* **a** well supplied (with some commodity or stock). **b** depending on a rise in prices for profit.
a long face, a sad expression.
in the long (or **short**) **run.** See RUN.
—adv. **1** throughout the whole length of: *all night long.* **2** for a long time: *a reform long advocated.* **3** at a point of time far distant from the time indicated: *long before, long since.*
as long as or **so long as,** provided that.
—n. **1** a long time: *He hasn't worked there for long.* **2** a long sound, syllable, or signal: *Morse code consists of longs and shorts.*
before long, soon; in a short time.
the long and the short of it, the sum total (of something); substance; upshot: *The long and the short of it is that she'll be looking for another job.* ⟨OE *lang*⟩ **—ˈlong•ness,** *n.*

long[2] [lɒŋ] *v.* wish very much; have a strong desire: *to long for peace.* ⟨OE *langian* < *lang* long[1]⟩

long. longitude.

lon•gan [ˈlɒŋgən] *n.* **1** a tree (*Euphoria longana*) native to Asia, having edible fruit like litchis. **2** the fruit of this tree. ⟨< NL *longanum* < Chinese *lung-yen* dragon's eye⟩

long•boat [ˈlɒŋ,bout] *n. Nautical.* the largest and strongest boat carried by a merchant sailing ship.

long•bow [ˈlɒŋ,bou] *n.* a bow drawn by hand and shooting a long feathered arrow. A longbow is usually between 170 cm and 185 cm long.
draw the longbow, tell exaggerated stories.

long•cloth [ˈlɒŋ,klɒθ] *n.* a kind of fine, soft cotton cloth.

long–dis•tance [ˈlɒŋ ˈdɪstəns] *adj., n.* *—adj.* **1** of or having to do with telephone service to another town, city, etc. **2** for or over great distances; travelling great distances: *a long-distance moving van.*
—n. an operator or exchange that takes care of long-distance calls.

long division *Arithmetic.* division involving numbers containing usually two or more digits, and in which the steps of the process are written down in full.

long dozen thirteen; baker's dozen.

long–drawn [ˈlɒŋ ˈdrɒn] *adj.* lasting a long time; prolonged to great length: *the long-drawn howl of a coyote, a long-drawn speech.*

long•ear sunfish [ˈlɒŋ,ir] a freshwater food fish (*Lepomis megalotis*) found from the Maritimes to Manitoba, and in some lakes in British Columbia, having a small mouth and a bright orange belly. The female lays its eggs in nests which are cared for by the male. It grows to about 12 cm long.

lon•gev•i•ty [lɒnˈdʒɛvəti] *n.* long life. ⟨< L *longaevitas* < *longaevus* long-lived < *longus* long + *aevum* age⟩

long–finned smelt [ˈlɒŋ ˈfɪnd] a fish (*Spirinchus dilatus*) found in Pacific coastal waters, spawning in freshwater streams. It is small and not common, although good to eat.

long•hair [ˈlɒŋ,hɛr] *n., adj. Informal.* *—n.* **1** a person who is interested in intellectual or artistic things, especially one who prefers classical music to popular music or jazz. **2** hippie.
—adj. Also, **long-haired,** of, suitable for, or referring to longhairs: *longhair music.*

long•hand [ˈlɒŋ,hænd] *n.* ordinary writing, not shorthand or typewriting.

long–hand•led underwear [ˈlɒŋ ˈhændəld] *Cdn. Slang.* warm underwear having ankle-length legs and, usually, long sleeves.

long–head•ed [ˈlɒŋ ,hɛdɪd] *adj.* **1** having foresight and good sense; shrewd. **2** having a long head.

long–headed coneflower a meadow wildflower (*Ratibida columnifera*) having bright yellow petals, and blooming in summer across Canada and south to the prairies. It was used by the First Nations people to make a yellowish orange dye.

long•horn [ˈlɒŋ,hɔrn] *n.* **1** a breed of cattle having very long horns, formerly common in the SW United States. **2** a type of orange Cheddar cheese. Also called **longhorn cheese.**

long•house [ˈlɒŋ,hʌus] *n. Cdn.* a large dwelling of certain First Nations peoples, especially the Iroquois, in which several families of a community lived together. Compare PLANK HOUSE.

longhouse marriage *Cdn.* among non-Christian Iroquois, a wedding ceremony conducted according to the ancient traditions.

longhouse religion *Cdn.* the traditional religious beliefs of the Iroquois people.

long•ing [ˈlɒŋɪŋ] *n., adj., v.* *—n.* an earnest desire: *She was filled with a longing to see her family.*
—adj. having or showing such desire: *a longing look, longing eyes.*
—v. ppr. of LONG[2]. **—ˈlong•ing•ly,** *adv.* **—ˈlong•ing•ness,** *n.*
☛ *Syn. n.* See note at DESIRE.

long•ish [ˈlɒŋɪʃ] *adj.* rather long.

lon•gi•tude ['lɒŋgɪ,tjud] *or* ['lɒŋgɪ,tud], ['lɒndʒɪ,tjud] *or* ['lɒndʒɪ,tud] *n.* **1** *Geography.* a distance east or west on the earth's surface, measured in degrees from a certain meridian. On maps, lines running between the North and South Poles represent longitudes. Usually the meridian through Greenwich, England, is used to measure longitude. See EQUATOR for picture. Compare LATITUDE. **2** *Archaic.* length. ⟨ME < L *longitudo* length < *longus* long⟩

lon•gi•tu•di•nal [,lɒndʒə'tjudənəl], [,lɒndʒə'tudənəl], [,lɒŋgə'tjudənəl], *or* [,lɒŋgə'tudənəl] *adj.* **1** of or having to do with length or the lengthwise dimension: *longitudinal measurements.* **2** running lengthwise: *longitudinal stripes.* **3** of or dealing with changes in an individual or group over an extended period of time: *a longitudinal study.* **4** of longitude.
—,lon•gi'tu•di•nal•ly, *adv.*

long•johns or **long–johns** ['lɒŋ,dʒɒnz] *n.pl. Informal.* **1** underpants with long legs. **2** LONG UNDERWEAR.

long jump **1** an athletic event or contest in which contestants try to jump over as much ground as possible. The long jump from a running start is one of the Olympic track and field events. **2** a jump of this kind. **3 standing long jump,** a long jump from a standing start. The standing long jump is often included in school field meets.

long•line ['lɒŋ,laɪn] *n.* a fishing line, sometimes several kilometres long, that has many baited hooks, used for deep-sea fishing.

long•lin•er ['lɒŋ,laɪnər] *n. Cdn.* a fishing vessel that uses longlines.

long–lived ['lɒŋ 'lɪvd] *or* ['lɒŋ 'laɪvd] *adj.* living or lasting a long time.

long measure LINEAR MEASURE.

long•nose gar ['lɒŋ,nouz] a freshwater fish (*Lepisosteus osseus*) found in the St. Lawrence River and the Great Lakes. It is green with yellowish spotted fins, and has sharp teeth. It grows to a length of about one metre.

longnose sucker a freshwater fish (*Catostomus catostomus*) found across Canada in deep water, and reaching a mass of 2.5 kg.

Long Parliament in England, the Parliament that assembled in 1640, was expelled by Cromwell in 1653, reassembled in 1659, and was dissolved in 1660.

long–play•ing ['lɒŋ 'pleiɪŋ] *adj.* designating or of a microgroove phonograph record designed to be played at 33⅓ revolutions per minute.

long–range ['lɒŋ 'reindʒ] *adj.* **1** looking ahead; future: *long-range plans.* **2** capable of covering a great distance: *long-range missiles.*

long–run ['lɒŋ 'rʌn] *adj.* lasting a long time: *a long-run theatre show.*

long•shore ['lɒŋ,ʃɔr] *adj.* **1** of or having to do with longshoremen or the waterfront. **2** employed or found along the shore.

long•shore•man ['lɒŋ'ʃɔrmən] *or* ['lɒŋ,ʃɔrmən] *n.* **-men.** a man whose work is loading and unloading ships. ⟨for *alongshoreman*⟩

long shot **1** *Informal.* a bet, or wager, against great odds, but which therefore carries great possible winnings. **2** *Informal.* any venture or undertaking involving great risk or only slight chance of success, but offering great rewards if successful. **3** a motion picture or television scene photographed from a distance.
by a long shot, by any means; to any degree *(used with a negative)*: *The campaign isn't over by a long shot.*

long–sight•ed ['lɒŋ ,səitɪd] *adj.* **1** far-sighted; focussing at more than the right distance. **2** having foresight; wise.
—'long-'sight•ed•ly, *adv.* **—'long-'sight•ed•ness,** *n.*

long slide *Cdn. Curling.* a style of play in which the curler takes a long slide along the ice when delivering his or her stone from the hack.

long•spur ['lɒŋ,spɜr] *n.* any of various finches (genera *Rhyncophanes* and *Calcarius*) of the Arctic and the North American plains, having a long claw on the hind toe.

long–stand•ing ['lɒŋ ,stændɪŋ] *adj.* having lasted for a long time: *a long-standing feud.*

long–suf•fer•ing ['lɒŋ 'sʌfrɪŋ] *adj., n.* —*adj.* enduring trouble, pain, or injury long and patiently.
—*n.* long and patient endurance of trouble, pain, or injury.
—'long-'suf•fer•ing•ly, *adv.*

long suit **1** *Card games.* the suit in which one has most cards. **2** something in which a person excels; a strong point: *Patience is not her long suit.*

long–term ['lɒŋ 'tɜrm] *adj.* **1** lasting or intended to last for a long time: *our long-term plans and ambitions, a long-term lease.* **2** falling due in several years: *a long-term loan.*

long–term memory memory of far distant events, such as over a lifetime. Compare SHORT-TERM MEMORY.

long ton the British ton, 2240 pounds (about 1.02 tonnes).

long–tongued ['lɒŋ 'tʌŋd] *adj.* **1** having a long tongue. **2** talking much or too much.

lon•gueur [lɒŋ'gɜr]; *French,* [lɔ̃'gœʀ] *French. n.* a long and tedious period of time or a long or boring section in a book, motion picture, etc. ⟨< F *longueur,* literally, length⟩

long underwear underwear consisting of ankle-length underpants and a top with long or short sleeves, the pants and top often made in one piece.

long–waist•ed ['lɒŋ 'weistɪd] having a long upper body with a low waist: *a long-waisted woman, a long-waisted dress.* Compare SHORT-WAISTED.

long wave a radio wave that is between 1000 metres and 300 kilohertz. **—'long-,wave,** *adj.*

long•ways ['lɒŋ,weiz] *adv.* lengthwise.

long–wind•ed ['lɒŋ 'wɪndɪd] *adj.* **1** capable of long effort without getting out of breath: *A long-distance runner must be long-winded.* **2** talking or writing at great lengths; long and tiresome: *a long-winded speaker, a long-winded speech.*
—'long-'wind•ed•ly, *adv.* **—'long-'wind•ed•ness,** *n.*

long•wise ['lɒŋ,waɪz] *adv.* lengthwise.

loo[1] [lu] *n.* a kind of card game in which forfeits are paid into a pool. ⟨short for *lanterloo* < F *lanturelu,* a meaningless word in the refrain of an old French song⟩
☛ *Hom.* LIEU.

loo[2] [lu] *n. Esp. Brit. Informal.* TOILET (defs. 1 and 2). ⟨Perhaps abbrev. from Water*loo,* substituting for *water closet*⟩
☛ *Hom.* LIEU.

look [lʊk] *v., n.* —*v.* **1** try to see; turn the eyes (*often used with* **at**): *He looked this way.* **2** direct a gaze at: *to look someone in the eyes.* **3** examine; pay attention to (*used with* **at**): *You must look at all the facts.* **4** search: *I looked everywhere for my socks. He looked through the drawer, trying to find his keys.* **5** appear equal to: *He doesn't look his age.* **6** seem; appear: *She looks pale. I look like a fool.* **7** have a view; face: *Our house looks upon a garden.* **8** express or suggest by looks: *She looked her dismay.*
look after, attend to; take care of.
look alive, *Informal.* hurry: *You'd better look alive if you don't want to be late for the concert.*
look around or **round,** consider many possibilities.
look askance at, regard with disfavour.
look at, examine; pay attention to.
look back, a recollect; think about the past. **b** have regrets or second thoughts.
look bad, seem improper.
look black, seem hopeless: *After he lost his job, his future looked black.*
look daggers, look angrily: *He looked daggers at me when I divulged his age.*
look down on, despise; scorn.
look for, a seek or search for. **b** expect: *We'll look for you tonight.* **c** act so as to cause: *You're just looking for trouble.*
look forward to, expect, especially with pleasure: *We look forward to seeing you. When the crops failed, they knew they had to look forward to a bad winter.*
look in, make a short visit: *She said she'd look in on her way back.*
look into, investigate: *She promised to look into the matter.*
look on, a watch without taking part: *The teacher conducted the experiment while we looked on.* **b** regard; consider: *I look on her as a very able person.*
look (oneself), seem like oneself; look well: *She has been quite ill and still doesn't look herself.*
look out, be careful; watch out: *Look out for cars as you cross the street.*
look out for, take care of: *Ernie had always looked out for his little sister.*
look over, examine; inspect: *The police officer looked over the speeder's driver's licence.*
look sharp or **snappy,** *Informal.* be quick; be alert.
look through, a direct the gaze through: *to look through a window, to look through a microscope.* **b** examine: *She looked through the merchandise carefully.*
look to, a attend to; take care of. **b** turn to for help.

look up, a find; refer to: *She looked up the word in the dictionary.* **b** *Informal.* call on; visit: *Look me up when you come to town.* **c** *Informal.* of things, get better; improve: *Hopefully, things will look up soon.*
look up to, respect; admire.
—n. **1** a glance; the act of looking: *He took a quick look at the magazine.* **2** a search. **3** appearance; aspect. **4 looks,** *pl.* **a** personal appearance: *to have good looks.* **b** *Informal.* general aspect or appearance: *the looks of a situation.* ⟨OE lōcian⟩

look–a•like ['lʊk ə,ləik] *n.* **1** a person who or thing that closely resembles one that is famous or popular, especially as used for promotional purposes or for prestige. **2** (*adjl.*) that is such a person or thing.

look•er ['lʊkər] *n.* **1** a person who looks. **2** *Slang.* a person who is good-looking; an attractive person: *She's a real looker.*

look•er–on ['lʊkər 'ɒn] *n., pl.* **look•ers-on.** a person who watches without taking part; spectator.

looking glass mirror.

look•out ['lʊk,ʌut] *n.* **1** a careful watch. **2** a person or group that keeps such a watch. **3** a place from which to watch, as for forest fires, ships, etc.: *A crow's-nest is a lookout.* **4** what is seen ahead; outlook. **5** *Informal.* something to be cared for or worried about: *That is his lookout.*
be on the lookout *(for),* watch (for); watch out (for): *Be on the lookout for trouble. He was always on the lookout for bargains.*

lookout tower *Cdn.* a high tower from which a trained forestry employee watches for forest fires and reports the position so that action may be taken to fight them.

look–see ['lʊk ,si] *n. Slang.* a quick search or survey: *She went to the book sale to have a look-see.* ⟨< pidgin English⟩

loom¹ [lum] *n., v. —n.* a machine for weaving cloth.
—v. weave on a loom. ⟨OE *(ge)lōma* implement⟩

loom² [lum] *v.* appear dimly or vaguely as a large, often threatening shape: *An iceberg loomed through the thick, grey fog.*
loom large, seem important. ⟨origin uncertain⟩

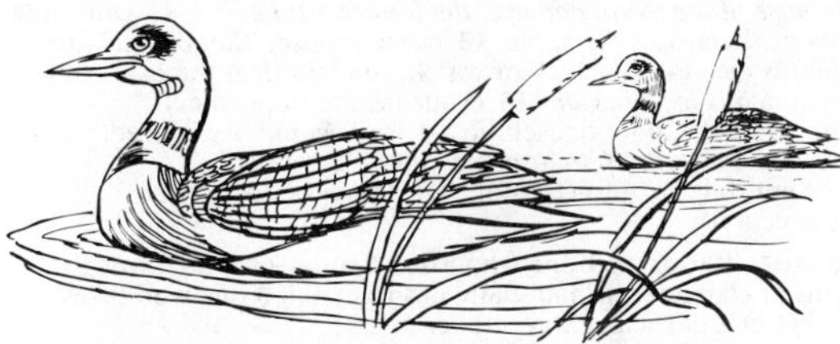

Common loons—about 80 cm long including the tail

loon¹ [lun] *n.* any of a genus (*Gavia*, constituting the order Gaviiformes) of diving birds of northern regions having mainly black-and-white or grey-and-white plumage, a straight, pointed bill, and a long body with the legs set far back on it. The common loon (*G. immer*) is found throughout most of Canada, but generally in more or less remote areas. It has a haunting cry. ⟨earlier *loom* < ON *lómr*⟩
☛ *Hom.* LUNE.

loon² [lun] *n. Informal* a crazy or stupid person. ⟨Cf. MDu. *loen* stupid fellow⟩
☛ *Hom.* LUNE.

loon•y¹ ['luni] *adj.* **loon•i•er, loon•i•est;** *n., pl.* **loon•ies.** *Slang.*
—adj. crazy.
—n. a crazy person; lunatic. ⟨var. of obs. *luny* < *lunatic*⟩
—'loon•i•ness, *n.*

loon•y² ['luni] *n., pl.* **loon•ies.** *Informal.* a Canadian one-dollar coin. A loon is pictured on its obverse. Also, **loonie.**

loop [lup] *n., v. —n.* **1** the shape of a curved string, ribbon, bent wire, etc. that crosses itself. In cursive handwriting, *b, g, h,* and *l* often have loops. **2** a thing, bend, course, or motion shaped somewhat like this: *The road makes a wide loop around the lake.* **3** a fastening or ornament formed of cord, etc. bent and crossed. **4** a turn like the cursive letter *l*, especially one made by an airplane. **5** *Computer technology.* a program, routine, or instruction that repeats continuously. **6** a turning place at the end of a bus line. **7** a complex figure made by a figure skater.
throw or **knock for a loop,** *Informal.* surprise very much: *Her proposal threw him for a loop.*
—v. **1** make a loop or loops in. **2** fasten with a loop: *She looped the sail to the mast with rope.* **3** encircle with a loop. **4** form a loop or loops. **5** make a vertical turn or revolution in an airplane.
loop the loop, turn over and over; make a loop in the air. ⟨ME *loupe*, ? < Celtic; cf. Gælic *lub* loop, bend⟩
☛ *Hom.* LOUPE.

loop•hole ['lup,houl] *n.* **1** a small opening in a wall to shoot through, look through, or let in light and air. **2** a means of escape or evasion; especially, something in a law, contract, etc. that is ambiguous or unclear, which makes it possible to avoid the intent or consequences of the law, etc. ⟨? < MDu. *lupen* to peer⟩

loose [lus] *adj.* **loos•er, loos•est;** *v.* **loosed, loos•ing;** *adv., n.*
—adj. **1** not firmly set or fastened: *a loose tooth, a loose thread.* **2** not tight: *loose clothing.* **3** not bound together: *loose papers.* **4** not packaged or put up in a container, etc.: *loose tea; loose chocolate.* **5** free; not shut in or up: *We leave the dog loose at night.* **6** not close or solid; having spaces: *loose earth, cloth with a loose weave.* **7** not strict or exact: *a loose translation from another language, loose thinking.* **8** having or showing too little control or restraint: *loose conduct, a loose tongue.* **9** lewd or unchaste. **10** *Informal.* not tense; relaxed. **11** *Informal.* not employed; not appropriated: *loose hours, loose funds.* **12** *Chemistry.* of a chemical element, free; uncombined.
—v. **1** set free; let go: *They loosed the prisoners.* **2** shoot (an arrow, bullet, etc.). **3** make loose; untie; unfasten. **4** relax.
—adv. in a loose manner.
break loose, a separate from anything; break a connection or relation. **b** run away; free oneself. **c** *Slang.* go on a spree.
cast loose, unfasten; separate.
cut loose, a break loose; **b** abandon restraint: *She works hard during the week, but cuts loose on weekends.*
let, set, or **turn loose,** set free; release; let go.
—n.
on the loose, *Informal.* **a** free; unconfined: *The prisoner was on the loose for a week before she was recaptured.* **b** on a spree. **c** absent without leave. ⟨ME < ON *lauss*⟩ **—'loose•ly,** *adv.* **—'loose•ness,** *n.*

loose end **1** something left hanging loose: *There's a loose end hanging from the hem.* **2** usually, **loose ends,** *pl.,* unfinished detail; relatively minor things that remain to be done: *We've finished the main job, but there are still a few loose ends to tie up.*
at loose ends, in an unsettled or disorganized condition or situation: *She has finished university, but is still at loose ends about what she wants to do.*

loose–joint•ed ['lus 'dʒɔɪntɪd] *adj.* **1** having loose joints; loosely built. **2** able to move very freely.

loose–leaf ['lus ,lif] *adj., n. —adj.* of a notebook, etc., having pages or sheets that can be taken out and replaced: *a loose-leaf binder.*
—n. **looseleaf,** collectively, sheets of lined paper with holes punched in the margin for use in a ring binder.

loose–limbed ['lus 'lɪmd] *adj.* having flexible and supple arms and legs.

loos•en ['lusən] *v.* **1** make loose or looser; untie; unfasten: *The doctor loosened the stricken man's collar.* **2** become loose or looser.
loosen up, a warm up one's muscles with exercise. **b** be or become more tolerant or relaxed: *She has loosened up considerably in the last three years.* **—'loos•en•er,** *n.*

loose•strife ['lus,strəif] *n.* **1** any of a genus (*Lythrum*) of herbs, especially a common and problematic weed having long, showy spikes of purple flowers. **2** (*adjl.*) designating a family (Lythraceae) of mainly tropical plants that includes the purple loosestrife and henna. **3** any of a genus (*Lysimachia*) of plants of the primrose family having leafy stems and spikes of yellow, white, or rose flowers. ⟨literal translation of L *lysimachia* < Gk. *Lysimachos* (as if < *lyein* to loose + *machē* battle), the supposed discoverer⟩

loose–tongued ['lus ,tʌŋd] *adj.* talking too much; irresponsible in speech.

loot [lut] *n., v. —n.* **1** spoils; plunder; booty: *loot taken by soldiers from a captured town.* **2** *Slang.* **a** money or other capital: *That's a lot of loot to spend for a CD player!* **b** gifts received.
—v. plunder; rob: *The jewellery store was looted by burglars.* ⟨< Hind. *lūt*⟩ **—'loot•er,** *n.*
☛ *Hom.* LUTE.
☛ *Syn. n.* **1.** See note at PLUNDER.

lop¹ [lɒp] *v.* **lopped, lop•ping. 1** cut (*usually used with* **off**): *We lopped off a big chunk of cheese.* **2** trim by cutting off branches, twigs, etc.: *to lop a tree.* ⟨origin uncertain⟩

lop² [lɒp] *v.* **lopped, lop•ping.** 1 hang loosely; droop. 2 flop. ⟨origin uncertain⟩

lope [loup] *v.* **loped, lop•ing;** *n.* —*v.* run with a long, easy stride: *The coyote loped along the trail.*
—*n.* a long, easy stride. ⟨ME < ON *hlaupa* leap⟩ **—'lop•er,** *n.*

lop–eared ['lɒp ˌird] *adj.* having ears that hang loosely or droop.

lo•per•a•mide [lə'pɛrəˌmaɪd] *n.* a drug used to treat diarrhea.

lop•sid•ed ['lɒpˌsaɪdɪd] *adj.* larger or heavier on one side than the other; unevenly balanced; leaning to one side.
—'lopˌsid•ed•ly, *adv.* **—'lopˌsid•ed•ness,** *n.*

lop•stick ['lɒpˌstɪk] *n. Cdn.* See LOBSTICK.

lo•qua•cious [lə'kweiʃəs] *adj.* talking much; fond of talking.
—lo'qua•cious•ly, *adv.* **—lo'qua•cious•ness,** *n.*
☛ *Syn.* See note at TALKATIVE.

lo•quac•i•ty [lə'kwæsəti] *n.* an inclination to talk a great deal; talkativeness. ⟨< L *loquacitas* < *loquax* talkative < *loqui* talk⟩

lo•quat ['loukwɒt] *or* ['loukwæt] *n.* 1 an evergreen tree (*Eriobotrya japonica*) of the rose family native to China and Japan, having small, yellow, edible, plumlike fruit. 2 the fruit of this tree. ⟨< Cantonese *lo kwat* rush orange⟩

lo•ran ['lɔrən] *n.* a device by which a navigator can determine his or her geographical position by utilizing signals sent out from two or more radio stations. ⟨*lo*ng *ra*nge *n*avigation⟩

lo•rat•a•dine [lə'rætəˌdin] *n.* a drug used to treat certain allergies.

lo•raz•e•pam [lə'ræzəˌpæm] *n.* a tranquillizing and sedative drug.

lord [lɔrd] *n., v.* —*n.* 1 a ruler, master, or chief; a person of great power. 2 a feudal superior. 3 **the Lord, a** God. **b** Christ. 4 in the United Kingdom, a man entitled by courtesy to the title of lord: *A baron is a lord.* 5 **Lord, a** in the United Kingdom, a titled nobleman or peer of the realm belonging to the House of Lords. **b** a title used in writing or speaking to or of noblemen of certain ranks: *Lord Beaverbrook was born in Ontario.* **c** a title given by courtesy to men holding certain positions: *Lord Chief Justice.* 6 **the Lords,** the House of Lords; the upper house of the British Parliament. 7 *Archaic.* a husband.
—*v.* 1 rule proudly or absolutely. 2 raise to the rank of lord.
lord it over, domineer over. ⟨OE *hlāford* < *hlāfweard* bread keeper < *hlāf* loaf + *weard* keeper, ward. Cf. LADY.⟩
—'lordˌlike, *adj.*

lord and lady (duck) *Cdn.* HARLEQUIN DUCK.

Lord Chamberlain in the United Kingdom, a government officer and the official in charge of the royal household.

Lord Chancellor or **Lord High Chancellor** in the United Kingdom, the highest-ranking official of state, with the exception of the royal princes and the Archbishop of Canterbury. He is chairman of the House of Lords, keeper of the Great Seal, and a cabinet member by political appointment.

lord•ling ['lɔrdlɪŋ] *n.* a little or unimportant lord.

lord•ly ['lɔrdli] *adj.* **-li•er, -li•est;** *adv.* —*adj.* 1 like or suitable for a lord; grand; magnificent. 2 haughty; insolent; scornful.
—*adv.* in a lordly manner. **—'lord•li•ness,** *n.*

Lord Mayor in the United Kingdom, the title of the mayors of London and of some other large cities.

lor•do•sis [lɔr'dousɪs] *n., pl.* **-ses** [-siz]. *Pathology.* a forward curvature of the spine. ⟨< Gk. *lordos* bent back + E *-osis*⟩

lords–and–la•dies ['lɔrdz ən 'leidiz] *n.* cuckoopint.

Lord's Day *Christianity.* Sunday.

Lord's Day Alliance of Canada *Cdn.* a national organization of Anglican, Baptist, Methodist, and Presbyterian churches founded in 1888 for preserving Sunday as a day of rest.

lord•ship ['lɔrdʃɪp] *n.* 1 the rank or position of a lord. 2 Often, **Lordship,** *Brit.* a title used in speaking to or of a lord: *your Lordship, his Lordship.* 3 rule; ownership.

Lord's Prayer in the Bible, a prayer given by Jesus to His disciples.

Lord's Supper 1 LAST SUPPER. 2 the Christian service in memory of this; Holy Communion. Also called (def. 2) **Lord's Table.**

lore [lɔr] *n.* 1 the facts and stories about a certain subject. 2 learning; knowledge. ⟨OE *lār.* Related to LEARN.⟩

Lor•e•lei ['lɔrəˌlaɪ] *n. German legend.* a siren of the Rhine whose beauty and singing distracted sailors and caused them to wreck their ships. ⟨< G, var. of *Lurlei,* a cliff overlooking the Rhine River thought to be where the siren lived⟩

lor•gnette [lɔr'njɛt] *n.* 1 eyeglasses without sidepieces, mounted on a handle. 2 opera glasses mounted on a handle. ⟨< F *lorgnette* < *lorgner* look sidelong at, eye < OF *lorgne* squinting⟩

lo•ris ['lɔrɪs] *n.* any of several small, slow-moving, nocturnal primates (genera *Loris* and *Nycticebus* of the family Lorisidae) of the forests of S and SE Asia, having soft, grey or brown fur, very large eyes, short index fingers, and no tail. ⟨< F *loris,* ? < Du. *loeris* booby⟩

lorn [lɔrn] *adj.* 1 *Poetic.* forsaken; forlorn. 2 *Archaic.* lost; ruined. ⟨OE *-loren,* pp. of *-lēosan* lose. Related to FORLORN.⟩

lor•ry ['lɔri] *n., pl.* **-ries.** 1 a long, flat wagon without sides. 2 *Brit.* motor truck. ⟨Cf. dial. E *lurry* pull, lug⟩
☛ *Hom.* LORY.

lo•ry ['lɔri] *n., pl.* **-ries.** any of a number of small, brightly coloured parrots native to Australia, New Guinea, and nearby islands, most of which have a fringed, brushlike tongue tip for feeding on nectar and soft fruits. ⟨< Du., var. of *lori, loeri* < Malay *luri*⟩
☛ *Hom.* LORRY.

lose [luz] *v.* **lost, los•ing.** 1 not have any longer; have taken away from one by accident, carelessness, gambling, parting, death, etc.: *to lose one's life.* 2 be unable to find: *to lose one's way, to lose a book.* 3 fail to keep or maintain; cease to have: *to lose patience, to lose all fear.* 4 get rid of (something unwanted): *Try to lose weight.* 5 miss; fail to get, catch, see, hear, or understand: *to lose a train, to lose a few words of what was said, to lose a sale.* 6 fail to win: *to lose a bet.* 7 be defeated: *Our team lost.* 8 bring to destruction; ruin: *The ship and its crew were lost.* 9 let pass without use or profit; waste: *to lose an opportunity, lose time. The hint was not lost on her.* 10 suffer loss: *to lose on a contract.* 11 be or become worse off in money, in numbers, etc.: *Because of the storm damage, the farmer lost heavily.* 12 cause the loss of: *Delay lost the battle.* 13 cause to lose: *That one act lost him his job.* 14 of a clock or watch, run less than the exact time: *My watch is losing again.* 15 evade; shake (a pursuer).
lose (oneself), **a** let oneself go astray; become bewildered. **b** become absorbed: *to lose oneself in a good book.*
lose out, fail; be unsuccessful. ⟨OE *losian* be lost < *los* destruction⟩

los•er ['luzər] *n.* 1 one who loses. 2 a person who, through fault of character, is habitually unsuccessful. 3 one who takes defeat in a particular way: *a poor loser.*

los•ing ['luzɪŋ] *adj., v.* —*adj.* 1 that cannot be won: *a losing game.* 2 who or that loses: *the losing team.*
—*v.* ppr. of LOSE.

los•ings ['luzɪŋz] *n.pl.* losses.

loss [lɒs] *n.* 1 a losing or being lost. 2 a person or thing lost: *The fire was finally put out, but her house was a complete loss.* 3 the amount lost. 4 the harm or disadvantage caused by losing something. 5 a defeat: *Our team had two losses and one tie out of ten games played.* 6 *Military.* **a** the losing of soldiers by death, capture, or wounding. **b** the losing of ships, planes, tanks, etc. in combat. 7 in insurance, the occurrence of death, property damage, or other contingency against which a person is insured under circumstances that make the insurer liable under the contract. 8 *Electricity.* the reduction in power, measured by the difference between the power input and power output, in an electric circuit, device, system, etc., corresponding to the transformation of electric energy into heat.
at a loss, a puzzled; uncertain; in difficulty: *He was at a loss for words.* **b** unable: *She was at a loss to explain the reason for her anxiety.* ⟨OE *los*⟩

loss leader an article sold at a loss in order to attract customers into a store.

lost [lɒst] *v., adj.* —*v.* pt. and pp. of LOSE.
—*adj.* 1 no longer had or kept: *lost friends.* 2 no longer to be found; missing: *lost articles.* 3 no longer visible, audible, or recognizable: *He was soon lost in the crowd.* 4 attended with defeat: *a lost battle.* 5 not used, or for any reason not able to be used, to good purpose; wasted: *lost time.* 6 having gone astray: *We were soon lost in the forest.* 7 destroyed or ruined. 8 bewildered: *She looked completely lost.* 9 absorbed; rapt; engrossed (*used with* **in**): *lost in thought.*
get lost, *Slang.* go away: *The older boys told him to get lost.*
lost on, wasted on: *Sarcasm is lost on her.*
lost to, a no longer possible or open to: *The chance of promotion*

was lost to him. **b** no longer belonging to: *After that incident, her son was lost to her.* **c** insensible to: *He was lost to all sense of duty.*

lost cause an undertaking already defeated or one certain to be defeated.

lost sheep a person who has strayed from the right sort of conduct or religious belief.

lot [lɒt] *n., adv., v.* **lot•ted, lot•ting.** *—n.* **1** a large number or amount; a great many or a great deal: *a lot of books, a lot of money. There is a lot of truth in what he said.* **2 lots,** *Informal.* a large number or amount: *He has lots of money. There were lots of people.* **3** a number of persons or things considered as a group; collection or set: *This lot of ballots still has to be counted.* **4** a plot of ground, especially one having fixed boundaries, as a subdivision of a block in a town or city: *a vacant lot. Our house is on a corner lot.* **5** a film studio together with the surrounding property. **6** an object used to decide something by chance: *We drew lots to decide who should be captain.* **7** such a method of deciding: *divide property by lot.* **8** a choice made in this way: *The lot fell to me.* **9** what one gets by lot; one's share. **10** one's fate; fortune: *a happy lot.* **11** an item or items for sale at an auction: *When is this lot being sold?*
cast or **draw lots,** use lots to decide something.
cast or **throw in** (one's) **lot with,** share the fate of; become a partner with.
—adv. **lots,** *Informal.* much: *This table is lots nicer than that one.*
—v. divide into lots. ⟨OE *hlot*⟩

loth [louθ] See LOATH.

Lo•thar•i•o [lou'θɛriou] *n., pl.* **-thar•i•os.** a man who professes love to many women; rake; libertine. ⟨< *Lothario,* a character in Nicholas Rowe's *The Fair Penitent*⟩

lo•ti ['louti] *n., pl.* **ma•lo•ti.** the main unit of currency in Lesotho, divided into 100 lisente. See table of money in the Appendix.

lo•tic ['loutɪk] *adj.* **1** of or having to do with a river or rivers. **2** living in a river or rivers. ⟨< L *lotus* a washing < *lautus,* pp. of *lavare* to wash⟩

lo•tion ['louʃən] *n.* a liquid medicine or cosmetic which is applied to the skin. Lotions are used to relieve pain, to heal, to cleanse, or to beautify the skin. ⟨< L *lotio, -onis,* a washing, ult. < *lavere* wash⟩

lo•tos ['loutəs] See LOTUS.

lot•ter•y ['lɒtəri] *n., pl.* **-ter•ies. 1** a scheme for distributing prizes by lot or chance. In a lottery a large number of tickets are sold, only some of which win prizes. **2** a distribution by chance of success, fortune, happiness, etc.: *the lottery of life.* ⟨< Ital. *lotteria* < *lotto* lot. See LOTTO.⟩

lot•to ['lɒtou] *n.* a game played by drawing numbered pieces from a bag or box and covering the corresponding numbers, images, etc. on cards. ⟨< Ital. *lotto* lot, ult. < Gmc. Akin to LOT.⟩

lot•us ['loutəs] *n.* **1** any of various tropical, Old World water lilies, especially the Egyptian white lotus (*Nymphaea lotus*) which was sacred to the ancient Egyptians and was often represented in art and architecture. **2** an Asian aquatic plant (*Nelumbo nucifera*) that is the sacred lotus of Hinduism and Buddhism. **3** the fruit eaten by the ancient Greek lotus-eaters that was supposed to cause a dreamy and contented forgetfulness. It is thought to have been the fruit of a tree of the buckthorn family. **4** any of a genus (*Lotus*) of plants of the pea family found in many parts of the world. **5** an ancient painting or sculpture of one of these plants. Also, **lotos.** ⟨< L < Gk. *lōtos* the lotus plant⟩

lo•tus–eat•er ['loutəs ,itər] *n.* a person who leads a life of dreamy, indolent ease.

lotus land *Cdn. Informal.* British Columbia, especially Vancouver. ⟨so called because of its laid-back way of life⟩

loud [laʊd] *adj., adv. —adj.* **1** strong in sound; noisy: *The music is too loud.* **2** producing a loud sound; making a noise: *He has a very loud voice.* **3** clamorous; insistent: *They were loud in their demands for higher pay.* **4** *Informal.* showy, flashy, or vulgar: *loud clothes.*
—adv. in a loud manner: *She blew the bugle loud and long. Don't talk so loud.*
out loud, loud enough to be heard; not to oneself or in a whisper; aloud: *She repeated her lines out loud to herself.* ⟨OE *hlūd*⟩ **—'loud•ly,** *adv.* **—'loud•ness,** *n.*

☛ *Syn. adj.* **1, 2. Loud,** NOISY = making much or intense sound. **Loud** emphasizes the idea of being not quiet, low, or soft, and suggests strength or intensity of sound. *The speaker's voice was quite loud enough to be heard in the back of the room.* **Noisy** means disagreeably loud or harsh, and emphasizes continued loudness or disturbances of sound: *The people next door are noisy.*

loud•hail•er ['laʊd,heilər] *n.* a megaphone with an electric amplifier; bullhorn.

loud•ish ['laʊdɪʃ] *adj.* rather loud.

loud•mouth ['laʊd,mʌuθ] *n., pl.* **-mouths** [,maʊðz]. *Slang.* a loudmouthed person.

loud•mouthed ['laʊd,mʌuθt] *or* ['laʊd,maʊðd] *adj.* offensively noisy; given to talking too loudly.

loud•speak•er ['laʊd,spikər] *n.* a device for amplifying the sound of a speaker's voice, music, etc.

lough [lɒk] *or* [lɒx] *n. Irish.* **1** lake. **2** an arm of the sea; bay or inlet. ⟨< Irish Gaelic *loch*⟩

lou•is d'or [,lui 'dɔr] **1** a French gold coin varying in value, first issued during the reign of Louis XIII and continued up to the Revolution. **2** a later French gold coin worth 20 francs. ⟨< F *louis d'or* gold louis⟩

Lou•i•si•an•a [lu,izi'ænə] *n.* a southern state of the United States.

Louisiana Purchase an extensive region that the United States bought from France in 1803. It extended from the Mississippi River to the Rocky Mountains and from Canada to the Gulf of Mexico.

Lou•is Qua•torze ['lui kə'tɔrz]; *French,* [lwika'tɔʀz] **1** a style in architecture, art, and decoration developed in France during the reign of King Louis XIV (1643-1715). **2** of or having to do with this style. **3** something, especially a piece of furniture, in this style. ⟨< F *Louis Quatorze* Louis the Fourteenth⟩

Lou•is Quinze ['lui 'kænz], *French,* [lwi'kɛ̃z] **1** a style in architecture, art, and decoration developed in France during the reign of King Louis XV (1715-1774). **2** of or having to do with this style. **3** something, especially a piece of furniture, in this style. ⟨< F *Louis Quinze* Louis the Fifteenth⟩

Lou•is Seize ['lui 'sɛz]; *French,* [lwi'sɛz] **1** a style in architecture, art, and decoration developed in France during the reign of King Louis XVI (1774-1792). **2** of or having to do with this style. **3** something, especially a piece of furniture, in this style. ⟨< F *Louis Seize* Louis the Sixteenth⟩

lounge [laʊndʒ] *v.* **lounged, loung•ing;** *n. —v.* **1** stand, stroll, sit, or lie at ease and lazily. **2** pass time indolently; idle at one's ease.
—n. **1** the act or state of lounging. **2** a comfortable and informal room as in a theatre, ship, hotel, or club, in which one can lounge and be at ease. **3** a sofa having a headrest at one end but no back. **4** a bar featuring comfortable chairs, etc. and, often, live music. ⟨< 15c. Scottish dial.; ? < *lungis* laggard⟩
—'loung•er, *n.*

loupe [lup] *n.* an eyepiece fitted with a magnifying glass for use by jewellers, watchmakers, etc. ⟨< F⟩
☛ *Hom.* LOOP.

loup garou ['lu gə'ru] *Cdn.* werewolf. ⟨< F *loup* (< L *lupus* wolf) + *garou* werewolf < OF *garolf* < Frankish **werwulf*⟩

loup–marin [lu mə'rɛ̃] *n. Cdn. French.* a seal. ⟨< F, literally, marine wolf⟩

lour [laʊr] *v. or n.* See LOWER[2].

louse [lʌus] *n., pl.* **lice** or (for def. 3) **lous•es** ['lʌusəz]; *v.* **loused, lous•ing.** *—n.* **1** any of a large group of small, wingless insects constituting two orders (Anoplura and Mallophago, sometimes classified as suborders within the order Phthiraptera), that are parasites of mammals (including humans) and birds. **2** any of various similar but unrelated insects or other arthropods. **3** *Slang.* a mean, contemptible person; heel.
—v. delouse.
louse up, *Slang.* make a mess; spoil; botch: *We loused up the filing so badly, we had to do it all over again.* ⟨OE *lūs*⟩

Louse Town *Cdn. Slang.* Klondike City, Yukon Territory.

louse•wort ['lʌus,wɜrt] *n.* any of a genus (*Pedicularis*) of plants of the figwort family found in north temperate regions, having spikes of white, yellow, or mauve flowers.

lous•y ['laʊzi] *adj.* **lous•i•er, lous•i•est. 1** *Slang.* inferior; bad; poor: *The job isn't bad, but the pay is lousy. That was a lousy movie.* **2** *Slang.* nasty; dirty; mean: *a lousy swindler.* **3** *Slang.* well-supplied (with): *lousy with money.* **4** infested with lice.
—'lous•i•ly, *adv.* **—'lous•i•ness,** *n.*

lout [lʌut] *n.* an awkward, stupid person; boor. ⟨? < ON *lútr* bent down, stooping⟩

lout•ish ['lʌutɪʃ] *adj.* awkward and stupid; boorish.
—'lout•ish•ly, *adv.* **—'lout•ish•ness,** *n.*

lou•vre or **lou•ver** ['luvər] *n.* **1** a window or other opening covered with louvre boards. **2** a ventilating slit. ⟨ME < MF *louvier*⟩ **—'lou•vred,** *adj.*

louvre boards or **louver boards** horizontal strips of wood, glass, etc. set slanting in a window or other opening, so as to keep out rain or light but provide ventilation.

lov•a•ble ['lʌvəbəl] *adj.* inspiring love; endearing. Also, **loveable. —,lov•a'bil•i•ty,** *n.* **—'lov•a•ble•ness,** *n.* **—'lov•a•bly,** *adv.*

lov•age ['lʌvɪdʒ] *n.* a plant (*Levisticum officinale*) of the umbel family, native to Europe, and formerly used in medicine. ⟨ME *loveache,* altered < OF *levesche* < LL *levisticum* for L *ligusticum,* plant native to Liguria, a country in Cisalpine Gaul⟩

lo•vas•ta•tin [lou'væstətɪn] *n.* a drug used to lower blood cholesterol levels.

love [lʌv] *n., v.* **loved, lov•ing.** *—n.* **1** a deep feeling of fondness and friendship; great tenderness, affection, or devotion: *love of one's family, love for a sweetheart.* **2** an instance of such feeling: *first love.* **3** this feeling as a subject for literature or art, etc., or as a personified influence. **4** language representing affection: *Give Mother my love.* **5 Love, a** Venus. **b** Cupid or Eros. **6** a loved one; sweetheart. **7** selfless care and concern; kindness; generosity; good will. **8** a strong liking: *a love of books.* **9** sexual passion. **10** godly affection, devotion, and fellowship. **11** *Tennis, etc.* no score.
fall in love (with), begin to love; come to feel love (for).
for love, a for nothing; without pay. **b** for pleasure; not for money.
for the love of, for the sake of; because of.
in love, feeling love, usually romantic.
make love, a be intimate sexually. **b** behave like lovers; woo.
no love lost, dislike; animosity: *There is no love lost between the two brothers.*
not for love or money, not on any terms.
—v. **1** have a deep feeling of fondness and friendship for; have great tenderness or affection for or devotion to: *She loves her mother.* **2** be in love with; feel sexual passion for. **3** be in love; fall in love. **4** make love to. **5** like very much; take great pleasure in: *He loves music. Most people love ice cream.* **6** value; hold dear: *I love my freedom.* ⟨OE *lufu,* n., *lufian,* v.⟩
☛ *Syn. n.* **1. Love,** AFFECTION = a feeling of warm liking and tender attachment. **Love,** an emotion, emphasizes strength, depth, sincerity, and warmth of feeling, suggesting also tenderness, devotion, loyalty, or passion: *Every person needs to give and receive love.* **Affection** applies to a less strong feeling, suggesting tenderness and warm fondness: *I like my teacher, but feel no affection for her.*
☛ *Usage.* See note at LIKE.

love•a•ble ['lʌvəbəl] *adj.* See LOVABLE. **—,love•a'bil•i•ty, —'love•a•ble•ness,** *n.* **—'love•a•bly,** *adv*

love affair **1** a romantic relationship between two people who are not married to each other. **2** a lively or intense interest in or enthusiasm about something: *a love affair with the opera.*

love apple formerly, the tomato. ⟨Cf. F *pomme d'amour,* G *Liebesapfel*⟩

love•bird ['lʌv,bɜrd] *n.* **1** any of various small parrots, especially an African genus (*Agapornis*), often kept as cage birds, that appear to show great affection for their mates. **2 lovebirds,** *pl.* two people very obviously in love with each other.

love child a child born out of wedlock.

love feast **1** a meal eaten together by the early Christians as a symbol of love and fellowship. **2** a religious ceremony imitating this. **3** a banquet or other gathering to promote good feeling.

love game *Tennis.* a game in which one's opponent does not win a point.

love handles *Informal.* a roll of flesh around a person's middle, just below the waist.

love–in–i•dle•ness ['lʌv ɪn 'aɪdəlnɪs] *n.* wild pansy.

love knot an ornamental knot or bow of ribbon, or a carved imitation of one, as a token of love. Also, **lover's knot**.

love•less ['lʌvlɪs] *adj.* **1** not loving. **2** not loved. **—'love•less•ly,** *adv.* **—'love•less•ness,** *adj.*

love–lies–bleed•ing ['lʌv ,laɪz 'blidɪŋ] *n.* an amaranth (*Amaranthus caudatus*) that is a popular garden plant, having long, drooping, tassel-like spikes of dark red flowers.

love•lock ['lʌv,lɒk] *n.* **1** a long lock of hair, often tied with a ribbon, worn by courtiers in the 17th and 18th centuries. **2** any separate lock of hair, such as one worn on the forehead.

love•lorn ['lʌv,lɔrn] *adj.* suffering because of love; forsaken by the person whom one loves. **—'love,lorn•ness,** *n.*

love•ly ['lʌvli] *adj.* **-li•er, -li•est. 1** having beauty, harmony, or grace; inspiring admiration or affection: *a lovely woman. He is a lovely person.* **2** *Informal.* very pleasing; delightful: *a lovely holiday.* **—'love•li•ness,** *n.*
☛ *Syn.* **1.** See note at BEAUTIFUL.

love•making ['lʌv,meikɪŋ] *n.* **1** the attentions of courtship. **2** sexual intimacy.

love match a marriage for love, not for money or social position.

lov•er ['lʌvər] *n.* **1** a person who is in love with another. **2 lovers,** *pl.* two people who are in love with each other. **3** a person who loves illicitly; paramour. **4** a person in terms of his or her physical skill at lovemaking: *a good lover.* **5** a person having a strong liking for or devotion to something: *a lover of books, a lover of humanity.* **—'lov•er•less,** *adj.* **—'lov•er,like,** *adj.*

lover's knot See LOVE KNOT.

love seat a small couch, or chesterfield, seating two persons.

love set *Tennis.* a set in which the winner does not lose a game.

love•sick ['lʌv,sɪk] *adj.* languishing because of love.

lov•ing ['lʌvɪŋ] *adj., v. —adj.* feeling or showing love; affectionate; fond.
—v. ppr. of LOVE. **—'lov•ing•ly,** *adv.* **—'lov•ing•ness,** *n.*

loving cup a large cup having two or more handles, passed around for all to drink from.

lov•ing–kind•ness ['lʌvɪŋ 'kaɪndnɪs] *n.* **1** deep affection and tenderness that inspires kindness. **2** kind behaviour arising from love.

low¹ [lou] *adj., adv., n. —adj.* **1** not high or tall: *A low wall enclosed the garden. This stool is very low.* **2** rising but slightly from a surface: *low relief.* **3** of less than average or ordinary height, depth, amount, or degree: *The river is low this year.* **4** near the ground, floor, or base: *a low shelf.* **5** lying or being below the general level: *low ground.* **6** almost used up; short: *Supplies were low. Our furnace oil is low.* **7** not loud; soft: *We heard a low sound.* **8** small in amount, degree, force, value, etc.: *a low price.* **9** not advanced in development, organization, complexity, etc.: *Bacteria are low organisms.* **10** lacking in dignity or elevation: *low thoughts.* **11** humble: *She rose from a low position to president of the company. He is of low birth.* **12** lacking health or strength; sick or weak: *Her mother is very low.* **13** unfavourable; poor: *He had a low opinion of their abilities.* **14** depressed or dejected: *low spirits.* **15** mean or base: *a low trick.* **16** coarse; vulgar: *low language, low company.* **17** near the horizon: *a low sun.* **18** near the equator: *low latitudes.* **19** of a dress or its neckline, cut so as to leave the neck and part of the breast exposed. **20** of a bow, made with the upper body deeply bent. **21** *Informal.* short of money: *Can you lend me twenty dollars? I'm a bit low right now.* **22** *Music.* not high in the scale; deep in pitch: *a low note.* **23** *Phonetics.* of a vowel, pronounced with the tongue held low and relatively flat; open. *Examples*: [æ], [ɑ], [ɒ]. **24** in the Anglican Church, maintaining Low-Church practices.
—adv. **1** at or to a low position, amount, rank, degree, pitch, etc.: *The lamp hangs too low. The sun sank low. Supplies are running low. He bowed low.* **2** in a low manner.
lay low, bring down; overthrow: *The first blow laid him low.*
lie low, *Informal.* stay hidden; keep still: *The robbers will lie low for a time.*
—n. **1** that which is low. **2** a low position or state. **3** an arrangement of the gears in motor vehicles used for the lowest speed. **4** *Meteorology.* an area of low barometric pressure. ⟨ME < ON *lágr*⟩ **—'low•ness,** *n.*
☛ *Hom.* LO.
☛ *Syn. adj.* **10, 15, 16.** See note at BASE².

low² [lou] *v., n. —v.* make the sound of a cow mooing; moo.
—n. the sound a cow makes; mooing. ⟨OE *hlōwan*⟩
☛ *Hom.* LO.

low blow **1** *Boxing.* an illegal hit below the belt. **2** any unfair or unjust action.

low•born ['lou,bɔrn] *adj.* of humble birth; born into a family of low social rank.

low•boy ['lou,bɔɪ] *n.* a chest or side table with drawers, about the height of a table and having fairly short legs.

low•bred ['lou,brɛd] *adj.* coarse; rude; vulgar.

low•brow ['lou,braʊ] *n., adj. Informal. —n.* a person lacking in appreciation of intellectual or artistic things.
—adj. **1** being a lowbrow; incapable of culture. **2** fit for lowbrows.

low–bush cranberry ['lou ,bʊʃ] *Cdn.* **1** a shrub (*Viburnum edule*). **2** its fruit.

low–cal ['lou 'kæl] *adj. Informal.* low-calorie: *a low-cal dressing.*

low–cal•o•rie ['lou 'kæləri] *adj.* being low in calories; containing few calories.

Low Church a party in the Anglican Church, laying little stress on church authority and ceremonies, being more like other Protestant denominations, and less like the Roman Catholic Church. Compare HIGH CHURCH.

low comedy broadly humorous comedy.

Low Countries the Netherlands, Belgium, and Luxembourg. **—'low-,coun•try,** *adj.*

low–cut ['lou 'kʌt] *adj.* having a low neckline.

low•down ['lou,daʊn] *n. Slang.* the actual facts or truth: *Can you give me the lowdown on what happened at the meeting?*

low–down ['lou 'daʊn] *adj.* **1** *Informal.* low; mean; nasty: *a low-down trick.* **2** in low spirits; depressed.

low•er¹ ['louər] *v., adj., adv.* *—v.* **1** let down or haul down: *to lower the flag.* **2** reduce in amount, degree, force, etc.: *to lower the volume of a radio.* **3** sink; become lower: *The sun lowered slowly.* **4** *Music.* depress in pitch. **5** bring down in rank, station, or estimation; degrade; dishonour.
lower oneself, a behave improperly. **b** condescend: *She could hardly lower herself to speak to us.*
—adj. or adv. the comparative of LOW¹. ⟨< *low¹*⟩

low•er² ['laʊər] *v., n.* *—v.* **1** become or appear dark and threatening. **2** frown or scowl.
—n. a frowning or threatening appearance or look. Also, **lour.** ⟨ME *loure(n)* to frown⟩

lower bound ['louər] *Mathematics.* a number no greater than any other in a set.

Lower Canada ['louər] *Cdn.* **1** a traditional name for the province of Québec. **2** until 1841, the official name of the region between the Ottawa River and New Brunswick, now included in the province of Québec. Lower Canada was lower down the St. Lawrence River than Upper Canada. *Abbrev.*: L.C.

lower case ['louər] *Printing.* small letters, not capital.

low•er–case ['louər ˌkeis] *adj. Printing.* in small letters, not capitals. *Abbrev.*: l.c.

Lower Chamber or **lower chamber** ['louər] LOWER HOUSE.

lower class ['louər] Often, **lower classes,** *pl.* the people having the lowest social, political, and economic status, characterized especially by lower average incomes and a lower level of education than that of the middle class.

low•er–class ['louər 'klæs] *adj.* of, having to do with, or belonging to the lower class.

lower criticism ['louər] textual criticism.

Lower House or **lower house** ['louər] the more representative branch of a bicameral legislature. The members of the Lower House of a legislature are usually elected.

low•er•ing ['laʊərɪŋ] *adj., v.* *—adj.* **1** dark and threatening: *a lowering sky.* **2** frowning or scowling.
—v. ppr. of LOWER². Also, **louring. —'low•er•ing•ly,** *adv.*

Lower Lakes ['louər] *Cdn.* the most southerly of the Great Lakes, Lakes Erie and Ontario.

low•er•most ['louər,moust] *adj.* lowest.

lower regions ['louər] hell; Hades.

Lower Town ['louər] *Cdn.* **1** the part of a town lying closest to the waterfront, usually the oldest part of the town and that where many business establishments are located; specifically, this part of Québec City. **2** in Ottawa, Ontario, that part of the city lying downstream from the point where the Rideau Canal meets the Ottawa River, now a predominantly French-Canadian district.

lower world ['louər] **1** hell; Hades. **2** earth (versus heaven).

lowest common denominator 1 *Mathematics.* LEAST COMMON DENOMINATOR. **2** the level of the feelings, tastes, or opinions supposedly common to the majority of people.

lowest terms fraction *Mathematics.* a fraction whose numerator and denominator have no factor in common.

low frequency the range of radio frequencies between 30 and 300 kilohertz. Low frequency is the range next above very low frequency. *Abbrev.*: LF, L.F., or l.f. **—'low-'fre•quen•cy,** *adj.*

Low German 1 the Germanic dialects of the Low Countries (Dutch, Flemish, etc.) and especially of N Germany. **2** the group of west Germanic dialects from which English, Flemish, Dutch, Frisian, etc. are derived.

low–grade ['lou 'greid] *adj.* of poor quality; inferior: *low-grade wood.*

low–key ['lou 'ki] *adj.* played down; subdued or restrained: *a low-key attack on government policy.*

low•land ['loulənd] *or* ['lou,lænd] *n.* **1** land that is lower and flatter than the neighbouring country. **2** *(adjl.)* of or in the lowlands. **3 the Lowlands,** *pl.* a low, flat region in S and E Scotland.

Low•land•er ['louləndər] *or* ['lou,lændər] *n.* a native of the Lowlands of Scotland.

lowland fir a fir tree (*Abies grandis*) growing in low elevations on Vancouver Island and the Lower Mainland, having shiny, dark green leaves composed of many narrow leaflets, and bearing large cones. Also called **grand fir.**

Low Latin Latin as spoken in the Middle Ages.

low•life ['lou,ləif] *n., pl.* **-lifes** [-,ləifs]; *adj., Slang.* *—n.* **1** a debased or vile person; a criminal. **2** immoral people or surroundings.
—adj. **1** resembling a lowlife; debased; immoral. **2** crude; cheap.

low•lin•er ['lou,laɪnər] *n.* **1** the boat in a Maritime fishing fleet making the smallest catch within a specified time. **2** the captain of such a boat.

low•ly ['louli] *adj.* **-li•er, -li•est;** *adv.* *—adj.* **1** low in rank, station, or position: *a lowly servant, a lowly occupation.* **2** modest in feeling, behaviour, or condition; humble; meek: *He held a lowly opinion of himself.*
—adv. humbly; meekly. **—'low•li•ness,** *n.*
☛ *Syn. adj.* **2.** See note at HUMBLE.

Low Mass a Mass that is recited, not sung, and is simpler in form than a High Mass.

low–mind•ed ['lou ˌmaɪndɪd] *adj.* having or showing a low or vulgar mind. **—'low-'mind•ed•ly,** *adv.* **—'low-'mind•ed•ness,** *n.*

low–necked ['lou 'nɛkt] *adj.* of a dress, etc., cut low so as to show the neck, part of the bosom, and shoulders or back.

low–pitched ['lou 'pɪtʃt] *adj.* **1** having a deep tone: *a low-pitched musical instrument.* **2** having little slope; not steep: *a low-pitched roof.*

low–pres•sure ['lou 'prɛʃər] *adj.* **1** having or using relatively little pressure: *a low-pressure laminate.* **2** having a low barometric pressure: *There is a low-pressure region to the south.* **3** not forceful; easygoing: *a low-pressure sales pitch.*

low profile an attitude concerned with keeping quiet about one's work or reputation: *to keep a low profile.*

low relief bas-relief. See RELIEF for picture.

low–rise ['lou ˌraɪz] *adj., n.* *—adj.* of a building, having only a few storeys: *Only low-rise apartments are permitted in this area of the city.*
—n. a low-rise building.

low–spir•it•ed ['lou 'spɪrətɪd] *adj.* sad; depressed. **—'low-'spir•it•ed•ly,** *adv.* **—'low-'spir•it•ed•ness,** *n.*

low spirits sadness; depression.

Low Sunday in the Christian calendar, the Sunday after Easter.

low–tension ['lou 'tɛnʃən] *adj. Electricity.* operating at a low voltage: *low-tension wires.*

low tide 1 the lowest level of the tide. **2** the time when the tide is lowest: *The boat must have left sometime after low tide.* **3** the lowest point of anything.

low water 1 the lowest level of water in a lake or river. **2** LOW TIDE.

low–water mark ['lou 'wɒtər] **1** a mark showing low water. **2** the lowest point of anything.

lox¹ [lɒks] *n.* thinly sliced smoked salmon. ⟨< Yiddish *laks* < MHG *lacs* salmon⟩

lox² [lɒks] *n.* LIQUID OXYGEN. ⟨< *l*iquid *ox*ygen⟩

loy•al ['lɔɪəl] *adj.* **1** faithful to love, promise, or duty. **2** faithful to one's sovereign, government, or country: *a loyal citizen.* ⟨< F *loyal* < L *legalis* legal < *lex, legis* law. Doublet of LEGAL.⟩ **—'loy•al•ly,** *adv.* **—'loy•al•ness,** *n.*
☛ *Syn.* See note at FAITHFUL.

loy•al•ist ['lɔɪəlɪst] *n., adj.* *—n.* **1** a person who supports the existing government or sovereign, especially in time of revolt. **2 Loyalist,** *Cdn.* **a** UNITED EMPIRE LOYALIST. **b** any of the colonists who remained loyal to Great Britain during the American Revolution, or their descendants. **3 Loyalist,** in Spain, a person loyal to the Republic during the Civil War (1936-1939). *—adj.* 1 of, being, or having to do with a loyalist or loyalists. 2 **Loyalist,** of, being, or having to do with a Loyalist or Loyalists.

Loyalist Province *Cdn.* New Brunswick. ⟨because originally settled by United Empire Loyalists⟩

Loyal Orange Association or **Lodge** a Protestant organization, named after William, Prince of Orange, who became King William III of England.

loy•al•ty ['lɔɪəlti] *n., pl.* **-ties.** loyal feeling or behaviour; faithfulness.

loz•enge ['lɒzɪndʒ] *n.* 1 a small tablet of medicine or a piece of candy: *Cough drops are sometimes called lozenges.* 2 a design or figure shaped like this ⟨◊⟩; diamond. ⟨ME < OF *losenge*, ult. < LL *lausa* slab < Celtic⟩

LP a long-playing phonograph record. ⟨< a trademark⟩

L.P.P. LABOUR PROGRESSIVE PARTY.

Lr lawrencium.

LRC light, rapid, comfortable (designating a type of railway train).

LRT light rapid transit.

L.S. or **LS** LEADING SEAMAN.

LSD LYSERGIC ACID DIETHYLAMIDE.

L/Sgt. LANCE-SERGEANT.

LSI an electronic circuit on a small semiconductor chip, having hundreds or thousands of microcircuits. ⟨< *l*arge-*s*cale *i*ntegration⟩

Lt. or **Lt** lieutenant.

Lt.Cdr. LIEUTENANT-COMMANDER.

Lt.Col. LIEUTENANT-COLONEL.

Ltd. limited.

Lt.Gen. LIEUTENANT-GENERAL.

Lt.Gov. LIEUTENANT-GOVERNOR.

Lu lutetium.

lu•au ['luaʊ] *n.* a Hawaiian feast, usually including entertainment. ⟨< Hawaiian *lu'au*⟩

Lu•ba ['lubə] *n.* a Bantu language used as a lingua franca in central Zaire.

lub•ber ['lʌbər] *n.* 1 a big, clumsy, stupid fellow. 2 *Nautical.* a clumsy sailor. ⟨ME *lober*⟩

lub•ber•ly ['lʌbərli] *adj., adv. —adj.* 1 loutish; clumsy; stupid. 2 *Nautical.* awkward in the work of a sailor.
—adv. in a lubberly manner. **—'lub•ber•li•ness,** *n.*

lubber's line *Navigation.* on a compass, a line aligned with the bow of a ship or aircraft that shows direction.

lube [lub] *n. Informal.* 1 a lubricant. 2 lubrication, as of machinery parts. ⟨short form⟩

lu•bri•cant ['lubrəkənt] *n., adj. —n.* a substance such as oil, grease, or graphite for putting on surfaces that slide or move against one another, such as parts of machines, in order to reduce friction and make the surfaces move smoothly and easily.
—adj. lubricating.

lu•bri•cate ['lubrə,keit] *v.* **-cat•ed, -cat•ing.** 1 put a lubricant on. 2 make slippery or smooth. 3 make easy and smooth: *to lubricate the peace talks.* ⟨< L *lubricare* < *lubricus* slippery⟩

lu•bri•ca•tion [,lubrə'keiʃən] *n.* 1 a lubricating or being lubricated. 2 oil, grease, etc. used for lubricating.

lu•bri•ca•tor ['lubrə,keitər] *n.* a person or thing that lubricates, especially a lubricant or device for applying a lubricant to machinery.

lu•bric•i•ty [lu'brɪsəti] *n., pl.* **-ties.** 1 oily smoothness; slipperiness. 2 shiftiness. 3 lewdness. ⟨< LL *lubricitas* < L *lubricus* slippery, slimy⟩

lu•cent ['lusənt] *adj. Archaic.* 1 shining; luminous. 2 letting the light through; clear. ⟨< L *lucens, -entis*, ppr. of *lucere* shine⟩ **—'lu•cen•cy,** *n.* **—'lu•cent•ly,** *adv.*

lu•cerne [lu'sɜrn] *n.* alfalfa. ⟨< F *luzerne* < Provençal *luzerno*, ult. < L *lux, lucis* light⟩

lu•ces ['lusiz] *n.* a pl. of LUX.

lu•cid ['lusɪd] *adj.* 1 easy to understand: *a lucid explanation.* 2 shining; bright. 3 having a clear mind; using reason: *Insane persons sometimes have lucid intervals.* 4 clear; transparent: *a lucid stream.* ⟨< L *lucidus* < *lux, lucis* light⟩ **—'lu•cid•ly,** *adv.* **—lu'cid•i•ty, 'lu•cid•ness,** *n.*

Lu•ci•fer ['lusəfər] *n.* 1 in the Bible, the chief rebel angel who was cast out of heaven; Satan, especially before his fall. 2 the planet Venus when it is the morning star. 3 **lucifer,** a match that lights by friction. ⟨< L *lucifer* the morning star, literally, bringing light < *lux, lucis* light + *ferre* bring⟩

Lu•cite ['lusəit] *n. Trademark.* a clear, plastic compound used for airplane windows, ornaments, etc. ⟨< L *lux, lucis* light⟩

luck [lʌk] *n., v. —n.* 1 that which seems to happen or come to one by chance; chance. 2 good fortune: *Lots of luck to you. She thinks a horseshoe brings luck.*
down on (one's) **luck,** *Informal.* having bad luck; unlucky.
in luck, having good luck; lucky: *I'm in luck today; I found a five-dollar bill.*
out of luck, having bad luck; unlucky.
push or **crowd one's luck,** try to take advantage of a situation; take unnecessary chances when things are going favourably: *You've won every game so far, but don't push your luck.*
try (one's) **luck,** see what one can do: *Try your luck with this puzzle.*
worse luck, unfortunately.
—v.
luck out, *Informal.* be lucky. ⟨ME < MDu. *(ghe)luc*, MLG *(ge)lucke*⟩

luck•less ['lʌklɪs] *adj.* having or bringing bad luck. **—'luck•less•ly,** *adv.* **—'luck•less•ness,** *n.*

luck•y ['lʌki] *adj.* **luck•i•er, luck•i•est.** 1 having good luck: *She was lucky to win the lottery.* 2 bringing good luck: *a lucky day, a lucky charm.* 3 happening by good fortune; fortunate: *a lucky coincidence.* **—'luck•i•ly,** *adv.* **—'luck•i•ness,** *n.*
☛ *Syn.* See note at FORTUNATE.

lu•cra•tive ['lukrətɪv] *adj.* bringing in money; profitable. ⟨ME < L *lucrativus* < *lucrari* to gain < *lucrum* gain⟩ **—'lu•cra•tive•ly,** *adv.* **—'lu•cra•tive•ness,** *n.*

lu•cre ['lukər] *n. Archaic, poetic, or facetious.* money. ⟨ME < L *lucrum*⟩

lu•cu•brate ['lukjə,breit] *or* ['lukə,breit] *v.* **-brat•ed, -brat•ing.** 1 write or study laboriously or late at night. 2 write in a scholarly way. **—'lu•cu,bra•tor,** *n.*

lu•cu•bra•tion [,lukjə'breiʃən] *or* [,lukə'breiʃən] *n.* 1 study carried on late at night. 2 laborious study. 3 a learned or carefully written production, especially one that is laboured and dull. ⟨< L *lucubratio, -onis* < *lucubrare* work at night⟩

Lu•cul•li•an [lu'kʌliən] *adj.* rich; luxurious; magnificent. ⟨< *Lucullus* (110?-57? B.C.), a wealthy Roman famous for his luxurious banquets⟩

Lud•dite ['lʌdəit] *n.* 1 any of a group of English workers who smashed machinery (1811-1816) as a protest against mechanization and the resulting lowered wages. 2 any person opposed to technological progress. ⟨said to be named after Ned *Ludd,* a Leicestershire worker who smashed machinery c. 1779⟩ **—'Lud•dism** or **'Lud•dit,ism,** *n.*

lu•di•crous ['ludəkrəs] *adj.* amusingly absurd; ridiculous. ⟨< L *ludicrus* < *ludus* sport⟩ **—'lu•di•crous•ly,** *adv.* **—'lu•di•crous•ness,** *n.*

luff [lʌf] *v., n. Nautical. —v.* turn a ship's bow to the wind.
luff the helm, move the helm so that the bow of the ship turns toward the wind.
—n. 1 the act of turning the bow of a ship toward the wind. 2 the forward edge of a fore-and-aft sail. ⟨ME; cf. Du. *loef*⟩

Luft•waf•fe ['lʊft,vafə] *n. German.* the German air force, especially under the Nazis in World War II. ⟨< G *Luft* air + *Waffe* weapon⟩

lug[1] [lʌg] *v.* **lugged, lug•ging.** 1 pull along or carry with effort; drag. 2 *Nautical.* of a ship, carry (sail) beyond the limit of safety in a strong wind. ⟨ME *luggen*; cf. Swedish *lugga* pull by the hair⟩

lug[2] [lʌg] *n.* 1 *Esp. Scottish.* ear. 2 earflap. 3 a projecting part used to hold or grip something. 4 a flange or stud projecting from the outer surface of a wheel to increase traction on soft ground: *Tractors having lugs should stay off paved highways.* 5 *Slang.* a clumsy or stupid person. ⟨< Scand.; cf. Swedish *lugg* forelock⟩

lug[3] [lʌg] *n.* lugsail.

lug[4] [lʌg] *n.* lugworm. ⟨origin uncertain; cf. Du. *log* slow, heavy⟩

luge [luʒ] *n.* a small sled which a person rides lying on his or her back, used in downhill races over snow or ice, often on a specially designed course. ⟨< F *luge* sled⟩

lug•gage ['lʌgɪdʒ] *n.* 1 suitcases, bags, etc. packed with belongings for a trip; baggage. 2 suitcases, bags, etc. for use on trips: *I bought a new set of luggage.* ⟨< lug[1]⟩
☛ *Syn.* See note at BAGGAGE.

lug•ger ['lʌgər] *n. Nautical.* a boat with lugsails.

lug•sail ['lʌg,seil] *or* ['lʌgsəl] *n. Nautical.* a four-cornered sail held by a yard that slants across the mast.

lu•gu•bri•ous [lə'gubriəs] *adj.* sad; mournful, especially in an exaggerated or affected way. ⟨< L *lugubris* < *lugere* mourn⟩ **—lu'gu•bri•ous•ly,** *adv.* **—lu'gu•bri•ous•ness,** *n.*

lug•worm ['lʌg,wɜrm] *n.* any of a genus (*Arenicola*) of marine annelid worms that burrow in the sand along the seashore or on the sea bottom, having a row of tufted gills along each side of the body. Lugworms are often used for bait. ⟨< *lug*[4]⟩

luke•warm ['luk'wɔrm] *adj.* **1** of a liquid, neither hot nor cold; fairly warm. **2** showing little enthusiasm; half-hearted: *a lukewarm greeting.* ⟨expansion of dial. *luke* lukewarm < dial. *lew*; cf. OE *hlēo* shelter (warm place)⟩ **—'luke'warm•ly,** *adv.* **—'luke'warm•ness,** *n.*

lull [lʌl] *v., n.* —*v.* **1** hush to sleep: *The mother lulled the crying baby.* **2** make or become calm or more nearly calm: *The wind lulled.* **3** set at rest: *to lull one's suspicions, to lull people into a false sense of security.*
—*n.* a temporary period of less noise or activity; brief calm: *a lull in a storm.* ⟨ME *lulle(n)*, perhaps imitative; cf. Swedish *lulla*, G *lullen*, L *lallāre* to sing lullaby⟩ **—'lull•er,** *n.* **—'lull•ing•ly,** *adv.*

lul•la•by ['lʌlə,baɪ] *n., pl.* **-bies. 1** a song to lull a baby to sleep. **2** any soothing song or piece of music. ⟨< *lull* + *by* as in *good-bye*⟩

lum•ba•go [lʌm'beigou] *n.* an injury of the muscles in the lower back producing pain, sometimes intense. Lumbago can be caused by a sprain, lifting something that is too heavy, a sudden twisting movement, cold and damp, etc. ⟨< LL < L *lumbus* loin⟩

lum•bar ['lʌmbər] *or* ['lʌmbɑr] *adj.* of, having to do with, or referring to the loins or a vertebra, artery, nerve, etc. in this part of the body. See SPINAL COLUMN for picture. ⟨< NL *lumbaris* < L *lumbus* loin⟩
☛ *Hom.* LUMBER ['lʌmbər].

lum•ber[1] ['lʌmbər] *n., v.* —*n.* **1** timber, logs, beams, boards, etc. roughly cut and prepared for use. **2** *Brit.* household articles no longer in use; old furniture, etc. that takes up room.
—*v.* **1** *Cdn.* cut and prepare lumber. **2** *Brit.* fill up or obstruct by taking space that is wanted for something else.
lumber with, *Brit. Informal.* burden with. ⟨original meaning 'useless goods', ? < *lombard* pawnshop⟩ **—'lum•ber•er,** *n.* **—'lum•ber•less,** *adj.*
☛ *Hom.* LUMBAR.

lum•ber[2] ['lʌmbər] *v.* move along heavily and noisily. ⟨ME *lomeren* < Scand.; cf. Swedish dial. *loma* walk heavily⟩ **—'lum•ber•ing•ly,** *adv.*
☛ *Hom.* LUMBAR.

lum•ber•ing ['lʌmbərɪŋ] *n.* the business of cutting and preparing timber for use.

lum•ber•jack ['lʌmbər,dʒæk] *n. Cdn.* **1** CANADA JAY. **2** logger.

lum•ber•man ['lʌmbərmən] *n., pl.* **-men.** a man whose business is buying and selling timber or lumber.

lum•ber•yard ['lʌmbər,jɑrd] *n.* a place where lumber is stored and sold.

lu•men ['lumən] *n., pl.* **-mi•na** [-mənə]. **1** *Optics.* an SI unit for measuring the rate of emission or transmission of light rays from a given light source. One lumen is the rate of emission in a cone of one steradian of a light source having an intensity of one candela. *Symbol*: lm **2** *Anatomy.* the inner space or passage in a blood vessel or within a cell wall. ⟨< NL, special uses of L *lūmen* light, window⟩

lu•mi•nar•y ['lumə,nɛri] *n., pl.* **-nar•ies. 1** the sun, moon, or other light-giving body. **2** a distinguished person, especially one who enlightens. ⟨ME < Med.L *luminarium* < L *lumen, -minis* light⟩

lu•mi•nesce [,lumə'nɛs] *v.* **-nesced, -nesc•ing.** exhibit luminescence. ⟨back formation from *luminescent*⟩

lu•mi•nes•cence [,lumə'nɛsəns] *n.* an emission of light by a process other than incandescence; any light produced at relatively low temperatures by chemical or electrical action, friction, etc. Luminescence includes phosphorescence, fluorescence, and the light produced by fireflies. ⟨< L *lumen, luminis* light + E *-escence* a beginning to be < L *-escentia*⟩

lu•mi•nes•cent [,lumə'nɛsənt] *adj.* **1** of or having to do with luminescence. **2** producing or capable of producing light by luminescence. ⟨< L *lumen, luminis* + *escent*⟩

lu•mi•nif•er•ous [,lumə'nɪfərəs] *adj.* producing or transmitting light. ⟨< L *lumen, luminis* light + E *-ferous*⟩

lu•mi•nos•i•ty [,lumə'nɒsəti] *n., pl.* **-ties. 1** the quality or state of being luminous. **2** something that is luminous. **3** *Astronomy.* the total amount of radiation emitted by a heavenly body in a given time.

lu•mi•nous ['lumənəs] *adj.* **1** shining by its own light: *The sun and stars are luminous.* **2** full of light; bright. **3** treated with some substance that glows in the dark: *The numbers on some watches are luminous.* **4** easily understood; clear; enlightening: *a luminous explanation.* ⟨ME < L *luminosus* < *lumen* light⟩ **—'lu•mi•nous•ly,** *adv.* **—'lu•mi•nous•ness,** *n.*

luminous flux *Optics.* the rate of flow of light, or luminous energy, measured in lumens.

lum•ma ['lʌmə] *n.* a unit of currency in Armenia, equal to 1/100 of a dram. See table of money in the Appendix.

lum•mox ['lʌməks] *n. Informal.* an awkward, stupid person. ⟨origin uncertain⟩

lump[1] [lʌmp] *n., v.* —*n.* **1** a solid mass of no particular shape: *a lump of coal.* **2** a small cube or oblong piece of sugar. **3** a swelling; bump: *a lump on the head.* **4** a lot; mass. **5** (*adjl.*) not divided or in parts; in a single lot or mass: *a lump payment.* **6** *Informal.* an awkward, dull, or stupid person. **7 lumps,** *pl. Informal.* a beating or defeat; punishment or retribution; one's just desserts: *The outspoken mayor had to take her lumps from the press.*
—*v.* **1** make lumps of, on, or in. **2** form into a lump or lumps; become lumpy: *If you don't stir the pudding, it will lump.* **3** put together; deal with in a mass or as a whole: *We will lump all our expenses.* ⟨ME < Scand.; cf. Danish *lump(e)*⟩

lump[2] [lʌmp] *v. Informal.* put up with; endure: *If you don't like it, you can lump it.* ⟨origin uncertain⟩

lump•ec•to•my [lʌm'pɛktəmi] *n.* the surgical removal of a tumour in the breast, without removing the whole breast.

lump•ish ['lʌmpɪʃ] *adj.* **1** like a lump; heavy and clumsy. **2** stolid; stupid. **—'lump•ish•ly,** *adv.* **—'lump•ish•ness,** *n.*

lump sugar small blocks of sugar shaped like cubes, dominoes, etc.

lump sum a relatively large sum of money given in payment at one time: *He paid off the last $500 of his loan in a lump sum.* **—'lump-'sum,** *adj.*

lump•y ['lʌmpi] *adj.* **lump•i•er, lump•i•est. 1** full of lumps: *lumpy gravy.* **2** covered with lumps: *lumpy ground.* **3** heavy and clumsy: *a lumpy animal.* **4** of water in a lake, etc., rough; having choppy waves. **—'lump•i•ly,** *adv.* **—'lump•i•ness,** *n.*

Lu•na ['lunə] *n.* **1** *Roman mythology.* the goddess of the moon. **2** the moon. ⟨< L *luna* moon⟩

lu•na•cy ['lunəsi] *n., pl.* **-cies. 1** insanity. **2** extreme folly. ⟨< *lunatic*⟩

luna moth a large North American saturniid moth (*Actias luna*) having light green wings with crescent-shaped markings.

lu•nar ['lunər] *adj.* **1** of or having to do with the moon: *a lunar eclipse.* **2** like the moon in shape. **3** measured by the revolutions of the moon: *a lunar month.* **4** designed for use on the moon: *a lunar vehicle.* ⟨< L *lunaris* < *luna* moon⟩

lunar caustic *Chemistry.* SILVER NITRATE.

lunar eclipse an eclipse of the moon when it lies within the earth's shadow.

lunar module an independent unit designed for use on the moon: *A lunar module may be part of a lunar vehicle.*

lunar month the period of one complete revolution of the moon around the earth; the interval between one new moon and the next, about 29½ days.

lunar vehicle a vehicle designed for use on the moon.

lunar year a period of twelve lunar months.

lu•nate ['luneit] *adj.* crescent-shaped. ⟨< L *lunatus* crescent-shaped < *luna* moon⟩ **—'lu•nate•ly,** *adv.*

lu•na•tic ['lunə,tɪk] *n., adj.* —*n.* **1** an insane person. **2** an extremely foolish person.
—*adj.* **1** insane. **2** for insane people. **3** extremely foolish; idiotic: *a lunatic search for buried treasure.* ⟨ME < LL *lunaticus* < L *luna* moon⟩

lunatic fringe *Informal.* members of the periphery of any group, whose zeal in some cause, movement, etc. goes far beyond the views, etc. held by the majority of members.

lunch [lʌntʃ] *n., v.* —*n.* **1** a light meal between breakfast and dinner: *We usually have lunch at noon.* **2** a light meal eaten at

any time: *We had a lunch at bedtime.* **3** food for lunch: *Leave your lunch in the locker.*
out to lunch, *Slang.* crazy.
—*v.* eat lunch. ⟨shortened form of *luncheon*⟩ **—'lunch•er,** *n.* **—'lunch•less,** *adj.*

lunch•eon ['lʌntʃən] *n., v.* —*n.* **1** a lunch. **2** a formal meal taken at noon.
—*v.* eat luncheon. ⟨< dial. *luncheon* hunk, large lump of food < dial. *lunch* lump, formed after obs. synonym *nuncheon*⟩ **—'lunch•eon•less,** *adj.*

lunch•eon•ette [,lʌntʃə'nɛt] *n.* a restaurant that serves lunches.

lunch•room ['lʌntʃ,rum] *or* ['lʌntʃ,rʊm] *n.* **1** a public dining room; restaurant serving light meals. **2** a room in a plant, school, etc. where employees, teachers, or students may eat the lunches they have brought. Also, **lunch-room.**

lunch•time ['lʌntʃ,taɪm] *n.* the time when lunch is served and eaten, usually around midday.

lune [lun] *n.* **1** anything shaped like a crescent or a half moon. **2** *Geometry.* a crescent-shaped figure formed on a sphere by two great semicircles intersecting at two points. ⟨< F < L *luna* moon⟩
☛ *Hom.* LOON.

lu•nette [lu'nɛt] *n.* **1** *Architecture.* **a** a crescent-shaped opening or space in a vaulted ceiling, dome, wall, etc. **b** a painting, piece of sculpture, etc. that fills this space. **c** an arched or rounded opening, window, etc. **2** a projecting part of a rampart, shaped like an arch. ⟨< F *lunette,* dim. of *lune* moon < L *luna*⟩

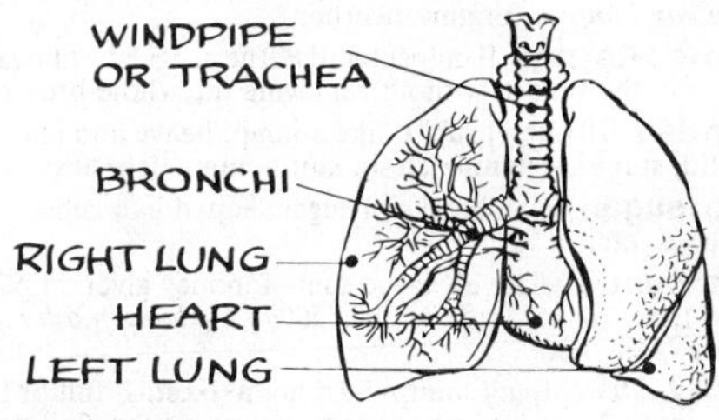

Human lungs seen from the front

lung [lʌŋ] *n.* **1** in vertebrates, one of the pair of breathing organs by means of which the blood receives oxygen and is relieved of carbon dioxide. **2** any of various similar organs in invertebrates. **3** a mechanical device for supplying respiration.
at the top of one's lungs, as loudly as possible: *She shouted at the top of her lungs, but no one seemed to hear her.* ⟨OE *lungen*⟩

lunge[1] [lʌndʒ] *n., v.* **lunged, lung•ing.** —*n.* any sudden forward movement; thrust: *The catcher made a lunge toward the ball.*
—*v.* move suddenly forward; thrust. ⟨ult. < F *allonger,* ult. < L *ad-* toward + *longus* long⟩ **—'lung•er,** *n.*

lunge[2] [lʌndʒ] *n., v.* **lunged, lung•ing.** —*n.* **1** a long rope used for training or exercising a horse. **2** the training of a horse with such a rope. **3** a ring or circular exercise track for training horses.
—*v.* train, exercise, or move (a horse tied with a lunge) around a circular track. ⟨< F *longe* cord, halter < OF *loigne*⟩

lunge[3] or **'lunge** [lʌndʒ] *n. Cdn. Informal.* muskellunge.

lung•fish ['lʌŋ,fɪʃ] *n., pl.* **-fish** or **-fish•es.** any of six species of freshwater fishes, the only living members of the subclass Dipnoi, having an air-breathing lung as well as gills and found in the rivers of South America, Africa, and Australia.

lung•wort ['lʌŋ,wɜrt] *n.* any of several plants (genus *Pulmonaria*) of the borage family, especially a common European perennial (*P. officinalis*) having blue flowers and spotted leaves, formerly used in medicine in the treatment of lung diseases.

lu•ni•so•lar [,lunə'soulər] *adj.* caused by or having to do with both the sun and the moon.

lun•ker ['lʌŋkər] *n. Informal.* anything considered large for its kind, especially a game fish. ⟨origin uncertain⟩

Lu•per•ca•li•a [,lupər'keiliə] *n.* in ancient Rome, a fertility festival celebrated on February 15. ⟨< *Lupercus,* a rural god⟩

lu•pine[1] or **lu•pin** ['lupən] *n.* **1** any of a genus (*Lupinus*) of plants of the pea family found in the western hemisphere and the Mediterranean, having long spikes of brightly coloured flowers, palmate compound leaves, and flat pods with bean-shaped seeds. **2** the seed of this plant, used as food. ⟨< L *lupinus, lupinum.* See LUPINE[2].⟩

lu•pine[2] ['lupaɪn] *adj.* of or like a wolf or wolves. ⟨ME < L *lupinus* < *lupus* wolf⟩

lu•pus ['lupəs] *n.* **1** a skin disease, also called **lupus vulgaris,** caused by the tubercle bacillus. **2** a chronic immunological disorder, also called **lupus erythematosus,** affecting either the skin only or the skin as well as the joints, nervous system, kidneys, and lungs. ⟨< L *lupus* wolf⟩

Lu•pus ['lupəs] *n., gen.* **-pi** [-paɪ]. *Astronomy.* the Wolf, a southern constellation near Scorpius.

lurch[1] [lɜrtʃ] *n., v.* —*n.* **1** a sudden leaning or roll to one side: *The car gave a lurch and overturned.* **2** a stagger.
—*v.* **1** lean or roll suddenly to one side. **2** stagger. ⟨origin uncertain⟩ **—'lurch•ing•ly,** *adv.*

lurch[2] [lɜrtʃ] *n. Archaic* (*except in* **leave in the lurch**). *Games.* a condition in which one player scores nothing or is badly beaten.
leave in the lurch, leave in a helpless condition or a difficult situation. ⟨< F *lourche,* the name of a game⟩

lurch•er ['lɜrtʃər] *n.* **1** a prowler; petty thief; poacher. **2** *Brit.* a mongrel hunting dog much used by poachers.

lure [lur] *n., v.* **lured, lur•ing.** —*n.* **1** attraction: *the lure of the sea.* **2** something that allures, entices, or tempts. **3** a decoy; bait.
—*v.* **1** lead away or into something by awakening desire; attract; tempt. **2** attract with a bait. ⟨ME < OF *loire* < Gmc.⟩
—'lur•er, *n.* **—'lur•ing•ly** *adv.*
☛ *Syn. v.* **1. Lure,** ALLURE, ENTICE = attract or tempt. **Lure,** commonly in a bad sense, means tempt by arousing desire, usually to lead into something bad or not to one's advantage: *The hope of high profits lured him into questionable dealings.* **Allure,** seldom in a bad sense, means tempt by appealing to the senses and feelings and by offering pleasure or advantage: *The Caribbean allures many tourists.* **Entice,** in a good or bad sense, means tempt by appealing to hopes and desires and by using persuasion: *We enticed the kitten down from the tree.*

Lu•rex ['lurɛks] *n. Trademark.* aluminum thread covered with plastic.

lu•rid ['lʊrɪd] *adj.* **1** lighted up with a red or fiery glare: *The sky was lurid with the flames of the burning city.* **2** causing horror; gruesome; terrible: *a lurid crime.* **3** sensational: *The newspaper carried a lurid account of the kidnapping.* **4** very pale and wan in appearance; livid. **5** glaring in brightness or colour: *Her dress was a lurid yellow.* ⟨< L *luridus*⟩

lurk [lɜrk] *v.* **1** stay about without arousing attention; wait out of sight. **2** be hidden. ⟨apparently < *lour* lower[2]⟩ **—'lurk•er,** *n.* **—'lurk•ing•ly,** *adv.*
☛ *Syn.* **1. Lurk,** SKULK = keep out of sight or move in a secret or furtive way. **Lurk** means lie hidden and waiting or move about so as to keep from arousing attention, usually but not always suggesting an evil purpose: *A tiger was lurking in the jungle.* **Skulk** suggests sneakiness and fear, cowardice, or shame: *The cattle thieves skulked in the woods until the posse had passed.*

lus•cious ['lʌʃəs] *adj.* **1** delicious; richly sweet: *a luscious peach.* **2** very pleasing to the senses, especially those of taste and smell. ⟨ME; ? var. of *delicious*⟩ **—'lus•cious•ly,** *adv.* **—'lus•cious•ness,** *n.*
☛ *Syn.* **1.** See note at DELICIOUS.

lush[1] [lʌʃ] *adj.* **1** tender and juicy; growing thick and green: *Lush grass grows along the river banks.* **2** characterized by abundant growth: *We passed many lush fields.* **3** abundant. **4** rich in ornament; flowery: *lush description.* ⟨late ME *lusch* slack; akin to OE *lysu* bad *lēas* lax, MLG *lasch* slack, Icel. *löskr* weak, Gothic *lasiws* weak⟩ **—'lush•ly,** *adv.* **—'lush•ness,** *n.*

lush[2] [lʌʃ] *n., v. Slang.* —*n.* **1** a person who habitually drinks excessive amounts of alcoholic liquor, especially an alcoholic. **2** alcoholic liquor.
—*v.* drink (alcoholic liquor). ⟨? < *lush*[1]⟩

lust [lʌst] *n., v.* —*n.* **1** sexual desire, especially when very intense. **2** any very strong desire; craving: *a lust for power, a lust for revenge. Her lust for life shows in everything she does.*
—*v.* feel a very strong or excessive desire (*usually used with* **after** *or* **for**): *A miser lusts after gold.* ⟨OE *lust* pleasure⟩

lus•ter ['lʌstər] See LUSTRE.

lus•ter•ware ['lʌstər,wɛr] See LUSTREWARE.

lust•ful ['lʌstfəl] *adj.* **1** full of lust. **2** *Archaic.* lusty.
—'lust•ful•ly, *adv.* **—'lust•ful•ness,** *n.*

lus•tral ['lʌstrəl] *adj.* **1** of or used in ceremonial purification. **2** occurring every five years. ⟨< L *lūstrālis.* See LUSTRUM.⟩

lus•trate ['lʌstreit] *v.* **-trat•ed, -trat•ing.** purify by a ceremonial method, such as washing, sacrifice, etc. ⟨< L *lustrare* brighten, clean < *lustrum* lustrum⟩ **—lus'tra•tion,** *n.* **—'lus•tra•tive** ['lʌstrətɪv], *adj.*

lus•tre ['lʌstər] *n., v.,* **-tred, -tring.** *—n.* **1** a bright shine on the surface: *the lustre of pearls.* **2** brightness: *Her eyes lost their lustre.* **3** fame; glory; brilliance. **4** a kind of china or pottery that has a lustrous metallic, often iridescent surface. **5** a thin fabric of cotton and wool that has a lustrous surface.
—v. finish or shine with a lustre or gloss. Also, **luster.** ⟨< F < Ital. *lustro* < *lustrare* < L *lustrare* illuminate⟩
—'lus•tre•less, *adj.*

lus•tre•ware ['lʌstər,wɛr] *n.* a kind of earthenware or china that has a lustrous, often iridescent glaze. Also, **lusterware.**

lus•trous ['lʌstrəs] *adj.* having lustre; shining; glossy: *lustrous satin.* **—'lus•trous•ly,** *adv.* **—'lus•trous•ness,** *adj.*

lus•trum ['lʌstrəm] *n., pl.* **-trums** or **-tra** [-trə]. **1** in ancient Rome, a ceremonial purification, performed every five years. **2** a period of five years. ⟨< L, akin to *luere* to atone for, avert by expiation (literally, get rid of by washing), *lavāre* to wash⟩

lust•y ['lʌsti] *adj.* **lust•i•er, lust•i•est.** strong and healthy; full of vigour and enthusiasm. **—'lust•i•ly,** *adv.* **—'lust•i•ness,** *n.*

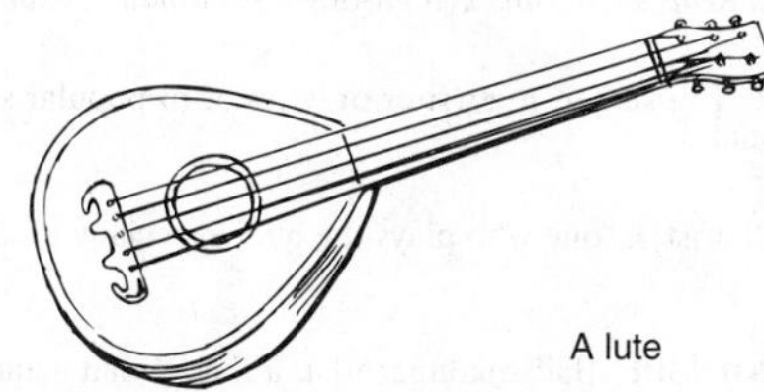
A lute

lute [lut] *n.* a stringed musical instrument like a large mandolin, much used in the 1500s and 1600s. ⟨ME < OF < Provençal *laut* < Arabic *al'ud* the lute⟩
☛ *Hom.* LOOT.

lu•ten•ist ['lutənɪst] *n.* one who plays the lute, especially a skilled player.

lu•te•ti•um [lu'tiʃəm] *n. Chemistry.* a rare, metallic chemical element. *Symbol*: Lu; *at.no.* 71; *at.mass* 174.97. Also, esp. formerly, **lutecium.** ⟨< NL < L *Lutetia* Paris⟩

Lu•ther•an ['luθərən] *n., adj. —n.* **1** a member of any of the churches that together constitute the largest Protestant denomination, originating in the 1520s as a result of the teachings of Martin Luther (1483-1546), and whose tenets traditionally include the belief that a person can be saved not by good works but only by faith, through the redemption of Christ, and that the individual can come to God on his or her own, with the Bible as a sufficient guide to truth. **2** a follower of Martin Luther.
—adj. **1** of or having to do with Luther or his doctrines. **2** of or having to do with a Lutheran church.

Lu•ther•an•ism ['luθərə,nɪzəm] *n.* the doctrines or religious principles of Martin Luther and his followers or the Lutheran churches.

lu•thi•er ['lutiər] *n.* **1** one who makes lutes. **2** one who makes and repairs stringed instruments. ⟨< F *luth* lute < OF *leut*⟩

lux [lʌks] *n., pl.* **lux•es** or **lu•ces** ['lusiz]. *Optics.* an SI unit for measuring illumination by a source of light per unit area on a surface. One lux is the illumination of one lumen over an area of one square metre. *Symbol*: lx ⟨< L *lūx* light[1]⟩

lux•ate ['lʌkseit] *v.* **-at•ed, -at•ing.** dislocate; put out of joint. ⟨< L *luxare* dislocate⟩ **—lux'a•tion,** *n.*

luxe [lʊks], [luks], *or* [lʌks]; *French,* [lyks] *n.* an elegant or luxurious quality. ⟨< F < L *luxus* extravagance⟩

Lux•em•bourg ['lʌksəm,bɜrg] *n.* a small country in W Europe.

lux•u•ri•ance [lʌg'ʒʊriəns] *or* [lʌk'ʃʊriəns] *n.* the quality or state of being luxuriant; rich abundance.

lux•u•ri•ant [lʌg'ʒʊriənt] *or* [lʌk'ʃʊriənt] *adj.* **1** growing in a vigorous and healthy way; thick and lush: *In spring the grass on our lawn is luxuriant. She has a luxuriant head of hair.* **2** producing abundantly. **3** rich in ornament. ⟨< L *luxurians, -antis,* ppr. of *luxuriare.* See LUXURIATE.⟩ **—lux'u•ri•ant•ly,** *adv.*
☛ *Usage.* Do not confuse **luxuriant** and LUXURIOUS; they are related words with very different meanings.

lux•u•ri•ate [lʌg'ʒʊri,eit] *or* [lʌk'ʃʊri,eit] *v.* **-at•ed, -at•ing. 1** indulge oneself luxuriously; take great delight; revel (*in*): *luxuriating in a hot bath.* **2** grow very abundantly. ⟨< L *luxuriare* < *luxuria* luxury < *luxus* excess⟩

lux•u•ri•ous [lʌg'ʒʊriəs] *or* [lʌk'ʃʊriəs] *adj.* **1** giving luxury; very comfortable and beautiful. **2** fond of luxury; tending toward luxury; self-indulgent. **—lux'u•ri•ous•ly,** *adv.* **—lux'u•ri•ous•ness,** *n.*
☛ *Usage.* See note at LUXURIANT.

lux•u•ry ['lʌkʃəri] *or* ['lʌgʒəri] *n., pl.* **-ries. 1** an abundance of the comforts and beauties of life beyond what is really necessary. **2** the use of the best and most costly food, clothes, houses, furniture, and amusements. **3** anything that one enjoys, usually something choice and costly. **4** something pleasant but not necessary. **5** emotional comfort: *the luxury of knowing he was always there for her.* **6** the thing giving emotional comfort: *Introspection was a luxury she could not afford.*
in the lap of luxury. See LAP. ⟨< L *luxuria* < *luxus* excess⟩

lwei [lwei] *or* [lə'wei] *n.* a unit of currency in Angola, equal to 1/100 of a kwanza. See table of money in the Appendix.

LXX Septuagint.

-ly[1] *adverb-forming suffix.* **1** in a —— manner: *cheerfully = in a cheerful manner.* **2** in —— ways or respects: *financially = in financial respects.* **3** to a —— degree or extent: *greatly = to a great degree.* **4** in, to, or from a —— direction: *northwardly = to or from the north.* **5** in a —— place: *thirdly = in the third place.* **6** at a —— time: *recently = at a recent time.* ⟨OE *-līce* < *-līc* -ly[2]⟩

-ly[2] *adjective-forming suffix.* **1** like a ——: *a ghostly form = a form like a ghost.* **2** like that of a ——; characteristic of a ——: *a brotherly kiss = a kiss like that of a brother.* **3** suited to a ——; fit or proper for a ——: *sisterly kindness = kindness suited to a sister.* **4** of each or every ——; occurring once per ——: *daily = of every day.* **5** being a ——; that is a ——: *a heavenly home = a home that is a heaven.* ⟨OE *-līc,* suffixal use of LIKE[1]⟩

ly•can•thrope ['ləikən,θroup] *or* [ləi'kænθroup] *n.* werewolf. ⟨< Gk. *lykánthrōpos* wolf-man (< *lýkos* wolf + *ánthrōpos* man)⟩

ly•can•thro•py [ləi'kænθrəpi] *n.* **1** a mental illness causing one to believe one is a wolf. **2** the supposed power to turn oneself into a wolf. **—,ly•can'throp•ic** [,ləikən'θrɒpɪk], *adj.*

ly•cée [li'sei] *n., pl.* in France, a secondary school maintained by the government. ⟨< F < L *Lyceum.* Doublet of LYCEUM.⟩

ly•ce•um [ləi'siəm] *or* ['ləisiəm] *n.* **1** a lecture hall; a place where lectures are given. **2 Lyceum,** an ancient outdoor grove and gymnasium near Athens, where Aristotle taught. ⟨< L *Lyceum* < Gk. *Lykeion* (def. 2), from the nearby temple of Apollo, *Lykeios.* Doublet of LYCÉE.⟩

ly•chee ['lɪtʃi] *n.* See LITCHI.

lych–gate ['lɪtʃ ,geit] See LICH-GATE.

ly•co•po•di•um [,ləikə'poudiəm] *n.* **1** any of a large genus (*Lycopodium*) of chiefly creeping club mosses having needlelike evergreen leaves. The **ground cedar** (*L. complanatum*) and **shining club moss** (*L. lucidulum*) are two lycopodiums found in Canada. **2** a fine, yellow powder made from the spores of certain lycopodiums, used in medicine and for making fireworks. ⟨< NL < Gk. *lykos* wolf + *pous, podos* foot⟩

lydd•ite ['lɪdəit] *n. Chemistry.* a high explosive, consisting chiefly of picric acid. ⟨< *Lydd,* a town in SE England⟩

Lyd•i•an ['lɪdiən] *n., adj. —n.* **1** a native or inhabitant of Lydia, an ancient kingdom in W Asia Minor. **2** the extinct Anatolian language of the Lydians.
—adj. of or having to do with Lydia, its people, their language, or their music.

lye [laɪ] *n. Chemistry.* any strong, alkaline substance obtained by leaching wood ashes, especially sodium hydroxide or potassium hydroxide. Lye is used in making soap and in cleaning. ⟨OE *lēag*⟩
☛ *Hom.* LIE.

ly•ing[1] ['laɪɪŋ] *n., adj., v. —n.* the telling of a lie; the habit of telling lies.
—adj. false; untruthful: *a lying report.*
—v. ppr. of LIE[1].

ly•ing[2] ['laɪɪŋ] *v.* ppr. of LIE[2].

ly•ing–in ['laɪɪŋ 'ɪn] *n., adj. —n.* confinement in childbirth.
—adj. having to do with childbirth: *a lying-in hospital.*

Lyme disease [laɪm] a disease borne by ticks and characterized by recurrent skin rash, fever, etc. and later by arthritis and heart failure. ⟨after *Lyme,* Connecticut where first diagnosed⟩

lymph [lɪmf] *n. Anatomy, physiology.* a nearly colourless liquid in the tissues of the body, resembling blood plasma and containing white blood cells but no red blood cells. ⟨< L *lympha* clear water⟩

lym•phat•ic [lɪm'fætɪk] *adj., n. —adj.* **1** of lymph; carrying lymph. **2** sluggish; lacking energy.
—n. a vessel that contains or carries lymph.
—lym'phat•i•cal•ly, *adv.*

lymph node or **gland** one of the rounded masses of tissue lying along the course of the lymphatic vessels, in which the lymph is purified and lymphocytes are formed.

lym•pho•blast ['lɪmfə,blæst] *n. Physiology.* a cell type that develops into lymphocytes. It can be cultured from blood for genetic studies. **—,lym•pho'blas•tic,** *adj.*

lym•pho•cyte ['lɪmfə,səit] *n. Physiology.* one of the colourless cells of lymph produced in the lymph nodes, a variety of leucocyte. ⟨< L *lympha* clear water + E *-cyte* hollow body (< Gk. *kytos*)⟩ **—,lym•pho'cyt•ic** [,lɪmfə'sɪtɪk], *adj.*

lymph•oid ['lɪmfɔɪd] *adj.* **1** of, having to do with, or resembling lymph or lymphocytes. **2** of, having to do with, or resembling lymphatic tissue.

lynch [lɪntʃ] *v.* kill, usually by hanging, through mob action and without a proper trial. ⟨See LYNCH LAW⟩ **—'lynch•er,** *n.* **—'lynch•ing,** *n.*

lynch law the punishment of an accused person without a lawful trial, usually by putting him or her to death. ⟨originally *Lynch's law* < William *Lynch* (1742-1820), a Virginia magistrate⟩

lynx [lɪŋks] *n., pl.* **lynx•es** or *(esp. collectively)* **lynx** *for 1-3; gen.* **Lyn•cis** ['lɪnsɪs] *for 4.* **1** a medium-sized wildcat (*Felis lynx*) of Eurasia and N North America, having long legs with large paws, tufted ears, and a short tail. See also CANADA LYNX. **2** any of several other closely related wildcats, such as the bobcat or caracal. **3** the silky fur of the lynx. **4 Lynx,** a constellation in the northern hemisphere near Ursa Major. ⟨ME < L < Gk.⟩ **—'lynx,like,** *adj.*
☛ *Hom.* LINKS.

lynx–eyed ['lɪŋks,aɪd] *adj.* having sharp eyes; sharp-sighted.

Ly•on hypothesis ['laɪən] *Genetics.* the principle that, in somatic cells of mammalian females, one X chromosome is inactivated and appears in interphase cells as the SEX CHROMATIN. ⟨after Mary *Lyon* (1925-), British geneticist⟩

Ly•on•i•za•tion [,laɪənaɪ'zeiʃən] *n. Genetics.* the inactivation of one X chromosome in the cells of females.

ly•on•naise [,laɪə'neiz]; *French,* [ljɔ'nɛz] *adj.* fried with pieces of onion: *lyonnaise potatoes.* ⟨< F *lyonnaise* < *Lyon* Lyons, a city in E France⟩

Ly•ra ['laɪrə] *n., gen.* **-rae** [-ri] *or* [-raɪ]. a small, northern constellation thought of as arranged in the shape of a lyre. It contains the star Vega.

ly•rate ['laɪreit] *adj.* shaped like a lyre.

A lyre

lyre [laɪr] *n.* an ancient, stringed musical instrument resembling a small harp. ⟨ME < L < Gk. *lyra*⟩

lyre•bird ['laɪr,bɜrd] *n.* either of two Australian birds (*Menura superba* and *M. alberti*) that make up a separate family (Menuridae) of passerine birds. The adult males have a long tail that is lyre-shaped when spread.

lyr•ic ['lɪrɪk] *n., adj. —n.* **1** a short poem expressing personal emotion. Love poems, patriotic songs, laments, and hymns are all lyrics. **2 lyrics,** *pl.* the words for a song.
—adj. **1** having to do with a lyric or lyrics (def. 1): *a lyric poet.* **2** characterized by a spontaneous expression of feeling. **3** of or suitable for singing with a light, flexible voice. **4** having a light, melodic singing voice: *a lyric soprano.* **5** of or for the lyre. ⟨< L *lyricus* < Gk. *lyrikos* of a lyre⟩

lyr•i•cal ['lɪrɪkəl] *adj.* **1** showing or expressing great enthusiasm and emotion: *She was lyrical in her praise of the new auditorium.* **2** lyric. **—'lyr•i•cal•ly,** *adv.* **—'lyr•i•cal•ness,** *n.*

lyr•i•cism ['lɪrɪ,sɪzəm] *n.* **1** a lyric style, quality, or form of expression: *Keats's lyricism.* **2** high-flown sentiments; exuberance.

lyr•i•cist ['lɪrɪsɪst] *n.* **1** a writer of lyrics or of popular songs. **2** a lyric poet.

lyr•ist ['laɪrɪst] *n.* one who plays the lyre, especially a skilled player.

Ly•sen•ko•ism [lə'sɛŋkou,ɪzəm] *n.* a theory that acquired characteristics are hereditary. ⟨after T.D. *Lysenko* (1898-1976), Soviet agronomist who promulgated it for political reasons⟩

ly•ser•gic acid [lə'sɜrdʒɪk] *Chemistry.* a crystalline compound produced synthetically or as an extract from ergot. *Formula*: $C_{16}H_{16}N_2O_2$

lysergic acid di•eth•yl•am•ide [daɪ'ɛθələmaɪd] a drug that can produce hallucinations and schizophrenic symptoms. *Formula*: $C_{20}H_{25}N_3O$ *Abbrev.*: LSD

ly•sin ['ləisɪn] *n. Biochemistry.* any of a class of substances that are developed in blood serum, and that are capable of causing the dissolution or destruction of bacteria, blood corpuscles, and other cellular elements. ⟨< Gk. *lysis* a loosening + E *-in*⟩

ly•sine ['ləisin] *n. Biochemistry.* a basic amino acid vital to nutrition. *Formula*: $NH_2(CH_2)_4CH(NH_2)COOH$.

Ly•sol ['ləisɒl] *n. Trademark.* a brown, oily liquid containing cresols and soap, used as a disinfectant and antiseptic. ⟨< Gk. *lysis* a loosening + L *oleum* oil⟩

ly•so•so•mal disease [,ləisə'souməl] a disease in which there is a genetic defect in one of the enzymes contained in lysosomes, leading to storage of an abnormal substance. An example is **Tay-Sachs disease.**

ly•so•some ['ləisə,soum] *n. Biochemistry.* part of a cell which contains digestive enzymes capable of digesting living organisms such as bacteria, and which also helps to decompose the cell after death. ⟨< Gk. *lysis* a breaking down + *soma* body⟩

lyt•ta ['lɪtə] *n., pl.* **lyt•tas** or **lyt•tae** ['lɪti] *or* ['lɪti]. a thin strip of cartilage in the tongue of a dog and some other carnivores.

M m *M m*

m or **M** [ɛm] *n., pl.* **m's** or **M's. 1** the thirteenth letter of the English alphabet. **2** any speech sound represented by this letter. **3** a person or thing identified as *m*, especially the thirteenth in a series. **4 M**, the Roman numeral for 1000. **5** *Printing.* an em, a unit of measure. **6** something shaped like the letter M. **7** any device, such as a printer's type, a lever, or a key on a keyboard, that produces an M or an m. **8** (*adjl.*) of or being an M or an m.

m 1 metre(s). **2** milli- (an SI prefix). **3** mass.

m. or **M. 1** minute. **2** masculine. **3** male. **4** mile. **5** married. **6** minim. **7** month. **8** manual. **9** *Currency.* mill. **10** modulus. **11** noon (for L *meridies*). **12** medium. **13** morning.

M 1 mega- (an SI prefix). **2** *Currency.* mark.

M. 1 Monday. **2** Monsieur. **3** Master (in titles). **4** Mass.

M' a variant of *Mac* or *Mc*.

ma [mɑ] *or* [mɒ] *n. Informal.* mamma; mother.
☛ *Hom.* MAW [mɒ].

MA *Psychology.* mental age.

MA or **ma** milliamperes.

ma'am [mæm] *or* [mɑm]; *unstressed,* [məm] *n.* madam.

Maas•tricht Treaty ['mɑstrɪxt] an agreement involving closer union among European countries.

mac [mæk] *n.* mackintosh; a raincoat.

Mac [mæk] *n. Cdn. Informal.* a McIntosh apple.

ma•ca•bre [mə'kɑbər], [mə'kɑb], *or* [mə'kɑbrə] *adj.* gruesome; horrible; ghastly. ⟨< F⟩

ma•ca•co [mə'kakou] *or* [mə'keikou] *n., pl.* **-cos.** any of several lemurs (genus *Lemur*), especially *L. macaco*, the male of which is black and the female brown. ⟨< Pg. < native African⟩

mac•ad•am [mə'kædəm] *n.* **1** material for making roads, consisting of small, broken stones of nearly uniform size which are mixed with a binding agent such as tar or asphalt. Several layers of macadam are put down to make a road, each layer rolled until solid and smooth before the next layer is laid down. **2** pavement made with layers of macadam. ⟨after John L. *McAdam* (1756-1836), a Scottish engineer⟩

ma•ca•da•mia [,mækə'deimiə] *n.* **1** an Australian tree of the genus *Macadamia*. **2** Usually, **macadamia nut**, the edible seed of this tree. ⟨< NL, after J. *Macadam* (d. 1865), Australian chemist⟩

mac•ad•am•ize [mə'kædə,maɪz] *v.* **-ized, -iz•ing.** construct or surface (a road) with macadam. **—mac,ad•am•i'za•tion,** *n.*

Ma•ca•nese [,mækə'niz] *n., adj. —n.* a native or inhabitant of Macao.
—adj. of or having to do with Macao.

Ma•cao [mə'kaʊ] *n.* a Portuguese colony in China.

ma•caque [mə'kɑk] *or* [mə'kæk] *n.* any of a genus (*Macaca*) of short-tailed or tailless Old World monkeys found mainly in Asia. The rhesus monkey and the Barbary ape are macaques. ⟨< F < Pg. *macaco* monkey⟩

mac•a•ro•ni [,mækə'rouni] *n., pl.* **-nis** or **-nies. 1** flour paste that has been dried, usually in the form of hollow tubes, to be cooked for food. **2** formerly, an English dandy. ⟨< earlier Ital. *maccaroni*, pl., ult. < LGk. *makaria* barley broth⟩

mac•a•ron•ic [,mækə'rɒnɪk] *adj.* **1** composed of a mixture of languages, especially of Latin and English. **2** mixed; jumbled. ⟨< Med.L *macarōnicus* < dial. Ital. *maccarone* MACARONI + L *-icus*⟩ **—,mac•a'ron•i•cal•ly,** *adv.*

mac•a•roon [,mækə'run] *n.* a very sweet, chewy cookie, usually made of egg whites, sugar, and ground almonds or coconut. ⟨< F < Ital. *maccarone*, sing. of *maccaroni.* See MACARONI.⟩

ma•caw [mə'kɒ] *n.* any parrot belonging to either of two genera (*Ara* and *Anodorhynchus*) of large, brilliantly coloured, tropical American parrots having a long, loose tail and a large, deep, hooked bill. ⟨< Pg. *macao* parrot< origin uncertain⟩

mac•ca•boy ['mækə,bɔɪ] *n.* a rose-scented snuff. ⟨earlier *Macaubao* < F *macouba* a kind of aromatic tobacco; named after *Macouba*, the place in N Martinique where it is made⟩

Mac•don•ald Brier [mək'dɒnəld] *Cdn.* the Canadian national curling championship.

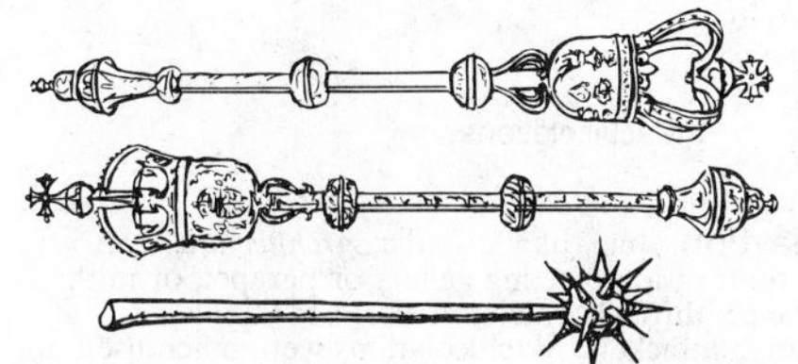

The maces of the Canadian Senate and the House of Commons

A medieval mace

mace¹ [meis] *n.* **1** a staff used as a symbol of authority. **2** the bearer of a mace. **3** in the Middle Ages, a war club having a heavy metal head. ⟨ME < OF < VL *mattea* < L *matteola* kind of hammer⟩

mace² [meis] *n.* a spice made from the dried outer covering of nutmegs. ⟨ME < OF *macis* < L *macir* reddish rind of an Indian root < Gk. *makir*⟩

Mace [meis] *n. Trademark.* a liquid chemical similar in effect to tear gas, producing tears and temporary blindness, dizziness, etc. when sprayed in a person's face. It has been used by some police forces, etc. for controlling riots.

mace•bear•er ['meis,bɛrər] *n.* an official who carries a ceremonial mace in procession. Also, **macer.**

mac•é•doine [,mæsə'dwɑn]; *French,* [mase'dwan] *n.* a mixture of vegetables or fruits, sometimes in jelly. ⟨< F a special use of *macédoine* Macedonian⟩

Ma•ce•do•nia [,mæsə'douniə] *n.* **1** a country in E Europe, part of the former Yugoslavia. **2** a northern region of Greece. **3** an ancient kingdom in SE Europe, north of ancient Greece.

Ma•ce•do•ni•an [,mæsə'douniən] *n., adj. —n.* **1** a native or inhabitant of Macedonia. **2** the Slavic language of Macedonia.
—adj. of or having to do with Macedonians or their language.

ma•cer ['meisər] *n.* macebearer.

mac•er•ate ['mæsə,reit] *v.* **-at•ed, -at•ing. 1** soften by soaking for some time. **2** break up or soften (food) by the digestive process. **3** grow or cause to grow thin. ⟨< L *macerare* soften⟩ **—,mac•er'a•tion,** *n.* **—'mac•er,a•tor,** *n.* **—'mac•er•a•tive,** *adj.*

Mach [mɑk] *or* [mæk] *n.* MACH NUMBER.

ma•chet•e [mə'ʃɛti] *or* [mə'tʃɛti]; *Spanish,* [ma'tʃete] *n.* a large, heavy knife, used as a tool and weapon in South America, Central America, and the West Indies. ⟨< Sp., ult. < L *mactare* kill⟩

Mach•i•a•vel•li•an or **Mach•i•a•vel•i•an** [,mækiə'vɛliən] *adj., n. —adj.* **1** of or having to do with Niccolo Machiavelli (1469-1527), an Italian statesman and writer who wrote *The Prince*, a detailed study of how force, deceit, and other unscrupulous methods were used to gain and hold power. **2** of or having to do with the crafty political methods described by Machiavelli. **3** characterized by subtle or unscrupulous cunning; crafty; wily; astute.
—n. a person who uses such crafty political methods as were described by Machiavelli. **—,Mach•i•a'vel•li•an,ism,** *n.*

ma•chic•o•late [mə'tʃɪkə,leit] *v.* **-lat•ed, -lat•ing.** provide with machicolations.

ma•chic•o•lat•ed [mə'tʃɪkə,leitɪd] *adj.* having machicolations.

Machicolations

ma•chic•o•la•tion [mə,tʃɪkə'leiʃən] *n. Architecture.* **1** an opening in the floor of a projecting gallery or parapet, or in the roof of an entrance, through which missiles, hot liquids, etc. might be cast upon attackers. Machicolations were much used in medieval fortified structures. **2** a projecting gallery or parapet with such openings. ⟨< Med.L *machicolatio, -onis* < OF < Provençal *machacol* projection, balcony < *macar* crush (< Gmc.) + *col* neck < L *collum*⟩

mach•i•nate ['mækə,neit] *or* ['mæʃə,neit] *v.* **-nat•ed, -nat•ing.** contrive or devise artfully or with evil purpose; plot; intrigue. ⟨< L *machinari* < *machina.* See MACHINE.⟩ **—'mach•i,na•tor,** *n.*

mach•i•na•tion [,mækə'neiʃən] *or* [,mæʃə'neiʃən] *n.* **1** the act of machinating. **2** Usually, **machinations,** *pl.* a secret or cunning scheme, especially one with an evil purpose: *He could not have been overthrown without the machinations of his enemies.*

ma•chine [mə'ʃin] *n., v.* **-chined, -chin•ing.** *—n.* **1** a device consisting of an arrangement of interrelated fixed and moving parts powered mechanically, electrically, or electronically, designed to do a particular kind of work: *a sewing machine, a calculating machine.* **2** (*adjl.*) of or having to do with a machine or machines: *the machine age, machine action.* **3** (*adjl.*) produced by or with a machine, not by hand: *machine printing.* **4** *Mechanics.* a device for transmitting power, energy, or motion or changing its direction. Levers and pulleys are simple machines. **5** a coin-operated dispenser: *a cigarette machine.* **6** a motor vehicle, aircraft, bicycle, etc. **7** a person or group that acts mechanically, without thinking or feeling. **8** a highly organized group of people, especially a group controlling a political organization: *the Liberal machine.*
—v. make or finish by machine. ⟨< F < L *machina* < Gk. *machana,* dial. var. of *mēchanē* device, means⟩ **—ma'chin•er,** *n.* **—ma'chine,like,** *adj.*

machine bolt a bolt for connecting metal parts.

machine gun a gun that uses small-arms ammunition automatically and can keep up a rapid fire of bullets.

ma•chine–gun [mə'ʃin ,gʌn] *v.* **-gunned, -gun•ning.** fire at with a machine gun.

machine language *Computer technology.* a language for specifying instructions in terms of numbers that, in their binary form, can be used directly by the central processing unit of a computer.

ma•chine–made [mə'ʃin ,meid] *adj.* made by machinery, not by hand.

machine readable *Computer technology.* of data, which can be read and used by a computer.

ma•chin•er•y [mə'ʃinəri] *n., pl.* **-er•ies. 1** machines: *There is a lot of machinery in a shoe factory.* **2** the parts or works of a machine: *He examined the machinery of his watch.* **3** any combination of persons or things by which something is kept going or something is done: *Police officers, judges, courts, and prisons are the machinery of the law.*

machine screw a screw for connecting metal parts.

machine shed *Cdn.* a farm building in which implements are kept.

machine shop a workshop where machines or parts of machines are made or repaired.

machine tool an electrically or mechanically driven tool, such as a lathe, drill, or punch press, used in manufacturing machinery.

machine–tool [mə'ʃin ,tul] *v.* manufacture (machinery) with a machine tool.

ma•chin•ist [mə'ʃinɪst] *n.* **1** a person skilled in using machine tools. **2** a person who runs a machine. **3** a person who makes and repairs machinery.

ma•chis•mo [mɑ'tʃizmou] *or* [mə'tʃɪzmou] *n.* exaggerated or aggressive masculinity; a macho quality or condition. ⟨< Sp. *macho* male⟩

Mach•me•ter ['mɑk,mitər] *or* ['mæk,mitər] *n. Aeronautics.* an instrument for indicating the air speed of an aircraft as a Mach number.

Mach number a number representing the ratio of the speed of an object to the speed of sound in the same medium. Mach number 1 equals the speed of sound, Mach number 2 is twice the speed of sound, and Mach number 0.5 is half the speed of sound. ⟨after Ernst *Mach* (1838-1916), an Austrian physicist⟩

ma•cho ['mɑtʃou] *adj., n. —adj.* robust and virile in an exaggerated way; proudly or aggressively masculine: *a macho swagger, a macho image.*
—n. **1** a man who is proudly or aggressively masculine. **2** manhood; virility. ⟨< Sp. *macho* male⟩

—machy *suffix.* fighting: *logomachy.* ⟨< Gk. *-machia, machē* battle⟩

mac•in•tosh ['mækən,tɒʃ] See MACKINTOSH.

mack•er•el ['mækərəl] *n., pl.* **-el** or **-els. 1** an important marine food fish (*Scomber scombrus*) of the N Atlantic coastal regions and the Mediterranean, having a rounded, torpedo-shaped, green and silver body and a deeply forked tail. **2** any of various other fishes of the same family (Scombridae), such as the **Spanish mackerel** (genus *Scomberomorus*) of warm seas or the **Pacific mackerel** (*Scomber japonicus*). ⟨ME < AF *makerel*⟩

mackerel sky a sky spotted with small, white fleecy clouds.

mack•i•naw ['mækə,nɒ] *n. Cdn.* **1** MACKINAW COAT. **2** MACKINAW BLANKET. **3** MACKINAW BOAT. ⟨< Cdn.F *Mackinac* < *Michilimackinac* Mackinac Island < Algonquian (Ojibwa) *mitchimakinak* large turtle⟩

mackinaw blanket *Cdn.* a kind of thick, woollen blanket that often has bars of colour, used in the North and West by First Nations people, trappers, etc.

mackinaw boat *Cdn.* a large, heavy, flat-bottomed boat, formerly used in the region of the Upper Great Lakes.

mackinaw coat or **jacket** *Cdn.* a kind of short coat made of heavy, woollen cloth, often plaid.

mack•in•tosh ['mækɪn,tɒʃ] *n.* **1** raincoat. **2** waterproof, rubberized cloth. Also, **macintosh.** ⟨< Charles *Macintosh* (1766-1843), the inventor⟩ **—'mack•in,toshed,** *adj.*

mack•le ['mækəl] *n., v.* **mack•led, mack•ling.** *—n.* a blur such as a double impression in printing.
—v. make such a blur. Also, **macule**. ⟨var. of earlier *macle, makle,* late ME *macule* spot, blemish < L *macula*⟩
☛ *Hom.* MACLE.

ma•cle ['mækəl] *n. Crystallography.* **1** a discoloration in a mineral. **2** a twin; two crystals that are interwoven. ⟨< F < L *macula* spot, blemish⟩
☛ *Hom.* MACKLE.

mac•ra•mé ['mækrə,mei] *n.* a type of decorative openwork made by knotting coarse thread or cord into patterns. ⟨< F < Ital. *macramè* kind of fringe on hand towels < Turkish *makrama* napkin, face towel < Arabic *migrama* embroidered veil⟩

mac•ro ['mækrou] *n. Computer technology.* a set of detailed computer instructions that can be generated or invoked by a single instruction. Also called **macro instruction.**

macro– *combining form.* large; long; large-scale: *macrocosm.* Compare MICRO-. ⟨< Gk. *makro-, makrós*⟩

mac•ro•bi•ot•ic [,mækroubaɪ'ɒtɪk] *adj.* of food, regarded as healthful. **—,mac•ro•bi'ot•i•cal•ly,** *adv.*

mac•ro•bi•ot•ics [,mækroubaɪ'ɒtɪks] *n.* a dietary theory which promotes a regime of food consisting mainly of whole grains; a form of vegetarianism (*used with a singular verb*).

mac•ro•ceph•a•ly [,mækrou'sɛfəli] *n.* excessive cranial capacity. ⟨< Gk. *makroképhalos* large-headed < *makro-* large + *kephalē head*⟩

mac•ro•cli•mate ['mækrou,klaɪmɪt] *n.* the climate of an extensive geographic area. **—,mac•ro•cli'mat•ic** [-klaɪ'mætɪk], *adj.* **—,mac•ro•cli'mat•i•cal•ly,** *adv.*

mac•ro•cosm ['mækrə,kɒzəm] *n.* **1** universe. **2** any system composed of smaller units. ⟨< F *macrocosme* < Med.L

macrocosmus < Gk. *makros* great + *kosmos* world⟩
—,mac•ro'cos•mic, *adj.* **—,mac•ro'cos•mi•cal•ly,** *adv.*

mac•ro•cyte ['mækrə,səit] *n. Pathology.* an abnormally large blood cell. **—,mac•ro'cyt•ic** [,mækrə'sɪtɪk] *adj.*

mac•ro•don•tia [,mækrə'dɒnʃə] *n.* the condition of having unusually large teeth. Also called **megadontia.**

mac•ro–e•co•nom•ics [,mækrou ,ikə'nɒmɪks] *or* [,ɛkə'nɒmɪks] *n.* the study of the economy of a country as a whole (*used with a singular verb*). Compare MICRO-ECONOMICS. **—,mac•ro-,e•co'nom•ic,** *adj.*

mac•ro–ev•o•lu•tion [,mækrou ,ɛvə'luʃən] *or* [,ivə'luʃən] *n.* the evolution of a complete species.

mac•ro•gam•ete [,mækrou'gæmit] *or* [,mækrougə'mit] *n. Zoology.* the larger of two gametes in protozoans, normally the female cell.

mac•ro•mol•e•cule [,mækrə'mɒlə,kjul] *n. Chemistry.* a very large molecule, consisting of hundreds of repeating monomers. **—,mac•ro•mo'lec•u•lar** [,mækroumə'lɛkjələr], *adj.*

ma•cron ['meikrɒn] *or* ['mækrɒn] *n.* a short, horizontal line (¯) placed over a vowel letter to identify a sound differing from that represented by the same letter without such a mark. *Example*: ā. ⟨< Gk. *makron*, neut. adj., long⟩

mac•ro•nu•cle•us [,mækrou'njukliəs] *or* [,mækrou'nukliəs] *Zoology. n.* a large non-reproducing nucleus in the cells of ciliated protozoans. **—,mac•ro'nu•cle•ar,** *adj.*

mac•ro•nu•tri•ent [,mækrou'njutriənt] *or* [,mækrou'nutriənt] *n. Botany* an element such as nitrogen that is needed in large quantity for plant growth.

mac•rop•ter•ous [mæ'krɒptərəs] *adj. Zoology.* having large fins or wings. ⟨< Gk. *makrópteros* long-winged < *makros* great + *pteron* wing⟩
—mac'rop•ter•y, *n.*

mac•ro•scop•ic [,mækrə'skɒpɪk] *adj.* **1** that can be seen with the naked eye. **2** having to do with large groups. **—,mac•ro'scop•i•cal•ly,** *adv.*

mac•ro•spo•ran•gi•um [,mækrouspə'rændʒiəm] *n., pl.* **-gi•a** [-dʒiə]. *Botany.* megasporangium.

mac•ro•spore ['mækrə,spɔr] *n. Botany.* megaspore.

ma•cru•ran [mə'krʊrən] *adj.* belonging or pertaining to the suborder *Macrura*, comprising the crustaceans. ⟨< NL < Gk. *makros* great + *oura* tail⟩

mac•u•la ['mækjələ] *n., pl.* **-lae** [-,li] *or* [-,laɪ]. a blemish caused by lack of pigment in the skin. ⟨late ME < L: spot, blemish⟩ **—'mac•u•lar,** *adj.*

macula lutea ['lutiə] *n.* that part of the retina that produces acute and clear vision. ⟨< L, literally, yellow spot⟩

macular degeneration *Ophthalmology.* degeneration of the central part of the retina, causing lack of clear vision.

mac•u•late *adj.* ['mækjəlɪt]; *v.* ['mækjə,leit] *adj., v.* **-lat•ed, -lat•ing.** *—adj.* stained or blemished.
—v. stain or blemish. **—,mac•u'la•tion,** *n.*

mac•ule ['mækjul] *n., v.* **-uled, -ul•ing.** See MACKLE.

mad [mæd] *adj.* **mad•der, mad•dest. 1** out of one's mind; crazy; insane. **2** angry: *The article made him mad enough to write a letter to the editor.* **3** much excited; wild: *The dog made mad efforts to catch up with the automobile.* **4** foolish; unwise: *a mad undertaking.* **5** very lively: *a mad party.* **6** blindly and unreasonably fond: *mad about boats.* **7** having rabies; rabid: *a mad dog.*
like mad, *Slang.* furiously; very hard or fast: *I ran like mad to catch the train.*
mad as a hatter, or **mad as a March hare,** completely crazy. ⟨OE *(ge)mæded, gemæden* to hurt, drive mad⟩
☛ *Syn.* **1. Mad,** CRAZY, and INSANE have similar meanings. All three words have been commonly used at some time to describe someone who is mentally ill. This is still proper use in legal contexts for the word **insane:** *an institution for criminally insane people.* **Mad** is most often used to mean just very reckless or foolish: *Crossing the Pacific on a raft seems a mad thing to do.* **Crazy** usually suggests a more wild or disturbed state: *She was nearly crazy with fear.*

Mad•a•gas•can [,mædə'gæskən] *n., adj. —n.* a native or inhabitant of Madagascar.
—adj. of or having to do with Madagascar.

Mad•a•gas•car [,mædə'gæskər] *n.* an island country in the Indian Ocean, properly called the Democratic Republic of Madagascar.

mad•am ['mædəm] *n., pl.* **mad•ams** or (for def. 1) **mes•dames** [mei'dɑm]. **1** a polite or formal title used in speaking to a woman (*used alone, not with a name*): *The line is busy, madam; would you care to hold?* **2** a formal title for a woman, used before the name of her rank or office: *Madam Chairman, Madam Prime Minister.* **3** a woman who runs a brothel. ⟨ME *madame* < OF *ma dame* my lady⟩

ma•dame [mə'dæm] *or* ['mædəm]; *French,* [ma'dam] *n., pl.* **mes•dames** [mei'dɑm]; *French,* [me'dam]. **1** a French title of respect for a married woman; Mrs. **2** a title often used by female singers, artists, etc. *Abbrev.*: Mme. ⟨< F; see MADAM⟩

mad•cap ['mæd,kæp] *adj., n. —adj.* impulsive, wild, or foolish: *a madcap escapade.*
—n. a person who habitually does impulsive, wild, or foolish things.

mad•den ['mædən] *v.* **1** make crazy. **2** make very angry or excited. **—'mad•den•ing,** *adj.* **—'mad•den•ing•ly,** *adv.*

mad•der¹ ['mædər] *n.* **1** a perennial vine (*Rubia tinctorum*) native to Europe and Asia, having loose clusters of small, funnel-shaped, yellow flowers. **2** the root of this plant, formerly used for making a red dye. **3** the dye made from this root; alizarin. **4** bright red. **5** *(adjl.)* designating the family (Rubiaceae) of mostly tropical and subtropical herbs, shrubs, and trees that includes the madder, gardenia, coffee tree, cinchona, etc. ⟨OE *mædere*⟩

mad•der² ['mædər] *adj.* comparative of MAD.

mad•ding ['mædɪŋ] *adj. Archaic.* **1** mad; acting as if mad: *the madding crowd.* **2** making mad.

made [meid] *v., adj. —v.* pt. and pp. of MAKE.
—adj. **1** built; formed. **2** specially prepared. **3** artificially produced: *made land.* **4** invented: *a made word.* **5** certain of success; successful: *a made man.*
☛ *Hom.* MAID.

Ma•dei•ra or **ma•dei•ra** [mə'dirə] *n.* a kind of wine made on the island of Madeira off the west coast of Africa.

Mad•e•li•not [,mædə'linou] *n.* a native or inhabitant of the Magdalen Islands in the Gulf of St. Lawrence.

mad•e•moi•selle [,mædəmə'zɛl]; *French,* [madmwa'zɛl] *n., pl.* **mad•e•moi•selles** [,mædəmə'zɛlz] *or* **mes•de•moi•selles** [medmwa'zɛl]. a French title of respect for an unmarried woman; Miss. *Abbrev.*: Mlle. ⟨< F; OF *ma damoisele* my noble young lady⟩

made–to–meas•ure ['meid tə 'mɛʒər] *adj.* of clothing, made to the buyer's own measurements.

made–to–or•der ['meid tu 'ɔrdər] *adj.* **1** made according to the buyer's wishes. **2** completely appropriate.

made–up ['meid 'ʌp] *adj.* **1** put together. **2** invented; not real: *a made-up story.* **3** painted, powdered, etc. with cosmetics: *made-up lips.*

mad•house ['mæd,hʌus] *n.* **1** formerly, an asylum for the insane. **2** a place of uproar and confusion: *The arena was a madhouse after the home team won the championship game.*

Mad•i•son Avenue ['mædəsən] **1** in New York City, a street where many of the major U.S. advertising agencies have their offices. **2** the U.S. advertising industry, its techniques, language, influence, etc.

mad•ly ['mædli] *adv.* **1** insanely; wildly. **2** with desperate haste or intensity; furiously: *The girl pedalled madly to get to school on time.* **3** foolishly. **4** *Informal.* very; very much: *They were madly in love.*

mad•man ['mæd,mæn] *or* ['mædmən] *n., pl.* **-men.** *Informal.* **1** a man who is insane. **2** a man whose behaviour is so foolish or unconventional as to appear irrational.

mad money *Informal.* **1** a small amount of money kept for minor emergencies; originally, money carried by a woman or girl on a date to enable her to get home on her own if necessary. **2** pocket money for frivolous spending.

mad•ness ['mædnɪs] *n.* **1** the state or condition of being mad; insanity; rage: *In her madness, she struck her best friend.* **2** folly: *It was madness to take a sailboat out in that storm.*

Ma•don•na [mə'dɒnə] *n. Christianity.* **1** Usually, **the Madonna,** Mary, the mother of Jesus. **2** a picture or statue of her. ⟨< Ital. *madonna* my lady⟩

Madonna lily a garden lily (*Lilium candidum*) having large, pure white, bell-shaped flowers. It is the floral emblem of Québec.

Madonna lily

ma•dras [mə'drɑs], [mə'dræs], *or* ['mædrəs] *n.* **1** a medium or lightweight cloth in a close, plain weave, usually of cotton or silk, in white or with brightly coloured woven stripes, checks, or plaids. Madras is used for shirts, dresses, etc. **2** a light, open-weave cloth with a heavier woven pattern, used for curtains, etc. **3** a large, colourful silk or cotton scarf, worn as a turban. ⟨< *Madras,* a city in S India⟩

ma•dra•sa or **ma•dra•sah** [mə'dræsə] *n.* a school for children or adults in which Islamic subjects are taught, especially the Koran, the Arabic language, the Hadith, and jurisprudence. ⟨< Arabic⟩

mad•re•pore ['mædrə,pɔr] *n.* any of various tropical stony corals (genus *Madrepora*) that form coral reefs. ⟨< F < Ital. *madrepora* < *madre* mother (< L *mater*) + *poro,* ult. < Gk. *poros,* kind of stone⟩ —**,mad•re'por•ic, ,mad•re•po'rit•ic,** or **,mad•re'po•ri•an,** *adj.*

mad•ri•gal ['mædrəgəl] *n.* **1** a short poem, often about love, that can be set to music. **2** a medieval or Elizabethan song with parts for several voices, sung without instrumental accompaniment. **3** any song. ⟨< Ital. < LL *matricale* original, chief < *matrix* womb⟩ —**'mad•ri•gal•ist,** *n.*

mad•ri•lene or **mad•ri•lène** ['mædrə,lɛn] *or* [,mædrə'lɛn] *n.* a consommé flavoured with tomato, usually served cold. ⟨< F *madrilène* of Madrid, Spain < Sp. *madrileño*⟩

ma•dro•ña [mə'drounə] *n.* arbutus. ⟨< Sp.⟩

mad•wom•an ['mæd,wʊmən] *n., pl.* **-wom•en.** *Informal.* **1** a woman who is insane. **2** a woman whose behaviour is so foolish or unconventional as to appear irrational.

mad•wort ['mæd,wɜrt] *n.* any plant of the genus *Alyssum*.

Mae•ce•nas [məi'sinəs] *or* [mɪ'sinəs] *n.* a generous patron of literature or art. ⟨< *Maecenas* (circa 70-8 B.C.), a Roman statesman and patron of literature⟩

mael•strom ['meilstrəm] *n.* **1** a great or turbulent whirlpool. **2** a violent confusion of feelings, ideas, or conditions. **3 Maelstrom,** a dangerous whirlpool off NW Norway. ⟨< earlier Du. *maelstroom* < *malen* grind + *stroom* stream⟩

mae•nad ['minæd] *n.* **1** *Greek and Roman mythology.* a female follower of Bacchus (or Dionysus), who participated in the wild, orgiastic rites that were characteristic of the worship of this god. **2** a frenzied woman. Also, **menad.** ⟨< L *maenas, -adis* < Gk. *mainas, -adis*⟩ —**mae'nad•ic,** *adj.* —**'mæ•nad,ism,** *n.*

ma•es•to•so [,məi'stousou] *or* [,mɑɛ'stousou]; *Italian,* [mae'stoso] *adj., adv., n. Music.* —*adj. or adv.* stately; with dignity.
—*n.* a stately movement or passage; a composition to be played or sung in this way. ⟨< Ital. < L *mājestās* majesty⟩

ma•es•tro ['məistrou]; *Italian,* [ma'estro] *n., pl.* **-tros** or *(Italian)* **ma•es•tri** [ma'estri]. **1** a great composer, teacher, or conductor of music. **2** a master of any art. ⟨< Ital. < L *magister* master⟩

Mae West ['mei 'wɛst] an inflatable vest worn as a life preserver by an aviator in flying over water. ⟨< *Mae West* (1892-1980), a buxom American actress⟩

maf•e•nide ['mæfə,naɪd] *n.* an antibacterial cream used to treat severe burns. Also, **maphenide.**

Ma•fi•a ['mɑfiə] *or* ['mæfiə] *n.* **1** a worldwide, secret organization of criminal elements engaged in illicit activities such as racketeering and gambling. **2 mafia,** any group that is thought to dominate in an underhanded way some segment or aspect of society: *an intellectual mafia.* **3 mafia,** a hostile attitude toward authority. Also, **Maffia.** ⟨< Ital.(Sicilian) *mafia* boldness⟩

ma•fi•o•so [,mɑfi'ousou] *n., pl.* **-si** [-si]. a member of the Mafia.

mag. **1** magazine. **2** magnet; magnetism. **3** *Astronomy.* magnitude.

mag•al•drate ['mægəl,dreit] *n.* an antacid drug used to treat heartburn, indigestion, and acid stomach.

mag•a•zine [,mægə'zin] *or* ['mægə,zin] *n.* **1** a publication issued at regular intervals, especially weekly or monthly, which contains stories, articles, photographs, etc. by various contributors. **2** a section of a newspaper having similar articles. **3** a regular television program having several informational items. **4** a room in a fort or warship for keeping gunpowder and other explosives. **5** a place for storing goods or supplies, such as a warehouse or military supply depot. **6** a holder in or on a repeating or automatic gun for the cartridges to be fed into the gun chamber. **7** a lightproof space in or container on a camera for holding film or plates. ⟨< F *magasin* < Ital. *magazzino,* ult. < Arabic *makhzan* storehouse⟩

mag•da•lene ['mægdə,lin] *n.* any woman who has reformed from a sinful life, especially a repentant prostitute. ⟨after Mary *Magdalene,* in the Bible⟩

Mag•da•le•ni•an [,mægdə'liniən] *adj.* of a Paleolithic culture in Europe. ⟨< F *Magdalánien,* Latinization of *La Madeleine,* a prehistoric station in SW France⟩

mage [meidʒ] *n. Archaic.* magician. ⟨< OF < L *magus.* See MAGI.⟩

Mag•el•lan•ic cloud [,mædʒə'lænɪk] *Astronomy.* either of two small galaxies; the closest galaxy to the Milky Way.

Ma•gen Da•vid ['mɑgən 'deivɪd], [mɑ'gein dɑ'vid], *or* ['mɒgən 'dɒvɪd] STAR OF DAVID. ⟨< Hebrew *māghēn dāwīdh,* literally, shield of David⟩

ma•gen•ta [mə'dʒɛntə] *n., adj.* —*n.* **1** a purplish red dye. **2** a purplish red.
—*adj.* purplish red. ⟨< dye named after Battle of *Magenta,* Italy, 1859, because it was discovered in that year⟩

mag•got ['mægət] *n.* a fly in the earliest, legless stage, just after leaving the egg. Maggots often live in decaying matter. ⟨ME *magot,* early ME *mathek* < Scan.; cf. Icel. *mathkr,* Danish *maddik*⟩ —**'mag•go•ty,** *adj.*

Mag•i ['mædʒaɪ] *or* ['meidʒaɪ] *n.* pl. of MAGUS. **1** in the Bible, the three wise men who, according to the New Testament, brought gifts to the infant Jesus. **2** priests of ancient Persia. ⟨< L *magi,* pl. of *magus* < Gk. *magos* < OPersian⟩ —**'Ma•gi•an** ['mædʒiən] *or* ['meidʒiən], *adj.*

mag•ic ['mædʒɪk] *n., adj.* —*n.* **1** the use of charms, spells, etc. to try to call up spirits or other occult powers and through them to control natural forces or change the normal course of events. **2** something that produces results as if by magic; mysterious influence; unexplained power; enchantment: *the magic of music.* **3** the art of illusion; conjuring: *She made the rabbit disappear by magic.*
—*adj.* **1** made or done by magic or as if by magic: *A magic palace stood in place of their hut.* **2** having supernatural powers: *a magic wand.* **3** producing a feeling of rapture or enchantment: *magic moments.* **4** produced by sleight of hand: *I know some magic tricks.* ⟨ME < OF *magique,* ult. < Gk. *magikos* < *magos* astrologer < OPersian⟩

mag•i•cal ['mædʒəkəl] *adj.* **1** of, used in or done by magic. **2** like magic; mysterious; unexplained. —**'mag•i•cal•ly,** *adv.*

magic eye any of several electronic monitoring devices, used for checking the functioning of machinery, for activating mechanisms, for operating traffic signals, etc.

ma•gi•cian [mə'dʒɪʃən] *n.* **1** a person skilled in the use of magic, especially a sorcerer. **2** a person skilled in the use of sleight of hand to entertain: *The magician pulled three rabbits out of her hat.* ⟨ME < OF *magicien*⟩

magic lantern a device with a lamp and lenses for throwing a picture upon a screen, in magnified form, from a glass slide. A magic lantern is an early form of projector.

Magic Marker *Trademark.* a thick pen with a broad felt tip, used for marking boxes, writing on flipcharts, etc.

Ma•gi•not line ['mæʒə,nou] an elaborate system of defences built by France against Germany after the First World War. ⟨after André *Maginot* (1877-1932), a French minister of war⟩

mag•is•te•ri•al [,mædʒə'stiriəl] *adj.* **1** of or suited to a magistrate: *A judge has magisterial rank.* **2** showing authority: *The captain spoke with a magisterial voice.* **3** imperious; domineering; overbearing. ⟨< Med.L *magisterialis,* ult. < L *magister* master⟩ —**,mag•is'te•ri•al•ly,** *adv.*

mag•is•tra•cy ['mædʒəstrəsi] *n., pl.* **-cies.** **1** the position, rank, or duties of a magistrate. **2** magistrates as a group. **3** a district under a magistrate.

ma•gi•stral ['mædʒəstrəl] *adj.* **1** specified or prescribed by a physician. **2** *Rare.* magisterial.

mag•is•trate ['mædʒə,streit] *or* ['mædʒəstrɪt] *n.* a government official appointed to hear and decide cases in a magistrate's court or similar lower court. ⟨< L *magistratus*, ult. < *magister* master⟩

magistrate's court a court that has limited jurisdiction, dealing with minor civil and criminal cases. In Canada, magistrate's courts are established by provincial legislation.

Mag•le•mo•se•an or **Mag•le•mo•si•an** [,mæglə'mousiən], [,mæglə'mouʃən], *or* [,mæglə'mouʒən] *adj.* of a Mesolithic forest culture of N Europe. ⟨after *Maglemose* site of a Mesolithic station in Denmark⟩

mag•ma ['mægmə] *n.* **1** any soft, pastelike mixture of mineral or organic substances. **2** *Geology.* the very hot, fluid substance that is found below the earth's crust and from which lava and igneous rocks are formed. **3** *Pharmacy.* a suspension of insoluble or almost insoluble material in a small volume of water. ⟨< L *magma* dregs of an unguent < Gk. *magma* an unguent, ult. < *massein* knead, mould⟩ **—mag'mat•ic,** *adj.* **—'mag•ma,tism,** *n.*

Mag•na Car•ta or **Char•ta** ['mægnə 'kɑrtə] **1** the great charter, guaranteeing personal and political liberties, forcibly secured from King John of England by the barons at Runnymede on June 15, 1215. **2** any fundamental constitution guaranteeing civil and political rights. ⟨< Med.L *magna charta* great charter⟩

mag•na cum lau•de ['mægnə kʊm 'laʊdei] *or* [kʌm 'lɔdei] with high honours. ⟨< L *magna cum laude* with great praise⟩

mag•na•nim•i•ty [,mægnə'nɪməti] *n., pl.* **-ties. 1** the quality of being magnanimous. **2** a magnanimous act.

mag•nan•i•mous [mæg'nænəməs] *adj.* **1** noble in soul or mind; generous and forgiving; free from mean or petty feelings or acts. **2** showing or arising from a generous spirit: *a magnanimous attitude toward a conquered enemy.* ⟨< L *magnanimus* < *magnus* great + *animus* spirit⟩ **—mag'nan•i•mous•ly,** *adv.* **—mag'nan•i•mous•ness,** *n.*

mag•nate ['mægneit] *or* ['mægnɪt] *n.* an important or powerful person, especially in business or industry: *an oil magnate.* ⟨< LL *magnas*, *-atis* < L *magnus* great⟩
☛ *Hom.* MAGNET ['mægnɪt].

mag•ne•sia [mæg'niʒə], [mæg'niziə], *or* [mæg'niʃə] *n.* **1** magnesium oxide, a white, tasteless powder, used in medicine as a laxative, and in making fertilizers and some building materials. *Formula*: MgO **2** magnesium. ⟨ME < Med.L < Gk. *hē Magnēsia lithos* the Magnesian stone (from *Magnesia*, in Thessaly)⟩ **—mag'ne•sian,** *adj.*

mag•ne•site ['mægnə,sɔit] *n.* a mineral carbonate of magnesium, occurring in white crystalline or granular masses, used industrially in making steel, etc. *Formula*: $MgCO_3$ ⟨< *magnes(ium)* + *-ite*⟩

mag•ne•si•um [mæg'niʒəm], [mæg'niziəm], *or* [mæg'niʃəm] *n. Chemistry.* a light, silver-white metallic chemical element that burns with a dazzling white light. Magnesium is used in metal alloys, fireworks, etc. *Symbol*: Mg; *at.no.* 12; *at.mass.* 24.31. ⟨< NL < *magnesia.* See MAGNESIA.⟩

magnesium chloride a salt from seawater, used as a source of magnesium.

magnesium gluconate ['glukə,neit] a magnesium supplement.

magnesium hydroxide 1 *Chemistry.* a white, crystalline, slightly water-soluble powder. **2** MILK OF MAGNESIA.

magnesium oxide *Chemistry.* magnesia.

magnesium sulphate 1 *Chemistry.* a white, water-soluble salt used in making matches and explosives. *Formula*: $MgSO_4$ **2** an anticonvulsant drug.

mag•net ['mægnɪt] *n.* **1** a mass or piece of iron, steel, etc. that has the property, or power, of attracting iron and some other metals to it. **2** an artificially magnetized piece of iron, steel, etc.: *a horseshoe magnet.* **3** anything that attracts: *The rabbits in our backyard were a magnet that attracted all the children in the neighbourhood.* ⟨ME < OF *magnete* < L < Gk. *hē Magnētis lithos* the magnet. Related to MAGNESIA.⟩
☛ *Hom.* MAGNATE.

mag•net•ic [mæg'nɛtɪk] *adj.* **1** having the properties of a magnet. **2** of or having to do with magnetism; producing magnetism. **3** of or having to do with the earth's magnetism: *the magnetic meridian.* **4** capable of being magnetized or of being attracted by a magnet. **5** exerting a strong attractive power or charm: *a magnetic personality.* **—mag'net•i•cal•ly,** *adv.*

magnetic bottle *Physics.* an arrangement of magnetic fields used to control a thermonuclear reaction by containing the hot plasma.

magnetic circuit *Physics.* **1** a circuit producing magnetism. **2** the closed path described by magnetic lines of force, comparable to an electric circuit.

magnetic compass a compass showing direction relative to the earth's magnetic field.

magnetic course *Nautical.* the course of a ship allowing no deviation from the compass.

magnetic declination or **deviation** or **variation** DECLINATION (def. 3).

magnetic disk *Computer technology.* a device containing or able to receive or store information in a computer. Magnetic disks can be hard or floppy.

magnetic equator an imaginary line around the earth, roughly at the equator, where the lines of force of the earth's magnetic field are parallel to the earth's surface. At this line a magnetic needle will show no inclination toward the vertical but will remain horizontal.

magnetic field 1 the region of magnetic influence, or force, around a magnet, a magnetic body such as the earth, or a body carrying an electric current. **2** the magnetic forces present in such a region: *a strong magnetic field.*

magnetic flux *Physics.* the strength of a magnetic field in an area, equivalent to the number of magnetic lines of force per unit area (in a plane perpendicular to the direction of the field), or **magnetic flux density**, times the size of the total area.

magnetic induction *Physics.* magnetic flux density.

magnetic ink character recognition *Computer technology.* the scanning and translation (by machine) of characters written with magnetic ink for input to a computer. *Abbrev.*: MICR

magnetic mine *Navy.* an underwater mine that is exploded by the action of the metal parts of an approaching ship upon a magnetic needle.

magnetic moment *Physics.* the ratio of the TORQUE (def. 1) on a magnet to the magnetic induction around it.

magnetic needle a slender bar of magnetized steel that forms the basic part of a compass. When mounted horizontally so that it can turn freely, it will show the direction of the magnetic field of the earth, pointing toward the magnetic poles, approximately north and south.

magnetic north the direction in which the magnetic needle of a compass points; north MAGNETIC POLE.

magnetic pole 1 one of the two poles of a magnet. **2 Magnetic Pole,** one of the two points on the earth's surface toward which a magnetic needle points. The **North Magnetic Pole** is approximately at 77.8° North latitude and 95° West longitude. The **South Magnetic Pole** is approximately at 64.7° South latitude and 154° East longitude.

mag•net•ics [mæg'nɛtɪks] *n.* the science of magnetism (*used with a singular verb*).

magnetic storm a temporary fluctuation in the earth's magnetic field.

magnetic tape a plastic or paper ribbon coated on one side with a substance that magnetizes easily, such as particles of iron oxide, used for recording sounds, pictures, and other kinds of information by electromagnetic means. Magnetic tape is used in computers, tape recorders, and videotape recorders.

magnetic variation DECLINATION (def. 3).

mag•net•ism ['mægnə,tɪzəm] *n.* **1** the properties of a magnet; manifestation of magnetic properties. **2** the branch of physics dealing with magnets and magnetic properties. **3** the power to attract or charm: *His magnetism was shown by the number of his friends and admirers.*

mag•net•ite ['mægnə,tɔit] *n.* an important iron ore that is strongly magnetic; black iron oxide; lodestone. *Formula*: Fe_3O_4

mag•net•ize ['mægnə,taɪz] *v.* **-ized, -iz•ing. 1** give the properties of a magnet to. An electric current in a coil around a bar of iron will magnetize the bar. **2** attract or influence like a magnet; charm: *Her beautiful voice magnetized the audience.* **—'mag•net,iz•a•ble,** *adj.* **—,mag•net•i'za•tion,** *n.* **—'mag•net,iz•er,** *n.*

mag•ne•to [mæg'nitou] *n., pl.* **-tos.** a small machine which uses a magnetic field to produce an electric current. In some internal-combustion engines, a magneto supplies an electric spark to explode the gasoline vapour. ⟨< *magneto-electric generator*⟩

mag•ne•to– *combining form.* magnetic; magnetism: *magneto-electricity.*

mag•ne•to–e•lec•tric [mæg,nitou ɪ'lɛktrɪk] *adj.* of, designating, or using electricity produced by magnetic means. Also, **magneto-electrical**.

mag•ne•to–el•ec•tri•ci•ty [mæg,nitou ɪlɛk'trɪsəti] *n.* electricity developed by the action of magnets as their magnetic fields move around a conductor.

mag•ne•to•hy•dro•dy•nam•ics [mæg,nitou,haɪdroudaɪ'næmɪks] *n. Physics.* the branch of physics dealing with fluids and their ability to conduct electricity.

mag•ne•tom•e•ter [,mægnə'tɒmətər] *n.* an instrument used to measure magnetic forces. **–,mag•ne•to'met•ric** [,mægnətou'mɛtrɪk], *adj.* **–,mag•ne'tom•e•try,** *n.*

mag•ne•ton ['mægnə,tɒn] *n. Physics.* a unit used for measuring atomic and subatomic particles with reference to their magnetic moment.

mag•ne•to•scop•ic [mæg,nitou'skɒpɪk] *adj.* having to do with audiotape or videotape.

mag•ne•to•sphere [mæg'nitə,sfir] *n.* **1** the region surrounding the earth in which ionized particles are controlled by the earth's magnetic field. **2** a similar region around any other celestial body, such as a planet.

mag•ne•to•stric•tion [mæg,nitou'strɪkʃən] *n. Physics.* the change undergone by any ferromagnetic material influenced by a magnetic field.

mag•ne•tron ['mægnə,trɒn] *n. Electronics.* a two-element vacuum tube holding electrons which are made to create radio waves by means of an external magnetic field.

magni– *combining form.* large; great: *magnify.* ⟨< L, combining form of *magnus*⟩

mag•ni•fic [mæg'nɪfɪk] *adj. Archaic.* **1** magnificent. **2** pompous. Also, **magnifical**. ⟨< L *magnificus* < *magnus* great + *facere* make⟩ **—mag'nif•i•cal•ly,** *adv.*

Mag•nif•i•cat [mæg'nɪfə,kæt] *or* [mɑn'jɪfə,kɑt] *n.* **1** a hymn of the Virgin Mary beginning "My soul doth magnify the Lord." **2** any music for this hymn. ⟨< L *magnificat* (it) magnifies (from the first word of the hymn)⟩

mag•ni•fi•ca•tion [,mægnəfə'keiʃən] *n.* **1** the act of magnifying. **2** a magnified condition. **3** the power to magnify. **4** a magnified copy, model, image, or picture.

mag•nif•i•cence [mæg'nɪfəsəns] *n.* the quality or state of being magnificent; grand beauty or splendour. ⟨< OF < L *magnificentia* < *magnificus* noble. See MAGNIFIC.⟩

mag•nif•i•cent [mæg'nɪfəsənt] *adj.* **1** richly coloured or decorated; splendid; grand; stately: *a magnificent royal palace, a magnificent ceremony.* **2** impressive; noble; exalted: *magnificent words, magnificent ideas.* **3** extraordinarily fine; superb: *a magnificent view of the mountains, a magnificent opportunity.* ⟨< OF *magnificent* < *magnificence* < L *magnificentia.* See MAGNIFICENCE.⟩ **—mag'nif•i•cent•ly,** *adv.*

☛ *Syn.* **Magnificent**, SPLENDID, SUPERB = impressive in dignity and beauty, brilliance, or excellence. **Magnificent** emphasizes impressive beauty and costly richness or stateliness of things like natural scenery, jewels, buildings, etc., and noble greatness of ideas: *Westminster Abbey is magnificent.* **Splendid** emphasizes impressive brilliance or shining brightness in appearance or character of things, people, or deeds: *She had a splendid record in the army.* **Superb** denotes the highest possible excellence, magnificence, splendour, richness, etc.: *We have a superb view of the ocean.*

mag•nif•i•co [mæg'nɪfə,kou] *n., pl.* **-coes. 1** a Venetian nobleman. **2** an important person. ⟨< Ital. < L *magnificus.* See MAGNIFIC.⟩

mag•ni•fi•er ['mægnə,faɪər] *n.* a person or thing that magnifies, especially a lens or combination of lenses that makes things appear larger than they really are.

mag•ni•fy ['mægnə,faɪ] *v.* **-fied, -fy•ing. 1** cause to look larger than the real size; increase the apparent size of (an object). **2** make too much of; go beyond the truth in telling. **3** *Archaic or poetic.* praise or glorify highly. ⟨< L *magnificare* esteem greatly, ult. < *magnus* great + *facere* make⟩ **–'mag•ni,fi•a•ble,** *adj.*

magnifying glass a lens or combination of lenses that makes objects appear larger than they really are.

mag•nil•o•quence [mæg'nɪləkwəns] *n.* **1** a high-flown, lofty style of speaking or writing; the use of pompous and unusual words, elaborate phrases, etc. **2** boastfulness. ⟨< L *magnus* great + *loquens*, ppr. of *loqui* speak⟩

mag•nil•o•quent [mæg'nɪləkwənt] *adj.* **1** using big and unusual words; expressed in high-flown language. **2** boastful. ⟨< *magniloquence*⟩ **—mag'nil•o•quent•ly,** *adv.*

mag•ni•tude ['mægnə,tjud] *or* ['mægnə,tud] *n.* **1** greatness of size, extent, importance, effect, etc.: *a problem of magnitude. The magnitude of the crime called for a long sentence.* **2** relative size, extent, importance, volume, etc.: *the magnitude of an angle or line, the magnitude of an earthquake.* **3** *Astronomy.* a measure of the brightness of a heavenly body, expressed as a numerical value. Stars of the first magnitude are the brightest; stars barely visible to the naked eye are of about the sixth magnitude. **4** *Mathematics.* a number assigned to a quantity so that it may be used as a basis of comparison for measuring similar quantities. **of the first magnitude**, of great importance or significance. ⟨< L *magnitudo* < *magnus* large⟩

mag•no•lia [mæg'noulia] *or* [mæg'noulja] *n.* **1** any of a genus (*Magnolia*) of shrubs and trees of North America and Asia having simple leaves and large white, pink, or purple flowers that bloom in early spring. In some magnolias, the flowers appear before the leaves. **2** (*adjl.*) designating a family (Magnoliaceae) of trees, shrubs, and a few vines that includes the magnolias and the tulip tree. **3** the flower of any of these. ⟨< NL < Pierre *Magnol* (1638-1715), a French botanist⟩

mag•num ['mægnəm] *n.* **1** a bottle that holds 2.3 L of alcoholic liquor. **2** the amount that it holds. ⟨< L *magnum*, neut. adj., great⟩

mag•num o•pus ['mægnəm 'oupəs] *Latin.* a great work of literature, music, or art, especially the greatest work of a particular artist, composer, or writer.

mag•pie ['mæg,paɪ] *n.* **1** any of several mainly black-and-white, long-tailed birds (genus *Pica*) of the same family as crows and jays, having a chattering call. The **black-billed magpie** (*Pica pica*) is common in western Canada. **2** a person who chatters. ⟨< *Mag*, for *Margaret* + *pie*[2]⟩

mag•uey ['mægwei] *or* [mə'gei] *n.* MESCAL (def. 3). ⟨< Sp. < Taino, an extinct American Indian language⟩

Ma•gus ['meigəs] *n.* sing. of MAGI.

Mag•yar ['mægjɑr] *or* ['mɑgjɑr]; *Hungarian,* ['mɒdjɔʀ] *n., adj.* *—n.* **1** a member of a people that make up most of the population of Hungary. **2** the Hungarian language. *—adj.* of or having to do with the Magyars or their language.

Ma•ha•bha•ra•ta [mə'hɑ'bɑrətə] *n.* one of the two great Hindu epics. The other is the Ramayana. ⟨< Skt.⟩

ma•ha•ra•jah [,mɑhə'rɑdʒə] *n.* any of certain ruling princes in India, especially a ruler of one of the former native states. Also, **maharaja.** ⟨< Skt. *maharaja* < *maha-* great + *raja* rajah⟩

ma•ha•ra•ni [,mɑhə'rɑni] *n.* **1** the wife of a maharajah. **2** a woman holding in her own right a rank equal to that of a maharajah. Also, **maharanee.** ⟨< Hind. *maharani* < Skt. *maha-* great + *rani* queen⟩

ma•hat•ma [mə'hɑtmə] *or* [mə'hætmə] *n.* in India and Tibet, a wise and holy person who has extraordinary powers. ⟨< Skt. *mahatman* < *maha-* great + *atman* soul⟩

Ma•ha•vi•ra [mə,hɑ'virə] *n.* the chief founder of the Jain religion, and a contemporary of Buddha.

Ma•ha•ya•na [,mɑhə'jɑnə] *n.* a major branch of Buddhism, the 'Northern School'. It regards Buddha as divine. ⟨< Skt. *maha* great + *yana* vehicle⟩

Mah•di ['mɑdi] *n., pl.* **-dis. 1** *Islam.* a messianic leader expected to establish a reign of righteousness before the end of the world. **2** any of several Islamic revolutionary leaders who have claimed this title in the past. ⟨< Arabic *mahdiy* one who is guided aright < *hada* lead aright⟩ **–'Mah•dist,** *n.*

mah–jong or **mah–jongg** ['mɑ 'dʒɒŋ] *or* ['mɑ 'ʒɒŋ] *n.* a western version of a Chinese game played with 136 or 144 dominolike pieces called tiles. Each player tries to form winning combinations by drawing or discarding. ⟨formerly a trademark *Mah-Jongg*, coined by Joseph Babcock, U.S. resident in Shanghai, who introduced the game in the U.S. after World War I. The name is from a Chinese word meaning 'sparrow'; one of the tiles has a figure of a sparrow.⟩

mahl•stick ['mɑl,stɪk] *or* ['mɒl,stɪk] *n.* a long stick used by artists to support the hand that holds the brush; the padded end of the stick rests against the canvas being painted. ⟨< Du. *maalstok*, literally, paint-stick⟩

ma•hog•a•ny [mə'hɒgəni] *n., pl.* **-nies,** *adj.* *—n.* **1** any of various tropical American trees (genus *Swietenia*) having large, compound leaves and hard yellowish brown to reddish brown wood, especially *S. mahagoni* or *S. macrophylla*, highly valued for timber. **2** any of various W African trees (genus *Khaya*) of the same family, having similar wood. **3** any of various other trees of the same family, also used for timber. **4** (*adjl.*) designating the

family (Meliaceae) of trees and shrubs that includes the mahoganies. 5 the wood of a mahogany, used for fine furniture, etc. 6 (*adjl.*) made of this wood: *a mahogany dresser.* 7 a medium reddish brown colour.
—*adj.* medium reddish brown. ⟨< obs. Sp. *mahogani*, probably of West Indian origin⟩

Ma•hom•et [mə'hɒmɪt] *n.* Mohammed.

Ma•hom•et•an [mə'hɒmətən] *adj. or n.* Muslim.
—Ma'hom•et•an,ism, *n.*

ma•hout [mə'hʌut] *n.* in India and the East Indies, the keeper and driver of an elephant. ⟨< Hind. *mahaut*⟩

maid [meid] *n.* 1 a woman servant: *a kitchen maid.* 2 a young, unmarried woman; girl. 3 a virgin. 4 See MAID OF HONOUR.
5 the Maid, Joan of Arc (1412-1431), a French heroine who led armies against the invading British and saved the city of Orléans. ⟨shortened from *maiden*⟩
☛ *Hom.* MADE.

maid•en ['meidən] *n., adj.* —*n.* 1 a young, unmarried woman; girl. 2 a virgin. 3 a racehorse that has never won a race.
—*adj.* 1 of, suited to, or characteristic of a maiden: *maiden grace, maiden blushes.* 2 unmarried: *a maiden aunt.* 3 first: *a ship's maiden voyage.* 4 new or untried; fresh: *maiden ground.*
5 *Cricket.* without any runs being scored: *a maiden over.* ⟨OE *mægden*⟩

maid•en•hair ['meidən,hɛr] *n.* any of a genus (*Adiantum*) of ferns having very slender stalks and delicate, finely divided fronds. Also called **maidenhair fern.**

maidenhair tree ginkgo.

maid•en•head ['meidən,hɛd] *n.* 1 hymen. 2 *Archaic.* maidenhood; virginity.

maid•en•hood ['meidən,hʊd] *n.* 1 the condition of being a maiden; virginity. 2 the time when one is a maiden.

maid•en•ly ['meidənli] *adj.* 1 of a maiden or maidenhood.
2 like or suitable for a maiden; gentle; modest.
—'maid•en•li•ness, *n.*

maiden name the surname a married woman used before her marriage; birth name: *Mrs. Madsen's maiden name was Drury.*

maid–in–waiting ['meid ɪn 'weitɪŋ] *n., pl.* **maids-in-waiting.** an unmarried, young woman who attends a queen or princess; a lady-in-waiting.

maid of all work *Informal.* a woman servant who does all kinds of housework.

maid of honour or **honor** 1 an unmarried woman who is the chief attendant of the bride at a wedding; bridal attendant.
2 an unmarried lady who attends a queen or princess. 3 a small tart containing almond paste and jam.

Maid of Or•lé•ans [,ɔrlei'ɑ̃] *or* ['ɔrliənz] Joan of Arc. See MAID (def. 5).

maid•serv•ant ['meid,sɜrvənt] *n.* a female servant.

mail¹ [meil] *n., v.* —*n.* 1 letters, postcards, papers, parcels, etc. sent or to be sent by post. 2 the system by which such items are sent, managed by the Post Office.
3 the collection or delivery of such items: *I'll finish this letter quickly so it can go in the afternoon mail.* 4 all that comes by one such delivery. 5 a train, boat, etc. that carries mail.
—*v.* post; send by mail; put in a mailbox: *He mailed the letter to his mother.* ⟨ME *male* < OF *malle* < Gmc.; cf. OHG *malaha* satchel, bag⟩
☛ *Hom.* MALE.

The Maid of Orléans (Joan of Arc)

mail² [meil] *n., v.* —*n.* 1 flexible armour made of metal rings, loops of chain, or small plates linked together. See ARMOUR for picture. 2 the hard, protective covering of some animals, such as turtles.
—*v.* cover or protect with mail. ⟨ME < OF *maille* < L *macula* a mesh in a net⟩ **—'mail•less,** *adj.*
☛ *Hom.* MALE.

mail•box ['meil,bɒks] *n.* 1 a public box for depositing outgoing mail that is to be collected by the post office. 2 a private box outside a dwelling, cubbyhole in an office, etc. where mail is delivered.

mail coach formerly, a stagecoach that carried mail.

mailed¹ [meild] *v.* pt. and pp. of MAIL.

mailed² [meild] *adj.* covered or protected with mail.

mailed fist military force; aggression, especially by one nation against another. **—'mailed-'fist,** *adj.*

mail•er ['meilər] *n.* 1 a person who mails letters, etc. 2 a machine for stamping or addressing letters, etc. 3 a container in which to mail things. Cylindrical mailers are often used for maps, photographs, etc.

mail•lot [mɑ'jou] *or* ['maɪjou]; *French,* [ma'jo] *n., pl.* **mail•lots** [mɑ'jouz] *or* ['maɪjouz]; *French,* [ma'jo]. *French.* 1 a bathing suit, especially a one-piece bathing suit. 2 a one-piece, tightly fitting garment worn by dancers, gymnasts, etc.

mail•man ['meil,mæn] *n., pl.* **-men.** a man whose work is carrying or delivering mail; letter carrier.

mail order an order for goods sent by mail.

mail–or•der ['meil ,ɔrdər] *adj.* of or having to do with mail orders or a business establishment that does business by mail.

mail–order house a business that receives orders for and sends goods requested by mail.

maim [meim] *v.* cause permanent damage to or loss of a part of the body; cripple; disable: *He lost two toes in the accident, but we were glad that he was not more seriously maimed.* ⟨ME *mayme,* var. of *mayhem*⟩ **—'maim•er,** *n.*

main [mein] *adj., n.* —*adj.* most important; largest: *the main street of a town.*
by main force or **strength,** by using full strength.
—*n.* 1 *Archaic.* physical strength. 2 a large pipe for water, gas, etc.: *a water main.* 3 *Poetic.* the open sea; ocean. 4 *Archaic.* the mainland.
in the main, for the most part; chiefly; mostly: *Her grades were excellent in the main.*
with might and main, with all one's force: *They argued with might and main.* ⟨OE *mægen* power⟩
☛ *Hom.* MANE.

main chance an opportunity offering the greatest possible gain.

main clause *Grammar.* a clause that can stand by itself as a sentence; independent clause. *Example: In* She came although I had warned her, She came *is the main clause.*

main drag *Cdn. Slang.* the chief thoroughfare of a town or city.

Maine [mein] *n.* a NE coast state of the United States.

main•frame ['mein,freim] *adj., n. Computer technology.* —*adj.* of or referring to a type of central computer with large capacity, serving several terminals.
—*n.* a mainframe computer. Compare MICROCOMPUTER, MINICOMPUTER.

main•land ['mein,lænd] *or* ['meinlənd] *n.* the principal part of a continent or land mass, apart from peninsulas and outlying islands.

main•land•er ['mein,lændər] *or* ['meinləndər] *n.* a person who lives on the mainland.

main•line ['mein,laɪn] *n., adj., v.* **-lined, lin•ing.** —*n.* the principal line of a railway, etc.
—*adj.* having a principal or dominant status.
—*v. Slang.* inject (a drug, such as heroin) directly into a principal vein. **—'main,lin•er,** *n.*

main•ly ['meinli] *adv.* for the most part; chiefly; mostly.

main•mast ['mein,mæst] *or* ['meinməst] *n. Nautical.* the principal mast of a sailing ship, usually the second one from the bow. See MAST¹, SCHOONER, and YAWL for pictures.

main•sail ['mein,seil] *or* ['meinsəl] *n. Nautical.* the largest sail on the mainmast of a ship. See SCHOONER and YAWL for pictures.

main sequence *Astronomy.* on a graph of stars, a diagonal line connecting a large series of stars of similar age and colour.
—'main-'se•quence, *adj.*

main•sheet ['mein,ʃit] *n. Nautical.* a rope that controls the angle at which the mainsail is set.

main•spring ['mein,sprɪŋ] *n.* 1 the principal spring in a clock, watch, etc. See ESCAPEMENT for picture. 2 the main cause, motive, or influence.

main•stay ['mein,stei] *n.* 1 *Nautical.* a supporting rope or wire extending from the maintop to the foot of the foremast. See

SCHOONER for picture. **2** the main support: *His friends were his mainstay through his time of trouble.*

main•stream ['mein,strim] *n., v.* —*n.* **1** the main current of a river, etc. **2** the main trend or direction of development of a fashion, body of opinion, activity, etc.: *She is not well-known to the critics because her painting is outside the mainstream of modern art.* **3** (*adjl.*) of or in the mainstream: *mainstream culture.*
—*v.* integrate (a child with a disability) into a regular class.

main street the chief road in a small town, especially through the downtown area where business establishments are located.

main•street•ing ['mein,stritɪŋ] *n. Cdn.* the act or practice, by a politician, etc. of walking about the main streets of a town or city in order to meet and greet potential supporters.
—'main,street, *v.*

main•tain [mein'tein] *v.* **1** keep; keep up; carry on: *to maintain a business, to maintain one's composure.* **2** keep from failing or declining; keep in good condition: *He employs a mechanic to maintain his fleet of trucks.* **3** pay the expenses of; provide for: *She maintains a family of four.* **4** uphold; argue for; keep to in argument or discussion: *to maintain an opinion.* **5** declare to be true: *He maintained that he was innocent.* ⟨ME < OF *maintenir* < L *manu tenere* hold by the hand⟩
—main'tain•a•ble, *adj.* **—main'tain•er,** *n.*
☛ *Syn.* **3.** See note at SUPPORT.

main•te•nance ['meintənəns] *n.* **1** a maintaining or being maintained; support: *A government collects taxes to pay for its maintenance.* **2** keeping in good repair; upkeep: *The army devotes much time to the maintenance of its equipment.* **3** enough to support life; means of living: *His small farm provides a maintenance, but not much more.* **4** *Law.* **a** the payment of money by a person after divorce to his or her former spouse for the support of the former spouse and any children. Maintenance is awarded by court order and usually stops if the supported person remarries. Compare ALIMONY. **b** the payment of money by a person for the support of children living apart from him or her, after separation or divorce of the parents.

main•top ['mein,tɒp] *n. Nautical.* a platform at the head of the lower mainmast of a square-rigged ship. See MAST[1] for picture.

main•top•gal•lant ['mein,tɒp'gælənt] *or* ['meintə'gælənt] *n. Nautical.* a mast, sail, or yard above the main-topmast.

main–top•mast [,mein 'tɒp,mæst] *or* [,mein 'tɒpməst] *n. Nautical.* the second section of the mainmast above the lower mainmast. See MAST[1] for picture.

main–top•sail [,mein 'tɒp,seil] *or* [,mein 'tɒpsəl] *n. Nautical.* the sail above the mainsail.

main verb *Grammar.* the verb in the MAIN CLAUSE.

main yard *Nautical.* the yard from which a square mainsail is suspended.

mai•son•ette or **mai•son•nette** [,meizə'nɛt] *n.* an apartment, especially one that occupies more than one floor. ⟨< F, dim. of *maison* house⟩

mai•tre d' [,meitər 'di] *or* [,meitrə 'di] *n., pl.* **mai•tre d's.** *Informal.* MAÎTRE D'HÔTEL (defs. 1 and 2).

maî•tre d'hô•tel ['meitər dou'tɛl]; *French,* [mɛtʀdo'tɛl] *n., pl.* **maîtres d'hôtel** ['meitər dou'tɛl]; *French,* [mɛtʀdo'tɛl]. **1** a butler or steward; major-domo. **2** headwaiter. **3** (*adjl.*) of a sauce, etc., containing melted butter, chopped parsley, and lemon juice. ⟨< F: master of the hotel⟩

maize [meiz] *n., adj.* —*n.* **1** *Brit.* CORN[1] (defs. 1 and 2); Indian corn. **2** yellow.
—*adj.* yellow. ⟨< Sp. *maiz,* of West Indian origin⟩
☛ *Hom.* MAZE.

Maj. or **Maj** MAJOR (def. *n.* 1).

ma•jes•tic [mə'dʒɛstɪk] *adj.* grand; noble; dignified; stately. Also, **majestical. —ma'jes•ti•cal•ly,** *adv.*

maj•es•ty ['mædʒəsti] *n., pl.* **-ties. 1** grandeur; nobility; dignity; stateliness: *We were much impressed by the majesty of the coronation ceremony.* **2** supreme power or authority: *the majesty of the law.* **3 Majesty,** a title used in speaking to or of a king, queen, emperor, empress, etc.: *Your Majesty, His Majesty, Her Majesty.* ⟨ME < OF < L *majestas*⟩

Maj.Gen. MAJOR-GENERAL.

ma•jol•i•ca [mə'dʒɒləkə] *or* [mə'jɒləkə] *n.* **1** a kind of enamelled Italian pottery, richly decorated in colour.
2 something made of this pottery. ⟨earlier *maiolica* < Ital. < Med.L, var. of LL *Majorica* Majorka, where it was made⟩

ma•jor ['meidʒər] *adj., n., v.* —*adj.* **1** larger; greater; more important: *Take the major share of the profits.* **2** of the first rank or order: *E.J. Pratt is a major poet.* **3** very serious or important: *a major disaster.* **4** of legal age. **5** of, having to do with, or designating a post-secondary student's principal subject or course of study. **6** *Music.* **a** of an interval, greater by a half step than the minor; having the difference of pitch which is found between the tonic and the second, third, sixth, or seventh tone (or step) of a major scale: *a major second.* **b** of a scale, key, or mode, in which the interval between the tonic and the third step is a major third (two whole steps): *C major scale or key.* **c** of a chord, especially a triad, containing a major third (two whole steps) between the root and the second tone or note.
—*n.* **1** an officer in the armed forces ranking next above a captain and below a lieutenant-colonel. *Abbrev.*: Maj. or Maj See chart of ranks in the Appendix. **2** a person of the legal age of responsibility. **3** the subject or course of study to which a post-secondary student gives the greatest part of his or her time and attention. **4** a post-secondary student who devotes most of his or her time and attention to a given subject: *She is a geology major.* **5** *Music.* a major interval, key, scale, chord, etc.: *The song ends on a major.* **6** *Hockey.* MAJOR PENALTY. **7** *Sports.* **the majors,** *pl.* the MAJOR LEAGUES.
—*v.* **1** of a post-secondary student, give most of one's time and attention to (a subject or course of study) (*used with* **in**): *to major in mathematics.* **2** focus on; specialize in (*used with* **in**). ⟨< L *major,* comparative of *magnus* great. Doublet of MAYOR.⟩

ma•jor–do•mo ['meidʒər 'doumou] *n., pl.* **-mos. 1** a man in charge of a royal or noble household. **2** a butler; steward. ⟨< Sp. or Ital. < Med.L *major domus* chief of the household⟩

ma•jor•ette [,meidʒə'rɛt] *n.* DRUM MAJORETTE.

ma•jor–gen•er•al ['meidʒər 'dʒɛnərəl] *n.* an officer in the armed forces ranking next above a brigadier-general and below a lieutenant-general. *Abbrev.*: M.Gen., MGen, or Maj.Gen. See chart of ranks in the Appendix.

major his•to•com•pat•i•bil•i•ty complex [,hɪstoukəm,pætə'bɪləti] HUMAN LEUKOCYTE ANTIGEN COMPLEX.

ma•jor•i•ty [mə'dʒɔrəti] *n., pl.* **-ties. 1** the larger number; greater part; more than half. **2** in a contest involving two or more candidates, the number of votes cast for one candidate by which his or her return exceeds the total number of votes for all other candidates: *If Smith received 12 000 votes, Adams 7000, and White 3000, Smith had a majority of 2000.* **3** the legal age of responsibility. In some provinces a person reaches his or her majority at the age of 18. **4** the rank or position of major in the armed forces.

major key *Music.* a key whose melody and harmony are based on a major scale. Compare MINOR KEY.

major league 1 *Baseball.* either of the two chief leagues of American professional baseball teams. **2** *Hockey.* the National Hockey League.

major mode *Music.* a key of a composition using the major scale. Compare MINOR MODE.

major penalty *Hockey.* a five-minute penalty awarded for certain serious infractions of the rules, including fighting and instances of highsticking, slashing, etc. that draw blood.

major premise See SYLLOGISM.

major scale *Music.* a scale having eight tones, with half steps instead of whole steps after the third and seventh tones. Compare MINOR SCALE.

major suit *Bridge.* a set of spades or hearts with high value.

major term *Logic.* the predicate of the major premise of a syllogism.

ma•jus•cule ['mædʒə,skjul] *or* [mə'dʒʌskjul] *n., adj.* —*n.* **1** a large letter, capital or uncial, in writing or printing. **2** writing or printing using such letters. Compare MINUSCULE.
—*adj.* of or being such a letter or writing. ⟨< F < L *majusculus,* dim. of *major* greater⟩ **—ma'jus•cu•lar,** *adj.*

make [meik] *v.* **made, mak•ing;** *n.* —*v.* **1** bring into being; put together; build; form; shape: *to make a new dress, to make a poem, to make a boat, to make a medicine.* **2** have the qualities needed for: *Wood makes a good fire.* **3** cause; bring about: *to make trouble, to make a noise.* **4** cause to; force to: *He made me go. Excess water made the lake rise.* **5** cause to be or become: *to make a room warm. They made him king.* **6** turn out to be; become: *She will make a good legislator.* **7** get ready for use; arrange: *to make a bed.* **8** get; obtain; acquire, earn: *to make a fortune, to make one's living.* **9** do; perform: *to make an attempt, to make a mistake.* **10** amount to; add up to; count as: *Two and two make four.* **11** think of as; figure to be: *I make the distance across the room 5 m.* **12** reach; arrive at: *The ship made port.*

13 go; travel: *Some airplanes can make 2000 km/h.* **14** cause the success of: *One big deal made the young businesswoman.*
15 *Informal.* get on; get a place on: *He made the football team.*
16 *Card games.* **a** win (a trick or hand). **b** state (the trump, or bid). **c** win a trick with (a card). **d** shuffle (the cards).
17 *Electricity.* close (a circuit). **18** *Sports and games.* score; have a score of. **19** engage in: *to make war.* **20** attend: *I can't make tonight's meeting.*
make after, follow; chase; pursue.
make as if, pretend that; act as if.
make away with, a get rid of. **b** kill. **c** steal: *The treasurer made away with the club's funds.*
make believe, pretend: *The girl liked to make believe she was a pirate.*
make fast, attach (something such as a boat) firmly.
make for, a go toward: *Make for the hills!* **b** rush at; attack. **c** help bring about: *Careful driving makes for fewer accidents.*
make fun. See FUN.
make good. See GOOD.
make good time, *Cdn.* travel at a swift pace; advance at a satisfactory rate.
make it, *Informal.* **a** succeed. **b** *Slang.* have sexual intercourse (with). **c** reach a destination: *Can you make it to the meeting?*
make like, *Slang.* **a** imitate; act the part of. **b** perform the services of: *to make like a cook.* **c** make as if.
make off, run away.
make off with, steal; take without permission: *He made off with some apples.*
make or break, cause to succeed or fail.
make out, a write out: *He made out his application for camp.* **b** show (to be); try to prove: *That makes me out a liar.* **c** understand: *The girl had a hard time making out the problem.* **d** see with difficulty; distinguish: *I can barely make out three ships near the horizon.* **e** *Informal.* get along; manage: *We must try to make out with what we have.* **f** *Slang.* engage in extensive kissing and caressing, and, often, sexual intercourse.
make over, a alter; make different: *to make over a dress.* **b** hand over; transfer ownership of: *Grandfather made over his farm to my mother.*
make ready, *Printing.* prepare (a form) for the press by levelling and adjusting type, plates, etc. to ensure a clear and even impression.
make something of, make an issue of.
make time, go with speed.
make tracks (for), *Cdn.* leave; start out (for a place), usually in haste.
make up, a put together: *to make up cloth into a dress.* **b** invent: *to make up a story.* **c** make satisfactory. **d** become friends again after a quarrel. **e** put paint, powder, etc. on (the face). **f** arrange (type, pictures, etc.) in the pages of a book, paper, or magazine: *to make up a page of type, to make up an edition of a newspaper.* **g** complete; fill out: *We need two more eggs to make up a dozen.* **h** go to form or produce; constitute: *Girls make up most of that class. The committee is made up of women.*
make up for, a give or do something in place of: *to make up for lost time.* **b** compensate for: *Her kindness more than makes up for her shyness.*
make up one's mind, decide.
make up to, try to get the friendship of; flatter.
—n. **1** the way in which a thing is made; a style, build, or character: *Do you like the make of that coat?* **2** a kind; brand: *What make of car is this?* **3** nature; character. **4** the act of making. **5** the amount made.
on the make, *Informal.* trying for success, profit, etc. ⟨OE *macian*⟩

☛ *Syn. v.* **1. Make,** CONSTRUCT, FASHION = put together or give form to something. **Make** is the general word, meaning 'bring something into existence by forming or shaping it or putting it together': *She made a cake.* **Construct** means 'put parts together in proper order, or build', and suggests a plan or design: *They constructed a bridge.* **Fashion** means 'give a definite form, shape, or figure to something', and usually suggests that the maker is inventive or resourceful: *He fashions beautiful totems out of argillite.*

make–be•lieve ['meik bɪ,liv] *n., adj. —n.* **1** pretence. **2** one who pretends.
—adj. pretended: *a make-believe world.*

make•fast ['meik,fæst] *n. Nautical.* something such as a post to which a boat may be tied.

mak•er ['meikər] *n.* **1** a person who or thing that makes. **2 Maker,** God.
meet (one's) **Maker,** die: *He has gone to meet his Maker.*

make–read•y ['meik ,rɛdi] *n. Printing.* the preparation of a form for the press by levelling and adjusting type, plates, etc. to ensure a clear and even impression.

make•shift ['meik,ʃɪft] *n., adj. —n.* **1** something used for a time in the place of the proper thing; a temporary substitute: *When the power went off, we used candles as a makeshift.* **2** the use of such substitutes.
—adj. **1** used for a time instead of the proper thing: *The boys made a makeshift tent out of a blanket.* **2** characterized by makeshifts: *makeshift endeavours.*

make–up or **make•up** ['meik ,ʌp] *n.* **1** the way of being put together; composition. The make-up of a magazine is either the arrangement of type, illustrations, etc. or the kind of articles, stories, etc. used. **2** one's nature or disposition; constitution: *a nervous make-up.* **3** the way in which an actor is dressed and painted to look his or her part. **4** the paint, powder, wigs, etc. used by actors taking part in a play: *His make-up was so effective that we didn't recognize him.* **5** face powder, lipstick, eye shadow, etc. used to beautify the face; cosmetics. **6** *(adjl.)* referring to a course or examination taken to make up for one missed or failed: *a make-up test.*

make•weight ['meik,weit] *n.* anything added to make up for some lack.

make–work ['meik ,wɜrk] *n., adj. —n.* **1** the finding of unnecessary jobs; featherbedding. **2** the providing of work for unemployed people.
—adj. **1** of or used for unnecessary work. **2** planned so as to provide work.

mak•ing ['meikɪŋ] *n., v. —n.* **1** the cause of a person's success; means of advancement: *Early hardships were the making of him.* **2** the material needed. **3** the qualities needed: *I see in him the making of a hero.* **4** something made. **5** the amount made at one time. **6 makings,** *pl. Informal.* **a** the tobacco and papers used in making one's own cigarettes. **b** ingredients; contributory factors.
in the making, in the process of being made; not yet fully developed.
—v. ppr. of MAKE.

–making *combining form.* that makes: *noise-making.*

ma•ku•ta [mɑ'kutɑ] *n.* pl. of LIKUTA.

mal– *combining form.* bad or badly; poor or poorly: *malnutrition, maltreat.* ⟨< F *mal-* < L *male* badly < *malus* bad⟩

mal•ab•sorp•tion [,mæləb'zɔrpʃən] *or* [,mæləb'sɔrpʃən] *n. Pathology.* the failure of the alimentary canal to absorb nutrients.

Malacca cane [mə'lækə] a light walking stick made of rattan. ⟨< *Malacca,* a state of Malaya⟩

mal•a•chite ['mælə,kəit] *n.* a green mineral, copper carbonate, used as an ore of copper and as a stone for making ornamental objects. *Formula:* $Cu_2(OH)_2CO_3$ ⟨< F < Gk. *malachē* mallow (from the similarity of colour)⟩

mal•a•col•o•gy [,mælə'kɒlədʒi] *n.* the science dealing with the study of molluscs. ⟨< F < *malacologie* < Gk. *malakos* soft⟩

mal•a•cos•tra•can [,mælə'kɒstrəkən] *adj.* any of the class (Malacostraca) of crustaceans. ⟨< Gk. *malakostrakos* soft-shelled < *malakos* soft⟩

mal•ad•just•ed [,mælə'dʒʌstɪd] *adj.* badly adjusted; especially, not in harmony with one's environment and conditions of life.

mal•ad•just•ment [,mælə'dʒʌstmənt] *n.* poor or unsatisfactory adjustment, especially to one's environment and conditions of life.

mal•ad•min•is•ter [,mæləd'mɪnəstər] *v.* administer badly; manage inefficiently or dishonestly. **—,mal•ad,min•is'tra•tion,** *n.* **—,mal•ad'min•is,tra•tor,** *n.*

mal•a•droit [,mælə'drɔɪt] *adj.* unskilful; awkward; clumsy. ⟨< F⟩ **—,mal•a'droit•ly,** *adv.* **—,mal•a'droit•ness,** *n.*

mal•a•dy ['mælədi] *n., pl.* **-dies. 1** a sickness or disease. **2** any unwholesome or disordered condition: *Poverty is a social malady.* ⟨ME < OF *maladie* < *malade* ill < L *male habitus* doing poorly⟩

Mal•a•ga ['mæləgə] *n.* **1** a kind of large, oval, white grape. **2** a kind of sweet white wine. ⟨< *Málaga,* a city and province in S Spain⟩

Mal•a•gas•y [,mælə'gæsi] *n., pl.* **-gas•y** or **-gas•ies** *for 1; adj. —n.* **1** a native or inhabitant of Madagascar. **2** the official language of Madagascar, belonging to the Malayo-Polynesian language family.
—adj. of or having to do with Madagascar, its people, or their language.

ma•la•gue•na [,mælə'geinjə] *or* [,mælə'gweinjə] *n.* **1** a Spanish folk dance. **2** the music for this dance. ⟨< Sp.⟩

mal•ai•ka [mæ'ləikɑ] *n. Islam.* angels; the heavenly counterparts of the evil jinn.

ma•laise [mæ'leiz] *n.* **1** a general but indefinite feeling of bodily discomfort and weakness, often the first signs of an illness. **2** a weakness or disorder tending toward disruption or decline: *Apathy is the malaise of democracy.* ⟨< F *malaise* < *mal-* ill + *aise* ease⟩

mal•a•mute ['mælə,mjut] *n. Cdn.* a breed of large, powerful dog having a heavy, grey or black-and-white coat, erect ears, and a tail that curls over the back. Malamutes have long been used as sled dogs in Alaska and the Canadian North. Also called **Alaskan malamute.** Also, **malemute.** ⟨< *Malemiut*, an Inuit people of W Alaska⟩

mal•a•pert ['mælə,pɜrt] *adj. Archaic.* too bold; impudent; saucy. ⟨ME < OF *malapert* < *mal* badly + *apert* adroit, expert⟩

Mal•a•prop ['mælə,prɒp] *n.* **Mrs. Malaprop,** in Richard Brinsley Sheridan's play *The Rivals,* a woman noted for her ridiculous misuse of words. ⟨< F *mal à propos.* See MALAPROPOS.⟩

mal•a•prop•ism ['mæləprɒ,pɪzəm] *n.* **1** a ridiculous misuse of words, especially by confusing words that sound somewhat alike, as in the confusion of *immortality* with *immorality* in *They believe in the immorality of souls.* **2** a misused word. ⟨after Mrs. *Malaprop*⟩

☛ *Usage.* **Malapropisms** are often unconscious, but are sometimes intentionally used for humorous effect.

mal•ap•ro•pos [,mælæprə'pou] *adj., adv. —adj.* inappropriate; at the wrong time or place.
—adv. inappropriately; inopportunely. ⟨< F *mal à propos*⟩

ma•lar ['meilər] *adj., n. Anatomy. —adj.* of the cheekbone.
—n. the zygomatic bone. ⟨< NL *malaris* < L *mala* jaw⟩

ma•lar•i•a [mə'lɛriə] *n.* **1** *Pathology.* a disease characterized by periodic chills followed by fever and sweating. Malaria is caused by microscopic parasitic animals in the red blood corpuscles, and is transmitted by the bite of anopheles mosquitoes that have bitten infected persons. **2** *Archaic.* unwholesome or poisonous air, especially that of marshes; miasma. ⟨< Ital. *malaria* < *mala aria* bad air⟩ **—ma'lar•i•al, ma'lar•i•an,** or **ma'lar•i•ous,** *adj.*

ma•lar•key or **ma•lar•ky** [mə'lɑrki] *n. Slang.* sheer nonsense. ⟨origin uncertain⟩

mal•ate ['mæleit] *or* ['meileit] *n. Chemistry.* an ester of malic acid.

ma•la•thi•on [,mælə'θaɪən] *or* [,mælə'θaɪɒn] *n.* **1** *Chemistry.* a very powerful insecticide recognizable by its pungent, unpleasant odour. *Formula:* $C_{10}H_{19}O_6PS_2$ **2** a preparation used to treat head lice. ⟨< *mal(ic) a(cid)* + *thio-* comb. form for sulphur < Gk. *theion*⟩

Ma•la•wi [mə'lɑwi] *n.* a country in SE Africa, formerly called Nyasaland.

Ma•la•wi•an [mə'lɑwiən] *n., adj. —n.* a native or inhabitant of Malawi.
—adj. of or having to do with Malawi.

Ma•lay [mə'lei] *or* ['meilei] *n., adj. —n.* **1** a member of a people living in the Malay peninsula, Borneo, and nearby islands. **2** the Austronesian language of the Malays.
—adj. of or having to do with the Malays or their language.

☛ *Hom.* MELEE ['meilei].

Mal•a•ya•lam [,mɑlə'jɑləm] *n.* a Dravidian language, spoken in SW India, closely related to Tamil.

Ma•lay•an [mə'leiən] *n. or adj.* Malay.

Ma•lay•o–Pol•y•ne•sian [mə'leiou ,pɒlɪ'niʒən] *n., adj.* Austronesian.

Ma•lay•sia [mə'leiʒə] *or* [mə'leiʃə] *n.* a country in SE Asia, comprising many small islands.

Ma•lay•sian [mə'leiʒən] *or* [mə'leiʃən] *n., adj. —n.* a native or inhabitant of Malaysia.
—adj. of or having to do with Malaysia, its people, or their languages.

mal•con•tent *adj.* ['mælkən,tɛnt] *or* [,mælkən'tɛnt]; *n.* ['mælkən,tɛnt] *adj., n. —adj.* discontented or rebellious.
—n. a discontented or rebellious person.

mal de mer [maldə'mɛʀ] *French.* seasickness.

mal de raquette [mæl də rə'kɛt] *Cdn.* a painful state of inflamed joints and muscles affecting snowshoers, caused by undue strain on the tendons of the leg.

Mal•dives ['mɒldaɪvz] *or* ['mældaɪvz] *n.* a country comprising a group of islands in the Indian Ocean.

Mal•div•i•an [mæl'dɪviən] *n., adj. —n.* a native or inhabitant of Maldives.
—adj. of or having to do with Maldives.

male [meil] *adj., n. —adj.* **1** of, having to do with, or being the sex that produces the gametes, or sperm cells, that fertilize the eggs of a female to produce young: *the male organs.* **2** of, having to do with, or characteristic of men or boys: *a male voice.* **3** made up of men and/or boys: *a male choir.* **4** designating a part of a machine or a connection, etc. that fits into a corresponding hollow part: *a male pipe fitting.*
—n. a person, animal, or plant that is male: *There were three puppies in the litter; two males and one female.* ⟨ME < OF *male, masle* < L *masculus,* dim. of *mas* male⟩ **—'male•ness,** *n.*

☛ *Hom.* MAIL.

☛ *Syn. adj.* **1. Male,** MASCULINE, MANLY = having to do with men or the gender to which they belong. **Male,** describing plants, animals, or human beings, suggests only sex: *We have a male avocado tree.* **Masculine** describes things or people and suggests qualities (especially strength, vigour, etc.) belonging to or characteristically associated with men and boys as distinguished from women and girls: *He is a big, masculine man.* **Manly** suggests the finer qualities of a man, such as courage and honour: *He is an upright, manly youth.*

male chauvinist *Informal.* a man who believes in the superiority of men over women, and acts according to that belief.

Mal•e•cite ['mælə,sɔit] *or* [,mælə'sit] *n., pl.* **-cite** or **-cites;** *adj.*
—n. a member of a First Nations people living in New Brunswick, eastern Québec, and northern Maine. The Malecite are an Algonquian people.
—adj. of or having to do with the Malecite.

mal•e•dic•tion [,mælə'dɪkʃən] *n.* the uttering of a curse; the calling down of evil on a person. ⟨ME < L *maledictio, -onis* < *maledicere* < *male* ill + *dicere* speak. Doublet of MALISON.⟩ **—,mal•e'dic•tive,** *adj.* **—,mal•e'dic•to•ry,** *adj.*

mal•e•fac•tion [,mælə'fækʃən] *n.* a crime or evil deed.

mal•e•fac•tor ['mælə,fæktər] *n.* a criminal or evildoer. ⟨ME < L *malefactor* < *malefacere* < *male* badly + *facere* do⟩

male fern a fern (*Dryopteris filix-mas*) yielding a drug used against tapeworms.

ma•lef•ic [mə'lɛfɪk] *adj.* causing disaster. ⟨< L *maleficus* evil-doing; wicked⟩

ma•lef•i•cence [mə'lɛfəsəns] *n.* harm; evil. ⟨< L *maleficentia* < *maleficus* wicked < *male* badly + *facere* do⟩

ma•lef•i•cent [mə'lɛfəsənt] *adj.* harmful; evil. ⟨< *maleficence*⟩

ma•le•ic acid [mə'liɪk] *Chemistry.* a solid used in the making of synthetic resins and as a preservative for oils. *Formula:* $H_4O_4C_4$ ⟨< F *maléique,* alteration of *malique.* See MALIC ACID.⟩

mal•e•mute ['mælə,mjut] *Cdn.* malamute.

ma•lev•o•lence [mə'lɛvələns] *n.* the wish that evil may happen to others; ill will; spite.

ma•lev•o•lent [mə'lɛvələnt] *adj.* having or showing vicious ill will; spiteful; malicious: *a malevolent smile.* ⟨< L *malevolens, -entis,* ult. < *male* ill + *velle* wish⟩ **—ma'lev•o•lent•ly,** *adv.*

mal•fea•sance [mæl'fizəns] *n. Law.* misconduct by a public official; violation of a public trust or duty: *A judge is guilty of malfeasance if he or she accepts a bribe.* Compare MISFEASANCE, NONFEASANCE. ⟨< F *malfaisance,* ult. < *mal-* badly + *faire* do⟩ **—mal'fea•sant,** *adj., n.*

mal•for•ma•tion [,mælfər'meiʃən] *n.* an irregular, faulty, or abnormal shape or structure: *A hunchback is a malformation of the spine.*

mal•formed [mæl'fɔrmd] *adj.* badly shaped; having an abnormal or faulty structure.

mal•func•tion [mæl'fʌŋkʃən] *n., v. —n.* an improper functioning; failure to work or perform: *a malfunction of an organ of the body, a malfunction in a machine.*
—v. function badly; work or perform improperly.

Ma•li ['mɑli] *n.* a country in W Africa, formerly French Sudan. See SENEGAL for map.

mal•ic acid ['mælɪk] *or* ['meilɪk] *Chemistry.* an acid found in apples and numerous other fruits. *Formula:* $C_4H_6O_5$ ⟨< F *malique* < L *malum* apple < Doric Gk. *malon*⟩

mal•ice ['mælɪs] *n.* **1** active ill will; a wish to hurt others; spite. **2** *Law.* intent to commit an act which will result in harm to another person without justification.
malice aforethought, *Law.* an unlawful act committed with intent. ⟨ME < OF < L *malitia* < *malus* evil⟩

☛ *Syn.* **1.** See note at SPITE.

ma•li•cious [mə'lɪʃəs] *adj.* showing active ill will; wishing to hurt others; spiteful: *malicious gossip.* **—ma'li•cious•ly,** *adv.* **—ma'li•cious•ness,** *n.*

ma•lign [mə'laɪn] *v., adj.* *—v.* speak evil of, often falsely; slander: *You malign him unjustly when you call him stingy, for he gives all he can afford to give.*
—adj. **1** evil; injurious: *Gambling often has a malign influence.* **2** hateful; malicious. **3** very harmful; threatening to be fatal. ⟨ME < OF *maligne, adj.* (v. < OF *malignier* < LL *malignare*) < L *malignus* < *malus* evil + *gen-* birth, nature⟩ **—ma'lign•er,** *n.* **—ma'lign•ly,** *adv.*

ma•lig•nan•cy [mə'lɪgnənsi] *n., pl.* **-cies. 1** a malignant condition, quality, or tendency. **2** malignant behaviour, character, action, etc. Also, **malignance.**

ma•lig•nant [mə'lɪgnənt] *adj.* **1** extremely evil, hateful, or malicious. **2** extremely harmful. **3** *Pathology.* of a disease, very infectious and dangerous: *malignant cholera.* **4** *Pathology.* of a tumour, cyst, etc., tending to grow and spread, causing harm to healthy tissues around it; cancerous. Compare BENIGN (def. 3). ⟨< LL *malignans, -antis* acting from malice < *malignus.* See MALIGN.⟩ **—ma'lig•nant•ly,** *adv.*

ma•lig•ni•ty [mə'lɪgnəti] *n., pl.* **-ties. 1** great malice; extreme hate. **2** great harmfulness; dangerous quality; deadliness. **3** a malignant act or feeling.

ma•lines or **ma•line** [mə'lin] *n.* **1** Mechlin lace. **2** a thin, stiff, silk net used in dressmaking. ⟨< F *malines,* after *Malines* (or Mechlin), a town in Belgium⟩

ma•lin•ger [mə'lɪŋgər] *v.* pretend to be sick in order to escape work or duty; shirk. ⟨< F *malingre* sickly < OF *mal-* badly (< L *male*) + *heingre* sick (< Gmc.)⟩ **—ma'lin•ger•er,** *n.*

mal•i•son ['mæləzən] *or* ['mæləsən] *n. Archaic.* a malediction; curse. Compare BENISON. ⟨ME < OF *maleison* < L *maledictio.* Doublet of MALEDICTION.⟩

mall [mɒl] *n.* **1** SHOPPING MALL. **2** a walk lined with stores; a place to walk in a shopping centre. **3** a shaded walk; a public walk or promenade. ⟨ME < OF *ma(i)l* mallet < L *malleus* hammer; originally, a mallet used in pall-mall (an old game); later, the game itself; then, a lane or alley in which the game was played⟩
☛ *Hom.* MAUL, MOLL.

mal•lard ['mælərd] *n., pl.* **-lards** or (*esp. collectively*) **-lard.** a wild duck (*Anas platyrhynchos*) common throughout much of the northern hemisphere, having greyish brown plumage with a conspicuous blue wing patch, the male in breeding plumage having a green head and neck, narrow white collar, and reddish brown breast. The mallard is the ancestor of most domestic breeds of duck. ⟨ME < OF *mallart,* probably < Gmc.⟩

mal•le•a•ble ['mæliəbəl] *adj.* **1** capable of being hammered or pressed into various shapes without being broken. Gold, silver, copper, and tin are malleable; they can be beaten into thin sheets. **2** adaptable; yielding: *A malleable person is easily persuaded to change her plans.* ⟨ME < OF < L *malleare* to hammer < *malleus,* n.⟩ **—,mal•le•a'bil•i•ty,** *n.* **—'mal•le•a•ble•ness,** *n.* **—'mal•le•a•bly,** *adv.*

mal•lee ['mæli] *n.* **1** an Australian eucalyptus shrub of the genus *Eucalyptus.* **2** the thick bush formed by such plants. ⟨< native Australian language⟩

mal•le•muck ['mælə,mʌk] *n.* albatross. ⟨< Du. *mallemok* < *mal* silly + *mok* seagull⟩

mal•let ['mælɪt] *n.* **1** a hammer having a head of wood, rubber, or other relatively soft material. **2** a long-handled, wooden mallet used to play croquet or polo. **3** a small, short-handled hammer with a soft head, used for playing percussion instruments. ⟨ME < OF *maillet,* dim. of *mail* < L *malleus* hammer⟩

mal•le•us ['mæliəs] *n., pl.* **mal•le•i** ['mæli,aɪ]. in mammals, the outermost of three small bones in the middle ear, shaped like a hammer. See EAR[1] for picture. ⟨< L *malleus* hammer⟩

mal•low ['mælou] *n.* **1** any of a genus (*Malva*) of herbs native to Europe, Asia, and N Africa, having lobed leaves and usually large, showy flowers. Some mallows are cultivated as garden flowers, but others have become naturalized in North America as weeds. **2** any of several other related herbs and shrubs. **3** (*adjl.*) designating a family (Malvaceae) of herbs, shrubs, and small trees found throughout the world, but especially in the tropics. The cotton plant, hollyhock, mallows, and hibiscus belong to the mallow family. ⟨OE *mealwe* < L *malva.* Doublet of MAUVE.⟩

malm [mɑm] *or* [mɒm] *n.* soft limestone. ⟨ME *malme* < OE *mealm* sand⟩
☛ *Hom.* MA'AM [mɑm].

malm•sey ['mɑmzi] *or* ['mɒmzi] *n.* a strong, sweet wine. ⟨ME < Med.L *malmasia,* from *Monembasia,* a town in Greece⟩

mal•nour•ished [mæl'nɜrɪʃt] *adj.* suffering from lack of food or nutritious food.

mal•nu•tri•tion [,mælnjə'trɪʃən] *or* [,mælnə'trɪʃən] *n.* poor nourishment; lack of nourishment. Malnutrition may come from eating the wrong kinds of food as well as from eating too little.

mal•oc•clu•sion [,mælə'kluʒən] *n.* failure of the upper and lower teeth to meet or close properly.

mal•o•dor•ous [mæl'oudərəs] *adj.* smelling bad. **—mal'o•dor•ous•ly,** *adv.* **—mal'o•dor•ous•ness,** *n.*

ma•lo•nic acid [mə'lounɪk] *or* [mə'lɒnɪk] *Chemistry.* a white, crystalline, water-soluble, dibasic acid that is easily decomposed by heat. *Formula:* $H_4O_4C_3$

ma•lo•ti [mɑ'louti] *n.* pl. of LOTI.

mal•peque [mæl'pik] *or* ['mælpɛk] *n. Cdn.* a variety of oyster, found in Malpeque Bay, Prince Edward Island.

Mal•pi•ghi•an [mæl'pɪgiən] *adj.* relating to Marcello Malpighi (1628-1694), Italian physiologist who discovered the capillary system.

Malpighian body or **corpuscle** *Anatomy.* **1** in the kidney, a cluster of capillaries inside the enlarged end of each of the tubules that carry urine. **2** a small mass of lymphatic tissue in the spleen.

Malpighian layer *Anatomy.* the deepest layer of the epidermis.

Malpighian tube one of the excretory tubes leading out of the digestive organs of insects.

mal•po•si•tion [,mælpə'zɪʃən] *n. Pathology.* abnormality in the position of the fetus.

mal•prac•tice [mæl'præktɪs] *n.* **1** criminal neglect or unprofessional treatment of a patient by a doctor. **2** wrong practice or conduct in any official or professional position. **—,mal•prac'ti•tion•er,** *n.*

malt [mɒlt] *n., v.* *—n.* **1** barley or other grain that is soaked in water until it sprouts and is then dried and aged. Malt has a sweet taste and is used in making beer and ale. **2** *Informal.* beer or ale. **3** MALTED MILK.
—v. **1** change or be changed into malt. **2** prepare with malt. ⟨OE *mealt*⟩ **—'malt•y,** *adj.*

Mal•ta ['mɒltə] *n.* an island country in the Mediterranean.

mal•tase ['mɒlteis] *or* ['mɒlteiz] *n. Biochemistry.* an enzyme which hydrolyzes maltose into sugar.

malted milk a sweet, cold drink made from milk, dried milk, and malt, mixed with ice cream and flavouring.

Mal•tese [mɒl'tiz] *n., pl.* **-tese;** *adj.* *—n.* **1** a native or inhabitant of Malta. **2** the language of the Maltese. It is a Semitic language, mostly Arabic, with many Italian loan words. **3** a breed of toy dog usually weighing 2 to 3 kg, having long, silky, white hair, a black nose, and black eyes. The Maltese is one of the oldest breeds of lap dog. **4** MALTESE CAT.
—adj. of or having to do with Malta, its people, or their language.

Maltese cat a bluish grey variety of domestic shorthair.

Maltese cross a cross with arms that broaden out from the centre and are often indented at the ends. See CROSS for picture.

malt extract a sugary substance obtained by soaking malt in water.

mal•tha ['mælθə] *n.* a viscous bitumen occurring naturally. ⟨< L < Gk., mixture of pitch and wax⟩

Mal•thu•sian [mæl'θuʒən] *or* [mæl'θuziən] *adj., n.* *—adj.* of or having to do with Malthus or his theory that the world's population tends to increase faster than the food supply.
—n. an advocate of Malthus' theory. ⟨< Thomas Robert *Malthus* (1766-1834), a British economist⟩

malt liquor any alcoholic drink made by fermenting malt.

malt•ose ['mɒltous] *n. Chemistry.* a white, crystalline sugar made by the action of diastase on starch. *Formula:* $C_{12}H_{22}O_{11} \cdot H_2O$

mal•treat [mæl'trit] *v.* treat roughly or cruelly; abuse: *Only vicious persons maltreat animals.* **—mal'treat•ment,** *n.*

malt•ster ['mɒltstər] *n.* a person who makes or sells malt.

malt sugar maltose.

malt vinegar a strong vinegar made from malt liquor.

mal•ver•sa•tion [,mælvər'seiʃən] *n.* corrupt conduct in a position of trust. ⟨< F *malversation* < *malverser* embezzle < L *maleversari* behave badly⟩

ma•ma or **mam•ma** ['mʌmə], ['mɑmə], *or* ['mɒmə]; *esp. Brit.,* [mə'mɑ] *n. Informal.* mother. ⟨reduplication of an infantile sound⟩

mam•ba ['mɑmbə] *or* ['mæmbə] *n.* any of a genus (*Dendroaspis*) of long, slender, very poisonous snakes of central and S Africa, belonging to the same family (Elapidae) as the cobras and coral snakes. ⟨< South African *m'namba*⟩

mam•bo ['mɑmbou], ['mɒmbou], *or* ['mæmbou] *n., pl.* **-bos;** *v.* —*n.* **1** a fast ballroom dance of Caribbean origin. **2** the music for such a dance.
—*v.* dance the mambo. ⟨< Haitian Creole⟩

Mam•e•luke ['mæmə,luk] *n.* **1** a member of a military group that ruled Egypt from about 1250 to 1517 and had great power until 1811. The Mamelukes were originally slaves. **2 mameluke,** in Muslim countries, a slave. ⟨< Arabic *mamluk* slave⟩

mam•ma¹ ['mʌmə], ['mɑmə], *or* ['mɒmə]; *esp. Brit.,* [mə'mɑ] *n.* See MAMA.

mam•ma² ['mæmə] *n., pl.* **mam•mae** ['mæmi] *or* ['mæmaɪ]. *Anatomy, zoology.* a milk-giving gland in female mammals. ⟨< L *mamma* breast⟩

mam•mal ['mæməl] *n.* any of a class (Mammalia) of warm-blooded, vertebrate animals, the females of which have glands (mammae) that produce milk for feeding their young. Human beings, horses, dogs, rats, and whales are all mammals. ⟨< NL *mammalia*, pl., ult. < L *mamma* breast⟩ **—'mam•mal,like,** *adj.*

mam•ma•lia [mə'meiliə] *n.* a class of vertebrates including 15 000 species.

mam•ma•li•an [mə'meiliən] *or* [mə'meiljən] *adj., n.* —*adj.* of or having to do with mammals.
—*n.* a mammal.

mam•mal•o•gist [mə'mælədʒɪst] *n.* a person trained in mammalogy, especially one whose work it is.

mam•mal•o•gy [mə'mælədʒi] *n.* the branch of zoology that deals with the study of mammals. ⟨< *mamma(lia)* + *-logy*⟩ **—,mam•ma'log•i•cal** [,mæmə'lɒdʒɪkəl], *adj.*

mam•ma•ry ['mæməri] *adj. Anatomy, zoology.* of or designating the mammae. The mammary glands secrete milk.

mammary gland *Anatomy, zoology.* an organ in female mammals that produces milk.

mam•mil•la [mæ'mɪlə] *n., pl.* **-mil•lae** [-'mɪli] *or* [-'mɪlaɪ]. **1** the nipple of the mamma, or breast. **2** anything shaped like a nipple.

mam•mil•late ['mæmə,leit] *adj.* **1** having a nipple or nipples. **2** shaped like a nipple. **—,mam•mil'la•tion,** *n.*

mam•mo•gram ['mæmə,græm] *n.* **1** a printout of a mammography. **2** an instance of mammography.

mam•mog•ra•phy [mə'mɒgrəfi] *n.* examination of the breasts by X ray for the early detection of tumours. ⟨< *mamma²* + *-graphy.* 20c.⟩ **—,mam•mo'graph•ic** [,mæmə'græfɪk], *adj.*

Mam•mon or **mam•mon** ['mæmən] *n.* **1** material wealth or possessions thought of as objects of worship. **2** material wealth or possessions thought of as an evil; greed for wealth. ⟨< L *mammona* < Gk. *mammōnas* < Aramaic *mamon* riches⟩ **—'Mam•mon,ism,** *n.*

mam•moth ['mæməθ] *n., adj.* —*n.* any of an extinct genus (*Mammuthus*) of elephants of the Pleistocene epoch having a hairy skin and very long, curved tusks.
—*adj.* huge; gigantic. ⟨< earlier Russian *mammot*⟩

mam•my ['mæmi] *n., pl.* **-mies.** *Informal.* mother.

man [mæn] *n., pl.* **men,** *v.* **manned, man•ning,** *interj.* —*n.* **1** an adult male person. **2** a person; human being: *Death comes to all men.* **3** the human race; humankind; Homo sapiens: *Man has existed for thousands of years.* **4** an extinct hominid: *Neanderthal man.* **5** men as a group; the average man: *The man of today likes to travel.* **6** a male follower, servant, or employee. **7** a male member of the armed forces, especially one who is not an officer (*usually used in the plural*). **8** a male member of a team, organization, etc. **9** *Informal.* a husband or lover. **10** one of the pieces used in chess, checkers, etc. **11** a man thought of as having all the best characteristics distinctive of manhood: *He was every inch a man.*
act the man, be courageous.
as a man, from a human point of view.
as one man, with complete agreement; unanimously.
be (one's) own man (or **woman**), **a** be free to do as one pleases. **b** have complete control of oneself.
man and boy, from boyhood on; as a youth and as an adult.
to a man, every one, without an exception; all: *We accepted his idea to a man.*
—*v.* **1** supply with a crew: *We can man ten ships.* **2** serve or operate; get ready to operate: *Man the guns.* **3** make (oneself) strong in anticipation; brace: *to man oneself for an ordeal.*
—*interj. Informal.* an exclamation of surprise, excitement, etc., or for effect: *Man, what a player!* ⟨OE *mann*⟩ **—'man•less,** *adj.*
☛ *Usage.* **Man,** GENTLEMAN. **Man** is now generally preferred to **gentleman,** unless a note of special courtesy or respect is desired.

Man. Manitoba.

M.A.N. MEMBER OF THE NATIONAL ASSEMBLY (for *M*embre de l'*A*ssemblée *N*ationale).

man about town a worldly man who spends much of his time in fashionable clubs, theatres, etc.

man•a•cle ['mænəkəl] *n., v.* **-cled, -cling.** —*n.* **1** Usually, **manacles,** *pl.* a handcuff; fetter for the hands. **2** any restraint.
—*v.* **1** put manacles on: *The pirates manacled their prisoners.* **2** restrain. ⟨ME < OF < L *manicula*, dim. of *manicae* sleeves, manacles < *manus* hand⟩

man•age ['mænɪdʒ] *v.* **-aged, -ag•ing. 1** control; conduct; handle; direct: *manage a business, manage a horse.* **2** conduct affairs. **3** succeed in accomplishing; contrive; arrange: *I finally managed to get the job done.* **4** get along: *manage on one's income.* **5** make use of. **6** get one's way with (a person) by craft or flattery. ⟨< Ital. *maneggiare* < *mano* hand < L *manus*⟩
☛ *Syn. v.* **1. Manage,** CONDUCT, DIRECT = guide or handle with authority. **Manage** emphasizes the idea of skilful handling of people and details so as to get results: *She manages a large department store.* **Conduct** emphasizes the idea of supervising the action of a group working together for something: *The Scouts are conducting a safety drive.* **Direct** emphasizes the idea of guiding the affairs or actions of a group by giving advice and instructions to be followed: *A lawyer directed our anti-noise campaign.*

man•age•a•ble ['mænədʒəbəl] *adj.* that can be managed. **—,man•age•a'bil•i•ty,** *n.* **—'man•age•a•ble•ness,** *n.* **—'man•age•a•bly,** *adv.*

managed currency a monetary system regulated by a government through its bank, and not by a gold standard.

man•age•ment ['mænɪdʒmənt] *n.* **1** control; handling; direction: *The new store failed because of bad management.* **2** the persons that manage a business or an institution: *The management of the store decided to keep it open every evening.* **3** managers regarded as a social class. **—,man•age'men•tal,** *adj.*

management consultant a specialist or expert who can be hired to examine the operations of a company and advise on planning, organization, and other management problems.

management information system *Computer technology.* computer software whose output is particularly useful to those who make managment decisions in an organization. *Abbrev.*: MIS

man•ag•er ['mænədʒər] *n.* **1** a person who manages: *a bank manager, an advertising manager.* **2** a person skilled in managing (affairs, time, money, etc.): *Mrs. Jones is not much of a manager, but the family gets along somehow.* **3** a person who directs the activities of a team, athlete, performer, etc.

man•a•ge•ri•al [,mænə'dʒiriəl] *adj.* of or like a manager; having to do with management. **—,man•a'ge•ri•al•ly,** *adv.* **—,man•a'ge•ri•al,ism,** *n.*

managing editor the supervisor of editorial work in a publishing company or newspaper.

man•a•kin ['mænəkɪn] *n.* a small bird of tropical America, of the family Pipridae.
☛ *Hom.* MANNEQUIN, MANIKIN, MANNIKIN.

ma•ña•na [mɑ'njɑnə] *or* [mɑ'njɑnɑ] *n. or adv.* tomorrow; some time in the future. ⟨< Sp.⟩

ma•nat [mɑ'nɑt] *n.* **1** the basic unit of money in Turkmenistan, divided into 100 tenesi. See table of money in the Appendix. **2** the basic unit of money in Azerbaijan, divided into 100 qepiq.

man–at–arms ['mæn ət 'ɑrmz] *n., pl.* **men-at-arms.** formerly, a soldier, especially one who was heavily armed and mounted on horseback.

man•a•tee ['mænə,ti] *or* [,mænə'ti] *n.* any of a small genus (*Trichechus*, constituting the family Trichechidae) of sea mammals found in the coastal waters of tropical America and Africa, having a whalelike body with a broad, rounded tail flipper. ⟨< Sp. *manati* < Carib lang.⟩

man•chet ['mæntʃɪt] *n. Archaic.* **1** bread made of the finest white flour. **2** a small loaf or roll of such bread. ⟨origin uncertain⟩

man–child ['mæn ˌtʃaɪld] *n., pl.* **men-children.** a young boy, especially a son.

Man•chu [mæn'tʃu] *or* ['mæntʃu] *n.* **1** a member of an Asiatic people, the original inhabitants of Manchuria, who conquered China in 1644 and ruled it until 1912. **2** their Altaic language.
–adj. of or having to do with the Manchus, their country, or their language.

Man•chu•ri•an [mæn'tʃʊriən] *n., adj. –n.* a native or inhabitant of Manchuria, an E Asian region that includes several Chinese provinces.
–adj. of or having to do with Manchuria.

man•ci•ple ['mænsəpəl] *n. Archaic.* a person who buys provisions for a college or other institution; steward. ⟨ME < OF < L *manicipium* office of purchaser < *manceps* buyer, ult. < *manu capere* take in hand⟩

man•da•la ['mʌndələ] *n.* in Oriental art, any stylized design, usually of gods, representing the cosmos. ⟨< Skt. *mandala* a circle⟩

man•da•mus [mæn'deiməs] *n. Law.* a written order from a higher court to a lower court, an official, a city, a corporation, etc. directing that a certain thing be done. ⟨< L *mandamus* we order⟩

Man•dan ['mændæn] *or* ['mændən] *n.* **1** an American Indian people of the plains, once famous as trackers in North Dakota. **2** the Siouan language of these people.

man•da•rin ['mændərɪn] *n.* **1** a kind of small, sweet orange having a thin, very loose, dark orange peel. Also called **mandarin orange. 2** the small, spiny citrus tree (*Citrus reticulata*; sometimes classified as *C. nobilis*) bearing this fruit. The mandarin is native to China. **3 Mandarin, a** formerly, in the Chinese Empire, the language of the court, government officials, and other educated people. Mandarin was a northern dialect. **b** the main language of modern China, the standard form being the one used in Beijing. **4** formerly, in the Chinese empire, an official of high rank. **5** a person of high position whose government work is not necessarily publicized but who has, or is thought to have, considerable political or social influence: *the mandarins of Ottawa.* **6** a Canadian woodland wildflower (*Streptopus roseus*) having tiny, pink flowers beneath the leaves, blooming in spring and summer. ⟨< Chinese Pidgin English < Pg. *mandar* order (< L *mandare*), blended with Malay *mantri* < Hind. < Skt. *mantrin* adviser⟩

man•da•rin•ate ['mændərənɪt] *or* ['mændərəˌneit] *n.* a group or establishment of mandarins.

mandarin collar a narrow collar that stands up straight and does not meet at the front.

mandarin orange MANDARIN (def. 1).

mandarin duck a waterfowl (*Aix galericulata*) of Asia, with a colourful plumage and crest.

man•da•tar•y ['mændəˌtɛri] *n., pl.* **-tar•ies. 1** a nation to which a mandate over another country has been given. **2** *Law.* a person to whom a mandate is given.

man•date *n.* ['mændeit] *or* ['mændɪt]; *v.* ['mændeit] *n., v.* **-dat•ed, -dat•ing.** *–n.* **1** a command or official order. **2** *Law.* an order from a higher court or official to a lower one. **3** a direction or authority given to a government by the votes of the people in an election: *The prime minister said she had a mandate to increase taxes.* **4** a commission given to one nation by a group of nations to administer the government and affairs of a territory, etc. **5** a territory, etc. under the administration of another nation.
–v. **1** put (a territory, etc.) under the administration of another nation. **2** order (something) to be done or put into effect; make mandatory: *The new curriculum will be mandated next fall.* ⟨< L *mandatum*, n. use of neut. pp. of *mandare* order⟩

man•da•to•ry ['mændəˌtɔri] *adj., n., pl.* **-ries.** *–adj.* **1** of, like, or having to do with a mandate; giving a command or order. **2** required by a command or order.
–n. mandatary. **–'man•daˌto•ri•ly,** *adv.*

Man•de ['mɑndei] *or* ['mɑndi] *n.* **1** a people of W Africa, in the Niger valley. **2** the Niger-Congo language of these people.

Man•de•an [mæn'diən] *n.* **1** a member of an ancient sect of Gnostics in Mesopotamia. **2** the dialect of Aramaic in which their texts were written. ⟨< Mandean *mandayya* < *manda* knowledge⟩

man•di•ble ['mændəbəl] *n.* **1** either member of the foremost pair of mouth parts of an insect, spider, lobster, etc., adapted for seizing and biting. **2** either the upper or lower part of the beak of a bird or of any other beaked animal, such as an octopus. **3** the jaw of a vertebrate, especially the lower jaw. ⟨< LL *mandibula* < L *mandere* chew⟩ **–man'dib•u•lar,** *adj.*

man•dib•u•late [mæn'dɪbjəlɪt] *or* [mæn'dɪbjəˌleit] *adj., n.* *–adj.* having mandibles.
–n. a mandibulate insect, as a beetle.

man•do•lin ['mændəlɪn] *or* [ˌmændə'lɪn] *n.* a musical instrument having a pear-shaped body, a neck with a fretted fingerboard, and several metal strings. It is usually played with a plectrum. ⟨< F < Ital. *mandolino*, dim. of *mandola*, ult. < Gk. *pandoura* three-stringed instrument⟩ **–ˌman•do'lin•ist,** *n.*

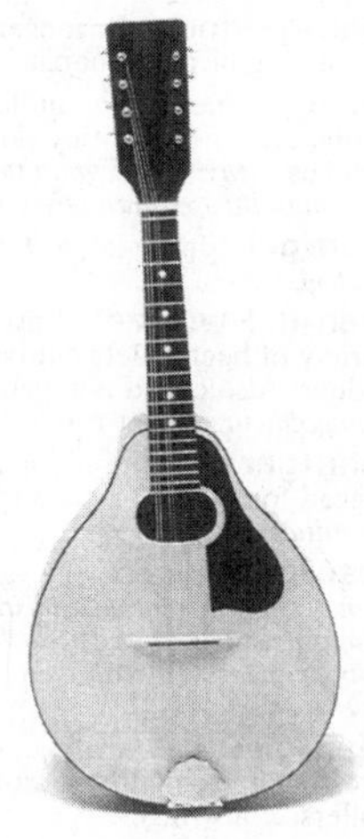

Mandolin

man•drag•o•ra [mæn'drægərə] *or* [ˌmændrə'gɔrə] *n.* mandrake. ⟨ME < L < Gk. *mandragoras*⟩

man•drake ['mændreik] *n.* **1** a Eurasian plant (*Mandragora officinarum*) of the nightshade family, having a short stalk, purplish flowers, and a thick, forked root formerly thought of as resembling the human form and therefore having magical powers. A drug used as a narcotic and sedative was also prepared from the root. **2** the root of this plant. **3** mayapple. ⟨by folk etymology < *mandragora*⟩

man•drel or **man•dril** ['mændrəl] *n.* **1** on a lathe, the spindle or bar that is inserted into a hole in a piece of work to support it while it is being turned. **2** a rod or core around which metal is shaped. ⟨< F *mandrin*⟩
☛ *Hom.* MANDRILL.

man•drill ['mændrəl] *n.* a large, terrestrial, Old World monkey (*Mandrillus sphinx*) of the forests of W Africa, having a stout body, short tail, and small, closely set eyes. The adult male has bare patches of red, blue, and pink skin on the face and buttocks. ⟨< *man* + *drill* baboon⟩
☛ *Hom.* MANDREL.

mane [mein] *n.* **1** the long, heavy hair growing on the back or around the neck of a horse, lion, etc. **2** long, profuse human hair. ⟨OE *manu*⟩ **–'mane•less,** *adj.*
☛ *Hom.* MAIN.

man–eater ['mæn ˌitər] *n.* **1** a tiger or other large member of the cat family that has acquired the habit of eating human flesh. **2** any of various sharks known to feed on human flesh, especially the white shark. **3** cannibal. **4** *Informal.* a sexually attractive and aggressive woman who preys on men.

ma•nège [mə'nɛʒ] *or* [mə'neiʒ] *n.* **1** the art of training or riding horses; horsemanship. **2** the movements of a trained horse. **3** a riding school. ⟨< F < Ital. *maneggio* < *maneggiare* manage⟩

ma•nes or **Ma•nes** ['meiniz] *n.pl.* **1** in the ancient Roman religion, the deified souls of dead ancestors, together with the gods of the lower world. **2** the spirit or shade of a particular person (*used with a singular verb*). ⟨< L: literally, the good ones⟩

ma•neu•ver [mə'nuvər] See MANOEUVRE.
–ma'neu•ver•a•ble, *adj.* **–maˌneu•ver•a'bil•i•ty,** *n.*

man Friday a faithful servant. ⟨< *Friday*, Robinson Crusoe's servant⟩

man•ful ['mænfəl] *adj.* having or showing courage, resolution, etc.; manly. **–'man•ful•ly,** *adv.* **–'man•ful•ness,** *n.*

man•ga•bey ['mæŋgəˌbei] *n.* an African monkey of the genus *Cercocebus.* ⟨after *Mangabey*, Madagascar⟩

man•ga•nate ['mæŋgəˌneit] *n. Chemistry.* a salt of manganic acid, such as potassium manganate, containing the radical MnO_4.

man•ga•nese ['mæŋgəˌniz] *or* ['mæŋgəˌnis] *n. Chemistry.* a hard, brittle, greyish white, metallic element. Substances containing manganese are used in making steel, glass, paints, and medicines. *Symbol*: Mn; *at.no.* 25; *at.mass* 54.94. ⟨< F *manganèse* < Ital. *manganese*, alteration of Med.L *magnesia.* See MAGNESIA.⟩

manganese dioxide *Chemistry.* an oxide of manganese. *Formula*: MnO_2

manganese steel manganese alloyed with steel, to increase its strength.

man•gan•ic [mæn'gænɪk] *adj. Chemistry.* having to do with bivalent manganese or any compound containing it.

man•gan•ite ['mæŋgə,nəit] *n.* a crystalline mineral form of manganese oxide. *Formula*: $Mn_2O_3H_2O$

man•ga•nous ['mæŋgənəs] *or* [mæn'gænəs] *adj. Chemistry.* containing bivalent manganese.

mange [meindʒ] *n.* an itchy skin disease of dogs, horses, cattle, etc., in which tiny skin sores form and the hair falls off in patches. ⟨ME < OF *manjue* or *mangeue* the itch < *mangier* eat < L *manducare, mandere* chew⟩

man•gel ['mæŋgəl] *n.* MANGEL-WURZEL.
☛ *Hom.* MANGLE.

man•gel–wur•zel ['mæŋgəl ,wɜrzəl] *n.* a large, coarse, yellow variety of beet widely cultivated, especially in Europe, for cattle fodder. Also called **mangel, mangold.** ⟨< G *Mangelwurzel*, var. of *Mangoldwurzel* beet root⟩

man•ger ['meindʒər] *n.* a box or trough in which hay can be placed for horses or cows to eat. ⟨ME < OF *mangeoire*, ult. < L *manducare* eat⟩

man•gle¹ ['mæŋgəl] *v.* **-gled, -gling. 1** cut or tear roughly: *His arm was badly mangled in the accident.* **2** do or play badly; ruin: *The music was too difficult for her, and she mangled it.* ⟨< AF *mangler*, ? < OF *mahaignier* < *mahaigne* injury. Cf. MAYHEM.⟩
☛ *Hom.* MANGEL.

man•gle² ['mæŋgəl] *n., v.* **-gled, -gling.** *—n.* **1** a machine for pressing and smoothing cloth by passing it between heated rollers. **2** a wringer.
—v. press with a mangle; put through a mangle. ⟨< Du. *mangel* < MDu. *mange* < LL *manganum* contrivance < Gk.⟩
☛ *Hom.* MANGEL.

man•go ['mæŋgou] *n., pl.* **-goes** or **-gos. 1** a juicy, sweet, usually oval-shaped fruit having a yellow, red, or greenish rind, yellow or orange flesh, and a single large flat seed in the centre. **2** a tropical Asian tree (*Mangifera indica*) of the cashew family that produces this fruit. The tree is widely cultivated throughout the tropics. ⟨< Pg. < Malay < Tamil *mankay*⟩

man•gold ['mæŋgould] *n.* MANGEL-WURZEL.

man•go•nel ['mæŋgə,nɛl] *n.* formerly, a machine used in war for throwing large stones, etc. ⟨ME < OF < VL *manganellum*, dim. of LL *manganum* deceive, contrivance < Gk. *manganon*⟩

man•go•steen ['mæŋgə,stin] *n.* **1** a SE Asian tree (*Garcinia mangostana*) bearing edible fruit. **2** the fruit of this tree, having a hard, reddish skin and sweet, juicy, whitish pulp. ⟨< Malay *mangustan*⟩

man•grove ['mæŋgrouv] *n.* **1** any of a genus (*Rhizophora*) of tropical evergreen trees or shrubs that grow in salt marshes and along coasts, having proplike roots that grow down from the branches, intertwining to form dense thickets. **2** any of various unrelated trees or shrubs with similar habits. ⟨< Sp. *mangle* < Malay *manggi-manggi*; influenced by *grove*⟩

man•gy ['meindʒi] *adj.* **-gi•er, -gi•est. 1** affected with or caused by the mange: *a mangy dog.* **2** shabby, dirty, scruffy, etc.: *a mangy old rug.* **3** contemptible. **—'man•gi•ness,** *n.* **—'man•gi•ly,** *adv.*

man•han•dle ['mæn,hændəl] *v.* **-dled, -dling. 1** treat roughly; pull or push about. **2** move by human strength without mechanical appliances.

Man•hat•tan [mæn'hætən] *n.* **1** Manhattan Island, an island in the Hudson River, on which much of New York City stands. **2** an American Indian people formerly living on Manhattan Island. **3** the Algonquian language of these people. **4** a cocktail made of vermouth, rye whisky, and bitters.

man•hole ['mæn,houl] *n.* a hole through which a worker may enter a sewer, steam boiler, etc.

man•hood ['mænhʊd] *n.* **1** the condition or time of being a man. **2** courage; manliness. **3** men as a group: *the manhood of Canada.*

man–hour ['mæn ,aʊr] *n.* an hour of work done by one person, used as a time unit in industry.

man•hunt ['mæn,hʌnt] *n.* an organized hunt for a criminal, escaped convict, etc.

ma•ni•a ['meiniə] *n.* **1** a form or phase of mental disorder characterized by extremes of joy or rage, uncontrolled and often violent activity, extravagant and irregular speech, etc., often followed by depression, as in manic-depressive psychosis. **2** an excessive fondness or enthusiasm; obsession or craze: *a mania for ice cream.* ⟨< L < Gk. *mania* madness⟩

-mania *combining form.* mania: *megalomania, Beatlemania.*

ma•ni•ac ['meini,æk] *n.* **1** a person who behaves in a wild, disorderly, or irresponsible way: *That driver is a maniac.* **2** a person who has an excessive fondness for something.

ma•ni•a•cal [mə'naɪəkəl] *adj.* **1** having to do with, characteristic of, or affected with mania. **2** like or characteristic of a maniac; frenzied or frantic. **—ma'ni•a•cal•ly,** *adv.*

man•ic ['mænɪk] *or* ['meinɪk] *adj., n. —adj.* of, designating, or affected with mania.
—n. a person affected with mania.

man•ic–de•pres•sive ['mænɪk dɪ'prɛsɪv] *adj., n. —adj.* designating a psychosis characterized by periods of extreme confidence, excitement, activity, etc. alternating with deep depression.
—n. a person affected with manic-depressive psychosis.

ma•ni•cot•ti [,mænə'kɒti] *n.* an Italian dish consisting of noodles stuffed with cheese and baked in a tomato sauce.

man•i•cure ['mænə,kjʊr] *v.* **-cured, -cur•ing;** *n. —v.* **1** care for (the fingernails and hands); especially, trim, clean, and polish (the fingernails). **2** trim closely and evenly: *to manicure a lawn.* **3** give a manicure to.
—n. a treatment for the hands and fingernails: *He made an appointment for a manicure at the salon.* ⟨< F < L *manus* hand + *cura* care⟩

man•i•cur•ist ['mænə,kjʊrɪst] *n.* a person whose work is to provide manicures.

man•i•fest ['mænə,fɛst] *adj., v., n. —adj.* clear to the eye or the mind; obvious: *The thief left so many clues that her guilt was manifest.*
—v. **1** show plainly; reveal; display. **2** prove; put beyond doubt. **3 a** record (an item) in a ship's manifest. **b** present the manifest of (a ship's cargo).
—n. **1** a list of a ship's cargo. **2** a list of passengers, freight, etc. on an airplane flight. **3** BILL OF LADING. ⟨< L *manifestus* palpable, near at hand; ult. < *manus* hand⟩ **—'man•i,fest•ly,** *adv.* **—'man•i,fest•ness,** *n.*

man•i•fes•ta•tion [,mænəfɛs'teiʃən] *n.* **1** a manifesting or being manifested. **2** something that manifests: *A brave deed is a manifestation of courage.* **3** a public demonstration. **4** the occurrence or occasion of a spiritualistic materialization: *No manifestation occurred at the first séance.*

man•i•fes•to [,mænə'fɛstou] *n., pl.* **-toes.** a public declaration of intentions, purposes, or motives by a person or group; proclamation. ⟨< Ital.; see MANIFEST⟩

man•i•fold ['mænə,fould] *adj., n., v. —adj.* **1** of many kinds; many and various: *manifold duties.* **2** having many parts or forms: *The hero was praised for his manifold goodness.* **3** doing many things at the same time.
—n. **1** a pipe or chamber having several openings for connection with other pipes. **2** a pipe in an internal-combustion engine, connecting the cylinders with a main inlet or outlet. **3** one of many copies.
—v. **1** make many copies of. **2** make manifold; multiply. ⟨OE *manigfeald*⟩

man•i•kin ['mænəkɪn] *n.* **1** a little man; dwarf. **2** mannequin. **3** an anatomical model of the human body, used in medical or art classes. Also, **mannikin.** ⟨< Du. *manneken*, dim. of *man* man⟩
☛ *Hom.* MANAKIN, MANNEQUIN.

ma•nil•a or **ma•nil•la** [mə'nɪlə] *n.* **1** MANILA HEMP. **2** MANILA PAPER. **3** MANILA ROPE. **4** (*adjl.*) made from manila paper or hemp: *a manila envelope.* ⟨< *Manila*, the capital of the Philippines⟩

Manila hemp a strong fibre made from the leafstalks of the abaca, used for making rope and fabrics.

Manila paper a strong, brown or brownish yellow wrapping paper, made originally from Manila hemp.

Manila rope a strong rope made from Manila hemp.

man in the street *Informal.* the average person.

man•i•oc ['mæni,ɒk] *or* ['meini,ɒk] *n.* cassava. ⟨< Sp., Pg. < Tupi-Guarani *manioca*⟩

ma•ni•ple ['mænəpəl] *n.* a division of a Roman legion, usually made up of 60 to 120 men. ⟨< Med.L *manipulus* < L, infantry company, literally, handful (*manus* hand + *-pulus* full)⟩ **—ma'nip•u•lar,** *adj., n.*

ma•nip•u•late [mə'nɪpjə,leit] *v.* **-lat•ed, -lat•ing. 1** handle or treat skilfully; handle: *The driver of an automobile manipulates levers and pedals.* **2** manage by clever use of personal influence, especially unfair influence: *She so manipulated the ball team that she was elected captain.* **3** change for one's own purpose or advantage: *The bookkeeper manipulated the company's accounts to* *cover up his theft.* ⟨back formation < *manipulation*⟩ **—ma'nip•u,la•tor,** *n.* **—ma'nip•u,lat•a•ble** or **ma'nip•u•la•ble,** *adj.*

ma•nip•u•la•tion [mə,nɪpjə'leiʃən] *n.* **1** skilful handling or treatment. **2** clever use of influence. **3** a clever or unfair change made for one's own purpose or advantage. ⟨< F, ult. < L *manipulus* handful < *manus* hand + root of *plere* to fill⟩

ma•nip•u•la•tive [mə'nɪpjələtɪv] *or* [mə'nɪpjə,leitɪv] *adj., n.* *—adj.* **1** of or having to do with manipulation. **2** done by manipulation. **3** tending to manipulate others.
—n., pl. **manipulatives.** *Education.* small items such as blocks, cards, and counters, which children can use to develop their reasoning skills.

man•i•to ['mænə,tou] *n., pl.* **-tos.** *Cdn.* manitou.

Man•i•to•ba [,mænə'toubə] *n.* a western province of Canada.

Manitoba fever *Cdn.* formerly, in the early 1880s, the excitement in western Canada which led to extensive migration to the newly opened-up province of Manitoba.

Manitoba maple *Cdn.* a medium-sized maple (*Acer negundo*) common on the Prairies, the only Canadian maple normally having compound leaves; box elder.

Man•i•to•ban [,mænə'toubən] *n., adj.* *—n.* a native or long-term resident of Manitoba.
—adj. of or having to do with Manitoba.

man•i•tou or **man•i•tu** ['mænə,tu] *n.* in the traditional religion of the Algonquian peoples: **1** any of the spirits representing the power that dwells within all things in nature, both weak and strong, and having both good and evil influence. **2** *Cdn.* Often, **Manitou,** the impersonal supreme being or supernatural force, author of life and all things; the chief of the manitous, called **gitche** (or **kitshe**) **manitou,** often translated as 'the Great Spirit'. ⟨< Algonquian⟩

man•kind [,mæn'kaɪnd] *for 1;* ['mæn,kaɪnd] *for 2; n.* **1** the human race; all human beings. **2** men collectively, as opposed to women.

man•like ['mæn,ləik] *adj.* **1** of an animal, having characteristics of a human being: *The chimpanzee is the most manlike of the apes.* **2** like or characteristic of a man or men. **3** suitable for a man; masculine.

man•ly ['mænli] *adj.* **-li•er, -li•est. 1** like a man; as a man should be; possessing qualities attributable to a man. **2** suitable for a man; masculine. **—'man•li•ness,** *n.*
☛ *Syn.* **1.** See note at MALE.

man–made ['mæn 'meid] *adj.* made by people; not occurring naturally; artificial or synthetic: *Nylon is a man-made fibre.*

man•na ['mænə] *n.* **1** in the Bible, the food that miraculously fell from heaven to the Israelites when they were starving in the wilderness. **2** the secretion from the ash tree (*Fraxinus ornus*), once used as a laxative. **3** food for the soul. **4** a much-needed thing that is unexpectedly supplied. ⟨ME < LL < Gk. < Hebrew *man* what?⟩

man•ne•quin ['mænəkɪn] *n.* **1** a model of a human figure, used by artists, tailors, stores, etc.: *Many clothing stores use mannequins for their window displays.* **2** a woman whose work is modelling clothes for designers, retail stores, etc. ⟨< F < Du. *manneken.* See MANIKIN.⟩
☛ *Hom.* MANIKIN, MANAKIN.

man•ner ['mænər] *n.* **1** the way something happens or is done: *The trouble arose in a curious manner.* **2** a way of acting or behaving: *She has a kind manner.* **3** a style or fashion: *He dresses in a strange manner.* **4** kind or kinds: *We saw all manner of birds in the forest. What manner of person was he?* **5 manners,** *pl.* **a** ways or customs: *Books and movies show us the manners of other times and places.* **b** ways of behaving toward others: *bad manners.* **c** polite behaviour: *It is nice to see a child with manners.*
by all manner of means, most certainly.
by no manner of means, not at all; under no circumstances.
in a manner of speaking, as one might say; in a way; so to speak.
to the manner born, a accustomed since birth to some way or condition, usually wealthy. **b** naturally suited to some activity. ⟨ME < AF *manere* < L *manuaria,* fem. of *manuarius* belonging to the hand, ult. < *manus* hand⟩
☛ *Hom.* MANOR.
☛ *Syn.* **1.** See note at WAY.

man•nered ['mænərd] *adj.* **1** having manners of a certain kind: *a well-mannered child.* **2** affected; artificial; having many mannerisms.

man•ner•ism ['mænə,rɪzəm] *n.* **1** too much use of some manner in speaking, writing, or behaving. **2** an odd little trick; an idiosyncratic habit; a peculiar way of acting. **3 Mannerism,** a style in art and architecture developed in Europe during the late 16th century, marked by the use of distortion and exaggeration as a conscious revolt against the classical principles of the Renaissance.

man•ner•ist ['mænərɪst] *n.* **1** a person given to mannerisms. **2** Often, **Mannerist,** an artist whose work is characterized by Mannerism. **—,man•ner'is•tic,** *adj.* **—,man•ner'is•ti•cal•ly,** *adv.*

man•ner•less ['mænərlɪs] *adj.* having bad manners. **—'man•ner•less•ness,** *n.*

man•ner•ly ['mænərli] *adj., adv.* *—adj.* having or showing good manners; polite.
—adv. politely. **—'man•ner•li•ness,** *n.*

man•ni•kin ['mænəkɪn] *n.* See MANIKIN.
☛ *Hom.* MANAKIN, MANNEQUIN.

man•nish ['mænɪʃ] *adj.* **1** peculiar to a man: *a mannish way of holding a baby.* **2** of women, their clothes or manners, generally associated with a man rather than a woman: *She has a mannish style of dress.* **—'man•nish•ly,** *adv.* **—'man•nish•ness,** *n.*

man•ni•tol ['mænə,tɒl] *n.* **1** a dietary supplement; an alcohol. *Formula*: $C_6H_8(OH)_6$ **2** a diuretic drug.

ma•noeu•vre [mə'nuvər] *n., v.* **-vred, -vring.** *—n.* **1** a planned movement of troops or warships: *The army practises warfare by holding manoeuvres.* **2** a skilful plan or movement; clever trick: *Her superior manoeuvres won the game.*
—v. **1** perform manoeuvres. **2** cause to perform manoeuvres. **3** plan skilfully; use clever tricks; scheme: *He is always manoeuvring to gain some advantage over others.* **4** force by skilful plans; get by clever tricks: *She manoeuvred her mother into letting her have a party.* **5** move or manipulate skilfully: *She manoeuvred her car through the heavy traffic with ease.* Also, **maneuver.** ⟨< F *manoeuvre,* ult. < L *manu operare* work by hand⟩ **—ma'noeuv•ra•ble,** *adj.* **—ma,noeuv•ra'bil•i•ty,** *n.*

Man of Galilee Jesus.

man of God 1 a holy man; saint; prophet. **2** clergyman.

man of letters 1 writer. **2** a man who has a wide knowledge of literature.

man of straw STRAW MAN.

man of the world a man who has a wide experience of different kinds of people and customs; a sophisticated and worldly-wise or practical man.

man–of–war [,mæn əv 'wɔr] *n., pl.* **men-of-war. 1** warship. **2 Portuguese man-of-war,** a stinging jellyfish of the genus *Physalia*.

man–of–war bird FRIGATE BIRD.

ma•nom•e•ter [mə'nɒmətər] *n.* an instrument for measuring the pressure of gases or liquids. ⟨< F < Gk. *manos* thin + *metron* measure⟩

man•o•met•ric [,mænə'metrɪk] *adj.* **1** having to do with a manometer. **2** having to do with the measurement of gas pressures. Also, **manometrical. —,man•o'met•ri•cal•ly,** *adv.* **—ma'nom•e•try,** *n.*

man•or ['mænər] *n.* **1** in the Middle Ages, a feudal estate, part of which was set aside for the lord and the rest divided among his peasants. If the lord sold his manor, the peasants or serfs were sold with it. **2** a large holding of land. **3** a large house on an estate, especially a manor house. ⟨ME < AF *maner* < L *manere* stay⟩
☛ *Hom.* MANNER.

manor house the house of the owner of a manor.

ma•no•ri•al [mə'nɔriəl] *adj.* of, having to do with, or forming a manor.

man–o'–war bird See FRIGATE BIRD.

man•pow•er ['mæn,paʊər] *n.* **1** the power supplied by human physical work. **2** strength thought of in terms of the number of persons needed or available for service in a particular region, for a particular type of work, etc. **3 Manpower,** *Informal.* the Canadian federal labour exchange.

man•qué [mɑŋ'kei]; *French,* [mɑ̃'ke] *adj. French.* frustrated or unfulfilled; that might have been (*used only after a noun*): *a novelist manqué teaching creative writing courses.* ⟨< F, pp. of *manquer* to miss; to be lacking⟩

man•rope ['mæn,roup] *n. Nautical.* on a ship, a rope used as a rail for support on a ladder.

man•sard ['mænsɑrd] *or* ['mænsərd] *n.* **1** a four-sided roof having two slopes on each side, with the lower much steeper than the upper. See ROOF for picture. **2** the upper storey formed by the lower slope of a mansard roof. ⟨< F *mansarde,* named after François *Mansard* (1598-1666), a French architect⟩

man•sard•ed ['mænsɑrdɪd] *adj.* of a roof, built with two slopes on each of four sides.

manse [mæns] *n.* a minister's house; parsonage. ⟨ME < Med.L *mansa* dwelling, n. use of fem. pp. of L *manere* stay⟩

man•serv•ant ['mæn,sɜrvənt] *n., pl.* **men•serv•ants.** a male servant.

man•sion ['mænʃən] *n.* **1** a large, stately house. **2** *Oriental and medieval astronomy.* any of the 28 divisions of the moon's monthly course. ⟨ME < OF < L *mansio, -onis* < *manere* stay⟩

man–sized ['mæn ,saɪzd] *adj.* **1** suited to a man; large: *a man-sized meal.* **2** *Informal.* requiring the strength, skill, judgment, etc. of a mature man: *a man-sized problem.*

man•slaugh•ter ['mæn,slɒtər] *n.* **1** *Law.* the unlawful killing of another human being accidentally or without malice or premeditation. The driver of a car that accidentally hits and kills a pedestrian while the pedestrian has the right of way may be charged with manslaughter. **2** the killing of a human being or human beings.

man•sue•tude ['mænswə,tjud] *or* ['mænswə,tud] *n.* gentleness in behaviour. ⟨ME < L *mansuētūdō* tameness, mildness; ult. < *manus* hand + *suetus, suescēre* to grow accustomed⟩

man•ta ['mæntə] *n.* devilfish. Also called **manta ray.**

man•teau ['mæntou]; *French,* ['mɑ̃'to] *n. Obsolete.* a loose cloak.

man•tel ['mæntəl] *n.* **1** a shelf above a fireplace. See FIREPLACE for picture. **2** (*adjl.*) designed to rest on a mantel or similar surface: *a mantel radio.* **3** a decorative facing above and around a fireplace: *a mantel of tile.* ⟨var. of *mantle*⟩
☛ *Hom.* MANTLE.

man•tel•et ['mæntə,lɛt] *or* ['mæntəlɪt] *n.* **1** a short mantle or cape. **2** formerly, a large movable shelter, shield, or screen, used in war to protect soldiers firing a gun. ⟨ME < MF. See MANTLE.⟩

man•tel•piece ['mæntəl,pis] *n.* **1** a shelf above a fireplace. **2** MANTEL (def. 3).

man•tic ['mæntɪk] *adj.* prophetic. ⟨< Gk. *mantikós* of or for a soothsayer, prophetic < *mantis* prophet⟩

man•tid ['mæntɪd] *n.* mantis.

man•til•la [mæn'tɪlə] *or* [mæn'tiə]; *Spanish,* [man'tija] *n.* **1** a light scarf of lace, silk, etc. covering the hair and shoulders, worn especially by Spanish and Mexican women. **2** a short mantle or cape. ⟨< Sp. < L *mantellum* mantle⟩

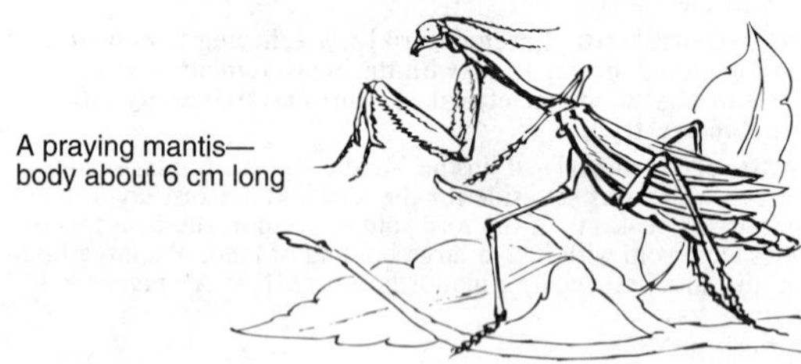
A praying mantis—body about 6 cm long

man•tis ['mæntɪs] *n., pl.* **-tis•es** or **-tes** [-'tiz]. any of a large family (Mantidae) of slow-moving, carnivorous, winged insects of tropical and warm temperate regions, having a long, slender, typically green body and having the habit of remaining still with their foremost pair of legs raised, suggesting a praying position. ⟨< NL use of Gk. *mantis* prophet (from its praying posture)⟩

man•tis•sa [mæn'tɪsə] *n. Mathematics.* the decimal part of a logarithm. In the logarithm 2.954 24, the characteristic is 2 and the mantissa is .954 24. ⟨< L *mantissa* addition < Etruscan⟩

mantis shrimp a burrowing crustacean, the squilla.

man•tle ['mæntəl] *n., v.* **-tled, -tling.** *—n.* **1** a loose cloak without sleeves. **2** anything that covers or conceals like a mantle: *The ground had a mantle of snow.* **3** *Geology.* the part of the earth's interior between the crust and the core, beginning at about 8 to 35 km from the surface and extending to a depth of about 2880 km and composed of very dense, solid rock believed to consist mainly of silicates of iron and magnesium. See CORE for picture. **4** a netlike sheath fixed around the flame of a gas lamp, made of a substance that glows with an intense white light when it becomes hot. **5** the plumage on the back and folded wings of a bird, especially when of a different colour from the rest of the plumage.
—v. **1** clothe, cover, or conceal with or as if with a mantle: *mantled in a heavy fur coat, mountaintops mantled with snow, jealousy mantled in an outward friendliness.* **2** become covered with a coating or scum: *The pond was mantled.* **3** redden; blush: *His cheeks mantled.* ⟨OE *mæntel* < L *mantellum* < L *mantellum* < *mantum* cloak⟩
☛ *Hom.* MANTEL.

mantle rock loose rock.

man–to–man ['mæn tə 'mæn] *adj., adv.* *—adj.* **1** honest; sincere; straightforward: *a man-to-man talk.* **2** *Sports.* referring to a defence system in which players do not guard zones but cover individual opponents.
—adv. honestly; sincerely.

man•tra ['mæntrə] *or* ['mɑntrə] *n. Hinduism or Buddhism.* **1** any of the metrical hymns of praise in the Veda. **2** a sacred word or formula used for incantation or meditation. ⟨< Skt., literally, instrument of thought, ult. < *man* to think. 19c.⟩

man•tu•a ['mæntʃuə] *n.* **1** a loose gown or cloak formerly worn by women. **2** mantle. ⟨< *Mantua,* a town in Italy⟩

man•u•al ['mænjuəl] *adj., n.* *—adj.* **1** of, having to do with, or using the hands: *manual labour. She has great manual dexterity.* **2** done or operated by hand, not automatically: *The car has a manual choke.* **3** lacking an external power source such as electricity: *a manual typewriter.*
—n. **1** a book that helps its readers to understand or use something; handbook. **2** an organ keyboard played with the hands. ⟨< L *manualis* < *manus* hand⟩ **—'man•u•al•ly,** *adv.*

manual training training in work done with the hands, especially in making things out of wood, metal, or plastic.

manual transmission a transmission in a motor vehicle in which the driver has control over changing gears.

ma•nu•bri•um [mə'njubriəm] *or* [mə'nubriəm] *n., pl.* **-bri•a** [-briə] or **-bri•ums.** *Anatomy, zoology.* a bone shaped like a handle. ⟨< NL < L, a handle < *manus* hand⟩ **—ma'nu•bri•al,** *adj.*

man•u•fac•to•ry [,mænjə'fæktəri] *n., pl.* **-ries.** *Archaic.* a factory.

man•u•fac•ture [,mænjə'fæktʃər] *v.* **-tured, -tur•ing;** *n.* *—v.* **1** make by hand or by machine: *This factory manufactures outboard motors.* **2** make into something useful: *Iron is manufactured into steel.* **3** invent; make up: *The dishonest lawyer manufactured evidence.*
—n. **1** the act of manufacturing. **2** the thing manufactured. ⟨< F < Med.L *manufactura* < L *manu facere* make by hand⟩

man•u•fac•tur•er [,mænjə'fæktʃərər] *n.* a person or company whose business is manufacturing; owner of a factory.

man•u•mis•sion [,mænjə'mɪʃən] *n.* a freeing or being freed from slavery. ⟨< L *manumissio, -onis* < *manu mittere.* See MANUMIT.⟩

man•u•mit [,mænjə'mɪt] *v.* **-mit•ted, -mit•ting.** set free from slavery. ⟨< L *manu mittere* release from control (lit., from the hand)⟩

ma•nure [mə'njʊr] *or* [mə'nʊr] *n., v.* **-nured, -nur•ing.** *—n.* a substance, especially animal waste, put in or on the soil as fertilizer. The dung from a stable is often used as manure.
—v. put manure in or on. ⟨ME < AF *maynoverer* work with the hands < OF *manuevre* hand-work (in F *manoeuvre*). See MANOEUVRE.⟩ **—ma'nur•er,** *n.*

ma•nus ['meinəs] *n., pl.* **ma•nus.** *Anatomy, zoology.* the end of the forelimb in vertebrates; hand, foot, or claw. ⟨ < L *manus* hand⟩

man•u•script ['mænjə,skrɪpt] *n.* **1** a book or paper written by hand or with a typewriter or computer. **2** especially of an unpublished book, article, etc., the condition of being handwritten or typewritten: *His last book was three years in manuscript.* **3** a book, document, etc. written by hand before the introduction of printing. **4** (*adjl.*) of or being a manuscript: *a manuscript version. Abbrev.*: MS., MS, ms., or ms ⟨< Med.L < L *manu scriptus* written by hand⟩

man•wise ['mæn,waɪz] *adv.* in the manner of a man.

Manx [mæŋks] *adj.* of or having to do with the Isle of Man, its people, or their language.
—n. **1 the Manx,** *pl.* the people of the Isle of Man. **2** the Celtic language of the Manx, now extinct.

Manx cat a breed of domestic cat that is tailless and has a thick undercoat and a longer-haired outer coat.

Manx•man ['mæŋksmən] *n., pl.* **-men.** a native or inhabitant of the Isle of Man.

Manx•wo•man ['mæŋks,wʊmən] *n., pl.* **-wom•en.** a female native or inhabitant of the Isle of Man.

man•y ['mɛni] *adj.* **more, most;** *n. —adj.* in great number; numerous: *many years ago. Many people have said so.*
one too many for, more than a match for.
—n. a large number of people or things: *There were many at the fair.*
a good many, a fairly large number.
a great many, a very large number.
the many, a most people. **b** the common people. ⟨OE *manig*⟩

man•y•plies ['mɛni,plaɪz] *n. Zoology.* the third stomach of a cow or other ruminant; omasum (*used with a singular verb*). ⟨< *many* + *plies*, pl. of *ply*, n.⟩

man•y–sid•ed ['mɛni 'saɪdɪd] *adj.* **1** having many sides. **2** having many interests or abilities.

man•za•nil•la [,mænzə'niljə], [,mænzə'niə], *or* [,mænzə'nɪlə]; *Spanish* [,manzə'nijə] a very dry sherry originating in Spain. ⟨< Sp., camomile⟩

man•za•ni•ta [,mænzə'nitə] *n.* any of several evergreen shrubs and trees (genus *Arctostaphylos*) of the heath family that are native to the Pacific coastal areas of North America. ⟨< Sp. *manzanita*, dim. of *manzana* apple⟩

Mao•ism ['maʊɪzəm] *n.* Marxism-Leninism as interpreted and developed by Mao Tse-tung (1893-1976) and practised in the People's Republic of China during his leadership, from 1949 until his death.

Mao•ist ['maʊɪst] *n., adj. —n.* a follower of Mao Tse-tung. *—adj.* of or having to do with Maoism or Maoists.

Mao jacket [maʊ] *n.* a blue or grey jacket cut like a shirt, having many pockets and a stand-up collar, as worn by Mao Tse-tung.

Ma•o•ri ['maʊri] *or* ['mɑouri] *n., pl.* **-ris;** *adj. —n.* **1** a member of a Polynesian people of New Zealand. **2** the Polynesian language of the Maoris.
—adj. of or having to do with the Maoris or their language.

map [mæp] *n., v.* **mapped, map•ping.** *—n.* **1** a drawing representing the earth's surface or part of it, usually showing countries, cities, rivers, seas, lakes, mountains, and roads. **2** a drawing representing part of the sky, showing the position of the stars. **3** a maplike drawing of anything: *a highway map, a road map.* See also GENE MAP, LINKAGE MAP.
off the map, *Informal.* of no importance; of no account.
put on the map, *Informal.* give prominence to; make well-known.
—v. **1** make a map of; show on a map. **2** plan; arrange in detail: *to map out the week's work.* **3** transfer, represent, etc., by or as if by a mathematical transformation. ⟨< Med.L *mappa mundi* map of the world; special use of < L *mappa* napkin⟩
☛ *Syn.* **Map,** CHART, ATLAS = a drawing representing a surface or area. A **map** may refer especially to a plan of roads or other routes on land, while **chart** is used especially for plans showing air or sea routes. An ATLAS is a book of maps covering a large area or the whole world.

ma•phen•ide ['mæfə,naɪd] *n.* See MAFENIDE.

ma•ple ['meipəl] *n.* **1** any of a large genus (*Acer*) of trees and shrubs found throughout the north temperate regions of the world, having usually lobed leaves that grow in opposite pairs and dry fruits with normally two winglike extensions, each containing a seed. Two of the most common Canadian maples are the sugar maple and the Manitoba maple. **2** the light-coloured, hard, close-grained wood of certain maples, valued for making furniture, flooring, etc. **3** (*adjl.*) made of maple wood. **4** (*adjl.*) designating a family (Aceraceae) of trees and shrubs consisting of the maples and several trees of central and southern China. All the trees of the maple family have winged seeds. **5** (*adjl.*) made of or flavoured with maple sugar or syrup: *maple ice cream, maple candy.* ⟨OE *mapeltrēow* maple tree⟩ **—'ma•ple,like,** *adj.*

Maple

maple bush *Cdn.* a grove of sugar maple trees.

maple cake *Cdn.* a block or mould of maple sugar.

maple camp *Cdn.* the place in a sugar bush where sugaring-off takes place, including the building and equipment.

maple candy *Cdn.* candy made from maple sap.

maple leaf 1 a leaf of the maple tree. **2** this leaf as a Canadian emblem. A red maple leaf on a white background is in the centre of the Canadian flag.

Maple Leaf (flag) *Cdn.* the flag of Canada.

maple producer *Cdn.* a person who operates a sugar bush, producing maple sugar and maple syrup.

maple sugar *Cdn.* sugar made from the sap of the sugar maple.

maple syrup *Cdn.* syrup made from the sap of the sugar maple.

ma•quette [mæ'kɛt] *or* [mə'kɛt] *n.* a sculptor's or architect's small model of a planned project. ⟨< F < Ital. *macchietta* a little sketch, dim. of *macchia* < *macchiare* to sketch < L *maculare* to stain < *macula* a spot⟩

ma•quis [mɑ'ki]; *French,* [ma'ki] *n., pl.* **-quis** [-ki]. **1 a** scrubby bush consisting mainly of low-growing evergreens such as myrtle, heath, and ilex, found on islands and along the coast of the Mediterranean. **b** an area or region characterized by such vegetation. **2** Usually, **Maquis, a** the French underground resistance movement against the Germans in World War II. **b** a member of, or a guerrilla fighter in, this movement. **c** (*adjl.*) of or having to do with the Maquis or their tactics. ⟨< F < *maquis* bushy land < Ital. *macchia* thicket; with reference to the cover bandits take in bushy regions⟩

mar [mɑr] *v.* **marred, mar•ring.** spoil the beauty of; damage; injure. ⟨OE *merran* waste⟩

mar. 1 married. **2** marine. **3** maritime.

Mar. March.

mar•a•bou ['mærə,bu] *or* ['mɛrə,bu] *n.* **1** a large black-and-white stork (*Leptoptilos crumeniferus*) of Africa that feeds mainly on carrion and refuse. **2** a furlike trimming made from the soft, downy feathers of marabous or, sometimes, of other birds. ⟨< F *marabout*⟩

mar•a•bout ['mærə,but] *or* ['mærə,bu], ['mɛrə,but] *or* ['mɛrə,bu] *n. Islam.* **1** a holy man or hermit, especially in N Africa. **2** a shrine or tomb of a holy man. ⟨< F < Pg. *marabuto* < Arabic *murabit*⟩ **—'mar•a,bout•ism,** *n.*

ma•ra•ca [mə'rɑkə] *or* [mə'rækə] *n.* a percussion instrument resembling a rattle, consisting of a gourd or gourd-shaped body containing seeds or pebbles and attached to a handle, usually played in pairs. ⟨< Pg. < Tupi⟩

ma•ras•ca [mə'ræskə] *n.* **1** a European tree (*Prunus cerasus marasca*) bearing bitter, red cherries from which maraschino is made. **2** the cherry. ⟨< Ital., var. of *amarasca* < *amaro* < L *amārus* bitter⟩

mar•a•schi•no [,mærə'ʃinou] *or* [,mɛrə'ʃinou], [,mærə'skinou] *or* [,mɛrə'skinou] *n.* a strong, sweet liqueur made from marasca cherries. ⟨< Ital. See MARASCA.⟩

maraschino cherries cherries preserved in a syrup flavoured with or similar to maraschino.

ma•ras•mus [mə'ræzməs] *n. Pathology.* a wasting away of the body because of failure to assimilate food. ⟨< NL < Gk. *marasmos* a wasting away < *marainein* to weaken⟩
—ma'ras•moid, *adj.*

Ma•ra•tha [mə'rɑtə] *n.* a Seytho-Dravidian people of SW India.

Ma•ra•thi [mə'rɑti] *n.* the Indic language of the Maratha.

mar•a•thon ['mærə,θɒn] *or* ['mɛrə,θɒn] *n.* **1** a long-distance foot race, officially measured at 42.195 km. It is an Olympic event. **2** any long-distance race or endurance contest: *a marathon swim, a dance marathon.* ⟨< *Marathon*, where the Greeks defeated the Persians in 490 B.C. A Greek messenger ran 37 km from Marathon to Athens to bring news of the victory. The official distance for the Olympic marathon is from a decision by the British Olympic Committee at the 1908 London Games to make the race the distance from Windsor Castle to the royal box at the London Stadium.⟩

ma•raud [mə'rɒd] *v.* go about in search of plunder; make raids for booty. ⟨< F *marauder* < *maraud* rascal⟩
—ma'raud•er, *n.*

mar•ble ['mɑrbəl] *n., v.* **-bled, -bling.** *—n.* **1** a hard, crystallized, metamorphic limestone that may be white, coloured, or mottled or streaked, and that is capable of taking a high polish. It is extensively used for sculpture and building. **2** something made of marble, especially a sculpture. **3** (*adjl.*)

made of marble: *a marble statue.* **4** (*adjl.*) resembling marble; white, hard, cold, streaked, mottled, or unfeeling: *a marble heart, a marble cake.* **5** a small ball of glass, clay, stone, etc. used in games. **6 marbles,** a game played with such little balls (used with a singular verb). **7 marbles,** *pl. Slang.* wits, common sense, or brains: *to lose one's marbles. He seems quite nice, but I don't think he's got all his marbles.*
—*v.* colour in imitation of the patterns in marble: *Binders marble the edges of some books.* ⟨ME < OF *marbre* < L *marmor* < Gk. *marmaros* gleaming stone⟩ **—'mar•ble,like,** *adj.*

marble cake a cake made by mixing dark and light batters in streaks, giving a marblelike appearance when cooked.

mar•ca•site ['mɑrkə,sɔit] *n.* **1** a native iron disulphide, white iron pyrites, similar to and of the same composition as ordinary pyrites. Marcasite is often used in jewellery. *Formula*: FeS_2 **2** a piece of jewellery made from this material. ⟨< Med.L *marcasita* < Arabic *marqashita* < Aramaic⟩ **—,mar•ca'sit•i•cal** [,mɑrkə'sɪtɪkəl], *adj.*

mar•cel [mɑr'sɛl] *n., v.* **-celled, -cel•ling.** —*n.* a series of regular waves put in the hair, a popular style in the 1920s.
—*v.* put a series of regular waves in (the hair). ⟨after *Marcel* Grateau (1852-1936), the French hairdresser who originated it⟩ **—mar'cel•ler,** *n.*

mar•ces•cent [mɑr'sɛsənt] *adj. Botany.* of buds and blossoms, withering but not fallen. ⟨< L *marcescent, marcēscens, marcēre* to wither⟩

march[1] [mɑrtʃ] *v., n.* —*v.* **1** walk as soldiers do, in time and with steps of the same length. **2** walk or proceed steadily. **3** cause to march or go: *The police officer marched the thief off to jail.* **4** advance or progress inexorably.
—*n.* **1** the movement of troops: *The army is prepared for the march.* **2** the act or fact of marching. **3** *Music.* **a** a composition to march to, having a regular, strongly accented metre, usually in 4/4 time. **b** any composition or part of a composition having similar characteristics: *She enjoyed listening to marches.* **4** the distance marched. **5** a long, hard walk. **6** a demonstration or protest made by walking. **7** inexorable advance or progress: *History records the march of events.*
on the march, moving forward; advancing inexorably.
steal a march on, gain an advantage over without being noticed. ⟨< OF *marchier* to tread < origin uncertain⟩ **—'march•er,** *n.*

march[2] [mɑrtʃ] *n.* **1** the land along the border of a country; frontier. **2 the Marches,** *pl.* the districts along the border between England and Scotland, or between England and Wales. ⟨ME *marche*, OE *gemearc gemierce* boundary + OF *marche* < Gmc.; cf. Gothic *marka* boundary⟩

March [mɑrtʃ] *n.* the third month of the year. It has 31 days. ⟨ME < OF *marche* < L *Martius* (month) of Mars⟩

March brown **1** a striped mayfly (*Ecdyurus venosus*). **2** an angler's fly made to resemble this fly.

mar•che•sa [mɑr'keizə] *n., pl.* **mar•che•se** [-zi]. the wife or widow of a marchese.

mar•che•se [mɑr'keizei] *n., pl.* **mar•che•si** [-zi]. an Italian noble ranking above a count and below a prince. ⟨< Ital.⟩

marching orders a command to move on or to leave.

mar•chion•ess ['mɑrʃənɪs] *or* [,mɑrʃə'nɛs] *n.* **1** the wife or widow of a marquis. **2** a woman with a rank equal to that of a marquis. ⟨< Med.L *marchionissa* < *marchio* marquis < *marcha, marca* march[2] < Gmc.⟩

march•pane ['mɑrtʃ,pein] *n.* marzipan.

march•past ['mɑrtʃ,pæst] *n.* a display, especially a military parade, in which troops, etc. march past a reviewing stand.

Mar•cion•ism ['mɑrʃə,nɪzəm] *n.* a Gnostic movement of the 2nd and 3rd centuries A.D. that rejected the Old Testament. **—'Mar•cion•ist** or **'Mar•cion,ite,** *n.*

Mar•co•ni rig [mɑr'kouni] *Nautical.* a fore-and-aft rig used in racing vessels. ⟨< Guglielmo *Marconi* (1874-1937), inventor of wireless telegraphy, because of its physical resemblance to the device⟩

Mar•di Gras ['mɑrdi 'grɑ] **1** the last day before Lent; Shrove Tuesday. **2** a traditional public carnival celebrating this day, especially in New Orleans. ⟨< F *mardi gras* fat (that is, meat-eating) Tuesday⟩

mare[1] [mɛr] *n.* a fully mature female horse, donkey, etc. ⟨OE *mere*⟩
☛ *Hom.* MAYOR.

mare[2] ['mɑrei] *or* ['mɛrei] *n., pl.* **ma•ri•a** ['mɑriə] *or* ['mɛriə]. *Astronomy.* one of the dark areas on the moon and Mars, thought by Galileo to be seas. ⟨< L *mare* sea⟩

mare clausum ['mɑrei 'klaʊsəm] *Latin.* a body of water controlled by one nation for navigational purposes. ⟨< L, closed sea⟩

mare liberum ['mɑrei 'libərəm] *Latin.* a sea that is open to all nations. ⟨< L, free sea⟩

ma•rem•ma [mə'rɛmə] *n., pl.* **-me** [mi]. an area of marsh near the sea. ⟨< Ital. < L *maratima, maratimus* maritime⟩

mare's–nest ['mɛrz ,nɛst] *n.* **1** something supposed to be a great discovery that turns out to be a mistake or joke. **2** *Informal.* a situation that is disordered or confused.

mare's–tail ['mɛrz ,teil] *n.* **1** a water plant (*Hippuris vulgaris*) having tiny flowers and many circles of narrow, hairlike leaves around the stems. **2** horsetail. **3** a long wisp of cirrus cloud.

mar•gar•ic acid [mɑr'gærɪk] *or* [mɑr'gɛrɪk] *Chemistry.* a fatty acid obtained from lichens or made synthetically. *Formula*: $C_{17}H_{34}O_2$ ⟨< Gk. *márgaron* pearl + *-ic*⟩

mar•ga•rine ['mɑrdʒərɪn], ['mɑrdʒə,rin], *or* [,mɑrdʒə'rin] *n.* a compound of vegetable oils, used for cooking or as a spread, often as a substitute for butter. Also, **margarin.** ⟨< F⟩

mar•gar•ite ['mɑrgə,rɔit] *n.* a mineral related to mica, having a translucent lustre, found in sheets of monoclinic crystals. *Formula*: $CaAl_4Si_2O_{10}(OH)_2$ ⟨ME < L < *margarīta* < Gk. *margarítēs, márgaron* pearl + *itēs*⟩

mar•gay ['mɑrgei] *n.* a small wildcat (*Felix wiedii*) rather like an ocelot, native to Brazil and the SW U.S. ⟨< F, alteration of *margaia* < Pg. *maracajá* < Tupi *mbaracaiá*⟩

marge[1] [mɑrdʒ] *n. Archaic.* an edge; border. ⟨< F < L *margō.* See MARGIN.⟩

marge[2] [mɑrdʒ] *n. Informal.* margarine. ⟨shortened form⟩

mar•gin ['mɑrdʒən] *n., v.* —*n.* **1** an edge; border: *the margin of a lake.* **2** the blank space around the writing or printing on a page. **3** the space left at the left-hand side, or sometimes on both sides, by a person writing or keyboarding. **4** an extra amount; amount beyond what is necessary: *We allow a margin of 15 minutes when we want to catch a train.* **5** the difference between the cost and selling price of stocks, etc. **6** *Business.* **a** the money or security deposited with a broker to protect him or her from loss on contracts undertaken for the real buyer or seller. **b** the amount of such a deposit. **c** the transaction itself, financed by both the broker and his or her customer: *When you buy on margin, you put up only part of the total cost and the broker lends you the remainder.* **d** the customer's profit or loss in such a transaction. **7** the point at which an economic activity yields just enough return to cover its costs and below which the activity will result in a loss. **8** a condition beyond which something ceases to exist or be possible; limit: *the margin of subsistence, the margin of consciousness.*
—*v.* **1** provide with a margin. **2** *Business.* **a** deposit a margin upon (stock, etc.). **b** secure by a margin. ⟨ME < L *margo, -ginis* edge⟩

mar•gin•al ['mɑrdʒənəl] *adj.* **1** written or printed in a margin. **2** of or being a margin, edge, or border: *marginal forests.* **3** at, on, or near a margin, border, or limit. **4** barely useful, acceptable, or profitable: *marginal knowledge, marginal land.* **5** minimal; slight. **6** of, having to do with, or obtained from goods produced and marketed so as to barely cover costs. **—,mar•gin'al•i•ty,** *n.*

mar•gi•na•li•a [,mɑrdʒə'neiliə] *or* [,mɑrdʒə'neiljə] *n.pl.* notes written in the margin or margins of a manuscript, book, etc. ⟨< NL, neuter pl. of L *marginalis*⟩

mar•gin•al•ly ['mɑrdʒənəli] *adv.* **1** in the margin. **2** slightly: *She is marginally better today.*

mar•gin•ate ['mɑrdʒə,neit] *v.* **-at•ed, -at•ing.** provide with margins. **—'mar•gin,at•ed,** *adj.* **—,mar•gin'a•tion,** *n.*

mar•grave ['mɑrgreiv] *n.* **1** a German nobleman whose rank corresponds to that of a British marquis. **2** formerly, the title of certain princes of the Holy Roman Empire. Originally, a margrave was a German military governor of a border province. ⟨< MDu. *markgrave* count of the marches⟩

mar•grav•i•ate [mɑr'greiviɪt] *n.* the territory governed by a margrave. Also, **margravate** ['mɑrgrəvɪt].

mar•gra•vine ['mɑrgrə,vin] *n.* the wife or widow of a margrave.

mar•gue•rite [,mɑrgə'rit] *n.* **1** a garden plant (*Chrysanthemum frutescens*) of the composite family having daisylike flowers with white or pale yellow rays around a yellow disk. **2** any of various other composite plants with daisylike flowers, such as the **ox-eye daisy.** ⟨< F, daisy, pearl < L *margarīta* pearl < Gk. See MARGARITE.⟩

ma•ri•a•chi [ˌmɑri'ɑtʃi] *n.* one of a band of strolling musicians in Mexico. ⟨< Mexican Sp.< F *mariage* marriage⟩

Ma•ri•a•nas trench or **trough** [ˌmæri'ænəz] *or* [ˌmɛri'ænəz] a depression in the floor of the Pacific Ocean SE of the Marianas, a chain of islands in the western Pacific.

mar•i•gold ['mærɪˌgould] *or* ['mɛrɪˌgould] *n.* **1** any of various plants (genus *Tagetes*) of the composite family native to tropical and subtropical America that are widely cultivated for their showy yellow, orange, or red flowers. **2** any of various other yellow-flowered plants, such as the **pot marigold** or **marsh marigold. 3** the flower of any of these plants. ⟨ME < (the Virgin) *Mary* + *gold*⟩

mar•i•jua•na or **mar•i•hua•na** [ˌmærə'wɒnə] *or* [ˌmɛrə'wɒnə] *n.* **1** hemp. **2** the dried leaves and flower clusters of the female hemp plant, especially when smoked as a cigarette for its intoxicating effect. Compare CANNABIS, HASHISH. ⟨< Mexican Sp. *mariguana, marihuana*⟩

ma•rim•ba [mə'rɪmbə] *n.* an African and Latin American percussion instrument resembling a xylophone but having resonators below the bars. ⟨< Bantu⟩

ma•ri•na [mə'rinə] *n.* a place on a waterfront where pleasure boats may be moored and where fuel and equipment may be bought. ⟨< Ital. *marina* shore, coast < L *marina.* See MARINE.⟩

mar•i•nade *n.* [ˌmærə'neid] *or* [ˌmɛrə'neid]; *v.* ['mærəˌneid] *or* ['mɛrəˌneid] *n., v.* **-nad•ed, -nad•ing.** *—n.* **1** a spiced vinegar or wine in which meat, fish, etc. are soaked before being cooked. Food may be marinaded both to give it flavour and to make it tender. **2** meat or fish soaked in such vinegar or wine.
—v. marinate. ⟨< F *marinade* < *mariner* marinate⟩

ma•ri•na•ra [ˌmɑrə'nɑrə], [ˌmærə'nɑrə], *or* [ˌmærə'nɛrə], [ˌmɛrə'nɑrə] *or* [ˌmɛrə'nɛrə] *n.* an Italian sauce made of tomatoes and spices.

mar•i•nate ['mærəˌneit] *or* ['mɛrəˌneit] *v.* **-nat•ed, -nat•ing. 1** soak in brine or marinade. **2** soak in oil and vinegar. ⟨< F *mariner* < *marin* marine⟩

ma•rine [mə'rin] *adj., n. —adj.* **1** of the sea; found in the sea; produced by the sea: *Whales are marine animals.* **2** of or having to do with shipping; maritime: *marine law.* **3** of or having to do with a navy; naval: *marine power.* **4** for use at sea, on a ship, etc.: *marine supplies, a marine engine.* **5 a** of or having to do with ships, sailors, etc.: *marine lore.* **b** of or having to do with navigation at sea: *a marine compass.*
—n. **1** shipping; a fleet: *our merchant marine.* **2** a soldier formerly serving only at sea, now also participating in land and air action: *Canada has no marines.* **3** a picture showing a sea scene. ⟨< F < L *marina*, fem. *mare* sea⟩
☛ *Hom.* MOREEN.

marine highway *Cdn.* a connected series of waterways, as the St. Lawrence Seaway.

mar•i•ner ['mærənər] *or* ['mɛrənər] *n.* one who navigates or helps to navigate or run a ship; sailor; seaman. ⟨ME < AF *mariner* < OF *marin* < L *marinus* < *mare* sea⟩

marine railway *Cdn.* a device consisting of a cable-drawn cradle equipped to run on rails up and down a ramp, used for launching and landing boats or for moving boats from one water level to another.

mar•i•o•nette [ˌmæriə'nɛt] *or* [ˌmɛriə'nɛt] *n.* a small doll or puppet made to imitate a person or an animal and moved by strings. A marionette show is often given on a miniature stage. See PUPPET for picture. ⟨< F *marionette*, ult. < *Marie* Mary⟩

Mar•i•po•sa lily [ˌmærə'pousə] *or* [ˌmɛrə'pousə]; [ˌmærə'pouzə] *or* [ˌmɛrə'pouzə] **1** any of a genus (*Calochortus*) of plants of the lily family found in W North America, having tuliplike flowers, usually white with yellow, purple, or lilac markings. **2** the flower of any of these plants. ⟨< Sp. *mariposa* butterfly⟩

mar•i•tal ['mærətəl] *or* ['mɛrətəl] *adj.* **1** of or having to do with marriage: *marital vows, a marital relationship.* **2** *Archaic.* of or having to do with a husband. ⟨< L *maritalis* < *maritus* married man. See MARRY.⟩ **—'mar•i•tal•ly,** *adv.*

mar•i•time ['mærəˌtaɪm] *or* ['mɛrəˌtaɪm] *adj.* **1** on or near the sea: *Halifax is a maritime city.* **2** living near the sea: *Many maritime peoples live from fishing.* **3** of or having to do with the sea or with shipping and sailing: *Ships and sailors are governed by maritime law.* **4 Maritime,** of or having to do with the Maritime Provinces. ⟨< L *maritimus* < *mare* sea⟩

Maritime Command *Cdn.* a major organizational element of the Canadian Forces, whose role is to provide operationally ready maritime forces to patrol and control Canadian territorial waters and adjacent ocean areas and to meet Canada's international defence commitments. It was formerly known as the Royal Canadian Navy.

Maritime Provinces *Cdn.* the provinces along the east coast of Canada, including New Brunswick, Nova Scotia, and Prince Edward Island.
☛ *Usage.* The **Maritime Provinces** and **Maritimes** do not usually include Newfoundland; the **Atlantic Provinces** include the Maritime provinces and Newfoundland.

Mar•i•tim•er ['mærəˌtaɪmər] *or* ['mɛrəˌtaɪmər] *n. Cdn.* a native or long-term resident of the Maritime Provinces.

Mar•i•times ['mærəˌtaɪmz] *or* ['mɛrəˌtaɪmz] *n.* MARITIME PROVINCES.

mar•jo•ram ['mɑrdʒərəm] *n.* any of various plants (genera *Majorana* and *Origanum*) of the mint family, especially sweet marjoram, whose fragrant leaves are used for flavouring in cooking. ⟨ME < OF *majorane* < Med.L *majorana, majoraca,* alteration of L *amaracus* < Gk. *amárakos* marjoram⟩

mark[1] [mɑrk] *n., v. —n.* **1** a trace or impression made by some object on the surface of another. A line, dot, spot, stain, or scar is a mark. **2** an object, arrow, line, dot, etc. put as a guide or sign: *a mark for pilots, the starting mark in a race, a question mark.* **3** something that indicates a quality or characteristic: *Courtesy is a mark of good breeding. She has the mark of a leader.* **4** a cross or other sign made by a person who cannot write, instead of signing his or her name: *Make your mark here.* **5** a letter or number to show how well one has done; grade or rating: *My mark in arithmetic was B.* **6** something to be aimed at; target; goal. **7** what is usual, proper, or expected; standard: *A tired person does not feel up to the mark.* **8** influence; impression: *A great man leaves his mark on whatever he does.* **9** *Informal.* a person who is an easy prey for pickpockets, tricksters, etc.; sucker; gull. **10** *Archaic.* a border or frontier. **11** in the Middle Ages, a tract of land held in common by a community.
beside the mark, a not hitting the thing aimed at. **b** not to the point; not relevant. **c** not precise or accurate.
hit the mark, a succeed in doing what one tried to do. **b** be exactly right.
make (one's) **mark,** succeed; become famous.
miss the mark, a fail to do what one tried to do. **b** be not exactly right.
of mark, important or famous: *a woman of mark.*
wide of the mark, a inaccurate. **b** irrelevant.
—v. **1** make a mark on by stamping, cutting, writing, etc.: *Be careful not to mark the table.* **2** show by means of a sign: *Mark all the large cities on this map. This post marks the city limits.* **3** put a sign on (something), as a tag, label, brand, or seal, to show the price, quality, maker, owner, etc. **4** show clearly; make plain: *A tall pine marks the beginning of the trail. A frown marked her displeasure.* **5** set off; give interest or importance to: *Many important inventions mark the last 150 years.* **6** give grades to; rate. **7** *Archaic.* give attention to; notice; observe; see: *Mark how carefully he moves. Mark well my words.* **8** keep (the score); record. **9** select as if by mark: *She was marked for promotion.*
mark down, a write down; note down. **b** mark for sale at a lower price.
mark off or **out,** make lines, etc. to show the position of or to separate.
mark out for, set aside for; select for.
mark time, a move the feet as in marching, but remaining in the same spot. **b** suspend progress temporarily. **c** go through the motions without accomplishing anything.
mark up, a spoil the look of by making marks on: *Don't mark up the desks.* **b** mark for sale at a higher price. ⟨OE *mearc*⟩
☛ *Syn. n.* **3. Mark,** SIGN, TOKEN can all refer to an indication of something not visible or readily apparent. **Mark** particularly suggests an indication of the character of the thing: *Generosity is often a mark of greatness.* **Sign** is the general word, applying to any indication, as of a quality, idea, mental or physical state, etc.: *We could see no sign of life.* **Token** applies especially to something that stands as a reminder or promise of something else, as of a feeling, event, etc.: *This gift is a token of my love.*
☛ *Hom.* MARQUE.

mark[2] [mɑrk] *n.* **1** the basic unit of money in Germany, equal to 100 pfennigs; DEUTSCHE MARK. See table of money in the Appendix. **2** MARKKA. **3** a coin worth one mark. ⟨< G⟩
☛ *Hom.* MARQUE.

marked [mɑrkt] *adj., v. —adj.* **1** having a mark or marks on it. **2** very noticeable; very clear; easily recognized: *There is a marked difference between a grape and an orange.* **3** distinguished or singled out as if by a mark: *marked for success.*
—v. pt. and pp. of MARK[1]. **—'mark•ed•ly** ['mɑrkɪdli], *adv.* **—'mark•ed•ness,** *n.*

marked man a person, such as a suspected criminal, who is picked out as someone to watch or take action against: *After he was reported as having been near the scene of the murder, John was a marked man.*

mark•er ['mɑrkər] *n.* **1** a person who or thing that marks, especially a FELT PEN. **2** MARK[2] (def. 2). **3** a person or thing that keeps the score in games. **4** bookmark. **5** *Slang.* a pledge of future payment: *You hold my marker for $350.*

mar•ket ['mɑrkɪt] *n., v.* —*n.* **1** a meeting of people for the purpose of buying and selling: *There is a fruit and vegetable market here every Saturday.* **2** the people so gathered. **3** a space or building in which provisions, cattle, etc. are shown for sale. **4** a store for the sale of provisions: *a meat market.* **5** trade, especially as regards a particular article: *the cotton market.* **6** the opportunity to buy or sell: *lose one's market.* **7** the demand (for goods): *There was not enough cheese to supply the market.* **8** a region where goods can be sold: *Africa is a new market for many products.* **9** (*adjl.*) of or having to do with a market or markets: *market research, market variations.*

be in the market for, be a possible buyer of: *He is in the market for a new bike.*

play the market, speculate on the stock exchange.

price out of the market, lose business by setting a price above that of competitors or above what buyers will pay: *The firm priced itself out of the market. We must not price our book out of the market.*

—*v.* **1** buy or sell in a market. **2** sell: *He cannot market the goods he makes.* **3** carry or send to market. **4** shop at a grocery store or supermarket; buy food. ⟨ME < ONF < L *mercatus* trade, ult. < *merx, mercis* merchandise⟩ **—'mar•ket•er,** *n.*

mar•ket•a•ble ['mɑrkətəbəl] *adj.* **1** that can be sold. **2** in demand. **—,mar•ket•a'bil•i•ty,** *n.*

market garden a farm where vegetables are raised for market. **—market gardener. —market gardening.**

mar•ket•ing ['mɑrkətɪŋ] *n.* **1** the business or process of planning and implementing a strategy for the promotion, sale, and distribution of goods or services. **2** (*adjl.*) of or having to do with marketing: *a marketing seminar.* **3** grocery shopping: *I have to do the marketing for our dinner.*

market order an order to a broker to sell stocks at the prevailing price.

mar•ket•place ['mɑrkɪt,pleis] *n.* **1** a place where a market is held. **2** the world of business and commerce.

market price or **value** the price that an article brings when sold; current price.

market research research carried out by companies who ask consumers what they buy and what they would like, as a guide to production and advertising. **—market researcher.**

market value MARKET PRICE.

mark•ing ['mɑrkɪŋ] *n., v.* —*n.* **1** a mark or marks. **2** the arrangement of marks: *I like the marking on your cat's coat.*
—*v.* ppr. of MARK.

mark•ka ['mɑrkkə] *n., pl.* **-kaa** [-kɑ]. **1** the basic unit of money in Finland, divided into 100 pennia. See table of money in the Appendix. **2** a coin worth one markka. ⟨< Finnish⟩

marks•man ['mɑrksmən] *n., pl.* **-men.** a person who shoots, especially one who shoots well; sharpshooter: *She is a noted marksman.*

marks•man•ship ['mɑrksmən,ʃɪp] *n.* skill in shooting.

mark•up ['mɑrk,ʌp] *n.* **1** an increase in the price of an article. **2** the amount of this increase. **3** the percentage or amount added to the cost to take care of profit and overhead when establishing the selling price of a commodity; the difference between the cost price and the selling price.

marl [mɑrl] *n.* **1** soil containing clay, magnesium, and calcium carbonate, used in making cement and as a fertilizer. **2** *Archaic.* earth. ⟨ME < OF *marle* < Med.L *margila* < L *marga,* probably < Celtic⟩ **—mar'la•cious,** *adj.* **—'marl•y,** *adj.*

mar•lin ['mɑrlən] *n.* any of several large marine food and game fishes (genera *Makaira* and *Tetrapturus*) related to the sailfishes. ⟨short for *marlinespike*⟩
☛ *Hom.* MARLINE.

mar•line ['mɑrlən] *n. Nautical.* a small cord that sailors wind around the ends of a rope to keep it from fraying. ⟨< Du. *marlijn* < *marren* tie + *lijn* line⟩
☛ *Hom.* MARLIN.

mar•line•spike or **mar•lin•spike** ['mɑrlən,spəik] *n. Nautical.* a pointed steel spike used, like a fid, for separating strands of rope or wire in splicing.

mar•ma•lade ['mɑrmə,leid] *n.* a preserve resembling jam, made of oranges or other citrus fruit. The peel is usually sliced and boiled with the fruit. ⟨< F < Pg. *marmelada* < *marmelo* quince < L < Gk. *melimêlon* < *meli* honey + *mêlon* apple⟩

marmalade plum 1 a tree (*Calocarpum zapota*) native to tropical America and having edible fruit. **2** the fruit of this tree.

mar•mite ['mɑrməit] *or* ['mɑrmit] *n.* **1** a large, covered, earthenware pot. **2** the broth made in such a pot. ⟨< F⟩

mar•mo•re•al [mɑr'mɔriəl] *adj.* **1** of marble. **2** like marble; cold; smooth; white. Also, **marmorean.** ⟨< L *marmoreus* < *marmor* marble⟩ **—mar'mo•re•al•ly,** *adv.*

mar•mo•set ['mɑrmə,sɛt] *or* ['mɑrmə,zɛt] *n.* any of numerous small, squirrel-like monkeys (family Callithricidae, especially genus *Callithrix*) of South and Central America, having claws instead of nails, a long, furry tail, and, in many species, brightly coloured fur and long tufts of hair around the head. The **pygmy marmoset** (*Cebuella pygmaea*) is the smallest monkey, measuring only about 20 cm long, including the tail. ⟨< OF *marmouset* grotesque figurine < *merme* under age < L *minimus* very small, influenced by Gk. *mormotos* fearful⟩

mar•mot ['mɑrmət] *n.* any of a genus (*Marmota*) of burrowing rodents of the northern hemisphere belonging to the same family as squirrels and chipmunks, having a thickset body, broad, flat head, short, strong legs, and a relatively short, furry tail. ⟨< F *marmotte* < *marmottaine* < Med.L *mus (muris) montanus* mouse of the mountains⟩

mar•o•cain ['mærə,kein] *or* ['mɛrə,kein] *n.* a crepelike dress fabric of silk woven with cotton or wool. ⟨< F *marocain* relating to Morocco < *Maroc* Morocco⟩

ma•roon[1] [mə'run] *n. or adj.* dark brownish red. ⟨< F < Ital. *marrone* chestnut⟩

ma•roon[2] [mə'run] *v., n.* —*v.* **1** put (a person) ashore in a lonely place and leave him or her there: *Pirates used to maroon people on desert islands.* **2** leave in a lonely, helpless position.
—*n.* **1** a descendant of escaped black slaves living in the West Indies and Surinam. **2** an escaped black slave, an ancestor of these people. **3** a person who is marooned. ⟨< Am.Sp. *cimarron* wild⟩ **—ma'roon•er,** *n.*

mar•plot ['mɑr,plɒt] *n.* a person who spoils some plan by meddling or blundering.

marque[1] [mɑrk] See LETTERS OF MARQUE. ⟨< F < Provençal *marca* reprisal < *marcar* seize as a pledge, ult. < Gmc.⟩
☛ *Hom.* MARK.

marque[2] [mɑrk] *n.* a make or brand of a product, especially an automobile.
Hom. MARK.

mar•quee [mɑr'ki] *n.* **1** a large tent, often one put up for some outdoor entertainment or wedding or other party. **2** a rooflike shelter over an entrance, especially to a theatre or cinema. ⟨< F *marquise* (misunderstood as plural) < OF *(tente) marquise* a large tent for officers, literally, for a marquis⟩
☛ *Hom.* MARQUIS.

mar•que•try ['mɑrkətri] *n., pl.* **-tries.** decoration made with thin pieces of wood, ivory, metal, etc. fitted together to form a design on furniture. ⟨< F *marqueterie* < *marqueter* inlay < *marque* mark[1] < Gmc.⟩

mar•quis ['mɑrkwɪs] *or* [mɑr'ki] *n.* a nobleman ranking below a duke and above an earl or count. ⟨ME < OF *marquis, marchis* < *marche* march[2] < Gmc.⟩
☛ *Hom.* MARQUEE [mɑr'ki].

mar•quis•ate ['mɑrkwɪzɪt] *n.* the position or rank of marquis.

mar•quise [mɑr'kiz] *n.* **1** marchioness. **2** a gem of a pointed, oval shape, or a ring set with such a stone. **3** MARQUEE (def. 2). ⟨< F *marquise,* fem. of *marquis*⟩

mar•qui•sette [,mɑrkə'zɛt] *or* [,mɑrkwə'zɛt] *n.* a very thin fabric with square meshes, made of cotton, silk, rayon, nylon, etc. and often used for window draperies. ⟨< F *marquisette,* dim. of *marquise* marquise⟩

Marquis of Queens•ber•ry Rules ['kwinz,bɛri] a code of fair play in boxing, established in 1869 by the eighth Marquis of Queensberry. ⟨after Sir John Sholto Douglas (1844-1900), 8th Marquis of *Queensberry*⟩

mar•ram grass ['mærəm] *or* ['mɛrəm] a beach grass (*Ammophila arenaria*) often planted to stabilize shifting dunes. ⟨< ON *marr* sea + *halmr* grass⟩

mar•riage ['mærɪdʒ] *or* ['mɛrɪdʒ] *n.* **1** married life; living together as husband and wife: *We wished the bride and groom a happy marriage.* **2** the ceremony of being married; a marrying; a wedding. **3** a close union: *the marriage of words and melody.* ⟨ME < OF *mariage* < *marier.* See MARRY[1].⟩

☛ *Syn.* **1, 2. Marriage,** MATRIMONY, WEDDING = the state of being married or the act of marrying. **Marriage** is the general and common word applying to the institution, the legal and spiritual relation, the state of being married, or, less often, the ceremony. **Matrimony** is the formal and religious word, and applies especially to the spiritual relation or the religious ceremony (sacrament). **Wedding** is the common word for the ceremony or celebration.

mar•riage•a•ble ['mærədʒəbəl] *or* ['mɛrədʒəbəl] *adj.* fit for marriage; old enough to marry. **—,mar•riage•a'bil•i•ty,** *n.*

marriage of convenience a marriage for money, position, or citizenship, not for love.

marriage portion dowry.

mar•ried ['mærid] *or* ['mɛrid] *adj., n., v. —adj.* **1** living together as husband and wife. **2** having a husband or wife. **3** of marriage; of husbands and wives. **4** closely united; combined (*with*); devoted (*to*): *The painter was married to his art. The author's sensitivity is married with wit in this book.*
—n. a person who is married (*usually used in the plural*): *a roomful of young marrieds.*
—v. pt. and pp. of MARRY.

married quarters housing provided for married members of the armed forces, married students in residence, etc.

mar•row ['mærou] *or* ['mɛrou] *n.* **1** the soft tissue that fills the cavities of most bones. **2** the inmost or essential part: *He was chilled to the marrow.* **3** VEGETABLE MARROW. **4** vigour; energy. ⟨OE *mearg*⟩

mar•row•bone ['mærou,boun] *or* ['mɛrou,boun] *n.* **1** a bone containing marrow, often used to make soup. **2 marrowbones,** *pl.* **a** knees. **b** crossbones.

mar•row•fat ['mærou,fæt] *or* ['mɛrou,fæt] *n.* a kind of pea that has a large seed.

marrow squash VEGETABLE MARROW.

mar•ry[1] ['mæri] *or* ['mɛri] *v.* **-ried, -ry•ing. 1** join as husband and wife: *The minister married them.* **2** take as husband or wife: *John planned to marry Grace.* **3** become married; take a husband or wife: *She married late in life.* **4** give in marriage (*often used with* **off**): *They married their son off to a young lawyer.* **5** unite closely. ⟨ME < OF *marier* < L *maritare* < *maritus* husband, formed after *marita* woman with husband < *mas, mari-* a male⟩

☛ *Hom.* MERRY ['mɛri].

mar•ry[2] ['mæri] *or* ['mɛri] *interj. Archaic.* an exclamation showing surprise, indignation, etc. ⟨< (the Virgin) *Mary*⟩

☛ *Hom.* MERRY ['mɛri].

Mars [mɑrz] *n.* **1** *Roman mythology.* the god of war, son of Jupiter and Juno, corresponding to the Greek god Ares. **2** war personified. **3** the planet next beyond the earth and the fourth in order from the sun.

Mar•sa•la [mɑr'sɑlə] *n.* a dark, sweet, fortified wine originally made in Marsala, Sicily.

Mar•seil•laise [,mɑrsə'leiz]; *French,* [maʀsɛ'jɛz] *n.* the national anthem of France, written in 1792 during the French Revolution. ⟨< *Marseilles,* France; because first sung by a group of men from Marseilles⟩

mar•seilles [mɑr'seilz] *n.* a thick cotton cloth woven in figures or stripes, used for bedspreads, etc. ⟨< *Marseilles,* France⟩

marsh [mɑrʃ] *n.* **1** an area of wet, muddy land sometimes partly covered with water and having plant life that consists mainly of grasses and sedges. **2** *Cdn., esp. Maritimes.* reclaimed marshland. ⟨OE *mersc* < *mere* lake⟩

mar•shal ['mɑrʃəl] *n., v.* **-shalled** or **-shaled, -shal•ling** or **-shal•ing.** *—n.* **1** any of various kinds of officer: *a fire marshal.* **2** in the armed forces of certain countries, an officer of a high, or the highest, rank: *a field marshal.* **3** a person who arranges the order of march in a parade: *a parade marshal.* **4** a person in charge of events or ceremonies.
—v. **1** arrange or order properly or effectively: *He spent a lot of time marshalling his arguments for the debate.* **2** conduct with ceremony: *We were marshalled before the king.* **3** arrange in military order; prepare for war: *to marshall the troops.* ⟨ME < OF *mareschal* < LL *mariscalcus* groom < Gmc., literally, horse servant⟩ **—'mar•shal•ler** or **'mar•shal•er,** *n.*

☛ *Hom.* MARTIAL.

Marshall Islands a country of several islands in the Pacific Ocean.

marsh bittern *Cdn.* the American bittern (*Botaurus lentiginosus*).

marsh dike or **dyke** *Cdn.* a dike or dam equipped with a gate which functions as a valve releasing flood water from behind but preventing seawater from entering at high tide.

marsh gas a gas formed by the decomposition of organic substances in marshes; methane.

marsh hawk *Cdn.* a slate grey or brownish hawk (*Circus cyaneus hudsonius*).

marsh hen *Cdn.* MARSH BITTERN.

marsh•land ['mɑrʃ,lænd] *n.* marshy land.

marsh•mal•low ['mɑrʃ,mɛlou] *or* ['mɑrʃ,mælou] *n.* **1** a soft, spongy confection originally made from the root of the marsh mallow, now made from corn syrup, sugar, gelatin, and flavouring. **2** a piece of this confection, covered with powdered sugar: *a bag of marshmallows.* ⟨OE *merscmealwe*; originally made from the root of the marsh mallow⟩

marsh mallow a perennial herb (*Althaea officinalis*) of the mallow family native to Europe, Asia, and N Africa, found in marshy areas, having toothed leaves and pink flowers and a root that secretes a gummy substance originally used to make marshmallow. The marsh mallow has become naturalized in eastern North America.

marsh marigold a perennial marsh plant (*Caltha palustris*) of the buttercup family having roundish leaves and bright yellow flowers.

marsh rabbit or **hare** *Cdn.* muskrat, especially when eaten as food.

marsh•y ['mɑrʃi] *adj.* **marsh•i•er, marsh•i•est. 1** soft and wet like a marsh. **2** having many marshes. **3** of marshes. **—'marsh•i•ness,** *n.*

Mar•ston's trout ['mɑrstənz] a deep red fish (*Salvelinus marstoni*) common in lakes in Québec and New Brunswick, related to the arctic char. Its tail fin is forked.

mar•su•pi•al [mɑr'supiəl] *n., adj. —n.* any of an order (Marsupialia) of mammals typically lacking a placenta, and whose young are born at a very early stage of development, continuing their growth outside the womb while attached to the mother's nipples, usually inside a pouch, or marsupium. Kangaroos, bandicoots, wombats, and opossums are marsupials.
—adj. **1** of, having to do with, or belonging to the order Marsupialia. **2** of, having to do with, or like a pouch.

mar•su•pi•um [mɑr'supiəm] *n., pl.* **-pi•a** [-piə]. a pouch or fold of skin on the abdomen of a female marsupial for carrying the young. ⟨< L < Gk. *marsupion,* dim. of *marsipos* pouch⟩

mart [mɑrt] *n.* a market; a centre of trade. ⟨late ME < MDu., var. of *markt* market⟩

mar•ta•gon ['mɑrtəgən] *n.* a lily (*Lilium martagon*) having pink-spotted flowers. ⟨< Turk *martagán* turban⟩

Mar•tel•lo tower [mɑr'tɛlou] a fort like a round tower, formerly built on coasts for defence against invasion: *There are Martello towers in Kingston harbour.* Also, **martello tower.** ⟨< alteration (influenced by Ital. *martello* hammer) of Cape *Mortella,* Corsica, where such a tower was built⟩

mar•ten ['mɑrtən] *n., pl.* **-tens** or (*esp. collectively*) **-ten. 1** any of several small carnivorous mammals (genus *Martes*) related to the weasels, but larger, having a long, slender body and short legs. Martens spend most of their time in trees and are active mainly at night. **2** the valuable fur of the marten. ⟨ME < Du. *martren* < OF *martrine,* ult. < Gmc.⟩

☛ *Hom.* MARTIN.

mar•tens•ite ['mɑrtən,zəit] *n. Metallurgy.* a combination of iron with one percent of carbon, used in carbon steel tools. ⟨after A. *Martens* (1850-1914), German metallurgist⟩

Mar•tha ['mɑrθə] *n. Archaic.* a practical woman who leads a busy, active life. ⟨in the Bible, the sister of Lazarus and Mary⟩

mar•tial ['mɑrʃəl] *adj.* **1** of war; suitable for war: *martial music.* **2** fond of fighting; warlike; brave: *a man of martial spirit.* ⟨ME < L *Martialis* < *Mars, Martis* Mars⟩ **—'mar•tial•ly,** *adv.*

☛ *Syn.* **1, 2.** See note at MILITARY.

☛ *Hom.* MARSHAL.

martial art any form of exercise, especially Oriental, used for self-defence, such as karate, judo, etc.

martial law temporary rule by the army or militia with special military courts instead of by the usual civil authorities. Martial law is declared during a time of trouble or war.

☛ *Usage.* See note at MILITARY LAW.

Mar•tian ['mɑrʃən] *adj., n. —adj.* of the planet or god Mars. *—n.* a supposed inhabitant of the planet Mars. ⟨< L *Martius* of Mars⟩

mar•tin ['mɑrtən] *n.* any of various swallows, such as the

black-and-white **house martin** (*Delichon urbica*) of Europe. See also PURPLE MARTIN. ⟨< F *Martin*, the bird being supposed to migrate at Martinmas⟩
☛ *Hom.* MARTEN.

mar•ti•net [ˌmɑrtəˈnɛt] *or* [ˈmɑrtəˌnɛt] *n.* a person who enforces very strict discipline. ⟨after Jean *Martinet*, a 17c. French general⟩

mar•tin•gale [ˈmɑrtənˌgeil] *n.* **1** the strap of a horse's harness that prevents the horse from rising on its hind legs or throwing back its head. **2** *Nautical.* a rope or spar that steadies the jib boom on a ship. ⟨< F *martingale*, ? ult. < *Martigues*, name of a town⟩

mar•ti•ni [mɑrˈtini] *n.* a cocktail made of gin and dry vermouth. ⟨< *Martini* and Rossi, vermouth and wine makers⟩

Mar•tin•mas [ˈmɑrtənməs] *n.* November 11, a Christian church festival in honour of Saint Martin (1250-1300).

mart•let [ˈmɑrtlɪt] *n.* **1** *Heraldry.* a bird with no feet used as a crest to indicate a fourth son. **2** the martin.

mar•tyr [ˈmɑrtər] *n., v.* —*n.* **1** a person who chooses to die or suffer rather than renounce his or her faith; a person who is put to death or made to suffer greatly for his or her religion or other beliefs. **2** a person who suffers great pain or anguish. **3** a person who puts on a false appearance of suffering or makes a display of self-denial in order to attract sympathy or attention.
—*v.* **1** put (a person) to death or torture because of his or her religion or other beliefs. **2** cause to suffer greatly; torture. ⟨OE < L < Gk. *martyr* witness⟩ —**ˈmar•tyrˌlike,** *adj.*

mar•tyr•dom [ˈmɑrtərdəm] *n.* **1** the state of being a martyr. **2** the death or suffering of a martyr. **3** great suffering; torment.

mar•ty•ry [ˈmɑrtəri] *n.* a shrine or similar building in honour of a martyr.

mar•vel [ˈmɑrvəl] *n., v.* **-velled** or **-veled, -vel•ling** or **-vel•ing.**
—*n.* something wonderful; an astonishing thing: *Television and the airplane are among the marvels of invention.*
—*v.* **1** be filled with wonder; be astonished: *She marvelled at the beautiful sunset.* **2** express wonder: *I marvel that you dare show your face here again.* ⟨ME < OF *merveillier* < VL < L *mirabilia* wonders, ult. < *mirus* strange⟩

mar•vel•lous or **mar•vel•ous** [ˈmɑrvələs] *adj.* **1** causing wonder; extraordinary. **2** improbable. **3** *Informal.* excellent; splendid; fine: *a marvellous time.* —**ˈmar•vel•lous•ly** or **ˈmar•vel•ous•ly,** *adv.* —**ˈmar•vel•lous•ness** or **ˈmar•vel•ous•ness,** *n.*
☛ *Syn.* **1.** See note at WONDERFUL.

mar•vel–of–Pe•ru [ˈmɑrvəl əv pəˈru] *n.* FOUR-O'CLOCK.

Marx•i•an [ˈmɑrksiən] *adj., n.* Marxist.

Marx•ism [ˈmɑrksɪzəm] *n.* the political and economic theories of Karl Marx (1818-1883) and Friedrich Engels (1820-1895), German writers on social philosophy, who interpreted history as a continuing economic class struggle and believed that the eventual result would be the establishment of a classless society and communal ownership of all natural and industrial resources. Also, **Marxianism.**

Marx•ist [ˈmɑrksɪst] *n., adj.* —*n.* a follower or disciple of Karl Marx or an advocate of Marxism.
—*adj.* of or having to do with Karl Marx or Marxism.

Mar•y [ˈmɛri] *n.* in the Bible, the mother of Jesus.

Mary Jane *Slang.* marijuana.

Ma•ry•land [ˈmɛrɪlənd] *n.* a SE coast state of the United States.

mar•zi•pan [ˈmɑrzəˌpæn] *or* [ˈmɑrdzəˌpæn] *n.* a paste of ground almonds and sugar, often moulded into various forms. Also, **marchpane.** ⟨< G < Ital. *marzapane*, a medieval coin < Arabic⟩

Ma•sai [ˈmɑsaɪ] *or* [məˈsaɪ] *n., pl.* **Ma•sai** or **Ma•sais. 1** a tall hunting and cattle-raising people native to East Africa. **2** a member of this people. **3** their Nilo-Hamitic language.

masc. masculine.

mas•car•a [mæˈskærə] *or* [mæˈskɛrə] *n.* a cosmetic preparation for darkening the eyelashes. ⟨< Sp. *máscara* mask. See MASQUERADE.⟩

mas•con [ˈmæskɒn] *n.* one of several regions on the moon where gravity is increased as if by a concentration of dense matter under the surface. ⟨< *mas*(*s*) + *con*(*centration*)⟩

mas•cot [ˈmæskɒt] *or* [ˈmæskət] *n.* **1** an animal, person, or thing supposed to bring good luck. **2** any person, animal, or thing adopted as a symbol by a group: *The regiment's mascot is a goat.* ⟨< F *mascotte* < Provençal *mascotto*, dim. of *masco* witch < Gmc.⟩

mas•cu•line [ˈmæskjəlɪn] *adj., n.* —*adj.* **1** of men; male. **2** like a man; manly; strong; vigorous. **3** having qualities suited to a man; mannish. **4** *Grammar.* of the gender to which names of male things normally belong. *Soleil*, *Canada*, and *argent* are masculine French nouns. Compare FEMININE, NEUTER.
—*n. Grammar.* **1** the masculine gender. **2** a word or form in the masculine gender. ⟨< L *masculinus*, ult. < *mas* male⟩
—**ˈmas•cu•line•ly,** *adv.* —**ˌmas•cuˈlin•i•ty,** *n.*
☛ *Syn. adj.* **1, 2.** See note at MALE.

masculine rhyme a rhyme in which the final syllables are stressed, as in *disdain* and *complain.*

ma•ser [ˈmeizər] *n.* a device for amplifying microwaves to produce a very narrow, intense beam of radiation. ⟨*m*icrowave *a*mplification by *s*timulated *e*mission of *r*adiation⟩

mash [mæʃ] *n., v.* —*n.* **1** a soft mixture; soft mass. **2** a warm mixture of bran or meal and water for horses and cattle. **3** any of various mixtures of ground grain, often supplemented with proteins, antibiotics, etc., used as feed for poultry, livestock, etc. **4** crushed malt or meal soaked in hot water for making beer. **5** a similar preparation of rye, corn, barley, etc., used to make whisky.
—*v.* **1** beat into a soft mass; crush to a uniform mass. **2** mix (crushed malt or meal) with hot water in brewing. ⟨OE *māsc-*⟩
—**ˈmash•er,** *n.*

mas•jid [ˈmʌsdʒɪd] *or* [ˈmæsdʒɪd] *n.* mosque. Also, MUSJID. ⟨< Arabic⟩

mask [mæsk] *n., v.* —*n.* **1** a covering for the face, worn for disguise or in fun: *a Halloween mask.* **2** anything that hides or disguises: *He hid his evil plans under a mask of friendship.* **3** *Rare.* a masked person. **4** a covering for the face, worn for protection from cold, etc.: *a ski mask.* **5** a covering for the nose and mouth, worn for protection against infection: *a surgical mask.* **6** a device covering the nose and mouth, designed to aid breathing, purify air before it is inhaled, apply anesthetic, etc.: *a gas mask, an oxygen mask.* **7** a clay, wax, or plaster likeness of a person's face. **8** the hollow figure of a human head worn by Greek and Roman actors to identify the character represented and increase the volume of the voice. **9** See MASQUE. **10** a carved or moulded face or head, usually grotesque, used as an architectural ornament. **11** a cosmetic preparation spread over the entire face and left on for a certain time to recondition the skin.
—*v.* **1** cover (the face) with a mask. **2** hide; disguise: *A smile masked his disappointment.* **3** cover with masking tape: *We masked the edges of the window panes before painting the wood.* ⟨< F *masque* < Med.L *mascus*, *masco* ghost, *masca* witch < origin uncertain⟩ —**ˈmask•er,** *n.* —**ˈmaskˌlike,** *adj.*
☛ *Hom.* MASQUE.

masked [mæskt] *adj., v.* —*adj.* **1** wearing a mask: *a masked gunman.* **2** hidden or disguised; not apparent: *masked jealousy.*
—*v.* pt. and pp. of MASK.

masked ball a formal dance at which masks are worn.

masking tape adhesive paper tape used to cover areas that are not to be painted.

mas•kin•onge [ˈmæskəˌnɒndʒ] *n., pl.* **mas•kin•onge.** *Cdn.* muskellunge. ⟨< Cdn.F *masquinongé* < Algonkian, akin to Cree *mashkinonche* great pike⟩

ma•so [ˈmɑsou] *n. Cdn.* licorice. Also, **masu.** ⟨< Inuktitut⟩

mas•och•ism [ˈmæsəˌkɪzəm] *or* [ˈmæzəˌkɪzəm] *n.* **1** a condition in which abnormal sexual pleasure results from being beaten, dominated, etc. Compare SADISM. **2** a tendency to experience pleasure from being mistreated, dominated, etc. ⟨< Leopold Von Sacher-*Masoch* (1836-1895), an Austrian novelist who described the condition in his books⟩
—**ˈmas•och•ist,** *n.* —**ˌmas•oˈchis•tic,** *adj.* —**ˌmas•oˈchis•ti•cal•ly,** *adv.*

ma•son [ˈmeisən] *n.* **1** a person whose work is building with stone, brick, or similar materials. **2** Usually, **Mason,** Freemason. ⟨ME < OF *masson* < LL *machio, -onis*, probably < Gmc.⟩

mason bee any bee of the genus *Anthidium*, that builds nests made of clay.

Ma•son•ic [məˈsɒnɪk] *adj.* of or having to do with Freemasons or Freemasonry. Also, **masonic.**

Ma•son•ite [ˈmeisəˌnəit] *n. Trademark.* a wood fibre pressed into sheets and used in building.

Mason jar a wide-mouthed glass jar with a top that screws on and a rubber seal, used especially for home bottling and preserving. ⟨after John L. *Mason*, an American inventor who patented such a jar. 19c.⟩

ma•son•ry ['meisənri] *n., pl.* **-ries. 1** the work done by a mason; stonework, brickwork, etc. **2** something constructed of stone, brick, etc., such as a chimney or wall. **3** the trade or skill of a mason. **4** Usually, **Masonry,** Freemasonry.

masque [mæsk] *n.* **1** an amateur dramatic entertainment in which fine costumes, scenery, music, and dancing are more important than the story. Masques were often given in England in the 16th and 17th centuries, at court and at the homes of nobles. **2** the play written for such an entertainment. **3** a masked ball; masquerade. ⟨< F *masque.* See MASK.⟩
☛ *Hom.* MASK.

mas•quer•ade [ˌmæskə'reid] *n., v.* **-ad•ed, -ad•ing.** *—n.* **1** a party or dance at which masks and fancy costumes are worn. **2** the costume and mask worn at such a party or dance. **3** a false pretence; disguise. **4** a going about or acting under false pretences.
—v. **1** take part in a masquerade. **2** disguise oneself; go about under false pretences: *The king masqueraded as a beggar to find out if his people really liked him.* ⟨earlier *masquerada* < Sp. *mascarada,* equivalent to *mascara* mask⟩ **—ˌmas•quer'ad•er,** *n.*

mass[1] [mæs] *n., v. —n.* **1** a lump: *a mass of dough.* **2** a large quantity together: *a mass of flowers.* **3** the majority; greater part. **4** (*adjl.*) done or occurring on a large scale: *mass buying, a mass protest.* **5** bulk; size. **6** *Physics.* a measure of the amount of matter a body contains. The greater the mass of an object, the more force is needed to give it a particular acceleration. The mass of water is not changed by freezing it or changing it into steam, even though the volume changes. **7** a piece of metal having a specified mass, used to weigh something on a balance. **8** an expanse of colour, light, shade, etc. in a painting. **9** *Pharmacy.* a thick, pasty preparation from which pills are made. **10 the masses,** the common people; the general population: *Most television programs are entertainment for the masses.* **11** (*adjl.*) of, having to do with, or for the general population: *mass culture, a book designed for a mass market.*
in the mass, as a whole; without distinguishing parts or individuals.
—v. form or collect into a mass; assemble. ⟨ME < OF < L *massa* kneaded dough < Gk. *maza* barley bread < *massein* knead⟩

Mass or **mass[2]** [mæs] *n.* **1** the central service of worship in the Roman Catholic Church and in some other Christian churches; Holy Eucharist as a sacrifice. The ritual of the Mass consists of various prayers and ceremonies. **2** a piece of music written for or suggested by certain parts of the Mass. ⟨OE *mæsse* < LL *missa* < L *mittere* send away⟩

Mas•sa•chu•sett [ˌmæsə'tʃusɪt] *n.* **1** a member of an American Indian people formerly living in Massachusetts. **2** the Algonquian language of these people, now extinct.

Mas•sa•chu•setts [ˌmæsə'tʃusɪts] *n.* a NE coast state of the United States.

mas•sa•cre ['mæsəkər] *n., v.* **-cred, -cring.** *—n.* a wholesale, pitiless slaughter of people or animals.
—v. kill (many people or animals) needlessly or cruelly; slaughter in large numbers. ⟨< F *massacre,* in OF *macecle* shambles⟩

mas•sage [mə'sɑʒ] *or* [mə'sɑdʒ] *n., v.* **-saged, -sag•ing.** *—n.* a rubbing and kneading of the body to stimulate the circulation of the blood and make the muscles and joints more supple: *A thorough massage relaxes tired muscles.*
—v. give a massage to. ⟨< F *massage,* ult. < *masse* mass⟩

massage parlour 1 an establishment offering therapeutic body rubs to people in need of massage. **2** a euphemism for a brothel, etc.

mas•sa•sau•ga [ˌmæsə'sɒgə] *n. Cdn.* a small rattlesnake (*Sistrurus catenatus*) found in southern Ontario and the E United States. ⟨< *Mississauga* River, Ontario < Algonquian (Ojibwa) < *misi* great + *sauk* river mouth⟩

mass defect *Physics.* of an atom, the amount by which the sum of its constituent particles is greater than the mass of their atomic nucleus.

mas•sé [mæ'sei] *or* ['mæsei] *n. Billiards.* a stroke in which the cue ball is hit on its side so as to roll in a curve. ⟨< F, pp. of *masser* strike from above⟩

mass–energy equation *Physics.* the equivalence expressed by the EINSTEIN EQUATION $E = mc^2$.

mas•se•ter [mə'sitər] *n. Anatomy.* the muscle that raises the lower jaw. ⟨< NL < Gk. *masseter* chewer < *masasthai* to chew⟩

mas•seur [mæ'sɜr] *or* [mə'sɜr]; *French,* [ma'sœʀ] *n.* a man whose work is massaging. ⟨< F⟩

mas•seuse [mæ'sɜz] *or* [mə'suz]; *French,* [ma'søz] *n.* a woman whose work is massaging. ⟨< F⟩

mass hysteria *Psychology.* a condition of a crowd of people among whom excitement, rage, or sometimes illness, spreads rapidly.

mas•si•cot ['mæsɪˌkɒt] *n.* monoxide of lead, used as a pigment in its form as a yellow powder. *Formula:* PbO ⟨< F < Ital. *massicotto* < Sp. *mazacote* soda ash, mortar⟩

mas•sif ['mæsɪf]; *French,* [ma'sif] *n. Geology.* **1** a main part or mass of a mountain range, surrounded by depressions. **2** a large block of the earth's crust that has shifted as a unit and is bounded by faults. ⟨< F n. use of *massif* massive⟩

mas•sive ['mæsɪv] *adj.* **1** big and heavy; large and solid; bulky: *a massive building, a massive wrestler.* **2** giving the impression of being large and broad: *a massive forehead.* **3** imposing; impressive. **4** in or by great numbers; broad in scope; extensive: *a massive assault, massive retaliation.* **5** of gold, silver, plate, etc., solid rather than hollow. **6** much larger or more than usual: *a massive dose.* **7** *Mineralogy.* not definitely crystalline. **8** *Geology.* without definite structural divisions. **—'mas•sive•ly,** *adv.* **—'mas•sive•ness,** *n.*

mass•less ['mæslɪs] *adj. Physics.* having no mass. **—'mass•less•ness,** *n.*

mass market the general population considered as a homogeneous market for goods or services. Goods produced for the mass market have to appeal to the average consumer. **—'mass-'mar•ket,** *adj.*

mass marketing the production and distribution of goods intended to be sold to large numbers of people.

mass media the various modern means of communication that reach a vast audience, such as television, radio, movies, and the press.

mass meeting a large public gathering of people to hear or discuss some matter of common interest, or to demonstrate on such a matter.

mass noun *Grammar.* a noun that stands for something which cannot be counted, such as *milk, happiness.*
☛ *Usage.* a mass noun cannot be used with an indefinite article or in the plural.

mass number *Physics.* the whole number that most closely indicates the mass of an isotope, equal to the sum of the protons and neutrons in the nucleus.

mass–pro•duce ['mæs prə'djus] *or* ['mæs prə'dus] *v.* **-duced, -duc•ing.** make or manufacture anything by mass production. **—'mass-pro'duc•er,** *n.*

mass production the making of goods in large quantities by machinery.

mass psychology *Psychology.* the study of the actions of large crowds or numbers of people.

mass society *Sociology.* a society of people who tend to relate to one another impersonally, move around a lot, move up and down the social scale, view events as if from the outside, and conform to the norms of the society.

mass spectrograph *Physics.* a mass spectrometer for recording a mass spectrum on a photographic plate.

mass spectrometer an instrument which separates ions according to their relative charge and mass by passing them through electric or magnetic fields, so as to show the quantity of each type of ion present (**mass spectrum**).

mass•y ['mæsi] *adj.* **mass•i•er, mass•i•est.** *Archaic or poetic.* massive. **—'mass•i•ness,** *n.*

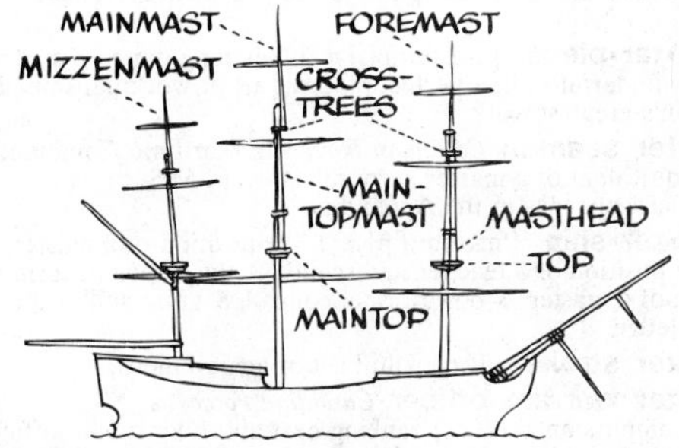

mast[1] [mæst] *n.* **1** a long pole of wood or steel set upright to

support the sails and rigging of a ship. **2** any upright pole: *a flag mast, a TV mast.*
before the mast, *Archaic.* serving as an ordinary sailor. Sailors (not officers) used to sleep in the forward part of the ship. ⟨OE *mæst*⟩ **—'mast•less,** *adj.* **—'mast,like,** *adj.*

mast² [mæst] *n.* acorns, chestnuts, beechnuts, etc. that have accumulated on the ground. Pigs eat mast. ⟨OE *mæst*⟩

mas•ta•ba ['mæstəbə] *n.* an ancient Egyptian tomb, oblong in shape, with sloping sides and flat top, set over a mummy chamber or burial pit. ⟨< Arabic *mastabah* bench⟩

mas•tec•to•my [mæ'stɛktəmi] *n.* the surgical removal of a breast. ⟨< Gk. *mastos* breast + E *-ectomy*⟩

mas•ter ['mæstər] *n., v. —n.* **1** a person who has power or authority; one in control; employer; owner. **2** the man at the head of a household. **3** the captain of a merchant ship. **4** a male teacher, especially in a private school. **5** a great artist. **6** a picture or painting by a great artist: *an old master.* **7** a person who knows all about his or her work; expert. **8** a skilled worker, or artisan, qualified to teach apprentices. **9 the Master,** Jesus. **10** a title of respect for a boy: *Master James Smith.* **11** (*adjl.*) of or by a master. **12** (*adjl.*) main; controlling: *a master switch, a master plan.* **13** See MASTER KEY. **14** victor. **15** a court officer appointed to assist the judge. **16** an initial recording, mould, stencil, etc. used for making duplications.
—v. **1** become master of; conquer; control. **2** become expert in; become skilful at. ⟨< OF *maistre,* OE *mægester* < L *magister*; cf. *magis* more⟩ **—'mas•ter•dom,** *n.* **—'mas•ter,hood,** *n.* **—'mas•ter•less,** *adj.*

mas•ter–at–arms ['mæstər ət 'ɑrmz] *n., pl.* **mas•ters-at-arms.** a naval police officer who keeps order on a ship and takes charge of prisoners.

master builder 1 a person skilled in planning buildings; architect. **2** a person who directs the construction of buildings; contractor.

master class *Music.* instruction in performance of advanced music students, usually conducted one-on-one by a recognized musician, with an audience.

master corporal *Canadian Forces.* a non-commissioned officer ranking next above a corporal and below a sergeant. *Abbrev.*: M.Cpl. or MCpl See chart of ranks in the Appendix.

master file *Computer technology.* a file, usually kept on a hard disk, that serves as permanent storage of needed data.

mas•ter•ful ['mæstərfəl] *adj.* **1** fond of power or authority; domineering. **2** expert; skilful; masterly: *The actor gave a masterful performance.* **—'mas•ter•ful•ly,** *adv.* **—'mas•ter•ful•ness,** *n.*

master hand 1 an expert. **2** expertise: *to show a master hand in building.*

master key a key that opens all the different locks in a particular building, apartment block, etc.; passkey.

mas•ter•ly ['mæstərli] *adj., adv. —adj.* expert; skilful: *Emily Carr was a masterly painter.*
—adv. expertly; skilfully. **—'mas•ter•li•ness,** *n.*

master mechanic a skilled mechanic who supervises other mechanics.

mas•ter•mind ['mæstər,maɪnd] *n., v. —n.* a person who plans and directs a complex project.
—v. plan and direct (a complex project).

master of ceremonies a person in charge of a ceremony or entertainment who announces the successive events and makes sure that they take place in the proper order. *Abbrev.*: M.C.

mas•ter•piece ['mæstər,pis] *n.* **1** anything done or made with wonderful skill; a perfect piece of art or workmanship. **2** a person's greatest work.

master seaman *Canadian Forces.* in Maritime Command, the equivalent of a master corporal. *Abbrev.*: M.S. or MS See chart of ranks in the Appendix.

mas•ter•ship ['mæstər,ʃɪp] *n.* **1** the position of a master. **2** the position of a teacher in a school. **3** the duties or term of office of a master. **4** power; rule; control. **5** great skill; expert knowledge.

master stroke a very skilful act or achievement.

master warrant officer *Canadian Forces.* a non-commissioned officer ranking next above a warrant officer and below a chief warrant officer. *Abbrev.*: M.W.O. or MWO See chart of ranks in the Appendix.

master work masterpiece.

mas•ter•y ['mæstəri] *n.* **1** power such as a master has; rule; control. **2** the upper hand; victory: *Two teams competed for mastery.* **3** great skill; expert knowledge: *Our teacher has a mastery of many subjects.*

mast•head ['mæst,hɛd] *n.* **1** *Nautical.* the top of a ship's mast. A crow's-nest near the masthead of the lower mast is used as a lookout. See MAST for picture. **2** the part of a newspaper or magazine that gives the title, the names of the owners and editors, and the publication address.

mas•tic ['mæstɪk] *n.* **1** a yellowish resin used in making varnish, chewing gum, and incense, and as an astringent. **2** any of various cements or mortars. **3** the evergreen tree (*Pistacia lentiscus*) which yields the resin; mastic tree. ⟨ME *mastyk* < L *masticha* < Gk. *mastichē* chewing gum; akin to *mastichân* to gnash the teeth⟩

mas•ti•cate ['mæstə,keit] *v.* **-cat•ed, -cat•ing. 1** chew. **2** crush or knead (rubber, etc.) to a pulp. ⟨< LL *masticare* < Gk. See MASTIC.⟩ **—'mas•ti•ca•ble** ['mæstəkəbəl], *adj.* **—,mas•ti'ca•tion,** *n.*

mas•ti•ca•tor ['mæstə,keitər] *n.* **1** an animal or organ that chews. **2** a machine for cutting things into small pieces.

mas•ti•ca•to•ry ['mæstəkə,tɔri] *adj., n., pl.* **-ries.**
—adj. of chewing; used in chewing.
—n. a substance chewed to increase the flow of saliva.

mastic tree a small evergreen tree (*Pistacia lentiscus*) of Mediterranean regions.

mas•tiff ['mæstɪf] *n.* a breed of large, strong dog having a short, thick coat, drooping ears, and hanging jowls. ⟨ME < OF *mastin,* ult. < L *mansuetus* tame; influenced by OF *mestif* mongrel⟩

mas•ti•tis [mæ'stəitəs] *n.* inflammation of a breast or, in cows, sheep, etc., of the udder. ⟨< Gk. *mastos* breast + E *-itis.* 19c.⟩ **—ma'stit•ic** [mæ'stɪtɪk], *adj.*

masto– *prefix.* breast: *mastopathy.* Also (*esp. before a vowel*) **mast-.** ⟨< Gk. *mastos* breast⟩

mas•to•don ['mæstə,dɒn] *n.* any of several extinct elephantlike mammals (genus *Mammut,* also called *Mastodon*) that flourished from the Miocene to the Pleistocene epochs in the forests of Europe, Asia, and North America. ⟨< NL < Gk. *mastos* breast + *odōn* tooth; from the nipplelike projections on its molars⟩

mas•to•don•tic [,mæstə'dɒntɪk] *adj.* **1** having teeth like a mastodon. **2** characteristic of the mastodons. Also, **mastodonic** [-'dɒnɪk].

mas•toid ['mæstɔɪd] *n.* the projection of bone behind the ear. ⟨< Gk. *mastoeidēs* < *mastos* breast + *eidos* form⟩

mas•toid•i•tis [,mæstɔɪ'dəitɪs] *n.* inflammation of the mastoid.

mas•to•pa•thy [mæ'stɒpəθi] *n., pl.* **-thies.** *Pathology.* any disease of the breast.

mas•tur•bate ['mæstər,beit] *v.* **-bat•ed, -bat•ing.** engage in masturbation. ⟨< L *masturbari*⟩ **—'mas•tur,ba•tor,** *n.*

mas•tur•ba•tion [,mæstər'beiʃən] *n.* the manipulation of the genitals to induce sexual gratification. **—,mas•tur'ba•tion•al,** *adj.* **—'mas•tur•ba,to•ry,** *adj.*

ma•su ['mɑsu] *n.* See MASO.

mat¹ [mæt] *n., v.* **mat•ted, mat•ting.** *—n.* **1** a piece of coarse fabric like a rug, made of woven grass, straw, rope, etc. **2** a piece of material to put under a dish, vase, lamp, etc. **3** a large, thick pad on the floor of a ring, etc. to protect wrestlers or gymnasts. **4** anything packed or tangled thickly together: *a mat of weeds, a mat of hair.*
—v. **1** cover with mats. **2** pack or tangle together like a mat: *The swimmer's wet hair was matted. The fur collar mats when it gets wet.* ⟨OE *matt* < LL *matta*⟩
☛ *Hom.* MATTE.

mat² [mæt] *adj., n., v.* **mat•ted, mat•ting.** *—adj.* dull; not shiny.
—n. **1** a dull surface or finish. **2** a border for a picture, usually between the picture and the frame.
—v. **1** give a dull finish to. **2** put a mat around. Also (*adj., n.*), **matte.** ⟨< F *mat,* originally adj., dull, dead < *mater* subdue, checkmate⟩
☛ *Hom.* MATTE.

mat³ [mæt] *n.* MATRIX (def. 2).
☛ *Hom.* MATTE.

mat. 1 matinee. **2** matins. **3** maturity.

Mat•a•be•le [,mætə'bili] *n.* a member of a Zulu,

Bantu-speaking people who were driven out of the Transvaal in 1837 by the Boers; Ndebele.

mat•a•dor ['mætə,dɔr] *n.* the chief performer in a bullfight. The matador kills the bull with his sword. ⟨< Sp. < L *mactātor* slayer < *mactāre* to kill⟩

match[1] [mætʃ] *n.* **1** a short, slender piece of wood or pasteboard tipped with a mixture that takes fire when rubbed on a rough or specially prepared surface. **2** a cord prepared to burn at a uniform rate, for firing guns and cannon. ⟨ME < OF *mesche*, probably ult. < Gk. *myxa* lamp wick, influenced by VL *muccare* snuff < L *muccus* mucus⟩

match[2] [mætʃ] *n., v.* *—n.* **1** a person or thing equal to another. **2** a person or thing like another. **3** two persons or things that are alike and go well together: *Those two horses make a good match.* **4** a game; contest: *a boxing match, a tennis match.* **5** marriage: *She made a good match.* **6** a person considered as a possible spouse.
—v. **1** be equal to; be a match for. **2** be alike; go well together. **3** be the same as. **4** find one like; get a match for. **5** make like; fit together. **6** put in opposition; oppose. **7** marry. ⟨OE *(ge)mæcca* companion⟩ **—'match•a•ble,** *adj.* **—'match•er,** *n.*

match•board ['mætʃ,bɔrd] *n.* a board cut to fit with other boards having the same groove on one side and a tongue on the other.

match•book ['mætʃ,bʊk] *n.* a small paper folder to hold safety matches, having a striking surface on the cover.

match•box ['mætʃ,bɒks] *n.* a stiff cardboard box for matches, usually having a striking surface on one side.

match•less ['mætʃlɪs] *adj.* so great or wonderful that it cannot be equalled. **—'match•less•ly,** *adv.* **—'match•less•ness,** *n.*

match•lock ['mætʃ,lɒk] *n.* an old type of gun fired by lighting the charge of powder with a wick or cord.

match•mak•er[1] ['mætʃ,meikər] *n.* **1** a person who arranges, or tries to arrange, marriages for others. **2** a person who arranges contests, prize fights, races, etc. ⟨*match[2]* + *maker*⟩ **—'match,mak•ing,** *n., adj.*

match•mak•er[2] ['mætʃ,meikər] *n.* a person who makes matches for lighting. ⟨*match[1]* + *maker*⟩ **—'match,mak•ing,** *n., adj.*

match play **1** *Golf.* a form of competition in which the game is won by the winner of the greatest number of holes rather than by the player or side taking the fewest strokes. **2** a play in any match, as in tennis or hardball. **—match player.**

match point *Tennis, golf, etc.* the final point needed to win a match.

match•stick ['mætʃ,stɪk] *n.* a small, thin stick of wood from which a match is made.

match•wood ['mætʃ,wʊd] *n.* **1** wood for making matches. **2** splinters; tiny pieces.

mate[1] [meit] *n., v.* **mat•ed, mat•ing.** *—n.* **1** one of a pair. **2** either of two animals or birds (male and female) who have come together as a pair: *The eagle mourned its dead mate.* **3** a husband or wife. **4** *Nautical.* a ship's officer next below the captain. On large ships there is usually more than one mate: a first mate, a second mate, and, sometimes, a third mate. **5** assistant. **6** a companion or fellow worker: *John and Bill were mates in the army.*
—v. **1** put, bring, or come together as a pair: *Birds mate in the spring.* **2** marry. ⟨apparently < MLG *mate* messmate. Akin to MEAT.⟩ **—'mate•less,** *adj.*

mate[2] [meit] *n., v.* **mat•ed, mat•ing;** *interj. Chess.*
—n. a checkmate.
—v. checkmate; defeat.
—interj. checkmate. ⟨ME < OF *mater* checkmate < *mat* checkmated, defeated < Arabic. Related to MAT[2].⟩

ma•té or **ma•te[3]** ['mɑtei], ['mætei], *or* [mɑ'tei] *n.* **1** a stimulating beverage made from the dried aromatic leaves of a South American holly (*Ilex paraguariensis*). Maté is a popular drink in many South American countries. **2** the dried leaves, containing caffeine, from which the drink is made. **3** the plant itself. ⟨< Sp. < Quechua *mati* calabash dish⟩

ma•te•lote ['mætəlout]; *French,* [mat'lɔt] *n.* a highly seasoned stew made of fish and wine. ⟨< F *matelot* sailor⟩

ma•ter ['meitər] *or* ['mɑtər] *n. Informal.* mother. ⟨< L⟩

ma•ter•fa•mil•i•as [,meitərfə'mɪliəs] *or* [,mɑtərfə'miliəs] *n.* the mother of a family. ⟨< L⟩

ma•te•ri•al [mə'tiriəl] *n., adj.* *—n.* **1** what a thing is made from; substance of anything manufactured or built: *building materials, raw material.* **2** cloth: *I have enough material for a jacket and pants.* **3** anything serving as crude or raw matter for working upon or developing: *His files contain enough material for a score of books.* **4** a person thought of in terms of his or her potential in a given field or occupation: *Her coach is sure that she is Olympic material.* **5** written or printed material; information; documents.
—adj. **1** having to do with whatever occupies space; of matter; physical; corporeal. **2** of the body: *Food and shelter are material comforts.* **3** having to do with the things of this world rather than with intellectual or spiritual things. **4** that matters; important: *Hard work is a material factor in success.* **5** *Law.* likely to influence a case: *material evidence.* **6** *Philosophy.* concerning matter rather than form. ⟨ME < OF < LL *materialis* < *materia* timber, matter < *mater* trunk (of a tree). Doublet of MATÉRIEL.⟩
☛ *Syn. n.* See note at SUBSTANCE.

ma•te•ri•al•ism [mə'tiriə,lɪzəm] *n.* **1** *Philosophy.* the doctrine that matter is the fundamental reality and that all thought, feeling, etc. can be explained in terms of physical laws. **2** a tendency to care more for material possessions, physical well-being, etc. than for intellectual or spiritual needs.

ma•te•ri•al•ist [mə'tiriəlɪst] *n.* **1** a person who advocates materialism. **2** a person who cares more for material possessions and physical well-being than for intellectual or spiritual needs. **—ma,te•ri•al'is•tic,** *adj.* **—ma,te•ri•al'is•ti•cal•ly,** *adv.*

ma•te•ri•al•i•ty [mə,tiri'ælɪti] *n.* **1** a being material. **2** physical substance.

ma•te•ri•al•ize [mə'tiriə,laɪz] *v.* **-ized, -iz•ing. 1** become an actual fact; be realized: *Our plans for the party did not materialize.* **2** give material form to: *The inventor materialized her ideas by building a model.* **3** appear or cause to appear in material or bodily form: *A spirit materialized from the smoke of the magician's fire.* **—ma,te•ri•al•i'za•tion,** *n.* **—ma'te•ri•al,iz•er,** *n.*

ma•te•ri•al•ly [mə'tiriəli] *adv.* **1** with regard to material things; physically: *He improved materially and morally.* **2** considerably; greatly. **3** *Philosophy.* in matter or substance; not in form.

ma•te•ri•a med•i•ca [mə'tiriə 'mɛdɪkə] **1** drugs or other substances used in medicine. **2** the branch of medical science dealing with these drugs and substances. ⟨< NL *materia medica* medical material⟩

ma•té•ri•el [mə,tiri'ɛl] *n.* everything used by an army, organization, undertaking, etc.; equipment. ⟨< F *matériel* material < L *materialis.* Doublet of MATERIAL.⟩

ma•ter•nal [mə'tɜrnəl] *adj.* **1** of or like a mother; motherly. **2** related on the mother's side of the family: *maternal grandparents.* **3** received or inherited from a mother. ⟨< F *maternel* < L *maternus* < *mater* mother⟩ **—ma'ter•nal•ly,** *adv.*

maternal inheritance *Genetics.* inheritance of a trait from the mother.

ma•ter•ni•ty [mə'tɜrnəti] *n., adj.* *—n.* **1** motherhood; the condition of being a mother. **2** motherliness; qualities of a mother. **3** *Informal.* MATERNITY LEAVE: *She's on maternity.*
—adj. **1** for an expectant mother: *a maternity dress.* **2** for women in and after childbirth: *a maternity ward.*

maternity hospital a hospital providing facilities for childbirth and care for the mothers and their newborn babies.

maternity leave paid leave of absence from work for a mother before and after the baby is born.

math [mæθ] *n. Informal.* mathematics.

math. **1** mathematical. **2** mathematician.

math•e•mat•i•cal [,mæθə'mætəkəl] *or* [,mæθ'mætəkəl] *adj.* **1** of or having to do with mathematics. **2** exact; accurate. **—,math•e'mat•i•cal•ly,** *adv.*

mathematical logic SYMBOLIC LOGIC.

math•e•ma•ti•cian [,mæθəmə'tɪʃən] *n.* a person trained in mathematics, especially one whose work it is.

math•e•mat•ics [,mæθə'mætɪks] *n.* (*used with a singular verb*). the science dealing with the measurement, properties, and relationships of quantities. Mathematics includes arithmetic, algebra, geometry, calculus, etc. ⟨pl. of *mathematic* < L *mathematicus* < Gk. *mathēmatikos,* ult. < *manthanein* learn⟩

mat•i•née or **mat•i•nee** [,mætə'nei] *or* ['mætə,nei] *n.* a performance held in the afternoon, especially a dramatic or musical one. ⟨< F *matinée* < *matin* morning⟩

matinée or **matinee idol** an actor idolized by women.

ma•tins ['mætənz] *n.pl.* **1** *Roman Catholic Church.* the first of the seven canonical hours in the breviary. **2** *Anglican Church.* morning service; morning prayers. **3** Also, **matin.** *Poetic.*

morning song. ⟨ME < OF < LL *matutinus* of or in the morning < *Matuta* dawn goddess⟩

ma•tri•arch ['meitri,ɑrk] *n.* **1** a mother who is the ruler of a family or tribe. **2** a venerable old woman. ⟨< *matri-* (< L *mater, matris* mother) + (*patri*)*arch*⟩

ma•tri•ar•chal [,meitri'ɑrkəl] *adj.* **1** of a matriarch or matriarchy. **2** suitable for a matriarch.

ma•tri•ar•chate ['meitri,ɑrkɪt] *or* ['meitri,ɑrkeit] *n.* a society governed by women.

ma•tri•ar•chy ['meitri,ɑrki] *n., pl.* **-chies.** a form of social organization in which the mother is the ruler of a family or tribe and in which descent is traced through the mother.

mat•ric [mə'trɪk] *n. Esp. Brit. Informal.* matriculation.

matric. matriculation.

ma•tri•ces ['meitrə,siz] *or* ['mætrə,sɪz] *n.* pl. of MATRIX.

ma•tri•cid•al [,mætrə'saɪdəl] *or* [,meitrə'saɪdəl] *adj.* of, having to do with, or involving matricide.

ma•tri•cide ['mætrə,saɪd] *or* ['meitrə,saɪd] *n.* **1** the act of killing one's own mother. **2** a person who kills his or her mother. ⟨< L *matricidium* the murder of one's mother < *mater* mother + *-cidium* act of killing (for def. 1); < L *matricida* one who murders his mother < *mater* + *-cida* killer (for def. 2). 16c.⟩

ma•tric•u•late [mə'trɪkjə,leit] *v.* **-lat•ed, -lat•ing. 1** enrol as a student in a college or university. **2** enrol as a candidate for a degree. ⟨< LL *matricula,* dim. of L *matrix, -icis* register⟩ **—ma'tric•u,la•tor,** *n.*

ma•tric•u•la•tion [mə,trɪkjə'leiʃən] *n.* **1** an examination held at the end of secondary school or as a university entrance requirement. **2** the necessary qualification for university entrance. **3** the act of matriculating or the state of being matriculated.

ma•tri•foc•al [,mætrə'foukəl] *or* [,meitrə'foukəl] *adj.* of a society in which women are dominant.

ma•tri•lin•e•al [,mætrə'lɪniəl] *or* [,meitrə'lɪniəl] *adj.* of, having to do with, or designating descent or kinship through the maternal line: *a matrilineal tradition.* Compare PATRILINEAL. **—,ma•tri'lin•e•al•ly,** *adv.*

ma•tri•loc•al [,mætrə'loukəl] *or* [,meitrə'loukəl] *adj.* in early societies, having to do with the home of a wife's clan or kin.

mat•ri•mo•ni•al [,mætrə'mouniəl] *adj.* of marriage; having to do with marriage. **—,mat•ri•mo•ni•al•ly,** *adv.*

mat•ri•mo•ny ['mætrə,mouni] *n., pl.* **-nies. 1** married life. **2** the act of marrying; the rite or ceremony of marriage. **3** the relation between married persons. ⟨< L *matrimonium* < *mater* mother⟩

☛ *Syn.* **2, 3.** See note at MARRIAGE.

ma•trix ['meitrɪks] *or* ['mætrɪks] *n., pl.* **ma•tri•ces** ['meitrə,siz] *or* ['mætrə,sɪz] or **ma•trix•es. 1** that which gives origin or form to something enclosed within it. A mould for a casting, a main clause, or the rock in which gems are embedded is called a matrix. **2** *Printing.* a mould for casting faces of type. **3** a series of related things, as mathematical terms or electronic elements, arranged in a rectangular array of rows and columns. **4** *Archaic.* womb. ⟨< L *matrix* womb⟩

ma•tron ['meitrən] *n.* **1** a married woman or widow, especially a staid or dignified woman of middle age or older. **2** a woman who manages the household affairs or supervises the inmates of a school, hospital, prison, or other institution. ⟨ME < OF < L *matrona* < *mater* mother⟩

ma•tron•ly ['meitrənli] *adj.* like a matron; suitable for a matron; dignified. **—'ma•tron•li•ness,** *n.*

matron of honour or **honor** a married woman who is the chief attendant of the bride at a wedding; bridal attendant.

mat•ro•nym•ic [,mætrə'nɪmɪk] *adj., n. —adj.* derived from the name of a female ancestor.
—n. a name so derived.

matte[1] [mæt] *n.* an impure mixture of sulphides produced during the smelting of a sulphide ore. ⟨< F dial. *mate* lump⟩

☛ *Hom.* MAT.

matte[2] [mæt] *n.* See MAT[2].

☛ *Hom.* MAT.

mat•ted[1] ['mætɪd] *adj., v. —adj.* formed into a mat; entangled in a thick mass: *a matted growth of shrubs.*
—v. pt. and pp. of MAT. ⟨< *mat*[1]⟩

mat•ted[2] ['mætɪd] *adj.* having a dull finish. ⟨< *mat*[2]⟩

mat•ter ['mætər] *n., v. —n.* **1** the material of which something is made or composed; substance. **2** the substance of the material world; the opposite of mind or spirit. Matter occupies space. **3** what is said or written, thought of apart from the way in which it is said or written; content: *There was very little matter of interest in his speech.* **4** grounds or cause; basis: *If a person is robbed, he or she has matter for complaint to the police.* **5** an instance or case; a thing or concern: *a matter of fact, a matter of record, a matter of business.* **6** things written or printed: *reading matter.* **7** an amount or quantity: *a matter of 20 km.* **8** importance; significance. **9** mail: *Letters are first-class matter.* **10** a substance secreted by a living body, especially pus. **11** *Printing.* **a** something to be printed; copy. **b** type that has been composed.
as a matter of fact. See FACT.
for that matter, so far as that is concerned.
matter of life and death, something of crucial importance; something on which a lot depends.
matter of opinion, a debatable assertion or belief.
no matter, a it is not important; let it go. **b** regardless of: *He wants a bicycle, no matter what it costs.*
what is the matter? what is wrong?
—v. **1** be important: *Nothing seems to matter when you are very sick.* **2** form or discharge pus. ⟨ME < AF *matere* < L *materia,* originally, timber⟩

☛ *Syn. n.* **1.** See note at SUBSTANCE.

matter of course something that follows inevitably, as a result of logic or custom. **—'matter-of-'course,** *adj.*

mat•ter–of–fact ['mætər əv 'fækt] *adj.* **1** dealing with facts; not imaginative or fanciful: *a matter-of-fact report.* **2** not apologetic or equivocal; forthright. **—'mat•ter-of-'fact•ly,** *adv.* **—'mat•ter-of-'fact•ness,** *n.*

matter of record *Law.* something that is on record in a law court and can be established by producing the record.

mat•ting ['mætɪŋ] *n., v. —n.* fabric of grass, straw, hemp, or other fibre, for covering floors, for mats, for wrapping material, etc.
—v. ppr. of MAT.

mat•tock ['mætək] *n.* a tool like a pickaxe, but having a flat, adzelike blade on one or both sides. It is used for loosening soil and cutting roots. ⟨OE *mattuc*⟩

mat•tress ['mætrɪs] *n.* a thick, more or less soft or resilient pad consisting of padded, coiled springs or material such as foam rubber, cotton, or straw encased in a covering of strong cloth and used to form a bed or part of a bed. An **air mattress** is inflated. ⟨ME *materas* < OF < Ital. *materasso* < Arabic *almatrah* cushion⟩

mat•u•rate ['mætʃə,reit] *v.* **-rat•ed, -rat•ing. 1** *Pathology.* discharge pus; fester. **2** ripen; mature. ⟨< L *maturare* < *maturus* ripe⟩ **—ma'tur•a•tive** [mə'tʃʊrətɪv], *adj.*

mat•u•ra•tion [,mætʃə'reiʃən] *n.* **1** a discharge of pus; festering. **2** a ripening; a maturing. **3** *Biology.* the final stages in the preparation of germ cells for fertilization. **—,mat•u'ra•tion•al,** *adj.*

ma•ture [mə'tʃʊr] *or* [mə'tjʊr] *adj., v.* **-tured, -tur•ing.** *—adj.* **1** ripe or full-grown: *Grain is harvested when it is mature.* **2** having or showing full development of the body, mind, etc.: *a mature face, mature thinking.* **3** brought by time, treatment, etc. to the condition of full excellence: *mature wine, mature cheese.* **4** fully worked out; carefully and completely thought out: *By next year we will have a mature plan for the subway.* **5** due; payable: *a mature loan.*
—v. **1** come or bring to full growth; ripen: *The apples are maturing rapidly. We need more sun to mature the crops.* **2** of the body, mind, etc., come or bring to full development: *The experience has matured her understanding.* **3** make or become ready or complete: *to mature a plan.* **4** fall due; become payable: *The bonds will mature in ten years.* ⟨< L *maturus* ripe⟩ **—ma'ture•ly,** *adv.* **—ma'ture•ness,** *n.* **—ma'tur•er,** *n.*

ma•tu•ri•ty [mə'tʃʊrəti] *or* [mə'tjʊrəti] *n.* **1** a state of ripeness; full development. **2** a being completed or ready: *When their plans reached maturity, they were able to begin.* **3** a falling due; the time a debt is payable.

ma•tu•ti•nal [mə'tjutənəl] *or* [mə'tutənəl] *adj.* occurring in the morning; early in the day; having to do with the morning. ⟨< LL *matutinalis* < *matutinus* of or in the morning. See MATINS.⟩ **—ma'tu•ti•nal•ly,** *adv.*

matz•o ['mɑtsou] *n., pl.* **matz•oth** ['mɑtsout] or **matz•os** ['mɑtsouz]. a thin piece of unleavened bread, eaten by Jews especially during the Passover. ⟨< Hebrew *matstsōth,* pl. of *matstsāh,* a cake of unleavened bread⟩

maud•lin ['mɒdlɪn] *adj.* **1** sentimental in a weak, silly way: *maudlin sympathy.* **2** sentimental and tearful as a result of drinking too much alcoholic liquor. ⟨alteration of Mary *Magdalene*, often painted as weeping⟩

mau•gre ['mɒgər] *prep. Archaic.* in spite of; notwithstanding. Also, **mauger.** ⟨ME < OF *maugre*, originally n., ill will < L *malus* bad + *gratus* pleasing⟩

maul [mɒl] *v., n.* —*v.* beat and pull about; handle roughly; bruise and lacerate: *The lion mauled its keeper badly.*
—*n.* a very heavy hammer or mallet. ⟨ME *mallen* < OF *maillier*⟩
☛ *Hom.* MALL, MOLL.

maund [mɒnd] *n.* a unit of mass in India and other parts of Asia, varying with the locality. The standard is 37.5 kg. ⟨< Hind. *man* < Skt. *manā*⟩

maun•der ['mɒndər] *v.* **1** talk in a rambling, foolish way. People who maunder talk much but say little of value. **2** move or act in an aimless, confused manner: *The injured man maundered about in a daze.* ⟨origin uncertain⟩ **—'maun•der•er,** *n.*

Maun•dy Thursday ['mɒndi] the Thursday before Easter. ⟨*Maundy*, ME < OF *mande* < L *mandatum* a command⟩

Mau•ri•ta•nia [,mɔrə'teiniə] *n.* a country in NW Africa, properly called the Islamic Republic of Mauritania. See SENEGAL for map. **—,Mau•ri'ta•ni•an,** *adj.*

Mau•ri•tius [mɔ'rɪʃəs] *n.* an island country in the Indian Ocean, since 1968 a member of the Commonwealth.
—Mau'ri•tian, *adj.*

Mauritius parakeet a bird (*Psittacula echo*) having bright green plumage, found only in a small area of Mauritius. It is an endangered species as its forest habitat is being cleared.

mau•so•le•um [,mɒzə'liəm] *or* [,mɒsə'liəm] *n., pl.* **-le•ums, -le•a** [-'liə]. **1 Mausoleum,** at Halicarnassus, the magnificent tomb of King Mausolos of Caria, in ancient times a kingdom in SW Asia Minor. The tomb was one of the seven wonders of the ancient world. **2** a large, magnificent tomb. **3** a structure built to entomb many bodies. ⟨< L < Gk. *Mausōleion*⟩

mauve [mouv] *or* [mɒv] *n. or adj.* delicate, pale purple. ⟨< F < L *malva* mallow. Doublet of MALLOW.⟩

ma•ven or **ma•vin** ['meivən] *n.* a person who knows all about a certain subject; expert: *a railway maven.* ⟨< Yiddish < Hebrew, connoisseur⟩

mav•er•ick ['mævərɪk] *n.* **1** a calf or other animal not marked with an owner's brand. **2** *Informal.* one who refuses to affiliate with a regular political party. **3** *Informal.* any person or organization that is unconventional or unwilling to conform; a rebel. ⟨probably after Samuel *Maverick* (1803-1870), a Texan who did not brand his cattle⟩

ma•vis ['meivɪs] *n.* the song thrush of Europe. ⟨ME < OF *mauvis* < Celtic⟩

ma•vour•neen or **ma•vour•nin** [mə'vʊrnin] *or* [mə'vɔrnin] *n. Irish.* my darling. ⟨< Irish *mo mhuirnín*⟩

maw [mɒ] *n.* **1** the mouth and throat of an animal, especially a carnivorous animal. **2** the stomach of an animal or bird.
3 anything thought of as resembling this in appetite: *Nations continue to pour wealth into the maw of war.* ⟨OE *maga*⟩
☛ *Hom.* MA.

mawk•ish ['mɒkɪʃ] *adj.* **1** sickening. **2** sickly sentimental; weakly emotional. ⟨originally, maggoty < *mawk* maggot < ON *mathkr*⟩ **—'mawk•ish•ly,** *adv.* **—'mawk•ish•ness,** *n.*

max. maximum.

max•i ['mæksi] *n. Informal.* **1** a maxi-skirt. **2** anything else that is the biggest of a series or of its kind.

maxi– *combining form.* large; great; long: *maxi-skirt.* ⟨< *maximum*⟩

max•il•la [mæk'sɪlə] *n., pl.* **max•il•lae** [mæk'sɪli] *or* [mæk'sɪlaɪ]. **1** in vertebrates, the jaw; jawbone; upper jawbone.
2 either of a pair of appendages just behind the mandibles of insects, crabs, etc. ⟨< L *maxilla* jaw⟩

max•il•lar•y ['mæksə,lɛri] *or* [mæk'sɪləri] *adj., n., pl.* **-lar•ies.**
—*adj.* of or having to do with the jaw or jawbone.
—*n.* the maxilla. ⟨< L *maxillāris* of or belonging to the jaw⟩

max•il•li•ped [mæk'sɪlə,pɛd] *n.* one of two appendages behind the mandibles in crabs and other similar crustaceans. ⟨< *maxilla* + L *pes, pedis* foot⟩ **—,max•il•li'ped•a•ry,** *adj.*

max•im ['mæksəm] *n.* a short rule of conduct; proverb; statement of a general truth: *"Look before you leap" is a maxim.* ⟨ME *maxime* < OF < LL *maxima (propositio)* axiom, literally, greatest proposition⟩

max•i•ma ['mæksəmə] *n.* a pl. of MAXIMUM.

max•i•mal ['mæksəməl] *adj.* being the greatest possible.
—'max•i•mal•ly, *adv.*

max•i•mize ['mæksə,maɪz] *v.* **-mized, -miz•ing. 1** increase or intensify as much as possible; make as great as possible. **2** treat or make seem as great or important. ⟨< *maximum* + *-ize*⟩
—,max•i•mi'za•tion, *n.* **—'max•i,miz•er,** *n.*

max•i•mum ['mæksəməm] *n., pl.* **-mums** or **-ma;** *adj.* —*n.*
1 the largest or highest amount; upper limit: *He had decided that he would spend a maximum of $1000 at the auction.*
2 *Mathematics.* the greatest value of a function within a given interval of the domain of the function.
—*adj.* largest; highest; greatest possible: *The maximum score on the test is 100.* ⟨< L *maximum*, neut. adj., superlative of *magnus* great⟩

max•i–skirt ['mæksi ,skɜrt] *n.* a long skirt, reaching well below the knee.

max•well ['mækswɛl] *or* ['mækswəl] *n. Electricity.* a unit of magnetic flux. *Abbrev.:* Mx ⟨after J.C. *Maxwell* (1831-1879), Scottish physicist⟩

may [mei] *auxiliary v.* **might.** *May* is used to express:
1 possibility, opportunity, or permission: *You may enter.* **2** a wish or prayer: *May you be very happy.* **3** contingency, especially in clauses expressing condition, concession, purpose, result, etc.: *I write that you may know my plans.* **4** *Archaic.* ability or power. ⟨OE *mæg*⟩
☛ *Usage.* See note at CAN.

May [mei] *n.* the fifth month of the year. It has 31 days. ⟨< L *Maius*⟩

ma•ya ['mɑjə] *or* ['maɪə] *n. Hinduism.* illusory nature of the sense world, often personified as a woman. ⟨< Skt.⟩

Ma•ya ['mɑjə] *or* ['maɪə] *n., pl.* **Ma•ya** or **Ma•yas. 1** a member of any of a large group of peoples mainly of Yucatán, Belize, and Guatemala, who speak Mayan languages. **2** a member of the branch of the Maya living in Yucatán. The ancient Maya are famous for the remarkable civilization they developed, which flourished between about A.D. 250 and 900. **3** a Mayan language of the ancient Maya.

Ma•yan ['mɑjən] *or* ['maɪən] *n., adj.* —*n.* **1** a language family of Mexico and Central America. **2** Maya.
—*adj.* of or having to do with the Maya or their language.

may•ap•ple or **May apple** ['mei,æpəl] *n. Cdn.* **1** a perennial herb (*Podophyllum peltatum*) of the barberry family found in E North America, having a single large, white flower and an edible, yellowish, oval fruit. **2** the fruit of this plant.

may•be ['meibi] *or* ['mɛbi] *adv.* possibly; perhaps; it may be so.
☛ *Usage.* **Maybe, may be. Maybe** is an adverb meaning 'perhaps'; **may be** is a verb form: *Maybe you'll have better luck next time. She may be the next mayor.*

May•day ['mei,dei] *n.* an international signal of distress, used in emergencies by ships and aircraft. ⟨< pseudo-French *m'aidez* help me⟩

May Day May 1, traditionally celebrated as a festival of spring, accompanied by the crowning of a May queen, and dancing around the Maypole. It is now celebrated as Labour Day in some countries.

may•est ['meiəst] *v. Archaic.* second person singular, present tense of MAY. *Thou mayest* means *you may.* Sometimes, **mayst.**

may•flow•er ['mei,flaʊər] *n.* **1** *Cdn.* TRAILING ARBUTUS.
2 any of various other flowering plants that bloom in spring, such as the hawthorn. **3 Mayflower,** the ship on which the Pilgrim Fathers came to America in 1620.

may•fly ['mei,flaɪ] *n., pl.* **-flies. 1** any of an order (Ephemeroptera) of insects, the larva of which is aquatic and the adult having large, membranous, triangular forewings, small hind wings, and a slender body. The mayfly lives as a larva for two or more years, but only a day or two as a winged adult. **2** an artificial fishing fly made in imitation of this insect.

may•hap [,mei'hæp] *or* ['mei,hæp] *adv. Archaic.* perhaps. ⟨for *it may hap*⟩

may•hem ['meihɛm] *or* ['meiəm] *n.* **1** *Law.* the crime of maiming or injuring a person so that he or she is less able to defend himself or herself. **2** confusion and willful violence. ⟨< AF *mahaym* maim; origin uncertain⟩

May•ing ['meiɪŋ] *n.* the celebration of May Day; taking part in May festivities.

may•n't ['meiənt] *or* [meint] may not.

ma•yo ['meiou] *n. Informal.* mayonnaise: *Hold the mayo.*

may•on•naise [,meiə'neiz] *or* ['meiə,neiz] *n.* a thick dressing for salads, made of egg yolks, vegetable oil, vinegar or lemon juice, and seasoning. ⟨< F *mayonnaise*, ult. < *Mahón*, a seaport in Minorca, captured by the Duc de Richelieu, whose chef introduced the *Mahonnaise* after his master's victory⟩

may•or ['meiər] *or* [mɛr] *n.* the person at the head of the government of a city, town, or village. ⟨ME < OF *maire, maor* < L *major.* Doublet of MAJOR.⟩
☛ *Hom.* MARE [mɛr].

may•or•al•ty ['meiərəlti] *or* ['mɛrəlti] *n., pl.* **-ties. 1** the position of mayor. **2** a mayor's term of office.

May•pole or **may•pole** ['mei,poul] *n.* **1** a high pole decorated with flowers and ribbons, around which merrymakers dance on May Day. **2** *Cdn.* lobstick.

May queen a girl crowned with flowers and honoured as queen on May Day.

mayst MAYEST [meist].

May thorn a European hawthorn tree (*Crataegus monogyna*) having deeply lobed leaves, short thorns, and single-seeded fruits.

May•time ['mei,taɪm] *n.* the month of May.

May tree hawthorn.

May wine a mixture of three German wines, flavoured with woodruff (*Asperula odorata*).

Maz•da•ism ['mæzdə,ɪzəm] *n.* Zoroastrianism. ⟨See ORMAZD⟩

maze [meiz] *n.* **1** a network of paths through which it is hard to find one's way. **2** any complicated arrangement, as of streets, buildings, etc. **3** a state of confusion; muddled condition. ⟨var. of *amaze*⟩
☛ *Hom.* MAIZE.

ma•zer ['meizər] *n.* a goblet of metal or of hard wood. ⟨ME *maser* < OF *masere* maple wood < Gmc. as in OHG *masar* gnarled growth on oaks, ON *mösurr* maple⟩

maz•in•dol ['mæzən,dɒl] *n.* a drug used to treat obesity.

ma•zu•ma [mə'zumə] *n. Slang.* money. ⟨< Yiddish *mezumen* < Hebrew *mezūmān* set, fixed⟩

ma•zur•ka or **ma•zour•ka** [mə'zɜrkə] *or* [mə'zʊrkə] *n.* **1** a lively Polish dance. **2** the music for this dance, in 3/4 or 3/8 time. ⟨< Polish *mazurka*, a dance of *Mazur* (*Mazovia*), a province of Poland⟩

maz•y ['meizi] *adj.* **maz•i•er, maz•i•est.** like a maze, intricate: *mazy paths.* **—'maz•i•ly,** *adv.* **—'maz•i•ness,** *n.*

maz•zard ['mæzərd] *n.* a wild sweet cherry tree (*Prunus avium*) used mainly in grafting.

MB 1 *Cdn.* MEDAL OF BRAVERY. **2** Manitoba (*used esp. in computerized address systems*). **3** *Computer technology.* megabyte.

mbar millibar or millibars.

M.B.E. Member of (the Order of) the British Empire.

M•bun•du [əm'bʊndu] *n.* **1** a people of S Angola. **2** the Bantu language of these people.

mc millicycle.

Mc megacycle.

MC *Cdn.* Member of the Order of Canada.

M.C. 1 MILITARY CROSS. **2** Member of Congress. **3** MASTER OF CEREMONIES. **4** Medical Corps.

McCar•thy•ism [mə'kɑrθi,ɪzəm] *n.* **1** the act or practice of making sensational public accusations of political disloyalty or corruption, usually with little evidence. **2** the practice of holding public investigations, supposedly to reveal Communist sympathy or activity. ⟨< Senator Joseph R. *McCarthy* (1909-1957), chairman of the U.S. Senate Permanent Investigations Committee⟩

Mc•Coy [mə'kɔɪ] *n. Informal.*
the real McCoy, a genuine person or thing. ⟨origin uncertain⟩

Mc•In•tosh ['mækɪn,tɒʃ] *n. Cdn.* a bright red winter apple having crisp, white flesh. Also called **McIntosh Red.** ⟨< John *McIntosh* (1777-?), an Ontario farmer, who transplanted several wild trees in 1796, of which one lived to produce the apple that bears his name⟩

MCpl. or **MCpl** MASTER CORPORAL.

Md mendelevium.

M.D. Municipal District.

mdse. merchandise.

MDu. Middle Dutch.

M. du C. *Cdn.* Médaille du Canada.

me [mi] *pron.* the objective form of I: *The dog bit me. Give me a bandage.* ⟨OE *mē*⟩
☛ *Usage.* It is good English to say *It is me* (or *It's me*) in speech, though some people consider *It is I* to be correct in writing. Except in written conversation, *It's me* rarely occurs in writing.

ME or **M.E.** MIDDLE ENGLISH.

M.E. 1 Mechanical Engineer. **2** Mining Engineer. **3** Methodist Episcopal.

mead¹ [mid] *n. Poetic.* meadow. ⟨OE *mǣd*⟩
☛ *Hom.* MEED, MEDE.

mead² [mid] *n.* an alcoholic drink made from fermented honey. ⟨OE *medu*⟩
☛ *Hom.* MEED.

mead•ow ['mɛdou] *n.* **1** a piece of grassy land; a field where hay is grown. **2** low, wet, grassy land near a stream. **3** *Cdn., B.C.* an expanse of grassland, usually more or less surrounded by trees, in the uplands and valleys of the mountains. ⟨OE *mǣdwe*, oblique case of *mǣd* mead¹⟩ **—'mead•ow•less,** *adj.*

mead•ow•lark ['mɛdou,lɑrk] either of two North American songbirds (*Sturnella neglecta* and *S. magna*) of the same family as the blackbirds and orioles, both having mottled brown upper parts and yellow under parts, with a black crescent on the breast. The bubbling song of the western meadowlark (*S. neglecta*) is very different from the high whistle of the eastern meadowlark.

Meadowlark

mead•ow•sweet ['mɛdou,swit] *n.* **1** any of several North American plants (genus *Spiraea*) of the rose family having clusters of small, fragrant flowers. **2** a Eurasian plant (*Filipendula ulmaria*) of the rose family having dense clusters of small, fragrant, whitish flowers.

mead•ow•y ['mɛdoui] *adj.* **1** like a meadow. **2** of meadows.

mea•ger ['migər] *adj.* See MEAGRE.

mea•gre ['migər] *adj.* **1** poor or scanty: *a meagre meal.* **2** thin or lean: *a meagre face.* **3** without fullness or richness; deficient in quality. Also, **meager.** ⟨ME < OF *maigre* < L *macer* thin⟩ **—'mea•gre•ly,** *adv.* **—'mea•gre•ness,** *n.*
☛ *Syn.* **1.** See note at SCANTY.

meal¹ [mil] *n.* **1** breakfast, lunch, dinner, supper, or tea. **2** the food served or eaten at any one time. ⟨OE *mǣl*⟩

meal² [mil] *n.* **1** ground grain, especially corn meal. **2** anything ground to a powder. ⟨OE *melu*⟩

meal ticket 1 a ticket authorizing a person to obtain a meal. **2** *Slang.* someone or something that provides a living for oneself, another, or others.

meal•time ['mil,taɪm] *n.* the usual time for eating a meal.

meal train *Cdn.* a cat-train made up of sleds carrying the cooking, eating, and sleeping quarters of a work party in the wilderness.

meal•y ['mili] *adj.* **meal•i•er, meal•i•est. 1** like meal; dry and powdery. **2** of meal. **3** covered with meal. **4** pale. **5** mealy-mouthed. **—'meal•i•ness,** *n.*

meal•y–mouthed ['mili ,maʊðd] *or* [,mʌuθt] *adj.* unwilling to tell the truth in plain words; using soft, insincere words. **—'meal•y-,mouth•ed•ly** ['mili ,mʌuθɪdli], *adv.* **—'meal•y-,mouth•ed•ness,** *adj.*

mealy pudding a Scottish dish comprising a boiled sausage, oats, finely chopped onion, etc.

mean¹ [min] *v.* **meant, mean•ing. 1** refer to; signify; denote: *What does this word mean?* **2** indicate or intend to express: *Keep out; that means you.* **3** convey; communicate: *What is that look supposed to mean?* **4** have as a purpose; have in mind; intend: *I do not mean to go.* **5** have intentions of some kind; be minded or disposed: *She means well.* **6** design for a definite purpose: *This toy is meant for young children.* **7** destine: *Fate meant us for each other. He was meant to be a teacher.*
mean well by, have kindly feelings toward. ⟨OE *mǣnan*⟩
☛ *Hom.* MIEN, MESNE.
☛ *Syn.* **4.** See note at INTEND.

mean² [min] *adj.* **1** low in quality or grade; poor. **2** low in social position or rank; humble: *A peasant is of mean birth.* **3** of

little importance or value: *the meanest flower.* **4** of poor appearance; shabby: *a mean house.* **5** small-minded; ignoble: *mean thoughts.* **6** stingy: *mean about money.* **7** *Informal.* humiliated; ashamed: *to feel mean.* **8** *Informal.* hard to manage; troublesome; bad-tempered: *a mean horse.* **9** selfish and ill-tempered; vicious; unkind. **10** *Informal.* in poor physical condition; unwell: *I feel mean today.* **11** *Slang.* expert; done or handled with skill: *She still plays a mean guitar.*
no mean, very good; very well: *He is no mean artist.* ⟨OE *(ge)mæne* common⟩ **—'mean•ly,** *adv.* **—'mean•ness,** *adj.*
☛ *Hom.* MIEN, MESNE.

mean³ [min] *adj.* **1** halfway between the two extremes of a set of values; average: *The mean temperature for July in Yarmouth is 16.4°C.* **2** intermediate in kind, quality, or degree. **3** having a value intermediate between the values of other quantities: *a mean diameter.*
—n. **1** the average; arithmetic mean: *The grades this year have been consistently above the mean for the course.* **2** a condition, quality, or course of action halfway between two extremes or opposites; a medium: *the golden mean.* **3** *Mathematics.* **means,** *pl.* **a** all the terms between the first and last terms of an arithmetic progression. **b** the two middle terms of a proportion of four terms: *The means in the proportion* 8:4 = 4:2 *are* 4 *and* 4. **4 means,** what a thing is done by; the method or methods or the agency by which something is brought about (*used with a singular or plural verb*): *by fair means. She thinks of her car as simply a means of transportation.* **5 means,** *pl.* **a** money resources: *to live within one's means.* **b** wealth; riches: *a woman of means.*
by all means, certainly; without fail.
by any means, in any possible way; at any cost.
by means of, by the use of; through; with: *I found my dog by means of a notice in the paper.*
by no means, certainly not; not at all; under no circumstances; in no way: *This work is by no means easy.*
means to an end, a way of getting or doing something. ⟨ME < OF *meien* < L *medianus* middle < *medius*⟩
☛ *Hom.* MIEN, MESNE.
☛ *Usage.* **Means** meaning 'what a thing is done by' is plural in form and singular or plural in use: *A means of communication is lacking. The means of helping others are never lacking.* **Means** meaning 'wealth' is plural in form and in use: *His means permit him to live comfortably.*

me•an•der [mi'ændər] *v., n.* *—v.* **1** follow a winding course: *A brook meanders through the meadow.* **2** wander aimlessly: *We meandered through the park.*
—n. **1** a winding course. **2** an aimless wandering. ⟨< L < Gk. *Maiandros*, the name of a winding river in Asia Minor⟩ **—me'an•der•er,** *n.* **—me'an•der•ing•ly,** *adv.*

mean deviation *Statistics.* average deviation; the arithmetic mean of deviation from the median in a statistical distribution.

mean distance *Astronomy.* in the orbit of a planet, the average of the distances it reaches from its focus.

mean•ie ['mini] *n. Informal.* a mean or unkind person.

mean•ing ['miniŋ] *n., adj., v.* *—n.* what is meant or intended; significance.
—adj. that means something; expressive: *a meaning look.*
—v. ppr. of MEAN. **—'mean•ing•ly,** *adv.*
☛ *Syn. n.* **Meaning,** SENSE, PURPORT = what is expressed or meant. **Meaning** is the general word applying to the idea expressed or intended by a word, statement, gesture, action, painting, etc.: *The meaning of the sentence is clear.* **Sense** applies to the meaning of something said or written, especially to a particular meaning of a word: *In what sense did you mean that?* In other senses this word is not a synonym of **meaning. Purport,** formal, means the main idea or general drift of a longer statement: *That was the purport of the president's address.*

mean•ing•ful ['miniŋfəl] *adj.* full of meaning; having much meaning; significant. **—'mean•ing•ful•ly,** *adv.* **—'mean•ing•ful•ness,** *n.*

mean•ing•less ['miniŋlɪs] *adj.* **1** without meaning; not making sense. **2** not significant. **—'mean•ing•less•ly,** *adv.* **—'mean•ing•less•ness,** *n.*

mean•ness ['minnɪs] *n.* **1** a being mean. **2** a mean act.

mean solar time time measured by the MEAN SUN so as to give equal 24-hour days throughout the year.

means test an inquiry into the income and assets of a person applying for public funds.

mean sun a theoretical sun moving at a uniform rate along the celestial equator like the real sun, and used in computing mean solar time.

meant [mɛnt] *v.* pt. and pp. of MEAN¹.

mean•time ['min,taɪm] *n., adv.* *—n.* the time between: *The carnival opens Friday; in the meantime we will make our costumes.* *—adv.* meanwhile.

mean•while ['min,waɪl] *adv., n.* *—adv.* **1** in the time or period between: *Classes finish at 12 and start again at 2; meanwhile we can swim and have lunch.* **2** at the same time, especially in a different place.
—n. meantime.

mea•sles ['mizəlz] *n.* (*used with a singular verb*). **1** an infectious disease characterized by a bad cold, fever, and a breaking out of small, red spots on the skin. **2** a similar but much less severe disease, properly called **German measles. 3** a disease of pigs and cattle caused by the larvae of tapeworms. ⟨ME *meseles*, pl. of *mesel* spot characteristic of measles; akin to MDu. *masel*⟩

mea•sly ['mizli] *adj.* **-sli•er, -sli•est. 1** of or like measles. **2** having measles. **3** *Slang.* scanty; meagre; small: *He earns a measly $5 per hour.* **4** *Slang.* poor; unsatisfactory: *a measly performance.*

meas•ur•a•ble ['mɛʒərəbəl] *adj.* **1** capable of being measured; mensurable. **2** large enough to be measured; perceptible. **—,meas•ur•a'bil•ity,** *n.* **—'meas•ur•a•bly,** *adv.*

meas•ure ['mɛʒər] *v.* **-ured, -ur•ing;** *n.* *—v.* **1** find out the extent, size, quantity, capacity, etc. of (something); estimate by some standard: *to measure a room.* **2** be of specified dimensions: *This brick measures 5 cm × 10 cm × 20 cm.* **3** get or take by measuring; mark off or out in metres, litres, etc.: *Measure off 2 m of silk. Measure out a kilogram of potatoes.* **4** take measurements; find out sizes or amounts. **5** admit of measurement; be measurable. **6** serve as a measure of. **7** assess; estimate: *to measure a person's character by his or her actions.* **8** adjust (*to*): *He measured his expenses to his income.* **9** *Poetic.* travel over; traverse.
measure (one's) **length,** *Archaic.* fall, be thrown, or lie flat on the ground.
measure out, a distribute by measuring. **b** distribute carefully.
measure swords, a fight with swords. **b** take part in a duel, battle, debate, etc.
measure up, have the necessary features; meet a required standard: *The party did not measure up to her expectations.*
—n. **1** the act or process of finding extent, size, quantity, capacity, etc. of something, especially by comparison with a standard. **2** the size, dimensions, quantity, etc. thus ascertained: *His waist measure is 70 cm.* **3** an instrument for measuring: *A ruler is a linear measure.* **4** a system of measuring: *dry measure.* **5** a unit or standard of measuring. *Centimetre*, *kilogram*, *litre*, and *hour* are common measures. **6** any standard of comparison, estimation, or judgment. **7** a quantity or degree that should not be exceeded; reasonable limit: *to be angry beyond measure.* **8** quantity; extent; degree; proportion: *The measure of her courage was remarkable.* **9** rhythm, as in poetry or music: *the stately measure of blank verse.* **10** a metrical unit; foot of poetry. **11** *Music.* **a** a unit of rhythm, consisting of one strong beat and one or more weak beats. **b** the notes contained between two bar lines; a bar. **12** a dance or dance movement. **13** a course of action; procedure: *take measures to relieve suffering.* **14** a legislative enactment. **15** *Mathematics.* a quantity contained in another a certain number of times without remainder. **16** a definite quantity measured out: *to drink a measure.*
beyond measure, immeasurable; immeasurably.
for good measure, as something extra.
full measure, all it should be.
in some (or **a**) **measure,** to some degree; partly.
made to measure, of a garment, custom-made according to the customer's measurements.
take measures, do something; act: *The police are taking measures to counteract street fighting.*
take (someone's) **measure,** judge someone's character or someone's abilities.
tread a measure, *Archaic.* dance. ⟨ME *mesure* < OF mesurer < L *mensura*, n., *mensurare*, v. < *mensus*, pp. of *metiri* to measure⟩ **—'meas•ur•er,** *n.*

meas•ured ['mɛʒərd] *adj., v.* *—adj.* **1** regular; uniform. **2** rhythmical. **3** written in poetry, not in prose. **4** deliberate and restrained, not hasty or careless.
—v. pt. and pp. of MEASURE. **—'meas•ured•ly,** *adv.* **'meas•ured•ness,** *adj.*

meas•ure•less ['mɛʒərlɪs] *adj.* too great to be measured; unlimited; vast. **—'meas•ure•less•ly,** *adv.* **—'meas•ure•less•ness,** *n.*

meas•ure•ment ['mɛʒərmənt] *n.* **1** the act or process of measuring or finding the size, quantity, or amount: *The measurement of length by a metre-stick is easy.* **2** the size found by measuring: *The measurements of the room are 6 m by 4.5 m.* **3** a system of measuring or of measures.

measuring cup a pitcher, usually of glass or plastic, marked with a graduated scale for making measurements.

measuring worm the larva of any geometrid moth. It moves by bringing the rear end of its body forward, forming a loop, and then advancing the front end. Also called **inchworm.**

meat [mit] *n.* **1** animal flesh used as food. Fish and poultry are not usually called meat. **2** *Poetic.* food of any kind: *meat and drink.* **3** the part of anything that can be eaten: *the meat of a nut.* **4** the essential part or parts; substance; food for thought: *the meat of an argument, the meat of a book.* **5** *Archaic.* a meal: *Say grace before meat.* **6** *Slang.* something a person finds easy and pleasant: *Something to do with electronics would be more his meat than a job in commerce.* ⟨OE *mete*⟩ **—'meat•less,** *adj.*
☛ *Hom.* MEET, METE.

meat•ball ['mit,bɒl] *n.* ground meat shaped into a ball before cooking.

meat hawk *Cdn.* CANADA JAY.

meat loaf ground meat mixed with breadcrumbs and spices, baked in a loaf pan and sliced for eating. Also, **meatloaf.**

meat packing the business of slaughtering animals and preparing their meat for transportation and sale.

me•a•tus [mi'eitəs] *n., pl.* **-tus•es** or **-tus.** *Anatomy.* a passage, duct, or opening, especially in a bone or bony structure, as the ear, nose, etc. ⟨< L *meatus* path < *meare* to pass⟩

meat•y ['miti] *adj.* **meat•i•er, meat•i•est. 1** of meat; having the flavour of meat. **2** like meat. **3** full of meat. **4** full of substance; giving food for thought: *The speech was very meaty; it contained many valuable ideas.* **5** heavily fleshed. **—'meat•i•ly,** *adv.*

me•ben•da•zole [mə'bɛndə,zoul] *n.* a drug used to treat pinworm and other infestations.

Mec•ca ['mɛkə] *n.* **1** the birthplace of Mohammed and holy city of the Muslims. **2 mecca,** a place that many people visit: *a tourist mecca.* **3 mecca,** a place that many people long for as a goal. **—'Mec•can,** *adj.*

mech. **1** mechanical. **2** mechanism.

me•chan•ic [mə'kænɪk] *n.* **1** a worker skilled with tools. **2** a worker who repairs machinery. ⟨< L *mēchanicus* < Gk. *mēchanikos* < *mēchanē* machine⟩

me•chan•i•cal [mə'kænəkəl] *adj.* **1** having to do with machinery or mechanisms. **2** made or worked by machinery. **3** like a machine; like that of a machine; automatic; without expression: *Her reading is very mechanical.* **4** of, having to do with, or in accordance with the science of mechanics. **—me'chan•i•cal•ly,** *adv.* **—me'chan•i•cal•ness,** *n.*

mechanical advantage the ratio of the output of a machine to the input.

mechanical drawing *Mechanics.* drawing done with the help of rulers, scales, compasses, etc., such as an architect's plans.

mechanical engineering the branch of engineering that deals with the design, production, and use of machines and machinery.

mech•a•ni•cian [,mɛkə'nɪʃən] *n.* a worker skilled in making and repairing machines.

me•chan•ics [mə'kænɪks] *n.* (*used with a sing. verb in 1 & 2*) **1** the branch of physics dealing with motion and the effect of forces on bodies to produce motion or a state of balance; it includes kinematics, kinetics, and statics. **2** the application of the principles of mechanics to the design, construction, and operation of machinery. **3** the mechanical or technical part of something; technique: *the mechanics of playing the piano.* **4** MECHANISM (def. 2).

mechanic's lien the right of a mechanic to possess (something, such as a vehicle) when repair bills are not paid.

mech•a•nism ['mɛkə,nɪzəm] *n.* **1** a machine or its working parts: *Something must be wrong with the mechanism of our refrigerator.* **2** the system of parts working together as the parts of a machine do: *The bones and muscles are parts of the mechanism of the body.* **3** the means or way by which something is done; machinery: *Committees are a useful mechanism for getting things done.* **4** a mechanical aspect; technique. **5** *Psychology.* **a** the arrangements in the mind or brain that determine thought, feeling, or action in regular and predictable ways. **b** a response unconsciously selected to protect oneself or find satisfaction for an unfulfilled desire: *a defence mechanism.* **6** *Philosophy.* the theory that everything in the universe is produced by mechanical or material forces.

mech•a•nist ['mɛkənɪst] *n.* **1** a person who believes that all the changes in the universe are the effects of physical and chemical forces. **2** *Rare.* a mechanician.

mech•a•nis•tic [,mɛkə'nɪstɪk] *adj.* **1** of or having to do with mechanists, mechanism, mechanics, or mechanical theories. **2** mechanical; automatic: *mechanistic behaviour.* **—,mech•a'nis•ti•cal•ly,** *adv.*

mech•a•nize ['mɛkə,naɪz] *v.* **-nized, -niz•ing. 1** make mechanical. **2** do by machinery, rather than by hand: *Much housework can be mechanized.* **3** replace people or animals by machinery in (a business, etc.). **4** equip (a military unit) with armoured vehicles, tanks, and other machines. **—,mech•a•ni'za•tion,** *n.* **—'mech•a,niz•er,** *n.*

mech•a•no•ther•a•py [,mɛkənou'θɛrəpi] *n.* medical treatment by the use of massage or similar manual or mechanical therapy. **—,mech•a•no'ther•a•pist,** *n.*

Mech•lin ['mɛklɪn] *n.* a fine lace with the pattern clearly outlined by a distinct thread. ⟨< *Mechlin,* a city in N Belgium, where this lace is made⟩

me•co•ni•um [mə'kouniəm] *n.* the first feces of a newborn baby, formed while still in the uterus. It is very dark and sticky. ⟨< NL < L, poppy juice (it is the same colour) < Gk. *mekon* poppy⟩

me•cop•te•ran [mɪ'kɒptərən] *n.* any flesh-eating, four-winged insect of the order Mecoptera. **—me'cop•ter•ous,** *adj.*

med. **1** medical. **2** medieval. **3** medium.

Med. Medieval.

Canadian and Commonwealth medals

med•al ['mɛdəl] *n.* a small, flat piece of metal stamped with a figure and an inscription: *The captain won a medal for bravery. She won the gold medal for having the highest marks in the school. A medal was struck to commemorate the coronation.* ⟨< F < Ital. *medaglia,* ult. < L *metallum* metal⟩
☛ *Hom.* MEDDLE.

med•al•ist ['mɛdəlɪst] *n.* See MEDALLIST.

me•dal•lion [mə'dæljən] *n.* **1** a large medal. **2** a round or oval design or ornament, such as a design on a book or a pattern in lace. **3** a round or oval piece of cooked meat. ⟨earlier, *medaille* < F < Ital. *medaglione* large medal⟩

med•al•list ['mɛdəlɪst] **1** a person who designs or makes medals. **2** a person who has won a medal. Also, **medalist.**

Medal of Bravery *Cdn.* a decoration awarded for an act of outstanding courage involving personal risk. It is one of a series of three Canadian bravery decorations, the other two being the Cross of Valour (the highest award) and the Star of Courage. *Abbrev.:* MB

Medal of Service a Canadian award for civilian service, now superseded by the Order of Canada.

med•dle ['mɛdəl] *v.* **-dled, -dling.** busy oneself with something or with other people's affairs without being authorized or needed. ⟨ME < OF *medler,* ult. < L *miscere* mix⟩ **—'med•dler,** *n.* **—'med•dling•ly,** *adv.*
☛ *Hom.* MEDAL.
☛ *Syn.* **Meddle,** TAMPER, INTERFERE = concern oneself unnecessarily or unduly with someone or something. **Meddle** emphasizes busying oneself, without right or permission, with something not one's own affair or strictly the affair of another: *That old busybody is always meddling in someone's business.* **Tamper** emphasizes meddling in order to alter or experiment with a thing or improperly influence a person: *Don't tamper with electrical appliances.* **Interfere** suggests meddling in a way that disturbs or hinders: *She interferes when we scold the children.*

med•dle•some ['mɛdəlsəm] *adj.* fond of meddling in other people's affairs; meddling. **—'med•dle•some•ly,** *adv.* **—'med•dle•some•ness,** *n.*

Mede [mid] *n.* a native or inhabitant of Media, an ancient country in SW Asia, south of the Caspian Sea. ⟨< L *Medus,* pl. *Medi* < Gk. *Medos,* pl. *Medoi*⟩

Me•de•a [mə'diə] *n. Greek mythology.* a sorceress who helped Jason get the Golden Fleece. They were married but she was later deserted by him. Medea then killed their children as well as her rival, burned her palace, and fled to Athens.

me•de•vac ['mɛdə,væk] *n.* AIR AMBULANCE. Also, **medivac.**

Med.Gk. Medieval Greek.

me•di•a[1] ['midiə] *n.* a pl. of MEDIUM.
☛ *Usage.* See note at MEDIUM.

me•di•a[2] ['midiə] *n., pl.* **-di•ae** [-di,i] *or* [-di,aɪ]. *Anatomy.* the centre layer of an artery or lymphatic vessel. ⟨< LL, n. use of fem. sing. of L *medius* mid⟩

me•di•ae•val [,mɛdi'ivəl], [mɛd'ivəl], *or* [,midi'ivəl] *adj.* See MEDIEVAL.

me•di•al ['midiəl] *adj.* **1** in the middle. **2** having to do with a mathematical mean or average. **3** average; ordinary. **4** *Phonetics.* in the middle of a word or between other sounds: *a medial vowel. Medial* [t] *is often voiced, as in* latter. ⟨< LL *medialis* < L *medius* middle⟩ **—'me•di•al•ly,** *adv.*

me•di•an ['midiən] *adj., n. —adj.* **1** of, having to do with, or in the middle; middle. **2** having to do with or designating the plane that divides something into two equal parts. **3** *Statistics.* of a median; having as many above as below a certain number: *The median age of the population was found to be 21, while the average age was found to be 25.*
—n. **1** the middle number of a series: *The median of* 1, 3, 4, 8, 9 *is* 4. **2** a measurement so chosen that half the numbers in the series are above it and half are below it: *The median of* 1, 3, 4, 8, 9, 10 *is* 6. **3** a line or point in the middle. **4** on a highway, a central strip of grass or pavement separating the lanes used by traffic proceeding in opposite directions. ⟨< L *medianus* < *medius* middle⟩

Me•di•an ['midiən] *adj., n. —adj.* of Media, an ancient country in SW Asia south of the Caspian Sea, or the Medes, or their Iranian language or culture.
—n. Mede.

me•di•ant ['midiənt] *n. Music.* the third tone of a scale, halfway from the tonic or keynote to the dominant. ⟨< Ital. *mediante* < LL *medians, -antis,* pres. part. of *mediari.* See MEDIATE.⟩

me•di•ate *v.* ['midi,eit]; *adj.* ['midiɪt] *v.* **-at•ed, -at•ing;** *adj.*
—v. **1** be a go-between; act in order to bring about an agreement between persons or sides: *to mediate between labour and management.* **2** hold an intermediate position. **3** effect by intervening; settle by intervening. **4** be a connecting link between: *Canada is often said to mediate between the United States and the United Kingdom.* **5** be the medium for effecting (a result), conveying (a gift, etc.), or communicating (an idea).
—adj. **1** connected, but not directly; connected through some other person or thing. **2** intermediate. ⟨< LL *mediari* be in the middle, intervene < L *medius* middle⟩ **—'me•di,a•tor,** *n.* **—'me•di•a•tive,** *adj.*

me•di•a•tion [,midi'eiʃən] *n.* a mediating; the act of effecting an agreement; friendly intervention.

me•di•a•to•ry ['midiə,tɔri] *adj.* mediating; having to do with mediation.

med•ic[1] ['mɛdɪk] *n. Informal.* **1** physician. **2** a medical student. **3** a member of the medical branch of any of the armed forces. ⟨shortened form of *medical*⟩

med•ic[2] ['mɛdɪk] *n.* any of a genus (*Medicago*) of herbs of the pea family, such as alfalfa, having purple or yellow flowers. ⟨< L *medica* < Gk. *(poa) Mēdikē* Median (herb)⟩

med•i•ca•ble ['mɛdəkəbəl] *adj.* capable of being cured or relieved by medical treatment.

med•i•cal ['mɛdɪkəl] *adj., n. —adj.* of or having to do with healing or with the science and art of medicine: *medical advice, medical schools, medical treatment.*
—n. Informal. MEDICAL EXAMINATION. ⟨< Med.L *medicalis* < L *medicus* doctor⟩ **—'med•i•cal•ly,** *adv.*

medical examination an examination of a person by a physician to determine state of health, physical fitness, etc.

medical examiner **1** a physician appointed by a public body to perform autopsies. **2** a physician appointed by a company to perform medical examinations of its employees.

medical genetics the area of human genetics concerned with the study of genes that affect health.

med•i•ca•ment ['mɛdəkəmənt] *or* [mə'dɪkəmənt] *n.* a substance used to cure or heal; medicine. ⟨< L *medicamentum,* ult. < *medicus* healing⟩

med•i•care ['mɛdə,kɛr] *n. Cdn.* a government-sponsored program of health insurance, usually covering hospital costs, doctors' fees, and other medical expenses. ⟨< *medi(cal)* + *care*⟩

med•i•cate ['mɛdə,keit] *v.* **-cat•ed, -cat•ing. 1** treat with medicine. **2** put medicine on or in. ⟨< L *medicatus, medicare* < *medicus* healing⟩ **—'med•i•ca•tive,** *adj.*

med•i•cat•ed ['mɛdə,keitɪd] *adj., v. —adj.* containing medicine: *medicated gauze.*
—v. pt. and pp. of MEDICATE.

med•i•ca•tion [,mɛdə'keiʃən] *n.* **1** treatment with medicine. **2** putting medicine on or in: *The doctor was responsible for the medication of the wound.* **3** MEDICINE (def. 1).

Med•i•ci ['mɛdɪtʃi] *n.* a rich, famous, and powerful family of Florence, Italy, during the 15th and 16th centuries.

me•dic•i•nal [mə'dɪsənəl] *adj.* having value as medicine; healing; helping; relieving. **—me'dic•i•nal•ly,** *adv.*

med•i•cine ['mɛdəsɪn] *n.* **1** any substance such as a drug, used to cure disease or improve health. **2** the science and art of treating or curing disease and sickness and improving or maintaining health. **3** the branch of this discipline that deals with the non-surgical treatment of disease. **4** *Cdn.* among First Nations peoples: **a** an object or ceremony traditionally believed to have power over natural or supernatural forces. **b** magical power.
give (someone) **a taste of their own medicine,** treat (someone) as they have treated others.
take (one's) **medicine,** accept a punishment or other disagreeable result of one's own actions. ⟨< L *medicina* < *medicus* doctor⟩

medicine bag *Cdn.* a bag or pouch, often decorated with beadwork, used by First Nations people to carry various objects believed to have magical powers in protecting the bearer from harm.

medicine ball a large, heavy, leather ball tossed from one person to another for exercise.

medicine man a man traditionally believed by aboriginal peoples to have magic power over diseases, evil spirits, and other things.

medicine wheel *Cdn.* a circle of stones found at old First Nations and American Indian encampments on the North American prairies and believed to be associated with the religious life of those who constructed them.

medicine woman *Cdn.* among aboriginal peoples, a woman believed to have magic power over diseases, evil spirits, and other things.

med•i•co ['mɛdə,kou] *n., pl.* **-cos.** *Informal.* **1** a doctor. **2** a medical student. ⟨< Ital. *medico* or Sp. *médico* physician, learned borrowing from L *medicus.* See MEDIC[1].⟩

me•di•e•val [,mɛdi'ivəl], [mɛd'ivəl], *or* [,midi'ivəl] *adj.* **1** belonging to or having to do with the Middle Ages, the period from about A.D. 500 to about A.D. 1500: *medieval customs.* **2** like that of the Middle Ages. Also, **mediaeval.** ⟨< L *medium* middle + *aevum* age⟩ **—,me•di'e•val•ly,** *adv.*

me•di•e•val•ism [,mɛdi'ivə,lɪzəm], [,mɛ'divə,lɪzəm], *or* [,midi'ivə,lɪzəm] *n.* **1** the spirit, ideals, and customs of the Middle Ages; medieval thought, religion, and art. **2** devotion to medieval ideals; adoption of medieval customs. **3** a medieval belief or custom. Also, **mediaevalism.**

me•di•e•val•ist [,mɛdi'ivəlɪst], [mɛd'ivəlɪst], *or* [,midi'ivəlɪst] *n.* **1** a person who knows much about the Middle Ages. **2** a person who is in sympathy with medieval ideals, customs, etc. Also, **mediaevalist.**

Medieval Latin the Latin language from about A.D. 700 to about A.D. 1500.

Me•di•na [mə'dinə] *n.* the city in Saudi Arabia where Mohammed's tomb lies.

me•di•o•cre [,midi'oukər] *adj.* neither good nor bad; average; ordinary, but less than satisfactory: *a mediocre cake, a mediocre student.* ⟨< F < L *mediocris,* originally, middling < *medius* middle⟩

me•di•oc•ri•ty [,midi'ɒkrəti] *n., pl.* **-ties. 1** mediocre quality. **2** mediocre ability or accomplishment. **3** a mediocre person. ⟨< L *mediocritas*⟩

med•i•tate ['mɛdə,teit] *v.* **-tat•ed, -tat•ing. 1** think quietly and deeply; reflect: *Monks meditate on holy things.* **2** think about; consider; plan; intend. ⟨< L *meditari*⟩
☛ *Syn.* **2.** See note at THINK.

med•i•ta•tion [,mɛdə'teiʃən] *n.* **1** continued thought; reflection. **2** contemplation on sacred or solemn subjects, especially as a devotional exercise. **3** a contemplative or devotional writing or talk.

med•i•ta•tive ['mɛdə,teitɪv] *adj.* **1** fond of meditating. **2** expressing meditation. **—'med•i,ta•tive•ly,** *adv.* **—'med•i,ta•tive•ness,** *n.*

Med•i•ter•ra•ne•an [,mɛdətə'reiniən] *or* [,mɛdətə'reinjən] *adj.* of or having to do with the Mediterranean Sea or the lands around it. ⟨< L *mediterraneus* < *medius* middle + *terra* land⟩

me•di•um ['midiəm] *adj., n., pl.* **-di•ums** or **-di•a.** *—adj.* **1** having a middle position; moderate. **2** (*advl.*) moderately: *medium loud.*
—n. **1** that which is in the middle; neither one extreme nor the other; middle condition. **2** a substance or agent through which anything acts; a means: *Radio is a medium of communication.* **3** a means of artistic expression: *The sculptor did some carving in stone, but his favourite medium was wood.* **4** a substance in which something can live; environment: *Water is the medium in which fish live.* **5 a** a nutritive substance, either liquid or solid, such as agar or gelatin, in or upon which bacteria, fungi, and other micro-organisms are grown for study. **b** a substance used for displaying, preserving, etc. organic specimens. **6** a liquid with which paints are mixed. **7** a person through whom spirits of the dead can supposedly communicate with the living. **8** a middle-sized person or thing, especially with regard to clothing: *I think you're a medium.* ⟨< L *medium* neut. adj., middle⟩
☛ *Usage.* **Mediums** is the only plural used when the reference is to persons (defs. 7 and 8). MEDIA is the only plural used for def. 3 and also is usual for defs. 2, 4, and 5. Careful writers and speakers avoid using **media** as a singular or **medias** as a plural: *She gave up the medium of painting and took to other media instead.*

medium frequency the range of radio frequencies between 300 and 3000 kilohertz. Medium frequency is the range next above low frequency.

medium of exchange whatever is given in exchange for goods or services; money or its equivalent.

me•di•um–sized ['midiəm ,saɪzd] *adj.* neither large nor small of its kind: *a medium-sized car.*

medivac ['mɛdə,væk] See MEDEVAC.

Med.L MEDIEVAL LATIN.

med•lar ['mɛdlər] *n.* **1** a small tree (*Mespilus germanica*) of the rose family native to Europe and Asia, bearing an edible brown fruit that resembles a crab apple. **2** the fruit of this tree, which is fit to eat only when it has become overripe. ⟨ME < OF *meslier* (the tree) < *mesle* (its fruit), ult. < L *mespilum* < Gk. *mespilon*⟩

med•ley ['mɛdli] *n., pl.* **-leys;** *adj. —n.* **1** a mixture of things that ordinarily do not belong together. **2** *Music.* a vocal or instrumental composition made up of tunes, usually familiar, or excerpts from other pieces.
—adj. made up of parts that are not alike; mixed. ⟨ME *medlee* < OF *meslee* < *mesler* to mix, fight. See MEDDLE. Doublet of MELEE.⟩

Médoc or **Me•doc** [mei'dɒk] *n.* a red wine, a type of claret. ⟨< *Médoc,* a district in SW France, where it is made⟩

med•ro•ges•tone [,mɛdrə'dʒɛstoun] *n.* a synthetic, orally active progestogen used to re-establish normal menstrual cycles.

med•rox•y•pro•ges•ter•one [mɛ,drɒksiprou'dʒɛstə,roun] a drug used to treat menstrual disorders and certain forms of cancer. *Formula:* $C_{24}H_{34}O_4$

med•ry•sone ['mɛdrə,soun] *n.* a drug used as drops to treat certain eye conditions.

me•dul•la [mə'dʌlə] *n., pl.* **-dul•las** or **-dul•lae** [-'dʌli] *or* [-'dʌlaɪ]. **1** *Anatomy.* **a** MEDULLA OBLONGATA. **b** bone marrow. **c** the innermost part of an organ or structure. The medulla of the adrenal gland produces the hormone adrenaline. **2** *Botany.* the pith of plants. ⟨< L *medulla* marrow⟩

medulla ob•lon•ga•ta [,ɒblɒŋ'gɑtə] *or* [,ɒblɒŋ'geitə] *Anatomy.* the lowest part of the brain, at the top end of the spinal cord. See BRAIN for picture. ⟨< NL *medulla oblongata* prolonged medulla⟩

med•ul•lar•y ['mɛdə,lɛri], ['mɛdʒə,lɛri], *or* [mə'dʌləri] *adj.* of, having to do with, or like medulla or the medulla oblongata.

me•du•sa [mə'djusə] *or* [mə'dusə], [mə'djuzə] *or* [mə'duzə] *n., pl.* **-sas, -sae** [-si] *or* [-saɪ], [-zi] *or* [-zaɪ]. *Zoology.* **1** one of two main body forms in which coelenterates exist; it is the gamete-producing form with a jellylike, umbrella-shaped body, the typical form of the jellyfish. **2** jellyfish. ⟨< *Medusa*⟩ **—me'du•san,** *adj.* **—me'du•soid,** *adj.*

Me•du•sa [mə'djusə] *or* [mə'dusə], [mə'djuzə] *or* [mə'duzə] *n., pl.* **-sas.** *Greek mythology.* a horrible monster, one of the three Gorgons. She had snakes for hair, and anyone who looked upon her was turned to stone. She was killed by Perseus. **—Me'du•sa,like,** *adj.*

meed [mid] *n. Poetic.* what one deserves; reward. ⟨OE *mēd*⟩
☛ *Hom.* MEAD.

meek [mik] *adj.* **1** patient; not easily angered; mild. **2** submitting when ordered about or injured by others: *The boy was meek as a lamb when he was reproved.* ⟨ME *meke, meoc* < Scand.; cf; Icel. *mjūkr* soft, mild, meek⟩ **—'meek•ly,** *adv.* **—'meek•ness,** *n.*
☛ *Syn.* **1.** See note at GENTLE. **2.** See note at HUMBLE.

meer•schaum ['mirʃəm], ['mirʃɒm], *or* ['mirʃaʊm] *n.* **1** a very soft, light magnesium silicate used to make tobacco pipes, etc. *Formula:* $H_4Mg_2S_{13}O_{10}$ **2** a tobacco pipe made of this material. ⟨< G *meerschaum* sea foam⟩

meet[1] [mit] *v.* **met, meet•ing;** *n. —v.* **1** come face to face; come face to face with; encounter: *Their cars met on the narrow road.* **2** come together; come into contact or connection (with); join up: *where two streets meet. Sword met sword in battle.* **3** be united; join in harmony: *His is a nature in which courage and caution meet.* **4** receive; welcome: *The hosts met their guests at the door.* **5** come into company with by arrangement; keep an appointment (with): *Meet me at one o'clock.* **6** be introduced to; become acquainted: *Have you met my sister?* **7** be present at the arrival of: *to meet a boat.* **8** satisfy; comply with; respond to: *to meet obligations, objections, etc.* **9** pay: *to meet bills, debts, etc.* **10** confront; oppose; deal with: *The champion boxer will meet his challenger next spring.* **11** fight: *The two knights met in single combat.* **12** face directly: *He met her glance with a smile.* **13** experience: *She met open scorn before she won fame.* **14** assemble; convene: *Parliament will meet next month.*
meet halfway, compromise (with).
meet the eye or **the ear,** be seen or heard.
meet up with, meet.
meet with, a come across; find. **b** have or get: *The plan met with approval.* **c** talk with face to face.
—n. **1** a meeting or gathering; especially, a competition: *a racing meet, an athletic meet.* **2** the people at such a gathering, or the place where it is held. ⟨OE *mētan*⟩ **—'meet•er,** *n.*
☛ *Hom.* MEAT, METE.

meet[2] [mit] *adj. Archaic.* suitable; proper; fitting: *It is meet that you should help your friends.* ⟨OE *(ge)mǣte*⟩ **—'meet•ly,** *adv.* **—'meet•ness,** *n.*
☛ *Hom.* MEAT, METE.

meet•ing ['mitɪŋ] *n., v. —n.* **1** a coming together: *He looked forward to a meeting with his sister.* **2** a gathering or assembly for business discussion, social purposes, etc. **3** an assembly of people for worship. **4** the place where things meet; junction: *a meeting of roads.*
—v. ppr. of MEET[1].
☛ *Syn.* **2. Meeting,** ASSEMBLY, GATHERING = a coming together of a group of people. **Meeting** applies especially to the coming together of a body of people to discuss or arrange business or action: *The club held a meeting.* **Assembly,** more formal, emphasizes coming or calling together of a large group for a common purpose, such as social pleasure, religious worship, or, particularly, joining in deliberation or action, often political or military: *The totalitarian regime declared the rally an unlawful assembly.* **Gathering** suggests a less formal or less organized coming together: *There was a large gathering at her house.*

meeting house **1** a building used for worship by certain religious groups, such as Quakers. **2** any building used for meetings.

mega– *combining form.* **1** great; large: *megalith.* **2** *SI prefix.* million: *megavolt.* Compare GIGA-, KILO-. Symbol: M ⟨< Gk. *megas* great, large, vast, powerful⟩

meg•a•buck ['mɛgə,bʌk] *n. Slang.* **1** a million dollars. **2** a vast amount of money.

meg•a•byte ['mɛgə,bəit] *n. Computer technology.* A measure of the storage capacity of a computer system, roughly equal to one million bytes. *Abbrev.*: MB

meg•a•ce•phal•ic [,mɛgəsə'fælɪk] *adj.* large-headed; having a skull with a cranial capacity above the average. Also, **megacephalous** [,mɛgə'sɛfələs]. ⟨< *mega-* + Gk. *kephalē* head + E *-ic*⟩ **—,meg•a'ceph•a•ly,** *n.*

meg•a•cu•rie ['mɛgə,kjuri] *n.* one million curies.

meg•a•cy•cle ['mɛgə,səikəl] *n.* megahertz. ⟨< *mega-* one million times (< Gk. *megas* great) + *cycle*⟩

meg•a•death ['mɛgə,dɛθ] *n.* the death of one million persons. ⟨< *mega-* one million times (< Gk. *megas* great) + *death*⟩

meg•a•don•tia [,mɛgə'dɒnʃə] *n.* macrodontia.

meg•a•dose ['mɛgə,dous] *n.* a dose of a vitamin or drug many times the normal size.

meg•a•hertz ['mɛgə,hɜrts] *n., pl.* **meg•a•hertz.** an SI unit for measuring frequency, equal to one million hertz. *Symbol*: MHz

meg•a•hype ['mɛgə,həip] *n. Informal.* an extremely aggressive advertising campaign.

meg•a•joule ['mɛgə,dʒul] *n. Physics.* one million joules. *Symbol*: MJ

meg•a•lith ['mɛgə,lɪθ] *n.* a stone of great size, especially in ancient construction work or in monuments left by people of prehistoric times. ⟨< Gk. *megas* great + *lithos* stone⟩ **—,meg•a'lith•ic,** *adj.*

megalo– *combining form.* large; extravagant; exaggerated: *megalomania.* ⟨< Gk. *megas, -galou*⟩

meg•a•lo•car•dia [,mɛgəlou'kɑrdiə] *n. Pathology.* enlargement of the heart.

meg•a•lo•ma•ni•a [,mɛgəlou'meiniə] *n. Psychiatry.* a mental illness characterized by delusions of greatness, wealth, etc. **—,meg•a•lo•ma'ni•a•cal** [,mɛgəloumə'naɪəkəl] *or* **,meg•a•lo'man•ic** [,mɛgəlou'mænɪk] *or* [,mɛgəlou'meinɪk], *adj.*

meg•a•lo•ma•ni•ac [,mɛgəlou'meini,æk] *n.* a person who has megalomania.

meg•a•lop•o•lis [,mɛgə'lɒpəlɪs] *n.* **1** a city of great or overpowering size, especially one thought of as a centre of the power, wealth, and influence of a country. **2** a heavily populated urban and industrial area made up of several cities. ⟨< Gk. *mega, megalou* great + *polis* city⟩

meg•a•lo•pol•i•tan [,mɛgələ'pɒlɪtən] *n., adj. —n.* an inhabitant of a megalopolis.
—adj. having to do with a megalopolis.

meg•a•lo•saur ['mɛgələ,sɔr] *n.* an extinct giant dinosaur of the genus *Megalosaurus,* of the Jurassic period. **—,meg•a•lo'sau•ri•an,** *adj., n.*

meg•a•par•sec [,mɛgə'pɑrsɛk] *n. Astronomy.* one million parsecs. *Symbol*: Mpc

meg•a•phone ['mɛgə,foun] *n.* a large, funnel-shaped horn used to increase the loudness of the voice or the distance at which it can be heard. **—,meg•a'phon•ic** [,mɛgə'fɒnɪk], *adj.* **—,meg•a'phon•i•cal•ly,** *adv.*

meg•a•pod ['mɛgə,pɒd] *adj.* having large feet.

meg•a•pode ['mɛgə,poud] *n.* any bird of the family Megapodidae, found in Australia and the South Pacific, having large feet.

Meg•a•ra ['mɛgərə] *n.* **1** a city in the Megaris region of ancient Greece. **2** *Classical mythology.* the wife of Hercules and daughter of Creon. Her children were killed by Hercules.

meg•a•spo•ran•gi•um [,mɛgəspə'rændʒiəm] *n., pl.* **-gi•a** [-dʒiə]. *Botany.* a sporangium containing megaspores.

meg•a•spore ['mɛgə,spɔr] *n. Botany.* the larger of the two spores formed by heterosporous plants, that produces the female gametophyte, as in ferns. Compare MICROSPORE.

meg•a•spo•ro•phyl or **meg•a•spo•ro•phyll** [,mɛgə'spɔrəfɪl] *n. Botany.* a sporophyl that produces only megasporangia.

meg•a•there ['mɛgə,θir] *n.* any of the extinct genus *Megatherium* of giant sloths, which grew in length to about 6 m. ⟨< NL *megathērium* < Gk. *mega-* large + *thērion* wild beast⟩

meg•a•ton ['mɛgə,tʌn] *n.* a measure of atomic power equivalent to the energy released by one million tons of high explosive, specifically TNT. ⟨< *mega-* + *(1000-kilo)ton*⟩ **—,meg•a'ton•ic** [,mɛgə'tɒnɪk], *adj.*

meg•a•vi•ta•min ['mɛgə,vəitəmɪn] *n.* an abnormally large amount of any vitamin.

meg•a•volt ['mɛgə,voult] *n. Electricity.* one million volts.

meg•a•watt ['mɛgə,wɒt] *n. Electricity.* one million watts. *Symbol:* MW

me•gil•lah [mə'gɪlə] *or, for 3,* [mɛgi'lɑ] *n., pl.* **-gil•lahs** *or (for 3)* **-gil•loth** [-gi'lout]. **1** *Slang.* a long-winded explanation or story: *Don't give me a long megillah.* **2** a boringly complex situation, **3** a scroll containing one of the books of the Apocrypha. Also, **megilla.** ⟨< Yiddish *megile* scroll⟩

meg•ohm ['mɛg,oum] *n. Electricity.* one million ohms. *Symbol*: MΩ ⟨< *mega-* + *ohm*⟩

me•grim ['migrɪm] *n. Archaic.* **1** migraine. **2** a whim; fancy. **3 megrims,** *pl.* morbid low spirits. ⟨var. of *migraine*; influenced by *grim*⟩

mei•o•sis [maɪ'ousɪs] *n., pl.* **-ses** [-siz]. **1** *Biology.* the division of a living germ cell to produce gametes. Meiosis consists of two successive divisions of the nucleus of the parent cell, producing four haploid daughter cells (gametes); it also involves the interchange of genetic information between the maternal and paternal chromosome pairs, so that each daughter cell carries slightly different genes. Compare MITOSIS. **2** *Rhetoric.* understatement; litotes. ⟨< NL *meiosis* < Gk. *meiōsi* a lessening < *meioein* lessen < *meiōn* less⟩ **—mei'ot•ic** [maɪ'ɒtɪk], *adj.* **—mei'o•ti•cal•ly,** *adv.*

Meis•sen ['məisən]; *German,* ['maɪsən] *n.* a kind of porcelain. ⟨< *Meissen,* a city in Germany, where it is made⟩

Meis•ter•sing•er ['məistər,sɪŋər] *or* ['maɪstər,zɪŋər] *n.* a member of one of the guilds, established in the principal German cities in the 14th, 15th, and 16th centuries for the cultivation of poetry and music. ⟨< G, master singer⟩

mel•a•mine ['mɛlə,min] *or* ['mɛləmɪn] *n.* **1** *Chemistry.* a white, crystalline compound used to make a synthetic thermosetting resin. *Formula*: $C_3H_6N_6$ **2** the resin made from melamine or the hard, strong plastic made from the resin, used for making moulded articles, adhesives, and surface coatings. ⟨< *mel(am),* a chemical compound + *amine*⟩

melan– var. of MELANO- before a vowel: *melanin.*

mel•an•cho•li•a [,mɛlən'kouliə] *or* [,mɛlən'kouljə] *n. Psychiatry.* a mental disorder characterized by great depression of spirits and gloomy fears. ⟨< LL < Gk. *melancholia* < *melas* black + *cholē* bile⟩ **—,mel•an'cho•li,ac,** *n.*

mel•an•chol•ic [,mɛlən'kɒlɪk] *adj.* **1** melancholy; gloomy. **2** having melancholia. **—,mel•an'chol•i•cal•ly,** *adv.*

mel•an•chol•y ['mɛlən,kɒli] *n., pl.* **-chol•ies;** *adj. —n.* **1** sadness; low spirits; a tendency to be sad. **2** sober thoughtfulness; pensiveness. **3** *Archaic.* black bile, the one of the four humours of ancient physiology, believed to cause low spirits.
—adj. **1** sad; gloomy. **2** causing sadness; depressing: *a melancholy scene.* **3** expressive of sadness: *a melancholy smile.* **4** lamentable; deplorable: *a melancholy fact.* **5** soberly thoughtful; pensive.

Mel•a•ne•sian [,mɛlə'niʒən] *or* [,mɛlə'niʃən] *adj., n. —adj.* **1** of or designating a major race of humans that includes most of the peoples traditionally inhabiting Melanesia, a group of islands in the southwestern Pacific, especially New Guinea, New Britain, and the Solomon Islands. **2** of or having to do with Melanesia or the peoples, cultures, or languages of Melanesia.
—n. **1** a member of the Melanesian race. **2** a native or inhabitant of Melanesia. **3** a group of Austronesian languages widely spoken in Melanesia. ⟨< Gk. *melas* black + *nesos* island⟩

mé•lange [me'lɑ̃ʒ] *n., pl.* **-langes** [-'lɑ̃ʒ] *French.* a mixture; medley. ⟨< F *mélange* < *mêler* mix⟩

me•lan•ic [mə'lænɪk] *adj.* **1** of, having to do with, or characterized by melanism. **2** *Pathology.* melanotic.

mel•a•nin ['mɛlənɪn] *n. Biochemistry.* the dark brown or black pigment present in the skin, hair, and eyes of humans and animals. **—'mel•a•nin,like,** *adj.*

mel•a•nism ['mɛlə,nɪzəm] *n.* **1** the condition in an individual or type of organism of having a large amount of melanin, producing black or nearly black fur, feathers, skin, etc. **2** melanosis. **—,mel•a'nis•tic,** *adj.*

mel•a•nite ['mɛlə,nəit] *n. Mineralogy.* a type of black garnet.
☛ *Hom.* MELINITE.

melano– *combining form.* black: *melanosis.* Also, (*esp. before a vowel*) **melan-** ⟨< Gk., combining form of *mélas* black⟩

mel•a•no•ma [,mɛlə'noumə] *n., pl.* **-mas** or **-mata** [-mətə]. *Pathology.* a malignant tumour developed from cells that form melanin, usually occurring in the skin.

mel•a•no•sis [,mɛlə'nousɪs] *n. Pathology.* abnormal, dark brown or black pigmentation of tissues or organs caused by melanins or, sometimes, other substances resembling melanins. Melanosis of the skin can occur in pregnancy or as a result of sunburn.

mel•a•not•ic [,mɛlə'nɒtɪk] *adj. Pathology.* of, having to do with, or affected with melanosis.

Mel•ba toast ['mɛlbə] very thin, crisp toast. ⟨after Dame Nellie *Melba* (Helen Armstrong, 1861-1931), Australian soprano⟩

meld¹ [mɛld] *v., n. —v.* **1** merge; blend; combine. **2** become merged, blended, or combined.
—n. a blend or combination. ⟨blend of *melt* + *weld*⟩

meld² [mɛld] *v., n. —v.* in canasta, pinochle, etc. announce and show (cards for a score).
—n. **1** the act of melding. **2** the cards that can be melded. ⟨< G *melden* announce⟩

Mel•e•a•ger [ˌmɛli'eidʒər] *n. Greek mythology.* the hero who killed the Calydonian boar. He was one of the Argonauts.

me•lee or **mê•lée** [mɛ'lei] *or* ['mɛlei], [mei'lei] *or* ['meilei]; *French,* [mɛ'le] *n.* **1** a confused fight; hand-to-hand fight among a number of fighters. 2 any similar state of hectic confusion. ⟨< F *mêlée* (in OF *meslee*). Doublet of MEDLEY.⟩
☛ *Hom.* MALAY ['meilei].

mel•ic ['mɛlɪk] *adj.* to be sung. ⟨< L *melicus* < Gk. *melikos* < *melos* song⟩

mel•i•nite ['mɛlə,nəit] *n. Chemistry.* a powerful explosive containing picric acid. ⟨< F < Gk. *mēlinos* quince yellow < *mēlon* quince⟩
☛ *Hom.* MELANITE.

mel•io•rate ['miljə,reit] *or* ['miliə,reit] *v.* **-rat•ed, -rat•ing.** improve. ⟨< LL *meliorare* < L *melior* better⟩
—,mel•io'ra•tion, *n.* **—'mel•io,ra•tor,** *n.* **—'mel•io•ra•ble,** *adj.* **—'mel•io•ra•tive,** *adj.*

mel•io•rism ['miljə,rɪzəm] *or* ['miliə,rɪzəm] *n.* the doctrine that human effort can improve the state of the world, socially, economically, and spiritually. **—'mel•io•rist,** *n.* **—,mel•io'ris•tic,** *adj.*

mel•ior•i•ty [mil'jɔrəti] *or* [mili'ɔrəti] *n.* superiority.

mel•lif•er•ous [mə'lɪfərəs] *adj.* producing honey. ⟨< L *mellifer* honey-bearing < *mel* honey + *ferre* bear + E *-ous*⟩

mel•lif•lu•ent [mə'lɪfluənt] *adj.* mellifluous.
—mel'lif•lu•ence, *n.* **—mel'lif•lu•ent•ly,** *adv.*

mel•lif•lu•ous [mə'lɪfluəs] *adj.* sweetly or smoothly flowing: *a mellifluous speech.* ⟨< LL *mellifluus* < L *mel* honey + *fluere* to flow⟩ **—mel'lif•lu•ous•ly,** *adv.* **—mel'lif•lu•ous•ness,** *n.*

mel•lo•phone ['mɛlə,foun] *n.* althorn. ⟨< *mellow* + *phone*⟩

mel•low ['mɛlou] *adj., v.* *—adj.* **1** soft and full-flavoured from ripeness; sweet and juicy: *a mellow apple.* **2** fully matured: *mellow wine.* **3** soft, warm, and rich: *a violin with a mellow tone, a mellow light in a picture, mellow colour.* **4** rich; loamy: *mellow soil.* **5** softened and made wise by age and experience. **6** affected by liquor or drinking; slightly tipsy. **7** *Informal.* laid back; relaxed.
—v. make or become mellow. ⟨var. of OE *mearu* soft, tender⟩
—'mel•low•ly, *adv.* **—'mel•low•ness,** *n.*

me•lo•de•on [mə'loudiən] *n.* a small reed organ in which air is sucked inward by a bellows. ⟨pseudo-Gk. form of earlier *melodium* < *melody*⟩

me•lod•ic [mə'lɒdɪk] *adj.* **1** having to do with melody. **2** melodious. **3** *Music.* of a minor scale in which the sixth and seventh notes are sharpened on the way up, and restored on the way down. ⟨< F *mélodique* < LL *melodicus*⟩ **—me'lod•i•cal•ly,** *adv.*

me•lo•di•ous [mə'loudiəs] *adj.* **1** sweet-sounding; pleasing to the ear; musical: *a melodious voice.* **2** producing melody: *a melodious bird.* **3** having a melody: *a melodious song.*
—me'lo•di•ous•ly, *adv.* **—me'lo•di•ous•ness,** *n.*

mel•o•dist ['mɛlədɪst] *n.* a composer or singer of melodies.

mel•o•dize ['mɛlə,daɪz] *v.* **-dized, -diz•ing. 1** make melodies. **2** blend into harmony. **3** set to a melody. **—'mel•o,diz•er,** *n.*

mel•o•dra•ma ['mɛlə,dræmə] *or* ['mɛlə,drɑmə] *n.* **1** a sensational drama with exaggerated appeal to the emotions and, usually, a happy ending. **2** any sensational writing, speech, or action with exaggerated appeal to the emotions. ⟨< F < Gk. *melos* song, music + *drama* drama⟩ **—,mel•o'dram•a,tize,** *v.*

mel•o•dra•mat•ic [,mɛlədrə'mætɪk] *adj.* of, like, or suitable for melodrama; sensational and exaggerated.
—,mel•o•dra'mat•i•cal•ly, *adv.*
☛ *Syn.* See note at DRAMATIC.

mel•o•dra•mat•ics [,mɛlədrə'mætɪks] *n.pl.* **1** melodramatic writing. **2** melodramatic behaviour.

mel•o•dy ['mɛlədi] *n., pl.* **-dies. 1** any agreeable succession of sounds. **2** musical quality: *the melody of good speech.* **3** *Music.* **a** a succession of single tones, arranged in a rhythmical pattern; tune. **b** the main tune in a harmonized composition; air. **4** a poem to be sung to music. ⟨ME < OF < LL < Gk. *melōidia,* ult. < *melos* song + *ōidē* song⟩

mel•oid ['mɛlɔɪd] *n., adj.* *—n.* a beetle of the family Meloidae. *—adj.* belonging to the family Meloidae. ⟨< Mod.L *Meloidæ* < *meloe* oil beetle⟩

mel•on ['mɛlən] *n.* **1** the large, thick-skinned, juicy fruit of any of various plants of the gourd family, such as the watermelon or muskmelon. **2** any plant producing such fruits. **3** a deep pink colour. **4** *Slang.* an extra dividend for stockholders.
cut or **split a melon,** *Slang.* divide extra profits among those considered to have a claim on them. ⟨ME < OF < LL *melo, -onis,* short for L *melopepo* < Gk. *mēlopepōn* < *mēlon* apple + *pepōn* gourd⟩ **—'mel•on,like,** *adj.*

Mel•pom•e•ne [mɛl'pɒməni] *n. Greek mythology.* the Muse of tragedy.

melt [mɛlt] *v.* **melt•ed, melt•ed** or **mol•ten, melt•ing;** *n.*
—v. **1** change or be changed from solid to liquid: *Great heat melts iron. The ice melted quickly.* **2** dissolve: *Sugar melts in water.* **3** disappear or cause to disappear gradually: *As the sun came out, the clouds melted away.* **4** blend or merge gradually: *In the rainbow, the green melts into blue, the blue into violet.* **5** waste away; dwindle: *Her wealth melted away.* **6** make or become gentle, tender, etc.: *Pity for his wounded enemy melted his heart.*
—n. **1** the act or process of melting. **2** the state of being melted. **3** a melted metal. **4** a quantity of metal melted at one operation or over a specified period, especially a single charge in smelting. **5** a sandwich with a layer of melted cheese in it or over it. ⟨OE *meltan*⟩ **—'melt•er,** *n.* **—,melt•a'bil•i•ty,** *n.* **—'melt•a•ble,** *adj.* **—'melt•ing•ly,** *adv.* **—'melt•ing•ness,** *n.*
☛ *Syn.* **1. Melt,** DISSOLVE, THAW = change from a solid state. **Melt** suggests a gradual change caused by heat, by which a solid softens, loses shape, and finally becomes liquid: *The warm air melted the butter.* **Dissolve** emphasizes a breaking up of a solid into its smallest parts, caused by putting it in a liquid that reduces it and of which it becomes a part: *Dissolve some salt in a glass of water.* **Thaw,** used only of frozen things, means 'change to the unfrozen state': *She thawed the frozen fruit. The lake thaws in April.*

melt•age ['mɛltɪdʒ] *n.* **1** what is produced by a melting process. **2** the process.

melt•down ['mɛlt,daʊn] *n.* a situation in a nuclear reactor resulting from a failure of the cooling system so that heat generated by the reaction is not removed, and the metal holder for the bundles of fuel melts. If this happened, the reaction could no longer be controlled and would speed up, producing more heat and ending in a violent reaction, possibly an explosion.

melting point *Physical chemistry.* the temperature at which a solid substance melts.

melting pot 1 a pot or other vessel to melt something in. **2** a country or city thought of as a place in which various races or sorts of people are assimilated. North America is often called a melting pot.

mel•ton ['mɛltən] *n.* a smooth, heavy woollen cloth. Overcoats are often made of melton. ⟨< *Melton (Mowbray),* a town in central England⟩

melt•wa•ter ['mɛlt,wɒtər] *n.* water from melting glaciers or snows.

mem [mɛm] *n.* the fourteenth letter of the Hebrew alphabet. See table of alphabets in the Appendix.

mem•ber ['mɛmbər] *n.* **1** a person belonging to a group: *a member of our club.* **2** Usually, **Member,** a person elected to a legislative body: *Write to your local Member.* **3** *Mathematics.* **a** one of the objects that belongs to a set. **b** the expression on one side or the other of an equation. In 1 + 5 = 6, the left member is 1 + 5, and the right member is 6. **4** limb; a part of a human or animal body or of a plant, especially a leg, arm, wing, or branch. **5** the penis. ⟨ME < OF < L *membrum* limb, part⟩
—'mem•ber•less, *adj.*

Member of Parliament *Cdn.* in Canada, a title given to each of the representatives elected to the Federal Parliament in Ottawa. *Abbrev.:* MP or M.P.

Member of the Provincial Parliament *Cdn.* in Ontario, a member of the Legislative Assembly. *Abbrev.:* MPP or M.P.P.

Member of the House of Assembly *Cdn.* in Newfoundland, a member of the Legislative Assembly. *Abbrev.:* MHA or M.H.A.

Member of the Legislative Assembly *Cdn.* a title given to each of the representatives elected to the legislatures of most Canadian provinces. *Abbrev.:* MLA or M.L.A.

Member of the National Assembly *Cdn.* in Québec, a member of the provincial legislature. *Abbrev.:* MNA or M.N.A.

mem•ber•ship ['mɛmbər,ʃɪp] *n.* **1** the fact or status of being a member. **2** the members. **3** the number of members.

mem•brane ['mɛmbrein] *n.* **1** *Biology.* a thin, soft sheet or layer of animal tissue, lining or covering some part of the body: *One kind of membrane lines the stomach and another covers the front of the eyeball.* **2** a similar layer of plant tissue. **3** a thin, pliable sheet of any of various materials, such as plastic, used to line or cover something or connect parts. ⟨< L *membrana* < *membrum* member⟩ **—'mem•brane•less,** *adj.*

membrane bone any bone developing from membranous tissue.

mem•bra•nous ['mɛmbrənəs] *or* ['mɛmbreinəs] *adj.* **1** of or like membrane. **2** characterized by the formation of a membrane. In **membranous croup,** a membrane forms in the throat and hinders breathing.

me•men•to [mə'mɛntou] *n., pl.* **-tos** or **-toes. 1** something serving as a reminder, warning, or remembrance: *These postcards are mementos of our trip abroad.* **2 Memento,** *Roman Catholic Church.* either of two prayers beginning *Memento* (Remember) in the canon of the Mass, in which the living and the dead respectively are commemorated. ⟨< L *memento* remember!⟩

memento mori ['mɔri] an object serving as a reminder of death. ⟨< L, literally, remember that you must die⟩

Mem•non ['mɛmnɒn] *n.* **1** *Greek mythology.* an Ethiopian king killed by Achilles. **2** a huge statue of an Egyptian king at Thebes, Egypt.

mem•o ['mɛmou] *n., pl.* **mem•os.** *Informal.* memorandum.

mem•oir ['mɛmwɑr] *or* ['mɛmwɔr] *n.* **1** biography. **2** a report of a scientific or scholarly study. **3 memoirs,** *pl.* **a** a record of facts and events written from personal knowledge or special information. **b** a record of a person's own experiences; autobiography. ⟨< F *mémoire* < L *memoria.* Doublet of MEMORY.⟩

mem•oir•ist ['mɛmwɑrɪst] *or* ['mɛmwɔrɪst] *n.* an author of memoirs.

mem•o•ra•bil•i•a [,mɛmərə'bɪliə] *or* [,mɛmərə'biliə] *n.pl.* things or events worth remembering. ⟨< L *memorabilia,* pl. of *memorabilis.* See MEMORABLE.⟩

mem•o•ra•ble ['mɛmərəbəl] *adj.* worth remembering; not to be forgotten; notable. ⟨< L *memorabilis,* ult. < *memor* mindful⟩ **—'mem•o•ra•bly,** *adv.* **—,mem•o•ra'bil•i•ty,** *n.*

mem•o•ran•da [,mɛmə'rændə] *n.* a pl. of MEMORANDUM.

mem•o•ran•dum [,mɛmə'rændəm] *n., pl.* **-dums** or **-da** [-də]. **1** a short written statement for future use; a note to aid the memory. **2** an informal letter, note, or report. **3** a diplomatic communication consisting of a summary of facts and arguments on some issue or arrangement that concerns two or more governments. **4** *Law.* an informal document recording the terms of a transaction. ⟨< L *memorandum* (thing) to be remembered⟩

me•mo•ri•al [mə'mɔriəl] *n., adj.* *—n.* **1** something that is a reminder of some important event or person, such as a statue, an arch or column, a book, or a holiday. **2** a statement sent to a government or person in authority, usually giving facts and asking that some wrong be corrected.
—adj. helping people to remember some person, thing, or event: *We have memorial services on Remembrance Day.* ⟨ME < OF < L *memorialis* < *memoria.* See MEMORY.⟩ **—me'mo•ri•al•ly,** *adv.*

me•mo•ri•al•ist [mə'mɔriəlɪst] *n.* **1** a person who writes memorials. **2** memoirist.

me•mo•ri•al•ize [mə'mɔriə,laɪz] *v.* **-ized, -iz•ing. 1** preserve the memory of; commemorate. **2** submit a MEMORIAL (def. 2) to; petition. **—me'mo•ri•al,iz•er,** *n.* **—me,mo•ri•al•i'za•tion,** *n.*

me•mo•ri•am [mə'mɔriəm] *n.* See IN MEMORIAM.

mem•o•rize ['mɛmə,raɪz] *v.* **-rized, -riz•ing.** commit to memory; learn by heart. **—'mem•o,riz•a•ble,** *adj.* **—,mem•o•ri'za•tion,** *n.* **—'mem•o,riz•er,** *n.*

mem•o•ry ['mɛməri] *n., pl.* **-ries. 1** the ability to remember. **2** the act of remembering; remembrance. **3** what a person remembers. **4** a person, thing, or event that is remembered. **5** the length of time during which the past is remembered: *This has been the hottest summer within living memory.* **6** reputation after death. **7** *Computer technology.* the part of a computer that stores data.
in memory of, as a help in remembering; as a remembrance of: *On November 11 we observe a two-minute silence in memory of those who died fighting for their country.* ⟨ME < OF < L *memoria* < *memor* mindful. Doublet of MEMOIR.⟩

☛ *Syn.* **2. Memory,** RECOLLECTION = the act or fact of remembering. **Memory** emphasizes the ability to keep in the mind or call back something once learned, experienced, or otherwise known: *That vacation lives in her memory.* **Recollection,** applying to the act or to what is remembered, emphasizes calling back to mind, often with effort, something not thought of for a long time or forgotten: *I have little recollection of my childhood.*

memory bank **1** everything that a person remembers. **2** the collected archives of an organization or nation.

mem•sa•hib ['mɛm,sɑɪb] *or* [,mɛm'sɑɪb] *n.* **1** formerly, a title of respect used in the Indian subcontinent when speaking to or of a married European lady, especially the wife of a British colonial official. **2** a title of respect used in the Indian subcontinent when speaking to or of any European woman. ⟨< Hind. *mem-sahib* < *mem* (< E *ma'am*) + *sahib* sir⟩

men [mɛn] *n.* pl. of MAN.

men•ace ['mɛnɪs] *n., v.* **-aced, -ac•ing.** *—n.* a threat: *In dry weather forest fires are a menace.*
—v. threaten: *Floods menaced the valley towns with destruction.* ⟨late ME < MF < L *minācia,* ult. < *minaz* jutting out, threatening⟩ **—'men•ac•er,** *n.* **—'men•ac•ing•ly,** *adv.*

☛ *Syn. v.* See note at THREATEN.

me•nad ['minæd] See MAENAD.

men•a•di•one [,mɛnə'daɪoun] *or* [,mɛnədaɪ'oun] *n.* vitamin K used medicinally. *Formula:* $C_{11}H_8O_2$

mé•nage or **me•nage** [mei'nɑʒ]; *French,* [me'naʒ] *n., pl.* **-nages** [-'nɑʒɪz]; *French* [-'naʒ]. **1** a household; domestic establishment. **2** housekeeping. ⟨< F⟩

ménage a trois [menaʒa'tʀwa] *n. French.* **1** a living arrangement consisting of a married couple plus the lover of one them. **2** any continuous relationship, usually sexual, involving three people who live together.

me•nag•er•ie [mə'nædʒəri] *or* [mə'nɑʒəri] *n.* **1** a collection of wild animals kept in cages for exhibition. **2** the place where such animals are kept. ⟨< F *ménagerie,* literally, management of a household⟩

men•ar•che [mə'nɑrki] *n. Physiology.* the time of a girl's first menstruation, at puberty, usually at about the age of 12 years. ⟨< Gk. *mēn* month + *archē* beginning⟩

me•nat ['meinɑt] *n.* an amulet worn by the ancient Egyptians for protection by the gods and as a fertility charm. ⟨< Egyptian *mnyt*⟩

mend [mɛnd] *v., n.* *—v.* **1** put in good condition again; make whole; repair: *to mend a flat tire.* **2** set right; improve: *He should mend his manners.* **3** get back one's health.
—n. **1** a place that has been mended. **2** a mending; improvement.
on the mend, a improving. **b** getting well. ⟨var. of *amend*⟩ **—'mend•a•ble,** *adj.* **—'mend•er,** *n.*

☛ *Syn. v.* **1. Mend,** REPAIR[1], PATCH = put in good or usable condition again. **Mend** = make whole again something that has been broken, torn, or worn, but is now seldom used of large things: *She mended the broken vase with cement.* **Repair** = make right again something damaged, run down, decayed, weakened, etc.: *She repaired the electric toaster.* **Patch** = mend by putting a piece (or amount) of material on or in a hole, tear, or worn place: *He patched his torn trousers.*

men•da•cious [mɛn'deiʃəs] *adj.* **1** lying; untruthful. **2** false; untrue. ⟨< L *mendax* lying + E *-acious*⟩ **—men'da•cious•ly,** *adv.* **—men'da•cious•ness,** *n.*

men•dac•i•ty [mɛn'dæsəti] *n., pl.* **-ties. 1** the habit of telling lies; untruthfulness. **2** a lie.

Men•de ['mɛndei] *or* ['mɛndi] *n.* **1** a member of a people living in Sierra Leone and Liberia. **2** the Niger-Congo language of these people.

men•de•le•vi•um [,mɛndə'liviəm] *n. Chemistry.* a rare, radioactive, synthetic chemical element, produced as a by-product of nuclear fission. *Symbol:* Md; *at.no.* 101; *at.mass* 258.10; *half-life* approx. 60 days. ⟨after Dmitri Ivanovich *Mendeleev* (1834-1907), a Russian chemist⟩

Men•de•li•an [mɛn'diliən] *or* [mɛn'diljən] *adj.* of or having to do with the laws of heredity, especially single-gene inheritance, formulated by Gregor Mendel (1822-1884), an Austrian monk and biologist.

Mendel's laws ['mɛndəlz] *Genetics.* the two basic principles of heredity formulated by Gregor Mendel, whose investigations laid the foundations for the science of genetics. The **Law of Segregation** states that each cell of an individual has a pair of factors (now called genes) for each inherited characteristic and that these pairs separate during meiosis so that each gamete carries only one unit of each pair. The **Law of Independent Assortment** states that the pairs of factors (genes) are segregated independently of each other, without influence from any other pair. This is now known not to be always true, since the genes on the same chromosome are affected by linkage (the tendency to be segregated together).

men•di•can•cy ['mɛndəkənsi] *n.* the act of begging; the state of being a beggar.

men•di•cant ['mɛndəkənt] *adj., n.* *—adj.* **1** begging: *mendicant friars.* **2** pertaining to or characteristic of a beggar.

—*n.* **1** a beggar. **2** a mendicant friar. ⟨< L *mendicans, -antis* < *mendicus* beggar⟩

men•di•ci•ty [mɛn'dɪsəti] *n.* mendicancy.

mend•ing ['mɛndɪŋ] *n., v.* —*n.* **1** the act of a person who mends. **2** items, such as garments, to be mended.
—*v.* ppr. of MEND.

Men•e•la•us [,mɛnə'leiəs] *n. Greek mythology.* a king of Sparta, husband of Helen, and brother of Agamemnon.

men•folk ['mɛn,fouk] *n.pl. Informal.* **1** men collectively. **2** a particular group of men, such as the male members of a family.

men•ha•den [mɛn'hɛidən] *n., pl.* **-den.** a marine fish (*Brevoortia tyrannus*) of the herring family found along the Atlantic coast of North and South America, valued as a source of fish meal, oil, and fertilizer. ⟨< Algonquian⟩

men•hir ['mɛnhir] *n.* MONOLITH (def. 2). ⟨< F < Breton *men* stone + *hir* long⟩

me•ni•al ['miniəl] *or* ['minjəl] *adj., n.* —*adj.* suited to or belonging to a servant; low; mean.
—*n.* **1** a servant who does the humblest and most unpleasant tasks. **2** a low, mean, or servile person; flunky. ⟨ME < *meynie* household < OF *mesnie* < VL *mansionata* < L *mansio* habitation < *manere* remain⟩ **—'me•ni•al•ly,** *adv.*

Ménière's disease [mein'jɛrz] *n.* a disease characterized by vertigo, nausea, ringing in the ears, and gradual loss of hearing. ⟨after P. *Ménière* (1799-1862), French physician⟩

me•nin•ges [mə'nɪndʒiz] *n.pl., sing.* **me•ninx** ['minɪŋks]. *Anatomy.* the three membranes that surround the brain and spinal cord. ⟨< NL pl. of < Gk. membrane *mēninx*⟩ **—me'nin•ge•al,** *adj.*

men•in•gi•tis [,mɛnɪn'dʒəitɪs] *n. Pathology.* a serious disease in which the meninges are inflamed. ⟨< NL < Gk. *mēninx, -ingos* membrane + *-itis*⟩ **—,men•in'git•ic** [,mɛnɪn'dʒɪtɪk], *adj.*

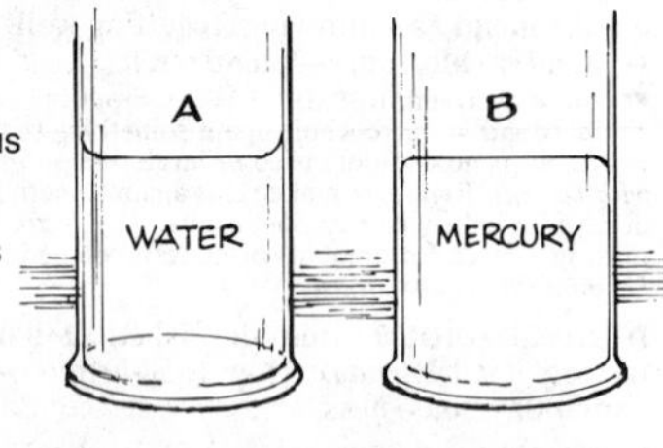

A: The concave meniscus of a column of water

B: The convex meniscus of a column of mercury

me•nis•cus [mə'nɪskəs] *n., pl.* **-nis•cus•es, -nis•ci** [-'nɪsaɪ] *or* [-'nɪskaɪ], ['nɪsi] *or* [-'nɪski]. **1** the curved upper surface of a column of liquid, produced by surface tension. The meniscus is concave when the walls of the container are made wet by the liquid (i.e., if there is capillary attraction) and convex when they are not (i.e., if there is capillary repulsion). **2** *Optics.* a lens that is concave on one side and convex on the other. See CONCAVE and CONVEX for pictures. **3** a crescent or crescent-shaped body. ⟨< NL < Gk. *mēniskos,* dim. of *mēnē* moon⟩

Men•non•ite ['mɛnə,nəit] *n., adj.* —*n.* **1** a member of any of several Christian churches having their roots within the radical left wing of the Reformation, whose tenets include pacificism and the rejection of infant baptism in favour of the baptism of adult believers. **2** a member of a Pennsylvania Dutch Mennonite group, especially a group characterized by adherence to a simple lifestyle and rejection of modern technology.
—*adj.* of or having to do with Mennonites: *Mennonite cooking.* ⟨after *Menno* Simons (1492-1559), a Dutch leader of the Mennonites⟩

me•no ['meinou] *adv. Music.* less. ⟨< Ital. < L *minus* less⟩

me•nom•i•nee [mə'nɒməni] *n. Cdn.* wild rice. ⟨< Cree⟩

men•o•pause ['mɛnə,pɒz] *n.* the period in a woman's life during which menstruation ceases permanently, usually between the ages of 45 and 55; change of life. ⟨< NL < Gk. *mēn* month + *pausis* pause⟩ **—,men•o'pausal,** *adj.*

men•o•rah or **Men•o•rah** [mə'nɔrə] *n.* a candelabrum used in Jewish worship. The seven-branched menorah is used in temple services; the nine-branched one is used during Hanukkah. ⟨< Hebrew *manorah*⟩

men•or•rhea [,mɛnə'riə] *n.* menstrual bleeding. Also, **menorrhoea.** ⟨< Gk. *men* month + *-rrhoia* ult. < *rhein* flow⟩

men's [mɛnz] *n.* **1** a range of sizes of clothing made for men. **2** clothing in these sizes. **3** a department of a store which sells men's clothing.

Men•sa ['mɛnsə] *n. Astronomy.* **1** the Table, a southern constellation between Hydrus and Volans. **2** a worldwide organization promoting friendship and fellowship among people having IQs in the top two percent. ⟨< L *mensa* table, symbolizing the concept of round table discussion among equals⟩

men•sal[1] ['mɛnsəl] *adj.* used at a table. ⟨< L *mensalis* < *mensa* table⟩

men•sal[2] ['mɛnsəl] *adj.* monthly. ⟨< L *mensis* month⟩

men•serv•ants ['mɛn,sɜrvənts] *n.* pl. of MANSERVANT.

men•ses ['mɛnsiz] *n.pl.* menstruation. ⟨< L *menses,* pl. of *mensis* month⟩

Men•she•vik or **men•she•vik** ['mɛnʃə,vɪk] *n., pl.* **-viks** or **-vi•ki** [-,viki]; *adj.* —*n.* in Russia, a member of the conservative wing of the Social Democratic Party, opposed to the more radical Bolsheviks from 1903 to 1917.
—*adj.* of or having to do with the Mensheviks or Menshevism. ⟨< Russian *Menshevik* < *menshe* less; because it was at one time the minority wing of the Party. Compare BOLSHEVIK.⟩

men•stru•al ['mɛnstruəl] *or* ['mɛnstrəl] *adj.* **1** of or having to do with menstruation. **2** monthly.

men•stru•ate ['mɛnstru,eit] *or* ['mɛnstreit] *v.* **-at•ed, -at•ing.** have a period; undergo menstruation. ⟨< LL *menstruare,* ult. < *mensis* month⟩

men•stru•a•tion [,mɛnstru'eiʃən] *or* [mɛn'streiʃən] *n.* the regular discharge of blood, secretions, and sloughed-off tissue from the uterus through the vagina, normally occurring about every four weeks in non-pregnant women from puberty to menopause. **—'men•stru•ous,** *adj.*

men•stru•um ['mɛnstruəm] *n., pl.* **-stru•ums, -stru•a** [-struə]. a liquid that dissolves solids; a solvent. ⟨< Med.L *menstruum,* neut. of L *menstruus* monthly⟩

men•sur•a•ble ['mɛnʃərəbəl] *or* ['mɛnsərəbəl] *adj.* measurable. ⟨< LL *mensurabilis* < L *mensurare.* See MEASURE, v.⟩ **—,men•sur•a'bil•i•ty,** *n.*

men•sur•al ['mɛnʃərəl] *adj. Music.* having notes of a fixed rhythmic value.

men•su•ra•tion [,mɛnʃə'reiʃən] *or* [,mɛnsə'reiʃən] *n.* **1** the act, art, or process of measuring. **2** the branch of mathematics that deals with finding lengths, areas, and volumes. ⟨< LL *mensuratio, -onis,* ult. < L *mensura.* See MEASURE.⟩ **—'men•su•ra•tive,** *adj.* **—,men•su'ra•tion•al,** *adj.*

mens•wear ['mɛnz,wɛr] *n., adj.* —*n.* **1** men's clothing. **2** cloth suitable for making men's clothing.
—*adj.* of or made from this kind of cloth: *menswear terylene.*

-ment *noun-forming suffix.* **1** the act or state or fact of ——ing: *enjoyment, management.* **2** the state or condition or fact of being ——ed: *amazement, astonishment.* **3** the product or result of ——ing: *pavement.* **4** a means or instrument for ——ing: *inducement.* ⟨< F < L *-mentum*⟩

men•tal ['mɛntəl] *adj.* **1** of, having to do with, or involving the mind: *mental processes, mental alertness.* **2** done by or in the mind, without being spoken or written down: *a mental calculation. She accepted the invitation but with the mental reservation to leave early.* **3** of or having to do with a disorder of the mind that affects thoughts, feelings, and behaviour: *mental illness, a mental patient.* **4** designating a place for the care and treatment of people with mental illness: *a mental hospital.* ⟨< LL *mentalis* < L *mens, mentis* mind⟩ **—'men•tal•ly,** *adv.*

mental age *Psychology.* an estimate of the level of mental development as measured against the chronological age at which this development is reached by the average person.

mental health **1** a psychological condition of well-being and good adjustment to the demands of society and life. **2** a branch of the medical field dealing with the attainment or maintenance of such well-being.

mental illness the condition of having a neurosis or more severe psychiatric illness.

men•tal•ism ['mɛntə,lɪzəm] *n. Philosophy.* the doctrine that the fundamental reality is mind and the material world exists only as a perception of the mind. **—,men•tal'is•tic,** *adj.* **—,men•tal'is•ti•cal•ly,** *adv.*

men•tal•ist ['mɛntəlɪst] *n.* **1** a person who believes in mentalism. **2** mind reader.

men•tal•i•ty [mɛn'tæləti] *n., pl.* **-ties. 1** mental capacity; mind: *The boy was of average mentality for his age.* **2** attitude or outlook: *the Eastern mentality.*

mental reservation an unexpressed qualification of a statement.

mental telepathy telepathy.

men•thol ['mɛnθɒl] *n. Chemistry, pharmacy.* a white, crystalline substance obtained from oil of peppermint, used in medicine. *Formula:* $C_{10}H_{20}O$ ⟨< G < L *menta* mint + *oleum* oil⟩

men•tho•lat•ed ['mɛnθə,leitɪd] *adj.* containing menthol.

men•tion ['mɛnʃən] *v., n.* —*v.* speak about; refer to.
not to mention, in addition to; besides.
—*n.* a short statement; reference.
make mention of, speak of; refer to. ⟨ME < OF < L *mentio, -onis*⟩ **—'men•tion•a•ble,** *adj.* **—'men•tion•er,** *n.*

men•tor ['mɛntɔr] *or* ['mɛntər] *n.* a wise and trusted adviser. ⟨< *Mentor,* a faithful friend of Odysseus. Disguised as Mentor, the goddess Athena acted as the teacher and adviser of Odysseus' son Telemachus⟩

men•u ['mɛnju] *n.* **1** a list of the food served at a meal; bill of fare. **2** the food served. **3** *Computer technology.* in computer programs, a list of topics, operations, etc. that allows the user to make a selection. ⟨< F *menu* small, detailed < L *minutus* made small. Doublet of MINUTE[2].⟩

menu-driven ['menju ,drɪvən] *adj. Computer technology.* of software, relying extensively on menus to guide users to choose programs.

me•ow [mi'aʊ] *n., v.* —*n.* the sound made by a cat.
—*v.* make the sound of a cat. Also, **miaow, miaou.** ⟨imitative⟩

me•pe•ri•dine [mə'pɛrɪ,din] *n.* an analgesic and sedative drug. *Formula:* $C_{15}H_{21}NO_2$

me•phen•y•toin [mə'fɛnə,toɪn] *n.* an anticonvulsant drug used to treat epilepsy.

Meph•i•stoph•e•les [,mɛfə'stɒfə,liz] *n.* **1** in the Faust legend, the devil. **2** in medieval Christian theology, one of the seven chief devils.

Meph•is•to•phe•li•an [,mɛfɪstou'filiən] *or* [mə,fɪstə'filiən] *adj.* **1** like Mephistopheles; wicked and crafty; sardonic; scoffing. **2** of or having to do with Mephistopheles. Also, **Mephistophelean.**

me•phit•ic [mə'fɪtɪk] *adj.* **1** having an offensive smell. **2** noxious; poisonous; pestilential. ⟨< LL *mephiticus* < *mephitis* stench⟩ **—me'phit•i•cal•ly,** *adv.*

me•phi•tis [mə'fəitɪs] *n.* **1** a foul or offensive smell. **2** a poisonous vapour arising from the earth, as poison gas. ⟨< L < Gk.⟩

me•pro•ba•mate [mə'proubə,meit] *or* [,mɛprou'bæmeit] *n.* a tranquillizing drug.

mer•can•tile ['mɜrkən,taɪl] *adj.* **1** of or having to do with merchants or trade; commercial: *a successful mercantile venture.* **2** engaged in trade or commerce: *a mercantile firm.* **3** of or having to do with mercantilism. ⟨< F < Ital. *mercantile* < *mercante* merchant⟩

mercantile system mercantilism.

mer•can•til•ism ['mɜrkəntə,lɪzəm] *or* ['mɜrkəntaɪ,lɪzəm] *n.* a theory or system of political economy that stressed the holding of gold and other precious metals, a greater volume of exports than imports, and the exploitation of colonies. Mercantilism replaced feudalism. **—'mer•can•til•ist,** *n., adj.*

mer•cap•tan [mər'kæptæn] *n. Chemistry.* any organic compound containing sulphur. ⟨< L, short for *corpus mercurium captans* body capturing mercury⟩

mer•cap•to•pu•rine [mər,kæptou'pjʊrin] *n.* a drug used to treat leukemia. *Formula:* $C_5H_4N_4S$

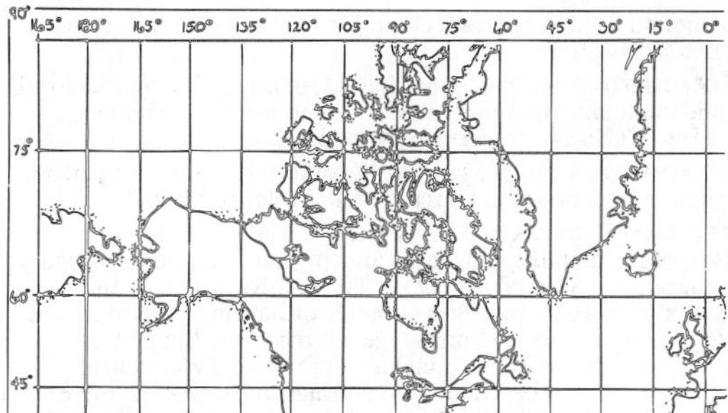

A Mercator projection of part of the Northern Hemisphere

Mer•ca•tor projection [mər'keitər] a method of drawing maps with straight instead of curved lines for latitude and longitude. ⟨after Gerhardus *Mercator* (1512-1594), a Flemish map maker⟩

mer•ce•nar•y ['mɜrsə,nɛri] *adj., n., pl.* **-nar•ies.**
—*adj.* **1** working for money only; acting with money as the sole motive. **2** done only for money or gain.
—*n.* a soldier serving for pay in a foreign army. ⟨ME < L *mercenarius* < *merces* wages⟩ **—'mer•ce,nar•i•ly,** *adv.* **—'mer•ce,nar•i•ness,** *n.*

mer•cer ['mɜrsər] *n. Brit.* a dealer in textile fabrics, especially fine silks, etc. ⟨ME < AF < OF *mercier* merchant, ult. < L *merx, mercis* goods. See MARKET.⟩ **—'mer•cer•y,** *n.*

mer•cer•ize ['mɜrsə,raɪz] *v.* **-ized, -iz•ing.** treat (cotton thread or cloth) with a chemical solution that strengthens it, makes it hold dyes better, and gives it a silky lustre. ⟨after John *Mercer* (1791-1866), a British calico printer, who patented the process in 1850⟩

mer•chan•dise *n.* ['mɜrtʃən,dəis] *or* ['mɜrtʃən,daɪz]; *v.* ['mɜrtʃən,daɪz] *n., v.* **-dised, -dis•ing.** —*n.* goods for sale; wares; articles bought and sold.
—*v.* **1** buy and sell; trade. **2** strive for increased sales or greater acceptance of goods, services, etc. by attractive display, advertising, etc. ⟨ME < OF *marchandise* < *marchand* merchant⟩ **—'mer•chan,dis•er,** *n.*

mer•chant ['mɜrtʃənt] *n., adj.* —*n.* **1** a person who buys and sells commodities for profit. **2** storekeeper.
—*adj.* trading; having to do with trade: *merchant ships.* ⟨ME < OF *marchant,* ult. < L *merx, mercis* wares⟩ **—'mer•chant,like,** *adj.*

mer•chant•a•ble ['mɜrtʃəntəbəl] *adj.* marketable. ⟨ME < obs. v. *merchant* + *-able*⟩

mer•chant•man ['mɜrtʃəntmən] *n., pl.* **-men.** a ship used in commerce.

merchant marine 1 ships used in commerce. **2** the sailors who work on such ships, thought of as a group: *John's brother is in the merchant marine.*

merchant vessel a ship used in commerce.

Mer•cian ['mɜrʃən] *or* ['mɜrsiən] *adj., n.* —*adj.* of Mercia, in ancient times an Anglo-Saxon kingdom in central England, its people, or their dialect.
—*n.* **1** a native or inhabitant of Mercia. **2** the dialect of Anglo-Saxon spoken in Mercia. **3** the dialect of Middle English resulting from this type of Anglo-Saxon.

mer•ci•ful ['mɜrsəfəl] *adj.* having mercy; showing or feeling mercy; full of mercy. **—'mer•ci•ful•ly,** *adv.* **—'mer•ci•ful•ness,** *n.*

mer•ci•less ['mɜrsəlɪs] *adj.* without mercy; having or showing no mercy: *a merciless attack.* **—'mer•ci•less•ly,** *adv.* **—'mer•ci•less•ness,** *n.*

mer•cu•ri•al [mər'kjʊriəl] *adj., n.* —*adj.* **1** sprightly; quick. **2** changeable; fickle. **3** caused by the use of mercury: *mercurial poisoning.* **4** containing mercury: *a mercurial ointment.* **5** affected by the planet Mercury. **6** of or having to do with the god Mercury.
—*n.* a drug containing mercury. **—mer'cu•ri•al•ly,** *adv.*

mer•cu•ric [mər'kjʊrɪk] *adj. Chemistry.* of compounds, containing mercury with a valence of two.

mercuric chloride *Chemistry.* a poisonous, crystalline

compound used as a disinfectant, for engraving metals, etc. *Formula*: $HgCl_2$

Mer•cu•ro•chrome [mər'kjʊrə,kroum] *n. Trademark.* a red liquid containing mercury, used as an antiseptic. *Formula*: $C_{20}H_8Br_2HgNa_2O_6$ ⟨< *mercury* + *chrome*⟩

mer•cu•rous [mər'kjʊrəs] *or* ['mɜrkjərəs] *adj. Chemistry.* of compounds, containing mercury with a valence of one.

mer•cu•ry ['mɜrkjəri] *n., pl.* **-ries. 1** *Chemistry.* a heavy, silver-white, metallic chemical element that is liquid at ordinary temperatures. *Symbol*: Hg; *at.no.* 80; *at.mass* 200.59. **2** the column of mercury in a thermometer or barometer. **3 Mercury, a** *Roman mythology.* the messenger of the gods, the god of commerce, skill of hands, quickness of wit, and eloquence, corresponding to the Greek god Hermes. **b** *Astronomy.* the planet that is the smallest in the solar system and nearest to the sun. ⟨< L *Mercurius* Mercury⟩

mer•cy ['mɜrsi] *n., pl.* **-cies. 1** more kindness than justice requires; kindness beyond what can be claimed or expected: *The judge showed mercy to the young offender.* **2** kindly treatment; pity. **3** something to be thankful for; blessing: *It's a mercy that they arrived safely through the storm.*
at the mercy of, in the power of: *Without shelter we were at the mercy of the storm.* ⟨ME < OF *merci* < L *merces* reward⟩
☛ *Syn.* **1. Mercy,** CLEMENCY = kindness or mildness shown to an enemy, an offender, etc. **Mercy** = compassion shown by refraining from punishing severely those deserving severity or from treating harshly enemies and others in one's power: *The guard showed mercy to the prisoners.* **Clemency** is a term often used in a legal sense that suggests showing mercy because of mildness of disposition rather than from sympathy: *That judge's clemency is well-known.*

mercy flight *Cdn.* especially in the North, an aircraft flight to fetch a seriously ill or injured person to hospital for treatment.

mercy killing euthanasia.

mercy seat in the Bible: **1** the gold covering on the Ark of the Covenant, regarded as the resting place of God. **2** the throne of God.

mere[1] [mir] *adj. superl.* **mer•est.** nothing more than; only; simple: *The cut was a mere scratch.* ⟨< L *merus* pure⟩
☛ *Hom.* MIR.

mere[2] [mir] *n. Poetic or dialect.* lake; pond. ⟨OE⟩
☛ *Hom.* MIR.

mere•ly ['mirli] *adv.* simply; only; and nothing more; and that is all.

me•ren•gue [mə'rɛŋ,gei] *n.* **1** a fast, rhythmic Caribbean dance in duple time. **2** music for this dance. ⟨< Sp.⟩

mer•e•tri•cious [,mɛrə'trɪʃəs] *adj.* **1** attractive in a showy way; alluring by false charms: *A wooden building painted to look like marble is meretricious.* **2** plausible but not genuine. **3** of or having to do with a prostitute. ⟨< L *meretricius* < *meretrix, -tricis* prostitute < *mereri* earn⟩ **—,mer•e'tri•cious•ly,** *adv.* **—,mer•e'tri•cious•ness,** *n.*

mer•gan•ser [mər'gænsər] *n., pl.* **-sers** or (*esp. collectively*) **-ser.** any of several large diving ducks (genera *Mergus* and *Lophodytes*) having a long, slender bill with a hooked top and sharp, toothlike projections along the edges which help to catch and hold fish. ⟨< NL *merganser* < *mergus* diver + *anser* goose⟩

merge [mɜrdʒ] *v.* **merged, merg•ing. 1** combine or cause to combine into one: *The brothers decided to merge their two businesses.* **2** come or bring together gradually or smoothly; blend: *merging cultures, merging traffic. The distant walker merged with the darkness.* **3** *Computer technology.* combine (two or more files, pieces of information, etc.). ⟨< L *mergere* dip⟩

merg•er ['mɜrdʒər] *n.* **1** the act of merging; combination: *One big company was formed by the merger of four small ones.* **2** any combination of two or more companies.

me•rid•i•an [mə'rɪdiən] *n., adj. —n.* **1** *Geography.* **a** an imaginary circle passing through any place on the earth's surface and through the North and South Poles. **b** the half of such a circle from pole to pole. All the places on the same meridian have the same longitude. See EQUATOR for picture. **2** the highest point that the sun or a star reaches in the sky. **3** the highest point; the time of greatest success and happiness: *The meridian of life is the prime of life.* **4** one of a series of north-south lines used as a basis of land surveys. See also FIRST MERIDIAN.
—adj. **1** highest; greatest. **2** around midday. ⟨ME < OF < L *meridianus*, ult. < *medius* middle + *dies* day⟩

me•rid•i•o•nal [mə'rɪdiənəl] *adj., n. —adj.* **1** southern; southerly; characteristic of the south or people living there, especially of southern France. **2** of, having to do with, or resembling a meridian. **3** along a meridian; in a north-south direction: *a meridional flow of air, a meridional chain of weather stations.*
—n. an inhabitant of the south, especially the south of France. ⟨< LL *meridionalis* < L *meridies* noon, south < *medius* middle + *dies* day; patterned after *septentrionalis* northern⟩
—me'rid•i•o•nally, *adv.*

me•ringue [mə'ræŋ] *n.* **1** a mixture of egg white and sugar, beaten until stiff: *Meringue is often spread on pies, puddings, etc. and lightly browned in the oven.* **2** a small cake, tart shell, etc. made of this mixture. ⟨< F⟩

me•ri•no [mə'rinou] *n., pl.* **-nos. 1** a breed of sheep, originating in Spain, having long, fine wool. **2** the wool of this sheep. **3** a soft yarn made from it. **4** a thin, soft cloth made from this yarn or some substitute. **5** (*adjl.*) made of this wool, yarn, or cloth. ⟨< Sp.⟩

me•ri•stem ['mɛrə,stɛm] *n. Botany.* the area at the tip of a stem or root where cells divide and grow. ⟨< Gk. *meristos, merizein* to divide into parts < *meris* part, share⟩ **—,mer•i•ste'mat•ic,** *adj.* **—,mer•i•ste'mat•i•cal•ly,** *adv.*

mer•it ['mɛrɪt] *n., v. —n.* **1** goodness; worth or value. **2** anything that deserves praise or reward. **3** Usually, **merits,** *pl.* actual facts or qualities, whether good or bad: *The judge will consider the case on its merits.*
—v. deserve. ⟨< F < L *meritum* earned⟩ **—'mer•it•less,** *adj.*
☛ *Syn. n.* **1. Merit,** WORTH = the goodness or value of someone or something. **Merit** emphasizes the idea of something earned, and suggests an excellence in accomplishment or quality that deserves praise: *The merits of your plan outweigh the defects.* **Worth** emphasizes inherent excellence or value, apart from any connections or conditions affecting its usefulness, value, or importance: *The worth of the new drugs is certain, although all their uses are not yet known.*

mer•i•toc•ra•cy [,mɛrə'tɒkrəsi] *n., pl.* **-cies. 1** an elite class of people distinguished for their high intellect or talent rather than for birth or wealth. **2** leadership or rule by such a group. **3** a social or educational system in which individuals achieve high status on the basis of intellect or talent.

mer•i•to•ri•ous [,mɛrə'tɔriəs] *adj.* deserving reward or praise; having merit; worthy. **—,mer•i'to•ri•ous•ly,** *adv.* **—,mer•i'to•ri•ous•ness,** *n.*

merle or **merl** [mɜrl] *n. Poetic.* the common European blackbird. ⟨< F < L *merula*⟩

mer•lin ['mɜrlən] *n.* the usual European name for the pigeon hawk. Merlins are often trained for falconry. ⟨ME < AF *merilun* < OF *esmeril* < Gmc.⟩
☛ *Hom.* MERLON.

Mer•lin ['mɜrlən] *n. Arthurian legend.* the magician who was adviser to King Arthur.

mer•lon ['mɜrlən] *n.* the solid part between two openings in a battlement. See FORT for picture. ⟨< F < Ital. *merlone*⟩
☛ *Hom.* MERLIN.

mer•maid ['mɜr,meid] *n.* **1** an imaginary sea maiden having the form of a fish from the waist down. **2** *Informal.* a girl or woman who is a good swimmer. ⟨ME *mermayde.* See MERE[2], MAID.⟩

mer•man ['mɜr,mæn] *or* ['mɜrmən] *n., pl.* **-men. 1** an imaginary man of the sea having the form of a fish from the waist down. **2** *Informal.* a boy or man who is a good swimmer. ⟨ME. See MERE[2], MAN.⟩

mero– *combining form.* part; partial: *meropia.* ⟨< Gk. *méros* part⟩

me•ro•blast•ic [,mɛrə'blæstɪk] *adj. Embryology.* of an egg, undergoing partial division. ⟨< Gk. *meros* part + *blastos* sprout⟩ **—,mer•o'blas•ti•cal•ly,** *adv.*

me•ro•pi•a [mə'roupiə] *Opthalmology.* partial blindness.

Mer•o•vin•gi•an [,mɛrə'vɪndʒiən] *adj., n. —adj.* designating or having to do with the Frankish line of kings, beginning with Clovis, who reigned in France from about A.D. 500 to 751.
—n. one of these kings.

mer•ri•ment ['mɛrimənt] *n.* laughter and gaiety; fun; mirth; merry enjoyment.

mer•ry ['mɛri] *adj.* **-ri•er, -ri•est. 1** full of fun; loving fun. **2** happy; joyful: *a merry holiday.* **3** *Archaic.* pleasant; delightful.
make merry, laugh and be happy; have fun. ⟨OE *myrge*⟩ **—'mer•ri•ly,** *adv.* **—'mer•ri•ness,** *n.*
☛ *Syn.* **1.** See note at GAY.
☛ *Hom.* MARRY.

mer•ry–an•drew [,mɛri 'ændru] *n.* a clown; buffoon.

mer•ry–go–round ['mɛri gou ,raʊnd] *n.* **1** a set of figures with seats on a circular platform that is driven round and round by machinery and that people ride for fun. **2** any whirl or rapid round: *The holidays were a merry-go-round of parties.*

mer•ry•mak•er ['mɛri,meikər] *n.* a person who is being merry; a person engaged in merrymaking.

mer•ry•mak•ing ['mɛri,meikɪŋ] *n., adj.* —*n.* **1** laughter and gaiety; fun. **2** a joyous festival; merry entertainment.
—*adj.* gay and full of fun; engaged in merrymaking.

mer•ry•thought ['mɛri,θɒt] *n. Brit.* wishbone.

me•sa ['meisə] *n. U.S.* an isolated, flat-topped hill or upland with steep sides, similar to a butte, but usually wider. ⟨< Sp. < L *mensa* table⟩

mé•sal•li•ance [mei'zæliəns]; *French,* [meza'ljɑ̃s] *n. French.* a misalliance; marriage with a person of lower social position.

mes•cal [mɛ'skæl] *n.* **1** an alcoholic drink made from the fleshy leaves of any of various agaves. **2** any agave from which this drink is made. **3** a small, spineless cactus (*Lophophora williamsii*) of Mexico and the SW United States having buttonlike tubercles that yield mescaline and are used especially among Mexican Indian peoples for their stimulating and hallucinogenic effects. ⟨< Sp. < Nahuatl *mexcalli* liquor⟩

mes•cal•ine ['mɛskə,lin] *or* ['mɛskəlɪn] *n.* a narcotic drug that produces hallucinations and is chemically related to LSD, derived from MESCAL (def. 3). Also, **mescalin.** *Formula:* $C_{11}H_{17}NO_3$

mes•dames [mei'dæm] *or* [mei'dɑm]; *French,* [mɛ'dam] *n.* pl. of MADAME.

mes•de•moi•selles [meidmwə'zɛl]; *French,* [medmwa'zɛl] *n.* pl. of MADEMOISELLE.

me•seems [mi'simz] *v.* **-seemed.** *Archaic.* it seems to me.

mes•en•ceph•a•lon [,mɛzən'sɛfə,lɒn] *n., pl.* **-la** [-lə] or **-lons.** the midbrain. **—,mes•en•ce'phal•ic** [,mɛzənsə'fælɪk], *adj.*

mes•en•ter•y ['mɛsən,tɛri] *or* ['mɛzən,tɛri] *n., pl.* **-ter•ies.** *Anatomy.* a membrane that enfolds and supports an internal organ, attaching it to the body wall or to another organ.
⟨< Med.L < Gk. *mesenterion* < *mesos* middle + *enteron* intestine⟩ **—,mes•en'ter•ic,** *adj.*

mesh [mɛʃ] *n., v.* —*n.* **1** one of the open spaces of a net, sieve, or screen: *This net has one-centimetre meshes.* **2** a fabric of thread, cord, wire, etc. knitted, knotted, or woven in an open texture with small holes: *We found an old fly swatter made of wire mesh.* **3** the act of meshing. **4 meshes, a** web; network: *Seaweed was caught in the meshes of the net.* **b** snares.
in mesh, in gear; fitted together.
—*v.* **1** catch or be caught in a net. **2** engage or become engaged: *The teeth of the small gear mesh with the teeth of a larger one.* **3** be in harmony: *Their ideas do not mesh.* ⟨Cf. OE *mǣscre* net⟩

me•shu•ga [mə'ʃʊgə] *adj. Slang.* crazy; mad. Also, **meshugga.** ⟨< Yiddish *meshuge* < Hebrew *meshugga*⟩

me•si•al ['miziəl] *adj.* near the middle. ⟨< Gk. *mesos* middle + E *-ial*⟩

me•sit•y•lene [mɪ'sɪtə,lin] *n.* a hydrocarbon found in petroleum and coal tar. *Formula:* $C_6H_3(CH_3)_3$

mes•mer•ic [mɛz'mɛrɪk] *or* [mɛs'mɛrɪk] *adj.* hypnotic. **—mes'mer•i•cal•ly,** *adv.*

mes•mer•ism ['mɛzmə,rɪzəm] *or* ['mɛsmə,rɪzəm] *n.* hypnotism. ⟨after Franz Anton *Mesmer* (1734-1815), an Austrian physician who popularized it⟩

mes•mer•ist ['mɛzmərɪst] *or* ['mɛsmərɪst] *n.* hypnotist.

mes•mer•ize ['mɛzmə,raɪz] *or* ['mɛsmə,raɪz] *v.* **-ized, -iz•ing.** hypnotize. **—'mes•mer,iz•er,** *n.*

mes•na ['mɛznə] *n.* a drug used to treat certain conditions of the urinary tract.

mesne [min] *adj. Law.* intermediate or intervening. ⟨< ME < AF var. of *meen* mean⟩
☛ *Hom.* MEAN, MIEN.

meso– *combining form.* middle: *mesocarp, mesoderm, mesomorph.* Also, before vowels, **mes-.** ⟨< Gk. *mesos* middle⟩

Mes•o•am•er•i•ca [,mɛzouə'mɛrɪkə] *or* [,mɛsouə'mɛrɪkə] *n.* Central America, from Mexico to Panama.

mes•o•blast ['mɛzə,blæst] *or* ['mɛsə,blæst] *n.* the early stage of development of the mesoderm.

mes•o•carp ['mɛzə,karp] *or* ['mɛsə,karp] *n. Botany.* the middle layer of the pericarp, such as the fleshy part of a peach or plum. ⟨< *meso-* + Gk. *karpos* fruit⟩

mes•o•ce•phal•ic [,mɛzousə'fælɪk] *or* [,mɛsousə'fælɪk] *adj.* having a head size intermediate between brachycephalic and dolichocephalic. **—'mes•o,ceph•al,** *n.* **—,mes•o'ceph•al•y,** *n.*

mes•o•derm ['mɛzə,dɜrm] *or* ['mɛsə,dɜrm] *n. Biology.* the middle layer of cells in an embryo. ⟨< *meso-* + Gk. *derma* skin⟩

mes•o•lith•ic or **Mes•o•lith•ic** [,mɛzə'lɪθɪk] *or* [,mɛsə'lɪθɪk] *adj.* of or relating to the period in the Stone Age between the neolithic and the paleolithic periods. ⟨< *meso-* + Gk. *lithos* stone + E *-ic*⟩

mes•o•morph ['mɛzə,mɔrf] *or* ['mɛsə,mɔrf] *n.* **1** a human body type characterized by a medium frame, medium height, and the capacity for good, even muscular development. It is one of three basic body types. Compare ECTOMORPH, ENDOMORPH. **2** a person having such a body structure. ⟨< *meso-* + Gk. *morphē* form, shape⟩

mes•o•mor•phic [,mɛzə'mɔrfɪk] *or* [,mɛsə'mɔrfɪk] *adj.* of, having to do with, or being a mesomorph. **—,mes•o'mor•phism** or **'mes•o,mor•phy,** *n.*

me•son ['misɒn] *or* ['mɛsɒn], ['mizɒn] *or* ['mɛzɒn] *n. Physics.* a highly unstable particle in the nucleus of an atom, having a positive, neutral, or negative charge and a very short lifetime (about a millionth of a second or less). Theoretically, mesons exert nuclear forces of attraction. ⟨< Gk. *meson,* neut. of adj. *mesos* middle⟩

mes•o•phyll ['mɛzəfɪl] *or* ['mɛsəfɪl] *n. Botany.* the soft tissue inside a leaf that aids photosynthesis. **—,mes•o'phyl•lic** or **,mes•o'phyl•lous,** *adj.*

mes•o•phyte ['mɛzə,fəit] *or* ['mɛsə,fəit] *n.* a plant that thrives under high humidity.

Mes•o•po•ta•mi•a [,mɛsəpə'teimiə] *or* [,mɛsəpə'teimjə] *n.* an ancient country in SW Asia, between the Tigris and Euphrates Rivers, now part of Iraq. **—,Mes•o•po'ta•mi•an,** *adj.* or *n.*

me•so•rid•a•zine bes•y•late [,mɛsə'rɪdə,zin 'bɛsə,leit] *n.* a drug used to treat schizophrenia and some other conditions.

mes•o•sphere ['mɛzə,sfir] *or* ['mɛsə,sfir] *n.* the layer of the earth's atmosphere lying above the stratosphere, extending from about 50 km to about 85 km above the earth's surface, and characterized by a decrease in temperature with increasing altitude, to about −90°C at the point where the thermosphere begins.

mes•o•tho•rax [,mɛzə'θɔræks] *or* [,mɛsə'θɔræks] *n., pl.* **-tho•rax•es** or **-tho•ra•ces** [-'θɔrə,siz]. the middle part of an insect's thorax.

mes•o•tho•ri•um [,mɛzə'θɔriəm] *or* [,mɛsə'θɔriəm] *n. Chemistry.* **1** a product of thorium in decay. **2** an isotope of radium and actinium.

mes•o•tron ['mɛzə,trɒn] *or* ['mɛsə,trɒn] *n. Physics.* meson. ⟨< *meson* + (*elec*)*tron*⟩ **—,mes•o'tron•ic,** *adj.*

Mes•o•zo•ic [,mɛzə'zouɪk] *or* [,mɛsə'zouɪk] *adj., n. Geology.* —*adj.* **1** of, having to do with, or designating the era before the present era, beginning about 245 million years ago. The Mesozoic era is the age of reptiles. See geological time chart in the Appendix. **2** of, having to do with, or designating the system of rocks formed during this era.
—*n.* the Mesozoic era or its rocks. ⟨< *meso-* + Gk. *zōē* life + E *-ic*⟩

mes•quite [mɛ'skit] *or* ['mɛskit] *n.* a spiny tree or shrub (*Prosopis juliflora*) of the pea family found in the southwestern United States and Mexico, bearing sugary pods of seeds used as fodder. ⟨< Sp. *mezquite* < Nahuatl *mizquitl*⟩

mess [mɛs] *n., v.* —*n.* **1** a dirty or untidy mass or group of things; a dirty or untidy condition: *There was a mess of dirty dishes in the sink.* **2** *Informal.* a person in a dirty or untidy state. **3** confusion or difficulty: *His affairs are in a mess.* **4** an unpleasant or unsuccessful affair or state of affairs: *He made a mess of his final examinations.* **5** a group of people who eat together regularly, especially such a group in the armed forces. **6** a meal for such a group or the place where it is eaten: *The officers are at mess now.* **7** in the armed forces: **a** an organization for social purposes: *He was secretary of the sergeants' mess.* **b** the dining room, lounge, etc. used by members of such an organization. **8** *Archaic.* a portion of food; portion of soft food: *a mess of porridge, a mess of fish.* **9** food that does not look or taste good.
—*v.* **1** make dirty or untidy: *He messed up his book by scribbling on the pages.* **2** make a failure of; spoil: *He messed up his chances of winning the race.* **3** take one's meals *(with).*
mess around (or **about**), *Informal.* **a** busy oneself without seeming to accomplish anything; putter. **b** *Slang.* waste time.
mess up, a spoil (something). **b** *Informal.* commit a misdeed: *I'm*

sorry I got so angry; I really messed up. ⟨ME < OF *mes* < LL *missus* (course) put (i.e., on the dinner table), pp. of *mittere* send⟩

mes•sage ['mɛsɪdʒ] *n.* **1** information or instructions sent from one person to another. **2** an official speech or writing: *On Christmas Day we listened to the Queen's message to the Commonwealth.* **3** a lesson or moral implied in a work or works of fiction, a motion picture, play, etc. **4** inspired words: *the message of a prophet.* **5** the business entrusted to a messenger; mission; errand: *His message completed, he went on his way.* **6** a radio or television commercial. **7** sermon. **8** *Communication theory.* gist; what is conveyed or expressed; meaning.
get the message, a understand. **b** take the hint. ⟨ME < OF, ult. < L *missus*, pp. of *mittere* send⟩

mes•sa•line [,mɛsə'lin] *or* ['mɛsə,lin] *n.* a thin, soft, silk cloth with a surface like satin. ⟨< F⟩

Mes•sei•gneurs or mes•sei•gneurs [mesɛ'njœʀ] *n. French.* pl. of MONSEIGNEUR.

mes•sen•ger ['mɛsəndʒər] *n.* **1** a person who carries a message or goes on an errand. **2** a sign that something is coming; forerunner: *Dawn is the messenger of day.* **3** a government official employed to carry dispatches; courier. **4** *Nautical.* a chain for hauling in a cable. ⟨ME *messanger*, earlier *messager* < OF *messagier* < *message.* See MESSAGE.⟩

messenger RNA *Genetics.* that segment or type of RNA that carries the code for the synthesis of protein from the DNA to the ribosomes. *Abbrev.*: mRNA

mess hall in the armed forces, a place where a group of people eat together regularly.

Mes•si•ah [mə'saɪə] *n.* **1** *Judaism.* according to some interpretations of the writings of the ancient Hebrew prophets, the deliverer promised to the Hebrews, who would establish a kingdom of righteousness on earth. **2** *Christianity.* Jesus Christ, the fulfillment of these prophecies. **3 messiah,** a person thought of as a great saviour or liberator of a people or country. ⟨var. of LL *Messias* < Gk. < Hebrew *mashiah* anointed⟩ **—,Mes•si'an•ic** [,mɛsi'ænɪk], *adj.* **—,Mes•si'an•i•cal•ly,** *adv.*

mes•sieurs ['mɛsərz] *French,* [mes'jø] *n.* pl. of MONSIEUR. gentlemen. See note at MESSRS.

mess jacket a tight-fitting jacket of waist length.

mess•man ['mɛsmən] *n., pl.* **-men.** a waiter on a ship.

mess•mate ['mɛs,meit] *n.* especially in the armed services, one of a group of people who eat together regularly.

Messrs. ['mɛsərz] *n.* pl. of MR.: *Messrs. Rankin and Grant.*
☛ *Usage.* **Messrs.** is also sometimes used in addressing firms (*Messrs. Elken, Marci, and Company*).

mes•su•age ['mɛswɪdʒ] *n. Law.* a dwelling with adjoining lands and buildings. ⟨< AF *mesuage*, prob. misspelling of OF *mesnage* household, ménage⟩

mess•y ['mɛsi] *adj.* **mess•i•er, mess•i•est. 1** in a mess; untidy; dirty. **2** badly done. **3** confused and complicated; difficult: *a messy situation.* **—'mess•i•ness,** *n.* **—'mes•si•ly,** *adv.*

mes•ti•zo [mɛ'stizou] *n., pl.* **-zos** or **-zoes.** a person of mixed blood, especially the child of a Spaniard and an American Indian. Also, feminine, **mestiza.** ⟨< Sp., ult. < L *mixtus* mixed⟩

met [met] *v.* pt. and pp. of MEET[1].

met. 1 metaphor. **2** metaphysics. **3** meteorological. **4** metronome. **5** metropolitan.

meta– *prefix.* **1** behind, beyond, or after: *metalanguage.* **2** change of state or place: *metamorphosis.* **3** between or among: *metatarsal.* **4** transposed or reciprocal: *metathesis.* **5** similar in chemical composition: *metaphosphate.* Also, before a vowel, **met-.** ⟨< Gk. *meta* with, after⟩

met•a•bol•ic [,mɛtə'bɒlɪk] *adj.* having to do with metabolism. **—,met•a'bol•i•cal•ly,** *adv.*

me•tab•o•lism [mə'tæbə,lɪzəm] *n. Biology, physiology.* the processes of building up food into living matter and using living matter so that it is broken down into simpler substances or waste matter, giving off energy. ⟨< Gk. *metabolē* change < *meta-* into a different position + *bolē* a throwing⟩

me•tab•o•lite [mə'tæbə,ləit] *n. Biology, physiology.* any organic compound produced by metabolism.

me•tab•o•lize [mə'tæbə,laɪz] *v.* **-lized, -liz•ing. 1** subject to or change by metabolism. **2** produce or perform metabolism. **—me,tab•o,liz•a'bil•i•ty,** *n.* **—me'tab•o,liz•a•ble,** *adj.*

met•a•car•pal [,mɛtə'kɑrpəl] *adj., n. Anatomy. —adj.* of or having to do with the metacarpus.
—n. a metacarpal bone.

met•a•car•pus [,mɛtə'kɑrpəs] *n., pl.* **-pi** [-paɪ] *or* [-pi]. **1** *Anatomy.* the part of the hand between the wrist (the carpus) and the fingers (the phalanges), containing five long bones. See ARM[1] for picture. **2** *Zoology.* the corresponding part in the foreleg of an animal; the long bone or bones between the knee (the carpus) and the paw or hoof (the phalanges). ⟨< NL, ult. < Gk. *meta-* after + *karpos* wrist⟩

met•a•cen•tre ['mɛtə,sɛntər] *n.* in a floating object such as a buoy, the centre of gravity of that portion that is not under water. Its position above the centre of gravity of the whole object ensures stability. **—,met•a'cen•tric,** *adj.* **—,met•a•cen'tric•i•ty** [,mɛtəsɛn'trɪsəti], *n.*

met•a•chro•mat•ism [,mɛtə'kroumə,tɪzəm] *n.* a change in colour of an object subjected to changing conditions.

met•a•cy•mene [,mɛtə'saɪmin] *n.* See CYMENE.

met•a•gal•ax•y [,mɛtə'gæləksi] *n., pl.* **-ax•ies.** *Astronomy.* all the galaxies making up the universe. **—,met•a•ga'lac•tic** [,mɛtəgə'læktɪk], *adj.*

met•a•gen•e•sis [,mɛtə'dʒɛnəsɪs] *n.* ALTERNATION OF GENERATIONS. **—,met•a•ge'net•ic** [-dʒə'nɛtɪk], *adj.* **—,met•a•ge'net•i•cal•ly,** *adv.*

me•tag•na•thous [mə'tægnəθəs] *adj.* of birds, having a crossed beak. **—me'tag•na,thism,** *n.*

met•al ['mɛtəl] *n., v.* **-alled** or **-aled, -all•ing** or **-al•ing.** *—n.* **1** a substance that is usually shiny, a good conductor of heat and electricity, and can be made into wire, or hammered into sheets. Gold, silver, iron, copper, lead, tin, and aluminum are metals. **2** an alloy or mixture of these, such as steel or brass. **3** (*adjl.*) made of metal or a mixture of metals: *a metal container, a metal coin.* **4** *Chemistry.* any element that can form a salt by replacing the hydrogen of an acid, or any mixture of such elements. **5** broken stone, cinders, etc. used for roads and roadbeds. **6** the melted material that becomes glass or pottery. **7** material; substance: *Cowards are not made of the same metal as heroes.* **8** *Printing.* **a** TYPE METAL. **b** the state of being set or composed in type. **9** the aggregate number, mass, or power of the guns of a warship.
—v. furnish, cover, or fit with metal. ⟨ME < OF < L < Gk. *metallon*, originally, mine⟩ **—'met•al,like,** *adj.*
☛ *Hom.* METTLE.

met•a•lang•uage ['mɛtə,læŋgwɪdʒ] *n.* language or a symbolic system used in talking about language or in discussing another language.

metal fatigue the deterioration and breakdown of metal as a result of slight but constant stress, such as continual tapping, vibration, etc.

met•a•ling•uis•tics [,mɛtəlɪŋ'gwɪstɪks] *n.* (*used with a singular verb*). the study of the relationship between language and other aspects of culture. **—,met•a•lin'guis•ti•cal•ly,** *adv.*

me•tal•lic [mə'tælɪk] *adj.* **1** of, having to do with, or being a metal: *a metallic element.* **2** made of or containing a metal: *a metallic compound.* **3** that resembles or suggests metal; having a lustre, hardness, etc. like metal: *metallic blue, a metallic voice.* **—me'tal•li•cal•ly,** *adv.* **—,met•al'lic•i•ty** [,mɛtə'lɪsəti], *n.*

met•al•lif•er•ous [,mɛtə'lɪfərəs] *adj.* containing or yielding metal: *metalliferous rocks.* ⟨< L *metallifer* < *metallum* metal + *ferre* to bear⟩

met•al•lize or **met•al•ize** ['mɛtə,laɪz] *v.* **-lized, -liz•ing** or **-ized, -iz•ing. 1** treat or coat with metal. **2** make metallic. **—,met•al•li'za•tion** or **,met•al•i'za•tion,** *n.*

met•al•lur•gist ['mɛtə,lɜrdʒɪst]; *also, esp. Brit.,* [mə'tælərdʒɪst] *n.* a person who is trained in metallurgy, especially one whose work it is.

met•al•lur•gy ['mɛtə,lɜrdʒi]; *also, esp. Brit.,* [mə'tælərdʒi] *n.* the science or art of working with metals. It includes the separation and refining of metals from their ores, the production of alloys, and the shaping and treatment of metals by heat, rolling, etc. ⟨< NL *metallurgia*, ult. < Gk. *metallon* metal + *ergon* work⟩ **—,met•al'lur•gic** or **,met•al'lur•gi•cal,** *adj.* **—,met•al'lur•gi•cal•ly,** *adv.*

met•al•work ['mɛtəl,wɜrk] *n.* **1** things made out of metal. **2** the act of making things out of metal. **—'met•al,work•er,** *n.* **—'met•al,work•ing,** *n.*

met•a•math•e•mat•ics [,mɛtə,mæθə'mætɪks] *n.* the logic of mathematical systems (*used with a singular verb*). **—,met•a,math•e'mat•i•cal,** *adj.* **—,met•a,math•e•ma'ti•cian,** *n.*

met•a•mor•phic [,mɛtə'mɔrfɪk] *adj.* **1** having to do with or characterized by change of form. **2** *Geology.* designating rock that has derived from either igneous or sedimentary rock that has undergone changes in composition, texture, or internal structure through the action of pressure, heat, moisture, etc. Slate is a metamorphic rock formed from shale.

met•a•mor•phism [ˌmɛtəˈmɔrfɪzəm] *n.* **1** a change of form. **2** *Geology.* a change in the structure of a rock caused by pressure, heat, etc.

met•a•mor•phose [ˌmɛtəˈmɔrfouz] *or* [ˌmɛtəˈmɔrfous] *v.* **-phosed, -phos•ing. 1** change in form; transform: *The witch metamorphosed people into animals.* **2** change the form or structure of by metamorphosis or metamorphism. **3** undergo metamorphosis or metamorphism.

met•a•mor•pho•sis [ˌmɛtəˈmɔrfəsɪs] *n., pl.* **-ses** [-ˌsiz]. **1** a complete change of form, structure, or substance, as if by magic. **2** the changed form. **3** a dramatic change of character, appearance, or condition. **4** *Zoology.* a marked change in the form, and usually the habits, of an animal in its development after the embryonic stage. Tadpoles become frogs by metamorphosis; they lose their tails and grow legs. **5** *Botany.* the structural or functional modification of a plant organ or structure during the course of its development. **6** *Pathology.* the degeneration or abnormal modification of tissue. ⟨< L < Gk. *metamorphōsis*, ult. < *meta-* over + *morphē* form⟩

met•a•phase [ˈmɛtəˌfeiz] *n. Biology.* the second stage of MITOSIS, in which the nuclear membrane disintegrates, and the split chromosomes are contracted and deeply stained, and form a straight line.

met•a•phor [ˈmɛtəˌfɔr] *or* [ˈmɛtəfər] *n.* an implied comparison between two different things; a figure of speech in which a word or phrase that ordinarily means one thing is used of another thing in order to suggest a likeness between the two. *Examples*: a copper sky, a heart of stone. Compare SIMILE.
mix metaphors, use two or more incompatible metaphors in the same expression. ⟨< F < L < Gk. *metaphora* transfer, ult. < *meta-* over + *pherein* carry⟩ **—ˌmet•aˈphor•ic** or **ˌmet•aˈphor•i•cal,** *adj.* **—ˌmet•aˈphor•i•cal•ly,** *adv.*

☛ *Usage.* **Metaphor,** SIMILE. Both are figures of speech that make comparisons. A **simile** says explicitly that one thing is like another, using a word such as **like** or **as:** *This play reflects reality as a mirror does.* A **metaphor** compares implicitly by speaking of one thing as if it were another: *This play is a mirror of reality. This play uses a bent mirror to reflect a warped reality.* Metaphors are unconscious and frequent in ordinary speech; similes are more conscious and literary.

met•a•phys•i•cal [ˌmɛtəˈfɪzəkəl] *adj.* **1** of metaphysics; about the real nature of things. **2** highly abstract; hard to understand. **3** concerned with abstract thought or subjects: *a metaphysical mind.* **4** of or having to do with a group of English poets of the 1600s whose verse is characterized by abstruse, highly developed comparisons and the use of unexpected or elaborate imagery to express very powerful emotion.
—ˌmet•aˈphys•i•cal•ly, *adv.*

met•a•phy•si•cian [ˌmɛtəfəˈzɪʃən] *n.* a person expert in or familiar with metaphysics.

met•a•phys•ics [ˌmɛtəˈfɪzɪks] *n.* (*used with a singular verb*). **1** the branch of philosophy that tries to explain reality and knowledge; philosophical study of the real nature of the universe. **2** the more abstruse or speculative divisions of philosophy, thought of as a unit. **3** *Informal.* any process of reasoning thought of as abstruse or extremely subtle. ⟨ME < Med.L *metaphysica* < Med.Gk. *(ta) metaphysika* for Gk. *ta meta ta physika* those (works) after the Physics; with reference to the philosophical works of Aristotle⟩

me•tas•ta•sis [məˈtæstəsɪs] *n., pl.* **-ses** [-ˌsiz] **1** *Pathology.* the spread or transfer of disease from one part of the body to another, especially the transfer of malignant cells of a tumour to another part of the body via the bloodstream or lymphatic system. **2** a change or transformation, such as a change of theme or subject in rhetoric. **—ˌmet•aˈstat•ic** [ˌmɛtəˈstætɪk], *adj.* **—ˌmet•aˈstat•i•cal•ly,** *adv.* ⟨< LL < Gk. *metastasis* removal, ult. < *meta-* + *histanai* place⟩

me•tas•ta•size [mɛˈtæstəˌsaɪz] *v.* **-sized, -siz•ing.** undergo metastasis: *Has the cancer metastasized?*

met•a•tar•sal [ˌmɛtəˈtɑrsəl] *adj., n.* *—adj.* of or having to do with the metatarsus.
—n. a metatarsal bone: *The human foot has five metatarsals.*
—ˌmet•aˈtar•sal•ly, *adv.*

met•a•tar•sus [ˌmɛtəˈtɑrsəs] *n., pl.* **-si** [-saɪ] *or* [-si]. **1** *Anatomy.* the part of the foot between the heel and ankle (the tarsus) and the toes (the phalanges), containing five long bones. The metatarsus includes the instep and arch of the foot. See LEG for picture. **2** *Zoology.* the corresponding part in the foot of a bird and in the hind leg of an animal; the long bone or bones between the hock (the tarsus) and the paw or hoof (the phalanges). In a hoofed animal such as the horse, the metatarsus is called the cannon bone. ⟨< NL < Gk. *meta-* after + *tarsos* flat of the foot⟩

me•tath•e•sis [məˈtæθəsɪs] *n., pl.* **-ses** [-ˌsiz]. **1** *Phonology.* the transposition of sounds, syllables, or letters in a word. *Example*: aks *for* ask. **2** *Chemistry.* the interchange of atoms between two molecules. **3** a transposition; reversal. ⟨< LL < Gk. *metathesis* transposition, ult. < *meta-* over + *tithenai* set⟩ **—ˌmet•aˈthet•ic** [ˌmɛtəˈθɛtɪk] or **ˌmet•aˈthet•i•cal,** *adj.*

met•a•zo•a [ˌmɛtəˈzouə] *n.* pl. of METAZOON.

met•a•zo•an [ˌmɛtəˈzouən] *n., adj.* *—n.* any animal belonging to a large zoological group (Metazoa), including all animals having a body composed of many cells arranged into different tissues and organs with specialized functions. This group includes most of the phyla in the animal kingdom.
—adj. of, having to do with, or designating this group of animals. ⟨< NL *Metazoa* ult. < Gk. *meta-* after + *zōion* animal⟩

met•a•zo•on [ˌmɛtəˈzouən] *n., pl.* **-zo•a** [-ˈzouə]. metazoan.

mete[1] [mit] *v.* **met•ed, met•ing. 1** (*usually used with* **out**) give to each a share of; distribute; allot. **2** *Archaic.* measure. ⟨OE *metan*⟩
☛ *Hom.* MEAT, MEET.

mete[2] [mit] *n.* **1** boundary. **2** a boundary stone. ⟨late ME < MF < L *meta* goal-mark, turning post⟩
☛ *Hom.* MEAT, MEET.

me•tem•psy•cho•sis [ˌmɛtəmsəiˈkousɪs] *or* [məˌtɛmpsəˈkousɪs] *n., pl.* **-ses** [-siz]. the passing of the soul at death into a new body of another person or animal. Some Oriental philosophies, such as Hinduism and Buddhism, teach that by metempsychosis a person's soul lives again in an animal's body. ⟨< L < Gk. *metempsychosis* < *meta-* over + *empsychoein* animate, ult. < *en* in + *psychē* soul⟩ **—ˌme•tem•psyˈchot•ic** [-səiˈkɒtɪk], *adj.*

me•te•or [ˈmitiər] *or* [ˈmitiɔr] *n.* a mass of stone or metal that comes toward the earth from outer space at enormous speed; shooting star. Meteors become so hot from the friction of the air that they glow and usually burn up. ⟨ME < Med.L < Gk. *meteōron* (thing) in the air, ult. < *aeirein* lift⟩
—ˈme•te•orˌlike, *adj.*

me•te•or•ic [ˌmitiˈɔrɪk] *adj.* **1** of meteors. **2** flashing like a meteor; brilliant and soon ended. **3** of the atmosphere: *Wind and rain are meteoric phenomena.* **—ˌme•teˈor•i•cal•ly,** *adv.*

me•te•or•ite [ˈmitiəˌrəit] *n.* a mass of stone or metal that has fallen to the earth from outer space; fallen meteor.
—ˌme•te•orˈit•ic [ˌmitiəˈrɪtɪk] or **ˌme•te•orˈit•i•cal,** *adj.*

me•te•or•o•graph [ˌmitiˈɔrəˌgræf] *or* [ˈmitiərəˌgræf] *n.* an instrument that records various meteorological factors at the same time. **—ˌme•te•or•oˈgraph•ic,** *adj.* **—ˌme•te•oˈrog•ra•phy** [ˌmitiəˈrɒgrəfi], *n.*

me•te•or•oid [ˈmitiəˌrɔɪd] *n. Astronomy.* any of the solid bodies in outer space seen as meteors on entering the earth's atmosphere.

me•te•or•o•log•i•cal [ˌmitiərəˈlɒdʒəkəl] *adj.* **1** of or having to do with the atmosphere and weather. **2** of or having to do with meteorology. Also, **meteorologic.**
—ˌme•te•or•oˈlog•i•cal•ly, *adv.*

me•te•or•ol•o•gist [ˌmitiəˈrɒlədʒɪst] *n.* a person trained in meteorology, especially one whose work it is.

me•te•or•ol•o•gy [ˌmitiəˈrɒlədʒi] *n.* the science of the atmosphere and atmospheric conditions, especially as they relate to the weather. ⟨< Gk. *meteōrologia* < *meteōron* (thing) in the air + *-logos* treating of⟩

meteor shower *Astronomy.* all the meteors to be seen when the earth passes through a group of them.

me•ter[1] [ˈmitər] See METRE[2].

me•ter[2] [ˈmitər] *n., v.* *—n.* a device that measures, or that measures and records: *a parking meter, a water meter.*
—v. measure with a meter. ⟨< *-meter*⟩
☛ *Hom.* METRE.

-meter *combining form.* **1** a device for measuring: *speedometer, thermometer.* **2** verse having a specified number of metrical feet per line: *pentameter, hexameter.* ⟨< NL *-metrum* < Gk. *metron* measure⟩

met•for•min [mɛtˈfɔrmɪn] *n.* a drug used to treat certain forms of diabetes.

meth•ac•ry•late [mɛ'θækrə,leit] *n. Chemistry.* an ester of methacrylic acid.

meth•a•cryl•ic acid [,mɛθə'krılık] a clear liquid acid that produces a clear product when its ester is polymerized. *Formula*: CH_2:C(CH_3)COOH

meth•a•done ['mɛθə,doun] *n.* a synthetic, narcotic drug similar to morphine but less habit-forming. It is used for the relief of pain and as a substitute narcotic in the treatment of heroin addiction. *Formula*: $C_{21}H_{27}NO$ ⟨< *di*methyl + *a*mino + *d*iphenyl + *-one.* 20c.⟩

meth•am•phet•a•mine [,mɛθæm'fɛtə,min] *or* [,mɛθæm'fɛtəmın] *n.* an amphetamine derivative used as a mood-elevating drug. *Formula*: $C_{10}H_{15}N$ ⟨< *methyl* + *amphetamine.* 20c.⟩

meth•ane ['mɛθein] *n. Chemistry.* a colourless, odourless, highly flammable gas, the simplest of the hydrocarbons. Methane comes from marshes, petroleum wells, volcanoes, and coal mines. *Formula*: CH_4 ⟨< *methyl*⟩

me•than•o•gen [mə'θænədʒən] *n.* any of that group of monerans that take in carbon dioxide and give off methane, such as those found in swamps, the stomachs of ruminants, etc. **—me,than•o'gen•ic,** *adj.*

meth•a•nol ['mɛθə,nɒl] *n. Chemistry.* a colourless, poisonous, volatile, flammable liquid obtained from the destructive distillation of wood or from the catalytic treatment of carbon monoxide and hydrogen. It is extensively used as a fuel, antifreeze, solvent, etc. *Formula*: CH_3OH ⟨< *methane* + *-ol*⟩

meth•a•zo•la•mide [,mɛθə'zoulə,maıd] *n.* a drug used to treat certain forms of glaucoma.

me•theg•lin [mə'θɛglın] *n.* an alcoholic drink made from fermented honey, herbs, and water; a kind of mead. ⟨< Welsh *meddyglyn, meddyg* healing (< L *medicus*) + *llyn* liquor⟩

me•then•a•mine [mə'θɛnə,min] *or* [mə'θɛnəmın] *n.* an antiperspirant and antibacterial drug.

me•thim•a•zole [mə'θımə,zoul] *or* [mə'θaımə,zoul] *n.* a drug used to treat hyperthyroidism.

me•thinks [mi'θıŋks] *v.* **-thought.** *Archaic.* it seems to me. ⟨OE *mē thyncth*⟩

me•tho•car•ba•mol [,mɛθou'karbə,mɒl] *n.* a drug used as a skeletal muscle relaxant. *Formula*: $C_{11}H_{15}NO_5$

meth•od ['mɛθəd] *n.* **1** a set way of doing something involving various ordered steps. **2** order or system in getting things done or in thinking: *If you used more method, you wouldn't waste so much time.* **3 Method, a** an acting technique in which the actor attempts to think and feel like the character he or she is playing. **b** (*adjl.*) using the method: *a method actor.*
method in (one's) **madness,** system and sense underlying apparent folly. ⟨< L < Gk. *methodos,* originally, pursuit < *meta-* after + *hodos* a travelling⟩ **—'meth•od,less,** *adj.*
☛ *Syn.* **1.** See note at WAY.

me•thod•i•cal [mə'θɒdəkəl] *adj.* **1** done or arranged according to a method or order: *a methodical procedure.* **2** tending to act according to a method: *a methodical thinker.* Also, **methodic. —me'thod•i•cal•ly,** *adv.* **—me'thod•i•cal•ness,** *n.*
☛ *Syn.* See note at ORDERLY.

Meth•od•ism ['mɛθə,dızəm] *n.* the doctrines or religious principles of the Methodist churches.

Meth•od•ist ['mɛθədıst] *n., adj.* *—n.* **1** a member of any of the churches that grew out of a reform movement within the Church of England, led by John Wesley (1703-1791) and his brother Charles (1707-1788), both clergymen; these churches' tenets historically include acceptance of the Bible as the basic guide for faith and religious practice, with emphasis on faith through individual conversion, the leading of a holy life in which good works are important, and the possibility of full salvation for all people. See also UNITED CHURCH OF CANADA. **2 methodist,** a stickler for systematic procedure.
—adj. of or having to do with Methodists or Methodism.

meth•od•ize ['mɛθə,daız] *v.* **-ized, -iz•ing.** reduce to a method; arrange with method. **—'meth•od,iz•er,** *n.*

meth•od•ol•o•gy [,mɛθə'dɒlədʒi] *n.* **1** a system or body of procedures, methods, and rules used in a particular field or discipline. **2** the branch of logic that deals with the analysis of such procedures and methods. ⟨< NL *methodologia* < Gk. *methodos* method + *-logia* science⟩ **—,meth•od•o'log•i•cal** [,mɛθədə'lɒdʒəkəl], *adj.* **—,meth•od•o'log•ic•al•ly,** *adv.* **—,meth•od'ol•o•gist,** *n.*

me•tho•hex•i•tal [,mɛθou'hɛksətəl] *n.* an anesthetic drug. *Formula*: $C_{14}H_{17}N_2NaO_3$

me•thought [mi'θɒt] *v.* pt. of METHINKS.

me•thox•a•mine [mə'θɒksə,min] *n.* a drug used to raise blood pressure.

meth•sux•i•mide [mɛθ'sʌksə,maıd] *n.* an anticonvulsant drug used to treat petit mal epilepsy.

Me•thu•se•lah [mə'θuzələ] *n. Informal.* a very old man. ⟨in the Bible, a man said to have lived 969 years.⟩

me•thy•clo•thi•a•zide [,mɛθəklou'θaıə,zaıd] *n.* a diuretic drug.

meth•yl ['mɛθəl] *n. Chemistry.* a univalent, hydrocarbon radical that occurs in many organic compounds. *Formula*: CH_3 ⟨< F *méthyle,* ult. < Gk. *methy* wine + *hylē* wood⟩ **—meth'yl•ic,** *adj.*

methyl acetate *Chemistry.* a solvent in the form of a very volatile liquid. *Formula*: $CH_3OCH_2OCH_3$

methyl alcohol *Chemistry.* a colourless, poisonous, flammable liquid obtained from the distillation of wood or from the catalytic treatment of carbon monoxide and hydrogen. It is widely used as a fuel, a solvent, etc. *Formula*: CH_3OH

meth•yl•a•mine [,mɛθələ'min] *or* [,mɛθəl'æmın] *n. Chemistry.* one of three derivatives of ammonia. *Formula*: CH_3NH_2

meth•yl•ate ['mɛθə,leit] *n. Chemistry.* any compound containing the methyl group. **—'meth•yl•a•tor,** *n.*

methyl bromide *Chemistry.* a poisonous solvent. *Formula*: CH_3Br

meth•yl•cel•lu•lose [,mɛθəl'sɛljə,lous] *n.* a bulk-forming laxative.

methyl chloride *Chemistry.* a colourless gas used as a refrigerant and as a local anesthetic. *Formula*: CH_3Cl

meth•yl•do•pa [,mɛθəl'doupə] *n.* a drug used to lower blood pressure.

meth•yl•ene ['mɛθə,lin] *n. Chemistry.* a bivalent organic radical derived from methane. *Formula*: CH_2

methylene blue 1 *Chemistry.* a blue analine dye used as a stain in isolating bacteria for microscopic examination. **2** *Pharmacy.* a diagnostic aid for renal deficiency. *Formula*: $C_{16}H_{18}ClN_3S$

meth•yl•phen•i•date [,mɛθəl'fɛnı,deit] *or* [,mɛθəl'finı,deit] *n.* a central nervous system stimulant used to control hyperactivity in some children.

meth•yl•sal•i•cy•late [,mɛθəl'sæləsə,leit] *n.* a local anesthetic in an ointment form for muscular and joint pains.

meth•yl•tes•tos•ter•one [,mɛθəltɛs'tɒstə,roun] *n.* a drug used to treat certain male hormone deficiencies.

me•thy•ser•gide [,mɛθı'sɜrdʒaıd] *n.* a drug used to treat migraine and cluster headaches.

me•tic•u•lous [mə'tıkjələs] *adj.* extremely or excessively careful about small details. ⟨< L *meticulosus* < *metus* fear⟩ **—me'tic•u•lous•ly,** *adv.* **—me'tic•u•lous•ness,** *n.*

mé•tier [mei'tjei] *or* ['meitjei] *n.* **1** a trade; profession. **2** the kind of work for which one has special ability. ⟨< F < L *ministerium.* Doublet of MINISTRY.⟩

Mé•tis or **Me•tis** ['meiti], or [mei'ti], *n., pl.* **-tis;** *adj. Cdn.* *—n.* a person of mixed blood, especially a person of French and North American Indian ancestry belonging to or descended from the people who established themselves in the valleys of the Red, Assiniboine, and Saskatchewan Rivers during the 19th century, forming a cultural group distinct from both Europeans and Indians.
—adj. of or having to do with the Métis. ⟨< Cdn.F < F *métis* < LL *misticius, mixticius* of mixed blood⟩

Mé•tisse [mei'tis] *n., pl.* **-tisses** [-'tis] or [-'tisız]. *Cdn. Rare.* a female Métis. ⟨< Cdn.F⟩

me•to•cu•rine [,mɛtou'kjʊrin] *n.* a drug used as a skeletal muscle relaxant.

me•to•la•zone [mə'toulə,zoun] *n.* a diuretic drug.

Metonic cycle [mı'tɒnık] *Astronomy.* a period of 235 lunar months (about 19 years), after which the phases of the moon occur just as in the preceding period. ⟨after *Meton,* an Athenian astronomer of the 5c. B.C.⟩

met•o•nym ['mɛtə,nım] *n.* any word used in metonymy.

me•ton•y•my [mə'tɒnəmi] *n. Rhetoric.* the use of the name of one thing for that of another which it naturally suggests. *Example*: *In* The pen is mightier than the sword, pen *is used to mean* power of literature *and* sword *is used to mean* military force. ⟨< LL < Gk. *metonymia*, literally, change of name < *meta-* over + dial. *onyma* name⟩ **—ˌmet•o'nym•ic** or **ˌmet•o'nym•i•cal,** *adj.*

met•o•pe ['mɛtə,pi] *or* ['mɛtoup] *n. Architecture.* one of the square spaces, often decorated, between triglyphs in a Doric frieze. ⟨< L < Gk. *metopē* < *meta-* between + *opē* opening⟩

me•top•ic [mə'tɒpɪk] *adj. Anatomy.* of or pertaining to the forehead. ⟨< Gk. *metopon* forehead⟩

me•to•pro•lol [,mɛtə'proulɒl] *or* [mə'tɒprə,lɒl] *n.* a drug used to lower blood pressure. *Formula*: $C_{15}H_{25}HO_3$

me•tre¹ ['mitər] *n.* **1** *Prosody.* the rhythmical pattern resulting from the arrangement of stressed and unstressed syllables in regularly recurring groups (feet). **2** *Music.* the combining of beats or notes into rhythmic groups, or the pattern formed in this way; TIME (def. 14). Also, **meter.** ⟨OE *meter* < L *metrum* poetic metre < Gk. *metron* measure, metre⟩
☛ *Hom.* METER².

me•tre² ['mitər] *n.* an SI unit for measuring length. A twin bed is about 1 m wide. The metre is one of the seven base units in the SI. *Symbol*: m Also, **meter.** ⟨< F *mètre* < L < Gk. *metron* measure⟩
☛ *Hom.* METER².

-metre *combining form.* METRE²: *kilometre, millimetre.* ⟨< NL *-metrum* < Gk.⟩

me•tre–kil•o•gram–sec•ond ['mitər 'kɪlə,græm 'sɛkənd] *adj.* designating the system of SI units in which the metre, the kilogram, and the second are the principal units of length, mass, and time. *Abbrev.*: mks

metre–stick ['mitər ,stɪk] *n.* a measuring stick that is one metre long and is marked off in centimetres and millimetres.

met•ric ['mɛtrɪk] *adj.* **1** of or having to do with the metre or the SI system of measurement. **2** metrical. ⟨(def. 1) < F *métrique* < *mètre* < L < Gk. *metron* measure; (def. 2) < L *metricus* < Gk. *metrikos* < *metron* measure, metre⟩

met•ri•cal ['mɛtrəkəl] *adj.* **1** of or having to do with metre; having a regular arrangement of stresses; written in verse, not in prose: *a metrical translation of Homer.* **2** of, having to do with, or used in measurement. **—'met•ri•cal•ly,** *adv.* **—me'tric•i•ty** [mɛ'trɪsəti], *n.*

met•ri•cate ['mɛtrə,keit] *v.* **-cat•ed, -cat•ing.** change into or express in a metric system of measurement.

met•ri•ca•tion [,mɛtrə'keiʃən] *n.* the act or process of converting from an existing system of measurement into a metric one.

metric hundredweight fifty kilograms (about 110 lbs).

metric system a decimal system of measurement, that is, one based on tens, traditionally using the metre as the basic unit of length, the kilogram as the basic unit of mass, and the litre as the basic unit of volume or capacity. The metric system adopted by Canada is the new, simplified international version established in 1960, called the International System of Units (SI). It has a total of seven base units and two supplementary units from which all the other units are derived:

Quantity	Name	Symbol
length	metre	m
mass	kilogram	kg
time	second	s
electric current	ampere	A
thermodynamic temperature	kelvin	K
amount of substance	mole	mol
luminous intensity	candela	cd
plane angle	radian	rad
solid angle	steradian	sr

metric ton tonne.

me•triz•a•mide [mə'trɪzə,maɪd] *n.* a contrast medium used in medical diagnosis.

met•ro ['mɛtrou] *n. Informal.* **1** the territory of a METROPOLITAN (*adj.*, def. 3) government. **2** any metropolitan area. **3** the subway train system in Montréal. **4** *Cdn.* metropolitan Toronto. ⟨< F *métro*, short for *chemin de fer metropolitain* metropolitan railway⟩

me•trol•o•gist [mə'trɒlədʒɪst] *n.* one trained in metrology, especially one whose work it is.

me•trol•o•gy [mə'trɒlədʒi] *n., pl.* **-gies. 1** the science of weights and measures. **2** a system of weights and measures. ⟨< Gk. *metron* measure + E *-logy*⟩ **—,me•tro'log•i•cal,** *adj.* **—,me•tro'log•i•cal•ly,** *adv.*

me•tro•ni•za•dole [,mɛtrə'naizə,doul] *n.* a drug used to treat certain forms of cancer. *Formula*: $C_6H_9N_3O_3$

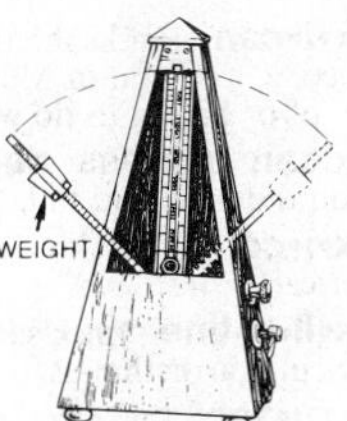

A metronome. The beat is regulated by the movable weight on the inverted pendulum. The higher the weight is moved, the slower the rate of swing of the pendulum and therefore, the slower the beat.

met•ro•nome ['mɛtrə,noum] *n.* a timing device having a battery or a pendulum that can be adjusted to tick at different speeds. A metronome is mainly used by persons practising musical instruments to help them keep time. ⟨< Gk. *metron* measure + *-nomos* regulating < *nemein* regulate⟩ **—,met•ro'nom•ic** [,mɛtrə'nɒmɪk] or **,met•ro'nom•i•cal,** *adj.* **—,met•ro'nom•i•cal•ly,** *adv.*

me•trop•o•lis [mə'trɒpəlɪs] *n.* **1** the most important city of a country or region: *London is the metropolis of England.* **2** a large city; important centre: *Montréal is a busy metropolis.* **3** the chief diocese of an ecclesiastical province; the see of a metropolitan bishop. ⟨< LL < Gk. *mētropolis* < *mētēr* mother + *polis* city⟩

met•ro•pol•i•tan [,mɛtrə'pɒlətən] *adj., n.* *—adj.* **1** of, having to do with, or characteristic of a large city or large cities: *metropolitan newspapers.* **2** constituting a metropolis: *a metropolitan centre.* **3** designating a form of municipal government based on a federation of several adjacent municipalities that together form a large urban area. **4** of or being such a federation. **5** of or having to do with the chief diocese of a church or province. **6** of or constituting the mother city or the mainland territory of the parent state: *metropolitan France.*
—n. **1** a person who lives in a large city and knows its ways. **2** *Eastern Orthodox Church.* the head of an ecclesiastical province, ranking next above an archbishop and below a patriarch. **3** *Roman Catholic and Anglican Churches.* an archbishop having authority over the bishops of an ecclesiastical province. **—,met•ro'pol•i•tan,ism,** *n.*

metropolitan area the area or region including a large city and its suburbs, especially one under a federated municipal government.

met•ro•pol•i•tan•i•za•tion [,mɛtrə,pɒlətənaɪ'zeiʃən] *or* [,mɛtrə,pɒlətənə'zeiʃən] *n. Cdn.* the state or condition of being formed into a metropolitan administrative area, as in Metropolitan Toronto.

-metry *combining form.* the process of measuring: *biometry.* ⟨< Gk. *-metria* < *metron* measure⟩

met•tle ['mɛtəl] *n.* **1** disposition or temperament. **2** spirit; courage.
on (one's) **mettle,** ready to do one's best. ⟨var. of *metal*⟩
☛ *Hom.* METAL.

met•tle•some ['mɛtəlsəm] *adj.* full of mettle; spirited; courageous.

me•tump [mə'tʌmp] *n. Cdn. Archaic.* tumpline. ⟨? < Abenaki⟩

Mev [mɛv] *n.* megaelectronvolt.

mew¹ [mju] *n., v.* *—n.* the sound made by a cat or kitten.
—v. make such a sound. ⟨imitative⟩
☛ *Hom.* MU.

mew² [mju] *n.* a sea gull, especially *Larus canus.* Also called **mew gull.** ⟨OE *mǣw*⟩
☛ *Hom.* MU.

mew³ [mju] *n., v.* *—n.* **1** a cage in which hawks are kept, especially while moulting. **2** a place of retirement or concealment; secret place; den.
—v. **1** cage (a hawk), especially at moulting time. **2** shut up in a cage; conceal; confine. **3** *Archaic.* change (feathers, etc.); moult. ⟨ME < OF *mue* < *muer* molt < L *mutare*⟩
☛ *Hom.* MU.

mewl [mjul] *v.* cry like a baby; whimper. ⟨imitative⟩
☛ *Hom.* MULE.

mews [mjuz] *n. Esp. Brit.* **1** stables built around a court or alley. **2** such stables converted into dwellings: *an apartment in a mews.* ⟨originally pl. of *mew³*⟩
☛ *Hom.* MUSE.

Mex. 1 Mexico. **2** Mexican.

Mex•i•can ['mɛksəkən] *n., adj.* *—n.* **1** a native or inhabitant of Mexico. **2** a person of Mexican descent.
—adj. of or having to do with Mexico or its people.

Mexican hairless dog a little dog with no hair except for a tuft on the head and tail.

Mex•i•co ['mɛksəkou] *n.* a country in southern North America.

mex•il•e•tine [mɛk'sılə,tin] *n.* a drug used to suppress certain ventricular arrhythmias.

me•zu•zah [mə'zuzə] *n. Judaism.* a piece of parchment inscribed with scriptural passages and kept in a small case or tube affixed to the doorpost of some Jewish homes as a sign and reminder of faith in God. ⟨< Hebrew *mezûzāh* doorpost⟩

mez•za•nine ['mɛzə,nin] *n.* **1** a partial storey between two main floors of a building. It is usually just above the ground floor. **2** in a theatre, the lowest balcony, or its front section. ⟨< F < Ital. *mezzanino* < *mezzano* middle < L *medianus.* See MEDIAN.⟩

mez•zo ['mɛtsou], ['mɛdzou], *or* ['mɛzou] *adj., n.* *—adj.* **1** *Music.* middle; medium; half. **2** *Informal.* mezzo-soprano.
—n. Informal. mezzo-soprano. ⟨< Ital. < L *medius* middle⟩

mez•zo•for•te [,mɛtsou'fɔrtei], [,mɛdzou'fɔrtei], *or* [,mɛzou'fɔrtei] *adj. or adv. Music.* moderately loud; half as loud as forte. ⟨< Ital.⟩

mez•zo–so•pran•o ['mɛtsou sə'prænou], ['mɛdzou-], *or* ['mɛzo-] *n., pl.* **-pran•os;** *adj.* *—n.* **1** an adult female singing voice having an intermediate range between soprano and alto. **2** a singer who has such a voice.
—adj. having to do with, having the range of, or designed for a mezzo-soprano.

mez•zo•tint ['mɛtsou,tınt] *or* ['mɛzou,tınt] *n., v.* *—n.* **1** an engraving on copper or steel made by polishing and scraping away parts of a roughened surface. **2** a print made from such an engraving. **3** this method of engraving.
—v. engrave in mezzotint. ⟨< Ital. *mezzotinto* half-tint⟩

mf. or **mf** mezzoforte.

MF MIDDLE FRENCH.

mfg. manufacturing.

mfr. manufacturer.

mg milligram(s).

Mg magnesium.

M.Gen. or **MGen** MAJOR-GENERAL.

Mgr. **1** manager. **2** Monsignor. **3** Monseigneur.

MHA or **M.H.A.** MEMBER OF THE HOUSE OF ASSEMBLY.

MHG MIDDLE HIGH GERMAN.

MHz megahertz.

mi [mi] *n. Music.* **1** the third tone of an eight-tone major scale. **2** the tone E. See DO[2] for picture. ⟨See GAMUT⟩

mi. **1** mile(s). **2** mill(s).

M.I.5 *Brit.* the branch of Military Intelligence dealing with security and counter-espionage in the United Kingdom.

Mi•a•mi [maı'æmi] *n., pl.* **Mi•a•mis** or **Mi•a•mi, 1** a member of a Native American people now living in Oklahoma. **2** the Algonquian language of these people.

Mi•ao [mi'aʊ] *n.* **1** a member of a people of SE China and neighbouring regions of Laos, Thailand, and North Vietnam. **2** the Miao-Yao language of these people. Also called **Hmong.**

mi•aow or **mi•aou** [mi'aʊ] See MEOW.

mi•as•ma [maı'æzmə] *or* [mi'æzmə] *n., pl.* **-mas, -ma•ta** [-mətə]. **1** a poisonous vapour rising from the earth and infecting the air. The miasma of swamps was formerly supposed to cause disease. **2** an atmosphere or influence that infects or corrupts: *a miasma of evil thoughts.* ⟨< NL < Gk. *miasma* pollution < *miainein* pollute⟩ **—mi'as•mal** or **,mi•as'mat•ic,** *adj.* **—mi'as•mic,** *adj.*

mi•ca ['məikə] *n.* a mineral that divides into thin, partly transparent layers; isinglass. Mica withstands heat and is used for insulation. ⟨< L *mica* grain, crumb⟩ **—'mi•ca,like,** *adj.*

mice [məis] *n.* pl. of MOUSE.

Mich•ael•mas ['mıkəlməs] *n. Esp. Brit.* September 29, a Christian festival in honour of the archangel Michael. ⟨OE *(Sanct) Michaeles masse* (St.) Michael's mass⟩

Michaelmas daisy a tall aster bearing small, purple flowers blooming in September.

Mi•chi•gan ['mıʃəgən] *n.* a northern state of the United States.

Michigan lily a marshland wildflower (*Lilium michiganense*) closely related to the Canada lily, having broad petals with brown spots. It blooms in summer in Ontario and Manitoba, and south to Tennessee. It is an endangered species.

mick•ey ['mıki] *n. Slang.* **1** MICKEY FINN. **2** *Cdn.* a half bottle of liquor or wine. **3** the detonator of a bomb. ⟨< *Mickey* (nickname for *Michael*) once a slang term for an Irishman⟩

Mickey Finn or **mickey finn** *Slang.* **1** a pill, etc., such as chloral hydrate, put into an alcoholic drink in order to drug it. **2** a drink so drugged. ⟨origin unknown⟩

Mickey Mouse *Informal.* not worthwhile or serious; insignificant or trivial: *a Mickey Mouse rehabilitation program, a school offering Mickey Mouse courses.* ⟨from the name of Walt Disney's movie cartoon character⟩

mick•le ['mıkəl] *adj., adv., n. Archaic or dialect.* much. ⟨OE *micel*⟩

Mic•mac or **Mi'k•maq** ['mık,mæk] *n., pl.* **-mac, -maq,** or **-macs;** *adj.* *—n.* **1** a member of a First Nations people living in the Maritimes. **2** the Algonquian language of the Micmac.
—adj. of or having to do with the Micmac or their language. ⟨< Algonquian *migmac,* literally, allies⟩
☛ *Spelling.* Members of this people group prefer the spelling **Mi'kmaq.**

mi•con•a•zole [məi'kɒnə,zoul] *n.* an antifungal drug in a cream form.

MICR MAGNETIC INK CHARACTER RECOGNITION.

mi•cro ['məikrou] *n. Computer technology.* microcomputer.

micro– *combining form.* **1** very small: *micro-organism, microfilm.* Compare MACRO–. **2** abnormally small: *microcephalic.* **3** done with or involving the use of a microscope: *microbiology.* **4** SI prefix. millionth: *microsecond.* ⟨< Gk. *mikros* small⟩

mi•cro•an•al•y•sis [,məikrouə'næləsıs] *n.* the analysis of quantities less than a milligram in mass.

mi•cro•bar ['məikrə,bɑr] *n.* one millionth of a BAR[2].

mi•cro•bar•o•graph [,məikrə'bærə,græf] *or* [,məikrə'bɛrə,græf] *n. Meteorology.* an instrument for recording very minor fluctuations in atmospheric pressure.

mi•crobe ['məikroub] *n.* a micro-organism, especially a disease-producing bacterium. ⟨< F < Gk. *mikros* small + *bios* life⟩ **—'mi•crobe•less,** *adj.* **—mi'cro•bi•al** or **mi'cro•bic,** *adj.*

mi•cro•bi•ol•o•gy [,məikroubaı'ɒlədʒi] *n.* the biology of micro-organisms. **—,mi•cro,bi•o'log•i•cal,** *adj.* **—,mi•cro,bi•o'log•i•cal•ly,** *adv.* **—,mi•cro•bi'ol•o•gist,** *n.*

mi•cro•ceph•a•ly [,məikrou'sɛfəli] *n.* an abnormally small head. **—,mi•cro'ceph•a•lous** or **,mi•cro•ce'phal•ic,** *adj.*

mi•cro•chem•is•try [,məikrou'kɛməstri] *n.* the branch of chemistry dealing with minute samples or quantities. **—,mi•cro'chem•i•cal,** *adj.*

mi•cro•chip ['məikrə,tʃıp] *n. Computer technology.* a very small piece of semiconducting material containing the information for a computer circuit.

mi•cro•cir•cuit ['məikrou,sɜrkıt] *n.* an integrated circuit or other miniature electronic circuit. **—,mi•cro'cir•cuit•ry,** *n.*

mi•cro•cli•mate ['məikrou,klaımıt] *n.* the climate of one place in an area, studied so as to compare it with the rest of the area. **—,mi•cro,cli•ma'tol•o•gy,** *n.*

mi•cro•cline ['məikrə,klaın] *n.* a mineral of the feldspar group. *Formula*: $KAlSi_3O_8$

mi•cro•coc•cus [,məikrou'kɒkəs] *n., pl.* **-coc•ci** [-'kɒkaı], [-'kɒksaı], *or* [-'kɒksi]. any of a genus (*Micrococcus*) of spherical bacteria, including species which cause the fermentation of milk. Micrococci are not generally disease-producing bacteria.

mi•cro•com•put•er ['məikroukəm,pjutər] *n. Computer technology.* a miniature, portable computer capable of carrying out only one operation at a time. Compare MAINFRAME, MINICOMPUTER.

mi•cro•cop•y ['məikrou,kɒpi] *n., pl.* **-cop•ies;** *v.* **-cop•ied, cop•y•ing.** *—n.* a copy made on microfilm.
—v. make a copy of on microfilm.

mi•cro•cosm ['məikrou,kɒzəm] *n.* **1** a little world; universe in miniature. **2** a person or community thought of as a miniature representation of the universe. ⟨< F < LL *microcosmus* < LGk. *mikros kosmos* little world⟩ **—,mi•cro'cos•mic,** *adj.* **—,mi•cro'cos•mi•cal•ly,** *adv.*

mi•cro•crys•tal•line [,məikrou'krıstə,laın], [,məikrou'krıstə,lin], *or* [,məikrou'krıstələn] *adj.* designating a solid composed of crystals of microscopic size: *Chalcedony is a* *microcrystalline variety of quartz.* **—ˌmi•cro,crys•tal'lin•i•ty** [ˌməikrouˌkrɪstə'lɪnəti], *n.*

mi•cro•dot ['məikrouˌdɒt] *n.* a photograph of a document, etc. reduced to the size of a tiny dot.

mi•cro–e•co•nom•ics [ˌməikrou ˌikə'nɒmɪks] *or* [ˌməikrou ˌɛkə'nɒmɪks] *n.* the economy of one particular product or a single consumer *(used with a singular verb)*. Compare MACRO-ECONOMICS. **—ˌmi•cro,e•co'nom•ic,** *adj.*

mi•cro–e•lec•tron•ics or **mi•cro•e•lec•tron•ics** [ˌməikrou ɪlɛk'trɒnɪks] *or* [ˌməikrou ˌilɛk'trɒnɪks] *n.* *(used with a singular verb)* the branch of electronics that deals with the theory, manufacture, and use of electronic components of miniature size. **—ˌmi•cro-e•lec'tron•ic** or **ˌmi•cro•e•lec'tron•ic,** *adj.*

mi•cro•far•ad [ˌməikrou'færəd] *or* [ˌməikrou'fɛrəd] *n.* *Electricity.* one-millionth of a farad. *Symbol*: µF

mi•cro•fiche ['məikrouˌfiʃ] *n., pl.* **-fich•es** [-ˌfiʃ] *or* [-ˌfiʃɪz]. a single sheet of microfilm, usually the same size as a filing card, carrying microcopies of numerous pages of printed matter. ⟨< *micro-* + F *fiche* card⟩

mi•cro•film ['məikrouˌfɪlm] *n., v. —n.* **1** a film for making very small photographs of pages of a book, newspapers, documents, etc. to preserve them in a very small space. **2** a photograph made on such film.
—v. photograph on microfilm.

mi•cro•groove ['məikrouˌgruv] *n.* a narrow groove used on long-playing phonograph records.

mi•cro•light ['məikrouˌləit] *n.* a lightweight, one-seater aircraft with a very small engine. Also called **ultralight.**

mi•crom•e•ter¹ [məi'krɒmətər] *n.* **1** an instrument for measuring very small distances, angles, objects, etc. Certain kinds are used with a microscope or telescope. **2** MICROMETER CALLIPER. ⟨< F *micromètre*⟩

mi•cro•me•ter² ['məikrəˌmitər] See MICROMETRE.

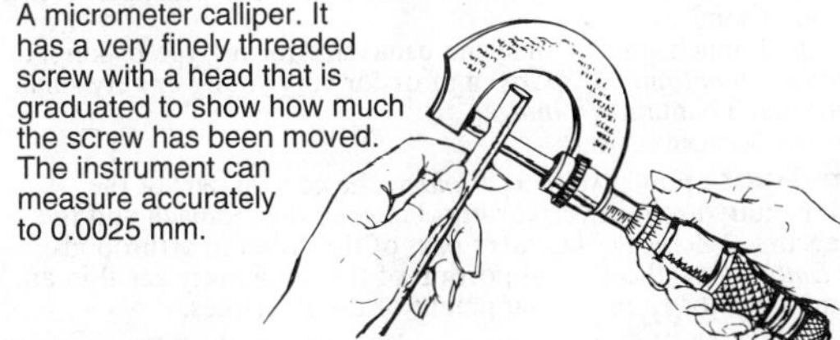
A micrometer calliper. It has a very finely threaded screw with a head that is graduated to show how much the screw has been moved. The instrument can measure accurately to 0.0025 mm.

micrometer calliper or **caliper** a calliper having an adjusting screw with a fine thread, capable of making very accurate measurements.

mi•cro•me•tre ['məikrouˌmitər] *n.* one-millionth of a metre. The micrometre is used for measuring the size of bacteria and for other very precise measurements in technology, engineering, and science. *Symbol*: µm Also, **micrometer.**

mi•cron ['məikrɒn] *n., pl.* **mi•crons** or **mi•cra** ['məikrə]. micrometre. ⟨< NL < Gk. *micron*, neut. adj., small⟩

Mi•cro•ne•sia [ˌməikrou'niʒə] *or* [ˌməikrou'niʃə] *n.* a country comprising many islands in the Pacific, east of the Philippines and north of Australia.

Mi•cro•ne•sian [ˌməikrou'niʒən] *or* [ˌməikro'niʃən] *adj., n.* *—adj.* **1** of or designating a major race of people that includes the traditional inhabitants of Micronesia. This race, most closely related to the Polynesian race, is distinguished by a combination of biological characteristics, including dark skin and wavy or woolly hair. **2** of or having to do with Micronesia or its peoples or their languages.
—n. **1** a native or inhabitant of Micronesia. **2** a member of the Micronesian race. **3** a group of Austronesian languages spoken in Micronesia. ⟨< *micro-* + Gk. *nesos* island⟩

mi•cro–or•gan•ism or **mi•cro•or•gan•ism** [ˌməikrou 'ɔrgəˌnɪzəm] *n.* any of a great number of one-celled organisms too small to be seen with the naked eye, most of which contain no chlorophyl, including the bacteria, viruses, yeasts, algae, fungi, and protozoans. Because micro-organisms do not clearly show basic characteristics identifying them as either plants or animals, some biologists group them into a separate kingdom.

mi•cro•phone ['məikrəˌfoun] *n.* an instrument for increasing the loudness of sounds or for transmitting sounds. Microphones change sounds into variations of an electric current and are used in recording and in radio and television broadcasting.
—ˌmi•cro'phon•ic [ˌməikrə'fɒnɪk], *adj.*

mi•cro•pho•to•graph [ˌməikrə'foutəˌgræf] *n.* a very small photograph, as on microfilm, that has to be magnified for viewing. **—ˌmi•cro,pho•to'graph•ic,** *adj.*
—ˌmi•cro•pho'tog•ra•phy [ˌməikroufə'tɒgrəfi], *n.*

mi•cro•phys•ics [ˌməikrou'fɪzɪks] *n.* the branch of physics dealing with the structure of molecules, atoms, electrons, and other minute particles of matter *(used with a singular verb)*.
—ˌmi•cro'phys•i•cal, *adj.*

mi•cro•pro•ces•sor [ˌməikrou'prousɛsər] *or* [ˌməikrou'prɒsɛsər] *n.* *Computer technology.* an integrated circuit consisting of usually a single chip of semiconductor that carries out instructions in a computer or other electronic device.

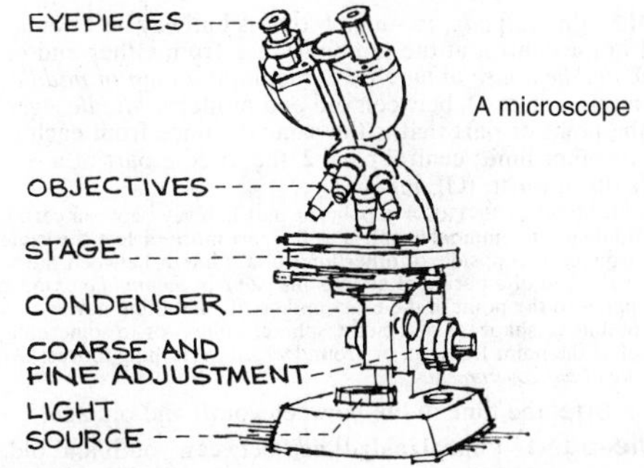

A microscope

mi•cro•scope ['məikrəˌskoup] *n.* an instrument with a lens or combination of lenses for making small things look larger. ⟨< NL *microscopium* < Gk. *mikros* small + *-skopion* means of viewing < *skopeein* look at⟩

mi•cro•scop•ic [ˌməikrə'skɒpɪk] *adj.* **1** that cannot be seen without using a microscope; tiny. **2** like a microscope; suggesting a microscope: *a microscopic eye for mistakes.* **3** of or having to do with a microscope. Also, **microscopical. —ˌmi•cro'scop•i•cal•ly,** *adv.*

mi•cros•co•pist [məi'krɒskəpɪst] *n.* a person trained in the use of the microscope.

mi•cros•co•py [məi'krɒskəpi] *n.* **1** the use of a microscope. **2** microscopic investigation.

mi•cro•sec•ond ['məikrəˌsɛkənd] *n.* one-millionth of a second. *Symbol*: µs

mi•cro•spore ['məikrəˌspɔr] *n.* *Botany.* **1** a small spore from which a male gametophyte develops. Compare MEGASPORE. **2** in seed plants, a pollen grain. **—ˌmi•cro'spor•ic** or **ˌmi•cro'spor•ous,** *adj.*

mi•cro•wave ['məikrouˌweiv] *n.* **1** a very short electromagnetic wave, especially one having a wavelength between one and one hundred centimetres. **2** MICROWAVE OVEN.

microwave oven an oven in which food is cooked by means of the heat produced by microwaves penetrating the food.

mic•tu•rate ['mɪktʃəˌreit] *v.* **-rat•ed, -rat•ing.** urinate. ⟨< L *micturīre* < *mictus*, *mingere*⟩

mid¹ [mɪd] *adj.* in the middle; middle. ⟨OE *midd*⟩

mid² or **'mid** [mɪd] *prep. Poetic.* amid. ⟨var. of *amid*⟩

mid– *combining form.* middle; mid; the middle point or part of: *midair.* ⟨ME, OE. See MID¹.⟩

mid. middle.

mid•air or **mid–air** ['mɪd 'ɛr] *n.* **1** the sky; air: *The parachute floated in midair.* **2** uncertainty; doubt: *With the contract still in midair, the board recessed.* **3** (*adjl.*) in midair: *a midair collision of two jets.*

Mi•das ['maɪdəs] *n.* **1** *Greek legend.* a king of Phrygia whose touch turned everything to gold. Unable to eat or drink, and seeing his daughter turned to gold, he begged that his gift be removed, and he was permitted to wash it away. **2** *Informal.* a man of great moneymaking ability.
the Midas touch, the ability to make money easily.
—'Mi•das,like, *adj.*

mid–At•lan•tic ['mid æt'læntɪk] *adj.* **1** in the middle of the

Atlantic Ocean: *a mid-Atlantic storm.* **2** characterized by both British and Canadian or American usage: *a mid-Atlantic accent.*

mid•brain ['mɪd,brein] *n.* the middle part of the brain.

mid•con•ti•nent ['mɪd'kɒntənənt] *n.* the middle part of a continent.

mid•course ['mɪd'kɔrs] *n.* **1** the middle of any course. **2** the middle of the curve of a rocket in flight, between the cessation of powered flight and the start of re-entry. **3** *Aerospace.* the middle of a space flight, between leaving the earth's gravitational pull and arrival at another planet or other destination.

mid•day ['mɪd,dei] *n.* **1** the middle of the day; noon. **2** (*adjl.*) of or like midday: *the midday meal.* ⟨OE *middæg*⟩

mid•den ['mɪdən] *n.* **1** KITCHEN MIDDEN. **2** *Dialect.* a dunghill; refuse heap. ⟨apparently < Scand.; cf. Danish *mödding,* alteration of *mög dynge* muck heap⟩

mid•dle ['mɪdəl] *adj., n.* —*adj.* **1** that is halfway between; located in the centre; at the same distance from either end or side; *the middle house in the row.* **2** medium: *a man of middle size.* **3** intermediate. **4** between old and modern: *Middle Ages.*
—*n.* **1** the point or part that is the same distance from each end or side or other limit; central part. **2** the middle part of a person's body; waist. ⟨OE *middel*⟩

☛ *Syn. n.* **1. Middle,** CENTRE = a point or part halfway between certain limits. **Middle** most commonly applies to the part more or less the same distance from each end, side, or other limit of a thing or between the beginning and end of a period of action: *She came in the middle of the day.* **Centre** applies to the point in the exact middle of something having a definite outline or shape, as of a circle, sphere, square, or to something thought of as the point from, to, or around which everything moves: *Ottawa is the centre of our government.*

middle age the time of life between youth and old age.

mid•dle–aged ['mɪdəl 'eidʒd] *adj.* between youth and old age.

Middle Ages the period of European history between ancient and modern times, from about A.D. 500 (or from A.D. 476, the date of the fall of Rome) to about A.D. 1450.

middle–age spread weight gain in the middle years of life, especially on the waist and hips, due to the body's diminishing capacity to change calories by metabolism.

mid•dle•brow ['mɪdəl,braʊ] *n., adj.* —*n.* a person whose intellectual and cultural interests are conventional and conservative; one who is neither a highbrow nor a lowbrow.
—*adj.* of, appealing to, or suitable for middlebrows.

middle C *Music.* **1** the note on the first added line below the treble staff and the first above the bass staff. **2** the tone corresponding to this notation.

middle class people between the aristocracy or the very wealthy and the working class.

mid•dle–class ['mɪdəl 'klæs] *adj.* of or characteristic of the middle class; bourgeois.

middle distance **1** the part of a landscape or scene between the foreground and the background. **2** *Sports.* a category of footrace between the sprints and the distance races, especially a race of 800 m or 1500 m. —**'middle-'distance,** *adjl.*

middle ear *Anatomy.* a cavity between the eardrum and the inner ear, containing a chain of three tiny bones which transmit sound waves. See EAR[1] for picture.

Middle East the region between the E Mediterranean and India, including Egypt, Sudan, Israel, Lebanon, Iran, Iraq, Kuwait, Jordan, Bahrain, Syria, Saudi Arabia, and Turkey.

☛ *Usage.* See note at NEAR EAST.

Middle English **1** the period in the development of the English language between Old English and Modern English, lasting from about 1100 to about 1500. **2** the language of this period. Chaucer wrote in Middle English. *Abbrev.:* ME

middle finger the finger between the forefinger and the ring finger; the longest finger.
middle finger salute, an offensive gesture made by pointing the middle finger upward.

Middle French the French language from 1400 to 1600. *Abbrev.:* MF

Middle High German the High German language from 1100 to 1450. *Abbrev.:* MHG

Middle Low German the Low German language from 1100 to 1450. *Abbrev.:* MLG

mid•dle•man ['mɪdəl,mæn] *n., pl.* **-men.** a trader or merchant who buys goods from the producer and sells them to a retailer or directly to the consumer.

middle management the mid-level of supervisory management in a company, between managers and workers.

mid•dle•most ['mɪdəl,moust] *adj.* in the exact middle; nearest the middle. Also, **midmost**.

mid•dle–of–the–road ['mɪdəl əv ðə 'roud] *adj.* not extreme; moderate. —**'mid•dle-of-the-'road•er,** *n.*

Middle Path *Buddhism.* a way of life midway between materialism and self-denial, aspired to by most of the faithful.

middle school a school midway between elementary and high school, usually comprising grades six through eight.

middle term *Logic.* a term in the major and minor premises of a syllogism but not in the conclusion, as *tree* in the example at SYLLOGISM.

mid•dle•weight ['mɪdəl,weit] *n.* **1** a boxer weighing between 71 kg and 75 kg. **2** any person or thing of average mass.

mid•dling ['mɪdlɪŋ] *adj., adv., n.* —*adj.* medium in size, quality, grade, etc.
—*adv. Informal or dialect.* moderately; fairly.
—*n.* **middlings,** *pl.* **a** products of medium size, quality, grade, or price. **b** coarse particles of ground wheat mixed with bran. ⟨< *middle*⟩

mid•dy ['mɪdi] *n., pl.* **-dies. 1** MIDDY BLOUSE. **2** *Informal.* a midshipman. ⟨< *midshipman*⟩

middy blouse a loose blouse like a sailor's, having a collar with a broad flap at the back.

Mid•gard ['mɪd,gard] *n. Norse mythology.* the earth.

midge [mɪdʒ] *n.* **1** any of a family (Chironomidae) of small, two-winged flies usually found in swarms around ponds and streams. Midges resemble mosquitoes, but do not bite. **2** any of various similar insects which do bite. **3** a very small person or animal. ⟨OE *mycg*⟩

midg•et ['mɪdʒɪt] *n., adj.* —*n.* **1** a person very much smaller than normal. **2** anything much smaller than the usual size for its type or kind.
—*adj.* **1** much smaller than the usual size for its type or kind: *a midget submarine.* **2** *Sports.* **a** of or for very young or very small players. **b** bantam. ⟨< *midge*⟩

☛ *Syn.* See note at DWARF.

mid•gut ['mɪd,gʌt] *n.* **1** *Zoology.* the central part of the alimentary canal in vertebrates, between the stomach and the caecum. **2** *Zoology.* the latter part of the colon in arthropods. **3** *Embryology.* the central portion of the alimentary canal in an embryo prior to the development of the intestines.

Mi•di [mi'di] *n.* the south, especially the south of France. ⟨< F, literally, midday⟩

mid•i•ron ['mɪd,aɪərn] *n. Golf.* a club with a steel or iron head having a face of medium slope.

mid•land ['mɪdlənd] *n., adj.* —*n.* the middle part of a country; the interior.
—*adj.* in or of the midland.

mid•life crisis ['mɪd,ləɪf] a turning point during the middle years of life, brought about by stressful events such as menopause or children leaving home.

mid•most ['mɪd,moust] *adj.* middlemost.

mid•night ['mɪd,nəit] *n.* **1** the middle of the night; especially 12 o'clock at night. **2** (*adjl.*) of, at, or like midnight; very dark: *midnight blue.*
burn the midnight oil, work or study far into the night: *I'll have to burn the midnight oil tonight if I want to get my project done.*

midnight sun the sun seen at midnight in the arctic and antarctic regions during the summer.
land of the midnight sun, the Arctic or Antarctic in summer.

mid•point ['mɪd,pɔɪnt] *n.* a point at or near the centre or middle: *the midpoint of a line, the midpoint of a career.*

mid•rib ['mɪd,rɪb] *n. Botany.* the central vein or rib of a leaf, running from the base to the tip.

mid•riff ['mɪdrɪf] *n.* **1** the muscular wall separating the chest cavity from the abdomen; diaphragm. **2** the middle portion of the human body. **3** part of a woman's garment covering or revealing the midriff. ⟨OE *midhrif* < *midd* mid + *hrif* belly⟩

mid•ship ['mɪd,ʃɪp] *adj.* in or of the middle of a ship.

mid•ship•man ['mɪd,ʃɪpmən] *n., pl.* **-men. 1** a person training for a naval commission; officer cadet. **2** formerly, a boy who assisted the officers of a ship.

mid•ships ['mɪd,ʃɪps] *adv.* amidships.

midst [mɪdst] *n., prep.* *–n.* the middle.
in our (or **your** or **their**) **midst,** among us (or you or them): *a traitor in our midst.*
in the midst of, a in the middle of; among or surrounded by: *The bomb fell in the midst of the crowd.* **b** during: *The announcement was made in the midst of the program.*
–prep. amidst; amid. Also, **'midst** (for prep.). ⟨OE *tō middes* in the middle; and < *mid* + *-est*⟩

mid•stream ['mɪd'strim] *n.* the middle of a stream.

mid•sum•mer ['mɪd'sʌmər] *or* ['mɪd,sʌmər] *n.* **1** the middle of summer. **2** the time around June 21, the summer solstice. **3** (*adjl.*) of or in the middle of summer.

mid•term ['mɪd,tɜrm] *n.* **1** the middle of a term. **2** an examination held in the middle of a term or semester. **3** (*adjl.*) of or in the middle of a term.

mid•town ['mɪd'taʊn] *or* ['mɪd,taʊn] *n., adj.* *–n.* the most central location in a city or town.
–adj. of or located in midtown.

mid•Vic•to•ri•an ['mɪdvɪk'tɔriən] *adj., n.* *–adj.* **1** in Britain, of or having to do with the middle period of Queen Victoria's reign, from about 1850 to 1890. **2** like this period; old-fashioned; strict in morals.
–n. **1** a person who lived during the middle period of Queen Victoria's reign. **2** a person with old-fashioned ideas and tastes, and strict in morals.

mid•way *adv.* ['mɪd'wəi]; *adj., n.* ['mɪd,wei] *adv., adj., n.* *–adv. or adj.* halfway; in the middle: *midway between the two towns* (*adv.*), *a midway point on the chart* (*adj.*).
–n. **1** a middle way or course. **2** at a fair or exhibition, the place for games, rides, and other amusements. ⟨OE *midweg*⟩

mid•week ['mɪd,wik] *n., adj.* *–n.* the middle of the week.
–adj. in the middle of the week. **–,mid'week•ly,** *adv.*

mid•wife ['mɪd,wəif] *n., pl.* **-wives.** a person who helps women in childbirth. ⟨OE *mid* with + *wīf* woman⟩

mid•wife•ry [mɪd'wɪfəri] *or* ['mɪd,wəifəri] *n.* the science and art of helping women in childbirth.

mid•win•ter ['mɪd'wɪntər] *n.* **1** the middle of winter. **2** the time around December 21, the winter solstice. **3** (*adjl.*) of or in the middle of winter.

mid•year ['mɪd,jir] *adj., n.* *–adj.* happening in the middle of the year.
–n. **1** the middle of the year. **2** **midyears,** *pl. Informal.* midyear examinations.

mien [min] *n.* one's manner of holding the head and body; a way of acting and looking: *The manager had the mien of a soldier.* ⟨probably < *demean*; influenced by F *mine* expression < Celtic⟩
☛ *Hom.* MEAN, MESNE.

mi•fe•pris•tone [,mɪfə'pristoun] *n.* an artificial steroid drug, RU 486, used as a contraceptive. *Formula*: $C_{29}H_{35}NO_2$

miff [mɪf] *n., v. Informal.* *–n.* a peevish fit; petty quarrel.
–v. be or make offended; have a petty quarrel. ⟨origin uncertain⟩

might[1] [məit] *v.* pt. of MAY. ⟨OE *mihte*⟩
☛ *Hom.* MITE.
☛ *Usage.* See note at COULD.

might[2] [məit] *n.* great power; strength.
with might and main, with all one's strength. ⟨OE *miht*⟩
☛ *Hom.* MITE.

might•i•ly ['məitəli] *adv.* **1** in a mighty manner; powerfully; vigorously. **2** very much; greatly.

might•y ['məiti] *adj.* **might•i•er, might•i•est;** *adv.*
–adj. **1** having or showing strength or power; powerful: *a mighty ruler, a mighty blow.* **2** (*noml.*) **the mighty,** *pl.* all those who are mighty. **3** very great: *a mighty famine.*
–adv. Informal. very; extremely: *a mighty cold day.*
–'might•i•ness, *n.*
☛ *Syn. adj.* **1. Mighty,** POWERFUL = having or showing great strength or force. **Mighty** in this sense is now used chiefly for effect, suggesting overwhelming strength or force or a power above all others: *The mighty battleship steamed into port.* **Powerful** = having the strength, energy, or authority to do great things or showing great force: *A heavy truck needs a powerful engine.*

mi•gnon [mɪn'jɒn] *or* ['mɪnjɒn]; *French,* [mi'njɔ̃] *adj.* small and pretty; dainty. ⟨< F⟩ **–'mig•nonne,** *fem.*

mi•gnon•ette [,mɪnjə'nɛt] *n.* any of a genus (*Reseda*) of plants, especially an annual plant (*R. odorata*) widely grown for its pointed clusters of fragrant, greenish yellow flowers. ⟨< F⟩

mi•graine ['maigrein] *n.* a severe, recurring type of headache usually affecting only one side of the head and often accompanied by nausea and vomiting, dizziness, and sensitivity of the eyes to light. ⟨< F < LL < Gk. *hemikrania* < *hemi-* half + *kranion* skull⟩ **–'mi•grain•ous,** *adj.*

mi•grant ['maigrənt] *n., adj.* *–n.* a person, animal, bird, or plant that migrates.
–adj. migrating: *Migrant workers were hired for the harvest.*

mi•grate ['maigreit] *v.* **-grat•ed, -grat•ing. 1** move from one place to settle in another. **2** go from one region to another with the change in the seasons. Many birds migrate to warmer countries in the winter. ⟨< L *migrare*⟩ **–'mi•gra•tor,** *n.*

mi•gra•tion [mai'greiʃən] *n.* **1** migrating. **2** a number of people or animals migrating together. **3** *Chemistry* **a** a movement of one or more atoms from one place to another within the molecule. **b** the movement of ions between the two electrodes during electrolysis. **–mi'gra•tion•al,** *adj.*

mi•gra•to•ry ['maigrə,tɔri] *adj.* **1** migrating; that migrates. **2** of migration. **3** wandering.

mi•ka•do [mə'kɑdou] *n., pl.* **-dos.** the ancient title of the emperor of Japan. ⟨< Japanese *mikado* < *mi* august, honourable + *kado* door, gate⟩

Mi•ka•su•ki [,mikɑ'suki] *n.* a language of the Seminole people.

mike [məik] *n. Informal.* microphone.

Mi'kmaq ['mɪkmæk] *n., pl.* **-maq.** See MICMAC.

mil [mɪl] *n.* **1** a unit for measuring length, equal to 0.001 inch (25.4 µm). The mil was used for measuring the diameter of wires. **2** a unit of money in Cyprus, equal to 1/1000 of a pound. See table of money in the Appendix. **3** a coin worth one mil. ⟨< L *mille* thousand⟩
☛ *Hom.* MILL.

mil. 1 military. **2** militia. **3** mileage. **4** million.

mi•la•dy [mɪ'leidi] *n., pl.* **-dies. 1** my lady. **2** an English Lady.

mil•age ['mailɪdʒ] See MILEAGE.

Mi•lan or **mi•lan** [mə'læn] *or* ['mɪlən] *n.* a finely woven straw used for hats. ⟨< *Milan,* Italy, where it is made⟩

milch [mɪltʃ] *adj.* giving milk; kept for the milk it gives: *a milch cow.* ⟨OE *-milce* milking < *mioluc* milk⟩

mild [maild] *adj.* **1** gentle; kind: *a mild old gentleman.* **2** warm; temperate; moderate; not harsh or severe: *a mild climate, a mild winter.* **3** soft or sweet to the senses; not sharp, sour, bitter, or strong in taste: *mild cheese, a mild cigar.* ⟨OE *milde*⟩ **–'mild•ly,** *adv.* **–'mild•ness,** *n.*
☛ *Syn.* **1.** See note at GENTLE.

mil•dew ['mɪldju] *or* ['mɪldu] *n., v.* *–n.* **1** any of various fungi that attack plants or grow on food, paper, cloth, leather, etc., especially in damp conditions. **2** any of various plant diseases caused by such fungi. **3** a thin, furry coating or discoloration caused by the growth of such fungi, especially on cloth, paper, etc.
–v. affect or become affected with mildew. ⟨OE *mildēaw* honeydew⟩ **–'mil,dew•y,** *adj.*

mile [mail] *n.* **1** a non-metric unit for measuring distance or length on land, equal to about 1.609 km; statute mile. **2** NAUTICAL MILE. **3** **miles,** *pl.* a relatively great distance: *The sun went down, but we were still miles from home. From here you can see for miles. Abbrev.*: mi. ⟨OE *mīl* < L *milia (passuum),* pl. of *mille* (gen. pl. of *passus*) a thousand (paces)⟩

mile•age ['mailɪdʒ] *n.* **1** the total number of miles travelled: *What's the mileage on your car?* **2** the length, extent, or distance of a road, journey, etc., expressed in miles. **3** the distance a motor vehicle can go on a given amount of fuel: *We get good mileage on our new car.* **4** an allowance for travelling expenses at a fixed rate per unit of distance: *She gets mileage on trips she makes for the company.* **5** the profit or use a person gets or can get out of something: *He's getting a lot of mileage out of that one joke.* **6** a rate charged per mile, as on a toll highway or for a rental car.

mile•post ['mail,poust] *n.* a post set up to show the distance in miles to a certain place.

mile•stone ['mail,stoun] *n.* **1** a stone set up to show the distance in miles to a certain place. **2** an important event: *The invention of printing was a milestone in the progress of education.*

mil•foil ['mɪl,fɔil] *n.* **1** yarrow. **2** WATER MILFOIL. ⟨ME < OF < L *millefolium* < *mille* thousand + *folium* leaf⟩

mil•i•a ['mɪliə] *n.* pl. of MILIUM.

mi•lieu [mɪ'lju]; *French,* [mi'ljø] *n.* surroundings; environment.

mil•i•tant ['mɪlətənt] *adj., n.* *–adj.* **1** aggressive; fighting; warlike. **2** aggressively active in serving a cause or in spreading a belief: *a militant environmentalist.*

—*n.* a person aggressively active in serving a cause or in spreading a belief. ⟨< L *militans, -antis* serving as a soldier, ult. < *miles* soldier⟩ —'**mil•i•tan•cy,** *n.* —'**mil•i•tant•ly,** *adv.*

mil•i•tar•ism ['mɪlətə,rɪzəm] *n.* **1** the policy of making military organization and power very strong. **2** the political condition in which the military interest is predominant in government or administration. **3** military spirit, ideals, and organizational style.

mil•i•ta•rist ['mɪlətərɪst] *n.* **1** a person who believes in a powerful military organization. **2** an expert in military matters. —,**mil•i•ta'ris•tic,** *adj.* ,**mil•i•ta'ris•ti•cal•ly,** *adv.*

mil•i•ta•rize ['mɪlətə,raɪz] *v.* **-rized, -riz•ing. 1** make the military organization of (a country) very powerful. **2** fill with military spirit and ideals. —,**mil•i•ta•ri'za•tion,** *n.*

mil•i•tar•y ['mɪlə,tɛri] *adj.* **1** of or having to do with soldiers or war. **2** done by soldiers. **3** fit for soldiers. **4** suitable for war; warlike: *military valour.* **5** belonging to the armed forces.
6 (*noml.*) **the military,** the armed forces; soldiers: *The military did rescue work during the flood.* ⟨< L *militaris* < *miles* soldier⟩ —,**mil•i'tar•i•ly,** *adv.* —'**mil•i,tar•i•ness,** *n.*
☛ *Syn. adj.* **1. Military,** MARTIAL, WARLIKE = having to do with war. **Military** describes anything to do with affairs of war or the armed forces: *She studied military history.* **Martial** emphasizes the glory and pomp of war or the gallantry of fighting soldiers: *Troops paraded in martial array.* **Warlike** suggests a fighting nature, and especially describes acts, feelings, words, etc. threatening or fit for war: *The Vikings were a warlike people.*

Military Cross an award for bravery for officers of the army up to the rank of captain. *Abbrev.*: M.C.

military law a system of regulations governing the armed forces and others in military service.
☛ *Usage.* **Military law** is not to be confused with MARTIAL LAW, which replaces CIVIL LAW in times of emergency and applies to civilians as well as military personnel.

Military Medal an award for bravery for members of the armed forces.

military police soldiers who act as police in an army. *Abbrev.*: MP or M.P.

Military Regime in Canada, the period of military rule between 1759 and 1764.

mil•i•tate ['mɪlə,teit] *v.* **-tat•ed, -tat•ing.** act; work; operate (*against*): *Bad weather militated against the success of the picnic.* ⟨< L *militare* serve as a soldier < *miles* soldier⟩

mi•li•tia [mə'lɪʃə] *n.* a part of an army made up of citizens who are not regular soldiers but who undergo training for emergency duty or national defence; the reserve army. ⟨< L *militia* < *miles* soldier⟩

mi•li•tia•man [mə'lɪʃəmən] *n., pl.* **-men.** a soldier in the militia.

mil•i•um ['mɪliəm] *n., pl.* **mil•i•a** ['mɪliə]. a small white nodule on the skin, the result of a plugged sebaceous gland. Newborns often have milia on the face. ⟨< NL < L, millet⟩

Mil•i•um ['mɪliəm] *n. Trademark.* a fabric or material sprayed with a metal solution and used as insulation in clothing, draperies, etc.

milk [mɪlk] *n., v.* —*n.* **1** the white liquid secreted by the mammary glands of female mammals for the nourishment of their young. **2** cow's milk or goat's milk, used as a drink or to make puddings, butter, cheese, etc. **3** any kind of liquid resembling this, such as the white juice of a plant, tree, or nut: *coconut milk.*
cry over spilt milk, waste sorrow or regret on what has happened and cannot be remedied.
—*v.* **1** draw milk from; strip of milk: *She used to milk twenty cows a day.* **2** yield or produce milk. **3** extract as if by milking. **4** drain contents, strength, information, wealth, etc. from: *The dishonest treasurer milked the club treasury.* **5** draw juice, poison, etc. from: *to milk a snake.* ⟨OE *mioluc*⟩ —'**milk•less,** *adj.*

milk bar a store or counter specializing in dairy products such as ice cream, milk shakes, yogurt, etc.

milk•er ['mɪlkər] *n.* **1** a cow, goat, etc. that gives a specified quantity or quality of milk: *a good milker.* **2** a person who or machine that milks.

milk•ing ['mɪlkɪŋ] *n., v.* —*n.* **1** the amount of milk obtained at one time. **2** one of the regularly scheduled times when cows are milked on a farm.
—*v.* ppr. of MILK.

milk leg *Pathology.* a painful swelling of the leg caused by thrombosis in the veins, often caused by infection during childbirth.

milk•maid ['mɪlk,meid] *n.* a woman or girl whose job it is to milk cows, or who works in a dairy.

milk•man ['mɪlk,mæn] *n., pl.* **-men.** a man who sells or delivers milk.

milk of human kindness natural sympathy and affection.

milk of magnesia a milky-white medicine in water, used as a laxative and antacid. *Formula*: $Mg(OH)_2$

milk shake a drink consisting of milk, flavouring, and often ice cream, shaken or beaten until frothy.

milk snake a small, harmless grey-and-brown snake (*Lampropeltis triangulum*, also called *L. doliata*) of North America. Milk snakes eat small rodents such as rats and mice.

milk•sop ['mɪlk,sɒp] *n.* a weak person; a coward.

milk sugar lactose.

milk tooth one of the first set of teeth; a temporary tooth of a young child or animal. ⟨from their whiteness⟩

milk•vetch ['mɪlk,vɛtʃ] *n.* a Canadian wildflower (*Astragalus adsurgens*) having purple flowers and not poisonous like other plants of this genus. It blooms in summer on the southern Prairies and south to Colorado.

milk•weed ['mɪlk,wid] *n.* any of various weeds whose stem contains a white juice that looks like milk; especially, any of a genus (*Asclepias*) of mainly North American perennial plants with milky juice and pointed pods that burst open when ripe, releasing tufted seeds.

milk–white ['mɪlk 'wəit] *adj.* white as milk. Also, **milky-white.**

milk•y ['mɪlki] *adj.* **milk•i•er, milk•i•est. 1** like milk; white as milk; whitish. **2** of milk; containing milk. **3** mild; weak; timid. —'**milk•i•ness,** *n.*

Milky Way 1 a broad band of faint light that stretches across the sky at night. It is made up of countless stars, too far away to be seen separately without a telescope. **2** the galaxy in which these countless stars are found. The earth, sun, and all the planets around the sun are part of the Milky Way. ⟨ME, translation of L *via lactea*⟩

mill[1] [mɪl] *n., v.* —*n.* **1** a machine for grinding or crushing: *A flour mill grinds wheat into flour. A coffee mill grinds coffee beans.* **2** a building containing a machine for grinding grain. **3** a building where manufacturing is done: *A paper mill makes paper from wood pulp.* **4** any institution or establishment regarded as mass-producing something. **5** *Slang.* a boxing match or fist fight.
go through the mill, *Informal.* **a** get a thorough training or experience. **b** learn by hard or painful experience.
put through the mill, *Informal.* **a** test; examine; try out. **b** teach by hard or painful experience.
—*v.* **1** grind: *Some wheat will be milled before it is exported.* **2** manufacture. **3** cut a series of fine notches or ridges on the edge of (a coin): *A dime is milled.* **4** of people or animals in a group, move around in a confused or aimless way (*often used with* **around** *or* **about**): *There were many people milling around after the parade.* ⟨OE *mylen* < LL *molinum* < L *mola* millstone⟩ —'**mill•a•ble,** *adj.*
☛ *Hom.* MIL.

mill[2] [mɪl] *n.* \$.001, or 1/10 of a cent. Mills are used in accounting, but not as coins. ⟨short for L *millesimum* one thousandth < *mille* thousand⟩
☛ *Hom.* MIL.

mill•dam ['mɪl,dæm] *n.* **1** a dam built in a stream to supply water power for a mill. **2** a pond made by such a dam.

mil•len•ni•um [mə'lɛniəm] *n., pl.* **mil•len•ni•ums** or **mil•len•ni•a** [mə'lɛniə]. **1** a period of a thousand years: *The world is many millenniums old.* **2 the millennium,** the period of a thousand years during which, according to the Bible, Christ is expected to reign on earth. **3** a period of righteousness and happiness. ⟨< NL < L *mille* thousand + *annus* year⟩ —**mil'len•ni•al,** *adv.*

mil•le•pede ['mɪlə,pid] See MILLIPEDE.

mil•le•pore ['mɪlə,pɔr] *n.* any of an order (Milleporina) of tropical hydrozoans having a calcareous skeleton and living in colonies which often form reefs. Millepores pass through a free-swimming medusa stage. ⟨< NL *millepora* < L *mille* thousand + *porus* pore⟩

mill•er ['mɪlər] *n.* **1** a person who owns or runs a mill, especially a flour mill. **2** a moth whose wings look as if they were powdered with flour.

mil•les•i•mal [mə'lɛsəməl] *adj., n.* —*adj.* **1** thousandth. **2** consisting of thousandth parts.
—*n.* a thousandth part. ⟨< L *millesimus* thousandth part < *mille* thousand⟩

mil•let ['mɪlɪt] *n.* **1** any of various annual grasses grown for grain or fodder, such as the East Indian grass (*Panicum miliaceum*), widely cultivated for grain in Europe, Asia, and Africa. **2** the small seed of any of these plants, used especially for cereals and unleavened breads. ⟨< F, ult. < L *milium*⟩

milli– *SI prefix.* thousand; thousandth: *millilitre.* ⟨< L *mille*⟩

mil•li•am•pere [,mɪli'æmpir] *n.* one one-thousandth of an ampere. *Symbol*: mA

mil•liard ['mɪljərd] *or* ['mɪljɑrd] *n. Brit.* a thousand million; a billion; 1 000 000 000. ⟨< F < L *mille* thousand⟩

mil•li•bar ['mɪlə,bɑr] *n.* an SI unit for measuring pressure, equal to 0.1 kilopascals. Atmospheric pressure readings are sometimes given in millibars. *Symbol*: mbar

mil•lieme [mil'jɛm] *n.* **1** a unit of money in Egypt and Sudan, equal to 1/100 of a piastre and 1/1000 of a pound. See table of money in the Appendix. **2** a coin worth one millieme. ⟨< F⟩

mil•li•gram ['mɪlə,græm] *n.* one thousandth of a gram. The milligram is used for very small masses, such as the amount of vitamins and minerals contained in a serving of food. *Symbol*: mg Also, **milligramme.**

mil•li•li•tre ['mɪlə,litər] *n.* one thousandth of a litre. Cooking measures are graduated in millilitres. *Symbol*: mL Also, **milliliter.**

mil•lim [mə'lim] *or* ['mɪlim] *n.* **1** a unit of money in Tunisia, equal to 1/1000 of a dinar. See table of money in the Appendix. **2** a coin worth one millim.

mil•li•me•tre ['mɪlə,mitər] *n.* one thousandth of a metre. A dime is about one millimetre thick. *Symbol*: mm Also, **millimeter.**

mil•li•ner ['mɪlənər] *n.* a person who makes, trims, or sells women's hats. ⟨var. of *Milaner*, a dealer in goods from Milan, Italy, famous for straw⟩

mil•li•ner•y ['mɪlənəri] *or* ['mɪlə,nɛri] *n.* **1** women's hats. **2** the business of making, trimming, or selling women's hats.

mill•ing ['mɪlɪŋ] *n., v.* —*n.* **1** the business or process of grinding grain in a mill. **2** manufacturing. **3** the business or process of cutting notches or ridges on the edge of a coin. **4** such notches or ridges. **5** the random movement of a crowd.
—*v.* ppr. of MILL[1].

mil•lion ['mɪljən] *n. or adj.* **1** one thousand thousand; 1 000 000. **2** a very large number; very many. ⟨ME < OF < Ital. *milione*, ult. < L *mille* thousand⟩

mil•lion•aire ['mɪljə,nɛr] *or* [,mɪljə'nɛr] *n.* **1** a person whose wealth is equal to more than a million dollars, pounds, etc. **2** any very wealthy person. ⟨< F⟩

mil•lion•fold ['mɪljən,fould] *adv. or adj.* a million times as much or as many.

mil•lionth ['mɪljənθ] *adj. or n.* **1** last in a series of a million. **2** one of a million equal parts.

mil•li•pede ['mɪlə,pid] *n.* any of a class (Diplopoda) of arthropod having a cylindrical, segmented body armoured with hard plates, and with most segments bearing two pairs of legs each. Also, **millepede.** ⟨< L *millepeda* < *mille* thousand + *pes, pedis* foot⟩

mil•li•sec•ond ['mɪlə,sɛkənd] *n.* one thousandth of a second. *Symbol*: ms

mill•pond ['mɪl,pɒnd] *n.* a pond supplying water to drive a mill wheel.

mill•race ['mɪl,reis] *n.* **1** a current of water that drives a mill wheel. **2** the channel in which it flows to the mill.

mill rate *Cdn.* a rate used for calculating municipal taxes. A mill rate of 45.6 means that a property owner pays a tax of 45.6 mills ($0.045 6) for every dollar of the assessed value of his or her property.

mill•stone ['mɪl,stoun] *n.* **1** either of a pair of round, flat stones used for grinding corn, wheat, etc. **2** a heavy burden: *The old house was a millstone around her neck.* **3** anything that grinds or crushes.

mill•stream ['mɪl,strim] *n.* the stream in a millrace.

mill wheel a wheel that is turned by water and supplies power for a mill.

mill•work ['mɪl,wɜrk] *n.* **1** doors, windows, mouldings, etc. made in a planing mill. **2** the work done in a mill.
—'mill,work•er, *n.*

mill•wright ['mɪl,rəit] *n.* **1** a person who designs, builds, or sets up mills or machinery for mills. **2** a mechanic who sets up and takes care of the machinery in a factory, etc.

milque•toast ['mɪlk,toust] *n.* an extremely timid person. ⟨< Mr. *Milquetoast*, a comic-strip character⟩

milt [mɪlt] *n.* **1** the sperm cells of male fishes together with the milky fluid containing them. **2** the reproductive gland in male fishes. ⟨for older *milk*; influenced by *milt* spleen (OE *milte*), and perhaps by Du. *milt* milt of fish, spleen⟩

Mil•ton•ic [mɪl'tɒnɪk] *adj.* **1** of or having to do with John Milton (1608-1674), an English poet. **2** resembling Milton's literary style; solemn and majestic.

Mi•mas ['maɪməs] *or* ['mimǝs] *n.* **1** *Roman mythology.* one of the Gigantes, killed by Hercules. **2** *Astronomy.* a satellite of the planet Saturn.

mime [maɪm] *n., v.* **mimed, mim•ing.** —*n.* **1** a form of drama in which the actors use movement and gestures but no words; pantomime. **2** communication through gestures but without the use of words: *She told her story in mime.* **3** an actor communicating through gestures only. **4** in ancient Greece and Rome: **a** a coarse farce using funny actions and gestures. **b** an actor in such a farce.
—*v.* communicate through gestures without the use of words. ⟨< L < Gk. *mimos*⟩ **—'mim•er,** *n.*

mim•e•o•graph ['mɪmiə,græf] *n., v.* —*n.* a machine for making copies of written or typewritten material, or of drawings, by means of stencils.
—*v.* make (copies) on a mimeograph. ⟨< *Mimeograph*, a former trademark < Gk. *mimeesthai* imitate + E *-graph*⟩

mi•me•sis [mɪ'misɪs] *or* [maɪ'misɪs] *n.* **1** mimicry or imitation. **2** *Biology.* protective colouring or markings in a plant, animal, etc., imitating the surroundings or another organism, so as to be concealed from predators. **3** the imitation or representation of reality in art or literature. **4** *Pathology.* the assuming of the symptoms of one disease by another disease. ⟨< Gk. *mimēsis* < *mimeisthai* imitate < *mimos* mime⟩

mi•met•ic [mɪ'mɛtɪk] *or* [maɪ'mɛtɪk] *adj.* **1** imitative: *mimetic gestures.* **2** mimic or make-believe. **3** having to do with or exhibiting mimesis. ⟨< Gk. *mimetikos* < *mimeesthai* imitate⟩

mim•ic ['mɪmɪk] *v.* **-icked, -ick•ing;** *n., adj.* —*v.* **1** make fun of by imitating. **2** copy closely; imitate: *A parrot can mimic a person's voice.* **3** represent imitatively, as by drawing; simulate. **4** of things, be an imitation of. **5** resemble closely: *Some insects mimic leaves.*
—*n.* **1** a person who or thing that imitates. **2** a performer whose act is mimicking.
—*adj.* **1** not real, but imitated or pretended for some purpose: *a mimic battle.* **2** imitative. ⟨< L *mimicus* < Gk. *mimikos* < *mimos* mime⟩ **—'mim•ick•er,** *n.*

mim•ic•ry ['mɪmɪkri] *n., pl.* **-ries. 1** the act of mimicking. **2** mimesis.

mi•mo•sa [mɪ'mousə] *or* [mɪ'mouzə] *n.* any of a genus (*Mimosa*) of shrubs, trees, and herbs found in tropical and warm regions, having compound, fernlike leaves that in some species are sensitive to touch or to changes in light or temperature. See also SENSITIVE PLANT. ⟨< NL *mimosa* < L *mimus* mime < Gk. *mimos*; from mimicry of animal reactions⟩

min minute(s).

min. minimum.

mi•na ['maɪnə] *n., pl.* **mi•nae** ['maɪni] *or* ['maɪnaɪ] or **mi•nas.** a unit of weight and value used by the ancient Greeks, Egyptians, and others. ⟨< L < Gk. *mna* < Semitic; cf. Babylonian *manū*⟩
☛ *Hom.* MYNA.

mi•na•cious [mɪ'neiʃəs] *adj.* menacing; threatening. ⟨< L *minax, minacis*, ult. < *minae* projecting points, threats⟩
—mi'na•cious•ly, *adv.* **—mi'na•cious•ness,** *n.*

Min•a•ma•ta disease [,mɪnə'mætə] *or* [,mɪnə'mɑtə] a disease caused by methyl mercury poisoning as a result of eating contaminated fish, and characterized by slurred speech, numbness, and progressive paralysis. ⟨< *Minamata*, a fishing settlement in Japan, where the disease first appeared in the 1950s⟩

min•a•ret [ˌmɪnəˈrɛt] *or* [ˈmɪnəˌrɛt] *n.* a slender, high tower of a Muslim mosque, having one or more projecting balconies, from which a muezzin or crier calls the people to prayer. ⟨< F or Sp. < Arabic *manāret* lighthouse⟩

min•a•to•ry [ˈmɪnəˌtɔri] *adj.* menacing; threatening. ⟨< LL *minatorius* < L *minari* threaten, ult. < *minae* projecting points, threats⟩

mince [mɪns] *v.* **minced, minc•ing;** *n.* *—v.* **1** chop or grind into very small pieces. **2** speak or move in a prim, affected way. **3** soften or moderate (words, etc.), as when stating unpleasant facts: *The judge addressed the jury bluntly, without mincing words.*
not to mince matters, to speak plainly and frankly.
—n. **1** meat cut or ground up into very small pieces. **2** mincemeat. **3** (*adjl.*) made with mincemeat: *mince pie.* ⟨ME < OF *mincier*, ult. < L *minutus* small⟩

mince•meat [ˈmɪnsˌmit] *n.* **1** a mixture of chopped apples, raisins, currants, etc., flavoured with spices, used as a filling for pies. **2** minced meat.
make mincemeat of, *Informal.* reduce as if into little pieces; cut down; defeat overwhelmingly: *Our team made mincemeat of the rest of the league.*

mince pie a pie filled with MINCEMEAT (def. 1).

minc•ing [ˈmɪnsɪŋ] *adj., v.* *—adj.* too polite or nice; affectedly elegant or dainty: *a mincing courtier.*
—v. ppr. of MINCE. **—ˈminc•ing•ly,** *adv.*

mind [maɪnd] *n., v.* *—n.* **1** that part of a person which knows, thinks, remembers, feels, and wills. **2** intellect. **3** a person who has intelligence: *a great mind.* **4** the intellectual powers or capacities of a body of persons: *the popular mind.* **5** reason; sanity: *be out of one's mind.* **6** mental or physical activity in general, as opposed to matter. **7** a conscious or intelligent agency or being: *the doctrine of a mind creating the universe.* **8** a way of thinking and feeling: *change one's mind.* **9** one's desire, purpose, intention, or will. **10** remembrance or recollection; memory: *Keep the rules in mind.*
bear in mind, keep one's attention on; remember.
be in (or **of**) **two** (**many,** etc.) **minds,** vacillate between two (many, etc.) intentions or opinions.
be of one mind, agree.
call to mind, a recall. **b** remember.
give (someone) **a piece of** (one's) **mind,** speak to angrily or without holding back.
have a mind of (one's) **own,** have definite or decided opinions, inclinations, or purposes.
have a mind to, intend to; think of favourably: *I have a mind to watch hockey tonight.*
have half a mind (to), be somewhat inclined.
have in mind, a remember. **b** think of; consider. **c** intend; plan.
keep in mind, remember.
know (one's) **(own) mind,** know what one really thinks, wishes, or intends.
make up (one's) **mind,** decide; resolve.
on (one's) **mind,** in one's thoughts; troubling one.
pass out of mind, be forgotten.
put (someone) **in mind** (of), remind.
set (one's) **mind on, a** want very much. **b** concentrate on.
speak (one's) **mind,** give one's frank opinion.
take (one's) **mind off,** distract one's attention from; divert from (something unpleasant).
to (one's) **mind,** in one's opinion; to one's way of thinking.
—v. **1** bear in mind; give heed to: *Mind my words!* **2** take notice; observe. **3** be careful concerning: *Mind the step.* **4** be careful. **5** look after; take care of; tend: *Mind the baby.* **6** obey: *Mind your father and mother.* **7** feel concern about; object to: *We mind parting from a friend.* **8** feel concern; object: *Do you mind?* **9** *Archaic or dialect.* remember. **10** *Archaic or dialect.* remind.
mind the store. See STORE. ⟨OE *(ge)mynd*⟩ **—ˈmind•er,** *n.*
mind you, a however; on the other hand. **b** even; moreover: *Paid me in full—and on time, mind you!*
☛ *Syn. n.* **1, 2. Mind,** INTELLECT= the part of a human being that enables him or her to know, think, and act effectively. **Mind** in general usage is the inclusive word, meaning the part that knows, thinks, feels, wills, remembers, etc., thought of as distinct from the body: *To develop properly, the mind needs training and exercise.* **Intellect** applies to the knowing and thinking powers of the mind, as distinct from the powers of feeling and will: *Many motion pictures appeal to the feelings rather than the intellect.*

mind•ed [ˈmaɪndɪd] *adj., v.* *—adj.* **1** having a certain kind of mind (*usually used in combination*); *high-minded, strong-minded.* **2** inclined; disposed: *I am minded to stay home today.*
—v. pt. and pp. of MIND.

mind•ful [ˈmaɪndfəl] *adj.* having in mind: *Mindful of your advice, I went slowly.* **—ˈmind•ful•ly,** *adv.* **—ˈmind•ful•ness,** *n.*

mind•less [ˈmaɪndlɪs] *adj.* **1** without intelligence; stupid. **2** not taking thought; careless. **3** not requiring the use of intelligence: *trapped in a mindless job.* **—ˈmind•less•ly,** *adv.* **—ˈmind•less•ness,** *n.*

mind reader a person who professes to be able to perceive another's thoughts directly.

mind's eye imagination. ⟨coined by Shakespeare in *Hamlet*⟩

mine[1] [maɪn] *pron., adj.* *—pron.* a possessive form of I; that which belongs to or is associated with me: *The dog is mine. These are his boots; mine are over there.*
of mine, belonging to or associated with me: *She's a friend of mine. My mother found some old essays of mine.*
—adj. Archaic. my (*used only before a vowel or* h, *or after a noun*): *mine eyes, mine heart, sister mine.* ⟨OE *mīn*⟩
☛ *Usage.* See note at MY.

mine[2] [maɪn] *n., v.* **mined, min•ing.** *—n.* **1** a large hole or space dug in the earth to get out valuable minerals: *a coal mine, a gold mine.* **2** a rich or plentiful source: *a mine of information.* **3** an underground passage in which an explosive is placed to blow up the enemy's forts, etc. **4** a container holding an explosive charge that is put under water and exploded by propeller vibrations **(acoustic** or **sonic mine),** or by magnetic attraction **(magnetic mine),** or laid on the ground or shallowly buried and exploded by contact with a vehicle, etc. **(land mine).**
—v. **1** dig a mine; make a hole, space, passage, etc. below the earth. **2** dig into (the earth, a hill, etc.) for coal, ore, etc. **3** get (metal, etc.) from a mine. **4** make (passages, etc.) by digging. **5** put explosive mines in or under; lay explosive mines. **6** destroy secretly; ruin slowly; undermine. ⟨< F < Celtic⟩

mine•field [ˈmaɪnˌfild] *n.* **1** an area throughout which explosive mines have been laid. **2** the pattern of mines in such an area.

min•er [ˈmaɪnər] *n.* **1** a person who works in a mine: *a coal miner.* **2** a soldier who lays explosive mines.
☛ *Hom.* MINOR.

min•er•al [ˈmɪnərəl] *n.* **1** any inorganic, naturally occurring, solid chemical element or compound having a crystalline structure. **2** any natural substance that is neither plant nor animal. **3** a substance obtained by mining, especially an ore. **4** (*adjl.*) of, having to do with, or containing minerals: *mineral water. There are mineral deposits at the mouth of the river.* ⟨ME < OF *mineral*, ult. < *mine* mine[2] < Celtic⟩

min•er•al•ize [ˈmɪnərəˌlaɪz] *v.* **-ized, -iz•ing. 1** convert into mineral substance; petrify. **2** transform (metal) into an ore. **3** impregnate or supply with mineral substances. **4** search for minerals. **—ˌmin•er•al•iˈza•tion,** *n.* **—ˈmin•er•alˌiz•er,** *n.*

mineral kingdom one of the three broad divisions of the natural world. The mineral kingdom includes all non-living, or inorganic, things. Compare ANIMAL KINGDOM and PLANT KINGDOM.

min•er•al•o•gist [ˌmɪnəˈrɒlədʒɪst] *or* [ˌmɪnəˈrælədʒɪst] *n.* a person trained in mineralogy, especially one whose work it is.

min•er•al•o•gy [ˌmɪnəˈrɒlədʒi] *or* [ˌmɪnəˈrælədʒi] *n.* the science that deals with the physical and chemical properties of minerals, their classification, and the form and structure of their crystals. **—ˌmin•er•alˈog•i•cal** [ˌmɪnərəˈlɒdʒəkəl] or **ˌmin•er•alˈog•ic,** *adj.* **—ˌmin•er•alˈog•i•cal•ly,** *adv.*

mineral oil any oil derived from a mineral substance, especially a colourless, odourless, tasteless oil obtained from petroleum, used as a laxative and as a base for cold creams, etc.

mineral right a right both to the mineral deposits in a given piece of land and to the royalties accruing from their extraction.

mineral water water containing mineral salts or gases. People drink mineral water for its healthful properties.

Mi•ner•va [məˈnɜrvə] *n. Roman mythology.* the goddess of wisdom, the arts, and defensive war, corresponding to the Greek goddess Athena.

min•e•stro•ne [ˌmɪnəˈstrouni] *n.* a soup containing vegetables, vermicelli, etc. ⟨< Ital.⟩

mine•sweep•er [ˈmaɪnˌswipər] *n.* a warship equipped for dragging a harbour or the sea to remove or disarm enemy mines.

Ming [mɪŋ] *n.* **1** a kind of fine porcelain. **2** something made of this porcelain. **3** *(adjl.)* of or designating this porcelain: *a Ming vase.* ⟨< *Ming,* a dynasty that ruled China 1368-1644, when this porcelain was made⟩

Ming

min•gle ['mɪŋgəl] *v.* **-gled, -gling. 1** mix or blend: *The Fraser and Thompson Rivers join and mingle their waters near Lytton, B.C.* **2** associate: *to mingle with important people.* ⟨ME *mengele(n)* < OE *mengan* mix⟩ **—'min•gler,** *n.*

min•i ['mɪni] *n. Informal.* something small, short, etc. for its kind, such as a miniskirt, minicar, or minibus: *She was wearing a mini.* ⟨< *miniature*⟩

mini– *combining form.* small for its kind; very small, very short, etc.: *miniskirt, minicar, minicomputer.* ⟨combining form of MINIATURE⟩

min•ia•ture ['mɪnətʃər] *or* ['mɪniətʃər] *n., adj. —n.* **1** a small model or copy: *In the museum there is a miniature of the ship* Victory. **2** a very small painting, usually a portrait.
in miniature, on a small scale; reduced in size.
—adj. done or made on a very small scale; tiny: *She had miniature furniture for her doll house.* ⟨< Ital. *miniatura* < Med.L *miniare* illuminate (a manuscript) < L *miniare* paint red < *minium* red lead; confused with L *minutus* small⟩

miniature camera a camera using narrow film (35 mm or smaller).

min•ia•tur•ize ['mɪnətʃə,raɪz] *or* ['mɪniətʃə,raɪz] *v.* **-ized, -iz•ing.** reduce to a very small size: *to miniaturize electronic devices.* **—,min•i•a•tur•i'za•tion,** *n.*

min•i•bike ['mɪni,bəik] *n.* a small motorcycle.

min•i•bus ['mɪni,bʌs] *n.* a small bus used for short runs, as between an airport and a hotel, etc.

min•i•car ['mɪni,kɑr] *n.* a very small automobile, such as a small subcompact.

min•i•com•pu•ter ['mɪnikəm,pjutər] *n. Computer technology.* a computer midway between a microcomputer and a mainframe in size, cost, and power.

min•i•fy ['mɪnə,faɪ] *v.* **-fied, -fy•ing.** make small or less important. ⟨< L *minor,* neuter of *minus* less + E *-fy*⟩ **—,min•i•fi'ca•tion,** *n.*

min•im ['mɪnəm] *n.* **1** a unit for measuring liquids, equal to one-sixtieth of a fluid dram (about 0.06 cm^3). The minim is the smallest unit in the imperial system of liquid measure. **2** a very small amount. **3** something very small or insignificant. **4** *Music. Brit.* a half note. ⟨< L *minimus* smallest⟩

min•i•ma ['mɪnəmə] *n.* a pl. of MINIMUM.

min•i•mal ['mɪnəməl] *adj.* least possible; very small; having to do with a minimum: *The article claimed that the side effects of the drug were minimal.* **—'min•i•mal•ly,** *adv.*

minimal pair *Linguistics.* two speech forms in a given language that are distinguished by a single phonetic feature, phoneme, or morpheme, as *tie* and *die* in English.

min•i•mize ['mɪnə,maɪz] *v.* **-mized, -miz•ing. 1** reduce to the least possible amount or degree: *The polar explorers took every precaution to minimize the dangers of their trip.* **2** state at the lowest possible estimate; make the least of: *The ungrateful woman minimized the help others had given her.*
—,min•i•mi'za•tion, *n.* **—'min•i,miz•er,** *n.*

min•i•mum ['mɪnəməm] *n., pl.* **-mums** or **-ma** [-mə]. **1** the least amount or smallest quantity possible or permitted: *I need a minimum of eight hours sleep a night.* **2** *Mathematics.* the least value of a function within a given interval of the domain of the function. **3** *(adjl.)* least possible; lowest: *a minimum rate. Eighteen is the minimum age for voting in federal elections.* ⟨< L *minimum* smallest (thing)⟩
☛ *Usage.* **Minimum** has two plurals: *minimums* and *minima.* The first is more common in informal English.

minimum wage the lowest wage paid or allowed, especially the wage fixed by law as the lowest that can be paid to any employed person or to certain categories of employed persons.

min•ing ['maɪnɪŋ] *n., v. —n.* **1** the act, process, or business of extracting coal, ore, etc. from mines. **2** *(adjl.)* of or having to do with this process or business: *a mining camp, a mining town.* **3** the act or process of laying explosive mines.
—v. ppr. of MINE.

min•ion ['mɪnjən] *n.* **1** a person willing to do whatever he or she is ordered, especially a servile or obsequious follower. **2** a darling; favourite: *the king's minion.* **3** *Printing.* a size of type, 7-point. ⟨< F *mignon* dainty⟩
☛ *Hom.* MINYAN.

min•i–ser•ies ['mɪni ,siriz] *n.* a television drama in serial form.

min•i•skirt ['mɪni,skɜrt] *n.* a very short skirt ending well above the knees. **—'min•i,skirt•ed,** *adj.*

min•is•ter ['mɪnɪstər] *n., v. —n.* **1** a member of the clergy serving a church; pastor. **2** a member of the cabinet who is in charge of a government department: *the Minister of Labour.* **3** a person sent to a foreign country to represent his or her own government; a diplomat ranking below an ambassador: *the British Minister to France.* **4** a person or thing employed in carrying out (purpose, will, etc.): *The storm which killed the murderer seemed the minister of God's vengeance.* **5** *Archaic.* a servant.
—v. **1** act as a servant or nurse; be of service (*to*): *She ministers to the sick.* **2** be helpful; give aid; contribute. **3** *Archaic.* furnish; supply. ⟨< L *minister* servant < *minus* less; patterned after *magister* master⟩

min•is•te•ri•al [,mɪnɪ'stiriəl] *adj.* **1** of, having to do with, or suitable for a minister of religion or the ministry. **2** of or having to do with a government minister or ministry. **3** having to do with or characteristic of administrative functions of government; executive. **4** acting as an agent; instrumental.
—,min•is'te•ri•al•ly, *adv.*

minister plenipotentiary *pl.* **ministers plenipotentiary.** plenipotentiary.

minister without portfolio a cabinet minister who is not connected with any particular cabinet post or department.

min•is•trant ['mɪnɪstrənt] *adj., n. —adj.* ministering.
—n. one who ministers. ⟨< L *ministrans, -antis,* ppr. of *ministrare* < *minister* servant⟩

min•is•tra•tion [,mɪnɪ'streiʃən] *n.* the act or process of ministering: *ministration to the sick.* **—'min•is•tra•tive,** *adj.*

min•is•try ['mɪnɪstri] *n., pl.* **-tries. 1** the office, duties, or time of service of a minister. **2** the ministers of a church. **3** the ministers of a government. **4** in the United Kingdom, Europe, Canada, etc.: **a** a government department under a minister. **b** the offices of such a department. **5** a ministering or serving. ⟨< L *ministerium* office, service < *minister.* See MINISTER. Doublet of METIER.⟩

min•i•van ['mɪni,væn] *n.* a motor vehicle able to seat several passengers, whose rear seats can be removed or folded down to accommodate cargo.

min•i•ver ['mɪnəvər] *n.* a white or spotted white fur formerly much used for lining and trimming garments worn by members of the medieval nobility and still sometimes used on ceremonial robes. ⟨ME < OF *menu vair* small vair (a type of fur used in the 14c. and the animal from which it was obtained); *menu* < L *minutus* made small (see MINUTE[2]); *vair* < L *varius* variegated⟩

mink [mɪŋk] *n., pl.* **mink** or **minks. 1** any of several semiaquatic mammals (genus *Mustela*) closely related to and resembling the weasels, having thick, soft, lustrous fur generally ranging in colour from brown to almost black. The common North American mink is **M. vison. 2** the fur of a mink, one of the most valuable commercial furs. **3** a coat or other garment made of this fur. ⟨apparently < Scand.; cf. Swedish *mänk*⟩ **—'mink,like,** *adj.*

min•ne•sing•er or **Min•ne•sing•er** ['mɪnə,sɪŋər] *or* ['mɪnə,zɪŋər] *n.* a German lyrical poet and singer in the 12th, 13th, and 14th centuries. ⟨< G *Minnesinger* love singer⟩

Min•ne•so•ta [,mɪnə'soutə] *n.* a northern state of the United States.

min•now ['mɪnou] *n.* **1** any of various small, freshwater cyprinid fishes, such as a common, small-scaled Eurasian species (*Phoxinus phoxinus*). **2** *(adjl.)* designating the family (Cyprinidae) of chiefly freshwater, mostly very small fishes that includes the minnows, goldfish, chubs, daces, shiners, breams, and carp. **3** any of various other small fishes or the young of larger fishes, especially when used as live bait. ⟨ME *minwe*; cf. OE *myne*⟩

Mi•no•an [mə'nouən] *adj., n. —adj.* of, having to do with, or designating a Bronze Age culture of Crete that flourished between about 2500 B.C. and 1100 B.C.
—n. a native or inhabitant of Crete during this period. ⟨< *Minos*⟩

mi•no•cy•cline [ˌmɪnou'səiklin] *or* [ˌmɪnou'səiklɪn] *n.* an antibiotic drug. *Formula*: $C_{23}H_{27}N_3O_7$

mi•nor ['maɪnər] *adj., n., v. —adj.* **1** smaller; lesser; less important: *a minor fault, a minor poet.* **2** under legal age. **3** *Music.* **a** of an interval, less by a half step than the corresponding major interval. **b** of or designating a scale, mode, or key whose third tone is minor in relation to the tonic.
—n. **1** a person who is legally considered not an adult. In various provinces, minors are under 18, 19, or 21 years of age. A minor cannot make legal contracts and needs the consent of a parent or guardian to marry. **2** *Music.* a minor interval, key, scale, chord, etc. **3** a subject or course of study to which a student gives much time and attention, but less than to his or her major subject.
4 *Hockey.* MINOR PENALTY. **5 the minors,** *pl. Sports.* the MINOR LEAGUES.
—v. have or take as a minor subject of study (*used with* **in**): *to minor in Chemistry.* ⟨< L *minor* lesser⟩
☛ *Hom.* MINER.

Mi•nor•ca [mə'nɔrkə] *n.* a breed of large chicken originally developed in Spain. ⟨< *Minorca*, one of the Balearic Islands⟩

mi•nor•i•ty [mə'nɔrəti] *or* [maɪ'nɔrəti] *n., pl.* **-ties. 1** a smaller number or part; less than half: *The minority must often accept what the majority decides to do.* **2** a group within a country, state, etc. that differs in race, religion, or national origin from the larger part of the population. **3** (*adj.*) of or constituting a minority: *a minority group, etc.* **4** (*adj.*) belonging to a minority: *a minority opinion.* **5** the condition or time of being under the legal age of responsibility.

minor key *Music.* a key whose melody and harmony are based on a minor scale. Compare MAJOR KEY.

minor league any professional sports league or association, as in baseball or hockey, other than the major leagues.

mi•nor–league ['maɪnər 'lig] *adj.* **1** of or having to do with minor leagues. **2** *Informal.* inferior; second rate; not top quality.

minor mode *Music.* a key of a composition using the minor scale. Compare MAJOR MODE.

minor penalty *Hockey.* a two-minute penalty awarded for certain infractions of the rules, such as highsticking, hooking, slashing, tripping, etc. The referee may award a major penalty for many such infractions, especially when injury results.

minor premise See SYLLOGISM.

minor scale *Music.* a scale having eight tones with half steps instead of whole steps after the second and fifth tones. Compare MAJOR SCALE.

Mi•nos ['maɪnəs] *or* ['maɪnɒs] *n. Greek mythology.* a son of Zeus and Europa who was a king and lawgiver of Crete. After his death, Minos became a judge in Hades.

Min•o•taur ['mɪnəˌtɔr] *n. Greek mythology.* a monster with a bull's head and a man's body, kept in the Labyrinth of Crete and fed with human flesh. The Minotaur was killed by Theseus. ⟨< L < Gk. *Minotauros* < *Minos* Minos + *tauros* bull⟩

mi•nox•i•dil [mɪ'nɒksədɪl] *n.* a hair growth stimulant.

min•ster ['mɪnstər] *n. Esp. Brit.* **1** the church of a monastery. **2** a large or important church; cathedral. ⟨OE *mynster* < LL *monasterium.* Doublet of MONASTERY.⟩

min•strel ['mɪnstrəl] *n.* **1** any of a class of medieval entertainers, especially a singer or musician who sang or recited poetry, often composed by himself, and accompanied himself on a harp or lute. **2** formerly, a singer or musician in the household of a lord. **3** *Poetic.* any musician or poet. ⟨ME < OF < LL *ministerialis* < L *ministerium.* See MINISTRY.⟩

min•strel•sy ['mɪnstrəlsi] *n., pl.* **-sies. 1** the art or practice of a minstrel. **2** a collection of songs and ballads. **3** a company of minstrels.

mint[1] [mɪnt] *n.* **1** any of a genus (*Mentha*) of strongly scented herbs, especially any of several species used for seasoning or flavouring food, such as peppermint or spearmint. **2** any of several other plants of the same family. **3** (*adj.*) designating a family (Labiatae) of plants found especially in the Old World, having square stems and aromatic leaves that have been used in cooking and medicine since ancient times. The mint family includes lavender, peppermint, sage, rosemary, savory, and thyme. **4** a piece of candy flavoured with mint, especially peppermint or spearmint. ⟨OE *minte* < L *menta* < Gk. *minthē*⟩

mint[2] [mɪnt] *n., v. —n.* **1** a place where money is made by government authority. Mints also often make special commemorative coins and medals. **2** (*adj.*) of a stamp or coin, in perfect condition, as issued. **3** *Informal.* a large sum or amount, especially of money: *She made a mint when she sold her house.* **4** a place where anything is made or fabricated.
in mint condition, without a blemish; as good as new: *an old car in mint condition.*
—v. **1** make (coins, medals, etc.): *This quarter was minted in 1938.* **2** make or fabricate; originate. ⟨OE *mynet* coin < L *moneta* mint, money. Doublet of MONEY.⟩ **—'mint•er,** *n.*

mint•age ['mɪntɪdʒ] *n.* **1** a minting; coinage. **2** the product of minting; output of a mint. **3** a charge for coining; cost of coining. **4** a stamp or character impressed on a coin.

mint jelly or **sauce** a jelly or sauce made with chopped mint leaves and served as an accompaniment to roast lamb.

min•u•end ['mɪnjuˌɛnd] *n. Mathematics.* a number or quantity from which another is to be subtracted. In 100–23 = 77, the minuend is 100. ⟨< L *minuendus* be made smaller < *minus* less⟩

min•u•et [ˌmɪnju'ɛt] *n.* **1** a slow, stately dance, popular in the 1700s. **2** the music for it. ⟨< F *menuet*, dim. of *menu* small⟩

mi•nus ['maɪnəs] *prep., n., adj. —prep.* **1** decreased by; reduced by; less: *Five minus two is three.* **2** *Informal.* without or lacking: *a book minus its cover.*
—n. the sign (–) meaning that the quantity following it is to be subtracted.
—adj. **1** showing subtraction. The minus sign is –. **2** less than (*never used before a noun*): *A mark of B minus is not as high as B.* **3** less than zero; negative: *a minus quantity. The temperature this morning was minus thirteen degrees.* ⟨< L *minus* less⟩

mi•nus•cule ['mɪnəˌskjul] *or* [mə'nʌskjul] *adj., n. —adj.* **1** minute; very small. **2** *Paleography.* of or written in small letters, or in minuscules.
—n. **1** a lower case letter. **2** *Paleography.* **a** the small, cursive script developed from the uncial, about A.D. 600-800. **b** a letter in this script. Compare MAJUSCULE. ⟨< F *minuscule*, learned borrowing from L *minuscula (littera)* slightly smaller (letter) < *minus* less⟩

min•ute[1] ['mɪnɪt] *n., v.* **min•ut•ed, min•ut•ing.** *—n.* **1** an SI unit for measuring time, equal to sixty seconds or one-sixtieth of an hour. *Symbol*: min **2** any short period of time; moment: *It will only take me a minute to put the dishes away. He paused for a minute to listen.* **3** a point in time: *Come here this minute!*
4 *Geometry.* an SI unit for measuring plane angles, equal to sixty seconds or one-sixtieth of a degree.
Symbol: ′ **5** a memorandum or written record. **6 minutes,** *pl.* the official record of the proceedings at a meeting of a society, board, committee, etc.
up to the minute, up to date.
—v. put in the minutes: *Have you minuted that?* ⟨ME < OF < LL *minuta* small part < L *minuta*, fem. of *minutus*, adj. See MINUTE[2].⟩
☛ *Syn.* **2, 3. Minute,** MOMENT, INSTANT = a point or extremely short period of time. **Minute** usually suggests a measurable, although very short, amount of time: *May I rest a minute?* **Moment** is more vague, suggesting a very brief period that is noticeable but not measurable or definite: *I'll be with you in a moment.* **Instant,** often used interchangeably with *moment,* is more definite and particularly suggests a point of time or a period too brief to be noticed: *Come this instant!*

mi•nute[2] [maɪ'njut], [maɪ'nut], *or* [mɪ'njut] *adj.* **1** very small; tiny: *a minute speck of dust.* **2** going into or concerned with very small details: *a minute observer, minute instructions.*
3 unimportant; petty. ⟨ME < L *minutus* made small < *minus* less. Doublet of MENU.⟩ **—mi'nute•ness,** *n.*

minute hand ['mɪnɪt] on a watch or clock, the longer of the two hands, indicating the minutes. It moves around the dial once every hour.

mi•nute•ly [maɪ'njutli], [maɪ'nutli], *or* [mɪ'njutli] *adv.* in minute manner, form, degree, or detail.

minute steak ['mɪnɪt] a thin slice of beef that is very quick to cook.

mi•nu•ti•ae [mɪ'njuʃiˌi] *or* [mɪ'nuʃiˌi], [mɪ'njuʃiˌaɪ] *or* [mɪ'nuʃiˌaɪ] *n.pl.* very small matters; trifling details. ⟨< L *minutiae* trifles, pl. of *minutia* smallness < *minutus.* See MINUTE[2].⟩

minx [mɪŋks] *n.* a bold or impudent girl. ⟨? < LG *minsk*, impudent woman; cf. G *Mensch* person⟩ **—'minx•ish,** *adj.*

min•yan ['mɪnjən] *or* [min'jɑn] *n., pl.* **min•yan•im** [mɪn'jɒnɪm] *or* [ˌminjɑ'nim]. *Judaism.* a quorum of ten adults needed to hold a service, a funeral, etc.
☛ *Hom.* MINION ['mɪnjən].

Mi•o•cene ['maɪəˌsin] *n., adj. Geology. —n.* **1** a period of the Cenozoic era, beginning approximately 24 million years ago. **2** the rocks formed in this period. See geological time chart in the Appendix.

—*adj.* of or having to do with this period or the rocks formed during it. ⟨< Gk. *meiōn* less + *kainos* new⟩

mip•ku ['mɪpku] *n. Cdn.* dried caribou meat. ⟨< Inuktitut⟩

mir [mir] *n.* a peasant village community in Imperial Russia. ⟨< Russian⟩
☛ *Hom.* MERE.

Mi•ra ['maɪrə] *n. Astronomy.* a first magnitude star in the constellation Cetus, the first variable star discovered. ⟨< NL *Mira* < L *mira* wonderful⟩

mir•a•cle ['mirəkəl] *n.* **1** a wonderful happening that is contrary to or independent of the known laws of nature: *It would be a miracle if the earth stood still in the sky for an hour.*
2 something marvellous; a wonder. **3** a remarkable example: *a miracle of patience.* **4** MIRACLE PLAY. ⟨ME < OF < L *miraculum,* ult. < *mirus* wonderful⟩

miracle drug a new drug that treats conditions previously thought untreatable.

miracle play any of a class of medieval religious dramas dealing with the lives of the saints.

mi•rac•u•lous [mə'rækjələs] *adj.* **1** contrary to or independent of the known laws of nature; suggesting a miracle; supernatural: *a miraculous cure.* **2** wonderful; marvellous: *Meeting you here is miraculous good fortune.* **3** able to produce a miracle. ⟨< Med.L *miraculosus* < L *miraculum.* See MIRACLE.⟩ **—mi'rac•u•lous•ly,** *adv.* **—mi'rac•u•lous•ness,** *n.*

mi•rage [mə'rɑʒ] *n.* **1** a misleading appearance in which some distant scene is viewed as being close and, often, inverted. In a mirage, the actual scene is reflected by layers of air of different temperatures. **2** an illusion; a thing that does not exist. ⟨< F *mirage* < *mirer* look at carefully, *se mirer* look at oneself in a mirror, see reflected < L *mirare,* var. of *mirari* wonder (at), admire⟩

mire [maɪr] *n., v.* **mired, mir•ing.** *—n.* **1** soft, deep mud; slush. **2** a bog; swamp.
—v. **1** stick or cause to stick in mire: *He mired his car and had to go for help.* **2** soil with mud or mire. **3** hamper or hold back, as if in a mire; involve in difficulties: *She got mired in a traffic jam.* ⟨ME < ON *mýrr*⟩

mirk [mɜrk] See MURK.

mir•ror ['mirər] *n., v. —n.* **1** a looking glass; a surface that reflects light. **2** whatever reflects or gives a true description: *This book is a mirror of Laurier's life.* **3** a model; example; pattern: *That knight was a mirror of chivalry.*
—v. **1** reflect as a mirror does: *The still water mirrored the trees along the bank.* **2** give a true description or picture of: *The book mirrored colonial life in Canada.* ⟨ME < OF *mirour,* ult. < L *mirari* wonder, admire⟩ **—'mir•ror,like,** *adj.*

mirth [mɜrθ] *n.* merriment or gaiety accompanied by laughter: *Her sides shook with mirth.* ⟨OE *myrgth* < *myrge* merry⟩

mirth•ful ['mɜrθfəl] *adj.* laughing and merry. **—'mirth•ful•ly,** *adv.* **—'mirth•ful•ness,** *n.*

mirth•less ['mɜrθlɪs] *adj.* without mirth; joyless; gloomy. **—'mirth•less•ly,** *adv.* **—'mirth•less•ness,** *n.*

mir•y ['maɪri] *adj.* **mir•i•er, mir•i•est. 1** muddy; swampy. **2** dirty; filthy. **—'mir•i•ness,** *n.*

MIS MANAGEMENT INFORMATION SYSTEM.

mis– *prefix.* **1** bad: *misinformation, misgovernment.* **2** badly: *misbehave, mismanage.* **3** wrong: *mispronunciation.* **4** wrongly: *misunderstand, mislabel.* ⟨OE *mis(s)-*, or in borrowed words < OF *mes-* < OHG *missi-, missa-*⟩

mis•ad•ven•ture [,mɪsəd'vɛntʃər] *n.* an unfortunate accident; an instance of bad luck; misfortune: *By some misadventure, the letter got lost.*

mis•al•li•ance [,mɪsə'laɪəns] *n.* an unsuitable alliance or association, especially in marriage.

mis•al•ly [,mɪsə'laɪ] *v.* **-lied, -ly•ing.** ally unsuitably.

mis•an•dry [mɪ'sændri] *or* ['mɪsændri] *n.* hatred of men or of males. ⟨< Gk. *misos* hatred + *aner, andros* man⟩ **—mis'an•drist,** *n.*

mis•an•thrope ['mɪsən,θroup] *or* ['mɪzən,θroup] *n.* a hater of people; person who dislikes or distrusts human beings. ⟨< Gk. *misanthrōpos* < *miseein* hate + *anthrōpos* < person⟩ **—,mis•an'throp•ic** [-'θrɒpɪk], *adj.* **—,mis•an'throp•i•cal•ly,** *adv.*

mis•an•throp•ist [mɪ'sænθrəpɪst] *or* [mɪ'zænθrəpɪst] *n.* misanthrope.

mis•an•thro•py [mɪ'sænθrəpi] *or* [mɪ'zænθrəpi] *n.* a hatred, dislike, or distrust of human beings.

mis•ap•pli•ca•tion [,mɪsæplə'keɪʃən] *n.* a wrong application; a misapplying or being misapplied.

mis•ap•ply [,mɪsə'plaɪ] *v.* **-plied, -ply•ing.** apply wrongly; make a wrong application or use of. **—,mis•ap'pli•er,** *n.*

mis•ap•pre•hend [,mɪsæprɪ'hɛnd] *v.* misunderstand.

mis•ap•pre•hen•sion [,mɪsæprɪ'hɛnʃən] *n.* a misunderstanding; wrong idea.

mis•ap•pro•pri•ate [,mɪsə'proupri,eit] *v.* **-at•ed, -at•ing.** make use of for oneself without authority or right: *The treasurer had misappropriated the club funds.*

mis•ap•pro•pri•a•tion [,mɪsə,proupri'eiʃən] *n.* **1** a dishonest use of something as one's own. **2** any act of putting something to a wrong use.

mis•be•came [,mɪsbɪ'keim] *v.* pt. of MISBECOME.

mis•be•come [,mɪsbɪ'kʌm] *v.* **-came, -come, -com•ing.** be unbecoming to; be unfit for.

mis•be•got•ten [,mɪsbɪ'gɒtən] *adj.* **1** begotten unlawfully; illegitimate: *a misbegotten child.* **2** poorly done or conceived; pitiable: *She was ready to throw out the whole misbegotten plan.*

mis•be•have [,mɪsbɪ'heiv] *v.* **-haved, -hav•ing.** behave oneself badly: *The child was punished for misbehaving at the party.*

mis•be•hav•iour or **mis•be•hav•ior** [,mɪsbɪ'heivjər] *n.* bad behaviour.

mis•be•lief [,mɪsbɪ'lif] *n.* a false or erroneous belief.

mis•be•liev•er [,mɪsbɪ'livər] *n.* one who holds a wrong or erroneous belief.

mis•brand [mɪs'brænd] *v.* brand or mark incorrectly.

misc. 1 miscellaneous. **2** miscellany.

mis•cal•cu•late [mɪs'kælkjə,leit] *v.* **-lated, -lat•ing.** calculate wrongly; judge or count wrongly: *Her arrow fell short because she had miscalculated the distance.* **—,mis•cal•cu'la•tion,** *n.* **—mis'cal•cu,la•tor,** *n.*

mis•call [mɪs'kɒl] *v.* call by a wrong name.

mis•car•riage [mɪs'kærɪdʒ] *or* [mɪs'kɛrɪdʒ]; *for def. 2,* ['mɪskɛrɪdʒ] *n.* **1** a failure: *The jury was biassed, and the trial resulted in a miscarriage of justice.* **2** the involuntary expulsion of a fetus from the womb before it has developed enough to survive. A pregnant woman might have a miscarriage because of a defect in the fetus, or an accident or illness. **3** a failure to arrive: *the miscarriage of a letter.*

mis•car•ry [mɪs'kæri] *or* [mɪs'kɛri] *v.* **-ried, -ry•ing. 1** go wrong: *John's plans miscarried, and he could not come.* **2** have a MISCARRIAGE (def. 2). **3** fail to arrive.

mis•cast [mɪs'kæst] *v.,* **-cast, -casting.** cast in an unsuitable role: *The young actor was badly miscast as a grandfather.*

mis•ce•ge•na•tion [,mɪsədʒə'neiʃən] *or* [mɪ,sɛdʒə'neiʃən] *n.* marriage or sexual relations between a man and woman of different races, especially between a white person and one of another race. ⟨< L *miscere* mix + *genus* race⟩

mis•cel•la•ne•ous [,mɪsə'leiniəs] *adj.* **1** formed or consisting of different things or parts, not arranged in a particular pattern or system: *a miscellaneous collection of stamps. She writes a newspaper column of miscellaneous comments.*
2 having or showing various qualities, interests, etc.; many-sided: *a miscellaneous writer.* ⟨< L *miscellaneus* < *miscellus* mixed, ult. < *miscere* mix⟩ **—,mis•cel'la•ne•ous•ly,** *adv.* **—,mis•cel'la•ne•ous•ness,** *n.*
☛ *Syn.* **1. Miscellaneous,** INDISCRIMINATE = including various things or kinds, without plan or order in selection. **Miscellaneous,** describing a group or mass, emphasizes the idea of mixing, and means 'of varied nature, usually gathered together without special order, plan, or care in selection': *A person's miscellaneous expenses include stamps and haircuts.* **Indiscriminate,** applying chiefly to actions, feelings, methods, purposes, etc., emphasizes lack of selection or judgment in selection, and means 'including all, good and bad, deserving and undeserving, etc. without distinction': *Indiscriminate buying is wasteful.*

mis•cel•la•ny [mə'sɛləni] *or* ['mɪsɛ,ləini] *n., pl.* **-nies. 1** a miscellaneous collection; a mixture of various things.
2 miscellanies, *pl.* a collection of separate articles, etc. in one book. ⟨< L *miscellanea,* neut. pl. of *miscellaneus.* See MISCELLANEOUS.⟩

mis•chance [mɪs'tʃæns] *n.* misfortune; bad luck.

mis•chief ['mɪstʃɪf] *n.* **1** action or conduct that causes trouble or harm, often not intentionally: *A child's mischief with matches may cause a serious fire. She's always getting into mischief.*
2 merry teasing; playful mocking or fooling: *Her eyes were full of mischief.* **3** harm or injury, especially when done by a person: *He'll try to do you a mischief if you meddle.* **4** a person who causes annoyance, irritation, or harm: *He's a little mischief.* ⟨ME

< OF *meschief*, ult. < *mes-* bad (see MIS-) + *chever* come to an end < *chief* head < L *caput*⟩

mis•chief–mak•ing ['mɪstʃɪf ,meikɪŋ] *adj., n.* —*adj.* stirring up trouble by tale-bearing, inciting quarrels, gossiping, etc.
—*n.* the act or practice of stirring up trouble.
—'mis•chief-,mak•er, *n.*

mis•chie•vous ['mɪstʃəvəs] *adj.* **1** causing or tending to cause harm or annoyance: *mischievous gossip, mischievous behaviour.* **2** full of pranks and teasing fun: *mischievous children, a mischievous look.* **—'mis•chie•vous•ly,** *adv.*
—'mis•chie•vous•ness, *n.*

mis•ci•ble ['mɪsəbəl] *adj.* especially of liquids, capable of being mixed to form a substance having the same composition throughout. Water and alcohol are miscible; water and oil are not. ⟨< L *miscere* mix⟩ **—,mis•ci'bil•i•ty,** *n.*

mis•con•ceive [,mɪskən'siv] *v.* **-ceived, -ceiv•ing.** have a wrong idea about; misunderstand.

mis•con•cep•tion [,mɪskən'sɛpʃən] *n.* a mistaken idea or notion; incorrect conception.

mis•con•duct *n.* [mɪs'kɒndʌkt]; *v.* [,mɪskən'dʌkt] *n.* **1** bad or dishonest management, especially by a public or government official or a member of the military: *The ambassador was censured by the government for misconduct of diplomatic affairs.* **2** bad behaviour; improper conduct. **3** *Hockey.* a ten-minute penalty awarded for improper behaviour, such as insulting the referee or using foul or abusive language. **4** *Law.* **a** adultery. **b** malfeasance.
—*v.* **1** manage badly or dishonestly. **2** behave (oneself) badly.

mis•con•struc•tion [,mɪskən'strʌkʃən] *n.* the act or process of misconstruing or an instance of this; a taking in the wrong sense; misinterpretation: *Such vague and ambiguous statements are open to misconstruction.*

mis•con•strue [,mɪskən'stru] *v.* **-strued, -stru•ing.** take in a wrong sense; misinterpret: *Shyness is sometimes misconstrued as rudeness.*

mis•count *v.* [mɪs'kaʊnt]; *n.* ['mɪs,kaʊnt] *v., n.* —*v.* count incorrectly.
—*n.* an incorrect count.

mis•cre•ant ['mɪskriənt] *adj., n.* —*adj.* **1** morally base; depraved. **2** *Archaic.* unbelieving; heretical.
—*n.* **1** villain. **2** *Archaic.* an unbeliever; heretic. ⟨ME < OF *mescreant* < *mes-* wrongly (see MIS-) + *creant*, ppr. of *creire* believe < L *credere*⟩

mis•cue *n.* ['mɪskju] *or* [mɪs'kju]; *v.* [mɪs'kju] *n., v.* **-cued, -cu•ing.** —*n.* **1** a bad stroke in which the cue slips and does not hit the ball squarely. **2** *Informal.* mistake; slip-up.
—*v.* **1** make a miscue. **2** *Theatre.* miss one's cue; respond to a wrong cue.

mis•date [mɪs'deit] *v.* **-dat•ed, -dat•ing.** date wrongly; put a wrong date on or assign to a wrong date: *to misdate a document, to misdate an event.*

mis•deal *v.* [mɪs'dil]; *n.* ['mɪsdil] *v.* **-dealt, -deal•ing;** *n. Card games.* —*v.* deal incorrectly.
—*n.* an incorrect deal.

mis•dealt [mɪs'dɛlt] *v.* pt. and pp. of MISDEAL.

mis•deed [mɪs'did] *or* ['mɪsdid] *n.* a bad or wicked act; offence.

mis•de•mean [,mɪsdɪ'min] *v. Rare.* behave badly.

mis•de•mean•our or **mis•de•mean•or** [,mɪsdɪ'minər] *n.* **1** an offence or wrong deed, especially a minor one. **2** *Law. Esp. U.S.* a minor criminal offence, less serious than a felony. A misdemeanour is similar to a summary conviction offence in Canada.

mis•di•ag•nose [,mɪsdaɪəg'nous] *or* [,mɪsdaɪəg'nouz] *v.,* **-nosed, -nos•ing.** diagnose incorrectly.

mis•did [mɪs'dɪd] *v.* pt. of MISDO.

mis•di•rect [,mɪsdə'rɛkt] *or* [,mɪsdaɪ'rɛkt] *v.* direct incorrectly.

mis•di•rec•tion [,mɪsdə'rɛkʃən] *or* [,mɪsdaɪ'rɛkʃən] *n.* **1** a misdirecting or being misdirected. **2** a wrong direction.

mis•do [mɪs'du] *v.* **-did, -done, -do•ing.** do wrongly or improperly. ⟨OE *misdōn*⟩ **—mis'do•er,** *n.*

mis•do•ing [mɪs'duɪŋ] *n., v.* —*n.* wrongdoing; misdeed.
—*v.* ppr. of MISDO.

mis•done [mɪs'dʌn] *v.* pp. of MISDO.

mis•doubt [mɪs'dʌut] *v., n. Archaic.* —*v.* **1** have doubts about; distrust. **2** suspect; fear.
—*n.* suspicion; distrust; doubt.

mise en scène [mizɑ̃'sɛn] *French.* the general direction of a play or film, including staging, lighting, etc.

mis•em•ploy [,mɪsəm'plɔɪ] *v.* use wrongly or improperly.
—,mis•em'ploy•ment, *n.*

mi•ser ['maɪzər] *n.* a person who loves money for its own sake, especially one who lives poorly in order to save money and keep it. A miser dislikes spending money, except to gain more money. ⟨< L *miser* wretched⟩

mis•er•a•ble ['mɪzərəbəl] *adj.* **1** unhappy; wretched: *A sick child is often miserable.* **2** causing trouble or unhappiness: *a miserable cold.* **3** poor; pitiful: *They live in a miserable, cold house.* **4** pitiable; deplorable; sorry: *a miserable failure, miserable sinners.* ⟨< L *miserabilis*, ult. < *miser* wretched⟩
—'mis•er•a•ble•ness, *n.* **—'mis•er•a•bly,** *adv.*
☛ *Syn.* **1.** See note at WRETCHED.

Mis•e•re•re [,mɪzə'rɛrei] *or* [,mɪzə'riri] *n.* **1** the 51st Psalm in the Revised and Authorized versions of the Bible (the 50th Psalm in the Douay version). **2** a musical setting for it.
3 miserere, a speech, prayer, etc. for mercy. ⟨< L *miserere* have pity, the first word of this psalm in the Vulgate⟩

mi•ser•ly ['maɪzərli] *adj.* of or like a miser; stingy.
—'mi•ser•li•ness, *n.*

mis•er•y ['mɪzəri] *n., pl.* **-er•ies. 1** a miserable, extremely unhappy state of mind. **2** a cause of this. **3** poor, mean, or miserable conditions: *Some very poor people live in misery, without beauty or comfort around them.* **4** *Informal.* a wretched or miserable person: *She's an old misery.* ⟨< L *miseria* < *miser* wretched⟩

mis•fea•sance [mɪs'fizəns] *n. Law.* the wrongful performance of a lawful act; wrongful and injurious exercise of lawful authority. Compare MALFEASANCE and NONFEASANCE. ⟨ME < OF *mesfaisance* < *mes-* wrong (see MIS-) + *faire* do < L *facere*⟩

mis•file [mɪs'faɪl] *v.,* **-filed, -filing.** file (papers, etc.) incorrectly: *We couldn't find the document as it had been misfiled.*

mis•fire [mɪs'faɪr] *v.* **-fired, -fir•ing;** *n.* —*v.* **1** of a firearm, missile, etc., fail to discharge or go off. **2** of an internal-combustion engine, fail to ignite properly or at the right moment. **3** fail to have an intended effect; go wrong: *The robber's scheme misfired.*
—*n.* a failure to discharge or explode properly, or to be carried out as planned.

mis•fit *n.* ['mɪsfɪt]; *v.* [mɪs'fɪt] *n., v.* **-fit•ted, -fit•ting.** —*n.* **1** a bad fit, such as of a garment. **2** a person who is not suited to his or her environment or does not get along well with other people.
—*v.* fit badly.

mis•for•tune [mɪs'fɔrtʃən] *n.* **1** bad luck. **2** a piece of bad luck; unlucky accident.
☛ *Syn.* **1, 2. Misfortune,** ADVERSITY, MISHAP = bad luck. **Misfortune** applies to either an unfortunate condition, ordinarily not one's own fault, or a particular turning of affairs against one, or an unlucky happening: *She had the misfortune to break her arm.* **Adversity** applies chiefly to a condition of great and continued misfortune, marked by serious accidents, hardships, and distress: *Displaced persons have experienced adversity.* **Mishap** applies to a minor accident or unlucky accident: *Breaking a dish is a mishap.*

mis•gave [mɪs'geiv] *v.* pt. of MISGIVE.

mis•give [mɪs'gɪv] *v.* **-gave, -giv•en, -giv•ing.** cause to feel doubt, suspicion, or anxiety: *My heart misgave me.*

mis•giv•en [mɪs'gɪvən] *v.* pp. of MISGIVE.

mis•giv•ing [mɪs'gɪvɪŋ] *n., v.* —*n.* a feeling of doubt, suspicion, or anxiety: *We started off through the storm with some misgivings.*
—*v.* ppr. of MISGIVE.

mis•gov•ern [mɪs'gʌvərn] *v.* govern or manage badly.
—mis'gov•ern•ment, *n.* **—mis'gov•er•nor,** *n.*

mis•guid•ance [mɪs'gaɪdəns] *n.* bad or wrong guidance.

mis•guide [mɪs'gaɪd] *v.* **-guid•ed, -guid•ing.** lead into mistakes or wrongdoing; mislead.

mis•guid•ed [mɪs'gaɪdɪd] *adj., v.* —*adj.* erring or misled in thought or action: *He mixed everything up in a well-meaning but misguided attempt to help.*
—*v.* pt. and pp. of MISGUIDE.

mis•han•dle [mɪs'hændəl] *v.* **-dled, -dling. 1** handle roughly or harshly; maltreat: *to mishandle a horse.* **2** manage badly or ignorantly; mismanage: *to mishandle a business deal.*

mis•hap ['mɪshæp] *or* [mɪs'hæp] *n.* an unlucky accident.
☛ *Syn.* See note at MISFORTUNE.

mis•hear [mɪs'hir] *v.* **-heard, -hearing.** hear (especially words) inaccurately: *You must have misheard me, I said 'same' not 'shame'.*

mis•heard [mɪs'hɜrd] *v.* pt. and pp. of MISHEAR.

mish•mash ['mɪʃ,mæʃ] *n.* jumble; hodgepodge: *a mishmash of styles.* ⟨origin uncertain⟩

Mish•nah or **Mish•na** ['mɪʃnə] *n., pl.* **Mish•na•yoth** [,mɪʃnə'jout] or **Mish•na•yos** [,mɪʃnə'jous]. *Judaism.* the collection of the interpretations and discussions of the law of Moses by the Jewish rabbis, completed about A.D. 200; the oral law of the Hebrews. The Mishna is the first part of the Talmud. ⟨< post-Biblical Hebrew *mishnah* instruction < *shanah* teach, learn < Hebrew *shanah* repeat⟩ **—Mish'na•ic** [mɪʃ'neiɪk] or **'Mish•nic,** *adj.*

mis•in•form [,mɪsɪn'fɔrm] *v.* give incorrect or misleading information to. **—,mis•in'form•er,** *n.* **—,mis•in•for'ma•tion** [,mɪsɪnfər'meiʃən], *n.*

mis•in•ter•pret [,mɪsɪn'tɜrprɪt] *v.* interpret wrongly; give a wrong meaning to: *to misinterpret a signal.*
—,mis•in'ter•pret•a•ble, *adj.* **—,mis•in,ter•pre'ta•tion,** *n.*
—,mis•in'ter•pret•er, *n.*

mis•judge [mɪs'dʒʌdʒ] *v.* **-judged, -judg•ing. 1** judge or estimate wrongly: *The archer misjudged the distance to the target and her arrow fell short.* **2** judge unfairly; have an unjust opinion: *The teacher soon discovered that she had misjudged the girl's capabilities.* **—mis'judg•er,** *n.* **—mis'judg•ing•ly,** *adv.*
—mis'judg•ment or **mis'judge•ment,** *n.*

mis•la•bel [mɪs'leibəl] *v.* **-la•belled, -label•ling.** label (something) incorrectly: *I got such a bargain—the $500 dress had been mislabelled $200!*

mis•laid [mɪs'leid] *v.* pt. and pp. of MISLAY.

mis•lay [mɪs'lei] *v.* **-laid, -lay•ing.** put (something) in a place and then forget where it is: *Mother is always mislaying her glasses.* **—mis'lay•er,** *n.*

mis•lead [mɪs'lid] *v.* **-led, -lead•ing.** cause to go in a wrong direction or to do or believe in something that is wrong: *Her cheerfulness misled us into believing that everything was all right. He was accused of misleading his followers.* **—mis'lead•er,** *n.*

mis•lead•ing [mɪs'lidɪŋ] *adj., v. —adj.* tending to mislead; deceptive or deceiving: *misleading advertising. The calmness of the sea was misleading.*
—v. ppr. of MISLEAD. **—mis'lead•ing•ly,** *adv.*

mis•led [mɪs'lɛd] *v.* pt. and pp. of MISLEAD.

mis•like [mɪs'ləik] *v.* **-liked, -lik•ing. 1** dislike. **2** *Archaic.* displease.

mis•man•age [mɪs'mænɪdʒ] *v.* **-aged, -ag•ing.** manage badly. **—mis'man•ag•er,** *n.* **—mis'man•age•ment,** *n.*

mis•match *v.* [mɪs'mætʃ]; *n.* ['mɪsmætʃ] *—v.* match incorrectly or unsuitably, or fail to match: *He was wearing a mismatched pair of socks.*
—n. a poor or unsuitable match: *That marriage is definitely a mismatch.*

mis•mate [mɪs'meit] *v.* **-mat•ed, -mat•ing.** mate unsuitably.

mis•name [mɪs'neim] *v.* **-named, -nam•ing.** call by a wrong or unsuitable name: *The slow horse was misnamed 'Lightning'.*

mis•no•mer [mɪs'noumər] *n.* **1** a wrong or unsuitable name or term: *'Lightning' is a misnomer for that slow old horse.* **2** an error in naming a person in a legal document. ⟨ME < AF < OF *mesnommer* < *mes-* wrongly (see MIS-) + *nommer* to name < L *nominare*⟩

mi•sog•a•my [mɪ'sɒgəmi] *n.* a hatred of marriage. ⟨< Gk. *misos* hatred + *gamos* marriage; formed on the pattern of *misogyny, misanthrope,* etc.⟩ **—,mis•o'gam•ic** [,mɪsə'gæmɪk], *adj.* **—mi'sog•a•mist,** *n.*

mi•sog•y•ny [mɪ'sɒdʒəni] *n.* a hatred of women. ⟨< Gk. *misogynia* < *misogynēs* woman-hater < *misos* hatred + *gynē* woman⟩ **—mi'sog•y•nist,** *n.* **—mi'sog•y•nous,** *adj.*

mi•sop•ro•stol [məi'sɒprə,stɒl] *n.* a drug used to treat certain ulcers.

mis•place [mɪs'pleis] *v.* **-placed, -plac•ing. 1** put in the wrong place: *a misplaced adjective.* **2** put (something) in a place and then forget where it is; mislay. **3** place (one's affections, trust, etc.) on an unworthy or unsuitable object. **—mis'place•ment,** *n.*

mis•play *n.* ['mɪsplei]; *v.* [mɪs'plei] *—n.* a wrong or unskilful play, as in a game: *A misplay in the last quarter almost cost us the game.*
—v. play wrongly or unskilfully.

mis•print *n.* ['mɪs,prɪnt]; *v.* [mɪs'prɪnt] *n., v. —n.* a mistake in printing.
—v. print incorrectly.

mis•pri•sion [mɪs'prɪʒən] *n.* **1** a wrongful action or omission, especially by a public official. **2** *Law.* the failure of an individual to give to the proper authorities information which he or she knows may lead to the apprehension of a felon: *misprision of treason.* ⟨ME < AF < OF *mesprision* < *mesprendre* mistake, act wrongly < *mes-* wrongly (see MIS-) + *prendre* take < L *prehendere*⟩

mis•prize [mɪs'praɪz] *v.* **-prized, -priz•ing.** despise; undervalue; slight. ⟨ME < OF *mesprisier* < *mes- wrongly* (see MIS-) + *prisier,* var. of *preisier* praise, ult. < L *pretium* price⟩

mis•pro•nounce [,mɪsprə'naʊns] *v.* **-nounced, -nounc•ing.** pronounce in a way considered incorrect. **—,mis•pro'nounc•er,** *n.* **—,mis•pro,nun•ci'a•tion** [,mɪsprə,nʌnsi'eiʃən], *n.*

mis•quo•ta•tion [,mɪskwou'teiʃən] *n.* **1** the act of misquoting. **2** an incorrect quotation.

mis•quote [mɪs'kwout] *v.* **-quot•ed, -quot•ing.** quote incorrectly. **—mis'quot•er,** *n.*

mis•read [mɪs'rid] *v.* **-read** [-'rɛd], **-read•ing. 1** read wrongly: *I misread tapering as papering and got the whole sentence wrong.* **2** misinterpret; misunderstand: *She misread his silence as agreement.* **—mis'read•er,** *n.*

mis•rep•re•sent [,mɪsrɛprɪ'zɛnt] *v.* **1** represent falsely; give a wrong or untrue idea of, especially in order to deceive: *She misrepresented the car when she said it was in good running order.* **2** be a bad or inadequate representative of: *His new novel misrepresents his status as a writer.* **—,mis•rep•re•sen'ta•tion,** *n.* **—,mis•rep•re'sen•ta•tive,** *adj.* **—,mis•rep•re'sent•er,** *n.*

mis•rule [mɪs'rul] *n., v.* **-ruled, -rul•ing.** *—n.* **1** bad or unwise rule. **2** disorder.
—v. rule badly; misgovern.

miss[1] [mɪs] *v., n. —v.* **1** fail to hit (a target): *He fired twice, but both shots missed. She missed the mark.* **2** fail to find, get, meet, attend, catch, hear, do, solve, etc.: *miss a train.* **3** let slip by; not seize: *I missed my chance.* **4** escape or avoid: *barely miss being hit.* **5** notice the absence of: *I did not miss my purse till I got home.* **6** feel keenly the absence of: *He missed his mother when she went away.* **7** fail to work properly; misfire: *The car was missing on two cylinders.* **8** leave out: *to miss a word in reading.* **9** lack: be without (*used only in progressive tenses*): *The bicycle is missing one pedal.*
miss one's guess, guess wrongly.
—n. a failure to hit, attain, etc.
a miss is as good as a mile, a close or narrow miss is in effect no better or worse than a wide miss.
give (something) **a miss,** *Slang.* not go to (an event or function) on purpose. ⟨OE *missan*⟩

miss[2] [mɪs] *n., pl.* **miss•es. 1** a girl or young woman. **2 Miss,** a title put before a girl's or unmarried woman's name: *Miss Brown, the Misses Brown, the Miss Browns.* **3 Miss,** a form of address used in place of the name of a girl or an unmarried woman: *I beg your pardon, Miss.* **4** a title given to a female winner of certain competitions: *Miss Canada.* ⟨short for *mistress*⟩

mis•said [mɪs'sɛd] *v.* pt. and pp. of MISSAY.

mis•sal ['mɪsəl] *n.* **1** *Roman Catholic Church.* a book containing the prayers, etc. for celebrating the Mass throughout the year. **2** any book of devotions, prayers, etc. ⟨< Med.L *missale* < LL *missa* Mass⟩
☛ *Hom.* MISSILE.

mis•say [mɪs'sei] *v.* **-said, -say•ing.** *Archaic.* **1** speak ill of; slander. **2** say wrongly. **3** speak wrongly.

mis•sense mutation ['mɪssɛns] *Genetics.* a mutation that changes a codon specific for one amino acid so that it codes for a different amino acid.

mis•shape [mɪs'ʃeip] *v.* **-shaped, -shaped** or **-shap•en, -shap•ing.** shape badly; deform; make in the wrong shape.

mis•shap•en [mɪs'ʃeipən] *adj., v. —adj.* badly shaped; deformed.
—v. a pp. of MISSHAPE. **—mis'shap•en•ly,** *adv.*
—mis'shap•en•ness, *n.*

mis•sile ['mɪsaɪl] *or* ['mɪsəl] *n.* **1** an object that is thrown or shot at a target, such as a stone, arrow, bullet, etc. **2** a self-propelled rocket containing explosives: *Missiles can be launched from land, air, or water.* ⟨< L *missilis,* ult. < *mittere* send⟩
☛ *Hom.* MISSAL ['mɪsəl].

mis•sile•man ['mɪsəlmən] *n., pl.* **-men.** *Esp. U.S.* a person whose work is designing, building, or operating guided missiles.

miss•ing ['mɪsɪŋ] *adj., v.* —*adj.* **1** out of the usual or a known place; lost or gone: *The missing ring was found under the dresser.* **2** absent: *Only two students were missing from class today. Two soldiers are missing, presumed killed.* **3** lacking or wanting: *It was quite a good dinner, but there was something missing.*
—*v.* ppr. of MISS.

mis•sion ['mɪʃən] *n.* **1** a sending or being sent on some special work; errand. **2** a group of persons sent on some special business: *She was one of a mission sent by our government to France.* **3** the business on which a person or group is sent: *Their mission was to blow up the bridge.* **4 a** an organization for the spread of a religious faith or for humanitarian work motivated by such belief; a society, etc. that recruits and sends missionaries. **b** the station or headquarters of such a mission. **5** a program or course of religious services for converting unbelievers or stimulating faith and zeal. **6 missions,** *pl.* organized missionary work, especially of Christian churches. **7** a district or local church served by a priest or pastor from a nearby parish. **8** a place where persons may go for aid, such as food, clothing, shelter, or counsel. **9** a particular purpose in life; calling: *He felt that his mission was to take care of his brother's children.* ⟨< L *missio, -onis* < *mittere* send⟩

mis•sion•ar•y ['mɪʃə,nɛri] *n., pl.* **-ar•ies. 1** a person sent by a church, etc. on a religious mission: *Many Christian churches have missionaries working at home or abroad.* **2** a person who works to advance some cause or idea: *a missionary for science.* **3** (*adjl.*) of, having to do with, or characteristic of missions or missionaries: *He spoke with missionary zeal of a new social order.*

mission furniture heavy, plain, dark furniture.

mission statement a paper issued by an organization, such as a university, government, corporation, etc. setting forth its objectives, goals, and future plans.

mis•sis ['mɪsəz] *n.* See MISSUS.

miss•ish ['mɪsɪʃ] *adj.* prim; prudish; affected.
—'miss•ish•ness, *n.*

Mis•sis•sip•pi [,mɪsə'sɪpi] *n.* **1** a southern state of the United States. **2** a very long river in the United States.

Mis•sis•sip•pi•an [,mɪsə'sɪpiən] *adj., n.* —*adj.* **1** of or having to do with Mississippi or the Mississippi River. **2** *Geology.* having to do with or designating the early Carboniferous period of the Paleozoic era in North America. See geological time chart in the Appendix.
—*n.* **1** a native or inhabitant of Mississippi. **2** *Geology.* the Mississippian period or rock system.

mis•sive ['mɪsɪv] *n. Literary.* a written message; letter. ⟨< Med.L *missivus,* ult. < L *mittere* send⟩

Mis•sou•ri [mə'zʊri] *n.* **1** a midwestern state of the United States. **2** a member of an American Indian people now living in Nebraska. **3** the Siouan language of these people.

mis•spell [mɪs'spɛl] *v.* **-spelled** or **-spelt, -spell•ing.** spell incorrectly. **—mis'spell•ing,** *n.*

mis•spelt [mɪs'spelt] *v.* a pt. and a pp. of MISSPELL.

mis•spend [mɪs'spɛnd] *v.* **-spent, -spend•ing.** spend foolishly or wrongly; waste: *the old man regretted having misspent his youth.* **—mis'spend•er,** *n.*

mis•spent [mɪs'spɛnt] *v.* pt. and pp. of MISSPEND.

mis•state [mɪs'steit] *v.* **-stat•ed, -stat•ing.** make incorrect or misleading statements about. **—mis'state•ment,** *n.* **—mis'stat•er,** *n.*

mis•step [mɪs'stɛp] *or* ['mɪsstɛp] *n.* **1** a wrong step: *A single misstep would have plunged her into the abyss.* **2** an error in judgment; blunder: *A misstep now could ruin his career.*

mis•sus ['mɪsəz] *n.* Often, **the missus,** *Informal.* wife: *You'll have to ask the missus about that. Are you going to bring your missus along?* Also, **missis.**
☛ *Usage.* See note at MRS.

miss•y ['mɪsi] *n., pl.* **missies.** *Informal.* little miss; miss.

mist [mɪst] *n., v.* —*n.* **1** a cloud of very fine drops of water in the air; fog. **2** anything that dims, blurs, or obscures: *The ideas were lost in a mist of long words.* **3** a haze before the eyes due to illness or tears.
—*v.* **1** come down in mist; rain in very fine drops. **2** become covered with or as if with mist (*often used with* **over** *or* **up**): *The bathroom window has misted.* **3** cover with or as if with mist: *Tears misted her eyes.* ⟨OE⟩

mis•tak•a•ble [mɪ'steikəbəl] *adj.* that may be mistaken or misunderstood. **—mis'tak•a•bly,** *adv.*

mis•take [mɪ'steik] *n., v.* **-took, -tak•en, -tak•ing.** —*n.* an error; blunder; misunderstanding of the meaning or use of something: *I used your towel by mistake.*
and no mistake, without a doubt; surely.
—*v.* **1** make a mistake regarding; misunderstand what is seen or heard: *She gave me the address but I mistook the street name and got lost.* **2** take wrongly; take to be some other person or thing: *I mistook that stick for a snake.* ⟨ME < ON *mistaka*⟩
☛ *Syn. n.* See note at ERROR.

mis•tak•en [mɪ'steikən] *adj., v.* —*adj.* **1** wrong in opinion; having made a mistake: *A mistaken person should admit his or her error.* **2** wrong; wrongly judged; misplaced: *It was a mistaken kindness to give that girl more candy.*
—*v.* pp. of MISTAKE. **—mis'tak•en•ly,** *adv.*

mis•ter ['mɪstər] *n.* **1 Mister,** the spoken form of MR., a title for a man, used before his last name or the name of his rank or office: *He always called his teacher 'Mister'.* **2** *Informal.* a title used in speaking to a man (*used alone, not with a name*): *Hey, mister! You dropped your wallet.* **3** *Informal.* husband: *How's your mister these days?* ⟨var. of *master*⟩
☛ *Usage.* When used as a title before a name or office, **Mister** is generally written in its abbreviated form: MR. Compare with the note at MRS.

mis•te•ri•o•so [mɪ,stiri'ousou] *adv. Music.* mysteriously. ⟨< Ital.⟩

mis•time [mɪs'taɪm] *v.* **-timed, -tim•ing. 1** say or do at the wrong time. **2** misstate the time of.

mis•tle•toe ['mɪsəl,tou] *n.* **1** any of various evergreen plants of the genera *Viscum* and *Phoradendron* that grow as parasites on certain trees; especially, a European shrub *V. album* often growing on apple trees, having yellow flowers and small, waxy white berries, traditionally used as a Christmas decoration. **2** (*adjl.*) designating the family (Loranthaceae) of parasitic plants that includes the mistletoes. **3** a sprig of mistletoe used as a Christmas decoration. ⟨OE *misteltān* < *mistel* mistletoe + *tān* twig⟩

Mistletoe

mis•took [mɪs'tʊk] *v.* pt. of MISTAKE.

mis•tral ['mɪstrəl] *or* [mɪs'trɑl] *n.* a cold, dry, northerly wind common in S France and neighbouring regions. ⟨< F < Provençal *mistral,* originally, dominant < L *magistralis* < *magister* master⟩

mis•trans•late [,mɪstrænz'leit] *or* [mɪs'trænzleit], [,mɪstræns'leit] *or* [mɪs'trænsleit] *v.* **-lat•ed, -lat•ing.** translate incorrectly. **—,mis•trans'la•tion,** *n.*

mis•treat [mɪs'trit] *v.* treat badly; abuse. **—mis'treat•ment,** *n.*

mis•tress ['mɪstrɪs] *n.* **1** a woman who has power or authority, such as the female head of a household or institution. **2** a woman or girl as owner or possessor: *The dog was sitting outside the door, waiting for its mistress.* **3** a woman having a thorough knowledge or mastery (of something): *mistress of the difficult art of fencing. She is mistress of the situation.* **4** a state or country that is in control or can rule; a personification of power: *Britain was mistress of the seas.* **5** a woman who has a continuing sexual relationship with a man who supports her, without being legally married to him. **6** *Archaic or poetic.* a woman loved and courted by a man; sweetheart: *"My mistress' eyes are nothing like the sun."* **7** *Brit.* a female teacher: *the dancing mistress.*
8 Mistress, *Archaic or dialect.* a title for a woman, used before the name. It is replaced in modern use by **Mrs.** (pronounced ['mɪsəz]), **Miss,** or **Ms.** ⟨ME < OF *maistresse* < *maistre.* See MASTER.⟩

mis•tri•al [mɪs'traɪəl] *n.* **1** a trial declared void in law because of some error or serious misconduct in the proceedings. **2** a trial that is inconclusive because the jury has failed to reach a verdict.

mis•trust [mɪs'trʌst] *v., n.* —*v.* have no confidence or trust in; doubt: *She mistrusted her ability to learn to swim.*
—*n.* a lack of trust or confidence; distrust. **—mis'trust•er,** *n.* **—mis'trust•ing•ly,** *adv.*

mis•trust•ful [mɪs'trʌstfəl] *adj.* lacking confidence; distrustful; doubting; suspicious. **—mis'trust•ful•ly,** *adv.*

mist•y ['mɪsti] *adj.* **mist•i•er, mist•i•est. 1** full of or covered with mist: *misty hills, misty air.* **2** not clearly seen or outlined: *a* *misty shape in the distance.* **3** as if seen through a mist; vague; indistinct: *a misty idea.* ⟨OE *mistig*⟩ **—'mist•i•ly,** *adv.* **—'mist•i•ness,** *n.*

mis•un•der•stand [ˌmɪsʌndər'stænd] *v.* **-stood, -stand•ing.** understand wrongly; take in a wrong sense; give the wrong meaning to. **—ˌmis•un•der'stand•er,** *n.*

mis•un•der•stand•ing [ˌmɪsʌndər'stændɪŋ] *n., v.* *—n.* **1** a failure to understand; a mistake as to meaning; wrong understanding. **2** a disagreement: *After their misunderstanding, they scarcely spoke to each other for months.*
—v. ppr. of MISUNDERSTAND. **—ˌmis•un•der'stand•ing•ly,** *adv.*

mis•un•der•stood [ˌmɪsʌndər'stʊd] *v., adj.* *—v.* pt. and pp. of MISUNDERSTAND.
—adj. not understood or properly appreciated: *As a child, he had always felt misunderstood.*

mis•us•age [mɪs'jusɪdʒ] *or* [mɪs'juzɪdʒ] *n.* **1** a wrong or improper usage, especially of words. **2** ill usage; harsh treatment.

mis•use *v.* [mɪs'juz]; *n.* [mɪs'jus] *v.* **-used, -us•ing;** *n.* *—v.* **1** use for the wrong purpose: *He misuses his knife at the table by lifting food with it.* **2** abuse; ill-treat: *She misuses her sled dogs by driving them too hard.*
—n. wrong, improper, or harsh usage: *the misuse of public funds, a misuse of words.*

Mit•chell's satyr ['mɪtʃəlz] a butterfly (*Neonympha mitchellii*) found in wetlands in Indiana and Michigan, and having spots and decorative striped borders on the wings. It is an endangered species.

mite [məit] *n.* **1** any of a large number of tiny arachnids (order Acarina) that are often parasites on plants or animals, and some of which carry diseases. Some species are so small they cannot be seen with the naked eye. **2** any very small object or creature: *I'm not really hungry, but I'll have just a mite of toast. I have a two-year-old, a darling little mite.* **3** a small coin or a small sum of money: *Though poor herself, she gave her mite to charity.*
4 *Informal.* bit; tad: *She's a mite greedy.* ⟨OE, defs. 2-4 influenced by MDu. *mite*⟩
☛ *Hom.* MIGHT.

mi•ter ['məitər] See MITRE.

mi•tered ['məitərd] See MITRED.

Mith•ra•ic [mɪθ'reiɪk] *adj.* of or having to do with Mithras or his cult.

Mith•ras ['mɪθræs] *n.* **1** *Persian mythology.* the god of light, truth, and justice, often taken as representing the sun. He became the object of an extensive cult during the late Roman Empire. **2** in Zoroastrianism, the angel of light who aided Ahura Mazda. ⟨< Gk. *Mithras* < *OPersian Mithra*⟩

mit•i•gate ['mɪtəˌgeit] *v.* **-gat•ed, -gat•ing.** make or become less severe, painful, or harsh; make or become mild or milder; soften or moderate: *to mitigate a person's anger, to mitigate pain, to mitigate the effects of war.* ⟨< L *mitigare* < *mitis* gentle⟩
—'mit•iˌga•tor, *n.* **—'mit•i•ga•ble** ['mɪtəgəbəl], *adj.*
—'mit•iˌgat•ed•ly, *adv.* **—ˌmit•i'ga•tion,** *n.* **—'mit•iˌga•tive,** *adj.*

mi•to•chon•dri•a [ˌməitou'kɒndriə] *n.* pl. of MITOCHONDRION.

mi•to•chon•dri•al [ˌməitou'kɒndriəl] *adj.* of or having to do with mitochondria.

mitochondrial disease one of several diseases caused by mutation in mitochondrial DNA.

mitochondrial inheritance the pattern of inheritance shown by mitochondrial diseases, which are transmitted only by the mother to children of both sexes.

mi•to•chon•dri•on [ˌməitou'kɒndriən] *n., pl.* **-dri•a.** *Biology.* any of the many organelles with their own unique DNA, in the cytoplasm of cells, important in cellular respiration. ⟨< NL < Gk. *mitos* a thread + *chondrion* small cartilage < *chondros* cartilage⟩ **—ˌmi•to'chon•dri•al,** *adj.*

mi•to•gen ['məitədʒən] *n.* an agent that initiates or increases the rate of mitosis. ⟨< *mito(sis)* + *-gen*⟩

mi•to•my•cin [ˌməitou'məisɪn] *n.* a drug used to treat certain forms of intestinal cancer.

mi•to•sis [məi'tousɪs] *or* [mɪ'tousɪs] *n.* *Biology.* the division of the nucleus of a living animal or plant cell to produce two daughter nuclei that are identical to the parent. In mitosis, each chromosome is exactly duplicated, forming two chromatids which separate and move apart, after which a new nuclear membrane forms around each group of daughter chromosomes and these daughter nuclei are then in most cases separated into two individual, identical daughter cells. Compare MEIOSIS. ⟨< NL < Gk. *mitos* thread⟩ **—mi'tot•ic** [məi'tɒtɪk] *or* [mɪ'tɒtik], *adj.*
—mi'tot•i•cal•ly, *adv.*

mi•to•tane ['məitəˌtein] *n.* a drug used to treat certain forms of cancer.

mi•tox•an•trone [məi'tɒksənˌtroun] *n.* a drug used to treat certain forms of cancer.

mi•tral valve ['məitrəl] *Anatomy.* the valve between the left atrium and the left ventricle of the heart that prevents a flow of blood from going back to the atrium during systole.

mi•tre ['məitər] *n., v.* **mi•tred, mi•tring.** *—n.* **1** a tall, pointed, folded cap worn by bishops and abbots during certain ceremonies as a symbol of office. **2** the official headdress of the ancient Jewish high priests. **3** MITRE JOINT. **4** the bevel on either of the pieces in a mitre joint. **5** a finished or hemmed corner on a garment, tablecloth, etc. made by joining the seam allowances of the sides in a diagonal seam.
—v. **1** bestow a mitre on; make a bishop. **2** join or prepare (ends of wood) for joining in a mitre joint. **3** finish (a corner of a hem) in a mitre. Also, **miter.** ⟨ME < OF < L < Gk. *mitra* headband⟩

mitre box *Carpentry.* a box designed to guide a saw in cutting a mitre joint.

mi•tred ['məitərd] *adj., v.* *—adj.* **1** having a mitre joint.
2 wearing a bishop's mitre. Also, **mitered.**
—v. pt. and pp. of MITRE.

mitre joint a right-angled joint made by cutting the ends of two pieces of wood, etc. on equal slants and fitting them together. Picture frames usually have mitre joints at the corners. See JOINT for picture.

mi•tre•wort ['məitərˌwɜrt] *n.* either of two species of the genus *Mitella,* a Canadian wildflower with green petals. It blooms in summer in damp places across Canada and northern U.S., and also in Asia.

mitt [mɪt] *n.* **1** mitten. **2** a padded, oversized glove used for catching the ball in baseball, etc.: *a catcher's mitt.* **3** a knitted or lace hand covering that resembles a glove but does not cover the fingers. **4** a mittenlike covering or pad worn over the hand, designed for a particular use: *a bath mitt, oven mitts.* **5** *Slang.* a hand. ⟨short for *mitten*⟩

mit•ten ['mɪtən] *n.* **1** a kind of winter glove covering the four fingers together and the thumb separately. **2** MITT (def. 3). ⟨< F *mitaine* half glove, ult. < L *medius* middle⟩

mix [mɪks] *v.* **mixed, mix•ing;** *n.* *—v.* **1** put together; stir well together: *mix ingredients to make a cake.* **2** prepare by blending different things: *to mix a cake.* **3** join: *mix business and pleasure.* **4** be mixable: *Milk and water mix.* **5** get along together; make friends easily: *She found it difficult to mix with strangers. He doesn't mix very well.* **6** confuse or muddle (*usually used with* **up**): *Don't mix me up; I'm trying to count. She got her facts mixed.*
—n. **1** mixture. **2** *Informal.* a mixed condition; mess. **3** an already mixed preparation: *a cake mix.* **4** ginger ale, soda water, etc. to mix with alcoholic drinks. ⟨< *mixt* mixed < F < L *mixtus,* pp. of *miscere* mix⟩ **—ˌmix•a'bil•i•ty,** *n.* **—'mix•a•ble,** *adj.*
☛ *Syn. v.* **1. Mix,** BLEND = put two or more things together. **Mix** emphasizes forming a mass or compound in which the parts or ingredients are well scattered or spread into one another: *Mix the dry ingredients before adding a liquid.* **Blend** = mix thoroughly and smoothly together, or one thing little by little into the other, so that each part loses its separate and distinct existence and the whole has the qualities of both (or all): *Blend the flour into the melted butter.*

mixed [mɪkst] *adj., v.* *—adj.* **1** put together or formed by mixing; composed of different parts or elements; of different kinds combined: *mixed emotions.* **2** of different classes, kinds, etc.; assorted: *mixed candy.* **3** of or for persons of both sexes: *mixed company. She sings in the mixed chorus.*
mixed up, involved; concerned, especially in something dishonest or disreputable (*used with* **in** *or* **with**): *She was mixed up in a plot to overthrow the king.*
—v. pt. and pp. of MIX.

mixed bag *Informal.* a collection of different people or things; assortment: *The people at the party were really a mixed bag.*

mixed blessing an advantage that has some disadvantageous aspects.

mixed doubles *Tennis, etc.* a match for two couples, each a man and a woman.

mixed farm a farm on which both crops and livestock are raised. **—mixed farming.**

mixed grill a dish consisting of several different kinds of meat, such as liver, sausage, and lamb chop, broiled or grilled, served with vegetables.

mixed marriage a marriage between persons of different races or religions.

mixed media 1 the use of various types of visual and audio media together. 2 a technique of drawing or painting using several different media, as ink, chalk, and pencil, oil, impasto, etc.

mixed metaphor a metaphor in which two or more different images or ideas get confused. *Example*: The horse sailed down the course at full throttle.

mixed number a number consisting of a whole number and a fraction, such as 1 ½, 16 ⅔.

mixed train a train having both freight and passenger cars.

mixed–up ['mɪkst 'ʌp] *adj.* bewildered; emotionally unbalanced: *a mixed-up youth*.

mix•er ['mɪksər] *n.* **1** an apparatus or appliance for mixing foods, etc. **2** a person whose work is mixing ingredients. **3** a person who gets along well with others, making friends easily: *She is a good mixer.* **4** MIX (def. 4). **5** *Electronics.* a device which combines various input signals into one output signal. **6** a person who equalizes the amplification of different sounds, as of voices and instruments, to create a balanced effect. **7** an informal party where people can mingle.

mixing valve a valve controlling both hot and cold water so as to produce water of the desired temperature.

Mix•tec ['mistɛk] *n.* **1** a member of an American Indian people living in Mexico. **2** the Mixtecan language of these people.

Mix•tec•an [mis'tɛkən] *n.* an Oto-Manguean language family of Mexico.

mix•ture ['mɪkstʃər] *n.* **1** a mixing or being mixed. **2** something made by mixing: *The mixture is put into a greased dish and baked. Green is a mixture of blue and yellow.* **3** *Chemistry.* a substance consisting of two or more ingredients that keep their individual chemical properties and can be separated by non-chemical means: *A sugar-and-water mixture can be separated by boiling off the water.* Compare COMPOUND[1] (def. 2). ⟨< L *mistura* < *miscere* mix⟩

mix–up ['mɪks,ʌp] *n. Informal.* **1** confusion; mess. **2** a confused fight.

miz•zen ['mɪzən] *n.* **1** a fore-and-aft sail on the mizzenmast. See YAWL for picture. **2** mizzenmast. ⟨< F < Ital. *mezzana* < L *medianus* in the middle < *medius* middle⟩

miz•zen•mast ['mɪzən,mæst] *or* ['mɪzənməst] *n.* the mast next behind the mainmast on a sailing ship or sailboat. See MAST[1] and YAWL for pictures.

mk. mark.

mks METRE-KILOGRAM-SECOND.

mkt. market.

mL millilitre(s).

MLA or **M.L.A.** MEMBER OF THE LEGISLATIVE ASSEMBLY.

MLG MIDDLE LOW GERMAN.

Mlle or **Mlle.** *pl.* **Mlles** or **Mlles.** Mademoiselle.

mm millimetre(s).

MM. or **MM** Messieurs.

M.M. MILITARY MEDAL.

Mme or **Mme.** *pl.* **Mmes** or **Mmes.** Madame.

MMM *Cdn.* Member of the Order of Military Merit.

Mn manganese.

MNA or **M.N.A.** MEMBER OF THE NATIONAL ASSEMBLY.

mne•mon•ic [nɪ'mɒnɪk] *adj., n.* *—adj.* **1** aiding or intended to aid memory: *a set of mnemonic symbols.* **2** of or having to do with memory: *great mnemonic power.*
—n. a device to aid the memory. **—mne'mon•i•cal•ly,** *adv.* ⟨< Gk. *mnēmonikos* < *mnamnasthai* remember⟩

Mne•mos•y•ne [nɪ'mɒsə,ni] *or* [nɪ'mɒzə,ni] *n. Greek mythology.* the goddess of memory and mother of the Muses.

mo [mou] *interj. Brit. Informal.* moment: *I won't be a mo.* ⟨short for MOMENT⟩
☛ *Hom.* MOT, MOW.

mo. month(s).

Mo molybdenum.

M.O. **1** MONEY ORDER. **2** Medical Officer.

mo•a ['mouə] *n.* any of several extinct, flightless birds of New Zealand (family Dinornithidae), most of them very large, including one species that stood about 3.5 m tall. The moas looked something like the modern kiwi or the ostrich. ⟨< Maori⟩

moan [moun] *n., v.* *—n.* **1** a long, low sound of suffering. **2** any similar sound: *the moan of the wind.* **3** complaint or lamentation.
—v. **1** make moans. **2** utter with a moan. **3** complain: *She was always moaning about her luck.* **4** grieve or lament: *He moaned the loss of his friends.* ⟨ME *man*; cf. OE *mǣnan* complain⟩ **—'moan•ing•ly,** *adv.*
☛ *Syn. v.* **1.** See note at GROAN.

moat [mout] *n., v.* *—n.* **1** a deep, wide ditch dug around a castle or town as a protection against enemies. Moats were usually kept filled with water. See CASTLE for picture. **2** a similar ditch used to separate areas in a zoo.
—v. surround with a moat. ⟨ME *mote* < OF mound⟩
☛ *Hom.* MOTE.

mob [mɒb] *n., v.* **mobbed, mob•bing.** *—n.* **1** a large number of people; crowd: *There was a great mob at the gate, waiting to get in.* **2** an uncontrollable crowd, easily moved to destructive or riotous action: *The crowd had turned into an ugly mob.* **3** *Slang.* **a** a gang of criminals. **b the mob,** the Mafia. **4 the mob, a** the common mass of people, thought of as lacking taste, culture, judgment, etc.; the masses; rabble.
—v. **1** attack with violence, as a mob does. **2** crowd around too closely in excessive eagerness, curiosity, etc.: *Autograph hunters mobbed the singer outside her hotel.* ⟨shortened form of L *mobile vulgus* fickle common people⟩

mob•cap ['mɒb,kæp] *n.* a large, loose cap, fitting down over the ears, formerly worn indoors by women. ⟨< obs. *mob* muffle the head⟩

mo•bile[1] ['moubaɪl] *or* ['moubəl] *adj.* **1** capable of moving or of being moved around: *A car is a mobile machine.* **2** easily changed; quick to change from one position to another: *mobile features, a mobile mind.* **3** allowing or undergoing movement from one social class to another: *a mobile society, mobile professionals.* ⟨< L *mobilis* movable < *movere* move⟩

mo•bile[2] ['moubaɪl] *or* ['moubil] *n.* an artistic construction of small metal, plastic, wood, or paper shapes suspended from a balanced arrangement of more or less horizontal bars or wires, etc. so that the shapes will move in a current of air. ⟨< *mobile[1]*⟩

Mobile Command *Cdn.* a major organizational element of the Canadian Forces, whose role is to maintain combat-ready land forces to meet Canada's national and international defence commitments; the land services for defence.

mobile home **1** a large trailer used as a more or less permanent home. Compare MOTOR HOME. **2** a prefabricated house which is moved to the chosen site.

mo•bil•i•ty [mou'bɪləti] *n.* a being mobile; ability or readiness to move or be moved.

mo•bi•lize ['moubə,laɪz] *v.* **-lized, -liz•ing. 1** call (troops, warships, etc.) into active military service; organize for war. **2** assemble and prepare for war: *The troops mobilized quickly.* **3** put into action or active use: *mobilize the wealth of a country.* ⟨< F *mobiliser* < *mobile* mobile⟩ **—'mo•bi,liz•a•ble,** *adj.* **—,mo•bi•li'za•tion,** *n.* **—'mo•bi,liz•er,** *n.*

Mö•bi•us strip ['meibiəs], ['moubiəs], *or* ['mibiəs]; *German,* ['mœbiʊs] a one-sided, continuous surface, bounded by a continuous curve, made by twisting one end of a long, narrow, rectangular strip through 180° and joining it to the other end. Also, **Moebius strip.** ⟨< A.F. *Möbius* (1790-1868), German mathematician⟩

mob•ster ['mɒbster] *n. Slang.* a member of a gang of criminals.

moc•ca•sin ['mɒkəsən] *or* ['mɒkəzən] *Cdn. n.* **1** a soft, heelless leather shoe or boot having the bottom and sides made of a single piece of leather which is joined in a puckered seam to the rounded piece forming the top. Moccasins were the traditional footwear of many American Indian and First Nations peoples. **2** a shoe or slipper similar in construction or appearance. ⟨< Algonquian⟩

moccasin dance *Cdn. Slang.* a dance, often held outdoors or in a rink, for which moccasins are worn.

moccasin flower *Cdn.* any of several lady's-slippers, especially one (*Cypripedium acaule*) having pink or, sometimes, white flowers, found from Newfoundland to Alberta and south to Georgia and Alabama.

Moccasin flowers

moccasin telegraph *Cdn. Informal.* **1** GRAPEVINE (def. 2). **2** formerly, the sending of messages by First Nations runner.

mo•cha ['moukə] *n., adj.* —*n.* **1** a choice variety of coffee originally coming from the Arabian peninsula. **2** a flavouring made from strong coffee or a mixture of coffee and cocoa or chocolate. **3** (*adjl.*) flavoured with mocha. **4** a soft suede leather made from sheepskin, used especially for gloves. **5** a dark brown; chocolate brown.
—*adj.* dark chocolate brown. ⟨< *Mocha*, a port in SW Yemen⟩

mock [mɒk] *v., adj., n.* —*v.* **1** laugh at; make fun of. **2** make fun of by copying or imitating. **3** imitate; copy. **4** scoff. **5** make light of; pay no attention to. **6** deceive or disappoint.
—*adj.* not real; sham or imitation: *a mock battle.*
—*n.* **1** an action or speech that mocks. **2** a person or thing scorned or deserving scorn.
make mock of, ridicule. ⟨ME < OF *mocquer*⟩ —**'mock•er,** *n.*
☛ *Syn. v.* **1.** See note at RIDICULE.

mock•er•nut hickory ['mɒkər,nʌt] a rare tree (*Carya tomentosa*) found only at the western end of Lake Erie, having compound leaves that are fragrant when crushed, and bearing edible nuts.

mock•er•y ['mɒkəri] *n., pl.* **-er•ies. 1** a making fun; ridicule. **2** a person or thing to be made fun of: *He had become a mockery in the village.* **3** a poor copy or imitation. **4** a travesty: *The trial was a mockery of justice.*
make mockery of, ridicule.

mock–he•ro•ic ['mɒk hɪ'rouɪk] *adj., n.* —*adj.* imitating or burlesquing what is heroic. Pope's *Rape of the Lock* is a mock-heroic poem.
—*n.* an imitation or burlesque of what is heroic.

mock•ing ['mɒkɪŋ] *adj., v.* —*adj.* that mocks; ridiculing or mimicking: *mocking laughter.*
—*v.* ppr. of MOCK. —**'mock•ing•ly,** *adv.*

mock•ing•bird ['mɒkɪŋ,bərd] *n.* a North American songbird (*Minus polyglottos*) related to the thrashers, famous for being able to imitate the songs of other birds. It is especially common in the southern United States.

mock orange or **mock–orange** ['mɒk 'ɔrɪndʒ] any of a genus (*Philadelphus*) of shrubs of the saxifrage family having showy white, sometimes fragrant flowers. Several species of mock orange are widely grown in temperate regions as ornamentals.

mock sun parhelion.

mock turtle soup a soup made in imitation of green turtle soup.

mock–up ['mɒk ,ʌp] *n.* a full-sized model of an aircraft, machine, piece of landscape, etc., built accurately to scale and used for display or for teaching or experimental purposes.

mo•cock ['mɑkɑk] *or* [mə'kɑk] *n. Cdn.* a box or container made of birchbark, often used to hold maple sugar, wild rice, berries, etc. ⟨< Algonquian/Ojibwa *makak*⟩

mod•a•cryl•ic [,mɒdə'krɪlɪk] *adj.* designating any of various synthetic fibres made by copolymerization of acrylonitrile with modifying materials such as vinyl chloride. Modacrylic fibres contain between 35 percent and 85 percent of acrylonitrile. ⟨shortened form of *modified acrylic*⟩

mo•dal ['moudəl] *adj., n.* —*adj.* **1** *Grammar.* of, having to do with, or being a verb form or auxiliary verb that characteristically expresses action, state, or quality in terms of possibility, probability, power, etc. rather than simple fact. *Can, may, will, should, ought,* etc. are modal verbs. **2** of or having to do with mode, manner, or form. **3** *Music.* of or in one of the modes that preceded the modern diatonic scales.
—*n. Grammar.* MODAL AUXILIARY. ⟨< Med.L *modalis* < L *modus* measure⟩

modal auxiliary *Grammar.* an auxiliary verb, such as *may, can, must, would,* and *should,* used with a verb expressing action, state, or quality to indicate possibility, probability, obligation, etc.

mo•dal•i•ty [mou'dæləti] *n.* **1** the fact, state, or quality of being modal. **2** form. **3** mode; method. **4** *Medicine.* a therapeutic method or apparatus, especially physiotherapy or electrotherapy. **5** *Logic.* a proposition having some qualification, such as contingency, necessity, possibility, or impossibility.

mode[1] [moud] *n.* **1** the manner or way in which a thing is done. **2** *Grammar.* MOOD[2]. **3** *Music.* **a** any of various arrangements of the tones of an octave. **b** either of the two main scale systems in modern music: *major and minor modes.* **c** any of various Greek or medieval scales, each having a different pattern of intervals: *The keyboard of the modern piano represents the Dorian mode.* **4** *Logic.* **a** the form of a proposition with reference to the necessity, contingency, possibility, or impossibility of its content. **b** any of the various forms of valid syllogisms, depending on the quantity and type of their constitutent propositions. **5** the actual mineral composition of a sample of igneous rock, stated quantitatively in percentages by mass. **6** *Computer technology.* the state of a device or program indicating the type of operations it is ready to perform: *The printer is in letter-quality mode.* ⟨< L *modus* measure⟩

mode[2] [moud] *n.* the style, fashion, or custom that prevails; the way most people are behaving, talking, dressing, etc. ⟨< F < L *modus* mode[1]⟩

Mod.E MODERN ENGLISH.

mod•el ['mɒdəl] *n., v.* **-elled** or **-eled, -el•ling** or **-el•ing;** *adj.* —*n.* **1** a small copy: *a model of a ship.* **2** a figure, object, etc. in clay, wax, etc. that is to be copied in marble, bronze, etc.: *a model for a statue.* **3** a particular style or design of a thing: *Some car makers produce a new model every year.* **4** a descriptive hypothesis: *the Copernican model of the universe.* **5** a thing or person to be imitated: *The boy wrote so well that the teacher used his composition as a model for the class.* **6** a person, especially a woman, who poses for artists, photographers, etc. **7** a person employed to help sell clothing by wearing it for customers to see. **8** a figure of an item not yet made that serves as a plan for producing the finished item: *City Hall has displayed a model of what the new stadium will look like.*
on the model of, analogous(ly) to; in imitation of.
—*v.* **1** make; shape; fashion; design; plan: *model a bird's nest in clay.* **2** in drawing or painting, show the effects of light and shade on objects or figures to make them appear three-dimensional. **3** make models; design: *model in clay.* **4** follow as a model; form (something) after a particular model: *He modelled himself on his father.* **5** be a model (of). **6** work as a model; display (clothes) by wearing them: *That woman usually models evening gowns.*
—*adj.* **1** used or serving as a model. **2** just right or perfect, especially in conduct: *a model child.* ⟨< F < Ital. *modello,* dim. of *modo* mode[1]⟩ —**'mod•el•ler** or **'mod•el•er,** *n.*
☛ *Syn. n.* **5. Model,** EXAMPLE, PATTERN = someone or something to be copied or followed. **Model** applies to a person or thing thought especially worth copying or imitating: *This famous surgeon is Andrea's model.* **Example** applies to a person, to his or her conduct, or to actions of his or hers that are likely for some reason to be imitated: *He follows his father's example.* **Pattern** applies particularly to a fine example or model set up worth imitating or following closely: *Her book gives a pattern for behaviour.*

mod•el•ling or **mod•el•ing** ['mɒdəlɪŋ] *n., v.* —*n.* **1** the act or occupation of a model: *He is interested in fashion modelling. Modelling is the best teaching technique.* **2** the making of solid forms or figures in clay, wax, etc., especially by pressing and shaping with the hands. **3** in drawing or painting, the showing of the effects of light and shade on objects or figures to give a three-dimensional appearance.
—*v.* ppr. of MODEL.

mo•dem ['moudəm] *n. Computer technology.* a device which enables a computer to receive and send data over telephone lines. ⟨< *mo*(*dulator*) + *dem*(*odulator*)⟩

mod•er•ate *adj., n.* ['mɒdərɪt]; *v.* ['mɒdə,reit] *adj., n., v.* **-at•ed, -at•ing.** —*adj.* **1** kept or keeping within proper bounds; not extreme: *moderate expenses, moderate styles.* **2** not violent; calm or gentle: *moderate winds.* **3** fair; medium; not very large or good: *a moderate profit.*
—*n.* a person who holds moderate opinions.
—*v.* **1** make or become less extreme or violent: *The wind is moderating.* **2** act as moderator; preside (over). ⟨< L *moderatus,* pp. of *moderare* regulate < *modus* measure⟩ —**'mod•er•ate•ly,** *adv.* —**'mod•er•ate•ness,** *n.*
☛ *Syn. adj.* **1, 2. Moderate,** TEMPERATE mean 'not extreme in any way', and are often interchangeable. But **moderate** emphasizes freedom from excess, not going beyond or above the proper, right, or reasonable limit: *He is a moderate eater.* **Temperate** emphasizes restraint, holding back within limits, especially with regard to the feelings or appetites: *He feels things deeply, but is always temperate in speech.*

moderate breeze *Meteorology.* a wind with a speed between 20 km/h and 28 km/h. See chart of Beaufort scale in the Appendix.

moderate gale *Meteorology.* a wind with a speed between 50 km/h and 61 km/h. See chart of Beaufort scale in the Appendix.

mod•er•a•tion [ˌmɒdəˈreiʃən] *n.* **1** freedom from excess; proper restraint; temperance. **2** a moderating or moving away from an extreme: *The rain brought moderation to the uncomfortably hot weather.* **3** calmness; lack of violence.
in moderation, within limits; not going to extremes: *He eats sweets in moderation.*

mod•e•ra•to [ˌmɒdəˈrɑtou] *adj., adv., n. Music.*
—adj. or adv. in moderate time.
—n. a moderate movement or passage; a composition to be played or sung at this tempo. ⟨< Ital. < L *moderātus* moderate⟩

mod•er•a•tor [ˈmɒdəˌreitər] *n.* **1** a presiding officer; chairperson. **2** an arbitrator; mediator. **3** the chief elected officer of certain churches, such as the United Church of Canada. **4** material used in a nuclear reactor to slow down nuclear fission.

mod•ern [ˈmɒdərn] *adj., n. —adj.* **1** of the present time or times not long past: *Television is a modern invention. We speak modern English.* **2** using or involving recent techniques, ideas, etc.; up-to-date; not old-fashioned: *Do you like modern jazz?*
—n. **1** a person of the present time or of times not long past: *He is studying English dramatists, specializing in the moderns.* **2** a person who has modern ideas and tastes. ⟨< LL *modernus* < L *modo* just now (originally, with measure, ablative of *modus* measure)⟩ **—ˈmod•ern•ly,** *adv.* **—ˈmod•ern•ness,** *n.*
☛ *Syn. adj.* **1.** See note at NEW.

Modern English the English language from about 1500 to the present.

Modern French the French language from about 1600 to the present.

Modern Greek the Greek language from about 1500 to the present.

Modern Hebrew the adaptation of ancient Hebrew spoken as a native language in present-day Israel.

mod•ern•ism [ˈmɒdərˌnɪzəm] *n.* **1** modern attitudes, methods, etc. or sympathy with what is modern. **2** Usually, **Modernism,** the tendency to interpret the teachings of the Bible or the Christian church in accordance with modern scientific theories. **3** a modern word, phrase, or practice.

mod•ern•ist [ˈmɒdərnɪst] *n.* **1** a person who holds modern views or follows modern techniques or ideas. **2** Usually, **Modernist,** a person who advocates or adheres to theological Modernism.

mod•ern•is•tic [ˌmɒdərˈnɪstɪk] *adj.* **1** of or having to do with modernism or modernists. **2** following modern styles, methods, etc., especially in art or music. **—ˌmod•ernˈis•ti•cal•ly,** *adv.*

mo•der•ni•ty [məˈdɜrnəti] *or* [mouˈdɜrnəti] *n., pl.* **-ties. 1** a being modern. **2** something modern. **3** modern times.

mod•ern•i•za•tion [ˌmɒdərnəˈzeiʃən] *or* [ˌmɒdərnaɪˈzeiʃən] *n.* **1** a modernizing or being modernized. **2** something modernized; a modernized version.

mod•ern•ize [ˈmɒdərˌnaɪz] *v.* **-ized, -iz•ing. 1** make modern; bring up to present ways or standards. **2** adopt modern ideas, techniques, etc. **—ˈmod•ernˌiz•er,** *n.*

mod•est [ˈmɒdɪst] *adj.* **1** having or showing a moderate estimate of one's own abilities or merits: *a modest reply. She is very modest about her accomplishments.* **2** unassertive or diffident: *modest behaviour.* **3** proper and respectable in dress and conduct. **4** not extreme or excessive: *a modest request.* **5** not pretentious, gaudy, etc.: *a modest living room.* ⟨< L *modestus* in due measure < *modus* measure⟩ **—ˈmod•est•ly,** *adv.*
☛ *Syn.* **Modest,** DEMURE = not bold or pushing oneself forward in the presence of others. **Modest** emphasizes a sense of fit and proper behaviour and a lack of conceit that hold a person back from calling attention to himself or herself: *I like a modest boy, one who is neither shy nor bold.* **Demure,** usually applied to women, now chiefly suggests an unnatural modesty or pretended shyness thought to be attractive and put on for effect: *She sipped her soda and looked demure.*

mod•es•ty [ˈmɒdɪsti] *n., pl.* **-ties. 1** the quality or condition of being modest. **2** simplicity.

mod•i•cum [ˈmɒdəkəm] *n.* a small or moderate quantity: *a modicum of good sense.* ⟨< L *modicum,* neut., moderate < *modus* measure⟩

mod•i•fi•ca•tion [ˌmɒdəfəˈkeiʃən] *n.* **1** a slight or partial change in form: *a modification in plans.* **2** a reduction; a making less; moderation. **3** a limitation or qualification of a statement. **4** a modified form or variety: *The most recent modification of the long-range missile performs flawlessly.* **5** *Biology.* a change in an animal or plant caused by environment and not inheritable.

mod•i•fi•er [ˈmɒdəˌfaɪər] *n.* **1** a person or thing that modifies. **2** *Grammar.* a word or group of words that limits the meaning of another word or group of words. In *a very tight coat,* the adjective *tight* is a modifier of *coat,* and the adverb *very* is a modifier of *tight.*

mod•i•fy [ˈmɒdəˌfaɪ] *v.* **-fied, -fy•ing. 1** change somewhat: *to modify the terms of a lease.* **2** make less; reduce or moderate: *to modify one's demands.* **3** *Grammar.* limit the meaning of; qualify. Adverbs modify verbs, adjectives, and other adverbs. **4** *Biology.* bring about or make important structural changes in (a part), usually resulting in a different function or orientation of the part. The tusk of a narwhal is a modified tooth. In birds, the front limbs have become modified for flight. ⟨< L *modificare* limit < *modus* measure + *facere* make⟩ **—ˈmod•iˌfi•a•ble,** *adj.*

mod•ish [ˈmoudɪʃ] *adj.* fashionable; stylish. **—ˈmod•ish•ly,** *adv.* **—ˈmod•ish•ness,** *n.*

mo•diste [mouˈdist] *n.* a maker of or dealer in women's clothes, hats, etc.; dressmaker or milliner. ⟨< F⟩

Mo•dred [ˈmoudrɪd] *n. Arthurian legend.* King Arthur's treacherous nephew, who led the rebellion against Arthur. Also called **Mordred**.

mod•u•lar [ˈmɒdʒələr] *or* [ˈmɒdjələr] *adj.* **1** of, having to do with, or based on a module or modulus. **2** designed or constructed in standardized sizes or units that can be interchanged and fitted together in a variety of ways: *modular storage units, modular furniture.*

mod•u•late [ˈmɒdʒəˌleit] *or* [ˈmɒdjəˌleit] *v.* **-lat•ed, -lat•ing. 1** regulate; adjust; vary; soften; tone down. **2** alter (the voice) for expression. **3** *Music.* change from one key to another. **4** *Radio.* **a** vary the frequency of (electrical waves). **b** change (a radio current) by adding sound waves to it. ⟨< L *modulari,* ult. < *modus* measure⟩

mod•u•la•tion [ˌmɒdʒəˈleiʃən] *or* [ˌmɒdjəˈleiʃən] *n.* **1** a modulating or being modulated. **2** *Music.* a change from one key to another. **3** *Electronics.* a varying of high-frequency waves to match a signal.

mod•u•la•tor [ˈmɒdʒəˌleitər] *or* [ˈmɒdjəˌleitər] *n.* **1** a person who or thing that modulates. **2** a device for varying the range of frequency of a signal or wave in radio, television, etc.

mod•ule [ˈmɒdʒul] *or* [ˈmɒdjul] *n.* **1** a standard or unit for measuring. **2** the size of some part taken as a unit of measure. **3** a standardized piece or component. **4** an independent unit that forms part of a larger, complex structure, program, etc. The command module of a spacecraft can function independently. ⟨< L *modulus,* dim. of *modus* measure. Doublet of MOULD[1].⟩

mod•u•lus [ˈmɒdʒələs] *or* [ˈmɒdjələs] *n., pl.* **-li** [-ˌlaɪ] *or* [-ˌli]. *Mathematics.* **1** of a complex number, the numerical length of the vector representing the complex number. **2** the number by which a logarithm to a certain base is multiplied, to give the corresponding logarithm to another base. **3** an integer which can be divided exactly into the difference between two other integers. *Example*: a modulus of 4 and 14 is 5.

mo•dus o•pe•ran•di [ˈmoudəs ˌɒpəˈrændaɪ] *or* [ˌɒpəˈrændi] *Latin.* a method or manner of working.

mo•dus vi•ven•di [ˈmoudəs vəˈvendaɪ] *or* [vəˈvendi] *Latin.* **1** a mode of living; a way of getting along. **2** a temporary arrangement while waiting for a final settlement.

Moebius strip See MÖBIUS STRIP.

mo•gul[1] [ˈmougʌl], [ˈmougəl], *or* [mouˈgʌl] *n.* **1 Mogul,** a Mongolian, especially one of the Mongol conquerors of India in the 16th century or one of their descendants. **2** an important or influential person; magnate. ⟨< Arabic and Persian *Mugul* < the native name *Mongol*⟩

mo•gul[2] [ˈmougəl] *n.* a mound or bump of hard snow on a ski run. ⟨< Norwegian⟩

M.O.H. Medical Officer of Health.

mo•hair [ˈmouhɛr] *n.* **1** cloth or yarn made from the long, silky hair of the Angora goat, sometimes blended with other fibres, such as wool or cotton. **2** the hair of the Angora goat. **3** (*adj.*) made of mohair or covered with it: *mohair yarn, a mohair coat.* ⟨ult. < Arabic *mukhayyar*; conformed to *hair*⟩

Mo•ham•med [mou'hɑmɪd] *or* [mou'hæmɪd] *n.* A.D. 570?-632, a prophet and the founder of Islam, one of the world's great religions. His words are preserved in the Koran. Also, **Muhammad.**

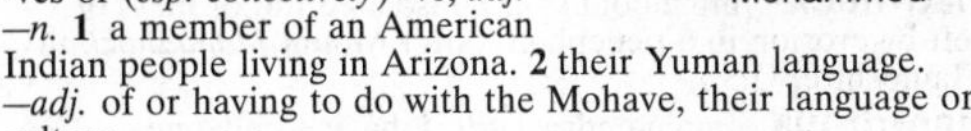

Mohammed

Mo•ham•med•an [mou'hɑmədən] *or* [mou'hæmədən] *adj., n. —adj.* of or having to do with Mohammed or Islam.
—n. Muslim.

Mo•ham•med•an•ism [mou'hɑmədə,nɪzəm] *or* [mou'hæmədə,nɪzəm] *n.* Islam.

Mo•ha•ve [mou'hɑvi] *n., pl.* **-ves** or (*esp. collectively*) **-ve;** *adj.* *—n.* **1** a member of an American Indian people living in Arizona. **2** their Yuman language.
—adj. of or having to do with the Mohave, their language or culture.

Mo•hawk ['mouhɒk] *n., pl.* **-hawks** or (*esp. collectively*) **-hawk;** *adj. —n.* **1** a member of a First Nations people now living mainly in southern Ontario and Québec. The Mohawk belonged to the Iroquois Confederacy. **2** the Iroquoian language of the Mohawk.
—adj. **1** of or having to do with the Mohawk or their language. **2** of or being a haircut leaving only a central raised portion: *a Mohawk cut.*

Mo•hi•can [mou'hikən] *n., pl.* **-cans** or (*esp. collectively*) **-can;** *adj. —n.* a member of either of two closely related American Indian peoples of the eastern United States, the **Mahican** of the upper Hudson River valley and the **Mohegan** of southeastern Connecticut.
—adj. of or having to do with either of these peoples.
⟨< Algonquian, wolf⟩

Mo•hole ['mou,houl] *n.* a drilling project for geological study of the earth's crust down through the Mohorovicic discontinuity. ⟨< *Mo*(*horovicic*) + *hole.* See MOHOROVICIC DISCONTINUITY.⟩

Mo•ho•ro•vi•cic discontinuity [,mouhə'rouvə,tʃɪtʃ] *Geology.* a rock layer separating the earth's crust and its mantle at a depth of about 10 km under ocean beds and about 32 km on land. ⟨after Andrija *Mohorovicic,* a Yugoslavian geologist who discovered it in 1909⟩

moi•dore ['mɔɪdɔr] *n.* a former gold coin of Portugal, worth about $6.50. ⟨< Pg. *moeda d'ouro* coin of gold⟩

moi•e•ty ['mɔɪəti] *n., pl.* **-ties. 1** half. **2** an indefinite part: *Only a moiety of high-school graduates go to college.* ⟨ME < OF < LL *medietas* half < L *medietas* the middle < *medius* middle⟩

moil [mɔɪl] *v., n. —v.* work hard; drudge.
—n. **1** hard work; drudgery. **2** trouble; confusion. ⟨ME < OF *moillier* moisten < L *mollis* soft⟩

moiré or **moire** [mwɑ'rei], [mwɑr], *or* [mɔ'rei] *n., adj. —n.* **1** cloth having an irregular, wavy finish; watered fabric. **2** the watery pattern itself.
—adj. having such a finish; watered: *moiré taffeta.* ⟨< F *moire,* alteration of E *mohair*⟩

moist [mɔɪst] *adj.* **1** slightly wet; damp. **2** humid. **3** filled with tears: *His eyes were moist, but he did not cry.* ⟨ME < OF *moiste* < LL *muccidus* mouldy, musty < L *mucus* mucus⟩ **—'moist•ly,** *adv.* **—'moist•ness,** *n.*
☛ *Syn.* **1.** See note at DAMP.

moist•en ['mɔɪsən] *v.* make or become moist: *He moistened his dry lips. Her eyes moistened with tears.*

mois•ture ['mɔɪstʃər] *n.* a slight wetness; water or other liquid spread in very small drops in or on something.

mo•ksha ['moukʃə] *n. Buddhism, Hinduism, Jainism.* spiritual release and freedom from the ongoing cycle of death and rebirth; the final state of mystical bliss. ⟨< Skt.⟩

mol MOLE[4].

mo•lar[1] ['moulər] *n., adj. —n.* a tooth with a broad surface for grinding. A person's back teeth are molars. See TEETH for picture.
—adj. **1** pulverizing by friction; grinding or capable of grinding. **2** of or having to do with the molar teeth. ⟨< L *molaris* < *mola* mill⟩

mo•lar[2] ['moulər] *adj.* **1** *Physics.* of mass, pertaining to a body of matter as a whole. **2** *Chemistry.* of, having to do with, or measured by the *mole*[4]. ⟨both ult. < L *moles* mass⟩

mo•las•ses [mə'læsɪz] *n.* a sweet syrup obtained in making sugar from sugar cane. ⟨< Pg. < LL *mellaceum* must < *mel* honey⟩

mold [mould] See MOULD.

mold•board ['mould,bɔrd] See MOULDBOARD.

mold•er ['mouldər] See MOULDER.

mold•ing ['mouldɪŋ] See MOULDING.

Mol•do•va [mɒl'douvə] *n.* a country in E Europe.

mold•y ['mouldi] See MOULDY.

mole[1] [moul] *n.* a small, permanent spot on the skin, usually brown and slightly raised. ⟨OE *māl*⟩

A star-nosed mole—about 13 cm long excluding the tail

mole[2] [moul] *n.* **1** any of a family (Talpidae) of small, burrowing, insect-eating mammals having a thick body covered with soft fur, short legs with the front feet modified for digging, small, weak eyes, and a long, pointed snout. **2** *Cdn., esp. Prairies.* POCKET GOPHER. ⟨ME *molle*⟩ **—'mole,like,** *adj.*

mole[3] [moul] *n.* **1** a barrier built of stone to break the force of waves; breakwater. **2** a harbour formed by a mole. ⟨< L *moles* mass⟩

mole[4] [moul] *n. Chemistry.* an SI base unit for measuring amounts of substances that take part in chemical reactions. One mole of an element, compound, etc. corresponds to its molecular weight, or the amount that contains particles equal in number to AVOGADRO'S NUMBER, 6.02×10^{23}. *Symbol:* mol ⟨< G *Mol,* abbrev. of *Molekül* molecule⟩

mo•lec•u•lar [mə'lɛkjələr] *adj.* of, having to do with, produced by, or consisting of molecules.

molecular biology the area of biology that seeks to interpret biological phenomena at the molecular level.

molecular disease any disease in which the basic defect is a molecular abnormality.

molecular genetics the area of genetics in which genetic phenomena are investigated at the molecular level.

mol•e•cule ['mɒlə,kjul] *n.* **1** *Chemistry.* the smallest part, or unit, into which a substance can be divided without chemical change. A molecule of an element consists of one or more similar atoms. A molecule of a compound consists of two or more different atoms. **2** any very small bit or particle. ⟨< NL *molecula,* dim. of L *moles* mass⟩

mole•hill ['moul,hɪl] *n.* a small mound or ridge of earth raised up by moles burrowing under the ground.
make a mountain (out) of a molehill, give great importance to something which is really insignificant, especially a hindrance or obstacle.

mole•skin ['moul,skɪn] *n.* **1** the skin of the mole used as fur. **2** a strong cotton fabric used for sports and work clothing. **3 moleskins,** *pl.* pants made of this fabric.

mo•lest [mə'lɛst] *v.* **1** annoy, meddle with, or persecute, especially so as to injure: *It is cruel to molest animals.* **2** make improper sexual advances to: *to molest a child.* ⟨< OF < L *molestare* < *molestus* troublesome < *moles* burden⟩
—mo'lest•er, *n.* **—,mo•les'ta•tion** [,moulə'steiʃən] *or* [,mɒlə'steiʃən], *n.*

moll [mɒl] *n. Slang.* **1** a female companion of a criminal or vagrant. **2** a prostitute. ⟨short for *Molly,* familiar var. of *Mary*⟩
☛ *Hom.* MALL, MAUL

mol•li•fy ['mɒlə,faɪ] *v.* **-fied, -fy•ing. 1** soothe; appease: *The angry child refused all our attempts to mollify him.* **2** soften or mitigate: *His anger was finally mollified.* ⟨< F < LL *mollificare* < *mollis* soft + *facere* make⟩ **—,mol•li•fi'ca•tion,** *n.* **—'mol•li,fi•er,** *n.* **—'mol•li,fi•a•ble,** *adj.*

mol•lusc or **mol•lusk** ['mɒləsk] *n.* any of a phylum (Mollusca) of invertebrate animals having soft, unsegmented bodies covered with a mantle that in most species produces a hard shell. Abalones, chitons, clams, cockles, limpets, mussels, nautiluses, octopuses, oysters, scallops, slugs, snails, and whelks are molluscs. ⟨< F < L *molluscus* soft (of a nutshell)⟩

mol•ly•cod•dle ['mɒli,kɒdəl] *n., v.* **-dled, -dling.** *—n.* a person accustomed to being fussed over and pampered; milksop.

—*v.* coddle; pamper. ⟨< *Molly* (familiar var. of *Mary*) + *coddle*⟩ **—'mol•ly,cod•dler,** *n.*

Mo•loch ['moulɒk] *or* ['mouləkl] *n.* **1** an ancient Canaanite god to whom children were sacrificed by their parents. **2** anything thought of as requiring frightful sacrifice: *War is a Moloch.* **3 moloch,** a lizard (*Moloch horridus*) of Australian deserts, having spines and looking much like the horned lizard.

Mol•o•tov cocktail ['mɒlə,tɒf] a simple incendiary hand grenade consisting usually of a gasoline-filled bottle with a short fuse or wick that is ignited just before being thrown. ⟨after V.M. *Molotov* (1890-1986), Russian statesman⟩

molt [moult] See MOULT.

mol•ten ['moultən] *adj.* **1** of metal, rock, etc., made liquid by heat; melted: *molten steel, molten lava.* **2** *Archaic.* made by melting and casting: *a molten image.*
—*v. Archaic.* a pp. of MELT.

mo•ly ['mouli] *n., pl.* **mo•lies. 1** a mythical herb with a milk-white flower and a black root, having magic properties. Hermes gave Odysseus moly to counteract the spells of Circe. **2** a European wild garlic (*Allium moly*). ⟨< L < Gk.⟩

mo•lyb•de•nite [mə'lɪbdə,nəit] *or* [,mɒlɪb'dinəit] *n.* a sulphide mineral of molybdenum that occurs in soft, bluish silver flakes resembling graphite. It is the chief ore of molybdenum. *Formula*: MoS_2

mo•lyb•de•nous [mə'lɪbdənəs] *or* [,mɒlɪb'dinəs] *adj.* **1** of molybdenum. **2** containing divalent molybdenum.

mo•lyb•de•num [mə'lɪbdənəm] *or* [,mɒlɪb'dinəm] *n. Chemistry.* a heavy, silver-white, metallic chemical element of the chromium group. Molybdenum occurs only in combination and is used to harden steel. *Symbol*: Mo; *at.no.* 42, *at.mass* 95.94. ⟨< NL < L *molybdaena* < Gk. *molybdaina* < *molybdos* lead⟩

mom [mʌm] *or* [mɒm] *n. Informal.* mother.

mo•ment ['moumənt] *n.* **1** a very short, indefinite space of time: *In a moment, all was changed.* **2** a particular point of time: *We both arrived at the same moment.* **3 the moment,** the present point of time; right now: *He's busy at the moment.* **4** a definite state, period, or turning point in a course of events. **5** a period of temporary excellence or distinction: *He has his moments.* **6** importance or significance: *a matter of moment.* **7** *Physics.* **a** a tendency to cause motion, especially rotation around an axis or point. **b** the product of a given quantity (such as force) and its distance from an axis or point. Moment of force is measured in newton metres. ⟨< L *momentum* < *movere* move. Doublet of MOMENTUM.⟩
☛ *Syn.* **1.** See note at MINUTE.

mo•men•ta [mou'mɛntə] *n.* a pl. of MOMENTUM.

mo•men•tar•i•ly [,moumən'tɛrəli] *or* ['moumən,tɛrəli] *adv.* **1** for a moment: *hesitate momentarily.* **2** at every moment; from moment to moment: *The danger was momentarily increasing.* **3** at any moment: *We expect him to arrive momentarily.*

mo•men•tar•y ['moumən,tɛri] *adj.* lasting only a moment. **—'mo•men,tar•i•ness,** *n.*

mo•ment•ly ['moumәntli] *adv. Rare.* momentarily.

moment of truth 1 the moment when a critical decision must be made or action taken: *The guard turned and saw him and he knew that this was the moment of truth.* **2** the moment in a bullfight when the matador faces the bull to kill it.

mo•men•tous [mou'mɛntəs] *adj.* very important: *a momentous decision. Her graduation was a momentous occasion.* **—mo'men•tous•ly,** *adv.* **—mo'men•tous•ness,** *n.*

mo•men•tum [mou'mɛntəm] *n., pl.* **-tums** or **-ta** [-tə]. **1** the force with which a body moves, the product of its mass and its velocity. A falling object gains momentum as it falls. **2** the impetus resulting from movement: *The runner's momentum carried her beyond the finish line.* **3** the power (of a campaign, social movement, etc.) to continue its advance or maintain its force. ⟨< L *momentum* moving power. Doublet of MOMENT.⟩

mo•met•a•sone [mə'mɛtə,soun] *n.* a drug used in a cream or lotion form to treat certain skin conditions.

mom•ism ['mɒmɪzəm] *n.* an excessively sentimental elevation of motherhood. ⟨< *mom* + *-ism* (coined by Philip Wylie, a U.S. author, born 1902)⟩

mom•my ['mʌmi] *or* ['mɒmi] *n. Informal.* mother; mom.

Mo•mus ['mouməs] *n., pl.* **-mi** [-maɪ]. **1** *Greek mythology.* the god of mockery, who was banished from heaven for his ridicule and criticism of the gods. **2** any critical person; fault-finder. ⟨< L *Momus* < Gk. *Momos*, special use of *momos* blame, ridicule⟩

Mon [moun] *n., pl.* **Mon** or **Mons. 1** a member of a people living in E Myanmar. **2** the Mon-Khmer language of these people.

mon– *combining form.* the form of MONO- used before a vowel.

mon. 1 monetary. **2** monastery.

Mon. Monday.

Mon•a•co ['mɒnə,kou] *n.* a very small principality on the Mediterranean coast between France and Italy.

mon•ad ['mɒnæd] *or* ['mounæd] *n.* **1** *Philosophy.* a fundamental metaphysical unit or entity, first propounded by Leibnitz. **2** *Biology.* a one-celled organism, especially a flagellate protozoan. **3** *Chemistry.* an atom, element, or radical having a valence of one. **4** unit; one. ⟨< LL < Gk. *monas, -ados* unit < *monos* alone⟩

mo•nad•nock [mə'nædnɒk] *n.* an isolated hill or mass of rock left by erosion in a peneplain. ⟨after Mount *Monadnock* in New Hampshire, U.S.⟩

mo•nan•drous [mə'nændrəs] *adj.* **1** having only one husband at a time. **2** *Botany.* **a** of a flower, having only one stamen. **b** of a plant, having monandrous flowers. ⟨< Gk. *monandros* < *monos* single + *anēr, andros* husband⟩

mon•arch ['mɒnərk] *or* ['mɒnɑrk] *n.* **1** a ruler or sovereign head of state with the title of king or queen, or emperor or empress. **2** a person or thing having supreme power or pre-eminence. **3** MONARCH BUTTERFLY. ⟨< LL < Gk. *monarchēs* < *monos* alone + *archein* rule⟩

mo•nar•chal [mə'nɑrkəl] *adj.* of, having to do with, characteristic of, or suitable for a monarch; royal; regal. Also, **monarchial. —mo'nar•chal•ly,** *adv.*

monarch butterfly a butterfly (*Danaus plexippus*) native to Canada but wintering in California and Mexico, having orange and black wings with white spots. The larvae eat the leaves of milkweed.

mo•nar•chi•cal [mə'nɑrkəkəl] *adj.* of, having to do with, or characteristic of a monarch or monarchy. Also, **monarchic. —mo'nar•chi•cal•ly,** *adv.*

mon•ar•chism ['mɒnər,kɪzəm] *n.* **1** the principles of monarchy. **2** attachment to monarchy.

mon•ar•chist ['mɒnərkɪst] *n.* a person who supports or favours government by a monarch.

mon•ar•chy ['mɒnərki] *n., pl.* **-chies. 1** government by or under a monarch. **2** a nation governed or headed by a monarch. ⟨ME < LL < Gk. *monarchia* < *monos* alone + *archein* rule⟩

mon•as•ter•y ['mɒnə,stɛri] *n., pl.* **-ter•ies. 1** a building or buildings where monks or nuns live and work according to religious rules. **2** the monks or nuns who live in such a building. ⟨ME < LL *monasterium* < Gk. *monastērion*, ult. < *monos* alone. Doublet of MINSTER.⟩ **—,mon•as'te•ri•al** [,mɒnə'stiriəl], *adj.*

mo•nas•tic [mə'næstɪk] *adj., n.* —*adj.* **1** of or having to do with monks or nuns: *monastic vows.* **2** of or having to do with monasteries. **3** like that of monks or nuns: *He lives an almost monastic life.*
—*n.* a monk or nun. ⟨< LL *monasticus* < LGk. *monastikos*, ult. < *monos* alone⟩ **—mo'nas•ti•cal•ly,** *adv.*

mo•nas•ti•cal [mə'næstəkəl] *adj.* monastic.

mo•nas•ti•cism [mə'næstə,sɪzəm] *n.* the system or condition of living according to fixed rules under religious vows, usually in a monastery or convent.

mon•au•ral [mɒn'ɔrəl] *adj.* MONOPHONIC (def. 1).

Mon•day ['mʌndei] *or* ['mʌndi] *n.* the second day of the week, following Sunday. ⟨OE *mōn(an)dæg* day of the moon, a translation of LL *lunae dies* (whence F *lundi*)⟩

mo•ne•cious [mə'niʃəs] See MONOECIOUS.

Mo•nel metal [mou'nɛl] *Trademark.* a silver-coloured alloy containing 67 percent nickel and 28 percent copper, made from ore having the metals in this proportion. ⟨< Ambrose *Monel*, an American manufacturer⟩

mon•er•an [mə'nirən] *n.* a member of the KINGDOM (def. 3) **Monera** of living things, comprising the bacteria, blue-green algae, and other prokaryotes. ⟨< NL < Gk. *moneres* single < *monos* alone⟩

mon•e•tar•ism ['mɒnətə,rɪzəm] *or* ['mʌnətə,rɪzəm] *n.* **1** the theory that economic growth, the control of inflation, and the creation of jobs depend primarily on the regulation of the money supply (monetary policy), especially through the control of interest rates. **2** economic policy based on this theory.

mon•e•tar•ist ['mɒnətə,rɪst] *or* ['mʌnətə,rɪst] *n.* a person who advocates or practises monetarism.

mon•e•tar•y [ˈmɒnəˌtɛri] *or* [ˈmʌnəˌtɛri] *adj.* **1** of or having to do with the currency of a country: *The monetary unit in Canada is the dollar.* **2** of money: *a monetary reward.* ⟨< LL *monetarius* < *moneta.* See MONEY.⟩ **—ˈmon•eˌtar•i•ly,** *adv.*

☛ *Syn.* **2.** See note at FINANCIAL.

mon•e•tize [ˈmɒnəˌtaɪz] *or* [ˈmʌnəˌtaɪz] *v.* **-tized, -tiz•ing.** **1** legalize as money. **2** coin into money. **—ˌmon•e•tiˈza•tion,** *n.*

mon•ey [ˈmʌni] *n., pl.* **-eys** or **-ies. 1** officially issued coins and paper notes used as a standard medium of exchange: *I have five dollars left in American money.* **2** a particular form or denomination of money. **3** a sum of money used for a particular purpose or belonging to a particular person. **4** wealth: *She has a lot of money.* **5** wealthy people collectively. **6** **money** or **moneys, a** sums of money: *The treasurer was responsible for the moneys entrusted to him.* **b** more than one kind of money: *He had a collection of the moneys issued by different countries.* **7** any object or material serving as a medium of exchange and a measure of value, as cheques drawn on a bank, or nuggets or the dust of a precious metal.

for my money, *Informal.* for my choice; in my opinion; as I see it.

in the money, doing well financially.

make money, a earn or receive money. **b** become rich. ⟨ME < OF *moneie* < L *moneta* mint, money < *Juno Moneta,* in whose temple money was coined. Doublet of MINT².⟩ **—ˈmon•ey•less,** *adj.*

☛ *Usage.* **Money.** Exact sums of money that are not round amounts are usually written in figures: *72 cents; $4.98; $5; $168.75; $42 810.* Round or approximate amounts are more likely to be written in words: *two hundred dollars, a million and a half dollars.* In factual books or articles involving frequent references to sums of money, however, figures are often used throughout.

mon•ey•bags [ˈmʌniˌbægz] *n. Slang.* a wealthy person.

mon•ey•chang•er [ˈmʌniˌtʃeindʒər] *n.* a person whose business is to exchange money, usually that of one country for that of another. Also, **money changer, money-changer.**

mon•eyed [ˈmʌnid] *adj.* **1** having money; wealthy: *a moneyed family.* **2** consisting of or representing money or people having money: *moneyed resources, moneyed interests.* Also, **monied.**

mon•ey•grub•ber [ˈmʌniˌgrʌbər] *n. Informal.* a person whose main or sole concern is making or saving money. **—ˈmon•eyˌgrub•bing,** *adj., n.*

mon•ey•lend•er [ˈmʌniˌlɛndər] *n.* a person whose business is lending money at interest.

mon•ey–mak•er [ˈmʌni ˌmeikər] *n.* **1** a person who is clever at making money or one who is paid well. **2** a product, investment, etc. that yields large profits.

mon•ey–mak•ing [ˈmʌni ˌmeikɪŋ] *n., adj.* *—n.* the gaining or accumulating of wealth.

—adj. **1** engaged in gaining wealth. **2** very profitable; lucrative.

money of account a monetary denomination used in reckoning, especially one not issued as a coin. In Canada, the mill is a money of account but not a coin. The nickel is a coin, but not a money of account.

money order an order issued by a post office or bank for the payment of a particular amount of money by a post office or bank in another place. One can buy a money order in one town and mail it to a person in another town, where that person can cash it.

mon•ey•wort [ˈmʌniˌwɜrt] *n.* a plant (*Lysimachia nummularia*) of the primrose family, having yellow flowers.

-monger *combining form.* **1** a dealer in——; a person who sells——: *fishmonger.* **2** a person who exploits——; a person who spreads or busies himself or herself with——: *scandalmonger.* ⟨OE *mangere,* ult. < L *mango* trader < Gk.⟩

mon•go [ˈmɒŋgou] *n., pl.* **-gos** or **-go.** a unit of money in Mongolia, equal to ¹⁄₁₀₀ of a tugrik. See table of money in the Appendix. ⟨< Mongolian⟩

Mon•gol [ˈmɒŋgəl], [ˈmɒŋgɒl], *or* [ˈmɒŋgoul] *n., adj.* *—n.* **1** a member of an Asiatic people now inhabiting Mongolia. **2** the language of the Mongols; Mongolian. **3** Asiatic.

—adj. **1** of or having to do with the Mongols or their language. **2** Asiatic.

Mon•go•lia [mɒŋˈgouliə] *n.* **1** a country in central Asia, properly called the Mongolian People's Republic. **2** a vast region in Asia including the Mongolian People's Republic and parts of China and Siberia.

Mon•go•li•an [mɒŋˈgouliən] *n., adj.* *—n.* **1** a native or inhabitant of the Mongolian People's Republic or of Mongolia. **2** the Altaic language of the Mongols. **3** Mongoloid.

—adj. **1** of, having to do with, or designating the Mongolian People's Republic, Mongolia, the Mongols, or the language of the Mongols. **2** Mongoloid.

Mon•gol•ic [mɒŋˈgɒlɪk] *n.* **1** a branch of the Altaic family of languages, including Mongolian and Kalmuck. **2** Mongoloid.

mon•gol•ism [ˈmɒŋgəˌlɪzəm] *n. Obsolete.* DOWN SYNDROME.

Mon•gol•oid [ˈmɒŋgəˌlɔɪd] *adj., n.* *—adj.* belonging to or like the Mongols.

—n. MONGOL (def. 3).

mon•goose [ˈmɒŋgus] *n., pl.* **-goos•es. 1** any of a genus (*Herpestes*) of small, carnivorous mammals of tropical Africa and Asia, especially a slender, ferretlike species (*H. nyula*) of India, used for destroying rats, and noted for its ability to kill certain poisonous snakes without being harmed. **2** any of various other related mammals of Asia and Africa. ⟨< Marathi (lang. of W. India) *mangus*⟩

Mongoose

mon•grel [ˈmɒŋgrəl] *or* [ˈmʌŋgrəl] *n., adj.* *—n.* an animal or plant of mixed breed, especially a dog.

—adj. of mixed breed, race, origin, nature, etc.: *He habitually used a mongrel speech that was half English and half French.* ⟨Cf. OE *gemang* mixture⟩

monied [ˈmʌnid] See MONEYED.

mon•ies [ˈmʌniz] *n.* a pl. of MONEY.

mon•i•ker or **mon•ick•er** [ˈmɒnəkər] *n. Informal.* a person's name, nickname, signature, or other identifying mark or sign, such as initials. ⟨origin uncertain⟩

mon•ism [ˈmɒnɪzəm] *or* [ˈmounɪzəm] *n. Philosophy.* **1** the doctrine that the universe can be explained by one substance or principle. **2** the doctrine that reality is an indivisible, universal, organic entity. ⟨< NL < Gk. *monos* single⟩ **—ˈmon•ist,** *n.* **—moˈnis•tic,** *adj.* **—moˈnis•ti•cal•ly,** *adv.*

mo•ni•tion [mouˈnɪʃən] *or* [məˈnɪʃən] *n.* **1** a warning or sign of danger. **2** a formal warning from a bishop or religious court to correct an offence. ⟨< L *monitio, -onis* < *monere* warn⟩

mon•i•tor [ˈmɒnətər] *n., v.* *—n.* **1** a person, piece of equipment, etc. that checks, reminds, or gives warning. **2** in schools, a pupil with special duties, such as helping to keep order and taking attendance. **3** a device used for checking and listening to radio and television transmissions, telephone messages, etc. as they are being recorded or broadcast. **4** any of a genus (*Varanus,* constituting the family Varanidae) of large, tropical lizards of Africa, S Asia, and Australia. **5** *Computer technology.* a device which provides a video display of a computer's output.

—v. **1** check the quality, etc. of (a radio or television broadcast, etc.) by means of a receiver. **2** test the intensity of radiation, especially of that produced by radioactivity. **3** act as a monitor (of). ⟨< L *monitor* < *monere* admonish⟩

mon•i•to•ri•al [ˌmɒnəˈtɔriəl] *adj.* **1** of, having to do with, or using a monitor or monitors. **2** monitory. **—ˌmon•iˈto•ri•al•ly,** *adv.*

mon•i•tor•ship [ˈmɒnətərˌʃɪp] *n.* the office, work, or period of service of a MONITOR (def. 2).

mon•i•to•ry [ˈmɒnəˌtɔri] *adj., n., pl.* **-ries.** *—adj.* admonishing; warning.

—n. a letter containing admonition.

monk [mʌŋk] *n.* a man who has taken certain vows to live his life in a way prescribed by a religious brotherhood. Monks usually live in monasteries. ⟨OE *munuc* < LL < LGk. < Gk. *monachos* individual < *monos* alone⟩ **—ˈmonkˌlike,** *adj.*

mon•key [ˈmʌŋki] *n., pl.* **-keys;** *v.* **-keyed, -key•ing.** *—n.* **1** any of the smaller, usually long-tailed and tree-living primates, as distinguished from humans, apes, lemurs, etc. There are two main groups: the **Old World monkeys,** comprising a single family (Cercopithecidae) that includes langurs and baboons and some tailless species, such as the macaques; and the **New World monkeys,** comprising the family Cebidae, which includes many arboreal species with prehensile tails, and the family Callithricidae, which includes the marmosets. **2** any primate, excluding the lemurs and humans. **3** a person, especially a child, who is full of mischief.

—v. Informal. play; fool; trifle: *Don't monkey with the TV set.*

⟨probably < MLG *Moneke*, son of Martin the Ape in the story of Reynard⟩ **—'mon•key,like,** *adj.*

monkey bars **1** an open structure of vertical and horizontal pipes or bars, designed for children to climb and play on. Many playgrounds have monkey bars. **2** a structure of horizontal bars built against a wall, as in a gymnasium, used for climbing exercises.

monkey business *Informal.* **1** silly or mischievous acts: *Those kids are always full of monkey business.* **2** deceitful or treacherous acts: *There must have been some monkey business, because a few of the files were missing.*

monkey flower a western North American wildflower (*Mimulus lewisii*) of wet areas, having pink or red flowers.

monkey jacket a short, close-fitting jacket, formerly worn by sailors, now worn only as part of a military dress uniform.

monkey puzzle tree a coniferous tree (*Araucaria araucana*), having branches like arms, and edible nuts, native to South America.

mon•key•shines ['mʌŋki,ʃaɪnz] *n.pl. Informal.* mischievous tricks and jokes; pranks: *Those kids have been up to their monkeyshines again.*

monkey wrench an adjustable wrench, similar to a pipe wrench, but having smooth jaws.
throw a monkey wrench into, *Informal.* hinder; disrupt; upset (plans, operations, etc.)

Mon–Khmer ['moun kə'mɛr] *n.* a language family of SE Asia.

monk•ish ['mʌŋkɪʃ] *adj.* **1** of or having to do with monks. **2** like or characteristic of monks or their way of life. **—'monk•ish•ly,** *adv.* **—'monk•ish•ness,** *n.*

monks•hood ['mʌŋks,hʊd] *n.* any of several aconites having flowers shaped somewhat like the hoods worn by monks.

mon•o[1] ['mɒnou] *n. Informal.* mononucleosis.

mon•o[2] ['mɒnou] *adj. Informal.* MONOPHONIC (def. 1).

mono– *combining form.* one; single: *monogamy, monosyllable, monotone.* Also, before vowels, **mon-**. ⟨< Gk. *monos* single⟩

mon•o•ba•sic [,mɒnou'beisɪk] *adj.* of an acid, having only one atom of hydrogen replaceable by an atom or radical of a base in forming salts.

mon•o•car•pic [,mɒnou'kɑrpɪk] *adj.* bearing fruit only once in its life cycle. ⟨< *mono-* + Gk. *karpos* fruit⟩

Mo•noc•er•os [mə'nɒsərəs] *n. Astronomy.* the Unicorn, a constellation in the southern hemisphere between Canis Major and Orion. ⟨< Gk. *monokeros* < *mono-* single + *keros* horn⟩

mon•o•chord ['mɒnə,kɔrd] *n.* **1** a sounding board with a single string, used for measuring musical intervals. **2** a harmonious combination of sounds. **3** harmony; agreement.

mon•o•chro•mat•ic [,mɒnoukrə'mætɪk] *adj.* **1** of one colour only: *a monochromatic colour scheme in shades of blue.* **2** *Optics.* consisting of only one wavelength of light or other radiation.

mon•o•chro•ma•tism [,mɒnə'kroumə,tɪzəm] *n.* colour blindness in which everything is seen in shades of grey or, sometimes, of some other colour. **—,mon•o'chro•mat,** *n.*

mon•o•chrome ['mɒnə,kroum] *n.* a painting, drawing, etc. in a single colour or shades of a single colour. ⟨< Gk. *monochrōmos* < *monos* single + *chrōma* colour⟩

mon•o•cle ['mɒnəkəl] *n.* an eyeglass for one eye. ⟨< F < LL *monoculus* one-eyed < Gk. *monos* single + L *oculus* eye⟩ **—'mon•o•cled,** *adj.*

mon•o•coque ['mɒnə,kɒk] *n.* **1** a racing car whose body and chassis are one piece. **2** a boat whose hull is one piece. **3** an aircraft in which all the stress is borne by the outer shell. ⟨< F < *mono-* mono- + *coque* shell⟩

mon•o•cot ['mɒnə,kɒt] *n.* monocotyledon.

mon•o•cot•y•le•don [,mɒnə,kɒtə'lidən] *n.* any flowering plant having a single seed leaf (cotyledon) in the embryo, including grasses, lilies, orchids, and palms. Compare DICOTYLEDON. **—,mo•no,co•ty'le•don•ous,** *adj.*

mo•noc•u•lar [mə'nɒkjələr] *adj.* **1** of, involving, or affecting only one eye: *monocular vision.* **2** suitable for or adapted to only one eye: *a microscope with a monocular eyepiece.*

mon•o•cul•ture ['mɒnə,kʌltʃər] *n. Agriculture.* the use of land for the cultivation of a single product.

mon•o•dy ['mɒnədi] *n., pl.* **-dies. 1** a mournful song. **2** a plaintive poem in which one person laments another's death. **3** *Music.* **a** a style of composition that has only one predominating melody or part. **b** a composition written in such a style. ⟨< LL < Gk. *monōidia*, ult. < *monos* single + *aeidein* sing⟩ **—'mon•o•dist,** *n.*

mo•noe•cious [mə'niʃəs] *adj.* **1** *Botany.* having the stamens and the pistils in separate flowers on the same plant. **2** *Zoology.* having both male and female organs in the same individual; hermaphroditic. Also, **monecious.** ⟨< NL *Monoecia*, pl., class name < Gk. *monos* single + *oikos* house⟩

mo•nog•a•mist [mə'nɒgəmɪst] *n.* a person who practises or believes in monogamy. **—mo,nog•a'mis•tic,** *adj.*

mo•nog•a•mous [mə'nɒgəməs] *adj.* **1** practising or advocating monogamy. **2** of or having to do with monogamy. **—mo'nog•a•mous•ly,** *adv.*

mo•nog•a•my [mə'nɒgəmi] *n.* **1** the practice or condition of being married to only one person at a time. **2** *Zoology.* the habit of having only one mate. ⟨< L < Gk. *monogamia* < *monos* single + *gamos* marriage⟩

mon•o•gen•e•sis [,mɑnə'dʒɛnəsɪs] *n. Biology.* **1 a** the hypothetical descent of all living things from one cell or organism. **b** the hypothetical descent of all humans from one original pair. **2** asexual reproduction. **—,mon•o•ge'net•ic,** *adj.*

mon•o•gram ['mɒnə,græm] *n.* a design made by combining letters, usually the initials of a person's name. Monograms are often used on notepaper, table linen, clothing, jewellery, etc. ⟨< LL *monograma* < LGk. *monogrammon*, neut., consisting of a single letter < Gk. *monos* single + *gramma* letter⟩ **—,mon•o'gram•mic,** *adj.*

mon•o•graph ['mɒnə,græf] *n., v.* —*n.* a scholarly book or article on one aspect of a subject.
—*v.* write a monograph on; treat in a monograph. **—,mon•o'graph•ic,** *adj.* **—,mon•o'graph•i•cal•ly,** *adv.*

mo•nog•y•ny [mə'nɒdʒəni] *n.* **1** the practice or state of having one wife at a time. **2** *Botany.* of a flower, the condition of having one pistil. **3** *Zoology.* the condition of having only one mate at a time. **4** of bees or wasps, the condition of having only one queen at a time. ⟨< *mono-* + Gk. *gynē* woman + E *-y*[3]⟩ **—mo'nog•y•nous,** *adj.*

mon•o•lin•gual [,mɒnə'lɪŋgwəl] *or* [,mɒnə'lɪŋgjuəl] *adj.* knowing or using only one language: *a monolingual person, a monolingual conversation.*

mon•o•lith ['mɒnə,lɪθ] *n.* **1** a single large block of stone. **2** a monument, column, statue, etc. formed of a single large block of stone. **3** an organization that is massive, uniform, and therefore rigid and unyielding in its attitudes and policy. ⟨< L < Gk. *monolithos* < *monos* single + *lithos* stone⟩ **—,mon•o'lith•ic,** *adj.*

mon•o•logue ['mɒnə,lɒg] *n.* **1** a long speech by one person in a group. **2** an entertainment by a single speaker. **3** a scene or short play for one actor, often written to tell a story, to show character, or to describe a humorous or dramatic situation. **4** a part of a play in which a single actor speaks alone. ⟨< F < LGk. *monologos* < *monos* single + *logos* speech, discourse⟩ **—'mon•o,logu•ist,** *n.*

mon•o•ma•ni•a [,mɒnə'meiniə] *n.* an excessive concern with or interest in one thing or idea.

mon•o•ma•ni•ac [,mɒnə'meini,æk] *n.* a person having an excessive interest in one thing or idea. **—,mon•o•ma'ni•a•cal** [,mɒnəmə'naɪəkəl], *adj.*

mon•o•mer ['mɒnəmər] *n. Chemistry.* a chemical compound consisting of single molecules that can join together to form a polymer or copolymer. ⟨< *mono-* + *-mer* (as in *polymer*). 20c.⟩ **—,mon•o'mer•ic** [,mɒnə'mɛrɪk], *adj.*

mon•o•me•tal•lic [,mɒnoumə'tælɪk] *adj.* **1** using one metal only. **2** having to do with monometallism.

mon•o•met•al•lism [,mɒnou'mɛtə,lɪzəm] *n.* the use of one metal only as the standard of money values.

mo•no•mi•al [mou'noumiəl] *or* [mə'noumiəl] *adj., n.* —*adj.* consisting of a single word or term.
—*n.* **1** a name consisting of a single word. **2** *Algebra.* an expression consisting of a single term. z, a^3b^4, and $\frac{m_1m_2}{d^2}$ are monomials. Compare BINOMIAL, POLYNOMIAL. ⟨< *mono-* + *-nomial*, modelled after *binomial*⟩

mon•o•mo•le•cu•lar [,mɒnoumə'lɛkjələr] *adj.* having the thickness of one molecule.

mon•o•morph•ic [,mɒnə'mɔrfɪk] *adj.* **1** *Biology.* having only one form. **2** having uniform structure. Also, **monomorphous.**

mon•o•nu•cle•ar [,mɒnə'njukliər] *or* [,mɒnə'nukliər] *adj.* with one nucleus.

mon•o•nu•cle•o•sis [ˌmɒnəˌnjukli'ousɪs] *or* [ˌmɒnəˌnukli'ousɪs] *n.* an infectious disease characterized by an abnormal increase of leucocytes. Also called **infectious mononucleosis.**

mon•o•pho•bia [ˌmɒnə'foubiə] *n.* abnormal fear of being alone. **—'mon•oˌphobe,** *n.* **—ˌmon•o'pho•bic,** *adj.*

mon•o•phon•ic [ˌmɒnə'fɒnɪk] *adj.* **1** in sound reproduction or recording, having only one channel for transmission of sound: *a monophonic record.* **2** *Music.* having a single melody, with little or no accompaniment or harmonization.

mo•noph•o•ny [mə'nɒfəni] *n.* music having one line of melody. ⟨< Gk. *monos* alone + *phone* sound⟩

mon•oph•thong ['mɒnəfˌθɒŋ] *or* ['mɒnəpˌθɒŋ] *n.* a single vowel sound; a vowel without a glide. ⟨< Gk. *monophthongos* < *monos* single + *phthangos* sound⟩

mo•no•phyl•lous [ˌmɒnə'fɪləs] *adj.* having only one leaf. ⟨< Gk. *monophyllos* < *monos* single + *phyllon* leaf⟩

mon•o•plane ['mɒnəˌplein] *n.* an airplane having one set of wings. Most modern planes are monoplanes.

mon•o•ple•gia [ˌmɒnə'plidʒiə] *n.* paralysis of one part of the body. **—ˌmon•o'ple•gic,** *adj.*

mo•nop•o•list [mə'nɒpəlɪst] *n.* **1** a person who has a monopoly. **2** a person who favours monopoly. **—moˌnop•o'lis•tic,** *adj.* **—moˌnop•o'lis•ti•cal•ly,** *adv.*

mo•nop•o•lize [mə'nɒpəˌlaɪz] *v.* **-lized, -liz•ing. 1** have or get exclusive possession or control of. **2** occupy wholly; keep entirely to oneself. **—mo'nop•oˌliz•er,** *n.*

mo•nop•o•ly [mə'nɒpəli] *n., pl.* **-lies. 1** control of a commodity or service for a particular market, with little or no competition: *The new dairy bought out the other two dairies in town and now has a monopoly on milk.* Compare OLIGOPOLY. **2** such control granted by a government: *An inventor has a monopoly on the manufacture and sale of her invention for a certain number of years.* **3** a commodity or service that one company, etc. has a monopoly on: *In some countries, the telephone service is a government monopoly.* **4** a company having a monopoly. **5** the exclusive possession or control of something: *No one has a monopoly on virtue.* ⟨< L < Gk. *monopōlion* < *monos* single + *pōleein* sell⟩

mo•nop•so•ny [mə'nɒpsəni] *n.* a situation in which one buyer bids for the product of several sellers. ⟨< Gk. *monos* alone + *opsonia* shopping, purchase⟩

mon•o•rail ['mɒnəˌreil] *n.* **1** a single rail serving as a complete track for a wheeled vehicle. **2** a railway in which cars run on a single rail.

mon•o•sac•char•ide [ˌmɒnou'sækəˌraɪd] *or* [ˌmɒnou'sækərɪd] *n.* a simple sugar such as glucose or fructose, that cannot be decomposed by hydrolysis.

mon•o•so•di•um glu•ta•mate [ˌmɒnə'soudiəm 'glutəˌmeit] a white, crystalline powder made from various vegetable proteins and used for seasoning foods. *Formula*: $C_5H_8NNaO_4 \cdot H_2O$ *Abbrev.*: MSG

mon•o•sperm•ous [ˌmɒnou'spɜrməs] *adj.* having only one seed.

mon•o•stich ['mɒnəˌstɪk] *n.* one line of poetry, especially an epigram.

mon•o•stome ['mɒnəˌstoum] *adj.* having only one stoma.

mo•no•stro•phe ['mɒnəˌstroufi], ['mɒnəˌstrouf], *or* [mə'nɒstrəfi] *n.* a poem in which all the verses follow the same metrical pattern. **—ˌmon•o'stroph•ic,** *adj.*

mon•o•syl•lab•ic [ˌmɒnəsə'læbɪk] *adj.* **1** having only one syllable. **2** consisting of a word or words of one syllable each.

mon•o•syl•la•ble ['mɒnəˌsɪləbəl] *n.* a word of one syllable. *Yes* and *no* are monosyllables.

mon•o•the•ism ['mɒnəθiˌɪzəm] *or* ['mɒnəˌθiɪzəm] *n.* the doctrine or belief that there is only one God. ⟨< *mono-* + Gk. *theos* god⟩ **—'mon•o•the•ist,** *n.* **—ˌmon•o•the'is•tic,** *adj.* **—ˌmon•o•the'is•ti•cal•ly,** *adv.*

mo•no•tint ['mɒnouˌtɪnt] *n.* monochrome.

mon•o•tone ['mɒnəˌtoun] *n.* **1** sameness of tone, of style of writing, of colour, etc. **2** a person who cannot produce the correct musical intervals in singing and so cannot follow a melody; someone who is tone-deaf. **3** (*adjl.*) continuing on one tone; of one tone, style, or colour.

mo•not•o•nous [mə'nɒtənəs] *adj.* **1** continuing in the same tone: *She spoke in a monotonous voice.* **2** tedious or wearying because of lack of variety: *monotonous food, monotonous work.* **—mo'not•o•nous•ly,** *adv.* **—mo'not•o•nous•ness,** *n.*

mo•not•o•ny [mə'nɒtəni] *n.* **1** sameness of tone or pitch. **2** a wearisome sameness.

mon•o•treme ['mɒnəˌtrim] *n.* any of an order (Monotremata) of lower mammals comprising the platypus and echidna, which lay eggs. ⟨< *mono-* + Gk. *trēma* hole⟩

mo•not•ri•chate [mə'nɒtrəkɪt] *or* [mə'nɒtrɪˌkeit] *adj.* describing bacteria having one flagellum at one end only. Also, **monotrichous.**

mon•o•type ['mɒnəˌtəip] *n., v.* **-typed, -typ•ing.** *—n.* **1 Monotype,** *Trademark.* a set of two machines (keyboard machine and casting machine) for setting and making type in separate letters, using a coded tape. **2** *Biology.* the sole type of its group. A single species constituting a genus is a monotype. **3 a** a print from a metal plate on which a picture has been painted in colour with oil or printing ink, which is transferred to paper by a rubbing process. **b** the method of producing such a print. *—v.* set with a Monotype machine.

mon•o•va•lent [ˌmɒnə'veilənt] *adj. Chemistry.* having a valence of one.

mon•ox•ide [mə'nɒksaɪd], [mən'ɒksɪd], *or* ['mɒnəkˌsaɪd] *n. Chemistry.* an oxide containing one oxygen atom in each molecule.

mon•o•zy•got•ic [ˌmɒnəzaɪ'gɒtɪk] *adj.* arising from a single zygote.

monozygotic twins a pair of twins derived from a single fertilized ovum. See TWIN. Monozygotic twins are identical.

Mon•roe Doctrine [mən'rou] the doctrine that European nations should not interfere with Latin American nations or try to acquire more territory in Latin America. ⟨< James *Monroe* (1758-1831), president of the United States from 1817 to 1825⟩

Mon•sei•gneur or **mon•sei•gneur** [mɔ̃sɛ'njœʀ] *n., pl.* **Mes•sei•gneurs** or **mes•sei•gneurs** [mesɛ'njœʀ]. *French.* **1** a title of honour given to princes, bishops, and other persons of importance, usually used in front of a title of office. **2** a person having this title. ⟨< F < *mon* my + *seigneur* lord⟩

mon•sieur [mə'sjø] *n., pl.* **mes•sieurs** [mɛ'sjø]. *French.* Mr.; sir. ⟨< F *monsieur,* earlier *mon sieur* my lord⟩

Mon•si•gnor or **mon•si•gnor** [mɒn'sinjər]; *Italian,* [ˌmonsi'njɔr] *n., pl.* **Mon•si•gnors** or **mon•si•gnors;** *Italian,* **Mon•si•gno•ri** or **mon•si•gno•ri** [ˌmonsi'njɔri]. *Roman Catholic Church.* **1** a title given to certain dignitaries. **2** a person having this title. ⟨< Ital. *monsignor,* half-translation of F *monseigneur* monseigneur⟩

mon•soon [mɒn'sun] *n.* **1** a large wind system that reverses its direction with the seasons, especially a wind of the Indian Ocean and SE Asia that blows from the southwest from April to October and from the northeast during the rest of the year. **2** in India and adjacent regions, the season when the monsoon blows from the southwest, characterized by heavy rains. ⟨< Du. < Pg. < Arabic *mausim* season⟩ **—mon'soon•al,** *adj.*

mons pubis ['mɒnz 'pjubɪs] *pl.* **montes pubis** ['mɒntiz] *Anatomy.* the mound of flesh, covered with pubic hair, at the base of the abdomen of the adult human. ⟨< L⟩

mon•ster ['mɒnstər] *n., adj. —n.* **1** an imaginary creature of strange appearance: *Mermaids and centaurs are monsters.* **2** a huge creature or thing. **3** a person who is extremely evil or cruel: *The man in charge of the slaves was a monster.* *—adj.* huge. ⟨ME < OF *monstre* < L *monstrum* divine warning < *monstrare* show⟩ **—'mon•sterˌlike,** *adj.*

monster house an overlarge house occupying most of a city or rural lot.

mon•strance ['mɒnstrəns] *n. Roman Catholic Church.* a receptacle in which the consecrated Host is shown for adoration. ⟨< Med.L *monstrantia* < L *monstrare* show⟩

mon•stros•i•ty [mɒn'strɒsəti] *n., pl.* **-ties. 1** the state or character of being monstrous. **2** a monster or something monstrous.

mon•strous ['mɒnstrəs] *adj., adv. —adj.* **1** huge; enormous. **2** unnaturally formed or shaped; like a monster. **3** shocking; horrible; dreadful. *—adv. Informal.* very; extremely. **—'mon•strous•ly,** *adv.* **—'mon•strous•ness,** *n.*

mons veneris ['mɒnz 'vɛnərɪs] *pl.* **montes veneris** ['mɒntiz] *Anatomy.* the mons pubis of the human female. ⟨< NL⟩

mon•tage [mɒn'tɑʒ]; *French,* [mɔ̃'taʒ] *n.* **1** the combination of several distinct pictures to make a composite picture. **2** a composite picture so made. **3** in motion pictures or television, the use of a sequence of rapidly changing pictures to suggest an emotional reaction, a state of mind, etc. **4** any combining or blending of different elements: *His latest novel is a montage of biography, history, and fiction.* ⟨< F *montage* < *monter* mount⟩

Mon•ta•gnais [ˌmɒntə'njei] *n., pl.* **-gnais** [-'njei] *or* [-'njeiz] or **-gnaises** [-'njeiz]. Innu. ⟨< F < *montagne* mountain⟩

Mon•ta•na [mɒn'tænə] *n.* a northwestern state of the United States, bordering British Columbia, Alberta, and Saskatchewan.

mon•te ['mɒnti] *n.* a Spanish gambling game played with cards. ⟨< Sp. *monte* mountain, i.e., of cards⟩

Mon•te•ne•grin [ˌmɒntə'nigrɪn] *adj., n. —adj.* of or having to do with Montenegro, a former kingdom in S Europe, or its people.
—n. a native or inhabitant of Montenegro.

Mon•te•rey Jack [ˌmɒntə'rei] a mild, light yellow cheese. ⟨< *Monterey* County, California, where it was first made⟩

month [mʌnθ] *n.* **1** one of the twelve parts into which the year is divided. **2** the period of time from any day of one month to the corresponding day of the next month: *It will take us about a month to finish the project.* **3** *Astronomy.* **a** the time it takes the moon to make one complete revolution around the earth; lunar month. **b** the time from one new moon to the next, about 29.53 days; synodical month. **c** one twelfth of a solar year, about 30.41 days; solar month. **d** a sidereal month (29.531 days). ⟨OE *mōnath.* Related to MOON.⟩

☛ *Usage.* **Months.** In reference matter and informal writing, the names of months with more than four letters are abbreviated in dates: *Jan. 21, 1951,* but *June 30, 1950.* When only the month or month and year are given, abbreviations are rare: *January 1950. Every January she tries again.* In formal writing, the names of the months are not abbreviated. In the newer digital system, the months are shown as numbers: 1950 04 30.

month•ly ['mʌnθli] *adj., adv., n., pl.* **-lies.** *—adj.* **1** of a month; for a month. **2** done, happening, payable, etc. once a month.
—adv. once a month; every month.
—n. **1** a magazine published once a month. **2** menstrual period.

Mont•ré•al canoe [ˌmʌntri'ɒl] *Cdn.* formerly, the largest canoe of the fur trade, used especially on the Great Lakes and the St. Lawrence River. It was up to 12 m long and could carry a cargo of over four tonnes. Also called **canot du maître.**

mon•u•ment ['mɒnjəmənt] *n.* **1** something set up to preserve the memory of a person or an event. A monument may be a building, pillar, arch, statue, tomb, or stone. **2** anything that keeps alive the memory of a person or an event. **3** an enduring or prominent instance or example: *The professor's publications were monuments of learning.* **4** something set up to mark a boundary. ⟨< L *monumentum* < *monere* remind⟩

mon•u•men•tal [ˌmɒnjə'mɛntəl] *adj.* **1** of or serving as a monument. **2** like a monument; weighty, lasting, and important: *The British North America Act is a monumental document.* **3** very great: *monumental ignorance, a monumental achievement.*
—ˌmon•u'men•tal•ly, *adv.*

moo [mu] *n., pl.* **moos;** *v.* **mooed, moo•ing.** *—n.* the sound made by a cow.
—v. make the sound of a cow. ⟨imitative⟩
☛ *Hom.* MOUE, MU.

mooch [mutʃ] *v. Slang.* **1** sneak; skulk; rove about. **2** steal, usually food. **3** beg; get (something) at another person's expense. **4** *Cdn.* fish for big fish by drifting with light tackle. ⟨origin uncertain⟩ **—'mooch•er,** *n.*

mooched herring herring used as bait in mooching; see MOOCH (def. 4).

mood¹ [mud] *n.* **1** a state of mind or feeling. **2 moods,** *pl.* fits of depression or bad temper. ⟨OE *mōd* spirit⟩

mood² [mud] *n. Grammar.* the form of a verb that shows whether the act or state expressed is thought of as fact, or as something else, such as command, possibility, or wish. The indicative mood is used for statements or questions of facts; the imperative mood is used for commands. The subjunctive mood is used for possibilities. ⟨alteration of *mode;* influenced by *mood¹*⟩

mood•y ['mudi] *adj.* **mood•i•er, mood•i•est. 1** likely to have changes of mood; temperamental: *He's a very moody person so it's hard to say how he'll react.* **2** often having gloomy moods. **3** sullen or gloomy: *He sat there in moody silence.* **—'mood•i•ly,** *adv.* **—'mood•i•ness,** *n.*

moo•la or **moo•lah** ['mulɑ] *n. Slang.* money.

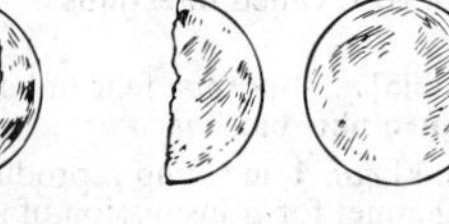

moon [mun] *n., v. —n.* **1** a heavenly body that revolves around the earth from west to east once in approximately 29½ days with reference to the sun or 27⅓ days with reference to the stars. It shines by the sun's reflected light. **2** the moon at a certain period of time: **new moon** (visible as a slender crescent), **half moon** (visible as a half circle), **full moon** (visible as a circle), **old moon** (waning). **3** *Cdn.* a lunar month; about a month or 29 days. **4** moonlight. **5** something shaped like the moon. **6** a natural or artificial satellite: *the moons of Jupiter.*
once in a blue moon. See BLUE.
—v. wander about or gaze idly or listlessly. ⟨OE *mōna*⟩
—'moon,like, *adj.*

moon•beam ['mun,bim] *n.* a ray of moonlight.

moon•calf ['mun,kæf] *n.* a foolish or absent-minded person.

moon•eye ['mun,aɪ] *n., pl.* **-eye** or **-eyes. 1** *Cdn.* a medium-sized, olive and silver freshwater fish (*Hiodon tergisus*) of northern North America having a deep, laterally compressed body, a deeply forked tail, and large, golden eyes set far forward on the head. **2** (*adjl.*) designating the family Hiodontidae, whose only living members are the mooneye and the closely related goldeye.

moon•less ['munlɪs] *adj.* **1** lacking the light of the moon: *a moonless night.* **2** having no satellite: *a moonless planet.*

moon•light ['mun,ləit] *n., v. —n.* **1** the light of the moon. **2** (*adjl.*) having the light of the moon: *a moonlight night.* **3** (*adjl.*) while the moon is shining; by night: *a moonlight swim.*
—v. Informal. work at a second job, usually at night, in order to supplement the wages earned at a regular job.
—'moon,light•er, *n.* **—'moon,light•ing,** *n.*

moon•lit ['mun,lɪt] *adj.* lighted by the moon.

moon•quake ['mun,kweik] *n.* an agitation of the surface of the moon, of the same kind as an earthquake.

moon•rise ['mun,raɪz] *n.* **1** the rising of the moon above the horizon. **2** the time when the moon rises above the horizon.

moon•scape ['mun,skeip] *n.* **1** a view of the details of the surface of the moon. **2** a barren and desolate area on earth thought of as resembling the surface of the moon.

moon•shine ['mun,ʃaɪn] *n.* **1** *Informal.* intoxicating liquor made unlawfully, or smuggled. **2** empty talk; empty show; nonsense. **3** moonlight.

moon•shin•er ['mun,ʃaɪnər] *n. Informal.* **1** a person who makes intoxicating liquor contrary to law. **2** a person who follows an unlawful trade at night.

moon•shot ['mun,ʃɒt] *n.* the action or an instance of launching a spacecraft to the moon.

moon•stone ['mun,stoun] *n.* **1** a translucent, whitish variety of feldspar having a pearly lustre. **2** a gem made from this stone.

moon•struck ['mun,strʌk] *adj.* dazed; crazed.

moon•y ['muni] *adj.* **moon•i•er, moon•i•est. 1** of the moon. **2** like the moon; crescent-shaped. **3** dreamy; listless.

moor¹ [mur] *v.* **1** put or keep (a ship, etc.) in place by means of ropes or chains fastened to the shore or to anchors. **2** be made secure by ropes, anchors, etc. ⟨ME *more(n);* cf. OE *mærels* mooring rope⟩

moor² [mur] *n. Brit.* open wasteland, usually hilly or high up. ⟨OE *mōr*⟩

Moor [mur] *n.* a member of a people of mixed Arab and Berber descent who conquered Spain in the 8th century A.D. The present-day Moors are a nomadic people of Mauritania and nearby areas. ⟨ME < OF *More, Maure* < L < Gk. *Mauros*⟩

moor•age ['murɪdʒ] *n.* **1** a mooring or being moored. **2** a place for mooring. **3** the charge for its use.

moor•cock ['mur,kɒk] the male of the red grouse.

moor•fowl ['mur,faʊl] *n. Archaic.* RED GROUSE.

moor•hen ['mur,hɛn] **1** the female of the red grouse. **2** *Esp. Brit.* the common gallinule.

moor•ing ['murɪŋ] *n., v. —n.* **1** a place where a ship or aircraft is made fast. **2 moorings,** *pl.* **a** the ropes, cables, anchors, etc. by which a ship, etc. is made fast. **b** that which gives stability and security.
—v. ppr. of MOOR¹.

mooring mast the mast to which an airship is moored.

Moor•ish ['murɪʃ] *adj.* of or having to do with the Moors or their culture: *Moorish architecture.*

moor•land ['mur,lænd] *or* ['murlənd] *n. Brit.* an area of moors.

A bull moose and his cow. The bull is about 210 cm high at the shoulder; antler spread up to 180 cm.

moose [mus] *n., pl.* **moose.** a large mammal (*Alces alces*), the largest living member of the deer family, having long legs, high, humped shoulders, a long head with a large snout, and, in the male, large, palmate antlers. In North America it is found across Canada and south to parts of the N United States. In Europe, this animal is called an elk. ⟨< Algonquian⟩
☛ *Hom.* MOUSSE.

moose•ber•ry ['mus,bɛri] *n. Cdn.* **1** a shrub (*Viburnum opulus*). **2** the reddish, tart berry of this plant. **3** *West.* a related shrub (*Viburnum edule*). **4** the fruit of this plant.

moose•bird ['mus,bɜrd] *n. Cdn.* CANADA JAY.

moose call *Cdn.* a device made to imitate the call of a moose, to entice a moose to come within the hunter's range.

moose camp *Cdn.* a browsing area where a group of moose or deer tread down the snow, remaining there for protection and warmth until the fodder within easy reach is exhausted.

moose country *Cdn.* a region in which moose are numerous.

moose•fly ['mus,flaɪ] *n. Cdn.* any one of several species of horsefly, especially of the genus *Chrysops*.

moose hair *Cdn.* a tuft of hair between the shoulders of a moose, used by First Nations people for decoration of various kinds.

moose•hide ['mus,haɪd] *n. Cdn.* the hide of the moose, valued as leather.

moose lily *Cdn.* the yellow, or pond, lily (*Nuphar advena*).

moose maple *Cdn.* a small maple tree (*Acer pensylvanicum*) found in central and eastern Canada.

moose•meat ['mus,mit] *n. Cdn.* the flesh of the moose, used as food.

moose•milk ['mus,mɪlk] *n. Cdn. Slang.* **1** a drink made of rum or other liquor and milk. **2** in the North, home-distilled liquor.

moose pasture *Cdn. Slang.* mining claims that are considered worthless.

moose willow *Cdn.* a shrub (*Cornus stolonifera*) with conspicuous red stems, the inner bark of which was often used in the making of kinnikinik; red-osier dogwood.

moose•wood ['mus,wʊd] *n. Cdn.* the striped maple tree (*Acer pensylvanicum)* having large leaves that are a favourite forage of deer and moose, and flowers in drooping clusters.

moose yard *Cdn.* a space in the woods where moose in winter tread down the snow, remaining there for protection and warmth, feeding on tender shoots and saplings.

moot [mut] *adj., v., n.* —*adj.* debatable; doubtful: *a moot point.*
—*v.* **1** argue. **2** bring forward (a point, subject, case, etc.) for discussion.
—*n.* an assembly. ⟨OE *(ge)mōt* meeting⟩

moot court a mock court held in a law school to give students practice.

mop¹ [mɒp] *n., v.* **mopped, mop•ping.** —*n.* **1** a bundle of coarse yarn, rags, sponge, etc. fastened at the end of a stick, for cleaning floors, dishes, etc. **2** something like a mop: *He is going to have his mop of hair cut before he goes for his interview.*
—*v.* **1** wash or wipe up; clean with a mop. **2** wipe.
mop up, a finish. **b** *Military.* clear out or rid (an area, town, etc.) of scattered or remaining enemy troops. ⟨probably < OF *mappe* < L *mappa* napkin⟩ —**'mop•per,** *n.*

mop² [mɒp] *v.* **mopped, mop•ping;** *n.* —*v. Archaic or poetic.* grimace.
mop and mow, make faces.
—*n. Archaic or poetic.* a grimace. ⟨Cf. Du. *moppen* to pout⟩

mope [moup] *v.* **moped, mop•ing;** *n.* —*v.* be listless, silent, and sad.
—*n.* a person who mopes. ⟨? related to MOP²⟩ —**'mop•er,** *n.*

mo•ped ['mou,pɛd] *n.* a motorized bicycle.

mop•ish ['moupɪʃ] *adj.* inclined to mope; sad and listless.

mop•pet ['mɒpɪt] *n. Informal.* child. ⟨< obs. *mop* doll⟩

mop–up ['mɒp ,ʌp] *n. Informal.* **1** a finishing off or a wiping out; a clean-up. **2** in battle, the finishing off of an action in an area by the killing or capture of enemy troops.

mo•quette [mou'kɛt] *n.* a thick, velvety carpet or upholstery. ⟨< F⟩

mo•raine [mə'rein] *n.* a mass or ridge of rocks, dirt, etc. deposited at the sides or end of a glacier after being carried down or pushed aside by the pressure of the ice. ⟨< F⟩
—**mo'rain•al** or **mo'rain•ic,** *adj.*

mor•al ['mɔrəl] *adj., n.* —*adj.* **1** good in character or conduct; virtuous according to civilized standards of right and wrong; right; just: *a moral act, a moral man.* **2** capable of understanding right and wrong: *A little baby is not a moral being.* **3** having to do with character or with the difference between right and wrong: *a moral question.* **4** based on the principles of right conduct rather than on law or custom. **5** teaching a good lesson; having a good influence: *a moral book.* **6** being so by virtue of its psychological effect: *a moral victory. We gave moral support to the team by cheering loudly.* **7** depending on considerations of what generally occurs; resting upon grounds of probability: *moral evidence, moral arguments.*
—*n.* **1 morals,** *pl.* **a** character or behaviour in matters of right and wrong: *The boy's morals were excellent.* **b** one's principles in regard to conduct. **2** the lesson, inner meaning, or teaching of a fable, a story, or an event: *The moral of the story was "Look before you leap."* ⟨ME < L *moralis* < *mos, moris* custom (pl., manners)⟩ —**'mor•al•ly,** *adv.*
☛ *Syn. adj.* **1. Moral,** ETHICAL = in agreement with a standard of what is right and good in character or conduct. **Moral** means right and good according to the customary rules and accepted standards of society: *He leads a moral life.* **Ethical** particularly suggests agreement with principles of right conduct or good living expressed in a system or code, especially of the branch of philosophy dealing with moral conduct or of a profession or business: *It is not considered ethical for doctors to advertise.*
☛ *Usage.* **Moral,** MORALE. **Moral** (a lesson) and **morale** (mental condition as regards courage, confidence, enthusiasm, etc.) are often confused: *He understood the moral of the story. The general was pleased with the morale of his soldiers.*

moral certainty a probability so great that it might just as well be a certainty.

mo•rale [mə'ræl] *n.* the mental condition or attitude as regards courage, confidence, enthusiasm, etc.: *The morale of the team was low after its defeat.* ⟨< F *moral,* mistakenly spelt *morale* in English to keep the pronunciation⟩
☛ *Usage.* See note at MORAL.

mor•al•ist ['mɔrəlɪst] *n.* **1** a person who thinks much about moral duties, sees the moral side of things, and leads a moral life. **2** a person who teaches, studies, or writes about morals. **3** a person concerned with regulating or improving the morals of others. —**'mor•al,ism,** *n.*

mor•al•is•tic [,mɔrə'lɪstɪk] *adj.* **1** moralizing; teaching the difference between right and wrong. **2** of or having to do with moralism or moral teaching. —**,mo•ral'is•ti•cal•ly,** *adv.*

mo•ral•i•ty [mə'rælәti] *n., pl.* **-ties. 1** the rightness or wrongness of an action. **2** the doing of right; virtue. **3** a system of morals; a set of rules or principles of conduct. **4** moral instruction; a moral lesson or precept. **5** MORALITY PLAY. **6** (*adjl.*) of or belonging to a MORALITY SQUAD: *a morality officer.*

morality play a form of drama popular during the 15th and 16th centuries, in which vices and virtues were personified.

morality squad a police division that deals with the enforcement of laws concerning gaming and prostitution.

mor•al•ize ['mɔrə,laɪz] *v.* **-ized, -iz•ing. 1** think, talk, or write about questions of right and wrong. **2** point out the moral lesson

or inner meaning of. **3** improve the morals of.
—,mor•al•i'za•tion, *n.* **—'mor•al,iz•er,** *n.*

moral philosophy ETHICS (def. 1).

mo•rass [mə'ræs] *n.* **1** a piece of low, marshy ground; swamp. **2** a difficult situation; a puzzling mess. ⟨< Du. *moeras* < OF *marais* < Gmc.⟩

mor•a•to•ri•um [,mɔrə'tɔriəm] *n., pl.* **-ri•ums, -ri•a** [-riə]. **1** a legal authorization to delay payments of money due. **2** the period during which such authorization is in effect. **3** a temporary pause in action, negotiation, etc. of any action. ⟨< NL < L *morari* delay < *mora* a delay⟩

Mo•ra•vi•an [mɔ'reiviən] *n., adj.* —*n.* **1** a native or inhabitant of Moravia, a region in the Czech Republic. **2** the Czech dialect spoken by Moravians. **3** a member of the Moravian church.
—*adj.* **1** of or having to do with Moravia, its people, or their dialect. **2** of, having to do with, or designating the Protestant church which developed from a 15th century reform movement in Moravia and Bohemia under the leadership of John Hus.

mo•ray ['mɔrei] *or* [mə'rei] *n.* any of numerous eels (family Muraenidae) found in warm seas, having a heavy, often brilliantly coloured body and a large mouth with strong, sharp teeth. ⟨< Pg. *moreia* < L *murena*, var. of *muraena* < Gk. *muraina*⟩

mor•bid ['mɔrbɪd] *adj.* **1** unhealthy; not wholesome: *His mother thinks his liking for horror movies is morbid.* **2** caused by disease; characteristic of disease; diseased: *Cancer is a morbid growth.* **3** horrible; frightful: *the morbid details of a murder.* ⟨< L *morbidus* < *morbus* disease⟩ **—'mor•bid•ly,** *adv.*
—'mor•bid•ness, *n.*

mor•bid•i•ty [mɔr'bɪdəti] *n.* **1** a morbid state or quality. **2** the proportion of sickness in a certain group or locality: *Morbidity statistics show that tuberculosis is on the decline in Canada.*

mor•da•cious [mɔr'deiʃəs] *adj.* **1** having the habit of biting. **2** bitter in manner. ⟨< L *mordax* given to biting⟩

mor•dan•cy ['mɔrdənsi] *n.* a mordant quality; sharpness.

mor•dant ['mɔrdənt] *adj., n.* —*adj.* **1** biting; cutting; sarcastic: *Their mordant criticisms hurt his feelings.* **2** in dyeing, that fixes colours.
—*n.* **1** a substance that fixes colours. **2** an acid that eats into metal. ⟨< OF *mordant*, ppr. of *mordre* bite < L *mordere*⟩
☛ *Hom.* MORDENT.

mor•dent ['mɔrdənt] *n. Music.* a short trill of the written note with the note below it. ⟨< G < Ital. *mordente* biting < L *mordens*, ppr. of *mordere* to bite⟩
☛ *Hom.* MORDANT.

Mor•dred ['mɔrdrɛd] *n.* Modred.

more [mɔr] *adj.* (*used as comparative of* **much** *and* **many,** *with the superlative* **most**), *n., adv.* —*adj.* **1** greater in number, quantity, amount, degree, or importance: *more men, more help.* **2** further; additional: *Take more time.*
—*n.* **1** a greater number, quantity, amount, or degree: *The more they have, the more they want.* **2** an additional amount: *Tell me more.*
—*adv.* **1** in or to a greater extent or degree: *It hurts more to beg than to borrow.* **2** in addition; further; longer; again: *Sing once more.*
be no more, be dead.
more or less, a rather; somewhat: *Most people are more or less selfish.* **b** approximately: *The distance is 5 km, more or less.* ⟨OE *māra*⟩
☛ *Usage.* **More** and MOST are often used before adjectives and adverbs to form comparatives and superlatives. **More** and **most** are put before all adjectives and adverbs of three syllables or more, and before some adjectives and most adverbs of two syllables. Other adjectives and adverbs, apart from a few irregular ones, use **-er** and **-est** to form the comparative and superlative.

mo•reen [mə'rin] *n.* a strong, heavy, woven fabric used for curtains and upholstery, made of wool, cotton, or a mixture of wool and cotton, and usually having a watered finish. ⟨? related to MOIRÉ⟩
☛ *Hom.* MARINE.

mo•rel¹ [mə'rɛl] *n.* any of a genus (*Morchella*) of edible fungus having a fleshy, pitted head on a stalk. ⟨< F *morille* < Gmc.⟩

mo•rel² [mə'rɛl] *n.* any nightshade, especially the black nightshade (*Solanum nigrum*). ⟨ME < OF *morel* dark brown⟩

mo•rel•lo [mə'rɛlou] *n.* a variety of very dark red sour cherry. ⟨< amarelle; influenced by Ital. *morello* blackish⟩

more•o•ver [mɔr'ouvər] *adv.* also; besides: in addition to that: *His power is absolute and, moreover, hereditary.*

mo•res ['mɔreiz] *or* ['mɔriz] *n.pl. Sociology.* customs prevailing among a people or a social group that are accepted as right; traditional rules; ways; manners. ⟨< L *mores* customs, manners⟩

Mo•resque [mə'rɛsk] *adj.* Moorish; in the Moorish style.

Mor•gan ['mɔrgən] *n.* a North American breed of small, strong saddle horse, usually of a dark colour. ⟨after Justin *Morgan* (1747-1798), owner of the sire⟩

mor•ga•nat•ic [,mɔrgə'nætɪk] *adj.* designating or having to do with a form of marriage in which a man of high rank marries a woman of lower rank with an agreement that neither she nor her children shall have any claim to his rank or property. ⟨< NL *morganaticus* < Med.L *(matrimonium ad) morganaticam* (marriage with) morning gift, ult. < OHG *morgangeba* < *morgan* morning + *geban* give; the 'morning gift' to the bride on the day after the wedding was her only share in her husband's goods and rights⟩ **—,mor•ga'nat•i•cal•ly,** *adv.*

Mor•gan le Fay ['mɔrgən lə 'fei] *Arthurian legend.* a fairy and King Arthur's half sister, usually represented as trying to harm him at every opportunity.

morgue [mɔrg] *n.* **1** a place, usually in a police station or hospital, in which unclaimed bodies of dead persons are kept until they can be identified. **2** that part of a hospital where autopsies are performed. **3** *Informal.* in a newspaper office, the reference library. ⟨< F⟩

mor•i•bund ['mɔrə,bʌnd] *adj.* dying. ⟨< L *moribundus*, ult. < *mori* die⟩ **—,mor•i'bun•di•ty,** *n.* **—'mor•i,bund•ly,** *adv.*

mo•ri•on¹ ['mɔri,ɒn] *n.* a helmet without a visor, shaped somewhat like a hat with a high crest, worn especially by Spanish foot soldiers in the 1500s and 1600s. ⟨< F < Sp. *morrion* < *morra* crown of head⟩

mo•ri•on² ['mɔri,ɒn] *n.* a kind of dark brown or black quartz. ⟨< L *morion*, misreading of *mormorion* crystal⟩

Mor•mon ['mɔrmən] *n., adj.* —*n.* **1** a member of The Church of Jesus Christ of Latter-day Saints, founded in the United States in 1830 by Joseph Smith. **2 The Book of Mormon,** a sacred book of The Church of Jesus Christ of Latter-day Saints.
—*adj.* of or having to do with the Mormons or their religion. ⟨< the name of the narrator of 'The Book of Mormon'⟩
—'Mor•mon,ism, *n.*

morn [mɔrn] *n. Poetic.* dawn or morning. ⟨OE *morgen*⟩
☛ *Hom.* MOURN.

mor•nay ['mɔrnei] *n.* a rich white cheese sauce. Also, **mornay sauce, Mornay sauce.** ⟨origin uncertain⟩

morn•ing ['mɔrnɪŋ] *n., adj.* —*n.* **1** the early part of the day, ending at noon. **2** the first or early part of anything: *the morning of life.*
—*adj.* of, for, or in the morning. ⟨ME *morwening* < *morwen* morn (OE *morgen*) + *-ing*; patterned on *evening*⟩
☛ *Hom.* MOURNING.

morning coat a man's coat used for formal daytime wear, cut away diagonally from the waist in front, tapering down to the knees at the back; cutaway; tailcoat; swallow-tailed coat.

morning dress **1** informal, simple garments for wearing in the house; housedress. **2** formal wear for men in the daytime, often worn at weddings. It includes striped trousers, a cutaway coat, and a silk hat.

morn•ing–glo•ry ['mɔrnɪŋ ,glɔri] *n., pl.* **-ries. 1** any of numerous twining plants (genus *Ipomoea*) having showy, trumpet-shaped, blue, mauve, pink, or white flowers and heart-shaped leaves. **2** (*adjl.*) designating a family (Convolvulaceae) of herbs, shrubs, and trees that includes the morning-glories. **3** the flower of any of these plants.

morning sickness a feeling of nausea, often accompanied by vomiting, that occurs in the morning during pregnancy, especially in the first few months.

morning star a planet, especially Venus, seen in the eastern sky before sunrise.

Mo•ro ['mɔrou] *n., pl.* **Mo•ros. 1** a member of any of various peoples of Muslim Malays in the S Philippine Islands. **2** the language of these people. ⟨< Sp. *Moro* a Moor⟩

Mo•roc•can [mə'rɒkən] *n., adj.* —*n.* a native or inhabitant of Morocco.
—*adj.* of or having to do with Morocco or its people.

mo•roc•co [mə'rɒkou] *n., pl.* **-cos. 1** a fine leather made from goatskins, used in binding books. **2** a leather imitating this. ⟨< *Morocco*, where it was first made⟩

Mo•roc•co [mə'rɒkou] *n.* a country in NW Africa.

mo•ron ['mɔrɒn] *n.* **1** *Informal.* a stupid or annoyingly ignorant person; dullard; dunce. **2** in a former system for classifying mentally retarded people, a person unable to develop mentally to the normal level of an adult. ⟨< Gk. *mōron*, neut. of *mōros* foolish, dull⟩ **—mo'ron•ic** [mə'rɒnɪk], *adj.* **—mo'ron•i•cal•ly,** *adv.*

mo•rose [mə'rous] *adj.* gloomy, sullen; ill-humoured: *He has a morose expression.* ⟨< L *morosus*, originally, set in one's ways < *mos, moris* habit⟩ **—mo'rose•ly,** *adv.* **—mo'rose•ness,** *n.*

morph [mɔrf] *n., v.* *—n.* **1** *Linguistics.* **a** allomorph. **b** an isolable form, or sequence of phonemes, whose morphemic status is not established. **2** *Biology.* any of the distinct forms of a species, as, for example, the worker bee versus the queen bee of a species of bee.
—v. Slang. undergo a radical change in form. ⟨< Gk. *morphē* form⟩

-morph *combining form.* form.

mor•pheme ['mɔrfim] *n. Linguistics.* the smallest meaningful element of a language or dialect, such as *un-*, *-ing*, *do*, *make*, or *snow* in English. Simple words, bases, and affixes are morphemes. ⟨< Gk. *morphē* form + E *-eme* as in *phoneme*⟩ **—mor'phem•ic,** *adj.* **—mor'phem•i•cal•ly,** *adv.*

Mor•phe•us ['mɔrfiəs] *or* ['mɔrfjus] *n. Greek mythology.* the god of dreams; popularly thought of as the god of sleep. ⟨ME < L *Morpheus* fashioner or moulder < Gk. *morphē* form, shape, in allusion to the forms seen in dreams⟩

mor•phine ['mɔrfin] *n.* a bitter, crystalline addictive drug made from opium, used to dull pain and to cause sleep. *Formula:* $C_{17}H_{19}NO_3$ Also, **morphia.** ⟨< F < G *Morphin* < *Morpheus*⟩

mor•phin•ism ['mɔrfɪ,nɪzəm] *n.* **1** a morbid condition caused by habitual use of morphine. **2** the morphine habit.

mor•pho•gen•e•sis [,mɔrfə'dʒɛnəsɪs] *n. Embryology.* the development of form during prenatal life. **—,mor•pho•ge'ne•tic** [,mɔrfoudʒə'nɛtɪk] or **,mor•pho'gen•ic,** *adj.*

mor•phol•o•gy [mɔr'fɒlədʒi] *n.* **1** the branch of biology that deals with the forms and structure of animals and plants. **2** the form and structure of an organism or of one of its parts. **3** the branch of linguistics that deals with the forms of words. **4** the system of word-forming elements and processes of a language. The morphology of English is very different from that of French. **5** the study of forms in any science, as in physical geography or geology. ⟨< Gk. *morphē* form + E *-logy*⟩ **—,mor•pho'log•ic•al** [,mɔrfə'lɒdʒɪkəl] or **,mor•pho'log•ic,** *adj.* **—,mor•pho'log•i•cal•ly,** *adv.* **—mor'phol•o•gist,** *n.*

mor•pho•pho•neme [,mɔrfou'founim] *n. Linguistics.* **1** a set of phonemes that express the same morpheme, as the plural *-s* expressed as [s], [z], [ɪz] in *lots, loads, lasses.* **2** an abstraction of the phonemes expressing different allomorphs of the same morpheme, as the [f] in *scarf* relates to the [v] in *scarves.*

mor•pho•pho•nem•ics [,mɔrfoufə'nimɪks] *n. Linguistics.* the study of the relationship between morphemes and the phonemes which represent them. Also called **morphonology, morphophonology.**

Morris chair or **morris chair** an armchair with an adjustable back. ⟨after William *Morris* (1834-1896), an English poet and painter, who invented it⟩

morris dance **1** an old English dance performed by people, usually men, in costumes. **2** the music for such a dance. ⟨*morris*, ME *morys* Moorish⟩ **—morris dancer.**

mor•row ['mɔrou] *n. Archaic or poetic.* the following day or time: *We expected her on the morrow.* ⟨ME *morwe*, var. of *morwen* morn, OE *morgen*⟩

Morse [mɔrs] *adj., n.* *—adj.* having to do with or designating the Morse code, or a telegraph system using it.
—n. the MORSE CODE. ⟨< Samuel F.B. *Morse* (1791-1872), American inventor of the telegraph⟩

Morse code a signalling system by which letters, numbers, etc. are represented by dots, dashes, and spaces or by long and short sounds or flashes of light.

mor•sel ['mɔrsəl] *n.* **1** a small bite; mouthful. **2** a piece; fragment. **3** a dish of food; tidbit: *a dainty morsel.* **4** something to be enjoyed, disposed of, or endured: *This decision was a bitter morsel.* ⟨ME < OF *morsel*, dim. of *mors* a bite, ult. < L *morsum*, pp. of *mordere* bite⟩

mort [mɔrt] *n. Hunting.* a note sounded on a horn at the death of the quarry. ⟨< F *mort* death < L *mors, mortis*⟩

mor•ta•del•la [,mɔrtə'dɛlə] *n.* an Italian cooked meat, served cold. ⟨< Ital. < L *murtatum* seasoned with myrtle < *murtus* myrtle⟩

mor•tal ['mɔrtəl] *adj., n.* *—adj.* **1** sure to die sometime. **2** of humans; of mortals. **3** of death. **4** causing death: *a mortal wound, a mortal illness.* **5** causing spiritual death: *mortal sin.* **6** lasting until death: *a mortal enemy, a mortal battle.* **7** very great; deadly: *mortal terror.*
—n. **1** a being that is sure to die sometime. All living creatures are mortals. **2** a human being. ⟨< L *mortalis* < *mors, mortis* death⟩ **—'mor•tal•ly,** *adv.*
☛ *Syn. adj.* 4. See note at FATAL.

mor•tal•i•ty [mɔr'tæləti] *n.* **1** mortal nature; the state of being sure to die sometime. **2** a loss of life on a large scale: *The mortality from automobile accidents is very serious.* **3** the death rate; number of deaths per thousand cases of a disease, or per thousand persons in the population.

mortality table an actuarial table used by insurance companies to predict how many people will die at a given age, based on statistics of a given population.

mortal sin *Christian theology.* a sin so serious that it can cause spiritual death. Compare VENIAL SIN.

mor•tar[1] ['mɔrtər] *n., v.* *—n.* a mixture of lime, cement, sand, and water, used for holding bricks or stones together.
—v. plaster or fix with mortar. ⟨ME < OF *mortier* < L *mortarium*⟩

mor•tar[2] ['mɔrtər] *n.* **1** a bowl of very hard material, in which substances may be pounded to a powder. See PESTLE for picture. **2** a very short artillery piece for shooting shells at high angles. ⟨ME < OF *mortier* < L *mortarium*⟩

mor•tar•board ['mɔrtər,bɔrd] *n.* **1** a flat, square board used by masons to hold mortar. **2** an academic cap with a close-fitting crown topped by a stiff, flat, cloth-covered square piece, worn by faculty and students in some schools and universities on ceremonial occasions, particularly graduation. ⟨because thought to resemble a bricklayer's flat mortarboard⟩

mort•gage ['mɔrgɪdʒ] *n., v.* **-gaged, -gag•ing.** *—n.* **1** a claim on property, given to a person, bank, or firm that has loaned money in case the money is not repaid when due. **2** a document that gives such a claim.
—v. **1** give a lender a claim to (one's property) in case a debt is not paid when due. **2** put under some obligation; pledge: *Faust mortgaged his soul to the devil.* ⟨ME < OF *mortgage* < *mort* dead (< L *mortuus*) + *gage* pledge, GAGE[1] < Gmc.⟩

mort•ga•gee [,mɔrgə'dʒi] *n.* the person, bank, or company to whom property is mortgaged; the creditor in a mortgage.

mort•gag•er or **mort•ga•gor** ['mɔrgədʒər] *n.* a person or company whose property is mortgaged; the debtor in a mortgage.

mor•tice ['mɔrtɪs] *n., v.* **-ticed, -tic•ing.** See MORTISE.

mor•ti•cian [mɔr'tɪʃən] *n. Esp. U.S.* UNDERTAKER (def. 1). ⟨< *mort*(*uary*) + *-ician*, probably an analogy with *physician*⟩

mor•ti•fi•ca•tion [,mɔrtəfə'keiʃən] *n.* **1** extreme embarrassment; shame: *The boy was overcome with mortification when he spilled milk on his host's suit.* **2** the cause of such feelings. **3** the control and subjection of one's physical desires and feelings through self-denial or endurance of pain. **4** *Pathology.* gangrene.

mor•ti•fied ['mɔrtə,faɪd] *adj., v.* *—adj.* ashamed; humiliated.
—v. pt. and pp. of MORTIFY.
☛ *Syn. adj.* See note at ASHAMED.

mor•ti•fy ['mɔrtə,faɪ] *v.* **-fied, -fy•ing.** **1** make ashamed or embarrassed; humiliate: *They were mortified by their cousin's rudeness to their friend.* **2** control or overcome (one's physical desires and feelings) through self-denial or the endurance of pain. **3** *Pathology.* become affected with or cause gangrene. ⟨ME < OF *mortifier* < L *mortificare* kill < *mors, mortis* death + *facere* make⟩ **—'mor•ti,fi•er,** *n.*

mor•tise ['mɔrtɪs] *n., v.* **-tised, -tis•ing.** *—n.* a hole in one piece of wood cut to receive a projection on another piece, called the **tenon,** so as to form a joint **(mortise and tenon joint).** See JOINT for picture.
—v. fasten by a mortise: *Some furniture is mortised together, not nailed.* Also, **mortice.** ⟨ME < OF *morteise* < Arabic *murtazz* fastened⟩

mort•main ['mɔrtmein] *n. Law.* an inalienable possession; the condition of lands or tenements held without right to sell them or give them away. ⟨ME < OF *mortemain*, translation of Med.L *mortua manus* dead hand; with reference to corporations as not being persons⟩

mor•tu•a•ry ['mɔrtʃu,ɛri] *n., pl.* **-ries;** *adj.* *—n.* **1** that part of a funeral parlour or of a cemetery where bodies of dead people await burial. **2** a morgue.

—*adj.* of death or burial. ⟨ME < AF < Med.L *mortuarium*, ult. < L *mors, mortis* death⟩

mortuary pole a kind of totem pole erected to the memory of certain First Nations chiefs, whose remains were kept in a box at the top of the pole.

mos. months.

Detail of a mosaic in the Galla Placidia Mausoleum in Ravenna, Italy, dating from the 5th century A.D.

mo•sa•ic [mou'zeiɪk] *n.* **1** a picture or design made of small pieces of stone, glass, wood, etc. of different colours, set together or inlaid: *Mosaics are used in floors, walls, ceilings, etc.* **2** the art or process of making such pictures or designs. **3** something made up of varied parts or elements, like a mosaic: *Canada is often called a cultural mosaic.* **4** (*adjl.*) of, having to do with, or used for mosaic or mosaics. **5** any of several viral diseases of plants that cause the leaves to become mottled with small yellow or brownish spots. Mosaic occurs especially in tobacco, corn, and sugar cane. **6** *Genetics.* an individual made up of tissues of two or more genetic types, as a result of mutation at an early stage of embryological development. ⟨< F *mosaïque* < Ital. < Med.L *mosaicus*, var. of *musaicus* of the Muses, artistic⟩

Mo•sa•ic [mou'zeiɪk] *adj.* of Moses or of writings ascribed to him.

mo•sa•i•cism [mou'zeiɪ,sɪzəm] *n. Genetics.* the state of being a MOSAIC (def. 6).

Mosaic law **1** the ancient law of the Hebrews, ascribed to Moses. **2** the part of the Bible where these laws are stated.

Mo•selle [mou'zɛl] *n.* **1** a dry white wine produced near the Moselle River in Germany. **2** a similar wine produced elsewhere.

mo•sey ['mouzi] *v.* **-seyed, -sey•ing.** *Slang.* move in an aimless or leisurely manner; amble. ⟨probably < Sp. *vamos* let's go⟩

Moslem ['mɒzləm] *n., adj.* See MUSLIM.

mosque [mɒsk] *n.* a Muslim place of worship. ⟨< F < Ital. < Arabic *masjid* < *sajada* prostrate oneself⟩

mos•qui•to [mə'skitou] *n., pl.* **-toes** or **-tos.** any of a large family (Culicidae) of two-winged insects, the females of which have mouthparts adapted for piercing the skin of humans and animals and sucking their blood. Some species transmit serious diseases, such as malaria, yellow fever, one type of sleeping sickness, etc. ⟨< Sp. *mosquito*, dim. of *mosca* < L *musca* fly⟩

mosquito hawk *Cdn.* the common nighthawk (*Chordeiles minor*) which feeds on flying insects.

moss [mɒs] *n.* **1** any of a class (Musci) of flowerless and rootless plants usually growing as low, dense, carpetlike masses on tree trunks, rocks, moist ground, etc. See also PEAT MOSS. **2** a mass of these plants growing together. **3** any of various other plants resembling mosses, such as reindeer moss, club moss, or Spanish moss. ⟨OE *mos* bog⟩ **—'moss,like,** *adj.*

moss agate a variety of agate that has brown, black, or green mosslike markings.

moss•back ['mɒs,bæk] *n. Slang.* a person whose ideas are out of date; fogey.

moss bag *Cdn.* a kind of bag of leather or cloth used by certain First Nations peoples to carry a baby. Packed with dry moss, which serves as a diaper, it is laced up in front and usually carried strapped to a cradle-board.

moss basket *Cdn.* a moss bag attached to a cradle-board.

moss campion an Arctic wildflower (*Silene acaulis*) having many small purplish pink flowers forming a carpet. It blooms in summer from Newfoundland to Alaska, in mountainous regions of the U.S., and in the Alps and in northern Europe. Also called **moss pink.**

moss heather *Cdn.* WHITE HEATHER (*Cassiope mertensiana*).

moss rose a cultivated variety of cabbage rose having very fragrant, usually pink flowers and having a mosslike growth on the calyx and stem.

moss•y ['mɒsi] *adj.* **moss•i•er, moss•i•est. 1** covered with moss: *a mossy bank.* **2** like moss; *mossy green.* **3** as if moss-covered. **—'moss•i•ness,** *n.*

most [moust] *adj.* (superlative of **many** and **much**), *n., adv.* (superlative of **much**). —*adj.* **1** greatest in quantity, amount, measure, degree, or number: *The winner gets the most money.* **2** the majority of; almost all: *Most children like candy.*
for the most part, mainly or usually.
—*n.* the greatest quantity, amount, degree, or number: *He did most of the work.*
at (the) most, not more than.
make the most of, make the best use of.
—*adv.* **1** in or to the greatest extent or degree: *Which movie did you like most?* **2** to a very great degree: *a most persuasive argument.* **3** *Informal.* almost; nearly: *We go there most every week.* ⟨OE *māst*⟩

☛ *Usage.* **Most,** ALMOST. **Most** is a common informal shortening of **almost:** *A drop in prices will appeal to most everybody.* It is sometimes used in writing conversation and in informal style, but is ordinarily out of place in written English.

☛ *Usage.* See note at MORE.

-most *suffix.* superlative: *foremost, inmost, topmost, uttermost.* ⟨ME < OE *-mest*; influenced by *most*⟩

most•ly ['moustli] *adv.* almost all; for the most part; mainly.

mot [mou] *n.* (*usually preceded by* **bon**) a clever or witty remark. ⟨< F < L *muttum* grunt, word. Doublet of MOTTO.⟩

☛ *Hom.* MO, MOW.

mote[1] [mout] *n.* a speck of dust. ⟨OE *mot*⟩

☛ *Hom.* MOAT.

mote[2] [mout] *v. Archaic.* may; might. ⟨OE *mōtan.* Related to MUST[1].⟩

☛ *Hom.* MOAT.

mo•tel [mou'tɛl] *n.* a kind of hotel consisting of a building or group of buildings having rooms that can be reached directly from an outdoor parking area. ⟨< *mo(tor)* + *(ho)tel*⟩

mo•tet [mou'tɛt] *n. Music.* a polyphonic composition having a sacred theme, usually sung unaccompanied. ⟨ME < OF *motet*, dim. of *mot* word⟩

moth [mɒθ] *n., pl.* **moths** [mɒðz] *or* [mɒθs]. any of a large number of mostly nocturnal insects (order Lepidoptera) having broad wings that in most species are held flat on the back when at rest, feathery or threadlike antennae, usually a fairly stout body, and caterpillar larvae that in most species feed on plants. Compare BUTTERFLY. ⟨OE *moththe*⟩

moth•ball ['mɒθ,bɒl] *n., v.* —*n.* a small ball made of naphthalene, or some other strong-smelling substance, used for putting in garments or in clothes closets to keep moths away.
in mothballs, *Informal.* **a** in protective storage. **b** in an inactive state or condition: *The plans for expansion have been put in mothballs.* Also called **camphor ball.**
—*v.* **1** put in protective storage: *to mothball a ship.* **2** set aside or postpone for an indefinite period: *to mothball a project.*

moth–eat•en ['mɒθ ,itən] *adj.* **1** eaten by moths; having holes made by moths. **2** worn-out; out-of-date.

moth•er[1] ['mʌðər] *n., v.* —*n.* **1** a female parent. **2** (*adjl.*) of, like, or being a mother: *mother love. We saw a mother squirrel with three babies.* **3** the cause; source: *Necessity is the mother of invention.* **4** MOTHER SUPERIOR. **5** a woman exercising authority and responsibility like that of a mother. **6** *Informal.* an old or elderly woman (*used especially as a title or form of address*). **7** (*adjl.*) native or innate: *mother courage. Scotland is my mother country and English is my mother tongue.*
—*v.* **1** be mother of; give birth to or produce. **2** act as mother to; care for and protect as a mother does: *mothering a tearful child.* **3** acknowledge oneself the mother or originator of. ⟨OE *mōdor*⟩ **—'moth•er•less,** *adj.* **—'moth•er•less•ness,** *n.*

moth•er[2] ['mʌðər] *n.* a stringy, sticky substance, consisting of bacteria that is formed in vinegar or on the surface of liquids that are turning to vinegar. ⟨special use of *mother*[1]⟩

mother•board ['mʌðər,bɔrd] *n. Computer technology.* a circuit board, usually of a small computer, that contains the major electronic components and usually expansion slots. Also, **mother board.**

Mother Car•ey's chicken ['kɛriz] *Cdn.* **1** STORMY PETREL. **2** any of various petrels. ⟨origin unknown⟩

mother church a church from which or by which other churches have been formed.

mother country 1 the country where a person was born. 2 a country in relation to its colonies.

Mother Goose 1 the imaginary author of a book of fairy tales by Charles Perrault (1628-1703), a French author, published in 1697. 2 the imaginary author of English nursery rhymes, actually of folk origin and first published in book form by John Newbury (1713-1767). Mother Goose is a traditional character of nursery tales in Europe.

moth•er•hood ['mʌðər,hʊd] *n.* 1 the state of being a mother. 2 mothers (*used with a singular verb*): *The motherhood of our city wants more day-care centres.*

Mother Hub•bard ['hʌbərd] 1 the subject of a well-known Mother Goose nursery rhyme beginning "Old Mother Hubbard went to the cupboard." 2 a woman's full, loose gown. 3 *Cdn.* a parka made from duffle cloth, covered with a cotton cover in a bright print, edged at hood and cuffs with wolverine fur.

moth•er–in–law ['mʌðər ɪn ,lɒ] *n., pl.* **moth•ers-in-law.** the mother of one's husband or wife.

moth•er•land ['mʌðər,lænd] *n.* 1 one's native country. 2 the land of one's ancestors.

mother lode the main vein of ore in an area or mine.

moth•er•ly ['mʌðərli] *adj.* 1 of, suitable for, or characteristic of a mother: *motherly advice.* 2 like a mother; kindly: *She's a warm, motherly person.* **—'moth•er•li•ness,** *n.*

moth•er–of–pearl ['mʌðər əv 'pɜrl] *n.* the hard, smooth, pearly lining of certain marine shells, such as that of the pearl oyster and abalone. Mother-of-pearl is used to make buttons and ornaments.

Mother's Allowance *Cdn.* FAMILY ALLOWANCE.

Mother's Day the second Sunday of May, set apart in Canada and the United States in honour of mothers: *The children brought their mother breakfast in bed on Mother's Day.*

mother ship a whaling ship, fishing vessel, spacecraft, etc. that acts as a base or supply point for one or more smaller craft.

mother superior a woman who is in charge of a convent of nuns.

mother tongue 1 one's native language. 2 a language to which other languages owe their origin.

mother wit natural intelligence; common sense.

moth•proof ['mɒθ,pruf] *adj., v. —adj.* treated chemically so as to keep moths away: *The carpet is mothproof.*
—v. make mothproof: *to mothproof a fibre.*

moth•y ['mɒθi] *adj.* **moth•i•er, moth•i•est.** 1 containing moths. 2 having holes made by moths.

mo•tif [mou'tif] *n.* 1 *Art or literature.* a subject for development or treatment; dominant, usually recurring idea or feature; theme: *The Cinderella motif is found in the literature of many countries.* 2 a distinctive, often repeated figure in a decorative design. 3 *Music.* **a** a recurring melodic or rhythmic fragment of a theme or subject. **b** LEITMOTIF. ⟨< F < Med.L *motivus* moving. Doublet of MOTIVE.⟩

mo•tile ['moutaɪl] *or* ['moutəl] *adj. Biology.* able to move about; capable of motion. ⟨< L *motus* moved + E *-ile*, capable of (< L *-ilis*)⟩ **—mo'til•i•ty** [mou'tɪləti], *n.*

mo•tion ['mouʃən] *n., v. —n.* 1 the condition or state of moving: *Everything is either in motion or at rest.* 2 a movement or a change of position or place: *He swayed with the motion of the moving train.* 3 a formal proposal for action made in a meeting, etc. 4 *Law.* an application made to a court or judge for an order, ruling, etc. 5 *Music.* **a** the melodic progression of a single part or voice from one pitch to another. **b** the progression of two or more parts or voices with relation to each other.
go through the motions, act mechanically without commitment.
in motion, moving; going.
—v. 1 make a movement, as of the hand or head, to show one's meaning: *She motioned her disagreement.* 2 show (a person) what to do by such a motion: *He motioned me out.* ⟨< L *motio, -onis* < *movere* move⟩

mo•tion•less ['mouʃənlɪs] *adj.* without motion or incapable of motion. **—'mo•tion•less•ly,** *adv.* **—'mo•tion•less•ness,** *n.*

motion picture 1 a movie; a series of pictures on a continuous strip of film, projected on a screen in such rapid succession that the viewer gets the impression that the images are moving. 2 a story or drama told by this means.

motion sickness nausea and dizziness caused by motion, such as the pitching and rolling of a ship or boat, the swaying, etc. of a train or car, or the swinging of a hammock.

mo•ti•vate ['moutə,veit] *v.* **-vat•ed, -vat•ing.** make (someone) want to act; provide with a motive: *His offer to help was motivated by a desire to please.*

mo•ti•va•tion [,moutə'veiʃən] *n.* 1 the act or process of furnishing with an incentive or inducement to action. 2 the incentive or inducement itself, often specifically that arising from one's own interests or desires: *She doesn't have the motivation to do her homework.* **—,mo•ti'va•tion•al,** *adj.*

mo•tive ['moutɪv] *n., adj. —n.* 1 the thought or feeling that makes one act: *His motive in going away was a wish to travel.* 2 motif.
—adj. that makes something move. ⟨< Med.L *motivus* moving, impelling < L *motus*, pp. of *movere* move. Doublet of MOTIF.⟩
☛ *Syn. n.* **1.** See note at REASON.

motive power 1 power used to impart motion to machinery; any source of mechanical energy: *The motive power of a train is now a diesel engine.* 2 all the locomotives of a railway collectively.

mot juste [mo'ʒyst] *French.* a word or phrase that exactly fits the situation.

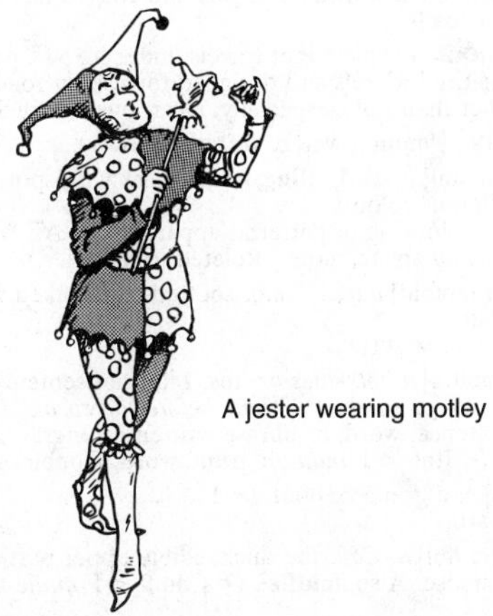

A jester wearing motley

mot•ley ['mɒtli] *adj., n., pl.* **-leys.** *—adj.* made up of different colours or of different things or people; varied: *a motley collection of old books and toys, a motley crew.*
—n. a suit of more than one colour worn by clowns: *At the party she wore motley.* ⟨ME *motteley*, apparently < AF **motelé* < OE *mot* mote[1]⟩

mo•tor ['moutər] *n., v. —n.* 1 *Electricity.* a machine that converts electrical energy into mechanical energy, used to operate another machine: *the motor of a pump.* 2 an internal-combustion engine. 3 a car or truck. 4 (*adjl.*) powered by a motor: *a motor car.* 5 (*adjl.*) of, by, or by means of automobiles: *a motor tour.* 6 (*adjl.*) causing or having to do with motion or action; functioning like a motor: *Motor nerves arouse muscles to action.* 7 something that causes or imparts motion or activity.
—v. 1 travel or transport by automobile. 2 *Slang.* move or go quickly. ⟨< L *motor* mover < *movere* move⟩ **—'mo•tor•less,** *adj.*

motor area the part of the brain that is believed to control muscular movement.

mo•tor•bike ['moutər,bəik] *n. Informal.* a motorcycle, especially a small, lightweight one.

mo•tor•boat ['moutər,bout] *n.* a boat that is propelled by a motor.

mo•tor•bus ['moutər,bʌs] *n.* bus.

mo•tor•cade ['moutər,keid] *n.* a procession or parade of automobiles. ⟨< *motor* + (*caval*)*cade*⟩

motor car automobile.

motor coach bus.

mo•tor•cy•cle ['moutər,səikəl] *n., v.* **-cy•cled, -cy•cling.** *—n.* a two-wheeled motor vehicle, sometimes having a sidecar with a third supporting wheel.
—v. travel by motorcycle. **—'mo•tor,cy•clist,** *n.*

motor generator an apparatus consisting of a combination of motor and generator, used to reduce voltage, etc.

motor home a large motor vehicle built on a truck chassis, having a completely enclosed body that is equipped for use as a travelling home. Compare MOBILE HOME.

motor hotel or **inn** a hotel for accommodating motorists, somewhat more elaborate than a motel and usually consisting of several floors of rooms and suites.

mo•tor•ist ['moutərɪst] *n.* a person who drives or travels by automobile.

mo•tor•ize ['moutə,raɪz] *v.* **-ized, -iz•ing. 1** furnish with a motor. **2** supply with motor-driven vehicles in place of horses and horse-drawn vehicles. **3** equip (infantry) with motor-driven transport vehicles, especially trucks. **—,mo•tor•i'za•tion,** *n.*

motor lodge motel.

mo•tor•man ['moutərmən] *n., pl.* **-men.** the driver of a streetcar or subway train.

motor scooter a light, two-wheeled motor vehicle steered by handlebars attached to the front wheel and having a seat for the rider with a broad footboard in front of it.

motor truck a truck with an engine and chassis made for carrying heavy loads.

motor vehicle a vehicle that travels under its own power, having rubber-tired wheels and designed for use on roads and highways rather than rails; especially, a car, bus, or truck.

mo•tor•way ['moutər,wei] *n. Brit.* expressway.

mot•tle ['mɒtəl] *v.* **-tled, -tling;** *n.* *—v.* mark with spots or streaks of different colours.
—n. a mottled colouring or pattern. ⟨apparently < AF **moteler* speckle < OE *mot* speck, mote[1]. Related to MOTLEY.⟩

mot•tled ['mɒtəld] *adj., v.* *—adj.* spotted or streaked with different colours.
—v. pt. and pp. of MOTTLE.

mot•to ['mɒtou] *n., pl.* **-toes** or **-tos. 1** a brief sentence adopted as a rule of conduct: *"Think before you speak" is a good motto.* **2** a sentence, word, or phrase written or engraved on some object. ⟨< Ital. < L *muttum* grunt, word. Doublet of MOT.⟩

moue [mu] *n.* a grimace; pout. ⟨< F⟩
☛ *Hom.* MOO, MU.

mou•fle ['mufəl] *n. Cdn.* the thick, edible upper part of the snout of the moose. Also, **muffle**[2]. ⟨< Cdn.F < F *mufle* flabby face⟩

mouf•lon or **mouf•flon** ['muflɒn] *n.* **1** a wild sheep (*Ovis musimon*) of the mountainous regions of Sardinia and Corsica, having a dark, reddish brown coat used as fur. The adult male has large, curved horns. **2** the wool of this sheep. ⟨< F < Corsican Ital. < LL *mufro*⟩

mou•jik [mu'ʒɪk] *or* ['muʒɪk] See MUZHIK.

mou•lage [mu'lɑʒ] *n.* **1** the making of a cast or mould of a footprint or other evidence connected with criminal investigation. **2** the mould itself. **3** a rubber or wax model of a body injury used in physiotherapy. ⟨< F⟩

mould[1] or **mold** [mould] *n., v.* *—n.* **1** a hollow shape in which anything is formed or cast: *Molten metal is poured into a mould to harden into shape.* **2** the shape or form which is given by a mould. **3** the model according to which anything is shaped. **4** something shaped in a mould: *a mould of pudding.* **5** the nature or character of anything. **6** the shape or frame on or about which something is made.
—v. **1** form; shape: *We mould statues out of clay.* **2** make or form into shape: *We are moulding clay to make model animals. Her character was moulded by suffering.* ⟨ME < OF *modle* < L *modulus.* Doublet of MODULE.⟩

mould[2] or **mold** [mould] *n., v.* *—n.* **1** a woolly or furry growth of fungus that appears on food and other animal or vegetable substances when they are left too long in a moist place. **2** any fungus that produces mould.
—v. make or become covered with mould: *The boots moulded in the cellar.* ⟨ME *mould,* earlier *muwle(n),* probably influenced by *mould*[3]⟩

mould[3] or **mold** [mould] *n.* **1** soft, rich, crumbly soil; earth mixed with decaying leaves, manure, etc.: *Many wildflowers grow in the forest mould.* **2** *Archaic.* ground; earth. ⟨OE *molde*⟩

mould•board or **mold•board** ['mould,bɔrd] *n.* a curved metal plate on a plough, that turns over the earth from the furrow.

mould•er[1] or **mold•er** ['mouldər] *v.* turn into dust by natural decay; crumble; waste away. ⟨probably < *mould*[3]⟩

mould•er[2] or **mold•er** ['mouldər] *n.* a person who or thing that moulds, especially a person who shapes something or one who makes moulds for casting. ⟨< *mould*[1]⟩

mould•ing or **mold•ing** ['mouldɪŋ] *n., v.* *—n.* **1** something produced by shaping or casting. **2** *Architecture.* a decorative shaping or contour given to a cornice along the top of a wall, to the jamb of a door or window, etc. **3** a shaped strip of wood or plaster, such as that often used around the upper walls of a room. Mouldings may be simply ornamental, or they may be used to support pictures, to cover electric wires, etc.
—v. ppr. of MOULD.

moulding board or **molding board** a board used for kneading bread, rolling cookies, etc.

mould•y or **mold•y** [mouldi] *adj.* **mould•i•er** or **mold•i•er, mould•i•est** or **mold•i•est. 1** covered with mould. **2** musty; stale: *a mouldy smell.* **3** outdated. **—'mould•i•ness** or **'mold•i•ness,** *n.*

mou•lin [mu'lɛ̃] *n. Geology.* a nearly vertical cavity in a glacier, worn by water falling through a crevice. ⟨< F *moulin,* literally, mill; from the noise sometimes made by the rushing water⟩

moult or **molt** [moult] *v., n.* *—v.* **1** shed the feathers, skin, shells, or horns periodically before a new growth. Birds and snakes moult. **2** shed (feathers, etc.): *The snake moulted its skin.*
—n. the act or process of moulting. ⟨ME *mout* < OE *mūtian* (as in *bemūtian* exchange for) < L *mutare* change⟩

mound [maʊnd] *n., v.* *—n.* **1** a bank or heap of earth or stones. **2** a small hill. **3** *Baseball.* the slightly elevated ground from which a pitcher pitches. **4** a pile or heap of anything.
—v. **1** enclose with a mound. **2** heap up. ⟨OE *mund* protection; meaning influenced by *mount*[2]⟩

Mound Builders people who lived in North America long ago, from the Great Lakes region to Florida. They built mounds of earth to bury their dead or for defence.

mound•er [maʊndər] *n. Cdn.* a member of a surveying team responsible for setting up boundary markers.

mount[1] [maʊnt] *v., n.* *—v.* **1** go up; ascend: *to mount stairs.* **2** move or proceed upward: *A flush mounted to her brow.* **3** raise; increase; rise in amount: *The cost of living mounts steadily.* **4** get up on: *mount a platform.* **5** get on a horse; get up on something: *mount and ride away.* **6** put on a horse; furnish with a horse: *The police who patrol this park are mounted.* **7** put in proper position or order for use: *The scientist mounted the sample on a slide for her microscope.* **8** fix in a proper setting, backing, support, etc.: *to mount a picture on cardboard.* **9** have or carry (guns) as a fortress or ship does. **10** provide (a play) with scenery and costumes. **11 a** post (a guard). **b** go on (guard) as a sentry or watch does. **12** set or place upon an elevation: *a small house mounted on poles.* **13** plan and begin to carry out: *to mount a campaign to get elected.*
—n. **1** a horse provided for riding. **2** an act or occasion of riding a horse, especially in a race. **3** the act or manner of mounting. **4** that on which anything is mounted, fixed, supported, or placed: *the mount for a picture.* ⟨ME < OF *monter* < L *mons, montis* mountain⟩ **—'mount•a•ble,** *adj.* **—'mount•less,** *adj.*
☛ *Syn. v.* **1.** See note at CLIMB.

mount[2] [maʊnt] *n. Poetic* (*except before a proper name*). a mountain or high hill: *Mount Robson.* ⟨OE *munt* < L *mons, montis*⟩

moun•tain ['maʊntən] *n.* **1** a very high, steep, often rocky hill: *Mount Robson is Canada's highest mountain.* **2 mountains,** *pl.* a series of such hills: *You can sometimes see the mountains from here. They stayed at a lodge in the mountains.* **3** (*adjl.*) of, having to do with, or resembling a mountain or mountains: *mountain air.* **4** (*adjl.*) living, growing, or found on mountains: *mountain plants.* **5** a large heap or pile of anything: *a mountain of rubbish.* **6** a huge amount: *a mountain of difficulties.*
make a mountain (out) **of a molehill.** See MOLEHILL. ⟨ME < OF *montaigne* < *mont* < L *mons, montis*⟩

mountain alder a western Canadian tree (*Alnus tenuifolia*) related to the speckled alder, having thin, smooth leaves without impressed veins, and bearing small nuts with narrow wings.

mountain ash any of several trees (genus *Sorbus*) of the rose family having pinnate leaves, white flowers, and bright red berries. Also called **rowan.**

mountain avens 1 any of a small genus (*Dryas*) of woody, evergreen plants of the rose family found especially in northern and mountainous regions, having horizontal branches, small, leathery leaves, and white or yellow, roselike flowers. The white mountain avens (*D. octopetala*) is the official flower of the Northwest Territories. **2** the flower of any of these plants.

mountain badger HOARY MARMOT.

mountain cat **1** cougar. **2** bobcat. **3** *Cdn.* lynx.

mountain chain a connected series of mountains.

mountain clematis a rare wildflower (*Clematis verticillaris*) with purple flowers. It blooms in spring in rocky woods from Québec to Manitoba and south to North Carolina, Iowa, and Ohio.

mountain cranberry a low-growing, creeping, evergreen shrub (*Vaccinium vitis-idaea*) found in dry and mountainous north temperate regions, bearing edible red berries. The North American mountain cranberry is a subspecies (*V. vitis-idaea minus*), generally smaller than the typical European shrub.

mountain cutthroat trout *Cdn.* a spotted trout (*Salmo clarki alpestris*) found in mountain streams in British Columbia, having a brown back with a grey belly and a streak of pink and a red streak under the lower jaw.

moun•tain•eer [,maʊntə'nir] *n., v.* —*n.* **1** a person who lives in the mountains. **2** a person skilled in mountain climbing. **3 Mountaineer,** a Montagnais or Naskapi.
—*v.* climb mountains.

mountain goat **1** a shaggy, white mountain antelope (*Oreamnos americanus*) of the Cordilleran region of NW North America, having a stocky body with high shoulders, a long, low-slung head, relatively short, black, backward-curving horns, and hooves with thick, spongy pads. **2** *Cdn.* a goatlike mammal (*Oreamnos montanus*) found in the western mountains and related to the European chamois.

Mountain goats

mountain hemlock a western Canadian evergreen shrub or tree (*Tsuga mertensiana*), having narrow leaves like needles, and bearing broad, cylindrical cones.

mountain juneberry a serviceberry (*Amelanchier bartramiana*) growing as a shrub with oval leaves and showy white flowers, common across southern Canada.

mountain Kamloops trout KAMLOOPS TROUT.

mountain laurel an evergreen shrub (*Kalmia latifolia*) of the heath family found in E North America, having glossy leaves and clusters of pink or white flowers.

mountain lion *Cdn.* cougar.

moun•tain•ous ['maʊntənəs] *adj.* **1** covered with mountain ranges: *mountainous country.* **2** huge: *a mountainous wave.*

mountain phacelia an Arctic wildflower (*Phacelia sericea*) having purple flowers.

mountain plover a bird (*Eupoda montana*) of the U.S. plains having a slender, black bill, long brownish yellow legs, a greyish brown back, white chest, and white stripes on the forehead. It is an endangered species.

mountain range a row of connected mountains; series of mountains.

mountain saxifrage an Arctic wildflower (*Saxifraga oppositifolia*) having tiny purple flowers.

mountain sheep **1** bighorn. **2** any of several other wild sheep inhabiting mountains.

mountain sickness sickness caused by the rarefied air at high altitudes. The common symptoms are difficulty in breathing, headache, and nausea.

moun•tain•side ['maʊntən,saɪd] *n.* the side or face of a mountain: *The whole mountainside was covered with trees.*

moun•tain•top ['maʊntən,tɒp] *n.* the top or summit of a mountain.

moun•te•bank ['maʊntə,bæŋk] *n.* **1** a person who sells quack medicines in public, appealing to the audience by tricks, stories, jokes, etc. **2** anybody who tries to deceive people by tricks, stories, and jokes. ⟨< Ital. *montambanco* for *monta in banco* mount-on-bench⟩

mount•ed ['maʊntɪd] *adj., v.* —*adj.* **1** on horseback. **2** supplied with a means of transportation, including trucks, tanks, etc. **3** in a position for use: *a mounted gun.* **4** having a proper support or setting: *a mounted photograph.*
—*v.* pt. and pp. of MOUNT[1].

Mount•ie or **mount•ie** ['maʊnti] *n., pl.* **-ies.** *Cdn. Informal.* a member of the ROYAL CANADIAN MOUNTED POLICE.

mount•ing ['maʊntɪŋ] *n., v.* —*n.* a support, setting, or the like. The mounting of a photograph is the paper or cardboard on which it is pasted.
—*v.* ppr. of MOUNT[1].

mourn [mɔrn] *v.* **1** grieve. **2** feel or show sorrow over: *The girl mourned her dead grandmother.* ⟨OE *murnan*⟩ **—'mourn•er,** *n.*
☛ *Hom.* MORN.

mourners' bench a front seat reserved for repenting sinners at a religious revival meeting.

mourn•ful ['mɔrnfəl] *adj.* **1** sad; sorrowful. **2** gloomy; dreary. **—'mourn•ful•ly,** *adv.* **—'mourn•ful•ness,** *n.*

mourn•ing ['mɔrnɪŋ] *n., adj.* —*n.* **1** the act of sorrowing; lamentation. **2** the wearing of black or some other colour (white in the Orient), or the draping of buildings, the flying of flags at half-mast, etc. as outward signs of sorrow for a person's death. **3** clothes, decorations, draperies, etc. worn or displayed to show such sorrow: *The widow was dressed in mourning.* **4** the period during which such signs of sorrow are shown.
—*adj.* of or used in mourning. **—'mourn•ing•ly,** *adv.*
☛ *Hom.* MORNING.

mourning cloak a butterfly (*Nymphalis antiopa*) having purple wings bordered with yellow, common in Europe and N America; Camberwell beauty.

mourning dove a North American wild dove (*Zenaidura macroura*) having brown plumage and a long, pointed tail. It has a slow and mournful-sounding call.

mouse *n.* [mʌus]; *v.* [mʌus] *or* [maʊz] *n., pl.* **mice** [maɪs]; *v.* **moused, mous•ing.** —*n.* **1** a small rodent (*Mus musculus*) native to the Old World but now common throughout North America, having a pointed snout, large ears, and a long, scaly tail. Mice live mainly in or near buildings. Also called **house mouse. 2** any of various other small, Old World rodents of the same family (Muridae). **3** any of numerous small, New World rodents (family Cricetidae) resembling the house mouse but usually having a long tail more or less covered with hair, such as the **deer mouse. 4** *Informal.* a shy, timid person. **5** *Computer technology.* a hand-held input device for a computer that controls the location of an object or a cursor on a screen and allows commands to be entered. The location of the object or cursor is changed by moving the mouse correspondingly on the desktop. Commands are entered by depressing buttons on the mouse.
—*v.* **1** of a cat, owl, etc., hunt for or catch mice. **2** search or move carefully or stealthily, as a cat does. ⟨OE *mūs*⟩
—'mouse,like, *adj.*

mouse deer chevrotain.

mouse ear *Cdn.* the soft, feltlike bud of the pussy willow.

mous•er ['mʌusər] *or* ['maʊzər] *n.* an animal that catches mice: *Our cat is a good mouser.*

mouse•trap ['mʌus,træp] *n.* a trap for catching mice. **build a better mousetrap, a** make a more excellent item. **b** make something for which there is a great demand.

mous•ey ['mʌusi] *adj.* **mous•i•er, mous•i•est.** See MOUSY.

mous•ing ['mʌusɪŋ] *or* ['maʊzɪŋ] *n. Nautical.* a lashing of small line joining the shank of a hook to the point to keep the hook from jumping or slipping out of a ringbolt or eye.

mous•sa•ka [mu'sɑkə] *or* [,musə'kɑ] *n.* a Greek dish consisting of layers of ground beef and eggplant, covered with a béchamel sauce and baked. ⟨< Mod.Gk.⟩

mousse [mus] *n.* **1** a chilled or frozen dessert made with sweetened whipped cream or gelatin: *chocolate mousse.* **2** finely ground, cooked meat or fish mixed with cream and other ingredients and poached, steamed, or set with gelatin. **3** any other substance with a foamy texture, such as hair setting lotion. ⟨< F *mousse* foam < Gmc.⟩
☛ *Hom.* MOOSE.

mousse•line [mus'lin] *n.* a fine, sheer, somewhat crisp fabric resembling muslin, originally made of silk, but now usually made of rayon. It is used especially for evening dresses. ⟨< F, muslin⟩

mousse•line de laine [muslində'lɛn] *French.* a fine, light, woollen fabric used for dresses.

mousse•line de soie [muslində'swɑ] *French.* a fine, sheer silk fabric with a crisp finish.

mous•tache ['mʌstæʃ] *or* [mə'stæʃ] See MUSTACHE.

mous•y ['mʌusi] *adj.* **mous•i•er, mous•i•est. 1** resembling or suggesting a mouse in being timid, drab in colour, quiet, etc.:

mousy hair. **2** infested with mice. Also, **mousey.** **—'mous•i•ly,** *adv.* **—'mous•i•ness,** *n.*

mouth *n.* [mʌuθ]; *v.* [maʊð] *n., pl.* **mouths** [maʊðz]; *v.* *—n.* **1** *Anatomy.* the opening through which a person or an animal takes in food; space in the head containing the tongue and teeth. **2** the part of the face around the mouth; the lips. **3** an opening suggesting a mouth: *the mouth of a cave.* **4** a part of a river, creek, etc. where its waters are emptied into some other body of water: *the mouth of the St. Lawrence River.* **5** a grimace. **6** a person or an animal requiring food or support: *He has seven mouths to feed in his family.* **7 a** the mouth as the source of spoken words. **b** utterance of words; speech: *get news by mouth, give mouth to one's thoughts.*
down in the mouth, *Informal.* in low spirits; discouraged.
have a big mouth, *Informal.* have a tendency to talk indiscreetly or excessively.
laugh on the other side or **wrong side of** (one's) **mouth.** See LAUGH.
open (one's) **big mouth,** *Informal.* talk indiscreetly or out of turn.
put (one's) **money where** (one's) **mouth is,** support one's words with concrete actions.
shoot off (one's) **mouth,** *Slang.* talk freely and indiscreetly, boastfully, or disrespectfully.
the horse's mouth. See HORSE.
—v. **1** utter (words) in an affected or pompous way. **2** speak oratorically. **3** utter (words) without sincerity or understanding: *She mouthed an apology for her poor manners.* **4** form (words) with the lips without speaking. **5** make grimaces. **6** accustom (a horse) to the bit and bridle.
mouth off, *Slang.* talk freely and indiscreetly, boastfully, or disrespectfully. ⟨OE *mūth*⟩ **—'mouth,like,** *adj.* **—'mouth•less,** *adj.*

–mouthed *combining form.* having a ——mouth: *small-mouthed.*

mouth•er ['maʊðər] *n. Informal.* a long-winded talker.

mouth•ful ['mʌuθfʊl] *n., pl.* **-fuls. 1** the amount that the mouth can easily hold. **2** what is taken into the mouth at one time. **3** a small amount. **4** *Slang.* an important or significant statement: *You said a mouthful.* **5** a long word which is difficult to pronounce.

mouth organ **1** harmonica. **2** panpipe.

mouth•part ['mʌuθ,pɑrt] *n.* usually, **mouthparts,** *pl.,* a structure or appendage near or around the mouth of arthropods, variously adapted for piercing, sucking, biting, grasping, etc.

mouth•piece ['mʌuθ,pis] *n.* **1** the part of a musical instrument that is placed against or in the mouth of the player. **2** the part of a bit that goes in a horse's mouth. **3** a piece placed at or forming the mouth of something: *the mouthpiece of a telephone, the mouthpiece of a pipe.* **4** a person, newspaper, etc. used by other persons or groups to express their views: *That newspaper is just a mouthpiece for the government.*

mouth–to–mouth ['mʌuθ tə 'mʌuθ] *adj.* of, having to do with, or designating a method of artificial resuscitation in which the rescuer places his or her mouth closely over the mouth of a person who has stopped breathing and forces his or her breath into the person's lungs.

mouth•wash ['mʌuθ,wɒʃ] *n.* an antiseptic liquid for rinsing the inside of the mouth or gargling.

mouth–wa•ter•ing ['mʌuθ ,wɒtərɪŋ] *adj.* very appealing, especially to the appetite; very appetizing: *a mouth-watering menu, a mouth-watering bowl of fruit.*

mouth•y ['mʌuθi] *or* ['maʊði] *adj.* **mouth•i•er, mouth•i•est. 1** impudent; given to rude and disrespectful talk. **2** loud-mouthed; ranting; bombastic. **—'mouth•i•ly,** *adv.* **—'mouth•i•ness,** *n.*

mou•ton ['mutɒn] *n.* **1** fur made from sheepskin that is pressed and dyed to look like beaver or seal. **2** (*adjl.*) made of mouton: *mouton coats.* ⟨< F⟩

mov•a•ble ['muvəbəl] *adj., n.* *—adj.* **1** that can be moved. **2** that can be carried from place to place as personal possessions can. **3** changing from one date to another in different years: *Easter is a movable holy day.*
—n. **1** a piece of furniture that is not a fixture but can be moved to another house. **2** a thing that can be moved, removed, or set in motion. **3** Usually, **movables,** *pl. Law.* personal property. Also, **moveable. —,mov•a'bil•i•ty,** *n.* **—'mov•a•ble•ness,** *n.* **—'mov•a•bly,** *adv.*

move [muv] *v.* **moved, mov•ing;** *n.* *—v.* **1** change the place or position of: *Do not move your hand. The chess player moved a pawn.* **2** change place or position: *The child moved in his sleep. We moved out to the veranda for coffee.* **3** change one's place of living or working: *We move to the country next week.* **4** put or keep in motion: *The wind moves the leaves.* **5** of the bowels, empty or cause to be emptied. **6** act: *God moves in a mysterious way.* **7** impel; rouse; excite: *What moved you to do this?* **8** affect with emotion; excite to tender feeling: *The sad story moved him to tears.* **9** make a formal request, application, or proposal; propose: *Mr. President, I move that we adjourn.* **10** sell or be sold: *These pink dresses are moving slowly.* **11** make progress: *The train moved slowly.* **12** exist; be active: *She moved in the best society.* **13** turn; swing; operate: *Most doors move on a hinge.* **14** carry oneself: *move with dignity and grace.* **15** *Informal.* start off; depart: *It's time to be moving.*
move heaven and earth. See HEAVEN.
move in (or **out**), move oneself, one's family, one's belongings, etc. into (or out of) a place to live or work.
—n. **1** *Games.* **a** the moving of a piece: *That was a good move.* **b** a player's turn to move: *It's your move now.* **2** the act of moving; movement. **3** an action, regarded strategically.
get a move on, *Slang.* **a** make haste; hurry up. **b** begin to move.
make one's move, take strategic action.
on the move, moving about: *They are restless and always on the move.* ⟨ME < AF < L *movere*⟩
☛ *Syn. v.* **8. Move,** ACTUATE = rouse a person to action or to act in a certain way. **Move,** the general word, does not suggest whether the thing that rouses is an outside force or influence or an inner urge or personal motive: *Praise moved him to work harder.* **Actuate,** a formal word, always implies a powerful inner force, like a strong feeling, desire, principle, etc.: *He was actuated by desire for praise.*

move•ment ['muvmənt] *n.* **1** the act or fact of moving. **2** the moving parts of a machine; a special group of parts that move on each other. The movement of a watch consists of many little wheels. **3** *Music.* **a** the kind of rhythm of a composition: *a waltz movement.* **b** its speed. **c** one section of a long composition: *the second movement of a symphony.* **4** the suggestion of action or progress in a novel, painting, etc. **5** a program by a group of people to bring about some one thing: *the movement for peace.* **6** a change in the market price, as of stocks or commodities. **7 a** an emptying of the bowels. **b** the matter discharged by it.

mov•er ['muvər] *n.* a person or thing that moves, especially a person whose work is moving furniture, etc. from one residence or place of work to another: *The movers will be here tomorrow.*

mov•ie ['muvi] *n.* a motion picture; film.

mov•ie•go•er ['muvi,gouər] *n.* a person who goes to movies.

mov•ing ['muvɪŋ] *adj., v.* *—adj.* **1** capable of or characterized by movement. **2** of or having to do with changing a place of residence or work: *a moving company, moving expenses.* **3** causing a strong emotional response; touching: *a moving story.*
—v. ppr. of MOVE. **—'mov•ing•ly,** *adv.*

moving sidewalk a path on an endless belt which moves forward mechanically and fairly slowly, as in airports.

moving staircase escalator.

mow[1] [mou] *v.* **mowed, mowed** or **mown, mow•ing. 1** cut down with a machine or scythe. **2** cut down the grass or grain from. **3** cut down grass, etc.: *The gardeners are mowing today.* **4** destroy at a sweep or in large numbers, as if by mowing: *The machine guns mowed down our soldiers.* ⟨OE *māwan*⟩ **—'mow•er,** *n.*
☛ *Hom.* MO, MOT [mou].

mow[2] [maʊ] *or* [mou] *n.* **1** the place in a barn where hay, alfalfa, grain, or straw is piled or stored. **2** a pile of hay, grain, etc. in a barn. ⟨OE *mūga*⟩
☛ *Hom.* MO, MOT [mou].

mow[3] [maʊ] *or* [mou] *v. or n. Archaic.* grimace. ⟨ME < OF *moue*⟩
☛ *Hom.* MO, MOT [mou].

mow•ing ['mouɪŋ] *n., v.* *—n.* **1** the act or process of cutting grass with a scythe or machine. **2** meadowland. **3** the hay mowed at one time.
—v. ppr. of MOW.

mown [moun] *v.* a pp. of MOW[1].

mox•ie ['mɒksi] *n. Slang.* **1** courage; bravery; nerve. **2** know-how; skill; experience. ⟨< earlier *Moxie,* a former trademark for a soft drink (because the drink supposedly gave courage)⟩

Mo•zam•bique [,mouzəm'bik] *n.* a country in SE Africa, formerly Portuguese East Africa.

Moz•za•rel•la or **moz•za•rel•la** [,mɒtsə'rɛlə] *or* [,mɒzə'rɛlə] *n.* a mild, soft Italian cheese, used especially in the making of pizza. ⟨< Ital.⟩

MP or **M.P.** **1** MEMBER OF PARLIAMENT. **2** MILITARY POLICE. **3** Mounted Police. **4** Metropolitan Police.

mph or **m.p.h.** miles per hour.

MPP or **M.P.P.** MEMBER OF THE PROVINCIAL PARLIAMENT.

Mr. or **Mr** ['mɪstər] *pl.* **Messrs.** MISTER. a title for a man, used before his last name or the name of his rank or office: *Mr. Einola, Mr. Speaker, Mr. Chief Justice.* ⟨abbrev. of MISTER⟩

☛ *Usage.* See note at MISTER. **Mr.** is written out only when it represents informal usage and when it is used without a name: *"They're only twenty-five cents for two, mister."*

MRI magnetic resonance imaging, a technique that produces an image of an object in cross-section, used for diagnostic purposes.

mRNA MESSENGER RNA.

Mrs. or **Mrs** ['mɪsɪz] *pl.* **Mrs.** or **Mesdames** [mei'dæm]. a title for a married woman, used before her name: *Mrs. Perlman.* ⟨< abbrev. of MISTRESS, female equivalent of MASTER, when used as a title before a name. The pronunciation became weakened to ['mɪsɪz] in this usage.⟩

☛ *Usage.* Even when used in writing to represent conversation or to talk about the word itself, it is rarely written out in full: *"Did you say Miss Jarvis?" "No. Mrs." I think* Mrs. *sounds so formal.* The form MISSUS is used only for writing the word with its informal meaning of 'wife': *That's my missus over there.* Compare with note at MR.

Ms. or **Ms** [mɪz] a title used in front of the name of a woman or girl: *Ms. Jackson.*

☛ *Usage.* **Ms.** is a form made up in the early 1950s to parallel **Mr.** and **Mrs.** Unlike them, it is not an abbreviation, but it imitates them in being followed by a period. Like **Mr.**, but unlike **Mrs.** or **Miss, Ms.** does not identify a woman as being married or unmarried.

ms millisecond(s).

MS MULTIPLE SCLEROSIS.

MS., MS, ms., or **ms** manuscript.

M.S. or **MS** MASTER SEAMAN.

MSG MONOSODIUM GLUTAMATE.

Msgr. 1 Monsignor. 2 Monseigneur.

m'sieur [mə'sjœ] *n. French.* monsieur.

M.S.M. Meritorious Service Medal.

MSS., MSS, mss., or **mss** manuscripts.

Mt. *pl.* **Mts.** Mount; Mountain.

mtg. 1 meeting. 2 mortgage.

mtge. mortgage.

Mtl. Montréal.

Mtn. *pl.* **Mtns.** Mountain.

Mt.Rev. Most Reverend.

mu [mju] *or* [mu] *n.* the twelfth letter of the Greek alphabet (Μ, μ).

☛ *Hom.* MEW [mju], MOO, MOVE [mu].

much [mʌtʃ] *adj., adv.* **more, most;** *n.* —*adj.* in great quantity, amount, or degree: *much money, much time.*
—*adv.* **1** to a great extent or degree: *much pleased.* **2** nearly; about: *This is much the same as the others.* **3** often; a lot: *Do you go out much?*
—*n.* **1** a great deal: *Much of this is not true.* **2** a great, important, or notable thing or matter: *The rain did not amount to much.*
a bit (or **too**) **much,** far-fetched or unreasonable.
as much as, a to the same extent as: *I like you as much as your sister.* **b** in effect: *She as much as told him to get lost.*
make much of, treat, represent, or consider as of great importance.
much as, a although: *Much as I like opera, I had to decline her invitation.* **b** in almost the same way as.
much of a size, height, etc., nearly the same size, height, etc.
not much of a, not a very good: *This is not much of a game.*
too much for, more than a match for; more than one can cope with, stand, or bear: *The work is too much for him. Their team was too much for ours.* ⟨var. of OE *micel*⟩

much–needed ['mʌtʃ 'nidɪd] *adj.* in great demand; really necessary: *We gave the dog a much-needed bath.*

much•ness ['mʌtʃnɪs] *n.* greatness; magnitude.
much of a muchness, much alike; nearly equivalent.

mu•ci•lage ['mjusəlɪdʒ] *n.* **1** a gummy substance used to make things stick together. **2** a substance in plants that resembles glue or gelatin. ⟨< F < LL *mucilago* musty juice < L *mucus* mucus⟩

mu•ci•lag•i•nous [,mjusə'lædʒənəs] *adj.* **1** sticky; gummy. **2** containing mucilage. —**,mu•ci'lag•i•nous•ly,** *adv.*

mu•cin ['mjusɪn] *n. Biochemistry.* any of a group of proteins that are the main constituent of mucus. —**'mu•cin,oid,** *adj.* —**'mu•cin•ous,** *adj.*

muck [mʌk] *n., v.* —*n.* **1** dirt; filth; mud. **2** anything filthy, dirty, or disgusting. **3** moist farmyard manure. **4 a** well-decomposed peat, used as manure. **b** a heavy soil containing a high percentage of this. **5** *Placer mining. Cdn.* unwanted earth, rock, etc. that is dug out or otherwise removed. **6** *Informal.* mess; untidy condition.
—*v.* **1** soil or make dirty. **2** put muck on. **3** *Mining.* remove unwanted earth, rock, etc.
muck around or **about,** waste time; putter or go around aimlessly: *She's mucking around in the basement.*
muck out, clean out (a stable, mine, etc.).
muck up, *Informal.* mess up; ruin or spoil. ⟨ME < ON *myki* cow dung⟩

muck•er ['mʌkər] *n.* **1** *Slang.* a vulgar, ill-bred person. **2** *Mining, etc.* one who removes muck.

muck•rake ['mʌk,reik] *v.* **-raked, -ra•king.** hunt out and expose real or imagined corruption or misconduct of prominent people, public officials, etc. —**'muck,rak•er,** *n.*

muck•y ['mʌki] *adj.* **muck•i•er, muck•i•est. 1** of muck; like muck. **2** filthy; dirty.

mu•cous ['mjukəs] *adj.* **1** of or like mucus. **2** containing or secreting mucus. ⟨< L *mucosus* < *mucus* mucus⟩ —**mu'cos•i•ty** [mju'kɒsəti], *n.*

☛ *Hom.* MUCUS.

mucous membrane the tissue that lines the nose, throat, and other cavities of the body that are open to the air.

mu•cus ['mjukəs] *n.* a slimy substance that is secreted by and moistens the mucous membranes. A cold in the head causes a discharge of mucus. ⟨< L⟩

☛ *Hom.* MUCOUS.

mud [mʌd] *n., v.* **mud•ded, mud•ding.** —*n.* **1** soft, sticky, wet earth. **2** any place, situation, etc. that is mean or degrading. **3** *Cdn.* muskeg, bog mud, etc. applied to the runners of a dogsled so that it freezes into a smooth-sliding surface.
clear as mud, incomprehensible; obscure.
drag in the mud, defame; sully.
here's mud in your eye, a friendly toast.
(one's) **name is mud,** one is in disgrace.
—*v.* cover with mud; put mud on. ⟨ME *mudde*⟩

mud dauber any of various solitary wasps (family Sphecidae, especially genus *Sceliphron*) that construct their nests of mud, usually in the form of several long, narrow, adjacent cells. Mud daubers are black and yellow, with the abdomen connected to the thorax by a long, thin waist.

mud•dle ['mʌdəl] *v.* **-dled, -dling;** *n.* —*v.* **1** mix or mess up; cause confusion or disorder in; bungle (*often used with* **up**): *to muddle a piece of work. She was trying to help, but she only muddled it up.* **2** make confused or stupid; befog. **3** make (water, etc.) muddy. **4** think or act in a confused, blundering way.
muddle through, manage somehow; succeed in one's object in spite of lack of skill or foresight: *Don't worry, I'll muddle through.*
—*n.* a mess; disorder; confusion.
make a muddle of, bungle. ⟨< *mud*⟩ —**'mud•dle•ment,** *n.* —**'mud•dling•ly,** *adv.*

mud•dle–head•ed ['mʌdəl ,hɛdɪd] *adj.* confused or scatterbrained: *You're awfully muddle-headed today.* —**'mud•dle-,head•ed•ness,** *n.*

mud•dler ['mʌdlər] *n.* **1** one who muddles or muddles through. **2** a thin plastic or metal stick for stirring drinks or other liquids.

mud•dy ['mʌdi] *adj.* **-di•er, -di•est;** *v.* **-died, -dy•ing.** —*adj.* **1** full of or covered with mud: *a muddy sidewalk, muddy water.* **2** of or like mud: *The dog left muddy footprints on the floor.* **3** suggesting or resembling mud; dull, impure, etc.: *a muddy colour, a muddy flavour.* **4** confused; not clear: *muddy thinking.*
—*v.* make or become muddy: *Erosion muddied the river. Don't muddy the issue.*
muddy the water, confuse matters. —**'mud•di•ly,** *adv.* —**'mud•di•ness,** *n.*

mud•fish ['mʌd,fɪʃ] *n.* bowfin.

mud flat the level, low-lying land bordering a stream.

mud•guard ['mʌd,gɑrd] *n.* a guard or shield so placed as to protect riders or passengers from the mud thrown up by the moving wheels of a vehicle.

mud hen coot, especially a North American species, *Fulica americanus.*

mud•pie ['mʌd,paɪ] *n.* **1** a shape made of mud by the use of a small pail. **2** a dessert dish containing chocolate ice cream.

mud puppy any of a genus (*Necturus*) of North American

aquatic salamanders, especially one species (*N. maculosus*) having fluffy, red external gills on either side of the head.

mud room *Cdn.* in a school or other building, a room near the entrance in which overshoes, boots, etc. are deposited before entering.

mud•sill ['mʌd,sɪl] *n.* the lowest sill of a structure, usually one placed in or on the ground.

mud•sling•ing ['mʌd,slɪŋɪŋ] *n.* the use of offensive charges, misleading or slanderous accusations, etc. against an opponent in a political campaign, public meeting, or the like.

mud trout BROOK TROUT.

mud turtle any of a genus (*Kinosternon*) of freshwater turtles of North America.

mues•li ['mjuzli] *n.* a breakfast cereal made of rolled oats, dried fruit and nuts, etc.

mu•ez•zin [mju'ɛzən] *n.* a crier who, at certain hours, calls Muslims to prayer. ⟨< Arabic *mu'adhdhin* < *adhana* proclaim⟩

muff [mʌf] *n., v.* *—n.* **1** a cylindrical covering of fur or other material into which the hands are thrust from both ends to keep them warm. **2** a clumsy failure to catch and hold a ball that comes into one's hands. **3** awkward handling; bungling.
—v. **1** fail to catch and hold (a ball) when it comes into one's hands. **2** handle awkwardly; bungle: *My brother muffed his chance to get that job.* ⟨< Du. *mof* < F *moufle* mitten < OF *moufle* thick glove (cf. Med.L *muffula*), probably < Gmc. Related to MUFFLE.⟩

muf•fin ['mʌfən] *n.* **1** a small, round kind of quick bread made of wheat flour, cornmeal, etc., and egg, often eaten with butter. **2** *Brit.* a round, flat, spongy cake, usually eaten toasted and with butter, in Canada usually called **English muffin.** ⟨< LG *muffen* small cakes⟩

muf•fle[1] ['mʌfəl] *v.* **-fled, -fling;** *n.* *—v.* **1** wrap or cover up in order to keep warm and dry. **2** wrap or cover in order to soften or stop the sound: *A bell can be muffled with cloth.* **3** keep (a person, organization, etc.) from expressing (something); stifle; suppress: *All opposition had been muffled.* **4** dull or deaden (a sound): *a muffled cry for help.*
—n. **1** a muffled sound. **2** something that muffles. ⟨ME < OF *mofler* stuff (cf. OF *enmouflé*, pp., wrapped up) < *moufle* thick glove. Related to MUFF.⟩

muf•fle[2] ['mʌfəl] **1** the bare, thick part of the upper lip and nose in certain animals. **2** See MOUFLE.

muf•fler ['mʌflər] *n.* **1** a wrap or scarf worn around the neck for warmth. **2** a device attached to an automobile or similar engine in order to reduce the noise of the exhaust. **3** anything used to deaden sound.

muf•ti ['mʌfti] *n.* **1** ordinary clothes, not a uniform: *The retired general appeared in mufti.* **2** a Muslim official who assists a judge by formal exposition of the religious law. **3** in Turkey, the official head of the state religion, or one of this official's deputies. ⟨< Arabic *mufti* judge (apparently because of the informal costume traditional for the stage role of a *mufti*)⟩

mug [mʌg] *n., v.* **mugged, mug•ging.** *—n.* **1** a usually large and heavy earthenware or metal drinking cup with a handle, used without a saucer. **2** the amount a mug holds. **3** *Slang.* the face. **4** *Slang.* the mouth. **5** *Slang.* a ruffian; hoodlum; petty criminal.
mug shot a police photograph of a suspect.
—v. **1** attack and rob a person. **2** make a photograph of (a person's face) for police purposes. **3** *Slang.* make faces, especially before an audience or camera: *He loves to mug for the camera.* ⟨Cf. Norwegian *mugge; n.* defs. 3 and 4 derive from the common shape of mugs in earlier times⟩

mug•ger[1] ['mʌgər] *n.* one who attacks and robs people.

mug•ger[2] ['mʌgər] *n.* a large, freshwater crocodile (*Crocodylus palustris*) of India and Sri Lanka, having a broad snout. ⟨< Hind. *magar* < Old Icelandic *mugga*⟩

mug•ging ['mʌgɪŋ] *n., v.* *—n.* an instance of attacking and robbing.
—v. ppr. of MUG.

mug•gy ['mʌgi] *adj.* **-gi•er, -gi•est.** hot and humid; damp and close. ⟨< dial. *mug.* drizzle < Scand.; cf. ON *mugga* fine rain⟩ **—'mug•gi•ly,** *adv.* **—'mug•gi•ness,** *n.*

mug•ho pine ['mjugou] *or* ['mugou] a dwarf form of the Swiss mountain pine tree (*Pinus mugo*) having flexible leaves about 1 cm long, growing in pairs. ⟨< F *mugho* < Ital. *mugo*⟩

mug–up ['mʌg ,ʌp] *n.* a light meal, especially one taken at a break in a journey.

mug•wump ['mʌg,wʌmp] *n.* **1** *Informal.* any indecisive person. **2** *U.S.* an independent in politics. ⟨< Algonquian *mukquomp* great man⟩

Mu•ham•mad [mʊ'hɑməd] *or* [mʊ'hæməd] *n.* See MOHAMMED.

mu•jik [mu'ʒik] *or* ['muʒɪk] *n.* See MUZHIK.

muk•luk ['mʌklʌk] *n. Cdn.* **1** a high, waterproof boot, often made of sealskin, worn by Inuit and others in the North. **2** *Informal.* any similar boot. ⟨< Inuktituk *muklok* bearded seal, a large seal⟩

muk•tuk ['mʌktʌk] *n. Cdn.* the thin outer skin of the beluga, used as food (often eaten raw) in the Arctic. ⟨< Inuktitut⟩

mu•lat•to [mjə'lɑtou] *or* [mjə'lætou], [mə'lɑtou] *or* [mə'lætou] *n., pl.* **-toes. 1** a person having one white and one black parent. **2** a person having both European and African ancestors. ⟨< Sp. and Pg. *mulato* < *mulo* mule < L; from the mule's hybrid origin⟩

mul•ber•ry ['mʌl,bɛri] *n., pl.* **-ries;** *adj.* *—n.* **1** any of a genus (*Morus*) of trees and shrubs having edible, usually purple, berrylike fruit. The leaves of the white mulberry of Europe and Asia are used for feeding silkworms. **2** the fruit of a mulberry. **3** (*adj.*) designating a family (Moraceae) of mainly tropical trees, shrubs, and herbs that includes the mulberry, fig, and breadfruit trees, as well as the hop vine and hemp. **4** a dark reddish purple.
—adj. dark reddish purple. ⟨OE *mōrberie* < L *morum* mulberry + OE *berie* berry⟩

mulch [mʌltʃ] *n., v.* *—n.* straw, leaves, loose earth, etc. spread on the ground around trees or plants. Mulch is used to protect roots from cold or heat, to prevent evaporation of moisture from the soil, to control weeds, or to enrich the soil.
—v. **1** cover with mulch. **2** use or prepare for use as mulch. ⟨OE *mylsc* mellow⟩

mulct [mʌlkt] *v., n.* *—v.* **1** deprive (someone) of (something) by fraud or deceit; swindle: *He was mulcted of his money by a shrewd trick.* **2** punish by a fine.
—n. a fine; penalty. ⟨< L *mulctare*, erroneous var. of *multare* < *multa* a fine⟩

mule[1] [mjul] *n.* **1** the sterile, hybrid offspring of a donkey and a horse, especially of a male donkey and a mare, used as a beast of burden. It has the form and size of a horse, but the large ears, small hoofs, and tufted tail of a donkey. Compare HINNY. **2** any hybrid animal or plant, especially one that is sterile. **3** *Informal.* a stupid or stubborn person. **4** a kind of spinning machine. ⟨ME < OF < L *mulus*⟩
☛ *Hom.* MEWL.

Mule

mule[2] [mjul] *n.* a loose slipper covering only the toes and part of the instep, and leaving the rest of the foot and the heel uncovered. ⟨< F < Du. *muil* < L *mulleus* shoe of red leather⟩
☛ *Hom.* MEWL.

mule deer a deer (*Odocoileus hemionus*) of W North America that has very long ears and a white tail with a black tip. The mule deer is larger than the white-tailed deer.

mule–skin•ner ['mjul ,skɪnər] *n. Informal.* muleteer. ⟨*mule*[1] + *skinner*, so called because the driver figuratively skins his horses, mules, etc. with his whip⟩

mu•le•teer [,mjulə'tir] *n.* a driver of mules. ⟨< F *muletier* < *mulet*, dim. of OF *mul* mule < L *mulus*⟩

mule train a line of pack mules or of carts pulled by mules.

mul•ish ['mjulɪʃ] *adj.* like a mule; stubborn; obstinate. **—'mul•ish•ly,** *adv.* **—'mul•ish•ness,** *n.*

mull[1] [mʌl] *v. Informal.* think (about); reflect; turn over in one's mind (*used with* **over**): *He mulled over his problems.* ⟨origin uncertain⟩

mull[2] [mʌl] *v.* make (wine, beer, or cider) into a hot drink, with sugar, spices, etc. ⟨origin uncertain⟩

mull[3] [mʌl] *n.* a thin, soft muslin. ⟨for *mulmul* < Hind., Persian *malmal*⟩

mul•lah ['mʌlə], ['mʊlə], *or* ['mulə] *n.* a title of respect for a Muslim who is learned in Islamic theology and the sacred law. ⟨< Turkish, Persian, Hind. *mulla* < Arabic *maula*⟩

mul•lein ['mʌlən] *n.* any of a genus (*Verbascum*) of plants of the figwort family having coarse, woolly leaves and spikes of yellow, pink, or white flowers. Some mulleins are common weeds; others are grown as garden flowers. Also, **mullen.** ⟨ME < AF *moleine*⟩

mul•let [ˈmʌlɪt] *n., pl.* **-let** or **-lets. 1** any of a family (Mugilidae) of important food fishes of small or medium size, having soft fins and a streamlined, rounded body. Mullet are found in fresh water and salt water. Also called **grey mullet. 2** any of a family (Mullidae) of brightly coloured, medium-sized saltwater fishes having barbels on the lower jaw. Some species are valued as food fish. Also called **red mullet.** ⟨ME < OF *mulet* < L *mullus* red mullet < Gk. *myllos*⟩

mul•li•gan [ˈmʌləgən] *n. Slang.* a stew of meat or, sometimes, fish and vegetables. ⟨origin uncertain⟩

mul•li•ga•taw•ny [ˌmʌləgəˈtɒni] *n.* a soup made of chicken or meat stock and flavoured with curry. ⟨< Tamil *milagu-tanni* pepper water⟩

mul•lion [ˈmʌljən] *n.* a vertical bar between the panes of a window, the panels in the wall of a room, or the like. ⟨alteration of ME *muniall, monial* < OF *moi(e)nel,* earlier *meienel* in the middle < *meien* in the middle < L *medianus* < *medius*⟩ **—ˈmul•lioned,** *adj.*

multi– *combining form.* **1** having or consisting of several or many: *multicoloured, multiform.* **2** involving or affecting several or many: *multinational.* **3** several or many times more than; several or many times over: *multimillionaire.* ⟨< L *multi-* < *multus* much, many⟩
☛ *Pronun.* See note at ANTI-.

mul•ti•cel•lu•lar [ˌmʌltiˈsɛljələr] *adj.* having more than one cell.

mul•ti•col•oured or **mul•ti•col•ored** [ˈmʌltiˌkʌlərd] *adj.* having many colours.

mul•ti•cul•tur•al [ˌmʌltiˈkʌltʃərəl] *adj.* **1** of or having a number of distinct cultures existing side by side in the same country, province, etc.: *Canada is a multicultural country.* **2** designed for a country, province, etc. having a number of distinct cultures existing side by side: *multicultural programs.*

mul•ti•cul•tur•al•ism [ˌmʌltiˈkʌltʃərəˌlɪzəm] *n.* **1** the fact or condition of being multicultural: *She wrote a report on multiculturalism in the schools.* **2** a policy supporting or promoting the existence of a number of distinct cultural groups side by side within a country, province, etc.: *Canada has a federal minister responsible for multiculturalism.*

mul•ti•dis•ci•pli•na•ry [ˌmʌltiˈdɪsəpləˌnɛri] *adj.* combining a number of subject fields; requiring expertise from several different areas.

mul•ti•eth•nic [ˌmʌltiˈɛθnɪk] *adj.* comprising people from many nations.

mul•ti•fac•tor•ial [ˌmʌltifækˈtɔriəl] *adj.* due to multiple factors.

multifactorial inheritance *Genetics.* the pattern of inheritance shown by traits that are caused by the combined action of genes with minor effects, sometimes combined with environmental effects. This is characteristic of many types of normal variation, such as stature, and of many common congenital malformations.

mul•ti•far•i•ous [ˌmʌltəˈfɛriəs] *adj.* having many different kinds; extremely varied: *multifarious talents.* ⟨< L *multifarius*⟩ **—ˌmul•tiˈfar•i•ous•ly,** *adv.* **—ˌmul•tiˈfar•i•ous•ness,** *n.*

mul•ti•fo•cals [ˈmʌltiˌfoukəlz] *n.pl.* trifocals.

mul•ti•fold [ˈmʌltəˌfould] *adj.* manifold.

mul•ti•form [ˈmʌltəˌfɔrm] *adj.* having many different shapes, forms, or kinds.

mul•ti–in•farct dementia [ˈmʌlti ɪnˈfɑrkt] loss of memory due to repeated small strokes.

mul•ti•lat•er•al [ˌmʌltiˈlætərəl] *adj.* **1** having many sides; many-sided. **2** involving two or more nations, parties, etc.: *a multilateral trade agreement.* **—ˌmul•tiˈlat•er•al•ly,** *adv.*

mul•ti•lin•gual [ˌmʌltiˈlɪŋgwəl] *or* [ˌmʌltiˈlɪŋgjuəl] *adj.* **1** able to speak several languages well: *The company needs several multilingual sales representatives.* **2** expressed in or containing several languages: *a multilingual conversation, a multilingual dictionary.* **—ˌmul•tiˈlin•gual•ly,** *adv.*

mul•ti•lin•gual•ism [ˌmʌltiˈlɪŋgwəˌlɪzəm] *or* [ˌmʌltiˈlɪŋgjuəˌlɪzəm] *n.* the ability to speak several languages: *Multilingualism is common in some ethnic groups.*

mul•ti•me•di•a [ˌmʌltiˈmidiə] *adj.* **1** using, involving, or including several media together: *a multimedia sales presentation, a multimedia art exhibition.* **2** *Computer technology.* making use of sound, graphics, scanned photos, text, etc. simultaneously or within a single piece of software.

mul•ti•mil•lion•aire [ˌmʌltiˈmɪljəˌnɛr] *or* [ˌmʌltiˌmɪljəˈnɛr] *n.* a person whose wealth amounts to many millions of dollars, pounds, etc.

mul•ti•na•tion•al [ˌmʌltiˈnæʃənəl] *adj., n. —adj.* **1** of, having to do with, or involving several nations: *a multinational empire, a multinational agreement.* **2** of a business organization, having divisions in several nations: *a multinational food corporation.* **3** of or having to do with a multinational business organization.
—n. a multinational company: *Several large multinationals have already located in this area.*

mul•ti•nu•cle•ar [ˌmʌltiˈnjukliər] *or* [ˌmʌltiˈnukliər] *adj.* having many nuclei.

mul•tip•a•rous [mʌlˈtɪpərəs] *adj. Biology.* producing more than one offspring at a birth. ⟨< NL *multiparus* < L *multus* much, many + *parere* bring forth⟩

mul•ti•phase [ˈmʌltiˌfeiz] *adj.* having several phases.

mul•ti•ple [ˈmʌltəpəl] *adj., n. —adj.* of, having, or involving many parts, elements, relations, etc.: *a man of multiple interests.*
—n. **1** *Mathematics.* a number or quantity that contains another number or quantity a certain number of times without a remainder: *Twelve is a multiple of three. The kilometre is a multiple of the metre.* **2** a submultiple: *Ten is a multiple of one hundred.* ⟨< F < LL *multiplus* manifold⟩

multiple alleles *Genetics.* the occurrence in a population of multiple alternative forms of a gene at a single place on the chromosome (locus). Some gene loci are known to have hundreds of alleles; for example, the cystic fibrosis locus has more than 300 known alleles.

multiple sclerosis a disease of the brain and spinal cord that usually eventually results in permanent paralysis. The cause of multiple sclerosis is a growth of fibrous tissue in the brain or on the spinal cord. *Abbrev.:* MS

multiple star *Astronomy.* three or more stars that appear to be only one, and have one gravitational centre.

mul•ti•plex [ˈmʌltəˌplɛks] *adj., n. —adj.* **1** manifold; multiple. **2** *Genetics.* of or having to with a family in which more than one individual has a specific trait. **3** *Radio, television, etc.* capable of carrying two or more distinct signals simultaneously: *multiplex telegraphy.*
—n. a building that houses more dwellings than a duplex. ⟨< L *multiplex* < *multus* much + *-plex* -fold⟩ **—ˈmul•tiˌplex•er,** *n.*

mul•ti•pli•cand [ˌmʌltəpləˈkænd] *n. Mathematics.* the number or quantity to be multiplied by another. In 5 times 497, the multiplicand is 497. ⟨< L *multiplicandus,* gerundive of *multiplicare.* See MULTIPLY.⟩

mul•ti•pli•cate [ˈmʌltəpləkɪt] *or* [ˈmʌltɪplɪˌkeit] *adj. Rare.* multiple.

mul•ti•pli•ca•tion [ˌmʌltəpləˈkeiʃən] *n.* **1** a multiplying or being multiplied. **2** *Mathematics.* the operation of multiplying one number by another.

mul•ti•plic•i•ty [ˌmʌltəˈplɪsəti] *n., pl.* **-ties. 1** the fact or condition of being multiple. **2** a manifold variety. **3** a great many: *a multiplicity of interests.* ⟨< LL *multiplicitas* < L *multiplex.* See MULTIPLEX.⟩

mul•ti•pli•er [ˈmʌltəˌplaiər] *n.* **1** the number by which another number is to be multiplied. In 5 times 83, the multiplier is 5. **2** a person or thing that multiplies.

mul•ti•ply [ˈmʌltəˌplaɪ] *v.* **-plied, -ply•ing. 1** increase or cause to increase in number or amount: *As we climbed up the mountain, the dangers and difficulties multiplied.* **2** *Mathematics.* take (a number or quantity) a given number of times. To multiply 16 by 3 means to take 16 three times, making a total of 48. **3** increase by procreation. **4** produce (animals or plants) by propagation. ⟨ME < OF *multiplier* < L *multiplicare* < *multiplex.* See MULTIPLEX.⟩ **—ˈmul•tiˌpli•a•ble,** *adj.*

mul•ti•ra•cial [ˌmʌltiˈreiʃəl] *adj.* involving, comprising, or representing many different races: *a multiracial society.*

mul•ti•stage [ˈmʌltiˌsteidʒ] *adj.* **1** of a rocket or missile, having several sections, each of which lifts it to a greater height before burning out and dropping off. **2** having a number of stages for the completion of a process: *a multistage investigation.*

mul•ti•task•ing [ˈmʌltiˌtæskɪŋ] *n. Computer technology.* a feature of an operating system allowing it to run more than one application simultaneously.

mul•ti•tude [ˈmʌltəˌtjud] *or* [ˈmʌltəˌtud] *n.* **1** a great many; crowd. **2 the multitude,** the common people. ⟨< L *multitudo* < *multus* much⟩

mul•ti•tu•di•nous [ˌmʌltəˈtjudənəs] *or* [ˌmʌltəˈtudənəs] *adj.* **1** forming a multitude; very numerous. **2** including many parts, elements, items, or features. **—ˌmul•ti'tu•di•nous•ly,** *adv.* **—ˌmul•ti'tu•di•nous•ness,** *n.*

mul•ti•va•lent [ˌmʌltəˈveilənt] *or* [mʌlˈtɪvələnt] *adj. Chemistry.* polyvalent. **—ˌmul•ti'va•lence,** *n.*

mul•ti•va•ri•ate [ˌmʌltəˈvɛriɪt] *adj. Statistics.* involving more than one variable.

mul•ti•ver•si•ty [ˌmʌltəˈvɜrsəti] *n., pl.* **-ties.** a large university housing many faculties, schools, or colleges.

mum¹ [mʌm] *adj., interj. —adj.* silent; saying nothing.
—interj. be silent! say nothing!
mum's the word, keep silent. ⟨ME; ? imitative⟩

mum² [mʌm] *n. Esp. Brit.* See MOM.

mum³ [mʌm] *v.* **mummed, mum•ming. 1** be a mummer; act or play in a mask or disguise. **2** masquerade. **3** *Archaic.* act in a dumb show. ⟨perhaps back formation < *mommyng* mummer's play. See MUMMER.⟩

mum⁴ [mʌm] *n. Informal.* chrysanthemum.

mum•ble [ˈmʌmbəl] *v.* **-bled, -bling;** *n. —v.* **1** speak indistinctly, as people do when they move their lips only slightly. **2** chew as a person does who has no teeth.
—n. a mumbling sound. ⟨ME *momele(n)*, ? < *mum¹*⟩
—'mum•bler, *n.* **—'mum•bling•ly,** *adv.*
☛ *Syn. v.* **1.** See note at MURMUR.

mum•bo jum•bo [ˈmʌmbou ˈdʒʌmbou] **1** a foolish or meaningless ritual; ceremonial nonsense. **2** meaningless or unintelligible language; gibberish. **3** an object foolishly worshipped or feared. ⟨? < a West African language⟩

mum•mer [ˈmʌmər] *n.* **1** a person who wears a mask, fancy costume, or disguise for fun. **2** an actor. **3** an actor in one of the rural plays traditionally performed in England, Newfoundland, and elsewhere at Christmas. ⟨ME < OF *momeur* < *momer* mask oneself⟩

mum•mer•y [ˈmʌməri] *n., pl.* **-mer•ies. 1** a performance of mummers. **2** any useless or silly show or ceremony. ⟨< OF *mommerie*⟩

mum•mi•chog [ˈmʌmɪˌtʃɒg] *n.* a fish (*Fundulus heteroclitus*) of Atlantic coastal waters which often enters fresh water, having a blunt snout, rounded body, and rounded tail fin. It is very hardy and can live for a long time without oxygen. ⟨< Algonquian⟩

mum•mi•fy [ˈmʌməˌfaɪ] *v.* **-fied, -fy•ing. 1** make (a dead body) into a mummy; make like a mummy. **2** dry or shrivel up. **—ˌmum•mi•fi'ca•tion,** *n.*

mum•my¹ [ˈmʌmi] *n., pl.* **-mies. 1** a dead body preserved from decay by the ancient Egyptian method. Egyptian mummies have lasted more than 3000 years. **2** a dead human or animal body dried and preserved by nature. ⟨< F *momie* < Med.L *mumia* < Arabic *mumiya* mummy < *mum* wax⟩

mum•my² [ˈmʌmi] *n., pl.* **-mies.** *Esp. Brit.* See MOMMY.

mumps [mʌmps] *n.pl.* (*used with a singular verb*) a contagious disease caused by a virus, characterized especially by inflammation and swelling of the salivary glands below the ears and by difficulty in swallowing. It is generally a childhood disease. ⟨pl. of obs. *mump* grimace⟩
☛ *Usage.* **Mumps** is plural in form and singular in use: *Mumps is dangerous when caught by adults.*

munch [mʌntʃ] *v.* chew vigorously and steadily; chew noisily: *A horse munches its oats.* ⟨apparently imitative⟩

Mun•da [ˈmʊndə] *n.* an Austro-Asiatic language spoken in NE India.

mun•dane [mʌnˈdein] *or* [ˈmʌndein] *adj.* **1** ordinary; everyday; humdrum: *mundane matters of business.* **2** of this world, not of heaven; earthly. ⟨< F < L *mundanus* < *mundus* world⟩

mung bean [mʌŋ] an annual bean grown for forage or as a source of bean sprouts. ⟨< obs. *mungo* < Tamil *mungu*⟩

mun•go [ˈmʌŋgou] *n.* SHODDY (defs. 1, 2). ⟨origin uncertain⟩

mu•nic•i•pal [mjuˈnɪsəpəl] *adj.* **1** of or having to do with the affairs of a city, town, or other municipality. **2** run by a municipality: *municipal affairs.* **3** having local self-government: *a municipal district.* ⟨< L *municipalis*, ult. < *munia* official duties + *capere* take on⟩

municipal district *Cdn. Alberta and Territories.* a large rural municipality.

mu•nic•i•pal•i•ty [mjuˌnɪsəˈpæləti] *or* [ˌmjunəsəˈpæləti] *n., pl.* **-ties.** a city, town, county, district, township, or other area having local self-government.

mu•nic•i•pal•ly [mjuˈnɪsəpli] *adv.* by a city or town; with regard to a city or town or to municipal affairs.

mu•nif•i•cent [mjuˈnɪfəsənt] *adj.* **1** extremely generous. **2** characterized by great generosity: *a munificent reward.* ⟨< L *munificentia* < *munificus* generous, ult. < *munus* gift + *facere* make⟩ **—mu'nif•i•cence,** *adj.* **—mu'nif•i•cent•ly,** *adv.*

mu•ni•ment [ˈmjunəmənt] *n.* **1 muniments,** *pl. Law.* a document or documents kept as evidence of inheritance, title to property, etc. **2** *Archaic.* a defence; protection. ⟨< Med.L *munimentum* document, title deed < L *munimentum* defence, fortification < *munire* fortify < *moenia* walls⟩

mu•ni•tion [mjuˈnɪʃən] *n., v. —n.* **1** Usually, **munitions,** *pl.* material used in war: *Munitions are military supplies, such as guns, powder, or bombs.* **2** (*adjl.*) having to do with military supplies. A munitions plant is a factory for making munitions.
—v. provide with military supplies: *to munition a fort.* ⟨< L *munitio, -onis* < *munire* fortify < *moenia* walls⟩

mu•on [ˈmjuɒn] *n. Physics.* a highly unstable, elementary particle of the lepton group having a positive or negative charge and a mass equal to about 207 times the mass of an electron. Cosmic-ray showers detected on earth are composed mainly of muons. ⟨short for *mu meson*; it was formerly classified as a meson. 20c.⟩

mu•pi•ro•cin [mjuˈpirəsɪn] *n.* an antibiotic drug used in an ointment form.

mu•ral [ˈmjʊrəl] *adj., n. —adj.* **1** on, in, or for a wall. A mural painting is painted on a wall of a building. **2** of, having to do with, or like a wall.
—n. a painting done directly on a wall or a large photograph, etc. attached directly to a wall. ⟨< F < L *muralis* < *murus* wall⟩

mu•ral•ist [ˈmjʊrəlɪst] *n.* a designer or painter of murals.

mur•der [ˈmɜrdər] *n., v. —n.* **1** *Law.* the unlawful killing of a person by another. In Canada, **first-degree murder** is the intentional and unlawful killing of one person or the accidental killing of one person by someone committing any of certain crimes (such as kidnapping, hijacking of an aircraft, or rape). **2** an instance of such a crime: *There has never been a murder in this town.* **3** *Informal.* something very hard, disagreeable, or dangerous: *The traffic was murder last night. The last part of the climb is murder.* **4** of crows, a group.
murder will out, a a murder cannot be hidden. **b** any great wrong will be found out.
scream or **yell bloody** (or **blue**) **murder,** scream or yell very loudly.
—v. **1** *Law.* commit the crime of murder against: *Cain murdered his brother.* **2** do (something) very badly; spoil or ruin: *She really murders that song.* ⟨var. of *murther*⟩ **—'mur•der•er,** *n.*
☛ *Syn. v.* **1.** See note at KILL.

mur•der•ous [ˈmɜrdərəs] *adj.* **1** able or likely to kill: *a murderous blow.* **2** ready or intending to murder: *a murderous villain.* **3** causing or characterized by murder or bloodshed: *a murderous plot.* **4** *Informal.* very dangerous, unpleasant, or difficult. **—'mur•der•ous•ly,** *adv.* **—'mur•der•ous•ness,** *n.*

mu•rex [ˈmjʊrɛks] *n., pl.* **mu•rex•es** or **mu•ri•ces** [-ˌsiz]. a tropical shellfish with a spiny shell, formerly used as a source of purple dye, found only in warm oceans. ⟨< NL < L⟩

mu•ri•ate [ˈmjʊriˌeit] *n.* a chloride, especially potassium chloride, used for fertilizer. ⟨< F *muriate* < L *muria* brine⟩

mu•ri•at•ic acid [ˌmjʊriˈætɪk] See HYDROCHLORIC ACID. ⟨< L *muriaticus* < *muria* brine⟩

mu•ri•cate [ˈmjʊrəkɪt] *or* [ˈmjʊrəˌkeit] *adj. Botany, zoology.* of a surface, having short points. ⟨< L *mūricātus* murexlike⟩

mu•rine [ˈmjʊrɪn] *or* [ˈmjʊraɪn] *adj.* having to do with rodents (family Muridae). ⟨< L *mūrīnus* of mice⟩

murk [mɜrk] *n., adj. —n.* darkness; gloom.
—adj. Poetic. dark; gloomy. Also, **mirk.** ⟨ME *mirke* < Scand.; cf. Icel. *myrkr* dark, darkness⟩

murk•y [ˈmɜrki] *adj.* **murk•i•er, murk•i•est. 1** dark or gloomy. **2** very thick and obscure; misty; hazy: *murky smoke.* **3** obscure in meaning: *murky prose.* **—'murk•i•ly,** *adv.* **—'murk•i•ness,** *n.*

mur•mur [ˈmɜrmər] *n., v. —n.* **1** a soft, low, indistinct sound that rises and falls a little but goes on without breaks: *the murmur of a stream, of little waves, or of voices in another room.* **2** *Medicine.* a sound in the heart or lungs, especially an abnormal sound due to a leaky valve in the heart. **3** a softly spoken word or speech. **4** a complaint made under the breath, not aloud.
—v. **1** make a soft, low, indistinct sound. **2** utter in a murmur.

3 complain under the breath; grumble. ⟨< L⟩ —**'mur•mur•er,** *n.* —**'mur•mur•ing•ly,** *adv.*

☛ *Syn. v.* **2. Murmur,** MUMBLE, MUTTER = speak indistinctly. **Murmur** = speak too softly to be clearly heard or plainly understood: *She murmured her thanks.* **Mumble** = speak with the lips partly closed, so that the sounds are not properly formed or articulated: *I'm not hard of hearing; you just mumble.* **Mutter** = mumble in a low voice, as if not wanting to be heard, and especially suggests complaint or anger: *She muttered some rude remarks.*

mur•mur•a•tion [,mɜrmə'reiʃən] *n.* **1** a muttering. **2** a group of starlings.

Mur•phy bed ['mɜrfi] a bed that may be folded or swung up into a wall cabinet when not in use. ⟨after Wm. *Murphy* U.S. inventor⟩

mur•rain ['mɜrən] *n.* **1** an infectious disease of cattle. **2** *Archaic.* a pestilence; plague. ⟨ME < OF *morine,* ult. < L *mori* die⟩

murre [mɜr] *n.* **1** any of a small genus (*Uria*) of black-and-white sea birds belonging to the auk family. **2** *Rare.* razorbill. ⟨origin uncertain⟩

☛ *Hom.* MYRRH.

mur•re•let ['mɜrlɪt] *n.* either of two species of small seabirds (*Brachyramphus marmoratus* or *Synthliboramphus antiquus*).

mur•rey ['mɜri] *n., adj.* mulberry.

murrhine glass ['mɜrɪn] *or* ['mɜraɪn] glass decorated with precious stones. ⟨< L *murrhinus* < *murra* < Iranian⟩

mur•ther ['mɜrðər] *n. or v. Archaic.* murder. ⟨OE *morthor*⟩ —**'mur•ther•er,** *n.*

mus. 1 music. **2** museum.

Mus•ca ['mʌskə] *n. Astronomy.* the Fly, a constellation in the southern hemisphere near Carina. ⟨< L, fly⟩

mus•ca•dine ['mʌskə,din] *n.* a grape (*Vitis rotundifolia*) of the S U.S. with a purple skin. ⟨< *muscatel*⟩

mus•ca•ri [mə'skɑri] *n.* GRAPE HYACINTH. ⟨< NL genus name, ? < Mod.Gk. *moschari* grape hyacinth⟩

mus•cat ['mʌskæt] *or* ['mʌskət] *n.* **1** any of several varieties of grapevine that produce sweet, highly scented, white grapes used especially for wine or raisins but also as table grapes. **2** muscatel. ⟨< F < Provençal *muscat* having the fragrance of musk < *musc* musk < LL *muscus.* See MUSK.⟩

mus•ca•tel [,mʌskə'tɛl] *n.* **1** a rich, sweet, fortified dessert wine made from muscat grapes. **2** the raisin from muscat grapes. ⟨< MF, dim. of *muscat* < Provençal. See MUSCAT.⟩

mus•cid ['mʌsɪd] *adj., n.* —*adj.* belonging to the Muscidae, the family of dipterous insects such as the housefly.
—*n.* any of these insects.

mus•cle ['mʌsəl] *n., v.* **-cled, -cling.** —*n.* **1 a** a kind of animal tissue consisting of long cells that contract and relax to produce movement. **b** an organ made up of a bundle of muscle tissue, attached at either end to a particular bone or joint, which moves or stops the movement of a part of the body. **2** strength: *It takes muscle to move a piano.* **3** *Informal.* power or influence, especially when based on force or the threat of force: *The organization has enough muscle to get its way with the city council.*
not move a muscle, keep perfectly still.
—*v. Informal.* move or gain by using force or the threat of force: *He muscled his way past the doorman.*
muscle in, *Slang.* force oneself into a situation when one is not wanted: *Why should she muscle in on our meeting?* ⟨< F < L *musculus,* dim. of *mus* mouse; from the way in which certain muscles move when they are tensed and relaxed⟩ —**'mus•cle•less,** *adj.* —**'mus•cly,** *adj.*

☛ *Hom.* MUSSEL.

mus•cle–bound ['mʌsəl ,baʊnd] *adj.* having some of the muscles stiff or tight, usually as a result of too much or too little exercise.

mus•cle•man ['mʌsəl,mæn] *or* ['mʌsəlmən] *n., pl.* **-men. 1** *Informal.* a brawny, muscular man. **2** *Slang.* a ruffian; strong-arm man.

muscle sense *Physiology.* the sense by which muscular movements are perceived, through nerve cells.

mus•co•va•do [,mʌskə'veidou] *or* [,mʌskə'vɑdou] *n.* raw sugar from the juice of sugar cane by evaporation. ⟨< Pg. (*açucar*) *mascavado* separated (sugar) < *mascavar* separate⟩

Mus•co•vite ['mʌskə,vəit] *n., adj.* —*n.* **1** a native or inhabitant of Muscovy or of Moscow. **2** Russian. **3 muscovite,** the common, light-coloured variety of mica.
—*adj.* of or having to do with Muscovy, Moscow, or Russia, or its inhabitants.

Mus•co•vy ['mʌskəvi] *n.* **1** formerly, a grand duchy of the 13th to 16th centuries, that had Moscow as its capital. **2** *Archaic.* Russia.

Muscovy duck a large, crested, greenish black duck (*Cairina moschata*) native to tropical America, but now widely domesticated. ⟨for *musk duck*⟩

mus•cu•lar ['mʌskjələr] *adj.* **1** of or having to do with muscle or the muscles: *a muscular strain, muscular activity.* **2** having well-developed muscles; strong: *a muscular arm.* **3** consisting of muscle. —**,mus•cu'lar•i•ty,** *n.* —**'mus•cu•lar•ly,** *adv.*

muscular dystrophy *Pathology.* a disease characterized by progressive wasting away of muscle fibres; one of several disorders in which a defect in a gene leads to muscle wasting and weakness.

mus•cu•la•ture ['mʌskjələtʃər] *or* ['mʌskjələ,tʃʊr] *n.* a system or arrangement of muscles. ⟨< F⟩

muse [mjuz] *v.* **mused, mus•ing. 1** think in a dreamy way; think; meditate. **2** look thoughtfully. **3** say thoughtfully. ⟨ME < OF *muser* loiter⟩ —**'mus•er,** *n.*

☛ *Hom.* MEWS.

Muse [mjuz] *n.* **1** *Greek mythology.* one of the nine goddesses of the fine arts and sciences, daughters of Zeus and Mnemosyne. Their names are Calliope, Clio, Erato, Euterpe, Melpomene, Polyhymnia, Terpsichore, Thalia, and Urania. **2 muse,** a spirit that inspires a poet or composer. ⟨ME < OF < L *Musa* < Gk. *Mousa*⟩

mu•sette [mju'zɛt] *n.* **1 a** a gentle pastoral air written for a bagpipe, or imitating the effect of a bagpipe. **b** a dance for this air. **2** a kind of bagpipe. **3** MUSETTE BAG. ⟨< F < OF *musette* < *muse* bagpipe < *muser* play the musette⟩

musette bag a small bag carried by means of a shoulder strap, used by soldiers and hikers to carry food, belongings, etc.

mu•se•um [mju'ziəm] *n.* the building or rooms where a collection of objects illustrating science, history, art, or other subjects is kept and displayed. ⟨< L < Gk. *mouseion* seat of the Muses < *Mousa* Muse⟩

mush[1] [mʌʃ] *n.* **1** *Esp. U.S.* cornmeal boiled in water. **2** any soft, thick mass. **3** *Informal.* weak sentiment; sentimentality; maudlin talk. ⟨var. of *mash;* cf. Du. *moes*⟩

mush[2] [mʌʃ] *n., v. Cdn.* —*n.* **1** a command to advance given to sled dogs. **2** a journey made by dogsled, especially while driving the team from behind the sled.
—*v.* **1** urge (sled dogs) onward by shouting commands: *She mushed her dog team through the blinding storm.* **2** follow a dogsled on foot: *For six days he mushed across the barren lands.* ⟨< F *marche* (*donc*), a command to dogs < *marcher* go, walk⟩ —**'mush•er,** *n.*

mush•room ['mʌʃrum] *or* ['mʌʃrʊm] *n., v.* —*n.* **1** the large, often umbrella-shaped fruiting body of any of various fungi (class Basidiomycetes, especially of order Agaricales). Many mushrooms are edible. Compare TOADSTOOL. **2** anything shaped or growing like a mushroom. **3** (*adjl.*) of or like a mushroom in shape or rapid growth: *a mushroom town, growing out of control.* **4** (*adjl.*) made with mushrooms: *mushroom soup.*
—*v.* **1** grow very fast: *His business mushroomed when he opened the new store.* **2** of a bullet, flatten at the end on impact against something very hard. ⟨ME < OF *mousseron* < LL *mussirio, -onis*⟩

mushroom cloud a rapidly rising, mushroom-shaped cloud of radioactive matter that follows a nuclear explosion.

mush•y ['mʌʃi] *adj.* **mush•i•er, mush•i•est. 1** like mush; pulpy. **2** *Informal.* weakly sentimental. —**'mush•i•ly,** *adv.* —**'mush•i•ness,** *n.*

mu•sic ['mjuzɪk] *n.* **1** the art and science of organizing sounds of varying pitch and volume into rhythmical, harmonic, and melodic patterns to produce a composition having structure and unity. **2** such an organization of sounds; a musical composition or compositions. **3** written or printed music; a score or composition set down on paper using special signs and symbols to indicate tone, rhythm, etc.: *a songbook with words and music.* **4** a pleasant sound or succession of sounds: *the music of the wind.* **5** responsiveness to, or appreciation of, music: *She had music in her blood.*
face the music, *Informal.* accept difficulties or punishment resulting from one's actions.
set to music, compose a melody to accompany (a poem, etc.) ⟨ME < OF *musique* < L *musica* < Gk. *mousikē (technē)* art of the Muse < *Mousa* Muse⟩ —**'mu•sic•less,** *adj.*

mu•si•cal ['mjuzəkəl] *adj., n.* —*adj.* **1** of or having to do with music: *musical knowledge, musical instruments.* **2** like music;

melodious and pleasant. **3** set to music or accompanied by music. **4** fond of music. **5** skilled in music; talented as a musician.
—n. **1** a stage entertainment or motion picture in which a story is told through music, singing, and dancing as well as dialogue. **2** *Archaic.* musicale. **—'mu•si•cal•ly,** *adv.* **—,mu•si'cal•i•ty,** *n.*

musical chairs **1** an elimination game in which players march to music around chairs numbering always one fewer than the players. When the music stops, everyone rushes to sit down and the person left standing is eliminated. **2** a situation in which a number of people exchange positions.

musical comedy a light and amusing play in which plot and characterization are less important than singing, dancing, and costumes.

mu•si•cale [,mjuzə'kæl] *n.* a social gathering to enjoy music. ⟨< F *musicale,* short for *soirée musicale* musical evening⟩

musical instrument **1** any stringed, wind, or percussion instrument, as a violin, trumpet, or drum, employed, or designed to be employed, in producing music or musical sounds. **2** an electronic instrument used to produce, not reproduce, musical sounds.

music box a box or case containing apparatus for producing music mechanically, usually a revolving cylinder set with pins that strike the tuned teeth of a comblike strip, or bar, of steel.

music drama **1** a type of opera in which words and music are intimately linked, the music's prime purpose being to indicate dramatic development, character, mood, etc. Wagner's 'Lohengrin' is a music drama. **2** any opera.

music hall *Esp. Brit.* **1** a theatre for singing, dancing, variety shows, etc.; vaudeville theatre. **2** vaudeville entertainment. **—'mu•sic-,hall,** *adj.*

mu•si•cian [mju'zɪʃən] *n.* a person trained in music, especially one who earns a living by playing, conducting, composing, or singing music: *An orchestra is made up of many musicians.*

music of the spheres music once supposed to be made by the movement of celestial bodies.

mu•si•col•o•gy [,mjuzə'kɒlədʒi] *n.* the study of the forms, principles, literature, and history of music. **—,mu•si•co'log•i•cal** [,mjusəkə'lɒdʒəkəl], *adj.* **—,mu•si•co'log•i•cal•ly,** *adv.* **—,mu•si'col•o•gist,** *n.*

music synthesizer an electronic instrument capable of producing musical sounds.

music video a short videotape featuring a piece of music such as a rock song.

mus•jid ['mʌsdʒɪd] *n.* See MASJID.

musk [mʌsk] *n.* **1** a substance with a strong and lasting odour, used as a perfume base and fixative. It is obtained from a special gland in the abdomen of the male musk deer. **2** a similar substance produced by any of various other animals, such as the mink, civet, or muskrat. **3** a synthetic substance with similar characteristics. **4** the odour of musk or something like it in heaviness or persistence. **5** any plant whose leaves or flowers smell like musk, such as the musk rose. ⟨ME < OF < LL *muscus* < LGk. *moschos* < Persian *mushk* < Skt. *mushka* testicle⟩

musk deer a small, hornless deer (*Moschus moschiferus*) of central Asia, the male of which has a gland containing musk.

mus•keg ['mʌskɛg] *n. Cdn.* **1** a swamp or marsh. **2** an area of bog composed of decaying plant life, especially moss. There are vast regions of muskeg in northern Alberta. ⟨< Algonquian; cf. Cree *muskak* swamp⟩

mus•kel•lunge ['mʌskə,lʌndʒ] *n., pl.* **-lunge.** *Cdn.* a very large freshwater fish (*Esox masquinongy*) of the pike family. The muskellunge is highly valued as a food and game fish. ⟨< Algonquian (Objibwa) *mashkinonge* great pike⟩

mus•ket ['mʌskɪt] *n.* an old type of long-barrelled gun used by soldiers before rifles were invented. See FIREARM for picture. ⟨< F *mousquet* < Ital. *moschetto,* originally a kind of hawk < *mosca* fly < L *musca*⟩

mus•ket•eer [,mʌskə'tir] *n.* a soldier armed with a musket.

mus•ket•ry ['mʌskɪtri] *n.* **1** muskets collectively. **2** the act of shooting with muskets. **3** soldiers armed with muskets.

mus•kie ['mʌski] *n. Cdn. Informal.* muskellunge.
☛ *Hom.* MUSKY.

musk•mel•on ['mʌsk,mɛlən] *n.* **1** any of several varieties of melon with a musky odour, the fruits of varieties of an annual trailing vine (*Cucumis melo*) of the gourd family, having a hard, rough or smooth rind and sweet, juicy, pale orange, green, or yellowish flesh. **2** any of the vines that bear such fruits.

Musk-oxen—
about 150 cm high
at the shoulder

musk–ox or **musk•ox** ['mʌsk ,ɒks] *n., pl.* **-ox** or **-ox•en.** *Cdn.* a large, heavy-set, bovid mammal (*Ovibos moschatus*) native to N Canada, Alaska, and NW Greenland, having a brown, shaggy coat, large, downward-curving horns, and a musky odour.

musk•rat ['mʌsk,ræt] *n., pl.* **-rats** or (*esp. collectively*) **-rat.** *Cdn.* **1** a water rodent (*Ondatra zibethica*) native to North America, related to and resembling the voles, but larger, having webbed hind feet, a scaly, laterally compressed tail, and dark brown, glossy fur. **2** the fur of a muskrat. **3** (*adjl.*) made of this fur: *a muskrat coat.* ⟨< *musquash* by folk etymology⟩

musk rose a rose (*Rosa moschata*) native to the Mediterranean region, having white flowers with a musky scent.

musk•y ['mʌski] *adj.* **musk•i•er, musk•i•est.** of, like, or having an odour of musk: *a musky perfume.*
☛ *Hom.* MUSKIE.

Mus•lim ['mʌzləm] *or* ['mʊslɪm] *n., adj.* *—n.* a believer in Islam.
—adj. of or having to do with Islam or its doctrines or the Islamic culture. Also, **Moslem.** ⟨< Arabic *muslim* one who submits < *aslama* submit. Related to SALAAM.⟩

mus•lin ['mʌzlən] *n.* **1** a cotton cloth in a plain weave, made in a wide variety of weights ranging from sheer to heavy or coarse, and used for dresses, sheets, curtains, etc. **2** (*adjl.*) made of muslin. ⟨< F < Ital. *mussolina* < *Mussolo* Mosul, city in Iraq⟩

mus•pike ['mʌs,pəik] *n. Cdn.* a hybrid game fish crossbred from muskellunge and pike.

mus•quash ['mʌskwɒʃ] *n., pl.* **-quash.** *Cdn.* muskrat. ⟨< Algonquian⟩

Mus•queam ['mʌskwəm] *n.* a First Nations band living in Vancouver.

muss [mʌs] *v., n. Informal.* *—v.* put into disorder; rumple; rumple or disarrange (*often used with* **up**): *The child's clothes were mussed. Don't muss up my hair.*
—n. disorder; a mess. ⟨var. of *mess*⟩

mus•sel ['mʌsəl] *n.* **1** any of a family (Mytilidae) of marine bivalve molluscs having a dark, elongated shell. The common edible mussel is *Mytilus edulis.* **2** any of a superfamily (Unionacea) of freshwater, bivalve molluscs having a flattened, green, blue, or brown shell which in many species has a pearly lining used for making buttons, etc. ⟨OE *muscle, musle* < L *musculus* mussel, muscle. See MUSCLE.⟩
☛ *Hom.* MUSCLE.

Mus•sul•man ['mʌsəlmən] *n., pl.* **-mans.** *Archaic.* Muslim. ⟨< Persian *musulmān,* adj., Mohammedan < *muslim* a Muslim < Arabic *muslim.* See MUSLIM.⟩

muss•y ['mʌsi] *adj.* **muss•i•er, muss•i•est.** *Informal.* untidy; messy; rumpled. **—'muss•i•ly,** *adv.* **—'mus•si•ness,** *n.*

must[1] [mʌst]; *unstressed,* [məst] *aux.v., n., adj.* *—aux.v.* **1** be forced to; need to: *We must eat to live.* **2** be obliged to; ought to; should: *I must go home soon.* **3** be certain to: *I must seem very rude.* **4** be supposed or expected to: *You must have that book.*
—n. something necessary; obligation: *This rule is a must.*
—adj. Informal. demanding attention or doing; necessary: *a must item, must legislation.* ⟨OE *mōste,* pt. of *mōtan* MOTE[2]⟩
☛ *Usage.* **Must.** In literary English, when motion is implied, the auxiliary verb **must** is sometimes used without the main verb it modifies: *We must to horse. We must away.*

must[2] [mʌst] *n.* the unfermented juice of the grape; new wine. ⟨OE < L *(vinum) mustum* fresh (wine)⟩

must[3] [mʌst] *n., v.* *—n.* a musty condition; mould.
—v. make musty; become musty. ⟨< *musty*⟩

mus•tache ['mʌstæʃ] *or* [mə'stæʃ] *n.* **1** the hair that grows on a man's upper lip, especially when groomed and not shaved smooth. **2** the hair growing on any person's upper lip. **3** the hairs or bristles growing near the mouth of an animal. Also, **moustache.** ⟨< F < Ital. < Med.L *mustacia* < Gk. *mystax* upper lip, mustache⟩ **—'mus•tached,** *adj.*

mus•ta•chio [mə'stɑʃou] *or* [mə'stɑʃiou] *n., pl.* **-chios.** a large or fancy mustache. ⟨< Sp. *mostacho* and Ital. *mostaccio*⟩

mus•tang ['mʌstæŋ] *n.* the small, wild or half-wild horse of the North American plains. ⟨< Sp. *mestengo* untamed⟩

mus•tard ['mʌstərd] *n.* **1** a yellow powder or paste used as seasoning to give food a pungent taste. **2** any of several plants (genus *Brassica*) of the mustard family, whose seeds are ground for this seasoning. **3** a dark yellow colour. **4** designating a family (Cruciferae) of plants having cross-shaped flowers and pointed pods. Some plants of the mustard family are the mustards, cabbage, horseradish, radish, turnip, and broccoli.
cut the mustard, *Slang.* do what is required; perform adequately. ⟨ME < OF *moustarde,* ult. < L *mustum* MUST[2]⟩

mustard gas a poison gas that causes burns, blindness, and death. *Formula*: $(ClCH_2CH_2)_2S$

mustard oil any oil obtained from mustard seeds.

mustard plaster a poultice made of mustard and water, or of mustard, flour, and water, used as a counter-irritant in the treatment of chest colds, bronchitis, etc.

mus•ter ['mʌstər] *v., n.* *—v.* **1** assemble; gather together; collect: *muster soldiers.* **2** summon: *muster up courage.*
muster in, enlist.
muster out, discharge.
—n. **1** an assembly; collection. **2** a bringing together of people or troops for review or service. **3** the list of those mustered. Also called **muster roll. 4** the number mustered.
pass muster, be inspected and approved; come up to the required standards. ⟨ME < OF *mostrer* < L *monstrare* show < *monstrum* portent⟩

mus•ter•ing ['mʌstərɪŋ] *n., v.* *—n.* **1** a gathering. **2** a group of storks.
—v. ppr. of MUSTER.

must•n't ['mʌsənt] must not.

mus•ty ['mʌsti] *adj.* **-ti•er, -ti•est. 1** having a smell or taste suggesting mould or damp; mouldy: *a musty room, musty crackers.* **2** stale; out-of-date: *musty laws.* **3** lacking vigour; dull: *a musty old fellow.* ⟨? < *moisty* < *moist* + *-y*[1]⟩ **—'mus•ti•ly,** *adv.* **—'mus•ti•ness,** *n.*

mu•ta•ble ['mjutəbəl] *adj.* **1** liable to change: *mutable customs.* **2** capable of or liable to undergo mutation. **3** fickle: *a mutable person.* ⟨< L *mutabilis* < *mutare* change⟩ **—,mu•ta'bil•i•ty** or **'mu•ta•ble•ness,** *adj.* **—'mu•ta•bly,** *adv.*

mu•ta•gen ['mjutədʒən] *n.* anything that causes biological mutation by causing changes in DNA.

mu•ta•gen•ic [,mjutə'dʒɛnɪk] *adj.* able to cause mutation. **—,mu•ta'gen•i•cal•ly,** *adv.*

mu•tant ['mjutənt] *adj., n.* *—adj.* of, having to do with, or produced by mutation.
—n. a new variety of plant or animal resulting from mutation. ⟨< L *mutans,* ppr. of *mutare* to change⟩

mu•tate ['mjuteit] *or* [mju'teit] *v.* **-tat•ed, -tat•ing. 1** change. **2** *Biology.* produce mutations. **3** *Phonetics.* change by umlaut. **—'mu•ta•tive** ['mjutətɪv], *adj.*

mu•ta•tion [mju'teiʃən] *n.* **1** a change; alteration. **2** *Biology.* **a** a sudden, permanent, heritable change in the genetic structure of an animal or plant that produces a new feature or characteristic. **b** a new variety of animal or plant resulting from such a change. **3** *Phonetics.* umlaut. ⟨< L *mutatio, -onis* < *mutare* change⟩ **—mu'ta•tion•al,** *adj.* **—mu'ta•tion•al•ly,** *adv.*

mutation rate *Genetics.* the frequency of mutation at a single locus, expressed as the frequency of mutations per gamete.

mu•ta•tis mu•tan•dis [mju'teitɪs mju'tændɪs] *or* [mu'tɑtis mu'tɑndis] *Latin.* with the necessary changes.

mute [mjut] *adj., n., v.* **mut•ed, mut•ing.** *—adj.* **1** not making any sound; silent. **2** unable to speak; dumb. **3** of alphabetical letters, not pronounced. The *e* in *mute* is mute. **4** unspoken: *mute hostility.*
—n. **1** a person who cannot speak. **2** a clip or some other device put in or on a musical instrument to soften the sound. **3** a silent letter.
—v. **1** soften or deaden the sound of: *He muted the strings of his violin.* **2** lessen the intensity of (a colour, flavour, etc.) ⟨< L *mutus*⟩ **—'mute•ly,** *adv.* **—'mute•ness,** *n.*
☛ *Syn. adj.* **1, 2.** See note at DUMB.

mu•ti•late ['mjutə,leit] *v.* **-lat•ed, -lat•ing. 1** cut, tear off, or destroy a part of (a living body): *Many of the victims of the accident had been badly mutilated.* **2** tear, break, cut off, or remove or deface some part of (something) so as to damage or ruin it: *The book had been mutilated by someone who had torn some pages and written on others. The story had been mutilated by an editor.* ⟨< L *mutilare* < *mutilus* maimed⟩ **—'mu•ti,la•tor,** *n.* **—,mu•ti'la•tion,** *n.*

mu•ti•neer [,mjutə'nir] *n.* a person who takes part in a mutiny. ⟨< MF *mutinier*⟩

mu•ti•nous ['mjutənəs] *adj.* **1** rebelling against authority, especially the authority of a superior officer or officers on a ship or in the armed forces: *a mutinous crew.* **2** of or having to do with mutiny: *mutinous talk.* **3** unruly. **—'mu•ti•nous•ly,** *adv.*

mu•ti•ny ['mjutəni] *n., pl.* **-nies;** *v.* **-nied, -ny•ing.** *—n.* an open rebellion against lawful authority, especially by sailors or soldiers against their officers.
—v. take part in a mutiny; rebel. ⟨< obs. *mutine* revolt < OF *mutiner* < *mutin* rebellious, ult. < L *movere* move⟩

mutt [mʌt] *n. Slang.* **1** a dog, especially a mongrel. **2** a stupid person. ⟨origin uncertain⟩

mut•ter ['mʌtər] *v., n.* *—v.* **1** speak softly and indistinctly with lips partly closed: *He was muttering to himself as he counted.* **2** complain; grumble. **3** say in low and indistinct tones, especially when expressing secret anger or discontent: *"I'll get even with her," he muttered.*
—n. **1** the act of muttering. **2** muttered words. ⟨ME *mutere(n)*; probably imitative⟩ **—'mut•ter•er,** *n.* **—'mut•ter•ing•ly,** *adv.*
☛ *Syn. v.* **1.** See note at MURMUR.

mut•ton ['mʌtən] *n.* the meat from a mature sheep. ⟨ME < OF *moton* < Med.L *multo, -onis,* ram < Celtic⟩

mutton chop 1 a small piece of mutton, usually from the ribs or loin, for broiling or frying. **2 mutton chops,** *pl.* side whiskers shaped somewhat like mutton chops, narrow at the top, in front of the ears, and broad at the bottom, along the sides of the lower jaw.

mu•tu•al ['mjutʃuəl] *adj., n.* *—adj.* **1** done, said, felt, etc. by each toward the other; given and received: *mutual promises, mutual dislike.* **2** having the same relation each to the other: *mutual enemies.* **3** *Informal.* belonging to each of several: *our mutual friend.* **4** of or having to do with MUTUAL INSURANCE: *a mutual company.*
—n. **1** a mutual insurance company. **2** MUTUAL FUND. ⟨< L *mutuus* reciprocal⟩ **—'mu•tu•al•ly,** *adv.*
☛ *Usage.* See note at COMMON.
☛ *Hom.* MUTUEL.

mutual fund a financial fund that invests the pooled capital of its members in diversified securities.

mutual insurance or **plan** a system of insurance by which the policyholders own the company and share the gains and losses of a common fund.

mu•tu•al•ism ['mjutʃuə,lɪzəm] *n. Biology.* a relationship between two species of organisms in which both species benefit from the association. Compare AMENSALISM, COMMENSALISM, and PARASITISM.

mu•tu•al•i•ty [,mjutʃu'æləti] *n.* the state or quality of being mutual; reciprocity; mutual dependence.

mu•tu•al•ize ['mjutʃuə,laɪz] *v.* **-ized, -iz•ing.** make mutual.

mu•tu•el ['mjutʃuəl] *n.* PARI-MUTUEL.
☛ *Hom.* MUTUAL.

muu•muu ['mu,mu]; *Hawaiian,* ['muu 'muu] *n.* a woman's long, loose, flowing gown that is gathered at the neckline. ⟨< Hawaiian⟩

Mu•zak ['mjuzæk] *n. Trademark.* music that is transmitted by telephone or FM radio, used by restaurants, offices, public areas, etc.

mu•zhik [mu'ʒik] *or* ['muʒɪk] *n.* a Russian peasant. Also, **moujik, mujik.** ⟨< Russian⟩

muz•zle ['mʌzəl] *n., v.* **-zled, -zling.** *—n.* **1** the nose, mouth, and jaws of a four-footed animal. **2** a cover of straps or wires for putting over an animal's head to keep it from biting or eating. **3** the open front end of a firearm. **4** *Informal.* anything preventing free expression.
put a muzzle on, prevent persons, newspapers, etc. from expressing free opinions.
—v. Informal. **1** put a muzzle on. **2** compel to keep silent about something; prevent from expressing views: *The government*

muzzled the newspapers during the recent rebellion. ⟨ME < OF *musel* < *muse* muzzle⟩ **—'muz•zler,** *n.*

muz•zle•load•er ['mʌzəl,loudər] *n.* a muzzleloading gun.

muz•zle•load•ing ['muzəl,loudɪŋ] *adj.* of firearms, loaded by putting gunpowder in through the open front end of the barrel and ramming it down.

muz•zy ['mʌzi] *adj. Informal.* **1** mentally confused; muddled. **2** vague; blurred; indistinct. ⟨? blend of *mu(ddle)* + *(fu)zzy*⟩ **—'muz•zi•ly,** *adv.* **—'muz•zi•ness,** *n.*

M.V.O. Member of the (Royal) Victorian Order.

MVP *Sports.* most valuable player.

M.W.O. or **MWO** MASTER WARRANT OFFICER.

Mx maxwell.

my [maɪ] *adj., interj.* *—adj.* **1** a possessive form of **I**; of, belonging to, or made or done by me or myself: *I hurt my arm. Please hand me my coat. I'm getting a new watch for my graduation.* **2** a word used as part of any of certain formal titles when using the title to address the person holding it: *The horses are ready, my lord.* **3** *Informal:* a word used before certain other words in addressing a person: *my boy, my dear fellow.*
—interj. Informal. a word used as an exclamation of surprise, often together with another word: *My, what a big cat!* ⟨OE *mīn*⟩
☛ *Usage.* **My,** MINE are the possessive forms of **I. My** is a determiner and is always followed by a noun: *This is my hat.* **Mine** stands alone: *This hat is mine.*

my•al•gia [maɪ'ældʒiə] *n.* muscular rheumatism.

my•al•ism ['maɪə,lɪzəm] *n.* a type of witchcraft practised in the West Indies. ⟨< *myal* a native word⟩ **—'my•al,** *adj.*

My•an•mar ['mjʌnmɑ] *or* ['mjænmɑr] *n.* a country in SE Asia on the Bay of Bengal, formerly called Burma.

my•as•the•nia gra•vis ['maɪəs,θiniə 'grævɪs] a chronic but treatable neurological disorder characterized by muscle weakness. ⟨< *myo-* + *asthenia*; *gravis* < L, heavy⟩

my•ce•li•um [məi'siliəm] *n., pl.* **-li•a** [-liə]. the vegetative body of a fungus, consisting of a mass of white, threadlike fibres spread through a nutritive body or substance, such as soil or organic matter. ⟨< NL < Gk. *mýkēs* mushroom⟩

My•ce•nae•an [,məisə'niən] *n., adj.* *—n.* a native or inhabitant of Mycenae, a city in ancient Greece.
—adj. of or having to do with Mycenae, its people or the civilization that flourished there.

-mycete *combining form.* fungus. ⟨< NL < Gk. *mykētes*, pl. of *mýkēs* mushroom, fungus⟩

myco- *prefix.* fungus: *mycology.* ⟨< Gk. *mýkēs* mushroom, fungus⟩

my•col•o•gy [məi'kɒlədʒi] *n.* the branch of botany that deals with fungi. ⟨< Gk. *mýkēs* fungus + E *-logy*⟩ **—,my•co'log•i•cal** [,məikə'lɒdʒəkəl], *adj.* **—my•co'log•i•cal•ly,** *adv.* **—my'col•o•gist,** *n.*

my•e•lin ['maɪələn] *n. Anatomy.* a soft, white substance consisting of lipids and protein that forms a sheath around the axon of certain nerve fibres. ⟨< Gk. *myelos* narrow + *-in*⟩

my•el•i•tis [,maɪə'ləitɪs] *n. Pathology.* inflammation of the spinal cord or of the bone marrow.

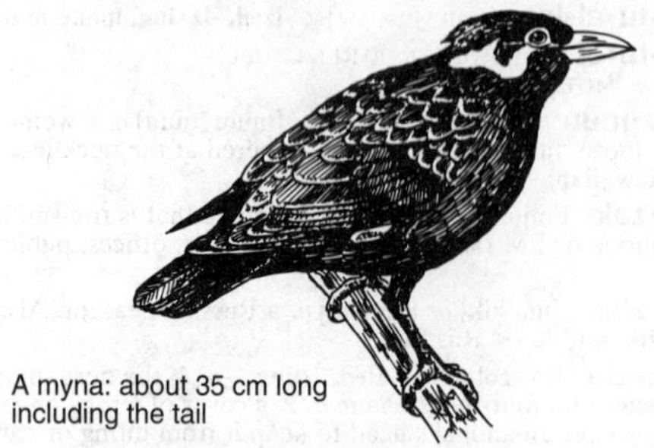
A myna: about 35 cm long including the tail

my•na or **my•nah** ['maɪnə] *n.* any of various tropical Asian starlings (especially genera *Acridotheres* and *Gracula*), some of which can be trained to mimic human speech and are kept as cage birds. ⟨< Hind. *maina*⟩
☛ *Hom.* MINA.

myo- *combining form.* muscle: *myology.* ⟨< Gk. *mys* mouse, muscle⟩

my•o•car•di•al [,maɪou'kɑrdiəl] *adj.* of or having to do with the myocardium.

myocardial infarction *Pathology.* the destruction of an area of the heart muscle as a result of a stoppage or insufficiency of blood supply to that area, usually caused by blockage of a coronary artery. Compare CORONARY THROMBOSIS.

my•o•car•di•um [,maɪou'kɑrdiəm] *n., pl.* **-di•a** [-diə]. *Anatomy.* the muscular middle layer of the wall of the heart.

my•o•graph ['maɪə,græf] *n.* an instrument that records the movement of muscles. **—,my•o'graph•ic** [,maɪə'græfɪk], *adj.* **—,my•o'graph•i•cal•ly,** *adv.* **—my'og•ra•phy** [maɪ'ɒgrəfi], *n.*

my•o•lo•gy [maɪ'ɒlədʒi] *n.* that branch of anatomy dealing with muscles. **—,my•o'log•i•cal** [,maɪə'lɒdʒəkəl] or **,my•o'log•ic,** *adj.* **—my'ol•o•gist,** *n.*

my•ope ['maɪoup] *n.* a myopic person.

my•o•pi•a [maɪ'oupiə] *n.* **1** near-sightedness. **2** short-sightedness: *intellectual myopia.* ⟨< NL < Gk. *myōps*, ult. < *myein* shut + *ōps* eye⟩

my•op•ic [maɪ'ɒpɪk] *adj.* **1** near-sighted. **2** lacking foresight.

my•o•sin ['maɪəsɪn] *n. Biochemistry.* a protein in muscle.

my•o•so•tis [,maɪə'soutɪs] *n.* the forget-me-not or other plant of the genus *Myosotis.* ⟨< NL < L *myosotis* < Gk. *myosotis* (the plant) mouse-ear⟩

my•o•to•nia [,maɪə'touniə] *n.* a muscular disorder resulting in muscle spasms or abnormal muscle tension. ⟨< *myo-* + *ton(ic)* + -ia⟩ **—,my•o'ton•ic** [-'tɒnɪk], *adj.*

myria- *prefix.* ten thousand: *a myriametre = 10 000 m* ⟨< Gk. *myrías*⟩

myr•i•ad ['miriəd] *n., adj.* *—n.* **1** a very large, indefinite number: *myriads of stars.* **2** *Archaic.* ten thousand.
—adj. **1** countless: *We saw myriad stars that summer night.* **2** highly varied; having many aspects or elements. ⟨< LL < Gk. *myrias, -ados* ten thousand, myriad⟩

myr•i•a•pod ['miriə,pɒd] *n.* any of a group (formerly the taxonomic class Myriapoda) of arthropods having a wormlike body with many segments and many legs. Centipedes and millipedes are myriapods. ⟨< Gk. *myrias* myriad + *pous, podos* foot⟩

myr•me•co•lo•gy [,mɜrmə'kɒlədʒi] *n.* that part of entomology dealing with the study of ants. **—,myr•me•co'log•i•cal** [,mɜrməkə'lɒdʒəkəl], *adj.* **—,myr•me'col•o•gist,** *n.*

Myr•mi•don ['mɜrmə,dɒn] *n.* **1** *Greek mythology.* a member of a warlike people of ancient Thessaly who accompanied Achilles, their king, to the Trojan War. **2 myrmidon,** an obedient and unquestioning follower.

my•rob•a•lan [maɪ'rɒbələn] *or* [mɪ'rɒbələn] *n.* **1** CHERRY PLUM. **2** a tropical tree (genus *Terminalia*) or its dried fruit, used in dyeing and tanning. **3** a dye extracted from this fruit.

myrrh [mɜr] *n.* **1** a fragrant, gummy substance with a bitter taste, used in medicines, perfumes, and incense. It is obtained from a shrub that grows in Arabia and E Africa. **2** the shrub from which it is obtained. ⟨OE *myrre* < L *myrrha* < Gk. *myrra*, ult. < Semitic⟩
☛ *Hom.* MURRE.

myr•tle ['mɜrtəl] *n.* **1** any of a genus (*Myrtus*) of evergreen shrubs, especially the common myrtle (*M. communis*) of southern Europe, having shiny leaves, fragrant white flowers, and black berries. **2** designating a family (Myrtaceae) of evergreen trees and shrubs. The myrtle family includes the myrtle, pimento or allspice, clove, and eucalyptus. **3** a low, creeping evergreen vine having blue flowers; periwinkle. ⟨ME < OF *mirtile*, dim. of L *myrtus* < Gk. *myrtos*⟩

my•self [maɪ'sɛlf] *pron., pl.* **our•selves. 1** a reflexive pronoun, the form of *I* used as an object when it refers to the same person as the subject: *I hurt myself. I told myself that it didn't really matter.* **2** a form of *I* or *me* added for emphasis: *I will go myself.* **3** my usual self: *I'm sorry I shouted; I'm not myself today.*

My•si•a ['mɪʃiə] *n.* in ancient times, a country in Asia Minor.

mys•te•ri•ous [mɪ'stiriəs] *adj.* **1** full of mystery; hard to explain or understand; secret; hidden. **2** suggesting mystery. **—mys'te•ri•ous•ly,** *adv.* **—mys'te•ri•ous•ness,** *n.*
☛ *Syn.* **1. Mysterious,** INSCRUTABLE = hard to explain or understand. **Mysterious** describes a person, thing, or situation about which there is something secret, hidden, or unknown that arouses curiosity, conjecture, or wonder: *She had a mysterious telephone call.* **Inscrutable** describes a thing that is so mysterious or such a riddle that it is impossible to make out its meaning, or a person who keeps his or her feelings, thoughts, and

intentions completely hidden: *His mother began to cry, but his father's face was inscrutable.*

mys•ter•y[1] ['mɪstəri] *n.* **-ter•ies. 1** a secret; something that is hidden or unknown. **2** secrecy; obscurity. **3** a story, play, etc. of suspense, telling of the development and solution of a crime or crimes: *a writer of mysteries.* **4** something that is not explained or understood: *the mystery of the migration of birds.* **5** a religious idea or doctrine that human reason cannot understand. **6** a secret religious rite to which only initiated persons are admitted. **7** MYSTERY PLAY. **8 a** a sacramental rite of the Christian religion. **b** the Eucharist; Communion; Mass. ⟨ME < L < Gk. *mystērion* < *mystēs* an initiate < *myein* close (i.e., the lips or eyes)⟩

mys•ter•y[2] ['mɪstəri] *n., pl.* **-ter•ies.** *Archaic.* **1** a craft; trade. **2** a craft or merchant association; a guild. ⟨< Med.L *misterium* for L *ministerium* ministry; form influenced by MYSTERY[1]⟩

mystery play a medieval, religious play based on the Bible, centring mainly on the life, death, and resurrection of Christ. These plays were called mystery plays because they dealt with the Christian mysteries (See MYSTERY[1], def. 5).

mys•tic ['mɪstɪk] *adj., n. —adj.* **1** mystical. **2** having to do with the ancient religious mysteries or other occult rites: *mystic arts.* **3** of or having to do with mystics or mysticism. **4** of hidden meaning or nature; enigmatical; mysterious.
—n. a person who believes that truth or God can be known intuitively or directly through spiritual insight, especially as cultivated by meditation, spiritual exercises, etc. ⟨< L < Gk. *mystikos* < *mystēs* an initiate. See MYSTERY[1].⟩

mys•ti•cal ['mɪstəkəl] *adj.* **1** having a spiritual meaning that is beyond human understanding: *the mystical food of the sacrament.* **2** spiritually symbolic: *The lamb and the dove are mystical symbols of the Christian religion.* **3** of or concerned with mystics or mysticism: *a mystical experience.* **4** of or having to do with secret rites open only to the initiated; cryptic. **—'mys•ti•cal•ly,** *adv.* **—'mys•ti•cal•ness,** *n.*

mys•ti•cism ['mɪstə,sɪzəm] *n.* **1** the beliefs, practices, or mode of thought of mystics. **2** the doctrine that truth or God may be known intuitively or directly through spiritual insight, independent of the mind.

mys•ti•fy ['mɪstə,faɪ] *v.* **-fied, -fy•ing. 1** bewilder; puzzle; perplex: *The magician's tricks mystified the audience.* **2** make mysterious; involve in mystery. ⟨< F *mystifier* < *mystique* mystic (< L *mysticus*; see MYSTIC) + *-fier* < L *-ficare* make < *-ficus* making < *facere* make⟩ **—'mys•ti,fi•er,** *n.* **—,mys•ti•fi'ca•tion,** *n.* **—'mys•ti,fied•ly,** *adv.* **—'mys•ti,fy•ing•ly,** *adv.*

mys•tique [mɪ'stik] *n.* **1** an aura of mystery and awe associated with a particular person, profession, skill, institution, etc. **2** a mystical or peculiar way of interpreting reality.

myth [mɪθ] *n.* **1** a traditional story about superhuman beings, such as gods, goddesses, heroes, and monsters, usually explaining the origin of natural events and forces, cultural practices, etc. **2** MYTHOLOGY (defs. 1 and 2). **3** an invented story. **4** an imaginary person or thing: *Her wealthy aunt was a myth invented to impress her friends.* **5** an opinion, belief, or ideal that has little or no basis in fact or truth. ⟨< NL < LL < Gk. *mythos* word, story⟩
☛ *Usage.* See note at LEGEND.

myth. mythology.

myth•i•cal ['mɪθəkəl] *adj.* **1** of, like, or in myths: *a mythical interpretation of nature, mythical monsters.* **2** not real; made-up; imaginary. Also, **mythic. —'myth•i•cal•ly,** *adv.*

myth•i•cize ['mɪθə,saɪz] *v.* **-cized, -ciz•ing.** treat as a myth. **—'myth•i,ciz•er,** *n.*

my•thog•ra•pher [mɪ'θɒgrəfər] *n.* MYTHOLOGIST (def. 1).

myth•o•log•i•cal [,mɪθə'lɒdʒəkəl] *adj.* of or having to do with mythology. **—,myth•o'log•i•cal•ly,** *adv.*

my•thol•o•gist [mɪ'θɒlədʒɪst] *n.* **1** one who writes, records, or compiles myths. **2** a person knowledgable about or studying mythology.

my•thol•o•gy [mɪ'θɒlədʒi] *n., pl.* **-gies. 1** a body of myths relating to a particular culture or person: *Greek mythology.* **2** myths collectively: *Mythology is an aspect of religion.* **3** the study of myths. ⟨< LL < Gk. *mythologia* < *mythos* word, story + *logos* word, discourse⟩

myth•o•ma•nia [,mɪθə'meiniə] *n. Psychiatry.* compulsive exaggeration.

myth•os ['mɪθɒs] *n.* **1** MYTHOLOGY (defs. 1 and 2). **2** ethos; the beliefs and attitudes typical of a certain group, time, etc.

myxo– *combining form.* mucus or slime: *myxoma.*

myx•o•ma [mɪk'soumə] *n., pl.* **-mas** or **-ma•ta** [-mətə]. *Pathology.* a soft tumour comprising mucus and connective tissue.

myx•o•ma•to•sis [,mɪksoumə'tousɪs] *n.* a highly infectious and usually fatal disease of rabbits, characterized by the growth of many skin tumours. ⟨< Gk. *myxa* mucus + E *-oma* + *-osis*⟩

N n *N n*

n or **N** [ɛn] *n., pl.* **n's** or **N's. 1** the fourteenth letter of the English alphabet. **2** any speech sound represented by this letter. **3** a person or thing identified as n, especially the fourteenth in a series. **4** *Printing.* an en. **5** *Mathematics.* an indefinite number. See NTH. **6** something shaped like the letter N. **7** (*adj.*) of or being an N or an n. **8** any device, such as a printer's type, a lever, or a key on a keyboard, that produces an n or an N.

n nano- (an SI prefix).

n. 1 born (for L *natus*). **2** name. **3** noun. **4** neuter. **5** nominative. **6** new. **7** number. **8** *Chemistry.* normal. **9** *Business.* net. **10** noon.

N 1 nitrogen. **2** north; northern. **3** noun. **4** newton(s).

N. 1 north; northern. **2** new. **3** noon. **4** November. **5** National; Nationalist. **6** Norse. **7** Navy.

Na sodium (for L *natrium*).

n/a *Banking.* no account.

N.A. 1 North America. **2** not applicable. **3** not available. Also (defs. 2, 3), **N/A.**

NAACP *U.S.* National Association for the Advancement of Colored People.

nab [næb] *v.* **nabbed, nab•bing.** *Informal.* **1** catch or seize suddenly; grab. **2** arrest: *The police soon nabbed the thief.* ⟨earlier *nap*, probably < Scand.; cf. Swedish *nappa* catch, snatch⟩

na•bob ['neibɒb] *n.* **1** a provincial governor under the Mogul empire in India. **2** a wealthy man, originally one who had returned to Europe after making a fortune in India. **3** any important or powerful person. ⟨< Hind. *nabab*, colloquial var. of *nav(v)ab.* See NAWAB.⟩ **—'na•bob•ism,** *n.*

na•celle [nə'sɛl] *n.* an enclosed part on an aircraft for an engine or for passengers or crew. ⟨< F < L *navicella*, double dim. of *navis* ship⟩

na•cho ['nɑtʃou] *n.,pl.* **na•chos.** a highly spiced, baked tortilla chip. ⟨< Sp.⟩

na•cre ['neikər] *n.* mother-of-pearl. ⟨< F < OItal. *naccara* < Arabic < *naqqārah* shell, drum⟩

nac•re•ous ['neikriəs] *adj.* **1** of or pertaining to nacre. **2** pearly.

Na–Dene [nɑ 'deini] *or* [,nɑ dei'nei] *n.* an American Indian language grouping including Tlingit, Haidan, and Athapaskan.

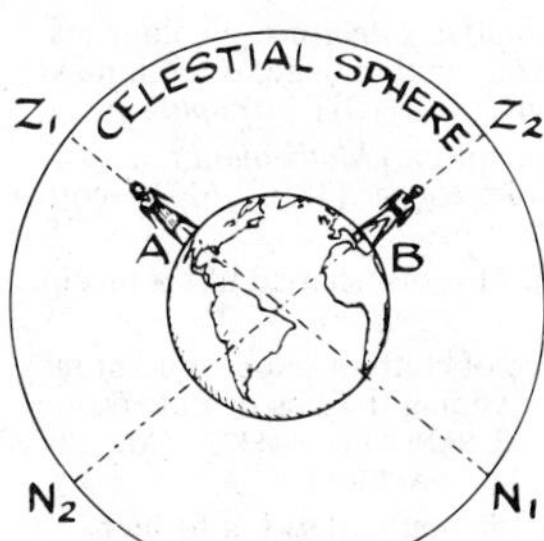

The zenith and nadir for observer A are Z_1 and N_1. For observer B, the zenith and nadir are Z_2 and N_2.

na•dir ['neidər] *or* ['neidir] *n.* **1** *Astronomy.* the point in the heavens directly beneath the place where one stands; point opposite the zenith. **2** the lowest point: *the nadir of his career.* Compare ZENITH. ⟨ME < OF < Arabic *nadir* opposite (i.e., to the zenith)⟩ **—'na•dir•al,** *adj.*

nae•vus ['nivəs] *n.* birthmark. Also, **nevus.** ⟨< L⟩

NAFTA 1 North American Free Trade Agreement. **2** North American free trade area.

nag[1] [næg] *v.* **nagged, nag•ging. 1** find fault with or annoy by peevish complaints: *He's always nagging at me to walk faster. If you nag her too much she won't do anything.* **2** continue to cause annoyance, irritation, or pain: *a nagging headache. The thought kept nagging at the back of my mind that I had left the door unlocked.* ⟨< Scand.; cf. Icelandic *nagga* grumble. Akin to GNAW.⟩ **—'nag•ger,** *n.* **—'nag•ging•ly,** *adv.*

nag[2] [næg] *n.* **1** *Informal.* a horse, especially one that is old and worn out. **2** a small riding horse; pony. **3** *Slang.* a racehorse regarded as useless. ⟨ME; cf. Du. *negge*⟩

Na•hua•tl ['nɑwɑtəl] *n., adj. —n.* any of a group of Uto-Aztecan languages spoken by the Aztecs, Toltecs, and other Indian peoples of central Mexico and parts of Central America. *—adj.* of or having to do with this group of languages.

nai•ad ['naɪæd] *or* ['neiæd] *n., pl.* **-ads, -a•des** [-ə,diz]. **1** *Greek and Roman mythology.* a nymph guarding a stream or spring. **2** a plant of the genus *Naias.* **3** a larval form of the dragonfly. ⟨< L < Gk. *Naias, -ados* (related to *naein* flow)⟩

na•if or **na•ïf** [nɑ'if] *adj., n. —adj.* naïve. *—n.* a naïve person.

nail [neil] *n., v. —n.* **1** a slender piece of metal with a head on one end and a point on the other, to be hammered into or through pieces of wood or other material to hold them together. **2** the hard, horny substance covering the upper side of the end of a finger or toe. **3** a claw or talon.

hard as nails, a tough; physically fit. **b** without pity; merciless.

hit the nail on the head, *Informal.* guess or understand correctly; say or do something just right.

on the nail, especially of making a payment, at once; immediately.

—v. **1** fasten with a nail or nails. **2** *Informal.* hold or keep fixed. **3** *Informal.* catch; seize. **4** *Informal.* secure by prompt action. **5** *Informal.* detect and expose (a lie, etc.).

nail down, a fix in place with nails: *The shingles were nailed down with a hammer.* **b** *Informal.* win, settle, or get with certainty: *He nailed down first place in the singing competition.* ⟨OE *nægel*⟩ **—'nail•er,** *n.*

nail file a small file, usually flat, for smoothing or shaping fingernails.

nail•head ['neil,hɛd] *n.* the flat top of a metal nail.

nail polish a liquid applied to fingernails with a brush, that hardens into a high gloss, often coloured.

nail•set ['neil,sɛt] *n.* a tool for driving nails beneath the surface.

nail varnish NAIL POLISH.

nain•sook ['neinsʊk] *or* ['nænsʊk] *n.* a very soft, fine, mercerized cotton cloth in a plain weave. ⟨< Hind. *nainsukh* < *nain* eye + *sukh* pleasure⟩

nai•ra ['naɪrə] *or* [nɑ'ɛrə] *n.* **1** the basic unit of money in Nigeria, divided into 100 kobo. See table of money in the Appendix. **2** a note worth one naira.

na•ïve or **na•ive** [nɑɪ'iv] *or* [nɑ'iv] *adj.* **1** simple in nature; like a child; artless. **2** not sophisticated; inexperienced; showing a lack of informed judgment: *She was naïve to believe their promises.* ⟨< F *naïve*, fem. of *naïf* < L *nativus.* Doublet of NATIVE.⟩ **—na'ïve•ly** or **na'ive•ly,** *adv.* **—na'ïve•ness** or **na'ive•ness,** *n.*

na•ïve•té or **na•ive•té** [nɑɪ'ivtei], [nɑɪ'ivə,tei], *or* [nɑ'ivtei] *n.* **1** the quality of being naïve; unspoiled freshness. **2** a naïve action, remark, etc. ⟨< F⟩

na•ïve•ty or **na•ive•ty** [nɑɪ'ivti] *n., pl.* **-ties.** naïvete.

na•ked ['neikɪd] *adj.* **1** with no clothes on: *The boys enjoyed swimming naked.* **2** bare; not covered; stripped of usual cover: *The trees stood naked in the snow.* **3** not protected; exposed: *a naked sword.* **4** without addition of anything else; plain: *the naked truth.* **5** of seeds, not in ovaries. **6** *Law.* not supported by any evidence. **7** *Zoology.* lacking any protective covering such as feathers.

naked eye, the eye alone, not helped by any glass, telescope, or microscope: *too small to be seen with the naked eye.* ⟨OE *nacod*⟩ **—'na•ked•ly,** *adv.* **—'na•ked•ness,** *n.*

☛ *Syn.* **1, 2.** See note at BARE[1].

N.Am. North America.

nam•a•ble ['neiməbəl] *adj.* that can be named. Also, **nameable.**

nam•ay•cush [,næmə'kʊʃ] *n., pl.* **-cush.** *Cdn. Rare.* lake trout. ⟨< Algonquian⟩

nam•by-pam•by ['næmbi 'pæmbi] *adj., n., pl.* **-bies.** *Informal. —adj.* weakly simple or sentimental; insipid: *That valentine is too namby-pamby.* *—n.* **1** namby-pamby talk or writing. **2** a namby-pamby person.

⟨alteration of *Nam*, short for *Am*brose Philips (1674-1749), an English poet ridiculed by Alexander Pope⟩

name [neim] *n., v.* **named, nam•ing.** *—n.* **1** the word or words by which an individual person, group, animal, place, or, sometimes, thing is known and spoken to or about: *Our dog's name is Sparky. Did they mention him by name? The name of the town is Aurora.* **2** a word or words used to identify a type or class of animal, plant, thing, etc.: *What's the name of that plant?* **3** a word or words applied descriptively; an appellation, title, or epithet: *to give someone the name of friend.* **4** the persons grouped under one name; family or clan. **5** reputation: *He made a name for himself as a writer.* **6** (*adjl.*) having a reputation that is known by a name: *The plumber buys all her supplies from name manufacturers.* **7** a famous person or thing: *She's a name in the industry.* **8** a symbol of divinity, such as IHS.
call names, insult by using bad names; swear at.
drop names, mention famous people one has met.
in name only, supposed to be but not really so.
in the name of, a on the authority of; acting for: *He bought the car in the name of his father.* **b** for the sake of: *We did it in the name of charity.*
know (only) by name, know only by hearing about: *I know her by name but I've never met her.*
to (one's) **name,** belonging to one: *I've got only about $10 to my name.*
—v. **1** give a name to: *They named the baby Mary.* **2** call by name; mention by name: *Three persons were named in the report.* **3** give the right name for; identify: *Can you name these flowers?* **4** mention or speak of; state: *She named several reasons for her decision.* **5** specify or fix: *to name a price.* **6** nominate; appoint: *Jim was named captain of the team.* **7** choose; settle on: *They named the day for their wedding.*
name after or **for,** give someone or something the same name as. ⟨OE *nama*⟩ **—'nam•er,** *n.*

☛ *Syn. n.* **3. Name,** TITLE = a word or words that describe or characterize. **Name** is used of a descriptive or characterizing word or phrase applied to a person or thing because of certain qualities or acts or to express an attitude toward him or her (or it): *'Gastown' was an old name for Vancouver.* **Title** is used of a descriptive or characterizing name given to a book, song, play, etc. or to a person as a sign of honour, rank, office, occupation: *His title is Secretary.* Of these two words, only **title** is used to describe rank or position.

name•a•ble ['neiməbəl] See NAMABLE.

name brand a product or brand of product identified and backed by the name and reputation of the manufacturer or distributor: *He usually buys name brands.* **—'name-,brand,** *adj.*

name–caller ['neim ,kɒlər] *n.* someone who often indulges in name-calling.

name–call•ing ['neim ,kɒlɪŋ] *n.* the act or fact of giving a bad name to a person; slandering; defamation.

name day 1 the feast day of the saint whose name one bears. **2** the day on which a child is named; baptismal day.

name–drop•ping ['neim ,drɒpɪŋ] *n.* the act or habit of mentioning the names of famous people frequently in familiar or casual conversation, so as to convey the impression, often false, that one has met them or is familiar with them.
—'name-,drop•per, *n.*

name•less ['neimlɪs] *adj.* **1** having no name: *a nameless baby.* **2** having no acknowledged paternal name. **3** not marked with a name: *a nameless grave.* **4** not named; unknown: *a book by a nameless writer.* **5** that cannot be named or described: *a strange, nameless longing.* **6** not fit to be mentioned: *nameless crimes.* **7** unknown to fame; obscure. **—'name•less•ly,** *adv.*
—'name•less•ness, *n.*

name•ly ['neimli] *adv.* that is to say: *Only two students got a perfect mark, namely, Jamil and Jeanne.*

name of the game the main objective.

name•plate ['neim,pleit] *n.* a strip of metal, wood, plastic, etc. mounted on a door, wall, etc. or set on a desk or table and imprinted with the name of the occupant.

name•sake ['neim,seik] *n.* a person having the same name as another; especially, one named after another. ⟨for *name's sake*⟩

Na•mi•bia [nə'mɪbiə] *n.* a country in SW Africa, formerly German Southwest Africa.

na•na ['nænə] *n. Informal.* grandmother.

nan•keen [næn'kin] *n.* **1** a firm, yellow or buff cotton cloth originally woven in China from a native cotton having a yellowish colour. **2 nankeens,** *pl.* trousers made of nankeen. ⟨alteration of *Nanking*, China⟩

nan•ny ['næni] *n., pl.* **-nies. 1** a woman with special training hired to look after the children of a family. **2** *Informal.* NANNY GOAT. ⟨< *Nan*, dim. of *Anna*, feminine name⟩

nan•ny goat a female goat.

nano– *SI prefix.* one billionth: *nanosecond. Symbol:* n ⟨< Gk. *nanos* dwarf⟩

na•no•me•tre ['nænou,mitər] *n.* one billionth of a metre.

na•nook ['nænuk] *n. Cdn.* **1** polar bear. **2 Nanook of the North,** character in a book, *My Eskimo Friends* (1924), by Robert Joseph. ⟨< Inuktitut *nanuq*⟩

na•no•sec•ond ['nænou,sɛkənd] *n.* one billionth of a second.

Nansen bottle ['nænsən] *or* ['nɑnsən] a container for taking samples of ocean water at predetermined depths. ⟨after Fridtjof *Nansen,* Norwegian arctic explorer (1861-1930)⟩

na•nuk ['nænuk] See NANOOK.

na•nuq ['nænuk] See NANOOK.

na•os ['neiɒs] *n., pl.* **na•oi** ['neiɔi] **1** a Greek temple. **2** the enclosed area of a Greek temple, with a statue of a god. ⟨< Gk.⟩

nap[1] [næp] *n., v.* **napped, nap•ping.** *—n.* a short sleep.
—v. take a short sleep.
catch napping, find off guard; take unprepared: *The test caught me napping.* ⟨OE *hnappian* sleep lightly⟩

nap[2] [næp] *n., v.* **napped, nap•ping.** *—n.* **1** a fuzzy or furry surface on cloth or leather, consisting of fibres that have been raised by brushing, as on flannel, or sheared threads or loops, as on velvet. **2** the direction in which these fibres lie on the surface, when smoothed down.
—v. raise the nap on (textiles or leather). ⟨ME *noppe* < MDu. or MLG⟩ **—'nap•less,** *adj.* **—'nap•less•ness,** *n.* **—napped,** *adj.*

na•palm ['nei,pɒm], ['nei,pɑm], *or* ['næpɒm] *n., v. Military.* *—n.* **1** a chemical substance used to thicken gasoline for use in certain military weapons, especially incendiary bombs. **2** the thickened gasoline.
—v. attack or destroy with napalm. ⟨< *na*phthenic and *palm*itic acids, used in its manufacture⟩

nape [neip] *n.* the back of the neck. ⟨ME; origin uncertain⟩

na•per•y ['neipəri] *n.* tablecloths, serviettes, and doilies; table linen. ⟨ME < OF *naperie* < *nape* < L *mappa* napkin⟩

naph•tha ['næpθə] *or* ['næfθə] *n.* any of various colourless, often highly flammable liquids distilled from petroleum, coal tar, etc. used as a solvent, paint thinner, etc. ⟨< L < Gk. *naphtha,* originally, a flammable liquid issuing from the earth < Iranian *neft*⟩ **—'naph•thous,** *adj.*

naph•tha•lene ['næpθə,lin] *or* ['næfθə,lin] *n. Chemistry.* a white, crystalline hydrocarbon, usually prepared from coal tar, used in mothballs and in the manufacture of organic compounds such as dyes. *Formula:* $C_{10}H_8$ Also, **naphthaline.** ⟨< *naphtha*⟩

naph•thene ['næpθin] *or* ['næfθin] *n. Chemistry.* one of a group of hydrocarbon compounds. *Formula:* C_nH_{2n}
—naph'the•nic, *adj.*

naph•thol ['næpθɒl] *or* ['næfθɒl] *n. Chemistry.* a colourless, crystalline substance obtained from naphthalene, used in making dyes, as an antiseptic, etc. *Formula:* $C_{10}H_7OH$ ⟨< *naphtha*⟩

Na•pier•i•an logarithm [nə'piriən] *Mathematics.* a logarithm with *e* as a base. ⟨< John *Napier* (1550–1617), Scottish mathematician⟩

na•pi•form ['neipə,fɔrm] *adj.* of roots, shaped like a turnip. ⟨< L *napus* turnip⟩

nap•kin ['næpkɪn] *n.* **1** a piece of cloth or paper used at meals for protecting the clothing or for wiping the lips or fingers; serviette. **2** *Brit.* a baby's diaper. **3** SANITARY NAPKIN. ⟨ME *napekyn*, dim. of OF *nape* cloth. See NAPERY.⟩

na•po•le•on [nə'pouliən] *or* [nə'pouljən] *n.* **1** a former French gold coin worth 20 francs. **2** a kind of pastry with a cream or jam filling. **3** a card game like euchre. ⟨< *Napoleon* Bonaparte (1769-1821), Emperor of France (1804-1815)⟩

Na•po•le•on•ic [nə,pouli'ɒnɪk] *adj.* of, having to do with, or resembling Napoleon Bonaparte (1769-1821), Emperor of France (1804-1815).

Napoleonic code the basis of civil law in France, Québec, and other places.

nap•pie[1] or **nap•py**[1] ['næpi] *n., pl.* **-pies.** a small dish used for serving fruit; a fruit dish. ⟨ME *nap* a bowl⟩

nap•pie[2] or **nap•py**[2] *n., pl.* **-pies.** *Brit.* a baby's diaper or napkin. ⟨< *napkin*⟩

nar•ce•ine ['nɑrsi,in] *n. Pharmacy.* a white, crystalline narcotic derived from opium. ⟨< NL *narcē* < Gk. *narkē* numbness + E *ine*⟩

nar•cis•sism ['nɑrsə,sɪzəm] *n.* excessive absorption in one's own personal comfort, importance, etc.; self-love. **—'nar•cis•sist,** *n.* **—,nar•cis'sis•tic,** *adj.*

nar•cis•sus [nɑr'sɪsəs] *n., pl.* **-cis•sus•es, -cis•si** [-'sɪsaɪ] *or* [-'sɪsi]. **1** any of a genus (*Narcissus*) of plants of the amaryllis family having yellow, white, or pink, spring-blooming flowers with a central trumpet-shaped or cup-shaped corona, especially any of several species having mainly white flowers with a relatively short corona. See also DAFFODIL, JONQUIL. **2** the flower of any of these plants. **3 Narcissus,** *Greek mythology.* a beautiful youth who fell in love with his own reflection in the water of a spring. He pined away from unrequited love and was changed into the flower called narcissus. ⟨< L < Gk. *narkissos*; associated (from the sedative effect of the plant) with *narkē* numbness⟩

Narcissuses

narco– *combining form.* stupor: *narcoanalysis.* ⟨< Gk. *narkē* numbness, stiffness⟩

nar•co•an•al•y•sis [,nɑrkouə'næləsɪs] *n.* psychoanalysis while the patient is sleepy as a result of drugs.

nar•co•lep•sy ['nɑrkə,lɛpsi] *n.* a pathological condition marked by periods of sudden, deep sleep. **—,nar•co'lep•tic,** *adj.*

nar•co•sis [nɑr'kousɪs] *n.* a stupor or state of insensibility, brought about by narcotics or other chemicals. ⟨< NL < Gk. *narkōsis* < *narkoein* benumb. See NARCOTIC.⟩

nar•cot•ic [nɑr'kɒtɪk] *n., adj. —n.* **1** any of a group of drugs, including opium and its derivatives and similar compounds, that have a strong pain-killing effect and produce drowsiness, dullness, or sleep, and that have the potential for physiological dependence with prolonged use. **2** any drug subject to legal restrictions because of its narcotic or mood-altering effects or its potential for psychological or physiological dependence. **3** something that numbs, soothes, or dulls.
—adj. **1** of, having to do with, or being a narcotic: *narcotic drugs.* **2** induced by a narcotic: *a narcotic stupor.* **3** producing mental lethargy or dullness; soporific. **4** of, involving, or intended for the treatment of drug addicts. ⟨ME < Med.L < Gk. *narkōtikos* < *narkoein* benumb < *narkē* numbness⟩

nard [nɑrd] *n.* spikenard. ⟨ME < L < Gk. *nardos* < Phoenician < Skt.⟩

nar•es ['nɛriz] *n.* pl. of **nar•is** ['nɛrɪs]. *Anatomy.* the nostrils; nasal passages. ⟨< L *nares*, pl.⟩ **—'na•ri•al,** *adj.*

nar•ghi•le or **nar•gi•le** ['nɑrgə,li] *or* ['nɑrgə,lei] *n.* hookah. Also, **nargileh.** ⟨ult. < Persian *nargileh* < *nargil* coconut, the original material used in making the pipe⟩

Nar•ra•gan•sett [,nærə'gænsɪt] *or* [,nɛrə'gænsɪt] *n., adj. —n.* **1** a member of a Native American people living in Rhode Island. **2** the extinct Algonquian language of these people.
—adj. of or having to do with the Narragansett, their language or culture.

nar•rate [nə'reit], ['næreit], *or* ['nɛreit] *v.* **-rat•ed, -rat•ing. 1** tell (a story): *A strange tale was narrated by the old hunter.* **2** tell the story of (events). **3** provide the narration for (a film, etc.): *The travelogue was narrated by a local journalist.* ⟨< L *narrare* relate⟩

nar•ra•tion [næ'reiʃən], [nɛ'reiʃən], *or* [nə'reiʃən] *n.* **1** the act or process of narrating. **2** the verbal accompaniment to certain kinds of films, television programs, etc.: *the narration for a travelogue.* **3** something narrated; narrative.
☛ *Syn.* **3.** See note at NARRATIVE.

nar•ra•tive ['nærətɪv] *or* ['nɛrətɪv] *n., adj. —n.* **1** a report, account, story, etc. **2** the part of a literary work that describes the sequence of events, as distinguished from dialogue, etc. **3** the art or technique of narrating; storytelling.
—adj. having to do with or in the form of a narrative: *Earl Birney's 'David' is a narrative poem.*
☛ *Syn. n.* **1. Narrative,** NARRATION = something told as a story. **Narrative** chiefly applies to what is told, a story or an account of real events or experiences told like a story in connected and interesting form: *The account of her trip through the Near East made an interesting narrative.* **Narration** chiefly applies to the act of telling a story or relating an experience or a series of events, and emphasizes the way in which the narrative is put together and presented: *Her narration of their trip was interesting.*

nar•ra•tor ['næreitər], ['nɛreitər], *or* [nə'reitər] *n.* a person who narrates.

nar•row ['nærou] *or* ['nɛrou] *adj., n., v. —adj.* **1** not wide; having little width; of less than the specified, understood, or usual width: *a narrow ribbon. A path 30 cm wide is narrow.* **2** limited in extent, space, amount, range, scope, opportunity, etc.: *He had only a narrow circle of friends.* **3** close; with a small margin: *a narrow escape.* **4** lacking sympathy; not tolerant; prejudiced: *A person who says that all modern art is rubbish has a narrow mind about art.* **5** close; careful; minute: *a narrow scrutiny.* **6** with barely enough to live on: *to live in narrow circumstances.* **7** *Phonetics.* **a** pronounced with tense articulation; tense. **b** indicating minute details of pronunciation: *a narrow transcription.*
—n. **narrows,** *pl.,* the narrow part of a river, strait, sound, valley, pass, etc.
—v. **1** make or become narrow; decrease in width: *The road narrows here.* **2** fix the limits of (*often used with* **down**): *At last we could narrow our search to three places.* ⟨OE *nearu*⟩ **—'nar•row•ly,** *adv.* **—'nar•row•ness,** *n.*

nar•row•cast ['nærou,kæst] *or* ['nɛrou,kæst] *v., n. —v.* broadcast (a radio or television program) to a limited audience, such as over cable.
—n. the program so broadcast.

nar•row gauge *n.* a width of railway track less than 143.5 cm apart, narrower than the standard gauge. Compare BROAD GAUGE. **—'nar•row-,gauge,** *adj.*

nar•row–mind•ed ['nærou 'maɪndɪd] *or* ['nɛrou 'maɪndɪd] *adj.* lacking understanding; blind to other points of view; prejudiced. **—'nar•row-'mind•ed•ly,** *adv.* **—'nar•row-'mind•ed•ness,** *n.*

narrow squeak *Informal.* a narrow escape.

nar•thex ['nɑrθɛks] *n. Architecture.* **1** a portico or vestibule in ancient churches. **2** a vestibule leading into the nave of a church. ⟨< Gk.⟩ **—nar'the•cal** [nɑr'θikəl], *adj.*

nar•whal ['nɑrwəl] *n.* a whale (*Monodon monoceros*) of the arctic seas. The male has a long tusk extending forward from a tooth in the upper jaw. Also, **narwal.** ⟨< Danish or Swedish *narval* < ON *nár* corpse + *hval* whale⟩

NASA National Aeronautics and Space Administration.

na•sal ['neizəl] *adj., n. —adj.* **1** of, in, or from the nose: *nasal bones, nasal discharge, nasal passages.* **2** *Phonetics.* spoken through the nose with the mouth passage closed. **3** of a voice, characterized by resonance produced through the nose: *a nasal voice.*
—n. Phonetics. a speech sound produced by expelling air through the nose. The sounds of [m], [n], and [ŋ], as in *mouth, nose,* and *sing,* are nasals. ⟨< L *nasus* nose⟩ **—na'sal•i•ty** [nei'zæləti], *n.* **—'na•sal•ly,** *adv.*

na•sal•ize ['neizə,laɪz] *v.* **-ized, -iz•ing.** *Phonetics.* **1** utter or speak with a nasal sound. Many vowels in French and Portuguese are nasalized, such as [ɛ̃], [ɑ̃], [ɔ̃], and [œ̃]. **2** produce nasal sounds. **—,na•sal•i'za•tion,** *n.*

nas•cent ['næsənt] *or* ['neisənt] *adj.* **1** in the process of coming into existence; just beginning to exist, grow, or develop. **2** *Chemistry.* **a** having to do with the state or condition of an element at the instant it is set free from a combination. **b** of an element, being in a free or uncombined state: *nascent chlorine.* ⟨< L *nascens, -entis,* ppr. of *nasci* be born⟩

NASDAQ National Association of Securities Dealers Automated Quotations.

Nas•ka•pi ['næskə,pi] *n., pl.* **Nas•ka•pi** or **Nas•ka•pis. 1** a member of an Algonquian people of northern Québec and the interior of Labrador. **2** the Cree dialect spoken by the Naskapi.
—adj. of or having to do with the Naskapi or their dialect.
☛ *Usage.* These people, together with the Montagnais, prefer to call themselves **Innu.**

na•so•front•al [,neizou'frʌntəl] *adj. Anatomy.* having to do with the nasal and frontal bones.

na•so•phar•ynx [,neizou'færɪŋks] *n., pl.* **-pha•ryn•ges** [-fə'rɪndʒiz]. the part of the pharynx above and behind the velum. **—,na•so•pha'ryn•ge•al,** *adj.*

nas•tic ['næstɪk] *adj.* of plant growth or movement, occurring as a result of external stimulus but independent of its direction. ⟨< Gk. *nastos* close-pressed < *nassein* press⟩

na•stur•tium [nə'stɜrʃəm] *n.* **1** any of a genus (*Tropaeolum*) of plants having showy yellow, orange, or red flowers, and sharp-tasting seeds and leaves. **2** the flower of any of these plants. ⟨< L *nasturtium* < *nasus* nose + *torquere* twist; from its pungent odour⟩

nas•ty ['næsti] *adj.* **-ti•er, -ti•est. 1** disgustingly dirty, etc.; physically repugnant: *a nasty smell. There was a nasty, slimy mess at the bottom of the pit.* **2** sordid, vile, or obscene: *a nasty mind, a nasty story of betrayal.* **3** very unpleasant or disagreeable: *nasty weather. She has a nasty temper.* **4** rather serious or dangerous: *a nasty wound, a nasty accident.* **5** difficult or frustrating: *a nasty problem.* **6** selfish; spiteful; disagreeable: *My brother is a nasty man.* ⟨ME; cf. Du. *nestig*⟩ **—'nas•ti•ly,** *adv.* **—'nas•ti•ness,** *n.*

nat. 1 national. **2** native. **3** natural; naturalist.

na•tal ['neitəl] *adj.* **1** of, having to do with, or present at birth: *a natal star. Your natal day is your birthday.* **2** *Poetic.* native. ⟨ME < L *natalis,* ult. < *nasci* be born. Doublet of NOËL.⟩

na•tal•i•ty [nei'tæləti] *n.* See BIRTH RATE.

na•tant ['neitənt] *adj.* swimming; floating; represented as swimming. ⟨< L *natans, -antis,* ppr. of *natare* float, swim, ult. < *nare* float⟩

na•ta•tion [nei'teiʃən] *or* [nə'teiʃən] *n.* **1** the art of swimming. **2** the act of swimming. **—na'ta•tion•al,** *adj.*

na•ta•to•ri•al [,neitə'tɔriəl] *or* [,nætə'tɔriəl] *adj.* having to do with, adapted for, or characterized by swimming: *Ducks are natatorial birds.* Also, **natatory** ['nætə,tɔri] *or* [nə'teitəri]. ⟨< LL *natatorialis,* ult. < L *natare* swim. See NATANT.⟩

na•ta•to•ri•um [,neitə'tɔriəm] *or* [,nætə'tɔriəm] *n., pl.* **-ri•ums, -ri•a** [-riə]. a swimming pool, especially an indoor one. ⟨< LL⟩

Nat•chez ['nætʃɪz] *n.* **1** a member of a Native American people now living in Oklahoma. **2** the extinct language of these people, the only member of its family.

na•tes ['neitiz] *n.pl.* buttocks; bottom. ⟨< L *nates,* pl. of *natis;* akin to Gk. *noton* the back⟩

nathe•less ['neiθlɪs] *or* ['næθlɪs] *adv., prep. Archaic.*
—adv. nevertheless.
—prep. notwithstanding. Also, **nathless.** ⟨OE *nā thȳ læs* never the less⟩

na•tion ['neiʃən] *n.* **1** a community of people occupying and possessing a defined territory and united under one government; especially, such a community that is politically independent; country; state. **2 the nation, a** the people of such a community: *The prime minister appealed to the nation to support the government's policy of restraint.* **b** the territory of such a community: *The entire nation experienced unusually cold weather over the weekend.* **3** a people having the same descent and social and political history and, usually, sharing a common language; race or people: *the Scottish nation, the French-Canadian nation.* **4** a confederacy of First Nations peoples: *The Iroquois Nation included the Seneca, Mohawk, Oneida, Onondaga, and Cayuga tribes, and later the Tuscarora.* **5** one of the peoples making up such a confederacy. ⟨< L *natio, -onis* stock, race, ult. < *nasci* be born⟩

☛ *Syn.* **1.** See note at PEOPLE.

☛ *Usage.* Def. 1, referring to people under an independent government, is the primary meaning of **nation** in English. But def. 3, referring to people with common ties of birth, language, and culture, has in recent years become more widely established. In Canada this use of the word has been reinforced by similar uses of the word **nation** in Canadian French.

na•tion•al ['næʃənəl] *adj., n.* *—adj.* **1** of a nation; affecting or belonging to a whole nation: *national laws, a national disaster.* **2** strongly upholding one's own nation; patriotic. **3** extending throughout the nation; having chapters, branches, or members in every part of the nation. **4** set up and kept up by the federal government: *a national park.*
—n. a citizen of a nation: *Each year many nationals of Canada visit the United States.*

National Assembly *Cdn.* in Québec, the group of representatives elected to the provincial legislature; legislative assembly.

na•tion•al•ism ['næʃənə,lɪzəm] *n.* **1** patriotic feelings or efforts. **2** the desire and plans for national independence. **3** the desire of a people to preserve its own language, religion, traditions, etc.

na•tion•al•ist ['næʃənəlɪst] *n., adj.* *—n.* **1** an upholder of nationalism; a person who believes in nationalism. **2 Nationalist,** a member of a political party supporting national independence or a strong national government.
—adj. **1** nationalistic. **2 Nationalist,** of, having to do with, or being a political party supporting national independence or a strong national government: *the Nationalist platform.*

na•tion•al•is•tic [,næʃənə'lɪstɪk] *adj.* **1** of or having to do with nationalism or nationalists. **2** supporting nationalism: *a very nationalistic speech.* **—,na•tion•al'is•ti•cal•ly,** *adv.*

na•tion•al•i•ty [,næʃə'næləti] *n., pl.* **-ties. 1** the fact of belonging to a nation: *His passport showed that his nationality was Canadian.* **2** the condition of being an independent nation; nationhood. **3** an ethnic group: *There are 46 nationalities benefiting from the Heritage Language program.*

na•tion•al•ize ['næʃənə,laɪz] *v.* **-ized, -iz•ing. 1** make national. **2** bring (land, industries, railways, etc.) under the control or ownership of a nation. **3** make into a nation. **—,na•tion•al•i'za•tion,** *n.*

na•tion•al•ly ['næʃənəli] *adv.* **1** in a national manner; as a nation. **2** throughout the nation: *The opposition leader's speech was broadcast nationally.*

national park land kept by the government of a country for people to enjoy because of its beautiful scenery, historical interest, etc.

National Socialist German Workers' Party the political party, led by Adolf Hitler, that controlled Germany from 1933 to 1945. See also NAZI.

na•tion•hood ['neiʃən,hʊd] *n.* the condition or state of being a nation; the fact of having national existence: *A country's nationhood is sometimes threatened by civil wars.*

na•tion•wide ['neiʃən'waɪd] *adj. or adv.* throughout the nation: *a nationwide election. The RCMP polices remote areas nationwide.*

na•tive ['neitɪv] *n., adj.* *—n.* **1** a person born in a certain place or country: *She is a native of Montréal.* **2** a member of a people who are the traditional or original inhabitants of a region or country, as contrasted with explorers, settlers, visitors, etc.; aboriginal; in Canada, a member of the First Nations. **3** an indigenous animal or plant.
—adj. **1** born in a certain place or country: *Frederick is a native son of Winnipeg.* **2** belonging to or associated with one by birth: *one's native land.* **3** belonging to one because of his or her country or the nation to which he or she belongs: *one's native language.* **4** born in a person; natural: *native ability, native courtesy.* **5** of, having to do with, or designating people who are the traditional or original inhabitants of a region or country; aboriginal; in Canada, having to do with a member or members of the First Nations: *the native peoples of Canada, native customs, native rights.* **6** originating, grown, or produced in a certain place: *The Manitoba maple is native to Canada.* **7** found pure in nature: *native copper.* **8** found in nature; not produced: *Native salt is refined for use.* **9** *Computer technology.* of programming, included at the point of manufacture or shipping: *a native spell check, native anti-virus software.*
go native, of a conqueror, settler, visitor, etc., give up one's own culture and live as the natives do. ⟨adj. < L *nativus* innate, ult. < *nasci* be born, 14c; n. < Med.L *nativus* a native < L *nativus* adj.; 15c. Doublet of NAÏVE.⟩ **—'na•tive•ly,** *adv.* **—'na•tive•ness,** *n.*

☛ *Syn. adj.* **4. Native,** NATURAL = belonging to someone or something by birth or nature. **Native** emphasizes the idea of being born in a person, as contrasted with being acquired: *He has native artistic talent.* **Natural** emphasizes being part of the nature of a person, animal, or thing, belonging by birth or because of essential character: *Sugar has natural sweetness.*

na•tive–born ['neitɪv 'bɔrn] *adj.* born in a particular town, country, etc.: *My father is a native-born Canadian, but my mother was born in Iceland.*

na•tiv•ism ['neitə,vɪzəm] *n.* **1** the protection and perpetuation of a native culture, especially in opposition to assimilation by another culture. **2** a policy of favouring the native inhabitants of a country over immigrants. **3** *Philosophy.* the doctrine of innate ideas. **—'na•tiv•ist,** *n.* **—'na•tiv•ist** or **,na•tiv'is•tic,** *adj.*

na•tiv•i•ty [nə'tɪvəti] *or* [nei'tɪvəti] *n., pl.* **-ties. 1 Nativity, a** the birth of Christ. **b** a picture showing the newborn infant Jesus, usually with Mary and Joseph and often with animals, shepherds, and the three Wise Men grouped around them. **c** Christmas. **2** birth. **3** horoscope. ⟨ME < OF *nativite* < LL *nativitas*⟩

natl. national.

NATO ['neitou] *n.* North Atlantic Treaty Organization.

na•tro•lite ['nætrə,ləit] *or* ['neitrə,ləit] *n.* a hydrous silicate of sodium and aluminum; a white zeolite. *Formula:* $Na_2Al_2Si_3O_{10} \cdot 2H_2O$ ⟨< *natron* + *-lite*⟩

na•tron ['neitrɒn] *or* ['neitrən] *n.* native sodium carbonate. *Formula:* $Na_2CO_3 \cdot 10H_2O$ ⟨< F < Sp. < Arabic *natrun* < Gk. *nitron* < Semitic. Doublet of NITRE.⟩

nat•ter ['nætər] *v.* **1** talk on at length; chatter. **2** mutter discontentedly; fret. ⟨< earlier *gnatter*; origin uncertain⟩

nat•ty ['næti] *adj.* **-ti•er, -ti•est.** *Informal.* trim and tidy; neatly smart in dress or appearance: *a natty uniform, a natty young officer.* ⟨origin uncertain⟩ **—'nat•ti•ly,** *adv.* **—'nat•ti•ness,** *n.*

nat•u•ral ['nætʃərəl] *adj., n. —adj.* **1** produced by nature; based on some state of things in nature: *Scenery has natural beauty.* **2** not artificial: *Coal and oil are natural products.* **3** instinctive; inborn: *natural ability.* **4** coming or occurring in the ordinary course of events; normal: *a natural death.* **5** in accordance with the nature of things or the circumstances of the case: *a natural response.* **6** instinctively felt to be right and fair: *natural law, natural rights.* **7** like nature; true to nature: *The picture looked natural.* **8** free from affectation or restraint: *a natural manner.* **9** of or having to do with nature: *the natural sciences.* **10** concerned with natural science. **11** based on what is learned from nature: *natural religion.* **12** *Music.* **a** neither sharp nor flat; without sharps and flats. **b** neither sharped nor flatted: *C natural.* **c** having the pitch affected by the natural sign. **d** produced without the aid of valves or keys, as in brass instruments. **13** by birth, but not legally recognized; illegitimate: *a natural son.* **14** related by birth rather than by adoption: *Who are her natural father and mother?* **15** of food, having little interference such as processing or additives. **16** of a colour near but not quite white. **17** *Mathematics.* having 1 as the base of the system (applied to a function or number belonging or referred to such a system).
—n. **1** that which is natural. **2** *Music.* **a** a natural tone or note. **b** a sign (♮) used to cancel the effect of a preceding sharp or flat. **c** a white key on a keyboard instrument. **3** *Archaic.* a half-witted person. **4** *Informal.* a person who seems especially suited for something: *He's a natural for the football team.* **5** *Informal.* a sure success. **6** a colour near but not quite white. ⟨ME < L *naturalis* < *natura.* See NATURE.⟩ **—'nat•u•ral•ness,** *n.*
☛ *Syn. adj.* **3.** See note at NATIVE.

natural childbirth childbirth with a minimum or no use of anesthetic and with the conscious participation of the mother, who may have learned techniques for relaxation and has done exercises designed to facilitate the process of labour and delivery.

natural gas a combustible gas commonly used as a fuel, that occurs dissolved in petroleum and is also found in separate natural deposits in the earth. Natural gas consists of methane and other hydrocarbons.

natural gender *Grammar.* grammatical gender based on the actual sex, or lack of sex, of the thing denoted by the noun. Thus *king* is masculine, *queen* is feminine, and *palace* is neuter.

natural history **1** the study of animals, plants, minerals, and other things in nature. **2** a book or article on some aspect of nature.

nat•u•ral•ism ['nætʃərə,lɪzəm] *n.* **1** a style in art and literature characterized by a realistic and objective portrayal of nature, life, etc. **2** the principles of certain 19th-century writers, especially in France, who strove for a type of realism that stressed the unpleasant and sordid aspects of life. **3** action based on natural instincts. **4** *Philosophy.* a view of the world which posits the existence only of natural elements and forces, excluding the supernatural or spiritual. **5** the doctrine that all religious truth is derived from the study of nature.

nat•u•ral•ist ['nætʃərəlɪst] *n., adj. —n.* **1** a person who studies animals and plants; a field biologist. **2** a person who supports or practises naturalism.
—adj. naturalistic.

nat•u•ral•is•tic [,nætʃərə'lɪstɪk] *adj.* **1** of, having to do with, or characterized by naturalism: *a naturalistic painting.* **2** of natural history or naturalists. **3** imitating nature.
—,nat•u•ral'is•ti•cal•ly, *adv.*

nat•u•ral•ize ['nætʃərə,laɪz] *v.* **-ized, -iz•ing.** **1** grant the rights of citizenship to (persons native to other countries); admit (a foreigner) to citizenship: *My father is a naturalized Canadian but my mother was born here.* **2** adopt (a foreign word or custom): *The French word* chauffeur *has been naturalized in English.* **3** introduce and make at home in another country: *The English sparrow has become naturalized in parts of Canada.* **4** make natural; free from conventional characteristics. **5** regard or explain as natural rather than supernatural. **6** become like a native. **—,nat•u•ral•i'za•tion,** *n.*

natural law **1** a law, or the laws, of nature. **2** a rule of conduct supposedly based on reason inherent in nature.

nat•u•ral•ly ['nætʃərəli] *adv.* **1** in a natural way: *to speak naturally.* **2** by nature: *a naturally obedient child.* **3** as might be expected; of course.

natural magnet a piece of magnetite; lodestone.

natural number any of the numbers used in counting; 1, 2, 3, 4, 5, etc.; any whole number other than zero.

natural parent the biological parent of a child or children; the one who begot or bore the child or children.

natural philosophy NATURAL SCIENCE.

natural resource a kind of material or means that is supplied by nature and is useful or necessary to people: *Minerals and water power are natural resources.*

natural science any of the sciences that deal with nature and the physical world, including biology, chemistry, physics, and geology.

natural selection the process by which animals and plants best adapted to their environment tend to survive and produce similar offspring.

na•ture ['neitʃər] *n.* **1** the world; all things except those made by humans. **2** the sum total of the forces at work throughout the universe: *the laws of nature.* **3 Nature,** the personification of all natural facts and forces. **4** the natural world, with all its plants and animals: *She loved to go to the forest and enjoy nature in all its colour and beauty.* **5** the instincts or inherent tendencies directing conduct: *It is against nature for a mother to kill her child.* **6** reality: *true to nature.* **7** a primitive, wild condition; condition of human beings before social organization. **8** the qualities or abilities with which a person or animal is born; character; way or manner: *It is the nature of birds to fly. She has a kind nature.* **9** sort; kind. **10** physical being; vital powers: *food sufficient to sustain nature.* **11** *Theology.* moral nature unaffected by grace.
by nature, because of the essential character of the person or thing.
of or **in the nature of,** having the nature of; being a kind of: *The company president was something in the nature of an autocrat.*
⟨ME < OF < L *natura* birth, character, ult. < *nasci* be born⟩

–natured *combining form.* having a specified kind of nature: *ill-natured = having a disagreeable nature.*

nature study the study of animals, plants, and other things and events in nature.

nature trail a trail through a conservation area, park, or game sanctuary providing opportunities for the enjoyment and study of nature. Nature trails often have signs, information boards, and displays at intervals along the way.

nature worship a system of religion that includes the worship of natural forces.

na•tur•o•path ['nætʃərə,pæθ] *n.* a person who practises the treatment of disease by means of naturopathy.

na•tur•op•a•thy [,nætʃə'rɒpəθi] *n.* a system or method of treating diseases and disorders without the use of surgery or synthetic drugs, relying instead on natural forces such as good nutrition, and on the use of natural herbal medicines.
—,na•tur•o'path•ic [,nætʃərə'pæθɪk], *adj.*

naught [nɒt] *n.* nothing: *All his work went for naught.* ⟨OE *nāwiht* < *nā* no + *wiht* wight⟩
☛ *Hom.* KNOT[1], NOT, NOUGHT.

naugh•ty ['nɒti] *adj.* **-ti•er, -ti•est.** **1** bad; not obedient. **2** improper; indelicate. ⟨ME *naught* wickedness⟩ **—'naugh•ti•ly,** *adv.* **—'naugh•ti•ness,** *n.*
☛ *Hom.* KNOTTY.

nau•pli•us ['nɒpliəs] *n., pl.* **nau•pli•i** [-pli,aɪ]. the first stage of the larvae of certain crustaceans, when they become able to swim. ⟨< L, a kind of shellfish⟩

nau•se•a ['nɒziə], ['nɒʒə], *or* ['nɒʃə] *n.* **1** the feeling that one has when about to vomit. **2** extreme disgust; loathing. ⟨< L < Gk. *nausia* < *naus* ship. Doublet of NOISE.⟩

nau•se•ant ['nɒziənt], ['nɒsiənt], ['nɒʃiənt], *or* ['nɒʒiənt] *n.* an agent for inducing nausea.

nau•se•ate ['nɒzi,eit], ['nɒsi,eit], ['nɒʒi,eit], *or* ['nɒʃi,eit] *v.* **-at•ed, -at•ing.** **1** cause nausea in; make sick. **2** feel nausea; become sick. **3** cause to feel loathing. ⟨< L *nauseare*⟩
—'nau•se,at•ing•ly, *adv.* **—,nau•se'a•tion,** *n.*

nau•se•ous ['nɒziəs] *or* ['nɒʃəs] *adj.* **1** causing nausea; sickening. **2** affected with nausea or disgust. **3** disgusting; loathsome. ⟨< L *nauseosus*⟩ **—'nau•seous•ly,** *adv.*

naut. nautical.

nau•ti•cal ['nɒtɪkəl] *adj.* of or having to do with ships, sailors, or navigation. ⟨< L < Gk. *nautikos,* ult. < *naus* ship⟩
—'nau•ti•cal•ly, *adv.*

nautical mile a unit for measuring distance in air and sea navigation, equal to 1853.25 m.

nau•ti•loid ['nɒtə,lɔid] *n.* a mollusc of the subclass Nautiloidea, which includes the nautilus.

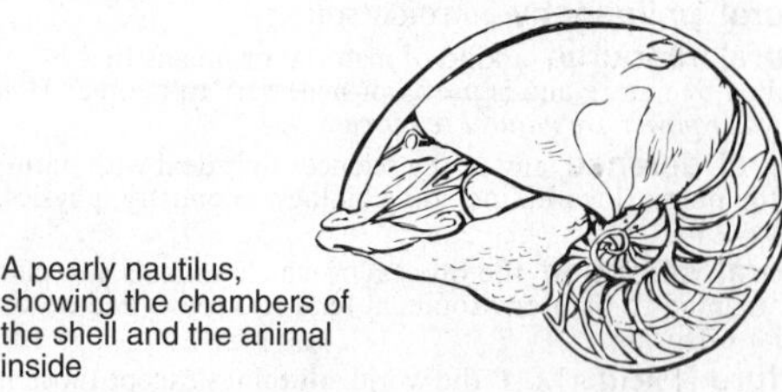

A pearly nautilus, showing the chambers of the shell and the animal inside

nau•ti•lus ['nɒtələs] *n., pl.* **-lus•es, -li** [-,laɪ] *or* [-,li]. **1** any of a genus (*Nautilus*) of cephalopod molluscs comprising six species found in the S Pacific and Indian Oceans, which are the only living representatives of a subclass of cephalopods that flourished millions of years ago. The nautilus has a pearly-lined, chambered shell coiled in a flat spiral; the animal lives in the outermost chamber. Also called **pearly nautilus. 2** PAPER NAUTILUS. **3 Nautilus. a** *Trademark.* a type of weightlifting equipment using weight resistance in proportion to muscular strength. **b** the first nuclear-powered submarine to be launched by the U.S. Navy. ⟨< Gk. *nautilos* sailor⟩

nav. 1 naval. **2** navigation. **3** navigable.

Nav•a•ho or **Nav•a•jo** ['nævə,hou] *n., pl.* **-ho** or **-hos, -jo** or **-jos. 1** a member of an American Indian people of New Mexico, Arizona, and Utah; Na-Dene. **2** the Athapascan language of the Navaho.
—adj. of or having to do with the Navaho or their language.

na•val ['neivəl] *adj.* **1** of, having to do with, or for warships or the navy: *a naval officer, naval supplies.* **2** having a navy: *Canada is among the naval powers.* ⟨< L *navalis* < *navis* ship⟩
—'na•val•ly, *adv.*
☛ *Hom.* NAVEL.

nave¹ [neiv] *n.* the main part of a cross-shaped church between the side aisles. The nave extends from the main entrance to the transepts. See BASILICA and TRANSEPT for pictures. ⟨< Med.L < L *navis* ship⟩
☛ *Hom.* KNAVE.

nave² [neiv] *n.* the central part of a wheel; hub. ⟨OE *nafu*⟩
☛ *Hom.* KNAVE.

na•vel ['neivəl] *n.* **1** the small scar, usually a hollow, in the middle of the abdomen, marking the place where the umbilical cord was attached before and at birth. **2** a central point; middle. ⟨OE *nafela.* Related to NAVE².⟩
☛ *Hom.* NAVAL.

navel orange a seedless orange having a small growth that resembles a navel in shape and contains a small, secondary fruit.

nav•i•ga•ble ['nævəgəbəl] *adj.* **1** that ships can travel on: *The St. Lawrence River is deep enough to be navigable.* **2** seaworthy. **3** that can be steered. **—,nav•i•ga'bil•i•ty,** *n.* **—'nav•i•ga•bly,** *adv.*

nav•i•gate ['nævə,geit] *v.* **-gat•ed, -gat•ing. 1** sail, manage, or steer (a ship, aircraft, etc.). **2** sail on or over (a sea, river, etc.): *Many ships navigate the St. Lawrence Seaway each year.* **3** travel by water; sail. **4** convey (goods) by water. **5** sail through (the air) in an aircraft, etc. **6** plot the position and course of (a ship, aircraft, vehicle, etc.) **7** move along; find one's way: *The snowplough could hardly navigate along the icy streets.* ⟨< *navigare* < *navis* ship + *agere* drive⟩

nav•i•ga•tion [,nævə'geiʃən] *n.* **1** the act or process of navigating. **2** the science of determining the position, course, and distance travelled of a ship, aircraft, or spacecraft. **3** traffic by ship, especially commercial shipping. **—,nav•i'ga•tion•al,** *adj.*

nav•i•ga•tor ['nævə,geitər] *n.* **1** a person who is qualified to navigate, especially one whose work is navigating ships or aircraft: *They took on a special navigator to guide the ship through the dangerous waters. She served as a navigator in the air force.* **2** a person who sails the seas as an explorer: *a story of one of the early navigators.* ⟨< L⟩

nav•jo•te [,nɑvdʒou'ti] *n.* in Zoroastrianism, the initiation ceremony in which boys and girls, before puberty, are instructed concerning their religious duties and are received into full membership.

nav•vy ['nævi] *n., pl.* **-vies.** *Esp. Brit.* an unskilled labourer who works on canals, railways, roads, etc. ⟨< *navigator*⟩

na•vy ['neivi] *n., pl.* **-vies;** *adj. —n.* **1** all the ships of war of a country, together with their personnel. **2** Often, **Navy,** the branch of the armed forces of a nation comprising warships and personnel, as well as all the organization for their maintenance. In Canada, the function of a navy is served by the Maritime Command of the Canadian Forces. **3** a dark blue. **4** *Archaic.* a fleet of ships.
—adj. having the colour navy. ⟨ME < OF *navie,* ult. < L *navis* ship⟩

navy bean the small, white seed of a variety of kidney bean commonly used in baked bean dishes, soups, etc. ⟨from its former extensive use in the U.S. navy⟩

navy blue a dark blue. ⟨from the colour of the navy uniform⟩

na•wab [nə'wɒb] *n.* **1** formerly, in India, a title of a governor or nobleman. **2** in Pakistan, a title of a distinguished Muslim. ⟨< Hind. *nav(v)ab* < Arabic *nuwwab,* pl. of *nā'ib* deputy⟩

Naw Ruz [nɑ ruz] *n.* in Bahaism and Zoroastrianism, the New Year festival celebrated at the vernal equinox.

nay [nei] *adv., n. —adv.* **1** *Archaic.* no. **2** *Formal.* not only that, but also: *We are willing, nay, eager to go.*
—n. **1** no; a denial or refusal. **2** a negative vote or voter. ⟨ME < ON *nei* < *ne* not + *ei* ever⟩
☛ *Hom.* NÉE, NEIGH.

nay•say•er ['nei,seiər] *n.* one who usually expresses a negative view.

Naz•a•rene [,næzə'rin] *or* ['næzə,rin] *n., adj. —n.* **1** a native or inhabitant of Nazareth, the boyhood home of Jesus. **2 the Nazarene,** Jesus. **3** an early Christian.
—adj. of or having to do with the Nazarenes or with Nazareth.

Naz•a•rite ['næzə,rəit] *n.* **1** among the ancient Hebrews, a Jew who had taken certain strict religious vows. **2** a native of Nazareth. Also, **Nazirite.**

Na•zi ['nætsi] *or* ['nɑtsi] *n., pl.* **Na•zis. 1** a member or supporter of the National Socialist German Workers' Party which controlled Germany from 1933 to 1945, under the leadership of Adolf Hitler. Compare FASCIST. **2** (*adjl.*) of or having to do with the Nazis. ⟨< G *Nationalsozialist* National Socialist⟩
☛ *Usage.* **Nazi** was a political nickname for the National Socialist German Workers' Party in Germany and is capitalized like **Conservative** or **Liberal.** The type of party represented by the Nazis is usually referred to as fascist or totalitarian.

Na•zi•fy or **na•zi•fy** ['nætsə,faɪ] *or* ['nɑtsə,faɪ] *v.* **-fied, -fy•ing. 1** place under control of the Nazis. **2** indoctrinate with Nazi views. **—,Na•zi•fi'ca•tion** or **,na•zi•fi'ca•tion,** *n.*

Nazirite ['næzə,rəit] See NAZARITE.

Na•zism ['nætsɪzəm] *or* ['nɑtsɪzəm] *n.* the doctrines and policies of the Nazi party, based on the idea of the innate superiority of the 'Aryan' race, especially the Nordic type of that race, and its destiny and responsibility to rule the world. Nazism also glorified strength and discipline within an authoritarian hierarchy having at its apex an infallible leader, or Führer. Also, **Nazi•ism** [-si,ɪzəm]

Nb niobium.

NB New Brunswick (*used esp. in computerized address systems*).

N.B. New Brunswick.

N.B. or **n.b.** NOTA BENE.

n/c no charge.

NCO or **N.C.O.** non-commissioned officer.

n.d. 1 no date. **2** not dated.

Nd neodymium.

NDP or **N.D.P.** NEW DEMOCRATIC PARTY.

Ne neon.

NE, N.E., or **n.e.** northeast; northeastern.

Ne•an•der•thal [ni'ændər,θɒl] *or* [ni'ændər,tɒl] *adj., n. —adj.* of or having to do with Neanderthal humans.
—n. an extinct people widespread in Europe, N Africa, and parts of Asia in the early Stone Age. ⟨< *Neanderthal,* a valley in W Germany, where evidence of this people was found⟩

neap [nip] *adj., n. —adj.* of, having to do with, or designating a NEAP TIDE.
—n. NEAP TIDE. ⟨OE *nēp*⟩

Ne•a•pol•i•tan [,niə'pɒlətən] *n., adj. —n.* a native or inhabitant of Naples, a city in Italy.

—adj. of or having to do with Naples. ⟨< L *Neapolitanus* < *Neapolis* Naples < Gk.⟩

Neapolitan ice cream ice cream consisting of several flavours in layers, usually chocolate, strawberry, and vanilla.

neap tide the tide that occurs when the difference in height between high and low tide is least; lowest level of high tide. Neap tide occurs at the first and last quarters of the moon, that is, about twice a month. ⟨ME *neep* < OE *nep* in *nepflod* neap tide⟩

near [nir] *adv., adj., prep., v. —adv.* **1** at or to a place or time not far away; close by: *The train drew near.* **2** closely: *peoples near allied.* **3** *Informal.* all but; almost: *near crazy with fright.*
come near (doing), almost do: *I came near forgetting my glasses again.*
near at hand, a within easy reach: *My pen is always near at hand.* **b** not far in the future: *The time for decision is near at hand.*
—adj. **1** close by; not distant: *The near house is yellow; the far one red.* **2** intimate; familiar: *a near friend.* **3** closely related: *a near relative.* **4** approximating or resembling closely: *near silk, near beer.* **5** on the left-hand side (*used of a horse, team of horses, vehicle, etc.*): *the near foreleg. The near horse is a bit stronger than the off horse.* Compare OFF (adj. def. 10). **6** short; direct: *Go by the nearest route.* **7** stingy. **8** by a close margin: *a near escape.*
—prep. at or to a place, time, or condition not far away; close to: *Our house is near the river. They were both near tears.*
—v. come or draw near; approach: *The ship neared the land.* ⟨OE *nēar*, comparative of *nēah* nigh⟩ **—'near•ness,** *n.*

near•by ['nir'baɪ] *adv. or adj.* near; close at hand: *They live in a nearby house. They live nearby.*

Near East **1** the countries of SW Asia (including Saudi Arabia, Israel, Lebanon, Iran, etc.) and Egypt. **2** MIDDLE EAST.
☛ *Usage.* The term **Middle East,** which often refers to a broader area, is now more commonly used than **Near East.**

near–letter quality *Computer technology.* a level of print quality in which the characters are almost as clear and well-formed as those of a good typewriter. In a character of near-letter quality, the dots that form it are still slightly visible to the unaided eye. Compare LETTER QUALITY.
—near-letter-quality, *adj.*

near•ly ['nirli] *adv.* **1** almost: *I nearly missed the train.* **2** closely: *a matter that concerns you very nearly.*

near–miss ['nir 'mɪs] *n.* **1** a narrow escape from danger. **2** anything approaching, but not quite fulfilling, excellence or perfection.

near–sight•ed ['nir ˌsəitɪd] *adj.* having a condition of the eyes in which the visual images of distant objects come to a focus before they reach the retina, so that they are not clear. A near-sighted person has better vision for nearby objects than for distant objects. Compare FAR-SIGHTED. **—'near-'sight•ed•ly,** *adv.* **—'near-'sight•ed•ness,** *n.*

neat[1] [nit] *adj.* **1** clean and in order: *a neat desk, a neat room, a neat dress.* **2** able and willing to keep things in order: *He's a very neat person.* **3** well-formed; in proportion: *a neat design.* **4** skilful; clever: *a neat trick.* **5** especially of alcoholic liquor, not having anything mixed in it; undiluted; straight: *She prefers her whisky neat.* **6** *Informal.* very pleasing; fine: *a neat party.* **7** NET.[2] ⟨< F *net* < L *nitidus* gleaming < *nitere* shine⟩ **—'neat•ly,** *adv.* **—'neat•ness,** *n.*
☛ *Syn.* **1. Neat,** TIDY, TRIM = in good order. **Neat** emphasizes cleanness and absence of disorder or litter: *Her clothes are always neat.* **Tidy** emphasizes orderliness and showing painstaking care in having a place for everything and everything in its place: *She keeps her room tidy.* **Trim** adds the idea of being pleasing in appearance, sometimes suggesting smartness, sometimes good proportion, clean lines, and compactness: *That is a trim sailing boat.*

neat[2] [nit] *n.pl. or sing. Archaic.* cattle; oxen. ⟨OE *nēat*⟩

neat•en ['nitən] *v.* make neat; tidy up.

neath or **'neath** [niθ] *prep. Poetic.* beneath.

neat•herd ['nitˌhɜrd] *n. Archaic.* cowherd.

neat's–foot oil ['nits ˌfʊt] an oil obtained from the feet and shinbones of cattle by boiling. Neat's-foot oil is used to soften leather.

neb [nɛb] *n. Scottish.* **1** a bill; beak. **2** a person's mouth or nose. **3** an animal's snout. **4** the tip of anything; nib. ⟨OE *nebb*⟩

Ne•bras•ka [nə'bræskə] *n.* a midwestern state of the United States.

neb•u•la ['nɛbjələ] *n., pl.* **-lae** [-ˌli] *or* [-ˌlaɪ] or **-las.** **1** *Astronomy.* **a** a cloudlike cluster of stars or a mass of dust particles visible in the sky at night. **b** an exterior galaxy. **2** *Pathology.* **a** a cloudlike spot on the cornea of the eye. **b** liquid medication used by spraying. ⟨< L *nebula* mist⟩ **—'neb•u•lar,** *adj.*

neb•u•lar hypothesis ['nɛbjələr] the hypothesis that the solar system developed from a luminous mass of gas.

ne•bu•lize ['nɛbjəˌlaɪz] *v.* **-lized, -lizing.** ATOMIZE (def. 2). **—ˌneb•u•li'za•tion,** *n.*

neb•u•los•i•ty [ˌnɛbjə'lɒsəti] *n., pl.* **-ties. 1** the quality or state of being nebulous. **2** cloudlike matter; nebula.

neb•u•lous ['nɛbjələs] *adj.* **1** hazy; vague; indistinct: *Our holiday plans are still somewhat nebulous.* **2** of, having to do with, or resembling a nebula; nebular. ⟨< L *nebulosus* < *nebula* mist⟩ **—'neb•u•lous•ly,** *adv.* **—'neb•u•lous•ness,** *n.*

nec•es•sar•i•ly [ˌnɛsə'sɛrəli] *or* ['nɛsəˌsɛrəli] *adv.* because of necessity; because it must be; invariably or inevitably: *Leaves are not necessarily green. War necessarily causes misery and waste.*

nec•es•sar•y ['nɛsəˌsɛri] *adj., n., pl.* **-sar•ies.** *—adj.* that must be, be had, or be done; inevitable; required; indispensable: *Death is a necessary end.*
—n. **1** something essential; something that cannot be done without: *a necessary of life.* **2 necessaries,** *pl. Law.* the things, as food, shelter, clothing, etc., required to support a dependent or similar person in a way suitable to his or her station in life. ⟨< L *necessarius* < *necesse* unavoidable, ult. < *ne-* not + *cedere* withdraw⟩
☛ *Syn. adj.* **Necessary,** INDISPENSABLE, ESSENTIAL = needed or required. **Necessary** applies to whatever is needed but only because of circumstances: *Work is a necessary part of life.* **Indispensable** implies that, without the thing referred to, the intended result or purpose cannot be achieved: *Determination is indispensable for success.* **Essential** implies that the existence or proper functioning of something depends on the thing referred to: *Good health is essential to happiness.*

ne•ces•si•tar•i•an [nəˌsɛsə'tɛriən] *adj., n. —adj.* of or having to do with necessitarianism.
—n. an advocate of necessitarianism.

ne•ces•si•tar•i•an•ism [nəˌsɛsə'tɛriəˌnɪzəm] *n. Philosophy.* the theory that every event in the universe is causally determined and cannot occur by chance. The theory of necessitarianism applied to the human will is identical with determinism.

ne•ces•si•tate [nə'sɛsəˌteit] *v.* **-tat•ed, -tat•ing. 1** make necessary: *His broken leg necessitated an operation.* **2** *Archaic.* compel; force. **—neˌces•si'ta•tion,** *n.* **—ne'ces•siˌta•tive,** *adj.*

ne•ces•si•tous [nə'sɛsətəs] *adj.* **1** very poor; needy. **2** necessary; essential. **3** urgent. **—ne'ces•si•tous•ly,** *adv.* **—ne'ces•si•tous•ness,** *n.*

ne•ces•si•ty [nə'sɛsəti] *n., pl.* **-ties. 1** the fact of being necessary; extreme need: *We understand the necessity of eating.* **2** the quality of being necessary. **3** anything that cannot be done without: *Water is a necessity.* **4** that which forces one to act in a certain way: *Necessity often drives people to do disagreeable things.* **5** that which is inevitable: *Night follows day as a necessity.* **6** need; poverty: *This poor family is in great necessity.*
of necessity, because it must be: *We left early of necessity; there are no buses at night.* ⟨< L *necessitas* < *necesse.* See NECESSARY.⟩

neck [nɛk] *n., v. —n.* **1** the part of the body that connects the head with the shoulders. **2** the part of a garment that goes around the neck. **3** any narrow part like a neck. **4** a narrow strip of land. **5** the slender part of a bottle, flask, retort, or other container: *the neck of a vase.* **6** *Architecture.* the lowest part of the capital of a column. **7** the long slender part of a violin or similar instrument, extending from the body to the head; fingerboard. **8** the part of a tooth between the crown and the root. **9** a slender or constricted part of a bone or organ. **10** *Racing.* the length of the neck of a horse or other animal as a measure.
get it in the neck, *Slang.* receive a severe scolding, defeat, etc.
lose by a neck, a lose a horse race by the length of a head and neck. **b** lose narrowly.
neck and neck, a abreast. **b** being equal or even in a race or contest: *The two horses ran neck and neck for a kilometre.*
neck of the woods, *Informal.* locality or region: *There are few good roads in this neck of the woods.*
neck or nothing, venturing all.
risk (one's) **neck,** put (oneself) in a dangerous position; risk one's life.
stick (one's) **neck out,** *Informal.* put (oneself) in a dangerous or vulnerable position by foolish or zealous action.
win by a neck, a win a horse race by the length of a head and neck. **b** win by a close margin.
—v. Informal. exchange passionate embraces, kisses, and caresses. ⟨OE *hnecca*⟩

neck•band ['nɛkˌbænd] *n.* **1** a band worn around the neck.

2 the part of a shirt, blouse, etc. to which the collar is attached. 3 the part of a garment that fits the neck.

neck•cloth ['nɛk,klɒθ] *n.* a cloth worn round the neck; cravat.

neck•er•chief ['nɛkərtʃɪf] *n.* a cloth worn round the neck.

neck•lace ['nɛklɪs] *n.* a string of jewels, gold, silver, beads, etc. worn around the neck as an ornament.

neck•line ['nɛk,laɪn] *n.* the line formed by the neck opening of a garment: *a plain neckline, a low neckline.*

neck•piece ['nɛk,pis] *n.* a separate article of clothing, such as a scarf, worn around the neck: *a fur neckpiece.*

neck•tie ['nɛk,taɪ] *n.* TIE (n. def. 2).

neck•wear ['nɛk,wɛr] *n.* collars, ties, and other articles that are worn around the neck.

nec•ro– *combining form.* dead; corpse; death: *necrophobia, necrobiosis.* Also, **necr-** *before vowels.* ⟨< Gk. *nekr-, nekro-* < *nekros* corpse⟩

nec•ro•bi•o•sis [,nɛkroubaɪ'ousɪs] *n. Medicine.* the natural death of cells and tissues as distinguished from death by injury.

ne•crol•a•try [nə'krɒlətri] *n.* worship of the dead.

ne•crol•o•gy [nə'krɒlədʒi] *n., pl.* **-gies. 1** a list of persons who have recently died. **2** a notice of a person's death; obituary. ⟨< Med.L *necrologia* < Gk. *nekros* dead body + *logos* count, reckoning⟩ **—,nec•ro'log•i•cal** [,nɛkrə'lɒdʒɪkəl], *adj.* **—,nec•ro'log•i•cal•ly,** *adv.* **—nec'ro•lo•gist,** *n.*

nec•ro•man•cy ['nɛkrə,mænsi] *n.* **1** a supposed foretelling of the future by communicating with the dead. **2** magic; enchantment; sorcery. ⟨ME < OF < Med.L *nigromantia* < L *necromantia* < Gk. *nekromanteia* < *nekros* dead body + *manteia* divination; confusion with L *niger* 'black' led to interpretation as 'black art'⟩ **—'nec•ro,man•cer,** *n.* **—,nec•ro'man•tic,** *adj.* **—,nec•ro'man•ti•cal•ly,** *adv.*

nec•ro•phil•i•a [,nɛkrə'fɪliə] *or* [,nɛkrə'filjə] *n. Psychiatry.* an attraction toward death; a morbid fascination with dead bodies. **—'nec•ro,phile** ['nɛkrə,faɪl], *n.* **—,nec•ro'phil•i,ac,** *adj., n.*

nec•ro•pho•bi•a [,nɛkrə'foubiə] *n. Psychiatry.* an abnormal fear of death or dead bodies. **—,nec•ro'pho•bic,** *adj.*

ne•crop•o•lis [nə'krɒpəlɪs] *n., pl.* **-lis•es. 1** cemetery. **2** an ancient burial ground. ⟨< NL < Gk. *nekropolis* < *nekros* dead body + *polis* city⟩

nec•rop•sy ['nɛkrɒpsi] *n., pl.* **-sies.** autopsy.

ne•cro•sis [nə'krousɪs] *n., pl.* **-ses** [-siz]. **1** the death of body cells or of a portion of tissue or an organ, resulting from irreversible damage caused by an outside agent. **2** any of various bacterial diseases of plants characterized by spots of decayed tissue. ⟨< NL < Gk. *necrosis,* ult. < *nekros* dead body⟩ **—ne'crot•ic** [nə'krɒtɪk], *adj.*

nec•tar ['nɛktər] *n.* **1** *Greek mythology.* **a** the drink of the gods. **b** the food of the gods. **2** any delicious drink. **3** *Botany.* a sweet liquid found in many flowers. Bees gather nectar and make it into honey. ⟨< L < Gk. *nektar*⟩ **—'nec•tar,like,** *adj.* **—'nec•tar•ous,** *adj.*

nec•tar•ine [,nɛktə'rin] *or* ['nɛktə,rin] *n.* **1** a fruit (*Prunus persica nectarina*) like a peach but having a smooth skin. **2** the tree it grows on. ⟨< *nectar*⟩

nec•ta•ry ['nɛktəri] *n., pl.* **-ries.** *Botany.* the part of a flower that secretes nectar. **—nec'ta•ri•al** [-'tɛriəl], *adj.*

née or **nee** [nei] *adj.* born. ⟨< F *née,* fem. pp. of *naître* be born < L *nasci*⟩

☛ *Usage.* **Née** is placed after the name of a married woman who has changed her name, to show her birth name: *Mrs. Sing, née Adams.*

☛ *Hom.* NAY, NEIGH.

need [nid] *n., v.* —*n.* **1** want; lack of a necessary thing: *The loss by our team showed the need of practice.* **2** a useful or desired thing that is lacking: *In the desert their need was water.* **3** necessity; something that has to be; requirement: *There is no need to hurry.* **4** a situation or time of difficulty: *a friend in need.* **5** extreme poverty.

have need to, *Dialect.* be required to; should or must.

if need be, if the necessity arises: *I'll do it myself if need be.*

—*v.* **1** have need of; want; require: *to need money.* **2** must; should; have to; ought to: *He need not go. Need she go?* **4** be in want: *Give to those that need.* ⟨OE *nēd*⟩ **—'need•er,** *n.*

☛ *Hom.* KNEAD.

☛ *Syn. v.* **1.** See note at LACK.

need•ful ['nidfəl] *adj.* needed; necessary. **—'need•ful•ly,** *adv.* **—'need•ful•ness,** *n.*

nee•dle ['nidəl] *n., v.* **-dled, -dling.** —*n.* **1** a slender tool, pointed at one end and having a hole, or eye, at the other to pass a thread through, used in sewing. **2** a similar tool on a sewing machine, having the hole at the pointed end. **3** a slender rod used in knitting. **4** a thin steel pointer on a compass or on electrical machinery. **5** a slender, hollow tube with a sharp point, used for injecting or extracting something; hypodermic syringe: *The doctor jabbed the needle into my arm.* **6** injection: *The doctor gave him a needle.* **7** an instrument resembling a needle, used in etching and engraving. **8** an indicator on a gauge. **9** a phonograph needle; stylus. **10** any of various small objects resembling a needle in sharpness: *needles of broken glass, ice, etc.* **11** a slender, needle-shaped rod that controls the opening of a valve. **12** NEEDLE VALVE. **13** *Botany.* the needle-shaped leaf of the fir, pine, spruce, or larch. **14** a pillar; obelisk: *Cleopatra's Needle.* **15** *Mineralogy and chemistry.* a crystal or spicule like a needle in shape. **16** *Geology.* a pinnacle of rock tapering to a point.

a needle in a haystack, something very difficult to find.

give (someone) **the needle,** *Informal.* tease; goad.

—*v.* **1** sew with a needle. **2** *Informal.* tease; goad or incite: *The boys needled him into losing his temper.* ⟨OE *nǣdl*⟩ **—'nee•dle,like,** *adj.*

nee•dle•fish ['nidəl,fɪʃ] *n.* any of a family (Belonidae) of sea fishes having a long, pipelike body, a long snout, and many sharp teeth.

nee•dle•point ['nidəl,pɔɪnt] *n.* **1** embroidery done on canvas, using straight, even stitches to cover the entire surface, giving a tapestrylike effect. **2** (*adjl.*) of, designating, or made or decorated with such embroidery. **3** POINT LACE.

need•ler ['nidlər] *n. Informal.* a person who nags or irritates others; heckler.

need•less ['nidlɪs] *adj.* not needed; unnecessary. **—'need•less•ly,** *adv.* **—'need•less•ness,** *n.*

needle valve a valve whose very small opening is controlled by a slender, needle-shaped rod.

nee•dle•wom•an ['nidəl,wʊmən] *n., pl.* **-wom•en.** a woman who does needlework, especially one who earns her living by sewing.

nee•dle•work ['nidəl,wɜrk] *n.* **1** work done with a needle, especially handwork such as embroidery, needlepoint, or fine hand sewing. **2** the art or practice of such work.

need•n't ['nidənt] need not.

needs [nidz] *adv.* because of necessity; necessarily: *A soldier must needs go where duty calls.* ⟨OE *nēdes,* originally gen. of *nēd* need⟩

need•y ['nidi] *adj.* **need•i•er, need•i•est.** very poor; not having enough to live on. **—'need•i•ness,** *n.*

ne'er [nɛr] *adv. Poetic.* never.

ne'er–do–well ['nɛr du ,wɛl] *n., adj.* —*n.* a worthless fellow; good-for-nothing person.
—*adj.* worthless; good-for-nothing.

ne•far•i•ous [nɪ'fɛriəs] *adj.* very wicked; villainous. ⟨< L *nefarius,* ult. < *ne-* not + *fas* right, originally, (divine) decree < *fari* speak⟩ **—ne'far•i•ous•ly,** *adv.* **—ne'far•i•ous•ness,** *n.*

neg. negative.

ne•gate [nɪ'geit] *v.* **-gat•ed, -gat•ing.** deny; nullify. ⟨< L *negare* say no⟩ **—ne'gat•or,** *n.*

ne•ga•tion [nɪ'geiʃən] *n.* **1** a denying; denial: *Shaking the head is a sign of negation.* **2** the absence or opposite of some positive thing or quality: *Darkness is the negation of light.* **3** *Linguistics.* the formation of a negative sentence: *Negation takes different forms in different languages.* ⟨< L *negatio, -onis* < *negare* say no⟩ **—ne'ga•tion•al,** *adj.*

neg•a•tive ['nɛgətɪv] *adj., n., adv., v.* **-tived, -tiv•ing.**
—*adj.* **1** saying no: *His answer was negative.* **2** consisting only in the absence of something: *Not being unkind is only negative kindness.* **3** not positive, optimistic, or helpful: *a negative attitude.* **4** *Mathematics, physics.* **a** counting down from zero; minus: *Three below zero is a negative quantity.* **b** measured or proceeding in the opposite direction to that considered positive. **5** *Chemistry, physics.* having more electrons than protons: *a negative particle.* **6** *Electricity.* of, having to do with, or characterized by the kind of electricity produced on resin when it is rubbed with silk. **7** *Photography.* showing the lights and shadows reversed: *the negative image on a photographic plate.* **8** *Biology.* opposing (a stimulus): *The shoot has a negative stimulus to gravity.* **9** *Chemistry.* having a tendency to gain electrons, and thus to become charged with negative electricity, as an element or radical. **10** showing an absence of the germs, symptoms, etc. of

an illness. **11** *Psychology.* resisting suggestions; very unco-operative.
—n. **1** an affix, word, or statement that says no or denies. **2** the side that says no or argues against a question being debated; side opposing the affirmative. **3** a negative quality or characteristic. **4** *Mathematics.* a minus quantity, sign, etc. **5** *Electricity.* the negative element in an electric cell. **6** *Photography.* an image in which the lights and shadows are reversed and from which prints can be made. **7** the right of veto.
in the negative, a in favour of denying (a request, suggestion, etc.): *His behaviour showed him to be in the negative.* **b** expressing disagreement by saying no; denying: *Most of the replies were in the negative.*
—adv. Radio communication. no.
—v. **1** say no to; deny; vote against. **2** disprove. **3** make useless; counteract; neutralize. ⟨< L *negativus* < *negare* say no⟩
—'neg•a•tive•ly, *adv.* **—'neg•a•tive•ness** or **ˌneg•a'tiv•i•ty,** *n.*
☛ *Usage.* **Double negatives.** Two negatives should not be used in a sentence where only one is required. *She won't tell us nothing* should be corrected to *She won't tell us anything.* Double negatives were used in and before Shakespeare's time, but they are no longer accepted in standard English. They are common in Black English. See also note at HARDLY.

negative sign MINUS (*n.*).

neg•a•tiv•ism ['nɛgətɪˌvɪzəm] *n.* **1** a tendency to say or do the opposite of what is suggested. **2** *Psychology.* a type of behaviour marked by resistance to suggestion. **3** an attitude characterized by doubt or pessimism instead of acceptance or optimism. **—'neg•a•tiv•ist,** *n., adj.* **—ˌneg•a•tiv'ist•ic,** *adj.*

ne•glect [nɪ'glɛkt] *v., n. —v.* **1** give too little care, respect, or attention to: *to neglect one's health. He neglected his lawyer's advice.* **2** leave undone; not attend to: *The maid neglected her work.* **3** omit; fail: *Don't neglect to water the plants.*
—n. **1** the act or fact of neglecting; disregard: *His neglect of the truth was astonishing.* **2** a lack of attention to what should be done. **3** the state of being neglected. ⟨< L *neglectus,* pp. of *negligere, neglegere,* var. of *neclegere* < *nec* not (< *ne-* not + *que* and) + *legere* pick up⟩ **—ne'glect•er** or **ne'glect•or,** *n.* **—ne'glect•ed•ly,** *adv.* **—ne'glect•ing•ly,** *adv.*
☛ *Syn. v.* **1.** See note at SLIGHT. *—n.* **1. Neglect,** NEGLIGENCE = lack of proper care or attention. **Neglect** applies especially to the act or fact of giving too little care or attention to one's duty or work or leaving it undone: *That car has been ruined by neglect.* **Negligence** applies especially to the quality of being inclined to neglect, possessed by a person or group or shown by inattentiveness to work or duty or carelessness in doing it: *Many accidents in industry are caused by the negligence of workers.*

ne•glect•ful [nɪ'glɛktfəl] *adj.* careless; negligent. **—ne'glect•ful•ly,** *adv.* **—ne'glect•ful•ness,** *n.*

né•gli•gé [neigli'ʒei]; *French,* [negli'ʒe] *n. French.* negligee.

neg•li•gee [ˌnɛglə'ʒei] *or* ['nɛgləˌʒei] *n., adj. —n.* **1** a woman's loose, often sheer, dressing gown. **2** easy, informal dress or attire.
—adj. not fully dressed. ⟨< F *négligée,* fem. pp. of *négliger* neglect⟩

neg•li•gence ['nɛglədʒəns] *n.* **1** a lack of proper care or attention; neglect: *Because of the owner's negligence the house was in great need of repair.* **2** carelessness; indifference. **3** *Law.* failure to take due care, as required by law, resulting in damage to property or injury to a person or persons. ⟨< L *negligentia* < *negligere.* See NEGLECT.⟩
☛ *Syn.* **1.** See note at NEGLECT.

neg•li•gent ['nɛglədʒənt] *adj.* **1** neglectful; given to neglect; showing neglect. **2** careless; indifferent: *His negligent behaviour resulted in an accident.* ⟨< L *negligens, -entis,* ppr. of *negligere.* See NEGLECT.⟩ **—'neg•li•gent•ly,** *adv.*

neg•li•gi•ble ['nɛglədʒəbəl] *adj.* that can be disregarded; of little importance; trifling: *a negligible difference in price.* **—'neg•li•gi•bly,** *adv.* **—ˌneg•li•gi'bil•i•ty,** *n.*

ne•go•ti•a•ble [nɪ'gouʃəbəl] *or* [nɪ'gouʃiəbəl] *adj.* **1** capable of being negotiated or sold; whose ownership can be transferred. **2** that can be got past, through, or over. **—neˌgo•tia'bil•i•ty,** *n.*

ne•go•ti•ate [nɪ'gouʃiˌeit] *v.* **-at•ed, -at•ing. 1** talk over and arrange terms; parley; confer; consult: *The rebels negotiated for peace with the government.* **2** arrange for: *They finally negotiated a peace treaty.* **3** transfer, assign, or sell ownership in return for equivalent value. **4** get past or over: *The car negotiated the sharp curve by slowing down.* ⟨< L *negotiare* < *negotium* business < *neg-* not + *otium* ease⟩ **—ne'go•tiˌa•tor,** *n.*

ne•go•ti•a•tion [nɪˌgouʃi'eiʃən] *n.* **1** a talking over and arranging; arrangement: *Negotiations for the new school are finished.* **2** the act of negotiating. **—ne'go•tia,to•ry,** *adj.*

Ne•gri•to [nɪ'gritou] *n., pl.* **-tos** or **-toes.** a member of any of several dark-skinned peoples living in the Philippines and other islands in SE Asia. The Negritos are very small people, averaging less than 150 cm tall. ⟨< Sp. *negrito,* dim. of *negro* Negro⟩ **—Ne'grit•ic** [-'grɪtɪk], *adj.*

neg•ri•tude ['nɛgrəˌtjud] *or* ['nɛgrəˌtud], ['nigrəˌtjud] *or* ['nigrəˌtud] *n.* **1** the condition of being a Black. **2** awareness of and pride in Black or African culture and heritage.

Ne•gro ['nigrou] *n., pl.* **-groes;** *adj. —n.* **1** one of the major races of the world, especially the people of Africa. **2** a member of this race.
—adj. of or having to do with Negroes. ⟨< Sp. *negro* < L *niger* black⟩

Ne•groid ['nigrɔɪd] *adj., n. —adj.* having to do with or like the Negro race.
—n. a member of the Negro race.

ne•gus ['nigəs] *n.* a drink made of wine, hot water, sugar, lemon, and nutmeg. ⟨after Colonel Francis *Negus* (died 1732), its English inventor⟩

Ne•gus ['nigəs] *n.* the title of the ruler of Ethiopia. ⟨< Amharic⟩

neigh [nei] *n., v. —n.* the sound that a horse makes; whinny.
—v. make the sound that a horse makes or one like it; whinny. ⟨OE *hnǣgan*⟩
☛ *Hom.* NAY, NÉE.

neigh•bour or **neigh•bor** ['neibər] *n., v. —n.* **1** a person who lives near another: *We asked our next-door neighbours to take in our mail while we were away. Their nearest neighbours are 20 km away.* **2** a person or thing that is near another: *The big tree brought down several of its smaller neighbours as it fell.* **3** (*adjl.*) living or situated near or next to another; neighbouring. **4** a fellow human being.
—v. **1** be near or next to; adjoin. **2** be friendly with. ⟨OE *nēahgebūr* < *nēah* nigh + *gebūr* dweller, countryman⟩ **—'neigh•bour•less** or **'neigh•bor•less,** *adj.*

neigh•bour•hood or **neigh•bor•hood** ['neibərˌhʊd] *n., adj. —n.* **1** the region near some place or thing; vicinity. **2** a place; district: *Is your new house in an attractive neighbourhood?* **3** the people of a place or district: *The whole neighbourhood came to the big party.* **4** neighbourly feeling or conduct. **5** (*adjl.*) of or having to do with a neighbourhood: *a neighbourhood newspaper.* **6** nearness.
in the neighbourhood of, *Informal.* somewhere near; about: *The car cost in the neighbourhood of $29 000.*
neighbourhood of a point, *Mathematics.* a set of points around a specified point within a given distance of it.
—adj. of or having to do with a neighbourhood: *a neighbourhood newspaper.*

neigh•bour•ing or **neigh•bor•ing** ['neibərɪŋ] *adj.* living or being near; bordering; adjoining; near.

neigh•bour•ly or **neigh•bor•ly** ['neibərli] *adj.* of, having to do with, or characteristic of neighbours who get along with each other; especially, sociable or kindly: *a neighbourly chat, a neighbourly atmosphere.* **—'neigh•bour•li•ness** or **'neigh•bor•li•ness,** *n.*

nei•ther ['niðər] *or* ['naɪðər] *conj., adj., pron. —conj.* **1** not either: *Neither you nor I will go.* **2** nor yet: *"They toil not, neither do they spin."*
—adj. not either: *Neither statement is true.*
—pron. not either: *Neither of the statements is true.* ⟨ME *neither* < *ne* not + *either*⟩

nek•ton ['nɛktɒn] *or* ['nɛktən] *n.* all of the marine animals that swim independently of currents. ⟨< G < Gk. *nēktón* swimming⟩ **—nec'ton•ic,** *adj.*

nel•son ['nɛlsən] *n.* either of two holds in wrestling. See HALF NELSON and FULL NELSON. ⟨origin uncertain⟩

ne•lum•bo [nə'lʌmbou] *n., pl.* **-bos.** a plant of the genus *Nelumbo,* such as a lotus. ⟨< NL < Singhalese *nelumbu*⟩ **—ne'lum•bi•an,** *adj.*

nemato– *combining form.* threadlike: *nematocyst.* ⟨< Gk. *nēmat-, nêma* thread, yarn, that which is spun⟩

nem•a•to•cyst ['nɛmətəˌsɪst] *or* [nə'mætəˌsɪst] *n. Zoology.* one of the tiny, stinging organs of jellyfish and other coelenterates. Each nematocyst contains a coiled thread that can be projected as a sting. **—ˌnem•a•to'cyst•ic,** *adj.*

nem•a•tode ['nɛməˌtoud] *n.* any of a class (Nematoda) of worms having a long, unsegmented, round body. Some nematodes, such as hookworms, pinworms, and trichinae, are parasites in human beings and animals. ⟨< NL *Nematoda,* pl., ult. < Gk. *nēma, -atos* thread < *neein* spin⟩

nem•a•tol•o•gy [ˌnɛmə'tɒlədʒi] *n.* the study of nematodes. **—ˌnem•a•to'log•i•cal** [ˌnɛmətə'lɒdʒɪkəl], *adj.* **—ˌnem•a'tol•o•gist,** *n.*

nem. con. unanimously. ⟨for L *nemine contradicente,* with no one contradicting⟩

Ne•me•an lion [nɪ'miən] *or* ['nimiən] *Classical mythology.* the lion killed by Hercules as one of his twelve tasks.

ne•mer•te•an [nɪ'mɜrtiən] *n., adj.* *—n.* ribbon worm. *—adj.* of or having to do with the nemerteans or ribbon worms. Also, **nemertinean** [ˌnɛmər'tɪniən]. ⟨< NL *Nemertea,* the class name < Gk. *Nēmertēs,* a sea nymph + E *-an, -ian*⟩

nem•er•tine ['nɛmər,taɪn] *or* ['nɛmər,tɪn] *n., adj.* *—n.* ribbon worm; nemertean. *—adj.* of or having to do with the nemertines, or ribbon worms.

nem•e•sis ['nɛməsɪs] *n., pl.* **-ses** [-ˌsiz]. **1 Nemesis,** *Greek mythology.* the goddess of vengeance and retribution; the punisher of excessive pride. **2** just punishment for evil deeds. **3** a person who punishes another for evil deeds; the agent of just punishment. **4** any person or thing that seems to have the power to defeat: *When he saw his opponent, he knew he had met his nemesis.* **5** *Astronomy.* a hypothetical companion star to the sun, responsible for meteor showers. ⟨< Gk. *Nemesis* < *nemein* give what is due⟩

neo– *combining form.* **1** new; recent: *Neozoic.* **2** *Chemistry.* an isomer with a carbon atom attached to four other carbon atoms. ⟨< Gk. *neos*⟩

ne•o–ars•phen•a•mine [ˌniou ɑrs'fɛnə,min] *n. Pharmacy.* a yellow powder containing arsenic, used in treating syphilis and yaws.

Ne•o•cene ['niə,sin] *n., adj. Geology.* *—n.* **1** the later division of the Tertiary period, comprising the Miocene and Pliocene epochs. **2** the rocks formed during this division. *—adj.* of or having to do with this division or the rocks formed during it. ⟨*neo-* + Gk. *kainos* recent⟩

ne•o•clas•sic [ˌniou'klæsɪk] *adj.* of or having to do with neoclassicism. Also, **neoclassical. —ˌne•o'clas•si•cist,** *n.*

ne•o•clas•si•cism [ˌniou'klæsə,sɪzəm] *n.* **1** *Arts.* the revival of classical ideals of form, proportion, and restraint. **2** *Literature.* a similar style or movement, especially that which prevailed in 18th-century England. **3** *Music.* a 20th-century movement marked by a return to the style of classical composers such as Johann Sebastian Bach.

ne•o•co•lo•ni•al•ism [ˌniouka'louniə,lɪzəm] *n.* **1** the control of former colonies by economic means. **2** the use of economic power to influence a nation. **—ˌne•o•co'lo•ni•al,** *adj.* **—ˌne•o•co'lo•ni•al•ist,** *n.*

Ne•o–Dar•win•ism [ˌniou 'dɑrwɪ,nɪzəm] *n. Biology.* the theory of NATURAL SELECTION. **—ˌNe•o•Dar'win•i•an,** *adj., n.* **—ˌNe•o-'Dar•win•ist,** *n.*

ne•o•dym•i•um [ˌniou'dɪmiəm] *n. Chemistry.* a metallic chemical element of the lanthanide series found in certain rare minerals. *Symbol:* Nd; *at.no.* 60; *at.mass* 144.24. ⟨< *neo-* + *(di)dymium*⟩

ne•o•fas•cism [ˌniou'fæʃɪzəm] *n.* any movement to restore the former beliefs or principles of fascism. **—ˌne•o'fas•cist,** *n., adj.*

ne•o•gen•e•sis [ˌniou'dʒɛnəsɪs] *n.* the regeneration of tissue.

Ne•o–Im•pres•sion•ism [ˌniou ɪm'prɛʃə,nɪzəm] *n.* pointillism. **—ˌNe•o•Im'pres•sion•ist,** *n., adj.*

Ne•o–La•marck•ism [ˌniou lə'mɑrkɪzəm] *n. Biology.* an extension of LAMARCKISM to include the theory that genetic change can be influenced by environment. **—ˌNe•o-La'marck•i•an,** *adj., n.* **—ˌNe•o-La'marck•ist,** *n.*

ne•o•lin•guis•tics [ˌnioulɪŋ'gwɪstɪks] *n.* a school of linguistics which denies attempts to trace languages back to a common ancestor, and emphasizes the transmission of language elements through space (*used with a singular verb*).

ne•o•lith ['niə,lɪθ] *n.* a Neolithic stone implement.

Ne•o•lith•ic [ˌniə'lɪθɪk] *adj.* of the later Stone Age, when polished stone weapons and tools were first made and used, marked also by the appearance of settled agriculture and of accompanying social development. ⟨< *neo-* + Gk. *lithos* stone⟩

ne•ol•o•gism [nɪ'ɒlə,dʒɪzəm] *n.* **1** a new word; new meaning for an old word. **2** the use of new words or new meanings for old words. ⟨< F < Gk. *neos* new + *logos* word⟩ **—ne'ol•o•gist,** *n.* **—ne,ol•o'gis•tic** or **,ne•ol•o'gis•ti•cal,** *adj.*

ne•ol•o•gize [ni'ɒlə,dʒaɪz] *v.* **-gized, -giz•ing. 1** create new words or new meanings. **2** create new doctrines of religion.

ne•ol•o•gy [ni'ɒlədʒi] *n.,* pl. **-gies.** neologism. **—ˌne•o'log•i•cal** [ˌniə'lɒdʒɪkəl], *adj.* **—ˌne•o'log•i•cal•ly,** *adv.*

ne•o•my•cin [ˌniou'maɪsən] *n. Pharmacy.* an antibiotic or mixture of antibiotics produced by a bacterium (*Streptomyces fradiae*) found in the soil. ⟨< *neo-* + Gk. *mykēs* fungus⟩

ne•on ['niɒn] *n. Chemistry.* an inert chemical element that is a colourless, odourless gas found in very small quantities in the atmosphere. Neon is used in electric lights and signs because it gives off a glow when electricity is passed through it in a low-pressure tube. *Symbol:* Ne; *at.no.* 10; *at.mass* 20.17. ⟨< NL < Gk. *neon,* neut., new⟩

ne•o•na•tal [ˌniou'neitəl] *adj.* of, having to do with, or affecting the newborn child, especially a child less than a month old: *neonatal distress, a neonatal hospital unit.* **—ˌne•o'na•tal•ly,** *adv.*

ne•o•nate ['niou,neit] *n.* a newborn child, especially one less than a month old. ⟨< NL *neonatus* < *neo-* + L *natus* born⟩

ne•o•na•tol•o•gy [ˌniounə'tɒlədʒi] *n.* the care of newborns, especially children born prematurely. **—ˌne•o•na'tol•o•gist,** *n.*

ne•o–Na•zi [ˌniou 'nætsi] *or* ['nɑtsi] *n., adj.* *—n.* **1** a member of a political party favouring neo-Nazism. **2** a person who supports neo-Nazism. *—adj.* of or having to do with neo-Nazism or neo-Nazis.

ne•o–Na•zism [ˌniou 'nætsɪzəm] *or* ['nɑtsɪzəm] *n.* a movement to restore the principles and beliefs of Nazism. Also, **neo-Naziism** [-si,ɪzəm].

neon lamp an electric light containing neon, that glows when a current passes through it.

neon sign an electric sign containing neon, that glows when a current passes through it.

neon tetra a small, tropical fish (*Hyphessobrycon innesi*) with blue and red markings.

ne•o–or•tho•dox•y [ˌniou 'ɔrθə,dɒksi] *n.* a 20th-century Protestant movement intended to revive an older theology.

ne•o•phyte ['niə,fəit] *n.* **1** a new convert; one recently admitted to a religious body. **2** a beginner; novice. ⟨< L < Gk. *neophytos* < *neos* new + *phyein* to plant⟩ **—ˌne•o'phyt•ic** [ˌniə'fɪtɪk], *adj.*

ne•o•plasm ['niə,plæzəm] *n. Pathology.* an abnormal growth of tissue; tumour.

Ne•o•pla•to•nism [ˌniou'pleitə,nɪzəm] *n.* a combination of Christianity with Platonism. **—Ne•o•pla'ton•ic** [ˌnioupla'tɒnɪk], *adj.*

ne•o•prene ['niə,prin] *n. Chemistry.* a synthetic rubber made from chloroprene.

ne•ot•e•ny [ni'ɒtəni] *n. Zoology.* the ability of larvae to be sexually mature. **—ne'ot•e•nous,** *adj.*

ne•o•ter•ic [ˌniə'tɛrɪk] *adj., n.* *—adj.* new. *—n.* a new or modern thinker. **—ˌne•o'ter•i•cal•ly,** *adv.*

Ne•o•tro•pi•cal [ˌniou'trɒpəkəl] *adj.* having to do with a biogeographical area running south from the Tropic of Cancer.

Ne•o•zo•ic [ˌniə'zouɪk] *adj. Geology.* designating or having to do with the period from the end of the Mesozoic to the present; Cenozoic. ⟨< *neo-* + Gk. *zōē* life⟩

Nep•al [nə'pɒl], [nə'pɑl], *or* [nə'pæl] *n.* a kingdom between India and China.

Nep•al•ese [ˌnɛpə'liz] *n., adj.* *—n.* a native or inhabitant of Nepal. *—adj.* of or having to do with Nepal or its people.

Nep•a•li [nə'pɒli], [nə'pɑli], *or* [nə'pæli] *n.* **1** the language of Nepal. **2** a native or inhabitant of Nepal; Nepalese.

ne•pen•the [nɪ'pɛnθi] *n.* **1** a drug or potion used by the ancients to bring forgetfulness of trouble or sorrow. **2** anything that brings forgetfulness. ⟨< L < Gk. *nēpenthēs* < *nē-* not + *penthos* grief⟩

neph•e•lom•e•ter [ˌnɛfə'lɒmətər] *n. Physical chemistry.* a device to measure the size and concentration of particles in a liquid by analysing the light reflected by the liquid. **—ˌneph•ə•lo'met•ric** [ˌnɛfələ'mɛtrɪk] or **ˌneph•e•lo'met•ri•cal,** *adj.* **—ˌneph•e•lo'met•ri•cal•ly,** *adv.* **—ˌneph•e'lom•e•try,** *n.*

neph•ew ['nɛfju]; *esp. Brit.* ['nɛvju] *n.* **1** the son of one's brother or sister. **2** the son of one's brother-in-law or sister-in-law. ⟨ME < OF *neveu* < L *nepos*⟩

nepho– *combining form.* cloud: *nephology.* ⟨< Gk. *néphos*⟩

ne•phol•o•gy [nɛ'fɒlədʒi] *n.* the study of cloud formations and of clouds. **—ˌneph•o'log•i•cal** [ˌnɛfə'lɒdʒɪkəl], *adj.* **—ne'phol•o•gist,** *n.*

ne•phrid•i•um [nɪ'frɪdiəm] *n., pl.* **-phrid•i•a** [-'frɪdiə]. *Zoology.* **1** an excretory organ in most invertebrates. **2** the part of the embryo that develops into a kidney. **—ne'phrid•i•al,** *adj.*

neph•rite ['nɛfrəit] *n.* a silicate of calcium and either magnesium or iron; one of the two varieties of jade. It is not as hard or as valuable as jadeite, the other variety of jade. ⟨< G *Nephrit* < Gk. *nephros* kidney (from its supposed value in curing kidney disease)⟩

ne•phrit•ic [nɪ'frɪtɪk] *adj.* **1** *Anatomy.* of, having to do with, or located near the kidneys; renal. **2** *Pathology.* of, having to do with, or affected with nephritis.

ne•phri•tis [nɪ'frəitɪs] *n. Pathology.* acute or chronic inflammation of the kidney, caused by infection, degeneration of tissue, or disease of the blood vessels. ⟨< LL < Gk. *nephritis* < *nephros* kidney⟩

nephro– *combining form.* kidney: *nephron.* Also (*especially before a vowel*), **nephr-**. ⟨< Gk. *néphros* kidney⟩

neph•ron ['nɛfrɒn] *n. Anatomy, zoology.* any of the minute, tubular structures in the kidney, responsible for filtering out wastes from the blood.

ne plus ul•tra [ni plʌs 'ʌltrə] *or* [nei plʊs 'ʊltrə] the highest or furthest point or state attainable; the height of excellence or achievement. ⟨literally, 'not more beyond', said to have been inscribed on the Pillars of Hercules, the two rocks forming the western exit from the Mediterranean⟩

nep•o•tism ['nɛpəˌtɪzəm] *n.* the showing of too much favour by one in power to his or her relatives, especially by giving them desirable appointments. ⟨< F < Ital. *nepotismo* < *nepote* nephew⟩ **—'nep•o•tist,** *n.* **—ˌnep•o'tis•tic,** *adj.*

Nep•tune ['nɛptjun] *or* ['nɛptun] *n.* **1** *Roman mythology.* the god of the sea, corresponding to the Greek god Poseidon. **2** the ocean. **3** *Astronomy.* the fourth largest planet in the solar system and the eighth in distance from the sun. It is too far from the earth to be seen with the naked eye.

Nep•tu•ni•an [nɛp'tjuniən] *or* [nɛp'tuniən] *adj.* **1** having to do with the sea or with the god Neptune. **2** *Astronomy.* having to do with the planet Neptune. **3** formed by the action of water.

nep•tu•ni•um [nɛp'tjuniəm] *or* [nɛp'tuniəm] *n. Chemistry.* a radioactive chemical element similar to uranium, obtained as a by-product in the production of plutonium. *Symbol*: Np; *at.no.* 93; *at.mass* 237.05; *half-life* about 2.1 million years. ⟨< *Neptune*⟩

nerd [nɜrd] *n. Slang.* **1** an ineffectual and foolish person. **2** an intelligent but obsessive person concerned exclusively with one non-social activity: *a computer nerd.* ⟨probably from *Slang. nut,* an idiot⟩

Ne•re•id or **ne•re•id** ['niriɪd] *n. Greek mythology.* any of the fifty daughters of Nereus. The Nereids were sea nymphs who attended Poseidon.

ne•re•is ['niriɪs] *n.* any marine worm of the genus *Nereis.*

Ne•re•us ['nirjus] *or* ['niriəs] *n. Greek mythology.* a sea god, father of the Nereids.

ne•rit•ic [nɪ'rɪtɪk] *adj.* having to do with the waters of a shoreline. ⟨< *Nereus*⟩

neritic zone CONTINENTAL SHELF.

ner•ka ['nɜrkə] *n.* sockeye. ⟨? a native name⟩

ne•ro•li ['nɛrəli] *or* ['nirəli] *n.* an oil distilled from orange flowers and used in making perfumes. ⟨< the Princess of *Neroli*⟩

nerv•ate ['nɜrveit] *adj. Botany.* of leaves, having veins.

ner•va•tion [nər'veiʃən] *n.* the arrangement of veins or ribs in a leaf or an insect's wing; venation.

nerve [nɜrv] *n., v.* **nerved, nerv•ing.** *—n.* **1** *Physiology.* a fibre or bundle of fibres connecting the brain or spinal cord with the eyes, ears, muscles, glands, etc., or with other nerves. **2** *Dentistry.* one of these fibres in the pulp of a tooth. **3** mental strength; courage: *The diver lost his nerve and wouldn't go off the high board.* **4** strength; vigour; energy. **5** *Informal.* rude boldness; impudence. **6** *Botany, zoology.* a vein of a leaf or an insect's wing. **7 nerves,** *pl.* **a** NERVOUS SYSTEM. **b** nervousness. **c** an attack of nervousness.

get on (someone's) **nerves,** annoy or irritate someone.

have (got) (one's) **nerve,** show bravado; be cheeky: *She's got her nerve pushing in front of us like that.*

strain every nerve, exert oneself to the utmost.

—v. put strength or courage in (oneself): *The soldiers nerved themselves for the battle.* ⟨< L *nervus* sinew, tendon⟩

nerve cell *Anatomy, physiology.* **1** the basic functional unit of nerve tissue, that conducts nervous impulses; neuron. **2** the cell body of a neuron, excluding its fibres.

nerve centre **1** a group of nerve cells closely connected with one another and having a common function. **2** a source of leadership or energy; a control centre or headquarters: *the economic nerve centre of the nation.*

nerve fibre *Anatomy, physiology.* one of the long, threadlike fibres of a nerve cell that conduct impulses toward or away from the body of the nerve cell.

nerve gas *Chemical warfare.* a gas containing invisible particles that penetrate the skin and attack the central nervous system, causing extreme weakness or death.

nerve impulse *Physiology.* the progression of chemical and electrical disturbance along a nerve fibre.

nerve•less ['nɜrvlɪs] *adj.* **1** without strength or vigour; feeble; weak. **2** without courage or firmness. **3** without nerves. **4** self-controlled. **—'nerve•less•ly,** *adv.*

nerve–wrack•ing or **nerve–rack•ing** ['nɜrv ˌrækɪŋ] *adj.* trying to the limit of endurance; exasperating.

nerv•ous ['nɜrvəs] *adj.* **1** of the nerves: *The brain is a part of the nervous system of the body.* **2** having delicate or easily excited nerves. **3** having or proceeding from nerves that are out of order: *a nervous patient, a nervous tapping of the fingers.* **4** deriving from a tense or quickened condition of the nerves: *nervous energy.* **5** restless; uneasy; timid. **6** having nerves. **7** strong; sinewy. ⟨< L *nervosus* sinewy < *nervus* sinew, tendon⟩ **—'nerv•ous•ly,** *adv.* **—'nerv•ous•ness,** *n.*

nervous breakdown (not in technical use) a psychiatric disorder requiring treatment, characterized by extreme physical and mental fatigue, irritability or depression, chronic aches and pains of a general nature, local digestive and circulatory disturbances of uncertain origin, etc.

nervous exhaustion a mild form of, or a beginning stage of a nervous breakdown, characterized especially by fatigue and depression.

nervous system *Anatomy, zoology.* the system in the body of an animal or human being that receives and interprets different stimuli and conducts impulses to the glands, muscles, etc. concerned. In vertebrates, the nervous system includes the brain, spinal cord, ganglia nerves, and the parts of the sense organs that receive the stimuli.

ner•vure ['nɜrvjʊr] *n. Botany, zoology.* **1** a vein of a leaf. **2** a rib of an insect's wing. ⟨< F⟩

nerv•y ['nɜrvi] *adj.* **nerv•i•er, nerv•i•est. 1** *Slang.* rude and bold. **2** showing courage or firmness. **3** *Archaic or poetic.* strong; vigorous. **4** nervous; excitable. **—'ner•vi•ly,** *adv.* **—'ner•vi•ness,** *n.*

nes•cience ['nɛʃəns], ['nɛʃiəns], *or* ['nɛsiəns] *n.* lack of knowledge; ignorance. ⟨< LL *nescientia,* ult. < L *ne-* not + *scire* know⟩ **—'nes•cient,** *adj.*

ness [nɛs] *n. Archaic.* a cape or promontory. ⟨ME *nasse* < OE *næs,* akin to OE *nosu* nose⟩

–ness *noun-forming suffix.* **1** the quality, state, or condition of being ——: *preparedness = the state of being prepared.* **2** ——action; ——behaviour: *carefulness = careful action* or *careful behaviour.* ⟨OE *-nes(s)*⟩

☛ *Usage.* **-ness** is a living suffix and can be freely used to form new words.

Nes•sus ['nɛsəs] *n. Greek mythology.* a centaur shot by Hercules with a poisoned arrow. Hercules was himself fatally poisoned by a shirt steeped in the blood of Nessus.

nest [nɛst] *n., v.* *—n.* **1** a structure or place used by birds for laying eggs and rearing young. **2** a place used by insects, fish, turtles, rabbits, etc. for depositing eggs or young. **3** a snug abode, retreat, or resting place. **4** a place where evil or harmful persons gather; a den: *a nest of thieves.* **5** the birds, animals, or insects living in a nest. **6** a set or series from large to small such that each fits within another: *a nest of drinking cups, a nest of tables.* **7** *Informal.* a base for guided missiles. **8** a group of rabbits.

feather (one's) **nest,** make things comfortable for oneself; look after one's own interest, especially financially.

—v. **1** build or have a nest. **2** place or fit together in a nest: *The tables were nested and placed along the wall.* **3** hunt for birds' nests. ⟨OE⟩ **—'nest•a•ble,** *adj.* **—'nestˌlike,** *adj.* **—'nest•er,** *n.*

nest egg **1** a natural or artificial egg left in a nest to induce a hen to continue laying eggs there. **2** something, usually a sum of money, as the beginning of a fund or as a reserve: *When he got married, he had already saved quite a nest egg.*

nes•tle ['nɛsəl] *v.* **-tled, -tling. 1** settle oneself or be settled comfortably and cosily: *to nestle down in a big chair, a house nestling among trees.* **2** press close (together) in love or for comfort: *The mother nestled her baby in her arms.* **3** make or have a nest; settle in a nest. ⟨OE *nestlian* < *nest* nest⟩ **—'nes•tler,** *n.*

nest•ling ['nɛstlɪŋ] *or* ['nɛslɪŋ] *n.* **1** a bird too young to leave the nest. **2** a young child.

Nes•tor ['nɛstər] *n.* **1** *Greek mythology.* a king who in his old age served as counsellor for the Greeks at the siege of Troy. **2** Sometimes, **nestor,** a wise old man; a patriarch or leader.

net[1] [nɛt] *n., v.* **net•ted, net•ting.** *—n.* **1** an open fabric made of string, cord, thread, or wire, knotted together in such a way as to leave holes regularly arranged: *Veils are made of very fine net.* **2** a piece of such a fabric used for some special purpose: *a fish net, a hair net, a tennis net.* **3** anything like a net; a set of things that cross each other; network. **4** a lacelike cloth. **5 the Net,** *Computer technology.* the Internet. **6** a trap or snare. **7** *Tennis, badminton, etc.* a ball that hits the net.
—v. **1** catch in or as if in a net: *net a fish.* **2** cover, confine, or protect with or as if with a net. **3** make into a net. **4** make with net. **5** *Tennis, badminton, etc.* hit (a ball) into the net. ⟨OE *nett*⟩ **—'net,like,** *adj.*

net[2] [nɛt] *adj., n., v.* **net•ted, net•ting.** *—adj.* **1** real or actual; clear and free from deductions or additions. A net gain or profit is the actual gain after all working expenses have been paid. The net weight of a glass jar of candy is the weight of the candy itself. **2** final: *the net result.*
—n. the net weight, profit, price, etc.
—v. gain (after all deductions, etc.): *The sale netted me a good profit.* ⟨< F. See NEAT[1].⟩ **—net•ta•ble,** *adj.*

net asset value the net value of shares in a company's portfolio.

neth•er ['nɛðər] *adj.* lower: *nether garments, nether regions.* ⟨OE *neothera*⟩

Neth•er•land•er ['nɛðər,lændər] *n.* a native or inhabitant of the Netherlands.

Neth•er•lands ['nɛðər,ləndz] *n.* **the Netherlands,** a small country in NW Europe, on the North Sea, also called Holland.

neth•er•most ['nɛðər,moust] *adj.* lowest.

net•su•ke ['nɛtsəki] *or* ['nɛtsəkei] *n.* a little toggle used in Japan to fasten something to a kimono sash. ⟨< Japanese⟩

net•ting ['nɛtɪŋ] *n., v. —n.* **1** a netted or meshed material: *mosquito netting, wire netting for window screens.* **2** the process of making a net. **3** the act of fishing with a net or nets.
—v. ppr. of NET.

net•tle ['nɛtəl] *n., v.* **-tled, -tling.** *—n.* **1** any of a genus (*Urtica*) of plants of the nettle family having sharp hairs on the leaves and stems that sting the skin when touched. **2** any of various other prickly or stinging plants. **3** (*adjl.*) designating the family (Urticaceae) of mainly tropical plants that includes the nettles. Most plants of the nettle family have stinging hairs.
—v. **1** sting with or as if with nettles. **2** sting the feelings of; irritate; make angry: *She was nettled by the boy's frequent interruptions.* ⟨OE *netele*⟩ **—'net•tle,like,** *adj.*

net•tle•some ['nɛtəlsəm] *adj.* **1** annoying. **2** easily annoyed.

net ton SHORT TON.

net•work ['nɛt,wɜrk] *n., v. —n.* **1** a netting; net. **2** any netlike combination or system of lines or channels: *a network of vines, a network of highways.* **3** a group of radio or television stations so connected that the same program may be broadcast by all: *the French network of CBC radio.* **4** *Computer technology.* a system of communication links interconnecting a set of computers and peripheral devices.
—v. **1** connect into a network. **2** meet with friends or colleagues to exchange ideas or further one's own interests.

net•work•ing ['nɛt,wɜrkɪŋ] *n., v. —n.* **1** a system of sharing information. **2** the design or implementation of a computer network.
—v. ppr. of NETWORK.

Neuf•châ•tel [,nuʃə'tɛl] *or* ['nuʃə,tɛl] *n.* a soft, white cheese made from milk or cream. ⟨after *Neufchâtel*, the town in N France where it is made⟩

neumes [njumz] *or* [numz] *n.pl.* **1** the signs used in the notation of plainsong in medieval times. **2** the signs used in transcribing Gregorian chant. ⟨ME < ML *neuma* < Gk. *pneuma* breath⟩

neu•ral ['njʊrəl] *or* ['nʊrəl] *adj.* of, having to do with, or affecting a nerve or the nervous system. ⟨< Gk. *neuron* nerve⟩ **—'neu•ral•ly,** *adv.*

neu•ral•gia [njʊ'rældʒə] *or* [nʊ'rældʒə] *n.* pain, usually sharp, along the course of a nerve. ⟨< NL < Gk. *neuron* nerve + *algos* pain⟩ **—neu'ral•gic,** *adj.*

neu•ras•the•ni•a [,njʊrəs'θiniə] *or* [,nʊrəs'θiniə] *n. Pathology.* nervous breakdown. ⟨< NL < Gk. *neuron* nerve + *astheneia* weakness⟩

neu•ras•then•ic [,njʊrəs'θɛnɪk] *or* [,nʊrəs'θɛnɪk] *adj., n. Pathology. —adj.* having to do with or suffering from neurasthenia.
—n. a person suffering from neurasthenia.
—,neu•ras'then•i•cal•ly, *adv.*

neu•rec•to•my [njʊ'rɛktəmi] *or* [nʊ'rɛktəmi] *n., pl.* **-mies.** removal of a nerve by surgery.

neu•ri•lem•ma [,njʊrə'lɛmə] *or* [,nʊrə'lɛmə] *n.* the outer covering of nerve fibres. Also, **neurolemma.** ⟨< NL *neuro-* + Gk. *eilema*⟩

neu•ri•tis [njʊ'rəitɪs] *or* [nʊ'rəitɪs] *n. Pathology.* inflammation of a nerve or nerves, causing muscular atrophy. ⟨< NL < Gk. *neuron* nerve + *-itis*⟩ **—neu'rit•ic** [njʊ'rɪtɪk] *or* [nʊ'rɪtɪk], *adj.*

neuro– *combining form.* nerve; sinew; tendon: *neurology.* Also (*esp. before a vowel*), **neur-.** ⟨< Gk. *neuron*⟩

neu•ro•blast ['njʊrou,blæst] *or* ['nʊrou,blæst] *n. Embryology.* one of the cells in the embryo of vertebrates that become nerve cells in the spinal cord.

neu•ro•gen•ic [,njʊrə'dʒɛnɪk] *or* [,nʊrə'dʒɛnɪk] *adj. Medicine.* originating in a nerve.

neu•ro•gli•a [njʊ'rɒgliə] *or* [nʊ'rɒgliə] *n. Anatomy.* the tissue that binds the central nervous system.

neu•ro•lem•ma [,njʊrə'lɛmə] *or* [,nʊrə'lɛmə] *n.* See NEURILEMMA.

neu•ro•lin•guis•tics [,njʊroulɪŋ'gwɪstɪks] *or* [,nʊroulɪŋ'gwɪstɪks] *n.* the study of the relationship between neurology and language (*used with a singular verb*).

neu•rol•o•gist [njʊ'rɒlədʒɪst] *or* [nʊ'rɒlədʒɪst] *n.* a person trained in neurology, especially a physician who specializes in the diagnosis and treatment of diseases of the nervous system.

neu•rol•o•gy [njʊ'rɒlədʒi] *or* [nʊ'rɒlədʒi] *n.* the study of the nervous system and its diseases. ⟨< Gk. *neuron* nerve + E *-logy*⟩ **—,neu•ro'log•i•cal** [,njʊrə'lɒdʒɪkəl] *or* [,nʊrə'lɒdʒɪkəl], *adj.* **—,neu•ro'log•i•cal•ly,** *adv.*

neu•ro•mus•cu•lar [,njʊrou'mʌskjələr] *or* [,nʊrou'mʌskjələr] *adj.* having to do with nerves as well as muscles.

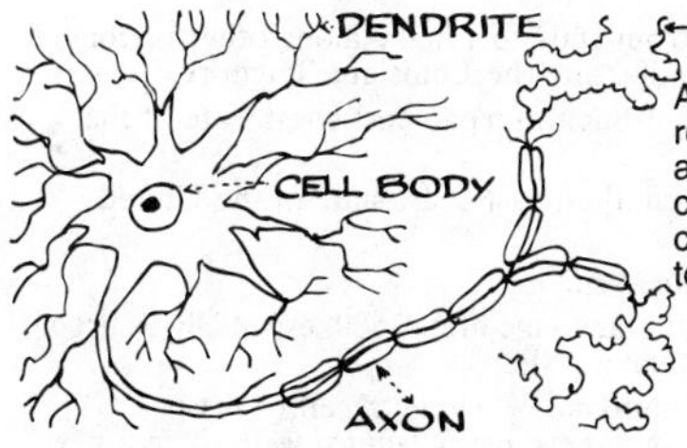

A neuron. The dendrites receive nerve impulses and carry them to the cell body. The axon carries impulses away to another cell.

neu•ron ['njʊrɒn] *or* ['nʊrɒn] *n. Anatomy.* one of the conducting cells of which the brain, spinal cord, and nerves are composed. The neuron is the basic functional unit of nervous tissue. It consists of a cell body, containing the nucleus, and its outgrowths, some of which may be very long. Also, **neurone.** ⟨< Gk. *neuron* nerve, cord, sinew⟩ **—neu'ron•ic** [njʊ'rɒnɪk] *or* [nʊ'rɒnɪk], *adj.*

neu•ro•path ['njʊrou,pæθ] *or* ['nʊrou,pæθ] *n. Psychiatry.* NEUROTIC (*n.*).

neu•ro•pa•thol•o•gy [,njʊroupə'θɒlədʒi] *or* [,nʊroupə'θɒlədʒi] *n.* the pathology of the nervous system. **—,neu•ro•pa'thol•o•gist,** *n.*

neu•ro•pa•thy [njʊ'rɒpəθi] *or* [nʊ'rɒpəθi] *n.* any diseased condition of the nervous system. **—,neu•ro'path•ic** [njʊrou'pæθɪk] *or* [nʊrou'pæθɪk], *adj.* **—,neu•ro'path•i•cal•ly,** *adv.*

neu•ro•phys•i•ol•o•gy [,njʊrou,fɪzi'ɒlədʒi] *or* [,nʊrou,fɪzi'ɒlədʒi] *n.* the branch of physiology dealing with the nervous system. **—,neu•ro,phys•i'ol•o•gist,** *n.* **—,neu•ro,phys•i•o'log•i•cal,** *adj.* **—,neu•ro,phys•i•o'log•i•cal•ly,** *adv.*

neu•ro•psy•chi•a•try [,njʊrousəi'kaɪətri] *or* [,nʊrousəi'kaɪətri] *n.* the branch of medicine dealing with neurology and psychiatry. **—,neu•ro,psy•chi'at•ric** [-,səiki'ætrɪk], *adj.* **—,neu•ro•psy'chi•a•trist,** *n.*

neu•rop•te•ran [njʊ'rɒptərən] *or* [nʊ'rɒptərən] *n.* an insect of the order Neuroptera, such as the lacewing.

neu•ro•sis [njʊ'rousɪs] *or* [nʊ'rousɪs] *n., pl.* **-ses** [-siz]. any of various, usually comparatively mild, mental disorders having no demonstrable physical basis and characterized chiefly by anxiety and obsessive behaviour. ⟨< NL < Gk. *neuron* nerve⟩

neu•ro•sur•ge•ry [,njʊrou'sɜrdʒəri] *or* [,nʊrou'sɜrdʒəri] *n.* surgery of the nervous system, especially of the brain. **—,neu•ro'sur•gi•cal,** *adj.* **—,neu•ro'sur•geon,** *n.*

neu•rot•ic [njʊ'rɒtɪk] *or* [nʊ'rɒtɪk] *adj., n. —adj.* **1** of, having to do with, or having a neurosis. **2** *Informal.* having or showing a tendency toward erratic behaviour or obsession with certain unrealistic ideas.
—n. a neurotic person. **—neu'rot•i•cal•ly,** *adv.* **—neu'rot•i,cism** [-tɪ,sɪzəm], *n.*

neu•rot•o•my [njʊ'rɒtəmi] *or* [nʊ'rɒtəmi] *n., pl.* **-mies.** the surgical treatment of a nerve by cutting to relieve pain. **—,neu•ro'tom•i•cal** [,njʊrə'tɒmɪkəl] *or* [,nʊrə'tɒmɪkəl], *adj.*

neu•ro•trans•mit•ter [,njʊroutrænz'mɪtər] *or* [,nʊroutrænz'mɪtər] *n.* a chemical substance such as serotonin, which passes messages between nerve cells in the brain.

neut. neuter.

neu•ter ['njutər] *or* ['nutər] *adj., n., v. —adj.* **1** *Grammar.* belonging to or designating the grammatical gender that includes words for a great many inanimate things and also some words for persons or animals of which the sex is not specified. In German, the words *Kind* (child), *Haus* (house), and *Licht* (light) are neuter. French has no neuter gender. Compare FEMININE, MASCULINE. **2** *Zoology.* of insects, etc., having no sex organs or having non-functional or underdeveloped sex organs: *Worker bees are neuter.* **3** *Botany.* of flowers, having neither stamens nor pistils; sterile. **4** taking no sides; neutral.
—n. **1** *Grammar.* **a** the neuter gender. **b** a word or form in the neuter gender. **2** *Zoology.* a neuter insect, etc. **3** a castrated domestic animal. **4** *Botany.* a flower having neither stamens nor pistils.
—v. castrate or spay (an animal). ⟨< L *neuter* < *ne-* not + *uter* either⟩

neu•tral ['njutrəl] *or* ['nutrəl] *adj., n. —adj.* **1** not taking part in a quarrel, contest, or war: *Switzerland was neutral during the last two wars in Europe.* **2** of or belonging to a neutral country or neutral zone: *a neutral port.* **3** being neither one thing nor the other; indefinite. **4** having little or no colour; greyish. **5** *Chemistry.* neither acid nor alkaline. **6** *Electricity.* neither positive nor negative. **7** *Biology.* not developed in sex.
—n. **1** a neutral person or country; one not taking part in a quarrel or war. **2** *Machinery.* the position of gears when they do not transmit motion from the engine to the wheels or other working parts. ⟨< L *neutralis* < *neuter.* See NEUTER.⟩
—'neu•tral•ly, *adv.*

neu•tral•ism ['njutrə,lɪzəm] *or* ['nutrə,lɪzəm] *n.* a policy, or the support of a policy, of remaining neutral, especially in international conflicts.

neu•tral•ist ['njutrəlɪst] *or* ['nutrəlɪst] *n.* **1** a person who practises or advocates neutralism. **2** (*adjl.*) practising or advocating neutralism: *a neutralist country.*

neu•tral•i•ty [njʊ'træləti] *or* [nʊ'træləti] *n.* **1** the quality or state of being neutral. **2** the policy of not taking part in a quarrel, contest, or war.

neu•tral•ize ['njutrə,laɪz] *or* ['nutrə,laɪz] *v.* **-ized, -iz•ing. 1** make neutral; keep from taking part in a conflict. **2** take away the power or effect of (something) by using an opposite power or force. Bases neutralize acids. **3** in magnetism or electricity, render neither positive nor negative. **4** *Phonetics.* reduce (a vowel) to schwa. **—,neu•tral•i'za•tion,** *n.* **—'neu•tral,iz•er,** *n.*

neutral spirits ethyl alcohol above 190 proof used in some alcoholic blends.

neutral vowel schwa.

neu•tri•no [njʊ'trinou] *or* [nʊ'trinou] *n., pl.* **-nos.** *Physics.* an elementary particle that has no electric charge and is believed by scientists to have no mass, and that interacts only weakly with matter. Neutrinos are produced in the process of radioactive decay.

neutro– *combining form.* neutral: *neutrophil.* ⟨< LL < L *neutr-*⟩

neu•tron ['njutrɒn] *or* ['nutrɒn] *n. Physics.* a nuclear particle having almost the same mass as a proton but having no electric charge, found in the nucleus of every kind of atom except that of hydrogen. ⟨< *neutral* neither positively nor negatively charged + *-on* (after *electron, proton*)⟩

neutron bomb a nuclear bomb designed to explode with relatively little force but to produce intense radiation over a wide area, thus causing great loss of life but relatively little destruction of property.

neutron star a very dense, rapidly rotating star composed of the remains of a collapsed supernova.

neu•tro•phil ['njutrə,fɪl] *or* ['nutrə,fɪl] *n., adj. —n.* a granular leukocyte easily stained by neutral dyes.
—adj. easily stained by neutral dyes.

Ne•va•da [nə'vædə] *or* [nə'vɑdə] *n.* a southwestern state of the U.S.

né•vé [nei'vei] *or* ['neivei] *n.* **1** granular snow that is compacted and partly converted into ice, found at the surface on the upper part of a glacier. **2** a field of this snow. ⟨< F, ult. < L *nix, nivis* snow⟩

nev•er ['nɛvər] *adv.* **1** not ever; at no time: *He never had to work for a living.* **2** in no case; not at all; to no extent or degree: *He was never the better for his experience. If we're careful, she'll never be the wiser.*
never mind, a pay no attention to; forget about: *Never mind the noise. Never mind your coats.* **b** it doesn't matter; forget it: *Never mind; I'll do it myself.* ⟨OE *nǣfre* < *ne* not + *ǣfre* ever⟩

nev•er•more [,nɛvər'mɔr] *adv.* never again.

nev•er•the•less [,nɛvərðə'lɛs] *adv.* however; nonetheless; for all that; in spite of it: *She was very tired; nevertheless, she kept on working.*

ne•vus ['nivəs] *n.* See NAEVUS.

new [nju] *or* [nu] *adj., adv. —adj.* **1** not existing before; having been made, grown, thought of, or produced only a short time ago: *a new invention, a new idea, a new house.* **2** now first used; not worn or used up: *a new path.* **3** beginning again: *The new moon is the moon when seen as a thin crescent.* **4** as if new; fresh: *go on with new courage. After taking a shower he felt a new man.* **5** different; changed: *He is a new man now.* **6** not familiar: *a new country to me.* **7** not yet accustomed: *new to the work.* **8** later; modern; recent: *new dances.* **9** just come; having just reached the position: *a new arrival, a new president.* **10** being the later or latest of two or more things of the same kind: *New France, New Testament.* **11** further; additional; more: *She sought new information on the subject.* **12** having been known only a short time, though existing before: *a new galaxy. The detective*

uncovered several new facts. **13** recently gained or bought: *a new dress, a new car.* **14 New,** of languages, modern.
—adv. **1** newly; recently or lately; freshly: *new-mown hay.* **2** again; anew. ⟨OE *nīwe*⟩ **—'new•ness,** *n.*
☛ *Hom.* GNU, KNEW.
☛ *Syn. adj.* **1. New,** NOVEL[1], MODERN = having only now or recently come into existence or knowledge. **New** describes something now existing, made, seen, or known for the first time: *They own a new house.* **Novel** adds and emphasizes the idea of being unusual, strikingly different, or strange, not of the ordinary kind: *Their house has a novel dining room.* **Modern** describes people and things belonging to or characteristic of the present time, or recent times, and sometimes suggests being up-to-date, not old-fashioned: *The architecture is modern.*

New Age **1** a cultural movement of the late 20th century, characterized by spiritual sensitivity and a belief in reincarnation. **2** a style of popular instrumental music designed to produce a relaxed mood.

new•born ['nju,bɔrn] *or* ['nu,bɔrn] *adj., n. —adj.* **1** recently or only just born: *a newborn baby.* **2** ready to start a new life; born again.
—n. a newborn baby: *clothes for the newborns.*

New Bruns•wick ['brʌnzwɪk] a Maritime province of Canada.

New Bruns•wick•er ['brʌnzwɪkər] *Cdn.* a native or long-term resident of New Brunswick.

New•burg ['njubɜrg] *or* ['nubɜrg] *adj.* of seafood, cooked in a rich sauce of cream, butter, and wine.

New Caledonia an early name for that part of British Columbia lying between the Rocky Mountains and the Coast Range, including some parts of the western U.S.

New Canadian **1** a person who has recently arrived in Canada from another country and plans to become a Canadian citizen. **2** a person originally from another country who has recently become a Canadian citizen.

New•cas•tle ['nju,kæsəl] *or* ['nu,kæsəl] *n.*
carry coals to Newcastle, a waste one's time, effort, etc. **b** bring something to a place where it is not needed (as coal to Newcastle, England, where it is plentiful).

new•com•er ['nju,kʌmər] *or* ['nu,kʌmər] *n.* a person who has just come or who came not long ago.

New Democratic Party a Canadian political party with socialist ties. It was formed in 1961 from the old CCF party with the assistance and support of the Canadian Labour Congress.

new•el ['njuəl] *or* ['nuəl] *n.* **1** the post at the top or bottom of a stairway that supports the railing. **2** the central post of a winding stairway. ⟨ME< OF *nouel*, ult. < L *nux* nut; influenced by OF *noel* bud, ult. < L *nodus* knot⟩

New Englander a native or inhabitant of New England, the NE part of the United States.

New England of Canada *Cdn.* formerly, the Eastern Townships of Québec, first settled by New England immigrants.

new•fan•gled ['nju,fæŋgəld] *or* ['nu,fæŋgəld] *adj.* lately come into fashion; new; novel: *She's always coming up with newfangled ideas.* ⟨ME *newefangle* < *newe* new + *fange(n)* take⟩

new–fash•ioned ['nju 'fæʃənd] *or* ['nu 'fæʃənd] *adj.* of a new fashion; lately come into style.

New•fie ['njufi] *or* ['nufi] *n. Cdn. Informal.* a Newfoundlander.

New•found•land[1] [,njufənd'lænd] *or* [,nufənd'lænd], ['njufəndlənd] *or* ['nufəndlənd], *or* [nju'faʊndlənd] *n.* the easternmost Canadian province, including Labrador.

New•found•land[2] ['njufəndlənd] *or* ['nufəndlənd], [,nju'faʊndlənd] *or* [,nu'faʊndlənd] *n.* a breed of very large, intelligent dog resembling a Saint Bernard, having a shaggy, often black, coat. Also, **Newfoundland dog.** ⟨< *Newfoundland*, where this powerful swimming dog was originally trained to rescue people from drowning⟩

A Newfoundland dog

New•found•land•er [,njufənd'lændər] *or* [,nufənd'lændər], ['njufənd,lændər] *or* ['nufənd,lændər] *n.* a native or long-term resident of Newfoundland.

New France the name of the territory in North America belonging to France from 1609 to 1763. Among other regions, it included Québec, Acadia, and the Louisiana Territory.

New Hamp•shire ['hæmpʃər] an east coast state of the United States.

New Jer•sey ['dʒɜrzi] an east coast state of the United States.

New Jerusalem heaven.

New Latin the Latin language after 1500, especially as used for scientific terms. *Abbrev.*: NL

new•ly ['njuli] *or* ['nuli] *adv.* **1** lately; recently: *newly discovered.* **2** once again; anew: *newly painted walls.* **3** in a new way: *newly arranged furniture.*

new•ly•wed ['njuli,wɛd] *or* ['nuli,wɛd] *n.* a newly married person.

New Mexico a southwestern state of the United States.

new moon **1** the phase of the moon when it is between the earth and the sun, so that its dark side is toward the earth and its face is invisible. **2** the thin crescent that appears at sunset two or three days after this phase, with the hollow side on the left. See MOON for picture. **3** the time of the new moon.

new–mown ['nju 'moun] *or* ['nu 'moun] *adj.* of grass, freshly cut: *the scent of new-mown hay.*

news [njuz] *or* [nuz] *n.* (*used with a singular verb*). **1** something told as having just happened; information about something that has just happened or will soon happen: *The news that he had been fired was a tremendous shock to his friends.* **2** a report of a current happening or happenings in a newspaper, on television, radio, etc.
break the news, make something known; tell something for the first time. ⟨ME *newes*, pl. of *newe* that which is new, adj. used as n.⟩

news•a•gent ['njuz,eidʒənt] *or* ['nuz,eidʒənt] *n.* a person who owns or manages a shop selling newspapers, magazines, etc.

news•boy ['njuz,bɔɪ] *or* ['nuz,bɔɪ] *n.* a boy who sells newspapers.

news•cast ['njuz,kæst] *or* ['nuz,kæst] *n., v. —n.* a radio or television program devoted to current events, news bulletins, etc. *—v.* broadcast (news).

news•cast•er ['njuz,kæstər] *or* ['nuz,kæstər] *n.* **1** a newspaperman or newspaperwoman. **2** a person who delivers a newscast.

news•girl ['njuz,gɜrl] *or* ['nuz,gɜrl] *n.* a girl who sells newspapers.

news•hound ['njuz,haʊnd] *or* ['nuz,haʊnd] *n. Informal.* a news reporter.

news•let•ter ['njuz,lɛtər] *or* ['nuz,lɛtər] *n.* **1** a written or printed letter presenting an informal or confidential coverage of the news. **2** an account of the activities of a society or company.

news magazine **1** a magazine, usually one published weekly, that reports, comments on, and interprets the news and current events. **2** a similar regular television program.

news•mon•ger ['njuz,mʌŋgər] *or* ['nuz,mʌŋgər], ['njuz,mɒŋgər] *or* ['nuz,mɒŋgər] *n.* a person who gathers and spreads misleading news; a gossip. **—'news,mon•ger•ing** or **'news,mon•ger•y,** *n.*

news•pa•per ['njuz,peipər] *or* ['nuz,peipər], ['njus,peipər] *or* ['nus,peipər] *n.* **1** a publication consisting of folded sheets of paper usually printed daily or weekly and containing news stories and pictures, advertisements, and other reading matter of general interest. **2** the company or organization that publishes a newspaper: *She used to work for a newspaper.* **3** the printed sheets making up a newspaper: *The plants were wrapped in newspaper.*

news•pa•per•man ['njuz,peipər,mæn] *or* ['nuz,peipər,mæn], ['njus-] *or* ['nus-] *n., pl.* **-men. 1** a newspaper reporter, editor, etc. **2** the owner or publisher of a newspaper.

news•pa•per•wom•an ['njuz,peipər,wʊmən] *or* ['nuz,peipər,wʊmən], ['njus-] *or* ['nus-] *n., pl.* **-wom•en. 1** a female newspaper reporter, editor, etc. **2** the owner or publisher of a newspaper.

new•speak ['nju,spik] *or* ['nu,spik] *n.* ambiguous or contradictory language deliberately intended to mislead or confuse. ⟨coined by English writer George Orwell in the novel *1984*, pub. 1949⟩

news•print ['njuz,prɪnt] *or* ['nuz,prɪnt], ['njus,prɪnt] *or* ['nus,prɪnt] *n.* a soft, cheap, coarse paper made from wood pulp, the kind on which newspapers are usually printed.

news•reel ['njuz,ril] *or* ['nuz,ril] *n.* a motion picture showing current events.

news release PRESS RELEASE.

news•room ['njuz,rum] *or* ['nuz,rum], ['njuz,rʊm] *or* ['nuz,rʊm] *n.* a room or section of a newspaper office or radio or television station where news is collected and edited for publication or broadcasting.

news•stand ['njuz,stænd] *or* ['nuz,stænd] *n.* a place where newspapers and magazines are sold.

New Style the present method of reckoning time, according to the Gregorian calendar. It was adopted in Britain in 1752. Compare OLD STYLE.

news•wor•thy ['njuz,wɜrði] *or* ['nuz,wɜrði] *adj.* having the qualities of news; interesting or important enough to the general public to be included in a newspaper or newscast: *The reporter tried to think of an angle that would make the basically ordinary story newsworthy.*

news•y ['njuzi] *or* ['nuzi] *adj.* **news•i•er, news•i•est;** *n., pl.* **news•ies.** *Informal. –adj.* full of news.
–n. a newsboy or newsgirl.

newt [njut] *or* [nut] *n.* any of various small salamanders (family Salamandridae, especially genera *Triturus* and *Diemectylus*), the males of which develop an enlarged crest, or fin, on the back and tail during the breeding season. Most adult newts are aquatic only during the breeding season; some, like the **red-spotted newt** (*Diemectylus viridescens*) of E North America, become permanently aquatic after a terrestrial stage lasting two or three years. ⟨OE *efete*; ME *an ewt* taken as *a newt*⟩

New Testament the second part of the Christian Bible, containing the Gospels, the Acts of the Apostles, the Epistles, and the Revelation of St. John.

new•ton ['njutən] *or* ['nutən] *n. Physics.* an SI unit for measuring force. One newton is the force required to give an acceleration of one metre per second squared to a mass of one kilogram. *Symbol*: N ⟨after Sir Isaac *Newton.* See NEWTONIAN.⟩

New•to•ni•an [nju'touniən] *or* [nu'touniən] *adj.* of, having to do with, or according to Sir Isaac Newton (1642-1727), the English scientist and mathematician, or his discoveries: *Newtonian physics.*

newton metre *Physics.* an SI unit for measuring torque or moment of force. *Symbol*: N·m

new–world ['nju 'wɜrld] *or* ['nu 'wɜrld] *adj.* of or having to do with the Western Hemisphere.

New World 1 the western hemisphere. 2 (*adjl.*) of, having to do with, or found in the New World: *New World monkeys have tails adapted for grasping and holding on.*

new year 1 the year approaching or newly begun. 2 **New Year** or **New Year's,** the first day or days of the year.

New Year's Day January 1, observed as a legal holiday in many countries, including Canada.

New York 1 a northeastern state of the United States. 2 the largest city in the United States.

New Zea•land ['zilənd] a country of islands in the S Pacific Ocean, near Australia.

New Zea•land•er ['ziləndər] a native or inhabitant of New Zealand.

next [nɛkst] *adj., prep., adv. –adj.* following at once; nearest: *We'll catch the next train.*
–prep. nearest to: *We live in the house next the church.*
next to, a immediately following or adjacent to: *Who was the girl next to you?* **b** almost; nearly: *Chairs like these cost next to nothing. It was next to impossible to move in the crowd.* **c** following in order of preference: *Next to eating I like sleeping.*
–adv. in the place, time, or position that is nearest: *I am going to do my arithmetic problems next. When you next come, bring your guitar.* ⟨OE *nēhst*, superlative of *nēah* nigh⟩

next door in or at the next house: *The woman next door owns two Saint Bernards.*
next door to, almost; very close to: *His silence was next door to an admission of guilt.* **–'next-'door,** *adj.*

next of kin the nearest blood relative or relative by marriage.

nex•us ['nɛksəs] *n., pl.* **nex•us. 1** a connection; link. **2** a connected series. ⟨< L *nexus*, ult. < *nectere* bind⟩

Nez Per•cé ['nɛz 'pɜrs]; *French,* [nepɛʀ'se] *n., pl.* **Nez Per•cés** ['nɛz 'pɜrsɪz]; *French,* [ne pɛʀ'se] **1** a member of an American Indian people living in Idaho, Oregon, and Washington. **2** the language of the Nez Percés. ⟨< F *nez percé*, literally, pierced nose⟩

Nez Percé horse appaloosa.

NF Newfoundland (*used esp. in computerized address systems*).

N.F. 1 Norman French. 2 New France. 3 Newfoundland.

NFB or **N.F.B.** National Film Board.

Nfld. Newfoundland.

N.G. or **n.g.** no good.

ngul•trum [əŋ'gʊltrəm] *n.* **1** the major unit of currency in Bhutan, equal to 100 chetrums. **2** a coin or note worth one ngultrum. See table of money in the Appendix.

ngwee [əŋ'gwei] *or* [əŋ'gwi] *n., pl.* **ngwee. 1** a unit of money in Zambia, equal to 1/100 of a kwacha. **2** a coin worth one ngwee. See table of money in the Appendix.

NHL or **N.H.L.** National Hockey League.

Ni nickel.

ni•a•cin ['naɪəsɪn] *n.* NICOTINIC ACID. ⟨< *ni(cotinic) ac(id)*⟩

nib [nɪb] *n.* **1** the point of a pen. **2** point or tip of anything. **3** a bird's bill. ⟨var. of *neb*⟩

nib•ble ['nɪbəl] *v.* **-bled, -bling;** *n. –v.* **1** eat away with quick, small bites, as a rabbit or a mouse does. **2** bite gently or lightly: *A fish nibbles at the bait.* **3** eat little or lightly.
nibble at, *Informal.* **a** be interested in: *The management are nibbling at my suggestion.* **b** take apart or attack, as if by taking small bites: *critics nibbling at a new play.*
–n. **1** an act of nibbling: *We've been fishing all morning and haven't had a nibble.* **2** a small piece, especially of food: *I just want a nibble of the cake.* ⟨Cf. LG *nibbelen*⟩ **–'nib•bler,** *n.*

Ni•be•lung ['nibə,lʊŋ] *n., pl.* **-lungs** or **-lung•en** [-,lʊŋən]. **1** *Germanic mythology.* any of a race of northern dwarfs: *Siegfried and his followers captured the treasure of the Nibelungs.* **2** one of Siegfried's followers. **3** one of the Burgundian kings in the Nibelungenlied.

Ni•be•lung•en•lied ['nibə,lʊŋən,lid]; *German,* ['nibə,lʊŋən,lit] *n.* a German epic poem based on Germanic legends, written in the 13th century in S Germany by an unknown author. ⟨< G, literally, Lay of the Nibelungs⟩

nib•lick ['nɪblɪk] *n. Golf.* a former term for the number 9 iron golf club. ⟨< Scottish, dim. of *nib*⟩

nibs [nɪbz] *n. Slang.* **1** a person in authority. **2 his** (or **her**, etc.) **nibs,** *Facetious.* a title of pretended respect for someone who is, or supposes himself or herself to be, of importance: *How is his nibs today?* ⟨origin uncertain⟩

Nic•a•ra•gua [,nɪkə'rɑgwə] *n.* a republic of Central America.

Nic•a•ra•guan [,nɪkə'rɑgwən] *n., adj. –n.* a native or inhabitant of Nicaragua.
–adj. of or having to do with Nicaragua or its people.

nic•co•lite ['nɪkə,ləit] *n.* a nickel ore, nickel arsenide.

nice [nəis] *adj.* **nic•er, nic•est. 1** pleasing; agreeable; satisfactory: *a nice day, a nice ride, a nice child.* **2** thoughtful; kind: *He was nice to us.* **3** fine; subtle; precise: *a nice distinction, a nice shade of meaning.* **4** delicately skilful; requiring or using care, skill, or tact: *a nice problem, a nice solution to a tricky*

problem. **5** exacting; particular; hard to please; fastidious; dainty: *nice in his eating.* **6** proper; suitable. **7** scrupulous: *too nice to be a crook.* **8** refined; cultured: *nice manners.* **9** *Archaic.* modest; reserved. ⟨ME < OF *nice* silly < L *nescius* ignorant < *ne-* not + *scire* know⟩ **—'nice•ly,** *adv.* **—'nice•ness,** *n.*
☛ *Hom.* GNEISS.

Ni•cene [nəi'sin] *or* ['nəisin] *adj.* of or having to do with Nicaea, an ancient town in Asia Minor.

Nicene Council either of two general ecclesiastical councils that met at Nicaea, the first in A.D. 325 to deal with the Arian heresy, the second in A.D. 787 to consider the question of images.

Nicene Creed a formal statement of the chief tenets of Christian belief, based on that adopted by the first Nicene Council, and generally accepted throughout western Christendom.

ni•ce•ty ['nəisəti] *n., pl.* **-ties. 1** exactness; accuracy; delicacy: *Television sets require nicety of adjustment.* **2** a fine point; small distinction; detail. **3** the quality of being very particular; daintiness; refinement. **4** something dainty or refined.
to a nicety, just right: *cakes browned to a nicety.* ⟨ME < OF *nicete* < *nice.* See NICE.⟩

niche [niʃ] or [nɪtʃ] *n.* **1** a recess or hollow in a wall for a statue, vase, etc. **2** a suitable place or position; place for which a person is suited: *John will find his niche in the world.* **3 a** the space occupied by an organism in its habitat. **b** the role of an organism or species including its behaviour, position in the food chain, etc. ⟨< F *niche,* ult. < L *nidus* nest⟩

Nich•o•las ['nɪkələs] See SAINT NICHOLAS.

Ni•chrome ['nəi,kroum] *n. Trademark.* an alloy of iron and chromium with a base of nickel.

nick [nɪk] *n., v. —n.* a place where a small bit has been cut or broken out; notch; groove: *She cut nicks in a stick to keep count of her score.*
in the nick of time, just in time; barely in time.
—v. **1** make a nick or nicks in: *I nicked the edge of the plate while washing it.* **2** cut into or wound slightly: *The bullet just nicked his arm.* **3** hit, guess, catch, etc. exactly. ⟨origin uncertain⟩

nick•el ['nɪkəl] *n., v.* **-elled** or **-eled, -el•ling** or **-el•ing.** *—n.* **1** *Chemistry.* a hard, malleable, silvery-white metallic element that is resistant to rust, used mainly in alloys. *Symbol*: Ni; *at.no.* 28; *at.mass* 58.71. **2** a five-cent piece. **3** five cents: *The paper costs a nickel a sheet.*
—v. cover or coat with nickel. ⟨< Swedish < G *Kupfernickel,* literally, copper, devil; the ore resembles copper but yields none⟩

nick•el–and–dime ['nɪkəl ən 'dɑɪm] *v.* **-dimed, dim•ing.** *Informal.* **1** spend very little or too little (on). **2** haggle (with) over trifling amounts.

nick•el•ic [nɪ'kɛlɪk] *or* ['nɪkəlɪk] *adj. Chemistry.* containing trivalent nickel.

nick•el•if•er•ous [,nɪkə'lɪfərəs] *adj.* of ores, containing nickel.

nick•el•o•de•on [,nɪkə'loudiən] *n.* **1** in the early days of motion pictures, a place of amusement with motion picture exhibitions, etc., to which the price of admission was five cents. **2** juke box, especially one that started on the insertion of a nickel. ⟨< *nickel* + *odeon*, var. of *odeum* < L < Gk. *oideion* music hall < *ōidē* song⟩

nick•el•ous ['nɪkələs] *adj. Chemistry.* containing bivalent nickel.

nickel plate a thin coating of nickel deposited by electrolysis of a solution containing nickel on a metal object to prevent rust, improve the appearance, etc. **—'nick•el-,plate,** *v.*

nickel silver a hard, tough, silvery-white alloy of copper, zinc, and nickel used to make utensils, wire, etc.

nickel steel an alloy of copper, zinc, and nickel used for tableware.

nick•er ['nɪkər] *v.* of a horse, emit a soft sound; neigh.

nick–nack ['nɪk ,næk] *n.* See KNICK-KNACK.

nick•name ['nɪk,neim] *n., v.* **-named, -nam•ing.** *—n.* **1** a short or familiar form of a proper name: *'The Alex' is a nickname for the Royal Alexandra Theatre. Elizabeth's nickname is 'Betty'.* **2** a name used instead of a proper name: *Roy's nickname was 'Buzz'.*
—v. give a nickname to: *They nicknamed the fast runner 'Speedy'.* ⟨ME *ekename* < *eke* an addition, OE *ēaca* + *name* name, OE *nama*; *an ekename* taken as *a nekename*⟩

ni•co•ti•a•na [nɪ,kouʃi'ænə *or* [nɪ,kouʃi'ɑnə] *n.* any of several flowering tobacco plants of the genus *Nicotiana,* grown for its perfume.

ni•co•tin•a•mide [,nɪkə'tinə,maɪd] *or* [,nɪkə'tinə,maɪd] *n. Biochemistry.* the amide of nicotinic acid that is a component of the vitamin B_{12} complex. *Formula*: $C_6H_6N_2O$

nic•o•tine ['nɪkə,tin] *n. Chemistry.* a poisonous alkaloid contained in the leaves of tobacco. *Formula*: $C_{10}H_{14}N_2$ ⟨< F < NL *herba nicotiana* Nicot's plant, after Jacques *Nicot* (1530-1600), a French ambassador to Portugal, who introduced tobacco into France about 1560⟩ **—'nic•o,tine•less,** *adj.*

nic•o•tin•ic acid [,nɪkə'tɪnɪk] *Biochemistry.* an acid of the vitamin B complex found in meat, eggs, wheat germ, etc.; niacin. A deficiency of nicotinic acid can cause pellagra. *Formula*: $C_6H_5NO_2$

ni•co•tin•ism ['nɪkəti,nɪzəm] *or* [,nɪkə'tinɪzəm] *n.* nicotine poisoning.

nic•ti•tate ['nɪktə,teit] *v.* **-tat•ed, -tat•ing.** wink. Also, **nictate.** ⟨< Med.L *nictitare* blink repeatedly < *nictare* blink⟩

nictitating membrane in reptiles, birds, and some other animals, a thin membrane inside the lower eyelid or at the inside corner of the eye, that can be extended across the eye. Also called **third eyelid.**

ni•da•na [nɪ'dɑnə] *n. Buddhism.* any one of the twelve ways of Samsara, the cycle of birth and death, often represented as twelve spokes of a wheel.

Nid•hogg ['nidhɒg] *n. Norse mythology.* a serpent in Niflheim that chews on the sacred tree.

ni•dic•o•lous [naɪ'dɪkələs] *adj.* of birds, staying in the nest for a long time after hatching. ⟨< L *nidus* nest + E *-colous* < L *colere* cultivate⟩

ni•dif•u•gous [naɪ'dɪfjʊgəs] *adj.* of fledglings, leaving the nest soon after hatching. ⟨< L *nidus* nest + *fugere* flee⟩

ni•di•fy ['nɪdə,faɪ] *v.,* **-fied, -fy•ing.** build a nest. ⟨< L *nidificare* to build a nest < *nidus* nest⟩

ni•dus ['naɪdəs] *n., pl.* **ni•di** ['naɪdaɪ] *or* **ni•dus•es. 1** a nest. **2** the place in an organism where another organism can breed. ⟨< L⟩ **—'ni•dal,** *adj.*

niece [nis] *n.* **1** the daughter of one's brother or sister. **2** a daughter of a brother or sister of one's spouse. ⟨ME < OF *niece,* ult. < L *neptis* granddaughter⟩

ni•el•lo [ni'ɛlou] *n., pl.* **ni•el•li** [nɪ'ɛli]; *v.* **-loed, -lo•ing.**
—n. **1** one of the black alloys of sulphur, copper, and silver, used to fill in a design cut into another metal. **2** a surface decorated with niello.
—v. inlay with niello.

Ni•fl•heim ['nɪvəl,heim] *n. Norse mythology.* a cold and black place where those who died of illness or old age went. Those killed in battle went to Valhalla. ⟨< ON, literally, mist home⟩

Ni•ger ['naɪdʒər]; *French,* [ni'ʒɛʀ] *n.* a republic in NW Africa, properly called the Republic of Niger.

Ni•ger–Con•go ['naɪdʒər 'kɒŋgou] *n.* a family of languages of Africa that includes the Bantu languages and most of the languages of the coastal regions of W Africa.

Ni•ge•ri•a [naɪ'dʒiriə] *n.* a republic in W Africa.

Ni•ge•ri•an [naɪ'dʒiriən] *n., adj. —n.* a native or inhabitant of Nigeria.
—adj. of or having to do with Nigeria or its people.

nig•gard ['nɪgərd] *n., adj. —n.* a stingy person.
—adj. stingy. ⟨ME < earlier *nig* < Scand. + E pejorative suffix *-ard*, as in *drunkard*; cf. ON *hnöggr* stingy⟩

nig•gard•ly ['nɪgərdli] *adj., adv. —adj.* **1** stingy. **2** meanly small or scanty: *a niggardly gift.*
—adv. stingily. **—'nig•gard•li•ness,** *n.*

nig•gle ['nɪgəl] *v.* **-gled, -gling. 1** be concerned with petty or trifling things or details. **2** irritate or worry. ⟨apparently < Scand.; cf. dial. Norwegian *nigla*⟩ **—'nig•gler,** *n.* **—'nig•gling,** *adj.*

nigh [naɪ] *adv., adj.* **nigh•er, nigh•est** or **next;** *prep. Archaic, poetic, or dialect. —adv.* **1** near: *Dawn was nigh.* **2** nearly: *He was nigh dead with fright.*
—adj. or prep. near. ⟨OE *nēah*⟩

night [nəit] *n.* **1** the period of darkness between evening and morning; the time between sunset and sunrise. **2** the darkness of night; the dark: *She went out into the night.* **3** the darkness of ignorance, sin, sorrow, old age, death, etc.: *the night of despair.* **4** nightfall: *We expect to get back before night.* **5** (*adjl.*) of or having to do with night: *cold night winds.* **6** (*adjl.*) working or for use at night: *a night light.* **7** (*advl.*) **nights,** regularly or habitually in the nighttime: *He works nights.*
make a night of it, celebrate until very late at night. ⟨OE *niht*⟩
—'night•less, *adj.* **—'night,like,** *adj.*
☛ *Hom.* KNIGHT.

night blindness the inability to see well in dim light, as at night. Also called **nyctalopia.**

night–bloom•ing cereus ['nəit,blumɪŋ] a flowering cactus of the genera *Selenicereus* or *Hylocereus,* having a large bloom that opens at night.

night•cap ['nəit,kæp] *n.* **1** a cap for wearing in bed. **2** a drink taken just before going to bed. **3** *Informal.* the last event in a sports program, especially the second baseball game of a double-header.

night•club ['nəit,klʌb] *n.* a place for dancing, eating, and entertainment, open only at night.

night•crawl•er ['nəit,krɒlər] *n. Esp. U.S.* dew-worm.

night•dress ['nəit,drɛs] *n.* nightgown.

night•fall ['nəit,fɒl] *n.* the coming of night.

night•gown ['nəit,gaʊn] *n.* **1** a loose garment for women and girls, for wearing in bed. **2** nightshirt.

night•hawk ['nəit,hɒk] *n.* **1** any of a genus (*Chordeiles*) of North American goatsuckers having dark, mottled plumage. The **common nighthawk** (*C. minor*) is a familiar bird throughout most of Canada. **2** *Informal.* NIGHT OWL.

night heron a nocturnal heron of the genus *Nycticorax.*

night•ie ['nəiti] *n. Informal.* nightgown. Also, **nighty.**

night•in•gale ['nəitən,geil] *or* ['nəitɪŋ,geil] *n.* **1** any of several thrushes (genus *Luscinia*) of Europe and Asia noted for the sweet song of the male; especially, a small, reddish brown bird (*L. megarhynchos*) having a varied song with loud and soft notes which it sings by night or day. **2** any of various other birds noted for their song. ⟨for *nightgale,* OE *nihtegale* < *niht* night + *galan* sing⟩

night•jar ['nəit,dʒɑr] *n.* **1** a common European goatsucker (*Caprimulgus europaeus*) having greyish brown, mottled and barred plumage and noted for its chirring call. **2** *Esp. Brit.* any goatsucker.

night latch a door lock opened by a key from the outside or by a knob from the inside.

night light a small lamp that provides a dim light, used especially beside the bed of a child or of a sick person at night.

night•light•ing ['nəit,ləitɪŋ] *n.* jacklighting.
—'night,light•er, *n.*

night•long ['nəit,lɒŋ] *adj., adv. —adj.* lasting all night. *—adv.* through the whole night.

night•ly ['nəitli] *adj., adv. —adj.* **1** done, happening, or appearing every night. **2** done, happening, or appearing at night. *—adv.* **1** every night: *Performances are given nightly except on Sunday.* **2** at night; by night.
☛ *Hom.* KNIGHTLY.

night•mare ['nəit,mɛr] *n.* **1** a frightening dream. **2** a very unpleasant or frightening experience: *The dust storm was a nightmare.* **3** a sight, object, or person such as might be seen in a nightmare. ⟨ME < OE *niht* night + *mare* female incubus oppressing men during sleep⟩

night•mar•ish ['nəit,mɛrɪʃ] *adj.* like a nightmare; strange and horrifying; causing fear. **—'night,mar•ish•ly,** *adv.* **—'night,mar•ish•ness,** *n.*

night owl *Informal.* a person who often stays up late.

night person NIGHT OWL.

night school a school held in the evening for persons who work during the day.

night•shade ['nəit,ʃeid] *n.* **1** any of various plants of the nightshade family having berries that are often poisonous. The **common nightshade,** also called **bittersweet,** and the **deadly nightshade,** also called **belladonna,** both have poisonous berries. **2** (*adjl.*) designating a family (Solanaceae) of mainly tropical herbs, shrubs, and trees having flowers in clusters and fruit in the form of a capsule or berry. The tomato, potato, eggplant, peppers, and hemp belong to the nightshade family. ⟨OE *nihtscada*⟩

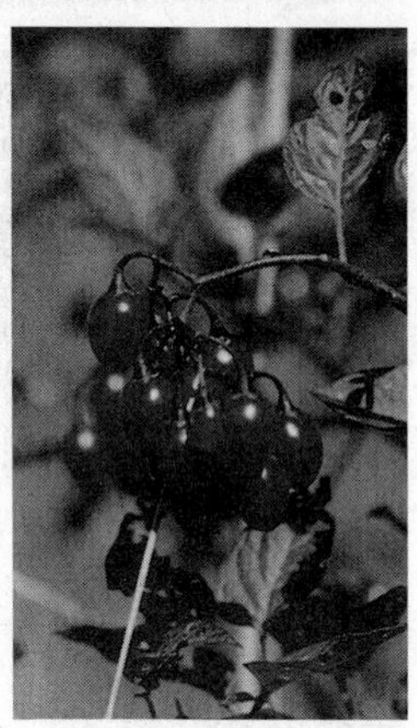
Nightshade

night shift **1** a working period during the night. **2** the workers who work at night.

night•shirt ['nəit,ʃɜrt] *n.* a loose garment for wearing in bed.

night soil human excrement used as fertilizer.

night•spot ['nəit,spɒt] *n. Informal.* nightclub.

night stand a small table at the side of a bed.

night•stick ['nəit,stɪk] *n.* a police officer's stick or club; billy; truncheon.

night terror *Psychiatry.* a feeling of extreme fear experienced on partial waking, often accompanied by palpitations and sweating, not the result of a nightmare but of the person's total inability to orient himself or herself.

night•time ['nəit,taɪm] *n.* the time between evening and morning.

night watch **1** a watch or guard kept during the night. **2** the person or persons keeping such a watch. **3** a period or division of the night.

night watchman a person who guards a store, factory, etc. at night.

nigh•ty ['nəiti] See NIGHTIE.

ni•gres•cence [naɪ'grɛsəns] *n.* **1** the process of becoming black. **2** blackness of hair or skin. ⟨< L *nigrescens,* ppr. of *nigrescere* to turn black⟩ **—ni'gres•cent,** *adj.*

nig•ri•fy ['nɪgrə,faɪ] *v.* **-fied, -fy•ing.** make black. ⟨< L *nigrificare* to blacken⟩

nig•ri•tude ['nɪgrə,tjud] *or* ['nɪgrə,tud], ['naɪgrə,tjud] *or* ['naɪgrə,tud] *n.* blackness. ⟨< L *nigritudo* blackness < *niger* black⟩

nig•ro•sine ['naɪgrə,sin] *or* ['naɪgrəsɪn] *n.* a dye, blue or black, used in making inks or for dyeing cloth.

ni•hil ['naɪhɪl] *or* ['nihɪl] *n. Latin.* nothing; a thing of no value.

ni•hil•ism ['naɪə,lɪzəm] *or* ['niə,lɪzəm] *n.* **1** the entire rejection of the usual beliefs in religion, morals, government, laws, etc. **2** *Philosophy.* the denial of all existence. **3** the use of violent methods against a ruler. **4 Nihilism,** the beliefs of a 19th-century Russian revolutionary party, that advocated the removal of the old society by violence and terror. ⟨< L *nihil* nothing⟩
—'ni•hil•ist, *n.* **—,ni•hil'is•tic,** *adj.*

ni•hi•li•ty [naɪ'hɪləti] *or* [ni'hɪləti] *n.* nothingness; lack of existence.

Ni•hon ['ni'hɒn] *n.* the official Japanese name for Japan.

Ni•hon Sho•ki ['ni'hɒn 'ʃouki] *n.* in Shintoism, an account of Japan's history and imperial ancestry from mythic origins to the 7th century. It is one of the highly revered texts of the Shinto religion.

Ni•ke ['nəiki] *or* ['nikei] *n. Greek mythology.* the goddess of victory, usually represented with outspread wings. ⟨< Gk. *nike* victory⟩

nil [nɪl] *n.* nothing. ⟨< L *nil,* a shortened form of *nihil*⟩

Nile green [naɪl] a light to vivid green.

Ni•lo–Sa•har•an [,naɪlou sə'hærən] *or* [sə'hɛrən] *n.* a large language family of Africa, extending from Chad to Kenya.

Ni•lot•ic [naɪ'lɒtɪk] *adj., n. —adj.* **1** having to do with the Nile Valley. **2** of or having to do with the Nilotic group of languages. *—n.* a Nilo-Saharan group of languages including Dinka, Masai, Luo, and Nandi.

nim•ble [ˈnɪmbəl] *adj.* **-bler, -blest. 1** able to move lightly and quickly; agile: *Her nimble fingers flew over the piano keys.* **2** quick to understand; clever: *a nimble mind.* ⟨ME *nymel* < OE *niman* take⟩ **—ˈnim•ble•ness,** *n.* **—ˈnim•bly,** *adv.*

nim•bo•stra•tus [ˌnɪmbouˈstreitəs] *or* [ˌnɪmbouˈstrætəs] *n., pl.* **-ti** [-taɪ] *or* [-ti]. a low, dark grey cloud layer that brings rain or snow. ⟨< L *nimbus* cloud + E *stratus*⟩

nim•bus [ˈnɪmbəs] *n., pl.* **-bus•es** or **-bi** [-baɪ] *or* [-bi]. **1** a light disk or other radiance about the head of a divine or sacred person in a picture. **2** a bright cloud surrounding a god, person, or thing. **3** a rain cloud. ⟨< L *nimbus* cloud⟩

ni•mi•e•ty [nɪˈmaɪəti] *n., pl.* **-ties. 1** excess; over-abundance. **2** an instance of this. ⟨< L *nimietas nimis* too much⟩

ni•mi•ny–pi•mi•ny [ˈnɪməni ˈpɪməni] *adj. Informal.* affectedly delicate. ⟨imitative of affected pronunciation⟩

Nim•rod [ˈnɪmrɒd] *n.* **1** in the Bible, a king who was a great builder and a mighty hunter. **2** any enthusiastic hunter.

nin•com•poop [ˈnɪnkəm,pup] *or* [ˈnɪŋkəm,pup] *n.* a fool; simpleton. ⟨origin uncertain⟩

nine [naɪn] *n., adj. —n.* **1** one more than eight; 9. **2** the numeral 9: *The 9 is bigger than the other numerals.* **3** the ninth in a set or series, especially a playing card having nine spots: *the nine of clubs.* **4** *Baseball.* a team of nine players. **5** *Golf.* the first or last nine holes of an eighteen-hole course. **6** any set or series of nine persons or things. **7 the Nine,** the Muses.

dressed (up) **to the nines,** *Informal.* very formally or elaborately dressed: *I showed up in my jeans and found that everyone else was dressed to the nines.*

—adj. **1** being one more than eight. **2** being ninth in a set or series (*used mainly after the noun*): *Chapter Nine was very exciting.* ⟨OE *nigon*⟩

nine days' wonder anything that causes a short period of excitement and great interest.

nine–eight [ˈnaɪn ˈeit] *adj. Music.* indicating or having nine eighth notes in a bar or measure.

nine•fold [ˈnaɪn,fould] *adj., adv. —adj.* **1** nine times as much or as many. **2** having nine parts.

—adv. nine times as much or as many.

nine•pins [ˈnaɪn,pɪnz] *n.* **1** a game in which nine large, wooden pins are set up to be bowled down with a ball (*used with a singular verb*): *Ninepins resembles tenpins.* **2** the pins used in this game.

nine•teen [ˈnaɪnˈtin] *n., adj. —n.* **1** nine more than ten; 19. **2** the numeral 19: *The nineteen is bigger than the other numbers.* **3** the nineteenth in a set or series. **4** a set or series of nineteen persons or things.

—adj. **1** being nine more than ten; 19: *He lived there for nineteen years.* **2** being nineteenth in a set or series (*used after the noun*): *Chapter Nineteen.* ⟨OE *nigontēne*⟩

nine•teenth [ˈnaɪnˈtinθ] *adj. or n.* **1** next after the 18th; last in a series of 19; 19th. **2** one, or being one, of 19 equal parts.

nine•ti•eth [ˈnaɪntiɪθ] *adj. or n.* **1** next after the 89th; last in a series of 90; 90th. **2** one, or being one, of 90 equal parts.

nine•ty [ˈnaɪnti] *n., pl.* **-ties;** *adj. —n.* **1** nine times ten; 90. **2 nineties,** *pl.* the years from ninety through ninety-nine, especially of a century or of a person's life: *She was in her nineties when she died.*

—adj. being nine times ten; 90. ⟨OE *nigontig*⟩

Nin•e•veh [ˈnɪnəvə] *n.* an ancient city of Assyria. Its ruins are on the Tigris River, opposite Mosul in N Iraq.

nin•ny [ˈnɪni] *n., pl.* **-nies.** fool. ⟨? < *an innocent* naïve, simple person; 16c.⟩

ninth [naɪnθ] *adj. or n.* **1** next after the eighth; last in a series of nine; 9th. **2** one, or being one, of nine equal parts.

ninth chord *Music.* a chord combining the third, fifth, seventh, and ninth above the tonic.

Ni•o•be [ˈnaɪoubi] *or* [ˈnaɪəbi] *n. Greek mythology.* a mother whose fourteen beautiful children were slain because she boasted about them. Turned by Zeus into a stone fountain, she weeps forever for her children. **—ˌNi•oˈbe•an** *adj.*

ni•o•bic [naɪˈoubɪk] *or* [naɪˈɒbɪk] *adj. Chemistry.* containing niobium in its pentavalent form.

ni•o•bi•um [naɪˈoubiəm] *n. Chemical.* a rare, steel grey, metallic chemical element that resembles tantalum in chemical properties. Formerly, COLUMBIUM. *Symbol*: Nb; *at.no.* 41; *at.mass* 92.91. ⟨< NL; after *Niobe*⟩

ni•o•bous [naɪˈoubəs] *adj. Chemistry.* containing niobium in its trivalent form.

nip[1] [nɪp] *v.* **nipped, nip•ping;** *n. —v.* **1** squeeze tight and suddenly; pinch; bite: *The crab nipped my toe.* **2** take off by biting, pinching, or snipping. **3** stop or spoil the growth, progress, or fulfilment of: *a new government policy designed to nip inflation.* **4** injure or make numb with cold: *The cold wind nipped our ears. The flowers were all nipped by frost.*

nip in the bud, stop or spoil at the very beginning: *All her plans were nipped in the bud by the sudden death of her benefactor.*

—n. **1** a tight squeeze or pinch; sudden bite. **2** stinging cold; chill: *There was a nip in the air.* **3** a strong, sharp flavour; tang: *cheese with a nip.* **4** a small bit: *a nip of bread.* **5** an injury caused by frost.

nip and tuck, *Informal.* in a race or contest, so evenly matched that the issue remains in doubt till the end. ⟨ME *nyppen*; cf. Du. *nijpen*⟩

nip[2] [nɪp] *n., v.* **nipped, nip•ping.** *—n.* a small drink: *a nip of brandy.*

—v. drink nips. ⟨for *nipperkin* a small vessel; origin uncertain⟩

ni•pa [ˈnipə] *or* [ˈnəipə] *n.* a palm tree (*Nipa fruticens*) of the East Indies, whose foliage is used for thatching and whose fruit is edible.

nip•per [ˈnɪpər] *n.* **1** a person or thing that nips, especially a big claw of a lobster or crab. **2** *Informal.* a small boy. **3 nippers,** *pl.* pincers, forceps, pliers, or any tool that nips.

nip•ple [ˈnɪpəl] *n.* **1** the round projection in the centre of the mammary gland which, in females, contains the outlet of the milk ducts. **2** the mouthpiece of a baby's bottle. **3** something shaped or used like a nipple. ⟨earlier *neble*, probably dim. of *neb* peak, tip⟩ **—ˈnip•ple•less,** *adj.*

Nip•pon [ˈnɪpɒn], [nɪˈpɒn], *or* [niˈpɒn] *n.* Japan. **—ˌNip•ponˈese,** *adj.*

nip•py [ˈnɪpi] *adj.* **-pi•er, -pi•est. 1** chilly; biting: *nippy weather.* **2** sharp; pungent: *nippy cheese.*

nip–up [ˈnɪp ˌʌp] *n.* a springing to the feet from a supine position.

nir•va•na or **Nir•va•na** [nərˈvænə] *or* [nərˈvɑnə] *n.* **1** *Buddhism.* the enlightened level of being of a person who has overcome the desires and the pain of worldly existence; a peaceful, pure, and deathless state which becomes complete and perfect when the body dies. The desires of life are thought of as a fever and nirvana is the extinguishing or cooling of this fever. **2** *Hinduism.* freedom of the soul; reunion with the universal soul reached by the suppression of individual existence. **3** freedom from care and pain. ⟨< Skt. *nirvāna* extinction < *nis-* out + *vā-* blow⟩

Ni•san [niˈsɑn], [ˈnɪsən], *or* [ˈnisɑn] *n.* in the Hebrew calendar, the first month of the ecclesiastical year, and the seventh month of the civil year.

Ni•sei [ˈniˈsei] *n., pl.* **-sei.** a native-born Canadian or United States citizen whose parents were Japanese immigrants. ⟨< Japanese *nisei* second generation < *ni* two + *sei* generation⟩

ni•si [ˈnəisaɪ] *or* [ˈnisi] *conj. Law.* not yet final: *a decree nisi.* ⟨< L *nisi* if not, unless⟩

Nis•sen hut [ˈnɪsən] a prefabricated shelter for soldiers, semicylindrical in shape, made of corrugated iron, with a concrete floor. Compare QUONSET HUT. ⟨after Lt.Col. Peter N. *Nissen* (1871-1930), who designed it⟩

ni•sus [ˈnəisəs] *n., pl.* **-sus.** an effort; striving toward a goal. ⟨< L⟩

nit[1] [nɪt] *n.* the egg or the young of a louse or similar insect. ⟨ME *nite,* OE *hnitu*⟩ **—ˈnit•ty,** *adj.*

☛ *Hom.* KNIT.

nit[2] [nɪt] *n. Esp. Brit. Informal.* nitwit.

☛ *Hom.* KNIT.

nitch•ie [ˈnɪtʃi] *n. Cdn.* **1** in First Nations use, a friend (especially of another First Nations person). **2** *Rare.* a small pony used by First Nations people; cayuse. ⟨< Algonquian⟩

ni•ter [ˈnəitər] See NITRE.

nit–pick [ˈnɪt ˌpɪk] *v.* engage in nit-picking. **—ˈnit-ˌpick•er,** *n.*

nit–pick•ing [ˈnɪt ˌpɪkɪŋ] *n. or adj.* criticizing and complaining in a petty manner; criticizing unimportant details; faultfinding: *You're being a little nit-picking in your criticism.*

ni•trate [ˈnəitreit] *n., v.* **-trat•ed, -trat•ing.** *—n.* **1** *Chemistry.* a salt or ester of nitric acid. **2** POTASSIUM NITRATE or SODIUM NITRATE, used as a fertilizer.

—v. **1** treat with nitric acid or a nitrate. **2** convert into a nitrate. **—niˈtra•tion,** *n.*

ni•tre ['nəitər] *n.* **1** potassium nitrate, obtained from potash, used in making gunpowder; saltpetre. *Formula*: KNO_3 **2** sodium nitrate or Chile saltpetre, used as a fertilizer. *Formula*: $NaNO_3$ Also, **niter.** ⟨< F < L *nitrum* < Gk. *nitron.* Doublet of NATRON.⟩

ni•tric ['nəitrɪk] *adj. Chemistry.* of or containing nitrogen, especially with a higher valence than in corresponding nitrous compounds. ⟨< F *nitrique*⟩

nitric acid *Chemistry.* a clear, colourless, highly corrosive liquid. Nitric acid is used as an oxidizing agent and in making dyes, fertilizers, and explosives. *Formula*: HNO_3

nitric oxide *Chemistry.* a poisonous gas produced during the manufacture of nitric acid. *Formula*: NO

ni•tride ['nəitraɪd] *or* ['nəitrɪd] *n. Chemistry.* a compound of nitrogen with a more electropositive element or radical, such as phosphorus, boron, or a metal.

ni•tri•fy ['nəitrə,faɪ] *v.* **-fied, -fy•ing. 1** oxidize (ammonia compounds, etc.) to nitrites or nitrates, especially by bacterial action. **2** impregnate (soil, etc.) with nitrates. **3** combine or treat with nitrogen or one of its compounds. ⟨< F *nitrifier*⟩ **—,ni•tri•fi'ca•tion,** *n.* **—'ni•tri,fi•er,** *n.* **—'ni•tri,fi•a•ble,** *adj.*

ni•trile ['nəitrɪl] *or* ['nəitraɪl] *n. Chemistry.* any compound of trivalent nitrogen in a cyanide group.

ni•trite ['nəitrəit] *n. Chemistry.* a salt or ester of nitrous acid.

ni•tro– *Chemistry. combining form.* indicating the presence of the univalent group NO_2: *nitrobenzene.*

ni•tro•bac•te•ri•a [,nəitroubæk'tiriə] *n., pl. sing.* **-te•ri•um** ['tiriəm]. bacteria in soil that produce nitrification.

ni•tro•ben•zene [,nəitrou'bɛnzin] *or* [,nəitroubɛn'zin] *n. Chemistry.* a poisonous, yellowish liquid obtained from benzene by the action of nitric acid, used as a solvent, etc. *Formula*: $C_6H_5NO_2$

ni•tro•cel•lu•lose [,nəitrou'sɛljə,lous] *n. Chemistry.* a polymer obtained from cellulose; guncotton.

ni•tro•gen ['nəitrədʒən] *n. Chemistry.* a colourless, odourless, tasteless, gaseous chemical element that forms about four-fifths of the earth's atmosphere by volume. *Symbol*: N; *at.no.* 7; *at.mass* 14.01. ⟨< F *nitrogène* < Gk. *nitron* native sodium carbonate + *-genēs* born, produced⟩ **—ni'trog•e•nous** [nəi'trɒdʒənəs], *adj.*

nitrogen cycle the cycle of chemical changes that returns nitrogen to its original form after its use by plants and bacteria.

nitrogen dioxide *Chemistry.* a brown gas found in automobile exhaust fumes. *Formula*: NO_2

nitrogen fixation the conversion of atmospheric nitrogen into compounds containing nitrogen by natural agencies, thus providing nitrogen for plants to use.

ni•tro•gen•ize ['nəitrədʒə,naɪz] *or* [nəi'trɒdʒə,naɪz] *v.* **-ized, -iz•ing. 1** combine with nitrogen. **2** treat with nitrogen. **—,ni•tro•gen•i'za•tion** or **,ni•tro•ge'na•tion,** *n.*

ni•tro•glyc•er•in or **ni•tro•glyc•er•ine** [,nəitrou'glɪsərɪn] *n. Chemistry.* a heavy, oily, explosive liquid made by treating glycerin with nitric and sulphuric acids. Nitroglycerin is used in dynamite and in medicine. *Formula*: $C_3H_5(NO_3)_3$

ni•trom•e•ter [nəi'trɒmətər] *n.* a device for measuring the amount of nitrogen in a substance. **—,ni•tro'met•ric,** *adj.*

ni•trous ['nəitrəs] *adj. Chemistry.* **1** of or containing nitrogen, especially with a lower valence than in corresponding nitric compounds. **2** of or containing nitre. ⟨< L *nitrosus* < *nitrum.* See NITRE.⟩

nitrous acid *Chemistry.* an acid found only in solution. *Formula*: HNO_2

nitrous oxide *Chemistry.* a colourless, nonflammable gas having a sweet taste and smell, used as an anesthetic, especially in dentistry. Also called **laughing gas.** *Formula*: N_2O

nit•ty–grit•ty ['nɪti 'grɪti] *n. Informal.* basic reality; actual fact or essence: *Let's get down to the nitty-gritty of who is going to pay for the broken window.*

nit•wit ['nɪt,wɪt] *n. Slang.* a stupid or scatterbrained person. ⟨< *nit*[2] + *wit*⟩

ni•val ['naɪvəl] *adj.* of or growing in snow. ⟨< L *nivalis* < *nix, nivis* snow⟩

niv•e•ous ['nɪviəs] *adj.* snowy. ⟨< L *niveus*⟩

nix[1] [nɪks] *n., interj., v. Slang. —n. or interj.* **1** no. **2** nothing. *—v.* reject or veto: *The city council nixed the proposal.* ⟨< G *nix,* dial. var. of *nichts* nothing⟩

nix[2] [nɪks] *n., pl.* **nix•es.** *Germanic mythology.* a water sprite. ⟨< colloquial Du. or G⟩

nix•ie ['nɪksi] *n. German mythology.* a female nix. ⟨< G *Nixe*⟩

Ni•zam [nɪ'zæm] *or* [nɪ'zɑm] *n.* formerly, the title of the ruler of Hyderabad, India. ⟨< Urdu and Turkish *nizām* < Arabic *nizām* order, arrangement⟩

NL New Latin.

NLQ *Computer technology.* NEAR-LETTER QUALITY.

NMR NUCLEAR MAGNETIC RESONANCE.

NNE or **N.N.E.** north-northeast.

NNW or **N.N.W.** north-northwest.

no[1] [nou] *n., pl.* **noes;** *adj., adv. —n.* **1** a word used to deny, refuse, or disagree. **2** a denial; refusal. **3** a negative vote or voter: *The noes have it.*
—adj. not any; not a: *He has no friends.* ⟨var. of *none*⟩
—adv. **1** a word used to deny, refuse, or disagree: *Will you come with us? No.* **2** not in any degree; not at all: *He is no better.* **3** not, chiefly in phrases like *whether or no.* ⟨OE *nā* < *ne* not + *ā* ever⟩
☛ *Hom.* KNOW, NOH.
☛ *Usage.* See note at YES.

no[2] [nou] NOH.
☛ *Hom.* KNOW.

No nobelium.

No. 1 north; northern. **2** Also, **no.**, number (for L *numero,* ablative of *numerus* number).
☛ *Usage.* **No.** The abbreviation **No.** for **number** (from the Latin *numero* by number) is usually written with a capital. It is appropriate chiefly in business and technical English, although nowadays it is usually replaced by the symbol #.

no–ac•count ['nou ə'kaʊnt] *adj., n. Informal. —adj.* no good; worthless: *a no-account swindler.*
—n. a good-for-nothing person; a person of no importance at all.

nob [nɒb] *n. Slang.* **1** head. **2** a person of wealth or social importance. ⟨? var. of *knob*⟩
☛ *Hom.* KNOB.

nob•by ['nɒbi] *adj.* **-bi•er, -bi•est.** *Slang.* **1** smart; fashionable; elegant. **2** first-rate.
☛ *Hom.* KNOBBY.

No•bel•ist [nou'bɛlɪst] *n.* one who has won a Nobel prize.

no•bel•i•um [nou'biliəm] *n.* an artificial radioactive element. *Symbol*: No; *at.no.* 102; *at.mass* 253; *half-life* approx. 180 s. ⟨< Alfred B. *Nobel,* who established the Nobel prizes⟩

No•bel prize [nou'bɛl] any of a group of prizes for physics, chemistry, physiology or medicine, literature, economic sciences, and the promotion of peace, established by Alfred B. Nobel (1833-1896), a Swedish chemist, engineer, and philanthropist, to be given annually to the person or persons who have contributed most in each of these fields. The prizes were first awarded in 1901.

no•bil•i•ty [nou'bɪləti] *n., pl.* **-ties. 1** people of noble rank. Earls, marquises, and counts belong to the nobility. **2** noble birth; noble rank. **3** noble character or quality: *the nobility of an act.* ⟨ME < OF < L *nobilitas*⟩

no•ble ['noubəl] *adj.* **-bler, -blest;** *n. —adj.* **1** high and great by birth, rank, or title. **2** high and great in character; showing greatness of mind; illustrious; outstanding: *a noble person, a noble deed.* **3** excellent; fine; splendid; magnificent: *Niagara Falls is a noble sight.* **4** of metals, resisting oxidation or corrosion. Gold is a noble metal. **5** *Chemistry.* of certain gaseous elements, chemically inert. Helium, neon, etc. are noble gases.
—n. **1** a person high and great by birth, rank, or title: *A duke is a noble.* **2** a former British gold coin worth one-third of a pound. ⟨< F < L *nobilis* renowned⟩ **—'no•ble•ness,** *n.*
☛ *Syn. adj.* **3.** See note at GRAND.

noble gas *Chemistry.* any of the inert gases: argon, helium, neon, krypton, radon, xenon.

no•ble•man ['noubəlmən] *n., pl.* **-men.** a man who belongs to the nobility; a man of noble rank or birth.

no•blesse o•blige [nou'blɛs ou'bliʒ]; *French,* [nɔblɛsɔ'bliʒ] *French.* the unwritten expectation that persons of noble rank should behave nobly.

no•ble•wom•an ['noubəl,wʊmən] *n., pl.* **-wom•en.** a woman who belongs to the nobility; a woman of noble birth or rank.

no•bly ['noubli] *adv.* **1** in a noble manner. **2** splendidly; magnificently. **3** of noble ancestry: *nobly born.*

no•bod•y ['nou,bʌdi], ['nou,bɒdi], *or* ['noubədi] *pron., n., pl.* **-bod•ies.** *—pron.* no one; no person.
—n. a person of no importance.
☛ *Usage.* **Nobody,** NOTHING, NOWHERE are written as single words.

Nobody and **nothing** are singular, although informally **nobody** is sometimes followed by a plural pronoun: *Nothing is further from the truth. Nobody thinks that his or her own dog is a nuisance.* Informal: *Nobody thinks their own dog is a nuisance.* See also the note at EVERYBODY.

no•cent ['nousənt] *adj.* **1** harmful. **2** guilty. ⟨< L *nocens*, ppr. of *nocere* to do harm⟩

nock [nɒk] *n., v.* —*n.* a notch on a bow or arrow for the bowstring.
—*v.* **1** make such a notch in. **2** fit (an arrow) to the bowstring for shooting. ⟨ME *nocke*⟩
☛ *Hom.* KNOCK.

noc•tam•bu•lism [nɒk'tæmbjə,lɪzəm] *n.* sleepwalking. ⟨< L *nox, noctis* night + *ambulare* to walk⟩

nocti– or **noct–** *combining form.* night: *noctambulism.*

noc•ti•lu•ca [,nɒktə'lukə] *n., pl.* **-lucae** [-'lusi] any marine organism of the genus *Noctiluca,* which glow. ⟨< *nocti-* + L *lucere* shine⟩

noc•ti•lu•cent [,nɒktə'lusənt] *adj.* glowing at night. **—,noc•ti'lu•cence,** *n.*

noc•tu•id ['nɒktʃuɪd] *n.* a moth of the family Noctuidae, which fly at night.

noc•tule ['nɒktjul] *or* ['nɒktul] *n.* a bat of the genus *Nyctalus.* ⟨< F < Ital. *nottola* a bat, owl < L *noctua* a night owl⟩

noc•tur•nal [nɒk'tɜrnəl] *adj.* **1** of, belonging to, or occurring at night: *a nocturnal journey. The stars are a nocturnal sight.* **2** of animals, active during the night instead of the day: *The owl is a nocturnal bird.* **3** of plants, having flowers that open only at night: *One species of cereus cactus is nocturnal.* ⟨< LL *nocturnalis*, ult. < L *nox, noctis* night⟩ **—noc'tur•nal•ly,** *adv.*

noc•turne ['nɒktərn] *n.* **1** *Music.* a dreamy or pensive composition. **2** a painting of a night scene. ⟨< F⟩

nod [nɒd] *v.* **nod•ded, nod•ding;** *n.* —*v.* **1** bow (the head) slightly and raise it again quickly. **2** show agreement by nodding: *I asked him if the baby was asleep and he nodded.* **3** express by bowing the head: *to nod consent.* **4** let the head fall forward and bob about when sleepy or falling asleep. **5** be sleepy; become careless and dull: *She was beginning to nod before the meeting was halfway through.* **6** droop, bend, or sway back and forth: *Trees nod in the wind.*
nod off, fall asleep.
—*n.* a nodding of the head.
get (or **give**) **the nod,** *Informal.* **a** receive or give approval. **b** receive or give a victory or decision to. ⟨ME *nodden*; origin uncertain⟩

nod•al ['noudəl] *adj.* having to do with, located near, or being a node: *the nodal joints of a stem.* **—no'dal•i•ty** [nou'dæləti], *n.*

nod•ding ['nɒdɪŋ] *adj., v.* —*adj.* casual; slight: *a nodding acquaintance.*
—*v.* ppr. of NOD.

nod•dle ['nɒdəl] *n. Slang.* the head. ⟨ME *nodel, nodul*; origin uncertain⟩

nod•dy ['nɒdi] *n., pl.* **-dies.** a fool. ⟨origin uncertain⟩

node [noud] *n.* **1** a knot; knob; swelling. **2** *Botany.* a joint in a stem; the part of a stem from which leaves grow. See STEM[1] for picture. **3** *Physics.* a point, line, or plane in a vibrating body at which there is comparatively no vibration. **4** a knotlike swelling or mass of specialized tissue on the body or an organ: *a lymph node.* **5** *Geometry.* a point at which a curve intersects itself so that each of the branches has a distinct tangent. **6** a central point in a system; point of concentration. **7** a complication or predicament in the plot or character development of a story, play, etc. **8** *Astronomy.* either of the two points at which the orbit of a heavenly body intersects the path of the sun or the orbit of another heavenly body. ⟨< L *nodus* knot⟩

nod•i•cal ['nɒdɪkəl] *adj. Astronomy.* of or having to do with a node or the nodes.

no•dose ['noudous] *or* [nou'dous] *adj.* having nodes. **—no'dos•i•ty** [nou'dɒsəti], *n.*

nod•u•lar ['nɒdʒələr] *adj.* having nodules.

nod•ule ['nɒdʒul] *n.* **1** a small knot, knob, or swelling. **2** a small, rounded mass or lump: *nodules of pure gold.* **3** *Botany.* a tubercle. ⟨< L *nodulus*, dim. of *nodus* knot⟩

no•du•lose ['nɒdʒə,lous] *adj.* having nodules.

no•dus ['noudəs] *n., pl.* **-di** [-daɪ]. a difficult situation. ⟨< L *nodūs* a knot⟩

no•ël [nou'ɛl] *n.* **1** a Christmas song; carol. **2 Noël,** Christmas. ⟨< F < L *natalis* natal (i.e., the natal day of Christ) < *nasci* be born. Doublet of NATAL.⟩

no•e•sis [nou'isɪs] *n.* the use of reason. ⟨< Gk. *noesis* thought, intelligence < *noein* to think⟩ **—no'et•ic** [nou'ɛtɪk], *adj.*

no–fault ['nou ,fɒlt] *adj.* of, having to do with, or designating a type of automobile insurance under which a person is compensated by his or her own insurance company for injury or damage due to an accident, regardless of who is to blame for the accident.

nog•gin ['nɒgən] *n.* **1** a small mug. **2** a small measure of liquor, usually one GILL[2]. **3** *Informal.* a person's head. ⟨origin uncertain⟩

noh [nou] *n.* the classical drama of Japan. Also, **no.**
☛ *Hom.* KNOW, NO.

no–hit•ter ['nou 'hɪtər] *n. Baseball.* a game in which the pitcher prevents the opposing team from gaining any base hits.

no–holds–barred ['nou 'houldz 'bɑrd] *adj. Informal.* **1** without rules or restrictions; unrestrainedly violent: *a no-holds-barred fight.* **2** complete; utmost: *a no-holds-barred effort.*

no•how ['nou,haʊ] *adv. Informal.* in no way; not at all.
☛ *Hom.* KNOW-HOW.

noil [nɔɪl] *n.* **1** a short fibre combed out during the preparation of wool, cotton, or silk yarn. **2** the waste material composed of these fibres. ⟨origin uncertain⟩

noise [nɔɪz] *n., v.* **noised, nois•ing.** —*n.* **1** a sound that is not musical or pleasant; loud or harsh sound: *The noise of the traffic kept me awake.* **2** any sound: *the noise of rain on the roof.* **3** a din of voices and movements; loud shouting; outcry; clamour. **4** *Physics.* a group of sound waves which are not periodic and which are produced by irregular vibrations; sound of no single fundamental frequency but many non-harmonic frequency components of varying amplitudes randomly placed. **5** any undesired or unintended disturbance in a radio or television signal.
—*v. Archaic.* spread the news of; tell: *It was noised abroad that the king was dying.* ⟨ME < OF *noise* < L *nausea.* Doublet of NAUSEA.⟩
☛ *Syn. n.* **1, 3. Noise,** DIN, UPROAR = disagreeably loud, confused, or harsh and clashing sound. **Noise** applies to any disagreeably unmusical or loud sound made by one or more people or things: *The noise kept me awake.* **Din** applies to a prolonged and deafening confusion of clanging or piercing noises: *The din of machines and factory whistles hurt my ears.* **Uproar** applies especially to the tumult, shouting, and loud noises of a crowd: *You should have heard the uproar when officials called back the touchdown.*

noise•less ['nɔɪzlɪs] *adj.* making little or no noise: *a noiseless electric fan.* **—'noise•less•ly,** *adv.* **—'noise•less•ness,** *n.*

noise•mak•er ['nɔɪz,meikər] *n.* a person or thing that makes noise, especially a horn, rattle, etc. used to make noise at a party, sports event, etc.

noi•sette [nwɑ'zɛt] *n.* a lean cut of meat, especially lamb. ⟨< F dim of *noix* choice cut of meat⟩

noisette rose a climbing rose (*Rosa noisettiana*) having fragrant pink, white, or yellow flowers. ⟨after P. *Noisette*, 19c. American horticulturist⟩

noi•some ['nɔɪsəm] *adj.* **1** offensive; disgusting; smelling bad: *a noisome slum.* **2** harmful; injurious: *a noisome pestilence.* ⟨< *noy* (var. of *annoy*) + *-some[1]*⟩ **—'noi•some•ly,** *adv.* **—'noi•some•ness,** *n.*

nois•y ['nɔɪzi] *adj.* **nois•i•er, nois•i•est. 1** making much noise: *a noisy boy.* **2** full of noise: *a noisy street.* **3** characterized by noise; accompanied by much noise: *a noisy quarrel, a noisy game.* **—'nois•i•ly,** *adv.* **—'nois•i•ness,** *n.*
☛ *Syn.* See note at LOUD.

nom. nominative.

no•mad ['noumæd] *n.* **1** a member of a people that moves from place to place so as to have pasture for its cattle or to be near its own food or water supply. The Inuit have traditionally been nomads. **2** (*adjl.*) nomadic: *nomad peoples, a nomad way of life.* **3** wanderer. ⟨< L < Gk. *nomas, -ados*, ult. < *nemein* to pasture⟩ **—'no•mad•ism,** *n.*

no•mad•ic [nou'mædɪk] *adj.* of, having to do with, or designating nomads or their way of life. Many North American First Nations peoples were traditionally nomadic. **—no'mad•i•cal•ly,** *adv.*

no–man's–land or **no man's land** ['nou ,mænz ,lænd] *n.* **1** in war, the land or area between opposing armies. **2** a tract of land to which no one has a recognized or established claim. **3** any area of involvement or operation that is not clearly defined or is ambiguous or inconsistent: *a legal no-man's-land.*

nom de guerre [ˌnɒm də ˈgɛr]; *French,* [nɔ̃dəˈgɛʀ] *French.* an assumed name under which to pursue a profession, undertaking, or the like. ⟨literally, war name⟩

nom de plume [ˌnɒm də ˈplum] a pen name; name used by a writer instead of the person's real name. ⟨formed in E from F words; literally, pen name⟩

no•men•cla•tor [ˈnoumənˌkleitər] *n.* one who gives names, as in a classification.

no•men•cla•ture [ˈnoumənˌkleitʃər] *or* [nouˈmɛnklətʃər] *n.* a system of names or terms used in a particular field of science, art, etc.: *the nomenclature of music, the international Latin nomenclature for animals and plants.* ⟨< L *nomenclatura* < *nomen* name + *calare* to call⟩

nom•i•nal [ˈnɒmənəl] *adj., n.* —*adj.* **1** being so in name only; not real: *The president is the nominal head of the club, but the secretary really runs its affairs.* **2** so small that it is not worth considering; unimportant compared with the real value: *We paid a nominal rent for the cottage—$25 a month.* **3 a** giving the name or names: *a nominal roll of the pupils in our room.* **b** mentioning specifically by name: *a nominal appeal.* **c** assigned to a person by name: *a nominal share of stock.* **4** of, having to do with, or being a name. **5** *Grammar.* of, having to do with, being, or used as a noun. *Day* is the nominal root of *daily, daybreak,* and *Sunday.*
—*n. Grammar.* a word or group of words used as a noun. *Rich* and *poor* in the phrase *the rich and the poor* are nominals. ⟨< L *nominalis* < *nomen, -inis* name⟩

nom•i•nal•ism [ˈnɒmənəˌlɪzəm] *n. Philosophy.* the doctrine that abstractions exist only as names. **—ˈnom•i•nal•ist,** *n.* **—ˌnom•i•nalˈis•tic,** *adj.* **—ˌnom•i•nalˈis•ti•cal•ly,** *adv.*

nom•i•nal•ly [ˈnɒmənəli] *adv.* **1** in name; as a matter of form; in a nominal way only. **2** by name.

nominal value PAR VALUE.

nom•i•nate [ˈnɒməˌneit] *v.* **-nat•ed, -nat•ing. 1** name as candidate for an office; propose for an office or award: *Lynn Conroy has been nominated as Liberal candidate in our riding.* **2** appoint to an office or duty: *The prime minister nominated her Secretary of State.* ⟨< L *nominare,* ult. < *nomen* name⟩ **—ˈnom•iˌna•tor,** *n.*

nom•i•na•tion [ˌnɒməˈneiʃən] *n.* **1** the naming of someone as a candidate for an office or award. **2** a selection for office or duty; appointment to office or duty. **3** a being nominated.

nom•i•na•tive [ˈnɒmənətɪv] *or* [ˈnɒməˌneitɪv] *adj., n.* —*adj.* **1** of, having to do with, or being the grammatical case, found in many languages, that shows that a noun, pronoun, or adjective is part of the subject of a sentence. The English personal pronouns *I, he, she, we,* and *they* correspond to the nominative case in languages such as German and Latin because they are special forms used only as subjects in a sentence. **2** appointed to an office. **3** bearing a person's name, as on shares.
—*n. Grammar.* **1** the nominative case. **2** a word or construction in the nominative case. *Abbrev.:* nom. ⟨< L *nominativus*⟩

nom•i•nee [ˌnɒməˈni] *n.* a person who is nominated.

noml. *Grammar.* nominal.

nomo– *combining form.* custom; law: *nomogram.* ⟨< Gk. *nómos* law, custom⟩

no•mo•gram [ˈnɒməˌgræm] *n.* **1** a set of lines on a graph, each sealed for different variables in such a way that a straight line connecting known values will yield the unknown values at its intersection with the differently sealed lines. **2** any chart showing numerical relationships. Also, **nomograph.**

no•mog•ra•phy [nouˈmɒgrəfi] *n.* **1** NOMOLOGY (def. 1). **2** the science of making nomograms. **—ˌno•moˈgraph•ic,** *adj.* **—ˌno•moˈgraph•i•cal•ly,** *adv.*

no•mol•o•gy [nouˈmɒlədʒi] *n.* **1** the art or science of drafting laws. **2** the formulation of laws of nature in science. **—ˌnom•oˈlog•i•cal,** *adj.*

–nomy *combining form.* distribution; arrangement; management: *astronomy.* ⟨< Gk. *nomía* law⟩

non– *prefix.* not; opposite of; lack of: *nonconformity, nonflammable, non-smoking.* ⟨< L *non* not < OL *ne-* not + *oinom* one⟩

non–ac•cept•ance [ˌnɒn ækˈsɛptəns] *n.* a failure or refusal to accept.

non•age [ˈnɒnɪdʒ] *or* [ˈnounɪdʒ] *n.* **1** the condition of being under the legal age of responsibility; minority. **2** an early stage; period before maturity. ⟨ME < AF *nonnage* < *non-* not (< L) + *age* age < VL *aetaticum* < L *aetas*⟩

non•a•ge•nar•i•an [ˌnɒnədʒəˈnɛriən] *or* [ˌnounədʒəˈnɛriən] *n., adj.* —*n.* a person who is 90 years old or between 90 and 100 years old.
—*adj.* 90 years old or between 90 and 100 years old. ⟨< L *nonagenarius* of ninety⟩

non–ag•gres•sion [ˌnɒn əˈgrɛʃən] *n.* absence of aggression: *a pact of non-aggression.*

non•a•gon [ˈnɒnəˌgɒn] *n.* a polygon having nine sides and nine interior angles. ⟨< L *nonus* ninth + Gk. *gōnia* angle⟩

non•a•ligned [ˌnɒnəˈlaɪnd] *adj.* of a country, not allied with other countries; especially, not allied with any of the great powers. **—ˌnon•aˈlign•ment,** *n.*

non–ap•pear•ance [ˌnɒn əˈpirəns] *n.* the fact of not appearing; failure to appear, especially in court as a witness or defendant.

non–at•tend•ance [ˌnɒn əˈtɛndəns] *n.* failure to be present.

non–cap•i•tal murder [nɒn ˈkæpətəl] formerly, in Canada, murder not punishable by death.

nonce [nɒns] *n., adj.* —*n.* the one, or particular, occasion or purpose.
for the nonce, for the present time or occasion.
—*adj.* serving a single occasion: *a nonce word, nonce use.* ⟨ME *(for then) ones,* (for the) once, taken as *(for the) nones*⟩

nonce word a word formed and used for a single occasion.

non•cha•lance [ˌnɒnʃəˈlɒns] *or* [ˈnɒnʃəˌlɒns] *n.* cool unconcern or indifference: *Eleanor received the prize with pretended nonchalance.*

In each of the words below **non-** *means* not *or, for nouns,* no *or* not a.

ˌnon-aˈbra•sive
ˌnon-abˈsorb•ent
ˌnon-ac•aˈdem•ic
non-ˈac•id
ˌnon-aˈcid•ic
non-ˈac•tive
ˌnon-adˈdic•tive
ˌnon-adˈher•ence
ˌnon-adˈhe•sive
ˌnon-adˈja•cent
ˌnon-adˈjust•a•ble
ˌnon-adˈmin•isˌtra•tive
ˌnon-ad•vanˈta•geous
ˌnon-aesˈthet•ic
non-ˈAf•ric•an
ˌnon-agˈgres•sive
ˌnon-aˈgree•ment
ˌnon-ag•riˈcul•tur•al
ˌnon-al•coˈhol•ic
ˌnon-al•lerˈgen•ic
ˌnon-alˈler•gic
ˌnon-al•phaˈbet•ic
ˌnon-Aˈmer•i•can
ˌnon-an•aˈlyt•ic
non-ˈap•pli•ca•ble
non-aˈquat•ic
non-ˈAr•ab
non-ˈAr•a•bic
ˌnon•aˌris•toˈcrat•ic
ˌnon-arˈtis•tic
ˌnon-As•iˈat•ic
ˌnon-asˈser•tive
ˌnon-asˈsess•a•ble
ˌnon-asˈsign•a•ble
ˌnon-asˌsim•iˈla•tion
ˌnon-asˈso•ci•a•tive
ˌnon-athˈlet•ic
ˌnon-at•mosˈpher•ic
ˌnon-atˈtrib•u•tive
ˌnon-auˈthor•iˌta•tive
non-ˈau•toˌmat•ed
ˌnon-au•toˈmat•ic
ˌnon-aˌvail•aˈbil•i•ty
ˌnon-bacˈte•ri•al
non-ˈbas•ic
ˌnon-beˈliev•er
ˌnon-beˈliev•ing
ˌnon-belˈlig•er•ent
non-ˈBib•li•cal
non-ˈblack
non-ˈbreak•a•ble
non-ˈBrit•ish
non-ˈBud•dhist
non-ˈburn•a•ble
ˌnon-calˈcar•e•ous
ˌnon-caˈlor•ic
ˌnon-Caˈna•di•an
non-ˈcan•cer•ous
ˌnon-cap•i•talˈis•tic
ˌnon-car•boˈhy•drate
non-ˈcar•boˌnat•ed
ˌnon-carˈniv•o•rous
ˌnon-cat•eˈgo•ri•cal
non-ˈCath•o•lic
ˌnon-Cauˈca•sian
non-ˈCau•caˌsoid
non-ˈcel•lu•lar
non-ˈcen•sored
non-ˈcen•tral
ˌnon-ceˈre•bral
non-ˈcer•tiˌfied

non•cha•lant [ˌnɒnʃəˈlɒnt] *or* [ˈnɒnʃəˌlɒnt] *adj.* coolly unconcerned or indifferent: *She remained quite nonchalant during all the excitement.* ⟨< F *nonchalant* < *non-* not (< L) + *chaloir* be warm < L *calere*⟩ **—ˌnon•chaˈlant•ly,** *adv.*

non–com [ˈnɒn ˌkɒm] *n. Informal.* a non-commissioned officer.

non–com•bat•ant [ˌnɒn kəmˈbætənt] *or* [nɒn ˈkɒmbətənt] *n., adj. —n.* **1** a person in the armed forces who is not a fighter. Military surgeons, nurses, chaplains, etc. are non-combatants. **2** a civilian in wartime.
—adj. **1** not fighting. **2** having civilian status in wartime.

non–com•mis•sioned [ˌnɒn kəˈmɪʃənd] *adj.* without a commission; not commissioned. Corporals and sergeants are non-commissioned officers.

non•com•mit•tal [ˌnɒnkəˈmɪtəl] *adj.* not committing oneself; not saying yes or no. *I will think it over* is a noncommittal answer. **—ˌnon•comˈmit•tal•ly,** *adv.*

non–com•pli•ance [ˌnɒn kəmˈplaɪəns] *n.* the fact of not complying; failure to comply. **—ˌnon-comˈpli•ant,** *adj.*

non com•pos men•tis [ˈnɒn ˈkɒmpəs ˈmɛntɪs] *Latin. Law.* mentally unable to manage one's own affairs; legally insane.

non–con•duc•tor [ˌnɒn kənˈdʌktər] *n.* a substance that does not readily allow heat, electricity, or sound to pass through it. Rubber is a non-conductor of electricity. **—ˌnon-conˈduct•ing,** *adj.*

non•con•form•ist [ˌnɒnkənˈfɔrmɪst] *n.* **1** a person who does not conform to accepted practices, conventions, etc. **2** Often, **Nonconformist,** a person who does not conform to an established church, especially a Protestant in England who does not belong to the Church of England.

non•con•form•i•ty [ˌnɒnkənˈfɔrməti] *n.* **1** a lack of conformity; failure or refusal to conform. **2** a failure or refusal to conform to an established church. **3** Usually, **Nonconformity,** in England, the principles or practices of Protestants who do not belong to the Church of England.

non–co–op•er•a•tion [ˌnɒn kou ˌɒpəˈreiʃən] *n.* **1** a failure or refusal to co-operate. **2** a refusal to co-operate with a government for political reasons. **—ˌnon-co-ˈop•er•a•tive,** *adj.*

non–dair•y [nɒn ˈdɛri] *adj.* designating a synthetic product used as a substitute for cream or milk or whipped cream, etc.: *a non-dairy whipped topping, a non-dairy creamer for coffee.*

non•de•script [ˈnɒndəˌskrɪpt] *or* [ˌnɒndəˈskrɪpt] *adj., n. —adj.* **1** having no distinctive or outstanding features; uninteresting or drab. **2** not easily classified; not of any one particular kind: *eyes of nondescript shade, neither brown, blue, nor grey.*
—n. a nondescript person or thing. ⟨< *non-* + L *descriptus* described⟩

non–dis•junc•tion [ˌnɒn dɪsˈdʒʌŋkʃən] *n. Biology.* the failure of paired chromosomes to separate in mitosis. If non-disjunction occurs during meiosis, gametes with extra or missing chromosomes are formed, and can give rise to individuals with extra or missing chromosomes, as in Down syndrome.

none[1] (nʌn) *pron., adv. —pron.* **1** not any: *We have none of that paper left.* **2** no one; not one: *None of these is a typical case.* **3** no persons or things: *None have arrived.*
—adv. to no extent; in no way; not at all: *Our supply is none too great.* ⟨OE *nān* < *ne* not + *ān* one⟩
☛ *Hom.* NUN.
☛ *Usage.* **None,** NO ONE. **None** is a single word, but **not one** or **no one** is often used instead of **none** for emphasis. **None** may be either singular or plural: *As only ten jurors have been chosen so far, none of the witnesses were called* (or *was called.*) *I have heard the whole story, and none of it is true. I read three books on the subject, no one of which was helpful.*

none[2] [noun] *n.* sing. of NONES[2].
☛ *Hom.* KNOWN.

non•e•go [nɒnˈigou] *or* [nɒnˈɛgou] *n.* whatever is not part of the conscious self.

non•en•ti•ty [nɒnˈɛntəti] *n., pl.* **-ties. 1** a person or thing of little or no importance. **2** something that does not exist. **3** non-existence.

In each of the words below **non-** *means* not *or, for nouns,* no *or* not a.

non-ˈcharge•a•ble
non-ˈchem•i•cal
ˌnon-Chiˈnese
non-ˈChris•tian
non-ˈcit•i•zen
non-ˈciv•iˌlized
non-ˈclas•sic
non-ˈclas•si•cal
ˌnon-clas•siˈfi•a•ble
non-ˈclas•siˌfied
non-ˈcler•i•cal
non-ˈclin•i•cal
non-ˈclot•ting
ˌnon-coˈag•uˌlat•ing
ˌnon-coˈer•cive
non-ˈcog•ni•tive
ˌnon-colˈlab•or•a•tive
ˌnon-colˈlaps•i•ble
ˌnon-colˈlect•a•ble
ˌnon-colˈlect•i•ble
ˌnon-colˈle•giate
non-ˈcom•bat
ˌnon-comˈbin•ing
ˌnon-comˈbust•i•ble
ˌnon-comˈmer•cial
ˌnon-comˈmu•ni•ca•ble
ˌnon-comˈmu•ni•cant
ˌnon-comˈmu•niˌcat•ing
ˌnon-comˈmu•niˌca•tive
non-ˈcom•mu•nist
non-ˈcom•pe•ten•cy
non-ˈcom•pe•tent
ˌnon-comˈpet•ing
ˌnon-comˈpet•i•tive
ˌnon-comˈply•ing
ˌnon-com•preˈhend•ing
ˌnon-comˈpres•si•ble
ˌnon-comˈpul•sion
ˌnon-comˈpul•so•ry
ˌnon-conˈcil•i•aˌto•ry
ˌnon-conˈclu•sive
ˌnon-conˈcur•rence
ˌnon-conˈcur•rent
ˌnon-conˈdu•cive
ˌnon-conˈduc•tive
ˌnon-con•fiˈden•tial
ˌnon-conˈflict•ing
ˌnon-conˈform•ance
ˌnon-conˈform•ing
ˌnon-conˈgen•i•tal
ˌnon-conˈnec•tive
non-ˈcon•scious
ˌnon-conˈsec•u•tive
ˌnon-conˈsent
ˌnon-conˈserv•a•tive
ˌnon-con•stiˈtu•tion•al
ˌnon-conˈstrain•ing
ˌnon-conˈstruc•tive
ˌnon-conˈta•gious
ˌnon-conˈtem•poˌra•ry
ˌnon-conˈten•tious
ˌnon-conˈtig•u•ous
ˌnon-con•tiˈnent•al
ˌnon-conˈtin•u•ance
ˌnon-conˈtin•u•ous
non-ˈcon•traˌband
ˌnon-con•traˈdic•to•ry
ˌnon-conˈtrib•u•ting
ˌnon-conˈtrib•uˌto•ry
ˌnon-conˈtrol•la•ble
ˌnon-con•troˈver•sial
ˌnon-conˈven•tion•al
ˌnon-conˈver•gent
ˌnon-conˈver•sant
ˌnon-conˈvert•i•ble
ˌnon-conˈvic•tion
ˌnon-co-ˈop•er•a•tive
ˌnon-co-ˈor•diˌnat•ing
non-ˈcor•por•ate
ˌnon-corˈrec•tive
ˌnon-cor•reˈspond•ing
ˌnon-corˈrob•o•ra•tive
ˌnon-corˈrod•ing
ˌnon-corˈros•ive
ˌnon-creˈa•tive
non-ˈcred•i•ble
non-ˈcrim•i•nal
non-ˈcrit•i•cal
non-ˈcru•cial
non-ˈcrys•talˌline
non-ˈcul•pa•ble
non-ˈcul•tiˌvat•ed
non-ˈcu•mu•la•tive
non-ˈcur•rent
non-ˈcy•clic
ˌnon-Darˈwin•i•an
ˌnon-deˈcay•ing
ˌnon-deˈcep•tive
ˌnon-deˈcid•u•ous
ˌnon-deˈduct•i•ble
ˌnon-deˈfam•aˌto•ry
ˌnon-deˈfen•sive
ˌnon-deˈfin•ing
ˌnon-deˈgrad•a•ble
ˌnon-deˈhis•cent
ˌnon-deˈliv•e•ry
ˌnon-deˈmand
ˌnon-de•moˈcrat•ic
ˌnon-deˈmon•stra•ble
ˌnon-deˌnom•iˈna•tion•al
ˌnon-de•partˈment•al
ˌnon-deˈpar•ture
ˌnon-deˈpen•dence
ˌnon-deˈrog•aˌto•ry
ˌnon-deˈstruc•tive
ˌnon-deˈtach•a•ble
non-ˈdet•oˌnat•ing
ˌnon-deˈvel•op•ment
ˌnon-deˈvo•tion•al
ˌnon-dic•taˈto•ri•al
ˌnon-diˈdac•tic
ˌnon-dif•feˌren•tiˈa•tion
ˌnon-dip•loˈmat•ic
ˌnon-diˈrec•tion•al
ˌnon-diˈrec•tive
non-ˈdir•i•gi•ble
ˌnon-disˈcharg•ing
ˌnon-disˈcrim•iˌnat•ing
ˌnon-disˌcrim•iˈna•tion
ˌnon-disˈcrim•i•naˌto•ry
ˌnon-disˈpa•rag•ing
ˌnon-disˈpos•al
ˌnon-disˈtinc•tive
ˌnon-disˈtri•bu•tive
ˌnon-diˈver•gent
ˌnon-diˈvis•i•ble
ˌnon-doc•triˈnaire
ˌnon-dogˈmat•ic
ˌnon-doˈmes•tiˌcat•ed
ˌnon-draˈmat•ic
non-ˈdrink•er
non-ˈdriv•er
non-ˈdry•ing
non-ˈdu•ti•a•ble
non-ˈearn•ing
ˌnon-e•coˈnom•ic
non-ˈed•ible
non-ˈed•u•ca•ble
ˌnon-ed•uˈca•tion•al
ˌnon-efˈfect•ive
ˌnon-ef•fiˈca•cious
ˌnon-efˈfic•ient
ˌnon-eˈlas•tic
ˌnon-eˈlec•tive
ˌnon-eˈlec•tric
non-ˈel•i•gi•ble
ˌnon-eˈmo•tion•al
ˌnon-emˈphat•ic
ˌnon-emˈpi•ri•cal
ˌnon-enˈdem•ic
ˌnon-enˈforce•a•ble
ˌnon-enˈforce•ment
non-ˈEng•lish
ˌnon-eˈphem•er•al
non-ˈe•qual
ˌnon-eˈquiv•a•lent

nones[1] [nounz] *n.pl.* in the ancient Roman calendar, the ninth day before the ides, counting both days, this being the 7th of March, May, July, and October, and the 5th of the other months. ⟨< L *nonae*, originally fem. pl. of *nonus* ninth⟩

nones[2] [nounz] *n.pl.* **1** the first of the seven Christian canonical hours. **2** the service or services for it. ⟨pl. of *none*[2], OE *nōn* < L *nona.* Doublet of NOON.⟩

non–es•sen•tial [ˌnɒn əˈsɛnʃəl] *adj., n. —adj.* not essential; not necessary.
—n. a person or thing not essential.

none•such [ˌnʌnˈsʌtʃ] *or* [ˈnʌnˌsʌtʃ] *n.* **1** a person or thing without equal or parallel; paragon. Also, **nonsuch. 2** a medic (*Medicago lupulina*) having black pods; black medic.

no•net [nouˈnɛt] *n. Music.* **1** a group of nine performers. **2** a composition for such a group.

none•the•less [ˌnʌnðəˈlɛs] *adv.* nevertheless.

non•e•vent [ˌnɒnɪˈvɛnt] *n.* a happening that is unimportant.

non•fea•sance [nɒnˈfizəns] *n. Law.* the failure to perform some act that duty requires to be done. Compare MALFEASANCE and MISFEASANCE.

non–fic•tion [nɒn ˈfɪkʃən] *n.* prose literature that is not a novel, short story, or other form of writing based on imaginary people and events. Biographies, histories, and scientific reports are non-fiction.

non–fig•ur•a•tive [nɒn ˈfɪgjərətɪv] *or* [nɒn ˈfɪgərətɪv] *adj.* **1** *Painting, sculpture, etc.* non-objective; having abstract as opposed to traditional or recognizable forms. **2** not figurative; literal: *a non-figurative use of a word.* **—non'fig•ur•a•tive•ly,** *adv.*

non•flam•ma•ble [nɒnˈflæməbəl] *adj.* not easily set on fire and not fast-burning if set on fire; not flammable.
☛ *Usage.* See note at FLAMMABLE.

non–ful•fil•ment or **non–ful•fill•ment** [ˌnɒn fʊlˈfɪlmənt] *n.* a failure to fulfil; failure to be fulfilled.

non•func•tion•al [nɒnˈfʌŋkʃənəl] *adj.* having no proper use. **—non'func•tion•al•ly,** *adv.*

no•nil•lion [nouˈnɪljən] *n.* **1** in North America, the number represented by 1 plus 30 zeros. **2** in the United Kingdom, the number represented by 1 plus 54 zeroes. **—no'nil•lionth,** *n., adj.*

non–in•ter•ven•tion [ˌnɒn ɪntərˈvɛnʃən] *n.* **1** a refraining from intervening. **2** the systematic avoidance of any interference by a nation in the affairs of other nations or of its own states, etc. **—ˌnon•in•ter'ven•tion•ist,** *adj., n.*

non•join•der [nɒnˈdʒɔɪndər] *n. Law.* the omission of a necessary part of a lawsuit.

non–ju•ror [nɒn ˈdʒʊrər] *n.* **1** one who refuses to take a required oath. **2 Non-juror,** in England, one of those members of the clergy of the Church of England who in 1689 refused to swear allegiance to William and Mary.

non–liv•ing [nɒn ˈlɪvɪŋ] *adj.* not living.

non–met•al [nɒn ˈmɛtəl] *n. Chemistry.* any chemical element not having the character of a metal. Carbon and nitrogen are non-metals.

non–me•tal•lic [ˌnɒn məˈtælɪk] *adj. Chemistry.* not like a metal. Carbon, oxygen, sulphur, and nitrogen are non-metallic chemical elements.

non–mor•al [nɒn ˈmɔrəl] *adj.* having no relation to morality; neither moral nor immoral.

In each of the words below **non-** *means* not *or, for nouns,* no *or* not a.

ˌnon-es'tab•lish•ment
ˌnon-e'ter•nal
non-'eth•i•cal
ˌnon-Eu'clid•e•an
ˌnon-Eu•ro'pe•an
ˌnon-ex'change•a•ble
ˌnon-ex'clu•sive
ˌnon-ex'cu•sa•ble
ˌnon-ex'ec•u•tive
ˌnon-ex'empt
ˌnon-ex'ist•ence
ˌnon-ex'ist•ent
ˌnon-ex'ot•ic
ˌnon-ex'pen•da•ble
ˌnon-ex'pe•ri•enced
ˌnon-exˌpe•ri'ment•al
ˌnon-ex'plo•sive
ˌnon-ex'port•a•ble
ˌnon-ex'tend•ed
ˌnon-ex'ter•nal
ˌnon-ex•tra'dit•a•ble
non-'fac•tu•al
non-'fad•ing
non-'Fas•cist
non-'fat
non-'fa•tal
non-'fat•ten•ing
non-'fed•er•al
non-'fed•erˌat•ed
non-'fer•rous
non-'fer•tile
non-'fes•tive
non-'feu•dal
non-'fic•tion•al
ˌnon-fic'ti•tious
non-'fig•u•ra•tive
ˌnon-fi'nan•cial
non-'fi•nite
non-'fireˌproof
non-'fis•cal
non-'fis•sion•a•ble
non-'flex•i•ble
non-'flow•er•ing
non-'fluc•tuˌat•ing
non-'flu•id
non-'fly•ing
non-'form•al
non-'frau•du•lent
non-'freez•ing
non-'French
non-'func•tion•al
non-'func•tion•ing
ˌnon-fun•da'ment•al
non-'fus•i•ble
non-'gas•e•ous
ˌnon-ge'net•ic
non-'Ger•man
ˌnon-gov•ern'ment•al
non-'gran•u•lar
non-'Greek
ˌnon-gre'ga•ri•ous
non-'hab•it•a•ble
ˌnon-har'mon•ic
ˌnon-har'mo•ni•ous
non-'haz•ard•ous
ˌnon-Hel'len•ic
ˌnon-he'red•iˌtar•y
non-'her•it•a•ble
ˌnon-his'tor•ic
ˌnon-his'tor•i•cal
non-'hos•tile
non-'hu•man
non-'hu•mor•ous
ˌnon-i'den•ti•cal
ˌnon-i'den•ti•ty
ˌnon-id•i•o'mat•ic
ˌnon-im'ag•iˌnar•y
ˌnon-im'mune
non-'im•muˌnized
ˌnon-im'mu•ni•ty
ˌnon-im'pe•ra•tive
ˌnon-im'pe•ri•al
ˌnon-im•por'ta•tion
ˌnon-im'preg•nat•ed
ˌnon-in'clu•sion
ˌnon-in'clu•sive
ˌnon-in•de'pen•dent
non-'in•dexed
non-'In•di•an
ˌnon-in'dict•a•ble
ˌnon-in'dict•ment
non-ˌIndo-Eu•ro'pe•an
ˌnon-in'dus•trial
ˌnon-in'fal•li•ble
ˌnon-in'fect•ed
ˌnon-in'fec•tious
ˌnon-in'flam•ma•ble
ˌnon-in'flam•maˌto•ry
ˌnon-in'fla•tionˌar•y
ˌnon-in'flect•ed
ˌnon-in'flec•tion•al
ˌnon-in'form•a•tive
ˌnon-in'her•ent
ˌnon-in'her•it•a•ble
ˌnon-in'ju•ri•ous
ˌnon-in'stinc•tive
ˌnon-in•sti'tu•tion•al
ˌnon-in'struc•tion•al
ˌnon-in•stru'ment•al
non-'in•teˌgrat•ed
ˌnon-in•tel'lec•tu•al
ˌnon-in'tel•li•gent
ˌnon-in•ter'change•a•ble
ˌnon-in•ter'fer•ence
ˌnon-in•ter'sect•ing
ˌnon-in'tox•i•cant
ˌnon-in'tox•iˌcat•ing
ˌnon-in'tu•i•tive
ˌnon-in'volve•ment
non-'i•onˌized
non-'Ir•ish
non-'ir•ri•ga•ble
non-'ir•ri•tant
non-'ir•riˌtat•ing
ˌnon-Is'lam•ic
non-'Is•ra•elˌite
ˌnon-I'tal•i•an
ˌnon-Ja•pa'nese
non-'Jew•ish
ˌnon-ju'di•cial
non-'ko•sher
non-'lam•iˌnat•ed
non-'La•tin
non-'leaf•y
non-'le•gal
non-'le•thal
non-'li•censed
non-'lim•it•ing
non-'lin•e•ar
non-'li•quid
non-'li•ter•al
non-'lit•erˌar•y
non-'lit•er•ate
ˌnon-li'tur•gi•cal
non-'liv•ing
non-'lo•cal
non-'log•i•cal
non-'lu•mi•nous
ˌnon-mag'net•ic
ˌnon-ma'lig•nant
non-'mal•le•a•ble
non-'ma•ri•tal
non-'mar•iˌtime
non-'mar•ket•a•ble
non-'mar•ry•ing
non-'mar•tial
ˌnon-ma'te•ri•al
ˌnon-maˌte•ri•al'is•tic
ˌnon-ma'ter•nal
ˌnon-math•e'mat•i•cal
ˌnon-me'chan•i•cal
non-'med•i•cal
ˌnon-me'dic•i•nal
ˌnon-me'lod•ic
ˌnon-me'lo•di•ous
non-'melt•ing
non-'mem•ber
non-'mem•ber•ship
ˌnon-met•ro'pol•i•tan
non-'mi•graˌto•ry
non-'mil•i•tant
non-'mil•iˌtar•y
non-'min•er•al
ˌnon-min•is'te•ri•al
non-'mo•bile
non-'mor•tal
non-'Mus•lim
non-'mo•tile
non-'moun•tain•ous
non-'mus•cu•lar
non-'mu•si•cal
non-'mys•ti•cal
non-'myth•i•cal
non-'na•tion•al
non-'na•tive
non-'nat•u•ral
non-'nau•ti•cal
non-'na•val
non-'na•vi•ga•ble
ˌnon-ne'ces•si•ty
ˌnon-ne'go•ti•a•ble
non-'neu•tral

no–no ['nou ,nou] *n. Informal.* an action, form of behaviour, etc. that is ill-advised or forbidden.

non•pa•reil [,nɒnpə'rɛl] *adj., n.* —*adj.* having no equal.
—*n.* **1** a person or thing having no equal. **2** a kind of apple. **3** *Printing.* a size of type; 6-point. This sentence is in nonpareil. ⟨< F *nonpareil* < *non-* not (< L) + *pareil* equal, ult. < L *par*⟩

non–par•ti•san [nɒn 'pɑrtəzən] *or* ['pɑrtə,zæn] *adj.* not partisan; not controlled by or supporting any single faction or political party.

non–pay•ment [nɒn 'peimənt] *n.* a failure to pay; condition of not being paid.

non–per•form•ance [,nɒn pər'fɔrməns] *n.* the fact of not performing; failure to perform: *non-performance of duty.*

non•per•son ['nɒn,pɜrsən] *n.* someone who is ignored, especially by a government or organization, or treated as if non-existent.

non•plus [nɒn'plʌs] *or* ['nɒnplʌs] *v.* **-plussed** or **-plused, -plus•sing** or **-plus•ing;** *n.* —*v.* puzzle completely; make unable to say or do anything: *We were nonplussed to see two roads leading off to the left where we had expected only one.*
—*n.* a state of being nonplussed. ⟨< L *non plus* no further⟩

non•pre•scrip•tion [,nɒnprɪ'skrɪpʃən] *adj.* of drugs, available over the counter, without a doctor's prescription: *nonprescription cough medicine.*

non–pro•duc•tive [,nɒn prə'dʌktɪv] *adj.* **1** failing to produce; unproductive. **2** not directly connected with production. —**,non-pro'duc•tive•ness,** *n.*

non–prof•it [nɒn 'prɒfɪt] *adj.* not conducted for the purpose of making a profit: *a non-profit organization.*

non–pros [,nɒn 'prɒs] *v.* **-prossed, -pros•sing.** *Law.* enter a judgment of NON PROSEQUITUR against.

non pro•se•qui•tur [,nɒn prou'sɛkwətər] *n. Law.* the judgment against a plaintiff who does not appear in court. ⟨< L: literally, he does not pursue⟩

non–re•new•able [,nɒn rɪ'njuəbəl] *or* [,nɒn rɪ'nuəbəl] *adj.* **1** not able to be made new again. **2** that cannot be replaced: *Oil is a non-renewable resource because once extracted from an oil well and used up, it is gone forever.*

non–rep•re•sen•ta•tion•al [,nɒn rɛprɪzɛn'teiʃənəl] *adj.* not intended to represent or resemble natural objects; abstract: *non-representational art.* —**,non-,rep•re•sen'ta•tion•al,ism,** *n.*

non–res•i•dent [nɒn 'rɛzədənt] *adj., n.* —*adj.* **1** not residing in a particular place. **2** not residing where official duties require one to reside.
—*n.* a non-resident person. —**non-'res•i•dence** or **non-'res•i•den•cy,** *n.*

non–re•sist•ance [,nɒn rɪ'zɪstəns] *n.* **1** the state or condition of being non-resistant. **2** the principles or practice of not resisting established authority, even when it is unjust or tyrannical.

non–re•sist•ant [,nɒn rɪ'zɪstənt] *adj., n.* —*adj.* **1** not resistant to the bad effects of something, such as an insecticide or a disease-producing organism. **2** not resisting; practising non-resistance.
—*n.* a person who practises non-resistance.

non–re•stric•tive [,nɒn rɪ'strɪktɪv] *adj.* **1** *Grammar.* adding descriptive detail. Modifiers which do not limit the meaning of a noun but add a descriptive detail are non-restrictive modifiers. **2** that does not restrict.

non–sched•uled [,nɒn 'skɛdʒʊld] *or* ['ʃɛdʒʊld] *adj.* not according to a set plan, program, or schedule: *a non-scheduled flight, a non-scheduled stop.*

non–sec•tar•i•an [,nɒn sɛk'tɛriən] *adj.* not connected with any religious denomination.

non•sense ['nɒnsɛns] *or* ['nɒnsəns] *n.* **1** words, ideas, or acts without meaning: *The magician talks nonsense as she is doing the tricks.* **2** foolish talk or doings; a plan or suggestion that is foolish: *It is nonsense to say that we can walk that far in an hour.* **3** impudent or silly behaviour or conduct: *She doesn't take any nonsense from her employees.* ⟨< *non-* + *sense*⟩

nonsense mutation *Genetics.* a single-based change in DNA resulting in a codon that terminates the chain.

In each of the words below **non-** *means* not *or, for nouns,* no *or* not a.

,non-nu'tri•tious
non-'nu•tri•tive
,non-o'be•di•ence
,non-ob'jec•tive
,non-ob'lig•a,to•ry
,non-ob'ser•vance
,non-oc•cu'pa•tion•al
,non-oc'cur•rence
non-'o•dor•ous
,non-of'fi•cial
non-'op•er,at•ing
,non-op•er'a•tion•al
non-'op•er•a•tive
,non-or'gan•ic
,non-or•i'en•tal
non-'or•tho,dox
non-'ox•y•gen,at•ed
,non-pa'cif•ic
non-'pal•a•tal
non-'pa•pal
non-'par•al,lel
,non-par•a'sit•ic
,non-pa'ren•tal
,non-pa'rish•ion•er
,non-par•lia'men•ta•ry
,non-pa'ro•chi•al
,non-par'ti•ci•pant
,non-par,tic•i'pa•tion
non-'pas•ser,ine
,non-pa'ter•nal
non-'pay•ing
non-'pay•ment
,non-per'cep•tu•al
non-'per•ish•a•ble
non-'per•ma•nent
non-'per•me•a•ble
,non-per'mis•si•ble
,non-per•pen'dic•u•lar
,non-per'sist•ence
,non-per'sist•ent
,non-phil•o'soph•i•cal
non-'phy•si•cal
non-'plau•si•ble
,non-po'et•ic
non-'poi•son•ous
,non-po'lit•i•cal
non-'po•rous
,non-pos'ses•sion
non-'prac•ti•cal
non-'pre•cious
non-'pred•a,to•ry
,non-pre'dict•a•ble
,non-pre•fer'en•tial
non-'preg•nant
,non-pre'hen•sile
,non-prej•u'di•cial
,non-pre'scrip•tive
,non-pre'serv•a•ble
,non-pres•er'va•tion
,non-pre'serv•a•tive
non-'pre•va•lent
,non-pro'duc•er
,non-pro'duc•ing
,non-pro'fes•sion•al
,non-pro•fes'so•ri•al
non-'prof•it•a•ble
,non-prof•i'teer•ing
,non-pro'gres•sive
,non-pro'hib•i•tive
,non-pro'lif•ic
,non-pro'phet•ic
,non-pro'por•tion•al
,non-pro'pri•e,ta•ry
,non-pro'tec•tive
non-'pro•tein
non-'Prot•es•tant
non-'prov•en
non-'pub•lic
non-'pun•ish•a•ble
non-'ra•cial
non-'ra•di,at•ing
non-'rad•i•cal
,non-ra•di•o'ac•tive
non-'ra•tion•al
,non-re'act•ive
non-'read•er
,non-re•al'is•tic
,non-re'al•i•ty
,non-re'cip•ro•cal
,non-rec•og'ni•tion
,non-re'cov•er•a•ble
,non-re'cur•rent
,non-re'cur•ring
,non-re'fill•a•ble
,non-re'flec•tive
,non-re'gen•er,at•ing
non-'reg•i,ment•ed
non-'reg•is•tered
non-'reg•is•tra•ble
non-'reign•ing
,non-re'li•gious
,non-re'mis•sion
,non-re'mov•a•ble
,non-re'mu•ner•a•tive
,non-re'new•a•ble
,non-re'pay•a•ble
,non-rep•re'sent•a•tive
,non-re•pro'duc•tive
,non-res•i'den•tial
,non-re'sid•u•al
non-'res•o•nant
,non-re'strict•ed
,non-re'ten•tive
,non-re'trace•a•ble
,non-re'trac•tile
,non-ret•ro'ac•tive
,non-re'turn•a•ble
,non-re'veal•ing
,non-re'vers•i•ble
,non-re'volv•ing
,non-rhe'to•ri•cal
non-'rhym•ing
non-'rhyth•mic
non-'rig•id
,non-rit•u•al'is•tic
non-'ri•val
non-'Ro•man
,non-ro'man•tic
,non-ro'tat•ing
non-'roy•al
non-'ru•ral
non-'Rus•sian
non-'sac•red
,non-sac•ri'fi•cial
non-'sal•a•ble
non-'sal•a•ried
non-'sal•u,tar•y
non-'sat•u,rat•ed
,non-Scan•di'na•vi•an
,non-scho'las•tic
,non-sci•en'tif•ic
non-'scor•ing
non-'sea•son•al
non-'sec•ret
non-'sec•tion•al
non-'sec•u•lar
non-'sed•en,tar•y
,non-se'di•tious
non-'seg•re,gat•ed
,non-se'lec•tive
,non-Se'mit•ic

non•sen•si•cal [nɒn'sɛnsɪkəl] *adj.* foolish; absurd. **—non'sen•si•cal•ly,** *adv.*

non–sep•a•ra•tist [nɒn 'sɛpərətɪst] *n.* in Québec, a person who is against the separating of that province from Confederation.

non seq. NON SEQUITUR.

non se•qui•tur [nɒn 'sɛkwətər] **1** a statement or reply that has no direct relationship with what has just been said. **2** *Logic.* an inference or conclusion that does not follow from the premises. *Example*: All cats have fur. Amelia has fur. Therefore, Amelia is a cat. ⟨< L *non sequitur* it does not follow⟩

non–skid ['nɒn 'skɪd] *adj.* made so as to prevent skidding: *non-skid tires.*

non–slip ['nɒn 'slɪp] *adj.* non-skid.

non–stand•ard ['nɒn 'stændərd] *adj.* **1** not conforming to regulations, accepted specifications, etc. **2** outside the generally accepted pattern; different from what is held to be normal.
☛ *Usage.* See note at STANDARD.

non–starter [nɒn 'stɑrtər] *n. Informal.* **1** something expected that does not happen. **2** a useless idea.

non–stop ['nɒn 'stɒp] *adj. or adv.* without stopping: *We took a non-stop flight from Toronto to Rome. We worked non-stop from noon till supper time.*

non•such ['nɒn,sʌtʃ] See NONESUCH.

non•suit [,nɒn'sut] *n., v. —n. Law.* **1** a judgment given against a person beginning a lawsuit who neglects to prosecute, or who fails to show a legal case, or who fails to bring sufficient evidence. **2** the termination of a suit by the plaintiff's voluntary withdrawal.
—v. stop by a nonsuit.

non–sup•port [,nɒn sə'pɔrt] *n.* failure to support, especially the failure to provide for someone for whom one is legally responsible.

non–trea•ty ['nɒn 'triti] *adj. Cdn.* of First Nations people, not under the terms of a treaty with the Canadian government but living, usually, on a reserve.

non trop•po [,noun 'troupou] *Music.* not too much. ⟨< Ital.⟩

non–un•ion [nɒn 'junjən] *adj.* **1** not belonging to a trade union. **2** made by other than union labour. **3** not recognizing or favouring trade unions.

non–un•ion•ism [nɒn 'junjə,nɪzəm] *n.* the theories or practices of those opposed to trade unions.

non–un•ion•ist [nɒn 'junjənɪst] *n.* **1** a person who is opposed to trade unions. **2** a person who does not belong to a trade union.

non–vi•o•lence [nɒn 'vaɪələns] *n.* **1** the absence of violence. **2** passive non-co-operation with authority, as opposed to violence, used as a means of gaining political ends.

non–vi•o•lent [nɒn 'vaɪələnt] *adj.* **1** free from violence: *a non-violent demonstration.* **2** supporting or practising non-violence. **—non-'vi•o•lent•ly,** *adv.*

non–vot•er [nɒn 'voutər] *n.* a person who does not vote or does not have the right to vote.

non–white [nɒn 'wəit] *n., adj. —n.* a person who does not belong to the European, or white, race.
—adj. of, having to do with, or designating non-whites.

noo•dle ['nudəl] *n.* **1** *Informal.* a very stupid person; fool. **2** *Slang.* the head. ⟨origin uncertain⟩

noo•dles ['nudəlz] *n.pl.* **1** a food made of flour and water, or flour and eggs, a kind of pasta resembling macaroni, but made in flat strips. **2 noodle, a** a single strip of this pasta. **b** (*adjl.*) made of or with noodles: *noodle soup.* ⟨< G *Nudel*⟩

nook [nʊk] *n.* **1** a cosy little corner. **2** a hidden spot; sheltered place. ⟨ME *noke*⟩

noon [nun] *n.* **1** twelve o'clock in the daytime; the middle of the day. **2** (*adjl.*) of noon. ⟨OE *nōn* < L *nona (hora)* ninth (hour), 3 p.m.; the meaning shifted with a change in time of church service. Doublet of NONE[2] (see NONES[2]).⟩

noon•day ['nun,dei] *n.* **1** noon; midday. **2** (*adjl.*) of noon: *the noonday meal.*

no one or **no–one** ['nou ,wʌn] no person; nobody.
☛ *Usage.* See note at NONE.

noon hour **1** noon; the time around noon. **2** lunch hour: *I'll see you at noon hour.*

noon–hour ['nun ,aʊr] *adj.* taking place at lunchtime: *There will be a noon-hour concert tomorrow.*

noon•tide ['nun,taɪd] *n.* **1** noon. **2** the highest point or best part: *the noontide of her career.*

noon•time ['nun,taɪm] *n.* noon.

noose [nus] *n., v.* **noosed, noos•ing.** *—n.* **1** a loop with a slip-knot that tightens as the string or rope is pulled. Nooses are used especially in lassos and snares. **2** anything that restricts or snares like a noose. **3 the noose,** death by hanging.
—v. **1** catch in a noose or as if in a noose; snare. **2** make a noose with or in. ⟨probably < OF *nos* < Provençal *nous* < L *nodus* knot⟩
☛ *Hom.* NOUS.

Noot•ka ['nʊtkə] *or* ['nutkə] *n.* **Noot•ka** or **-kas;** *adj. —n.* **1** a member of a First Nations people living mainly on Vancouver Island. **2** the Wakashan language of the Nootka.
—adj. of or having to do with the Nootka or their language.
☛ *Usage.* The Nootka prefer to call themselves Nuu Chah-nulth.

Nootka cypress *Cdn.* YELLOW CYPRESS. ⟨< *Nootka* Sound, Vancouver Island, B.C.⟩

In each of the words below **non-** *means* not *or, for nouns,* no *or* not a.

non-'sen•si•tive
non-'sen•so•ry
non-'se•ri•ous
non-'sex•u•al
,non-Shake'spear•i•an
non-'shar•ing
non-'shrink•a•ble
,non-sig'nif•i•cant
non-'sink•a•ble
non-'skilled
non-'Sla•vic
non-'smok•er
non-'smok•ing
non-'so•cial
non-'so•cial•ist
non-'sol•id
non-'sol•u•ble
non-'Span•ish
non-'spar•ing
non-'speak•ing
non-'spe•cial•ist
non-'spe•cial•ized
,non-spe'cif•ic
non-'spec•u•la•tive
non-'spher•i•cal
non-'spir•it•u•al
non-'sport•ing
non-'spot•ted
non-'stain•a•ble
non-'stain•ing
non-'stand•ard,ized
non-'start•ing
non-'stat•ic
non-'sta•tion,ar•y
,non-sta'tis•ti•cal
non-'stat•u,to•ry
,non-stra'te•gic
non-'stretch•a•ble
non-'strik•er
non-'strik•ing
non-'struc•tur•al
non-'stu•dent
,non-sub'mis•sive
,non-sub'scrib•er
,non-suc'cess•ful
,non-suc'ces•sive
,non-sup'por•ter
,non-sup'port•ing
non-'sur•gi•cal
,non-sus'tain•ing
non-'swim•mer
,non-sym'bol•ic
,non-sym'met•ri•cal
non-'sym•pa,thiz•er
,non-sym'phon•ic
,non-symp•to'mat•ic
,non-syn'tact•ic
,non-sys•tem'at•ic
non-'tax•a•ble
non-'teach•a•ble
non-'tech•ni•cal
non-'tem•po•ral
,non-ter'res•tri•al
,non-ter•ri'to•ri•al
,non-the'at•ri•cal
,non-the'ist•ic
,non-the•o'log•i•cal
,non-ther•a'peut•ic
non-'think•ing
non-'tox•ic
,non-tra'di•tion•al
non-'trag•ic
,non-trans'fer•a•ble
,non-tran'si•tion•al
,non-trans'par•ent
non-'trea•son•a•ble
non-'trop•i•cal
non-'typ•i•cal
,non-ty'ran•ni•cal
non-'ul•cer•ous
,non-un•der'stand•a•ble
non-'u•ni,form
,non-u•ni'ver•sal
non-'ur•ban
non-'us•a•ble
non-'us•age
,non-u,til•i'ta•ri•an
non-'use
non-'us•er
non-'vas•cu•lar
,non-ve'ne•re•al
non-'ven•om•ous
non-'ve•nous
non-'ver•bal
,non-ver•i'fi•a•ble
,non-ver'na•cu•lar
non-'ver•ti•cal
non-'vet•er•an
non-'vi•a•ble
,non-'vi•bra,to•ry
,non-vi'car•i•ous
,non-vi•o'la•tion
non-'vis•u•al
non-'vo•cal
,non-vo'cal•ic
,non-vo'ca•tion•al
non-'vol•a,tile
,non-vol'can•ic
non-'vol•un,tar•y
non-'vot•ing
non-'wood•y
non-'work•er
non-'work•ing
non-'wo•ven
non-'yield•ing

no•pal ['noupəl] *n.* a cactus of the genus *Nopalea.* ⟨< Sp. < Nahuatl *nopálli*⟩

no–par ['nou ˌpɑr] *adj.* having no PAR VALUE: *no-par stock.*

nope [noup] *adv. Informal.* no.

nor [nɔr]; *unstressed,* [nər] *conj.* and not; or not; neither; and not either. *Nor* is used: **1** with a preceding *neither* or negative: *Not a boy nor a girl stirred. She is neither friend nor foe.* **2** *Poetic.* with preceding *neither* or *not* left out: *"Great brother, thou nor I have made the world."* **3** *Poetic.* instead of *neither* as correlative to a following *nor: "Drake nor Devil nor Spaniard feared."* ⟨OE (unstressed) *nā(hwæ)ther* < *ne* not + *ā(hwæ)ther* either⟩

Nor. **1** Norway; Norwegian. **2** Norman. **3** North.

NORAD ['nɔræd] North American Air Defence (Command).

nor•ad•ren•a•lin [ˌnɔrə'drɛnəlɪn] *n.* norepinephrine.

Nor•dic ['nɔrdɪk] *adj., n. —adj.* **1** of, having to do with, or designating the Germanic peoples of northern Europe, especially of Scandinavia. **2** of, having to do with, or designating a type of people characterized by tall stature, blond hair, blue eyes, and long heads. **3** of or designating cross-country as opposed to downhill skiing.
—n. a person who is Nordic. ⟨< F *nordique* < *nord* north < Gmc.⟩

nor•ep•in•eph•rine [ˌnɔrɛpɪ'nɛfrɪn] *or* [ˌnɔrɛpɪ'nɛfrin] *n.* a hormone and neurotransmitter. *Formula:* $C_8H_{11}NO_3$

Nor•folk jacket ['nɔrfək] a loose-fitting, belted jacket having pleats at the front and back. ⟨after *Norfolk,* a county in England⟩

norm [nɔrm] *n.* the standard for a certain group; type; model; pattern: *In mathematics this class is above the norm for the senior year.* ⟨< L *norma* a rule, pattern⟩

Nor•ma ['nɔrmə] *n. Astronomy.* a constellation in the southern hemisphere, between Circinus and Scorpius.

nor•mal ['nɔrməl] *adj., n. —adj.* **1** of the usual standard or type; regular; usual: *The normal temperature of the human body is 37°C. It's normal for children to be energetic.* **2** *Geometry.* being at right angles; perpendicular. **3** *Chemistry.* **a** of an acidic or basic solution, containing the equivalent of one gram of hydrogen ion per litre. **b** of or denoting an aliphatic hydrocarbon or hydrocarbon derivative. **c** not found in association, as molecules. **4** *Medicine, psychology.* of average intelligence, mental or physical health, etc.; not diseased, defective, or disturbed.
—n. **1** the usual state or level: *two kilograms above normal.* **2** *Geometry.* a line or plane that is at right angles to another. ⟨< L *normalis* < *norma* a rule, pattern⟩ **—nor'mal•i•ty** [nɔr'mæləti], *n.*

nor•mal•cy ['nɔrməlsi] *n.* a normal condition.

nor•mal•ize ['nɔrməˌlaɪz] *v.* **-ized, -iz•ing.** make normal. **—ˌnor•mal•i'za•tion,** *n.* **—'nor•mal,iz•er,** *n.*

nor•mal•ly ['nɔrməli] *adv.* **1** in the normal way; regularly. **2** if things are normal.

normal school formerly, a school where people were trained to be elementary school teachers. ⟨after F *école normale*⟩

Nor•man ['nɔrmən] *n., adj. —n.* **1** a native or inhabitant of Normandy in France. **2** a member of the Scandinavian people who conquered Normandy in the 10th century A.D. **3** a member of the Norman-French people who conquered England in 1066. **4** NORMAN FRENCH.
—adj. of or having to do with the Normans or Normandy: *The rounded arch is characteristic of Norman architecture.* ⟨< OF *Normans,* pl. of *Normant* < Gmc.⟩

Norman Conquest the conquest of England by the Normans in 1066, under the leadership of William the Conqueror.

Norman French **1** the dialect of French spoken by the medieval Normans, especially as spoken by the Norman conquerors of England. **2** a form of this dialect used as the language of law in England until the late 17th century. **3** the dialect of the modern-day inhabitants of Normandy. **—'Nor•man-'French,** *adj.*

nor•ma•tive ['nɔrmətɪv] *adj.* of, following, or establishing a norm or standard: *normative grammar, a normative statement.* **—'nor•ma•tive•ly,** *adv.*

Norn [nɔrn] *n. Norse mythology.* one of the three goddesses of fate, who ruled over gods and men.

Norse [nɔrs] *n., adj. —n.* **1 the Norse,** *pl.* **a** the people of ancient Scandinavia; Norsemen. **b** the people of Norway. **2** the language of the ancient Scandinavians, often called Old Norse.
—adj. **1** of or having to do with ancient Scandinavia, its people, or their language. **2** of or having to do with Norway or its people. ⟨< Du. *Noorsch* Norwegian⟩

Norse•man ['nɔrsmən] *n.* **-men.** a member of a people that lived in ancient Scandinavia. The Vikings were Norsemen.

nor•te•ño [nɔr'teinjou] *n., adj. —n.* **1** a North American living north of Mexico. **2** a resident of the northern part of Mexico, near the border with the U.S. **3** a style of music popular among northern Mexicans, characterized by an accordion played in traditional simple rhythms.
—adj. of or having to do with people living north of Mexico.

north [nɔrθ] *n., adj., adv. —n.* **1** the direction to which a compass needle points; direction to the right as one faces the setting sun. **2** Also, **North,** the part of any country toward the north. **3 the North,** in Canada, the northern parts of the provinces from Québec westward and the territory lying north of these provinces.
—adj. **1** toward the north: *We have a north view from our bedroom.* **2** from the north: *a north wind.* **3** in the north; northern: *north China.*
north of, farther north than.
—adv. toward the north: *They drove north.* ⟨OE⟩

North American **1** a native or inhabitant of North America. **2** of or having to do with North America or its people.

north•bound ['nɔrθˌbaʊnd] *adj.* going toward the north.

North canoe *Cdn.* formerly, a canoe used by the fur brigades on the rivers of the north and northwest. It was about 7.5 m long and carried three or four passengers and about a tonne of cargo.

North Carolina [ˌkærə'laɪnə] *or* [ˌkɛrə'laɪnə] a southeastern state of the U.S.

North Country **1** the northern parts of North America. **2** northern England.

North Dakota [də'koutə] a northern state of the U.S.

north•east [ˌnɔrθ'ist] *adj., n., adv. —adj.* **1** halfway between north and east. **2** lying toward or situated in the northeast. **3** of, at, in, toward, or from the northeast: *a northeast wind.* **4** directed toward the northeast.
—n. **1** a northeast direction. **2** a place that is in the northeast part or direction.
—adv. **1** toward the northeast. **2** from the northeast. **3** in the northeast.

north•east•er [ˌnɔrθ'istər] *n.* a wind or storm from the northeast.

north•east•er•ly [ˌnɔrθ'istərli] *adj. or adv.* **1** toward the northeast. **2** from the northeast.

north•east•ern [ˌnɔrθ'istərn] *adj.* of, at, in, to, toward, or from the northeast.

north•east•ward [ˌnɔrθ'istwərd] *adv., adj., n. —adv. or adj.* **1** toward the northeast. **2** northeast. Also (adv.), **northeastwards.**
—n. the northeast.

north•east•ward•ly [ˌnɔrθ'istwərdli] *adj., adv.*
—adj. **1** toward the northeast. **2** of winds, from the northeast.
—adv. toward the northeast.

north•east•wards [ˌnɔrθ'istwərdz] *adv.* See NORTHEASTWARD.

north•er ['nɔrðər] *n.* a wind or storm from the north.

north•er•ly ['nɔrðərli] *adj., adv., n., pl.* **-lies.** *—adj.* **1** toward the north. **2** from the north: *a northerly wind.* **3** of the north.
—adv. **1** toward the north. **2** from the north.
—n. a storm or a wind from the north.

north•ern ['nɔrðərn] *adj.* **1** toward the north. **2** from the north: *a northern breeze.* **3** of or in the north: *He has travelled in northern countries.* **4** of or in the Canadian North: *Churchill is a northern port.* ⟨OE *northerne*⟩

Northern Cross *Astronomy.* a constellation in the northern hemisphere, comprising six stars in the constellation Cygnus, in the form of a cross.

Northern Crown *Astronomy.* the northern constellation Corona Borealis.

north•ern•er ['nɔrðərnər] *n.* **1** a native or inhabitant of the north. **2 Northerner,** *Cdn.* a native or inhabitant of the Far North.

Northern Hemisphere that half of the earth north of the equator.

northern lights the streamers and bands of light that appear in the northern sky at night; AURORA BOREALIS.

north•ern•most ['nɔrðərn,moust] *adj.* farthest north.

northern pike a common game fish (*Esox lucius*) of the pike family having a long, slender body and large head, found throughout most of Canada.

northern service officer *Cdn.* a federal government officer in charge of a district in the Far North.

Northern Spy a type of apple that is especially good for making pies.

North Germanic a subdivision of the Germanic languages that comprises Danish, Norwegian, Swedish, and Icelandic, along with their related dialects.

north•ing ['nɔrθɪŋ] *or* ['nɔrðɪŋ] *n.* **1** the distance measured in a northerly direction. **2** progress to the north.

north•land ['nɔrθ,lænd] *or* ['nɔrθlənd] *n.* **1** Usually, **Northland,** *Cdn.* the northern regions of Canada; the Far North. **2** a northern region or country. ⟨OE⟩ **—'north,land•er,** *n.*

North•man ['nɔrθmən] *n., pl.* **-men. 1** Norseman. **2** a native or inhabitant of northern Europe, especially Norway.

north–northeast ['nɔrθ ,nɔrθ'ist] *n., adj., adv.* —*n.* a compass direction halfway between north and northeast.
—*adj.* or *adv.* in, to, or from this direction.

north–northwest ['nɔrθ ,nɔrθ'wɛst] *n., adj., adv.* —*n.* a compass direction halfway between north and northwest.
—*adj.* or *adv.* in, to, or from this direction.

North Pole the northern end of the earth's axis. See EQUATOR for picture.

North Star the bright star almost directly above the North Pole.

North•um•bri•an [nɔr'θʌmbriən] *n., adj.* —*n.* **1** a native or inhabitant of Northumbria, an ancient kingdom in N England. **2** a dialect of Old English spoken in Northumbria. **3** a native or inhabitant of Northumberland. **4** the Northumberland dialect.
—*adj.* **1** of or having to do with Northumbria, its people, or their dialect. **2** of or having to do with Northumberland, its people, or their dialect.

north•ward ['nɔrθwərd] *adv., adj., n.* —*adv.* toward the north; north: *Rocks lay northward of the ship's course.* Also, **northwards.**
—*adj.* toward the north; north: *the northward slope of a hill.*
—*n.* a northward part, direction, or point.

north•ward•ly ['nɔrθwərdli] *adj., adv.* —*adj.* **1** toward the north. **2** of winds, from the north.
—*adv.* toward the north.

north•wards ['nɔrθwərdz] *adv.* See NORTHWARD.

north•west [,nɔrθ'wɛst] *adj., n., adv.* —*adj.* **1** halfway between north and west. **2** lying toward or situated in the northwest. **3** of, at, in, to, toward, or from the northwest: *a northwest wind.* **4** directed toward the northwest.
—*n.* **1** a northwest direction. **2** a place that is in the northwest part or direction. **3 Northwest,** *Cdn.* the general region of Canada north and west of the Great Lakes.
—*adv.* **1** toward the northwest. **2** from the northwest. **3** in the northwest.

North West Company a loosely organized group of companies and individuals formed in Montréal during the late 18th century to promote the fur trade in Canada. It was absorbed by the Hudson's Bay Company in 1821.

north•west•er [,nɔrθ'wɛstər] *n.* **1** a wind or storm from the northwest. **2 Northwester,** *Cdn.* formerly, a wintering partner or employee of the North West Company. Also, **Nor'Wester.**

north•west•er•ly [,nɔrθ'wɛstərli] *adj. or adv.* **1** toward the northwest. **2** of winds, from the northwest.

north•west•ern [,nɔrθ'wɛstərn] *adj.* of, at, in, to, toward, or from the northwest.

North West Mounted Police *Cdn.* a former name of the Royal Canadian Mounted Police. *Abbrev.:* NWMP or N.W.M.P.

Northwest Passage *Cdn.* a route for ships from the Atlantic to the Pacific along the northern coast of North America.

Northwest Rebellion *Cdn.* an armed uprising of Métis and First Nations peoples in Saskatchewan in 1885, springing from grievances similar to those that led to the Red River Rebellion.

Northwest Territories *Cdn.* a large area of land lying to the northeast of Canada, having a territorial government.

north•west•ward [,nɔrθ'wɛstwərd] *adj., adv., n.* —*adj. or adv.* northwest; toward the northwest. Also (adv.), **northwestwards.**
—*n.* the northwest.

north•west•ward•ly [,nɔrθ'wɛstwərdli] *adj., adv.* —*adj.* **1** toward the northwest. **2** of winds, from the northwest.
—*adv.* toward the northwest.

north•west•wards [,nɔrθ'wɛstwərdz] *adv.* See NORTHWESTWARD.

Nor•way ['nɔrwei] *n.* a kingdom in N Europe, on the Scandinavian peninsula.

Norway maple a tall tree (*Acer platanoides*) first cultivated in Norway and widely grown.

Nor•way pine RED PINE.

Norway spruce an evergreen tree (*Picea abies*) of northern regions.

Nor•we•gian [nɔr'widʒən] *n., adj.* —*n.* **1** a native or inhabitant of Norway. **2** the language of the Norwegians.
—*adj.* of or having to do with Norway, its people, or their language.

Norwegian elkhound a breed of medium-sized hunting dog having a thick, grey coat, pointed ears, and a curled tail. Also called **elkhound.**

nor'west•er [nɔr'wɛstər] *n.* **1** a heavy, waterproof oilskin coat worn by sailors. **2 Nor'Wester,** *Cdn.* Northwester.

Nos. or **nos.** numbers.

nose [nouz] *n., v.* **nosed, nos•ing.** —*n.* **1** the part of the face or head just above the mouth, serving as the opening for breathing and as the organ of smell. **2** a similar organ in other animals; muzzle; snout. **3** the sense of smell: *a dog with a good nose.* **4** a faculty for perceiving or detecting: *A reporter must have a nose for news.* **5** a part that stands out. The bow of a ship or airplane is often called the nose.
count noses, find out how many people are present.
follow (one's) **nose, a** go straight ahead. **b** be guided by one's instinct. **c** be guided by one's sense of smell.
lead by the nose, *Informal.* have complete control over.
look down (one's) **nose at,** *Informal.* feel contempt for.
on the nose, a exactly. **b** solidly. **c** of a bet on a horse, that it will win.
pay through the nose, *Informal.* pay a great deal too much.
poke (one's) **nose into,** pry into; meddle in.
put (someone's) **nose out of joint,** *Informal.* **a** take someone's place in another's favour. **b** destroy someone's hopes, plans, etc.
thumb (one's) **nose,** put one's thumb to one's nose in scorn.
turn up (one's) **nose at,** *Informal.* treat with contempt or scorn.
under (one's) **nose,** in plain sight; very easy to notice.
—*v.* **1** discover by smelling; smell out. **2** smell; sniff. **3** rub with the nose. **4** push with the nose or forward end. **5** make (one's way) front end first: *The little boat nosed carefully between the rocks.* **6** search (*for*); pry (*into*).
nose out, find out by looking around quietly or secretly. ⟨OE *nosu*⟩ **—'nose•less,** *adj.* **—'nose,like,** *adj.*

nose bag a bag containing food, to be hung over a horse's head; feedbag.

nose•band ['nouz,bænd] *n.* the part of a bridle that goes over the animal's nose.

nose•bleed ['nouz,blid] *n.* a bleeding from the nose.

nose cone a protective, cone-shaped cap at the forward end of a spacecraft, designed to streamline the craft and to provide protection against the intense heat encountered especially on re-entry into the earth's atmosphere.

nose–dive ['nouz ,daɪv] *n., v.* **-dived, -div•ing.** —*n.* **1** a swift plunge straight downward by an aircraft. **2** a sudden, sharp drop.
—*v.* **1** of an aircraft, plunge swiftly downward. **2** take a sharp, sudden drop: *The price of gasoline nose-dived overnight.*

no–see–em or **no–see–um** [nou 'si əm] *n. Cdn.* any of various tiny, two-winged insects (genus *Culicoides*) that have a nasty bite.

nose•gay ['nouz,gei] *n.* a bunch of flowers; a small bouquet. ⟨< *nose* + *gay,* obs. n., something gay or pretty⟩

nose•guard ['nouz,gɑrd] *n.* a part on a helmet, such as a football helmet, that covers and protects the nose.

nose guard *Football.* a player on a team's line of defence who tackles the centre on the line of the opposing team. Also, **nose tackle.**

nose job cosmetic surgery, usually to reduce the size of the nose; rhinoplasty.

nose•piece ['nouz,pis] *n.* **1** the part of a helmet that covers and protects the nose. **2** a noseband for an animal. **3** the bridge of a pair of eyeglasses.

nose ring a ring, usually metal, in the nose of an animal such as a bull, for leading it.

nos•ey ['nouzi] *adj.* **nos•i•er, nos•i•est.** *Informal.* too curious about other people's business; prying; inquisitive. Also, **nosy.** **—'no•si•ly,** *adv.* **—'no•si•ness,** *n.*

Nosey Park•er ['pɑrkər] *Informal.* a person showing a persistent and offensive curiosity about things which do not concern him or her.

nosh [nɒʃ] *n., v. Slang. —n.* a snack or tidbit.
—v. eat or chew: *noshing on a cookie.* ⟨< Yiddish *nash n.* a snack and *nashn v.* to nibble. Cf. G *naschen* to nibble⟩

no–show ['nou 'ʃou] *n. Informal.* **1** a passenger on an airline who fails to claim his or her seat. **2** anyone who fails to show up for a reservation, appointment, etc.

noso– *combining form.* disease: *nosology.* ⟨< Gk. *nósos* disease, sickness, malady⟩

no•sog•ra•phy [nə'sɒgrəfi] *n.* the description of diseases in a systematic way. **—no'sog•ra•pher,** *n.* **—,no•so'graph•ic** [,nɒsə'græfɪk], *adj.* **—,no•so'graph•i•cal•ly,** *adv.*

no•so•lo•gy [nə'sɒlədʒi] *n.* the classification of diseases. **—,nos•o'log•i•cal** [,nɒsə'lɒdʒɪkəl], *adj.* **—,nos•o'log•i•cal•ly,** *adv.* **—no'sol•o•gist,** *n.*

nos•tal•gia [nə'stældʒə] *or* [nə'stældʒiə] *n.* **1** homesickness. **2** a yearning for something in the past; sentimental longing for the return of a past period or of some former condition or circumstance: *She thought with nostalgia of how they used to go hiking in the hills.* ⟨< NL < Gk. *nostos* homecoming + *algos* pain⟩

nos•tal•gic [nə'stældʒɪk] *adj.* of, having to do with, producing, or characterized by nostalgia: *A nostalgic film about the sixties.* **—nos'tal•gi•cal•ly,** *adv.*

nos•toc ['nɒstɒk] *n.* algae of the genus *Nostoc,* found in fresh water. ⟨< NL; coined by Paracelsus, 16c. Swiss physician⟩

nos•tril ['nɒstrəl] *n.* either of the two external openings in the nose. Air is breathed into the lungs through the nostrils. ⟨OE *nosthyrl* < *nosu* nose + *thyrel* hole⟩

nos•trum ['nɒstrəm] *n.* **1** a medicine of secret ingredients prepared and recommended by the same person, usually without scientific evidence of its effectiveness. **2** a pet scheme for producing wonderful results; cure-all. ⟨< L *nostrum* ours; because usually prepared by the person recommending it⟩

nos•y ['nouzi] *adj.* **nos•i•er, nos•i•est.** See NOSEY.

not [nɒt] *adv.* a word used to make a negative statement or to express denial, refusal, etc.: *That is not true.* ⟨unstressed var. of *nought*⟩
☛ *Hom.* KNOT[1], NAUGHT, NOUGHT.

no•ta be•ne ['noutə 'bɛni] *or* ['bene] *Latin.* note well; observe what follows; take notice. *Abbrev.:* N.B. or n.b.

no•ta•bi•lia [,noutə'bɪliə] *n.pl.* matters worthy of notice. ⟨< L⟩

no•ta•bil•i•ty [,noutə'bɪləti] *n., pl.* **-ties. 1** the quality of being notable; distinction. **2** a prominent person: *There were several notabilities at the reception.*

no•ta•ble ['noutəbəl] *adj., n. —adj.* **1** worthy of notice; striking; remarkable; important: *a notable event, a notable book, a notable painter.* **2** that can be noted or perceived; perceptible; appreciable: *a notable quantity.*
—n. an important or famous person: *Many notables attended the Governor General's levee.* ⟨ME < OF < L *notabilis* < *notare* note < *nota* a mark⟩ **—'no•ta•ble•ness,** *n.* **—'no•ta•bly,** *adv.*

no•tar•i•al [nou'tɛriəl] *adj.* **1** of or having to do with a notary public. **2** made or done by a notary public. **—no'ta•ri•al•ly,** *adv.*

no•ta•rize ['noutə,raɪz] *v.* **-rized, -riz•ing.** certify (a contract, deed, will, etc.) as a notary public or other legal official.

no•ta•ry ['noutəri] *n., pl.* **-ries. 1** NOTARY PUBLIC. **2** *Cdn.* in Québec, a lawyer who has the same training as a barrister but who is not permitted to plead in court. ⟨< L *notarius* clerk, ult. < *nota* note⟩

notary public *pl.* **notaries public.** a person authorized to certify deeds and contracts, take oaths, and attend to certain other legal matters. *Abbrev.:* N.P.

no•ta•tion [nou'teiʃən] *n.* **1** a set of signs or symbols used to represent numbers, quantities, or other values. In arithmetic we use the Arabic notation (1, 2, 3, 4, etc.). **2** the representing of numbers, quantities, words, or other values by symbols or signs. Music and chemistry have special systems of notation. Shorthand is a system of notation. **3** a note to assist memory; record; jotting. **4** the act of noting. ⟨< L *notatio, -onis* < *notare* to note < *nota* a mark⟩ **—no'ta•tion•al,** *adj.*

notch [nɒtʃ] *n., v. —n.* **1** a V-shaped nick or cut made in an edge or on a surface: *The marooned survivors cut notches on a stick to keep count of the days.* **2** a deep, narrow pass or gap between mountains. **3** *Newfoundland.* an entrance to a harbour. **4** a grade; step; degree.
—v. **1** make a notch or notches in. **2** record by notches; score; tally. ⟨< MF *oche* < OF *oschier* notch; *an och* taken as *a noch*⟩

Musical notes (def. 7)

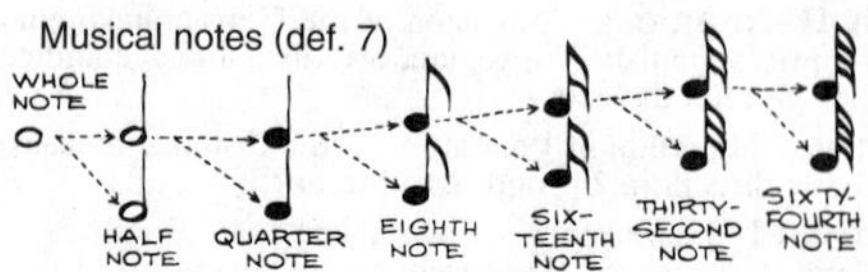

note [nout] *n., v.* **not•ed, not•ing.** *—n.* **1** a short sentence, phrase, or single word written down to remind one of something; memorandum: *Her notes helped her remember what the speaker said.* **2** a written observation. **3** a comment or piece of information in a book, often added to help students. **4** a brief letter. **5** a formal letter from one government to another; diplomatic or official communication in writing: *England sent a note of protest to France.* **6** a single sound of definite pitch made by a musical instrument or voice. **7** *Music.* **a** a written sign to show the pitch and length of a sound. **b** any one of the keys of a keyboard instrument: *to strike the wrong note.* **8** a bird's song or call. **9** a song; melody; tune. **10** a tone of voice or way of expression: *There was a note of anxiety in her voice.* **11** a sign, token, or proof of genuineness; characteristic or distinguishing feature. **12** distinction, importance, or consequence: *a woman of note.* **13** *Business.* a written promise to pay a certain sum of money at a certain time. **14** a certificate of a government or bank that may be used as money.
compare notes, exchange ideas or opinions.
make a note of, write down as something to be remembered.
of note, a that is important, great, or notable: *a writer of note.* **b** of being noticed: *worthy of note.*
strike the right note, say or do something suitable.
take note of, give attention to or notice: *Take note of the time, please; we must not be late.*
take notes, write down things to be remembered.
—v. **1** write down as a thing to be remembered. **2** observe carefully; give attention to; take notice of: *Now note what I do next.* **3** mention specially. **4** indicate, signify, or denote. ⟨ME < OF < L *nota* mark⟩ **—'note•less,** *adj.* **—'not•er,** *n.*

note•book ['nout,bʊk] *n.* **1** a book in which to write notes of things to be learned or remembered. **2** *Computer technology.* a small laptop computer.

not•ed ['noutɪd] *adj., v. —adj.* conspicuous or well-known; celebrated; famous: *Hercules was noted for his strength. Shakespeare is a noted English author.*
—v. pt. and pp. of NOTE.
☛ *Syn.* See note at FAMOUS.

note•pad ['nout,pæd] a pad of paper for taking notes.

note•paper ['nout,peipər] *n.* paper used for writing letters.

note•wor•thy ['nout,wɜrði] *adj.* worthy of notice; remarkable: *noteworthy achievement.* **—'note,wor•thi•ness,** *n.*

noth•ing ['nʌθɪŋ] *n., adv. —n.* **1** not anything; no thing: *Nothing arrived by mail.* **2** something that does not exist: *create a world out of nothing.* **3** a thing of no importance or value; person of no importance: *People regard him as a nothing.* **4** zero; nought.
make nothing of, a be unable to understand. **b** fail to use or do. **c** treat as unimportant or worthless.
nothing less than, just the same as.
think nothing of, a consider as easy to do. **b** treat as unimportant or worthless. **c** do without scruple: *He thinks nothing of taking pencils home from the office.*
—adv. not at all: *She is nothing like her sister in looks.* ⟨< *no* + *thing*⟩
☛ *Usage.* See note at NOBODY.

noth•ing•ness ['nʌθɪŋnɪs] *n.* **1** the fact of being nothing; non-existence. **2** being of no value; worthlessness. **3** an unimportant or worthless thing. **4** unconsciousness.

no•tice ['noutɪs] *n., v.* **-ticed, -tic•ing.** *—n.* **1** observation;

attention: *escape one's notice.* **2** advance information; warning: *The whistle blew to give notice that the boat was about to leave.* **3** a written or printed sign; paper posted in a public place. **4** a warning or announcement that one will end an agreement with another at a certain time: *The servant gave notice.* **5** a paragraph or article about something: *The new book got a favourable notice.*
serve notice, give warning; inform; announce.
take notice, give attention; observe; see.
–v. **1** take notice of; give attention to; perceive: *I noticed a big difference at once.* **2** mention; refer to. ⟨< F < L *notitia* < *notus* known⟩

no•tice•a•ble ['noutɪsəbəl] *adj.* **1** easily seen or noticed: *The class has made noticeable improvement.* **2** *Archaic.* worth noticing; noteworthy. **–'no•tice•a•bly,** *adv.*

no•ti•fi•ca•tion [,noutəfə'keiʃən] *n.* **1** a notifying. **2** a notice: *Have you received a notification of the meeting?*

no•ti•fy ['noutə,faɪ] *v.* **-fied, -fy•ing.** give notice to; let know; inform; announce to: *Our teacher notified us that there would be a test on Monday.* ⟨ME < OF < L *notificare* < *notus* known + *facere* make⟩ **–'no•ti,fi•er,** *n.* **–'no•ti,fi•a•ble,** *adj.*
☛ *Syn.* See note at INFORM.

no•tion ['nouʃən] *n.* **1** an idea; understanding: *He has no notion of what I mean.* **2** an opinion; view; belief: *It is a common notion that red hair means a quick temper.* **3** intention: *He has no notion of risking his money.* **4** an inclination; whim: *She had a notion to visit her grandmother.* **5 notions,** *pl.* small, useful articles, such as pins, needles, thread, tape, etc. ⟨< L *notio, -onis,* ult. < *noscere* know⟩ **–'no•tion•less,** *adj.*
☛ *Syn.* **1.** See note at IDEA.

no•tion•al ['nouʃənəl] *adj.* **1** having to do with ideas or opinions. **2** in one's imagination or thought only; not real. **–,no•tion'al•i•ty** [,nouʃə'næləti], *n.* **–'no•tion•al•ly,** *adv.*

noto– *combining form.* the back: *notochord.* ⟨< Gk. *nóton* the back⟩

no•to•chord ['noutə,kɔrd] *n. Biology.* **1** a rodlike structure that is the primitive cartilaginous backbone of the lowest vertebrates. **2** a similar structure in the embryos of higher vertebrates. ⟨< Gk. *nōton* back + E *chord*[2]⟩
–,no•to'chord•al, *adj.*

No•to•gaea [,noutə'dʒiə] *n.* the biogeographical area including Australia, New Zealand, and the SW Pacific Islands. ⟨< Gk. *noto(s)* the south + *gaia* earth⟩

no•to•ri•e•ty [,noutə'raɪəti] *n., pl.* **-ties. 1** a being famous for something bad; ill fame: *A crime or scandal brings much notoriety to those involved in it.* **2** the state of being widely known. **3** a well-known person.

no•to•ri•ous [nou'tɔriəs] *adj.* **1** widely known because of some unfavourable or bad quality, action, etc.: *a notorious criminal, a notorious gossip. He is notorious for being late.* **2** widely known. ⟨< Med.L *notorius* < L *notus* known⟩ **–no'to•ri•ous•ly,** *adv.* **–no'to•ri•ous•ness,** *n.*

no•tor•nis [nou'tɔrnɪs] *n.* a rare, flightless bird of the genus *Notornis,* living in New Zealand. ⟨< Gk. *noto(s)* the south + *ornis* bird⟩

No•tre Dame [,noutrə 'dɑm] *or* [,noutər'deim]; *French,* [nɔtʀə'dam] **1** *French.* Our Lady, the Virgin Mary. **2** in Paris, France, a famous cathedral.

no–trump ['nou 'trʌmp] *adj., n. Bridge, etc. –adj.* of a contract, hand, etc., played or suitable for playing without trumps.
–n. **1** a declaration or bid to play with no suit as trumps. **2** a hand that is so played.

not•with•stand•ing [,nɒtwɪθ'stændɪŋ] *or* [,nɒtwɪð'stændɪŋ] *prep., conj., adv. –prep.* in spite of: *He bought it notwithstanding the high price.*
–conj. in spite of the fact that: *Notwithstanding there was a need for haste, he still delayed.*
–adv. in spite of it; nevertheless: *It is raining; but I shall go, notwithstanding.*

nou•gat ['nugət] *or* ['nugɑ] *n.* a kind of soft candy made from sugar paste, containing nuts and sometimes fruit. ⟨< F < Provençal *noga,* ult. < L *nux, nucis* nut⟩

nought [nɒt] *n., adv. –n.* **1** zero; 0. **2** naught; nothing.
–adv. Archaic. in no way; not at all. ⟨See NAUGHT⟩
☛ *Hom.* KNOT[1], NOT, NAUGHT.

noughts and crosses *Brit.* tick-tack-toe.

nou•me•non ['numə,nɒn] *or* ['naʊmə,nɒn] *n., pl.* **-na** [-nə]. *Philosophy.* **1** an object not as perceived by the senses but by the intellect. **2** an object perceivable only to the intellect. Compare PHENOMENON. ⟨< Gk. *nooúmenon* a thing being perceived, *noêin* to perceive⟩ **–'nou•me•nal,** *adj.* **–'nou•me•nal•ly,** *adv.*

noun [naʊn] *n., adj. Grammar. –n.* a word used as the name of a person, place, thing, quality, event, etc. Words like *Christopher, table, school, kindness, skill,* and *party* are nouns.
–adj. used as a noun. ⟨ME < AF *nom* < L *nomen* name⟩

noun clause *Grammar.* a subordinate clause that acts as a noun. *Example:* I know *that you will come with us.*

noun phrase *Grammar.* a phrase consisting of a noun plus any modifiers. *Example:* the small white duck.

nour•ish ['nɜrɪʃ] *v.* **1** make grow, or keep alive and well, with food; feed: *Milk nourishes a baby.* **2** maintain; foster: *nourish a hope.* ⟨ME < OF *noriss-,* a stem of *norir* < L *nutrire* feed⟩ **–'nour•ish•er,** *n.* **–'nour•ish•a•ble,** *adj.* **–'nour•ish•ing•ly,** *adv.*

nour•ish•ment ['nɜrɪʃmənt] *n.* **1** food. **2** the act of nourishing or the condition of being nourished.

nous [nus] *or* [nʌus] *n.* reason, especially divine reason or reason as a universal governing principle. ⟨< Gk. *noos* mind⟩
☛ *Hom.* NOOSE [nus].

nou•veau riche ['nuvou 'riʃ]; *French,* [nuvo'ʀiʃ] *pl.,* **nou•veaux riches** ['nuvou'riʃ]. *French.* one who has recently become rich; often, one who makes a vulgar display of his or her wealth.

Nov. November.

no•va ['nouvə] *n., pl.* **no•vae** ['nouvi] *or* ['nouvaɪ] or **no•vas.** *Astronomy.* a star that suddenly becomes brighter (several times its normal magnitude) and then gradually fades away. ⟨< L *nova* (*stella*) new (star)⟩

no•vac•u•lite [nou'vækjə,ləit] *n.* a very hard stone used for sharpening blades. ⟨< L *novacula* razor⟩

No•va Sco•tia ['nouvə 'skouʃə] a Maritime province of Canada.

No•va Sco•tia duck tolling retriever *Cdn.* a breed of retriever developed in Nova Scotia in the early 19th century, having a fairly long, sleek, reddish coat. These dogs are trained to lure and retrieve waterfowl; they run and play along the water's edge, arousing the curiosity of the birds so that they approach within shooting range.

No•va Sco•tian ['nouvə 'skouʃən] *n., adj. –n.* a native or long-term resident of Nova Scotia.
–adj. of or having to do with Nova Scotia.

no•va•tion [nou'veiʃən] *n. Law.* the renegotiation of a debt or similar obligation. ⟨< L *novātiō, novātus* renewed⟩

nov•el[1] ['nɒvəl] *adj.* **1** of a new kind or nature: *a novel experience.* **2** strikingly new; original: *Red snow is a novel idea to us.* ⟨ME < OF L *novellus,* dim. of *novus* new⟩
☛ *Syn.* See note at NEW.

nov•el[2] ['nɒvəl] *n.* **1** a fictional story with characters and a plot, long enough to fill one or more volumes. **2 the novel,** the branch of literature having to do with such works: *He is studying the novel.* ⟨< Ital. *novella* < L *novella* new things, neut. pl. of *novellus* (see NOVEL[1]); intermediate meaning probably 'a composition showing originality'⟩ **–'nov•el,like,** *adj.*

nov•el[3] ['nɒvəl] *n.* **1** Usually, **Novels,** *Roman law.* amendments made to the Justinian code by the Emperor Justinian and his successors. **2** *Civil law.* an amendment to a statute. ⟨< LL *novella* (*constitūtiō*) a new (regulation order)⟩

nov•el•ette [,nɒvə'lɛt] *n.* a short novel.

nov•el•ist ['nɒvəlɪst] *n.* a writer of novels.

nov•el•is•tic [,nɒvə'lɪstɪk] *adj.* of or like novels.
–,nov•el'is•ti•cal•ly, *adv.*

nov•el•ize ['nɒvə,laɪz] *v.* **-ized, iz•ing.** convert (a play, motion-picture script, etc.) into the form of a novel.
–,nov•el•i'za•tion, *n.*

no•vel•la [nou'vɛlə]; *Italian,* [no'vɛlla] *n.* **no•vel•las, no•vel•le** *Italian,* [no'vɛlle]. **1** a short novel or an extended short story. **2** originally, a short prose narrative, often satirical or moralistic. ⟨< Ital.⟩

nov•el•ty ['nɒvəlti] *n., pl.* **-ties. 1** newness; novel character: *After the novelty of the game wore off, Maria lost interest.* **2** a new or unusual thing: *Staying up late was a novelty to the children.* **3 novelties,** *pl.* small, unusual articles; toys, cheap jewellery, etc. ⟨ME < OF *novelte* < L *novellitas* < *novellus.* See NOVEL[1].⟩

No•vem•ber [nou'vɛmbər] *n.* the eleventh month of the year. It has 30 days. ⟨< L *November* < *novem* nine; from the order of the early Roman calendar⟩

no•ve•na [nou'vinə] *n., pl.* **-nas, -nae** [-ni] *or* [-naɪ]. *Roman Catholic Church.* a religious exercise consisting of prayers or services on nine days, or nine corresponding days in consecutive months, usually as a petition or supplication for some special purpose: *a novena of nine first Fridays.* ⟨< Med.L *novena,* ult. < L *novem* nine⟩

nov•ice ['nɒvɪs] *n.* **1** one who is new to what he or she is doing; beginner. **2** a person who has been received into a religious order or community but has not yet taken final vows. Before becoming a monk or a nun, a person is a novice. ⟨ME < OF < L *novicius* < *novus* new⟩

no•vi•ti•ate or **no•vi•ci•ate** [nou'vɪʃiɪt] *or* [nou'vɪʃi,eit] *n.* **1** a period of probation and preparation before taking final vows in a religious order or community. **2** novice. **3** a house or rooms occupied by religious novices. **4** the state or period of being a beginner in anything. ⟨< Med.L *novitiatus,* ult. < *novus* new⟩

no•vo•caine or **no•vo•cain** ['nouvə,kein] *n.* **1** an alkaloid compound, used as a local anesthetic; procaine. **2 Novocain,** *Trademark.* a brand of product containing procaine. ⟨< L *novus* new + E *(co)caine*⟩

now [naʊ] *adv., n., conj., interj.* —*adv.* **1** at the present time: *He is here now.* **2** at once: *Do it now!* **3** then; next: *Now you see it; now you don't. We have signed the petition and it now goes to the school principal.* **4** at the time referred to: *The clock now struck three.* **5** under the present circumstances; as things are; as it is: *I would believe almost anything now.* **6 Now** is also used to introduce, emphasize, lessen the severity of a sentence, or sometimes just to fill in: *Now what do you mean? Oh, come now!*
just now. See JUST[1].
now and again, from time to time; once in a while.
now and then, from time to time; once in a while.
—*n.* the present; this time.
—*conj.* since; inasmuch as: *Now I am older, I have changed my mind.*
—*interj.* an expression of mild rebuke or of sympathy. ⟨OE *nū*⟩

now•a•days ['naʊə,deiz] *adv., n.* —*adv.* at the present day; in these times.
—*n.* the present day; these times.

no•way ['nou,wei] *adv.* nowise. Also, **noways.**

no way *Slang.* in no way; definitely not or definitely no: *No way could he pass an exam like that!*

no•ways ['nou,weiz] *adv.* noway.

no•where ['nou,wɛr] *adv., n.* —*adv.* in no place; at no place; to no place.
—*n.* a non-existent place. ⟨OE *nāhwǣr*⟩
☛ *Usage.* See note at NOBODY.

no–win ['nou 'wɪn] *adj.* losing or unsuccessful for all parties concerned: *The constitutional debate is a no-win situation.*

no•wise ['nou,waɪz] *adv.* in no way; not at all.

nox•ious ['nɒkʃəs] *adj.* **1** extremely harmful; poisonous: *Fumes from the exhaust of an automobile are noxious.* **2** morally hurtful; corrupting. ⟨< L *noxius* < *noxa* hurt < *nocere* hurt⟩ **—'nox•ious•ly,** *adv.* **—'nox•ious•ness,** *n.*

noz•zle ['nɒzəl] *n.* **1** a tip or spout put on a hose, pipe, can, etc. to allow one to control the outward flow of liquid or gas, often made so that the user can adjust the force and shape of that flow: *She adjusted the nozzle so that the water came out in a fine spray.* **2** *Slang.* nose. ⟨dim. of *nose*⟩

Np neptunium.

NP NOUN PHRASE.

N.P. NOTARY PUBLIC.

n.p.t. normal pressure and temperature.

nr. near.

NRC or **N.R.C.** National Research Council.

ns nanosecond.

Ns *Meteorology.* nimbo-stratus.

NS Nova Scotia (*used esp. in computerized address systems*).

N.S. **1** Nova Scotia. **2** NEW STYLE.

n.s. **1** new series. **2** not specified.

NSF or **nsf** not sufficient funds.

N.S.O. or **NSO** NORTHERN SERVICE OFFICER.

NT Northwest Territories (*used esp. in computerized address systems*).

N.T. New Testament.

nth [ɛnθ] *adj. Mathematics.* being of the indefinitely large or small value or amount denoted by *n: the nth power.*
to the nth degree or **power, a** to any degree or power. **b** *Informal.* to the utmost: *She was dressed to the nth degree for the occasion.*

nt.wt. net weight.

nu [nju] *or* [nu] *n.* the thirteenth letter (N, ν) of the Greek alphabet.

nu•ance ['njuɑns] *or* ['nuɑns], [nju'ɑns] *or* [nu'ɑns]; *French,* [ny'ɑ̃s] *n.* **1** a shade of expression, meaning, feeling, etc. **2** a shade of colour or tone. ⟨< F⟩

nub [nʌb] *n.* **1** a knob; protuberance. **2** a lump or small piece. **3** the point or gist of anything. ⟨apparently var. of *knob*⟩

nub•bin ['nʌbɪn] *n.* **1** a small lump or piece. **2** a small or imperfect ear of corn. **3** an undeveloped fruit. ⟨dim. of *nub*⟩

Nu•bi•an ['njubiən] *or* ['nubiən] *n., adj.* —*n.* **1** a native or inhabitant of Nubia, an ancient region of NE Africa. **2** any of several languages spoken in this region.
—*adj.* of or having to do with Nubia, its people, or the languages spoken there.

nu•bile ['njubaɪl] *or* ['nubaɪl], ['njubəl] *or* ['nubəl] *adj.* of a girl or young woman: **1** old or mature enough to be married. **2** sexually developed and attractive. ⟨< L *nubilis* marriageable < *nubere* take a husband⟩ **—nu'bil•i•ty** [-'bɪləti], *n.*

nu•cel•lus [nju'sɛləs] *or* [nu'sɛləs], *n., pl.* **nu•cel•li** [-laɪ] *or* [-li]. *Botany.* the centre of the seed of a plant, containing the embryonic sac. ⟨< NL⟩ **—nu'cel•lar,** *adj.*

nu•cha ['njukə] *or* ['nukə] *n., pl.* **-chae** [-ki] *or* [-kaɪ]. the nape of the neck. ⟨< ML < Arabic *nukhā* spinal marrow⟩

nu•cle•ar ['njukliər] *or* ['nukliər] *adj.* **1** of, having to do with, or contained within the nucleus of a cell: *nuclear membranes.* **2** of or having to do with the nuclei of atoms: *nuclear physics, nuclear energy.* **3** of, having to do with, or using nuclear energy: *a nuclear submarine, the nuclear age.* **4** of, having to do with, involving, or possessing nuclear weapons: *nuclear disarmament, nuclear nations.* **5** of, having to do with, or forming any kind of nucleus: *the nuclear family.*

nuclear emulsion an emulsion used to photograph the path of cosmic ray particles.

nuclear energy the energy released by any nuclear reaction; atomic power.

nuclear family *Anthropology.* a parent or parents and their child or children living together, without people from other generations or other branches of the family.

nuclear fission FISSION (def. 3).

nuclear fuel a fissile substance that will sustain a chain reaction.

nuclear fusion FUSION (def. 4).

nuclear magnetic resonance absorption of radio waves by atomic nuclei placed in a magnetic field, used to study molecular structure and biochemical reactions. *Abbrev.:* NMR

nuclear medicine the use of radioactive isotopes in the diagnosis and treatment of disease.

nuclear physics the branch of physics that is concerned with the internal structure and reactions of atomic nuclei.
—nuclear physicist.

nuclear power electrical or motive power from nuclear energy produced in a reactor.

nuclear reactor an apparatus for producing controlled nuclear energy instead of an explosion as in a bomb. Energy and neutrons are released when an atom splits on being struck by a neutron. A chain reaction starts as these additional neutrons hit more atoms. In a reactor this chain reaction is slowed down by means of control rods which absorb many of the neutrons. (In a bomb the reaction is uncontrolled and happens very fast, producing an explosion.)

nuclear winter a great cooling of the earth's temperature after a nuclear war, in which, it is thought, the sun's rays would be blocked by dense smoke and so all plant life would die, leading to human and animal starvation.

nu•cle•ase ['njukli,eis] *or* ['nukli,eis], ['njukli,eiz] *or* ['nukli,eiz] *n. Biochemistry.* any enzyme able to hydrolyze nucleic acids.

nu•cle•ate *v.* ['njukli,eit] *or* ['nukli,eit]; *adj.* ['njukliɪt] *or* ['nukliɪt] *v.* **-at•ed, -at•ing;** *adj.* —*v.* form into a nucleus or around a nucleus.
—*adj.* having a nucleus. ⟨< LL *nucleare* become full of kernels < L *nucleus* kernel⟩ **—,nu•cle'a•tion,** *n.* **—'nu•cle,a•tor,** *n.*

nu•cle•i ['njukli,aɪ] *or* ['nukli,aɪ] *n.* a pl. of NUCLEUS.

nu•cle•ic acid [nju'kliɪk] *or* [nju'kleiɪk], [nu'kliɪk] *or* [nu'kleiɪk] *Biochemistry.* any of a group of complex acids, including DNA and RNA, found especially in the nuclei of cells. All nucleic acids are composed of phosphoric acid, a carbohydrate, and a base, and are essential to life.

nucleo– *combining form.* **1** nucleus: *nucleoplasm.* **2** nucleic acid: *nucleoprotein.*

nu•cle•o•lus [nju'kliələs] *or* [nu'kliələs] *n., pl.* **-li** [-ˌlaɪ] *or* [-ˌli]. *Biology.* a small structure, usually round, found within the nucleus in most cells. See CELL for picture. Also, **nucleole.** ⟨< LL *nucleolus*, dim. of L *nucleus* kernel⟩ **—nu'cle•o•lar,** *adj.*

nu•cle•on ['njukli,ɒn] *or* ['nukli,ɒn] *n. Physics.* one of the atomic particles that make up the nucleus of an atom, such as a neutron or proton. **—,nu•cle'on•ic,** *adj.*

nu•cle•on•ics [,njukli'ɒnɪks] *or* [,nukli'ɒnɪks] *n.pl.* the study and science of the behaviour and characteristics of nucleons (*used with a singular noun*).

nu•cle•o•plasm ['njukliə,plæzəm] *or* ['nukliə,plæzəm] *n. Biology.* the protoplasm of a cell nucleus. **—,nu•cle•o'plas•mic** or **,nu•cle•o•plas'mat•ic** [-plæz'mætɪk], *adj.*

nu•cle•o•pro•tein [,njukliə'proutin], [,nukliə'proutin], *or* [,njukliə'proutiɪn] *n. Biochemistry.* any compound of a protein with a nucleic acid, found in all life.

nu•cle•o•side ['njukliə,saɪd] *or* ['nukliə,saɪd] *n. Biochemistry.* a compound of a sugar with a purine base. ⟨< *nucleo-* + *-ose* + *-ide*⟩

nu•cle•o•tide ['njukliə,taɪd] *or* ['nukliə,taɪd] *n. Biochemistry.* a molecule that is the unit of structure of nucleic acid, composed of a base which is either a purine (adenine or guanine) or a pyrimidine, a five-carbon sugar, and a phosphate group. A polymer of many nucleotides is a nucleic acid. ⟨< *nucleoside*⟩

nu•cle•us ['njukliəs] *or* ['nukliəs] *n., pl.* **-cle•i** [-kli,aɪ] or **-cle•us•es. 1** a beginning to which additions are to be made. **2** a central part or thing around which other parts or things are collected: *The family is the nucleus of our society.* **3** *Physics.* the group of particles forming the central part of an atom and carrying a positive electric charge, consisting of protons and neutrons (except for the hydrogen atom, which contains only a proton) and, sometimes, other particles. The nucleus makes up most of the mass of an atom but only a tiny fraction of its size. **4** *Chemistry.* a basic, stable group of atoms in a compound: *the benzene nucleus.* **5** *Biology.* a mass of protoplasm found in most plant and animal cells, without which a cell cannot grow and divide. See CELL for picture. **6** *Anatomy.* a group of nerve cells in the central nervous system. **7** *Astronomy.* the dense, central part of a comet's head. **8** *Meteorology.* a particle of dust, etc., upon which water vapour condenses so as to form a drop. ⟨< L *nucleus* < *nux, nucis* nut⟩

nude [njud] *or* [nud] *adj., n. —adj.* **1** uncovered or naked; especially, with the clothing removed. **2** being the colour of light-coloured, or fair, skin.
—n. **1** a representation of a naked person in painting, sculpture, photography, etc. **2** a naked person.
in the nude, without clothes on; naked: *The girls went swimming in the nude.* ⟨< L *nudus*⟩ **—'nude•ness,** *n.*
☛ *Syn. adj.* **1.** See note at BARE[1].

nudge [nʌdʒ] *v.* **nudged, nudg•ing;** *n. —v.* **1** push slightly or jog with the elbow to attract attention. **2** prod; stimulate: *to nudge one's memory, to nudge a person into action.* **3** approach closely: *She is nudging forty.*
—n. a slight push or jog. ⟨origin uncertain⟩ **—'nudg•er,** *n.*

nudi– *combining form.* naked; bare: *nudibranch.* ⟨< L *nūdus* naked⟩

nu•di•branch ['njudɪ,bræŋk] *or* ['nudɪ,bræŋk] *n.* a marine mollusc of the suborder Nudibranchia, having no shell.

nu•di•bran•chi•ate [,njudi'bræŋkiɪt] *or* [,nudi'bræŋkiɪt], [,njudɪ'bræŋki,eit] *or* [,nudɪ'bræŋki,eit] *n., adj. —n.* a nudibranch. *—adj.* having to do with the Nudibranchia.

nud•ism ['njudɪzəm] *or* ['nudɪzəm] *n.* the cult or practice of going naked, especially for the sake of one's health. **—'nud•ist,** *n., adj.*

nu•di•ty ['njudəti] *or* ['nudəti] *n., pl.* **-ties. 1** nakedness. **2** something naked.

nu•ga•to•ry ['njugə,tɔri] *or* ['nugə,tɔri] *adj.* **1** trifling; worthless. **2** of no force; invalid. **3** ineffective; useless. ⟨< L *nugatorius* < *nugari* trifle < *nugae* trifles⟩

nug•get ['nʌgɪt] *n.* **1** a lump, especially a small lump of gold in its natural state. **2** anything small but valuable: *a few nuggets of truth.* ⟨? < *nug* lump⟩

nui•sance ['njusəns] *or* ['nusəns] *n.* a thing that or person who annoys, troubles, offends, or is disagreeable: *Flies are a nuisance.* ⟨ME < OF *nuisance* < *nuire* harm < L *nocere*⟩

nuisance ground *Cdn.* in the West, a garbage dump; a place where worn-out and useless material is thrown.

nuisance tax a tax that is annoying because it is collected in very small amounts from the consumer.

nuke [njuk] *or* [nuk] *n., v.* **nuked, nuking.** *—n. Slang.* **1** a nuclear weapon. **2** nuclear reactor.
—v. **1** destroy with or as if with atomic bombs. **2** cook or heat in a microwave oven.

null [nʌl] *adj.* **1** not binding; of no effect; as if not existing: *A promise obtained by force is legally null.* **2** unimportant; useless; meaningless; valueless. **3** not any; zero.
null and void, without legal force or effect; worthless. ⟨< L *nullus* < *ne-* not + *ullus* any⟩

null allele *Genetics.* an allele that either makes no gene product or makes a non-functional product.

null hypothesis *Statistics.* a hypothesis that assumes that two variables are unrelated.

nul•li•fy ['nʌlə,faɪ] *v.* **-fied, -fy•ing. 1** make not binding; render void; *nullify a law.* **2** make unimportant, useless, or meaningless; destroy; cancel: *The difficulties of the plan nullify its advantages.* ⟨< L *nullificare* < *nullus* not any + *facere* make⟩
—,nul•li•fi'ca•tion, *n.* **—'nul•li,fi•er,** *n.*

nul•li•ty ['nʌləti] *n., pl.* **-ties. 1** futility; nothingness. **2** a mere nothing. **3** something that is null, such as a nullified law or agreement. ⟨< Med.L *nullitas* < L *nullus* not any⟩

null set *Mathematics.* an empty set; a set with no members.

numb [nʌm] *adj., v. —adj.* having lost the power of feeling or moving: *My fingers are numb with cold.*
—v. **1** make numb. **2** dull the feelings of: *The old lady was numbed with grief when her grandchild died.* ⟨ult. < OE *numen* taken, seized⟩ **—'numb•ly,** *adv.* **—'numb•ness,** *n.*

num•ber ['nʌmbər] *n., v. —n.* **1** a word or symbol used in counting. Two, fourteen, twenty-six, second, fourteenth, twenty-sixth, 2, 14, and 26 are all numbers. **2** the amount of units; sum; total: *The number of your fingers is ten.* **3** a quantity: *a number of reasons.* **4** a collection or company: *the number of saints.* **5** the particular number that indicates the place of a person or object in a series, and is a means of identifying it: *an apartment number, a licence number, a telephone number. Symbol:* # **6** a single item on a program, etc.: *The program consisted of four musical numbers.* **7** a song or other piece of music: *She sings many old numbers.* **8** a single issue of a periodical. **9** *Informal.* any thing or person thought of as standing apart from a collection or company: *That dress is the most fashionable number in the store.* **10** *Grammar.* **a** a system for varying the form of nouns, pronouns, adjectives, and often verbs to indicate reference to one or more than one person or thing. English distinguishes only singular and plural number. Some languages also distinguish dual number. **b** a form or group of forms indicating this. **c** in such a system, the category to which a particular noun, adjective, etc. belongs: *Verbs must agree with their subjects in person and number.* **11 numbers,** *pl.* **a** arithmetic. **b** many: *Numbers were turned away.* **c** numerical preponderance; a being more: *win a battle by force of numbers.* **d** *Archaic.* poetry. **e** a group of musical notes or measures.
a number of, several; many.
beyond number, too many to count.
(someone's) **number is up,** *Informal.* someone is doomed.
without number, too many to be counted.
—v. **1** mark with a number; assign a number to; distinguish with a number: *The pages of this book are numbered.* **2** be able to show; have: *This city numbers a million inhabitants.* **3** amount to: *a crew numbering twenty women.* **4** include as one of a class or collection: *I number you among my best friends.* **5** fix the number of; limit: *His days in office are numbered.* **6** count. ⟨ME < OF *nombre* < L *numerus*⟩ **—'num•ber•er,** *n.*
☛ *Syn. n.* **2. Number,** SUM = the total of two or more persons, things, or units taken together. **Number** applies to the total reached by counting the persons or things in a group or collection: *Only twelve came, a smaller number than usual.* **Sum** applies to the total reached by adding figures or things: *The sum of two and two is four.*
☛ *Usage.* **Number** is a collective noun, requiring a singular or plural verb according to whether the total or the individual units are meant: *A number of tickets have already been sold. The number of tickets sold is astonishing.* See also the note at AMOUNT.
☛ *Usage.* **Numbers.** Usage varies in writing numbers that are parts of consecutive sentences. In general, newspapers and informal writing have figures for numbers over ten, words for smaller numbers; a more formal style is to spell out all numbers that can be written in one or two words.

Informal: *four, ten, 15, 92, 114.* Formal: *four, ten, fifteen, ninety-two, 114.* Practice within a piece of writing should be consistent.

number cruncher *Informal.* **1** a very powerful computer. **2** a researcher who relies on statistics.

number crunching *Informal* **1** carrying out long, complicated, tedious, repetitive numerical calculations on the computer. **2** relying on statistics.

num•ber•less ['nʌmbərlɪs] *adj.* **1** very numerous; too many to count: *There are numberless fish in the sea.* **2** without a number.

number one **1** *Informal.* oneself: *He worries too much about number one.* **2** the first or best in a series.

numb•fish ['nʌm,fɪʃ] *n.* ELECTRIC RAY.

numb•skull ['nʌm,skʌl] *n.* numskull.

nu•men ['njumɪn] *or* ['numɪn] *n., pl.* **-mi•na** [-mənə]. **1** *Roman mythology.* the presiding spirit of a place. **2** creative energy. ⟨< L: a nod, command⟩

nu•mer•a•ble ['njumərəbəl] *or* ['numərəbəl] *adj.* that can be counted.

nu•mer•a•cy ['njumərəsi] *or* ['numərəsi] *n.* **1** the ability to think in quantitative terms. **2** the ability to cope confidently with the mathematical demands of adult life.

nu•mer•al ['njumərəl] *or* ['numərəl] *n.* a word, figure, or group of figures standing for a number. 2, 15, and 100 are Arabic numerals. II, XV, and C are Roman numerals for 2, 15, and 100. ⟨< LL *numeralis* < L *numerus* number⟩

nu•mer•ate *v.* ['njumə,reit] *or* ['numə,reit]; *adj.* ['njumərɪt] *or* ['numərɪt] *v.* **-at•ed, -at•ing;** *adj.* *—v.* **1** enumerate. **2** read (a numerical expression): *Our computer numerates easily.*
—adj. able to work with figures; the mathematical equivalent of literate. ⟨< L *numerare* < *numerus* number⟩

nu•mer•a•tion [,njumə'reiʃən] *or* [,numə'reiʃən] *n.* **1** the process or a method of numbering, counting, or calculating. **2** the expression in words of a written numeral.

nu•mer•a•tor ['njumə,reitər] *or* ['numə,reitər] *n.* **1** *Arithmetic.* in a fraction, the number above the line: *In* 3/8, 3 *is the numerator and* 8 *is the denominator.* **2** a person or thing that makes a count, takes a census, etc. ⟨< LL *numerator* a counter⟩

nu•mer•i•cal [nju'mɛrəkəl] *or* [nu'mɛrəkəl] *adj.* **1** of or having to do with a number or numbers; in numbers; by numbers. **2** shown by numbers, not by letters. *Example*: 10 *is a numerical quantity;* bx *is a literal or algebraic quantity.* **3** *Mathematics.* of a mathematical quantity, designating the value in figures without considering the sign: *The numerical value of* +4 *is less than that of* –7, *though its algebraic value is more.* Also, **numeric. —nu'mer•i•cal•ly,** *adv.*

nu•mer•ol•o•gy [,njumə'rɒlədʒi] *or* [,numə'rɒlədʒi] *n.* a system of foretelling the future, based on the supposed influence of numbers. **—,nu•mer•o'log•i•cal** [,njumərə'lɒdʒɪkəl] *or* [,numərə'lɒdʒɪkəl], *adj.* **—,nu•mer'ol•o•gist,** *n.*

nu•mer•ous ['njumərəs] *or* ['numərəs] *adj.* **1** very many: *He has numerous acquaintances.* **2** consisting of great numbers: *He has a numerous circle of acquaintances.* ⟨< L *numerosus*⟩ **—'nu•mer•ous•ly,** *adv.* **—'nu•mer•ous•ness,** *n.*

Num•ic ['nʌmɪk] *n., adj.* *—n.* a branch of the Uto-Aztecan family of languages, including Comanche, Northern and Southern Paiute, Ute, etc.
—adj. of or having to with the Numic languages.

Nu•mid•ia [nju'mɪdiə] *or* [nu'mɪdiə] *n.* an ancient country in N Africa.

Nu•mid•i•an [nju'mɪdiən] *or* [nu'mɪdiən] *n., adj.* *—n.* **1** a native or inhabitant of Numidia. **2** the language of Numidia.
—adj. of or having to do with Numidia, its people, or their language.

nu•mi•nous ['njumɪnəs] *or* ['numɪnəs] *adj.* **1** concerning a numen. **2** mystical; evoking a spiritual response.

nu•mis•mat•ic [,njumɪz'mætɪk] *or* [,numɪz'mætɪk] *adj.* **1** of numismatics or numismatists. **2** of coins and medals. **—,nu•mis'mat•i•cal•ly,** *adv.*

nu•mis•mat•ics [,njumɪz'mætɪks] *or* [,numɪz'mætɪks] *n.* the study or collection of coins and medals (*used with a singular verb*). ⟨< F < L *numisma* coin < Gk. *nomisma* < *nomizein* have in use⟩

nu•mis•ma•tist [nju'mɪzmətɪst] *or* [nu'mɪzmətɪst] *n.* **1** a person knowledgable about or studying numismatics. **2** a person who collects coins or medals.

num•mu•lar ['nʌmjələr] *adj.* circular like some coins. ⟨< L *nummulī* petty cash, *nummus* money⟩

num•skull ['nʌm,skʌl] *n. Informal.* a stupid person; blockhead. ⟨for *numb skull*⟩

nun[1] [nʌn] *n.* a woman who is a member of a religious order and lives a life of prayer, worship, and service, such as teaching or nursing. ⟨OE *nunne* < LL *nonna*, fem. of *nonnus* monk⟩
☛ *Hom.* NONE[1].

nun[2] [nun] *or* [nʊn] *n.* the fifteenth letter of the Hebrew alphabet. See table of alphabets in the Appendix.

nu•na•tak ['nunə,tæk] *n.* an isolated mountain peak or hill rising above the surrounding glacial ice. ⟨< Inuktitut⟩

Nu•na•vut ['nʊnəvʊt] *n.* an area in central and eastern Northwest Territories, governed by First Nations and Inuit people.

Nunc Di•mit•tis ['nʌŋk dɪ'mɪtɪs] *or* [nʊŋk] **1** the canticle of Simeon, beginning "Lord, now lettest thou thy servant depart in peace." **2 nunc dimittis,** a dismissal; leave to go. ⟨< L *Nunc dimittis* now dost thou dismiss, the first words as given in the Vulgate⟩

nun•ci•a•ture ['nʌnʃiətʃər] *n.* the office of a nuncio.

nun•ci•o ['nʊnsiou] *or* ['nʌnʃiou] *n., pl.* **-ci•os.** an ambassador from the Pope to a government. ⟨< Ital. < L *nuntius* messenger⟩

nun•cu•pa•tive ['nʌŋkjə,peitɪv] *or* [nʌŋ'kjupətɪv] *adj.* of a will, given orally before witnesses. ⟨< L *nuncupativus* < *nomen* name + *-ceps* taking⟩

nun•ner•y ['nʌnəri] *n., pl.* **-ner•ies.** a building or buildings where nuns live; convent.

nun•ny bag ['nʌni] *Cdn.* in Newfoundland, a kind of haversack, often made of sealskin.

nun's veiling a thin, plain-woven, woollen fabric, used mainly for women's dresses.

nup•tial ['nʌpʃəl] *or* ['nʌptʃəl] *adj., n.* *—adj.* of marriage or weddings.
—n. **nuptials,** *pl.* a wedding; the wedding ceremony. ⟨< L *nuptialis*, ult. < *nubere* take a husband⟩ **—'nup•tial•ly,** *adv.*

nurse [nɜrs] *n., v.* **nursed, nurs•ing.** *—n.* **1** a person who takes care of the sick, the injured, or the old, or is trained to do this. **2** a woman who cares for and brings up the young children or babies of another person. **3** one who feeds and protects.
—v. **1** be a nurse; act as a nurse; work as a nurse. **2** act as a nurse for; wait on or try to cure (the sick); take care of (sick, injured, or old people). **3** cure or try to cure by care: *She nursed a bad cold by going to bed.* **4** take care of and bring up (another's baby or young child). **5** make grow; nourish and protect: *to nurse a plant, to nurse a hatred in the heart.* **6** use or treat with special care: *He nursed his sore arm by using it very little.* **7** hold closely; clasp fondly. **8** feed milk to (a baby) at the breast. **9** suck milk from the breast. ⟨ME < OF *nurrice* < L *nutricia* < *nutrire* feed, nourish⟩

nurse•ling ['nɜrslɪŋ] See NURSLING.

nurse•maid ['nɜrs,meid] *n.* a maid employed to care for children.

nurs•er ['nɜrsər] *n.* a baby's bottle.

nurs•er•y ['nɜrsəri] *n., pl.* **-er•ies.** **1** a room set apart for the use of babies and children. **2** a baby's bedroom. **3** a day-care centre. **4** NURSERY SCHOOL. **5** a piece of ground or place where young plants are grown for transplanting or sale. **6** a place or condition that helps something to grow and develop: *Slums are often nurseries of disease.*

nurs•er•y•maid ['nɜrsəri,meid] *n.* nursemaid.

nurs•er•y•man ['nɜrsərimən] *n., pl.* **-men.** a man who grows or sells young trees and plants.

nursery rhyme a short, traditional poem for young children. "Humpty Dumpty sat on a wall" is the beginning of a famous nursery rhyme.

nursery school a school for young children, usually for those under five.

nur•sing ['nɜrsɪŋ] *n., v.* *—n.* **1** the occupation of a nurse. **2** the training needed to be a nurse.
—v. ppr. of NURSE.

nursing home **1** a residence providing personal or nursing care for old, chronically ill, or disabled persons. **2** *Brit.* a private hospital.

nursing station 1 in a hospital, a location serving as a base and office area for the nurses on duty on a floor or part of a floor. 2 *Cdn.* in the North, a small hospital for emergency cases, served by nurses and visited periodically by a doctor.

nurs•ling ['nɜrslɪŋ] *n.* 1 a baby that is being nursed. 2 any person or thing that is under tender care. Also, **nurseling.**

nur•ture ['nɜrtʃər] *v.* **-tured, -tur•ing;** *n.* *—v.* 1 bring up; care for; rear: *She nurtured the child as if he had been her own.* 2 nourish: *Minerals in the soil nurture the plants.*
—n. 1 the act or process of raising or rearing; a bringing up; training; education. 2 food; nourishment. 3 the sum of environmental factors acting on a person, as opposed to genetic makeup: *Is one's character due to nature or nurture?* ⟨ME < OF *nourture* < LL *nutritura* a nursing, suckling < L *nutrire* nurse⟩ **—'nur•tur•er,** *n.*

nu•sa [nu'sɑ] *n.* a ceremonial wand waved by Shinto priests in purification rituals.

nut [nʌt] *n., v.* **nut•ted, nut•ting;** *adj.* *—n.* 1 a dry fruit or seed with a hard, woody, or leathery shell and a kernel inside. Some nuts, including walnuts, almonds, and pecans, are good to eat. See FRUIT for picture. 2 the kernel of a nut. 3 a small square or six-sided block, usually metal, having a threaded hole in the centre, by means of which it is screwed on to a bolt to hold the bolt in place. 4 a piece at the upper end of a violin, cello, etc. over which the strings pass. 5 *Slang.* the head. 6 *Slang.* an eccentric or crazy person. 7 *Slang.* an enthusiast: *a car nut.*
hard nut to crack, *Informal.* a difficult question, person, problem, or undertaking.
off one's nut, *Slang.* crazy.
—v. gather nuts.
—adj. **nuts,** *Slang.* eccentric or crazy. ⟨OE *hnutu*⟩ **—'nut,like,** *adj.*

nut•crack•er ['nʌt,krækər] *n.* 1 an instrument for cracking the shells of nuts. 2 any of several birds of the same family as the crow, that feed on nuts.

nut•gall ['nʌt,gɒl] *n.* a lump or ball that swells up on an oak tree where it has been injured by an insect; gall.

nut•hatch ['nʌt,hætʃ] *n.* any of a family (Sittidae) of small songbirds having a strong, straight, pointed bill, long, pointed wings, and a short tail, and typically having plumage that is greyish blue above and white or reddish on the under parts. ⟨ME *notehache,* literally, nut hacker; from the birds' habit of opening nuts by hammering them with the bill until the shell is broken⟩

nut•let ['nʌtlɪt] *n.* 1 a small nut. 2 the stone of a peach, plum, cherry, etc.

nut•meat ['nʌt,mit] *n.* the kernel of a nut.

Ripe nutmegs on the tree

nut•meg ['nʌtmɛg] *n.* 1 a hard, spicy seed about as big as a marble, obtained from the fruit of an East Indian tree. Nutmeg is grated and used for flavouring food. 2 the tree. ⟨ME; half-translation of OF **nois mugue*, var. of *nois muguete*, originally, nut smelling like musk *(nois* < L *nux*; *mugue*, ult. < LL *muscus)*⟩

nut•pick ['nʌt,pɪk] *n.* a small, pointed tool for getting the meat of a nut.

nut pine piñon.

nu•tri•a ['njutriə] *or* ['nutriə] *n.* 1 the durable, valuable, beaverlike fur of the coypu. 2 (*adjl.*) made of this fur: *a nutria coat.* 3 coypu. ⟨< Sp. < L *lutra*⟩

nu•tri•ent ['njutriənt] *or* ['nutriənt] *n., adj.* *—n.* a nutritive substance.
—adj. nourishing. ⟨< L *nutriens, -entis,* ppr. of *nutrire* nourish⟩

nu•tri•ment ['njutrəmənt] *or* ['nutrəmənt] *n.* nourishment; food. ⟨< L *nutrimentum* < *nutrire* nourish⟩ **—,nu•tri'ment•al** [,njutrə'mɛntəl] *or* [,nutrə'mɛntəl], *adj.*

nu•tri•tion [nju'trɪʃən] *or* [nu'trɪʃən] *n.* 1 food; nourishment: *A balanced diet gives good nutrition.* 2 the series of processes by which food is changed to living tissues. **—nu'tri•tion•al** or **nu'tri•tion,ar•y,** *adj.* **—nu'tri•tion•al•ly,** *adv.*

nu•tri•tion•ist [nju'trɪʃənɪst] *or* [nu'trɪʃənɪst] *n.* an expert in nutrition, especially one whose work it is.

nu•tri•tious [nju'trɪʃəs] *or* [nu'trɪʃəs] *adj.* valuable as food; nourishing. ⟨< L *nutritius, nutricius* < *nutrix* nurse < *nutrire* nourish⟩ **—nu'tri•tious•ly,** *adv.* **—nu'tri•tious•ness,** *n.*

nu•tri•tive ['njutrətɪv] *or* ['nutrətɪv] *adj.* 1 having to do with foods and the use of foods. Digestion is part of the nutritive process. 2 nutritious. **—'nu•tri•tive•ness,** *n.* **—'nu•tri•tive•ly,** *adv.*

nuts and bolts *Informal.* practical details: *Anna knows the nuts and bolts of producing a book.*

nut•shell ['nʌt,ʃɛl] *n.* 1 the shell of a nut. 2 something extremely small in size or scanty in amount.
in a nutshell, in very brief form; in a few words: *Let me tell you the whole story in a nutshell.*

nut•ting ['nʌtɪŋ] *n., v.* *—n.* the act of looking for nuts; gathering nuts.
—v. ppr. of NUT.

nut•ty ['nʌti] *adj.* **-ti•er, -ti•est.** 1 containing many nuts: *nutty cake.* 2 producing many nuts. 3 like nuts; tasting like nuts. 4 *Slang.* eccentric; crazy. 5 *Slang.* very interested or enthusiastic (*used with* **about**): *nutty about line dancing.* **—'nut•ti•ly,** *adv.* **—'nut•ti•ness,** *n.*

nux vom•i•ca ['nʌks 'vɒməkə] 1 the poisonous seed of an Asian tree (*Strychnos nux-vomica*), containing strychnine and other poisonous alkaloids. 2 a drug prepared from these seeds, formerly used in medicine. 3 the tree itself. ⟨< Med.L *nux vomica* vomiting nut < L *nux* nut + *vomere* vomit⟩

nuz•zle ['nʌzəl] *v.* **-zled, -zling.** 1 poke or rub with the nose; press the nose against (something): *The calf nuzzles its mother.* 2 nestle; snuggle; cuddle. 3 burrow or dig with the nose. ⟨< *nose*; influenced by *nestle*⟩

NW or **N.W.** northwest; northwestern.

NWMP or **N.W.M.P.** *Cdn.* NORTH WEST MOUNTED POLICE.

N.W.T. NORTHWEST TERRITORIES.

nyc•ta•lo•pia [,nɪktə'loupiə] *n.* NIGHT BLINDNESS. ⟨< Gk. *nyx, nyct-* night + *alaos* blind + *-opia*⟩

nyc•tit•ro•pism [nɪk'tɪtrə,pɪzəm] *n. Botany.* the tendency of the leaves of certain plants to change their position at night. **—,nyc•ti'trop•ic** [,nɪktɪ'trɒpɪk], *adj.*

ny•lon ['naɪlɒn] *n.* 1 an extremely strong and durable, plastic substance, used to make textiles, utensils, bristles, etc. 2 **nylons,** *pl.* stockings made of nylon. 3 (*adjl.*) made of nylon: *Many toothbrushes have nylon bristles.* ⟨< *Nylon*, formerly a trademark⟩

nymph [nɪmf] *n.* 1 *Greek and Roman mythology.* one of a group of minor goddesses of nature, beautiful maidens living in seas, rivers, springs, hills, woods, or trees. 2 *Poetic.* a beautiful or graceful young woman. 3 any of certain insects in the stage of development between larva and adult. It resembles the adult but has no wings. ⟨ME < OF < L < Gk. *nymphē*⟩ **—'nymph,like, 'nym•phal,** or **'nym•phe•an** ['nɪmfiən], *adj.*

nym•pha•lid ['nɪmfəlɪd] *n.* a butterfly of the family Nymphalidae.

nymph•et [nɪm'fɛt] *or* ['nɪmfət] *n.* an attractive young girl who is at or close to the age of puberty and shows herself to be aware of her sexuality. ⟨< MF *nymphette*⟩

nym•pho•lep•sy ['nɪmfə,lɛpsi] *n.* **1** an obsession to get the impossible. **2** a frenzy caused by seeing nymphs.

nym•pho•ma•ni•a [,nɪmfə'meiniə] *n. Psychiatry.* excessive, uncontrollable sexual desire in a woman. ⟨< Gk. *nymphē* nymph, bride + E *mania*⟩

nym•pho•ma•ni•ac [,nɪmfə'meini,æk] *adj., n. —adj.* **1** of or having to do with nymphomania. **2** having nymphomania. *—n.* a woman who has nymphomania.

ny•stag•mus [nɪ'stægməs] *n.* an involuntary, rapid, rhythmic movement of the eyeball, usually associated with disease of the eye. ⟨< NL < Gk. *nystagmos* drowsiness < *nystazein* to be sleepy⟩

Oo *Oo*

o or **O**[1] [ou] *n., pl.* **o's** or **O's. 1** the fifteenth letter of the English alphabet. **2** any speech sound represented by this letter. **3** a person or thing identified as *o*, especially the fifteenth in a series. **4** zero. **5 O,** the type of human blood not containing either of the antigens A or B. It is one of the four blood types in the ABO system. **6** something shaped like the letter O. **7** any device, such as a printer's type, a lever, or a key on a keyboard that produces an o or an O. **8** (*adjl.*) of or being an O or o.
☛ *Hom.* OH, OWE.

O[2] [ou] See OH.
☛ *Hom.* OWE.
☛ *Usage.* **O** is usually used only before a name or something treated as a name: *O Canada. O Happy Day!* In other cases, the spelling generally used is **Oh.**

o' [ə] *or* [ou] *prep.* **1** of: *man-o'-war.* **2** on.

o– *prefix.* the form of *ob-* occurring before *m*, as in *omit.*

o. 1 octavo. **2** *Baseball.* out.

O oxygen.

O. 1 Ocean. **2** October. **3** Octavo.

oaf [ouf] *n., pl.* **oafs.** a clumsy and usually stupid or boorish person. ⟨orig. = elf's child, or changeling < dial. *aufe, aulfe,* ult. < ON *álfr* elf. 17c.⟩

oaf•ish ['oufɪʃ] *adj.* clumsy and stupid. **–'oaf•ish•ly,** *adv.* **–'oaf•ish•ness,** *n.*

oak [ouk] *n.* **1** any of a genus (*Quercus*) of deciduous or evergreen trees or shrubs of the beech family, having usually lobed or toothed leaves and bearing single-seeded nuts called acorns. **2** the hard, durable wood of an oak, valued for the construction of buildings, furniture, etc. **3** (*adjl.*) made of oak: *an oak desk.* **4** any of various trees or shrubs resembling oaks in some way, such as poison oak. **5** the leaves of an oak, used as decoration. **6** something made of oak. ⟨OE *āc*⟩ **–'oak,like,** *adj.*

An oak leaf

oak apple a lump or ball on an oak leaf or stem resulting from injury by an insect.

oak•en ['oukən] *adj. Archaic or poetic.* made of oak wood: *the old oaken bucket.*

oak gall OAK APPLE.

oa•kum ['oukəm] *n.* a loose fibre obtained by untwisting and picking apart old ropes, used for stopping up the seams or cracks in ships. ⟨OE *ācumba* offcombings⟩

oak wilt a fungus disease of oak trees (*Chalara quercina*).

OAP old age pensioner.

oar [ɔr] *n., v.* *–n.* **1** a long pole with a broad, flat blade at one end, used for rowing or steering a boat. **2** a person who rows in a crew: *She's the best oar in our crew.*
put (one's) **oar in,** meddle; interfere.
rest on (one's) **oars,** stop working or trying and take a rest.
–v. row. ⟨OE *ār*⟩
☛ *Hom.* O'ER, OR, ORE.

oar•fish ['ɔr,fɪʃ] *n.* a marine fish (*Regalecus glesne*) with a thin body up to 10 m long.

oar•lock ['ɔr,lɒk] *n.* a support for an oar; rowlock. ⟨OE *ārloc*⟩

oars•man ['ɔrzmən] *n., pl.* **-men. 1** a man who rows. **2** a man who rows well.

oars•wom•an ['ɔrz,wʊmən] *n., pl.* **-wom•en. 1** a woman who rows. **2** a woman who rows well.

OAS or **O.A.S.** Organization of American States.

o•a•ses [ou'eisiz] *or* ['ouə,siz] *n.* pl. of OASIS.

o•a•sis [ou'eisɪs] *or* ['ouəsɪs] *n., pl.* **-ses** [-siz] *or* [-,siz]. **1** a fertile spot in the desert: *Water is always available at an oasis.* **2** any fertile spot in a barren land; any pleasant place in a desolate region. ⟨< L < Gk. *oasis,* apparently < Egyptian⟩

oast [oust] *n.* **1** a kiln for drying hops or malt. **2** a kiln for curing tobacco.

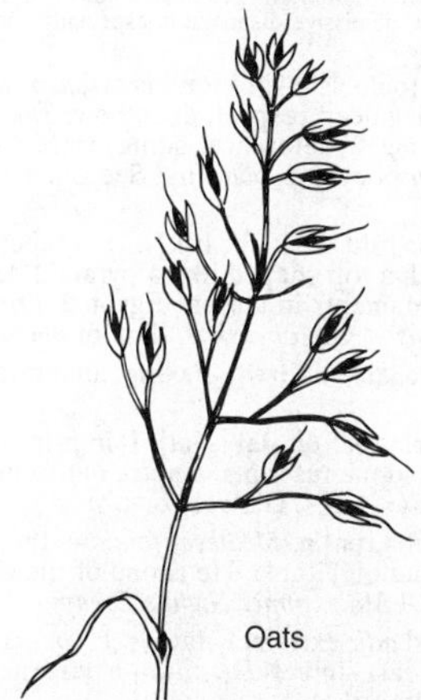

Oats

oat [out] *n.* **1** Usually, **oats,** *pl.* a tall cereal grass (*Avena sativa*), widely cultivated for its edible seeds. **2 oats,** *pl.* the seeds of the oat plant. **3** any of various other grasses of the same genus. **4** *Poetic.* a musical pipe made of an oat straw.
feel (one's) **oats,** *Slang.* **a** be lively or frisky. **b** feel pleased or important and show it.
sow (one's) **wild oats.** See WILD OATS. ⟨OE *āte*⟩ **–'oat,like,** *adj.*

oat•cake ['out,keik] *n.* a thin cake made of oatmeal.

oat•en ['outən] *adj.* made of oats, oat straw, or oatmeal.

oath [ouθ] *n., pl.* **oaths** [ouðz] *or* [ouθs]. **1** a solemn promise or statement that something is true, especially such a promise made to a judge, coroner, etc. A person who tells lies after taking an oath can be punished by the law. **2** the name of God or some holy person or thing used as an exclamation to add force or to express anger. **3** a curse; swear word.
take oaths or **take** (someone's) **oath,** certify or attest an oath: *A notary public is authorized to take oaths.*
take oath or **take an oath,** make an oath; promise or state solemnly.
under oath, bound by an oath: *He gave his evidence under oath.* ⟨OE *āth*⟩

oat•meal ['out,mil] *n.* **1** oats made into meal; ground oats. **2** rolled oats. **3** porridge made from rolled or ground oats.

ob– *prefix.* **1** against; in the way; opposing; hindering, as in *obstruct.* **2** inversely; contrary to the usual position, as in *oblate.* **3** toward; to, as in *obvert.* **4** on; over, as in *obscure.* **5** intensified action, as in *obdurate.* Also: **o-,** before *m*; **oc-,** before *c*; **of-,** before *f*; **op-,** before *p*; **os-,** in some cases before *c* and *t.* ⟨< L⟩

ob. 1 died (for L *obiit*; used on tombstones, etc.). **2** oboe.

ob•bli•ga•to [,ɒblə'gɑtou] *adj., n., pl.* **-tos.** *Music.* *–adj.* accompanying a solo, but having a distinct character and independent importance.
–n. an obbligato part or accompaniment. Also, **obligato.** ⟨< Ital. *obbligato,* literally, obliged⟩

ob•cor•date [ɒb'kɔrdeit] *adj. Botany.* heart-shaped and joining the stem at the pointed end.

ob•du•rate ['ɒbdjərɪt] *adj.* **1** stubborn; unyielding: *an obdurate refusal.* **2** hardened in feelings or heart; not repentant: *an obdurate criminal.* ⟨< L *obduratus,* pp. of *obdurare* < *ob-* against + *durare* harden⟩ **–'ob•du•ra•cy,** *n.* **–'ob•du•rate•ly,** *adv.* **–'ob•du•rate•ness,** *n.*

O.B.E. Officer (of the Order) of the British Empire.

o•be•di•ence [ou'bidiəns] *or* [ou'bidjəns] *n.* **1** the act or habit of doing what one is told; submission to authority or law: *Our puppy is already learning obedience. Soldiers act in obedience to orders.* **2** a sphere of ecclesiastical authority. **3** people under such authority.

obedience training the training of a dog to obey commands.

o•be•di•ent [ou'bidiənt] *adj.* doing what one is told; willing to obey. ⟨< F < L *oboediens, -entis*, ppr. of *oboedire* obey⟩ **—o'be•di•ent•ly,** *adv.*

☛ *Syn.* **Obedient,** COMPLIANT, DOCILE = acting as another asks or commands. **Obedient** emphasizes being willing to follow instructions and carry out orders of someone whose authority one acknowledges: *an obedient servant.* **Compliant** emphasizes bending easily, sometimes too easily, to another's will. Compliant people are not ideal leaders. **Docile** emphasizes having a submissive disposition, especially a willingness to be taught: *a docile horse.*

o•bei•sance [ou'beisəns] *or* [ou'bisəns] *n.* **1** a movement of the body expressing deep respect; deep bow: *The men made obeisance to the king.* **2** deference; homage. ⟨ME < OF *obeisance* obedience < *obeir* obey < L *oboedire.* See OBEY.⟩ **—o'bei•sant,** *adj.*

ob•e•lisk ['ɒbə,lɪsk] *or* ['oubə,lɪsk] *n.* **1** a tapering, four-sided shaft of stone with a top shaped like a pyramid. Obelisks were often used as monuments in ancient Egypt. **2** *Printing.* dagger (†). ⟨< L *obeliscus* < Gk. *obeliskos,* dim. of *obelos* a spit⟩

ob•e•lize ['ɒbə,laɪz] *v.* **-lized, -liz•ing.** annotate with an obelus.

ob•e•lus ['ɒbələs] *n., pl.* **-lai** [-,laɪ]. **1** in printing, an obelisk (dagger †). **2** in old manuscripts, a mark (÷) to indicate a spurious passage. ⟨< LL < Gk. *obelos* spit⟩

O•ber•on ['oubə,rɒn] *n. Medieval folklore.* the king of the fairies and husband of Titania. He is one of the chief characters in Shakespeare's *A Midsummer Night's Dream.*

o•bese [ou'bis] *adj.* extremely fat. ⟨< L *obesus* < *ob-* in addition + *edere* eat⟩ **—o'bese•ly,** *adv.* **—o'bese•ness,** *n.* **—o'be•si•ty** [ou'bisəti], *n.*

o•bey [ou'bei] *v.* **1** do what one is told: *The dog obeyed immediately when told to sit.* **2** follow the orders of: *They obeyed their father.* **3** act in accordance with; comply with: *to obey the laws.* **4** yield to the control of: *A car obeys the driver.* ⟨ME *obeien* < F *obéir* < L *oboedire* < *ob-* to + *audire* give ear⟩ **—o'bey•er,** *n.*

ob•fus•cate ['ɒbfə,skeit] *or* [ɒb'fʌskeit] *v.* **-cat•ed, -cat•ing. 1** confuse; stupefy: *A person's mind may be obfuscated by liquor.* **2** darken; obscure. ⟨< L *obfuscare* < *ob-* + *fuscus* dark⟩ **—,ob•fus'ca•tion,** *n.* **—'ob•fus,ca•tor,** *n.*

o•bi ['oubi] *n., pl.* **o•bis** or **o•bi.** a long, broad sash worn around the waist of a kimono by Japanese women and children. See KIMONO for picture. ⟨< Japanese⟩

ob•i•ter dic•tum ['ɒbətər] *or* ['oubətər 'dɪktəm] *pl.* **ob•i•ter dic•ta** ['dɪktə]. **1** an incidental remark. **2** *Law.* an incidental opinion given by a judge. ⟨< L *obiter dictum* said by the way⟩

o•bit•u•ar•y [ou'bɪtʃu,ɛri] *n., pl.* **-ar•ies;** *adj.* *—n.* a notice of death, often with a brief account of the person's life.
—adj. of a death; recording a death. ⟨< Med.L *obituarius,* ult. < L *obire (mortem)* meet (death) < *ob-* up to + *ire* go⟩ **—o'bit•u,ar•ist,** *n.*

obj. object; objective; objection.

ob•ject *n.* ['ɒbdʒɪkt] *or* ['ɒbdʒɛkt]; *v.* [əb'dʒɛkt] *n., v.* *—n.* **1** anything that can be seen or touched; thing; article. **2** a person or thing toward which feeling, thought, or action is directed: *an object of charity.* **3** something aimed at; end; purpose. **4** *Grammar.* a word or group of words toward which the action of the verb is directed or to which a preposition expresses some relation. In *He threw the ball to his sister, ball* is the object of *threw,* and *sister* is the object of *to.* **5 a** anything that can be presented to the mind: *objects of thought.* **b** a thing with reference to the impression it makes on the mind: *an object of pity.*
—v. **1** make objections; be opposed; feel dislike: *I made my suggestion, but Jean objected. Many people object to loud noise.* **2** give a reason against something; bring forward in opposition; oppose: *Mother objected that the weather was too wet to play outdoors.* ⟨< Med.L *objectum* thing presented to the mind or thought, neut. of L *objectus,* pp. of *obicere* throw before, put in the way of < *ob-* against + *jacere* throw⟩ **—ob'ject•ing•ly,** *adv.* **—ob'jec•tor,** *n.*

object glass *Optics.* See OBJECTIVE (def 4).

ob•jec•ti•fy [əb'dʒɛktə,faɪ] *v.* **-fied, -fy•ing.** make objective; externalize: *Experiments in chemistry objectify the teaching. Kind acts objectify kindness.* **—ob,jec•ti•fi'ca•tion,** *n.*

ob•jec•tion [əb'dʒɛkʃən] *n.* **1** something said in objecting; reason or argument against something: *One of his objections to the plan was that it would cost too much.* **2** a feeling of disapproval or dislike. **3** the act of objecting: *What is the basis for your objection?* **4** a ground or cause of objecting.

ob•jec•tion•a•ble [əb'dʒɛkʃənəbəl] *adj.* **1** likely to be objected to. **2** unpleasant; disagreeable. **—ob'jec•tion•a•bly,** *adv.*

ob•jec•tive [əb'dʒɛktɪv] *n., adj.* *—n.* **1** something aimed at: *My objective this summer will be learning to play tennis better.* **2** something real and observable. **3** *Grammar.* **a** the grammatical form of an English pronoun that shows that it is an object of a verb or preposition, corresponding to the dative and accusative cases in German and Latin. **b** a word or construction in this form. **4** *Optics.* the lens or set of lenses in a microscope or telescope that is nearest to the object being viewed and that forms the image of the object. See MICROSCOPE for picture.
—adj. **1** existing outside the mind as an actual object and not merely in the mind as an idea; real. Buildings and landscapes are objective; ideas and feelings are subjective. **2** dealing with facts or objects, not with the thoughts and feelings of the speaker, writer, painter, etc.; impersonal: *A scientist must be objective in experiments. The report was not objective, but was biassed in favour of the one firm.* Compare SUBJECTIVE (def. 2). **3** *Grammar.* of, having to do with, or being the objective. The six English pronouns with special objective forms are *me, us, him, her, them,* and *whom.* Compare SUBJECTIVE (def. 4). **4** *Medicine.* of symptoms, observable or perceptible by people other than the patient. **5** *Art.* **a** of a work of art, representing or resembling natural objects; not abstract. **b** in perspective, designating or of the object of which the delineation is required: *an objective point.* **6** being the object of endeavour. **—ob'jec•tive•ly,** *adv.* **—ob'jec•tive•ness,** *n.* **—,ob•jec'tiv•i•ty** [,ɒbdʒɛk'tɪvɪti], *n.*

object lesson 1 instruction conveyed by means of material objects. **2** a practical illustration of a principle: *Most street accidents are object lessons in the dangers of carelessness.*

ob•jet d'art [,ɒbʒei 'dɑr]; *French,* [ɔbʒɛ'daʀ] *pl.* **ob•jets d'art** [ɔbʒɛ'daʀ] *French.* a small picture, vase, etc. of some artistic value.

ob•jur•gate ['ɒbdʒər,geit] *or* [əb'dʒɜrgeit] *v.* **-gat•ed, -gat•ing.** reproach vehemently; upbraid violently; berate. ⟨< L *objurgare* < *ob-* against + *jurgare* scold⟩ **—,ob•jur'ga•tion,** *n.* **—'ob•jur,ga•tor,** *n.* **—ob'jur•ga,to•ry** [əb'dʒɜrgə,tɔri], *adj.*

ob•lan•ce•o•late [ɒb'lænsiəlɪt] *or* [ɒb'lænsiə,leit] *adj. Botany.* tapering at the base, as a leaf.

ob•late[1] ['ɒbleit] *or* [ou'bleit] *adj.* flattened at the poles; having an equatorial diameter greater than the polar diameter. The earth is an oblate spheroid. Compare PROLATE. ⟨< NL *oblatus* < L *ob-* inversely + *(pro)latus* prolate⟩ **—'ob•late•ly,** *adv.* **—'ob•late•ness,** *n.*

ob•late[2] ['ɒbleit] *or* [ou'bleit] *n., adj.* *—n. Roman Catholic Church.* a member of any of various secular institutes devoted to religious work.
—adj. dedicated to religious work. ⟨< Med.L *oblatus,* noun use of pp. of L *offerre* offer⟩

ob•la•tion [ə'bleiʃən] *n.* **1** an offering to God or a god. **2** the offering of bread and wine in the Christian Communion service. ⟨< LL *oblatio, -onis* < *ob-* up to + *latus,* pp. of *ferre* bring⟩ **—ob'la•tion•al** or **'ob•la,to•ry** ['ɒblə,tɔri], *adj.*

ob•li•gate ['ɒblə,geit] *v.* **-gat•ed, -gat•ing.** bind morally or legally; pledge: *A witness in court is obligated to tell the truth.* ⟨< L *obligare* < *ob-* to + *ligare* bind. Doublet of OBLIGE.⟩ **—'ob•li•ga•ble** ['ɒbləgəbəl], *adj.* **—'ob•li,ga•tor,** *n.*

ob•li•ga•tion [,ɒblə'geiʃən] *n.* **1** a duty under the law or due to a promise or contract, social relationship, etc.: *a person's obligation to family. It is her obligation to pay for the damage. He is under obligation to paint our house first.* **2** a binding legal agreement; bond; contract: *The firm was not able to meet its obligations.* **3** being in debt for a favour, service, or the like. **4** a service; favour; benefit: *An independent person likes to repay all obligations.* **—,ob•li'ga•tion•al,** *adj.*

☛ *Syn.* **1.** See note at DUTY.

ob•li•ga•to [,ɒblə'gɑtou] See OBBLIGATO.

ob•lig•a•to•ry [ə'blɪgə,tɔri] *or* ['ɒbləgə,tɔri] *adj.* binding morally or legally; required: *Attendance at school is obligatory.* ⟨< LL *obligatorius*⟩ **—ob'lig•a,to•ri•ly,** *adv.*

o•blige [ə'blaɪdʒ] *v.* **o•bliged, o•blig•ing. 1** bind by a promise, contract, duty, etc.; compel; force: *The law obliges parents to send their children to school.* **2** put under a debt of thanks for a favour or service: *She obliged us with a song.* **3** do a favour (to): *She asked for a cup of tea and he obliged immediately.*
be obliged, be grateful to someone for a service: *I am obliged to you for letting me stay so long at your house.* ⟨ME < OF *obliger* < L *obligare.* Doublet of OBLIGATE.⟩ **—o'blig•ed•ly** [ə'blaɪdʒədli], *adv.* **—o'blig•er,** *n.*

ob•li•gee [ˌɒblə'dʒi] *n.* **1** *Law.* one to whom another is bound by contract; creditor. **2** one under obligation to another.

o•blig•ing [ə'blaɪdʒɪŋ] *adj.* willing to do favours; helpful. **—o'blig•ing•ly,** *adv.* **—o'blig•ing•ness,** *n.*

ob•lique [ə'blik] *adj., n., v.* **-liqued, -liqu•ing.** *—adj.* **1** not vertical or horizontal; not perpendicular or parallel; slanting. **2** *Geometry.* **a** containing no right angle: *an oblique triangle.* **b** having the axis not perpendicular to the base: *an oblique cone.* **3** not straightforward; indirect: *an oblique glance, an oblique movement.* **4** underhanded or evasive: *oblique dealings.* **5** *Grammar.* of or designating any case other than nominative or vocative. **6** *Botany.* having unequal sides: *an oblique leaf.*
—n. something oblique, especially a stroke or line.
—v. have or advance in an oblique direction; angle or slant. ⟨< L *obliquus*⟩ **—ob'lique•ness,** *n.*

oblique angle any angle that is not a right angle. See ANGLE[1] for picture.

ob•liq•ui•ty [ə'blɪkwəti] *n., pl.* **-ties. 1** indirectness or crookedness of thought or behaviour, especially conduct that is not upright and moral. **2** being oblique. **—ob'liq•ui•tous,** *adj.*

ob•lit•er•ate [ə'blɪtəˌreit] *v.* **-at•ed, -at•ing.** remove all traces of; blot out; destroy: *Heavy rain obliterated the footprints.* ⟨< L *oblit(t)erare* < *ob literas (scribere)* (draw) across the letters⟩ **—obˌlit•er'a•tion,** *n.* **—ob'lit•erˌa•tor,** *n.* **—ob'lit•er•a•tive,** *adj.*

ob•liv•i•on [ə'blɪviən] *n.* **1** the condition of being entirely forgotten: *Many ancient cities have long since passed into oblivion.* **2** the condition of being unaware of what is going on; forgetfulness. ⟨< L *oblivio, -onis* < *oblivisci* forget, originally, even off, smooth out + *ob-* + *levis* smooth⟩

ob•liv•i•ous [ə'blɪviəs] *adj.* **1** forgetful; not mindful; unaware (*used with* **to** *or* **of**): *The book was so interesting that I was oblivious of my surroundings.* **2** bringing or causing forgetfulness. ⟨< L *obliviosus*⟩ **—ob'liv•i•ous•ly,** *adv.* **—ob'liv•i•ous•ness,** *n.*

ob•long ['ɒblɒŋ] *adj., n.* *—adj.* **1** longer than broad or round: *an oblong loaf of bread, an oblong tablecloth.* **2** of a plane figure, having four sides and four right angles, but not square; rectangular with adjacent sides unequal.
—n. a rectangle that is not square. See QUADRILATERAL for picture. ⟨< L *oblongus* < *ob-* + *longus* long⟩

ob•lo•quy ['ɒbləkwi] *n., pl.* **-quies. 1** public reproach; abuse; blame. **2** disgrace; shame. ⟨< LL *obloquium,* ult. < L *ob-* against + *loqui* speak⟩ **—ob'lo•qui•al** [ɒb'loukwiəl], *adj.*

ob•nox•ious [əb'nɒkʃəs] *adj.* very disagreeable; offensive; hateful: *His disgusting table manners made him obnoxious to us.* ⟨< L *obnoxiosus,* ult. < *ob-* + *noxa* injury⟩ **—ob'nox•ious•ly,** *adv.* **—ob'nox•ious•ness,** *n.*
☛ *Syn.* See note at HATEFUL.

o•boe ['oubou] *n.* **1** a wooden musical wind instrument in which a thin, poignant tone is produced by a double reed. **2** a reed stop in an organ that produces a tone like that of the oboe. ⟨< Ital. < F *hautbois* hautboy⟩

An oboe

o•bo•ist ['oubouɪst] *n.* one who plays the oboe, especially a skilled player.

ob•o•vate [ɒb'ouveit] *adj.* *Botany.* of a leaf, egg-shaped with the narrow end attached to the stalk. Also, **obovoid** [ɒb'ouvɔɪd].

obs. 1 obsolete. **2** observation; observatory.

ob•scene [əb'sin] *adj.* **1** grossly indecent or lewd: *an obscene dance, an obscene remark.* **2** *Law.* of written or printed material, etc., tending to deprave or corrupt. **3** repugnant; highly offensive: *an obscene display of wealth.* ⟨< L *obscenus*⟩ **—ob'scene•ly,** *adv.*

ob•scen•i•ty [əb'sɛnəti] *or* [əb'sinəti] *n., pl.* **-ties. 1** the quality or state of being obscene. **2** something that is obscene, such as an utterance or an act.

ob•scu•rant•ism [ˌɒbskjə'ræntɪzəm] *or* [əb'skjʊrənˌtɪzəm] *n.* **1** opposition to progress and the spread of knowledge and enlightenment. **2** an artistic or literary style characterized by deliberate complexity and obscurity. ⟨< L *obscurans, -antis,* ppr. of *obscurare* to obscure < *obscurus* obscure⟩ **—ob•scu'rant•ist,** *n., adj.*

ob•scu•ra•tion [ˌɒbskjə'reiʃən] *n.* obscuring or being obscured.

ob•scure [əb'skjʊr] *adj.* **-scur•er, -scur•est;** *v.* **-scured, -scur•ing.** *—adj.* **1** not clearly expressed: *an obscure passage in a book.* **2** not expressing meaning clearly: *an obscure style of writing.* **3** not well-known; attracting no notice: *an obscure little village, an obscure poet, an obscure position in the government.* **4** not easily discovered; hidden: *an obscure path, an obscure meaning.* **5** not distinct; not clear: *an obscure form, obscure sounds, an obscure view.* **6** dark; dim: *an obscure corner.* **7** indefinite: *an obscure brown, an obscure vowel.*
—v. **1** hide from view; make obscure; dim; overshadow: *Clouds obscure the sun. Her modest talents were obscured by the razzle-dazzle of her rival.* **2** confuse; make unclear: *All their talk just obscures the issue.* ⟨ME < OF < L *obscurus* < *ob-* over + *scur-* cover⟩ **—ob'scure•ly,** *adv.* **—ob'scure•ness,** *n.* **—ob'scur•er,** *n.*
☛ *Syn. adj.* **1. Obscure,** VAGUE, AMBIGUOUS = not clearly expressed or understood. **Obscure** suggests that the meaning of something is hidden from the understanding, because it is not plainly expressed or the reader lacks the knowledge necessary for understanding. Much legal language is obscure. **Vague** suggests not definite, too general in meaning or statement or not clearly and completely thought out. No one can be sure what a vague statement means. **Ambiguous** means so expressed that more than one meaning is possible: *The ambiguity of the passage makes several interpretations possible.*

ob•scu•ri•ty [əb'skjʊrəti] *n., pl.* **-ties. 1** a lack of clearness; difficulty in being understood: *The obscurity of the cave inscription made its meaning escape us.* **2** something obscure; something hard to understand; doubtful or vague meaning: *The movie had so many obscurities that we didn't enjoy it.* **3** the state or condition of being unknown: *The premier rose from obscurity to fame.* **4** a little-known person or place. **5** a lack of light; dimness.

ob•se•quies ['ɒbsəkwiz] *n.pl.* funeral rites or ceremonies; stately funeral. ⟨ME < OF < Med.L *obsequiae,* pl., for L *exsequiae* < *ex-* out + *sequi* follow⟩

ob•se•qui•ous [əb'sikwiəs] *adj.* polite or obedient from hope of gain or from fear; servile; fawning: *Obsequious courtiers greeted the king.* ⟨< L *obsequiosus,* ult. < *ob-* after + *sequi* follow⟩ **—ob'se•qui•ous•ly,** *adv.* **—ob'se•qui•ous•ness,** *n.*

ob•serv•a•ble [əb'zɜrvəbəl] *adj.* **1** that can be or is noticed; noticeable; easily seen. **2** that can be or is observed: *Lent is observable by most Christian churches.* **—ob'serv•a•bly,** *adv.* **—obˌserv•a'bil•i•ty,** *n.*

ob•serv•ance [əb'zɜrvəns] *n.* **1** the act of observing or keeping laws or customs: *the observance of the Sabbath.* **2** an act performed as a sign of worship or respect; a religious ceremony. **3** a rule or custom to be observed. **4** *Archaic.* respectful attention or service. **5** an observation.

ob•serv•ant [əb'zɜrvənt] *adj.* **1** quick to notice; watchful; observing: *If you are observant in the fields and woods, you will find many flowers that others fail to notice.* **2** careful in observing (a law, rule, custom, etc.): *observant of the traffic rules.* ⟨< L *observans, -antis,* ppr. of *observare.* See OBSERVE.⟩ **—ob'serv•ant•ly,** *adv.*

ob•ser•va•tion [ˌɒbzər'veiʃən] *n.* **1** the act, habit, or power of seeing and noting: *His keen observation helped him to become a good scientist.* **2** the fact of being seen; being seen; notice: *The tramp escaped observation.* **3** something seen and noted. **4** the act of watching for some special purpose; study: *The observation of nature is important in science.* **5** a remark; comment.
☛ *Usage.* **Observation,** OBSERVANCE are sometimes confused because both are related to the verb **observe. Observation,** connected with the meaning 'watch closely', applies especially to the act or power of noticing things or watching closely, or to being watched or noticed: *An observatory is a building designed for the observation of the stars.* **Observance,** connected with the meaning 'keep', applies to the act of keeping and following customs or duties, or to a rule, rite, etc. kept or celebrated: *You go to church for the observance of religious duties.* **Observation** sometimes means 'observance', but this meaning is obsolete or rare.

ob•ser•va•tion•al [ˌɒbzər'veiʃənəl] *adj.* of, having to do with, or founded on observation, rather than on experiment. **—ˌob•ser'va•tion•al•ly,** *adv.*

observation car a railway passenger car having large windows, a glass dome, or an open platform at one end, to enable passengers to view the scenery easily.

ob•serv•a•to•ry [əb'zɜrvəˌtɔri] *n., pl.* **-ries. 1** a place or building equipped with a telescope, etc. for observing the stars and other heavenly bodies. **2** a place or building for observing facts or happenings of nature. **3** a high place or building giving a wide view.

ob•serve [əb'zɜrv] *v.* **-served, -serv•ing. 1** see and note; notice: *I observed nothing queer in his behaviour.* **2** examine for some special purpose; study: *An astronomer observes the stars.* **3** remark; comment: *"Foul weather," the captain observed.* **4** keep; follow in practice: *to observe silence, to observe a rule.* **5** show regard for; celebrate: *to observe the Sabbath.* ⟨ME < OF < L *observare* < *ob-* over + *servare* watch, keep⟩ **—ob'serv•ed•ly,** *adv.*

☛ *Syn.* **1.** See note at SEE[1].

ob•serv•er [əb'zɜrvər] *n.* **1** one who watches or examines. **2** one who follows or celebrates a rule, custom, etc.: *an observer of the Sabbath.* **3** one who attends a meeting as a guest but can take no official part in it. **4** someone sent to report on a situation by a body such as the United Nations.

ob•serv•ing [əb'zɜrvɪŋ] *adj., v.* — *adj.* observant. —*v.* ppr. of OBSERVE. **—ob'serv•ing•ly,** *adv.*

ob•sess [əb'sɛs] *v.* fill the mind of greatly; keep the full attention of; haunt: *The fear that someone might steal her money obsesses her.* ⟨< L *obsessus,* pp. of *obsidere* besiege⟩ **—ob'ses•sor,** *n.*

ob•ses•sion [əb'sɛʃən] *n.* **1** obsessing or being obsessed; the influence of a feeling, idea, or impulse that a person cannot escape. **2** the feeling, idea, or impulse itself. **3** *Psychiatry.* a compelling or fixed idea or feeling, usually irrational, over which a person has little conscious control; compulsion. **—ob'ses•sion•al,** *adj.* **—ob'ses•sion•al•ly,** *adv.*

ob•ses•sive [əb'sɛsɪv] *adj.* of, having to do with, or causing obsession. **—ob'ses•sive•ly,** *adv.*

ob•sid•i•an [əb'sɪdiən] *n.* a hard, dark, glassy rock that is formed when lava cools; volcanic glass. ⟨< L *obsidianus,* mistaken reading for *obsianus;* after *Obsius,* its discoverer⟩

ob•so•les•cence [,ɒbsə'lɛsəns] *n.* the condition or state of passing out of use; getting out of date; a becoming obsolete.

ob•so•les•cent [,ɒbsə'lɛsənt] *adj.* **1** passing out of use; tending to become out-of-date: *Fountain pens are obsolescent.* **2** *Biology.* gradually disappearing; imperfectly or slightly developed: *obsolescent organs.* ⟨< L *obsolescens, -entis,* ppr. of *obsolescere* fall into disuse, ult. < *ob-* + *solere* be usual, be customary⟩ **—,ob•so'les•cent•ly,** *adv.*

ob•so•lete [,ɒbsə'lit] *adj.* **1** no longer in use. *Eft,* meaning *again,* is an obsolete word. **2** out-of-date: *We still use this machine although it is obsolete.* ⟨< L *obsoletus,* pp. of *obsolescere.* See OBSOLESCENT.⟩ **—'ob•so•lete•ly,** *adv.* **—'ob•so•lete•ness,** *n.*

ob•sta•cle ['ɒbstəkəl] *n.* something that stands in the way or stops progress: *Blindness is an obstacle in most occupations.* ⟨ME < OF < L *obstaculum* < *ob-* in the way of + *stare* stand⟩

☛ *Syn.* **Obstacle,** OBSTRUCTION, HINDRANCE = something that gets in the way of action or progress. **Obstacle** suggests an object, condition, etc. that stands in the way and must be removed or overcome before someone or something can continue toward a goal: *A tree fallen across the road was an obstacle to our car.* **Obstruction** applies especially to something that blocks a passage: *The enemy built obstructions in the road.* **Hindrance** applies to a person or thing that holds back or makes progress difficult: *Noise is a hindrance to studying.*

obstacle course 1 a course to be crossed that includes several obstacles, such as walls or ditches. **2** *Informal.* any procedure fraught with difficulties.

ob•stet•ric [əb'stɛtrɪk] *adj.* having to do with the care of women in childbirth.

ob•stet•ri•cal [əb'stɛtrɪkəl] *adj.* obstetric; of or having to do with obstetrics. **—ob'stet•ri•cal•ly,** *adv.*

ob•ste•tri•cian [,ɒbstə'trɪʃən] *n.* a physician who specializes in obstetrics.

ob•stet•rics [əb'stɛtrɪks] *n.* the branch of medicine and surgery concerned with caring for and treating women before, during, and after childbirth (*used with a singular verb*). ⟨< L *obstetrica,* fem. *obstetrix, -tricis* midwife < *ob-* by + *stare* stand⟩

ob•sti•na•cy ['ɒbstənəsi] *n., pl.* **-cies. 1** stubbornness; being obstinate. **2** an obstinate act.

ob•sti•nate ['ɒbstənɪt] *adj.* **1** not giving in; stubborn: *The obstinate girl would go her own way, in spite of all warnings.* **2** hard to control or treat: *an obstinate cough.* ⟨ME < L *obstinatus,* pp. of *obstinare,* ult. < *ob-* by + *stare* stand⟩ **—'ob•sti•nate•ly,** *adv.* **—'ob•sti•nate•ness,** *n.*

☛ *Syn.* **1. Obstinate,** STUBBORN = fixed in purpose or opinion. **Obstinate** suggests a persistent holding to a purpose, opinion, or way of doing something, sometimes unreasonably or contrarily: *The obstinate man refused to obey orders.* **Stubborn,** often interchangeable with *obstinate,* especially suggests a quality of character that makes a person resist attempts to change his or her mind: *She is stubborn as a mule.* **Stubborn** is used more often than **obstinate** to describe animals or things.

ob•strep•er•ous [əb'strɛpərəs] *adj.* **1** noisy; boisterous. **2** unruly; disorderly. ⟨< L *obstreperus* < *ob-* against + *strepere* make a noise⟩ **—ob'strep•er•ous•ly,** *adv.* **—ob'strep•er•ous•ness,** *n.*

ob•struct [əb'strʌkt] *v.* **1** make hard to pass through; block up: *Fallen trees obstruct the road.* **2** be in the way of; hinder: *Trees obstruct our view of the ocean.* ⟨< L *obstructus,* pp. of *obstruere* < *ob-* in the way of + *struere* pile⟩ **—ob'struct•er** or **ob'struct•or,** *n.*

ob•struc•tion [əb'strʌkʃən] *n.* **1** anything that obstructs; something in the way; obstacle: *The soldiers had to get over such obstructions as ditches and barbed wire. Anger is an obstruction to clear thinking.* **2** the act of obstructing or the state of being obstructed.

☛ *Syn.* **1.** See note at OBSTACLE.

ob•struc•tion•ism [əb'strʌkʃə,nɪzəm] *n.* the deliberate hindering of the progress of business in a meeting, legislature, etc.

ob•struc•tion•ist [əb'strʌkʃənɪst] *n.* one who hinders (progress, legislation, reform, etc.). **—ob,struc•tion'is•tic,** *adj.*

ob•struc•tive [əb'strʌktɪv] *adj.* tending or serving to obstruct; blocking; hindering. **—ob'struc•tive•ly,** *adv.* **—ob'struc•tive•ness,** *n.*

ob•stru•ent ['ɒbstruənt] *adj., n.* —*adj.* **1** *Medicine.* producing an obstruction. **2** *Phonetics.* of a sound, made by blocking the progress of air. —*n.* **1** *Medicine.* a drug to close the open passages of the body. **2** *Phonetics.* any consonant sound made by blocking the progress of air; a stop, fricative, or affricate.

ob•tain [əb'tein] *v.* **1** get or procure through diligence or effort; come to have: *He worked hard to obtain the prize. We study to obtain knowledge.* **2** be in use; be customary: *Different rules obtain in different schools.* ⟨ME < OF < L *obtinere* < *ob-* to + *tenere* hold⟩ **—ob'tain•a•ble,** *adj.* **—ob'tain•er,** *n.* **—ob'tain•ment,** *n.*

☛ *Syn.* **1.** See note at GET.

ob•tect [ɒb'tɛkt] *adj.* covered by a hardened secretion. ⟨< L *obtectus,* pp. of *obtegere* to cover⟩

ob•test [ɒb'tɛst] *v.* entreat. **—,ob•tes'ta•tion,** *n.*

ob•trude [əb'trud] *v.* **-trud•ed, -trud•ing. 1** put forward unasked and unwanted; force: *Don't obtrude your opinions on others.* **2** come unasked and unwanted; force oneself; intrude. **3** push out; thrust forward: *A turtle obtrudes its head from its shell.* ⟨< L *obtrudere* < *ob-* toward + *trudere* thrust⟩ **—ob'trud•er,** *n.*

ob•tru•sion [əb'truʒən] *n.* **1** an obtruding. **2** something obtruded. ⟨< LL *obtrusio, -onis* < L *obtrudere.* See OBTRUDE.⟩

ob•tru•sive [əb'trusɪv] *adj.* **1** too noticeable; not blending or fitting in: *obtrusive colours.* **2** protruding. **3** intrusive or pushy. **—ob'tru•sive•ly,** *adv.* **—ob'tru•sive•ness,** *n.*

ob•tund [ɒb'tʌnd] *v.* make less intense: *Anesthetics can obtund the reflexes for some time after the patient regains consciousness.* ⟨< L *obtundere* to beat at⟩ **—ob'tund•ent,** *adj.*

ob•tu•rate ['ɒbtjʊ,reit] *or* ['ɒbtʊ,reit] *v.* **-rat•ed, -rat•ing.** close up. ⟨< L *obturatus,* pp. of *obturare* to block⟩ **—,ob•tu'ra•tion,** *n.* **—'ob•tu,ra•tor,** *n.*

ob•tuse [əb'tjus] *or* [əb'tus] *adj.* **1** not sharp or acute; blunt. **2** having more than 90° of angle but less than 180°. **3** slow in understanding; stupid: *He was too obtuse to take the hint.* **4** not sensitive; dull: *One's hearing often becomes obtuse in old age.* ⟨< L *obtusus,* pp. of *obtundere* < *ob-* on + *tundere* beat⟩ **—ob'tuse•ly,** *adv.* **—ob'tuse•ness,** *n.*

obtuse angle an angle greater than 90° but less than 180°; an angle greater than a right angle.

ob•verse *n.* ['ɒbvərs]; *adj.* [ɒb'vɜrs] *or* ['ɒbvərs] *n., adj.* —*n.* **1** the side of a coin, medal, etc. that has the principal design. Opposed to REVERSE. **2** the face of anything that is meant to be turned toward the observer; front. **3** a counterpart. **4** *Logic.* a proposition derived through obversion; the negative (or affirmative) counterpart of a given affirmative (or negative) proposition. —*adj.* **1** turned toward the observer. **2** being a counterpart to something else. **3** having the base narrower than the top or tip: *an obverse leaf.* ⟨< L *obversus,* pp. of *obvertere* < *ob-* toward + *vertere* to turn⟩ **—ob'verse•ly,** *adv.*

ob•ver•sion [ɒb'vɜrʒən] *or* [ɒb'vɜrʃən] *n. Logic.* a form of reasoning which gets a negative from an affirmative, or vice versa.

ob•vert [ɒb'vɜrt] *v.* **1** turn (something) toward an object. **2** *Logic.* change (a proposition) to its obverse. **3** present another side of. ⟨< L *obvertere.* See OBVERSE.⟩

ob•vi•ate ['ɒbvi,eit] *v.* **-at•ed, -at•ing. 1** meet and dispose of; clear out of the way; remove: *to obviate a difficulty, to obviate danger, to obviate objections.* **2** foresee something and thus make it unnecessary. ⟨< LL *obviare* < *obvius* in the way. See OBVIOUS.⟩ **—,ob•vi'a•tion,** *n.* **—'ob•vi,a•tor,** *n.*

ob•vi•ous ['ɒbviəs] *adj.* easily seen or understood; clear to the eye or mind; not to be doubted; plain: *It is obvious that two and two make four.* ⟨< L *obvius* < *obviam* in the way < *ob* across + *via* way⟩ **—'ob•vi•ous•ly,** *adv.* **—'ob•vi•ous•ness,** *n.*

☛ *Syn.* **Obvious,** APPARENT, EVIDENT = plain to see, easy to understand. **Obvious** suggests standing out so prominently that the eye or mind cannot miss it: *His exhaustion was obvious when he fell asleep standing up.* **Apparent** means plainly to be seen as soon as one looks (with eye or mind) toward it: *A change in government policy is now apparent.* **Evident** means plainly to be seen because all the apparent facts point to it: *The damage by the storm was evident in the ruined buildings.*

ob•vo•lute ['ɒbvə,lut] *adj. Botany.* of leaves or petals, folded over one another. **—,ob•vo'lu•tion,** *n.* **—'ob•vo,lu•tive,** *adj.*

oc– a form of **ob-** before *c,* as in *occasion.*

OC *Cdn.* Officer of the Order of Canada.

O.C. Officer in Charge; Officer Commanding.

Oc. or **oc.** ocean.

oc•a•ri•na [,ɒkə'rinə] *n.* a simple wind instrument having an oval body with six to eight finger holes and a protruding, whistlelike mouthpiece on one side. ⟨probably dim. of Ital. *oca* goose; with reference to the shape⟩

Oc•cam's razor ['ɒkəmz] See OCKHAM'S RAZOR.

oc•ca•sion [ə'keiʒən] *or* [ou'keiʒən] *n., v. —n.* **1** a particular time: *We have met Mr. Smith on several occasions.* **2** a special event: *The jewels were worn only on great occasions.* **3** a good chance; opportunity. **4** a cause; reason: *The dog that was the occasion of the quarrel had run away.*
improve the occasion, take advantage of an opportunity.
on occasion, now and then; once in a while.
—v. cause; bring about: *Her queer behaviour occasioned talk.* ⟨< L *occasio, -onis,* ult. < *ob-* in the way of + *cadere* fall⟩

oc•ca•sion•al [ə'keiʒənəl] *adj.* **1** happening or coming now and then, or once in a while: *We had fine weather except for an occasional thunderstorm.* **2** caused by or used for some special time or event: *She composed a piece of occasional music to be played at the opening concert in the new auditorium.* **3** for use as called for, not forming part of a set: *occasional chairs.*

oc•ca•sion•al•ly [ə'keiʒənəli] *adv.* now and then; once in a while; at times.

Oc•ci•dent ['ɒksədənt] *n.* **1** the countries in Europe and America; the West. Compare ORIENT. **2 occident,** the west. ⟨< L *occidens, -entis,* ppr. of *occidere* fall toward, go down < *ob-* toward + *cadere* fall; with reference to the setting sun⟩

Oc•ci•den•tal [,ɒksə'dɛntəl] *adj., n. —adj.* **1** Western; of the Occident. **2 occidental,** western.
—n. a native of the West. Europeans are Occidentals. Compare ORIENTAL.

Oc•ci•den•tal•ism [,ɒksə'dɛntə,lɪzəm] *n.* anything that is Occidental in character. **—,Oc•ci'den•tal•ist,** *n.*

Oc•ci•den•tal•ize [,ɒksə'dɛntə,laɪz] *v.* **-ized, -iz•ing.** make Occidental; westernize. **—,Oc•ci,den•tal•i'za•tion,** *n.*

oc•cip•i•tal [ɒk'sɪpətəl] *adj., n. Anatomy. —adj.* of or having to do with the back part of the head or skull.
—n. OCCIPITAL BONE. ⟨< Med.L *occipitalis* < L *occiput.* See OCCIPUT.⟩ **—oc'cip•i•tal•ly,** *adv.*

occipital bone *Anatomy.* the compound bone forming the lower back part of the skull.

occipital lobe *Anatomy.* the rear part of either hemisphere of the brain.

oc•ci•put ['ɒksəpət] *n., pl.* **oc•ci•puts** or **oc•cip•i•ta** [ɒk'sɪpətə]. *Anatomy.* the back part of the head or skull. ⟨< L *occiput* < *occipitium* < *ob-* behind + *caput* head⟩

oc•clude [ə'klud] *v.* **-clud•ed, -clud•ing. 1** stop up (a passage, pores, etc.); close. **2** shut in, out, or off. **3** *Chemistry.* absorb and retain (gases). Platinum occludes hydrogen. **4** *Dentistry.* meet closely. The teeth in the upper jaw and those in the lower jaw should occlude. **5** *Meteorology.* force (air) to rise, such as when a cold front overtakes and pushes under a warm front. ⟨< L *occludere* < *ob-* up + *claudere* close⟩ **—oc'clu•dent,** *adj.*

occluded front *Meteorology.* the front created when a cold front overtakes a warm front, forcing the air up.

oc•clu•sion [ə'kluʒən] *n.* an occluding or being occluded. ⟨< L *occlusus,* pp. of *occludere.* See OCCLUDE.⟩

oc•cult [ə'kʌlt] *or* ['ɒkʌlt] *adj., n. —adj.* **1** beyond the bounds of ordinary knowledge; mysterious. **2** outside the laws of the natural world; magical: *Astrology and alchemy are occult sciences.*
—n. **the occult,** occult studies or beliefs. ⟨< L *occultus* hidden, pp. of *occulere* < *ob-* up + *celare* cover⟩

oc•cul•ta•tion [,ɒkʌl'teiʃən] *n.* **1** a hiding of one heavenly body by another passing between it and the observer: *the occultation of a star by the moon.* **2** a disappearance from view or notice.

oc•cult•ism [ə'kʌltɪzəm] *n.* **1** a belief in occult powers. **2** the study or use of occult sciences. **—oc'cult•ist,** *n.*

oc•cu•pan•cy ['ɒkjəpənsi] *n., pl.* **-cies.** the act or fact of occupying; holding (land, houses, a pew, etc.) by being in possession.

oc•cu•pant ['ɒkjəpənt] *n.* **1** a person who occupies: *the occupant of a chair. Who is the present occupant of this apartment?* **2** the person in actual possession of a house, office, etc. ⟨< L *occupans, -antis,* ppr. of *occupare.* See OCCUPY.⟩

oc•cu•pa•tion [,ɒkjə'peiʃən] *n.* **1** one's business or employment; trade: *Teaching is a teacher's occupation.* **2** an occupying or being occupied; possession: *the occupation of a town by the enemy.* ⟨< L *occupatio, -onis* < *occupare.* See OCCUPY.⟩

☛ *Syn.* **1. Occupation,** BUSINESS, EMPLOYMENT = work a person does regularly or to earn a living. **Occupation** = work of any kind one does regularly or for which one is trained: *By occupation he is a homemaker.* **Business** = work done for profit, often for oneself, especially in commerce, banking, merchandising, etc.: *My business is real estate.* **Employment** = work done for another, for which one is paid: *He has no employment.*

oc•cu•pa•tion•al [,ɒkjə'peiʃənəl] *adj.* of or having to do with occupation, especially of or having to do with trades, callings, etc.: *occupational diseases.* **—,oc•cu'pa•tion•al•ly,** *adv.*

occupational disease a disease that results from a particular occupation: *Silicosis (black lung) is an occupational disease of coal miners.*

occupational therapy *Medicine.* the treatment of persons having disabilities through specific types of activities, work, etc. to promote rehabilitation.

oc•cu•py ['ɒkjə,paɪ] *v.* **-pied, -py•ing. 1** take up; fill: *The building occupies an entire block.* **2** keep busy; engage; employ: *Sports often occupy her attention.* **3** take possession of: *The enemy occupied our fort.* **4** keep possession of; have; hold: *The judge occupies an important position.* **5** live in: *The owner and her family occupy the house.* ⟨ME < OF < L *occupare* seize < *ob-* onto + *capere* grasp⟩ **—'oc•cu,pi•er,** *n.*

oc•cur [ə'kɜr] *v.* **-curred, -cur•ring. 1** take place; happen: *Storms often occur in winter.* **2** be found; exist: E *occurs in English more than any other letter.* **3** come to mind; suggest itself: *Did it occur to you to close the window?* ⟨< L *occurrere* < *ob-* in the way of + *currere* run⟩

oc•cur•rence [ə'kɜrəns] *n.* **1** an occurring: *The occurrence of storms delayed our trip.* **2** event: *an unexpected occurrence.*
☛ *Syn.* **2.** See note at EVENT.

OCdt OFFICER CADET.

o•cean ['ouʃən] *n.* **1** the great body of salt water that covers almost three-fourths of the earth's surface. **2** any of its four main divisions—the Atlantic, Pacific, Indian, and Arctic Oceans. **3** a vast expanse or quantity: *oceans of trouble.* ⟨< L *oceanus* < Gk. *ōkeanos*⟩

o•cean•ar•i•um [,ouʃə'nɛriəm] *n., pl.* **-i•ums** or **-i•a** [-iə]. a large saltwater aquarium for ocean fish and other animals.

ocean bed the bottom of the ocean.

o•cean–go•ing ['ouʃən ,gouɪŋ] *adj.* of, having to do with, or designed for travel on the ocean: *an ocean-going ship.*

ocean greyhound a swift ship, especially an ocean liner.

O•ce•an•i•a [,ouʃi'æniə] *n.* Australia, New Zealand, and other islands of the Pacific Ocean.

o•ce•an•ic [,ouʃi'ænɪk] *adj.* **1** of the ocean. **2** living in the ocean. **3** like the ocean; wide; vast.

O•ce•a•nid [ou'siənɪd] *n., pl.* **O•ce•a•nids** or **O•ce•an•i•des** [,ousi'ænɪ,diz]. *Greek mythology.* a sea nymph; daughter of Oceanus, the ocean god.

o•cean•og•ra•pher [ˌouʃə'nɒgrəfər] *n.* a person skilled in oceanography, especially one whose work it is.

o•cean•o•graph•ic [ˌouʃənə'græfɪk] *adj.* of or having to do with oceanography. **—ˌo•cean•o'graph•i•cal•ly,** *adv.*

o•cean•og•ra•phy [ˌouʃə'nɒgrəfi] *n.* the branch of physical geography dealing with oceans and ocean life.

o•cean•o•lo•gy [ˌouʃə'nɒlədʒi] *n.* oceanography. **—ˌo•cean'ol•o•gist,** *n.* **—ˌo•cean•o'log•i•cal,** *adj.*

ocean sunfish globefish.

O•ce•a•nus [ou'siənəs] *n. Greek mythology.* **1** the god of the sea before Poseidon. Oceanus was a Titan and the father of the Oceanids. **2** the great body of water that was believed to encircle the earth and that was the source of all rivers and lakes.

oc•el•late ['ɒsəˌleit] *or* [ou'sɛlɪt] *adj.* having or marked with ocelli. Also, **ocellated.**
☛ *Hom.* OSCILLATE [ɒsəˌleit].

o•cel•lus [ou'sɛləs] *or* [ɒ'sɛləs] *n., pl.* **-cel•li** [-'sɛlaɪ] *or* [-'sɛli]. **1** a small, simple eye of insects and some other invertebrates. **2** an eyelike spot or marking, such as the spot on any of the tail feathers of a peacock. ⟨< L *ocellus,* dim. of *oculus* eye⟩ **—o'cel•lar,** *adj., adv.*

o•ce•lot ['ɒsəˌlɒt] *or* ['ousəˌlɒt] *n.* a medium-sized New World mammal (*Felis pardalis*) of the cat family found from Texas south to central South America, having a buff coat spotted and striped with black. ⟨< F < Mexican *ocelotl*⟩

och•lo•cra•cy [ɒk'lɒkrəsi] *n.* mob rule. ⟨< Gk. *ochlokratia* < *ochlos* mob + *-kratia* -cracy⟩ **—'och•loˌcrat** ['ɒkləkræt], *n.* **—ˌoch•lo'crat•ic,** *adj.*

o•chre ['oukər] *n., adj. —n.* **1** any of various clays ranging in colouring from pale yellow to orange, brown, and red, used as pigments. **2** a pale brownish yellow.
—adj. pale brownish yellow. Also, **ocher.** ⟨ME < OF *ocre* < L < Gk. *ōchra* < *ōchros* pale yellow⟩ **—'o•chre•ous** ['oukərəs], *adj.*

Ockham's razor a maxim that the simplest solution to a problem is the best one of all proposed. Also, **Occam's razor.** ⟨< William of *Ockham* (c.1285-c.1349), English philosopher⟩

o'clock [ə'klɒk] the time expressed in units of one hour: *It is one o'clock.* ⟨contraction of *of the clock*⟩

OCR OPTICAL CHARACTER RECOGNITION.

oct. octavo.

oct– *combining form.* the form of **octo-** or **octa-** before vowels, as in *octet.*

Oct. October.

octa– *combining form.* a variant of **octo-**: *octagon.*

oc•tad ['ɒktæd] *n.* **1** a group of eight. **2** anything with a valence of eight. ⟨< Gk. *oktas* group of eight⟩

oc•ta•gon ['ɒktəˌgɒn] *or* ['ɒktəgən] *n.* a polygon having eight sides. ⟨< Gk. *oktagōnos* < *oktō* eight + *gōnia* angle⟩

oc•tag•o•nal [ɒk'tægənəl] *adj.* having eight interior angles and eight sides.

oc•ta•he•dral [ˌɒktə'hidrəl] *adj.* having eight plane faces.

oc•ta•hed•rite [ˌɒktə'hidrəit] *n.* anatase. ⟨< LL *octahedros* eight-sided < Gk. *oktaedron*⟩

oc•ta•he•dron [ˌɒktə'hidrən] *n., pl.* **-drons, -dra** [-drə]. a polyhedron having eight faces. ⟨< Gk. *oktaedron,* neut. of *oktaedros* < *oktōs* eight + *hedra* seat, base⟩

oc•ta•me•ter [ɒk'tæmətər] *n. Prosody.* a passage of poetry with eight metrical feet to the line.

oc•tan ['ɒktən] *adj.* taking place every eighth day. ⟨< F *octane* < L *octo* eight⟩

oc•tane ['ɒktein] *n. Chemistry.* any of a group of colourless, liquid hydrocarbons obtained from petroleum. *Formula*: C_8H_{18} ⟨< *oct-* eight (< Gk. *oktō*) + *-ane,* chemical suffix < L *-anus,* adj. suffix⟩

octane number the number indicating the quality of a motor fuel, based on its antiknock properties.

Oc•tans ['ɒktænz] *n. Astronomy.* a constellation that includes the south celestial pole. Also, **Octant** ['ɒktænt].

oc•tant ['ɒktənt] *n.* **1** an eighth of a circle. **2** an instrument used in navigation, using an angle of 45°.

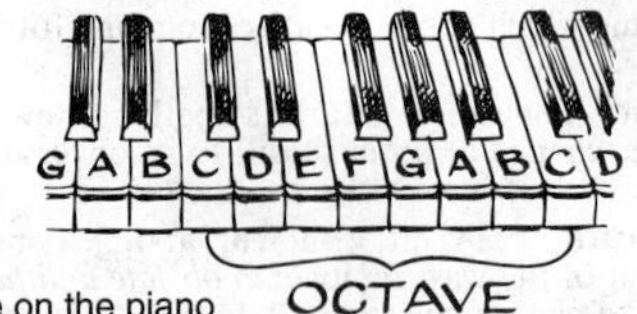

An octave on the piano

oc•tave ['ɒktɪv] *or* ['ɒkteiv] *n.* **1** *Music.* **a** the interval between a tone and another tone having twice or half as many vibrations. From middle C on a piano or organ to the C above it is an octave. **b** the eighth tone above or below a given tone, having twice or half as many vibrations per second. **c** the series of tones or of keys of an instrument, filling the interval between a tone and its octave. **d** the combination of a tone and its octave. **e** an organ stop making the keys produce additional tones an octave above those normally played. **2** a group of eight. **3** *Prosody.* **a** an eight-line stanza. **b** the first eight lines of a sonnet; octet. **4 a** the eighth day after a festival. **b** the period between the festival and the eighth day. **5** *Fencing.* a parry that rotates. ⟨< L *octavus* eighth < *octo* eight⟩ **—oc'ta•val** [ɒk'teivəl], *adj.*

oc•ta•vo [ɒk'teivou] *or* [ɒk'tævou] *n., pl.* **-vos. 1** the page size of a book in which each leaf is one-eighth of a whole sheet of paper. **2** a book having this size, usually about 15 cm by 24 cm. ⟨< Med.L *in octavo* in an eighth⟩

oc•ten•ni•al [ɒk'tɛniəl] *adj.* **1** lasting eight years. **2** happening every eighth year. **—oc'ten•ni•al•ly,** *adv.*

oc•tet [ɒk'tɛt] *n.* **1** a musical composition for eight voices or instruments. **2** eight singers or players. **3** *Prosody.* **a** the first eight lines of a sonnet. **b** an eight-line stanza; octave. **4** any group of eight. Also, **octette.** ⟨< *oct-* eight + *-et,* patterned on *duet,* etc.⟩

oc•til•lion [ɒk'tɪljən] *n.* **1** in Canada, the United States, and France, 1 followed by 27 zeros. **2** in the United Kingdom and Germany, 1 followed by 48 zeros. ⟨< F < L *octo* eight + F *million* million⟩

octo– *combining form.* eight: *octopus.* ⟨< Gk. *oktō*⟩

Oc•to•ber [ɒk'toubər] *n.* the tenth month of the year. October has 31 days. ⟨< L *October* < *octo* eight; from the order of the early Roman calendar⟩

oc•to•ge•nar•i•an [ˌɒktədʒə'nɛriən] *n., adj. —n.* a person who is 80 years old or between 80 and 90 years old.
—adj. 80 years old or between 80 and 90 years old. ⟨< L *octogenarius* containing eighty⟩ **—ˌoc•to•ge'nar•i•an•ism,** *n.*

oc•to•na•ry ['ɒktəˌnɛri] *adj.* **1** having to do with the number eight. **2** made up of eight groups each made up of eight. ⟨< L *octonarius* consisting of eight⟩

oc•to•pod ['ɒktəˌpɒd] *n.* any of an order (Octopoda) of cephalopods, including octopuses and the paper nautilus, having eight armlike tentacles with suckers and lacking an internal shell. ⟨< NL *Octopoda* name of order < Gk. *oktopoda* neuter pl. of *octopous* eight-footed⟩

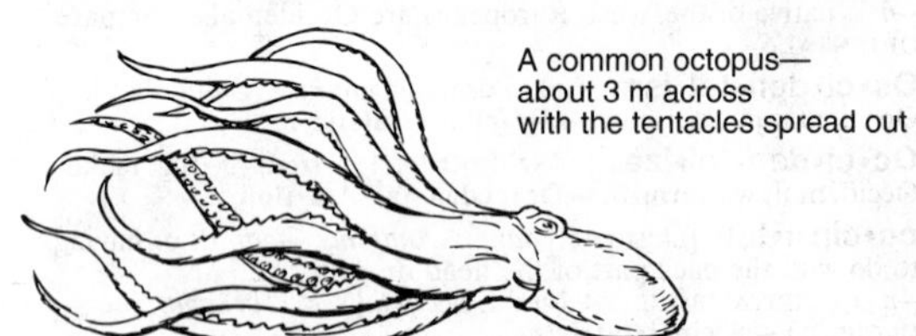
A common octopus— about 3 m across with the tentacles spread out

oc•to•pus ['ɒktəpəs] *n., pl.* **-pus•es** or **-pi** [-ˌpaɪ]. **1** any of a genus (*Octopus*) of marine cephalopods having a soft, rounded body, large, highly developed eyes, a beaklike mouth, and eight muscular arms, or tentacles, bearing rows of suckers.
2 something that resembles an octopus in being able to reach out and grasp, especially a large organization with many far-reaching branches: *The octopus of organized crime threatens the business life of every major city.* ⟨< NL < Gk. *oktopous* < *oktō* eight + *pous* foot⟩

oc•to•roon [ˌɒktə'run] *n.* a person having one-eighth African ancestry. ⟨< *octo-* eight + (*quad*)*roon*⟩

oc•to•syl•la•ble [ˌɒktə'sɪləbəl] *n.* **1** a line of verse with eight syllables. **2** a word of eight syllables. **—ˌoc•to•syl'la•bic,** *adj.*

oc•tre•o•tide ['ɒktriə,taɪd] *n.* a drug used to treat cancerous and other tumours.

oc•tu•ple [ɒk'tjupəl] *or* [ɒk'tupəl], ['ɒktjəpəl] *or* ['ɒktəpəl] *adj., n. —adj.* **1** having eight parts. **2** eightfold.
—n. a quantity exceeding another by eight times.

oc•tyl di•meth•yl PABA ['ɒktɪl daɪ'mɛθɪl] a sunscreen.

oc•u•lar ['ɒkjələr] *adj., n. —adj.* **1** of or having to do with the eye: *an ocular muscle.* **2** like an eye. **3** received by actual sight; seen.
—n. the eyepiece of a telescope, microscope, etc. ⟨< LL *ocularis* of the eyes < L *oculus* eye⟩ **—'oc•u•lar•ly,** *adv.*

oc•u•lar•ist ['ɒkjələrɪst] *n.* a person who makes and fits artificial eyes.

oc•u•list ['ɒkjəlɪst] *n.* a physician who specializes in the treatment of the eyes; ophthalmologist. ⟨< F *oculiste*⟩
☛ *Usage.* See note at OPHTHALMOLOGIST.

oc•u•lo•mo•tor [,ɒkjəlou'moutər] *adj.* moving the eyeball.

oculomotor nerve one of the nerves moving the eyeball.

od 1 olive drab. **2** overdrawn. **3** outside diameter.

OD ['ou'di] *n., pl.* **OD's;** *v.* **OD'd, OD'ing.** *Slang. —n.* an overdose of a narcotic.
—v. take an overdose (*used with* **on**).

O.D. OFFICER OF THE DAY.

o•da•lisque or **o•da•lisk** ['oudə,lɪsk] *n.* **1** a female concubine in an Oriental harem. **2** a painting of such a woman. ⟨< F < Turkish *odaliq* < *odah* room in a harem; influenced by suffix *-isque* -ish⟩

odd [ɒd] *adj.* **1** not divisible by two; being an odd number. **2** of or having an odd number: *The odd pages are always on the right in an open book.* **3** being one of a matched pair or set when the other or others are missing: *an odd glove in the drawer, some odd volumes of an encyclopedia.* **4** being a small, leftover or additional quantity or amount: *odd bits of lace, a few odd dollars in her purse.* **5** occasional, extra, or random: *He earns a living doing odd jobs around town.* **6** somewhat more than a quantity, distance, etc. specified in round numbers (*used in compounds*): *The whole job should cost 300-odd dollars. We still had 20-odd kilometres to go.* **7** peculiar or strange: *It's odd that she's not back yet. He had an odd expression on his face.* **8** remote or secluded. ⟨ME < ON *odda-*⟩ **—'odd•ness,** *n.*
☛ *Syn.* 7. See note at STRANGE.

odd•ball ['ɒd,bɒl] *n., adj. Slang. —n.* a person whose behaviour is eccentric or unconventional.
—adj. eccentric; unconventional.

odd•i•ty ['ɒdəti] *n., pl.* **-ties. 1** strangeness; queerness; peculiarity. **2** a strange, queer, or peculiar person or thing.

odd lot *Stock exchange.* in transactions, an amount less than the usual.

odd•ly ['ɒdli] *adv.* queerly; strangely.

odd man out *n.* **1** one who does not fit into a group. **2** one who is left out of a group. **3 a** a person chosen by lot to do something special. **b** a method of selection used to choose such a person.

odd•ment ['ɒdmənt] *n.* a thing left over; an extra bit.

odd number a number that has a remainder of 1 when divided by 2: *Three, five, and seven are odd numbers.*

odd–pin•nate ['ɒd 'pɪneit] *or* ['pɪnɪt] *adj. Botany.* pinnate but with a single leaf at the end.

odds [ɒdz] *n.pl. or sing.* **1** a difference in favour of one as against another; advantage. In betting, odds of 3 to 1 mean that 3 will be paid if the bet is lost for every 1 that is received if the bet is won. **2** *Games.* an extra allowance given to the weaker side. **3** things that are odd, uneven, or unequal. **4** difference: *It makes no odds when she goes.*
at odds, quarrelling or disagreeing: *The two boys had been at odds for months.*
odds and ends, things left over; extra bits; odd pieces; scraps; remnants.
the odds are, the chances are; the probability is: *The odds are we'll win since they will be without their best player.*

odds–on ['ɒdz 'ɒn] *adj.* having the odds in one's favour; having a good chance to win in a contest.

ode [oud] *n.* a lyric poem full of noble feeling expressed with dignity, often addressed to some person or thing: *Ode to a Nightingale.* ⟨< F < LL *ode* < Gk. *ōidē*, ult. < *aeidein* sing⟩

-ode¹ *combining form.* path; road: *anode, electrode.* ⟨< Gk. *-odos, hodós*⟩

-ode² *combining form.* like; similar: *phyllode.* ⟨< Gk. *ōdēs*⟩

O•din ['oudən] *n. Norse mythology.* the chief deity and god of wisdom, culture, war, and the dead; the Saxon god *Woden.* ⟨< ON *Othinn,* related to OE *Woden*⟩

o•di•ous ['oudiəs] *adj.* very displeasing; hateful; offensive: *odious behaviour.* ⟨ME < OF < L *odiosus* < *odium* hate⟩ **—'o•di•ous•ly,** *adv.* **—'o•di•ous•ness,** *n.*
☛ *Syn.* See note at HATEFUL.

o•di•um ['oudiəm] *n.* **1** hatred; dislike. **2** reproach; blame. ⟨< L *odium* < *odisse* hate⟩

o•do•graph ['oudə,græf] *n.* **1** pedometer. **2** odometer.

o•dom•e•ter [ou'dɒmətər] *n.* an instrument for measuring the distance a vehicle travels by counting the number of wheel revolutions. ⟨< F *odomètre* < Gk. *hodometron* < *hodos* way + *metron* a measure⟩

odont– var. of ODONTO- before a vowel: *odontoid.*

–odont var. of ODONTO- as final element of compounds.

odonto– *combining form.* tooth: *odontology.* Also, **odont-** and **-odont.** ⟨< Gk. *odoús, odōn* tooth⟩

o•don•to•blast [ou'dɒntə,blæst] *n.* a cell in the outer surface of pulp in a tooth that produces dentine. ⟨< *odonto-* + Gk. *blastos* sprout⟩

o•don•toid [ou'dɒntɔɪd] *adj.* **1** like a tooth. **2** designating or having to do with the projection from the second vertebra of the neck. ⟨< Gk. *odontoeides* toothlike⟩

o•don•tol•o•gy [,oudɒn'tɒlədʒi] *n.* the branch of anatomy dealing with the structure, development, and diseases of the teeth; dentistry. ⟨< Gk. *odous, -ontos* tooth + E *-logy*⟩

odor ['oudər] *n.* See ODOUR.

o•dor•ant ['oudərənt] *n.* something that smells.

o•dor•if•er•ous [,oudə'rɪfərəs] *adj.* giving forth an odour; fragrant. ⟨ME < L *odorifer* < *odor* odour + *ferre* bear⟩ **—,o•dor'if•er•ous•ly,** *adv.* **—,o•dor'if•er•ous•ness,** *n.*

o•dor•ous ['oudərəs] *adj.* giving forth an odour; having an odour; sweet-smelling; fragrant: *Spices are odorous.* ⟨< L *odorous*⟩ **—'o•dor•ous•ly,** *adv.* **—'o•dor•ous•ness,** *n.*

o•dour or **o•dor** ['oudər] *n.* **1** a smell or scent: *the odour of roses, the odour of garbage.* **2** repute: *They were in bad odour because of a suspected theft.* **3** a taste or quality characteristic or suggestive of something: *There is no odour of impropriety about the case.* **4** *Archaic.* a fragrance or perfume. ⟨ME < AF < L⟩ **—'o•dour•ful** or **'o•dor•ful,** *adj.* **—'o•dour•less** or **'o•dor•less,** *adj.*
☛ *Syn.* **1.** See note at SMELL.

O•dys•se•us [ou'dɪsiəs] *n. Greek mythology.* a king of Ithaca, the shrewdest of the Greek leaders in the Trojan War, who spent ten years in adventurous wanderings before returning home. Latin name: **Ulysses.**

Od•ys•sey ['ɒdəsi] *n., pl.* **-seys. 1** a long, Greek epic poem by Homer, describing the ten years of wandering of Odysseus after the Trojan War and his final return home. **2** Also, **odyssey,** any long series of wanderings. **—,Od•ys'se•an,** *adj.*

Oe oersted.

OE OLD ENGLISH.

OECD or **O.E.C.D.** Organization for Economic Co-operation and Development.

oec•u•men•i•cal [,ɛkjə'mɛnɪkəl] See ECUMENICAL.

Oed•i•pus ['idəpəs] *or* ['ɛdəpəs] *n. Greek mythology.* a king of Thebes who killed his father and married his mother, unaware of their identity. When he learned what he had done, he blinded himself and passed the rest of his life wandering miserably.

Oedipus complex *Psychology.* the tendency of a son to be attracted to his mother (or a daughter, her father) and to oppose his father (her mother).

oe•no•phile ['inə,faɪl] *n.* a lover of fine wines. ⟨< Gk. *oinos* wine + F *phile*⟩

o'er [ɔr] *adj., prep., or adv. Poetic.* over.
☛ *Hom.* OAR, OR, ORE.

oer•sted ['ɜrstɛd] *n. Electricity.* an electromagnetic unit equal to the intensity of magnetism one centimetre from a unit magnetic pole. *Symbol:* Oe

oe•soph•a•gus [ɪ'sɒfəgəs] *n., pl.* **-gi** [-,dʒaɪ] *or* [-,dʒi]. See ESOPHAGUS.

oeu•vre ['œvʀ] *French. n.* all the works in the lifetime of a composer, writer, artist, etc.

of [ʌv] *or* [ɒv]; *unstressed,* [əv] *prep.* **1** belonging to; associated with; forming a part of: *the children of a family.* **2** made from: *a house of bricks.* **3** that has; containing; with: *a house of six rooms.* **4** that has as a quality: *a look of pity.* **5** that is; named: *the city of Vancouver.* **6** away from; from: *north of Brandon. She came of a noble family.* **7** in regard to; concerning; about: *to think well of someone.* **8** that has as a purpose: *the hour of prayer.* **9** by: *the writings of Shakespeare.* **10** as a result of; through: *to die of grief.* **11** among: *a mind of the finest.* **12** during: *of late years.* **13** in telling time, before: *ten minutes of six.* **14** in; as to: *She is sixteen years of age.* **15** like: *smelling of onions.* **16** *Of* connects nouns having the meaning of a verb with what would be the object of the verb: *The eating of fruit.* ⟨OE (unstressed) *of.* Cf. OFF.⟩

☛ *Usage.* In informal English **of** is sometimes used unnecessarily to make such double prepositions as *inside of, outside of.* This usage is usually avoided in formal writing. Using **of** after **off** is not normally acceptable in standard English: *She stepped off the sidewalk* (not *off of*).

of– *prefix.* the form of **ob-** occurring before *f,* as in *offer.*

OF OLD FRENCH.

off [ɒf] *prep., adv., adj., interj., n.* —*prep.* **1** not in the usual or correct position on; into a position not on: *A button is off his coat. I fell off the curb.* **2** from; away from; far from: *You are off the road.* **3** of ships at sea, just away from: *The ship anchored off Victoria.* **4** supported by; using the resources of: *He lived off his relatives.*
—*adv.* **1** from the usual or correct position, condition, etc.: *He took off his hat.* **2** away; at a distance; to a distance: *to go off on a journey.* **3** distant in time: *Christmas is only five weeks off.* **4** so as to stop or lessen: *Turn the water off. The game was called off.* **5** without work: *an afternoon off.* **6** in full; wholly: *Pay off the debt.* **7** on one's way: *The train started and we were off on our trip.*
be off, go away; leave quickly.
off and on, at some times and not at others; now and then.
—*adj.* **1** no longer due to take place: *Our trip to Europe is off.* **2** not connected; stopped: *The electricity is off.* **3** not spent working: *He pursues his hobby during off hours.* **4** in a specified condition in regard to money, property, etc.: *How well off are the Smiths?* **5** not very good; not up to average: *Bad weather made last summer an off season for fruit.* **6** deteriorated in quality, etc.: *The milk seems to be off.* **7** possible but not likely: *I came on the off chance that I would find you.* **8** in error; wrong: *Your figures are way off.* **9** more distant; farther: *the off side of a wall.* **10** on the right-hand side (used of a horse, team of horses, vehicle, etc.): *the off wheel. The off horse doesn't pull as well as the near horse.* Compare NEAR (def. 5). **11** seaward.
—*interj.* go away! stay away!
off with, a take off. **b** cut off: *Off with his head!* **c** away with: *Off with you!*
—*n. Cricket.* the side opposite to the batsman. Compare LEG (def. 6a). ⟨OE (stressed) *of.* Cf. OF.⟩

☛ *Usage.* Avoid using the double preposition **off of.** See note at OF.

off. office; officer; official.

of•fal [ˈɒfəl] *n.* **1** the waste parts of an animal killed for food. **2** garbage; refuse. ⟨< *off* + *fall*⟩

☛ *Hom.* AWFUL.

off–and–on [ˈɒf ən ˈɒn] *adj. Informal.* intermittent; uncertain.

off–bal•ance [ˈɒfˈbæləns] *adj.* unsteady; unprepared.

off•beat [ˈofˈbit] *or* [ˈɒf,bit] *n., adj.* —*n. Music.* a beat that has relatively little stress.
—*adj.* **1** *Music.* of or having to do with offbeats. **2** *Informal.* unconventional; not usual; odd.

off–break [ˈɒf ,breik] *n. Cricket.* a ball bowled so as to deviate to the leg side from the off side.

off•cast [ˈɒf,kæst] *adj., n.* —*adj.* rejected; cast off.
—*n.* a person or thing that is cast off or rejected.

off–col•our or **off–col•or** [ˈɒf ˈkʌlər] *adj.* **1** defective in colour. **2** somewhat improper: *an off-colour joke.* **3** not well: *She was feeling off-colour yesterday.*

of•fence [əˈfɛns], [ouˈfɛns], *or, for defs. 5-7,* [ˈɒfɛns] *n.* **1** a breaking of the law; sin. Offences against the law are punished by fines or imprisonment. **2** something that offends or causes displeasure: *Rudeness is always an offence.* **3** the condition of being offended; hurt feelings; anger: *He tried not to cause offence.* **4** the act of offending or hurting someone's feelings: *No offence was intended.* **5** the act of attacking: *The army proved weak in offence.* **6** an attacking team or force. **7** *Football, hockey, etc.* the attacking part of a team. Also, **offense.**
give offence, offend.
take offence, be offended. ⟨ME *offens* < OF < L *offensum* offence, annoyance; and ME *offense* < OF < L *offensa* hurt, injury, wrong; both L nouns < L *offendere.* See OFFEND.⟩

☛ *Syn.* **1.** See note at CRIME.

of•fence•less [əˈfɛnslɪs] *adj.* **1** without offence; incapable of offence or attack. **2** not offending; inoffensive. Also, **offenseless.**

of•fend [əˈfɛnd] *v.* **1** hurt the feelings of; make angry; displease. **2** give offence; cause displeasure. **3** sin; do wrong. ⟨ME < OF < L *offendere* < *ob-* against + *-fendere* strike⟩
—of'fend•a•ble *or* **of'fend•i•ble,** *adj.* **—of'fend•ed•ly,** *adv.* **of'fend•ed•ness,** *n.*

of•fend•er [əˈfɛndər] *n.* **1** a person who offends. **2** a person who does wrong or breaks a law.

of•fense [əˈfɛns], [ouˈfɛns], *or* [ˈɒfɛns] See OFFENCE.

of•fense•less [əˈfɛnslɪs] See OFFENCELESS.

of•fen•sive [əˈfɛnsɪv] *adj., n.* —*adj.* **1** giving offence; irritating; annoying: *"Shut up" is an offensive retort.* **2** unpleasant; disagreeable; disgusting: *Bad eggs have an offensive odour.* **3** ready to attack; attacking: *an offensive army.* **4** used for attack; having to do with attack: *offensive weapons, an offensive war for conquest.*
—*n.* **1** the position or attitude of attack: *The army took the offensive.* **2** an attack: *An offensive against polio was begun when the proper vaccine was developed.* **—of'fen•sive•ly,** *adv.* **—of'fen•sive•ness,** *n.*

of•fer [ˈɒfər] *v., n.* —*v.* **1** hold out to be taken or refused; present: *He offered us his help.* **2** present for sale: *to offer suits at reduced prices.* **3** say one is willing; volunteer: *He offered to help us.* **4** bring forth for consideration; propose: *She offered a few ideas to improve the plan.* **5** present in worship: *to offer prayers.* **6** give; show: *The enemy offered resistance to our soldiers' attack.* **7** present itself; occur: *I will come if the opportunity offers.* **8** have as an advantageous feature: *The hotel offers a pool and shopping concourse. Self-employment offers independence and adventure.* **9** present to sight or notice. **10** bid as a price: *He offered twenty dollars for our old stove.*
—*n.* **1** the act of offering: *an offer of money, an offer to sing, an offer of marriage, an offer of $360 000 for a house.* **2** a thing that is offered. **3** *Law.* a proposal from one person to another which, if accepted, will become a contract. **4** an attempt or show of intention. ⟨OE *offrian* < L *offerre* < *ob-* to + *ferre* bring⟩
—'of•fer•a•ble, *adj.* **—'of•fer•er** or **'of•fer•or,** *n.*

☛ *Syn.* —*v.* **1. Offer,** PROFFER, TENDER[2] = hold out something to someone to be accepted. **Offer** is the common word meaning 'hold out' something to be taken or refused as one chooses or pleases: *She offered him coffee.* **Proffer** is the literary word, usually suggesting volunteering or offering with warmth, courtesy, or earnest sincerity: *He refused the proffered hospitality.* **Tender** is a formal word meaning 'offer formally' something like actions or services, not objects: *He tendered his resignation.*

of•fer•ing [ˈɒfərɪŋ] *or* [ˈɒfrɪŋ] *n., v.* —*n.* **1** the act of one who offers. **2** something offered. **3** a sacrifice of an animal, etc. made to a deity.
—*v.* ppr. of OFFER.

of•fer•to•ry [ˈɒfər,tɔri] *n., pl.* **-ries. 1** a collection, usually of money, at a religious service. **2** the verses said or the music sung or played while the offering is received. **3 a** *Roman Catholic Church.* the part of the Mass at which bread and wine are offered to God. **b** *Anglican Church.* a similar offering of bread and wine to God. **c** the prayers said or sung at this time. ⟨< LL *offertorium* place to which offerings were brought⟩

off•hand *adv.* [ˈɒfˈhænd]; *adj.* [ˈofˈhænd] *or* [ˈɒf,hænd] *adv., adj.* —*adv.* without previous thought or preparation: *The carpenter could not tell offhand how much the work would cost.*
—*adj.* Also, **offhanded. 1** done or made on the spur of the moment without previous thought or planning: *His offhand remarks were often very funny.* **2** casual; informal. **3** impolite; without due courtesy: *The boy's offhand ways angered his mother.*
—'off'hand•ed•ly, *adv.* **—'off'hand•ed•ness,** *n.*

of•fice [ˈɒfɪs] *n.* **1** the place in which the work of a business or profession is done; a room or rooms in which to do such work: *The executive offices were on the second floor.* **2** a position, especially in the public service: *The MP was appointed to the office of Minister of Defence.* **3** the duty of one's position; one's job or work: *A teacher's office is teaching.* **4** the staff or persons carrying on work in an office: *Half the office is on vacation.* **5** an administrative department of a governmental organization. **6** an act of kindness or unkindness; attention; service; injury: *Through the good offices of a friend, she was able to get a job.* **7** a religious ceremony or prayer: *the Communion office, last offices.* ⟨ME < OF < L *officium* service < *opus* work + *facere* do⟩

office automation *Computer technology.* the use of computer technology (word processing, electronic mail, etc.) to increase the efficiency with which tasks commonly done in an office environment can be carried out.

of•fice•hold•er ['ɒfɪs,houldər] *n.* a person who holds a public office; government official.

of•fi•cer ['ɒfəsər] *n., v.* *—n.* **1** a person who commands others in the armed forces, such as a colonel, a lieutenant, or a captain. **2** the captain of a ship or any of that captain's chief assistants. **3** a person who holds an office in the government, the church, the public service, etc.: *a health officer, a police officer.* **4** a person appointed or elected to an administrative position in a company, club, society, etc. **5** in some organizations, any member above the lowest rank.
—v. **1** provide with officers. **2** direct; conduct; manage. ⟨ME < AF *officer,* OF *officier* < Med.L *officiarius* < L *officium* service⟩ **—'of•fi•cer•less,** *adj.* **—'of•fi•cer,ship,** *n.*

officer cadet a person training for a commission in the armed forces; CADET (def. 1). *Abbrev.:* OCdt

Officer of the Day *Military.* an officer who has charge, for the time being, of the guards, prisoners, barracks, etc. *Abbrev.:* O.D.

office seeker a person who tries to obtain a public office.

of•fi•cial [ə'fɪʃəl] *n., adj.* *—n.* **1** a person who holds a public position or who is in charge of some public work or duty: *Postmasters are government officials.* **2** a person holding office; officer: *bank officials.*
—adj. **1** of or having to do with an office or officers: *Police officers wear an official uniform.* **2** having authority: *An official record is kept of the proceedings of Parliament.* **3** being an official: *Each province has its own official representatives in Parliament.* **4** suitable for a person in office: *the official dignity of a judge.* **5** formal or ceremonial, involving community leaders: *The princess was given an official welcome to the city.* **6** holding office. ⟨< LL *officialis* < *officium* service⟩ **—of'fi•cial•ly,** *adv.*

of•fi•cial•dom [ə'fɪʃəldəm] *n.* **1** the position or domain of officials. **2** officials collectively.

of•fi•cial•ese [ə,fɪʃə'liz] *n.* pompous, involved, or obscure language thought of as characteristic of official statements, reports, etc.

of•fi•cial•ism [ə'fɪʃə,lɪzəm] *n.* **1** official methods or systems. **2** an excessive attention to official routine.

of•fi•cial•ize [ə'fɪʃə,laɪz] *v.* **-ized, -iz•ing.** make official. **—of,fi•cial•i'za•tion,** *n.*

of•fi•ci•ate [ə'fɪʃi,eit] *v.* **-at•ed, -at•ing. 1** perform the duties of any office or position: *The president officiates as chair at all club meetings.* **2** perform the duties of a priest, minister, or rabbi, etc.: *The bishop officiated at the cathedral.* **3** do anything as a ritual or ceremony: *to officiate in carving the Thanksgiving turkey.* **4** serve as a referee or umpire in a sport. ⟨< Med.L *officiare* < L *officium* service⟩

of•fic•i•nal [ə'fɪsənəl] *adj., n.* *—adj.* **1** kept in stock by druggists. **2** recognized by the pharmacopoeia.
—n. a drug that is kept in stock. ⟨< Med.L *officinalis* < L *officina* shop, storeroom, ult. < *opus* work + *facere* do⟩ **—of'fic•i•nal•ly,** *adv.*

of•fi•cious [ə'fɪʃəs] *adj.* too ready to offer services or advice; minding other people's business; fond of meddling. ⟨< L *officiosus* dutiful < *officium* service⟩ **—of'fi•cious•ly,** *adv.* **—of'fi•cious•ness,** *n.*

off•ing ['ɒfɪŋ] *n.* **1** the more distant part of the sea as seen from the shore. **2** a position at a distance from the shore.
in the offing, a just visible from the shore; within sight; not far off. **b** due to come, happen, etc. soon but at a time as yet unspecified: *There is a general election in the offing.*

off•ish ['ɒfɪʃ] *adj. Informal.* inclined to keep aloof; distant and reserved in manner. **—'off•ish•ness,** *n.*

off–key ['ɒf 'ki] *adj.* **1** *Music.* not in the correct musical key; inharmonious. **2** *Informal.* improper; ill-timed: *an off-key remark.*

off–line ['ɒf 'laɪn] *adv., adj.* *—adv. Computer technology.* by means not controlled by a computer: *The customer mailing labels will be produced off-line.*
—adj. Computer technology. involving or designating processing not controlled by a computer.

off•load ['ɒf,loud] *v.* unload: *The ferry will offload cars at the terminal..*

off•print ['ɒf,prɪnt] *n., v.* *—n.* a separate reprint or reproduction of a story, article, etc. from a journal, book, etc.; printed excerpt.
—v. reprint separately as an excerpt.

off–put•ting ['ɒf ,pʊtɪŋ] *adj. Informal.* likely to deter one.

off•scour•ings ['ɒf,skaʊrɪŋz] *n.pl.* **1** filth; refuse. **2** low, worthless people.

off–screen ['ɒf 'skrin] *adj., adv.* *—adj.* **1** not seen on a movie or television screen: *an off-screen commentary.* **2** not engaged in acting for movies or television.
—adv. so as not to be seen on a movie or television screen.

off–sea•son ['ɒf ,sizən] *n., adj.* *—n.* the slack or slow season of a business, sport, etc.
—adj. in or for the off-season: *Off-season hotel rates are usually low.*

off•set *v.* [,ɒf'sɛt]; *n.* ['ɒf,sɛt] *v.* **-set, -set•ing;** *n.* *—v.* **1** make up for; counterbalance; compensate for: *The better roads offset the greater distance.* **2** balance (one thing) by another as an equivalent: *We offset the greater distance by the better roads.* **3** form an offset. **4** *Printing.* make an offset.
—n. **1** something that makes up for something else; compensation. **2** *Botany.* a short side shoot from a main stem or root that starts a new plant. **3** any offshoot. **4** *Printing.* **a** the process in which an inked impression is first made on a rubber roller and then on the paper, instead of directly on the paper. **b** an impression made by such a process. **5** *Surveying.* a short distance measured perpendicularly from a main line. **6** *Architecture.* a ledge formed on a wall by lessening its thickness above. **7** an abrupt bend in a pipe or bar to carry it past some obstruction.

off•shoot ['ɒf,ʃut] *n.* **1** *Botany.* a shoot or branch growing out from the main stem of a plant, tree, etc. **2** anything coming, or thought of as coming, from a main part, stock, race, etc.

off•shore ['ɒf'ʃɔr] *adj., adv.* *—adj.* **1** off or away from the shore: *an offshore wind.* **2** done or working away from the shore: *offshore fisheries.*
—adv. toward the water; from the shore: *The wind was blowing offshore.*

off•side or **off–side** ['ɒf'saɪd] *adj.* **1** away from one's own or the proper side; being on the wrong side. **2** *Football, hockey, etc.,* of a player on the offensive, being ahead of the ball or puck and being penalized.

off•spring ['ɒf,sprɪŋ] *n. sing.* or *pl.* **1** the young of a person, animal, or plant; descendant: *Every one of Mr. Kelly's offspring had red hair.* **2** a result; effect. ⟨OE *ofspring*⟩

off–stage ['ɒf 'steidʒ] *adj., adv.* *—adj.* **1** away from the part of the stage that the audience can see. **2** not spent performing: *Much of her off-stage life is spent in her garden.*
—adv. when not performing: *Off-stage, she is a shy and retiring stamp collector.*

off–street ['ɒf 'strit] *adj.* away from the street: *More off-street parking will ease downtown traffic congestion.*

off–the–cuff ['ɒf ðə 'kʌf] *adj. Informal.* not prepared beforehand; impromptu: *The minister's speech was off-the-cuff, not a formal statement.*

off–the–rec•ord ['ɒf ðə 'rɛkərd] *adj.* **1** not to be written in the minutes or proceedings (of a meeting, conference, etc.). **2** not for publication or release as news.

off–track ['ɒf 'træk] *adj.* **1** not conducted at a race track: *off-track betting.* **2** out of the way; off the beaten track.

off–white ['ɒf 'wəit] *n., adj.* *—n.* a very pale beige or light grey, almost white.
—adj. almost white.

off year ['ɒf ,jir] *n.* a year of lower returns or of poor conditions in business, farming, etc. **—'off-,year,** *adj.*

oft [ɒft] *adv. Archaic or Poetic.* often. ⟨OE⟩

of•ten ['ɒfən] *or* ['ɒftən] *adv.* in many cases; many times; frequently: *Blame is often misdirected. He comes here often.* ⟨ME *often* oft, the form of *ofte* before a vowel⟩

of•ten•times ['ɒfən,taɪmz] *or* ['ɒftən,taɪmz] *adv.* often.

oft•times ['ɒft,taɪmz] *adv. Poetic.* often.

o•gee [ou'dʒi] *or* ['oudʒi] *n.* **1** an S-shaped curve or line. **2** *Architecture.* a moulding with such a curve. **3** OGEE ARCH. ⟨< F *ogive*⟩

ogee arch *Architecture.* a form of pointed arch, each side of which has the curve of an ogee.

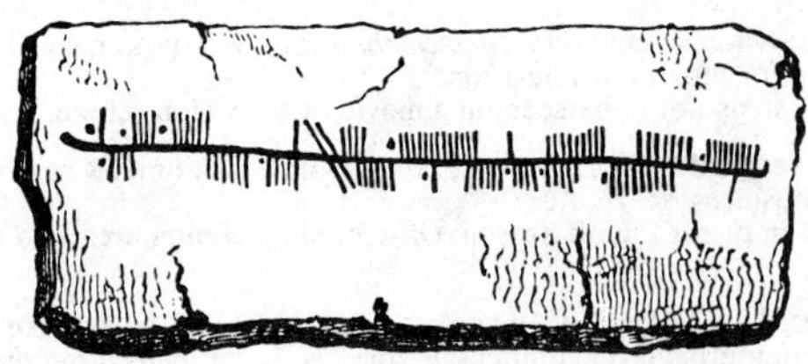

Ogham script on a stone found near Ennis

og•ham or **og•am** ['ɒgəm] *or* ['ouəm] *n.* an alphabetical writing system used on monuments by the ancient Celts in Ireland and Great Britain from about the 4th or 5th century A.D. to the early 7th century. ⟨< Old Irish *ogam*, associated with *Ogma*, legendary inventor of this writing system. 17c.⟩

o•give ['oudʒaɪv] *or* [ou'dʒaɪv] *n.* **1** *Architecture.* **a** a pointed arch. **b** a diagonal rib across a vault. **2** *Statistics.* a distribution graph or curve showing cumulative frequencies. ⟨< MF; origin uncertain⟩

Og•la•la [ɒg'lɑlə] *n.* **1** a member of an American Indian people now living in South Dakota. **2** the Dakota language of these people.

o•gle ['ougəl] *v.* **o•gled, o•gling;** *n.* —*v.* look (at) with desire; make eyes (at): *He is always ogling.*
—*n.* an ogling look. ⟨< Du. *oogelen* < *oog* eye⟩ —**'o•gler,** *n.*

O•go•po•go [,ougou'pougou] *n. Cdn.* a famed monster reported as being seen from time to time in Okanagan Lake, B.C. ⟨< a name from a British music hall song, applied first to the monster in 1912⟩

o•gre ['ougər] *n.* **1** *Folklore.* a giant or monster that supposedly eats people. **2** a brutal or terrifying person. ⟨< F⟩

o•gre•ish ['ougərɪʃ] *adj.* like an ogre.

o•gress ['ougrɪs] *n.* a female ogre.

oh [ou] *interj.* **1** a word used before names in addressing persons: *Oh Mary, look!* **2** an expression of surprise, joy, grief, pain, and other feelings. Also, **O.**

☛ *Hom.* O, OWE.

☛ *Usage.* **Oh** is the preferred form in Modern English, except occasionally in poetry and rhetoric, or in formal invocations such as prayers. Thus "O my prophetic soul My uncle!" (*Hamlet* I v 40).

O–Ha•rai ['ou hæ'raɪ] *n.* in Shinto, the purification ceremony observed in June and December, during which believers receive absolution from the sun goddess, Amaterasu. It is proclaimed traditionally by the Japanese emperor. ⟨< Japanese⟩

OHG OLD HIGH GERMAN.

O•hi•o [ou'haɪou] *n.* a midwestern state of the United States.

ohm [oum] *n. Electricity.* an SI unit for measuring the resistance of a conductor to an electric current sent through it. A conductor has a resistance of one ohm if it takes a potential difference of one volt to send a current of one ampere through it. *Symbol*: Ω. ⟨after Georg Simon *Ohm* (1787-1854), a German physicist⟩ —**'ohm•ic,** *adj.*

ohm•met•er ['oum,mitər] *n. Electricity.* a device for measuring the resistance of a conductor in ohms.

OHMS or **O.H.M.S.** On Her (or His) Majesty's Service.

Ohm's law *Electricity.* the law that states that the electric current (I) in a circuit is in direct proportion to the voltage (V) and inversely proportional to the resistance (R).
Equation: V = IR

o•ho [ou'hou] *interj.* an exclamation expressing a taunt, surprise, or exultation.

–oid *suffix.* resembling; like: *alkaloid, planetoid.* ⟨< Gk. *-oeidēs* < *eidos* form⟩

oil [ɔɪl] *n., v.* —*n.* **1** any of several kinds of thick, fatty, or greasy liquids that are lighter than water, that burn easily, and that dissolve in alcohol, but not in water. Mineral oils are used for fuel; animal and vegetable oils are used in cooking, medicine, and in many other ways. Essential or volatile oils, such as oil of peppermint, are distilled from plants, leaves, flowers, etc. and are thin and evaporate very quickly. **2** petroleum. **3** any substance that resembles oil in some respect. Sulphuric acid is sometimes called oil of vitriol. **4** Often, **oils,** *pl.* OIL PAINT. **5** OIL PAINTING.
pour oil on troubled waters, make things calm and peaceful.
strike oil, a find oil by boring a hole in the earth. **b** find something very profitable; have good luck.
—*v.* **1** become oil: *Butter oils when heated.* **2** put oil on or in. **3** make smooth or oily. **4** seek to persuade by bribery, flattery, etc.: *The failing student oiled the teacher to change the grade.* ⟨ME < ONF *olie* < L *oleum* < Gk. *elaion*⟩

oil burner 1 a furnace, ship, etc. that uses oil for fuel. **2** the part of such a furnace in which the fuel oil is atomized, mixed with air, and burned.

oil cake a mass of linseed, cottonseed, etc. from which the oil has been pressed. Oil cakes are used as a food for cattle and sheep or as a fertilizer.

oil•can ['ɔɪl,kæn] *n.* a can for oil, especially one with a narrow spout or a nozzle, for oiling machinery, etc.

oil•cloth ['ɔɪl,klɒθ] *n.* **1** a cloth made waterproof and glossy on one side by coating it with a mixture of oil, clay, and colouring. Oilcloth is used to cover shelves, tables, etc. **2** oilskin.

oil colour or **color 1** OIL PAINT. **2** a painting done in oil colours.

oil•er ['ɔɪlər] *n.* **1** a person or thing that oils. **2** a can with a long spout used in oiling machinery. **3** OIL TANKER. **4 oilers,** *pl. Cdn.* oilskins or other waterproof clothing.

oil field an area where petroleum has been found.

oil of turpentine a colourless, inflammable, volatile oil made from turpentine, used in mixing paints.

oil of vitriol *Chemistry.* See SULPHURIC ACID.

oil paint paint made by mixing pigment with an oil, such as linseed oil.

oil painting 1 a picture painted with oil paints. **2** the art of painting with oil paints.

oil pan the bottom of the crankcase serving as an oil reservoir.

oil•pa•per ['ɔɪl,peipər] *n.* paper treated with oil to make it transparent and waterproof.

oil sand *Cdn.* any area of sand or rock, especially sandstone, that contains large deposits of oil.

oil•seed ['ɔɪl,sid] *n.* any vegetable crop, such as canola, which yields oil.

oil shale *Geology.* a shale from which petroleum is distilled.

oil•skin ['ɔɪl,skɪn] *n.* **1** cloth treated with oil to make it waterproof. **2 oilskins,** *pl.* a coat and trousers made of this cloth.

oil slick 1 a film of oil on water. **2** a similar film on the surface of a road.

oil•stone ['ɔɪl,stoun] *n.* a fine-grained stone used for sharpening tools, the rubbing surface of which is oiled.

oil tanker a ship having special tanks to transport oil.

oil well a well drilled in the earth to get oil.

oil•y ['ɔɪli] *adj.* **oil•i•er, oil•i•est. 1** of oil: *an oily smell.* **2** containing oil: *oily salad dressing.* **3** covered or soaked with oil. **4** like oil; smooth; slippery. **5** too smooth; suspiciously or disagreeably smooth: *an oily smile, an oily manner.*
—**'oil•i•ness,** *n.* —**'oil•i•ly,** *adv.*

oint•ment ['ɔɪntmənt] *n.* a substance made from oil or fat, often containing medicine, used on the skin to heal or to make it soft. Cold cream and salve are ointments. ⟨ME < OF *oignement*, ult. < L *unguere* anoint; form influenced by *anoint*⟩

O•jib•wa or **O•jib•way** [ou'dʒɪbwei] *or* [ou'dʒɪbwɑ] *n., pl.* **-wa** or **-was, -way** or **-ways;** *adj.* —*n.* **1** a member of a First Nations people living in the region around Lake Superior and westward. The Ojibwa traditionally occupied an area stretching from the Ottawa Valley to the prairies. **2** an Algonquian language spoken by the Ojibwa, Algonquins, Ottawas, and Salteaux.
—*adj.* of or having to do with the Ojibwa or their language.

OK or **O.K.** ['ou'kei] *adj., adv., v.* **OK'd** or **O.K.'d, OK'ing** or **O.K.'ing;** *n., pl.* **OK's** or **O.K.'s.** *Informal.* —*adj. or adv.* all right; correct; approved: *The new schedule is OK.*
—*v.* endorse; approve.
—*n.* approval: *The supervisor has given us her OK.* Also, **okay.** ⟨origin uncertain⟩

O•ka ['oukə] *n. Cdn.* a cheese, cured with brine, made by Trappist monks in Oka, Québec.

o•ka•pi [ou'kɑpi] *n., pl.* **-pis** or **-pi.** an African mammal (*Okapia johnstoni*) related to and resembling the giraffe, but smaller and having a much shorter neck. ⟨< an African lang.⟩

o•kay ['ou'kei] See OK.

O•ki•na•wa rail [,oukə'nɑwə] a flightless bird (*Rallus* *okinawae*), native to forests on Okinawa, a W Pacific Island, and reaching a length of 30 cm. It is an endangered species.

Ok•la•ho•ma [,ouklə'houmə] *n.* a southwestern state of the United States.

o•kra ['oukrə] *n.* **1** a tall, annual herb (*Hibiscus esculentus*) of the mallow family having heart-shaped, lobed leaves and long, tapering seed pods. The okra is native to Africa but is commonly cultivated in the United States and other countries. **2** the unripe, tender pods of this plant, used as a vegetable and for thickening soups; gumbo. ⟨< West African lang.⟩

–ol *combining form.* containing, derived from, or like an alcohol or phenol: *glycerol.* ⟨< (*alcoh*)*ol*⟩

o•lal•lie [ou'lɑli] *n. Cdn.* **1** any of several berries, especially the salmonberry. **2** the bush such berries grow on. ⟨< Chinook jargon, berry⟩

old [ould] *adj.* **old•er** or (def. 3) **eld•er, old•est** or (def. 3) **eld•est;** *n.* *—adj.* **1** having existed long; dating from a relatively long time ago: *an old house, an old debt. They are old friends.* **2** of (a specified) age: *She is one year old today.* **3** advanced in age: *an old woman. He doesn't look at all old.* **4** (*noml.*) **the old, a** people who are old (*used with a plural verb*): *The old often have interesting stories to tell.* **b** things that are old (*used with a singular verb*): *The old gives way to the new.* **5** Often, **Old,** designating the earlier or earliest of two or more periods, types, etc.; not new: *Old English, the Old Testament. They're still using the old edition.* **6** showing the effects of age or use: *Are you still wearing that old coat?* **7** former: *an old student of hers. Infantile paralysis is an old name for polio.* **8** familiar: *an old excuse, good old Tony.* **9** experienced: *an old hand, old in wrongdoing.* **10** *Informal.* a word used as an intensifier: *any old day. We had a high old time at the party.*
—n. **1** a time long ago: *the heroes of old.* **2** a person of a specified age (*used in compounds*): *a six-year-old.* ⟨OE *ald*⟩
—'old•ness, *n.*

☛ *Syn. adj.* **1. Old,** ELDERLY, ANCIENT = having existed a long time. **Old,** describing people, animals, or things, suggests not young or new but having been alive, in existence, or in a particular state for a long or relatively long time: *We are old friends.* **Elderly,** describing people, means 'past middle age and getting old': *He is an elderly man, about seventy.* **Ancient** suggests having come into existence or use, or having existed or happened, in the distant past: *Jerusalem is an ancient city.*

☛ *Usage.* See note at ELDER[1].

old age the last part of life, when a person is old; the years of life from about 70 on.

Old Bai•ley ['beili] in London, England, the chief court for trying criminal cases.

old–boy network an exclusive group of people of a similar educational and social background, expected to give help to one another. Also, **old girls' network.**

Old Country the native land of persons living elsewhere: *To many New Canadians, Britain is the Old Country.*

old•en ['ouldən] *adj. Poetic.* of old; old; ancient.

Old English **1** the language of the people of England up to about 1100 A.D.; Anglo-Saxon. **2** *Printing.* gothic, or black-letter, type, especially a style of this type used in England up to about the 18th century.

Old English sheepdog a breed of English working dog, having a long, shaggy, blue or grizzly grey coat and docked tail.

old fashioned a cocktail made of whisky, sugar, and bitters with a slice of orange and a cherry, mixed with soda and served cold.

old–fash•ioned ['ould 'fæʃənd] *adj.* **1** of an old fashion; out-of-date in style, construction, etc.: *an old-fashioned dress.* **2** keeping to old ways, ideas, etc.: *an old-fashioned housekeeper.*

old–fo•gey or **old–fo•gy** ['ould 'fougi] *adj.* out-of-date; behind the times. Also, **old-fogeyish** or **old-fogyish.**

Old French the French language from about A.D. 800 to about 1400.

old gold dark yellow.

Old Guard **1** the imperial guard of Napoleon I. It made the last French charge at Waterloo. **2** Usually, **old guard,** the conservative members of a country, community, organization, etc.

old hand an expert; a very skilled or experienced person.

Old Har•ry ['hæri] *or* ['hɛri] the Devil.

old hat **1** *Informal.* well-known; familiar. **2** old-fashioned; out-of-date.

Old High German the form of the German language that was spoken in S Germany from about A.D. 800 to 1100. Modern standard German is descended from Old High German.

old home week *Cdn. Informal.* a time of festivity when former residents of a community or members of a family return for the celebrations.

Old Icelandic OLD NORSE (def. 2).

old•ie ['ouldi] *n. Informal.* an old thing or person: *They asked the band to play some oldies.*

old•ish ['ouldɪʃ] *adj.* somewhat old.

Old Latin the Latin language before the 2nd century B.C.

old–line ['ould ,laɪn] *adj.* **1** keeping to old ideas and ways; conservative. **2** having a long history; established.

old–line party *Cdn.* either the Liberal or the Progressive Conservative Party, as opposed to more recently founded, smaller parties on the Canadian political scene.

Old Low German collectively, the earliest forms of the Low German dialects, up to about A.D. 1100.

old maid **1** a woman who has not married and seems unlikely to do so. **2** a prim, fussy person: *What an old maid he is!* **3** a very simple card game.

old–maid•ish ['ould 'meidɪʃ] *adj.* like, suggesting, or befitting an old maid; prim; fussy.

Old Man of the Sea **1** in *The Arabian Nights,* a horrible old man who clung to the back of Sinbad. **2** any person or thing that is hard to get rid of.

old master **1** any great painter who lived before 1800. **2** a painting by such a painter.

old moon the moon when seen as a thin crescent with the hollow side on the right; waning crescent. See MOON for picture.

Old Nick [nɪk] *Informal.* the Devil.

Old Norse **1** the northern branch of Germanic which is the parent of the modern Scandinavian languages. **2** the Icelandic language from about 900 to about 1600.

Old North French collectively, the dialects of Old French spoken in the northern areas of France.

Old Persian Persian recorded in cuneiform script, probably of the 6th century B.C.

Old Prussian a language of the Baltic branch of the Indo-European language family, spoken in East Prussia until about 1700.

old rose dark pink.

Old Saxon the form of Low German spoken by the Saxons in NW Germany from about A.D. 800 to about 1100.

old school any group of people who have old-fashioned or conservative ideas. **—'old-,school,** *adj.*

old school tie **1** a tie bearing the sign of one of the British private schools. **2** the social relationship among alumni of the British private schools, including conservatism in dress and attitudes.

old squaw ['ould 'skwɒ] *n. Cdn.* a common marine duck (*Clangula hyemalis*) of the northern hemisphere, the male having distinctive plumage, with a large, white patch on each side of the dark brown head and neck in summer and a brown-and-grey patch on each side of the white head and neck in winter.

old•ster ['ouldstər] *n. Informal.* an old or older person.

Old Stone Age paleolithic.

Old Style **1** the method of reckoning time according to the Julian calendar, used before the adoption of the Gregorian calendar. Compare NEW STYLE. **2 old style,** *Printing.* a style of type characterized by slanting serifs and only slight distinction between light and heavy strokes. *Example*: old style

Old Testament the sacred Scriptures of the Hebrews, as constituting the first part of the Christian Bible. It contains the religious and social laws of the Hebrews, a record of their history, their important literature, and writings of their prophets.

old–time ['ould 'taɪm] *adj.* of or like former times.

old–tim•er ['ould 'taɪmər] *n. Informal.* **1** a person who has long been a resident, member, or worker in a place, group, or community. **2** a person who favours old ideas and ways.

old•wife ['ould,wəif] *n.* **1** OLD SQUAW. **2** ALEWIFE[1].

old–world ['ould 'wɜrld] *adj.* **1** of or having to do with the ancient world: *an old-world mammoth.* **2** belonging to or characteristic of a former period: *old-world courtesy.* **3** of, having to do with, or characteristic of the Old World; especially, having a picturesque or charming quality associated with Europe, N Africa, etc.: *an old-world market.*

Old World 1 Europe, Asia, and Africa. 2 (*adjl.*) of, having to do with, or found in the Old World: *Pythons are the Old World equivalent of the New World boas.*

–ole *suffix.* a diminutive suffix in technical use: *vacuole.* ⟨< F < L *-olus.* var. of *-ulus*⟩

o•le•ag•i•nous [,ouli'ædʒənəs] *adj.* oily. ⟨< L *oleaginus* of the olive < *olea* olive, alteration of *oliva.* See OLIVE.⟩ **–,o•le'ag•i•nous•ly,** *adv.* **–,o•le'ag•i•nous•ness,** *n.*

o•le•an•der ['ouli,ændər] *or* [,ouli'ændər] *n.* a poisonous evergreen shrub (*Nerium oleander*) of the dogbane family, native to the Mediterranean but widely cultivated in warm regions for its fragrant red, pink, or white flowers. ⟨< Med.L⟩

o•le•as•ter [,ouli'æstər] *or* ['ouli,æstər] *n.* 1 any of several shrubs (genus *Elaeagnus*) cultivated for their attractive silvery foliage and also often planted as hardy windbreaks. The Russian olive and silverberry are oleasters. 2 (*adjl.*) designating the family of shrubs and trees that includes the oleasters, buffalo berry, etc.

o•le•ate ['ouli,eit] *n. Chemistry.* a salt of oleic acid.

o•lec•ra•non [ou'lɛkrə,nɒn] *or* [,oulə'kreinɒn] *n. Anatomy.* FUNNY BONE (def. 1). ⟨< Gk. *olekranon* < *olene* elbow + *kranion* head⟩

o•le•fin ['ouləfɪn] *n.* any unsaturated hydrocarbon. **–,o•le'fin•ic,** *adj.*

o•le•ic [ou'liɪk], ['oulіɪk], *or* [ou'leiɪk] *adj.* 1 having to do with oil. 2 derived from oil.

o•le•ic acid *Chemistry.* an oily liquid obtained by hydrolyzing various animal and vegetable oils and fats. *Formula*: $C_{17}H_{33}COOH$ ⟨*oleic* < L *oleum* oil⟩

o•le•in ['ouliɪn] *n. Chemistry.* an ester of oleic acid and glycerin. Lard, olive oil, and cottonseed oil are mostly olein. *Formula*: $(C_{17}H_{33}CO_2)_3C_3H_5$ ⟨< L *oleum* oil⟩

o•le•o ['ouliou] *n.* margarine.

oleo– *combining form.* oil: *oleograph.* ⟨< L *oleum* oil⟩

o•le•o•graph ['ouliə,græf] *n.* a lithograph printed to look like an oil painting. **–,o•le•o'graph•ic,** *adj.*

o•le•o•mar•ga•rine [,ouliou'mɑrdʒərɪn] *or* [,ouliou'mɑrdʒə,rin] *n.* margarine. Also, **oleomargarin.** ⟨< L *oleum* oil + E *margarine*⟩

o•le•o•res•in [,ouliou'rɛzən] *n.* a natural or prepared solution of resin in oil. ⟨< L *oleum* oil + E *resin*⟩

ol•fac•tion [ɒl'fækʃən] *or* [oul'fækʃən] *n.* 1 the act of smelling. 2 the sense of smell. ⟨< L *olfactus,* pp. of *olfacere* smell at < *olere* emit a smell + *facere* make⟩

ol•fac•to•ry [ɒl'fæktəri] *or* [oul'fæktəri] *adj., n., pl.* **-ries.** *–adj.* having to do with smelling; of smell. The nose is an olfactory organ.
–n. an olfactory organ.

olfactory nerve *Anatomy.* either of the two sets of nerves that recognize smell.

o•lib•a•num [ou'lɪbənəm] *n.* frankincense. ⟨ME< ML for LL *libanus* < Gk. *libanos*⟩

ol•i•garch ['ɒlə,gɑrk] *n.* one of a small number of persons holding the ruling power in a state. ⟨< Gk. *oligarches*⟩

ol•i•gar•chic [,ɒlə'gɑrkɪk] *adj.* of an oligarchy or oligarchs; having to do with rule by a few. Also, **oligarchical.** **–,ol•i'gar•chi•cal•ly,** *adv.*

ol•i•gar•chy ['ɒlə,gɑrki] *n., pl.* **-chies.** 1 a form of government in which a few people have the power. 2 a country or state having such a government. Ancient Sparta was really an oligarchy, though it had two kings. 3 the ruling few. ⟨< Gk. *oligarchia,* ult. < *oligos* few + *archos* leader⟩

ol•i•go– *combining form.* few: *oligopoly.* Also, before vowels, **olig-.** ⟨< Gk. *olígos* little, few⟩

Ol•i•go•cene ['ɒləgou,sin] *n., adj. Geology. –n.* 1 an epoch of the Cenozoic era, beginning approximately 37 million years ago. 2 the rocks formed in this epoch. See geological time chart in the Appendix.
–adj. of or having to do with this epoch or rocks formed during it. ⟨< Gk. *oligos* small, little + *kainos* new, recent⟩

ol•i•go•clase ['ɒlɪgou,kleis] *n. Mineralogy.* any of the triclinic feldspars.

ol•i•gop•o•ly [,ɒlə'gɒpəli] *n.* a market situation in which a few large producers control an industry so that there is limited competition and each producer is able to calculate the direct effect on the other firms of its own decisions with respect to pricing, etc. Compare MONOPOLY. ⟨< Gk. *oligos* few + E (*mono*)*poly*⟩ **–,ol•i'gop•o•list,** *n.* **–,ol•i,gop•o'lis•tic,** *adj.*

ol•i•gop•so•ny [,ɒlɪ'gɒpsəni] *n.* a period of economic activity in which there are so few buyers that they control the market. ⟨< Gk. *oligos* few + *opsonia* buying of provisions⟩ **–,ol•i,gop•so'nis•tic,** *adj.*

ol•i•go•troph•ic [,ɒləgou'trɒfɪk] *or* [,ɒləgou'troufɪk] *adj. Ecology.* of a lake or river, deficient in plant nutrients and plant life and rich in oxygen throughout its depth, thus able to support a large fish population. Compare EUTROPHIC. ⟨< Gk. *oligos* little, few + *trophikos* nourishing < *trophē* food, nourishment. 20c.⟩

ol•i•got•roph•y [,ɒlə'gɒtrəfi] *n. Ecology.* the condition or state of being oligotrophic.

ol•i•va•ceous [,ɒlə'veiʃəs] *adj.* OLIVE GREEN.

ol•i•va•ry ['ɒlə,vɛri] *adj.* 1 shaped like an olive. 2 *Anatomy.* having to do with either of the olive-shaped tissues on each side of the medulla oblongata.

ol•ive ['ɒlɪv] *n., adj. –n.* 1 a subtropical evergreen tree (*Olea europaea*) having narrow, leathery, greyish green leaves, fragrant white flowers, and edible fruits that are bluish black when ripe. 2 the fruit of this tree, which is also the source of olive oil. 3 the wood of this tree, used for ornamental carving, etc. 4 (*adjl.*) designating the family of trees and shrubs of tropical and warm temperate regions that includes the olive and many species cultivated as ornamentals, such as lilac, forsythia, and jasmine. 5 a branch or wreath of olive leaves, used as a symbol of peace. 6 a medium to dark yellowish green colour. 7 a yellowish brown colour (*used to describe complexions*).
–adj. having the colour olive: *olive skin.* ⟨ME < OF < L *oliva* < Gk.* *elaiwa,* dial. var. of *elaia*⟩

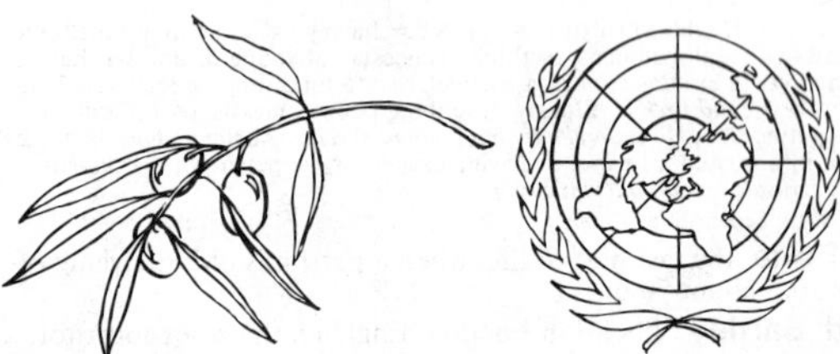

An olive branch with olives

The emblem of the United Nations, using olive branches as a symbol of peace

olive branch 1 a branch of the olive tree as an emblem of peace. 2 anything offered as a sign of peace.

olive drab a greenish brown, or cloth of this colour, especially as used for military uniforms.

olive green a greenish yellow colour.

o•liv•e•nite [ou'lɪvə,nəit] *or* ['ɒləvə,nəit] *n.* arsenite of copper.

olive oil oil pressed from olives, used in cooking, in medicine, etc.

Ol•i•ver ['ɒləvər] *n.* one of Charlemagne's heroic followers and the close friend of Roland, with whom he engaged in a fight which neither of them could win. See also ROLAND.

ol•i•vine ['ɒlə,vin] *or* [,ɒlə'vin] *n.* chrysolite, especially when greenish. ⟨< *olive*; from the colour⟩ **–,ol•i'vin•ic** [,ɒlə'vɪnɪk], *adj.*

Ol•mec ['ɒlmɛk] *or* ['oulmɛk] *n.* 1 a member of an ancient people who lived in Mexico. 2 the language of these people.

ol•o•gy ['ɒlədʒi] *n., pl.* **-gies.** *Informal.* any science or branch of knowledge. ⟨< connective *-o-* + *-logy*⟩

ol•sal•a•zine [ɒl'sælə,zin] *n.* a drug used to treat colitis.

O•lym•pi•a [ə'lɪmpiə] *or* [ou'lɪmpiə] *n.* in ancient Greece, a plain where games were held every four years in honour of Zeus.

O•lym•pi•ad or **o•lym•pi•ad** [ə'lɪmpi,æd] *or* [ou'lɪmpi,æd] *n.* 1 in ancient Greece, a period of four years reckoned from one celebration of the Olympic games to the next, by which Greeks computed time from 776 B.C. 2 the celebration of the modern Olympic games. ⟨< L < Gk. *Olympias, -ados,* ult. < *Olympus,* a mountain in NE Greece⟩

O•lym•pi•an [ə'lɪmpiən] *or* [ou'lɪmpiən] *adj., n. –adj.* 1 having to do with Olympia or with Mount Olympus. 2 like a

god; heavenly. **3** rather too gracious; magnificent; superior: *Olympian calm, Olympian manners.*
—n. **1** any of the major Greek gods. **2** a contender in the Olympic games.

Olympian games OLYMPIC GAMES.

O•lym•pic [ə'lɪmpɪk] *or* [ou'lɪmpɪk] *adj., n. —adj.* **1** of or having to do with Olympia in ancient Greece: *the Olympic games.* **2** of or having to do with Mount Olympus. **3** of or having to do with the Olympic Games: *an Olympic pool. Tennis is an Olympic event.*
—n. **Olympics,** *pl.* the OLYMPIC GAMES.

Olympic games **1** in ancient Greece, contests in athletics, poetry, and music, held every four years by the Greeks in honour of Zeus. **2** a modern event including only the athletic contests of these games. They were revived in 1896 and are held once every four years in a different country, and athletes from many nations compete in them. In 1924 the winter games were begun.

O•lym•pus [ə'lɪmpəs] *or* [ou'lɪmpəs] *n.* heaven. ⟨< Mount *Olympus,* in Greece, regarded as the home of the ancient Greek deities⟩

O.M. ORDER OF MERIT.

–oma *combining form.* a tumour or growth: *carcinoma.* ⟨< Gk. noun suffix *-ōma, -ōmatos*⟩

O•man [ou'mɑn] *n.* a sultanate in SE Arabia.

o•ma•sum [ou'meisəm] *n., pl.* **-sa** [-sə]. the third stomach of a cow or other ruminant. The omasum receives the food when it is swallowed the second time. ⟨< L⟩

om•buds•man ['ɒmbədzmən] *or* [ɒm'bʌdzmən] *n., pl.* **-men.** a government official appointed to receive and investigate citizens' grievances against the government. The office of ombudsman originated in the Scandinavian countries. ⟨< Swedish⟩

o•meg•a [ou'meigə], [ou'migə], [ou'mɛgə], *or* ['oumɪgə] *n.* **1** the last of any series; end. **2** the last letter of the Greek alphabet (Ω or ω). ⟨< LGk. *o mega* big *o*⟩

om•e•lette or **om•e•let** ['ɒmlɪt] *or* ['ɒmlɪt] *n.* a food dish of eggs beaten with milk or water, cooked, and folded over. Omelettes are sometimes filled with chopped meat, mushrooms, or some other filling.

o•men ['oumən] *n., v. —n.* **1** a sign of what is to happen; an object or event that is believed to mean good or bad fortune: *Spilling salt is said to be an omen of misfortune.* **2** prophetic meaning: *Some people consider a black cat a creature of ill omen.*
—v. be a sign of; presage: *to omen disaster.* ⟨< L⟩
☛ *Syn. n.* **1.** See note at SIGN.

o•mep•ra•zole [ou'mɛprə,zoul] *n.* a drug used to treat ulcers.

om•i•cron ['oumə,krɒn] *or* ['ɒmə,krɒn] *n.* the fifteenth letter of the Greek alphabet (Ο or *o*). ⟨< Gk. *o micron* small *o*⟩

om•i•nous ['ɒmənəs] *adj.* of bad omen; unfavourable; threatening: *The watchdog gave an ominous growl.* ⟨< L *ominosus* < *omen* omen⟩ **—'om•i•nous•ly,** *adv.* **—'om•i•nous•ness,** *n.*

o•mis•si•ble [ou'mɪsəbəl] *adj.* able or allowed to be left out.

o•mis•sion [ou'mɪʃən] *n.* **1** an omitting or being omitted. **2** anything omitted: *His song was the only omission from the program.* ⟨< LL *omissio, -onis* < L *omittere.* See OMIT.⟩

o•mis•sive [ou'mɪsɪv] *adj.* showing omissions.

o•mit [ou'mɪt] *v.* **o•mit•ted, o•mit•ting. 1** leave out: *You have omitted a letter in this word.* **2** fail to do; neglect: *Mary omitted to make her bed.* ⟨< L *omittere* < *ob-* by + *mittere* let go⟩

OMM *Cdn.* Officer of the Order of Military Merit.

om•ma•tid•i•um [,ɒmə'tɪdiəm] *n., pl.* **-tid•ia** [-'tɪdiə]. *Zoology.* one of the parts of the compound eye of an arthropod. ⟨< NL < Gk. *ommat-* < *omma* eye⟩

omni– *combining form.* all: *omnidirectional; omnipotence.* ⟨< L *omnis*⟩

om•ni•bus ['ɒmnə,bʌs] *or* ['ɒmnəbəs] *n., pl.* **-bus•es;** *adj.*
—n. **1** a large passenger vehicle having seats inside and sometimes also on the upper level; bus. **2** a volume of works by a single author, or of similar works by several authors: *a Hemingway omnibus, a science fiction omnibus.*
—adj. covering many things at once: *an omnibus law.* ⟨< L *omnibus* for all⟩

om•ni•di•rec•tion•al [,ɒmnidə'rɛkʃənəl] *adj.* receiving or sending signals in all directions.

om•ni•far•i•ous [,ɒmnə'fɛriəs] *adj.* of all forms, varieties, or kinds. ⟨< LL *omnifarius,* < L *omnis* all + *fas, faris,* originally, pronouncement < *fari* speak⟩

om•nip•o•tence [ɒm'nɪpətəns] *n.* complete power; unlimited power: *the omnipotence of God.* ⟨< LL *omnipotentia*⟩

om•nip•o•tent [ɒm'nɪpətənt] *adj., n. —adj.* having all power; almighty: *an omnipotent ruler.*
—n. **the Omnipotent,** God. ⟨< L *omnipotens, -entis* < *omnis* all + *potens* being able⟩ **—om'nip•o•tent•ly,** *adv.*

om•ni•pres•ent [,ɒmnə'prɛzənt] *adj.* present everywhere at the same time. ⟨< Med.L *omnipraesens, -entis* < L *omnis* all + *praesens* present⟩ **—,om•ni'pres•ence,** *n.*

om•ni•range ['ɒmnɪ,reindʒ] *n.* a radio network that gives an aircraft information on bearings, now superseded by LORAN.

om•nis•cience [ɒm'nɪsiəns] *or* [ɒm'nɪʃəns] *n.* knowledge of everything; complete or infinite knowledge. ⟨< Med.L *omniscientia* < L *omnis* all + *scientia* knowledge⟩

om•nis•cient [ɒm'nɪsiənt] *or* [ɒm'nɪʃənt] *adj.* knowing everything; having complete or infinite knowledge.
—om'nis•cient•ly, *adv.*

om•ni•um–gath•er•um ['ɒmniəm 'gæðərəm] *n.pl.* a miscellaneous collection; a confused mixture. ⟨< L *omnium* of all + *gatherum,* pseudo-Latin form from E *gather*⟩

om•ni•vore ['ɒmnə,vɔr] *n.* a creature that eats every kind of food: *Human beings are omnivores.*

om•niv•o•rous [ɒm'nɪvərəs] *adj.* **1** eating every kind of food. **2** eating both animal and vegetable food: *The human being is an omnivorous animal.* **3** taking in everything; fond of all kinds. An omnivorous reader reads all kinds of books. ⟨< L *omnivorus* < *omnis* all + *vorare* eat greedily⟩ **—om'niv•o•rous•ly,** *adv.* **—om'niv•o•rous•ness,** *n.*

om•pha•los ['ɒmfələs] *n.* **1** the navel. **2** a centre. ⟨< Gk. *omphalos* navel⟩

OMR *Computer technology.* OPTICAL MARK RECOGNITION.

on [ɒn] *prep., adv., adj. —prep.* **1** above and supported by: *The book is on the table.* **2** touching so as to cover, be around, etc.: *There's new paint on the ceiling. Put the ring on her finger.* **3** close to; along the edge of: *a house on the shore. He lives on the next street.* **4** in the direction of; toward: *The workers marched on the capital.* **5** against; upon: *the picture on the wall.* **6** by means of; by the use of: *This news is on good authority.* **7** in the condition of; in the process of; in the way of: *on half pay, on purpose, on duty.* **8** at the time of; during: *They greeted us on our arrival.* **9** in relation to; in connection with; concerning: *a book on animals.* **10** for the purpose of: *He went on an errand.* **11** in addition to: *Defeat on defeat discouraged them.* **12** among: *I am on the committee.* **13** carried by: *He had a gun on him.* **14** paid by: *Have a drink on me.*
—adv. **1** on something: *The walls are up, and the roof is on.* **2** to something: *Hold on, or you may fall.* **3** toward something: *Some played; the others looked on.* **4** farther; more; longer: *March on.* **5** in or into a condition, process, manner, action, etc.: *Turn the gas on.* **6** from a time; forward: *later on, from that day on.*
and so on, and more of the same.
be on about, talk a lot about.
on and off, at some times and not others; now and then.
on and on, without stopping.
—adj. taking place or going to take place: *The race is on.* ⟨OE⟩
☛ *Hom.* AWN.
☛ *Usage.* **on to, onto.** See note at ONTO.

ON[1] Ontario (*used esp. in computerized address systems*).

ON[2] OLD NORSE.

o•na•ger ['ɒnədʒər] *n.* a small, wild ass, brown with a white belly and a black stripe on its back, found in central Asia. ⟨< L < Gk. *onagros* < *onos* ass + *agros* field⟩

o•nan•ism ['ounə,nɪzəm] **1** removal of the penis from the vagina during sexual intercourse, so that ejaculation takes place outside the female's body. **2** masturbation. ⟨< *Onan,* a biblical character⟩

once [wʌns] *adv., n., conj., adj. —adv.* **1** one time: *He comes once a day.* **2** at some one time in the past; formerly: *a once powerful nation.* **3** even a single time; ever: *If the facts once became known everybody would laugh at her.*
once and again, repeatedly.
once and for all or **once for all,** finally.
once in a while, now and then; at one time or another.
once or twice, a few times.
once over, a single time over.
once upon a time, long ago (*used to begin a fairy tale*).
—n. a single occasion: *Once is enough.*

all at once, a suddenly: *All at once there was a loud crack of thunder.* **b** simultaneously.
at once, a immediately: *Come at once.* **b** at the same time; simultaneously: *Everyone shouted at once.*
for once, for one time at least.
just this once, for this time only.
—conj. whenever or if ever; after: *Once you cross the river, you are safe.*
—adj. former: *a once friend.* ⟨OE ānes < ān one⟩

once–o•ver ['wʌns ˌouvər] *n. Informal.* **1** a short, quick look. **2** a quick, superficial job: *He gave the furniture a once-over with a dust cloth.*

on•co•gene ['ɒŋkəˌdʒin] *n. Genetics.* a gene that can convert a normal cell into a malignant cell. Compare PROTO-ONCOGENE. ⟨< Gk. *onkos* swelling + E *gene*⟩

on•col•o•gy [ɒŋ'kɒlədʒi] *n.* the branch of medicine dealing with the study and treatment of tumours. ⟨< Gk. *onkos* swelling, tumour + E *-logy.* 19c.⟩ **—ˌon•co'log•ic** [ˌɒŋkə'lɒdʒɪk] or **ˌon•co'log•i•cal,** *adj.* **—on'col•o•gist,** *n.*

on•com•ing ['ɒnˌkʌmɪŋ] *adj., n. —adj.* approaching: *oncoming winter.*
—n. approach: *the oncoming of the storm.*

one [wʌn] *n., adj., pron. —n.* **1** the first and lowest natural number; 1. **2** the numeral 1: *What does the 1 in the margin mean?* **3** a single person or thing: *a table for one.* **4** the first in a set or series; especially, a playing card or side of a die having one spot; ace. **5** a one-dollar bill: *They have ones and fives in the States but no twos.*
at one, in agreement: *The two judges were at one about the winner.*
make one, a form or be the one of a number, assembly, or party. **b** join together; unite in marriage.
one and all, everyone.
one by one, one after another.
one up on, *Informal.* in a position of advantage over: *to be one up on someone.*
—adj. **1** being a single unit or individual: *one apple.* **2** some: *One day he will be sorry.* **3** the same: *They held one opinion.* **4** joined together; united: *They replied in one voice.* **5** being the first in a set or series (*used mainly after the noun*): *We'll start with Chapter One.* **6** a certain: *One John Smith was elected.*
all one, a exactly the same: *They are all one in their love of hockey.* **b** making no difference: *It is all one to me whether you stay or go.*
one or two, a few.
—pron. **1** some person or thing: *One of the poems was selected for the book.* **2** any person or thing: *One must work hard to achieve success.* **3** the same person or thing: *Dr. Jekyll and Mr. Hyde were one.* **4** the person or thing previously mentioned: *She has a black purse and a white one.*
one and the same, the very same.
one or two, a few. ⟨OE (*stressed*) ān. Cf. A[1], AN[1].⟩
☛ *Usage.* The use of the impersonal pronoun **one** is characteristically formal, especially if it must be repeated. Informal: *You can't be too careful, can you?* Formal: *One can't be too careful, can one?*

–one *suffix.* a ketone: *acetone.* ⟨< Gk.⟩

one–acter ['wʌn 'æktər] *n.* a one-act play.

one another each of several in an action or relation that is reciprocal: *They struck at one another. They were in one another's way.*
☛ *Usage.* **One another,** EACH OTHER. As a reciprocal pronoun, **one another** is usually used with reference to more than two, **each other** with reference to two: *The members of the team support one another. The two hate each other.* In informal English the two are interchangeable.

one–base hit ['wʌn 'beis] *Baseball.* a hit which allows the batter to reach first base.

one–celled ['wʌn 'sɛld] *adj.* having only one cell.

one–flowered wintergreen ['wʌn 'flaʊərd] a Canadian wildflower (*Moneses uniflora*) having delicate white flowers, blooming in summer in damp woods in the north, and south to New Mexico.

one–horse ['wʌn 'hɔrs] *adj.* **1** drawn or worked by a single horse: *a one-horse sleigh.* **2** using or having only a single horse: *a one-horse farmer.*
one-horse town, *Informal.* a town of little scope, capacity, or importance; minor.

O•nei•da [ou'naidə] *n., pl.* **-da** or **-das;** *adj. —n.* **1** a member of an American Indian people belonging to the Five Nations confederacy, originally of New York State and later living in SW Ontario and Wisconsin. **2** the Iroquoian language of the Oneida.
—adj. of or having to do with the Oneida or their language.

o•nei•ric [ou'naɪrɪk] *adj.* having to do with dreams. ⟨< Gk. *oneiros* dream + *-ic*⟩

o•nei•ro•man•cy [ou'naɪrəˌmænsi] *n.* the use of dreams to foretell the future. ⟨< Gk. *oneiros* dream + E *-mancy* < F *-mancie*, ult. < Gk. *mantcia* soothsaying⟩

one–legged ['wʌn 'lɛgd] *or* ['lɛgɪd] *adj.* **1** having only one leg. **2** of an argument or viewpoint, limited. **3** lacking some important element, so as to be ineffective: *a one-legged law.*

one–lin•er ['wʌn ˌlaɪnər] *n.* a one-line joke.

one–man ['wʌn 'mæn] *adj.* **1** of or by only one man: *one-man rule, a one-man art show.* **2** made for or to be used by one person: *a one-man space ship.* **3** showing loyalty to or affection for one person only: *one-man dog.*

one•ness ['wʌnnɪs] *n.* **1** the quality of being one in number or the only one of its kind; singleness. **2** the quality of being the same in kind; sameness. **3** the fact of forming one whole; unity. **4** agreement in mind, feeling, or purpose; harmony.

one–night stand ['wʌn 'nəit] **1** a single performance in one place, as by a touring theatrical company or band. **2** *Informal.* a single sexual meeting, lasting only one night.

one–on–one ['wʌn ɒn 'wʌn] *adj., adv. —adj.* involving single persons; consisting of individual confrontation or interaction: *a one-on-one meeting.*
—adv. individually: *I'd like to meet him one-on-one.*

one–piece ['wʌn ˌpis] *adj.* of a garment, consisting of a single piece: *a one-piece swimsuit.*

on•er•ous ['ounərəs] *or* ['ɒnərəs] *adj.* **1** burdensome; oppressive: *an onerous task.* **2** *Law.* in a contract, entailing a legal obligation greater than the benefits. ⟨< L *onerosus* < *onus* burden⟩ **—'on•er•ous•ly,** *adv.* **—'on•er•ous•ness,** *n.*

one•self [wʌn'sɛlf] *pron.* **1** a reflexive pronoun, the form of **one** used as an object when it refers to the same person as the subject: *One might ask oneself if it is worth the trouble.* **2** a form of **one** added for emphasis: *One has to do the real work oneself.* **3** one's usual self: *It's nice to be oneself again after an illness.*

one–shot ['wʌn 'ʃɒt] *adj. Informal.* being the only one, not part of a series; being or involving a single act, attempt, etc.: *a one-shot effort.*

one–sid•ed ['wʌn 'saɪdɪd] *adj.* **1** seeing only one side of a question; partial; unfair; prejudiced. **2** uneven; unequal: *If one team is much better than the other, a game is one-sided.* **3** having but one side. **4** on only one side. **5** having one side larger or more developed than the other.

one's self oneself.

one•step ['wʌnˌstɛp] *n., v.* **-stepped, -step•ping.** *—n.* **1** a ballroom dance in 2/4 time, much like a quick walk. **2** the music for such a dance.
—v. dance the onestep.

one–time ['wʌn ˌtaɪm] *adj.* of the past; former: *my one-time best friend.*

one–to–one ['wʌn tə 'wʌn] *adj.* **1** *Mathematics.* **a** having proportional amounts on both sides. **b** allowing for one member of a class to pair with only one of another class. **2** one–on–one.

one–track ['wʌn 'træk] *adj.* **1** having only one track. **2** *Informal.* understanding or preoccupied with only one thing at a time: *a one-track mind.*

one–two ['wʌn 'tu] *n.* **1** *Boxing.* a knockout punch. **2** a concluding argument.

one up **1** winning. **2** beating an opponent by one score: *At half-time we were one up on our rivals.* **3** one each: *The score was one up at half-time.*

one–up•man•ship [ˌwʌn 'ʌpmənˌʃɪp] *n. Informal.* the art or practice of getting the better of someone else in business, social life, etc.

one–way ['wʌn 'wei] *adj.* moving or allowing movement in only one direction: *one-way traffic, a one-way flight.*

one–wom•an ['wʌn 'wʊmən] *adj.* **1** of or by one woman only: *a one-woman play.* **2** made for or to be used by one woman: *a one-woman canoe.* **3** showing loyalty to or affection for one woman only: *a one-woman man.*

on•go•ing ['ɒnˌgouɪŋ] *adj.* actually going on; in process; continuing: *This is not an isolated crime, but part of an ongoing social problem.*

on•ion ['ʌnjən] *n.* **1** a commonly cultivated herb (*Allium cepa*) of the lily family, having an edible bulb with a very sharp, strong taste and smell. The many varieties of onion include the Spanish onion, Bermuda onion, and green onion. See BULB for picture.

2 the bulb of this plant, used as a vegetable or seasoning: *Fried onions do not have the sharp taste of raw onions.*
know one's onions, *Informal.* be well-informed. ⟨< F *oignon* < L *unio, -onis* onion, kind of pearl⟩ **—'on•ion,like,** *adj.*

onion rings transverse slices of onion battered and deep-fried.

on•ion•skin ['ʌnjən,skɪn] *n.* **1** the thin, papery outer skin of an onion: *Onionskins can be used to make a yellow dye.* **2** a thin, glossy, translucent paper.

on–line ['ɒn 'laɪn] *adj., adv.* *—adj. Computer technology.* involving or designating interactive processing done while directly connected to a computer: *Her flight to Winnipeg was booked through the on-line reservation system.*
—adv. Computer technology. by means controlled by a computer.

on•look•er ['ɒn,lʊkər] *n.* a person who watches without taking part; spectator.

on•look•ing ['ɒn,lʊkɪŋ] *adj. or n.* watching; seeing; noticing.

on•ly ['ounli] *adj., adv., conj.* *—adj.* **1** by itself or themselves; one and no more; these and no more; sole, single, or few of the kind or class: *an only son. Those were the only clothes he owned. This is the only road along the shore.* **2** best; finest: *As far as she is concerned, he is the only writer.*
—adv. **1** merely; just: *He sold only two.* **2** and no one or nothing more; and that is all: *Only he remained. I did it only through friendship.*
if only, I wish: *If only wars would cease!*
only too, very: *She was only too glad to help us.*
—conj. **1** except that; but: *I would have gone only I didn't have the money.* **2** it must be added that; however: *We camped right beside a stream, only the water was not fit to drink.* ⟨OE *ānlīc*⟩
☛ *Syn. adj.* **1.** See note at SINGLE.
☛ *Usage.* To avoid uncertainty, **only** as an adverb should be placed immediately before the word or words it modifies. The following three sentences all have different meanings: *He only wrote to his parents last week* (he didn't telephone). *He wrote only to his parents last week* (not to anyone else). *He wrote to his parents only last week* (just last week).

on•o•mas•tic [,ɒnə'mæstɪk] *adj.* having to do with names. ⟨< Gk. *onomastikos* < *onomazein* to name⟩

on•o•mas•ti•con [,ɒnə'mæstɪ,kɒn] *n.* **1** a list of names. **2** a list of technical terms pertaining to one subject area.

on•o•mas•tics [,ɒnə'mæstɪks] *n.* the study of names (*used with a singular verb*).

on•o•mat•o•poe•ia [,ɒnə,mætə'piə] *n.* **1** the naming of a thing or action by imitating the sound associated with it, as in *buzz, hum, cuckoo, slap, splash.* **2** the adaptation of the sound to the sense for rhetorical effect, as in 'the murmuring of innumerable bees'. ⟨< L < Gk. *onomatopoiia* < *onoma, -matos* word, name + *-poios* making⟩ **—,on•o,mat•o'poe•ic** or **,on•o,mat•o•po'et•ic** [,ɒnə,mætəpou'ɛtɪk], *adj.* **—,on•o,mat•o•po'et•i•cal•ly,** *adv.*

On•on•da•ga [,ɒnən'dɑgə] *or* [,ɒnən'deigə] *n., pl.* **-ga** or **-gas;** *adj.* *—n.* **1** a member of an American Indian people belonging to the Five Nations confederacy, living mainly in New York State. **2** the Iroquoian language of the Onondaga.
—adj. of or having to do with the Onondaga or their language. ⟨< Iroquois *Onnonta' gé*, a place name meaning 'on top of the hill'⟩

on•rush ['ɒn,rʌʃ] *n.* a violent forward movement: *He was knocked down by the onrush of water.* **—'on,rush•ing,** *adj.*

on•set ['ɒn,sɛt] *n.* **1** an attack: *The onset of the enemy took us by surprise.* **2** the beginning: *the onset of a disease, the onset of winter.*

on•shore ['ɒn'ʃɔr] *adv. or adj.* **1** toward the land: *an onshore wind.* **2** on the land: *an onshore patrol.*

on•side ['ɒn'saɪd] *adj. or adv.* in a position allowed by the rules of a game.

on–site ['ɒn 'səit] *adj.* on the spot; at the actual location: *an on-site inspection.*

on•slaught ['ɒn,slɒt] *n.* a vigorous attack: *The attackers were driven back by a sudden onslaught from within the city.* ⟨< MDu. *aanslag* < *aan* on + *slag* stroke⟩

on•stage ['ɒn'steidʒ] *adj., adv.* *—adj.* being part of a scene: *the onstage characters.*
—adv. on or onto the stage: *She carried the sword onstage.*

on–stream ['ɒn 'strim] *adj.* operating: *The new factory is on-stream.*

Ont. Ontario.

On•tar•i•an [ɒn'tɛriən] *n., adj.* *—n.* a native or long-term resident of Ontario.
—adj. of or having to do with Ontario.

On•ta•ri•o [ɒn'tɛriou] *n.* an eastern province of Canada.

on•to ['ɒntu]; *before consonants often* ['ɒntə] *prep.* **1** on to; to a position on: *throw a ball onto the roof, get onto a horse, a boat driven onto the rocks.* **2** *Informal.* familiar with or aware of: *Are you onto your new job yet? We're onto her tricks.*
☛ *Usage.* **Onto, on to.** When **on** is an adverb and **to** is a preposition, they should be written as two words: *The rest of us drove on to the city.* When the two words are combined to make a compound preposition, they are usually written solid: *The team trotted onto the floor. They looked out onto the park.*

onto– *combining form.* being, existence: *ontogenesis.* ⟨< Gk. *ōn, ontos* ppr. of *einai* to be⟩

on•to•gen•e•sis [,ɒntə'dʒɛnəsɪs] *n.* ontogeny. ⟨< *onto-* + Gk. *-geneia* origin < *-genēs* born, produced⟩ **—,on•to•ge'net•ic** [,ɒntədʒə'nɛtɪk], *adj.*

on•tog•e•ny [ɒn'tɒdʒəni] *n. Biology.* the development of an individual organism. ⟨< Gk. *ōn, ontos* being + *-geneia* origin < *-genēs* born, produced⟩

on•tol•o•gy [ɒn'tɒlədʒi] *n.* the part of philosophy that deals with the nature of reality and being. ⟨< NL *ontologia* < Gk. *ōn, ontos* being + *-logos* treating of⟩ **—,on•to'log•i•cal** [,ɒntə'lɒdʒɪkəl], *adj.* **—,on•to'log•i•cal•ly,** *adv.* **—on'tol•o•gist,** *n.*

o•nus ['ounəs] *n.* a burden; responsibility: *Since he made the accusation, the onus is on him to prove it.* ⟨< L⟩

on•ward ['ɒnwərd] *adv. or adj.* going toward the front; on or further on; forward: *The army marched onward. She continued her onward course.* Also, **onwards.**

on•yx ['ɒnɪks] *n.* a translucent variety of quartz in layers of different colours. Onyx is used as a semiprecious stone, especially for making cameos. ⟨< L < Gk. *onyx* nail, claw⟩

o•o•cyte ['ouə,səit] *n. Biology.* a stage in the development of the mature ovum from the primordial germ cell. In human females, there are about 2.5 million oocytes at the time of birth. ⟨< Gk. *oion* egg + *kytos* a hollow⟩

oo•dles ['udəlz] *n.pl. Informal.* large or unlimited quantities; heaps; loads: *oodles of money.* ⟨< *huddle* a mass of things⟩

o•og•a•mous [ou'ɒgəməs] *adj. Biology.* having to do with reproduction by oogamy.

o•og•a•my [ou'ɒgəmi] *n. Biology.* the fertilization of female gametes.

o•o•gen•e•sis [,ouə'dʒɛnəsɪs] *n. Biology.* the development of mature ova from primordial germ cells, through a sequence of developmental stages. **—,o•o•ge'net•ic** [,ouədʒə'nɛtɪk], *adj.*

Ook•pik ['ukpɪk] *n. Cdn. Trademark.* a doll resembling an owl, invented by an unnamed Inuit artist in 1963, and soon adopted as a symbol of Canadian handicraft exhibits abroad. ⟨< Inuktitut *ukpik* snowy owl⟩

oo•li•chan ['ulə,kɑn] *or* ['uləkən] *n., pl.* **-chan** or **-chans.** *Cdn.* a small, highly valued food fish (*Thaleichthys pacificus*) of the smelt family found along the Pacific coast of North America, having a slender body and very oily, rich flesh. Oolichan spend most of their lives in the sea, but swim into freshwater rivers to spawn, after which they die. Also, **eulachon, oolachan.** ⟨< Chinook jargon⟩

oolichan oil or **grease** *Cdn.* a clear, edible oil rendered from the oolichan and being a highly valuable food and trade item among the Coast and Inland First Nations people of British Columbia.

o•o•lite or **o•ö•lite** ['ouə,ləit] *n. Geology.* rock, usually limestone, consisting of small, rounded grains cemented together. ⟨< F *oölithe* < Gk. *ōon* egg + *lithos* stone⟩

o•ol•o•gy [ou'ɒlədʒi] *n.* that part of ornithology that studies birds' eggs. **—,o•o'log•i•cal** [,ouə'lɒdʒɪkəl], *adj.* **—o'ol•o•gist,** *n.*

oo•long ['ulɒŋ] *n.* tea made from leaves that have been partially fermented before being dried in ovens. Oolong is greenish brown in colour. ⟨< Chinese *wu-lung* black dragon⟩

oo•loo ['ulu] *Cdn.* See ULU.

oo•mi•ak ['umi,æk] *Cdn.* See UMIAK.

oomph [umf] *n. Slang.* **1** extreme vigour. **2** sex appeal.

o•o•phyte ['ouə,fəit] *n. Botany.* the phase during which sex organs are developed in plants. ⟨< Gk. *ōon* egg + E *-phyte*⟩

o•o•sphere ['ouə,sfir] *n. Botany.* an egg ready for fertilization.

o•o•spore ['ouə,spɔr] *n. Botany.* a spore developed by parthenogenesis or by means of a fertilized oosphere.

o•o•the•ca [,ouə'θikə] *n., pl.* **-cae** [-si]. the capsule enclosing the eggs of some insects and molluscs.

o•o•tid ['ouətɪd] *n. Biology.* one of the four sections into which an ovum divides. ⟨< Gk. *ōon* egg + E *-id*⟩

ooze[1] [uz] *v.* **oozed, ooz•ing;** *n.* —*v.* **1** pass slowly through small openings; leak slowly and quietly: *Blood oozed from her scraped knee. The mud oozed into her boots.* **2** leak slowly and quietly: *The news of their failure oozed to the public.* **3** disappear or drain away: *His courage oozed away as he waited.* **4** give out slowly: *The cut oozed blood.*
—*n.* **1** a slow flow. **2** something that oozes. **3** an infusion of vegetable matter for tanning leather. ⟨OE *wōs* juice⟩

ooze[2] [uz] *n.* **1** a soft mud or slime, especially that at the bottom of a pond, lake, river, or ocean. **2** muddy ground. ⟨OE *wāse* mud⟩

ooz•y[1] ['uzi] *adj.* **ooz•i•er, ooz•i•est.** oozing. ⟨< *ooze[1]*⟩ **—'ooz•i•ly,** *adv.* **—'ooz•i•ness,** *n.*

ooz•y[2] ['uzi] *adj.* **ooz•i•er, ooz•i•est.** containing ooze; muddy and soft; slimy. ⟨< *ooze[2]*⟩ **—'ooz•i•ly,** *adv.* **—'ooz•i•ness,** *n.*

op [ɒp] *n.* **1** OP ART. **2** (*adjl.*) of or designating op art: *an op artist.*

op– the form of **ob-** before *p*, as in *oppress.*

op. 1 opus; opera. **2** opposite. **3** operation.

OP, O.P., or **o.p. 1** out of print. **2** opposite prompt (side of the stage).

O.P. 1 Order of Preachers (Dominican). **2** observation post.

o•pac•i•ty [ou'pæsəti] *n., pl.* **-ties. 1** the quality or state of being opaque: *Onionskin has less opacity than bond paper.*
2 something opaque: *A cataract is an opacity of the lens of the eye.* ⟨< L *opacitas* < *opacus* dark⟩

o•pal ['oupəl] *n.* a mineral, an amorphous form of silica that is softer and less dense than quartz, found in many varieties and colours, certain of which have a peculiar rainbowlike play of colours and are valued for gems. **Black opals** are green and blue with brilliant coloured lights; some are so dark as to seem almost black. **Milk opals** are milky white with rather pale lights. **Fire opals** are similar with more red and yellow lights. ⟨< L *opalus* < Gk. *opallios* < Skt. *upala* precious stone⟩

o•pal•esce [,oupə'lɛs] *v.* **-esced, -esc•ing.** exhibit a play of colours like that of the opal. ⟨< *opal* + *-esce* begin to be, become (< L *-escere*)⟩

o•pal•es•cent [,oupə'lɛsənt] *adj.* showing a play of colours like that of the opal. **—,o•pal'es•cence,** *n.*

o•pal•ine ['oupə,laɪn], ['oupə,lin], *or* ['oupəlɪn] *adj., n.*
—*adj.* of or like opal.
—*n.* milk glass, an opaque white glass.

o•paque [ou'peik] *adj., n.* —*adj.* **1** not letting light through; not transparent: *Muddy water is opaque.* **2** not shining; dark; dull. **3** obscure; hard to understand. **4** stupid.
—*n.* something opaque. ⟨< L *opacus* dark, shady⟩ **—o'paque•ly,** *adv.* **—o'paque•ness,** *n.*

opaque projector an apparatus for projecting written, drawn, or printed material onto a screen or wall. An opaque projector projects images directly from paper or books rather than from transparencies.

op art a style of drawing and painting that creates optical illusions of motion and depth by means of complex geometrical designs. ⟨shortened from *optical art*, on analogy with *pop art*⟩

op.cit. in the book, passage, etc. previously referred to. ⟨for L *opere citato* in the work cited⟩

OPEC Organization of Petroleum Exporting Countries.

o•pen ['oupən] *adj., n., v.* —*adj.* **1** not shut; not closed; letting (anyone or anything) in or out: *an open drawer. Open windows let in the fresh air.* **2** not having its lid, cover, gate, etc. closed: *an open box, an open cage.* **3** not closed in: *an open field.* **4** unfilled; not taken up: *have an hour open. The position is still open.* **5** that may be entered, used, shared, competed for, etc. by all: *an open meeting, an open market.* **6** accessible or available: *the only course still open.* **7** ready for business or for admission of the public: *The exhibition is now open. This store stays open till 9:30 p.m.*
8 without restriction or prohibition: *open season for hunting.*
9 *Informal.* allowing liquor, gambling, etc.: *an open town.*
10 undecided; not settled: *an open question.* **11** having no cover, roof, etc.; letting in air freely: *an open car.* **12** not covered or protected; exposed: *open to temptation.* **13** not obstructed: *an open view.* **14** unprejudiced; ready to consider new ideas: *an open mind.* **15** exposed to general view, knowledge, etc.; not secret: *open disregard of rules.* **16** having spaces or holes: *open ranks, cloth of open texture.* **17** *Music.* **a** of an organ pipe, not closed at the upper end. **b** of a string on a violin, cello, etc., not stopped by the finger. **c** of a note, produced by such a pipe or string, or without aid of slide, key, etc. **18** *Phonetics.* **a** designating a vowel uttered with relatively wide opening between the tongue and the roof of the mouth, such as [ɑ]. **b** designating a syllable that ends with a vowel sound, as in *to.* **19** unreserved, candid, or frank: *an open face.* **20** that is spread out; expanded: *an open flower, an open newspaper.* **21** generous; liberal: *Give with an open hand.*
22 free from frost: *an open winter.* **23** free from hindrance, especially from ice: *open water on the lake, a river or harbour now open.* **24** *Electricity.* of an electric circuit, not complete or closed. **25** of a city, town, etc., unfortified; protected from enemy attack under international law: *In World War II Rome was declared an open city.* **26** *Computer technology.* ready for use.
open to, a ready to take; willing to consider: *open to suggestion.* **b** liable to; vulnerable to: *open to criticism.* **c** to be had or used by: *open to the public.*
—*n.* **1 the open, a** the open country, air, sea, etc.: *I spent the afternoon out in the open and got badly sunburned.* **b** public view or knowledge: *It would be better to bring the problem out into the open.* **2** a competition, tournament, etc. open to anyone who wishes to enter. **3** an opening.
—*v.* **1** cause to become open; move or remove so as to allow entry or exit: *Open the door. I can't open the vent. We opened the lid and looked in the box.* **2** open the lid, cover, etc. of: *to open a parcel, to open a cage.* **3** establish or set going: *She has opened a new store.* **4** begin; start: *School opens today.* **5** begin the proceedings of; initiate formally: *to open negotiations. The Queen opened Parliament.* **6** have or make entrance; allow entry: *This hall opens into the bedrooms.* **7** become open or more open; become accessible: *The valley opens wide lower down.* **8** cause to be open or more open; make accessible: *Open a path through the woods.* **9** clear of obstructions; make (a passage, etc.) clear.
10 make or become accessible to knowledge, sympathy, etc.; enlighten or become enlightened: *to open a person's eyes. She opened her heart to them.* **11** uncover; lay bare; expose to view; disclose. **12** come to view. **13** expand, extend, or spread out; make or become less compact: *The ranks opened.* **14** cut into: *open a wound.* **15** come apart, especially so as to allow passage or show the contents: *The wound opened. The clouds opened and the sun shone through.* **16** *Law.* make the first statement of (a case) to the court or jury. **17** *Computer technology.* in software, prepare for use: *open a window on a screen, open a file.*
open up, a make or become open. **b** unfold; spread out. **c** open a way to and develop: *The early settlers opened up the West.* ⟨OE. Related to UP.⟩ **—'o•pen•ly,** *adv.* **—'o•pen•ness,** *n.*

open admissions *Education.* the policy of admitting anyone to an educational institution, such as a university, without reference to academic record.

open air the out-of-doors.

o•pen–air ['oupən 'ɛr] *adj.* outdoor: *an open-air festival.*

o•pen–and–shut ['oupən ən 'ʃʌt] *adj. Informal.* simple and direct; obvious; straightforward: *The Crown attorney was sure they had an open-and-shut case against the defendant.*

open book someone or something that is easy to discover or interpret; something not hidden: *Her opinions are an open book.*

open chain *Chemistry.* an arrangement of atoms in linear sequence to form certain compounds of carbon and silicon.

open classroom *Education.* a system of instruction in which several classes share a large, open area, suitable for individualized teaching.

open door 1 freedom of access; unrestricted admission. **2** a policy of a country giving all other countries an equal chance to trade with it.

o•pen–end ['oupən 'ɛnd] *adj.* **1** allowing for change or revision: *an open-end mortgage.* **2** of or having to do with investment groups that issue or recall shares on demand, since the capital is open, not fixed.

o•pen–end•ed ['oupən 'ɛndɪd] *adj.* **1** having no set boundary or limit; not rigidly defined or controlled; adaptable to a changing situation or need; having no single right answer: *an open-ended agreement. The audience participated in an open-ended discussion after the speech. Open-ended questions are best for children.* **2** not closed at either end: *an open-ended cylinder.*
—'o•pen-'end•ed•ness, *n.*

o•pen•er ['oupənər] *n.* **1** a person who or thing that opens, especially a device for opening bottles, cans, letters, etc.
2 *Informal.* the first game of a scheduled series. **3 openers,** *Card games.* cards of high enough value to allow the player holding them to open the bidding.
for openers, *Informal.* as a beginning.

o•pen–eyed ['oupən ,aɪd] *adj.* **1** having eyes wide open as in wonder. **2** having the eyes open; watchful or vigilant; observant. **3** done or experienced with the eyes open.

o•pen–face ['oupən ˌfeis] *adj.* of a sandwich, made without the top slice of bread.

o•pen–faced ['oupən ˌfeist] *adj.* **1** open-face. **2** not having the face or surface covered. **3** of a watch, having no cover over the dial. **4** having a frank and honest face. **5** honest; ingenuous.

o•pen–hand•ed ['oupən 'hændɪd] *adj.* generous; liberal. **—'o•pen-'hand•ed•ly,** *adv.* **—'o•pen-'hand•ed•ness,** *n.*

open–heart ['oupən 'hɑrt] *adj.* designating surgery on the heart while its functions are performed by mechanical means.

o•pen–heart•ed ['oupən 'hɑrtɪd] *adj.* **1** candid; frank; unreserved. **2** kindly; generous. **—'o•pen-'heart•ed•ly,** *adv.* **—'o•pen-'heart•ed•ness,** *n.*

o•pen–hearth ['oupən 'hɑrθ] *adj.* having an open hearth; using a furnace with an open hearth.

open–hearth process a process of making steel in a furnace in which the flame is directed onto the raw material, the impurities becoming oxidized.

open house **1** an informal social event open to all to come and go as they wish: *They dropped in at their neighbour's open house before leaving for Christmas.* **2** an occasion when a school, university, factory, etc. is opened for inspection by the public: *The art college has an open house every spring to display student work and demonstrate the facilities of the college.* **3** a time when a house for sale is open to inspection by buyers and agents. **keep open house,** offer food, or food and lodging, to all visitors.

o•pen•ing ['oupənɪŋ] *n.* **1** an open or clear space; gap; hole: *an opening in a wall, an opening in the forest.* **2** the first part; beginning: *the opening of a lecture.* **3** an official ceremony to mark the beginning of a new business, institution, etc.: *The opening of the new city hall was last week. Were you there for the opening?* **4** a job, place, or position that is open or vacant. **5** a favourable chance or opportunity: *She waited for an opening to ask to borrow the car.* **6** *Law.* the statement of the case made by the lawyer to the court or jury before adducing evidence.

open letter a letter addressed to a particular person but intended for publication in a newspaper, magazine, etc.

o•pen–line ['oupən 'laɪn] *adj.* hot-line: *an open-line radio show.*

open marriage a marriage in which the partners agree that each is permitted sexual relationships with other people.

open mind a mind ready to consider new arguments or ideas: *A politician ought to keep an open mind.*

o•pen–mind•ed ['oupən 'maɪndɪd] *adj.* having or showing a mind open to new arguments or ideas. **—'o•pen-'mind•ed•ly,** *adv.* **—'o•pen-'mind•ed•ness,** *n.*

o•pen–mouthed ['oupən ˌmaʊðd] *or* [ˌmʌuθt] *adj.* **1** having the mouth open. **2** gaping with surprise or astonishment. **3** greedy, ravenous, or rapacious. **4** vociferous or clamorous: *open-mouthed hounds.* **5** having a wide mouth: *an open-mouthed pitcher.* **—'o•pen-'mouth•ed•ly,** *adv.* **—'o•pen-'mouth•ed•ness,** *n.*

o•pen–pit ['oupən 'pɪt] *adj.* worked on from the exposed surface, or slightly below the surface; not underground: *open-pit mining.*

open position *Music.* any harmony in which the notes of a chord are widely spaced.

open question a matter that has not been decided and on which differences of opinion are accepted.

open season **1** a period during which it is legal to hunt and kill fish or game that is protected by law at other times. **2** a situation in which anyone can criticize or attack a given person, group, etc. with seeming impunity (*used with* **on**): *open season on tourists.*

open secret a matter that is supposed to be secret but that everyone knows about: *It's an open secret that he has applied for another job.*

open sesame **1** in the *Arabian Nights*, the magic words that opened the door of the robbers' den in the story of Ali Baba. **2** anything that obtains easy access: *Her education was an open sesame to the position as researcher.*

open shop a factory, shop, or other establishment that will employ both union and non-union workers. Compare CLOSED SHOP, PREFERENTIAL SHOP.

open syllable a syllable that ends with a vowel sound. *Examples*: *free-* in *freedom*, *o-* in *open.* Compare CLOSED SYLLABLE.

Open University an organization offering university-level courses by distance education, using radio, tapes, and mail, and often having no admission requirements.

open water **1** water free of obstructions. **2** *Cdn.* especially in the North: **a** the time when rivers and lakes become free of ice; break-up: *At open water he got twenty beaver and two otter.* **b** the period during which rivers and lakes are free of ice; the time between break-up and freeze-up: *We have good hunting here during open water.*

o•pen•work ['oupənˌwɜrk] *n.* ornamental work in cloth, metal, etc. that has openings in the material.

op•er•a[1] ['ɒpərə] *n.* **1** a kind of drama set to music, in which the words are sung by the performers rather than spoken, usually to an orchestral accompaniment. **2** the art of creating or performing operas: *the history of opera.* **3** a performance of an opera. **4** the music of an opera. **5** a company that performs opera. **6** a theatre where operas are performed. ⟨< Ital. *opera*, for *opera in musica* a (dramatic) work to music; *opera* < L *opera* effort (related to OPUS)⟩

op•er•a[2] ['ɒpərə] *n.* a pl. of OPUS.

op•er•a•ble ['ɒpərəbəl] *adj.* **1** fit for, or admitting of, a surgical operation. **2** fit or able to be operated.

o•pé•ra bouffe ['ɒpərə 'buf]; *French,* [ɔpeʀa'buf] **1** comic opera; light opera. **2** an absurd situation; ridiculous arrangement. ⟨< F *opéra bouffe* comic opera⟩

o•pé•ra co•mique ['ɒpərə kɔ'mik]; *French,* [ɔpeʀakɔ'mik] opera that has spoken dialogue as well as arias, etc.

opera glasses small, low-powered binoculars for use at the opera, in theatres, etc.

opera hat a man's tall, collapsible hat worn with formal clothes.

opera house **1** a theatre where operas are performed. **2** any theatre.

op•er•and ['ɒpəˌrænd] *n. Mathematics.* any symbol or quantity that is subject to an operation. ⟨< L *operandum*, gerundive of *operari.* See OPERATE.⟩

op•er•ate ['ɒpəˌreit] *v.* **-at•ed, -at•ing. 1** be at work; run: *The machinery operates night and day.* **2** keep at work; drive: *Who operates this elevator?* **3** direct the working of as owner or manager; manage: *That company operates factories in seven countries.* **4** take effect; produce an effect; work; act: *Several causes operated to bring on the war. The medicine operated quickly.* **5** *Medicine.* perform a surgical operation: *Will they have to operate? The doctor operated on the injured man immediately.* **6** carry on military movements. **7** buy and sell stocks and bonds: *to operate in stocks or grain futures.* ⟨< L *operare* < *opus* a work, or *opera* effort⟩

op•er•at•ic [ˌɒpə'rætɪk] *adj.* of, like, or having to do with the opera: *operatic music.* **—ˌop•er'at•i•cal•ly,** *adv.*

operating system *Computer technology.* a collection of computer programs that provide the overall control of a computer system by directing the detailed operation of its hardware and software: *She entered a command that caused the operating system to load the word processing software from disk.*

op•er•a•tion [ˌɒpə'reiʃən] *n.* **1** working: *The operation of a railway requires many people.* **2** the way a thing works: *the operation of a machine.* **3** an action; activity: *the operation of brushing one's teeth.* **4** *Medicine.* a treatment for injury or disease, in which instruments are used to cut into the body in order to remove, replace, or repair an organ or part: *She had her operation yesterday and is doing well.* **5** movements of soldiers, ships, supplies, etc. for military purposes. **6** *Mathematics.* something done to a number or quantity. Addition, subtraction, multiplication, and division are the four commonest operations in arithmetic. **7** a commercial transaction, especially one that is speculative and on a large scale: *operations in stocks or wheat.* **in operation, a** running; working; in action. **b** in use or effect.

op•er•a•tion•al [ˌɒpə'reiʃənəl] *adj.* **1** of or having to do with any kind of operation. **2** of equipment, in working order. **3** of a military operation, ready or equipped to perform a certain mission. **—ˌop•er'a•tion•al•ly,** *adv.*

operations research the analysis of a process to determine its efficiency.

op•er•a•tive ['ɒpərətɪv] *or* ['ɒpəˌreitɪv] *adj., n.* *—adj.* **1** operating; effective: *the laws operative in a community.* **2** having to do with work or productiveness: *operative departments of a manufacturing establishment.* **3** of, concerned

with, or resulting from a surgical operation. **4** relevant; of note: *the operative word in a sentence.*
—n. **1** a person who operates a machine. **2** a private detective or secret agent. **—'op•er•a•tive•ly,** *adv.* **—'op•er•a•tive•ness,** *n.*

op•er•a•tor ['ɒpə,reitər] *n.* **1** a person who operates something, especially: **a** a skilled worker who runs a machine, telephone exchange, telegraph, etc. **b** the owner or manager of a business, factory, etc. **2** *Informal.* a person who is skilled in avoiding problems or restrictions or manipulating people for his or her own needs. **3** a person who speculates in stocks or a commodity. **4** *Mathematics.* a symbol denoting a specific operation.

o•per•cu•late [ou'pɜrkjəlɪt] *or* [ou'pɜrkjə,leit] *adj.* having an operculum.

o•per•cu•lum [ou'pɜrkjələm] *n., pl.* **-la** [-lə] or **-lums.** *Biology.* any lidlike part or organ; any flap covering an opening. ⟨< L *operculum* < *operire* cover⟩ **—o'per•cu•lar,** *adj.*

op•er•et•ta [,ɒpə'rɛtə] *n., pl.* **-tas.** a short, amusing opera with some words spoken rather than sung. ⟨< Ital. *operetta,* dim. of *opera* opera⟩

o•phid•i•an [ou'fɪdiən] *n., adj. —n.* snake.
—adj. of, having to do with, or like snakes. ⟨< NL *Ophidia* an order of reptiles < Gk. *ophidion,* dim. of *ophis* serpent⟩

oph•i•ol•o•gy [,ɒfi'ɒlədʒi] *or* [,oufi'ɒlədʒi] *n.* the branch of herpetology dealing with snakes. ⟨< Gk. *ophis* snake + E *-logy*⟩

o•phite ['ɒfəit] *or* ['oufəit] *n.* **1** any rock, such as serpentine, having a mottled green colour. **2** any green rock of diabase. ⟨< L *ophites* < Gk. *ophites* < *ophis* snake⟩ **—o'phit•ic** [ou'fɪtɪk], *adj.*

Oph•i•u•chus [,ɒfi'jukəs] *or* [,oufi'jukəs] *Astronomy. n.* a constellation in the equatorial region, close to Hercules and Scorpius; the Serpent Bearer. ⟨< L < Gk., holding a snake⟩

oph•thal•mi•a [ɒf'θælmiə] *or* [ɒp'θælmiə] *n.* an acute infection of the eyeball or the membrane covering the front of the eyeball. Also, **ophthalmitis.** ⟨< LL < Gk. *ophthalmia* < *ophthalmos* eye; cf. *ōps* eye, *thalamos* chamber⟩

oph•thal•mic [ɒf'θælmɪk] *or* [ɒp'θælmɪk] *adj.* **1** of or having to do with the eye. **2** having to do with or affected with ophthalmia.

oph•thal•mi•tis [,ɒfθæl'məitɪs] *or* [,ɒpθæl'məitɪs] *n.* See OPHTHALMIA.

ophthalmo– *combining form.* the eye: *opthalmology.* ⟨< Gk. *ophthalmós*⟩

oph•thal•mol•o•gist [,ɒfθæl'mɒlədʒɪst] *or* [,ɒpθæl'mɒlədʒɪst], [,ɒfθə'mɒlədʒɪst] *or* [,ɒpθə'mɒlədʒɪst] *n.* a physician who specializes in ophthalmology.

☛ *Usage.* An **ophthalmologist** (or **oculist**), an OPTOMETRIST, and an OPTICIAN all have to do with the health of the eyes. An **ophthalmologist** is a doctor who is trained to treat diseases of the eye as well as recommending corrective lenses. An **optometrist** is not a doctor but is trained to examine eyes and recommend corrective lenses. An **optician** prepares, fits, and sells glasses and contact lenses.

oph•thal•mol•o•gy [,ɒfθæl'mɒlədʒi] *or* [,ɒpθæl'mɒlədʒi], [,ɒfθə'mɒlədʒi] *or* [,ɒpθə'mɒlədʒi] *n.* the branch of medicine that deals with the structure, functions, and diseases of the eye. ⟨< Gk. *ophthalmos* eye + E *-logy*⟩

oph•thal•mo•scope [ɒf'θælmə,skoup] *or* [ɒp'θælmə,skoup] *n.* an instrument for examining the interior of the eye or the retina. ⟨< Gk. *ophthalmos* eye + E *-scope*⟩

–opia *combining form.* a specified defect or condition of the eye: *myopia.* ⟨< Gk. *-ōpia, ōps* eye⟩

o•pi•ate ['oupiɪt] *or* ['oupi,eit] *n., adj. —n.* **1** any powerful drug containing opium or a derivative of opium (such as morphine) and used especially to dull pain or to bring sleep. **2** anything that quiets.
—adj. **1** containing opium or a derivative. **2** bringing sleep or ease. ⟨< Med.L *opiatus* < L *opium* opium⟩

o•pine [ou'pain] *v.* **o•pined, o•pin•ing.** express or have an opinion; suppose: *He opined that the weather would improve by evening.* ⟨< F < L *opinari*⟩ **—o'pin•er,** *n.*

o•pin•ion [ə'pɪnjən] *n.* **1** an appraisal or judgment formed in the mind about the truth or probability of something: *I prefer to learn the facts and form my own opinion.* **2** a view or impression: *She has a poor opinion of such shoddy construction.* **3** a formal judgment made by an expert; professional advice. **4** *Law.* a statement by a judge or jury of the reasons for the decision of the court. ⟨ME < OF < L *opiniō*; akin to *opinārī* to opine⟩

☛ *Syn.* **1. Opinion,** VIEW = what a person thinks about something. **Opinion** is the general word and particularly suggests a carefully thought-out conclusion based on facts, but without the certainty of knowledge: *I try to learn the facts and form my own opinions.* **View** applies to a particular way of looking at something, and especially suggests a personal opinion affected by personal leanings or feelings: *His views are conservative.*

o•pin•ion•at•ed [ə'pɪnjə,neitɪd] *adj.* obstinate or conceited with regard to one's opinions; dogmatic. **—o'pin•ion,at•ed•ly,** *adv.* **—o'pin•ion,at•ed•ness,** *n.*

o•pin•ion•a•tive [ə'pɪnjə,neitɪv] *adj.* **1** based on opinion. **2** opinionated. **—o'pin•ion,at•ive•ly,** *adv.* **—o'pin•ion,at•ive•ness,** *n.*

op•is•thog•na•thous [,ɒpɪs'θɒgnəθəs] *adj., Zoology.* having receding jaws. ⟨< Gk. *opisthen* behind + *gnathos* jaw⟩

o•pi•um ['oupiəm] *n.* **1** a powerful, addictive drug that causes sleep and eases pain, made from the dried juice extracted from the unripe seed capsules of the opium poppy. **2** anything that has a dulling or tranquillizing effect. ⟨ME < L < Gk. *opion,* dim. of *opos* vegetable juice⟩

opium poppy a poppy (*Papaver somniferum*) whose unripe pods are the source of opium.

o•pos•sum [ə'pɒsəm] *n.* any of a family (Didelphidae) of New World marsupials, especially an arboreal species (*Didelphis marsupialis*) found in wooded regions near water from southern Ontario south to Argentina, having light grey to black fur, a pointed snout, and a hairless prehensile tail. It feigns death when in danger. Also called **possum.** ⟨< Algonquian⟩

An opossum

opossum shrimp a small crustacean of the order Mysidacea, the female of which carries her eggs in a pouch between her legs.

op•pi•dan ['ɒpɪdən] *adj., n. —adj.* of a town; urban.
—n. a resident of a town. ⟨< L *oppidanus* < *oppidum* town⟩

op•pi•late ['ɒpə,leit] *v.* **-lat•ed, -lat•ing.** obstruct, usually by filling up. ⟨< L *oppilare* stop up < *ob-* against + *pilare* pack down⟩ **—,op•pi'la•tion,** *n.*

op•po•nen•cy [ə'pounənsi] *n.* **1** being an opponent. **2** an act of opposing.

op•po•nent [ə'pounənt] *n., adj. —n.* a person who is on the other side in a fight, game, or argument; a person fighting, struggling, or speaking against another.
—adj. opposing. ⟨< L *opponens, -entis* < *ob-* against + *ponere* place⟩

☛ *Syn. n.* **Opponent,** ANTAGONIST, ADVERSARY = someone against a person or thing. **Opponent** applies to someone on the other side in an argument, game, or other contest, or against a proposed plan, law, etc., but does not suggest personal ill will: *She defeated her opponent in the election.* **Antagonist,** more formal, suggests active, personal, and unfriendly opposition, often in a fight for power or control: *Hamlet and his uncle were antagonists.* **Adversary** now usually means a definitely hostile antagonist actively blocking or openly fighting another: *Gamblers found a formidable adversary in the new chief of police.*

op•por•tune [,ɒpər'tjun] *or* [,ɒpər'tun] *adj.* **1** fortunate; well-chosen; suitable; favourable: *You have come at a most opportune moment.* **2** occurring at the right time: *an opportune meeting.* ⟨< L *opportunus* favourable (of wind) < *ob portum (ferens)* (bringing) to port⟩ **—,op•por'tune•ly,** *adv.* **—,op•por'tune•ness,** *n.*

☛ *Syn.* See note at TIMELY.

op•por•tun•ism [,ɒpər'tjunɪzəm] *or* [,ɒpər'tunɪzəm] *n.* the policy or practice of taking advantage of opportunities and particular circumstances, especially with little regard for principles. **—,op•por'tun•ist,** *n.* **—,op•por•tun'is•tic,** *adj.* **—,op•por•tun'is•ti•cal•ly,** *adv.*

op•por•tu•ni•ty [,ɒpər'tjunəti] *or* [,ɒpər'tunəti] *n., pl.* **-ties.** a good chance; favourable time; convenient occasion.

op•pos•a•ble [ə'pouzəbəl] *adj.* **1** capable of being opposed or resisted. **2** capable of being placed opposite something else. The human thumb is opposable to the fingers. **—op,pos•a'bil•i•ty,** *n.*

op•pose [ə'pouz] *v.* **-posed, -pos•ing. 1** act, fight, speak, or struggle against; try to hinder or stop; resist: *The residents opposed the widening of the street. The army's advance was fiercely opposed.* **2** put against as a defence, reply, or contrast: *Let us oppose good nature to anger.* **3** put in contrast: *to oppose European and North American culture.* **4** put in front of; cause to face: *to oppose one's finger to one's thumb.* ⟨ME < OF *opposer* < *op-* (< L *ob-*) against + *poser* put (see POSE[1])⟩ **—op'pos•er,** *n.*

☛ *Syn.* **Oppose,** RESIST, WITHSTAND = act or stand against someone or

something. **Oppose** means set oneself against a person or thing, especially an idea, plan, etc., but does not suggest the nature, purpose, form, or effectiveness of the action or stand taken: *We opposed the plan because of the cost.* **Resist** suggests making a stand and actively striving against an attack or force of some kind: *The bank messenger resisted the attempt to rob him.* **Withstand** emphasizes holding firm against attack: *The bridge withstood the flood.*
☛ *Hom.* APPOSE.

op•posed [ə'pouzd] *adj., v.* —*adj.* placed in opposition; contrary or contrasted: *The two brothers had strongly opposed characters.*
—*v.* pt. and pp. of OPPOSE.
as opposed to, in contrast to: *I prefer fish as opposed to meat. We talked of the merits of train travel as opposed to air travel.*

op•po•site ['ɒpəzɪt] *or* ['ɒpəsɪt] *adj., n., prep.* —*adj.* **1** placed face to face, back to back, or at the other end or side: *the opposite side of the street. The map is opposite page 37. The printing on the opposite side of the page shows through to this side.* **2** as different as can be; just contrary: *Sour is opposite to sweet.* **3** *Botany.* of leaves, flowers, etc. growing singly and directly opposite each other along either side of a stem. Compare ALTERNATE.
—*n.* a thing that or person who is opposite: *Black is the opposite of white.*
—*prep.* **1** opposite to: *opposite the church.* **2** in a motion picture or play, acting as the leading lady or man of (an actor of the opposite sex): *She played opposite a famous actor in her first starring role.* ⟨< L *oppositus,* pp. of *opponere* < *ob-* against + *ponere* place⟩ —**'op•po•site•ly,** *adv.* —**'op•po•site•ness,** *n.*
☛ *Syn. adj.* **2. Opposite,** CONTRARY = completely different (from each other). **Opposite** particularly suggests two things thought of as standing one at each end of a line, so far apart in position, nature, meaning, etc. that they can never be brought together: True *and* false *have opposite meanings.* **Contrary** particularly suggests two things going in opposite directions, or set against each other, often in strong disagreement or conflict: *Your statement is contrary to the facts.*

opposite number a person in an organization who holds a position equal to that of a person in another organization.

op•po•si•tion [,ɒpə'zɪʃən] *n.* **1** action against; resistance: *The mob offered opposition to the police.* **2** contrast: *His views were in opposition to mine.* **3** the political party or parties not in power: *In parliament or a legislature, the party having the second largest number of elected members is called the official opposition.* **4** any opponent or group of opponents: *Our team easily defeated the opposition.* **5** the act of placing opposite: *the opposition of the thumb to the fingers.* **6** an opposite direction or position. **7** *Astronomy.* the position of two heavenly bodies when their longitude differs by 180°. ⟨< L *oppositio, -onis* < *opponere.* See OPPOSITE.⟩ —**,op•po'si•tion•al** or **,op•po'si•tion,ar•y,** *adj.* —**,op•po'si•tion•less,** *adj.*

op•press [ə'prɛs] *v.* **1** govern harshly; keep down unjustly or by cruelty: *A good government will not oppress the poor.* **2** weigh down; lie heavily on; burden: *A fear of trouble ahead oppressed my spirits.* ⟨< Med.L *oppressare,* ult. < L *ob-* against + *premere* press⟩

op•pres•sion [ə'prɛʃən] *n.* **1** cruel or unjust treatment; tyranny; persecution; despotism: *The oppression of the people by the dictator caused the war. They fought against oppression.* **2** a heavy, weary feeling. **3** a burden.

op•pres•sive [ə'prɛsɪv] *adj.* **1** harsh; severe; unjust. **2** hard to bear; burdensome. —**op'pres•sive•ly,** *adv.* —**op'pres•sive•ness,** *n.*

op•pres•sor [ə'prɛsər] *n.* a person who is cruel or unjust to people over whom he or she has authority or power.

op•pro•bri•ous [ə'proubriəs] *adj.* expressing scorn, reproach, or abuse: *Coward, liar, and thief are opprobrious names.* ⟨< LL *opprobriosus*⟩ —**op'pro•bri•ous•ly,** *adv.* —**op'pro•bri•ous•ness,** *n.*

op•pro•bri•um [ə'proubriəm] *n.* disgrace or reproach caused by conduct considered shameful or vicious; infamy; scorn; abuse. ⟨< L *opprobrium,* ult. + *ob-* at + *probrum* infamy, reproach⟩

op•pugn [ə'pjun] *v.* contradict; oppose. ⟨ME < L *oppugnāre*⟩ —**op'pugn•er,** *n.*

op•pug•nant [ə'pʌgnənt] *adj.* antagonistic. —**op'pug•nan•cy,** *n.*

-opsis *combining form.* likeness: *coreopsis.* ⟨< Gk. *ópsis* appearance, sight⟩

op•so•nin ['ɒpsənɪn] *n. Bacteriology.* a substance in the blood serum that weakens bacteria and other foreign cells so that the white blood cells can destroy them more easily. ⟨< L *opsonium* relish (meat, fish) < Gk. *opsonion* to buy food⟩ —**op'son•ic** [ɒp'sɒnɪk], *adj.*

op•so•nize ['ɒpsə,naɪz] *v.* **-nized, -niz•ing.** form opsonins in. —**,op•so•ni'za•tion,** *n.*

opt [ɒpt] *v.* make a choice, especially in favour of something; decide: *She opted to stay. The class opted for a field trip.*
opt in, choose to join.
opt out (of), decide to leave; choose to drop out of some activity or organization: *Several nations wanted to opt out of the alliance.* ⟨< L *optare* choose, desire⟩

opt. 1 optative. **2** optical; optics. **3** optional.

op•ta•tive ['ɒptətɪv] *adj., n. Grammar.* —*adj.* **1** expressing a wish: *"Oh! that I had wings to fly!" is an optative expression.* **2** of the form of the subjunctive mood used to express a wish. In *Oh, that she were here, were* is an optative subjunctive.
—*n.* **1** the optative mood. **2** a verb in the optative mood. ⟨< LL *optativus* < L *optare* wish⟩ —**'op•ta•tive•ly,** *adv.*

op•tic ['ɒptɪk] *adj., n.* —*adj.* of the eye or the sense of sight.
—*n. Informal.* the eye. ⟨< Med.L *opticus* < Gk. *optikos* < *op-* see⟩

op•ti•cal ['ɒptɪkəl] *adj.* **1** of or having to do with the eye or the sense of sight; visual: *an optical illusion. Being near-sighted is an optical defect.* **2** made to assist sight or according to the principles of optics: *A microscope is an optical instrument. An optical telescope uses light waves, but a radio telescope uses radio waves.* **3** of or having to do with optics. —**'op•ti•cal•ly,** *adv.*

optical character recognition *Computer technology.* the ability of a photo-electric machine to read letters and numbers *Abbrev.*: OCR

optical double (star) DOUBLE STAR.

optical fibre a fibre of glass or plastic used to allow the operator to see or record images of something beneath the surface, as the lungs; the glass or acrylic fibre used in FIBRE OPTICS.

optical illusion a drawing so made that the eye is deceived. See ILLUSION for picture.

optical mark recognition *Computer technology.* the use of optical technology to scan and translate marks (usually made in special locations on special forms) for input to a computer.

optical maser a maser that produces visible radiation.

optic axis a path through a crystal allowing access to a light ray.

optical microscope a microscope using beams of light. Compare ELECTRON MICROSCOPE.

op•ti•cian [ɒp'tɪʃən] *n.* a person who prepares, fits, and sells glasses and contact lenses that have been prescribed by an optometrist or an ophthalmologist. ⟨< F *opticien*⟩
☛ *Usage.* See note at OPHTHALMOLOGIST.

optic nerve *Anatomy.* the cranial nerve that conducts visual stimuli from the eye to the brain. See EYE for picture.

op•tics ['ɒptɪks] *n.* (*used with a singular verb*) the science that deals with light and vision.

op•ti•mal ['ɒptəməl] *adj.* most favourable or desirable; optimum. —**'op•ti•mal•ly,** *adv.*

op•ti•mism ['ɒptə,mɪzəm] *n.* **1** a tendency to look on the bright side of things and make the best of any situation or event as it comes about. **2** a belief that everything will turn out for the best. **3** *Philosophy.* the doctrine that the existing world is the best of all possible worlds. ⟨< NL *optimismus* < L *optimus* best⟩

op•ti•mist ['ɒptəmɪst] *n.* **1** a person who tends to look on the bright side of things, making the best of any situation or event as it comes about. **2** a person who believes that everything in life will turn out for the best. **3** a person who believes in the doctrine of optimism.

op•ti•mis•tic [,ɒptə'mɪstɪk] *adj.* **1** inclined to look on the bright side of things. **2** hoping for the best. **3** having to do with optimism. —**,op•ti'mis•ti•cal•ly,** *adv.*

op•ti•mize ['ɒptə,maɪz] *v.* **-mized, -miz•ing.** make the most of; make as satisfactory or effective as possible: *She checked every detail of design to optimize the effect of the advertisement.* —**,op•ti•mi'za•tion,** *n.*

op•ti•mum ['ɒptəməm] *n., pl.* **-ma** [-mə] or **-mums;** *adj.*
—*n.* the best or most favourable point, degree, amount, etc. for a particular purpose.
—*adj.* most favourable, desirable, or satisfactory; best: *an optimum temperature for growth.* ⟨< L *optimus* best, superlative of *bonus* good⟩

op•tion ['ɒpʃən] *n., v.* —*n.* **1** the right or power to choose: *We have the option of rejecting this offer and waiting for a better one.* **2** the act of choosing: *to make an option.* **3** something chosen or

that may be chosen: *One of the options open to her was to accept a grant to study abroad. One of the options offered with this car model is air conditioning.* **4** a right to buy something at a certain price within a certain time: *to hold an option on land.*
—*v.* obtain or grant an option in reference to (something). ⟨< L *optio, -onis*⟩

op•tion•al ['ɒpʃənəl] *adj.* involving an option; not required or standard: *optional equipment on a car.* —**ˌop•tion'al•i•ty** [ˌɒpʃə'næləti], *n.* —**'op•tion•al•ly,** *adv.*

option play *Football.* a play which allows a fullback to pass or run with the ball.

op•tom•e•ter [ɒp'tɒmətər] *n.* any machine for measuring defects of vision. ⟨< Gk. *optos* visible + *meter*⟩

op•tom•e•trist [ɒp'tɒmətrɪst] *n.* a person who is qualified to practise optometry. An optometrist does not prescribe drugs or surgery.
☛ *Usage.* See note at OPHTHALMOLOGIST.

op•tom•e•try [ɒp'tɒmətri] *n.* the art or profession of examining the eyes for defects in vision and prescribing lenses or exercises to correct such defects. ⟨< Gk. *optos* seen + E *-metry*⟩

op•u•lence ['ɒpjələns] *n.* **1** wealth; affluence. **2** luxuriant abundance; lavishness.

op•u•lent ['ɒpjələnt] *adj.* **1** wealthy; affluent. **2** abundant and luxuriant; lavish. ⟨< L *opulens, -entis* < *ops* power, resources⟩ —**'op•u•lent•ly,** *adv.*

o•pun•tia [ou'pʌnʃiə] *or* [ou'pʌnʃə] *n.* any cactus of the genus *Opuntia*; PRICKLY PEAR.

o•pus ['oupəs] *n., pl.* **o•pus•es** or **op•er•a** ['ɒpərə]. a literary work or musical composition: *The violinist played his own opus, No. 16.* ⟨< L⟩
☛ *Usage.* **Opera, opuses.** Because the Latin plural is identical with **opera** 'musical drama', it is now generally replaced, except in learned use, by **opuses.**

o•pus•cule [ou'pʌskjul] *n.* a minor work. ⟨< L *opusculum* < *opus* work⟩

or[1] [ɔr]; *unstressed,* [ər] *conj.* **1** a word used to indicate: **a** a choice, alternative, or difference: *Do you prefer coffee or tea? We intend to go, whether or not they do. Either the blue or the brown would be suitable.* **b** equivalence of two words: *This is the termination or end.* **c** approximate quantity, etc.: *They'll be gone for three or four days.* **2** if not, then; otherwise: *Hurry, or you'll be late.* ⟨OE (unstressed) *ā(hwæ)ther* < *ā* ever + *hwæther* either, whether⟩
☛ *Hom.* OAR, O'ER, ORE.

or[2] [ɔr] *prep. or conj. Archaic.* before; ere. ⟨OE *ār* early, confused with OE *ǣr* ere⟩
☛ *Hom.* OAR, O'ER, ORE.

or[3] [ɔr] *n. Heraldry.* gold or yellow. ⟨< F < L *aurum* gold⟩
☛ *Hom.* OAR, O'ER, ORE.

-or *suffix.* **1** a person or thing that ——s: *actor, accelerator, orator, survivor, sailor.* **2** an act, state, condition, quality, characteristic, etc., especially in words from Latin: *error, horror, terror.* ⟨< L⟩
☛ *Spelling.* **-or, -our.** The suffix **-or** entered English directly from Latin: *horror, terror.* With a few words, the spelling **-our** was also introduced from French: *colour, labour, neighbour.* British English prefers **-our** in such words, but American English prefers **-or.** In Canada, both spellings are acceptable but **-our** is the more frequent, and is the variant given first in this dictionary.

o.r. owner's risk.

OR or **O.R. 1** operating room. **2** orderly room.

o•ra ['ɔrə] *n.* pl. of OS².

or•a•cle ['ɔrəkəl] *n.* **1** in ancient times: **a** an answer given by a god through a priest or priestess to some question. **b** the place where the god gave answers. A famous oracle was at Delphi. **c** the priest, priestess, or other means by which the god's answer was given. **2** a person who gives wise advice. **3** something regarded as a reliable and sure guide. ⟨ME < OF < L *oraculum* < *orare*, originally, recite solemnly⟩

o•rac•u•lar [ɔ'rækjələr] *adj.* **1** of or like an oracle. **2** with a hidden meaning that is difficult to make out. **3** very wise. —**o'rac•u•lar•ly,** *adv.*

o•ral ['ɔrəl] *adj., n.* —*adj.* **1** spoken; using speech. **2** of the mouth. **3** taken by mouth: *oral medicine.*
—*n.* a spoken examination: *a PhD oral.* ⟨< L *os, oris* mouth⟩ —**'o•ral•ly,** *adv.*
☛ *Hom.* AURAL.
☛ *Usage.* **Oral,** VERBAL. Strictly, **oral** means 'spoken', and **verbal,** used as an adjective, means 'in (written or spoken) words'; but **verbal** has been used so long with the same sense as **oral** that in many contexts they are interchangeable: *He gave an oral report. They had only a verbal agreement.*

or•ange ['ɔrɪndʒ] *n., adj.* —*n.* **1** a round, reddish yellow, edible citrus fruit having a bitter rind and a sweet or tangy, juicy pulp. **2** any of several citrus trees that produce such fruit. The **sweet orange** (*Citrus sinensis*), cultivated in many varieties, is one of the most important commercial species. See also MANDARIN (def. 1). **3** any fruit or tree that suggests an orange. **4** a colour made by mixing red and yellow. **5** a soft drink flavoured with orange juice or a synthetic substitute.
—*adj.* **1** of or like an orange. **2** of or having the colour orange. ⟨ME < OF *orenge* < Sp. *naranja* < Arabic < Persian *narang*; in OF blended with the word *or* meaning 'gold'⟩ —**'or•ange,like,** *adj.* —**'or•ang•y** or **'or•ange•y,** *adj.*

Or•ange ['ɔrɪndʒ] *n.* a princely family of Europe that ruled the former principality of Orange in W Europe, now a part of SE France. William III of England was of this family, and so is the present royal family of the Netherlands.

or•ange•ade [ˌɔrɪndʒ'eid] *or* [ˌɔrɪn'dʒeid] *n.* a drink made of orange juice, sugar, and water.

Orange Association LOYAL ORANGE ASSOCIATION.

orange hawkweed a perennial weed (*Hieracium aurantiacum*) having bright orange flowers, growing in summer in central and eastern Canada and on the Pacific coast. Also called **devil's paintbrush.**

orange honeysuckle a Canadian vine (*Lonicera ciliosa*) having showy orange-red flowers, and twining over trees up to 6 m high. It blooms in spring in British Columbia and Montana and south to California.

Or•ange•ism ['ɔrɪnˌdʒɪzəm] *n.* the principles and practices of the LOYAL ORANGE ASSOCIATION.

Or•ange•man ['ɔrɪndʒmən] *n., pl.* **-men. 1** a member of a secret society, formed in the north of Ireland in 1795, to uphold the Protestant religion and Protestant control in Ireland. **2** a member of the LOYAL ORANGE ASSOCIATION. **3** any Irish Protestant.

Orange Order LOYAL ORANGE ASSOCIATION.

orange pekoe a black tea that comes from Sri Lanka or India.

or•ange•ry ['ɔrɪndʒri] *n.* a greenhouse for orange trees.

orange stick a slim stick, formerly of orangewood, used by manicurists to clean the fingernails or push back the cuticles.

or•ange•wood ['ɔrɪndʒˌwʊd] *n.* the wood of the orange tree, having a very fine grain.

o•rang•u•tan, o•rang–u•tan, or **o•rang•u•tang** [ɔ'ræŋəˌtæn] *or* [ɔ'ræŋgəˌtæŋ] *n.* a large anthropoid ape (*Pongo pygmaeus*) of the forests of Borneo and Sumatra, having very long arms and long, reddish brown hair. Orangutans live much of the time in trees and eat fruits and leaves. Also, **orangoutang** or **orang-outang.** ⟨< Malay *orangutan* < *orang* man + *utan* wild⟩

An orangutan

o•rate [ɔ'reit] *or* ['ɔreit] *v.* **-rat•ed, -rat•ing.** make an oration; talk in a grand manner. ⟨< *oration*⟩

o•ra•tion [ɔ'reiʃən] *n.* **1** a formal public speech delivered on a special occasion. **2** a speech given in an overly formal or affected style. ⟨< L *oratio, -onis* < *orare* speak formally. Doublet of ORISON.⟩
☛ *Syn.* See note at SPEECH.

or•a•tor ['ɔrətər] *n.* **1** a person who makes an oration. **2** a person who can speak very well in public.

or•a•tor•i•cal [ˌɔrə'tɔrəkəl] *adj.* **1** of oratory; having to do with orators or oratory: *an oratorical contest.* **2** characteristic of orators or oratory: *an oratorical manner.* —**ˌor•a'tor•i•cal•ly,** *adv.*

or•a•to•ri•o [,ɔrə'tɔri,ou] *n., pl.* **-ri•os. 1** a musical drama performed without action, costumes, or scenery, for solo voices, chorus, and orchestra. Oratorios are usually based on Biblical or historical themes. Handel's *Messiah* is an oratorio. **2** the art of creating or performing oratorios. **3** a performance of an oratorio. **4** the music of an oratorio. ⟨< Ital. *oratorio*, originally, place of prayer < LL *oratorium.* Doublet of ORATORY².⟩

or•a•to•ry¹ ['ɔrə,tɔri] *n.* **1** the art of public speaking. **2** skill in public speaking; fine speaking. **3** language used in public speaking; words appropriate to fine speaking. ⟨< L *(ars) oratoria* oratorical (art), ult. < *orare* plead, speak formally⟩

or•a•to•ry² ['ɔrə,tɔri] *n., pl.* **-ries.** a small chapel; a room set apart for prayer. ⟨< LL *oratorium* < *orare* pray. Doublet of ORATORIO.⟩

orb [ɔrb] *n., v.* *—n.* **1** a sphere, especially a heavenly body such as the sun, moon, or a star. **2** a jewelled sphere, especially a symbol of royal power. **3** *Esp. poetic.* the eyeball or eye. *—v.* **1** form into a circle or sphere. **2** *Archaic or poetic.* encircle; enclose. ⟨< L *orbis* circle⟩ **—'orb,like,** *adj.*

or•bic•u•lar [ɔr'bɪkjələr] *adj.* **1** spherical; globular. **2** circular; disk-shaped: *an orbicular leaf.* ⟨< LL *orbicularis* < L *orbiculus,* dim. of *orbis* circle⟩ **—or,bic•u'lar•i•ty,** *n.* **—or'bi•cu•lar•ly,** *adv.*

or•bic•u•late [ɔr'bɪkjəlɪt] *or* [ɔr'bɪkjə,leit] *adj.* orbicular; rounded. Also, **orbiculated.** ⟨< L *orbiculatus* < *orbiculus.* See ORBICULAR.⟩ **—or'bic•u•late•ly,** *adv.* **—or,bic•u'la•tion,** *n.*

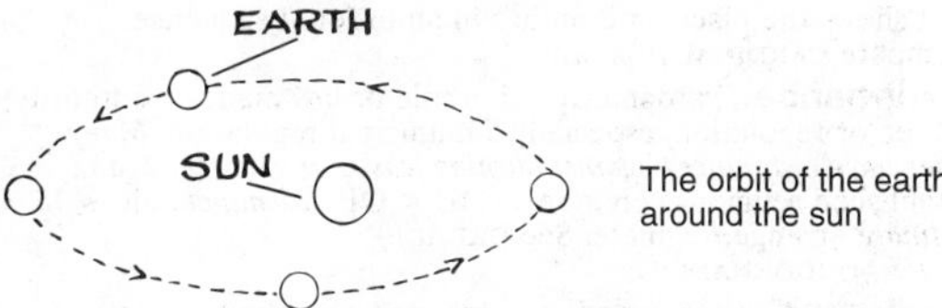

The orbit of the earth around the sun

or•bit ['ɔrbɪt] *n., v.* *—n.* **1** the curved path, usually elliptical, of a heavenly body, planet, or satellite around another body in space: *the earth's orbit around the sun, the moon's orbit around the earth, the orbit of a satellite around the earth.* See ECLIPTIC for another picture. **2** the regular course of life or experience. **3** *Anatomy.* the bony cavity or socket in which the eyeball is set. *—v.* **1** travel in an orbit around: *Many artificial satellites are orbiting the earth.* **2** put into an orbit: *They plan to orbit a new weather satellite.* ⟨< L *orbita* wheel track < *orbis* wheel, circle⟩ **—'or•bit•er,** *n.* **—'or•bit•al** or **'or•bit,a•ry,** *adj.*

orc [ɔrk] *n.* grampus. ⟨< F *orque* < L *orca*⟩

or•ca ['ɔrkə] *n.* KILLER WHALE. ⟨< L⟩

or•chard ['ɔrtʃərd] *n.* **1** an area, often enclosed, in which fruit trees are grown. **2** the trees in an orchard. ⟨OE *ortgeard* < *ort-* (apparently < L *hortus* garden) + *geard* yard¹⟩

orchard grass a European bunch grass (*Dactylis glomerata*) widely cultivated as a pasture grass and also for hay.

or•chard•ist ['ɔrtʃərdɪst] *n.* one who cultivates an orchard.

or•ches•tra ['ɔrkɪstrə] *n.* **1** a relatively large group of musicians, including especially players of violins and other stringed instruments, organized to perform music together. Compare BAND. **2** all the instruments played together by the musicians in such a group. **3** the part in a theatre just in front of the stage, where the musicians sit to play. **4** the main floor of a theatre, especially the part near the front. ⟨< L < Gk. *orchēstra* the space where the chorus of dancers performed, ult. < *orcheesthai* dance⟩

or•ches•tral [ɔr'kɛstrəl] *adj.* of, composed for, or performed by an orchestra. **—or'ches•tral•ly,** *adv.*

or•ches•trate ['ɔrkɪs,treit] *v.* **-trat•ed, -trat•ing. 1** compose or arrange (music) for performance by an orchestra. **2** arrange or control all the various stages or elements of (something) to achieve a particular end or effect. **—,or•ches'tra•tion,** *n.* **—'or•ches,trat•or,** *n.*

or•chid ['ɔrkɪd] **1** any of a large family (Orchidaceae) of perennial plants, some of which grow on other plants, obtaining their food and moisture from the air. Most orchids have showy, often brilliantly coloured flowers with three petals, one of which is much larger and shaped somewhat like a lip. **2** the flower of an orchid: *Cultivated varieties of tropical orchids are much valued for corsages.* **3** a light purple. *—adj.* light purple. ⟨< NL *orchideae,* ult. < L < Gk. *orchis* testicle; from shape of root⟩

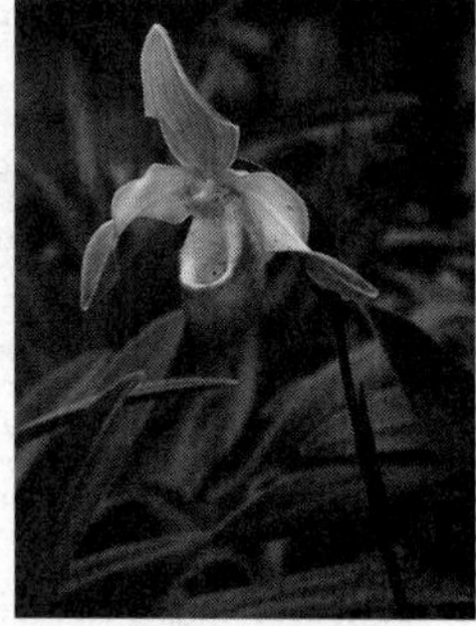
An orchid

or•chid•o•lo•gy [,ɔrkɪ'dɒlədʒi] *n.* that branch of botany dealing with orchids.

or•chil ['ɔrkɪl] *or* ['ɔrtʃɪl] *n.* **1** a lichen yielding a violet dye. **2** the dye itself. ⟨< OF⟩

or•chis ['ɔrkɪs] *n.* orchid. ⟨< L < Gk. *orchis* plant with roots like testicles⟩

or•ci•pre•na•line [,ɔrsɪ'prɛnə,lin] *n. Pharmacy.* a drug used to treat bronchial spasms associated with asthma, bronchitis, lung cancer, and other conditions.

Or•cus ['ɔrkəs] *n. Roman mythology.* **1** Hades. **2** the god of the underworld, equivalent to the Greek Pluto.

or•dain [ɔr'dein] *v.* **1** order or establish by law or by decree: *The law ordains that convicted murderers shall be imprisoned.* **2** officially appoint or consecrate as a member of the Christian clergy. ⟨ME < OF < L *ordinare* < *ordo, -inis* order⟩ **—or'dain•er,** *n.* **—or'dain•a•ble,** *adj.* **—or'dain•ment,** *n.*

or•deal [ɔr'dil], [ɔr'diəl], *or* ['ɔrdil] *n.* **1** a severe test or experience. **2** an ancient method of establishing the guilt or innocence of an accused person by making him or her do something dangerous such as putting his or her hand in a fire or taking poison. It was supposed that an innocent person would be given divine protection and so would escape harm. ⟨OE *ordǣl* judgment⟩

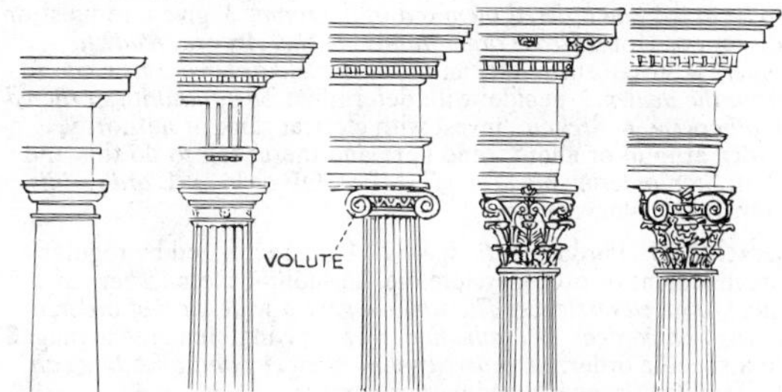

Order (def. 21): columns and entablatures illustrating the five orders of classical Greek and Roman architecture

or•der ['ɔrdər] *n., v.* *—n.* **1** the way one thing follows another: *in order of size, in alphabetical order.* **2** a condition in which every part or piece is in its right place: *to put a room in order.* **3** a condition; state: *My affairs are in good order.* **4** the way the world works; the way things happen: *the order of nature.* **5** the state or condition of things in which the law is obeyed and there is no trouble: *The police officer tried hard to keep order.* **6** the principles and rules by which a meeting is run. **7** a telling what to do; command: *The orders of the captain must be obeyed.* **8** a spoken or written request for goods that one wants to buy or receive: *a grocery order.* **9** the goods so requested or brought to a checkout: *Mother asked when they would deliver our order.* **10** the direction of a court or judge made in writing and not included in a judgment. **11** a paper saying that money is to be given or paid, or something handed over: *a money order.* **12** a kind or sort: *to have ability of a high order.* **13** *Biology.* a major category in the classification of plants and animals, more specific than a class and more general than a family. Butterflies, moths, and skippers belong to the insect order Lepidoptera. See classification chart

in the Appendix. **14** a social rank, grade, or class: *all orders of society.* **15** a rank or position in the Christian church: *the order of bishops.* **16** Usually, **orders,** HOLY ORDERS. **17** a group of people banded together for some purpose or united by something they share in common: *the Franciscan Order.* **18** a society to which one is admitted as an honour: *the Order of the Golden Fleece, the Order of Canada.* **19** a modern fraternal organization: *the Order of Freemasons, the Imperial Order Daughters of the Empire.* **20** a badge worn by those belonging to an honorary order.
21 *Architecture.* any of five types of column and entablature forming the basis of the five classical styles of architecture. The five orders are Doric, Ionic, and Corinthian of ancient Greek origin, and Tuscan and Composite of ancient Roman origin.
22 the regular form of worship for a given occasion. **23** a portion or serving of food served in a restaurant, etc.: *I'd like one order of toast, please.*
by order, according to an order given by the proper person: *by order of the premier.*
call to order, a ask to be quiet and start work: *She called the meeting to order.* **b** a pronouncement by a chairperson to be quiet and start work: *He issued a call to order and welcomed the members.*
in order, a in the right arrangement or condition: *Are all the pages in order?* **b** working properly. **c** allowed by the rules of a meeting, etc.
in order that, so that; with the purpose that: *The teacher spoke clearly in order that everyone could hear her.*
in order to, as a means to; with a view to; for the purpose of: *She worked hard in order to qualify for the scholarship.*
in short order, quickly: *They got the broken window replaced in short order.*
made to order, a made or as if made to fit a certain person or place; **b** made according to the buyer's specifications: *They had the couch made to order.*
on order, having been ordered but not yet received.
on the order of, resembling; similar to: *a house on the order of ours.*
out of order, a in a wrong arrangement or condition: *These pages are out of order.* **b** not working properly: *The radio is out of order.* **c** against the rules of a meeting, etc.: *Your motion is out of order.*
take holy orders, become a member of the Christian clergy.
tall order, *Informal.* something difficult to do.
—v. **1** put in order; arrange: *to order one's affairs.* **2** tell what to do; command; bid: *The judge ordered the people in the courtroom to be quiet. She ordered them out of the room.* **3** give a request or directions (for): *Please order dinner for me. Are you ready to order?* **4** give a store, etc. an order for: *He ordered a new car from the dealer.* **5** decide; will; determine: *The authorities ordered it otherwise.* **6** *Archaic.* invest with clerical rank or authority.
order around or **about,** send here and there; tell to do this and that: *Stop ordering me around.* ⟨ME < OF *ordre* < L *ordo, -inis* row, rank⟩ **—'or•der•er,** *n.*

or•dered ['ɔrdərd] *adj., v.* *—adj.* **1** characterized by regular arrangement or order; systematic, harmonious, etc.: *They led a quiet, ordered existence. The window gave a wide view of ordered lawns and gardens.* **2** *Mathematics, etc.* having elements arranged in a specific order: *an ordered set of rules. A point on a line can be identified by an ordered pair of numbers.*
—v. pt. and pp. of ORDER.

or•der–in–coun•cil ['ɔrdər in 'kaʊnsəl] *n., pl.* **or•ders-in-coun•cil.** *Cdn.* a regulation made by the federal cabinet under the authority of the Governor General or by a provincial cabinet under the authority of the lieutenant-governor of that province.

or•der•ly ['ɒrdərli] *adj., n., pl.* **-lies.** *—adj.* **1** in order; with regular arrangements, method, or system: *an orderly arrangement of dishes on shelves, an orderly mind.* **2** keeping order; well-behaved or regulated: *an orderly class.* **3** concerned with carrying out orders; being on duty.
—n. **1** *Military.* a person who attends a superior officer to carry messages, etc. **2** a hospital attendant who keeps things clean and in order. **—'or•der•li•ness,** *n.*
☛ *Syn. adj.* **1. Orderly,** METHODICAL, SYSTEMATIC = following a plan of arrangement or action. **Orderly** suggests lack of confusion and arrangement of details or things in proper relation to each other according to some rule or scheme: *The chairs are in orderly rows.* **Methodical** suggests an orderly way of doing something, following step by step a plan carefully worked out in advance or regularly followed: *Police made a methodical search for the weapon.* **Systematic** adds to **methodical** and emphasizes the idea of thoroughness and completeness: *The committee began a systematic investigation of crime.*

orderly officer OFFICER OF THE DAY.

Order of Canada *Cdn.* an order established in 1967 to honour Canadians for outstanding achievement and service to their country or to humanity at large. Memberships are awarded by the Governor General, in three categories: companion (CC), officer (OC), and member (CM).

Order of Good Cheer *Cdn.* formerly, a convivial fraternity organized by Champlain in 1604 to promote recreation and relaxation in the first French colony in Canada, at St. Croix Island in 1604, and from 1605 at Port Royal, Nova Scotia.

order of magnitude **1** magnitude expressed as a power of ten. **2** a range of values from a stated unit to one ten times as large.

Order of Merit a highly prestigious British order, limited to 24 members.

Order of Military Merit *Cdn.* an order established in 1972 to recognize conspicuous merit and exceptional service by members of the Canadian Forces, both regular and reserve. Memberships are awarded by the Governor General, in three levels: commander (CMM), officer (OMM), and member (MMM).

Order of the British Empire a British honour for services rendered.

Order of the Garter the oldest and highest order of British knighthood, established about 1344. It includes the sovereign.

or•di•nal ['ɔrdənəl] *adj., n.* *—adj.* **1** showing order or position in a series. **2** *Biology.* of or having to do with an order of animals or plants.
—n. **1** ORDINAL NUMBER. **2 Ordinal,** a book of special forms for certain Christian church ceremonies. ⟨ME < LL *ordinalis* < L *ordo, -inis* order⟩ **—'or•di•nal•ly,** *adv.*

ordinal number a number, such as first, second, twentieth, that shows the place an item has in an ordered sequence. Compare CARDINAL NUMBER.

or•di•nance ['ɔrdənəns] *n.* **1** a rule or law made by authority; decree or regulation, especially a municipal regulation: *Many cities have ordinances against burning leaves or garbage.* **2** an established religious ceremony. ⟨ME < OF *ordenance,* ult. < L *ordinare* arrange, regulate. See ORDAIN.⟩
☛ *Hom.* ORDONNANCE.

or•di•nand ['ɔrdɪ,nænd] *n.* someone who is being ordained.

or•di•nar•i•ly [,ɔrdə'nɛrəli] *or* ['ɔrdə,nɛrəli] *adv.* **1** usually; regularly. **2** to the usual extent or in the usual way.

or•di•nar•y ['ɔrdə,nɛri] *adj., n., pl.* **-nar•ies.** *—adj.* **1** usual; customary; normal: *She ate her ordinary breakfast of cereal, toast, and coffee.* **2** not special; common; everyday; average: *an ordinary person, an ordinary situation.* **3** somewhat below the average: *The speech was ordinary and tiresome.*
—n. **1** *Archaic.* **a** a meal served at a fixed price. **b** an inn or the dining room of an inn. **2** a person who has authority in his or her own right, especially a bishop or a judge. **3** a form for saying Mass. **4** *Heraldry.* a bearing of the earliest, simplest, and commonest kind, usually bound by straight lines, such as the bend.
in ordinary, in regular service: *physician in ordinary to the king.*
out of the ordinary, unusual; not regular or customary: *It wasn't anything out of the ordinary for her to jog 15 km.* ⟨< L *ordinarius* < *ordo, -onis* row, rank⟩ **—'or•di,nar•i•ness,** *n.*
☛ *Syn. adj.* **1.** See note at COMMON.

ordinary seaman **1** *Canadian Forces.* in Maritime Command, a person of the lowest rank, equivalent to a private. See chart of ranks in the Appendix. **2** a person of similar rank in the naval forces of other countries. *Abbrev.*: O.S. or OS

or•di•nate ['ɔrdənɪt] *or* ['ɔrdə,neit] *n. Mathematics.* the second number in an ordered pair; the vertical coordinate, or *y*-value, in a system of Cartesian coordinates. Compare ABSCISSA. ⟨< L *ordinatus,* pp. of *ordinare.* See ORDAIN.⟩

or•di•na•tion [,ɔrdə'neiʃən] *n.* **1** the act or ceremony of admitting a person to the ministry of the Christian church. **2** the state of being admitted as a minister in a Christian church. ⟨< L *ordinatio, -onis* < *ordinare.* See ORDAIN.⟩

ord•nance ['ɔrdnəns] *n.* **1** artillery; big guns or cannon. **2** military weapons and equipment of all kinds. ⟨var. of *ordinance*⟩

or•don•nance ['ɔrdənəns]; *French,* [ɔRdɔ'nɑ̃s] *n.* the arrangement of parts of a plan for a building. ⟨< F⟩ **—'or•don•nant,** *adj.*
☛ *Hom.* ORDINANCE.

Or•do•vi•cian [,ɔrdə'vɪʃən] *n., adj. Geology.* *—n.* **1** an early period of the Paleozoic era, beginning approximately 500 million years ago. **2** the rocks formed in this period. See geological time chart in the Appendix.

—adj. of or having to do with an early Paleozoic period or the rocks formed during it. ⟨< L *Ordovices* an ancient Celtic tribe in Wales where this rock abounds⟩

or•dure ['ɔrdʒər] *or* ['ɔrdjʊr] *n.* **1** filth; dung. **2** vile language. ⟨ME < OF *ordure* < *ord* filthy < L *horridus* horrid⟩ **—'or•dur•ous,** *adj.*

ore [ɔr] *n.* a naturally occurring mineral containing a valuable substance such as metal: *Iron ore is mined and worked to extract the iron it contains.* ⟨OE *ār* brass⟩
☛ *Hom.* OAR, O'ER, OR.

ø•re ['ørə] *n.* a unit of money in Norway and Denmark, equal to 1/100 of a krone. See table of money in the Appendix. ⟨< Danish, Norwegian, Swedish, ult. < L *aureus* a gold coin⟩

ö•re ['ørə] *n.* a unit of money in Sweden, equal to 1/100 of a krona. See table of money in the Appendix. ⟨See ØRE.⟩

O•re•ad or **o•re•ad** ['ɔri,æd] *n. Greek mythology.* a mountain nymph. ⟨< L *Oreas, -adis,* < Gk. *Oreias* < *oros* mountain⟩

ore•bod•y ['ɔr,bɒdi] *n., pl.* **-bod•ies.** a vein or bed of ore.

o•reg•a•no [ə'rɛgə,nou] *or* [,ɔrə'gænou] *n.* the dried leaves and flowering tops of any of several perennial herbs (genus *Origanum*) of the mint family, especially *O. vulgare,* used as a seasoning. Oregano has a flavour like sweet marjoram, but more pungent; it is used especially in Latin and Mediterranean dishes. ⟨< Sp. *orégano* < L < Gk. *origanon* wild marjoram⟩

Or•e•gon ['ɔrə,gɒn] *or* ['ɔrəgən] *n.* a Pacific northwest coast state of the United States.

Oregon fir DOUGLAS FIR.

Oregon question *Cdn.* the dispute (1818-1846) between Britain and the United States over the Oregon territory, settled by division at the present British Columbia-Washington border.

Oregon territory *Cdn.* formerly, the vast region lying between California and Alaska on the Pacific coast of North America, that part south of the 49th parallel being ceded to the United States by Britain in 1846.

Oregon Treaty *Cdn.* the 1846 treaty settling the Oregon question, officially called the Washington Treaty.

O•res•tes [ɔ'rɛstiz] *n. Greek mythology.* the son of Agamemnon and Clytemnestra, who killed his mother because she had murdered his father. He was pursued by the Furies for his crime.

org. 1 organic. **2** organized.

or•gan ['ɔrgən] *n.* **1** a large musical wind instrument consisting of sets of pipes of different diameters and lengths which are sounded by forcing air through them by means of keys and pedals; pipe organ. **2** an instrument in which a similar sound is produced by electronic means. **3** any of various other instruments such as a mouth organ or harmonium. **4** any structure in an animal or plant, such as an eye, lung, stamen, or pistil, that is composed of different cells and tissues organized to perform some particular function. **5** a group or organization that performs a particular function within a larger group or organization: *A court is an organ of government.* **6** a means of giving information or expressing opinions; a newspaper or magazine that speaks for and gives the views of a political party or some other group or organization. ⟨ME < OF < L *organum* < Gk. *organon* instrument < *ergon* work⟩

or•gan•dy or **or•gan•die** ['ɔrgəndi] *n., pl.* **-dies.** a very fine, thin, sheer cotton cloth with a crisp finish, woven in a plain weave with tightly twisted yarns. Organdy is used for dresses, curtains, blouses, trimming, etc. ⟨< F *organdi*⟩

or•gan•elle [,ɔrgə'nɛl] *n. Biology.* a separate, membrane-bound structure within the cytoplasm of a cell, such as a cilium or centriole, that functions as an organ. ⟨< NL *organella,* dim. of L *organum* organ⟩

organ grinder a person who plays a hand organ by turning a crank.

or•gan•ic [ɔr'gænɪk] *adj.* **1** of, having to do with, or affecting a bodily organ: *an organic disease.* **2** of, having to do with, or characteristic of beings having organs or an organized physical structure; of, having to do with, or characteristic of animals and plants: *organic substances, organic nature.* **3** made up of related and co-ordinated parts; organized: *Every part of an organic whole depends on every other part.* **4** forming part of the basic structure of something; fundamental: *The music is not just background but an organic part of the film.* **5** of, designating, or containing compounds of carbon: *Organic compounds exist naturally as constituents of animals and plants.* **6** designating the branch of chemistry dealing with such compounds. **7** obtained from animals or plants: *organic fertilizer.* **8** designating a method of raising plants or animals without using chemical fertilizers, pesticides, or drugs: *organic gardening.* **9** of vegetables, meat, etc. produced in this way: *organic beef.* **10** designating the basic laws of any organization, including a government. ⟨< L *organicus* < Gk. *organikos* < *organon* instrument⟩ **—or'gan•i•cal•ly,** *adv.*

organic chemistry the branch of chemistry that deals with compounds of carbon. Organic chemistry teaches us about foods and fuels.

or•gan•ism ['ɔrgə,nɪzəm] *n.* **1** a living body having organs or an organized structure in which each part has a particular function but all depend on each other; an individual animal or plant. **2** a very tiny animal or plant. **3** a complex structure made of related parts that work together and are dependent on each other and on the whole structure, especially one that can grow or change. A community may be spoken of as a social organism. **—,or•gan'is•mic** or **,or•gan'is•mal,** *adj.* **—,or•gan'is•mi•cal•ly,** *adv.*

or•gan•ist ['ɔrgənɪst] *n.* a person who plays the organ, especially a skilled player.

or•gan•i•za•tion [,ɔrgənə'zeiʃən] *or* [,ɔrgənaɪ'zeiʃən] *n.* **1** a group of persons united for some purpose. Churches, clubs, and political parties are organizations. **2** the act of organizing; the grouping and arranging of parts to form a whole: *The organization of a big picnic takes time and thought.* **3** the way in which a thing's parts are arranged to work together: *The organization of the nervous system is very complicated.* **4** something made up of related parts, each having a special duty: *A tree is an organization of roots, trunk, branches, leaves, and fruit.* **—,or•gan•i'za•tion•al,** *adj.* **—,or•gan•i'za•tion•al•ly,** *adv.*

or•gan•ize ['ɔrgə,naɪz] *v.* **-ized, -iz•ing. 1** arrange to work or come together as a whole: *The general organized his soldiers into a powerful fighting force.* **2** plan and lead, get started, or carry out: *The explorer organized an expedition to the North Pole.* **3** arrange in a system: *She organized her thoughts. He organized his stamp collection.* **4** *Informal.* make oneself ready to do what is required: *Please wait—I'm not organized yet.* **5** bring or form into a labour union; unionize: *to organize the workers in a plant, to organize the garment industry.* ⟨ME < LL *organizare* < L *organum* < Gk. *organon.* See ORGAN.⟩ **—'or•gan,iz•a•ble,** *adj.* **—'or•gan,iz•er,** *n.*

organized labour or **labor** workers who belong to labour unions.

organo– *combining form.* **1** a biological organ. **2** having to do with organs: *organogenesis.* ⟨< Gk. *organon* organ⟩

or•ga•no•gen•e•sis [,ɔrgənou'dʒɛnəsɪs] *n. Biology.* the origin and development of biological organs. **—,or•ga•no•ge'net•ic** [,ɔrgənoudʒə'nɛtɪk], *adj.* **—,or•ga•no•ge'net•i•cal•ly,** *adv.*

or•ga•no•gra•phy [,ɔrgə'nɒgrəfi] *n., pl.* **-phies.** the description of the organs of plants and animals. **—,or•ga•no'graph•ic** or **,or•ga•no'graph•i•cal,** *adj.*

or•ga•no•lep•tic [,ɔrgənə'lɛptɪk] *or* [ɔr,gænə'lɛptɪk] *adj.* **1** having to do with the organs of sense. **2** perceived by such an organ. ⟨< Gk. *organon* organ + *leptikos* < *leptos* < lambainein seize⟩

or•ga•nol•o•gy [,ɔrgə'nɒlədʒi] *n.* the branch of biology that deals with the structure and function of the organs of plants and animals. **—,or•ga•no'log•i•cal** or **,or•ga•no'log•ic,** *adj.* **—,or•ga'nol•o•gist,** *n.*

or•ga•no•me•tal•lic [,ɔrgə,noumə'tælɪk] *or* [ɔr,gænoumə'tælɪk] *adj.* denoting an organic compound containing a metal.

or•ga•non ['ɔrgə,nɒn] *n., pl.* **-na** [-nə] or **-nons.** *Epistemology.* a set of principles of investigation of knowledge.

or•ga•no•ther•a•py [,ɔrgənou'θɛrəpi] *or* [ɔr,gænou'θɛrəpi] *n.* the treatment of disease by means of extracts from biological organs, such as insulin.

or•ga•not•ro•pism [,ɔrgə'nɒtrə,pɪzəm] *n.* the attraction of certain chemical compounds to specific biological organs.

or•gan•za [ɔr'gænzə] *n.* a silky cloth of silk, rayon, nylon, etc. that is more crisp and sheer than organdy. ⟨< L *Organzi,* a former city in Asia where it was made.⟩

or•gan•zine ['ɔrgən,zin] *n.* a thread of raw silk used as a warp. ⟨< F *organsin* < Ital. *organzino*⟩

or•gasm ['ɔrgæzəm] *n.* **1** the climax or culmination of sexual excitement. **2** an instance of frenzied excitement or behaviour.

⟨< NL *orgasmus* < Gk. *orgasmos* < *orgaein* swell⟩ **—or'gas•mic** or **or'gas•tic,** *adj.*

or•geat ['ɔrʒæt] *n.* a flavouring made of almond and orange. ⟨< F < Pg. *orjat,* derivative of *orge* barley < L *hordeum*⟩

or•gi•as•tic [,ɔrdʒi'æstɪk] *adj.* of, having to do with, or of the nature of orgies; wild; frenzied. ⟨< Gk. *orgiastikos,* ult. < *orgia* secret rites⟩ **—,or•gi'as•ti•cal•ly,** *adv.*

or•gy ['ɔrdʒi] *n., pl.* **-gies. 1** a wild, drunken, or licentious revelry. **2** something resembling an orgy in lack of control; excessive indulgence in something: *an orgy of destruction, an orgy of bloodshed.* **3** Usually, **orgies,** *pl.* secret rites or ceremonies in the worship of certain Greek and Roman gods, especially Dionysus, the god of wine, celebrated with drinking, wild dancing, and singing. ⟨< MF *orgie* < L < Gk. *orgia* secret rites⟩

o•ri•bi ['ɔrəbi] *n.* a small African antelope (*Ourebia ourebia*). ⟨< Afrikaans < ? Hottentot *arab*⟩

o•ri•el ['ɔriəl] *n.* a bay window projecting from a wall, usually in an upper storey, and supported by a bracket. ⟨ME < OF *oriol* porch⟩
☛ *Hom.* ORIOLE.

o•ri•ent *n., adj.* ['ɔriənt]; *v.* ['ɔri,ɛnt] *n., adj., v.* *—n.* **1 the Orient, a** the Far East. China, Japan, Korea, and Vietnam are in the Orient. **b** *Archaic.* the regions lying to the east of Europe and the Mediterranean Sea, including Asia Minor and the Indian subcontinent as well as the Far East. Compare OCCIDENT. **2 the orient,** *Poetic.* the east. Compare OCCIDENT. **3** the lustre of a pearl. **4** a pearl of great value.
—adj. **1** *Poetic.* eastern or Oriental. **2** lustrous; shining: *an orient pearl.* **3** *Archaic.* rising in the east.
—v. **1** put or build facing east. **2** place in a certain position or face or tend in a certain direction: *The building is oriented north and south. She is oriented toward a career in business.* **3** find the direction or position of. **4** adjust to a reference system such as the points of the compass.
orient oneself, find the right relationship with one's surroundings; adjust to a new situation: *It takes a while to orient yourself in a strange city.* ⟨< L *oriens, -entis,* ppr. of *oriri* rise, with reference to the rising sun⟩

O•ri•en•tal [,ɔri'ɛntəl] *adj., n.* *—adj.* Sometimes, **oriental,** of, having to do with, or characteristic of the Orient or its inhabitants: *Oriental music.*
—n. a native or inhabitant of the Orient. Compare OCCIDENTAL.

Oriental cedar a small tree or shrub (*Thuja orientalis*) growing widely in Asia, having wingless seeds, often planted in Canada as an ornamental.

O•ri•en•tal•ism or **o•ri•en•tal•ism** [,ɔri'ɛntə,lɪzəm] *n.* **1** a custom, habit, etc. that is characteristic of Oriental peoples. **2** a knowledge of Oriental languages, literature, etc.

O•ri•en•tal•ist or **o•ri•en•tal•ist** [,ɔri'ɛntəlɪst] *n.* a person who specializes in the study of Oriental languages, literature, cultures, history, etc.

O•ri•en•tal•ize [,ɔri'ɛntə,laɪz] *v.* **-ized, -iz•ing.** make or become Oriental.

Oriental poppy a poppy (*Papaver orientale*) having scarlet and black flowers.

o•ri•en•tate ['ɔriən,teit] *v.* **-tat•ed, -tat•ing.** orient. ⟨< F *orienter* to orient⟩

o•ri•en•ta•tion [,ɔriən'teiʃən] *n.* **1** the act or process of orienting or the state of being oriented. **2** a change in position of an organism or part of an organism in response to an external stimulus, such as light. **3** the homing instinct of certain animals. **4** a general tendency or direction of interest or thought: *Her orientation toward the dramatic shows clearly in her dress designs.*

or•i•en•teer [,ɔriən'tir] *v., n.* *—v.* find one's way through unfamiliar territory by means of a map or compass or both.
—n. a person who participates in the sport of orienteering.

or•i•en•teer•ing [,ɔriən'tirɪŋ] *n.* the sport or practice of finding one's way through unfamiliar territory by means of a map or compass or both, usually involving a given starting and finishing point with a series of checkpoints in between. ⟨< Swedish *orientera* orient + *-ing*⟩

or•i•fice ['ɔrəfɪs] *n.* an opening, such as a mouth, hole, or vent through which something may pass. ⟨< F < L *orificium* < *os, oris* mouth + *facere* make⟩

or•i•flamme ['ɔrə,flæm] *n.* **1** the red banner carried as a military ensign by the early kings of France. **2** any banner used as an ensign or standard. **3** anything that is bright, colourful, or showy. ⟨ME < OF *orieflambe;* ult. < L *aurum* gold + *flamma* flame⟩

orig. 1 origin. **2** originally.

or•i•ga•mi [,ɔrɪ'gæmi] *or* [,ɔrɪ'gɑmi] *n.* **1** a kind of paper sculpture developed by the Japanese in which paper is folded in a great variety of simple or intricate ways to make birds, flowers, etc. **2** one of these paper sculptures. ⟨< Japanese *ori* a folding + *gami* paper⟩

or•i•gin ['ɔrədʒɪn] *n.* **1** the thing from which anything comes; source; beginning: *the origin of a quarrel, the origin of a disease.* **2** parentage or ancestry: *a man of humble origin. The word* beef *is of French origin.* **3** *Mathematics.* the intersection of co-ordinate axes or planes. **4** *Anatomy.* the firmer or larger of the two points of attachment of a muscle. ⟨< L *origo, -ginis* < *oriri* rise⟩

o•rig•i•nal [ə'rɪdʒənəl] *adj., n.* *—adj.* **1** belonging to the beginning; first; earliest: *the original settlers.* **2** fresh and unusual; novel: *She has written a very original story. They thought up several original games for the party.* **3** able to do, make, or think something new; inventive. **4** not copied, imitated, or translated from something else: *This is the original manuscript.*
—n. **1** the first version or actual thing from which something is copied, imitated, or translated: *This sculpture is a plaster copy; the original is in Rome.* **2** the language in which a book was first written: *She has read* War and Peace *in the original.* **3** an unusual or eccentric person. **4** *Archaic.* originator.

o•rig•i•nal•i•ty [ə,rɪdʒə'næləti] *n.* **1** the quality or state of being original: *Several experts questioned the originality of the manuscript.* **2** freshness or novelty of style, etc.: *The furniture has a striking originality of design.* **3** the ability to do, make, or think up something new: *He is known for his originality in thinking up plots.*

o•rig•i•nal•ly [ə'rɪdʒənəli] *adv.* **1** by origin: *The family was originally Irish.* **2** at first; in the first place: *The house was originally small.* **3** in an original manner.

original sin *Christian theology.* the state of sin in which all human beings exist from conception because of Adam's disobedience to the word of God.

o•rig•i•nate [ə'rɪdʒə,neit] *v.* **-nat•ed, -nat•ing. 1** cause to be; invent. **2** come into being; begin; arise. ⟨< F *origination* < L *originatio* etymology⟩ **—o'rig•i,na•tor,** *n.* **—o,rig•i'na•tion,** *n.*

o•rig•i•na•tive [ə'rɪdʒənətɪv] *or* [ə'rɪdʒə,neitɪv] *adj.* inventive; creative. **—o'rig•i•na•tive•ly,** *adv.*

o•ri•ole ['ɔriəl] *or* ['ɔri,oul] *n.* **1** any of a genus (*Icterus*) of New World songbirds belonging to the same family (Icteridae) as the bobolink, meadowlark, and blackbirds, the adult males having black and orange, yellow, or reddish brown plumage, the females mainly yellowish. **2** any of a family (Oriolidae) of Old World songbirds, especially any of a genus (*Oriolus*) that includes the yellow-and-black **golden oriole** of Europe and Asia. The orioles of North America were given their name by early settlers from the British Isles because of their resemblance to the golden oriole. Orioles common in Canada include the **Baltimore oriole, Bullock's oriole,** and the **Orchard oriole.** ⟨< NL *oriolus* < OF, ult. < L *aurum* gold⟩
☛ *Hom.* ORIEL ['ɔriəl].

O•ri•on [ɔ'raɪən] *n.* **1** *Greek and Roman mythology.* a hunter loved by the goddess Diana, who was accidentally killed by her and placed among the stars after his death. **2** *Astronomy.* a constellation near the equator of the heavens, suggesting a man with a belt around his waist and a sword by his side.

or•i•son ['ɔrəzən] *n. Archaic or poetic.* prayer. ⟨ME < OF < LL *oratio, -onis* prayer < L *oratio* speech < *orare* pray. Doublet of ORATION.⟩

Ork•ney•man ['ɔrknɪmən] *n., pl.* **-men.** *Cdn. Fur trade.* formerly, a native of the Orkney Islands of Scotland serving in the fur trade, especially with the Hudson's Bay Company.

Or•lon ['ɔrlɒn] *n. Trademark.* a synthetic acrylic fibre used in a number of fabrics. Orlon is used for knitted clothing, rugs, draperies, etc.

or•lop ['ɔrlɒp] *n.* the lowest deck of a warship. Also, **orlop deck.** ⟨late ME < MLG *overlōp* covering *over-* over + *-loopen* to run, extend⟩

Or•mazd ['ɔrmæzd] *n.* the chief deity of Zoroastrianism. ⟨< Persian < Arestan *ahura* god + *mazdah* wise⟩

or•mo•lu ['ɔrmə,lu] *n.* an alloy of copper and zinc, used to imitate gold. Ormolu is used in decorating furniture, clocks, etc. ⟨< F *or moulu* ground gold⟩

or•na•ment *n.* ['ɔrnəmənt]; *v.* ['ɔrnə,mɛnt] *n., v.* *—n.* **1** something used to add beauty, especially a beautiful object or part that has no particular function in itself: *Jewellery and vases are ornaments.* **2** the use of ornaments; ornamentation:

Ornament played an important part in rococo architecture. **3** a person or an act, quality, etc. that adds beauty, grace, or honour: *He was an ornament to his time.* **4** Usually, **ornaments,** *pl.* things used in Christian church services, such as the organ, bells, silver plate, etc. **5** *Music.* an additional note or notes introduced as an embellishment but not essential to the harmony or melody.
—v. add beauty to; make more pleasing or attractive; decorate: *A single brooch ornamented her dress.* ⟨ME < OF < L *ornamentum* < *ornare* adorn⟩ **—'or•na,ment•er,** *n.*
☛ *Syn. v.* See note at DECORATE.

or•na•men•tal [,ɔrnə'mɛntəl] *adj.* **1** of or having to do with ornament: *ornamental purposes.* **2** used for ornament; decorative: *an ornamental staircase, ornamental plants.*
—,or•na•men'tal•i•ty, *n.* **—,or•na'men•tal•ly,** *adv.*

or•na•men•ta•tion [,ɔrnəmɛn'teiʃən] *n.* **1** the act of ornamenting or the condition of being ornamented. **2** decorations; ornaments.

or•nate [ɔr'neit] *adj.* **1** much adorned; much ornamented: *She liked ornate furniture.* **2** characterized by the use of elaborate figures of speech, flowery language, etc.: *an ornate style of writing.* ⟨< L *ornatus*, pp. of *ornare* adorn⟩ **—or'nate•ly,** *adv.* **—or'nate•ness,** *n.*

or•ner•y ['ɔrnəri] *adj. Informal or dialect.* having an irritable or mean disposition; tending to be hard to get along with: *an ornery horse. He was born ornery.* ⟨contraction of *ordinary*⟩ **—'or•ner•i•ness,** *n.*

or•nith•ic [ɔr'nɪθɪk] *adj.* having to do with birds.

ornitho– *combining form.* bird: *ornithology.* ⟨< Gk. *ornīth-*, *órnīs* bird⟩

or•ni•thol•o•gist [,ɔrnə'θɒlədʒɪst] *n.* a person trained in ornithology, especially one whose work it is.

or•ni•thol•o•gy [,ɔrnə'θɒlədʒi] *n., pl.* **-gies. 1** a branch of zoology dealing with birds. **2** an article or book on this subject. ⟨< NL *ornithologia* < Gk. *ornis, -nithos* bird + *-logos* treating of⟩ **—,or•ni•tho'log•i•cal** [,ɔrnəθə'lɒdʒɪkəl], *adj.* **—,or•ni•tho'log•i•cal•ly,** *adv.*

oro–[1] *combining form.* mountain: *orogeny.* ⟨< Gk., combining form of *óros*⟩

oro–[2] *combining form.* mouth: *oropharynx.* ⟨< L, combining form of *ōs*⟩

o•rog•e•ny [ɔ'rɒdʒəni] *n. Geology.* the creation of mountains by the movements of the earth's crust. Also, **orogenesis.**
—,or•o'gen•ic [,ɔrə'dʒɛnɪk] or **,or•o•ge'net•ic,** *adj.*

o•rog•ra•phy [ɔ'rɒgrəfi] *n.* the branch of physical geography dealing with mountains and mountain ranges. **—,or•o'graph•ic** [,ɔrə'græfɪk] or **,or•o'graph•i•cal,** *adj.* **—,or•o'graph•i•cal•ly,** *adv.*

o•ro•ide ['ɔrou,aɪd] *n.* a cheap alloy of copper, zinc, and tin, intended to look like gold. ⟨< F⟩

o•rol•o•gy [ɔ'rɒlədʒi] *n.* the study of mountains.
—,o•ro'log•i•cal, *adj.* **—o'rol•o•gist,** *n.*

o•ro•phar•ynx [,ɔrou'færɪŋks] *n., pl.* **-pha•ryn•ges** [-fə'rɪndʒiz] or **phar•ynx•es. 1** that part of the pharynx lying between the soft palate and the epiglottis, visible through the open mouth. **2** the pharynx proper, as distinct from the nasopharynx and the laryngeal pharynx.

o•ro•tund ['ɔrə,tʌnd] *adj.* **1** strong, full, rich, and clear in voice or speech; sonorous. **2** pompous; bombastic. ⟨alteration of L *ore rotundo*, literally, with round mouth⟩ **—,o•ro'tun•di•ty** [,ɔrə'tʌndəti], *n.*

or•phan ['ɔrfən] *n., v.* *—n.* **1** a child whose parents are dead or, sometimes, a child who has lost one parent. **2** (*adjl.*) of or for such children: *an orphan home.* **3** (*adjl.*) without a father or mother or both. **4** in printing, a word or line of text left alone at the top of a page.
—v. make an orphan of. ⟨< LL < Gk. *orphanos* bereaved⟩

or•phan•age ['ɔrfənɪdʒ] *n.* **1** a home for orphans. **2** the condition of being an orphan.

or•phe•na•drine [ɔr'fɛnə,drin] *n.* a muscle relaxant drug used to treat muscle spasm. Orphenadrine hydrochloride is used to treat Parkinson's disease.

Or•phe•us ['ɔrfiəs] *or* ['ɔrfjəs] *n. Greek mythology.* the son of Calliope and Apollo, who played his lyre so sweetly that animals and even trees and rocks followed him. With his music he charmed Pluto into releasing his wife Eurydice from Hades, but he lost her again when he disobeyed Pluto's order not to look back at her before reaching Earth. **—'Or•phe•an,** *adj.*

Or•phic ['ɔrfɪk] *adj.* **1** of or having to do with Orpheus or the religious or philosophical cults associated with his name. **2** Often, **orphic, a** mystic; oracular. **b** melodious or entrancing. ⟨< Gk. *Orphikos* < *Orpheus* Orpheus + *-ikos* -ic⟩
—'Or•phi•cal•ly, *adv.*

or•phrey ['ɔrfri] *n.* elaborate embroidery decorating ecclesiastical dress. ⟨< OF < ML *aurifrisium*, var. of *auriphrigium*, for L *aurum Phrygium* gold embroidery, literally Phrygium gold⟩

or•pi•ment ['ɔrpəmənt] *n.* arsenic trisulphide. *Formula*: As_2S_3 ⟨ME < OF < L *auripigmentum* pigment of gold⟩

or•pine ['ɔrpaɪn] *n.* sedum. ⟨ME *orpin* < MF *orpiment.* See ORPIMENT.⟩

Or•ping•ton ['ɔrpɪŋtən] *n.* a breed of large buff, white, or black chickens. ⟨< *Orpington*, a town in Kent, England⟩

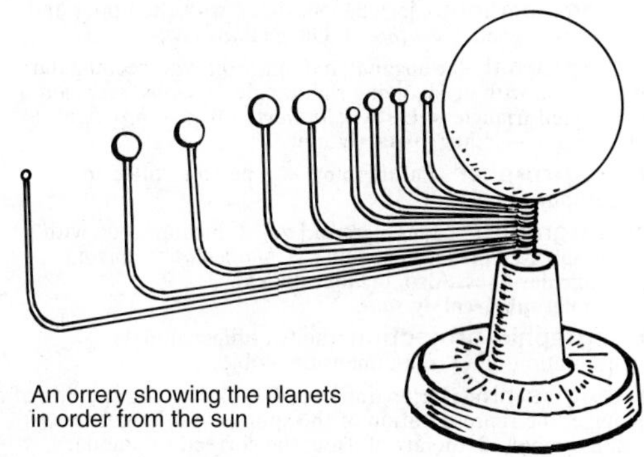
An orrery showing the planets in order from the sun

or•rer•y ['ɔrəri] *n., pl.* **-rer•ies.** a device with balls representing various planets, that are moved by clockwork to illustrate motions of the solar system. ⟨after Charles Boyle, Earl of *Orrery* (1676-1731), who first had such a device made⟩

or•ris ['ɔrɪs] *n.* **1** any of several European irises, especially *Iris florentina*, having fragrant rootstocks which are used in making perfumes, etc. **2** the rootstock of this plant. Also (def. 2), **orrisroot.** ⟨apparently an alteration of *iris*⟩

or•thi•con ['ɔrθə,kɒn] *n.* IMAGE ORTHICON.

ortho– *combining form.* **1** straight; upright: *orthopterous.* **2** correct; accepted: *orthodox.* **3** correcting irregularities in; corrective: *orthodontics.* ⟨< Gk. *orthos* straight⟩

or•tho•cen•tre ['ɔrθə,sɛntər] *n. Geometry.* the point at which the three altitudes of a triangle intercept.

or•tho•chro•mat•ic [,ɔrθəkrə'mætɪk] *or* [,ɔrθoukrə'mætɪk] *adj.* reproducing colours of nature accurately.

or•tho•clase ['ɔrθə,kleis] *or* ['ɔrθə,kleiz] *n.* feldspar. ⟨< *ortho-* + Gk. *klasis* fracture⟩

or•tho•cy•mene [,ɔrθou'saɪmin] *n.* See CÝMENE.

or•tho•don•tics [,ɔrθə'dɒntɪks] *n.* (*used with a singular verb*). the branch of dentistry that deals with the straightening and adjusting of irregular or crooked teeth. Also, **orthodontia** [-'dɒnʃə]. ⟨< NL < Gk. *orthos* straight + *odōn, odontos* tooth⟩ **—,or•tho'don•tic,** *adj.*

or•tho•don•tist [,ɔrθə'dɒntɪst] *n.* a dentist who specializes in orthodontics.

or•tho•dox ['ɔrθə,dɒks] *adj.* **1** conforming to established doctrine, especially in religion: *orthodox views, an orthodox Muslim.* **2** conforming to custom; conventional: *The orthodox Christmas dinner is turkey and plum pudding.* **3 Orthodox, a** of, having to do with, or designating the Eastern Orthodox Church or any of its member churches. **b** of, having to do with, or designating the branch of Judaism following most closely the ancient laws, customs, and traditions. ⟨< LL < Gk. *orthodoxos* < *orthos* correct + *doxa* opinion < *dokeein* think⟩

Orthodox Church EASTERN ORTHODOX CHURCH.

Orthodox Judaism Judaism involving strict adherence to dietary laws, the keeping of the Sabbath, study of the Torah, daily synagogue attendance, and the keeping of holy days.

or•tho•dox•y ['ɔrθə,dɒksi] *n., pl.* **-dox•ies.** the holding of correct or generally accepted beliefs; orthodox practice, especially in religion; a being orthodox.

or•tho•ep•ic [,ɔrθou'ɛpɪk] *adj.* **1** relating to correct pronunciation. **2** describing the relationship between spelling and pronunciation: *orthoepic rules.* **—ˌor•tho'ep•i•cal•ly,** *adv.*

or•tho•e•py [ɔr'θouəpi] *or* ['ɔrθouˌɛpi] *n.* **1** the standard pronunciation of a language. **2** the part of grammar that deals with pronunciation; phonology. ⟨< Gk. *orthoepeia* < *orthos* correct + *epos* utterance⟩ **—or'tho•e•pist,** *n.*

or•tho•gen•e•sis [ˌɔrθou'dʒɛnəsɪs] *n.* **1** *Biology.* the theory, no longer accepted, that the evolutionary development of one species into another takes place in a fixed direction that is determined solely by internal factors and not influenced by external, or environmental, factors. **2** *Sociology.* the theory, no longer accepted, that all human cultures pass through the same stages of development in the same order. **—ˌor•tho•ge'net•ic** [-dʒə'nɛtɪk], *adj.* **—ˌor•tho•ge'net•i•cal•ly,** *adv.*

or•thog•na•thous [ɔr'θɒgnəθəs] *adj.* with the upper and lower jaws aligned. ⟨< *ortho-* + Gk. *gnathos* jaw⟩

or•thog•o•nal [ɔr'θɒgənəl] *adj. Mathematics.* rectangular; having to do with or involving right angles. ⟨< obs. *orthogon* a right-angled triangle < L < Gk. *orthogōnios* < *orthos* right + *gōnia* angle⟩ **—or'thog•o•nal•ly,** *adv.*

or•thog•ra•pher [ɔr'θɒgrəfər] *n.* a person skilled in orthography.

or•tho•graph•ic [ˌɔrθə'græfɪk] *adj.* **1** having to do with orthography. **2** correct in spelling. **3** *Mathematics.* having perpendicular lines. Also, **orthographical.** **—ˌor•tho'graph•i•cal•ly,** *adv.*

orthographic projection the two-dimensional representation of a three-dimensional object.

or•thog•ra•phy [ɔr'θɒgrəfi] *n., pl.* **-phies. 1** the spelling of a language; the representation of the sounds of a language by written symbols. **2** the art of using the correct, or standard, spelling. **3** the study of letters and spelling. **4** any system using symbols to represent the sounds of a language. **5** ORTHOGRAPHIC PROJECTION. ⟨< L < Gk. *orthographia* < *orthos* correct + *graphien* write⟩

or•tho•mo•lec•u•lar [ˌɔrθoumə'lɛkjələr] *adj.* of or having to do with a theory according to which diseases, especially certain mental disorders, are caused by molecular abnormalities which can be corrected by megavitamin therapy, diet, etc.

or•tho•pe•dic [ˌɔrθə'pidɪk] *adj.* of, having to do with, or used in orthopedics: *Orthopedic shoes are worn to help correct deformities of the feet.* Also, **orthopaedic.**

or•tho•pe•dics [ˌɔrθə'pidɪks] *n.* (*used with a singular verb*) the branch of surgery that deals with deformities, diseases, and injuries of bones and joints. Also, **orthopaedics.** ⟨< Gk. *orthos* correct + *paideia* rearing of children < *pais, paidos* child⟩

or•tho•pe•dist [ˌɔrθə'pidɪst] *n.* a surgeon who specializes in orthopedics. Also, **orthopaedist.**

or•tho•psy•chi•a•try [ˌɔrθousəi'kaɪətri] *or* [ˌɔrθousɪ'kaɪətri] *n.* the diagnosis and treatment of incipient mental disorders. **—ˌor•thoˌpsy•chi'at•ric** [ˌɔrθouˌsaiki'ætrɪk], *adj.* **—ˌor•tho•psy'chi•a•trist,** *n.*

or•thop•ter•an [ɔr'θɒptərən] *n., adj. —n.* any of a large order (Orthoptera) of mostly plant-eating insects having two pairs of wings, the membranous hind wings covered by hard, narrow front wings or, in some species, having no wings at all. Crickets, grasshoppers, and cockroaches are orthopterans.
—adj. of or designating this order of insects. ⟨< NL < Gk. *orthos* straight + *pteron* wing⟩

or•thop•ter•ous [ɔr'θɒptərəs] *adj.* of or having to do with the orthopterans or the order they belong to.

or•tho•rhom•bic [ˌɔrθou'rɒmbɪk] *adj.* of a crystal, of or having to do with a system having three unequal axes at right angles to each other.

or•tho•scope ['ɔrθəˌskoup] *n.* an instrument for examining the eye.

or•tho•scop•ic [ˌɔrθə'skɒpɪk] *adj.* having normal vision.

or•thot•ic [ɔr'θɒtɪk] *n., adj. —n.* a device used to aid a foot or other part which has some orthopedic problem.
—adj. of or having to do with orthotics.

or•thot•ics [ɔr'θɒtɪks] *n.* the branch of medicine dealing with the manufacture and fitting of devices for the correction of orthopedic problems (*used with a singular verb*).

or•tho•trop•ic [ˌɔrθə'trɒpɪk] *adj. Botany.* growing along a vertical axis.

or•thot•ro•pism [ɔr'θɒtrəˌpɪzəm] *n. Botany.* orthotropic tendency or growth.

or•thot•ro•pous [ɔr'θɒtrəpəs] *adj. Botany.* growing straight.

or•to•lan ['ɔrtələn] *n.* **1** a European bunting (*Emberiza hortulana*) considered a table delicacy in the autumn, when it grows fat. **2** any of several other small birds considered delicacies, such as the bobolink. ⟨< F < Provençal < L *hortulanus* of gardens < *hortus* garden⟩

-ory *suffix.* **1** ——ing: *compensatory, contradictory.* **2** of or having to do with ——; of or having to do with ——ion: *advisory, auditory.* **3** characterized by ——ion: *adulatory.* **4** serving to ——: *expiatory.* **5** tending to ——; inclined to ——: *conciliatory.* **6** a place for ——ing; establishment for ——ing: *depository.* **7** other meanings: *conservatory, desultory.* ⟨< L *-orius, -orium*⟩

o•ryx ['ɔrɪks] *n., pl.* **o•ryx•es** ['ɔrɪksəz] or (*esp. collectively*) **o•ryx.** any of a genus (*Oryx*) of large African antelope having long, nearly straight horns. ⟨ME < L < Gk. *oryx* antelope, pickaxe; with reference to pointed horns⟩

os[1] [ɒs] *n., pl.* **os•sa** ['ɒsə]. *Latin.* bone.

os[2] [ɒs] *n., pl.* **o•ra** ['ɔrə]. *Latin.* a mouth; opening.

os- *prefix* the form of **ob-** (from the form *obs-*) occurring in some cases before *c* and *t*, as in *oscine, ostensible.*

o/s out of stock.

Os osmium.

O.S. OLD STYLE.

O.S. or **OS** ORDINARY SEAMAN.

O•sage [ou'seidʒ] *or* ['ouseidʒ] *n.* **1** a member of an American Indian people now living in Oklahoma. **2** the Siouan language of these people.

Osage orange [ou'seidʒ] **1** a small, thorny, North American tree (*Maclura pomifera*) of the mulberry family having small, glossy, oval leaves and hard, orange wood. The osage orange is often planted as an ornamental tree. **2** the inedible yellow fruit of this tree.

Os•can ['ɒskən] *n.* **1** a member of an ancient people living in Italy. **2** the Italic language of these people.

Os•car ['ɒskər] *n.* a small statuette awarded annually by the American Academy of Motion Picture Arts and Sciences for the best performances, production, photography, etc. during the year. ⟨< from its alleged resemblance to an Academy official's Uncle *Oscar*⟩

os•cil•late ['ɒsəˌleit] *v.* **-lat•ed, -lat•ing. 1** swing to and fro like a pendulum. **2** move or travel to and fro between two points. **3** vary between opposing opinions, purposes, theories, etc. **4** *Physics.* vary regularly above and below a mean value, as an electric current. **5** cause to oscillate. ⟨< L *oscillare*⟩
☛ *Hom.* OCELLATE.

os•cil•la•tion [ˌɒsə'leiʃən] *n.* **1** the fact or process of oscillating. **2** a single swing of an oscillating body. **3** *Physics.* **a** a single forward and backward surge of a charge of electricity. **b** a rapid change in electromotive force. **c** a single complete cycle of an electric wave.

os•cil•la•tor ['ɒsəˌleitər] *n.* a person or thing that oscillates, especially a device for producing the oscillations that give rise to an alternating electric current.

os•cil•la•to•ry ['ɒsələˌtɔri] *adj.* characterized by or involving oscillation.

os•cil•lo•gram [ə'sɪləˌgræm] *or* ['ɒsələˌgræm] *n.* the recording made by an oscillograph.

os•cil•lo•graph [ə'sɪləˌgræf] *or* ['ɒsələˌgræf] *n.* an instrument for recording oscillations.

os•cil•lo•scope [ə'sɪləˌskoup] *n.* an electronic instrument for representing wave oscillations on the screen of a cathode-ray tube. Tuning pianos and checking motors can be done with very great accuracy by means of oscilloscopes.

os•cine ['ɒsɪn] *or* ['ɒsaɪn] *n., adj. —n.* any of a suborder of the passerine birds that includes most songbirds, including the larks, swallows, and finches. Oscines have well-developed, specialized vocal organs and most species sing.
—adj. of or designating this order of birds. ⟨< L *oscines,* pl., < *ob-* to + *canere* sing⟩

os•ci•tan•cy ['ɒsɪtənsi] *n., pl.* **-cies. 1** drowsiness. **2** the act of yawning. ⟨< L *oscitans* ppr. of *oscitare* to gape, yawn < *os* mouth + *citare* to put in motion⟩

os•cu•lant ['ɒskjələnt] *adj.* **1** forming a connection between two groups having something in common. **2** supporting; embracing.

os•cu•late ['ɒskjəˌleit] *v.* **-lat•ed, -lat•ing. 1** kiss. **2** come into close contact. **3** *Geometry.* **a** have three or more points coincident with: *A plane or a circle is said to osculate when it has three coincident points in common with the curve.* **b** of two curves, surfaces, etc., osculate each other. ⟨< L *osculari* < *osculum* little mouth, kiss, dim. of *os* mouth⟩

os•cu•la•tion [ˌɒskjəˈleiʃən] *n.* **1** the act of kissing. **2** a kiss. **3** *Geometry.* a contact between two curves, surfaces, etc. at three or more common points.

os•cu•la•to•ry [ˈɒskjələˌtɔri] *adj.* **1** kissing. **2** coming into close contact.

os•cu•lum [ˈɒskjələm] *n., pl.* **-la** [-lə]. in a sponge, an opening for expelling water. ⟨< NL < L *osculum* < *os* mouth⟩ **—ˈos•cu•lar,** *adj.*

–ose[1] *suffix.* **1** full of; having much or many: *verbose.* **2** inclined to; fond of: *jocose.* **3** like: *schistose.* ⟨< L *-osus*⟩

–ose[2] *suffix.* used to form chemical terms, especially names of sugars and other carbohydrates, as in *fructose*, *lactose*, and of protein derivations, as in proteose. ⟨< F *-ose* in *glucose*⟩

o•sier [ˈouʒər] *n.* **1** any of various willows, especially a common willow (*Salix viminalis*) of Europe and Asia having long, slender, straight branches used in making baskets, furniture, etc. **2** a branch or twig of an osier. **3** (*adj.*) made of osier. **4** RED-OSIER DOGWOOD. ⟨< F⟩

O•si•ris [ouˈsaɪrɪs] *n.* one of the most important gods of ancient Egypt, a god of fertility and also ruler of the lower world and the dead.

–osis *combining form.* **1** denoting an act, process, state, or condition: *osmosis.* **2** *Medicine.* denoting an abnormal or diseased condition: *neurosis.* ⟨< Gk.⟩

Os•man•li [ɒzˈmænli] *or* [ɒsˈmænli] *n., pl.* **-lis;** *adj.* *—n.* **1** an Ottoman. **2** the language of the Ottoman Turks.
—adj. Ottoman. ⟨< Turkish *Osmanli* belonging to *Osman*, Arabic *Othman.* See OTTOMAN.⟩

os•mic [ˈɒzmɪk] *adj. Chemistry.* containing osmium.

os•mi•um [ˈɒzmiəm] *n. Chemistry.* a hard, heavy, greyish metallic element of the platinum group, used for electric light filaments, as a catalyst, and in hard alloys. Osmium is the heaviest metal known. *Symbol:* Os; *at.no.* 76; *at.mass* 190.2. ⟨< NL < Gk. *osmē* smell, odour; from the odour of one of the osmium oxides⟩

os•mo•sis [ɒzˈmousɪs] *or* [ɒsˈmousɪs] *n.* **1** *Physical chemistry.* the tendency of a fluid separated from a more concentrated solution by a porous partition to pass through the partition until the concentration on each side is the same. Nutrients dissolved in fluids pass in and out of plant and animal cells by osmosis. **2** *Informal.* a process of gradual, often unconscious absorption that suggests osmosis: *He thought he could learn German by osmosis, without taking a course.* ⟨Latinized var. of *osimose* < Gk. *ōsmos* a thrust⟩ **—os'mot•ic** [ɒzˈmɒtɪk] *or* [ɒsˈmɒtɪk], *adj.* **—os'mot•i•cal•ly,** *adv.*

os•mun•da [ɒsˈmʌndə] *n.* a fern of the genus *Osmunda*, having erect fronds.

os•na•burg [ˈɒznəˌbɜrg] *n.* a coarse cotton fabric.

os•prey [ˈɒspri] *or* [ˈɒsprei] *n., pl.* **-preys.** **1** a large, long-winged, brown-and-white hawk (*Pandion haliaetus*) that feeds on fish. **2** an ornamental feather, used for trimming hats, etc. ⟨ult. < L *ossifraga* < *os* bone + *frangere* break⟩

Ospreys

os•sa [ˈɒsə] *n., pl.* of OS[1].

Os•sa [ˈɒsə] *n.* a mountain in NE Greece. In Greek legend, when the giants made war on the gods, they piled Mount Ossa on Mount Olympus and Mount Pelion on Mount Ossa in an attempt to reach heaven.

os•se•in [ˈɒsiɪn] *n.* the residue of bone used in making glue.

os•se•ous [ˈɒsiəs] *adj.* consisting of or resembling bone; bony. ⟨< L *osseus* < *os, ossis* bone⟩

Os•si•an [ˈɒsiən] *or* [ˈɒʃən] *n. Irish legend.* a legendary Gaelic warrior and poet of about the 3rd century A.D.

os•si•fi•ca•tion [ˌɒsəfəˈkeiʃən] *n.* **1** the process of developing or changing into bone. **2** a mass of tissue that has been ossified; a part that is ossified. **3** a settling into a conventional, rigid, or unimaginative condition.

os•si•fy [ˈɒsəˌfaɪ] *v.* **-fied, -fy•ing.** **1** change into bone; become bone: *The soft parts of a baby's skull ossify as the baby grows older.* **2** harden; make or become fixed and rigid, or very conservative: *The once free and spontaneous exchange of ideas among the group members had ossified into mere ritual.* ⟨< L *os, ossis* bone + E *-(i)fy*⟩ **—ˈos•si,fi•er,** *n.*

os•su•ary [ˈɒsjuˌɛri] *or* [ˈɒʃuˌɛri] *n., pl.* **-ar•ies.** an urn, vault, or other place to hold the bones of the dead. ⟨< LL *ossuarium*, neuter of *ossuarius* of bones⟩

os•te•al [ˈɒstiəl] *adj.* bony.

os•te•i•tis [ˌɒstiˈəitɪs] *n. Pathology.* inflammation of bone or tissue of the bone.

os•ten•si•ble [ɒˈstɛnsəbəl] *adj.* apparent; pretended; professed: *They were sure that the ostensible reason for her resignation was not the true one.* ⟨< F < L *ostendere* show < *os-* < *obs-* toward + *tendere* stretch⟩ **—os'ten•si•bly,** *adv.*

os•ten•sive [ɒˈstɛnsɪv] *adj.* **1** ostensible. **2** directly or manifestly demonstrative. **—os'ten•sive•ly,** *adv.*

os•ten•ta•tion [ˌɒstənˈteiʃən] *or* [ˌɒstɛnˈteiʃən] *n.* **1** a showing off; display intended to impress others. **2** a group of peacocks. ⟨< L *ostentatio, -onis,* ult. < *ob-* toward + *tendere* stretch⟩

os•ten•ta•tious [ˌɒstənˈteiʃəs] *or* [ˌɒstɛnˈteiʃəs] *adj.* having or showing a desire to attract notice and arouse admiration or envy, etc.: *an ostentatious display of wealth.* **—,os•ten'ta•tious•ly,** *adv.*

osteo– *combining form.* bone: *osteoarthritis.* Also, before vowels, **oste-.** ⟨< Gk. *osteon* bone⟩

os•te•o•ar•thri•tis [ˌɒstiouɑrˈθrəitɪs] *n. Pathology.* arthritis caused by joint and cartilage degeneration.

os•te•o•blast [ˈɒstiəˌblæst] *n. Anatomy.* a cell from which bone develops. ⟨< *osteo-* + *-blast* < Gk. *blastos* sprout⟩

os•te•oid [ˈɒstiˌɔɪd] *adj.* like bone.

os•te•ol•o•gy [ˌɒstiˈɒlədʒi] *n.* **1** the branch of anatomy that deals with the skeleton. **2** the bony structure or system of bones of an animal or major part of an animal, as the head, trunk, etc. ⟨< *osteo-* + *-logy*⟩ **—,os•te•o'log•i•cal,** *adj.* **—,os•te'ol•o•gist,** *n.*

os•te•o•my•e•li•tis [ˌɒstiouˌmaɪəˈləitɪs] *n. Pathology.* inflammation of the bone or bone marrow. ⟨< *osteo-* + Gk. *myelos* marrow + E *-itis*⟩

os•te•o•path [ˈɒstiəˌpæθ] *n.* a person who practises osteopathy. Also, **osteopathist** [ˌɒstiˈɒpəθɪst]. ⟨< *osteopathy*⟩

os•te•op•a•thy [ˌɒstiˈɒpəθi] *n.* a system of medical practice based on the theory that the muscles and bones of the body are closely interrelated with all other parts of the body and that many diseases can be treated by manipulating the bones and muscles. ⟨< Gk. *osteon* bone + E *-pathy*⟩ **—,os•te•o'path•ic** [ˌɒstiəˈpæθɪk], *adj.* **—,os•te•o'path•i•cal•ly,** *adv.*

os•te•o•plas•ty [ˈɒstiəˌplæsti] *n.* the surgical repair of bone. **—,os•te•o'plas•tic,** *adj.*

os•te•o•po•ro•sis [ˌɒstioupəˈrousɪs] *n.* a bone condition common especially in older women, characterized by loss of bone mass and easily broken bones, owing to loss of calcium.

os•ti•na•to [ˌɒstəˈnɑtou] *n., pl.* **-tos.** *Music.* a phrase repeated over and over in the same voice or pitch. ⟨< Ital. *ostinato*, literally, obstinate < L *obstinatus*⟩

os•ti•ole [ˈɒstiˌoul] *n.* a small opening. ⟨< L *ostiolum* little door⟩

ost•ler [ˈɒslər] *n.* hostler.

os•tra•cism [ˈɒstrəˌsɪzəm] *n.* **1** an ancient Greek method of banishing an unpopular or dangerous citizen for a number of years by popular vote, without a trial or formal accusation. **2** the act or state of being shut out from society, from favour, from privileges, or from association with one's fellows.

os•tra•cize [ˈɒstrəˌsaɪz] *v.* **-cized, -ciz•ing.** **1** banish by the ancient Greek method of ostracism. **2** shut out from society, from favour, from privileges, etc. ⟨< Gk. *ostrakizein* < *ostrakon* tile, potsherd, originally used in balloting⟩ **—ˈos•tra,ciz•a•ble,** *adj.* **—,os•tra•ci'za•tion,** *n.* **—ˈos•tra,ciz•er,** *n.*

os•tra•cod [ˈɒstrəˌkɒd] *n.* any of a subclass (Ostracoda) of tiny, mainly freshwater crustaceans having a two-valved shell. ⟨< Gk. *ostrakodes* having a shell < *ostrakon* shell⟩

os•trich [ˈɒstrɪtʃ] *n.* **1** a very large, two-toed, flightless bird (*Struthio camelus*) of Africa, the largest living bird, having dark plumage on the body, with the head, neck, thighs, and legs bare, and strong legs which enable it to run very fast. Ostriches have large, showy tail plumes valued for ornamentation. **2** *Informal.* a person who avoids facing reality or an approaching danger (from the ostrich's supposed habit of burying its head in the sand to avoid oncoming danger). ⟨ME < OF < LL *avis struthio* < L *avis* bird, LL *struthio* < Gk. *strouthiōn* < *strouthos* ostrich⟩

ostrich fern a tall fern (*Matteuccia struthiopteris*) having long, soft, bright green, sterile fronds and short, fertile fronds. The fiddleheads of this fern are a popular delicacy, especially in Nova Scotia and New Brunswick.

Os•tro•goth ['ɒstrə,gɒθ] *n.* a member of the eastern division of Goths that overran the Roman Empire and controlled Italy from A.D. 493 to 555. ⟨< LL *Ostrogothi*, earlier *Austrogothi* < Gmc.; probably originally 'the splendid Goths', but later taken as 'the eastern Goths'⟩ **–,Os•tro'goth•ic,** *adj.*

Os•ty•ak ['ɒsti,æk] *n.* **1** a member of a Finno-Ugric people of Siberia. **2** the language of these people.

O.T. OLD TESTAMENT.

oth•er ['ʌðər] *adj., pron., adv. –adj.* **1** remaining: *John is here, but the other boys are at school.* **2** additional or further: *I have no other books with me.* **3** not the same as one or more already mentioned: *Come some other day.* **4** different: *I would not have him other than he is.*

every other, every second; alternate: *She buys cream every other day.*

no or **none other than,** no one less than: *The presentation was made by none other than the prime minister.*

the other day (night, etc.), recently.

–pron. **1** the other one; not the same ones: *Each praises the other.* **2** another person or thing: *There are others to be considered.*

of all others, more than all others.

–adv. otherwise; differently: *I can't do other than to go.*

other than, apart from; except for: *Other than Peter, no one knew.* ⟨OE *ōther*⟩

other half **1** a different stratum of society: *seeing how the other half lives.* **2** *Informal.* one's spouse.

oth•er•ness ['ʌðərnɪs] *n.* the quality or state of being separate, distinct, or special in nature, character, etc.

oth•er•wise ['ʌðər,waɪz] *adv., adj., conj. –adv.* **1** in a different way; differently: *I could not do otherwise.* **2** in other ways: *He is noisy, but otherwise a very nice boy.* **3** under other circumstances; in a different condition: *He reminded me of what I should otherwise have forgotten.*

–adj. different: *It might have been otherwise.*

–conj. or else; if not: *Come at once; otherwise you will be too late.* ⟨< *other* + *wise*²⟩

other world the world to come; life after death.

oth•er•world•ly ['ʌðər'wɜrldli] *adj.* **1** of or devoted to another world, such as the world of the mind or imagination, or the world to come. **2** supernatural; weird. **–'oth•er'world•li•ness,** *n.*

o•tic ['outɪk] *or* ['ɒtɪk] *adj. Anatomy.* of or pertaining to the ear; auricular. ⟨< Gk. *ōtikós* < *ous*, *otos* ear⟩

–otic *combining form.* **1** causing: *narcotic.* **2** having: *sclerotic.* ⟨< Gk. *-ōtikós*⟩

o•ti•ose ['ouʃi,ous] *or* ['outi,ous] *adj.* **1** at leisure; lazy or idle: *an otiose individual sunning himself in the park.* **2** ineffective; futile: *otiose excuses.* **3** having no real function; superfluous: *The article was wordy and full of otiose comments and digressions.* ⟨< L *otiosus* < *otium* leisure⟩ **–'o•ti,ose•ly,** *adv.* **–,o•ti'os•i•ty,** *n.*

o•ti•tis [ou'təitɪs] *n. Pathology.* inflammation of the ear, especially the middle ear (**otitis media**).

oto– *prefix.* the ear: *otology.* ⟨< Gk. *oûs*, *otos* ear⟩

o•to•la•ryn•gol•o•gy [,outou,lærɪŋ'gɒlədʒi] *or* [-,lɛrɪŋ'gɒlədʒi] *n.* the study of diseases of the ear and throat. **–,o•to,la•ryn'gol•o•gist,** *n.*

o•tol•o•gist [ou'tɒlədʒɪst] *n.* a physician who specializes in otology.

o•tol•o•gy [ou'tɒlədʒi] *n.* the branch of medicine dealing with the ear and its diseases, including their diagnosis and treatment. ⟨< *oto-* + *-logy*⟩ **–,o•to'log•i•cal** [,outə'lɒdʒɪkəl], *adj.*

O•to–Man•gue•an ['outou 'mæŋgiən] *n.* a family of American Indian languages spoken in Mexico, including Otomi, Zapotec, and Mixtec.

o•to•rhi•no•lar•yn•gol•o•gy [,outou,raɪnou,lærɪŋ'gɒlədʒi] *or* [-,lɛrɪŋ'gɒlədʒi] *n.* the study of diseases of the ear, nose, and throat. **–,o•to,rhi•no,lar•yn'gol•o•gist,** *n.*

ot•ta•va ri•ma [ou'tɑvə 'rimə] *pl.* **rimas.** a stanza of eight lines with the lines according to the rhyme scheme *a b a b a b c c.* In Italian each line normally has eleven syllables; in English, ten. ⟨< Ital. *ottava rima* octave rhyme⟩

Ot•ta•wa ['ɒtə,wɒ] *or* ['ɒtəwə] *n., pl.* **-was** or **-wa;** *adj.* *–n.* **1** the capital city of Canada, in Ontario. **2** a member of an American Indian people living in southern Ontario and Michigan. **3** the dialect of Ojibwa spoken by the Ottawas.

–adj. of or having to do with the Ottawas or their language.

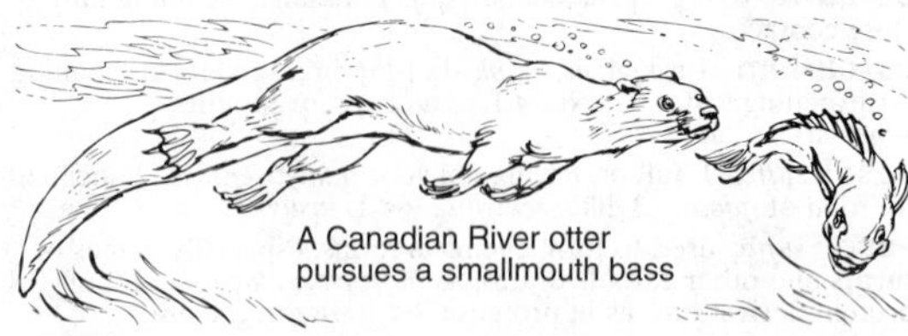

A Canadian River otter pursues a smallmouth bass

ot•ter ['ɒtər] *n., pl.* **-ters** or *(esp. collectively)* **-ter. 1** any of several fish-eating water mammals of the weasel family having a long, lithe body, long neck, small ears, and webbed feet with claws. The common North American river otter is *Lutra canadensis.* The large sea otter of the N Pacific coasts is *Enhydra lutris.* **2** the short, thick, glossy brown fur of an otter. ⟨OE *oter*⟩

Ot•ter ['ɒtər] *n. Cdn. Trademark.* a famous light monoplane much used in bush flying in the Canadian North, manufactured by DeHavilland Aircraft of Canada Ltd.

ot•to ['ɒtou] *n.* attar.

ot•to•man ['ɒtəmən] *n., pl.* **-mans. 1** a low, cushioned seat without back or arms. **2** a cushioned footstool. **3** a heavy, corded fabric of silk or rayon, often with cotton or wool.

Ot•to•man ['ɒtəmən] *n., adj. –n.* a Turk.

–adj. **1** Turkish. **2** having to do with the dynasty called the Ottoman Empire. ⟨< F < Ital. *Ottomano* < Arabic *Othmani* belonging to *Othman*, the name of the founder of the empire⟩

Ottoman Empire a former empire of the Turks in SE Europe, SW Asia, and N Africa; Turkish Empire.

oua•na•niche [,wɑnə'nɪʃ] *or* [,wɑnə'niʃ] *n., pl.* **-niche.** *Cdn.* a landlocked Atlantic salmon native to Lac St-Jean and some other freshwater lakes in Québec and Ontario. The ouananiche was formerly thought to be a subspecies of the Atlantic salmon, or even a separate species. Compare KOKANEE. ⟨< Cdn.F < Algonquian (Montagnais *wananish* little salmon)⟩

ou•bli•ette [,ubli'ɛt] *n.* a secret dungeon having a trapdoor in the ceiling as its only entrance. ⟨< F *oubliette* < *oublier* forget⟩

ouch [ʌutʃ] *interj.* an exclamation expressing sudden pain.

ought¹ [ɒt] *auxiliary verb. Ought* is used with an infinitive to express: **1** duty or obligation: *You ought to obey your parents.* **2** rightness or appropriateness: *The theatre ought to allow children in free.* **3** a wise or sensible course: *I ought to go before it rains.* **4** an expectation by others: *At your age you ought to know better.* **5** likelihood: *The fastest one ought to win the race.*

☛ *Hom.* AUGHT.

☛ *Usage.* **Ought. Had ought** and **hadn't ought** are not used in careful English: *He ought* (not *had ought*) *to dress more carefully. She ought to have been more careful.*

ought² [ɒt] *n., adv. Archaic.* See AUGHT.

ought³ [ɒt] *n. Informal. Esp. Brit.* nought; zero; the cipher 0. ⟨var. of *nought, a nought* taken as *an ought*⟩

☛ *Hom.* AUGHT.

oughtn't ['ɒtənt] *v.* ought not: *She oughtn't to have said that.*

ou•gi•ya [u'gijə] *n.* a unit of currency of Mauritania, divided into five khoum. See table of money in the Appendix. ⟨< Arabic⟩

Oui•ja ['widʒə] or ['widʒi] *n. Trademark.* a device consisting of a small board on legs that rests on a larger board marked with words, letters of the alphabet, or other characters. The person wishing an answer to questions rests his or her fingers lightly on the small board which may then move and touch letters or words. Ouijas are used at spiritualistic meetings and as games. ⟨< F *oui* yes + G *ja* yes⟩

ounce¹ [aʊns] *n.* **1** a unit for measuring mass, one-sixteenth of a pound (about 28 g) in avoirdupois and one-twelfth of a pound (about 31 g) in troy weight. **2** a unit for measuring liquids, equal to one-twentieth of a pint; fluid ounce (about 28 cm³). **3** a little bit; very small amount: *an ounce of prevention. He hadn't an ounce of strength left.* ⟨ME < OF *unce* < L *uncia* twelfth part. Doublet of INCH.⟩

ounce[2] [aʊns] *n.* SNOW LEOPARD. ⟨ME < OF *once* for *lonce* < L *lynx* lynx < Gk.⟩

our [aʊr] *or* [ɑr] *adj.* a possessive form of **we:** of, belonging to, or made or done by us or ourselves: *Would you like to see our garden? We went to get our coats.* ⟨OE *ūre*⟩
☛ *Hom.* ARE [ɑr], HOUR [aʊr].
☛ *Usage.* **Our, ours** are the possessive forms of **we. Our** is a determiner and is always followed by a noun: *This is our car.* **Ours** is a pronoun and stands alone: *This car is ours.*

Our Lady the VIRGIN MARY.

ours [aʊrz] *or* [ɑrz] *pron.* a possessive form of **we**: that which belongs to us: *That car is ours. They got their tickets yesterday, but ours haven't come yet.*
of ours, belonging to or associated with us: *They're friends of ours.*
☛ *Usage.* See note at OUR.

our•self [aʊr'sɛlf] *or* [ɑr'sɛlf] *pron.* myself (used when **we** is used as the subject instead of **I,** as by a sovereign, writer, or judge): *"We shall ourself reward the victor," said the queen.*

our•selves [aʊr'sɛlvz] *or* [ɑr'sɛlvz] *pron.pl.* **1** a reflexive pronoun, the form of **we** used as an object when it refers to the same people as the subject: *We cannot see ourselves as others see us.* **2** a form of **we** or **us** added for emphasis: *We ourselves are responsible for what happened.* **3** our usual selves: *We weren't ourselves when we let them get away with that.*

–ous *adjective-forming suffix.* **1** having; having much; full of: *joyous, perilous.* **2** characterized by: *blasphemous, parsimonious, zealous.* **3** having the nature of: *murderous, idolatrous.* **4** of or having to do with: *monogamous.* **5** like: *thunderous.* **6** committing or practising: *bigamous.* **7** inclined to: *amorous.* **8** *Chemistry.* implying a larger proportion of the element indicated than *-ic* implies. *Stannous* means containing tin in larger proportions than a corresponding *stannic* compound. ⟨ME < OF < L *-osus*; often used to represent L *-us*, adj. (e.g., *omnivorus* omnivorous) or Gk. *-os*, adj. (e.g., *anonymos* anonymous)⟩

ou•sel ['uzəl] See OUZEL.

oust [ʌust] *v.* force out; drive out. ⟨< AF *ouster* (cf. F *ôter*) < L *obstare* block, hinder < *ob-* in the way of + *stare* stand. Related to OBSTACLE.⟩

oust•er [ʌustər] *n.* the act of ousting, especially an illegal eviction or dispossession.

out [ʌut] *adv., adj., n., prep., v., interj. —adv.* **1** away; forth: *to rush out.* **2** not in or at a place, position, state, etc.: *That dress is out of fashion.* **3** into the open air: *He went out at noon.* **4** to or at an end: *to fight it out.* **5** from the usual place, condition, position, etc.: *Put the light out. The boy turned his pockets out.* **6** completely; effectively: *to fit out.* **7** so as to project or extend: *to stand out.* **8** into or in existence, activity, or outward manifestation: *Fever broke out. Flowers are out.* **9** aloud; loudly: *Speak out.* **10** to others: *Give out the books.* **11** from a number, stock, store, source, cause, material, etc.; from among others: *Pick out an apple for me. She picked out a new coat.* **12** in the wrong: *to be out in one's calculations.* **13** from a state of composure, satisfaction, or harmony: *to feel put out.* **14** at a money loss of: *to be out ten dollars.* **15** *Baseball, etc.* not in play; no longer at bat or on base.
out and away, by far: *She is out and away the best player.*
out and out, thoroughly: *out and out discouraged.*
out of, a from within: *He came out of the house.* **b** not within; away from; outside of; beyond: *out of town, 60 km out of Calgary. The boat has gone out of sight.* **c** having no more of: *We are out of coffee.* **d** so as to take away: *She was cheated out of her money.* **e** from: *My dress is made out of silk.* **f** from among: *We picked our puppy out of that litter.* **g** because of: *I went only out of curiosity.*
out of hand. See HAND.
—adj. **1** not in possession or control: *The Liberals are out, the Conservatives in.* **2** not in use, action, fashion, etc.: *The fire is out. Full skirts are out this season.* **3** without money, supplies, etc.: *Have you any cigarettes left? No, I'm right out.* **4** *Baseball, cricket, etc.* of a player or side, not allowed to continue in play. **5** external; exterior; outer; outlying: *an out island.* **6** not usual: *an out size.* **7** of a homosexual, no longer secretive about his or her sexuality.
out for, looking for; trying to get: *We have a holiday and are out for a good time.*
out of, of animals, borne by (a female).
out to, eagerly or earnestly trying to: *Their team is out to make the finals.*
—n. **1** one who is out. **2** something wrong. **3** that which is omitted. **4** a defence or excuse: *to have an out for stealing.* **5** *Baseball.* an instance of putting out or being put out.
at outs or **on the outs,** quarrelling; disagreeing: *to be on the outs with a friend.*
—prep. **1** out from; forth from: *He went out the door.* **2** *Informal.* out along: *Drive out Main Street.*
—v. **1** *Archaic.* go or come out: *Murder will out.* **2** *Archaic.* put out: *Please out the fire.* **3** disclose the homosexual orientation of.
—interj. an exclamation of indignation, reproach, etc.: *Out with you!* ⟨OE *ūt*⟩

out– *prefix.* **1** outward; forth; away: *outburst, outgoing.* **2** outside; at a distance: *outbuilding, outfield, outlying.* **3** more than; longer than: *outbid, outlive, outnumber.* **4** better than: *outdo, outrun.* ⟨ME; OE *ūt*⟩

out•age ['ʌutɪdʒ] *n.* **1** a time of interrupted service, especially a suspension of gas, electric, or water power. **2** an interruption or failure in service, function, or use.

out–and–out ['ʌut ən 'ʌut] *adj.* thorough: *That is an out-and-out lie.*

out•back ['ʌut,bæk] *n.* **1** in Australia, the unsettled part of the interior; back country. Also, **Outback**. **2** any similarly unsettled area.

out•bal•ance [,ʌut'bæləns] *v.* **-anced, -anc•ing.** outweigh.

out•bid [,ʌut'bɪd] *v.* **-bid, -bid** or **-bid•den, -bid•ding.** bid higher than (someone else).

out•bluff [,ʌut'blʌf] *v.* defeat (someone) by bluffing better.

out•board ['ʌut,bɔrd] *adj., adv., n. —adj. or adv.* **1** outside the hull of a ship or boat. **2** away from the middle of a ship or boat. *—n.* **1** a boat equipped with an OUTBOARD MOTOR. **2** the motor itself.

outboard motor a portable internal-combustion engine with an attached propeller, that is mounted on the outside of the stern of a small boat or canoe.

out•bound ['ʌut,baʊnd] *adj.* outward bound.

out•brave [,ʌut'breiv] *v.* **-braved, -brav•ing. 1** face bravely. **2** be braver than.

out•break ['ʌut,breik] *n.* **1** a breaking out; sudden occurrence or increase: *outbreaks of anger, an outbreak of flu.* **2** a riot; public disturbance.

out•breed•ing ['ʌut,bridɪŋ] *n.* the mating of unrelated individuals. Compare INBREEDING.

out•build•ing ['ʌut,bɪldɪŋ] *n.* a shed or building built near a main building: *Barns are outbuildings on a farm.*

out•burst ['ʌut,bɜrst] *n.* a bursting forth: *an outburst of laughter, anger, smoke, etc.*

out•cast ['ʌut,kæst] *n., adj. —n.* a person or animal cast out from home and friends: *Criminals are outcasts of society.*
—adj. being an outcast; homeless; friendless.

out•class [,ʌut'klæs] *v.* be of higher class than; be much better than: *He is a good runner, but his younger brother definitely outclasses him.*

out•climb [,ʌut'klaɪm] *v.* climb better or higher than (someone).

out•come ['ʌut,kʌm] *n.* a result or consequence: *The outcome of the election was in doubt until the very end.*

out•crop *n.* ['ʌut,krɒp]; *v.* [,ʌut'krɒp] *n., v.* **-cropped, -crop•ping.** *—n.* **1** a coming to the surface of the earth: *the outcrop of a vein of coal.* **2** the part that comes to the surface: *The outcrop that we found proved to be very rich in gold.*
—v. come to the surface; appear.

out•cross ['ʌut,krɒs] *n., v.* crossbreed.

out•cry ['ʌut,kraɪ] *n., pl.* **-cries. 1** crying out; a sudden cry or clamour. **2** a strong protest: *There was a public outcry against the proposal to widen the street into a four-lane highway.*

out•dance [,ʌut'dæns] *v.* **-danced, -danc•ing.** dance better or longer than (someone).

out•dat•ed [,ʌut'deitɪd] *adj.* out-of-date; old-fashioned: *The coal-oil lamp is outdated.*

out•did [,ʌut'dɪd] *v.* pt. of OUTDO.

out•dis•tance [,ʌut'dɪstəns] *v.* **-tanced, -tanc•ing.** leave behind; outstrip: *She outdistanced all the other runners and won the race.*

out•do [,ʌut'du] *v.* **-did, -done, -do•ing.** do more or better than; surpass.
☛ *Syn.* See note at EXCEL.

out•done [,ʌut'dʌn] *v.* pp. of OUTDO.

out•door ['ʌut'dɔr] *adj.* done, used, or living outdoors: *outdoor games.*

out•doors ['ʌut'dɔrz] *adv., n. —adv.* out in the open air; not indoors: *The minute it stopped raining, they all went outdoors.*
—n. **the outdoors,** the world outside of buildings; the open air (*used with a singular verb*): *We spend most of the summer in the outdoors.*

out•doors•man [ˌʌut'dɔrzmən] *n., pl.* **-men.** a man who enjoys the outdoors and spends much time in outdoor activities or sports.

out•doors•y [ˌʌut'dɔrzi] *adj. Informal.* of, having to do with, or fond of the outdoors or outdoor activities: *She's an outdoorsy person who likes going on hikes.*

out•draw [ˌʌut'drɒ] *v.* **out•drew, out•drawn. 1** be more popular than; attract more interest or a larger following than: *Hockey usually outdraws curling as a spectator sport in this town.* **2** draw a pistol or revolver more quickly than: *He could outdraw anyone in the territory.*

out•drawn [ˌʌut'drɒn] *v.* pp. of OUTDRAW.

out•drew [ˌʌut'dru] *v.* pt. of OUTDRAW.

out•drink [ˌʌut'drɪŋk] *v.* **-drank, -drunk.** drink more than (someone).

out•er ['ʌutər] *adj.* **1** of or on the outside: *The outer door is locked.* **2** farther out; farther from the centre: *the outer suburbs of the city.*

outer ear the outer, visible part of the ear that serves to direct sound waves toward the eardrum; EXTERNAL EAR. See EAR[1] for picture.

out•er•most ['ʌutərˌmoust] *adj.* farthest out.

outer space 1 space immediately beyond the earth's atmosphere: *The moon is in outer space.* **2** space between the planets or between the stars. **—'out•er-'space,** *adj.*

out•er•ware ['ʌutərˌwɛr] *n.* clothing intended to be seen. Compare UNDERWEAR.

out•face [ˌʌut'feis] *v.* **-faced, -fac•ing. 1** face boldly; defy. **2** stare at (a person) until he or she stops staring back; browbeat; abash.

out•fall ['ʌutˌfɒl] *n.* the mouth or outlet of a stream, sewer, etc. where it discharges into a lake or the sea.

out•field ['ʌutˌfild] *n. Baseball.* **1** the part of the field beyond the diamond or infield. **2** the three players in the outfield. Compare INFIELD.

out•field•er ['ʌutˌfildər] *n. Baseball.* a player stationed in the outfield.

out•fit ['ʌutˌfɪt] *n., v.* **-fit•ted, -fit•ting.** *—n.* **1** all the articles or equipment necessary for any undertaking or purpose: *a sailor's outfit, the outfit for a camping trip.* **2** a group or organization thought of as a single unit; a military company, business firm, ranch, etc.: *They were in the same outfit during the war. He worked for the same outfit for five years.* **3** a set of clothes to be worn together; ensemble: *a bride's outfit, a summer outfit.* **4** *Cdn.* a vehicle and its team, such as a sled and dogs. **5** *Cdn.* formerly, **a** the annual shipment of trading goods and supplies sent by a fur company to its trading posts; also, any part of this shipment dispatched to or received by any particular post. **b** the trading goods and supplies taken into the interior by fur-company employees.
—v. **1** furnish with everything necessary for any purpose; equip: *John outfitted himself for camp.* **2** supply: *The whole family was outfitted with new coats last winter.*

out•fit•ter ['ʌutˌfɪtər] *n.* **1** a person or company that provides outfits, such as a dealer in camping supplies, a shop selling men's or women's clothing, etc. **2** *Cdn.* a guide and manager of an expedition, such as a hunting or exploring party in the wilderness.

out•flank [ˌʌut'flæŋk] *v.* **1** go or extend beyond the flank of (an opposing army, etc.); turn the flank of. **2** get the better of; circumvent: *They outflanked us and won the debate.*

out•flow ['ʌutˌflou] *n.* **1** a flowing out: *the outflow from a waterpipe, an outflow of sympathy.* **2** that which flows out.

out•fox [ˌʌut'fɒks] *v.* get the better of; outsmart: *The escaped convict outfoxed his pursuers.*

out•gen•er•al [ˌʌut'dʒɛnərəl] *v.* **-alled** or **-aled, -al•ling** or **-al•ing.** be a better general than; get the better of by superior strategy.

out•go ['ʌutˌgou] *n., pl.* **-goes.** what goes out; what is paid out; an amount that is spent.

out•go•ing ['ʌutˌgouɪŋ] *for defs. 1 and 2;* [ˌʌut'gouɪŋ] *for def. 3. adj.* **1** departing; outward bound: *outgoing ships, the outgoing mail.* **2** retiring or withdrawing from office: *A dinner was held for the outgoing president.* **3** friendly; sociable: *She is very outgoing and enjoys giving parties.*

out•grew [ˌʌut'gru] pt. of OUTGROW.

out•grow [ˌʌut'grou] *v.* **-grew, -grown, -grow•ing. 1** grow too large for. **2** grow beyond or away from; get rid of by growing older: *outgrow early friendships, outgrow a babyish habit.* **3** grow or increase faster than: *She outgrew her twin sister. The population was rapidly outgrowing the food supply.*

out•grown [ˌʌut'groun] *v.* pp. of OUTGROW.

out•growth ['ʌutˌgrouθ] *n.* **1** a natural development, product, or result: *This big store is an outgrowth of the little shop started ten years ago.* **2** an offshoot; something that has grown out of something else: *A corn is an outgrowth on a toe.* **3** a growing out or forth: *the outgrowth of new leaves in the spring.*

out•guess [ˌʌut'gɛs] *v.* get the better of by anticipating a person's actions: *She outguessed her competitor and got her proposal accepted.*

out•haul ['ʌutˌhɒl] *n. Nautical.* a rope used to extend a sail.

out•house ['ʌutˌhʌus] *n.* **1** an outdoor toilet. **2** a separate building used in connection with a main building.

out•ing ['ʌutɪŋ] *n.* a short pleasure trip; walk or airing; holiday spent outdoors or away from home.

outing flannel a cotton cloth woven to look like flannel.

out•land•er ['ʌutˌlændər] *n.* **1** a foreigner; alien. **2** *Informal.* an outsider; stranger.

out•land•ish [ˌʌut'lændɪʃ] *adj.* **1** not familiar; queer; strange or ridiculous. **2** looking or sounding foreign. **3** geographically remote. **—ˌout'land•ish•ly,** *adv.* **—ˌout'land•ish•ness,** *n.*

out•last [ˌʌut'læst] *v.* **1** last longer than. **2** outlive.

out•law ['ʌutˌlɒ] *n., v. —n.* **1** a person outside the protection of the law; exile; outcast. **2** a lawless person; criminal. **3** an unbroken horse.
—v. **1** make or declare (a person) an outlaw. **2** make or declare illegal: *A group of nations agreed to outlaw war.* **3** ban. **4** deprive of legal force. An outlawed debt is one that cannot be collected because it has been due too long. ⟨OE *ūtlaga* < ON *útlagi*⟩

out•law•ry ['ʌutˌlɒri] *n., pl.* **-ries. 1** the condition of being outlawed. In the early Middle Ages outlawry was used as a punishment in England. **2** the condition of being an outlaw.

out•lay *n.* ['ʌutˌlei]; *v.* [ˌʌut'lei] *n., v.* **-laid, -lay•ing.**
—n. **1** spending; laying out of money, energy, etc.: *a large outlay for clothing.* **2** the amount spent.
—v. expend: *outlay money in improvements.*

out•let ['ʌutˌlɛt] *or* ['ʌutlɪt] *n.* **1** a means or place of letting out or getting out; way out: *the outlet of a lake, an outlet for one's energies.* **2** a market for a product. **3** a store selling the products of a particular manufacturer: *The shoe manufacturer had several retail outlets.* **4** a place in a wall, etc. for inserting an electric plug to make connection with an electric circuit.

out•li•er ['ʌutˌlaɪər] *n.* **1** a person, place, or thing that is detached from the main body or system. **2** *Geology.* a formation surrounded by older strata and exposed because of erosion, denudation, etc.

out•line ['ʌutˌlaɪn] *n., v.* **-lined, -lin•ing.** *—n.* **1** the line that shows the shape of an object; line that bounds a figure: *We saw the outlines of the mountains against the evening sky.* **2** a drawing or style of drawing that gives only outer lines. **3** a general plan; rough draft: *Make an outline before trying to write a composition.* **in outline, a** with only the outline shown. **b** with only the main features.
—v. **1** draw the outer line of. **2** indicate or define the outline of: *hills outlined against the sky.* **3** give a plan of; sketch: *She outlined their trip abroad.* **—'outˌlin•er,** *n.*

☛ *Syn. n.* **1. Outline,** CONTOUR, PROFILE = the line or lines showing the shape of something. **Outline** applies to the line marking the outer limits or edge of an object, figure, or shape: *We could see the outline of a man.* **Contour** emphasizes the shape shown by the outline: *The contours of his face are rugged.* **Profile** applies to the side view of something seen in outline, especially against a background: *You would stand up straight if you could see your profile when you slouch.*

out•live [ˌʌut'lɪv] *v.* **-lived, -liv•ing.** live or last longer than; survive: *The idea was good once, but it has outlived its usefulness.*

out•look ['ʌutˌlʊk] *n.* **1** what one sees on looking out; view: *The room has a pleasant outlook.* **2** what seems likely to happen; prospect: *Because of the black clouds, the outlook for our picnic is not very good.* **3** a way of thinking about things; attitude of mind;

point of view: *a gloomy outlook on life.* **4** a lookout; tower or other high place to watch from.

out•ly•ing ['ʌut,laɪɪŋ] *adj.* lying outside the boundary; far from the centre; remote: *the outlying houses in the settlement.*

out•ma•noeu•vre [,ʌutmə'nuvər] *v.* **-vred, -vring. 1** get the better of by skilful manoeuvring; outwit: *They were outmanoeuvred in the negotiations and lost the contract.* **2** surpass in being manoeuvrable: *This car can outmanoeuvre any other car of its size on the market.* Also, **outmaneuver.**

out•mod•ed [,ʌut'moudɪd] *adj.* out-of-date.

out•most ['ʌut,moust] *adj.* outermost.

out•num•ber [,ʌut'nʌmbər] *v.* be more than; exceed in number: *They outnumbered us three to one.*

out–of–bounds ['ʌut əv 'baʊnds] *adj. or adv.* **1** *Sports.* outside the boundary line. **2** outside the established limits of use or entry.

out–of–date ['ʌut əv 'deit] *adj.* old-fashioned; not in present use.

out–of–door ['ʌut əv 'dɔr] *adj.* outdoor.

out–of–doors ['ʌut əv 'dɔrz] *adj., n., adv.* *—adj.* outdoor.
—n. or adv. outdoors.

out–of–the–way ['ʌut əv ðə 'wei] *adj.* **1** remote; unfrequented; secluded: *an out-of-the-way cottage.* **2** seldom met with; unusual: *out-of-the-way bits of information.*

out–of–town ['ʌut əv 'taʊn] *adj.* of, having to do with, or situated on land outside a city or town.

out•pace [,ʌut'peis] *v.* **-paced, -pac•ing. 1** run faster than. **2** outdo; excel.

out–pa•tient ['ʌut ,peiʃənt] *n.* a patient receiving treatment at a hospital or clinic but not staying there. Compare IN-PATIENT.

out•per•form [,ʌutpər'fɔrm] *v.* perform better or longer than.

out•play [,ʌut'plei] *v.* play better than.

out•point [,ʌut'pɔɪnt] *v.* **1** score more points than. **2** sail closer to the wind than.

out•port ['ʌut,pɔrt] *n. Cdn.* a small harbour, especially one of the isolated fishing villages along the coasts of Newfoundland.

out•port•er ['ʌut,pɔrtər] *n. Cdn.* a native or resident of an outport.

out•post ['ʌut,poust] *n.* **1** a guard, or small number of soldiers, placed at some distance from an army or camp to prevent surprise attack. **2** the place where they are stationed. **3** a settlement or village in an outlying place: *an outpost in the North, a distant outpost of civilization.* **4** anything thought of as an outpost or advance guard.

out•pour *n.* ['ʌut,pɔr]; *v.* [,ʌut'pɔr] *n., v.* *—n.* **1** a pouring out. **2** an uncontrolled expression of thoughts or feelings.
—v. pour out.

out•pour•ing *n.* ['ʌut,pɔrɪŋ]; *v.* [,ʌut'pɔrɪŋ] *n., v.* *—n.* **1** anything that is poured out. **2** an uncontrolled expression of thoughts or feelings.
—v. ppr. of OUTPOUR.

out•pro•duce [,ʌutprə'djus] *or* [,ʌutprə'dus] *v.* **-duced, -duc•ing.** produce more or better than (someone or another company).

out•put ['ʌut,pʊt] *n.* **1** the amount produced; product or yield: *the daily output of automobiles.* **2** a putting forth: *a sudden output of effort.* **3** *Computer technology.* information produced from the storage unit of a computer.

out•race [,ʌut'reis] *v.* **-raced, -rac•ing.** race faster than (someone).

out•rage *n.* ['ʌutreidʒ]; *v.* ['ʌutreidʒ] *or* [ʌut'reidʒ] *n., v.* **-raged, -rag•ing.** *—n.* **1** an act showing no regard for the rights or feelings of others. **2** an overturning of the rights of others by force; act of violence; offence; insult. **3** the hurt, angry feeling aroused by such treatment.
—v. **1** insult; offend greatly or arouse great anger in. **2** break (the law, a rule of morality, etc.) openly; treat as nothing at all. ⟨ME < OF *outrage,* ult. < L *ultra* beyond⟩

out•ra•geous [ʌut'reidʒəs] *adj.* shocking; very offensive or insulting. **—out'ra•geous•ly,** *adv.* **—out'ra•geous•ness,** *n.*

out•ran [,ʌut'ræn] *v.* pt of. OUTRUN.

out•rank [,ʌut'ræŋk] *v.* rank higher than.

ou•tré [u'trei] *adj.* passing the bounds of what is usual and considered proper; eccentric; bizarre. ⟨< F *outré,* pp. of *outrer* exaggerate, ult. < L *ultra* beyond⟩

out•reach *v.* [,ʌut'ritʃ]; *n.* ['ʌut,ritʃ] *v., n.* *—v.* **1** exceed or reach beyond: *Her accomplishments far outreached those of her predecessors.* **2** *Esp. poetic.* reach or stretch out; extend: *He outreached his arms.*
—n. **1** the act or fact of reaching out: *The social aid program has too little outreach into the community.* **2** the extent or limit of reach: *the outreach of the flood.*

out•rid•den [,ʌut'rɪdən] *v.* pp. of OUTRIDE.

out•ride [,ʌut'raɪd] *v.* **-rode, -rid•den, -rid•ing. 1** ride faster or better than. **2** of ships, last through (a storm).

out•rid•er ['ʌut,raɪdər] *n.* a servant or attendant riding on a horse before or beside a carriage or wagon, etc. A chuckwagon team consists of a driver and four outriders.

out•rig•ger ['ʌut,rɪgər] *n.* **1** a framework ending in a float, extending outward from the side of a light boat or canoe to prevent upsetting. **2** a boat or canoe with an outrigger. **3** a bracket extending outward from either side of a boat to hold a rowlock. **4** a boat equipped with such brackets. **5** a projecting spar, framework, or part: *an outrigger from a ship's mast to extend a sail, an outrigger from an airplane to support the rudder.*

out•right ['ʌut,rəit] *adv., adj.* *—adv.* **1** altogether; entirely; not gradually: *sell a thing outright.* **2** openly; without restraint: *I laughed outright.* **3** at once; on the spot: *She fainted outright.*
—adj. **1** complete; thorough: *an outright loss.* **2** downright; straightforward; direct: *an outright refusal.* **3** entire; total.

out•rode [,ʌut'roud] *v.* pt. of OUTRIDE.

out•run [,ʌut'rʌn] *v.* **-ran, -run, -run•ning. 1** run faster than. **2** leave behind; go beyond; pass the limits of: *I am afraid your story outruns the facts.*

out•sell [,ʌut'sɛl] *v.* **-sold, -sell•ing. 1** outdo in selling: *She can easily outsell any of the other sales reps.* **2** sell in greater amounts than; exceed in the number of items sold: *His second novel outsold his first by a wide margin.*

out•set ['ʌut,sɛt] *n.* a start; a beginning: *At the outset, it looked like a nice day.*

out•shine [,ʌut'ʃaɪn] *v.* **-shone, -shin•ing. 1** shine longer or more brightly than. **2** be more brilliant or excellent than; surpass.

out•shoot *v.* [,ʌut'ʃut]; *n.* ['ʌut,ʃut] *v.* **-shot, -shoot•ing;** *n.*
—v. **1** shoot better or farther than. **2** shoot forth.
—n. **1** projection. **2** offshoot.

out•side ['ʌut,saɪd] *or* [,ʌut'saɪd] *n., adj., adv., prep.* *—n.* **1** the side or surface away from the centre or inside: *the outside of a circle or a balloon. The cupboards were blue on the outside and white on the inside.* **2** the external appearance. **3** a space or position on the outer side or beyond a boundary or limit: *She opened the window from the outside.* **4** *Cdn.* the settled parts of Canada: *In the North, people refer to the rest of Canada as the outside.*
at the outside, at the most; at the limit: *It will take me a week, at the outside.*
outside in, so that what should be outside is inside; inside out.
—adj. **1** of, having to do with, on, or toward the outer part or surface: *The outside leaves are turning brown.* **2** not belonging to a certain group, set, district, etc.: *Outside people tried to get control of the business.* **3** being, acting, done, or originating without or beyond a wall, boundary, etc.: *Outside noises disturbed the class.* **4** maximum or extreme: *What is your outside estimate on costs?* **5** of a chance or possibility, slight; remote: *He had only an outside chance of winning the race.*
—adv. **1** on or to the outside. **2** outdoors.
—prep. out of; beyond the limits of: *Stay outside the house.*
outside of, *Informal.* with the exception of: *Outside of John, none of us liked the play.*

out•sid•er [,ʌut'saɪdər] *or* ['ʌut,saɪdər] *n.* **1** a person who does not belong to a particular group, company, party, etc. **2** *Cdn.* a person who does not live in the North: *The people of Whitehorse, Y.T., call the people of Edmonton outsiders.* **3** a person, horse, etc. believed to have no chance of winning a competition.

out•size ['ʌut,saɪz] *adj., n.* *—adj.* larger than the usual size.
—n. an article of clothing, etc. larger than the usual size.

out•skirts ['ʌut,skɜrts] *n.pl.* the outer parts or edges of a town, district, etc.; outlying parts.

out•smart [,ʌut'smɑrt] *v.* *Informal.* outdo in cleverness.

out•sold [,ʌut'sould] *v.* pt. and pp. of OUTSELL.

out•sourc•ing ['ʌut,sɔrsɪŋ] *n.* *Computer technology.* the use by one organization of another organization's computers and expertise to have data processing work done.

out•spo•ken [,ʌut'spoukən] *adj.* frank; not reserved: *an*

outspoken person, outspoken criticism. **—,out'spo•ken•ly,** *adv.* **—,out'spo•ken•ness,** *n.*
☛ *Syn.* See note at FRANK.

out•spread *adj.* ['ʌut,sprɛd]; *v.* [,ʌut'sprɛd] *adj., v.* **-spread, -spread•ing.** *—adj.* spread out; extended: *an eagle with outspread wings.*
—v. spread out; extend.

out•stand [,ʌut'stænd] *v.* **-stood, -stand•ing. 1** put out to sea. **2** be outstanding.

out•stand•ing [ʌut'stændɪŋ] *adj., v. —adj.* **1** standing out from others; well-known; important; excellent: *an outstanding basketball player, an outstanding performance.* **2** unpaid: *outstanding debts.* **3** needing attention; *outstanding letters.* **4** projecting.
—v. ppr. of OUTSTAND. **—out'stand•ing•ly,** *adv.*

out•stare [,ʌut'stɛr] *v.* outface.

out•sta•tion ['ʌut,steiʃən] *n.* a remote station or post.

out•stay [,ʌut'stei] *v.* **1** stay beyond the limit of; overstay: *He outstayed his welcome.* **2** stay longer than; have more staying power than: *She outstayed all the other buyers. He outstayed the other guests.*

out•stretch [,ʌut'strɛtʃ] *v.* extend.

out•stretched *adj.* ['ʌut,strɛtʃt]; *v.* [,ʌut'strɛtʃt] *adj., v. —adj.* stretched out; extended: *He welcomed his old friend with outstretched arms.*
—v. pt. and pp. of OUTSTRETCH.

out•strip [,ʌut'strɪp] *v.* **-stripped, -strip•ping. 1** go faster than; leave behind in a race. **2** do better than; excel.

out•swim [,ʌut'swɪm] *v.* **-swam, -swum, -swim•ming.** swim better, farther, or faster than (someone).

out•take ['ʌut,teik] *n.* part of a film which is discarded and does not appear in the finished film.

out•talk [,ʌut'tɒk] *v.* talk better, faster, longer, or louder than; get the better of by talking.

out•turn ['ʌut,tɜrn] output.

out•vote [,ʌut'vout] *v.* **-vot•ed, -vot•ing.** defeat in voting; cast more votes than.

out•walk [,ʌut'wɒk] *v.* walk farther or faster than (someone).

out•ward ['ʌutwərd] *adj., adv. —adj.* **1** going toward the outside; turned toward the outside: *an outward motion, an outward glance.* **2** outer: *to all outward appearances.* **3** on the surface; external: *an outward transformation.*
—adv. **1** toward the outside; away. **2** away from the dock, station, etc.: *That ship is outward bound.* **3** on the outside: *He folded the coat with the lining outward.* Also (*adv.*), **outwards.** ⟨OE *ūtweard*⟩ **—'out•ward•ness,** *n.*

out•ward•ly ['ʌutwərdli] *adv.* **1** on the outside or outer surface. **2** toward the outside. **3** as regards appearance or outward manifestation.

out•wards ['ʌutwərdz] *adv.* outward.

out•wash ['ʌut,wɒʃ] *n. Geology.* rock fragments or other glacial debris carried beyond the glacier by meltwater.

out•wear [,ʌut'wɛr] *v.* **-wore, -worn, -wear•ing. 1** wear longer than. **2** wear out. **3** outgrow.

out•weigh [,ʌut'wei] *v.* **1** weigh more than. **2** exceed in value, importance, influence, etc.: *The advantages of the plan outweigh its disadvantages.*

out West *Cdn.* in or to the Prairie Provinces of Canada, or British Columbia.

out•wit [,ʌut'wɪt] *v.* **-wit•ted, -wit•ting.** get the better of by being more intelligent; be too clever for: *The prisoner outwitted the guards and escaped.*

out•work *n.* ['ʌut,wɜrk]; *v.* [,ʌut'wɜrk] *n., v. —n.* a part of the fortifications of a place lying outside the main ones; a less important defence: *the outworks of a castle.*
—v. surpass in working; work harder or faster than.

out•worn [,ʌut'wɔrn] *adj., v. —adj.* **1** worn out. **2** out-of-date.
—v. pp. of OUTWEAR.

ou•zel ['uzəl] *n.* **1** RING OUZEL. **2** WATER OUZEL; DIPPER (def. 2). Also, **ousel.** ⟨OE *ōsle*⟩

ou•zo ['uzou] *n.* a strong, colourless, Greek alcoholic liquor flavoured with aniseed. ⟨< Mod.Gk. *ouzon*⟩

o•va ['ouvə] *n.* pl. of OVUM.

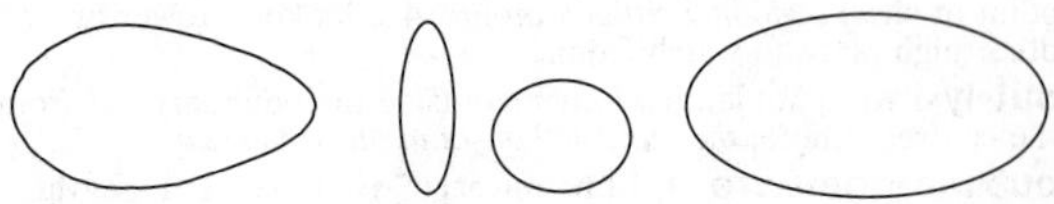

Ovals: the three on the right are ellipses

o•val ['ouvəl] *adj., n. —adj.* **1** egg-shaped. **2** shaped like an ellipse.
—n. something having an oval shape. ⟨ME < NL *ovalis* < L *ovum* egg⟩ **—'o•val•ly,** *adv.* **—'o•val•ness,** *n.*

o•var•i•an [ou'vɛriən] *adj.* of or having to do with an ovary.

o•va•ry ['ouvəri] *n., pl.* **-ries. 1** *Anatomy, zoology.* in female animals, the reproductive organ that produces the egg cells and, in vertebrates, female sex hormones. In mammals, there is one ovary on each side of the abdomen. **2** *Botany.* in a seed-bearing plant, the part of the pistil that contains the young seeds, called ovules. See FLOWER for picture. ⟨< NL *ovarium* < L *ovum* egg⟩

o•vate ['ouveit] *adj. Botany.* egg-shaped and attached at the broader end: *an ovate leaf.* See LEAF for picture. ⟨< L *ovatus* < *ovum* egg⟩

o•va•tion [ou'veiʃən] *n.* an enthusiastic public welcome; burst of applause. ⟨< L *ovatio, -onis* < *ovare* rejoice⟩

ov•en ['ʌvən] *n.* **1** a space in a stove or near a fireplace, for baking food. **2** a small furnace for heating or drying. ⟨OE *ofen*⟩

ov•en•bird ['ʌvən,bɜrd] *n.* **1** any of several small, brown songbirds (genus *Furnarius*) of South America that build a dome-shaped nest of clay and leaves or twigs, etc. The nest of an ovenbird has a side entrance and is often quite elaborate, with more than one chamber. **2** a North American songbird (*Seiurus aurocapillus*), a large wood warbler that builds a dome-shaped nest of leaves and plant fibres on the forest floor. This ovenbird's nest also has a side entrance.

ov•en•proof ['ʌvən,pruf] *adj.* able to stand the heat of an oven without cracking.

ov•en•ware ['ʌvən,wɛr] *n.* dishes made to be ovenproof.

o•ver ['ouvər] *prep., adv., adj., n. —prep.* **1** above in place or position: *the roof over one's head.* **2** above in authority, power, etc.: *We have a captain over us.* **3** on; upon: *a blanket lying over a bed.* **4** at or to all or various places on or in; round about; all through: *A blush came over her face. We will be travelling over Europe. Farms were scattered over the valley.* **5** above and to the other side of; across: *to leap over a wall.* **6** on the other side of: *lands over the sea.* **7** out and down from: *He fell over the edge of the cliff.* **8** more than; beyond: *It costs over ten dollars.* **9** from end to end of; along: *We drove over the new highway.* **10** during; in the course of: *over many years.* **11** in reference to; concerning; about: *He is troubled over his health.* **12** while engaged in or concerned with: *to fall asleep over one's work.* **13** by means of: *They spoke over the telephone.* **14** until the end of: *to stay over the weekend.* **15** because of (something in the way): *I fell over a toy in the hallway.*
over and above, besides; in addition to.
—adv. **1** above: *The cliff hung over.* **2** so as to cover the surface, or affect the whole surface: *Cover the tar over with sand until it has hardened.* **3** from side to side; to the other side; across any intervening space: *Go over to the store for me.* **4** from one to another: *Hand the money over.* **5** on the other side; at some distance: *over in Europe, over by the hill.* **6** down; out and down: *The ball went too near the edge and rolled over. When he lost his balance, he fell over.* **7** so as to bring the upper side or end down or under: *to turn over a page.* **8** again; in repetition: *ten times over. I'll have to do that assignment over.* **9** through a region, area, etc.: *to travel all over.* **10** from beginning to end: *to read a newspaper over.* **11** more; besides; in excess or addition: *He spent seventy cents and had thirty cents over.* **12** at or to some place: *He's over there at Bob's house. Can Julia stay over here tonight?*
over again, once more: *Let's do that over again.*
over against, a opposite to; in front of. **b** so as to bring out a contrast with.
over and over, again and again: *He keeps telling the same story over and over.*
over with or **over and done with,** *Informal.* finished; completed: *I have to get this homework over with today.*
—adj. **1** upper; higher up: *the over crust of a pie.* **2** at an end: *The play is over.*
—n. **1** an amount in excess; extra. **2** *Cricket.* **a** the number of balls (usually six) delivered between successive changes of bowlers. **b** the part of the game between such changes. ⟨OE *ofer*⟩
☛ *Syn. prep.* **1, 2. Over,** ABOVE = express a relation in which one thing is thought of as being higher than the other. **Over,** the opposite of **under,** suggests being directly higher or in the position or space immediately

higher up: *Carry the umbrella over your head. A sergeant is over a corporal.* **Above,** opposed to **below** and **beneath,** suggests being on or at or rising to a higher level, but seldom suggests being straight up or a direct connection: *The plane flew above the clouds. A general is above a sergeant.*

☛ *Usage.* **Over with.** Used in informal speech and writing to mean 'over' or 'finished'. Spoken: *I'd like to get this over with today.* More formal: *I'd like to get this finished today.*

o•ver– *prefix.* **1** too; too much; too long, etc.: *overcrowded, overfull, overburden, overpay, oversleep.* **2** extra: *oversize, overtime.* **3** other meanings: *overflow, overlord, overseas, overthrow.* ⟨ME; OE *ofer-*⟩

o•ver•a•chieve [ˌovərə'tʃiv] *v.* **-chieved, -chiev•ing.** do too much; perform better than expected or required. **—ˌo•ver•a'chieve•ment,** *n.* **—ˌo•ver•a'chiev•er,** *n.*

o•ver•act [ˌouvər'ækt] *v.* act to excess; overdo in acting; act (a part) in an exaggerated manner.

o•ver•ac•tive [ˌouvər'æktɪv] *adj.* too active; active to excess. **—ˌo•ver'ac•tive•ly,** *adv.*

o•ver•age¹ [ˌouvər'eidʒ] *adj.* over a specified age, especially too old to be of use, etc.

o•ver•age² ['ouvərɪdʒ] *n.* a surplus or extra amount, as of goods.

o•ver•all *adj., n.* ['ouvərˌɒl]; *adv.* [ˌouver'ɒl] *adj., adv., n.*
—adj. **1** from one end to the other: *The overall length of the house is 10 m.* **2** including everything: *an overall estimate.*
—adv. as a whole; generally: *Overall, it was a successful meeting.*
—n. **1 overalls,** *pl.* loose trousers, usually with a part that extends up over the chest, of strong, usually cotton, cloth worn over a top or over clothes to keep them clean. **2** *Esp. Brit.* a loose-fitting smock, etc. worn over other clothes to protect them.

o•ver•arch [ˌouvər'ɑrtʃ] *v.* **1** arch over; span with or like an arch: *The street was overarched by elm trees.* **2** curve like an arch.

o•ver•arm ['ouvərˌɑrm] *adj. or adv.* with the arm raised above the shoulder; overhand: *an overarm stroke, to throw overarm.*

o•ver•awe [ˌouvər'ɒ] *v.* **-awed, -aw•ing.** overcome or restrain with awe: *She was overawed by the grandeur of the estate.*

o•ver•bal•ance [ˌouvər'bæləns] *v.* **-anced, -anc•ing,** *n.*
—v. **1** be greater than in weight, importance, value, etc.: *The gains overbalanced the losses.* **2** cause to lose balance. **3** lose balance: *She overbalanced and fell from the wall.*
—n. an excess in weight.

o•ver•bear [ˌouvər'bɛr] *v.* **-bore, -borne, -bear•ing.** **1** overcome by weight or force; oppress; master: *His father overbore his objections.* **2** bear down by weight or force; overthrow; upset.

o•ver•bear•ing [ˌouvər'bɛrɪŋ] *adj., v.* *—adj.* **1** inclined to dictate; forcing others to one's own will; domineering. **2** overriding; of supreme importance.
—v. ppr. of OVERBEAR. **—ˌo•ver'bear•ing•ly,** *adv.*
☛ *Syn.* See note at PROUD.

o•ver•bid *v.* [ˌouvər'bɪd]; *n.* ['ouvərˌbɪd] *v.* **-bid, -bid** or **-bid•den, -bid•ding;** *n.* *—v.* **1** bid more than the value of (a thing). **2** bid higher than (a person).
—n. a bid that is too high.

o•ver•bite ['ouvərˌbəit] *n. Dentistry.* a condition in which the upper front teeth project over the lower ones.

o•ver•blouse ['ouvərˌblaʊz] *or* ['ouvərˌblʌus] *n.* a blouse for women, designed to be worn outside a skirt or pants instead of tucked in. An overblouse is usually slightly longer than a regular blouse.

o•ver•blown [ˌouvər'bloun] *adj.* **1** of a flower, past its peak of beauty; too fully open. **2** inflated or pompous; pretentious: *Her acceptance speech was filled with flowery, overblown sentiments.*

o•ver•board ['ouvərˌbɔrd] *adv.* from a ship or boat into the water: *He fell overboard.*
go overboard, go too far in an effort because of extreme enthusiasm: *She went overboard and bought more than she needed.*
throw overboard, *Informal.* get rid of; abandon or discard: *We had to throw all our plans overboard and start again from scratch.*

o•ver•book [ˌouvər'bʊk] *v.* issue tickets to or reservations on (a flight, performance, etc.) to more people than there is room for: *The airline had overbooked the flight and we had to wait for the next one.*

o•ver•bore [ˌovər'bɔr] *v.* pt. of OVERBEAR.

o•ver•borne [ˌouvər'bɔrn] *v.* pp. of OVERBEAR.

o•ver•build [ˌouvər'bɪld] *v.* **-built, -build•ing.** **1** build over (something). **2** build in (an area) more than is allowed.

o•ver•bur•den *v.* [ˌouvər'bɜrdən]; *n.* ['ouvərˌbɜrdən] *v., n.*
—v. overload.
—n. **1** too great a burden; something that overloads. **2** *Geology.* **a** rock, clay, etc. that overlays and hides a deposit of ore. **b** soil, gravel, or other material that overlays bedrock.

o•ver•came [ˌouvər'keim] *v.* pt. of OVERCOME.

o•ver•cap•i•tal•ize [ˌouvər'kæpətəˌlaɪz] *v.* **-ized, -iz•ing.** fix or estimate the capital of (a company, enterprise, etc.) at too high an amount. **—ˌo•verˌcap•i•tal•i'za•tion,** *n.*

o•ver•cast ['ouvərˌkæst] *adj., v.* **-cast, -cast•ing;** *n.*
—adj. **1** cloudy; dark; gloomy: *The sky was overcast before the storm.* **2** sad; gloomy: *Her face was overcast.* **3** sewn by overcasting.
—v. **1** cover or be covered with clouds or darkness. **2** sew over and through (the raw edges of a seam) with long stitches to prevent ravelling.
—n. mist or cloud cover.

o•ver•charge *v.* [ˌouvər'tʃɑrdʒ]; *n.* ['ouvərˌtʃɑrdʒ] *v.* **-charged, -charg•ing;** *n.* *—v.* **1** charge too high a price: *The grocer overcharged you for the eggs.* **2** load too heavily; fill too full: *The musket was overcharged and burst.*
—n. **1** a charge that is too high. **2** too heavy or too full a load.

o•ver•cloud [ˌouver'klaʊd] *v.* **1** cloud over; become clouded over; darken. **2** make or become gloomy.

o•ver•coat ['ouvərˌkout] *n.* a coat worn for warmth over regular clothing.

o•ver•come [ˌouvər'kʌm] *v.* **-came, -come, -com•ing.** **1** get the better of; win the victory over; conquer; defeat: *to overcome an enemy, one's faults, all difficulties.* **2** make weak or helpless: *to overcome by weariness.* **3** confuse or overwhelm: *The girl was so overcome by the noise and the lights that she couldn't speak.* ⟨OE *ofercuman*⟩
☛ *Syn.* **1.** See note at DEFEAT.

o•ver•com•pen•sate [ˌouvər'kɒmpənˌseit] *v.* **-sat•ed, -sat•ing.** go too far in trying, consciously or unconsciously, to make up for or get rid of a feeling of inferiority: *She overcompensated for her shyness at the party by insulting half the guests.*

o•ver•com•pen•sa•tion [ˌouvərˌkɒmpən'seiʃən] *n.* the act or an instance of overcompensating.

o•ver•cor•rec•tion [ˌouvərkə'rɛkʃən] *n.* **1** a correction in excess of what is required, as in steering a car. **2** an incorrect usage due to trying too hard to avoid an error. *Example*: for you and I *instead of* for you and me.

ˌo•ver•a'bound
ˌo•ver•a'bun•dance
ˌo•ver•a'bun•dant
ˌo•ver•ac'cen•tuˌate
ˌo•ver•acˌcu•mu'la•tion
ˌo•ver•ac'tiv•i•ty
ˌo•ver•a'dorned
ˌo•ver•af'fect
ˌo•ver•ag'gres•sive
ˌo•ver•am'bi•tious
ˌo•ver'an•aˌlyse
ˌo•ver'an•gry
ˌo•ver'an•iˌmat•ed
ˌo•verˌan•i'ma•tion
ˌo•ver•anx'i•e•ty
ˌo•ver'anx•ious
ˌo•ver•apˌpre•ci'a•tion
ˌo•ver•ap'pre•ci•a•tive
ˌo•verˌap•pre'hen•sive
ˌo•verˌar•gu'men•ta•tive
ˌo•ver•as'ser•tive
ˌo•ver•as'ser•tive•ness
ˌo•ver•as'sess•ment
ˌo•ver•as'sured
ˌo•ver•at'tached
ˌo•ver•at'ten•tive
ˌo•ver•at'ten•tive•ness
ˌo•ver'bold
ˌo•ver'brave
ˌo•ver'bulk•y
ˌo•ver'bur•den•some
ˌo•ver'bus•y
ˌo•ver'buy
ˌo•ver'care•ful
ˌo•ver'cas•u•al
ˌo•ver'cau•tion
ˌo•ver'cau•tious
ˌo•ver'cau•tious•ness
ˌo•verˌcen•tral•i'za•tion
ˌo•ver'cen•tralˌize
ˌo•ver•ce're•bral
ˌo•ver'civ•il
ˌo•ver'civ•iˌlize
ˌo•ver'com•mon
ˌo•ver•com'pet•i•tive
ˌo•ver•com'pla•cen•cy
ˌo•ver•com'pla•cent
ˌo•ver'com•plex
ˌo•ver'com•pliˌcate
ˌo•ver'con•fi•dence
ˌo•ver'con•fi•dent
ˌo•verˌcon•sci'en•tious
ˌo•ver•con'serv•a•tive
ˌo•ver•con'sid•er•ate
ˌo•ver•con'sume
ˌo•ver•con'sump•tion
ˌo•ver'cook
ˌo•ver'cool
ˌo•ver•cor'rect
ˌo•ver'crit•i•cal
ˌo•ver'crit•iˌcize

o•ver•crop [ˌouvər'krɒp] *v.* **-cropped, -crop•ping.** exhaust the fertility of (land) by excessive growth of crops.

o•ver•de•vel•op [ˌouvərdi'vɛləp] *v.* develop too much or too long. If a photograph is overdeveloped, it will be too dark. **—ˌo•ver•de'vel•op•ment,** *n.*

o•ver•do [ˌouvər'du] *v.* **-did, -done, -do•ing. 1** do or attempt too much: *She overdoes exercise. He overdid and became tired.* **2** exaggerate: *The funny scenes in the play were overdone.* **3** cook too much or too long; overcook: *Don't overdo the roast.* **4** exhaust; tire. ⟨OE *oferdōn*⟩

o•ver•done [ˌouvər'dʌn] *v., adj. —v.* pt. of OVERDO.
—adj. cooked too much: *overdone vegetables.*

o•ver•dose *n.* ['ouvərˌdous]; *v.* [ˌouvər'dous] *or* ['ouvərˌdous] *n., v.* **-dosed, -dos•ing.** *—n.* too big a dose.
—v. **1** give too large a dose to. **2** take too large a dose.

o•ver•draft ['ouvərˌdræft] *n.* **1** an overdrawing of a bank account. **2** the amount of the excess. **3** a current of air over fuel in a furnace.

o•ver•draw [ˌouvər'drɒ] *v.* **-drew, -drawn, -draw•ing. 1** draw from (a bank account) more money than one has there. **2** exaggerate: *The characters in the book were greatly overdrawn.*

o•ver•dress *v.* [ˌouvər'drɛs]; *n.* ['ouvərˌdrɛs] *v., n. —v.* dress or decorate too formally or elaborately or too warmly: *He decided not to wear his tuxedo because he did not want to risk being overdressed. It is not good for a baby to be overdressed.*
—n. a dress worn over another dress: *a sheer overdress.*

o•ver•drive ['ouvərˌdraɪv] *n.* **1** an arrangement of gears that reduces the power required to maintain a desired speed. **2** the gear setting in which this takes place.

o•ver•due [ˌouvər'dju] *or* [ˌouvər'du] *adj.* **1** late coming or arriving: *The plane is overdue.* **2** due but not yet paid: *This bill is overdue.*

o•ver•es•ti•mate *v.* [ˌouvər'ɛstəˌmeit]; *n.* [ˌouvər'ɛstəmɪt] *v.* **-mat•ed, -mat•ing;** *n. —v.* estimate at too high a value, amount, rate, etc.
—n. an estimate that is too high. **—ˌo•verˌes•ti'ma•tion,** *n.*

o•ver•ex•cite [ˌouvərɛk'səit] *v.* **-cit•ed, -cit•ing.** excite too much. **—ˌo•ver•ex'cit•a•ble,** *adj.* **—ˌo•ver•ex'cite•ment,** *n.*

o•ver•ex•ert [ˌouvərɛg'zɜrt] *v.* put forth too much effort; exert too much (*usually used with a reflexive pronoun*): *He hurt his back when he overexerted himself in gymnastics.*

o•ver•ex•er•tion [ˌouvərɛg'zɜrʃən] *n.* the act or an instance of overexerting: *The injury was the result of overexertion.*

o•ver•ex•pose [ˌouvərɛk'spouz] *v.* **-posed, -pos•ing. 1** expose to too much light or radiation: *to overexpose a film.* **2** show to the public too often: *She is overexposed in this movie.*

o•ver•ex•po•sure [ˌouvərɛk'spouʒər] *n.* **1** the act of overexposing or state of being overexposed: *an overexposure in photography, overexposure to the sun.* **2** an overexposed photograph.

o•ver•ex•tend [ˌouvərɛk'stɛnd] *v.* extend too far; especially, commit (oneself) beyond what one can pay, do, etc. **—ˌo•ver•ex'ten•sion,** *n.*

o•ver•fill [ˌouvər'fɪl] *v.* fill too full; fill so as to cause overflowing.

o•ver•fish [ˌouvər'fɪʃ] *v.* take too many fish from: *If you overfish these waters, the fisheries will be closed.*

o•ver•flight ['ouvərˌfləit] *n.* the act or fact of flying over an area, especially the territory of another country.

o•ver•flow *v.* [ˌouvər'flou]; *n.* ['ouvərˌflou] *v., n. —v.* **1** flow over the bounds: *Rivers often overflow in the spring.* **2** cover; flood: *The creek overflowed my garden.* **3** have the contents flowing over: *The bathtub is overflowing.* **4** flow over the top of: *The milk is overflowing the cup.* **5** extend out beyond; be too many for: *The crowd overflowed the little parlour and filled the hall.* **6** be very abundant: *an overflowing harvest, overflowing kindness.*
—n. **1** an overflowing: *The sink has an extra drain near the top to prevent an overflow.* **2** an excess: *We caught the overflow in a pail.* **3** an outlet or container for overflowing liquid. ⟨OE *oferflōwan*⟩

o•ver•flown [ˌouvər'floun] *v.* pp. of OVERFLY.

o•ver•fly [ˌouvər'flaɪ] *v.* **o•ver•flew, o•ver•flown, o•ver•fly•ing. 1** fly in an airplane above: *Be careful not to overfly enemy territory.* **2** fly in an airplane beyond: *The plane overflew its destination because of snow on the runway.*

o•ver•gar•ment ['ouvərˌgɑrmənt] *n.* an outer garment.

o•ver•grow [ˌouvər'grou] *v.* **-grew, -grown, -grow•ing. 1** grow over: *Vines had completely overgrown the wall.* **2** grow too fast; become too big. **3** outgrow; grow too big for.

o•ver•grown [ˌouvər'groun] *adj., v. —adj.* **1** grown too big: *an overgrown tree.* **2** covered by growing vegetation: *The wall is overgrown with vines.*
—v. pp. of OVERGROW.

o•ver•growth ['ouvərˌgrouθ] *n.* **1** too great or too rapid growth. **2** growth overspreading or covering something.

o•ver•hand ['ouvərˌhænd] *adj., adv., n., v. —adj.* **1** done or made with the hand brought forward and down from above the shoulder: *an overhand throw.* **2** done or made with the back of the hand upward or outward. **3** of or designating a method of sewing two edges together, with the stitches passing successively over the line formed by the two edges.
—adv. in an overhand manner: *to pitch overhand.*
—n. Sports. an overhand stroke or throw: *He's practising his overhand.*
—v. sew overhand.

overhand knot a knot made by forming a loop in a cord, etc. and passing the end of the cord through it. See KNOT for picture.

o•ver•hang *v.* [ˌouvər'hæŋ]; *n.* ['ouvərˌhæŋ] *v.* **-hung, -hang•ing;** *n. —v.* **1** project over: *Trees overhang the street to form an arch of branches.* **2** threaten or menace; impend: *The threat of an invasion overhung the city.*
—n. **1** something that projects: *The overhang of the roof shaded the flower bed beneath.* **2** the extent of projecting.

o•ver•haul *v.* [ˌouvər'hɒl]; *n.* ['ouvərˌhɒl] *v., n. —v.* **1** examine thoroughly so as to make any repairs or changes that are needed. **2** gain upon; overtake.
—n. a thorough examination to find problems, weaknesses, etc. and make necessary repairs or changes.

o•ver•head *adv.* [ˌouvər'hɛd]; *adj. or n.* ['ouvərˌhɛd] *adv., adj., n. —adv.* over or above one's head; aloft or on high: *the stars shining overhead, the flag raised overhead.*
—adj. **1** being, working, or passing overhead: *overhead wires.* **2** applying to one and all; general.
—n. general expenses of running a business, such as rent, lighting, heating, taxes, repairs.

overhead projector a projecting device in which transparencies are placed on a glass surface that is lit from below, the image being focussed and reflected onto a wall or screen by means of an overhead lens and mirror.

o•ver•hear [ˌouvər'hir] *v.* **-heard, -hear•ing.** hear when one is not supposed to hear: *They spoke so loudly that I could not help overhearing what they said.* ⟨OE *oferhīeran*⟩

o•ver•hung *adj.* ['ouvərˌhʌŋ]; *v.* [ˌouvər'hʌŋ] *adj., v. —adj.*

ˌo•ver'crowd
ˌo•ver'cul•tiˌvate
ˌo•ver'cu•ri•ous
ˌo•ver'dec•oˌrate
ˌo•ver•de'fen•sive
ˌo•verˌdef•er'en•tial
ˌo•ver•de'lib•erˌate
ˌo•ver'del•i•cate
ˌo•ver•de'pend•ence
ˌo•ver•de'pend•ent
ˌo•ver'de•tailed
ˌo•ver'dig•niˌfied
ˌo•ver'dil•i•gent
ˌo•ver•di'lute
ˌo•ver•diˌver•si•fi'ca•tion
ˌo•ver•di'ver•siˌfy
ˌo•ver'dram•aˌtize
ˌo•ver'drink
ˌo•ver'ea•ger
ˌo•ver'ear•nest
ˌo•ver'eat
ˌo•ver'ed•uˌcate
ˌo•ver•ef'fu•sive
ˌo•ver•e'lab•oˌrate
ˌo•ver•em'bel•lish
ˌo•ver•e'mo•tion•al
ˌo•ver'em•pha•sis
ˌo•ver'em•phaˌsize
ˌo•ver•em'phat•ic
ˌo•ver•en'thu•siˌasm
ˌo•ver•enˌthu•si'as•tic
ˌo•ver•ex'act•ing
ˌo•ver•ex'cit•a•ble
ˌo•ver•ex'cite
ˌo•ver'ex•erˌcise
ˌo•ver•ex'pand
ˌo•ver•ex'pan•sion
ˌo•ver•ex'pect•ant
ˌo•ver•ex'pen•di•ture
ˌo•ver•ex'plic•it
ˌo•ver•ex'u•ber•ant
ˌo•ver•fa'mil•iar
ˌo•ver•faˌmil•i'ar•i•ty
ˌo•ver•fas'tid•i•ous
ˌo•ver'fear•ful
ˌo•ver'fed
ˌo•ver'feed
ˌo•ver'fond
ˌo•ver'fre•quent
ˌo•ver'full
ˌo•verˌgen•er•al•i'za•tion
ˌo•ver'gen•er•alˌize
ˌo•verˌgen•er'os•i•ty
ˌo•ver'gen•er•ous
ˌo•ver'gen•er•ous•ly
ˌo•ver'greed•y
ˌo•ver'hast•y
ˌo•ver'heat

1 hung from above: *an overhung door.* 2 of the upper jaw, projecting beyond the lower jaw.
–v. pt. and pp. of OVERHANG.

o•ver•in•dulge [,ouvərɪn'dʌldʒ] *v.* **-dulged, -dulg•ing.** indulge to excess. **–,o•ver•in'dul•gent,** *adj.*

o•ver•joyed [,ouvər'dʒɔɪd] *adj.* filled with great joy: *He was overjoyed at finding them safe and sound.*

o•ver•kill ['ouvər,kɪl] *n.* **1** a capacity for destruction in excess of that required to destroy a target or enemy. **2** *Informal.* the act of overdoing something.

o•ver•lad•en [,ouvər'leidən] *adj.* overloaded.

o•ver•laid [,ouvər'leid] *v.* pt. and pp. of OVERLAY[1].

o•ver•lain [,ouvər'lein] *v.* pp. of OVERLIE.

o•ver•land ['ouvər,lænd] *or* ['ouverlənd] *adv. or adj.* on land; by land: *We travelled overland from Halifax to Montréal: It was a long overland trip.*

O•ver•land•er ['ouvər,lændər] *n. Cdn.* a person who went from eastern Canada to the Cariboo gold rush in 1862; ARGONAUT (def. 2).

o•ver•lap *v.* [,ouvər'læp]; *n.* ['ouvər,læp] *v.* **-lapped, -lap•ping;** *n.* *–v.* lap over; place or be placed so that one piece covers part of the next: *Shingles are laid to overlap each other.*
–n. **1** a lapping over. **2** the part or amount that overlaps: *Allow for an overlap of 10 cm.*

o•ver•lay[1] *v.* [,ouvər'lei]; *n.* ['ouvər,lei] *v.* **-laid, -lay•ing;** *n.*
–v. **1** lay or place (one thing) over or upon (another). **2** cover, overspread, or surmount with something; especially, finish with an ornamental layer of something: *The dome is overlaid with gold.*
–n. **1** something laid over something else; a covering. **2** an ornamental layer: *The lid of the box had a gold overlay.* **3** a sheet of transparent material having marks on it, that is keyed to a design, chart, or map over which it is placed to give additional information.

o•ver•lay[2] [,ouvər'lei] *v.* pt. of OVERLIE.

o•ver•leaf ['ouvər,lif] *adj., adv.* on the other side of the page: *Turn the page and write your name overleaf.*

o•ver•leap [,ouvər'lip] *v.* leap over; pass beyond.

o•ver•lie [,ouvər'laɪ] *v.* **-lay, -lain, -ly•ing. 1** lie over or upon. **2** smother (an infant or other newborn creature) by lying on it, as in sleeping.

o•ver•load *v.* [,ouvər'loud]; *n.* ['ouvər,loud] *v., n.* *–v.* load too heavily.
–n. too great a load.

o•ver•look [,ouvər'lʊk] *v.* **1** fail to see: *Here are the letters you overlooked.* **2** pay no attention to; excuse: *His boss said he would overlook the mistake.* **3** have a view of from above; be higher than: *This high window overlooks half the city.* **4** manage; look after and direct. **–'o•ver,look•er,** *n.*
☛ *Syn.* **1.** See note at SLIGHT.

o•ver•lord ['ouvər,lɔrd] *n.* **1** a person who is lord over another lord or other lords: *The duke was the overlord of barons and knights who held land from him.* **2** a ruler with absolute or dictatorial powers; despot.

o•ver•ly ['ouvərli] *adv.* overmuch; excessively; too: *overly sensitive to criticism.*

o•ver•mas•ter [,ouvər'mæstər] *v.* overcome; overpower.

o•ver•match [,ouvər'mætʃ] *v.* be more than a match for; surpass.

o•ver•much [,ouvər'mʌtʃ] *adj., adv., n.* *–adj. or adv.* too much.
–n. too great an amount.

o•ver•nice [,ouvər'nəis] *adj.* too fastidious. **–,o•ver'nice•ly,** *adv.* **–,o•ver'nice•ness,** *n.*

o•ver•night *adv., v.* [,ouvər'nəit]; *adj.,* ['ouvər,nəit] *adv., adj., v.* *–adv.* **1** for one night: *to stay overnight.* **2** at once; immediately; in a very short time: *Change will not come overnight.* **3** on the night before: *Preparations were made overnight for an early start.*
–adj. **1** done, occurring, etc. from one day to the next: *an overnight stop.* **2** for use for one night: *An overnight bag contains articles needed for one night's stay.* **3** of or having to do with the night before. **4** immediate; sudden; an overnight stay or stop.
–v. stay overnight: *We'll overnight in Calgary before moving on to Vancouver.*

overnight bag a bag or small suitcase used to carry articles needed for a night's stay.

o•ver•night•er [,ouvər'nəiter] *n.* OVERNIGHT BAG.

o•ver•pass *n.* ['ouvər,pæs]; *v.* [,ouvər'pæs] *n., v.* **-passed** or **-past, -pass•ing.** *–n.* a bridge over a road, railway, canal, etc.
–v. **1** pass over, across, or beyond. **2** overlook; disregard.

o•ver•play [,ouvər'plei] *v.* **1** play (a part, etc.) in an exaggerated manner. **2** overestimate or rely too much on the strength of (one's position, etc.): *She overplayed her price advantage, failed to guarantee quick delivery, and lost the contract.* **3** *Golf.* hit (the ball) past the green.
overplay (one's) **hand, a** *Cards.* be too confident in the hand one has been dealt; take risks. **b** try too hard; argue to excess.

o•ver•plus ['ouvər,plʌs] *n.* a surplus; too great an amount.

o•ver•pop•u•late [,ouvər'pɒpjə,leit] *v.* **-at•ed, -at•ing.** permit or cause (a city, region, etc.) to become too densely populated, resulting in deterioration of the environment, reduced standard of living, shortage of food, etc.
–,o•ver,pop•u'la•tion, *n.*

o•ver•pow•er [,ouvər'paʊər] *v.* **1** overcome; master; overwhelm: *overpower one's enemies.* **2** be so much greater than, that nothing else is felt, heard, etc.; drown: *Sudden anger overpowered every other feeling.* **–,o•ver'pow•er•ing•ly,** *adv.*

o•ver•price [,ouvər'prəis] *v.* **-priced, -pric•ing.** set too high a price on: *His paintings aren't selling well because they're overpriced.*

o•ver•print *v.* [,ouvər'prɪnt]; *n.* ['ouvər,prɪnt] *v., n.* *–v.* **1** print additional matter, revisions, etc. on (sheets already printed). **2** *Photography.* print (a positive) darker than desired.
–n. **1** anything overprinted. **2** any design or mark printed across a postage stamp to change its use, value, etc. **3** a postage stamp printed in this way.

o•ver•pro•duce [,ouvərprə'djus] *or* [,ouvərprə'dus] *v.* **-duced, -duc•ing. 1** produce more (of) than necessary. **2** produce more (of) than can be sold profitably.

o•ver•pro•duc•tion [,ouvərprə'dʌkʃən] *n.* **1** production of more than is needed. **2** production of more than can be sold at a profit.

o•ver•proof ['ouvər'pruf] *adj.* higher than 100 proof; containing more alcohol than proof spirit contains.

o•ver•pro•tect [,ouvərprə'tɛkt] *v.* protect too much; exercise more control over than is necessary or desirable in trying to shield from hurt, disappointment, etc.: *He had a hard time when he first left home because he had been overprotected as a child.*

o•ver•pro•tec•tive [,ouvərprə'tɛktɪv] *adj.* having or showing a tendency to overprotect: *an overprotective parent.*

,o•ver'hur•ried
,o•ver,i•de•al'is•tic
,o•ver•i'de•al,ize
,o•ver•im'ag•i•na•tive
,o•ver•im'pressed
,o•ver•im'pres•sion•a•ble
,o•ver•in'dulge
,o•ver•in'dul•gence
,o•ver•in'dus•tri•al,ize
,o•ver•in'flate
,o•ver'in•flu•ence
,o•ver,in•flu'en•tial
,o•ver•in'sis•tence
,o•ver•in'sist•ent
,o•ver•in'sure
,o•ver•in•tel'lec•tu•al
,o•ver•in'tense
,o•ver•in'vest
,o•ver'jeal•ous
,o•ver'large
,o•ver'lav•ish
,o•ver'long
,o•ver'mer•ry
,o•ver'mod•est
,o•ver'mourn•ful
,o•ver'neg•li•gent
,o•ver'nerv•ous
,o•ver•o'be•di•ent
,o•ver,op•ti'mist•ic
,o•ver'or•gan,ize
,o•ver•par'tic•u•lar
,o•ver'pay
,o•ver'pay•ment
,o•ver'plump
,o•ver,pop•u'la•tion
,o•ver'pop•u•lous
,o•ver'pow•er•ful
,o•ver'praise
,o•ver•pre'cise
,o•ver'prize
,o•ver'prom•i•nent
,o•ver'prompt
,o•ver'proud
,o•ver•pro'vide
,o•ver'pub•li,cize

o•ver•qual•i•fied [ˌouvərˈkwɒlɪˌfaɪd] *adj.* having more education, training, or experience than a job calls for.

o•ver•rate [ˌouvərˈreit] *v.* **-rat•ed, -rat•ing.** rate or estimate too highly: *The movie was overrated; it really wasn't very good.*

o•ver•reach [ˌouvərˈritʃ] *v.* **1** reach over or beyond. **2** reach too far. **3** get the better of by cunning: *to overreach someone in a bargain.* **4** cheat. **5** strain: *to overreach one's leg.*
overreach oneself, a fail or miss by trying for too much: *In trying to make peace between the two friends, she overreached herself.* **b** fail by being too crafty or tricky.

o•ver•re•act [ˌouvərriˈækt] *v.* react too strongly and unreasonably. **—ˌo•ver•re'ac•tion,** *n.*

o•ver•ride *v.* [ˌouvərˈraɪd]; *n.* [ˈouvərˌraɪd] *v.* **-rode, -rid•den, -rid•ing;** *n.* —*v.* **1** act in spite of: *to override advice or objections.* **2** prevail over: *The new rule overrides all previous ones.* **3** ride over; trample on. **4** ride over (a region, place, etc.). **5** tire out by riding; ride too much.
—*n.* an instance of overriding: *She showed the new clerk how to do a price override on the cash register.* ⟨OE *oferrīdan*⟩

o•ver•rule [ˌouvərˈrul] *v.* **-ruled, -rul•ing. 1** decide authoritatively against (an argument, objection, etc.); set aside: *The president overruled my plan.* **2** be stronger than; prevail over: *The majority overruled me.* **—ˌo•ver'rul•ing•ly,** *adv.*

o•ver•run *v.* [ˌouvərˈrʌn]; *n.* [ˈouvərˌrʌn] *v.* **-ran, -run, -run•ning;** *n.* —*v.* **1** spread over rapidly or in great numbers: *Weeds had overrun the old garden. The barn was overrun with rats.* **2** invade and conquer, occupy, or destroy: *Enemy troops overran most of the country.* **3** run or go beyond; exceed: *The speaker overran the time set for him.* **4** *Printing.* **a** carry over (words or lines of type) into another line or page to provide for addition or removal of other matter. **b** remake (columns, pages, etc.) by carrying over words, lines, etc.
—*n.* **1** an overrunning. **2** the amount overrunning or carried over, as a balance or surplus; an excess. **3** the amount of money by which a cost exceeds estimates.

o•ver•saw [ˌouvərˈsɒ] *v.* pt. of OVERSEE.

o•ver•sea *adv.* [ˌouvərˈsi]; *adj.* [ˈouvərˈsi] *adv. or adj.* overseas.
☛ *Hom.* OVERSEE [ˌouvərˈsi].

o•ver•seas *adv.* [ˌouvərˈsiz]; *adj.* [ˈouvərˈsiz] *adv., adj.*
—*adv.* **1** across the sea; beyond the sea; abroad: *to travel overseas.* **2** *Military.* serving across the sea: *My grandmother was overseas during the war.*
—*adj.* **1** done, used, or serving overseas: *overseas service.* **2** of countries across the sea; foreign: *overseas trade.*

o•ver•see [ˌouvərˈsi] *v.* **-saw, -seen, -see•ing.** look after and direct (work or workers); superintend; manage. ⟨OE *oferséon*⟩
☛ *Hom.* OVERSEA.

o•ver•se•er [ˈouvərˌsiər] *n.* **1** a person who oversees the work of others. **2** *Cdn.* in certain provinces, the head of a township council; reeve.

o•ver•sell [ˌouvərˈsɛl] *v.* **-sold, -sell•ing. 1** sell to excess; sell more of than can be delivered. **2** *Informal.* urge (a person) to buy (something) too aggressively or too long, often at the risk of losing a sale.

o•ver•set [ˌouvərˈsɛt] *v.* **-set, -set•ting.** overturn.

o•ver•sew [ˈouvərˌsou] *or* [ˌouvərˈsou] *v.* **-sewed** or **-sewn, -sew•ing.** sew overhand with close stitches.

o•ver•sexed [ˌouvərˈsɛkst] *adj.* having excessive sexual desire or capacity.

o•ver•shad•ow [ˌouvərˈʃædou] *v.* **1** be or appear more important than: *The boy overshadowed his older brother as a hockey player.* **2** cast a shadow over.

o•ver•shoe [ˈouvərˌʃu] *n.* a waterproof shoe or boot, often made of rubber, worn over another shoe to keep the foot dry and warm.

o•ver•shoot [ˌouvərˈʃut] *v.* **-shot, -shoot•ing. 1** of an aircraft, pass beyond the limit of (the runway or landing field) when trying to land. **2** shoot or go beyond (the target, mark, limit, etc.)
overshoot the mark, do too much.

o•ver•shot *adj.* [ˈouvərˌʃɒt]; *v.* [ˌouvərˈʃɒt] *adj., v.* —*adj.* **1** of a water wheel, driven by water flowing over it from above. See WATER WHEEL for picture. **2** of the upper jaw, projecting beyond the lower.
—*v.* pt. and pp. of OVERSHOOT.

o•ver•sight [ˈouvərˌsəit] *n.* **1** a failure to notice or think of something; an unintentional mistake or omission: *Through an oversight, the bill was not paid.* **2** watchful care.

o•ver•sim•pli•fi•ca•tion [ˌouvərˌsɪmpləfəˈkeiʃən] *n.* the act or fact of oversimplifying: *It is an oversimplification to say that her success is due to hard work.*

o•ver•sim•pli•fy [ˌouvərˈsɪmpləˌfaɪ] *v.* **-fied, -fy•ing.** simplify too much; simplify to the point of distortion: *She has oversimplified the problem; there are several important factors she did not even consider.*

o•ver•size [ˈouvərˌsaɪz] *adj., n.* —*adj.* **1** larger than the usual size; outsize. **2** too big: *an oversize sweater.*
—*n.* something that is oversize.

o•ver•skirt [ˈouvərˌskɜrt] *n.* **1** an outer skirt. **2** a separate skirt over the main skirt.

o•ver•sleep [ˌouvərˈslip] *v.* **-slept, -sleep•ing.** sleep beyond the time set for waking; sleep too long; sleep in: *I was late for work this morning because I overslept.*

o•ver•spend [ˌouvərˈspɛnd] *v.* **-spent, -spend•ing.** spend more than one should; buy extravagantly.

o•ver•spread [ˌouvərˈsprɛd] *v.* **-spread, -spread•ing.** spread over: *A smile overspread his broad face.*

o•ver•state [ˌouvərˈsteit] *v.* **-stat•ed, -stat•ing.** state too strongly; exaggerate. **—'o•ver,state•ment,** *n.*

o•ver•stay [ˌouvərˈstei] *v.* stay beyond the time or limits of: *to overstay one's welcome.*

o•ver•step [ˌouvərˈstɛp] *v.* **-stepped, -step•ping.** go beyond; exceed: *She overstepped the limits of politeness by asking such personal questions.*

o•ver•stock *v.* [ˌouvərˈstɒk]; *n.* [ˈouvərˌstɒk] *v., n.* —*v.* stock or supply with more than is needed or can readily be used: *Stores often have sales when they're overstocked.*
—*n.* too great a stock or supply.

o•ver•strung [ˈouvərˈstrʌŋ] *adj.* **1** too nervous or sensitive. **2** having the bass strings crossing the treble strings: *an overstrung piano.*

o•ver•stuff [ˌouvərˈstʌf] *v.* **1** stuff more than is necessary; stuff too much: *Don't overstuff the turkey.* **2** of furniture, upholster with very thick stuffing.

o•ver•stuffed [ˈouvərˈstʌft] *adj., v.* —*adj.* of furniture, having very thick stuffing: *a large, comfortable, overstuffed armchair.*
—*v.* pt. and pp. of OVERSTUFF.

o•ver•sub•scribe [ˌouvərsəbˈskraɪb] *v.* **-scribed, -scrib•ing.** subscribe (for) in excess of what is available or required.

o•ver•sub•scrip•tion [ˌouvərsəbˈskrɪpʃən] *n.* an oversubscribing.

o•ver•sup•ply *v.* [ˌouvərsəˈplaɪ]; *n.* [ˈouvərsəˌplaɪ] *v.* **-plied, -ply•ing;** *n., pl.* **-plies.** —*v.* supply more than is needed or wanted.
—*n.* an excessive supply.

o•vert [ouˈvɜrt] *or* [ˈouvərt] *adj.* open; evident; not hidden; public: *Hitting someone is an overt act.* ⟨ME < OF *overt*, pp. of *ovrir* open < L *aperire*⟩ **—o'vert•ly** or **'o•vert•ly,** *adv.*

o•ver•take [ˌouvərˈteik] *v.* **-took, -tak•en, -tak•ing. 1** come up with; catch up to: *If you hurry, you might be able to overtake her before she reaches her car.* **2** catch up with and pass: *They overtook us and arrived before we did.* **3** come upon suddenly: *A storm overtook the children.*

ˌo•ver'rash
ˌo•ver•re'fined
ˌo•ver•re'li•ance
ˌo•ver•re'li•gious
ˌo•ver,rep•re'sent•ed
ˌo•ver'right•eous
ˌo•ver'right•eous•ness
ˌo•ver'ripe
ˌo•ver•ro'man•ti,cize
ˌo•ver'scep•ti•cal
ˌo•ver'scru•pu•lous
ˌo•ver'sen•si•tive
ˌo•ver,sen•ti'ment•al
ˌo•ver'se•ri•ous
ˌo•ver•se'vere
ˌo•ver'sharp
ˌo•ver•so'lic•i•tous
ˌo•ver•so'phis•ti,cat•ed
ˌo•ver'spar•ing
ˌo•ver,spe•cial•i'za•tion
ˌo•ver'spe•cial,ize
ˌo•ver'spend
ˌo•ver'stim•u,late
ˌo•ver,stim•u'la•tion
ˌo•ver'strain
ˌo•ver'stretch
ˌo•ver'strict
ˌo•ver'stu•di•ous
ˌo•ver'stud•y
ˌo•ver'sub•tle
ˌo•ver•sus'cep•ti•ble
ˌo•ver•sus'pi•cious
ˌo•ver'sweet
ˌo•ver,sys•tem'at•ic
ˌo•ver'talk•a•tive

o•ver•task [ˌouvər'tæsk] *v.* give overly long or difficult tasks to.

o•ver•tax [ˌouvər'tæks] *v.* **1** tax too heavily. **2** put too heavy a burden on. **—ˌo•ver•tax'a•tion,** *n.*

o•ver–the–count•er ['ouvər ðə 'kaʊntər] *adj.* **1** of medicines, sold without a prescription. **2** of securities, sold privately and not on an exchange.

o•ver•threw [ˌouvər'θru] *v.* pp. of OVERTHROW.

o•ver•throw *v.* [ˌouvər'θrou]; *n.* ['ouvər,θrou] *v.* **-threw, -thrown, -throw•ing;** *n.* *—v.* **1** take away the power of; defeat: *to overthrow a government.* **2** put an end to; destroy: *to overthrow slavery.* **3** overturn; upset; knock down. **4** throw a ball over or past (the player or place aimed for).
—n. **1** a defeat; upset: *the overthrow of one's plans.* **2** a ball thrown over or past the player or place aimed for.

o•ver•thrown [ˌouvər'θroun] *v.* pp. of OVERTHROW.

o•ver•thrust ['ouvər,θrʌst] *n. Geology.* a fault in which rocks of an older, lower stratum are pushed on top of those of a newer, originally higher stratum.

o•ver•time *n., adv., adj.* ['ouvər,taɪm]; *v.* [ˌouvər'taɪm] *n., adv., adj., v.* **-timed, -tim•ing.** *—n.* **1** extra time; time beyond the regular hours. **2** wages for this period: *They don't pay overtime.* **3** *Sports.* a period or periods beyond the normal game time.
—adv. **1** beyond the regular hours: *She worked overtime.* **2** beyond the allotted or permitted time.
—adj. **1** of or for overtime: *overtime work.* **2** being beyond the allotted or permitted time: *overtime parking.*
—v. give too much time to: *to overtime a camera exposure.*

o•ver•tone ['ouvər,toun] *n.* **1** *Music.* a tone heard along with the main or fundamental tone and whose rate of vibration is an integral multiple of the main tone; harmonic. **2** a hint or suggestion of something felt, believed, etc.: *an overtone of anger.*

o•ver•took [ˌouvər'tʊk] *v.* pt. of OVERTAKE.

o•ver•top [ˌouvər'tɒp] *v.* **-topped, -top•ping. 1** rise above; be higher than. **2** surpass; excel.

o•ver•train [ˌouvər'trein] *v.* subject to or undergo excessive athletic training; train too hard or too much, with a resulting loss of proficiency.

o•ver•trump [ˌouvər'trʌmp] *v.* play a higher trump (than).

o•ver•ture ['ouvərtʃər] *or* ['ouvər,tʃʊr] *n.* **1** an introductory proposal or offer; the beginning of negotiations with another (*usually used in the plural*): *overtures for peace. She did not respond to his amorous overtures.* **2** *Music.* **a** a composition played by the orchestra as an introduction to an opera, oratorio, etc. **b** an independent orchestral composition having one movement. ⟨ME < OF < L *apertura* opening. Doublet of APERTURE.⟩

o•ver•turn *v.* [ˌouvər'tɜrn]; *n.* ['ouvər,tɜrn] *v., n.* *—v.* **1** turn over; upset: *The boat overturned.* **2** overthrow; destroy the power of: *The rebels overturned the government.*
—n. an overturning.
☛ *Syn. v.* **1.** See note at UPSET.

o•ver•view ['ouvər,vju] *n.* a brief, general survey.

o•ver•watch [ˌouvər'wɒtʃ] *v.* **1** watch over. **2** *Archaic.* make weary by watching.

o•ver•wea•ry [ˌouvər'wiri] *adj.* too tired.

o•ver•ween•ing [ˌouvər'winɪŋ] *adj.* thinking too much of oneself; conceited; self-confident; presumptuous. ⟨ppr. of *overween* < *over-* + *ween* expect (OE *wēnan*)⟩
—ˌo•ver'ween•ing•ly, *adv.*

o•ver•weigh [ˌouvər'wei] *v.* **1** be greater than in weight, importance, etc.; outweigh. **2** oppress; burden.

o•ver•weight *adj., n.* ['ouvər,weit]; *v.* [ˌouvər'weit] *adj., n., v.* *—adj.* **1** of a person or animal, having a mass that is too great in proportion to height and build. **2** totalling a greater mass than allowed by regulations: *overweight baggage.*
—n. more mass than is needed, desired, or specified; extra or excessive mass: *The butcher gave us overweight on this roast.*
—v. OVERWEIGH (def. 2).

o•ver•whelm [ˌouvər'wɛlm] *v.* **1** overcome completely; crush: *to overwhelm with grief.* **2** cover completely as a flood would: *A great wave overwhelmed the boat.* ⟨< *over-* + ME *whelmen* turn upside down < Gmc.; cf. ON *hvelfa* overturn⟩

o•ver•whelm•ing [ˌouvər'wɛlmɪŋ] *adj., v.* *—adj.* too many, too great, or too much to be resisted; overpowering: *an overwhelming majority of votes.*
—v. ppr. of OVERWHELM. **—ˌo•ver'whelm•ing•ly,** *adv.*

o•ver•wind [ˌouvər'waɪnd] *v.* **-wound, -wind•ing.** wind (a clock or watch) too tightly.

o•ver•win•ter [ˌouvər'wɪntər] *v.* spend the winter (in a place).

o•ver•work *n.* [ˌouvər'wɜrk] *or* ['ouvər,wɜrk]; *v.* [ˌouvər'wɜrk] *n., v.* *—n.* **1** too much or too hard work. **2** extra work.
—v. **1** work or cause to work too hard or too long: *She has a tendency to overwork her employees.* **2** *Informal.* use to excess: *to overwork a pose of childlike innocence.* **3** work too much upon (a book, speech, etc.); elaborate too much. **4** figure or decorate the surface of.

o•ver•wrap *n.* ['ouvər,ræp]; *v.* [ˌouvər'ræp] *n., v.* **-wrapped, -wrap•ping.** *—n.* a second, outside wrapper of transparent paper, cellophane, etc.
—v. wrap too much; use too much paper in wrapping.

o•ver•wrought [ˌouvər'rɒt] *adj.* **1** wearied or exhausted by too much excitement; overly excited: *overwrought nerves.* **2** decorated all over: *an overwrought platter.* **3** too elaborate.

ovi– *prefix.* egg: *oviduct.* ⟨< L; combining form of *ōvum* egg⟩

o•vi•duct ['ouvə,dʌkt] *n. Anatomy, zoology.* the tube through which the ovum, or egg, passes from the ovary. ⟨< NL *oviductus* < L *ovum* egg + *ductus* duct⟩

o•vif•er•ous [ou'vɪfərəs] *adj. Anatomy, zoology.* producing eggs.

o•vi•form ['ouvə,fɔrm] *adj.* egg-shaped. ⟨< L *ovum* egg + E *-form*⟩

o•vine ['ouvaɪn] *or* ['ouvɪn] *adj.* of, like, or having to do with sheep. ⟨< LL *ovinus* < *ovis* sheep⟩

o•vip•a•rous [ou'vɪpərəs] *adj. Zoology.* producing eggs that are hatched after leaving the body. Birds are oviparous. Compare OVOVIVIPAROUS. ⟨< L *oviparus* < *ovum* egg + *parere* bring forth⟩

o•vi•pos•it [ˌouvə'pɒzɪt] *or* ['ouvə,pɒzɪt] *v.* lay eggs. **—ˌo•vi•po'si•tion** [-pə'sɪʃən], *n.*

o•vi•pos•i•tor [ˌouvə'pɒzɪtər] *n.* an organ at the end of the abdomen of certain female insects, by which eggs are deposited. ⟨< L *ovum* egg + *positor* placer < *ponere* place⟩

o•vi•sac ['ouvə,sæk] *n. Zoology.* a capsule containing an egg.

o•void ['ouvɔɪd] *adj., n.* *—adj.* egg-shaped. Also, **ovoidal.**
—n. an egg-shaped object. ⟨< L *ovum* egg⟩

o•vo•vi•vi•par•ous [ˌouvəvə'vɪpərəs] *adj. Zoology.* producing eggs that hatch in the body. **—ˌo•voˌvi•vi'par•i•ty** [ˌouvə,vɪvə'pærəti] *or* [-'pɛrəti], *n.*

ov•u•lar ['ɒvjələr] *or* ['ouvjələr] *adj.* of or being an ovule.

ov•u•late ['ɒvjə,leit] *or* ['ouvjə,leit] *v.* **-lat•ed, -lat•ing.** *Biology.* **1** produce an ovum. **2** discharge the ovum from an ovary.

ov•u•la•tion [ˌɒvjə'leiʃən] *or* [ˌouvjə'leiʃən] *n. Biology.* **1** the period when an ovum or female germ cell is produced or formed. **2** the discharge of an ovum or ova from the ovary. ⟨ult. < NL *ovulum*, dim. of *ovum* egg⟩

ov•ule ['ɒvjul] *or* ['ouvjul] *n.* **1** *Biology.* a small ovum, especially one in an early stage of growth. **2** *Botany.* the part of a plant that develops into a seed. ⟨< NL *ovulum*, dim. of L *ovum* egg⟩

o•vum ['ouvəm] *n., pl.* **o•va** ['ouvə]. the mature female reproductive cell produced by the ovary of a plant or animal; a female gamete. A new plant or animal develops from a fertilized ovum. ⟨< L *ovum* egg⟩

owe [ou] *v.* **owed, ow•ing. 1** have to pay; be in debt to or for: *I owe the grocer $10.* **2** be in debt: *She is always owing for something.* **3** be obliged or indebted to or for. **4** have or cherish toward another: *to owe a grudge.* **5** be obliged to give or offer: *We owe friends our trust.* ⟨OE *āgan*⟩
☛ *Hom.* O, OH.

ˌo•ver'task
ˌo•ver'tech•ni•cal
ˌo•ver'tire
ˌo•ver'use
ˌo•verˌval•u'a•tion
ˌo•ver'val•ue
ˌo•ver'vi•o•lent
ˌo•ver'will•ing
ˌo•ver'wise
ˌo•ver'wor•dy
ˌo•ver'wor•ry
ˌo•ver'zeal•ous
ˌo•ver'zeal•ous•ness

ow•ing ['ouɪŋ] *adj., v. —adj.* due; owed: *to pay what is owing.*
—v. ppr. of OWE.
owing to, on account of; because of; due to; as a result of: *The ball game was called off owing to rain.*

A great grey owl—about 75 cm long including the tail

owl [aʊl] *n.* any of an order (Strigiformes) of birds of prey found throughout the world, having a very big head in proportion to the body, big eyes set in the front of the head, and a flexible neck which allows the head to be turned almost completely around to the back. Most owls are active at night. ⟨OE *ūle*⟩ **—'owl-,like,** *adj.*

owl•et ['aʊlɪt] *n.* **1** a young owl. **2** a small owl.

owl•ish ['aʊlɪʃ] *adj.* like or characteristic of an owl, especially in having large, unblinking eyes or a seemingly wise expression: *She gave me an owlish look.* **—'owl•ish•ly,** *adv.* **—'owl•ish•ness,** *n.*

own [oun] *adj., n., v. —adj.* **1** of oneself or itself; belonging to oneself or itself: *We have our own troubles. The house is her own.* **2** in closest blood relationship: *Own brothers have the same parents.*
—n. the one or ones belonging to oneself or itself.
come into (one's) **own, a** get what belongs to one. **b** get the success or credit that one deserves.
get one's own back, get revenge.
hold (one's) **own,** keep one's position; not be forced back.
of (one's) **own,** belonging to oneself.
on (one's) **own,** *Informal.* **a** on one's own account, responsibility, resources, etc. **b** alone: *The baby should never be left on her own.* **c** single: *Now she's divorced and on her own.*
—v. **1** possess: *She owns much land.* **2** acknowledge; admit, confess: *He owned his guilt. She owns to many faults.* **3** acknowledge as one's own: *His father will not own him.*
own up (to), confess; admit: *The prisoner owned up to the crime.*
⟨OE *āgen*, originally pp. of *āgan* owe⟩
☛ *Syn. v.* **1.** See note at HAVE.

own•er ['ounər] *n.* one who owns; proprietor: *the owner of the dog.* **—'own•er•less,** *adj.*

own•er•ship ['ounər,ʃɪp] *n.* the state of being an owner; the possessing (of something); right of possession.

ox [ɒks] *n., pl.* **ox•en. 1** a full-grown, castrated male of cattle, a member of the family Bovidae, usually at least three or four years old. Oxen are used as draft animals or for beef. Compare STEER². **2** any of the family Bovidae that includes cattle, the yak, and buffalo; bovine. ⟨OE *oxa*⟩ **—'ox,like,** *adj.*

oxa– *prefix.* the presence of an oxygen atom replacing carbon: *oxalic.* Also, before vowels, **ox-.**

ox•a•late ['ɒksə,leit] *n. v.* **-lat•ed, -lat•ing.** *Chemistry. —n.* a salt of oxalic acid.
—v. treat with oxalic acid.

ox•al•ic acid [ɒk'sælɪk] *Chemistry.* a poisonous, organic acid that occurs in wood sorrel and various other plants. It is used for bleaching, removing stains, making dyes, etc. *Formula*: $C_2H_2O_4$ ⟨< F < L *oxalis* sorrel² < Gk. *oxalis* < *oxys* sour⟩

ox•a•lis ['ɒksəlɪs] *or* [ɒk'sælɪs] *n.* WOOD SORREL. ⟨< L < Gk. *oxalis* < *oxys* sour⟩

ox•az•e•pam [ɒks'æzə,pæm] *n.* a drug used to relieve anxiety.

ox•blood ['ɒks,blʌd] *n.* a deep red.

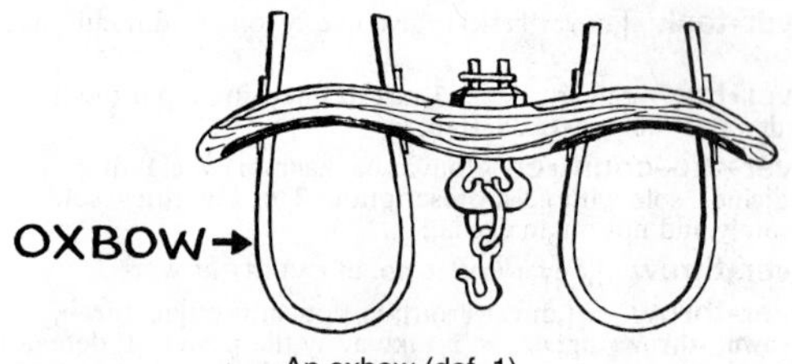

An oxbow (def. 1)

ox•bow ['ɒks,bou] *n.* **1** a U-shaped frame of wood or iron that forms the lower part of a yoke for an ox. The oxbow fits under and around the neck of the ox, with the upper ends inserted in the bar of the yoke. **2** a U-shaped bend in a river. **3** the land contained within such a bend.

oxbow lake a small pond or lake which originally formed an oxbow but which became a separated body of water when the river straightened its course.

Ox•bridge ['ɒks,brɪdʒ] *n., adj. —n.* the universities of Oxford and Cambridge, England.
—adj. of or having to do with the universities of Oxford and Cambridge: *Oxbridge attitudes.*

ox•cart ['ɒks,kɑrt] *n.* a cart drawn by an ox or oxen.

ox•en ['ɒksən] *n.* pl. of OX.

ox•eye ['ɒks,aɪ] *n.* a North American perennial plant (*Heliopsis helianthoides*) resembling a sunflower.

ox•eyed ['ɒks,aɪd] *adj.* having large, full eyes like those of an ox.

ox–eye daisy ['ɒks ,aɪ] the common North American daisy (*Chrysanthemum leucanthemum*), having large flower heads composed of tiny yellow disk flowers surrounded by white ray flowers. The ox-eye daisy was introduced to North America from Europe and has become a common weed.

ox•ford ['ɒksfərd] *n.* a kind of low shoe, laced over the instep. See SHOE for picture. ⟨< *Oxford*, a city in S England⟩

Ox•ford blue dark, sometimes purplish, blue.

oxford cloth a cotton cloth with a soft finish, in a plain or basket weave, used especially for shirts.

Oxford grey a very dark grey.

Oxford Movement 1 a movement in the Church of England, favouring High Church principles, which originated at Oxford University about 1833. **2** a modern religious movement that stresses public confession of one's faults and direct guidance by God.

ox•heart ['ɒks,hɑrt] *n.* a large, heart-shaped variety of sweet cherry.

ox•i•dant ['ɒksədənt] *n.* any reagent that oxidizes.

ox•i•dase ['ɒksə,deis] *or* ['ɒksə,deiz] *n. Biochemistry.* any animal or plant that is an oxidant.

ox•i•da•tion [,ɒksə'deiʃən] *n. Chemistry.* **1** the act or process of oxidizing; the combining of oxygen with another element to form one or more new substances. Burning is one kind of oxidation; rust is another. **2** the state or result of being oxidized.

ox•i•da•tion–re•duc•tion [,ɒksə'deiʃən rɪdʌkʃən] a reaction in which a molecule or an atom loses electrons to another molecule or atom; redox.

ox•ide ['ɒksaɪd] *n. Chemistry.* a compound of oxygen with another element or a radical. ⟨< F *oxide* (now *oxyde*) < *ox(ygène)* oxygen + *(ac)ide* acid⟩

ox•i•dize ['ɒksə,daɪz] *v.* **-dized, -diz•ing.** *Chemistry.* **1** combine with oxygen. When a substance burns or rusts, it is oxidized. **2** rust. **3** lose or cause to lose hydrogen. **4** change to a higher positive valence. **—,ox•i•di'za•tion,** *n.* **—'ox•i,diz•er,** *n.*

ox•lip ['ɒks,lɪp] *n.* a primrose (*Primula elatior*) of Europe and Asia, having clusters of pale yellow flowers. ⟨OE *oxanslyppe* < *oxan* ox's + *slyppe* slime⟩

Oxon. 1 Oxford. **2** Oxonian. **3** Oxfordshire.

Ox•o•ni•an [ɒk'souniən] *adj., n. —adj.* of or having to do with Oxford University or Oxford, England.
—n. **1** a member or graduate of Oxford University. **2** a native or inhabitant of Oxford, England. ⟨< Med.L *Oxonia* Oxford⟩

ox•pren•o•lol [ɒks'prɛnə,lɒl] *n.* a drug used to lower blood pressure.

ox•tail ['ɒks,teil] *n.* the tail of a cow, ox, or steer, skinned and cut up to make soup.

ox•tri•phyl•line [ɒks'trɪfə,lin] *n.* a drug used to treat asthma and bronchitis.

oxy–¹ *combining form.* **1** pointed: *oxymoron.* **2** acid: *oxygen.* ⟨< Gk. *oxys* sharp, acid⟩

oxy–² *combining form.* **1** oxygen, or containing oxygen or one of its compounds: *oxygenated.* **2** a product of oxidation: *oxysulphide.* ⟨< *oxygen*⟩

ox•y•a•cet•y•lene [,ɒksiə'sɛtə,lin] *adj.* of, having to do with, or using a mixture of oxygen and acetylene.

oxyacetylene torch a tool with a very hot flame for welding or cutting metals. It uses a mixture of oxygen and acetylene.

ox•y•ben•zone [,ɒksə'bɛnzoun] *n.* a sunblock.

ox•y•bu•ty•nin [,ɒksə'bjutənɪn] *n.* a drug used to treat certain bladder conditions.

ox•y•ceph•a•ly [,ɒksə'sɛfəli] *n. Pathology.* a birth defect causing the skull to be conical in shape. ⟨< G *Oxycephalie* < Gk. *oxykephalos* sharp-headed⟩ **—,ox•y•ce'phal•ic** [,ɒksəsə'fælɪk] or **,ox•y'ceph•a•lous,** *adj.*

ox•y•chlo•ro•sene [,ɒksə'klɔrə,sin] *n.* an antiseptic.

ox•y•co•done [,ɒksə'koudoun] *n.* an analgesic drug.

ox•y•gen ['ɒksədʒən] *n. Chemistry.* a colourless, odourless, tasteless gas that forms one-fifth of the air and is also combined in water and most mineral and organic substances. Oxygen is the most abundant of all elements and is essential to plant and animal life. *Symbol:* O; *at.no.* 8; *at.mass* 16.00. ⟨< F *oxygène*, intended as 'acidifying (principle)' < Gk. *oxys* sharp + *-genēs* born⟩ **—,ox•y'gen•ic** [-'dʒɛnɪk] or **ox'yg•e•nous** [ɒk'sɪdʒənəs], *adj.*

ox•y•gen•ate ['ɒksədʒə,neit] *v.* **-at•ed, -at•ing.** treat, combine, or supply with oxygen: *to oxygenate the blood.* **—,ox•y•gen'a•tion,** *n.* **—'ox•y•gen,a•tor,** *n.*

ox•y•gen•ize ['ɒksədʒə,naɪz] *v.* **-ized, -iz•ing.** oxygenate. **—'ox•y•gen,iz•a•ble,** *adj.*

oxygen mask a device worn over the nose and mouth through which oxygen is supplied from a storage tank. Oxygen masks are worn in unpressurized aircraft at high altitudes.

oxygen tent a small, clear plastic tent or canopy that can be placed over the head of a patient lying in bed and provided with a measured flow of oxygen.

ox•y•he•mo•glo•bin [,ɒksə'himə,gloubɪn] *n. Biochemistry.* a complex of oxygen with hemoglobin, taking oxygen from the lungs via the blood.

ox•y•hy•dro•gen [,ɒksə'haɪdrədʒən] *adj.* of, having to do with, or using a mixture of oxygen and hydrogen.

oxyhydrogen torch a tool with a very hot flame for welding or cutting metals. It uses a mixture of oxygen and hydrogen.

ox•y•me•ta•zo•line [,ɒksəmə'tæzə,lin] *n.* a decongestant drug.

ox•y•meth•a•lone [,ɒksə'mɛθə,loun] *n.* a drug used to treat anemia.

ox•y•mo•ron [,ɒksə'mɔrɒn] *n., pl.* **-mo•ra** [-'mɔrə]. a figure of speech in which contradictory words or connotations are placed together. *Example*: *Avoid accidents by* making haste slowly. ⟨< Gk. *oxymōron*, neuter of *oxymōros* pointedly stupid, foolish < *oxys* sharp + *mōros* stupid⟩ **—,ox•y•mo'ron•ic,** *adj.*

ox•y•mor•phone [,ɒksə'mɔrfoun] *n.* an analgesic drug. *Formula*: $C_{17}H_{19}NO_4$

ox•y•phen•bu•ta•zone [,ɒksəfɛn'bjutə,zoun] *n.* a drug used to treat arthritis.

ox•y•to•cin [,ɒksə'tousən] *n. Biochemistry.* a peptide hormone secreted by the pituitary gland, which in females causes the muscles of the uterus to contract during labour and also stimulates the release of milk from the breast of a nursing mother. *Formula*: $C_{43}H_{66}N_{12}O_{12}S_2$

o•yez or **o•yes** ['oujɛz], ['oujɛs], *or* [ou'jei] *interj. or n.* Hear! Attend! A cry uttered, usually three times, by a public or court crier to command silence and attention before a proclamation, etc. is made. ⟨ME < AF *oyez* hear ye! < *oyer* hear, var. of *oïr* < L *audire*⟩

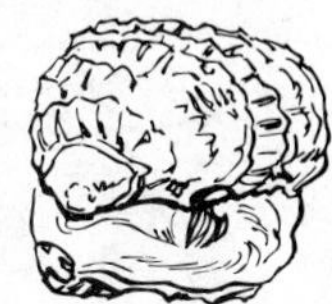

Common food oysters—
usually about 5 to 12 cm long

oys•ter ['ɔɪstər] *n.* **1** any of a family (Ostreidae) of bivalve molluscs having a rough, irregular shell; especially, any edible species of the genus *Ostrea.* **2** any of various other similar bivalve molluscs, such as the **pearl oysters** (family Aviculidae). **3** an oyster-shaped bit of dark meat in the hollow of the pelvic bone of a fowl. **4** *Informal.* a very uncommunicative person. **5** something from which to take or derive advantage: *The world is her oyster.* ⟨ME < OF *oistre* < L < Gk. *ostreon*⟩

oyster bed a place where oysters breed or are cultivated.

oyster catcher any of a small genus (*Haematopus*, constituting the family Haematopodidae) of shore birds resembling plovers, having a long, stout, wedge-shaped, red bill, long, pointed wings, and black or black-and-white plumage.

oyster crab a small crab (*Pinnotheres ostreum*) that lives within the shell of a live oyster, but without harm to its host.

oyster cracker a small, round or hexagonal, salted cracker eaten with oysters, soups, etc.

oyster farm a place where oysters are raised for the market.

oyster plant salsify.

oyster white pale yellow to light grey.

oz. ounce(s).

o•zone ['ouzoun] *n.* **1** a form of oxygen consisting of molecules composed of three atoms instead of the usual two, produced by electricity and present in the air, especially after a thunderstorm. *Formula*: O_3 **2** *Informal.* pure air that is refreshing. ⟨< F *ozone* < Gk. *ozein* smell + F *-one*, chemical suffix⟩

ozone layer ozonosphere.

ozone sickness a pathological condition caused by overexposure to ozone, as in smog and at high altitudes, characterized by drowsiness, smarting eyes, and chest pain.

o•zon•ic [ou'zɒnɪk] *or* [ou'zounɪk] *adj.* ozoniferous.

o•zo•nide ['ouzə,naɪd] *or* ['ouzou,naɪd] *n. Chemistry.* any chemical having ozone attached to an unsaturated compound.

o•zo•nif•er•ous [,ouzə'nɪfərəs] *adj.* of, having to do with, or containing ozone.

o•zon•ize ['ouzə,naɪz] *v.* **-nized, -niz•ing.** treat with ozone. **—,o•zo•ni'za•tion,** *n.*

o•zo•no•sphere [ou'zounə,sfir] *n.* a region of the upper stratosphere containing a relatively high concentration of ozone that protects earth from excessive ultraviolet radiation from the sun.

P p *P p*

p or **P** [pi] *n., pl.* **p's** or **P's. 1** the sixteenth letter of the English alphabet. **2** any speech sound represented by this letter. **3** a person or thing identified as *p*, especially the sixteenth in a series. **4** something shaped like the letter P. **5** (*adjl.*) of or being a P or p. **6** anything, such as a printer's type, a lever or a key on a keyboard, that produces a p or P.
mind (one's) **p's and q's,** be careful about what one says or does.

p 1 *Music.* piano (softly). **2** *Baseball.* pitcher. **3** *Brit.* penny; pence. **4** pressure. **5** pico- (an SI prefix). **6** *Knitting.* purl.

p. 1 page. **2** participle. **3** part. **4** past. **5** *Baseball.* pitcher. **6** peso. **7** peseta. **8** pint. **9** population. **10** *Brit.* penny; pence. **11** pressure.

P 1 phosphorus. **2** *Chess.* pawn. **3** power. **4** *Grammar.* **a** predicate. **b** phrase.

P. 1 pastor. **2** president. **3** priest. **4** prince. **5** Father (for F *père*; L *pater*).

P1 petty officer 1st class.

P2 petty officer 2nd class.

pa [pɒ] *or* [pɑ] *n. Informal.* papa; father.
☛ *Hom.* PAW [pɒ].

p.a. 1 PARTICIPIAL ADJECTIVE. **2** PER ANNUM.

Pa protactinium.

P.A. 1 PUBLIC ADDRESS (SYSTEM). **2** PRESS AGENT. **3** POWER OF ATTORNEY. **4** private account. **5** purchasing agent. **6** personal assistant.

pa'anga ['pɑŋgə] *or* [pɑ'ɑŋgə] *n., pl.* **pa'anga.** a monetary unit of Tonga, divided into 100 seniti. See table of money in the Appendix.

PABA PARA-AMINOBENZOIC ACID.

Pab•lum ['pæbləm] *n. Trademark.* a type of soft, bland, cooked cereal food for infants.

pab•u•lum ['pæbjələm] *n.* **1** food. **2** intellectual or spiritual nourishment; food for the mind. ⟨< L *pabulum* fodder⟩

pac [pæk] *n.* **1** a high laced boot, usually waterproof and lined, for cold weather wear. **2** a soft, heelless shoe worn as a liner inside a boot. ⟨shoepack⟩
☛ *Hom.* PACK.

Pac. Pacific.

pace[1] [peis] *n., v.* **paced, pac•ing.** *—n.* **1** rate of movement; speed: *a fast pace in walking.* **2** a step. **3** the length of a step in walking, used as a unit for measuring length or distance; about 76 cm. **4** a way of stepping; gait. The walk, trot, and canter are some of the paces of a horse. **5** a particular gait of some horses in which both legs on one side are raised at the same time.
change of pace, alteration of a set routine, focus of attention, etc.; variation in tempo, mood, order of presentation, etc.
go through (one's) **paces,** show off one's abilities, skills, etc.
keep pace with, keep up or up to date with.
off the pace, out of first place, as in golf: *There were several players three strokes off the pace.*
put (someone) **through** (his or her) **paces,** try someone out; find out what someone can do.
set the pace, a set a speed for others to keep up with. **b** be an example or model for others to follow.
—v. **1** set the pace for: *A motorboat will pace the training for the rowing match.* **2** walk over with regular steps: *to pace the floor.* **3** walk with regular steps. **4** measure by paces: *We paced off the distance.* **5** train (a horse) to a certain step, especially to lift and put down the feet on the same side together. **6** of a horse, move at a pace. **7** control the rate of progress of. **8** take the lead. ⟨ME < OF < L *passus* step⟩

pa•ce[2] ['pɑtʃei] *or* ['peisi] *prep.* with due respect to (*used to refer politely to someone with whom the speaker or writer disagrees*). ⟨< L *pax* peace. 19c.⟩

pace•mak•er ['peis,meikər] *n.* **1** *Medicine.* an electrical device for steadying or stimulating the heartbeat in cases where the natural pacemaker does not function properly. **2** a person who or thing that sets the pace for another, as in a race. **3** *Anatomy.* a node of specialized tissue near the top of the wall of the right auricle of the heart where the impulse that results in the heartbeat begins.

pac•er ['peisər] *n.* **1** a person who or thing that paces, especially a horse that normally runs by raising both legs on the same side at the same time. **2** a pacemaker.

pace•set•ter ['peis,sɛtər] *n.* a person who leads the way or serves as a model for others in fashion, ideas, etc.

pa•cha ['pæʃə], ['pɑʃə], *or* [pə'ʃɑ] *n.* See PASHA (def. 1).

pa•chin•ko [pə'tʃɪŋkou] *n.* a Japanese pinball game in which players can receive prizes other than money. ⟨imitative⟩

pa•chi•si [pə'tʃizi] *n.* Parcheesi.

pach•y•derm ['pækə,dɜrm] *n.* **1** any of several large, thick-skinned, hoofed mammals, such as the elephant, hippopotamus, or rhinoceros, that were formerly classified together. **2** a thick-skinned person; one who is not sensitive to criticism or ridicule. ⟨< F < Gk. *pachydermos* < *pachys* thick + *derma* skin⟩ **—,pach•y'der•mal,** *adj.*

pach•y•san•dra [,pækə'sændrə] *n.* any hardy evergreen plant of the genus *Pachysandra,* having low, dense-growing clumps of foliage, often used as a ground cover. ⟨< Gk. *pachys* thick + *aner, andros* man⟩

pa•cif•ic [pə'sɪfɪk] *adj.* **1** tending to make peace; making peace. **2** loving peace; not warlike: *a pacific nation.* **3** peaceful; calm; quiet: *a pacific nature.* **4 Pacific, a** of or having to do with the Pacific Ocean, the great ocean west of North and South America. **b** on, in, over, or near the Pacific Ocean: *a Pacific storm.* ⟨< L *pacificus,* ult. < *pax, pacis* peace + *facere* make⟩ **—pa'cif•i•cal•ly,** *adv.*

pa•cif•i•ca•to•ry [pə'sɪfəkə,tɔri] *adj.* tending to make peace; conciliatory.

Pacific Coast *Cdn.* that part of Canada that borders the Pacific Ocean, especially British Columbia.

Pacific crab apple *Cdn.* **1** a shrub or small tree (*Malus diversifolia*) growing only in British Columbia in damp areas of the coastal forest, having showy white, pink-streaked flowers. **2** the round, edible fruit of this shrub.

Pacific dogwood *Cdn.* a tree (*Cornus nuttallii*) bearing green flowers surrounded by white petal-like bracts, native to southern and eastern Vancouver Island and the adjacent Mainland Coast. It is the provincial flower of British Columbia.

Pacific lamprey a fish (*Entosphenus tridentatus*) which lives and feeds in salt water but returns to fresh water to spawn. It reaches a length of 60 cm and is found in coastal streams of British Columbia.

Pacific Northwest *Cdn.* that part of North America lying north of California and west of the Rocky Mountains, especially the coastal areas.

Pacific railway *Cdn.* formerly, the transcontinental railway completed in 1885 and later known as the Canadian Pacific Railway, linking eastern Canada with the Pacific Coast.

Pacific Rim the coastal areas and countries bordering the Pacific Ocean, especially with reference to trade and cultural relations, political agreements, etc.

Pacific salmon any of a small genus (*Oncorhynchus*) of important food and game fishes of the salmon and trout family, found in the Pacific Ocean. The five species of Pacific salmon found along the North American coast are sockeye, chum, coho, pink, and spring.

Pacific serviceberry a shrub or small tree (*Amelanchier florida*) related to other serviceberries of the same genus, having showy flowers in early spring, followed by edible purplish berries. It grows in British Columbia. Also, **service berry**.

Pacific silver fir AMABILIS FIR.

Pacific slope *Cdn.* the drainage basin of the North American rivers flowing into the Pacific Ocean.

Pacific willow a tree (*Salix lasiandra*) having dark green deciduous leaves, and growing from Alberta to the west coast, especially in the southern mainland of British Columbia and on Vancouver Island.

Pacific yew WESTERN YEW.

pac•i•fi•er ['pæsə,faɪər] *n.* **1** a person or thing that pacifies. **2** a rubber nipple or ring given to a baby to suck.

pac•i•fism ['pæsə,fɪzəm] *n.* the principle or policy of opposition to war or violence as a means of settling disputes; the refusal to take up arms or to resist violence by force.

pac•i•fist ['pæsəfɪst] *adj., n. –adj.* of or having to do with pacifism or pacifists.
–n. a person who is strongly opposed to conflict, especially war.

pac•i•fis•tic [,pæsə'fɪstɪk] *adj.* of or pertaining to pacifism or pacifists. **–,pac•i'fis•ti•cal•ly,** *adv.*

pac•i•fy ['pæsə,faɪ] *v.* **-fied, -fy•ing. 1** make calm; quiet down: *Can't you pacify that screaming baby?* **2** bring order to; make submissive: *Soldiers were sent to pacify the country.* **3** reduce the anger of; make peace with. ⟨< L *pacificare* < *pax, pacis* peace + *facere* make⟩ **–,pac•i•fi'ca•tion,** *n.*
☛ *Syn.* **1.** See note at APPEASE.

pack [pæk] *n., v., adj. –n.* **1** a bundle of things wrapped up or tied together for carrying. **2** the amount packed: *This year's pack of fish is larger than last year's.* **3** a set; lot; a number of things together: *a pack of thieves, a pack of nonsense, a pack of lies.* **4** a group of dogs, etc. trained to run and hunt together. **5** a number of wild animals running or hunting together: *a pack of wolves.* **6** a package containing a standard number: *a pack of cigarettes, a six-pack of beer.* **7** a complete set of playing cards, usually 52. **8** a large area of floating pieces of ice pushed together; ICE PACK (def. 1): *A ship forced its way through the pack.* **9** something put on the body or skin as a treatment. A cloth soaked in hot or cold water or a soothing lotion is often used as a pack. **10** a company or troop of Cubs or Brownies. **11** backpack.
–v. **1** put together in a bundle, box, bale, etc.: *Pack your clothes in this bag.* **2** put things together in a bundle, box, bale, etc.: *Are you ready to pack?* **3** fill with things; put one's things into: *Pack your trunk.* **4** fit together closely; admit of storing and shipping: *These goods pack well.* **5** press or crowd closely together: *A hundred people were packed into one small room.* **6** press together; make firm: *The heavy trucks packed the snow on the highway.* **7** fill (a space) with all that it will hold: *to pack a small theatre with a large audience.* **8** become packed; crowd together. **9** become relatively compact: *Some mud will pack easily to make bricks.* **10** put into a container to be sold or stored: *Meat, fish, and vegetables are often packed in cans.* **11** make tight with something that water, steam, air, etc. cannot leak through. **12** *Cdn.* load (an animal) with a pack; burden. **13** *Informal.* carry: *to pack a gun.* **14** *Cdn.* carry in a pack, on a pack animal, or by truck: *He packed his supplies into the bush.* **15** cover, surround, or protect with closely applied materials: *The fish was packed in ice.* **16** treat with a therapeutic pack: *to pack the gum after a tooth extraction.* **17** *Informal.* have as a power or capacity: *That guy packs quite a punch.* **18** arrange unfairly. To pack a jury or a convention is to fill it unfairly with those who will favour one side.
pack in, *Cdn.* **a** carry in one's supplies, especially on the back. **b** deliver goods by packing.
pack it in, a give up or abandon an activity: *They packed it in for the day.* **b** stop annoying someone.
pack off, send away: *The child was packed off to bed.*
pack up, *Informal.* **a** stop working; cease operating; fail: *One of the aircraft's engines packed up.* **b** die. **c** assemble or pack one's things in preparation for leaving.
send packing, send away abruptly.
–adj. **1** trained to carry goods or supplies: *a pack dog, a pack mule.* **2** used for supporting or carrying a pack: *a packsack, a packsaddle.* **3** having the characteristics of a pack: *pack ice.* ⟨ME < MLG *packe*⟩ **–'pack•a•ble,** *adj.*

pack•age ['pækɪdʒ] *n., v.* **-aged, -ag•ing.** *–n.* **1** a bundle of things packed or wrapped together; a box with things packed in it; parcel. **2 a** a box, can, bottle, jar, case, or other receptacle for packing goods, especially one designed for a particular commodity and printed with matter intended both to identify it and to attract buyers. **b** such a package with its contents, as offered for sale. **3** a finished product contained in a unit ready for immediate use: *a computer package.* **4** a group of related items or elements, such as goods, services, laws, articles of agreement in a negotiation, etc., offered, provided, sold, accepted, or rejected as a unit, often as an indivisible unit: *Our Montréal package includes transportation, hotel, and meals for a week.* **5** (*adj.*) constituting such a package: *a package tour.* **6** *Computer technology.* software and related materials (manuals, etc.) designed to perform a specific type of task and usually sold as a unit: *a word-processing package.*
–v. **1** put in a package. **2** make a package or packages out of: *to wrap and package Christmas presents.* **–'pack•ag•er,** *n.*

package deal a bargain, sale, or business deal in which a number of items are presented as a single offer.

package tour an arrangement for a holiday including airfare, hotel(s), and, sometimes, activities.

pack•ag•ing ['pækədʒɪŋ] *n., v. –n.* **1** the design and manufacture of packages. **2** the process of putting goods into such packages. **3** such packages collectively.
–v. ppr. of PACKAGE.

pack animal an animal used for carrying loads or packs.

pack•board ['pæk,bɔrd] *n. Cdn.* a light wooden or metal frame, usually covered with canvas and attached to the back by shoulder straps, used for carrying heavy loads.

pack•er ['pækər] *n.* **1** a person who or thing that packs, especially: **a** a person or company whose business is packing meat, fruit, vegetables, etc. to be sold at wholesale: *a meat packer.* **b** a person who or machine that puts things in containers for storage, preservation, or sale. **2** *Cdn.* someone who carries goods on a pack animal or on his or her own back. **3** someone who packs goods in a store after purchase. **4** *Cdn.* a person who transports goods and supplies to remote places by truck or other vehicle.

pack•et ['pækɪt] *n.* **1** a small package; parcel. **2** PACKET BOAT. **3** *Cdn.* a party carrying mail and other special deliveries between trading posts. **4** *Informal.* a lot of money. ⟨< AF *pacquet*, dim. of ME *pakke* back⟩

packet boat a boat that carries mail, passengers, and goods regularly on a fixed route, usually along a river or the coast.

pack horse a horse used to carry packs of goods.

pack ice *Cdn.* ice pushed by wind or current into a solid mass.

pack•ing ['pækɪŋ] *n., adj., v. –n.* **1** material used to pack or to make watertight, steamtight, etc.: *the packing around the valves of a radiator.* **2** the business of preparing and packing meat, fish, fruit, vegetables, etc. to be sold. **3** gauze or other sterilized material used to fill a wound or cavity to allow drainage and prevent closure. **4** *Cdn.* the transportation of goods on the backs of people or animals.
–adj. of snow, of such consistency that it packs and binds together easily.
–v. ppr. of PACK.

packing house or **plant** a place where meat, fruit, vegetables, etc. are prepared and packed to be sold.

pack•man ['pækmən] *n., pl.* **-men.** formerly, a person who transported goods on his own back; a peddler.

pack mule a mule used for carrying loads.

pack rat 1 a wood rat; especially, a large, bushy-tailed species (*Neotoma cinerea*) found especially in the Rocky Mountains and the interior of British Columbia, well-known for picking up and hoarding objects of various kinds. **2** *Informal.* a person who has a tendency to hoard objects, especially useless ones.

pack•sack ['pæk,sæk] *n.* a bag of canvas, nylon, or leather for carrying gear, clothing, etc. when hiking or on the trail, usually worn strapped to the back; knapsack.

pack•sad•dle ['pæk,sædəl] *n.* a saddle specially adapted for supporting the load on a pack animal.

Pack Scouter *Cdn.* an adult responsible for the operation of a pack of Cubs.

pack strap *Cdn.* tumpline.

pack•thread ['pæk,θrɛd] *n.* a strong thread or twine for sewing or tying up packages.

pack train a line or group of animals carrying loads.

pack•y ['pæki] *adj.* **pack•i•er, pack•i•est.** *Cdn.* packing.

pact [pækt] *n.* an agreement; compact: *The two nations signed a peace pact.* ⟨< L *pactum*, originally, pp. of *pacisci* covenant⟩

pad¹ [pæd] *n., v.* **pad•ded, pad•ding.** *–n.* **1** something soft used for comfort, protection, or stuffing; cushion. **2** a soft, stuffed saddle. **3** one of the cushionlike parts on the bottom side of the feet of dogs, foxes, and some other animals. **4** the foot of such animals. **5** a large floating leaf of a water lily or similar water plant. **6** a number of sheets of paper fastened along an edge or edges; tablet: *a writing pad.* **7** a cloth soaked with ink to use with a rubber stamp; stamp pad. **8** the launching platform for a rocket or missile; launching pad: *The artificial satellite rose from the pad at midnight.* **9** *Slang.* a place where a person sleeps, such as a bed, a room, an apartment, etc. **10** SANITARY NAPKIN.
–v. **1** fill with something soft; stuff. **2** make (a paper or speech) longer by using unnecessary words just to fill space or time: *Don't pad your compositions.* **3** increase the amount of (a bill, expense account, etc.) by false entries. ⟨origin uncertain⟩

pad² [pæd] *v.* **pad•ded, pad•ding;** *n. –v.* **1** walk; tramp; trudge. **2** walk or trot softly, with a muffled sound: *a wolf padding through the bush.*
–n. **1** a dull or muffled sound, as of footsteps on the ground: *We*

heard the pad of hoofs on the path. **2** a slow horse for riding on a road. ⟨< Du. or LG. Akin to PATH.⟩

pad•ded cell ['pædɪd] in a psychiatric hospital, a room having padded walls to prevent a violent patient from injuring himself or herself.

pad•ding ['pædɪŋ] *n., v.* —*n.* **1** material used to pad with, such as foam rubber, cotton or synthetic fibre, or straw. **2** unnecessary words used to make a speech or a written paper longer.
—*v.* ppr. of PAD.

pad•dle[1] ['pædəl] *n., v.* **-dled, -dling.** —*n.* **1** a short oar with a broad blade at one end or both ends, used without resting it against the boat. **2** a similar but smaller object with a rounded blade and a short handle, used as a racket for table tennis, etc. **3** the act of paddling; a turn at the paddle. **4** one of the broad boards fixed around a water wheel or a paddle wheel to push, or be pushed by, the water. **5** a paddle-shaped piece of wood used for stirring, for mixing, for beating clothes, etc. **6** a special handle with a wheel, by which the user can control the action in electronic games. **7** *Cdn.* a canoe journey; the distance that can be covered by a canoe in a specified time: *a short paddle away.*
—*v.* **1** move (a boat or canoe) with a paddle or paddles. **2** use a paddle to move a canoe, etc. **3** row gently. **4** *Informal.* beat with a paddle or something similar; spank. **5** stir, mix, etc. with a paddle.
paddle one's own canoe, act independently; look after one's own affairs. ⟨origin uncertain⟩ —**'pad•dler,** *n.*

pad•dle[2] ['pædəl] *v.* **-dled, -dling. 1** move the hands or feet about in water. **2** wade barefoot in water: *Children love to paddle at the beach.* ⟨apparently < *pad*[2]⟩ —**'pad•dler,** *n.*

pad•dle•fish ['pædəl,fɪʃ] *n., pl.* **-fish** or **-fish•es.** either of two large freshwater fishes, *Polyodon spathula* of the Mississippi River valley and *Psephurus gladius* of the Yangtze River valley, comprising the family Polyodontidae. Both species have a smooth, scaleless body and a very long, flat snout resembling a spatula.

paddle wheel a wheel having an arrangement of paddles around its rim, used for propelling a boat.

pad•dle•wheel•er ['pædəl,wilər] *n.* a boat propelled by means of one or more PADDLE WHEELS.

paddling song ['pædlɪŋ] *Cdn.* BOAT SONG.

pad•dock ['pædək] *n., v.* —*n.* **1** a small field near a stable or house, used for exercising animals or as a pasture. **2** an enclosure at a racetrack for saddling and displaying horses before they race.
—*v.* enclose or confine in a paddock. ⟨var. of *parrock,* OE *pearroc* enclosed space, fence < Med.L *parricus* enclosure. Doublet of PARK.⟩

pad•dy ['pædi] *n., pl.* **-dies. 1** rice, especially before threshing or in the husk. **2** a field of rice. ⟨< Malay *padi*⟩

paddy wagon *Slang.* PATROL WAGON.

pad•lock ['pæd,lɒk] *n., v.* —*n.* a removable lock having a hinged bar that is passed through a loop or eye in the door, box, etc. to be locked, and is then snapped shut.
—*v.* **1** fasten with such a lock. **2** secure (a building) against entrance, by any means.

pa•dre ['pɑdrei] *n.* **1** father. It is used as a name for a priest. **2** a chaplain in the armed forces. **3** a chaplain at certain universities. ⟨< Ital., Sp., Pg. < L *pater* father⟩

pae•an ['piən] *n.* a song of praise, joy, or triumph. Also, **pean.** ⟨< L < Gk. *paian* hymn to Apollo (called *Paian*)⟩
☛ *Hom.* PEON ['piən].

paed•er•ast ['pɛdə,ræst] See PEDERAST.

paed•er•as•ty ['pɛdə,ræsti] See PEDERASTY.

pae•dol•o•gy [pi'dɒlədʒi] See PEDOLOGY[1].

pa•el•la [pɑ'jɛlə]; *Spanish,* [pa'elja] *or* [pa'eja] a Spanish dish made of rice flavoured with saffron, chicken, shrimps, vegetables, etc.

pa•gan ['peigən] *n., adj.* —*n.* a person who is not a Christian, Jew, or Muslim; a heathen. The ancient Greeks and Romans were pagans.
—*adj.* **1** of or having to do with the pagans: *pagan customs.* **2** not religious. ⟨< L *paganus* rustic (at a time when Christianity was accepted by the urban population), in LL, heathen < *pagus* village⟩
☛ *Usage.* Both **pagan** and HEATHEN have a basic connotation of 'unenlightened' or 'unbelieving'. People belonging to established religions other than Christian, Jewish, and Muslim object to being called pagan. **Heathen,** in particular, is sometimes used as a term of insult. The words, therefore, are best used in historical contexts: *Julius Caesar was a pagan. The Goths were heathen.*

pa•gan•dom ['peigəndəm] *n.* the pagan world; pagans collectively.

pa•gan•ism ['peigə,nɪzəm] *n.* **1** pagan beliefs and practices. **2** a pagan religion. **3** the quality or state of being pagan.

page[1] [peidʒ] *n., v.* **paged, pag•ing.** —*n.* **1** one side of a leaf or sheet of paper: *The book has 350 pages.* **2** a leaf or sheet of paper, especially in a book, magazine, etc.: *The page was torn. Write on only one side of the page.* **3** what is printed, written, or pictured on one side of a leaf: *This page is hard to read.* **4** type arranged for printing a page. **5** a written record: *the pages of history.* **6** an event or period worth recording: *a glorious page in the history of the country.* **7** *Computer technology.* **a** a relatively small unit of storage, made up of one or more blocks. **b** a block of stored program instructions. **c** in word processing, part of a document. **d** a file on the WORLD WIDE WEB.
—*v.* **1** number the pages of: *Make sure you page your essay.* **2** make up (already typeset copy) into pages. **3** turn pages rapidly in scanning (*used with* **through**): *You need only page through this book to understand it.* ⟨< F < L *pagina* < *pangere* fasten⟩

page[2] [peidʒ] *n., v.* **paged, pag•ing.** —*n.* **1** a servant, often a boy, who runs errands, carries hand luggage, etc. for guests at hotels, etc. **2** a young person employed to carry messages, books, etc. for members of the House of Commons, the Senate, or a legislative assembly. **3** a young man who attends a person of rank. **4** formerly, a young man preparing to be a knight.
—*v.* **1** try to get a message to a person by means of an announcement, by a page, an electronic pager, or on a public address system. **2** act as a page to. ⟨ME < OF < Ital. *paggio,* ult. < Gk. *paidion* lad, dim. of *pais, paidos* child⟩

pag•eant ['pædʒənt] *n.* **1** an elaborate spectacle; procession in costume; pomp; display: *The coronation of the new king was a splendid pageant.* **2** a public entertainment that represents scenes from history, legend, or the like. **3** empty show, not reality. ⟨ME *pagent, pagen* < Med.L *pagina* movable scaffold fixed with planks, serving as a stage < L *pangere* fix⟩

pag•eant•ry ['pædʒəntri] *n., pl.* **-ries. 1** a splendid show; gorgeous display; pomp and ceremony. **2** mere show; empty display.

page•boy ['peidʒ,bɔɪ] *n.* **1** a boy serving as a page. **2** a hairstyle in which the hair, usually about shoulder length, is curled smoothly under at the ends.

pag•er ['peidʒər] *n.* a small, portable electric device used to page someone; beeper.

pag•i•nate ['pædʒə,neit] *v.,* **pag•i•nat•ed, pag•i•nat•ing.** number the pages of (books, etc.).

pag•i•na•tion [,pædʒə'neiʃən] *n.* **1** the act of numbering the pages of books, etc. **2** the figures with which pages are numbered. **3** the number and arrangement of pages in a book, etc., as described in a bibliography or catalogue.

A pagoda in the Chinese style of architecture

pa•go•da [pə'goudə] *n.* a temple having many storeys, usually an odd number, with a roof curving upward from each storey. Pagodas are found especially in India and the Far East, often constructed over a sacred relic. ⟨< Pg. *pagode* < Tamil *pagavadi* < Skt. *bhagavati* of a goddess < *bhagavat* a deity⟩

pa•ho•e•ho•e [pə'houi,houi] *n.* in Hawaii, lava that has hardened with a smooth, undulating surface. ⟨< Hawaiian⟩

paid [peid] *adj., v.* —*adj.* **1** receiving money; hired. **2** no longer owed; settled. **3** cashed.
—*v.* a pt. and pp. of PAY[1].
☛ *Usage.* **Paid,** PAYED. **Paid** is the spelling of the past tense and past participle of *pay*[1] (He *paid* his bills) in all senses except 'let out' (They *payed out* the rope), and occasionally in that sense also.

pail [peil] *n.* **1** a fairly large, usually cylindrical container with outward sloping sides, for carrying liquids, having a wide top and a handle that is attached at each side and arches over the top. **2** the amount a pail holds: *It will take a pail of milk to fill all those jugs.* **3** a pail and its contents: *We need milk; go get a pail from the barn.* ⟨OE *pægel* and < OF *paielle*, both < Med.L *pagella* a measure, dim. of L *pagina*, originally, something fixed⟩
☛ *Hom.* PALE.

pail•ful ['peil,fʊl] *n., pl.* **-fuls.** the amount that fills a pail.

pail•lasse [pæl'jæs] *or* ['pæljæs] *n.* See PALLIASSE. ⟨< F *paillasse* < *paille* straw < L *palea*⟩

pail•lette [pæl'jɛt], [paɪ'jɛt], [pei'ɛt], *or* [pə'lɛt]; *French,* [pa'jɛt] *n.* **1** a small shiny ornament used as decoration on women's clothing; spangle. **2** a small piece of metal or foil as an ornament on enamel work. ⟨< F *paillette*, dim. of *paille* straw⟩

pain [pein] *n., v.* —*n.* **1** an unpleasant sensation in the body or a particular part of it, due to some stimulus of the nerve endings from injury, disorder, or disease: *A cut usually causes pain. She felt a sharp pain in her back.* **2** mental suffering; grief: *The memory still gave her pain.* **3 pains,** *pl.* **a** care; effort; trouble to do something: *He said he would not interfere, because he would get nothing but trouble for his pains.* **b** the throes of childbirth; spasms of labour: *The pains had started.* **4** *Archaic* (*except in* **on** *or* **under pain of**). punishment; penalty.
be at pains, make a conscientious effort: *She was at great pains to make them understand.*
on or **under pain of,** subject to the penalty of (if a given command is not fulfilled): *They were ordered never to return on pain of death.*
pain in the neck, *Slang.* a very troublesome or irritating thing or person.
take pains, be careful: *She took pains to do a good job.*
—*v.* cause to suffer; give rise to pain; ache: *His tooth was paining him a great deal.* ⟨ME < OF *peine* < L *poena* penalty < Gk. *poinē*⟩
☛ *Hom.* PANE.
☛ *Syn. n.* **Pain,** ACHE = a feeling of being hurt, bodily or mentally. **Pain** particularly suggests a sharp hurt of any degree from a sudden jab in one spot to a very severe and sometimes long-lasting hurt of the whole body, or, figuratively, a sorrow that causes severe mental suffering: *I have a pain in my side.* **Ache** means a steady, usually dull hurt, and, when used figuratively, suggests longing for something.

pained [peind] *adj., v.* —*adj.* **1** distressed, grieved, mentally hurt, etc. **2** showing pain: *a pained face.*
—*v.* pt. and pp. of PAIN.

pain•ful ['peinfəl] *adj.* **1** causing pain; unpleasant; hurting: *a painful illness, a painful duty.* **2** feeling pain: *My finger is painful where I trapped it in the door.* **3** difficult: *Balancing accounts can be a painful job.* **4** produced with difficulty: *a long, painful speech by the bride's father.* —**'pain•ful•ly,** *adv.* —**'pain•ful•ness,** *n.*

pain•kill•er ['pein,kɪlər] *n.* anything, especially a drug, that relieves pain. —**'pain,kil•ling,** *adj.*

pain•less ['peinlɪs] *adj.* causing or producing no pain: *The treatment is painless.* —**'pain•less•ly,** *adv.* —**'pain•less•ness,** *n.*

pains•tak•ing ['peinz,teikɪŋ] *adj.* **1** very careful. **2** using or showing great care or effort on the part of the doer.
—**'pains,tak•ing•ly,** *adv.*

paint [peint] *n., v.* —*n.* **1 a** a mixture of a solid colouring matter and liquid that can be put on a surface to dry as a coloured coating. **b** the solid colouring matter alone; pigment: *a box of paints.* **c** a dried coat of paint: *There is a mark on the fresh paint.* **2** any cosmetic that colours or tints, such as blusher or lipstick.
—*v.* **1** cover or decorate with paint: *to paint a house.* **2** use paint. **3** represent (an object, etc.) in paint. **4** make pictures with paint: *She spends her weekends painting.* **5** picture vividly in words. **6** put on (antiseptic) so as to cover: *The doctor painted iodine on the cut.* **7** use cosmetics to colour or tint.
paint black, represent as evil or wicked: *not so black as he is painted.* ⟨ME < OF *peint*, pp. of *peindre* paint < L *pingere*⟩

paint•brush ['peint,brʌʃ] *n.* **1** a brush for applying paint. **2** INDIAN PAINTBRUSH.

paint•ed–cup ['peintɪd 'kʌp] *n.* INDIAN PAINTBRUSH.

painted trillium a wildflower (*Trillium undulatum*) having red markings at the base of each wavy-edged petal. It can grow to a height of 30 cm, and blooms in forests in May and June.

paint•er[1] ['peintər] *n.* **1** a person who paints pictures; artist. **2** a person who paints houses, woodwork, etc. ⟨< OF *peintour*, ult. < L *pictor* < *pingere* to paint⟩

paint•er[2] ['peintər] *n.* a rope, usually fastened to the bow of a boat, for tying it to a ship, pier, etc. ⟨prob. < OF *pentoir* hanging cordage, ult. < L *pendere* hang⟩

paint•er[3] ['peintər] *n. Dialect.* cougar. ⟨variant of *panther*⟩

paint•er•ly ['peintərli] *adj.* **1** of, having to do with, or characteristic of a painter. **2** of or designating a style of painting that emphasizes the qualities peculiar to the medium of paint, such as texture or masses of colour, as opposed to linear elements.

painter's colic ['peintərz] a type of lead poisoning characterized by acute intestinal pain. ⟨from the inhalation by painters of fumes from lead-based paint⟩

paint•ing ['peintɪŋ] *n., v.* —*n.* **1** the art or occupation of using paints to create pictures or other artistic compositions. **2** a work produced by the art of painting. **3** the act or process of applying paint to a surface.
—*v.* ppr. of PAINT.

pair [pɛr] *n., pl.* **pairs** or (*sometimes after a numeral*) **pair;** *v.* —*n.* **1** a set of two; two that go together: *a pair of shoes, a pair of horses.* **2** a single thing consisting of two parts that cannot be used separately: *a pair of scissors, a pair of pants.* **3** two people who are married or are engaged to be married. **4** two partners in a dance. **5** two animals that are mated. **6** *Card games.* **a** two cards of the same value in different suits, viewed as a unit in one's hand: *a pair of sixes, jacks, etc.* **b** in games using a multiple deck, two identical cards. **7** in a legislative body: **a** two members on opposite sides who arrange not to vote on a certain question. **b** the arrangement thus made.
—*v.* **1** arrange or be arranged in pairs. **2** join in marriage. **3** of animals, mate. **4** in a legislative body, form or cause to form a voting pair.
pair off or **up,** arrange or form into pairs: *The guests paired off for the first dance.* ⟨< F *paire* < L *paria*, neut. pl., equals⟩
☛ *Hom.* PARE, PEAR, PÈRE.
☛ *Syn. n.* **1. Pair,** COUPLE = two of the same kind. **Pair** applies to two things that belong together because they go together to make a set, because they are used together and each is needed to make the other useful, or because they are so well matched they seem to belong together: *I bought a new pair of gloves.* **Couple** applies to any two of the same kind: *I bought a couple of shirts.* **Couple** is also used of people: *the happy couple.*
☛ *Usage.* **Pair.** In informal usage the plural of **pair** is sometimes **pair** when it comes after a number: *six pair of socks.* Some people now consider this usage non-standard.
☛ *Usage.* When a **pair** is thought of as a unit, it takes a singular verb: *This pair of shoes is getting old.* When a **pair** is thought of as referring to two individual items, it takes a plural verb: *The pair of vases were both chipped.*

pair•ing ['pɛrɪŋ] *n., v.* —*n.* **1 a** the grouping of individual competitors or teams in a tournament into opposing pairs. **b pairs,** *pl.* the list of such groupings. **2** in a legislative body, the act of arranging a PAIR (def. 7).
—*v.* ppr. of PAIR.

pair skating a form of competitive skating in which a man and a woman perform choreographed moves on ice, including acrobatic movements to music. Also, **pairs.**

pai•sa ['pəisɑ] *n., pl.* **pai•se** ['pəisei] in India, **pai•sa** in Nepal, **pai•sas** in Pakistan. **1** a unit of money in India, Nepal, and Pakistan, equal to 1/100 of a rupee. **2** a coin worth one paisa. See table of money in the Appendix. ⟨< Hind.⟩

pais•ley ['peizli] *n., pl.* **-leys;** *adj.* —*n.* **1** an elaborate, colourful fabric design of curving lines and figures: *silk paisley.* **2** something made of this fabric.
—*adj.* made of fabric having a paisley design; having a design like paisley. ⟨< *Paisley*, a city in Scotland, where woollen shawls having this design were first made⟩

Pai•ute [paɪ'ut] *or* ['paɪut] *n.* **1** a member of an American Indian people living in SW U.S. **2** either of two Uto-Aztecan languages spoken by these people.

pa•ja•mas [pə'dʒæməz] *or* [pə'dʒɑməz] See PYJAMAS.

Pak•i•stan ['pækə,stæn] *n.* properly, the Islamic Republic of Pakistan, a country in S Asia between India and Afghanistan, on the Arabian Sea, formerly called West Pakistan.

Pak•i•stan•i [,pækə'stæni] *n., adj.* —*n.* **1** a native or inhabitant of Pakistan. **2** *Cdn.* a Canadian resident born in Pakistan or descended from Pakistanis.
—*adj.* of or having to do with Pakistan or its people.

pal [pæl] *n., v.* **palled, pal•ling.** *Informal.* —*n.* a comrade; mate; partner; chum; accomplice.
—*v.* associate as pals. ⟨< Romany *pal* brother, var. of *pral* or *plal*, ult. < Skt. *bhratr* brother⟩

pal•ace ['pælɪs] *n.* **1** the official home of a king, queen, bishop, or some other important person. **2** a very fine house or official building: *the palace of justice.* **3** a gaudy or pretentious place of entertainment: *an old movie palace.* ⟨ME < OF *palais*

< L *Palatium* Palatine Hill, the site of the Roman emperor's palace⟩

pal•a•din [ˈpælədɪn] *n.* **1** one of the twelve knights in attendance on Charlemagne. **2** a knightly defender. ⟨< F < Ital. *paladino*⟩

palaeo– See PALEO-.

pa•laes•tra [pəˈlɛstrə] *n., pl.* **pa•laes•tras** or **pa•laes•trae** [pəˈlɛstri]. **1** in ancient Greece, a public place for physical exercise and training. **2** a wrestling school. ⟨< L < Gk. *palaistra* < *palaiein* wrestle⟩

pal•an•quin or **pal•an•keen** [ˌpælənˈkin] *n.* a covered couch, or litter, for one person, carried by means of poles resting on the shoulders of four or six men. They were formerly used in E Asia. ⟨< Pg. *palanquim*; cf. Skt. *palyanka* couch⟩

pal•at•a•ble [ˈpælətəbəl] *adj.* agreeable to the taste; pleasing. **—ˈpal•at•a•bly,** *adv.*

pal•a•tal [ˈpælətəl] *adj., n. —adj.* **1** of or having to do with the palate. **2** *Phonetics.* designating a sound made with the blade of the tongue near or in contact with the hard palate. The [j] in *yet* is palatal.
—n. Phonetics. a palatal sound. ⟨< F < L *palatum* palate⟩

pal•a•tal•ize [ˈpælətəˌlaɪz] *v.* **-ized, -iz•ing.** *Phonetics.* change into or pronounce as a palatal sound. **—ˌpal•a•tal•iˈza•tion,** *n.*

pal•ate [ˈpælɪt] *n.* **1** the roof of the mouth. The bony part in front is the **hard palate;** the fleshy part at the back is the **soft palate. 2** the sense of taste: *The new ice cream flavour pleased the children's palates.* **3** a liking. ⟨< L *palatum*⟩
☛ *Hom.* PALETTE, PALLET.

pa•la•tial [pəˈleiʃəl] *adj.* like or fit for a palace; magnificent: *a palatial apartment.* ⟨< L *palatium* palace⟩ **—paˈla•tial•ly,** *adv.*

pa•lat•i•nate [pəˈlætənɪt] *or* [pəˈlætəˌneit] *n.* **1** a territory under the rule of a count palatine. See PALATINE (def. 1). **2** an inhabitant or native of a palatinate. **3 the Palatinate,** a region in Germany, west of the Rhine.

pal•a•tine [ˈpæləˌtaɪn] *or* [ˈpælətɪn] *adj., n. —adj.* **1** having royal rights in one's own territory. A count palatine was subject only to the emperor or king. **2** belonging to or having to do with a lord having such rights. **3** palatial. **4 Palatine,** of the Palatinate.
—n. **1** a lord having royal rights in his own territory. **2 Palatine,** a native or inhabitant of the Palatinate. **3 Palatine,** the Palatine Hill. ⟨< L *palatinus*, adj., < *palatinum* palace⟩

Palatine Hill one of the seven hills on which the city of Rome was built.

pa•lav•er [pəˈlævər] *or* [pəˈlɑvər] *n., v. —n.* **1** a parley or conference, especially (in historical use) between European travellers or explorers and African natives. **2** empty or idle talk. **3** smooth, persuading talk; fluent talk; flattery. **4** fuss and bother.
—v. **1** talk idly. **2** talk fluently or flatteringly (to). ⟨< Pg. *palavra* < L *parabola* story, parable. Doublet of PARABLE, PAROLE.⟩

pa•laz•zo [pəˈlɑtsou] *n., pl.* **pa•laz•zi** [-lɑtsi]. **1** *Italian.* a palace or mansion. **2 palazzos** or **palazzo pants,** a type of women's pants with long, full, or flared legs; a long divided skirt; culottes.

pale[1] [peil] *adj.* **pal•er, pal•est;** *v.* **paled, pal•ing.**
—adj. **1** without much colour; whitish: *Her face is still pale after her illness.* **2** not intense or bright; faint or dim: *pale blue. The streetlight gave a pale light in the fog.* **3** lacking vigour; feeble: *a pale foreign policy.*
—v. **1** turn or cause to turn pale: *Helen's face paled at the bad news.* **2** appear weaker or less significant by comparison: *Our present troubles pale beside those of other countries.* ⟨ME < OF < L *pallidus* < *pallere* be pale. Doublet of PALLID.⟩ **—ˈpale•ly,** *adv.* **—ˈpale•ness,** *n.*
☛ *Hom.* PAIL.
☛ *Syn. adj.* **1. Pale,** PALLID, WAN = with little or no colour. **Pale,** describing the face of a person, means 'without much natural or healthy colour', and describing things, 'without much brilliance or depth': *She is pale and tired-looking. The walls are pale green.* **Pallid,** chiefly describing the face, suggests having all colour drained away as by sickness or weakness: *Her pallid face shows her suffering.* **Wan** emphasizes the idea of a faintness and whiteness coming from a weakened or unhealthy condition: *The starved refugees looked wan.*

pale[2] [peil] *n., v.* **paled, pal•ing.** *—n.* **1** a long, narrow board pointed at the top, used for fences; picket. **2** enclosure. **3** a territory with fixed bounds, under a particular jurisdiction or subject to particular restrictions. **4** a boundary; the limits within which one has a right to protection: *Murder is an act outside the pale of society.* **5** *Heraldry.* a broad vertical stripe in the middle of an escutcheon.
beyond the pale, outside the norm of usual behaviour: *Their bad behaviour at the concert was completely beyond the pale.*
—v. enclose with pales. ⟨ME < OF *pal* < L *palus.* Doublet of POLE[1].⟩
☛ *Hom.* PAIL.

pale– *combining form.* the form of **paleo-** usually used before vowels, as in *paleontology.*
☛ *Hom.* PAIL.

pale corydalis a Canadian wildflower (*Corydalis sempervivens*) having pink and yellow flowers which bloom from May to September in rocky places.

paleo– *combining form.* **1** old; ancient: *paleography = ancient writing.* **2** of a relatively early time division: *Paleocene = the earliest epoch of the Tertiary period.* **3** having to do with (something specified) of a remote time period: *paleoanthropology, paleogeography.* Also, **palaeo-.** ⟨< Gk. *palaio-* < *palaios* ancient⟩

Pa•le•o•cene [ˈpeiliəˌsin] *or* [ˈpæliəˌsin] *n., adj. Geology.*
—n. **1** the oldest epoch of the Tertiary period, before the Eocene. See geological time chart in the Appendix. **2** the rocks formed during this period.
—adj. of or having to do with this epoch, its strata, etc. ⟨< *paleo-* + Gk. *kainos* new⟩

pa•le•og•ra•pher [ˌpeiliˈɒgrəfər] *or* [ˌpæliˈɒgrəfər] *n.* a person trained in paleography, especially one whose work it is.

pa•le•og•ra•phy [ˌpeiliˈɒgrəfi] *or* [ˌpæliˈɒgrəfi] *n.* **1** ancient writing or ancient forms of writing. **2** the study of ancient writings to determine their dates, origins, meaning, etc. **—ˌpa•le•oˈgraph•ic,** *adj.*

Pa•le•o•lith•ic [ˌpeiliəˈlɪθɪk] *or* [ˌpæliəˈlɪθɪk] *n., adj. —n.* the earlier part of the Stone Age, characterized by the use of stone, flint, and later, bone tools.
—adj. of or having to do with this period.

pa•le•on•tol•o•gist [ˌpeiliənˈtɒlədʒɪst] *or* [ˌpæliənˈtɒlədʒɪst] *n.* a person trained in paleontology, especially one whose work it is.

pa•le•on•tol•o•gy [ˌpeiliənˈtɒlədʒi] *or* [ˌpæliənˈtɒlədʒi] *n.* the science that deals with the forms of life existing long ago in other geological periods, as known from fossil remains of animals and plants.

Pa•le•o•zo•ic [ˌpeiliəˈzouɪk] *or* [ˌpæliəˈzouɪk] *adj., n. Geology. —adj.* **1** of, having to do with, or designating the era before the Mesozoic era, beginning about 600 million years ago. The Paleozoic era is the age of fishes. See geological time chart in the Appendix. **2** of, having to do with, or designating the system of rocks formed during this era.
—n. the Paleozoic era or its rock system. ⟨< *paleo-* + Gk. *zōē* life⟩

Pal•es•tine [ˈpæləˌstaɪn] *n.* **1** a former ancient territory on the E coast of the Mediterranean Sea in SW Asia, also known as the **Holy Land. 2** the British Mandate of this area (1923-1948), including parts of modern Egypt, Israel, and Jordan.

Palestine Liberation Organization an organization representing the Palestinian people of Israel, Lebanon, Jordan, and Syria. *Abbrev.:* PLO or P.L.O.

Pal•es•tin•ian [ˌpæləˈstɪniən] *n., adj. —n.* a native or inhabitant of Palestine.
—adj. of or having to do with natives or inhabitants of Palestine.

pal•ette [ˈpælɪt] *n.* **1** a thin board, usually oval or oblong, with a thumb hole at one end, used by painters to lay and mix colours on. **2** a set of colours on this board. **3** the range or quality of colour used by an artist: *Gauguin used a bright palette.* ⟨< F *palette* < L *pala* spade⟩
☛ *Hom.* PALATE, PALLET.

palette knife a tool used by artists for mixing colours on a palette, etc. and consisting of a thin, flexible, blunt-tipped steel blade set into a handle.

pal•frey [ˈpɒlfri] *n., pl.* **-freys.** *Archaic or poetic.* a gentle riding horse, especially one used by ladies. ⟨ME < OF *palefrey* < LL *paraveredus* < Gk. *para-* beside + L *veredus* light horse < Celtic⟩

Pa•li [ˈpɑli] *n.* the religious language of Buddhism.

pa•li•mo•ny [ˈpæləˌmouni] *n. Informal.* money paid to a lover on the breakup of the relationship. ⟨modelled on *alimony*⟩

pal•imp•sest [ˈpælɪmpˌsɛst] *n.* a piece of parchment or other writing material from which one writing has been erased to make room for another; a manuscript with one text written over another. ⟨< L < Gk. *palimpsestos* scraped again, ult. < *palin* again + *psaein* rub smooth⟩

pal•in•drome ['pælın,droum] *n.* a word, phrase, sentence, or number which reads the same backward as forward. The sentence *Madam, I'm Adam* is a palindrome, as is the number 1 234 321 ⟨< Gk. *palindromos* a running back < *palin* again, back + *dromos* a running, related to *dramein* run⟩

pal•ing ['peilıŋ] *n., v. —n.* **1** a fence of pales. **2** pales collectively, as fencing material. **3** a pale in a fence. **4** the act of constructing a fence of pales.
—v. ppr. of PALE.

pal•i•node ['pælə,noud] *n.* **1** a retraction in verse of something said in a previous poem by the same author. **2** any retraction or recantation. ⟨< Gk. *palin* again, back + *ōidē* song, ode⟩

pal•i•sade [,pælı'seid] *or* ['pælə,seid] *n., v.* **-sad•ed, -sad•ing.** *—n.* **1** a high fence of heavy, pointed wooden stakes set firmly in the ground, built especially for defence. **2** one of the stakes used in such a fence. **3** Usually, **palisades,** *pl.* a line of high, steep cliffs.
—v. furnish or surround with a palisade. ⟨< F *palissade* < Provençal *palissada* < L *palus* stake⟩

palisade layer *Botany.* the **palisade parenchyma,** a layer of cells shaped like cylinders, lying below the upper epidermis of many leaves and serving to produce chlorophyll.

pal•ish ['peilıʃ] *adj.* somewhat pale.

pall[1] [pɒl] *n.* **1** a heavy cloth, often made of velvet, spread over a coffin, a hearse, or a tomb. **2** a dark, gloomy covering: *A pall of smoke shut out the sun from the city.* ⟨OE *pæll* < L *pallium* cloak⟩
☛ *Hom.* PAWL, POL.

pall[2] [pɒl] *v.* **1** become distasteful or very tiresome. **2** cloy (*used with* **on**): *The thought of sitting through another long lecture palled on her.* ⟨var. of *appall*⟩
☛ *Hom.* PAWL, POL.

Pal•la•di•an[1] [pə'leidiən] *adj.* of, having to do with, or based on the classical Roman style of architecture as modified by the Italian architect Andrea Palladio (1518-1580).

Pal•la•di•an[2] [pə'leidiən] *adj.* **1** of or having to do with the goddess Pallas Athena. **2** Also, **palladian,** concerning learning, study, or wisdom.

Palladian window a window consisting of a central section with a rounded top, with a flat-topped section on either side on which the arch of the central section rests.

pal•la•di•um[1] [pə'leidiəm] *n. Chemistry.* a rare, silver-white metallic chemical element, harder than platinum. *Symbol*: Pd; *at.no.* 46; *at.mass* 106.4. ⟨< NL; after the asteroid *Pallas*⟩

pal•la•di•um[2] [pə'leidiəm] *n., pl.* **-di•a** [-diə]. **1** anything regarded as an important safeguard. **2 Palladium,** in Troy, the statue of Pallas Athena, on which the safety of the city was supposed to depend. ⟨< L < Gk. *palladion*, dim. of *Pallas*⟩

Pal•las ['pæləs] *n.* **1** a title of the Greek goddess Athena. **2** *Astronomy.* the second largest and fourth brightest asteroid, and the second to be discovered (1802).

pall•bear•er ['pɒl,bɛrər] *n.* a person who accompanies or helps to carry the coffin at a funeral.

pal•let[1] ['pælıt] *n.* **1** a straw bed. **2** a small, hard, or inferior bed. ⟨ME < OF *paillet* < *paille* straw < L *palea*⟩
☛ *Hom.* PALATE, PALETTE.

pal•let[2] ['pælıt] *n.* **1** an instrument with a flat wooden blade, used by potters, etc. **2** *Mechanics.* a projection on a pawl. See ESCAPEMENT for picture. **3** a portable platform on which goods can be stacked and transported from place to place in a factory, warehouse, etc. **4** *Bookbinding.* a tool used to stamp letters on binding. **5** PALETTE (def. 1). ⟨var. of *palette*⟩
☛ *Hom.* PALATE, PALETTE.

pal•let•ed ['pælətıd] *adj.* of the binding of a book, bearing the name of the binder.

pal•let•ize ['pælə,taız] *v.* **-ized, -iz•ing. 1** supply with pallets: *to palletize a truck.* **2** transport by means of pallets.

pal•liasse [pæl'jæs], ['pæljæs], *or* ['pæli,æs] *n.* a straw-filled mattress. Also, **paillasse.** ⟨< F *paillasse* < Ital. *pagliaccio*, ult. < L *palea* straw. 18c.⟩

pal•li•ate ['pæli,eit] *v.* **-at•ed, -at•ing. 1** lessen without curing; mitigate: *to palliate a disease.* **2** make appear less serious; excuse: *to palliate a fault.* ⟨< L *palliare* cover with a cloak < *pallium* cloak⟩ **—,pal•li'a•tion,** *n.*

pal•li•a•tive ['pæliətıv] *or* ['pæli,eitıv] *adj., n. —adj.* **1** useful to lessen or soften; mitigating; excusing. **2** serving to control pain: *Palliative care is given to people who are not likely to live.*
—n. something that lessens, softens, mitigates, or excuses.

pal•lid ['pælıd] *adj.* lacking colour; having less colour than normal or usual; pale: *a pallid face.* ⟨< L *pallidus.* Doublet of PALE[1].⟩
☛ *Syn.* See note at PALE[1].

pal•li•um ['pæliəm] *n.* **1** a large rectangular cloak worn by men in ancient Greece and Rome. **2** a woollen garment worn by the pope and conferred by him on archbishops. **3** an altar cloth. **4** *Anatomy.* the whole cerebral cortex. ⟨< L, cloak⟩

pall–mall ['pɛl 'mɛl], ['pæl 'mæl], *or* ['pɒl 'mɒl] *n.* **1** a 17th century game in which the player uses a mallet to drive a wooden ball through a raised hoop at the end of a playing alley. **2** the playing alley used in this game. ⟨< MF *pallemaille* < Ital. *pallamaglio* < *palla* ball + *maglio* mallet⟩

pal•lor ['pælər] *n.* a lack of colour from fear, illness, death, etc.; paleness. ⟨< L⟩

palm[1] [pɒm] *or* [pɑm] *n., v. —n.* **1** the inside of the hand between the wrist and the fingers. **2** the part of a glove or mitten covering the palm. **3** a broad, flat part resembling a palm, such as the blade of an oar or paddle or the flattened part of an antler of a moose, etc. **4** the width of the hand as a unit for measuring length; about 10 cm.
grease the palm of, bribe.
have an itching palm, be greedy for money.
—v. **1** conceal in the hand: *The magician palmed a nickel.* **2** touch or stroke with the palm or hand; handle.
palm off, pass off or get accepted by fraud or deceit: *The book he palmed off on me turned out to have some pages missing.* ⟨ME < OF < L *palma*⟩

palm[2] [pɒm] *or* [pɑm] *n.* **1** any of a family (Palmae) of mainly tropical and subtropical trees, shrubs, and vines, most species having a tall, pillarlike trunk crowned by very large, fan-shaped or feather-shaped leaves. **2** a leaf of a palm tree used as a symbol of victory or triumph. **3** a victory; triumph.
bear or **carry off the palm,** be the victor; win: *Althea Gibson was the first black woman to bear off the palm in both tennis and golf.*
yield the palm to, admit defeat by. ⟨OE < L *palma* palm tree, from the spreading shape of the leaves. See PALM[1].⟩

pal•mar ['pælmər] *or* ['pɒlmər] *adj.* of, in or corresponding to the palm of the hand. ⟨< L *palmaris* a hand's breadth⟩

pal•mate ['pælmeit] *or* ['pɒlmeit] *adj.* **1** shaped like a hand with the fingers spread out; having lobes radiating from a central point: *a palmate leaf, palmate antlers.* See LEAF for picture. **2** of the feet of many water birds, having the front toes joined by a web; webbed. ⟨< L *palmatus* < *palma* palm (of the hand)⟩

pal•ma•tion [pæl'meiʃən], [pɒl'meiʃən], *or* [pɑ'meiʃən] *n.* a palmate formation or structure; one division of a palmate structure.

palm•er[1] ['pɒmər] *or* ['pɑmər] *n.* **1** formerly, a pilgrim returning from the Holy Land bringing a palm branch as a token. **2** pilgrim. ⟨ME < AF < Med.L *palmarius* < L *palma* palm tree⟩

palm•er[2] ['pɒmər] *or* ['pɑmər] *n.* a person who palms or conceals something. ⟨< *palm[1]*⟩

pal•mer–worm ['pɒmər ,wɜrm] *or* ['pɑmər ,wɜrm] *n.* any of various caterpillars that injure or destroy fruit trees by eating the leaves, especially a small green caterpillar that is the larva of a North American moth (*Dichomeris ligulella*). ⟨< *palmer[1]*; so named from its wandering habits⟩

pal•met•to [pæl'mɛtou] *or* [pɒl'mɛtou] *n., pl.* **-tos** or **-toes.** any of a genus (*Sabal*) of mainly small palms found in the Caribbean, Central America, and the SE United States, having fan-shaped leaves. ⟨< Sp. *palmito*, dim. of *palma* palm tree⟩

palm•ist ['pɒmıst] *or* ['pɑmıst] *n.* a person who practises palmistry.

palm•is•try ['pɒmıstri] *or* ['pɑmıstri] *n.* the art or practice of telling a person's future or reading his or her character from the lines and marks in the palm of the hand. ⟨ME *pawmestry*, *palmestrie* < *paume*, *palme* palm (of the hand) + a word element of uncertain origin⟩

palm leaf a leaf of a palm tree, used for making hats, baskets, fans, etc.

palm oil an edible yellow fat obtained from the fruit of any of several palms, used especially to make soap and candles.

Palm Sunday the Sunday before Easter Sunday; the yearly Christian celebration commemorating Jesus' triumphal entry into Jerusalem.

palm•y ['pɒmi] *or* ['pɑmi] *adj.* **palm•i•er, palm•i•est.** **1** abounding in palm trees. **2** flourishing; prosperous.

pal•o•mi•no [,pælə'minou] *n., pl.* **-nos.** a horse of mainly Arabian stock, having a cream, golden, or tan coat and a white or ivory mane and tail. ⟨< Sp.⟩

A palomino

pa•loo•ka [pə'lukə] *n. Slang.* **1** a poor or inferior boxer. **2** a stupid lout, especially a muscular one. ⟨coined word⟩

palp [pælp] *n.* palpus. ⟨< F *palpe*⟩ **—'pal•pal,** *adj.*

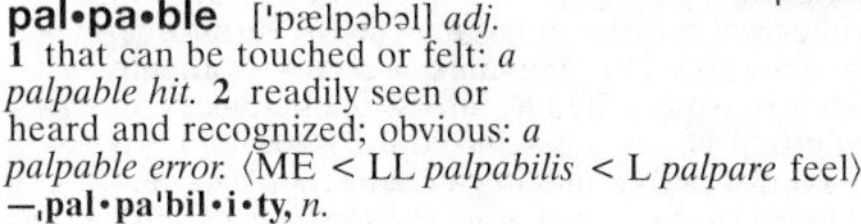

pal•pa•ble ['pælpəbəl] *adj.* **1** that can be touched or felt: *a palpable hit.* **2** readily seen or heard and recognized; obvious: *a palpable error.* ⟨ME < LL *palpabilis* < L *palpare* feel⟩ **—,pal•pa'bil•i•ty,** *n.*

pal•pa•bly ['pælpəbli] *adv.* **1** plainly; obviously. **2** to the touch.

pal•pate¹ ['pælpeit] *v.* **-pat•ed, -pat•ing.** examine or feel with the hands, especially for purposes of medical diagnosis. ⟨< L *palpatus*, pp. of *palpare* feel, pat⟩ **—pal'pa•tion,** *n.*

pal•pate² ['pælpeit] *adj.* having a palpus or palpi.

pal•pi ['pælpaɪ] *or* ['pælpi] *n.* pl. of PALPUS.

pal•pi•tate ['pælpə,teit] *v.* **-tat•ed, -tat•ing. 1** beat very rapidly; throb: *Your heart palpitates when you are excited.* **2** quiver; tremble: *His body palpitated with terror.* ⟨< L *palpitare* throb < *palpare* pat⟩

pal•pi•ta•tion [,pælpə'teiʃən] *n.* **1** very rapid beating of the heart. **2** a quivering; trembling.

pal•pus ['pælpəs] *n., pl.* [-paɪ] *or* [-pi]. a jointed feeler that is an organ of touch or taste, attached to one of the mouthparts of insects, crustaceans, etc. ⟨< L *palpus* the palm of the hand, rel. to *palpāre* feel⟩

pals•grave ['pɒlz,greiv] *or* ['pælz,greiv] *n.* a count palatine in Germany. ⟨< Du. *paltsgrave* < L *palatium* palace + *graaf* count⟩

pal•sied ['pɒlzid] *adj.* **1** having or affected by palsy. **2** shaking; trembling.

pal•sy ['pɒlzi] *n., pl.* **-sies;** *v.* **-sied, -sy•ing.** *—n.* **1** paralysis, especially when accompanied by uncontrollable tremors of the body or a part of the body. **2** paralysis.
—v. paralyse. ⟨ME *palesie* < OF *paralysie* < L < Gk. *paralysis.* Doublet of PARALYSIS.⟩

pal•ter ['pɒltər] *v.* **1** talk or act insincerely; trifle deceitfully. **2** act carelessly; trifle: *Do not palter with a decision involving life and death.* **3** deal crookedly; use tricks and dodges in bargaining. **4** haggle. ⟨origin uncertain⟩

pal•try ['pɒltri] *adj.* **-tri•er, -tri•est. 1** almost worthless; trifling. **2** petty; mean. ⟨? < dial. *palt* trash; possibly < LG *paltrig* ragged, torn⟩ **—'pal•tri•ly,** *adv.* **—'pal•tri•ness,** *n.*

pal•y•no•log•i•cal [,pælənə'lɒdʒəkəl] *adj.* of or having to do with palynology. **—,pal•y•no'log•i•cal•ly,** *adv.*

pal•y•nol•o•gist [,pælə'nɒlədʒɪst] *n.* a person trained in palynology, especially one whose work it is.

pal•y•nol•o•gy [,pælə'nɒlədʒi] *n.* the branch of science dealing with living and fossil plant spores and pollen.

pam•pas ['pɑmpəs] *or* ['pæmpəz]; *Spanish,* ['pampas] *n.pl.* **1** the vast, almost treeless plains of South America south of the Amazon and east of the Andes, especially in central Argentina. **2** (*adjl.*) of or found on the pampas: *pampas dwellers, pampas grass.* ⟨< Sp. *pampas*, pl., < Quechua *pampa* a plain⟩

Pampas grass

pam•pas grass any of various very tall, reedlike grasses (especially *Cortaderia selloana*) of South America having silvery plumes often used for decorative purposes.

pam•per ['pæmpər] *v.* **1** indulge too much; allow too many privileges to: *to pamper a child, to pamper one's appetite.* **2** treat very kindly; give the best of everything to: *Let our hotel staff pamper you.* ⟨ME *pampere(n)*⟩ **—'pam•per•er,** *n.*

pam•pe•ro [pæm'pɛrou] *n.* a cold, dry, southwesterly wind that reaches the pampas of Argentina from the Andes. ⟨< Sp.⟩

pam•phlet ['pæmflɪt] *n.* a short printed work, usually with no binding or having a stapled paper cover: *an advertising pamphlet, a pamphlet on the care of hamsters.* ⟨ME < Anglo-L *panfletus*, for *Pamphilet*, the popular name for the 12c. poem, 'Pamphilus, seu de Amore' (Pamphilus, or About Love)⟩

pam•phlet•eer [,pæmflə'tir] *n., v. —n.* a writer of pamphlets, especially those containing political propaganda or used for religious proselytizing.
—v. write and issue such pamphlets.

pan¹ [pæn] *n., v.* **panned, pan•ning.** *—n.* **1** a dish for cooking and other household uses, usually broad and shallow. **2** anything like this. Gold and other metals are sometimes obtained by washing ore in pans and the dishes on a pair of scales are called pans. **3** the contents of a pan: *a pan of potatoes.* Also, **panful. 4** any area shaped like a pan, such as a small natural or artificial hollow in the ground. **5** in old guns, the hollow part of the lock that held a little gunpowder to set the gun off. **6** hard subsoil. **7** ICE PAN. **8** *Slang.* the human face. **9** *Slang. Baseball.* the home plate. **10** *Informal.* a severely critical review of a play, film, etc.
—v. **1** cook in a pan. **2** wash in a pan: *to pan gold.* **3** wash (gravel, sand, etc.) in a pan to get gold. **4** yield gold by this method. **5** *Informal.* criticize severely.
pan out, 1 *Informal.* turn out well. **2** *Cdn. Gold mining.* to yield gold. ⟨OE *panne*⟩

pan² [pæn] *v.* **panned, pan•ning.** move (a film, video, or television camera) so as to take in a whole scene, follow a moving character or object, etc. ⟨< *pan(orama)*⟩

Pan [pæn] *n. Greek mythology.* the god of forests, pastures, flocks, and shepherds, represented as a man having the horns, ears, and legs of a goat and playing upon a reed pipe, or panpipe.

PAN peroxyacetyl nitrate, an irritant found in smog.

pan– *combining form.* all or every, as in *Pan-American, pandemonium.* ⟨< Gk. *pan*, neut. of *pas* all⟩

pan•a•ce•a [,pænə'siə] *n.* a remedy for all diseases or ills; cure-all. ⟨< L < Gk. *panakeia*, ult. < *pan-* all + *akos* cure⟩ **—,pan•a'ce•an,** *adj.*

pa•nache [pə'næʃ] *or* [pə'nɑʃ] *n.* **1** behaviour marked by dash or flair; swagger; verve. **2** an ornamental plume or bunch of feathers, especially on a helmet. ⟨< F *panache* < MF *penache* < Ital. *pennaccio*, var. of *pennachio* < *penna* feather < L⟩

Pan–Af•ri•can [,pæn 'æfrəkən] *adj.* of or for all African peoples: *Pan-African freedom.*

Pan–Af•ri•can•ism [,pæn 'æfrəkə,nɪzəm] *n.* **1** the theory of or movement toward a political union of all African peoples. **2** belief in or support of such a theory or movement.

pan•a•ma ['pænə,mɑ] *n.* **1** a fine hat woven from the young leaves of a palmlike plant of Central and South America. **2** the leaves from which the hat is made. Also called **Panama hat.**

Pan•a•ma ['pænə,mɑ] *n.* a country on the Isthmus of Panama, in Central America.

Pan•a•ma•ni•an [ˌpænə'meiniən] *n., adj. —n.* a native or inhabitant of Panama.
—adj. of or having to do with Panama or its people.

Pan–A•mer•i•can [ˌpæn ə'mɛrəkən] *adj.* **1** of all Americans. **2** including all the countries of North, Central, and South America.

Pan–A•mer•i•can•ism [ˌpæn ə'mɛrəkəˌnɪzəm] *n.* the notion or policy that all North, South, and Central American countries should co-operate for the improvement of their economic, political, and cultural welfare.

Pan American Union a permanent body, the central office of the Organization of American States.

pan•a•tel•la or **pan•a•tel•a** [ˌpænə'tɛlə] *n.* a long, slender cigar with a rounded end. ⟨< Am.Sp. *panetela* long, thin biscuit < Ital. *panatella*, dim. of *pane* bread⟩

pan•broil ['pænˌbrɔɪl] *v.* cook with little or no fat in a heavy frying pan over high heat.

pan•cake ['pænˌkeɪk] *n., v.* **-caked, -cak•ing.** *—n.* **1** a thin, flat cake of batter, fried in a pan or on a griddle. **2** PANCAKE LANDING.
—v. of an aircraft, make or cause to make a PANCAKE LANDING.

pancake ice *Cdn.* ice that has newly formed in flat, thin pieces usually between 30 cm to 2 m in diameter, which do not interfere with shipping.

Pancake Day Shrove Tuesday, the day before Ash Wednesday at the beginning of Lent. ⟨from the custom of eating pancakes on this day, before fasting for Lent⟩

pancake landing a quick landing in which an aircraft is levelled off at a higher altitude than for a normal landing, a manoeuvre that causes it to stall and drop almost straight down while remaining in a horizontal position.

pan•chro•mat•ic [ˌpænkrou'mætɪk] *adj.* sensitive to all colours: *a panchromatic photographic film.*
—pan'chro•maˌtism, *n.*

pan•cre•as ['pæŋkriəs] *or* ['pænkriəs] *n. Anatomy, zoology.* a large gland near the stomach that secretes digestive enzymes into the small intestine and the hormone insulin into the blood. The pancreas of animals, when used for food, is called sweetbread. ⟨< NL < Gk. *pankreas* < *pan-* all + *kreas* flesh⟩
—ˌpan•cre'at•ic [ˌpænkri'ætɪk], *adj.*

pan•cre•i•tis [ˌpæŋkri'əitɪs] *or* [ˌpænkri'əitɪs] *n. Pathology.* inflammation of the pancreas.

pan•da ['pændə] *n.* **1** a large, black-and-white, bearlike mammal (*Ailuropoda melanoleuca*) found in the bamboo forests of Tibet. Zoologists differ on whether the panda is more closely related to the bears or the raccoons. Also called **giant panda. 2** a small, mainly reddish brown mammal (*Ailurus fulgens*) found in the Himalayas, having a bushy tail, white face with a reddish stripe on each side, and soft, thick fur. This panda, also called the **lesser panda,** or **common panda,** belongs to the same family as the raccoon. ⟨< native Nepali name⟩

pan•dect ['pændɛkt] *n.* **1** Often, **pandects,** *pl.* a complete body of laws. **2** a comprehensive digest. **3 Pandects,** *pl.* a digest of Roman civil law in 50 books, made by order of Justinian in the 6th century A.D. ⟨< L < Gk. *pandektēs* < *pan-* all + *dechesthai* receive⟩

pan•dem•ic [pæn'dɛmɪk] *adj., n. —adj.* of a disease, affecting a large proportion of the population over an extensive geographical area: *a pandemic outbreak of influenza.*
—n. a disease that has become pandemic.

pan•de•mo•ni•um [ˌpændə'mouniəm] *n.* **1** wild or chaotic disorder and confusion. **2** any place or scene displaying these characteristics. ⟨< NL < Gk. *pan-* all + *daimōn* demon; coined by Milton⟩

pan•der ['pændər] *n., v. —n.* **1** a person who caters to or exploits the weaknesses of others; one who helps people indulge evil designs or base passions. **2** one who acts as a pimp in a sexual relationship. Also, **panderer.**
—v. **1** act as a pander; supply material or opportunity for vices: *The newspaper pandered to people's liking for sensational stories.* **2** pimp. ⟨< *Pandarus* (Ital. *Pandoro*) a character in a story told by Boccaccio and Chaucer⟩

Pan•do•ra [pæn'dɔrə] *n. Greek mythology.* the first woman, created by Hephaestus, to punish humans for having learned the use of fire. Curiosity led her to open a box **(Pandora's box)** and thus let out all sorts of ills into the world; only Hope remained at the bottom.

pan•dow•dy [pæn'daʊdi] *n., pl.* **-dies.** *Esp. U.S.* a deep apple pie with top crust only. ⟨origin uncertain⟩

pane [pein] *n.* **1** a sheet of glass enclosed in a frame as part of a larger entity such as a window or door. **2** the sheet of glass itself. **3** a panel of a larger construction such as a door, wainscot, wall, etc. **4** a flat side or surface of anything such as a bolthead, diamond, nut, etc. **5** a sheet or a large portion of a sheet of stamps. ⟨ME < OF *pan* < L *pannus* piece of cloth⟩
☛ *Hom.* PAIN.

pan•e•gyr•ic [ˌpænə'dʒaɪrɪk] *or* [ˌpænə'dʒirɪk] *n.* **1** something written or spoken in praise of a person or thing; eulogy. **2** enthusiastic or extravagant praise. ⟨< L < Gk. *panēgyrikos* < *pan-* all + *agyris* assembly⟩ **—ˌpan•e'gyr•i•cal,** *adj.* **—ˌpan•e'gyr•i•cal•ly,** *adv.*

pan•e•gyr•ist [ˌpænə'dʒaɪrɪst] *or* [ˌpænə'dʒirɪst] *n.* a person who praises enthusiastically or extravagantly.

pan•el ['pænəl] *n., v.* **-elled** or **-eled, -el•ling** or **-el•ing.** *—n.* **1** a separate strip or surface that is usually set off in some way from what is around it. A panel is often sunk below, raised above or loose from the rest, and used for a decoration. Panels may be in a door or other woodwork, on large pieces of furniture, or made as parts of a dress. **2** a long, narrow picture, hanging, or design. **3** a list of persons called as jurors; the members of a jury. **4** a small group of persons selected for a special purpose, such as holding a discussion, judging a contest, or participating in a quiz: *The panel gave its opinion on the recent election.* **5 a** one section of a switchboard. **b** a board containing the instruments, controls, or indicators used in operating an automobile, aircraft, computer, or other mechanism. **6** PANEL TRUCK. **7** a thin pad placed under, or used as, a saddle.
—v. arrange in panels; furnish or decorate with panels. ⟨ME < OF *panel* piece < VL *pannellus* < L *pannus* piece of cloth⟩

panel discussion the discussion of a particular issue by a selected group of people, usually experts, before an audience.

panel heating a method of heating a building by means of panels containing heating pipes in the walls, ceiling, or floor.

pan•el•ing ['pænəlɪŋ] See PANELLING.

pan•el•ling or **pan•el•ing** ['pænəlɪŋ] *n., v. —n.* panels joined together to make a single surface, especially wooden panels forming a decorative wall surface: *We have pine panelling in the study.*
—v. ppr. of PANEL.

pan•el•list or **pan•el•ist** ['pænəlɪst] *n.* one of a group of persons making up a panel.

panel truck a small, light motor truck with a completely enclosed body.

pan•fish ['pænˌfɪʃ] *n.* any small food fish suitable for frying whole in a pan.

pan–fry ['pæn ˌfraɪ] *v.* **-fried, -fry•ing.** fry in a frying pan or skillet: *to pan-fry fish.*

pan•ful ['pænˌfʊl] *n.* the contents of a pan: *a panful of potatoes.*

pang [pæŋ] *n.* **1** a sudden, short, sharp pain or feeling: *the pangs of a toothache.* **2** a sudden feeling of distress or anguish: *a pang of remorse.* ⟨origin uncertain⟩

Pan•glos•si•an [pæn'glɒsiən] *or* [pæŋ'glɒsiən] *adj.* characterized by extreme or foolish optimism, especially in the face of adversity. ⟨after Dr. *Pangloss*, a character in Voltaire's *Candide*⟩

pan•go•lin [pæŋ'goulən] *n.* any of an order (Pholidota, usually considered to consist of a single genus, *Manis*) of tropical Asian and African mammals having a body covered with an armour of overlapping horny scales, a long, toothless snout, and a long, wormlike tongue used for catching termites, ants, and other insects for food. Pangolins curl up into a ball when they feel threatened. Also called **scaly anteater.** ⟨< Malay *peng-goling* roller⟩

pan•han•dle[1] ['pænˌhændəl] *n.* **1** the handle of a pan. **2** a narrow strip of land projecting like a handle: *the Alaska Panhandle.*

pan•han•dle[2] ['pænˌhændəl] *v.* **-dled, -dling.** *Informal.* actively beg from passers-by on the street. ⟨? < *panhandler* < *pan* receptacle used for collecting money + *handler*⟩
—'panˌhan•dler, *n.*

Pan•hel•len•ic or **pan•hel•len•ic** [ˌpænhə'lɛnɪk] *adj.* **1** of or having to do with all Greece or all Greek people. **2** *Esp. U.S.* of or having to do with all college fraternities and sororities with names made up of Greek letters.

pan•ic ['pænɪk] *n., adj., v.* **-icked, -ick•ing.** *—n.* **1** a sudden fear that causes an individual or entire group to lose self-control;

unreasoning fear: *When the theatre caught fire, there was a panic.* **2** a sudden and widespread fear that the financial system will collapse, leading to frantic attempts to withdraw cash, liquidate assets, etc. **3** *Slang.* a very amusing person or thing: *That child's costume is a panic.*
—adj. **1** of, showing, or caused by unreasoning fear: *panic terror, panic haste, panic selling of stocks.* **2** Often, **Panic,** of or having to do with the god Pan or the fear he was thought to induce.
push (or **press** or **hit**) **the panic button,** *Informal.* react with panic in the face of a supposed emergency.
—v. **1** lose control of oneself through fear. **2** cause panic in. **3** *Slang.* amuse greatly. ⟨< F < L *panicus* < Gk. *panikos* of god Pan (who caused fear)⟩

panic attack an attack of sudden intense fear, accompanied by palpitations and sweating, often occurring during the night.

panic disorder *Psychiatry.* a disease characterized by sudden attacks of anxiety, fear, sweating, etc., especially during the night or in crowds.

pan ice *Cdn.* See ICE PAN.

pan•ick•y ['pænɪki] *adj.* **1** affected with panic; panic-stricken. *He began to get panicky as the deadline approached.* **2** liable to panic.

pan•i•cle ['pænəkəl] *n. Botany.* a loose, diversely branching flower cluster; compound raceme: *a panicle of oats.* See INFLORESCENCE for picture. ⟨< L *panicula*, dim. of *panus* a swelling, thread wound on a bobbin, ear of millet; cf. Gk. *pēnos* web⟩

panicled dogwood ['pænəkəld] a shrub (*Cornus racemosa*) having white fruits on red stems and very thin grey branches.

pan•ic–strick•en ['pænɪk ˌstrɪkən] *adj.* frightened out of one's wits; demoralized by fear.

pa•nic•u•late [pə'nɪkjəlɪt] *or* [pə'nɪkjəˌleit] *adj. Botany.* growing in a panicle; arranged in panicles.

Pan•ja•bi [pʌn'dʒɑbi] *n.* See PUNJABI.

pan•jan•drum [pæn'dʒændrəm] *n.* a mock title for an official of imaginary or exaggerated importance or power. ⟨coined by Samuel Foote (1720-1777), an English dramatist⟩

pan juice the natural juice given off by meat while roasting.

panne [pæn] *n.* a lightweight velvet whose pile is laid flat. ⟨< F < OF *penne* < L *penna* feather⟩

pan•ner ['pænər] *n.* a prospector who seeks gold by panning.

pan•ni•er ['pæniər] *n.* **1** a basket, especially one of a pair of considerable size to be slung across the shoulders or across the back of a beast of burden. **2** formerly, a frame to stretch out the skirt of a woman's dress at the hips. **3** puffed drapery about the hips. ⟨ME < OF < L *panarium* bread basket < *panis* bread⟩

pa•no•cha [pə'noutʃə] *n.* **1** a coarse, dark brown sugar from Mexico. **2** penuche. ⟨< Mexican Sp.⟩

pan•o•plied ['pænəplid] *adj.* covered with or dressed or arrayed in a panoply.

pan•o•ply ['pænəpli] *n., pl.* **-plies. 1** a complete suit of armour. **2** complete equipment or covering: *the panoply of war.* **3** any splendid display, especially involving ceremonial dress and equipment: *the panoply of an academic convocation or a coronation.* ⟨< Gk. *panoplia* < *pan-* all + *hopla* arms⟩

pan•o•ram•a [ˌpænə'ræmə] *n.* **1** a wide, unbroken view of a surrounding region. **2** a complete survey of some subject: *a panorama of the development of the snowmobile.* **3** a presentation of a landscape or other scene surrounding the spectator on all sides or gradually unrolled to pass continuously before the spectator's eyes. **4** a continuously passing or changing scene: *the panorama of city life.* ⟨< *pan-* + Gk. *horama* view⟩

pan•o•ram•ic [ˌpænə'ræmɪk] *adj.* of or like a panorama: *a panoramic view.* **—ˌpan•o'ram•i•cal•ly,** *adv.*

pan•pipe ['pænˌpəip] *n.* **1** Sometimes, **Panpipe,** an early instrument made of reeds or tubes of different lengths, fastened together in the order of their length. The reeds or tubes were closed at one end; the player blew across their tops. **2** Usually, **panpipes,** *pl.* a similar instrument as used in modern instrumental music. Also, **Pan's pipes.**

pan•so•phism ['pænsəˌfɪzəm] *n.* a claim to universal knowledge and wisdom. ⟨< Gk. *pansophos* all-wise⟩ **—'pan•so•phist,** *n.*

Pan's pipes See PANPIPE.

pan•sy ['pænzi] *n., pl.* **-sies. 1** a common flowering garden plant (*Viola tricolour hortensis*) of the violet family, having large, showy flowers with velvety petals of several colours, usually combinations of blue, yellow, and white. The pansy is a hybrid derived mainly from the wild pansy of Europe. **2** the flower of this plant. **3** *Slang.* **a** a homosexual man or boy. **b** an effeminate man or boy. ⟨< F *pensée* thought < *penser* think. Related to PENSIVE.⟩

pant [pænt] *v., n.* *—v.* **1** breathe hard and quickly. **2** speak with short, quick breaths: *"Come quickly! Come quickly!" panted Elsa.* **3** long eagerly. **4** throb; pulsate.
—n. **1** a short, quick breath. **2** a puffing (sound): *the pant of an engine.* ⟨ME < OF *pantoisier* < VL *phantasiare* be oppressed with nightmare, ult. < L < Gk. *phantasia* appearance, image⟩

pan•ta•lettes or **pan•ta•lets** [ˌpæntə'lɛts] *n.pl.* **1** long underpants extending to the ankles and having a ruffle at the bottom of each leg that showed beneath the skirt, worn by women and girls in the early 19th century. **2** detachable ruffles for this garment. ⟨dim. < *pantaloon*⟩

pan•ta•loon [ˌpæntə'lun] *n.* **1** a clown. **2 Pantaloon,** in traditional Italian COMMEDIA DELL'ARTE and in pantomime, a thin, foolish old man wearing pantaloons and slippers with attached stockings. **3 pantaloons,** *pl. Archaic.* close-fitting pants. ⟨< F < Ital. *Pantalone*, a comic character in early Italian comedies; originally a Venetian < *Pantaleone* the patron saint of Venice⟩

pan•the•ism ['pænθiˌɪzəm] *n.* **1** the belief that God and the universe are identical. **2** the worship of the gods of all cultures together.

pan•the•ist ['pænθiɪst] *n.* a person who believes in pantheism. **—ˌpan•the'ist•ic,** *adj.* **—ˌpan•the'ist•i•cal•ly,** *adv.*

pan•the•on ['pænθiˌɒn] *or* ['pænθiən] *n.* **1 Pantheon,** in Rome, a temple for all the gods, built about 27 B.C. and later used as a Christian church. **2** a temple dedicated to all the gods. **3** all the gods of a people, especially those that are officially recognized. **4** a public building containing tombs or memorials of the illustrious dead of a nation. **5** a group of illustrious people. ⟨ME < L < Gk. *pantheion* < *pan-* all + *theos* god⟩

pan•ther ['pænθər] *n., pl.* **-thers** or *(esp. collectively)* **-ther. 1** a leopard, especially one of the black colour phase. **2** *Esp. Cdn.* cougar. **3** jaguar. ⟨ME < OF < L *panthera* < Gk. *panthēr*⟩

pan•tie ['pænti] *n.* **1** panties. **2** pantie-girdle. Also, **panty.**

pan•tie–gir•dle ['pænti ˌgɜrdəl] *n.* a woman's girdle in the shape of panties.

pan•ties ['pæntiz] *n.pl.* **1** an undergarment worn by women and girls, covering the lower part of the torso and having separate leg holes or short legs. **2** a similar undergarment for babies and young children. ⟨dim. of PANTS⟩

pan•ti•hose ['pæntiˌhouz] See PANTYHOSE.

pan•tile ['pænˌtaɪl] *n.* **1** a roofing tile which is straight lengthwise but shaped like an unequal S in its width, so that the large curve of one tile overlaps the small curve of the next. **2** a tapered semi-circular roofing tile laid alternately convex or concave side up so as to overlap with neighbouring tiles.

pant leg the leg of a pair of pants.

pan•to•graph ['pæntəˌgræf] *n.* an instrument for copying plans, drawings, etc. on any scale desired, consisting of a diamond-shaped jointed framework. ⟨< Gk. *pas, pantos* all + E *-graph*⟩ **—pan'tog•ra•pher** [pæn'tɒgrəfər], *n.* **—ˌpan•to'graph•ic,** *adj.* **—ˌpan•to'graph•i•cal•ly,** *adv.* **—pan'tog•ra•phy,** *n.*

pan•to•mime ['pæntəˌmaɪm] *n., v.* **-mimed, -mim•ing.** *—n.* **1** a play without words, in which the actors express themselves by gestures. **2** gestures without words. **3** *Brit.* a lavish stage entertainment, usually presented at Christmas and based on a fairy story or other traditional tale, featuring singing, dancing, and clowning. **4** MIME (def. 3).
—v. express by gestures. ⟨< L < Gk. *pantomimos* < *pas, pantos* all + *mimos* mimic⟩ **—ˌpan•to'mim•ic** [ˌpæntə'mɪmɪk], *adj.*

pan•to•mim•ist ['pæntəˌmaɪmɪst] *n.* **1** an actor in a pantomime. **2** a writer of pantomimes.

pan•to•then•ic acid [ˌpæntə'θɛnɪk] *Biochemistry.* an oily acid belonging to the vitamin B complex and found in all living tissues. *Formula*: $C_9H_{17}NO_5$

pan•to•there ['pæntəˌθir] *n.* an extinct mammal which lived during the Mesozoic Era: *Pantotheres may be the ancestors of marsupials.*

pan•try ['pæntri] *n., pl.* **-tries. 1** a small airy room used for storing food that must be kept cold. **2** a similar room in which food, dishes, silverware, table linen, etc. are kept. ⟨ME < OF *paneterie*, ult. < L *panis* bread⟩

pants [pænts] *n.pl.* **1** an outer garment for the lower body, reaching from the waist to the ankles or, sometimes, to the knees, and covering each leg separately; trousers. **2** the lower part of a pair of pyjamas. **3** panties. ⟨short for *pantaloons*⟩

pant•suit ['pænt,sut] *n.* a suit for women, consisting of long pants and a matching jacket or overblouse.

pan•ty ['pænti] *n., pl.* **-ties.** See PANTIE.

pan•ty•hose ['pænti,houz] *n.pl.* a garment for women, consisting of sheer stockings knitted in one piece with a pantie-like top of the same or slightly heavier material. Also, **panty-hose, pantihose.**

pan•ty•waist ['pænti,weist] *n.* **1** a child's garment consisting of short pants and shirt buttoned together. **2** *Informal.* sissy.

pan•zer ['pænzər] *or* ['pæntsər]; *German,* ['pantsəʀ] *adj. German military.* armoured; mechanized and armoured. A German panzer division consists largely of tanks. ⟨< G *Panzer* armour⟩

pap [pæp] *n.* **1** soft food for infants or invalids. **2** ideas or facts watered down to a characterless consistency. ⟨Cf. LG *pappe*⟩

pa•pa ['pɑpə] *or* ['pɒpə] *n.* father; daddy. ⟨< F⟩

pa•pa•cy ['peipəsi] *n., pl.* **-cies. 1** the position, rank, or authority of the Pope. **2** the time during which a pope rules. **3** all the popes. **4** government by the Pope. ⟨< Med.L *papatia* < LL *papa* pope. See POPE.⟩

Pap•a•go ['pɑpə,gou] *n.* **1** a member of a Native American people living near Tucson, Arizona. **2** the Uto-Aztecan language of these people.

pa•pa•in [pə'peiɪn] *or* [pə'paɪɪn] *n. Chemistry.* an enzyme derived from papaya fruit, used chiefly as a meat tenderizer and as an aid to good digestion. It also has some medicinal uses.

pa•pal ['peipəl] *adj.* **1** of or having to do with the Pope: *a papal letter.* **2** of or having to do with the papacy. **3** of or having to do with the Roman Catholic Church: *papal ritual.* ⟨< Med.L *papalis* < LL *papa* pope. See POPE.⟩ **—'pa•pal•ly,** *adv.*

pa•pa•raz•zi [,pɑpə'rɑtsi]; *Italian,* [papa'rattsi] *n.pl., sing.* **paparazzo.** a horde of photographers and reporters who hound celebrities. ⟨< Ital. *paparazzo.* a slang word for photographer⟩

pa•pa•ve•rine [pə'pævə,rin] *n.* a muscle relaxant and anti-spasmodic drug derived from opium and also used as a local anesthetic. *Formula:* $C_{20}H_{21}NO_4$

pa•paw ['pɒpɒ] *n.* See PAWPAW. ⟨< Sp. *papaya.* See PAPAYA.⟩

pa•pa•ya [pə'pɑjə] *or* [pə'paɪjə] *n.* **1** a treelike plant (*Carica papaya*) native to tropical America but widely cultivated in warm regions, having a straight, unbranched, palmlike trunk, large palmately lobed leaves, and large, round or oval edible fruit. **2** the fruit of this tree, having juicy, orange or dark yellow flesh. It may be eaten raw or cooked, and yields papain. ⟨< Sp. *papaya* < Carib. 15c.⟩

pa•per ['peipər] *n., adj., v.* **—*n.* 1** a material in the form of thin sheets made from wood pulp, rags, etc. and used for writing, printing, wrapping packages, etc. **2** a piece or sheet of paper. **3** a piece or sheet of paper with writing or printing on it; document: *Important papers were stolen.* **4 papers,** *pl.* a collection of documents such as correspondence, journals, or miscellaneous writing, of an individual: *The Pearson papers are in the National Archives.* **5** a wrapper, container, or sheet of paper containing something: *What's inside that paper?* **6** newspaper. **7** an article; essay: *Professor Burgos read a paper on the teaching of English.* **8** a written examination. **9** a written promise to pay money; note. **10** PAPER MONEY. **11 papers,** *pl.* documents telling who or what a person is. **12** wallpaper.
on paper, a in writing or in print. **b** in theory: *The plan looks all right on paper but it may not work.*
—adj. **1** made of paper: *paper dolls.* **2** having to do with or used with paper: *a paper clip.* **3** like paper; thin: *almonds with paper shells.* **4** of, consisting of, or carried on by means of pamphlets, books, or letters to newspapers: *paper warfare.* **5** existing only on paper: *When he tried to sell, his paper profits disappeared.*
—v. **1** cover with paper, especially wallpaper. **2** *Slang.* fill (a place of entertainment) with an audience admitted mostly by free passes: *To get a crowd at the concert they had to paper the house.* ⟨ME < AF *papir* < L < Gk. *papyros.* Doublet of PAPYRUS.⟩ **—'pa•per•er,** *n.*

pa•per•back ['peipər,bæk] *n., adj.* **—*n.*** a book with a flexible paper binding and cover, especially one that is small and relatively inexpensive.
—adj. **1** (of a book) bound in a flexible paper cover: *a paperback mystery.* **2** of, for, or pertaining to paperbacks: *the paperback market.*

paper birch *Cdn.* the white birch (*Betula papyrifera*), the bark of which was used to make canoes or as a surface for writing.

pa•per•board ['peipər,bɔrd] *n.* a thick type of cardboard, such as that used for cartons, etc.

pa•per•bound ['peipər,baʊnd] *adj.* PAPERBACK (def. 1).

pa•per•boy ['peipər,bɔɪ] *n.* a boy who delivers or sells newspapers.

paper clip a flat clip of flexible, bent wire or plastic, used to slip over the edge of a small bundle of loose sheets to hold them together.

pa•per•girl ['peipər,gɜrl] *n.* a girl who delivers or sells newspapers.

pa•per•hang•er ['peipər,hæŋər] *n.* **1** a person whose work is applying wallpaper to walls. **2** *Slang.* a person who makes a business of passing counterfeit bills or forged cheques.

paper knife a blunt knife with a blade of metal, wood, ivory, etc., used to slit open letters or uncut pages of books.

pa•per•mak•er ['peipər,meikər] *n.* a person who makes or manufactures paper. **—'pa•per•mak•ing,** *n.*

paper money money made of paper, not metal. A five-dollar bill is paper money.

paper nautilus any of a genus (*Argonauta*) of marine cephalopod molluscs belonging to the same order as the octopus, especially *A. argo,* found in warm seas, the female of which produces a very thin, paperlike shell in which the young are hatched and which the animal casts off afterward.

paper profits profits existing on paper but not yet realized.

paper tiger a person, country, organization, etc. apparently posing a threat but actually weak or powerless.

pa•per•weight ['peipər,weit] *n.* a small, heavy object put on loose papers to keep them from being scattered.

pa•per•white ['peipər,wɔit] *n.* a type of narcissus with white petals.

pa•per•work ['peipər,wɜrk] *n.* work done on or with paper, such as writing, filing, or other clerical work: *She hates all the paperwork involved in her job.*

pa•per•y ['peipəri] *adj.* thin, like paper.

pap•e•terie ['pæpətri]; *French,* [pap'tʀi] *n.* a set of stationery, such as notepaper and envelopes, in a box or other package. ⟨< F⟩

pa•pier–mâ•ché [,peipər mæ'ʃei]; *French,* [papjema'ʃe] *n.* **1** a paper pulp mixed with some stiffener and used for modelling. It becomes hard and strong when dry. **2** (*adjl.*) made of papier-mâché. ⟨< F *papier mâché* chewed paper⟩

pa•pil•la [pə'pɪlə] *n., pl.* **-pil•lae.** [-'pɪlaɪ] *or* [-'pɪli]. **1** a small, nipplelike projection. **2** a small vascular process at the root of a hair or feather. **3** one of certain small protuberances concerned with the senses of touch, taste, or smell: *the papillae on the tongue.* ⟨< L *papilla* nipple⟩

pap•il•lar•y ['pæpə,lɛri] *adj.* of, like, or having papillae.

pap•il•lo•ma [,pæpə'loumə] *n., pl.* **-ma•ta** [-mətə]. a benign tumour, such as a wart or polyp, on mucous membranes or the skin. ⟨< *papilla* + *-oma.* 19c.⟩

pa•pil•lon ['pæpə,lɒn] *or* ['pæpə,jɒn] *n.* one of a breed of toy spaniels having long, silky hair, and fringed ears carried so that they resemble the wings of a butterfly. ⟨< F *papillon* butterfly⟩

pap•il•lose ['pæpə,lous] *adj.* having many papillae.

papoose [pə'pus] *n.* **1** formerly, a small child or baby of First Nations parents. Now considered derogatory. **2** *Cdn.* a beaver cub or young beaver. Also, **pappoose.** ⟨< Algonquian *papeisses* < *peisses* child⟩

pap•pus ['pæpəs] *n., pl.* **pap•pi** ['pæpaɪ] *or* ['pæpi]. *Botany.* an appendage to a seed, often made of down or bristles. Dandelion and thistle seeds have pappi. ⟨< NL < Gk. *pappos*⟩

pap•py ['pæpi] *adj.* **-pi•er, -pi•est.** like pap; soft; mushy.

pap•ri•ka [pə'prikə] *or* ['pæprəkə] *n.* **1** a kind of mild, red-coloured pepper made of the dried, ground-up pods of any of various sweet pepper plants. **2** a pod of pepper used for making paprika. **3** the plant on which these peppers grow. ⟨< Hungarian < Serbian *pàprika* < *pàpar* pepper, ult. < L *piper* pepper⟩

Pap smear or **test** [pæp] a test for early stages of cancer of the uterus or cervix, consisting of a microscopic examination of castoff cells found in vaginal fluid, using a special staining technique that separates abnormal cells from normal ones. ⟨named after George *Papanicolaou* (1883-1962), the U.S. scientist who devised it. 20c.⟩

Pap•u•an ['pɑpuən] *n., adj. —n.* **1** any or all of a group of very different languages spoken in New Guinea, New Britain, and the Solomon Islands in the SW Pacific. **2** a member of any of the Papuan-speaking peoples who live in this area.
—adj. of or having to do with Papua New Guinea, the peoples living there, or their languages.

Pap•ua New Guinea ['pɑpuə nju 'gɪni] a country of islands in the Pacific, north of Australia.

pa•py•rus [pə'paɪrəs] *n., pl.* **-ri** [-raɪ] *or* [-ri]. **1** a tall water plant (*Cyperus papyrus*) of the Nile valley from which the ancient Egyptians, Greeks, and Romans made a kind of paper to write on. **2** a writing material made from the pith of the papyrus plant. **3** an ancient record written on papyrus. ⟨< L < Gk. *papyros.* Doublet of PAPER.⟩

par [pɑr] *n., adj. —n.* **1** equality; an equal level: *The gains and losses are about on a par. He is quite on a par with the rest of his family in intelligence.* **2** an average or normal amount, degree, or condition: *A sick person feels below par.* **3** the value of a bond, a note, a share of stock, etc., that is printed on it; face value: *That stock is selling above par.* **4** the established normal value of the money of one country in terms of the money of another country: *Some American hotels accept the Canadian dollar at par.* **5** *Golf.* the number of strokes set as an expert score for any one hole. The sum of the par scores for each hole on a golf course is par for that particular course.
—adj. **1** average; normal. **2** of or at par.
par for the course, *Informal.* that which is normal or to be expected. ⟨< L *par* equal. Doublet of PEER[1].⟩
☛ *Hom.* PARR.

par– *prefix.* the form of **para-** before vowels and *h*, as in *parenthesis*, *parhelion.*

par. **1** paragraph. **2** parallel. **3** parenthesis. **4** parish.

pa•ra ['pɑrɑ] *n.* a unit of money in Serbia, equal to ¹⁄₁₀₀ of a dinar. See table of money in the Appendix.

para–¹ *prefix.* **1** beside, near, or beyond: *parathyroid, parapsychology.* **2** functionally disordered: *paranoia.* Also, **par-** before vowels and *h.* ⟨< Gk. *para-* < *para*, prep.⟩

para–² *combining form.* **1** a defence or protection against: *parachute* (protection against a fall), *parasol* (protection against the sun). **2** that uses a parachute: *paratrooper.* ⟨< F < Ital. < *para*, imperative of *parare* ward off, defend against < L *parare* prepare against⟩

para. paragraph.

par•a–a•mi•no•ben•zo•ic acid [,pærə ə,minoubɛn'zouɪk] *or* [,pɛrə-] *Chemistry.* a yellowish, crystalline acid belonging to the vitamin B complex, found especially in yeast and liver, and used in suntan lotions labelled PABA, because of its capacity to absorb ultraviolet rays. *Formula*: $C_7H_7NO_2$

par•a•bi•o•sis [,pærəbaɪ'ousɪs] *or* [,pɛrəbaɪ'ousɪs] *n.* **1** *Biology.* the anatomical union of two individuals, in which they share a common blood circulation, occurring naturally as in Siamese twins, or produced for experimental purposes in animals. **2** a reversible suspension of a vital life process, as in the temporary loss of excitability of a nerve cell. **3** the cohabitation of more than one species, as in a mixed flock of birds.

par•a•bi•ot•ic [,pærəbaɪ'ɒtɪk] *or* [,pɛrəbaɪ'ɒtɪk] *adj.* of or having to do with parabiosis. **—,par•a•bi'ot•i•cal•ly,** *adv.*

par•a•ble ['pærəbəl] *or* ['pɛrəbəl] *n.* a short, simple story used to teach some truth or moral lesson: *Jesus often taught in parables.* ⟨< L *parabola* < Gk. *parabolē* comparison < *para-* alongside + *bolē* a throwing. Doublet of PALAVER, PARABOLA, PAROLE.⟩
☛ *Syn.* See note at ALLEGORY.

pa•rab•o•la [pə'ræbələ] *n., pl.* **-las.** *Geometry.* a plane curve formed by the intersection of a cone with a plane parallel to a side of the cone. See CONE for picture. ⟨< NL < Gk. *parabolē* juxtaposition. See PARABLE.⟩

par•a•bol•ic¹ [,pærə'bɒlɪk] *or* [,pɛrə'bɒlɪk] *adj.* **1** having to do with or resembling a parabola. **2** dish-shaped, as a TV satellite dish.

par•a•bol•ic² [,pærə'bɒlɪk] *or* [,pɛrə'bɒlɪk] *adj.* of, having to do with, or expressed in a parable. **—,par•a'bol•i•cal•ly,** *adv.*

pa•rab•o•lize [pə'ræbə,laɪz] *v.* **-lized, -liz•ing.** tell in parables.

par•a•cen•tric [,pærə'sɛntrɪk] *or* [,pɛrə'sɛntrɪk] *adj.* **1** beside a central point. **2** *Genetics.* beside the centromere of a chromosome.

par•a•chute ['pærə,ʃut] *or* ['pɛrə,ʃut] *n., v.* **-chut•ed, -chut•ing.** *—n.* **1** an apparatus made to give a slow, gradual fall to a person or thing that jumps or is dropped from an aircraft. The top of a parachute resembles that of an umbrella and is made from nylon or silk. **2** anything resembling or used like a parachute.
—v. **1** come or send down by, or as if by, a parachute; airdrop. **2** *Cdn.* **a** *Politics.* introduce (a non-resident candidate, usually a well-known figure) into a riding in an attempt to win the seat. **b** bring in (an outsider) to do a specific job or act in a specific capacity, especially at a senior level. ⟨< F *parachute* < *para-* (< Ital. *para* guard against, ult. < L *parare* prepare) + *chute* a fall⟩

par•a•chut•ist ['pærə,ʃutɪst] *or* ['pɛrə,ʃutɪst] *n.* a person who uses a parachute, especially one who is skilled in making descents with a parachute.

par•a•cy•mene [,pærə'saɪmin] *or* [,pɛrə'saɪmin] *n.* See CYMENE.

pa•rade [pə'reid] *n., v.* **-rad•ed, -rad•ing.** *—n.* **1** a march for display; procession: *The circus had a parade.* **2** a group of people walking for display or pleasure. **3** a place where people walk for display or pleasure. **4** a great show or display: *A modest man will not make a parade of his wealth.* **5** a military display or review of troops. **6** PARADE SQUARE.
—v. **1** march through with display: *The performers and animals paraded the streets.* **2** march in procession; walk proudly as if in a parade. **3** make a great show of. **4** come together in military order for review or inspection. **5** assemble (troops) for review. ⟨< F < Sp. *parada*, ult. < L *parare* prepare⟩ **—pa'rad•er,** *n.*

parade ground *Esp. U.S.* PARADE SQUARE.

parade square the area where troops parade, drill, etc.

par•a•digm ['pærə,daɪm] *or* ['pɛrə,daɪm], ['pærə,dɪm] *or* ['pɛrə,dɪm] *n.* **1** a pattern; example. **2** *Grammar.* **a** an example of a noun, verb, pronoun, etc. in all its inflections. **b** a display of such an arrangement. *Example*: horse, horse's, horses, horses'. ⟨< L < Gk. *paradeigma* pattern, ult. < *para-* side by side + *deiknunai* to show⟩ **—,par•a•dig'mat•ic,** *adj.*

par•a•di•sa•ic•al [,pærədə'seiəkəl] *or* [,pɛrədə'seiəkəl] *adj.* paradisiacal. ⟨alt. of *paradisiacal* on the pattern of Judaic, Mosaic, etc.⟩

par•a•dise ['pærə,dəis] *or* ['pɛrə,dəis] *n.* **1** heaven. **2** a place or condition of great happiness. **3** a place of great beauty. **4** Also, **Paradise,** the Garden of Eden. ⟨ME < OF < L *paradisus* < Gk. *paradeisos* < OPersian *pairidaeza* park < *pairi* around + *daeza* wall⟩

par•a•di•si•ac•al [,pærədə'saɪəkəl] *or* [,pɛrədə'saɪəkəl] *adj.* of, having to do with, or resembling paradise.

par•a•dor ['pærə,dɔr] *or* ['pɛrə,dɔr]; *Spanish,* [pɑʀɑ'ðɔʀ] a Spanish inn owned by the government, often formerly a castle or great house, offering accommodation and food at reasonable prices. ⟨< Sp.⟩

par•a•dox ['pærə,dɒks] *or* ['pɛrə,dɒks] *n.* **1** a statement that may be true but seems to say two opposite things. *Examples*: More haste, less speed. The child is father to the man. **2** a statement that is false because it says two opposite things. **3** a person or thing that seems to be full of contradictions. **4** any inconsistent or contradictory fact, action, or condition. ⟨< L < Gk. *paradoxos* < *para-* contrary to + *doxa* opinion⟩
☛ *Syn.* **1.** See note at EPIGRAM.

par•a•dox•i•cal [,pærə'dɒksəkəl] *or* [,pɛrə'dɒksəkəl] *adj.* **1** of or involving a paradox. **2** having the habit of using paradoxes. **—,par•a'dox•i•cal•ly,** *adv.*

par•a•drop ['pærə,drɒp] *or* ['pɛrə,drɒp] *v.* **-dropped, -drop•ping;** *n.* airdrop.

par•af•fin ['pærəfɪn] *or* ['pɛrəfɪn] *n., v. —n.* **1 a** a flammable, white, waxy substance that is a mixture of hydrocarbons obtained especially from petroleum or shale, used for making candles and for coating or sealing. **b** any of various other mixtures of hydrocarbons. **2** *Chemistry.* any hydrocarbon of the methane series. **3** *Esp. Brit.* kerosene.
—v. treat with paraffin. ⟨< G < L *parum* not very < *affinis* related; from its small affinity for other substances⟩
—,par•af'fin•ic, *adj.*

par•af•fine ['pærəfɪn] *or* ['pɛrəfɪn] *n., v.* **-fined, -fin•ing.** See PARAFFIN.

par•a•gen•e•sis [,pærə'dʒɛnəsɪs] *or* [,pɛrə'dʒɛnəsɪs] *n.* the order in which associated minerals in rocks or veins have crystallized, including formations affected by deposits in contact.

par•a•gon ['pærə,gɒn] *or* ['pɛrə,gɒn], ['pærəgən] *or* ['pɛrəgən] *n.* **1** a model of excellence or perfection. **2** a flawless diamond weighing 100 carats or more. ⟨< OF < Ital. *paragone* touchstone < Med.Gk. *parakonē* whetstone⟩

par•a•graph ['pærə,græf] *or* ['pɛrə,græf] *n., v.* *—n.* **1** a group of sentences relating to the same idea or topic and forming a distinct part of a chapter, letter, or other piece of writing. A paragraph begins on a new line and is usually indented. **2** a separate note or item of news in a newspaper. **3** a sign (¶) used to show where a paragraph begins or should begin. It is used mostly in correcting or drafting written work, and may also mark material referred to elsewhere.
—v. **1** divide into paragraphs. **2** write paragraphs about. ⟨< LL < Gk. *paragraphos* line (in the margin) marking a break in sense < *para-* beside + *graphein* write⟩ **—'par•a,graph•er,** *n.*

Par•a•guay ['pærə,gwaɪ] *or* ['pɛrə,gwaɪ], ['pærə,gwei] *or* ['pɛrə,gwei] *n.* **1** a country in central South America. **2** a river of South America.

Par•a•guay•an [,pærə'gwaɪən] *or* [,pɛrə'gwaɪən], [,pærə'gweiən] *or* [,pɛrə'gweiən] *n., adj.* *—n.* a native or inhabitant of Paraguay.
—adj. of or having to do with Paraguay or its people.

Paraguay tea maté.

par•a•keet ['pærə,kit] *or* ['pɛrə,kit] *n.* any of various small parrots, most of which have slender bodies and long tails. Also, **parrakeet.** ⟨< OF *paroquet,* apparently alteration of *perrot* parrot < *Perrot,* dim. of *Pierre* Peter⟩

par•a•lan•guage ['pærə,læŋgwɪdʒ] *or* ['pɛrə,læŋgwɪdʒ] *n.* aspects of vocal utterances not strictly part of language, as volume, tempo, and vocal quality, sometimes also facial expressions and gestures. **—,pa•ra•lin'guis•tic,** *adj.*

par•a•leip•sis [,pærə'ləipsɪs] *or* [,pɛrə'ləipsis] paralipsis.

par•a•lep•sis [,pærə'lɛpsɪs] *or* [,pɛrə'lɛpsɪs] paralipsis.

par•a•lip•sis [,pærə'lɪpsɪs] *or* [,pɛrə'lɪpsɪs] *n., pl.* **par•a•lip•ses** [-siz] a rhetorical device for emphasizing a point by omitting all but a passing reference to it: *not to mention the danger involved.* ⟨< Gk. *para* alongside + *leipein* to leave⟩

par•al•lac•tic [,pærə'læktɪk] *or* [,pɛrə'læktɪk] *adj.* of or having to do with parallax.

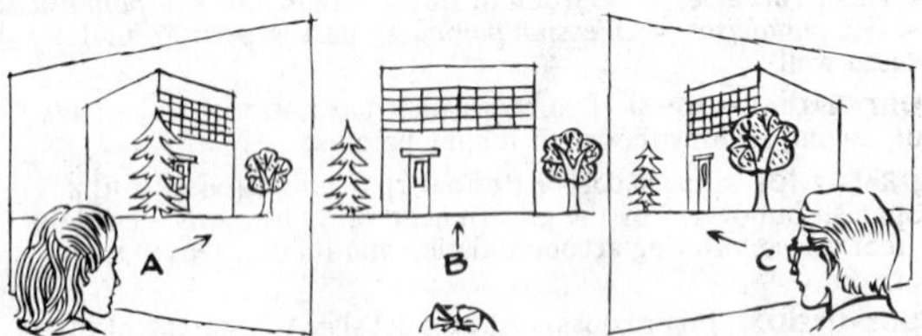

Parallax. The trees appear to be in different positions in relation to the building when viewed from different points.

par•al•lax ['pærə,læks] *or* ['pɛrə,læks] *n.* **1** the apparent change or amount of change in the direction or position of an object as seen from two different points. **2** *Astronomy.* the apparent change in angle of a celestial body with reference to a fixed object, caused by its being viewed from the surface rather than the centre of the earth (**diurnal** or **geocentric parallax**), or from the earth rather than the sun (**annual** or **heliocentric parallax**). ⟨< Gk. *parallaxis* deviation, ult. < *para-* + *allasein* to change⟩

par•al•lel ['pærə,lɛl] *or* ['pɛrə,lɛl] *adj., n., v.* **-lelled** or **-leled, -lel•ling** or **-lel•ing.** *—adj.* **1** at or being the same distance apart everywhere, like the two rails of a railway track. See QUADRILATERAL for picture. **2** similar; corresponding: *parallel points in the characters of different people.* **3** having component parts located or attached in parallel, as in machine or electric tools. **4** *Grammar.* characterized by a succession of syntactically similar phrases or clauses.
—n. **1** a parallel line or surface. **2** *Geography.* **a** any of the imaginary circles around the earth parallel to the equator, marking degrees of latitude: *The 49th parallel marks much of the boundary between Canada and the United States.* **b** any of the markings on a map that represent these circles. **3** something like or similar to another: *Their experience was an interesting parallel to ours.* **4** a comparison to show likeness: *Draw a parallel between this winter and last winter.* **5** *Electricity.* an arrangement of the wiring of batteries, lights, etc. in which all the positive poles or terminals are joined to one conductor, and all the negative to the other. **6** the condition of being parallel.
—v. **1** be at the same distance from throughout the length: *The street parallels the railway.* **2** cause to be or run parallel. **3** be like; be similar to: *Your story closely parallels what they told me.* **4** find a case which is similar or parallel to: *Can you parallel that for friendliness?* **5** compare in order to show likeness. ⟨< L < Gk. *parallēlos* < *para allēlōn* beside one another⟩

parallel bars *Gymnastics.* an apparatus consisting of two parallel wooden bars mounted horizontally on upright posts, used for various exercises.

par•al•lel•e•pi•ped [,pærə,lɛlə'pəipɪd] *or* [,pɛrə,lɛlə'pəipɪd] *n.* a geometric solid whose faces are all parallelograms. A parallelepiped is a six-sided prism. ⟨< Gk. *parallēlepipedon* body with parallel surfaces < *parallēlos* parallel + *epipedon* a plane surface⟩

par•al•lel•ism ['pærəlɛl,ɪzəm] *or* ['pɛrəlɛl,ɪzəm], ['pærələ,lɪzəm] *or* ['pɛrələ,lɪzəm] *n.* **1** the quality or state of being parallel. **2** a likeness; correspondence; agreement. **3** in writing, balance between parts of a sentence or paragraph, obtained by echoing structure or style.

par•al•lel•o•gram [,pærə'lɛlə,græm] *or* [,pɛrə'lɛlə,græm] *n.* a four-sided plane figure having opposite sides parallel and equal. Squares, oblongs, rhombuses, and rhomboids are parallelograms. See QUADRILATERAL for picture. ⟨< Gk. *parallēlogrammon,* neut. < *parallēlos* parallel + *grammē* line⟩

par•a•lyse or **par•a•lyze** ['pærə,laɪz] *or* ['pɛrə,laɪz] *v.* **-lysed** or **-lyzed, -lys•ing** or **-lyz•ing. 1** affect with a lessening or loss of the power of motion or feeling in a part of the body: *His left arm was paralysed after the accident.* **2** make powerless or ineffective; cripple: *The whole project was paralysed when the funds were cut off.* **3** stun or deaden: *paralysed with fear.*

pa•ral•y•sis [pə'ræləsɪs] *n., pl.* **-ses** [-,siz]. **1** a lessening or loss of the power of motion or sensation in any part of the body. **2** a condition of powerlessness or helpless inactivity; a crippling: *The war caused a paralysis of trade.* ⟨< L < Gk. *paralysis,* ult. < *para-* from beside + *lyein* to loosen, disable. Doublet of PALSY.⟩

par•a•lyt•ic [,pærə'lɪtɪk] *or* [,pɛrə'lɪtɪk] *adj., n.* *—adj.* **1** of, having to do with, or like paralysis. **2** having paralysis: *a paralytic limb.*
—n. a person affected with paralysis.

par•a•lyze ['pærə,laɪz] *or* ['pɛrə,laɪz] *v.* See PARALYSE.

par•a•me•ci•um [,pærə'miʃiəm] *or* [,pɛrə'miʃiəm], [,pærə'misiəm] *or* [,pɛrə'misiəm] *n., pl.* **-ci•a** [-ʃiə] *or* [-siə] any of a genus (*Paramecium*) of free-swimming protozoans shaped somewhat like the sole of a slipper, completely covered with cilia and having a groove along one side leading into the mouth cavity. ⟨< NL < Gk. *paramēkēs* oblong < *para-* on one side + *mēkos* length⟩

par•a•med•ic [,pærə'mɛdɪk] *or* [,pɛrə'mɛdɪk] *n.* a person trained in paramedical work.

par•a•med•i•cal [,pærə'mɛdəkəl] *or* [,pɛrə'mɛdəkəl] *adj.* of, having to do with, or designating auxiliary medical personnel such as medical technicians, X-ray technicians, or ambulance drivers, or the work they do.

pa•ram•e•ter [pə'ræmətər] *n.* **1** *Mathematics.* a quantity that is constant in a particular calculation or case but varies in other cases. **2** any of a set of measurable features or properties that determine the characteristics or behaviour of something: *parameters of space and time.* **3** any limiting or defining element or feature: *They found the parameters of their life too restricting.* ⟨< NL *parametrum* < Gk. *para-* beside + *métron* meter⟩

par•a•mil•i•tar•y [,pærə'mɪlə,tɛri] *or* [,pɛrə'mɪlə,tɛri] *adj.* **1** of or designating a group, unit, etc. organized along military lines and functioning as a civil force or an auxiliary military force: *a paramilitary police force.* **2** of or for such a force: *paramilitary training.*

par•am•ne•sia [,pæræm'niʒə] *or* [,pɛræm'nɪʒə] *n.* *Psychology.* **1** a distortion of the memory in which fantasy is confused with fact. **2** failure to recollect the correct meaning of a word. **3** DÉJÀ VU.

par•a•mount ['pærə,maʊnt] *or* ['pɛrə,maʊnt] *adj., n.* *—adj.* chief in importance; above others; supreme: *Truth is of paramount importance.*
—n. an overlord; supreme ruler. ⟨< AF *paramont* above < *par* by (< L *per*) + *amont* up < L *ad montem* to the mountain⟩
☛ *Syn. adj.* See note at DOMINANT.

par•amour ['pærə,mʊr] *or* ['pɛrə,mʊr] *n.* **1** a person who takes the place of a husband or wife illegally. **2** lover. ⟨ME < OF *paramour* < *par amour* by love < L *per amorem*⟩

par•a•noi•a [,pærə'nɔɪə] *or* [,pɛrə'nɔɪə] *n.* **1** a serious mental illness characterized by the firm belief that one is being persecuted or by delusions of grandeur. **2** an irrational but not pathological feeling of persecution. ⟨< NL < Gk. *paranoia*, ult. < *para-* amiss + *nous* mind⟩

par•a•noi•ac [,pærə'nɔɪæk] *or* [,pɛrə'nɔɪæk] *adj. or n.* paranoid.

par•a•noid ['pærə,nɔɪd] *or* ['pɛrə,nɔɪd] *adj., n.* *—adj.* **1** of, like, or showing paranoia. **2** having an extreme tendency to mistrust people and suspect them of ill will or bad intentions.
—n. a person with paranoia.

par•a•nor•mal [,pærə'nɔrməl] *or* [,pɛrə'nɔrməl] *adj.* that cannot be explained in normal scientific terms: *paranormal phenomena, a paranormal experience.* **—,par•a'nor•mal•ly,** *adv.*

par•a•pet ['pærəpət] *or* ['pɛrəpət] *n.* **1** a low wall or mound of stone, earth, etc., to protect soldiers. See FORT for picture. **2** a low wall at the edge of a balcony, roof, bridge, etc. ⟨< Ital. *parapetto* < *para* defend (< L *parare* prepare) + *petto* breast < L *pectus*⟩

par•a•pet•ed ['pærə,pɛtəd] *or* ['pɛrə,pɛtəd] *adj.* having a parapet or parapets.

par•a•pher•nal•ia [,pærəfə'neiljə] *or* [,pɛrəfə'neiljə], [,pæəfər'neiliə] *or* [,pɛrəfər'neiljə] *n.pl.* (*often used with a singular verb*) **1** personal belongings. **2** equipment; outfit. ⟨< Med.L *paraphernalia*, ult. < Gk. *parapherna* < *para*, besides + *phernē* dowry⟩
☛ *Usage.* **Paraphernalia** can be used with either a singular or a plural verb.

par•a•phrase ['pærə,freiz] *or* ['pɛrə,freiz] *v.* **-phrased, -phras•ing;** *n.* *—v.* state the meaning of (a passage) in other words.
—n. an expression of the meaning of a passage in other words. ⟨< F < L < Gk. *paraphrasis* < *para-* alongside of + *phrazein* say⟩
☛ *Hom.* PERIPHRASE ['pɛrə,freiz].

par•a•phras•tic [,pærə'fræstɪk] *or* [,pɛrə'fræstɪk] *adj.* marked by the use of paraphrase.
☛ *Hom.* PERIPHRASTIC [,pɛrə'fræstɪk].

par•a•ple•gi•a [,pærə'plidʒiə] *or* [,pɛrə'plidʒiə] *n.* paralysis of the legs and the lower part of the trunk. ⟨< NL < Gk. *paraplēgia* paralysis of one side of the body⟩

par•a•ple•gic [,pærə'plidʒɪk] *or* [,pɛrə'plidʒɪk] *n., adj.* *—n.* a person affected with paraplegia.
—adj. having to do with, or affected with, paraplegia.

par•a•prax•is [,pærə'præksɪs] *or* [,pɛrə'præksɪs] *n., pl.* **-prax•es** [-'præksiz]. *Psychology.* an action not completed according to conscious intention, such as a slip of the tongue or pen, misplacement of objects, forgetfulness or other errors, thought to be caused by conflicting conscious and unconscious wishes.

par•a•psy•chol•o•gy [,pærəsəi'kɒlədʒi] *or* [,pɛrəsəi'kɒlədʒi] *n.* the study of mental phenomena not explainable in terms of known physical laws, such as clairvoyance, telepathy, and psychokinesis.
—,par•a,psy•cho'log•i•cal, *adj.*

par•a•site ['pærə,səit] *or* ['pɛrə,səit] *n.* **1** a plant or animal living in, with, or on another from which it receives food or other benefit; the host receives no benefit and may be harmed. Lice and tapeworms are parasites on animals and mistletoe is a parasite on oak trees. **2** a person who lives on others without making any useful and fitting return. **3** in ancient Greece and Rome, a person who ate at the table or at the expense of another, earning meals by flattery or wit. ⟨< L < Gk. *parasitos* < *para-* alongside of + *sitos* food⟩

par•a•sit•ic [,pærə'sɪtɪk] *or* [,pɛrə'sɪtɪk] *adj.* **1 a** having the characteristics of a parasite. **b** living off others, with or without their consent. **2** caused by the action of parasites, as a growth or disease. Also, **parasitical. —,par•a'sit•i•cal•ly,** *adv.*

par•a•sit•ism ['pærəsəi,tɪzəm] *or* ['pɛrəsəi,tɪzəm], ['pærəsə,tɪzəm] *or* ['pɛrəsə,tɪzəm] *n. Biology.* a form of symbiosis in which one organism lives in or on another organism. Compare AMENSALISM, COMMENSALISM, and MUTUALISM.

par•a•si•tol•o•gy [,pærəsəi'tɒlədʒi] *or* [,pɛrəsəi'tɒlədʒi], [,pærəsə'tɒlədʒi] *or* [,pɛrəsə'tɒlədʒi] *n.* the branch of biology that deals with the study of parasites and their habits.

par•a•si•to•sis [,pærəsəi'tousɪs] *or* [,pɛrəsəi'tousɪs], [,pærəsə'tousɪs] *or* [,pɛrəsə'tousɪs] *n. Medicine.* any diseased condition caused by parasites.

par•a•sol ['pærə,sɒl] *or* ['pɛrə,sɒl] *n.* a light umbrella used as a protection from the sun. ⟨< F < Ital. *parasole* < *para* ward off + *sole* sun⟩

parasympathetic nervous system [,pærə,sɪmpə'θɛtɪk] *or* [,pɛrə,sɪmpə'θɛtɪk] that part of the autonomic nervous system arising in the cranial and sacral regions and operating in opposition to the sympathetic nervous system in such functions as contracting the pupil of the eye or slowing the heartbeat.

par•a•syn•the•sis [,pærə'sɪnθəsɪs] *or* [,pɛrə'sɪnθəsɪs] *n. Linguistics.* a process of word formation in which: **a** a derivational suffix is added to a compound or phrase. *Example*: open-minded *is* open mind + ed, *not* open + minded. **b** both a prefix and a derivational suffix are added to a word or stem. *Example*: unhappiness *is* un + happy + ness.

par•a•tac•tic [,pærə'tæktɪk] *or* [,pɛrə'tæktɪk] *adj.* having the characteristics of, or involving the use of, parataxis.

par•a•tax•is [,pærə'tæksɪs] *or* [,pɛrə'tæksɪs] *n. Grammar.* the placing together of two or more related clauses, phrases, etc. without a connecting word. *Example*: Let's go, it's getting late. ⟨< Gk. *parataxis* a placing beside⟩

par•a•thy•roid [,pærə'θaɪrɔɪd] *or* [,pɛrə'θaɪrɔɪd] *adj., n. Anatomy.* *—adj.* **1** near the thyroid gland. **2** of, having to do with, or caused by the PARATHYROID GLANDS.
—n. PARATHYROID GLAND. ⟨< *para-*[1] + *thyroid*⟩

parathyroid gland *Anatomy.* any of four small glands situated near or embedded in the thyroid gland and producing a hormone for the metabolism of calcium and phosphorus. The hormone of the parathyroid gland is necessary for life.

par•a•troop•er ['pærə,trupər] *or* ['pɛrə,trupər] *n.* a soldier trained to use a parachute for descent from an aircraft into a battle area. ⟨< *para(chute)* + *trooper*⟩

par•a•troops ['pærə,trups] *or* ['pɛrə,trups] *n.pl.* troops moved by air and landed by parachutes in a battle area.

par•a•ty•phoid [,pærə'təifɔɪd] *or* [,pɛrə'təifɔɪd] *n., adj. Pathology.* *—n.* an infectious disease having symptoms similar to but usually milder than those of typhoid fever, caused by any bacteria of the genus *Salmonella* other than *S. typhi.*
—adj. of or pertaining to paratyphoid. ⟨< *para*[1]*-* + *typhoid*⟩

par av•i•on [paʀa'vjɔ̃] *French.* by air mail.

par•boil ['pɑr,bɔɪl] *v.* **1** boil till partly cooked. **2** overheat. ⟨< F < LL *perbullire* < *per-* thoroughly + *bullire* boil; *par-* confused with *part*⟩

Par•ca ['pɑrkə] *n. Roman mythology.* the goddess of childbirth and destiny.

Par•cae ['pɑrsi] *or* ['pɑrkaɪ] *n.pl. Roman mythology.* the Fates.

par•cel ['pɑrsəl] *n., v.* **-celled** or **-celed, -cel•ling** or **-cel•ing.** *—n.* **1** a bundle of things wrapped or packed together; package. **2** a container with things packed in it. **3** a piece: *a parcel of land.* **4** a group; lot; pack. **5** a piece or unit, especially of something for sale.
—v. make a parcel of.
parcel out, divide into or distribute in portions. ⟨ME < OF *parcelle*, ult. < L *particula*, dim. of *pars*, *partis* part⟩
☛ *Syn. n.* **1.** See note at BUNDLE.

parcel post 1 a class of postal service for sending heavy or large parcels. **2** mail handled by this service.

parch [pɑrtʃ] *v.* **1** make hot and dry or thirsty: *The fever parched her.* **2** dry by heating; roast slightly: *Corn is sometimes parched.* ⟨ME *parchen*, *perchen*; origin uncertain⟩

Par•chee•si or **Par•che•si** [pɑr'tʃizi] *n. Trademark.* a game resembling backgammon, played by moving pieces according to throws of dice. ⟨< Hind. *pachisi* < *pachis* twenty-five (highest throw)⟩

parch•ment ['pɑrtʃmənt] *n.* **1** the skin of sheep, goats, etc. prepared for use as a writing material. **2** a manuscript or document written on parchment. **3** a kind of paper that looks like parchment. ⟨ME < OF *parchemin* < VL *particaminum*, blending of *parthica (pellis)* Parthian (leather) and *pergamina* of Pergamum, a city in Greece, where it originated⟩

pard [pɑrd] *n. Archaic.* leopard; panther. ⟨ME < OF < L < Gk. *pardos*⟩

par•don ['pɑrdən] *n., v.* *—n.* **1** forgiveness: *He asked his mother's pardon for having insulted her.* **2** a setting free from punishment. **3** a legal document setting a person free from punishment. **4** a papal indulgence.
I beg your pardon! I am extremely sorry!
—v. **1** forgive; excuse; overlook: *to pardon someone's bad manners.* **2** set free from punishment: *to pardon a criminal.* ⟨ME

< OF *pardon* < *pardonner* to pardon < LL *perdonare* < L *per-* thoroughly + *donare* give < *donum* gift⟩
☛ *Syn. v.* **1.** See note at EXCUSE.
☛ *Usage.* See note at EXCUSE.

par•don•a•ble ['pɑrdənəbəl] *adj.* that can be pardoned; excusable. **—'par•don•a•bly,** *adv.*

par•don•er ['pɑrdənər] *n.* **1** in the Middle Ages, a person authorized by the church to sell papal pardons, called indulgences. **2** a person who pardons.

pare [pɛr] *v.* **pared, par•ing. 1** trim by cutting away irregular bits: *to pare a corn.* **2** cut or shave off the outer skin or layer of; peel: *to pare an apple.* **3** cut away or lessen little by little: *We're trying to pare expenses.* ⟨ME < OF < L *parare* make ready. Doublet of PARRY.⟩
☛ *Hom.* PAIR, PEAR, PÈRE.

par•e•gor•ic [ˌpærə'gɔrɪk] *or* [ˌpɛrə'gɔrɪk] *n., adj. —n.* a soothing medicine containing camphor and a little opium.
—adj. soothing. ⟨< LL < Gk. *parēgorikos* soothing, ult. < *para-* at the side of + *-agoros* speaking⟩

paren. parenthesis.

pa•ren•chy•ma [pə'rɛŋkəmə] *n.* **1** *Botany.* a soft tissue of higher plants composed of thin-walled, unspecialized, living cells that make up much of the substance of the softer parts of leaves, the pulp of fruits, the pith of stems, etc. **2** *Zoology.* the essential, functional tissue of an animal organ, as distinguished from its connective or supporting tissue. ⟨< Gk. *parenchyma* < *para-* beside + *en-* in + *chyma* what is poured⟩ **—ˌpar•en'chym•a•tous** [ˌpærən'kɪmətəs], *adj.*

par•ent ['pɛrənt] *n., v. —n.* **1** a mother, father; any ancestor or progenitor. **2** any animal or plant that produces offspring or seed. **3** a source; cause: *Danger is often the parent of fear.* **4** a business enterprise having subsidiary companies in which it has a controlling interest.
—v. take care of a child or children: *Young mothers learn to parent by experience.* ⟨ME < OF < L *parens, -entis,* originally active pp. of *parere* bring forth⟩

par•ent•age ['pɛrəntɪdʒ] *n.* **1** descent from parents; family line; ancestry. **2** the state of being a parent.

pa•ren•tal [pə'rɛntəl] *adj.* of or having to do with a parent or parents; like a parent's: *parental advice.* **—pa'ren•tal•ly,** *adv.*

parental leave a leave of absence from a job for a parent to look after a new baby.

par•en•ter•al [pɑr'ɛntərəl] *adj.* **1** situated or occurring outside of the intestines. **2** of a drug, food, etc., taken into the body otherwise than by way of the digestive tract, especially by injection. ⟨< *para-* + *-enter-* (< Gk. *entera* intestines) + *-al.* 20c.⟩

pa•ren•the•ses [pə'rɛnθəˌsiz] *n.* pl. of PARENTHESIS.

pa•ren•the•sis [pə'rɛnθəsɪs] *n., pl.* **-ses** [-siz]. **1** *Grammar.* a word, phrase, or sentence inserted within a sentence to explain or qualify something, and usually set off by brackets, commas, or dashes. A parenthesis is not grammatically essential to the sentence it is in. **2** an often irrelevant episode or digression; an interlude. **3** either or both of two curved lines ( ) used to set off such an expression or to indicate that a group of symbols in mathematics, chemistry, or symbolic logic is to be regarded as a single term. ⟨< L < Gk. *parenthesis,* ult. < *para-* beside + *en-* in + *thesis* a placing⟩

pa•ren•the•size [pə'rɛnθəˌsaɪz] *v.* **-sized, -siz•ing. 1** insert as or in a parenthesis. **2** put between the marks of parenthesis. **3** put many parentheses in.

par•en•thet•ic [ˌpærən'θɛtɪk] *or* [ˌpɛrən'θɛtɪk] *adj.* **1** qualifying; explanatory. **2** in parentheses. **3** using parentheses. Also, **parenthetical. —ˌpar•en'thet•i•cal•ly,** *adv.*

par•ent•hood ['pɛrəntˌhʊd] *n.* the state of being a parent.

par•ent•ing ['pɛrəntɪŋ] *n., adj. —n.* **1** the work of raising children. **2** the skills and abilities necessary for this work.
—adj. of or concerning parenting: *Her parenting skills are quite remarkable.*

Parent–Teacher Association an organization of the teachers in a school and the parents or guardians of their students, having the mutual aims of promoting co-operation and furthering the effectiveness of the educational program. *Abbrev.*: PTA or P.T.A.

pa•re•sis [pə'risɪs], ['pærəsɪs], *or* ['pɛrəsɪs] *n.* **1** an incomplete paralysis resulting from spinal cord disease, muscular dystrophy, etc., affecting the ability to move but not the ability to feel. **2** a psychosis due to extensive destruction of brain tissue that is a late manifestation of syphilis, generally characterized by mental deterioration, seizures, speech defects, and progressive paralysis. Also called **general paresis** or **general paralysis of the insane.** ⟨< NL < Gk. *paresis* a letting go, ult. < *para-* by + *hienai* let go⟩

pa•ret•ic [pə'rɛtɪk] *or* [pə'ritɪk] *adj., n. —adj.* of, having to do with, or caused by paresis.
—n. a person suffering from paresis.

par ex•cel•lence [pɑr ˌɛksə'lɑns]; *French* [paʀɛksɛ'lɑ̃s] beyond comparison; above all others of the same sort.

par•fait [pɑr'fei]; *French,* [paʀ'fɛ] *n.* **1** ice cream with syrup or crushed fruit and whipped cream, served in a tall glass. **2** a rich ice cream, containing eggs and whipped cream, frozen unstirred. ⟨< F *parfait* perfect⟩

par•fleche ['pɑrˌflɛʃ] *or* [ˌpɑr'flɛʃ] *n. Cdn.* **1** rawhide made from buffalo skin that has been soaked in lye to remove the hair and then dried in the sun. **2** an article, such as a shield or bag, made from this rawhide. ⟨< Cdn.F *parflèche,* apparently < F *parer* to parry, ward off + *flèche* arrow⟩

par•he•lic [pɑr'hilɪk] *adj.* of, having to do with, or resembling a parhelion.

parhelic circle *Meteorology.* a luminous ring in the sky in a plane parallel to the horizon and at the same altitude as the sun, caused by the reflection of light by ice crystals in the atmosphere. Compare HALO (def. 1).

par•he•li•on [pɑr'hiliən] *or* [pɑr'hiljən] *n., pl.* **-he•li•a** [-'hiliə] *or* [-'hiljə] a bright, often coloured spot that sometimes appears to either side of the sun on the parhelic circle. Also called **mock sun.** ⟨< L < Gk. *parēlion* < *para-* beside + *hēlios* sun⟩

pa•ri•ah [pə'raɪə] *n.* **1** an outcast. **2** a member of a low caste in S India and Burma. ⟨< Tamil *paraiyar,* pl. or *paraiyan* drummer; because this caste provided the drummers at festivals⟩

pa•ri•e•tal [pə'raɪətəl] *adj., n. —adj.* of, having to do with, or forming the walls of a body cavity: *Two parietal bones form part of the sides and top of the skull.*
—n. a parietal bone or plate. ⟨< LL *parietalis* < L *paries, -etis* wall⟩

parietal lobe *Anatomy.* the middle part of each hemisphere of the brain, between the frontal and occipital lobes.

par•i–mu•tu•el [ˌpæri 'mjutʃuəl] *or* [ˌpɛri 'mjutʃuəl] *n.* **1** a system of betting on horse races in which those who have bet on the winning horses divide all the money bet. **2** a machine for recording such bets. ⟨< F *pari-mutuel* mutual wager; *pari* < *parier* bet < L *pariare* make equal < *par* equal⟩

par•ing ['pɛrɪŋ] *n., v. —n.* a part pared off; skin; rind.
—v. ppr. of PARE.

par•i pas•su [ˌpɑri 'pæsu], [ˌpæri 'pæsu], *or* [ˌpɛri 'pæsu] *Latin.* at an equal rate of progress; side by side; equally.

Par•is ['pærɪs] *or* ['pɛrɪs] *n. Greek legend.* a son of Priam, king of Troy. His abduction of Helen, the wife of King Menelaus of Sparta, caused the Trojan war.

Paris green *Chemistry.* a very poisonous, emerald green powder used as an insecticide and pigment. It is a compound of copper, arsenic, and acetic acid.

par•ish ['pærɪʃ] *or* ['pɛrɪʃ] *n.* **1** a district that has its own church and clergy; part of a diocese or other administrative district. **2** the people of a parish. **3** the members of the congregation of a particular church. **4** in New Brunswick, a political unit similar to a township. **5** in Québec, a civil district, a municipality similar to a township and related to a religious parish. **6** in the United Kingdom, a civil district. ⟨ME < OF *paroisse* < LL *parochia* < Gk. *paroikia,* ult. < *para-* near + *oikos* dwelling⟩
☛ *Hom.* PERISH ['pɛrɪʃ].

pa•rish•ion•er [pə'rɪʃənər] *n.* a member of a parish. ⟨earlier *parishion* < OF *paroissien*⟩

Pa•ri•sian [pə'rɪʒən] *or* [pə'rɪʒən] *n., adj. —n.* a native or inhabitant of Paris, the capital of France.
—adj. of or having to do with Paris or its people.

par•i•ty[1] ['pærɪti] *or* ['pɛrɪti] *n.* **1** equality; similarity or close correspondence with regard to state, position, condition, value, quality, degree, etc. **2** an equality between the market prices received by farmers for their commodities and the prices that they have to pay for labour, taxes, etc. **3** *Mathematics.* a condition existing between two integers when both are odd or both even. ⟨< L *paritas* < *par* equal⟩

par•i•ty[2] ['pærɪti] *or* ['pɛrɪti] *n. Obstetrics.* the condition or fact of having borne offspring. ⟨< L *parere* to bear or bring forth⟩

park [pɑrk] *n., v. —n.* **1** a piece of land in or near a city, town, etc. set apart for public recreation: *Let's have a picnic in the park.* **2** a large area of land kept as a recreation area (for camping, picnicking, hiking, canoeing, etc.) and as a refuge for wildlife: *Canada has fine national and provincial parks.* **3** the grounds around a fine house, usually in the country. **4** PARKING LOT. **5** a space where army vehicles, supplies, and artillery are put when an army camps. **6** a commercially operated recreation area with amusements, facilities for picnicking, swimming, etc. **7** PARKLAND (defs. 2, 3).
—v. **1** leave (an automobile, etc.) for a time in a certain place. **2** arrange (army vehicles, artillery, etc.) in a park. **3** *Informal.* place, put, or leave: *Just park your books on the table.* ⟨ME < OF *parc* < Med.L *parricus* enclosure. Doublet of PADDOCK.⟩

par•ka ['pɑrkə] *n. Cdn.* **1** a fur jacket with a hood, worn in the North. **2** a long, warm winter jacket of wool, nylon, etc., with a hood and usually shorter than the original Inuit type. Also, **parkae, parky, parki.** ⟨< Inuktitut (Aleutian Inuit) *purka* skin, outer coat < Russian, hide or pelt < Samoyed⟩

par•kade [pɑr'keid] *n. Cdn.* a multistoreyed structure for parking a large number of automobiles. ⟨blend of *park* and *arcade*⟩

park•ette [pɑr'kɛt] *n. Cdn.* a small park in a city, rarely larger and often smaller than a city block, usually containing flower beds and one or more park benches.

parking lot an area used for parking motor vehicles.

parking meter a device containing a coin-operated clock mechanism for indicating the amount of parking time that has been bought for a vehicle and the passing of that time.

par•kin•son•ism ['pɑrkənsə,nɪzəm] *n.* **1** PARKINSON'S DISEASE. **2** any neurological disorder, with or without tremor, characterized by muscular rigidity.

Par•kin•son's disease ['pɑrkənsənz] *Pathology.* a progressive disorder of the central nervous system occurring especially in men over the age of fifty and characterized by tremors, muscular rigidity, and impaired muscular co-ordination. ⟨named after James *Parkinson* (1755-1824), the English surgeon who first described it. 19c.⟩

Parkinson's Law satirical statements expressed as a law of economics or physics, such as the one stating that work expands to fill the time available for its completion. ⟨after C. Northcote *Parkinson* (1909-1993), the British economist who proposed it⟩

park•land ['pɑrk,lænd] *n.* **1** land kept free from houses, factories, etc. and maintained as a public park: *Parklands are intended to preserve the scenic beauty of the countryside.* **2** *Cdn.* the region between the foothills of the Rockies and the prairie. **3** *Cdn.* the wooded region between the northern forests and the three Prairie Provinces.

park ranger a government official who patrols and helps maintain a national or provincial park.

park•way ['pɑrk,wei] *n.* a broad road through an area kept up as a park, made attractive by grass, trees, flowers, etc.: *There is a beautiful parkway running through Ottawa.*

par•lance ['pɑrləns] *n.* a way of speaking; idiom: *The will was written in legal parlance.* ⟨< OF *parlance* < *parler* speak. See PARLEY.⟩

par•lan•do [pɑr'lɑndou] *adj. or adv. Music.* sung as if speaking or reciting. ⟨< Ital., ppr. of *parlare* speak⟩

par•lay ['pɑrlei] *or* ['pɑrli] *v., n. —v.* **1** risk (an original bet and its winnings) on another bet. **2** build up (something) by taking risks with it: *She parlayed a few hundred dollars into a fortune.*
—n. a series of bets made by parlaying. ⟨alteration of *paroli* < F < Ital. *paroli* grand cast at dice⟩
☛ *Hom.* PARLEY ['pɑrli].

par•ley ['pɑrli] *n., pl.* **-leys;** *v.* **-leyed, -ley•ing.** *—n.* a conference or informal talk, especially one with an enemy to discuss terms of surrender, exchange of prisoners, etc.
—v. discuss terms, especially with an enemy. ⟨< F *parlée* < a pp. of *parler* speak, ult. < L *parabola* parable⟩
☛ *Hom.* PARLAY ['pɑrli].

par•lia•ment ['pɑrləmənt] *n.* **1 Parliament, a** the national lawmaking body of Canada, consisting of the Senate and the House of Commons. **b** the national lawmaking body of the United Kingdom, consisting of the House of Lords and the House of Commons. **c** the lawmaking body of a country or colony having the British system of government. **2** a formal or official assembly convened to discuss public or national affairs. **3** the sitting members of a Parliament from one election to the next. ⟨ME < OF *parlement* < *parler* speak. See PARLEY.⟩

Parliament Buildings, Ottawa

par•lia•men•tar•i•an [,pɑrləmən'tɛriən] *n.* **1** a person skilled in parliamentary procedure or debate. **2 Parliamentarian,** a person who supported the Parliamentary forces under Oliver Cromwell against Charles I of England; Roundhead.

par•lia•men•ta•ry [,pɑrlə'mɛntəri] *adj.* **1** of a parliament: *parliamentary authority.* **2** according to the rules and customs of a parliament or other lawmaking body: *Our debating society is run by the rules of parliamentary procedure.* **3** done by a parliament. **4** having a parliament: *a parliamentary democracy.*

parliamentary secretary *Cdn.* a member of the House of Commons appointed to assist a Cabinet Minister in his or her parliamentary work.

Parliament Hill **1** the location of the Parliament buildings in Ottawa. **2** the government or Parliament of Canada: *the latest pronouncement from Parliament Hill.*

par•lour or **par•lor** ['pɑrlər] *n.* **1** a room for receiving or entertaining guests; sitting room or living room. **2** a room or rooms specially furnished or equipped for a certain kind of business; shop: *a beauty parlour, a funeral parlour.* **3** a place where refreshments of various kinds are sold: *an ice-cream parlour, a beer parlour.* ⟨ME < AF *parlour* < *parler* speak. See PARLEY.⟩

parlour car or **parlor car** *Archaic.* CLUB CAR.

par•lour•maid or **par•lor•maid** ['pɑrlər,meid] *n.* a maid who answers the door, waits on guests, etc.

par•lous ['pɑrləs] *adj., adv. Archaic. —adj.* **1** perilous: *a parlous state.* **2** very clever; shrewd.
—adv. extremely. ⟨var. of *perilous*⟩

Par•ma violet ['pɑrmə] a variety of violet (*Viola odorata*) which yields an oil used to make perfumes.

Par•me•san ['pɑrmə,zɑn], ['pɑrməzən], *or* ['pɑrmə,zæn] *n.* a very hard, dry Italian cheese with a sharp flavour, usually used in grated form. ⟨< *Parma,* Italy⟩

par•mi•gia•na [,pɑrmə'ʒɑnə] *adj.* containing or prepared with Parmesan cheese. ⟨< Ital.⟩

Par•nas•si•an [pɑr'næsiən] *adj., n. —adj.* **1** of or concerning Mount Parnassus. **2** of or concerning the art of poetry. **3** pertaining to the Parnassians.
—n. one of a group of 18th century French poets who believed in art for art's sake and were primarily concerned with form.

Par•nas•sus [pɑr'næsəs] *n.* **1** the fabled mountain of poets, the summit of which is supposed to be their goal. **2** a collection of poems or BELLES-LETTRES. **3** a centre of literary activity, especially poetic.
try to climb Parnassus, try to write poetry. ⟨< Mount *Parnassus* in S Greece, in ancient times sacred to Apollo and the Muses⟩

pa•ro•chi•al [pə'roukiəl] *adj.* **1** of or in a parish: *a parochial school.* **2** narrow; limited: *a parochial viewpoint.* ⟨ME < OF < LL *parochialis* < *parochia* parish. See PARISH.⟩
—pa'ro•chi•al•ly, *adv.*

pa•ro•chi•al•ism [pə'roukiə,lɪzəm] *n.* a parochial character or tendency; narrowness of interests or views.
—pa'ro•chi•al•ist, *n.*

parochial school **1** a local school maintained by a church. **2** an independent school receiving little or no tax support, especially one supported by the Roman Catholic Church.

par•o•dist ['pærədɪst] *or* ['pɛrədɪst] *n.* a writer of parodies.

par•o•dy ['pærədi] *or* ['pɛrədi] *n., pl.* **-dies;** *v.* **-died, -dy•ing.** *—n.* **1** a humorous imitation of a serious writing. A parody follows the form of the original, but changes its sense to nonsense or satire, thus making fun of the characteristics of the

original. **2** the art of writing parodies. **3** any work of art that makes fun of another. **4** a poor imitation.
—v. **1** make fun of by imitating; make a parody of. **2** imitate poorly. ⟨< L < Gk. *parōidia* < *para-* beside + *ōidē* song⟩ **—pa'rod•ic** [pə'rɒdɪk] or **pa'rod•i•cal,** *adj.*

pa•role [pə'roul] *n., v.* **-roled, -rol•ing.** *—n.* **1** a conditional release from prison before the full term is served: *The prisoner was released on parole.* **2** conditional freedom allowed in place of imprisonment. **3** word of honour: *The prisoner of war gave his parole not to try to escape.*
out on parole, released from prison under certain conditions such as reporting to a parole officer, not associating with known criminals, etc.
—v. give a parole: *The boys were paroled on condition that they report to the judge every three months.* ⟨< F *parole* word < L *parabola* parable. Doublet of PARABLE, PARABOLA, PALAVER.⟩ **—pa'rol•a•ble,** *adj.*

pa•rol•ee [pərou'li] *n.* one who is released from prison on parole.

pa•rot•id [pə'rɒtɪd] *adj., n. —adj.* near the ear. The **parotid glands,** one in front of each ear, supply saliva to the mouth through the **parotid ducts.**
—n. a parotid gland. ⟨< L < Gk. *parōtis, -idos* < *para-* beside + *ous, ōtos* ear⟩

-parous *combining form.* bearing or bringing forth: *oviparous = laying eggs; viviparous = bearing live young.* ⟨< L *-parus* bearing⟩

par•ox•ysm ['pærək,sɪzəm] *or* ['pɛrək,sɪzəm] *n.* **1** a sudden attack or increase of symptoms of a disease; convulsion: *a paroxysm of coughing.* **2** a sudden violent emotion, etc.: *a paroxysm of rage.* ⟨< Med.L < Gk. *paroxysmos,* ult. < *para-* + *oxynein* render acute⟩

par•ox•ys•mal [,pærək'sɪzməl] *or* [,pɛrək'sɪzməl] *adj.* of, like, or having paroxysms. **—,par•ox'ys•mal•ly,** *adv.*

par•quet [pɑr'kei] *n., v.* **-queted** [-'keid], **-quet•ing** [-'keiɪŋ]; *adj. —n.* a flooring made of inlaid pieces of wood, often of different kinds, fitted together to form a pattern.
—v. furnish with a parquet floor: *to parquet a room.*
—adj. made of parquet: *a parquet floor.* ⟨< F *parquet,* dim. of *parc* park⟩

par•quet•ry ['parkɪtri] *n., pl.* **-ries.** woodwork of small pieces of wood, often in different shapes and of different kinds, arranged in a geometric pattern. Parquetry is used especially for floors.

parr [pɑr] *n., pl.* **parr** or **parrs.** a young salmon before it leaves fresh water and enters the sea. Parr have dark vertical markings on the sides. Compare SMOLT. ⟨< Scottish dial.⟩
☛ *Hom.* PAR.

par•ra•keet ['pærə,kit] *or* ['pɛrə,kit] *n.* See PARAKEET.

par•ri•cide ['pærə,saɪd] *or* ['pɛrə,saɪd] *n.* **1** the crime of killing one's parent or a close relative. **2** a person who commits parricide. Compare PATRICIDE. ⟨< F < L *parricidium* the murder of a kinsman < **parus* kinsman + *-cidium* the act of killing (for def. 1); < F < L *parricida* one who murders a kinsman < **parus* + *-cida* killer (for def. 2)⟩ **—,par•ri'cid•al,** *adj.*

par•rot ['pærət] *or* ['pɛrət] *n., v. —n.* **1** any of a family (Psittacidae, constituting the order Psittaciformes) of birds of the tropics and southern temperate regions, having a stout, hooked bill and, usually, brightly coloured plumage. Parrots are excellent mimics. **2** a person who repeats words or acts without understanding them.
—v. **1** repeat without understanding. **2** repeat the words of without understanding: *He just parrots his elder brother.* ⟨< F *Perrot,* dim. of *Pierre* Peter⟩ **—'par•rot,like,** *adj.*

parrot fever psittacosis.

par•ry ['pæri] *or* ['pɛri] *v.* **-ried, -ry•ing;** *n., pl.* **-ries.** *—v.* **1** ward off; turn aside; evade (a thrust, stroke, weapon, question, etc.): *He parried the sword with his dagger.* **2** dodge; counter: *She parried our question by asking us one.*
—n. the act of parrying. ⟨< F *parez,* imperative of *parer* < Ital. *parare* ward off < L *parare* prepare. Doublet of PARE.⟩
☛ *Hom.* PERRY ['pɛri].

parse [pɑrs] *v.* **parsed, pars•ing. 1** *Grammar.* **a** analyse (a sentence) grammatically, describing the function of each part. **b** describe (a word) grammatically, telling what part of speech it is, its form, and its use in a sentence. **2** *Computer technology.* analyse (a string) for the purpose of associating groups of characters with syntactic structures in the underlying grammar: *This program will parse English but not Swahili.* ⟨< L *pars (orationis)* part (of speech)⟩ **—'pars•a•ble,** *adj.* **—'pars•er,** *n.*

par•sec ['pɑr,sɛk] *n. Astronomy.* a unit used with the SI for measuring distance in interstellar space, equal to about 3.26 light years. *Symbol:* pc ⟨< *par(allax)* + *sec(ond)*[2]⟩

Par•si or **Par•see** ['pɑrsi] *or* [pɑr'si] *n.* in India, a member of a Zoroastrian sect, descended from Persians who first settled there early in the 8th century A.D. ⟨< Persian and Hind. *Parsi* a Persian⟩ **—'Par•si,ism** or **'Par•see,ism,** *n.*

Par•si•fal ['pɑrsəfəl] *or* ['pɑrsə,fɑl] *n.* See PARZIFAL.

par•si•mo•ni•ous [,pɑrsə'mouniəs] *adj.* too economical; stingy. **—,par•si'mo•ni•ous•ly,** *adv.* **—,par•si'mo•ni•ous•ness,** *n.*

par•si•mo•ny ['pɑrsə,mouni] *n.* **1** carefulness in using money; thrift. **2** extreme carefulness in using money; stinginess. ⟨< L *parsimonia* < *parcere* spare⟩

pars•ley ['pɑrsli] *n., pl.* **-leys. 1** a Mediterranean plant (*Petroselinum crispum*) widely cultivated for its aromatic leaves, which are used for flavouring and also for garnishing meats, etc. **2** (*adjl.*) designating the family (Umbelliferae, also called Apiaceae) of plants mainly of north temperate regions that includes parsley and other plants used as herbs and spices, such as dill, caraway, and cumin, as well as a number of common vegetables such as the carrot, celery, and parsnip. ⟨OE *petersilie,* also < OF *peresil;* both < VL *petrosilium* < L < Gk. *petroselinon* < *petros* rock + *selinon* parsley⟩ **—'pars•leyed,** *adj.*

pars•nip ['pɑrsnɪp] *n.* **1** a plant (*Pastinaca sativa*) of the parsley family, native to Europe and Asia but widely cultivated for its long, tapering, fleshy, whitish root. **2** the root of this plant, usually eaten as a cooked vegetable. ⟨ME < OF *pasnaie* < L *pastinaca* (cf. *pastinare* dig); form infl. by ME *nep* turnip⟩

par•son ['pɑrsən] *n.* **1** a minister in charge of a Christian parish; rector. **2** any member of the Christian clergy; minister. ⟨< Med.L *persona* parson < L *persona* person, character. Doublet of PERSON.⟩

par•son•age ['pɑrsənɪdʒ] *n.* the house provided for a minister by his or her church.

parson bird tui.

Parson's table a square or rectangular table designed so that the four straight legs, of the same thickness as the top, extend down flush with the corners of the top so as to appear seamless; often constructed of a lightweight material such as plastic. ⟨< *Parson's* School of Design, New York⟩

part [pɑrt] *n., v., adj., adv. —n.* **1** something less than the whole: *What part of the chicken do you like best?* **2** each of several equal quantities into which a whole may be divided: *A dime is a tenth part of a dollar.* **3** a thing that helps to make up a whole: *spare parts. A radio has many parts.* **4** a share: *Everyone must do her part.* **5** a side in a dispute or contest: *He always takes his family's part.* **6** a character in a play, motion picture, etc.; role: *She played the part of Juliet.* **7** the words spoken by a character: *Actors have to learn their parts quickly.* **8** a role played by a person in real life. **9** a dividing line left in combing one's hair. **10** *Music.* **a** one of the voices or instruments. The four parts in singing are soprano, alto, tenor, and bass. **b** the music for one voice or instrument. **11** ability; talent: *a man of parts.* **12 parts,** *pl.* a region; district; place: *They have travelled much in foreign parts. I was born in these parts.* **13** concern or interest: *Her part in the matter was unclear.*
for (one's) **part,** as far as one is concerned: *For my part, I'd rather just forget it.*
for the most part, mostly: *The attempts were for the most part unsuccessful.*
in good part, in a friendly or gracious way: *She took the teasing in good part.*
in part, in some measure or degree; to some extent; partly.
on (someone's) **part** or **on the part of** (someone), done by or proceeding from someone: *We had never heard of any improprieties on the minister's part.*
part and parcel, a necessary or essential part: *Practising is part and parcel of learning to play the piano.*
play a part, a behave out of one's own character, with the intention of deceiving: *After murdering her husband, she played the part of the grieving widow.* **b** share in any activity; be an influential factor: *The lack of available jobs played a part in her decision to return to school.*
take part, take or have a share; participate.
—v. **1** divide into two or more pieces. **2** force apart; divide: *The police officer on horseback parted the crowd.* **3** go apart; separate: *The friends parted in anger.* **4** make a dividing line in (the hair): *He parts his hair on the right.*
part from, go away from; leave.

part with, give up; let go.
—adj. less than the whole: *part-time.*
—adv. in some measure or degree; partly. ⟨OE < L *pars, partis;* ME < OF *part,* n., and *partir* (< L *partire*), v., < L *pars, partis*⟩

☛ *Syn. n.* **1. Part,** PORTION, PIECE = something less than the whole. **Part** is the general word and means an element, fraction, or member of a whole, considered apart from the rest: *Save part of the roast for tomorrow night.* **Portion** means a part thought of not so much in relation to the whole from which it is taken as an amount or quantity assigned as a share: *Give a portion of each day to recreation.* **Piece** means a separate part, often thought of as complete in itself: *The child ate a big piece of cake.*

☛ *Usage.* **On the part of** is often a rather clumsy substitute for **by, among, for,** and the like: *In recent years there has been a noticeable feeling on the part of (among) students that education is all-important.*

part. 1 participle. 2 particular.

par•take [pɑr'teik] *v.* **-took, -tak•en, -tak•ing. 1** to take part or share in common with others; participate (in): *The children looked forward to partaking in the ceremony.* **2** take or have a share or part (*used with* **of**): *Would you care to partake of dessert?* **3** have to some extent the nature or character (*of*): *Her graciousness partakes of condescension.* ⟨< *partaker,* for *part-taker*⟩
—par'tak•er, *n.*

☛ *Syn.* **2.** See note at SHARE.

par•tak•en [pɑr'teikən] *v.* pp. of PARTAKE.

par•terre [pɑr'tɛr] *n.* **1** the part of the main floor of a theatre under the balcony. **2** an ornamental arrangement of flower beds and paths in a garden. ⟨< F *parterre* < *par terre* on the ground⟩

par•the•no•gen•e•sis [ˌpɑrθənou'dʒɛnəsɪs] *n. Biology.* reproduction by the development of an unfertilized ovum, occurring especially among the lower plants and invertebrate animals. ⟨< Gk. *parthenos* virgin + *genesis* origin, source⟩
—ˌpar•the•no•ge'net•ic [ˌpɑrθənoudʒə'nɛtɪk], *adj.*

Par•the•non ['pɑrθəˌnɒn] *or* ['pɑrθənən] *n.* in Athens, the temple of Athena on the Acropolis, regarded as the finest example of Doric architecture. ⟨< L < Gk. *Parthenon* < *hē parthenos* the Virgin, i.e., Athena⟩

Par•thi•an ['pɑrθiən] *n., adj. —n.* a native or inhabitant of Parthia, an ancient Asian kingdom that is now part of Iran.
—adj. of or having to do with Parthia or its people.

Par•thi•an shot a sharp parting remark or action. Parthian archers used to aim at their enemies while fleeing or pretending to flee.

par•tial ['pɑrʃəl] *adj.* **1** not complete; not total: *a partial loss.* **2** inclined to favour one side more than another; favouring unfairly; biassed: *A father should not be partial to any one of his children.* **3** having a liking; favourably inclined (*used with* **to**): *Most young people are partial to sports.* ⟨< LL *partialis* < L *pars, partis* part⟩

partial derivative *Mathematics.* the derivative of a function which has two or more variables with respect to one of the variables; the other variables are treated as constants.

partial fractions *Algebra.* a set of fractions whose algebraic sum is a given fraction: $\frac{1}{x^2-1} = \frac{A}{x-1} + \frac{B}{x+1}$

par•ti•al•i•ty [ˌpɑrʃi'æləti] *n., pl.* **-ties. 1** a favouring of one more than another or others; the quality or state of being partial. **2** a particular liking; fondness: *Children often have a partiality for candy.*

par•tial•ly ['pɑrʃəli] *adv.* **1** in part; not generally or totally; partly. **2** in a partial manner; with undue bias.

☛ *Syn.* **1.** See note at PARTLY.

Par•tic•i•pac•tion [pɑrˌtɪsə'pækʃən] *n. Cdn.* a private, non-profit organization whose purpose is to encourage and motivate the general public to become physically fit through participation in regular exercise. It is partly funded by the federal government.

par•tic•i•pant [pɑr'tɪsəpənt] *n., adj. —n.* one who participates.
—adj. participating.

participant observation *Sociology, anthropology.* a method of study in which the researcher takes part in the life of the group he or she is studying.

par•tic•i•pate [pɑr'tɪsəˌpeit] *v.* **-pat•ed, -pat•ing.** have a share; take part: *The teacher participated in the children's games.* ⟨< L *participare,* ult. < *pars, partis* part + *capere* take⟩
—parˌtic•i'pa•tion, *n.* **—par'tic•iˌpa•tor,** *n.*

☛ *Syn.* See note at SHARE.

par•ti•ci•pa•to•ry [pɑr'tɪsəpəˌtɔri] *adj.* allowing participation: *participatory children's theatre, participatory democracy.*

par•ti•cip•i•al [ˌpɑrtə'sɪpiəl] *adj. Grammar.* of, having to do with, or formed from a participle.

par•ti•ci•ple ['pɑrtəˌsɪpəl] *n. Grammar.* a verb form not marked for tense, used principally as part of a verb phrase or as an adjective. *Examples: The children are* watching *television. The* dripping *tap has been* fixed. *The* broken *vase was my favourite.* ⟨ME < OF *participle,* var. of *participe* < L *participium* a sharing. Related to PARTICIPATE.⟩

par•ti•cle ['pɑrtəkəl] *n.* **1** a very small bit: *I had a particle of dust in my eye.* **2** *Physics.* **a** a minute mass of matter that while still having inertia and attraction is treated as a point without length, breadth, or thickness. **b** one of the fundamental units of matter, as the electron, neutron, photon, or proton; elementary particle. **3** *Grammar* **a** an invariable word that cannot be easily classified as to part of speech, used to express a syntactic and/or semantic relationship in a phrase or sentence. *Examples: Please look* over *this paper;* Pick *up your toys.* **b** a derivational affix. *Examples:* un- *in* untrue, -ful *in* careful. ⟨< L *particula,* dim. of *pars, partis* part⟩

par•ti•cle•board ['pɑrtəkəlˌbɔrd] *n.* a kind of board used in building, furniture-making, etc., made of sawdust or small pieces of wood pressed together with a synthetic resin or similar binding agent.

par•ti–col•oured or **par•ti–col•ored** ['pɑrti ˌkʌlərd] *adj.* coloured differently in different parts; partly of one colour or tint, partly of another or others. ⟨*parti-* < F *parti* divided, pp. of *partir* < L *partire* < *pars, partis* a part⟩

par•tic•u•lar [pər'tɪkjələr] *adj., n. —adj.* **1** apart from others; considered separately; single: *That particular chair is already sold.* **2** belonging to some one person, thing, group, occasion, etc.: *A particular characteristic of a skunk is its smell.* **3** different from others; unusual; special: *a particular friend.* **4** hard to please; wanting everything to be just right; very careful: *She is very particular; nothing but the best will do.* **5** giving details; full of details: *a particular account of the game.* **6** *Logic.* describing a proposition that refers to an indefinite part of a whole class; not universal.
—n. **1** an individual part; item; point: *The work is complete in every particular.* **2** *Logic.* a proposition referring to an indefinite individual or group within a general class. *Example:* Some cats *have blue eyes.* **3** Often, **particulars,** *pl.* a detail or specific item of information: *The police should be informed of the particulars of the break-in.*
in particular, especially. ⟨ME < OF < L *particularis* < *particula.* See PARTICLE.⟩

☛ *Syn. adj.* **2.** See note at SPECIAL. *—n.* **1, 3.** See note at ITEM.

par•tic•u•lar•i•ty [pərˌtɪkjə'lærəti] *or* [pərˌtɪkjə'lɛrəti] *n., pl.* **-ties. 1** a detailed quality; minute detail. **2** special carefulness. **3** attentiveness to details. **4** a particular feature or trait. **5** the quality of being hard to please. **6** the quality or fact of being particular.

par•tic•u•lar•ize [pər'tɪkjələˌraiz] *v.* **-ized, -iz•ing. 1** mention particularly or individually; treat in detail; specify. **2** mention individuals; give details. **—par'tic•u•larˌiz•er,** *n.*
—parˌtic•u•lar•i'za•tion, *n.*

par•tic•u•lar•ly [pər'tɪkjələrli] *or* [pər'tɪkjəˌlɛrli] *adv.* **1** in a high degree; especially. **2** in a particular or specific manner. **3** in detail; minutely.

☛ *Syn.* **1.** See note at ESPECIALLY.

part•ing ['pɑrtɪŋ] *n., adj., v. —n.* **1** a departure; going away; taking leave. **2** a division; separation. **3** a place or thing that divides or separates: *Her hair is arranged with a side parting.* **4** death.
—adj. **1** given, taken, spoken, done, etc. on going away: *a parting request, a parting shot.* **2** departing. **3** dividing; separating. **4** dying.
—v. ppr. of PART.

parting shot a violent denunciation, criticism, threat, etc. made on departing.

par•ti pris [ˌpɑrti 'pri]; *French,* [paʀti'pʀi] an attitude decided upon in advance.

Parti Québécois [pɑr'ti ˌkeibɛk'wɑ] *Cdn.* a major political party in Québec, formed as a separatist party in 1968.

Parti rouge ['pɑrti 'ruʒ]; *French,* [paʀti'ʀuʒ] *Cdn.* the name of a radical French-Canadian political party of the mid-19th century, inspired by Louis Joseph Papineau, that supported universal suffrage, called for the abolition of the seigneurial system, and opposed political action by the Church. It later became the Québec wing of the Liberal Party.

par•ti•san ['partə,zæn] *or* ['partəzən] *n., adj.* —*n.* **1** a strong supporter of a person, party, or cause, especially one whose support is based on feeling rather than on reasoning. **2** a member of light, irregular troops; guerrilla.
—*adj.* of or like a partisan. Also, **partizan.** ⟨< F < Ital. *partigiano* < *parte* part⟩

par•ti•san•ship ['partəzən,ʃɪp] *n.* **1** strong loyalty to a party or cause. **2** the act of taking sides.

par•ti•ta [par'titə] *n. Music.* **1** an instrumental suite common in the 18th century. **2** a set of variations. ⟨< Ital.⟩

par•ti•tion [par'tɪʃən] *n., v.* —*n.* **1** a division into parts: *the partition of a man's wealth when he dies.* **2** one of the parts of a whole. **3** something that separates, especially a thin inside dividing wall or membrane.
—*v.* **1** divide into parts: *The empire was partitioned after the emperor's death.* **2** separate by a partition (*often used with* **off**): *A corner of the basement was partitioned off for a washroom.* ⟨< L *partitio, -onis* < *partire.* See PART.⟩

par•ti•tive ['partətɪv] *n., adj.* —*n. Grammar.* a word or phrase referring to a part of a collective or mass. *Some, few,* and *any* are partitives.
—*adj.* **1** expressing a part of a collective or mass: *a partitive determiner.* **2** serving to separate or make a division.
—**'par•ti•tive•ly,** *adv.*

partitive genitive a genitive case that denotes part of a whole.

par•ti•zan ['partə,zæn] *or* ['partəzən] See PARTISAN.

part•ly ['partli] *adv.* in part; in some measure or degree.
☛ *Syn.* **Partly,** PARTIALLY = in part or to a certain extent, not wholly or totally. **Partly** = not wholly or entirely but only in part or in some measure or degree: *They are partly to blame.* **Partially** = not totally or generally but affecting only one part or to only a limited extent: *She is partially paralysed.*

part•ner ['partnər] *n., v.* —*n.* **1** a member of a partnership. **2** associate or colleague: *The thief climbed through the window while his partner watched the street.* **3** spouse. **4** either person of a couple dancing together. **5** *Sports and games.* either of two players playing together against another pair. **6** one who shares: *My sister was the partner of my walks.*
—*v.* be a partner of. ⟨var. of *parcener* < AF *parconier* < *parçon* partition < L *partitio, -onis*; influenced by PART⟩
—**'part•ner•less,** *adj.*

part•ner•ship ['partnər,ʃɪp] *n.* **1** a legal association of two or more persons in a business enterprise. The members of a partnership share the risks and profits of their business. **2** the people associated in a partnership. **3** the state or office of being a partner: *She was rewarded with a partnership.* **4** the relationship of partners; association: *the partnership of marriage.*

part of speech *Grammar.* one of the nine form classes into which words are grouped according to their use or function in sentences. The main parts of speech in English are noun, pronoun, adjective, verb, adverb, preposition, conjunction, interjection, and article.
☛ *Usage.* **Parts of speech.** One of the fundamental facts of English grammar is that a word may function as more than one part of speech: In *spell the word,* we use **word** as a noun; in *How will I word the message?,* **word** is the verb.

par•took [par'tʊk] *v.* pt. of PARTAKE.

par•tridge ['partrɪdʒ] *n.* **-tridg•es** or *(esp. collectively)* **-tridge. 1** any of numerous medium-sized game birds (family Phasianidae) native to the Old World. The **Hungarian partridge** was introduced to Canada from Europe in the early 20th century. **2** any of various North American game birds resembling the partridge, such as the ruffed grouse or the quail. **3** *Cdn.* the ptarmigan, *Lagopus lagopus.* ⟨ME < OF *perdriz* < L < Gk. *perdix*⟩

par•tridge•ber•ry ['partrɪdʒ,bɛri] *n., pl.* **-ries. 1** a North American trailing evergreen plant (*Mitchella repens*) of the madder family having fragrant white flowers and scarlet berries. Also, **twinberry. 2** the edible but insipid berry of this plant.

part song a song consisting of parts for two or more voices in harmony, with one voice carrying the melody. Part songs are usually sung without accompaniment.

part time part of the time; on a part-time basis: *They're working part-time this year.*

part–time ['part 'taɪm] *adj.* using or working only part of the standard or usual number of hours: *a part-time job, part-time employees.*

par•tu•ri•ent [par'tjʊriənt] *or* [par'tʊriənt] *adj.* **1** bringing forth young; about to give birth to young. **2** of or having to do with parturition. **3** about to produce an idea, literary work, etc.

par•tu•ri•tion [,partʃə'rɪʃən] *or* [,partjə'rɪʃən] *n.* the act or process of giving birth to young. ⟨< L *parturitio, -onis* < *parturire* be in labour, ult. < *parere* bear⟩

par•ty ['parti] *n., pl.* **-ties;** *v.* **-tied, -ty•ing.** —*n.* **1** a group of people doing something together: *a sewing party, a dinner party, a scouting party of three soldiers.* **2** a gathering for pleasure: *On her birthday she had a party and invited her friends.* **3** a group of people having similar political aims and opinions, organized together to gain influence and control: *the Liberal, Conservative, or New Democratic Party.* **4** (*adjl.*) of, for, or having to do with a party. **5** one who takes part in, aids, or knows about: *She was a party to our plot.* **6** each of the persons or sides in a contract, lawsuit, etc. **7** *Law.* person. **8** any one of two or more persons or families using the same telephone line.
—*v.* hold, attend, or take part in a party or parties: *partying till dawn.*
party away, spend or use up in partying: *We partied the night away. She partied all her money away.* ⟨ME < OF *partie* < a pp. of *partir* divide < L *partire* < *pars, partis* part⟩
☛ *Usage.* See note at PERSON.

party line 1 a telephone line by which two or more subscribers are connected with the exchange by one circuit. **2** the official policy or policies of a political party: *The members of parliament were not expected to vote along party lines on the issue.* **3** a boundary line between two adjacent properties.

par•ty–lin•er ['parti 'laɪnər] *n.* a person who follows closely the officially adopted policies of his or her political party.

party politics politics based on political parties and their policies, regardless of public interest.

party pooper someone who spoils a party by refusing to take part in the usual activities or attitudes.

party wall *Law.* a wall dividing adjoining properties. Each owner has certain rights in it.

party whip a political official whose job it is to organize party members to vote on a certain issue.

par•ure [pə'rʊr]; *French,* [pa'RYR] *n.* a matching set of jewellery such as necklace, earrings, bracelet, etc. ⟨< F *parer* < L *parare* prepare⟩

par value the value of a stock, bond, note, etc. printed on it; face value.

Par•va•ti ['parvəti] *n. Hinduism.* a goddess, the wife of Shiva and a kindly form of the Mother Goddess.

par•ve•nu [,parvə'nju] *or* [,parvə'nu], ['parvə,nju] *or* ['parvə,nu] *n., adj.* —*n.* a person who has risen quickly to a position of wealth or power, but is not yet socially accepted in this new position; upstart.
—*adj.* like or characteristic of a parvenu. ⟨< F *parvenu,* pp. of *parvenir* arrive < L *pervenire* < *per-* through + *venire* come⟩

par•vis ['parvɪs] *n. Architecture.* **1** an enclosed vacant area in front of a building, usually a church. **2** a colonnade or portico in front of a church. ⟨< F *parevis* < L *paradisus* paradise, from the space in front of St. Peter's Church in Rome⟩

Par•zi•fal ['partsɪ,fæl] *n. German legend.* a knight who successfully sought the Holy Grail. As **Parsifal,** he is the hero of an opera by Wagner. Compare PERCEVAL.

pas [pa] *n. French.* **1** *Dancing.* a step or series of steps in ballet. **2** the right to precede; right of precedence.

pas•cal [pæ'skæl] *n.* an SI unit for measuring pressure or stress, equal to the pressure produced by the force of one newton applied to an area of one square metre. *Symbol*: Pa ⟨after Blaise *Pascal* (1623-1662), a French mathematician⟩
☛ *Hom.* PASCAL.

PASCAL [pæ'skæl] *n. Computer technology.* a high-level programming language. ⟨after Blaise *Pascal* (1623-1662), French mathematician who built the first mechanical calculator⟩
☛ *Hom.* PASCAL.

pas•chal ['pæskəl] *adj.* **1** of or having to do with the Passover. **2** of or having to do with Easter; used in Easter celebrations. ⟨ME < OF < LL *paschalis* < L *pascha* < Gk. < Aramaic *paskhā,* related to Hebrew *pesach* Passover⟩

paschal lamb 1 among the ancient Jews, the sacrificial lamb killed and eaten on the first day of Passover. **2** *Christianity.* Jesus. **3** AGNUS DEI (def. 1). ⟨< OF *pasche,* alteration of L *pascha,* ult. < Hebrew *pesach* Passover⟩

pas de chat ['pa də 'ʃa]; *French,* [pad'ʃa] *n. Ballet.* a light, springing jump of one foot over the other, supposedly catlike. ⟨< F, literally, cat's step⟩

pas de deux ['pɑ də 'dʊ]; *French,* [pad'dø] **1** *Ballet.* a dance for two people. **2** in classical ballet, a set of five dances for a ballerina and her partner. ⟨< F, literally, step for two⟩

pa•sha ['pæʃə], ['pɑʃə], *or* [pə'ʃɑ] *n.* **1** formerly, in Turkey, a title of honour or rank, placed after the name. Also, **pacha. 2** a high Turkish official, military or civil. ⟨< Turkish *pasha,* var. of *basha* < *bash* head⟩

Pash•to ['pʌʃtou] *or* ['pɑʃtou] *n.* an Indo-European language of the Iranian branch, spoken in Pakistan and Afghanistan. It is an official language of Afghanistan. Also, **Pushtu.**

pasque–flow•er ['pæsk ˌflaʊər] *n.* any of various anemones, especially a Eurasian species, *Anemone pulsatilla,* widely cultivated as a garden flower. The prairie crocus is also sometimes called a pasque-flower. ⟨< F *passefleur* < *passer* excel + *fleur* flower, altered to *pasque-flower* Easter flower (< OF *pasque* Easter, related to PASCHAL) because it blooms at Easter time; 16c.⟩

Pasque-flowers

pas•quin•ade [ˌpæskwə'neid] *n., v.* **-ad•ed, -ad•ing.** *—n.* a publicly posted satirical writing; lampoon. *—v.* attack by lampoons. ⟨< F < Ital. *pasquinata* < *Pasquino,* the name of a statue on which lampoons were posted⟩

pass [pæs] *v., n. —v.* **1** go by; move past: *The parade passed. We passed the big truck. Two hours passed slowly.* **2** move on; go: *The sales representative passed from house to house.* **3** go from one to another: *Money passes from person to person. Her estate passed to her children.* **4** cause to go from one to another; hand: *Pass me the salt. The old coin was passed around for everyone to see.* **5** get through or by: *We passed the dangerous section of the road successfully.* **6** go across or over: *The horse passed the stream.* **7** put or direct (a rope, string, etc.): *He passed a rope around his waist for support.* **8** go away; depart: *The pain will soon pass.* **9** overtake and leave behind: *She soon passed the other runners.* **10** cause to go, move onward, or proceed: *to pass troops in review.* **11** discharge from the body. **12** be successful in (an examination, a course, etc.): *Most of the class passed Latin.* **13** ratify or enact: *to pass a bill or law.* **14** be approved by (a law-making body, etc.): *The new law passed the city council.* **15** go beyond; exceed; surpass: *His strange story passes belief.* **16** come to an end; die: *King Arthur passed in peace.* **17** use; spend: *We passed the days pleasantly.* **18** change: *Water passes from a liquid to a solid state when it freezes.* **19** take place; happen: *Tell me all that passed.* **20** give approval to: *The inspector passed the item after examining it.* **21** express; pronounce: *A judge passes sentence on guilty persons.* **22** give a judgment or opinion: *The judges passed on each contestant.* **23** go without notice: *He was rude, but let that pass.* **24** let something go without action; decline to respond, take, etc. **25** leave out; omit. **26** *Football, hockey, etc.* transfer (the ball, etc.). **27** *Card games.* give up a chance to play a hand, refuse to play a hand, or refuse to bid. **28** *Fencing.* make a thrust.
bring to pass, accomplish; cause to be.
come to pass, take place; happen.
pass as or **for,** be accepted as: *Use silk, or a material that will pass as silk. She could pass for twenty.*
pass away, a come to an end. **b** die.
pass (something) **by,** fail to notice; overlook; disregard.
pass off, a go away. **b** take place; be done. **c** cause to be accepted under false pretenses.
pass on, a pass from one person to another. **b** die.
pass one's lips, a be uttered. **b** be eaten or drunk.
pass out, a hand out or circulate: *The teacher passed out the report cards.* **b** *Informal.* faint; lose consciousness.
pass over, a fail to notice; overlook; disregard: *The teacher passed over my mistake.* **b** ignore the claims of (a person) to promotion, a post, honour, etc. **c** die.
pass the time of day, greet and chat with someone.
pass up, a give up; renounce: *to pass up a chance at revenge.* **b** fail to take advantage of.
—n. **1** the act of passing; passage: *The invading army made a swift pass through the country.* **2** success in an examination, etc.; passing an examination but without honours. **3** a note, licence, etc. allowing one to do something: *He needed a pass to enter the fort.* **4** free ticket: *a pass to the circus.* **5** state; condition: *Things have come to a strange pass when young children give orders to their parents.* **6** a motion of the hands. **7** a sleight-of-hand motion; manipulation; trick. **8** a narrow road, path, way, channel, etc.; a narrow passage through mountains. **9** *Football, hockey, etc.* a transference of a ball, puck, etc. **10** *Fencing.* a thrust. **11** *Card games.* a decision not to bet, raise, double, etc. **12** *Informal.* a sexual approach; an attempt to kiss, etc.: *He made a pass at her as soon as they were alone.* ⟨ME < OF *passer,* ult. < L *passus* step⟩ **—'pass•er,** *n.*

pass. 1 passive. **2** passenger.

pass•a•ble ['pæsəbəl] *adj.* **1** fairly good; tolerable; mediocre: *a passable performance. Her French is passable, but not very fluent.* **2** that can be crossed or travelled on: *the roads are just barely passable.* **3** that can be freely circulated; current; valid: *passable currency.* **4** of a proposed law, able to be passed. ⟨< F *passable* < *passer* to pass⟩ **—'pass•a•ble•ness,** *n.*

pass•a•bly ['pæsəbli] *adv.* fairly; moderately; to some extent.

pas•sage ['pæsɪdʒ] *n.* **1** a hall or way through a building; passageway. **2** a means of passing; way through: *to ask for passage through a crowd.* **3** right, liberty, or leave to pass: *The guard refused us passage.* **4** a passing: *the passage of time.* **5** transition or movement from one place to another; migration: *birds of passage.* **6** a piece from a speech, writing, or musical composition: *a passage from the first symphony of Beethoven.* **7** a journey, especially by sea: *We had a stormy passage across the Atlantic.* **8** change or progression from one state or condition to another: *rites of passage.* **9** a ticket that entitles the holder to transportation, especially by boat: *to secure a passage for Europe.* **10** a making into law by a favouring vote of a legislature: *the passage of a bill.* **11** PASSAGE OF ARMS. **12** *Music.* a phrase or other division of a composition. **13** an alley or narrow lane. **14** an opening into, through, or out of something: *the nasal passages.* ⟨ME < OF *passage* < *passer* pass. See PASS.⟩

passage of arms an exchange of blows; quarrel.

pas•sage•way ['pæsɪdʒˌwei] *n.* a way along which one can pass; passage. Halls and alleys are passageways.

pas•sant ['pæsənt] *adj. Heraldry.* of a beast, represented as walking with the head facing the viewer and the forepaw on the far side raised: *a lion passant.* Compare RAMPANT (def. 4). ⟨ME < OF *passant* walking, ppr. of *passer.* See PASS.⟩

pass•book ['pæsˌbʊk] *n.* bankbook.

pas•sé [pæ'sei]; *French,* [pa'se] *adj.* **1** past one's prime. **2** no longer useful or fashionable; out-of-date: *That expression is passé.* ⟨< F *passé* passed⟩

pas•sen•ger ['pæsəndʒər] *n.* a traveller in a train, motor vehicle, boat, or aircraft who has nothing to do with its operation. ⟨ME < OF *passagier* < *passage.* See PASSAGE.⟩

passenger pigeon a migratory wild pigeon (*Ectopistes migratorius*) of North America that was hunted to extinction by humans. Passenger pigeons were abundant in E North America in the early 19th century, but by the early 20th century the species was extinct.

passe par•tout [ˌpæs pɑr'tu] **1** a method of framing a picture whereby the picture, the glass, the mat, and the backing are bound together by strips of paper (often decorative) pasted around the edges. **2** paper prepared for this purpose. **3** something that passes or allows one to pass everywhere. ⟨< F *passe partout* pass everywhere⟩

pass•er–by ['pæsər 'baɪ] *n., pl.* **pass•ers-by.** a person who passes by: *The robbery was seen by a passer-by who called the police.*

pas•ser•ine ['pæsərɪn], ['pæsəˌraɪn], *or* ['pæsəˌrin] *adj., n. —adj.* of, having to do with, or designating an order (Passeriformes) of birds, including more than half of all the existing species in the world. Passerine birds are perching birds and, because most of them sing, they are also called songbirds. *—n.* a bird belonging to this order. ⟨< L *passerinus* < *passer* sparrow⟩

pas seul [pɑ'sœl] *French.* a dance for one person; solo dance.

pas•sim ['pæsɪm] *adv. Latin.* here and there; in various places.
☛ *Usage.* **Passim** is used in footnotes in referring to material found throughout a book, article, series, etc.

pass•ing ['pæsɪŋ] *adj., n., v. —adj.* **1** going past or by: *A passing motorist drove them to a service station.* **2** not lasting; fleeting: *a passing idea, a passing fashion.* **3** superficial or incidental: *a passing remark.* **4** that is now happening: *the passing scene.* **5** designating satisfactory completion of a course of study

or examination: *The passing grade for the course is B–.* **6** of or designating a track, lane, etc. for passing another vehicle, etc.
—n. **1** the act of one who or that which passes: *the passing of summer. They mourned her passing.* **2** a means or place of passing.
in passing, incidentally; by the way: *She mentioned in passing that she was planning a trip to the Far East.*
—v. ppr. of PASS.

pas•sion [ˈpæʃən] *n.* **1** very strong feeling: *Love and hate are passions.* **2** a violent anger; rage: *He flew into a passion.* **3** intense love or sexual desire. **4** a very strong liking or devotion: *a passion for music.* **5** the object of a passion: *Music is her passion.* **6** *Archaic.* suffering. **7** Usually, **the Passion, a** the sufferings of Jesus on the cross or after the Last Supper. **b** the story of these sufferings in the Bible. **c** a musical setting or a series of paintings, etc. of this. ⟨ME < OF < L *passio, -onis,* ult. < *pati* suffer⟩ **—ˈpas•sion•less,** *n.*
☛ *Syn.* **1.** See note at FEELING.

pas•sion•ate [ˈpæʃənɪt] *adj.* **1** affected with or easily moved to strong emotion: *a passionate believer in freedom, a passionate person.* **2** caused by or showing strong emotion; emotionally intense or vehement: *a passionate defence of the accused man.* **3** affected with or influenced by strong sexual desire. ⟨< Med.L *passionatus* < L *passio, -onis.* See PASSION.⟩ **—ˈpas•sion•ate•ly,** *adv.* **—ˈpas•sion•ate•ness,** *n.*

pas•sion•flow•er [ˈpæʃən,flaʊər] *n.* **1** any of a genus (*Passiflora*) of mainly tropical vines having showy red, purple, white, or yellow flowers and, in some species, edible fruit. **2** (*adjl.*) designating the family Passifloraceae of tropical, tendril-climbing plants.

passion fruit the edible fruit of the passionflower.

Passion Play or **passion play** a play representing the sufferings and death of Christ. A Passion Play is given every ten years at Oberammergau, West Germany.

Passion Sunday in the Christian calendar, the second Sunday before Easter Sunday; the Sunday before Palm Sunday. It is the fifth Sunday in Lent.

Passion Week the second week before Easter; the fifth week in Lent, between Passion Sunday and Palm Sunday.

pas•sive [ˈpæsɪv] *adj., n. —adj.* **1** not acting in return; being acted on without itself acting: *a passive victim.* **2** characterized by lack of motivation, response, or initiative: *a passive disposition.* **3** *Grammar.* of or designating a form (called the passive voice) of a verb that shows the grammatical subject of a clause as the recipient of the action expressed in the verb. In *The window was broken by John, was broken* is passive; the subject *the window* receives the action represented by the verb *was broken.* Compare ACTIVE (def. 8). **4** produced or induced by an outside agency: *passive exercise.* **5** *Chemistry.* not readily entering into chemical combination; inert; inactive.
—n. Grammar. **1** the passive voice. **2** a verb in the passive voice, consisting in English of a form of the verb **be** followed by a past participle: *My coat was cleaned only last week.*. ⟨< L *passivus,* ult. < *pati* suffer⟩ **—ˈpas•sive•ly,** *adv.* **—ˈpas•sive•ness** or **pasˈsiv•i•ty,** *n.*

passive immunity immunity resulting from the presence of antibodies not produced by the organism itself but injected or, in infants, transferred from the mother via the placenta or breastmilk.

passive resistance resistance to a government or other authority, especially by non-violent refusal to co-operate, often in the form of hunger strikes, sit-ins, etc.

pass•key [ˈpæs,ki] *n., pl.* **-keys. 1** a key for opening several locks; master key. **2** a private key.

Pass•o•ver [ˈpæs,oʊvər] *n.* an annual Jewish holiday in memory of the escape of the Hebrews from Egypt, where they had been slaves. It is so called because, according to the Bible, a destroying angel 'passed over' the houses of the Hebrews when it killed the first-born child in every Egyptian home. See PASCHAL LAMB (def. 1). ⟨from the *passing over* of the destroying angel⟩

pass•port [ˈpæspɔrt] *n.* **1** an official document identifying the citizenship of the holder, and giving the holder permission to leave and return to the country issuing the document and to travel abroad under the protection of its government. **2** anything that gives one admission or acceptance: *An interest in gardening was a passport to my aunt's favour.* ⟨< F *passeport* < *passer* pass + *port* harbour⟩

pass•word [ˈpæs,wɜrd] *n.* **1** a secret word or phrase that identifies a person speaking it and allows him or her to pass. **2** *Computer technology.* a personal code which enables its possessor to use a computer by keying in the code and which protects computer files from interference by other users.

past [pæst] *adj., n., prep., adv., —adj.* **1** gone by; ended: *Our troubles are past.* **2** just gone by: *The past year was full of trouble.* **3** having served a term in office: *a past president.* **4** of former times. **5** *Grammar.* of or designating a verb form expressing actions, happenings, or states that have ended or been completed at the time of utterance of a statement, etc.: *the past tense, a past participle.*
—n. **1** time gone by; time before: *Life began far back in the past.* **2** a past life or history: *Our country has a glorious past.* **3** a person's past life, especially if hidden or unknown or of questionable morality: *He was a man with a past; no one knew that he had been in prison.* **4** the past tense or a verb form in it.
—prep. **1** beyond; farther on than: *The arrow went past the mark.* **2** after; later than: *ten past two. It is past noon.* **3** beyond in number, amount, or degree. **4** beyond the ability, range, scope, etc. of: *absurd fancies that are past belief.*
not put it past (someone), believe someone capable of something.
—adv. so as to pass by or beyond: *The cars go past once an hour.*
☛ *Usage.* **Past** is not a verb. The past tense of the verb **pass** is **passed.**

pas•ta [ˈpɑstə] *or* [ˈpæstə] *n.* **1** a type of flour paste used to make foods such as spaghetti, macaroni, ravioli, or noodles. **2** food or foods made of this paste. ⟨< Ital. < LL. See PASTE.⟩

paste [peist] *n., v.* **past•ed, past•ing.** *—n.* **1** a mixture, such as flour and water, that will stick paper together, stick it to a wall, etc. **2** dough for pastry; PASTA (def. 1). **3** a soft, doughlike mixture. Pottery is made from a paste of clay and water. **4 a** a hard, glassy material used in making imitations of precious stones. **b** an artificial gem made of this material. **5** a soft, jellylike candy. **6** a preparation of meat, fish, etc. used for filling sandwiches or spreading on canapes: *liver paste, chicken paste.*
—v. **1** stick with paste: *to paste a label on a box.* **2** cover by pasting: *to paste a wall with notices.* **3** *Slang.* hit with a hard, sharp blow. ⟨ME < OF < LL *pasta* < Gk. *pasta* porridge < *passein* sprinkle⟩ **—ˈpast•er,** *n.*

paste•board [ˈpeist,bɔrd] *n., adj. —n.* **1** a stiff material made of sheets of paper pasted together or of paper pulp pressed and dried. **2** *Slang.* a ticket or card.
—adj. **1** made of pasteboard. **2** flimsy; sham.

pas•tel [pæˈstɛl] *n., adj. —n.* **1** a kind of crayon made of ground colouring matter and gum, used in drawing. **2** a drawing made with such crayons. **3** the art of drawing with pastels. **4** a soft, pale shade of some colour.
—adj. of a colour, soft and pale: *pastel blue.* ⟨< F < Ital. *pastello* < LL < Gk. *pasta.* See PASTE.⟩

pas•tern [ˈpæstərn] *n.* **1** the part of a horse's foot between the fetlock and the hoof. See HORSE for picture. **2** a corresponding part in other animals. ⟨ME < OF *pasturon,* dim. of *pasture* tether for a horse, ult. < L *pastor.* See PASTOR.⟩

paste–up [ˈpeist ,ʌp] *n.* **1** a sheet of paper or other material on which things are pasted to form a working diagram, design or plan. **2** collage.

pas•teur•ize [ˈpæstʃə,raɪz] *or* [ˈpæstjə,raɪz] *v.* **-ized, -iz•ing.** heat (milk, beer, etc.) to a high temperature and chill it quickly to destroy harmful bacteria without causing a major chemical change to the substance itself. ⟨after Louis *Pasteur* (1822-1895), a French chemist⟩ **—,pas•teur•iˈza•tion,** *n.*

pas•tiche [pæˈstiʃ] *n.* **1** a piece of writing, music, or other artistic creation consisting mainly of bits borrowed from various sources, or intended to caricature a certain artist's style. **2** an unlikely or incongruous mixture of materials, styles, etc.; a hodge-podge. ⟨< F < Ital. *pasticcio* pie⟩

pas•tille [pæˈstil] *n.* **1** a flavoured or medicated lozenge. **2** a small roll or cone of aromatic paste, burnt as a disinfectant, incense, etc. **3** PASTEL (defs. 1, 2). Also, **pastil** [ˈpæstəl]. ⟨< F < L *pastillus* roll, aromatic lozenge, dim. of *panis* bread⟩

pas•time [ˈpæs,taɪm] *n.* something that causes the time to pass pleasantly; a form of amusement or recreation. Games and sports are pastimes. ⟨< *pass* + *time*⟩

past master 1 one who has filled the office of master in a society, lodge, etc. **2** a person who has much experience in any profession, art, etc.

pas•tor [ˈpæstər] *n.* **1** a priest or minister in charge of a church or other Christian community. **2** a person serving as a spiritual guide or mentor to several people. ⟨< L *pastor* shepherd, ult. < *pascere* feed⟩

pas•tor•al [ˈpæstərəl] *adj., n. —adj.* **1** of or having to do with shepherds or country life. **2** simple or naturally beautiful like the

country: *a pastoral scene.* **3** of a pastor or his or her duties. **4** of or having to do with pastoral literature or a pastoral.
—n. **1 a** a play, poem, or picture dealing in an idealized and conventionalized manner with rural life, formerly with the lives of shepherds specifically. **b** such writing as a genre. **2** a letter from a bishop to the clergy or to the people of his or her Christian church district. ⟨< L *pastoralis* < *pastor.* See PASTOR.⟩ **—'pas•tor•al•ly,** *adv.*
☛ *Syn. adj.* **1.** See note at RURAL.

pas•tor•ale [ˌpæstəˈræl], [ˌpæstəˈrɑl], *or* [ˌpæstəˈrɑli] *n. Music.* **1** any piece of music composed in a simple and idyllic style intended to suggest rural life and scenes. **2** an opera, cantata, or especially a section of such based on pastoral themes. **3** a forerunner of opera in which a dramatic performance on a pastoral theme was interspersed with incidental music of a pastoral nature. ⟨< Ital.⟩

pas•tor•ate [ˈpæstərɪt] *n.* **1** the position or duties of a Christian pastor. **2** the term of service of a Christian pastor. **3** pastors as a group.

past participle *Grammar.* in English, a participle used: **a** with the auxiliary verb *have* to form perfect tenses. *Examples*: *It* has *rained every day. They* had *been swimming.* **b** with the auxiliary verb *be* to form the passive voice in English. *Example*: *The cheese* was *eaten by the rat.* **c** as an adjective indicating a completed state. *Examples*: broken *glass, a* locked *door.*

past perfect *Grammar.* **1** in English, a periphrastic verb tense employing the preterite of the verb *have* with a past participle and showing that an event was completed before a given past time. In *Anne had learned to read before she went to school, had learned* is in the past perfect. *Past perfect* and *pluperfect* mean the same. **2** a verb in this tense. The past perfect of *see* is *had seen*.

pas•tra•mi [pəˈstrɑmi] *n.* smoked and highly seasoned beef, especially from a shoulder cut. ⟨< Yiddish⟩

pas•try [ˈpeistri] *n., pl.* **-tries. 1** a paste or dough of flour and lard, butter, or shortening, used to make pie crusts, tarts, etc.: *Pastry has a flaky texture when it is baked.* **2** food made wholly or partly of this paste: *He eats too much pastry.* **3** in general, all fancy baked goods, such as petits fours, sweet rolls, etc. **4** an individual item of pastry; a pie, tart, etc. ⟨< *paste* + *-ry*⟩

past tense *Grammar.* **1** a tense expressing time gone by, or a former action or state. **2** a verb form in the past tense. *Examples*: *The moose* ran *headlong into the swamp. Beavers* built *a dam in the pond this spring.*

pas•tur•age [ˈpæstʃərɪdʒ] *n.* **1** the growing grass and other plants for cattle, sheep, or horses to feed on. **2** pasture land. **3** the pasturing of cattle, etc. **4** the right to pasture cattle, etc. on certain land. ⟨< OF *pasturage*, ult. < *pasture.* See PASTURE.⟩

pas•ture [ˈpæstʃər] *n., v.* **-tured, -tur•ing.** *—n.* **1** a grassy field or hillside; grasslands on which cattle, sheep, or horses can feed. **2** grass and other growing plants.
put out to pasture, a put (animals) in a pasture to graze. **b** *Slang.* allow or force (older employees or members of an organization) to retire or be less active: *It's time that group was put out to pasture.*
—v. **1** put (cattle, sheep, etc.) out to pasture. **2** of cattle, sheep, etc., feed on (growing grass, etc.). **3** of land, provide (animals) with pasture: *This field will pasture twenty cattle.* ⟨ME < OF *pasture* < LL *pastura*, ult. < L *pascere* feed⟩

past•y[1] [ˈpeisti] *adj.* **past•i•er, past•i•est.** of or like paste in appearance or texture; especially, pale and flabby. ⟨< *paste*⟩ **—'past•i•ness,** *n.*

pas•ty[2] [ˈpæsti] *n., pl.* **-ties.** *Esp. Brit.* a small pastry, usually filled with fish or meat, especially game, occasionally vegetables or fruit: *a venison pasty, an onion pasty.* ⟨ME < OF *pastee* < *paste* paste < LL *pasta.* See PASTE. Doublet of PATTY.⟩

pat[1] [pæt] *v.* **pat•ted, pat•ting;** *n. —v.* **1** strike or tap lightly with the hand or a flat object, for the purpose of shaping or applying: *He patted the plaster into the crack. She patted the dough into a flat cake.* **2** tap lightly with the hand as a sign of sympathy, approval, or affection: *to pat a dog.* **3** walk or run with quick, light footsteps.
pat on the back, praise; compliment.
—n. **1** a light stroke or tap with the hand or with something flat. **2** the sound made by patting. **3** a small mass, especially of butter.
pat on the back, a compliment. ⟨ME patte⟩

pat[2] [pæt] *adj., adv. —adj.* **1** apt; suitable; to the point: *a pat reply.* **2** so perfect as to seem glib or memorized; tritely apt.
—adv. **1** aptly; exactly; suitably. **2** glibly; tritely.
have (down) pat or **know pat,** *Informal.* have perfectly; know thoroughly: *John has the history lesson pat.*
stand pat, *Informal.* keep the same position; hold to things as they are and refuse to change: *Many people were angry with the government but the prime minister stood pat.* ⟨probably special use of *pat[1]*⟩

pat. patent; patented.

pa•ta•ca [pəˈtɑkə] *n.* the main unit of currency in Macao, divided into 100 avos. See table of money in the Appendix.

Pat•a•go•nia [ˌpætəˈgouniə] *or* [ˌpætəˈgounjə] *n.* a tableland area of S South America between the Andes and the Atlantic, covering the southern parts of Argentina and Chile, especially Argentina.

Pat•a•go•ni•an [ˌpætəˈgouniən] *or* [ˌpætəˈgounjən] *n., adj.*
—n. a native or inhabitant of Patagonia.
—adj. of or having to do with Patagonia or its people.

patch [pætʃ] *n., v. —n.* **1** a piece of some material put on to mend a hole or a tear, or to strengthen a weak place. **2** a protective pad or dressing applied to a sore or wound: *The doctor ordered him to wear a patch over his right eye.* **3** a small piece of cloth, especially one used for patchwork. **4** a tiny bit of black cloth that women used to wear on their faces to hide a blemish or to set off their fair skin. **5** a small area different from that around it: *a patch of brown on the skin.* **6** a piece of ground: *a garden patch.* **7** a connection or hookup between two circuits or pieces of electronic equipment such as radio circuits or telephone lines. **8** *Military.* a small square or rectangle of coloured fabric worn on the sleeve just below the shoulder, indicating affiliation with a particular military unit. **9** a small membrane made of fibre or plastic which releases a substance gradually through the skin: *a nicotine patch, an allergen patch.*
—v. **1** put on a patch; mend, protect, or cover with a patch or patches: *to patch a torn sleeve, to patch a leaky pipe.* **2** put together or mend hastily or poorly (*usually used with* **up** *or* **together**): *to patch up a costume for Halloween.* **3** form or make with patches: *to patch a quilt.* **4** put an end to; settle (*usually used with* **up**): *to patch up a quarrel.* **5** connect circuits (*usually with* **through**): *I'll patch you through to the main office.*
patch together, improvise a temporary solution for: *We could patch together a plan that will do for the time being.*
patch up, put together or mend hastily or poorly: *I can patch it up for now, but it won't hold for long.* ⟨ME *pacche*, ? var. of *pece* piece. See PIECE.⟩ **—'patch•er,** *n.*
☛ *Syn. v.* **1.** See note at MEND.

patch fox *Cdn.* CROSS FOX.

patch logging *Cdn.* a system of logging by which only patches of trees in a stand are cut down, the surrounding trees being left intact to ensure natural reseeding of the cutover patch.

patch•ou•li or **patch•ou•ly** [ˈpætʃʊli] *or* [pəˈtʃuli] *n.* **1** any of several Asian trees (genus *Pogostemon*) of the mint family having leaves that yield an essential oil used for perfumes. **2** a perfume with a heavy fragrance, made from this oil. ⟨< Tamil⟩

patch•work [ˈpætʃˌwɜrk] *n.* **1** pieces of cloth of various colours or shapes sewed together. **2** sewing things in this way: *She enjoys patchwork.* **3** (*adj.*) made in this way: *a patchwork quilt.* **4** anything like this: *From the airplane, we saw a patchwork of fields and woods.*

patch•y [ˈpætʃi] *adj.* **patch•i•er, patch•i•est. 1** abounding in or characterized by patches: *a patchy lawn.* **2** occurring in, forming or resembling patches. **3** not consistent or regular; not uniform in quality, etc.: *a patchy performance.* **—'patch•i•ly,** *adv.* **—'patch•i•ness,** *n.*

patd. patented.

pate [peit] *n.* **1** the top of the head; head: *a bald pate.* **2** brains. ⟨ME; origin uncertain⟩

pâ•té [pæˈtei] *or* [pɑˈtei]; *French,* [pɑˈte] *n.* **1** a meat paste, usually highly seasoned. **2** a pastry case filled with chicken, sweetbreads, oysters, etc.; patty. **3** PÂTÉ DE FOIE GRAS. ⟨< F < OF *paste* paste⟩

pâté de foie gras [pæˈtei də ˌfwɑ ˈgrɑ]; *French,* [pɑtedfwaˈgʀɑ] *French.* a rich paste made from the livers of specially fattened geese.

pa•tel•la [pəˈtɛlə] *n., pl.* **-tel•las, -tel•lae** [-ˈtɛli] *or* [-ˈtɛlaɪ]. **1** kneecap. See LEG for picture. **2** an ancient Roman small pan or shallow vessel. **3** *Biology.* a panlike or cuplike formation or structure. ⟨< L *patella*, dim. of *patina* pan. See PATEN.⟩

pa•tel•lar [pəˈtɛlər] *adj.* of or having to do with the kneecap.

pat•en [ˈpætən] *n.* **1** the plate on which the bread is placed at the celebration of the Christian Eucharist or Mass. **2** a plate or

flat piece of metal. Also, **patina, patine.** ⟨ME < OF < L *patena* or *patina* pan, dish < Gk. *patanē*⟩
☛ *Hom.* PATTEN.

pa•ten•cy ['peitənsi] *or* ['pætənsi] *n.* **1** a being patent; obviousness. **2** *Medicine.* the state of being not blocked or obstructed.

pat•ent *n., adj. 1 & 2, v.* ['pætənt] *or* ['peitənt]; *adj. 3* ['peitənt] *n., adj., v. —n.* **1** a right given by a government to a person by which he or she is the only one allowed to make, use, or sell a new invention for a certain number of years. **2** an invention that is protected by a patent. **3** an official document from a government giving a right or privilege.
—adj. **1** protected by a patent: *a patent lock.* **2** appointed or granted by LETTERS PATENT. **3** evident; plain: *She smiled at the patent ineptness of their scheme.*
—v. **1** get a patent for: *The designer patented her latest invention.* **2** grant a patent to (someone) or for (something). ⟨< L *patens, -entis,* ppr. of *patere* lie open⟩ **—'pat•ent•a•ble,** *adj.*

pat•ent•ee [,pætən'ti] *n.* **1** a person to whom a patent is granted. **2** a person licensed to use another's patent.

patent leather leather with a very glossy, smooth surface, usually black, made by a process formerly patented.

pa•tent•ly ['peitəntli] *or* ['pætəntli] *adv.* **1** plainly; clearly; obviously. **2** openly.

patent medicine a product advertised and sold without prescription as a remedy for certain ailments or illnesses.

Patent Office a government office that issues patents.

pa•ter•fa•mil•i•as [,pætərfə'mɪliəs] *or* [,peitərfə'mɪliəs] *n., pl.* **patres familias** ['pætreis fə'mɪliəs]. a father or head of a family. ⟨< L *paterfamilias* < *pater* father + OL *familias,* gen., of a family⟩

pa•ter•nal [pə'tɜrnəl] *adj.* **1** of, having to do with, or like a father; fatherly. **2** related on the father's side of the family: *a paternal aunt.* **3** received or inherited from one's father: *Mary's blue eyes were a paternal inheritance.* ⟨< LL *paternalis,* ult. < L *pater* father⟩ **—pa'ter•nal•ly,** *adv.*

paternal inheritance *Genetics.* inheritance of a trait from the father.

pa•ter•nal•ism [pə'tɜrnə,lɪzəm] *n.* the principle or practice of managing the affairs of a country or group of people as a father manages the affairs of his children. **—pa'ter•nal•ist,** *n.* **—pa,ter•nal'is•tic,** *adj.* **—pa,ter•nal'is•ti•cal•ly,** *adv.*

pa•ter•ni•ty [pə'tɜrnəti] *n.* **1** the fact or state of being a father; fatherhood. **2** paternal origin. **3** authorship or origin generally. ⟨< LL *paternitas* < L *paternus* fatherly < *pater* father⟩

pat•er•nos•ter ['pætər'nɒstər] *or* ['peitər'nɒstər] *n.* **1** Usually, **Paternoster,** the Lord's Prayer, especially in Latin. **2** one of the beads of a rosary, usually every eleventh, on which the Lord's Prayer is said. **3** any fixed set of words used as a prayer or charm. The **devil's paternoster** is a muttered curse or imprecation. ⟨< L *pater noster* our father⟩

path [pæθ] *n., pl.* **paths** [pæðz]. **1** a track made by people or animals walking. It is usually too narrow for automobiles or wagons. **2** a way made to walk upon or to ride horses, bicycles, etc. upon: *He laid stone for a garden path.* **3** a line along which a person or thing moves; route; track: *The moon has a regular path through the sky.* **4** a way of acting or behaving; way of life: *"Some choose paths of glory, some choose paths of ease."* ⟨OE *pæth*⟩ **—'path•less,** *n.*

Pa•than [pə'tɒn] *n.* one of the Pashto-speaking peoples of N Pakistan and Afghanistan. ⟨< Hind. *Pathan,* ult. < Afghani *Paštó* the Pashto language⟩

pa•thet•ic [pə'θɛtɪk] *adj.* **1** arousing pity and compassion; pitiful: *A lost child is a pathetic sight.* **2** arousing contempt; pitifully inadequate or unsuccessful: *a pathetic attempt to be funny.* Also, **pathetical.** ⟨< LL < Gk. *pathētikos,* ult. < *pathein* suffer⟩ **—pa'thet•i•cal•ly,** *adv.*

pathetic fallacy the attribution of human emotions and characteristics to nature or inanimate things, especially as a figure of speech. *Examples*: *a killing rain, a stubborn cold.*

path•find•er ['pæθ,faɪndər] *n.* **1** a person who finds a path or way, especially through a wilderness. **2 Pathfinder,** a member, aged 12 to 15, of the Girl Guides.

patho– *combining form.* disease: *pathology.* ⟨< Gk. *pathos* disease, suffering⟩

path•o•gen ['pæθədʒən] *n.* a disease-causing agent. Also, **pathogene.** ⟨< Gk. *pathos* disease + *gen-* produce⟩

path•o•gen•ic [,pæθə'dʒɛnɪk] *adj.* having to do with pathogeny; producing disease.

pa•thog•e•ny [pə'θɒdʒəni] *n.* the production of disease.

path•o•log•i•cal [,pæθə'lɒdʒəkəl] *adj.* **1** of pathology; dealing with diseases or concerned with diseases: *pathological studies.* **2** due to disease or accompanying disease: *a pathological condition of the blood cells.* **3** caused or controlled by an obsession; compulsive: *a pathological hatred of cats. He's a pathological liar.* Also, **pathologic. —,path•o'log•i•cal•ly,** *adv.*

pa•thol•o•gist [pə'θɒlədʒɪst] *n.* a medical doctor who is a specialist in pathology.

pa•thol•o•gy [pə'θɒlədʒi] *n., pl.* **-gies. 1** the study of the nature and causes of disease and of the changes in the body caused by them. **2** unhealthy conditions and processes caused by disease. **3** any deviation from a normal or sound condition.

pa•thos ['peiθɒs] *n.* **1** the quality in experience or events, or in literature, art, or music that arouses a feeling of pity or sadness. **2** the feeling aroused; pity, sadness, etc. ⟨< Gk. *pathos* suffering, feeling⟩

path•way ['pæθ,wei] *n.* path.

–pathy *combining form.* **1** a feeling: *telepathy.* **2** a disorder or disease: *neuropathy.* **3** the treatment of disease: *osteopathy.* ⟨< Gk. *-patheia*⟩

pa•tience ['peiʃəns] *n.* **1** the ability to accept calmly things that trouble or annoy, or that require long waiting or effort. **2** long, hard work; steady effort. **3** a card game played by one person; solitaire. ⟨ME < OF < L *patientia* < *patiens, -entis.* See PATIENT.⟩
☛ *Syn.* **1. Patience,** FORBEARANCE, FORTITUDE = power to endure, without complaining, something unpleasant or painful. **Patience** suggests calmness and self-control in enduring suffering or trouble, in waiting, or in doing something requiring steady effort: *Teachers need patience.* **Forbearance** suggests uncommon patience and self-control in keeping oneself from doing or saying something when greatly tried or provoked: *I admire their forbearance.* **Fortitude** sometimes suggests patience but emphasizes strength and firmness of character and indicates calm courage in facing danger or enduring hardship: *With fortitude the disabled veteran learned a new trade.*

pa•tient ['peiʃənt] *adj., n. —adj.* **1** having or showing patience: *patient suffering.* **2** with steady effort or long, hard work: *patient research.*
—n. **1** a person or animal who is being treated by a doctor, dentist, veterinarian, etc. **2** *Grammar.* a person or thing receiving action or affected by it. In the sentence *The tree was blown down by the wind, the tree* is the patient. ⟨ME < OF < L *patiens, -entis* suffering⟩ **—'pa•tient•ly,** *adv.*

pat•i•na[1] ['pætənə] *or* [pə'tinə] *n.* **1** a film or encrustation, usually green, formed naturally over time on the surface of copper or bronze. **2** a smooth surface appearance produced by age and exposure on substances such as wood or stone: *The old table had a beautiful glossy patina.* **3** an appearance or aura assumed by something as a result of association, etc.: *the patina of success.* ⟨< Ital. *patina* coating < L *patina* dish, pan⟩

pat•i•na[2] ['pætənə] *n.* paten.

pat•ine ['pætən] *or* [pə'tin] *n.* **1** paten. **2** any coloured coating resulting from age; PATINA[1].
☛ *Hom.* PATTEN ['pætən].

pat•i•o ['pætiou] *n., pl.* **-i•os. 1** an inner court or yard open to the sky. **2** a terrace for outdoor meals, lounging, etc. ⟨< Sp.⟩

pa•tis•se•rie [pə'tɪsəri]; *French,* [patis'ʀi] *n.* **1** a bakery specializing in fancy or French pastry. **2** a single item of such pastry.

pat•ois [pæ'twɑ] *or* ['pætwɑ]; *French,* [pa'twa] *n., pl.* **pat•ois** [pæ'twɑz] *or* ['pætwɑz]; *French,* [pa'twa]. **1** a dialect different from the standard language of a country or district, especially one spoken in rural areas. **2** the special language characteristic of a particular group; jargon. ⟨< F *patois* < OF *patoier* handle clumsily < *pate* paw < Gmc.⟩

patri– *combining form.* father: *patrimony.* Also, before vowels, **patr-.** ⟨< L *pater* father < Gk.⟩

pa•tri•arch ['peitri,ɑrk] *n.* **1** the father and ruler of a family or tribe. In the Bible, Abraham, Isaac, and Jacob are patriarchs. **2** a person thought of as the father or founder of something. **3** a venerable old man. **4** in the early Christian church, a bishop of the highest rank. **5** a high-ranking bishop or other high religious official in certain churches, especially the Roman Catholic Church and the Eastern Orthodox Church. **6** the oldest male in a group. ⟨< L < Gk. *patriarchēs* < *patria* family + *archos* leader⟩ **—'pa•tri,ar•chal,** *adj.*

pa•tri•ar•chate ['peitri,ɑrkɪt] *n.* **1** the position, dignity, authority, or residence of a church patriarch. **2** a church district under a patriarch's authority. **3** patriarchy.

pa•tri•ar•chy ['peitri,ɑrki] *n., pl.* **-chies. 1** a form of social organization in which the father is head of the family and in which descent is reckoned in the male line, the children belonging to the father's clan. **2** a family, community, or tribe governed by a patriarch or the eldest male. **3** any type of social institution dominated by men. **4** systemic male domination.

pa•tri•ate ['peitri,eit] *or* ['pætri,eit] *v.* **-at•ed, -at•ing.** *Cdn.* bring (government, decision-making powers, etc.) under the direct control of the people of a given region, nation, etc.: *The British parliament voted in 1982 to patriate the Canadian constitution.* ⟨back formation from *repatriate*⟩ **—,pa•tri'a•tion,** *n.*

pa•tri•cian [pə'trɪʃən] *n., adj.* *—n.* **1** in ancient Rome, **a** a member of the early senatorial aristocracy. **b** later, a member of the nobility. Compare PLEBEIAN (def. 1). **2** in the late Roman Empire, a member of the honorary nobility, a title conferred by the Emperor. **3** a person of noble birth or high social rank; aristocrat. **4** any person of good background, education, and manners or refined taste.
—adj. **1** of or having to do with patricians. **2** noble; aristocratic. ⟨< L *patricius*, adj. < *patres* senators (literally, fathers) of Rome⟩

pat•ri•cide ['pætrə,saɪd] *or* ['peitrə,saɪd] *n.* **1** the crime of killing one's father. **2** one who kills his or her father. Compare PARRICIDE. ⟨def. 1: < LL *patricidium* < L *pater* father + *-cidium* act of killing; def. 2: < Med.L *patricida* < L *pater* father + *-cida* killer⟩ **—,pat•ri'cid•al,** *adj.*

pat•ri•lin•e•al [,pætrə'lɪniəl] *or* [,peitrə'lɪniəl] *adj.* of or designating inheritance, descent, or kinship through the male line. Compare MATRILINEAL.

pat•ri•mo•ny ['pætrə,mouni] *n., pl.* **-nies. 1** property inherited from one's father or ancestors. **2** property belonging to a church, monastery, or convent. **3** any heritage. ⟨ME < OF < L *patrimonium* < *pater* father⟩ **—,pat•ri'mo•ni•al,** *adj.*

pa•tri•ot ['peitriət] *or* ['pætriət] *n.* a person who loves and loyally supports the interests and rights of his or her country. ⟨< LL < Gk. *patriōtēs*, ult. < *patris* fatherland⟩

pa•tri•ot•ic [,peitri'ɒtɪk] *or* [,pætri'ɒtɪk] *adj.* inspired by love and loyal support for one's country: *a patriotic speech. She is very patriotic.* **—,pa•tri'ot•i•cal•ly,** *adv.*

pa•tri•ot•ism ['peitriə,tɪzəm] *or* ['pætriə,tɪzəm] *n.* love and loyal support for the interests and rights of one's country.

pa•tris•tic [pə'trɪstɪk] *adj.* having to do with the early leaders, or fathers, of the Christian church or with their writings. **—pa'tris•ti•cal•ly,** *adv.*

pa•trol [pə'troul] *v.* **-trolled, -trol•ling;** *n.* *—v.* **1** make the rounds as a watchman or a police officer does. **2** go around (a town, camp, etc.) to watch or guard.
—n. **1** a person or group of persons who patrol: *The patrol was changed at midnight.* **2** a making of the rounds to watch or guard: *He was on patrol last night.* **3** a group of soldiers, ships, or aircraft, sent to find out all they can about the enemy. **4** one of the subdivisions of a troop of Scouts or a company of Girl Guides. There are up to eight people in a patrol, including a patrol leader and a second. ⟨< F *patrouiller* paddle in mud⟩

patrol car a police car used for patrolling roads or districts.

patrol leader 1 the person in charge of a military patrol. **2** the boy or girl in charge of a patrol of Scouts or Girl Guides.

pa•trol•man [pə'troulmən] *n., pl.* **-men** [-mən]. a man who patrols, especially a police officer who patrols a certain district.

patrol wagon a closed van or truck used by the police for carrying prisoners.

pa•tron ['peitrən] *n., adj.* *—n.* **1** one who buys regularly at a given store or goes regularly to a given restaurant, hotel, etc. **2** a person, especially one having social or political influence, who sponsors or supports another person or a cause, institution, etc.: *a patron of the arts.* **3** a guardian saint or god; an otherworldly protector. **4** in ancient Rome, **a** an influential man who took certain persons under his protection. **b** one who had freed a slave but kept some sort of paternal control over him or her.
—adj. guarding; protecting: *a patron saint.* ⟨ME < OF < L *patronus* < *pater* father⟩

pa•tron•age ['peitrənɪdʒ] *or* ['pætrənɪdʒ] *n.* **1** the regular business given to a store, hotel, etc. by customers. **2** the favour, encouragement, or support given by a patron. **3** favour, kindness, etc. given in a haughty, condescending way: *an air of patronage.* **4** the power to give jobs or favours: *the patronage of a premier, mayor, or reeve.* **5** jobs or favours given in return for political support. **6** the act of handing out jobs or favours in this way.

pa•tron•ess ['peitrənɪs] *or* ['pætrənɪs] *n.* **1** a woman, especially one having social or political influence, who sponsors or supports another person or a cause, institution, etc. **2** a woman who is a guardian saint or a goddess.

pa•tron•ize ['peitrə,naɪz] *or* ['pætrə,naɪz] *v.* **-ized, -iz•ing. 1** be a regular customer of; give regular business to. **2** act as a patron toward; support or protect: *to patronize the ballet.* **3** be helpful to in a haughty, condescending way, as if to a very young child or an inferior: *Children do not like being patronized by adults.* **—'pa•tron,iz•er,** *n.* **—'pa•tron,iz•ing•ly,** *adv.*

patron saint a saint regarded as the special guardian of a person, church, city, etc.

pat•ro•nym•ic [,pætrə'nɪmɪk] *n., adj.* *—n.* a name derived from the name of a father or ancestor, especially through the use of a patronymic affix. *MacDonald*, meaning *Son of Donald*, and *Williamson,* meaning *son of William,* are patronymics.
—adj. deriving or indicating derivation from the name of a father or other progenitor. ⟨< LL < Gk. *patrōnymikos* < *patēr* father + dial. *onyma* name⟩

pat•sy ['pætsi] *n., pl.* **-sies.** *Informal.* **1** one who is easily victimized or deceived. **2** a scapegoat or fall guy. ⟨origin uncertain⟩

pat•ten ['pætən] *n.* **1** a wooden overshoe with a thick sole. **2** a kind of wooden sandal or overshoe, mounted on an iron ring, to raise the foot above wet ground. ⟨ME < OF *patin* < *pate* paw < Gmc.⟩
☛ *Hom.* PATEN, PATINE.

pat•ter[1] ['pætər] *v., n.* *—v.* **1** make rapid taps: *bare feet pattering along the floor. The rain pattered against the window.* **2** move or run with light, rapid steps: *She pattered down the stairs.*
—n. a series of quick taps or the sound they make: *the patter of hail on the roof.* ⟨< *pat[1]*⟩

pat•ter[2] ['pætər] *n., v.* *—n.* **1** rapid and easy talk, such as that of a magician, comedian, or circus barker. **2** the specialized vocabulary of a certain group, especially thieves, etc.; cant. **3** rapid speech, usually for comic effect, introduced into a song.
—v. talk or say rapidly and easily, without much thought: *to patter a prayer.* ⟨var. of *pater* in *paternoster*⟩

pat•tern ['pætərn] *n., v.* *—n.* **1** an arrangement of shapes, lines, colours, etc.; design: *wallpaper with a floral pattern, frost patterns on the windows, a checkered pattern of sunlight and shade on the lawn.* **2** a model or guide for making something: *a paper dressmaking pattern.* **3** a fine example; model to be followed. **4** a configuration suggesting a design: *the pattern of events, traffic patterns.* **5** a standard group of traits, qualities, movements, acts, etc. that characterize a type or individual: *a behaviour pattern, speech patterns.* **6** form and style in a work of literature or music: *the pattern of a Haydn symphony.* **7** a wooden or metal form used in a foundry to make a mould. **8** something that represents a class or type; example; specimen. **9** a predictable or predetermined route or direction of movement: *the flight pattern.*
—v. **1** make or do according to a pattern; model (often used with **after** or **on**): *She patterned herself after her mother.* **2** form into or decorate with a pattern. ⟨ME < OF *patron* pattern, patron < L *patronus* (See PATRON); with reference to a client's copying his or her patron⟩
☛ *Syn. n.* **3.** See note at MODEL.

pat•ty ['pæti] *n., pl.* **-ties. 1** a small pie or filled pastry. **2** a small, flat, usually round cake of chopped food: *hamburger or chicken patties.* **3** a small, round, flat piece of candy: *a peppermint patty.* ⟨< F *pâté* < OF *pastee.* Doublet of PASTY[2].⟩

patty pan 1 a small pan for baking little cakes, patties, etc. **2** a type of summer squash vaguely resembling this pan.

PAU PAN-AMERICAN UNION.

pau•ci•ty ['pɒsəti] *n.* **1** a small number. **2** a small amount; scarcity; lack. ⟨< L *paucitas* < *paucus* few⟩

Paul Bunyan *North American folklore.* a giant lumberjack who did many incredible deeds, often assisted by his giant blue ox, Babe.

Pau•li exclusion principle ['paʊli] *Physics.* the principle that two similar subatomic particles cannot have the same quantum numbers and hence cannot be in the same space at the same time. ⟨after W. *Pauli*, U.S. physicist (1900–1955)⟩

Paul•ine ['pɒlaɪn] *or* ['pɒlin] *adj.* **1** of, having to do with, or written by the Apostle Paul. **2** of his doctrines or writings, especially the epistles attributed to him in the New Testament.

paunch [pɒntʃ] *n.* **1** the belly; abdomen. **2** a large, protruding belly; POT BELLY. **3** the first stomach of a cud-chewing animal; rumen. ⟨ME < ONF *panche* < L *pantex, -ticis*⟩

paunch•y ['pɒntʃi] *adj.* having a big paunch.
—'paunch•i•ness, *n.*

pau•per ['pɒpər] *n.* **1** a very poor person. **2** a person supported by charity or by public welfare. ⟨< L *pauper* poor. Doublet of POOR.⟩
☛ *Hom.* POPPER.

pau•per•ism ['pɒpə,rɪzəm] *n.* poverty.

pau•per•ize ['pɒpə,raɪz] *v.* **-ized, -iz•ing.** make a pauper of.
—,pau•per•i'za•tion, *n.* **—'pau•per,iz•er,** *n.*

pause [pɒz] *v.* **paused, paus•ing;** *n.* *—v.* **1** stop for a time; wait. **2** dwell; linger: *to pause upon a word.*
—n. **1** a moment of silence; stop; rest. **2** a brief stop in speaking or reading. **3** any punctuation mark indicating such a stop. **4** a momentary hesitation or slight delay. **5** *Music.* **a** the holding of a note, chord, or rest beyond its written time value. The length of a pause is at the discretion of the performer. **b** the symbol for this (𝄐) or (𝄑), written above or below the note or rest. **6** a break in the rhythm of a line of poetry; caesura.
give (one) **pause,** cause (one) to reconsider or be unsure. ⟨ME < OF < L *pausa* < Gk. *pausis* < *pauein* to stop⟩
—'paus•er, *n.*
☛ *Syn. v.* **1.** See note at STOP.

pa•vane or **pa•van** [pə'væn], [pə'vɑn], *or* ['pævən] *n.* **1** a slow, stately dance, usually in 4/4 time, popular in the 16th and 17th centuries. **2** the music for this dance. ⟨< MF < Sp. *pavana* < OItal. *padovana* Paduan (dance) < *Padova* Padua⟩

pave [peiv] *v.* **paved, pav•ing.** cover (a street, sidewalk, etc.) with pavement.
pave the way, prepare a smooth or easy way; facilitate progress or development: *The maps made by the earliest explorers paved the way for those who followed.* ⟨ME < OF *paver,* ult. < L *pavire* beat, tread down⟩ **—'pav•er,** *n.*

pave•ment ['peivmənt] *n.* **1** a covering, or surface, for streets, sidewalks, etc., made of stones, gravel, concrete, asphalt, etc. **2** the material used for paving. **3** a paved road, etc. **4** *Brit.* sidewalk. ⟨ME < OF *pavement,* ult. < L *pavimentum* a beaten-down floor < *pavire* beat, tread down⟩

pa•vil•ion [pə'vɪljən] *n., v.* *—n.* **1** a building, usually open-sided, used for shelter, pleasure, etc.: *a bathing pavilion.* **2** a large tent, often luxurious, for entertainment or shelter. **3** a light, ornamental building, usually open-fronted, for the players and spectators of outdoor games: *a cricket pavilion.* **4** any building that houses an exhibition at a fair. **5** a part of a building higher and more decorated than the rest. **6** any of the group of detached or semidetached buildings forming an institution, such as a hospital.
—v. furnish with a pavilion; enclose or shelter in a pavilion. ⟨ME < OF < L *papilio, -onis* tent, butterfly⟩

pav•ing ['peivɪŋ] *n., v.* *—n.* **1** the material for pavement. **2** pavement.
—v. ppr. of PAVE.

pav•iour or **pav•ior** ['peivjər] *n.* **1** a person who paves; paver. **2** material used for paving.

Pa•vo ['peivou] *n. Astronomy.* the Peacock, a constellation in the southern hemisphere, between Triangulum Australe and Indus. ⟨< L, peacock⟩

paw [pɒ] *n., v.* *—n.* **1** the foot of an animal having claws. Cats and dogs have paws. **2** *Informal.* a hand, especially when large or clumsy.
—v. **1** strike at or touch with a paw: *The kitten pawed the ball of yarn.* **2** scrape or strike with or as if with a hoof: *The horse was pawing the ground, eager to go.* **3** handle or touch awkwardly, rudely, or too intimately. **4** grab at or for wildly: *He pawed the air in an effort to keep himself from falling.* ⟨ME < OF *powe* < Gmc.⟩
☛ *Hom.* PA [pɒ].

pawl [pɒl] *n.* a pivoted bar arranged to catch in the teeth of a ratchet wheel or the like so as to allow rotation in only one direction. See RATCHET WHEEL for picture. ⟨origin uncertain⟩
☛ *Hom.* PALL, POL.

pawn¹ [pɒn] *v., n.* *—v.* **1** give (something) as security that borrowed money will be repaid: *He pawned his watch to buy food until he could get work.* **2** stake; pledge; risk.
—n. **1** something left as security. **2** a pledge. **3** a person held as security that demands will be met; hostage.
in pawn, in another's possession as security: *His watch is in pawn to the man who lent him money.* ⟨ME < OF *pan*⟩

pawn² [pɒn] *n.* **1** *Chess.* one of the 16 pieces, 8 black and 8 white, of lowest value. **2** a person or thing used by someone to further his or her own purposes: *She used her friends and colleagues as pawns in her race for political power.* ⟨ME < AF *paon,* var. of OF *peon* < LL *pedo, pedonis* foot soldier < L *pes, pedis* foot. Doublet of PEON. Related to PIONEER.⟩

pawn•bro•ker ['pɒn,broukər] *n.* a person who lends money at interest on articles that are left as security for the loan.

Paw•nee [pɒ'ni] *n., adj.* *—n.* **1** a member of a confederacy of Native American peoples of Caddoan stock, now living in N Oklahoma. **2** the Caddoan language of the Pawnees.
—adj. of or having to do with the Pawnees, their language or their culture.

pawn•shop ['pɒn,ʃɒp] *n.* a pawnbroker's shop.

pawn ticket a receipt given in return for a pawned object or objects.

paw•paw ['pɒ,pɒ] *n.* **1** a small North American tree (*Asimina triloba*) of the custard-apple family bearing oblong, yellowish, edible fruit with many beanlike seeds. **2** the fruit of this tree. **3** papaya. Also, **papaw.**

pax vo•bis•cum ['pæks vou'bɪskəm] *or* [wo'bɪskʊm] *Latin.* peace be with you.

pay¹ [pei] *v.* **paid** or (*obsolete except for def. 10*) **payed, pay•ing;** *n., adj.* *—v.* **1** give (a person) what is due for goods, services, work, etc. **2** give (money, etc.) that is due. **3** give money for: *Pay your way.* **4** hand over the amount of: *pay a debt.* **5** give; make; offer: *to pay attention, to pay compliments, to pay a visit.* **6** be profitable (to); be worthwhile (for): *Crime does not pay. It wouldn't pay me to take that job.* **7** yield as a return: *That stock pays four percent.* **8** reward or punish: *She paid them for their insults by causing them trouble.* **9** suffer; undergo: *The one who does wrong must pay the penalty.* **10** let out (a rope, etc.) (*used with* **out**).
pay as you go, pay or discharge obligations as they are incurred.
pay back, a return (borrowed money). **b** give the same treatment as received: *I'll pay her back for her hospitality by inviting her for dinner.* **c** take revenge on; retaliate: *I'll pay you back yet!*
pay down, a pay (part of the price) at the time of purchase, used in instalment buying. **b** pay off or in full.
pay off, a give all the money that is owed; pay in full. **b** get even with; get revenge on. **c** *Informal.* bribe. **d** *Nautical.* fall off to leeward.
pay up, pay; especially, pay in full.
—n. **1** money or equivalent given for goods, services, or work; wages; salary. **2** a reward; punishment; a return for favours or hurts: *Dislike is the pay for being mean.* **3** the act of paying; payment, especially of wages: *rate of pay.* **4** the condition of being paid, or receiving wages: *workers in a person's pay or employment.*
in the pay of, paid by and working for.
—adj. **1** containing enough metal, oil, etc. to be worth mining, drilling, etc.: *a pay lode.* **2** made operable or accessible by the use of coins or credit cards: *a pay phone.* **3** concerning a service or facility for which a fee or subscription is paid: *pay TV.* ⟨ME < OF *paier* < L *pacare* pacify < *pax, pacis* peace⟩
☛ *Hom.* PE.
☛ *Syn. v.* **1. Pay,** COMPENSATE, REMUNERATE = give someone money or its equivalent in return for something. **Pay** is the common word and means 'give someone money due for goods, work, or services': *He paid the lawyer.* **Compensate** suggests making up for time spent, things lost, service given, etc.: *The railway compensated the farmer for her cow.* **Remunerate** suggests giving a reward in return for services, trouble, etc. and, like **compensate,** is used especially as being more polite than **pay** and as not suggesting crudely that money is expected or due: *The club remunerated the lecturer.*
☛ *Usage.* See note at PAID.

pay² [pei] *v.* **payed, pay•ing.** cover (a ship's bottom, seams, rope, etc.) with tar, pitch, or another waterproof substance. ⟨ME < OF *peier* < L *picare* < *pix, picis* pitch⟩
☛ *Hom.* PE.

pay•a•ble ['peiəbəl] *adj.* **1** required to be paid; due: *accounts payable.* **2** that may or can be paid: *that bill is payable at any chartered bank.* **3** of a mine or other business, profitable.
4 payables, *pl.* accounts payable.

pay•day ['pei,dei] *n.* a day on which wages are paid or pay cheques issued.

pay dirt **1** earth, gravel, or ore containing enough metal to be worth mining. **2** *Informal.* something that yields a profit or beneficial result. **3** *Placer mining.* gold-bearing gravel. Also, **pay gravel.** Compare PAYSTREAK, PAY ZONE.
hit or **strike pay dirt,** find a source of wealth or success.

pay•ee [pei'i] *n.* a person to whom money is paid or is to be paid.

pay•load ['pei,loud] *n.* **1** the part of a vehicle's load that produces revenue. **2** the warhead, instruments, etc. carried by a missile or rocket.

pay•mas•ter ['pei,mæstər] *n.* a man whose job is to pay wages.

pay•ment ['peimənt] *n.* **1** the act or fact of paying. **2** the amount paid: *a monthly payment of $30.* **3** reward or punishment: *He said his child's good health was payment enough.*

pay•mis•tress ['pei,mɪstrəs] *n.* a woman whose job is to pay wages.

pay•nim or **Pay•nim** ['peinɪm] *n. or adj. Archaic.* **1** pagan; heathen. **2** Muslim; Saracen. ⟨ME < OF *paienisme* < LL *paganismus* < L *paganus* rustic. See PAGAN.⟩

pay•off ['pei,ɒf] *n.* **1** a paying of wages. **2** the time of such payment. **3 a** returns for an enterprise, specific action, etc. **b** *Informal.* a dividing of the returns from some undertaking among those having an interest in it. **4** a bribe. **5** *Slang.* the climax of a story, situation, etc., often unexpected.

pay phone a coin-operated telephone.

pay•roll ['pei,roul] *n.* **1** an employer's list of persons to be paid, together with the amount that each is to receive. **2** the total amount to be distributed among these persons.

pays d'en haut or **Pays d'en Haut** [peidɑ̃'o] *Cdn. French.* **1** formerly, the vast region north and west of Lake Superior, as known by the fur traders and explorers; NORTHWEST (*n.* def. 3). **2** upcountry.

pays sau•vage or **Pays Sau•vage** [peiso'vaʒ] *Cdn. French.* formerly, a region inhabited by First Nations peoples; Indian country.

pay•streak ['pei,strik] *n.* a profitable deposit or stratum of gold-bearing gravel. Compare PAY DIRT (def. 3), PAY ZONE.

payt. payment.

pay TV 1 a cable television service for which extra payment is made. **2** a coin-operated television set.

pay zone *Cdn. Hardrock mining.* a profitable stratum or vein of mineral-bearing ore. Compare PAYSTREAK.

Pb lead (for L *plumbum*).

PBS Public Broadcasting Service.

PBX Private Branch (Telephone) Exchange.

pc. 1 piece. **2** price.

p.c. 1 percent. **2** postcard. **3** PETTY CASH. **4** *Pharmacy.* after eating (for L *post cibum*).

P.C. 1 POLICE CONSTABLE. **2** PROGRESSIVE CONSERVATIVE. **3** PRIVY COUNCIL; PRIVY COUNCILLOR. **4** POLITICALLY CORRECT.

PC 1 PERSONAL COMPUTER. **2** POLITICALLY CORRECT.

PCB *pl.* **PCB's.** POLYCHLORINATED BIPHENYL.

PCP phenylcyclohexylpiperidine, a psychedelic drug capable of causing severe mental or emotional derangement, and sometimes fatal; angel dust.

pct. percent.

pd. paid.

p.d. 1 per day (for L *per diem*). **2** *Electricity.* potential difference.

Pd palladium.

P.D. 1 per day (for L *per diem*). **2** Postal District. **3** *Esp. U.S.* Police Department.

PDT or **P.D.T.** Pacific Daylight Time.

pe [pei] *n.* the eighteenth letter of the Hebrew alphabet. See table of alphabets in the Appendix.
☛ *Hom.* PAY.

PE PRINCE EDWARD ISLAND (*used esp. in computerized address systems*).

P.E. 1 PHYSICAL EDUCATION. **2** PROTESTANT EPISCOPAL. **3** Petroleum Engineer.

pea [pi] *n.* **1** an annual vine (*Pisum sativum*) grown in many varieties for its smooth, round, protein-rich seeds borne in pods. **2** the seed of this plant, used as a vegetable when green or for soups, etc. when ripened and dried. **3** any of various plants that are related to or resemble the garden pea (*usually used in compounds*): *chick pea, sweet pea.* **4** (*adjl.*) designating a very large family (Leguminosae, also called Fabaceae) of herbs, climbing plants, shrubs, and trees found throughout the world, having usually compound leaves and bearing fruit in the form of oblong pods that split open evenly along the middle when ripe and in which the seeds are arranged in rows. The bean, pea, clover, alfalfa, wisteria, and rosewood are some members of the pea family. **5** especially in the West Indies, the fresh or dried seed of a legume, especially any of various beans or peas. **6** something resembling a pea.
(as) like as two peas (in a pod), exactly alike. ⟨ME *pees, pese,* originally sing., later taken as a pl. < OE *pise* < LL *pisa* < L pl. of *pisum* pea < Gk. *pison*⟩
☛ *Hom.* PEE.

peace [pis] *n., interj. —n.* **1** freedom from war or strife of any kind. **2** public quiet, order, and security. **3** an agreement between contending parties to end a war: *to sign the peace, the Peace of Paris.* **4** quiet; calm; stillness: *peace of mind.*
at peace, a not in a state of war. **b** not quarrelling. **c** in a state of quietness; quiet; peaceful.
hold or **keep** (one's) **peace,** be silent.
keep the peace, refrain, or prevent others, from disturbing the (public) peace; maintain public order.
make peace, a effect a reconciliation between persons or parties at variance. **b** arrange peace with a nation at the close of a war.
make (one's) **peace with,** come to accept or be reconciled to (something or someone).
—interj. **1** keep still! be silent! **2** a call of greeting or farewell. ⟨ME < OF *pais* < L *pax, pacis*⟩
☛ *Hom.* PIECE.

peace•a•ble ['pisəbəl] *adj.* **1** liking peace; keeping peace. **2** peaceful. **—'peace•a•ble•ness,** *n.* **—'peace•a•bly,** *adv.*

peace•ful ['pisfəl] *adj.* **1** free of turmoil, commotion, or conflict; quiet; calm: *a peaceful day, a peaceful scene.* **2** keeping peace: *peaceful neighbours.* **3** of or having to do with peace or a time of peace: *peaceful uses for nuclear energy.* **4** without violence or force: *to settle a dispute by peaceful means.* **—'peace•ful•ly,** *adv.* **—'peace•ful•ness,** *n.*
☛ *Syn.* **1. Peaceful,** PLACID, SERENE = quiet and calm. **Peaceful** suggests a state of deep inner quiet, coming from release or freedom from everything that disturbs or excites: *It was peaceful in the mountains.* **Placid** suggests contentment and absence of excitement, especially associated with a disposition or nature that stays even and calm in the midst of excitement: *Placid cows grazed beside the highway.* **Serene** suggests a state of peacefulness and calmness that is above all disturbance: *She is always cool, gracious, and serene.*

peace•keep•ing ['pis,kipɪŋ] *n.* the preserving of peace, especially the enforcement of peace between hostile nations by means of an international body. **—'peace,keep•er,** *n.*

peace•mak•er ['pis,meikər] *n.* a person who makes peace, especially by reconciling conflicts or quarrels between individuals or groups.

peace•mak•ing ['pis,meikɪŋ] *n., adj. —n.* the act of making peace, especially between warring nations or disunited countries. *—adj.* of or having to do with the act of peacemaking: *The Canadian Armed Forces are known worldwide for their peacemaking abilities.*

peace offering 1 an offering made to obtain peace. **2** in old Jewish custom, an offering of thanksgiving to God.

peace officer a person responsible for preserving public peace, such as a mayor, justice of the peace, or police officer, or an officer of a prison.

peace pipe calumet.

Peace River Block or **country** *Cdn.* a settled region of rolling plains in northern British Columbia and Alberta, lying in the fertile valley of the Peace River.

peace•time ['pis,taɪm] *n.* **1** a time of peace. **2** (*adjl.*) of or having to do with a time of peace.

peach[1] [pitʃ] *n., adj. —n.* **1** a juicy, roundish fruit having a soft, pinkish yellow, fuzzy skin and a rough stone, or pit. **2** the small tree (*Prunus persica*) of the rose family that bears peaches. It is cultivated in temperate regions. See also NECTARINE. **3** a yellowish pink colour. **4** *Informal.* a person or thing especially admired or liked.
—adj. having the colour peach. ⟨ME < OF *pesche,* ult. < L *Persicum (malum)* Persian apple < Gk.⟩

peach[2] [pitʃ] *v. Slang.* give secret information; turn informer. ⟨ME, var. of *appeach* < AF var. of OF *empechier* hinder < LL *impedicare* < L *in-* on + *pedica* shackle. Cf. IMPEACH.⟩

peach•leaf willow ['pitʃ,lif] a willow tree (*Salix amygdaloides*) which grows tall in Manitoba and Ontario, but remains a shrub elsewhere. Its leaves are about 10 cm long with a pale underside.

peach•y ['pitʃi] *adj.* **peach•i•er, peach•i•est. 1** like a peach, as in colour or texture. **2** *Slang.* fine; wonderful. **—'peach•i•ness,** *n.*

pea•cock ['pi,kɒk] *n., pl.* **-cocks** or (*esp. collectively*) **-cock;** *v.,*

adj. —*n.* **1** the male of a peafowl, a large bird having iridescent green, blue, and gold plumage, with a very large tail that can be erected and spread out like a fan. Most of the upper tail feathers have an eyelike spot at the tip. **2** peafowl. **3** a person who is vain and fond of showing off.
—*v.* strut, showing off like a peacock.
—*adj.* bright blue green. ⟨ult. < OE *pēa* (< L *pavo* peafowl) + *cock[1]*⟩

peacock blue a bright or iridescent greenish blue.

peacock copper *Cdn.* bornite, a copper-iron sulphide with a purplish tarnish like peacock feathers.

pea•fowl ['pi,faʊl] *n.* any of several large, brightly coloured birds of the same family (Phasianidae) as pheasants, found in S Asia and Africa. The males of the **blue peafowl** (*Pavo cristatus*) of India and Sri Lanka and the **green peafowl** (*P. muticus*) of Burma and Java have the characteristic iridescent plumage. Both sexes of the rare **Congo peafowl** (*Afropavo congensis*) of Africa have bright plumage.

pea green light yellowish green.

pea•hen ['pi,hɛn] *n.* an adult female peafowl.

pea jacket a short, double-breasted coat of thick woollen cloth, worn especially by sailors. ⟨< Du. *pij-jekker* < *pij* a coarse woollen cloth + *jekker* jacket⟩

peak [pik] *n., v.* —*n.* **1** the pointed top of a mountain or hill. **2** a mountain that stands alone. **3** the highest level or degree; maximum or high point: *the peak of a career, the peak of an election campaign.* **4** (*adjl.*) of or being a peak, or maximum: *peak output.* **5** any pointed end or top: *the peak of a beard, the peak of a roof.* **6** a projecting brim at the front of a cap; visor. **7** *Nautical.* **a** the narrow part of a ship's hold at the bow or the stern. **b** the upper rear corner of a four-sided fore-and-aft sail. **8** promontory; headland. **9** a downward point formed by the hairline in the middle of the forehead; widow's peak.
—*v.* **1** *Nautical.* tilt up: *to peak a gaff.* **2** come or cause to come to a maximum or high point: *The unemployment rate peaked in February. Their election campaign peaked too early.* ⟨var. of *pick[2]*⟩
☛ *Hom.* PEEK, PIQUE.

peaked[1] *adj.* [pikt] *or* ['pikɪd]; *v.* [pikt] *adj., v.* —*adj.* having a peak; pointed: *a peaked hat.*
—*v.* pt. and pp. of PEAK.

peak•ed[2] ['pikɪd] *adj.* sickly in appearance; wan; thin. ⟨< obs. *peak*, v., become pale and sickly; origin unknown⟩

peal [pil] *n., v.* —*n.* **1** the loud, prolonged ringing of bells. **2** any loud, long, usually reverberating sound: *a peal of thunder, peals of laughter.* **3** a set of tuned bells, usually hung in a tower. **4** a complete series of changes rung on a given number of bells: *to ring a peal.*
—*v.* **1** sound out in a peal; ring: *The bells pealed.* **2** cause (bells) to ring in peals. **3** give forth loudly. ⟨ME *pele*⟩
☛ *Hom.* PEEL.

pe•an ['piən] See PAEAN.

pea•nut ['pi,nʌt] *or* ['pinət] *n.* **1** an annual plant (*Arachis hypogaea*) of the pea family having yellow flowers whose stalks later grow down into the ground where the ovary ripens and the pods are formed. **2** one of these pods, containing from one to three seeds that are roasted and eaten as nuts and also yield an oil used in cooking, etc. **3** one of the seeds. **4 peanuts,** *Slang.* something of little value, especially a small amount of money: *It costs peanuts to run this car.* **5** *Slang.* a small or unimportant person.

peanut butter a spread made from roasted, ground peanuts, used as a filling for sandwiches, etc.

pear [pɛr] *n.* **1** a sweet, juicy, edible fruit rounded at both ends and smaller toward the stem end. **2** the widely cultivated tree (*Pyrus communis*) of the rose family that bears this fruit. **3** *Informal.* especially in the West Indies, avocado. ⟨OE *pere* < LL *pira* < L *pirum*⟩
☛ *Hom.* PAIR, PARE, PÈRE.

pearl [pɜrl] *n., adj., v.* —*n.* **1** a white or off-white rounded bead formed inside the shells of oysters and other bivalve molluscs from deposits of calcite around an irritant nucleus such as a grain of sand. Pearls are valued as gems when the lustre and colour are of high quality. **2** a similar gem made artificially. **3** anything that looks like a pearl, such as a dewdrop or a tear. **4** a very fine one of its kind. **5** a very pale bluish grey. **6** mother-of-pearl. **7** *Printing.* a size of type; 5 point.
cast pearls before swine, offer or display something very fine to a person who cannot appreciate it.
—*adj.* **1** of or concerning pearls. **2** made of or set with pearls: *a pearl necklace.* **3** very pale bluish grey. **4** formed into small, round pieces like pearls: *pearl tapioca.* **5** made from mother-of-pearl: *pearl buttons.*
—*v.* **1** hunt or dive for pearls. **2** adorn or set with or as with pearls, or with mother-of-pearl. **3** make pearly in colour or lustre. **4** convert or reduce to small, round pieces. ⟨ME < OF *perle* < VL *perla*⟩
☛ *Hom.* PURL.

pearl•ash ['pɜrl,æʃ] *n.* potassium carbonate, usually made by refining potash.

pearl dace a fish (*Margariscus margarita*) found across Canada. It is black or dark brown on the back and silver on the sides.

pearl grey a soft, pale, bluish grey.

pearl•ized ['pɜrlaɪzd] *adj.* made to resemble mother-of-pearl: *pearlized earrings.*

pearl onion a small, sweet onion, often pickled for use as a garnish.

pearl oyster any of several oysters of the family Pteridae, of the coasts of eastern Asia, Panama, and southern California, producing valuable pearls.

pearl•y ['pɜrli] *adj.* **pearl•i•er, pearl•i•est. 1** like a pearl; having the colour or lustre of pearls: *pearly teeth.* **2** like mother-of-pearl. **3** adorned with or containing many pearls. **—'pearl•i•ness,** *n.*

pearly nautilus NAUTILUS (def. 1).

pear–shaped ['pɛr ,ʃeipt] *adj.* **1** shaped like a pear, being rounded and smaller at the top than at the bottom, which may bulge. **2** of the human voice, especially sung tones, full, clear, and resonant.

pea•sant ['pɛzənt] *n., adj.* —*n.* a person who lives in the country and works on the land, especially a farm labourer or tenant farmer.
—*adj.* of peasants: *peasant labour.* ⟨ME < AF var. of OF *paysant* < *pays* country, ult. < L *pagus* district⟩

peas•ant•ry ['pɛzəntri] *n.* **1** peasants collectively. **2** the rank or condition of a peasant.

peas•cod ['piz,kɒd] See PEASECOD.

pease [piz] *n. Archaic.* pea (*sometimes treated as a plural*). ⟨OE *pise* < LL *pisa* < L *pisum* < Gk. *pison*⟩

pease•cod ['piz,kɒd] *n.* the pod of a pea. Also, **peascod.**

pea•shoot•er ['pi,ʃutər] *n.* a toy blowgun for shooting dried peas or other small objects.

pea soup 1 a thick soup made from dried peas, meat (usually ham), and other vegetables, and, in Canada, associated especially with Québec. **2** peasouper.

pea•soup•er ['pi,supər] *n. Informal.* a thick, heavy fog. Also, **peasoup.**

peat [pit] *n.* vegetable matter consisting of mosses and other plants that have decomposed in water and become partly carbonized, used as fertilizer and as a fuel when dried. **2** a block of peat used as fuel. **3** PEAT MOSS. ⟨ME *pete* < Anglo-L *peta*; origin uncertain⟩ **—'peat•y,** *adj.*

peat bog a bog composed of peat and from which peat moss and peat for fuel are harvested.

peat moss 1 any of a genus (*Sphagnum*) of mosses that grow only in wet, acid areas; sphagnum. Peat moss forms peat when it dies and decomposes together with other plants. **2** any peat composed of the residues of mosses and used as garden mulch.

A logger using a peavey to move a log

pea•vey ['pivi] *n., pl.* **-veys.** *Cdn.* a strong pole or lever, 1.5 to 2 m long, fitted at one end with a sharp point of iron or steel and a hinged semicircular hook, used by loggers for handling logs in a drive, during booming operations, etc. Also, **peavy.**

Compare CANT-HOOK. ⟨origin uncertain; possibly from a Joseph *Peavey*, who has been claimed as the inventor⟩

pea•vy ['pivi] *n., pl.* **-vies.** See PEAVEY.

peb•ble ['pɛbəl] *n., v.* **-bled, -bling.** *—n.* **1** a small stone, usually worn smooth and round by being rolled about by water. **2** a rough, uneven surface on leather, paper, etc.
—v. **1** prepare (leather) so that it appears to be covered with pebbles. **2** pelt with pebbles. ⟨OE *pæbbel* (in place names)⟩
—'peb•ble,like, *adj.*

peb•bly ['pɛbli] *adj.* **1** having many pebbles; covered with pebbles. **2** having a rough, uneven surface.

pe•can [pi'kæn], ['pikæn], *or* [pɪ'kɑn] *n.* **1** a large hickory tree (*Carya pecan*, also called *C. illinoensis*) of the S United States and Mexico having deeply furrowed bark and hard wood and bearing olive-shaped, edible nuts. **2** the nut of this tree, having a thin, smooth shell and a sweet, oily kernel. **3** the wood of the pecan tree. ⟨< Algonquian *pakan* hard-shelled nut⟩

pec•ca•dil•lo [,pɛkə'dɪlou] *n., pl.* **-loes** or **-los.** a slight sin or fault. ⟨< Sp. *pecadillo*, dim. of *pecado* sin < L *peccatum*⟩

pec•cant ['pɛkənt] *adj.* **1** sinful; sinning; morally guilty. **2** faulty; breaking an ordinance, rule, or established practice. ⟨< L *peccare* to sin⟩ **—'pec•ca•ble,** *adj.*

pec•ca•ry ['pɛkəri] *n., pl.* **-ries** or *(esp. collectively)* **-ry.** either of two small, piglike animals (*Tayassu tajacu* or *T. albirostris*) of North and South America having sharp tusks, small, erect ears, and a very short tail. The peccaries constitute the family Tayassuidae, and are distantly related to pigs. ⟨< Carib *pakira*⟩

peck[1] [pɛk] *n.* **1** a unit for measuring volume of grain, fruit, etc., equal to eight quarts or one-fourth of a bushel (about 9.09 dm^3). **2** a container for measuring, holding just a peck. **3** a great deal: *a peck of trouble.* ⟨ME *pec*; origin uncertain⟩

peck[2] [pɛk] *v., n. —v.* **1** strike and pick with the beak or with something pointed like a beak. **2** make by striking with the beak or with something pointed: *Woodpeckers peck holes in trees.* **3** aim with a beak; make a pecking motion. **4** strike at and pick up with the beak: *A hen pecks corn.* **5** *Informal.* kiss lightly and hurriedly. **6** find fault.
peck at, a try to peck. **b** *Informal.* eat only a little, bit by bit: *She just pecked at her food.* **c** keep criticizing.
—n. **1** a stroke made with the beak. **2** a hole or mark made by pecking. **3** *Informal.* a hurried or casual kiss: *She gave him a peck on the cheek as she hurried out the door.* ⟨akin to *pick*[1]⟩

pecking order **1** an order of superiority established in flocks of chickens, etc., each bird enjoying the right of dominating those weaker than itself. **2** any similar hierarchy or order of precedence in human society.

peck•ish ['pɛkɪʃ] *adj. Informal.* somewhat hungry.

pecs [pɛks] *n. Slang.* pectoral muscles, especially those well developed by strenuous exercise.

pec•ten ['pɛktən] *n., pl.* **-tens** or **-tin•es** [-tə,niz]. *Zoology.* a comblike part; especially, a membrane in the eyes of birds and reptiles that has parallel folds suggesting the teeth of a comb. ⟨< L *pecten* < *pectere* to comb⟩
☛ *Hom.* PECTIN.

pec•tin ['pɛktən] *n. Biochemistry.* a water-soluble carbohydrate of high molecular weight that occurs in ripe fruits, especially apples, and is used to stiffen jams and jellies, as well as in certain pharmaceuticals and cosmetics. ⟨< Gk. *pēktos* congealing, curdling < *pēgnynai* make stiff⟩ **—'pec•tic,** *adj.*
☛ *Hom.* PECTEN.

pec•tin•ate ['pɛktə,neit] *adj.* having parallel toothlike projections like those on a comb. ⟨See PECTEN⟩

pec•to•ral ['pɛktərəl] *adj., n. —adj.* **1** of, in, or on the breast or chest: *the pectoral muscles.* **2** worn on the chest: *a pectoral cross.* **3** good for diseases of the lungs.
—n. **1** a medicine for the lungs. **2** something, such as an ornament, worn on the breast. ⟨< L *pectoralis* < *pectus, pectoris* chest⟩

pectoral fin one of the two fins behind the head of a fish, corresponding to the forelimbs of the higher vertebrates.

pec•u•late ['pɛkjə,leit] *v.* **-lat•ed, -lat•ing.** steal (money or goods entrusted to one); embezzle. ⟨< L *peculari* embezzle < *peculium* property < *pecu* money, cattle⟩ **—,pec•u'la•tion,** *n.* **—'pec•u,la•tor,** *n.*

pe•cul•iar [pɪ'kjuljər] *adj.* **1** strange; odd; unusual: *The dog's peculiar behaviour frightened the children.* **2** belonging to only one person or thing; unique; special; particular: *Some minerals are peculiar to the Canadian Shield.* ⟨< L *peculiaris* of one's own < *peculium*. See PECULATE.⟩ **—pe'cul•iar•ly,** *adv.*
☛ *Syn.* **1.** See note at STRANGE.

pe•cu•li•ar•i•ty [pɪ,kjuli'ærəti] *or* [pɪ,kjuli'ɛrəti] *n., pl.* **-ties.** **1** the quality or state of being peculiar. **2** a peculiar feature, characteristic, thing, etc.: *They had grown used to the professor's peculiarities.*

pe•cu•ni•ar•y [pɪ'kjuni,ɛri] *adj.* of or having to do with money; in the form of money. ⟨< L *pecuniarius* < *pecunia* money < *pecu* money, cattle⟩

ped•a•gog ['pɛdə,gɒg] See PEDAGOGUE.

ped•a•gog•i•cal [,pɛdə'gɒdʒɪkəl] *or* [,pɛdə'goudʒɪkəl] *adj.* of teachers or teaching; of pedagogy. Also, **pedagogic.**
—,ped•a'gog•i•cal•ly, *adv.*

ped•a•gogue ['pɛdə,gɒg] *n.* **1** *Archaic.* teacher; schoolmaster. **2** a narrow-minded or pedantic teacher. Also (*esp. U.S.*), **pedagog.** ⟨ME < OF < L < Gk. *paidagōgos* < *pais, paidos* boy + *agōgos* leader⟩

ped•a•go•gy ['pɛdə,gɒdʒi] *or* ['pɛdə,goudʒi] *n., pl.* **-gies.** **1** the profession of teaching. **2** the science or art of teaching. **3 a** a method of teaching a particular subject or area: *second language pedagogy.* **b** the method or techniques used by a particular teacher or school: *This is usual Montessori pedagogy.*

ped•al *n., v., adj. 2* ['pɛdəl]; *adj. 1* ['pɛdəl] *or* ['pidəl] *n., v.* **-alled** or **-aled, -al•ling** or **-al•ing;** *adj. —n.* a lever worked by the foot; the part on which the foot is placed to move any kind of machinery. Organs and pianos have pedals for changing the tone. The two pedals of a bicycle, pushed down one after the other, make it go.
—v. **1** work or use the pedals of; move by pedals: *to pedal a bicycle up a hill.* **2** work pedals: *She pedalled frantically to catch up with the others.*
—adj. **1** *Zoology.* of or having to do with the foot or feet, as of a mollusc. **2** of, worked, or propelled by pedals: *a pedal boat.* ⟨< F < Ital. < L *pedale* (thing) of the foot < *pes, pedis* foot⟩
☛ *Hom.* PEDDLE.

pe•dal•fer [pə'dælfər] *n.* soil lacking calcium and magnesium because of high humidity. ⟨< Gk. *pedon* soil + L *al(umen)* alum + L *ferrum* iron⟩

pedal pushers formerly, calf-length slacks worn by women and girls, originally for bicycle riding.

ped•ant ['pɛdənt] *n.* **1** a person who displays his or her knowledge in an unnecessary or tiresome way. **2** a narrow-minded teacher or scholar who places too much emphasis on detail and precision in the use or presentation of knowledge at the expense of common sense. ⟨< Ital. *pedante*, ult. < Gk. *paideuein* educate < *pais, paidos* boy⟩

pe•dan•tic [pə'dæntɪk] *adj.* **1** displaying one's knowledge more than is necessary. **2** tediously learned; scholarly in a dull and narrow way. **—pe'dan•ti•cal•ly,** *adv.*

ped•ant•ry ['pɛdəntri] *n., pl.* **-ries.** **1** an insistence on the use of arbitrary rules and excessive precision in the display of knowledge; the characteristics of a pedant. **2** an instance or example of such characteristics.

ped•ate ['pɛdeit] *adj.* **1** *Zoology.* **a** having a foot or feet. **b** footlike. **c** having divisions like toes. **2** *Botany.* of a leaf, palmately divided into three main parts, the two outer or lateral lobes being divided again into smaller parts somewhat like toes. ⟨< L *pedatus* < *pes, pedis* foot⟩

ped•dle ['pɛdəl] *v.* **-dled, -dling.** **1** carry from place to place and sell. **2** sell or deal out in small quantities: *to peddle candy, to peddle gossip.* **3** travel about with things to sell. ⟨apparently a back formation from *peddler*⟩
☛ *Hom.* PEDAL.

ped•dler ['pɛdlər] *n.* a person who travels about selling things that he or she carries in a pack, in a cart, or on a truck. Also, **pedlar.** ⟨ME *pedlere* < *pedder* < *ped* basket⟩

ped•er•ast ['pɛdə,ræst] *n.* a man who practises pederasty.
—,ped•er'as•tic, *adj.* **—,ped•er'as•ti•cal•ly,** *adv.*

ped•er•as•ty ['pɛdə,ræsti] *n.* the practice of homosexual relations by a man with a boy. ⟨< NL *paederastia* < Gk. < *pais, paidos* boy + *erastēs* lover. 17c.⟩

ped•es•tal ['pɛdɪstəl] *n.* **1** the base supporting a column or pillar. See COLUMN for picture. **2** the base or foot of a statue or a large vase, lamp, etc. **3** any foundation or support, especially when used to display something.
put or **set on a pedestal,** idolize; glorify, idealize, or romanticize: *The newly engaged couple put each other on a pedestal.* ⟨< F < Ital. *piedestallo* < *pie* foot (< L *pes, pedis*) + *di* of + *stallo* stall[1] (< Gmc.)⟩

pe•des•tri•an [pə'dɛstriən] *n., adj.* *—n.* a person who goes on foot; walker.
—adj. **1** going on foot; walking. **2** of or for pedestrians: *a pedestrian crossing.* **3** without imagination; dull; slow: *a pedestrian style in writing.* ⟨< L *pedester, -tris* on foot < *pes, pedis* foot⟩

pe•des•tri•an•ism [pə'dɛstriə,nɪzəm] *n.* **1** the quality or characteristic of being dull or commonplace: *The politician's speeches were famous for their pedestrianism.* **2** walking.

pe•di•a•tri•cian [,pidiə'trɪʃən] *n.* a physician who is a specialist in pediatrics.

pe•di•at•rics [,pidi'ætrɪks] *n.* (*used with a singular verb*) the branch of medicine dealing with children's diseases and the care and development of babies and children. ⟨pl. of *pediatric* < Gk. *pais, paidos* child + *iatreia* medical treatment < *iaesthai* heal⟩ **—,pe•di'at•ric,** *adj.*

ped•i•cab ['pɛdə,kæb] *n.* a three-wheeled, pedal-operated vehicle having a seat over the rear wheels for one or two passengers and a seat in front for the driver. Pedicabs are available for hire in some countries in the Far East and in some major tourist centres in North America. ⟨< L *pes, pedis* foot + *cab*⟩

ped•i•cel ['pɛdəsəl] *n.* **1** *Biology.* a plant stalk that supports a single flower or spore-bearing organ. **2** *Zoology.* a short, narrow structure joining organs or parts; stalk. ⟨< NL *pedicellus*, ult. < L *pes, pedis* foot⟩

ped•i•cle ['pɛdəkəl] pedicel.

pe•dic•u•lar [pə'dɪkjələr] *adj.* **1** of or pertaining to lice. **2** infested with lice; lousy. ⟨< L *pedicularis* < *pediculus,* dim. of *pedis* louse⟩

pe•dic•u•lo•sis [pə,dɪkjə'lousɪs] *n. Pathology.* the state of being infested with lice.

ped•i•cure ['pɛdə,kjur] *n.* **1** a treatment for the feet, toes, and toenails, especially a cosmetic treatment including trimming and polishing of the toenails. **2** the care of the feet, toes, and toenails.

ped•i•cur•ist ['pɛdə,kjʊrɪst] *n.* a person whose work is giving pedicures.

ped•i•gree ['pɛdə,gri] *n.* **1** the list of ancestors of a person or animal; family tree. **2** ancestry; line of descent. **3** derivation, as from a source: *the pedigree of a word.* **4** the recorded line of descent of a purebred animal. **5** (*adj.*) of an animal, purebred: *a pedigree cat.* ⟨apparently < F *pied de grue* foot of a crane; from appearance of 3-branched mark used in genealogies⟩

ped•i•greed ['pɛdə,grid] *adj.* having a known pedigree.

ped•i•ment ['pɛdəmənt] *n.* **1** *Classical architecture.* a low, triangular, gablelike part forming the front of a building with a two-pitched roof, especially over a portico. **2** a similar form used as a decoration on any building, piece of furniture, etc. ⟨earlier *periment, peremint,* probably alteration of *pyramid*⟩ **—'ped•i,ment•ed** [-,mɛntɪd] or **,ped•i'ment•al,** *adj.*

ped•lar ['pɛdlər] *n.* **1** peddler. **2** Often, **Pedlar,** formerly, in the usage of the men of the Hudson's Bay Company, **a** a COUREUR DE BOIS, especially one who competed for trade in Rupert's Land. **b** after 1776, a member of the NORTH WEST COMPANY. **c** an American trader.

ped•o•cal ['pɛdə,kæl] *n.* soil high in calcium and magnesium because of low humidity. ⟨< Gk. *pedon* soil + L *calx, calcis* lime⟩

ped•o•dont•ics [,pɛdə'dɒntɪks] *n.* a branch of dentistry concerned with the care and treatment of children's teeth and mouths. ⟨< Gk. *paido* child + L *dons, dontis* tooth⟩

ped•o•gen•e•sis [,pɛdə'dʒɛnəsɪs] *n.* the formation of soil.

pe•dol•o•gist[1] [pɪ'dɒlədʒɪst] *n.* a person trained in the study of children, especially one whose work it is.

pe•dol•o•gist[2] [pɪ'dɒlədʒɪst] *n.* a person trained in the study of soils, especially one whose work it is.

pe•dol•o•gy[1] [pɪ'dɒlədʒi] *n.* the study of the growth and development of children. ⟨< Gk. *pais, paidos* boy, child + *-ology*⟩ **—,ped•o'log•i•cal** [,pɛdə'lɒdʒəkəl], *adj.*

pe•dol•o•gy[2] [pɪ'dɒlədʒi] *n.* the study of soils, including their formation and characteristics. ⟨< Russian *pedologiya* < Gk. *pedan* ground + *-ologeia*⟩ **—,ped•o'log•i•cal** [,pɛdə'lɒdʒəkəl], *adj.*

pe•dom•e•ter [pɪ'dɒmətər] *n.* an instrument for recording the number of steps taken and thus measuring the distance travelled. ⟨< F *pédomètre* < L *pes, pedis* foot + Gk. *metron* measure⟩

ped•o•phile ['pɛdə,faɪl] *or* ['pidə,faɪl] *n.* an adult who has pedophilia.

ped•o•phil•ia [,pɛdə'fɪliə] *or* [,pidə'fɪliə] *n.* the abnormal sexual attraction of an adult for young children.

pe•dun•cle [pɪ'dʌŋkəl] *n.* **1** *Biology.* a plant stalk that supports a solitary flower or a flower cluster. See STEM for picture. **2** *Zoology.* a narrow structure connecting an organ or part to a larger part or the whole body; PEDICEL (def. 2). **3** *Anatomy.* a stalklike bundle of nerve fibres connecting various areas of the brain. **4** *Pathology.* the narrow, stalklike base of a polyp or tumour. ⟨< NL *pedunculus,* dim. of L *pes, pedis* foot⟩

pe•dun•cu•lar [pɪ'dʌŋkjələr] *adj.* of or having to do with a peduncle.

pe•dun•cu•late [pɪ'dʌŋkjəlɪt] *or* [pɪ'dʌŋkjə,leit] *adj.* having a peduncle; growing on a peduncle.

pee [pi] *v.* **peed, pee•ing;** *n. Slang.* *—v.* urinate.
—n. **1** urine. **2** the act of urinating. ⟨euphemism for *piss,* from the initial letter *p*⟩
☛ *Hom.* PEA.

peek [pik] *v.* **1** look quickly or secretly: *He pretended to have his eyes covered, but I could see he was peeking between his fingers. She peeked around the corner.* **2** look through a small narrow hole or crack: *I peeked through the hole in the fence.*
—n. a quick or secret look: *We took a peek through the crack in the door.* ⟨ME *piken;* origin uncertain⟩
☛ *Hom.* PEAK, PIQUE.

peel[1] [pil] *n., v.* *—n.* the rind or outer covering of certain fruits or vegetables.
—v. **1** remove skin, rind, or bark from: *to peel an orange.* **2** pull or tear off (rind, etc.): *to peel the bark from a tree.* **3** come off, especially in flakes or layers: *My skin is peeling from the sunburn.* **4** *Informal.* undress: *She peeled quickly and dove into the lake.* **5** remove (*used with* **off**): *to peel off a bandage. We peeled off our shirts and lay in the sun.* **6** veer off; change direction (*used with* **off**): *Each motorcycle in the line peeled off as it reached its station.*
keep (one's) **eyes peeled,** *Informal.* be on the alert: *Keep your eyes peeled for cars turning off the highway here.* ⟨var. of obs. *pill;* ME *pele(n)* < OE *pilian* and OF *peler,* both < L *pilare* strip of hair < *pilus* body hair⟩ **—'peel•er,** *n.*
☛ *Hom.* PEAL.

peel[2] [pil] *n.* a long-handled shovel used to put bread, pies, etc. into an oven or take them out. ⟨ME < OF *pele* < L *pala* spade⟩
☛ *Hom.* PEAL.

peel[3] [pil] *n.* a fortified tower used as a residence and for defence, commonly built in the counties on the border of England and Scotland in the 16th century. ⟨< AF *pel* stockade < OF *stake* < L *palus* stake. See PALE[2].⟩
☛ *Hom.* PEAL.

peel•ing ['pilɪŋ] *n., v.* *—n.* a piece or strip, as of rind or skin, peeled or pared off: *potato peelings.*
—v. ppr. of PEEL.

peen [pin] *n., v.* *—n.* a usually rounded or wedge-shaped end opposite the striking face of the head of a hammer.
—v. strike with a peen in order to flatten, shape, or bend. ⟨apparently related to Norwegian *pann* sharpened end of a hammer and Swedish *pana* to beat out⟩

peep[1] [pip] *v., n.* *—v.* **1** look through a small or narrow hole or crack. **2** look quickly or secretly; peek. **3** emerge or show slightly, as if peeping: *violets peeping through the leaves. Her toe peeped through a hole in her sock.*
—n. **1** a look through a hole or crack: *Take a peep through that fence and you can see the new kittens.* **2** a small hole or crack to look through. **3** a quick or secret look; peek: *to take a peep into the refrigerator.* **4** the first glimpse or coming out: *at the peep of day.* ⟨? var. of *peek*⟩

peep[2] [pip] *n., v.* *—n.* **1** a short, high sound such as that made by a baby bird; cheep: *the peeps of newly hatched chicks.* **2** a slight, feeble utterance, especially of protest: *I don't want to hear another peep out of you.*
—v. **1** make a short, high sound like a baby bird. **2** speak in a small, weak voice. ⟨imitative⟩

peep•er[1] ['pipər] *n. Slang.* **1** a person or thing that peeps; voyeur. **2** *Informal.* an eye: *Close your peepers, now, and go to sleep.* **3** *Slang.* a private investigator. ⟨< late ME *pepen, pipen* < OF *piper* < L *pipare*⟩

peep•er[2] ['pipər] *n.* **1** any of several frogs that make peeping noises. **2** any person or thing that makes a peeping noise.

peep•hole ['pip,houl] *n.* a hole through which one may peep.

Peeping Tom a man who derives pleasure or satisfaction from secretly watching women undressing, etc. ⟨from the name of the Coventry tailor who, according to legend, spied on Lady Godiva as she rode naked through the streets⟩

peep show a film or an exhibition of objects or pictures viewed through a small opening usually having a magnifying glass.

peep sight a type of rear sight for a firearm, consisting of a disk containing a small hole through which the front sight and the target are aligned.

peer[1] [pir] *n.* **1** a person of the same age, social situation, ability, etc. as another; equal: *a jury of one's peers. He is so fine a man that it would be hard to find his peer.* **2** a member of the peerage; a noble. Dukes, marquesses, earls, viscounts, and barons are British peers. ⟨ME < OF *per* < L *par* equal. Doublet of PAR.⟩
☛ *Hom.* PIER.

peer[2] [pir] *v.* **1** look closely to see clearly, as a near-sighted person does: *She peered at the tag to read the price.* **2** come out slightly; peep out: *The sun was peering from behind a cloud.* **3** *Poetic.* appear. ⟨apparently a var. of *appear*⟩
☛ *Hom.* PIER.

peer•age ['pirɪdʒ] *n.* **1** all the titled persons of a country; the body of peers. **2** the rank or dignity of a peer. **3** a book giving a list of the peers of a country with their genealogy, titles, etc.

peer•ess ['pirɪs] *n.* **1** a woman who is a member of the peerage; noblewoman. **2** the wife or widow of a peer.

peer group 1 the people of approximately the same age, social status, etc. within a culture or community: *peer group pressure. As a boy, he was heavily influenced by his peer group at school.* **2** all those people of the same age, status, etc. regarded as a sociological entity having a homogeneous value system.

peer•less ['pirlɪs] *adj.* without an equal; matchless: *He was a peerless leader.* **—'peer•less•ly,** *adv.* **—'peer•less•ness,** *n.*

peer of the realm any of the class of peers of the United Kingdom who are entitled by birth to sit in the House of Lords.

peeve [piv] *v.* **peeved, peev•ing;** *n. Informal.* *—v.* make cross; annoy: *Their attitude really peeves me.*
—n. an annoyance: *Her pet peeve is people who don't say "Thank you."*

pee•vish ['pivɪʃ] *adj.* cross; fretful; complaining. ⟨ME *pevysh*; origin uncertain⟩ **—'pee•vish•ly,** *adv.* **—'pee•vish•ness,** *n.*

pee•wee ['piwi] *n.* **1** a very small person or thing. **2** *Juvenile sports.* a player aged between 8 and 12. **3** *Cdn. Lumbering.* an undersized log. ⟨imitative of the cry of the *pewee*, a small bird⟩
☛ *Hom.* PEWEE.

peg [pɛg] *n., v.* **pegged, peg•ging.** *—n.* **1** a pin or small bolt of wood, metal, etc. used to fasten parts together, to hang things on, to plug a hole, to make fast a rope or string, to mark the score in a game, etc. **2** a step; degree: *When the mayor gave that land for a park, he went up several pegs in everyone's estimation.* **3** a small drink of alcoholic liquor. **4** clothespin. **5** a leg or foot, especially a wooden one.
a square peg in a round hole a person in a position for which he or she is totally unsuited.
off the peg, *Esp. Brit.* of clothing, ready-made as opposed to custom-made.
take (someone) **down a peg,** lower the pride of; humble.
—v. **1** fasten or hold with pegs. **2** mark with pegs. **3** work hard and steadily (*usually used with* **away**): *pegging away at one's studies.* **4** *Informal.* aim; throw. **5** *Informal.* identify or categorize: *She has been pegged as a militant feminist.* **6** keep (a price, commodity, interest, etc.) at a set level: *The price of the shares was pegged at $25.00.* ⟨ME *pegge*; (*n.*), *peggen* (*v.*) < MDu. *pegge* related to L *baculum* stick⟩ **—'peg,like,** *adj.* **—'peg•less,** *adj.*

Peg•a•sus ['pɛgəsəs] *n.* **1** *Greek mythology.* a winged horse that stamped his hoof and thus caused the Hippocrene, the fountain of the Muses, to flow on Mount Helicon. **2** poetic genius or inspiration. **3** *Astronomy.* a northern constellation near Andromeda.

Peg•board ['pɛg,bɔrd] *n. Trademark.* a board with evenly spaced holes in which pegs or hooks are inserted to hold tools, displays, etc.

peg leg 1 a wooden leg. **2** *Informal.* a person who has a wooden leg.

peg top a wooden top spinning on a metal peg.

P.E.I. PRINCE EDWARD ISLAND.

peign•oir [pɛn'wɑr] *or* ['pɛnwɑr], [pein'wɑr] *or* ['peinwɑr] *n.* **1** a woman's dressing gown. **2** negligee. ⟨< F *peignoir* < *peigner* < L *pectinare* comb < *pecten* a comb⟩

pej•o•ra•tion [,pɛdʒə'reiʃən] *or* [,pidʒə'reiʃən] *n.* **1** depreciation; worsening; lessening of worth. **2** *Linguistics.* semantic change in which a word's meaning lowers, becoming less approved or less respectable. *Example: the word* imbecile, *originally with a meaning of* feeble in body, *now means* feeble in mind.

pe•jo•ra•tive [pɪ'dʒɔrətɪv], ['pɛdʒərətɪv], *or* ['pidʒərətɪv] *adj., n.* *—adj.* **1** tending to make worse; disparaging; depreciatory. **2** *Linguistics.* of a word whose basic meaning has changed over time for the worse.
—n. a pejorative word, suffix, or phrase. ⟨< L *pejoratus* < *pejor* worse⟩ **—pe'jo•ra•tive•ly,** *adv.*

pek•an ['pɛkən] *n.* FISHER (def. 1). ⟨< Cdn.F *pécan, pékan* < Abenaki *pekane*⟩

Pe•kin [pi'kɪn] *or* ['pikɪn] *n.* a breed of large white ducks, originally from China, raised primarily for their meat. ⟨< F *Pékin* Beijing, the capital of China⟩

Pe•kin•ese [,pikə'niz] *n., pl.* **-ese;** *adj.* *—n. or adj.* Pekingese.

Pe•king duck [pi'kɪŋ] in Chinese cookery, a dish of roasted duck prepared by blowing hot air between the skin and the flesh, brushing with a mixture of sugar and water, and hanging to dry before cooking. It is prized for its crisp skin, and may be served in several courses.

Pe•king•ese *n. 1* [,pikə'niz] *or* [,pikɪŋ'iz]; *n. 2 & 3, adj.* [,pikɪŋ'iz] *n., pl.* **-ese;** *adj.* *—n.* **1** a breed of small dog with long, soft hair and a broad, flat nose, originally developed in China. **2** a native or inhabitant of Peking, the capital of the People's Republic of China. **3** the Chinese dialect spoken in Peking.
—adj. of or having to do with Peking, its people, or their dialect. ⟨< *Peking* Beijing, the capital of China⟩
☛ *Usage.* **Peking** is now officially spelled **Beijing** and pronounced [,bei'ʒɪŋ], ['bei'ʒɪŋ], *or* [bei'ʒɪŋ].

Peking man a type of early human (*Homo erectus*) known from a fossil skeleton discovered at Zhou Koudian near Peking, China, in the 1930s and 1940s. Dating from the middle Pleistocene age, the skeleton was lost during World War II.

pe•koe ['pikou] *n.* a kind of black tea. ⟨< Chinese *pek-ho* white down; because the leaves are picked young with the 'down' still on them⟩
☛ *Hom.* PICOT.

pel•age ['pɛlɪdʒ] *n.* the hair, fur, wool, or other soft covering of a mammal. ⟨< F < OF *peil* hair < L *pilus*⟩

Pe•la•gi•an [pə'leidʒiən] *or* [pə'leidʒən] *n., adj.* *—n.* a follower of Pelagius, an English monk circa A.D. 360-420, who denied original sin and therefore the need of divine grace for virtue and salvation.
—adj. of or having to do with Pelagius and his followers, or their beliefs. **—Pe'la•gi•an,ism,** *n.*

pe•lag•ic [pə'lædʒɪk] *adj.* of, having to do with, or living in the ocean or the open sea. ⟨< L < Gk. *pelagikos* < *pelagos* sea⟩

pel•ar•go•ni•um [,pɛlɑr'gouniəm] *n.* any plant of the genus *Pelargonium*, having rounded leaves and brightly coloured flowers. The domesticated varieties are commonly called geranium. ⟨< NL < Gk. *pelargos* stock + (*gera*)*nium*⟩

Pe•las•gi•an [pə'læzdʒiən], [pə'læzdʒən], *or* [pə'læzgiən] *n., adj.* *—n.* a prehistoric people who inhabited the Aegean Islands, Greece, and Asia Minor; also called **Pelasgi.**
—adj. of or having to do with the Pelasgians. **—Pe'las•gic,** *adj.*

pelf [pɛlf] *n.* money or riches, thought of as bad or degrading. ⟨ME < OF *pelfre* spoils⟩

pel•i•can ['pɛləkən] *n.* any of a small genus (*Pelacanus*, constituting the family Pelecanidae) of large, fish-eating, web-footed aquatic birds having a very long bill with a distensible pouch on the underside for scooping up and holding food. The largest species are among the largest flying birds. ⟨ME, OE *pellican* < LL *pelicanus*, var. of *pelecanus* < Gk. *pelekan*⟩

A pelican

pe•lisse [pə'lis] *n.* **1** a coat lined or trimmed with fur. **2** a woman's long cloak. ⟨< F *pelisse*, ult. < LL *pelliceus* of fur < *pellis* skin⟩

pel•lag•ra [pə'lægrə] *or* [pə'leigrə] *n. Pathology.* a disease associated chiefly with a deficiency of nicotinic acid in the diet, characterized by burning and itching skin, diarrhea and vomiting, and, in severe cases, nervous and mental disorders. ⟨< Ital. < L *pellis* skin; apparently patterned after *podagra* gout in the feet (< Gk.)⟩

pel•let ['pɛlɪt] *n.* **1** a little ball of paper, mud, medicine, compressed food for animals, etc. **2** bullet. **3** a piece of small shot, previously lead but now probably steel. **4** a stone missile, formerly used in catapults and cannons. ⟨ME < OF *pelote* < L *pila* ball. Related to PLATOON.⟩ **—'pel•let,like,** *adj.*

pel•let•ize ['pɛlə,taɪz] *v.* **-ized, -iz•ing. 1** form (a substance, usually concentrate ore) into pellets. **2** make pellets. **—,pel•let•i'za•tion,** *n.* **—'pel•let,iz•er,** *n.*

pel•li•cle ['pɛləkəl] *n.* **1** a very thin skin; membrane; scum. **2** *Photography.* a thin, somewhat reflective coating, as on an emulsion. **3** *Zoology.* a non-living membrane secreted by animal cells such as protozoans. ⟨< L *pellicula,* dim. of *pellis* skin⟩ **—pel•lic•u•lar** [pɛ'lɪkjələr], *adj.*

pell–mell or **pell•mell** ['pɛl 'mɛl] *adv., adj., n.* *—adv.* **1** in a rushing, tumbling mass or crowd. **2** in headlong haste.
—adj. headlong; tumultuous.
—n. violent disorder or confusion. ⟨< F *pêle-mêle,* latter element apparently < *mêler* mix⟩

pel•lu•cid [pə'lusɪd] *adj.* **1** transparent; clear: *a pellucid stream.* **2** clearly expressed; easy to understand: *pellucid language.* ⟨< L *pellucidus,* ult. < *per-* through + *lucere* to shine⟩ **—pel'lu•cid•ly,** *adv.* **—,pel•lu'cid•i•ty** or **pel'lu•cid•ness,** *n.*

Pel•o•pon•ne•sian [,pɛləpə'niʒən] *or* [,pɛləpə'niʃən] *n., adj.* *—n.* a native or inhabitant of Peloponnesus, a peninsula in S Greece.
—adj. of or having to do with the Peloponnesus or its people.

Pel•o•pon•ne•sus [,pɛləpə'nisəs] *n.* a peninsula that constitutes the southern part of Greece.

pe•lo•ta [pə'loutə] *n.* **1** a game of Basque or Spanish origin played on a walled court with a hard ball that is struck with a curved wicker racket fastened to a glove on the hand. **2** the game of JAI ALAI. **3** the ball used in playing jai alai or pelota. ⟨< Sp. *pelota* < *pella* ball < L *pila*⟩

pelt[1] [pɛlt] *v., n.* *—v.* **1** throw things at; attack; assail: *The bride was pelted with flowers.* **2** beat heavily: *The rain came pelting down.* **3** throw: *The clouds pelted rain upon us.* **4** run quickly; hurry: *The thief pelted down the street.*
—n. **1** *Rare.* the act of pelting. **2** a vigorous blow; a whack.
at full pelt, fast: *The horse is coming at full pelt.* ⟨ME *pelten,* ? var. of *pulten* hasten, thrust < L *pultare* strike⟩ **—'pelt•er,** *n.*

pelt[2] [pɛlt] *n.* **1** the skin of a fur-bearing animal before it has been dressed or tanned. **2** *Facetious.* human skin. ⟨probably < *peltry*⟩
☛ *Syn.* **1.** See note at SKIN.

pelt•ry ['pɛltri] *n., pl.* **-ries. 1** pelts; skins; furs. **2** a pelt. ⟨< AF var. of OF *peleterie* < *pel* skin < L *pellis*⟩

pel•vic ['pɛlvɪk] *adj.* of, having to do with, or located in or near the pelvis.

pelvic fin either of a pair of fins on the lower surface of a fish, corresponding to the hind limbs of the higher vertebrates.

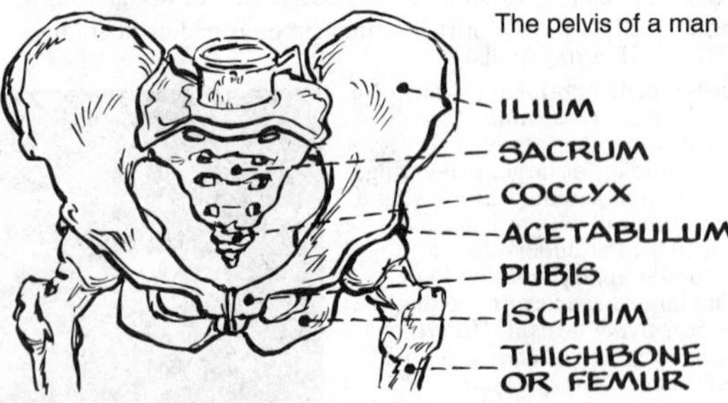

The pelvis of a man

pel•vis ['pɛlvɪs] *n., pl.* **-vis•es** or **-ves** [-viz]. *Anatomy, zoology.* **1** the basin-shaped structure in many vertebrates formed by the hipbones and the end of the backbone. The pelvis supports the spinal column and rests on the legs. **2** the cavity of the pelvis. **3** the funnel-shaped part of the kidney that receives urine before it is passed into the ureter. ⟨< L *pelvis* basin⟩

pem•bi•na ['pɛmbənə] *or* [pɛm'binə] *n. Cdn.* highbush cranberry. See CRANBERRY (def. 3). Also, **pimbina.** ⟨< Cdn.F *pimbina* < ? Cree *nipiminān*⟩

pembina cart formerly, a simple two-wheeled cart used by the early settlers of the Canadian West. ⟨? < *Pembina* (now Cavalier), a town in North Dakota, probably after *pembina* growing in its valleys⟩

pem•mi•can ['pɛməkən] *n.* **1** *Cdn.* dried, lean meat pounded into a paste with melted fat and sometimes berries. Pemmican was the usual food of the voyageurs because it would keep for a long time under almost any conditions. **2** a similar mixture prepared as a concentrated high energy food to be used as emergency rations such as those used on Arctic expeditions. ⟨< Cree *pimii* fat, grease + *kan* prepared⟩

pen[1] [pɛn] *n., v.* **penned, pen•ning.** *—n.* **1** a writing instrument supplying a continuous flow of ink, such as a fountain pen, ballpoint, or felt-tipped pen. **2** a small metal instrument with a split point used with a holder, for writing with ink; nib. **3** such an instrument together with its holder. **4** writing or a style of writing: *She makes her living by her pen.* **5** a writer; author: *a knowledgeable pen.*
—v. write: *He penned a few lines to his parents.* ⟨ME < OF < L *penna* feather⟩ **—'pen,like,** *adj.*

pen[2] [pɛn] *n., v.* **penned** or **pent, pen•ning.** *—n.* **1** a small, closed area for cows, sheep, pigs, chickens, etc. **2** the animals in a pen. **3** any small place of confinement. **4** a dock or slip, often protected by a concrete superstructure, for docking and reconditioning submarines.
—v. **1** shut in a pen. **2** confine closely: *I kept the dog penned in a corner while they hunted for the leash.* ⟨OE *penn*⟩ **—'pen,like,** *adj.*

pen[3] [pɛn] *n. Slang.* penitentiary.

pen[4] [pɛn] a female swan. ⟨origin unknown⟩

Pen. or **pen.** peninsula.

pe•nal ['pinəl] *adj.* **1** of, having to do with, or given as punishment: *penal laws, penal labour.* **2** liable to be punished: *Robbery is a penal offence.* **3** used as a prison or place of punishment: *a penal colony.* ⟨ME < L *poenalis* < *poena* punishment < Gk. *poinē* penalty⟩ **—'pe•nal•ly,** *adv.*

penal code a collection of the laws and the punishments for breaking them.

pe•nal•ize ['pinə,laɪz] *or* ['pɛnə,laɪz] *v.* **-ized, -iz•ing. 1** declare punishable by law or by rule; set a penalty for: *The City Council has penalized loud noises late at night. Murder is penalized in most societies.* **2** inflict a penalty on; punish: *The player was penalized by having to forfeit a point.* **3** put under a handicap: *Our team was penalized five yards.*

pen•al•ty ['pɛnəlti] *n., pl.* **-ties. 1** a punishment for breaking a law or rule: *The penalty for speeding is a fine of fifty dollars.* **2** a disadvantage imposed on a side or player for breaking the rules of a sport or game: *The team was given six penalties in last night's game.* **3** a disadvantage attached to some act or condition: *the penalties of old age.* **4** a handicap imposed on someone for breach of contract, such as withdrawing invested funds before maturity: *The penalty for cashing this bond before the due date is $100.*

penalty box *Cdn. Hockey or lacrosse.* a special bench where penalized players serve their penalties.

pen•al•ty–kill•er ['pɛnəlti ,kɪlər] *n. Cdn. Hockey.* a player put on the ice when his or her team is shorthanded as the result of a penalty, to check the opposing forwards closely and to control the puck as much as possible in order to prevent any scoring by the opposite side. Also, **penalty killer. —'pen•al•ty-,kill•ing,** *n.,* or **penalty killing.**

pen•ance ['pɛnəns] *n.* **1** any act done as a punishment borne to show sorrow for sin, to make up for a wrong done, and to obtain pardon for sin. **2** *Roman Catholic Church.* the sacrament that includes contrition, confession, satisfaction, and absolution.
do penance, perform some act, or undergo some penalty, in repentance for sin. ⟨ME < OF *pen(e)ance* < L *paenitentia* penitence. Doublet of PENITENCE.⟩

pe•na•tes or **Pe•na•tes** [pə'nɑtiz] *n.pl.* in ancient Rome, the gods of the household. Compare LARES. ⟨< L *penates* < *penus* interior of the house⟩

pence [pɛns] *n. Brit.* a pl. of PENNY.

pen•chant ['pɛntʃənt] *n.* a strong taste or liking; inclination (*used with* **for**): *a penchant for taking long walks.* ⟨< F *penchant,* ppr. of *pencher* incline, ult. < L *pendere* hang⟩

pen•cil ['pɛnsəl] *n., v.* **-cilled** or **-ciled, -cil•ling** or **-cil•ing.** *—n.* **1** a pointed tool to write or draw with, consisting of a tube of wood, metal, plastic, etc., having a long, thin piece of graphite or some coloured material in the centre. **2** an object of like shape.

3 a stick of colouring matter. 4 an artist's paintbrush. 5 a set of lines, planes, light rays, or the like, coming to a point or extending through a given point and satisfying a given condition or equation. 6 the skill or style of an artist.
—v. **1** mark, write, or draw with a pencil. **2** mark (something) with a pencil: *She pencilled her eyebrows carefully.*
pencil in, book, as by writing on a calendar: *When can I pencil you in for an interview?*
pencil pusher, *Informal,* a person such as a bookkeeper or clerk whose work entails much writing or manual record-keeping. ⟨ME < OF *pincel*, ult. < L *penicillus* paintbrush, double dim. of *penis*, originally, tail. Doublet of PENICILLIUM⟩ **—'pen•cil-,like,** *adj.*
☛ *Hom.* PENSILE ['pɛnsəl].

pend [pɛnd] *v.* remain undecided or unsettled. ⟨< L *pendere* hang⟩

pend•ant ['pɛndənt] *n., adj.* *—n.* **1** a hanging ornament, especially one attached to an earring, necklace, or bracelet. **2** an ornament hanging down from a ceiling or roof. Pendants were common in later Gothic architecture. **3** an attachment by which something is suspended. Also, **pendent.**
—adj. pendent. ⟨ME < OF *pendant*, ppr. of *pendre* hang, ult. < L *pendere*⟩ **—'pend•ant,like,** *adj.*

pend•ent ['pɛndənt] *adj., n.* *—adj.* **1** hanging: *the pendent branches of a willow.* **2** overhanging. **3** pending.
—n. a pendant. ⟨ME < L *pendens, -entis*, ppr. of *pendere* hang⟩ **—'pen•den•cy,** *n.*

pend•ing ['pɛndɪŋ] *adj., prep., v.* *—adj.* waiting to be decided or settled: *The agreement was pending.*
—prep. **1** while waiting for; until: *Pending their return, let us get everything ready.* **2** during: *pending the investigation.*
—v. ppr. of PEND.

pen•drag•on or **Pen•drag•on** [pɛn'drægən] *n.* the chief leader, the title of ancient British chiefs. King Arthur's father, Uther, was surnamed Pendragon. ⟨< Welsh *pendragon* < *pen* chief, head + *dragon* war leader, dragon⟩

pen•du•lous ['pɛndʒələs] *or* ['pɛndjələs] *adj.* **1** hanging downward: *pendulous jowls.* **2** suspended so as to swing freely. ⟨< L *pendulus* < *pendere* hang⟩ **—'pen•du•lous•ly,** *adv.* **—'pen•du•lous•ness,** *n.*

pen•du•lum ['pɛndʒələm] *or* ['pɛndjələm] *n.* a body or mass hung from a fixed point so as to move to and fro under the forces of gravity and momentum. The movement of the works of a tall clock is often timed by a pendulum. See METRONOME for picture. ⟨< NL *pendulum*, neut. < L *pendulus.* See PENDULOUS.⟩

Pe•nel•o•pe [pə'nɛləpi] *n. Greek legend.* the faithful wife of Odysseus. She waited twenty years for his return from the Trojan War in spite of the entreaties of her many suitors. She told them she would remarry when she had finished the weaving on which she was working, but each night she undid the work she had done during the day.

pe•ne•plain ['pinə,plein] *or* ['pɛnə,plein] *n. Geology.* a formerly mountainous or hilly area reduced nearly to a plain by erosion. ⟨< L *paene* almost + E *plain*⟩

pen•e•tra•ble ['pɛnətrəbəl] *adj.* that can be penetrated. ⟨< L *penetrabilis*⟩ **—,pen•e•tra'bil•i•ty** or **'pen•e•tra•ble•ness,** *n.* **—'pen•e•tra•bly,** *adv.*

pen•e•trance ['pɛnətrəns] *n. Genetics.* the proportion of individuals having the genotype for a certain trait who express the trait phenotypically. Compare EXPRESSIVITY.

pen•e•trant ['pɛnətrənt] *n., adj.* *—n.* **1** a thing or person that penetrates. **2** lotion, cream, etc., that penetrates the skin.
—adj. sharp; acute; penetrating.

pen•e•trate ['pɛnə,treit] *v.* **-trat•ed, -trat•ing. 1** pass into or through: *The bullet penetrated the wall.* **2** pierce through: *Our eyes could not penetrate the darkness.* **3** make a way through something: *Even where the trees were thickest, the sunshine penetrated.* **4** soak through; spread through: *The smell penetrated the whole house.* **5** see into; understand: *I could not penetrate the mystery.* **6** affect or impress (the mind or feelings) very much. ⟨< L *penetrare*, ult. < *penitus* inmost⟩
☛ *Syn.* **1. Penetrate,** PIERCE = go into or through something. **Penetrate** means go deeply into something, or into it and out the other side, and suggests the driving force or keenness of what goes in: *The bullet penetrated the board.* **Pierce** means stab through the surface, or pass right through, with a sharp-pointed object or something sharp and cutting, as a knife: *The dagger pierced his side.*

pen•e•trat•ing ['pɛnə,treitɪŋ] *adj., v.* *—adj.* **1** sharp; piercing: *a penetrating scream.* **2** acute or keen: *a penetrating insight.* **3** that can penetrate: *a penetrating medication.*
—v. ppr. of PENETRATE. **—'pen•e,trat•ing•ly,** *adv.*

pen•e•tra•tion [,pɛnə'treiʃən] *n.* **1** the act or power of penetrating. **2** the act of entering a country or becoming a member of an organization and gaining influence there. **3** the depth to which something penetrates. **4** the ability to understand deeply: *a mind of great acuteness and penetration.*
☛ *Syn.* **4.** See note at INSIGHT.

pen•e•tra•tive ['pɛnə,treitɪv] *adj.* penetrating; piercing, acute, or keen. **—'pen•e,tra•tive•ly,** *adv.* **—'pen•e,tra•tive•ness,** *n.*

P.Eng. Professional Engineer.

pen•guin ['pɛŋgwɪn] *n.* any of a family (Spheniscidae, constituting the order Sphenisciformes) of flightless sea birds native to the cold regions of the southern hemisphere, having webbed feet, legs set far back on the body so that they walk erect, and wings modified into flippers for diving and swimming. ⟨? < Breton *penguin* white head; cf. Welsh *pen* head + *gwyn* white⟩

Penguins

pen•hold•er ['pɛn,houldər] *n.* **1** the handle or holder for a pen nib. **2** a stand or rack for a pen or pens.

pen•i•cil•lin [,pɛnə'sɪlən] *n.* any of a group of very powerful antibiotic drugs (general formula $C_9H_{11}N_2O_4SR$), made from a penicillium mould or produced synthetically. ⟨< *penicillium*⟩

pen•i•cil•li•um [,pɛnə'sɪliəm] *n., pl.* **-cil•li•ums** or **-cil•li•a** [-'sɪliə]. any of a genus (*Penicillium*) of fungi typically occurring as green or blue mould on stale food or on damp natural fabrics or leather. Some species are used in making cheese; others are a source of penicillin. ⟨< L *penicillus* small brush or tail, double dim. of *penis* tail. Doublet of PENCIL.⟩

pen•in•su•la [pə'nɪnsələ] *or* [pə'nɪnsjələ] *n.* a piece of land almost surrounded by water, or extending far out into the water. Nova Scotia is a peninsula. ⟨< L *paeninsula* < *paene* almost + *insula* island⟩

pen•in•su•lar [pə'nɪnsələr] *or* [pə'nɪnsjələr] *adj.* of, in, or like a peninsula.

pe•nis ['pinɪs] *n., pl.* **-nis•es** or **-nes** [-niz]. the male sexual organ, which, in mammals, is also the organ through which urine is excreted. ⟨< L *penis* penis, originally, tail⟩

pen•i•tence ['pɛnətəns] *n.* sorrow for sinning or doing wrong; repentance. ⟨ME < OF *penitence* < L *paenitentia* < *paenitere* repent. Doublet of PENANCE.⟩

pen•i•tent ['pɛnətənt] *adj., n.* *—adj.* sorry for sinning or doing wrong; repenting.
—n. **1** a person who is sorry for sin or wrongdoing. **2** *Roman Catholic Church.* a person who confesses and does penance for his or her sins under the direction of a priest or confessor. **—'pen•i•tent•ly,** *adv.*

pen•i•ten•tial [,pɛnə'tɛnʃəl] *adj., n.* *—adj.* **1** of, showing, or having to do with penitence: *The penitential psalms express remorse for sin.* **2** of or having to do with penance.
—n. **1** a person performing or undergoing penance; penitent. **2** a book or code of church canons on penance, its imposition, etc.

pen•i•ten•tia•ry [,pɛnə'tɛnʃəri] *n., pl.* **-ries;** *adj.* *—n.* a prison, especially a federal prison for persons convicted of serious crimes.
—adj. **1** making one liable to punishment in a prison: *a penitentiary offence.* **2** used for punishment, discipline, and reformation: *penitentiary measures.* **3** of penance; penitential. **4** concerning or located in a penitentiary: *the penitentiary library.*

pen•knife ['pɛn,naɪf] *n., pl.* **-knives.** a small pocketknife, originally used for sharpening or making the quills for pens.

pen•man ['pɛnmən] *n., pl.* **-men** [-mən]. **1** a person whose handwriting is good. **2** a person who writes; author.

pen•man•ship ['pɛnmən,ʃɪp] *n.* **1** skill in writing with pen, pencil, etc. **2** style of handwriting.

pen name a name used by a writer instead of his or her real name: *Mark Twain* was the pen name of *Samuel Clemens.*

pen•nant ['pɛnənt] *n.* **1** a flag, usually long and narrow and tapering to a point or swallowtail, used on ships for signalling, as a school banner, etc. **2** a flag or other trophy competed for in an athletic contest: *Our team won the baseball pennant.* ⟨blend of *pennon* and *pendant*⟩

pen•nate ['pɛneit] *adj.* **1** having wings; having feathers. **2** pinnate. ⟨< L *pennatus* < *penna* feather, wing⟩

pen•ni ['pɛni] *n., pl.* **-ni•a** [-niə], or **-nis. 1** a unit of money in Finland, worth 1/100 of a markka. **2** a coin worth one penni. See table of money in the Appendix. ⟨< Finnish < G *Pfennig* penny⟩
☛ *Hom.* PENNY.

pen•ni•less ['pɛnilɪs] *adj.* having no money; very poor. **—'pen•ni•less•ness,** *n.*
☛ *Syn.* See note at POOR.

pen•non ['pɛnən] *n.* **1** a long, triangular or swallow-tailed flag, originally carried on the lance of a knight; now used for signalling, or as a school banner, etc.; pennant. **2** any similarly shaped flag or banner. **3** any flag or banner. **4** a wing or pinion. ⟨ME < OF *penon,* ult. < L *penna* feather⟩

Penn•syl•va•nia [,pɛnsəl'veinjə] *n.* a northern state of the U.S.

Pennsylvania Dutch 1 the descendants of 17th- and 18th-century immigrants to SE Pennsylvania from S Germany and Switzerland. **2** people of this stock who settled in Upper Canada after the American Revolution. **3** the German dialect spoken by the Pennsylvania Dutch. **4** the form of folk art associated with the Pennsylvania Dutch, characterized by stylized painted or carved flowers, birds, hearts, etc.

Penn•syl•va•ni•an [,pɛnsəl'veinjən] *n., adj. —n.* **1** a native or inhabitant of Pennsylvania. **2** *Geology.* the Pennsylvanian period or rock system.
—adj. **1** of or having to do with the state of Pennsylvania. **2** *Geology.* of or having to do with the later Carboniferous period of the Paleozoic era in North America. See geological time chart in the Appendix.

pen•ny ['pɛni] *n., pl.* **pen•nies** or *esp. Brit.* (*collectively for defs 2, 3*) **pence. 1** in Canada and the United States, one cent. **2** a unit of money in the United Kingdom and Ireland equal to one one-hundredth of a pound. *Abbrev.:* p. **3** formerly, a unit of money in the United Kingdom and other Commonwealth countries equal to one-twelfth of a shilling. *Symbol:* d. **4** a coin worth one penny. **5** a piece or sum of money: *I wouldn't give them a penny.*
a pretty penny, *Informal.* a large sum of money: *That must have cost a pretty penny!*
turn an honest penny, earn money honestly. ⟨OE *pen(d)ing, penig;* cf. ON *penning* and G *Pfennig* < OHG *pfenning*⟩
☛ *Hom.* PENNI.

pen•ny–dog ['pɛni ,dɒg] *Cdn. Slang. n.* PENNY STOCK.

pen•ny–pinch•ing ['pɛni ,pɪntʃɪŋ] *adj., n. —adj.* excessively thrifty; too careful about spending money; miserly.
—n. excessive thrift. **—'pen•ny-,pinch•er,** *n.*

pen•ny•roy•al ['pɛni,rɔɪəl] *or* [,pɛni'rɔɪəl] *n.* **1** a European mint (*Mentha pulegium*) having small, aromatic leaves and mauve flowers. **2** a strongly aromatic North American plant (*Hedcoma pulegioides*) of the same family. **3** an oil obtained from either of these plants, traditionally used in medicine. ⟨apparently alteration of earlier *puliall royal; puliall* < OF *pouliol* < VL dim. of L *puleium* pennyroyal⟩

penny stock *Finance.* common stock that sells for under a dollar a share.

pen•ny•weight ['pɛni,weit] *n.* a unit for measuring mass, equal to 24 grains or one-twentieth of an ounce in troy weight (about 1.56 g). *Abbrev.:* dwt.

pen•ny–wise ['pɛni 'waɪz] *adj.* thrifty in regard to small sums.
penny-wise and pound-foolish, thrifty in small expenses and wasteful in big ones.

pen•ny•worth ['pɛni,wɜrθ] *n.* **1** as much as can be bought for a penny. **2** a small amount.

Pe•nob•scot [pɪ'nɒbskɒt] *n.* **1** a member of a Native American people living in Maine. **2** the Abenaki dialect of these people.

pe•nol•o•gy [pi'nɒlədʒi] *n.* the study of the treatment of criminals and the management of prisons. Penology is a branch of criminology. ⟨< Gk. *poinē* punishment + E *-logy*⟩

pen pal a person with whom one develops a friendship through correspondence, without ever having met the person.

pen•sile ['pɛnsaɪl] *or* ['pɛnsəl] *adj.* **1** hanging; pendent. **2** of birds, building a hanging nest. ⟨< L *pensilis* < *pendere* hang⟩
☛ *Hom.* PENCIL ['pɛnsəl].

pen•sion¹ ['pɛnʃən] *n., v. —n.* **1** money other than wages paid regularly to a person under certain conditions. Pensions are paid to people who have retired from regular work because of old age, sickness, or injury, or for long service or special merit. **2** an allowance given by a patron to an artist.
—v. give a pension to.
pension off, cause to retire from service with a pension. ⟨ME < OF < L *pensio, -onis* < *pendere* weigh, pay⟩ **—'pen•sion•a•ble,** *adj.* **—'pen•sion•less,** *adj.*

pen•sion² [pɑ̃'sjɔ̃] *n. French.* **1** boarding house. **2** accommodation; board and lodging. **3** payment for board and lodging. ⟨< OF *pension* rent, payment. See PENSION¹.⟩

pen•sion•er ['pɛnʃənər] *n.* a person who receives or lives on a pension, especially an old-age pension.

pen•sive ['pɛnsɪv] *adj.* **1** thoughtful in a serious or sad way. **2** melancholy. ⟨ME < OF *pensif* < *penser* think < L *pensare* weight, ponder < *pendere* weigh⟩ **—'pen•sive•ly,** *adv.* **—'pen•sive•ness,** *n.*

pen•stock ['pɛn,stɒk] *n.* **1** a channel for carrying water to a water wheel. **2** a gate for controlling the flow of water, etc. ⟨< *pen²* + *stock,* in the sense of 'trough'⟩

pent [pɛnt] *adj., v. —adj.* closely confined; shut (*used with* **in** *or* **up**): *He was pent up in the house most of the winter because of illness.*
—v. a pt. and a pp. of PEN².

penta– *combining form.* five: *pentagon.* Also, **pent-** before vowels. ⟨< Gk. *penta-* < *pente* five⟩

pen•ta•cle ['pɛntəkəl] *n.* **1** a symbol, frequently in the shape of a five-pointed star, used in magic. **2** pentagram.

pen•tad ['pɛntæd] *n.* **1** a group of five. **2** a five-year period of time. **3** the number five. **4** *Chemistry.* a pentavalent radical or element. **5** *Climatology.* five consecutive days.

pen•ta•dac•tyl [,pɛntə'dæktəl] *adj.* **1** having five fingers on each hand and five toes on each foot. **2** having five fingerlike projections. ⟨< Gk. *pente* five + *daktylos* finger⟩

pen•ta•gon ['pɛntə,gɒn] *n.* **1** a polygon having five sides and five interior angles. **2 the Pentagon,** in the United States: **a** a building in the shape of a pentagon that is the headquarters of the Department of Defense, just outside Washington, D.C. in Arlington, VA. **b** the Department of Defense, its policies, etc. ⟨< LL < Gk. *pentagōnon* < *pente* five + *gōnia* angle⟩ **—pen'tag•o•nal** [pɛn'tægənəl], *adj.*

pen•ta•gram ['pɛntə,græm] *n.* **1** a five-pointed star formed by extending the sides of a regular pentagon until they meet; pentacle. **2** any figure of five lines.

pen•ta•he•dron [,pɛntə'hidrən] *n., pl.* **-drons, -dra** [-drə]. a polyhedron having five faces. ⟨< Gk. *pente* five + *hedra* base⟩ **—,pen•ta'he•dral,** *adj.*

pen•tam•e•ter [pɛn'tæmətər] *n.* **1** a line of verse consisting of five metrical feet. *Example:* Óh! what | a rógue | and peás- | ant sláve | am Í! **2** unrhymed verse, each line having five iambic feet; HEROIC VERSE; BLANK VERSE. **3** (*adjl.*) designating such a line of verse or verse consisting of such lines. ⟨< L < Gk. *pentametros* < *pente* five + *metron* meter⟩

pen•tane ['pɛntein] *n. Chemistry.* any of three hydrocarbons of the methane series. *Formula:* C_5H_{12} ⟨< Gk. *pente* five⟩

pen•tar•chy ['pɛntɑrki] *n., pl.* **-chies. 1** government by five leaders. **2** a governing body consisting of five members. **3** a federated group of five nations or states, each having its own ruler or government.

Pen•ta•teuch ['pɛntə,tjuk] *or* ['pɛntə,tuk] *n.* the first five books of the Christian or Jewish scriptures. *Genesis, Exodus, Leviticus, Numbers,* and *Deuteronomy* make up the Pentateuch. ⟨< L < Gk. *pentateuchos* < *pente* five + *teuchos* vessel, book⟩

pen•tath•lete [pɛn'tæθlit] *n.* an athlete who competes in a pentathlon.

pen•tath•lon [pɛn'tæθlən] *or* [pɛn'tæθlɒn] *n.* **1** an athletic contest in track and field, consisting of five different events: discus throw, javelin throw, long jump, 200 m dash, and 1500 m run. The athlete having the highest total score wins. **2** *Olympic Games.* the **modern pentathlon**, comprising a 5000 m cross-country equestrian steeplechase, a 4000 m cross-country run, a 300 m swim, foil fencing, and pistol shooting. ⟨< Gk. *pentathlon* < *pente* five + *athlon* contest⟩

pen•ta•ton•ic [,pɛntə'tɒnɪk] *adj. Music.* having five tones in the scale: *The black notes of the piano form a pentatonic scale.*

pen•ta•val•ent [,pɛntə'veilənt] *or* [pɛn'tævələnt] *adj. Chemistry.* **1** having a valence of five. **2** having five valences; quinquevalent.

pen•taz•o•cine [pɛn'tæzə,sin] *n.* an analgesic drug derived from coal tar and used instead of morphine because it is less addictive. *Formula*: $C_{19}H_{27}NO$

Pen•te•cost ['pɛntə,kɒst] *n.* **1** the seventh Sunday after Easter, a Christian festival commemorating the descent of the Holy Spirit upon the Apostles. Also called **Whitsunday. 2** a Jewish religious holiday, about seven weeks after the Passover, celebrating the harvest and also the giving of the law to Moses. ⟨OE < LL *pentecoste* < Gk. *pentēkostē (hēmera)* fiftieth (day)⟩

Pen•te•cos•tal or **pen•te•cos•tal** [,pɛntə'kɒstəl] *adj., n.* *—adj.* **1** of or having to do with Pentecost. **2** of or having to do with certain fundamentalist Protestant denominations which emphasize the charismatic gifts.
—n. a member of any of these denominations.

pent•house ['pɛnt,hʌus] *n.* **1** an apartment or house built on the top of a building. **2** a luxury apartment on the top floor of a highrise. **3** a sloping roof projecting from a building. **4** a shed with a sloping roof attached to a building. ⟨ME *pentis* < OF *apentis*, ult. < L *appendere* append < *ad-* on + *pendere* hang⟩

pen•to•bar•bi•tal sodium [,pɛntou'bɑrbə,tɒl] an odourless, water-soluble barbiturate used medicinally as a sedative and hypnotic. *Formula*: $C_{11}H_{17}N_2O_3Na$

pent–up ['pɛnt 'ʌp] *adj.* confined; restrained; checked; contained: *pent-up anger, pent-up emotions.*

pe•nu•che or **pe•nu•chi** [pə'nutʃi] *n.* a candy or fudge made of brown sugar, butter, milk, and nuts. ⟨< Mexican Sp. *panocha* brown or raw sugar⟩

pe•nult [pɪ'nʌlt] *or* ['pinʌlt] *n.* **1** the next to the last syllable in a word. **2** the next to the last thing in a series. ⟨< L *paenultima (syllaba)* next-to-last (syllable) < *paene* almost + *ultimus* last⟩

pe•nul•ti•mate [pɪ'nʌltəmɪt] *adj., n.* *—adj.* **1** next to the last. **2** of or having to do with the penult.
—n. the penult.

pe•num•bra [pɪ'nʌmbrə] *n., pl.* **-brae** [-bri] *or* [-braɪ] or **-bras. 1** the partial shadow outside the complete shadow formed by the sun, moon, etc. during an eclipse. See ECLIPSE for picture. **2** the greyish outer part of a sunspot. ⟨< NL *penumbra* < L *paene* almost + *umbra* shadow⟩

pe•nu•ri•ous [pə'njʊriəs] *or* [pə'nʊriəs] *adj.* **1** characteristic of or suffering from penury; poor: *penurious surroundings, penurious times.* **2** mean about spending or giving money; stingy. **—pe'nu•ri•ous•ly,** *adv.* **—pe'nu•ri•ous•ness,** *n.*

pen•u•ry ['pɛnjəri] *n.* great poverty. ⟨< L *penuria*⟩

Pe•nu•ti•an [pə'njuʃən] *or* [pə'nuʃən], [pə'njutiən] *or* [pə'nutiən] *n.* a linguistic phylum of distantly related languages found on the west coast of North and Central America, especially in California. ⟨coined in 1913 by R.B. Dixon and A.L. Kroeber, from *pene* + *uti*, schematized bases for 'two' in two subgroups of those languages⟩

pe•on ['piɒn] *or* ['piən] *n.* **1** in Latin America, a person doing work that requires little skill. **2** in India, a native police officer. **3** any of various workers, etc. in India or Sri Lanka, such as a foot soldier, attendant, or unskilled labourer. ⟨< Sp. < LL *pedo, -onis* foot soldier. Doublet of PAWN[2]. Related to PIONEER.⟩
☛ *Hom.* PAEAN ['piən].

pe•on•age ['piənɪdʒ] *n.* the condition or service of a peon.

pe•o•ny ['piəni] *n., pl.* **-nies. 1** any of a genus (*Paeonia*) of perennial herbaceous or shrubby plants, many of which are cultivated for their large, showy pink, red, or white flowers. **2** the flower of any of these plants. ⟨ult. < Gk. *paiōnia* < *Paiōn* physician of the gods; from the plant's use in medicine⟩

peo•ple ['pipəl] *n., pl.* (*functioning as singular for def. 2*), *v.* **-pled, -pling.** *—n.* **1** men, women, and children; persons. **2** an ethnic group; nation. **3** the body of citizens of a state; the public. **4** the persons of a place, class, or group: *city people, Prairie people.* **5** the common people; the lower classes. **6** persons in relation to a superior: *A king rules over his people.* **7** *Informal.* family; relatives. **8** human beings considered indefinitely: *People will do the most surprising things. She's afraid of what people will think.*
—v. fill or supply with inhabitants; populate or stock: *Canada was very largely peopled by Europeans.* ⟨ME < AF < L *populus*⟩
☛ *Syn. n.* **2. People,** RACE, NATION = a group of persons thought of as a unit larger than a family or community. **People** emphasizes cultural and social unity, applying to a group united by a common culture, common ideas, and a feeling of unity arising from common responsibilities and interests: *The Pennsylvania Dutch are a people, not a nation.* **Race** refers to biological unity, having common descent and common physical characteristics: *The Japanese belong to the Asiatic race.* **Nation** emphasizes political unity, applying to a group united, or at one time united, under one government: *Norwegians are a people and a nation, not a race.* However, **nation** is often used of a group united by history, language, and culture.

pep [pɛp] *n., v.* **pepped, pep•ping.** *Informal. —n.* spirit; energy; enthusiasm.
—v. fill or inspire with energy, etc.; put new life into (*used with* **up**): *to pep up a party.* ⟨short for *pepper*⟩

pep•lum ['pɛpləm] *n., pl.* **-lums. 1** a short flared, gathered piece of material attached to the waistline of a jacket, blouse, or dress and extending to the hips. **2** in ancient Greece, a full garment worn by women. ⟨< L < Gk. *peplos*⟩ **—'pep•lumed,** *adj.*

pep•per ['pɛpər] *n., v. —n.* **1** a seasoning with a hot taste, made from the ground-up berries of a tropical woody vine. See BLACK PEPPER and WHITE PEPPER. **2** any of a genus (*Piper*) of tropical climbing shrubs having fragrant leaves; especially, *Piper nigrum*, which bears the red berries from which white and black pepper are made. **3** (*adjl.*) designating the family (Piperaceae) of plants that includes pepper and cubeb. **4** any of various capsicums, especially one species (*Capsicum frutescens*) grown in numerous varieties for its mild or hot-tasting fruit. **5** the fruit of any of these capsicums. See RED PEPPER, SWEET PEPPER.
—v. **1** season or sprinkle with black, white, or red pepper. **2** sprinkle thickly: *His face is peppered with freckles.* **3** hit with small objects sent thick and fast: *We peppered the enemy with shot.* ⟨OE *pipor* < L *piper* < Gk. *peperi*⟩

pep•per–and–salt ['pɛpər ən 'sɒlt] *adj.* black and white finely mixed: *a pepper-and-salt coat.*

pep•per•box ['pɛpər,bɒks] *n.* PEPPER SHAKER.

pep•per•corn ['pɛpər,kɔrn] *n.* a dried berry of the pepper plant (*Piper nigrum*). ⟨OE *piporcorn*⟩

pep•per•grass ['pɛpər,græs] *n.* any of a genus (*Lepidium*) of plants of the mustard family, especially garden cress.

pepper grinder PEPPER MILL.

pep•per•idge ['pɛpərɪdʒ] *n.* black gum.

pepper mill a hand mill used to grind peppercorns.

pep•per•mint ['pɛpər,mɪnt] *n.* **1** a common herb (*Mentha piperita*), a species of mint yielding a sweet-smelling oil used in medicine and as a flavouring. **2** the oil of this herb. **3** a candy flavoured with peppermint oil.

pep•per•o•ni [,pɛpə'rouni] *n.* a spicy Italian sausage, often put on a pizza. ⟨< Ital. *peperoni*, pl. of *peperone* Cayenne pepper plant < *pepe* pepper < L *piper*⟩

pepper pot 1 a highly seasoned soup or stew made of meat (usually tripe), vegetables, and sometimes dumplings. **2** a West Indian stew of meat or fish with vegetables, highly seasoned with cassava juice and hot spices. **3** *Brit.* PEPPER SHAKER.

pepper shaker a container with holes in the top for sprinkling pepper on food.

pep•pery ['pɛpəri] *adj.* **1** of, like, or full of pepper: *a peppery stew.* **2** sharp; pungent. **3** having a hot temper; easily made angry. **4** fiery or stinging in speech or writing.
—'pep•per•i•ness, *n.*

pep pill *Informal.* any of various stimulant drugs, such as amphetamine, in pill form.

pep•py ['pɛpi] *adj.* **-pi•er, -pi•est.** *Informal.* full of pep; energetic; lively. **—'pep•pi•ness,** *n.*

pep rally *Informal.* a meeting organized to stimulate support and enthusiasm for a team, cause, campaign, etc.

pep•sin ['pɛpsən] *n.* **1** an enzyme in the gastric juice of the stomach that helps to digest meat, eggs, cheese, and other proteins. **2** a medicine containing this enzyme, used to help digestion. ⟨< Gk. *pepsis* digestion⟩

pep talk a short, emotional talk intended to encourage a person or group in some activity: *The coach gave us a pep talk before the game.*

pep•tic ['pɛptɪk] *adj.* **1** promoting digestion; digestive. **2** of or having to do with pepsin. **3** having to do with or caused by the action of digestive juices: *a peptic ulcer.* ⟨< L < Gk. *peptikos* < *peptos* cooked, digested⟩

pep•ti•dase ['pɛptə,deis] *n.* any of a group of enzymes that convert peptides to amino acids by hydrolysis.

pep•tide ['pɛptaid] *n. Biochemistry.* any of a group of compounds consisting of two or more amino acids chemically bonded, or linked, together. ⟨< G *peptid.* See PEPTONE.⟩

pep•tone ['pɛptoun] *n. Biochemistry.* any of a class of diffusible, soluble substances into which meat, eggs, cheese, and other proteins are changed by the action of pepsin in digestion. ⟨< G *Pepton* < Gk. *pepton*, neut. of *peptos* cooked, digested⟩
—pep'ton•ic [-'tɒnɪk], *adj.*

Pé•quiste [pei'kist] *n. Cdn.* a member or supporter of the Parti Québécois. Also, **péquiste.**

Pe•quot ['pikwɒt] *n., adj.* —*n.* **1** a member of a Native American people living in Connecticut. **2** the Algonquian language of these people.
—*adj.* of or having to do with the Pequots, their language, or their culture.

per [pər]; *stressed,* [pɜr] *prep.* **1** for each: *We need 125 g of ground beef per person.* **2** by; through; by means of: *The letter was sent per messenger.* **3** according to: *a payment calculated per number of children in the family. The order was sent out as per instructions.* ⟨< L⟩
☛ *Usage.* **Per,** the Latin for **through, by, by the, among,** is found chiefly in business or technical English: *$280 per week, 45 revolutions per minute.* The English equivalent is usually more appropriate in general English: *$280 a week, eight hours a day.*
☛ *Hom.* PURR [pɜr].

per– *prefix.* **1** through or throughout: *perforate, pervade.* **2** thoroughly or utterly: *perceive, perfect.* **3** *Chemistry.* the maximum or a large amount of: *peroxide.* **4** away; to destruction: *perjure, pervert.* ⟨< L⟩

per. **1** person. **2** period.

per•am•bu•late [pər'æmbjə,leit] *v.* **-lat•ed, -lat•ing. 1** walk through, over, etc.: *perambulating the street.* **2** walk about from place to place. **3** walk through or around and inspect. ⟨< L *perambulare* < *per-* through + *ambulare* walk⟩
—per,am•bu'la•tion, *n.* **—per'am•bu•la,to•ry** [pe'ræmbjələ,tɔri], *adj.*

per•am•bu•la•tor [pər'æmbjə,leitər] *n.* **1** *Brit.* a baby carriage. **2** a person who perambulates.

per an•num [pər 'ænəm] *Latin.* yearly; for each year: *Her salary was $29 000 per annum.*

per•cale [pər'keil] *or* [pər'kæl] *n.* a smooth, firm cotton cloth in a plain weave made in different grades. High-grade percale with a very close weave and a lustrous finish is used for bed linen. ⟨< F < Persian *pargālah* fragment, scrap⟩

per cap•i•ta [pər 'kæpətə] for each person: *$40 for eight people amounts to $5 per capita.* ⟨< L *per capita* by heads⟩

per•ceive [pər'siv] *v.* **-ceived, -ceiv•ing. 1** be aware of through the senses; see, hear, taste, smell, or feel. **2** take in with the mind; observe: *I perceived that I could not make them change their minds.* ⟨ME < OF *perceivre* < L *percipere* < *per-* fully + *capere* grasp⟩ **—per'ceiv•er,** *n.* **—per'ceiv•a•ble,** *adj.* **—per'ceiv•a•bly,** *adv.*
☛ *Syn.* **1, 2.** See note at SEE[1].

per•cent or **per cent** [pər'sɛnt] *n.* **1** hundredths; parts in each hundred. Five percent (5%) is 5 out of each 100, or 5/100 of the whole. Five percent of 40 is 2. *Symbol:* % **2** for each hundred; in each hundred: *Seven percent of the students failed.* **3** *Informal.* percentage: *A large percent of the apple crop was ruined.* ⟨for Ital. *per cento* or LL *per centum*⟩
☛ *Usage.* **Percent,** whether written as one word or two, is not followed by a period. The one-word form is more common, possibly through the influence of **percentage** and **percentile.**

per•cent•age [pər'sɛntɪdʒ] *n.* **1** the rate or proportion of each hundred; part of each hundred: *What percentage of children were absent?* **2** a part; proportion: *A large percentage of students finish high school now.* **3** an allowance, commission, discount, rate of interest, etc., figured by percent. **4** *Slang.* advantage or profit: *What's the percentage in that?*

per•cen•tile [pər'sɛntaɪl] *or* [pər'sɛntəl] *n.* **1** any value in a series of points on a scale arrived at by dividing a group into a hundred equal parts in order of magnitude: *A student at the fiftieth percentile is at a point halfway between the top and the bottom of the group.* **2** any one of the parts thus described.

per centum [pər 'sɛntəm] *or* [pər 'kɛntʊm] *Latin.* PERCENT (def. 1).

per•cept ['pɜrsɛpt] *n.* **1** that which is perceived. **2** the result, in the mind, of perceiving; impression. ⟨< L *perceptum,* pp. neut. of *percipere* perceive. See PERCEIVE.⟩

per•cep•ti•ble [pər'sɛptəbəl] *adj.* that can be perceived; especially, great enough to be perceived. **—per,cep•ti'bil•i•ty,** *n.*

per•cep•ti•bly [pər'sɛptəbli] *adv.* in a perceptible way or amount; to a perceptible degree.

per•cep•tion [pər'sɛpʃən] *n.* **1** the act of perceiving: *My perception of the change came in a flash.* **2** the power of perceiving: *a keen perception.* **3** PERCEPT (def. 2). ⟨< L *perceptio, -onis* < *percipere* perceive. See PERCEIVE.⟩

per•cep•tive [pər'sɛptɪv] *adj.* **1** having to do with perception. **2** having the power of perceiving; insightful: *Her comments about the election were unusually perceptive.* **—per'cep•tive•ly,** *adv.* **—per'cep•tive•ness,** *n.*

per•cep•tu•al [pər'sɛptʃuəl] *adj.* of or having to do with perception. **—per'cep•tu•al•ly,** *adv.*

Per•ce•val ['pɜrsəvəl] *n. Arthurian legend.* one of only three Knights of the Round Table to see the Holy Grail. In the earliest legends about the Quest for the Holy Grail, Perceval is the main hero. Also, **Percevale, Percival.** Compare PARZIFAL.

perch[1] [pɜrtʃ] *n., v.* —*n.* **1** a bar, branch, or anything else on which a bird can come to rest. **2** a rather high place or position. **3** a former unit for measuring length; rod; pole (about 5.03 m). **4** a unit for measuring area; square rod (about 25.3 m^2). **5** a unit for measuring the volume of stone (about 7 m^3). **6** a pole joining the axles of a horse-drawn vehicle.
—*v.* **1** alight and rest: *A robin perched on our porch railing.* **2** sit, especially on something rather high: *The child perched on a stool.* **3** place or situate high up: *The village was perched on a high hill.* ⟨ME < OF *perche* < L *pertica* pole⟩ **—'perch•er,** *n.*

perch[2] [pɜrtʃ] *n., pl.* **perch** or **perch•es. 1** any of a genus (*Perca*) of small freshwater food fishes, especially the **yellow perch** (*P. flavescens*) of North America or a similar European species. **2** (*adjl.*) designating a family (Percidae) of freshwater fishes including the perches, darters, and the walleye. Fishes of the perch family have two dorsal fins, the first having spiny rays and the second having soft rays. **3** any of various similar freshwater or saltwater fishes, especially of the families Centrarchidae and Serranidae. ⟨ME < OF *perche* < L < Gk. *perkē*⟩

per•chance [pər'tʃæns] *adv. Archaic or poetic.* perhaps. ⟨ME < AF *par chance* < *par* by (< L *per*) + *chance* < L *cadentia* a falling < *cadere* fall⟩

Per•che•ron ['pɜrtʃə,rɒn] *or* ['pɜrʃə,rɒn] *n.* a breed of large, strong draft horse originally developed in France. ⟨< F *Percheron* < *Le Perche,* a district in France⟩

per•chlor•ate [pər'klɔreit] *n. Chemistry.* a salt or ester of perchloric acid.

per•chlor•ic acid [pər'klɔrɪk] *Chemistry.* a colourless liquid acid of chlorine that is a strong oxidizing agent; it is used chiefly as a reagent in analytical chemistry, for making solid propellants, etc. *Formula:* $HClO_4$

per•chlo•ro•eth•yl•ene [pər,klɔrou'ɛθə,lin] *n. Chemistry.* a chlorinated hydrocarbon, the most common solvent used in dry cleaning. *Formula:* C_2Cl_4

per•cip•i•ent [pər'sɪpiənt] *adj., n.* —*adj.* capable of perceiving, especially quickly or keenly; discerning.
—*n.* a person who perceives. ⟨< L *percipiens, -entis,* ppr. of *percipere.* See PERCEIVE.⟩ **—per'cip•i•ence,** *n.* **—per'cip•i•ent•ly,** *adv.*

Percival or **Percivale** ['pɜrsəvəl] See PERCEVAL.

per•co•late ['pɜrkə,leit] *v.* **-lat•ed, -lat•ing. 1** drip or drain through small holes or spaces. **2** filter through; permeate: *Water percolates sand. The idea finally percolated through to my tired brain.* **3** make (coffee) in a percolator. **4** of coffee, bubble up and drip through in a percolator. ⟨< L *percolare,* ult. < *per-* through + *colum* strainer⟩
—,per•co'la•tion, *n.*

per•co•la•tor ['pɜrkə,leitər] *n.* **1** a kind of coffee pot in which boiling water continually bubbles up through a tube and drips down through ground coffee. **2** anything that percolates.

per•cus•sion [pər'kʌʃən] *n., adj.* —*n.* **1** the striking of one body against another with force; stroke; blow. **2** the shock made by the striking of one object against another with force. **3** the striking of sound upon the ear. **4** *Medicine.* the technique of tapping a part of the body to find out the condition of the parts underneath by the resulting sound. **5** *Music.* the section of an orchestra or band composed of PERCUSSION INSTRUMENTS.
—*adj.* made up of or written for a percussion instrument: *a percussion quintet.* ⟨< L *percussio, -onis* < *per-* (intensive) + *quatere* strike, beat⟩ **—per'cus•sive,** *adj.*

Percussion (def. 5)

percussion cap a small cap containing powder that explodes when struck by the hammer of a gun.

percussion instrument a musical instrument played by

striking it, such as a drum (except tympani) or cymbal, or by shaking it, as maracas or a tambourine.

per•cus•sion•ist [pər'kʌʃənɪst] *n.* one who plays percussion instruments, especially a skilled player.

per di•em [pər 'diəm] *or* ['daɪəm] *Latin.* **1** per day; for each day: *The room rate is $75.00 per diem.* **2** a daily allowance: *We were given a per diem of $85.00.* ⟨< L *per diem* per day⟩

per•di•tion [pər'dɪʃən] *n.* **1** the loss of one's soul and the joys of heaven; eternal death. **2** hell. **3** *Archaic.* utter loss. ⟨< L *perditio, -onis* < *perdere* destroy < *per-* (intensive) + *dare* give⟩

père [pɛr] *n.* **1** father; senior. Used after a French surname: *Dumas père.* **2** the title of certain French-speaking priests: *Père Lachaise.* ⟨< F, father⟩

☛ *Hom.* PAIR, PEAR, PARE.

per•e•grin ['pɛrəgrɪn] *n. or adj.* See PEREGRINE.

per•e•gri•nate ['pɛrəgrə,neit] *v.* **-nat•ed, -nat•ing. 1** travel; journey, especially on foot. **2** travel across or through (a place); follow (a route); traverse. ⟨< L *peregrinari* < *peregrinus.* See PEREGRINE.⟩ **—,per•e•gri'na•tion,** *n.* **—'per•e•gri,na•tor,** *n.*

per•e•grine ['pɛrəgrɪn] *or* ['pɛrə,grin] *adj., n. —adj.* **1** wandering or migratory. **2** *Archaic.* foreign; coming from abroad.
—n. PEREGRINE FALCON. ⟨< L *peregrinus* from foreign parts, ult. < *per-* outside + *ager (Romanus)* the (Roman) territory. Doublet of PILGRIM.⟩

peregrine falcon a large falcon (*Falco peregrinus*) of worldwide distribution, much used in falconry.

per•emp•to•ry [pə'rɛmptəri] *or* ['pɛrəmp,tɔri] *adj.* **1** imperious; dogmatic: *a peremptory teacher.* **2** allowing no denial or refusal: *a peremptory command.* **3** leaving no choice; decisive; final; absolute: *a peremptory decree.* **4** *Law.* **a** not admitting of debate or discussion. **b** not requiring that cause be shown. ⟨< L *peremptorius* deadly, that puts an end to, ult. < *per-* (intensive) + *emere,* originally, take⟩ **—per'emp•to•ri•ly,** *adv.* **—per'emp•to•ri•ness,** *n.*

per•en•ni•al [pə'rɛniəl] *adj., n. —adj.* **1** lasting through the whole year: *a perennial stream.* **2** lasting for a very long time; enduring: *the perennial beauty of the hills.* **3** having underground parts that live more than two years; producing flowers and seeds from the same root structure year after year: *perennial garden plants.* **4** perpetual; recurring again and again.
—n. a perennial plant. Roses are perennials. Compare ANNUAL and BIENNIAL. ⟨< L *perennis* lasting < *per-* through + *annus* year⟩ **—per'en•ni•al•ly,** *adv.*

perf. 1 perfect. **2** perforated.

per•fect *adj., n.* ['pɜrfɪkt]; *v.* [pər'fɛkt] *adj., v., n. —adj.* **1** without defect; faultless: *Perfect work is the result when attention is given to detail.* **2** as excellent as can be beyond practical or theoretical improvement. In this sense it can be used comparatively: *a more perfect love.* **3** completely skilled; expert: *a perfect golfer.* **4** having all its parts; complete: *The set was perfect; nothing was missing or broken.* **5** entire; utter: *She was a perfect stranger to us.* **6** *Grammar.* of a verb form, showing an action, state, or event thought of as being completed. There are three periphrastic perfect tenses. See PRESENT, PERFECT, PAST PERFECT, and FUTURE PERFECT. **7** *Bookbinding.* of a method in which pages are glued to the spine and not sewn. **8** exact; precise; correct in every detail: *a perfect copy.* **9** *Botany.* having both stamens and pistils. **10** *Music.* **a** having to do with the intervals or original consonances of unison, a fourth, fifth, and octave, as contrasted with the major intervals of a third and sixth. **b** of a cadence, consisting of a dominant chord followed by a tonic chord. Also called **authentic.** Compare PLAGAL.
—v. remove all faults from; make perfect; improve; add the finishing touches to: *The formula was perfected at last. We will perfect our plan as it is tried out.*
—n. Grammar. **1** the PERFECT TENSE. **2** a verb form in this tense. *Have eaten* is the perfect of *eat.* ⟨ME < OF < L *perfectus* completed, pp. of *perficere* < *per-* thoroughly + *facere* make, do⟩ **—per'fect•er,** *n.* **—'per•fect•ness,** *n.*

per•fect•i•ble [pər'fɛktəbəl] *adj.* capable of becoming, or being made, perfect. **—per,fect•i'bil•i•ty,** *n.*

perfecting press *Printing.* a rotary press that prints both sides of a sheet in a single operation.

per•fec•tion [pər'fɛkʃən] *n.* **1** a perfect condition; faultlessness; highest excellence. **2** a perfect person or thing. **3** a making complete or perfect: *The perfection of our plans will take another week.*
to perfection, perfectly: *He played the violin concerto to perfection.*

per•fec•tion•ism [pər'fɛkʃə,nɪzəm] **1** a striving for absolute perfection in what one does. **2** a doctrine that a state of freedom from sin can and should be achieved on earth.

per•fec•tion•ist [pər'fɛkʃənɪst] *n.* **1** a person who is not content with anything that is not perfect or nearly perfect. **2** a person who believes it possible to lead a sinless life. **—per,fec•tion'ist•ic,** *adj.*

per•fect•ive [pər'fɛktɪv] *adj., n. —adj. Grammar.* indicating an aspect of verbs that expresses a completed action, state, or event.
—n. **1** the perfective aspect. **2** a verb in the perfective aspect.

per•fect•ly ['pɜrfɪktli] *adv.* **1** in a perfect manner or to a perfect degree; completely and faultlessly: *a perfectly drawn circle.* **2** to an adequate extent: *This skirt is still perfectly good.*

perfect number *Mathematics.* a positive number that is equal to the sum of its factors. Six is a perfect number because its factors, 1, 2, and 3, add up to 6.

per•fec•to [pər'fɛktou] *n., pl.* **-tos.** a thick cigar that tapers at both ends. ⟨< Sp. *perfecto* perfect⟩

perfect participle *Grammar.* **1** the past participle preceded by the present participle of *have* (*having*), expressing action completed before the time of speaking or acting. In *Having written the letter, she mailed it, having written* is a perfect participle. **2** the past participle. In *When she had written the letter, she mailed it, written* may be called the perfect participle.

perfect square *Mathematics.* a number (rational or polynomial) that is the exact square of another number: *9 is the perfect square of 3;* $a^2 + 2ab + b^2$ *is the perfect square of* $(a + b)$.

perfect tense the form of a verb which shows that the action is completed now (PRESENT PERFECT); was completed in the past (PAST PERFECT); is to be completed in the future (FUTURE PERFECT).

per•fer•vid [pər'fɜrvɪd] *adj.* very fervid; ardent.

per•fid•i•ous [pər'fɪdiəs] *adj.* deliberately faithless; treacherous. ⟨< L *perfidiosus* < *perfidia.* See PERFIDY.⟩ **—per'fid•i•ous•ly,** *adv.* **—per'fid•i•ous•ness,** *n.*

per•fi•dy ['pɜrfədi] *n., pl.* **-dies.** a breaking faith; base treachery; being false to a trust. ⟨< L *perfidia,* ult. < *per-* away + *fides* faith⟩

per•fo•li•ate [pər'foulirt] *or* [pər'fouli,eit] *adj. Botany.* having the stem apparently passing through the leaf: *a perfoliate leaf.* ⟨< NL *perfoliatus* < L *per-* through + *folium* leaf⟩

per•fo•rate *v.* ['pɜrfə,reit]; *adj.* ['pɜrfərɪt] *or* ['pɜrfə,reit] *v.* **-rat•ed, -rat•ing;** *adj. —v.* **1** make a hole or holes through: *The bullets perforated the target.* **2** make a series of small holes through in order to make separation easier: *Sheets of postage stamps are perforated.*
—adj. pierced. ⟨< L *perforare* < *per-* through + *forare* bore⟩ **—'per•fo•ra•tive,** *adj.* **—'per•fo,ra•tor,** *n.*

per•for•a•tion [,pɜrfə'reiʃən] *n.* **1** a hole bored or punched through something: *He removed the coupon by tearing along the perforations.* **2** a perforating or being perforated.

per•force [pər'fɔrs] *adv. Formal or archaic.* by necessity; necessarily. ⟨< F *par* by + *force*⟩

per•form [pər'fɔrm] *v.* **1** do; carry out or execute (an action): *Perform your duties well.* **2** put into effect; fulfil: *Perform your promise.* **3** go through, especially publicly; render: *to perform a piece of music.* **4** act, play an instrument, sing, dance, or do tricks in public. **5** carry out or execute a stated or understood action, function, or process: *They performed particularly well last night. She is performing very capably as CEO.* ⟨< AF *perfourmer,* var. of OF *parfournir* < *par-* completely + *-fournir* furnish, finish; influenced by *forme* form⟩

☛ *Syn.* **2. Perform,** EXECUTE, DISCHARGE = carry out or put into effect. **Perform** = carry out a process, usually one that is long or that requires effort, attention, or skill: *The surgeon performed an operation.* **Execute** = put into effect a plan or proposal or carry out an order: *The nurse executed the doctor's orders.* **Discharge** = carry out an obligation or duty, by performing or executing the acts or steps necessary to relieve oneself of the responsibility: *She gave a large party to discharge all her social obligations.*

☛ *Usage.* See note at DO[1].

per•form•ance [pər'fɔrməns] *n.* **1** a performing: *in the performance of one's regular duties.* **2** the thing performed; act; deed. **3** the giving of a play, concert, circus, or other show: *The evening performance is at eight o'clock.* **4** the manner of operation or the efficiency (of something) with regard to the fulfilment of its intended purpose: *The performance of my new car is far beyond expectation.* **5** (*adjl.*) designed for highly efficient performance.

performance art a collaborative art form combining

elements of several artistic media such as painting, film, video, music, dance, and drama. It originated in the 1970s, apparently as a development of the 1960s artistic 'happenings'.

per•form•a•tive [pər'fɔrmətɪv] *adj., n. —adj.* **1** of or concerning performance. **2** of, being, or based on a performative.
—n. **1** *Linguistics, philosophy.* **a** a verbal expression which, when used in the first person, in itself performs the act that it is describing. *Promise, accuse, swear,* etc. are performatives. **b** a performative utterance. *Example: I swear I did not do it.* **2** a conventionalized gesture having a conventional linguistic meaning, as a wave of the hand indicating 'hello', 'goodbye', 'come here', (in English) shaking the head for 'no' and nodding for 'yes'. These gestures vary from culture to culture. Performatives are the first step in most children's language acquisition.

per•form•er [pər'fɔrmər] *n.* a person who performs, especially one who performs for the entertainment of others; player.

performing arts any of the arts such as dance, drama, singing, and instrumental music that are performed before an audience.

per•fume *n.* ['pɜrfjum] *or* [pər'fjum]; *v.* [pər'fjum] *n., v.* **-fumed, -fum•ing.** *—n.* **1** the scent of something that smells sweet: *the perfume of flowers.* **2** a substance having a sweet smell, especially one prepared from essences of flowers or from synthetic substances and applied to the skin or clothes to produce a pleasant scent.
—v. **1** fill with a sweet odour: *Flowers perfumed the air.* **2** put a sweet-smelling substance on. ⟨< F *parfum,* n., and *parfumer,* v., < OItal. < L *per-* through + *fumare* smoke; 16c.⟩

per•fum•er [pər'fjumər] *n.* **1** a maker or seller of perfumes. **2** a person or thing that perfumes.

per•fum•er•y [pər'fjuməri] *n., pl.* **-er•ies. 1** the products made by a perfumer; perfumes. **2** the art or process of making perfumes. **3** a place where perfumes are made or sold.

per•func•to•ry [pər'fʌŋktəri] *adj.* **1** done merely for the sake of getting rid of the duty; mechanical; indifferent: *The little girl gave her face a perfunctory washing.* **2** acting in a perfunctory way: *The new nurse was perfunctory in the performance of his duties; he did not really care about his work.* ⟨< LL *perfunctorius,* ult. < L *perfungi* perform < *per-* to the end + *fungi* execute⟩ **—per'func•to•ri•ly,** *adv.* **—per'func•to•ri•ness,** *n.*

per•fuse [pər'fjuz] *v.* **-fused, -fus•ing. 1** overspread (something) with a vapour, fluid, colour, etc.; permeate; suffuse. **2** cause (something) to flow through or spread over. ⟨< L *perfusus,* pp. of *perfundere* pour out < *per-* (intensive) + *fundere* pour out⟩ **—per'fu•sion,** *n.* **—per'fu•sive** [pər'fjusɪv], *adj.*

per•go•la ['pɜrgələ] *n.* an arbour formed by vines, etc. growing over an open roof of latticework or rafters supported by posts. ⟨< Ital. < L *pergula,* probably dim. of **perga* timber work⟩

per•haps [pər'hæps] *or* [pər'æps] *adv.* maybe; possibly. ⟨ME *per happes* by chances (pl. of *hap* chance)⟩

pe•ri ['piri] *n., pl.* **pe•ris. 1** *Persian mythology.* a beautiful fairy descended from fallen angels and shut out from paradise until forgiven. **2** any fairylike or elfin being; a lovely and graceful person. ⟨< Persian *parik* < Avestan *pairika* lit., winged⟩

peri– *prefix.* **1** around; surrounding: *periscope, periphery.* **2** near: *perigee, perihelion.* ⟨< Gk.⟩

per•i•anth ['pɛri,ænθ] *n. Botany.* the envelope of a flower, including the calyx and the corolla. ⟨< NL < Gk. *peri-* around + *anthos* flower⟩

per•i•car•di•ac [,pɛrɪ'kɑrdi,æk] *adj.* pericardial.

per•i•car•di•al [,pɛrɪ'kɑrdiəl] *adj.* **1** of, having to do with, or affecting the pericardium. **2** around the heart.

per•i•car•di•tis [,pɛrɪkɑr'dəitɪs] *n. Pathology.* an inflammation of the pericardium.

per•i•car•di•um [,pɛrɪ'kɑrdiəm] *n., pl.* **-di•a** [-diə]. *Anatomy.* the membranous sac enclosing the heart and the roots of the great blood vessels. ⟨< Gk. *pericardion* < *peri-* around + *kardia* heart⟩

per•i•carp ['pɛrɪ,kɑrp] *n. Botany.* the walls of a ripened ovary or fruit, sometimes consisting of three layers, the epicarp, mesocarp, and endocarp; seed vessel. ⟨< NL < Gk. *perikarpion* < *peri-* around + *karpos* fruit⟩ **—,per•i'car•pi•al** or **,per•i'car•pic,** *adj.*

per•i•cen•tric [,pɛrɪ'sɛntrɪk] *adj.* **1** around a centre. **2** *Genetics.* on both sides of the centromere of a chromosome.

Per•i•cle•an [,pɛrɪ'kliən] *adj.* of or having to do with Pericles, an Athenian statesman (d. 429 B.C.), or with the period of his leadership.

per•i•cra•ni•um [,pɛrɪ'kreiniəm] *n., pl.* **-ni•a** [-niə]. *Anatomy.* the membrane covering the bones of the skull. ⟨< Gk. *perikranion* < *peri-* around + *kranion* skull⟩

per•i•cy•cle ['pɛrɪ,səikəl] *n. Botany.* the outermost layer of the stele in the stems and roots of most plants, after becoming multilayered. **—,per•i'cy•clic** [-'səiklɪk] *or* [-'sɪklɪk], *adj.*

per•i•cyn•thi•on [,pɛrɪ'sɪnθiən] *n.* the point in the lunar orbit of an earth-launched spacecraft where it is nearest to the moon. Compare APOCYNTHION, APOLUNE, PERILUNE. ⟨< *peri-* + *-cynthion* < *Cynthia* (goddess of) the moon⟩

per•i•derm ['pɛrɪ,dɜrm] *n. Botany.* the soft growing tissue between the wood and the bark of plants; the cork-producing tissue of the stem, with the cork layers.

per•i•dot ['pɛrɪdou] *or* ['pɛrɪ,dɒt] *n.* a pale green transparent gemstone, a variety of olivine. ⟨< F *péridot* < OF *peritot*⟩

per•i•gee ['pɛrɪ,dʒi] *n.* **1** the point in the orbit of a satellite of the earth or an orbiting vehicle where it comes closest to the earth. Compare APOGEE. **2** the lowest or closest point of anything. ⟨< F < NL < Gk. *perigeion* < *peri-* near + *gē* earth⟩ **—,per•i'ge•an** or **,peri'ge•al,** *adj.*

per•i•he•li•on [,pɛrɪ'hiliən] *or* [,pɛrɪ'hiljən] *n., pl.* **-he•li•a** [-'hiliə] *or* [-'hiljə]. the point in the orbit of a planet or other heavenly body where it is closest to the sun. Compare APHELION. ⟨< NL < Gk. *peri-* near + *hēlios* sun⟩

per•il ['pɛrəl] *n., v.* **-illed** or **-iled, -il•ling** or **-il•ing.** *—n.* a chance of harm; exposure to danger or the risk of being injured or destroyed.
—v. put in danger; expose to risk. ⟨ME < OF < L *periculum*⟩
☛ *Syn. n.* See note at DANGER.

per•il•ous ['pɛrələs] *adj.* dangerous; full of peril: *a perilous journey.* ⟨< AF *perillous* < L *periculosus*⟩ **—'per•il•ous•ly,** *adv.* **—'per•il•ous•ness,** *n.*

per•i•lune ['pɛrɪ,lun] *n.* the point in the lunar orbit of a moon-launched spacecraft where it is nearest to the moon. Compare APOCYNTHION, APOLUNE, PERICYNTHION. ⟨< *peri-* + *-lune* < L *luna* moon⟩

pe•rim•e•ter [pə'rɪmətər] *n.* **1** the outer boundary of a plane figure or an area: *the perimeter of a circle. A fence marks the perimeter of a field.* **2** the distance around such a boundary. The perimeter of a square equals four times the length of one side. **3** an optical instrument for testing the scope of peripheral vision. **4** *Military.* a fortified boundary strip. ⟨< L < Gk. *perimetros* < *peri-* around + *metron* measure⟩ **—,pe•ri'met•ric** [,pɛrɪ'mɛtrɪk], *adj.* **—pe'rim•e•try,** *n.*

per•i•morph ['pɛrɪ,mɔrf] *n.* a crystal of a mineral of one type enclosing that of another type.

per•i•nat•al [,pɛrɪ'neitəl] *adj.* concerning or occurring during the period surrounding the time of birth, from the twentieth week of gestation to the end of the fourth week of life outside the womb.

per•i•na•tol•o•gy [,pɛrənei'tɒlədʒi] *n.* the study of the health of newborn babies.

per•i•ne•al [,pɛrɪ'niəl] *adj.* of or having to do with the perineum.

per•i•neph•ri•um [,pɛrɪ'nɛfriəm] *n., pl.* **-nia** [-niə]. *Anatomy.* the envelope of tissue surrounding the kidney.

per•i•ne•um [,pɛrɪ'niəm] *n., pl.* **-ne•a** [-'niə]. *Anatomy.* **1** the area of the body at the outlet of the pelvis, reaching from the anus to the vulva in females and to the scrotum in males. **2** the region included in the opening of the pelvis. ⟨< LL < Gk. *perinaion* < *peri-* around + *inein* discharge⟩

per•i•neu•ri•um [,pɛrɪ'njʊriəm] *or* [,pɛrɪ'nʊriəm] *n. Anatomy.* a sheath of connective tissue enclosing a bundle of nerve fibres that make up a peripheral nerve.

pe•ri•od ['pirjəd] *n., adj., interj.* *—n.* **1** a span of time, especially one having certain features or conditions: *He visited us for a short period.* **2** a portion of time marked off by events that happen again and again; the time after which the same things begin to happen again. A month, from new moon to new moon, is a period. **3** *Geology.* a subdivision of an era. **4** the portion of a game during which there is actual play: *There are three twenty-minute periods in a hockey game.* **5** one of the portions of time into which a school day is divided. **6** the time needed for a disease to run its course. **7** an occurrence of menstruation. **8** the punctuation mark (.) that indicates the end of a declarative sentence or an abbreviation; full stop. **9** the pause at the end of a sentence. **10** a complete sentence, especially one that is

impressively well-composed and balanced; a PERIODIC SENTENCE: *The orator spoke in stately periods.* **11** an end; termination; final stage. **12** *Physics.* the interval of time between the recurrence of like phases in a vibration or other periodic motion or phenomenon. **13** *Astronomy.* the length of time it takes a planet to orbit the sun. **14** *Music.* a group of related phrases, usually composed of eight or sixteen measures and ending with a conclusive cadence.
—adj. characteristic of a certain period of history: *period furniture.*
—interj. **1** *Informal.* that's it! that's final! *The discussion is over, period!* **2** simply; categorically: "He dislikes noisy babies?" "No, he dislikes babies, period." ⟨< L < Gk. *periodos* a going around, cycle < *peri-* around + *hodos* a going⟩

☛ *Usage.* **Period.** A period coming at the end of a quotation, of any length, from a single word to a full sentence, is generally placed inside the quotation marks: *"The longer you put it off," he said, "the harder it's going to be."*

pe•ri•od•ic [ˌpiriˈɒdɪk] *adj.* **1** occurring, appearing, or done again and again at regular intervals: *periodic attacks of malaria.* **2** happening every now and then: *a periodic fit of clearing up one's desk.* **3** having to do with a period. **4** expressed in formal sentences whose meanings are not complete without the final words.

periodic acid *Chemistry.* one of a series of crystalline acids, such as HIO_4 or H_5IO_6, derived from iodic acid (I_2O_7) by the addition of water molecules, and used as an oxidizing agent. ⟨< *per* + *iodic*⟩

pe•ri•od•i•cal [ˌpiriˈɒdəkəl] *n., adj. —n.* a magazine that appears at regular intervals.
—adj. **1** of or having to do with periodicals. **2** published at regular intervals, less frequent than daily. **3** periodic.

pe•ri•od•i•cal•ly [ˌpiriˈɒdɪkli] *adv.* **1** every now and then. **2** at regular intervals.

pe•ri•o•dic•i•ty [ˌpiriəˈdɪsəti] *n., pl.* **-ties.** a periodic character; the tendency to happen at regular intervals.

periodic law *Chemistry.* the law stating that, when the chemical elements are arranged in the order of their atomic numbers, the elements with similar chemical properties appear at regular intervals.

periodic sentence a complex sentence with the MAIN CLAUSE at the end. In *When he was ready, he left the room, he left the room* is the main clause.

periodic table *Chemistry.* a table in which the elements, arranged in the order of their atomic masses, are shown in related groups. See table of elements in the Appendix.

per•i•o•don•tal [ˌpɛriəˈdɒntəl] *adj. Dentistry.* **1** of or affecting the tissues or structures around the teeth: *periodontal disease.* **2** situated around a tooth. ⟨< *peri-* + Gk. *odon, odontos* tooth⟩

per•i•o•don•tia [ˌpɛriəˈdɒnʃə] *n.* periodontics.

per•i•o•don•tics [ˌpɛriəˈdɒntɪks] *n.* (*used with a singular verb*) the branch of dentistry dealing with diseases of the tissues and structures around the teeth.
—ˌper•i•oˈdon•tic, *adj.*

per•i•o•don•tist [ˌpɛriəˈdɒntɪst] *n.* a dentist who is a specialist in periodontics.

per•i•o•don•ti•tis [ˌpɛriədɒnˈtəitɪs] *n.* bacterial inflammation of the periodontal tissue.

per•i•o•don•tol•o•gy [ˌpɛriədɒnˈtɒlədʒi] *n.* periodontics.

period piece a work of art, as a painting, a building, or literature, that calls to mind a particular period of history.

per•i•os•te•um [ˌpɛriˈɒstiəm] *n., pl.* **-te•a** [-tiə]. *Anatomy.* the dense fibrous membrane closely covering the surface of bones except at the joints. ⟨< NL < LL < Gk. *periosteon* < *peri-* around + *osteon* bone⟩ **—perˈi•os•te•al,** *adj.*

per•i•os•ti•tis [ˌpɛriəˈstəitɪs] *n. Pathology.* inflammation of the periosteum. **—ˌper•i•oˈstit•ic** [ˌpɛriəˈstɪtɪk], *adj.*

per•i•pa•tet•ic [ˌpɛrɪpəˈtɛtɪk] *adj., n. —adj.* **1** walking about; travelling from place to place; itinerant. **2 Peripatetic,** having to do with the philosophy of Aristotle, who taught while walking.
—n. **1** a person who wanders or travels about from place to place. **2 Peripatetic,** a disciple of Aristotle. ⟨< L < Gk. *peripatētikos* < *peri-* around + *pateein* walk; with reference to Aristotle's manner of teaching⟩ **—ˌper•i•paˈtet•i•cal•ly,** *adv.*

pe•riph•er•al [pəˈrɪfərəl] *adj., n. —adj.* **1** of, having to do with, or forming a periphery. **2** incidental or minor; superficial: *peripheral issues.* **3** *Anatomy.* of, having to do with, or situated on or near the surface of the body: *peripheral nerves.* **4** *Computer technology.* having to do with auxiliary or supplementary hardware that is connected to a computer to make up a computer system. Printers, monitors, and disk drives are peripheral devices.
—n. Computer technology. a peripheral device. **—peˈriph•er•al•ly,** *adv.*

peripheral nervous system all the nerves outside the brain and spinal cord. Compare CENTRAL NERVOUS SYSTEM.

peripheral vision the area of vision outside the line of direct sight; the outer part of the field of vision.

pe•riph•er•y [pəˈrɪfəri] *n., pl.* **-er•ies.** **1** an outside boundary; perimeter. The periphery of a circle is called the circumference. **2** an area outside the centre or main area; outer parts: *the periphery of a city.* **3** *Anatomy.* the area surrounding a nerve ending, such as a sense organ or muscle. **4** *Geometry.* the external surface, especially of something round. ⟨< LL < Gk. *periphereia* < *peri-* around + *pherein* carry⟩

pe•ri•phrase [ˈpɛrəˌfreiz] *n.* periphrasis.
☛ *Hom.* PARAPHRASE.

pe•riph•ra•sis [pəˈrɪfrəsɪs] *n., pl.* **-ses** [-ˌsiz]. **1** a roundabout way of speaking or writing; circumlocution. *The wife of your father's brother* is a periphrasis for *your aunt.* **2** an expression using auxiliaries that has the same essential syntactic function as a single inflected word. *Examples*: *has gone = went, of the dog = dog's.* Also, **periphrase.** ⟨< L < Gk. *periphrasis*, ult. < *peri* around + *phrazein* speak⟩

per•i•phras•tic [ˌpɛrəˈfræstɪk] *adj.* **1** expressed in a roundabout way. **2** *Grammar.* formed by using auxiliaries or particles rather than inflection. *Examples*: *of John* (periphrastic genitive) rather than *John's*; *did run* (periphrastic conjugation) rather than *ran.* **—ˌper•iˈphras•ti•cal•ly,** *adv.*
☛ *Hom.* PARAPHRASTIC.

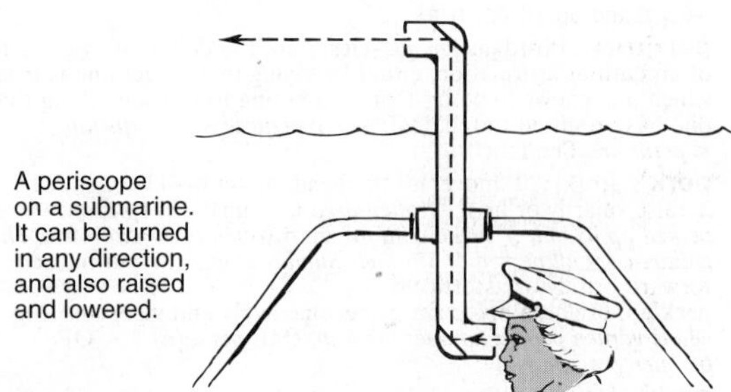

A periscope on a submarine. It can be turned in any direction, and also raised and lowered.

per•i•scope [ˈpɛrɪˌskoup] *n.* an instrument consisting of a tube with an arrangement of mirrors or prisms that permits a person to see things that are otherwise out of sight. Periscopes are used to get a view of the surface from a trench or a submerged submarine, to see around a corner or over the heads of people in a crowd, etc. See SUBMARINE for picture. ⟨back formation from *periscopic*⟩

per•i•scop•ic [ˌpɛrɪˈskɒpɪk] *adj.* **1** giving distinct vision obliquely as well as in a direct line. **2** of or having to do with periscopes. ⟨< Gk. *periskopeîn* to look about + *-ic*⟩

per•ish [ˈpɛrɪʃ] *v.* **1** die or be destroyed: *Many soldiers perished in the battle. The building perished in the flames.* **2** decay; become spoiled: *Fruit perishes quickly in hot weather.* ⟨ME < OF *periss-*, a stem of *perir* < L *perire* < *per-* (intensive) + *ire* go⟩
☛ *Syn.* See note at DIE.
☛ *Hom.* PARISH [ˈpɛrɪʃ].

per•ish•a•ble [ˈpɛrɪʃəbəl] *adj., n. —adj.* likely to spoil or decay: *Fresh fruit is perishable.*
—n. Usually, **perishables,** *pl.* things that are likely to spoil or decay, especially fresh food. **—ˌper•ish•aˈbil•i•ty** or **ˈper•ish•a•ble•ness,** *n.*

per•i•stal•sis [ˌpɛrɪˈstælsɪs] *or* [ˌpɛrɪˈstɒlsɪs] *n., pl.* **-ses** [-siz]. *Physiology.* the successive wavelike contractions of the alimentary canal or other hollow muscular organ, by which its contents are forced onward. ⟨< NL < Gk. *peristalsis*, ult. < *peri-* around + *stellein* wrap⟩

per•i•stal•tic [ˌpɛrɪˈstæltɪk] *or* [ˌpɛrɪˈstɒltɪk] *adj. Physiology.* of or having to do with peristalsis. **—ˌper•iˈstal•ti•cal•ly,** *adv.*

per•i•style [ˈpɛrɪˌstaɪl] *n.* **1** a row of columns surrounding a building, court, etc. **2** a space or court so enclosed. ⟨< F < L < Gk. *peristylon* < *peri* around + *stylos* pillar⟩

per•i•to•ne•al [,pɛrɪtə'niəl] *adj.* of or having to do with the peritoneum.

per•i•to•ne•um or **per•i•to•nae•um** [,pɛrɪtə'niəm] *n., pl.* **-ne•a** or **-nae•a** [-'niə]. *Anatomy.* the smooth, transparent membrane that lines the walls of the abdomen of a mammal and covers the abdominal organs. ⟨< LL < Gk. *peritonaion,* neut. adj., stretched over, ult. < *peri-* around + *teinein* stretch⟩

per•i•to•ni•tis [,pɛrɪtə'nəitɪs] *n. Pathology.* inflammation of the peritoneum.

per•i•wig ['pɛrɪ,wɪg] *n.* a wig, especially that worn by men in the 17th and 18th centuries, frequently powdered and with the hair gathered back with a ribbon into a 'club' or tail; peruke. ⟨earlier *perewyke* < F *perruque.* Cf. PERUKE.⟩

per•i•win•kle[1] ['pɛrɪ,wɪŋkəl] *n.* any of several evergreen plants (genus *Vinca*) of the dogbane family having trailing stems and blue or white flowers. ⟨< L *pervinca;* influenced by *periwinkle*[2]⟩

per•i•win•kle[2] ['pɛrɪ,wɪŋkəl] *n.* **1** any of various edible marine snails (family Littorinidae), especially the common periwinkle (*Littorina littorea*) native to N Europe, having a thick, cone-shaped, spiral shell. **2** the shell of any of these animals. ⟨OE *pīnewincle; pīne-* ? < L *pina* mussel < Gk. *pinē*⟩

periwinkle blue a light, pretty blue much used for clothing.

per•jure ['pɜrdʒər] *v.* **-jured, -jur•ing.** make (oneself) guilty of perjury; swear falsely; lie when under oath (*used with a reflexive pronoun*): *The witness perjured himself at the trial.* ⟨ME < AF < L *perjurare* < *per-* through + *jurare* swear < *jus, juris* right (n.)⟩ **—'per•jur•er,** *n.*

per•jured ['pɜrdʒərd] *adj., v. —adj.* **1** guilty of perjury: *a perjured witness.* **2** characterized by or involving perjury: *perjured evidence.*
—v. pt. and pp. of PERJURE.

per•ju•ry ['pɜrdʒəri] *n., pl.* **-ries.** *Law.* the deliberate violation of an oath or affirmation, either by saying that something is true which one knows to be false or by omitting to tell something that one has promised to tell. ⟨ME < AF *perjurie* < L *perjurium* < *perjurare.* See PERJURE.⟩

perk[1] [pɜrk] *v.* **1** move, lift the head, or act briskly or saucily. **2** raise smartly or briskly (*often used with* **up**): *The sparrow perked up its tail.* **3** make trim or smart (*often used with* **out**): *The children are all perked out in their Sunday clothes.* **4** put oneself forward briskly or assertively.
perk up, brighten up; make or become lively and vigorous: *The whole garden perked up after the rain.* ⟨ME *perke(n)* ? < OF *perquer* perch⟩

perk[2] [pɜrk] *v. Informal.* **1** percolate: *to perk a pot of coffee. We could hear the coffee perking.* **2** be in a state of activity; go well: *a tax measure to keep the economy perking.* ⟨short for *percolate*⟩

perk[3] [pɜrk] *n. Informal.* perquisite: *enjoying perks such as free theatre tickets.*

perk•y ['pɜrki] *adj.* **perk•i•er, perk•i•est.** smart; brisk; saucy; pert. **—'perk•i•ly,** *adv.* **—'perk•i•ness,** *n.*

per•lite ['pɜrləit] *n.* volcanic glass with a pearl-like lustre, showing minute concentric circles, used for insulation and as a planting medium. ⟨< F *perle* pearl⟩ **—per'lit•ic** [pər'lɪtɪk], *adj.*

perm [pɜrm] *n., v. —n. Informal.* PERMANENT WAVE.
—v. give (hair) a permanent wave.

per•ma•frost ['pɜrmə,frɒst] *n. Cdn.* ground or subsoil that is permanently frozen. ⟨blend of *permanent* + *frost*⟩

permafrost line *Cdn.* the line marking the southern boundary of the permafrost, roughly from the Ontario shore of Hudson Bay northwest, passing north of Lake Athabaska and along the north shore of Great Slave Lake.

permafrost pit *Cdn.* a storage pit for food, making use of the refrigerative properties of permafrost.

per•ma•nence ['pɛrmənəns] *n.* the state or condition of being permanent; lasting quality or condition.

per•ma•nen•cy ['pɜrmənənsi] *n., pl.* **-cies. 1** permanence. **2** something that is permanent.

per•ma•nent ['pɜrmənənt] *adj., n. —adj.* lasting; intended to last; not for a short time only: *a permanent filling in a tooth. After doing odd jobs for a week, he got a permanent position as office boy.*
—n. Informal. PERMANENT WAVE. ⟨< L *permanens, -entis* staying to the end, ppr. of *permanere* < *per-* through + *manere* stay⟩ **—'per•ma•nent•ly,** *adv.*
☛ *Syn. adj.* See note at LASTING.

permanent married quarters government housing for married members of the armed forces and their immediate families. *Abbrev.:* P.M.Q.'s

permanent press 1 a chemical treatment given to a fabric to make it resistant to creases and, often, to provide a garment with permanent pleats, etc. **2** the condition of a fabric so treated: *Articles with permanent press shouldn't need ironing.* **3** (*adjl.*) **permanent-press,** designating fabric or a garment that has been treated in this way.

permanent tooth one of the second set of teeth in a mammal that follow the baby teeth, or milk teeth.

permanent wave a wave produced in the hair by chemicals or heat, that lasts even after the hair has been washed many times.

per•man•ga•nate [pər'mæŋgə,neit] *n. Chemistry.* a salt of an acid containing the negative radical M_nO_4, strongly acidic in nature and usually of a deep purple colour. A solution of potassium permanganate is used as an antiseptic.

per•me•a•bil•i•ty [,pɜrmiə'bɪləti] *n.* **1** *Physics.* a measure of the ease with which magnetic induction can be established by a magnetic field. **2** a measure of the ease with which liquid or gas can filter through a porous material, such as water through porous sedimentary rock.

per•me•a•ble ['pɜrmiəbəl] *adj.* that can be permeated: *A sponge is permeable by water.* ⟨< LL *permeabilis* < L *permeare.* See PERMEATE.⟩

per•me•ate ['pɜrmi,eit] *v.* **-at•ed, -at•ing. 1** spread through the whole of; penetrate throughout; pass into or through and affect all of: *Smoke permeated the house. Water will not permeate this fabric.* **2** spread or diffuse itself: *Anger permeated through the crowd.* ⟨< L *permeare* < *per-* through + *meare* pass⟩ **—,per•me'a•tion,** *n.*

per men•sem [pər 'mɛnsəm] *Latin.* by the month.

per•meth•rin [pər'mɛθrɪn] *n.* an insecticide derived from pyrethrin, produced in chrysanthemums, which is less poisonous to humans than other insecticides. It is used to treat infestations of head lice.

Per•mi•an ['pɜrmiən] *n., adj. Geology. —n.* **1** a late period of the Paleozoic era, beginning approximately 235 million years ago. **2** the rocks formed in this period. See chart of geological time periods in the Appendix.
—adj. of or having to do with this period or the rocks formed during it. ⟨< *Perm,* a former province in E Russia where such rocks are found⟩

per mill [pər 'mɪl] per thousand; for every thousand: *The average occurrence of this structural defect is one per mill.*

per•mis•si•ble [pər'mɪsəbəl] *adj.* that may be permitted; allowable. **—per'mis•si•bly,** *adv.* **—per,mis•si'bil•i•ty,** *n.*

per•mis•sion [pər'mɪʃən] *n.* consent; leave; permitting: *They asked the teacher's permission to leave early.* ⟨< L *permissio, -onis* < *permittere.* See PERMIT.⟩

per•mis•sive [pər'mɪsɪv] *adj.* **1** not strict in discipline; allowing a great deal of freedom; lenient; indulgent: *a permissive society, permissive parents.* **2** permitting; giving permission: *a permissive statute.* **3** *Archaic.* optional. **—per'mis•sive•ly,** *adv.* **—per'mis•sive•ness,** *n.*

per•mit *v.* [pər'mɪt]; *n.* ['pɜrmɪt] *or* [pər'mɪt] *v.* **-mit•ted, -mit•ting;** *n. —v.* **1** allow (a person, etc.) to do something: *Permit me to explain.* **2** let (something) be done or occur: *The law does not permit smoking in this store.*
—n. **1** an official printed and/or stamped order giving the recipient permission to do something: *a parking permit, a hunting permit.* **2** permission. **3** *Cdn.* **a** a license to buy and consume a specified amount of liquor, often for medicinal or religious purposes, in an area where the consumption of liquor is otherwise prohibited. **b** the quantity of liquor one is allowed to purchase with such a government permit. ⟨< L *permittere* < *per-* through + *mittere* let go⟩
☛ *Syn. v.* **Permit,** ALLOW = let someone or something do something. **Permit** emphasizes the idea of expressing willingness or giving consent: *His parents permitted him to have a car when he was eighteen.* **Allow** often means not to forbid or prevent, without necessarily giving permission or approval: *That teacher allows too much noise in the room.*

per•mu•ta•tion [,pɜrmjə'teiʃən] *n.* **1** alteration; extensive or radical alteration; complete rearrangement. **2** the process by which such alteration, etc., is arrived at. **3** *Mathematics.* **a** a changing of the order of a set of things; an arranging in different orders. **b** such an arrangement or group. The permutations of *a, b,* and *c* are *abc, acb, bac, bca, cab, cba.* ⟨< L *permutatio, -onis* < *permutare* < *per-* across + *mutare* change⟩

per•mute [pər'mjut] *v.* **-mut•ed, -mut•ing.** alter the order or arrangement of; especially, alter successively in all possible ways. ⟨< L *permutare.* See PERMUTATION.⟩

per•ni•cious [pər'nɪʃəs] *adj.* **1** that will destroy or ruin; causing harm or damage; injurious: *pernicious habits.* **2** fatal: *a pernicious disease.* ⟨< L *perniciosus*, ult. < *per-* thoroughly + *nex, necis* death⟩ **—per'ni•cious•ly,** *adv.* **—per'ni•cious•ness,** *n.*

pernicious anemia *Pathology.* a severe disease characterized by a continued decrease in the number of red blood cells and, often, white cells and platelets in the blood. It is unrelated to iron deficiency and is caused by a deficiency of vitamin B_{12}, usually due to the body's inability to absorb the vitamin from food.

per•nick•e•ty [pər'nɪkɪti] *adj. Informal.* **1** overly fastidious; fussy. **2** requiring precise and careful handling. ⟨origin uncertain⟩

Per•nod [pɛr'nou] *n. Trademark.* a French alcoholic liquor flavoured with aniseed; a drink of this.

per•o•gy [pə'rougi] *n., pl.* **-gies.** a dumplinglike pastry with a meat, cheese, or other filling. Also, **pierogi, pirogi, pyrohy.** ⟨< Ukrainian < Old Slavic *pir* feast + *og*⟩

per•o•rate ['pɛrə,reit] *v.* **-rat•ed, -rat•ing. 1** make a formal conclusion to a speech. **2** speak at length; make a long and majestic speech. ⟨< L *perorare.* See PERORATION.⟩

per•o•ra•tion [,pɛrə'reiʃən] *n.* **1** the last part of an oration or discussion, summing up what has been said. **2** a long speech, usually employing high-flown and pompous language. ⟨< L *peroratio, -onis* < *perorare* < *per-* to a finish + *orare* speak formally⟩

per•ox•ide [pə'rɒksaɪd] *n., v.* **-id•ed, -id•ing.** *—n.* **1** *Chemistry.* an oxide of a given element or radical that contains the greatest, or an unusual, amount of oxygen. **2** HYDROGEN PEROXIDE.
—v. bleach (hair) by applying hydrogen peroxide.

per•pen•dic•u•lar [,pɜrpən'dɪkjələr] *adj., n.* *—adj.* **1** at right angles to the plane of the horizon; vertical; upright. **2** very steep: *a perpendicular cliff.* **3** *Geometry.* at right angles to a given line, plane, or surface. One line is perpendicular to another when it makes a 90° angle with the other. **4** Often, **Perpendicular,** of or designating a late stage of medieval English Gothic architecture characterized by a marked emphasis on vertical lines.
—n. **1** a perpendicular line, plane, or surface. **2** a perpendicular position. **3** an instrument used for locating the vertical line from any point. ⟨< L *perpendicularis* < *perpendiculum* plumb line, ult. < *per-* + *pendere* hang⟩ **—,per•pen'dic•u•lar•ly,** *adv.* **—,per•pen,dic•u'lar•i•ty** [-'lærəti], *n.*

per•pe•trate ['pɜrpə,treit] *v.* **-trat•ed, -trat•ing.** do or commit (crime, fraud, or anything bad or foolish). ⟨< L *perpetrare* < *per-* (intensive) + *patrare* perform⟩ **—,per•pe'tra•tion,** *n.* **—'per•pe,tra•tor,** *n.*

per•pet•u•al [pər'pɛtʃuəl] *adj., n.* *—adj.* **1** lasting forever or for all time: *the perpetual orbit of the moon.* **2** lasting throughout life: *a perpetual income.* **3** continuous; never ceasing: *a perpetual stream of visitors; perpetual motion.* **4** *Horticulture.* being in bloom more or less continuously throughout the year or the season.
—n. a hybrid rose that is perpetual. ⟨< L *perpetualis* < *perpetuus* < *perpes, -etis* continuous < *per-* to the end + *petere* seek⟩ **—per'pet•u•al•ly,** *adv.*

perpetual calendar 1 a calendar or table that allows one to find out the day of the week for any given date over a wide range of years. **2** a desk calendar that can be adjusted so as to be used for each of several years.

perpetual motion *Mechanics.* the movement of a hypothetical machine that can run forever, creating its own power source.

per•pet•u•ate [pər'pɛtʃu,eit] *v.* **-at•ed, -at•ing.** make perpetual; cause to last indefinitely: *attempts to perpetuate a species. The Brock Monument was built to perpetuate the memory of a great man.* ⟨< L *perpetuare* < *perpetuus.* See PERPETUAL.⟩ **—per,pet•u'a•tion,** *n.* **—per'pet•u,a•tor,** *n.*

per•pe•tu•i•ty [,pɜrpə'tʃuəti], [,pɜrpə'tjuəti], *or* [,pɜrpə'tuəti] *n., pl.* **-ties. 1** the state of being perpetual; endless time. **2** a perpetual possession, tenure, or position. **3** *Law.* **a** of an estate, the quality or condition of being inalienable perpetually or longer than the legal time limit. **b** the estate so restricted. **4** a perpetual annuity.
in perpetuity, forever. ⟨< F < L *perpetuitas* < *perpetuus.* See PERPETUAL.⟩

per•plex [pər'plɛks] *v.* **1** trouble with doubt; make unable to think clearly or logically; puzzle: *The problem is hard enough to perplex even the instructor.* **2** complicate (something). ⟨back formation from *perplexed*⟩ **—per'plex•ing,** *adj.* **—per'plex•ing•ly,** *adv.*
☛ *Syn.* **1.** See note at PUZZLE.

per•plexed [pər'plɛkst] *adj., v.* *—adj.* **1** not knowing what to do or how to act; puzzled and confused: *She was greatly perplexed by her friend's strange manner.* **2** confusing; complicated: *This is a highly perplexed problem.*
—v. pt. and pp. of PERPLEX. ⟨< L *perplexus* confused, ult. < *per-* completely + *plectere* intertwine⟩ **—per'plex•ed•ly** [pər'plɛksədli], *adv.*

per•plex•i•ty [pər'plɛksəti] *n., pl.* **-ties. 1** a perplexed condition; confusion; the state of being puzzled or not knowing what to do or how to act. **2** something that perplexes.

per•qui•site ['pɜrkwɪzɪt] *n.* **1** anything desirable received in addition to regular pay and that results directly from one's position, especially something promised or expected: *Included among the maid's perquisites were expensive dresses cast off by her mistress.* **2** a tip. **3** something expected or due as an exclusive right, by virtue of status, position, etc. ⟨< Med.L *perquisitum* (thing) gained, ult. < L *per-* thoroughly + *quaerere* seek⟩

per•ry ['pɛri] *n.* an alcoholic drink resembling cider, made from the juice of pears. ⟨ME *pereye, perrye* < OF *peré*, ult. < L *pirum* pear⟩
☛ *Hom.* PARRY.

per se [pər 'sei] *Latin.* by, of, or in itself; intrinsically.

per•se•cute ['pɜrsə,kjut] *v.* **-cut•ed, -cut•ing. 1** treat badly; do harm to again and again; oppress, especially for religious, racial, or political reasons: *Christians were persecuted in ancient Rome. Children are often persecuted by other children because they seem different.* **2** annoy: *persecuted with endless questions.* ⟨< *persecution*⟩ **—'per•se,cu•tor,** *n.* **—'per•se,cu•tive** or **'per•se•cu,to•ry,** *adj.*
☛ *Usage.* Both **persecute** and PROSECUTE come from the same Latin word *sequi*, meaning 'follow' or 'pursue'. But **persecute** means to pursue or harass a person (or other creature) with the idea of doing harm, while **prosecute** means to bring someone before a court of law or to pursue a plan, a job, or idea in the sense of carrying it out or bringing it to completion.

per•se•cu•tion [,pɜrsə'kjuʃən] *n.* **1** the act or practice of persecuting. **2** the condition or state of being persecuted. ⟨< L *persecutio, -onis*, ult. < *per-* perseveringly + *sequi* follow⟩

Per•seids ['pɜrsiɪdz] *n.pl. Astronomy.* brilliant and extensive showers of meteors occurring each year in mid-August and appearing to originate in the constellation Perseus.

Per•seph•o•ne [pər'sɛfə,ni] *n. Greek mythology.* the daughter of Zeus and Demeter, who was carried off by Pluto to become his wife and queen of the underworld. Persephone corresponds to the Roman goddess Proserpina.

Per•se•us ['pɜrsiəs] *or* ['pɜrsjus] *n.* **1** *Greek mythology.* a Greek hero, the son of Zeus and Danae, who slew the Gorgon Medusa and rescued Andromeda from a sea monster.
2 *Astronomy.* a constellation in the northern sky between Taurus and Cassiopeia.

per•se•ver•ance [,pɜrsə'virəns] *n.* **1** a sticking to a purpose or an aim; never giving up what one has set out to do; persistence. **2** *Theology.* especially in Calvinism, the continuance of the elect in a state of grace to the end of their lives, thus ensuring eternal salvation.
☛ *Syn.* **1.** See note at PERSISTENCE.

per•se•ve•rate [pər'sɛvə,reit] *v.* **-rat•ed, -rat•ing.** be repeated persistently; display perseveration.

per•se•ve•ra•tion [pər,sɛvə'reiʃən] *n.* **1** of an idea, experience, etc., the tendency to recur or persist. **2** in a person, the tendency to pursue a mental activity without being able to change to another. **3** *Psychiatry.* abnormal, persistent, often involuntary repetition of actions or words. ⟨< L *perseveratio, -onis*⟩

per•se•vere [,pɜrsə'vir] *v.* **-vered, -ver•ing.** continue steadily in doing something hard; persist: *The early explorers persevered in their efforts to find a westerly route to India.* ⟨< F < L *perseverare* < *per-* very + *severus* strict⟩ **—,per•se'ver•ing•ly,** *adv.*

Per•sia ['pɜrʒə] *n.* **1** the official name of Iran before 1935. **2** the Persian Empire, an ancient state covering at its height (circa 500 B.C.) an area extending from Egypt and the Aegean to the Indus River; conquered circa 328 B.C. by Alexander the Great.

Per•sian ['pɜrʒən] *n., adj.* *—n.* **1** a native or inhabitant of Persia (or Iran). **2** the language of Persia (or Iran). **3** PERSIAN CAT.

—adj. **1** of or having to do with Persia (or Iran), its people, or their language. **2** of, resembling, or pertaining to a Persian cat: *the typical flat Persian face.*

Persian carpet a handwoven rug made in Iran, having tight weaving, designs of flowers, animals, or birds, and bright colours.

Persian cat a longhaired breed of cat, thought to have originated in Asia Minor.

A Persian cat

Persian Gulf States the oil-producing nations and emirates situated on or near the Persian Gulf. These include Bahrain, Iran, Iraq, Kuwait, Oman, Saudi Arabia, and the United Arab Emirates.

Persian lamb **1** the lamb of the karakul sheep, native to central Asia. **2** the very curly, black or grey fur of newborn lambs of this sheep, used to make coats and hats and to trim clothing and accessories. **3** a coat or other garment made from this fur.

Persian violet any of several plants of the genus *Exacum*, native to Eurasia as *E. affine*, having shiny leaves and fragrant blue flowers. It is popular as a houseplant.

Persian walnut a tree (*Juglans regia*), also known as **English walnut**, valued for its dark, beautifully grained wood which is often used for fine furniture. It bears edible nuts. It has been planted in Canada, but is not hardy.

per•si•flage ['pɜrsɪˌflɑʒ] *n.* **1** a frivolous or flippant style of treating a subject in speech or writing. **2** light, bantering speech or writing: *Enough persiflage; we must be serious about this.* ⟨< F *persiflage* < *persifler* banter, apparently < *per-* (< L) + *siffler* whistle, hiss < L *sibilare*⟩

per•sim•mon [pər'sɪmən] *n.* **1** any tree of the genus *Diospyrus*, of the ebony family, particularly *D. virginia* in North America. **2** the fruit of any of these trees, typically orange-red in colour and sweet-tasting when ripe. ⟨< Virginian Algonquian, *pessemins, pichamins*, etc.⟩

per•sist [pər'sɪst] *or* [pər'zɪst] *v.* **1** continue firmly; refuse to stop or be changed: *He persists in eating with his fingers. She persisted till she had solved the difficult problem.* **2** last; stay; endure, especially past a usual, normal, or expected time: *The cold weather will persist for some time.* **3** say again and again; maintain. ⟨< *persistere* < *per-* to the end + *sistere* stand⟩

per•sist•ence [pər'sɪstəns] *or* [pər'zɪstəns] *n.* **1** the quality or state of being persistent or the act of persisting. **2** the continuing existence or continuance of an effect after the cause is removed, as of images on the retina.

☛ *Syn.* **1. Persistence,** PERSEVERANCE = a holding fast to a purpose or course of action. **Persistence,** having a good or bad sense according to one's attitude toward what is done, emphasizes holding stubbornly or obstinately to one's purpose and continuing firmly and often annoyingly against disapproval, opposition, advice, etc.: *By persistence many people won religious freedom.* **Perseverance,** always in a good sense, emphasizes refusing to be discouraged by obstacles or difficulties and continuing steadily with courage and patience: *Perseverance leads to success.*

per•sist•en•cy [pər'sɪstənsi] *or* [pər'zɪstənsi] *n.* persistence.

per•sist•ent [pər'sɪstənt] *or* [pər'zɪstənt] *adj.* **1** persisting; having lasting qualities, especially in the face of dislike, disapproval, or difficulties: *a persistent worker, a persistent beggar.* **2** lasting; going on; continuing: *a persistent headache that lasted for three days.* **3** *Botany.* continuing without withering, as a calyx which remains after the corolla has withered; permanent. **4** *Zoology.* permanent; not lost or altered during development or over time: *persistent horns.* **—per'sist•ent•ly,** *adv.*

per•snick•e•ty [pər'snɪkɪti] *adj.* pernickety.

per•son ['pɜrsən] *n.* **1** a man, woman, or child; human being: *Any person who wishes may come to the fair.* **2** a human body: *The person of the monarch was well guarded.* **3** bodily appearance: *He kept his person neat and trim.* **4** the self, being, or personality of an individual: *Consider the person who said that.* **5** *Grammar.* **a** a reference in discourse to the speaker, the person spoken to, or another person or thing, indicated by a distinction of form in pronouns and, in many languages, verbs. **b** any of the three groups of pronoun or verb forms indicating distinction of person: **first person** (speaker), **second person** (person spoken to), or **third person** (person or thing spoken about). In *I asked her where she met you*, the pronoun *I* is the singular form for the first person, *her* and *she* are singular forms for the third person, and *you* is the singular or plural form for the second person. **6** *Christianity.* any of the three modes of being in the Trinity (Father, Son, and Holy Spirit). **7** *Law.* a human being, or an entity such as a corporation, a partnership, or occasionally a collection of property, as the estate of a dead person, recognized by the law as capable of having legal rights and duties.

in person, by or with one's own action or presence; personally: *You may phone in your order or shop in person. The artist was there in person.* ⟨ME < OF < L *persona* character, mask worn by actor. Doublet of PARSON.⟩

☛ *Syn.* **Person,** INDIVIDUAL, PARTY. **Person** is the ordinary word for a human being of either sex: *A well-known person came into the room.* **Individual** emphasizes the person's uniqueness: *A strange individual came into the room.* Unlike **person, individual** can also be applied to animals and objects: *Our cat is a fascinating individual.* The phrase **a person** is often used instead of the impersonal pronoun **one:** *Exercise makes a person hungry.* It is, as a rule, awkward and pretentious to use **individual** in this way. **Party** is used especially in legal documents to refer to one of the people or groups of people involved in a contract, agreement, etc.

per•so•na [pər'sounə] *n., pl.* **-nas** or **-nae** [-ni] *or* [-naɪ]. **1** a character or personality that a person adopts and presents to the public: *In private life the premier drops his public persona. Some novelists display a different persona in each of their books.* **2** Usually, **personae,** *pl.* the characters in a novel, play, etc. **3** *Jungian psychology.* the technique or system by which a person adapts to his or her environment in life in accordance with his or her own inner needs. **4** person.

per•son•a•ble ['pɜrsənəbəl] *adj.* having a pleasing appearance and personality; attractive: *a personable young woman.*

per•son•age ['pɜrsənɪdʒ] *n.* **1** a person of importance. **2** person. **3** a character in a book, play, etc. ⟨< MF⟩

per•so•na gra•ta [pər'sounə 'grɑtə], ['grætə], *or* ['greitə] *Latin.* an acceptable person, said especially of foreign diplomats acceptable to the governments of the countries to which they are assigned.

per•son•al ['pɜrsənəl] *adj., n.* *—adj.* **1** of or for an individual; involving individuals: *personal opinion, a personal letter, personal relationships.* **2** private; intimate: *personal details, a personal question.* **3** done in person; directly by oneself, not through others or by letter: *a personal visit.* **4** of the body or bodily appearance: *personal beauty.* **5** being a person; having personality: *a personal God.* **6** inclined to make remarks or to ask questions which are too searching or intimate: *Don't be too personal.* **7** *Grammar.* showing person. *I, we, thou, you, he, she, it,* and *they* are **personal pronouns. 8** *Law.* of or having to do with possessions, other than land or buildings, that can be moved.
—n. **1** a short paragraph in a newspaper about or directed toward a particular person or persons. **2** Usually, **personals,** *pl.* such notices appearing in the classified advertisement section of the newspaper. ⟨< LL *personalis*⟩

personal computer a small, relatively inexpensive computer designed for use by individuals at home or in their place of business, chiefly for such applications as word processing, data management, video games, etc. *Abbrev.*: PC

personal effects personal belongings normally worn or carried, such as clothing, cosmetics, etc.

personal equation **1** individual tendencies for which allowance should be made. **2** the allowance or correction so made.

per•son•al•i•ty [ˌpɜrsə'nælәti] *n., pl.* **-ties. 1** the personal or individual quality that makes one person be different or act differently from another; the perceptible qualities of character that impress one's identity on others; the fact of being a particular person: *Although identical, the twins are quite unlike in personality.* **2** the pleasing or attractive qualities of a person: *He is popular because he has a lot of personality.* **3** a remark made about or against some person. **4** a person of importance or renown; a person who regularly faces the public in his or her work: *a television personality, personalities of the stage and screen. The Royal personalities have been in the news a lot lately.* **5** the quality or state of being a person, not a thing. **6** the sum of the qualities or characteristics perceived as being distinctive of a group, place, nation, etc.: *Vancouver has quite a different personality from Toronto.*

☛ *Syn.* **1.** See note at CHARACTER.

per•son•al•ize ['pɜrsənəˌlaɪz] *v.* **-ized, -iz•ing. 1** make personal or individual; especially, mark with one's name, etc.: *Personalized stationery has the owner's monogram, name, or name and address stamped on it.* **2** personify.
–ˌper•son•al•i'za•tion, *n.*

per•son•al•ly ['pɜrsənəli] *adv.* **1** in person; not by the aid of others: *The hostess personally saw to the comforts of her guests.* **2** as far as oneself is concerned: *Personally, I don't believe a word* *of it.* **3** as a person: *We like him personally, but dislike his way of living.* **4** as being meant for oneself: *She intended no insult to you; do not take what she said personally.*

personal pronoun *Grammar.* a pronoun standing for the person or persons speaking (*I, we*); the person or persons addressed (*thou, you*); or the person or persons being spoken about (*he, she, they, it*).

personal property property that is not land, buildings, mines, or forests; movable possessions.

per•son•al•ty [ˈpɜrsənəlti] *n., pl.* **-ties.** *Law.* personal property. ⟨< AF < LL *personalitas* personality⟩

per•so•na non gra•ta [pərˈsounə nɒn ˈgrɑtə], [ˈgrætə], *or* [ˈgreitə] *Latin.* **1** a person who is not acceptable, usually said of diplomats not acceptable to the governments of the foreign countries to which they have been assigned: *The second secretary was declared a persona non grata because of her anti-government statements.* **2** *Informal.* a person who is disapproved of, unacceptable, or unwanted: *I was definitely a persona non grata at that feminist meeting. Abbrev.*: p.n.g. or P.N.G.

per•son•ate [ˈpɜrsə,neit] *v.* **-at•ed, -at•ing. 1** act the part of (a character in a play, etc.). **2** give a personality or personal characteristics to; personify. **3** *Law.* pretend to be (someone else), especially for purposes of fraud; impersonate. ⟨< obs. *personate*, adj., feigned < L *personatus*, < *persona* a mask⟩ **—ˈper•son,a•tor,** *n.* **—ˈper•son•a•tive,** *adj.* **—,per•so'na•tion,** *n.*

per•son•i•fi•ca•tion [pər,sɒnəfɪˈkeiʃən] *n.* **1** representation in speech, writing, or visual art, of a thing or idea as a person or as having human qualities. Personification is a common type of figure of speech. The expression *Duty calls us* involves a personification of the idea of duty. **2** a person or thing seen as a striking example or embodiment of a quality, etc.: *A miser is the personification of greed.*

per•son•i•fy [pərˈsɒnə,faɪ] *v.* **-fied, -fy•ing. 1** regard or represent in speech, writing, or visual art as a person or as having human qualities: *The sea is often personified in poetry.* **2** be the incarnation of; embody: *She personifies kindness.*

per•son•nel [,pɜrsəˈnɛl] *n.* **1** persons employed in any work, business, or service. **2** (*adjl.*) of or relating to a division in a business that deals with employee hiring, firing, and benefits; human resources: *the personnel department.* ⟨< F *personnel* personal; adj. used as n.⟩

per•spec•tive [pərˈspɛktɪv] *n.* **1 a** the art of picturing objects on a flat surface so as to give the appearance of distance. **b** a drawing or picture in perspective. **2** (*adjl.*) drawn so as to show the proper perspective. **3** the effect of distance on the appearance of objects: *Railway tracks seem to meet at the horizon because of perspective.* **4** the effect, as of calmness, objectivity, etc., that the distance of events has on the mind: *If you distanced yourself from the whole situation for a while, you could get some perspective on it.* **5** a view of things or facts in which they are in the right relation to one another: *This editorial puts the crisis in perspective.* **6** a view in front; distant view. **7** a mental viewpoint; consideration: *My perspective on this matter is quite different from yours.* ⟨< Med.L *perspectiva (ars)* (science) of optics, ult. < L *per-* through + *specere* look⟩ **—perˈspec•tive•ly,** *adv.*

per•spi•ca•cious [,pɜrspɪˈkeiʃəs] *adj.* keen in observing and understanding; discerning: *a perspicacious judgment.* ⟨< L *perspicax, -acis* sharp-sighted, ult. < *per-* through + *specere* look⟩ **—,per•spiˈca•cious•ly,** *adv.*

per•spi•cac•i•ty [,pɜrspɪˈkæsəti] *n.* keen perception; discernment; wisdom and understanding in dealing with people or with facts.

per•spi•cu•i•ty [,pɜrspɪˈkjuəti] *n.* clearness in expression; ease in being understood: *The premier was noted for the perspicuity of his speeches.*

per•spic•u•ous [pərˈspɪkjuəs] *adj.* clear; easily understood: *a perspicuous style.* ⟨< L *perspicuus*, ult. < *per-* through + *specere* look⟩ **—perˈspic•u•ous•ly,** *adv.* **—perˈspic•u•ous•ness,** *n.*

per•spi•ra•tion [,pɜrspəˈreiʃən] *n.* **1** SWEAT (*n.* def. 1). **2** a sweating or perspiring.

☛ *Syn.* **1.** See note at SWEAT.

per•spire [pərˈspaɪr] *v.* **-spired, -spir•ing.** SWEAT (*v.* def. 1). ⟨< L *perspirare* < *per-* through + *spirare* breathe⟩

per•suade [pərˈsweid] *v.* **-suad•ed, -suad•ing. 1** cause (a person) to do something by urging, arguing, etc.; prevail upon: *I knew I should study but they persuaded me to go to the movies with them.* **2** cause (a person) to believe something by urging, arguing, etc.; convince: *They finally persuaded him of the truth of the rumour. We tried to persuade her that we had known all along what she was up to.* ⟨< L *persuadere* < *per-* strongly + *suadere* urge⟩ **—perˈsuad•er,** *n.* **—perˈsuad•a•ble,** *adj.*

☛ *Syn.* **1. Persuade,** CONVINCE = get someone to do or believe something. **Persuade** emphasizes winning someone over to a desired belief or action by appealing to his or her feelings as well as to his or her mind. **Convince** emphasizes overcoming a person's objections or disbelief by proof or arguments appealing to his or her reason and understanding: *I have convinced her that she needs a vacation, but I cannot persuade her to take one.*

per•sua•si•ble [pərˈsweisəbəl] *or* [pərˈsweizəbəl] *adj.* that can be persuaded; open to persuasion. **—per,sua•siˈbil•i•ty,** *n.*

per•sua•sion [pərˈsweiʒən] *n.* **1** a persuading: *All our persuasion was of no use; she would not come.* **2** the power of persuading. **3** a firm belief: *The two brothers were of different political persuasions.* **4 a** a religious belief; creed: *All Christians are not of the same persuasion.* **b** a body of persons holding a particular religious belief; sect; denomination. **5** *Facetious.* kind; sort: *lawyers, and others of that persuasion.* ⟨ME < L *persuasio, -onis* < *persuadere.* See PERSUADE.⟩

per•sua•sive [pərˈsweisɪv] *or* [pərˈsweizɪv] *adj.* able to persuade; effective in persuading: *The sales representative had a very persuasive way of talking.* **—perˈsua•sive•ly,** *adv.* **—perˈsua•sive•ness,** *n.*

pert [pɜrt] *adj.* **1** too forward or free in speech or action; saucy; bold. **2** *Informal.* lively; in good health or spirits. **3** chic and sprightly; jaunty. ⟨for *apert*, ME < OF *apert* open < L *apertus*; influenced by OF *aspert* expert⟩ **—ˈpert•ly,** *adv.* **—ˈpert•ness,** *n.*

per•tain [pərˈtein] *v.* **1** belong or be connected as a part, possession, etc.: *We own the house and the land pertaining to it.* **2** refer; be related (*to*): *an editorial pertaining to the coming election.* **3** be appropriate; belong: *We had turkey and everything else that pertains to Thanksgiving Day.* ⟨ME < OF < L *pertinere* < *per-* across + *tenere* reach⟩

perth•ite [ˈpɜrθəit] *n.* a type of feldspar. ⟨< *Perth*, Ontario, where it occurs⟩

per•ti•na•cious [,pɜrtəˈneiʃəs] *adj.* **1** holding firmly to a purpose, action, or opinion; very persistent: *A bulldog is a pertinacious fighter.* **2** stubborn to excess; obstinate or perverse. **3** obstinately or persistently continuing; not yielding to treatment: *a pertinacious cough.* ⟨< L *pertinacia* firmness < *per-* very + *tenax, -acis* tenacious⟩ **—,per•tiˈna•cious•ly,** *adv.* **—,per•tiˈna•cious•ness,** *n.*

per•ti•nac•i•ty [,pɜrtəˈnæsəti] *n.* the quality of being pertinaceous: *The patient's pneumonia exhibited great pertinacity. His pertinacity is what finally got him the interview.*

per•ti•nence [ˈpɜrtənəns] *n.* being to the point; fitness; relevance: *The pertinence of the student's replies showed intelligence.* Also, **pertinency.**

per•ti•nent [ˈpɜrtənənt] *adj.* having to do with what is being considered; relating to the matter in hand; to the point. ⟨< L *pertinens, -entis*, ppr. of *pertinere* pertain. See PERTAIN.⟩ **—ˈper•ti•nent•ly,** *adv.*

☛ *Syn.* **Pertinent,** RELEVANT = relating to the matter in hand. **Pertinent** means directly to the point of the matter, belonging properly and fittingly to what is being considered and helping to explain or solve it: *The committee asked for all the pertinent information about the events leading up to this situation.* **Relevant** means having some bearing on the problem or enough connection with it to have some significance: *Even seemingly unimportant incidents might be relevant.*

per•turb [pərˈtɜrb] *v.* **1** disturb greatly; make uneasy or troubled: *The management was perturbed at the possibility of another strike.* **2** throw into confusion; disorder; unsettle. **3** *Astronomy.* disturb or cause perturbation in (the orbit of a celestial body). ⟨< L *perturbare* < *per-* thoroughly + *turbare* confuse⟩ **—perˈturb•er,** *n.* **—perˈturb•ing•ly,** *adv.*

per•tur•ba•tion [,pɜrtərˈbeiʃən] *n.* **1** perturbing or being perturbed. **2** something that perturbs; disturbance. **3** *Astronomy.* a slight deviation in the orbit of a celestial body, caused by the attraction of another body or bodies. **—,per•turˈba•tion•al,** *adj.*

per•tus•sis [pərˈtʌsɪs] *n. Pathology.* WHOOPING COUGH. ⟨< L *per* through + *tussis* a cough⟩

Pe•ru [pəˈru] *n.* a country on the western coast of South America.

pe•ruke [pəˈruk] *n.* a wig, especially a style of wig commonly worn by European men in the 17th and 18th centuries; periwig. ⟨< F *perruque* < It. *perruca*⟩

pe•rus•al [pəˈruzəl] *n.* a perusing; reading: *the perusal of a letter.*

pe•ruse [pəˈruz] *v.* **-rused, -rus•ing. 1** read thoroughly and carefully. **2** read. **3** examine, inspect, or consider in detail. ⟨ME *perusen*, orig., use up < L *per-* to the end + E *use*⟩

Pe•ru•vi•an [pə'ruviən] *n., adj.* *—n.* a native or inhabitant of Peru.
—adj. of or having to do with Peru, or its people.

Peruvian bark a bark yielding quinine; cinchona.

per•vade [pər'veid] *v.* **-vad•ed, -vad•ing. 1** go or spread throughout; be throughout: *The odour of pines pervades the air.* **2** be found throughout (the body of a work, etc.), so as to characterize, flavour unmistakably, etc.: *The author's anger at injustice pervades the whole novel.* ⟨< L *pervadere* < *per-* through + *vadere* go⟩ **—per'vad•er,** *n.* **—per'vad•ing•ly,** *adv.* **—per'va•sion** [pər'veiʒən], *n.* **—per'va•sive** [pər'veisɪv], *adj.* **—per'va•sive•ly,** *adv.* **—per'va•sive•ness,** *n.*

per•verse [pər'vɜrs] *adj.* **1** contrary and willful; stubborn: *The perverse child did just what we told her not to do.* **2** characterized by or proceeding from such a disposition: *a perverse mood.* **3** persistent in wrong. **4** wicked. **5** not correct; wrong: *perverse reasoning.* **6** twisted in mind; of a distorted character, especially now as regards sexual morality. ⟨< L *perversus* turned away, pp. of *pervertere.* See PERVERT.⟩ **—per'verse•ly,** *adv.* **—per'verse•ness** or **per'vers•i•ty,** *n.*

per•ver•sion [pər'vɜrʒən] *or* [pər'vɜrʃən] *n.* **1** a turning or being turned to what is wrong; change to what is unnatural, abnormal, or wrong: *A tendency to eat sand is a perversion of appetite.* **2** a twisted or distorted shape or character: *perversion of facts.* **3** any of various sexual preferences and practices that are considered abnormal.

per•vert *v.* [pər'vɜrt]; *n.* ['pɜrvərt] *v., n.* *—v.* **1** lead or turn from the right way or from the truth: *Reading unwholesome books may pervert our taste for good books.* **2** give a wrong meaning to: *His enemies perverted his friendly remark and made it into an insult.* **3** use for improper purposes or in an improper way: *A clever criminal perverts his talents.* **4** change from what is natural or normal, now especially what is generally accepted or defined by law as natural or normal in sexual behaviour.
—n. a perverted person, now especially one who practises sexual perversion. ⟨< L *pervertere* < *per-* (intensive) + *vertere* turn⟩ **—per'vert•er,** *n.* **—per'vert•i•ble,** *adj.* **—per'vert•ed•ly,** *adv.* **—per'vert•ed•ness,** *n.*

per•vi•ous ['pɜrviəs] *adj.* **1** giving passage or entrance; permeable: *Sand is easily pervious to water.* **2** open to influence, argument, etc.; accessible: *pervious to reason.* ⟨< L *pervius* < *per-* through + *via* way⟩ **—'per•vi•ous•ness,** *n.*

Pe•sach ['peisɑx] *or* ['pɛsɑx] Passover. ⟨< Hebrew *pesah*⟩

pe•se•ta [pə'seitə] *n.* **1** the basic unit of money in Spain, divided into 100 centimos. See table of money in the Appendix. **2** a coin or note worth one peseta. ⟨< Sp., dim. of *peso*⟩

pe•se•wa [pə'seiwɑ] *n.* **1** a unit of money in Ghana, equal to 1/100 of a cedi. See table of money in the Appendix. **2** a coin worth one pesewa.

pes•ky ['pɛski] *adj.* **-ki•er, -ki•est.** *Informal.* troublesome; annoying: *How can we get rid of these pesky wasps?* ⟨? alteration of *pesty* < *pest*⟩

pe•so ['peisou] *n., pl.* **-sos. 1** the basic unit of money in Argentina, Chile, Colombia, Cuba, Dominican Republic, Guinea-Bissau, and Mexico, divided into 100 centavos. **2** the basic unit of money in Uruguay, divided into 100 centesimos. See table of money in the Appendix. **3** a coin or note worth one peso. **4** a former gold coin of Spain and its colonies. ⟨< Sp. < L *pensum,* pp. of *pendere* weigh⟩

peso bo•li•vi•a•no [bə,lɪvi'ɑnou] the monetary unit of Bolivia, equal to 1/1000 of a boliviano or 100 centavos. See table of money in the Appendix.

pes•si•mism ['pɛsə,mɪzəm] *n.* **1** a tendency to look on the dark side of things or to see difficulties and disadvantages. **2** a belief that things naturally tend to evil, or that life is not worthwhile. **3** *Philosophy.* the doctrine that this world is the worst of all possible worlds. ⟨< L *pessimus* worst + *-ism*⟩

pes•si•mist ['pɛsəmɪst] *n.* **1** a person inclined to see all the difficulties and disadvantages or to look on the dark side of things. **2** a person who thinks that life holds more evil than good, and so is not worth living. **3** *Philosophy.* a believer in pessimism.

pes•si•mis•tic [,pɛsə'mɪstɪk] *adj.* of, having to do with, or characterized by pessimism: *a pessimistic outlook on life.* **—,pes•si'mis•ti•cal•ly,** *adv.*
☛ *Syn.* See note at CYNICAL.

pest [pɛst] *n.* **1** any thing or person that causes trouble, annoyance, or destruction; nuisance: *Mosquitoes are pests.* **2** *Archaic.* pestilence. ⟨< F *peste* < L *pestis* plague⟩

pes•ter ['pɛstər] *v.* **1** annoy; trouble; vex: *If we sit outside we'll be pestered by flies.* **2** bother with repeated requests or demands; keep after: *He kept pestering his older sister till she gave in and took him along.* ⟨apparently < OF *empestrer* hobble (an animal); influenced by *pest*⟩ **—'pes•ter•er,** *n.* **—'pest•er•ing•ly,** *adv.* **—'pes•ter•some,** *adj.*
☛ *Syn.* See note at TEASE.

pest•house ['pɛst,hʌus] *n. Archaic.* a hospital for persons ill with highly infectious and dangerous diseases.

pes•ti•cide ['pɛstə,saɪd] *n.* any chemical agent or other substance used to destroy plant or animal pests.

pes•tif•er•ous [pɛ'stɪfərəs] *adj.* **1** bringing disease or infection. **2** bringing moral evil: *the pestiferous influence of a bad example.* **3** pestilential. **4** *Informal.* troublesome; annoying. ⟨< L *pestiferus* < *pestis* plague + *ferre* bring⟩

pes•ti•lence ['pɛstələns] *n.* **1** a deadly epidemic infectious disease, especially bubonic plague. **2** anything that is extremely destructive or deadly in its effect.

pes•ti•lent ['pɛstələnt] *adj.* **1** bringing contagious, often epidemic and fatal disease; pestilential: *Rat bites may be pestilent.* **2** harmful to morals; destroying peace: *a pestilent den of vice, the pestilent effects of war.* **3** troublesome; annoying: *Those pestilent rabbits have eaten all the lettuce plants.* ⟨< L *pestilens, -entis* < *pestis* pest⟩ **—'pes•ti•lent•ly,** *adv.*

pes•ti•len•tial [,pɛstə'lɛnʃəl] *adj.* **1** of, having to do with, or causing pestilence. **2** morally or socially harmful. **3** irritating. **—,pes•ti'len•tial•ly,** *adv.*

A neolithic mortar and pestle, made of stone

pes•tle ['pɛsəl] *n., v.* **-tled, -tling.** *—n.* **1** a club-shaped tool used for pounding or crushing substances into a powder in a mortar. **2** any of various mechanical appliances for pounding, stamping, pressing, etc., as a vertically moving or pounding part in a machine.
—v. pound or crush with a pestle. ⟨ME < OF *pestel* < L *pistillum,* ult. < *pinsere* pound. Doublet of PISTIL.⟩

pes•to ['pɛstou] *n.* a sauce typically prepared by grinding together garlic, pine nuts, fresh basil, olive oil, and Parmesan cheese, usually served with pasta, meat, or fish. ⟨< Ital., pp. of *pestare* grind, pound⟩

pet[1] [pɛt] *n., adj., v.* **pet•ted, pet•ting.** *—n.* **1** an animal kept as a favourite and treated with affection. **2** a darling; a favourite.
—adj. **1** treated as a pet. **2** showing affection: *a pet name.* **3** darling; favourite. **4** *Informal.* particular; special: *a pet aversion, a pet theory, a pet phrase.*
—v. **1** treat as a pet. **2** stroke; pat; touch lovingly and gently. **3** *Informal.* caress and fondle passionately. **4** yield to the wishes of; indulge. ⟨< Scots Gaelic *peata,* poss. back formation from ME *pety* small. See PETTY.⟩

pet[2] [pɛt] *n.* a fit of peevishness; a state of fretful discontent. ⟨origin uncertain⟩

peta– ['pɛtə] *SI prefix.* one quadrillion; 10^{15}: *petametre.* *Symbol:* P

pet•al ['pɛtəl] *n.* one of the parts of a flower that are often coloured; one of the parts of a corolla. A daisy has many petals. See FLOWER for picture. ⟨< NL < Gk. *petalon* leaf, originally neut. adj., outspread⟩ **—'pet•al-,like** or **'pet•al,oid,** *adj.*

pe•tard [pɪ'tɑrd] *n.* an explosive device formerly used in warfare to break down a door or gate or to breach a wall. It was fastened to the gate, etc. and ignited.
hoist with (one's) **own petard,** injured or destroyed by one's own scheme or device for the ruin of others. ⟨< F *pétard* < *péter* break wind, ult. < L *pedere*⟩

pet•cock ['pɛt,kɒk] *n.* a small tap or valve for draining a pipe or cylinder, releasing pressure, etc. ⟨< obs. *pet* < F *péter* break wind + *cock*[1]⟩

pe•te•chia [pə'tikiə] *n., pl.* **-chi•ae** [-ki,i] *or* [-ki,aɪ]. *Medicine.* a small, purple-coloured hemorrhage in the skin or mucous membrane. ⟨< NL < Ital. *petecchia* miser, in pl., spots on skin⟩

pe•ter ['pitər] *v. Informal.* gradually fail or come to an end; give out or become exhausted (*used with* **out**): *We were forced to ration our food as supplies began to peter out.* ⟨origin unknown⟩

Pe•ter•bor•ough or **Pe•ter•bor•o** ['pitər,bɜrə] *n. Cdn.* a type of canoe made from wood or birchbark, formerly manufactured at Lakefield, Ontario, by the Peterborough Canoe Company. Also, **Peterborough canoe.**

Pe•ter•head or **pe•ter•head** ['pitər,hɛd] *n. Cdn.* a decked launch or large whaleboat equipped with a single sail and a small motor, much used by Inuit and others in the E Arctic. Also, **Peterhead boat, Peterhead launch, Peterhead schooner.** ⟨< *Peterhead*, Scotland, where early boats of this type were made⟩

Peter Pan collar a small collar with rounded ends, often white, worn on a high neckline on girls' and women's clothing. ⟨after *Peter Pan*, titular hero of a play by J.M. Barrie, traditionally portrayed as wearing such a collar⟩

Peter Principle a satirical 'law' maintaining that in any organizational structure, employees tend to be promoted until they reach their individual level of incompetence. ⟨< J. *Peter*, Canadian educator⟩

Pe•ter•sham ['pitərʃəm] *n.* **1** a rough, heavy woollen fabric used for men's overcoats and jackets. **2** any coat or jacket made from this cloth. **3** a narrow corded belting used for lining the waistbands of skirts and trousers. ⟨< Lord *Petersham* (1780–1851)⟩

pet•i•o•late ['pɛtiə,leit] *adj. Zoology.* having a petiole or peduncle.

pet•i•ole ['pɛti,oul] *n.* **1** *Botany.* the slender stalk by which a leaf is attached to the stem. See STEM for picture. **2** *Zoology.* a stalklike part. A petiole connects the thorax and abdomen of a wasp. ⟨< L *petiolus*, dim. of *pes, pedis* foot⟩ **–,pet•i'ol•ar,** *adj.*

pet•i•o•lule ['pɛtiə,lul] *or* ['pɛtioul,jul] *n. Botany.* a small petiole such as the stalk of a leaflet in a compound leaf.

pet•it ['pɛti] *adj.* petty (*now used only in legal phrases*): *petit larceny.* ⟨< F *petit* < VL stem *pit-* little. Doublet of PETTY.⟩
☛ *Hom.* PETTY.

petit bourgeois *French.* **1** a member of the lower middle class. **2** See PETITE BOURGEOISIE.

pe•tite [pə'tit] *adj.* little; of small size; tiny, especially with reference to a woman or girl. ⟨< F *petite*, fem. of *petit* little⟩

petite bourgeoisie that part of the bourgeoisie having the lowest social status and least wealth; the lower middle class.

pet•it four ['pɛti 'fɔr]; *French,* [pəti'fuʀ] *pl.* **pet•its fours** ['pɛti 'fɔrz]; *French,* [pəti'fuʀ]. a small fancy cake with decorative frosting. ⟨< F *petit four* little oven⟩

pe•ti•tion [pə'tɪʃən] *n., v.* *–n.* **1** a formal request to a superior or to one in authority for some privilege, right, benefit, etc.: *The people signed a petition asking the city council for a new sidewalk.* **2** *Law.* a written application for an order of court for some action by a judge. **3** prayer. **4** that which is requested or prayed for. **5** the act of formally asking or humbly requesting.
–v. **1** ask for earnestly; make a petition (to): *They petitioned the mayor to use his influence with the city council. The residents petitioned for a crosswalk.* **2** pray. ⟨< L *petitio, -onis* < *petere* seek⟩ **–pe'ti•tion•er,** *n.* **–pe'ti•tion,ar•y,** *adj.*

petit jury *Law.* TRIAL JURY. Compare GRAND JURY.

petit larceny *U.S. Law.* in some states, a theft in which the value of the property stolen is less than a certain amount fixed by law.

pe•tit mal [pə'ti 'mæl] *Pathology.* a mild type of epilepsy characterized by brief attacks of unconsciousness as short as a few seconds, unaccompanied by convulsions. Compare GRAND MAL. ⟨< F, literally, small illness⟩

petit point **1** a small, diagonal needlepoint stitch used for fine, allover embroidery. **2** embroidery done with such stitches. Petit point is usually done with embroidery floss. ⟨< F *petit* small + *point* stitch⟩

Pe•trarch•an sonnet [pə'trɑrkən] a sonnet of 14 lines, of which eight form the octave (rhyming abba abba) and six form the sestet, with varying rhyme schemes. ⟨after *Petrarch*, Ital. name *Francesco Petrarca* (1304–1374), lyricist + scholar⟩

pet•rel ['pɛtrəl] *n.* any of various small, web-footed sea birds (order Procellariiformes) having thick, usually black-and-white plumage, long, pointed wings, and a hooked bill. Petrels roam far out at sea between breeding seasons. See also STORMY PETREL. ⟨apparently dim. of St. *Peter*, who walked on a lake⟩
☛ *Hom.* PETROL.

pet•ri•chor ['pɛtrɪ,kɔr] *n.* a yellowish oil trapped in rocks and soil. ⟨< Gk. *petros* stone + *khor* the liquid that flowed in the veins of the gods⟩

Petri dish or **petri dish** ['pitri] a round, shallow glass container with a loose cover, used in laboratories to hold bacterial and other micro-organic cultures. ⟨< Julius *Petri* (1852-1922), the German bacteriologist who invented it⟩

pet•ri•fac•tion [,pɛtrə'fækʃən] *n.* **1** the process of petrifying. **2** the condition or quality of being petrified. **3** something petrified. **–,pet•ri'fact•ive,** *adj.*

pet•ri•fi•ca•tion [,pɛtrəfə'keiʃən] *n.* petrifaction.

pet•ri•fied ['pɛtrə,faɪd] *adj., v.–adj.* **1** turned to stone by having cells replaced with mineral deposits: *petrified wood.* **2** immobilized by fear.
–v. pt. and pp. of PETRIFY.

Petrified Forest an ancient forest in Arizona whose trees have turned to stone.

pet•ri•fy ['pɛtrə,faɪ] *v.* **-fied, -fy•ing. 1** replace animal or vegetable cells with mineral deposits; turn into stone or stony substance (*usually used in the passive*): *Many types of wood and bone become petrified over time.* **2** make or become stiff, dull, etc.; deaden. **3** paralyse with fear, horror, or surprise: *They heard a footstep upstairs and stopped, petrified with fear.* ⟨< F *pétrifier*, ult. < L *petra* rock, stone < Gk. *petros*⟩

petro– *combining form.* **1** rock: *petroglyph = a rock carving.* **2** petroleum: *petrochemical = a chemical made of or from petroleum.* **3** of the petroleum business: *petrodollars.* ⟨< Gk. *petra* rock, *petros* stone⟩

pet•ro•chem•i•cal [,pɛtrou'kɛmɪkəl] *n., adj. –n.* any of various important chemicals made from petroleum or natural gas, used in the manufacture of plastics, synthetic fibres, paints, etc.
–adj. of or having to do with petrochemicals or petrochemistry.

pet•ro•chem•is•try [,pɛtrou'kɛmɪstri] *n.* **1** the branch of chemistry dealing with petroleum and petrochemicals. **2** the chemistry of rocks.

pet•ro•dol•lar ['pɛtrou,dɒlər] *n.* Usually, **petrodollars,** *pl.* money earned from the sale of petroleum and available as dollars, especially when thought of as a source of economic or political power.

pet•ro•glyph ['pɛtrə,glɪf] *n.* a carving or inscription on rock, especially a prehistoric one: *There are some interesting petroglyphs on the shores of Lake Superior depicting animals.* ⟨< F *petroglyphe* < Gk. *petra* rock + *glyphē* a carving⟩ **–,pet•ro'glyph•ic,** *adj.*

pet•ro•graph ['pɛtrə,græf] *n.* a painting or inscription on rock.

pe•trog•ra•phy [pɪ'trɒgrəfi] *n.* a branch of petrology dealing mainly with the detailed description and classification of rocks. ⟨< Gk. *petra* rock, *petros* stone + E *-graphy*⟩ **–pe'trog•ra•pher,** *n.* **–,pe•tro'graph•ic,** *adj.* **–,pe•tro'graph•i•cal•ly,** *adv.*

pet•rol ['pɛtrəl] *n. Brit.* gasoline. ⟨< F < Med.L *petroleum.* Shortening of *petroleum.*⟩
☛ *Hom.* PETREL.

pet•ro•la•tum [,pɛtrə'leitəm] *n.* **1** a salve or ointment made from petroleum. **2** mineral oil. ⟨< NL *petroleum* + L *-atum.* See -ATE[1].⟩

pe•tro•le•um [pə'trouliəm] *n.* a combustible, usually dark-coloured liquid, a kind of oil that occurs in deposits within the rock strata of many parts of the world and consists of a complex mixture of hydrocarbons and small amounts of many other substances. Petroleum is processed to produce gasoline, fuel oils, kerosene, paraffin, lubricants, etc. ⟨< Med.L < Gk. *petra* rock, *petros* stone + L *oleum* oil⟩

petroleum jelly a smooth, greasy, odourless, and tasteless substance obtained from petroleum, used as an ointment and as a lubricant.

pe•trol•o•gist [pɪ'trɒlədʒɪst] *n.* a person trained in petrology, especially one whose work it is.

pe•trol•o•gy [pɪ'trɒlədʒi] *n.* the branch of geology that deals with rocks, including their origin, history, structure, chemical composition, classification, etc. **–,pet•ro'log•i•cal** [,pɛtrə'lɒdʒɪkəl], *adj.* **–,pet•ro'log•i•cal•ly,** *adv.*

PET scan positron emission tomography, a type of imaging that shows ongoing processes of brain activity such as blood flow, glucose metabolism, etc. **–PET scanner.**

pet•ti•coat ['pɛti,kout] *n.* **1** a skirt worn beneath a dress or outer skirt by women or girls. **2** a skirt. **3** (*adjl.*) female; feminine: *petticoat government.* ⟨originally, *petty coat* little coat⟩

pet•ti•fog ['pɛtɪ,fɒg] *v.* **-fogged, -fog•ging. 1** use petty, underhanded, or dishonest methods: *a pettifogging lawyer.* **2** quibble over small details. ⟨back formation from *pettifogger*⟩

pet•ti•fog•ger ['pɛtɪ,fɒgər] *n.* **1** a lawyer who uses petty, underhanded, or dishonest methods; shyster. **2** any person who uses petty, underhanded, or dishonest methods. **3** a person who quibbles over small details. ⟨apparently < *petty* + obs. *fogger* (origin unknown)⟩ **—'pet•ti,fog•ge•ry,** *n.*

pet•tish ['pɛtɪʃ] *adj.* peevish; cross: *a pettish reply, a pettish child.* ⟨< *pet*[2]⟩ **—'pet•tish•ly,** *adv.* **—'pet•tish•ness,** *n.*

pet•ty ['pɛti] *adj.* **-ti•er, -ti•est. 1** having little importance or value; small: *She insisted on telling me all her petty troubles.* **2** mean; narrow-minded; making a fuss over small matters. **3** lower in rank or importance; subordinate; minor: *a petty official, a petty offence.* ⟨ME < OF *petit* < VL stem *pit-* little. Doublet of PETIT.⟩ **—'pet•ti•ly,** *adv.* **—'pet•ti•ness,** *n.*
☛ *Hom.* PETIT.

petty cash 1 small sums of money spent or received. **2** a sum of money kept on hand to pay small expenses.

petty jury PETIT JURY.

petty larceny PETIT LARCENY.

petty officer 1 *Canadian Forces.* in Maritime Command, either of two ranks: petty officer 2nd class (*abbrev.*: P2), equivalent to a sergeant; and petty officer 1st class (*abbrev.*: P1), equivalent to a warrant officer. See chart of ranks in the Appendix. **2** a naval non-commissioned officer of similar rank in other countries. *Abbrev.*: P.O. or PO

pet•u•lance ['pɛtʃələns] *n.* the quality or state of being irritated by trifles; peevishness; bad humour. Also, **petulancy.**

pet•u•lant ['pɛtʃələnt] *adj.* peevish; subject to little fits of bad temper; irritable over trifles. ⟨< L *petulans, -antis,* ult. < *petere* seek, aim at⟩ **—'pet•u•lant•ly,** *adv.*

Pe•tun [pə'tun] *n., pl.* **Pe•tun. 1** a member of an extinct First Nations people who lived between Lakes Huron and Ontario, noted for their tobacco cultivation and trade. **2** the Iroquoian dialect of this people. ⟨< Cdn.F < MF *petun* tobacco⟩

pe•tu•nia [pə'tjunjə] *or* [pə'tunjə] *n.* **1** any of a genus (*Petunia*) of tropical American plants of the nightshade family cultivated for their large white, red, purple, or blue funnel-shaped flowers. **2** the flower of any of these plants. ⟨< NL < F *petun* tobacco < Tupi⟩

pew [pju] *n.* in a church, a bench for people to sit on, having a back and often fastened to the floor. In some churches the pews are separated by partitions. ⟨ME < OF *puie* < L *podia,* pl. of *podium* elevated place, balcony. See PODIUM.⟩

pe•wee ['piwi] *n.* any of several small North American flycatchers (genus *Contopus*) having greyish olive plumage. ⟨imitative⟩
☛ *Hom.* PEEWEE.

pe•wit ['piwɪt] *or* ['pjuɪt] *n.* **1** lapwing. **2** *U.S.* pewee. ⟨imitative⟩

pew•ter ['pjutər] *n.* **1** any of various alloys composed mainly of tin; especially, a dull alloy containing lead, formerly used for eating and cooking utensils. **2** dishes or other utensils made of pewter. **3** (*adjl.*) made of pewter. ⟨ME < OF *peutre*⟩

pey•o•te [pei'outi]; *Spanish,* [pe'jote] *n.* **1** any of several New World cactuses (genus *Logophora*), especially mescal. Also, **peyotl. 2** mescaline. ⟨< Mexican Sp. *peyote* < Nahuatl *peyotl,* literally, a caterpillar; from the mescal's soft, furry centre⟩

pf. 1 pfennig. **2** preferred (stock). **3** pianoforte.

pfd. preferred.

pfen•nig ['fɛnɪg]; *German,* ['pfɛnɪç] *n., pl.* **pfen•nigs, pfen•ni•ge** ['fɛnɪgə]; *German,* ['pfɛnɪgə]. **1** a unit of money in Germany, equal to 1/100 of a mark. **2** a coin worth one pfennig. ⟨< G⟩

pfg. pfennig.

pg. page.

PG 1 Parental Guidance, a movie rating informing parents that children of all ages may attend but that there may be some scenes or language considered unsuitable for young children. **2** paying guest. **3** postgraduate. **4** *Informal.* pregnant.

PG–13 Parental Guidance under thirteen, a movie rating informing parents that some scenes or language may be considered unsuitable for children under the age of thirteen.

pH *Chemistry.* a symbol used to express acid or alkaline content, used in testing water and soils, for various applications in industry, etc. A pH of 14 denotes high alkaline content, and a pH of 0 indicates high acidity; pH 7 is taken as neutral. ⟨< *p*otential of *H*ydrogen⟩

Ph phenyl.

pha•ce•lia [fə'siliə] *n.* a Canadian mountain wildflower (*Phacelia sericea*) having purple flower spikes. It blooms all summer in the western mountains.

Phae•dra ['fidrə] *n. Greek mythology.* the wife of Theseus, who falls in love with her stepson Hippolytus and, when he rejects her advances, falsely accuses him of attacking her.

Pha•ë•thon ['feiə,θɒn] *or* ['feiəθən] *n. Greek mythology.* the son of Helios, who tried for one day to drive the sun, his father's chariot. He so nearly set the earth on fire that Zeus had to strike him dead with a thunderbolt.

pha•e•ton ['feiətən] *or* ['feitən] *n.* **1** a light, four-wheeled carriage with or without a top. **2** an early open automobile of the touring-car type. ⟨< F *phaéton,* after *Phaëthon,* son of Helios⟩

-phage *combining form.* eating; devouring: *bacteriophage.* ⟨< Gk. *-phagos*⟩

phago– *combining form.* eating; devouring: *phagocyte.* Also, **phag-** before vowels.

phag•o•cyte ['fægə,sait] *n. Physiology.* a white blood corpuscle, or leucocyte, capable of absorbing and destroying waste or harmful material, such as disease microbes. ⟨< Gk. *-phagos* -eating + E *-cyte* cell (< Gk. *kytos* hollow container)⟩

-phagous *combining form.* eating or devouring ——: *anthropophagous = man-eating.*

-phagy *combining form.* practice or habit of eating or devouring ——: *icthyophagy = habit of eating fish.*

pha•lange [fə'lændʒ], ['fælәndʒ], *or* ['feilәndʒ] *n., pl.* **pha•lan•ges** [fə'lændʒiz]. *Anatomy, zoology.* PHALANX (def. 4).

pha•lan•ger [fə'lændʒər] *n.* any of various Australasian tree-climbing marsupials (family Phalangeridae) having thick, woolly fur and a long tail which in many species is prehensile. ⟨< NL < Gk. *phalangion* spiderweb < *phalanx, -angos* spider; with reference to webbed toes⟩

pha•lan•ges [fə'lændʒiz] *n.* **1** pl. of PHALANGE. **2** a plural of PHALANX. The bones of the fingers and toes are called the phalanges. See ARM and LEG for pictures.

pha•lanx ['fælæŋks] *or* ['feilæŋks] *n., pl.* **pha•lanx•es** or **pha•lan•ges** [fə'lændʒiz] (for def. 1), **pha•lanx•es** (defs. 2, 3), **pha•lan•ges** (def. 4). **1** in ancient Greece, a special battle formation of infantry fighting in close ranks with their shields joined and long spears overlapping each other. **2** a compact or closely massed body of persons, animals, or things: *a phalanx of trees.* **3** a number of persons united for a common purpose: *They were opposed in the debate by a phalanx of Conservative MPs.* **4** *Anatomy, zoology.* any one of the bones of the fingers or toes. ⟨< L < Gk.⟩ **—pha'lan•ge•al,** *adj.*

phal•a•rope ['fælə,roup] *n.* any of three species, constituting a family (Phalaropodidae) of shore birds resembling sandpipers, having a long, slender bill and lobed toes adapted for swimming. Phalaropes are noted for their reversal of the typical male and female roles: the female is larger and more brightly coloured than the male; the male rears the young. ⟨< F < NL, ult. < Gk. *phalaros* white-crested + *pous, podos* foot⟩

phal•lic ['fælɪk] *adj.* **1** of or having to do with a phallus; symbolic of male generative power. **2** of or having to do with phallicism. ⟨< Gk. *phallikós* < *phallós* penis, phallus⟩

phal•li•cism ['fælə,sɪzəm] *n.* worship of the phallus as symbolic of the generative power of nature or of male generative power.

phal•lus ['fæləs] *n., pl.* **phal•li** ['fælai] or **phal•lus•es. 1** an image or model of the penis, symbolizing the generative power of nature. **2** *Anatomy.* **a** the penis or the clitoris. **b** the undifferentiated embryonic tissue that develops into either of these organs. ⟨< L *phallus* < Gk. *phallós* penis, phallus⟩

Phan•er•o•zo•ic [,fænərə'zouɪk] *n., adj.* —*n.* the geologic eon that comprises the Paleozoic, Mesozoic, and Cenozoic eras. —*adj.* of or having to do with this eon. ⟨< Gk. *phaneros* visible (< *phanein* appear) + *zōē* life⟩

phan•tasm ['fæn,tæzəm] *n.* **1** a thing seen only in one's imagination; unreal fancy: *the phantasms of a dream.* **2** a supposed appearance of an absent person, living or dead. **3** a deceiving likeness (of something). ⟨< L < Gk. *phantasma* image, ult. < *phainein* show. Doublet of PHANTOM.⟩

phan•tas•ma•go•ria [fæn,tæzmə'gɔriə] *n.* **1** a shifting scene of real things, illusions, imaginary fancies, deceptions, and the like: *the phantasmagoria of a dream.* **2** a display of optical illusions in which figures increase or decrease in size, fade away, and pass into each other. **3** any swiftly changing scene comprising many elements. ⟨< Gk. *phantasma* image + ? *ageirein* assemble⟩ **—phan,tas•ma'go•ri•cal** or **phan,tas•ma'go•ric,** *adj.*

phan•tas•mal [fæn'tæzməl] *adj.* of, having to do with, or being a phantasm; unreal; imaginary. Also, **phantasmic**.

phan•ta•sy ['fæntəsi] *or* ['fæntəzi] *n., pl.* **-sies.** See FANTASY.

phan•tom ['fæntəm] *n., adj. —n.* **1** an illusory image of the mind: *phantoms of a dream.* **2** a vague, dim, or shadowy appearance; ghost; illusion or spectre. **3** a mere show; appearance without material substance: *a phantom of a government.*
—adj. like a ghost; unreal: *a phantom ship.* ⟨ME < OF *fantosme* < VL < Gk. *phantasma* image. Doublet of PHANTASM.⟩

Phar•aoh ['færou] *or* ['fɛrou] *n.* a title given to the kings of ancient Egypt.
☛ *Hom.* FARO, FARROW.

Phar•aon•ic or **phar•aon•ic** [fæ'rɒnɪk] *or* [fɛ'rɒnɪk], [,færei'ɒnɪk] *or* [,fɛrei'ɒnɪk] *adj.* **1** like a Pharaoh: *Pharaonic splendour.* **2** overwhelmingly large or impressive: *a home of pharaonic size.* **3** tyrannical; oppressive: *pharaonic behaviour.*

Phar•i•sa•ic [,færə'seiɪk] *or* [,fɛrə'seiɪk] *adj.* **1** of or having to do with the Pharisees. **2 pharisaic, a** making an outward show of religion or morals without the real spirit; hypocritical. **b** thinking oneself more moral than others. Also, **pharisaical.**
—,phar•i'sa•i•cal•ly, *adv.*

Phar•i•sa•ism ['færəsei,ɪzəm] *or* ['fɛrəsei,ɪzəm] *n.* **1** the doctrine and practice of the Pharisees. **2 pharisaism, a** rigid observance of the external forms of religion without genuine piety; hypocrisy. **b** self-righteousness.

Phar•i•see ['færə,si] *or* ['fɛrə,si] *n.* **1** in ancient times, a member of a Jewish sect that was very strict in keeping to the tradition and laws of its religion. **2 pharisee, a** a person who makes a show of religion rather than following its spirit. **b** a person who considers himself or herself much better than others. ⟨OE *farisē* < L *pharisaeus* < Gk. *pharisaios* < Aramaic *perishaiya* separated⟩

phar•i•see•ism ['færəsi,ɪzəm] *or* ['fɛrəsi,ɪzəm] *n.* pharisaism.

phar•ma•care ['fɑrmə,kɛr] *n. Cdn.* a program administered by some provincial governments whereby the cost to the patient of prescription drugs is partially or completely subsidized. The amount of subsidy may depend on factors such as age, welfare status, and the condition for which the drug is prescribed. ⟨< *pharma(ceutical)* + *care*⟩

phar•ma•ceu•ti•cal [,fɑrmə'sutəkəl] *adj., n. —adj.* **1** of or having to do with pharmacy or pharmacists. **2** of or having to do with drugs: *pharmaceutical treatment.* Also, **pharmaceutic.**
—n. a medicinal drug; pharmaceutical preparation. ⟨< LL < Gk. *pharmakeutikos,* ult. < *pharmakon* drug, poison⟩

phar•ma•ceu•tics [,fɑrmə'sutɪks] *n.* (*used with a singular verb*) PHARMACY (def. 1).

phar•ma•cist ['fɑrməsɪst] *n.* a person who is qualified to prepare and dispense medicinal drugs; druggist.

phar•ma•co•ge•net•ics [,fɑrməkədʒə'nɛtɪks] *n.* the study of genetic variation in response to drugs.

phar•ma•col•o•gist [,fɑrmə'kɒlədʒɪst] *n.* a person trained in pharmacology, especially one whose work it is.

phar•ma•col•o•gy [,fɑrmə'kɒlədʒi] *n.* the science of drugs, including their sources and properties, and their preparation, uses, and effects. ⟨< Gk. *pharmakon* drug + E *-logy*⟩
—,phar•ma•co'log•i•cal, *adj.* **—,phar•ma•co'log•i•cal•ly,** *adv.*

phar•ma•co•poe•ia [,fɑrməkə'piə] *n.* **1** a book containing an official list and description of drugs and medicines. **2** a stock or collection of drugs. ⟨< Gk. *pharmakopoiia* < *pharmakon* drug + *poieein* make⟩

phar•ma•cy ['fɑrməsi] *n., pl.* **-cies. 1** the art and practice of preparing and dispensing drugs and medicines. **2** a drugstore. **3** the department of a hospital where drugs, medicines, etc. are prepared. ⟨< LL < Gk. *pharmakeia,* ult. < *pharmakon* drug⟩

Pha•ros ['fɛrɒs] *n.* **1** a small peninsula near Alexandria in N Egypt, site of an ancient lighthouse that was one of the Seven Wonders of the Ancient World. **2** the lighthouse that stood on this site. **3 pharos,** any lighthouse or beacon intended to guide sailors.

pha•ryn•gal [fə'rɪŋgəl] *adj.* pharyngeal.

pha•ryn•ge•al [fə'rɪndʒiəl], [,færɪn'dʒiəl], *or* [,fɛrɪn'dʒiəl] *adj., n. —adj.* **1** having to do with the pharynx. **2** located or produced in the region of the pharynx.
—n. Phonetics. a speech sound produced in the region of the pharynx. Also, **pharyngal.**

phar•yn•gi•tis [,færɪn'dʒəitɪs] *or* [,fɛrɪn'dʒəitɪs] *n. Pathology.* an inflammation of the mucous membrane of the pharynx. ⟨< NL < Gk. *pharynx, -yngos* pharynx + *-itis*⟩

pharyngo– *combining form.* referring to the pharynx or the pharyngeal cavity: *pharyngoscope.* ⟨< Gk.⟩

pha•ryn•go•scope [fə'rɪŋgə,skoup] *n.* an instrument used to examine the pharynx. **—pha,ryn•go'scop•ic** [fə,rɪŋgə'skɒpɪk], *adj.* **—,pha•ryn'go•sco•py** [,færɪŋ'gɒskəpi] *or* [,fɛrɪŋ'gɒskəpi], *n.*

phar•ynx ['færɪŋks] *or* ['fɛrɪŋks] *n., pl.* **phar•ynx•es** or **pha•ryn•ges** [fə'rɪndʒiz]. *Anatomy.* in vertebrates, the muscular tube connecting the mouth cavity with the esophagus. The pharynx is part of the alimentary canal. See WINDPIPE for picture. ⟨< NL < Gk. *pharynx* throat⟩

phase [feiz] *n., v. —n.* **1** one of the changing states or stages of development of a person or thing. The pupa is a phase in the life cycle of the moth. **2** one side, part, or view (of a subject): *What phase of mathematics are you studying now?* **3** *Astronomy.* the shape of the moon or of a planet as it is seen at a given time. The last quarter is a phase of the moon. **4** *Physics.* a particular stage or point in a recurring sequence of movements or changes, considered in relation to a starting point or normal position. The current in all parts of a series circuit is in the same phase. **5** *Zoology.* **a** a marked variation, especially in colour of fur, plumage, etc. in an individual animal or a subgroup of animals that distinguishes it from typical members of the group to which it belongs. A leopard of the black colour phase is usually called a panther. **b** an individual or subgroup distinguishable in this way. The blue goose is a colour phase of the snow goose. **6** *Biology.* one of the distinct states in meiosis or mitosis.
—v. plan or carry out (an enterprise or project) in orderly stages: *They phased the troop withdrawal so as to avoid civic disruption.*
phase in, bring about (an innovation or reform of existing conditions) in orderly stages.
phase out, eliminate (an old system, order, etc.) gradually, in planned stages. ⟨< NL < Gk. *phasis* appearance < *phainein* show⟩
☛ *Hom.* FAZE.

phase•out ['feiz,ʌut] *n.* a gradual withdrawal; a planned discontinuation; the act of phasing out: *The phaseout went off without a hitch.*

-phasia *combining form.* a speech disorder as specified by the initial element: *aphasia, dysphasia.* ⟨< NL < Gk. *phanai* speak⟩

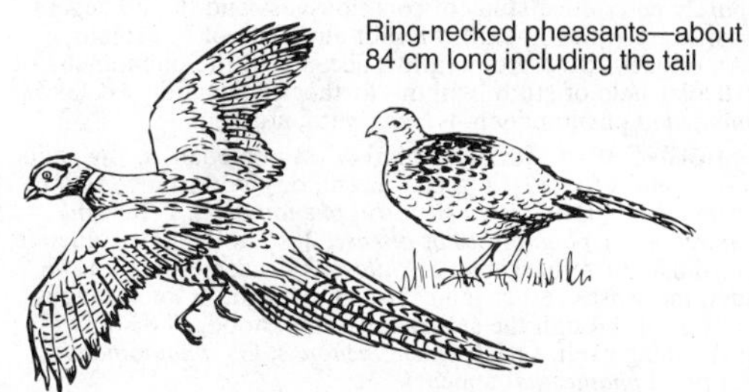
Ring-necked pheasants—about 84 cm long including the tail

pheas•ant ['fɛzənt] *n., pl.* **-ants** or (*esp. collectively*) **-ant. 1** any of various large, long-tailed game birds (family Phasianidae) native to the Old World, the male of which has brightly coloured plumage, especially the **ring-necked pheasant** (*Phasianus colchicus*). **2** any of various other Old or New World birds of the same order (Galliformes), such as various partridges or grouse; especially, in Canada, the sharp-tailed and ruffed grouse. ⟨ME < AF < Provençal *faisan* < L < Gk. *phasianos,* literally, Phasian; with reference to the river Phasis in Colchis⟩

phe•nac•e•tin [fə'næsətɪn] *n. Pharmacy.* a white, crystalline powder used to relieve fever and pain. *Formula*: $C_{10}H_{13}NO_2$ ⟨< Gk. *phainein* show + E *acet(ic)*⟩

phen•a•zine ['fɛnə,zin] *n. Chemistry.* a yellow, crystalline base used chiefly in making dyes. *Formula*: $C_6H_4N_2C_6H_4$

phen•cy•cli•dine [fɛn'səiklə,din] *n.* an anesthetic drug, an animal tranquillizer, used illicitly in various forms as a hallucinatory agent; PCP; angel dust.

phe•net•ic [fə'nɛtɪk] *adj. Biology.* based on the perceptible similarities and differences between organisms without regard to apparent genealogy. ⟨< Gk. *phanein* to show⟩
☛ *Hom.* PHONETIC.

phe•no•bar•bi•tal [ˌfinouˈbɑrbəˌtɒl] *n. Pharmacy.* a white, crystalline barbiturate drug used as a hypnotic or sedative. *Formula*: $C_{12}H_{12}N_2O_3$

phe•no•cop•y [ˈfinouˌkɒpi] *n., pl.* **-ies.** *Genetics.* a mimic of a phenotype usually determined by a certain genotype, produced instead by the interaction of environment with a different genotype.

phe•nol [ˈfinɒl] *or* [ˈfinoul] *n. Chemistry.* a white, crystalline compound produced from coal tar or chlorobenzine; CARBOLIC ACID. *Formula*: C_6H_5OH ⟨< Gk. *phainein* show + E *-ol*⟩

phe•nol•ic [fəˈnɒlɪk] *adj., n.* *—adj.* of, like, or pertaining to phenol.
—n. Chemistry. any of a group of synthetic plastics or resins, used in varnishes, coatings, etc.

phe•nol•o•gy [fɪˈnɒlədʒi] *n.* the study of the relationship between climate and naturally recurring phenomena such as the budding of plants and the migration of birds and other animals. ⟨a contraction of *phenomenology*⟩ **—pheˈnol•o•gist,** *n.*

phe•nol•phthal•ein [ˌfinɒlˈθælin] *or* [ˌfinɒlfˈθælin] *n. Chemistry, pharmacy.* a white or yellowish crystalline compound used in testing acidity, making dyes, and as a laxative. Its solution is red when basic, colourless when acid. *Formula*: $C_{20}H_{14}O_4$

phe•nom [fəˈnɒm] *n. Slang.* one who displays extraordinary talent or skill, as a sports or pop music star: *a football phenom.* ⟨shortened form for *phenomenon*⟩

phe•nom•e•na [fəˈnɒmənə] *n.* pl. of PHENOMENON.

phe•nom•e•nal [fəˈnɒmənəl] *adj.* **1** of or having to do with a phenomenon or phenomena. **2** having the nature of or being a phenomenon. **3** extraordinary: *a phenomenal memory.* **—pheˈnom•e•nal•ly,** *adv.*

phe•nom•e•nal•ism [fəˈnɒmənəˌlɪzəm] *n. Philosophy.* the theory that knowledge is limited to physical and mental phenomena (things as they are experienced) and either that there is no reality behind the phenomena or that there is a reality, but it is unknowable. **—pheˈnom•e•nal•ist,** *n.* **—pheˌnom•e•nalˈist•ic,** *adj.*

phe•nom•e•no•log•i•cal [fəˌnɒmənəˈlɒdʒɪkəl] **1** of or having to do with phenomenology or phenomenalism. **2** of or having to do with a phenomenon or phenomena; phenomenal. **—pheˌnom•e•noˈlog•i•cal•ly,** *adv.*

phe•nom•e•nol•o•gy [fəˌnɒməˈnɒlədʒi] *n.* **1** *Philosophy.* the purely descriptive study of consciousness and the objects of consciousness (phenomena), without any attempt to explain causes, origins, etc. **2** a descriptive account of the phenomena of a particular field of study, with no further explanation. ⟨< Gk. *phainomenon* phenomenon + *logos* word, study⟩

phe•nom•e•non [fəˈnɒməˌnɒn] *or* [fəˈnɒmənən] *n.* **-na** (defs. 1 & 3) or **-nons** (def. 2). **1** a fact, event, or circumstance that can be observed: *Lightning is an electrical phenomenon. Fever and inflammation are phenomena of disease.* **2** something or someone extraordinary or remarkable. **3** *Philosophy.* **a** something known through the senses rather than through thought. **b** something as it is observed through the senses and understood, as distinct from the thing itself. ⟨< LL *phænomenon* < Gk. *phainomenon,* neut. ppr. of *phainesthai* appear⟩

phe•no•type [ˈfinəˌtəip] *n. Genetics.* **1** the physical, especially visible, characteristics or properties of an organism as determined by the interaction of its genetic inheritance (genotype) and its environment. **2** a group of organisms sharing such characteristics or properties. **3** any member of such a group. **4** the expression of a particular genotype. ⟨< Gk. *phaino-* < *phainein* show + E *type*⟩ **—ˌphe•noˈtyp•ic** [-ˈtɪpɪk], *adj.*

phen•yl [ˈfɛnəl] *or* [ˈfinəl] *n. Chemistry.* a univalent radical derived from benzene, that forms the basis of phenol, aniline, and other aromatic compounds. *Formula*: C_6H_5 *Abbrev.*: Ph
☛ *Hom.* FENNEL.

phen•yl•al•a•nine [ˌfɛnəlˈæləˌnin] *or* [ˌfinəlˈæləˌnin] *n. Biochemistry.* a water soluble crystalline amino acid occurring in proteins, especially egg white and skim milk, and necessary for the nutrition of humans and most other animals. *Formula*: $C_6H_5CH_2CH(NH_2)COOH$

phen•yl•bu•ta•zone [ˌfɛnəlˈbjutəˌzoun] *or* [ˌfinəlˈbjutəˌzoun] *n. Pharmacy.* a potent white powder used as an analgesic painkiller and to reduce inflammation in rheumatoid arthritis, gout, etc. *Formula*: $C_{19}H_{20}N_2O_2$

phen•yl•ke•to•nu•ria [ˌfɛnəlˌkitəˈnjʊriə] *or* [ˌfinəlˌkitəˈnjʊriə] *n. Pathology.* a genetic disorder caused by faulty metabolism of phenylalanine. If left untreated, the accumulation of toxic metabolic substances causes severe mental retardation in infants. *Abbrev.*: PKU ⟨< *phenyl* + Gk. *keton* acetone + *ourein* < *ouron* urine⟩ **—ˌphen•ylˌke•toˈnur•ic,** *adj.*

pher•o•mone [ˈfɛrəˌmoun] *n. Biochemistry.* a chemical substance exuded by certain organisms, such as insects, that serves as a means of communication with others of the same species, affecting their behaviour, etc. ⟨< Gk. *pherein* carry + E *(hor)mone*⟩ **—ˌpher•oˈmon•al,** *adj.*

phew [fju] *interj.* an exclamation of disgust, impatience, surprise, relief, etc.
☛ *Hom.* FEW.

phi [faɪ] *or* [fi] *n.* the twenty-first letter of the Greek alphabet (Φ, ϕ).
☛ *Hom.* FIE.

phi•al [ˈfaɪəl] *n.* a small bottle; vial. ⟨ME *fiole* < OF < Prov. *fiola* < LL < L *phiala* < Gk. *phialē* a broad flat vessel⟩

Phi Be•ta Kap•pa [ˈfaɪ ˈbeitə ˈkæpə] *or* [ˈbitə] *U.S.* **1** an honour society composed of college students and graduates who have ranked high in scholarship. **2** a member of this society: *Their son is a Phi Beta Kappa.*

Phil. **1** philosophy. **2** Philippine.

phi•lan•der [fəˈlændər] *v.* make love without serious intentions; flirt. ⟨originally n., < Gk. *philandros* < *philos* loving + *anēr, andros* man; apparently taken as 'lover', used as a character name in drama and poetry⟩ **—phiˈlan•der•er,** *n.*

phil•an•throp•ic [ˌfɪlənˈθrɒpɪk] *adj.* of, having to do with, or characterized by philanthropy; charitable; benevolent. **—ˌphil•anˈthrop•i•cal•ly,** *adv.*

phi•lan•thro•pist [fəˈlænθrəpɪst] *n.* a person who practises philanthropy, especially a wealthy person who supports charitable organizations, etc.

phi•lan•thro•py [fəˈlænθrəpi] *n., pl.* **-pies. 1** love of people, especially as shown by practical kindness and active efforts to help humanity: *Charitable institutions appeal to one's philanthropy.* **2** a philanthropic act, institution, etc. ⟨< LL < Gk. *philanthrōpia,* ult. < *philos* loving + *anthrōpos* man⟩

phi•lat•e•list [fəˈlætəlɪst] *n.* a person who makes a hobby of philately; stamp collector.

phi•lat•e•ly [fəˈlætəli] *n.* the collecting and studying of postage stamps and, often, envelopes or postcards with postmarked stamps on them; stamp collecting. ⟨< F *philatélie,* ult. < Gk. *philos* loving + *ateleia* exemption from tax; the stamp indicated the tax was paid⟩ **—ˌphil•aˈtel•ic** [ˌfɪləˈtɛlɪk], *adj.*

-phile *combining form.* a lover of ——; a person who is fond of ——: *discophile = a person who is fond of records, or discs.* Also, **-phil.** ⟨< F *-phile,* ult. < Gk. *philos* loving⟩

phil•har•mon•ic [ˌfɪlhɑrˈmɒnɪk] *or* [ˌfɪlɑrˈmɒnɪk] *adj., n.* *—adj.* **1** devoted to music; loving music. A musical club is often called a philharmonic society. **2** given by a philharmonic society: *a philharmonic concert.*
—n. **1** a philharmonic society or concert. **2 Philharmonic,** a symphony orchestra: *the London Philharmonic.* ⟨< F *philharmonique,* ult. < Gk. *philos* loving + *harmonia* music⟩

-philia *combining form.* **1** tendency toward ——: *hemophilia.* **2** extraordinarily strong or unnatural attraction toward ——: *Anglophilia, necrophilia.* ⟨< Gk. *philia* friendship, attraction⟩

Phi•lip•pic [fəˈlɪpɪk] *n.* **1** any of several orations by Demosthenes denouncing King Philip II of Macedonia and arousing the Athenians to resist Philip's growing power. **2** any of several orations by the Roman statesman, Cicero, denouncing Mark Antony. **3 philippic,** a bitter attack in words. ⟨< L *Philippicus* < Gk. *Philippikos* having to do with *Phillipos* Philip⟩

Phil•ip•pine [ˈfɪləˌpin] *adj.* of or having to do with the Philippines or its inhabitants. Also, **Filipine, Filipino.**

Phil•ip•pines, the [ˈfɪləˌpinz] *n.* a country consisting of 7083 islands in the SW Pacific Ocean, SE of China.

Phi•lis•ti•a [fəˈlɪstiə] *n.* **1** the land of the ancient Philistines. **2** a place inhabited or frequented by people with uncultured tastes.

Phi•lis•tine [fəˈlɪstən], [ˈfɪləˌstin], *or* [ˈfɪləˌstaɪn] *n., adj.* *—n.* **1** a member of the non-Semitic people who inhabited ancient Philistia. **2** Sometimes, **philistine,** a person who has commonplace ideas and tastes and is indifferent to or contemptuous of artistic or intellectual values.
—adj. **1** of the Philistines. **2** Usually, **philistine,** smugly commonplace and uncultured. ⟨< LL *Philistini,* pl, < Gk. *Philistinoi* < Hebrew *p'lishtim,* rel. to *Palestine*⟩

Phil•lips [ˈfɪlɪps] *n. Trademark.* a type of screwdriver (**Phillips screwdriver**) having a cross-shaped tapered tip designed to fit into the **Phillips screw,** which has two slots crossed at right angles at the centre of the head. ⟨after N.F. *Phillips* (d. 1958), its inventor⟩

phil•is•tin•ism [ˈfɪləstə,nɪzəm] *or* [fəˈlɪstə,nɪzəm] *n.* the character, habits, or views of persons indifferent to artistic or intellectual values. Also, **Philistinism.**

philo– *combining form,* loving; attracted to; disposed toward: *philology.* ⟨< Gk. *philos* loving⟩

phil•o•den•dron [,fɪləˈdɛndrən] *n., pl.* **-drons** or **-dra** [-drə]. any of a genus (*Philodendron*) of tropical plants of the arum family that are cultivated for their thick, glossy leaves. Philodendrons are popular house plants because they thrive with little care. ⟨< NL *Philodendron* the genus name < Gk. *philodendron,* neut. of *philodendros* < *philos* fond of + *dendron* tree, because it clings to trees⟩

phi•lol•o•gist [fəˈlɒlədʒɪst] *n.* a person trained in philology, especially one whose work it is.

phi•lol•o•gy [fəˈlɒlədʒi] *n.* **1** the historical and comparative study of languages, especially through literature and written documents. Compare LINGUISTICS. **2** the study of old literary texts, to find out their age, meaning, etc. **3** formerly, linguistics, especially comparative and historical. **4** originally, love of scholarship and writing. ⟨< L < Gk. *philologia,* ult. < *philos* loving + *logos* word, speech, story⟩ **—,phil•o'log•i•cal** [,fɪləˈlɒdʒɪkəl], *adj.* **—,phil•o'log•i•cal•ly,** *adv.*

Phil•o•mel [ˈfɪlə,mɛl] *n. Poetic.* nightingale. Also, **philomel.** ⟨< L *philomela* < Gk. *philomēlā*⟩

Phil•o•me•la [,fɪləˈmilə] *n.* **1** *Greek mythology.* an Athenian princess who was turned into a nightingale and, as a bird, continued to lament the tragedy of her life. **2** *Poetic.* nightingale.

phil•o•pro•gen•e•tive [,fɪlouprouˈdʒɛnɪtɪv] *adj.* **1** prolific in the production of offspring. **2** concerning or characterized by love of offspring, especially one's own.

phi•los•o•pher [fəˈlɒsəfər] *n.* **1** a person who studies philosophy. **2** a person who has a system of philosophy. **3 a** a person who shows the calmness of philosophy under difficult conditions, accepting life and making the best of it. **b** a person who likes to philosophize. ⟨ME *philosophre* < OF *philosophe* < L *philosophus* < Gk. *philosophos* lover of wisdom < *philos* loving + *sophos* wise⟩

philosophers' stone an imaginary stone, substance, or chemical preparation sought after by alchemists in the belief that it had the power to change base metals into gold or silver.

phil•o•soph•ic [,fɪləˈsɒfɪk] *adj.* **1** of or having to do with philosophers or philosophy. **2** devoted to or skilled in philosophy: *a philosophic society.* **3** like a philosopher, especially in being wise or in taking a calm, patient attitude in the face of trouble: *a philosophic person.* Also, **philosophical.** **—,phil•o'soph•i•cal•ly,** *adv.*

phi•los•o•phize [fəˈlɒsə,faɪz] *v.* **-phized, -phiz•ing. 1** think or reason as a philosopher does; try to understand and explain things: *philosophizing about life and death.* **2** moralize; express truisms or otherwise engage in more or less superficial philosophical talk. **—phi'los•o,phiz•er,** *n.*

phi•los•o•phy [fəˈlɒsəfi] *n., pl.* **-phies. 1** the study of the truth or principles underlying all knowledge; study of the most general causes and principles of the universe. **2** an explanation or theory of the universe: *Hegelian philosophy.* **3** any of the three main branches of study into which philosophy is normally divided: natural philosophy, moral philosophy, and metaphysical philosophy. **4** a system for guiding life, such as a body of principles of conduct, religious beliefs, or traditions. **5** a set of broad, general principles of a particular subject: *a philosophy of history, the philosophy of science.* **6** a treatise covering these principles. **7** a calm and reasonable attitude; the practice of accepting things as they are and making the best of them. ⟨< L < Gk. *philosophia* love of wisdom, ult. < *philos* loving + *sophos* wise⟩

phil•tre [ˈfɪltər] *n., v.* **-tred, -tring.** *—n.* **1** a potion, drug, or charm supposed to arouse sexual love, especially toward a particular person. **2** any magic drink.
—v. bewitch or arouse by means of a philtre. Also, **philter.** ⟨< F < L *philtrum* < Gk. *philtron* love charm, ult. < *philos* loving⟩
☛ *Hom.* FILTER.

phle•bi•tis [fləˈbaitɪs] *n. Pathology.* inflammation of the wall of a vein. ⟨< NL < Gk. *phleps, phlebos* vein + *-itis*⟩ **—phle'bit•ic** [-ˈbɪtɪk], *adj.*

phle•bot•o•mist [fləˈbɒtəmɪst] *n.* a specialist in phlebotomy.

phle•bot•o•my [fləˈbɒtəmi] *n.* the opening of a vein to let blood; bleeding. ⟨ME *flebotomia* < OF *flebothomie* < LL < Gk. *phlebotomia,* ult. < *phleps, phlebos* vein + *-tomos* cutting⟩ **—phle'bot•om,ize,** *v.*

phlegm [flɛm] *n.* **1** the thick discharge of mucus from the nose and throat during a cold or other respiratory disease. **2** the one of the four humours of ancient physiology believed to cause sluggishness. **3** sluggishness or indifference. **4** coolness or calmness. ⟨ME *fleume* < OF < LL < Gk. *phlegma* clammy humour (resulting from heat) < *phlegein* burn⟩ **—'phleg•my,** *adj.*

phleg•mat•ic [flɛgˈmætɪk] *adj.* **1** sluggish or indifferent. **2** cool or calm: *John is phlegmatic; he never seems to get excited about anything.* ⟨< LL *phlegmaticus* < Gk. *phlegmatikos* < *phlegma.* See PHLEGM.⟩ **—phleg'mat•i•cal•ly,** *adv.*

phlo•em or **phlo•ëm** [ˈflouəm] *n.* the soft tissue in the vascular system of plants or trees, consisting mainly of sieve tubes and parenchyma cells, that serves to transport and store food materials and help support the plant. Compare XYLEM. ⟨< G < Gk. *phloos* bark (var. of *phloios*) + *-ema*⟩

phlo•gist•ic [fləˈdʒɪstɪk] *adj.* **1** of or having to do with phlogiston. **2** *Pathology.* inflammatory.

phlo•gis•ton [fləˈdʒɪstɒn] *or* [fləˈdʒɪstən] *n.* a non-existent element causing flammability, once thought to exist in all things that burn. ⟨< NL < Gk. *phlogiston,* neut. adj., flammable, ult. < *phlox, phlogos* flame⟩

phlox [flɒks] *n.* **1** any of a genus (*Phlox*) of annual or perennial plants cultivated for their showy clusters of red, white, or purple flowers. **2** (*adjl.*) designating the family (Polemoniaceae) of plants that includes phlox and Jacob's-ladder. ⟨< L < Gk. *phlox,* a kind of plant, literally, flame⟩

-phobe *combining form.* a person who has irrational hatred or fear of ——: *Anglophobe = a person who hates or fears the English or England.* ⟨< L < F *phobe,* learned borrowing < L *phobus* < Gk. *phobos* panic, fear⟩

pho•bi•a [ˈfoubiə] *n.* an irrational, exaggerated fear of or aversion to a particular thing or situation.

-phobia *combining form.* extreme or irrational hatred or fear of ——: *claustrophobia.* ⟨< Gk. *phobia* < *phobos.* See -PHOBE.⟩

pho•bic [ˈfoubɪk] *adj.* of, having to do with, or having a phobia.

Pho•bos [ˈfoubəs] *n. Astronomy.* the larger of the two satellites or moons of Mars, the other being Deimos.

pho•cine [ˈfousaɪn] *or* [ˈfousɪn] *adj. Zoology.* of or having to do with seals.

phoe•be [ˈfibi] *n.* any of several North American flycatchers (genus *Sayornis*), such as the **eastern phoebe** (*S. phoebe*), having a greyish brown back, yellowish white under parts, and a small crest. ⟨imitative, but spelling adapted to that of *Phoebe*⟩

Phoe•be [ˈfibi] *n.* **1** *Greek mythology.* Artemis, goddess of the moon. **2** *Poetic.* the moon. **3** the ninth, outermost satellite of Saturn.

Phoe•bus [ˈfibəs] *n.* **1** *Greek mythology.* Apollo, god of the sun. **2** *Poetic.* the sun.

Phoe•ni•cia [fəˈniʃə] *n.* an ancient area of city-states at the E end of the Mediterranean, in the general region of Syria, Lebanon, and Israel.

Phoe•ni•cian [fəˈniʃən] *n., adj.* *—n.* **1** a native or inhabitant of Phoenicia. **2** the Semitic language of ancient Phoenicia.
—adj. of or having to do with Phoenicia, its people, or their language.

phoe•nix [ˈfinɪks] *n.* **1** a mythical bird, the only one of its kind, said to live 500 or 600 years, burn itself to ashes on a funeral pyre, and rise again from the ashes, fresh and beautiful, for another long life; a symbol of immortality. **2** someone or something of great beauty and wonder, or that has come, renewed or restored, through calamity or apparent destruction. **3** *Astronomy.* **Phoenix,** a southern constellation between Grus and Eridanus. ⟨ME < OF *fenix* < L *phoenix* < Gk. *phoinix,* probably < Egyptian *bonū, bennu* heron⟩

phon•ate [ˈfouneit] *v.* **-at•ed, -at•ing. 1** *Phonetics.* produce a speech sound or sounds, especially a voiced continuant or a vowel. **2** vocalize. **—pho'na•tion,** *n.*

phone[1] [foun] *n., v.* **phoned, phon•ing.** *Informal.* telephone. ⟨shortened form⟩

phone[2] [foun] *n. Phonetics.* a speech sound considered as a physical event without reference to its function in the sound system of any language. ⟨< Gk. *phōnē* sound⟩

-phone *combining form.* **1** sound: *telephone = sound from far.* **2 a** speaker. **b** speaking: *the Anglophone community.* **3** a telephone with ——: *speakerphone.* ⟨< Gk. *phōnē* sound⟩

phone book *Informal.* telephone book; telephone directory.

pho•neme ['founim] *n. Linguistics.* one of a set of sounds used to distinguish the individual words of a language from one another. The words *cat* and *bat* are contrasted by their initial phonemes [k] and [b]. A phoneme comprises several different sounds (allophones), the differences between which cannot be used to distinguish one word from another. The *p* in *pit* and the *p* in *spit*, though differing in pronunciation, belong to the one English phoneme [p]. ⟨< Gk. *phōnēma* a sound < *phōnein* to sound < *phōnē* voice⟩

pho•nem•ic [fə'nimɪk] *adj.* having to do with phonemes: *a phonemic transcription.* **—pho,nem•i•ci'za•tion,** *n.*

pho•nem•ics [fə'nimɪks] *n.* (*used with a singular verb*) the description of the phonemes of a language or of phonemic systems in general. Compare PHONETICS.

pho•net•ic [fə'nɛtɪk] *adj.* **1** of or having to do with speech sounds as they are actually produced, without reference to their occurrence in the sound system of a language: *phonetic laws.* **2 a** representing the sounds of speech. In this dictionary the phonetic symbol [ə] stands for the vowel sound in the second syllable of *taken, pencil, lemon, circus.* **b** of a system of spelling, having each sound represented by one letter and each letter representing one sound: *a phonetic alphabet.* ⟨< NL < Gk. *phōnētikos*, ult. < *phōnē* sound⟩ **—pho'net•i•cal•ly,** *adv.*
☛ *Hom.* PHENETIC.

pho•ne•ti•cian [,founə'tɪʃən] *n.* a person trained in phonetics, especially one whose work it is.

pho•net•ics [fə'nɛtɪks] *n.* (*used with a singular verb*) *Linguistics.* **1** the scientific study, description, and classification of speech sounds in general. Compare PHONEMICS. **2** the study of all the sounds of a particular language. **3** a system of symbols for transcribing these sounds.

phon•ic ['fɒnɪk] *or* ['founɪk] *adj.* **1** of or having to do with sound; acoustic. **2** of sounds made in speech; phonetic. **3** of or having to do with phonics. ⟨< Gk. *phōnē* sound⟩
—'phon•i•cal•ly, *adv.*

phon•ics ['fɒnɪks] *or* ['founɪks] *n.* (*used with a singular verb*) **1** a method of teaching people to read or pronounce words by learning the relationship between the sounds of the language and the letters or groups of letters used to represent them. **2** the science of sound; acoustics.

phono– *combining form.* sound or sounds: *phonology.* ⟨< Gk. *phōnē* sound⟩

pho•no•gram ['founə,græm] *n.* a character or symbol representing a single speech sound, syllable, or word.
—,pho•no'gram•ic, *adj.* **—,pho•no'gram•i•cal•ly,** *adv.*

pho•no•graph ['founə,græf] *n.* RECORD PLAYER.

pho•no•graph•ic [,founə'græfɪk] *adj.* **1** for, having to do with, or produced by a phonograph. **2** of or having to do with phonography. **—,pho•no'graph•i•cal•ly,** *adv.*

pho•nog•ra•phy [fə'nɒgrəfi] *n.* **1** the art of writing according to sound; phonetic spelling. **2** phonetic shorthand.

pho•no•log•i•cal rule [,founə'lɒdʒɪkəl] a principle of phonology that one sound or group of sounds is substituted for another in a given phonological environment.

pho•nol•o•gist [fə'nɒlədʒɪst] *n.* a person trained in phonology, especially one whose work it is.

pho•nol•o•gy [fə'nɒlədʒi] *n.* **1** the study of human speech sounds, especially of their systems and rules of interaction and historical changes in particular languages. **2** the sounds and sound system of a given language at a particular time.
—,pho•no'log•i•cal [,founə-] *or* [,fɒnə-], *adj.*
—,pho•no'log•i•cal•ly, *adv.*

pho•nom•e•ter [fə'nɒmətər] *n.* an instrument for measuring the intensity of sound. **—,pho•no'met•ric** [,founə'mɛtrɪk], *adj.*
—pho'nom•e•try, *n.*

pho•non ['founɒn] *n. Physics.* one unit, or quantum, of vibrational energy, usually associated with the transfer of heat energy among atoms in crystalline materials. ⟨< *phon*(*o*)- + *-on* as in *photon*⟩

pho•ny ['founi] *adj.* **-ni•er, -ni•est;** *n., pl.* **-nies.** *Informal.*
—adj. not genuine; counterfeit; fake.
—n. a fake; pretender. Also, **phoney** (*pl.* **-neys**) ⟨< ? var. of *fawney*, a gilt brass ring used by swindlers < Irish Gaelic *fáinne* ring⟩ **—'pho•ni•ness,** *n.*

-phony *combining form* (*used to construct abstract nouns from nouns ending in* **-phone**). ——sound: *telephony* < *telephone.*

phoo•ey ['fui] *interj. Slang.* an exclamation of contempt or distaste. ⟨< Yiddish < G *pfui*⟩

-phore *combining form.* a thing that carries ——: *semaphore = a device that carries signals.* ⟨< Gk. *-phoros* < *pherein* carry⟩

phos•gene ['fɒsdʒin] *or* ['fɒz,dʒin] *n. Chemistry.* a colourless, poisonous gas, a compound of carbon monoxide and chlorine; carbonyl chloride. *Formula*: $COC1_2$ ⟨< Gk. *phōs* light + *-genēs* born⟩

phos•phate ['fɒsfeit] *n. Chemistry.* **1** a salt or ester of an acid containing phosphorus. **2** *Agriculture.* a fertilizer containing such salts. **3** a drink made of carbonated water flavoured with fruit syrup, and containing a little phosphoric acid. ⟨< F *phosphate* < *phosphore* phosphorus⟩ **—phos'phat•ic** [fɒs'fætɪk], *adj.*

phos•phat•u•ria [,fɒsfə'tjʊriə] *or* [,fɒsfə'tʊriə] *n. Pathology.* the presence of excessive phosphates in the urine.

phos•phide ['fɒsfaɪd] *n. Chemistry.* a compound of phosphorus with another element or a radical.

phos•phine ['fɒs,fin] *n.* **1** *Chemistry.* a colourless, flammable, poisonous gas, hydrogen phosphide, having the smell of garlic. *Formula:* PH_2 **2** a synthetically produced yellow dye.

phos•phite ['fɒsfəit] *n. Chemistry.* a salt or ester of phosphorous acid.

phospho– *combining form.* indicating the presence of phosphorous acid or phosphoric acid in the substance indicated: *phospholipid*. Also, especially before a vowel, **phos-.** ⟨< *phosphorus*⟩

phos•pho•lip•id [,fɒsfou'lɪpɪd] *n. Biochemistry.* any of a group of lipids or fatty compounds, such as lecithin, composed of phosphoric esters and found in living cells; subjected to hydrolysis, they yield phosphoric acid, an alcohol, fatty acids, and a nitrogenous base.

phos•phor ['fɒsfər] *n.* **1** a phosphorescent substance, especially one that emits light when subjected to radiation. See CATHODE RAY TUBE and VACUUM TUBE for pictures. **2** phosphorus. **3** any phosphorescent or fluorescent substance. ⟨< F *phosphore* < NL *phosphorus.* See PHOSPHORUS.⟩

Phos•phor ['fɒsfər] *n. Poetic.* Venus; the morning star. ⟨< L *Phosphorus* < Gk. *Phōsphóros* the morning star⟩

phos•pho•rate ['fɒsfə,reit] *v.* **-rat•ed, -rat•ing.** *Chemistry.* combine or impregnate with phosphorus.

phos•pho•resce [,fɒsfə'rɛs] *v.* **-resced, -resc•ing.** be luminous without noticeable heat.

phos•pho•res•cence [,fɒsfə'rɛsəns] *n.* **1** a giving out of light without burning or by very slow burning that seems not to emit heat. **2** such light. **3** the property of a substance that causes this. **4** *Physics.* light given off by a substance as a result of the absorption of certain rays, as X rays or ultraviolet rays, and continuing for a period of time after the substance has ceased to be exposed to these rays. **—,phos•pho'res•cent,** *adj.*

phos•pho•ret•ted or **phos•pho•ret•ed** [,fɒsfə'rɛtɪd] See PHOSPHURETTED.

phos•phor•ic [fɒs'fɔrɪk] *adj. Chemistry.* of, having to do with, or containing phosphorus, especially with a higher valence than in phosphorous compounds.

phosphoric acid *Chemistry.* any of three oxygen acids of phosphorus derived from phosphorus pentoxide (P_2O_5) and water, used especially in preparing phosphates for fertilizers, in rust-proofing metals, and in flavouring soft drinks: orthophosphoric acid (H_3PO_4), metaphosphoric acid (HPO_3), and pyrophosphoric acid ($H_4P_2O_7$).

phos•phor•ism ['fɒsfə,rɪzəm] *n. Pathology.* chronic phosphoric poisoning.

phos•phor•ite ['fɒsfə,rəit] *n.* **1** a sedimentary rock containing phosphate minerals in sufficient quantity to be used as a base for commercial fertilizers, phosphorous chemicals, etc. **2** a sedimentary rock containing calcium phosphate.

phos•pho•rous ['fɒsfərəs] *adj. Chemistry.* of, having to do with, or containing phosphorus, especially with a lower valence than in phosphoric compounds.
☛ *Hom.* PHOSPHORUS.

phosphorous acid *Chemistry.* a colourless, unstable, crystalline acid used especially in making compounds and as a chemical reducing agent. *Formula*: H_3PO_3

phos•pho•rus ['fɒsfərəs] *n. Chemistry.* **1** a common, non-metallic chemical element occurring especially in

phosphorite. It has three main allotropic forms: white phosphorus is poisonous, extremely flammable, and luminous in the dark; red phosphorus is nonpoisonous and less flammable; black phosphorus is the most stable form. *Symbol*: P; *at.no.* 15; *at.mass* 30.97. **2 phosphorus–32,** a radioactive isotope of phosphorus used in biochemical research, the diagnosis of certain diseases, and as a chemotherapeutic agent. ⟨< L *phosphoros* morning star < Gk. *phōsphoros* light-bringing < *phōs* light + *pherein* bring⟩
☛ *Hom.* PHOSPHOROUS.

phos•phu•ret•ted or **phos•phu•ret•ed** ['fɒsfjə,rɛtɪd] *adj. Chemistry.* combined with phosphorus. Also, **phosphoretted.**

phot [fɒt] *n. Optics.* a unit of illumination equivalent to one lumen per square centimetre. ⟨< Gk. *phōs, phōtos* light⟩

phot. photograph; photographic; photography.

pho•tic ['foutɪk] *adj.* **1** of or having to do with light. **2** *Biology.* pertaining to the effect of light on organisms, or their generation of light.

pho•to ['foutou] *n., pl.* **-tos.** *Informal.* photograph.

photo– *combining form.* **1** light: *photometry.* **2** photographic or photograph: *photo-engraving.* ⟨< Gk. *phōs, phōtos* light⟩

pho•to•bi•ot•ic [,foutoubaɪ'ɒtɪk] *adj. Biology.* existing or thriving only in the presence of light.

pho•to•chem•i•cal [,foutou'kɛmɪkəl] *adj.* **1** of, having to do with, or resulting from the chemical action of light or other radiant energy. **2** of or having to do with photochemistry: *photochemical studies.* **—,pho•to'chem•i•cal•ly,** *adv.*

pho•to•chem•is•try [,foutou'kɛmɪstri] *n.* the branch of chemistry dealing with the chemical changes produced by light and other electromagnetic radiation.

pho•to•chro•mic [,foutə'kroumɪk] *adj.* referring to chemically treated materials such as glass or plastic, capable of turning dark or changing colour when exposed to light, and returning to normal when the source of light is removed: *photochromic eyeglasses.*

pho•to•com•po•si•tion [,foutou,kɒmpə'zɪʃən] *n. Printing.* any method of print composition using photography; phototypesetting.

pho•to•cop•i•er ['foutou,kɒpiər] *n.* a machine or instrument for making photocopies.

pho•to•cop•y ['foutou,kɒpi] *n., pl.* **-cop•ies;** *v.* **-cop•ied, -cop•y•ing.** *—n.* a photographic reproduction of a document or other printed matter.
—v. make a photocopy (of).

pho•to•de•grad•a•ble [,foutoudɪ'greidəbəl] *adj.* referring to substances such as certain plastics or insecticides that decompose when exposed to light, especially ultraviolet light.

pho•to•dis•in•te•gra•tion [,foutoudɪs,ɪntə'greiʃən] *n. Physics.* the destruction of a nucleus caused by the absorption of a photon.

pho•to•dis•so•ci•a•tion [,foutoudɪ,sousi'eiʃən] *n.* the breakdown of a chemical compound into simpler components by radiant energy.

pho•to•dy•nam•ics [,foutoudaɪ'næmɪks] *n.* (*used with a singular verb*) **1** the science dealing with the study of light and its activating effects on living organisms, as in phototropism in plants. **2** the effects themselves.

pho•to•e•lec•tric [,foutouɪ'lɛktrɪk] *adj.* of or having to do with the electrical effects produced by light or other electromagnetic radiation.

photo•electric cell *Electronics.* a cell in which variations in electric current are produced by variations in the light falling upon it; electric eye: *Photoelectric cells can be used to open doors automatically, set off alarms, etc.*

pho•to•e•lec•tron [,foutouɪ'lɛktrɒn] *n. Physics.* an electron emitted from a system by a photon striking it, or as a result of radiation.

pho•to•e•mis•sion [,foutouɪ'mɪʃən] *n.* the emission of electrons on exposure to light or other electromagnetic radiation.

pho•to•en•grave [,foutouɛn'greiv] *v.* **-graved, -grav•ing.** produce by photoengraving. **—,pho•to•en'grav•er,** *n.*

pho•to•en•grav•ing [,foutouɛn'greivɪŋ] *n., v. —n.* **1** production of printing plates by a photomechanical process that reproduces photographs on a relief printing plate. **2** a plate so produced. **3** a picture printed from it.
—v. ppr. of PHOTOENGRAVE.

photo finish **1** *Sports.* a finish so close that a photograph is required to decide the winner. **2** any contest decided by a narrow margin of victory.

pho•to•fin•ish•ing [,foutou'fɪnɪʃɪŋ] *n.* the development of exposed photographic film.

pho•to•flash ['foutou,flæʃ] *n., adj. Photography. —n.* flashbulb. Also, **photoflash lamp.**
—adj. of or having to do with the use of a lamp or light electrically synchronized with the shutter of the camera.

pho•to•flood lamp ['foutou,flʌd] an electric lamp that gives very bright, sustained light for taking pictures. Also, **photoflood.**

pho•to•gene ['foutou,dʒin] *n. Ophthalmology.* after-image.

pho•to•gen•ic [,foutə'dʒɛnɪk] *adj.* **1** looking or likely to look attractive in photographs or motion pictures: *a photogenic face. Julia is very photogenic; her grad photos are stunning.* **2** *Biology.* phosphorescent; luminescent. Certain bacteria are photogenic. **3** due to or caused by light. ⟨< *photo-* + Gk. *gen-* producing, produced (by)⟩ **—,pho•to'gen•i•cal•ly,** *adv.*

pho•to•gram ['foutə,græm] *n.* a silhouette photograph produced without the use of a camera by placing an object directly onto photosensitive paper and exposing it to light.

pho•to•gram•me•try [,foutə'græmətri] *n.* the process of making maps or surveys with the help of photographs, especially aerial photographs. ⟨< *photogram,* obs. var. of *photograph* + *-metry*⟩ **—,pho•to'gram•me•trist,** *n.*

pho•to•graph ['foutə,græf] *n., v. —n.* a picture or image made with a camera.
—v. **1** take a photograph of. **2** take photographs. **3** look (clear, natural, etc.) in a photograph: *She does not photograph well; she always looks startled.*

pho•tog•ra•pher [fə'tɒgrəfər] *n.* **1** a person who takes photographs. **2** a person whose business is taking photographs.

pho•to•graph•ic [,foutə'græfɪk] *adj.* **1** of or like a photograph, especially as regards realism and precise detail: *photographic accuracy.* **2** used in the process of photography: *photographic plates.* **3** produced by means of photography: *a photographic record of our holiday.* **4** remembering or recalling in precise detail: *a photographic memory.*
—,pho•to'graph•i•cal•ly, *adv.*

pho•tog•ra•phy [fə'tɒgrəfi] *n.* the making of photographs.

pho•to•gra•vure [,foutəgrə'vjʊr] *or* [,foutə'greivjʊr] *n.* **1** any one of several photochemical processes by which photographs are reproduced on an intaglio plate from which ink reproductions are made. **2** the plate so made. **3** a print made from this plate.

pho•to•jour•nal•ism [,foutou'dʒɜrnə,lɪzəm] *n.* **1** journalism in which photographs, rather than written material, are used to present the majority of news items. **2** news photography.

pho•to•ki•ne•sis [,foutoukɪ'nisɪs] *n.* movement occurring in response to exposure to light.

pho•tol•y•sis [fou'tɒləsɪs] *n.* chemical decomposition of substances due to the influence of light.

pho•to•me•chan•i•cal [,foutoumə'kænɪkəl] *adj.* relating to or designating any of various mechanical methods, such as photoengraving or phototype, used for making printing plates with the aid of photography. **—,pho•to•me'chan•i•cal•ly,** *adv.*

pho•tom•e•ter [fou'tɒmətər] *n. Optics.* an instrument for measuring the intensity of light or the relative illuminating power of different lights.

pho•to•met•ric [,foutə'mɛtrɪk] *adj.* having to do with photometry or a photometer. **—,pho•to'met•ri•cal•ly,** *adv.*

pho•tom•e•try [fou'tɒmətri] *n.* **1** the branch of physics dealing with the measurement of the intensity of light. **2** the measurement of the intensity of light, especially by means of a photometer.

pho•to•mi•cro•graph [,foutə'məikrə,græf] *n.* a photograph of an object as seen through a microscope.
—,pho•to,mi•cro'graph•ic, *adj.* **—,pho•to•mi'crog•ra•phy,** *n.*

pho•to•mon•tage [,foutoumɒn'tɑʒ] *or* [,foutoumɒn'tæʒ] *n. Photography.* a montage composed of photographs.

pho•ton ['foutɒn] *n. Physics.* a quantum or unit particle of light, having a momentum equal to its energy and moving with the velocity of light. ⟨< *phot(o electr)on*⟩

pho•to•neg•a•tive [,foutou'nɛgətɪv] *adj.* **1** *Biology.* of or having to do with anything that responds negatively to light, such as an earthworm. **2** *Physics.* of or having to do with a substance in which the conductivity decreases when it absorbs electromagnetic radiation.

pho•to–off•set [,foutou 'ɒf,sɛt] *n.* a method of printing in which a photographic image is produced on a metal plate from which inked impressions are transferred to a rubber surface and thence to paper.

pho•to•pho•bia [ˌfoutəˈfoubiə] *n.* **1** *Pathology.* an abnormal intolerance for light, as in certain eye conditions or diseases such as measles. **2** an abnormal fear of light.

pho•to•pia [fouˈtoupiə] *n. Ophthalmology.* normal vision after adaptation to light; vision in bright light.

pho•to•play [ˈfoutəˌplei] *n.* MOTION PICTURE (def. 2).

pho•to–re•con•nais•sance [ˈfoutou rəˈkɒnəsəns] *n.* reconnaissance made by aerial photographs.

pho•to•sen•si•tive [ˌfoutouˈsɛnsətɪv] *adj.* sensitive to light; easily stimulated by light or other radiant energy. **—ˌpho•toˌsen•siˈtiv•i•ty,** *n.*

pho•to•sen•si•tize [ˌfoutouˈsɛnsəˌtaɪz] *v.* **-tized, -tiz•ing.** make (something) sensitive to light.

pho•to•set [ˈfoutouˌsɛt] *v.* **-set, -set•ting.** *Printing.* set for printing by photocomposition.

pho•to•sphere [ˈfoutəˌsfir] *n.* **1** *Astronomy.* the dazzling surface of the sun as seen from the earth. **2** a sphere of light or radiance. **—ˌpho•toˈspher•ic** [-ˈsfɛrɪk], *adj.*

pho•to•stat [ˈfoutəˌstæt] *n., v.* **-stat•ted** or **-stat•ed, -stat•ting** or **-stat•ing.** *—n.* **1 Photostat,** *Trademark.* a special camera for making copies of maps, drawings, pages of books, etc. directly on specially prepared paper. **2** a copy made with this camera. *—v.* make a copy of using a Photostat camera. ⟨< *photo-* light + Gk. *-statēs* that brings to a stop⟩ **—ˌpho•toˈstat•ic,** *adj.*

pho•to•syn•the•sis [ˌfoutəˈsɪnθəsɪs] *n. Biology, biochemistry.* the process by which plant cells make sugar from carbon dioxide and water in the presence of chlorophyl and light. **—ˌpho•to•synˈthet•i•cal•ly,** *adv.*

pho•to•tax•is [ˌfoutəˈtæksɪs] *n. Biology.* free movement of an organism toward or away from light.

pho•to•te•leg•ra•phy [ˌfoutoutəˈlɛgrəfi] *n.* **1** telegraphy by means of light, as with a heliograph. **2** the electronic transmission of facsimiles of photographs.

pho•to•the•ra•py or **photo therapy** [ˌfoutouˈθɛrəpi] *n.* treatment of disease by means of light rays.

pho•tot•ro•pism [fouˈtɒtrəˌpɪzəm] *or* [ˌfoutouˈtroupɪzəm] *n. Botany.* a tendency to turn or grow toward or away from light. ⟨< *photo-* + Gk. *-tropos* turning⟩

pho•to•type [ˈfoutəˌtəip] *n. Printing.* **1** a block on which a photograph is reproduced so that it can be printed. **2** the process used in making such a block. **3** a picture printed from such a block.

pho•to•type•set•ting [ˌfoutəˈtəipsɛtɪŋ] *n.* photocomposition.

pho•to•vol•ta•ic [ˌfoutouvɒlˈteiɪk] *adj.* **1** of or having to do with the production of voltage or electric current by means of light or other electromagnetic radiation. **2** producing or utilizing such voltage or electric current. In a **photovoltaic cell** an electric current is produced when a junction between two dissimilar materials, such as a metal and a semiconductor, is exposed to electromagnetic radiation.

phras•al [ˈfreizəl] *adj.* of, having to do with, or consisting of a phrase: *a phrasal verb.* **—ˈphras•al•ly,** *adv.*

phrasal verb a verb used in combination with an adverb or preposition, or both, whose meaning cannot be obtained from the meanings of the separate words. In *She looked up the word, looked up* is a phrasal verb, but in *She looked up the stairs, looked up* is not.

phrase [freiz] *n., v.* **phrased, phras•ing.** *—n.* **1** a combination of words that has meaning: *He spoke in simple phrases so that the children understood him.* **2** a short, often used expression. *Call up* is the common phrase for *make a telephone call to.* **3** a short, striking expression. *Examples*: *From sea to sea. Atoms for peace. A war to end wars.* **4** *Grammar.* a group of words not containing a subject and finite verb and used as a unit in a clause or sentence. In *He went to the house,* the words *to the house* form a prepositional phrase. **5** *Music.* a short part of a composition, usually containing four or eight measures. **6** *Dance.* a connected series of movements making up a section of a choreographic pattern. *—v.* **1** express in a particular way: *She phrased her excuse politely.* **2** *Music.* mark off or bring out the phrases of (a composition). ⟨< L < Gk. *phrasis* < *phrazein* express⟩

phrase•book [ˈfreizˌbʊk] *n.* a collection of idioms and everyday phrases used in a foreign language, with their translations.

phra•se•o•log•i•cal [ˌfreiziəˈlɒdʒɪkəl] *adj.* **1** of or having to do with phraseology. **2** characterized by a special phraseology, or by the choice of particular words, expressions, etc. **—ˌphra•se•oˈlog•i•cal•ly,** *adv.*

phra•se•ol•o•gy [ˌfreiziˈɒlədʒi] *n., pl.* **-gies.** the selection and arrangement of words; the particular way in which a person expresses himself or herself in language.
☛ *Syn.* See note at DICTION.

phras•ing [ˈfreizɪŋ] *n., v.* *—n.* **1 a** the style of wording or verbal expression; phraseology. **b** the grouping of spoken words by pauses. **2** *Music.* **a** a grouping or dividing into phrases. **b** the playing of phrases. **c** the style in which the composition is phrased. *—v.* ppr. of PHRASE.

phra•try [ˈfreitri] *or* [ˈfrætri] *n., pl.* **-tries. 1** in ancient Athens, each of the subdivisions of a tribe. **2** *Anthropology.* a similar tribal division among certain preindustrial peoples. ⟨< Gk. *phratria* < *phratēr* clansman, brother⟩

phre•net•ic [frəˈnɛtɪk] *adj.* See FRENETIC. ⟨ME *frenetik* < OF *frenetique* < L *phreneticus* < Gk. *phrenetikos* < *phrenitis* disease of the mind < *phrēn* mind. Doublet of FRANTIC.⟩ **—phreˈnet•i•cal•ly,** *adv.*

phren•ic [ˈfrɛnɪk] *adj.* **1** *Anatomy.* of or having to do with the diaphragm. **2** *Physiology.* of or having to do with the mind or mental activity. ⟨< Gk. *phrien* midriff, heart; mind, mental capacity⟩

phre•nol•o•gy [frɪˈnɒlədʒi] *n.* a now rejected theory that the shape of the skull shows what sort of mind and character a person has; practice of reading character from the shape of the skull. ⟨< Gk. *phrēn* mind + E *-logy*⟩ **—ˌphren•oˈlog•i•cal** [ˌfrɛnəˈlɒdʒɪkəl], *adj.* **—phreˈnol•o•gist,** *n.*

Phryg•i•an [ˈfrɪdʒiən] *n., adj.* *—n.* **1** a native or inhabitant of Phrygia, an ancient country in west central Asia Minor. **2** the Indo-European language of the ancient Phrygians. *—adj.* of or having to do with Phrygia, its people, or their language.

phthis•ic [ˈtɪzɪk] *n. Archaic.* phthisis.

phthis•i•cal [ˈtɪzɪkəl] *adj.* having to do with, having the nature of, or affected by phthisis.

phthi•sis [ˈθəisɪs], [ˈtəisɪs], *or* [ˈfθəisɪs] *n. Pathology.* any wasting disease, such as pulmonary tuberculosis or consumption. ⟨< L < Gk. *phthisis* a decay < *phthinein* waste away⟩

phy•lac•ter•y [fəˈlæktəri] *n., pl.* **-ter•ies. 1** either of two small black leather cases containing texts from the Jewish law, worn on the forehead and left arm by Orthodox and Conservative Jews during morning prayers to remind them to keep the law. **2** reminder. **3** a charm worn as a protection. ⟨ME *filaterie* < LL *philaterium* < Gk. *phylaktērion* safeguard, ult. < *phylax, phylakos* watchman⟩

phy•le [ˈfaili] *n., pl.* **-lae** [-li] *or* [-laɪ]. in ancient Greece: **1** a clan or tribe. **2** in Athens, a large political subdivision. ⟨< Gk.⟩

phyl•lo [ˈfɪlou] *n.* a flaky pastry made in layers with butter, used for Greek pastries, etc. ⟨< Mod.Gk. *phyllon* a thin sheet < Gk. *phyllon* a leaf⟩

phyl•lox•e•ra [fəˈlɒksərə] *or* [ˌfɪləkˈsirə] *n., pl.* **phyl•lox•e•rae** [-səri] *or* [-ˈsiri] any of a genus (*Phylloxera*) of small insects, especially *P. vitifolia,* which destroys grapevines by feeding on the plant juices. ⟨< NL < Gk. *phyllon* leaf + *xēros* dry⟩

phy•lo•gen•e•sis [ˌfailouˈdʒɛnəsɪs] *n.* phylogeny.

phy•log•e•ny [faɪˈlɒdʒəni] *n., pl.* **-nies. 1** the history of a division, group, or race of organisms. **2** the origin and development of anything, especially of an animal or plant. **3** the historical development of a group of non-living things such as a family of languages. ⟨< G < Gk. *phylon* race + *-geneia* origin⟩ **—ˌphy•loˈgen•ic** [ˌfailəˈdʒɛnɪk] or **ˌphy•lo•geˈnet•ic,** *adj.* **—ˌphy•lo•geˈnet•i•cal•ly,** *adv.*

phy•lum [ˈfailəm] *n., pl.* **-la** [-lə]. *Biology.* a major category in the classification of animals, more general than a class. It corresponds to a division in the classification of plants. See classification chart in the Appendix. ⟨< NL < Gk. *phylon* race, stock⟩

phys ed or **phys•ed** PHYSICAL EDUCATION.

phys•i•at•rics [ˌfɪziˈætrɪks] *n.* (*used with a singular verb*) a branch of medicine concerned with physiotherapy.

phys•ic [ˈfɪzɪk] *n., v.* **-icked, -ick•ing.** *Archaic.* *—n.* **1** a

medicine, especially one that moves the bowels. **2** the art of healing; science and practice of medicine.
—v. **1** move the bowels of. **2** give medicine to. **3** act like a medicine on; cure. ⟨ME *fisike* < OF *fisique* < L < Gk. *physikē (epistēmē)* (knowledge) of nature, ult. < *phyein* produce⟩

phys•i•cal [ˈfɪzɪkəl] *adj., n. —adj.* **1** of the body: *physical exercise.* **2** pertaining to natural science and natural philosophy. **3** sexual or carnal: *a physical attraction.* **4** requiring or characterized by aggressive or rough bodily activity: *Hockey is a very physical sport.* **5** of matter; material: *The tide is a physical force.* **6** according to the laws of nature: *It is a physical impossibility to stop the earth's movement around the sun.* **7** of the science of physics.
—n. Informal. a complete or general medical examination: *my annual physical.* **—ˈphys•i•cal•ly,** *adv.* **—ˌphys•iˈcal•i•ty** [ˌfɪzɪˈkælɪti], *n.*

physical anthropology the branch of anthropology that deals with the evolution of human bodily structure and its variations.

physical chemistry the branch of chemistry that deals with the physical properties of substances and their relations to chemical composition and changes.

physical education **1** instruction in how to exercise and take care of the body, especially as a course at school or university. **2** a course in gymnastics, athletics, etc.

physical geography the branch of geography that deals with the study of land forms, climate, winds, and all other topographical features of the earth.

phys•i•cal•ism [ˈfɪzɪkəˌlɪzəm] *n. Philosophy.* a theory holding that all referential terms in meaningful statements, except analytical statements as in logic and mathematics, must refer to the observable properties of physical objects and events.
—ˈphys•i•cal•ist, *n.*

physical science **1** physics. **2** physics, chemistry, geology, astronomy, and other sciences dealing with inanimate matter.

physical therapy physiotherapy.

physical training the practice of doing exercises of various kinds so as to keep the body in good condition.

phy•si•cian [fəˈzɪʃən] *n.* **1** any legally qualified doctor of medicine. **2** a medical doctor as distinct from a surgeon. **3** one who is skilled in the healing arts. ⟨ME < OF *fisicien* < L *physica.* See PHYSIC.⟩

phys•i•cist [ˈfɪzəsɪst] *n.* a person trained in physics, especially one whose work it is.

phys•i•co•chem•i•cal [ˌfɪzɪkouˈkɛmɪkəl] *adj.* **1** of or having to do with both physics and chemistry. **2** of or having to do with physical chemistry. **—ˌphys•i•coˈchem•i•cal•ly,** *adv.*

phys•ics [ˈfɪzɪks] *n.* (*used with a singular verb*) **1** originally, natural philosophy. **2** the science that deals with matter and energy and their relationships, excluding chemical and biological change. Physics deals with matter, energy, motion, and force. **3** the physical properties and processes of a specific thing: *the physics of a machine.* ⟨pl. of *physic* (< Gk. *ta physika* the natural things)⟩

physio– *combining form.* **1** having to do with nature or natural features and processes: *physiography.* **2** of or having to do with physical form or function: *physiology.* Also, **physi-** before vowels. ⟨< Gk. *physis* nature⟩

phys•i•og•no•my [ˌfɪziˈɒnəmi] *or* [ˌfɪziˈɒgnəmi] *n., pl.* **-mies. 1** the kind of features or type of face one has; one's face. **2** the art of estimating character from the features of the face or the form of the body. **3** the general aspect or looks of a countryside, a situation, etc. ⟨ME *fisionomie* < MF *phisonomie* < LL *phisonomia* < Gk. *physiognōmonia* < *physis* nature + *gnōmōn* judge, one who knows⟩ **—ˌphys•iˈog•no•mist,** *n.*
—ˌphys•i•ogˈnom•i•cal [ˌfɪziəˈnɒmɪkəl] *or* [ˌfɪziəgˈnɒmɪkəl], *adj.*

phys•i•og•ra•pher [ˌfɪziˈɒgrəfər] *n.* a person trained in physiography, especially one whose work it is.

phys•i•og•ra•phy [ˌfɪziˈɒgrəfi] *n.* **1** PHYSICAL GEOGRAPHY. **2** geomorphology. **3** the description of nature in general.
—ˌphys•i•oˈgraph•ic [ˌfɪziəˈgræfɪk], *adj.*
—ˌphys•i•oˈgraph•i•cal•ly, *adv.*

phys•i•o•log•i•cal [ˌfɪziəˈlɒdʒɪkəl] *adj.* **1** having to do with physiology: *Digestion is a physiological process.* **2** having to do with the normal or healthy functioning of an organism: *Food and sleep are physiological needs.* **—ˌphys•i•oˈlog•i•cal•ly,** *adv.*

phys•i•ol•o•gist [ˌfɪziˈɒlədʒɪst] *n.* a person trained in physiology, especially one whose work it is.

phys•i•ol•o•gy [ˌfɪziˈɒlədʒi] *n.* **1** the science dealing with the normal functions of living things or their parts: *animal physiology, plant physiology.* **2** all the functions and activities of a living thing or of one of its parts. ⟨< F *physiologie* < L < Gk. *physiologia* < *physis* nature + *-logos* treating of⟩

phy•si•o•ther•a•pist [ˌfɪziəˈθɛrəpɪst] *n.* a person trained in physiotherapy, especially one whose work it is.

phys•i•o•ther•a•py [ˌfɪziəˈθɛrəpi] *n.* the treatment of diseases and defects by physical remedies, such as massage, special exercises, or electrical treatment such as ultrasound (rather than by drugs).

phy•sique [fɪˈzik] *n.* the body; bodily structure, organization, or development: *a man of strong physique.* ⟨< F *physique* physical⟩

phys•o•stig•mine [ˌfəisouˈstɪgmin] *or* [ˌfəisouˈstɪgmɪn] *n. Pharmacy.* a crystalline alkaloid obtained from the Calabar bean and used in the treatment of Alzheimer's disease and glaucoma. *Formula*: $C_{15}H_{21}N_3O_2$

–phyte *combining form.* a growth; plant: *epiphyte.* ⟨< Gk. *phyton* plant⟩

phyto– *combining form.* a plant; plants: *phytobiology.* Also, **phyt-** before vowels. ⟨< Gk. *phyton* plant⟩

phy•to•bi•ol•o•gy [ˌfəitoubaɪˈɒlədʒi] *n.* the branch of biology that deals with plants.

phy•to•chem•is•try [ˌfəitouˈkɛmɪstri] *n.* the chemistry of plants.

phy•to•gen•e•sis [ˌfəitouˈdʒɛnəsɪs] *n.* the science of the evolution and development of plants. Also, **phytogeny.**

phy•to•ge•net•ic [ˌfəitoudʒəˈnɛtɪk] *adj.* **1** of or having to do with phytogenesis. **2** of plant or vegetable origin.

phy•to•gen•ic [ˌfəitəˈdʒɛnɪk] *adj.* of plant origin.

phy•tog•e•ny [fəiˈtɒdʒəni] *n.* phytogenesis.

phy•to•ge•og•ra•phy [ˌfəitoudʒiˈɒgrəfi] *n.* the science that deals with the geographical distribution of plant life.

phy•tog•ra•phy [fəiˈtɒgrəfi] *n.* the branch of botany that deals with the description of plants.

phy•tol•o•gy [fəiˈtɒlədʒi] *n.* a former term for botany.

phy•to•pa•thol•o•gist [ˌfəitoupəˈθɒlədʒɪst] *n.* a person trained in phytopathology, especially one whose work it is.

phy•to•pa•thol•o•gy [ˌfəitoupəˈθɒlədʒi] *n.* the science that deals with diseases of plants. **—ˌphy•toˌpath•oˈlog•i•cal** [ˌfəitouˌpæθəˈlɒdʒɪkəl], *adj.*

phy•to•plank•ton [ˌfəitouˈplæŋktən] *n.* microscopic plants, mainly one-celled algae, that are a constituent of plankton.

pi[1] [paɪ] *n., pl.* **pis. 1** *Mathematics.* the ratio of the circumference of any circle to its diameter, equal to about 3.141 592. The circumference of a circle equals pi times the diameter of the circle ($C = \pi d$). *Symbol*: π **2** the sixteenth letter of the Greek alphabet (Π, π). ⟨def. 1, use of Gk. letter to mean Gk. *periphereia* periphery. See PERIPHERY.⟩
☛ *Hom.* PIE.

pi[2] [paɪ] *n., v.* **pied, pi•ing.** *—n.* **1** printing types in disorder. **2** any confused mixture.
—v. mix up (type). Also, **pie.** ⟨extended use of *pie*[1]⟩
☛ *Hom.* PIE.

pi•affe [pjæf] *or* [piˈæf] *n., v.* **pi•affed, pi•af•fing.** *Dressage.*
—n. a movement in which the horse executes a cadenced trot in place, with a stressed elevation of the legs.
—v. **1** of the horse, execute a piaffe. **2** cause (a horse) to perform the piaffe. ⟨< F *piaffer* strut⟩

pi•a ma•ter [ˈpaɪə ˈmeitər] *Anatomy.* the innermost of three membranes enveloping the brain and spinal cord. ⟨< Med.L *pia mater* pious mother, a wrong translation of Arabic *al ʼumm al raqīqah* thin or tender mother⟩

pi•an•ism [ˈpiəˌnɪzəm] *or* [piˈænˌɪzəm] *n.* **1** the skill and technique of a pianist. **2** a pianist's performance.

pi•a•nis•si•mo [ˌpiəˈnɪsəˌmou] *adj., adv., n. Music. —adj.* very soft.
—adv. very softly.
—n. a very soft movement or passage; composition to be played or sung very softly. *Abbrev.*: pp. ⟨< Ital. *pianissimo,* superlative of *piano* soft. See PIANO[2].⟩

pi•an•ist [ˈpiənɪst] *or* [piˈænɪst] *n.* a person who plays the piano, especially a skilled player.

pi•an•o[1] [piˈænou] *n., pl.* **-an•os.** a large musical instrument having metal strings that sound when struck by felt-covered hammers operated by the keys on a keyboard. A standard size piano has a range of over seven octaves. ⟨short for *pianoforte*⟩

pi•a•no² [pi'ɑnou] *adj., adv., n. Music. —adj.* soft.
—adv. softly.
—n. a soft movement or passage; composition to be played or sung softly. *Abbrev.*: p. ⟨< Ital. *piano* < L *planus* plain, flat. Doublet of PLAIN¹ and PLAN.⟩

piano accordion an accordion having a keyboard for the right hand and buttons on the other side for producing chords with the left hand.

pi•an•o•for•te [pi,ænou'fɔrti] *or* [pi'ænou,fɔrt] *n.* PIANO¹. ⟨< Ital. *pianoforte* < *piano* soft + *forte* loud⟩

piano player **1** one who plays a piano. **2** a mechanical device that makes the keys of a PLAYER PIANO work.

pi•as•tre [pi'æstər] *n.* **1** a unit of money in Egypt and Syria, equal to 1/100 of a pound. **2** a unit of money in Lebanon, equal to 1/100 of a livre. **3** kurus. **4** a coin worth one piastre. Also, **piaster.** **5** a former Spanish silver peso. See table of money in the Appendix. ⟨< Ital. *piastra* metal plate < L⟩

pi•az•za [pi'ætsə] *for 1,* [pi'æzə] *for 2 & 3. n.* **1** in Italy, an open public square in a town. **2** a large porch or veranda along one or more sides of a house. **3** a covered walk or arcade in front of a building or around a public square. ⟨< Ital. *piazza* < L *platea* < Gk. *plateia (hodos)* broad (way). Doublet of PLACE and PLAZA.⟩

pib•gorn ['pɪb,gɔrn] *n.* an ancient Welsh musical instrument played by blowing. ⟨< Welsh *pib* pipe + *gorn* horn⟩

pi•broch ['pibrɒk] *or* ['pibrɒx] *n.* a piece of music, usually warlike or sad, played on the bagpipe. ⟨< Scots Gaelic *piobaireachd* pipe music, ult. < *piob* pipe⟩

pi•ca¹ ['pəikə] *n.* **1** *Printing.* a size of type, 12 point. **2** this size of type used as a measure; about 4.2 mm. **3** a size of typewriter type, larger than elite, corresponding to 12-point printing type. There are 10 pica characters to the inch (2.5 cm). ⟨< Anglo-L *pica*, the name of a book of rules concerning holy days, supposed (? erroneously) to be printed in pica⟩
☛ *Hom.* PIKA.

pi•ca² ['pəikə] *n. Pathology.* an abnormal craving to eat substances considered to be non-foods such as chalk, common in pregnancy, malnutrition, etc. ⟨< L, magpie⟩

pica³ ['pəikə] *n. Cdn.* See PIKA.

pic•a•dor ['pɪkə,dɔr] *n.* one of the horseback riders who begin a bullfight by irritating the bull and weakening its neck and shoulder muscles with pricks of their lances. ⟨< Sp. *picador* < *picar* pierce⟩

pic•a•resque [,pɪkə'rɛsk] *adj.* **1** referring to a type of fiction originating in Spain and recounting the exploits of a roguish hero in a series of satiric or humorous episodes: *a picaresque novel.* **2** relating to rogues and vagabonds. ⟨< Sp. *picaresco* < *picaro* rogue⟩

pic•a•roon [,pɪkə'run] *n., v. —n.* **1** a rogue; thief; brigand. **2** a pirate. **3** a piratical or privateering ship.
—v. act or cruise as a brigand or pirate. ⟨< Sp. *picarón* < *picaro* rogue⟩

pic•a•yune [,pɪkə'jun] *adj., n. —adj.* **1** small; trifling; of little value: *It was a lot of effort for such picayune results.* **2** mean; petty; small-minded.
—n. **1** a coin of small value, such as a penny or nickel. **2** anything trivial. ⟨< Louisiana F *picaillon* coin worth 5 cents < Provençal *picaioun* coin⟩

Pic•ca•dil•ly Circus [,pɪkə'dɪli] a traffic circle and open square in the West End of London, England, centred on a statue of Eros, and famous for its theatres and entertainment centres. Piccadilly, the street leading to Piccadilly Circus, is traditionally known for fashionable shops, clubs, restaurants, etc.

pic•ca•lil•li ['pɪkə,lɪli] *n.* a relish made of chopped pickles, onions, tomatoes, etc. and hot spices. ⟨origin uncertain; ? < *pickle*⟩

A piccolo

pic•co•lo ['pɪkə,lou] *n., pl.* **-los.** a small wind instrument of the flute family, pitched an octave higher than the ordinary flute. ⟨< Ital. *piccolo* small⟩

pic•co•lo•ist ['pɪkə,louɪst] *n.* one who plays the piccolo, especially a skilled player.

pice [pəis] *n., pl.* **pice. 1** the Nepalese paisa. **2** a former monetary unit of British India, equal to 1/4 of an anna.

pick¹ [pɪk] *v., n. —v.* **1** choose; select: *I picked a winning horse at the races.* **2** pull off with the fingers; gather: *We pick fruit and flowers.* **3** be picked: *Cherries pick easily.* **4** pierce, dig into, or break up with something pointed: *to pick ground, rocks, etc.* **5** use a pick (on). **6** use something pointed to remove things from: *to pick one's teeth, to pick a bone.* **7** steal the contents of: *to pick someone's pocket.* **8** prepare for use by removing feathers, waste parts, etc.: *to pick a chicken.* **9** pull apart: *The stuffing in the pillow has matted and needs to be picked.* **10** use the fingers on with a plucking motion: *to play the banjo by picking its strings.* **11** seek and find occasion for; look for and hope to find: *to pick a quarrel, to pick flaws.* **12** take up (seeds, small pieces of food, etc.) with the bill or teeth, as a bird or squirrel does. **13** eat (food) in small pieces, slowly, or without appetite.
pick a lock, open a lock with a pointed instrument, wire, etc.
pick and choose, be very particular about choosing.
pick apart, find flaws in; criticize severely.
pick at, a pull on with the fingers: *The invalid picked at the blankets.* **b** eat only a little of at a time. **c** *Informal.* find fault with; nag.
pick off, a shoot one at a time. **b** *Baseball.* catch (a runner) off base and throw him or her out. **c** remove by picking.
pick on, a *Informal.* find fault with; nag: *The teacher picked on the student for always being late.* **b** *Informal.* annoy; tease: *The big boys picked on the new boy during recess.* **c** bully; take advantage of. **d** select: *Why did he pick on this colour scheme?*
pick (one's) **way** or **pick** (one's) **steps,** move with great care and caution over treacherous ground, in a difficult situation, etc.
pick out, a choose; select: *Pick out a dress you would like to wear.* **b** distinguish something or someone from the surroundings: *Can you pick me out in this group picture?* **c** make out (the sense or meaning). **d** select the notes of (a tune) one by one, especially laboriously, on a keyboard, etc., and so play it. **e** embellish, especially by lines or spots of contrasting colour following outlines, etc.: *The main pattern was picked out in gold leaf.* **f** remove or extract by picking.
pick over, a look over carefully and make selections. **b** sort and clean: *The berries need to be picked over before we can eat them.*
pick (someone's) **brains, a** find out and turn to one's own advantage, or use as one's own, the ideas, skills, etc. of another. **b** ask someone's advice.
pick up, a take up: *The child picked up a stone. She picked up the chance to make some money by baby-sitting.* **b** summon (courage, etc.). **c** get by chance: *to pick up a bargain.* **d** give (a person) fresh energy, courage, etc.: *A good dinner will pick you up.* **e** acquire (a particular skill); become skilful at; master: *She picked up the trumpet after just a few lessons.* **f** learn without being taught: *Some people pick up games easily.* **g** take up into a vehicle or ship: *The bus picked up passengers at every other corner.* **h** get and take along with one: *to pick up a coat at the cleaners.* **i** *Informal.* improve; recover: *He seemed to pick up quickly after his fever.* **j** receive (radio signals, etc.). **k** succeed in seeing, hearing, etc.: *to pick up a radio program from Paris.* **l** go faster; increase in speed. **m** *Esp. U.S.* tidy up; put in order. **n** arrest. **o** of a dog, find and follow (a scent). **p** take (a check) with intent to pay it: *Who'll pick up the tab?* **q** *Informal.* meet (someone) casually, with intention of a sexual encounter.
pick up on, notice and understand.
—n. **1** a choice or selection. **2** the best or most desirable part. **3** the amount of a crop gathered at one time. **4** something held in the fingers and used to pluck the strings of a musical instrument; plectrum. **5** the act of picking; a blow with a pointed

instrument. **6** a turn to choose: *It's your pick.* ⟨ME *picke(n)*; cf. OE *pīcung* pricking⟩

pick² [pɪk] *n.* **1** pickaxe. **2** a sharp-pointed tool. Ice is broken into pieces with a pick. ⟨ME *picke*, var. of *pike* pike², OE *pīc*⟩

pick³ [pɪk] *v., n. —v. Weaving.* cast (a shuttle).
—n. **1** one cast of the shuttle in a loom. **2** one of the filling or weft yarns. ⟨ME *pykken*, var. of *picchen* pitch¹⟩

pick⁴ *n. Cdn. Informal.* pickerel. Also, **picker.**

pick•a•back ['pɪkə,bæk] *adv.* piggyback.

pick•axe ['pɪk,æks] *n.* a heavy metal tool that is pointed at one or both ends and has a long wooden handle, used for breaking up dirt, rocks, etc.; pick. Sometimes, **pickax.** ⟨alteration of ME *picois* < OF *picois* (Cf. OF *pic* pike¹)⟩

picked [pɪkt] *adj., v. —adj.* **1** with waste parts removed and ready for use. **2** specially chosen or selected for merit: *a crew of picked men.*
—v. pt. and pp. of PICK.

pick•er ['pɪkər] *n.* **1** a person who gathers, picks, or collects. **2** a tool for picking anything. **3 a** a machine for separating and cleaning the fibres of cotton, wool, etc. **b** a person who runs such a machine.

pick•er•el ['pɪkərəl] *n., pl.* **-el** or **-els. 1** any of three small fishes of the pike family (*Esox niger, E. americanus americanus*, and *E. americanus vermiculatus*). **2** WALLEYE (def. 7). ⟨dim. of pike³⟩

pick•er•el•weed ['pɪkərəl,wid] *n.* any of various aquatic plants (family Pontederiaceae, especially genus *Pontederia*) having arrow-shaped leaves and blue or purple flowers.

pick•et ['pɪkɪt] *n., v. —n.* **1** a pointed stake or peg placed upright to make a fence, to tie a horse to, etc. **2 a** a small body of troops, or a single person, posted at some place to watch for the enemy and guard against surprise attack. **b** a ship or plane patrolling the defence perimeter. **3 a** a person stationed by a labour union near a place of work where there is a strike. Pickets try to prevent employees from working or customers from buying. **b** a participant in a demonstration.
—v. **1** enclose with pickets; fence. **2** tie to a picket. **3** station as pickets. **4** station pickets at or near: *to picket a factory during a strike.* **5** act as a picket. ⟨< F *piquet*, dim. of *pic* a pike. See PIKE¹.⟩ **—'pick•et•er,** *n.*

picket fence a fence made of pickets.

picket line a group or line of people picketing a business, etc.

pick•ings ['pɪkɪŋz] *n.pl.* **1** the amount picked. **2** things left over; scraps. **3** things stolen or received dishonestly. **4** profits; returns; gains: *That investment brought in pretty slim pickings.*

pick•le ['pɪkəl] *n., v.* **-led, -ling.** *—n.* **1** a cucumber or other vegetable preserved in brine, vinegar, or some other liquid. **2** the liquid in which foods can be preserved. **3** *Informal.* a problematic situation; difficulty. **4** a chemical bath for removing surface scale from metal castings, etc.
—v. **1** preserve in pickle: *to pickle beets.* **2** clean (metal, etc.) with a chemical, such as acid. ⟨< MDu. *pekel*⟩

pick•lock ['pɪk,lɒk] *n.* **1** a person who picks locks; burglar; thief. **2** an instrument for picking locks; lock pick.

pick–me–up ['pɪk mi ,ʌp] *n. Informal.* a stimulant or tonic.

pick•pock•et ['pɪk,pɒkɪt] *n.* a person who steals from people's pockets, especially in crowded public places.

pick•up ['pɪk,ʌp] *n.* **1** a picking up: *the daily pickup of mail.* **2** *Informal.* improvement or power of acceleration: *a pickup in business. This car hasn't much pickup.* **3** a going faster; increase in speed; acceleration. **4** something obtained or secured without planning and as chance offers, such as a bargain or a hurried meal: *We'll just have a quick pickup before we catch the plane.* **5** (*adjl.*) using or made up of available material, personnel, etc., without planning or organizing beforehand: *a pickup meal, a pickup team.* **6** *Sports.* a catching or hitting of a ball very soon after it has bounced on the ground. **7** *Radio and television.* **a** the reception of sound waves or images and their conversion into electrical waves for broadcasting. **b** an apparatus for such reception. **c** the place where it occurs. **d** the electrical system for connecting to the broadcasting station or studio a program originating outside. **8** a small truck for collecting and delivering light loads. Also, **pickup truck. 9** anything that is picked up. **10** (*adjl.*) of or for picking up: *a pickup schooner plying along the coast.* **11** in a record player: **a** the device in the arm that converts the vibrations of the stylus into sound. **b** the arm itself. **12** a very small microphone, especially one attached to a musical instrument. **13** *Informal.* a person met casually and usually unintroduced, as in a restaurant or bar, often in the hope that a sexual encounter will result.

Pick•wick•i•an [pɪk'wɪkiən] *adj.* **1** of, having to do with, or characteristic of Samuel Pickwick, the kindly, genial hero of Dickens' *Pickwick Papers,* or his club. **2** given a special meaning for the occasion: *words used in a Pickwickian sense.*

pick•y ['pɪki] *adj.* **pick•i•er, pick•i•est.** *Informal.* too fussy or particular; inclined to find fault with trifles.

pic•nic ['pɪknɪk] *n., v.* **-nicked, -nick•ing.** *—n.* **1** a pleasure trip with a meal in the open air. **2** any outdoor meal. **3** *Informal.* a pleasant time or experience; very easy job.
—v. **1** go on a picnic. **2** eat in picnic style. ⟨< F *piquenique*⟩ **—'pic•nick•er,** *n.*

picnic shelter *Cdn.* a shelter erected at a roadside picnic ground or campsite for the convenience of travellers and picnickers.

picnic shoulder or **ham** a smoked shoulder of pork, cut to resemble a ham. See PORK for picture.

pico– *SI prefix.* one one-trillionth; 10^{-12}: *picofarad. Symbol*: p ⟨< Sp. *pico* small quantity⟩

pi•cot ['pikou] *n., v. —n.* one of a number of fancy loops in embroidery, tatting, etc. or along the edge of lace, ribbon, etc.
—v. trim with picots. ⟨< F *picot*, dim. of *pic* pick¹. See PIKE¹.⟩
☛ *Hom.* PEKOE.

pi•co•tee [,pɪkə'ti] *n.* a variety of a flower, usually a carnation or tulip, having a border of a colour darker than the main colour. ⟨< F *picoté*, pp. of *picoter* mark, prick < *picot*, dim. of *pic* pick¹⟩

pic•rate ['pɪkreit] *n. Chemistry.* a salt or ester of picric acid.

pic•ric acid ['pɪkrɪk] *Chemistry.* a yellow, intensely bitter acid used as a dye and in explosives. *Formula*: $C_6H_3N_3O_7$ ⟨< Gk. *pikros* bitter⟩

Pict [pɪkt] *n.* a member of a people of disputed origin, formerly living in Scotland, especially N Scotland. ⟨< LL *Picti*, painted ones, pl. of *pictus*, pp. of *pingere* to paint⟩

Pict•ish ['pɪktɪʃ] *adj., n. —adj.* of or having to do with the Picts.
—n. the language of the Picts, known chiefly from place names and fragmentary inscriptions, thought to be pre-Indo-European with some Celtic influence.

pic•to•gram ['pɪktə,græm] *n.* pictograph.

pic•to•graph ['pɪktə,græf] *n.* **1** a picture used as a sign or symbol. **2** a chart or graph on which symbols are used to represent quantities such as population or production of goods. ⟨< L *pictus* painted + E *-graph*⟩ **—,pic•to'graph•ic,** *adj.* **—,pic•to'graph•i•cal•ly,** *adv.*

pic•tog•ra•phy [pɪk'tɒgrəfi] *n.* written communication using a system of pictures.

Pic•tor ['pɪktər] *n. Astronomy.* a southern constellation between Dorado and Columba.

pic•to•ri•al [pɪk'tɔriəl] *adj., n. —adj.* **1** having to do with pictures; expressed in pictures. **2** making a picture for the mind; vivid. **3** illustrated by pictures: *a pictorial history.* **4** having to do with painters or painting.
—n. a magazine in which pictures are an important feature. ⟨< L *pictorius* < *pictor* painter⟩ **—pic'to•ri•al•ly,** *adv.*

pic•ture ['pɪktʃər] *n., v.* **-tured, -tur•ing.** *—n.* **1** a drawing, painting, portrait, or photograph; a print of any of these. **2** a scene. **3** a mental image; a visualized conception; idea: *to have a clear picture of the problem.* **4** something beautiful: *She was the picture in her new dress.* **5** image; likeness: *Michael is the picture of his father.* **6** an example; embodiment: *She was the picture of despair.* **7** a vivid description. **8** movie; film: *Let's see a picture tonight.* **9** an image on a screen. **10** a tableau, as in a theatrical production. **11** *Informal.* state of affairs; condition; situation: *the employment picture.*
in or **out of the picture,** part or not part of any given situation.
picture perfect, so attractive that one would want its likeness to be preserved.
the big picture, a comprehensive and coherent view of a topic, situation, etc.
—v. **1** draw, paint, etc.; make into a picture. **2** form a picture of in the mind; imagine: *It is hard to picture life a hundred years ago.* **3** show by words; describe vividly: *The speaker pictured the suffering of the poor.* ⟨ME < L *pictura*, ult. < *pingere* to paint⟩

picture hat a woman's hat having a very wide brim, originally often trimmed with ostrich feathers, now more often with flowers.

pic•tur•esque [,pɪktʃə'rɛsk] *adj.* **1** quaint, interesting, or pretty enough to be used as the subject of a picture: *a picturesque old mill.* **2** making a picture for the mind; vivid. ⟨< F *pittoresque* < Ital. *pittoresco* in the style of a painter < *pittore* painter < L *pictor*; influenced by *picture*⟩ **—ˌpic•tur'esque•ly,** *adv.* **—ˌpic•tur'esque•ness,** *n.*

picture tube a cathode ray tube that produces a transmitted picture on a television screen.

picture window a large window that seems to frame the view seen through it.

picture writing **1** the recording of events or expressing of ideas by pictures. **2** the pictures so used.

pid•dle ['pɪdəl] *v.* **-dled, -dling;** *n.* *—v.* **1** do anything in a trifling or ineffective way. **2** *Informal.* urinate.
—n. Informal. urine. ⟨origin uncertain⟩ **—'pid•dler,** *n.*

pid•dling ['pɪdlɪŋ] *adj., v.* *—adj.* trifling; petty.
—v. ppr. of PIDDLE.

pid•dock ['pɪdək] *n.* any of a family (Pholadidae) of bivalve molluscs that bore holes in soft rocks, wood, clay, etc. Compare TEREDO. ⟨possibly related to OE *puduc* wart⟩

pid•gin ['pɪdʒən] *n.* **1** an auxiliary language developed as a result of long-term contact between speakers of two or more different languages who need to communicate for purposes of trade, religion, etc. A pidgin has a simplified grammar and phonology and a basic vocabulary drawn from the various contributing languages, and is no one's mother tongue. Compare CREOLE. **2** in a loose sense, any extremely simplified or broken form of a language, especially between speakers of different languages. ⟨< Chinese Pidgin English pronunciation of *business*⟩
☛ *Hom.* PIGEON.

pidgin English **1** originally, Chinese Pidgin English. **2** any of a number of English-based pidgins spoken in the South Pacific and West Africa. **3** any very simple or broken English used for communication.

pie[1] [paɪ] *n.* **1** food consisting of an upper crust, an under crust, or both, made from pastry or a mixture of fine crumbs, sugar, and butter, usually baked, having a filling of meat, fruit, custard, etc. **2** a layer cake with a filling of whipped cream, jelly, etc.: *Boston cream pie.* **3** something desirable that may be divided into portions.
as easy as pie, extremely easy to do. ⟨ME *pye*; origin uncertain⟩
☛ *Hom.* PI.

pie[2] [paɪ] *n.* magpie. ⟨ME < OF < L *pica*⟩
☛ *Hom.* PI.

pie[3] [paɪ] *n. v.* **pied, pie•ing.** See PI[2]. ⟨? extended use of *pie[1]*⟩
☛ *Hom.* PI.

pie•bald ['paɪˌbɒld] *adj., n.* *—adj.* spotted in two colours, especially black and white.
—n. a spotted animal, especially a horse. ⟨apparently < *pie[2]* + *bald*; with reference to dark colour of magpie⟩

piece [pis] *n., v.* **pieced, piec•ing.** *—n.* **1** one of the parts into which a thing is divided or broken; bit: *a piece of wood. The cup broke in pieces.* **2** a portion; part; small quantity: *a piece of land, a piece of bread.* **3** a single item from a set or class: *a piece of luggage. This set of china has 144 pieces.* **4** a coin: *A nickel is a five-cent piece.* **5** an example; instance. **6** a single work of art: *a piece of music, a piece of poetry.* **7** a unit of work forming a single job: *These workers are paid by the piece.* **8** a gun; cannon. **9** a standard quantity in which goods are made: *She bought the whole piece of muslin.* **10** a share; financial interest: *a piece of the action.* **11** *Checkers, chess, etc.* a figure, disk, block, etc. used in playing. **12** a snack between meals. **13** *Cdn.* formerly, a package of goods or furs weighing about 40 kg, the standard load carried by the fur brigades.
go to pieces, a fall apart; break up: *Another ship had gone to pieces on the rocks.* **b** break down; collapse: *When his business failed, he went completely to pieces.*
of a piece, of the same kind; in keeping: *That plan is of a piece with the rest of their silly suggestions.*
piece of (one's) **mind,** *Informal.* **a** candid opinion. **b** a scolding: *He gave the taxi-driver a piece of his mind for coming late.*
speak or **say** (one's) **piece,** voice one's opinions.
—v. **1** make or repair by adding or joining pieces: *She had to piece the skirt to make it come out.* **2** join the pieces of: *We can piece the vase so the break won't show.* **3** eat between meals: *The child was always piecing.* ⟨ME *pece* < OF < Med.L *petia* fragment < Celtic⟩ **—'piec•er,** *n.*
☛ *Hom.* PEACE.
☛ *Syn. n.* **2.** See note at PART.

pièce de ré•sis•tance [ˌpjɛs də reɪzɪ'stɑns]; *French,* [pjɛsdəʀesi'stɑ̃s] **1** the chief dish of a meal. **2** the most important or outstanding item in any collection or series.

piece•meal ['pisˌmil] *adv., adj.* *—adv.* **1** piece by piece; a little at a time: *work done piecemeal.* **2** piece from piece; to pieces; into fragments.
—adj. done piece by piece. ⟨ME *pecemele* < *pece* piece + *-mele* < OE *mæl* part, measure⟩

piece of eight a former Spanish coin equal to eight reals.

piece•work ['pisˌwɜrk] *n.* work paid for the amount done, not by the time it takes. **—'piece,work•er,** *n.*

pie•crust ['pəiˌkrʌst] *adj.* having a fluted edge like that of a pie crust: *a piecrust table.*

pie crust pastry used for the bottom or top of a pie.

pied [paɪd] *adj.* **1** having patches of two or more colours; many-coloured. **2** spotted. **3** wearing a costume of two or more colours. ⟨< *pie[2]*; with reference to magpie's plumage⟩

pied–à–terre [pjeta'tɛʀ] *n., pl.* **pieds-à-terre.** *French.* a house or apartment kept for occasional use: *They live on a ranch but have a pied-à-terre in Vancouver.* ⟨literally, foot on (the) ground⟩

pied•mont ['pidˌmɒnt] *n., adj.* *—n.* an area of land at the base of a mountain or mountains: *the piedmont of Alberta.*
—adj. near the base of a mountain or mountains: *the piedmont area of Alberta, a piedmont stream.* ⟨after *Piedmont*, Italy < L *Pedimontium* < *pedi(s)* (gen. of *pes* foot) + *monti(s)* (gen. of *mons* mountain)⟩

Pied Piper *Folklore.* a piper who appeared in the German town of Hamelin, promising to rid the town of rats. The rats followed his piping out of the town, but when the townspeople refused to pay him, he enticed the children out of the town with his piping, and they were never seen again.

pie–eyed ['paɪ ˌaɪd] *adj. Slang.* drunk.

pie–faced ['paɪ ˌfeist] *adj. Informal.* looking stupid.

Pie•gan ['pigæn] *n., pl.* **-gan** or **-gans.** a member of a First Nations people of the Plains, one of the three Algonquian tribes of the Blackfoot confederacy.

pie–in–the–sky ['paɪ ɪn ðə 'skaɪ] *n., adj.* *—n. Slang.* **1** unrealistic promises of benefits or rewards in the distant future: *Most of that party's platform is pie-in-the-sky.* **2** utopian plans unlikely to come to fruition: *Their dream house on the Riviera is so much pie-in-the-sky.*
—adj. unrealistic; hopelessly utopian: *They made a lot of pie-in-the-sky suggestions.*

pier [pir] *n.* **1** a structure supported on columns extending into the water, used as a walk or a landing place for ships. **2** breakwater. **3** one of the solid supports on which the arches of a bridge rest; any solid support of masonry. **4** the solid part of a wall between windows, doors, etc. ⟨ME *per* < Med.L *pera* prob. ult. < L *petra* stone⟩
☛ *Hom.* PEER.

pierce [pirs] *v.* **pierced, pierc•ing. 1** make a hole in; bore into or through: *A nail pierced the tire of our car.* **2** go into; go through: *A tunnel pierces the mountain.* **3** sound so loudly and keenly in (air, ears) as to be almost painful to the hearer: *A sharp cry pierced the air.* **4** penetrate with the eye or mind: *to pierce a disguise, to pierce a mystery.* **5** affect sharply with some feeling: *a heart pierced with grief.* ⟨ME *percen* < OF *percer*, ult. < L *pertusus* pierced, pp. of *pertundere* < *per-* through + *tundere* beat⟩
☛ *Syn.* **1.** See note at PENETRATE.

pierc•ing ['pirsɪŋ] *adj., v.* *—adj.* that pierces; penetrating; sharp; keen: *piercing cold, a piercing look.*
—v. ppr. of PIERCE. **—'pierc•ing•ly,** *adv.* **—'pierc•ing•ness,** *n.*

pier glass a tall mirror, such as that originally used to fill the space, or pier, between two windows.

Pi•er•i•an [paɪ'iriən] *adj.* of or having to do with the Muses. ⟨< *Pieria*, in ancient Thessaly, supposed home of the Muses⟩

Pierian spring the supposed fountain of knowledge and poetic inspiration.

pie•ro•gi [pə'rougi] *n., pl.* **-gies.** See PEROGY.

Pi•er•rot [ˌpiə'rou] *or* [pjə'rou]; *French,* [pjɛ'ʀo] *n., pl.* **-rots** [-'roz]; *French,* [-'ʀo] a clown who is a traditional character in French pantomime. He has his face whitened and wears white pantaloons and, usually, a white jacket with big buttons. ⟨< F *Pierrot*, dim. of *Pierre* Peter⟩

pie social *Cdn.* a social event to which those attending bring pies to raise money for some charitable purpose.

pi•e•tà or **Pi•e•tà** [piei'tɑ] *or* [pi'eitɑ] *n. Art.* a representation of the Virgin holding the dead Christ in her arms. ⟨< Ital. *pietà* pity < L *pietas* piety⟩

pi•e•tism ['paɪə,tɪzəm] *n.* **1** an emphasis on personal piety at the expense of neglecting corporate or social righteousness. **2** pretended piety. **3 Pietism,** a 17th-century movement for reviving piety in the Lutheran Church. ⟨< G *Pietismus*⟩
—'pi•e•tist, *n.* **—,pi•e'tis•tic,** *adj.* **—,pi•e'tis•ti•cal•ly,** *adv.*

pi•e•ty ['paɪəti] *n., pl.* **-ties. 1** the condition of being pious or of having reverence for God; devotion to religion; holiness. **2** a dutiful regard for one's parents. **3** a pious act, remark, belief, etc. ⟨ME < OF *piete* < L *pietas* < *pius* pious. Doublet of PITY.⟩

pi•e•zo•e•lec•tric [paɪ,izouɪ'lɛktrɪk] *adj.* of certain crystals, alternately enlarging and growing smaller as a result of mechanical stress when subjected to an alternating electric current. ⟨< *piezo*-pressure (< Gk. *piezein* press) + *electric*⟩

pif•fle ['pɪfəl] *n., v.* **pif•fled, pif•fling,** *interj. Informal.* *—n.* silly talk; nonsense.
—v. talk nonsense.
—interj. nonsense! ⟨? related to OE *pyffan* puff⟩

pif•fling ['pɪflɪŋ] *adj. Informal.* insignificant; trifling; piddling.

pig [pɪg] *n., v.* **pigged, pig•ging.** *—n.* **1** a cloven-hoofed domestic mammal (*Sus scrofa*) having a long snout, a stout, heavy body, and short legs; swine. Pigs are raised for their meat. **2** any other mammal of the same family (Suidae). **3** a young swine. **4** pork. **5** *Informal.* a dirty, disagreeable person. **6** *Informal.* a person who eats a lot, often with bad table manners. **7** metal, such as iron, cast in an oblong shape for storage or transportation; PIG IRON. **8** *Slang.* a rude or arrogant person.
buy a pig in a poke, buy something without seeing or knowing its real nature or value.
make a pig of (oneself), *Informal.* overindulge oneself in eating.
—v. **1** of a sow, give birth; farrow. **2** *Informal.* Also, **pig it,** live in poor, dirty, or crowded conditions.
pig out, *Informal.* eat to the point of discomfort; overindulge in food. ⟨OE *picg* (in *picg-bred* mast[2], literally, pig-bread); origin uncertain⟩

pig bed *Metallurgy.* a bed of sand into which molten metal is poured to mould PIGS (def. 7).

One kind of pigeon: about 38 cm long including the tail

pi•geon ['pɪdʒən] *n.* **1** any of a family (Columbidae) of birds having a stout body and small head. Many domesticated varieties of pigeon are bred from the wild **rock pigeon. 2** CLAY PIGEON. **3** *Slang.* a person who is easily tricked. **4** *Informal.* a usually attractive girl or young woman. ⟨ME *pejon* < OF *pijon* < VL < LL *pipio, -onis* squab; from the sound (cf. L *pipiare* cheep)⟩
☛ *Hom.* PIDGIN.

pigeon hawk a pigeon-sized falcon (*Falco columbarius*) found throughout the N hemisphere, having mainly blue-grey plumage with a white-barred tail. Its usual European name is **merlin.**

pi•geon•hole ['pɪdʒən,houl] *n., v.* **-holed, -hol•ing.** *—n.* **1** a small place built, usually as one of a series, for a pigeon to nest in. **2** one of a set of boxlike compartments for holding papers and other articles in a desk, a cabinet, etc.
—v. **1** put in a pigeonhole; put away. **2** classify and lay aside in memory for future reference. **3** assign to a category; classify, often in a rigid or stereotypical way. **4** put aside with the idea of dismissing, forgetting, or neglecting: *The city council pigeonholed the request for a new park.*

pi•geon–toed ['pɪdʒən ,toud] *adj.* having the toes or feet turned inward.

pi•geon•wing ['pɪdʒən,wɪŋ] *n.* **1** a figure in skating outlining the shape of a pigeon's wing. **2** a fancy dance step executed by jumping and striking the feet together with the knees apart, so that the space between the legs has roughly the shape of a pigeon's wing.

pig•ger•y ['pɪgəri] *n., pl.* **-ger•ies.** *Esp. Brit.* PIGPEN (def. 1).

pig•gish ['pɪgɪʃ] *adj.* like a pig; greedy; filthy. **—'pig•gish•ly,** *adv.* **—'pig•gish•ness,** *n.*

pig•gy ['pɪgi] *n., pl.* **-gies.** *Informal.* a little pig.

pig•gy•back ['pɪgi,bæk] *n., adv., adj., v.* *—n.* **1** a carrying or being carried on the back or shoulders: *He gave the child a piggyback.* **2** the act or process of transporting loaded truck trailers on flatcars.
—adv. or adj. **1** on the back or shoulders: *a piggyback ride.* **2** by piggyback.
—v. carry by piggyback.

piggy bank 1 a small container in the shape of a pig, with a slot in the top for coins. **2** any coin bank.

pig–head•ed ['pɪg ,hɛdɪd] *adj.* stupidly obstinate or stubborn.
—'pig-,head•ed•ness, *n.*

pig iron crude iron as it first comes from the blast furnace or smelter, usually cast into oblong masses called pigs.

pig Latin a children's jargon, in one form of which the syllable *-ay* [ei] is added to the end of a word, any initial consonant being placed immediately before this ending. *Examples*: oodgay = good, offay = off, ordway = word.

pig•let ['pɪglət] *n.* a little pig; baby pig.

pig•ment ['pɪgmənt] *n.* **1** a colouring matter, especially a powder or some easily pulverized dry substance, that, when mixed with oil, water, or other liquid vehicle, constitutes a paint. **2** *Biology.* the natural colouring matter of a cell or tissue. ⟨ME < L *pigmentum*, ult. < *pingere* paint. Doublet of PIMENTO.⟩
—'pig•ment,ize, *v.*

pig•men•tar•y ['pɪgmən,tɛri] *adj.* of, producing, or containing pigment.

pig•men•ta•tion [,pɪgmən'teiʃən] *n. Biology.* **1** a deposit of pigment in the tissue of a living animal or plant, causing coloration or discoloration. **2** the colouring of an animal or plant resulting from pigment in the tissues.

pig•my ['pɪgmi] See PYGMY.

pig•nut ['pɪg,nʌt] *n.* **1** the bitter nut of any of several North American hickory trees, such as *Carya glabra.* **2** a tree bearing such nuts. **3** earthnut.

pig•pen ['pɪg,pɛn] *n.* **1** a pen where pigs are kept. **2** a filthy place.

pig•skin ['pɪg,skɪn] *n.* **1** the skin of a pig. **2** leather made from it. **3** *Informal.* the ball used in playing Canadian or American football.

pig•stick•ing ['pɪg,stɪkɪŋ] *n.* the hunting of wild boars, usually from horseback and using a spear as the weapon.

pig•sty ['pɪg,staɪ] *n., pl.* **-sties.** pigpen.

pig•tail ['pɪg,teil] *n.* **1 pigtails,** *pl.* **a** two usually short bunches of loose hair, one sticking down on either side of the head. **b** braids. **2** a twist of tobacco.

pig•weed ['pɪg,wid] *n.* **1** any of several North American amaranths that are troublesome weeds, especially **red-root pigweed** (*A. retroflexus*), having hairy leaves and stems and small green flowers. **2** a tall, annual plant (*Axyris amaranthoides*) of the goosefoot family, native to Asia but now a common Canadian weed, especially in the Prairies. Also called **Russian pigweed.**

pi•ka [pəikə] *n.* any of a family (Ochotonidae) of small, short-eared, short-legged, tailless mammals resembling guinea pigs but belonging to the same order as rabbits and hares. All 14 living species, found in the mountainous regions of W North America and Asia, belong to the genus *Ochotona.* ⟨< Tungus (Siberia) *piika*, probably imitative of its cry⟩
☛ *Hom.* PICA.

pike[1] [pəik] *n., v.* **piked, pik•ing.** *—n.* a weapon having a long wooden handle and a pointed metal head, once carried by foot soldiers; spear.
—v. kill, pierce, or wound with or as with a pike. ⟨< F *pique* < *piquer* pierce < *pic* a pick < Gmc.⟩

pike[2] [pəik] *n.* a sharp point; spike. ⟨ME *pike* OE *pīc* pick, pickaxe⟩

pike[3] [pəik] *n.* **1** a large, long freshwater food and game fish (*Esox lucius*) having a long, narrow, pointed head with many sharp teeth. Also called **northern pike. 2** (*adjl.*) designating a family (Esocidae) of freshwater food and game fishes found in North America, Europe, and Asia. The pike family is made up of one genus (*Esox*), which includes the pike, muskellunge, and pickerel. **3** pickerel. ⟨apparently < *pike[2]* (because of the shape of its snout)⟩

pike[4] [pəik] *n.* turnpike.

pike•man ['pəikmən] *n., pl.* **-men** [-mən]. a soldier armed with a pike.

pike•perch or **pike–perch** ['pəik,pɜrtʃ] *n. Cdn.* WALLEYE (def. 7); doré.

pike–pole or **pike•pole** ['pəik ,poul] *n. Cdn.* a long pole with a pike or spike at one end, especially one used by loggers to direct floating logs.

pik•er ['pəikər] *n. Slang.* a person who does things in a small or cheap way. ⟨origin uncertain⟩

pike•staff ['pəik,stæf] *n., pl.* **-staves** [-,steivz]. **1** the staff or shaft of a pike or spear. **2** a staff with a metal point or spike, used by travellers on foot.

pi•laf or **pi•laff** [pɪ'lɑf] *or* ['pilɑf] *n.* pilau.

pi•las•ter [pə'læstər] *n.* a rectangular pillar, especially when it forms part of a wall from which it projects slightly. ⟨< F *pilastre* < Ital. *pilastro* < L *pila* pillar⟩

pi•lau or **pi•law** [pɪ'laʊ] *or* [pɪ'lɒ], ['pilaʊ] *or* ['pilɒ] *n.* a dish consisting of steamed or boiled rice flavoured with spices and often including chopped meat, poultry, or fish. ⟨< Turkish < Persian *pilāw.* 17c.⟩

pil•chard ['pɪltʃərd] *n.* **1** an important European food fish (*Sardina pilchardus*) of the herring family. **2** any of various other fishes of the herring family, such as *Sardinops sagax* of Pacific coastal waters from Alaska to Baja California and from Peru to Chile. ⟨origin uncertain⟩

pile[1] [paɪl] *n., v.* **piled, pil•ing.** *—n.* **1** many things lying one upon another in a more or less orderly way: *a pile of wood.* **2** a heap; mass like a hill or mound: *a pile of dirt.* **3** pyre. **4** a large structure or mass of buildings. **5** Often, **piles,** *pl. Informal.* a large amount or number: *piles of dishes to wash, a pile of work to do.* **6** *Informal.* a large amount of money: *He made a pile on that deal.* **7** NUCLEAR REACTOR. **8** *Electricity.* **a** a series of plates of different metals, arranged alternately with cloth or paper wet with acid between them, for producing an electric current. **b** any similar arrangement for producing an electric current; battery.
—v. **1** make into or as if into a pile; heap (*often used with* **up**): *We piled the blankets in a corner.* **2** accumulate or become heaped in or as if in a pile (*usually used with* **up**): *Snow had piled up against the door. A lot of work had piled up while we were away.* **3** load with a pile of something: *They piled her plate with spaghetti.* **4** move or press forward in a group, especially in a rushed or confused way (*used with* **in, into, out, off,** *etc.*): *to pile out into the street. Two more players piled into the scrimmage.* **5** collide; destroy or be destroyed (*often used with* **up**): *The sailboat had piled up on the rocky shore.*
pile (something) **on,** *Informal.* employ (description, flattery, humour, etc.) in great amounts or to excess: *Some authors like to pile on the sex and violence. It's nice to be complimented, but she really piles it on.* ⟨ME < OF < L *pila* pillar⟩ **—'pil•er,** *n.*

pile[2] [paɪl] *n., v.* **piled, pil•ing.** *—n.* **1** a heavy beam driven upright into the earth, often under water, to help support a bridge, wharf, building, etc. **2** *Heraldry.* a wedge-shaped or triangular bearing entering from one edge of the escutcheon.
—v. furnish with piles; drive piles into. ⟨OE *pīl* stake < L *pilum* javelin⟩

pile[3] [paɪl] *n.* **1** the surface of certain fabrics woven with loops of yarn which may be uncut, as in towelling, or cut, as in velvet, carpeting, etc. **2** the cut or uncut loops that form the surface. **3** a soft, fine hair or down. ⟨< L *pilus* hair⟩

pi•le•ate ['paɪliɪt] *or* ['pɪliɪt], ['paɪli,eit] *or* ['pɪli,eit] *adj. Botany, zoology.* having a pileus.

pi•le•at•ed ['paɪli,eitɪd] *or* ['pɪli,eitɪd] *adj.* **1** of a bird, having a crest: *a pileated woodpecker.* **2** pileate.

pileated woodpecker a large bird (*Dryocopus pileatus*) having black-and-white plumage and a pronounced red crest on the head.

piled [paɪld] *adj., v. —adj.* having a soft, thick nap.
—v. pt. and pp. of PILE.

pile driver a machine for driving down piles or stakes, usually a tall framework in which a heavy weight is raised to a height and then allowed to fall upon the pile.

pi•le•ous ['paɪliəs] *or* ['pɪliəs] *adj.* furry; hairy.
☛ *Hom.* PILEUS.

piles [paɪlz] *n.pl.* a swelling of blood vessels at the anus, often painful; hemorrhoids. ⟨ME *pyle,* sing., ? < L *pila* ball⟩

pi•le•um ['paɪliəm] *or* ['pɪliəm] *n., pl.* **-le•a** [-liə]. the top of a bird's head, from the base of the bill to the nape.

pile–up ['paɪl ,ʌp] *n. Informal.* **1** a collision involving several or many vehicles: *Five people were killed in the pile-up on the parkway yesterday.* **2** a great mass or jumble of people or things: *a pile-up on the football field.*

pi•le•us ['paɪliəs] *or* ['pɪliəs] *n., pl.* **-le•i** [-li,aɪ]. **1** *Botany.* the umbrella-shaped fruiting body of a mushroom or similar fungus. **2** *Zoology.* the umbrella-shaped bell of a jellyfish. **3** pileum. **4** a brimless skullcap worn in ancient Greece and Rome. ⟨< LL special use of L *pileus* skullcap < Gk. *pilós* felt, felt cap⟩
☛ *Hom.* PILEOUS.

pile•wort ['paɪl,wɜrt] *or* ['paɪl,wɔrt] *n.* **1** fireweed. **2** the lesser celandine. **3** a North American figwort (*Scraphularia marilandica*). ⟨< *piles,* for its purported medicinal properties⟩

pil•fer ['pɪlfər] *v.* steal in small quantities; steal. ⟨ME < MF *pelfrer* rob⟩ **—'pil•fer•er,** *n.* **—'pil•fer•age,** *n.*
☛ *Syn.* See note at STEAL.

pil•grim ['pɪlgrəm] *n.* **1** a person who goes on a journey to a sacred or holy place as an act of religious devotion. **2** a traveller; wanderer. **3 Pilgrim,** one of the British Puritan settlers who founded Plymouth Colony (in what is now Massachusetts) in 1620. ⟨ME < AF *pelegrim, var. of OF *pelerin* < Med.L *peregrinus* pilgrim < L *peregrinus* foreigner. Doublet of PEREGRINE.⟩

pil•grim•age ['pɪlgrəmɪdʒ] *n.* **1** a pilgrim's journey; journey to some sacred place as an act of religious devotion. **2** a long journey, especially one to see or visit a special place, etc. **3** life thought of as a journey. ⟨ME < OF *pelerinage* < *peleriner* go as a pilgrim⟩

pili– *combining form.* hair: *piliform.* ⟨< L *pilus*⟩

pi•lif•er•ous [pə'lɪfərəs] *adj.* producing or having hair.

pil•i•form ['pɪlə,fɔrm] *adj.* resembling hair.

pil•ing ['paɪlɪŋ] *n., v. —n.* **1** piles or heavy beams driven into the ground, etc. **2** a structure made of piles.
—v. ppr. of PILE.

Pil•i•pi•no [,pɪlɪ'pinou] *n.* a language essentially the same as Tagalog, that has been declared the official language of the Philippines.

pill [pɪl] *n., v. —n.* **1** medicine in a small, solid, usually rounded mass intended to be swallowed whole. **2 the pill** or **the Pill,** any of various pills for contraception; an oral contraceptive. **3** *Slang.* a baseball or golf ball. **4** something unpleasant that has to be endured: *Our defeat was a bitter pill.* **5** *Slang.* an unpleasant or boring person.
—v. of knitted or brushed woven fabric, become matted into small balls: *This sweater is pilling badly.* ⟨late ME *pylle* < L *pilula,* dim. of *pila* ball⟩

pil•lage ['pɪlɪdʒ] *v.* **-laged, -lag•ing;** *n. —v.* rob with violence; plunder: *Pirates pillaged the towns along the coast.*
—n. plunder; robbery. ⟨ME < OF *pillage* < *piller* plunder < VL *pileare* flay⟩ **—'pil•lag•er,** *n.*

pil•lar ['pɪlər] *n.* **1** a slender, upright structure; column. Pillars are usually made of stone, wood, or metal and used as supports or ornaments for a building. **2** anything slender and upright like a pillar. **3** an important support or supporter; an influential and dependable member: *He is a pillar of the community.*
from pillar to post, a from one thing or place to another without any definite purpose. **b** from one predicament or bad solution to another, often under harassment. ⟨ME < OF *piler,* ult. < L *pila* pillar, pile[1]⟩

pil•lared ['pɪlərd] *adj.* **1** having pillars. **2** formed into pillars.

Pillars of Hercules two high points of land at the eastern end of the Strait of Gibraltar, one on either side of the strait. The point on the European side is the Rock of Gibraltar and the one on the African side is Jebel Musa.

Pillars of Islam the five bases of the Islamic faith: confession, prayer, almsgiving, fasting, and the pilgrimage to Mecca.

pill•box ['pɪl,bɒks] *n.* **1** a box, usually shallow and often round, for holding pills. **2** a small, low fortress with very thick walls and roof, having machine guns, anti-tank weapons, etc. **3** a small, round, brimless hat with a low, flat crown: *Royal Military College cadets wear pillboxes.* See HAT for picture.

pil•lion ['pɪljən] *n., adv. —n.* a pad attached behind a saddle on a horse or motorcycle for a passenger to sit on.
—adv. on a pillion: *to ride pillion.* ⟨< Scots Gaelic *pillin* or *pillean,* dim. of *pell* cushion < L *pellis* skin⟩

pil•lo•ry ['pɪləri] *n., pl.* **-ries;** *v.* **-ried, -ry•ing.** *—n.* **1** formerly, a device used for the public punishment of an offender, consisting of a wooden frame with holes through which the person's head and hands were put and which was then locked in place. **2** exposure to public ridicule, scorn, or abuse.
—v. **1** formerly, put in a pillory as punishment. **2** expose to

public ridicule, scorn, or abuse. ⟨< OF *pellori* < Provençal *espilori*; origin uncertain⟩

pil•low ['pɪlou] *n., v.* *—n.* **1** a fabric bag or case filled with feathers, down, or some other soft material, usually used to support the head when resting or sleeping. **2** anything used for a similar purpose. **3** a pad on which a kind of lace is made. **4** a supporting piece or part, such as the block on which the inner end of a bowsprit rests.
—v. **1** rest on or as if on a pillow: *He pillowed his head on a pile of leaves.* **2** be a pillow for. ⟨OE *pyle, pylu,* ult. < L *pulvinus*⟩ **—'pil•low,like** or **'pil•lo•wy,** *adj.*

pil•low•case ['pɪlou,keis] *n.* a removable cover for a pillow, usually made from cotton or linen.

pillow sham an ornamental cover for a bed pillow, often trimmed with ruffles, lace, etc.

pil•low•slip ['pɪlou,slɪp] *n.* pillowcase.

pi•lo•car•pine [,pɪlou'kɑrpin] *n. Pharmacy.* an oil or crystalline alkaloid, $C_{11}H_{16}N_2O_2$, obtained from jaborandi. It is used in its hydrochloride or nitrate form to treat glaucoma.

pi•lose ['paɪlous] *adj.* covered with soft hair; hairy. ⟨< L *pilosus* shaggy < *pilus* hair⟩ **—pi'los•i•ty** [paɪ'lɒsəti], *n.*

pi•lot ['paɪlət] *n., v.* *—n.* **1** a person trained to operate the controls of an aircraft or spacecraft in flight. **2** a person who steers a ship; a person at the helm. **3** one whose business is steering ships in or out of a harbour or through dangerous waters. A ship takes on a pilot before coming into a strange harbour. **4** (*adjl.*) of or having to do with a pilot: *The crash was the result of pilot error.* **5** a guide or leader. **6** a device that controls the action of one part of a machine, motor, etc. **7** cowcatcher. **8** a television show produced to serve as a sample of a projected series. **9** (*adjl.*) serving as an advance or experimental version or sample of some action, operation, device, etc.: *a pilot project, a pilot film.* **10** (*adjl.*) that serves to activate, guide, or control: *a pilot star for navigation.* **11** PILOT LIGHT.
—v. **1** act as the pilot of; steer. **2** guide or lead: *The manager piloted us through the big factory.* **3** use as an advance or experimental version: *to pilot a book in a school.* ⟨< F < Ital. *pilota*⟩

pi•lot•age ['paɪlətɪdʒ] *n.* **1** the act of piloting. **2** a pilot's expertise or duties. **3** the fee paid for a pilot's service.

pilot balloon a small balloon used for visual observation of wind velocity.

pilot biscuit or **bread** SHIP BISCUIT.

pilot film PILOT (def. 8).

pilot fish **1** a tropical or subtropical marine fish (*Naucrates ductor*) of the same family as the pompano, that often accompanies a shark. **2** any of various other fishes that act in a similar way.

pilot house an enclosed place on the deck of a ship, sheltering the steering wheel and the person at the helm.

pi•lot•ing ['paɪlətɪŋ] *n., v.* *—n.* the directing of the course or position of a ship or plane using landmarks, buoys, and other navigational devices.
—v. ppr. of PILOT.

pilot lamp **1** an electric lamp used to indicate the position of a circuit breaker or a switch. **2** in conjunction with a control, an electric light indicating whether or not the current is on.

pilot light a small flame kept burning all the time and used to light a main burner whenever the gas is turned on. Gas stoves and gas water heaters have pilot lights.

pilot officer *Commonwealth excluding Canada.* an air-force officer of the lowest commissioned rank, junior to a flying officer. *Abbrev.:* P.O.

pilot whale any of a genus (*Globicephala*) of small, mostly black, toothed whales found in most seas. Some authorities recognize only one species in the genus; others recognize two or three different species.

Pil•sen•er ['pɪlzənər] *or* ['pɪlznər] *n.* a pale lager beer. ⟨< G *Pilsener* < *Pilsen,* a city in Czechoslovakia⟩

Pilt•down man ['pɪlt,daʊn] a supposed type of prehistoric person of which fossil remains found at Piltdown, Sussex, were thought to be the most ancient yet discovered in England; they are now generally considered to have been a hoax.

PIM *Computer technology.* personal information manager, a hand-held computer for keeping track of dates, addresses and phone numbers, messages, etc.

Pi•ma ['pimə] *n.* **1** a member of a Native American people living in southern Arizona and northern New Mexico. **2** the Uto-Aztecan language of these people. ⟨< Am.Sp. *pima* < 16c. Pima *pim a daita* nothing⟩ **—'Pi•man,** *adj.*

Pima cotton a variety of fine, smooth, long-staple cotton derived from Egyptian cotton and grown in the SW United States. Its chief use is in the manufacture of shirts. ⟨< *Pima* County, Arizona⟩

pi•men•to [pɪ'mɛntou] *n., pl.* **-tos. 1** any of various sweet red peppers, the fruit of a capsicum, especially *C. annuum,* used especially as a relish and as stuffing for green olives. Pimentos are also dried and ground up to make paprika. **2** a small evergreen tree (*Pimenta officinalis*) of the myrtle family native to the West Indies. **3** a spice made from the dried berries of the West Indian pimento; allspice. ⟨< Sp. *pimienta* pepper, *pimiento* capsicum < Med.L *pigmentum* spice < LL *pigmentum* vegetable juice < L *pigmentum* pigment. Doublet of PIGMENT.⟩

pi•mien•to [pɪ'mjɛntou] *or* [pɪ'mɛntou] *n., pl.* **-tos.** PIMENTO (def. 1). ⟨< Sp. *pimiento.* See PIMENTO.⟩

pi•mo•la [pɪ'moulə] *n.* an olive stuffed with red sweet pepper. ⟨? < *pimento*⟩

pimp [pɪmp] *n., v.* *—n.* **1** a person, especially a man, who solicits for or manages one or more prostitutes and takes part of their earnings. **2** a man who procures sexual entertainment for others; pander.
—v. be or act as a pimp. ⟨origin unknown⟩

pim•per•nel ['pɪmpər,nɛl] *or* ['pɪmpərnəl] *n.* **1** any of a genus (*Anagallis*) of plants of the primrose family, especially the **scarlet pimpernel** (*A. arvensis*), having scarlet, purple, or white star-shaped flowers that close in cloudy or rainy weather. **2** the flower of any of these plants. ⟨ME < OF *pimprenele,* ult. < VL *piperinus* of peppercorns < L *piper* pepper⟩

pim•ple ['pɪmpəl] *n.* a small, inflamed swelling in the skin, containing pus. A pimple is a small abscess. ⟨Cf. OE *piplian* grow pimply⟩ **—pim•pled,** *adj.*

pim•ply ['pɪmpli] *adj.* **-pli•er, -pli•est.** having pimples.

pin [pɪn] *n., v.* **pinned, pin•ning.** *—n.* **1** a short, slender piece of wire with a point at one end and a head at the other, used for fastening things together. **2** a kind of badge with a pin or clasp to fasten it to the clothing. **3** a brooch. **4** any of various fastenings consisting essentially or in part of a slender, often pointed, bar or wire: *a safety pin, a hatpin, a bobby pin.* **5** a peg made of wood, metal, or plastic used to fasten things together, hold something, hang things on, etc.: *a clothes pin.* **6** BELAYING PIN. **7** a peg that holds an oar in place. **8** in a stringed musical instrument, a peg to which a string is fastened. **9** *Bowling.* any of the bottle-shaped pieces of wood used as targets. **10 pins,** *Informal.* legs: *She's getting better, but is still a little shaky on her pins.* **11** *Wrestling.* a position in which a person controls an opponent completely, especially by holding both the opponent's shoulders to the ground. **12** *Golf.* a stick for the flag marking a hole on a course. **13** something small or worthless. **14** a tingling sensation in a part of the body that had become numb due to lack of circulation. **15** a metal rod used to hold the pieces of a broken bone together. **16** *Computer technology.* **a** a short piece of wire that forms part of an electronic connection: *She was careful not to bend the pins on the memory chips while installing the chips in her computer.* **b** one of a set of short pieces of wire used by the print head of some dot matrix printers to produce characters.
on pins and needles, very anxious or uneasy.
—v. **1** fasten with a pin or pins; put a pin through. **2** fasten or attach firmly to or on; tack; fasten as if with pins. **3** hold fast in one position: *When the tree fell, it pinned her shoulder to the ground.* **4** *Wrestling.* gain control over (an opponent) by holding his or her shoulders to the ground.
pin down, a hold or bind to an undertaking or pledge. **b** fix firmly; determine with accuracy; establish.
pin (someone's) **ears back,** scold; reprove; find fault with (someone) in a forceful manner.
pin on, *Informal.* fix blame for (something) on: *The police could not pin the crime on him.* ⟨OE *pinn* peg⟩ **—'pin,like,** *adj.*

pi•ña co•la•da ['pinjə] *or* ['pinə kə'lɑdə] **1** a cool mixed drink made of coconut milk, pineapple juice, and rum or vodka. **2** a flavour of food such as ice cream or soft drinks that tastes like the drink but is non-alcoholic.

pin•a•fore ['pɪnə,fɔr] *n.* **1** a garment like a full apron worn by children or women to protect other clothes. **2** *Esp. Brit.* a sleeveless dress usually worn over a blouse or sweater; jumper. ⟨< *pin,* v. + *afore*⟩

pi•ña•ta [pi'njɑtə] *or* [pɪn'jɑtə] *n.* a Mexican papier-mâché or clay figure, usually of an animal such as a donkey, filled with candies. Children, usually blindfolded, hit the piñata with sticks until it breaks open, to get at the candy.

pin•ball ['pɪn,bɒl] *n.* a game in which a ball rolls down a board, which is studded with pins or pegs, into numbered compartments.

pinball machine a gambling device used for playing pinball.

pince–nez [,pɪns 'nei] *or* [,pæns 'nei], ['pɪns ,nei] *or* ['pæns ,nei]; *French,* [pɛ̃s'ne] *n.* eyeglasses kept in place by a spring that pinches the nose. ⟨< F *pince-nez* pinch-nose⟩

pin•cer ['pɪnsər] *n.* **1** a claw of a crab, lobster, etc., resembling a pair of pincers; chela. **2 pincers,** *pl.* a tool for gripping and holding tight, made like scissors but with jaws instead of blades. **3 pincers,** *pl. Military.* a manoeuvre in which two parts of a military force converge on the enemy from opposite sides. Also called **pincer movement** or **pincers movement. —'pin•cer,like,** *adj.* ⟨ME < AF < OF *pynceour* < *pincier* to pinch⟩

pinch [pɪntʃ] *v., n.* —*v.* **1** squeeze between two hard edges or squeeze with thumb and forefinger. **2** squeeze or press so as to hurt: *My finger is pinched in the drawer.* **4** cause sharp discomfort or distress to. **5** cause to shrink or become thin: *a face pinched by hunger.* **6** limit closely; stint: *to be pinched for space.* **7** *Horticulture.* nip off the end of (a plant) to encourage branching and improve the quality of the bloom or fruit (*often used with* **back, out,** *or* **off**). **8** be stingy. **9** be stingy with: *The miser knew how to pinch pennies.* **10** *Slang.* arrest. **11** *Slang.* steal; pilfer.
—*n.* **1** a squeeze between two hard edges; a squeeze with thumb and forefinger. **2** sharp pressure that hurts. **3** as much as can be taken up with the tips of finger and thumb: *a pinch of salt.* **4** sharp discomfort or distress: *the pinch of hunger.* **5** a time of special need; emergency. **6** *Slang.* an arrest. **7** *Slang.* a theft. ⟨ME < ONF < OF *pincier*⟩ **—'pinch•er,** *n.*

pinch bar a kind of crowbar or lever with a pointed projecting end used as a fulcrum to move heavy objects such as large wheels.

pinch•beck ['pɪntʃ,bɛk] *n., adj.* —*n.* **1** an alloy of zinc and copper, used in imitation of gold. **2** something not genuine; an imitation.
—*adj.* **1** made of pinchbeck. **2** not genuine; sham. ⟨after Christopher *Pinchbeck* (1670?-1732), the inventor⟩

pinch•cock ['pɪntʃ,kɒk] *n.* a clamp used to control the flow of fluid through a flexible tube by constricting it.

pin cherry a North American wild cherry (*Prunus pensylvanica*) having shiny, bright green leaves, small, five-petalled, white flowers, and small, bright red, sour fruit used for jellies and preserves.

pinch•ers ['pɪntʃərz] *n.pl.* PINCERS (def. 2).

pinch–hit ['pɪntʃ ,hɪt] *v.* **-hit, -hit•ting. 1** *Baseball.* bat for another player, especially when a hit is badly needed. **2** take another's place in an emergency. **—'pinch,hit•ter,** *n.*

pinch•pen•ny ['pɪntʃ,pɛni] *adj., n., pl.* **-nies.** *Informal.* —*adj.* too thrifty; overfrugal; mean with money.
—*n.* a niggardly or miserly person.

pin curl a curl kept in place by a hairpin or clip.

pin•cush•ion ['pɪn,kʊʃən] *n.* a small cushion to stick pins in for use as needed.

Pin•dar•ic [pɪn'dærɪk] *or* [pɪn'dɛrɪk] *adj.* of, having to do with, or in the style of Pindar (522?-443? B.C.), a Greek lyric poet.

pin•dling ['pɪndlɪŋ] *adj. Informal.* puny; sickly. ⟨? euphemistic var. of *piddling*⟩

pine[1] [paɪn] *n.* **1** any of a large genus (*Pinus*) of evergreen trees found in many parts of the northern hemisphere, having long, needlelike leaves growing in tufts from the stems. The **soft pines** include the white pines; the **hard pines** include the ponderosa, red, and jack pines. **2** the wood of any of these trees. **3** (*adjl.*) made of pine: *a pine floor.* **4** (*adjl.*) designating a family (Pinaceae) of evergreen trees, including pines, larches, spruces, firs, and true cedars. ⟨OE *pīn* < L *pinus*⟩ **—'pine,like,** *adj.*

pine[2] [paɪn] *v.* **pined, pin•ing. 1** long eagerly; yearn. **2** waste away with pain, hunger, grief, or desire. ⟨OE *pīnian* < *pīn*, n., torture < L *poena* penalty < Gk. *poinē*⟩

pin•e•al ['pɪniəl] *adj.* **1** resembling a pine cone in shape. **2** of or having to do with the PINEAL BODY. ⟨< F < L *pinea* pine cone < *pinus* pine⟩

pineal body or **pineal gland** a small body present in the brain of vertebrates, whose function has not been definitely established. It secretes the hormone melatonin.

pine•ap•ple ['paɪn,æpəl] *n.* **1** a perennial plant (*Ananas comosus*) native to tropical and subtropical America but widely cultivated in other warm regions as well, for its large, edible fruit. **2** the fruit of this plant, resembling a large pine cone and having juicy, sweet, yellow flesh. **3** (*adjl.*) designating the tropical and subtropical American family (Bromeliaceae) of plants that includes the pineapple and Spanish moss. **4** *Slang.* a hand grenade or bomb.

pine cone the cone of a pine tree or of any of various other members of the pine family, such as spruce or fir.

pine•drops ['paɪn,drɒps] *n.sing. or pl.* a purplish, leafless plant (*Pterospora andromedea*) of North America that has clusters of white or red flowers and is a parasite on the roots of pine trees.

pine grosbeak a large grosbeak (*Pinicola enucleator*) common in the northern parts of Canada and Eurasia.

pine marten marten.

pine needle the very slender, needlelike leaf of a pine tree or of other members of the pine family, such as spruce or fir.

pine nut the edible seed of any of several pine trees found in the SW United States and in Mexico, used in making pastry, etc. or eaten roasted.

pin•er•y ['paɪnəri] *n., pl.* **-er•ies. 1** a forest or plantation of pine trees. **2** a place where pineapples are grown.

pine siskin a small North American finch (*Spinus pinus*) having streaky, greyish brown and yellowish plumage. It is found in coniferous and mixed forests from S Alaska, across Canada, and south to Mexico.

pine tar a brownish black, semisolid tar obtained by distilling pine wood and used especially in roofing materials, paints, and varnishes, and as an antiseptic.

pine•y ['paɪni] *adj.* **pin•i•er, pin•i•est.** See PINY.

pin•feath•er ['pɪn,fɛðər] *n. Ornithology.* an undeveloped feather just emerging through the skin. A pinfeather looks like a small stub.

pin•fold ['pɪn,fould] *n., v.* —*n.* a place where stray animals, especially cattle, are kept; pound.
—*v.* confine in a pinfold. ⟨OE *pundfald* < *pund-* pound[3] + *fald* fold[2]; later influenced by ME *pind* enclose < OE *pyndan*⟩

ping [pɪŋ] *n., v.* —*n.* a sound like that of a rifle bullet whistling through the air or striking an object.
—*v.* produce this sound or cause it to be produced. ⟨imitative⟩

ping•er ['pɪŋər] *n.* **1** a sound mechanism for warding off whales. **2** *Placer mining. Slang.* a small piece of gold, larger than dust, that pings in the pan used for separating gold from gravel.

pin•go ['pɪŋgou] *n., pl.* **ping•os** or **ping•oes.** *Cdn.* a cone-shaped or dome-shaped mound or hill of peat or soil, usually with a core of ice, found in tundra regions and produced by the pressure of water or ice accumulating underground and pushing upward. ⟨< Eskimo⟩

Ping–Pong ['pɪŋ ,pɒŋ] *n. Trademark.* TABLE TENNIS.

pin•guid ['pɪŋgwɪd] *adj.* fatty or oily. ⟨< L *pinguis* fat⟩ **—pin'guid•i•ty,** *n.*

pin•head ['pɪn,hɛd] *n.* **1** the head of a pin. **2** something very small or unimportant. **3** *Informal.* a very stupid person.

pin•head•ed ['pɪn,hɛdɪd] *adj. Informal.* very stupid or silly: *That was a pinheaded thing to do.*

pin•hole ['pɪn,houl] *n.* **1** a tiny hole made by or as if by a pin. **2** a hole made for a pin or peg to go into.

pin•ion[1] ['pɪnjən] *n., v.* —*n.* **1** the outermost segment of a bird's wing. **2** *Poetic.* a bird's wing. **3** any one of the stiff flying feathers of a bird's wing.
—*v.* **1** cut off or tie the pinions of (a bird) to prevent its flying. **2** bind: *His arms were pinioned behind his back.* **3** bind the arms of or bind (*to* something): *The thieves pinioned her securely. He was pinioned to the chair.* ⟨ME < OF *pignon*, ult. < L *pinna* feather⟩
☛ *Hom.* PIÑON.

pin•ion[2] [pɪn'jən] *n. Machinery.* **1** a small gear with teeth that fit into those of a larger gear or rack. See DIFFERENTIAL and GEAR for pictures. **2** a spindle with teeth that engage with a gear. ⟨< F *pignon* < OF *pignon* battlement, ult. < L *pinna* pinnacle⟩
☛ *Hom.* PIÑON.

pink[1] [pɪŋk] *n., adj.* —*n.* **1** a colour made by mixing red and white. Pink may vary from a very pale, light colour to a vivid, almost red colour. **2 a** any of a genus (*Dianthus*) of plants native to Europe, Asia, and Africa, having long, slender leaves, stems with swollen joints, and sepals joined together to form a tube

below the petals. **b** the flower of any of these plants. **3** the highest degree or condition of excellence: *An athlete needs to be in the pink of health.* **4** *Informal.* a person who is somewhat sympathetic to Communist doctrine. **5** PINK SALMON. **6** the scarlet coat worn by the official huntsmen and male members of the hunt in fox-hunting. Also, **pink coat.**
—adj. **1** of or having the colour pink: *a pink rose.* **2** designating a family (Caryophyllaceae) of annual or perennial herbs having flowers with four or five petals, simple leaves, and stems with swollen joints. Pinks, chickweeds, and baby's-breath belong to the pink family. **3** *Informal.* somewhat sympathetic to Communist doctrine. **4** *Informal.* over-refined; exquisite; smart: *a pink tea.* ⟨The flower gets its name from the serrated edges of its petals (see PINK²). The colour is named after the flower.⟩

pink² [pɪŋk] *v.* **1** prick or pierce with a sword, spear, or dagger. **2** cut the edge of (cloth) with special shears, leaving a serrated or notched edge that prevents unravelling. **3** ornament with small, round holes. **4** adorn. **5** irritate or hurt, especially by criticism: *The singer was somewhat pinked by the critiques in the press.* ⟨ME *pynke(n)* < OE *pynca* point⟩

pink–col•lar ['pɪŋk 'kɒlər] *adj.* referring to types of jobs traditionally performed by women, such as nursing, secretarial work, salesclerking, etc.

pink er•y•thro•ni•um [,ɛrɪ'θrouniəm] a wild lily (*Erythronium revolutum*) having pink petals and sepals. It blooms in spring on Vancouver Island and in the NW U.S.

pink•eye ['pɪŋk,aɪ] *n. Pathology.* an acute, highly contagious type of conjunctivitis of humans and some domestic animals.

pink gin a cocktail made from gin and Angostura bitters, usually without ice.

pink•ie ['pɪŋki] *n. Informal.* the smallest finger. Also, **pinky.**

pinking shears shears for pinking cloth.

pink•ish ['pɪŋkɪʃ] *adj.* somewhat pink.

pink lady **1** a cocktail made with gin, grenadine, and egg white, shaken with ice. **2** a female hospital volunteer whose duties include escorting patients to their rooms, taking around the book cart, etc., so called from the colour of their uniform.

pink lady's slipper a Canadian orchid (*Cypripedium acaule*) having pink or white flowers which are difficult for bees to enter. It blooms from April to July across Canada and south to Georgia and Alabama.

pink monkey flower a perennial wildflower (*Mimulus lewisii*) having pink flowers and growing in large clumps. It blooms in summer throughout western North America.

pink prairie clover a wild clover (*Petalostemum purpureum*) having pink flowers and blooming in summer on the prairies.

pink rhododendron a wildflower (*Rhododendron macrophyllum*).

pink salmon the smallest Pacific salmon (*Onchorhynchus gorbuscha*), found along the coast especially from the Columbia River north to Alaska. The pink salmon is blue and silver in colour and has pink flesh.

pink slip *Informal.* notice of dismissal or termination of employment. ⟨< the colour of the paper on which the notice is often printed⟩

pink tea *Cdn.* **1** a formal afternoon tea or reception. **2** a social gathering of any sort, especially one attended by women.

pin money **1** money set aside for buying extra or minor things. **2** formerly, an allowance of money given to a wife for her own use.

pin•na ['pɪnə] *n., pl.* **pin•nae** ['pɪni] *or* ['pɪnaɪ] or **pin•nas.** **1** *Zoology.* a projecting body part such as a feather, wing, or fin. **2** *Anatomy.* the upper part of the external ear. **3** *Botany.* one of the main divisions of a pinnate leaf; leaflet. ⟨< L, feather⟩ **—'pin•nal,** *adj.*

pin•nace ['pɪnɪs] *n.* **1** a ship's boat. **2** a very small schooner. ⟨< F < Ital. *pinaccia* or Sp. *pinaza,* ult. < L *pinus* pine¹⟩

pin•na•cle ['pɪnɪkəl] *n., v.* **-cled, -cling.** *—n.* **1** *Architecture.* a slender turret or spire, used especially in Gothic buildings at the top of a buttress. **2** a high peak or point of rock. **3** the highest point of development or achievement: *at the pinnacle of her fame.*
—v. **1** put on a pinnacle. **2** furnish with pinnacles. ⟨ME *pinacle* < OF < LL *pinnaculum,* dim. of *pinna* feather, wing, point⟩

pin•nate ['pɪnɪt] *or* ['pɪneit] *adj.* **1** like a feather, especially in having parts arranged on opposite sides of an axis. **2** *Botany.* **a** of a leaf, consisting of leaflets arranged on opposite sides of the leaf stalk. The Manitoba maple has pinnate leaves. **b** of a leaf, having a pattern of veins resembling a feather. ⟨< L *pinnatus* < *pinna* feather⟩ **—'pin•nate•ly,** *adv.*

pin•nat•ed grouse ['pɪneitəd] PRAIRIE CHICKEN.

pin•ni•ped ['pɪnə,pɛd] *n., adj. —n.* any of an order (Pinnepedia) of aquatic mammals having a streamlined body and limbs modified into flippers, and including seals, sea lions, and the walrus.
—adj. of, having to do with, or belonging to this order.

pin oak a tree (*Quercus palustris*) of the oak family, native to the deciduous forests of southern Ontario. The flowers appear before the leaves, which have hairy undersides.

pi•noch•le or **pi•noc•le** ['pinʌkəl] *or* ['pinɒkəl] *n.* **1** a game played with 48 cards, in which points are scored according to the value of certain combinations of cards. **2** a combination of the jack of diamonds and the queen of spades in this game. ⟨origin uncertain⟩

pi•ñon ['pɪnjən] *or* ['pinjoun] *n.* **1** any of several small pines, such as *Pinus cembroides* or *P. monophylla,* of the Rocky Mountains in the SW United States and N Mexico, producing large, edible, nutlike seeds. **2** the seed of this tree. **3** the wood of this tree, which smells pleasant when burning. Also, **pinyon.** ⟨< Sp. *piñón* < *piña* pine cone⟩
☛ *Hom.* PINION ['pɪnjən].

pi•not [pi'nou] *n.* **1** any of several viniferous grapes, either red (**pinot noir** [nwar]) or white (**pinot blanc** [blɑ̃]), grown originally in Alsace and Burgundy, but now common in the wine-producing areas of Canada and the United States. **2** the wines produced from these grapes. ⟨< F, little pine, from the cluster's shape⟩

pin•point ['pɪn,pɔɪnt] *n., v. —n.* **1** the point of a pin. **2** something very small or sharp: *We could see a pinpoint of light through a hole in the blind.* **3** (*adjl.*) extremely fine or precise: *pinpoint bombing, pinpoint accuracy.* **4** (*adjl.*) very small; minute.
—v. aim at or locate precisely: *to pinpoint the heart of the problem.*

pin•prick ['pɪn,prɪk] *n., v. —n.* **1** a tiny puncture or prick from a pin or something like a pin. **2** a minor irritation.
—v. puncture or prick with or as if with a pin.

pin•scher ['pɪnʃər] *n.* DOBERMAN PINSCHER.

pin•stripe ['pɪn,strəip] *n.* **1** a fine stripe. **2** cloth having fine stripes. **3** a garment made of such cloth.

pint [paɪnt] *n.* **1** a unit for measuring liquids, equal to half a quart (about 0.57 dm³). *Abbrev.*: p., pt. **2** a container holding a pint. **3** this amount of liquid: *He drank a whole pint.* ⟨< F *pinte* < MDu. *pinte* plug⟩

pin•tail ['pɪn,teil] *n.* **1** a slender North American duck (*Anas acuta*) having grey, white, and brown plumage, the adult male having a white stripe running up each side of the neck just behind the head and two long black feathers in the centre of the tail. **2** PINTAILED GROUSE. **3** SHARP-TAILED GROUSE.

pin•tailed grouse ['pɪn,teild] a common grouse of the Prairies, having a pointed tail.

pin•tle ['pɪntəl] *n.* a pin or bolt, especially an upright one on which something turns, as in a hinge. ⟨OE *pintel* penis⟩

pin•to ['pɪntou] *adj., n., pl.* **-tos.** *—adj.* marked with patches of black and white or another dark colour; pied; piebald.
—n. **1** a piebald horse. **2** PINTO BEAN. ⟨< Sp. *pinto* painted⟩

pinto bean a variety of bean (*Phaseolus vulgaris*) with mottled seeds, grown chiefly in the southern U.S. but common throughout North America as a food.

pint–sized ['paɪnt ,saɪzd] *adj. Informal.* small.

pin–up ['pɪn ,ʌp] *n.* **1** a picture of a sexually attractive person put up on a wall, especially by admirers who have not met the person. **2** a person who has posed for such pictures or is considered a suitable subject for them. **3** (*adjl.*) of or having to do with pin-ups: *a pin-up calendar.*

pin•wale corduroy ['pɪn,weil] a lightweight corduroy having very fine wales.

pin•wheel ['pɪn,wil] *n.* **1** a toy made of a wheel fastened to a stick by a pin so that it revolves in the wind. **2** a kind of firework that revolves when lighted.

pin•worm ['pɪn,wɜrm] *n.* any of various small, threadlike worms (family Oxyuridae) that are intestinal parasites in vertebrates, especially one (*Enterobius vermicularis*) that infests the rectum and large intestine of human beings, most commonly children.

pin•y ['paɪni] *adj.* **pin•i•er, pin•i•est.** **1** abounding in or covered with pine trees: *piny mountains.* **2** having to do with or suggesting pine trees: *a piny fragrance.* Also, **piney.**

Pin•yin ['pɪn'jɪn] *n.* the system for the romanization of Chinese words: *Peking in Pinyin becomes Beijing.* Also, **pinyin.**

pi•on ['paɪɒn] *n. Physics.* a meson having no electric charge and a mass about 264 times that of an electron, or a positive or negative charge and a mass 273 times that of an electron. ⟨shortened form of *pi (me)son*⟩

pi•o•neer [,paɪə'nir] *n., v.* —*n.* **1** a person who settles in a region that has not been settled before. **2** a person who goes first or does something first and so prepares a way for others. **3** *Ecology.* a plant or animal species that establishes itself successfully in a barren area. **4** *Military.* a member of an engineering unit whose job it is to go in advance of other troops, preparing camps, roads, trenches, etc. **5** a railway track-laying machine that works at the END OF STEEL.
—*v.* prepare or open up (a field or way) for others; take the lead: *Astronauts are pioneering in exploring outer space.* ⟨< F *pionnier* < OF *peon* foot soldier < LL *pedo, pedonis,* < L *pes, pedis* foot. Related to PAWN[2], PEON.⟩

pi•os•i•ty [paɪ'ɒsɪti] *n., pl.* **-ties. 1** an excessive, obvious, or insincere show of piety; sanctimoniousness. **2** an instance of excessive piety. ⟨modelled on *religious, religiosity*⟩

pi•ous ['paɪəs] *adj.* **1** having or showing reverence for God; religious: *a pious person, a pious act.* **2** showing religious scruples in a smug or ostentatious way: *pious platitudes about work and duty.* **3** of deeds, thoughts, etc., deriving from real or pretended devotion or moral motives. **4** pertaining to that which is religious or sacred rather than secular or profane. **5** *Archaic.* dutiful to parents. ⟨< L *pius*⟩ —**'pi•ous•ly,** *adv.* —**'pi•ous•ness,** *n.*

☛ *Syn.* **1. Pious,** DEVOUT = religious. **Pious** emphasizes showing religion or reverence for God by carefully observing religious duties and practices, such as going to church, and sometimes suggests that more religion is shown than felt: *They are pious enough to go to church in the morning but they gossip all afternoon.* **Devout** emphasizes feeling true reverence that usually is expressed in prayer or devotion to religious observances, but may not be outwardly shown at all: *They are devout Christians and good people.*

pip[1] [pɪp] *n.* the seed of an apple, orange, etc. ⟨short for *pippin*⟩

pip[2] [pɪp] *n.* **1** a contagious disease of poultry, etc. characterized by thick mucus in the mouth and throat and, often, a scale or crust on the tongue. **2** *Informal.* any slight, unspecified illness of human beings: *I've got a touch of the pip this morning.*
give (someone) **the pip,** *Brit. Informal.* cause irritation or disgust: *His superior attitude gives me the pip.* ⟨ME < MDu. < VL *pippita* < L *pituita* phlegm⟩

pip[3] [pɪp] *n.* **1** one of the spots on playing cards, dominoes, or dice. **2** in the British army, etc., one of the stars of rank worn on the shoulders of certain officers: *A captain wears three pips, a lieutenant two.* **3** a single rootstock or a portion of the rootstock of certain plants such as the lily of the valley or peony. ⟨var. of *peep*[2]; origin uncertain⟩

pip[4] [pɪp] *v.* **pipped, pip•ping. 1** peep; chirp. **2** of a young bird, break through (the shell). ⟨? var. of *peep*[2]⟩

pipe [pəip] *n., v.* **piped, pip•ing.** —*n.* **1** a tube through which a liquid or gas flows. **2** a tube with a bowl of clay, wood, etc. at one end, for smoking. **3** the quantity of tobacco a pipe will hold. **4** a musical wind instrument with a single tube into which the player blows. **5 pipes,** *pl.* **a** a set of musical tubes: *the pipes of Pan.* **b** bagpipe. **c** the voice, especially the singing voice. **6** any one of the tubes in a pipe organ. **7** a shrill sound, voice, or song. **8** a boatswain's whistle. **9** a cask for wine. **10** anything shaped like a tube. **11** *Mining.* **a** a deposit of ore in the shape of a cylinder. **b** in South Africa, a vertical cylindrical matrix in which diamonds are found. **12** an eruptive passage opening into the crater of a volcano. **13** a unit of measure of volume equivalent to the capacity of one cask of wine (two hogsheads or 126 gallons, approximately 441 L). **14** *Cdn.* formerly, in the fur trade: **a** a rest period on a journey, originally one in which to smoke a pipe. **b** a spell of travelling between rest periods.
put that in your pipe and smoke it, see if you can accept that.
—*v.* **1** carry by means of a pipe or pipes. **2** supply with pipes. **3** transmit (music, speech, etc.) by electric or electronic means, especially from one room or part of a building to another (*used with* **in**): *The background music for the reception will be piped in.* **4** play on a pipe. **5** make a shrill noise; sing or speak in a shrill voice. **6** sing; utter. **7** give (orders, signals), etc., with a pipe or whistle. **8** of hardening metal, develop a longitudinal cavity or depression in the head of an ingot. **9** announce the arrival and departure of (someone) by playing a boatswain's pipe: *The admiral was piped on board.* **10** summon by a pipe: *All hands were piped on deck.* **11** trim (a dress, etc.) with PIPING (def. 5).
pipe down, *Slang.* be quiet; stop talking, crying, etc.
pipe up, a begin to play (music). **b** *Slang.* speak, especially in a piping voice. ⟨OE *pīpe,* n., *pīpian,* v., < Gmc. < VL < L *pipare* chirp; certain meanings reinforced by F⟩ —**'pipe,like,** *adj.*

pipe clay a fine white clay used for making tobacco pipes, whitening shoes, etc.

pipe cleaner a short length of fine twisted wire covered with small tufts of yarn, used to clean a smoker's pipe and in some handicrafts.

pipe dream *Informal.* an impractical idea.

pipe•fish ['pəip,fɪʃ] *n.* any of various small fishes of the same family (Syngnathidae) as the seahorses, having a long, slender body and a long, tubular snout with a small mouth.

pipe fitter a worker who installs, repairs, and maintains pipe systems.

pipe fitting 1 a joint or coupling such as an elbow or a tee used to connect pieces of pipe. **2** the work of a pipe fitter.

pipe•ful ['pəip,fʊl] *n., pl.* **-fuls.** the quantity sufficient to fill the bowl of a pipe.

pipe•line ['pəip,laɪn] *n., v.* **-lined, -lin•ing.** —*n.* **1** a line of pipes for carrying gas, oil, or other liquids. **2** a direct channel for supplying information, etc.: *He's got a pipeline into the manager's office and always knows what's going on.* **3** a flow of materials through a series of productive processes.
—*v.* **1** carry by a pipeline. **2** provide with a pipeline.

pipe•lin•er ['pəip,laɪnər] *n.* a person working on a PIPELINE (def. 1).

pipe of peace *Cdn.* peace pipe; calumet.

pipe organ a large musical wind instrument consisting of sets of pipes of different diameters and lengths which are sounded by forcing air through them by means of keys and pedals. Pipe organs usually have two or more keyboards, as well as a variety of stops and pedals for producing many different varieties of sound.

pip•er ['pəipər] *n.* a person who plays on a pipe or bagpipe.
pay the piper, pay for one's pleasure; bear the consequences (from the proverb *He who pays the piper calls the tune,* meaning 'the one who pays has the right to be in control').

pi•per•a•zine [pɪ'pɛrəzɪn], [pɪ'pɛrə,zin], *or* ['pɪpərə,zin] *n.* a drug used to treat infestations of pinworm or roundworm. ⟨< L *piper* pepper⟩

pi•per•ine ['pɪpərin] *n.* a colourless, crystalline alkaloid found in pepper. *Formula:* $C_{17}H_{19}NO_3$ ⟨L *piper* pepper + *-ine*[2]⟩

pipe•stone ['pəip,stoun] *n.* any of various types of argillaceous stone suitable for making tobacco pipes or calumets.

pi•pette [pɪ'pɛt] *or* [pəi'pɛt] *n., v.* **-et•ted, -et•ting.** —*n.* a slender pipe or tube for transferring or measuring liquids.
—*v.* transfer or measure (a liquid) using a pipette. ⟨< F *pipette,* dim. of *pipe* pipe⟩

pipe wrench a wrench with adjustable, toothed jaws set at right angles to the handle, used especially for turning pipes, rods, and similar curved surfaces.

pip•ing ['pəipɪŋ] *n., adj., v.* —*n.* **1** a quantity or system of pipes. **2** material that can be used for pipes. **3** the music of a pipe. **4** a shrill sound or call: *the piping of frogs in the spring.* **5** a narrow band of material, sometimes containing a cord, used for trimming along edges and seams of clothing, cushions, etc. **6** ornamental lines of icing, meringue, etc.
—*adj.* shrill.
piping hot, very hot.
—*v.* ppr. of PIPE.

piping plover a bird (*Charadrius melodus*) with webbed feet, being pale greyish brown on the upper parts and having a black bar on the head. It has a whistling call that sounds like 'queep'. It is found in the southern prairies, SW Ontario, and Nova Scotia. It is an endangered species.

pip•it ['pɪpɪt] *n.* any of a genus (*Anthus*) of songbirds found in open country, having streaked brownish or greyish plumage, a slender bill, very long hind toenails, and a fairly long tail that the birds habitually wag up and down when perching. Pipits resemble larks. ⟨imitative⟩

pip•kin ['pɪpkɪn] *n.* a small earthen pot. ⟨? dim. of *pipe*⟩

pip•pin ['pɪpɪn] *n.* any of several varieties of apple having a yellowish green skin. ⟨ME < OF *pepin*⟩

pip•sis•se•wa [pɪp'sɪsəwə] *n.* any of a genus (*Chimaphila*) of small evergreen plants of the wintergreen family, whose jagged, leathery leaves were formerly used in medicine as a tonic, diuretic, etc. Some authorities classify the pipsissewas in the heath family. ⟨< Algonquian⟩

pip•squeak ['pɪp,skwik] *n. Slang.* a small or insignificant person or thing. ⟨name given to a small German high-speed shell of World War I, so named because of its sound in flight⟩

pi•quant ['pikənt] *or* [pi'kɑnt] *adj.* **1** sharp or pungent in an agreeable way; pleasantly stimulating to the taste: *a piquant sauce.* **2** pleasantly stimulating to the mind, etc.; intriguing: *a piquant bit of news.* ⟨< F *piquant* pricking, stinging⟩
—'pi•quan•cy, *n.* **—'pi•quant•ly,** *adv.*

pique [pik] *n., v.* **piqued, pi•quing.** *—n.* a feeling of anger at being slighted; wounded pride: *She left the party in a fit of pique.*
—v. **1** cause a feeling of anger or resentment in; wound the pride of: *It piqued him that they had gone ahead with their plans without consulting him.* **2** arouse; stir up: *The curiosity of the children was piqued by the locked trunk.*
pique (oneself) **on** or **upon,** feel proud about. ⟨< F *pique,* n., and *piquer,* v., prick, sting < *pic* a pick (< Gmc.)⟩
☛ *Hom.* PEAK, PEEK.

pi•qué [pi'kei] *n.* a cloth, usually cotton or a cotton blend, woven with raised, narrow lengthwise ribs or cords, sometimes also having a honeycomb, waffle, or bird's-eye pattern. ⟨< F *piqué* quilted, pp. of *piquer* stitch, prick⟩

pi•quet [pɪ'kei] *or* [pɪ'kɛt] *n.* a complicated card game for two people, played with a deck of 32 cards. ⟨< F⟩

pi•ra•cy ['paɪrəsi] *n., pl.* **-cies. 1** robbery on the high seas. **2** the act of publishing, reproducing, or using a book, play, musical composition, etc. without permission. **3** *Informal.* the charging of excessively high prices: *the price of the dress was sheer piracy.* ⟨ME < Med.L < Gk. *peirateia*⟩

pi•ra•gua [pə'rɑgwə] *or* [pə'rægwə] *n.* pirogue. ⟨< Sp. < Carib, dugout⟩

pi•ra•nha [pə'rɑnə] *or* [pə'rænə] *n., pl.* **-nhas** or (*esp. collectively*) **-nha.** any of various small carnivorous freshwater fishes (genus *Serrasalmus*) of tropical America noted for their voracity. Schools of piranhas will attack and devour human beings or large animals. ⟨< Portuguese *piranha* < Tupi (Brazil) *pira nya,* toothed fish⟩

pi•rate ['paɪrɪt] *n., v.* **-rat•ed, -rat•ing.** *—n.* **1** one who attacks and robs ships; a robber on the high seas. **2** a ship used by pirates. **3** a person who publishes, reproduces, or uses a book, play, musical composition, etc. without permission. **4** a person or group that operates an illegal radio or television station.
—v. **1** be a robber on the high seas; plunder; rob. **2** publish, reproduce, use, or broadcast illegally or without permission. ⟨ME < L *pirata* < Gk. *peiratēs* < *peiraein* attack⟩ **—'pi•rate,like,** *adj.* **—pi'rat•ic** [paɪ'rætɪk] or **pi'rat•i•cal,** *adj.* **—pi'rat•i•cal•ly,** *adv.*

pir•o•gi [pə'rougi] *n.* See PEROGY.

pi•rogue [pə'roug] *n.* **1** a canoe hollowed from the trunk of a tree; dugout. **2** any canoe. **3** a two-masted, flat-bottomed sailing barge. Also, **piragua.** ⟨< F; probably < Carib. dial.⟩

pi•rosh•ki or **pi•rozh•ki** [pə'rʌʃki] *or* [pə'rɒʃki] *n.pl.* small pastry turnovers filled usually with a ground beef mixture. ⟨< Russian, sing. *pirozhok,* dim. of *pirogpie.*⟩

pir•ou•ette [,piru'ɛt] *n., v.* **-et•ted, -et•ting.** *—n.* a whirling about on one foot or on the toes, as in dancing.
—v. whirl in this way. ⟨< F *pirouette* spinning top⟩

pis al•ler [piza'le] *French.* the last resort; final resource.

pis•ca•to•ri•al [,pɪskə'tɔriəl] *adj.* of or having to do with fishing. ⟨< L *piscatorius,* ult. < *piscis* fish⟩
—,pis•ca'to•ri•al•ly, *adv.*

pis•ca•to•ry ['pɪskə,tɔri] *adj.* piscatorial.

Pis•ces ['pəisiz], ['pɪsiz], *or* ['pɪskiz] *n.* (*used with a singular verb*) **1** *Astronomy.* a northern constellation thought of as having the shape of two fishes with a ribbon connecting their tails. **2** *Astrology.* **a** the twelfth sign of the zodiac. The sun enters Pisces about February 21. See ZODIAC for picture. **b** a person born under this sign. **3** a taxonomic group that includes all fishes. ⟨< L *pisces,* pl. of *piscis* fish⟩

pis•ci•cul•ture ['pɪsɪ,kʌltʃər] *or* ['pəisɪ,kʌltʃər] *n.* the breeding and rearing of fish by artificial means, as in industry or science.

pis•cine ['pəisin], ['pɪsin], *or* ['pɪsɪn] *adj.* of, having to do with, or characteristic of a fish or fishes. ⟨< L *piscis* fish + E *-ine¹*⟩

Pis•cis Aus•tri•nus ['pəisɪs], ['pɪsɪs], *or* ['pɪskɪs ɒ'straɪnəs] *Astronomy.* a southern constellation between Aquarius and Grus.

pish [pɪʃ] *or* [pʃ] *interj., n., v. —interj. or n.* a sound made to express contempt or impatience.
—v. make such a sound.

pis•mire ['pɪs,maɪr] *n. Archaic.* ant. ⟨ME *pissemire* < *pisse* urine (from the formic acid discharged by ants, popularly regarded as urine) + *mire* ant < Scand.; cf. Norwegian *myre*⟩

pi•so ['pisou] *n.* the main unit of money in the Philippines, divided into 100 sentimos. See table of money in the Appendix.

pis•ta•chi•o [pɪ'stæʃi,ou] *n., pl.* **-chi•os;** *adj. —n.* **1** a small tree (*Pistacia vera*) of the cashew family that grows in warm climates. **2** the greenish, edible seed of this tree. **3** the flavour of the pistachio nut. **4** light, yellowish green.
—adj. having the colour or flavour pistachio. ⟨< Ital. < L *pistachium* < Gk. *pistakion* < *pistakē* the tree < OPersian⟩

pis•ta•reen [,pɪstə'rin] *n., adj. —n.* a former Spanish silver coin used as currency in the West Indies, the United States, and Canada during the 18th century.
—adj. petty; trifling. ⟨apparently < modification of Sp. *peseta* peseta⟩

piste [pist] *n.* **1** a downhill ski run. **2** the track or trail of an animal. **3** *Fencing.* a regulation strip on which fencers compete. ⟨< F, trail⟩

pis•til ['pɪstəl] *n. Botany.* the part of a flower that produces seeds, consisting of a base section called the ovary, a thinner middle section, the style, and, at the top, the stigma. A simple pistil, like that of the pea, consists of one carpel; a compound pistil, like that of the iris, consists of several carpels fused together. See FLOWER for picture. ⟨< NL *pistillum* < L *pistillum* pestle. Doublet of PESTLE.⟩
☛ *Hom.* PISTOL.

pis•til•late ['pɪstəlɪt] *or* ['pɪstə,leit] *adj. Botany.* **1** having a pistil or pistils. **2** having a pistil or pistils but no stamens.

pis•tol [pɪs'təl] *n.* a small, short gun capable of being held and fired with one hand. A revolver is a kind of pistol. See FIREARM for picture. ⟨< F *pistole* < G < Czech *pišťala*⟩
☛ *Hom.* PISTIL.

pis•tole [pɪ'stoul] *n.* **1** a former gold coin of Spain. **2** any of various other old European gold coins of about the same value. ⟨< F *pistole* coin, pistol. See PISTOL.⟩

pis•ton ['pɪstən] *n.* **1** in an engine, pump, etc., a short cylinder, or a flat, round piece of wood or metal, fitting closely inside a tube or hollow cylinder in which it is moved back and forth by the force of exploding vapour or steam. A piston receives or transmits motion by means of the piston rod that is attached to it. See CYLINDER and STEAM ENGINE for pictures. **2** in a wind instrument, a sliding valve that, when pressed by the fingers, lowers the pitch. ⟨< F < Ital. *pistone* < *pistare* pound, ult. < L *pistus,* pp. of *pinsere* pound⟩

piston ring a metal ring, split so it can expand, placed around a piston to ensure a tight fit.

piston rod a rod that moves, or is moved by, a piston.

pit¹ [pɪt] *n., v.* **pit•ted, pit•ting.** *—n.* **1** a hole or cavity in the ground. Deep pits are used to trap wild animals. A mine or the shaft of a mine is a pit. **2** a hollow on the surface of the body: *the armpit.* **3** a little hole or scar in the skin, such as is left by smallpox; pockmark. **4** the bottom of a body cavity: *the pit of the stomach.* **5** an unsuspected danger; a trap or snare; a pitfall. **6** *Brit.* **a** the main floor of a theatre, especially at the back, where the seats are cheap. **b** the people who sit there. **7** a usually sunken area in front of the stage of a theatre where the orchestra sits. **8** the part of the floor of an exchange where a particular kind of trading is done: *the wheat pit.* **9** an enclosed place where animals or birds are made to fight each other: *a bear pit.* **10** an area in a garage, often below floor level, for repairing and servicing automobiles. **11** an area alongside an automobile race track where cars are serviced or repaired during a race. **12 the pit,** hell.
the pits, *Slang.* the worst possible thing: *That exam was the pits.*
—v. **1** mark with small pits or scars. **2** set to fight or compete; match: *The man pitted his brains against the strength of the bear.* ⟨OE *pytt,* ult. < L *puteus* well⟩

pit² [pɪt] *n., v.* **pit•ted, pit•ting.** *—n.* the hard seed of a cherry, peach, plum, date, etc.; stone.
—v. remove pits from (fruit). ⟨< Du. *pit* kernel⟩

pi•ta ['pitə] *n.* a Mediterranean kind of round, flat bread forming a pocket which can be stuffed with meat, vegetables, etc. ⟨< Mod.Hebrew *pita* or Mod.Gk. *pitta*⟩

pit•a•pat ['pɪtə,pæt] *adv., n., v.* **-pat•ted, -pat•ting** *—adv.* with a quick succession of beats or taps.
—n. the movement or sound of something proceeding in a quick succession of beats or taps.
—v. go with pitapats.

pit bull terrier a powerful dog with a squat body, powerful jaws, and a smooth coat. Also, **pitbull.**

pitch¹ [pɪtʃ] *v., n.* —*v.* **1** throw; fling; hurl; toss: *The men were pitching horseshoes.* **2** pick up and fling (hay, straw, etc.) in a mass with a pitchfork onto a vehicle, into a barn, etc. **3 a** *Baseball.* throw (the ball) for the batter to hit. **b** *Golf.* loft (a ball) so that it lands with little roll. **4** *Slang.* sell or try to sell (a product, service, etc.) often by high-pressure means. **5** erect or set up: *to pitch a tent, to pitch camp.* **6** take up a position; settle. **7** fix firmly, in or as if in the ground. **8** fall or plunge forward: *The man lost his balance and pitched over the cliff.* **9 a** of a boat or ship, plunge with the bow rising and then falling: *The ship pitched about in the storm.* **b** of an aircraft, move in a similar way. **10** set at a certain point, degree, or level. **11** *Music.* determine the key of (a tune, instrument, etc.). **12** slope downward: *That roof is very steeply pitched.* **13** *Card games.* **a** indicate one's choice of trump by an opening lead of (a card of the suit chosen). **b** settle (the trump suit) thus. **14** *Cdn.* travel from one camping place to another; move on, especially in stages, camping en route.
pitch in, *Informal.* **a** contribute; join in: *If everyone pitches in, it won't take long to clean up the yard.* **b** begin to work vigorously: *All the boys pitched in to get the job done.*
pitch into, *Informal.* **a** attack. **b** start on vigorously: *The children pitched into their dinners as if they had never seen food before.*
pitch on or **upon,** choose; select.
—*n.* **1** a throw; fling; hurl; toss. **2** a point; position; degree: *The poor man has reached the lowest pitch of bad fortune.* **3** in music, speech, etc., the highness or lowness of a sound. The pitch of a sound is determined by the frequency of the waves producing the sound; a sound with a low pitch has a lower frequency than one with a high pitch. **4** *Music.* **a** the exact number of vibrations producing a particular tone. **b** a particular standard of pitch: *concert pitch.* **5** height. **6** the act or manner of pitching. **7** that which is pitched. **8** *Slang.* **a** a talk, argument, offer, plan, etc. used to persuade, as in selling, or to promote an idea, product, etc. **b** a television or radio commercial. **9 a** a place of pitching or encamping or taking up a position. **b** a spot in a street or market place where a peddler, street performer, etc. is regularly stationed. **10** the amount of slope. **11 a** *Machinery.* the distance between the successive teeth of a cogwheel. **b** the distance between two things in a machine. **12** the piece of ground on which certain games are played: *a cricket pitch, a horseshoe pitch.* **13** the movement of the longitudinal axis of an aircraft up or down from the horizontal plane. **14** a plunge forward or headlong; lurch. **15** a downward plunging of the fore part of a ship in a rough sea.
make a pitch for, *Informal.* make a persuasive request for; make a bid for. ⟨ME *picche(n)*⟩

pitch² [pɪtʃ] *n., v.* —*n.* **1** a black, sticky substance obtained from the distillation of tar, petroleum, etc., used to waterproof the seams of ships, cover roofs, make pavements, etc. **2** bitumen. **3** resin obtained from various evergreens, often used as medicine. **4** any of various artificial mixtures resembling pitch.
—*v.* cover or smear with pitch. ⟨OE *pic* < L *pix, picis*⟩

pitch–black ['pɪtʃ 'blæk] *adj.* very dark or black: *Her hair is pitch-black.*

pitch•blende ['pɪtʃ,blɛnd] *n.* a mineral consisting largely of uranium oxide, occurring in black, pitchlike masses. It is a source of radium, uranium, and actinium. ⟨half-translation of G *Pechblende*⟩

pitch–dark ['pɪtʃ 'dɑrk] *adj.* very dark; with no light at all: *It was pitch-dark in the room.*

pitched battle **1** a planned battle with lines of troops, etc., arranged beforehand. **2** an intense battle involving close combat.

pitch•er¹ ['pɪtʃər] *n.* **1** a container for holding and pouring liquids, with a lip on one side and a handle on the other; jug. **2** the amount that a pitcher holds. ⟨ME < OF *pichier*⟩

pitch•er² ['pɪtʃər] *n. Baseball.* the player who throws the ball to the batter. ⟨< *pitch¹*⟩

pitch•er•ful ['pɪtʃər,fʊl] *n., pl.* **-fuls.** the quantity sufficient to fill a pitcher.

A pitcher plant

pitcher plant *Cdn.* **1** any of a genus (*Sarracenia*) of herbs found in the bogs and peat barrens of northern and eastern Canada and the United States, having leaves modified into pitchers in which insects are trapped, to be digested by the plant by means of an enzyme secreted by the leaves. The species *S. purpurea* is the provincial flower of Newfoundland. **2** designating a family (Sarraceniaceae) of insect-eating plants of North and South America that includes the pitcher plants. **3** any of various other plants, especially of the Old World family Nepentheceae.

pitch•fork ['pɪtʃ,fɔrk] *n., v.* —*n.* a large fork with a long handle and two or three slightly curved prongs, used for lifting and throwing hay or straw.
—*v.* lift and throw with a pitchfork.

pitch–hole ['pɪtʃ ,houl] *n. Cdn.* pothole.

pitch•man ['pɪtʃ,mæn] *n., pl.* **-men** [-mən]. **1** *Informal.* a man who sells articles such as small toys on the street or at carnivals. **2** *Slang.* a high-pressure promoter or salesman: *a television pitchman.*

pitch•out ['pɪtʃ,ʌut] *n.* **1** *Baseball.* a ball purposely pitched too far outside the plate for the batter to hit, especially in anticipation of the catcher trying to prevent a stolen base. **2** *Football.* a lateral pass behind the line of scrimmage from one back to another.

pitch pine *Cdn.* any of various pines from which pitch or turpentine is obtained, especially a North American species (*Pinus rigida*) having yellowish green needles, reddish brown bark, and relatively hard, heavy, resinous wood.

pitch pipe a small musical pipe having one or more fixed tones, used to give the desired musical pitch for singing or for tuning an instrument.

pitch•y ['pɪtʃi] *adj.* **pitch•i•er, pitch•i•est. 1** full of pitch. **2** like pitch; sticky. **3** black.

pit•e•ous ['pɪtiəs] *adj.* to be pitied; moving the heart; deserving pity. ⟨ME < OF *pitos* < Med.L *pietosus* pitiful < L *pietas* pity; influenced in form by ME *pite* pity⟩
—'pit•e•ous•ly, *adv.* **—'pit•e•ous•ness,** *n.*
☛ *Syn.* See note at PITIFUL.

pit•fall ['pɪt,fɒl] *n.* **1** a hidden pit to catch animals in. **2** any trap or hidden danger, such as a likely error or difficulty.

pith [pɪθ] *n.* **1 a** *Botany.* the central, spongy tissue in the stems of certain plants. **b** a similar tissue occurring in other parts of plants, as that lining the skin of an orange. **2** *Zoology.* the soft inner substance of a bone, feather, etc. **3** an important or essential part: *the pith of a speech.* **4** strength; energy. ⟨OE *pitha*⟩

pit•head ['pɪt,hɛd] *n.* **1** the top of a mine shaft. **2** the area surrounding this, with its buildings, etc.

Pith•e•can•thro•pus [,pɪθə'kænθrəpəs] *or* [,pɪθəkæn'θroupəs] *n., pl.* **-pi** [-paɪ] *or* [-pi]. a type of extinct, prehistoric hominid, whose existence is assumed from remains found in Java in 1891 and 1892. ⟨< NL < Gk. *pithēkos* ape + *anthrōpos* man⟩ **—,pith•e'can•thro•pine,** *adj.*

pith helmet a sun hat shaped like a helmet, originally made from the dried pith of Bengal spongewood.

pith•y ['pɪθi] *adj.* **pith•i•er, pith•i•est. 1** full of substance, meaning, force, or vigour: *pithy phrases, a pithy speaker.* **2** of or like pith. **3** having much pith: *a pithy orange.* **—'pith•i•ly,** *adv.* **—'pith•i•ness,** *n.*

pit•i•a•ble ['pɪtiəbəl] *adj.* **1** to be pitied; moving the heart; deserving pity. **2** deserving contempt; to be scorned.
—'pit•i•a•ble•ness, *n.* **—'pit•i•a•bly,** *adv.*
☛ *Syn.* **1.** See note at PITIFUL.

pit•i•ful ['pɪtɪfəl] *adj.* **1** to be pitied; arousing pity: *The deserted children were a pitiful sight.* **2** deserving contempt; to be scorned: *a pitiful performance.* **3** *Archaic.* feeling or showing pity; compassionate. **—'pit•i•ful•ly,** *adv.* **—'pit•i•ful•ness,** *n.*
☛ *Syn.* **1. Pitiful,** PITEOUS, PITIABLE = arousing pity or to be pitied. **Pitiful** emphasizes the effect on others, that of arousing pity, made by someone or something felt to be touching or pathetic: *The starving children were pitiful.* **Piteous** emphasizes the quality in the thing itself that makes it appeal for pity and move the heart: *Their sad faces were piteous.* **Pitiable** emphasizes pity over something that causes indignity or shame: *Their bodies and clothes were in a pitiable condition.*

pit•i•less ['pɪtɪlɪs] *adj.* showing no pity or mercy: *a pitiless tyrant, a pitiless act.* **—'pit•i•less•ly,** *adv.* **—'pit•i•less•ness,** *n.*
☛ *Syn.* See note at CRUEL.

pit lamp *Cdn., esp. British Columbia.* **1** a kind of jacklight, so called because of its resemblance to the light on a miner's helmet. **2** engage in pitlamping or jacklighting.

pit•lamp•ing ['pɪt,læmpɪŋ] *n. Cdn., esp. British Columbia.* jacklighting.

pi•ton ['pitɒn] *or* [pɪ'tɒn]; *French,* [pi'tɔ̃] *n.* **1** an iron spike with a ring at one end, used in mountain climbing. It can be driven into a crack in rock or ice and used to secure a rope or as a step. **2** a sharply pointed mountain or rock peak. ⟨< F *piton* point, peak⟩

pit stop **1** *Auto racing.* a stop in the PIT (def. 11) for repairs, refuelling, etc. during a race. **2** *Informal.* a pause made during a journey to eat, drink, visit the rest room, etc. **3** any place where such a stop is made.

pit•tance ['pɪtəns] *n.* **1** a small allowance or wage. **2** a small amount or share. ⟨ME < OF *pitance,* ult. < L *pietas* piety⟩

pit•ted ['pɪtɪd] *adj., v.* —*adj.* **1** having the pits removed: *We bought pitted olives for the party.* **2** marked with pits: *This silver dish is pitted. His face was badly pitted with acne scars.*
—*v.* pt. and pp. of PIT.

pit•ter–pat•ter ['pɪtər ˌpætər] *n., adv., v.* —*n.* a rapid succession of light beats or taps, as of rain.
—*adv.* with a rapid succession of beats or taps.
—*v.* move or fall with a pitter-pattering sound.

pi•tu•i•tar•y [pə'tjuəˌtɛri] *or* [pə'tuəˌtɛri] *adj., n., pl.* **-tar•ies.**
—*adj.* of or having to do with the pituitary gland.
—*n.* **1** PITUITARY GLAND. **2** *Pharmacy.* medicine made from an extract of this gland. ⟨< L *pituitarius* < *pituita* phlegm⟩

pituitary body PITUITARY GLAND.

pituitary gland *Anatomy.* a small, oval endocrine gland situated at the base of the brain. It secretes hormones that promote growth, stimulate other glands, and regulate many other basic bodily functions. See BRAIN for picture.

pit viper any of a family (Crotalidae) of New World poisonous snakes that includes the rattlesnakes and the water moccasin, similar to the Old World vipers but having a heat-sensitive pit on each side of the head, by means of which they can sense the presence of warm-blooded animals. Some authorities classify pit vipers and vipers as constituting subfamilies within the single family Viperidae.

pit•y ['pɪti] *n., pl.* **pit•ies;** *v.* **pit•ied, pit•y•ing.** —*n.* **1** sympathy; sorrow for another's suffering or distress; a feeling for the sorrows of others. **2** a cause for pity or regret; something to be sorry for: *It is a pity to be kept in the house in good weather.*
have or **take pity on,** show pity for.
—*v.* feel pity for. ⟨ME < OF *pite* < L *pietas.* Doublet of PIETY.⟩
—'pit•y•ing•ly, *adv.*

☛ *Syn. n.* **1. Pity,** COMPASSION, SYMPATHY = a feeling for the sorrows or suffering of others. **Pity** suggests a feeling of sorrow for someone who is suffering or in sorrow or distress and who is often felt to be weak or unfortunate: *Nobody wants pity from friends.* **Compassion** adds the idea of tenderness, a sharing and understanding of feelings, and a strong desire to help or protect: *He had compassion for the sobbing child.* **Sympathy** emphasizes feeling with another in his or her sorrow: *He expects sympathy from his sister.*

più [pju] *adv. Music.* more. ⟨< Ital.⟩

piv•ot ['pɪvət] *n., v.* —*n.* **1** a shaft, pin, or point on which something turns. **2** a person, thing, etc. serving as a central point or having a central role or function. **3** *Hockey.* the player who plays centre in a forward line.
—*v.* **1** mount on, attach by, or provide with a pivot. **2** turn on a pivot or something like a pivot: *to pivot on one's heel.* ⟨< F⟩

piv•ot•al ['pɪvətəl] *adj.* of, having to do with, or serving as a pivot; being that on which something turns, hinges, or depends; very important. **—'piv•ot•al•ly,** *adv.*

pix•el ['pɪksəl] *or* ['pɪksɛl] *n.* any of the many tiny dots which make up an image on a computer or television screen. ⟨< *pict(ure)* + *el(ement)*⟩

pix•ie or **pix•y** ['pɪksi] *n., pl.* **pix•ies.** a fairy or elf. ⟨< SW Brit. dial. *pixey, pisky*⟩ **—'pix•ie•ish** or **'pix•y•ish,** *adj.*

pix•i•lat•ed ['pɪksəˌleitɪd] *adj.* whimsical; eccentric; crazy. ⟨< *pixie-led* + *-ated.* 20c.⟩ **—ˌpix•i'la•tion,** *n.*

pizz. *Music.* pizzicato.

pizza ['pitsə] *n.* an open pie, usually made of a layer of yeast dough covered with a savoury mixture of tomatoes, cheese, olives, etc. and baked. Sometimes called **pizza pie.** ⟨< Ital.; possible substitution for Mod.Gk. *pitta* cake⟩

pizza parlour pizzeria.

piz•zazz [pə'zæz] *n. Slang.* glamorous vitality or sparkle; dash and style: *a political leader with pizzazz, accessories to add pizzazz to a basic suit.* Also, **pizazz.** ⟨imitative⟩ **—piz'zaz•zy,** *adj.*

piz•ze•ri•a [ˌpitsə'riə] *n.* a place where pizzas are made and sold, for taking out or eating on the premises.

piz•zi•ca•to [ˌpɪtsə'kɑtou] *adj., adv., n., pl.* **-ti** [-ti]. *Music.*
—*adj.* played by plucking the strings of a musical instrument with the finger instead of using the bow.
—*adv.* in a pizzicato manner.
—*n.* a note or passage so played. ⟨< Ital. *pizzicato* picked⟩

pj's or **p.j.'s** ['piˌdʒeiz] *Informal.* pyjamas.

pk. **1** peck. **2** peak. **3** park. **4** pack.

pkg. package.

PKU phenylketonuria.

pl. **1** plural. **2** place. **3** plate.

PL/1 or **P/L1** *Computer technology.* a high-level computer programming language. ⟨< *P*rogramming *L*anguage 1⟩

pla•ca•ble ['plækəbəl] *or* ['pleikəbəl] *adj.* forgiving; easily quieted; mild. ⟨ME < OF < L *placabilis* < *placare* placate⟩ **—'pla•ca•ble•ness** or **ˌpla•ca'bil•i•ty,** *n.* **—'pla•ca•bly,** *adv.*

plac•ard ['plækərd] *or* ['plækɑrd] *n., v.* —*n.* a notice to be posted in a public place; poster.
—*v.* **1** put placards on or in: *The circus placarded the city with advertisements.* **2** give notice of with placards. **3** post as a placard. ⟨< F *placard* < *plaque* plaque⟩

pla•cate [plə'keit], ['pleikeit], *or* ['plækeit] *v.* **-cat•ed, -cat•ing.** soothe or satisfy the anger of; make peaceful: *to placate a person one has offended.* ⟨< L *placare*⟩ **—pla'cat•er,** *n.* **—pla'cat•ing•ly,** *adv.* **—pla'ca•tion,** *n.*

place [pleis] *n., v.* **placed, plac•ing.** —*n.* **1** a particular part of space, of a definite or indefinite size: *This would be a good place for a picnic.* **2** a city, town, village, district, etc. **3** a building or spot used for a certain purpose. A church is a place of worship. A store or office is a place of business. **4** a house or dwelling: *We all went to my place for supper after skating. They have a beautiful place in the country.* **5** a part or spot in something: *There's a sore place on my leg where I bumped the table.* **6** a particular page or other point in a book or other writing: *to mark one's place.* **7** reasonable ground or occasion: *There was no place for such behaviour.* **8** the proper, original, or usual position or location: *The book is back in its place on the shelf.* **9** a proper, suitable, or designated rank or position: *He has found his place in teaching. Somebody should put him in his place.* **10** a position in time: *The performance went too slowly in several places.* **11** a space or seat for a person: *Keep a place for me if you get there first.* **12** a post or office: *In his place as corresponding secretary he is responsible for sending out the notices.* **13** duty; business: *It is not my place to find fault.* **14** a step or point in order of proceeding: *In the first place, the room is too small; in the second place, it is too dirty.* **15** *Mathematics.* the position of a figure in a number or series: *in the third decimal place.* **16** a position among the leaders at the finish of a race or competition: *John won first place.* **17** the position second to the winner at the end of a horse race. **18** a short street or court. **19** an open space or square in a city, town, etc.
all over the place,, *Informal.* **a** everywhere. **b** very disordered, imprecise, inconsistent, etc.
give place, a make room. **b** yield; give way: *His anger gave place to remorse.*
go places, *Informal.* advance rapidly toward success; achieve success.
in place, a on or in the proper, original, or usual place: *dishes in place on the shelf, members of the chorus in place on the stage.* **b** fitting, appropriate, or timely. **c** ready for action or use: *All systems are in place for the first democratic election in this small country.*
in place of, instead of: *You can use water in place of milk in this recipe.*
know (one's) **place,** act according to one's (usually, inferior) position in life.
out of place, a not in the proper or usual place. **b** inappropriate or ill-timed.
put (someone) **in** (his, her, etc.) **place,** tell or show someone that he or she is unduly conceited.
take place, happen; occur.
—*v.* **1** put (in a spot, position, condition, or relation). **2** put in the proper order or position; arrange; dispose. **3** give the place, etc. associated with; identify: *I remember his name, but I cannot place him.* **4** assign to a date, rank, category, value, age, etc. **5** appoint (a person) to a post or office; find a situation, etc. for. **6** entrust to an appropriate person, firm, etc. for action, treatment, disposal, etc.: *to place an order, to place an ad. They placed their wills with their lawyer.* **7** *Sports.* **a** be among the leaders at the finish of a race or competition: *The horse failed to place in the first race and was eliminated.* **b** finish second in a race or competition, especially in a horse race. Compare WIN (def. 1) and SHOW (def. 16b). ⟨ME < OF < VL *plattia* < L < Gk. *plateia*

(hodos) broad (way) < *platys* broad. Doublet of PLAZA and PIAZZA.⟩

☛ *Hom.* PLAICE.

☛ *Syn. v.* **1.** See note at PUT.

pla•ce•bo [plə'sibou] *for 1, 2;* [plɑ'tʃeibou] *for 3. n., pl.* **-bos** or **-boes. 1** a pill, etc., containing no active substance, given to humour or satisfy a patient or to serve as a control in an experiment to test a new drug. **2** something said only to flatter or mollify. **3** *Roman Catholic Church.* the vespers of the office for the dead. ⟨< L *placebo* I shall please, the opening word of the church service⟩

place card a small card with a person's name on it, to indicate where the guest is to sit at the table.

place holder *Mathematics.* the symbol zero when used to indicate the place value of another digit. In the number 40, the 0 is a place holder (for the ones) indicating that the 4 is in the tens place.

place in the sun a favourable position; as favourable a position as any occupied by others.

place mat a usually oblong or oval mat of cloth, paper, plastic, etc. that serves as an individual table cover at a meal.

place•ment ['pleismənt] *n.* **1** a placing or being placed; location; arrangement. **2 a** the finding of work or a job for a person. **b** the job found. **3** *Football.* **a** a placing of the ball on the ground for a placement kick. **b** PLACEMENT KICK.

placement kick *Football.* a kick given to a ball after it has been placed on the ground.

place name a name of a place, city, area, country, etc.; any geographical name. Athens, Asia, Niagara Falls, Arctic Ocean are place names.

pla•cen•ta [plə'sɛntə] *n., pl.* **-tae** [-ti] *or* [-taɪ] or **-tas. 1** *Anatomy. Zoology.* the organ by which the fetus is attached to the wall of the womb and nourished. **2** *Botany.* the part of the ovary of flowering plants that bears the ovules. ⟨< NL < L *placenta* flat cake < Gk. *plakounta*, accus. < *plax, plakos* flat surface⟩ **—pla'cen•tal,** *adj.*

pla•cen•tate [plə'sɛnteit] *adj.* having a placenta.

plac•er¹ ['pleisər] *n.* a person who or thing that places.

plac•er² ['plæsər] *n. Mining.* a deposit of sand or gravel containing gold or other valuable minerals in particles that can be washed out. ⟨< Am.Sp. *placer* sandbank. Akin to PLAZA.⟩

placer mining the process of washing loose sand or gravel for gold or other minerals. Placer mining was a common practice in the Klondike.

place setting the dishes and cutlery required to set one person's place at a table.

place value *Mathematics.* the value of a digit according to its position in a number. In *582*, the place values are *5×100, 8×10, 2×1.*

plac•id ['plæsɪd] *adj.* calm; peaceful; quiet: *a placid lake.* ⟨< L *placidus* < *placere* please⟩ **—'plac•id•ly,** *adv.* **—pla'cid•i•ty** or **'plac•id•ness,** *n.*

☛ *Syn.* See note at PEACEFUL.

plack•et ['plækɪt] *n.* a finished opening or slit with some kind of fastening at the top of a skirt, the side or back of a dress, etc., to make it easy to put on and take off. ⟨? var. of *placard*⟩

plac•oid ['plækɔɪd] *adj.* having platelike scales that are periodically shed, as in sharks and cartilaginous fishes. ⟨< Gk. *plak* flat⟩

pla•gal ['pleigəl] *adj. Music.* of a cadence, consisting of a subdominant chord followed by a tonic chord. Compare PERFECT (def. 10b). < L *plagialis*, ult. < Gk. *plagios* sideways⟩

plage [plɑʒ] *n.* **1** a beach at a seaside resort. **2** *Astronomy.* a luminous area in the chromosphere of the sun appearing in the vicinity of a sunspot and visible on a spectroheliogram taken at the wavelength of the ionized calcium vapours. ⟨< F *plage* beach < L *plagia* shore < Gk. *plagios* slanting⟩

pla•gia•rism ['pleidʒə,rɪzəm] *n.* **1** the act of plagiarizing. **2** an idea, expression, plot, etc. taken from another and used as one's own. ⟨< L *plagiarius* kidnapper, ult. < *plaga* net⟩

pla•gia•rist ['pleidʒərɪst] *n.* a person who uses the ideas, expressions, plot, etc. of someone else and passes them off as his or her own. **—,pla•gia'rist•ic,** *adj.*

pla•gia•rize ['pleidʒə,raɪz] *v.* **-rized, -riz•ing.** take and use as one's own (the thoughts, writings, inventions, etc. of another); especially, to take and use (a passage, plot, etc.) from the work of (another writer). **—'pla•gia,riz•er,** *n.*

pla•gi•o•clase ['pleidʒiə,kleis] *n.* any of certain common minerals of the feldspar family, ranging from albite, which is acidic, to anorthite, which is basic. ⟨< Gk. *plagios* oblique + *klasis* a break < *klaein* to break⟩

pla•gi•o•trop•ic [,pleidʒiə'trɒpɪk] *adj. Botany.* growing divergent from the vertical line, so that the long axes of roots or branches slant away from the vertical. ⟨< Gk. *plagios* oblique, slanting + E *tropic*⟩

plague [pleig] *n., v.* **plagued, pla•guing.** *—n.* **1** a dangerous disease that spreads rapidly and often causes death. It occurs in several forms, one of which is BUBONIC PLAGUE. The plague is common in Asia and has several times swept through Europe. **2** any epidemic disease; pestilence. **3** a misfortune thought of as a punishment from God. **4** anything or anyone that torments, vexes, annoys, troubles, offends, or is disagreeable: *My hay fever is a plague this year.*

—v. **1** cause to suffer from a disease or calamity. **2** vex; annoy; bother: *Stop plaguing me for money.* ⟨ME < L *plaga* blow, pestilence < dial. Gk. *plaga* blow⟩

☛ *Syn. v.* **2.** See note at TEASE.

pla•guy ['pleigi] *adj. Informal.* troublesome; annoying. Also, **plaguey.**

plaice [pleis] *n., pl.* **plaice** or **plaic•es. 1** a red and brown European flounder (*Pleuronectes platessa*) that is a commercially important food fish. **2** a reddish or brownish flatfish (*Hippoglossoides platessoides*) of the same family (Pleuronectidae), found in the western North Atlantic. ⟨ME < OF < LL *platessa* flatfish < Gk. *platys* flat⟩

☛ *Hom.* PLACE.

plaid [plæd] *n.* **1** a pattern consisting of an evenly repeated design of broad and narrow unevenly spaced stripes crossing each other at right angles. **2** such a pattern as the distinctive identification of a Scottish clan or other group; tartan. **3** cloth woven or printed with a plaid. **4** *(adjl.)* having such a pattern: *a plaid dress.* **5** an oblong length of woollen cloth, usually woven with a tartan design, worn over the left shoulder as part of the traditional dress of the Scottish Highlanders. See KILT for picture. ⟨< Scots Gaelic *plaide*⟩ **—'plaid•ed,** *adj.*

plain¹ [plein] *adj., adv., n. —adj.* **1** easy to see, hear, or understand; clear: *The meaning is plain.* **2** that is clearly what the name expresses; unmistakable; downright; absolute: *plain foolishness.* **3** not intricate; uncomplicated: *plain sewing.* **4** frank and honest; straightforward: *plain speech. She believes in plain dealing.* **5** without ornament or decoration; simple: *a plain dress.* **6** without figured pattern, varied weave, or variegated colour: *a plain blue fabric.* **7** not rich or highly seasoned: *plain food.* **8** simple or ordinary in manner: *They're plain people.* **9** not good-looking: *a plain face.* **10** pure; not mixed with anything: *plain coffee.* **10** *Archaic* level; plane.

—adv. simply; clearly: *He's plain stubborn.*

—n. **1** Often, **plains,** *pl.* a large, more or less flat and treeless stretch of land: *Buffalo used to roam the North American plains.* See PLATEAU for picture. **2** a knitting stitch which raises a ridge on the back of the knitted fabric. Compare PURL² (defs. 1, 2). ⟨ME < OF < L *planus* flat. Doublet of PIANO², PLAN.⟩ **—'plain•ly,** *adv.* **—'plain•ness,** *n.*

☛ *Hom.* PLANE.

plain² [plein] *v. Archaic or dialect.* complain. ⟨ME < OF, ult. < L *plangere* lament⟩

☛ *Hom.* PLANE.

plain•chant ['plein,tʃænt] *n.* plainsong.

plain–clothes ['plein ,klouz] *or* [,klouðz] *adj., n. —adj.* wearing ordinary clothes, not a uniform, when on duty, as some police detectives.

—n. civilian clothes; non-uniform attire: *They're working in plain-clothes today.*

Plain People the Mennonites, Amish, etc. because of their plain and simple way of life and manner of dress.

plain sailing **1** sailing in a straightforward course. **2** a clear, simple course of action; easy, unobstructed progress: *We had some problems at first but after that it was plain sailing.*

plains buffalo a species of buffalo native to the great plains, smaller than the **wood buffalo.**

plains cottonwood a poplar tree (*Populus deltoides occidentalis*) having hairy winter buds, and leaves with a few teeth and a long tip.

Plains Cree a member of one of the two main branches of the Cree people. The Plains Cree migrated to the Prairies from the eastern woodlands.

Plains Indian a member of any of the First Nations peoples of varying linguistic stocks including the Assiniboine, Blackfoot, and Plains Cree, who formerly inhabited the Great Plains area and shared a number of cultural traits such as the nomadic following of a buffalo herd.

plains•man ['pleinzmən] *n., pl.* **-men. 1** a man who lived on or was familiar with the prairies in early times. **2** an inhabitant of the plains.

Plains of A•bra•ham ['eibrə,hæm] a plain originally outside and just west of Québec City but now enclosed by it, the site of the battle of 1759 between British and French troops that gave the British supremacy in North America.

plain•song ['plein,sɒŋ] *n.* **1** vocal music used in the Christian church from very early times, sung in unison and unaccompanied, employing a limited musical scale and free rhythm. **2** GREGORIAN CHANT. **3** any similar simple religious chant. **4** any unadorned melody.

plain–spo•ken ['plein 'spoukən] *adj.* plain or frank in speech.

plaint [pleint] *n.* **1** *Archaic or poetic.* lamentation. **2** *Law.* accusation or complaint. ⟨ME < OF *plainte* < L *planctus* lamentation < *plangere* lament⟩

plain•tiff ['pleintɪf] *n.* a person who begins a lawsuit. ⟨ME < OF *plaintif* complaining. See PLAINTIVE.⟩

plain•tive ['pleintɪv] *adj.* mournful; sad. ⟨ME < OF *plaintif,* ult. < L *planctus* complaint⟩ **—'plain•tive•ly,** *adv.* **—'plain•tive•ness,** *n.*

plait [pleit] *or* [plæt] *n. or v.* **1** braid. **2** *Rare.* pleat. ⟨ME < OF *pleit,* ult. < L *plicare* fold⟩
☛ *Hom.* PLATE [pleit], PLAT [plæt].

plan [plæn] *n., v.* **planned, plan•ning.** *—n.* **1** a way of making or doing something that has been worked out beforehand; a scheme or method for achieving an end: *a plan for attracting more tourists to the city.* **2** goal; aim: *Her plan was to have the business firmly established by the end of the year.* **3** a drawing or diagram made on a flat surface, especially one showing how a floor of a building is arranged and the relative size of all its rooms, etc. **4** a large-scale, detailed map of a small area such as a town or district, a property, a development site, etc.
—v. **1** think out beforehand how (something) is to be made or done; design, scheme, or devise (*sometimes with* **out**): *to plan a program.* **2** make plans. **3** have in mind as a purpose; intend: *We are planning to take a long vacation this year.* **4** make a drawing or diagram of.
plan on, a reckon on: *If we plan on 200 guests we'll be sure to have enough.* **b** intend: *I plan on going. He plans on an early start.* ⟨< F *plan,* literally, a plane < L *planus*; with reference to a sketch on a flat surface. Doublet of PLAIN[1], PIANO[2].⟩
☛ *Syn. n.* **1. Plan,** DESIGN, PROJECT = a proposed way of doing or making something. **Plan** is the general word meaning 'an arrangement of parts or a method of procedure worked out beforehand': *He has a plan for increasing production.* **Design** emphasizes careful arrangement of details according to the purpose, intention, or end in view: *They have a design for a rich, full life.* **Project** applies to a purposed plan, often having a particular practical goal and worked out according to specific times, places, etc.: *He introduced a project for slum clearance.*

pla•nar ['pleinər] *adj.* **1** of or having to do with a geometric plane or a point on a surface at which the curvature is zero. **2** level; flat.
☛ *Hom.* PLANER.

pla•nar•i•an [plə'nɛriən] *n.* any of an order (Tricladida) of free-living, mainly aquatic flatworms having three-branching intestines, a soft, flat body, and the power of growing again when cut apart. ⟨< NL *Planaria* < L *planus* flat; level + E *-an*⟩

pla•na•tion [plə'neiʃən] *n. Geology.* the process whereby a land area is reduced by erosion to a nearly flat surface.

plan•chette [plæn'ʃɛt] *or* [plæn'tʃɛt] *n.* **1** a small triangular or heart-shaped board supported on casters at two points and having a vertical pencil at the third. It is believed to produce automatic writing when a person rests his or her fingers lightly on the board. **2** a similar board without a pencil, such as that used with a Ouija board. ⟨< F *planchette,* dim. of *planche* plank⟩

Planck's constant [plæŋks] *or* [plaŋks] *Physics.* the fundamental constant (h) of quantum mechanics, giving the ratio of a quantum of radiant energy (E) to the frequency (v) of the radiation source (thus $E = hv$) and approximately equal to 6.625×10^{-27} erg-seconds or 10^{-34} joule-seconds. ⟨after Max K.E.L. *Planck* (1858-1947), German physicist⟩

plane[1] [plein] *n., adj., v.* **planed, plan•ing.** *—n.* **1** any flat or level surface. **2** a level of development, thought, conduct, achievement, etc.: *the intellectual plane. He keeps his work on a high plane.* **3** a thin, flat or curved supporting surface of an airplane; airfoil. **4** airplane. **5** *Geometry.* a surface such that if any two points on it are joined by a straight line, the line will be contained wholly in the surface.
—adj. **1** flat; level. **2** being wholly in a plane. Rectangles and circles are plane figures. **3** of or having to do with such figures: *plane geometry.*
—v. **1** glide as an airplane does. **2** of a speedboat, etc., rise slightly out of the water while moving; skim over the water. **3** travel by airplane. ⟨< L *planum* level place⟩
☛ *Hom.* PLAIN.

plane[2] [plein] *n., v.* **planed, plan•ing.** *—n.* carpenter's tool with a blade for smoothing or shaping wood.
—v. **1** make smooth or level by means of a plane; use a plane on. **2** remove with a plane. ⟨< F *plane,* ult. < LL *plana*⟩
☛ *Hom.* PLAIN.

plane[3] [plein] *n.* PLANE-TREE.
☛ *Hom.* PLAIN.

plane angle *Mathematics.* an angle formed by two straight lines lying on the same plane.

plane figure *Mathematics.* in geometry, a figure which lies in a single PLANE[1] (def. 5); a flat figure.

plane geometry *Mathematics.* a branch of geometry dealing with plane figures.

plane•load ['plein,loud] *n.* the load of people or cargo carried by an airplane: *a planeload of supplies.*

plan•er ['pleinər] *n.* a person or thing that planes, especially a machine for planing wood or for finishing flat surfaces on metal.
☛ *Hom.* PLANAR.

plan•et ['plænɪt] *n.* **1** *Astronomy.* one of the heavenly bodies (except comets and meteors) that move around the sun in regular paths. Mercury, Venus, the Earth, Mars, Jupiter, Saturn, Uranus, Neptune, and Pluto are planets in our solar system. **2** *Astrology.* a heavenly body, including the sun and the moon, thought to influence people's lives. ⟨< LL < Gk. *planētēs* < *planaesthai* wander⟩

plan•e•tar•i•um [,plænə'tɛriəm] *n., pl.* **-i•a** [-iə] or **-i•ums. 1** an apparatus that shows the movements of the sun, moon, planets, and stars by projecting lights on the inside of a dome. **2** a room or building with such an apparatus. ⟨< NL⟩

plan•e•tar•y ['plænə,tɛri] *adj.* **1** of, having to do with, or being a planet: *planetary influence, planetary motion.* **2** wandering; erratic. **3** of, having to do with, or belonging to the earth; terrestrial. **4** *Machinery.* of or designating an epicyclic gear train used for automobile transmissions.

plan•e•tes•i•mal [,plænə'tɛsəməl] *adj., n. Astronomy. —adj.* of or having to do with minute bodies in space that, according to a certain hypothesis (now rejected), move in planetary orbits and gradually unite to form the planets of a given planetary system.
—n. one of these minute bodies. ⟨< *planet* + (*infinit*)*esimal*⟩

plan•et•oid ['plænə,tɔɪd] *n. Astronomy.* a minor planet; asteroid.

plane–tree or **plane tree** ['plein ,tri] *n.* any of a genus (*Platanus*) making up a family (Platanaceae) of trees native to North America, Europe, and Asia, having large, broad, lobed leaves, spreading branches, and small fruits hanging in ball-shaped clusters from long stems; sycamore.

planet wheel *Machinery.* a gear revolving around and meshing with the sun gear in an epicyclic gear train. Also called **planet gear.**

planet X a hypothetical planet beyond the orbit of Pluto.

plan•gent ['plændʒənt] *adj.* **1** resounding loudly and mournfully, as a deep bell. **2** beating with a deep, loud sound. ⟨< L *plangens,* ppr. of *plangere* to bewail⟩

plan•ish ['plænɪʃ] *v.* **1** smooth or polish (metal) by hammering. **2** give a smooth finish to (metal or paper) by rolling. ⟨< OF *planiss* < *planir* to smooth⟩ **—'plan•ish•er,** *n.*

plan•i•sphere ['plænɪ,sfir] *n.* **1** a map or chart representing the whole or part of a sphere on a plane. **2** a map that is a projection on a plane of the celestial sphere, usually with the north or south celestial pole as the centre.

plank [plæŋk] *n., v. —n.* **1** a long, flat, thick piece of sawed timber. **2** an item or feature of the platform of a political party, etc. **3** a flat timber forming part of the outer side of a ship's hull. **4** anything that supports or saves in time of need (with allusion to the use of a plank to save a shipwrecked person from drowning).
walk the plank, be forced to walk off a plank extending from a

ship's side over the water. Pirates reputedly used to make their prisoners do this.
—*v.* **1** cover or furnish with planks. **2** cook and serve on a board. Steak is sometimes planked. **3** *Informal.* put or set with force; plunk (*used with* **down**): *He planked down the package.*
4 *Informal.* pay at once; pay on the spot (*used with* **down** *or* **out**): *She planked her money down.* ⟨ME *planke* < OF *planche* < L *planca* board⟩ **—'plank,like,** *adj.*

plank house among coastal First Nations peoples, a long rectangular communal building built of cedar and capable of housing several families, now used chiefly for ceremonial affairs. Compare LONGHOUSE.

plank•ing ['plæŋkɪŋ] *n., v.* —*n.* **1** the act of laying or covering with planks. **2** a quantity of planks together: *They bought planking for the floor of the shed.*
—*v.* ppr. of PLANK.

plank•ter ['plæŋktər] *n.* an individual planktonic organism. ⟨< Gk. *plankter* roamer⟩

plank•ton ['plæŋktən] *n.* the mass of very small or microscopic animal or plant life that floats or drifts near the surface of bodies of salt and fresh water, providing food for fish and other water animals. Plankton contains algae, protozoans, fish in a larval stage, etc. ⟨< G < Gk. *planktos* wandering, verbal adj. to *plazomai* wander⟩ **—plank'ton•ic** [-'tɒnɪk], *adj.*

plan•ner ['plænər] *n.* a person who plans, especially one whose job it is. Most cities have a city planner who looks after the arrangement of parks, residential and business areas, etc.

pla•no–con•cave ['pleinou 'kɒnkeiv] *or* [kɒn'keiv], ['kɒŋkeiv] *or* [kɒŋ'keiv] *adj.* flat on one side and concave on the other. See CONCAVE for picture. ⟨< L *planus* flat + E *concave*⟩

pla•no–con•vex ['pleinou 'kɒnvɛks] *or* [kɒn'vɛks] *adj.* flat on one side and convex on the other. See CONVEX for picture. ⟨< L *planus* flat + E *convex*⟩

pla•nog•ra•phy [plə'nɒgrəfi] *n. Printing.* the method or technique of printing from a flat surface, either directly or offset.

plant [plænt] *n., v.* —*n.* **1** any living thing that is not an animal, fungus, protist, or moneran. Trees, shrubs, herbs, algae, etc. are plants. They are generally characterized by the ability to process their own food from inorganic matter by photosynthesis, and by rigid cell walls that contain cellulose. **2** a living thing that has leaves, roots, and a soft stem, and is small in contrast with a tree or shrub. **3** a young tree, shrub, vine, or herb ready to be planted: *The farmer set out 100 cabbage plants.* **4** the buildings, machinery, etc. used in manufacturing: *There is an aluminum plant in Kingston.* **5** the workers at a plant: *The whole plant is on strike.* **6** the complete apparatus used for a specific mechanical operation or process: *the heating plant on a ship.* **7** buildings, equipment, etc. used for any purpose: *a college plant.* **8** *Slang.* a scheme to trap, trick, mislead, or deceive. **9** *Informal.* a person or thing placed so as to trap, lure, or deceive: *She claimed that the money found in her room was a plant.*
—*v.* **1** put or set in the ground to grow. **2** provide with seed or plants; stock; put seed in: *We planted our garden last weekend.* **3** deposit (young fish, spawn, oysters) in a river, lake, etc. **4** set firmly; put; place: *He planted his feet firmly apart and pulled hard.* **5** post; station: *to plant guards at an entrance.* **6** establish or set up (a colony, city, etc.). **7** implant (principles, doctrines, etc.). **8** *Slang.* deliver (a blow, etc.) with a definite aim. **9** *Informal.* place (a person or thing) so as to trap, lure, or deceive: *The evidence was planted.* **10** *Slang.* conceal. ⟨OE *plante* < L *planta* sprout⟩ **—'plant•a•ble,** *adj.* **—'plant,like,** *adj.*

Plan•tag•e•net [plæn'tædʒənɪt] *n.* a member of the royal family that ruled England from 1154 to 1485. The English kings from Henry II through Richard III were Plantagenets. ⟨< *planta genista* sprig of broom, worn as an identifying mark⟩

plan•tain[1] ['plæntən] *n.* **1** a tropical treelike plant (*Musa paradisiaca*) closely related to the banana, yielding an edible fruit similar to the common banana. **2** the fruit of this plant, larger and starchier than a banana. Plantains are not eaten raw; they are boiled or fried and also dried and ground up into meal or flour. ⟨< Sp. *plántano*⟩

plan•tain[2] ['plæntən] *n.* any of a genus (*Plantago*) of plants having spikes of tiny, greenish flowers and usually broad leaves that spread out from the base of the stem. Several species of plantain are common Canadian weeds. ⟨ME < OF < L *plantago, -ginis* < *planta* sole of the foot; from its flat leaves⟩

plantain lily any of several plants (genus *Hosta*) of the lily family native to Asia but widely cultivated as garden plants, having large, often wavy and variegated leaves and spikes of white, lilac, or blue flowers.

plan•tar ['plæntər] *adj.* of, having to do with, or on the sole of the foot: *plantar warts.* ⟨< L *plantaris* < *planta* sole of the foot⟩
☛ *Hom.* PLANTER.

plan•ta•tion [plæn'teiʃən] *n.* **1** a large farm or estate, especially in a tropical or semitropical country, on which cotton, tobacco, sugar, etc. are grown. The work on a plantation is usually done by labourers who live there. **2** a large group of trees or other plants that have been planted. **3** a colony; settlement: *Plantations were established in Newfoundland in the early 1600s.* **4** *Logging.* a reforested tract of land that has previously been cut over. ⟨< L *plantatio, -onis* a planting < *planta* sprout⟩

plant•er ['plæntər] *n.* **1** a person who owns or runs a plantation: *a cotton planter.* **2** a machine for planting. **3** a person who plants. **4** an enclosure in which flowers are planted alongside of a building. **5** a box, stand, or pot used for growing plants indoors, on a patio or balcony, etc. **6** *Cdn.* in Newfoundland, a small trader; a person who hires others to fish for him or her, advancing their supplies and taking a share of the catch. **7** an early settler; colonist.
☛ *Hom.* PLANTAR.

planter's punch a chilled drink made with rum, lime juice, sugar, and water or soda water.

plan•ti•grade ['plæntə,greid] *adj., n.* —*adj.* walking on the whole sole of the foot. A bear is a plantigrade animal.
—*n.* a plantigrade animal, as a bear or human. ⟨< F < LL *plantigradus* < L *planta* sole + *-gradus* walking⟩

plant kingdom **1** one of the broad divisions of the natural world, ranging from small plants to large trees. Members of the plant kingdom make use of photosynthesis to produce sugars for nourishment. Compare ANIMAL KINGDOM and MINERAL KINGDOM. **2** in present-day biology, one of the five divisions of living things. See also PROTIST, FUNGUS, and MONERAN.

plant louse aphid.

plaque [plæk] *n.* **1** an ornamental, inscribed tablet of metal, porcelain, wood, etc., fastened to a wall, door, or piece of furniture and intended basically to inform, but often simply decorative. **2** a flat, thin ornament or badge. **3** *Dentistry.* a thin film of saliva, mucus, etc., together with bacteria, that forms on the teeth. Plaque hardens into calculus, or tartar, if not removed. **4** *Medicine.* **a** an abnormal patch on the body, such as a spot of psoriasis. **b** an area marked by destruction or loss of the myelin sheath normally enveloping the nerve fibres, characteristic of multiple sclerosis. **5** a clear space in a bacterial culture, resulting from the localized destruction of cells by a virus. ⟨< F < Du. *plak* flat board⟩

plash [plæʃ] *v. or n.* splash. **—'plash•y,** *adj.*

plas•ma [plæzmə] *n.* **1** *Physiology.* the liquid part of blood or lymph, as distinguished from the corpuscles. **2** the watery part of milk, as distinguished from the globules of fat; whey. **3** *Physics.* a highly ionized gas, consisting of almost equal numbers of free electrons and positive ions. **4** *Biology.* protoplasm; cytoplasm.
5 a green, faintly translucent variety of quartz. Also (defs. 1, 2, 4 & 5), **plasm.** ⟨< LL < Gk. *plasma* something formed or moulded < *plassein* mould⟩

plasma membrane *Biology.* the extremely thin living membrane surrounding the cytoplasm of a cell.

plas•mid ['plæzmɪd] *n.* a self-replicating segment of DNA independent of the chromosomes, occurring in bacteria and yeast. Because of its ability to transfer genetic material from one cell to another and alter hereditary characteristics, it is used in recombinant DNA technology.

plas•min ['plæzmɪn] *n. Biochemistry.* a proteolytic enzyme, a derivative of blood plasma and capable of dissolving blood clots. Also called **fibrinolysin.**

plas•mo•di•um [plæz'moudiəm] *n., pl.* **-di•a** [-diə]. *Biology.*
1 any one-celled parasite of the genus *Plasmodium* found in red blood corpuscles, including the type that produces malaria in humans. **2** a multinuclear mass of protoplasm, a stage in the life cycle of certain moulds.

plas•mol•y•sis [plæz'mɒləsɪs] *n. Botany.* a reduction in volume of a plant cell as a result of a loss of water by osmosis.

–plast *combining form.* living substance; cell, etc.; a unit of protoplasm: *chloroplast, protoplast.* ⟨< Gk. *plastós* formed, moulded < *plassein* mould⟩

plas•ter ['plæstər] *n., v.* —*n.* **1** a soft mixture of lime, sand, and water that hardens in drying, used for covering walls or ceilings. **2** PLASTER OF PARIS. **3** a medicated or protective

dressing consisting of a pastelike substance spread on cloth, etc., that will stick to the body and protect cuts, relieve pain, etc.
—*v.* **1** cover (walls, ceilings, etc.) with plaster. **2** spread with anything thickly: *My shoes were plastered with mud.* **3** make smooth and flat: *He plastered his wet hair down.* **4** apply a plaster on. **5** apply like a plaster. ⟨ME, OE, OF *plastre* < Med.L *plastrum* < L *emplastrum* < Gk. *emplastron* < *en-* on + *plassein* mould⟩ **—'plas•ter,like,** *adj.*

plas•ter•board ['plæstər,bɔrd] *n.* a relatively thin board consisting of a layer of plaster between layers of pressed felt covered with paper, made in large sheets and used for walls and partitions.

plaster cast **1** a rigid casing made of layers of gauze soaked in wet plaster of Paris and formed around an arm or other part of the body to keep a broken bone in place. **2** a sculptor's model of a statue made of plaster of Paris.

plas•tered ['plæstərd] *adj., v.* —*adj. Slang.* drunk; intoxicated.
—*v.* pt. and pp. of PLASTER.

plas•ter•er ['plæstərər] *n.* a person who plasters walls, etc.

plas•ter•ing ['plæstərɪŋ] *n., v.* —*n.* a covering of plaster on walls, etc.
—*v.* ppr. of PLASTER.

plaster of Paris a mixture of powdered gypsum and water, which hardens quickly and is used for making moulds, cheap statuary, casts, etc. ⟨so named because it was originally made in Paris⟩

plas•tic ['plæstɪk] *n., adj.* —*n.* **1** any of various synthetic materials that harden and retain their shape after being moulded or shaped when subjected to heat, pressure, etc. Celluloid, Bakelite, vulcanite, and nylon are all plastics. **2** such a substance produced in a laboratory from raw materials such as petroleum, urea, phenol, or glycerin. Plastics may be rigid or soft and are often used in place of natural substances such as leather, wood, or metal. Some of the most widely used plastics are polyethylene, vinyl, styrene, and polyester. **3 plastics, a** the branch of chemistry that deals with the production and use of plastics (*used with a singular verb*): *The class is studying plastics.* **b** plastic articles.
4 *Informal.* credit card or cards.
—*adj.* **1** made of synthetic plastic: *plastic cups.* **2** moulding or giving shape to material. **3** concerned with moulding or modelling: *Sculpture is a plastic art.* **4** easily moulded or shaped: *Clay, wax, and plaster are plastic substances.* **5** easily influenced; impressionable: *Children's minds are incredibly plastic.* **6** showing lack of depth or originality; artificial or phoney; not natural or real: *a plastic hero, plastic food.* ⟨< L *plasticus* < Gk. *plastikos,* ult. < *plassein* form, shape⟩

plastic art **1** art producing three-dimensional works or effects. **2 a** art producing works that are carved or modelled, as sculpture. **b** visual art as distinct from music or writing.

plastic bomb a bomb made of a puttylike substance containing explosives, capable of adhering to walls, etc. and detonated by a fuse or an electrical timer.

Plas•ti•cine ['plæstɪ,sin] *or* [,plæstɪ'sin] *n. Trademark.* an oil-based modelling paste made in different colours, that remains soft and malleable. Plasticine is used especially by children.

plas•tic•i•ty [plæ'stɪsəti] *n.* the quality or state of being plastic; especially, the capacity for being moulded.

plas•ti•cize ['plæstə,saɪz] *v.* **1** make or become plastic.
2 treat with a plastic: *a plasticized fabric for raincoats.*
—,plas•ti•ci'za•tion, *n.* **—'plas•ti,ci•zer,** *n.*

plastic surgery a branch of surgery concerned with repairing or reconstructing parts of the body that are deformed or have been lost or injured, or with improving outward appearance, especially of the face. **—plastic surgeon.**

plas•tid ['plæstɪd] *n. Biology.* any of the structures found in some plant cells in which proteins and colouring matter are stored.

plas•tique [plæs'tik] *n.* **1** a PLASTIC BOMB. **2** a ballet and pantomime technique of making very slow movements and of posing like a statue.

plas•tron ['plæstrən] *n.* **1** a metal breastplate worn under a coat of mail. **2** a leather guard worn over the chest of a fencer.
3 an ornamental, detachable front of a woman's bodice.
4 *Zoology.* the ventral part of the shell of a turtle or tortoise.
⟨< F < Ital. *piastrone* < *piastra* plate of metal < Med.L *plastrum* plaster. See PLASTER.⟩

-plasty *combining form.* surgical repair or plastic surgery on or of the body part specified by the first element: *angioplasty, rhinoplasty.*

plat¹ [plæt] *n., v.* **plat•ted, plat•ting.** —*n.* **1** a map; chart; plan.
2 a small piece of ground; plot.
—*v.* map; chart; plan. ⟨ME < OF < VL < Gk. *platys* broad, flat; meaning of def. 2 from *plot*⟩
☛ *Hom.* PLAIT [plæt].

plat² [plæt] *n., v.* **plat•ted, plat•ting.** braid; plait. ⟨var. of *plait*⟩

plat du jour ['plɑ du 'ʒʊr]; *French,* [plady'ʒuʀ] in a restaurant, the special dish of the day.

plate [pleit] *n., v.* **plat•ed, plat•ing.** —*n.* **1** a dish, usually round, that is almost flat: *a dinner plate.* **2** plateful: *a plate of meat and potatoes.* **3** a part of a meal, served on or in a separate dish; course: *I ordered the cold plate.* **4** the dishes and food served to one person at a meal: *The dinner will cost $50 a plate.*
5 a tray or other container similar to a plate: *A plate is passed in church to receive the collection.* **6 a** dishes or containers made of or covered with a thin layer of silver or gold: *The family plate included an antique silver pitcher.* **b** the thin layer of silver or gold laid over a base metal such as copper or nickel silver: *The plate on this tray is wearing thin and the copper shows through.* **7** a thin, flat sheet or piece of metal: *The warship was covered with steel plates.* **8** armour made of such pieces of metal. **9** a platelike part, organ, or structure. Some animals and fishes have a covering of horny or bony plates. **10** a thin, flat piece of metal, plastic, etc., on which something is engraved. Plates are used for printing pictures. **11** something printed from such a piece of metal. **12** a metal copy of a page of type. **13** any full-page inserted illustration forming part of a book. **14** a thin sheet of glass coated with chemicals that are sensitive to light. Plates are sometimes used in taking photographs. **15** *Geology.* one of the enormous segments of which the crust of the earth appears to be composed, that float and move on the softer mantle below.
16 *Baseball.* **a** the place where the batter stands to hit a pitched ball; home base. **b** the place where the pitcher stands.
17 *Dentistry.* **a** the part of a set of false teeth that fits to the gums, and in which the teeth are fixed: *a partial plate, an upper plate.* **b** an orthodontic device of similar shape. **18** a thin cut of beef from the lower end of the ribs. See BEEF for picture.
19 *Electronics.* the anode of an electron tube, especially when flat. **20** a piece of timber laid horizontally to support rafters or studs. **21** a gold or silver cup or other prize given to the winner of a contest, especially a horse race. **22** a horse race in which the prize is (or was originally) such an object: *The Queen's Plate is the biggest race in the Canadian racing season.* Also, **plate race.**
on a plate. See PLATTER.
on (one's) **plate,** taking up one's time, effort, and attention.
—*v.* **1** cover with a thin layer of silver, gold, or other metal.
2 cover with metal plates for protection. **3** make a plate from (type) for printing. ⟨ME < OF *plate,* ult. < VL *plattus* flat < Gk. *platys*⟩
☛ *Hom.* PLAIT [pleit].

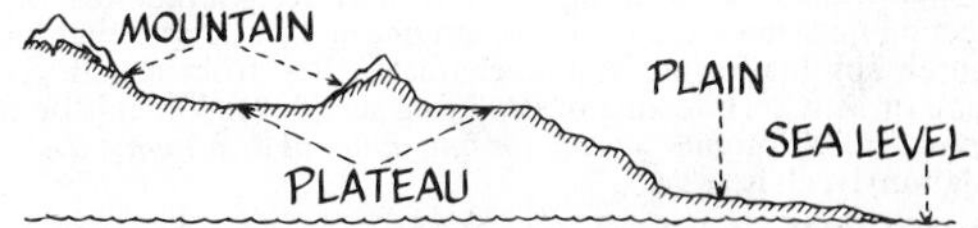

pla•teau [plə'tou] *n., pl.* **-teaus** or **-teaux** [-'touz]. **1** a large level or mainly level area of land in the mountains or rising sharply from the sea or a lowland area. Many plateaus have a very dry climate. **2** a period or level at which something is stabilized for a time, represented on a graph as a horizontal line; a period or state of levelling off: *Our volleyball team improved rapidly at first, but then we reached a plateau.* ⟨< F < OF *platel,* dim. of *plat* flat < VL *plattus.* See PLATE.⟩

plate block a block of four or more postage stamps with the serial number(s) of the printing plates (also called **plate number(s)**) in the margin.

plate•ful ['pleit,fʊl] *n., pl.* **-fuls.** the contents of a plate or as much or as many as a plate will hold: *a plateful of cookies.*

plate glass thick sheet glass that has been ground and polished to make it very smooth and clear. Plate glass is used for mirrors, large windows, etc.

plate•let ['pleitlɪt] *n.* one of the very tiny, colourless disks found in the blood of vertebrates, that assist in blood clotting.

plat•en ['plætən] *n.* **1** a flat metal plate in a printing press that presses the paper against the inked type. **2** the roller in a typewriter, against which the paper rests. ⟨< F *platine* < *plat* flat < VL *plattus.* See PLATE.⟩

plate tectonics *Geology.* the study of the structure of the earth's crust on the basis of the theory that the crust is made up of huge segments, called plates, that float on the mantle below, and whose individual movement is responsible for continental drift, mountain building, earthquakes, etc.

plat•form ['plætfɔrm] *n.* **1** a raised, level surface. There usually is a platform beside the track at a railway station. A public hall usually has a platform for speakers. **2** a plan of action or statement of principles of a group. A political party is said to have a platform. **3 a** an extra layer in a sole of a shoe, to give additional thickness. **b** a type of shoe having this sole.
4 *Computer technology*. the environment in which applications are run, consisting of the operating system, type of CPU or other hardware, the way a system is configured, or any combination of these factors. ⟨< F *plateforme* flat form⟩

platform rocker a rocking chair that rocks on a stable base.

plat•ing ['pleitɪŋ] *n., v.* —*n.* **1** a thin layer of silver, gold, or other metal. **2** a covering of metal plates.
—*v.* ppr. of PLATE.

pla•ti•nic [plə'tɪnɪk] *adj. Chemistry.* like, of, or containing platinum, especially in its tetravalent state.

pla•ti•noid ['plætə,nɔɪd] *adj., n.* —*adj.* resembling platinum.
—*n.* **1** any metal, such as iridium or paladium, with which platinum is associated. **2** an alloy of copper, nickel, and zinc with small amounts of tungsten or aluminum added.

plat•i•num ['plætənəm] *n., adj.* —*n.* **1** *Chemistry.* a heavy, precious, metallic chemical element that looks like silver or white gold and does not tarnish or melt easily. It is used as a catalyst, in jewellery, etc. *Symbol*: Pt; *at.no.* 78; *at.mass* 195.09.
2 a light grey colour, less bright than silver and having a faint bluish tinge.
—*adj.* designating an album or video of recorded music that has sold over two million copies: *The band's latest disc went platinum last week.* ⟨< NL *platinum*, ult. < Sp. *plata* silver⟩

platinum blond **1** the colour of whitish silver. **2** of hair, having this colour. **3** Or **platinum blonde,** a person having hair of this colour.

plat•i•tude ['plætə,tjud] *or* ['plætə,tud] *n.* **1** a dull or commonplace remark, especially one given out solemnly as if it were fresh and important. *Better late than never* is a platitude.
2 flatness; triteness; dullness. ⟨< F *platitude* < *plat* flat⟩
—,plat•i'tu•din,ize, *v.*

plat•i•tu•di•nous [,plætə'tjudənəs] *or* [,plætə'tudənəs] *adj.* characterized by, using, or being a platitude.
—,plat•i'tu•di•nous•ly, *adv.* **—,plat•i'tu•di•nous•ness,** *n.*

Pla•ton•ic [plə'tɒnɪk] *adj.* **1** of or having to do with Plato (d. 347? B.C.), a Greek philosopher, or his philosophy.
2 Usually, **platonic, a** having to do with or designating love or affection between a man and woman or any two people that has a purely spiritual or intellectual character, free from sexual desire or activity. **b** feeling or declaring such love. **3** idealistic or impractical: *a Platonic scheme for international disarmament.*
—pla'ton•i•cal•ly, *adv.*

Pla•to•nism ['pleitə,nɪzəm] *n.* **1** the doctrine or belief that physical objects are mere impermanent representations of permanent and unchanging ideas, or forms, which are the only true reality and the source of all knowledge. **2** any philosophy or doctrine based on that of Plato. **3** the doctrine or practice of platonic love.

Pla•to•nist ['pleitənɪst] *n.* a follower of Plato; person who believes in Plato's philosophy.

pla•toon [plə'tun] *n., v.* —*n.* **1** one of the formations of soldiers making up a company. A platoon is smaller than a company and larger than a section. **2** a small group of people sharing an activity or interest. **3** *Football, etc.* a group of players specially trained for a particular kind of play: *The coach sent in the punt-return platoon.*
—*v.* **1** divide into or use as platoons. **2** *Football, etc.* **a** alternate (players or teams). **b** be alternated with another player at a given position. ⟨< F *peloton* group, little ball, dim. of *pelote* ball. Related to PELLET.⟩

Platt•deutsch ['plɑt,dɔɪtʃ] *n.* the Low German vernacular dialects of northern Germany; LOW GERMAN (def. 1).

plat•ter ['plætər] *n.* a large, often oval or oblong plate, used especially for holding or serving a main dish such as meat or fish.
on a platter or **plate,** *Informal.* with no effort being required: *The position was practically handed to her on a platter.* ⟨ME < AF *plater* < OF *plat* plate < VL *plattus* flat. See PLATE.⟩

plat•y ['plæti] *n., pl.* **plat•ies** or **plat•ys.** a small, brightly coloured tropical fish, often kept in a home aquarium. ⟨shortened from NL *Platypoecilus* fish genus < Gk. *platys* flat + *poikilos* variegated⟩

plat•y•hel•minth [,plætə'hɛlmɪnθ] *n.* any of a phylum (Platyhelminthes) of flatworms, bilaterally symmetrical and having a soft body. ⟨< Gk. *platys* flat + *helmins* worm⟩

plat•y•pod ['plætɪ,pɒd] *adj., n.* —*adj.* of certain molluscs, having a wide foot.
—*n.* an animal with a wide foot. ⟨< Gk. *platys* flat + E *-pod*⟩

plat•y•pus ['plætəpəs] *n., pl.* **-pus•es** or **-pi** [-,paɪ]. a small, egg-laying water mammal (*Ornithorhynchus anatinus*) of Australia and Tasmania having a broad, flat, rubbery snout resembling a duck's bill, thick fur, four webbed feet, and a broad, flat tail. The platypus makes up a separate mammalian family. ⟨< NL < Gk. *platypous* < *platys* flat + *pous* foot⟩

A platypus

plat•yr•rhine ['plætɪ,raɪn] *or* ['plætɪrɪn] *adj., n.* —*adj.* **1** *Anthropology, zoology.* having a flat, broad nose. **2** of or having to do with the primate group Platyrrhini, comprising the New World monkeys.
—*n.* a platyrrhine animal. ⟨< Gk. *platys* flat + *rhis, rhinos* nose⟩

plau•dit ['plɒdɪt] *n.* **1** a round of applause. **2** Usually, **plaudits,** *pl.* enthusiastic expression of approval or praise: *He basked in the plaudits of the critics.* ⟨alteration of L *plaudite* applaud!⟩

plau•si•bil•i•ty [,plɒzə'bɪləti] *n.* **1** the quality or state of appearing true or reasonable. **2** something that appears true or reasonable.

plau•si•ble ['plɒzəbəl] *adj.* **1** appearing true, reasonable, or fair. **2** apparently worthy of confidence but often not really so: *a plausible liar.* ⟨< L *plausibilis* deserving applause, pleasing < *plaudere* applaud⟩ **—'plau•si•bly,** *adv.* **—'plau•si•ble•ness,** *n.*

play [plei] *n., v.* —*n.* **1** something done to amuse oneself; fun; sport; recreation. **2** a turn, move, or act in a game: *It is your play next. The centre made a brilliant play.* **3** the act of carrying on a game: *Play was slow in the first half of the game.* **4** a way of carrying on a game: *Slow play is frowned on in golf.* **5 a** a story written for or presented as a dramatic performance; drama. **b** a stage, radio, television, etc. performance of such a story.
6 action: *foul play.* **7** a light, quick movement or change: *the play of sunlight on leaves, the play of colour in an opal.* **8** freedom for action, movement, etc. **9** operation; working. **10** gambling.
11 the act of lightly or briskly wielding or plying (*used in compounds*): *swordplay.*
in play, a *Sports.* of a ball, in a position or condition to be legally played. **b** as a joke; jocularly.
out of play, *Sports.* of a ball, not in a position to be legally played.
—*v.* **1** have fun; do something in sport; take part in a game or active pastime: *children playing on the lawn, a kitten playing with its tail.* **2** do or perform for amusement or to deceive, make fun of, etc.: *to play a joke on someone. They played a mean trick.*
3 take part in (a game): *to play tag.* **4** take part in a game against. **5** put in the game; cause to play in a game: *Each coach played the best goalie.* **6** act on or as if on a stage; act a part: *to play in a tragedy.* **7** act the part of (a character in a play, etc.).
8 give theatrical performances in: *to play the larger cities.* **9** act in a specified way: *to play sick.* **10** make believe; pretend to be, in fun: *to play cowboys.* **11** be placed at (a given position) in a team game: *to play first base.* **12** make music: *The pianist played beautifully.* **13** produce (music) on an instrument: *to play a tune.*
14 perform on (a musical instrument): *to play a piano.* **15** of a musical instrument, radio, etc., produce sound: *We could hear the piano playing in the next apartment.* **16** send (someone) in a specified direction with music (*used with* **off, on, in,** etc.): *The governor general was played off the platform.* **17** move lightly or quickly: *A breeze played on the water.* **18** cause to act, move, or work; direct (on, over, along): *to play a hose on a burning building.* **19** put into action in a game: *Play your ten of hearts.*
20 operate with continued or repeated action: *A fountain played in the garden.* **21** allow (a hooked fish) to exhaust itself by pulling on the line. **22** do something foolishly or pointlessly; trifle: *Do not play with your food. Don't play with matches.*
23 gamble; bet. **24** bet on: *She plays the horses.*
play at, a pretend to be engaged in doing (something). **b** do (something) half-heartedly.
play down, make seem unimportant or less important; avoid or

reduce emphasis on: *The government tried to play down the unfavourable results of the opinion poll.*
played out, **a** exhausted. **b** finished; done with. **c** of a mine or gold field, exhausted of minerals.
play fair, **a** play according to the rules. **b** act in an honourable way.
play for time, stall a decision or event; delay acting so as to benefit oneself in the long run.
play into (someone's) **hands,** act so as to give a person an advantage over oneself.
play off, **a** pit (one person *against* another) by clever manipulation. **b** play an extra game or round to settle (a tie).
play on or **upon,** take advantage of; make use of: *She played on her mother's good nature.*
play out, play (drama, game, etc.) to the end.
play possum. See POSSUM.
play second fiddle, take an inferior role.
play up, make the most of; exploit: *The singer's agent played up her extensive background in classical music.*
play up to, *Slang.* try to get the favour of; flatter: *to play up to a famous person.* ⟨OE *plegan*, v., *plega*, n., exercise⟩
☛ *Syn. n.* **1. Play,** SPORT, GAME = activity or exercise of mind or body engaged in for recreation or fun. **Play** is the general word: *Play is as necessary as work.* **Sport** applies to any form of athletics or an outdoor pastime, whether it requires much or little activity or is merely watched for pleasure: *Fencing, swimming, fishing, and horse racing are his favourite sports.* **Game** applies especially to an activity in the form of a contest, mental or physical, played by certain rules: *Tennis and chess are games.*

play•a•ble ['pleiəbəl] *adj.* **1** that can be played. **2** fit to be played on: *The golf course is not playable after all that heavy rain.*

play–act ['plei ˌækt] *v.* **1** pretend; make believe. **2** perform in a play.

play–ac•tion pass ['plei ˌækʃən] *Football.* a play intended to deceive the opposition, in which the quarterback fakes a handoff to a back before throwing a forward pass.

play•back ['plei,bæk] *n.* a replaying of a tape recording or videotape, especially when it has just been made.

play•bill ['plei,bɪl] *n.* **1** a handbill or placard announcing a play. **2** the program of a play.

play•boy ['plei,bɔɪ] *n.* a man, usually rich, who devotes his time to the pursuit of pleasure and sexual promiscuity.

play–by–play ['plei baɪ 'plei] *adj.* giving each event or action as it happens or happened: *a play-by-play broadcast of a hockey game. They gave us a play-by-play account of their holiday.*

play•down ['plei,daʊn] *n.* playoff.

play•er ['pleiər] *n.* **1** a person who plays a game: *a baseball player.* **2** an actor in a theatre. **3** a person who plays a musical instrument; musician. **4** a device that plays: *a record player.*

player piano a piano that plays automatically using either electronic activation of the keys, or a pneumatic device that depresses the keys in response to perforations on a roll.

play•fel•low ['plei,fɛlou] *n.* playmate.

play•ful ['pleifəl] *adj.* **1** full of fun; fond of playing. **2** joking; not serious. **—'play•ful•ly,** *adv.* **—'play•ful•ness,** *n.*

play•go•er ['plei,gouər] *n.* a person who goes to the theatre often.

play•ground ['plei,graʊnd] *n.* **1** a place for outdoor play, especially an area equipped with swings, slides, etc. for children. **2** a popular or, sometimes, notorious place for leisure activity, such as a resort area: *The Riviera is a playground of the wealthy.*

play•house ['plei,hʌus] *n.* **1** a small house for children to play in. **2** a doll's house. **3** a theatre for live dramatic performances. ⟨OE *pleghūs*⟩

playing box *Lacrosse.* an area approximately the size of a hockey rink and enclosed with boards, in which box lacrosse is played.

playing card one of a set of small, oblong plastic or paper cards used in games, having one side marked with numbers and symbols for rank and group, or suit. Most sets, or decks, of playing cards consist of 52 cards with 13 cards in each of 4 suits.

playing field a piece of level ground where athletic events are held, often marked out for the playing of particular games such as soccer or field hockey.
level playing field, equal opportunity.

play•mate ['plei,meit] *n.* a person who plays with another; a playing companion.

play•off ['plei,ɒf] *n.* **1** an extra game or round played off to settle a tie. **2** one of a series of games played by the top teams in a league to determine the winner of the championship, of a special trophy, etc.

play on words pun; punning.

play•pen ['plei,pɛn] *n.* a small, portable enclosure for babies to play in.

play•room ['plei,rum] *or* ['plei,rʊm] *n.* a room for children to play in.

play therapy a method of therapy in which children express their emotions and hidden problems through play.

play•thing ['plei,θɪŋ] *n.* a thing to play with; toy.

play•time ['plei,taɪm] *n.* time for playing.

play•wright ['plei,rɔit] *n.* a writer of plays; dramatist.

play•writ•ing ['plei,rɔitɪŋ] *n.* the writing of plays; the art or profession of a dramatist.

pla•za ['plæzə] *n.* **1** a shopping centre. Also, **shopping plaza.** **2** a public square in a city or town. ⟨< Sp. *plaza* < L < Gk. *plateia (hodos)* broad (way). Doublet of PLACE and PIAZZA.⟩

plea [pli] *n.* **1** a request or appeal; asking: *a plea for pity.* **2** an excuse: *The man's plea was that he had not seen the signal.* **3** *Law.* **a** the answer made by a defendant to a charge against him or her in a court. **b** an argument or allegation of fact made in support of one side in a lawsuit. **c** a statement which alleges some new fact on the basis of which the suit should be dismissed, delayed, or barred, but does not answer the charge; special plea. ⟨ME < OF *plaid* < L *placitum* (that) which pleases⟩

plea bargain an arrangement between a prosecutor and a defendant before a case comes to trial, whereby the defendant pleads guilty to lesser charges in return for having graver charges dropped. This may be done to avoid a lengthy trial or to ensure the defendant's co-operation as a witness. **—'plea-ˌbar•gain,** *v.*

pleach [plitʃ] *v.* interweave (growing branches, vines, etc.); entwine. ⟨ME < OF *plechier*, ult. < L *plectere* weave⟩

plead [plid] *v.* **plead•ed** or **pled** [plɛd], **plead•ing. 1** offer reasons for or against something; argue. **2** ask earnestly; make an earnest appeal: *He pleaded for more time to finish his paper.* **3** offer as an excuse: *The woman pleaded poverty in defence of her shoplifting.* **4** *Law.* **a** act as counsel for; speak for: *She had a good lawyer to plead her case.* **b** conduct a case in court: *Who is pleading for the defence?* **c** answer to a charge in court: *Do you plead guilty or not guilty?* ⟨ME < OF *plaidier* < VL *placitare*, ult. < L *placere* please⟩ **—'plead•ing•ly,** *adv.*

plead•er ['plidər] *n.* a person who pleads, especially in a court of law.

plead•ings ['plidɪŋz] *n.pl. Law.* the claim made by the plaintiff, and the defendant's answer to it in a court.

pleas•ance ['plɛzəns] *n. Archaic.* **1** a pleasant place, usually an area with trees, fountains, and flowers, attached to a mansion. **2** pleasure; enjoyment. ⟨ME < OF *plaisance* < *plaisant* pleasing. See PLEASANT.⟩

pleas•ant ['plɛzənt] *adj.* **1** pleasing; agreeable; giving pleasure. **2** easy to get along with; friendly. **3** fair; not stormy: *pleasant weather.* ⟨ME < OF *plaisant*, ppr. of *plaisir* please < L *placere*⟩ **—'pleas•ant•ly,** *adv.* **—'pleas•ant•ness,** *n.*
☛ *Syn.* **1. Pleasant,** PLEASING, AGREEABLE = giving pleasure or satisfaction to the mind, feelings, or senses. **Pleasant** emphasizes that the person or thing described has certain qualities that give pleasure: *We spent a pleasant evening.* **Pleasing** emphasizes the effect on the one knowing or experiencing what is described: *It was pleasing to me because I wanted to see them.* **Agreeable** means pleasing because to a person's own taste or liking: *I think this cough medicine has an agreeable flavour.*

pleas•ant•ry ['plɛzəntri] *n., pl.* **-ries. 1** a good-natured joke; a witty remark: *His speech was full of pleasantries.* **2** lively, good-humoured talk; banter.

please [pliz] *v.* **pleased, pleas•ing. 1** give pleasure or satisfaction (to): *Toys please children. Such a fine meal cannot fail to please.* **2** wish; think fit: *Do what you please.* **3** be the will of: *It pleased her to remain anonymous.* **4** if you would be so kind or obliging (*used as a polite addition to requests or commands*): *Come here, please. Could you please tell me the time? Two orders of fish and chips, please. Please come in.*
be pleased, **a** be moved to pleasure: *He is pleased at the good news.* **b** *Formal.* be disposed; like; choose: *I will be pleased to go.*
if you please, **a** if you like. **b** with your permission (may be used as an ironic exclamation of indignation).
please God, if it is God's will.
please yourself, do what you like. ⟨ME < OF *plaisir* < L *placere*⟩

pleas•ing ['plizɪŋ] *adj., v.* —*adj.* giving pleasure; pleasant: *a pleasing manner.*
—*v.* ppr. of PLEASE. **—'pleas•ing•ly,** *adv.* **—'pleas•ing•ness,** *n.*
☛ *Syn.* See note at PLEASANT.

pleas•ur•a•ble ['plɛʒərəbəl] *adj.* pleasant; agreeable. **—'pleas•ur•a•bly,** *adv.* **—,pleas•ur•a'bil•i•ty** or **'pleas•ur•a•ble•ness,** *n.*

pleas•ure ['plɛʒər] *n., v.* *—n.* **1** a feeling of being pleased; enjoyment; delight. **2** something that pleases; cause of joy or delight. **3** worldly or sensual enjoyment. **4** one's will, desire, or choice: *What is your pleasure in this matter?*
at (one's) **pleasure,** as or when one pleases; at will; at discretion.
take (one's) **pleasure,** enjoy, take pleasure (*in*): *He takes his pleasure in hunting and fishing.*
—v. **1** give pleasure to; gratify, often in a sexual way. **2** find pleasure (*in*). ⟨ME < OF *plaisir,* nominal use of infinitive. See PLEASE.⟩ **—'pleas•ure•ful,** *adj.*
☛ *Syn.* **1. Pleasure,** DELIGHT, JOY = a feeling of satisfaction and happiness coming from having, experiencing, or expecting something good or to one's liking. **Pleasure** is the general word applying to this feeling whether or not it is shown in any way: *The compliment gave her pleasure.* **Delight** suggests great pleasure, usually shown or expressed in a lively way: *The children clapped their hands in delight.* **Joy** applies to a strong emotion of intense delight and happiness, expressing itself in gladness or rejoicing: *Success brought him joy.*

pleat [plit] *n., v.* *—n.* a flat, relatively narrow fold made by doubling material on itself. Pleats made in cloth, as in a skirt, are usually sewn at the top or pressed in place.
—v. fold or arrange in pleats. ⟨var. of *plait*⟩ **—'pleat•er,** *n.*

ple•be•ian [plə'biən] *n., adj.* *—n.* **1** a member of the plebs, or common people, of ancient Rome. Compare PATRICIAN (def. 1). **2** a member of the common people of any country. **3** a vulgar, coarse, or unrefined person.
—adj. **1** of or having to do with the common people of ancient Rome or any country. **2** vulgar or crude in manner or style. **3** ordinary; pedestrian in style. ⟨< L *plebeius* < *plebs* the common people⟩ **—ple'be•ian,ism,** *n.*

pleb•i•scite ['plɛbə,sait] *or* ['plɛbəsɪt] *n.* a direct vote by the qualified voters of a country, province, municipality, etc. on some question. Compare REFERENDUM. ⟨< L *plebiscitum* < *plebs* the common people + *scitum* decree⟩

plebs [plɛbz] *n., pl.* **ple•bes** ['plibiz]. in ancient Rome, the common people. ⟨< L⟩

plec•trum ['plɛktrəm] *n., pl.* **-trums, -tra** [-trə]. a small piece of ivory, horn, metal, etc., used for plucking the strings of a guitar, mandolin, lyre, zither, etc. Also, **plectron.** ⟨< L *plectrum* < Gk. *plēktron* < *plēssein* strike⟩

pled [plɛd] *v.* a pt. and a pp. of PLEAD.

pledge [plɛdʒ] *n., v.* **pledged, pledg•ing.** *—n.* **1** a solemn promise. **2** something that secures; SECURITY (def. 7): *The knight left a jewel as pledge for the borrowed horse.* **3** *Law.* the act of presenting goods, property, etc. to someone as security. **4** the condition of being held as security. **5** a promised donation. **6** a person who has promised to join an organization but is serving a probationary period before being granted membership. **7** something given to show favour or love or as a promise of something to come; sign; token. **8** the drinking of a health or toast.
take the pledge, promise not to drink alcoholic liquor.
—v. **1** promise solemnly. **2** cause to promise solemnly; bind by a promise. **3 a** accept tentative membership in an organization. **b** accept (someone) as a PLEDGE (def. 5). **4** give as security. **5** promise to donate (a sum). **6** drink to the health of; drink in honour of (someone) and wish (him or her) well: *The guests pledged the newly married couple in champagne.* ⟨ME < OF *plege* < Med.L *plebium* < Gmc. Cf. OE *plēon* to risk, G *pflegen* to look after. Related to PLIGHT[2].⟩ **—'pledg•er,** *n.*

pledg•ee [plɛ'dʒi] *n.* a person to whom a pledge is made or with whom something is deposited as a pledge.

-plegia *combining form.* paralysis: *hemiplegia.* ⟨< Gk. *plēge* blow, stroke⟩

Ple•iad ['pliæd] *or* ['plaiæd] *n.* any of the Pleiades.

Plé•iade [ple'jad] *French. n.* a small group, usually seven, of gifted people. ⟨< F a group of seven poets of the second half of 16c.⟩

Ple•ia•des ['pliə,diz] *or* ['plaiə,diz] *n.pl.* **1** *Astronomy.* a group of hundreds of stars in the constellation Taurus, of which only six can normally be seen with the naked eye. **2** *Greek mythology.* the seven daughters of Atlas who were turned into a group of stars. ⟨< L *Pleiades,* pl. of *Pleias* < Gk.⟩

Plei•o•cene ['plaiə,sin] *n. or adj.* See PLIOCENE.

plei•ot•ro•py [plei'ɒtrəpi] *n. Genetics.* multiple phenotypic effects produced by the expression of a single gene or gene pair.

Pleis•to•cene ['pləistə,sin] *n., adj. Geology.* *—n.* **1** the geological time period before the present period, beginning approximately one million years ago; ICE AGE (def. 2). **2** the deposits of gravel, etc. made in this period. See geological time chart in the Appendix.
—adj. of or having to do with this period or these deposits. ⟨< Gk. *pleistos* most + *kainos* recent⟩

ple•na•ry ['plinəri] *or* ['plɛnəri] *adj.* **1** complete; entire; absolute: *plenary powers.* **2** attended or to be attended by all qualified members: *a plenary session.* ⟨< LL *plenarius* < L *plenus* full⟩ **—'ple•na•ri•ly,** *adv.*

plen•i•po•ten•ti•ar•y [,plɛnəpə'tɛnʃəri] *or* [,plɛnəpə'tɛnʃi,ɛri] *n., pl.* **-ar•ies;** *adj.*
—n. a diplomatic agent having full power or authority.
—adj. having or giving full power and authority. ⟨< Med.L, ult. < L *plenus* full + *potens, -entis* powerful⟩

plen•i•tude ['plɛnɪ,tjud] *or* ['plɛnɪ,tud] *n.* **1** fullness; completeness: *in the plenitude of health and vigour.* **2** abundance: *a plenitude of food.* ⟨ME < OF < *plenitudo* < *plenus* full⟩

plen•te•ous ['plɛntiəs] *adj.* plentiful. **—'plen•te•ous•ly,** *adv.* **—'plen•te•ous•ness,** *n.*

plen•ti•ful ['plɛntɪfəl] *adj.* more than enough; abundant: *a plentiful supply of gasoline for the trip, a plentiful harvest.* **—'plen•ti•ful•ly,** *adv.* **—'plen•ti•ful•ness,** *n.*

plen•ty ['plɛnti] *n., pl.* **-ties;** *adj., adv.* *—n.* **1** a full supply; all that one needs; large enough number or quantity: *There is plenty of time.* **2** the quality or condition of being plentiful; abundance: *years of peace and plenty.*
—adj. enough; plentiful; abundant: *Six potatoes will be plenty.*
—adv. Informal. quite; fully: *plenty good enough.* ⟨ME *plente* < OF *plented, plentet* < L *plenitas* fullness < *plenus* full⟩

ple•num ['plinəm] *or* ['plɛnəm] *n., pl.* **-nums** or **-na** [-nə]. **1** an enclosed space containing a gas at a pressure higher than that of the surrounding atmosphere. **2** a metal box which connects a furnace or airconditioner to the ducts. **3** an assembly of all members, especially of a legislative body. **4** space completely filled by matter. **5** the quality or condition of being full. ⟨< NL < L *plenus* full⟩

pleo– *combining form.* more: *pleonasm.* ⟨< Gk. *pleion*⟩

ple•o•morph•ism [,pliə'mɔrfɪzəm] *n.* **1** *Zoology. Botany.* the existence of an organism in two or more forms in one life cycle. **2** POLYMORPHISM (def. 1). **—,ple•o'morph•ic,** *adj.*

ple•o•nasm ['pliə,næzəm] *n.* **1** the use of more words than are necessary to express an idea; redundancy; tautology. *Examples: The* two twins *arrived together. The* realization of *her dream* came true. **2** a redundant word or expression. ⟨< LL < Gk. *pleonasmos,* ult. < *pleon* more⟩ **—,ple•o'nas•tic,** *adj.* **—,ple•o'nas•ti•cal•ly,** *adv.*

ple•si•o•saur ['plisiə,sɔr] *n.* any of a suborder (Plesiosauria) of sea reptiles, now extinct, having a small head, long neck, and four flippers instead of legs. The plesiosaurs lived during the age of the dinosaurs. ⟨< NL *plesiosaurus* < Gk. *plēsios* near + *sauros* lizard⟩

pleth•o•ra ['plɛθərə] *n.* **1** excessive abundance or fullness; too much. **2** *Pathology. Archaic.* a condition of the body caused by an excess of red blood cells or an overall increase in the quantity of blood, characterized by swelling and a florid complexion. ⟨< NL < Gk. *plēthorē* < *plēthein* be full⟩

ple•thor•ic [plə'θɔrɪk] *or* ['plɛθərɪk] *adj.* having to do with or characterized by plethora; especially, swollen, overfull, or overstocked.

pleu•ra ['plʊrə] *n., pl.* **pleu•rae** ['plʊri] *or* ['plʊraɪ]. *Anatomy. Zoology.* in mammals, either of the thin membranes lining the two halves of the thorax and folded back over the surface of the lung on the same side. ⟨< NL < Gk. *pleura* rib⟩ **—'pleu•ral,** *adj.*

pleu•ri•sy ['plʊrɪsi] *n. Pathology.* inflammation of the pleura, in which varying amounts of fluid from the inflamed membrane enter the chest cavity. Pleurisy is usually accompanied by severe pain on breathing. ⟨ME < OF *pleurisie* < LL *pleurisis,* for L *pleuritis* < Gk. *pleuritis* < *pleura* rib⟩ **—pleu'rit•ic** [-'rɪtɪk], *adj.*

pleuro– *combining form.* side; rib; pleura, etc. Also, before vowels, **pleur–:** *pleuropneumonia.* ⟨< NL < Gk. *pleura* rib⟩

pleu•ro•dont ['plʊrə,dɒnt] *adj., n.* *—adj.* having teeth growing from the inner edge of the jaw instead of from individual sockets.
—n. a pleurodont animal, such as certain lizards.

pleu•ro•pneu•mo•nia [,plʊrounju'mounjə] *or* [,plʊrounu'mounjə] *n. Pathology.* pleurisy occurring in conjunction with pneumonia.

plew [plu] *n. Cdn.* See PLU.

-plex *combining form.* a building or series of buildings having —— units: *duplex, multiplex, cineplex.* ⟨< L *plex*, related to *plicare* fold, bend and to *plectere* braid, plait⟩

Plex•i•glas ['plɛksə,glæs] *n. Trademark.* a light, transparent, acrylic plastic, often used in place of glass. ⟨*pl*astic + fle*x*ible + *glas*s⟩

plex•us ['plɛksəs] *n., pl.* **-us•es** or **-us. 1** a network of nerves, blood vessels, etc. The **solar plexus** is a collection of nerves behind the stomach. **2** an interwoven combination of parts in a system; network. ⟨< L *plexus* < *plectere* twine, braid⟩
—'plex•al, *adj.*

pli•a•ble ['plaɪəbəl] *adj.* **1** easily bent; flexible; supple: *Willow twigs are pliable.* **2** easily influenced; yielding: *He is too pliable to be a good leader.* ⟨< F *pliable* < *plier* bend⟩ **—,pli•a'bil•i•ty** [,plaɪə'bɪlɪti], *n.*

pli•ant ['plaɪənt] *adj.* **1** bending easily; flexible; supple. **2** easily influenced; yielding. ⟨ME < OF *pliant* bending, ppr. of *plier.* See PLY[2].⟩ **—'pli•an•cy,** *adj.* **—'pli•ant•ly,** *adv.*
☛ *Syn.* **1.** See note at FLEXIBLE.

pli•cate ['pləikɪt] *or* ['pləikeit] *adj. Botany.* folded like a fan: *a plicate leaf.* ⟨< L *plicatus* folded⟩

pli•ca•tion [pləi'keiʃən] *or* [plə'keiʃən] *n.* **1** the act of folding. **2** the state of being folded. **3** *Geology.* a crumpling or folding of unstratified rocks. **4** *Surgery,* **a** the folding and attachment of an organ or a section of an organ to a second organ or tissue. **b** the tucking and suturing of stretched or weakened tissue so as to strengthen it.

pli•é [pli'ei] *n. Ballet.* a bending of the knees outward while the back remains straight. This can be done from all five positions of the feet.

pli•ers ['plaɪərz] *n.* (*usually used with a plural verb*) small pincers with long jaws, used for bending wire, holding small objects, etc. ⟨< *ply[1]*⟩

plight[1] [pləit] *n.* a difficult or dangerous condition or state. ⟨ME < AF *plit,* originally, manner of folding, ult. < L *plicare* fold; confused with *plight[2]*⟩
☛ *Syn.* See note at PREDICAMENT.

plight[2] [pləit] *v., n. —v.* pledge; promise.
plight (one's) **troth, a** *Archaic.* pledge one's word. **b** promise to marry.
—n. Archaic. pledge. ⟨ME, OE *pliht* danger, risk. Cf. Du. *plicht,* G *pflicht* duty, obligation. Related to PLEDGE.⟩

Plim•soll mark or **line** ['plɪmsəl] a mark or line painted on a ship's hull to show how heavily it may be loaded. This mark is required by law on British merchant ships and also on most other merchant ships. ⟨< Samuel *Plimsoll* (1824-1898), a member of Parliament, who had the law on overloading passed⟩

plink [plɪŋk] *v., n. —v.* **1** play on a musical instrument so as to produce a tinkling or clinking sound. **2** strike with such a sound.
—n. a tinkling or clinking sound.

plinth [plɪnθ] *n.* **1** *Architecture.* the lower, square part of the base of a column. See COLUMN for picture. **2** any square base, as of a pedestal, etc. ⟨< L < Gk. *plinthos*⟩

Pli•o•cene ['plaɪə,sin] *n., adj. Geology. —n.* **1** a geological time period beginning approximately 12 million years ago. **2** the rocks formed in this period. See geological time chart in the Appendix.
—adj. of or having to do with this period or the rocks formed during it. Also, **Pleiocene.** ⟨< Gk. *pleiōn* more + *kainos* recent⟩

plis•sé [pli'sei] *or* [plɪ'sei] *n., adj. —n.* **1** a textile finish giving a crinkled effect achieved by treating the fabric with caustic soda. **2** a fabric so treated.
—adj. having been treated in this way and having this finish (*follows the noun modified*): *cotton plissé, velvet plissé.*

PLO or **P.L.O.** PALESTINE LIBERATION ORGANIZATION.

plod [plɒd] *v.* **plod•ded, plod•ding;** *n. —v.* **1** walk slowly or heavily; trudge: *We plodded along the mountain path.* **2** proceed in a slow or dull way; work patiently with effort: *He plods away at his lessons until he learns them.*
—n. **1** the act of plodding or the course followed: *We went for a plod across the muddy fields.* **2** heavy footsteps; a heavy tread: *The plod of the horses' hooves could be heard in the distance.* ⟨? imitative⟩ **—'plod•der,** *n.* **—'plod•ding•ly,** *adv.*
☛ *Syn.* **1.** See note at WALK.

plonk[1] [plɒŋk] *v.* PLUNK (def. 2).

plonk[2] [plɒŋk] *n. Informal.* wine, especially cheap or inferior wine. ⟨origin uncertain, possibly < F (*vin*) *blanc*⟩

plop [plɒp] *n., v.* **plopped, plop•ping;** *adv. —n.* **1** a sound like that of a flat object striking water without a splash. **2** a fall that makes such a sound.
—v. **1** fall or drop with a sound like that of a flat object striking water without a splash: *The stone plopped into the water.* **2** fall or drop heavily: *She plopped into the first soft chair she came to. She plopped her books on the table.*
—adv. with a plop. ⟨imitative⟩

plo•sion ['plouʒən] *n. Phonetics.* **1** the forced release of air as the final stage of the articulation of a plosive consonant, either audible or inaudible. **2** the articulation of a plosive sound.

plo•sive ['plousɪv] *or* ['plouzɪv] *adj., n. Phonetics. —adj.* of a stop consonant, produced and characterized by a complete stoppage and sudden forced release of air, as in the consonants [p], [t], [k], etc.
—n. a sound so produced.

plot [plɒt] *n., v.* **plot•ted, plot•ting.** *—n.* **1** a secret plan, especially to do something wrong: *Two men formed a plot to rob the bank.* **2** the plan or main story of a play, novel, poem, etc. **3 a** a small piece of ground to be buried in: *a cemetery plot.* **b** any small piece of ground: *a garden plot.* **4** a map; diagram.
—v. **1** plan secretly with others; plan. **2** divide (land) into plots. **3** make a map or diagram of. **4** mark (something) on a map or diagram: *The nurse plotted the patient's temperature over several days.* **5** *Mathematics.* **a** determine the location of (a point) by means of its coordinates; mark (a point) on graph paper. **b** make (a curve) by connecting points marked out on a graph. **c** represent (an equation, etc.) by means of a curve drawn through points on a graph. ⟨OE *plot* patch of ground; meaning influenced by *complot* a joint plot (< F)⟩ **—'plot•less,** *adj.* **—'plot•less•ness,** *n.*
☛ *Syn. v.* **1. Plot,** CONSPIRE, SCHEME = plan secretly. **Plot** means to form secretly, alone or together with others, a carefully designed plan, usually harmful or treacherous, against a person, group, or country: *Enemy agents plotted to blow up the plant.* **Conspire** emphasizes the combining of one person or group with another, usually secretly, to carry out some act, especially treachery or treason: *They conspired to overthrow the government.* **Scheme** suggests careful planning, often in a crafty or underhand way, to gain one's own ends: *She schemed to become president.*

plot•ter ['plɒtər] *n.* **1** one who plots. **2** *Computer technology.* a computer-controlled device to produce diagrams and pictures on paper.

Plott hound [plɒt] an American dog having a grey or tawny coat with darker spots, used in hunting bears and wild boars. ⟨prob. after J. *Plott,* 18c. American dog breeder⟩

plough or **plow** [plaʊ] *n., v. —n.* **1** a farm implement used for cutting the soil and turning it over. **2** a machine for removing snow; snowplough.
—v. **1** turn over (soil) with a plough. **2** use a plough. **3** move as a plough does; advance slowly and with effort: *The ship ploughed through the waves. The student ploughed through two books to get material for an essay.* **4** remove with a plough or as if with a plough: *to plough up old roots.* **5** furrow: *to plough a field, wrinkles ploughed in one's face by time.* **6** cut the surface of (water). **7** *Brit. Slang.* reject (a candidate) or be rejected in an examination.
plough back, reinvest (profits) in the same business.
plough into, *Informal.* **a** hit hard or at speed and travel into: *The car went out of control and ploughed into the building.* **b** start (an activity) vigorously or with energy and determination: *to plough into one's homework. They ploughed into dinner as if they were starving.*
plough through, work one's way through: *The students must plough through a lot of material for their course work.*
plough under, a plough into the ground to enrich the soil. **b** defeat; destroy; overwhelm. ⟨OE *plōg*⟩ **—'plough•er** or **'plow•er,** *n.*

plough•boy or **plow•boy** ['plaʊ,bɔɪ] *n.* **1** a boy who guides the horses drawing a plough. **2** a country boy.

ploughing or **plowing match** *Cdn.* a competition among farmers to determine who is the most skilful at ploughing.

plough•man or **plow•man** ['plaʊmən] *n., pl.* **-men. 1** a man who guides a plough. **2** a farm worker.

plough•share or **plow•share** ['plaʊ,ʃɛr] *n.* the part of a plough that cuts the soil.

plov•er ['plʌvər] *or* ['plouvər] *n.* any of numerous shore birds (family Charadriidae) having a plump, compact body with brownish or greyish plumage, a fairly short bill and tail, long wings, and, usually, no hind toes. The killdeer is a plover. **2** UPLAND PLOVER. ⟨ME < AF *plover,* ult. < L *pluvia* rain from the belief that the bird calls before rain⟩

plow [plaʊ] *n., v.* See PLOUGH.

plow•boy ['plaʊ,bɔɪ] *n.* See PLOUGHBOY.

plow•man ['plaʊmən] *n., pl.* **-men.** See PLOUGHMAN.

plow•share ['plaʊ,ʃɛr] See PLOUGHSHARE.

ploy [plɔɪ] *n. Informal.* an action or words by which advantage over another may be gained: *He won the game by a clever ploy.* ⟨? < *employ*, n.⟩

plu [plu] *n., pl.* **plus** or **plues.** *Cdn.* a prime beaver skin or other fur of equivalent value. Also, **plew, plue** and (erroneously) **plus**. ⟨< Cdn.F < F *pelu* skin, pelt⟩

pluck [plʌk] *v., n.* —*v.* **1** pull off; pick: *to pluck flowers. She plucked a bit of lint from the blanket.* **2** pick or pull (at); tug or grasp: *to pluck the strings of a violin for a pizzicato passage. The child plucked at her sleeve.* **3** play (a musical instrument) by picking at the strings: *to pluck a banjo.* **4** pull off the feathers or hair from: *to pluck a chicken, to pluck one's eyebrows.* **5** *Slang.* rob; swindle.
pluck up (one's) **spirits** (or **courage** etc.), take courage: *He plucked up his spirits and carried on.*
—*n.* **1** the act of picking or pulling. **2** courage; boldness and spirit: *It took pluck to stand up to that bully.* **3** the heart, liver, and lungs of an animal as food. ⟨ME *plukken*, OE *pluccian*⟩

pluck•y ['plʌki] *adj.* **pluck•i•er, pluck•i•est.** having or showing courage. **—'pluck•i•ly,** *adv.* **—'pluck•i•ness,** *n.*

plug [plʌg] *n., v.* **plugged, plug•ging.** —*n.* **1** a piece of wood or some other substance used to stop up a hole. **2** a disk of rubber or metal for stopping the drain of a sink, basin, bathtub, etc. **3** a device used to make an electrical connection by sticking it into an outlet. **4** a place where a hose can be attached; hydrant. **5** SPARK PLUG (def. 1). **6** *Informal.* an advertisement or recommendation: *The interview was mainly a plug for her latest book. I'll put in a plug for you when I talk to the manager.* **7** a cake of pressed tobacco or a piece of this cut off for chewing. **8** *Informal.* a worn-out or inferior horse. **9** a lure for catching fish. **10** *Geology.* a cylindrical mass of igneous rock formed in the crater of an extinct volcano. **11** a small piece cut from a melon, cheese, etc. to test its readiness for eating.
pull the plug, *Informal.* **a** put an end to something: *The administration pulled the plug on our new project.* **b** disconnect the life-support systems to which a terminally ill patient is attached.
—*v.* **1** stop up or fill with a plug (*often used with* **up**): *to plug up a hole.* **2** insert the plug of (an electrical appliance or device) into an outlet (*used with* **in** *or* **into**): *Where can I plug in the hair dryer?* **3** of an electrical appliance or device, be able to be connected to (a certain type of outlet) (*used with* **into**): *They got a coffee maker that plugs into the cigarette lighter of the car.* **4** *Slang.* hit or shoot. **5** *Informal.* recommend or advertise, especially on a radio or television program: *to plug a new product.*
plug away (or **along**) **at,** *Informal.* work steadily at (something): *She plugged away at the project.*
plug up, clog. ⟨< MDu. *plugge*⟩ **—'plug•ger,** *n.* **—'plug•less,** *adj.* **—'plug,like,** *adj.*

plug hat *Informal.* formerly, a man's tall silk hat.

plug–in ['plʌg ,ɪn] *n., adj.* —*n. Informal.* a receptacle in a wall, etc. designed to receive a plug attached to an electrical appliance in order to complete the circuit and operate the appliance; electrical outlet: *There are only two plug-ins in the bedroom.*
—*adj.* designed to operate by being plugged into an electrical outlet: *a plug-in light fixture.*

plug–ug•ly ['plʌg 'ʌgli] *n., pl.* **-lies.** *Slang.* ruffian.

plum [plʌm] *n., adj.* —*n.* **1** any of various trees and shrubs (of genus *Prunus* of the rose family) producing roundish or oval, edible fruit with a smooth skin, juicy flesh, and a somewhat flat, oblong stone or pit. **2** the fruit of any of these trees or shrubs. Plums may be purple, red, green, or yellow when ripe. **3** any of various other trees bearing edible fruit resembling plums. **4** the fruit of any of these trees. **5** sugarplum. **6** a raisin when used in a pudding, cake, etc. **7** something very good or desirable, especially a job or position: *His new job is quite a plum.* **8** a dark reddish purple.
—*adj.* having the colour plum. ⟨OE *plūme* < VL *pruna* < L *prunum* < Gk. *proumnon.* Doublet of PRUNE[1].⟩ **—'plum,like,** *adj.*
☛ *Hom.* PLUMB.

plum•age ['plumɪdʒ] *n.* the feathers covering the body of a bird: *Many parrots have bright plumage.* ⟨ME < OF. See PLUME.⟩

plu•mate ['plumeit] *adj. Zoology.* resembling a feather in structure, as a hair with bristles or smaller hairs. ⟨< L *plumatus* feathered < *pluma* feather + E *-ate*[1]⟩

plumb [plʌm] *n., adj., adv., v.* —*n.* a small weight used on the end of a line to find the depth of water or to see if a wall is truly vertical.
out of plumb or **off plumb,** not truly vertical.
—*adj.* vertical.
—*adv.* **1** vertically. **2** *Informal.* completely; thoroughly.
—*v.* **1** test or adjust by a plumb line; test; sound: *Our line was not long enough to plumb the depths of the lake.* **2** get to the bottom of: *No one could plumb the mystery.* **3** furnish with plumbing. **4** work as a plumber. ⟨ME < OF *plomb* < L *plumbum* lead⟩
☛ *Hom.* PLUM.

plum•ba•go [plʌm'beigou] *n.* **1** graphite. **2** any of several shrubby plants of the genus *Plumbago* or genus *Ceretostigma*, grown for their ornamental flowers; leadwort. ⟨< L *plumbago* lead ore < *plumbum* lead⟩

plumb bob a plumb; plummet.

plumb•er ['plʌmər] *n.* a person whose work is putting in, maintaining, and repairing water pipes and fixtures in buildings. ⟨ME < OF *plummier* < L *plumbarius*, ult. < L *plumbum* lead⟩

plum•bic ['plʌmbɪk] *adj. Chemistry.* of or containing lead, especially in the tetravalent state.

plum•bif•er•ous [plʌm'bɪfərəs] *adj.* yielding or containing lead.

plumb•ing ['plʌmɪŋ] *n., v.* —*n.* **1** the work or trade of a plumber. **2** the water pipes and fixtures in a building or part of a building: *the bathroom plumbing.*
—*v.* ppr. of PLUMB.

plumb line **1** a line with a plumb at the end, used to find the depth of water or to test the vertical straightness of a wall. **2** any vertical line.

plum•bous ['plʌmbəs] *adj. Chemistry.* of or containing bivalent lead.

plume [plum] *n., v.* **plumed, plum•ing.** —*n.* **1** a large, long feather; feather. **2** a feather, bunch of feathers, or tuft of hair worn as an ornament on a hat, helmet, etc. **3** something resembling a plume, as on a plant or animal. **4** a moving column of something such as smoke or snow: *Snow rose in a plume from the snowblower.* **5** a narrow, jetlike flow of hot material from deep in the earth's mantle.
—*v.* **1** furnish with plumes. **2 a** smooth or arrange the feathers of: *The eagle plumed its wing.* **b** preen (feathers).
plume (oneself) **on,** be proud of; show pride concerning: *She plumed herself on her skill in dancing.* ⟨ME < OF < L *pluma*⟩ **—'plume,like,** *adj.*

plum•met ['plʌmɪt] *v., n.* —*v.* plunge; drop.
—*n.* a weight fastened to a line; plumb. ⟨ME < OF *plommet* < *plomb* lead. See PLUMB.⟩

plum•my ['plʌmi] *adj.* **1** like or full of plums: *a plummy flavour, a plummy cake.* **2** *Informal.* good; desirable: *She got herself a plummy part in the new play.* **3** of a voice, rich and full in tone.

plu•mose ['plumous] *adj.* **1** having feathers or plumes; feathered. **2** feathery; like a plume. ⟨< L *plumosus* < *pluma* feather⟩ **—'plu•mose•ly,** *adv.* **—plu'mos•i•ty** [plu'mɒsɪti], *n.*

plump[1] [plʌmp] *adj., v.* —*adj.* rounded out; full; attractively chubby.
—*v.* make or become plump (*often used with* **up**): *He plumped the pillows on the bed.* ⟨late ME *plompe* dull, rude < MFlemish; cf. MDu. *plomp*, MLG *plump* blunt, thick⟩ **—'plump•ness,** *n.*

plump[2] [plʌmp] *v., n., adv., adj.* —*v.* **1** fall or drop heavily or suddenly: *All out of breath, she plumped down on a chair.* **2 a** drop, let fall, etc.: *to plump down one's bags at the station.* **b** pay at once and in one lot: *to plump down $10.* **3** *Informal.* burst, collide, or plunge: *to plump out of a room, to plump into the water.*
plump for, a give one's complete support to; champion vigorously: *to plump for lower taxes.* **b** vote for.
—*n.* **1** *Informal.* a sudden plunge or collision; heavy fall. **2** *Informal.* the sound made by a plunge or fall.
—*adv.* **1** heavily or suddenly: *He ran plump into me.* **2** directly; bluntly.
—*adj.* direct; downright; blunt. ⟨ME *plumpen;* cf. Du. *plompen*, LG *plumpen*, and *plump*[1]; prob. imitative⟩

plum pudding a rich pudding containing raisins, currants, spices, etc., cooked by wrapping in a cloth and steaming or boiling, and traditionally served with Christmas dinner.

plum tomato an egg- or pear-shaped variety of tomato, low in acid and often used for cooking.

plu•mule ['plumjul] *n.* **1** *Botany.* the bud of a plant embryo that becomes the growing stem tip. See EMBRYO for picture. **2** a small, soft feather; a down feather. ⟨< L *plumula*, dim. of *pluma* feather⟩

plum•y ['plumi] *adj.* **1** having plumes or feathers. **2** adorned with a plume or plumes. **3** like a plume.

plun•der ['plʌndər] *v., n.* —*v.* rob by force; rob, especially in the course of warfare.
—*n.* **1** things taken in plundering; booty; loot: *They carried off the plunder in their ships.* **2** the act of plundering; pillaging or robbing by force. ⟨< G *plündern* < *Plunder* household goods⟩
—**'plun•der•er,** *n.* —**'plun•der•a•ble,** *adj.*
☛ *Syn. n.* **1. Plunder,** BOOTY, LOOT = things taken by force. **Plunder** applies to things carried off by invading soldiers during a war or by bandits and other robbers: *The soldiers returned home with their plunder.* **Booty** applies particularly to things carried off and shared later by a band of robbers: *The bandits fought over their booty.* **Loot** applies particularly to things carried off from bodies and buildings in a city destroyed in war or at the scene of a fire, wreck, etc., but is used also of anything taken by robbery or some other crime: *Much loot was sold after the great tornado.*

plunge [plʌndʒ] *v.* **plunged, plung•ing;** *n.* —*v.* **1** throw or thrust with force into something, especially a liquid: *He plunged his hand into the water.* **2** throw suddenly or violently into a certain condition: *to plunge the world into war, to plunge the room into darkness.* **3** throw oneself (into water, danger, a fight, etc.). **4** move or act recklessly or in great haste: *She plunged into the crowd.* **5** pitch or lurch suddenly and violently: *The ship plunged about in the storm.* **6** slope abruptly or steeply, as a cliff or road. **7** *Slang.* gamble heavily.
—*n.* **1** the act or an instance of plunging. **2** a place for diving. **3** a swim.
take the plunge, *Informal.* dare to do something which requires courage. ⟨ME < OF *plungier,* ult. < L *plumbum* lead⟩
☛ *Syn. v.* **1.** See note at DIP.

plung•er ['plʌndʒər] *n.* **1** a part of a machine that acts with a plunging motion. **2** a rubber suction cup on a long stick, used for unplugging stopped-up drains, toilets, etc. **3** *Informal.* a reckless gambler or speculator. **4** any person or thing that plunges.

plunk [plʌŋk] *v., n., adv.* —*v.* **1** hit or pluck so as to produce a short hollow or metallic sound: *to plunk a banjo string.* **2** put down or drop heavily or suddenly: *She plunked her books on the table.*
plunk down, hand over (payment): *He plunked down ten thousand dollars for the car.*
plunk for, *Informal.* plump for.
—*n.* the act or sound of plunking.
—*adv.* with a thud or twang: *She sat down plunk on the ground.* ⟨imitative⟩

plu•per•fect [plu'pɜrfɪkt] *or* ['plu,pɜrfɪkt] *n. or adj. Grammar.* PAST PERFECT. ⟨short for L *plus quam perfectum* more than perfect⟩

plupf. pluperfect.

plur. **1** plural. **2** plurality.

plu•ral ['plʊrəl] *adj., n.* —*adj.* **1** consisting of or pertaining to more than one: *plural citizenship.* **2** *Grammar.* signifying or denoting reference to more than one. Almost all English nouns and pronouns have a distinct form to indicate **plural number.** In languages having dual number (see DUAL), the plural number refers to more than two.
—*n. Grammar.* **1** the plural number. **2** a word or construction in the plural number. **3** a plural affix or morpheme: *German has four main plurals.* ⟨ME < L *pluralis* < *plus* more⟩

plu•ral•ism ['plʊrə,lɪzəm] *n.* **1** the quality or state of being plural. **2** *Philosophy.* the theory that ultimate being or reality consists of multiple essential principles or entities. **3 a** a condition of society in which a number of diverse cultural, religious, or racial groups maintain their diversity within a single nation or civilization. **b** the policy of actively promoting such a condition. **4** the practice or system in some churches of having two or more ecclesiastical offices held by one person.
—**'plu•ral•ist,** *n.* —**,plu•ral'is•tic,** *adj.* —**,plu•ral'is•ti•cal•ly,** *adv.*

plu•ral•i•ty [plʊ'rælɪti] *n., pl.* **-ties. 1** in a contest involving more than two candidates, the number of votes cast for the leading candidate when that number is more than for any other one, but not more than half the total number of votes for all candidates: *He won by only a plurality, not a majority.* **2** a greater number of votes cast for a candidate than for an opposing candidate. **3** a number that is greater than another. **4** a large number; multitude. **5** the state or fact of being plural or numerous.

plu•ral•ize ['plʊrə,laɪz] *v.* **-ized, -iz•ing.** make plural or express in the plural form. —**,plu•ral•i'za•tion,** *n.*

plu•ral•ly ['plʊrəli] *adv.* in the plural number; so as to express or imply more than one.

plus [plʌs] *prep., adj., n., conj.* —*prep.* added to: *Three plus two equals five.*
—*adj.* **1** and more; better than: *His mark was B plus.* **2** showing addition: *the plus sign.* **3** greater than zero; positive: *a plus quantity.* **4** *Informal.* additional; extra: *a plus value.* **5** *Electricity.* electrically positive.
—*n.* **1** the plus sign (+). **2** an added quantity; something extra; a gain. **3** a positive quantity. **4** an asset or advantage: *the members' hard work and co-operation was a big plus for the organizers.*
—*conj. Informal.* and in addition: *The work of an engineer requires intelligence plus experience.* ⟨< L *plus* more⟩

plus fours loose-fitting baggy trousers gathered below the knee, worn mainly for sports, especially golf.

plush [plʌʃ] *n., adj.* —*n.* cloth of silk, wool, cotton, etc., having a softer and longer pile than velvet.
—*adj.* **1** of, resembling, or made of plush: *plush toys, plush upholstery.* **2** luxurious and showy: *plush surroundings.* ⟨< MF *pluche*, ult. < L *pilus* hair⟩

plush•y ['plʌʃi] *adj.* **1** like or covered with plush. **2** luxurious; rich-looking: *a plushy apartment.* —**'plush•i•ly,** *adv.* —**'plush•i•ness,** *n.*

Plu•to ['plutou] *n.* **1** *Greek mythology.* the god of the lower world, also called Hades, corresponding to the Roman god Dis. **2** *Astronomy.* the planet in our solar system that is smallest and farthest from the sun.

plu•toc•ra•cy [plu'tɒkrəsi] *n., pl.* **-cies. 1** a system of government in which the rich rule. **2** a ruling class of wealthy people. ⟨< Gk. *ploutokratia* < *ploutos* wealth + *kratos* power⟩

plu•to•crat ['plutə,kræt] *n.* **1** a person who has power or influence because of great wealth. **2** any wealthy person.

plu•to•crat•ic [,plutə'krætɪk] *adj.* **1** having power and influence because of wealth. **2** of or having to do with plutocrats or plutocracy. —**,plu•to'crat•i•cal•ly,** *adv.*

Plu•to•ni•an [plu'touniən] *adj.* of or having to do with Pluto or the lower world.

Plu•ton•ic [plu'tɒnɪk] *adj.* **1** Plutonian; infernal. **2** *Geology.* of or having to do with the theory that the present condition of the earth's crust is mainly due to igneous action. **3 plutonic,** *Geology.* of or having to do with a class of igneous rocks that have solidified far below the earth's surface.

plu•to•ni•um [plu'touniəm] *n.* an extremely toxic, radioactive metallic element found naturally in trace amounts in uranium ores and produced in great amounts from uranium in nuclear reactors. The most important isotope of plutonium is plutonium-239 (half-life 24 360 years), used as a fuel in nuclear fission. *Symbol*: Pu; *at.no.* 94; *at.mass* 239.05; *half-life* 80 million years. ⟨< L *plutonium*, neut. < *Pluto, -onis* Pluto⟩

plu•vi•al ['pluviəl] *adj.* **1** of or having to do with rain. **2** characterized by much rain. **3** *Geology.* caused or formed by the action of rain. ⟨< L *pluvialis* < *pluvia* rain⟩

plu•vi•om•e•ter [,pluvi'ɒmətər] *n.* RAIN GAUGE. ⟨< L *pluvia* rain + E *-meter*⟩

plu•vi•ous ['pluviəs] *adj.* rainy; of rain. —**,plu•vi'os•i•ty** [,pluvi'ɒsəti], *n.*

ply[1] [plaɪ] *v.* **plied, ply•ing. 1** work with; use: *The dressmaker plies her needle.* **2** work steadily or busily at or on (something): *carpenters plying their trade. For three hours we plied the water with our paddles.* **3** set upon forcefully: *The messenger was plied with questions.* **4** supply with in a pressing manner: *to ply a person with food or drink.* **5** travel regularly along (a course or route) or between (specified places): *Boats ply the river. A bus plies between the airport and the hotel.* ⟨ult. var. of *apply*⟩

ply[2] [plaɪ] *n., pl.* **plies. 1** a thickness or layer, as of laminated wood or cloth: *three-ply plywood.* **2** a strand or twist, as of rope or yarn: *six-ply embroidery thread.* ⟨< F *pli* < OF *plier* < L *plicare* fold⟩

Ply•mouth Brethren ['plɪməθ] a Protestant evangelical sect that recognizes no formal creed or ministerial orders. It originated about 1830 in Plymouth, England.

Plymouth Rock a breed of medium-sized, white, grey, or grey-and-black chicken. ⟨< the rock at Plymouth, Massachusetts, on which the Pilgrims are said to have landed in 1620⟩

ply•wood ['plaɪ,wʊd] *n.* a kind of board made of several thin layers of wood glued together, with the grains in adjacent layers running at right angles to each other. Plywood is made in large sheets and is used for furniture, floors, walls, etc.

p.m. **1** after noon (for L *post meridiem*). **2** post-mortem.

Pm promethium.

P.M. ['pi 'ɛm] 1 PRIME MINISTER. 2 after noon (for L *post meridiem*). 3 Postmaster. 4 PROVOST MARSHAL. 5 Police Magistrate. 6 Paymaster.

PMO Prime Minister's Office.

PMQ's PERMANENT MARRIED QUARTERS.

PMS PRE-MENSTRUAL SYNDROME.

P/N or **p/n** PROMISSORY NOTE. Also, **PN, pn.**

PNE Pacific National Exhibition.

pneu•ma ['njumə] *or* ['numə] *n.* 1 the soul or vital spirit. 2 *Christian theology.* the spirit of God; the Holy Spirit. ⟨< Gk. *pneuma* breath < *pnein* to breathe⟩

pneu•mat•ic [nju'mætɪk] *or* [nu'mætɪk] *adj.* 1 relating to wind, air, or gas. 2 worked by air pressure: *a pneumatic drill.* 3 holding or inflated with compressed air: *a pneumatic tire.* 4 of or having to do with compressed air: *pneumatic pressure.* 5 of or having to do with pneumatics. ⟨< L *pneumaticus* < Gk. *pneumatikos* < *pneuma* + *-atos* wind⟩ **—pneu'mat•i•cal•ly,** *adv.*

pneu•mat•ics [nju'mætɪks] *or* [nu'mætɪks] *n.* (*used with a singular verb*) the branch of physics that deals with the pressure, elasticity, mass, etc. of air and other gases.

pneu•ma•tol•o•gy [,njumə'tɒlədʒi] *or* [,numə'tɒlədʒi] *n. Christian theology.* 1 any doctrine relating to the Holy Spirit. 2 the study of spiritual phenomena.

pneu•ma•tom•e•ter [,njumə'tɒmətər] *or* [,numə'tɒmətər] *n.* an instrument for measuring the capacity of the lungs in either inspiration or expiration.

pneumo– *combining form.* lungs(s); air; respiration: *pneumonitis.* Also, **pneumato-, pneumono-.** ⟨< Gk. *pneumon* lung⟩

pneu•mo•gas•tric [,njumou'gæstrɪk] *or* [,numou'gæstrɪk] *adj. Anatomy.* of or having to do with the lungs and stomach.

pneu•mo•nec•to•my [,njumə'nɛktəmi] *or* [,numə'nɛktəmi] *n., pl.* **-ies.** the surgical excision of a lung or part of a lung. Also, **pneumectomy.**

pneu•mo•nia [nju'mounjə] *or* [nu'mounjə] *n. Pathology.* a bacterial or viral disease in which the lungs are inflamed. ⟨< NL < Gk. *pneumonia* < *pneumōn* lung⟩

pneu•mo•ni•tis [,njumə'nəitɪs] *or* [,numə'nəitɪs] *n. Pathology.* inflammation of the lung.

p.n.g. or **P.N.G.** PERSONA NON GRATA.

Po polonium.

P.O. 1 POST OFFICE. 2 PETTY OFFICER. 3 PILOT OFFICER. 4 personnel officer. 5 postal order.

poach[1] [poutʃ] *v.* 1 trespass on (another's land or water), especially to hunt or fish. 2 take (game or fish) illegally. 3 trample (soft ground) into muddy holes. 4 of land, become soft, miry, and full of holes by being trampled. 5 sink into wet, heavy ground in walking. 6 a mix with water and reduce to a uniform consistency. b mix (paper pulp) thoroughly with bleach liquor. ⟨< MF *pocher* poke out < Gmc. Akin to POKE[1].⟩ **—'poach•er,** *n.*

poach[2] [poutʃ] *v.* 1 cook (eggs) by breaking them into boiling water or into a very small pan over boiling water. 2 cook (fish, etc.) by simmering in milk, water, wine, or stock. ⟨ME < OF *pochier* < *poche* cooking spoon < Celtic⟩ **—'poach•er,** *n.*

pock [pɒk] *n., v.* —*n.* 1 a pustule caused by a disease such as smallpox. 2 any mark or spot suggesting such a pustule. 3 pockmark.
—*v.* mark or pit with or as if with pocks. ⟨ME *pocke,* OE *pocc*⟩

pock•et ['pɒkɪt] *n., v.* —*n.* 1 a small, flat bag or pouch sewn into or onto clothing for carrying small articles such as a handkerchief, pocket watch, comb, or money. 2 (*adjl.*) small enough to go in a pocket: *a pocket calculator.* 3 a pouch attached to the inside of a suitcase, car door, etc. 4 *Billiards, etc.* one of the pouches at each corner and on each side of a pool or billiard table. 5 a hollow place: *She hid in a pocket in the side of the hill.* 6 *Geology.* a cavity in the earth containing ore, oil, water, etc. 7 a small deposit of ore: *The miner struck a pocket of silver.* 8 any current or condition in the air that causes an aircraft to drop suddenly. 9 a small, isolated area different from the surrounding area: *a few Liberal pockets in a Conservative riding.*
be out of pocket, a spend or lose (money). b be a loser.
in pocket, having or gaining money: *They were $100 in pocket at the end of the day.*
—*v.* 1 put in one's pocket: *He pocketed his change.* 2 shut in or hem in. 3 hold back; suppress; hide: *He pocketed his pride and said nothing.* 4 take and endure; put up with: *She pocketed the insult.* 5 take secretly or dishonestly: *The accountant pocketed all the profits.* 6 *Billiards, etc.* drive into a pocket. ⟨ME *poket* < AF *pokete,* dial. dim. of MF *poque, poche*⟩

pocket battleship a small, heavily armed and armoured battleship within the limits of tonnage and armament set by the Treaty of Versailles.

pocket billiards POOL[2] (def. 1).

pock•et•book ['pɒkɪt,bʊk] *n.* 1 Often, **pocket book,** a small, relatively inexpensive, paper-covered edition of a book; paperback. 2 a small case for carrying money, papers, etc. in a pocket. 3 financial resources: *The shoes were just too expensive for his pocketbook.* 4 *Esp. U.S.* a woman's purse.

pocket borough 1 *Cdn.* an electoral riding where support for one party is so strong as to virtually guarantee its candidate's election. 2 *Brit.* formerly (before 1832) in England, an electoral riding whose representation in Parliament was virtually under the control of one family or person.

pock•et•ful ['pɒkɪt,fʊl] *n., pl.* **-fuls.** as much as a pocket will hold: *a pocketful of change.*

pocket gopher any of various rat-sized rodents (of the family Geomyidae) found on the North American plains, having fur-lined, external cheek pouches, a heavy body, a broad, flat head, short legs, and a short tail.

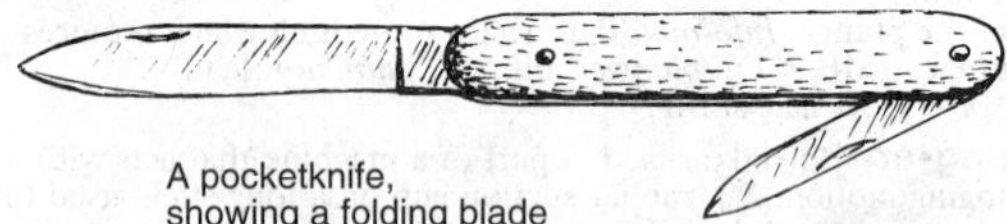
A pocketknife, showing a folding blade

pock•et•knife ['pɒkɪt,nəif] *n., pl.* **-knives.** a small knife with one or more blades that fold into the handle.

pocket money money for occasional or minor personal expenses.

pocket mouse any of a genus (*Perognathus*) of small, mouselike, North American rodents of the same family as the kangaroo rats, having large hind feet, small forefeet, and external cheek pouches. The **olive-backed pocket mouse** (*P. fasciatus*) of the southern Prairies is probably the smallest rodent found in Canada.

pock•et–size ['pɒkɪt ,saɪz] *adj.* 1 small enough to go in a pocket: *a pocket-size radio, camera, etc.* 2 *Informal.* small for its kind: *a pocket-size country* Also, **pocket-sized.**

pock•mark ['pɒk,mɑrk] *n., v.* —*n.* 1 a scar or pit in the skin, such as those left by smallpox or acne. 2 any small hollow suggesting such a scar: *The floor was covered with pockmarks made by spike-heeled shoes.*
—*v.* cover or scar with pockmarks.

pock•marked ['pɒk,mɑrkt] *adj.* having pockmarks.

po•co ['poukou] *adv. Music.* slightly; little. ⟨< Ital. *poco* < L *paucus* little, few⟩

po•co a po•co ['poukou ɑ 'poukou] *Music.* little by little; gradually. ⟨< Ital.⟩

pod[1] [pɒd] *n., v.* **pod•ded, pod•ding.** —*n.* 1 the fruit of a leguminous plant, such as beans or peas, consisting of a long, bivalve case that contains several seeds in a row and that splits along both sides when ripe, releasing the seeds. See FRUIT for picture. 2 the case itself, as distinct from the seeds. 3 any similar fruit or seedcase. 4 a streamlined cover over anything carried externally, especially on the wings or fuselage of an aircraft: *a gun pod or missile pod.* 5 a part of a spacecraft that can be detached from the main part.
—*v.* 1 produce pods. 2 fill out into a pod. ⟨origin uncertain⟩
—'pod,like, *adj.*

pod[2] [pɒd] *n.* 1 a small herd of whales, seals, etc. 2 a small flock of birds. ⟨origin unknown⟩

–pod *combining form.* having a foot or feet of the kind or number specified by the first element: *arthropod, octopod.* ⟨< Gk. *podos,* genetive of *pous* foot⟩

podg•y ['pɒdʒi] *adj.* **podg•i•er, podg•i•est.** pudgy. **—'podg•i•ness,** *n.*

po•di•a•try [pə'daɪətri] *n.* the branch of medicine dealing with the treatment of major foot disorders by means of surgery, drugs, or corrective devices; chiropody. ⟨< Gk. *pous, podos* foot + *iatreia* a healing⟩ **—po'di•a•trist,** *n.*

po•di•um ['poudiəm] *n., pl.* **-di•a** [-diə]. 1 a small raised platform, especially one used by an orchestra conductor. **2** lectern. **3** a low wall around the arena of an ancient amphitheatre, serving as a base for the tiers of seats. **4** *Architecture.* a projecting base or plinth supporting a wall, etc. ⟨< L < Gk. *podion*, dim. of *pous, podos* foot⟩

pod•zol ['pɒdzɒl] *n.* a type of leached, whitish grey soil usually found in moist, subpolar climates. Also, **podsol.** ⟨< Russian *podzol* < *pod* under + *zola* ashes⟩ **—pod'zol•ic,** *adj.*

po•em ['pouəm] *n.* **1** a piece of writing that uses language that is more evocative and concentrated than in prose or ordinary speech, in which the words and phrases often have a controlled rhythm and are usually arranged in lines to produce a pattern, with or without rhyme. **2** a composition showing great beauty or nobility of language or thought. **3** something very beautiful: *The runner was a poem in motion.* ⟨< MF *poeme* < L *poema* < Gk. *poēma*, var. of *poiēma* < *poieein* make, compose⟩

po•e•sy ['pouəzi] *or* ['pouəsi] *n., pl.* **-sies.** *Archaic.* poetry. ⟨ME < OF *poesie* < L *poesis* < Gk. *poēsis*, var. of *poiēsis* composition⟩

po•et ['pouɪt] *n.* **1** a person who writes poetry. **2** a person, especially a creative artist, who has great ability to feel and express beauty, emotion, etc.: *He is a poet with his paintbrush.* ⟨ME < OF *poete* < L *poeta* < Gk. *poētēs* composer, maker⟩

po•et•as•ter ['pouɪ,tæstər] *n.* a writer of rather poor poetry. ⟨< NL *poetaster* < L *poeta* + *-aster*, denoting inferiority⟩

po•et•ic [pou'ɛtɪk] *adj.* **1** of, having to do with, or characteristic of poets or poetry: *poetic imagery.* **2** written in verse: *Her poetic compositions are all very short.* **3** showing or inspiring beautiful or noble language, imagery, or thought: *a poetic description of a scene.* Also, **poetical. —po'et•i•cal•ly,** *adv.*

poetic justice ideal justice, in that the recompense is especially well-matched to the individual's behaviour and properly distributed, thought of as being characteristic of poets' philosophy, or of poetry.

poetic licence a freedom traditionally granted to poets and other writers to violate certain grammatical rules or to alter fact or history for effect within a poetic work. Also, **poetic license.**

po•et•ics [pou'ɛtɪks] *n.* (*used with a singular verb*). **1** the theory or study of poetry. **2 Poetics,** a collection of notes on aesthetics and poetic drama by Aristotle (4C. B.C.).

poet laureate *pl.* **poets laureate. 1** a poet appointed for life by the Crown to write poems in celebration of court and national events. The first poet laureate was Ben Jonson. **2** the official poet of any country, state, etc. **3** any widely respected or popularly acclaimed poet whose work is felt to express the essential culture of the community, or to speak on its behalf.

po•et•ry ['pouɪtri] *n.* **1** poetical works; poems: *a book of poetry.* **2** the art or theory of writing poems. Poetry uses many effects of sound, imagery, and vocabulary to achieve a heightened, intensive form of expression. **3** a poetic quality or its embodiment; poetic spirit or feeling: *Her skating is pure poetry.* ⟨ME *poetrie* < OF < LL *poetria* < L *poeta* poet. See POET.⟩

po•gey or **po•gy** ['pougi] *n., adj. —n. Cdn. Slang.* **1** money or forms of relief given by the government to unemployed persons, especially in times of extreme economic depression; dole. **2** the office providing such relief. **3** a hostel supervised by the local relief agency. **4** UNEMPLOYMENT INSURANCE.
on (the) pogey, drawing such relief.
—adj. obtained from the relief office: *pogey boots.* ⟨originally, hobo slang for 'workhouse'⟩

po•go stick ['pougou] a stick used to hop from place to place by jumping up and down on the spring-supported footrests near the bottom of the stick while holding the handle at the top.

po•grom [pou'grɒm], ['pougrəm], *or* [pou'grʌm] *n.* an organized, often officially sanctioned, massacre, especially of Jews. ⟨< Yiddish < Russian *pogrom* devastation⟩

poi [pɔɪ] *or* ['poui] *n.* a Hawaiian dish made from the root of the taro plant mixed with water, baked, pounded, and fermented.

poign•an•cy ['pɔɪnjənsi] *n., pl.* **-cies. 1** the quality or state of being poignant: *They were moved by the poignancy of his appeal for help.* **2** an instance of this.

poign•ant ['pɔɪnjənt] *adj.* **1** deeply affecting; causing sympathy; touching: *a poignant cry, a poignant story.* **2** painfully sharp to the feelings; piercing: *poignant suffering.* **3** stimulating; keen or intense: *a subject of poignant interest.* **4** sharp in taste or smell. ⟨ME < OF *poignant*, ppr. of *poindre* prick < L *pungere*⟩ **—'poign•ant•ly,** *adv.*

poi•lu ['pwɑlu]; *French,* [pwa'ly] *n. Slang.* a nickname for a French soldier. ⟨< F *poilu*, originally, hairy, ult. < L *pilus* hair⟩

poin•ci•a•na [,pɔɪnsi'ænə] *or* [,pɔɪnsi'ɑnə] *n.* **1** any of a genus (*Poinciana*) of tropical trees or shrubs of the pea family having showy red or orange flowers. **2** ROYAL POINCIANA. ⟨< NL *Poinciana*, the genus name < *de Poinci*, a governor of the Antilles in the 1600s, who wrote a natural history of the islands⟩

poin•set•ti•a [pɔɪn'sɛtə] *or* [pɔɪn'sɛtiə] *n.* a shrub (*Euphorbia pulcherrima*), a kind of spurge native to Mexico and Central America, having clusters of small flowers surrounded by large, petal-like, scarlet bracts. ⟨< NL; after Joel R. *Poinsett* (1779-1851), its discoverer⟩

point [pɔɪnt] *n., v. —n.* **1** a sharp end; something having a sharp end: *the point of a needle.* **2** a tiny, round mark; dot: *A period is a point. Use a point to set off decimals. Hebrew writing has vowel points.* **3** *Mathematics.* something that has position but no extension: *Two lines meet or cross at a point.* **4** a particular place or spot: *This is the point where we turned around and went back.* **5** a particular time or moment: *At this point they lost interest in the game.* **6** a particular or definite position, state, condition, or degree; stage: *boiling point.* **7** an item; detail: *She answered my questions point by point.* **8** a distinguishing mark or quality: *one's good points.* **9** a physical characteristic or feature of an animal. **10** the main idea; the important or essential thing: *I missed the point of the candidate's talk.* **11** force; effectiveness. **12** a particular aim, end, or purpose. **13 a** each of the 32 positions indicating direction, marked on the circumference of the card of a compass. **b** the interval (11 degrees 15 minutes) between any two adjacent points of the compass. **14** a wedge or tongue of land with a sharp end sticking out into the water, especially on a bend; cape. **15** a unit of credit, scoring, or measuring; unit of price quotations: *We're three points ahead. The stock has gone up half a point.* **16** *Printing.* a unit for measuring type; 1/12 of a pica (about 0.33 mm). **17** *Informal.* a hint; suggestion. **18** lace made with a needle. **19** *Brit.* a railway switch. **20** *Hockey.* a position at the opponents' blueline, taken by an offensive player when the puck is within their defensive zone, especially during a power play. **21** *Lacrosse.* **a** one of the defencemen playing out in front of the goalie. **b** the position played by such a player. **22** *Cricket.* **a** the position of a fielder playing to the offside and a short distance in front of the batsman. **b** a fielder playing this position. **23** *Hunting.* the attitude, usually with muzzle and tail pointing and one foreleg raised, assumed by a pointer or setter on finding game. **24 a** a tungsten or platinum piece, especially in the distributor of an automobile engine, for making or breaking the flow of current. **b** *Brit.* an electrical outlet; socket. **25** *Jewellery.* a unit of gem weight equal to 1/100 of a carat. **26** *Cdn.* one of the black or coloured markings woven into Hudson's Bay blankets, originally to indicate the size and weight.
at the point of, very near to; on the verge of: *at the point of death.*
beside the point, irrelevant.
in point, apt or relevant: *the case in point.*
in point of, as regards.
in point of fact, as a matter of fact: *In point of fact, they never left the house at all.*
make a point, convince a person that an idea or argument is reasonable or correct: *He is not a very good speaker, but he made his point.*
make a point of, be particular about: *He always makes a point of being on time.*
on point, *Ballet.* on the tips of the dancer's toeshoes: *Young dancers should not dance on point until the bones of their feet are fully formed.*
on the point of, just about; on the verge of: *She was on the point of going out when a neighbour came in.*
strain or **stretch a point, a** exceed the reasonable limit. **b** make a special exception: *Ordinarily, this is not allowed, but we can stretch a point for you.*
to the point, apt; appropriate: *The mayor's speech was brief and to the point.*
—v. **1** mark with points; punctuate. **2** give force to (speech, action, etc.). **3** align (the toes) with the leg by stretching one's foot out. **4** indicate position or direction, or direct attention with, or as if with, the finger. **5** show with the finger; call attention to (*used with* **at** *or* **out**): *She pointed out the suspect in the police line-up.* **6** direct (a finger, weapon, etc.). **7** have or face a specified direction: *The signboard points north.* **8** of a dog, show the presence of (game) by standing rigid and looking toward it, with head and tail in a straight line. **9** fill joints of (brickwork) with mortar or cement (*often used with* **up**): *They pointed up the stonework on the cathedral.* **10** of an abscess, come to a head. **11** sharpen: *to point a pencil.*
point off, mark off with points or dots.
point out, show or call attention to: *Please point out my mistakes.*

point up, put emphasis on; call or give special attention to. ⟨ME < OF *point* mark, moment and *pointe* sharp point, both ult. < L *punctum, pungere* prick⟩
☛ *Hom.* POINTE [pɔint].

point–blank ['pɔɪnt 'blæŋk] *adj.* **1** aimed straight at the mark, without allowing for the bullet, shell, etc. dropping from the original line of flight. **2** close enough for aim to be taken in this way: *He fired the gun from point-blank range.* **3** plain and blunt; direct: *a point-blank question.*
–adv. **1** straight at the mark. **2** from close range. **3** plainly and bluntly; directly: *One student gave excuses, but the other refused point-blank.* ⟨apparently < *point*, v. + *blank* (< F *blanc*) the white mark in the centre of a target⟩

point blanket *Cdn.* a Hudson's Bay Company blanket having black marks or 'points' woven in.

pointe [pwɛ̃t] *or* [pɔint]; *French,* [pwɛ̃t] *n. Ballet.* **1** the toe or the tip of the toe. **2** the reinforced toe of a ballet slipper. **3** a ballet position in which the dancer stands and moves on the tips of the toeshoes. **4** (*adjl.*) of, in, or indicating this position: *pointe work.* ⟨< F⟩
☛ *Hom.* POINT [pɔint].

point•ed ['pɔɪntɪd] *adj., v. –adj.* **1** sharpened to or having a point or points: *a pointed pencil, a pointed roof.* **2** sharp; piercing: *a pointed wit.* **3** directed; aimed: *a pointed remark.* **4** emphasized; conspicuous: *a pointed refusal.*
–v. pt. and pp. of POINT. **–'point•ed•ly,** *adv.* **–'point•ed•ness,** *n.*

point•er ['pɔɪntər] *n.* **1** a person or thing that points. **2** a long, tapering stick used in pointing things out on a map, chalkboard, etc. **3** a hand of a clock, meter, etc. **4** any of several breeds of hunting dog having short, smooth hair and trained to show where game is by standing rigid and looking toward it. **5** *Informal.* a useful hint or suggestion: *She gave him some pointers on improving his tennis.* **6** *Cdn.* **a** a river boat that is pointed at both bow and stern and is of shallow draft, designed for use in logging drives. **b** formerly, an inland freight bateau of shallow draft used in the fur trade.

poin•til•lism ['pwæntə,lɪzəm] *n.* a painting technique that developed from impressionism, using tiny dots, or points, of unmixed colour placed close together on a white background so that they blend together when seen from a distance. It was developed by the French painter Georges Seurat (1859-1891). ⟨< F *pointillisme* < *pointiller* mark with little dots or points⟩

poin•til•list ['pwæntə,lɪst] *n., adj. –n.* an artist who practises pointillism.
–adj. of or having to do with pointillism.

point lace lace made with a needle, using buttonhole stitch on a paper pattern. Also, **needlepoint lace.**

point•less ['pɔɪntlɪs] *adj.* **1** without a point; blunt. **2** without purpose or meaning. **3** in a game, not having scored a point. **–'point•less•ly,** *adv.* **–'point•less•ness,** *n.*

point man **1** *Cdn. Hockey.* a player assigned to play the POINT (def. 20). Also, **point player. 2** a front rider in a cattle drive.

point mutation *Genetics.* a single base pair substitution in DNA.

point of departure in a discussion, etc., a starting point.

point of honour or **honor** a matter that seriously affects a person's honour or principles: *It was a point of honour with her to give every applicant equal time.*

point of no return the stage in an action or event after which there is no turning back, so that one is obliged to continue.

point of order a question raised as to whether proceedings are according to the rules.

point–of–sale ['pɔɪnt əv seil] *adj.* designed for, operating at, etc., the checkout area in a store. Also, **point-of-purchase.**

point of view **1** a position from which objects are considered. **2** an attitude of mind.

point system **1** *Education.* a system of evaluating students' progress by assigning points to letter grades, then averaging the results. The average thus obtained is the **grade point average.** **2** *Printing.* a system for grading the sizes of type, etc. **3** any of various systems of writing for the blind, such as Braille, that employ combinations of raised dots to represent letters. **4** a system whereby motorists are assigned a set number of points for each infraction. When the points reach a certain total, the motorist's licence is suspended.

point–to–point ['pɔɪnt tə 'pɔɪnt] *n., adj. –n.* a steeplechase or cross-country race over a course marked by flags at the main points.
–adj. made in a direct line from one point or place to another.

poise [pɔɪz] *n., v.* **poised, pois•ing.** *–n.* **1** mental balance, composure, or self-possession: *She has perfect poise and never seems embarrassed.* **2** the way in which the body, head, etc. are held; carriage: *He admired the actor's poise.*
–v. **1** balance: *Poise yourself on your toes.* **2** hold or carry evenly or steadily: *The athlete poised the weight in the air before throwing it.* ⟨ME, n. < OF *pois, peis* < L *pensum* weight; v. < OF *poise, peise* < *peser* weigh < L *pensare*, intensive of *pendere* weigh⟩

poi•sha ['pɔɪʃɑ] *n.* a unit of money in Bangladesh, equal to ¹⁄₁₀₀ of a taka. See table of money in the Appendix.

poi•son ['pɔɪzən] *n., v., adj. –n.* **1** a drug or other substance that is dangerous to health and capable of causing death. Strychnine and arsenic are poisons. **2** anything dangerous or deadly: *Hate becomes a poison in the mind.*
–v. **1** kill or harm by poison: *The old lady was poisoned by her greedy relatives.* **2** put poison in or on: *Her hot milk was poisoned.* **3** have or exert a dangerous or harmful effect on: *Lies poison the mind. He poisoned his friend's mind against the girl.*
–adj. poisonous or poisoned: *a poison plant, a poison arrow.* ⟨ME < OF *poison* < L *potio, -onis* potion. Doublet of POTION.⟩ **–'poi•son•er,** *n.*

poison hemlock HEMLOCK (def. 3).

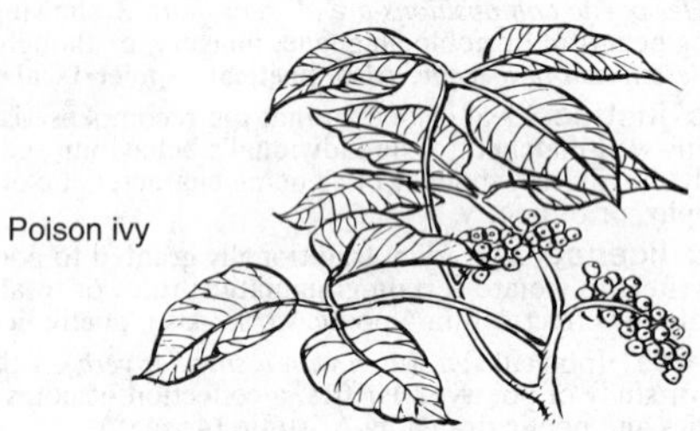
Poison ivy

poison ivy **1** a North American woody vine or shrub (*Rhus radicans*) of the cashew family, having greenish flowers, white berries, and leaves composed of three leaflets. It produces a toxic oil in its leaves, flowers, fruit, and bark that causes a severe rash on contact with the skin. **2** the rash. **3** any of several other plants of the genus *Rhus.*

poison oak **1** a plant (*Rhus diversiloba*) of the cashew family found along the Pacific coast of North America. The poison oak has leaflets shaped like oak leaves. **2** POISON SUMAC.

poi•son•ous ['pɔɪzənəs] *adj.* **1** containing poison; very harmful to health and capable of causing death. **2** having a dangerous or harmful effect: *a poisonous lie.* **–'poi•son•ous•ly,** *adv.* **–'poi•son•ous•ness,** *n.*

poi•son–pen ['pɔɪzən 'pɛn] *adj.* designating an abusive, insulting, or threatening letter, etc. written out of malice and usually anonymously.

poison sumac a shrub (*Rhus vernix*) of the cashew family found in swamps in E North America, having pinnate leaves with seven to thirteen leaflets, greenish flowers, and greenish white berries. Most people develop an itchy skin rash if they touch it.

Poisson distribution [pwɑ'soun]; *French,* [pwa'sɔ̃] *Statistics.* a frequency distribution which is a limiting form of the binomial probability distribution when the number of events is large and the probability of success becomes small. It is particularly useful in industrial quality control. ⟨< S.D. *Poisson* (1781-1840), French mathematician⟩

poke¹ [pouk] *v.* **poked, pok•ing;** *n. –v.* **1** push against with something pointed; jab: *He poked me in the ribs with his elbow.* **2** thrust; push: *He poked his head in the kitchen window.* **3** stir (a fire) with a poker. **4** *Informal.* punch: *He threatened to poke his brother in the nose.* **5** pry: *She's always poking into other people's business.* **6** make by piercing: *to poke a hole in something.* **7** go lazily; loiter: *poking along at 40 km/h.* **8** search or putter (*usually used with* **around** *or* **about**): *poking around in the attic.*
–n. **1** a poking; thrust; push. **2** *Informal.* a punch. **3** a slow, lazy person. **4** a projecting brim on the front of a POKE BONNET, or the bonnet itself. ⟨ME < MDu., MLG *poken* to thrust. Akin to POACH¹.⟩

poke² [pouk] *n.* **1** a bag or sack. **2** *Cdn.* a bag or small sack used to carry gold dust or nuggets. **3** *Cdn.* a sleeping bag. **4** *Slang.* money.
buy a pig in a poke, buy something without seeing it first. ⟨ME; akin to OE *pocca* bag, pocket. Akin to POUCH.⟩

poke³ [pouk] *n.* pokeweed. ⟨< Algonquian⟩

poke•ber•ry ['pouk,bɛri] *n., pl.* **-ries. 1** a berry of the pokeweed. **2** pokeweed.

poke bonnet a bonnet with a projecting brim at the front.

poke check *Hockey.* a defensive play made by holding the stick low along the ice and poking the puck out of the puck-carrier's control. **—'poke-,check,** *v.*

poke•lo•gan ['poukə,lougən] *n. Cdn., esp. Maritimes.* a small stagnant backwater or marshy place in a stream. Also, **logan.** ⟨< Algonquian⟩

pok•er¹ ['poukər] *n.* a person or thing that pokes, especially a metal rod for stirring a fire. ⟨< *poke¹*⟩

pok•er² ['poukər] *n.* any of several card games in which players bet that the value of the cards they hold in their hands is greater than that of the cards held by the other players. ⟨origin uncertain⟩

poker face *Informal.* **1** a face or facial expression that does not show one's thoughts or feelings, as of a poker player trying not to reveal the quality of his or her hand of cards. **2** a person having such a face or facial expression. **—'po•ker-,faced,** *adj.*

poke•root ['pouk,rut] *n.* pokeweed.

poke•weed ['pouk,wid] *n.* a tall North American perennial plant (*Phytolacca americana*) having juicy purple berries and a large, poisonous root. The red juice of the berries has been used as ink and to colour wine, candies, cloth, etc., but is now considered poisonous. ⟨*poke³* + *weed*⟩

pok•ey¹ or **pok•y¹** ['pouki] *n., pl.* **-eys** or **-ies.** *Slang.* jail.

pok•ey² or **pok•y²** ['pouki] *adj.* **pok•i•er, pok•i•est. 1** annoyingly slow or unenergetic: *a pokey old horse.* **2** small and shabby or cramped: *a pokey room.* **3** shabby or dowdy in dress. ⟨< *poke¹*⟩ **—'pok•i•ly,** *adv.* **—'pok•i•ness,** *n.*

pol [pɒl] *n. Slang.* a politician, especially one with experience and expertise.
☛ *Hom.* PALL, PAWL.

pol. 1 political. **2** politics.

Po•land ['poulənd] *n.* a republic in east central Europe, on the Baltic Sea.

Poland (China) 1 a breed of large American hogs, black with white markings. **2** any one of these hogs.

po•lar ['poulər] *adj.* **1** of, having to do with, or coming from the North or South Pole or the region around it: *the polar wastes, a polar wind.* **2** passing over the North or South Pole: *a satellite in polar orbit. We flew the polar route to Europe last year.* **3** of or having to do with the poles of a magnet, battery, etc. **4** directly opposite in character, like the poles of a magnet: *Good and evil are polar elements.* **5** *Chemistry.* ionizing when dissolved or fused. ⟨< Med.L *polaris* < L *polus* pole. See POLE².⟩

polar bear a large, white, semi-aquatic bear (*Thalarctos maritimus*) found in arctic regions.

polar front the line or region where cold air from the polar regions meets warm air from the temperate zones or tropics, usually producing strong winds and storms.

Po•lar•is [pə'lærɪs] *or* [pə'lɛrɪs] *n. Astronomy.* the North Star; polestar.

po•lar•i•scope [pə'lærɪ,skoup] *or* [pə'lɛrɪ,skoup] *n. Optics.* an instrument for showing the polarization of light, or for examining substances in polarized light. **—po,lar•i'scop•ic** [pə,lærɪ'skɒpɪk] *or* [pə,lɛrɪ'skɒpɪk], *adj.*

po•lar•i•ty [pə'lærɪti] *or* [pə'lɛrɪti] *n.* **1** *Physics.* **a** the possession of two opposed poles. A magnet or battery has polarity. **b** a positive or negative polar condition, as in electricity. **2** the possession or exhibition of two opposite or contrasted principles or tendencies. **4** *Linguistics.* the relation between antonyms that can be represented as a continuum, as *hot* and *cold* (but not *up* and *down*).

po•lar•i•za•tion [,poulərɪ'zeiʃən] *or* [,poulərai'zeiʃən] *n.* **1** the production or acquisition of polarity. **2** *Electricity.* a process by which gases produced during electrolysis are deposited on one or both electrodes of a cell, giving rise to a reverse electromotive force. **3** *Optics.* a state, or the production of a state, in which waves of light move or vibrate transversely in only one direction or plane or in two perpendicular planes. **4** the reduction of a complex but continuous spectrum of opinions, etc. or of the people holding them, to a pair of opposite extremes: *the polarization of the electorate on the issue of free trade.*

po•lar•ize ['poulə,raɪz] *v.* **-ized, -iz•ing. 1** give polarity to; cause polarization in. **2** become polarized; separate into opposing groups. ⟨< F *polariser*⟩

polar lights the **aurora borealis** in the northern hemisphere or the **aurora australis** in the southern hemisphere.

pol•der ['pouldər] *n.* an area of low, marshy land reclaimed from the sea or some other body of water and protected by dikes. ⟨< Du.⟩

pole¹ [poul] *n., v.* **poled, pol•ing.** *—n.* **1** a long, slender, usually cylindrical piece of wood, metal, etc.: *a telephone pole, a flagpole, a ski pole.* **2** a non-metric unit for measuring length, equal to a rod, or perch (about 5.03 m). **3** a non-metric unit for measuring area, equal to a square rod (about 25.3 m²). **4 a** a position on a racetrack nearest the infield. **b** (*adjl.*) referring to or having to do with such a position: *Tracy has drawn the pole position in the Vancouver Indy.*
—v. push or move by pushing with a pole: *to pole a raft. We poled down the river.* ⟨OE *pāl* < L *palus* stake. Doublet of PALE².⟩
☛ *Hom.* POLE, POLL.

pole² [poul] *n.* **1** either end of the earth's rotational axis. The North Pole and the South Pole are opposite each other. See EQUATOR for picture. **2** either of two parts or points where opposite forces are strongest. A magnet or battery has both a positive pole and a negative pole. **3** either end of the axis of any sphere. **4** either of two opinions, forces, etc., considered as being opposite extremes. **5** *Biology.* the point at either end of an ideal axis in a cell, nucleus, or ovum.
poles apart, very much different; in strong disagreement: *The two bargaining parties are still poles apart and there is no sign of a settlement.* ⟨ME < L *polus* < Gk. *polos*⟩
☛ *Hom.* POLE, POLL.

Pole [poul] *n.* **1** a native or inhabitant of Poland. **2** a person of Polish descent.

pole•axe ['poul,æks] *n., v.* **-axed, -ax•ing.** *—n.* an axe with a long handle and a hook or spike opposite the blade.
—v. fell with or as if with a poleaxe. Sometimes, **poleax.** ⟨ME *pollax* < *pol(le)* poll, head + *ax* axe⟩

pole bean any strain of vinelike beans of the common garden type, trained to grow up poles, trellises, etc. Compare BUSH BEAN.

pole bunk *Cdn.* a rudimentary bed or bunk, made of poles.

pole•cat ['poul,kæt] *n.* **1** a small, dark brown carnivorous European mammal (*Mustela putorius*) of the weasel family. **2** the North American skunk. **3** *Informal.* a mean or contemptible person. ⟨ME *polcat* < OF *poule* fowl, hen (< VL *pulla*, fem. to L *pullus* young fowl) + ME *cat* cat; so called because it preys on poultry⟩

po•lem•ic [pə'lɛmɪk] *n., adj.* *—n.* **1** a strong argument against or attack on an idea, belief, or opinion: *The book is nothing but a long polemic against conservatism.* **2** a line of argument; way of talking about things that reflects a particular argument: *the Marxist polemic.* **3** Usually, **polemics,** the art or practice of argument or controversy (*used with a singular or plural verb*): *This is not the time to indulge in polemics.*
—adj. of, having to do with, or actively engaged in controversy or disagreement: *a polemic writer.* Also, **polemical.** ⟨< Gk. *polemikos* belligerent < *polemos* war⟩ **—po'lem•i•cal•ly,** *adv.*

po•lem•i•cist [pou'lɛmɪ,sɪst] *n.* a person given to or skilful in polemics.

po•len•ta [pou'lɛntə] *n.* an Italian dish consisting of a thick cornmeal mush, usually baked or fried. ⟨< Ital. < L, pearl barley⟩

pole•star ['poul,stɑr] *n.* **1** Polaris, the North Star, formerly much used as a guide by sailors. **2** a guiding principle; guide. **3** a centre of attraction, interest, or attention.

pole vault 1 an athletic event or contest in which contestants jump, or vault, over a high, horizontal bar, with the aid of a long, flexible pole. The pole vault is one of the Olympic track and field events. **2** a vault of this kind.

pole–vault ['poul ,vɒlt] *v.* make a vault with the aid of a pole. **—'pole-,vault•er,** *n.*

po•lice [pə'lis] *n., v.* **-liced, -lic•ing.** *—n.* **1** the organized civil force of a country, province, state, or community whose duty is to guard people's lives and property, to preserve peace and order, and to arrest those who commit crimes. **2** the people who carry out this duty for a community: *The police arrived within 10*

minutes. **3** any organized body of people employed for a similar purpose. **4** the keeping of order in a military establishment or among military personnel.
—v. guard or keep order in: *to police the streets, to police an army camp.* ⟨< F *police* < LL *politia* administration of the state < Gk. *politeia* polity. Doublet of POLICY[1], POLITY.⟩

police constable a police officer of the lowest rank.

police court a court of limited jurisdiction, such as a magistrate's court.

police dog a dog trained for use in police work. German shepherds, Doberman pinschers, and Bouviers de Flandres are often used as police dogs.

police force the law-enforcing body of a country, province, state, or community.

po•lice•man [pə'lismən] *n., pl.* **-men. 1** a male member of a police force. **2** *Hockey. Slang.* a rugged player responsible for keeping opposing players from treating his teammates roughly.

police officer a member of a police force.

police post *Cdn.* a place where a detachment of the Royal Canadian Mounted Police is stationed: *They were 5 km from the nearest police post.*

police state a country strictly controlled by governmental authority, especially with the aid of a secret police organization.

police station the headquarters of the police of a particular area or district in a city, or of the local police force of a small community.

police village *Cdn.* in Ontario, an unincorporated village administered by a board of trustees. Also, **police town.**

po•lice•wom•an [pə'lis,wʊmən] *n., pl.* **-wom•en.** a female member of a police force.

pol•i•clin•ic [,pɒlɪ'klɪnɪk] *n.* the department of a hospital set aside for the treatment of outpatients. ⟨< G *Poliklinik* < Gk. *polis* city + G *klinik* clinic⟩

pol•i•cy[1] ['pɒləsi] *n., pl.* **-cies. 1** a plan of action; a course or method of action that has been deliberately chosen and that guides or influences future decisions: *Her actions were in accordance with company policy. The candidate explained his party's policy.* **2** practical wisdom; prudence: *It is poor policy to promise more than you can give.* ⟨ME < OF *policie* < L < Gk. *politeia* polity. Doublet of POLICE, POLITY.⟩

pol•i•cy[2] ['pɒləsi] *n., pl.* **-cies.** a written contract concerning insurance. ⟨< F < Ital. *polizza* < Med.L *apodixa* < Gk. *apodeixis* declaration⟩

pol•i•cy•hold•er ['pɒləsi,houldər] *n.* the owner of an insurance policy.

po•li•o ['pouli,ou] *n.* poliomyelitis.

po•li•o•my•e•li•tis [,pouliou,maiə'ləitɪs] *n. Pathology.* **1** an acute infectious disease caused by a virus, characterized by symptoms ranging from fever, headaches, vomiting, etc. to extensive permanent paralysis of muscles. **2** any inflammation of the grey matter of the spinal cord. ⟨< NL < Gk. *polios* grey + *myelos* marrow + *-itis*⟩

pol•ish ['pɒlɪʃ] *v., n. —v.* **1** make smooth and shiny by rubbing: *to polish shoes.* **2** become smooth and shiny: *This leather polishes well.* **3** remove by smoothing (*used with* **off** *or* **away**). **4** put into a better condition; improve (*often used with* **up**): *to polish a manuscript, to polish up one's French.* **5** make elegant; refine: *to polish one's manners.*
polish off, *Informal.* **a** get done with; finish. **b** consume eagerly.
—n. **1** a substance used to give smoothness or shine or to remove dirt, tarnish, etc.: *silver polish.* **2** shininess; smoothness: *The table has a high polish.* **3** culture; elegance; refinement: *a woman of breeding and polish.* **4** the act or process of polishing: *I gave the table a quick polish.* ⟨ME *polischen* < OF *poliss-*, a stem of *polir* < L *polire*⟩ **—'pol•ish•er,** *n.*

Pol•ish ['poulɪʃ] *n., adj. —n.* the West Slavic language of Poland.
—adj. of or having to do with Poland, its people, or their language.

Po•lit•bu•ro ['pɒlɪt,bjʊrou] *or* [pə'lɪt,bjʊrou] *n.* formerly, an executive committee of the Communist Party that controlled policy and matters of state in the Soviet Union, Bulgaria, and some other Communist countries.

po•lite [pə'ləit] *adj.* **1** having or showing good manners; behaving properly. **2** refined; elegant. ⟨< L *politus* polished⟩ **—po'lite•ly,** *adv.* **—po'lite•ness,** *n.*
☛ *Syn.* **1. Polite,** CIVIL, COURTEOUS = having the manners appropriate to good social relations. **Polite** suggests having and showing good manners at all times, and emphasizes following the rules for behaving properly: *That polite boy gave me his seat.* **Civil** means being just polite enough not to be rude: *All I expect is a civil answer.* **Courteous** adds to *polite* the idea of showing thoughtful attention to the feelings and wishes of others: *I go to that store because the clerks are courteous.*

pol•i•tic ['pɒlə,tɪk] *adj.* **1** characterized by prudence and practical wisdom; sensible and expedient: *It was not politic to arouse his irritation.* **2** scheming; crafty. **3** *Archaic.* political: *The state is a body politic.* ⟨ME *polytyk* < F *politique* < L *politicus* < Gk. *politikos*, ult. < *polis* city-state⟩ **—'pol•i•tic•ly,** *adv.*
☛ *Hom.* POLITICK.

po•lit•i•cal [pə'lɪtɪkəl] *adj.* **1** of or concerned with politics. **2** having to do with public affairs or government: *Treason is a political offence.* **3** of politicians or their methods. **4** having a definite system of government. **—po'lit•i•cal•ly,** *adv.*

political economy 1 a social science dealing with the ways in which political and economic processes are related to each other; the study of the economic problems of government. **2** *Archaic.* economics. **—political economist.**

politically correct anything that might be construed as avoiding racism, sexism, agism, etc. *Abbrev.*: P.C.

political party a registered group of people that tries to have its members elected to a legislature or government. Members of a political party have similar ideas about the running of business, industry, education, health care, social issues, etc.

political science a social science dealing with political institutions and processes, especially with the principles and conduct of government. **—political scientist.**

pol•i•ti•cian [,pɒlə'tɪʃən] *n.* **1** a person holding a political office. **2** a person active in politics, especially one seeking political office. **3** anyone, holding public office or not, regarded as being opportunistic and somewhat dishonest.
☛ *Syn.* **1. Politician,** STATESMAN = someone active or skilled in public or governmental affairs. **Politician** especially suggests the ability to deal with people and accomplish things for the good of the people and the country, but often is used slightingly or contemptuously to suggest an unprincipled person scheming for his or her own or the party's good: *All office-holders are politicians.* **Statesman,** always in a good sense, emphasizes sound judgment, shrewdness, far-sightedness, and skill in dealing with public problems and managing national affairs: *Churchill was a great statesman.*

po•lit•i•cize [pə'lɪtə,saɪz] *v.* **-cized, -ciz•ing. 1** make politically aware: *a politicized electorate.* **2** give a political character or tone to: *to politicize a social issue.* **3** talk about or take part in politics. **—po,lit•i•ci'za•tion,** *n.*

pol•i•tick ['pɒlə,tɪk] *v.* take part in political activity, especially in order to directly or indirectly solicit votes: *He's politicking in the Maritimes this week.* **—'pol•i,tick•er,** *n.*
☛ *Hom.* POLITIC.

po•lit•i•co [pə'lɪtə,kou] *n., pl.* **-cos.** politician. ⟨< Sp. *politico* or Ital. *politico* < L *politicus*⟩

pol•i•tics ['pɒlə,tɪks] *n.* **1** the science and art of government; political science (*used with a singular verb*). **2** the management and conduct of government as a business or profession (*used with a singular verb*): *Politics was her first and only career.* **3** the activities, practices, or policies entailed by or involved in this (*used with a plural or singular verb*): *party politics.* **4** methods or manoeuvres for gaining or keeping power, often suggesting scheming or dishonesty (*used with a singular or plural verb*): *The builder played politics to win the contract.* **5** views or opinions on the proper role of government (*used with a plural verb*): *Their politics are very conservative.* **6** the complex of relationships between people, especially as they involve authority or power (*used with a singular verb*): *the politics of volunteer organizations.*

pol•i•ty ['pɒləti] *n., pl.* **-ties. 1** political organization; government. **2** a particular form or system of government. **3** a community with a government; state. ⟨< obs. F *politie* < L *politia* < Gk. *politeia*, ult. < *polis* city-state. Doublet of POLICE, POLICY[1].⟩

pol•ka ['poulkə] *or* ['poukə] *n., v.* **-kaed, -ka•ing.** *—n.* **1** a kind of lively dance in four-four time, a skip or hop followed by three small steps. **2** the music for this dance.
—v. dance a polka. ⟨< F or G < Czech *pulka* half-step < *pul* half⟩

pol•ka dot 1 a dot or round spot repeated to form a regular pattern on cloth. **2** a pattern or fabric with such dots. **—'pol•ka-,dot** or **,pol•ka-'dot•ted,** *adj.*

poll [poul] *n., v. —n.* **1** a voting; collection of votes: *The class took a poll to decide where the picnic would be held.* **2** the number of votes cast: *If it rains on election day, there may be a light poll.* **3** the results of these votes. **4** a list of persons, especially a list of voters. **5** the place where votes are cast and counted: *The polls will be open till 8 o'clock tonight.* **6 a** a survey of public

opinion concerning a particular subject. **b** the results of such a survey. **7** the head, especially the part of it on which the hair grows.
—*v.* **1** receive (as votes): *The mayor polled a record vote.* **2** vote; cast (a vote): *They polled the proposed new tax out. The incumbent was polled in with a huge majority.* **3** take or register the votes of. **4** question or canvass in a public opinion poll. **5** cut off or cut short the hair, wool, horns, branches, etc. of. ⟨Cf. MDu. *pol(le)* top, MLG *pol* head⟩
☛ *Hom.* POLE.

pol•lack ['pɒlək] *n., pl.* **-lacks** or (*esp. collectively*) **lack.** See POLLOCK.

pol•lard ['pɒlərd] *n., v.* —*n* **1** a tree with the top branches severely cut back, so as to produce a dense growth of new shoots. **2** a tree that has been cut back in this manner. **3** a hornless or dehorned animal, such as a stag, goat, or ox.
—*v.* to severely cut back the branches of (a tree): *We should pollard that old elm.*

poll captain *Cdn.* in an election, a person charged with the responsibility of canvassing voters and reporting the estimated vote to party headquarters.

polled [pould] *adj.* of cattle, hornless.

pol•len ['pɒlən] *n.* a fine, yellowish powder formed in the anthers of flowers, consisting of tiny grains that are the male sex cells which fertilize the ovules. ⟨< L *pollen* mill dust⟩

pollen basket an area surrounded by stiff hairs on each hind leg of a honeybee, in which the bee collects pollen to carry back to the hive.

pollen count a count of pollen particles in the air, made to give information to allergic people.

pol•lex ['pɒlɪks] *n., pl.* **pol•li•ces** ['pɒlɪ,siz] the innermost digit of the forelimb; thumb. ⟨< L *pollex* thumb, big toe⟩

pol•li•nate ['pɒlə,neit] *v.* **-nat•ed, -nat•ing.** *Botany.* carry pollen from stamens to pistils of; shed pollen on. Many flowers are pollinated by bees. **—,pol•li'na•tion,** *n.*

polling booth a screened or otherwise enclosed space in a polling station where a voter marks his or her ballot in privacy.

polling station a room or building set up during an election as a place where the people living nearby may vote.

pol•li•wog ['pɒli,wɒg] *n.* tadpole. Also, **pollywog.** ⟨Cf. ME *polwigle* < *pol(le)* poll, head + *wigle* wiggle⟩

pol•lock ['pɒlək] *n., pl.* **-locks** or (*esp. collectively*) **-lock. 1** an important food fish (*Pollachius virens*) of the cod family, found in the N Atlantic Ocean, having a long body with a deep green back and pale belly and a small barbel under the jaw. **2** a closely related species (*Pollachius pollachius*) found in European coastal waters, having a brownish or olive back and lacking a barbel. It is a popular game fish but has no commercial value. Also, **pollack.**

poll•ster ['poulstər] *n.* a person who takes public opinion polls, especially one whose work it is.

poll tax a tax on every person, or on every person of a specified class, especially as a prerequisite to the right to vote; a tax levied on people and not on property.

pol•lu•tant [pə'lutənt] *n.* something that pollutes: *Automobile exhaust is a major air pollutant.*

pol•lute [pə'lut] *v.* **-lut•ed, -lut•ing. 1** make physically impure or unclean; especially, contaminate (the air, water, soil, etc.) with synthetic waste materials: *the polluted air of cities. The lake has been polluted with waste from a large factory.* **2** make morally impure; defile. ⟨< L *pollutus*, pp. of *polluere*⟩ **—pol'lut•er,** *n.*

pol•lu•tion [pə'luʃən] *n.* **1** the action of polluting or the condition of being polluted. **2** something that pollutes; pollutant: *That's not fog, that's pollution.*

Pol•lux ['pɒləks] *n.* **1** *Greek and Roman mythology.* one of the twin sons of Zeus and Leda. Pollux was immortal; his brother Castor was mortal. **2** *Astronomy.* one of the two brightest stars in the constellation Gemini. ⟨< L < Gk. *Polydeukēs*⟩

Pol•ly•an•na [,pɒli'ænə] *n.* one who is always cheerful, or overly cheerful, and always sees good in everything, even in the face of disaster. ⟨after *Pollyanna*, the heroine of stories by Eleanor H. Porter (1868-1920)⟩

pol•ly•wog ['pɒli,wɒg] See POLLIWOG.

po•lo ['poulou] *n.* **1** a game played by two teams of players on horseback, who use long-handled mallets to drive a wooden ball through the opposing team's goal. **2** WATER POLO. ⟨? ult. < Tibetan *pulu*⟩

pol•o•naise [,pɒlə'neiz] *or* [,poulə'nɛz] *n.* **1** a slow, stately dance in 3/4 time. **2** the music for such a dance. **3** a woman's overdress consisting of a bodice and a draped, cutaway overskirt. ⟨< F *polonaise*, fem. adj., literally, Polish⟩

po•lo•ni•um [pə'louniəm] *n. Chemistry.* a radioactive element that occurs naturally in trace amounts in uranium ores and is also produced artificially in nuclear reactors. The most commonly produced isotope is polonium-210 (half-life approximately 138 days), a highly radioactive and toxic material used as a heat and power source. *Symbol:* Po; *at.no.* 84; *at.mass* (210); *half-life* approximately 103 years. ⟨< NL < Med.L *Polonia* Poland, the homeland of Marie Curie (1867-1934), who, with her husband, discovered it⟩

pol•ter•geist ['poultər,gəist] *n.* a ghost or spirit that is essentially harmless but mischievous, supposedly responsible for unexplained happenings and noises such as door slamming, chain rattling, or rapping sounds on walls or tables. ⟨< G, literally, noise-ghost < *poltern* noisy + *geist* ghost⟩

pol•troon [pɒl'trun] *n., adj.* —*n.* a wretched coward.
—*adj.* marked by cowardice; cowardly. ⟨< F *poltron* < Ital. *poltrone* < *poltro* colt, ult. < L *pullus* young animal⟩

poly– *combining form.* **1** more than one; many; extensive: *polyangular.* **2** polymeric; polymerized: *polyethylene, polystyrene.* ⟨< Gk. *poly-* < *polys* much, many⟩

pol•y•am•ide [,pɒli'æmaɪd] *or* [,pɒli'æmɪd] *n. Chemistry.* any of a group of synthetic polymers containing two or more amide groups (-CONH-). The most common polyamides are the various forms of nylon.

pol•y•an•drous [,pɒli'ændrəs] *adj.* **1** having to do with or practising polyandry. **2** *Botany.* having many stamens.

pol•y•an•dry ['pɒli,ændri] *or* [,pɒli'ændri] *n.* the practice or condition of having more than one male mate at one time. Compare POLYGAMY and POLYGYNY. ⟨< Gk. *polyandria* < *polys* many + *anēr, andros* man, husband⟩ **—,pol•y'an•drist,** *n.*

pol•y•an•thus [,pɒli'ænθəs] *n.* **1** a hybrid primrose (*Primula polyantha*) cultivated in several varieties for its large, brightly coloured flowers. **2** a narcissus (*Narcissus tazetta*) having clusters of small yellow or white flowers. ⟨< NL < Gk. *polyanthos* < *polys* many + *anthos* flower⟩

pol•y•at•om•ic [,pɒliə'tɒmɪk] *adj. Chemistry.* of a molecule, having more than two atoms.

pol•y•car•pous [,pɒli'kɑrpəs] *adj. Botany.* consisting of many or several carpels. Also, **polycarpic.** ⟨< *poly-* + Gk. *karpos* fruit⟩

pol•y•cen•trism [,pɒli'sɛntrɪzəm] *n.* **1** the doctrine that many centres of power or ideology may exist within a single system. **2** the fact of the existence of such centres: *the polycentrism of the Communist bloc.*

pol•y•chlo•rin•at•ed biphenyl [,pɒli'klɔrə,neitɪd] PCB, one of a group of highly toxic isomers of biphenyl in chlorinated form, now banned in use.

pol•y•cho•to•my [,pɒli'kɒtəmi] *n., pl.* **-mies.** separation or division into many parts. Compare DICHOTOMY.
—,pol•y'chot•o•mous, *adj.*

pol•y•chro•mat•ic [,pɒlikrou'mætɪk] **1** having a variety of colours. **2** of or designating light or other electromagnetic radiation composed of more than one wavelength.

pol•y•chrome ['pɒli,kroum] *adj., n.* —*adj.* having to do with or made or decorated with several colours.
—*n.* **1** a work of art in several colours, especially a painted statue. **2** a combination of many colours. **—'pol•y,chro•my,** *n.*
—'pol•y,chro•mic, *adj.*

pol•y•clin•ic [,pɒli'klɪnɪk] *n.* a clinic or hospital designed for treating many different diseases.

pol•y•cot•y•le•don [,pɒli,kɒtə'lidən] *n. Botany.* a plant that has more than two cotyledons, such as the gymnosperm.
—,pol•y,cot•y'le•don•ous, *adj.*

pol•y•cy•clic [,pɒli'səiklɪk] *or* [,pɒli'sɪklik] *adj.* **1** *Biology.* having two or more whorls or rings. **2** *Chemistry.* of an organic compound, having two or more atomic rings in the molecule, usually fused.

pol•y•dac•tyl [,pɒli'dæktɪl] *adj., n.* —*adj.* **1** having many or several fingers and toes. **2** having more fingers and toes than is normal.
—*n.* a polydactyl person or animal: *Anne Boleyn had an extra finger; she was a polydactyl.*

pol•y•don•tia [,pɒli'dɒnʃiə] *or* [,pɒli'dɒnʃə] *n. Dentistry.* the condition of having more teeth than is normal.

pol•y•es•ter [,pɒli'ɛstər] *n.* **1** *Chemistry.* any of a group of synthetic organic polymers usually formed from glycols and certain acids, prepared in the form of plastics, fibres, etc. **2** thread, yarn, or fabric made of a polyester.

pol•y•eth•y•lene [ˌpɒli'ɛθəˌlin] *n. Chemistry.* any of various very strong, lightweight synthetic polymers of ethylene that are good insulators and are resistant to chemicals and moisture. Polyethylenes are used for electrical insulation, containers, and packaging, etc. Also, **polythene**. *Formula*: $(C_2H_4)_n$

po•lyg•a•mist [pə'lɪgəmɪst] *n.* a person who practises or favours polygamy.

po•lyg•a•mous [pə'lɪgəməs] *adj.* **1** having to do with or practising polygamy. **2** *Botany.* bearing both unisexual and hermaphrodite flowers on the same plant or on different plants of the same species. **3** *Zoology.* having more than one mate at one time: *Baboons are polygamous.* **—po'lyg•a•mous•ly,** *adv.*

po•lyg•a•my [pə'lɪgəmi] *n.* **1** the practice or condition of having more than one spouse at one time. Compare POLYGYNY and POLYANDRY. **2** *Zoology.* the practice of mating with several individuals of the opposite sex during one breeding season, usually one male with several females. ⟨< Gk. *polygamia* < *polys* many + *gamos* marriage⟩

pol•y•gen•e•sis [ˌpɒli'dʒɛnəsɪs] *n.* **1** *Biology.* an organ deriving from more than one kind of germ cell. **2** *Biology, anthropology.* origin in more than one line or species. **3** *Linguistics.* origin in more than one language family.

pol•y•gen•ic inheritance [ˌpɒli'dʒɛnɪk] *Genetics.* a pattern of inheritance determined by multiple genes with minor effects.

pol•y•glot ['pɒliˌglɒt] *adj., n. —adj.* **1** knowing several languages; multilingual. **2** written or expressed in several languages.
—n. **1** a person who knows several languages. **2** a book written in several languages. **3** a mixture or confusion of several languages. ⟨< Gk. *polyglōttos* < *polys* many + *glōtta* tongue⟩

pol•y•gon ['pɒliˌgɒn] *n. Geometry.* a closed plane figure having straight sides, especially one with more than four sides. ⟨< LL < Gk. < *polys* many + *gōnia* angle⟩

po•lyg•o•nal [pə'lɪgənəl] *adj. Geometry.* having three or more angles and sides.

pol•y•graph ['pɒliˌgræf] *n., v. —n.* **1** an instrument for recording various physiological responses (such as changes in blood pressure, respiration, etc.) to verbal stimuli. Polygraphs are often used as lie detectors; the physiological evidence is interpreted as indicating the probable truth or falsehood of specific statements made by the person being tested. **2** a device resembling a pantograph, for drawing or writing two or more copies of the same thing at the same time. **3** a versatile or prolific writer.
—v. test (someone) with a polygraph lie detector.
—ˌpol•y'graph•ic, *adj.* **—ˌpol•y'graph•i•cal•ly,** *adv.*

po•lyg•y•nist [pə'lɪdʒənɪst] *n.* one who practises or favours polygyny.

po•lyg•y•nous [pə'lɪdʒənəs] *adj.* **1** having to do with or practising polygyny. **2** *Botany.* having many pistils.

po•lyg•y•ny [pə'lɪdʒəni] *n.* **1** the practice or condition of having more than one wife or female mate at one time. Compare POLYGAMY and POLYANDRY. **2** *Botany.* the condition of having many pistils.

pol•y•he•dral [ˌpɒli'hidrəl] *adj.* **1** of or having to do with a polyhedron. **2** having many faces.

pol•y•he•dron [ˌpɒli'hidrən] *n., pl.* **-drons** or **-dra** [-drə]. a solid figure having four or more plane faces, all of which are polygons. The faces of a regular polyhedron are all identical polygons. A cube is a regular polyhedron with six square faces. See SOLID for picture. ⟨< NL < Gk. *polyedros* < *polys* many + *hedra* seat, side⟩

pol•y•math ['pɒliˌmæθ] *n.* a person of great and encyclopedic learning. ⟨< Gk. *polumathēs* very learned, ult. < *polu-* poly- + *manthanein* to learn. 17c. See MATHEMATICS.⟩
—ˌpol•y'math•ic, *adj.*

pol•y•mer ['pɒləmər] *n. Chemistry.* any of a large number of natural or synthetic, organic or inorganic compounds composed of very large molecules that are made up of many light, simple molecules chemically linked together. Cellulose and proteins are naturally occurring polymers; concrete, plastics, and glass are synthetic polymers.

pol•y•mer•ase ['pɒləməˌreiz] *or* ['pɒləməˌreis] *n. Biochemistry.* any of several enzymes that act as catalysts in the formation of polymers, especially in nucleic acids.

pol•y•mer•ic [ˌpɒlə'mɛrɪk] *adj. Chemistry.* of, having to do with, or being a polymer: *a polymeric compound.* ⟨< Gk. *polymerēs* < *polys* many + *meros* part⟩

po•lym•er•i•za•tion [pəˌlɪmərɪ'zeiʃən] *or* [pəˌlɪmərai'zeiʃən] *n. Chemistry.* the chemical union of many small, simple molecules into very large molecules to form a polymer. The molecules produced in polymerization contain repeating structural units of the simple molecules in the form of a chain or network.

po•lym•er•ize [pə'lɪməˌraɪz] *or* ['pɒləməˌraɪz] *v.* **-ized, -iz•ing.** *Chemistry.* **1** form into a polymer; make polymeric. **2** undergo polymerization.

pol•y•morph ['pɒliˌmɔrf] *n.* **1** *Zoology, botany.* a polymorphic organism. **2** *Chemistry.* **a** a substance able to crystallize in different forms. **b** any one of these forms.

pol•y•mor•phic [ˌpɒli'mɔrfɪk] *adj.* having, assuming, or passing through many or various forms, stages, etc.

pol•y•mor•phism [ˌpɒli'mɔrfɪzəm] *n.* **1** *Biology.* the occurrence of different forms or different colour types in one species. **2** *Chemistry.* the property of a compound of crystallizing in at least two distinct forms. **3** *Genetics.* the presence together in a population of two or more relatively common alleles of a specific gene.

pol•y•mor•phous [ˌpɒli'mɔrfəs] *adj.* polymorphic. ⟨< Gk. *polymorphos* < *polys* many + *morphē* form⟩
—ˌpol•y'mor•phous•ly, *adv.*

Pol•y•ne•sia [ˌpɒlə'niʒə] *or* [ˌpɒlə'niʃə] *n.* one of three divisions of Oceania, a group of islands bounded by New Zealand, Hawaii, and Easter Island.

Pol•y•ne•sian [ˌpɒlə'niʒən] *or* [ˌpɒlə'niʃən] *adj., n. —adj.* **1** of or designating a major cultural grouping that includes most of the peoples traditionally inhabiting Polynesia. The Polynesian grouping includes the Hawaiians, Maoris, Samoans, and Tahitians. **2** of or having to do with Polynesia, its peoples, or their languages.
—n. **1** a member of the Polynesian grouping. **2** a branch of the Malayo-Polynesian family of languages, including Hawaiian, Maori, etc.

pol•y•no•mi•al [ˌpɒli'noumiəl] *n., adj. —n.* **1** *Algebra.* an expression consisting of two or more terms. $ab + x^2y$ and $pq - p^2 + q$ are polynomials. Compare MONOMIAL. **2** *Biology.* a taxonomic name consisting of more than two terms, as for designating a subspecies.
—adj. consisting of two or more terms: *polynomial equations.* ⟨< *poly-* + *-nomial*, as in *binomial*⟩

pol•y•nu•cle•o•tide [ˌpɒli'njukliəˌtaɪd] *or* [ˌpɒli'nukliəˌtaɪd] *n. Genetics.* a sequence of many nucleotide units.

po•lyn•ya or **po•lyn•ia** [pə'lɪnjə] *n.* a fairly large area of open water surrounded by pack ice. ⟨< Russian⟩

pol•yp ['pɒlɪp] *n.* **1** *Zoology.* any of various small, simple water animals (of phylum Coelenterata) having a tubelike body that is closed at one end and has at the other end a mouthlike opening surrounded by tentacles for gathering in food. Polyps often grow in colonies, with their bases connected. Corals and sea anemones are polyps. **2** *Pathology.* a smooth, projecting growth arising from the surface of a mucous membrane. Also, **polypus**. ⟨< F < L < Gk. *polypous* < *polys* many + *pous* foot⟩

pol•y•pep•tide [ˌpɒli'pɛptaɪd] *or* [ˌpɒli'pɛptɪd] *n. Biochemistry.* a chain of amino acids forming a protein or part of a protein, joined together by peptide linkages and having a molecular mass of up to 10 000.

pol•y•pha•gia [ˌpɒli'feidʒiə] *n.* **1** *Pathology.* an excessive desire for food. **2** *Zoology.* the habit of eating or subsisting on many kinds of food. **—po'lyph•a•gous** [pə'lɪfəgəs], *adj.*

Pol•y•phe•mus [ˌpɒlə'fiməs] *n. Greek mythology.* in Homer's *Odyssey*, a Cyclops blinded by Odysseus.

polyphemus moth a large yellow-brown American silkworm moth (*Antheraea polyphemus*) having a prominent eyelike marking on each hind wing, and feeding on cherry, apple, and other trees.

pol•y•phon•ic [ˌpɒli'fɒnɪk] *adj.* **1** *Music.* of, having to do with, or characterized by polyphony: *polyphonic music.* **2** *Music.* of an instrument, capable of producing more than one tone at once, such as a piano. **3** producing many sounds; many-voiced. **4** *Phonetics.* representing more than one sound, as English *oo*, which represents [u] in *food* and [ʊ] in *good.*
—ˌpol•y'phon•i•cal•ly, *adv.*

po•lyph•o•ny [pə'lɪfəni] *n.* **1** *Music.* the combination of two or more independent melodies or musical parts so that they relate harmonically to each other; counterpoint. **2** a multiplicity of sounds. **3** *Phonetics.* the representation of more than one sound by the same letter or symbol. ⟨< Gk. *polyphōnia* < *polys* many + *phōnē* voice⟩

pol•y•ploid ['pɒlɪ,plɔɪd] *n. Genetics.* any multiple of the basic (haploid) chromosome number other than the normal diploid number.

pol•yp•ous ['pɒlɪpəs] *adj.* of or like a polyp. Also, **polypoid.**

pol•y•pro•pyl•ene [,pɒli'proupə,lin] *n. Chemistry.* a lightweight thermoplastic, similar to, but harder than, polyethylene, used for a wide variety of moulded articles, insulating materials, etc. It is a polymer of propylene. *Formula:* $(C_3H_6)_n$

pol•y•pus ['pɒlɪpəs] *n., pl.* **-pi** [-,paɪ] *or* [-,pi]. POLYP (def. 2).

pol•y•rhythm ['pɒli,rɪðəm] *n. Music.* **1** the simultaneous use of strongly contrasting rhythms within the same composition. **2** Usually, **polyrhythms,** *pl.* such rhythms. **—,pol•y'rhyth•mic,** *adj.* **—,pol•y'rhyth•mi•cal•ly,** *adv.*

pol•y•sac•cha•ride [,pɒli'sækə,raɪd] *or* [,pɒli'sækərɪd] *n. Chemistry.* any of a large group of natural carbohydrates, including starch, cellulose, and glycogen, whose molecules consist of two or more molecules of simple sugars linked together.

po•lys•e•my [pə'lɪsəmi] *n.* the fact or property of one word, having various meanings. The word *point* is a good example of polysemy. **—po'lys•e•mous,** *adj.*

pol•y•sty•rene [,pɒli'staɪrin] *n. Chemistry.* a synthetic organic polymer formed from styrene. It is a rigid, colourless, thermoplastic resin, resistant to acids, alkalis, and many solvents and having excellent insulating properties. Polystyrene is used as an insulator and for many moulded products such as dishes, toys, etc.

pol•y•sul•phide [,pɒli'sʌlfaɪd] *n. Chemistry.* a sulphide that contains two or more atoms of sulphur per molecule.

pol•y•syl•lab•ic [,pɒlɪsɪ'læbɪk] *adj.* **1** having three or more syllables. **2** of a style of writing or speaking, characterized by polysyllabic words. **—,pol•y•syl'lab•i•cal•ly,** *adv.*

pol•y•syl•la•ble ['pɒli,sɪləbəl] *n.* a word of three or more syllables.

pol•y•syn•the•sis [,pɒli'sɪnθəsɪs] *n., pl.* **-ses** [-,siz]. **1** the synthesis of several elements. **2** *Linguistics.* the combination of the subject, object, verb, and modifiers into one unit or expression whose elements have no separate existence as words, as in Inuktitut or certain First Nations languages. **—,pol•y•syn'thet•ic** [,pɒlɪsɪn'θɛtɪk], *adj.*

pol•y•tech•nic [,pɒli'tɛknɪk] *adj., n. —adj.* having to do with or giving instruction in many technical arts or applied sciences. *—n.* a polytechnic school. ⟨< F < Gk. *polytechnos* < *polys* many + *technē* art⟩

pol•y•the•ism ['pɒliθi,ɪzəm] *or* [,pɒli'θiɪzəm] *n.* belief in more than one god. The religion of the ancient Greeks was polytheism. ⟨< F *polythéisme,* ult. < Gk. *polys* many + *theos* god⟩ **—'pol•y•the•ist,** *n.* **—,pol•y•the'is•tic** or **,pol•y•the'is•ti•cal,** *adj.* **—,pol•y•the'is•ti•cal•ly,** *adv.*

pol•y•thene ['pɒlə,θin] *n.* polyethylene.

pol•y•ton•al [,pɒli'tounəl] *adj. Music.* using or having polytonality. **—pol•y'ton•al•ly,** *adv.*

pol•y•to•nal•i•ty [,pɒlitə'nælɪti] *n. Music.* **1** the use of several keys at the same time. **2** the sounds thus produced.

pol•y•un•sat•u•rate [,pɒliʌn'sætʃərɪt] *or* [,pɒliʌn'sætʃə,reit] *n.* any of a variety of polyunsaturated animal fats or vegetable oils. ⟨back formation from polyunsaturated⟩

pol•y•un•sat•u•rat•ed [,pɒliʌn'sætʃə,reitɪd] *adj.* having to do with or designating a class of vegetable and animal fats whose molecules consist of long carbon chains with many double bonds.

pol•y•ur•e•thane [,pɒli'jʊrə,θein] *n. Chemistry.* any of a group of synthetic organic polymers that may be rubbery, resinous, or fibrous. Polyurethanes are most often made in the form of flexible foams used for mattresses, cushions, etc. and rigid foams used for insulation, lightweight cores for aircraft wings, etc.

pol•y•va•lent [,pɒli'veilənt] *adj. Chemistry.* **1** having more than one valence. **2** *Bacteriology.* of a vaccine, effective against more than one micro-organism, toxin, etc. **—,pol•y'va•lence,** *adj.*

pol•y•vi•nyl [,pɒli'vaɪnəl] *adj. Chemistry.* of or having to do with a group of thermoplastic resins formed by the polymerization of vinyl.

polyvinyl chloride *Chemistry.* a colourless, synthetic thermoplastic material produced by the polymerization of vinyl chloride. It is widely used in a rigid form for moulded articles

and in a flexible form for tubing, electrical insulation, clothing, etc. *Abbrev.:* PVC

pol•y•wa•ter ['pɒli,wɒtər] *n. Chemistry.* a substance formerly mistakenly identified as a polymeric form of water, but now known to be water that contains ions of glass and quartz. Its boiling point is 1000°C.

pom•ace ['pʌmɪs] *n.* **1** apple pulp or similar fruit pulp before or after the juice has been pressed out. **2** the crushed matter that is left after the oil has been pressed out of fish, seeds, etc. ⟨ult. < Med.L *pomacium* cider < L *pomum* apple⟩
☛ *Hom.* PUMICE.

po•ma•ceous [pə'meiʃəs] *or* [pou'meiʃəs] *adj.* of, having to do with, bearing, or resembling apples or similar fruits. ⟨< NL *pomaceus* < L *pomum* apple⟩

po•made [pɒ'meid] *or* [pɒ'mɑd] *n.* a perfumed ointment for the scalp and hair. ⟨< F < Ital. *pomata* < L *pomum* fruit⟩

po•man•der ['poumændər] *or* [pə'mændər] *n.* **1** a ball of mixed aromatic substances formerly carried for perfume or as a guard against infection. **2** an orange or lemon studded with cloves. ⟨late ME *pomandre,* **pomambre* < Med.L *pomume ambre*⟩

pome [poum] *n.* an apple or any fruit like it; a fruit consisting of firm, juicy flesh surrounding a core that contains several seeds. Apples, pears, and quinces are pomes. See FRUIT for picture. ⟨ME < OF *pome,* ult. < L *pomum* apple⟩

Pomegranates. The one on the right is cut open showing the seeds.

pome•gran•ate ['pɒmə,grænɪt] *or* ['pɒm,grænɪt] *n.* **1** a fruit with a thick, leathery, red or brownish yellow skin, juicy red pulp, and many seeds. It has a pleasant tart taste. **2** the small tropical tree or bush (*Punica granatum*) that bears this fruit. ⟨ME < OF *pome grenate* < *pome* fruit (ult. < L *pomum*) + *grenate* having grains < L *granata,* fem. < *granum* grain⟩

pom•e•lo ['pɒməlou] *n.* **1** a large yellowish citrus fruit, similar to a grapefruit but sweeter. **2** the SE Asian tree it grows on (*Citrus maxima*). ⟨altered from Du. *pompelmoes* grapefruit⟩

Pom•er•a•nia [,pɒmə'reiniə] *n.* formerly a province of NE Germany on the Baltic Sea, now mainly in NW Poland.

Pom•er•a•ni•an [,pɒmə'reiniən] *n., adj. —n.* **1** a native or inhabitant of Pomerania. **2** a breed of small dog having a sharp nose, pointed ears, and long, thick, silky hair. *—adj.* of or having to do with Pomerania or its people.

pom•mel *n.* ['pɒməl] *or* ['pʌməl]; *v.* ['pʌməl] *n., v.* **-melled** or **-meled, -mel•ling** or **-mel•ing.** *—n.* **1** the part of a saddle that sticks up at the front. See SADDLE for picture. **2** a rounded knob on the hilt of a sword, dagger, etc. *—v.* pummel. ⟨ME < OF *pomel,* ult. < L *pomum* apple⟩ **—'pom•mel•ler** or **'pom•mel•er,** *n.*
☛ *Hom.* PUMMEL ['pʌməl].

pommel horse *Gymnastics.* a padded gymnastics horse, similar to a vaulting horse but with removable U-shaped handles, or pommels, on the top, used for gymnastic manoeuvres involving balancing, swinging, or rotating.

po•mol•o•gy [pou'mɒlədʒi] *n.* the science or practice of fruit growing. ⟨< NL *pomologia* < L *pomum* fruit + Gk. *-logos* treating of⟩ **—po'mol•o•gist,** *n.* **—po•mo'log•i•cal,** *adj.*

pomp [pɒmp] *n.* **1** a stately display; splendour; magnificence: *The king was crowned with great pomp.* **2** an excessively showy display. ⟨ME < OF < Gk. *pompē* parade⟩

pom•pa•dour ['pɒmpə,dɔr] *n.* **1** a woman's hairstyle in which the hair is puffed high over the forehead and turned under in a roll. **2** a man's hairstyle in which the hair is brushed straight up and back from the forehead. ⟨after Jeanne Antoinette Poisson,

Marquise de *Pompadour* (1721-1764), a mistress of Louis XV of France⟩

pom•pa•no ['pɒmpə,nou] *n., pl.* **-nos** or (*esp. collectively*) **-no.** **1** a saltwater food fish (*Trachinotus carolinus*) of the West Indies and neighbouring coasts of North America, having a deep body, no teeth, and a forked tail. **2** any of several related fishes. ⟨< Sp.⟩

Pom•pei•an [pɒm'peiən] *n., adj.* *—n.* a native or inhabitant of Pompeii, a city in ancient Italy.
—adj. of or having to do with Pompeii or its people.

Pom•peii [pɒm'peii] *or* [pɒm'pei] *n.* a city in ancient Italy, buried by an eruption of Mount Vesuvius in A.D. 79. Its ruins have been partly laid bare by excavation.

pom•pom ['pɒm,pɒm] *n.* **1** an ornamental ball or tuft of yarn, feathers, etc., used especially on clothing, hats, shoes, etc. **2** any of several varieties of chrysanthemum or dahlia having small, rounded flower heads. ⟨< F *pompon* < *pompe* pomp⟩
☛ *Hom.* POM-POM.

pom–pom ['pɒm ,pɒm] *n.* an automatic anti-aircraft gun, used especially on shipboard. ⟨imitative⟩
☛ *Hom.* POMPOM.

pom•pon ['pɒm,pɒn] *n.* **1** pompom. **2** *Horticulture.* a form of small round flower head characteristic of certain flowers such as chrysanthemums or dahlias.

pom•pos•i•ty [pɒm'pɒsəti] *n., pl.* **-ties. 1** the quality of being pompous; pompous behaviour, speech, etc.: *He is a good speaker, except for his tendency toward pomposity.* **2** a pompous act, gesture, remark, etc.

pom•pous ['pɒmpəs] *adj.* **1** having or showing a tendency to display oneself in an overly grand or self-important way: *a pompous speech. The band leader bowed in a pompous way.* **2** marked by pomp; splendid; magnificent. **3** of language, ostentatiously flowery or high-flown. ⟨< F *pompeux* < LL *pomposus*⟩ **—'pom•pous•ly,** *adv.* **—'pom•pous•ness,** *n.*

Pon•ca ['pɒŋkə] *n.* **1** a member of a Native American people living in Oklahoma and Nebraska. **2** the Siouan language of these people.

pon•cho ['pɒntʃou] *n., pl.* **-chos. 1** a cloak consisting basically of a large piece of cloth with a slit or hole in the middle for the head to go through, worn especially in Latin America. **2** a similar garment, especially one that is waterproof, worn by cyclists, hikers, etc. as a raincoat. ⟨< Sp. < Araucanian (S.Am.Ind.) *pontho*⟩

pond [pɒnd] *n.* **1** a body of still water, smaller than a lake. **2** *Cdn., esp. Nfld.* a lake. **3** *Cdn. Logging.* an expanse of quiet water where logs, often retained by a boom, are penned till needed. ⟨originally, var. of *pound*[3]⟩

pon•der ['pɒndər] *v.* consider carefully; think over; meditate. ⟨ME < OF < L *ponderare* weigh < *pondus, -deris* weight⟩ **—'pon•der•er,** *n.* **—'pon•der•ing•ly,** *adv.*

pon•der•a•ble ['pɒndərəbəl] *adj.* **1** capable of being evaluated, or mentally weighed. **2** capable of being weighed; having perceptible mass. **—,pon•der•a'bil•i•ty** [,pɒndərə'bɪləti], *n.*

pon•de•ro•sa pine [,pɒndə'rousə] **1** a large pine (*Pinus ponderosa*) found from southern British Columbia to California, usually 25 m to 30 m tall but sometimes reaching a height of about 50 m, having very long needles and large cones with prickles; YELLOW PINE. The ponderosa pine is one of the main timber-producing trees of W North America. **2** its yellowish wood. ⟨< L, fem. of *ponderosus* heavy. See PONDEROUS.⟩

pon•der•ous ['pɒndərəs] *adj.* **1** very heavy. **2** heavy and clumsy: *Slowly he lifted his ponderous bulk from the chair.* **3** overly serious and laboured: *a ponderous way of speaking.* ⟨ME < OF < L *ponderosus* < *pondus, -deris* weight⟩ **—'pon•der•ous•ly,** *adv.* **—'pon•der•ous•ness** or **,pon•der'os•i•ty** [,pɒndə'rɒsɪti], *n.*

pond hockey *Cdn.* **1** unorganized hockey played on frozen ponds, streams, etc. **2** *Slang.* poorly played hockey; hockey of a low standard.

pond lily WATER LILY.

pond scum free-floating freshwater algae that form a green scum on water.

pond•weed ['pɒnd,wid] *n.* any of a genus (*Potamogeton*) of aquatic plants found in ponds and slow streams, with some species occurring in brackish water, having jointed stems and, in many species, broad floating leaves and grasslike submerged leaves. Some species are entirely submerged.

pon•gee [pɒn'dʒi] *or* ['pɒndʒi] *n.* **1** a kind of soft, plain-woven silk, usually left in its natural brownish yellow colour. **2** any similar cloth, often made of cotton or rayon. ⟨< Mandarin Chinese *panchi* made at home⟩

pon•iard ['pɒnjərd] *n., v.* *—n.* dagger.
—v. stab with a poniard. ⟨< F *poignard*, ult. < L *pugnus* fist⟩

pons asinorum [,pɒnz ,æsɪ'nɔrəm] **1** *Geometry.* a proposition from the first book of Euclid, that if two sides of a triangle are equal, the angles opposite those sides are also equal. **2** any problem difficult for beginners to master. ⟨< L, bridge of asses⟩

pon•ti•fex ['pɒntə,fɛks] *n., pl.* **pon•tif•i•ces.** [pɒn'tɪfə,siz]. **1** in ancient Rome, a member of the principal college of priests. **2** pontiff. ⟨< L, a high priest of Rome, probably < *pons, pontis* bridge + *facere* make. Doublet of PONTIFF.⟩

pon•tiff ['pɒntɪf] *n.* **1** the Pope. **2** a bishop. **3** a high priest; chief priest. **4 Supreme Pontiff,** the Pope. ⟨< F *pontife* < L *pontifex* a high priest of Rome. Doublet of PONTIFEX.⟩

pon•tif•i•cal [pɒn'tɪfɪkəl] *adj., n.* *—adj.* **1** of or having to do with the Pope; papal. **2** of or having to do with a bishop. **3** pompous or dogmatic.
—n. Usually, **pontificals,** *pl.* the vestments and marks of dignity used by cardinals and bishops at certain ecclesiastical functions or ceremonies. **—pon'tif•i•cal•ly,** *adv.*

Pontifical Zouave a member of a force of volunteers from various countries, including Canada, recruited to fight for the Holy See in the 19th century when the independence of the Vatican was threatened by Piedmont. See also ZOUAVE.

pon•tif•i•cate *n.* [pɒn'tɪfəkɪt] *or* [pɒn'tɪfə,keit]; *v.* [pɒn'tɪfə,keit] *n., v.* **-cat•ed, -cat•ing.** *—n.* the office or term of office of a pontiff.
—v. **1** officiate as a pontiff, especially at Mass. **2** speak dogmatically and pompously: *Their parents loved to pontificate on the virtues of thrift.*

pon•tif•i•ces [pɒn'tɪfə,siz] *n.* pl. of PONTIFEX.

pon•til ['pɒntɪl] *n.* a steel or iron rod used as a glass blower's tool. Also called **pontil rod, punty.** ⟨< F *pontil* < Ital. *pontello*, diminutive < *punto* < L *punctum* a point⟩

pon•toon [pɒn'tun] *n.* **1** a low, flatbottomed boat. **2** such a boat, or some other floating structure, used as one of the supports of a temporary bridge. **3** a boat-shaped float on an aircraft, used for coming down on or taking off from water. ⟨< F *ponton* < L *ponto, -onis* < *pons, pontis* bridge⟩

pontoon bridge a temporary bridge supported by pontoons or other floating structures.

Pon•tus ['pɒntəs] *n.* an ancient country in NE Asia Minor, just south of the Black Sea. It became a Roman province. ⟨< L < Gk. *Pontos* Black Sea⟩

pon•y ['pouni] *n., pl.* **-nies;** *v.* *—n.* **1** a small horse, especially any of several breeds of very small, stocky, gentle horses, usually less than 130 cm high. **2** *Informal.* something that is small for its kind, especially a small liqueur glass or the amount it will hold. **3** *Slang.* a racehorse. **4** a literal translation of a text, especially such a translation of a Latin or other text used dishonestly by students in preparing or reciting lessons.
—v.
pony up, *Slang.* settle an account. ⟨< obs. F *poulenet*, ult. < L *pullus* foal⟩

pony express *U.S.* formerly, a system of carrying mail, etc. by riders on fast ponies or horses.

po•ny•tail ['pouni,teil] *n.* a hairstyle in which the main length is pulled back and held tightly against the head with a ribbon, elastic band, etc., the lock flowing free like a pony's tail.

pooch [putʃ] *n. Slang.* dog. ⟨origin uncertain⟩

pood [pud] *n.* a Russian unit for measuring mass, equal to about 16.4 kg. ⟨< Russian, ult. < L *pondus* weight⟩

poo•dle ['pudəl] *n.* a breed of intelligent, active dog having thick, curly, wool-like hair that is not shed and that is often clipped in any of several standard patterns. ⟨< G *Pudel*, short for *Pudelhund* < dial. *pudeln* splash water⟩ **—'poo•dle,like,** *adj.*

A poodle

poof [puf] *or* [pʊf] *n., interj.* *—n.* a sound resembling the puff of breath in blowing out a candle.
—interj. **1** an exclamation suggesting sudden or magical appearance, disappearance, or

transformation. **2** an expression of rejection or contempt. Also, **pouf.** ⟨imitative⟩

pooh [pu] *interj. or n.* an exclamation of contempt.

Pooh–Bah ['pu 'bɑ] *or* ['pu ˌbɑ] *n.* **1** a self-important, pompous person. **2** a person holding many insignificant offices. ⟨< *Pooh-Bah*, a character in Gilbert and Sullivan's *The Mikado*⟩

pooh–pooh ['pu 'pu] *v., interj.* —*v.* express contempt for; make light of.
—*interj.* an exclamation of contempt.

pool[1] [pul] *n.* **1** a small body of still water; a small pond. **2** a still, deep place in a stream: *Trout are often found in the pools of a brook.* **3** a large puddle of water or any other liquid: *There was a pool of grease under the car. The water stood in pools in the garden after the rain.* **4** a large tank made of concrete, plastic, etc., for swimming or bathing in; SWIMMING POOL. **5** a natural underground body of oil or gas, held in porous and permeable sedimentary rock. ⟨OE *pōl*⟩

pool[2] [pul] *n., v.* —*n.* **1** a game played on a billiard table with six pockets, using a cue ball and fifteen other numbered balls. The players try to drive the numbered balls into the pockets using cues and the cue ball. Compare SNOOKER. **2** the things or money put together by different persons for common advantage. **3** *Cdn.* in the West, a co-operative grain marketing organization among farmers. **4** a group of people, usually having the same skills, who are drawn upon as needed: *a secretarial pool.* **5** an arrangement between business firms to create a monopoly in order to control prices. **6** CAR POOL. **7** a fund raised by a group of persons for purposes of speculation, as in the stock market, commodities, etc. **8** the persons who form a pool. **9** the stake played for in some games. **10** the combined total of wagers of a group of betters.
—*v.* **1** put (things or money) together for common advantage: *The three students pooled their savings for a year to buy a boat.* **2** form a pool. ⟨< F *poule* booty, originally, hen < LL *pulla* chick; meaning influenced by *pool*[1]⟩

pool hall an establishment whose main attraction is a poolroom.

pool•room ['pul,rum] *or* ['pul,rʊm] *n.* a room or place in which the game of pool is played.

pool table a billiard table, having the usual six pockets but smaller than the standard table used for billiards or snooker.

pool train *Cdn.* formerly, a train operated over a line of track by more than one railway company. A pool train used to run between Toronto and Ottawa on CNR tracks as far as Brockville and on CPR tracks from there to Ottawa.

poop[1] [pup] *n., v.* —*n.* **1** a deck at the stern of a ship above the ordinary deck, often forming the roof of a cabin. Also, **poop deck.** **2** *Archaic.* the stern of a ship.
—*v.* of a wave, break over the stern of (a ship). ⟨late ME *pouppe* < MF < Ital. *poppa* < L *puppis* stern⟩

poop[2] [pup] *v. Slang.* make exhausted (*often used with* **out**): *All of us were pooped after the climb. That last dance pooped me out.* ⟨origin unknown⟩

poop[3] [pup] *n. Slang.* relevant or pertinent facts, especially the most recent or current inside information. ⟨by back formation from *poop sheet*⟩

poop[4] [pup] *n., v. Slang.* waste matter; feces; manure.
—*v.* defecate.

poop sheet *Slang.* a circular, press release, etc., containing a concise list of information about a particular subject.

poor [pur] *adj., n.* —*adj.* **1** not having enough income to maintain a standard of living regarded as normal in the community in which one lives: *They were poor, but never destitute.* **2** not good in quality; lacking something needed: *poor soil, a poor crop, a poor cook, poor health.* **3** scanty. **4** needing pity; unfortunate: *This poor child has been hurt.* **5** not favourable: *a poor chance for recovery.*
—*n.* **the poor,** (*used with a plural verb*) poor persons collectively. ⟨ME < OF *povre* < L *pauper.* Doublet of PAUPER.⟩
—**'poor•ness,** *n.*

☛ *Syn. adj.* **1. Poor,** PENNILESS, IMPOVERISHED = with little or no money or property. **Poor** has a rather wide range of meaning, from 'having no money or property at all and being dependent on charity for the necessities of life', to 'having no money to buy comforts or luxuries': *She is a poor widow.* **Penniless** suggests being without any money at all, but sometimes only temporarily: *He found himself penniless in a strange city.* **Impoverished** emphasizes being reduced to poverty from comfortable circumstances, even wealth: *The deposed king died alone and impoverished.*

poor box a box, usually in a church, into which donations for the assistance of the poor can be put.

poor•house ['pur,hʌus] *n.* formerly, a place in which paupers lived at public expense.

poor law formerly, a law providing for or regulating the relief or support of the poor through public funds.

poor•ly ['purli] *adv., adj.* —*adv.* in a poor manner; badly or inadequately.
—*adj. Informal.* in bad health; somewhat ill: *I feel poorly today.*

poor–mouth ['pur ˌmʌuθ] *n., v.* —*n.* a person who continually pleads poverty, often as an excuse for not paying bills, returning hospitality, etc.
—*v.* plead poverty; complain about lack of funds.

poor–spir•it•ed ['pur ˌspɪrɪtɪd] *adj.* having or showing a poor, cowardly, or abject spirit.

poor•will ['purwɪl] *n.* a small goatsucker (*Phalaenoptilus nuttalli*) of W North America having a short, rounded tail, mottled grey plumage, and bristles on the sides of its mouth. ⟨imitative⟩

pop[1] [pɒp] *v.* **popped, pop•ping;** *n., adv.* —*v.* **1** make a short, quick, explosive sound. **2** move, go, or come suddenly or unexpectedly. **3** thrust or put suddenly: *He popped a candy into his mouth.* **4** put (a question) suddenly. **5** *Informal.* shoot with a gun. **6** burst open with a pop. **7** heat or roast (popcorn) until it bursts with a pop. **8** of the eyes, bulge or open very wide: *The surprise made her eyes pop.* **9** *Baseball.* hit a short, high ball over the infield. **10** *Slang.* take (a drug or drugs) habitually, especially in pill form: *He used to pop a lot of pills.*
pop off, *Slang.* **a** fall asleep. **b** die. **c** complain or protest loudly and angrily. **d** leave quickly: *I must pop off now.*
pop the question, *Informal.* propose marriage.
—*n.* **1** a short, quick, explosive sound. **2** a gunshot. **3** *Esp. Cdn.* a non-alcoholic carbonated drink. **4** *Baseball.* a fly ball that can be easily caught. **5** *Slang.* attempt: *She got it on the first pop.*
a pop, each; per person: *Admission is $5 a pop.*
—*adv.* with a pop; suddenly. ⟨imitative⟩

pop[2] [pɒp] *adj., n. Slang.* —*adj.* aimed at or supposedly reflecting the tastes of the general population: *pop psychology.*
—*n.* **1** popular music. **2** POP ART.

pop[3] [pɒp] *n. Informal.* papa; father.

pop. **1** population. **2** popular.

pop art an art style, especially in painting and sculpture, based on that of advertising art, comic strips, etc. and using commonplace objects such as hamburgers or soup cans as subject matter.

pop•corn ['pɒp,kɔrn] *n.* **1** a variety of corn whose kernels burst open and puff out in a white mass when heated. Also called **popping corn.** **2** the white, puffed-out kernels, usually eaten salted and buttered.

Pope or **pope** [poup] *n.* **1** the supreme head of the Roman Catholic Church: *the Pope, the last three popes.* **2** a person having or behaving as if he had papal authority. **3 a** the Orthodox patriarch of Alexandria. **b** the Coptic patriarch of Alexandria. **c** in some Christian churches, a parish priest. ⟨OE *pāpa* < LL *papa* pope < L *papa* tutor, bishop < Gk. *pap(p)as* father⟩

pop•eye ['pɒp,aɪ] *n.* a prominent or bulging eye. —**'pop,eyed,** *adj.*

pop•gun ['pɒp,gʌn] *n.* a toy gun that shoots harmless pellets or a cork attached to the gun by a string, with a popping sound.

pop•in•jay ['pɒpɪn,dʒei] *n.* a vain, overtalkative person; conceited, silly person. ⟨ME < OF *papingay* parrot < Sp.; cf. Arabic *babaghā*⟩

pop•lar ['pɒplər] *n.* **1** any of a genus (*Populus*) of slender, fast-growing trees found mainly in north temperate regions, having oval or heart-shaped leaves, flowers in drooping catkins, and light, soft wood. **2** the wood of a poplar. Poplar is used for veneer, boxes, barrels, etc. ⟨ME < OF *poplier* < L *populus*⟩

poplar bluff *Cdn.* BLUFF[1] (def. 2).

pop•lin ['pɒplən] *n.* a strong, plain-woven fabric with a crosswise rib, used for sportswear, raincoats, etc. ⟨< F < Ital. *papalina*, fem., papal, perhaps from the one-time papal capital Avignon, France, where the fabric was first made⟩

pop•o•ver ['pɒp,ouvər] *n.* a very light and hollow muffin.

pop•per ['pɒpər] *n.* a person or thing that pops, especially a wire basket, metal pan or pot, or electrical appliance used for popping popcorn.
☛ *Hom.* PAUPER.

pop•pet ['pɒpɪt] *n.* **1** *Machinery.* a valve that controls the flow of water, gas, etc. by moving straight up and down instead of being hinged. **2** *Nautical.* **a** one of the small pieces of wood on the gunwale of a boat forming the rowlocks. **b** a timber placed beneath a ship's hull to support the ship in launching. **3** a bead that can be attached to other beads by a snap coupling to form a chain. Poppets are used especially to make necklaces, bracelets, etc. that are adjustable in length. **4** a small or dainty person, especially a pretty child, girl, etc.; pet. ⟨var. of *puppet*⟩

popping crease ['pɒpɪŋ] *Cricket.* a line in front of and parallel to the bowling crease, marking the limit to which a batsman may advance.

pop•py ['pɒpi] *n., pl.* **-pies;** *adj. —n.* **1** any of a genus (*Papaver*) of annual, perennial, or biennial plants having lobed leaves, a milky sap, showy flowers, and seeds in a capsule. Opium is made from the juice in the seed capsule of one species of poppy; other species are cultivated as garden plants. **2** the flower of a poppy. **3** a bright orange red.
—adj. **1** bright orange red. **2** designating a family (Papaveraceae) of plants having large, showy flowers, that includes the poppies and celandine. ⟨OE *popæg, papig,* ult. < L *papaver*⟩

pop•py•cock ['pɒpi,kɒk] *n. or interj. Informal.* nonsense; bosh. ⟨< Du. *pappekak* soft dung⟩

pop•py•seed ['pɒpi,sid] *n.* the very small, black seed of the poppy plant, used in baking or as a topping on breads, rolls, etc., and as a flavouring in salad dressings, sauces, etc.

pops[1] [pɒps] *adj., n. —adj.* of or in reference to a symphony orchestra that plays mainly light classics, music from popular stage shows or movies, etc., or to a concert featuring such music.
—n. a pops orchestra, concert, or series: *We have season tickets for the pops this year.*

pops[2] [pɒps] *n.* POP[3].

Pop•si•cle ['pɒpsɪkəl] *n. Trademark.* fruit-flavoured ice on a small stick.

pop•u•lace ['pɒpjəlɪs] *n.* the people in general; the masses. ⟨< F < Ital. *popolaccio,* ult. < L *populus* people⟩

pop•u•lar ['pɒpjələr] *adj.* **1** liked by most acquaintances or associates: *He was always popular with his co-workers.* **2** liked by a great many people: *The song quickly became popular.*
3 intended to appeal to the current tastes of the general public: *popular music, popular science.* **4** within the means of the average person: *popular prices.* **5** of or by the people; representing the people: *Canada has a popular government.* **6** widespread among many people; of people in general: *It is a popular belief that black cats bring bad luck.* ⟨< L *popularis* < *populus* people⟩
☛ *Syn.* **3, 6.** See note at GENERAL.

popular front or **Popular Front** a coalition of Communist, socialist, and moderate political parties against fascism in the 1930s, especially in France.

pop•u•lar•i•ty [,pɒpjə'lærɪti] *or* [,pɒpjə'lɛrɪti] *n.* the quality or state of being liked by most people.

pop•u•lar•ize ['pɒpjələ,raɪz] *v.* **-ized, -iz•ing. 1** change, especially by simplifying and presenting in an interesting form, so as to appeal to a great number of people instead of a special group: *to popularize the sciences.* **2** cause to be generally known and liked: *to popularize a tune.* **—,pop•u•lar•i'za•tion,** *n.* **—'pop•u•lar,iz•er,** *n.*

pop•u•lar•ly ['pɒpjələrli] *adv.* **1** by the people as a whole or in general: *The defendant was popularly believed to have been guilty, though she was acquitted.* **2** in a popular manner.

popular vote 1 the number of votes cast as opposed to seats won. **2** *U.S.* a vote by the qualified electorate as opposed to the electoral college.

pop•u•late ['pɒpjə,leit] *v.* **-lat•ed, -lat•ing. 1** inhabit: *This city is densely populated.* **2** furnish with inhabitants: *Europeans populated much of the Canadian West.* ⟨< Med.L *populare,* ult. < L *populus* people⟩

pop•u•la•tion [,pɒpjə'leiʃən] *n.* **1** the people of a city or a country: *The population was up in arms.* **2** the total number of such people. **3** a part of the inhabitants distinguished in any way from the rest: *the urban population, the Inuit population.* **4** the act or process of furnishing with inhabitants. **5** the total number of organisms of a specific kind in a given area: *the caribou population of the North.* **6** the total number of individuals or things from which samples are taken for statistical measurement.

population explosion a great and rapid increase in a population.

population genetics the study of genes in populations.

pop•u•lism ['pɒpjə,lɪzəm] *n.* a political movement supporting or appealing to the interests of ordinary people, or that section of society having little or no personal power or influence. ⟨< L *populus* people + E *-ism*⟩ **—'pop•u•list,** *n., adj.*

pop•u•lous ['pɒpjələs] *adj.* heavily populated; inhabited by many people: *a populous region.* ⟨ME < L *populosus* < *populus* people⟩ **—'pop•u•lous•ly,** *adv.* **—'pop•u•lous•ness,** *n.*

pop–up ['pɒp ʌp] *n., adj. —n.* **1 a** a folding picture having parts that stand up or out when it is unfolded, giving a three-dimensional effect. **b** any of these parts. **2** a book containing such pictures. **3** (*adjl.*) being or containing a pop-up or pop-ups.
—adj. characterized by a mechanical feature that automatically raises something at the proper time: *a pop-up toaster, a pop-up camera flash.*

por•bea•gle ['pɔr,bigəl] *n.* a large, voracious, viviparous and partly warm-blooded shark (*Lamna nasus*) of the North Atlantic and North Pacific Oceans. ⟨< Cornish *porgh-bugel*⟩

por•ce•lain ['pɔrsəlɪn] *n.* **1** a hard, white, translucent pottery fired at very high temperatures, consisting basically of kaolin, a fine, white clay that melts only at a very high temperature, quartz, and feldspar. Compare EARTHENWARE, STONEWARE.
2 articles made of porcelain: *We packed all the porcelain ourselves.* **3** (*adjl.*) made of porcelain. ⟨< F < Ital. *porcellana,* a kind of shell, ult. < L *porcus* hog; from the shell being shaped like a pig's back⟩

por•ce•lain•ize ['pɔrsələ,naɪz] *v.* **-ized, -iz•ing.** make into or coat with a substance resembling porcelain.
—,por•ce•lain•i'za•tion, *n.*

porch [pɔrtʃ] *n.* **1** a covered, sometimes enclosed, entrance to a building. **2** veranda. **3** a platform at the entrance to a house; stoop. **4** a SUN PORCH. ⟨ME < OF *porche* < L *porticus.* Doublet of PORTICO.⟩

por•cine ['pɔrsaɪn] *or* ['pɔrsən] *adj.* of, having to do with, or like pigs. ⟨< L *porcinus* < *porcus* pig⟩

por•cu•pine ['pɔrkjə,paɪn] *n.* any of a number of large, heavyset, short-legged rodents having long, sharp, barbed spines mixed in with the coarse hair of the back and tail. Porcupines make up two families: the New World family (Erethizontidae) of tree-dwelling porcupines and the Old World family (Hystricidae) of ground-dwelling porcupines. ⟨ME < OF *porc-espin,* ult. < L *porcus* pig + *spina* thorn⟩

porcupine fish any of various marine fishes (family Diodontidae, especially genus *Diodon*) having a spine-covered body that the fish can inflate into a ball as a means of defence when disturbed. Porcupine fish belong to the same order as the puffers.

pore[1] [pɔr] *v.* **pored, por•ing. 1** study long and steadily (*used with* **over**): *The historian pored over the magnificent old book for hours.* **2** meditate or ponder intently (*used with* **over**): *to pore over a problem.* **3** *Archaic.* gaze earnestly or steadily. ⟨origin uncertain⟩ **—'por•er,** *n.*
☛ *Hom.* POUR.

pore[2] [pɔr] *n.* a very tiny opening through which fluids may pass; especially, one of the openings in the skin of people or animals or in the leaves of plants through which fluids are absorbed or excreted. Sweat comes through the pores of our skin. See EPIDERMIS for picture. ⟨ME < OF < L < Gk. *poros,* literally, passage⟩ **—'pore,like,** *adj.*
☛ *Hom.* POUR.

por•gy ['pɔrgi] *n., pl.* **-gies** or (*esp. collectively*) **-gy. 1** any of various marine fishes (family Sparidae) found mainly in tropical and subtropical coastal waters, having a deep, compressed body with a single, long dorsal fin and a small mouth with strong teeth. **2** any of a variety of other similar fishes such as the menhaden. ⟨prob. altered form of Sp. or Pg. *pargo,* ult. < Gk. *phagros* sea bream⟩

po•rif•er•ous [pə'rɪfərəs] *adj.* **1** having pores. **2** *Zoology.* of or having to do with sponges, or **poriferans.**

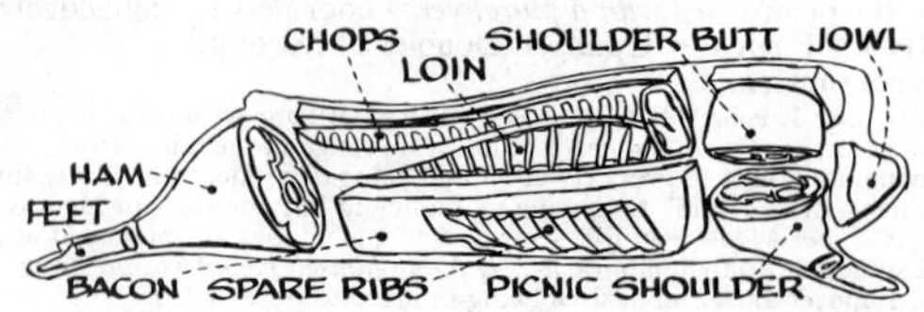

The main cuts of pork

pork [pɔrk] *n.* **1** the flesh of a pig, used for food. **2** *Slang.*

money from federal or provincial appropriations, taxes, licences, etc. spent to confer local benefits for political reasons. ⟨ME *porc* < OF < L *porcus* pig⟩

pork and beans canned haricot beans with pieces of salt pork, popular among campers.

pork barrel *Slang.* a term used to describe government appropriations for projects that may not be needed but are likely to appeal to certain constituents. **—'pork-ˌbar•rel,** *adj.*

pork duck *Cdn.* the common goldeneye (*Bucephila clangula*).

pork•er ['pɔrkər] *n.* a pig, especially one fattened to eat.

pork pie tourtière.

pork•pie ['pɔrk,pai] *n.* a hat having a low, flat crown resembling a pork pie.

pork•y ['pɔrki] *adj.* **1** of or like pork. **2** fat.

porn [pɔrn] *n., adj. —n.* pornography.
—adj. pornographic: *a porn movie*. Also, **porno.** ⟨shortened from *pornography, pornographic*⟩

por•nog•ra•pher [pɔr'nɒgrəfər] *n.* a person who produces pornography.

por•nog•ra•phy [pɔr'nɒgrəfi] *n.* writings, pictures, films, etc. gratuitously depicting nudity and sexual activity, especially when connected with violence and abuse. ⟨ult. < Gk. *pornē* harlot + *-graphos* writing about⟩ **—ˌpor•no'graph•ic** [ˌpɔrnə'græfɪk], *adj.* **—ˌpor•no'graph•i•cal•ly,** *adv.*

po•rous ['pɔrəs] *adj.* full of pores or tiny holes; permeable by water, air, etc. Cloth, blotting paper, and ordinary clay flowerpots are porous. **—'po•rous•ness** or **po'ros•i•ty** [pə'rɒsɪti], *n.*

por•phy•ria [pɔr'firiə] *or* [pɔr'faɪriə] *n. Pathology.* a genetic defect of blood pigment metabolism involving the presence of excess porphyrins in the blood and their excretion in the urine, as well as a dangerous sensitivity to sunlight.

por•phy•rin ['pɔrfərɪn] *n. Biochemistry.* a dark red, photosensitive pigment, a derivative of pyrrole and a component with iron and magnesium of heme and chlorophyl respectively. ⟨< Gk. *porphyra* purple⟩

por•phy•ry ['pɔrfəri] *n., pl.* **-ries. 1** a hard rock quarried in ancient Egypt, consisting of white or red feldspar crystals embedded in a fine-grained, dark red or purplish base. **2** any igneous rock in which crystals are scattered through a mass of fine-grained minerals. ⟨< F *porfire*, ult. < Gk. *porphyra* purple⟩

por•poise ['pɔrpəs] *n., pl.* **-pois•es** or (*esp. collectively*) **-poise;** *v.* **por•poised, por•pois•ing. 1** any of several small toothed whales (constituting genera *Phocaena, Phocaenoides*, and *Neomeris*) allied to the dolphins but smaller and having a blunt snout and flattened, spade-shaped teeth. Many authorities classify porpoises as forming a separate family (Phocaenidae), but others classify them in the same family (Delphinidae) as the dolphins, killer whale, etc. **2** DOLPHIN (def. 1).
—v. **1** move forward with an up-and-down motion, as a porpoise does. **2** of a motorboat, leap clear of the water after striking a wave at fast speed. ⟨ME < OF *porpeis*, ult. < L *porcus* hog + *piscis* fish⟩

por•ridge ['pɔrɪdʒ] *n.* a breakfast food made of oatmeal or other cereal boiled in water or milk until it thickens. ⟨var. of *pottage*⟩

por•rin•ger ['pɔrɪndʒər] *n.* a small dish, often having a handle, used for soup, porridge, etc. ⟨earlier *pottanger*, alteration of *potager* < OF *potager* < *potage.* See POTTAGE.⟩

Por•sild spruce ['pɔrsɪld] a variety of white spruce tree (*Picea glauca porsildii*) having smooth bark with resin blisters.

port[1] [pɔrt] *n.* **1** a harbour; a place where ships and boats can take shelter from storms. **2** a city or town with a harbour where ships and boats may take on or unload cargo. **3** See PORT OF ENTRY. **4** any place where one can find shelter. ⟨OE < L *portus*⟩
☛ *Syn.* **1.** See note at HARBOUR.

port[2] [pɔrt] *n.* **1** an opening in the side of a ship for letting in light and air; porthole. **2** an opening in a wall, ship's side, etc. through which guns may be fired. **3** the cover for such an opening. **4** an opening in machinery for steam, air, water, etc. to pass through. **5** *Curling. Lawn bowling.* an opening between stones or woods, large enough for another stone or wood to pass through. **6** *Electronics.* a point at which signals, energy, etc. enter or leave an electronic device. **7** *Computer technology.* a receptacle on a computer to which a communications cable can be connected. **8** *Archaic.* a gate or portal. ⟨< L *porta* gate⟩

port[3] [pɔrt] *n., adj., v. Nautical. —n.* the left side of a ship or aircraft when facing forward.
—adj. on the left side of a ship.
—v. turn or shift to the left side (*used mainly as a command*). Compare STARBOARD. ⟨< the docking in port toward the left side of the ship, as the steering oar prevented docking with the right side to the landing⟩

port[4] [pɔrt] *n., v. —n.* **1** a way of holding one's head and body; bearing. **2** the position of a weapon when ported.
—v. bring, hold, or carry (a rifle or sword) across and close to the body with the barrel or blade near the left shoulder. ⟨< F *port* < *porter* carry < L *portare*⟩

port[5] [pɔrt] *n.* a strong, sweet fortified wine that is usually ruby red or tawny, occasionally white. ⟨< *Oporto*, a city in Portugal⟩

port•a•ble ['pɔrtəbəl] *adj., n. —adj.* **1** capable of being carried by hand or readily moved about: *a portable typewriter.* **2** usable anywhere because it is run by its own batteries: *a portable TV set.* **3** capable of being transferred: *a portable pension.*
—n. **1** a portable radio, phonograph, etc. **2** a temporary building on the grounds of an overcrowded school, used as an extra classroom. ⟨< LL *portabilis* < L *portare* carry⟩ **—ˌport•a'bil•i•ty** [ˌpɔrtə'bɪlɪti], *n.*

portable pension a pension plan under which, if an employee changes jobs, pension contributions and entitlements continue unchanged.

por•tage *n. defs. 1-3, v.* [pɔr'tɑʒ]; *n. 4* ['pɔrtɪdʒ] *n., v.* **-taged, -tag•ing.**
—n. **1** the act of carrying boats, canoes, provisions, etc. overland from one stretch of water to another. **2** a place where such a carrying takes place. **3** an instance of such a carrying: *They made the trip without a single portage.* **4** the act or cost of transporting or carrying.
—v. **1** make a portage. **2** carry (a canoe, etc.) from one stretch of water to another; ⟨ME < OF *portage* < *porter* carry⟩

por•tal ['pɔrtəl] *n., adj. —n.* a door, gate, or entrance, especially an imposing one.
—adj. Anatomy. of or having to do with the large vein that carries blood from the intestines and stomach to the liver. ⟨< Med.L *portale* < L *porta* gate⟩

portal–to–portal pay ['pɔrtəl tə 'pɔrtəl] wages paid to an employee for the total time spent on the grounds or premises of the employer from the time of arrival to the time of leaving.

por•ta•men•to [ˌpɔrtə'mɛntou] *n., pl.* **-ti** [-ti]. *Music.* a smooth, legato movement gliding from one note or pitch to another without a break. ⟨< Ital. *portamento* < L *portare* carry⟩

port authority a commission federally appointed to manage a port.

port•cul•lis [pɔrt'kʌlɪs] *n.* a strong gate or grating of iron sliding up and down in grooves, used to close the gateway of a castle or fortress. ⟨ME < OF *porte coleice* sliding gate, ult. < L *porta* gate + *colare* filter through⟩

port de bras [ˌpɔr də 'brɑ]; *French,* [pɔʀdə'bʀa] *Ballet.* **1** the position of the arms. **2** the technique of moving the arms properly. **3** the exercises for developing this technique. ⟨< F⟩

Port du Salut ['pɔr də sæ'lu] *or* [sə'lu], ['pɔrt sæ'lu] *or* [sə'lu]; *French,* [pɔʀdysa'ly] a creamy, off-white cheese with a pale brown crust, originally made in a monastery at Port du Salut, France. Also called **Port Salut**.

porte–co•chere or **porte–co•chère** [ˌpɔrt kou'ʃɛr] *n.* **1** a covered extension at the door of a building under which carriages and automobiles stop so that persons getting in or out are sheltered. **2** an entrance for carriages, leading into a courtyard. ⟨< F *porte-cochère* coach gate⟩

porte–mon•naie ['pɔrt ˌmʌni]; *French,* [pɔʀtmɔ'nɛ] *n.* a purse; pocketbook; change-purse. ⟨< F *porte-monnaie* < *porter* carry + *monnaie* (small) change⟩

por•tend [pɔr'tɛnd] *v.* indicate beforehand; be a portent of (usually something bad): *Black clouds portend a storm.* ⟨ME < L *portendere* < *por-* before + *tendere* extend⟩

por•tent ['pɔrtɛnt] *n.* **1** a sign of something (usually bad) to come; omen: *The scandal was regarded as a portent of worse things to come.* **2** prophetic significance: *happenings of dire portent.* ⟨< L *portentum*, originally neut. pp. of *portendere.* See PORTEND.⟩

por•ten•tous [pɔr'tɛntəs] *adj.* **1** of, having to do with, or being a portent: *an event of portentous significance.* **2** amazing; extraordinary: *a portentous effort of will.* **3** self-important; pompous: *With a portentous clearing of the throat, he began to speak.* **—por'ten•tous•ly,** *adv.* **—por'ten•tous•ness,** *n.*

por•ter[1] ['pɔrtər] *n.* **1** a person employed to carry things, especially one who carries luggage for patrons at a hotel, airport, etc. **2** an attendant in a sleeping car or club car of a railway train. **3** a hospital employee who moves patients, supplies, etc. from one place to another. ⟨ME < OF *porteur*, ult. < L *portare* carry⟩

por•ter[2] ['pɔrtər] *n.* **1** a person who guards a door or entrance; doorkeeper. **2** janitor. ⟨ME < OF *portier* < LL *portarius* < L *porta* gate⟩

por•ter[3] ['pɔrtər] *n.* a heavy, dark brown beer made from browned or charred malt. ⟨short for *porter's ale* (i.e., ale for a *porter[1]*)⟩

por•ter•house ['pɔrtər,hʌus] *n.* a choice beefsteak containing the tenderloin. Also called **porterhouse steak.** ⟨possibly because made popular about 1814 by the keeper of a New York porterhouse (a place where porter and other liquors were sold)⟩

port•fo•li•o [pɔrt'fouliou] *n., pl.* **-li•os. 1** a briefcase; portable case for loose papers, drawings, etc. **2** the position and duties of office of a cabinet minister or a minister of state: *The Minister of Defence resigned her portfolio.* **3 a** holdings in the form of stocks, bonds, etc. **b** a list of such holdings. **4** a selection of works, such as drawings, academic papers, etc. ⟨< Ital. *portafoglio*, ult. < L *portare* carry + *folium* sheet, leaf⟩

port•hole ['pɔrt,houl] *n.* **1** an opening in a ship's side to let in light and air. **2** an opening in a wall, ship's side, etc., through which guns may be fired. **3** any similar opening in a furnace door.

por•ti•co ['pɔrtɪkou] *n., pl.* **-coes** or **-cos.** a porch or a covered walk having the roof supported by columns. ⟨< Ital. *portico* < L *porticus.* Doublet of PORCH.⟩

por•tière or **por•tiere** [pɔr'tjɛr] *n.* a curtain hung at a doorway. ⟨< F *portière* < *porte* door⟩

por•tion ['pɔrʃən] *n., v. —n.* **1** a part or share. **2** the quantity of food served for one person. **3** the part of an estate that goes to an heir. **4** dowry. **5** one's lot; fate.
—v. **1** divide into parts or shares. **2** give (a thing to a person) as his or her share; give a portion, inheritance, dowry, etc. to. ⟨ME < OF < L *portio, -onis*⟩ **—'por•tion•less,** *adj.*
☛ *Syn. n.* **1.** See note at PART.

Port•land cement ['pɔrtlənd] a kind of cement made by burning limestone and clay in a kiln. ⟨< Isle of *Portland*, a peninsula of S England⟩

port•ly ['pɔrtli] *adj.* **-li•er, -li•est. 1** stout; corpulent. **2** *Archaic.* stately; dignified. ⟨< *port[4]*⟩ **—'port•li•ness,** *n.*
☛ *Syn.* **1.** See note at FAT.

port•man•teau [,pɔrtmæn'tou] *or* [pɔrt'mæntou] *n., pl.* **-teaus** or **-teaux** [-touz]. **1** *Esp. Brit.* a travelling bag, especially a stiff, oblong one with two compartments opening like a book. **2** *(adjl.)* that combines two or more functions, types, etc. ⟨< F *portmanteau* < *porter* carry + *manteau* mantle⟩

portmanteau word *Linguistics.* a word that is made by combining parts of two other words; blend. *Smog* is a portmanteau word from *sm*oke and f*og*. *Brunch* is a portmanteau word from *br*eakfast and l*unch*. ⟨explanation devised by Humpty-Dumpty for Alice in Lewis Carroll's *Through the Looking-Glass*: "You see it's like a portmanteau – there are two meanings packed up into one word."⟩

port of entry any harbour, airport, etc. in a country that has customs facilities where goods and persons are cleared for entry into or exit from the country.

por•trait ['pɔrtrɪt] *or* ['pɔrtreit] *n.* **1** a depiction, usually a painting or photograph, of a person, especially when of the face or bust. **2** a picture in words; description. ⟨< F *portrait*, originally pp. of *portraire* portray⟩

por•trait•ist ['pɔrtrətɪst] *n.* a person who paints portraits.

por•trai•ture ['pɔrtrətʃər] *or* ['pɔrtrə,tʃʊr] *n.* **1** the act of portraying. **2** the art of making portraits. **3** a portrait or portraits. ⟨ME < OF *portraiture* < *portrait* portrait < *portraire.* See PORTRAY.⟩

por•tray [pɔr'trei] *v.* **1** describe or picture in words: *The book portrays life long ago.* **2** make a picture of. **3** represent on the stage. ⟨ME < OF *portraire* < L *protrahere* < *pro-* forth + *trahere* draw⟩ **—por'tray•er,** *n.*

por•tray•al [pɔr'treiəl] *n.* **1** a portraying by pictures or in words. **2** a picture or description.

Por•tu•gal ['pɔrtʃəgəl] *n.* a republic, formerly a kingdom, in SW Europe west of Spain on the Iberian peninsula and including the Azores and the Madeira Islands.

Por•tu•guese [,pɔrtʃə'giz] *or* ['pɔrtʃə,giz] *n., pl.* **-guese;** *adj. —n.* **1** a native or inhabitant of Portugal. **2** a person of Portuguese descent. **3** the Romance language of Portugal and Brazil.
—adj. of or having to do with Portugal, its people, or the Portuguese language.

Portuguese man-of-war any of various warm sea hydrozoans of the genus *Physalia*, having a large bladderlike sac with a sail-like structure on top which enables them to float, and long, dangling tentacles furnished with stinging cells.

por•tu•lac•a [,pɔrtʃə'lækə] *n.* any of a genus (*Portulaca*) of succulent herbs of the purslane family, mainly of tropical and subtropical regions, especially a trailing annual plant (*P. grandiflora*) cultivated in gardens for its showy, yellow, pink, red, purple, or white flowers. See also PURSLANE. ⟨< L *portulaca* purslane⟩

pose[1] [pouz] *n., v.* **posed, pos•ing.** *—n.* **1** a position of the body; a way of holding the body. **2** an attitude assumed for effect; pretence; affectation: *She takes the pose of being an invalid when really she is well and strong.* **3** formerly, in the fur trade, one of several stopping places established on a long portage. **4** the distance or track between any two of these stopping places.
—v. **1** hold a bodily position: *He posed for an hour for his portrait.* **2** put in a certain position: *The artist posed her before painting her picture.* **3** pretend; make a pretence, especially for effect: *He posed as a rich man though he owed more than he owned.* **4** put forward; state: *to pose a question.* ⟨< F *poser* < LL *pausare* pause < L *pausa* a pause; in Romance languages influenced by stem *pos-* of L *ponere* place (from meaning 'cause to pause, set down'); this influence spread to many compounds, e.g., *compose, dispose, oppose*⟩

pose[2] [pouz] *v.* **posed, pos•ing.** *Rare.* puzzle completely. ⟨var. of *appose*, var. of *oppose*⟩

Po•sei•don [pə'saɪdən] *n. Greek mythology.* the god of the sea and of horses, corresponding to the Roman god Neptune. He is usually represented carrying a trident.

pos•er[1] ['pouzər] *n.* a person who poses. ⟨< *pose[1]*⟩

pos•er[2] ['pouzər] *n.* a very puzzling problem. ⟨< *pose[2]*⟩

po•seur [pou'zɜr] *French*, [po'zœʀ] *n.* an affected person, one who puts on airs to impress others. ⟨< F *poseur* < *poser* pose⟩

posh [pɒʃ] *adj. Informal.* well-appointed; stylish; elegant. ⟨origin uncertain; the frequent explanation of its being the acronym of *port out, starboard home* (the best accommodation on ships to and from the East) is a later folk etymology⟩ **—'posh•ly,** *adv.* **—'posh•ness,** *n.*

pos•it ['pɒzɪt] *v.* lay down or assume as a fact or principle; affirm. ⟨< L *positus*, pp. of *ponere* set, place⟩

po•si•tion [pə'sɪʃən] *n., v. —n.* **1** a place where a thing or person is: *The house is in a sheltered position.* **2** a way of being placed: *Sit in a more comfortable position.* **3** the proper place. **4** a favourable condition with reference to place or circumstances: *The army manoeuvered for position before attacking.* **5** job. **6** a rank; standing, especially high standing: *The district manager was raised to the position of vice-president.* **7** a way of thinking; set of opinion; stand: *What is your position on this question?* **8** the place held by a player on a team: *My position on the hockey team was defence.* **9** a relationship with other people: *Your careless remark put me in an awkward position.* **10** *Ballet.* a way of placing the feet or arms: *fifth foot position.*
—v. put in position; place: *The general positioned his soldiers behind the line of trees.* ⟨< L *positio, -onis* < *ponere* set⟩
☛ *Syn.* **5. Position,** JOB, SITUATION = employment. **Position** is the formal word, but usually suggests white-collar work, in business or a profession: *He has a position in a bank.* **Job** is the informal and colloquial word applying to any kind of employment, but emphasizes the idea of having work to do: *He has a job on a ranch this summer.* **Situation** emphasizes the idea of a place to work, and now chiefly means a position or job wanted or applied for: *She desires a situation as housekeeper.*

po•si•tion•al [pə'zɪʃənəl] *adj.* of, having to do with, or dependent on position or context.

pos•i•tive ['pɒzətɪv] *adj., n. —adj.* **1** admitting of no question; without doubt; sure. **2** affirmative: *Do you think we can expect a positive answer?* **3** definite; emphatic: *a positive refusal.* **4** favourable or approving; optimistic; helpful or co-operative: *You should take a more positive attitude.* **5** that can be thought of as real and present: *Light is a positive thing; darkness is only the absence of light.* **6** showing that a particular disease, condition, germ, etc. is present. **7** that definitely does something or adds something; practical: *Don't just make criticisms; give us some positive help.* **8** tending in the direction thought of as that of increase or progress: *Motion in the direction in which the hands of a clock move is positive.* **9** greater than zero; plus: *Positive numbers are used to count things. Five above zero is a positive*

quantity. **10** *Electricity.* of the kind of electrical charge produced on glass by rubbing it with silk; lacking or losing electrons. **11** *Photography.* showing light and shadow or colour as it is in the subject photographed. **12** *Grammar.* of the simple form of an adjective or adverb, as distinct from the comparative and superlative. **13** *Biology.* moving or turning toward light, the earth, or any other stimulus. **14** *Chemistry.* having a tendency to lose electrons and thus become charged with positive electricity, as a chemical element or radical. **15** *Philosophy.* concerned with or based on matters of experience; not speculative or theoretical; empirical. **16** being so not by relation to or comparison with other things; absolute; unconditional (*often used informally as an intensifier*).
—n. **1** a positive degree or quantity. **2** *Electricity.* the positive terminal or plate in a battery, etc. **3** *Photography.* a positive photograph or a print made from a negative. **4** *Grammar.* the simple form of an adjective or adverb, as distinct from the comparative and superlative. *Fast* is the positive; *faster* is the comparative; *fastest* is the superlative. ⟨ME < OF < L *positivus,* ult. < *ponere* to set⟩ **—'pos•i•tive•ly,** *adv.* **—'pos•i•tive•ness,** *n.*

pos•i•tiv•ism ['pɒzətɪ,vɪzəm] *n.* **1** a philosophical system founded by Auguste Comte (1798-1857), a French philosopher and sociologist, which deals only with positive facts and phenomena, rejecting abstract speculation. **2** the state or quality of being positive; definiteness; assurance; dogmatism.

pos•i•tron ['pɒzə,trɒn] *n. Physics.* the antiparticle of the electron, having the same mass, etc. as the electron and an equal but opposite electric charge. ⟨< *positive* + (*elec*)*tron*⟩

pos•i•tro•ni•um [,pɒzə'trouniəm] *n.* a very short-lived entity like an atom, composed of a positron and an electron bound together, differing from hydrogen in that both particles have the same mass. The two particles annihilate each other to produce two or three photons.

po•so•lo•gy [pə'sɒlədʒi] *n.* the branch of pharmacology dealing with the study of drug dosages and their determination.

poss. **1** possessive; possession. **2** possibly; possible.

pos•se ['pɒsi] *n.* **1** a group of persons who could be summoned to help a law officer, especially in an emergency. Posses were often formed to capture criminals during frontier days in the American West. **2** a group so summoned. **3** *Cdn.* in western Canada, a troop of horses and riders trained for special exercises and drills, often giving exhibitions at stampedes and rodeos. ⟨< Med.L *posse* power < L *posse* be able⟩

pos•sess [pə'zɛs] *v.* **1** own; have: *The general possessed great wisdom.* **2** hold as property; hold; occupy. **3** control; influence strongly. **4** know (a language) well: *Anyone who possesses more than three languages is a polyglot.* **5** of a spirit, control: *The devil must have possessed those kids today.* **6** maintain; keep: *Possess your soul in patience.* **7** succeed in having sexual intercourse with (a woman): *Dracula's only normal desire was to possess Ermintrude.* **8** *Archaic.* take; win.
possess (someone) **of,** enable someone to have: *I will possess her of the facts as soon as possible.* ⟨ME < OF *possessier* < *possession* possession < L *possessio* < *possidere* possess⟩

pos•sessed [pə'zɛst] *adj.* **1** dominated by passion, or as by an evil spirit; lunatic; demoniac: *She fought like one possessed.* **2** owning or having as one's own: *The peacekeepers are possessed of great courage.* **3** maintaining poise and calm; unruffled: *She remained quite possessed throughout the gruelling interview.*

pos•ses•sion [pə'zɛʃən] *n.* **1** a possessing; holding. **2** ownership. **3** something possessed; property. **4** a territory under the rule of a country: *Ascension Island is a possession of the United Kingdom.* **5** domination by a particular feeling, idea, etc. **6** self-control: *Politicians should maintain their possession at all times.* **7** control by a spirit: *He was in a state of possession.*

pos•ses•sive [pə'zɛsɪv] *adj., n. —adj.* **1** of or having to do with possession: *the possessive instinct.* **2** having or showing a strong desire to own or dominate: *That boy's possessive nature has led him to take all his brother's toys. She is very possessive of her fiancé and glares at any woman who talks to him.* **3** *Grammar.* of, having to do with, or being the form of a noun or pronoun that shows that it refers to the possessor or source of something or to a part of a larger whole. *My* is the possessive form of *I* in *my books*; *bird's* is the possessive form of *bird* in *a bird's wing.*
—n. Grammar. **1** the possessive form. The English possessive corresponds roughly in meaning to the genitive case in German and Latin. **2** a word or construction in the possessive form. *Their* and *person's* are possessives. **—pos'ses•sive•ly,** *adv.* **—pos'ses•sive•ness,** *n.*

possessive adjective *Grammar.* a type of determiner used with a noun to show possession. In *My friend was late, my* is a possessive adjective.
☛ *Usage.* See note at POSSESSIVE PRONOUN.

possessive pronoun *Grammar.* **1** a pronoun in the possessive form. In *The book is hers, hers* is a possessive pronoun. **2** the genitive case of a personal pronoun; a POSSESSIVE ADJECTIVE derived from a pronoun.
☛ *Usage.* Many grammarians use the term **possessive pronoun** to include possessive adjectives as well. That is, they will call both **my** and **mine** possessive pronouns. Strictly speaking, *my* is a **determiner** or **possessive adjective,** while *mine* is a **possessive pronoun** because it stands for a noun phrase; in *The book is hers, hers* stands for 'her book'.

pos•ses•sor [pə'zɛsər] *n.* one who or that which occupies, owns, or controls: *the possessor of a lease. She is the proud possessor of a grand piano.*

pos•set ['pɒsɪt] *n.* a hot drink made of milk with ale, wine, etc., and spices. ⟨ME *possot*⟩

pos•si•bil•i•ty [,pɒsə'bɪlɪti] *n., pl.* **-ties. 1** the condition or fact of being possible: *There is a possibility that the train may be late.* **2** any thing or event that is possible, or considered as a possible choice: *He would be a good possibility for captain.*

pos•si•ble ['pɒsəbəl] *adj., n. —adj.* **1** that can happen or be done: *If it's at all possible, they'll come. It is possible to cure tuberculosis.* **2** that may be true or a fact: *It is possible that he left by the rear exit.* **3** that can be done, chosen, etc. properly: *the only possible candidate.*
—n. **1** a possible candidate, winner, etc. **2** a perfect score: *The shooter scored a possible on one target.* ⟨ME < L *possibilis* < *posse* be able⟩
☛ *Syn.* **1. Possible,** PRACTICABLE, FEASIBLE = capable of happening or being done. **Possible** means that with suitable conditions and methods something may exist, happen, or be done: *A cure for cancer is possible.* **Practicable** suggests that under present circumstances or by available means something (a plan, method, invention) can easily or effectively be carried out, done, or used: *The X-ray is a practicable way of discovering unsuspected diseases.* **Feasible** especially suggests something that is not yet tried but seems likely to be practicable: *Would compulsory X-rays be feasible?*

pos•si•bly ['pɒsəbli] *adv.* **1** by any possibility: *I cannot possibly go.* **2** perhaps: *Possibly you are right.*

pos•sum ['pɒsəm] *n.* **1** opossum. **2** *Australian.* a phalanger, especially *Trichosurus vulpecula.*
play possum, pretend to be dead or asleep. ⟨var. of *opossum*⟩

post¹ [poust] *n., v. —n.* **1** a length of timber, metal, etc. set upright, usually as a support or marker: *the posts of a door or bed, a hitching post.* **2** the post, line, etc. where a race starts or ends: *The horses are ready at the post.*
—v. **1** fasten (a notice) up in a place where it can easily be seen. **2** make known by, or as if by, a posted notice; offer publicly: *to post a reward.* **3** announce in a posted notice. **4** cover (a wall, etc.) with notices or bills. **5** put up notices warning people to keep out of (land or buildings): *When land is posted, no one may hunt there.* ⟨OE < L *postis*⟩

post² [poust] *n.* **1** a place where a soldier, police officer, etc. is stationed; a place where one is supposed to be when on duty. **2** a place where soldiers are stationed; a military station, fort, etc. **3** the soldiers occupying a military station. **4** a job or position: *She has a new post as district manager.* **5** a trading station, especially in an uncivilized or unsettled country: *a Hudson's Bay Company post.* **6** *Esp. Brit.* either of two bugle calls (**first post** and **last post**) calling soldiers to their quarters for the night. The last post is also played at military funerals and memorials such as Remembrance Day. **7** *Esp. U.S.* a local branch of a veterans' organization.
—v. **1** send to a station or post: *We posted guards at the door.* **2** appoint to a post, unit, etc. ⟨< F < Ital. < L *positus,* pp. of *ponere* station, place⟩

post³ [poust] *n., v., adv. —n.* **1** an established system for carrying letters, papers, packages, etc.; the mail: *to send by post.* **2** *Esp. Brit.* a single mail; the letters, etc. thus delivered: *this morning's post.* **3** *Brit.* LETTER CARRIER. **4** *Archaic.* a person, vehicle, or ship that carries mail. **5** *Brit.* POST OFFICE. **6** *Brit.* a letter box; MAILBOX (def. 1). **7** formerly, one of a series of fixed stations along a route for furnishing relays of men and horses for carrying letters, etc. and supplying service to travellers by post horse, post chaise, etc. **8** *Printing.* a size of printing paper, about 40 × 50 cm.
—v. **1** *Esp. Brit.* send by post; mail: *to post a letter.* **2** formerly, travel with post horses or by post chaise. **3** travel with haste; hurry. **4** of a rider on horseback, rise and fall in the saddle in rhythm with the horse's trot. **5** supply with up-to-date information; inform: *Keep me posted on any change in her condition.* **6** *Bookkeeping.* **a** transfer (an entry) from journal to ledger. **b** enter (an item) in due place and form. **c** make all requisite entries in (a ledger, etc.).

–*adv.* **1** by post. **2** speedily. ⟨< F < Ital. < L *posita*, fem. pp. of *ponere* place⟩

post– *prefix.* **1** after: *postgraduate, post-mortem, postscript.* **2** behind: *postjugular.* ⟨< L *post-* < *post* (prep. and adv.) after, behind⟩

post•age ['poustɪdʒ] *n.* **1** the amount paid on anything sent by mail. **2** the stamps or indicia showing the amount paid: *Did you put the right postage on that letter?*

postage meter a machine that prints marks on mail to indicate that postage has been paid, and that keeps a record of the cost of postage and the number of pieces processed.

postage stamp an official stamp for use on mail to show that postage has been paid.

post•al ['poustəl] *adj.* of or having to do with the mail or the post office.

postal card *Esp. U.S.* postcard.

postal code *Cdn.* the part of an address that uses a system of six alternating letters and numerals to identify a particular postal delivery route or point. The system is designed to speed the processing of machine-sorted mail: *The postal code of the CN Tower in Toronto is M5V 2T6.*

postal service POST OFFICE (def. 1).

postal station one of several branch post offices in a large community.

postal stationery any postal item issued by the Post Office, especially those already pre-stamped, such as aerograms, postcards, etc.

post–and–lin•tel ['poust ən 'lɪntəl] *adj. Architecture.* of or having to do with a type of construction based on the use of vertical supports and horizontal beams rather than vaults and arches.

post–and–rail ['poust ən 'reil] *n.* a fence made of rails set lengthwise between vertical posts in pairs side by side. Also, **post-and-rail fence.**

post•ax•ial [poust'æksiəl] *adj. Anatomy. Zoology.* pertaining to or situated behind the body's axis or the axis of a body part, especially a limb.

post bel•lum [,poust 'bɛləm] *Latin.* **1** after a war. **2** *U.S.* after the American Civil War. Compare ANTE BELLUM.
–post-'bel•lum, *adj.*

post•box ['poust,bɒks] *n. Esp. Brit.* a box into which letters, parcels, etc. are put for collection and delivery by the Post Office; mailbox.

post•boy ['poust,bɔɪ] *n.* formerly, a man who rode one of the horses drawing a carriage or coach; postilion.

post•card ['poust,kɑrd] *n.* a card used without an envelope for sending a short message by mail. Most postcards have a picture on one side.

post•ca•va [poust'keivə] *or* [poust'kɑvə] *n. Anatomy.* in vertebrates, the inferior VENA CAVA. Compare PRECAVA.

post chaise a hired carriage, changed at each post, that was used for travelling in the 18th and 19th centuries before the development of the railways.

post•code ['poust,koud] *n. Esp. Brit.* POSTAL CODE.

post•date [poust'deit] *or* ['poust,deit] *v.* **-dat•ed, -dat•ing.** **1** give (a letter, cheque, etc.) a later date than the actual date of writing. **2** follow in time.

post•di•lu•vi•an [,poustdə'luviən] *adj., n.* –*adj.* after the biblical Flood. Compare ANTEDILUVIAN.
–*n.* a person or thing existing after the Flood.

post•ed ['poustɪd] *adj., v.* –*adj.* **1** having posts. **2** informed. **3** *Bookkeeping.* entered in a ledger or some other due place and form.
–*v.* pt. and pp. of POST.

pos•ter ['poustər] *n.* **1** a large printed advertisement, or notice, often illustrated, put up in some public place; placard. **2** a large printed picture or message, used for room decoration. **3** a person who posts notices, etc.

poste restante [,poust rɛs'tɑnt]; *French,* [pɔstʀɛ'stɑ̃t] *Esp. Brit.* GENERAL DELIVERY. ⟨< F literally, standing mail⟩

pos•te•ri•or [pɒ'stiriər] *adj., n.* –*adj.* **1** situated behind; back; rear; hind. **2** later; coming after.
–*n. Informal.* the buttocks; rump. ⟨< L *posterior*, comparative of *posterus* subsequent < *post* after⟩

pos•ter•i•ty [pɒ'stɛrəti] *n.* **1** the generations of the future: *Posterity may travel to distant planets. Historical documents are preserved for posterity in the archives.* **2** all of a person's descendants. ⟨ME < OF < L *posteritas* < *posterus.* See POSTERIOR.⟩

pos•tern ['poustərn] *or* ['pɒstərn] *n., adj.* –*n.* **1** a back door or gate. **2** any small door or gate.
–*adj.* **1** of or like a postern. **2** rear; lesser: *The castle had a postern door.* ⟨ME < OF *posterne*, ult. < L *posterus* behind. See POSTERIOR.⟩

Post Exchange *Esp. U.S.* a general store at a military post or station that sells food and other goods to members of the armed forces and authorized civilians. *Abbrev.*: PX or P.X.

post–free ['poust 'fri] *adj.* postpaid.

post•grad•u•ate [poust'grædʒuɪt] *n., adj.* –*n.* a student who continues university studies at a level beyond that of a bachelor's degree.
–*adj.* **1** taking a course of study at such a level. **2** of or for postgraduates.

post•haste ['poust'heist] *adv.* very speedily; in great haste. ⟨< *post*[3] + *haste*⟩

post horse formerly, a horse hired for use in travelling by relay, each horse being changed for a fresh one after a certain distance.

post•hu•mous ['pɒstʃəməs] *adj.* **1** born after the death of the father: *a posthumous son.* **2** published after the death of the author. **3** happening after death: *posthumous fame.* ⟨< LL *posthumus*, var. of L *postumus* last, originally superlative of *post* after; *h* added by confusion with *humus* earth, in sense of 'burial'⟩

post•hu•mous•ly ['pɒstʃəməsli] *adv.* after death.

post•ie ['pousti] *n. Informal.* **1** a postal worker, especially an inside worker. **2** formerly, a letter carrier.

pos•til•ion or **pos•til•lion** [pɒ'stɪljən] *or* [pou'stɪljən] *n.* a person who rides one of the horses drawing a carriage or coach. ⟨< F *postillon*⟩

post–im•pres•sion•ism [,poust ɪm'prɛʃə,nɪzəm] *n.* a movement in painting in late 19th-century France which developed out of and went beyond the scientific naturalism of impressionism by stressing either formal structure or the expressive possibilities of colour as seen from a subjective viewpoint.

post–im•pres•sion•ist [,poust ɪm'prɛʃənɪst] *n., adj.* –*n.* an adherent or follower of post-impressionism.
–*adj.* of or having to do with post-impressionism or post-impressionists. **–,post-im,pres•sion'is•tic,** *adj.*

post•ing ['poustɪŋ] *n., v.* –*n.* a position to which a person has been posted, especially in the military and the diplomatic corps: *an ambassadorial posting. They should enjoy their new posting to London.*
–*v.* ppr. of POST.

post•lude ['poustlud] *n.* **1** a closing piece of music, especially a composition played at the end of a church service. **2** a final or concluding phase: *the postlude of an era.* ⟨blend of *post-* + *(pre)lude*⟩

post•man ['poustmən] *n., pl.* **-men.** *Esp. Brit.* a male LETTER CARRIER.

post•mark ['poust,mɑrk] *n., v.* –*n.* an official mark stamped on mail to cancel the postage stamp and record the place and date of mailing.
–*v.* stamp with a postmark.

post•mas•ter ['poust,mæstər] *n.* **1** the person in charge of a post office. **2** formerly, in the fur trade, a man between the ranks of Interpreter and Clerk who had been put in charge of a fur-trading post. **3** formerly, a person in charge of a station for post horses. **–'post,mas•ter•ship,** *n.*

Postmaster General *pl.* **Postmasters General.** *Cdn.* formerly, the federal cabinet minister responsible for the Post Office.

post•me•rid•i•an [,poustmə'rɪdiən] *adj.* occurring after noon; of or having to do with the afternoon.

post•mis•tress ['poust,mɪstrɪs] *n.* a woman in charge of a post office.

post•mod•ern [poust'mɒdərn] *adj.* coming after and usually in opposition to modernism in the 20th century, especially in architecture, literature, and the arts. **–post'mod•ern,ism,** *n.*

post–mor•tem [poust 'mɔrtəm] *adj., n.* –*adj.* of or having to do with an examination after death.

—n. an examination of a dead body; autopsy. ⟨< L *post mortem* after death⟩

post•na•tal [poust'neitəl] *adj.* **1** having to do with or for the mother of a newborn baby: *postnatal care, postnatal depression.* **2** having to do with the period just after birth: *postnatal diseases of children.*

post•nup•tial [poust'nʌpʃəl] *adj.* subsequent to marriage.

post–o•bit [ˌpoust 'oubɪt] *or* ['ɒbɪt] *n., adj. —n.* a written agreement signed by a borrower promising to pay a certain sum of money to the lender on the death of a person whose heir the borrower expects to be.
—adj. effective after a person's death. ⟨< L *post obitum* after death⟩

post office **1** Usually, **Post Office,** a government agency or department responsible for handling, transporting, and delivering mail. **2** a local office where mail is received and sorted for delivery or placement in individual boxes, and where stamps and money orders are sold, mail is registered or insured, etc. **3** a small office, located in a drugstore, etc., where stamps and money orders are sold and mail can be registered or insured, etc. *Abbrev.*: P.O.

post–op•er•a•tive [poust 'ɒpərətɪv] *or* ['ɒpəˌreitɪv] *adj.* of or occurring in the period immediately following a surgical operation: *a post-operative infection.* **—post-'op•er•a•tive•ly,** *adv.*

post•or•bit•al [poust'ɔrbɪtəl] *adj., n. —adj.* located behind the eye socket or orbit.
—n. a bone or scale thus located, as in some reptiles. Compare SUPRA-ORBITAL.

post•paid ['poustˌpeid] *or* ['poust'peid] *adj.* with the postage paid for in advance.

post•par•tum [poust'pɑrtəm] *adj.* having to do with the period following childbirth: *postpartum depression.*

post•pone [pous'poun] *v.* **-poned, -pon•ing. 1** put off till later; put off to a later time; delay. **2** *Grammar.* put (a sentence element) at or near the end of the sentence: *The verb in Latin is often postponed.* ⟨< L *postponere* < *post-* after + *ponere* put⟩ **—post'pone•ment,** *n.*
☛ *Syn.* **1.** See note at DELAY.

post•po•si•tion [ˌpoustpə'zɪʃən] *or* ['poustpəˌzɪʃən]. *n.* **1** the act of placing after. **2** the state of being placed after. **3** *Grammar.* **a** the placing of a word after the word it modifies, as in *governor general.* **b** the word so placed.

post•pos•i•tive [poust'pɒzətɪv] *adj., n. —adj.* of a modifier, coming after the word it modifies. An adjective coming immediately after its noun is a postpositive adjective. *Example*: the *President elect.*
—n. a postpositive modifier. **—post'pos•i•tive•ly,** *adv.*
☛ *Usage.* See note at ATTRIBUTIVE.

post•pran•di•al [poust'prændiəl] *adj.* after dinner: *postprandial speeches.* ⟨< *post-* + L *prandium* lunch⟩ **—post'pran•di•al•ly,** *adv.*

post•rid•er ['poustˌraɪdər] *n.* formerly, a person who travelled by means of relays of horses, especially one who carried mail. See also POST HORSE.

post road **1** a road or route over which mail is or was carried. **2** formerly, a road with stations providing post horses.

post•script ['pousˌskrɪpt] *n.* **1** an addition to a letter, written after the writer's name has been signed. **2** a supplementary part appended to any composition or literary work. ⟨< L *postscriptum,* originally neut. pp., < *post-* after + *scribere* write⟩

post–sec•on•da•ry ['poust 'sɛkənˌdɛri] *adj.* of or having to do with education beyond the secondary or high-school level.

post–test ['poust ˌtɛst] *n., v. —n.* a test taken after instruction to test what has been learned. Compare with PRE-TEST.
—v. give a post-test to.

post–trau•mat•ic stress disorder or **syndrome** [ˌpoust trə'mætɪk] a state of shock, with other symptoms, resulting from any form of severe stress, like battle fatigue.

pos•tu•lant ['pɒstʃələnt] *n.* **1** a candidate, especially for admission to a religious order. **2** a person who asks or applies for something; petitioner. ⟨< L *postulans, -antis,* ppr. of *postulare* demand⟩

pos•tu•late *n.* ['pɒstʃəlɪt]; *v.* ['pɒstʃəˌleit] *n., v.* **-lat•ed, -lat•ing.** *—n.* something taken for granted or assumed as a basis for reasoning; a fundamental principle or necessary condition: *One postulate of geometry is that a straight line may be drawn between any two points.*
—v. **1** take for granted; assume without proof as a basis for reasoning; require as a fundamental principle or necessary condition. **2** require; demand; claim. ⟨< L *postulatum,* originally pp. neut. of *postulare* demand⟩ **—ˌpos•tu'la•tion,** *n.* **—'pos•tuˌla•tor,** *n.*

pos•ture ['pɒstʃər] *n., v.* **-tured, -tur•ing.** *—n.* **1** a position of the body; way of holding the body: *Good posture is important for health.* **2** a condition; situation; state: *In the present posture of public affairs it is difficult to invest money safely.* **3** a mental or spiritual attitude.
—v. **1** take a certain posture: *The dancer postured before the mirror, bending and twisting her body.* **2** put in a certain posture. **3** adopt an attitude for effect. ⟨< F < Ital. < L *positura* < *ponere* place⟩ **—'pos•tur•al,** *adj.*

post•war ['poust'wɔr] *adj.* of, having to do with, or happening during the period immediately following a war: *a postwar construction boom.*

po•sy ['pouzi] *n., pl.* **-sies. 1** a flower. **2** a bunch of flowers; bouquet. **3** *Archaic.* a motto or line of poetry engraved within a ring. ⟨var. of *poesy.* 16c.⟩

pot [pɒt] *n., v.* **pot•ted, pot•ting.** *—n.* **1** a deep, usually round container made of metal, earthenware, glass, etc.: *a cooking pot, a flower pot, a coffee pot.* **2** a pot and what is in it; the amount a pot can hold: *a pot of jam.* **3** a container of alcohol or other drink: *a pot of ale.* **4** a basket used to catch fish, lobsters, etc. **5** *Informal.* a large sum of money. **6** *Informal.* all the money bet at one time; pool. **7** *Slang.* marijuana. **8** *Slang.* potbelly. **9** *Informal.* a trophy: *She has won a lot of pots at golf.* **10** *Billiards and snooker.* a successful shot: *What a super pot!*
go to pot, go to ruin: *After losing his job he took to drinking and went to pot.*
keep the pot boiling, *Informal.* **a** make a living. **b** keep things going in a lively way.
shoot or **trap for the pot,** kill animals for food.
sweeten the pot. See SWEETEN.
—v. **1** put into a plant pot: *to pot young tomato plants.* **2** cook and preserve in a pot. **3** take a pot shot at; shoot. **4** *Billiards and snooker.* successfully shoot (a ball) into one of the pockets: *There's only the black left to pot.* ⟨OE *pott* < VL *pottus* < LL *potus* cup < L *potus* a drinking⟩ **—'potˌlike,** *adj.*

pot. potential.

po•ta•ble ['poutəbəl] *adj., n. —adj.* fit for drinking.
—n. Usually, **potables,** *pl.* anything drinkable. ⟨< LL *potabilis* < L *potare* to drink⟩

po•tage [pɔ'taʒ] *n. French.* a soup, especially a thick soup.

pot•ash ['pɒtˌæʃ] *n.* **1** any of several substances, such as potassium carbonate, made from wood ashes and used in soap, fertilizers, etc. **2** any of several potassium salts, such as potassium chloride, mined and processed for use in agriculture and industry. **3** potassium, or a potassium oxide, especially K_2O. **4** POTASSIUM HYDROXIDE. ⟨< Du. *potasch,* literally, pot ash⟩

po•tas•sic [pə'tæsɪk] *adj.* having to do with or containing potassium.

po•tas•si•um [pə'tæsiəm] *n. Chemistry.* a soft, silver-white, metallic chemical element, occurring in nature only in compounds. *Symbol*: K; *at.no.* 19; *at.mass* 39.10. ⟨< NL < E *potash*⟩

potassium amide *Chemistry.* a crystalline compound produced by heating potassium in ammonia. *Formula*: KNH_2

potassium bromide *Chemistry.* a white, crystalline compound with a salty taste, used in medicine, photography, etc. *Formula*: KBr

potassium carbonate *Chemistry.* a white, crystalline compound that forms a strongly alkaline solution and is used especially in making glass and soap. *Formula*: K_2CO_3

potassium chlorate *Chemistry.* a colourless, crystalline compound used as an oxidizing agent in explosives, matches, etc. *Formula*: $KClO_3$

potassium chloride *Chemistry.* a crystalline compound that occurs naturally as a mineral, used in fertilizers. *Formula*: KCl

potassium cyanide *Chemistry.* a highly poisonous, white, crystalline compound used for removing gold from ore, electroplating, etc. *Formula*: KCN

potassium hydroxide *Chemistry.* a very strong alkali used especially in making soap and as a reagent. Also called **caustic potash.** *Formula*: KOH

potassium iodide *Chemistry.* a white, granular, water-soluble powder, or a transparent crystallizing salt, used chiefly as a laboratory reagent, in photographic emulsions, and in medicine, especially in the treatment of thyroid conditions. *Formula*: KI

potassium nitrate *Chemistry.* a colourless, crystalline compound used as an oxidizing agent, in gunpowder, in explosives, etc.; nitre; saltpetre. *Formula*: KNO_3

potassium permanganate *Chemistry.* a nearly black, crystalline compound used as an oxidizing agent, disinfectant, etc. *Formula*: $KMnO_4$

potassium sulphate *Chemistry.* a white, crystalline solid used in the manufacture of fertilizers and mineral water. *Formula*: K_2SO_4

po•ta•tion [pou'teiʃən] *n.* **1** the act of drinking. **2** a drink, especially of alcoholic liquor. ⟨ME < OF < L *potatio, -onis* < *potare* to drink⟩

po•ta•to [pə'teitou] *n., pl.* **1** a starchy tuber having crisp, whitish flesh or yellowish and a thin brown or red skin, widely eaten as a cooked vegetable. It is the traditional basic vegetable of North America and much of Europe. See TUBER for picture. **2** the plant *Solanum tuberosum*, a New World member of the nightshade family that produces these tubers. **3** SWEET POTATO. ⟨< Sp. *patata* < *Haitian*⟩

potato beetle a yellow-and-black striped beetle (*Leptinotarsa decemlineata*) that is a serious pest of potato plants. Also called **potato bug, Colorado potato beetle.**

potato bug POTATO BEETLE.

potato chip **1** a crisp, thin, dry slice of potato that has been fried in deep fat and is eaten cold as a snack. **2** FRENCH FRY.

pot•bel•lied ['pɒt,bɛlid] *adj.* **1** having a potbelly. **2** shaped like a potbelly: *a potbellied stove.*

pot•bel•ly ['pɒt,bɛli] *n.* a large, protruding belly; paunch.

potbelly stove or **potbellied stove** a squat, bulging stove on feet, that burns wood or coal.

pot•boiler ['pɒt,bɔɪlər] *n. Informal.* a mediocre work of literature, art, or music produced merely to make a living.

pot•bound ['pɒt,baʊnd] *adj.* of plants, having roots that have outgrown the size of the pot, so that the plant cannot continue growing without being replanted.

pot•bow ['pɒt,bou] *n. Cdn.* a piece of wood used to suspend a pot over an outdoor fire.

pot•boy ['pɒt,bɔɪ] *n. Esp. Brit.* a man or boy who works in a pub, serving customers, washing glasses, etc.

pot cheese **1** a kind of cottage cheese made from seasoned curds packed away in a crock in a warm place. **2** a coarse, dry cottage cheese.

po•ten•cy ['poutənsi] *n., pl.* **-cies. 1** the quality or state of being potent; power; strength: *the potency of an argument, the potency of a drug.* **2** the power or capacity to develop; potentiality. **3** sexual capability. ⟨< L *potentia* < *potens.* See POTENT.⟩

po•tent ['poutənt] *adj.* **1** having power or effectiveness in action; effective: *a potent remedy for a disease.* **2** of a drink, etc., strong: *potent tea.* **3** powerful or mighty: *a potent leader.* **4** of males, capable of having an erection and therefore of sexual intercourse. **5** convincing; persuasive in argument, etc. ⟨< L *potens, -entis,* ppr. of OL **potere* be powerful⟩ **—'po•tent•ly,** *adv.*

po•ten•tate ['poutən,teit] *n.* any person possessing great power, especially a ruler. The Roman emperors were potentates. ⟨ME < LL < L *potentatus* power, dominion < *potens, -entis.* See POTENT.⟩

po•ten•tial [pə'tɛnʃəl] *adj., n.* *—adj.* **1** possible as opposed to actual; capable of coming into being or action: *a potential danger.* **2** *Grammar.* of a verb or verb form expressing possibility, as in English by the use of modals such as *may, might, can, could,* etc.
—n. **1** something potential; possibility. **2** *Grammar.* **a** any verb construction that expresses possibility. **b** the category to which such forms belong; the potential mood or aspect. **3** *Electricity.* the amount of electrification of a point with reference to some standard. A current of high potential is used in transmitting electric power over long distances. **4** *Physics.* a type of function from which the intensity of a physical field can be mathematically derived. ⟨< LL *potentialis,* ult. < L *potens, -entis* potent⟩ **—po'ten•tial•ly,** *adv.*

☛ *Syn. adj.* **1.** See note at LATENT.

potential energy *Physics.* the energy that something has that is due to its structure, not to motion. A tightly coiled spring or a raised weight has potential energy.

po•ten•ti•al•i•ty [pə,tɛnʃi'æləti] *n., pl.* **-ties. 1** a potential state or quality; possibility as opposed to actuality; latent power or capacity. **2** something potential; a possibility.

po•ten•ti•ate [pə'tɛnʃi,eit] *v.* **-ated, -ating.** make more active or potent. **—po,ten•ti'a•tion,** *n.*

po•ten•ti•om•e•ter [pə,tɛnʃi'ɒmətər] *n. Electricity.* an instrument for measuring electromotive force. ⟨< *potential* + *-meter*⟩

pot•ful ['pɒt,fʊl] *n.* **1** as much or as many as a pot will hold: *a potful of potatoes.* **2** a large amount: *She made a potful of money on that deal.*

pot•head ['pɒt,hɛd] *n.* **1** *Cdn., esp. Nfld.* PILOT WHALE. Also **ca'aing whale. 2** *Slang.* a person who habitually smokes marijuana.

poth•er ['pɒðər] *n., v.* *—n.* **1** confusion; disturbance; fuss. **2** mental excitement: *She was all in a pother about chairing the meeting.*
—v. bother; fuss; worry. ⟨origin uncertain⟩

pot•herb ['pɒt,hɜrb] *or* ['pɒt,ɜrb] *n.* **1** any plant whose leaves and stems are boiled as a vegetable, such as spinach. **2** any plant used as seasoning in cooking. Sage and parsley are potherbs.

pot•hold•er ['pɒt,houldər] *n.* a small, thick pad used for protecting the hands when handling hot pots, pans, etc.

pot•hole ['pɒt,houl] *n.* **1** a deep, round hole, especially one made in the rocky bed of a river by stones and gravel being spun around in the current. **2** a hole in the surface of a road, especially one caused by frost or water damage. **3** *Cdn.* SLOUGH[1] (def. 1). **4** *Cdn.* DUGOUT (def. 4). **5** *Cdn.* a circular depression on any rock surface. **6** a deep cave extending vertically from the ground surface.

pothole trout *Cdn.* on the Prairies, trout introduced into sloughs or dugouts.

pot•hook ['pɒt,hʊk] *n.* **1** an S-shaped hook for hanging a pot or kettle over an open fire. **2** a rod with a hook for lifting hot pots, etc. **3** an S-shaped stroke, especially one made by children in learning to write.

pot•hunt•er ['pɒt,hʌntər] *n.* **1** a person who shoots anything he or she comes upon regardless of rules of sport. **2** a person who takes part in contests merely to win prizes. **3** a person who hunts for food or for profit.

po•tion ['pouʃən] *n.* a drink, especially one used as a medicine or poison, or in magic. ⟨< L *potio, -onis.* Doublet of POISON.⟩

pot•latch ['pɒtlætʃ] *n., v. Cdn., esp. West Coast.* *—n.* **1** among First Nations people of the west coast, especially the Kwa Kwa Ka'wakw (Kwakiutl), a large, festive gathering held to celebrate some special event or anniversary, at which the host presents gifts to his guests. Formerly, these gifts were valuable and were intended to show off the host's status. Potlatches were reciprocal, with each host trying to outdo the others. Because of the resulting increasing extravagance and frequent impoverishment, the Canadian government of the day outlawed potlatches in 1884 and they remained so until 1951. Present-day ceremonies emphasize the celebration aspects, although gifts are still given. **2** *Informal.* any party or celebration.
—v. **1** hold or take part in a potlatch. **2** give (something) with the expectation of a gift in return. **3** give things to others freely. ⟨< Chinook Jargon < Nootka *patshatl* gift⟩

pot•luck ['pɒt,lʌk] *n.* **1** whatever food happens to be ready or on hand for a meal. **2** a meal to which all present have contributed: *a potluck lunch.* **3** whatever comes one's way or is available: *Students are having to take potluck with their courses this year.*

potluck supper or **dinner** a meal to which each person brings a contribution, sometimes decided on beforehand by the host: *I was asked to bring a salad to Friday's potluck dinner.*

pot marigold a popular garden flower (*Calendula officinalis*) having large, double yellow or orange flowers. The flowers of the pot marigold were once used for flavouring in cakes, soups, etc.

pot•pie ['pɒt,paɪ] *n.* **1** a baked savoury pie, usually of meat, having only a top crust: *a chicken potpie.* **2** a soup with dumplings that may contain meat.

pot•pour•ri [,poupʊ'ri] *or* [,pɒtpʊ'ri] *n.* **1** a fragrant mixture of dried flower petals and spices. **2** a musical or literary medley. ⟨< F *potpourri,* translation of Sp. *olla podrida* rotten pot < L *olla* pot and VL *putrita,* fem. pp. of *putrire* rot < L *puter* soft, rotten⟩

pot roast a large piece of meat, usually beef, cooked slowly with a little liquid, in a deep, heavy, tightly covered dish.

pot•sherd ['pɒt,ʃɜrd] *n.* a broken piece of earthenware, especially an ancient one; shard. ⟨< *pot* + *sherd,* var. of *shard*⟩

pot shot 1 a quick shot at something from close range without careful aim. 2 a shot taken at game to provide a meal, with little regard to the rules of sport. 3 a passing or random criticism.

pot•tage ['pɒtɪdʒ] *n.* a thick soup. ⟨ME < OF *potage* < *pot* pot < VL *pottus.* See POT.⟩

pot•ted ['pɒtɪd] *adj.* 1 put into a pot. 2 cooked and preserved in pots or cans. 3 *Slang.* drunk; intoxicated. 4 *Esp. Brit.* being a condensed or summarized book, play, etc., often at the expense of quality: *a potted version of* War and Peace.

pot•ter[1] ['pɒtər] *n.* a person who makes pottery. ⟨OE *pottere* < *pott.* See POT.⟩

pot•ter[2] ['pɒtər] *v.* PUTTER[1]. ⟨< earlier *pote* poke, OE *potian* push. See PUT.⟩ —**'pot•ter•er,** *n.*

potter's field a burial ground for paupers, unknown persons, etc. ⟨with reference to the biblical story of Judas⟩

potter's wheel a horizontal disk that revolves by means of a treadle or motor and on which clay is moulded by hand into round objects such as vases or pots.

pot•ter•y ['pɒtəri] *n., pl.* **-ter•ies.** 1 pots, dishes, vases, or other earthenware, especially as distinct from porcelain or stoneware. Pottery is not as strong as stoneware and not as fine as porcelain. 2 the art or craft of making pottery. 3 a place where pottery is made. ⟨< OF *poterie* < *potier* potter < *pot* pot < VL *pottus.* See POT.⟩

pot•ty[1] ['pɒti] *n.* 1 a small seat that fits onto a regular toilet seat, for use by a child. 2 a child's chamber pot. 3 a child's chair for toilet training, having a hole in the seat with a pot fixed underneath. Also called **potty chair.** 4 *Baby talk.* a toilet. ⟨dim. of *pot,* sense 1⟩

pot•ty[2] ['pɒti] *adj. Informal.* 1 slightly mad; eccentric; mentally offbalance. 2 *Brit.* trivial; paltry: *That's a potty little thing to be arguing about!*

pouch [pʌutʃ] *n., v.* —*n.* 1 a bag or sack: *a letter carrier's pouch.* 2 *Anatomy. Zoology.* a baglike receptacle or cavity in any of various animals, such as that on the abdomen of a marsupial, in which the young are carried. 3 a loose fold of skin: *pouches under the eyes.* 4 a large bag that can be locked, used for transporting mail or government dispatches: *a diplomatic pouch.* 5 a small bag, often zippered, used for carrying tobacco or make-up.
—*v.* form a pouch or form into a pouch. ⟨ME < ONF *pouche* < Gmc. Akin to POKE[2].⟩ —**'pouch,like,** *adj.*

pouch•y ['pʌutʃi] *adj.* like a pouch, or having pouches; baggy. —**'pouch•i•ness,** *n.*

pouf [puf] *n., interj.* —*n.* 1 a woman's hairstyle popular in the 18th century and consisting of high rolls or puffs of hair. 2 a loose roll of hair. 3 a puffed or gathered part of a dress. 4 a soft hassock or ottoman. Also, **pouff** or **pouffe.** ⟨< F *pouf* a puff⟩
—*interj.* poof.

pou•lard [pu'lɑrd] *n.* a pullet that has been spayed to improve its eating qualities; a fattened hen. ⟨< MF *poularde* < *poule* hen + *-arde,* a noun suffix⟩

poult [poult] *n.* a young chicken, turkey, pheasant, etc. ⟨ME *poult,* short for *poullet* pullet⟩

poul•ter•er ['poultərər] *n.* a dealer in poultry. ⟨< obs. *poulter,* of the same meaning < OF *pouletier* < *poulet.* See POULTRY.⟩

poul•tice ['poultɪs] *n., v.* **-ticed, -tic•ing.** —*n.* a soft, moist mass of mustard, herbs, etc., applied to the body as a medicine. —*v.* put a poultice on. ⟨ult. < L *pultes,* pl. of *puls* mush⟩

poul•try ['poultri] *n.* domesticated birds, such as chickens, turkeys, ducks, and geese, raised for meat, eggs, or feathers. ⟨ME < OF *pouleterie* < *poulet,* dim. of *poule* hen < VL *pulla,* fem. to L *pullus* young fowl. Related to PULLET.⟩

poul•try•man ['poultrimən] *n., pl.* **-men.** 1 a person who raises poultry. 2 poulterer.

pounce[1] [paʊns] *v.* **pounced, pounc•ing;** *n.* —*v.* 1 come down with a rush and seize (*used with* **on**): *The cat pounced on the mouse.* 2 dash, come, or jump suddenly.
—*n.* 1 a sudden swoop or pouncing. 2 a claw or talon of a bird of prey. ⟨ME < *ponson, pounson,* dagger, pointed instrument < MF *poincon,* ult. < L *punctus,* pp. of *pungere* prick. Related to PUNCHEON[1], POINT.⟩

pounce[2] [paʊns] *n., v.* **pounced, pounc•ing.** —*n.* 1 a fine powder formerly used to prevent ink from spreading in writing, or to prepare parchment for writing. 2 a fine powder used for transferring a design through a stencil.
—*v.* 1 trace (a design) with pounce rubbed through perforations. 2 dust, smooth, or finish with pounce. ⟨< F *ponce* < L *pumex, -micis* pumice. Doublet of PUMICE.⟩

pound[1] [paʊnd] *n., pl.* **pounds** or (*esp. collectively*) **pound.** 1 a unit for measuring mass. In the avoirdupois system, formerly in general use in English-speaking countries, one pound equals 16 ounces (about 454 g). In the troy system, used for precious metals and gems, one pound equals 12 troy ounces (about 373 g). 2 the basic unit of money of the United Kingdom, divided into 100 pence; pound sterling. A pound was formerly divided into 20 shillings and 240 pence. *Symbol:* £ See money table in the Appendix. 3 the basic unit of money in certain other countries: in Egypt, Lebanon, and Syria, divided into 100 piastres; in Cyprus and Malta, divided into 100 cents. 4 a unit of money in Sudan, equal to 1⁄10 of a dinar. 5 the Turkish lira. 6 formerly, a monetary unit of Scotland originally worth an English pound, but which later declined to one shilling eight pence. Also called **pound Scots.** 7 a note or coin worth one pound. ⟨OE *pund* < L *pondo,* originally, *libra pondo* a pound by weight, ult. < *pendere* to weigh⟩

pound[2] [paʊnd] *v., n.* —*v.* 1 hit hard again and again; hit heavily: *He pounded the door with his fist.* 2 beat hard and repeatedly (*on*): *They pounded on the door, but no one heard.* 3 beat hard; throb: *After running fast, you can feel your heart pound.* 4 crush to powder or pulp by beating. 5 move quickly and heavily: *Marietta pounded down the hill to catch the bus.* 6 produce sound by pounding or as if by pounding: *We could hear drums pounding in the distance.* 7 forcefully instill (something) into (someone) by repetition: *I've been pounding a work ethic into him.*
pound (one's) **ear,** *Slang.* sleep.
pound the pavement, *Slang.* walk along the streets, as in looking for something or someone: *She pounded the pavement to no avail.*
—*n.* 1 the act of pounding. 2 a heavy or forcible blow. 3 the sound of a blow. ⟨OE *pūnian*⟩
☛ *Syn. v.* 1. See note at BEAT.

pound[3] [paʊnd] *n.* 1 an enclosed place for keeping stray or unlicensed animals, especially dogs, cats, etc., until claimed by the owners. Most cities and towns have a pound. 2 a place for keeping automobiles or other personal property until redeemed by the owners. 3 an enclosure for keeping or trapping animals. 4 an enclosure or trap for fish. 5 any place of confinement. ⟨OE *pund-*⟩

pound[4] [paʊnd] *n.* the button on a telephone marked with the symbol #. Also called **pound key.**

pound•age[1] ['paʊndɪdʒ] *n.* 1 a tax, commission, rate, etc. of so much per pound sterling or per pound of mass. 2 mass expressed in pounds.

pound•age[2] ['paʊndɪdʒ] *n.* 1 confinement in a pound. 2 the fee required for the release of an impounded animal.

pound•al ['paʊndəl] *n.* a foot-pound-second unit for measuring force, equal to about 0.138 newtons. ⟨< *pound*[1]⟩

pound cake a rich butter cake containing equal amounts of the principal ingredients. The original recipe for pound cake required one pound each of sugar, flour, and butter.

pound•er[1] ['paʊndər] *n.* a person or thing weighing, having, or associated with a specified number of pounds (*used in compounds*): *We caught a ten-pounder in the lake yesterday.* ⟨< *pound*[2]⟩

pound•er[2] ['paʊndər] *n.* a person or thing that pounds, especially an instrument such as a pestle for pounding or crushing. ⟨< *pound*[1]⟩

pound–fool•ish ['paʊnd 'fulɪʃ] *adj.* foolish or careless in regard to large sums of money.
penny-wise and pound-foolish. See PENNY-WISE.

pound net a fish trap using staked nets to make a rectangular enclosure or pound with a narrow opening, and from which escape is impossible. Compare WEIR (def. 2).

pound sterling the basic unit of money in the United Kingdom; POUND[1] (def. 2).

pour [pɔr] *v., n.* —*v.* 1 cause to flow in a steady stream: *I poured the milk from the bottle.* 2 flow in a steady stream: *The crowd poured out of the church. The rain poured down.* 3 pour tea or coffee at a formal reception. 4 express freely or without reserve: *The melancholy poet poured forth her sorrow in a song.*
it never rains but it pours, events of a kind, especially misfortunes, come all together or not at all.
pour it on, *Informal.* **a** to do or express something with great vigour and enthusiasm, especially in advancing one's interest, using persuasion, etc. **b** keep increasing one's score or advantage in a game, even when victory is no longer at issue. **c** offer profuse flattery. **d** go unduly fast; speed.

–*n.* **1** the act of pouring. **2** a heavy rain. ⟨ME *poure(n)*; origin uncertain⟩ **–'pour•er,** *n.*
☛ *Hom.* PORE.

pour•boire [pʊr'bwɑr]; *French,* [puʀ'bwaʀ] *n.* a gratuity; tip. ⟨literally, (money) for drinking⟩

pousse–ca•fé [,pus kæ'fei]; *French,* [puska'fe] *n.* **1** an after-dinner drink, served with coffee, composed of several liqueurs of different colours and varying specific gravities, poured so that the layers remain separate in the glass. **2** any liqueur served with coffee after dinner. ⟨literally, coffee-pusher⟩

pout¹ [pʌut] *v., n.* *–v.* **1** thrust or push out the lips, as a displeased or sulky child does. **2** show displeasure. **3** swell out; protrude.
–n. **1** a pushing out of the lips when displeased or sulky. **2** a fit of sullenness. ⟨ME *poute(n)*⟩

pout² [pʌut] *n., pl.* **pout** or **pouts.** a kind of freshwater catfish; eelpout. ⟨OE *-pūte,* as in *ælepūte* eelpout⟩

pout•er ['pʌutər] *n.* **1** a person who pouts. **2** a breed of domestic pigeon that has the ability to inflate its crop, producing a puffed-up breast.

pou•tine [pu'tin] *n. Cdn.* a Québécois dish consisting of French fries topped with gravy and cheese curds.

pout•y ['pʌuti] *adj. Informal.* inclined to pout.

pov•er•ty ['pɒvərti] *n.* **1** the condition of being poor or needy; the condition of not having enough income to maintain a standard of living regarded as normal in a community: *He died in poverty.* **2** the renunciation of the right to own property as an individual: *A person joining any of certain religious orders takes a vow of poverty.* **3** a lack of what is needed; inadequacy: *The poverty of the soil in this region makes farming difficult.* **4** scarcity; dearth: *a poverty of ideas.* ⟨ME < OF < L *paupertas* < *pauper* poor⟩
☛ *Syn.* **1. Poverty,** WANT, DESTITUTION = the condition of being in need. **Poverty** emphasizes being in actual need, owning nothing at all or having not enough for all the necessities of life: *Their tattered clothes and broken furniture indicated their poverty.* **Want** emphasizes extreme need, having too little to live on: *Welfare agencies help those in want.* **Destitution** emphasizes complete lack even of food and shelter, and often suggests having been deprived of possessions once had: *The Red Cross relieved the destitution following the floods.*

pov•er•ty–strick•en ['pɒvərti ,strɪkən] *adj.* extremely poor.

P.O.W. or **POW** prisoner of war.

pow•der ['paʊdər] *n., v.* *–n.* **1** a solid reduced to dust by pounding, crushing, or grinding. **2** something made or prepared as a special-purpose powder: *face powder, powders taken as medicine.* **3** gunpowder. **4** fine snow, usually newly fallen, good for skiing.
keep (one's) **powder dry,** *Informal.* stay ready for action (from the use of gunpowder in old muskets, cannon, etc.).
take a powder, *Slang.* leave; run off: *He took a powder as soon as things got rough.*
–v. **1** make into powder. **2** become powder. **3** sprinkle or cover with powder. **4** apply powder to (the face, etc.). **5** sprinkle (something in powder form). ⟨ME < OF *poudre* < L *pulvis, -veris* dust⟩ **–'pow•der•er,** *n.*

powder blue a pale blue colour.

powder burn a burn on the skin resulting from the explosion of gunpowder at close range.

powder flask formerly, a flask or case of horn, metal, or leather for carrying gunpowder.

powder horn a POWDER FLASK made of an animal's horn.

powder keg **1** a small cask for holding gunpowder or blasting powder. **2** something that is liable to explode or to erupt in violence: *The whole country was a powder keg after the death of the dictator.*

powder magazine a place where gunpowder is stored.

powder monkey **1** a person working with explosives, as in mines or oil fields. **2** formerly, a boy sailor who carried powder from the magazines to the artillery aboard a man-of-war.

powder puff a soft puff or pad for applying cosmetic or scented powder to the skin.

powder room a small rest room or lavatory for women, especially one having a dressing table for make-up, etc.

pow•der•y ['paʊdəri] *adj.* **1** of, like, or in the form of powder. **2** easily made into powder; crumbling: *powdery topsoil.* **3** covered with or as if with powder.

powdery mildew **1** any of various parasitic ascomycetous fungi of the order Erysiphales, producing a powderlike film on the host plant. **2** a plant disease caused by this mildew.

pow•er ['paʊər] *n., v., adj.* *–n.* **1** strength; might; force. **2** the ability to do or act: *I will give you all the help in my power.* **3** a particular ability: *Some students have great powers of concentration.* **4** control; authority; influence; right: *Parliament has the power to declare war.* **5** any person, thing, body, or nation having authority or influence: *Five powers held a peace conference.* **6** *Mechanics.* energy or force that can do work: *Running water produces power to run mills.* **7** electricity as a public utility: *The power is off.* **8** a simple machine. **9** *Physics.* the capacity for exerting mechanical force, as measured by the rate at which it is exerted or at which the work is done. In the SI, all power is expressed in watts or in multiples or sub-multiples of the watt. **10** *Mathematics.* the product of a number multiplied by itself: *16 is the 4th power of 2.* **11** the capacity of an instrument to magnify. The higher the power of a telescope or microscope the more details you can see. **12** Often, **powers,** *pl.* deity; divinity. **13** an order of angels.
in power, having control or authority: *the government in power.*
the powers that be, those who have control or authority.
–v. provide with power or energy: *a boat powered by an outboard motor.*
–adj. **1** operated by a motor; equipped with its own motor: *power tools, power steering.* **2** conveying electricity: *power lines.* ⟨ME < *poër,* n. < AF *poër,* var. of OF *poeir,* n. use of infinitive < VL *potere* for L *posse* be able⟩
☛ *Syn. n.* **1. Power,** STRENGTH, FORCE = ability to do something or capacity for something. **Power** is the general word applying to any physical, mental, or moral ability or capacity, whether used or not: *Every normal, healthy person has power to think.* **Strength** suggests a power within the person or thing, belonging to it as a quality, to do, bear, or resist much: *She has strength of character.* **Force** emphasizes the active use of power or strength to get something done or bring something about: *We had to use force to get into the house.*

pow•er•boat ['paʊər,bout] *n.* a motorboat, especially a boat propelled by an engine on board.

power dive *Aeronautics.* a dive of an aircraft, speeded up by the power of the engine.

po•wer–dive ['paʊər ,daɪv] *v.* **-dived** or **-dove, -dived, -div•ing.** *Aeronautics.* make a POWER DIVE.

pow•er–dress•ing ['paʊər ,drɛsɪŋ] *n.* cultivation of a powerful image by dressing in a style associated with high-level business professionals.

pow•er•ful ['paʊərfəl] *adj.* having great power or force; mighty; strong. **–'pow•er•ful•ly,** *adv.*
☛ *Syn.* See note at MIGHTY.

pow•er•house ['paʊər,hʌus] *n., adj.* *–n.* **1** a building containing boilers, engines, generators, etc. for generating electric power. **2** *Informal.* a person or group having great power, energy, drive, etc.: *That new teacher is a real powerhouse.*
–adj. of a person or group, powerful; effective; having potential for success.

pow•er•less ['paʊərlɪs] *adj.* without power; helpless. **–'pow•er•less•ly,** *adv.* **–'pow•er•less•ness,** *n.*

power loom a loom worked by steam, electricity, water power, etc.

power lunch *Informal.* a lunch over which high-level business negotiations are made.

power of attorney **1** a written statement giving one person legal power to act for another. *Abbrev.:* P.A. **2** the power so given: *She has power of attorney for her husband while he is abroad.*

power pack *Electricity.* a device that converts the voltage from a power line or battery to the voltage required by the elements of an electronic circuit, as in a radio or television set.

power plant **1** a building with machinery for generating power. **2** a motor; engine.

power play **1** *Hockey.* **a** a situation arising when one team has a temporary numerical advantage because of a penalty against the opposing team. **b** a special combination of players put on the ice when the opposition is shorthanded. **2** an action or stratagem in business or politics that attempts to achieve its goal by the use of power rather than finesse.

power politics international political strategy that uses the threat of superior military or economic power to advance national interests (*used with a singular or plural verb*).

power saw a saw powered by a motor.

power squadron an association of owners and operators of powerboats, yachts, etc. to promote safe boating, good seamanship, etc.

power station POWERHOUSE (def. 1).

power steering in a motor vehicle, a steering mechanism that uses power from the engine to increase the effect of the force used in turning the steering wheel.

power structure **1** the system of power and influence in a society, organization, etc. **2** those who, because of their economic, social, or political influence and position, are part of that system.

power tool a tool, such as a drill, worked by an electric or gasoline motor.

pow•wow ['paʊ,waʊ] *n., v.* —*n.* **1** among North American First Nations peoples, a celebration or ceremony, usually featuring feasting and dancing and certain rites, held before an expedition, hunt, council, or conference. **2** the hubbub and noise accompanying such a celebration. **3** a council or conference of or with a North American First Nations people. **4** *Informal.* any conference or meeting. **5** among some North American First Nations peoples, a medicine man. **6** a social gathering, as at a summer camp, usually featuring a campfire after dark.
—*v.* hold a powwow. ⟨< Algonquian⟩

pox [pɒks] *n.* **1** any of several diseases that are characterized by pustules, or pocks (*used especially in compounds*): *chicken pox, smallpox.* **2** Usually, **the pox**, syphilis.
a pox on (someone or something), *Archaic.* an exclamation of anger or impatience. ⟨var. of *pocks*, pl. of *pock.* See POCK.⟩

poz•zo•la•na [,pɒtsə'lɑnə] *n.* pozzuolana.

poz•zuo•la•na [,pɒtswə'lɑnə] *n.* **1** volcanic ash, etc., used by the ancient Romans in making mortar. **2** a cement additive, usually made from shale and containing silica, alumina, etc. ⟨< Ital. *pozzuolana*, n. use of fem. adj. < *Pozzuoli*, a seaport in S Italy, where it was first found⟩

pp. **1** pages. **2** PAST PARTICIPLE. **3** *Music.* pianissimo. **4** privately printed.

P.P. **1** PARCEL POST. **2** Parish Priest.

ppb or **p.p.b.** parts per billion.

ppd. **1** postpaid. **2** prepaid.

ppm or **p.p.m.** parts per million.

ppr. or **p.pr.** PRESENT PARTICIPLE.

P.P.S. **1** Often, **p.p.s.**, a second postcript (for L *post postscriptum*). **2** *Brit.* Parliamentary Private Secretary.

PQ or **P.Q.** **1** Parti Québécois. **2** Province of Québec (*used esp. in computerized address systems*).

pr. **1** pair. **2** price. **3** present. **4** prince. **5** printing. **6** pronoun.

Pr praseodymium.

P.R. PROPORTIONAL REPRESENTATION.

P.R. or **PR** PUBLIC RELATIONS.

praam [prɑm] *n.* PRAM[2].

prac•ti•ca•ble ['præktɪkəbəl] *adj.* **1** that can be done; capable of being put into practice; feasible: *a practicable idea.* **2** that can be used: *a practicable road.* ⟨< F *practicable* < *pratiquer* practise; influenced in English by obs. *practic.* See PRACTICAL.⟩ —**,prac•ti•ca'bil•i•ty**, *n.* —**prac•ti•ca•bly**, *adv.*
☛ *Syn.* **1.** See note at POSSIBLE. **Practicable**, PRACTICAL = able to be done or put into practice. **Practicable** emphasizes that it is possible (or not possible) for something to be done: *Building an apartment tower on soft marshland is not practicable.* **Practical** suggests that what can be done is (or is not) also reasonable or worthwhile: *Building on this drained swamp would cost too much for the project to be practical.* See also the note at IMPRACTICAL.

prac•ti•cal ['præktɪkəl] *adj.* **1** having to do with action or practice rather than thought or theory: *Earning a living is a practical matter.* **2** able to be put into practice with reasonable efficiency: *a practical plan.* **3** useful in practice: *His legal knowledge was not very practical when he became a chemist.* **4** having or showing good sense. **5** engaged in actual practice or work: *A practical farmer runs a farm.* **6** being such in effect; virtual: *So many of our soldiers were killed that our victory was a practical defeat.* ⟨< earlier *practic* < LL *practicus* < Gk. *praktikos* < *prassein* do⟩ —**'prac•ti•cal•ness**, *n.*
☛ *Syn.* **2.** See note at PRACTICABLE. **4.** See note at SENSIBLE.

prac•ti•cal•i•ty [,præktɪ'kælɪti] *n., pl.* **-ties.** **1** the quality of being practical; practical usefulness; a practical habit of mind. **2** a practical matter.

practical joke a kind of trick that depends for its effect or humour on someone being put at a disadvantage or embarrassed or abused in some way.

practical joker a person who plays practical jokes on others.

prac•ti•cal•ly ['præktɪkli] *adv.* **1** almost; nearly: *We're practically home.* **2** in effect; virtually: *They practically ran the show.* **3** in a practical way: *reacting very practically to the crisis.*

practical nurse a nurse whose occupation is to care for the sick, but who does not have the theoretical training required of a registered nurse.

prac•tice ['præktɪs] *n., v.* **-ticed, -tic•ing.** —*n.* **1** the doing of an action many times over in order to gain skill: *Practice makes perfect.* **2** the skill gained by experience or exercise: *He was out of practice at batting.* **3** the action or process of doing or being something: *Her plan is good in theory, but not in actual practice.* **4** the usual way; custom: *It is the practice at the factory to blow a whistle at noon.* **5** the working at or following of a profession or occupation: *engaged in the practice of law.* **6** the business of a doctor, dentist, or lawyer: *Dr. Adams sold her practice.* **7** *Archaic.* a scheme; plot. **8** *Law.* the established method of conducting legal proceedings. **9** a period set aside for practising: *He went to hockey practice last night.*
—*v.* See PRACTISE. ⟨ME < *practise*, v. < OF *practiser*, ult. < LL *practicus.* See PRACTICAL.⟩
☛ *Spelling.* **Practice** is one of two pairs of words that in Canadian English are usually spelled differently as nouns and verbs. The preferred spelling for the noun is **practice** and for the verb **practise.** For this reason the noun and verb are entered separately in this dictionary. The other pair is *licence* and *license*.
☛ *Syn.* **1.** See note at EXERCISE.

prac•ti•cum ['præktɪkəm] *n., pl.* **-cums** or **-ca** [-kə]. in schools and colleges: **1** a course in independent research or in practical work. **2** a practical part of a course, such as laboratory or field work. **3** in education, practice teaching. ⟨< NL *(collegium) practicum* practical course < Med.L *practicare* to practise⟩

prac•tise ['præktɪs] *v.* **-tised, -tis•ing.** **1** do (something) again and again so as to learn to do it well: *practise playing the piano.* **2** do as a rule; make a custom of; follow, observe, or use day after day: *to practise moderation. Practise what you preach.* **3** work at or follow as a profession, art, or occupation: *to practise medicine, to practise architecture.* **4** practise a profession, especially law, medicine, or dentistry: *My uncle practises in Thunder Bay.* **5** give training to; drill. **6** *Archaic.* scheme; plot. **7** take advantage of (*used with* **on**). Also, **practice.** ⟨See PRACTICE⟩ —**'prac•tis•er**, *n.*
☛ *Spelling.* See note at PRACTICE.

prac•tised ['præktɪst] *adj., v.* —*adj.* **1** experienced; skilled; expert; proficient. **2** acquired or perfected through practice.
—*v.* pt. and pp. of PRACTISE. Also, **practiced.**

prac•tis•ing ['præktəsɪŋ] *adj., v.* —*adj.* actively engaged in a particular profession or career or actively following a religion: *a practising lawyer, a practising Catholic.*
—*v.* ppr. of PRACTISE. Also, **practicing.**

prac•ti•tion•er [præk'tɪʃənər] *n.* a person engaged in the practice of an art or profession: *She was a medical practitioner for ten years; later she taught medicine.*

prae•fect ['prifɛkt] *n.* See PREFECT.

prae•no•men [pri'noumən] *n., pl.* **-nom•i•na** [-'nɒmənə]. in ancient Rome, the first or personal name of a citizen. ⟨< L *praenomen* < *prae-* before + *nomen* name⟩

prae•tor ['pritər] *or* ['pritɔr] *n.* in ancient Rome, a magistrate or judge, ranking next below a consul. Also, **pretor.** ⟨< L *praetor*, ult. < *prae-* before + *ire* go⟩

prae•to•ri•an [prɪ'tɔriən] *adj., n.* —*adj.* in ancient Rome: **1** of or having to do with a praetor. **2** having to do with or being the bodyguard of a commander or emperor.
—*n.* **1** a man having the rank of a praetor. **2** a soldier of the bodyguard of a commander or emperor. ⟨< L *praetorianus*⟩

prag•mat•ic [præg'mætɪk] *adj.* **1** of or concerned with practical results or values, not with theories or ideals: *He is a very pragmatic person.* **2** of or having to do with the philosophy of pragmatism. **3** having to do with the affairs of a state or community. **4** treating the facts of history systematically, with special reference to their causes and effects. Also, **pragmatical.** ⟨< L *pragmaticus* < Gk. *pragmatikos* efficient, ult. < *prassein* do⟩ —**prag'mat•i•cal•ly**, *adv.*

prag•mat•ics [præg'mætɪks] *n.* **1** *Logic. Philosophy.* a branch of semiotics dealing with the causal and other relationships between signs and symbols and their users. **2** *Linguistics.* the study and analysis of language in terms of the context of a situation, including the intent of the speaker and the relation between speaker and hearer.

pragmatic sanction an edict by a ruler that becomes a law of the land.

prag•ma•tism ['prægmə,tɪzəm] *n.* **1** the quality or condition of being pragmatic, or practical and matter-of-fact. **2** a philosophy that tests the value and truth of ideas by their practical consequences.

prag•ma•tist ['prægmətɪst] *n., adj.* —*n.* **1** a practical person **2** a person who believes in pragmatism.
—*adj.* of or having to to with pragmatism. —**,prag•ma'tis•tic,** *adj.*

prai•rie ['prɛri] *n., adj.* —*n.* **1** a large area of level or rolling land with grass but very few or no trees. **2 the Prairies,** *pl.* **a** the great, almost treeless, plain that covers much of central North America. **b** *Cdn.* the part of this plain that covers much of central and southern Manitoba, Saskatchewan, and Alberta.
—*adj.* Often, **Prairie,** of or having to do with the PRAIRIE PROVINCES. ⟨< F *prairie,* ult. < L *pratum* meadow⟩

prairie chicken **1** either of two grouse having brown-and-white, barred plumage: the **greater prairie chicken** (*Tympanuchus cupido*) of the central North American plains, formerly common in the Canadian Prairies but now rare; or the smaller, paler **lesser prairie chicken** (*T. pallidicinctus*) of the plains of the SW United States. **2** SHARP-TAILED GROUSE. **3** *Slang, esp. B.C.* a newcomer, especially one from the Prairies.

prairie crocus CROCUS (def. 2). See also PASQUE-FLOWER.

A prairie dog

prairie dog any of several North American burrowing rodents (genus *Cynomys*) found especially on the central plains, related to and resembling ground squirrels, but somewhat larger and stouter and having a shorter tail. Prairie dogs live in colonies often called 'towns'; in Canada, they occur only in extreme southern Saskatchewan. ⟨so-called because of its barklike cry⟩

prairie elk wapiti.

prairie fox a variety of the red fox (*Vulpes fulva*) found on the prairies.

prairie itch *Cdn.* a form of dermatitis caused by a freshwater hydra encountered in certain sloughs on the prairie.

prairie lily a North American wild lily (*Lilium philadelphicum*), orange-red in colour, found on the prairies and in open woods from Québec to British Columbia and south to New Mexico. The prairie lily is the provincial flower of Saskatchewan.

prairie oyster **1** a raw egg seasoned with Worcestershire sauce, swallowed whole. **2** *Cdn.* a testicle of a bull calf, prepared for eating.

Prairie Provinces Manitoba, Saskatchewan, and Alberta.

prairie rose a pink climbing rose (*Rosa setigera*) of the Prairies.

prairie schooner a large covered wagon used by pioneers in crossing the plains before the railways were built, especially in the United States.

prairie smoke a three-flowered avens (*Geum triflorum*) having deep pink sepals. It blooms in spring in dry fields and prairies.

prairie squint a squint characteristic of many western farmers who work long hours in the sun.

prairie squirrel or **gopher** the Richardson ground squirrel (*Spermophilus richardsonii*).

prairie sunflower a wild sunflower (*Helianthus petiolaris*) having large yellow flowers, blooming in summer in dry, open fields across North America.

prairie turnip **1** the edible root of one of the pea family (*Psoralea esculenta*), shaped like a large carrot and said to taste like a turnip. Used as a foodstuff by the Plains First Nations peoples, it was boiled, or pounded and then dried in the sun to yield a kind of flour. **2** the plant from which this root is obtained; breadroot.

prairie wolf coyote.

prairie wool *Cdn.* forage or pasturage composed of spear-grass, bunch-grass, and buffalo-grass.

praise [preiz] *n., v.* **praised, prais•ing.** —*n.* **1** the act of saying that a thing or person is good; words that tell the worth or value of a thing or person. **2** words or song setting forth the glory and goodness of God.
damn with faint praise. See DAMN.
sing the praise or **praises of,** praise with enthusiasm.
—*v.* **1** express approval or admiration of. **2** worship in words or song: *to praise God.* ⟨ME < OF *preisier,* ult. < L *pretium* price⟩ —**'prais•er,** *n.*

☛ *Syn. v.* **1.** Praise, APPROVE, COMMEND = think or speak well of. **Praise** means to express in a hearty or enthusiastic way one's high opinion or admiration of someone or something: *The coach praised the team for its fine playing.* **Approve** means to think or express a favourable opinion or admiration: *Everyone approved her idea.* **Commend** means to suggest a more formal expression of favourable opinion: *The mayor commended the teenagers for their quick thinking at the disaster.*

praise•wor•thy ['preiz,wɜrði] *adj.* worthy of praise; deserving approval. —**'praise,wor•thi•ly,** *adv.* —**'praise,wor•thi•ness,** *n.*

Pra•krit ['prɑkrɪt] *n.* any of the Indo-European vernacular languages or dialects of northern and central India, especially those of the ancient and medieval periods. ⟨< Skt. *prakrta* natural, common, vulgar. Cf. SANSKRIT.⟩

pra•line ['preilin] *or* ['prɒlin] *n.* **1** a brown candy made of sugar and nuts, usually pecans or almonds. **2** any similarly made candy. ⟨< F; invented by the cook of Marshal Duplessis-*Praslin* (1598-1675)⟩

pram[1] [præm] *n. Esp. Brit.* BABY CARRIAGE. ⟨shortened from *perambulator*⟩

pram[2] [præm] *n.* a small flatbottomed boat having a blunt, square bow. Also, **praam.** ⟨< Du. *praam*⟩

prance [præns] v. **pranced, pranc•ing;** *n.* —*v.* **1** spring about on the hind legs. Horses prance when they feel lively. **2** ride on a horse doing this. **3** move gaily or vainly; swagger. **4** caper; dance.
—*n.* the act of prancing. ⟨ME *prance(n), praunce(n)*; origin uncertain⟩ —**'pranc•er,** *n.* —**'pranc•ing•ly,** *adv.*

prang [præŋ] *v., n. Brit. Slang.* —*v.* **1** cause (a moving vehicle) to crash: *He pranged his old Triumph on a tree last week.* **2** collide with. **3** bomb heavily.
—*n.* **1** a collision. **2** a bombing raid.

prank[1] [præŋk] *n.* a piece of mischief; playful trick: *On April Fool's Day people play pranks on each other.* ⟨origin uncertain⟩

prank[2] [præŋk] *v.* **1** dress in a showy way; adorn. **2** make a show or display. ⟨Cf. MLG *prank* showiness⟩

prank•ish ['præŋkɪʃ] *adj.* **1** full of pranks; fond of pranks. **2** like a prank. —**'prank•ish•ly,** *adv.* —**'prank•ish•ness,** *n.*

prank•ster ['præŋkstər] *n.* a person who plays pranks.

pra•se•o•dym•i•um [,preiziou'dɪmiəm] *or* [,preisiou'dɪmiəm] *n. Chemistry.* a rare metallic chemical element of the same group as cerium. *Symbol*: Pr; *at.no.* 59; *at.mass* 140.91. ⟨< NL *praseodymium,* ult. < Gk. *prasios* bluish green + E *(di)dymium,* a rare element < Gk. *didymos* twin⟩

prat [præt] *n. Slang.* the rump or backside; buttocks. ⟨origin unknown. 16c.⟩

prate [preit] *v.* **prat•ed, prat•ing;** *n.* —*v.* talk a great deal in a foolish way; prattle; chatter.
—*n.* empty or foolish talk. ⟨late ME < Mdu. *praeten*⟩ —**'prat•er,** *n.* —**'prat•ing•ly,** *adv.*

prat•fall ['præt,fɒl] *n. Slang.* **1** a fall on the rump or backside, as part of a slapstick performance. **2** any laughable or disconcerting blunder.

prat•tle ['prætəl] *v.* **-tled, -tling;** *n.* —*v.* **1** talk as a child does; tell freely and carelessly. **2** talk or tell in a foolish way; prate. **3** make a sound like baby talk; babble.
—*n.* **1** foolish or childish talk. **2** a sound like baby talk; babble: *the prattle of a brook.* ⟨< *prate*⟩ —**'prat•tler,** *n.*

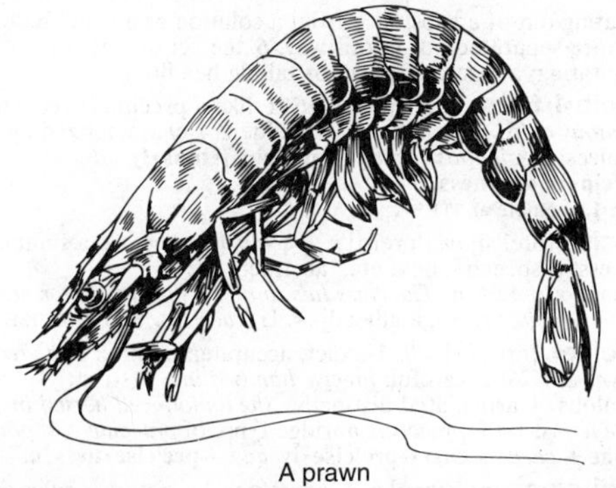
A prawn

prawn [prɒn] *n., v.* *–n.* **1** any of various long-bodied, marine decapod crustaceans (suborder Natantia, especially genera *Palaemon*, *Penaeus*, etc.). Compare SHRIMP. **2** any large, edible shrimp. Prawns may be up to 20 cm long.
–v. fish for or catch prawns. ⟨ME *prane*; origin uncertain⟩
–'prawn•er, *n.*

prax•is ['præksɪs] *n., pl.* **prax•is•es** or **prax•es** [-siz]. **1** the practice of an art, science, etc., as opposed to the theory or study of it. **2** established practice; custom. ⟨< Med.L < Gk. *prâxis* action, doing < *prassein* to do, practise. 16c.⟩

pray [prei] *v.* **1** speak to God in worship; enter into spiritual communion with God; offer worship. **2** make an earnest request to God or to any other object of worship: *to pray for help, to pray for one's family.* **3** ask earnestly: *They prayed that the kidnappers would let them go.* **4** ask earnestly for: *to pray someone's forgiveness.* **5** bring or get by praying. **6** *Archaic.* please: *Pray come with me.* ⟨ME *preien* < OF *preier* < L *precari* to beg, pray < *prex, precis* prayer⟩ **–'pray•ing•ly,** *adv.*
☛ *Hom.* PREY.

prayer¹ [prɛr] *n.* **1** an earnest request, especially one made to God. **2** the act of praying: *She was at prayer.* **3** the thing prayed for: *Our prayers were granted.* **4** a form of words to be used in praying. **5** a form of worship; religious service consisting mainly of prayers. **6** *Informal.* a chance or hope of success: *He doesn't have a prayer when it comes to getting that job.* ⟨ME *preiere* < OF, ult. < L *prex, precis* prayer⟩

pray•er² ['preiər] *n.* one who prays. ⟨late ME *preyare.* See PRAY, -ER¹.⟩

prayer book **1** a book of prayers. **2 Prayer Book,** the Book of Common Prayer, or the Book of Alternative Services, of the Anglican Church.

prayer•ful ['prɛrfəl] *adj.* **1** having the custom of praying often; devout. **2** like a prayer; earnest. **–'prayer•ful•ly,** *adv.* **–'prayer•ful•ness,** *n.*

prayer meeting a meeting for prayer and worship.

prayer rug a small rug used by Muslims to kneel on when praying.

prayer shawl a shawl with a fringe, traditionally worn over the head and shoulders by Jewish men for morning prayers; tallith.

prayer wheel a wheel or cylinder inscribed with prayers, each turn of the wheel counting as an uttered prayer, used by the Buddhists of Tibet.

praying mantis mantis.

pre– *prefix.* before in place, time, order, or rank: *prepay, preheat, prewar, premolar.* ⟨< L *prae-* before⟩

preach [pritʃ] *v.* **1** speak publicly on a religious subject. **2** deliver (a sermon). **3** make known by preaching; proclaim: *to preach the Gospel.* **4** advise or recommend strongly; urge: *The coach was always preaching exercise and fresh air.* **5** give earnest advice, usually in a meddling or tiresome way: *He is forever preaching about good table manners.* ⟨ME *prechen* < OF *prechier* < L *praedicare* declare, preach. Doublet of PREDICATE.⟩

preach•er ['pritʃər] *n.* a person who preaches; member of the clergy; minister.

preach•i•fy ['pritʃə,faɪ] *v.* **-fied, -fy•ing.** *Informal.* preach or moralize too much.

preach•ing ['pritʃɪŋ] *n., v.* *–n.* **1** what is preached; sermon(s). **2** the art of delivering sermons.
–v. ppr. of PREACH.

preach•ment ['pritʃmənt] *n.* **1** the act of preaching. **2** a long, tiresome sermon or speech.

preach•y ['pritʃi] *adj.* **preach•i•er, preach•i•est.** *Informal.* having or showing too great an inclination to preach or moralize.

pre•am•ble [pri'æmbəl] *n.* **1** a preliminary statement; introduction to a speech or a writing. The reasons for a law and its general purpose are often stated in a preamble. **2** a preliminary or introductory fact, act, or circumstance. ⟨< F < Med.L *praeambulum,* originally neut. adj., walking before, ult. < L *prae-* before + *ambulare* walk⟩

pre•am•pli•fi•er [pri'æmplə,faɪər] *n.* a device that amplifies very weak signals in the amplifier circuit of a radio, phonograph, etc. enabling them to be sent into the main amplifier.

pre•ar•range [,priə'reindʒ] *v.* **-ranged, -rang•ing.** arrange beforehand: *a prearranged meeting place, a prearranged signal.*
–,pre•ar'range•ment, *n.*

pre•as•sign [,priə'saɪn] *v.* assign beforehand: *The seats at the conference table were preassigned.*

pre•ax•ial [pri'æksiəl] *adj. Anatomy. Zoology.* located in front of the axis of the body or one of the limbs, especially the radial side of the upper limb and the tibial side of the lower.

preb•end ['prɛbənd] *n.* **1** the salary or stipend given to a member of the clergy connected with a cathedral or a collegiate church. **2** the particular property or church tax from which the money comes for this salary. **3** prebendary. ⟨ME *prebende* < OF < LL *praebenda* allowance < L *praebenda* (things) to be furnished < *praebere* furnish < *prae-* before + *habere* hold⟩

preb•en•dar•y ['prɛbən,dɛri] *n., pl.* **-dar•ies.** a member of the clergy who has a prebend.

prec. preceding.

Pre•cam•bri•an or **Pre–Cam•bri•an** [,pri'kæmbriən] *or* [,pri'keimbriən] *adj., n. Geology.* *–adj.* of, having to do with, or referring to the earliest era of geological time, including all the time before the Paleozoic era, or the rocks formed during this time. The CANADIAN SHIELD consists of Precambrian rock. See geological time chart in the Appendix.
–n. the Precambrian era or its rock system.

pre•can•cel [pri'kænsəl] *v.* **-celled** or **-celed, -cel•ling** or **-cel•ing;** *n.* *–v.* cancel (a postage stamp) before sale.
–n. a precancelled postage stamp.

pre•can•cer•ous [pri'kænsərəs] *adj.* showing pathological changes likely to lead to a malignancy.

pre•car•i•ous [prɪ'kɛriəs] *adj.* **1** not safe or secure; uncertain, risky, or dangerous: *a precarious hold on a branch. An active soldier leads a precarious life.* **2** poorly founded; doubtful; assumed: *a precarious opinion or conclusion.* **3** *Archaic.* dependent on the will or pleasure of another: *precarious tenure.* ⟨< L *precarius,* originally, obtainable by entreaty, ult. < *prex, precis* prayer⟩ **–pre'car•i•ous•ly,** *adv.* **–pre'car•i•ous•ness,** *n.*

pre•cau•tion [prɪ'kɒʃən] *n.* **1** something done beforehand to prevent harm or to secure good results: *Locking the door of a house is a precaution against theft.* **2** a taking care beforehand; foresight: *Proper precaution is necessary when taking a trip by car in winter.* ⟨< LL *praecautio, -onis* < L *praecavere* guard against beforehand < *prae-* before + *cavere* be on one's guard⟩

pre•cau•tion•ar•y [prɪ'kɒʃə,nɛri] *adj.* of or using precaution.

pre•ca•va [pri'keivə] *or* [pri'kɑvə] *n., pl.* **pre•ca•vae** [-vi] *or* [-vaɪ]. *Anatomy.* the superior VENA CAVA in vertebrates. Compare POSTCAVA.

pre•cede [prɪ'sid] *v.* **-ced•ed, -ced•ing.** **1** go or come before: *The rain was preceded by a violent windstorm. A band preceded the first float in the parade.* **2** be higher than in rank or importance: *A major precedes a captain.* ⟨< L *praecedere* < *prae-* before + *cedere* go⟩
☛ *Usage.* Do not confuse **precede** 'go or come before' with PROCEED 'move forward': *January precedes February. The year proceeds slowly.*

prec•e•dence ['prɛsɪdəns] *n.* **1** the act or fact of preceding. **2** a higher position or rank; greater importance; social superiority: *to take precedence over all others. The Royal dukes take precedence over all others except the Queen.* **3** the right to precede others in ceremonial affairs: *A major takes precedence over a captain. The Convocation procession is in reverse order of precedence, with the Chancellor coming last.*

prec•e•den•cy ['prɛsɪdənsi] *n., pl.* **-cies.** precedence.

prec•e•dent *n.* ['prɛsɪdənt]; *adj.* ['prɛsədənt] *or* [prɪ'sidənt] *n., adj.* *–n.* **1** a case that may serve as an example or reason for a later case. **2** *Law.* a judicial decision, case, proceeding, etc., that

serves as a guide or pattern in future similar or analogous situations.
—adj. preceding. ⟨< L *praecedens, -entis,* ppr. of *praecedere.* See PRECEDE.⟩

pre•ced•ing [prɪ'sidɪŋ] *adj., v. —adj.* going or coming before; previous: *the preceding page, the preceding year.*
—v. ppr. of PRECEDE.
☛ *Syn. adj.* See note at PREVIOUS.

pre•cen•tor [prɪ'sɛntər] *n.* a person who leads and directs the singing of a church choir or congregation. ⟨< LL *praecentor,* ult. < L *prae-* before + *canere* sing⟩

pre•cept ['prisɛpt] *n.* **1** a general rule of action or behaviour; maxim: *"If at first you don't succeed, try, try, try again" is a familiar precept.* **2** a teaching. ⟨< L *praeceptum,* originally neut. pp. of *praecipere* enjoin, anticipate < *prae-* before + *capere* take⟩ **—pre'cep•tive,** *adj.*

pre•cep•tor [prɪ'sɛptər] *or* [pri'sɛptər] *n.* an instructor; teacher. ⟨< L *praeceptor* < *praecipere.* See PRECEPT.⟩

pre•cep•to•ri•al [,prisɛp'tɔriəl] *adj.* **1** of a preceptor; like that of a preceptor. **2** using preceptors.

pre•cinct ['prisɪŋkt] *n.* **1** Usually, **precincts,** *pl.* a space enclosed by walls, a fence, etc.: *the school precincts.* **2** Often, **precincts,** *pl.* a boundary; limit. **3** a district within certain boundaries, for administration or other purposes: *a police precinct.* **4** Usually, **precincts,** *pl.* the area around a large public building, not necessarily enclosed: *the courthouse precincts.* ⟨< Med.L *praecinctum,* originally neut. pp. of *praecingere* enclose < *prae-* before + *cingere* gird⟩

pre•ci•os•i•ty [,prɛʃi'ɒsɪti] *n., pl.* **-ties.** too much refinement; affectation of language, style, or taste. ⟨< F *préciosité* < *précieux* precious⟩

pre•cious ['prɛʃəs] *adj., adv. —adj.* **1** worth much; valuable. See PRECIOUS METAL. **2** much loved; dear. **3** too fastidious; overrefined; affected. **4** *Informal.* very great; thoroughgoing: *a precious mess.*
—adv. Informal. very: *precious little money.* ⟨ME < OF *precios* < L *pretiosus* < *pretium* value⟩ **—'pre•cious•ness,** *n.*
☛ *Syn. adj.* **1.** See note at VALUABLE.

pre•cious•ly ['prɛʃəsli] *adv.* **1** at great cost. **2** in a valuable manner or degree. **3** extremely. **4** with extreme care in matters of detail. **5** affectedly.

precious metal a valuable metal such as gold, silver, or platinum.

precious stone a jewel; gem. Diamonds, rubies, emeralds, and sapphires are precious stones.

pre•cip [prɪ'sɪp] *or* ['prisɪp] *n. Informal.* precipitation. ⟨shortened form of *precipitation*⟩

prec•i•pice ['prɛsəpɪs] *n.* **1** a very steep cliff; an almost vertical slope; the face of a cliff. **2** a very dangerous situation; the brink of disaster. ⟨< F < L *praecipitium* < *praeceps, -cipitis* steep, literally, headlong < *prae-* first + *caput* head⟩

pre•cip•i•tance [prɪ'sɪpɪtəns] *n.* **1** headlong haste; rashness. **2** suddenness. Also, **precipitancy.**

pre•cip•i•tant [prɪ'sɪpɪtənt] *n., adj. —n. Chemistry.* a substance that causes another substance in solution in a liquid to be deposited in solid form; a precipitating agent.
—adj. precipitate. ⟨< L *praecipitans, -antis,* ppr. of *praecipitare.* See PRECIPITATE.⟩ **—pre'cip•i•tant•ly,** *adv.*

pre•cip•i•tate *v.* [prɪ'sɪpɪ,teit]; *adj.* [prɪ'sɪpɪtɪt]; *n.* [prɪ'sɪpɪtɪt] *or* [prɪ'sɪpɪ,teit] **-tat•ed, -tat•ing;** *adj., n. —v.* **1** hasten the beginning of; bring about suddenly: *to precipitate a war.* **2** throw headlong; hurl: *to precipitate a rock down a cliff.* **3** *Chemistry.* **a** separate (a substance) out from a solution as a solid. **b** be separated in this way. **4 a** condense from vapour in the form of rain, dew, etc. **b** be condensed in this way.
—adj. **1** very hurried; sudden: *A cool breeze caused a precipitate drop in the temperature.* **2** with great haste and force; plunging or rushing; hasty; rash: *precipitate actions.*
—n. a substance, usually crystalline, separated out from a solution as a solid. ⟨< L *praecipitare* < *praeceps* headlong. See PRECIPICE.⟩ **—pre'cip•i•tate•ly,** *adv.* **—pre'cip•i,ta•tor,** *n.* **—pre'cip•i•tate•ness,** *n.* **—pre'cip•i,ta•tive,** *adj.*

pre•cip•i•ta•tion [prɪ,sɪpɪ'teiʃən] *n.* **1** *Meteorology.* **a** the depositing of moisture in the form of rain, dew, or snow. **b** something that is precipitated, such as rain, dew, or snow. **c** the amount that is precipitated. **2** a hastening or hurrying. **3** a sudden bringing on: *the precipitation of a war without warning.* **4** unwise or rash speed; sudden haste. **5** *Chemistry. Physics.* **a** the separating out of a substance from a solution as a solid. **b** the substance separated out in this way. **6** the act or state of precipitating; a throwing down or falling headlong.

pre•cip•i•tous [prɪ'sɪpɪtəs] *adj.* **1** like a precipice; very steep: *precipitous cliffs.* **2** hasty; rash. **3** sudden. **4** characterized by precipices: *precipitous scenery.* **—pre'cip•i•tous•ly,** *adv.* **—pre'cip•i•tous•ness,** *n.*
☛ *Syn.* **1.** See note at STEEP.

pré•cis [prei'si] *or* ['preisi] *n., pl.* **-cis** [-siz]; *v. —n.* a summary of an essay, speech, book, etc.; abstract.
—v. make a précis of: *The class has to précis this article for next week.* ⟨< F *précis,* originally adj. < L *praecisus.* See PRECISE.⟩

pre•cise [prɪ'sɔɪs] *adj.* **1** exact; accurate; definite: *The precise sum was $31.28.* **2** careful: *precise handwriting.* **3** strict; scrupulous. **4** articulated distinctly: *She announced herself in precise terms.* ⟨< L *praecisus* abridged, pp. of *praecidere* < *prae-* in front + *caedere* cut⟩ **—pre'cise•ly,** *adv.* **—pre'cise•ness,** *n.*

pre•ci•sian [prɪ'sɪʒən] *n.* **1** a person who observes rules and forms strictly and punctiliously. **2** a 16th or 17th century English Puritan.
☛ *Hom.* PRECISION.

pre•ci•sion [prɪ'sɪʒən] *n.* **1** the quality or state of being precise; exactness: *the precision of a machine. The precision of the bookkeeper's calculations was amazing.* **2** the degree of refinement or exactness obtained. **3** (*adjl.*) designed for or marked by precision: *precision instruments, precision marching.*
☛ *Hom.* PRECISIAN.

pre•clin•i•cal [pri'klɪnɪkəl] *adj. Medicine.* of or in the stage of a disease prior to the appearance of symptoms.

pre•clude [prɪ'klud] *v.* **-clud•ed, -clud•ing.** shut out; make impossible; prevent: *Buying a house now would preclude any possibility of a holiday trip for the next few years.* ⟨< L *praecludere* < *prae-* before + *claudere* shut⟩

pre•clu•sion [prɪ'kluʒən] *n.* the act of precluding or the state of being precluded. ⟨< L *praeclusus,* pp. of *praecludere.* See PRECLUDE.⟩

pre•clu•sive [prɪ'klusɪv] *adj.* tending or serving to preclude. **—pre'clu•sive•ly,** *adv.*

pre•co•cious [prɪ'kouʃəs] *adj.* **1** developed much earlier than normal in knowledge, skill, etc.: *She was so precocious as a child that she was composing music at the age of three.* **2** of a plant, developing or maturing very early. ⟨< L *praecox, -ocis,* ult. < *prae-* before (its time) + *coquere* ripen⟩ **—pre'co•cious•ly,** *adv.* **—pre'co•cious•ness,** *n.*

pre•coc•i•ty [prɪ'kɒsɪti] *n.* precocious development; early maturity.

pre•cog•ni•tion [,prikəg'nɪʃən] *n.* **1** prior knowledge or cognition; foreknowledge. **2** *Scottish law.* **a** a preliminary examination of witnesses, etc. **b** the evidence taken at this examination. **—pre'cog•ni•tive** [pri'kɒgnətɪv], *adj.* ⟨< LL *præcognitio* < L *praecognitus* pp. of *praecognoscere* to foreknow, ult. < *prae-* before + *cognoscere* to know⟩

pre–Col•um•bi•an [,pri kə'lʌmbiən] *adj.* of or having to do with any period in the history of the Americas before the arrival of Columbus.

pre•con•ceive [,prikən'siv] *v.* **-ceived, -ceiv•ing.** form (an idea or opinion) before having any actual experience or knowledge: *Her first sea voyage didn't fit any of her preconceived notions of what it would be like.* **—,pre•con'ceived,** *adj.*

pre•con•cep•tion [,prikən'sɛpʃən] *n.* an idea or opinion formed beforehand.

pre•con•cert [,prikən'sɜrt] *v.* organize beforehand usually by agreement.

pre•con•di•tion [,prikən'dɪʃən] *n., v. —n.* something that must be fulfilled before something else can come about, take place, etc.; prerequisite.
—v. prepare or condition in advance: *You have been preconditioned to react that way from earliest association.*

pre–Con•fed•er•a•tion [,pri kən,fɛdə'reiʃən] *adj. Cdn.* of or relating to the period in Canada prior to 1867, when CONFEDERATION (def. 3) was established.

pre•con•scious [pri'kɒnʃəs] *adj., n. —adj.* **1** not present in, but capable of easy recall to the conscious mind. **2** happening before the development of consciousness.
—n. the preconscious part of the mind.

pre•cook [pri'kʊk] *v.* cook (food), partially or completely, ahead of time in order to shorten or simplify its final preparation.

pre•cur•sor [prɪ'kɜrsər] *n.* a forerunner: *A severe cough may* *be the precursor of pneumonia.* ⟨< L *praecursor*, ult. < *prae-* before + *currere* run⟩

pre•cur•so•ry [prɪ'kɜrsəri] *adj.* indicative of something to follow; introductory.

pred. predicate.

pre•da•cious [prɪ'deiʃəs] *adj.* living by preying; predatory. Also, **predaceous.** ⟨< L *praedari* rob < *praeda* prey⟩ **—pre'dac•i•ty** [prɪ'dæsəti] or **pre'da•cious•ness,** *n.*

pre•date [pri'deit] *v.* **-dat•ed, -dat•ing. 1** to come before in time: *His teaching career predated his entry into politics.* **2** assign something to a date before its actual date: *She predated her letter to make it look as if she had written it a week earlier.*

pre•da•tion [prɪ'deiʃən] *n.* the act or fact of preying on other animals.

pred•a•tor ['prɛdətər] *n.* **1** an animal that lives by killing and eating other animals. **2** a person who lives by exploiting or preying on others.

pred•a•to•ry ['prɛdə,tɔri] *adj.* **1** of or inclined to plundering or robbery: *Predatory highwaymen infested the highways.* **2** living by preying upon other animals. Hawks and owls are predatory birds. **3** tending to injure or exploit others for the sake of one's own interests, profit, etc. ⟨< L *praedatorius*, ult. < *praeda* prey⟩

pre•de•cease [,pridɪ'sis] *v.* **-ceased, -ceas•ing;** *n.* *—v.* die before (someone else): *Husbands frequently predecease their wives. King Henry VIII was predeceased by three of his six wives.*
—n. the fact of having died before someone else: *I leave everything to my husband; in the event of his predecease, everything is to be divided equally between my two children.*

pred•e•ces•sor ['prɛdɪ,sɛsər] *or* ['pridɪ,sɛsər] *n.* **1** a person holding a position or office before another: *Queen Victoria was the predecessor of Edward VII.* **2** something that came before another which has replaced it. **3** ancestor; forebear. ⟨< LL *praedecesor*, ult, < *prae-* before + *decedere* retire < *de-* from + *cedere* withdraw⟩

pre•des•ti•na•ri•an [pri,dɛstɪ'nɛriən]; *adj., n.* *—adj.* of or having to do with predestination.
—n. one who believes in predestination.

pre•des•ti•nate *v.* [pri'dɛstɪ,neit]; *adj.* [pri'dɛstənɪt] *v.* **-nat•ed, -nat•ing,** *adj.* *—v.* **1** decree or ordain beforehand. **2** foreordain by divine purpose.
—adj. predestinated. ⟨< L *praedestinare* appoint beforehand < *prae-* before + *destinare* make fast, ult. < *de-* + *stare* stand⟩

pre•des•ti•na•tion [pri,dɛstɪ'neiʃən] *n.* **1** an ordaining beforehand; destiny; fate. **2** an action of God in deciding beforehand what will happen. **3** a doctrine that by God's decree certain souls will be saved and others lost.

pre•des•tine [prɪ'dɛstɪn] *v.* **-tined, -tin•ing.** determine or settle beforehand, especially by predestination; foreordain: *predestined to failure and disappointment, predestined to rule.*

pre•de•ter•mine [,pridɪ'tɜrmɪn] *v.* **-mined, -min•ing. 1** determine or decide beforehand: *The time for the meeting was predetermined.* **2** direct or impel beforehand (to something): *Her love of children predetermined her to seek a career as a kindergarten specialist.* **—,pre•de,ter•mi'na•tion,** *n.*

pred•i•ca•ble ['prɛdɪkəbəl] *adj.* that can be predicated or affirmed. **—'pred•i•ca•bly,** *adv.*

pre•dic•a•ment [prɪ'dɪkəmənt] *n.* **1** an unpleasant, difficult, or dangerous situation. **2** *Archaic.* a specific condition, state, or situation. ⟨< LL *praedicamentum* quality, category < L *praedicare.* See PREDICATE.⟩

☛ *Syn.* **1. Predicament,** PLIGHT, DILEMMA= a difficult situation. **Predicament** suggests a position or situation that is hard to get out of or presents a problem difficult to solve: *The world is in a dangerous predicament.* **Plight** applies to an unfortunate state or condition, usually unhappy or miserable, often hopeless: *He is worried by the plight of his relatives in enemy-conquered territory.* **Dilemma** applies to a predicament forcing a choice between two things, both disagreeable: *She is faced with the dilemma of telling a lie or betraying her friend.*

pred•i•cate *n., adj.* ['prɛdɪkɪt]; *v.* ['prɛdɪ,keit] *n., adj., v.* **-cat•ed, -cat•ing.** *—n.* **1** *Grammar.* a word or words expressing what is said about the subject; that part of a sentence or clause that contains a finite verb. *Examples*: *We* work. *The committee* has organized a fund-raising drive. *She* is a journalist. **2** *Logic.* that which is said of the subject in a proposition.
—adj. Grammar. belonging to the predicate. In *Horses are strong, strong* is a **predicate adjective.**
—v. **1** found or base (a statement, action, etc.) on something. **2** declare, assert, or affirm to be real or true: *Most religions predicate life after death.* **3** connote; imply. **4** declare to be an attribute or quality (*of* some person or thing): *We predicate determination of those we admire and obstinacy of those we dislike.* **5** *Logic.* assert (something) about the subject of a proposition. ⟨< L *praedicatus*, pp. of *praedicare* < *prae-* before + *dicare* make known. Doublet of PREACH.⟩

☛ *Usage.* **Predicate.** The predicate of a clause or sentence is the verb with its modifiers, object, complement, etc. It may be a simple verb of complete meaning (The big bell *tolled*), a verb and adverbial modifier (The sun *went behind the cloud*), a transitive verb and its modifiers and object (He *finally landed the big fish*), or a linking verb and its complement (My sister *is an excellent skier).*

predicate adjective an adjective that is used in the predicate, either after a linking verb, as in *She is sad*, or after a direct object, as in *The news made her sad.*

predicate noun a noun used in the predicate, either after a linking verb, as in *She became queen*, or after a direct object, as in *They proclaimed her queen.*

pred•i•ca•tion [,prɛdɪ'keiʃən] *n.* **1** the act of predicating; affirming; assertion. **2** *Logic.* the assertion of something about the subject of a proposition. **3** that which is predicated.

pred•i•ca•tive ['prɛdɪkətɪv], ['prɛdɪ,keitɪv], *or* [prɪ'dɪkətɪv] *adj.* **1** predicating; expressing predication. **2** acting as a predicate. **—'pred•i•ca•tive•ly,** *adv.*

pred•i•ca•to•ry ['prɛdɪkə,tɔri] *adj.* of or having to do with preaching: *She wrote a textbook on predicatory theory.*

pre•dict [prɪ'dɪkt] *v.* tell beforehand; prophesy; forecast: *The weather office predicts rain for tomorrow. The publisher predicted that the novel would be a bestseller.* ⟨< L *praedictus*, pp. of *praedicere* < *prae-* before + *dicere* say⟩ **—pre'dic•tor,** *n.* **—pre'dict•a•ble,** *adj.* **—pre,dict•a'bil•i•ty,** *adv.*

pre•dic•tion [prɪ'dɪkʃən] *n.* **1** the act of predicting. **2** something predicted; prophecy: *The prediction came true.*

pre•dic•tive [prɪ'dɪktɪv] *adj.* foretelling; prophetic. **—pre'dic•tive•ly,** *adv.*

pre•di•gest [,pridaɪ'dʒɛst] *or* [,pridɪ'dʒɛst] *v.* **1** cause (food) to be partly digested beforehand by a natural or artificial process: *Predigested food is sometimes used for persons who are ill or whose digestion is impaired.* **2** simplify to make easier to use: *a predigested edition of* Gulliver's Travels *for children.* **—,pre•di'ges•tion,** *n.*

pre•di•lec•tion [,prɛdə'lɛkʃən] *or* [,pridə'lɛkʃən] *n.* a liking; preference. ⟨< F *prédilection*, ult. < L *prae-* before + *diligere* choose⟩

pre•dis•pose [,pridɪ'spouz] *v.* **-posed, -pos•ing. 1** give an inclination or tendency to; make liable or susceptible (*used with* **to**): *A cold predisposes a person to other viruses.* **2** put into a favourable or suitable frame of mind, emotional condition, etc.: *He is predisposed to be generous to his friends.* **3** dispose of, give away, or bequeath before the usual or specified time.

pre•dis•po•si•tion [,pridɪspə'zɪʃən] *or* [pri,dɪspə'zɪʃən] *n.* a previous inclination or tendency; susceptibility or liability: *a predisposition to look on the dark side of things.*

pred•ni•sone ['prɛdnɪ,soun] *n.* a chemical derivative or analogue of cortisone but with fewer side effects, used as an anti-inflammatory and immunosuppressive in the treatment of arthritis, organ transplants, and other conditions affecting the auto-immune system. *Formula*: $C_{21}H_{26}O_5$

pre•dom•i•nance [prɪ'dɒmənəns] *n.* the quality or state of being predominant.

pre•dom•i•nant [prɪ'dɒmənənt] *adj.* **1** having more power, authority, or influence than others; superior. **2** prevailing; most noticeable or frequent. **—pre'dom•i•nant•ly,** *adv.*

☛ *Syn.* **1.** See note at DOMINANT.

pre•dom•i•nate *v.* [prɪ'dɒmə,neit]; *adj.* [prɪ'dɒmənɪt] *v.* **-nat•ed, -nat•ing;** *adj.*
—v. be greater in power, strength, influence, frequency, or numbers.
—adj. predominant. **—pre'dom•i,nat•ing•ly,** *adv.* **—pre,dom•i'na•tion,** *n.* **—pre'dom•i,na•tor,** *n.*

pre–Dor•set [,pri 'dɔrsɪt] *n.* an Inuit culture of northeastern Canada and N Greenland, earlier than the Dorset and dating from about 2000 B.C.

pree•mie ['primi] *n. Informal.* a baby born prematurely. ⟨alteration of *prem*(*ature*) + *ie*⟩

pre–em•i•nence [pri 'ɛmənəns] *n.* the quality or state of being pre-eminent; superiority: *the pre-eminence of Edison among the inventors of his day.*

pre–em•i•nent [pri 'ɛmənənt] *adj.* standing out above all others; superior to others in some quality: *a pre-eminent scientist.* ⟨< L *praeeminens, -entis*, ppr. of *praeeminere* < *prae-* before + *eminere* stand out⟩ **—pre-'em•i•nent•ly,** *adv.*

pre-empt [pri 'ɛmpt] *v.* **1** secure before someone else can; acquire or take possession of beforehand: *The cat pre-empted the comfortable chair.* **2** take the place of: *The regular programs were pre-empted by the Grey Cup telecast.* **3** settle in (public land) with the right to buy it before others. ⟨< *pre-emption*⟩
—pre-'emp•tor, *n.*

pre-emp•tion [pri 'ɛmpʃən] *n.* **1** a pre-empting or being pre-empted. **2** *Cdn.* a piece of land available for or acquired by purchase under stipulated conditions and on the basis of a prior claim: *The city of Trail grew from the pre-emption of two men, Tipping and Hanna.* ⟨< *pre-* + L *emptio, -onis* buying < *emere* to buy⟩

pre-emp•tive [pri 'ɛmptɪv] *adj.* **1** having to do with pre-emption; being a pre-emption. **2** initiated to prevent someone from acting first: *The Allies launched a pre-emptive strike against the enemy.* **3** *Bridge.* referring to a high bid designed to obstruct opposing bids and make communication between one's opponents more difficult: *a pre-emptive bid.*
—pre-'emp•tive•ly, *adv.*

preen [prin] *v.* **1** of birds, smooth or arrange (the feathers) with the beak. **2** arrange or dress up (one's hair, clothing, etc.) in a fussy, self-satisfied way: *She preened in front of the mirror for fifteen minutes. He's always preening himself.*
preen oneself on, show pride and self-satisfaction in (an achievement or skill): *He preens himself on his dancing skill.*
⟨? var. of *prune* preen, dress carefully, influenced by ME *preonen* prick with a pin < OF *prēon* pin⟩

pre-ex•ist [,pri ɛg'zɪst] *v.* exist beforehand; exist before (something else). **—,pre-ex'ist•ence,** *n.*

pre-ex•ist•ent [,pri ɛg'zɪstənt] *adj.* existing before something else.

pref. **1** preface. **2** prefix. **3** preferred.

pre•fab ['pri,fæb] *n. Informal.* a prefabricated structure, especially a building.

pre•fab•ri•cate [pri'fæbrə,keit] *v.* **-cat•ed, -cat•ing. 1** make all standardized parts of at a factory, so that construction at the site consists mainly of assembling the various sections: *a prefabricated house.* **2** put together or prepare in advance, especially in an artificial way: *a prefabricated excuse.*
—,pre•fab•ri'ca•tion, *n.*

pref•ace ['prɛfɪs] *n., v.* **-aced, -ac•ing.** *—n.* **1** an explanatory introduction to a written work describing its scope, subject, purpose, etc. or giving background information. **2** the preliminary part of a speech.
—v. **1** introduce by written or spoken remarks; give a preface to. **2** be a preface to; begin. ⟨ME < OF *preface*, ult. < L *praefatio* < *prae-* before + *fari* speak⟩
☛ *Syn. n.* **1.** See note at INTRODUCTION.

pref•a•to•ry ['prɛfə,tɔri] *adj.* of, like, or given as a preface; introductory; preliminary. **—,pref•a'to•ri•ly,** *adv.*

pre•fect ['prifɛkt] *n.* **1** in ancient Rome, etc., a title of various military and civil officers. Also, **praefect. 2** in France, the chief administrative official of a department. **3** in Paris, France, the chief of police. **4** in some schools, a senior student who has some authority over other students; monitor. ⟨< L *praefectus*, originally pp. of *praeficere* put in charge < *prae-* in front + *facere* make⟩

pre•fec•ture ['prifɛktʃər] *n.* the office, jurisdiction, territory, or official residence of a prefect. ⟨< L *praefectura*⟩

pre•fer [prɪ'fɜr] *v.* **-ferred, -fer•ring. 1** like better; choose rather: *I will come later, if you prefer.* **2** put forward; present: *to prefer a claim to property. The constable preferred charges of speeding against the driver.* **3** promote; advance. **4** give priority to (a client, etc.). ⟨ME < MF *preferer* < L *praeferre* < *prae-* before + *ferre* carry⟩ **—pre'fer•rer,** *n.*

pref•er•a•ble ['prɛfərəbəl] *adj.* to be preferred; more desirable: *The teacher decided that going along was preferable to staying behind.* **—'pref•er•a•bly,** *n.*

pref•er•ence ['prɛfərəns] *n.* **1** a liking better; the favouring of one above another: *A teacher should not show preference for any one student.* **2** something preferred; first choice: *Her preference in reading is historical novels.* **3 a** in international trade, a granting of certain concessions, especially lower import tariffs, to another country or countries. **b** such a concession. **4** a prior right, power, or claim, as in payments of dividends.
☛ *Syn.* **1.** See note at CHOICE.

pref•er•en•tial [,prɛfə'rɛnʃəl] *adj.* of, having to do with, receiving, or showing preference: *preferential treatment, preferential tariffs.* **—,pref•er'en•tial•ly,** *adv.*
—,pref•er'en•tial,ism, *n.*

preferential shop an establishment or business giving preference to union members in hiring, promotion, etc. Compare CLOSED SHOP.

preferential voting a system of voting whereby the voter can indicate an order in the choice of candidates, as first, second, third, etc., so that if no one candidate gets a clear majority, the election may be determined by totalling the points for first choice, second choice, etc.

pre•fer•ment [prɪ'fɜrmənt] *n.* **1** advancement; promotion: *Captain White seeks preferment in the army.* **2** a position, office, or honour to which a person is advanced: *a sought-after preferment.* **3** the act of putting forward a charge or claim.

preferred stock stock that entitles holders to a fixed rate of return on their investments, with guaranteed priority over common stock in the payment of dividends and, usually, in the distribution of assets in the event of liquidation of the company.

pre•fig•ur•a•tion [,prifɪgjə'reiʃən] *or* [,prifɪgə'reiʃən] *n.* **1** the act of showing or suggesting or the fact of being shown or suggested beforehand by a figure or type. **2** that which prefigures.

pre•fig•ure [pri'fɪgjər] *or* [pri'fɪgər] *v.* **-ured, -ur•ing. 1** show or suggest beforehand by a figure or type: *The shadow of the gallows across his path prefigured his ultimate fate.* **2** imagine to oneself beforehand; foresee. ⟨ME < LL *praefigurare* < L *prae-* before + *figurare* form, shape < *figura* a form⟩
—pre'fig•ure•ment, *n.* **—pre'fig•ur•a•tive,** *adj.*
—,pre'fig•ur•a•tive•ly, *adv.* **—,pre'fig•ur•a•tive•ness,** *n.*

pre•fix *n.* ['prifɪks]; *v.* [pri'fɪks] *or* ['prifɪks] *n., v.* *—n.* **1** *Grammar.* a syllable, syllables, or full word put at the beginning of a word to change its meaning or to form a new word, as in *pre*paid, *under*line, *dis*appear, *un*like. **2** a title put before someone's name. *Example*: Dame *Joan Sutherland.*
—v. put before: *We prefix 'Mr.' to a man's name.* Compare SUFFIX. ⟨< L *praefixum*, neut. of *praefixus*, pp. of *praefigere* < *prae-* in front + *figere* fix⟩ **—'pre•fix•al,** *adj.* **—pre'fix•ion** [-'fɪkʃən], *n.*

pre•front•al [pri'frʌntəl] *adj. Anatomy.* in vertebrates, of or situated close to the front of the structure of the head or brain.

preg•na•ble ['prɛgnəbəl] *adj.* open to attack; assailable. ⟨ME < OF *prenable* < *prendre* < L *prendere*, shortened form of *prehendere* seize, take⟩ **—,preg•na'bil•i•ty,** *n.*

preg•nan•cy ['prɛgnənsi] *n., pl.* **-cies. 1** the state or condition of being pregnant. **2** the time this condition lasts. **3** the quality of being pregnant: *the pregnancy of his remarks.*

preg•nant ['prɛgnənt] *adj.* **1** having an embryo or fetus developing in the uterus; being with child or young. **2** filled; teeming; abounding: *a mind pregnant with ideas, a scheme pregnant with possibilities.* **3** filled with meaning; very significant: *a pregnant remark, a pregnant pause.* ⟨ME < L *praegnans, -antis* < *prae-* before + *gen-* bear⟩ **—'preg•nant•ly,** *adv.*

pre•heat [pri'hit] *v.* heat beforehand; especially, of an oven, heat to a particular temperature before placing something in it to cook.

pre•hen•sile [prɪ'hɛnsaɪl] *or* [prɪ'hɛnsəl] *adj.* adapted for seizing, grasping, or holding on: *New World monkeys have prehensile tails; Old World monkeys do not.* ⟨< F *préhensile*, ult. < L *prehendere* grasp⟩

pre•his•tor•ic [,prihɪ'stɔrɪk] *adj.* of, having to do with, or existing in periods before recorded history: *Fossils and artifacts provide us with information about prehistoric people and animals.*

pre•his•tor•i•cal [,prihɪ'stɔrəkəl] *adj.* prehistoric.
—,pre•his'tor•i•cal•ly, *adv.*

pre•his•to•ry [pri'hɪstəri] *n.* **1** all that occurred in time before the period of written history, deduced from anthropology, archaeology, geology, paleontology, etc. **2** a history or account of the background of a situation or event.

pre•ig•ni•tion [,priɪg'nɪʃən] *n.* ignition of the charge in an internal-combustion engine before the spark plug fires or before the intake valve is closed.

pre•judge [pri'dʒʌdʒ] *v.* **-judged, -judg•ing.** judge beforehand; judge without knowing all the facts. **—pre'judg•ment** or **pre'judge•ment,** *n.*

prej•u•dice ['prɛdʒədɪs] *n., v.* **-diced, -dic•ing.** *—n.* **1** an opinion or judgment based on irrelevant considerations or inadequate knowledge, either favourable or unfavourable, especially an unfavourable opinion or judgment: *a prejudice against doctors based on one unfortunate experience.*
2 unreasonable hostility toward a particular person, group, race,

nation, etc.: *the battle against prejudice. She was accused of prejudice.* **3** injury or disadvantage: *They feel that the new bylaw works to the prejudice of apartment dwellers.*
—v. **1** cause prejudice in: *The fact that I was her supervisor may prejudice me in her favour.* **2** injure or damage: *He was careful to say nothing that might prejudice their interests.* ⟨ME < OF < L *praejudicium* < *prae-* before + *judicium* judgment⟩

prej•u•diced ['prɛdʒədɪst] *adj., v. —adj.* having or showing a prejudice for or, more often, against a person, group, idea, or thing: *The judge's summary was prejudiced toward the accused. She is very prejudiced.*
—v. pt. and pp. of PREJUDICE.

prej•u•di•cial [,prɛdʒə'dɪʃəl] *adj.* causing prejudice or disadvantage; hurtful. **—,prej•u'di•cial•ly,** *adv.*

prel•a•cy ['prɛləsi] *n., pl.* **-cies. 1** the position or rank of a prelate. **2** prelates as a group. **3** church government by prelates.

pre•lap•sa•ri•an [,prilæp'sɛriən] *adj.* **1** *Christian theology.* occurring before the Fall. **2** referring to any period of carefree innocence. **3** old-fashioned: *Her ideas on birth control were positively prelapsarian.*

prel•ate ['prɛlət] *n.* a high-ranking member of the clergy, such as a bishop or abbot. ⟨ME *prelat* < OF < Med.L < L *praelatus* one preferred, originally pp. to L *praeferre* prefer. See PREFER.⟩ **—pre'lat•ic** [prɪ'lætɪk], *adj.*

prelim. preliminary.

pre•lim•i•nar•y [prɪ'lɪmə,nɛri] *adj., n., pl.* **-nar•ies.** *—adj.* coming before the main business; leading to something more important: *After preliminary remarks by the principal, the school play began.*
—n. **1** a preliminary step; something preparatory: *Intensive research is a necessary preliminary to any serious writing.* **2** a preliminary examination: *The Graduate Record Examination is a preliminary to admission to graduate school.* **3** a game or match as a run-up to the main one: *If the team makes it through the preliminaries, they will have achieved their goal.* ⟨< NL *praeliminaris*, ult. < L *prae-* before + *limen, -minis* threshold⟩ **—pre'lim•i,nar•i•ly,** *adv.*

pre•lims [prɪ'lɪmz] *n.pl. Informal.* **1** preliminary material in a book such as a dictionary, atlas, etc. The prelims include notes on etymology, style of entries, etc. **2** preliminaries. ⟨by clipping from *preliminary*⟩

pre•lit•er•ate [pri'lɪtərɪt] *adj.* having to do with or designating a society or culture that has not developed a written language.

prel•ude ['prɛljud], ['prilud], *or* ['preilud] *n., v.* **-ud•ed, -ud•ing.** *—n.* **1** anything serving as an introduction. **2** *Music.* **a** a composition, or part of it, that introduces another composition or part of a composition. **b** an independent instrumental composition, usually short. **c** a composition played at the beginning of a church service.
—v. **1** be a prelude or introduction to. **2** introduce with a prelude. ⟨< F < Med.L *praeludium*, ult. < L *prae-* before + *ludere* play⟩

pre•mar•i•tal [pri'mærɪtəl] *or* [pri'mɛrɪtəl] *adj.* existing or happening before marriage: *premarital counselling.*

pre•ma•ture [,primə'tʃʊr] *or* [,prɛmə'tʃʊr] *adj.* **1** born at less than 40 weeks of pregnancy. **2** happening, done, or coming before the proper time or too soon. ⟨< L *praematurus* < *prae-* before + *maturus* ripe⟩ **—,pre•ma'ture•ly,** *adv.* **—,pre•ma'tu•ri•ty** or **,pre•ma'ture•ness,** *n.*

pre•max•il•la [,primæk'sɪlə] *n., pl.* **-max•il•lae** [-mæk'sɪli] *or* [-mæk'sɪlaɪ]. *Anatomy. Zoology.* one of a pair of bones in the upper jaw of vertebrates, located between or in front of the maxillae and fused with them in adult humans. **—pre'max•il,lar•y** [pri'mæksə,lɛri] *or* [,pri•mæk'sɪləri], *adj.*

pre•med•i•cal [pri'mɛdɪkəl] *adj.* preparing for the study of medicine: *a premedical student.* Often shortened to **premed.**

pre•med•i•tate [pri'mɛdɪ,teit] *v.* **-tat•ed, -tat•ing.** think out, plan, or consider (something) ahead of time: *to premeditate a murder.* ⟨< L *praemeditari* < *prae-* before + *meditari* meditate⟩

pre•med•i•tat•ed [pri'mɛdɪ,teitɪd] *adj., v. —adj.* thought out or planned beforehand; characterized by conscious forethought and intent: *It looked more like accidental death than premeditated murder.*
—v. pt. and pp. of PREMEDITATE. **—pre'med•i,tat•ed•ly,** *adv.*

pre•med•i•ta•tion [,primɛdɪ'teiʃən] *n.* a previous deliberation or planning.

pre–men•stru•al syndrome [pri'mɛnstruəl] *or* ['mɛnstrəl] a set of symptoms experienced by many women just before their menstrual periods, characterized by bloating and irritability. *Abbrev.:* PMS

pre•mier ['primjər] *or* [prɪ'mir] *n., adj. —n.* **1** in Canada, the chief executive officer of a provincial government; the head of a provincial cabinet: *The ten premiers are attending a conference with the prime minister in Ottawa.* **2** the chief officer of any government; prime minister. The term *premier* is sometimes used in the United Kingdom to refer to the prime minister.
—adj. **1** first in rank or quality: *a novel of premier importance.* **2** first in time; earliest. ⟨< F *premier* first < L *primarius* primary < *primus* first⟩

premier danseur [pʀəmjedɑ̃'sœʀ] *French.* the principal male dancer in a ballet or ballet company.

pre•mière or **pre•miere** [prəm'jɛr], [prɪ'mir], *or* [prɛm'jɛr]; *French,* [pʀə'mjɛʀ] *n., v.* **-mièred** or **-miered, -mièr•ing** or **-mier•ing.** *—n.* **1** the first public performance or showing: *the première of a play.* **2** the leading actress in a theatrical cast or company.
—v. **1** give a first public performance or showing of: *The theatre group is premièring a new play by a Winnipeg playwright.* **2** have a first public performance: *The film is premièring at the festival tonight.* **3** appear for the first time: **a** as a star: *He premièred last year in a musical comedy.* **b** in publication: *The magazine premiered in September 1993.* ⟨< F *première*, originally fem. of *premier.* See PREMIER.⟩

pre•mière dan•seuse [pʀəmjɛʀdɑ̃'søz] *French.* the principal female dancer in a ballet or ballet company.

pre•mier•ship ['primjər,ʃɪp] *or* [prɪ'mirʃɪp] *n.* **1** the rank or office of a prime minister or premier. **2** the state of being first in any category.

pre•mil•len•ni•al [,primə'lɛniəl] *adj. Christian theology.* especially of the Second Coming, occurring before the millennium. **—,pre•mil'len•ni•al•ly,** *adv.*

pre•mil•len•ni•al•ism [,primə'lɛniə,lɪzəm] *n. Christian theology.* the doctrine that Christ will return before the millennium. **—,pre•mil'len•ni•al•ist,** *n., adj.*

prem•ise *n.* ['prɛməs]; *v.* ['prɛməs] *or* [prɪ'maɪz] *n., v.* **pre•mised, pre•mis•ing.** *—n.* **1** *Logic.* a statement assumed to be true and used to draw a conclusion. See also SYLLOGISM.
2 premises, *pl.* a house or building with its grounds. **3** *Law.* **a** something mentioned previously, such as the name of the party concerned, a description of the property, the price, etc. **b** the property forming the subject of a document.
—v. set forth as an introduction, assumption, or explanation; state beforehand. ⟨< Med.L *praemissa*, originally fem. pp., put before, ult. < L *prae-* before + *mittere* send⟩

pre•mi•um ['primiəm] *n., adj. —n.* **1** a reward; prize: *Some magazines give premiums to sales representatives who obtain new subscriptions.* **2** something more than the ordinary price or wages; an extra payment or charge: *They had to pay a considerable premium to get first-quality goods.* **3** money paid regularly for an insurance policy. **4** something given away or offered at a reduced price to purchasers of a product, service, etc. **5** the excess value of one form of money over another of the same nominal value. **6** an unusually high value: *The company puts a premium on accuracy of work.*
at a premium, much valued and in demand: *Good housing is at a premium these days.*
—adj. of a higher grade or quality. ⟨< L *praemium* reward < *prae-* before + *emere*, originally, take⟩

pre•mo•lar [pri'moulər] *n., adj. —n.* one of the permanent teeth in front of the molars; bicuspid.
—adj. having to do with or being a premolar.

prem•o•ni•tion [,prɛmə'nɪʃən] *or* [,primə'nɪʃən] *n.* **1** a feeling that something bad is about to happen; foreboding. **2** a forewarning. ⟨< obs. F < L *praemonitio, -onis*, ult. < *prae-* before + *monere* warn⟩

pre•mon•i•to•ry [pri'mɒnə,tɔri] *adj.* giving warning beforehand.

pre•na•tal [pri'neitəl] *adj.* **1** for or having to do with a woman who is expecting a child: *prenatal classes, prenatal care.* **2** before birth: *a prenatal diagnosis of defects.* **—pre'na•tal•ly,** *adv.*

pren•tice ['prɛntɪs] *n., adj. Archaic. —n.* apprentice.
—adj. of or like an apprentice; inexperienced; unskilled.

pre•nup•tial [pri'nʌpʃəl] *or* [pri'nʌptʃəl] *adj.* **1 a** before marriage: *a prenuptial contract.* **b** before a wedding: *a prenuptial party.* **2** *Zoology.* before mating.

pre•oc•cu•pa•tion [pri,ɒkjə'peiʃən] *n.* a preoccupying or being preoccupied; especially, complete absorption of the mind in something.

pre•oc•cu•pied [pri'ɒkjə,paɪd] *adj., v.* *—adj.* **1** lost in thought; with thoughts elsewhere: *He stood in the middle of the room, looking about him with a preoccupied air.* **2** having had a previous occupier: *Their supposedly new condo was actually preoccupied.* **3** referring to a taxonomic name previously used and so not available for a new variety.
—v. pt. and pp. of PREOCCUPY.

pre•oc•cu•py [pri'ɒkjə,paɪ] *v.* **-pied, -py•ing. 1** take up all the attention of; engross the mind of: *The problem of getting to Vancouver preoccupied her mind.* **2** occupy or take possession of beforehand or before others: *Our favourite seats had been preoccupied.*

pre•op•er•a•tive [pri'ɒpərə,tɪv] *or* [pri'ɒpə,reitɪv] *adj.* occurring in or referring to the preparatory period preceding a surgical operation.

pre•or•dain [,priɔr'dein] *v.* decide or settle beforehand; foreordain. **—,pre•or•di'na•tion,** *n.*

prep [prɛp] *adj., v.* **prepped, prep•ping;** *n.* *—adj. Informal.* preparatory.
—v. **1** attend a PREPARATORY SCHOOL: *They prepped at the local Montessori school.* **2** get training: *She prepped for her exams by extensive extra reading.* **3** prepare (a patient) for surgery.
—n. **1** PREPARATORY SCHOOL. **2** at private schools: **a** homework: *Have you done your prep yet?* **b** a time set aside for homework: *There were several students missing from prep tonight.* ⟨by clipping from *prep*aratory or *prep*aration⟩

prep. 1 preposition. **2** preparatory.

pre•pack•age [pri'pækɪdʒ] *v.* **-aged, -ag•ing.** package before sale according to certain weights, grades, prices, etc.

pre•paid [pri'peid] *v.* pt. and pp. of PREPAY.

prep•a•ra•tion [,prɛpə'reiʃən] *n.* **1** the act of preparing. **2** the state of being prepared; readiness. **3** anything done to prepare for something: *He made careful preparations for his holidays.* **4** a medicine, food, or other substance made by a special process: *The preparation included camphor.*

pre•par•a•tive [prɪ'pærətɪv] *or* [prɪ'pɛrətɪv] *adj., n.* *—adj.* preparatory.
—n. something that prepares.

pre•par•a•to•ry ['prɛpərə,tɔri], [prɪ'pærə,tɔri], *or* [prɪ'pɛrə,tɔri] *adj.* **1** of or for preparation; preparing. **2** as an introduction; preliminary.

preparatory school 1 *Cdn.* a private school at the elementary level. **2** *U.S.* a private secondary school that concentrates on preparing students for college.

pre•pare [prɪ'pɛr] *v.* **-pared, -par•ing. 1** put together or make from ingredients or parts: *They prepared a delicious meal for us. The witch prepared a magic brew.* **2** make or get ready for some purpose: *to prepare for school, to prepare someone for bad news.* **3** work out the details of; plan: *to prepare an adequate defence.* ⟨< L *praeparare* < *prae-* before + *parare* make ready⟩ **—pre'par•er,** *n.*

pre•pared•ness [prɪ'pɛrdnɪs] *or* [prɪ'pɛrɪdnɪs] *n.* **1** the state or quality of being prepared; readiness. **2** the possession of adequate military forces and defences to meet threats or outbreaks of war.

pre•pay [pri'pei] *v.* **-paid, -pay•ing.** pay or pay for in advance: *to prepay charges.* **—pre'pay•ment,** *n.*

pre•pense [prɪ'pɛns] *adj. Law.* planned beforehand; premeditated; deliberate (*usually placed after the noun*): *malice prepense.* ⟨ME, ult. < OF *purpenser* meditate (with prefix *pre-* substituted) < *pur-* (< L *pro-* before) + *penser* think. See PENSIVE.⟩

pre•pon•der•ance [prɪ'pɒndərəns] *n.* **1** a greater power, importance, or influence: *the preponderance of good over evil.* **2** a greater number or quantity: *a preponderance of oaks in the woods.*

pre•pon•der•ant [prɪ'pɒndərənt] *adj.* **1** having greater power, importance, or influence: *Greed is a miser's preponderant characteristic.* **2** having greater number or quantity; being prevalent: *Mixed farms are preponderant in the region.* **—pre'pon•der•ant•ly,** *adv.*

pre•pon•der•ate [prɪ'pɒndə,reit] *v.* **-at•ed, -at•ing. 1** be the chief or most important, influential, or numerous element or item; predominate: *Oaks and maples preponderate in our eastern woods.* **2** be weighed down, as one end of a balance. **3** *Archaic.* be heavier; weigh more. ⟨< L *praeponderare* outweigh, ult. < *prae-* before + *pondus, -deris* weight⟩

prep•o•si•tion [,prɛpə'zɪʃən] *n. Grammar.* a word that shows relationships of time, direction, position, etc. among other words or parts of a sentence. *With, for, by,* and *in* are prepositions in the following sentence: *A man* with *rugs* for *sale walked* by *our house* in *the morning.* ⟨< L *praepositio, -onis,* ult. < *prae-* before + *ponere* place⟩

prep•o•si•tion•al [,prɛpə'zɪʃənəl] *adj.* having to do with, containing, or having the nature or function of a preposition: *prepositional usage, a prepositional phrase.* **—,prep•o'si•tion•al•ly,** *adv.*

pre•pos•i•tive [pri'pɒzətɪv] *adj., n. Grammar.*
—adj. prefixed; placed before.
—n. a word placed before another as a modifier. In *the yellow ball, yellow* is a prepositive adjective. A preposition is a prepositive.

pre•pos•sess [,pripə'zɛs] *v.* **1** fill with a favourable feeling or opinion: *We were prepossessed by the child's modest behaviour.* **2** fill with a feeling or opinion.

pre•pos•sess•ing [,pripə'zɛsɪŋ] *adj., v.* *—adj.* making a favourable first impression; attractive; pleasing: *The performer's slightly scruffy appearance was not prepossessing.*
—v. ppr. of PREPOSSESS.

pre•pos•ses•sion [,pripə'zɛʃən] *n.* bias; prejudice; a favourable feeling or opinion formed beforehand.

pre•pos•ter•ous [prɪ'pɒstərəs] *adj.* contrary to nature, reason, or common sense; absurd; senseless: *It would be preposterous to shovel snow with a teaspoon.* ⟨< L *praeposterus* in reverse order, ult. < *prae-* before + *post* after⟩ **—pre'pos•ter•ous•ly,** *adv.* **—pre'pos•ter•ous•ness,** *n.*
☛ *Syn.* See note at RIDICULOUS.

pre•po•ten•cy [pri'poutənsi] *n.* **1** predominance; superiority. **2** *Biology.* the theory, now largely discounted, that one parent has a greater capacity than the other for transmitting certain characteristics to the offspring: *the prepotency of the Morgan horse.*

prep•py ['prɛpi] *n., pl.* **prep•pies;** *adj.,* **prep•pi•er, prep•pi•est.** *Informal.* *—n.* a student or graduate of a preparatory school.
—adj. of or like such a student or graduate; tending to be smart and self-opinionated: *preppy clothes. She has preppy attitudes.*

pre•print ['pri,prɪnt] *n., v.* *—n.* a part of a book or magazine printed ahead of publication.
—v. print ahead of publication: *This article has been preprinted.*

pre•puce ['pripjus] *n.* foreskin. ⟨< F < L *praeputium*⟩

pre•quel ['prikwəl] *n.* a novel, play, or film that prefigures an earlier work by the same author, showing the same characters at a younger age, and setting out the events that led up to those in the first work: *X is a prequel to Y.* ⟨coined by J.R.R. Tolkien, on the analogy of *sequel*⟩

Pre–Raph•a•el•ite [pri 'ræfiə,ləit] *or* [pri 'reifiə,ləit] *n.* **1** any Italian painter preceding Raphael (1483-1520), a famous Italian painter. **2** one of a group of English artists and poets formed in 1848, including Millais and Dante Gabriel Rossetti, who aimed to work in the Italian style of painting before the time of Raphael. **3** any modern artist following the style of Italian painting before Raphael.

pre•re•cord [,prirɪ'kɔrd] *v.* **1** *Radio and television.* record for later broadcast. **2** *Film.* record (music, sound effects, etc.) ahead of time for later inclusion, in order to make synchronization more efficient.

pre•re•cord•ed [,prirɪ'kɔrdɪd] *adj., v.* *—adj.* of commercial recording tapes, designating those which have images, sound, etc. recorded on them before sale: *It's easier to buy prerecorded videos than to copy them from the TV.*
—v. pt. and pp. of PRERECORD.

pre•req•ui•site [pri'rɛkwəzɪt] *n., adj.* *—n.* something that is necessary to achieve an end; something required as a condition before something else can be considered: *a high-school diploma is the usual prerequisite to university studies.*
—adj. required beforehand.

pre•rog•a•tive [prɪ'rɒgətɪv] *n., adj.* *—n.* a right or privilege that nobody else has: *The government has the prerogative of coining money.*
—adj. being or giving a prerogative: *The executive exercised its prerogative power.* ⟨< L *praerogativa,* originally fem. adj., asked to vote first, ult. < *prae-* before + *rogare* ask⟩
☛ *Syn. n.* See note at PRIVILEGE.

pres. present.

Pres. 1 president. 2 Presbyterian.

pres•age *n.* ['prɛsɪdʒ]; *v.* [prɪ'seidʒ] *or* ['prɛsɪdʒ] *n., v.* **pre•saged, pre•sag•ing.** *—n.* **1** something that foreshadows a future event; portent; omen: *a sure presage of evil.* **2** a feeling that something is about to happen; presentiment.
—v. **1** give warning of; foreshadow: *Some people think that a ring around the moon presages a storm.* **2** have or express a presentiment of: *The professor presaged a disaster from the experiment.* **3** have a presentiment; make a prediction. ⟨ME < OF < L *praesagium*, ult. < *prae-* before + *sagus* prophetic⟩
—pre'sag•er, *n.*

Presb. Presbyterian.

pres•by•o•pia [,prɛzbi'oupiə] *or* [,prɛsbi'oupiə] *n. Ophthalmology.* a form of farsightedness caused by diminishing elasticity of the crystalline lens and aliary muscle weakness, usually occurring after middle age. ⟨< Gk. *presbys* old + *opia, ops* eye⟩ **—,pres•by'op•ic** [-'ɒpɪk], *adj.*

pres•by•ter ['prɛzbɪtər] *or* ['prɛsbɪtər] *n.* **1** an elder in the early Christian church. **2** *Presbyterian Church, United Church of Canada.* a member of a presbytery. **3** a priest or minister in a church having an episcopal heirarchy. ⟨< L *presbyter* elder < Gk. *presbyteros*, comparative of *presbys* old.⟩ **—pres'byt•er,ate,** *n.* **—,pres•by'ter•i•al,** *adj.*

Pres•by•te•ri•an [,prɛzbɪ'tiriən] *or* [,prɛsbɪ'tiriən] *n., adj. —n.* a member of any of several Christian churches that constitute the main branch of the Reformed churches, whose government is by presbyters (elders) and whose doctrines emphasize the sovereignty of God and acceptance of the Bible as the only infallible rule of faith and life. The doctrines of these churches are more or less modified forms of Calvinism.
—adj. **1** of or having to do with Presbyterians or Presbyterianism. **2** belonging to the Presbyterian denomination. See also UNITED CHURCH OF CANADA. **3 presbyterian,** having to do with church government by presbyters.

Pres•by•te•ri•an•ism [,prɛzbɪ'tiriə,nɪzəm] *or* [,prɛsbɪ'tiriə,nɪzəm] *n.* **1** the doctrines or religious principles of the Presbyterian churches. **2 presbyterianism,** a system of church government by presbyters, all of equal rank.

pres•by•ter•y ['prɛzbɪ,tɛri] *or* ['prɛsbɪ,tɛri] *n., pl.* **-ter•ies.** **1** *Presbyterian Church, United Church of Canada.* **a** a local governing body composed of the ministers and representative lay members of the congregations of a given area. **b** the congregations or area under the jurisdiction of such a body. **2** the part of a church set aside for the clergy. **3** *Roman Catholic Church.* the residence of a parish priest.

pre•school ['pri,skul] *adj., n. —adj.* **1** of, for, or being the period in a child's life after infancy and before the child begins elementary school: *the preschool years, preschool activities.* **2** of, for, or designating a child of this age.
—n. a school for children of preschool age; NURSERY SCHOOL.
—'pre,school•er, *n.*

pre•sci•ence ['priʃiəns] *or* ['prɛʃiəns] *n.* a knowledge of things before they exist or happen; foreknowledge; foresight. ⟨< LL *praescientia* < L *praesciens*, ppr. of *praescire* foreknow < *prae-* before + *scire* know⟩

pre•sci•ent ['priʃiənt] *or* ['prɛʃiənt] *adj.* knowing beforehand; foreseeing. **—'pre•sci•ent•ly,** *adv.*

pre•scribe [prɪ'skraɪb] *v.* **-scribed, -scrib•ing. 1** lay down as a rule or guide; order; require: *to do what the law prescribes. Which textbooks are prescribed for this course?* **2** order as a remedy or treatment: *The doctor prescribed an antibiotic.* **3** give medical advice. **4** *Law.* **a** make or become invalid or outlawed because of the passage of time. **b** claim a right or title to something by virtue of long use and enjoyment of it. ⟨< L *praescribere* < *prae-* before + *scribere* write⟩

pre•script *n.* ['priskrɪpt]; *adj.* [prɪ'skrɪpt] *or* ['priskrɪpt] *n., adj. —n.* rule; order; direction.
—adj. prescribed. ⟨< L *praescriptum*, neut. of *praescriptus*, pp. of *praescribere.* See PRESCRIBE.⟩

pre•scrip•tion [prɪ'skrɪpʃən] *n., adj. —n.* **1** an order; direction. **2** a written direction or order for preparing and using a medicinal remedy or grinding lenses for eyeglasses: *a prescription for a cough. Symbol:* ℞ **3** the medicine that has been prescribed: *Did you use up the whole prescription?* **4** *Law.* **a** the possession or use of a thing long enough to give one a right or title to it. **b** the right or title thus established.
—adj. referring to drugs or prostheses available only with a doctor's prescription: *prescription drugs, prescription eyeglasses.*

pre•scrip•tive [prɪ'skrɪptɪv] *adj.* **1** that prescribes. **2** depending or based on legal prescription. **3** established by long use or custom. **—pre'script•ive•ly,** *adv.* **—pre'script•ive•ness,** *n.*

prescriptive grammar a style of grammar in which strict adherence to traditional rules is recommended.

pres•ence ['prɛzəns] *n.* **1** the fact or condition of being present in a place: *I knew of his presence in the other room.* **2** the place within immediate proximity and view of a person or thing: *She signed the statement in the presence of two witnesses. The messenger was admitted to the leader's presence.* **3** personal appearance and bearing, especially when impressive or imposing: *a woman of noble presence. He has no stage presence.* **4** a person who is present, especially one of high rank or great dignity. **5** a spirit or supernatural being felt to be near. ⟨ME < OF < L *praesentia* < *praesens* present. See PRESENT[1].⟩

presence chamber the room in which a king, president, or some very important person receives guests.

presence of mind the ability to think and act calmly and quickly when taken by surprise.

pres•ent[1] ['prɛzənt] *adj., n. —adj.* **1** being in a proper or expected place; at hand, not absent: *Every member of the class was present.* **2** at this time; being or occurring now; in progress: *present prices.* **3** *Grammar.* **a** designating the verb tense that expresses an action or state of the present time or the time of speaking, or a timeless state or habitual action. In the sentences *Many students have colds just now, The chemical symbol for water is H_2O, They go to California every winter* the words *have, is,* and *go* are verbs in the present tense. **b** any verb form carrying this meaning.
—n. **1** the present time: *At present people need courage.* **2** *Grammar.* the present tense or a verb form in that tense.
at present, now.
by these presents, *Formal.* by these words; by this document.
for the present, for the time being. ⟨ME < OF < L *praesens, -entis* < *prae-* before + *esse* be⟩
☛ *Syn. adj.* **2.** See note at CURRENT.

pre•sent[2] *v.* [prɪ'zɛnt]; *n.* ['prɛzənt] *v., n. —v.* **1** give formally: *They presented flowers to the singer after the performance.* **2** make a formal gift to (*used with* **with**): *The company presented him with a silver tray.* **3** bring before the mind; offer for consideration: *She presented reasons for her action.* **4** offer to view or notice: *The new City Hall presents a fine appearance.* **5** bring before the public: *The school presented a play.* **6** set forth in words: *present an argument, present an explanation.* **7** hand in or send in: *The grocer presented her bill.* **8** introduce socially: *Ms. Janzen, may I present Mr. Bindon?* **9** bring before a person of high rank: *She was presented to the Governor General.* **10** *Law.* **a** bring before a court, legislature, etc. for consideration: *to present a case.* **b** charge or indict (someone). **11** direct, point, or turn in a particular direction: *The handsome actor presented his profile to the camera.*
present arms, a salute by bringing a rifle, etc. to a vertical position in front of one's body. **b** the position itself. **c** the command to assume the position.
—n. something given; gift: *I got the CD player as a birthday present.* ⟨ME < OF < L *praesentare* < *praesens, -entis* present. See PRESENT[1].⟩ **—pre'sent•er,** *n.*
☛ *Syn. v.* **1.** See note at GIVE. **8.** See note at INTRODUCE.

pre•sent•a•ble [prɪ'zɛntəbəl] *adj.* **1** fit to be introduced or go into company; suitable in appearance, dress, manners, etc.: *It took him an hour to make himself presentable again after cleaning the basement.* **2** suitable to be offered or given: *That is a very presentable gift. Make the essay more presentable before you hand it in.* **—pre'sent•a•bly,** *adv.* **—pre,sent•a'bil•i•ty** or **pre'sent•a•ble•ness,** *n.*

pres•en•ta•tion [,prɛzən'teiʃən] *n.* **1** a giving: *the presentation of a gift.* **2** a gift. **3** a proposal for consideration. **4** an offering to be seen; showing: *the presentation of a play.* **5** a formal introduction, especially to somebody of high rank: *the presentation of a person to the Queen.* **6** a function at which a gift is presented: *A presentation was held when the manager retired.* **7** an expository talk accompanied by visual aids or demonstration: *Thirty percent of the grade for this course will be for the oral presentation. She gave a presentation on Mennonite culture.* **8** the act of presenting a member of the clergy to a bishop for naming and institution to a benefice.

pres•en•ta•tion•ism [,prɛzən'teiʃə,nɪzəm] *n. Philosophy.* the theory that in perception the mind is immediately aware of the things perceived with no intervening medium. Compare REPRESENTATIONALISM.

pres•ent–day ['prɛzənt 'dei] *adj.* of the present time.

pre•sen•ti•ment [prɪ'zɛntəmənt] *or* [prɪ'sɛntəmənt] *n.* a feeling or impression that something is about to happen;

premonition. ⟨< MF *presentiment*, ult. < L *prae-* before + *sentire* sense⟩

☛ *Usage.* Do not confuse **presentiment** with PRESENTMENT.

pres•ent•ly [ˈprɛzəntli] *adv.* **1** before long; soon: *The clock will strike presently.* **2** at present; now: *The prime minister is presently in Ottawa.* **3** *Archaic.* at once.

☛ *Syn.* **1.** See note at IMMEDIATELY.

pre•sent•ment [prɪˈzɛntmənt] *n.* **1** a bringing forward; offering to be considered. **2** a showing; offering to be seen. **3** a representation on the stage or by a portrait. **4** *Law.* a statement by a grand jury of an offence from their own knowledge. ⟨ME < OF *presentement* < *presenter* < L *praesentare.* See PRESENT[2].⟩

☛ *Usage.* Do not confuse **presentment** with PRESENTIMENT.

present participle *Grammar.* a participle that expresses the same time as that expressed by the finite verb of the clause. In the sentence *Saying good night, they started for home, saying* is a present participle expressing the same time as the verb *started.* In English, the present participle is also used to form the progressive aspect of the present and past tenses of verbs: *We are leaving now. They were arguing.* Present participles are also used as adjectives in an active sense: *running water, a cooling breeze* = *the water is running, the breeze is cooling.* In modern English the present participle always ends in **-ing.** *Abbrev.*: ppr. or p.pr.

present perfect *Grammar.* **1** a tense that expresses: **a** an action or a state that is completed at some indefinite time before the present. *Example*: *They* have gone. **b** an action begun in the past and continued in the present. *Example*: *They* have lived *here for six years.* The present perfect is formed in English with the present tense of *have* plus a past participle, as in *They have gone.* **2** a verb form in the present perfect.

pre•serv•a•ble [prɪˈzɜrvəbəl] *adj.* that can be preserved.

pres•er•va•tion [ˌprɛzərˈveiʃən] *n.* a preserving or being preserved: *the preservation of one's health. The artifacts were in an excellent state of preservation.*

pres•er•va•tion•ist [ˌprɛzərˈveiʃəˌnɪst] *n.* a person who advocates or supports positive measures taken to preserve aspects of the environment such as historic sites and buildings, natural areas, endangered species, etc.

pre•serv•a•tive [prɪˈzɜrvətɪv] *n., adj.* —*n.* any substance that will prevent decay or injury. Paint is a preservative for wood surfaces. Salt is a preservative for meat.
—*adj.* that preserves.

pre•serve [prɪˈzɜrv] *v.* **-served, -serv•ing;** *n.* —*v.* **1** keep from harm or change; keep safe; protect. **2** conserve and protect (wildlife) in a regulated area. **3** keep up; maintain. **4** keep from spoiling: *Ice helps to preserve food.* **5** prepare (food) to keep it from spoiling. Boiling with sugar, salting, smoking, and pickling are different ways of preserving food.
—*n.* **1** an area or region where wild animals, fish, or trees and plants are protected. **2** Usually, **preserves,** *pl.* fruit cooked with sugar and sealed from the air: *plum preserves.* **3** an activity or place regarded as the special domain of an individual or group: *In our library, all manuscript documents are the preserve of one retired history professor.* ⟨ME < OF < LL *praeservare* < L *prae-* before + *servare* keep⟩ **—pre'serv•a•ble,** *adj.*

pre•serv•er [prɪˈzɜrvər] *n.* a person or thing that preserves or protects from danger: *a life preserver.*

pre•set *v.* [priˈsɛt]; *n.* [ˈpriˌsɛt] *v.* **-set, -set•ting;** *n.* —*v.* set beforehand.
—*n.* a control that makes a preset device come on at the proper time.

pre•shrink [priˈʃrɪŋk] *v.* **-shrank, -shrunk, -shrink•ing.** **1** expose (fabric or a garment) before sale to conditions that cause shrinking, so that it will not shrink when washed or drycleaned after sale. **2** wash or dryclean (a piece of fabric) before a garment is cut from it. **—pre'shrunk,** *adj.*

pre•side [prɪˈzaɪd] *v.* **-sid•ed, -sid•ing.** **1** hold the place of authority; have charge of a meeting. **2** have authority; have control: *The manager presides over the business of the store.* **3** of a musician, be featured: *Chopin frequently presided at the piano at his friends' musical evenings.* ⟨< L *praesidere* < *prae-* before + *sedere* sit⟩ **—pre'sid•er,** *n.*

pres•i•den•cy [ˈprɛzɪdənsi] *n., pl.* **-cies.** **1** the office of president. **2** the time during which a president is in office. **3** **Presidency,** the office or time of office of a President. **4** *Mormon Church.* **a** a council of three people with local jurisdiction. **b** a council of three that is the highest authority in the Church, also called the **First Presidency.** **5** formerly, any of the three original provinces of British India: Bengal, Bombay, and Madras.

pres•i•dent [ˈprɛzɪdənt] *n.* **1** Often, **President,** the highest executive officer of a republic. **2** the head or presiding officer of a company, university, society, club, etc. **3** a person who presides. ⟨< L *praesidens, -entis* presiding, ppr. of *praesidere.* See PRESIDE.⟩

pres•i•dent e•lect [ˈprɛzɪdənt ɪˈlɛkt] *n.* a president who has been elected but has not yet taken office.

pres•i•den•tial [ˌprɛzɪˈdɛnʃəl] *adj.* of, having to do with, or belonging to a president or presidency. **—ˌpres•i'den•tial•ly,** *adv.*

pre•sid•i•um [prɪˈsɪdiəm] *n.* formerly, in the Soviet Union and other communist countries, a permanent executive committee set up at a high level of government to act for a larger body, such as a legislature, between sessions. ⟨< L *praesidium* a presiding over < *praesidere.* See PRESIDE.⟩

press[1] [prɛs] *v., n.* —*v.* **1** use force or weight steadily (against); push with steady force: *Press the button to ring the bell.* **2** squeeze; squeeze out. **3** clasp; hug. **4** make smooth; flatten: *Press clothes with an iron. I press flowers.* **5** put a crease in: *My father pressed my pants with an iron.* **6** of a fabric, lend itself to being ironed: *This cotton presses well.* **7** push forward; keep advancing: *The girl pressed on in spite of the wind.* **8** move by pushing steadily (up, down, against, etc.). **9** urge onward; cause to hurry. **10** crowd; throng: *The excited fans pressed up onto the stage.* **11** urge (a person); keep asking; entreat: *Because it was so stormy, we pressed our guest to stay all night.* **12** lay stress upon; insist on: *I hate to press the point, but I need the report tomorrow.* **13** constrain; compel; force. **14** urge for acceptance. **15** harass; oppress; trouble: *enemies pressing on every side.* **16** weigh heavily (upon the mind, a person, etc.) **17** demand prompt action; be urgent.

be hard pressed (to). See HARD PRESSED.

be pressed for, be constrained by the lack or scarceness of.

press the flesh, *Informal.* shake hands.

—*n.* **1** a pressing; pressure; push: *the press of ambition. She was kept busy by the press of many duties.* **2** a pressed condition. **3** any of various instruments or machines for exerting pressure. **4** a machine for printing; printing press. **5** an establishment for printing books, etc. **6** newspapers, magazines, and the people who work for them: *The concert was reported by the press.* **7** notice given in newspapers or magazines: *The star actor got good press for her performance.* **8** a crowd; throng. **9** a pressing forward or together; crowding. **10** urgency; hurry. **11** a cupboard for clothes, books, etc. **12** the act of smoothing or creasing with an iron: *Those pants need a good press.* **13** a crease. **14** *Basketball.* a defensive measure in which offensive players are closely guarded over the whole court. **15** *Weightlifting.* a lift in which the weight is pressed away from the body using the arms or legs.

go to press, begin to be printed: *The newspaper goes to press at midnight.* ⟨ME < OF < L *pressare*, ult. < *premere* press⟩ **—'press•er,** *n.*

press[2] [prɛs] *v., n.* —*v.* **1** force into service, usually naval or military. **2** make use of in other than the usual or intended way, especially in an emergency: *When the roof leaked, every container in the house was pressed into service as a rain-catcher.*
—*n.* **1** an impressment into service, usually naval or military. **2** an order for such impressment. ⟨obs. *prest* < OF *prester* furnish, ult. < L *praestro* ready⟩

press agent an agent in charge of publicity for a person, organization, etc.

press baron the chief executive or owner of a large newspaper or publishing company.

press box at a sports stadium, arena, racetrack, etc., an enclosed space set aside for reporters.

press conference a meeting for the giving of information to reporters by a person or group. Some press conferences are called to announce specific items of news, others to provide opportunities for reporters to question particular individuals.

press gallery **1** an area reserved for the news media, especially in a legislative assembly. **2** the group of reporters seated in such an area, especially those covering the sessions of a legislative assembly: *The prime minister's speech puzzled the press gallery.*

press gang in former times, a group of men whose job it was to obtain men, often by force, for service in the navy or army.

press•ing [ˈprɛsɪŋ] *adj., n., v.* —*adj.* **1** requiring immediate action or attention; urgent. **2** persistent, insistent, or importunate in making a request or demand.
—*n.* **1** the act of one that presses: *That dress needs a good pressing.* **2** **a** a number of identical articles made all at the same

time on a press, from a master or stamper, such as a batch of phonograph records. **b** one of a series so produced.
—v. ppr. of PRESS. **—'press•ing•ly,** *adv.*

press•man ['prɛsmən] *n., pl.* **-men.** a person who operates or has charge of a press, especially a printing press.

press release a story or statement officially prepared and released to the press by a government agency, public relations firm, etc. Also called **news release.**

press secretary a person responsible for media and public relations on behalf of a prominent figure or organization.

pres•sure ['prɛʃər] *n., v. —n.* **1** the continued action of a weight or force: *The pressure of the wind filled the sails of the boat.* **2** *Physics.* the force per unit of area: *The tires of a 3-speed bicycle need a pressure of about 300 kilopascals.* **3** a state of trouble or strain: *the pressure of poverty.* **4** a compelling force or influence: *He changed his mind under pressure from others.* **5** the need for prompt or decisive action; urgency: *the pressure of business.* **6** *Electricity.* ELECTROMOTIVE FORCE.
—v. force or urge by exerting pressure: *The opposition pressured the government into debating the matter.* ⟨ME < OF < L *pressura,* ult. < *premere* press⟩

pres•sure–cook ['prɛʃər ˌkʊk] *v.* cook in a PRESSURE COOKER.

pressure cooker **1** an airtight metal pot for cooking with steam under pressure. **2** *Informal.* something involving a great deal of pressure: *This job is a real pressure cooker.*

pressure group any business, professional, labour, or other group that attempts to further its interests in the federal or provincial legislatures or elsewhere through the use of lobbying, propaganda, etc.

pressure ice ridges of ice formed by vast areas of sea ice pressing against each other.

pressure point **1** any of a number of points on the surface of the body where an artery passes close under the skin and in front of a bony structure so that pressure applied at that point will check bleeding. **2** any point on the skin highly sensitive to pressure. **3** an area, issue, aspect of a situation, etc. that is sensitive to political or other pressure.

pressure ridge a ridge of PRESSURE ICE.

pres•sur•ize ['prɛʃəˌraɪz] *v.* **-ized, -iz•ing. 1** keep the atmospheric pressure inside (the cabin of an aircraft, spacesuit, etc.) at a normal level in spite of the altitude. **2** bring up to normal or near normal pressure. **3** place under high pressure.
—ˌpres•sur•i'za•tion, *n.*

press•work ['prɛsˌwɜrk] *n.* **1** the working or management of a printing press. **2** the work done by a printing press.

Pres•ter John ['prɛstər] a legendary Christian priest and king of the Middle Ages, said to have ruled a kingdom somewhere in Asia or Africa.

pres•ti•dig•i•ta•tion [ˌprɛstəˌdɪdʒə'teiʃən] *n.* sleight of hand. ⟨< F⟩

pres•ti•dig•i•ta•tor [ˌprɛstə'dɪdʒəˌteitər] *n.* a person skilled in sleight of hand. ⟨< F < L *praestigiator* juggler; form influenced by F *preste* quick and L *digitus* finger⟩

pres•tige [prɛ'stiʒ] *or* [prɛ'stidʒ] *n.* **1** good reputation, influence, or social status derived from achievements, associations, wealth, etc. **2** (*adjl.*) having or giving prestige: *prestige accessories for your desk.* ⟨< F *prestige* magic spell, ult. < L *praestigiae* tricks⟩

pres•ti•gious [prə'stɪdʒəs] *adj.* having or conferring prestige. **—pres'ti•gious•ly,** *adv.*

pres•tis•si•mo [prɛ'stɪsɪˌmou] *adv., adj., n. Music. —adv.* very quickly.
—adj. very quick.
—n. a very quick movement or passage; a composition to be played or sung at this tempo. ⟨< Ital. *prestissimo,* superlative of *presto* quick, quickly⟩

pres•to ['prɛstou] *adv., adj., n., pl.* **-tos;** *interj. —adv.* quickly.
—adj. quick.
—n. a quick movement or passage; a composition to be played or sung at this tempo.
—interj. used when something is produced rapidly, almost as if by magic. ⟨< Ital. *presto,* ult. < L *praesto,* adv., ready⟩

pre–stressed concrete ['pri 'strɛst] concrete that has been cast around steel cables which are under tension. The tension of the cables compresses the concrete, thus increasing its strength. The cables can also be bent to exert force in any direction in order to counteract the effect of the pressure of a load on the concrete.

pre•sum•a•ble [prɪ'zuməbəl] *or* [prɪ'zjuməbəl] *adj.* that can be presumed or taken for granted; probable; likely.
—pre'sum•a•bly, *adv.*

pre•sume [prɪ'zum] *or* [prɪ'zjum] *v.* **-sumed, -sum•ing. 1** take for granted without proving; presuppose: *The law presumes innocence until guilt is proved.* **2** take upon oneself; venture; dare: *May I presume to tell you what to do?* **3** take unfair advantage of (*used with* **on** *or* **upon**): *Don't presume on his good nature by borrowing from him every week.* **4** be good evidence for: *A signed receipt presumes payment.* **5** assume something is the case: *Dr. Livingstone, I presume.* ⟨ME < OF < L *praesumere* take for granted < *prae-* before + *sumere* take⟩ **—pre'sum•er,** *n.*
—pre'sum•ing•ly, *adv.*

pre•sum•ed•ly [prɪ'zumɪdli] *or* [prɪ'zjumɪdli] *adv.* as is or may be supposed.

pre•sump•tion [prɪ'zʌmpʃən] *n.* **1** the act of presuming. **2** something taken for granted; a conclusion based on good evidence: *Since he had the stolen jewels, the presumption was that he was the thief.* **3** a cause or reason for presuming; probability. **4** unpleasant boldness: *It is an unforgivable presumption to arrive for a visit without being invited.* **5** an inference based on proof: *This case is based on the presumption that she was elsewhere at the time of the murder.*
presumption of innocence, *Law.* a presumption that an accused person is innocent until proven guilty. ⟨ME < OF < L *praesumptio, -onis* < *praesumere.* See PRESUME.⟩

pre•sump•tive [prɪ'zʌmptɪv] *adj.* **1** based on likelihood; presumed: *heir presumptive.* **2** giving ground for presumption or belief: *The man's running away was regarded as presumptive evidence of his guilt.* **—pre'sump•tive•ly,** *adv.*

pre•sump•tu•ous [prɪ'zʌmptʃuəs] *adj.* acting without permission or right; too bold; forward. ⟨ME < OF < LL *praesumptuosus* < L *praesumptio* audacity (< *praesumere.* See PRESUME.), but modelled on *sumptuosus* expensive < *sumptus* expense⟩ **—pre'sump•tu•ous•ly,** *adv.* **—pre'sump•tu•ous•ness,** *n.*

pre•sup•pose [ˌprisə'pouz] *v.* **-posed, -pos•ing. 1** take for granted in advance; assume beforehand: *Let us presuppose that most people are motivated by good intentions.* **2** require as a necessary condition; imply: *A fight presupposes fighters.*

pre•sup•po•si•tion [ˌprisʌpə'zɪʃən] *n.* **1** the act of assuming beforehand. **2** a thing assumed beforehand.

pret. preterite.

pre•teen or **pre–teen** [ˌpri'tin] *n.* a young person before adolescence, usually aged 11 or 12 years.

pre•tence [prɪ'tɛns] *or* ['pritɛns] *n.* **1** a false appearance: *Under pretence of picking up the handkerchief, she took the money.* **2** a false claim: *The girls made a pretence of knowing the answer.* **3** a claim. **4** a pretending; make-believe: *His anger was all pretence.* **5** a showing off; display: *Her manner is free from pretence.* **6** anything done to show off. Also (*esp. U.S.*), **pretense.** ⟨ME < AF *pretense,* ult. < L *praetendere.* See PRETEND.⟩

pre•tend [prɪ'tɛnd] *v., adj. —v.* **1** make believe. **2** claim falsely: *She pretended to like the meal so she wouldn't offend the hostess.* **3** claim falsely to have: *He pretended illness.* **4** claim: *I don't pretend to be a musician.* **5** lay claim: *James Stuart pretended to the English throne.* **6** venture; attempt; presume: *I cannot pretend to judge between them.*
—adj. make-believe; simulated: *pretend pearls, pretend fur.* ⟨ME < OF < L *praetendere* < *prae-* before + *tendere* stretch⟩
☛ *Syn. v.* **2, 3. Pretend,** AFFECT[2], ASSUME = claim falsely to have or be something. **Pretend** means speak or act as if one has or feels something: *They pretended ignorance of the whole affair.* **Affect** emphasizes putting on some characteristic or feeling, for some intended effect: *When she applied for a job, she affected simplicity.* **Assume** suggests putting on the appearance of feeling something, to cover up one's real feelings: *He assumed a look of sorrow.*

pre•tend•ed [prɪ'tɛndɪd] *adj., v. —adj.* **1** that is claimed, especially falsely. **2** affected; feigned.
—v. pt. and pp. of PRETEND. **—pre'tend•ed•ly,** *adv.*

pre•tend•er [prɪ'tɛndər] *n.* **1** a person who pretends. **2** a person who makes claims to something without just right (*used with* **to**): *a pretender to the title.*

pre•tense [prɪ'tɛns] *or* ['pritɛns] *n. Esp. U.S.* See PRETENCE.

pre•ten•sion [prɪ'tɛnʃən] *n.* **1** a claim: *The young prince has pretensions to the throne.* **2** a putting forward of a claim. **3** a pretentious display.

pre•ten•tious [prɪ'tɛnʃəs] *adj.* **1** making claims to excellence or importance: *a pretentious person, book, or speech.* **2** doing things for show or to make a fine appearance; showy: *a pretentious style of entertaining guests.* ⟨< F *prétentieux*, ult. < L *praetendere.* See PRETEND.⟩ **—pre'ten•tious•ly,** *adv.* **—pre'ten•tious•ness,** *n.*

preter– *combining form.* beyond; past; more than: *preterhuman.* ⟨< L *praeter*⟩

pre•ter•hu•man [,pritər'hjumən] *adj.* beyond what is normally human; superhuman.

pret•er•ite or **pret•er•it** ['prɛtərɪt] *n., adj. Grammar. —n.* a verb form that expresses occurrence or existence in the past that stopped before the time of speaking; PAST TENSE. *Obeyed* is the preterite of *obey*; *spoke*, of *speak*; and *saw*, of *see.*
—adj. expressing past time. ⟨ME < OF < L *praeteritus*, ult. < *praeter-* past + *ire* go⟩

pre•ter•mit [,pritər'mɪt] *v.* **-mit•ted, -mit•ting. 1** leave out; omit. **2** let pass without notice. ⟨< L *praetermittere* < *praeter-* past + *mittere* let go⟩ **—,pre•ter'mis•sion,** *n.*

pre•ter•nat•u•ral [,pritər'nætʃərəl] *adj.* **1** out of the ordinary course of nature; abnormal. **2** due to something above or beyond nature; supernatural. ⟨< Med.L *praeternaturalis*, ult. < L *praeter-* beyond + *natura* nature⟩ **—,pre•ter'nat•u•ral•ly,** *adv.* **—,pre•ter'nat•u•ral,ism,** *n.*

pre–test *n.* ['pri ,tɛst]; *v* [pri 'tɛst] *n., v. —n.* a preliminary test. Pre-tests are sometimes given at the beginning of a course of study to determine the students' level of knowledge or comprehension. Compare POST-TEST.
—v. give a pre-test to.

pre•text ['pritɛkst] *n.* a false reason concealing the real reason; pretence; excuse: *He used his sore finger as a pretext for not going to school.* ⟨< L *praetextus*, ult. < *prae-* in front + *texere* weave⟩

pre•tor ['pritər] *or* ['pritɔr] *n.* See PRAETOR.

pret•ti•fy ['prɪtə,faɪ] *v.* **-fied, -fy•ing.** decorate, especially in an artificial or overly cute way. **—,pret•ti•fi'ca•tion,** *n.* **—'pret•ti,fi•er,** *n.*

pret•ty ['prɪti] *adj.* **-ti•er, -ti•est;** *n., pl.* **-ties;** *adv., v.* **-tied, -ty•ing.**
—adj. **1** attractive or pleasing. **2** not at all pleasing: *a pretty mess.* **3** too dainty or delicate. **4** *Archaic.* brave; bold; fine. **5** *Informal.* considerable in amount or extent: *I'll bet she paid a pretty price for those designer jeans.*
a pretty penny. See PENNY.
sitting pretty, *Slang.* well off; in a good position.
—n. a pretty person or thing.
—adv. fairly; rather: *It is pretty late.*
—v.
pretty up, *Informal.* make pretty. ⟨OE *prættig* cunning < *prætt* trick⟩ **—'pret•ti•ly,** *adv.* **—'pret•ti•ness,** *n.*

pret•zel ['prɛtsəl] *n.* a hard biscuit, usually made in the shape of a loose knot and salted on the outside. ⟨< G *Brezel* < Med.L *bracellus* bracelet, ult. < Gk. *brachion* arm⟩

pre•vail [prɪ'veil] *v.* **1** exist in many places; be in general use: *That custom still prevails.* **2** be the most usual or strongest: *Sadness prevailed in our minds.* **3** be the stronger; win the victory; succeed: *The knights prevailed against their foe.* **4** be effective.
prevail on, upon, or **with,** persuade. ⟨ME *prevayllen* to grow very strong < L *praevalere* to be more able, prevail < *prae-* before + *valere* have power⟩

pre•vail•ing [prɪ'veilɪŋ] *adj., v. —adj.* **1** having superior force or influence; victorious. **2** most usual, predominant, or noticeable: *prevailing westerly winds.* **3** in general use; most common.
—v. ppr. of PREVAIL. **—pre'vail•ing•ly,** *adv.*
☛ *Syn.* **3.** See note at CURRENT.

prev•a•lence ['prɛvələns] *n.* widespread occurrence; general use: *the prevalence of complaints about the weather.*

prev•a•lent ['prɛvələnt] *adj.* **1** widespread; general; common: *Colds are prevalent in the winter.* **2** predominant; victorious. ⟨< L *praevalens, -entis*, ppr. of *praevalere* prevail. See PREVAIL.⟩ **—'prev•a•lent•ly,** *adv.*

pre•var•i•cate [prɪ'værə,keit] *or* [prɪ'vɛrə,keit] *v.* **-cat•ed, -cat•ing. 1** turn aside from the truth in speech or act; lie. **2** equivocate; be evasive. ⟨< L *praevaricari* make a sham accusation, ult. < *prae-* before + *varicus* straddling < *varus* crooked⟩ **—pre'var•i,ca•tor,** *n.*

pre•var•i•ca•tion [prɪ,værə'keiʃən] *or* [prɪ,vɛrə'keiʃən] *n.* the act of prevaricating; departure from the truth; a lie.

pre•vent [prɪ'vɛnt] *v.* **1** keep *(from)*: *Illness prevented him from doing his work.* **2** keep from happening: *Rain prevented the game.* **3** hinder. ⟨< L *praeventus*, pp. of *praevenire* < *prae-* before + *venire* come⟩ **—pre'vent•er,** *n.* **—pre'vent•a•ble** or **pre'vent•i•ble,** *adj.*
☛ *Syn.* **Prevent,** HINDER[1], IMPEDE = get in the way of action or progress. **Prevent** = keep a person or thing from doing something or making progress by acting or setting up an obstacle to stop him, her, or it: *Business prevented her going.* **Hinder** = hold back, so that making, starting, going ahead, or finishing is late, difficult, or impossible: *An unbalanced diet hinders growth.* **Impede** = slow up movement and progress by putting something binding, fouling, etc. on or in the way: *Mud impedes the advance of troops.*

pre•vent•a•tive [prɪ'vɛntətɪv] *adj. or n.* preventive.

pre•ven•tion [prɪ'vɛnʃən] *n.* **1** a preventing: *the prevention of fire.* **2** something that prevents.

pre•ven•tive [prɪ'vɛntɪv] *adj., n. —adj.* that prevents: *preventive measures against disease.*
—n. something that prevents: *Vaccination is a preventive against flu.* **—pre'ven•tive•ly,** *adv.* **—pre'ven•tive•ness,** *n.*

preventive war an aggressive war waged against another nation, supposedly started in anticipation of attack by that nation.

pre•view ['pri,vju] *n., v. —n.* **1** a previous view, inspection, survey, etc. **2** an advance showing of a motion picture, play, etc. to a select audience. **3** TRAILER (def. 3).
—v. view beforehand.

pre•vi•ous ['priviəs] *adj.* **1** coming or going before; that came before; earlier. **2** *Informal.* quick; hasty; premature: *Don't be too previous about refusing.*
previous to, before: *Previous to her departure she gave a party.* ⟨< L *praevius* leading the way < *prae-* before + *via* road⟩
☛ *Syn.* **1. Previous,** PRECEDING, PRIOR = coming before something. **Previous** suggests earlier in time, made or done sometime earlier, or being the last one before the present: *I cannot go, for I have a previous engagement* (made before). **Preceding** means coming immediately before in a series of similar things, in order of time or in place: *Check the preceding statement.* **Prior** adds to **previous** the idea of coming first in order of importance: *I have a prior engagement* (one that has first call).

pre•vi•ous•ly ['priviəsli] *adv.* at a previous time: *I had not met him previously.*

previous question *Parliamentary procedure.* the question whether a vote shall be taken on the main question without further debate.

pre•vi•sion [pri'vɪʒən] *n.* **1** foresight; foreknowledge. **2** a prophetic vision or perception: *prevision of trouble.*

pre•vi•sion•al [pri'vɪʒənəl] *adj.* foreseeing; forecasting; of or having to do with prevision.

pre•vo•cal•ic [,privou'kælɪk] *adj. Phonetics.* immediately preceding a vowel.

pre•war ['pri'wɔr] *adj.* before a (given) war: *prewar prices.*

prex•y ['prɛksi] *n., pl.* **-ies.** *Esp. U.S. Slang.* president, especially of a college or university.

prey [prei] *n., v. —n.* **1** an animal hunted or seized for food, especially by another animal: *Mice and birds are the prey of cats.* **2** characterized by killing other animals: *a bird of prey.* **3** a person or thing injured; victim: *to be a prey to fear or disease.*
—v.
prey on or **upon, a** hunt or kill for food: *Cats prey on mice.* **b** be a strain upon; injure; irritate: *The memory of the accident prayed upon their minds.* **c** rob; plunder. **d** hunt. ⟨ME < OF < L *praeda*⟩
☛ *Hom.* PRAY.

pri•ap•ic [praɪ'æpɪk] *adj.* **1** phallic. **2** overly taken up with virility. **3** characterized by priapism. ⟨< L *Priapus* < Gk. *Priapos*, a god, the son of Dionysus and Aphrodite, who symbolizes male generative power⟩

pri•a•pism ['praɪə,pɪzəm] **1** *Pathology.* continuous erection of the penis, usually non-sexual, especially when due to a disease. **2** prurient or lascivious behaviour.

Prib•i•lof Islands ['prɪbə,lɒf] a group of four Alaskan islands in the Bering Sea, SW of Alaska and NW of the Aleutians. They are noted as the breeding ground of fur seals.

price [praɪs] *n., v.* **priced, pric•ing.** *—n.* **1** the amount for which a thing is sold or can be bought; cost to the buyer. **2** a reward offered for the capture of a person alive or dead: *Every*

member of the gang has a price on his head. **3** what must be given, done, undergone, etc. to obtain a thing: *We paid a heavy price for the victory, for we lost ten thousand soldiers.* **4** value; worth. **5** the lowest sum of money which someone will accept as an inducement or bribe, especially at the expense of integrity.
at any price, at any cost, no matter how great: *They wanted to win at any price.*
beyond or **without price,** so valuable that it cannot be bought or given a value in money; priceless.
—v. **1** put a price on; set the price of. **2** *Informal,* ask the price of; find out the price of: *to price a rug.* ⟨ME < OF *pris* < L *pretium*⟩
☛ *Syn. n.* **1. Price,** CHARGE, COST = the amount asked or paid for something. **Price** means the amount of money for which something is sold, but especially suggests what the seller asks for things: *The price of meat is high now.* **Charge** is the amount asked, especially for services: *There is no charge for delivery.* **Cost** suggests the amount paid for goods or services or whatever is given or spent, such as effort, to get anything: *The cost of building the house was high.*

price–earn•ings ratio [ˈprəis ˈɜrnɪŋz] the ratio of the current price of a share of common stock to the corporation's per share annual earnings, i.e., the current market price divided by the earnings per share over twelve months, used in stock valuation.

price fixing the establishment of ceiling prices at a predetermined level by a government or illegally by mutual consent of competing producers of a commodity.

price index a comparative index of the prices of goods and services, taking 100 as a base representing the prices of the same goods and services at a previous period arbitrarily selected.

price•less [ˈprəislɪs] *adj.* **1** beyond price; extremely valuable: *a priceless painting.* **2** *Informal.* delightfully amusing: *She told us a priceless story about her dog.* **—ˈprice•less•ness,** *n.*

price support a system by which the government guarantees a given price to farmers for their produce.

price tag **1** a ticket or tag on merchandise showing its price. **2** *Informal.* an estimated value, price, or cost.

price war a system in which sellers try to capture the market by repeatedly undercutting the prices of competitors.

pric•ey [ˈprəisi] *adj.* **pric•i•er, pric•i•est.** *Informal.* expensive: *It's a nice restaurant, but a bit too pricey for me.* Also, **pricy.**

prick [prɪk] *n., v.* *—n.* **1** a sharp point. **2** a little hole or mark made by a sharp point. **3** the act or an instance of jabbing or making a small hole with a sharp point. **4** a sharp pain.
kick against the pricks, make useless resistance that only hurts oneself.
—v. **1** jab or make a little hole in with a sharp point. **2** mark with a sharp point. **3** cause sharp pain to. **4** cause or feel a sharp pain. **5** raise or point erect: *The dog pricked his ears at the sound of footsteps.* **6** lame (a horse) by piercing its foot to the quick with a nail while shoeing. **7** *Archaic.* spur; urge on. **8** *Archaic.* ride fast.
prick out or **off,** transplant (seedlings) into larger individual containers with more room for growth.
prick up, point upward: *The cougar's ears pricked up.*
prick up (one's) **ears, a** point the ears upward. **b** give sudden attention; listen carefully: *The boy pricked up his ears when the teacher started talking about a trip.* ⟨OE *prica* point⟩ **—ˈprick•er,** *n.*

prick•le [ˈprɪkəl] *n., v.* **-led, -ling.** *—n.* **1** a small, sharp point; thorn; spine. **2** a prickly, tingling, or smarting sensation.
—v. **1** feel a tingling, prickly, or smarting sensation. **2** cause such a sensation in. ⟨OE *pricel* < *prica* point⟩

prick•ly [ˈprɪkli] *adj.* **-li•er, -li•est. 1** having many sharp points like thorns: *a prickly rosebush, the prickly porcupine.* **2** sharp and stinging; itching: *Heat sometimes causes a prickly rash on the skin.* **3** hard to deal with; likely to raise problems, controversy, etc.: *a prickly question.* **4** quick to take offence; easily angered: *He is a prickly individual.* **—ˈprick•li•ness,** *n.*

prick•ly–ash [ˈprɪkli ˈæʃ] a thorny plant (*Zanthoxylum americanum*) having alternate leaves, and thorns in pairs.

prickly heat a red, itching rash on the skin caused by inflammation of the sweat glands.

Prickly pear fruit in flower

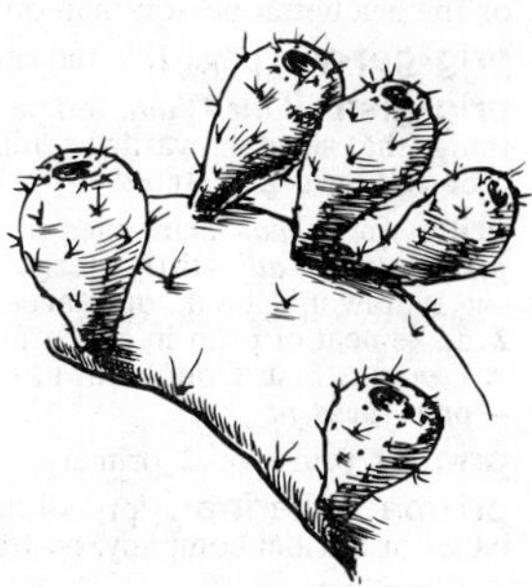

A prickly pear

prickly pear **1** any of a genus (*Opuntia*) of cactuses having spiny, flat or cylindrical joints, usually yellow flowers, and oval or pear-shaped fruit. It grows in the arid interior of British Columbia as well as in semi-desert areas of the U.S. **2** the pulpy, edible fruit of several of these cactuses.

prickly poppy chicalote.

prickly rose a common North American wild rose (*Rosa acicularis*) found along roadsides, on grassy slopes, and in clearings from Québec to Alaska and south to Colorado, having large pink flowers and leaves usually consisting of five leaflets. The prickly rose is the provincial flower of Alberta.

pric•y [ˈprəisi] *adj.* See PRICEY.

pride [praɪd] *n., v.* **prid•ed, prid•ing.** *—n.* **1** a high opinion of one's own worth or abilities; dignity; self-respect. **2** pleasure or satisfaction in something concerned with oneself: *to take pride in a hard job well done.* **3** something that one is proud of. **4** too high an opinion of oneself. **5** an acting as if better than or not needing others; scorn of others. **6** the best part; most flourishing period: *in the pride of adulthood.* **7** a group or company of lions.
—v.
pride oneself on, be proud about; indulge in pride about: *She prides herself on her mathematical ability.* ⟨OE *prȳde* < *prūd* proud⟩
☛ *Syn. n.* **1. Pride,** CONCEIT = a high opinion of oneself. **Pride** applies to a feeling of pleased satisfaction with what one is, has, or has done, and suggests either proper self-respect and personal dignity because of real worth or excessive self-love and arrogance because of imagined superiority: *Pride in oneself is necessary for a healthy outlook on life; excessive pride is unattractive.* **Conceit** suggests much too high an opinion of one's own abilities and accomplishments, and often implies an unpleasantly assertive manner: *Conceit makes criminals think they are too clever to be caught.*

pride•ful [ˈpraɪdfəl] *adj.* proud. **—ˈpride•ful•ly,** *adv.* **—ˈpride•ful•ness,** *n.*

prie–dieu [ˈpri ˈdjʊ]; *French,* [pʀiˈdjœ] *n. French.* a small desk for a prayer book, etc. with a lower piece on which to kneel. ⟨< F *prie-dieu,* literally, pray God⟩

pride of place the highest or most important position; first place: *In his affections, his wife holds pride of place.*

pri•er [ˈpraɪər] *n.* a person who pries; an inquisitive person.

pries [praɪz] *n., v.* *—n.* pl. of PRY.
—v. 3rd person singular, present tense of PRY.

priest [prist] *n.* **1** a special servant of a god, one who offers sacrifices and acts as an intermediary between the people and the god: *a priest of Apollo.* **2 a** a member of the clergy or minister of certain Christian churches. **b** a member of the clergy authorized to administer the sacraments and pronounce absolution. **3** a minister of any religion: *a Buddhist priest.* ⟨OE *prēost,* ult. < L *presbyter.* Related to PRESBYTER.⟩
—ˈpriest•less, *adj.*

priest•craft [ˈprist,kræft] *n.* **1** the training and abilities necessary for priesthood. **2** the unscrupulous use of a priestly office.

priest•ess [ˈpristɪs] *n.* formerly, a woman who served at an altar or in sacred rites: *a priestess of the goddess Diana.*

priest•hood [ˈprist,hʊd] *n.* **1** the position or rank of priest. **2** priests as a group.

priest•ly [ˈpristli] *adj.* **-li•er, -li•est. 1** of or having to do with a priest: *priestly duties.* **2** like a priest; suitable to a priest. **—ˈpriest•li•ness,** *n.*

prig [prɪg] *n.* someone who is smug and affected, and thinks he or she is a better person than others. ⟨origin uncertain⟩

prig•ger•y ['prɪgəri] *n.* the conduct or character of a prig.

prig•gish ['prɪgɪʃ] *adj.* too particular about being proper in things that show outwardly; priding oneself on being better than others. **—'prig•gish•ly,** *adv.* **—'prig•gish•ness,** *n.*

prim [prɪm] *adj.* **prim•mer, prim•mest;** *v.* **primmed, prim•ming.** *—adj.* stiffly precise, neat, proper, or formal.
—v. **1** draw up (the mouth, face, etc.) into a prim expression. **2** make neat or prim in appearance. ⟨< MF *prim* fine, delicate < L *primus* first. Doublet of PRIME[1]⟩ **—'prim•ly,** *adv.* **—'prim•ness,** *n.*

prim. **1** primitive. **2** primary.

pri•ma ballerina ['primə] the principal female dancer in a ballet or a ballet company. ⟨< Ital.⟩

pri•ma•cy ['praɪməsi] *n., pl.* **-cies. 1** the condition of being first in order, rank, importance, etc. **2** the position or rank of a PRIMATE (def. 2). **3** *Roman Catholic Church.* the supreme power of the Pope. ⟨ME *primacie* < OF < Med.L *primatia* < L *primas, -atis* of first rank. See PRIMATE.⟩

pri•ma don•na ['primə 'dɒnə] *pl.* **pri•ma don•nas. 1** the principal woman singer in an opera. **2** *Informal.* a temperamental person. ⟨< Ital. *prima donna* first lady⟩

pri•ma fa•ci•e ['primə] *or* ['praɪmə 'feiʃi,i], ['feiʃi,ei], *or* ['feiʃi] *Latin.* at first view; before investigation. ⟨< L ⟩

prima facie case or **evidence** *Law.* an argument or evidence sufficiently convincing in itself to establish a fact or presumption of a fact unless subsequently refuted.

pri•mal ['praɪməl] *adj.* **1** of early times; first; primeval. **2** chief; fundamental. ⟨< Med.L *primalis* < L *primus* first⟩ **—'pri•mal•ly,** *adv.*

pri•ma•ri•ly [praɪ'mɛrəli] *or* ['praɪmɛrəli] *adv.* **1** chiefly; principally: *Napoleon was primarily a general.* **2** at first; originally.

pri•ma•ry ['praɪmɛri] *or* ['praɪməri] *adj., n., pl.* **-ries.** *—adj.* **1** first in time; first in order. **2** from which others have come; original; fundamental. **3** first in importance; chief. **4** *Electricity.* of or having to do with the inducing circuit, coil, or current in an induction coil or the like. **5** *Ornithology.* of or having to do with one of the large flight feathers growing on the distal section of a bird's wing. **6** utilizing the crude products of nature as raw materials: *a primary industry.* **7** *Education.* of or having to do with grades 1, 2, and 3: *primary teachers.* **8** not involving an intermediary source. **9** *Chemistry.* involving or obtained from the replacement of one atom or group. **10** *Geology.* of rocks, formed directly by sedimentation, precipitation, or solidification, and not altered subsequently. **11** *Linguistics.* of derived forms, having a base that cannot be further broken down.
—n. **1** anything that is first in order, rank, or importance. **2** PRIMARY COLOUR. **3** *Electricity.* a primary coil or circuit. **4** *U.S.* PRIMARY ELECTION. **5** *Ornithology.* a primary feather. ⟨ME < L *primarius* first in rank < *primus* first⟩
☛ *Syn. adj.* **1.** See note at ELEMENTARY.

primary accent PRIMARY STRESS.

primary colour or **color** one of three colours that can be mixed together to make any other colour. Red, yellow, and blue are the primary colours in pigments; in light, they are red, green, and blue.

primary election *U.S.* an election to choose candidates for office from a certain political party.

primary school the first grades of elementary school, usually grades 1, 2, and 3, sometimes including kindergarten.

primary stress **1** the strongest stress or accent in the pronunciation of a word. **2** a mark, such as (') in ['praɪmɛri], used to show where this stress falls.

pri•mate ['praɪmeit] *or* ['praɪmɪt] *n.* **1** any of an order (Primates) of placental mammals that includes humans together with apes, monkeys, lemurs, lorises, etc. Primates are omnivorous and characterized especially by the use of the hands and by complex, flexible behaviour patterns. **2** an archbishop or bishop ranking above all other bishops in a country or church: *The Archibishop of Canterbury is the Primate of the Anglican Church throughout the world.* ⟨ME < OF < L *primas, -atis* of first rank < *primus* first⟩

pri•ma•tol•o•gy [,praɪmə'tɒlədʒi] *n.* the branch of zoology dealing with the study of primates, especially the great apes, monkeys, and early humans. **—,pri•ma'tol•o•gist,** *n.*

prime[1] [praɪm] *adj., n.* *—adj.* **1** first in rank; chief: *The minister's prime object was to lower the tax rate.* **2** first in time or order; fundamental. **3** first in quality; first-rate; excellent: *prime ribs of beef.* **4** *Mathematics.* **a** of or designating a PRIME NUMBER. **b** having no divisor in common with another number but 1: *16 is prime to 21.*
—n. **1** the best time; condition: *A person of forty is in the prime of life.* **2** the best part. **3** the first part; beginning. **4** springtime. **5** early adulthood; youth. **6** the second of the seven canonical hours, or the service for it, originally fixed for the first hour of the day (beginning at 6 a.m.). **7** a prime number. **8** *Mathematics.* **a** one of two or more different values of the same variable. **b** the mark (′) representing it, also standing for one of the sixty minutes of a degree. **9** *Music.* **a** the tonic, or keynote. **b** the interval between two tones of the same or different quality but identical pitch; unison. **c** a tone sung or played in unison with another. **10** PRIME RATE. ⟨ME < L *primus* first (def. 6 < OE *prīm* < L *prima hora* first hour). Doublet of PRIM.⟩ **—'prime•ness,** *n.*

prime[2] [praɪm] *v.* **primed, prim•ing. 1** prepare by putting something in or on. **2** supply (a gun) with powder. **3** cover (a surface) with a first coat of paint or oil so that the finishing coat of paint will not soak in. **4** equip (a person) with information, words, etc. **5** pour water into (a pump) to start action. ⟨probably < *prime*[1]⟩

prime meridian the meridian from which the longitude east and west is measured. It passes through Greenwich, England, and its longitude is 0°.

prime minister Often, **Prime Minister,** the chief minister in certain governments, usually the leader of the majority party in parliament; head of the cabinet: *The prime minister of Canada is the first minister of the federal government. Abbrev.*: P.M.

prime number *Mathematics.* an integer not exactly divisible by any whole number other than itself and 1; prime. The integers 2, 3, 5, 7, and 11 are prime numbers. Compare COMPOSITE NUMBER.

prim•er[1] ['prɪmər] *or* ['praɪmər] *n.* **1** a first book in reading. **2** a beginner's book in any subject. ⟨ME *prymer* < Med.L *primarius* < L *primarius* first in rank. See PRIMARY.⟩

prim•er[2] ['praɪmər] *n.* **1** a person who or thing that primes. **2** a cap or cylinder containing a little gunpowder, used for firing a charge of dynamite, etc. **3** a paint or sealant used for a first coat. ⟨< *prime*[2]⟩

prime rate the lowest rate of interest charged by a bank on commercial loans to its most preferred customers. Also called **prime lending** (or **interest**) **rate.**

prime time *Radio and television.* the period of the day when the largest audience can be expected, usually between 7 and 10 in the evening. **—'prime-'time,** *adj.*

pri•me•val [praɪ'mivəl] *adj.* **1** of or having to do with the earliest time: *In its primeval state the earth was without any form of life.* **2** ancient: *primeval forests untouched by the axe.* ⟨< L *primaevus* early in life < *primus* first + *aevum* age⟩ **—pri'me•val•ly,** *adv.*

prim•ing ['praɪmɪŋ] *n., v.* *—n.* **1** PRIMER[2] (defs. 2, 3). **2** the act of someone or something that primes.
—v. ppr. of PRIME.

prim•i•tive ['prɪmɪtɪv] *adj., n.* *—adj.* **1** of early times; of long ago: *Primitive people often lived in caves.* **2** first of the kind: *primitive Christians.* **3** very simple; such as people had early in human history; crude: *A primitive way of making fire is by rubbing two sticks together.* **4** original; primary. **5** *Biology.* **a** primordial. **b** representing or related to an ancient group or species.
—n. **1** an artist belonging to an early period, especially before the Renaissance. **2** an artist who imitates early painters, or who paints with directness and simplicity. **3** a picture by such an artist. **4 a** a person living in a very simple or pre-technological society. **b** a person living a simple non-technological lifestyle. **c** a person who lived in early times. **5** *Mathematics.* an algebraic or geometrical expression from which another is derived. **6** a word from which another is derived. ⟨ME < OF < L *primitivus*, ult. < *primus* first⟩ **—'prim•i•tive•ly,** *adv.* **—'prim•i•tive•ness,** *n.*

prim•i•tiv•ism ['prɪmɪtɪ,vɪzəm] *n.* **1** the condition of being primitive. **2** the theory or notion that primitive cultures are superior to technologically advanced cultures. **3** the principles, qualities, etc. of the art of primitive peoples or primitive artists. **—'prim•i•tiv•ist,** *n.* **—'prim•i•tiv•is•tic,** *adj.*

pri•mo•gen•i•tor [,praɪmə'dʒɛnɪtər] *n.* **1** an ancestor; forebear. **2** the earliest ancestor. ⟨< LL *primogenitor* < L *primus* first + *genitor* begetter⟩

pri•mo•gen•i•ture [,praɪmə'dʒɛnɪtʃər] *n.* **1** the state, condition, or fact of being the first-born of the children of the same parents. 2 *Law.* the right or principle of inheritance or succession by the first-born, especially the inheritance of a family estate by the eldest son. ⟨< Med.L *primogenitura*, ult. < L *primus* first + *gignere* beget⟩

pri•mor•di•al [praɪˈmɔrdiəl] *adj.* **1** existing at the very beginning; primitive. **2** *Biology.* formed first in the course of development: *primordial leaves.* **3** original; elementary: *primordial laws.* ⟨ME < LL *primordialis* < L *primordium* beginning⟩ **—pri'mor•di•al•ly,** *adv.*

pri•mor•di•um [praɪˈmɔrdiəm] *n., pl.* **-di•a** [-diə]. in the embryo, the first indication of development of an organ or part.

primp [prɪmp] *v.* dress (oneself) or arrange (one's hair or clothing) in a fussy or careful way, to make oneself look smart or showy: *to primp in front of a mirror.* ⟨apparently var. of *prim*, v. < *prim*, adj.⟩

prim•rose [ˈprɪm,rouz] *n., adj. —n.* **1** any of a genus (*Primula*) of popular perennial garden plants having large leaves and showy flowers of many different colours. **2** the flower of any of these plants. **3** a pale yellow, the colour of the common European primrose. **4** any of several other similar plants, such as the **evening primrose**.
—adj. **1** designating a family (Primulaceae) of plants found mainly in the northern hemisphere, having leaves that grow from the base of the plant and flowers growing in clusters. The primrose family includes the primroses, cyclamens, and loosestrife. **2** pale yellow in colour. **3** of or like a primrose; pleasant. ⟨< Med.L *prima rosa* first rose⟩

primrose path **1** a pleasant way; path of pleasure. **2** an irresponsible and hedonistic way of life. ⟨from Shakespeare's *Hamlet*, Act I Scene iii⟩

prim•u•la [ˈprɪmjələ] *n.* PRIMROSE (def. 1).

Pri•mus stove [ˈpraɪməs] *Trademark.* a portable stove that burns vaporized oil, used by campers, etc.

prin. **1** principal(ly). **2** principle.

prince [prɪns] *n.* a human male who is: **1** a member of a royal family; especially, in the United Kingdom, a son or grandson of the reigning monarch. **2** a sovereign. **3** a ruler of a small state subordinate to a king or emperor. **4** in certain countries, a high-ranking member of the nobility. **5** the greatest or best of a group; chief: *a merchant prince, a prince of artists.* **6** a generous, kind, and helpful person: *He's a real prince of a fellow.* ⟨ME < OF < L *princeps* chief < *primus* first + *capere* take⟩

Prince Albert a man's long, double-breasted coat. ⟨probably after either Prince Albert, consort of Queen Victoria, or their son, later King Edward VII⟩

prince consort a prince who is the husband of a queen or empress ruling in her own right.

prince•dom [ˈprɪnsdəm] *n.* **1** the territory ruled by a prince. **2** the position, rank, or dignity of a prince.

Prince Edward Island Canada's smallest province, an island in the Gulf of St. Lawrence.

Prince Edward Islander a native or long-term resident of Prince Edward Island.

prince•ling [ˈprɪnslɪŋ] *n.* a young, subordinate, or insignificant prince.

prince•ly [ˈprɪnsli] *adj.* **-li•er, -li•est.** **1** of a prince or his rank; royal. **2** like a prince; noble. **3** fit for a prince; magnificent: *He earns a princely salary.* **—'prince•li•ness,** *n.*

Prince of Darkness the Devil; Satan.

Prince of Peace a name for Jesus Christ, considered by Christians to be the Messiah.

prince of the blood a prince of a royal family.

Prince of Wales in the United Kingdom, a title conferred on the eldest son, or heir apparent, of the sovereign. Prince Charles was named Prince of Wales in 1956.

prince royal the eldest son of a reigning monarch.

prin•cess [ˈprɪnsɛs], [ˈprɪnsɪs], *or* [prɪnˈsɛs] *n.* **1** a daughter of a reigning monarch, or of the son of a reigning monarch. **2** the wife or widow of a prince. **3** a woman having the same rank as a prince. **4** any woman considered to have the characteristics, positive or negative, of a princess, in being: **a** accomplished, generous, charming, etc. or **b** snobbish, arrogant, spoiled, etc. ⟨< F *princesse*, fem. of *prince* prince⟩

prin•cesse or **prin•cess** [prɪnˈsɛs], [ˈprɪnsɛs], *or* [ˈprɪnsɪs] *adj.* of women's one-piece dresses, having an unbroken line from the shoulder to the hem, a fitted top, and a gently flaring skirt. ⟨< F *princesse* princess⟩

princess royal the eldest daughter of a reigning monarch. Princess Anne is the princess royal.

prin•ci•pal [ˈprɪnsəpəl] *adj., n. —adj.* most important; main; chief: *St. John's is the principal city in Newfoundland.*
—n. **1** a chief person; one who gives orders. **2** the head, or one of the heads, of a school, college, etc. **3** a sum of money that has been borrowed, as opposed to the interest payable on it. **4** the main body, or capital, of an investment or property, as opposed to the income received from it. **5** a person who hires another person to act for him or her. **6** a person directly responsible for a crime. **7** a person responsible for the payment of a debt that another person has endorsed or guaranteed. **8** a person taking a leading part, as in a play, opera, film, etc. **9** a soloist at a concert. **10** *Music.* **a** the lead player of any section of a symphony orchestra except the first violins. **b** any of the main stops of an organ. **c** the subject of a fugue. ⟨< L *principalis* < *princeps* chief. See PRINCE.⟩
☛ *Hom.* PRINCIPLE.
☛ *Usage.* **Principal,** PRINCIPLE. Do not confuse these two words of entirely different meaning. **Principal** as an adjective means 'chief', and as a noun, 'chief person' or 'main sum of money'. **Principle** is used only as a noun, meaning 'a basic idea' (*the principles of democracy*), or 'a rule of conduct' (*Good character depends upon high principles*).

prin•ci•pal•i•ty [,prɪnsəˈpæləti] *n., pl.* **-ties.** **1** a small state or country ruled by a prince. **2** a country from which a prince gets his title. **3** a supernatural power.

prin•ci•pal•ly [ˈprɪnsəpəli] *adv.* for the most part; above all; chiefly.
☛ *Syn.* See note at ESPECIALLY.

Principal Meridian *Cdn.* See FIRST MERIDIAN.

principal parts *Grammar.* the main parts of a verb, from which the rest can be derived. In English the principal parts are the present infinitive, past tense or preterite, and past participle. *Examples*: *go, went, gone; do, did, done; drive, drove, driven; push, pushed, pushed.*

prin•ci•pal•ship [ˈprɪnsəpəl,ʃɪp] *n.* the position or office of a principal.

prin•ci•pate [ˈprɪnsəpɪt] *n.* **1** a chief place or authority. **2** principality. ⟨ME < L *principatus* < *princeps* chief. See PRINCE.⟩

prin•ci•ple [ˈprɪnsəpəl] *n.* **1** a fact or belief on which other ideas are based: *Science is based on the principle that things can be explained.* **2 a** a rule of action or conduct: *I make it a principle to save some money each week.* **b** such rules collectively. **c** adherence to these rules; integrity. **3** uprightness; honour: *Joseph Howe was a man of principle.* **4** a rule of science explaining how things act: *the principle of the lever.* **5** a natural tendency; origin or source; a first cause or force. **6** the method of operation. **7** *Chemistry.* one of the elements that compose a substance, especially one that gives some special quality or effect: *the bitter principle in a drug.*
in principle, as regards the general idea or rule: *to approve something in principle.*
on principle, a according to a certain principle. **b** for reasons of right conduct. ⟨ME < OF < L *principium* < *princeps* chief. See PRINCE.⟩
☛ *Hom.* PRINCIPAL.
☛ *Usage.* See note at PRINCIPAL.

prin•ci•pled [ˈprɪnsəpəld] *adj.* showing, characterized by, or based on high moral principles: *a principled act of protest, a principled person.*

prink [prɪŋk] *v.* primp. ⟨origin uncertain⟩ **—'prink•er,** *n.*

print [prɪnt] *v., n. —v.* **1** use type, blocks, plates, etc. and ink or dye to reproduce (words, pictures, or designs) on paper or some other surface. **2** reproduce letters, words, or designs on with type, etc. **3** cause to be printed; publish. **4** produce (books, newspapers, etc.) by printing press. **5** make (words or letters) the way they look in print instead of in writing. **6** make with such letters: *Print your name clearly.* **7** stamp with designs, patterns, pictures, etc.: *Machines print wallpaper, cloth, etc.* **8** stamp; produce (marks or figures) by pressure; impress. **9** fix: *The scene is printed on my memory.* **10** produce by photocopying, etc.: *Please print five hundred copies of this poster.* **11** *Photography.* **a** produce (a photograph) by transmission of light through (a negative). **b** produce a photograph, print, or impress: *These negatives printed well considering their age.* **12** *Computer technology.* cause (a computer file) to be reproduced in printed form (*often used with* **out**): *I want this file printed out by tomorrow morning.*
—n. **1** printed words, letters, etc.: *This book has clear print.* **2** a printed condition. **3** printed publications; newspapers or magazines. **4** an edition or impression of a book, etc., made all

at one time. **5** a picture or design printed from an engraved block, plate, etc. **6** cloth with a pattern printed on it. **7** a garment made from such cloth: *I think I'll wear my pink print to the party tonight.* **8** a mark made by pressing or stamping: *the print of a foot.* **9** something that prints; a stamp or die. **10** something that has been marked or shaped by pressing or stamping. **11** *Photography.* a photograph produced from a negative.
in print, a in printed or published form. **b** of books, etc., still available for purchase from the publisher.
out of print, no longer sold by the publisher. ⟨ME *prente* < OF *priente*, ult. < L *premere* press⟩ **—'print•less,** *adj.*

print•a•ble ['prɪntəbəl] *adj.* **1** capable of being printed. **2** capable of being printed from. **3** fit to be printed. **—,print•a'bil•i•ty,** *n.*

printed circuit *Electronics.* an electrical circuit in which some of the components and the conductors have been printed or etched in fine lines with electrically conductive ink on an insulating board of dielectric material.

print•er ['prɪntər] *n.* **1** a person whose business or work is printing or setting type. **2** a machine or device used for printing, such as the part of a computer that produces printouts.

printer's devil formerly, an errand boy or apprentice in a printing office.

print•ing ['prɪntɪŋ] *n., v. —n.* **1** the art, process, or business of producing printed matter. **2** printed words, letters, etc. **3** all the copies printed at one time. **4** letters made like those in print.
—v. ppr. of PRINT.

printing press a machine for printing from types, plates, etc.

print•out ['prɪnt,ʌut] *n. Computer technology.* a printed record of the output of a computer, produced automatically.

print•wheel ['prɪnt,wil] *n.* a circular device holding characters for printing on a computer printer; DAISY WHEEL.

pri•or¹ ['praɪər] *adj.* **1** coming before; earlier: *I can't go with you because I have a prior engagement.* **2** of greater importance or higher rank: *He regretted not being able to work the extra hours, but considered his family a prior responsibility.*
prior to, coming before in time, order, or importance; earlier than; before. ⟨< L⟩
☛ *Syn.* **1.** See note at PREVIOUS.

pri•or² ['praɪər] *n.* the head of a priory or monastery for men. Priors usually rank below abbots. ⟨OE < Med.L *prior*, n. use of L *prior* prior¹⟩

pri•or•ate ['praɪərɪt] *n.* **1** the rank or office of a PRIOR². Also called **priorship. 2** priory.

pri•or•ess ['praɪərɪs] *n.* a woman who is the head of a convent or priory for women. Prioresses usually rank below abbesses in an abbey.

pri•or•i•tize [praɪ'ɔrə,taɪz] *v.* **-tized, -tiz•ing.** rank in order of priority.

pri•or•i•ty [praɪ'ɔrɪti] *n., pl.* **-ties. 1** the fact of being earlier in time. **2** a coming before in order or importance: *Fire engines and ambulances have priority over other traffic.* **3** governmental rating giving right of way to persons or things important in national defence, essential affairs of state, etc., in order of importance. **4** a preferential position allotted to any project, research, development, etc., giving it first claim to the necessary resources. **5** something of first importance: *Neatness is not a priority for her.*

pri•o•ry ['praɪəri] *n., pl.* **-ries.** a monastery, convent, etc. governed by a prior or prioress. A priory is often, but not necessarily, dependent on an abbey. ⟨ME < AF *priorie* < Med.L *prioria* < *prior.* See PRIOR².⟩

prise [praɪz] *v.* **prised, pris•ing.** *Brit.* See PRIZE⁴.

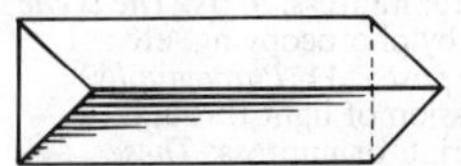
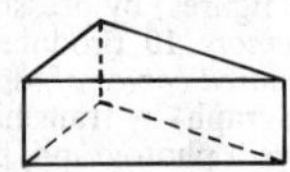

Prisms (def. 2)

prism ['prɪzəm] *n.* **1** *Geometry.* a polyhedron (geometric solid) whose bases, or ends, are parallel and of the same size and shape, and whose other faces are parallelograms. **2** *Optics.* a transparent prism having triangular bases and rectangular sides, used for separating white light into the colours of the spectrum. **3** any similar object. ⟨< LL < Gk. *prisma* < *priein* to saw⟩

pris•mat•ic [prɪz'mætɪk] *adj.* **1** of or like a prism. **2** formed by a transparent prism. **3** varied in colour.

pris•mat•i•cal•ly [prɪz'mætɪkəli] *adv.* by, or as if by, a prism.

prismatic colours or **colors** colours formed when white light is passed through a prism; red, orange, yellow, green, blue, indigo, and violet; the colours of the rainbow.

pris•on ['prɪzən] *n., v. —n.* **1** a public building in which criminals or those who have been arrested are detained. **2** any place where a person is shut up against his or her will. **3** a place that confines or restricts: *The small apartment was a prison to the big farm dog.* **4** time spent in prison: *Prison is too harsh a punishment for this young offender.*
—v. imprison. ⟨ME < OF < L *pre- hensio, -onis* arrest < *prehendere* seize⟩ **—'pris•on,like,** *adj.*

pris•on•er ['prɪzənər] *n.* **1** a person who is under arrest or held in a jail or prison. **2** a person who is confined against his or her will or who is not free to act.
prisoner of war, a person taken by the enemy in war.

priss [prɪs] *n., v. Informal. —n.* someone who is too precise and fussy, overnice, or prim and proper.
—v. behave in such a manner. ⟨back formation from *prissy*⟩

pris•sy ['prɪsi] *adj.* **-si•er, -si•est. 1** too precise and fussy. **2** too easily shocked; overnice. ⟨blend of *prim* and *sissy*⟩ **—'pris•si•ly,** *adv.* **—'pris•si•ness,** *n.*

pris•tine [prɪ'stin], ['prɪstin], ['prɪstən], *or* ['prɪstaɪn] *adj.* **1** as it was in its earliest time or state; original; primitive: *The colours of the paintings inside the pyramid had kept their pristine freshness.* **2** pure; undefiled: *We drank from the pristine waters of the mountain stream.* **—pris'tine•ly,** *adv.* ⟨< L *pristinus* former⟩

prith•ee ['prɪði] *interj. Archaic.* I pray thee: *Prithee, come hither.* ⟨alteration of *[I] pray thee*⟩

pri•va•cy ['praɪvəsi] *n., pl.* **-cies. 1** the condition of being private; the state of being away from others: *in the privacy of one's home.* **2** an absence of publicity; secrecy: *He told me his reasons in strict privacy.* **3** anyone's private affairs: *invasion of privacy.*

pri•vate ['praɪvɪt] *adj., n. —adj.* **1** not for the public; for just a few special people or for one: *a private car, a private house, a private letter.* **2** not public; individual; personal: *the private life of a monarch, my private opinion.* **3** secret; confidential: *a private drawer.* **4** secluded: *some private corner.* **5** having no public office: *a private citizen.* **6** secretive about one's personal life: *They are a very private couple.* **7** not owned or controlled by the government.
—n. **1** a person holding the lowest rank in the armed forces. *Abbrev.*: Pte. or Pte See chart of ranks in the Appendix.
2 privates, *pl.* private parts; genitals.
in private, a not publicly or openly; privately: *They met in private to discuss the salary increases.* ⟨ME < L *privatus* apart from the state, originally pp. of *privare* set apart, deprive < *privus* one's own. Doublet of PRIVY.⟩ **—'pri•vate•ly,** *adv.* **—'pri•vate•ness,** *n.*

private enterprise 1 the production and sale of goods, etc. by industries under private control and ownership rather than under government control or ownership. **2** a business operating under this system.

pri•va•teer [,praɪvə'tir] *n., v. —n.* **1** an armed ship owned by private persons and holding a government commission to attack and capture enemy ships. **2** the commander or one of the crew of a privateer. Also called (def. 2) **privateersman.**
—v. cruise as a privateer.

private eye *Informal.* a person who is not a member of a public police force but engages in detective work on behalf of private individuals or corporations; private investigator. Also, **P.I.**

private member backbencher.

private parts genitals.

private school a school that is under private or corporate management and is not part of the public school system of a province, state, or country, although it may be partially funded through grants. Also called **independent school.**

private sector privately owned business and industry.

pri•va•tion [praɪ'veiʃən] *n.* **1** the lack of the usual comforts or some of the necessities of life: *the privations of a life as an explorer. Privation led him to begin stealing.* **2** the state of being deprived; loss; absence: *She felt the loss of her husband as a real privation.* ⟨ME < L *privatio, -onis* < *privare* deprive. See PRIVATE.⟩

priv•a•tive ['prɪvətɪv] *adj., n. Grammar. —adj.* expressing deprivation or denial of something. In the word *unwise*, meaning 'not wise', *un-* is a privative prefix.

–n. a privative prefix or suffix. ⟨< L *privativus* < *privare* deprive. See PRIVATE.⟩

pri•va•tize ['praɪvə,taɪz] *v.* **-tized, -tiz•ing. 1** transfer (public property, services, etc.) from public or government control to private control. **2** make private or exclusive: *The club wants to privatize its membership.* **–,pri•va•ti'za•tion,** *n.*

priv•et ['prɪvɪt] *n.* any of a genus (*Ligustrum*) of Old World shrubs and small trees of the olive family having small, oval, dark green leaves, especially the common privet (*L. vulgare*), widely cultivated for hedges. ⟨origin uncertain⟩

priv•i•lege ['prɪvəlɪdʒ] *n., v.* **-leged, -leg•ing.**
–n. a special right, advantage, or favour.
–v. give a privilege to. ⟨ME < L *privilegium* law applying to one individual < *privus* individual + *lex* law⟩

☛ *Syn. n.* **Privilege,** PREROGATIVE = a special right. **Privilege** suggests a special right given to people as a favour or due them because of their position, age, sex, citizenship, etc. that often gives them an advantage over others: *Alumni have the privilege of buying football tickets at special rates.* **Prerogative** suggests a privilege or legal right belonging to a person by virtue of birth, office, position, etc., which always places him or her before or above others: *Calling an extraordinary meeting is the prerogative of the chair.*

priv•i•leged ['prɪvəlɪdʒd] *adj., v.* *–adj.* **1** having a privilege or privileges: *the privileged classes of society.* **2** *Law.* **a** not having to be revealed in a court of law: *Communication between a lawyer and client is privileged.* **b** of an utterance or other communication, not actionable as slander or libel.
–v. pt. and pp. of PRIVILEGE.

priv•i•ly ['prɪvəli] *adv.* in a private manner; secretly.

priv•y ['prɪvi] *adj., n., pl.* **priv•ies.** *–adj.* **1** private. **2** *Archaic.* secret; hidden.
privy to, having secret or private knowledge of.
–n. **1** a small outhouse used as a toilet. **2** *Law.* a person having a derivative interest or directly participating in a legal transaction. ⟨ME < OF *prive* < L *privatus.* Doublet of PRIVATE.⟩

privy council 1 a group of personal advisers to a ruler. **2 Privy Council, a** in Canada, the body of advisers to the Governor General, made up of the ministers of the federal cabinet and all former cabinet ministers. **b** in the United Kingdom, a body of advisers to the Queen, including members of the cabinet and certain commonwealth leaders. *Abbrev.:* P.C.

privy councillor or **councilor 1** a member of a privy council. **2 Privy Councillor,** a member of the Privy Council. Privy Councillors in Canada hold office for life, but can advise the Governor General only while they are cabinet ministers.

privy seal in the United Kingdom, the seal affixed to grants, etc. that are afterwards to receive the great seal, and to documents that do not require the great seal.

prix fixe ['pri 'fiks]; *French,* [pʀi'fiks]. a fixed price for a complete meal in a hotel or restaurant.

prize[1] [praɪz] *n., adj.* *–n.* **1** a reward won or offered in a contest or competition: *Prizes will be given for the three best stories.* **2** that which is won in a lottery, game of chance, or sweepstake. **3** something well worth working for.
–adj. **1** given as a prize. **2** that has won a prize. **3** worthy of a prize. ⟨alteration of ME *pris* < OF *pris* (see PRICE) under the influence of *prise.* See PRIZE².⟩

prize[2] [praɪz] *n.* a thing or person taken or captured in war, especially an enemy's ship and its cargo taken at sea. ⟨ME *prise* < OF *prise* seizure, alteration (under the influence of pp. *pris* seized) VL *presa* < stem of L *prensus,* pp. of *pre(he)ndere* seize⟩

prize[3] [praɪz] *v.* **prized, priz•ing. 1** value highly: *She prizes her best china.* **2** estimate the value of. ⟨ME < OF *prisier,* var. of *preisier* praise. See PRAISE.⟩

prize[4] [praɪz] *v.* **prized, priz•ing.** *Esp. Brit.* raise or move by force; PRY². ⟨< obs. *prize* lever < OF *prise* a taking hold, grasp. See PRIZE².⟩

prize court an international court that makes decisions concerning ships and other property captured at sea during a war.

prize•fight ['praɪz,fəit] *n.* a boxing match fought for money.

prize•fight•er ['praɪz,fəitər] *n.* a person who fights boxing matches for money. **–'prize,fight•ing,** *n.*

prize money 1 money obtained by the sale of ships and other property captured at sea in the course of a war, sometimes divided among those who made the capture. **2** in a race, contest, etc., the money offered as a prize.

prize ring 1 a square space enclosed by ropes, used for prizefights. **2** prizefighting.

pro[1] [prou] *adv., adj., prep., n., pl.* **pros.** *–adv.* in favour; affirmatively; so as to express approval.
–adj. in favour: *We were surprised by the number of pro responses. As regards the building proposal, I am very pro.*
–prep. in favour of: *pro anything foreign.*
–n. **1** a reason in favour. The pros and cons of a question are the arguments for and against it. **2** a person who votes for or favours something. **3** a vote in favour of something. ⟨< L *pro,* prep., in favour of; for⟩

pro[2] [prou] *n., pl.* **pros.** *Informal.* **1** a professional. **2** a prostitute.

pro–[1] *prefix.* **1** forward: *proceed, project.* **2** forth; out: *prolong, proclaim.* **3** on the side of; in favour of; in behalf of: *pro-British, pro-union.* **4** in place of; acting as: *pronoun, proconsul.* ⟨< L *pro,* prep.⟩

pro–[2] *prefix.* before; in front of: *prologue, proscenium.* ⟨< Gk. *pro,* prep.⟩

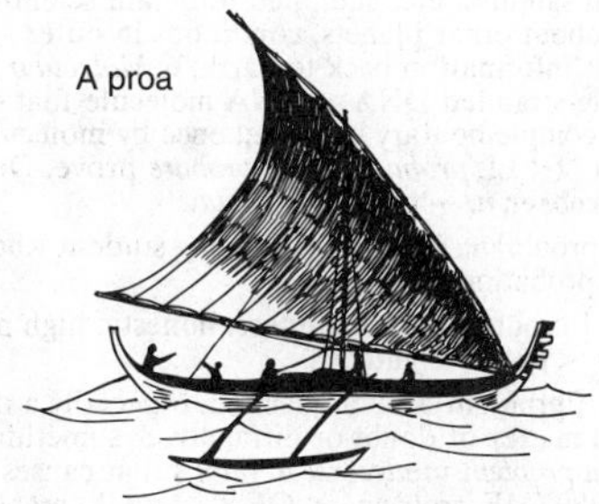
A proa

pro•a ['prouə] *n.* a swift Malay sailing boat built with one side flat and balanced by an outrigger. ⟨< Malay *prau*⟩

pro•act•ive [prou'æktɪv] *adj.* tending to take initiative or definitive action.

pro–am ['prou 'æm] *adj., n.* *–adj.* of or designating a sports tournament involving both professional and amateur players.
–n. a sports event in which: **a** both amateurs and professionals are entitled to play. **b** professionals play with amateurs often as the preliminary to a professional event.

prob•a•bil•i•ty [,prɒbə'bɪləti] *n., pl.* **-ties. 1** the quality or fact of being likely or highly possible; a good chance: *There is a probability that the field trip will be cancelled because of the weather.* **2** something likely to happen: *A storm is one of the probabilities for tomorrow.* **3** *Statistics.* the ratio $\frac{p}{p+q}$, where p is the probable number of occurrences and q is the probable number of non-occurrences.
in all probability, very likely, probably.

prob•a•ble ['prɒbəbəl] *adj.* **1** likely to happen: *Cooler weather is probable after this shower.* **2** likely to be as described: *the probable culprit. Something he ate is the probable cause of his pain.* ⟨ME < OF < L *probabilis* < *probare.* See PROVE.⟩ **–'prob•a•bly,** *adv.*

probable cause *Law.* reasonable grounds for assuming: **a** in a criminal case, that the accused is guilty. **b** in a civil case, that grounds for bringing the action exist.

pro•band ['proubænd] *n. Genetics.* the person through whom a family with a genetic disorder is first identified. ⟨< L *probandus,* gerund of *probare* test⟩

pro•bate ['proubeit] *n., adj., v.* **-bat•ed, -bat•ing.** *Law.* *–n.* **a** the official proving of a will as genuine. **b** the resultant judicial certification of the will. **c** a true copy of a will with a certificate that it has been proved genuine.
–adj. of or concerned with the probating of wills: *a probate court.*
–v. prove the genuineness of (a will) by legal process. ⟨ME < L *probatum,* originally neut. pp. of *probare* make good < *probus* good⟩

pro•ba•tion [prou'beiʃən] *n.* **1** a trial or testing of conduct, character, qualifications, etc.: *After a period of probation the novice became a nun.* **2** the time of trial or testing. **3** *Law.* **a** the system of letting convicted persons, especially young or first offenders, go free under the supervision of a probation officer. **b** the length of time that such a person is kept under supervision by a probation officer.

pro•ba•tion•al [prou'beiʃənəl] *adj.* probationary.

pro•ba•tion•ar•y [prou'beiʃə,nɛri] *adj.* **1** of or having to do with probation. **2** on probation.

pro•ba•tion•er [prou'beiʃənər] *n.* a person who is on probation.

probation officer an officer appointed to supervise offenders who have been placed on probation.

pro•ba•tive ['proubətɪv] *adj.* **1** giving proof or evidence. **2** used for a trial or test.

probe [proub] *v.* **probed, prob•ing;** *n.* *—v.* **1** search into; examine thoroughly; investigate: *to probe one's thoughts or feelings to find out why one acted as one did.* **2** search; penetrate: *to probe into the causes of crime.* **3** examine with a probe: *The doctor probed the wound to find the splinter.*
—n. **1** a thorough examination; investigation. **2** an investigation, usually by a legislative body, in an effort to discover evidences of law violation. **3** a slender instrument with a rounded end for exploring the depth or direction of a wound, cavity in the body, etc. **4** an instrument, often electronic, used to test or explore. **5** an artificial satellite, etc. equipped to obtain scientific information about other planets, conditions in outer space, etc. and radio this information back to earth. **6** *Molecular genetics.* a labelled single-stranded DNA or RNA molecule that can be used to identify a complementary base sequence by molecular hybridization. ⟨< LL *proba,* n., < L *probare* prove. Doublet of PROOF.⟩ **—'prob•er,** *n.* **—'prob•ing•ly,** *adv.*

pro•bie ['proubi] *n. Informal.* a nursing student who is on probation; a probationer.

pro•bi•ty ['proubɪti] *n.* uprightness; honesty; high principle. ⟨< L *probitas* < *probus* righteous⟩

prob•lem ['prɒbləm] *n.* **1** a question, especially a difficult question. **2** a matter of doubt or difficulty. **3** something to be worked out: *a problem in algebra.* **4** (*adjl.*) that causes difficulty: *a problem child.* ⟨ME *probleme* < OF < L < Gk. *problēma* < *proballein* propose < *pro-* forward + *ballein* throw⟩

prob•lem•at•ic [,prɒblə'mætɪk] *adj.* having the nature of a problem; difficult; uncertain; questionable.

prob•lem•at•i•cal [,prɒblə'mætəkəl] *adj.* problematic. **—,prob•lem'at•i•cal•ly,** *adv.*

pro bono [,prou 'bounou] designating the services provided free of charge by professional organizations or businesses to charitable groups, the poor, etc. ⟨< L⟩

pro bo•no pu•bli•co [prou 'bounou 'pʊblɪkou] *Latin.* for the public welfare.

pro•bos•cis [prou'bɒsɪs] *or* [prou'bɒskɪs] *n., pl.* **-bos•ci•des** [prou'bɒsɪdiz]. **1** an elephant's trunk. **2** any long, flexible snout such as that of an aardvark or tapir. **3** a tubular organ of some insects, such as flies or mosquitoes, adapted for piercing or sucking. **4** *Facetious.* a person's nose, especially when prominent. ⟨< L < Gk. *proboskis*⟩

proc. **1** proceedings. **2** procedure. **3** process.

pro•caine ['proukein] *or* [prou'kein] *n. Pharmacy.* a white or colourless, crystalline compound that is an ester of para-aminobenzoic acid, used in the form of its hydrochloride as a local anesthetic. *Formula:* $C_{13}H_{20}N_2O_2$

pro•car•y•ote [prou'kæriət] *or* [prou'kɛriət] *n.* See PROKARYOTE. **—,pro•car•y'ot•ic** [-'ɒtɪk], *adj.*

pro•ca•the•dral [,proukə'θidrəl] *n.* a church in temporary use as a cathedral.

pro•ce•dure [prə'sidʒər] *n.* **1** a way of proceeding; a method of doing things. **2** the customary manners or ways of conducting business: *parliamentary procedure, legal procedure.* ⟨< F *procédure* < *procéder* proceed⟩ **—pro'ce•dur•al,** *adj.* **—pro'ce•dur•al•ly,** *adv.*

pro•ceed *v.* [prə'sid]; *n.* ['prousid] *v., n.* *—v.* **1** go on after having stopped; move forward: *Please proceed with your story.* **2** be carried on; take place: *The trial may proceed.* **3** carry on any activity: *He proceeded to light his pipe.* **4** come forth; issue; go out: *Heat proceeds from fire.* **5** advance to a higher status: *She proceeded to office manager.* **6** begin and carry on an action at law.
—n. Usually, **proceeds,** *pl.* money obtained from a sale, etc.: *The proceeds from the school play will be used to buy a new curtain for the stage.* ⟨ME < OF < L *procedere* < *pro-* forward + *cedere* move⟩ **—pro'ceed•er,** *n.*

☛ *Syn. v.* **1.** See note at ADVANCE.

☛ *Usage.* See note at PRECEDE.

pro•ceed•ing [prə'sidɪŋ] *n., v.* *—n.* **1** an action; course of action; what is done. **2** the process of carrying out such action. **3 proceedings,** *pl.* **a** the action in a case in a law court: *The bank initiated proceedings against the embezzler.* **b** a record of what was done at the meetings of a society, club, etc.; minutes. **c** the published version of the papers presented at a conference, etc. *—v.* ppr. of PROCEED.

pro•cess¹ ['prousɛs] *or* ['prɒsɛs] *n., v., adj.* *—n.* **1** a set of actions or changes in a special order: *By what process is cloth made from wool?* **2** *Biology. Anatomy.* a part that grows out or sticks out: *the process of a bone.* **3** *Law.* **a** a written command or summons to appear in a court of law. **b** the proceedings in a legal case or action.
in (the) process, a in the course (*of*): *In process of time the house will be finished. In the process of looking for my keys I found many other mislaid items.* **b** in the course or condition of being done: *The author has just finished one book and has another in process.*
—v. **1** treat or prepare by some special method. **2** *Law.* start legal action against.
—adj. treated or prepared by some special method: *process cheese.* ⟨ME < OF *proces* < L *processus* progress < *procedere.* See PROCEED.⟩

pro•cess² [prə'sɛs] *v.* move in procession: *The graduands will process across the campus.* ⟨back formation from *procession*⟩

process cheese or **processed cheese** ['prousɛs] *or* ['prɒsɛs] a blend of cheddar or other natural cheeses and flavourings, powdered milk, emulsifier, etc.

pro•ces•sion [prə'sɛʃən] *n.* **1** something that moves forward; persons marching or riding: *A funeral procession filled the street.* **2** an orderly moving forward: *We formed lines to march in procession onto the platform.* ⟨early ME < Med.L *processio* a religious procession, literally, a marching on⟩

pro•ces•sion•al [prə'sɛʃənəl] *adj., n.* *—adj.* **1** of a procession. **2** used or sung in a procession.
—n. **1** processional music: *The choir and clergy marched into the church singing the processional.* **2** a book containing hymns, etc., for use in religious processions.

pro•ces•sor ['prousɛsər] *or* ['prɒsɛsər] *n.* **1** *Computer technology.* a computer or the part of a computer that processes data. **2** FOOD PROCESSOR. **3** any person or thing that processes.

process printing ['prousɛs] *or* ['prɒsɛs] a method of printing something in almost any colour by using a set of half-tone plates in a limited range of colours, usually yellow, magenta, cyan, and black, in various combinations.

pro•cès–ver•bal [prou'sɛ vər'bɑl]; *French,* [prɔsɛvɛʀ'bal] *n., pl.* **pro•cès–ver•baux** [-'bou]; *French,* [-'bo]. **1** a report of proceedings from a meeting; minutes. **2** *French law.* an official and authenticated written account of the facts surrounding a criminal or other charge. ⟨< F⟩

pro–choice ['prou 'tʃɔɪs] *adj.* referring to someone or something that supports the right to legal abortion: *pro-choice pamphlets.* **—'pro-'choic•er,** *n.*

pro•claim [prə'kleim] *v.* **1** make known publicly and officially; declare publicly: *War was proclaimed. The people proclaimed him king.* **2** formerly, **a** declare (a person) an outlaw; denounce. **b** subject (a place) to legal restrictions. **3** praise enthusiastically in public: *The crowds proclaimed the Queen as she rode to her coronation.* ⟨ME *proclamen* < L *proclamare* < *pro-* forth + *clamare* shout⟩

☛ *Syn.* **1.** See note at ANNOUNCE.

proc•la•ma•tion [,prɒklə'meiʃən] *n.* an official announcement; a public declaration: *A proclamation was issued to announce the forthcoming election.*

☛ *Syn.* **Proclamation,** EDICT = a notice or order issued by authority. **Proclamation** = an official public announcement by an executive or administrative officer, such as a president, premier, or mayor: *The Prime Minister issued a proclamation declaring martial law in the disaster area.* **Edict** = a public order or law proclaimed by the highest authority, usually a decree of a ruler or court with supreme or absolute authority: *The dictator issued an edict seizing the mines.*

pro•cliv•i•ty [prə'klɪvəti] *n., pl.* **-ties.** a tendency; inclination. ⟨< L *proclivitas,* ult. < *pro-* forward + *clivus* slope⟩

pro•con•sul¹ [prou'kɒnsəl] *n.* **1** in ancient Rome, the governor or military commander of a province, with duties and powers like those of a consul. **2** the governor of a British or French colony. ⟨ME < L *proconsul,* from the phrase *pro consule* in place of the consul⟩

pro•con•sul² [prou'kɒnsəl] *n.* a humanlike ape, a subgenus of *Dryopithecus* that lived during the Miocene period, approximately 25 million years ago, and was considered by some anthropologists to be a hominid ancestor. ⟨< name of a chimpanzee at the London Zoo in the 1930s⟩
—pro'con•su•lar, *adj.*

pro•con•su•late [prou'kɒnsəlɪt] *or* [prou'kɒnsjəlɪt] *n.* the position or term of a proconsul.

pro•con•sul•ship [prouˈkɒnsəl,ʃɪp] *n.* proconsulate.

pro•cras•ti•nate [prəˈkræstə,neit] *v.* **-nat•ed, -nat•ing.** put things off until later; delay; delay repeatedly. ⟨< L *procrastinare,* ult. < *pro-* forward + *cras* tomorrow⟩ **—proˈcras•ti,na•tor,** *n.*

pro•cras•ti•na•tion [prə,kræstəˈneiʃən] *n.* the act or habit of putting things off till later; delay.

pro•cre•ate [ˈproukri,eit] *v.* **-at•ed, -at•ing. 1** become father to; beget. **2** produce offspring. **3** bring into being; produce. ⟨< L *procreare* < *pro-* forth + *creare* create⟩ **—ˈpro•cre,a•tor,** *n.*

pro•cre•a•tion [,proukriˈeiʃən] *n.* **1** the act or fact of begetting; becoming a father. **2** production, especially of offspring.

pro•cre•a•tive [ˈproukri,eitɪv] *adj.* **1** begetting; bringing into being. **2** concerned with or having to do with procreation. **—ˈpro•cre,a•tive•ness,** *n.*

Pro•crus•te•an [prouˈkrʌstiən] *adj.* **1** of or having to do with Procrustes or his bed. **2** tending to produce conformity by violent or arbitrary means.

Pro•crus•tes [prouˈkrʌstiz] *n. Greek legend.* a robber who attacked travellers and either stretched them or cut off their legs to make them fit the length of his bed.

proc•tol•o•gy [prɒkˈtɒlədʒi] *n.* the branch of medicine dealing with the rectum and anus and diseases of that area. **—procˈtol•o•gist,** *n.* **—,proc•toˈlog•i•cal,** *adj.* ⟨< Gk. *proktos* anus, rectum + E *-ology*⟩

proc•tor [ˈprɒktər] *n., v.* —*n.* **1** in a university or school: **a** an official who keeps order. **b** a person who supervises students during an examination. **c** a prefect or monitor. **2** *Law.* a person employed to manage another's case in a court of law.
—*v.* serve as a proctor at (an examination). ⟨short for *procurator*⟩ **—procˈto•ri•al,** *adj.* **—ˈproc•tor,ship,** *n.*

proc•to•scope [ˈprɒktə,skoup] *n. Medicine.* an instrument used for direct visual examination of the interior of the rectum. ⟨< Gk. *proktos* anus, rectum + E *-scope*⟩ **—,proc•toˈscop•ic** [-ˈskɒpɪk], *adj.* **—procˈtos•co•py** [prɒkˈtɒskəpi], *n.*

pro•cum•bent [prouˈkʌmbənt] *adj.* **1** lying face down; prone; prostrate. **2** *Botany.* of a plant or stem, lying along the ground but not sending down roots. ⟨< L *procumbens, -entis,* ppr. of *procumbere* lean forward⟩

proc•u•ra•tor [ˈprɒkjə,reitər] *n.* **1** a person employed to manage the affairs of another; a person authorized to act for another; agent. **2** in ancient Rome, a financial agent or administrator of a province. ⟨< L *procurator* < *procurare.* See PROCURE.⟩ **—,proc•u•raˈto•ri•al,** *adj.*

pro•cure [prəˈkjʊr] *v.* **-cured, -cur•ing. 1** obtain by care or effort; get: *A friend procured a position in the bank for my cousin.* **2** bring about; cause: *to procure a person's death.* **3** obtain (persons) for prostitution. ⟨ME < OF < L *procurare* manage, ult. < *pro-* + *cura* care⟩ **—proˈcur•a•ble,** *adj.* **—proˈcure•ment,** *n.*

pro•cur•er [prəˈkjʊrər] *n.* a person who procures, especially one who obtains persons for prostitution.

pro•cur•ess [prəˈkjʊrɪs] *n.* a female keeper of a brothel; bawd.

Pro•cy•on [ˈprousi,ɒn] *n. Astronomy.* a star of the first magnitude in the constellation Canis Minor. ⟨< L < Gk. *Prokyon* < *pro-* before + *kyon* dog; because it rises before the Dog Star, Sirius⟩

prod [prɒd] *v.* **prod•ded, prod•ding;** *n.* —*v.* **1** a poke or jab with something pointed: *to prod an animal with a stick.* **2** stir up; urge on: *to prod a lazy boy to action by threats and entreaties.*
—*n.* **1** a poke or thrust. **2** a sharp-pointed stick; goad. **3** something that prods; a reminder. ⟨OE *prod-,* as in *prodbor* borer⟩ **—ˈprod•der,** *n.*

prod. product; produced.

prod•i•gal [ˈprɒdɪgəl] *adj., n.* —*adj.* **1** spending too much; wasting money or other resources; wasteful: *Canada has been prodigal of its forests.* **2** abundant; lavish or generous: *Millionaires are often not noted for their prodigal expenditures.* **3** returning, especially after a long absence or after leading a reckless and wasteful life.
—*n.* **1** a person who is wasteful or extravagant; spendthrift. **2** a returning wanderer, wastrel, etc.; PRODIGAL SON. ⟨< MF, back formation from *prodigalite* < LL *prodigalitas.* See PRODIGALITY.⟩ **—ˈprod•i•gal•ly,** *adv.*

prod•i•gal•i•ty [,prɒdɪˈgæləti] *n., pl.* **-ties. 1** wasteful or reckless extravagance. **2** rich abundance; profuseness. ⟨< LL *prodigalitas* (modelled on L *liberalitas* < *liber*) < L *prodigus* wasteful < *prodigere* drive forth, squander < *prod-* (var. of *pro-*) forth + *agere* drive⟩

prodigal son a person who is welcomed back into a family or group after having been away, especially one who has been gone for a long time or who returns repentant of having done wrong. ⟨< the story in the Bible of the wastrel son whose father welcomes him back⟩

pro•di•gious [prəˈdɪdʒəs] *adj.* **1** very great; huge; vast: *The ocean contains a prodigious amount of water.* **2** wonderful; marvellous: *a prodigious achievement.* ⟨< L *prodigiosus* < *prodigium* prodigy, omen⟩ **—proˈdi•gious•ly,** *adv.* **—proˈdi•gious•ness,** *n.*

prod•i•gy [ˈprɒdədʒi] *n., pl.* **-gies. 1** a marvel; wonder. A child prodigy is a child remarkably brilliant in some respect. **2** a marvellous example: *The warriors performed prodigies of valour.* **3** *Rare.* a wonderful sign or omen. ⟨< L *prodigium* omen⟩

pro•drome [ˈproudroum] *n. Pathology.* a premonitory symptom of disease. ⟨< NL *prodromus* < Gk. *prodromos* running before⟩ **—proˈdro•mal** or **proˈdrom•ic** [-ˈdrɒmɪk], *adj.*

pro•duce *v.* [prəˈdjus] *or* [prəˈdus]; *n.* [ˈprɒdjus] *or* [ˈprɒdus], [ˈproudjus] *or* [ˈproudus] *v.* **-duced, -duc•ing;** *n.* —*v.* **1** make; bring into existence: *The factory produces stoves.* **2** bring about; cause: *Hard work produces success.* **3** bring forth or yield (offspring, crops, products, dividends, interest, etc.): *Hens produce eggs.* **4** bring forward; show; present: *Produce your proof.* **5** bring (a play, film, etc.) before the public. **6** *Mathematics.* extend; continue (a line or plane).
—*n.* **1** what is produced; yield: *Vegetables are a garden's produce.* **2** fruit and vegetables. **3** (*adjl.*) of fruit and vegetables: *They own a produce market.* ⟨ME < L *producere* < *pro-* forth + *ducere* bring⟩

pro•duc•er [prəˈdjusər] *or* [prəˈdusər] *n.* **1** one who produces. **2** a person who grows or makes things that are to be used or consumed by others. **3** a person in charge of presenting a play, film, television program, etc., or of supervising a recording session.
☛ *Usage.* For def. 3, see note at DIRECTOR.

producer goods goods like machinery, raw materials, etc. that are used in the production or creation of other goods.

pro•duc•i•ble [prəˈdjusəbəl] *or* [prəˈdusəbəl] *adj.* capable of being produced. **—pro,duc•iˈbil•i•ty,** *n.*

prod•uct [ˈprɒdəkt] *or* [ˈprɒdʌkt] *n.* **1** that which is produced; result of work or of growth: *factory products, farm products.* **2** *Mathematics.* a number or quantity resulting from multiplying: *The product of 5 and 8 is 40.* **3** *Chemistry.* a substance obtained from another substance through chemical change. **4** a generic word used commercially to refer to any specific manufactured substance or article: *Squeeze a small amount of product into your hand.* ⟨ME < L *productus,* pp. of *producere.* See PRODUCE.⟩

pro•duc•tion [prəˈdʌkʃən] *n.* **1** the act of producing; creation; manufacture: *Their business is the production of automobiles.* **2** something that is produced: *The school play was a fine production.* **3** the total amount produced.
make a production (out) of, *Informal.* fuss or dwell on (something) needlessly: *The student made a big production out of the misprint on the examination paper.*

production line 1 a row of machines and equipment in a factory, along which workers oversee the various stages of production; assembly line. **2** *Hockey. Informal.* a forward line that scores a large number of goals.

production model an article in regular production; a standard or standardized product.

production number a part of a musical play, film, television show, etc. that is given spectacular presentation with elaborate scenery, costumes, dances, etc.: *The first act ended with a colourful production number.*

pro•duc•tive [prəˈdʌktɪv] *adj.* **1** capable of producing or bringing forth: *fields now productive only of weeds, hasty words that are productive of quarrels.* **2** producing food or other articles of commerce: *Farming is productive labour.* **3** producing abundantly; fertile: *a productive farm, a productive writer.* **—proˈduc•tive•ly,** *adv.* **—,pro•ducˈtiv•i•ty** [,prɒd-] or **proˈduc•tive•ness,** *n.*
☛ *Syn.* **3.** See note at FERTILE.

pro•em [ˈprouəm] *n.* a preface or introduction, especially to a book or speech. ⟨ME < OF *proeme* < L *procemium* < Gk. *procimion* prelude⟩ **—proˈe•mi•al** [-ˈimiəl], *adj.*

prof [prɒf] *n. Informal.* professor.

Prof. professor.

prof•a•na•tion [,prɒfəˈneiʃən] *n.* the act of showing

contempt or disregard toward something holy; mistreatment of something sacred.

pro•fan•a•to•ry [prəˈfænə,tɔri] *adj.* tending to treat with contempt or disregard.

pro•fane [prəˈfein] *adj., v.* **-faned, -fan•ing.** *—adj.* **1** with contempt or disregard for God or holy things: *profane language.* **2** not sacred; worldly: *Mozart wrote both religious and profane music.*
—v. **1** treat (holy things) with contempt or disregard: *Soldiers profaned the temple by stabling horses there.* **2** put to wrong or unworthy use. ⟨ME < OF < L *profanus* not sacred < *pro-* in front (outside) of + *fanum* shrine⟩ **—proˈfane•ly,** *adv.* **—proˈfane•ness,** *n.*

pro•fan•i•ty [prəˈfænɪti] *n., pl.* **-ties. 1** profane language or the use of it; swearing; profane conduct. **2** a profane utterance.

pro•fess [prəˈfɛs] *v.* **1** lay claim to; claim: *The embezzler professed the greatest respect for the law. I don't profess to be an expert.* **2** declare openly: *The soldiers professed their loyalty to their country.* **3** declare one's belief in: *Christians profess Christ and the Christian religion.* **4** make a solemn affirmation or avowal. **5** have as one's profession or business: *to profess law.* **6** receive or admit into a religious order. ⟨< *professed*⟩

pro•fessed [prəˈfɛst] *adj., v. —adj.* **1** alleged; pretended. **2** avowed or acknowledged; openly declared. **3** having taken the vows of, or been received into, a religious order.
—v. pt. and pp. of PROFESS. ⟨ME < L *professus,* ppr. of *profiteri* < *pro-* forth + *fateri* confess⟩

pro•fess•ed•ly [prəˈfɛsɪdli] *adv.* **1** avowedly. **2** ostensibly.

pro•fes•sion [prəˈfɛʃən] *n.* **1** an occupation requiring special postgraduate education and training, especially law, medicine, teaching, engineering, or the ministry. **2** the people collectively engaged in such an occupation. **3** the act of professing; open declaration: *I welcomed her profession of friendship.* **4** a declaration of belief in a religion. **5** the religion or faith professed. **6** the act of taking vows and entering a religious order.
the oldest profession, prostitution.

pro•fes•sion•al [prəˈfɛʃənəl] *adj., n. —adj.* **1** of or having to do with a profession; appropriate to a profession: *professional skill, a professional manner.* **2** engaged in a profession: *A lawyer or a doctor is a professional person.* **3** making a business or trade of something that others do for pleasure: *a professional ballplayer.* **4** undertaken or engaged in by professionals rather than amateurs: *a professional ballgame.* **5** making a business of something not properly to be regarded as a business: *a professional politician.*
—n. **1** a person who makes a business or trade of something that others do for pleasure. **2** someone who follows a profession: *Most of these students are the children of professionals.* **3** a person affiliated with a particular sports club such as golf, tennis, curling, as an instructor, contestant, etc. **4** an expert in some field: *She is practically a professional on the piano.*

pro•fes•sion•al•ism [prəˈfɛʃənə,lɪzəm] *n.* **1** professional character, spirit, or methods. **2** the standing, practice, or methods of a professional, as distinguished from those of an amateur.

pro•fes•sion•al•ize [prəˈfɛʃənə,laɪz] *v.* **-ized, -iz•ing.** make or become professional.

pro•fes•sion•al•ly [prəˈfɛʃənəli] *adv.* in a professional manner; in professional matters; because of one's profession.

pro•fes•sor [prəˈfɛsər] *n.* **1** a teacher of the highest rank in a university or college. **2** *Informal.* any teacher at a university or college. **3** a person who professes. **4** a person who declares belief in a religion. ⟨ME < L *professor* < *profiteri* profess. See PROFESSED.⟩ **—,prof•esˈso•ri•al** [,prɒfəˈsɔriəl], *adj.* **—,prof•esˈso•ri•al•ly,** *adv.*

pro•fes•sor•ate [prəˈfɛsərɪt] *n.* professoriate.

prof•es•sor•i•ate [,prɒfəˈsɔriɪt] *n.* **1** the office or term of service of a professor. **2** a group of professors.

pro•fes•sor•ship [prəˈfɛsər,ʃɪp] *n.* the position or rank of a professor.

prof•fer [ˈprɒfər] *v., n. —v.* offer for acceptance; present: *We proffered regrets at having to leave so early.*
—n. an offer made: *The counsellor's proffer of advice was accepted.* ⟨ME < AF < *pro-* forth (< L *pro-*) + *offrir* offer < L *offerre*⟩
☛ *Syn. v.* See note at OFFER.

pro•fi•cien•cy [prəˈfɪʃənsi] *n., pl.* **-cies.** the quality or condition of being proficient; knowledge; skill; expertness.

pro•fi•cient [prəˈfɪʃənt] *adj., n. —adj.* advanced in any art, science, or subject; skilled; expert: *She was very proficient in music.*
—n. an expert. ⟨< L *proficiens, -entis* making progress, ppr. of *proficere* < *pro-* forward + *facere* make⟩ **—proˈfi•cient•ly,** *adv.*
☛ *Syn. adj.* See note at EXPERT.

Profile of the Blackfoot leader Crowfoot

pro•file [ˈproufaɪl] *n., v.* **-filed, -fil•ing.** *—n.* **1** a side view, especially of the human face. **2** an outline. **3** a drawing of a transverse vertical section of a building, bridge, etc. **4** a concise description of a person's abilities, character, or career. **5** a chart or written report outlining the facts about someone or something: *Here is a profile of how the company will function after reorganization.*
—v. make a profile of. ⟨< Ital. *profilo* < *profilare* draw in outline < L *pro-* forth + *filum* thread⟩
☛ *Syn. n.* **2.** See note at OUTLINE.

prof•it [ˈprɒfɪt] *n., v. —n.* **1** Often, **profits,** *pl.* the gain from a business; what is left when the cost of goods and of carrying on the business is subtracted from the amount of money taken in. **2** advantage; benefit: *What profit is there in worrying?*
—v. **1** make a gain from a business; make a profit. **2** get advantage; gain; benefit: *Wise people profit by their mistakes.* **3** be an advantage or benefit (to). ⟨ME < OF < L *profectus* advance < *proficere.* See PROFICIENT.⟩ **—ˈprof•it•er,** *n.* **—ˈprof•it•less,** *adj.*
☛ *Hom.* PROPHET.
☛ *Syn. n.* **2.** See note at ADVANTAGE.

prof•it•a•ble [ˈprɒfətəbəl] *adj.* **1** yielding a financial profit: *a profitable deal.* **2** giving a gain or benefit; useful: *We spent a profitable afternoon in the library.* **—ˈprof•it•a•bly,** *adv.* **—,prof•it•aˈbil•i•ty** or **ˈprof•it•a•ble•ness,** *n.*

prof•i•teer [,prɒfəˈtir] *n., v. —n.* a person who makes an unfair profit by taking advantage of public necessity.
—v. seek or make excessive profits by taking advantage of public necessity.

pro•fit•er•ole [prəˈfɪtə,roul] *n.* a small cream puff having a rich filling, usually sweet, and often served with a sauce. ⟨< F, literally, little profit (as, a gift to a household servant)⟩

profit sharing the sharing of profits between employer and employees. **—ˈprof•it-,shar•ing,** *adj.*

prof•li•ga•cy [ˈprɒfləgəsi] *n.* **1** great wickedness; vice. **2** reckless extravagance.

prof•li•gate [ˈprɒfləgɪt] *adj., n. —adj.* **1** very wicked; shamelessly bad. **2** recklessly extravagant.
—n. a person who is very wicked or extravagant. ⟨< L *profligatus,* pp. of *profligare,* intensive of *profligere* ruin < *pro-* down + *fligere* strike, dash⟩ **—ˈprof•li•gate•ly,** *adv.*

pro for•ma [prou ˈfɔrmə] *adj., n. —adj.* **1** done in a set or perfunctory manner or for the sake of form. **2** providing or prescribing a set form or method: *a pro forma invoice, a pro forma balance sheet.*
—n. a document setting out the rules, method, or format by which something is to be done: *To have this directed studies course approved, you have to submit a pro forma.* ⟨< L, according to form, as a matter of form⟩

pro•found [prəˈfaʊnd] *adj.* **1** very deep: *a profound sigh, a profound sleep.* **2** deeply felt; very great: *profound despair, profound sympathy.* **3** having or showing great depth of knowledge or understanding: *a profound book, a profound thinker.* **4** low; carried far down; going far down: *a profound bow.* **5** radical or thoroughgoing; complete: *a profound reorganization.* ⟨ME < OF < L *profundus* < *pro-* toward + *fundus* bottom⟩ **—proˈfound•ly,** *adv.* **—proˈfound•ness,** *n.*

pro•fun•di•ty [prəˈfʌndəti] *n., pl.* **-ties. 1** the state or quality of being profound; great depth. **2** a very deep thing or place. ⟨< LL *profunditas* < L *profundus.* See PROFOUND.⟩

pro•fuse [prəˈfjus] *adj.* **1** very abundant: *profuse thanks.* **2** spending or giving freely; lavish; extravagant: *He was so profuse with his money that he is now poor.* ⟨ME < L *profusus* poured forth, pp. of *profundere* < *pro-* forth + *fundere* pour⟩ **—proˈfuse•ly,** *adv.* **—proˈfuse•ness,** *n.*

☛ *Syn.* **1, 2. Profuse,** LAVISH = occurring, spending, or given freely. **Profuse** suggests a quantity that is more than enough, poured out in streams, sometimes too freely: *They were profuse in their praise.* **Lavish** suggests pouring out in a flood, showing no attempt to limit the amount or to save, but implies excessive generosity or liberality: *It was a lavish display of gifts.*

pro•fu•sion [prəˈfjuʒən] *n.* **1** a great abundance: *There was a profusion of gulls on the breakwater.* **2** extravagance; lavishness.

pro•gen•i•tor [prouˈdʒɛnɪtər] *n.* **1** an ancestor in the direct line; forebear. **2** a source, predecessor, or precursor of anything. ⟨< L *progenitor* < *pro-* forth + *gignere* beget⟩

pro•gen•i•ture [prouˈdʒɛnɪtʃər] *n.* **1** begetting; birth. **2** offspring.

prog•e•ny [ˈprɒdʒəni] *n., pl.* **-nies.** children; offspring; descendants. ⟨ME < OF < L *progenies*, ult. < *pro-* forth + *gignere* beget⟩

pro•ges•ter•one [prəˈdʒɛstəˌroun] *n.* **1** *Biochemistry.* a natural steroid hormone that prepares the uterus for reception of the fertilized ovum and maintains pregnancy. *Formula:* $C_{21}H_{30}O_2$ **2** *Pharmacy.* a commercial preparation of this compound, obtained from the corpus luteum of pregnant sows or synthesized, used in the treatment of various uterine dysfunctions and as normal replacement therapy after menopause or complete hysterectomy. ⟨< *pro-* + *ge*(*station*) + *ster*(*ol*) + *-one*⟩

prog•na•thous [prɒgˈneiθəs] *or* [ˈprɒgnəθəs] *adj.* of a skull or a person, having the jaws protruding beyond the upper part of the face: *Early hominids usually had prognathous jaws.* Also, **prognathic** [prɒgˈnæθɪk]. ⟨< *pro-*[2] forward + Gk. *gnathos* jaw⟩ **—ˈprog•naˌthism,** *n.*

prog•no•sis [prɒgˈnousɪs] *n., pl.* **-ses** [-siz]. **1** *Medicine.* a forecast of the probable course of a disease. **2** an estimate of what will probably happen. ⟨< LL < Gk. *prognōsis*, ult. < *pro-* before + *gignōskein* recognize⟩

prog•nos•tic [prɒgˈnɒstɪk] *adj., n.* *—adj.* indicating something in the future.
—n. **1** an indication; sign. **2** a forecast; prediction. ⟨< Med.L < Gk. *prognōstikos* foretelling, ult. < *pro-* before + *gignōskein* recognize⟩

prog•nos•ti•cate [prɒgˈnɒstəˌkeit] *v.* **-cat•ed, -cat•ing.** predict from facts; forecast. **—progˌnos•tiˈca•tion,** *n.* **—progˈnos•tiˌca•tor,** *n.*

pro•gram or **pro•gramme** [ˈprougræm] *or* [ˈprougrəm] *n., v.* **-grammed, -gram•ming.** *—n.* **1** a list or schedule of items or events; list of performers, players, etc.: *a theatre program.* **2** the items composing an entertainment: *The entire program was delightful.* **3 a** a plan of what is to be done: *a school program, a business program, a government program.* **b** such a plan carried out: *To date this program has served over 900 people.* **4** *Computer technology.* **a** a set of instructions fed into a computer outlining precisely the steps to be performed by the machine in a specific operation. **b** a set of instructions arranged for any automatic machine to follow. **5** a unit of subject matter arranged in a series of small steps for PROGRAMMED LEARNING. **6** in education, a set of courses: *Each graduate student has an individual program.* **7** a presentation or performance, especially a radio or television show: *We listened to a radio program about mysteries.* **8** all activities sponsored by a community centre, summer camp, holiday resort, cruise, etc.
—v. **1** arrange or enter in a program. **2** draw up a program or plan (for). **3** *Computer technology.* prepare a set of instructions for (a computer or other automatic machine). **4** arrange in a series of small steps for programmed learning. ⟨< LL < Gk. *programma* proclamation, ult. < *pro-* forth + *graphein* write⟩

pro•gram•mat•ic [ˌprougrəˈmætɪk] *adj.* **1** of or having to do with a program, thus often somewhat predictable or mechanical. **2** of or having to do with PROGRAM MUSIC.

programmed learning a method of study by which a person works step by step at his or her own rate through a series of problems, checking the correctness of the response to each step before proceeding to the next.

pro•gram•mer [ˈprougræmər] *n.* a person who prepares a program or programs, especially for a computer or other automatic machine.

pro•gram•ming language [ˈprougræmɪŋ] *Computer technology.* a system of words and codes, like a language, which allows a person to put instructions into a computer in a form that the computer can recognize and process.

program music or **programme music** music that portrays or suggests a particular event, story, atmosphere, etc. Compare ABSOLUTE MUSIC.

pro•gress *n.* [ˈprougrɛs] *or* [ˈprɒgrɛs]; *v.* [prəˈgrɛs] *n., v.* *—n.* **1** an advance; growth; development; improvement: *the progress of science: The patient is making excellent progress.* **2** a moving forward or going ahead: *to make rapid progress on a journey.*
—v. **1** get better; advance; develop: *We progress in learning step by step.* **2** move forward; go ahead: *The building of the city hall has progressed a great deal this week.* ⟨< L *progressus*, ult. < *pro-* forward + *gradi* walk⟩

pro•gres•sion [prəˈgrɛʃən] *n.* **1** a moving forward or going ahead: *Creeping is a slow method of progression.* **2** *Mathematics.* a succession of quantities in which there is always the same relation between each quantity and the one succeeding it. 2, 4, 6, 8, 10 are in **arithmetical progression.** 2, 4, 8, 16 are in **geometrical progression. 3** *Music.* **a** a moving from one tone or chord to another. **b** a sequence of tones, chords, etc.

pro•gres•sive [prəˈgrɛsɪv] *adj., n.* *—adj.* **1** of, having to do with, or characterized by progress; interested in or using new ideas, etc. in order to advance to something better: *a progressive nation.* **2** Often, **Progressive,** favouring moderate social or political reform through government action. **3** moving forward; developing: *a progressive disease.* **4** *Education.* having to do with, based on, or designating an educational theory or system which places emphasis on the individual interests and capabilities of the child, encouraging self-expression in an informal classroom atmosphere: *a progressive approach.* **5** involving regular shifts of players, guests, or locations, as in card games, dances, dinners, etc. **6** *Grammar.* having to do with or designating a verb form that expresses action in progress at the time of speaking or at the time spoken of. *Is reading, was reading,* and *has been reading* are progressive forms of *read.* **7** increasing in proportion to the increase of something else: *A progressive income tax increases as a person's earnings increase.*
—n. **1** a person who favours or follows a progressive policy, as in politics or education. **2** *Grammar.* **a** the progressive form of a verb. **b** a verb in this form. **—proˈgres•sive•ly,** *adv.* **—proˈgres•sive•ness,** *n.*

Progressive Conservative *Cdn.* **1** a member of the Progressive Conservative Party. **2** a person who supports the policies of this party. *Abbrev.:* P.C.

Progressive Conservative Party *Cdn.* one of the principal political parties of Canada.

progressive jazz a style of jazz that evolved in the late 1940s and early 1950s, characterized by very complex and subtle harmonies and rhythms.

pro•gres•siv•ism [prəˈgrɛsəˌvɪzəm] *n.* the principles, doctrines, or beliefs of progressives.

pro•gres•siv•ist [prəˈgrɛsəvɪst] *n., adj.* *—n.* a person who favours or follows progressive policies; a progressive.
—adj. of or having to do with progressivists or progressivism.

pro•hib•it [prəˈhɪbɪt] *v.* **1** forbid by law or authority: *Picking flowers in this park is prohibited.* **2** prevent: *The high price prohibits my buying the bicycle.* ⟨ME < L *prohibitus*, pp. of *prohibere* < *pro-* away + *habere* keep⟩ **—proˈhib•i•tor,** *n.*

☛ *Syn.* **1.** See note at FORBID.

☛ *Usage.* **Prohibited** is followed by **from,** not **against:** *We are prohibited from smoking on school grounds.* The noun **prohibition** is followed by **against:** *The prohibition against smoking in laboratories is strictly enforced.*

pro•hi•bi•tion [ˌprouəˈbɪʃən] *n.* **1** the act of prohibiting or forbidding. **2** a law or order that prohibits. **3** a law or laws against making or selling alcoholic liquors. **4** the time during which such laws are enforced. **5 Prohibition, a** *U.S.* the period (1920–1933) when the sale, transport, and consumption of alcoholic beverages was forbidden by law. **b** *Cdn.* a period from about 1913 to 1927 when the manufacture, sale, and public consumption of alcohol was forbidden. The exact terms and duration varied from province to province.

☛ *Usage.* See note at PROHIBIT.

pro•hi•bi•tion•ist [ˌprouəˈbɪʃənɪst] *n.* one who favours laws against the manufacture and sale of alcoholic liquors.

pro•hib•i•tive [prəˈhɪbətɪv] *adj.* **1** prohibiting; preventing. **2** preventing or discouraging purchase: *The cost of the house was prohibitive.* **—proˈhib•i•tive•ly,** *adv.*

pro•hib•i•to•ry [prəˈhɪbəˌtɔri] *adj.* prohibitive.

proj•ect *n.* [ˈproudʒɛkt] *or* [ˈprɒdʒɛkt]; *v.* [prəˈdʒɛkt] *n., v.* *—n.* **1** a plan or undertaking; scheme; enterprise: *Flying in a heavy machine was once thought an impossible project.* **2** a major school

assignment, especially one involving individual research. **3** a government subsidized housing development.
—v. **1** plan; scheme. **2** stick out: *The rocky point projects far into the water.* **3** cause to stick out or protrude. **4** throw or cast forward: *A catapult projects stones.* **5** cause to fall on a surface: *Films are projected on the screen. The tree projects a shadow on the grass.* **6** *Geometry.* recast (a figure) by drawing straight lines or rays (parallel, converging, or diverging) through each point according to a fixed rule and reproducing them on another surface. **7** *Psychology.* treat as objective and external (what is essentially subjective). **8** cause (the voice) to be heard clearly at a distance: *Actors, singers, and teachers must all learn to project.* **9** extrapolate. ⟨< L *projectus*, pp. of *proicere*, *projicere* < *pro-* forward + *jacere* to throw⟩
☛ *Syn. n.* **1.** See note at PLAN.

pro•jec•tile [prə'dʒɛktaɪl] *or* [prə'dʒɛktəl] *n., adj. —n.* any object that is thrown, hurled, or shot, as a rocket, stone, or bullet.
—adj. **1** capable of being thrown, hurled, or shot. **2** forcing forward; impelling: *a projectile force.* **3** that can be thrust forward: *the projectile jaws of a fish.*

pro•jec•tion [prə'dʒɛkʃən] *n.* **1** a part that projects or sticks out: *rocky projections on the face of a cliff.* **2** a sticking out. **3** a throwing or casting forward: *the projection of a shell from a field gun.* **4** *Geometry.* **a** the projecting of a figure, etc. upon a surface. **b** the resulting new figure. **5** *Cartography.* a representation, upon a flat surface, of all or part of the surface of the earth. **6** a forming of projects or plans. **7** *Psychology and psychiatry.* a tendency to ascribe to others one's own impulses, attitudes, and emotions, and to treat these subjective reactions as objective and external realities, especially when doing so relieves guilt or other unpleasant emotions. **8** a forecast or extrapolation.

pro•jec•tion•ist [prə'dʒɛkʃənɪst] *n.* **1** a person who operates a film projector or slide projector. **2** a person who draws projections, especially a cartographer.

pro•jec•tor [prə'dʒɛktər] *n.* **1** an apparatus for projecting a picture on a screen. **2** a person who forms projects or makes projections.

pro•kar•y•ote [prou'kæriət] *or* [prou'kɛriət] *n. Biology.* a cell without a visible nucleus. A procaryote has genetic material in a streptococcic or chainlike configuration, but no nuclear membrane. Also, **procaryote. —pro,kar•y'ot•ic** [-'ɒtɪk], *adj.*

prol. prologue.

pro•lac•tin [prou'læktən] *n. Biochemistry.* a protein hormone produced by the front lobe of the pituitary gland. Prolactin stimulates the secretion of milk in some mammals, crop production in birds, and, in some mammals, the production of progesterone by the corpus luteum.

pro•lapse *n.* ['proulæps]; *v.* [prou'læps] *n., v.* **-lapsed, -laps•ing.** *—n. Pathology.* the falling down or slipping of an internal organ or part of an organ from its normal position, as with a prolapsed uterus.
—v. fall or slip out of place. ⟨< LL *prolapsus* a falling out of place⟩

pro•late ['prouleit] *adj.* elongated in the direction of the polar diameter; having a polar diameter greater than the equatorial diameter. A prolate spheroid is generated by the revolution of an ellipse about its longer axis. Compare OBLATE[1]. ⟨< L *prolatus*, pp. of *proferre* extend, bring forward < *pro-* forth + *ferre* bring⟩

pro•le•gom•e•non [,proulɪ'gɒmə,nɒn] *n., pl.* **-na** [-nə]. **1** preliminary remarks or discussion; introduction. **2** Often, **prolegomena,** *pl.* (*used with a singular verb*) a treatise or essay serving as a preface or foreword to a book. ⟨< NL < Gk. *prolegŏmenon*, pp. of *prolegein* say beforehand⟩

pro•le•tar•i•an [,proulə'tɛriən] *adj., n. —adj.* **1** of or belonging to the proletariat. **2** in ancient Rome, belonging to the poorest and lowest class.
—n. a person belonging to the proletariat. ⟨< L *proletarius* furnishing the state only with children < *proles* offspring < *pro-* forth + *alescere* grow⟩

pro•le•tar•i•at [,proulə'tɛriət] *n.* **1** the lowest class in economic and social status. The proletariat includes unskilled labourers, casual labourers, and tramps. **2** in ancient Rome, the poorest and lowest class, possessing no property. **3** in Marxist theory, the class of labourers who possess no capital or property and so must work for wages, especially in industry, in order to survive. ⟨< F *prolétariat*⟩

pro–life ['prou 'ləif] *adj.* defending the right to life of all human beings at every stage of development, especially by opposing abortion and, usually, euthanasia. **—'pro-'lif•er,** *n.*

pro•lif•er•ate [prə'lɪfə,reit] *v.* **-at•ed, -at•ing. 1** grow by reproducing (new parts) by multiplication as in budding or cell division, or by procreation. **2** produce (something) or be produced rapidly: *The administration is proliferating notices endlessly.* **—pro,lif•er'a•tion,** *n.*

pro•lif•er•ous [prə'lɪfərəs] *adj.* **1** growing or spreading rapidly. **2** *Botany.* **a** multiplying freely, as by budding, putting out side shoots, etc. **b** multiplying by budding or shooting from what should be the end, as a flower. **3** *Zoology.* like coral, reproducing by budding. ⟨< Med.L *prolifer* bearing offspring < *proles* offspring + *ferre* bear⟩

pro•lif•ic [prə'lɪfɪk] *adj.* **1** producing offspring abundantly: *prolific animals.* **2** producing much: *a prolific garden, a prolific imagination, a prolific writer.* ⟨< Med.L *prolificus* < L *proles* offspring + *facere* make⟩ **—pro'lif•i•cal•ly,** *adv.*

pro•lif•i•ca•cy [prə'lɪfəkəsi] *n.* the quality or state of being prolific.

pro•lix [prou'lɪks] *or* ['proulɪks] *adj.* using too many words; too long; tedious. ⟨ME < L *prolixus* stretched out < *pro-* forth + *lixus*, a pp. of *liquere* flow, be liquid⟩ **—pro'lix•i•ty** or **pro'lix•ness,** *n.*

PROLOG ['proulɒg] *n. Computer technology.* a high-level computer language whose program statements are written like those in formal logic. ⟨< *Pro*(*gramming in*) *Log*(*ic*)⟩

pro•logue ['proulɒg] *n.* **1** a speech or poem addressed to the audience by one of the actors at the beginning of a play, opera, etc. **2** an introduction to a novel, poem, or other literary work. **3** any introductory act or event. ⟨ME *prologe* < OF < L < Gk. *prologos* < *pro-* before + *logos* speech⟩

pro•long [prə'lɒŋ] *v.* make longer; draw out. Also, **prolongate.** ⟨ME *prolongen* < LL *prolongare* < *pro-* forth + *longus* long⟩ **—pro'long•er,** *n.*
☛ *Syn.* See note at LENGTHEN.

pro•lon•ga•tion [,proulɒŋ'geiʃən] *n.* **1** an extension; lengthening in time or space: *the prolongation of one's school days by graduate study.* **2** an added part.

prom [prɒm] *n. Informal.* a dance or ball given by a college or high-school class. ⟨short for *promenade*⟩

PROM [prɒm] *n. Computer technology.* a programmable read-only memory chip, having contents that can be programmed by a user or manufacturer to suit specific needs. ⟨from *p*rogrammable *r*ead-*o*nly *m*emory⟩

prom•e•nade [,prɒmə'neid] *or* [,prɒmə'nɑd] *n., v.* **-nad•ed, -nad•ing.** *—n.* **1** walk for pleasure or display: *The Easter promenade is well-known as a fashion show.* **2** a public place for such a walk. **3** a dance; ball. **4** a march of all the guests at the opening of a formal dance. **5** a square-dancing figure in which a couple or, usually, all the couples of a set march once around the square, circle, etc.
—v. **1** walk about or up and down for pleasure or for display: *He promenaded back and forth on the ship's deck.* **2** walk through. **3** take on a promenade. ⟨< F *promenade* < *promener* take for a walk⟩ **—,prom•e'nad•er,** *n.*

promenade deck an enclosed upper deck on a ship, where passengers can walk.

Pro•me•the•an [prə'miθiən] *adj.* of, having to do with, or suggestive of Prometheus; creative; boldly original.

Pro•me•the•us [prə'miθiəs] *n. Greek mythology.* the Titan who stole fire from heaven and taught people its use, for which Zeus punished him by chaining him to a rock.

pro•me•thi•um [prə'miθiəm] *n. Chemistry.* an artificially produced, radioactive metallic element, used as a power source, an X-ray source, in phosphorescent paint, etc. *Symbol:* Pm; *at.no.* 61; *at.mass* (147); *half-life* 17.7 years. ⟨< *Prometheus*⟩

prom•i•nence ['prɒmənəns] *n.* **1** the quality or fact of being prominent, distinguished, or conspicuous: *the prominence of athletics in some schools.* **2** something that juts out or projects, especially upward. A hill is a prominence. **3** *Astronomy.* an eruption of a relatively cool, flamelike tongue of solar gas arching from the chromosphere into the much hotter corona, and visible at the edge of the sun, especially during an eclipse.

prom•i•nent ['prɒmənənt] *adj.* **1** well-known; important: *a prominent citizen.* **2** easy to see: *A single tree in a field is prominent.* **3** standing out; projecting: *Some insects have prominent eyes.* ⟨< L *prominens*, *-entis*, ppr. of *prominere* project < *pro-* forward + *men-* jut⟩ **—'prom•i•nent•ly,** *adv.*
☛ *Syn.* **1.** See note at EMINENT. **2. Prominent,** CONSPICUOUS = attracting attention and easily seen. **Prominent** describes something that so stands out above its surroundings or from its background that it

attracts attention and is easy to see: *He put her picture in a prominent position on his desk.* **Conspicuous** describes something so plain that it is impossible not to see it, or so unusual, odd, loud, colourful, etc., that it attracts attention: *There was a conspicuous lack of warmth in his greeting.*

prom•is•cu•i•ty [ˌprɒmɪ'skjuɪti] *n., pl.* **-ties.** the fact, state, or condition or an instance of being promiscuous.

pro•mis•cu•ous [prə'mɪskjuəs] *adj.* **1** mixed and in disorder: *a promiscuous heap of clothing on your closet floor.* **2** making no distinctions; lacking discrimination, especially in sexual relations: *promiscuous behaviour.* **3** haphazard. ⟨< L *promiscuus* < *pro* for + *miscere* mix⟩ **—pro'mis•cu•ous•ly,** *adv.* **—pro'mis•cu•ous•ness,** *n.*

prom•ise ['prɒməs] *n., v.* **-ised, -is•ing.** *—n.* **1** the words by which one binds oneself to do or not to do something. **2** the thing promised. **3** an indication of what may be expected: *The clouds give promise of rain.* **4** an indication of future excellence; something that gives hope of success: *a young scholar who shows promise.*
—v. **1** make a promise of (something) to (a person, etc.). **2** give one's word; make a promise. **3** give indication of; give hope of; give ground for expecting: *The rainbow promises fair weather tomorrow.* ⟨< L *promissum,* originally neut. pp. of *promittere* promise < *pro-* before + *mittere* put⟩ **—'prom•is•er,** *n.*

Prom•ised Land ['prɒməst] **1** in the Bible and the Koran, the country promised by God to Abraham and his descendants; Canaan. **2** heaven. **3 promised land,** a place or condition of expected happiness: *Canada is a promised land for many immigrants.*

prom•is•ing ['prɒməsɪŋ] *adj., v. —adj.* likely to turn out well: *a promising student.*
—v. ppr. of PROMISE. **—'prom•is•ing•ly,** *adv.*

prom•is•so•ry ['prɒməˌsɔri] *adj.* containing a promise.

promissory note **1** a written promise to pay a stated sum of money to a certain person at a certain time. **2** a written promise, often given as a gift, to do or provide something for someone at a time to be chosen by the recipient. *Abbrev.:* P/N or p/n

pro•mo ['proumou] *n., adj. Informal. —n.* an advertisement on radio or television, etc. forming part of a campaign promoting a forthcoming product or program.
—adj. concerning or involving such a promotion. ⟨shortened form of *promotional piece*⟩

prom•on•to•ry ['prɒmənˌtɔri] *n., pl.* **-ries. 1** a high point of land jutting into a body of water; headland. **2** *Anatomy.* a prominent or projecting structure or part. ⟨< Med.L *promontorium,* var. of L *promunturium* < *pro-* forward + *mons, montis* mountain⟩

pro•mote [prə'mout] *v.* **-mot•ed, -mot•ing. 1** raise or advance in rank, condition, or importance: *Those who pass the test will be promoted to the next higher grade.* **2** help to grow or develop; help to success: *The United Nations has done much to promote peace.* **3** help to organize; start: *Several bankers promoted the new company.* **4** further the sale of (an article) by advertising. **5** *Slang.* obtain by trickery or in a crafty way. ⟨< L *promotus,* pp. of *promovere* < *pro-* forward + *movere* move⟩ **—pro'mot•ive,** *adj.*

☛ *Syn.* **2. Promote,** FURTHER = help something move toward a desired end. **Promote** emphasizes causing a movement, cause, scheme, or undertaking to move forward by giving open and active support and encouragement and helping it grow and develop: *The scholarships promote better understanding of the West Indies.* **Further** emphasizes helping a cause, project, etc. to keep going ahead: *Getting the scholarship will allow him to further his education.*

pro•mot•er [prə'moutər] *n.* **1** a person or thing that promotes. **2** one who organizes new companies and secures capital for them, or who sponsors concerts, sports events, etc. Compare IMPRESARIO. **3** *Chemistry.* a substance that, in small amounts, is able to speed up the effect of a catalyst.

pro•mo•tion [prə'mouʃən] *n.* **1** advancement or an advance in rank or importance: *The clerk was given a promotion and an increase in salary.* **2** the act or process of furthering the development, growth, or acceptance of something: *the promotion of peace, the promotion of a health campaign.* **3** publicity; advertising: *We are increasing our budget for promotion.*

pro•mo•tion•al [prə'mouʃənəl] *adj.* of, having to do with, or used in the promotion of a product, enterprise, etc.; pertaining to publicity. **—pro'mo•tion•al•ly,** *adv.*

prompt [prɒmpt] *adj., v., n. —adj.* **1** on time; quick: *Be prompt to obey.* **2** done at once; made without delay: *I expect a prompt answer.*
—v. **1** cause (someone) to do something: *His curiosity prompted him to ask questions.* **2** give rise to; suggest; inspire: *A kind thought prompted the gift.* **3** remind (a learner, speaker, actor, etc.) of the words or actions needed. **4** *Computer technology.* request input through a message on the screen.
—n. **1** an act of prompting. **2** something that prompts. **3** *(adjl.)* of a prompter; used in prompting: *a prompt box on a stage.* **4** *Business.* **a** a limit of time allowed for payment of goods purchased. **b** the contract determining this limit of time. **5** *Computer technology.* a message on the screen requesting input. ⟨ME < L *promptus,* originally pp. of *promere* bring forth < *pro-* forward + *emere,* originally, take. Doublet of PRONTO.⟩ **—'prompt•ly,** *adv.* **—'prompt•ness,** *n.*

☛ *Syn. adj.* **1.** See note at READY.

prompt•book ['prɒmptˌbʊk] *n.* an annotated copy of the script of a play with detailed instructions and cues for action, set, properties, lighting, etc., used by the stage manager, prompter, etc.

prompt•er ['prɒmptər] *n.* a person who supplies actors, speakers, etc. with their lines from off-stage, when they forget them.

promp•ti•tude ['prɒmptɪˌtjud] *or* ['prɒmptɪˌtud] *n.* promptness; readiness in acting or deciding.

prom•ul•gate ['prɒməlˌgeit] *or* [prə'mʌlgeit] *v.* **-gat•ed, -gat•ing. 1** proclaim formally; announce officially: *The monarch promulgated a decree.* **2** spread far and wide: *Schools try to promulgate knowledge and good habits.* ⟨< L *promulgare* < *pro-* forth + **mulgare,* intensive of *mulgere,* originally, press⟩ **—'prom•ulˌga•tor,** *n.* **—ˌprom•ul'ga•tion,** *n.*

pron. **1** pronoun. **2** pronunciation.

pro•nate ['prouneit] *v.* **-nat•ed, -nat•ing. 1 a** turn (the hand or forearm) so that the palm of the hand faces downward or backward. **b** turn (the foot) so that the weight falls on the inner edge when standing. **2** in vertebrates, rotate (any joint) in a similar manner: *Beginning tennis players are apt to pronate the wrist of the racket hand.* **—pro'na•tion,** *n.* **—pro'na•tor,** *n.*

prone [proun] *adj.* **1** inclined; liable (*to*): *prone to evil. He was prone to believe the worst of everyone.* **2** very likely to have (*used in compounds*): *She is accident-prone.* **3** lying face downward. Compare SUPINE. **4** lying flat. ⟨ME < L *pronus* < *pro-* forward⟩

prone•ness ['prounnɪs] *n.* **1** an inclination; tendency; preference. **2** a prone position.

prong [prɒŋ] *n., v. —n.* **1** one of the pointed ends of a fork, antler, etc. **2** a branch or fork of a small stream.
—v. pierce or stab with a prong. ⟨ME *prange;* origin uncertain⟩

pronged [prɒŋd] *adj., v. —adj.* having prongs.
—v. pt. and pp. of PRONG.

prong•horn antelope ['prɒŋˌhɔrn] *n., pl.* **-horns** or (*esp. collectively*) **-horn.** ANTELOPE (def. 2); the North American antelope. Also called **pronghorn, prongbuck.**

pro•nom•i•nal [prə'nɒmənəl] *adj. Grammar.* of or having to do with pronouns; having the nature of a pronoun. ⟨< LL *pronominalis* < L *pronomen.* See PRONOUN.⟩ **—pro'nom•i•nal•ly,** *adv.*

pro•noun ['prouˌnaʊn] *n. Grammar.* a word used to indicate without naming; a word used instead of a noun to refer to a noun or noun phrase mentioned in the immediate context. *I, we, you, he, it, they, who, whose, which, this, mine,* and *whatever* are pronouns in English. ⟨< F *pronom* < L *pronomen* < *pro-* in place of + *nomen* noun⟩

pro•nounce [prə'naʊns] *v.* **-nounced, -nounc•ing. 1** make the sounds of; speak: *Pronounce your words clearly.* **2 a** articulate or utter (a word or words) in the generally acceptable or standard way: *How do you pronounce* rhinoceros? **b** show acceptable pronunciation of (a word or words) by means of phonetic symbols: *a pronouncing dictionary.* **3** give an opinion or decision: *Only an expert should pronounce on this case.* **4** declare (a person or thing) to be: *The doctor pronounced her cured.* **5** declare formally or solemnly: *The judge pronounced sentence on the criminal.* ⟨ME < OF *pronuncier* < L *pronuntiare,* ult. < *pro-* forth + *nuntius* messenger⟩ **—pro'nounce•a•ble,** *adj.* **—pro'nounc•er,** *n.*

pro•nounced [prə'naʊnst] *adj., v. —adj.* strongly marked; decided: *She held pronounced opinions on gambling.*
—v. pt. and pp. of PRONOUNCE.

pro•nounc•ed•ly [prə'naʊnsɪdli] *adv.* in a pronounced manner; to a pronounced degree.

pro•nounce•ment [prə'naʊnsmənt] *n.* **1** a formal statement; declaration. **2** an opinion; decision.

pron•to ['prɒntou] *adv. Informal.* promptly; quickly; right away. ⟨< Sp. *pronto* < L *promptus* prompt. Doublet of PROMPT.⟩

pronun. pronunciation.

pro•nun•ci•a•men•to [prə,nʌnsiə'mɛntou] *n., pl.* **-tos.** a formal announcement; proclamation; manifesto. ⟨< Sp. *pronunciamiento* < *pronunciar* pronounce⟩

pro•nun•ci•a•tion [prə,nʌnsi'eiʃən] *n.* **1** the way of pronouncing. Most dictionaries give the pronunciation of each entry word. **2** the act or an instance of pronouncing. ⟨< L *pronuntiatio, -onis* < *pronuntiare.* See PRONOUNCE.⟩

proof [pruf] *n., adj., v. —n.* **1** a way or means of showing beyond doubt the truth of something. **2** the establishment of the truth of anything. **3** *Law.* evidence having probative weight. **4** the act of testing; trial. **5** the condition of having been tested and approved. **6** *Printing.* a trial impression from type. A book is first printed in proof so that errors can be corrected. **7** a trial print of an etching, photographic negative, etc. **8 a** the standard strength of alcoholic liquors, considered as 100; in Canada, 57.1 percent by volume of alcohol at 15.6°C. **b** strength with reference to this standard: *What proof is this brandy?* **9** *Numismatics.* one of a number of coins of a new issue that have been struck with special care, using a polished die on a polished or matte surface: *This silver dollar is a proof.*
—adj. **1** of tested strength or security against something: *Now we know that we are proof against being taken by surprise.* **2** of an alcoholic liquor, of standard strength: *proof spirit.*
—v. **1** treat (something) to make it resistant to water, etc.: *They proofed their boots with a special wax to keep their feet dry.* **2** proofread. **3** *Photography.* make a PROOF (def. 7) of: *We had better proof these negatives soon.* ⟨ME *profe* < OF *prueve* < LL *proba* < L *probare* prove. Doublet of PROBE.⟩
☛ *Syn. n.* **1.** See note at EVIDENCE.

-proof *suffix.* protected against; safe from: *fireproof, waterproof, bombproof.*

proof•read ['pruf,rid] *v.* **-read** [-,rɛd], **-read•ing.** read (printers' proofs, etc.) and mark errors to be corrected.

proof spirit an alcoholic liquor, or a mixture of alcohol with water, containing by volume a standard amount of ethyl alcohol at 15.6°C. In Canada and the United Kingdom, proof is 57.1 percent, and in the U.S., 50 percent.

prop[1] [prɒp] *v.* **propped, prop•ping;** *n. —v.* **1** hold up by placing a support under or against (*often used with* **up**): *to prop up the clothesline with a stick.* **2** support; sustain (*often used with* **up**): *to prop a failing cause.*
—n. a support; a thing or person used to support another: *Many branches are heavy with apples and need a prop.* ⟨Cf. MDu. *proppe*⟩

prop[2] [prɒp] *n. Informal.* any article, such as a table or a weapon, used in staging a play. ⟨short for *(stage) property*⟩

prop[3] [prɒp] *n. Informal.* a PROPELLER (def. 1). ⟨clipping of *propeller*⟩

prop. 1 proprietor. **2** properly. **3** property. **4** proposition.

prop•a•ga•ble ['prɒpəgəbəl] *adj.* able to be propagated.

prop•a•gan•da [,prɒpə'gændə] *n.* **1** systematic efforts to spread opinions or beliefs, especially by distortion and deception: *The Nazis were experts in propaganda.* **2** any plan or method for spreading opinions or beliefs. **3** the opinions or beliefs thus spread. ⟨< NL *congregatio de propaganda fide* congregation for the propagation of the faith⟩

prop•a•gan•dism [,prɒpə'gændɪzəm] *n.* the use of propaganda.

prop•a•gan•dist [,prɒpə'gændɪst] *n.* **1** a person who gives time or effort to the spreading of propaganda. **2** *(adjl.)* of propaganda or propagandists. **—,prop•a•gan'dis•tic,** *adj.*

prop•a•gan•dize [,prɒpə'gændaɪz] *v.* **-dized, -diz•ing. 1** propagate or spread (doctrines, etc.) by propaganda. **2** carry on propaganda. **3** subject (people) to propaganda; control by propaganda.

prop•a•gate ['prɒpə,geit] *v.* **-gat•ed, -gat•ing. 1** produce offspring; reproduce: *Trees propagate themselves by seeds.* **2** increase in number; multiply: *During this hard winter, potholes have propagated on all the city streets.* **3** cause to increase in number by the production of young. **4** spread (news, knowledge, etc.): *Don't propagate unkind reports.* **5** pass on; send further: *Sound is propagated by vibrations.* ⟨< L *propagare,* originally, plant slips < *pro-* widely + **pagare,* frequentative of *pangere* make fast⟩ **—'prop•a,ga•tor,** *n.*

prop•a•ga•tion [,prɒpə'geiʃən] *n.* **1** the breeding, reproduction, or multiplying of plants or animals: *Our propagation of poppies is by seed, and of roses by cuttings.* **2** the spreading of something, such as a belief; the act of making more widely known; dissemination: *the propagation of the principles of science.* **3** a passing on; a sending further; the act of spreading or extending: *the propagation of the shock of an earthquake.*

pro•pane [prou'pein] *or* ['proupein] *n. Chemistry.* a heavy, colourless hydrocarbon gas of the methane series, found in petroleum and used for fuel, refrigeration, etc. *Formula:* C_3H_8 ⟨blend of *prop(yl)* + *(meth)ane*⟩

pro pat•ri•a ['prou 'pætriə] *or* ['peitriə] *Latin.* for one's country or native land.

pro•pel [prə'pɛl] *v.* **-pelled, -pel•ling.** drive forward; force ahead: *to propel a boat by oars, a person propelled by ambition.* ⟨ME < L *propellere* < *pro-* forward + *pellere* push⟩ **—pro'pel•la•ble,** *adj.*

pro•pel•lant [prə'pɛlənt] *n.* **1** something that propels, such as the fuel of a missile or the explosive charge of a shell, or any inert gas under pressure that dispenses the contents of an aerosol container when the pressure is released. **2** a person who causes something to be driven forward.

pro•pel•lent [prə'pɛlənt] *adj., n. —adj.* propelling; driving forward.
—n. propellant.

pro•pel•ler [prə'pɛlər] *n.* **1** a device consisting of a revolving hub with blades, for driving forward boats and aircraft. **2** a person or thing that propels.

pro•pen•si•ty [prə'pɛnsɪti] *n., pl.* **-ties.** a natural inclination or bent; inclination: *Many academics have a propensity for wordiness.* ⟨< L *propensus* inclined, ult. < *pro-* forward + *pendere* hang⟩

prop•er ['prɒpər] *adj., n. —adj.* **1** correct; right; fitting: *Night is the proper time to sleep, and bed the proper place.* **2** strictly so called; in the strict sense of the word (*usually after the noun*): *The population of Vancouver proper does not include that of the suburbs.* **3** decent; respectable: *proper conduct.* **4** *Informal.* **a** complete; thorough. **b** fine; excellent. **5** *Archaic.* good-looking; handsome. **6** belonging exclusively or distinctively: *qualities proper to a substance.* **7** *Heraldry.* represented in its natural colours: *an eagle proper.* **8** genteel; overly concerned with correctness; prim: *He is a very proper old man and is easily scandalized.* **9** of prayers, readings, rites, etc., reserved for a particular day or days.
—n. Christianity. the parts of a liturgy, such as the mass, that vary according to the day and time of day. ⟨ME < OF < L *proprius*⟩

proper adjective *Grammar.* an adjective formed from a PROPER NOUN and always capitalized. *Example:* French *in the* French language.

proper fraction *Mathematics.* a fraction less than 1. $^2/_3$, $^1/_8$, and $^{199}/_{200}$ are proper fractions.

prop•er•ly ['prɒpərli] *adv.* **1** in a proper, correct, or fitting manner: *This job must be done properly.* **2** rightly; justly: *to be properly indignant at the offer of a bribe.* **3** strictly: *Properly speaking, a whale is not a fish.*

proper noun or **name** *Grammar.* a noun that identifies one particular person, place, organization, period of time, etc.; a name used to identify an individual. *Sarah, Calgary,* and *Renaissance* are proper nouns. Compare COMMON NOUN.
☛ *Spelling.* Proper nouns are always capitalized.

prop•er•tied ['prɒpərtid] *adj.* owning property.

prop•er•ty ['prɒpərti] *n., pl.* **-ties. 1** any thing or things owned; possession or possessions. **2** a piece of land or real estate: *She owns some property out West.* **3** the right to possess, use, and dispose of anything; ownership. **4** a quality or power belonging specially to something: *Soap has the property of removing dirt.* **5 properties,** *pl.* the furniture, weapons, etc., used in staging a play, film, or television scene. ⟨ME < OF *propriete* < L *proprietas* < *proprius* one's own⟩
☛ *Syn.* **1. Property,** GOODS, EFFECTS = what someone owns. **Property** suggests whatever someone legally owns, including land, buildings, animals, money, stocks, documents, objects, and rights: *Landed property is taxable.* **Goods** suggests movable personal property, as distinguished from land, buildings, etc., and applies chiefly to things of use in the house or on the land, such as furniture, furnishings, and implements, but never to money or papers, etc.: *Professional movers packed our goods.* **Effects** applies to personal possessions, including goods, clothing, jewellery, personal belongings, and papers: *I packed our other effects.*

pro•phase ['prou,feiz] *n. Biology.* the first stage of mitosis, in which changes take place in the nucleus of a cell.

proph•e•cy ['prɒfəsi] *n., pl.* **-cies. 1** a telling of what will happen; the foretelling of future events. **2** something told about the future. **3** a divinely inspired utterance, revelation, writing, etc. ⟨ME *prophecie* < OF < L < Gk. *prophēteia* < *prophētēs.* See PROPHET.⟩

proph•e•sy ['prɒfə,saɪ] *v.* **-sied, -sy•ing. 1** tell what will happen. **2** foretell; predict: *The sailor prophesied a severe storm.* **3** speak when or as if divinely inspired: *Jeremiah prophesied concerning the moral and spiritual depravity of his people.* **4** utter a prophecy. ⟨verb use and var. of *prophecy*⟩ **—'proph•e,si•er,** *n.*

proph•et ['prɒfɪt] *n.* **1** a person who tells what will happen. **2** someone whose preaching is believed to be inspired by, or to be the word of, God or a god: *Every religion has its prophets.* **3 the Prophet, a** Mohammed. **b** Joseph Smith, the founder of the Mormon religion. **4 the Prophets,** *pl.* **a** the twenty-one books that constitute the second main division of the Hebrew Bible, following the Pentateuch (the Law) and preceding the Hagiographa. **b** the subjects or authors of these books, including Isaiah, Micah, Jeremiah, etc. **c** in Christian use, the sixteen books of the Old Testament that are named after prophets. ⟨ME *prophete* < OF < L < Gk. *prophētēs,* ult. < *pro-* before + *phanai* speak⟩
☛ *Hom.* PROFIT.

pro•phet•ic [prə'fɛtɪk] *adj.* **1** belonging to a prophet; such as a prophet has: *prophetic power.* **2** containing prophecy: *a prophetic saying.* **3** giving warning of what is to happen; foretelling: *prophetic words.* **—pro'phet•i•cal•ly,** *adv.*

pro•phy•lac•tic [,proufə'læktɪk] *or* [,prɒfə'læktɪk] *adj., n.* *—adj.* **1** protecting from disease. **2** protective; preservative; precautionary.
—n. **1** *Medicine.* a medicine or treatment that protects against disease. **2** precaution. **3** a condom or other contraceptive device. ⟨< Gk. *prophylaktikos,* ult. < *pro-* before + *phylassein* guard < *phylax, -akos* a guard⟩ **—,pro•phy'lac•ti•cal•ly,** *adv.*

pro•phy•lax•is [,proufə'læksɪs] *or* [,prɒfə'læksɪs] *n.* **1** protection from disease. **2** treatment to prevent disease. **3** contraception; birth control. ⟨< NL < Gk. *pro-* before + *phylaxis* protection⟩

pro•pin•qui•ty [prou'pɪŋkwəti] *n.* **1** nearness in time or place, especially personal nearness. **2** nearness of blood; kinship. ⟨< L *propinquitas,* ult. < *prope* near⟩

pro•pi•ti•ate [prə'pɪʃi,eit] *v.* **-at•ed, -at•ing.** prevent or reduce the anger of; win the favour of; appease or conciliate. ⟨< L *propitiare,* ult. < *propitius* propitious. See PROPITIOUS.⟩ **—pro'pi•ti,a•tor,** *n.* **—pro'pi•ti•a•ble,** *adj.* **—pro'pi•ti•a•tive,** *adj.*

pro•pi•ti•a•tion [prə,pɪʃi'eiʃən] *n.* **1** the act of winning favour, reducing anger, etc. **2** something or someone that propitiates: *The flowers were a propitiation for my unkind words.*

pro•pi•ti•a•to•ry [prə'pɪʃiə,tɔri] *adj.* intended to win favour, reduce anger, etc.; offering appeasement; conciliatory: *a propitiatory offering.*

pro•pi•tious [prə'pɪʃəs] *adj.* **1** favourable: *It seemed propitious weather for our trip.* **2** favourably inclined; gracious: *Their propitious attitude toward the new system made it work.* ⟨< L *propitius,* originally, falling forward < *pro-* forward + *petere* go toward⟩ **—pro'pi•tious•ly,** *adv.* **—pro'pi•tious•ness,** *n.*

prop•jet ['prɒp,dʒɛt] *n.* turboprop.

pro•po•nent [prə'pounənt] *n.* **1** one who makes a proposal or proposition. **2** a favourer; supporter. ⟨< L *proponens, -entis,* ppr. of *proponere* set forth. See PROPOUND.⟩

pro•por•tion [prə'pɔrʃən] *n., v.* *—n.* **1** the relation in size, number, amount, or degree of one thing compared to another: *What's the proportion of flour to milk in your recipe?* **2** a proper relation between parts: *His short legs were out of proportion with his long body.* **3 proportions,** *pl.* size; extent; dimensions: *Canada has forests of huge proportions.* **4** a part; share: *A large proportion of British Columbia is mountainous.* **5** *Mathematics.* **a** an equality of ratios: *Example*: 4:2::10:5. **b** a method of finding the fourth term of such a proportion when three are known.
—v. **1** fit (one thing to another) so that they complement each other in size or scale: *The designs in that rug are well proportioned.* **2** adjust in proper proportion or relation. ⟨< L *proportio, -onis* < phrase *pro portione* in relation to the part⟩ **—pro'por•tion•er,** *n.* **—pro'por•tion•ment,** *n.*

pro•por•tion•al [prə'pɔrʃənəl] *adj., n.* *—adj.* in the proper quantitative relation; corresponding: *The increase in price is proportional to the improvement in the car.*
—n. *Mathematics.* one of the terms of a proportion.

pro•por•tion•al•ly [prə'pɔrʃənəli] *adv.* in proper quantitative relation.

proportional representation an electoral system in which the number of seats that each party or group is given is proportional to its share of the total number of votes cast.

pro•por•tion•ate *adj.* [prə'pɔrʃənɪt]; *v.* [prə'pɔrʃə,neit] *adj., v.* **-at•ed, -at•ing.** *—adj.* in the proper proportion; proportioned; proportional: *The money obtained by the bazaar was really not proportionate to the effort we put into it.*
—v. make proportionate; proportion. **—pro'por•tion•ate•ly,** *adv.* **—pro'por•tion•ate•ness,** *n.*

pro•por•tioned [prə'pɔrʃənd] *adj., v.* *—adj.* adjusted in proportion.
—v. pt. and pp. of PROPORTION.

pro•pos•al [prə'pouzəl] *n.* **1** something put forward for consideration; a suggestion, offer, plan, etc.: *a proposal to adjourn for lunch. Her proposal for a new bridge will be presented to the city council tomorrow.* **2** an offer of marriage. **3** the act of proposing: *Proposal is easier than performance.*
☛ *Syn.* **1. Proposal,** PROPOSITION = something put forward for consideration. **Proposal** indicates a suggestion, offer, plan, or terms put forward for consideration and acceptance or action, but emphasizes the idea of offering for acceptance or refusal or suggesting for consideration: *The young people made a proposal to the City Council.* **Proposition,** emphasizes the specific arrangement put forward as a proposal and how it is set forth, the statement of the terms, the details of the plan or scheme, especially from a contractual point of view: *The Council approved the idea, but not the proposition set forth.*

pro•pose [prə'pouz] *v.* **-posed, -pos•ing. 1** put forward for consideration, discussion, acceptance, etc.; suggest. **2** present (the name of someone) for office; membership, etc. **3** present as the object of (a toast to be drunk): *May I propose a toast to the chair?* **4** intend; plan: *She proposes to save half of all she earns.* **5** make an offer of marriage. ⟨< F *proposer* < *pro-* forth (< L) + *poser.* See POSE[1].⟩ **—pro'pos•er,** *n.*

prop•o•si•tion [,prɒpə'zɪʃən] *n., v.* *—n.* **1** something presented or offered for consideration; proposal. **2** assertion; statement. **3** *Logic.* a statement affirming or denying something, that is to be proved true or false. **4** *Mathematics.* a problem or theorem, usually together with its proof. **5** *Informal.* a person or thing to be dealt with: *He can be a difficult proposition if you don't approach him in the right way.* **6** *Informal.* a suggestion or invitation to engage in illicit sexual intercourse.
—v. *Informal.* make a suggestion to (someone), especially to engage in illicit sexual intercourse. ⟨< L *propositio, -onis* a setting forth < *proponere* < *pro-* forth + *ponere* put, place⟩
☛ *Syn. n.* **1.** See note at PROPOSAL.

pro•pound [prə'paʊnd] *v.* put forward; propose: *to propound a theory, a question, or a riddle.* ⟨earlier *propone* < L *proponere* < *pro-* before + *ponere* set⟩ **—pro'pound•er,** *n.*

pro•prae•tor or **pro•pre•tor** [prou'pritər] *or* [prou'pritɔr] *n.* in ancient Rome, an officer who, after having served as praetor, was sent to govern a province. ⟨< L⟩

pro•pran•o•lol [prou'prænə,lɒl] *n.* a beta-blocking drug inhibiting the activity of epinephrine and other similar substances, used to treat angina pectoris, irregular heartbeat, and hypertension. *Formula*: $C_{16}H_{21}NO_2$

pro•pri•e•tar•y [prə'praɪə,tɛri] *adj., n., pl.* **-tar•ies.** *—adj.* **1** belonging to a proprietor. **2** holding property. **3** owned by a private person or company; belonging to or controlled by a private person as property. A proprietary medicine is a patent medicine, that is, one which can be made and sold only by some one person or certain persons.
—n. **1** an owner. **2** a group of owners. **3** ownership; the holding of property. **4** formerly, the holder or group of holders of a grant from the English monarch. **5** a proprietary medicine. ⟨< LL *proprietarius* < L *proprietas* ownership. See PROPRIETY.⟩

proprietary colony any of certain British colonies in North America that were granted by the Crown, with full rights of self-government, to an individual or group.

pro•pri•e•tor [prə'praɪətər] *n.* an owner, especially of a business; manager. ⟨alteration of *proprietary*⟩

pro•pri•e•tor•ship [prə'praɪətər,ʃɪp] *n.* ownership.

pro•pri•e•ty [prə'praɪəti] *n., pl.* **-ties. 1** the quality of being proper; fitness. **2** proper behaviour: *She acted with propriety.* **3 proprieties,** *pl.* the conventional standards or requirements of proper behaviour: *Most of the proprieties are matters of common politeness.* ⟨< L *proprietas* appropriateness, peculiar nature (translation by Cicero of Gk. *idiōtēs*) < *proprius* one's own, proper (= Gk. *idios*)⟩

pro•pri•o•cep•tive [,proupriə'sɛptɪv] *adj. Physiology.* of or having to do with proprioceptors or the stimuli acting upon them.

pro•pri•o•cep•tor [,proupriə'sɛptər] *n. Physiology.* a receptor, located in subcutaneous tissues such as muscles, tendons, etc., that is sensitive to stimuli produced there by movement of the body or a body part.

pro•pul•sion [prə'pʌlʃən] *n.* **1** the act or process of driving forward or onward. **2** a propelling force or impulse: *the propulsion of jet engines.* ⟨< F⟩

pro•pul•sive [prə'pʌlsɪv] *adj.* propelling; driving forward or onward.

prop•y•lae•um [,prɒpə'liəm] *n., pl.* **-lae•a** [-'liə]. an elaborate or imposing gateway, entrance, or vestibule to a temple or other building. ⟨< L *propylaeum* < Gk. *propylaion* entrance⟩

pro•py•lene ['prɒpə,lin] *n. Chemistry.* a colourless hydrocarbon gas obtained from propane, similar in type and structure to ethylene. *Formula*: C_3H_6

propylene glycol *Chemistry.* a colourless, viscous, hygroscopic liquid used chiefly as an antifreeze, a solvent of fats, oils, etc. and in the manufacture of polyester resins. *Formula*: $C_3H_8O_2$

pro ra•ta ['prou 'rɑtə] *or* ['reitə] in proportion; according to the share, interest, etc. of each. ⟨< L *pro rata (parte)* according to the portion figured (for each); *rata* < *ratus*, pp. of *reri* count, figure⟩

pro•rate [,prou'reit] *or* ['prou,reit] *v.* **-rat•ed, -rat•ing.** distribute or access proportionally: *We prorated the money according to the number of days each had worked.* ⟨< *pro rata*⟩ **—,pro'ra•tion,** *n.*

pro•ro•ga•tion [,prourə'geiʃən] *n.* the discontinuance of the meetings of a lawmaking body without dissolving it.

pro•rogue [prou'roug] *v.* **-rogued, -rogu•ing.** discontinue the regular meetings of (a lawmaking body) for a time: *Parliament will be prorogued for the summer recess.* ⟨< F < L *prorogare* defer < *pro-* forward + *rogare* ask for⟩

pro•sa•ic [prou'zeiɪk] *adj.* like prose; matter-of-fact; ordinary; not exciting; unimaginative. ⟨< Med.L *prosaicus* < L *prosa.* See PROSE.⟩ **—pro'sa•i•cal•ly,** *adv.* **—pro'saic•ness,** *n.*

pro•sce•ni•um [prou'siniəm] *n., pl.* **-ni•a** [-niə]. **1** the part of the stage in front of the curtain. **2** the curtain and the framework that holds it **(proscenium arch)**. **3** the stage of an ancient theatre, or of a modern theatre having no curtain. ⟨< L *proscaenium* < Gk. *proskēnion* < *pro-* in front of + *skēnē* stage, originally, tent⟩

pro•sciut•to [prə'ʃutou]; *Italian,* [pro'ʃutto] *n.* a dried Italian ham, highly spiced and served finely sliced in appetizers, etc. ⟨< Ital. *prosciugare* dry out, ult. < LL⟩

pro•scribe [prou'skraɪb] *v.* **-scribed, -scrib•ing. 1** prohibit as wrong or dangerous; condemn: *to proscribe dancing and cardplaying.* **2** put outside of the protection of the law; outlaw. **3** forbid to come into a certain place; banish. **4** in former times, announce or publish (someone's name) as condemned to death, banishment, exile, etc. ⟨< L *proscribere* < *pro-* openly, publicly + *scribere* write⟩ **—pro'scrib•er,** *n.*

pro•scrip•tion [prou'skrɪpʃən] *n.* **1** the act of proscribing. **2** the state of being proscribed. ⟨< L *proscriptio, -onis* < *proscribere.* See PROSCRIBE.⟩

pro•scrip•tive [prou'skrɪptɪv] *adj.* proscribing; tending to proscribe. **—pro'scrip•tive•ly,** *adv.* **—pro'scrip•tive•ness,** *n.*

prose [prouz] *n., v.* **prosed, pros•ing.** *—n.* **1** the ordinary form of spoken or written language. **2** language not arranged in poetic metre: *This writer's prose is better than most people's poetry. Milton and Samuel Johnson are masters of the Latin style of prose.* **3** (*adjl.*) of or in prose. **4** dull, ordinary talk. **5** (*adjl.*) lacking imagination; matter-of-fact; commonplace.
—v. talk, utter, or write in a dull, commonplace way. ⟨< F < L *prosa (oratio)* straight (speech), ult. < *pro-* forward + *vertere* turn⟩

pros•e•cute ['prɒsə,kjut] *v.* **-cut•ed, -cut•ing. 1** *Law.* **a** bring before a court: *Reckless drivers will be prosecuted.* **b** bring a case before a court. **2** carry out; follow up: *The government prosecuted an inquiry into reasons for the company's failure.* **3** carry on (a business or occupation). ⟨ME < L *prosecutus*, pp. of *prosequi* pursue < *pro-* forth + *sequi* follow. Related to PURSUE.⟩
☛ *Usage.* See note at PERSECUTE.

pros•e•cu•tion [,prɒsə'kjuʃən] *n.* **1** *Civil Law.* **a** the carrying on of a lawsuit: *She abandoned her prosecution of the case for damages.* **b** *Criminal Law.* the side that institutes criminal proceedings against another. The prosecution makes charges against the defence. **2** a carrying out; following up: *In prosecution of his plan, he stored away a supply of food.*

pros•e•cu•tor ['prɒsə,kjutər] *n.* **1** *Criminal Law.* a lawyer who represents the state in the conducting of proceedings in a court of law against persons accused of crime. In Canada, such a person is a **Crown prosecutor,** who is a full-time or part-time officer of the court. **2** *Civil Law.* any person who carries on legal proceedings against another or others. **3** a person who carries out or follows up something.

pros•e•lyte ['prɒsə,ləit] *n., v.* **-lyt•ed, -lyt•ing.** *—n.* a convert from one opinion, religious belief, etc. to another.
—v. convert (someone) from one opinion, religious belief, etc. to another; proselytize. ⟨ME < LL < Gk. *prosēlytos* having arrived < *pros-* over + *ely-* come⟩ **—'pros•e,lyt•er,** *n.*

pros•e•lyt•ism ['prɒsələ,tɪzəm] *n.* the act or fact of making converts.

pros•e•lyt•ize ['prɒsələ,taɪz] *v.* **-ized, -iz•ing.** make converts; proselyte.

prose poem a written composition set out as prose, but having the highly concentrated, figurative and rhythmic language typical of poetry.

Pro•ser•pi•na [prou'sɜrpənə] *n. Roman mythology.* the daughter of Jupiter and Ceres and queen of the underworld, corresponding to the Greek goddess Persephone. Also, **Proserpine** ['prɒsər,paɪn] *or* [prou'sɜrpəni].

pro•sim•i•an [prou'sɪmiən] *adj., n. —adj.* of or having to do with the order Prosimii which includes lorises, lemurs, and bush babies.
—n. any member of this order.

pro•sit ['prouzɪt] *interj.* to your health! ⟨< L *prosit* may it benefit⟩

pros•o•dist ['prɒsədɪst] *n.* a person skilled in the technique of versification.

pros•o•dy ['prɒsədi] *n.* **1** the science of poetic metres and versification. **2** *Linguistics.* the stress and intonation patterns of an utterance. ⟨< L < Gk. *prosōidia* all the features (accent, modulation, etc.) that characterize speech < *pros* in addition to + *ōidē* song, poem⟩

pros•pect ['prɒspɛkt] *n., v. —n.* **1** anything expected or looked forward to. **2** the act of looking forward; expectation: *The prospect of a vacation is pleasant.* **3** the outlook for the future. **4** a person who may be a customer, candidate, etc.; prospective customer: *The sales rep had several prospects in mind.* **5** a view; scene: *The prospect from the mountain was grand.* **6** *Mining.* **a** a mining area or claim appearing to have attractive mineral deposits. **b** a site that a prospector works.
in prospect, expected; looked forward to.
—v. search (for minerals): *to prospect for gold, to prospect a region for silver.* ⟨< L *prospectus*, ult. < *pro-* forward + *specere* look⟩

pro•spec•tive [prə'spɛktɪv] *adj.* **1** probable; expected: *a prospective client.* **2** looking forward to the future: *a prospective suggestion.* **—pro'spec•tive•ly,** *adv.*

pros•pec•tor ['prɒspɛktər] *or* [prə'spɛktər] *n.* a person who explores or examines a region for gold, silver, oil, etc.

pro•spec•tus [prə'spɛktəs] *n.* a printed statement describing and advertising something, such as programs of study offered by a college, or funds, stocks, etc. of interest to investors. ⟨< L *prospectus.* See PROSPECT.⟩

pros•per ['prɒspər] *v.* **1** be successful; have good fortune; flourish. **2** make successful. ⟨ME < OF < L *prosperare* < *prosperus* prosperous⟩

pros•per•i•ty [prɒ'spɛrɪti] *n., pl.* **-ties.** a prosperous condition; good fortune; success.

pros•per•ous ['prɒspərəs] *adj.* **1** successful; thriving; doing well; fortunate. **2** favourable; helpful: *prosperous weather for growing wheat.* ⟨< L *prosperus* < *pro-* according to + *spes* hope⟩ **—'pros•per•ous•ly,** *adv.* **—'pros•per•ous•ness,** *n.*

pros•ta•cy•clin [,prɒstə'səiklɪn] *n. Biochemistry.* a prostaglandin derivative that forms in the walls of blood vessels and inhibits the formation of blood clots. *Formula*: $C_{20}H_{32}O_5$

pros•ta•glan•din [,prɒstə'glændɪn] *n.* **1** *Biochemistry.* any of a class of fatty acids found throughout the body that are involved in the control of body temperature, blood pressure, and other bodily functions. **2** *Pharmacy.* any commercial preparation of prostaglandin. ⟨< *prosta(te)* + *gland* + *-in*⟩

pros•tate ['prɒsteit] *n., adj. Anatomy. —n.* a large gland surrounding the male urethra in front of the bladder. It controls the release of urine and also secretes an alkaline fluid that is ejected with the semen, enhancing the motility of sperm.
—adj. designating or having to do with this gland. ⟨< Med.L < Gk. *prostatēs* one standing in front, ult. < *pro-* before + *stenai* stand⟩

pros•ta•tec•to•my [ˌprɒstəˈtɛktəmi] *n., pl.* **-mies.** surgical removal of all or part of the prostate.

pros•ta•tism [ˈprɒstəˌtɪzəm] *n. Pathology.* symptoms of prostate disorder, especially chronic disease or enlargement of the prostate.

pros•ta•ti•tis [ˌprɒstəˈtaitɪs] *n. Pathology.* inflammation of the prostate.

pros•the•sis [prɒsˈθisɪs] *or* [ˈprɒsθəsɪs] *n., pl.* **-ses** [-siz]. **1** the addition of a false tooth, artificial leg, etc. to the body. **2** the part itself. ⟨< LL < Gk. *prosthesis* addition, ult. < *pros* to + *tithenai* put⟩

pros•thet•ics [prɒsˈθɛtɪks] *n.* (*used with a singular verb*) the branch of dentistry or surgery pertaining to prosthesis. **—ˈpros•the•tist,** *n.*

pros•ti•tute [ˈprɒstəˌtjut] *or* [ˈprɒstəˌtut] *n., v.* **-tut•ed, -tut•ing.** *—n.* **1** any person who accepts payment for sexual acts: *a male prostitute.* **2** a person who gives up himself or herself or his or her talents to an unworthy cause.
—v. **1** offer (oneself or another person) for hire to engage in sexual acts. **2** give up (oneself or one's talents) to an unworthy cause: *He has prostituted his art by selling paintings that he knows are not well done.* ⟨< L *prostitutus,* pp. of *prostituere* prostitute < *pro-* publicly + *statuere* cause to stand⟩

pros•ti•tu•tion [ˌprɒstəˈtjuʃən] *or* [ˌprɒstəˈtuʃən] *n.* **1** the act or business of offering oneself or another person for hire to engage in sexual acts. **2** the act of giving up oneself or one's talents to an unworthy cause: *Churning out those cheap romances is a prostitution of her talents as a writer.*

pros•trate [ˈprɒstreit] *v.* **-trat•ed, -trat•ing;** *adj. —v.* **1** lay (oneself) down flat; cast (oneself) down submissively: *The captives prostrated themselves before the conqueror.* **2** make very weak or helpless; exhaust: *Sickness often prostrates people.*
—adj. **1** lying flat, with the face downward. **2** lying flat, exhausted. **3** helpless; overcome: *a prostrate enemy.* ⟨< L *prostratus,* pp. of *prosternere* < *pro-* forth + *sternere* strew⟩

pros•tra•tion [prɒˈstreiʃən] *n.* **1** the act of prostrating; bowing down low or lying face down in submission, respect, or worship. **2** the state or condition of being very much worn out in body or mind; exhaustion; dejection.

pros•y [ˈprouzi] *adj.* **pros•i•er, pros•i•est.** like prose; commonplace; dull; tiresome. **—ˈpros•i•ly,** *adv.* **—ˈpros•i•ness,** *n.*

Prot. Protestant.

pro•tac•tin•i•um [ˌproutækˈtɪniəm] *n. Chemistry.* a silver-grey, radioactive metallic element found in uranium ores. *Symbol:* Pa; *at.no.* 91; *at.mass* 231.04; *half-life* 32 500 years. ⟨< *proto-* (< Gk. *protos* first) + *actinium*⟩

pro•tag•o•nist [prəˈtægənɪst] *n.* **1** the main character in a play, story, or novel. **2** a person who takes a leading part; an active supporter. ⟨< Gk. *prōtagōnistēs* < *prōtos* first + *agōnistēs* actor < *agōn* contest < *agein* do⟩

pro•ta•no•pia [ˌproutəˈnoupiə] *n.* one of the types of red-green colour blindness, inherited as an X-linked recessive trait. Often shortened to **protan** [ˈproutæn]. ⟨< *proto-* + *an-* + *-opia*⟩

pro•te•an [ˈproutiən] *or* [prouˈtiən] *adj.* readily assuming different forms or characters; exceedingly variable. ⟨< *Proteus*⟩

pro•tect [prəˈtɛkt] *v.* **1** shield from harm or danger; shelter; defend; guard. **2** guard (home industry) by taxing competing foreign goods that are imported into the country. ⟨< L *protectus,* pp. of *protegere* < *pro-* in front + *tegere* to cover⟩
☛ *Syn.* **1.** See note at GUARD.

pro•tec•tion [prəˈtɛkʃən] *n.* **1** the act of protecting or condition of being kept from harm; defence: *We have police for our protection.* **2** a thing or person that prevents damage: *This old shirt is my protection against paint splatters.* **3** *Economics.* the system of taxing imported foreign goods so that people are more likely to buy goods made in their own country; the opposite of free trade. **4** something that assures safe passage through a region; a passport. **5** *Informal.* the payment of money to racketeers or gangsters as a form of tribute in order not to be molested.

pro•tec•tion•ism [prəˈtɛkʃəˌnɪzəm] *n. Economics.* the system or theory of PROTECTION (def. 3). **—proˈtec•tion•ist,** *n., adj.*

pro•tec•tive [prəˈtɛktɪv] *adj.* **1** being a defence; protecting: *the hard protective covering of a turtle.* **2** eager to protect. **3** preventing injury to those around: *a protective device on a machine.* **4** guarding against the competition of foreign-made goods by putting a high tax or duty on them: *a protective tariff.* **—proˈtec•tive•ly,** *adv.* **—proˈtec•tive•ness,** *n.*

protective coloration PROTECTIVE COLOURING.

protective colouring or **coloring** a colouring some animals have that makes them hard to distinguish from their surroundings, and so hides them from their enemies.

protective mimicry a close resemblance of an animal to its surroundings or to some different animal, that prevents its enemies from attacking it.

pro•tec•tor [prəˈtɛktər] *n.* **1** a person or thing that shields from harm or danger; defender. **2** the head of a kingdom when the monarch cannot rule.

pro•tec•tor•ate [prəˈtɛktərɪt] *n.* **1** a weak or underdeveloped country or territory under the partial control of a strong country. **2** such protection and control. **3** the position or term of a protector. **4** government by a protector. **5 Protectorate,** the period (1653-1659) during which Oliver and Richard Cromwell were Lords Protector of England.

pro•té•gé [ˈproutəˌʒei] *or* [ˌproutəˈʒei] *n.* a person under the patronage or protection of another. ⟨< F *protégé,* pp. of *protéger* < L *protegere.* See PROTECT.⟩ **—ˈpro•té,gée,** *n. fem.*

pro•te•id [ˈproutiɪd] *n. or adj.* protein.

pro•tein [ˈproutin] *n. Biochemistry.* a complex compound containing nitrogen that is a necessary part of the cells of animals and plants. Meat, fish, milk, cheese, eggs, and beans contain much protein. ⟨< L < Gk. *prōteios* of the first quality⟩

pro•tein•u•ria [ˌproutiˈnjʊriə] *n. Pathology.* the presence of abnormally large amounts of protein in the urine, often caused by kidney disease, but sometimes arising from other abnormal conditions or from excessive exercise.

pro tem. PRO TEMPORE.

pro tem•po•re [ˌprou ˈtɛmpəri] *or* [ˈtɛmpərei] *Latin.* for the time being; temporarily. Often shortened to **pro tem.**

Prot•er•o•zo•ic [ˌprɒtərəˈzouɪk] *or* [ˌproutərəˈzouɪk] *n., adj. Geology. —n.* **1** a very early era, beginning approximately 1200 million years ago. **2** the rocks formed in this era. See geological time chart in the Appendix.
—adj. of or having to do with this era or the rocks formed during it. ⟨< Gk. *proteros* prior + *zōē* life⟩

pro•test *n.* [ˈproutɛst]; *v.* [prəˈtɛst] *or* [ˈproutɛst] *n., v., —n.* **1** a statement that denies or objects strongly: *They yielded only after protest.* **2** a solemn declaration: *The accused man was judged guilty in spite of his protest of innocence.* **3** a declaration, especially by a taxpayer, disputing the legality of the payment or its amount. **4** a written statement by a notary public that a bill, note, cheque, etc. has been presented to someone who has refused to pay it or accept it. **5** *Sports.* an objection to a player or a play as illegal. **6** *(adjl.)* referring to a person or group making a protest: *The protest groups marched to Parliament Hill.*
under protest, unwillingly; though objecting.
—v. **1** make objections; object: *The boys protested against having girls in the game.* **2** object to: *to protest a decision.* **3** declare solemnly; assert: *The accused man protested his innocence.* **4** state that (a cheque, note, bill, etc.) has not been paid. ⟨ME < OF *protest* < *protester* protest < L *protestari,* ult. < *pro-* forth + *testis* witness⟩ **—proˈtest•er,** *n.* **—proˈtest•ing•ly,** *adv.*

Prot•es•tant *n.* (defs. 1 & 2), *adj.* (def. 1) [ˈprɒtəstənt]; *n.* (def. 3), *adj.* (def. 2) [ˈprɒtəstənt] *or* [prəˈtɛstənt] *n., adj. —n.* **1** a member or adherent of certain Christian churches that developed after the break with the Roman Catholic Church in the 16th century. Baptists, Presbyterians, some Anglicans, United Church members, and many others are Protestants. **2** generally, any Christian who is not a member of the Roman Catholic or Eastern Orthodox Churches. **3 protestant,** a person who protests.
—adj. **1** of Protestants or their religion. **2 protestant,** protesting. ⟨< L *protestans, -antis* ppr. of *protestari.* See PROTEST.⟩

Protestant Episcopal Church in the United States, a Protestant church having principles and beliefs similar to those of the Anglican Church of Canada. Also, **Episcopal Church.**

Prot•es•tant•ism [ˈprɒtəstənˌtɪzəm] *n.* **1** the religion of Protestants; their principles and beliefs. **2** Protestants or Protestant churches as a group.

prot•es•ta•tion [ˌprɒtɪˈsteiʃən] *or* [ˌproutiˈsteiʃən] *n.* **1** a solemn declaration: *to make a protestation of one's innocence.* **2** a protest.

Pro•te•us [ˈproutiəs] *n. Greek mythology.* a sea god who had the power of assuming many different forms.

pro•thal•li•um [prouˈθæliəm] *n., pl.* **-thal•li•a** [-ˈθæliə]. prothallus.

pro•thal•lus [prou'θæləs] *n., pl.* **-li** [-laɪ]. *Botany.* a tiny, flat, free-living plant body that is the gametophyte of a fern or other pteridophyte. It develops from a spore. ⟨< NL < Gk. *pro-* before + *thallos* sprout⟩

pro•tho•rax [prou'θɔræks] *n., pl.* **-tho•rax•es** or **-tho•ra•ces** [-'θɔrə,siz]. the anterior segment of an insect's thorax, bearing the first pair of legs. ⟨< F *prothorax* < NL < Gk. *pro-* + *thorax* chest, throat⟩

pro•throm•bin [prou'θrɒmbɪn] *n. Biochemistry.* a plasma protein that combines with calcium during blood coagulation to form thrombin. It is a precursor of thrombin synthesized in the liver when vitamin K is present.

pro•tist ['proutɪst] *n.* any organism of the group Protista.

Pro•tis•ta [prou'tɪstə] *n. Biology.* in some systems of classification, a kingdom of one-celled organisms having characteristics common to plants and animals alike, such as algae, bacteria, yeast, etc. ⟨< Gk. *protista*, neuter pl. super of *protos* first⟩

pro•ti•um ['proutiəm] *n. Chemistry.* the most common isotope of hydrogen and the lightest, having an atomic mass of 1. *Symbol*: H^1

proto– *combining form.* **1** first in time, importance, order, or rank: *prototype.* **2 a** being the parent form of a substance specified by the second element of the word. **b** being one of a series of compounds that has the least amount of the element specified. **3 Proto- a** designating the earliest reconstructed stage of a language: *Proto-Germanic.* **b** referring to the speakers of those languages, or any prehistoric peoples: *Proto-Indo-Europeans, Proto-hominids.*

pro•to•ac•tin•i•um [,proutouæk'tɪniəm] *n.* the former name of protactinium.

pro•to•col ['proutə,kɒl] *or* ['proutə,koul] *n.* **1** a first draft or record from which a document, especially a treaty, is prepared. **2** the rules of etiquette of the diplomatic corps. **3** the rules for any procedure. ⟨< OF < Med.L *protocollum* < Gk. *prōtokollon* a first leaf (with date and contents) glued onto a papyrus roll < *prōtos* first + *kolla* glue⟩

Pro•to–Ger•man•ic [,proutou dʒɜr'mænɪk] *n.* the reconstructed hypothetical language from which all the languages of the Germanic branch of the Indo-European language family are thought to be descended, including English.

pro•to•his•to•ry [,proutou'hɪstəri] *n.* archaeological history in the period immediately preceding that for which we have recorded history.

pro•ton ['proutɒn] *n. Physics. Chemistry.* a nuclear particle carrying one unit of positive electric charge, found in the nucleus of every kind of atom. An element is identified and classified according to the number of protons in the nucleus of each of its atoms; the number of protons gives the element its atomic number. ⟨< Gk. *prōton*, neut. adj., first⟩

proton synchrotron *Physics.* a synchrotron used for accelerating protons to very high energies.

pro•to–on•co•gene [,proutou 'ɒŋkə,dʒin] *n. Genetics.* a normal gene, involved in some aspect of cell division or proliferation, that if activated by mutation can become an oncogene.

pro•to•plasm ['proutə,plæzəm] *n. Biology.* living matter; a colourless substance somewhat like soft jelly or egg white that is the living substance of all plant and animal cells, consisting mainly of water, lipids, proteins, carbohydrates, and inorganic salts; the cytoplasm and nucleus. ⟨< G *Protoplasma* < Gk. *prōtos* first + *plasma* something moulded < *plassein* mould⟩ **—,pro•to'plas•mic,** *adj.*

pro•to•troph•ic [,proutə'trɒfɪk] *or* [,proutə'troufɪk] *adj.* capable of synthesizing its required growth factors from inorganic materials.

pro•to•type ['proutə,tɔip] *n.* the first or primary type of anything; the original or model: *A modern ship has its prototype in the hollowed log or skin boat.* ⟨< NL < Gk. *prōtotypon*, originally neut. of *prōtotypos* original, primitive < *prōtos* first + *typos* type, model⟩ **—,pro•to'typ•i•cal** or **'pro•to,typ•al,** *adj.*

pro•to•zo•an [,proutə'zouən] *n., pl.* **-zo•ans** or **-zo•a** [-'zouə]; *adj.* *—n.* any of a phylum (Protozoa) of minute, mostly microscopic, single-celled organisms found throughout the world in fresh water, in the oceans at all depths, and in the soil. Protozoans have traditionally been classified as simple animals, some of which have plantlike characteristics, but some authorities place them in a separate kingdom (Protista), along with algae and sometimes fungi.
—adj. of, having to do with, or belonging to the Protozoa.

pro•tract [prə'trækt] *v.* **1** draw out; lengthen in time: *to protract a visit.* **2** slide out; thrust out; extend. **3** draw by means of a scale and protractor. ⟨< L *protractus*, pp. of *protrahere* < *pro-* forward + *trahere* drag⟩ **—pro•tract•i•ble,** *adj.* **—pro'tract•ive,** *adj.*

pro•tract•ed [prə'træktɪd] *adj., v. —adj.* lengthened.
—v. pt. and pp. of PROTRACT. **—pro'tract•ed•ly,** *adv.* **—pro'tract•ed•ness,** *n.*

pro•trac•tile [prə'træktaɪl] *or* [prə'træktəl] *adj.* capable of being lengthened out, or of being thrust forth. The turtle has a protractile head.

pro•trac•tion [prə'trækʃən] *n.* **1** the act of drawing out; extension. **2** a drawing that has exactly the same proportions as the thing it represents.

pro•trac•tor [prə'træktər] *or* ['proutræktər] *n.* **1** an instrument for drawing or measuring angles. **2** a person or thing that protracts.

pro•trude [prə'trud] *v.* **-trud•ed, -trud•ing. 1** thrust forth; stick out: *The saucy child protruded his tongue.* **2** be thrust forth; project: *Her teeth protrude too far.* ⟨< L *protrudere* < *pro-* forward + *trudere* thrust⟩ **—pro'trud•ent,** *adj.*

pro•tru•sile [prə'trusaɪl] *or* [prou'trusəl] *adj.* capable of being thrust out or extended, as an elephant's trunk or the tongue of a hummingbird.

pro•tru•sion [prə'truʒən] *n.* **1** the act of protruding or the state of being protruded. **2** something that sticks out; projection. ⟨< L *protrusus*, pp. of *protrudere.* See PROTRUDE.⟩

pro•tru•sive [prə'trusɪv] *adj.* sticking out; projecting. **—pro'tru•sive•ly,** *adv.* **—pro'tru•sive•ness,** *n.*

pro•tu•ber•ance [prə'tjubərəns] *or* [prə'tubərəns] *n.* **1** a part that sticks out; bulge; swelling. **2** the act, fact, or state of bulging or sticking out.

pro•tu•ber•ant [prə'tjubərənt] *or* [prə'tubərənt] *adj.* bulging out; sticking out; prominent. ⟨< LL *protuberans*, *-antis* bulging, ppr. of *protuberare*, ult. < *pro-* forward + *tuber* lump⟩ **—pro'tu•ber•ant•ly,** *adv.*

pro•tu•ber•ate [prə'tjubə,reit] *or* [prə'tubə,reit] *v.* **-rat•ed, -rat•ing.** swell out or bulge, so as to form a rounded projection.

proud [praʊd] *adj.* **1** feeling honoured or gratified, or showing such a feeling: *I am proud to call them my friends.* **2** having a becoming sense of what is due to oneself, one's position, or character. **3** thinking too well of oneself; haughty; arrogant: *He was too proud to share a taxi with a stranger.* **4** such as to make a person proud; highly honourable, creditable, or gratifying: *a proud moment.* **5** proceeding from pride; due to pride: *a proud smile.* **6** imposing; stately; majestic; magnificent: *proud cities.* **7** of persons, of exalted rank or station: *proud nobles.* **8** full of spirit or mettle: *a proud war horse.*
do (someone or oneself) **proud,** honour or distinguish: *Her generosity did her proud.*
proud of, thinking well of; being well satisfied with; proud because of: *to be proud of oneself, to be proud of one's family.* ⟨OE *prūd* < OF *prod, prud* valiant < LL *prode* of use < L *prodesse* be useful⟩ **—'proud•ly,** *adv.* **—'proud•ness,** *n.*
☛ *Syn.* **1–3. Proud,** OVERBEARING, SUPERCILIOUS = having or showing a high opinion of oneself. **Proud** may mean either holding oneself above anything low, mean, or contemptible or thinking oneself better than others, but usually also suggests a haughty or conceited manner or appearance: *She has a strong, proud face.* **Overbearing** suggests being rudely dictatorial or haughtily insulting in behaviour and speech: *Promoted too quickly, the conceited youth became overbearing.* **Supercilious** suggests conceit, but emphasizes a coolly scornful attitude: *With a supercilious smile he refused our invitation.*

proud flesh *Pathology.* the formation of too many grainlike particles of flesh during the healing of a wound or sore.

prov. 1 province; provincial. **2** provisional. **3** provost.

Prov. 1 Provençal. **2** Provence. **3** Province. **4** Provost.

prove [pruv] *v.* **proved, proved** or **prov•en, prov•ing. 1** establish as true; make certain. **2** establish the genuineness or validity of, especially of a will. **3** be found (to be): *This book proved interesting. She proved to have a broken arm.* **4** try out; test; subject to some testing process.
prove oneself, a show oneself to be: *He proved himself honest.* **b** convince others by one's performance that one is worthy.
prove out, show or be shown as true, satisfactory, workable, etc.: *Their plan proved out in the end.* ⟨ME < OF *prover* < L *probare* < *probus* worthy⟩ **—'prov•a•ble,** *adj.*

prov•en ['pruvən] *adj., v. —adj.* known to be authentic: *Meat*

tenderizer is a proven treatment for bee stings.
—v. a pp. of PROVE.

prov•e•nance ['prɒvənəns] *n.* origin or source: *the provenance of a painting.*

Pro•ven•çal [,prouvɒn'sæl]; *French,* [prɔvɑ̃'sal] *n., adj. —n.* **1** a native or inhabitant of Provence, a region in SE France. **2** the language of Provence.
—adj. of or having to do with Provence, its people, or their language.

prov•en•der ['prɒvəndər] *n.* **1** dry food for animals, such as hay or corn. **2** *Informal.* food. ⟨ME < OF *provendre* < VL *probenda* < L *praebenda.* See PREBEND.⟩

pro•ve•ni•ence [prou'vinjəns] *n.* provenance. ⟨< L *proveniens, -entis,* ppr. of *provenire* to come forth⟩

prov•erb ['prɒvərb] *n.* **1** a short saying expressing a general truth, accepted and used for a long time. *Examples: A stitch in time saves nine. Look before you leap.* **2** an enigmatic statement. **3** a well-known example: *He is a proverb for carelessness.* **4 Proverbs,** a book of the Old Testament made up of sayings of the wise men of Israel, including Solomon. ⟨ME < OF < L *proverbium* < *pro-* forth + *verbum* word, originally, a speaking⟩
☛ *Usage.* See note at EPIGRAM.

pro•ver•bi•al [prə'vɜrbiəl] *adj.* **1** of proverbs; expressed in a proverb; like a proverb: *proverbial brevity, proverbial wisdom, a proverbial saying.* **2** that has become a proverb: *the proverbial stitch in time.* **3** well-known: *the proverbial loyalty of dogs.*
—pro'ver•bi•al•ly, *adv.*

pro•vide [prə'vaɪd] *v.* **-vid•ed, -vid•ing. 1** supply; furnish: *Sheep provide us with wool. Who will provide the costumes?* **2** supply means of support; arrange to supply means of support: *Parents provide for their children.* **3** take care for the future: *to provide against accident, to provide for old age.* **4** state as a condition beforehand: *Our club's rules provide that dues must be paid monthly.* ⟨< L *providere* < *pro-* ahead + *videre* see. Doublet of PURVEY.⟩ **—pro'vid•er,** *n.*

pro•vid•ed [prə'vaɪdɪd] *conj., v. —conj.* on the condition that; if: *She will go provided her friends can go also.*
—v. pt. and pp. of PROVIDE.

prov•i•dence ['prɒvədəns] *n.* **1** God's care and help. **2** an instance of God's care and help. **3** care or preparation for the future; good management. **4 Providence,** God.

prov•i•dent ['prɒvədənt] *adj.* **1** having or showing foresight; careful in providing for the future: *Provident parents lay aside money for their families.* **2** economical; frugal. ⟨ME < L *providens, -entis,* ppr. of *providere.* See PROVIDE.⟩
—'prov•i•dent•ly, *adv.*

prov•i•den•tial [,prɒvə'dɛnʃəl] *adj.* **1** fortunate: *Our delay seemed providential, for the train we had planned to take was wrecked.* **2** of or proceeding from divine power or influence.
—,prov•i'den•tial•ly, *adv.*

pro•vid•ing [prə'vaɪdɪŋ] *conj., v. —conj.* on the condition that; provided: *I shall go providing it doesn't rain.*
—v. ppr. of PROVIDE.

prov•ince ['prɒvəns] *n.* **1** *Cdn.* **a** one of the ten main political units, or divisions, which, together with the two Territories, make up Canada. **b** formerly, any one of the principal administrative subdivisions of British North America. **2** a similar political or administrative division in other countries. **3 the provinces,** *pl.* the parts of a country at a distance from the capital or the largest cities: *They were accustomed to city life and did not like living in the provinces.* **4** proper extent or scope of function or activity; sphere: *It was not within the province of the committee to make such decisions.* **5** an area or division of learning, art, government, etc.: *the province of science, the province of literature.* **6** in ancient Rome, a territory outside Italy, ruled by a Roman governor. **7** a large church district governed by an archbishop. ⟨ME < OF < L *provincia*⟩

pro•vin•cial [prə'vɪnʃəl] *adj., n. —adj.* **1** *Cdn.* of, associated with, or under the jurisdiction of a province, as opposed to the federal government of Canada: *Education is a provincial power in Canada, while justice is federal.* **2** of a province. **3** belonging or peculiar to some particular province or provinces rather than to the whole country; local: *provincial English, provincial customs.* **4** having or describing the manners, speech, dress, point of view, etc. of people living in the provinces. **5** lacking refinement or polish; narrow: *a provincial point of view.*
—n. **1** a person born or living in the provinces. **2** a person who lacks refinement or polish. **3** *Cdn.* a member of the provincial police. **—pro'vin•cial•ly,** *adv.*

pro•vin•cial•ism [prə'vɪnʃə,lɪzəm] *n.* **1** provincial manners, habits of thought, etc. **2** narrow-mindedness. **3** a word, expression, or way of pronunciation peculiar to a district of a country; localism. **—pro'vin•cial•ist,** *n.*

pro•vin•ci•al•i•ty [prə,vɪnʃi'ælɪti] *n., pl.* **-ties. 1** a provincial quality or character. **2** a provincial characteristic or trait.

pro•vin•cial•ize [prə'vɪnʃə,laɪz] *v.* **-ized, -iz•ing. 1** bring under the authority of a province. **2** give a provincial status or name to; make provincial.

provincial judge magistrate.

provincial legislature *Cdn.* PROVINCIAL PARLIAMENT.

provincial park *Cdn.* a tract of land established by a provincial government as a preserve for wildlife and as a holiday area: *Algonquin Park in Ontario is a well-known provincial park.*

provincial parliament *Cdn.* the parliamentary body of any Canadian province.

provincial police *Cdn.* in Ontario and Québec, a police force maintained by the provincial government.

provincial premier *Cdn.* PREMIER (def. 1).

provincial rights *Cdn.* the rights of provinces to exercise control in those areas designated as being under provincial jurisdiction in the British North America Act.

proving ground a place or context for testing or trying out something, such as a piece of new equipment, a new theory, etc.

pro•vi•sion [prə'vɪʒən] *n., v. —n.* **1** a statement making a condition: *A provision of the lease is that the rent must be paid promptly.* **2** a taking care for the future. **3** a way of taking care for the future; an arrangement made beforehand: *There is a provision for making the building larger if necessary.* **4** that which is made ready; supply; stock, especially of food; food. **5 provisions,** *pl.* a supply of food and drinks.
make provision, take care for the future; make arrangement beforehand.
—v. supply with provisions. ⟨ME < OF < *provisio, -onis* < *providere.* See PROVIDE.⟩
☛ *Syn. n.* **5.** See note at FOOD.

pro•vi•sion•al [prə'vɪʒənəl] *adj., n. —adj.* for the time being; temporary or conditional: *a provisional agreement, a provisional government.*
—n. a postage stamp issued for use until the regular issue is available.

pro•vi•sion•al•ly [prə'vɪʒənəli] *adv.* **1** for the time being; temporarily. **2** conditionally.

pro•vi•so [prə'vaɪzou] *n., pl.* **-sos** or **-soes.** a sentence or part of a sentence in a contract, or other agreement, that states a condition; condition: *He was admitted to the advanced course with the proviso that he was to be put back if he failed.* ⟨< L *proviso* it being provided < *providere.* See PROVIDE.⟩

pro•vi•so•ry [prə'vaɪzəri] *adj.* **1** containing a proviso; conditional. **2** provisional. **—pro'vi•so•ri•ly,** *adv.*

pro•vit•a•min [prou'vəitəmɪn] *n. Biochemistry.* a substance that, when ingested, can be transformed into a vitamin within the organism, as carotene is converted by the liver into vitamin A.

pro•vo•ca•teur [prə,vɒkə'tɜr]; *French,* [pʀɔvɔka'tœʀ] *n., adj.*
—n. one who stirs up trouble or provokes violence.
—adj. (*used after the noun*) that stirs up trouble. ⟨< F⟩

prov•o•ca•tion [,prɒvə'keiʃən] *n.* **1** the act of provoking. **2** something that stirs one up; a cause of anger: *Their insulting remarks were a provocation.* ⟨ME < OF < L *provocatio, -onis* < *provocare.* See PROVOKE.⟩

pro•voc•a•tive [prə'vɒkətɪv] *adj., n. —adj.* **1** irritating; vexing. **2** tending or serving to call forth action, thought, laughter, anger, etc.; stimulating: *a remark provocative of mirth.* **3** arousing sexual interest.
—n. something that rouses or irritates. **—pro'voc•a•tive•ly,** *adv.*
—pro'voc•a•tive•ness, *n.*

pro•voke [prə'vouk] *v.* **-voked, -vok•ing. 1** make angry; vex. **2** stir up; excite: *An insult provokes a person to anger.* **3** call forth; bring about; start into action; cause. ⟨< L *provocare* < *pro-* forth + *vocare* call⟩ **—pro'vok•er,** *n.*
☛ *Syn.* **1.** See note at IRRITATE.

pro•vok•ing [prə'voukɪŋ] *adj., v. —adj.* that makes angry, vexes, or excites; irritating.
—v. ppr. of PROVOKE. **—pro'vok•ing•ly,** *adv.*

pro•vo•lo•ne [,prouvə'louni]; *Italian,* [,provo'lone] *n.* a hard, sharp cheese having a smoky flavour. ⟨< Ital.⟩

pro•vost ['prouvoust], ['prouvou], *or* ['prɒvəst] *n.* **1** a person appointed to superintend, maintain discipline, administer, or

preside, such as the head of certain colleges or churches. **2** in Scotland, the chief magistrate of a town. ⟨partly OE *profost*, partly < OF *provost*, both < Med.L *propositus*, used for L *praepositus* placed in charge of, originally pp. of *praeponere* place before < *prae-* at the head of + *ponere* to place⟩
—'prov•ost,ship, *n.*

provost marshal ['prouvou] an officer in charge of the military police in a camp or region. *Abbrev.*: P.M.

prow [praʊ] *n.* **1** the pointed front part of a ship or boat; bow. See SCHOONER for picture. **2** the projecting front part of anything: *the prow of an aircraft.* ⟨< F *proue* < Ital. < L < Gk. *prōira*⟩

prow•ess ['praʊɪs] *n.* **1** bravery; daring. **2** brave or daring acts. **3** unusual skill or ability. ⟨ME < OF *proece* < *prod* valiant. See PROUD.⟩

prowl [praʊl] *v., n.* *—v.* **1** go about slowly and secretly hunting for something to eat or steal: *Many wild animals prowl at night.* **2** wander or cruise about (a place): *prowling the streets.*
—n. an act of prowling.
on the prowl, prowling about. ⟨ME *prolle(n)*; origin uncertain⟩
—'prowl•er, *n.*

prowl car SCOUT CAR (def. 1).

prox•em•ics [prɒks'imɪks] *n.* **1** *Sociology, Psychology.* the study of how people and animals use and structure their spatial requirements, and the effects of population density on their behaviour, etc. **2** *Linguistics.* the study of the symbolic and communicative role of spatial arrangements in a culture and its linguistic system.

prox•i•mal ['prɒksəməl] *adj. Anatomy.* situated toward the point of origin or attachment, as of a limb or bone. Compare DISTAL. ⟨< L *proximus* nearest⟩

prox•i•mate ['prɒksəmət] *adj.* **1** next; nearest. **2** near the exact amount; approximate. ⟨< pp. of Med.L **proximare* bring near < L *proximare* come near < *proximus* nearest⟩
—'prox•i•mate•ly, *adv.*

prox•im•i•ty [prɒk'sɪməti] *n.* nearness; closeness. ⟨< L *proximitas* < *proximus* nearest⟩

proximity fuse a tiny electronic device set in the nose of a projectile to make the shell explode at a certain distance from the target.

prox•i•mo ['prɒksə,mou] *adv. Archaic.* in or of the coming month: *on the 1st proximo.* ⟨short for L *proximo mense* during next month⟩

prox•y ['prɒksi] *n., pl.* **prox•ies. 1** the action of a deputy or substitute. In marriage by proxy, someone is substituted for the absent bridegroom or bride at the marriage service. **2** a person authorized to act for another: *John acted as a proxy for the child's godfather at the christening.* **3** a written statement authorizing a proxy to act or vote for a person. **4** the vote so given. ⟨ME *prokecye*, alteration of *procuracy* the office of proctor < Med.L *procuratia*, ult. < L *procurare.* See PROCURE.⟩

prude [prud] *n.* a person who shows excessive propriety or modesty, especially with regard to sexual matters. ⟨< F *prude* < *prudefemme* excellent woman < OF *prou, prod* excellent + *femme* woman⟩

pru•dence ['prudəns] *n.* **1** the exercising of careful thought before taking action; good judgment or discretion. **2** good management; economy.
☛ *Syn.* **1. Prudence,** FORESIGHT = thought in acting and planning. **Prudence** emphasizes common sense in directing oneself and one's affairs, giving thought to one's actions and their consequences, and usually suggests caution, watchfulness, and saving: *Prudence is wisdom in everyday life.* **Foresight** emphasizes ability to see what is likely to happen, and giving thought to being prepared: *They had the foresight to carry fire insurance.*

pru•dent ['prudənt] *adj.* **1** planning carefully ahead of time; taking no chances; sensible; discreet: *A prudent worker saves part of his or her wages.* **2** characterized by good judgment or good management: *a prudent policy.* ⟨ME < L *prudens, -entis*, var. of *providens.* See PROVIDENT.⟩ **—'pru•dent•ly,** *adv.*

pru•den•tial [pru'dɛnʃəl] *adj.* of, marked by, resulting from, or showing prudence. **—pru'den•tial•ly,** *adv.*

prud•er•y ['prudəri] *n., pl.* **-er•ies. 1** extreme modesty or propriety, especially when offensive. **2** a prudish act or remark.

prud•ish ['prudɪʃ] *adj.* like a prude; extremely proper or modest; too modest. **—'prud•ish•ly,** *adv.* **—'prud•ish•ness,** *n.*

prune[1] [prun] *n.* **1** a kind of dried sweet plum. **2** a plum suitable for drying. **3** *Slang.* a person thought to be unattractive, stupid, or unpleasant. ⟨ME < OF < VL *pruna* < L *prunum* < Gk. *proumnon.* Doublet of PLUM.⟩

prune[2] [prun] *v.* **pruned, prun•ing. 1** cut out useless or undesirable parts from: *to prune a wordy manuscript.* **2** cut superfluous or undesirable twigs or branches from (a bush, tree, etc.), in order to improve growth or productivity. **3** cut off or out. ⟨ME *pruynen* < OF *prooignier* < *por-* (< L *pro-*) + *rooignier* clip, originally, round off < L *rotundus* round⟩ **—'prun•er,** *n.*

pru•nel•la [pru'nɛlə] *n.* **1** a light worsted fabric in a twill weave, used for women's and children's clothing. **2** a smooth woollen cloth used for women's dresses and lawyers' robes.

pruning hook an implement with a long handle and a hooked blade, used for pruning vines, etc.

pru•ri•ent ['prʊriənt] *adj.* having, expressing, or exciting lustful thoughts or wishes. ⟨< L *pruriens, -entis*, ppr. of *prurire* itch, be wanton⟩ **—'pru•ri•ent•ly,** *adv.* **—'pru•ri•ence** or **'pru•ri•en•cy,** *n.*

pru•ri•tus [prʊ'raɪtɪs] *Pathology.* **1** itching. **2** a disorder characterized by an intense itching of the skin not accompanied by a rash or eruption. ⟨< L *pruritus* an itching < *prurire* to itch⟩

Prus•sian ['prʌʃən] *n., adj.* *—n.* **1** a native or inhabitant of Prussia, a former state on the Baltic Sea and later a part of Germany. **2** a member of a Baltic people formerly inhabiting East Prussia. **3** See OLD PRUSSIAN. **4** loosely, any German dialect of Prussia.
—adj. of or having to do with Prussia or Prussians.

Prussian blue a deep blue pigment, essentially a cyanogen compound of iron. ⟨so called from its discovery in Berlin, the capital of Prussia, in 1704⟩

prus•sic acid ['prʌsɪk] *Chemistry.* a deadly poison that smells like bitter almonds; hydrocyanic acid. ⟨< F *prussique* < *Prusse* Prussia⟩

pry[1] [praɪ] *v.* **pried, pry•ing;** *n., pl.* **pries.** *—v.* look or inquire into (other people's affairs) with curiosity, especially so as to give offence: *They accused her of prying into their affairs.*
—n. an inquisitive person. ⟨ME *prie(n)*; origin uncertain⟩

pry[2] [praɪ] *v.* **pried, pry•ing;** *n., pl.* **pries.** *—v.* **1** raise or move by force, especially by using a lever. **2** get with much effort: *We finally pried the secret out of him.*
—n. a lever for prying. ⟨< obs. *prize* a lever, taken as a pl. See PRIZE[4].⟩

pry•ing ['praɪɪŋ] *adj., v.* *—adj.* looking or searching curiously; inquisitive, especially offensively, about others' affairs.
—v. ppr. of PRY. **—'pry•ing•ly,** *adv.*
☛ *Syn.* See note at CURIOUS.

P.S. 1 postscript (for L *post scriptum*). **2** PRIVY SEAL. **3** PUBLIC SCHOOL. **4** public sale. **5** passenger steamer.

psalm [sɒm] *or* [sɑm] *n.* **1** a sacred song or poem. **2 Psalm,** any of the 150 sacred songs or hymns that together form a book of the Old Testament. **3 Psalms,** this book. ⟨OE *psalm, sealm* < LL < Gk. *psalmos*, originally, performance on a stringed instrument < *psallein* pluck⟩

psalm•book ['sɒm,bʊk] *or* ['sɑm,bʊk] *n.* a collection of metrical translations of the Psalms prepared for public worship.

psalm•ist ['sɒmɪst] *or* ['sɑmɪst] *n.* **1** the author of a psalm or psalms. **2 the Psalmist,** King David.

psalm•o•dy ['sɒmədi], ['sɑmədi], *or* ['sælmədi] *n.* **1** the act, practice, or art of singing psalms or hymns, or composing music for them. **2** psalms or hymns. ⟨ME < LL < Gk. *psalmōidia* < *psalmos* psalm + *ōidē* song⟩ **—'psalm•o•dist,** *n.* **—psal'mod•ic** [-'mɒdɪk], *adj.*

Psal•ter ['sɒltər] *n.* **1** the Book of Psalms. **2** a version of the Psalms for liturgical or devotional use, often with a musical score. **3** Usually, **psalter,** a prayer book containing such a version. ⟨ME < OF < L < Gk. *psaltērion.* See PSALTERY.⟩

psal•te•ri•um [sɒl'tiriəm] *or* [sæl'tiriəm] *n., pl.* **-te•ri•a** [-'tiriə]. *Zoology.* omasum. ⟨< L, psalter; because its many folds resemble pages⟩

psal•ter•y ['sɒltəri] *n., pl.* **-ter•ies.** an ancient and medieval musical instrument played by plucking the strings. ⟨OE *saltere* < L < Gk. *psaltērion*, originally, stringed instrument < *psallein* pluck⟩

PSAT ['pisæt] Preliminary Scholastic Aptitude Test.

pse•phol•o•gist [sɛ'fɒlə,dʒɪst] *n.* a person trained in psephology, especially one whose work it is.

pse•phol•o•gy [sɛ'fɒlədʒi] *n.* the study of election trends, based on the evaluation of statistical evidence. ⟨< Gk. *psephos* a pebble; the Athenians cast votes by means of pebbles⟩
—,pse•pho'log•i•cal, *adj.*

pseud [sud] *n., adj. Slang.* —*n.* someone who fatuously pretends to intellectual or artistic knowledge or who affects social pretensions; a fake or sham.
—*adj.* of, concerning, or characteristic of such a person: *I can't stand that couple's pseud behaviour.* ⟨clipping of *pseudo*⟩

pseud. pseudonym.

pseu•de•pig•ra•pha [sudə'pɪgrəfə] *n.* (*used with a plural verb*) certain books, not included in the Biblical canon or the Apocrypha, purporting to be Biblical in character. ⟨< Mod.L < Gk. *pseudepigraphos, pl. -a* having a false title⟩

pseu•do ['sudou] *adj.* **1** false; sham; pretended. **2** being so only in appearance. ⟨< Gk. *pseudēs* false⟩

pseudo– *combining form.* false; spurious: *pseudo-intellectual, pseudomorph.* Also, sometimes before a vowel, **pseud-.** ⟨< Gk.⟩

pseu•do•cy•e•sis [,sudousaɪ'isɪs] *n., pl.* **-cy•e•ses** [-siz] a condition in female mammals, caused by emotional imbalance or by a tumour, in which the body mimics the symptoms of pregnancy. Also called **false pregnancy.** ⟨< Gk. *pseudo-* + *kyesis* pregnancy < *kyein* be pregnant⟩ —**,pseu•do•cy'et•ic** [-'ɛtɪk], *adj.*

pseu•do•gene ['sudou,dʒin] *n. Genetics.* a gene, resembling a known gene at a different locus, that has undergone mutation and is not functional.

pseu•do•her•ma•phro•dite [,sudouhər'mæfrə,dəit] *n.* a person or animal having the internal reproductive organs of one sex and the external characteristics of the other.

pseu•do•morph ['sudou,mɔrf] *n.* **1** any irregular or false form. **2** a mineral having the outward form or appearance of another that it has replaced. —**,pseu•do'mor•phic** or **,pseu•do'mor•phous,** *adj.* —**,pseu•do'mor•phism,** *n.*

pseu•do•nym ['sudə,nɪm] *n.* a name used by an author instead of his or her real name. Ralph Connor is a pseudonym for Charles William Gordon. ⟨< Gk. *pseudonymon* < *pseudēs* false + dial. *onyma* name⟩ —**,pseu•do'nym•i•ty,** *n.*

pseu•don•y•mous [su'dɒnəməs] *adj.* done or written under, or using, a pseudonym: *a pseudonymous novel.*
—**pseu'don•y•mous•ly,** *adv.*

pseu•do•pod ['sudə,pɒd] *n.* any false limb, such as the extensions on an amoeba or the unsegmented legs of certain caterpillars, used for movement or to catch prey. ⟨< NL *pseudopodium* false limb⟩

pseu•do•preg•nan•cy [,sudou'pregnənsi] *n.* pseudocyesis.

psf or **p.s.f.** pounds per square foot.

pshaw [ʃɒ] *or* [pʃɒ] *interj. or n. Archaic or facetious.* an exclamation expressing impatience, contempt, etc.

psi[1] [saɪ], [psi], *or* [psaɪ] *n.* the twenty-third letter of the Greek alphabet (Ψ, ψ).

psi[2] [saɪ] *n.* psychic processes or phenomena, such as extrasensory perception, telepathy, clairvoyance, etc. Also called **psi phenomena.** ⟨< Gk. *psi,* the first letter of *psychē* soul, life⟩

psi[3] **or p.s.i.** pounds per square inch.

psi•lo•cybe ['saɪlə,saɪb] *or* ['sɪlə,saɪb] *n.* the mushroom *Psilocybe mexicana,* commonly called 'magic mushroom'. ⟨< NL < Gk. *psilos* bare + *kybe* head⟩

psi•lo•cy•bin [,saɪlə'saɪbɪn] *or* [,sɪlə'saɪbɪn] *n. Pharmacology.* a hallucinogenic crystalline solid obtained from the fungus *Psilocybe mexicana. Formula*: $C_{12}H_{17}N_2O_4P$

psit•ta•cine ['sɪtə,saɪn] *or* ['sɪtəsɪn] *adj.* of, having to do with, or resembling parrots. ⟨< L *psittacinus* parrotlike⟩

psit•ta•co•sis [,sɪtə'kousɪs] *n.* a contagious disease of parrots and other birds, communicable to people, in whom the symptoms are fever and pneumonia. ⟨< L *psittacus* parrot < Gk. *psittakos* parrot + *-osis* diseased condition⟩

pso•ri•a•sis [sə'raɪəsɪs] *n. Pathology.* a chronic, inflammatory skin disease characterized by scaly red patches, and highly resistant to treatment. ⟨< NL < Gk. *psoriasis* < *psorian* to have the itch⟩

psych or **psyche** [səik] *v.* **psyched, psych•ing;** *n. Informal.* —*v.* **1** psychoanalyse. **2** upset or excite emotionally (*often with* **up**).
psych out, *Informal.* **a** lose one's nerve: *The team psyched out at the mere thought of playing those giants.* **b** pretend to be mentally confused or disturbed in order to avoid a situation: *We could try psyching out to get out of writing the test!* **c** upset (someone): *Her remark psyched out her opponent.* **d** figure out or analyse mentally or intuitively: *She managed to psych it out for herself.*
psych up, *Informal.* prepare mentally or emotionally for a task, performance, etc.: *to psych oneself up for the opening-night performance.*
—*n.* psychology. ⟨shortened form of *psychoanalyse*⟩

psych. **1** psychology; psychological. **2** psychiatry; psychiatric.

psy•che ['səiki] *n.* **1** the human soul or spirit. **2** the mind. **3** *Psychiatry.* the mind considered as a functional entity; the mental or psychological structure of a person considered as a motive force. ⟨< L < Gk. *psychē* breath, life < *psychein* breathe, blow⟩

Psy•che ['səiki] *n. Greek and Roman mythology.* the human soul or spirit pictured as a beautiful young girl, usually with butterfly wings. Psyche was loved by Cupid, and was made immortal by Jupiter.

psy•che•de•li•a [,səikə'diliə] *n.* the way of life, ideas, objects, etc. associated with the use of psychedelic drugs: *a film dealing with psychedelia.*

psy•che•del•ic [,səikə'dɛlɪk] *adj., n.* —*adj.* **1** of, having to do with, or designating drugs that can produce abnormal changes in the mind, including intensified awareness of light, sound, colour, etc., often accompanied by hallucinations or delusions. LSD is a psychedelic drug. **2** produced by such a drug: *a psychedelic experience.* **3** suggesting or imitating the intensified or bizarre colours, sounds, etc. associated with the mental effects of psychedelic drugs: *a psychedelic pink miniskirt, psychedelic music.*
—*n.* **1** a psychedelic drug. **2** a person who uses psychedelic drugs. ⟨coined word; lit. 'mind-revealing', < Gk. *psychē* + *dēlein* to show + E *-ic*⟩

psy•chi•a•trist [sə'kaɪətrɪst] *or* [sɪ'kaɪətrɪst] *n.* a physician who specializes in psychiatry.

psy•chi•a•try [sə'kaɪətri] *or* [sɪ'kaɪətri] *n.* the branch of medicine dealing with the diagnosis and treatment of mental disorders. ⟨< *psycho-* + Gk. *iatreia* cure, ult. < *iaesthai* heal⟩ —**,psy•chi'at•ric** [,səiki'ætrɪk], *adj.* —**psy•chi'at•ri•cal•ly,** *adv.*

psy•chic ['səikɪk] *adj., n.* —*adj.* **1** of the soul or mind; mental: *illness due to psychic causes.* **2** outside the known laws of physics; supernatural. A psychic force or influence is believed by spiritualists to explain second sight, telepathy, table moving, tappings, etc. **3** especially susceptible to psychic influences.
—*n.* **1** a person supposed to be specially sensitive or responsive to psychic force or spiritual influences; a medium. **2** things that are psychic. ⟨< Gk. *psychikos* < *psychē* soul, mind⟩
—**'psy•chi•cal•ly,** *adv.*

psy•cho ['səikou] *n., pl.* **-chos;** *adj. Slang.* —*n.* a psychopath or psychotic.
—*adj.* psychopathic or psychotic. ⟨shortened form⟩

psycho– *combining form.* mind: *psychoanalysis.* Also, **psych-** before some vowels. ⟨< Gk. *psychē* soul, mind⟩

psy•cho•act•ive [,səikou'æktɪv] *adj.* referring to a drug having a profound effect on the mind.

psy•cho•an•a•lyse or **psy•cho•an•a•lyze** [,səikou'ænə,laɪz] *v.* **-lysed** or **-lyzed, -lys•ing** or **-lyz•ing.** examine or treat by psychoanalysis. —**,psy•cho'an•a,lys•er** or **,psy•cho'an•a,lyz•er,** *n.*

psy•cho•a•nal•y•sis [,səikouə'næləsɪs] *n.* **1** a method of studying human thought patterns, especially with a view to treating mental disorders, by which unconscious or subconscious forces that have impaired a person's ability to function satisfactorily in life are brought to the person's consciousness and their role in the person's life interpreted in order to enable him or her to deal with them. **2** the body of knowledge and theory that originated with the work of Sigmund Freud (1856-1939), an Austrian physician. —**,psy•cho,an•a'lyt•ic** [-,ænə'lɪtɪk] or **,psy•cho,an•a'lyt•i•cal,** *adj.*
—**,psy•cho,an•a'lyt•i•cal•ly,** *adv.*

psy•cho•an•a•lyst [,səikou'ænəlɪst] *n.* a person trained in psychoanalysis, especially one whose work it is.

psy•cho•an•a•lyze [,səikou'ænə,laɪz] *v.* See PSYCHOANALYSE.

psy•cho•bab•ble ['səikou,bæbəl] *n.* talk or writing that uses the jargon from psychology or psychiatry in a trite or superficial way.

psy•cho•chem•i•cal [,səɪkou'kɛməkəl] *adj., n.* —*adj.* of chemical compounds, capable of modifying people's behaviour, attitudes, etc.
—*n.* any chemical compound of this nature.

psy•cho•dra•ma ['səikou,dræmə] *or* ['səikou,drɑmə] *n. Psychiatry.* a type of group therapy, pioneered by Jacob Moreno in the 1930s and 1940s, in which participants improvise roles in a dramatization of emotionally charged situations.

psy•cho•dy•nam•ics [,səikoudaɪ'næmɪks] *n. Psychology.*

1 any clinical approach to personality that focusses on the dynamic interplay between conscious and unconscious motivation. 2 the total of motivational forces that affect human behaviour.

psy•cho•gen•ic [ˌsəikouˈdʒɛnɪk] *adj. Psychology.* originating in the mind or in a mental disorder: *a psychogenic disability.*

psy•cho•ki•ne•sis [ˌsəikoukɪˈnisɪs] *or* [ˌsəikoukaɪˈnisɪs] *n.* the control of the movement of physical objects by the force of the mind alone, without the use of any known physical energy.

psy•cho•lin•guis•tics [ˌsəikoulɪŋˈgwɪstɪks] *n.* (*used with a singular verb*) the branch of linguistics that deals with the interplay of mind and language, in both production and perception, and its effects on cognitive and social behaviours.

psy•cho•log•i•cal [ˌsəikəˈlɒdʒɪkəl] *adj.* **1** of the mind. **2** of or having to do with psychology or psychologists. **—ˌpsy•choˈlog•i•cal•ly,** *adv.*

psychological moment **1** the time psychologically most appropriate to achieve a desired end. **2** the critical moment.

psychological warfare systematic efforts to affect morale, loyalty, etc., especially of large national groups.

psy•chol•o•gist [səiˈkɒlədʒɪst] *n.* a person trained in psychology, especially one whose work it is.

psy•chol•o•gy [səiˈkɒlədʒi] *n., pl.* **-gies. 1** the study of the mind and the ways of thought. Psychology tries to explain why people act, think, and feel as they do. **2** a textbook or handbook of psychology. **3** the mental states and processes of a person or persons; mental nature and behaviour: *Mrs. Chang knew her husband's psychology.* ⟨< NL *psychologia* < Gk. *psychē* soul, mind + *-logos* treating of⟩ **—psyˈchol•oˌgize,** *v.*

psy•cho•met•ric [ˌsəikəˈmɛtrɪk] *adj.* of or having to do with psychometrics or psychometry. **—ˌpsy•choˈmet•ri•cal•ly,** *adv.*

psy•cho•me•tri•cian [ˌsəikəməˈtrɪʃən] *or* [səiˌkɒməˈtrɪʃən] *n.* psychometrist.

psy•cho•met•rics [ˌsəikouˈmɛtrɪks] *n.* (*used with a singular verb*) **1** the branch of psychology dealing with psychological testing and measurement. **2** the technique of making such tests or measurements, using statistical and mathematical formulae and methods.

psy•chom•e•trist [səiˈkɒməˌtrɪst] *n.* **1** a person trained in psychometrics, especially one whose work it is. **2** a person who engages in psychometry.

psy•chom•e•try [səiˈkɒmətri] *n.* **1** the psychic deduction of facts about the history of an object or about its owner by touching or being near the object. **2** psychometrics.

psy•cho•mo•tor [ˌsəikouˈmoutər] *adj.* of or having to do with muscular activity resulting from mental processes.

psy•cho•neu•ro•sis [ˌsəikounjʊˈrousɪs] *or* [ˌsəikounʊˈrousɪs] *n.* **-ses** [-siz]. neurosis. **—ˌpsy•cho•neuˈrot•ic** [-ˈrɒtɪk], *adj.*

psy•cho•path [ˈsəikəˌpæθ] *n.* one who has a particular mental illness usually characterized by amoral and antisocial behaviour.

psy•cho•path•ic [ˌsəikəˈpæθɪk] *adj.* **1** of or having to do with mental disorders manifesting themselves as abnormal and antisocial behaviour. **2** having such a mental disorder. **—ˌpsy•choˈpath•i•cal•ly,** *adv.*

psy•cho•path•o•log•i•cal [ˌsəikəˌpæθəˈlɒdʒɪkəl] *adj.* of or having to do with psychopathology.

psy•cho•pa•thol•o•gy [ˌsəikoupəˈθɒlədʒi] *n.* the science dealing with mental and behavioural disorders, including abnormal psychology and psychiatry.

psy•chop•a•thy [səiˈkɒpəθi] *n., pl.* **-thies. 1** mental disorder. **2** mental eccentricity or instability so extreme as to border on mental illness.

psy•cho•phys•i•ol•o•gy [ˌsəikouˌfɪziˈɒlədʒi] *n.* the branch of physiology that deals with the relationship between mental and physical processes.

psy•cho•ses [səiˈkousiz] *n.* pl. of PSYCHOSIS.

psy•cho•sis [səiˈkousɪs] *n., pl.* **-ses** [-siz]. any severe form of mental disturbance or disease, which may or may not have an organic basis. ⟨< NL < Gk. *psychosis* < *psychē* soul, mind⟩

psy•cho•so•mat•ic [ˌsəikousəˈmætɪk] *adj., n. —adj.* **1** of or having to do with both mind and body. **2** of or having to do with physical disorders caused by mental or emotional disturbances. *—n.* a person having symptoms of a psychosomatic disorder. **—ˌpsy•cho•soˈmat•i•cal•ly,** *adv.*

psychosomatic medicine the branch of medicine that deals with the interrelationships between physical disorders and mental or emotional disturbances.

psy•cho•sur•ge•ry [ˌsəikouˈsɜrdʒəri] *n.* brain surgery used to treat chronic mental disorders.

psy•cho•the•ra•peu•tics [ˌsəikouˌθɛrəˈpjutɪks] *n.* psychotherapy.

psy•cho•ther•a•pist [ˌsəikouˈθɛrəpɪst] *n.* a person trained in psychotherapy, especially one whose work it is.

psy•cho•ther•a•py [ˌsəikouˈθɛrəpi] *n.* the science or method of treating mental or physical disorders by psychological techniques.

psy•chot•ic [səiˈkɒtɪk] *adj., n. —adj.* of, having to do with, or affected with psychosis; unstable or mentally ill. *—n.* an unstable or mentally ill person.

psy•cho•tox•ic [ˌsəikouˈtɒksɪk] *adj.* referring to drugs or chemical substances such as alcohol that are capable of damaging the brain.

psy•cho•trop•ic [ˌsəikouˈtrɒpɪk] *or* [ˌsəikouˈtroupɪk] *adj.* of a drug, capable of acting on the mind. Tranquillizers and hallucinogens are psychotropic drugs.

psy•chrom•e•ter [səiˈkrɒmətər] *n.* a type of hygrometer having dry-bulb and wet-bulb thermometers, used for measuring humidity. ⟨< Gk. *psychros* cold + E *-meter*⟩ **—ˌpsy•chroˈmet•ric** [ˌsəɪkrəˈmɛtrɪk] or **ˌpsy•chroˈmet•ri•cal,** *adj.*

psyl•la [ˈsɪlə] *n.* any insect of a family (Psyllidae) of homopterous plant pests. ⟨< NL < Gk., flea⟩

psyl•li•um [ˈsɪliəm] *n.* **1** fleawort. **2** the seeds of this plant, used as a laxative. ⟨< NL < Gk. < *psylla* flea⟩

pt. **1** pint. **2** part. **3** point. **4** PAST TENSE. **5** preterite. **6** port.

Pt platinum.

P.T. PHYSICAL TRAINING.

PTA or **P.T.A.** PARENT-TEACHER ASSOCIATION.

Ptah [ptɑ] *or* [ptɑx] *n. Egyptian mythology.* the universal creator; the chief god, worshipped especially at Memphis.

ptar•mi•gan [ˈtɑrməgən] *n., pl.* **-gans** or (*esp. collectively*) **-gan.** any of several species of arctic and alpine grouse (genus *Lagopus*) having feathered feet and plumage that is mainly white in winter and mainly brown and grey in summer. ⟨< Scots Gaelic *tarmachan, p* added by mistaken analogy with Gk. *pteron* feather⟩

PT boat *U.S.* a small, fast motorboat that carries torpedoes, depth bombs, etc. ⟨< *Patrol Torpedo boat*⟩

Pte. or **Pte** *Military.* private.

pter•i•do•phyte [təˈrɪdəˌfəit] *n.* any of a major group of flowerless plants that have vascular tissue and reproduce by spores, including ferns, club mosses, and horsetails. In some classifications, these plants constitute the division Pteridophyta, but most authorities now classify them together with the flowering plants in the division Tracheophyta. See TRACHEOPHYTE. ⟨< Gk. *pteris, pteridos* fern + E *-phyte*⟩

ptero– *combining form.* wing; feather: *pterodactyl.*

A pterodactyl of 200 to 65 million years ago: wingspan up to 12 m

pter•o•dac•tyl [ˌtɛrəˈdæktəl] *n.* any of an order (Pterosauria) of extinct flying reptiles that lived during the Jurassic and Cretaceous periods, having membranous wings resembling those of a bat. ⟨< Gk. *pteron* wing + *daktylos* finger, toe⟩

pter•o•pod [ˈtɛrəˌpɒd] *n.* SEA BUTTERFLY.

pter•o•saur [ˈtɛrəˌsɔr] *n.* pterodactyl.

–pterous *suffix.* having —— (number of) wings: *dipterous = having two wings.* ⟨< Gk. *-pteros, pterón* wing⟩

P.T.O. or **p.t.o.** please turn (the page) over.

Ptol•e•ma•ic [ˌtɒləˈmeiɪk] *adj.* **1** of or having to do with Claudius Ptolemy, a Greek mathematician, astronomer, and geographer, who lived in the 2nd century A.D. The **Ptolemaic system** of astronomy taught that the earth was the fixed centre of the universe, around which the heavenly bodies moved. **2** of

or having to do with the Ptolemies. See PTOLEMY.
–,Ptol•e'ma•ist, *n.*

Ptol•e•my ['tɒləmi] *n., pl.* **-mies.** any of a certain family of Egyptian rulers who ruled Egypt from 323 to 30 B.C.

pto•maine or **pto•main** ['toumein] *or* [tou'mein] *n.* any of several chemical compounds produced by the decomposition of protein. Food poisoning is caused not by ptomaines, as formerly believed, but by bacteria or other sources of infection. ⟨< Ital. *ptomaina* < Gk. *ptōma* corpse⟩

ptomaine poisoning food poisoning caused by bacteria or poisons found in decaying food.

pto•sis ['tousɪs] *n. Pathology.* a drooping or prolapse of any organ, especially the upper eyelid. ⟨< Gk, a falling⟩ **–'ptot•ic** ['tɒtɪk], *adj.*

pty•a•lin ['taɪəlɪn] *n. Biochemistry.* an enzyme contained in the saliva of humans and of certain other animals that converts starch into dextrin and maltose, thus aiding digestion. ⟨< Gk. *ptyalon* saliva < *ptyein* spit⟩

pty•al•ism ['taɪə,lɪzəm] *n. Pathology.* excessive secretion of saliva.

Pu plutonium.

pub [pʌb] *n., v.* **pubbed, pub•bing.** *Informal.* –*n.* a beer parlour or tavern, especially one where food is served.
–*v.* visit or drink in a pub or pubs: *We went pubbing last night.* ⟨short for *public house*⟩

pu•ber•ty ['pjubərti] *n.* the physical beginning of manhood and womanhood; the stage in human development when the body becomes capable of sexual reproduction, and develops secondary sexual characteristics, usually at the age of about 14 in males and 12 in females. ⟨< L *pubertas* < *pubes* adult⟩

pu•bes[1] ['pjubiz] *n., pl.* **pu•bes.** *Anatomy.* **1** the area of the lower abdomen between the right and left iliac regions. **2** the hair that appears on the human body at puberty, especially that surrounding the external genitalia. ⟨< L⟩

pu•bes[2] ['pjubiz] *n.pl.* of PUBIS.

pu•bes•cent [pju'bɛsənt] *adj.* **1** arriving or arrived at puberty. **2** *Botany. Zoology.* covered with down or fine, short hair: *a pubescent stem or leaf.* ⟨< L *pubescens, -entis* reaching puberty < *pubes* adult⟩ **–pu'bes•cence,** *n.*

pu•bic ['pjubɪk] *adj.* having to do with the pubes or the pubis.

pu•bis ['pjubɪs] *n., pl.* **-bes** [-biz]. *Anatomy.* the lower, front portion of the hipbone. See PELVIS for picture. ⟨< NL *os pubis* bone of the groin⟩

publ. publisher; published.

pub•lic ['pʌblɪk] *adj., n.* –*adj.* **1** of, belonging to, or concerning the people as a whole: *public affairs.* **2** done, made, acting, etc. for the people as a whole: *public relief.* **3** open to all the people; serving all the people, especially when supported by government funds: *a public park.* **4** of or engaged in the affairs or service of the people: *a public official.* **5** known to many or all; not private: *The fact became public.*
go public, a issue shares for sale to the public, thus becoming a PUBLIC COMPANY. **b** reveal previously private or concealed information to the public.
–*n.* **a the public,** the people in general; all the people: *The public is not likely to accept more restraints.* **b** a particular group of people sharing an interest, etc.: *the reading public. A popular actor has a large public.*
in public, not in private or secretly; publicly; openly. ⟨< L *publicus,* ult. < *populus* the people; form influenced by *pubes* adult⟩

public address system an arrangement of loudspeakers used to carry speeches, messages, music, etc. to an audience in a large room, in different rooms of one building, or in the open air. *Abbrev.:* P.A. system.

pub•li•can ['pʌbləkən] *n.* **1** *Brit. Informal.* a keeper of a PUBLIC HOUSE. **2** in ancient Rome, a tax collector. ⟨< L *publicanus* < *publicum* public revenue, originally neut. of *publicus.* See PUBLIC.⟩

pub•li•ca•tion [,pʌblə'keiʃən] *n.* **1** a book, newspaper, or magazine; anything that is published. **2** the printing and selling of books, newspapers, magazines, etc. **3** the act of making known; the fact or state of being made known. ⟨< L *publicatio, -onis,* ult. < *publicus.* See PUBLIC.⟩

public company a company owned by shareholders whose shares can be freely traded on the Stock Exchange.

public defender *Esp. U.S.* a lawyer employed at the public expense to defend indigents accused of crime.

public domain **1** *Law.* of works, material, etc., never copyrighted or having an expired copyright. **2** lands belonging to the government.
in the public domain, of works, material, etc., available for unrestricted use because unprotected by copyright or patent: *Gilbert and Sullivan's operas are now in the public domain.*

public enemy a person who is a danger or menace to the public, usually a wanted criminal.

public funds money provided by the government.

public health a concern of government at all levels that deals with health issues that affect many people.

public house **1** *Brit.* a place where alcoholic liquor and often meals are sold to be consumed on the premises; saloon; tavern. **2** an inn; hotel.

pub•li•cist ['pʌbləsɪst] *n.* **1** a public relations expert or press agent. **2** a person skilled or trained in public law or in public affairs. **3** a writer on law, politics, or public affairs.

pub•lic•i•ty [pʌ'blɪsəti] *n.* **1** the act of bringing or the fact of being brought to public notice by special effort, through newspapers, signs, radio, TV, etc.: *the recent publicity about environmental concerns, a campaign of publicity for a new automobile.* **2** public notice: *the publicity that actors desire.* **3** the state of being public; being seen by or known to everybody: *in the publicity of the street.* **4** the business or industry of creating and distributing promotional material.

pub•li•cize ['pʌblə,saɪz] *v.* **-cized, -ciz•ing.** give publicity to.

public lending right an Act of Parliament that directs compensation in the form of royalties to an author whose books are borrowed from lending libraries.

pub•lic•ly ['pʌblɪkli] *adv.* **1** in a public manner; openly. **2** by the public.

public opinion the collective opinion of the people in a country, community, etc. on some issue, problem, etc.

public relations **1** the relations of an organization, institution, etc. with the public. **2** the activities an organization, institution, etc. undertakes to create and keep up a favourable public image of itself. *Abbrev.:* P.R. or PR **3** the art, business, or profession of promoting such an image.

public school **1 a** in Canada and the United States, a tax-supported school, especially an elementary school. **b** the building in which such a school is held. **2** in the United Kingdom, an endowed private boarding school.

public servant a member of the PUBLIC SERVICE (def. 1).

public service **1** CIVIL SERVICE; the body of employees of any level of government: *Public school teachers are in the public service.* **2** the business of supplying a service or commodity to a community, especially one subsidized by public funds or administered by public servants: *Bus service is a public service in most cities.* **3** a service given for the benefit of the community: *That church runs a drop-in centre as a public service.* **4** (*adjl.*) **public-service,** of or being a public service: *a public-service announcement.*

pub•lic-spir•it•ed ['pʌblɪk 'spirətɪd] *adj.* having or showing an unselfish desire for the public good.

public utility a company formed or chartered to render services to the public, such as a company furnishing electricity or gas, a railway, a streetcar or bus line, etc.

public works things built by the government at public expense and for public use, such as roads, docks, canals, and waterworks.

pub•lish ['pʌblɪʃ] *v.* **1** prepare, print, and offer (a book, paper, map, piece of music, etc.) for sale or distribution. **2** publish the work of: *Some Canadian writers are published abroad before being published in Canada.* **3** come into circulation; be published: *The newspapers here publish every weekday.* **4** make publicly or generally known: *Don't publish the faults of your friends.* **5** be the author of published books or articles: *In some universities, professors must publish every year to gain tenure.* ⟨ME < OF *publier,* ult. < L *publicus* (see PUBLIC); modelled after *punish,* etc.⟩ **–'pub•lish•a•ble,** *adj.*

pub•lish•er ['pʌblɪʃər] *n.* a person or company whose business is to publish books, newspapers, magazines, etc.

PUC or **P.U.C.** Public Utilities Commission.

puce [pjus] *n. or adj.* a brownish or dark purple. ⟨< F *puce* a flea < OF *pulce* < L *pulex, -licis*⟩

puck[1] [pʌk] *n.* **1** a mischievous spirit; goblin. **2** **Puck,** in

English folklore, a mischievous fairy who appears in Shakespeare's play *A Midsummer Night's Dream.* ⟨OE *pūca* goblin⟩

puck[2] [pʌk] *n.* a hard, black rubber disk used in hockey. ⟨< E dial. var. of *poke[1]*⟩

puck•a ['pʌkə] *adj.* See PUKKA.

puck–car•ri•er ['pʌk ,kæriər] *or* [,kɛriər] *n. Hockey.* the player in possession of the puck during play.

puck•chas•er ['pʌk,tʃeisər] *n. Slang.* a hockey player. Also, **puckpusher** and **puckster.**

puck•er ['pʌkər] *v., n.* —*v.* draw into wrinkles or irregular folds: *to pucker one's brow, to pucker cloth in sewing. The baby's lips puckered just before he began to cry.*
—*n.* an irregular fold; wrinkle: *There are puckers at the shoulders of this ill-fitting coat.* ⟨apparently < *poke[2]*⟩

puck•ish ['pʌkɪʃ] *adv.* mischievous; impish. —**'puck•ish•ly,** *adv.* —**'puck•ish•ness,** *n.*

puck sense *Hockey.* an intuitive ability to play hockey.

puck shy *Hockey.* of a goalie, afraid of being hit by the puck.

pud•ding ['pʊdɪŋ] *n.* **1** a soft dessert food, often having a milk base, and flavoured and sweetened: *rice pudding.* **2** a cakelike dessert, usually steamed or baked: *plum pudding.* **3** a kind of sausage, especially **blood pudding. 4** anything soft like a pudding. **5** *Brit.* dessert. ⟨Cf. F *boudin* stuffed sausage, ult. < L *botulus* sausage; cf. also OE *puduc* wart⟩

pud•dle ['pʌdəl] *n., v.* **-dled, -dling.** —*n.* **1** a small pool of standing water, especially dirty water. **2** a small pool of any liquid. **3** wet clay and sand stirred into a paste.
—*v.* **1** make wet or muddy. **2** mix up (wet clay and sand) into a thick paste. **3** use a waterproof mixture of wet clay and sand to stop water from running through: *Puddle up that hole.* **4** wade in shallow, dirty water. **5** *Metallurgy.* stir (melted iron) with an oxidizing agent to make wrought iron. ⟨ME *puddel*, dim. of OE *pudd* ditch⟩ —**'pud•dler,** *n.*

pud•dling ['pʌdlɪŋ] *n., v.* —*n. Metallurgy.* the act or process of converting pig iron into wrought iron by stirring the molten metal with an oxidizing agent.
—*v.* ppr. of PUDDLE.

pud•dly ['pʌdli] *adj.* **1** full of puddles. **2** like a puddle.

pu•den•dum [pju'dɛndəm] *n., pl* **-da** [-də]. *Anatomy.* the external genitalia of either sex, but especially those of the female; vulva. ⟨< NL, special use of neut. of *pudendus*, gerundive of *pudere* be ashamed⟩

pudg•y ['pʌdʒi] *adj.* **pudg•i•er, pudg•i•est.** short and fat or thick. ⟨Scots dial.⟩ —**'pudg•i•ly,** *adv.* —**'pudg•i•ness,** *n.*

pueb•lo ['pwɛblou] *or* ['pweiblou] *n., pl.* **-los** (defs. 1 and 2), **-lo** or **los** (def. 3). **1** a communal dwelling of certain Native American peoples of the SW United States, consisting of contiguous, flat-roofed houses of adobe or stone. **2** a Native American village or town in the SW United States. **3 Pueblo,** a member of any of several Native American peoples of the SW United States, who live or lived in pueblos. ⟨< Sp. *pueblo* people < L *populus*⟩

pu•er•ile ['pjʊraɪl] *or* ['pjʊrɪl], ['pjuə,raɪl] *or* ['pjuərɪl] *adj.* foolish for a grown person to say or do; childish. ⟨< L *puerilis* < *puer* boy⟩ —**'pu•er,ile•ly,** *adv.* —**'pu•er,ile•ness,** *n.*

pu•er•il•i•ty [pjʊ'rɪləti] *or* [,pjuə'rɪləti] *n., pl.* **-ties.** **1** childishness; foolishness. **2** a foolish or childish act, idea, or statement.

pu•er•per•al [pju'ɜrpərəl] *adj.* of or having to do with childbirth. ⟨< NL *puerperalis*, ult. < L *puer* child + *parere* bear⟩

puerperal fever a fever affecting women after childbirth, which used to cause many deaths. Modern aseptic practices have reduced its incidence.

Puer•to Ri•can ['pɔrtou'rikən] *or* ['pwɛrtə 'rikən] *n., adj.* —*n.* a native or inhabitant of Puerto Rico.
—*adj.* of or having to do with Puerto Rico or its inhabitants.

Puer•to Ri•co ['pɔrtou 'rikou] *or* ['pwɛrtou 'rikou] a country in the West Indies associated as a commonwealth with the U.S.

puff [pʌf] *v., n.* —*v.* **1** blow with short, quick blasts. **2** breathe quickly and with difficulty. **3** give out puffs; move with puffs: *The engine puffed out of the station.* **4** move or come in puffs: *Smoke puffed out of the chimney.* **5** smoke: *to puff a cigar.* **6 a** swell with fluid or air (*sometimes used with* **up**): *My ankles are puffed up in this heat.* **b** swell with pride or other emotion: *He puffed out his cheeks with anger.* **7** arrange in soft, round masses. **8** praise in exaggerated language: *They puffed her to the skies.*
—*n.* **1** a short, quick blast: *a puff of wind.* **2** a small quantity of air, smoke, etc., blown out in short, quick blasts. **3** a quick, hard breath. **4** the act or process of swelling. **5** a soft, round mass: *a puff of hair.* **6** a small pad for putting powder on the skin, etc. **7** a light pastry filled with whipped cream, jam, etc. **8** extravagant praise. **9** a portion of material gathered and held down at the edges but left full in the middle, as in a sleeve of a dress. **10** a quilted bedcover, usually filled with down, cotton, or wool. ⟨Cf. OE *pyffan*⟩

puff adder 1 a large, very poisonous viper (*Bitis arietans*) of the semi-arid regions of Africa, that gives warning by hissing loudly and inflating its body. **2** a similar snake (*B. inornata*), native to southern Africa.

puff•ball ['pʌf,bɒl] *n.* any of various fungi (order Lycoperdales, especially genera *Calvatia* and *Lycoperdon*) having a ball-shaped fruiting body which, when ripe, will give off a cloud of powdery spores when broken open. Some puffballs are edible when immature.

puffed–up ['pʌft 'ʌp] *adj.* **1** bloated; swollen. **2** conceited; vain. **3** inflated with air.

puff•er ['pʌfər] *n.* **1** a person who or thing that puffs. **2** any of various marine fishes (family Tetraodontidae) mainly of tropical and subtropical seas, having a beaklike snout and a prickly or spiny body which can be inflated with air or water into a globelike shape when the fish is disturbed. **3** *Informal.* a hand-held ventilator for asthmatics.

puf•fer•y ['pʌfəri] *n.* exaggerated praise or publicity. ⟨< *puff*, v. + *-ery.* 18c.⟩

puf•fin ['pʌfən] *n.* any of several northern diving birds of the auk family having a thickset body with the legs set far back on it, a short neck, and a high, laterally compressed bill which in breeding season becomes even larger and brighter, with yellow, red, and blue stripes. ⟨ME *poffin*; ? ult. < L *puff* (from its puffed-up appearance)⟩

puff pastry a very light, flaky, rich pastry used in making eclairs, cream puffs, sausage rolls, etc.

puff•y ['pʌfi] *adj.* **puff•i•er, puff•i•est. 1** puffed out; swollen: *Their eyes are puffy from crying.* **2** puffed up; vain. **3** blowing or breathing in puffs. **4** unhealthily chubby. —**'puff•i•ness,** *n.*

pug[1] [pʌg] *n.* **1** a breed of small, tan-coloured dog having a curly tail and turned-up nose. **2** PUG NOSE. ⟨origin uncertain⟩

pug[2] [pʌg] *n., v.* **pugged, pug•ging.** —*n.* the footprint of a game animal, sometimes called **pug mark.**
—*v.* track (game) by following its footprints. ⟨< Hind. *pag* footprint⟩

pu•gi•lism ['pjudʒə,lɪzəm] *n.* the art of fighting with the fists; boxing. ⟨< L *pugil* boxer⟩ —**'pu•gi•list,** *n.*

pu•gi•lis•tic [,pjudʒə'lɪstɪk] *adj.* of or having to do with pugilism or pugilists. —**,pu•gi•lis'ti•cal•ly,** *adv.*

pug•na•cious [pʌg'neiʃəs] *adj.* having the habit of fighting; fond of fighting; quarrelsome. ⟨< L *pugnax, -acis*, ult. < *pugnus* fist⟩ —**pug'na•cious•ly,** *adv.* —**pug'na•cious•ness,** *n.*

pug•nac•i•ty [pʌg'næsɪti] *n.* a fondness for fighting; quarrelsomeness.

pug nose a short, often thick turned-up nose.
—**'pug-,nosed,** *adj.*

pui•sne ['pjuni] *adj., n.* —*adj.* **1** designating a superior court judge of subordinate rank. The Supreme Court of Canada is composed of a chief justice and eight puisne judges. **2** *Law. Esp. Brit.* subsequent; later: *puisne mortgages.*
—*n.* a puisne judge. ⟨< AF < OF *puisné* born later. 16c. See PUNY.⟩
☛ *Hom.* PUNY.

pu•is•sant ['pwisənt] *or* ['pjuəsənt] *adj. Archaic or poetic.* powerful; mighty; strong. ⟨ME < OF *puissant* being powerful, ult. < var. of L *posse* be able⟩ —**'pu•is•sant•ly,** *adv.*
—**'pu•is•sance,** *n.*

pu•ka ['pukə] *n.* a small white shell found in Hawaii on the beach, and strung together to make necklaces.

puke [pjuk] *n., v. Slang.* vomit.

puk•ka ['pʌkə] *adj. Anglo-Indian.* **1** reliable; good: *We got a really pukka blender to replace the old one that overheated.* **2** solid; substantial. **3** permanent. Also, **pucka.** ⟨< Hind. *pakka* cooked, ripe⟩

pul [pul] *n.* a unit of money in Afghanistan, equal to 1/100 of an afghani. See table of money in the Appendix. ⟨< Persian⟩

pu•la ['pulɑ] *n.* a unit of money in Botswana, equal to 100 thebe. See table of money in the Appendix.

pul•chri•tude ['pʌlkrɪ,tjud] *or* ['pʌlkrɪ,tud] *n.* beauty. ⟨ME < L *pulchritudo* < *pulcher* beautiful⟩ **—,pul•chri'tu•di•nous,** *adj.*

pule [pjul] *v.* **puled, pul•ing.** cry in a thin voice, as a sick child does; whimper or whine. ⟨? imitative⟩

pu•li ['puli] *n., pl.* **pu•lis** or **pu•lik** ['pulik]. a breed of medium-sized Hungarian sheepdog with long, fine hair that often mats into cords, typically dull black, though any solid colour is acceptable.

Pu•lit•zer Prize ['pʊlɪtzər] *or* ['pjulɪtsər] in the United States, any one of various prizes given each year for the best American drama, novel, biography, history, book of verse, editorial, music, and cartoon. They were established by Joseph Pulitzer (1847-1911), an American journalist, and first awarded in 1917.

pull [pʊl] *v., n.* —*v.* **1** move (something) by grasping it and drawing toward oneself: *to pull a trigger. Pull the door open; don't push it.* **2** take hold of and tug: *He pulled at his tie.* **3** extract or pull away from an attachment: *to pull a plant out by its roots, to pull a tooth.* **4** be easily extracted: *This tooth will pull easily.* **5** move, usually with effort or force: *I pulled ahead of the others in the race. The car pulled out into traffic.* **6** pick; pluck: *to pull flowers.* **7** tear; rip: *The baby pulled the toy to pieces.* **8** stretch too far; strain: *The football player pulled a ligament in his leg.* **9** row: *Pull for the shore.* **10** be provided or rowed with: *The boat pulls eight oars.* **11** drink. **12** suck: *to pull at a cigar.* **13** *Informal.* indulge in; do; commit: *Don't pull any tricks. She pulled an armed robbery.* **14** *Golf.* hit (a ball) so that, in the case of a right-handed player, it curves to the left, and for a left-handed golfer, to the right. **15** *Printing.* take or make (an impression or proof).

pull apart, a separate into pieces by pulling. **b** be severely critical of: *to pull apart a term paper.*

pull down, *Informal.* receive as a salary: *She pulls down at least $80 000 in that job.*

pull for, *Informal.* give help, support, or encouragement to: *to pull for the underdog.*

pull in, a restrain; check. **b** *Informal.* arrest: *He was pulled in for speeding.* **c** arrive: *They pulled in this morning.* **d** stop: *Let's pull in at the next doughnut shop we see.*

pull off, *Informal.* do successfully: *They pulled off the merger in record time.*

pull (one's) **punches,** hold back, especially to keep from winning in a fight or other contest or conflict.

pull (oneself) **together,** gather one's faculties, energy, etc.: *I have to pull myself together if I want to get this job done on time.*

pull out (of), a withdraw from (a venture, undertaking, etc.) **b** leave: *The train pulled out of the station.*

pull over, steer or cause to steer a vehicle toward the curb and stop: *The police pulled me over because one tail-light was out.*

pull through, get through a difficult or dangerous situation.

pull together, work in harmony; get on together.

pull up, a tear up; uproot. **b** remove utterly. **c** bring or come to a halt; stop. **d** rebuke: *The professor pulled the disrespectful student up sharply.*

—*n.* **1** the act or effort of pulling. **2** a difficult climb, journey, or other effort: *It was a hard pull to get up the hill.* **3** handle, rope, ring, or other thing to pull by: *a curtain pull.* **4** a drink. **5** a suck: *a pull at a cigar.* **6** a force that attracts: *magnetic pull.* **7** *Golf.* a pulling of the ball to the left or right. **8** *Informal.* influence; advantage. **9** *Printing.* an impression or proof. ⟨OE *pullian*⟩ **—'pull•er,** *n.*

☛ *Syn. v.* **1. Pull,** TUG, JERK[1] = draw toward oneself. **Pull** = draw (or try to draw) toward or after oneself or in a particular stated or implied direction: *Pull the curtains across.* **Tug** = pull hard and, often, long, but not necessarily successfully: *The dog tugged at the tablecloth.* **Jerk** = pull, push, or twist quickly and suddenly: *She jerked her hand away. He jerked his hat off.*

pul•let ['pʊlɪt] *n.* a young hen, usually less than a year old. ⟨ME < OF *poulette,* dim. of *poule* hen < VL *pulla,* fem. of L *pullus* young animal or bird⟩

pul•ley ['pʊli] *n., pl.* **-leys. 1** a wheel with a grooved rim in which a rope, belt, or wire can run, making it possible to change the direction of the pull. **2** a set of such wheels used to increase the power applied. **3** a wheel used to transfer power by driving a belt that moves some other part of the machine. See GENERATOR for picture. ⟨ME < OF *poulie,* ult. < Gk. *polos* axle⟩

Pullman car ['pʊlmən] **1** a railway car with berths or small rooms for passengers to sleep in. **2** a railway car with especially comfortable seats. Also, **Pullman.** ⟨after George M. *Pullman* (1831-1897), an American inventor⟩

pull•o•ver ['pʊl,ouvər] *n., adj.* —*n.* a sweater put on by pulling it over the head.
—*adj.* referring to any upper garment put on in this manner: *pullover top, a pullover dress.*

pul•lu•late ['pʌljə,leit] *v.* **-lat•ed, -lat•ing. 1** of seeds or shoots, sprout or bud. **2** breed rapidly or profusely. **3** teem; swarm. ⟨< L *pullulare* to sprout < *pollulus,* dim. of *pullus* young animal or bird. 17c.⟩ **—,pul•lu'la•tion,** *n.*

pul•mo•nar•y ['pʌlmə,nɛri] *or* ['pʊlmə,nɛri] *adj.* **1** of or having to do with the lungs. Tuberculosis and pneumonia are pulmonary diseases. **2** having lungs. ⟨< L *pulmonarius* < *pulmo* lung⟩

pul•mon•ic [pʌl'mɒnɪk] *or* [pʊl'mɒnɪk] *adj.* pulmonary.

Pul•mo•tor ['pʌl,moutər] *or* ['pʊl,moutər] *n. Trademark.* a device used to restore natural breathing in persons rescued from suffocation or drowning. ⟨< L *pulmo* lung + E *motor*⟩

pulp [pʌlp] *n., v.* —*n.* **1** the soft part of any fruit or vegetable, especially after the juice or oil has been pressed out of it. **2** of a tooth, the soft inner part containing blood vessels and nerves. **3** a soft, moist mixture of ground-up wood, rags, or other material, from which paper is made. **4** any soft, wet mass. **5** poorly-written published material, printed usually on rough, cheap paper and often containing sensational stories or articles. **6** (*adjl.*) designating such material: *pulp fiction.*
—*v.* **1** reduce to pulp. **2** be reduced to pulp: *The wet newspaper pulped when we picked it up.* **3** remove pulp from. ⟨< L *pulpa*⟩ **—'pulp•less,** *adj.* **—'pulp,like,** *adj.*

pul•pit ['pʊlpɪt] *or* ['pʌlpɪt] *n.* **1** a platform or raised structure in a church from which the minister preaches. **2** members of the clergy as a group, or their sermons. ⟨ME < LL *pulpitum* < L *pulpitum* scaffold, platform⟩

pulp mill a mill producing pulp for paper.

pulp•wood ['pʌlp,wʊd] *n.* **1** wood reduced to pulp for making paper. **2** any soft wood suitable for making paper.

pulp•y ['pʌlpi] *adj.* **pulp•i•er, pulp•i•est.** of pulp; like pulp; soft. **—'pulp•i•ness,** *n.* **—'pulp•i•ly,** *adv.*

pul•sar ['pʌlsɑr] *n.* a body or mass of energy in space that emits regular, rapid, pulsating radio waves. ⟨< *pulse* + *-ar,* as in *quasar*⟩

pul•sate ['pʌlseit] *v.* **-sat•ed, -sat•ing. 1** beat; throb: *The patient's heart was pulsating rapidly.* **2** vibrate; quiver. ⟨< L *pulsare,* frequentative of *pellere* beat. Doublet of PUSH.⟩

pul•sa•tion [pʌl'seiʃən] *n.* **1** the action of beating or vibrating. **2** a single beat or vibration.

pulse[1] [pʌls] *n., v.* **pulsed, puls•ing.** —*n.* **1** the beating of the arteries caused by the rush of blood into them after each contraction of the heart. **2** the rate of this beating. **3** any series of regular, measured beats, waves, or vibrations: *the pulse in music, the pulse of an engine.* **4** one of the beats, waves, etc. in such a series. **5** *Physics, Electricity.* **a** a sudden, brief increase in the magnitude of a physical quantity, such as voltage or current, whose value is usually constant. **b** one of a series of such brief changes occurring at regular intervals and having a characteristic geometric shape when plotted on a graph. **c** (*adjl.*) of or having to do with a pulse: *pulse modulation, a pulse generator.* **6** feeling; sentiment: *the pulse of the nation.*
—*v.* **1** beat, throb, or vibrate: *a heart pulsing with excitement.* **2** cause (something) to pulsate. **3** *Electricity.* apply pulses to. **4** *Radio.* use pulses to modify (an electromagnetic wave). ⟨< L *pulsus* < *pellere* beat⟩

pulse[2] [pʌls] *n.* **1** the edible seeds of certain leguminous plants, such as peas, beans, lentils, etc. **2** a plant that produces such seeds. ⟨ME < OF < L *puls* porridge⟩

pulse•jet ['pʌls,dʒɛt] *n.* a type of jet engine into which the air necessary for the burning of the fuel is admitted in pulses by valves.

pul•sim•e•ter [pʌl'sɪmɪtər] *n. Medicine.* an instrument for measuring the rate and strength of the pulse.

pul•som•e•ter [pʌl'sɒmətər] *n.* **1** pulsimeter. **2** a pump without pistons, using the partial vacuum and sucking effect caused by condensing steam to raise water.

pul•ver•a•ble ['pʌlvərəbəl] *adj.* pulverizable.

pul•ver•i•za•ble ['pʌlvə,raɪzəbəl] *adj.* that can be pulverized.

pul•ver•ize ['pʌlvə,raɪz] *v.* **-ized, -iz•ing. 1** grind to powder or dust. **2** become dust. **3** break to pieces; demolish. ⟨< LL *pulverizare* < L *pulvis, -veris* dust⟩ **—,pul•ver•i'za•tion,** *n.* **—'pul•ver,iz•er,** *n.*

pu•ma ['pjumə] *n.* cougar. ⟨< Sp. < Quechua⟩

pum•ice ['pʌmɪs] *n., v.* **-iced, -ic•ing.** —*n.* Often, **pumice stone,** a light, spongy stone thrown up from volcanoes, used for cleaning, smoothing, and polishing.
—*v.* clean, smooth, or polish with pumice. ⟨ME < OF < L *pumex, -micis.* Doublet of POUNCE².⟩
☛ *Hom.* POMACE.

pum•mel ['pʌməl] *v.* **-melled** or **-meled, -mell•ing** or **-mel•ing.** beat; beat with the fists. Also, **pommel.**
☛ *Hom.* POMMEL ['pʌməl].

pump¹ [pʌmp] *n., v.* —*n.* **1** an apparatus or machine for forcing liquids or gases into or out of things. **2** *Informal.* the heart.
—*v.* **1** move (liquids, air, etc.) by a pump. **2** force air into by blowing or suctioning. **3** remove water, etc. (from) with a pump. **4** work a pump. **5** work as a pump does. **6** move up and down like a pump handle. **7** apply force (to) with an up and down motion. **8** *Physics.* inject or transfer energy into. **9** draw, force, supply, etc., as if by a pump. **10** *Informal.* get information out of; try to get information out of: *Don't let him pump you.*
pump iron, *Informal.* lift weights; do weightlifting exercises.
pump up, a inflate. **b** increase or strengthen; intensify; put more effort into. *The party decided that it needed to pump up its campaign.* **c** rouse to enthusiasm: *to pump up a team.* ⟨< F *pompe,* ? < Gmc.⟩ —**'pump•er,** *n.*

pump² [pʌmp] *n.* a low-cut shoe with no laces, straps, or other fastenings. See SHOE for picture. ⟨origin uncertain⟩

pumped [pʌmpt] *adj., v.* —*adj. Informal.* excited; enthusiastic.
—*v.* pt. and pp. of PUMP¹.

pump•er ['pʌmpər] *n.* a firetruck equipped with hoses and a water tank to pump water at the site of a fire.

pum•per•nick•el ['pʌmpər,nɪkəl] *n.* a heavy, dark, slightly sour bread made from unsifted rye flour. ⟨< G⟩

pump•kin ['pʌmpkɪn] *n.* **1** the edible fruit of any of certain trailing varieties of two plants (*Cucurbita pepo* and *C. moschata*) of the gourd family, usually very large and round or oblong in shape, with a smooth, orange or yellowish rind and golden flesh that is used as a vegetable and for pies, etc. **2** a vine that produces such fruits. ⟨alteration (with substitution of *-kin*) of earlier *pumpion* < MF *pompon* < L < Gk. *pepōn*⟩

pump•kin•seed ['pʌmpkɪn,sid] *n.* **1** the seed of a pumpkin. **2** a common North American freshwater sunfish (*Lepomis gibbosus*) having a golden brown to olive back and sides and a bronze to red-orange belly, with sides marked with blue, green, red, and orange spots and lines.

pun [pʌn] *n., v.* **punned, pun•ning.** —*n.* a humorous use of a word in which it can be taken as having two or more different meanings; a play on words. *Example*: *One berry to another: "If you hadn't been so* fresh, *we wouldn't be in this* jam.*"*
—*v.* make puns. ⟨? < first syllable of Ital. *puntiglio* verbal quibble⟩ —**'pun•ner,** *n.*

punch¹ [pʌntʃ] *v., n.* —*v.* **1** hit with the fist: *They punched each other like boxers.* **2** *Informal.* deliver with force or effectiveness. **3** *Esp. Western Canada and U.S.* herd or drive (cattle) while on horseback; work as a cowboy.
punch in, a record one's time of arrival by means of a time clock. **b** *Computer technology.* enter (data) into a computer.
punch out, a record one's time of departure by punching a time clock. **b** *Computer technology.* extract (data) from a computer.
punch up, *Computer technology.* use a keyboard to bring up (information) on a computer.
—*n.* **1** a quick thrust or blow. **2** *Informal.* vigorous force or effectiveness: *This story lacks punch.*
beat to the punch, be quicker than (someone) in doing something. ⟨? var. of *pounce¹*⟩ —**'punch•er,** *n.*

punch² [pʌntʃ] *n., v.* —*n.* **1** a tool for making holes. **2** a tool or apparatus for piercing, perforating, or stamping materials, impressing a design, forcing nails beneath a surface, driving bolts out of holes, etc.
—*v.* **1** make (a hole) with a punch or any pointed instrument. **2** pierce, cut, stamp, force, or drive with a punch: *The train conductor punched our tickets.* ⟨short for *puncheon¹*⟩
—**'punch•er,** *n.*

punch³ [pʌntʃ] *n.* a drink made of two or more liquids mixed together. ⟨probably < Hind. *panc* five (< Skt. *pañca*), from the number of ingredients in the drink⟩

Punch [pʌntʃ] *n.* a hooknosed, humpbacked doll, the main character in the puppet show *Punch and Judy.*
pleased as Punch, very much pleased. ⟨shortened form of *punchinello*⟩

Punch–and–Ju•dy show ['pʌntʃ ən 'dʒudi] a puppet show in which Punch quarrels violently with his wife Judy.

punch–drunk ['pʌntʃ ,drʌŋk] *adj.* **1** suffering from slight brain damage as a result of repeated blows to the head received in boxing. **2** *Informal.* behaving as if punch-drunk; appearing bewildered or dazed.

punched card a card on which information is recorded by means of holes punched according to a code, for use in processing data by machine, electronic computer, etc. Also called **punch card.**

pun•cheon¹ ['pʌntʃən] *n.* **1** a slab of timber, or a piece of a split log, with the face somewhat smoothed. **2** a short, upright piece of wood in the frame of a building. **3** a punching or stamping tool used by goldsmiths, etc. ⟨ME < OF *poinchon, ponson,* ult. < L *pungere* pierce⟩

pun•cheon² ['pʌntʃən] *n.* **1** a large cask for liquor. **2** the amount that it holds. ⟨ME < OF *poinchon*; origin uncertain⟩

pun•chi•nel•lo [,pʌntʃə'nɛlou] *n., pl.* **-los** or **-loes.** Often, **Pun•chi•nel•lo,** a clown; the prototype of Punch. ⟨< dial. Ital. *Pulcinella,* prob. ult. < L *pullus* chick⟩

punching bag a leather bag filled with air or stuffed, and hung up to be punched with the fists for exercise, especially in boxing training.

punch line a telling phrase, sentence, etc. that makes the point of a joke, story, or other narrative.

punch press a power-operated machine in which dies are fitted in order to cut, stamp, or press metal sheets by heavy blows under pressure.

punch–up ['pʌntʃ ,ʌp] *n. Informal.* a fight, especially with the fists, and often between more than two people.

punch•y ['pʌntʃi] *adj.* **punch•i•er, punch•i•est.** *Informal.* **1** forceful or incisive: *punchy talk.* **2** PUNCH-DRUNK.

punc•til•i•o [pʌŋk'tɪli,ou] *n., pl.* **-i•os. 1** a detail of honour, conduct, ceremony, etc. **2** care in attending to such details. ⟨< Ital. < Sp. *puntillo,* ult. < L *punctum* point⟩

punc•til•i•ous [pʌŋk'tɪliəs] *adj.* **1** very careful and exact: *A nurse should be punctilious in obeying the doctor's orders.* **2** paying strict attention to details of conduct and ceremony.
—**punc'til•i•ous•ly,** *adv.* —**punc'til•i•ous•ness,** *n.*
☛ *Syn.* **1.** See note at SCRUPULOUS.

punc•tu•al ['pʌŋktʃuəl] *adj.* **1** prompt; on time: *He is punctual to the minute.* **2** being a point; resembling a point. **3** *Grammar.* of or having to do with a verb or verb aspect expressing an action that occurs at a single point in time and may be repeated, as opposed to one that occurs over a period of time. *Rap, hit,* and *bite* are all punctual verbs. ⟨< Med.L *punctualis* < L *punctus* point⟩ —**'punc•tu•al•ly,** *adv.* —**'punc•tu•al•ness,** *n.* —**,punc•tu'al•i•ty,** *n.*

punc•tu•ate ['pʌŋktʃu,eit] *v.* **-at•ed, -at•ing. 1** use periods, commas, and other marks in writing or printing to help make the meaning clear. **2** put punctuation marks in. **3** interrupt now and then: *The crowd punctuated the politician's speech with boos.* **4** give point or emphasis to. ⟨< Med.L *punctuare* < L *punctus* point⟩

punc•tu•a•tion [,pʌŋktʃu'eiʃən] *n.* **1** the use of periods, commas, and other marks in writing or printing to help make the meaning clear. Punctuation does for writing and printing what pauses and changes in the pitch of voice do for speech. **2** PUNCTUATION MARKS. —**'punc•tu,a•tive,** *adj.*

punctuation marks marks used in writing or printing to help make the meaning of a sentence clear. Periods, commas, question marks, colons, semicolons, apostrophes, quotation marks, and exclamation marks are punctuation marks.

punc•ture ['pʌŋktʃər] *n., v.* **-tured, tur•ing.** —*n.* **1** a hole made by something pointed. **2** the act or process of puncturing. **3 a** a hole in a tire that is leaking air. **b** *Esp. Brit. Informal.* flat tire.
—*v.* **1** make a hole in with something pointed. **2** have or get a puncture: *I punctured the front tire of my bicycle on my way to work this morning.* **3** reduce, spoil, or destroy as if by a puncture. ⟨ME < L *punctura* < *pungere* prick⟩

pun•dit ['pʌndɪt] *n.* **1** a learned person; expert; authority, especially self-proclaimed; often used ironically. **2** a Hindu who is an expert in Sanskrit and in religion or philosophy. ⟨< Hind. < Skt. *pandita* learned⟩ —**'pun•dit•ry,** *n.*

pung [pʌŋ] *n. Maritimes and New England.* formerly, a low, horse-drawn sleigh with a boxlike body. ⟨shortened form of earlier *tom pung* < *tow-pung,* ult. < Algonquian; alteration of *toboggan*⟩

pun•gen•cy ['pʌndʒənsi] *n.* a pungent quality.

pun•gent ['pʌndʒənt] *adj.* **1** sharply affecting the organs of taste and smell: *a pungent pickle, the pungent smell of burning leaves.* **2** sharp; biting: *pungent criticism.* **3** stimulating to the mind; keen; lively: *a pungent wit.* **4** disagreeably sharp to the mind; distressing. **5** *Biology.* sharp-pointed; piercing. ⟨< L *pungens, -entis,* ppr. of *pungere* prick⟩ **—'pun•gent•ly,** *adv.*

Pu•nic ['pjunɪk] *adj.* **1** of or having to do with ancient Carthage or its inhabitants. **2** treacherous; faithless. ⟨< L *Punicus* < *Poenus* Carthaginian (Cf. Gk. *Phoinix*)⟩

pun•ish ['pʌnɪʃ] *v.* **1** cause pain, loss, or discomfort to (a person) because of some fault or offence: *The government punishes criminals.* **2** cause pain, loss, or discomfort for: *The law punishes crimes.* **3** *Informal.* deal with severely or roughly. **4** *Informal.* eat; use up: *The grandchildren certainly punished that last batch of cookies.* ⟨ME < OF *puniss-,* a stem of *punir* < L *punire* < *poena* penalty⟩ **—'pun•ish•er,** *n.*

pun•ish•a•ble ['pʌnɪʃəbəl] *adj.* **1** liable to punishment: *First-degree murder is punishable by life imprisonment.* **2** deserving punishment: *a punishable offence.* **—,pun•ish•a'bil•i•ty,** *n.*

pun•ish•ment ['pʌnɪʃmənt] *n.* **1** a punishing; being punished. **2** pain, suffering, or loss. **3** *Informal.* severe or rough treatment.

pu•ni•tive ['pjunətɪv] *adj.* **1** concerned with punishment. **2** inflicting punishment. **—'pu•ni•tive•ly,** *adv.* **—'pu•ni•tive•ness,** *n.*

pu•ni•to•ry ['pjunə,tɔri] *adj.* punitive.

Pun•ja•bi [pʌn'dʒɑbi] *n., adj.* *—n.* **1** a native or inhabitant of the Punjab. **2** an Indo-European language spoken in the Punjab, derived from Sanskrit. Also, **Panjabi.**
—adj. of or having to do with the Punjab, its people or their language.

punk¹ [pʌŋk] *n.* **1** decayed wood that smoulders when ignited, used as tinder. **2** a preparation that burns very slowly, especially one used to light fireworks. ⟨origin uncertain⟩

punk² [pʌŋk] *n., adj.* *—n.* **1** *Slang.* a young, inexperienced person, especially one regarded as presumptuous, ill-mannered, etc. **2** *Slang.* a hoodlum or petty gangster. **3** PUNK ROCK. **4** a person who follows or performs punk rock. **5** a style associated with punk rock music that is characterized by outrageous and grotesque clothing, make-up, and hairstyles.
—adj. **1** *Slang.* inferior in quality, condition, etc. **2** *Slang.* somewhat unwell: *I was feeling punk all day yesterday.* **3** of or designating punk. ⟨origin uncertain⟩

pun•kah or **pun•ka** ['pʌŋkə] *n.* in India and the East Indies, a fan, especially a large swinging fan hung from the ceiling and kept in motion by a servant or by machinery. ⟨< Hind. *pankha*⟩

punk rock a form of hard-driving, often deliberately offensive ROCK² (*n.* def. 2) music originating in the late 1970s, that expresses anger and discontent.

punk rocker **1** a member of a PUNK ROCK group. **2** a fan or groupie of such a group. **3** a person who dresses and acts like a member or fan of such a group. Also, **punker.**

pun•net ['pʌnət] *n. Esp. Brit.* a small, square basket, now often made of woven plastic, usually used to contain small fruits and vegetables: *a punnet of strawberries. I save my punnets from the store for when I pick berries.*

pun•ster ['pʌnstər] *n.* a person fond of making puns.

punt¹ [pʌnt] *v., n.* *—v. Football.* kick (a ball) before it touches the ground after being dropped from the hands.
—n. Football. such a kick: *The punt went over the goal line.* ⟨origin uncertain⟩ **—'punt•er,** *n.*

punt² [pʌnt] *n., v.* *—n.* a shallow, flat-bottomed boat having square ends, usually moved by pushing with a pole against the bottom of a river, etc.
—v. **1** propel (a boat) by pushing with a pole against the bottom of a river, etc. **2** use a punt; travel by punt: *We loved to punt on the river.* ⟨< L *ponto* punt (a kind of ship), pontoon⟩ **—'punt•er,** *n.*

punt³ [pʌnt] *v.* **1** *Card games.* bet against the banker. **2** *Esp. Brit.* bet or gamble. ⟨< F *ponter* < Sp. *puntar,* ult. < L *punctum* point⟩ **—'punt•er,** *n.*

pun•ty ['pʌnti] *n.* See PONTIL.

pu•ny ['pjuni] *adj.* **-ni•er, -ni•est.** **1** of less than usual size and strength; weak. **2** petty; not important. ⟨< OF *puisne* later-born < *puis* (ult. < L *postea*) afterward + *ne* born < L *natus*⟩ **—'pu•ni•ly,** *adv.* **—'pu•ni•ness,** *n.*
☛ *Hom.* PUISNE.

pup [pʌp] *n., v.* **pupped, pup•ping.** *—n.* **1** a young dog; puppy. **2** a young seal, etc. **3** *Informal.* a silly, conceited young man.
—v. give birth to a pup or pups. ⟨var. of *puppy*⟩

pu•pa ['pjupə] *n., pl.* **-pae** [-pi], [-paɪ], *or* [-pei] or **-pas.** **1** a stage between the larva and the adult in the development of many insects. **2** the form of an insect in this stage. Most pupae are inactive and some, such as those of many moths, are enclosed in a tough case or cocoon. ⟨< NL, special use of L *pupa* girl, doll⟩

pu•pal ['pjupəl] *adj.* of, having to do with, or in the form of a pupa.
☛ *Hom.* PUPIL.

pu•pate ['pjupeit] *v.* **-pat•ed, -pat•ing.** pass through the pupal stage: *Some moths pupate in shallow chambers they have constructed in the ground.* **—pu'pa•tion,** *n.*

pu•pil¹ ['pjupəl] *n.* a person who is learning in school or being taught by someone. ⟨< MF < L *pupillus, pupilla* ward < *pupus* boy, *pupa* girl⟩
☛ *Hom.* PUPAL.
☛ *Syn.* See note at STUDENT.

pu•pil² ['pjupəl] *n. Anatomy.* the opening in the centre of the iris of the eye which looks like a black spot. The pupil, which is the only place where light can enter the eye, expands and contracts, thus controlling the amount of light that strikes the retina. See EYE for picture. ⟨< L *pupilla,* originally, little doll, dim. of *pupa* girl, doll⟩
☛ *Hom.* PUPAL.

Two kinds of puppet. The hand puppet on the left is moved with the fingers. The marionette on the right is moved by means of strings; one set moves the head and arms and another moves the legs.

pup•pet ['pʌpɪt] *n.* **1** a figure made to look like a person or animal and moved by wires, strings, rods, or the hands. **2** any person who is not independent, who waits to be told how to act, or who does what somebody else says. **3** a small doll. ⟨earlier *poppet* < OF *poupette* < L *pupa* girl, doll⟩ **—'pup•pet,like,** *adj.*

pup•pe•teer [,pʌpɪ'tir] *n.* a person who designs or makes puppets or who manipulates puppets in puppet shows.

pup•pet•ry ['pʌpɪtri] *n.* the act of making and manipulating puppets.

Pup•pis ['pʌpɪs] *n. Astronomy.* the Stern, a southern constellation between Pyxis and Columba.

pup•py ['pʌpi] *n., pl.* **-pies.** **1** a young dog. **2** a young fox, wolf, etc. **3** *Informal.* a silly, conceited young man. ⟨probably < F *poupée* doll, ult. < L *pupa*⟩ **—'pup•py,like** or **'pup•py•ish,** *adj.* **—'pup•py,hood,** *n.*

puppy love sentimental love that often exists briefly between adolescent girls and boys.

pup tent a small, easily portable two-person tent.

Pu•ra•na [pʊ'rɑnə] *n.* any of 18 Hindu epic collections of legends and fables dealing with the gods, creation, genealogy, etc. ⟨< Skt., of old⟩ **—Pu'ra•nic,** *adj.*

pur•blind ['pɜr,blaɪnd] *adj.* **1** nearly blind. **2** slow to discern or understand. **3** originally, totally blind. ⟨earlier *pur blind* pure blind⟩ **—'pur,blind•ness,** *n.*

pur•chase ['pɜrtʃəs] *v.* **-chased, -chas•ing;** *n.* *—v.* **1** get by paying a price; buy. **2** get in return for something: *to purchase safety at the cost of happiness.* **3** *Law.* acquire (land or property) other than by inheritance.
—n. **1** the act of buying. **2** the thing bought. **3** a firm hold to help move something or to keep from slipping: *Wind the rope twice around the tree to get a better purchase.* **4** a lever, pulley, or other mechanical device for obtaining such a hold. **5** *Law.* the acquisition of land or property other than by inheritance. ⟨ME

< AF *purchacer* pursue < *pur-* forth (< L *pro-*) + *chacer* chase[1] < LL *captiare* < L *capere* take⟩ **—'pur•chas•er,** *n.*

pur•dah ['pɜrdə] *n.* among some Hindus and Muslims: **1** a curtain serving to screen women from the sight of men or strangers. **2** a veil worn by women to hide the face. **3** the condition of being kept hidden from men or strangers. ⟨< Hind. < Persian *pardah* veil, curtain⟩

pure [pjʊr] *adj.* **pur•er, pur•est;** *n.* *—adj.* **1** not mixed with anything else; unadulterated; genuine: *pure gold.* **2** perfectly clean; unpolluted: *pure air.* **3** perfect; correct; without defects: *Does anyone speak pure French?* **4** nothing else than; mere; sheer: *pure accident.* **5** with no evil; without sin; chaste: *a pure mind.* **6** abstract or theoretical (opposed to APPLIED): *pure mathematics.* **7** keeping the same qualities, characteristics, etc. from generation to generation; of unmixed descent: *a pure Indian family.* **8** *Phonetics.* of vowels, monophthongal.
—n. that which is pure. ⟨ME < OF < L *purus*⟩ **—'pure•ness,** *n.*

pure•bred ['pjʊr,brɛd] *adj., n.* *—adj.* designating an animal or plant whose ancestors are known to have all belonged to one breed and that will itself breed true to type: *purebred Holstein cows.*
—n. an animal or plant of this type.

pu•rée [pjʊ'rei] *or* ['pjʊrei] *n., v.* **-réed, -ré•ing.** *—n.* **1** food boiled soft and put through a sieve or blender. **2** a thick soup.
—v. make into a purée. ⟨< F *purée* < *purer* strain⟩

pure•ly ['pjʊrli] *adv.* **1** in a pure manner. **2** exclusively; entirely. **3** merely: *The forward scored the goal purely by chance.* **4** innocently; chastely.

pur•fle ['pɜrfəl] *v.* **-fled, -fling;** *n.* *—v.* **1** decorate with an ornamental border or edge. **2** adorn with metallic threads, laces, etc. **3** of a shrine, adorn with miniature architectural forms.
—n. an ornamental border, often inlaid, as on a table or the back of a stringed instrument. ⟨ME *purfilen* < OF *pourfiler,* ult. < L *filum* thread⟩

pur•ga•tion [pər'geiʃən] *n.* a purging; cleansing.

pur•ga•tive ['pɜrgətɪv] *n., adj.* *—n.* a medicine that empties the bowels; cathartic. Castor oil is a purgative.
—adj. purging. ⟨ME < L *purgativus* < *purgare.* See PURGE.⟩

pur•ga•to•ry ['pɜrgə,tɔri] *n., pl.* **-ries. 1** *Roman Catholic Church.* a temporary condition or place in which the souls of those who have died penitent are purified from sin or the effects of sin by punishment. **2** any condition or place of temporary suffering or punishment. ⟨< Med.L *purgatorium,* originally neut. adj., purging < L *purgare.* See PURGE.⟩ **—,pur•ga'to•ri•al,** *adj.*

purge [pɜrdʒ] *v.* **purged, purg•ing;** *n.* *—v.* **1** wash away all that is not clean from; make clean. **2** become clean. **3** clear of any undesired thing or person, such as air in a water pipe or opponents in a nation. **4** empty (the bowels). **5** *Medicine.* cause (someone) to have a bowel movement. **6** clear of ceremonial or moral defilement or guilt.
—n. **1** the act of purging. **2** a medicine that purges. **3** the elimination of undesired persons from a nation or party. ⟨ME < OF < L *purgare* cleanse, ult. < *purus* pure + *agere* drive⟩

pu•ri•fy ['pjʊrə,faɪ] *v.* **-fied, -fy•ing. 1** make free from impurities, contamination, etc.: *to purify water. The blood is purified in the lungs before it returns to the heart.* **2** make free from sin or guilt: *to purify the heart.* **3** make ceremonially clean: *to purify the altar.* **4** make free from blemish or corruption: *a country purified of sedition.* **5** become pure. ⟨ME < OF < L *purificare* < *purus* pure + *facere* make⟩ **—'pu•ri,fi•er,** *n.* **—pu'ri•fi•ca,to•ry,** *adj.* **—,pu•ri•fi'ca•tion,** *n.*

Pu•rim ['pjʊrɪm] *or* ['pʊrɪm]; *Hebrew,* [pu'rim] *n.* a Jewish religious festival, celebrated each year in February or March, commemorating Esther's deliverance of the Jews from being massacred by Haman. ⟨< Hebrew *purim,* pl. of *pur* lot⟩

pu•rine ['pjʊrin] *n.* **1** *Chemistry.* a white or colourless crystalline compound, the parent of a group of compounds of uric acid, including xanthine and caffeine. *Formula:* $C_5H_4N_4$
2 *Biochemistry.* any of several purine derivatives produced by the decomposition of nucleo-proteins, especially the bases adenine and guanine.

pur•ism ['pjʊrɪzəm] *n.* an insistence on purity and correctness, especially in language or art.

pur•ist ['pjʊrɪst] *n.* **1** a person who is very careful or too careful about purity and correctness, especially in language. A purist dislikes slang and all expressions that are not formally correct. **2** anyone overcareful about principles of purity in art. **—pu'ris•tic,** *adj.* **—pu'ris•ti•cal•ly,** *adv.*

Pu•ri•tan ['pjʊrətən] *n., adj.* *—n.* **1** during the 16th and 17th centuries, a member of a group in the Church of England who wanted simple forms of worship and stricter morals. **2 puritan,** a person who is very strict or too strict in morals and religion.
—adj. **1** of the Puritans. **2 puritan,** very strict or too strict in morals and religion. ⟨< LL *puritas* purity + E *-an*⟩

pu•ri•tan•i•cal [,pjʊrə'tænɪkəl] *adj.* of or like a puritan; very strict or too strict in morals or religion. **—,pu•ri'tan•i•cal•ly,** *adv.*

Pu•ri•tan•ism ['pjʊrətə,nɪzəm] *n.* the principles and practices of the Puritans.

pu•ri•ty ['pjʊrəti] *n.* **1** freedom from dirt, defilement, or mixture; clearness; cleanness. **2** freedom from evil; innocence. **3** freedom from foreign or inappropriate elements; correctness: *purity of style.* ⟨< LL *puritas* < *purus* pure⟩

purl[1] [pɜrl] *v., n.* *—v.* **1** knit with inverted stitches. **2** reverse (a stitch) in knitting: *To make a ribbed border, knit two stitches and then purl two alternately across each row.* **2** border (material) with small loops. **3** *Archaic.* embroider with gold or silver thread.
—n. **1** an inversion of stitches in knitting, producing a bumpy appearance. **2** a loop or chain of small loops along the edge of lace, braid, ribbon, etc. **3** a thread of twisted gold or silver wire. ⟨var. of obs. or dial. *pirl* twist (threads, etc.) into a cord⟩
☛ *Hom.* PEARL.

purl[2] [pɜrl] *v., n.* *—v.* flow with rippling motions and a murmuring sound: *A shallow brook purls.*
—n. a purling motion or sound. ⟨? < Scand.; cf. Norwegian *purla*⟩
☛ *Hom.* PEARL.

pur•lieu ['pɜrlu] *or* ['pɜrlju] *n.* **1** a piece of land on the border of a forest. **2** one's haunt or resort; one's domain. **3** any bordering, neighbouring, or outlying region or district. ⟨alteration of earlier *puraley* (influenced by F *lieu* place) < AF *puralee* < *poraler* go through < *por-* forth (< L *pro-*) + *aler* go⟩

pur•lin or **pur•line** ['pɜrlən] *n.* a horizontal beam running the length of a roof and supporting the top rafters of the roof. ⟨ME; ? < OF⟩

pur•loin [pər'lɔɪn] *or* ['pɜrlɔɪn] *v.* steal. ⟨ME < AF *purloigner* remove < *pur-* forth (< L *pro-*) + *loin* afar < L *longe*⟩ **—pur'loin•er,** *n.*

pur•ple ['pɜrpəl] *n., adj., v.* **-pled, -pling.** *—n.* **1** a colour made by mixing red and blue. **2** TYRIAN PURPLE. **3** a dye or pigment that produces purple. **4** cloth or clothing of this colour, especially as worn to symbolize noble or royal rank. **5** Usually, **the purple,** noble or royal rank. **6** the rank, position, or authority of a cardinal: *Monsignor Catelli has been elevated to the purple.*
born to the purple, of royal rank or high birth.
—adj. **1** of the colour purple. **2** deep red, as in the colour of a cardinal's robes. **3** noble or royal. **4** of rhetorical style, excessively elaborate and showy: *purple prose.*
turn purple, become very angry or furious.
—v. make or become purple. ⟨OE *purple,* var. of *purpure* < L *purpura* < Gk. *porphyra* a shellfish, or the purple dye from it⟩

purple clematis a rare wildflower (*Clematis verticillaris*) growing in spring in shady areas.

purple fringed orchid a wild orchid (*Habenaria psycodes*) having purple flower spikes up to a metre high, and growing in midsummer in damp, acid places.

purple loosestrife a wildflower (*Lythrum salicaria*) growing to a height of 2 m, and having purple flower spikes up to 30 cm long. It blooms in summer in wet places across the world, and is considered a pest.

purple martin a large New World swallow (*Progne subis*) having a stout bill and forked tail, the adult male having dark, glossy, purplish blue plumage.

purple milkvetch a wildflower (*Astragalus adsurgens*) having pale purple flowers and growing in summer on the prairies in large clumps. Related species are poisonous.

purple mountain saxifrage a tiny rock plant (*Saxifraga oppositifolia*) growing in clumps in arctic or high mountain areas.

pur•plish ['pɜrplɪʃ] *adj.* somewhat purple.

pur•port *v.* [pər'pɔrt]; *n.* ['pɜrpɔrt] *v., n.* *—v.* **1** claim; profess: *The document purported to be official.* **2** have as its main idea; mean.
—n. the meaning; main idea. ⟨ME < AF *purporter* < *pur-* forth (< L *pro-*) + *porter* carry < L *portare*⟩ **—pur'port•ed,** *adj.* **—pur'port•ed•ly,** *adv.*
☛ *Syn. n.* See note at MEANING.

pur•pose ['pɜrpəs] *n., v.* **-posed, -pos•ing.** *—n.* **1** something one intends to get or do; plan; aim; intention: *His purpose was to pass his exams.* **2** an object or end for which a thing is made, done, used, etc.: *What is the purpose of this machine?*

3 purposeful quality or character: *a man of purpose, a life of purpose.*
on purpose, intentionally; not by accident: *He tripped me on purpose.*
to good purpose, with good results.
to little (or **no**) **purpose,** with few (or no) results.
—v. plan; aim; intend. ⟨ME < OF *pourpos* < *pourposer* propose < *pour-* (< L *pro-*) + *poser* (see POSE[1])⟩
☛ *Syn. n.* **1.** See note at INTENTION.

pur•pose•ful ['pɜrpəsfəl] *adj.* having or showing a conscious purpose, determination, or intention: *She walked with a purposeful stride.* **—'pur•pose•ful•ly,** *adv.* **—'pur•pose•ful•ness,** *n.*

pur•pose•less ['pɜrpəslɪs] *adj.* lacking a purpose. **—'pur•pose•less•ly,** *adv.* **—'pur•pose•less•ness,** *n.*

pur•pose•ly ['pɜrpəsli] *adv.* on purpose; intentionally.

pur•pos•ive ['pɜrpəsɪv] *adj.* **1** having a function or use; useful: *purposive accuracy and precision.* **2** having or showing conscious intention; purposeful: *a purposive steadfastness.* **—'pur•pos•ive•ly,** *adv.*

purr [pɜr] *n., v. —n.* a low, murmuring sound such as a cat makes when pleased.
—v. **1** make a low, murmuring sound. **2** express by purring: *The kitten purred its contentment into my ear.* ⟨imitative⟩
☛ *Hom.* PER [pɜr].

purse [pɜrs] *n., v.* **pursed, purs•ing.** *—n.* **1** handbag: *She put her keys and gloves in her purse.* **2** a bag or case for carrying money, usually carried in a handbag or pocket. **3** anything shaped or used like a purse. **4** money; resources; treasury: *The family purse cannot afford a vacation.* **5** a sum of money offered as a prize or gift: *A purse was made up for the victims of the fire.*
—v. draw together; press into folds or wrinkles: *The elderly woman pursed her lips in disapproval.* ⟨OE *purs* < LL *bursa* < Gk. *byrsa* hide, skin. Doublet of BOURSE, BURSA.⟩

purse–proud ['pɜrs ˌpraʊd] *adj.* proud of being rich.

purs•er ['pɜrsər] *n.* an officer who keeps the accounts of a ship or airplane, pays wages, and attends to other matters of business.

purse seine a large fishing net held by two boats, one on each side of a school of fish, so that the ends can be pulled like a drawstring purse to enclose the fish. **—'purse-ˌseine,** *v.*

purse snatcher a petty thief who seizes women's purses by grabbing them on the run, sometimes knocking down the victim in the process.

purse strings strings pulled to close a purse.
control or **hold the purse strings,** control the spending of money.
tighten (or **loosen**) **the purse strings,** be more sparing (or generous) in spending money.

purs•lane ['pɜrslən] *or* ['pɜrslein] *n.* **1** any of various low-growing plants (genus *Portulaca*), especially a common, troublesome weed (*P. oleracea*) having prostrate reddish stems, fleshy leaves, and small yellow flowers. **2** (*adjl.*) designating the family (Portulacaceae) of herbs and a few small shrubs that includes purslane, portulaca, spring beauty, etc. ⟨ME < OF *porcelaine*, alteration of L *porcilaca*, var. of *portulaca*⟩

pur•su•ance [pər'suəns] *n.* a following or carrying out; pursuit of some plan, etc.: *to risk one's life in pursuance of one's duty.*

pur•su•ant [pər'suənt] *adj.* following; carrying out (*usually used with* **to**): *pursuant to your instructions.*

pur•sue [pər'su] *v.* **-sued, -su•ing. 1** follow to catch or kill; chase. **2** proceed along; follow in action; follow: *He pursued a wise course, taking no chances.* **3** strive for; try to get; seek: *to pursue pleasure.* **4** carry on; keep on with: *She pursued the study of French for four years.* **5** continue to annoy or trouble: *to pursue a person with questions.* ⟨ME < AF *pursuer*, ult. < L *prosequi.* See PROSECUTE.⟩ **—pur'su•a•ble,** *adj.* **—pur'su•er,** *n.*

pur•suit [pər'sut] *n.* **1** the act of pursuing. **2** an occupation or pastime.

pursuit plane a fighter aircraft that is capable of high speed and a high rate of climb, and that can be manoeuvred with ease.

pur•sui•vant ['pɜrswəvənt] *n.* **1** an assistant to a herald; officer below a herald in rank. **2** a follower; attendant. ⟨ME < OF *poursuivant*, originally ppr. of *poursuivre* pursue, follow, ult. < L *prosequi*⟩

pur•sy ['pɜrsi] *adj.* **-si•er, -si•est. 1** shortwinded or puffy. **2** fat. ⟨ME < AF *pursif*, var. of OF *polsif* < *polser* pant⟩ **—'pur•si•ness,** *n.*

pu•ru•lence ['pjʊrələns] *or* ['pjʊrjələns] *n.* the formation or discharge of pus. Also, **purulency.**

pu•ru•lent ['pjʊrələnt] *or* ['pjʊrjələnt] *adj.* **1** full of pus; discharging pus; like pus: *a purulent sore.* **2** corrupt; rotten. ⟨< L *purulentus* < *pus* pus⟩ **—'pu•ru•lent•ly,** *adv.*

pu•ru•sha ['pʊrəʃə] *n. Hinduism.* one's true self, unaffected by external influences. ⟨< Skt.⟩

pur•vey [pər'vei] *v.* supply (food or provisions); provide; furnish: *to purvey meat for an army, to purvey for a royal household.* ⟨ME < AF *porveier* < L *providere.* Doublet of PROVIDE.⟩

pur•vey•ance [pər'veiəns] *n.* **1** the act of supplying provisions. **2** provisions; supplies. **3** formerly, in England, the right of the king or queen to supplies, use of horses, and personal service.

pur•vey•or [pər'veiər] *n.* **1** a person who supplies provisions. **2** a person who supplies anything. **3** formerly, in Britain, an officer who provided or exacted food, etc. in accordance with the right of purveyance.

pur•view ['pɜrvju] *n.* a range of operation, activity, concern, etc.; scope; extent. ⟨ME < AF *purveu*, originally pp. of *proveier* purvey. See PURVEY.⟩

pus [pʌs] *n.* a liquid formed by inflammation of infected tissue in the body, consisting of white blood cells, bacteria, serum, etc. ⟨< L⟩

push [pʊʃ] *v., n. —v.* **1** move (something) away by pressing against it: *Push the door; don't pull it.* **2** move up, down, back, forward, etc. by pressing: *Push the cat outdoors.* **3** thrust: *Trees push their roots down into the ground.* **4** press hard: *to push with all one's might.* **5** go forward by force: *to push on at a rapid pace.* **6** force (one's way): *We had to push our way through the crowd.* **7** encourage strongly; pressure (a person); urge: *They pushed me to accept the job.* **8** continue with; follow up: *to push a claim. He pushed his plans cleverly.* **9** extend: *The Sahara Desert now pushes as far south as northern Niger and Chad.* **10** urge the use, sale, etc. of: *pushing her new book. He makes a fat living pushing drugs.*
push around, *Informal.* treat roughly or with contempt; bully.
push for, promote; support or advocate strongly.
pushed for, constrained by the lack or scarceness of.
push off, a move from shore: *We pushed off in the boat.*
push it, overdo it.
b *Informal.* go away; depart.
—n. **1** *Informal.* force; energy. **2** the act of pushing. **3** a hard effort; determined advance.
when push comes to shove, *Informal.* when the time comes to face a problem. ⟨ME < OF < L *pulsare* beat. Doublet of PULSATE.⟩
☛ *Syn. v.* **1. Push,** SHOVE = move someone or something by pressing against it. **Push** emphasizes pressing against the person or thing in order to move it ahead, aside, etc., away from oneself or something else: *She pushed the drawer shut.* **Shove** emphasizes moving someone or something out of the way by pushing roughly, or something hard to move or heavy by pushing it along with force and effort: *He shoved his way through the crowd. They shoved the piano across the room.*

push•ball ['pʊʃˌbɒl] *n.* **1** a game played with a large, heavy ball, usually about 180 cm in diameter. Two sides of players try to push the ball toward opposite goals. **2** the ball used.

push button a small button or knob that is pushed to close or open an electric circuit.

push–but•ton ['pʊʃ ˌbʌtən] *adj.* **1** operated by means of a push button or buttons: *a push-button telephone.* **2** using automated systems that can be operated from a distance or with little effort: *push-button cookery, push-button warfare.*

push•cart ['pʊʃˌkɑrt] *n.* a light cart pushed by hand.

push•chair ['pʊʃˌtʃɛr] *n. Brit.* STROLLER (def. 1).

push•er ['pʊʃər] *n.* **1** a person who or thing that pushes. **2** an airplane with propellers behind the wings rather than in front. **3** *Slang.* a person who sells drugs illegally.

push–o•ver ['pʊʃ ˌouvər] *n. Slang.* **1** something very easy to do. **2** a person very easy to beat in a contest. **3** a person easily influenced or swayed or unable to resist a particular appeal.

push•pin ['pʊʃˌpɪn] *n.* a type of thumbtack with a large, often highly coloured head, used for marking maps, charts, etc.

Push•tu ['pʌʃtu] *n.* Pashto.

push–up or **push•up** ['pʊʃ ˌʌp] *n.* **1** an exercise performed in a prone position, in which the person alternately raises and lowers the body by straightening and bending the arms while keeping the body and legs straight. **2** *Cdn.* a structure of grass and other vegetation pushed by a muskrat into a breathing-hole in the ice to keep it from freezing up; used also by the muskrat as a home or shelter.

push•y ['pʊʃi] *adj.* **push•i•er, push•i•est.** *Informal.* offensively forceful and aggressive.

pu•sil•la•nim•i•ty [ˌpjusələ'nɪmɪti] *n.* cowardliness; timidity.

pu•sil•lan•i•mous [ˌpjusə'lænəməs] *adj.* cowardly; timid; faint-hearted. ⟨< L *pusillanimus* < *pusillus* little + *animus* courage⟩ **—ˌpu•sil'lan•i•mous•ly,** *adv.*

puss¹ [pʊs] *n. Informal.* a cat. ⟨Cf. Du. *poes*, LG *puus*, *puss-katte*⟩

puss² [pʊs] *n. Slang.* the face; mouth. ⟨< Irish Gaelic *pus* mouth, lips⟩

puss•y¹ ['pʊsi] *n., pl.* **puss•ies. 1** a cat. **2** catkin. ⟨dim. of *puss*⟩

puss•y² ['pʌsi] *adj.* **-si•er, -si•est.** full of pus. ⟨< *pus* + *-y¹*⟩

puss•y•cat ['pʊsiˌkæt] *n.* **1** a cat. **2** a gentle person: *Many very large men are real pussycats, especially around small children.*

puss•y•foot ['pʊsiˌfʊt] *v., n., pl.* **-foots.** *Informal.* *—v.* **1** move softly and cautiously to avoid being noticed. **2** be cautious and timid about revealing one's opinions or committing oneself (*often used with* **around**).
—n. a person who pussyfoots.

pussy willow a North American willow (*Salix discolor*) having soft, furry, silvery grey catkins that appear before the leaves and are looked for as a harbinger of spring. Pussy willow branches with young catkins are often dried and kept for ornament.

pus•tu•lant ['pʌstʃələnt] *n., adj.* *—n.* a medication that causes pustulation.
—adj. causing the formation of pustules.

pus•tu•lar ['pʌstʃələr] *adj.* of, like, or having to do with pustules; characterized by pustules.

pus•tu•late *v.* ['pʌstʃəˌleit]; *adj.* ['pʌstʃəlɪt] *v.* **-lat•ed, -lat•ing;** *adj.* *—v.* form or cover with pustules.
—adj. having pustules. ⟨< L *pustulare* < *pustula* + E *-ate¹*⟩

pus•tu•la•tion [ˌpʌstʃə'leiʃən] *n.* the formation of pustules.

pus•tule ['pʌstʃul] *n.* **1** a pimple containing pus. **2** any swelling like a pimple or blister, such as the pustules of chicken pox. ⟨< L *pustula* < *pus* pus⟩

put [pʊt] *v.* **put, put•ting;** *n.* *—v.* **1** cause to be in some place or position; place; lay: *I put sugar in my tea. Put away your toys.* **2** cause to be in some state, condition, position, relation, etc.: *The murderer was put to death. Put your room in order.* **3** express: *The teacher puts things clearly.* **4** propose or submit for answer, consideration, deliberation, etc.: *The executive put several questions to the membership.* **5** take one's course; go; turn; proceed: *The ship put out to sea.* **6** throw or cast with an overhand motion from the shoulder: *to put the shot.* **7** set at a particular place, point, amount, etc. in a scale of estimation; appraise: *He puts the distance at 5 km.* **8** apply: *A doctor puts her skill to good use.* **9** impose: *to put a tax on gasoline.* **10** assign; attribute: *They put a wrong construction on my action.* **11** translate: *Putting Hemingway into French is a difficult task.* **12** set (words) to music: *Many composers have put Shakespeare's songs to music.* **13** spend (money) on a bet or investment: *Put your money on Somefun in the 3.30. Put your savings into blue chip stocks.*
put about, a put (a ship) on the opposite tack. **b** change direction.
put across, *Informal.* **a** carry out or express successfully. **b** cause to be accepted. **c** carry out by trickery.
put ahead, move the hands of (a clock or watch) forward: *We put the clocks ahead one hour in spring.*
put aside or **by, a** save for future use. **b** exclude from use or consideration.
put away, a lay aside for future use: *I've already put my winter clothes away for the summer.* **b** *Slang.* consume (food, drink, etc.) **c** *Informal.* kill (a pet or other domestic animal) to prevent suffering, etc.: *We had to put our dog away after it was hit by a car.* **d** *Slang.* commit to a prison, mental hospital, etc.: *The judge put him away for ten years.* **e** *Slang.* pawn. **f** *Archaic.* divorce.
put back, move the hands of (a clock or watch) back: *We put the clocks back one hour in the fall.*
put down, a put an end to; suppress. **b** write down. **c** pay as a down payment. **d** preserve (food). **e** snub; belittle. **f** put (an animal) to death humanely; put to sleep.
put forth, a stretch out: *She put forth a hand to touch his arm.* **b** grow; sprout; issue: *to put forth buds.* **c** use fully; exert: *to put forth effort.* **d** start, especially to sea. **e** publish.
put forward, suggest (a plan or idea).
put in, a *Informal.* spend (time). **b** do; accomplish: *They always put in a good day's work.* **c** enter port. **d** enter a place for safety, supplies, etc. **e** make (a claim, plea, or offer): *She put in for a loan.* **f** contribute.
put it on, *Slang.* pretend; exaggerate.
put it (or **her**) **there,** *Slang.* shake hands with me.
put off, a postpone: *Don't put off going to the dentist.* **b** go away; start out: *The ship put off for England.* **c** tell or cause to wait. **d** get rid of.
put on, a clothe or adorn oneself with; don: *She put on her new hat.* **b** assume or take on, especially as a pretence: *The naughty child put on an air of innocence.* **c** add to; increase: *The driver put on speed.* **d** apply or exert: *to put on pressure.* **e** present (an entertainment); produce: *The class put on a play.* **f** add to one's weight: *I put on five pounds last week.* **g** *Slang.* fool (someone): *Are you putting me on?*
put (someone) **on to,** inform (someone) about (something).
put out, a extinguish. **b** confuse; embarrass. **c** destroy (an eye, etc.). **d** cause to be out in a game. **e** dislocate: *I put my knee out when I fell.* **f** publish. **g** offend; provoke. **h** expel; dismiss. **i** spend; pay.
put over, *Informal.* **a** carry out successfully. **b** impose (something false or deceptive) on a person.
put through, carry out successfully.
put to flight, cause to flee.
put to it, a force to a course. **b** cause to have difficulty.
put up, a offer; give; show: *to put up a house for sale.* **b** make. **c** build or erect: *to put up a monument.* **d** lay aside. **e** put in its usual place. **f** prepare or pack up (food) for later use. **g** preserve (fruit, etc.). **h** give lodging or food to. **i** *Informal.* incite: *Who put you up to this?* **j** make available: *Their parents put up the money for the car.* **k** *Informal.* plan beforehand craftily. **l** offer as a candidate.
put up a fuss, express extreme displeasure.
put upon, impose upon; take advantage of; victimize.
put up with, bear with patience; tolerate.
stay put, stay in the same position: *The dog won't stay put.*
—n. a throw or cast. ⟨< late OE *putian* to push⟩
☛ *Syn. v.* **1, 2. Put,** PLACE, SET = cause someone or something to be in some place, position, condition, relation, etc. **Put** emphasizes the action of moving something into or out of a place or position or bringing it into some condition, state, or relation: *Put the groceries away.* **Place** emphasizes the idea of a definite spot, condition, etc. more than the action: *Place your hands behind your head.* **Set** suggests a more careful, purposeful, and directed 'putting': *Set the box down over there.*

pu•ta•tive ['pjutətɪv] *adj.* supposed; reputed: *the putative author of a book.* ⟨< L *putativus* < *putare* think⟩ **—'pu•ta•tive•ly,** *adv.*

put–down ['pʊt ˌdaʊn] *n. Informal.* **1** a slighting or belittling of a person or thing. **2** a comment, reply, etc. intended to snub or belittle.

put–on *adj.* ['pʊt 'ɒn]; *n.* ['pʊt ˌɒn] *adj., n.* *—adj.* assumed; affected; pretended.
—n. **1** a pretension or affectation. **2** *Slang.* a mischievous joke or trick played for fun; practical joke; hoax.

put•out ['pʊtˌʌut] *n. Baseball.* the play or action of putting out or retiring the batter or a base runner.

pu•tre•fac•tion [ˌpjutrə'fækʃən] *n.* decay; rotting.

pu•tre•fac•tive [ˌpjutrə'fæktɪv] *adj.* **1** causing putrefaction. **2** characterized by or having to do with putrefaction.

pu•tre•fy ['pjutrəˌfaɪ] *v.* **-fied, -fy•ing.** rot; decay. ⟨ME < OF < L *putrifieri*, ult. < *puter* rotten + *fieri* become⟩

pu•tres•cent [pju'trɛsənt] *adj.* **1** becoming putrid; rotting. **2** having to do with putrefaction. ⟨< L *putrescens*, *-entis*, ppr. of *putrescere* grow rotten, ult. < *puter* rotten⟩ **—pu'tres•cence,** *n.*

pu•trid ['pjutrɪd] *adj.* **1** rotten; foul. **2** causing, displaying, or coming from putrefaction. **3** thoroughly corrupt or depraved; extremely bad. **4** gangrenous: *putrid flesh.* **5** extremely unpleasant. ⟨< L *putridus*, ult. < *puter* rotten⟩ **—'pu•trid•ly,** *adv.* **—'pu•trid•ness,** *n.*

pu•trid•i•ty [pju'trɪdəti] *n.* **1** a putrid condition. **2** putrid matter.

putsch [pʊtʃ] *n.* a sudden, plotted political rebellion or uprising against the ruling faction. ⟨< Swiss G, violent blow⟩

putt [pʌt] *v., n. Golf.* *—v.* strike (a ball) gently and carefully in an effort to make it roll into the hole.
—n. the stroke itself. ⟨var. of *put*⟩

put•tee [pʌ'ti] *or* ['pʌti] *n.* **1** a long, narrow strip of cloth wound round the leg from ankle to knee, formerly worn by soldiers, sportsmen, etc. **2** a legging of leather or cloth reaching from ankle to knee, worn by soldiers, riders, etc. ⟨< Hind. *patti* bandage, strip⟩
☛ *Hom.* PUTTY ['pʌti].

put•ter¹ ['pʌtər] *v.* keep busy in a rather useless way. Also, **potter.** ⟨var. of *potter²*⟩ **—'put•ter•er,** *n.*

putt•er² ['pʌtər] *n. Golf.* **1** a person who putts. **2** a club with an upright face and a short, rigid shaft, used in putting. ⟨< *putt*⟩

put•ter³ ['pʊtər] *n.* one who or that which puts. ⟨< *put*⟩

putt•ing green ['pʌtɪŋ] that part of a golf course within about 18 m of a hole, except the hazards; the smooth turf or sand around a golf hole.

put•to ['putou] *n., pl.* **put•ti** [-ti]. *Fine Arts.* a representation of a cherubic infant, often male and winged. ⟨< Ital. boy < L *putus*⟩

putt–putt ['pʌt ,pʌt] *n., v.* **-put•ted, -put•ting.** *—n.* **1** the series of short, explosive sounds made by a small motor. **2** *Informal.* **a** a small boat or other vehicle run by such a motor. **b** the motor.
—v. move or travel by means of this type of motor. ⟨imitative⟩

put•ty ['pʌti] *n., pl.* **-ties;** *v.* **-tied, -ty•ing.** *—n.* **1** a soft mixture of whiting and linseed oil, used mainly for fastening panes of glass into window frames. **2** a pipe-joint compound. **3** the colour of putty, a kind of light grey.
—v. fix, cement, stop up, or cover with putty: *to putty holes in woodwork.* ⟨< F *potée*, originally, potful < *pot* pot⟩
—'put•ti•er, *n.*
☛ *Hom.* PUTTEE ['pʌti].

putty knife a tool with a broad, flexible blade used for applying and smoothing putty.

putty powder an abrasive consisting of powdered oxide of tin (stannic oxide) or tin and lead, used for polishing hard surfaces such as glass or metals.

put–up ['pʊt ,ʌp] *adj. Informal.* planned beforehand, or deliberately, in a secret or crafty manner: *a put-up job.*

puz•zle ['pʌzəl] *n., v.* **-zled, -zling.** *—n.* **1** a difficult problem. **2** a problem or task to be done for fun. **3** a puzzled condition. **4** a game such as a crossword puzzle, jigsaw puzzle, etc., requiring a solution.
—v. **1** make unable to answer, solve, or understand something; perplex. **2** put forth intense mental effort on something hard (*often used with* **over**): *They puzzled over their arithmetic.*
puzzle out, find out by thinking or trying hard: *to puzzle out the meaning of a sentence.* ⟨origin uncertain⟩ **—'puz•zler,** *n.* **—'puz•zled•ly,** *adv.* **—'puz•zling•ly,** *adv.*
☛ *Syn. v.* **1. Puzzle,** PERPLEX, BEWILDER = make a person uncertain what to think, say, or do. **Puzzle** suggests a problem having so many parts or sides and being so mixed up or involved that it is hard to understand or solve: *My friend's behaviour puzzles me.* **Perplex** adds the idea of troubling with doubt about how to decide or act: *The boy's obstinacy perplexes his parents.* **Bewilder** adds and emphasizes the idea of confusing and causing one to feel lost among all the various possibilities: *City traffic bewilders drivers from the country.*

puz•zle•ment ['pʌzəlmənt] *n.* **1** a puzzled condition. **2** something puzzling.

PVC POLYVINYL CHLORIDE.

pwt. pennyweight.

PX or **P.X.** *U.S.* POST EXCHANGE.

pya [pjɑ] *or* [pi'jɑ] *n.* **1** a unit of money in Myanmar, equal to 1/100 of a kyat. See table of money in the Appendix. **2** a coin worth one pya. ⟨< Burmese⟩

pyc•nom•e•ter [pɪk'nɒmətər] *n.* a vessel or container of precise volume used to measure the density of a liquid or powder. ⟨< Gk. *pyknos* thick, dense + E *-meter*⟩

py•e•li•tis [,paɪə'ləitɪs] *n. Pathology.* inflammation of the pelvis, or outlet, of a kidney. ⟨< Gk. *pyelos* basin + E *-itis*⟩

py•el•o•gram ['paɪələ,græm] *n.* an X-ray picture of the kidney and ureter taken after they have been filled with a radiopaque solution. ⟨< Gk. *pyelos* basin + E *-gram*⟩

py•e•lo•neph•ri•tis [,paɪələnə'frəitəs] *n. Pathology.* infection of one or both kidneys, often involving the kidney pelvis. ⟨< *pyelitis* + *nephritis*⟩

py•e•mi•a or **py•ae•mi•a** [paɪ'imiə] *n. Pathology.* a form of blood poisoning caused by bacteria that produce pus. ⟨< NL < Gk. *pyon* pus + *haima* blood⟩

Pyg•ma•li•on [pɪg'meiliən] *or* [pɪg'meiljən] *n. Greek mythology.* a sculptor who made a statue of a woman and then fell in love with it. Aphrodite gave the statue life, and it became Galatea.

pyg•my ['pɪgmi] *n., pl.* **-mies;** *adj. —n.* **1 Pygmy, a** a member of a small people of equatorial Africa, usually less than 150 cm tall. **b** a member of a race of dwarfs described by ancient authors as living in Ethiopia or India. **c** a Negrito of SE Asia or of the Philippines or Andaman Islands. **2** a very short or insignificant person. **3** anything that is unusually small for its kind; dwarf.
—adj. unusually or abnormally small or insignificant. Also, **pigmy.** ⟨< L < Gk. *pygmaioi*, originally pl. adj., dwarfish < *pygmē* cubit, fist⟩ **—'pyg•my,ism,** *n.*
☛ *Syn.* See note at DWARF.

py•ja•mas [pə'dʒæməz] *or* [pə'dʒɑməz] *n.pl., adj. —n.* **1** garments for sleeping or lounging in, consisting of a loose jacket or top and a pair of loose pants usually having an elastic or drawstring waist. **2** loose trousers worn by men and women in various Middle Eastern and Eastern countries.
—adj. **pyjama,** of, forming a part of, or like pyjamas: *pyjama pants.* Also (*esp. U.S.*), **pajama.** ⟨< Hind. < Persian *paejamah* < *pae* leg + *jamah* garment⟩

py•lon ['paɪlɒn] *n.* **1** a post or tower for guiding aircraft pilots. **2** a tall steel framework used to carry high-tension wires across country. **3** either of a pair of high supporting structures marking an entrance at either end of a bridge. **4** a small conical or pyramidal marker used to guide traffic, etc. **5** a gateway, particularly of an ancient Egyptian temple. **6** a structure attached under the wing of an aircraft for housing the engine fuel tank, etc. ⟨< Gk. *pylōn* gateway < *pylē* gate⟩

py•lo•rus [paɪ'lɔrəs] *n., pl.* **-ri** [-raɪ] *or* [-ri]. *Anatomy.* the opening that leads from the stomach into the intestine. ⟨< LL < Gk. *pylōros*, originally, gatekeeper < *pylē* gate + *-horos* watching (Cf. *horaein* see)⟩ **—py'lor•ic,** *adj.*

py•or•rhe•a or **py•or•rhoe•a** [,paɪə'riə] *n. Pathology.* **1** a discharge of pus. **2** a disease of the gums in which pockets of pus form about the teeth, the gums shrink, and the teeth become loose. Also, **pyorrhea alveolaris.** ⟨< NL < Gk. *pyon* pus + *rhoia* a flow < *rheein* flow⟩

py•ra•can•tha [,paɪrə'kænθə] *or* [,pɪrə'kænθə] *n.* any of a genus (*Pyracantha*) of thorn-bearing plants of the rose family, grown widely in both prostrate and upright varieties for their masses of bright orange and red berries in the late summer and early fall. Also, **firethorn.** ⟨< Gk. *purakantha* ult. < *pyr* fire + *akantha* thorn⟩

pyr•a•mid ['pɪrə,mɪd] *n., v. —n.* **1** *Geometry.* a solid having a polygon for its base and having triangular sides meeting in a point. See SOLID for picture. **2** any structure or object having a form similar to this. **3** any of the huge, massive stone pyramids, having four triangular sides, built by the ancient Egyptians to serve as royal tombs. **4** Also, **pyramid scheme**, a tiered network for direct marketing of goods, in which each tier of agents is recruited in larger numbers by, and charges a higher price than, the one above, passing a portion of the profits upward. Illegal in Canada if recruits are required to make large initial purchases of nonreturnable stock.
—v. **1** be or put in the form of a pyramid. **2** raise or increase (costs, wages, etc.) gradually. **3** increase (one's operations) in buying or selling stock on margin by using the profit to buy or sell more. ⟨< L < Gk. *pyramis, -idos* < Egyptian⟩

py•ram•i•dal [pɪ'ræmədəl] *adj.* shaped like a pyramid.

py•ran ['paɪræn] *or* [paɪ'ræn] *n. Chemistry.* either of two closed-chain compounds containing a ring having one oxygen and five carbon atoms. *Formula:* C_5H_6O

pyre [paɪr] *n.* **1** a pile of wood on which a dead body is burned as a funeral rite. **2** any large pile or heap of burnable material. ⟨< L < Gk. *pyra* < *pyr* fire⟩

py•rene¹ ['paɪrin] *n. Botany.* the stone of a drupe, such as an apple or pear, containing several seeds. ⟨< NL *pyrena* < Gk.⟩

py•rene² ['paɪrin] *n. Chemistry.* a colourless aromatic crystalline hydrocarbon consisting of four fused benzene rings, obtained from coal tar and thought to be carcinogenic. *Formula:* $C_{16}H_{10}$ ⟨< *pyro-* + *-ene*⟩

Pyr•e•ne•an [,pɪrə'niən] *adj.* of the Pyrenees, a mountain range between France and Spain.

py•re•thrin [paɪ'riθrɪn] *n.* the active ingredient of pyrethrum, a viscous, water-insoluble liquid obtained from pyrethrum flowers, used as an insecticide. *Formula:* $C_{21}H_{28}O_3$ or $C_{22}H_{28}O_5$

py•re•thrum [paɪ'riθrəm] *n.* **1** any of several Eurasian chrysanthemums cultivated for their showy red, white, or lilac flowers or as a source of insecticide. **2** an insecticide prepared from the dried flower heads of some of these plants. ⟨< L *pyrethrum* feverfew < Gk. *pyrethron*, probably < *pyr* fire⟩

py•ret•ic [paɪ'rɛtɪk] *adj.* **1** of or having to do with fever. **2** producing fever. **3** feverish. ⟨< NL < Gk. *pyretos* fever < *pyr* fire⟩

Py•rex ['paɪrɛks] *n. Trademark.* a kind of glassware that is highly resistant to heat.

py•rex•ia [paɪ'rɛksiə] *n. Pathology.* **1** a fever. **2** a feverish condition. ⟨< Gk. *pyrexis* feverishness < *pyressein* have fever < *pyr* fire⟩

pyr•i•dox•ine [ˌpirə'dɒksin] *or* [ˌpirə'dɒksən] *n.* vitamin B_6, essential to human nutrition, found in wheat germ, fish, liver, etc. *Formula*: $C_8H_{11}O_3N$

py•rite ['pairəit] *n.* a common mineral consisting of iron sulphide, having a yellow colour and a metallic glitter that suggests gold; FOOL'S GOLD. *Formula*: FeS_2 ⟨< L < Gk. *pyritēs* flint < *pyr* fire⟩

py•ri•tes [pai'rəitiz] *or* ['pairəits] *n., pl.* **-tes.** any of various compounds of sulphur and a metal: *Pyrite is the commonest pyrites.* **—py'rit•ic** [-'rɪtɪk], *adj.*

pyro– *combining form.* fire; heat: *pyrography.* ⟨< Gk. *pyr, pyros*⟩

py•ro•cat•e•chol [ˌpairou'kætəˌtʃɒl] *or* [ˌpairou'kætəˌkɒl] *n. Chemistry.* a white, crystalline phenol used as an antiseptic, photographic developer, etc.; catechol. *Formula*: $C_6H_4(OH)_2$ ⟨< *pyro* + *catechol*⟩

py•ro•chem•i•cal [ˌpairou'kɛmɪkəl] *adj.* referring to chemical activity at high temperatures.

py•ro•gen ['pairədʒən] *n. Medicine.* a fever-producing substance.

py•ro•gen•ic [ˌpairə'dʒɛnɪk] *adj.* **1** produced by heat. **2** producing heat. **3** igneous.

py•rog•ra•phy [pai'rɒgrəfi] *n.* the art of burning designs on wood, leather, etc. **—py'rog•ra•pher,** *n.* **—ˌpy•ro'graph•ic,** *adj.*

py•ro•hy [ˌpɛrə'hei] *or* [ˌpirə'hi] *n.pl.* **1** perogy. **2** verenyke.

py•rol•y•sis [pai'rɒləsɪs] *n.* **1** the chemical decomposition of a substance through the application of heat. **2** the resulting state of decomposition.

py•ro•mag•net•ic [ˌpairoumæg'nɛtɪk] *adj.* thermomagnetic.

py•ro•man•cy ['pairəˌmænsi] *n.* the practice of divination or of claiming to foretell the future by flames or the forms appearing in fire.

py•ro•ma•ni•a [ˌpairə'meiniə] *n.* an obsessive desire to set things on fire. **—ˌpy•ro'ma•ni•ac,** *n., adj.*

py•ro•ma•ni•a•cal [ˌpairoumə'naiəkəl] *adj.* **1** caused by a pyromaniac. **2** of or having a tendency toward pyromania.

py•ro•met•al•lur•gy [ˌpairə'mɛtəˌlɜrdʒi]; *also, esp. Brit.,* [ˌpairoumə'tælərdʒi] *n.* the branch of metallurgy involving processes that depend on high temperatures, such as smelting, sintering, and casting. **—ˌpy•roˌmet•al'lur•gi•cal,** *adj.*

py•rom•e•ter [pai'rɒmətər] *n.* an instrument used to measure high temperatures beyond the range of normal thermometers, using the radiation emitted by a hot body as the basis of measurement.

py•ro•nine ['pairəˌnin] *n. Histology.* any xanthine dye used as histological stain, especially for detecting the presence of R.N.A.

py•ro•pho•bia [ˌpairə'foubiə] an abnormal fear of fire.

py•ro•pho•tom•et•er [ˌpairoufou'tɒmətər] *n.* an optical pyrometer.

py•ro•sis [pai'rousɪs] *n. Pathology.* heartburn.

py•ro•tech•nic [ˌpairə'tɛknɪk] *adj.* **1** of or having to do with fireworks. **2** resembling fireworks; brilliant; sensational: *pyrotechnic eloquence.* **3** of or having to do with materials and devices activating various systems in spacecraft, by igniting or exploding on command. Also, **pyrotechnical.** **—ˌpy•ro'tech•ni•cal•ly,** *adv.*

py•ro•tech•nics [ˌpairə'tɛknɪks] *n.* **1** the making of fireworks. **2** the use of fireworks. **3** a display of fireworks. **4** a brilliant or sensational display. **—ˌpy•ro'tech•nist,** *n.*

py•rox•y•lin [pai'rɒksəlɪn] *n.* any of various substances made by nitrating certain forms of cellulose. Guncotton and the soluble cellulose nitrates used in making celluloid, collodion, etc. are pyroxylins. ⟨< *pyro-* + Gk. *xylon* wood⟩

pyr•rhic[1] ['pirɪk] *n., adj. —n.* in ancient Greece, a war dance imitating the motions of warfare.
—adj. of or having to do with this dance. ⟨< Gk. *pyrrhikhe* war dance⟩

pyr•rhic[2] ['pirɪk] *n., adj. —n. Prosody.* a metrical foot consisting of two unstressed syllables, also called a **dibrach.**
—adj. **1** consisting of two unstressed syllables. **2** made up of pyrrhics. ⟨extension of PYRRHIC[1]⟩

Pyr•rhic ['pirɪk] *adj.* of or having to do with Pyrrhus, King of Epirus.

Pyrrhic victory a victory won at too great cost. ⟨< *Pyrrhus*, King of Epirus in Greece, 300-272 B.C., who won a battle with an enormous loss of life⟩

pyr•rho•tite ['pairəˌtəit] *n.* a bronze-coloured, slightly magnetic iron sulphide, sometimes containing nickel. *Formula*: FeS ⟨< Gk. *pyrrhotēs* redness < *pyrrhos* fiery red < *pyr* fire (because of its colour) + E *-ite*[1]⟩

pyr•role [piroul] *n. Chemistry.* a colourless, toxic liquid, an organic component of chlorophyl. *Formula*: C_4H_5N

py•san•ka [pɪ'sæŋkə] *n., pl.* **pi•pan•ki** [pɪ'pæŋki]. a Ukrainian Easter egg, made by printing elaborate symbolic designs on a fresh egg that has been blown. The main colours used are black, white, red, orange, and yellow.

Py•thag•o•re•an [pəˌθægə'riən] *adj., n. —adj.* of or having to do with Pythagoras (582?-500? B.C.), a Greek philosopher and mathematician, his teachings, or his followers.
—n. a follower of Pythagoras.

Py•thag•o•re•an•ism [pəˌθægə'riəˌnɪzəm] *n.* the doctrines and philosophy of Pythagoras and his followers, especially the transmigration of souls and the belief that numbers are the ultimate elements of the universe.

Pythagorean theorem *Geometry.* the theorem that the square of the hypotenuse of a right-angled triangle is equal to the sum of the squares of the two adjacent sides.

Pyth•i•a ['pɪθiə] *n.* the priestess of Apollo at Delphi, who delivered the divine responses to questions asked of the oracle.

Pyth•i•an ['pɪθiən] *adj.* of or having to do with Apollo or the oracle at Delphi. ⟨< L < Gk. *Pythios* of Delphi (earlier called Pytho), or the Delphic Apollo⟩

Pythian games in ancient Greece, one of the great Panhellenic festivals, held every four years at Delphi in honour of Apollo.

Pyth•i•as ['pɪθiəs] *n. Roman legend.* a man famous for his devoted friendship with Damon, who pledged his life for him. **Damon and Pythias.** See DAMON.

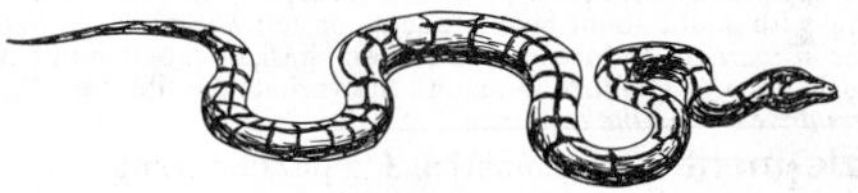

A python: length up to 9 m

py•thon ['pəiθɒn] *or* ['pəiθən] *n.* **1** any of a subfamily (Pythoninae) of large, nonvenomous, Old World snakes of the same family as the boas, that kill their prey by constriction but, unlike the boas, lay eggs rather than bearing live young. The **reticulated python** (*Python reticulatus*), which may reach a length of over 9 m, is one of the largest snakes in the world. **2** any large constricting snake. ⟨< L < Gk.⟩

py•tho•ness ['pəiθənɪs] *n.* **1** the priestess of Apollo at Delphi, who gave out the answers of the oracle. **2** any prophetess. ⟨earlier *phytoness* < OF < LL *pythonissa* < Gk. *pythōn* familiar spirit < *Pythō*, seat of the Delphic oracle⟩

py•thon•ic [pəɪ'θɒnɪk] *adj.* of or resembling a python.

py•u•ria [pai'jʊriə] *n. Pathology.* the presence of pus in the urine. ⟨< Gk. *pyon* pus + *ouria* urine⟩

pyx [pɪks] *n.* **1** *Ecclesiastical.* the box in which the bread of the Eucharist is kept or carried. **2** a box at the British mint in which specimen coins are kept to be tested for weight and purity. ⟨< L < Gk. *pyxis* < *pyxos* boxwood⟩

pyx•id•i•um [pɪk'sɪdiəm] *n., pl.* **pyx•id•i•a** [pɪk'sɪdiə]. *Botany.* the fruit of certain plants such as the plantain or portulaca, consisting of a dry seed capsule having a caplike upper part that falls off when the capsule is mature, releasing the seeds. ⟨< NL < Gk. *pyxidion*, dim. of *pyxis* box. See PYX.⟩

pyx•is ['pɪksɪs] *n., pl.* **pyx•i•des** ['pɪksɪˌdiz]. **1** pyxidium. **2** in ancient Greece and Rome a small container with a lid.

Pyx•is ['pɪksɪs] *n. Astronomy.* the Compass, a southern constellation between Puppis and Hydra.

Q q Q q

q or **Q** [kju] *n., pl.* **q's** or **Q's. 1** the seventeenth letter of the English alphabet. **2** any speech sound represented by this letter. **3** a person or thing identified as *q*, especially the seventeenth in a series. **4** (*adjl.*) of or being a Q or q. **5** any device, such as a printer's type, a lever, or a key on a keyboard, that produces a q or Q. **6** something shaped like a Q.

q. 1 quart(s). **2** quarterly.

Q 1 *Electronics.* the ratio of the reactance to the resistance, or of energy stored to energy lost in a resonant circuit or coil. Also called **Q-factor. 2** *Thermodynamics.* a heat unit equal to 10^{18} British Thermal Units or $1\ 055 \times 10^{21}$ joules. Also called **Q-unit.**

Q. 1 Queen. **2** question; query. **3** quarto. **4** quire. **5** quarterly.

qa•mu•tik ['kæmʊtɪk] *n. Cdn.* komatik.

Q and A or **Q & A** questions and answers in exchange.

Qa•tar [kə'tɑr] or ['kɑtɑr] *n.* an independent emirate on the Persian Gulf. Also, **Katar.**

QB 1 QUEEN'S BENCH. **2** *Chess.* queen's bishop. **3** *Football. Informal.* quarterback.

QC or **Q.C.** QUEEN'S COUNSEL.

Q.E.D. or **q.e.d. 1** which was to be demonstrated or proved (for L *quod erat demonstrandum*). **2** *Physics.* QUANTUM ELECTRODYNAMICS.

qe•piq [kə'pik] *n.* a unit of currency in Azerbaijan, equal to 1/100 of a manat. See table of money in the Appendix.

q.i.d. in prescriptions, four times a day (for L *quater in die*).

qin•dar [kɪn'dɑr] *n., pl.* **qin•dar•ka** [-kə]. a unit of money in Albania, equal to 1/100 of a lek. See table of money in the Appendix. ⟨< Albanian, akin to *quintal*⟩

qirsh [kɜrʃ] See QURSH.

qiv•i•ut ['kɪvi,ʊt] *n.* **1** the soft, silky underfur of the arctic muskox, used as a textile fibre. **2** the yarn spun from this fur. ⟨< Inuktitut⟩

QKt *Chess.* queen's knight.

ql quintal.

QM or **Q.M.** quartermaster.

QMG or **Q.M.G.** quartermaster-general.

qof [kɒf] *n.* the twenty-first letter of the Hebrew alphabet. See table of alphabets in the Appendix.
☛ *Hom.* COUGH.

QP *Chess.* queen's pawn.

qr. 1 quarter; quarterly. **2** quire.

Q.R. QUEEN'S REGULATIONS.

QR *Chess.* queen's rook.

q.s. in prescriptions, enough or as much as is sufficient (for L *quantum sufficit*).

qt. 1 quart(s). **2** quantity.

q.t. or **Q.T.** *Slang.* quiet.
on the q.t., very secretly; quietly.

Q–Tip ['kju ,tɪp] *n. Trademark.* a small stick tipped with cotton, for cleaning small areas such as a baby's ears, or for applying medicine.

qto. quarto.

qu. 1 quart. **2** quarterly. **3** question.

qua [kwei] *or* [kwɑ] *adv.* as; in the capacity of: *Qua father, he pitied the boy; qua judge, he condemned him.* ⟨< L *qua*, abl. fem. sing. of rel. pron., *qui* who⟩

quack¹ [kwæk] *n., v.* —*n.* **1** the sound a duck makes. **2** any similar sound.
—*v.* make the sound of a duck or one like it. ⟨imitative⟩

quack² [kwæk] *n., adj.* —*n.* **1** a person who practises as a doctor but lacks professional training. **2** an ignorant pretender to knowledge or skill of any sort.
—*adj.* **1** used by quacks. **2** not genuine: *quack medicine.* ⟨short for *quacksalver*⟩ **—'quack•ish,** *adj.*

quack•er•y ['kwækəri] *n., pl.* **-er•ies.** the practices or methods of a quack.

quack grass COUCH GRASS.

quack•sal•ver ['kwæk,sælvər] *n. Archaic.* a quack doctor; charlatan. ⟨< earlier Du. *quacksalver* < *quacken* boast of + *salf* salve⟩

quad¹ [kwɒd] *n. Informal.* a quadrangle on a college or university campus. ⟨by shortening⟩

quad² [kwɒd] *n. Informal.* quadruplet. ⟨by shortening⟩

quad³ [kwɒd] *n. Printing.* quadrat. ⟨by shortening⟩

quad⁴ [kwɒd] *adj., n. Informal.* —*adj.* quadraphonic.
—*n.* quadraphonics. ⟨by shortening⟩

quad. 1 quadrant. **2** quadruplicate.

quadr– prefix, variant of QUADRI- before a vowel: *quadrangle.*

Quad•ra•ges•i•ma [,kwɒdrə'dʒɛsəmə] *n.* **1** the first Sunday in Lent. Also, **Quadragesima Sunday. 2** *Archaic.* the forty days of Lent. ⟨< L *quadragesima*, fem. adj., fortieth⟩

quad•ra•ges•i•mal [,kwɒdrə'dʒɛsəməl] *adj.* **1** lasting 40 days, said of Lent or any other 40-day period. **2** suitable for or pertaining to Lent.

quad•ran•gle ['kwɒ,dræŋgəl] *n.* **1** a four-sided space or court wholly or nearly surrounded by buildings. **2** the buildings around a quadrangle. **3** a quadrilateral. ⟨< LL *quadrangulum* < L *quadri-* four + *angulus* angle⟩

quad•ran•gu•lar [kwɒ'dræŋgjələr] *adj.* like a quadrangle; having four corners or angles.

quad•rant ['kwɒdrənt] *n.* **1 a** a quarter of a circle or of its circumference. **b** anything having the shape of a quarter circle. **2** formerly, an instrument used in astronomy and navigation for measuring altitudes. Compare SEXTANT. **3** *Geometry and Astronomy.* one of the four sections into which a plane surface is divided by two perpendicular lines or coordinate axes, the sections being numbered clockwise from the upper right. ⟨< L *quadrans, -antis* a fourth⟩

quad•ra•phon•ics [,kwɒdrə'fɒnɪks] *n.* (*used with a singular verb*) a system for the high-fidelity recording or reproduction of sound using four transmission channels that feed four separate loudspeakers. **—,quad•ra'phon•ic,** *adj.*

qua•draph•o•ny [kwɒ'dræfəni] *n.* quadraphonics.

quad•rat ['kwɒdrət] *n. Printing.* a piece of metal used for wide spaces in setting type. ⟨var. of *quadrate*, n.⟩

quad•rate *adj., n.* ['kwɒdrɪt] *or* ['kwɒdreit]; *v.* ['kwɒdreit] *adj., n., v.* **-rat•ed, -rat•ing.** —*adj.* **1** square; rectangular. **2** *Zoology.* designating the quadrate bone.
—*n.* **1** something square or rectangular. **2** *Zoology.* one of a pair of bones or cartilages in the skulls of lower vertebrates such as birds or fish, to which the lower jaw is attached; the quadrate bone.
—*v.* **1** agree or conform (*often used with* **with**). **2** cause to become square or to conform; adapt. ⟨< L *quadratus* < *quadrus* square, ult. < *quattuor* four⟩

quad•rat•ic [kwɒ'drætɪk] *adj., n. Algebra.* —*adj.* involving a squared quantity or quantities, but none that are raised to powers higher than two.
—*n.* QUADRATIC EQUATION. **—quad'rat•i•cal•ly,** *adv.*

quadratic equation *Algebra.* an equation involving a square or squares, but no higher powers, of the unknown quantity or quantities. *Example*: $x^2 + 3x + 2 = 12$

quad•rat•ics [kwɒ'drætɪks] *n.* (*used with a singular verb*) the branch of algebra that deals with quadratic equations.

quad•ra•ture ['kwɒdrətʃər] *or* ['kwɒdrə,tʃʊr] *n.* **1** the act of squaring. **2** *Mathematics.* the finding of a square equal in area to a given surface bounded by a curve. **3** *Astronomy.* the position of any planet or star that is 90° away from another. ⟨< L *quadratura* < *quadratus.* See QUADRATE.⟩

quad•ren•ni•al [kwɒ'drɛniəl] *adj., n.* —*adj.* **1** occurring every four years: *a quadrennial election.* **2** of or lasting for four years.
—*n.* an event occurring every four years. ⟨< L *quadriennium* period of four years < *quadri-* four + *annus* year⟩
—quad'ren•ni•al•ly, *adv.*

quad•ren•ni•um [kwɒ'drɛniəm] *n.* a period of four years.

quadri– *prefix.* four; fourfold; four times: *quadrilateral.* Also, before a vowel, **quadr-.** ⟨< L⟩

quad•ri•cen•ten•ni•al [,kwɒdrəsɛn'tɛniəl] *adj., n.* —*adj.* marking or pertaining to the end or completion of a four hundred year period: *The year* A.D. *2267 will be the quadricentennial anniversary of Confederation.*

—n. a four hundredth anniversary or its celebration: *Canada will celebrate its quadricentennial in 2267.*

quad•ri•ceps ['kwɒdrə,sɛps] *n., pl.* **-ceps** or **-cep•ses** [-,sɛpsiz]. *Anatomy.* the large, four-part, extensor muscle of the front of the thigh.

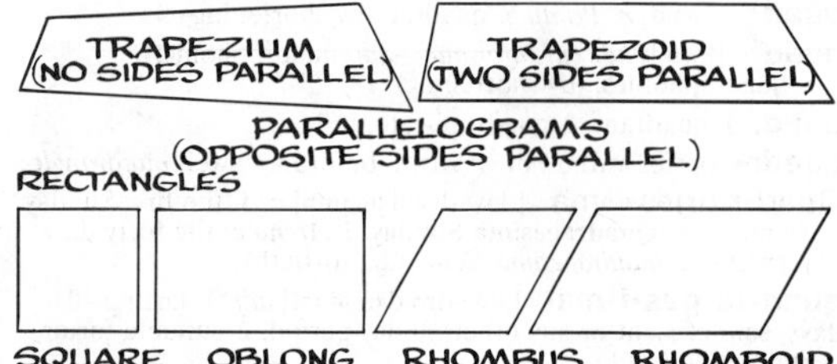

quad•ri•lat•er•al [,kwɒdrə'lætərəl] *adj., n. —adj.* having four sides and four interior angles.
—n. **1** a plane figure having four sides and four interior angles. **2** something having this form. ⟨< L *quadrilaterus* < *quadri-* four + *latus, -teris* side⟩

qua•drille [kwɒ'drɪl] *n.* **1** a square dance for four couples that has five parts or movements. **2** the music for such a dance. **3** an 18th century card game for four people. ⟨< F < Sp. *cuadrilla* troop < *cuadro* battle square < L *quadrus* square⟩

quad•ril•lion [kwɒ'drɪljən] *n., adj.* a cardinal number represented: **1** in Canada, the United States, and France by 1 followed by 15 zeros. **2** in the United Kingdom and Germany by 1 followed by 24 zeros. ⟨< F *quadrillon* < *quadri-* four (< L) + *million*⟩ **—quad'ril•lionth,** *adj., n.*

quad•ri•no•mi•al [,kwɒdrə'noumiəl] *adj., n. Algebra. —adj.* consisting of four terms.
—n. an expression having four terms. *Example:* $a^2 - ab + 4a - b^2$ ⟨< *quadri-* four (< L) + *-nomial*; modelled after *binomial*⟩

quad•ri•ple•gia [,kwɒdrə'plidʒiə] *or* [,kwɒdrə'plidʒə] *n. Pathology.* complete paralysis of all four limbs, or of the whole body from the neck down. **—,quad•ri'ple•gic,** *adj., n.*

quad•ri•va•lent [,kwɒdrə'veilənt] *or* [kwɒ'drɪvələnt] *adj., n. Chemistry. —adj.* **1** having a valence of four. **2** having four separate valences.
—n. a quadrivalent atom or element. **—,quad•ri'va•lence** or **,quad•ri'va•len•cy,** *n.* **—,quad•ri'va•lent•ly,** *adv.*

quad•riv•i•um [kwɒ'drɪviəm] *n., pl.* **quad•riv•i•a** [kwɒ'drɪviə]. in the Middle Ages, arithmetic, geometry, astronomy, and music, the more advanced group of the seven liberal arts. Compare TRIVIUM. ⟨< LL < L *quadrivium* crossroads < *quadri-* four + *via* way⟩

quad•roon [kwɒ'drun] *n.* a person having one-fourth African ancestry. ⟨< Sp. *cuarterón* < *cuarto* fourth < L *quartus*⟩

quadru– *prefix.* a variant of QUADRI- before labial consonants: *quadruple.*

quad•rum•vi•rate [kwɒ'drʌmvərɪt] *or* [-,reit] *n.* a governing or managing group consisting of four people.

quad•ru•ped ['kwɒdrə,pɛd] *n., adj. —n.* an animal, especially a mammal, that has four feet.
—adj. having four feet. ⟨< L *quadrupes, -pedis* < *quadru-* four + *pes, pedis* foot⟩

quad•ru•ple [kwɒ'drupəl], [kwɒ'drʌpəl], *or* ['kwɒdrəpəl] *adj., n., v.* **-pled, -pling.** *—adj.* **1** fourfold; consisting of four parts; including four parts or parties. **2** four times; four times as great. **3** *Music.* having four beats to each measure, with the first and third beats accented.
—n. a number, amount, etc., four times as great as another: *80 is the quadruple of 20.*
—v. make or become four times as great. ⟨< L *quadruplus* < *quadru-* four + *-plus* fold⟩ **—quad'ru•ply,** *adv.*

quad•ru•plet [kwɒ'druplɪt], [kwɒ'drʌplɪt], *or* ['kwɒdrəplɪt] *n.* **1** one of four children born at the same time from the same mother. **2** a group of four. ⟨< *quadruple,* adj., modelled on *triplet*⟩

quad•ru•plex ['kwɒdrə,plɛks] *or* [kwɒ'druplɛks] *adj., n. —adj.* **1** fourfold. **2** *Telegraphy.* of or having to do with a former system in which four messages, two in each direction, could be sent over one wire simultaneously.
—n. a four-unit apartment building. ⟨< L *quadruplex* fourfold < *quadru-* four + *-plex* fold⟩

quad•ru•pli•cate *adj., n.* [kwɒ'druplɪkɪt]; *v.* [kwɒ'druplə,keit] *adj., v.* **-cat•ed, -cat•ing;** *n. —adj.* **1** fourfold; quadruple. **2** designating or pertaining to the fourth of a set of copies.
—v. make fourfold; quadruple.
—n. one of four things, especially four copies of a document, exactly alike.
in quadruplicate, in four identical copies: *Please submit your résumé in quadruplicate.* ⟨< L *quadruplicatus,* ult. < *quadru-* four + *plicare* to fold⟩

quad•ru•pli•ca•tion [kwɒ,druplə'keiʃən] *n.* **1** a quadruplicating. **2** something quadruplicated.

quaes•tor ['kwɛstər] *or* ['kwistər] *n.* in ancient Rome: **1** an official in charge of the public funds; treasurer. **2** a public prosecutor in certain criminal cases. ⟨< L *quaestor* var. of *quaesitor* < *quaerere* inquire⟩

quaes•tor•ship ['kwɛstər,ʃɪp] *or* ['kwistər,ʃɪp] *n.* the position or term of office of a quaestor.

quaff [kwɒf] *or* [kwæf] *v., n. —v.* drink in large drafts; drink deeply and freely.
—n. an act of quaffing. ⟨origin uncertain⟩

quag [kwæg] *or* [kwɒg] *n.* a bog; quagmire.

quag•ga ['kwægə] *or* ['kwɒgə] *n.* an extinct, striped equine mammal (*Equus quagga*) of southern Africa, somewhat resembling a zebra. ⟨< Afrikaans < Hottentot⟩

quag•gy ['kwægi] *or* ['kwɒgi] *adj.* **-gier, -gi•est. 1** boggy; soft and marshy; swampy. **2** flabby; soft and wobbly: *quaggy flesh.* ⟨probably < *quag* bog⟩

quag•mire ['kwæg,maɪr] *n.* **1** soft, muddy ground; a boggy or miry place. **2** a difficult situation. ⟨< obs. *quag* to shake + *mire*⟩

qua•hog ['kwɒhɒg] *or* [kwə'hɒg] *n.* an edible clam (*Venus mercenaria*, also called *Mercenaria mercenaria*) of the Atlantic coast of North America, having a hard, thick, rounded shell. Also, **quahaug.** ⟨< Algonquian⟩

Quai d'Or•say [ki dɔr'sei]; *French,* [kedɔʀ'se] *n.* **1** a quay running along the south bank of the Seine in Paris, in which the French Ministry of Foreign Affairs is located along with other government offices. **2** the French Ministry of Foreign Affairs.

quail[1] [kweil] *n., pl.* **quails** or (*esp. collectively*) **quail. 1** any of various plump-bodied, small to medium-sized Old World game birds (subfamily Perdicinae, especially genus *Cortunix*) belonging to the same family as partridges and pheasants. **2** any of various New World birds (subfamily Odontophorinae) belonging to the same family and resembling Old World quail, but generally larger and more colourful and having no leg spurs. The commonest and best-known species is the bobwhite. ⟨ME < OF *quaille* < Gmc.⟩

A quail

quail[2] [kweil] *v.* be afraid; lose courage; shrink back in fear: *The slave quailed at his master's look.* ⟨ME; origin uncertain⟩

quaint [kweint] *adj.* **1** strange or odd in an interesting, pleasing, or amusing way: *Old photographs seem quaint to us today.* **2** unusual, fanciful, or whimsical. ⟨ME < OF *cointe* pretty < L *cognitus* known⟩ **—'quaint•ly,** *adv.* **—'quaint•ness,** *n.*

quake [kweik] *v.* **quaked, quak•ing;** *n. —v.* shake; tremble: *She quaked with fear.*
—n. **1** a shaking; trembling. **2** earthquake. ⟨OE *cwacian*⟩
☛ *Syn. v.* See note at SHIVER[1].

Quak•er ['kweikər] *n.* a member of a Christian group called the Society of Friends. Quakers favour simple religious services and refuse to fight in wars or take oaths. ⟨< *quake,* v.; said to refer to the fact that George Fox, the founder, bade his followers "tremble at the word of the Lord"⟩ **—'Quak•er•ish** or **'Quak•er•like,** *adj.*

Quak•er•ism ['kweikə,rɪzəm] *n.* the beliefs, principles, and customs of the Quakers.

qua•ky ['kweiki] *adj.* **qua•ki•er, qua•ki•est.** having a tendency to shake; tremulous; shaky. **—'qua•ki•ly,** *adv.* **—'qua•ki•ness,** *n.*

qual•i•fi•ca•tion [,kwɒləfə'keiʃən] *n.* **1** that which makes a person fit for a job, task, office, etc.: *Good eyesight is a necessary qualification for a crack shot.* **2** a modification; limitation; restriction: *The statement was made without any qualification. His pleasure had one qualification, that his friends could not enjoy it too.* **3** a necessary condition required by law or custom, which must be fulfilled before a right can be acquired or exercised, office held, etc.

qual•i•fied ['kwɒlə,faɪd] *adj.* **1** having the desirable or required qualifications; fitted; adapted: *He is fully qualified for his job.* **2** modified; limited; restricted: *Her qualified answer was, "I will go, but only if you will come with me."*

qual•i•fi•er ['kwɒlə,faɪər] *n.* **1** a person who or thing that qualifies. **2** *Grammar.* a word that qualifies or modifies the meaning of another word. Adjectives and adverbs are qualifiers.

qual•i•fy ['kwɒlə,faɪ] *v.* **-fied, -fy•ing. 1** make fit or competent: *to qualify oneself for a job.* **2** furnish with legal power; make legally capable. **3** characterize or describe by stating qualities or attributes. **4** change or modify the flavour or strength of. **5** satisfy criteria: *Can you qualify for the Scouts?* **6** *Sports.* gain the right to compete in a race, contest, or tournament. **7** make less strong; change somewhat; limit; modify: *Qualify your statement that dogs are loyal by adding "usually."* **8** *Grammar.* limit or modify the meaning of. ⟨< Med.L *qualificare* < L *qualis* of what sort + *facere* make⟩ **—'qual•i,fi•a•ble,** *adj.* **—'qual•i,fy•ing•ly,** *adv.*

qual•i•ta•tive ['kwɒlə,teitɪv] *adj.* concerned with quality or qualities. **—'qual•i,ta•tive•ly,** *adv.*

qualitative analysis 1 *Chemistry.* **a** the branch of chemistry dealing with the process of determining the chemical components of a substance. **b** the process itself. **2** in research, analysis of data based on factors of a non-statistical nature. Compare QUANTITATIVE ANALYSIS.

qual•i•ty ['kwɒləti] *n., pl.* **-ties. 1** something special about an object that makes it what it is; its basic character or nature: *One quality of iron is hardness; one quality of sugar is sweetness.* **2** a characteristic; attribute: *She has many fine qualities.* **3** grade of excellence; degree of worth: *That is a poor quality of cloth.* **4** nature; disposition; temper: *Trials often test a person's quality.* **5** character; position; relation: *Dr. Smith was present, but in the quality of a friend, not of a physician.* **6** fineness; merit; excellence: *Look for quality rather than quantity.* **7** *Logic.* the characteristic of a proposition that makes it positive or negative. **8** an accomplishment; attainment. **9** high rank; good or high social position. **10** people of high rank. **11** *Acoustics.* the character of a sound aside from pitch and volume or intensity. **12** *Phonetics.* the character of a vowel sound as determined by the configuration of the vocal tract. **13** *(adjl.)* of high standard: *This garage does quality repair work.* ⟨ME < OF < L *qualitas* < *qualis* of what sort⟩

qual•la ['kwɑlə] *n.* CHUM[3]. ⟨Salishan *kw'alux* striped⟩

qualm [kwɒm] *or* [kwɑm] *n.* **1** a sudden disturbing feeling in the mind; uneasiness; misgiving; doubt: *I tried the test with some qualms.* **2** a disturbance or scruple of conscience: *She felt some qualms at staying away from work.* **3** a momentary feeling of faintness or sickness, especially of nausea. ⟨OE *cwealm* pain⟩ **—'qualm•ish,** *adj.*

qua•mash ['kwɒ,mæʃ] *or* [kwə'mæʃ] *n.* camas.

quan•da•ry ['kwɒndəri] *n., pl.* **-ries.** a state of perplexity or uncertainty; dilemma. ⟨origin uncertain⟩

quan•ta ['kwɒntə] *n.* pl. of QUANTUM.

quan•tic ['kwɒntɪk] *n. Mathematics.* a rational, homogeneous integral function of two or more variables. ⟨< L *quantus* how much⟩

quan•ti•fi•er ['kwɒntə,faɪər] *n.* **1** *Logic.* a word, etc., such as *all* or *some,* that quantifies a proposition. **2** *Grammar.* a modifier that denotes the quantity of something. In the sentence *Few people really enjoy studying grammar, few* is a quantifier.

quan•ti•fy ['kwɒntə,faɪ] *v.* **-fied, -fy•ing. 1** determine the quantity of; count or measure. **2** *Prosody.* express the quantity of: *to quantify a syllable of verse.* **3** *Logic.* express explicitly the quantity or extent of, by using such words as *all, some,* or *most.* **4** express the quantity of; state in quantitative terms. ⟨< Med.L *quantificare* < L *quantus* how much + *facere* make⟩ **—,quan•ti'fi•a•ble,** *adj.* **—,quan•ti•fi'ca•tion,** *n.*

quan•ti•ta•tive ['kwɒntə,teitɪv] *adj.* **1** concerned with quantity. **2** that can be measured. **3** *Phonology.* having to do with the length of a spoken consonant or vowel. **4** pertaining to a system, usually prosodic or metrical, where syllables are classified as long or short rather than stressed or unstressed. **—'quan•ti,ta•tive•ly,** *adv.*

quantitative analysis 1 *Chemistry.* **a** the branch of chemistry dealing with the amount or proportion of each chemical component of a substance. **b** the process itself. **2** in research, analysis based on statistical methods. Compare QUALITATIVE ANALYSIS.

quantitative inheritance *Genetics.* the pattern of inheritance shown by traits determined by multiple factors with small additive effects.

quan•ti•ty ['kwɒntəti] *n., pl.* **-ties. 1** any particular or indeterminate amount (number, mass, bulk, etc.) of anything measurable: *Equal quantities of nuts and raisins were used in the cake.* **2** a large amount; a large number: *The baker buys flour in quantity. She owns quantities of books.* **3** something that is measurable. **4** *Music.* the length of a note. **5** *Prosody.* the length of a vowel sound or syllable. **6** *Mathematics.* **a** something having magnitude, or size, extent, amount, etc. **b** a figure or symbol representing this. ⟨< L *quantitas* < *quantus* how much⟩

quan•tize ['kwɒntaɪz] *v.* **-tized, -tiz•ing. 1** *Physics.* apply the principles of quantum mechanics to. **2** *Mathematics.* limit to values which are multiples of a base unit.

quan•tum ['kwɒntəm] *n., pl.* **-ta** [-tə]. **1** a portion, amount, or quantity. **2** *Physics.* **a** the smallest amount of energy capable of existing independently. **b** such a discrete amount of energy regarded as a unit. ⟨< L *quantum,* neut. adj., how much⟩

quantum chromodynamics *n. Physics.* the quantum theory describing the interactions of quarks and gluons. The colour of the quarks plays a role like that of an electric charge.

quantum electrodynamics *n. Physics.* the quantum theory dealing with the interaction of the electromagnetic field with electrons and positrons. *Abbrev.*: QED

quantum leap or **jump 1** *Physics.* a sudden change of an atom, electron, etc. from one discrete energy level or state to another. **2** any sudden major change or advance: *a quantum leap in electronic technology.*

quantum mechanics the branch of physics dealing with the interpretation of the behaviour of atoms and elementary particles, such as electrons, on the basis of the quantum theory.

quantum number *Physics.* **1** any number distinguishing among members of a family of elementary particles. **2** an integer, or half of an odd integer, expressing the physical quantity of a member of a quantum mechanical theory.

quantum theory *Physics.* the theory that whenever radiant energy is transferred, the transfer occurs in pulsations or stages rather than continuously, and that the amount of energy transferred during each stage is of a definite quantity.

quar•an•tine ['kwɔrən,tin] *or* [,kwɔrən'tin] *v.* **-tined, -tin•ing;** *n.* **—***v.* **1** isolate (people, ships, etc. carrying a communicable or infectious disease) usually for a specific length of time: *People with measles used to be quarantined for two weeks.* **2** isolate or exclude an undesirable person or group.
—*n.* **1** the state of being quarantined: *The house was in quarantine when the child had scarlet fever.* **2** detention, isolation, and other measures taken to prevent the spread of an infectious disease. **3** a place where people, animals, plants, ships, etc. are held until it is sure that they have no infectious diseases, insect pests, etc. **4** the period of such detention or isolation. **5** isolation, exclusion, and similar measures taken against an undesirable person, group, etc. ⟨< Ital. *quarantina* < *quaranta* forty < L *quadraginta*; with reference to 40 days as the original period of isolation⟩

quark [kwɔrk] *or, sometimes* [kwɑrk] *n. Physics.* any of the fundamental particles from which the composite particles called hadrons (including protons and neutrons) are formed, and which, together with leptons, are believed to be the basic constituents of all matter. Quarks differ from leptons in that they do not occur as free particles and in that they have fractional charges, either $+\frac{2}{3}$ or $-\frac{1}{3}$ of the charge of an electron. There is strong experimental evidence for the existence of fifteen quarks, with an additional three predicted but not yet seen. ⟨< a nonsense word coined by James Joyce in *Finnigan's Wake* and applied to these particles in 1963 by American physicist Murray Gell-Mann (b. 1929), who first postulated their existence⟩

quar•rel[1] ['kwɔrəl] *n., v.* **-relled** or **-reled, -rel•ling** or **-rel•ing.**
—*n.* **1** an angry dispute or disagreement; a breaking off of friendly relations. **2** a cause for a dispute or disagreement; reason for breaking off friendly relations: *A bully likes to pick quarrels.* **3** one's cause or side in a dispute or contest: *The knight took up the poor man's quarrel and fought his oppressor.*
—*v.* **1** dispute or disagree angrily; break off friendly relations. **2** find fault: *It is useless to quarrel with undeniable facts.* ⟨ME

< OF < L *querella*, var. of *querela* complaint < *queri* complain⟩ **—'quar•rel•ler** or **'quar•rel•er,** *n.*

☛ *Syn. n.* **1. Quarrel,** FEUD[1] = an angry disagreement or unfriendly relation between two people or groups. **Quarrel** particularly applies to a fight in words, an angry disagreement or dispute, soon over or ending in a fist fight or in severed relations: *The children had a quarrel over the division of the candy.* **Feud** suggests a long-lasting quarrel, marked by violent and sometimes murderous attacks and revenge when between two groups, by bitter hatred and unfriendly acts and verbal attacks when between individuals: *The senator and the columnist had carried on a feud for years.*

quar•rel[2] ['kwɔrəl] *n.* **1** a bolt or arrow with a square head, used with a crossbow. **2** a small, square or diamond-shaped pane of glass, used in latticed windows. **3** a stonemason's chisel. ⟨ME < OF < Med.L *quadrellus*, dim. of L *quadrus* square⟩

quar•rel•some ['kwɔrəlsəm] *adj.* too ready to quarrel; fond of fighting and disputing. **—'quar•rel•some•ly,** *adv.* **—'quar•rel•some•ness,** *n.*

quar•ri•er ['kwɔriər] *n.* a person who quarries stone.

quar•ry[1] ['kwɔri] *n., pl.* **-ries;** *v.* **-ried, -ry•ing.** *—n.* a place where stone is dug, cut, or blasted out for use in building or sculpture.
—v. **1** obtain (stone) from a quarry. **2** dig out by hard work, as if from a quarry. ⟨ME < Med.L *quareia*, ult. < L *quadrus* square⟩

quar•ry[2] ['kwɔri] *n., pl.* **-ries. 1** an animal chased in a hunt; prey or game. **2** anything hunted or eagerly pursued. ⟨ME < OF *cuiree* < *cuir* hide < L *corium*⟩

quar•ry[3] ['kwɔri] *n.* **1** QUARREL[2] (def. 2). **2** a square tile or stone.

quart [kwɔrt] *n.* **1** a non-metric unit for measuring volume or capacity, equal to two pints, 40 fluid ounces, one fourth of a gallon, or one eighth of a peck (about 1.14 L). **2** a container having a capacity of one quart. **3** such a container and its contents: *a quart of milk. Abbrev.*: qt. or qu. ⟨ME < OF < L *quarta*, fem. adj., fourth⟩

quar•tan ['kwɔrtən] *adj., n. —adj.* recurring every fourth day, by inclusive counting.
—n. a fever or ague with two days between attacks. ⟨< F < L *(febris) quartana* quartan (fever) < *quartus* fourth⟩

quar•ter ['kwɔrtər] *n., v. —n.* **1** one fourth; half of a half; one of four equal or corresponding parts. **2** in Canada, the United States, etc.: **a** one fourth of a dollar; 25 cents. **b** a coin worth 25 cents. **3** fifteen minutes; especially, the moment marking fifteen minutes before or after a specified hour: *They left at a quarter to three.* **4** one fourth of a year; three months: *Sales increased in the first quarter.* **5** one of the four phases of the moon. The quarters of the moon are four periods of about seven days each. **6** one fourth of any of various units of measure: *a quarter of a hectare of land.* **7** (*adjl.*) being or consisting of one of four equal or more or less equal parts: *a quarter package of peanuts.* **8** a region or district: *They live in the Latin Quarter of the city.* **9** a section of a community, group, etc.: *The bankers' theory was not accepted in other quarters.* **10** any of the four divisions of the horizon as marked off by the four main compass points: *What quarter is the wind blowing from?* **11** mercy or indulgence, as shown to a defeated opponent or enemy: *He asked no quarter and was given none.* **12 a** one of four parts, each including a leg, into which an animal's carcass is divided. **b** the leg and its adjoining parts.
13 *Nautical.* the part of a ship's side near the stern. **14** *Heraldry.* **a** one of four more or less equal parts into which a shield may be divided by two lines crossing at right angles. **b** a charge, or emblem, occupying the upper right fourth of a shield (from the bearer's point of view). **15** the part of a boot or shoe above the heel and below the top of either side of the foot from the middle of the back to the vamp. **16** *Music.* a QUARTER NOTE: *That note is held for two quarters.* **17** *Football, basketball, etc.* one of the four equal periods of play into which a game is divided.
18 quarters, *pl.* **a** a place to live or stay: *officers' quarters.* **b** proper position or station.
at close quarters, fighting, struggling, or living close together: *The two armies were at close quarters for several days. Three to a small apartment is living at close quarters.*
—v. **1** divide into quarters. **2** give a place to live in: *Soldiers were quartered in houses of the town.* **3** live or stay in a place. **4** cover (an area) by going over it from left to right and from right to left; search intensively. **5** cut the body of (a person or animal) into quarters. **6** *Nautical.* of a wind, blow on a ship's quarter.
7 *Heraldry.* place or bear (coats of arms) in quarters of a shield. ⟨ME < OF < L *quartarius* a fourth < *quartus* fourth⟩

quar•ter•back ['kwɔrtər,bæk] *n., v. —n.* **1** *Football.* the player whose position is immediately behind the centre of the line of scrimmage: *The quarterback usually directs the team's play in the field.* **2** a person who directs any group or activity.
—v. **1** play in this position; act as quarterback. **2** manage or direct any undertaking.

quarter day the day beginning or ending a quarter of the year.

quar•ter•deck ['kwɔrtər,dɛk] *n. Nautical.* **1** on a sailing vessel, the part of the upper deck between the mainmast and the stern, used especially by the officers of a ship. **2** on a modern naval vessel, a deck area designated as the ceremonial post of the commanding officer.

quar•tered ['kwɔrtərd] *adj., v. —adj.* **1** divided into quarters. **2** furnished with rooms or lodging. **3** *Heraldry.* divided or arranged in quarters. **4** of a log, quartersawed.
—v. pt. and pp. of QUARTER.

quar•ter•fi•nal ['kwɔrtər,faɪnəl] *n.* a stage in a sports tournament at which eight players or teams compete; the round preceding the semifinal round.

quarter horse a breed of horse orginally bred from thoroughbred stock for racing on quarter-mile tracks, now much used in Canada and the United States for working with cattle, playing polo, etc.

quar•ter–hour ['kwɔrtər 'aʊr] *n.* **1** fifteen minutes. **2** a point one-fourth or three-fourths of the way through an hour: *The bus leaves every 30 minutes on the quarter-hour.*

quar•ter•ing ['kwɔrtərɪŋ] *n., adj., v. —n.* **1** the act of dividing into fourths. **2** the act of assigning quarters, especially for soldiers. **3** *Heraldry.* **a** the division of a shield into quarters or parts. **b** one of such parts. **c** the coat of arms on a quartering.
—adj. **1** *Nautical.* of a wind, blowing on a ship's side near the stern. **2** lying at right angles.
—v. ppr. of QUARTER.

quar•ter•ly ['kwɔrtərli] *adj., adv., n., pl.* **-lies.** *—adj.*
1 happening, done, etc., at four regular intervals a year.
2 consisting of or pertaining to a quarter.
—adv. **1** once each quarter of a year. **2** *Heraldry.* with division into, or located in one of, the four quarters of an escutcheon.
—n. a magazine published four times a year: *The Society publishes a quarterly.*

quar•ter•mas•ter ['kwɔrtər,mæstər] *n.* **1** *Military.* **a** an officer who has charge of providing quarters, clothing, fuel, transportation, etc. for troops. **b** *Navy.* an officer on a ship who has charge of the steering, the compasses, signals, etc. *Abbrev.*: QM or Q.M. **2** the person in charge of ordering and distributing supplies for a summer camp, etc.

quar•tern ['kwɔrtərn] *n.* **1** a quarter; fourth part.
2 one-fourth of a pint; gill. ⟨ME < OF *quarteron* < *quart* fourth < L *quartus*⟩

quarter note *Music.* a note equal to one-fourth of a whole note. See NOTE for picture.

quarter rest *Music.* a rest lasting as long as a QUARTER NOTE. See REST[1] for picture.

quarter round a convex moulding whose cross section is a quarter of a circle.

quar•ter•saw ['kwɔrtər,sɒ] *v.* **-sawed, -sawed** or **-sawn, -saw•ing.** saw (a log) lengthwise into quarters and then into boards.

quarter section *Cdn.* a piece of land, usually square, containing 160 acres (about 65 hectares).

quarter sessions **1** formerly, a British court held quarterly before a recorder or two justices of the peace, having limited criminal and civil jurisdiction and empowered to hear appeals; replaced in 1972 by the CROWN COURT. **2** any of various courts held quarterly.

quar•ter•staff ['kwɔrtər,stæf] *n., pl.* **-staves. 1** a weapon consisting of a stout pole about 2 m long and tipped with iron, formerly used by English peasants and later by Scouts. **2** use of the quarterstaff in fighting or as a sporting exercise.

quar•ter•staves ['kwɔrtər,steivz] *n.* pl. of QUARTERSTAFF.

quarter tone or **step** *Music.* an interval of half a semitone.

quar•tet or **quar•tette** [kwɔr'tɛt] *n.* **1** a group of four musicians (singers or players). **2** a piece of music for four voices or instruments. **3** any group of four. ⟨< F < Ital. *quartetto* < *quarto* fourth < L *quartus*⟩

quar•tic ['kwɔrtɪk] *n. Algebra.* an equation of the fourth degree. Also called **biquadratic equation.**

quar•tile ['kwɔrtaɪl] *n. Statistics.* any of the three values of a variable that divide the items of a population into four equal groups with respect to the value of the variable.

quar•to ['kwɔrtou] *n., pl.* **-tos. 1** the page size of a book (about 24 × 30 cm) in which each leaf is one-fourth of a whole sheet of paper (about 48 × 60 cm). **2** (*adjl.*) having this size. **3** a book having this size. ⟨< Med.L *in quarto* in the fourth (of a sheet)⟩

quartz [kwɔrts] *n.* a very common, very hard, crystalline mineral consisting of silica, that is present in many rocks and solids in a variety of forms, many of which are used as gemstones. It occurs in the form of pure, colourless crystals (rock crystal) and impure, coloured crystals, such as amethyst, and also in microcrystalline forms, such as jasper, carnelian, and flint. *Formula*: SiO_2 ⟨< G *Quarz*⟩

quartz•ite ['kwɔrtsəit] *n.* a granular metamorphic rock consisting mostly of quartz.

quartz mining *Cdn.* the practice of mining mineral-bearing quartz.

qua•sar ['kweizɑr] *or* ['kweisɑr] *n. Astronomy.* any of various starlike bodies that are very distant from the earth and give off strong light and radio waves. ⟨blend of *quasi* and *stellar*⟩

quash[1] [kwɒʃ] *v.* put down completely; crush: *to quash a revolt.* ⟨ME < OF *quasser* < L *quassare* shatter, intensive of *quatere* to shake⟩

quash[2] [kwɒʃ] *v.* make void; annul: *The judge quashed the charges against the prisoner.* ⟨ME < OF *quasser* < LL *cassare* < *cassus* null; influenced in OF by *quasser* quash[1]⟩

qua•si ['kwɒzi], ['kweizaɪ], *or* ['kweisaɪ] *adj., adv.*
—adj. seeming; not real; halfway: *quasi humour.*
—adv. seemingly; not really; partly; almost. ⟨ME < L, equiv. to *quam* as + *si* if⟩

quasi– *combining form.* in some sense or to a certain extent: *quasi-historical, quasi-official.* ⟨< *quasi*⟩

quasi contract an obligation imposed in the absence of a contract to prevent enrichment of one party at the expense of another.

quasi–stellar radio source quasar.

quass [kwɑs] *or* [kvɑs] *n.* kvass.

quas•sia ['kwɒʃə] *n., adj. —n.* **1** a bitter drug obtained from the wood or bark of any of various tropical trees (genera *Quassia* and *Picrasma*) of the same family as the ailanthus, used as a tonic and medicine and also as an insecticide. **2** any of the trees whose wood or bark yields this drug. **3** the bark or wood of any of these trees.
—adj. designating the family Simaroubacae, order Sapindales, to which quassia and ailanthus belong. ⟨< NL; after *Quassi*, a Surinam slave who first used the bark as a fever remedy⟩

Qua•ter•na•ry [kwə'tɜrnəri] *or* ['kwɒtər,nɛri] *n., adj. Geology.* *—n.* **1** the period that includes the Pleistocene and Recent epochs. See geological time chart in the Appendix. **2** the deposits made in this period. **3 quaternary,** a group or set of four.
—adj. **1** of or having to do with this period or the deposits made during it. **2 quaternary,** of a compound or alloy, having four principal components. ⟨< L *quaternarius*, ult. < *quater* four times⟩

quat•rain ['kwɒtrein] *n.* a stanza or poem of four lines, usually having an alternating rhyme scheme *abab* or *abcb*, less frequently *abba*. ⟨< F *quatrain* < *quatre* four < L *quattuor*⟩

qua•tre ['kɑtər]; *French,* ['katʀ] *n.* the four in a card game or throw of dice.

quat•re•foil ['kætrə,fɔɪl] *or* ['kætər,fɔɪl] *n.* **1** a leaf or flower composed of four leaflets or petals. The four-leaf clover is a quatrefoil. **2** *Architecture.* an ornamental pane having four lobes that radiate from a common centre. ⟨ME < OF *quatre* four (< L *quattuor*) + *feuil* leaf < L *folium*⟩

quat•tro•cen•to [,kwɒtrə'tʃɛntou]; *Italian,* [,kwatro'tʃɛnto] *n.* the 15th century, with reference to the Italian art and literature of the time. ⟨< Ital., lit. four hundred (short for fourteen hundred)⟩ **—,quat•tro'cen•tist,** *n.*

qua•ver ['kweivər] *v., n. —v.* **1** shake tremulously; tremble: *The old man's voice quavered.* **2** sing or say in trembling tones. **3** trill in singing or in playing on an instrument.
—n. **1** a shaking or trembling, especially of the voice. **2** a trill in singing or in playing on an instrument. **3** *Music. Brit.* an eighth note. ⟨frequentative of ME *quave* shake, early ME *cwavie(n)*⟩ **—'qua•ver•ing•ly,** *adv.* **—'qua•ver•y,** *adj.*

quay [ki] *n.* a solid landing place where ships load and unload, often built of stone. ⟨ME < OF *kay* < Celtic⟩ **—'quay•age,** *n.*
☛ *Hom.* CAY [ki], KEY.

Que. Québec.

quean [kwin] *n.* **1** *Archaic.* a bold, impudent girl or woman; hussy. **2** prostitute. **3** *Scottish.* a girl or young woman. **4** *Slang.* QUEEN (def. 8). ⟨OE *cwene*⟩
☛ *Hom.* QUEEN.

quea•sy ['kwizi] *adj.* **-si•er, -si•est. 1** inclined to nausea; easily upset. **2** feeling nauseated. **3** tending to unsettle the stomach. **4** uneasy; uncomfortable: *a queasy conscience.* **5** squeamish; fastidious. ⟨origin uncertain⟩ **—'quea•si•ly,** *adv.* **—'quea•si•ness,** *n.*

Qué•bec [kwɪ'bɛk] *or* [kə'bɛk]; *French,* [ke'bɛk] *n.* an eastern province of Canada.

Québec hawthorn a tree (*Crataegus submollis*) having large white flowers, straight thorns, and red berries. It grows across Canada.

A Québec heater

Québec heater a type of heating stove that burns wood or coal in a tall, cylindrical firebox.

Qué•beck•er or **Qué•bec•er** [kwə'bɛkər] *or* [kə'bɛkər] *n.* a native or long-term resident of the province of Québec.

Qué•bé•cois [keibɛ'kwɑ]; *French,* [kebɛ'kwa] *n., pl.* **Qué•bé•cois.** a Québecker, especially a Francophone.

Qué•bé•coise [keibɛ'kwɑz]; *French,* [kebɛ'kwaz] *n., pl.* **Qué•bé•coises.** a female Québecker, especially a Francophone.

que•bra•cho [kei'brɑtʃou] *n.* **1** any of several South American hardwood trees (genus *Schinopsis*) of the cashew family, especially *S. lorentzii* and *S. balansae*, whose wood is valued as a source of tannin, and several other species that are important timber trees. **2** a South American hardwood tree (*Aspidosperma quebracho*) of the dogbane family whose bark is valued as a source of alkaloids used in medicine and tanning. **3** the wood or bark of any of these trees. ⟨< Sp. *quebracho*, literally, break-axe < *quebrar* break < L *crepare*⟩

Quech•ua ['kɛtʃwə] *n., pl.* **Quech•ua** or **Quech•uas. 1** the principal language of the Inca empire, still surviving as a dialect spoken in S Peru. **2** any of several related dialects and languages. **3** Quechuan. **4** a member of any of a group of Indian peoples of the Andes, including the peoples who constituted the dominant element in the Inca empire. Also, **Kechua.**

Quech•uan ['kɛtʃwən] *adj., n. —adj.* of or having to do with Quechua or the Quechua peoples.
—n. a family or subfamily of languages of the Andes in South America, including Quechua. Also, **Kechuan.**

queen [kwin] *n., v. —n.* **1** a female ruler. **2** QUEEN CONSORT. **3** a woman or girl judged to be first in importance or best in beauty or some other quality: *the queen of fashion, the queen of the May.* **4** *Entomology.* a fully developed egg-laying female in a colony of bees, ants, etc. There is usually only one queen in a hive of bees. **5** a playing card bearing a picture of a queen. **6** *Chess.* a piece that can move any number of squares in any straight or diagonal row. **7** the chief, best, finest, etc.: *The rose is the queen of flowers.* **8** *Slang.* a male homosexual, especially one who appears very effeminate.
—v. **1** be a queen or act like a queen. **2** make a queen of, especially in chess: *When the pawn reaches the last square, it is queened.*
queen it, *Informal.* behave pretentiously or domineeringly. ⟨OE cwēn⟩ **—'queen,like,** *adj.*
☛ *Hom.* QUEAN.

Queen Anne [æn] **1** a style of English architecture of the early 18th century, characterized by simple design and the use of red brick. **2** a style of upholstered furniture designed in England in the early 18th century.

Queen Anne's lace [ænz] a common biennial plant (*Daucus carota*) of the parsley family native to Europe and Asia but naturalized in North America and elsewhere, having lacelike, flat-topped clusters of small white flowers. The cultivated carrot is probably derived from this plant. Also called **wild carrot.**

queen bee **1** a fertile female bee, usually the only one in a hive. **2** a woman who is in a superior or prominent position.

Queen City *Cdn.* **1** Toronto, Ontario. **2** Regina, Saskatchewan. Also, **Queen City of the Plains. 3** Victoria, B.C. Also, **Queen City of British Columbia.**

queen consort the wife of a reigning king.

queen crab *Cdn.* a species of crab (*Chionoecetes opilio*) found on the east coast.

queen cup a wildflower (*Clintonia uniflora*) having six-petalled white flowers on a 10 cm stem, and found in damp coniferous forests on mountains in western North America.

queen•dom ['kwindəm] *n.* **1** the realm of a queen. **2** the position or dignity of a queen.

queen dowager the widow of a king.

queen•hood ['kwin,hʊd] *n.* the state of being a queen; the rank of a queen.

queen lady's slipper an orchid (*Cypripedium reginae*) having pink and white flowers, and blooming in summer in damp places. It is the provincial flower of Prince Edward Island.

queen•ly ['kwinli] *adj.* **-li•er, -li•est;** *adv. —adj.* **1** of a queen; fit for a queen. **2** like a queen; like a queen's.
—adv. in a queenly manner; as a queen does. **—'queen•li•ness,** *n.*

queen mother the widow of a former king and mother of a reigning king or queen.

queen post one of a pair of timbers extending vertically upward from the tie beam of a roof truss or the like, one on each side of its centre.

queen regent **1** a queen ruling in place of an absent or unfit monarch. **2** a queen ruling in her own right.

Queen's Bench [kwinz] in England, a division of the High Court of Justice. Also, during the reign of a king, **King's Bench.**

Queens•ber•ry rules See MARQUIS OF QUEENSBERRY RULES.

Queen's Birthday *Cdn.* VICTORIA DAY.

Queen's Counsel a lawyer who has been appointed counsel to the Crown and is entitled to wear a silk gown. In the U.K. the title is awarded to barristers on the basis of superior learning and talent, but in Canada, where it is a provincial option, it has been merely a formal appointment since the early 1900s. The appointment has been discontinued in Ontario. *Abbrev.*: QC or Q.C. Also, during the reign of a king, **King's Counsel.**

Queen's English the English that is recognized as correct and standard in the U.K. Also, during the reign of a king, **King's English.**

Queen's evidence *Law.* testimony given in court by an accomplice in a crime against his or her associate or associates. Also, during the reign of a king, **King's evidence**. Compare STATE'S EVIDENCE.
turn Queen's evidence, testify in court against one's associates in a crime.

queen–size ['kwin ,saɪz] *adj.* **1** of a bed or mattress, larger than double but smaller than king-size, usually 152 × 203 cm. **2** belonging to or made for a queen-size bed: *queen-size sheets*. Also, **queen-sized.** ⟨by analogy with *king-size*⟩

Queen's Park *Cdn.* **1** the Ontario government or legislature, so called after the park in which the buildings stand. **2** the legislative buildings located in this park, or the park itself.

Queen's Printer *Cdn.* **1** formerly, the publisher of a newspaper authorized by the government to print laws and proclamations as well as the debates and proceedings of Parliament. **2** in modern use, the printer of all government documents, federal and provincial.

Queen's Proctor *British law.* an officer of the crown having the right to intervene in certain divorce and nullity cases. Also, during the reign of a king, **King's Proctor**.

Queen's Regulations regulations for the armed forces (British, Canadian, etc.) issued by the government in the monarch's name. Also, during the reign of a king, **King's Regulations.**

queen truss a truss having queen posts but no king post.

queer [kwir] *adj., v., n. —adj.* **1** different from what is normal or usual; strange; odd; peculiar: *a queer remark, a queer noise, a queer reaction.* **2** *Informal.* eccentric or mildly crazy: *She's a little bit queer.* **3** *Informal.* not as it should be; causing doubt or suspicion: *There's something queer going on here.* **4** *Slang.* counterfeit; worthless: *queer money.* **5** not well; faint or giddy: *I started to feel queer and had to sit down.*
—v. **1** *Slang.* spoil; ruin: *to queer a deal.* **2** put (oneself or another) in an unfavourable or hopeless position.
—n. **1** *Informal.* a person who is strange or peculiar. ⟨< G *quer* oblique⟩ **—'queer•ly,** *adv.*

queer•ness ['kwirnɪs] *n.* **1** a queer nature or quality. **2** something strange or odd; a peculiarity of behaviour.

que•le•a ['kwiliə] *n.* any African bird of the genus *Quelea*, especially *Q. quelea.* In large flocks, it destroys grain crops.

quell [kwɛl] *v.* **1** put down (disorder, rebellion, etc.): *to quell a riot.* **2** put an end to; suppress: *to quell one's fears.* ⟨ME *quellen*, OE *cwellan* kill⟩

quench [kwɛntʃ] *v.* **1** put an end to; stop: *to quench a thirst.* **2** drown out; put out: *The rain quenched the fire.* **3** cool suddenly by plunging into water or other liquid: *Hot steel is quenched to harden it.* **4** subdue or suppress; destroy; quell: *Don't quench your natural feelings.* ⟨ME *quenchen*, OE *cwencean*⟩

quench•less ['kwɛntʃlɪs] *adj.* that cannot be quenched; inextinguishable; unquenchable: *quenchless thirst.*

que•nelle [kə'nɛl] *n.* a small ball of seasoned, finely minced meat or fish cooked in water or stock or fried as a croquette and often served with a sauce. ⟨< F < G *Knödel* dumpling < MHG *knode* knot. 19c.⟩

quer•cine ['kwɜrsɪn] *or* ['kwɜrsaɪn] *adj.* of or referring to an oak. ⟨< L *quercus* oak⟩

quern [kwɜrn] *n.* **1** a primitive hand mill for grinding grain, consisting commonly of two circular stones, the upper one being turned by hand. **2** a small hand mill used to grind pepper or other spices. ⟨OE *cweorn*⟩

quer•u•lous ['kwɛrələs] *or* ['kwɛrjələs] *adj.* **1** complaining; faultfinding; bad-tempered. **2** fretful; peevish. ⟨< L *querulus* < *queri* complain⟩ **—'quer•u•lous•ly,** *adv.* **—'quer•u•lous•ness,** *n.*

que•ry ['kwiri] *n., pl.* **-ries;** *v.* **-ried, -ry•ing.** *—n.* **1** a question; inquiry. **2** a doubt: *There was a query in his mind about the whole procedure.* **3** question mark, especially one used to express doubt about something written or printed: *a query in the margin.*
—v. **1** put as a question; ask: *"How long will that be?" she queried.* **2** ask questions of: *They queried him about his future plans.* **3** express doubt about: *She queried the wisdom of accepting the first offer.* **4** *Printing.* mark with a question mark, to express doubt. ⟨< Med.L *quere* < L *quaere* ask!⟩
☛ *Syn. n.* **1.** See note at QUESTION.

que•sa•dil•la [,keisə'dijə] *n.* a Mexican dish consisting of a crust covered with cheese and various items, rather like a pizza. ⟨< Mexican Sp. < *queso* cheese⟩

quest [kwɛst] *n., v. —n.* **1** the act or an instance of seeking or searching: *a quest for treasure. She descended to the cellar in quest of the sherry.* **2** an expedition or journey in search of something noble, ideal, or holy: *There are many stories about the quest for the Holy Grail.* **3** the object or goal of a search. **4** the participants in a quest.
—v. seek or hunt: *questing for gold in faraway places.* ⟨ME < OF < VL *quaesita* < L *quaerere* seek⟩

ques•tion ['kwɛstʃən] *n., v. —n.* **1** something asked; a sentence in interrogative form, addressed to someone to obtain information; inquiry. **2** a judicial examination or trial; interrogation. **3** a matter of doubt or dispute; controversy: *A question arose about the ownership of the property.* **4** a matter to be talked over, investigated, considered, etc.; problem: *the question of automation.* **5** a proposal to be voted on. **6** the taking of a vote on a proposal. **7** the act of asking or inquiring.
beg the question, a assume the truth of the very point one is trying to prove. **b** loosely, evade the issue.
beside the question, off the subject.
beyond question, without doubt; beyond dispute: *The statements in that book are true beyond question.*
call into or **in question,** dispute; challenge.
in question, a under consideration or discussion. **b** in dispute.
out of the question, not to be considered; impossible.
without question, a without a doubt; indisputably: *Leslie is without question the brightest student in the school.* **b** without challenging someone's authority: *to obey without question.*

—*v.* **1** ask questions of; seek information from. **2** ask; inquire. **3** doubt; challenge; dispute: *I question the truth of his story.* ⟨ME < OF < L *quaestio, -onis*, ult. < *quaerere* ask⟩ **—'ques•tion•er,** *n.* **— 'ques•tion•ing•ly,** *adv.* **—'ques•tion•less,** *adj.*

☛ *Syn. n.* **1. Question,** QUERY = something asked. **Question** applies to any request for information: *I have some questions about today's lesson.* **Query** applies in particular to a question raised as a matter of doubt or objection and seeking a specific or authoritative answer: *He put several queries concerning items in the budget.*

☛ *Syn. v.* **1. Question,** ASK, INTERROGATE = seek information from someone. **Ask** is the general word, and suggests nothing more: *I asked him why he did it.* **Question** often means ask a series of questions, sometimes formally and according to some plan: *I questioned the boy until he told all he knew.* **Interrogate** is a formal word meaning 'to question formally and methodically': *The intelligence officer interrogated the prisoners.*

ques•tion•a•ble ['kwɛstʃənəbəl] *adj.* **1** open to question or dispute; doubtful; uncertain. **2** of doubtful propriety, honesty, morality, respectability, or the like. **—'ques•tion•a•bly,** *adv.*

question mark a mark (?) put after a question or used to express doubt about something written or printed.

ques•tion•naire [ˌkwɛstʃə'nɛr] *n.* **1** a set of questions designed for obtaining statistical information: *The questionnaire was quite straightforward.* **2** a form containing such questions, usually having spaces for answers: *to fill out a questionnaire.* ⟨< F⟩

question time **1** in the House of Commons, a short period several times a week in which ministers answer questions submitted in advance by Members of Parliament. **2** a similar period in any assembly.

quet•zal [kɛt'sɑl] *n., pl.* **quetzales** [kɛt'sɑleis]. **1** a Central American bird (*Pharomachrus mocinno*) having brilliant gold-green and scarlet plumage. The male has long, flowing tail feathers. **2** the basic unit of money in Guatemala, divided into 100 centavos. Also, **quezal.** See table of money in the Appendix. **3** a note worth one quetzal. ⟨< Mexican Sp. < Nahuatl⟩

queue [kju] *n., v.* **queued, queu•ing.** *—n.* **1** a long line of people, automobiles, etc.; line-up. **2** *Computer technology.* a stored sequence of items such as messages, print jobs, etc., waiting to be processed in the order in which they were received. **3** a braid of hair hanging down the back.
—v. form or stand in a line while waiting to be served, etc. (*usually used with* **up**): *We had to queue up to get tickets.* ⟨< F < L *coda*, var. of *cauda* tail⟩
☛ *Hom.* CUE.

quib•ble ['kwɪbəl] *n., v.* **-bled, -bling.** *—n.* **1** an evasion of the main point, especially a petty one or one that depends on words that are vague or have a double meaning: *a legal quibble.* **2** a minor criticism or objection: *The meeting was delayed for several minutes because of a quibble about procedure.*
—v. use quibbles; resort to petty objections or evasions. ⟨apparently dim. of obs. *quib* quip < L *quibus* (dat. and abl. pl. of *qui* who, which), used in legal jargon⟩ **—'quib•bler,** *n.*

quiche [kiʃ] *n.* a kind of pie usually served as a main dish, consisting of a pastry shell filled with an egg and cream custard together with any of various other ingredients, such as ham, bacon, cheese, or seafood. ⟨< F < G dial. (Lorraine) *Küche*, dim. of *Kuchen* cake⟩

Qui•ché [ki'tʃei] *n.* a Mayan language spoken in Guatemala.

quiche Lor•raine [lə'rein] a quiche containing bacon, onion, and, usually, cheese.

quick [kwɪk] *adj., n., adv.* *—adj.* **1** fast and sudden; swift: *a quick turn.* **2** begun and ended in a short time: *a quick visit.* **3** coming soon; prompt: *a quick reply.* **4** not patient; hasty: *a quick temper.* **5** brisk: *a quick fire.* **6** acting quickly; ready; lively: *a quick wit.* **7** understanding or learning quickly: *a child who is quick in school.* **8** *Archaic.* alive; living. **9** acutely sensitive; keen; responsive: *a quick sense of hearing.* **10** nimble or deft: *quick fingers.* **11** eager or ready; not hesitating: *quick to help others.*
quick with child, *Archaic.* pregnant.
—n. **1** tender, sensitive flesh, especially the flesh under a fingernail or toenail: *The child bit his nails down to the quick.* **2** the tender, sensitive part of one's feelings: *Their insults cut him to the quick.* **3** *Archaic.* **the quick,** *pl.* living persons: *the quick and the dead.*
—adv. quickly: *Come quick!* ⟨OE *cwic* alive⟩ **—'quick•ness,** *n.* **—'quick•ly,** *adv.*

☛ *Syn. adj.* **1. Quick,** FAST[1], RAPID = done, happening, moving, or acting with speed. **Quick** especially describes the time of something done or made or happening with speed or without delay: *You made a quick trip.* **Fast** especially describes a characteristic of something moving or acting, and emphasizes the swiftness with which it acts or moves: *I took a fast plane.* **Rapid** emphasizes the rate of the action or movement, or series of movements, performed: *I had to do some rapid planning.*

quick bread bread, biscuits, etc. made with a leavening agent, usually baking powder or baking soda, that does not require the dough to be left to rise before baking.

quick•en ['kwɪkən] *v.* **1** make or become more rapid; accelerate: *He quickened his pace. His pulse quickened.* **2** make or become stimulated or animated: *Her interest quickened when the discussion turned to travel.* **3** of a child in the womb, show life by movements. **4** reach the stage of pregnancy in which the baby can be felt moving. **5** *Archaic.* cause to burn brighter: *to quicken hot ashes into flames.*

quick–fire ['kwɪk ˌfaɪr] *adj.* See RAPID-FIRE. Also, **quick-firing.**

quick–freeze ['kwɪk ˌfriz] *v.* **-froze, -fro•zen, -freez•ing.** freeze (food) quickly in preparation for storage, so that the ice crystals formed during the freezing process are too small to rupture the cells, thus preserving the natural juices and flavour of the food.

quick•hatch ['kwɪkˌhætʃ] *n. Cdn. Obsolete.* wolverine. ⟨< Algonkian Cree *$k^{w}ek^{w}uhakeo$*⟩

quick•ie ['kwɪki] *n. Informal.* **1** something made or done very quickly or superficially: *Her last film was just a quickie. Let's stop for coffee; we've got time for at least a quickie.* **2** an alcoholic drink consumed in a hurry. **3** (*adjl.*) done, made, etc. hastily or quickly.

quick kick *Football.* a punt kicked from a running play formation during a down other than the third, the objective being to catch the opposing players out of position and thus to gain ground.

quick•lime ['kwɪkˌlaɪm] *n.* a white, caustic, alkaline substance usually obtained by burning limestone and used for making calcium hydroxide, mortar, and cement; calcium oxide.

quick march **1** a march in QUICK TIME. **2** **Quick march!** an order to begin marching in QUICK TIME.

quick•sand ['kwɪkˌsænd] *n.* **1** soft, wet sand that will not support a heavy weight: *The horse was swallowed by the quicksand.* **2** a deep expanse of such sand.

quick•set ['kwɪkˌsɛt] *n. Esp. Brit.* **1** a plant or cutting, especially of hawthorn, set to grow in a hedge. **2** such plants collectively. **3** a hedge of such plants.

quick•sil•ver ['kwɪkˌsɪlvər] *n., adj., v.* *—n.* mercury.
—adj. unpredictable; prone to change unpredictably: *a quicksilver temperament.*
—v. amalgamate or coat with mercury. ⟨OE *cwicseolfor*, after L *argentum vivum* living silver⟩

quick•step ['kwɪkˌstɛp] *n.* **1** a lively dance step. **2** music in a brisk march rhythm, such as that used to accompany marching in QUICK TIME. **3** a step used in marching in QUICK TIME.

quick–tem•pered ['kwɪk 'tɛmpərd] *adj.* easily angered.

quick time a marching rate of 120 paces per minute, or about 5.5 km/h.

quick•wa•ter ['kwɪkˌwɒtər] *n. Cdn.* a stretch of a stream with sufficient fall to create a strong current but where there are no rapids.

quick–wit•ted ['kwɪk 'wɪtɪd] *adj.* having a quick mind; mentally alert. **—'quick-'wit•ted•ly,** *adv.* **—'quick-'wit•ted•ness,** *n.*

quid[1] [kwɪd] *n.* **1** a piece to be chewed. **2** a bite of chewing tobacco. ⟨OE *cwidu* cud⟩

quid[2] [kwɪd] *n., pl.* **quid.** *Brit. Slang.* one pound sterling: *She gets 180 quid a week.*
be quids in, *Brit. Slang.* have a lot of profit. ⟨probably from L *quid pro quo* something for something⟩

quid•nunc ['kwɪdˌnʌŋk] *n.* a newsmonger; gossip; inquisitive person. ⟨< L *quid nunc* what now⟩

quid pro quo [ˌkwɪd prou 'kwou] *Latin.* one thing in return for another; compensation. ⟨< L, something for something⟩

qui•es•cent [kwi'ɛsənt] *or* [kwaɪ'ɛsənt] *adj.* inactive; quiet; still; motionless. ⟨< L *quiescens, -entis*, ppr. of *quiescere* rest < *quies*, n., rest⟩ **—qui'es•cence,** *n.* **—qui'es•cent•ly,** *adv.*

qui•et ['kwaɪət] *adj., v., n., adv.* *—adj.* **1** moving very little; still: *a quiet river.* **2** with no or little noise: *quiet footsteps, a quiet room.* **3** saying little; reserved: *She is normally a quiet person, but injustice makes her voluble.* **4** calm; gentle; unobtrusive: *a quiet manner.* **5** not showy or bright: *Grey is a quiet colour.* **6** not active: *a quiet life in the country.* **7** not perturbed or excited; peaceful: *a quiet mind.* **8** out of the way; secluded: *a quiet spot in the country.*

—*v.* **1** make quiet: *The father quieted his frightened child.* **2** become quiet: *The wind quieted down.* **3** calm; allay; assuage: *The guide quieted our fears.*
—*n.* a state of rest or stillness; freedom from disturbance; peace: *to read in quiet, the quiet of early morning.*
—*adv.* in a quiet manner. ⟨ME < L *quietus* resting, pp. of *quiescere* rest < *quies* quiet. Doublet of COY and QUIT, adj.⟩ **—'qui•et•er,** *n.* **—'qui•et•ly,** *adv.* **—'qui•et•ness,** *n.*
☛ *Syn. adj.* **1.** See note at STILL[1].

qui•et•en ['kwaɪətən] *v.* **1** cause to become quiet; make still or peaceful: *The young riders quietened their excited horses.* **2** become quiet (*usually used with* **down**): *The wind finally quietened down.*

qui•et•ism ['kwaɪə,tɪzəm] *n.* **1** a form of religious mysticism requiring complete submission or abandonment of the will and withdrawal from worldly affairs to the point of indifference to one's fate. It was first proposed by the Spanish monk Molinus in the late 17th century. **2** mental or bodily passivity; apathy.

qui•e•tude ['kwaɪə,tjud] *or* ['kwaɪə,tud] *n.* quietness; stillness; calmness. ⟨< LL *quietudo* < L *quietus* quiet⟩

qui•e•tus [kwaɪ'itəs] *n.* **1** final extinction, riddance, or end: *to give an ugly rumour its quietus. The government's refusal of funds has given the quietus to the project.* **2** anything that effectively puts an end to something else; a finishing stroke. **3** release from life; death. **4** settlement or discharge of a debt, obligation, etc. ⟨< Med.L *quietus est* he is discharged < L *quietus est* he is at rest. See QUIET.⟩

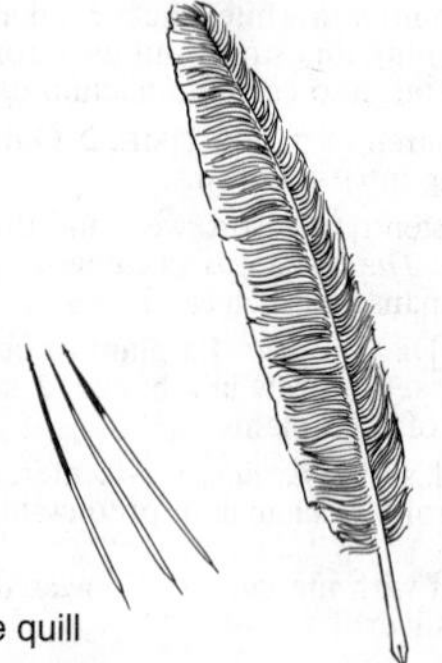
A porcupine quill
A feather made into a quill pen

quill [kwɪl] *n., v.* —*n.* **1** a large, stiff feather from the wing or tail of a bird. **2** the hollow stem of a feather. **3** anything made from the stem of a feather, such as a pen or toothpick. **4** *Cdn.* formerly, in the fur trade, a feather, especially a goose feather, used as a token by traders bartering with First Nations people. **5** one of the stiff sharp spines of a porcupine or hedgehog. **6** a musical pipe, especially one made from a hollow cane or reed. **7** a bobbin or spindle on which yarn is wound. **8** a roll of dried bark formed in drying, such as cinnamon.
—*v.* **1** arrange in cylindrical flutes or quillings. **2** wind on a spindle or bobbin. **3** cover or penetrate with, or as if with, quills like those of a hedgehog or porcupine. **4** remove a quill or quills from: *to quill a bird before roasting.* ⟨ME *quil*⟩

quill•back ['kwɪl,bæk] *n.* a North American freshwater fish (*Carpiodes cyprinus*), a kind of sucker having a very deep, laterally compressed, buff and white body and a dorsal fin with the first rays much elongated.

quil•ling ['kwɪlɪŋ] *n., v.* —*n.* **1** a fluted or pleated edging resembling quills. **2** quilled fabric.
—*v.* ppr. of QUILL.

quill pig *Cdn.* porcupine. Also **quilly pig.**

quilt [kwɪlt] *n., v.* —*n.* **1** a bed covering made of two layers of cloth with a filling between them that is held in place by lines of stitching, often in decorative patterns. The design is usually achieved by stitching together pieces of different fabrics in various colours. Quilts are usually filled with down or feathers or a batting of wool, cotton, or a synthetic fibre such as terylene. **2** any thick bed covering; a comforter. **3** anything quilted or similar to a quilt.
—*v.* **1** fill or pad like a quilt; stitch in layers with a padding between: *to quilt a jacket. I bought some quilted material for a vest.* **2** stitch with lines or patterns through layers of cloth: *to quilt a traditional design.* **3** make quilts: *They enjoy quilting.* ⟨ME < OF *cuilte* < L *culcita* cushion⟩ **—'quilt•er,** *n.*

quilt•ing ['kwɪltɪŋ] *n., v.* —*n.* **1** quilted work. **2** material that is quilted or used for making quilts. **3** the activity or act of making quilts. **4** QUILTING BEE.
—*v.* ppr. of QUILT.

quilting bee *Cdn.* a social gathering, usually of women, to work on a quilt.

qui•na•ry ['kwaɪnəri] *adj.* **1** occurring in sets of five. **2** pertaining to or consisting of five. **3** having reference to a numerical system based on the number five. ⟨< L *quinarius*, equiv. to *quiny* five + *arius* -ary⟩

quince [kwɪns] *n.* **1** a hard, yellowish, acid fruit, used for making preserves and jelly. **2** the Asiatic tree (*Cydonia oblonga*) it grows on, a member of the rose family. **3** japonica. ⟨originally pl. of ME *quyne* < OF *cooin* < L *cotoneum*⟩

quin•cen•te•na•ry [,kwɪnsɛn'tɛnəri] *or* [,kwɪnsɛn'tinəri] *n.* a 500th anniversary.

quin•cun•cial [kwɪn'kʌnʃəl] *adj.* of, having to do with, or being a quincunx.

quin•cunx ['kwɪnkʌŋks] *n.* **1** an arrangement or group of five objects with four forming the corners of a square or rectangle and the fifth in the centre, such as the five on a die or playing card. **2** a set of five stories. **3** *Botany.* an arrangement of five flower petals or leaves such that two are interior, two exterior, and one partly interior and partly exterior.

quin•el•la [kwɪ'nɛlə] *n.* **1** a system of betting that two horses in a particular race will occupy the first two places, though either horse may come first. **2** a race on which such bets may be made. ⟨< Am.Sp. *quiniela* < *quina* five; from the laying of such bets on the scores in a game with five players⟩

quin•ic acid ['kwɪnɪk] a white, crystalline, water-soluble acid, present in and prepared from cinchona bark, coffee beans, and the leaves of many plants. *Formula*: $C_7H_{12}O_6$

qui•ni•dine ['kwɪnɪ,din] *or* ['kwɪnɪdɪn] *n. Pharmacy.* a colourless crystalline alkaloid, isomeric with quinine ($C_{20}H_{24}N_2O_2$), obtained from the bark of certain species of cinchona and used to treat malaria and irregular heart rhythms.

qui•nine ['kwaɪnaɪn] *or* [kwɪ'nin] *n. Chemistry. Pharmacy.* **1** a bitter, colourless crystalline drug made from cinchona bark, used in medicine. *Formula*: $C_{20}H_{24}N_2O_2$ **2** any of various compounds of quinine that are used as medicine. ⟨< Sp. *quina* < Quechua *kina* bark⟩

quinine water TONIC (def. 3).

quinnat salmon ['kwɪnæt] *Cdn.* SPRING SALMON. ⟨< Salishan *t'kwinnat*⟩

qui•noi•dine [kwɪ'nɔɪdin] *or* [kwɪ'nɔɪdɪn] *n. Pharmacology.* a brownish black resinous substance consisting of a mixture of amorphous alkaloids, a by-product of the production of quinine and formerly used as a cheap substitute for it.

qui•none ['kwaɪnoun] *n.* any of various aromatic compounds, especially a yellow one, $C_6H_4O_2$, used as a pigment. ⟨< *quin(ine)* + *-one*⟩

Quin•qua•ges•i•ma [,kwɪŋkwə'dʒɛsəmə] *n.* the Sunday before the beginning of Lent; Shrove Sunday. ⟨< L, fiftieth⟩

quinque– *combining form.* five. Also, before vowels, **quinqu-**: *quinquennial.* ⟨< L⟩

quin•quen•ni•al [kwɪn'kwɛniəl] *or* [kwɪŋ'kwɛniəl] *adj., n.* —*adj.* **1** occurring every five years. **2** of or lasting for five years. —*n.* **1** something that occurs every five years. **2** something lasting five years. ⟨< L *quinquennium* < *quinque* five + *annus* year⟩ **—quin'quen•ni•al•ly,** *adv.*

quin•quen•ni•um [kwɪn'kwɛniəm] *or* [kwɪŋ'kwɛniəm] *n.* a period of five years.

quin•que•reme ['kwɪŋkwə,rim] *n.* an ancient Roman galley with five tiers of oars. ⟨< L *quinqueremis* < *quinque* five + *remus* oar⟩

quin•que•va•lent [,kwɪŋkwə'veilənt] *adj.* having five valences.

quin•sy ['kwɪnzi] *n. Pathology.* an abscess behind or on the tonsils, usually caused by a severe case of tonsillitis. ⟨ME < Med.L *quinancia* < Gk. *kynanchē*, originally, dog's collar < *kyon, kynos* dog + *anchein* choke⟩

quint [kwɪnt] *n. Informal.* quintuplet. ⟨by shortening⟩

quin•tain ['kwɪntən] *n.* **1** an object mounted on a post or crosspiece, used by knights as a target for tilting. **2** the sport of tilting at a quintain. ⟨ME *quyntain* < MF *quintaine* or Med.L *quintān*, of obscure origin⟩

quin•tal ['kwɪntəl] *or* ['kæntəl]. *n.* **1** *Cdn. Newfoundland.* **a** a unit used for weighing fish, especially cod, equal to 112 pounds (about 50.8 kg). **b** a quantity of fish weighing one quintal: *The first day they got 50 quintals of cod.* **c** a container holding 112 pounds or 50.8 kg, used for packing and shipping dried, salted cod. **2** a unit for measuring mass, equal to 100 pounds (about 45.4 kg). **3** a unit for measuring mass, equal to 100 kg. ⟨ME < Med.L *quintale* < Arabic *qintar* weight of a hundred pounds, probably ult. < L *centenarius* < *centum* hundred⟩

quin•tes•sence [kwɪn'tɛsəns] *n.* **1** the essence of a thing in its purest form. **2** the best example or representative of something: *Mother Theresa is the quintessence of goodness.* **3** in ancient and medieval philosophy, the fifth essence, ether, supposed to be the ultimate substance because it was that of which the heavenly bodies were composed, the other four being earth, air, fire, and water. ⟨ME < Med.L *quinta essentia* fifth essence⟩

quin•tes•sen•tial [,kwɪntə'sɛnʃəl] *adj.* having the nature of a quintessence; of the purest or most perfect kind: *the quintessential detective of modern fiction.*
—,quin•tes'sen•tial•ly, *adv.*

quin•tet or **quin•tette** [kwɪn'tɛt] *n.* **1** a group of five musicians who perform together. **2** a piece of music for five voices or instruments. **3** any group of five. ⟨< F < Ital. *quintetto* < *quinto* fifth < L *quintus*⟩

quin•til•lion [kwɪn'tɪljən] *n.* a cardinal number represented: **1** in Canada, the United States, and France by 1 followed by 18 zeros. **2** in the U.K. and Germany by 1 followed by 30 zeros.
—quin'til•lionth, *adj., n.* ⟨< L *quintus* fifth + E *million*⟩

quin•tu•ple [kwɪn'tjupəl], [kwɪn'tupəl], [kwɪn'tʌpəl], *or* ['kwɪntəpəl] *adj., v.* **-pled, -pling;** *n.* *—adj.* **1** fivefold; consisting of five parts. **2** five times as great or as many.
—v. make or become five times as great or as many: *He quintupled his investment.*
—n. a number, amount, etc. five times as great as another. ⟨< F *quintuple* < L *quintus* fifth; patterned on *quadruple*⟩

quin•tu•plet [kwɪn'tʌplɪt], [kwɪn'tjuplɪt], [kwɪn'tuplɪt], *or* ['kwɪntəplɪt] *n.* **1** one of five offspring born at one birth. **2** any group or combination of five. ⟨< *quintuple*, adj., modelled on *triplet*⟩

quin•tu•pli•cate *adj., n.* [kwɪn'tjupləkɪt] *or* [kwɪn'tupləkɪt]; *v.* [kwɪn'tjuplɪ,keit] *or* [kwɪn'tuplɪ,keit] *adj., n., v.* **-at•ed, -at•ing.**
—adj. **1** fivefold; occurring in five identical copies. **2** referring to the fifth of five identical copies.
—n. the fifth of five identical copies or things.
in quintuplicate, in five copies.
—v. **1** make or produce five identical copies of (something).
2 increase fivefold.

quip [kwɪp] *n., v.* **quipped, quip•ping.** *—n.* **1** a clever or witty saying, especially one made on the spur of the moment. **2** a sharp, cutting remark. **3** a quibble. **4** something odd or strange.
—v. make quips. ⟨for earlier *quippy* < L *quippe* indeed, I dare say⟩

qui•pu ['kipu] *or* ['kwɪpu] *n.* an ancient Peruvian counting and coding device, consisting of variously coloured and knotted strings attached to a cord. ⟨< Am.Sp. < Quechua⟩

quire[1] [kwaɪr] *n.* **1** 24 or, sometimes, 25 sheets of paper of the same size and quality; one-twentieth of a ream. **2** four sheets of paper folded to form a section of eight leaves, or 16 pages, as often done in medieval manuscripts. ⟨ME < OF *quaier*, ult. < L *quaterni* four each⟩
☛ *Hom.* CHOIR.

quire[2] [kwaɪr] *n. Archaic.* choir.

Quir•i•nal ['kwirənəl] *n., adj.* *—n.* **1** one of the seven hills upon which Rome was built. **2** a palace built on this hill, used from 1870-1946 as a royal residence and later as the presidential residence. **3** formerly, the Italian royal court or government, as distinguished from the Vatican (representing the papacy).
—adj. situated on or pertaining to the Quirinal. ⟨< L *Quirinalis* < *Quirinus*, an ancient Roman god of war⟩

quirk [kwɜrk] *n., v.* *—n.* **1** a peculiar trait; an odd mannerism or way of behaving: *She has some irritating quirks.* **2** an unexpected or sudden happening, action, etc.: *a quirk of fate.* **3** a sudden turn or curve, such as a flourish in writing. **4** a quibble or equivocation. **5** *Architecture.* an acute angle or deep groove in a moulding.
—v. form with a quirk or quirks. ⟨origin uncertain⟩

quirk•y ['kwɜrki] *adj.* characterized by a quirk or quirks; especially, odd, peculiar, or unexpected: *a quirky viewpoint.*
—'quirk•i•ly, *adv.* **—'quirk•i•ness,** *n.*

quirt [kwɜrt] *n., v.* *—n.* a riding whip with a short, stout handle and a lash of braided leather.
—v. strike with a quirt. ⟨< Sp. *cuarta*, originally, a long whip⟩

quis•ling ['kwɪzlɪŋ] *n.* **1** a person who collaborates with an enemy occupying his or her country, especially by serving in a puppet government. **2** a traitor. ⟨< Vidkun *Quisling* (1887-1945), a Norwegian army officer and politician, who co-operated with the Germans when they invaded Norway during World War II⟩

quit [kwɪt] *v.* **quit** or **quit•ted, quit•ting;** *adj.* *—v.* **1** stop: *The crew quit work when the whistle blew.* **2** stop doing something: *It's almost time to quit.* **3** leave: *He quit the room in anger.* **4** give up; let go: *She quit her job.* **5** pay back; pay off (a debt). **6** free; clear; rid. **7** *Archaic.* behave or conduct (oneself); ACQUIT (def. 4).
—adj. free; clear; rid: *I gave him money to be quit of him.* ⟨(v.) ME < OF *quiter* < Med.L *quietare* discharge < L *quietus.* See QUIET; (adj.) ME < OF *quite* < L *quietus.* Doublet of QUIET and COY.⟩

quitch or **quitch grass** [kwɪtʃ] *n.* COUCH GRASS. ⟨OE *cwice.* Related to QUICK.⟩

quit•claim ['kwɪt,kleim] *n., v.* *—n.* **1** the giving up of a claim. **2** a document stating that somebody gives up a claim; QUITCLAIM DEED.
—v. give up claim to (a right or title). ⟨ME < AF *quiteclamer* < OF *quite* + *clamer.* See QUIT, CLAIM.⟩

quitclaim deed *Law.* a deed or legal document by which one person gives up claim, title, or interest in a piece of property without guaranteeing that the claim, etc. is valid.

quite [kwəit] *adv.* **1** completely; wholly; entirely: *That's not quite true. I'm afraid it's quite impossible for me to go.* **2** really; positively: *It's quite the thing these days.* **3** *Informal.* to a considerable extent or degree: *This dress is quite nice but I like the other one better. She plays the piano quite well.*
quite a, a a considerable (number, amount, size, etc.); a considerably: *There are quite a few left. It cost quite a lot. We waited quite a long while.* **b** *Informal.* impressive or unusual: *That's quite a ring you have. He's quite a guy.*
quite so! true! ⟨originally adj., var. of *quit* in sense of 'clear'⟩
☛ *Usage.* **Quite.** The formal meaning of **quite** is 'entirely, wholly'. In informal English, it is generally used with the reduced meaning of 'to a considerable extent or degree'. Formal: *The fox was quite exhausted when we reached it.* Informal: *He is quite worried. I hiked quite a distance.* A number of convenient phrases with **quite** are good informal usage: *quite a few* people, *quite a little* time, and so on.

quit•rent ['kwɪt,rɛnt] *n.* under the feudal system, the rent paid in money, instead of services rendered. Also, **quit-rent.** ⟨< *quit*, adj. + *rent*[1]⟩

quits [kwɪts] *adj.* on even terms by repayment or retaliation (*never used before a noun*): *After the book was returned undamaged, the boys were quits.*
call it quits, stop doing something; end an association: *The mosquitoes got so bad that we finally had to call it quits and go home. Serbia and Croatia called it quits when the Yugoslav Republic broke up.*
cry quits, admit that things are now even; agree to stop quarrelling, etc. ⟨< *quit*, adj.⟩

quit•tance ['kwɪtəns] *n.* **1** a release from debt or obligation. **2** the paper certifying a release from debt; a receipt.
3 repayment. ⟨ME < OF *quitance* < *quiter* quit. See QUIT.⟩

quit•ter ['kwɪtər] *n. Informal.* a person who gives up too easily.

quiv•er[1] ['kwɪvər] *v., n.* *—v.* shake; shiver; tremble: *The singer's voice quivered. The dog quivered with excitement.*
—n. shaking or trembling: *A quiver of his mouth showed that he was about to cry.* ⟨Cf. OE *cwiferlīce* actively⟩
☛ *Syn. v.* See note at SHAKE.

quiv•er[2] ['kwɪvər] *n.* **1** a tubelike case for holding and carrying arrows. **2** the arrows in a quiver. ⟨ME < AF *quiveir*, probably < Gmc.⟩

qui vive [,ki 'viv] who goes there?
on the qui vive, watchful; alert. ⟨< F *qui vive?*, literally, (long) live who?; expecting a reply such as *Vive le roi!* Long live the king!⟩

Qui•xo•te [ki'houti] *or, occasionally,* ['kwɪksət]; *Spanish,* [ki'xote] *n.* See DON QUIXOTE.

quix•ot•ic [kwɪk'sɒtɪk] *adj.* characterized by very high but impractical ideals or extravagant chivalry. **—quix'ot•i•cal•ly,** *adv.* ⟨< *Don Quixote*⟩

quix•ot•ism ['kwɪksə,tɪzəm] *n.* an instance of a quixotic character or behaviour.

quiz [kwɪz] *n., pl.* **quiz•zes;** *v.* **quizzed, quiz•zing.** *—n.* **1** a short or informal test; a questioning: *a quiz in geography.* **2** *Archaic.* a person who makes fun of others.
—v. **1** give such a test to: *to quiz a class in history.* **2** question; interrogate: *The lawyer quizzed the witness.* **3** *Archaic.* make fun of. ⟨origin uncertain⟩ **—'quiz•zer,** *n.*

quiz•mas•ter ['kwɪz,mæstər] *n.* the person who asks questions of the contestants on a quiz show.

quiz show a radio or television program in which contestants are given prizes for answering questions correctly.

quiz•zi•cal ['kwɪzɪkəl] *adj.* **1** odd; queer; comical. **2** that suggests making fun of others; teasing: *a quizzical smile.* **3** perplexed or puzzled; slightly disbelieving: *She had a quizzical look on her face.* **—'quiz•zi•cal•ly,** *adv.*

quoin [kɔɪn] *or* [kwɔɪn] *n., v. —n.* **1** an external angle of a wall or building. **2** the stone forming an outside angle of a wall; a cornerstone. **3** a wedge-shaped piece of wood, metal, stone, etc., used for a number of architectural purposes such as a keystone or a piece in an arch.
—v. provide or secure with a quoin or quoins. Also, **coign, coigne.** ⟨var. of *coin*⟩
☛ *Hom.* COIN [kɔɪn].

quoit [kwɔɪt] *n., v. —n.* **1** a heavy, flattish ring of iron or circle of rope, rubber, etc., used in a game in which it is thrown at a peg stuck in the ground to encircle it or come as close to it as possible. **2 quoits,** the game in which quoits are thrown at a peg (*used with a singular verb*). Quoits is similar to horseshoes.
—v. **1** play quoits. **2** throw like a quoit. ⟨ME < OF *coite* cushion⟩

quon•dam ['kwɒndæm] *adj.* that once was; former: *the quondam king of Romania.* ⟨< L *quondam* at one time⟩

Quon•set hut ['kwɒnsɪt] *U.S. Trademark.* a prefabricated, largely metal building with a semicylindrical shape. Compare NISSEN HUT, the Canadian and British equivalent. ⟨< *Quonset,* Rhode Island, where such a building was first used at the naval air base⟩

quo•rum ['kwɔrəm] *n.* **1** the number of members of any society or assembly that must be present if the business done is to be legal or binding. The number is usually set by by-law. **2** any specially selected group. ⟨< L *quorum* of whom⟩

quot. quotation.

quo•ta ['kwoutə] *n.* **1** a share or proportion that is required of or due to a person or group: *Each club member was given a quota of tickets to sell for the banquet.* **2** a limited quantity or proportion that is allowed: *a government quota on imports.* ⟨< Med.L < L *quota pars* how large a part⟩

quot•a•ble ['kwoutəbəl] *adj.* suitable for or worth quoting: *a quotable comment.* **—,quot•a'bil•i•ty,** *n.* **—'quot•a•bly,** *adv.*

quo•ta•tion [kwou'teiʃən] *n.* **1** somebody's words repeated exactly by another person; a passage quoted from a book, speech, etc.: *From what author does this quotation come?* **2** the act or habit of quoting: *Quotation is a habit of some preachers.* **3** the stating of the current price of a stock, commodity, etc. **4** the price so stated: *today's quotation on wheat.*

quotation mark one of a pair of marks used to indicate the beginning and end of a quotation. The usual marks are (" ") for a quotation and (' ') for a quotation within a quotation.
☛ *Usage.* **Punctuation with quotation marks.** A punctuation mark at the end of a quotation is normally placed before the closing quotation mark if it is part of the quotation or precedes a phrase identifying the source. It is placed outside the quotation marks if its function is to punctuate the main sentence and not the quotation itself: *Her abrupt reply was "What do you think?" Have you heard him sing "If you could read my mind"? "The longer you put it off," he said, "the harder it's going to be."*

quote [kwout] *v.* **quot•ed, quot•ing;** *n. —v.* **1** repeat the exact words of; give words or passages from: *to quote Shakespeare. He often quotes his grandchildren's sayings.* **2** repeat exactly the words of another or a passage from a book: *She quoted from the lawyer's closing arguments.* **3** bring forward as an example or authority; cite: *The judge quoted various cases in support of her opinion.* **4** give (a price): *to quote a price on a home.* **5** enclose within quotation marks: *The dialogue in old books is not quoted.*
—n. **1** *Informal.* quotation. **2** *Informal.* QUOTATION MARK. ⟨< Med.L *quotare* to number chapters < L *quotus* which (in sequence)⟩ **—'quot•er,** *n.*
☛ *Syn. v.* **3. Quote,** CITE = bring forward as authority or evidence. Although the distinction is not always kept, **quote** means to bring forward the words of another, either repeated exactly or given in a summary, identifying the speaker: *The Commissioner was quoted as saying action will be taken.* **Cite** means to name as evidence or authority, but not to quote, a passage, author, or book, with exact title, page, etc.: *To support his argument he cited Article 68, Chapter 10, of the Charter of the United Nations.*

quoth [kwouθ] *v. Archaic.* said (*always precedes the subject*): *"I would never do anything so stupid," quoth he.* ⟨pt. of *queathe* (OE *cwethan* say)⟩

quoth•a ['kwouθə] *interj. Archaic.* indeed! (*used ironically or contemptuously in repeating the words of another*). ⟨from *quoth a* quoth he⟩

quo•tid•i•an [kwou'tɪdiən] *adj., n. —adj.* **1** reappearing daily; daily. **2** ordinary; commonplace; usual.
—n. a fever or ague that occurs daily. ⟨< L *quotidianus,* var. of *cotidianus* < *cotidie* daily < *quotus* which (in sequence) + *dies* day⟩

quo•tient ['kwouʃənt] *n. Mathematics.* the number obtained by dividing one number by another. In 26 ÷ 2 = 13, 13 is the quotient. ⟨< L *quotiens* how many times⟩

quo war•ran•to [kwou wə'ræntou] *Latin.* **1** a writ commanding a person to show by what authority a public office, privilege, franchise, etc. is held. **2** the legal proceedings taken against such a person as distinct from a private citizen. ⟨< Med.L *quo warranto* by what warrant⟩

Qur•an [kʊ'rɑn], [kə'rɑn], *or* [kə'ræn] *n.* Koran. Also, **Qu'ran.** ⟨< Arabic < *qurān* recitation < *qara'a* read⟩

qursh or **qurush** [kɜrʃ] *or* ['kʊrəʃ] *n.* **1** a unit of money in Saudi Arabia, worth 1/20 of a rial. **2** a coin worth one qursh. ⟨< Arabic *qirsh*⟩

q.v. see this word (for L *quod vide* which see).
☛ *Usage.* The abbreviation **q.v.** is also used as an instruction to refer to another book, article, etc. just mentioned. It is now often replaced in reference works by the English word **see.**

QWERTY keyboard ['kwɜrti] a keyboard for a typewriter, computer terminal, etc., having the alphabetical and numerical keys in the traditional order.

R r *R r*

r or **R** [ɑr] *n., pl.* **r's** or **R's. 1** the eighteenth letter of the English alphabet. **2** any speech sound represented by this letter. **3** a person or thing identified as *r*, especially the eighteenth in a series. **4** any device, such as a printer's type, a lever, or a key on a keyboard, that produces an r or R. **5** anything shaped like the letter R or r. **6** (*adjl.*) of or being an R or r.
the three R's, the basic elements of an education; reading, writing, and arithmetic.

r 1 ratio. **2** radius. **3** (in some Christian liturgies) respond or response. **4** *Physics.* resistance.

r. 1 railway. **2** rod. **3** ruble. **4** rupee. **5** road. **6** rare. **7** residence; resides. **8** retired. **9** ratio. **10** *Printing.* recto.

R Restricted, a film rating indicating that only those 18 years of age or older will be admitted.

R. 1 River. **2** *U.S.* Republican. **3** Railway; Railroad. **4** King (for L *rex).* **5** Queen (for L *regina).* **6** Royal. **7** Rabbi. **8** *Chemistry.* Radical. **9** Réaumur. **10** Rector. **11 R.** or **r.** roentgen(s). **12** rand.

Ra [rɑ] *n.* the Egyptian sun god and supreme deity, typically represented as a hawk-headed man bearing the sun on his head. ⟨< Egyptian *Rā* the sun⟩

Ra radium.

R.A. 1 Royal Academy; Royal Academician. **2** Royal Artillery.

rab•bet ['ræbɪt] *n., v.* **-bet•ed, -bet•ing.** *—n.* **1** a groove, slot, or recess made on the edge or surface of a board, etc. to receive the end or edge of another piece of wood shaped to fit it. **2** a joint so made, also called a **rabbet joint.** See JOINT for picture.
—v. **1** cut or form a rabbet in. **2** join or be joined with a rabbet. ⟨ME < OF *rabat* a beating down < *rabbatre.* See REBATE¹.⟩
☛ *Hom.* RABBIT.

rab•bi ['ræbaɪ] *n., pl.* **-bis. 1** a respectful title for a teacher or scholar of the Jewish law. **2** a Jewish religious leader, now especially the ordained head of a congregation. ⟨< L < Hebrew *rabbī* my master⟩

rab•bin•ate ['ræbɪnɪt] *or* ['ræbɪ,neit] *n.* **1** the position or office of rabbi. **2** rabbis collectively.

rab•bin•ic [rə'bɪnɪk] *adj.* **1** rabbinical. **2 Rabbinic,** RABBINIC HEBREW.

rab•bin•i•cal [rə'bɪnɪkəl] *adj.* of or having to do with rabbis, their learning, writings, etc., or the rabbinate. **—rab'bin•i•cal•ly,** *adv.*

Rabbinic Hebrew the Hebrew language as used by rabbis of the Middle Ages in their writings.

rab•bit ['ræbɪt] *n., v. —n.* **1** any of various gregarious burrowing mammals (family Leporidae, especially genera *Oryctolagus* and *Sylvilagus*) related to and resembling hares but generally smaller, with shorter ears, and bearing furless young whose eyes are closed at birth. The common European rabbit (*Oryctolagus cuniculus*) has been introduced into many parts of the world; the various domestic breeds have also been developed from this species. The common North American rabbits are the cottontails. **2** the fur of a rabbit. **3** the flesh of a rabbit, used as food. **4** WELSH RABBIT. **5** loosely, a hare. **6** *Track & Field.* a runner in a distance race who sets a fast pace early on so as to tire out a close competitor or to encourage a teammate to run faster. **7** *Sports. Informal.* a mediocre player, especially at golf or tennis.
—v. hunt or catch rabbits. ⟨ME *rabet;* cf. MDu. *robbe*⟩ **—'rab•bit,like,** *adj.*
☛ *Hom.* RABBET, REBATE² [ræbɪt].

rabbit dance *Cdn.* a dance commemorating the time when First Nations people heard the evil spirit come crashing through the bush to annihilate them. Pretending they were rabbits, they leaped, cavorted, and hopped accordingly. The ruse was successful; the evil one passed, leaving them unharmed.

rabbit ears *Informal.* a small indoor television antenna consisting of two rods of adjustable length attached to a small base in such a way that they can be swivelled apart to form a wide or narrow V.

rabbit fever tularemia.

rabbit punch a quick, hard blow to the base of the skull or the nape of the neck. This punch is illegal in organized boxing.

rabbit's foot the hind foot of a rabbit, especially the left one, carried as a good luck charm.

rab•bit–skin blanket ['ræbɪt ,skɪn] *Cdn.* a warm blanket or robe made by cutting the skins of rabbits, or hares, into long strips and weaving them together.

rab•ble¹ ['ræbəl] *n., v.* **rab•bled, rab•bling.** *—n.* a disorderly crowd; mob.
—v. attack or mob as a rabble. ⟨Cf. Du. *rabbelen* prattle⟩

rab•ble² ['ræbəl] *n., v.* **rabbled, rab•bling.** *Metallurgy. —n.* **1** an iron bar or mechanical device used in stirring or skimming molten metal. **2** any similar device.
—v. stir or skim using a rabble. ⟨< F *râble* < MF *raable* < L *rutabulum* tool for shifting hot coals⟩

rab•ble–rous•er ['ræbəl ,raʊzər] *n.* a person who tries to stir up groups of people to violence, as a form of social or political protest; demagogue.

rab•ble–rous•ing ['ræbəl ,raʊzɪŋ] *adj., n. —adj.* acting like a rabble-rouser; demagogic.
—n. the methods or actions of a rabble-rouser; demagoguery.

Rab•e•lai•si•an [,ræbə'leiʒən] *or* [,ræbə'leiziən] *adj.* of, having to do with, or suggesting François Rabelais (1495?-1553), a French writer of satire and humour; characterized by broad, coarse humour.

rab•id ['ræbɪd] *adj.* **1** of or affected with rabies: *a rabid dog.* **2** furious; raging. **3** unreasonably extreme; fanatical; violent: *a rabid idealist.* ⟨< L *rabidus* < *rabere* be mad⟩ **—'rab•id•ly,** *adv.* **—ra'bid•i•ty** or **'rab•id•ness,** *n.*

ra•bies ['reibiz] *n.* an acute, usually fatal, infectious viral disease of the central nervous system that can be transmitted to any warm-blooded animal, including humans, by the bite of an animal that has the disease. The usual symptoms of rabies are wild excitement and aggressiveness, followed by paralysis and death. ⟨< L *rabies* madness < *rabere* be mad⟩

rac•coon [rə'kun] *or* [ræ'kun] *n.* **1** any of a genus (*Procyon*) of small, greyish brown, carnivorous mammals having a thickset body, a long, bushy, ringed tail, a dark patch around the eyes, and a pointed snout, especially the common raccoon (*P. lotor*) of North and Central America and the West Indies. Raccoons live mainly in trees and are active at night. **2** the fur of a raccoon. **3** (*adjl.*) designating the family (Procyonidae) of mammals that includes the raccoons, the kinkajou, etc. Also, **racoon.** ⟨< Algonquian⟩

A raccoon

raccoon perch YELLOW PERCH.

race¹ [reis] *n., v.* **raced, rac•ing.** *—n.* **1** a contest of speed, as in running, driving, riding, sailing, etc. **2** Often, **races,** *pl.* a series of horse races run at a set time over a regular course. **3** any contest that suggests a race: *a political race.* **4** swift or relentless onward movement: *the race of life.* **5** a strong or fast current of water: *a mill race.* **6** the channel of a stream. **7** a channel leading water to or from a place where its energy is utilized. **8** a track, groove, etc. for a sliding or rolling part of a machine. **9** slipstream.
—v. **1** engage in a contest of speed: *Tomorrow we race against the top team in the province.* **2** try to defeat in a contest of speed; run a race with: *I'll race you to the corner.* **3** cause to take part in a race; use for racing. **4** run a horse or dog, etc. in a race: *"Does she ride?" "No, but she races."* **5** run, move, or go swiftly. **6** cause to run, move, or go swiftly. **7** of an engine, run too fast when idling. **8** run (an engine) at high speed without engaging the gears. ⟨ME < ON *rás*⟩

race² [reis] *n.* **1** *Anthropology.* a major grouping of human beings, distinguished biologically mainly by such hereditary traits as dominant blood types and resistance to particular diseases and also by skin colour, body proportions, etc. The three major races now generally recognized are the Caucasoid, Mongoloid, and

Negroid. **2** one of the major divisions of living things: *the human race, the race of birds.* **3** a group, class, or kind of people having some feature or quality in common: *the Scottish race, the Nordic race, the brave race of sailors.* **4** subspecies; variety. **5** the state or condition of belonging to a particular race: *Intelligence does not depend on race.* ⟨< F < Ital. *razza*⟩
☛ *Syn.* **1, 2.** See note at PEOPLE.

race•course [ˈreisˌkɔrs] *n.* **1** an open course or prepared track for racing; racetrack. **2** a millrace.

race•horse [ˈreisˌhɔrs] *n.* a horse bred or kept for racing.

ra•ce•mate [reiˈsimeit] *or* [ˈræsəˌmeit] *n. Chemistry.* **1** a salt or ester of racemic acid. **2** a racemic salt or compound.

ra•ceme [reiˈsim] *or* [rəˈsim] *n. Botany.* a type of inflorescence consisting of a simple flower cluster having the flowers on short stalks along a stem, the lower flowers blooming first. The lily of the valley, the currant, and the chokecherry have racemes. See INFLORESCENCE for picture. ⟨< L *racemus* cluster. Doublet of RAISIN.⟩

ra•ce•mic [reiˈsimɪk] *adj. Chemistry.* of a compound, consisting of an optically inactive mixture of two other substances of the same chemical composition as the mixture itself, one dextrorotatory and the other levorotatory. ⟨See RACEMIC ACID⟩

racemic acid *Chemistry.* a colourless, crystalline, optically inactive form of tartaric acid sometimes found in the juice of grapes along with dextrorotatory-tartaric acid. ⟨< *raceme*, because it is found in grapes⟩

rac•e•mize [ˈræsəˌmaɪz] *v.* **-mized, -mizing.** *Chemistry.* convert to a racemic compound. **—rac•e•mi'za•tion,** *n.*

rac•e•mose [ˈræsəˌmous] *adj.* **1** *Botany.* having the form or characteristics of a raceme. **2** *Anatomy.* of a gland, resembling a bunch of grapes.

rac•er [ˈreisər] *n.* **1** a person who races or an animal, vehicle, boat, or aircraft that is used for racing. **2** any of several harmless North American snakes (genera *Coluber* and *Mastigophis*) that can move very fast, especially the **blacksnake.**

race riot an outbreak of violence resulting from hostility or hatred between races.

race•run•ner [ˈreisˌrʌnər] *n.* a whip-tailed lizard (*Cnemidophorus sexlineatus*) that is extremely active and quick-moving, found in warm areas of the U.S. and South America.

race suicide the extinction of a people that results when, by deliberate limitation of the number of children, the birth rate falls below the death rate.

race•track [ˈreisˌtræk] *n.* **1** a track or course, usually oval in shape, on which races are run. **2** a place where races are held, including the track, viewing stands, etc.

race•way [ˈreisˌwei] *n.* **1** *Esp. Brit.* a millrace. **2** a racetrack. **3** RACE[1] (def. 8).

ra•chis [ˈreikɪs] *n., pl.* **ra•chis•es** or **rach•i•des** [ˈrækəˌdiz] *or* [ˈreikəˌdiz]. **1** *Botany.* the stem from which the individual flowers of a flower cluster or the leaflets of a compound leaf grow. **2** *Ornithology.* the shaft of a feather. **3** *Anatomy.* SPINAL COLUMN. ⟨< NL < Gk. *rhachis* backbone⟩

ra•chit•ic [rəˈkɪtɪk] *adj.* having to do with or affected with rickets; rickety.

ra•chi•tis [rəˈkəitɪs] *n. Pathology.* rickets. ⟨< NL < Gk. *rhachis* backbone + *-itis*⟩

ra•cial [ˈreiʃəl] *adj.* **1** of, having to do with, or characteristic of a human race: *racial traits.* **2** occurring between or involving two or more races: *racial tensions, racial harmony.*

ra•cial•ly [ˈreiʃəli] *adv.* in respect to race.

racing showshoe *Cdn.* a long, slender snowshoe used in showshoe races.

rac•ism [ˈreisɪzəm] *n.* **1** prejudice or discrimination against a person or group because of a difference of race or of cultural or ethnic background. **2** belief in the superiority of a particular race, based on the theory that human abilities, character, etc. are determined by race.

rac•ist [ˈreisɪst] *n., adj.* —*n.* one who favours or practises racism.
—*adj.* of or having to do with racism: *racist policies.*

rack[1] [ræk] *n., v.* —*n.* **1** a fixture with bars, shelves, or pegs to hold, arrange, or keep things on: *a towel rack, a hat rack, a baggage rack.* **2** a frame made of bars to hold hay and other food for cattle, etc. **3** a framework set on a wagon for carrying hay, straw, etc. **4** a pair, or set, of antlers. **5** a former instrument of torture that stretched the body of the victim. **6** a cause or condition of great suffering in body or mind. **7** a violent stretch or strain. **8** *Machinery.* a bar with pegs or teeth on one edge, into which teeth on the rim of a wheel can fit. See GEAR for picture. **9** *Billiards.* **a** a triangular frame used for arranging the balls. **b** the balls as arranged in this frame before the break.
off the rack, (of clothes) ready-made.
on the rack, in great pain; suffering very much.
—*v.* **1** hurt very much: *racked with grief. A toothache racked his jaw.* **2** stretch; strain. **3** torture on the rack.
rack (one's) **brains,** think as hard as one can.
rack up, a accumulate; score or gain (points, a victory, etc.). **b** *Billiards.* set up (the balls) in the rack. ⟨probably < MDu. or MLG *recke*⟩
☛ *Hom.* WRACK.

rack[2] [ræk] *n.* wreck; destruction (*now only in the phrase* **rack and ruin**).
go to rack and ruin, decay; become destroyed. ⟨var. of *wrack[1]*⟩
☛ *Hom.* WRACK.

rack[3] [ræk] *n., v.* —*n.* a horse's gait in which the feet move in lateral pairs, the forefeet as in a slow gallop, the hind feet as in a trot, each foot falling separately; SINGLE-FOOT. The rack is not a natural gait.
—*v.* go at a rack. ⟨origin uncertain⟩
☛ *Hom.* WRACK.

rack[4] [ræk] *n., v.* —*n.* a mass of flying, broken clouds driven by the wind.
—*v.* (of clouds) be driven by the wind. ⟨ME < Scand.; cf. Swedish dial. *rak* wreckage⟩
☛ *Hom.* WRACK.

rack[5] [ræk] *n.* **1** the neck portion of a forequarter of pork, veal, or mutton, sometimes made into a roast. See LAMB for picture. **2** a rib section of lamb, mutton, or veal. ⟨origin uncertain⟩
☛ *Hom.* WRACK.

rack•et[1] [ˈrækɪt] *n., v.* —*n.* **1** loud noise or talking; uproar; din: *Who's making all the racket?* **2** a dishonest scheme for getting money from people, especially by threatening violence. **3** *Informal.* any dishonest or fraudulent scheme or activity. **4** *Slang.* an easy, very profitable means of livelihood: *He has quite a racket going, with the edible wrapping paper he invented.* **5** *Slang.* any business or occupation: *What's your racket?*
stand the racket, hold out against strain or wear and tear.
—*v.* **1** make a din; move about in a noisy way. **2 a** take part in an exciting social life. **b** travel casually in search of adventure or excitement (*used with* **around**) ⟨formerly British slang (from early 19c.); ? imitative⟩

rack•et[2] or **rac•quet** [ˈrækɪt] *n.* **1 a** a light, wide bat used in games like tennis, badminton, and squash, consisting of a network of nylon, gut, etc. stretched in an open oval or round frame attached to a handle. **b** *Informal.* the paddle used in table tennis. **2** Usually, **racquets,** a game for two or four players with a ball and rackets, played in a walled court (*used with a singular verb*). **3** Usually, **racquet**. See RAQUETTE. ⟨< F *raquette* < Ital. < Arabic *rāḥa* palm of the hand⟩

rack•et•eer [ˌrækəˈtir] *n., v.* —*n.* a person who operates a racket, especially one who extorts money by threatening violence or by blackmail.
—*v.* obtain money, etc. by such means.

rack•et•eer•ing [ˌrækəˈtirɪŋ] *n.* the business of a racketeer.

rack•et•y [ˈrækəti] *adj.* **1** making a racket; noisy. **2** characterized by revelry or dissipation.

ra•con [ˈreiˌkɒn] *n.* RADAR BEACON. ⟨< *ra*(*dar* + *bea*)*con*⟩

rac•on•teur [ˌrækɒnˈtɜr]; *French,* [ʀakɔ̃ˈtœʀ] *n.* a person who is skilful at telling stories, anecdotes, etc. ⟨< F⟩

rac•on•teuse [ˌrækɒnˈtɜz]; *French,* [ˈʀakɔ̃ˈtøz] *n.* a female raconteur.

ra•coon [rəˈkun] *or* [ræˈkun] *n.* raccoon.

rac•quet [ˈrækɪt] *n.* RACKET[2].

rac•quet•ball [ˈrækɪtˌbɒl] *n.* an indoor game similar to handball, played by two or four players in a walled court, using a short racket and a hollow rubber ball about the size of a tennis ball.

rac•y [ˈreisi] *adj.* **rac•i•er, rac•i•est. 1** vigorous; lively. **2** having the distinctive quality characteristic of something in its best or original form: *racy flavour.* **3** having a strong or sharp taste or odour. **4** risqué; suggestive; slightly indecent: *a racy novel.* ⟨< *race[2]*, in the sense of particular class or special flavour⟩ **—'rac•i•ly,** *adv.* **—'rac•i•ness,** *n.*

rad¹ [ræd] *n.* a unit of nuclear radiation equal to 100 ergs of energy per gram, for measuring absorbed doses of radiation. ⟨< *rad(iation)*⟩

rad² [ræd] *n. Informal.* radiator.

rad³ [ræd] *adj. Slang.* excellent; terrific. ⟨short for *radical*⟩

rad⁴ *Mathematics.* **1** radical. **2** radian. **3** radius. **4** radix.

ra•dar ['reidɑr] *n.* **1** a system for determining the distance, direction, speed, etc. of unseen objects by the reflection of high-frequency radio waves. **2** an instrument used for this. ⟨short for *ra*dio *d*etecting *a*nd *r*anging⟩

radar beacon a beacon that transmits a radar signal in response to a signal from a ship or aircraft, which the navigator then uses to determine his or her position.

ra•dar•scope ['reidɑr,skoup] an oscilloscope displaying radar signals.

radar trap a police vehicle or apparatus, usually located in a hidden or unexpected place, that uses radar to detect road vehicles travelling faster than the speed limit.

rad•dle ['rædəl] *v.* **rad•dled, rad•dling.** interweave.

ra•di•al ['reidiəl] *adj., n.* —*adj.* **1** arranged like or in radii or rays from a centre: *radial symmetry. The petals of a daisy and the spokes of a wagon wheel have a radial form.* **2** *Anatomy.* of, having to do with, or near the bone in the arm called the radius. —*n.* **1** RADIAL TIRE. **2** something having a radial form or structure. —**'ra•di•al•ly,** *adv.*

radial engine an internal-combustion engine for an airplane, having radially arranged cylinders.

radial tire an automobile tire in which the plies of cord extending to the edges of the tire are at right angles to the centre line of the tread.

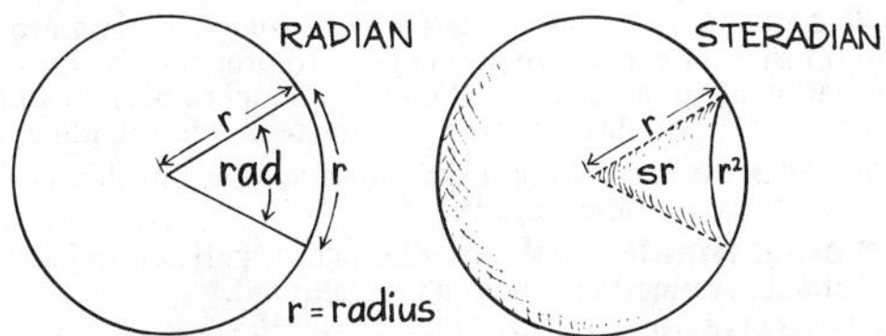

ra•di•an ['reidiən] *n.* an SI unit for measuring plane angles, equal to the angle formed between two radii of a circle that cut off an arc on the circumference equal in length to the radius. There are two pi (2 π) radians in a circle. The radian, which is used especially in mathematics, is one of the two supplementary units in the SI. *Symbol*: rad ⟨< *radius*⟩

ra•di•ance ['reidiəns] *n.* **1** the quality or state of being radiant. **2** vivid brightness: *the radiance of the sun, the radiance of a smile.* Also, **radiancy.**

ra•di•ant ['reidiənt] *adj., n.* —*adj.* **1** expressing or showing joy or good health: *a radiant smile.* **2** sending out rays of light or heat; shining; radiating: *The sun is a radiant body.* **3** bright with light. **4** sent off in rays from some source; radiated: *We get radiant energy from the sun.* **5** strikingly fine or splendid, as looks, beauty, etc., of the person.
—*n.* **1** *Physics.* a point or object from which light or heat radiates. **2** *Astronomy.* the point on the celestial sphere which appears to be the origin of a meteor shower. ⟨< L *radians, -antis,* ppr. of *radiare* beam < *radius* ray⟩ —**'ra•di•ant•ly,** *adv.*
☛ *Syn. adj.* See note at BRIGHT.

radiant energy *Physics.* a form of energy that is transmitted by electromagnetic waves and is perceived as heat, light, X rays, etc. The sun is our main source of radiant energy.

radiant flux *Physics.* the rate of flow of radiant energy.

radiant heating a method of heating a room, building, etc., by means of units consisting of pipes or wires concealed in walls, baseboards, or floors.

ra•di•ate *v.* ['reidi,eit]; *adj.* ['reidiɪt] *or* ['reidi,eit] *v.* **-at•ed, -at•ing;** *adj.* —*v.* **1** give out rays of: *The sun radiates light and heat.* **2** give out rays; shine. **3** issue in rays: *Heat radiates from those hot steam pipes.* **4** give out; send forth: *Her face radiates joy when she smiles.* **5** spread out from or as if from a centre: *Roads radiate from the city in every direction.*
—*adj.* **1** having rays or raylike parts emanating from a centre: *A daisy is a radiate flower.* **2 a** of parts, symmetrically radiating from a centre. **b** of an organism, having radial symmetry. ⟨ME < L *radiare.* See RADIANT.⟩ —**'ra•di•a•tive,** *adj.*

ra•di•a•tion [,reidi'eiʃən] *n.* **1** the act or process of giving out light, heat, or other radiant energy. **2** the energy radiated. **3** a radioactive ray or rays. Radiation is harmful to living tissues. **4** the process of using radiation from a radioactive material such as radium to treat disease by killing the diseased tissue. **5** *Informal.* the radiators of a central heating system referred to collectively, or their capacity: *The heating contractor will figure out how much radiation you need.* **6** the state of being radially arranged.

radiation sickness *Pathology.* a disease resulting from an overdose of radiation from radioactive materials. It is usually characterized by internal bleeding and changes in tissue structure.

ra•di•a•tor ['reidi,eitər] *or* (defs. 1 & 2) ['rædi,eitər] *n.* **1** a heating device consisting of a set of pipes through which steam or hot water passes. **2** a device for circulating coolant. The radiator of an automobile gives off heat very quickly and so cools the water inside it. **3** any person or thing that radiates or transmits something. **4** a radioactive person or thing. **5** *Radio.* the part of a transmitting antenna that produces electromagnetic waves.

rad•i•cal ['rædəkəl] *adj., n.* —*adj.* **1** going to the root; fundamental: *Cruelty is a radical fault. If he wants to reduce, he must make a radical change in his diet.* **2** advocating or favouring fundamental changes. **3 Radical,** of or having to do with certain 20th-century political parties, especially in Europe, whose programs range from somewhat leftist to conservative. **4** *Grammar.* of or pertaining to a root. **5** *Botany.* arising from the root or the base of the stem; basal. **6** *Mathematics.* having to do with or forming the root of a number or quantity.
—*n.* **1** a person who has radical views. **2 Radical,** a member of a Radical party. **3** *Chemistry.* an atom or group of atoms acting as a unit in reactions. Ammonium (NH_4) is a radical in NH_4OH and NH_4Cl. **4** *Mathematics.* **a** the sign ($\sqrt{}$) put before an expression to show that some root of it is to be extracted. **b** a quantity expressed as the root of another quantity, indicated by an expression written under a radical sign. **5** *Grammar.* a root. **6** anything fundamental or basic. ⟨ME < LL *radicalis* < L *radix, -icis* root⟩ —**'rad•i•cal•ly,** *adv.* —**'rad•i•cal•ness,** *n.*
☛ *Hom.* RADICLE.

rad•i•cal•ism ['rædɪkə,lɪzəm] *n.* **1** the condition or quality of being radical. **2** the principles or practices of radicals; extreme views.

rad•i•cal•ize ['rædɪkə,laɪz] *v.* **-ized, -iz•ing.** make radical. —**,rad•i•cal•i'za•tion,** *n.*

radical sign RADICAL (def. *n.* 4a).

rad•i•cand ['rædɪ,kænd] *n. Mathematics.* the quantity written beneath a radical sign.

ra•dic•chio [rə'dikjou] *n.* a variety of chickory, originally from Italy, having an oval head of purplish red, white-streaked leaves and a somewhat bitter taste, often used raw in salads.

rad•i•ces ['rædə,siz] *or* ['reidə,siz] *n.* a plural of RADIX.

rad•i•cle ['rædɪkəl] *n.* **1** *Botany.* **a** the lower end of the stem (hypocotyl) of a plant embryo, that develops into the main root. See EMBRYO for picture. **b** a small root; rootlet. **2** *Anatomy.* a small rootlike structure at the beginning of a vein or nerve. ⟨< L *radicula,* dim. of *radix, -icis* root⟩
☛ *Hom.* RADICAL.

ra•di•i ['reidi,aɪ] *n.* a pl. of RADIUS.

ra•di•o ['reidiou] *n., pl.* **-di•os;** *adj., v.* **-di•oed, -di•o•ing.**
—*n.* **1** the sending and receiving of sound in the form of electric signals by means of electromagnetic waves without connecting wires. **2** an apparatus for receiving and making audible the sounds so sent. **3** *Informal.* a message sent by radio. **4** the business of radio broadcasting: *She left the movies and got a job in radio.* **5** the branch of physics dealing with electromagnetic waves as used in communication.
—*adj.* **1** of, having to do with, used in, or sent by radio. **2** of or having to do with electric frequencies higher than 10 000 per second.
—*v.* **1** transmit or send out (a message) by radio. **2** send a message to (a person or place) by radio: *As soon as she got the information, she radioed headquarters.* ⟨independent use of *radio-,* abstracted from *radiotelegraphy,* etc.⟩

radio– *combining form.* **1** having to do with radio: *radiotelegraphy, radio-controlled.* **2** having to do with rays or radiation: *radiograph.* **3 a** having to do with radioactivity: *radioisotope.* **b** being a radioactive isotope of: *radiocarbon.* **4** of or having to do with a radius: *radiosymmetrical.* ⟨< *radius*⟩

ra•di•o•ac•tive [ˌreidiou'æktɪv] *adj. Physics. Chemistry.* giving off radiant energy in the form of alpha, beta, or gamma rays as a result of the breaking up of atoms. Radium, uranium, and thorium are radioactive metallic elements.

radioactive dating a method of determining the age of any earth material or artifact of organic origin by measuring the rate of decay of radioactive isotopes.

radioactive series a series of isotopes of certain elements, each of which disintegrates into the next until a stable element (usually lead) is reached. This disintegration may be either spontaneous or the result of the capture of electrons, and is called **radioactive decay**.

ra•di•o•ac•tiv•i•ty [ˌreidiouæk'tɪvɪti] *n. Physics. Chemistry.* **1** the property of being radioactive. **2** the radiation given off.

radio astronomy the branch of astronomy that studies objects in space by analysing radio waves given off by or reflected from them. **—radio astronomer.**

radio beacon a radio transmitter that sends out special radio signals to help ships, aircraft, etc. determine their position or come in safely when visibility is poor.

ra•di•o•bi•o•log•i•cal [ˌreidiouˌbaɪə'lɒdʒɪkəl] *adj.* **1** of or having to do with radiobiology. **2** of diseases, bodily conditions, etc., caused by radiation.

ra•di•o•bi•ol•o•gist [ˌreidioubaɪ'ɒlədʒɪst] *n.* a person trained in radiobiology, especially one whose work it is.

ra•di•o•bi•ol•o•gy [ˌreidioubaɪ'ɒlədʒi] *n.* the branch of biology that deals with the effects of radiation on living bodies.

ra•di•o•car•bon [ˌreidiou'kɑrbən] *adj. Chemistry.* radioactive carbon, especially carbon-14, used in finding out the age of ancient organic materials. The amount of radiocarbon in a piece of bone, fabric, etc. is an indication of how old it is.

ra•di•o•chem•i•cal [ˌreidiou'kɛmɪkəl] *adj.* of or having to do with radiochemistry.

ra•di•o•chem•ist [ˌreidiou'kɛmɪst] *n.* a person trained in radiochemistry, especially one whose work it is.

ra•di•o•chem•is•try [ˌreidiou'kɛmɪstri] *n.* the branch of chemistry dealing with radioactive phenomena and substances.

radio compass a direction finder in the form of a radio receiver having a directional antenna for determining the location of the receiver in relation to the transmitter.

radio control control by means of radio signals: *Our garage door is operated by radio control.*

ra•di•o–con•trolled ['reidiou kənˌtrould] *adj.* controlled from a distance by means of radio signals: *a radio-controlled model airplane.*

ra•di•o•el•e•ment [ˌreidiou'ɛləmənt] *n. Chemistry.* a radioactive element having no stable isotopes.

radio frequency any frequency of electromagnetic waves between about 10 kilohertz and 300 000 megahertz, i.e., on the spectrum between normally audible soundwaves and infrared light, used especially in transmitting radio and television signals. *Abbrev.*: RF, R.F., or r.f.

ra•di•o•gram ['reidiouˌgræm] *n.* **1** a message transmitted by radiotelegraphy. **2** radiograph.

ra•di•o•graph ['reidiouˌgræf] *n., v.* —*n.* a picture produced by X rays or other rays on a photographic plate, commonly called an X-ray photograph.
—*v.* make a radiograph of.

ra•di•og•ra•phy [ˌreidi'ɒgrəfi] *n.* the production of photographs by means of X rays. **—ˌra•di•o'graph•ic,** *adj.* **—ˌra•di'og•ra•pher,** *n.*

ra•di•o•i•so•tope [ˌreidiou'ɔisəˌtoup] *n.* a radioactive isotope, especially one produced artificially.

ra•di•o•lar•i•an [ˌreidiou'lɛriən] *n.* any of an order of marine protozoans having long, radiating projections and a shell of silica. ⟨< NL *Radiolaria* < LL *radiolus* little ray < L *radius* ray⟩

ra•di•o•log•i•cal [ˌreidiə'lɒdʒɪkəl] *adj.* **1** of or having to do with radiology. **2** of or having to do with the rays from radioactive substances. **—ˌra•di•o'log•i•cal•ly,** *adv.*

ra•di•ol•o•gist [ˌreidi'ɒlədʒɪst] *n.* a physician who specializes in radiology.

ra•di•ol•o•gy [ˌreidi'ɒlədʒi] *n.* the branch of medicine dealing originally with the use of radioactive substances and X rays in the diagnosis and treatment of disease; it now includes techniques such as ultrasound and other types of medical imaging.

ra•di•o•lu•cent [ˌreidiou'lusənt] *adj.* nearly transparent to X rays. **—ˌra•di•o'lu•cence,** *n.*

ra•di•ol•y•sis [ˌreidi'ɒləsɪs] *n. Chemistry.* chemical decomposition brought about by ionizing radiation. ⟨< *radio-* + *-lysis* a loosing (< Gk. *lyein* loose)⟩

ra•di•o•man ['reidiouˌmæn] *n., pl.* **-men. 1** a male radio operator or technician on an airplane, ship, etc. **2** a man who works in radio broadcasting.

ra•di•om•e•ter [ˌreidi'ɒmətər] *n.* an instrument for measuring radiant energy or the conversion of radiant energy into mechanical force, often consisting of a glass vessel containing vanes that are in a vacuum and rotate when exposed to light.

ra•di•o•met•ric [ˌreidiou'mɛtrɪk] *adj.* of, having to do with, or using a radiometer.

ra•di•om•e•try [ˌreidi'ɒmətri] *n.* the measurement of radiant energy by means of a radiometer.

ra•di•on•ics [ˌreidi'ɒnɪks] *n.* (radio) electronics.

ra•di•o•paque [ˌreidiou'peik] *adj.* not allowing the passage of X rays or other forms of radiant energy; visible in X-ray photographs and under fluoroscopy.

ra•di•o•phone ['reidiouˌfoun] *n.* a radiotelephone.

ra•di•o–pho•no•graph ['reidiou 'founəˌgræf] *n.* a unit combining a radio and a phonograph and sharing some of the components of the amplifier and speakers.

ra•di•os•co•py [ˌreidi'ɒskəpi] *n.* fluoroscopy. **—ˌra•di•o'scop•ic** [ˌreidiou'skɒpɪk], *adj.*

ra•di•o•sen•si•tive [ˌreidiou'sɛnsətɪv] *adj.* sensitive to or destructible by various forms of radiant energy such as X rays or rays from other radioactive material. **—ˌra•di•oˌsen•si'tiv•i•ty,** *n.*

ra•di•o•sonde ['reidiouˌsɒnd] *n. Meteorology.* a miniature radio transmitter carried up in a balloon to broadcast information about atmospheric humidity, temperature, pressure, etc. at various altitudes. ⟨< *radio* + F *sonde* depth, sounding⟩

radio source *Astronomy.* a supernova, quasar or other celestial source of radio waves.

ra•dio•sym•met•ri•cal [ˌreidiousə'mɛtrɪkəl] *adj.* radially symmetrical; symmetrical about a central point.

ra•di•o•tel•e•graph [ˌreidiou'tɛləˌgræf] *n., v.* —*n.* a telegraph worked by radio.
—*v.* telegraph by radio. **—ˌra•di•oˌtel•e'graph•ic,** *adj.*

ra•di•o•te•leg•ra•phy [ˌreidioutə'lɛgrəfi] *n.* the system of telegraphing by radio.

ra•di•o•tel•e•phone [ˌreidiou'tɛləˌfoun] *n., v.* **-phoned, -phon•ing.** —*n.* **1** a radio transmitter and receiver permitting two-way voice communication.
—*v.* telephone by radio.

ra•di•o•te•leph•o•ny [ˌreidioutə'lɛfəni] *n.* two-way radio communication by means of voice signals.

The main radio telescope at the National Research Council's radio astrophysical observatory near Penticton, B.C.

radio telescope *Astronomy.* an apparatus consisting of a radio receiver and an antenna, for the study of phenomena or bodies in outer space through observation of radio waves emanating from them.

ra•di•o•ther•a•py [ˌreidiou'θɛrəpi] *n.* the treatment of disease by means of radiation. **—ˌra•di•o'ther•a•pist,** *n.*

ra•di•o•ther•my ['reidiouˌθɜrmi] *n.* the treatment of disease or alleviation of pain by means of radiant heat. ⟨< *radio* + NL *-thermi* heat < Gk. *therme*⟩

radio wave an electromagnetic wave of radio frequency (between about 10 kilohertz and 300 000 megahertz).

rad•ish ['rædɪʃ] *n.* **1** an annual or biennial herb (*Raphanus sativus*) of the mustard family, widely cultivated for its thick, edible root. **2** the root of this plant, having red or white skin and crisp, hot-tasting, white flesh, eaten raw, in salads, etc. ⟨OE *rædic* < L *radix radicis* root. Doublet of RADIX.⟩

ra•di•um ['reidiəm] *n. Chemistry.* a rare, silvery-white, radioactive metallic element found in uranium ores, used in radiotherapy, in the manufacture of luminous paints, etc. *Symbol*: Ra; *at.no.* 88; *at.mass* 226.03; *half-life* 1620 years. ⟨< NL < L *radius* ray⟩

ra•di•us ['reidiəs] *n., pl.* **-di•i** [-di,aɪ] or **-di•us•es. 1 a** any line going straight from the centre to the outside of a circle or a sphere. See CIRCLE and RADIAN for pictures. **b** the length of such a line. **2** any radial or raylike part, such as a spoke in a wheel. **3** a circular area measured by the length of its radius: *The explosion could be heard within a radius of 10 km.* **4** the distance a ship or aircraft can travel to and return from without refuelling. **5** scope or range of influence, operation, experience, etc.: *beyond the radius of her influence.* **6** *Anatomy.* that one of the two bones of the forearm that is shorter and thicker and that is on the thumb side. See ARM[1] for picture. **7** *Zoology.* **a** a corresponding bone in the forelimb of vertebrates other than humans. **b** any of the lines around which the body of an animal is radially symmetrical. **c** a vein in an insect's wing. ⟨< L *radius* ray, spoke of a wheel. Doublet of RAY[1].⟩

radius vector *pl.* **radius vectors** or **radii vec•to•res** [vɛk'tɔriz]. *Mathematics.* a line joining a fixed point to a curve or a variable point. Its length is a factor in determining the position of such a variable point.

ra•dix ['reidɪks] *n., pl.* **rad•i•ces** ['rædə,siz] *or* ['reidə,siz] or **ra•dix•es. 1** a root; radical; source or origin. **2** *Mathematics.* a number taken as the base of a system of numbers, logarithms, or the like. The radix of the decimal system is ten. **3** *Linguistics.* a root form. **4** *Anatomy. Botany.* a root or radicle. ⟨< L *radis, radicis* root. Doublet of RADISH.⟩

RAdm., R.Adm, or **R.A.** REAR-ADMIRAL.

ra•dome ['reidoum] *n. Cdn.* a rigid, domed structure housing radar equipment, the antennae revolving with the structure. ⟨< *ra(dar)* + *dome*⟩

ra•don ['reidɒn] *n.* a rare, highly radioactive gaseous chemical element, the densest gas known, used as a source of alpha particles in radiotherapy. *Symbol*: Rn; *at.no.* 86; *at.mass* (222); *half-life* 3.82 days. ⟨< *radium*⟩

rad•u•la ['rædʒələ] *n., pl.* **-las** or **-lae** [-,li] *or* [-,laɪ]. a toothed strip of horny material on the tongue of molluscs for taking in food. ⟨< NL < L scraper < *radere* scrape⟩

RAF or **R.A.F.** Royal Air Force (of the United Kingdom).

raf•fi•a ['ræfiə] *n.* **1** a fibre from the leafstalks of a palm (*Raphia ruffia*) native to Madagascar, used in making baskets, mats, etc. **2** the tree itself, also called **raffia palm.** ⟨< Malagasy *rafia*⟩

raf•fish ['ræfɪʃ] *adj.* **1** crude; rowdy; vulgar. **2** rakishly unconventional. ⟨< *riffraff*⟩ **—'raf•fish•ly,** *adv.* **—'raf•fish•ness,** *n.*

raf•fle[1] ['ræfəl] *n., v.* **-fled, -fling.** *—n.* a lottery, often held for charity, in which many people each pay a small sum for a chance to win a prize.
—v. sell (an article) by a raffle (*usually used with* **off**): *to raffle off a quilt.* ⟨ME *rafle* a dice game < OF *rafle* plundering, stripping, ult. < Du. *rafelen* ravel, pluck⟩

raf•fle[2] ['ræfəl] *n. Nautical.* a tangled or jumbled mass, as of ropes, cables, canvas, etc. ⟨origin uncertain⟩

raft[1] [ræft] *n., v. —n.* **1** a platform made of logs, boards, etc. fastened together and used for transportation or support on water. **2** *Cdn. Logging.* **a** pieces of timber lashed together for floating downstream, as to a mill. **b** formerly, a larger formation of square timber, composed of smaller units called drams, as used on the Great Lakes and the streams of the St. Lawrence River system. **3** a shallow, flat-bottomed inflatable boat. **4** a floating ice formation resulting from the piling up of cakes of ice in layers.
—v. **1** send by or carry on a raft. **2** travel by or work on a raft. **3** make into a raft. **4** *Cdn.* of ice, be piled high, layer upon layer, as a result of pressure. **5** *Cdn. Logging.* drive (logs, timber, etc.) by means of a raft. ⟨ME < ON *raptr* log⟩

raft[2] [ræft] *n. Informal.* a large number; abundance. ⟨var. of *raff* heap < *riffraff*⟩

raf•ter[1] ['ræftər] *n.* a supporting beam, often slanting, of a roof. See FRAME for picture. ⟨OE *ræfter*⟩

raft•er[2] ['ræftər] *n.* **1** *Logging. Cdn.* raftsman. **2** a person who travels on a raft.

raf•tered ice ['ræftərd] *Cdn.* ice that has been caused to RAFT[1] (v. def. 4). Also, **rafted ice** or **rafting ice.**

rafts•man ['ræftsmən] *n., pl.* **-men. 1** a man who manages or works on a raft. **2** *Cdn. Logging.* formerly, a man employed in the rafting of timber.

rag[1] [ræg] *n.* **1** a torn or waste piece of cloth. **2** (*adjl.*) made from rags: *a rag doll, a rag rug.* **3** any small cloth used for cleaning, washing, etc. **4** anything like a rag, such as a fragment or scrap of something, of little or no value. **5** *Informal.* any article of cloth, such as a piece of clothing, a flag, or a theatre curtain. **6 rags,**
a *pl.* tattered or worn-out clothes. **b** *Informal.* any clothes: *I'll just toss a few rags into a suitcase and take off.* **7** *Informal.* a newspaper, especially one considered as inferior. ⟨ME < OE *ragg < ON *rögg* shaggy tuft⟩ **—'rag,like,** *adj.*

rag[2] [ræg] *v.* **ragged, rag•ging;** *n. —v. Slang.* **1** scold. **2** tease; torment. **3** *Brit.* play jokes (on).
rag the puck, *Hockey.* keep control of the puck by skilful stick-handling and elusive skating, usually as a means of killing time when one's own team is shorthanded.
—n. the act of ragging. ⟨origin uncertain⟩

rag[3] [ræg] *n., v.* **ragged, rag•ging.** *—n.* a piece of music in ragtime.
—v. play (a composition) in ragtime. ⟨< *ragtime*⟩

ra•ga ['rɑgə] *n.* **1** one of the traditional Hindu melodic formulas, with prescribed rhythms, intervals, and ornamentation, used as a basis for improvisation. **2** a composition so improvised. ⟨< Skt. *raga* colour, tone⟩

rag•a•muf•fin ['rægə,mʌfən] *n.* a ragged, dirty person, especially a child. ⟨< *Ragamoffyn*, a demon in the poem *Piers Plowman*, probably ult. < *rag*[1]⟩

rag•bag ['ræg,bæg] *n.* **1** a bag containing rags, scraps, etc. **2** a miscellaneous or motley collection.

rag doll 1 a doll made of cloth, especially scraps, and stuffed with some soft material. **2** a person who is limp, passive, unenergetic, etc.

rage [reidʒ] *n., v.* **raged, rag•ing.** *—n.* **1** violent anger: *a voice quivering with rage.* **2** a fit of violent anger: *be in a rage.* **3** violence: *the rage of a savage tiger.* **4** a movement, idea, or fashion that is popular for a short time (*especially in* **(all) the rage**): *There was a rage for hotpants in the 60s. That style of running shoe is all the rage now.* **5** great enthusiasm.
—v. **1** be furious with anger. **2** speak or move with furious anger. **3** act violently; move, proceed, spread, or continue with great violence: *A storm is raging. The epidemic raged across Europe.* ⟨ME < OF < VL *rabia* < L *rabies*⟩

☛ *Syn. n.* **1. Rage,** FURY = violent anger. **Rage** suggests anger so violent that it causes either complete loss of self-control or a bitter desire to get revenge: *In his rage the child broke his mother's favourite vase.* **Fury** suggests violent, uncontrollable, irrational action which is the expression of extreme anger and characterized by animal-like wildness: *In their fury the hoodlums went through the streets wrecking cars.*

rag•ged ['rægɪd] *adj.* **1** worn or torn into rags. **2** wearing torn or badly worn-out clothing: *a ragged beggar.* **3** not straight and tidy; rough: *an Airedale's ragged coat, a ragged garden.* **4** having loose shreds or bits: *a ragged wound.* **5** having rough or sharp points; uneven; jagged: *ragged rocks.* **6** harsh: *a ragged voice.* **7** faulty; imperfect; irregular: *ragged rhyme.*
run ragged, wear out or exhaust completely by stress, overwork, etc. **—'rag•ged•ly,** *adv.* **—'rag•ged•ness,** *n.*

ragged robin a perennial plant (*Lychnis floscuculi*) of Europe and Asia belonging to the pink family and whose pink or white flowers have ragged petals.

rag•ged•y ['rægɪdi] *adj. Informal.* rather ragged or tattered.

rag•gle–tag•gle ['rægəl ,tægəl] *adj. Informal.* ragtag.

ra•gi or **rag•gee** ['rægi] *n.* a cereal grass (*Eleusine coracana*) of Asia and Africa, cultivated for its grains which are a staple food. ⟨< Hind.⟩

rag•lan ['ræglən] *n.* **1** an overcoat having sleeves that continue up to the neckline so that there is no seam at the top of the arm. **2** (*adjl.*) of or having such sleeves. ⟨after Fitzroy James Somerset, Baron *Raglan* (1788-1855), a British field marshal⟩

raglan sleeve a sleeve that is cut to continue up to the neckline instead of ending at the shoulder.

rag•man ['ræg,mæn] *or* ['rægmən] *n., pl.* **-men.** a man who gathers, buys, or sells rags.

ra•gout [ræ'gu] *n., v.* **-gouted** [-'gud], **-gout•ing** [-'guɪŋ]. *—n.* a highly seasoned stew of meat and vegetables.
—v. cook together as a ragout. ⟨< F *ragoût* < *ragoûter* restore the appetite⟩

rag•pick•er ['ræg,pɪkər] *n.* a person who picks up rags and junk, usually to sell them.

rag•tag ['ræg,tæg] *adj., n.* —*adj.* **1** ragged or slovenly; down-at-heel. **2** motley; being an odd mixture of elements.
—*n.* rabble, especially in **ragtag and bobtail.**

rag•time ['ræg,taɪm] *n.* **1** an early (1890-1915) style of jazz performed especially on the piano, characterized by a strong, regular rhythm base in strict two-four time and a highly syncopated melody. **2** the syncopated beat characteristic of the melody of this music. ⟨origin uncertain⟩

rag•weed ['ræg,wid] *n.* **1** any of a genus (*Ambrosia*) of North American plants of the composite family, especially **common ragweed** (*A. artemesiifolia*), whose greenish flowers produce large amounts of the pollen that is one of the most important causes of hay fever in eastern North America. **2** an annual plant (*Iva xanthifolia*) of the composite family native to the North American plains, whose pollen is also an important cause of hay fever. Also called **false ragweed.**

rag•wort ['ræg,wɜrt] *n.* any of several weedy plants (genus *Senecio*) of the composite family, especially **tansy ragwort** (*S. jacobaea*), having daisylike yellow flowers and tall stems. It is native to Europe and Asia but has become a troublesome weed along the eastern and western coasts of North America.

rah [rɑ] *interj. or n.* hurrah.

raid [reid] *n., v.* —*n.* **1** an attack, especially a sudden attack. **2** a sudden attack by a small force having no intention of holding the territory invaded. **3** an entering and seizing things or people inside. **4** a deliberate attempt by speculators to force down prices on stock exchanges. **5** an aggressive attempt by a business firm or other institution to lure staff from a competitor.
—*v.* **1** attack suddenly. **2** force a way into; enter and seize what is in: *The police raided the gambling house.* **3** engage in a raid. ⟨northern form of OE *rād* a ride, road. Cf. ROAD.⟩ —**'raid•er,** *n.*

rail¹ [reil] *n., v.* —*n.* **1** a horizontal or slanting bar of wood or metal extending between posts, brackets, etc., and used as a barrier, guard, or support: *a stair rail. She leaned against the top rail of the fence.* **2** a steel bar or series of bars forming a continuous track for a train, etc. **3** railway: *They shipped their car by rail.* **4** *Nautical.* the upper part of the bulwarks of a ship. **5** a fence or railing, especially one of the two around the inside and outside boundaries of a racetrack. **6** the raised edge of a billiard table. **7** (*adjl.*) of or having to do with railways or travel by rail: *rail transport*.
off the rails, a off the right course; not functioning properly. **b** *Slang.* mentally deranged.
ride the rails, *Slang.* travel by train in a boxcar or otherwise not in a passenger car.
—*v.* supply or furnish with rails or a railing.
rail in, enclose within a fence.
rail off, separate by a fence. ⟨ME *raile* < OF *reille* < L *regula* straight rod. Doublet of RULE.⟩

rail² [reil] *v.* complain bitterly; use violent and abusive language: *He railed at his hard luck.* ⟨< F *railler*, ult. < LL *ragere* to scream. Doublet of RALLY².⟩ —**'rail•er,** *n.*

rail³ [reil] *n., pl.* **rails** or *(esp. collectively)* **rail. 1** any of numerous small or medium-sized wading birds (family Rallidae) having short wings and tail, a narrow body, and strong legs with very long toes that allow them to run over the mud of marshes and swamps. Rails have a harsh cry. **2** (*adjl.*) designating the family of birds that includes the rails and gallinules. ⟨< F *râle* < VL *rascla*; probably imitative⟩

rail fence *Cdn.* any of several kinds of fence made of rails split from logs, such as a SNAKE FENCE.

rail•head ['reil,hɛd] *n.* **1** the end or terminus of a railway. **2** *Cdn.* the farthest point to which the tracks of a railway under construction have been laid; END OF STEEL. **3** a point on a railway that serves as a depot for military supplies, etc.

rail•ing¹ ['reilɪŋ] *n., v.* —*n.* **1** a barrier made of rails, especially along the side of a staircase, the edge of a balcony, etc. **2** material for making rails, or rails collectively: *A pile of railing lay by the barn.*
—*v.* ppr. of RAIL¹.

rail•ing² ['reilɪŋ] *n., v.* —*n.* harsh complaints or reproaches.
—*v.* ppr. of RAIL².

rail•ler•y ['reiləri] *n., pl.* **-ler•ies. 1** good-humoured ridicule; joking; teasing. **2** a bantering remark. ⟨< F *raillerie* < *railler.* See RAIL².⟩

rail•road ['reil,roud] *n., v.* —*n. Esp. U.S.* railway. *Abbrev.*: R.R.
—*v.* **1** send or carry on a railway. **2** work on a railway: *He has been railroading all his life.* **3** *Informal.* rush (a person or thing) through or into something hastily, especially manipulatively so as to prevent fair and careful consideration: *to railroad a bill through a committee. The principal railroaded me into coaching volleyball this year.* **4** *Slang.* send to prison on insufficient or false evidence. —**'rail,road•er,** *n.*

rail•road•ing ['reil,roudɪŋ] *n., v.* —*n.* **1** the construction or operation of railways. **2** *Informal.* the act or process of hurrying (a thing or person) along.
—*v.* ppr. of RAILROAD.

rail•way ['reil,wei] *n.* **1** a road or track for trains, consisting of parallel steel rails along which the wheels of the locomotives and cars go. The rails of a railway are supported on heavy wooden crosswise beams called **ties. 2** tracks, stations, trains, and other property of a system of transportation that uses rails: *Canada's railway is subsidized by the government.* **3** the company or corporation which owns and operates such a system. *Abbrev.*: Ry. —**'rail•way•man,** *n.*

railway crossing a place where a railway track crosses a street or highway on the same level; LEVEL CROSSING.

railway town *Cdn.* a town or village located on a railway, especially one whose economy is based on it. Also, **railway village.**

rai•ment ['reimənt] *n. Poetic.* clothing; garments. ⟨short for *arraiment* < *array*⟩

rain [rein] *n., v.* —*n.* **1** water falling in the form of drops from clouds, produced by the rapid condensation of water vapour in low-lying clouds. **2 a** the fall of such drops: *The rain lasted all morning.* **b** rainy weather: *three straight weekends of rain.* **3** a thick, fast fall of anything: *a rain of bullets.* **4 the rains,** *pl.* the rainy season, as in tropical climates.
—*v.* **1** be the case that rain is falling (*used with the subject* **it**): *It was raining when we left.* **2** pour down like rain: *Tears rained down his cheeks. She rained curses on her arch rival.*
rain cats and dogs, *Informal.* rain very hard.
rained out, of an outdoor sports event, etc., cancelled because of rain: *The first game of the season was rained out.* ⟨OE *regn*⟩ —**'rain•less,** *adj.*
☛ *Hom.* REIGN, REIN.

rain•bow ['rein,bou] *n.* **1** an arch of coloured light, showing the different colours of the spectrum, seen in the sky when the sun's rays shine through rain, mist, or spray. The colours of the rainbow are violet, indigo, blue, green, yellow, orange, and red. **2** a similar phenomenon seen in the air, as through spray, or on the ground in an oil slick. **3** RAINBOW TROUT. **4** (*adjl.*) of or resembling a rainbow; multicoloured. ⟨OE *regnboga*⟩

rainbow darter a small fish (*Poecilchthys caeruleus*) native to Canada, of the perch family, living at the bottom of streams and feeding on insect larvae.

rainbow fish 1 guppy. **2** any of a number of brightly coloured saltwater fishes.

A rainbow trout, about 35 cm long

rainbow trout *Cdn.* a trout (*Salmo gairdneri*) of the rivers and streams of W North America, having a greenish back and whitish belly, with many black spots and a pinkish or reddish band along each side. This trout is so variable in appearance that it has several common names, depending on its habitat, etc. See also KAMLOOPS TROUT and STEELHEAD.

rain check 1 a ticket for future use, given to the spectators at a baseball game or other outdoor performance stopped by rain. **2** any similar ticket, such as that given by a store to guarantee to a customer for a limited time the advertised price on a sale item that is out of stock. **3** *Informal.* an understanding that an invitation which cannot presently be accepted will be renewed on a future occasion: *May I take a rain check on your invitation to dinner?*

rain cloud a low, dark grey cloud that brings rain.

rain•coat ['rein,kout] *n.* a waterproof or water-repellent coat worn for protection from rain.

rain•drop ['rein,drɒp] *n.* a drop of rain.

rain•fall ['rein,fɒl] *n.* **1** a shower or fall of rain: *There was a heavy rainfall during the night.* **2** the amount of water in the form of rain that falls in a particular area over a certain period of time. Rainfall is measured in millimetres.

rain forest a region of dense evergreen forest characterized by very tall trees and much undergrowth, where rainfall is very heavy throughout the year. The **tropical rain forests** of South America, Africa, and SE Asia are made up of broad-leaved evergreen trees, which form a continuous canopy over the undergrowth, and have many lianas and air plants.

rain gauge an instrument for measuring rainfall.

rain•mak•er ['rein,meikər] *n.* a person who tries to produce rain.

rain•mak•ing ['rein,meikɪŋ] *n.* the making of rain artificially or by supernatural means. One method is to seed a cloud with crystals of silver iodide, which expand with heat, collecting particles of moisture that are released from the cloud as rain.

rain•proof ['rein,pruf] *adj.* not letting rain through; impervious to rain: *The roof of our shed isn't rainproof any more.*

rain•storm ['rein,stɔrm] *n.* a storm with much heavy rain.

rain•wa•ter ['rein,wɒtər] *n.* water that has been collected from rain, not taken from a well, etc. Rainwater is soft, containing few minerals.

rain•wear ['rein,wɛr] *n.* clothing made to be worn in the rain, such as rubber boots, raincoats, etc.

rain•y ['reini] *adj.* **rain•i•er, rain•i•est. 1** having rain, especially much rain: *rainy weather, the rainy season.* **2** wet with rain: *rainy streets.* **3** of clouds or winds, bringing rain. **—'rain•i•ly,** *adv.* **—'rain•i•ness,** *n.*

rainy day a time of need, or of boredom or leisure, in the future: *to save for a rainy day. I think I'll save this filing job for a rainy day.*

raise [reiz] *v.* **raised, rais•ing;** *n.* *—v.* **1** lift up: *to raise one's hand.* **2** set upright: *to raise a totem pole.* **3** cause to rise or form: *to raise a cloud of dust. The lash raised a huge welt on his back.* **4** put or take into a higher position; make higher or nobler; elevate: *to raise a sales representative to manager.* **5** increase in degree, amount, price, pay, etc.: *to raise the rent.* **6** make louder or of higher pitch: *I cannot hear you; please raise your voice.* **7** *Games.* bid or bet more than (an opponent or partner): *I'll raise you five.* **8** gather together; collect; manage to get: *The leader raised an army.* **9** breed; grow: *The farmer raises crops and cattle.* **10** cause to appear; conjure up: *to raise the ghost of Napoleon.* **11** cause; bring about: *A funny remark raises a laugh.* **12 a** bring forward; mention: *The speaker raised an interesting point.* **b** utter, especially vigorously: *raise a cheer, raise an outcry.* **13** build; create; produce; start; set up: *to raise a monument, to raise a fund.* **14** rouse; stir up: *The dog raised a rabbit from the underbrush.* **15** bring up; rear: *Parents raise their children.* **16** cause to become light: *Yeast raises bread.* **17** bring back to life: *to raise the dead.* **18 a** put an end to: *Our soldiers raised the siege of the fort by driving away the enemy.* **b** break up and remove: *We raised camp at daybreak.* **19** come in sight of: *After a long voyage the ship raised land.* **20** falsify the value of (a cheque, note, etc.) by making the sum larger. **21** *Phonetics.* change the quality of (a vowel) by placing the blade of the tongue higher in the mouth. **22** establish radio or telephone contact with. **23** *Curling.* hit (a rock of one's own team) into a position nearer to the button or house.
raise Cain, the devil, mischief, the roof, etc. *Slang.* make a disturbance; create an uproar or confusion.
—n. **1** an act of raising. **2** a raised place; rise. **3** an increase in amount, price, pay, etc. **4** the amount of such an increase. ⟨ME < ON *reisa* < Gmc. causative of *rīsan* rise⟩
☛ *Hom.* RAZE.
☛ *Syn. v.* **1. Raise,** LIFT, ELEVATE = move to a higher position. **Raise** means to bring something to a high or, especially, vertical position or to move it up from a lower to a higher level: *Raise your right hand.* **Lift** means to take something, usually heavy, up from the ground or some other low level: *Please lift the table.* **Elevate** chiefly means 'to raise to a higher rank or nobler state': *Good reading elevates the mind.*

raised [reizd] *adj., v.* *—adj.* **1** having a surface design in low relief; embossed. **2** of cloth, having a fuzzy or pile surface. **3** leavened with yeast as opposed to baking powder or other agents: *Raised bread takes a long time to make.*
—v. pt. and pp. of RAISE.

rais•er ['reizər] *n.* a person who grows or raises things: *a cattle raiser.*
☛ *Hom.* RAZOR.

rai•sin ['reizən] *n.* a sweet dried grape. ⟨ME < OF < L *racemus* grape cluster. Doublet of RACEME.⟩

rai•son d'être [ʀɛzɔ̃'dɛtʀ] *French.* reason for being; justification.

raj [rɑdʒ] *n.* formerly, in India, sovereignty; dominion: *the British Raj.* ⟨< Hind. *rāj*⟩

ra•jah ['rɑdʒə] *or* ['rɑdʒɑ] *n.* a member of a hereditary class of noblemen and rulers in countries of southern Asia, including Malaysia and, formerly, India. Also, **raja.** ⟨< Hind. *rājā* < Skt.⟩

Raj•put ['rɑdʒput] *n.* a member of a Hindu military, land-owning, and ruling caste. ⟨< Hind. *rājput* < Skt. *rājaputra* king's son⟩

rake[1] [reik] *n., v.* **raked, rak•ing.** *—n.* **1** a long-handled tool having at one end a bar with teeth in it or a fan of long wooden or metal prongs. A rake is used for smoothing the soil or gathering together loose leaves, hay, or straw. **2** any of a number of similar tools with teeth.
—v. **1** move with a rake: *Rake the leaves off the grass.* **2** use a rake on (grass, earth, etc.): *to rake the lawn.* **3** use a rake: *It's no use trying to rake when it's this windy.* **4** scratch; scrape; make a long gash in: *He raked his arm on a loose nail.* **5** search carefully: *They raked the newspapers for descriptions of the accident.* **6** fire guns along the length of (a ship, line of soldiers, etc.): *The machine-gunners raked the streets as they entered the town.*
rake in, gather (something, especially money) in great amounts and very quickly.
rake over the coals, reprimand very severely.
rake up, a gather or bring together by or as if by raking: *She raked up enough money to rent a canoe.* **b** bring to light unpleasant facts about (someone's past, a public scandal, etc.). ⟨OE *raca*⟩

rake[2] [reik] *n.* a dissolute or debauched man, especially one who belongs to fashionable society. ⟨short for *rakehell*⟩

rake[3] [reik] *n., v.* **raked, rak•ing.** *—n.* **1** a slant; slope. A ship's smokestacks have a slight backward rake. **2** angle, as that between the wings and the body of an aircraft, or between the edge of a cutting tool and a plane perpendicular to the work surface.
—v. slope or cause to slope; incline: *This theatre's stage is steeply raked.* ⟨origin uncertain⟩

rake•hell ['reik,hɛl] *n. Archaic.* a libertine; roué. ⟨< *rake[1]* + *hell*; replacing ME *rakel* rash⟩

rake•off ['reik,ɒf] *n. Slang.* a commission or share of profits, especially when part of an illicit transaction.

ra•ki [rɑ'ki] *or* ['ræki] *n.* a strong alcoholic liquor made in the Middle East from grain and often flavoured with aromatics. ⟨< Turkish *raqi*⟩

rak•ish[1] ['reikɪʃ] *adj.* **1** smart; jaunty; dashing: *a hat set at a rakish angle.* **2** suggesting dash and speed: *She owns a rakish boat.* ⟨< *rake[3]*; influenced in def. 1 by association with *rakish[2]*⟩ **—'rak•ish•ly,** *adv.* **—'rak•ish•ness,** *n.*

rak•ish[2] ['reikɪʃ] *adj.* of, having to do with, or like a rake; immoral; dissolute; licentious. ⟨< *rake[2]*⟩ **—'rak•ish•ly,** *adv.* **—'rak•ish•ness,** *n.*

ra•ku [rɑ'ku] *n.* **1** a method of firing pottery with a lead glaze. **2** the rough, dark pottery so produced, used in the Japanese tea ceremony. ⟨< Japanese, pleasure, from the household stamp of the originator of the glaze⟩

rale or **râle** [rɑl] *n. Pathology.* an abnormal crackling or rattling sound produced along with the normal sounds of breathing when disease or infection of the lungs or bronchi is present. ⟨< F *râler* rattle⟩

rall. rallentando.

ral•len•tan•do [,rɑlɛn'tandou] *adj., adv., n. Music.* *—adj.* slackening; becoming slower.
—adv. gradually more slowly.
—n. **1** a gradual decrease in tempo. **2** a passage to be played or sung in this manner. ⟨< Ital. *rallentando* slowing down, ppr. of *rallentare* to abate⟩

ral•ly[1] ['ræli] *v.* **-lied, -ly•ing;** *n., pl.* **-lies.** *—v.* **1** bring or come together again; get in order again: *The commander was able to rally the fleeing troops. The scattered rebels rallied and made a fresh attack.* **2** pull together; revive: *He rallied all his energy for one last effort.* **3** come together in a body for a common purpose or action: *They rallied to the cause of the starving children.* **4** come to help a person, party, or cause: *She rallied to the side of her injured friend.* **5** recover health, strength, or confidence: *The sick man may rally now. The first few questions completely threw her off,*

but she rallied and fielded the rest with poise and assurance. **6** *Tennis, etc.* hit the ball back and forth several times. **7** *Finance.* of stocks, etc. go up sharply in price after a decline. **8** *Sports.* advance in score after falling behind.
—n. **1** the act or an instance of rallying; recovery. **2** a meeting or assembly of many people for a common purpose or action: *a political rally, a youth rally.* **3** an organized drive of motor vehicles along public roads, especially as a competition in driving skill. **4** *Tennis, etc.* a series of strokes between players before one player wins a point. ⟨< F *rallier* < *re-* again + *allier* ally⟩
—'ral•li•er, *n.*

ral•ly[2] ['ræli] *v.* **-lied, -ly•ing.** make fun of or tease in a good-natured way. ⟨< F *railler* rail[2]. Doublet of RAIL[2].⟩

ram [ræm] *n., v.* **rammed, ram•ming.** *—n.* **1** a male sheep. **2** a machine or part of a machine that strikes heavy blows. The ram on a pile driver is the weight that drives the piles into the ground. **3** BATTERING RAM. **4** formerly, the beak at the bow of a warship, used to break the sides of enemy ships. **5** a ship with such a beak. **6** the plunger of a force pump. **7** a pump in which the force of a descending column of water raises some of the water above its original level. **8 Ram,** *Astronomy. Astrology.* Aries.
—v. **1** butt (against or into); strike head on; strike violently: *One ship rammed the other ship. She turned the corner and rammed right into him.* **2** push hard; drive down or in by heavy force or effort: *He rammed the bolt into the wall.* **3** force acceptance or passage of: *trying to ram an unpopular bill through Parliament.* ⟨OE *ramm*⟩

RAM [ræm] *Computer technology.* the main memory of a computer, especially a microcomputer. ⟨< *r*andom-*a*ccess *m*emory⟩

Ra•ma ['rɑmə] *n. Hinduism.* an incarnation of the god Vishnu, depicted as the ideal ruler, representing grace and justice toward people.

Ram•a•dan or **Ram•a•zan** [,ramə'dɑn] *or* [,ramə'zɑn] *n.* **1** the ninth month of the Muslim year, during which fasting is rigidly practised daily from dawn until sunset. **2** the fasting itself. ⟨< Arabic *Ramadān*, originally, the hot month⟩

Ram•a•pith•e•cus [,ræmə'pɪθɪkəs] *n.* a genus of extinct hominid Miocene ape thought to be a possible human ancestor, known from fossils found in India and Pakistan.
—,ram•a'pith•e,cine [-,saɪn], [-,sin], *or* [-,sɪn], *adj., n.*

Ra•ma•ya•na [rɑ'mɑjənə] *n.* one of the two great epics of India, that tells the story of Rama, written in Sanskrit early in the Christian era. The other Sanskrit epic is the **Mahabharata.**

ram•ble ['ræmbəl] *v.* **-bled, -bling;** *n.* *—v.* **1** wander about for pleasure: *We rambled here and there through the woods.* **2** talk or write about first one thing and then another with no clear connections. **3** grow or spread irregularly in various directions: *Vines rambled over the wall.*
—n. **1** a walk for pleasure, with or without any definite route. **2** a loosely organized study or survey: *a ramble through Canadian history.* ⟨var. of ME *romblen*, a frequentative of *romen* roam⟩
☛ *Syn. v.* **1.** See note at ROAM.

ram•bler ['ræmblər] *n.* **1** a person or thing that rambles. **2** any of various climbing roses.

ram•bling ['ræmblɪŋ] *adj., v.* *—adj.* **1** wandering about. **2** going from one thing to another without clear connection; moving from one subject to another: *a rambling speech.* **3** climbing: *rambling roses.* **4** extending irregularly in various directions; not planned in an orderly way: *a rambling old house.*
—v. ppr. of RAMBLE.

ram•bunc•tious [ræm'bʌŋkʃəs] *adj.* uncontrollably exuberant; boisterous and unruly: *The kids were very rambunctious after travelling all day.* ⟨? a mock word formed from *ram* knock around + a var. of *bumptious*⟩

ram•bu•tan ['rɑmbə,tɑn] *or* [ræm'butən] *n.* **1** a tree (family Sapindaceae) of SE Asia bearing small red edible fruits with a spiny skin. **2** the fruit. ⟨< Malay *rambut* hair⟩

ram•e•kin or **ram•e•quin** ['ræməkɪn] *n.* **1** a small, separately cooked portion of some food, especially one topped with cheese and bread crumbs. **2** a small baking dish holding enough for one portion. ⟨< F *ramequin* < Du.⟩

ra•mi ['reimaɪ] *or* ['reimi] *n.* pl. of RAMUS.

ram•ie ['reimi] *or* ['ræmi] *n.* **1** a tall perennial plant (*Boehmeria nivea*) of the nettle family native to E Asia, having stalks that yield a strong, lustrous fibre. **2** the fibre from this plant, used for fabrics and cordage. **3** a similar fibre made of rayon, used for fabrics. ⟨< Malay *rami* plant⟩

ram•i•fi•ca•tion [,ræməfə'keiʃən] *n.* **1** an arrangement or configuration of branches or parts of a plant. **2** a dividing or branching out of anything. **3** a branch; part. **4** something that springs out like a branch. **5** a result, consequence, extension, etc.: *the ramifications of an idea.*

ram•i•form ['ræmə,fɔrm] *adj.* branched or branching; like a branch.

ram•i•fy ['ræmə,faɪ] *v.* **-fied, -fy•ing. 1** divide or spread out into branchlike parts. **2** have many complex and extensive effects. ⟨< MF *ramifier* < Med.L *ramificare* < L *ramus* branch + *facere* make⟩

ram•jet ['ræm,dʒɛt] *n.* the simplest type of jet engine, in which the fuel is fed into air that is compressed by the forward speed of the aircraft, missile, etc., instead of by means of a mechanical compressor.

ram•mer ['ræmər] *n.* a person or thing that rams, especially a device for driving or compacting something.

ra•mose ['reimous] *or* [rə'mous] *adj.* consisting of or having many branches; branching. ⟨< L *ramosus* < *ramus* branch⟩

ra•mous ['reiməs] *adj.* **1** ramose. **2** of or like a branch.

ramp[1] [ræmp] *n.* **1** a sloping walk or roadway connecting two different levels of a building, road, etc. **2** a movable stairway for going into or out of aircraft. **3** a sloping, often paved or cemented stretch from the shore into the water, for launching boats from a trailer. Also, **boat ramp.** ⟨< F *rampe* < *ramper.* See RAMP[2].⟩

ramp[2] [ræmp] *v., n.* *—v.* **1** rush wildly about; behave violently: *teenagers ramping in the park to work off energy.* **2** jump or rush with fury. **3 a** of beasts, rear on their hind feet. **b** *Heraldry.* of beasts, be depicted as RAMPANT (def. 4). **4** take a threatening stance.
—n. an act of ramping. ⟨< F *ramper* creep, climb, rear < Gmc.⟩

ramp[3] [ræmp] *n.* a wild leek (*Allium tricoccum*) found in E North America, having broad leaves at the bottom and a leafless stalk with rounded clusters of white flowers. The bulb is strong-tasting and is eaten raw or used as a seasoning. Also, **ramps.** ⟨< OE *hramsa*⟩

ram•page *n.* ['ræmpeidʒ]; *v.* [ræm'peidʒ] *or* ['ræmpeidʒ] *n., v.* **-paged, -pag•ing.** *—n.* a spell of violent behaviour often accompanied by rushing about wildly; wild outbreak: *The mad elephant went on a rampage and killed its keeper.*
on the rampage, acting hostilely, aggressively, or destructively: *She's been on the rampage ever since she heard about the pay cuts.*
—v. rush wildly about; behave violently; rage. ⟨? < *ramp[2]*⟩

ram•pa•geous [ræm'peidʒəs] *adj.* wild; unruly; boisterous.
—ram'pa•geous•ly, *adv.* **—ram'pa•geous•ness,** *n.*

ramp•an•cy ['ræmpənsi] *n.* the state of being rampant.

ramp•ant ['ræmpənt] *adj.* **1** growing without any check: *Rampant vines covered the fence.* **2** passing beyond restraint or usual limits; unchecked: *Anarchy was rampant after the dictator died.* **3** angry; excited; violent. **4** *Heraldry.* (*placed after the noun*) of a beast, represented as standing up on the left hind leg, with the forelegs raised, the right above the left, and the head and body in profile: *lions rampant.* Compare PASSANT. **5** of animals, rearing. **6** *Architecture.* of an arch, springing from a lower support on one side and resting on a higher one on the other.
run rampant, spread unchecked: *nasty rumours running rampant.* ⟨ME < OF *rampant* ramping⟩ **—'ramp•ant•ly,** *adv.*

ram•part ['ræmpɑrt] *or* ['ræmpərt] *n., v.* *—n.* **1** a wide bank of earth, usually with a parapet on top, built around a fort to help defend it. See FORT for picture. **2** anything that defends; defence; protection. **3** *Cdn.* in the Northwest: **a** a precipitous, high bank on either side of a river or stream flowing through a gorge or canyon. **b** the gorge itself. **c** the precipitous terrain adjacent to such gorges.
—v. furnish with a rampart or ramparts; protect as a rampart does. ⟨< F *rempart* < *remparer* fortify, ult. < L *re-* back + *ante* before + *parare* prepare⟩

ram•pike ['ræmpəik] *n. Cdn.* a tall, dead tree, especially one that has been blackened and stripped of its branches by fire. ⟨prob. Brit. dial. *rampick, rampike*, origin uncertain⟩

ram•rod ['ræm,rɒd] *n., v.* **-rod•ded, -rod•ding.** *—n.* **1** a rod for ramming down the charge in a gun that is loaded from the muzzle. **2** a rod for cleaning the barrel of a gun. **3** a person in charge who is an authoritarian or strict disciplinarian.
—v. Informal. force the passage or acceptance of: *to ramrod a bill through Parliament.*

ram•shack•le ['ræm,ʃækəl] *adj.* loose and shaky; likely to come apart: *ramshackle old buildings.* ⟨? ult. < *ransack*⟩

ra•mus ['reiməs] *n., pl.* **ra•mi** ['reimaɪ] *or* ['reimi]. *Botany.*

Zoology. Anatomy. a branch or branchlike part of a plant, vein, bone, feather, etc. ⟨< L *ramus* branch⟩

ran [ræn] *v.* pt. of RUN.

ranch [ræntʃ] *n., v.* —*n.* **1** a large farm with grazing land, for raising cattle, sheep, or horses in large numbers. **2** any farm, especially one used to raise one kind of animal or crop: *a mink ranch, a fruit ranch.* **3 a** the persons working or living on a ranch: *The entire ranch was at the party.* **b** the owners or lessees of a cattle ranch. **4** RANCH HOUSE. **5** rancherie.
—*v.* **1** work on or operate a ranch. **2** exploit (land) as rangeland for raising livestock: *Proposals have been made to ranch the central Arctic with caribou.* ⟨< Sp. *rancho* camp, mess⟩

ranch•er ['ræntʃər] *n.* a person who owns or operates a ranch.

ran•che•ra [ræn'tʃɛrə] *n.* **1** a style of cuisine involving baking with a spicy tomato and onion sauce: *chicken ranchera.* **2** a traditional style of Mexican music, using accordion, guitar, and snare drums. ⟨< Sp.⟩

ranch•er•ie ['ræntʃəri] *n. Cdn.* in British Columbia: **1 a** a village or settlement of First Nations people, especially the settled part of a First Nations reserve. **b** formerly, a settlement of KANAKAS. **2** RANCH HOUSE (def. 3). ⟨< Sp. *ranchería*⟩

ranch hand a person employed on a ranch, especially a cattle ranch.

ranch house **1** the main building on a ranch. **2** *Cdn.* on the West coast, a large communal dwelling or house of various coastal First Nations peoples. **3** a long, low, spacious, one-storey house.

ranch•ing ['ræntʃɪŋ] *n., v.* —*n.* **1** the raising of livestock by grazing the native grasslands on an extensive basis. **2** the raising of any of various animals for commercial purposes.
—*v.* ppr. of RANCH.

ranch•land ['ræntʃ,lænd] *n.* land used or suitable for ranching.

ranch•man ['ræntʃmən] *n., pl.* **-men.** a man who operates a ranch.

ran•cid ['rænsɪd] *adj.* **1** especially of fats or oils, stale; spoiled: *rancid butter.* **2** tasting or smelling like stale fat or butter: *a rancid odour.* ⟨< L *rancidus* < *rancere* be rank⟩
—'ran•cid•ly, *adv.* **—ran'cid•i•ty** or **'ran•cid•ness,** *n.*

ran•cor ['ræŋkər] See RANCOUR.

ran•cor•ous ['ræŋkərəs] *adj.* spiteful; bitterly malicious.
—'ran•cor•ous•ly, *adv.*

ran•cour or **rancor** ['ræŋkər] *n.* a deep-seated, bitter resentment or ill will; extreme hatred or spite. ⟨ME < OF < LL *rancour* rankness < L *rancere* be rank⟩

rand[1] [rænd] *n.* **1** the basic unit of money in South Africa, divided into 100 cents. See table of money in the Appendix. **2** a coin worth one rand. Compare KRUGERRAND. ⟨< Afrikaans < the *Rand,* the gold-mining district in the Transvaal⟩

rand[2] [rænd] *n.* a strip of leather put on the back section of a shoe sole before adding the heel. ⟨ME *rande* < DE *rand* edge, rim⟩

R & B RHYTHM AND BLUES. Also, **r & b.**

R and D or **R & D** *Informal.* research and development: *They're spending millions on R and D in the energy field.*

Rand formula *Cdn.* a part of many union agreements, stating that all employees must pay union dues, but actual membership in the union is voluntary. ⟨< Ivan C. *Rand,* justice of the Supreme Court of Canada, who proposed this in 1945 in settlement of a Ford Motor Co. strike⟩

ran•dom ['rændəm] *adj., n.* —*adj.* **1** done or happening by chance or with no plan or pattern. **2** of all different sizes and shapes; not regular or uniform: *wallpaper with a random pattern, masonry using random stones.* **3** *Statistics.* of or having to do with a method of statistical sampling in which each member of a set has an equal chance of being selected: *random sample.*
—*n.*
at random, by chance; with no plan or criterion: *She took a book at random from the shelf.* ⟨ME < OF *randon* rapid rush⟩
—'ran•dom•ly, *adv.* **—'ran•dom•ness,** *n.* **—'ran•dom,ize,** *v.*

☛ *Syn. adj.* **Random,** HAPHAZARD = made, done, happening, or arrived at by chance, not plan. **Random** emphasizes being undetermined by any particular criterion or pattern: *Random sampling is a basic statistical method.* **Haphazard** emphasizes being determined by chance, without giving any thought to fitness for a purpose or aim: *Because of her haphazard way of choosing clothes, she never looks well dressed.*

random access *Computer technology.* See DIRECT ACCESS.
—'ran•dom-'ac•cess, *adj.*

random assortment *Genetics.* independent assortment of non-allelic genes. See MENDEL'S LAWS.

ran•dom•ize ['rændə,maɪz] *v.* **-ized, -iz•ing.** make random, especially selection in a sample.

random mating *Genetics.* choice of mate without regard to genotype.

random variable *Statistics.* a variable, the values of which are assigned without reference to one another on the basis of a probability distribution.

random walk *Mathematics.* the path of a point or quantity, each successive move of which is randomly determined.

R & R *Informal.* **1** rest and recuperation or rest and relaxation (from *rest and recuperation leave* in the U.S. military): *After working very hard on several presentations, she repaired to her cottage for some R & R.* **2** rock-and-roll.

ran•dy ['rændi] *adj.* **-di•er, -di•est;** *n., pl.* **-dies.** —*adj.* **1** coarse and boisterous in behaviour. **2** lustful; lecherous.
—*n.* a randy person. ⟨origin uncertain⟩

ra•nee ['rɑni] See RANI.

rang [ræŋ] *v.* pt. of RING[2].

range [reindʒ] *n., v.* **ranged, rang•ing;** *adj.* —*n.* **1** the distance between certain limits; extent: *a range of prices from 5 cents to 25 dollars; the range of a person's experience.* **2** the distance a gun, etc. can shoot. **3** the maximum distance that can be travelled by a vehicle carrying a normal load without refuelling. **4** the distance from a gun, etc. to an object aimed at. **5** *Statistics.* a measure of the distribution of a sample, equalling the difference between the largest and smallest values. **6** *Music.* the extent, from lowest tone to highest, of the pitch of a voice, musical instrument, or piece of music: *He has an extraordinary range and can sing tenor just as well as bass.* **7** a place to practise shooting: *a rifle range.* **8** an area for doing flight tests with rockets. **9** rangeland. **10** the act of wandering or moving about: *a leisurely range over the countryside.* **11** a row or line of mountains. **12** a row; line. **13** a line of direction: *The two barns are in direct range with the house.* **14** a rank, class, or order. **15** the area in which certain plants or animals live. **16** an appliance that includes a stove and an oven: *an electric range, a gas range.* **17** *Cdn.* a row of lots, concessions, or townships.
—*v.* **1** vary within certain limits: *prices ranging from $5 to $10.* **2** have a given range: *This missile ranges 250 km.* **3** wander; rove; roam: *His eyes ranged over the crowd.* **4** wander over: *Buffalo once ranged these plains.* **5** pasture (cattle, sheep, etc.) on a range. **6** put in a row or other ordered formation: *We ranged the chairs across the stage.* **7** put in groups or classes: *The swimming classes are ranged by age and ability.* **8** take or have a position in a given class or group: *Her work ranges with the very best in the field.* **9** put or group on a given side of a conflict: *Loyal citizens ranged themselves with the king.* **10** align (a gun, telescope, etc.) with an object or target. **11** find the distance of (a target). **12** run in a line; extend: *a boundary ranging east and west.* **13** be found; occur (in a habitat): *a plant ranging from Canada to Mexico.*
—*adj.* of or on land for grazing. ⟨ME < OF *ranger* array, ult. < *renc* line. See RANK[1].⟩

☛ *Syn. n.* **1. Range,** SCOPE, COMPASS = the extent or limit of what something can do or take in. **Range** emphasizes the extent and variety that can be covered or taken in by something in operation or action, such as the mind, eye, a machine, force, etc.: *The car was out of his range of vision.* **Scope** emphasizes the idea of limits beyond which the understanding, view, application, etc. cannot extend: *Some technical terms are beyond the scope of this dictionary.* **Compass,** more formal, emphasizes the limits within which something can act or operate: *Geographical names are within its compass.*

range finder an instrument for determining the distance between an object or target and an observer, camera, gun, etc. Also, **rangefinder.**

range•land ['reindʒ,lænd] *n.* extensive areas of grassland suitable for grazing.

range–lil•y ['reindʒ ,lɪli] *n., pl.* **-lil•ies.** *Cdn.* the wild orange-red lily (*Lilium philadelphicum*).

rang•er ['reindʒər] *n.* **1** a person or thing that ranges; rover. **2** a person employed to guard a tract of forest; FOREST RANGER. **3** FIRE RANGER. **4** Often, **Ranger,** a soldier of certain regiments originally organized for fighting in the North American forests: *the Queen's Rangers.* **5 Ranger, a** a member, aged 15 or over, of the Girl Guides. **b** *Cdn.* in the North, a member of a First Nations or Inuit people who acts as a volunteer military scout or observer. **c** *Newfoundland.* formerly, a member of the Labrador Ranger Force.

rang•ette [rein'dʒɛt] *n.* a cooking stove smaller than a range, often with only two burners.

rang•y ['reindʒi] *adj.* **rang•i•er, rang•i•est. 1** slender and long-limbed: *a rangy horse.* **2** fitted for ranging or moving about; inclined to range about. **—'rang•i•ness,** *n.*

ra•ni ['rɑni] *n.* **1** in India, a queen or princess. **2** the wife or widow of a rajah. Also, **ranee.** ⟨< Hind. *rani* < Skt. *rajni*⟩

rank[1] [ræŋk] *n., v.* —*n.* **1** a row or line, especially of soldiers, placed side by side. **2 ranks,** *pl.* **a** private soldiers and junior non-commissioned officers. **b** RANK AND FILE. **3** a position; grade; class: *the military rank of colonel; people in the lowest ranks of society.* **4** a high position: *A duke is a man of rank.* **5** any of the horizontal rows of squares on a chessboard. Compare FILE[1] (def. 5). **6** a set of organ pipes of the same tonal colour. **7** an orderly arrangement or array.
pull rank, *Informal.* use one's superior position to take advantage of someone or get one's own way.
—*v.* **1** arrange in a row or line. **2** have a certain place or position in relation to other persons or things: *Bill ranked low in the test.* **3** assign a rank or position to: *Rank the continents in order of size.* **4** be more important than; outrank: *A major ranks a captain.* ⟨ult. < OF *renc* < Gmc.⟩ **—'rank•er,** *n.*

rank[2] [ræŋk] *adj.* **1** large and coarse: *rank grass.* **2** growing richly. **3** producing a dense but coarse growth: *rank swampland.* **4** having a strong, unpleasant smell or taste: *rank meat, rank tobacco.* **5** strongly marked; extreme: *rank ingratitude, rank nonsense.* **6** coarse; not decent. ⟨OE *ranc* proud⟩ **—'rank•ly,** *adv.* **—'rank•ness,** *n.*

rank and file 1 an armed force excluding its officers. **2** the members of an organization, society, or other group, excluding the leaders: *The union leaders were in favour of the offer but it was rejected by the rank and file.*

rank•ing ['ræŋkɪŋ] *adj., v., n.* —*adj.* **1** having the highest rank: *the ranking poet of the age, the ranking officer on a military base.* **2** recognized as being of high calibre or merit: *Most of the association members are ranking artists.*
—*v.* ppr. of RANK[1].
—*n.* **1** the act of making a list of people or things in order of their position relative to some standard or hierarchy. **2** the list itself: *DeMauro should make it to the top of the tennis ranking this year.* **3** a position in such a list.

ran•kle ['ræŋkəl] *v.* **-kled, -kling.** cause anger, bitterness, or irritation (in): *Even after all those years, the memory of the insult still rankled.* ⟨ME < OF *rancler,* var. of *draoncler* < Med.L *dracunculus* sore, dim. of L *draco* serpent < Gk. *drakōn*⟩

ran•sack ['rænsæk] *v.* **1** search through thoroughly: *I ransacked the whole closet, but couldn't find the belt.* **2** go through with the intent of plundering or robbing: *Burglars had ransacked the house.* ⟨ME < ON *rannsaka,* literally, search a house < *rann* house + *-saka* search⟩ **—'ran,sack•er,** *n.*

ran•som ['rænsəm] *n., v.* —*n.* **1** the price paid or demanded before a captive is set free: *The robber chief held the travellers as prisoners for ransom.* **2** the act of ransoming.
—*v.* **1** obtain the release of (a captive) by paying a price. **2** redeem. **3** release upon payment. ⟨ME < OF *ranson* < L *redemptio, -onis.* Doublet of REDEMPTION.⟩

rant [rænt] *v., n.* —*v.* speak wildly, extravagantly, violently, or noisily.
rant and rave, scold violently; speak wildly and extravagantly at great length.
—*n.* an extravagant, violent, or noisy speech. ⟨< MDu. *ranten*⟩ **—'rant•er,** *n.* **—'rant•ing•ly,** *adv.*

ra•nun•cu•lus [rə'nʌŋkjələs] *n.* any of various plants of the genus *Ranunculus,* including the common buttercup.

rap[1] [ræp] *n., v.* **rapped, rap•ping.** —*n.* **1** a quick, light blow; a light, sharp knock. **2** *Slang.* **a** blame; rebuke. **b** conviction; prison sentence.
beat the rap, *Slang.* escape conviction or prison sentence.
bum rap, *Slang.* an unfair judgment or penalty.
rap on the knuckles, *Informal.* an unduly light reprimand or punishment.
take the rap, *Slang.* pay the penalty; take the blame, often for someone else.
—*v.* **1** knock sharply; tap. **2** say sharply: *rap out an answer.* **3** *Slang.* rebuke; criticize; condemn. ⟨imitative⟩ **—'rap•per,** *n.*
☛ *Hom.* WRAP.

rap[2] [ræp] *n. Informal.* the least bit: *I don't care a rap.* ⟨originally, a counterfeit Irish half-penny⟩
☛ *Hom.* WRAP.

rap[3] [ræp] *v.* **rapped, rap•ping;** *n. Slang.* —*v.* **1** talk freely and informally; chat: *rapping till 2 in the morning.* **2** perform rap (*n.* 2).
—*n.* **1** a free, informal talk. **2 a** a type of popular music consisting of rhyming verse, often improvised, chanted or shouted to a strong, repetitive beat. **b** a composition of this type. ⟨origin uncertain⟩ **—'rap•per,** *n.*
☛ *Hom.* WRAP.

ra•pa•cious [rə'peiʃəs] *adj.* **1** seizing by force; plundering. **2** grasping; greedy; voracious. **3** of animals, living by the capture of prey. ⟨< L *rapax, -acis* grasping < *rapere* seize⟩ **—ra'pa•cious•ly,** *adv.* **—ra'pac•i•ty** [rə'pæsɪti] or **ra'pa•cious•ness,** *n.*

rape[1] [reip] *n., v.* **raped, rap•ing.** —*n.* **1** the crime of an individual having sexual intercourse with a person forcibly and without his or her consent. **2** any forcible or outrageous exploitation, destruction, or violation: *the rape of a country's natural resources.* **3** *Archaic or poetic.* the act or an instance of seizing and carrying off by force: *the rape of the Sabine women.*
—*v.* **1** force (someone) to have sexual intercourse; commit rape (on). **2** violate, destroy, or despoil. **3** *Archaic or poetic.* seize and carry off by force. ⟨< L *rapere* seize⟩

rape[2] [reip] *n.* a plant (*Brassica napus*) of the mustard family, native to Europe and Asia but widely cultivated for its seeds (rapeseed), which yield rapeseed oil, and as a forage crop for sheep and hogs. See also CANOLA. ⟨ME < L *rapa, rapum* turnip⟩

rape[3] [reip] *n.* the pulp, skins, stems of grapes that are left after squeezing the juice out to make wine. ⟨< F *râpe* < Med.L *raspa*⟩

rape oil RAPESEED OIL.

rape•seed ['reip,sid] *n.* the seed of the rape plant.

rapeseed oil an oil made from rapeseed and used as a cooking oil, fuel, or lubricant, and in making soap and synthetic rubber.

rap•id ['ræpɪd] *adj., n.* —*adj.* **1** quick; swift; moving, acting, or doing with speed: *a rapid worker.* **2** going on or forward at a fast rate: *rapid growth.*
—*n.* Usually, **rapids,** *pl.* a part of a river's course where the water rushes quickly, often over rocks near the surface. ⟨< L *rapidus* < *rapere* hurry away⟩ **—'rap•id•ly,** *adv.* **—'rap•id•ness,** *n.*
☛ *Syn. adj.* See note at QUICK.

rapid eye movement a rapid movement of the eyes under the closed lids that is characteristic of a particular stage of sleep during which a person dreams. *Abbrev.:* REM

rap•id–fire ['ræpɪd 'faɪr] *adj.* **1** firing or adapted for firing shots in quick succession. **2** rapid and lively; done or carried on quickly or sharply: *a rapid-fire style of speaking.*

ra•pid•i•ty [rə'pɪdəti] *n.* quickness; swiftness; speed.

rapid transit a system of fast public transportation by railway in urban areas, often underground or raised above the ground.

ra•pi•er ['reipiər] *n.* a light, straight, narrow, two-edged sword used for thrusting. See SWORD for picture. ⟨< MF *rapière* < *râpe* grater, rasp; with reference to the perforated guard⟩ **—'ra•pi•er,like,** *adj.*

rap•ine ['ræpin], ['ræpɪn], *or* ['ræpaɪn] *n.* a seizing by force and carrying off; plundering. ⟨< L *rapina*⟩

rap•ist ['reipɪst] *n.* a person who commits the crime of rape.

rap•pel [rə'pɛl] *or* [ræ'pɛl] *n., v.* **-pelled** or **-peled, -pel•ling** or **-pel•ing.** —*n.* a technique for descending a cliff, etc. by means of a double rope that is secured above and passed around the climber's body in such a way that he or she can control the rate of descent.
—*v.* **1** descend a cliff, etc. by this means. **2** *Military.* disembark from a hovering helicopter. ⟨< F *rappel* < *rappeler* to recall⟩

rap•pé pie ['ræpei] *Cdn. Maritimes.* a rich, nourishing dish popular among Acadians and others in the Maritimes. ⟨< Acadian F *tarte râpée,* literally grated pie⟩

rap•port [rə'pɔr]; *French,* [ʀa'pɔʀ] *n.* a connection or relationship, especially a harmonious or agreeable one: *He has no rapport with his students. There was good rapport among the leaders throughout the negotiations.* ⟨< F *rapport* < *rapporter* bring back⟩

rap•por•teur [,ræpɔr'tɜr]; *French,* [ʀapɔʀ'tœʀ] *n.* a person whose duty is to draw up reports, etc. on behalf of a committee, conference, etc., and present them, usually to a governing body; reporter or recorder. ⟨< F *rapporter* to bring back, report⟩

rap•proche•ment [,ræprʌʃ'mɑ̃]; *French,* [ʀaprɔʃ'mɑ̃] *n.* the establishment or renewal of friendly relations. ⟨< F *rapprochement* < *rapprocher* bring near⟩

rap•scal•lion [ræp'skæljən] *n.* a rascal; rogue; scamp. ⟨earlier *rascallion* < *rascal*⟩

rap sheet *Slang.* a record kept by law enforcement agencies of a person's arrests and convictions: *The RCMP had a long rap sheet on every member of the gang.*

rapt [ræpt] *adj.* **1** entranced or completely engrossed; lost in delight. **2** caused by or showing rapture or delight: *a rapt smile.* ⟨< L *raptus*, pp. of *rapere* seize⟩ **—'rapt•ly,** *adv.* **—'rapt•ness,** *n.*

rap•tor ['ræptər] *n.* BIRD OF PREY. ⟨< L *raptor* plunderer, robber < *rapere* seize⟩

rap•to•ri•al [ræp'tɔriəl] *adj.* **1** of, having to do with, or designating birds of prey. **2** adapted for seizing prey: *raptorial claws.* **3** predatory.

rap•ture ['ræptʃər] *n.* **1** a strong feeling that absorbs the mind; very great joy. **2** Often, **raptures,** *pl.* an expression of great joy. **3** a transporting or being transported, in body or spirit, to another plane of existence, specifically, as believed by some Christians, **the Rapture**, the taking up of the faithful to meet Christ in the air before his actual return to earth. ⟨< *rapt*⟩

rapture of the deep lightheadedness, euphoria, and an inability to think and react quickly, brought on by an increased nitrogen level in the body tissues and brain caused by an increase in air pressure. ⟨coined by Jacques Cousteau from F *ivresse des grandes profondeurs*⟩

rap•tur•ous ['ræptʃərəs] *adj.* full of rapture; expressing or feeling rapture. **—'rap•tur•ous•ly,** *adv.*

ra•quette [ræ'kɛt] *n. Cdn.* snowshoe. Also **raquet, racket, racquetté.** ⟨< Cdn.F⟩

ra•ra a•vis ['rɛrə 'eivɪs], pl. **ra•rae a•ves** ['rɛri 'eiviz] someone or something unusual or exceptional. ⟨< L, rare bird⟩

rare[1] [rɛr] *adj.* **rar•er, rar•est. 1** seldom seen or occurring; uncommon; unusual: *The whooping crane has become very rare. A solar eclipse is a rare event.* **2** unusually good or great: *Shakespeare had rare powers as a dramatist.* **3** thin; not dense: *The higher you go, the rarer the air becomes.* ⟨< L *rarus*⟩ **—'rare•ness,** *n.*

☛ *Syn.* **1. Rare,** SCARCE = not often or easily found. **Rare** describes something uncommon or unusual at any time because it seldom occurs or only a few specimens exist; it often suggests excellence or value above the ordinary: *The Gutenberg Bible is a rare book.* **Scarce** describes something usually or formerly common or plentiful, but not existing or produced in large enough numbers or quantities at the present time: *Water is becoming scarce in some parts of the country.*

rare[2] [rɛr] *adj.* **rar•er, rar•est.** of meat, not cooked much; cooked so that the inside is still red: *She prefers her steak rare.* ⟨OE *hrēr*⟩ **—'rare•ness,** *n.*

rare•bit ['rɛrbɪt] *n.* WELSH RABBIT. ⟨altered < *(Welsh) rabbit*⟩

rare earth *Chemistry.* **1** any of the oxides of rare-earth elements. **2** RARE-EARTH METAL. **—'rare-'earth,** *adj.*

rare–earth metal or **element** *Chemistry.* any of the rare metallic elements that have atomic numbers from 57 to 71 inclusive, such as the lanthanides, scandium, and yttrium.

rar•e•fac•tion [ˌrɛrə'fækʃən] *n.* the act or process of making less dense; the state of being made less dense. **—ˌrar•e'fac•tive,** *adj.*

rar•e•fy ['rɛrəˌfaɪ] *v.* **-fied, -fy•ing. 1** make less dense: *The air in the mountains is rarefied.* **2** become less dense. **3** refine or elevate; purify. **4** make subtle: *rarefied wit.* ⟨< L *rarefacere* < *rarus* rare + *facere* make⟩

rare•ly ['rɛrli] *adv.* **1** seldom; not often: *Horse-drawn delivery carts are rarely seen these days.* **2** unusually; unusually well: *a rarely carved panel.*

rar•ing ['rɛrɪŋ] *adj. Informal.* very eager: *raring to go, raring for a fight.* ⟨< *rare,* dialect var. of *rear*[2]⟩

rar•i•ty ['rɛrɪti] *n., pl.* **-ties. 1** something rare: *A thirty-year-old car is a rarity.* **2** the quality or state of being rare or scarce; scarcity. **3** a lack of density; thinness: *The rarity of mountain air is bad for people with weak hearts.* **4** unusual excellence: *The rarity of her thesis won her the Governor-General's medal.*

ras•cal ['ræskəl] *n.* **1** a dishonest person; rogue. **2** a mischievous person or animal. ⟨ME < OF *rascaille* < *rasque* filth, ult. < L *radere* scratch⟩

ras•cal•i•ty [ræ'skælɪti] *n., pl.* **-ties. 1** the character or actions of a rascal. **2** a rascally act.

ras•cal•ly ['ræskəli] *adj., adv. —adj.* of or characteristic of a rascal; mean, dishonest, mischievous, etc.
—adv. in a base or dishonest manner.

rash[1] [ræʃ] *adj.* too hasty or too bold; reckless; impetuous; taking or involving too much risk. ⟨ME *rasch* quick⟩ **—'rash•ly,** *adv.* **—'rash•ness,** *n.*

☛ *Syn.* **Rash,** RECKLESS = acting or speaking without due care or thought. **Rash** emphasizes being in too great a rush, speaking hastily or plunging into action without stopping to think: *You should never make rash promises.* **Reckless** emphasizes being without caution, acting carelessly without paying attention to possible consequences: *The dog was killed by a reckless driver.*

rash[2] [ræʃ] *n.* **1** an eruption of spots on the skin, usually temporary, as a symptom of a disease, infection, allergic reaction, etc.: *Perfumed soaps give me a rash.* **2** a sudden appearance of a large number of instances or cases of something unpleasant or unhappy: *There was a rash of angry letters following the publication of the article.* ⟨< OF *rasche* scurf, ult. < L *radere* scratch⟩

rash•er ['ræʃər] *n.* **1** a thin slice of bacon or ham for frying or broiling. **2** a serving of three or four such slices. ⟨origin uncertain⟩

rasp [ræsp] *v., n. —v.* **1** make a harsh, grating sound: *The file rasped on the scythe.* **2** utter with a grating sound: *to rasp out a command.* **3** have a harsh or irritating effect (on); grate. **4** scrape with a rasp or other rough instrument.
—n. **1** a harsh, grating sound or effect: *the rasp of crickets, a rasp in a person's voice.* **2** a coarse file with pointlike teeth. ⟨ME < OF *rasper* < Gmc.⟩ **—'rasp•er,** *n.* **—'rasp•ing•ly,** *adv.* **—'rasp•ish,** *adj.*

rasp•ber•ry ['ræzˌbɛri] *n., pl.* **-ries;** *adj. —n.* **1** any of several prickly shrubs (genus *Rubus*) of the rose family having pale pink flowers and red, purple, black, or yellow edible berries. **2** the juicy berry of any of these shrubs, an aggregate fruit consisting of small drupes crowded together around a fleshy receptacle. Red raspberries are the most common. **3** a dark purplish red colour. **4** *Slang.* a sound of derision made with the tongue and lips.
—adj. **1** made of or flavoured with raspberries. **2** having the colour raspberry. ⟨< earlier *raspis* raspberry (origin uncertain) + *berry*⟩ **—'rasp•ber•ry,like,** *adj.*

rasp•y ['ræspi] *adj.* **rasp•i•er, rasp•i•est. 1** harsh; rasping: *a raspy voice.* **2** irritable; short-tempered. **—'rasp•i•ly,** *adv.* **—'rasp•i•ness,** *n.*

Ras•ta•far•i•an [ˌræstə'færiən] *or* [ˌræstə'fɛriən] *n., adj. —n.* **1** a person who believes in Rastafarianism. **2** a person who identifies with Rastafarianism as a social and political movement.
—adj. of or having to do with Rastafarians or Rastafarianism. Also, **Rasta.**

Ras•ta•far•i•an•ism [ˌræstə'færiəˌnɪzəm] *or* [ˌræstə'fɛriəˌnɪzəm] *n.* a Jamaican religion based on the divinity of Haile Selassie (1892-1975), emperor of Ethiopia (1930-1936; 1941-1974), that stresses Africa as the home to which black people must return some day. Also, **Rasta.** ⟨< *Ras Tafari* Prince Tafari, the name and title of Haile Selassie before he became emperor⟩

ras•ter ['ræstər] *n.* a pattern of horizontal scanning lines traced by an electron beam on a television screen when there is no picture. ⟨< G *raster* screen < Med.L *rastrum* rake < L *radere* scrape⟩

rat [ræt] *n., v.* **rat•ted, rat•ting;** *interj. —n.* **1** any of numerous long-tailed Old World rodents (especially genus *Rattus*) related to and resembling the Old World mouse, but larger. Rats are now common disease-carrying pests in communities throughout the world. **2** any of various other rodents, such as the wood rat of North America. **3** *Slang.* a contemptible, disloyal person. **4** *Cdn. Northwest.* a muskrat. **5** a small pad over which a woman's hair is arranged to make it look thicker.
smell a rat, *Informal.* suspect a trick or scheme.
—v. **1** hunt for or catch rats. **2** *Cdn. Northwest.* trap muskrats. **3** *Slang.* betray, inform on, or desert one's friends or associates (*usually used with* **on**): *Most people wouldn't rat on their best friends.* **4** arrange or dress (the hair), as with a RAT (def. 5).
—interj.
rats, *Slang.* an exclamation of frustration, disappointment, disgust, etc. ⟨OE *rætt*⟩ **—'rat•tish,** *adj.*

rat•a•ble ['reitəbəl] *adj.* **1** capable of being rated. **2** assessed or calculated proportionally. Also, **rateable.**

rat•a•fi•a [ˌrætə'fiə] *n.* a liqueur made from fruit or brandy with fruit, and, often, almond flavouring. ⟨< Creole F of the West Indies⟩

ra•tan [rə'tæn] See RATTAN.

ra•ta•tou•ille [ˌrætə'tui]; *French,* [ʀata'twij] *n.* a vegetable dish (originally from Provence) made from eggplant, tomatoes, zucchini, onion, and garlic, flavoured with herbs. ⟨< F < *touiller* stir < L *tudiculare*⟩

ratch [rætʃ] *n.* ratchet.

ratch•et ['rætʃɪt] *n.* **1** a wheel or bar with teeth that strike against a catch fixed so that motion is permitted in one direction but not in the other. **2** the catch on such a device. **3** the entire device, wheel and catch or bar and catch. ⟨< F < Ital. *rocchetto,* ult. < Gmc.⟩

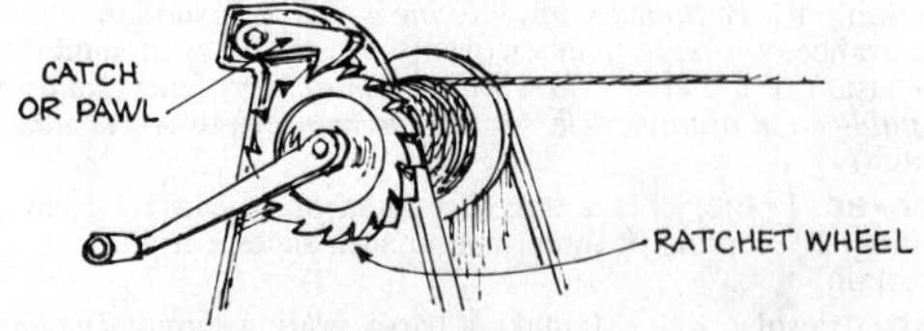

ratchet wheel a wheel with teeth and a catch that permits motion in only one direction.

rate[1] [reit] *n., v.* **rat•ed, rat•ing.** *—n.* **1** a quantity, amount, or degree measured in proportion to something else: *The rate of interest is 6 cents on the dollar. The car was going at the rate of 85 km/h.* **2** a price: *We pay the regular rate.* **3** speed or pace: *a rapid rate, a moderately slow rate.* **4** a class; grade; rating. **5** a local tax, often on property.
at any rate, a in any case; under any circumstances. **b** at least.
at that or **this rate,** in that or this case; under such conditions.
—v. **1** put a value on: *We rated the house as worth $75 000.* **2** consider; regard as: *He was rated one of the richest men in town.* **3** subject to a local tax. **4** fix at a certain rate. **5** put in a certain class or grade. **6** be regarded; be classed; rank. **7** *Informal.* have value; be worthy or be worthy of: *He doesn't rate. She rates the best seat in the house.* ⟨ME < OF < Med.L *rata (pars)* fixed (amount), pp. of L *reri* reckon⟩ **—'rat•er,** *n.*

rate[2] [reit] *v.* **rat•ed, rat•ing.** scold. ⟨ME *rate(n)*; ? < OF *rater, areter* scold < L *ad* + *reputare* count. See REPUTE.⟩

rate•a•ble ['reitəbəl] *adj.* See RATABLE.

ra•tel ['reitəl] *or* ['rɑtəl] *n.* a fierce, badgerlike carnivore (*Melivora capensis*) found in Africa and India. Also, **honey badger.** ⟨< Afrikaans < dial. Du. *raat* honeycomb, from the animal's fondness for honey⟩

rate•pay•er ['reit,peiər] *n.* a person who pays municipal taxes.

rat•fish ['ræt,fɪʃ] *n.* a chimaera (*Hydrolagus colliei*), one of a number of cartilaginous fishes of the family Chimaeridae, found in the E Pacific Ocean from Alaska to California.

rathe [reið] *adj. Archaic or poetic.* blossoming early: *the rathe primrose.* ⟨OE *hrathe*⟩

rath•er *adv.* ['ræðər]; *interj.* ['ræ'ðɜr] *adv., interj. —adv.* **1** more readily; more willingly; preferably: *I would rather go today than tomorrow.* **2** more properly or justly; with better reason: *This is rather for your parents to decide than for you.* **3** more precisely; more truly: *It was late Monday night or, rather, early Tuesday morning.* **4** in some degree; somewhat; more than a little: *rather good. She rather felt that this was unwise.* **5** on the contrary: *The sick man is no better today; rather, he is worse.*
had rather, would more willingly; prefer to.
—interj. Esp. Brit. Informal. yes, indeed! certainly! very much so! ⟨OE *hrathor*, comparative of *hrathe* quickly⟩

raths•kel•ler ['ræts,kɛlər], ['rɑts,kɛlər], *or* ['ræθs,kɛlər] *n.* a restaurant, usually below street level, selling alcoholic drinks. ⟨< G *Ratskeller, Rathskeller* < *Rat(haus)* town hall + *Keller* cellar⟩

rat•i•fi•ca•tion [,rætəfə'keiʃən] *n.* formal approval and sanction: *the ratification of a treaty by Parliament.*

rat•i•fy ['rætə,faɪ] *v.* **-fied, -fy•ing.** approve formally; confirm; authorize: *The two countries will ratify the agreement made by their representatives.* ⟨ME < OF < Med.L *ratificare,* ult. < L *ratus* fixed + *facere* make⟩ **—'rat•i,fi•er,** *n.*
☛ *Syn.* See note at APPROVE.

rat•ing[1] ['reitɪŋ] *n., v. —n.* **1** a rank; grade. **2** a position in a class or grade: *the rating of a seaman, the rating of a ship according to tonnage.* **3** in some navies, a sailor of the lowest rank; an ordinary seaman. **4** an amount fixed as a rate or grade: *a rating of 80% in English.* **5** a specification of an engine, furnace etc., expressing its performance limit, heat capacity, etc., usually in hp, W, or BTU. **6** a film classification recommending or restricting the age of viewers. **7** any survey of public taste, especially one taken to establish the popularity of one or more television programs. **8** a level of merit or popularity established by this or some other survey. **9** CREDIT RATING.
—v. ppr. of RATE[1].

rat•ing[2] ['reitɪŋ] *n., v. —n.* a scolding.
—v. ppr. of RATE[2].

ra•ti•o ['reiʃou] *n., pl.* **-ti•os. 1** the relative magnitude. *She has sheep and cows in the ratio of 10 to 3* means that she has ten sheep for every three cows, or 3⅓ times as many sheep as cows. **2** a quotient of two numbers or quantities. The ratio between two quantities is the number of times one contains the other. The ratio of 6 to 10 is 6/10. The ratio of 10 to 6 is 10/6. **3** *Finance.* the relative value of gold and silver in a bimetallic currency system. ⟨< L *ratio* reckoning < *reri* reckon. Doublet of RATION, REASON.⟩

ra•ti•oc•i•nate [,ræʃi'ɒsə,neit] *or* [,ræti'ɒsə,neit] *v.* **-nat•ed, -nat•ing.** carry on a process of reasoning; reason. ⟨< L *ratiocinari* < *ratio.* See RATIO.⟩ **—,ra•ti,oc•i'na•tion,** *n.* **—,ra•ti'oc•i,na•tor,** *n.*

ra•ti•oc•i•na•tive [,ræʃi'ɒsənətɪv] *or* [,ræti'ɒsənətɪv] *adj.* of, having to do with, or involving ratiocination.

ra•tion ['ræʃən] *or* ['reiʃən] *n., v. —n.* **1** (*often pl.*) a fixed allowance of food; daily allowance of food for a person or animal. **2** a portion of anything dealt out: *rations of sugar, of coal, etc.*
—v. **1** supply with rations: *to ration an army.* **2** allow only certain amounts to: *to ration citizens when supplies are scarce.* **3** distribute in limited amounts: *to ration food to the public in wartime.* ⟨< F < Med.L *ratio, -onis* < L *ratio* reckoning. See RATIO. Doublet of RATIO, REASON.⟩
☛ *Syn. n.* **1.** See note at FOOD.

ra•tion•al ['ræʃənəl] *adj.* **1** sensible; reasonable; reasoned out: *Angry people seldom act in a rational way.* **2** able to think logically as opposed to intuitively or emotionally: *As children grow older, they become more rational.* **3** able to think and reason clearly: *After the anesthetic wore off, she became quite rational again. As long as he takes his medication, he is perfectly rational.* **4** of reason; based on reasoning: *There is a rational explanation for thunder and lightning.* **5** *Mathematics.* **a** expressible as a fraction composed of whole numbers with a non-zero denominator. **b** involving no root that cannot be extracted. **c** of a function, capable of being expressed as the quotient of two polynomials. ⟨< L *rationalis* < *ratio.* See RATIO.⟩
—'ra•tion•al•ly, *adv.*
☛ *Syn.* **1-4.** See note at REASONABLE.

ra•tion•ale [,ræʃə'næl] *n.* the whys and wherefores; the fundamental reason or logical basis, or an explanation or statement of this. ⟨< L *rationale*, neut. of *rationalis.* See RATIONAL.⟩

ra•tion•al•ism ['ræʃənə,lɪzəm] *n.* **1** the principle or habit of accepting reason as the supreme authority in matters of opinion, belief, or conduct. **2** the philosophical doctrine that reason is in itself a source of knowledge, independent of the senses.

ra•tion•al•ist ['ræʃənə,lɪst] *n.* a person who believes in or follows rationalism.

ra•tion•al•is•tic [,ræʃənə'lɪstɪk] *adj.* of or having to do with rationalism or rationalists. **—,ra•tion•al'is•ti•cal•ly,** *adv.*

ra•tion•al•i•ty [,ræʃə'næləti] *n.* the quality or state of being rational: *the rationality of her explanation. Mr. Wallace is eccentric, but no one doubts his rationality.*

ra•tion•al•ize ['ræʃənə,laɪz] *v.* **-ized, -iz•ing. 1** make rational or conformable to reason. **2** treat or explain in a rational manner. **3** find (often unconsciously) an explanation or excuse for (one's desires or actions): *She rationalizes her gluttony by thinking, "I must eat enough to keep up my strength."* **4** think in a rational or rationalistic way. **5** *Mathematics.* eliminate radical signs from (an equation or expression) without changing the value. **—,ra•tion•al•i'za•tion,** *n.* **—'ra•tion•al,iz•er,** *n.*

rational number *Mathematics.* any number that can be expressed as an integer or as a ratio between two integers, excluding zero as a denominator. 2, 5, and ½ are rational numbers.

rational operation *Mathematics.* addition, subtraction, multiplication, or division.

rat•ite ['rætəɪt] *adj., n. —adj.* of or relating to a group of large, flightless birds (Ratitae) having a flat, unkeeled breastbone. The ostrich, cassowary, emu, and kiwi are ratites.
—n. any bird of this group. ⟨< L *ratitus* < *ratis* raft⟩

rat kangaroo any of a number of ratlike kangaroos of several genera, found in Australia.

rat•line or **rat•lin** ['rætlɪn] *n. Nautical.* one of the small ropes that cross the shrouds of a ship, used as steps for going aloft. See SHROUD for picture. ⟨ME, origin uncertain⟩

RA•TO or **ra•to** ['reitou] *n.* a unit consisting of one or more rockets, providing extra power to speed up an aircraft during take-off. ⟨< *r*ocket *a*ssisted *t*ake-*o*ff⟩

ra•toon [rə'tun] *n., v. —n.* a new shoot or sprout that grows from the root of a plant already cropped: *ratoons of banana trees.* —*v.* sprout after being cut. Also, **rattoon.** ⟨< Sp. *retoño* < *retoñar* to sprout⟩

rat race *Informal.* a fierce, frantic scramble or struggle, especially with reference to competing and keeping one's place in the business world.

rats•bane ['ræts,bein] *n.* any poison for rats. ⟨< *rat* + *bane*⟩

rat snake any of various large, non-poisonous colubrid snakes of the genus *Elaphe* found in E and SW North America, so called because they live chiefly on small rodents.

rat–tail ['ræt ,teil] *adj., n. —adj.* shaped like a rat's tail; long, thin, and tapered, or having a part that is long, thin, and tapered. —*n.* **1** GRENADIER (def. 3). **2** any of various implements with a long, tapering part. **3 a** any tail that is hairless like a rat's. **b** an animal having such a tail, especially a horse. **4** *Informal.* a masculine hairstyle with a lock of hair at the back of the head which is allowed to grow several centimetres longer than the rest.

rat•tan [rə'tæn] *n.* **1** any of several climbing palms (especially of genera *Calamus* and *Daemonorops*) having very long, jointed, pliable stems. **2** the stem of any of these palms, used for wickerwork, canes, etc. **3** a cane or switch made from a piece of such a stem. ⟨ult. < Malay *rotan*⟩

rat•ter ['rætər] *n.* **1** an animal or, sometimes, a person that catches rats: *Our terrier is a good ratter.* **2** *Slang.* a person who informs on or betrays his or her associates.

rat•tle ['rætəl] *v.* **-tled, -tling;** *n. —v.* **1** make a number of short, sharp sounds. **2** cause to rattle. **3** move with short, sharp sounds: *The cart rattled down the street.* **4** talk quickly, on and on (*usually used with* **on**): *to rattle on about something.* **5** say quickly (*often used with* **off**): *to rattle off a speech.* **6** *Informal.* confuse; upset: *She was so rattled that she forgot her speech.*
rattle around in, *Informal.* live or work in (a place) that is much larger than one needs.
—*n.* **1** a number of short, sharp sounds: *the rattle of empty bottles.* **2** a sound in the throat, occurring in some diseases of the lungs and also often just before death. **3** a racket; uproar. **4** a toy, instrument, etc. filled with pellets so that it makes a noise when it is shaken. **5 a** a series of horny pieces at the end of a rattlesnake's tail. **b** one of these pieces. ⟨ME *ratele(n)*; probably imitative⟩ —**'rat•tly,** *adj.*

rat•tle² ['rætəl] *v. Nautical.* furnish (a ship or its rigging) with ratlines (*often used with* **down**). ⟨< *rattling,* a former variant of *ratline*⟩

rat•tle•brain ['rætəl,brein] *n.* a giddy, foolish, unthinking person. —**'rat•tle,brained,** *adj.*

rat•tler ['rætlər] *n.* **1** a person or thing that rattles. **2** *Informal.* rattlesnake.

rat•tle•snake ['rætəl,sneik] *n.* any of the snakes constituting two genera (*Crotalus* and *Sistrurus*) of pit vipers that produce a whirring sound of warning by vibrating the end of the tail, which consists of a series of loosely connected horny segments.

rattlesnake root a white lettuce (*Prenanthes altissima*) growing to over 2 m tall, and having drooping white flowers. It blooms in late summer and early fall in damp eastern forests.

rat•tle•trap ['rætəl,træp] *n.* **1** something shaky, rickety, or rattling, especially an old, worn-out car. **2** (*adjl.*) rickety or rattling.

rat•tling ['rætlɪŋ] *adj., v. —adj.* **1** that rattles. **2** lively; very fast: *a rattling pace.* **3** *Informal.* great; very good. **4** (*advl.*) *Informal.* extremely; especially: *a rattling good time.*
—*v.* ppr. of RATTLE.

rat•toon [rə'tun] See RATOON.

rat–trap ['ræt ,træp] *n.* **1** a trap to catch rats. **2** a dirty, run-down building. **3** a holder for small items over the rear wheel of a bicycle, which secures the object by a spring-operated clamp like the one in a trap for catching rats. **4** a desperate situation.

rat•ty ['ræti] *adj.* **-ti•er, -ti•est. 1** of or like rats. **2** full of rats. **3** *Slang.* poor; shabby: *a ratty old jacket.* **4** *Slang.* angry or irritable: *The boss seems a little ratty this morning.*

rau•cous ['rɒkəs] *adj.* **1** hoarse; harsh-sounding: *the raucous caw of a crow.* **2** loud and disorderly; rowdy. ⟨< L *raucus*⟩ —**'rau•cous•ly,** *adv.* —**'rau•cous•ness,** *n.*

raun•chy ['rɒntʃi] *adj.* **-chi•er, -chi•est.** *Slang.* **1** lewd; indecent: *The entertainer's raunchy songs bordered on the obscene.* **2** smelly or dirty, especially from body odour: *She insists on wearing those raunchy sneakers. Phew! it's raunchy in this dressing room!* **3** boisterously and vulgarly exuberant: *Some of the Grey Cup fans got pretty raunchy at the game.* —**'raun•chi•ly,** *adv.* —**'raun•chi•ness,** *n.* ⟨origin uncertain⟩

rau•wol•fi•a [rɒ'wʊlfiə] *or* [raʊ'wʊlfiə] *n.* **1** any tree or shrub of the tropical genus *Rauwolfia,* mostly poisonous, but some of which have medicinal properties. **2** an extract from the roots of the plant *R. serpentina* of India, yielding alkaloids, especially reserpine, used in the treatment of hyperactivity and as a sedative. ⟨< NL after L. *Rauwolf,* 16c. German botanist⟩

rav•age¹ ['rævɪdʒ] *v.* **-aged, -ag•ing;** *n. —v.* lay waste; damage greatly; destroy: *The forest fire ravaged huge areas of country.* —*n.* **1** the act of ravaging. **2** the resulting destruction; great damage: *War causes ravage.* ⟨< F *ravager* < *ravir* ravish⟩ —**'rav•age•ment,** *n.* —**'rav•ag•er,** *n.*

rav•age² ['rævɪdʒ] *n. Cdn.* a place where a group of moose, deer, or other animals stay for a time feeding on the surrounding vegetation before moving on. ⟨< Cdn.F⟩

rave [reiv] *v.* **raved, rav•ing;** *n. —v.* **1** talk or utter wildly and incoherently, as when extremely excited, delirious, etc. **2** talk or utter with much, or too much, enthusiasm: *She raved about the food.* **3** howl; roar; rage: *The wind raved about the lighthouse.* —*n.* **1** the act or an instance of raving. **2** *Informal.* unrestrained praise, especially a highly enthusiastic review of a play, film, etc.: *The play got raves in the local press.* **3** a large, secret gathering of young people to dance and listen to highly synthesized music with a driving rhythm (**Third Wave**), regarded as an alternative to mainstream popular music. **4** (*adjl.*) unrestrainedly enthusiastic: *rave reviews.* ⟨ME *raven* < OF *raver,* var. of *rêver* dream⟩

rav•el ['rævəl] *v.* **-elled** or **-eled, -el•ling** or **-el•ing;** *n. —v.* **1** separate the threads of; fray: *The sweater was ravelled at the wrist.* **2** fray out; separate into threads: *When I washed my pants by machine, all the seams ravelled.* **3** tangle; involve; confuse. —*n.* **1** a ravelled thread or fibre. **2** a tangle or complication. ⟨probably < MDu. *ravelen*⟩

rav•el•ling or **rav•el•ing** ['rævəlɪŋ] *n., v. —n.* something ravelled out; a thread drawn from a woven or knitted fabric.
—*v.* ppr. of RAVEL.

ra•ven¹ ['reivən] *n., adj. —n.* **1** a very large passerine bird (*Corvus corax*) closely related to the crows, found throughout much of the northern hemisphere, having a large, straight bill and glossy black plumage. **2** any of various other large members of the same family. **3 Raven,** the trickster and divine culture-hero of Pacific Northwest First Nations folklore.
—*adj.* having the glossy black colour of a raven: *raven hair.* ⟨OE *hræfn*⟩

rav•en² ['rævən] *v., n. —v.* **1** devour (food or prey) greedily. **2** prey on; plunder. **3** go about in a predatory manner; prowl. —*n.* **1** plunder; rapine. Also, **ravin. 2** something captured; spoils or prey. ⟨ME *ravine* < OF *raviner* < *ravine* violent rush, robbery. Doublet of RAVINE.⟩

rav•en•ing ['rævənɪŋ] *adj., v. —adj.* **1** seeking eagerly for prey: *ravening wolves.* **2** greedy and hungry; voracious.
—*v.* ppr. of RAVEN².

rav•en•ous ['rævənəs] *adj.* **1** very hungry; famished: *The hikers were all ravenous by the time they stopped to eat.* **2** very eager or greedy: *ravenous hunger. The child was ravenous for praise.* **3** rapacious. ⟨ME < OF *ravineus* rapacious, violent < *ravine.* See RAVEN².⟩ —**'rav•en•ous•ly,** *adv.* —**'rav•en•ous•ness,** *n.*

rav•in ['rævən] See RAVEN².

ra•vine [rə'vin] *n.* a long, deep, narrow gorge worn by running water or by the action of glaciers. ⟨< F *ravine* < OF *ravine* violent rush, robbery. Doublet of RAVEN².⟩

rav•ing ['reivɪŋ] *adj., n., v. —adj.* **1** that raves; delirious; frenzied; raging. **2** *Informal.* remarkable; extraordinary: *a raving beauty.* **3** (*advl.*) so as to be or cause raving; furiously: *stark raving mad.*
—*n.* delirious, incoherent talk.
—*v.* ppr. of RAVE. —**'rav•ing•ly,** *adv.*

rav•i•o•li [,rævi'ouli] *n.* small, thin cases of pasta filled with chopped meat, cheese, etc., cooked in water and usually served with a highly seasoned tomato sauce. ⟨< Ital. *ravioli,* ult. < L *rapum* beet⟩

rav•ish ['rævɪʃ] *v.* **1** fill with delight; charm; enrapture: *to be ravished by the beauty of a scene.* **2** commit rape on. **3** *Archaic.* carry off by force. ⟨ME < OF *raviss-*, a stem of *ravir* < L *rapere* seize⟩ **–'rav•ish•er,** *n.*

rav•ish•ing ['rævəʃɪŋ] *adj., v.* *–adj.* totally delightful; enchanting: *jewels of ravishing beauty.*
–v. ppr. of RAVISH. **–'rav•ish•ing•ly,** *adv.*

rav•ish•ment ['rævɪʃmənt] *n.* **1** the act of ravishing. **2** rapture; ecstasy.

raw [rɒ] *adj.* **1** not cooked: *raw oysters.* **2** in the natural state; not manufactured, treated, or prepared: *raw materials, raw hides. Raw milk is milk that has not been pasteurized.* **3** unprocessed; unedited; unevaluated: *raw statistics, raw text.* **4** not experienced; not trained: *a raw recruit.* **5** unpleasantly damp or cold: *raw weather.* **6** with the skin off; sore: *a raw spot.* **7** uncivilized; brutal: *the raw frontier.* **8 a** having a crude quality; not refined in taste: *a raw piece of work, a raw story.* **b** so blunt or direct as to be harsh or coarse. **9** *Slang.* unjustly harsh; unfair: *a raw deal.*
–n.
in the raw, a in an unrefined or crude state: *experiencing life in the raw.* **b** *Slang.* naked: *to sleep in the raw.*
the raw, a raw or sore place or condition. ⟨OE *hrēaw*⟩
–'raw•ly, *adv.* **–'raw•ness,** *n.*
☛ *Syn. adj.* **2. Raw,** CRUDE = not processed or prepared for use. **Raw** applies to a material or natural product that has not yet been processed for use or shaped or made into something by treating, tanning, finishing, manufacturing, etc.: *Raw milk must be pasteurized to make it ready to drink.* **Crude** applies to a product in its natural state, not freed from impurities or prepared for use or greater usefulness and value by refining, tempering, or treating with chemicals and heat: *Crude rubber is treated with sulphur and heat to make it more elastic and durable.*

raw–boned ['rɒ ,bound] *adj.* **1** having little flesh on the bones; gaunt. **2** having a heavy, large, somewhat bony frame: *He was tall and raw-boned.*

raw•hide ['rɒ,haɪd] *n., v.* **-hid•ed, -hid•ing.** *–n.* **1** the untanned skin of cattle. **2** a rope or whip made of this skin. **3** *Cdn.* formerly, the dressed but untanned hide of an animal, usually buffalo, used to pack goods, especially ore, in, and lashed to rope tugs for hauling over ice and snow. **4** (*adjl.*) made of rawhide.
–v. whip or drive with a rawhide. **–'raw,hid•er,** *n.*

ra•win•sonde ['reiwɪn,sɒnd] *n. Meteorology.* **1** a radiosonde tracked by radar. **2** observation of atmospheric conditions, especially wind phenomena, at very high altitudes by radiosonde. ⟨< *ra(dio)* + *win(d)* + *(radio)sonde*⟩

raw material **1** material that can or will be treated, prepared, or manufactured into something else: *Petroleum is one of the basic raw materials of industry.* **2** a person or thing thought of as having potential for development, elaboration, training, etc.: *There is some good raw material for the football team among the new students.*

raw milk unpasteurized milk.

ray[1] [rei] *n., v.* *–n.* **1** a line or beam of light. **2** a line or stream of radiant energy in the form of heat, electricity, light, etc.: *X rays.* **3** a thin line like a ray, coming out from a centre. **4** any part like a ray. The petals of a daisy and the arms of a starfish are rays. **5** a slight trace; faint gleam: *Not a ray of hope pierced our gloom.* **6** *Geometry.* a straight line extending from a point.
–v. **1** send forth (something) in rays; radiate. **2** subject to rays or radiation. ⟨ME < OF *rai* < L *radius.* Doublet of RADIUS.⟩
–'ray•less, *adj.* **–'ray,like,** *adj.*
☛ *Hom.* RE[1] [rei].
☛ *Syn. n.* **1.** See note at BEAM.

ray[2] [rei] *n.* any of an order (Batoidea, also called Rajiformes) of fishes having a flattened body with the eyes and spiracles on the top of the head and the mouth and gill slits on the underside and having broad, winglike pectoral fins and a tapering tail often bearing one or more poisonous spines. See also ELECTRIC RAY, DEVILFISH, STINGRAY. ⟨ME < OF < L *raia*⟩
☛ *Hom.* RE[1] [rei].

ray flower one of the petal-like flowers forming the outside of the flower head of a composite plant. The flower head of a daisy consists of central disk flowers surrounded by ray flowers. See COMPOSITE for picture.

ray•on ['reiɒn] *n.* **1** any of a group of textile fibres made from cellulose. The cellulose in solution is extruded through minute holes and solidified in the form of filaments. **2** a yarn or fabric made from any of these fibres. **3** (*adjl.*) made of rayon. ⟨blend of *ray*[1] (because of its sheen) + *(cott)on*⟩

raze [reiz] *v.* **razed, raz•ing.** tear down; destroy completely; demolish: *The old school was razed and a new one was built in the same place.* ⟨< F *raser* scrape, ult. < L *radere*⟩
☛ *Hom.* RAISE.

ra•zor ['reizər] *n.* a cutting instrument used for shaving or cutting hair: *an electric razor, a safety razor.* ⟨ME < OF *rasor* < *raser* scrape, ult. < L *radere.* Related to RAZE.⟩
☛ *Hom.* RAISER.

ra•zor•back ['reizər,bæk] *n.* **1** a kind of thin, half-wild, mongrel hog with a ridged back. Razorbacks are common in the southern United States. **2** a finback whale; rorqual. **3** a sharp ridge on a hill, mountain, etc.

ra•zor•bill ['reizər,bɪl] *n.* a common North Atlantic auk (*Alca torda*) having a deep, curved, laterally compressed bill with a white line down the sides and black-and-white plumage.

ra•zor–billed auk ['reizər ,bɪld] razorbill.

razor clam any of various marine bivalve molluscs (family Solenidae) having a narrow, elongated shell resembling a straight razor, and a large, muscular foot adapted for burrowing deep in the sand in coastal waters.

razor shell RAZOR CLAM.

razz [ræz] *v., n. Slang.* *–v.* tease, ridicule, or heckle; make fun of: *Several people in the crowd were razzing the speaker. We razz her about the old car she drives.*
–n. a sound of disapproval or contempt; RASPBERRY (def. 4). ⟨< *raspberry*⟩

raz•zle–daz•zle ['ræzəl 'dæzəl] *n., adj., v.* **-zled, -zling.** *Slang.* *–n.* **1** confusing or bewildering activity, especially of a colourful and spectacular nature. **2** *Sports.* a deceptive play involving fast movement, crisscrossing, etc. by several players, intended to bewilder the opposing team.
–adj. bewildering; flashy.
–v. bewilder; confuse. ⟨varied reduplication of *dazzle*⟩

razz•ma•tazz ['ræzmə,tæz] *n. Slang.* **1** razzle-dazzle; excitement and fanfare. **2** doubletalk; equivocation: *political razzmatazz.* **3** (*adjl.*) characterized by excitement and fanfare: *the razzmatazz heyday of journalism.*

rb or **RB** *Football.* running back.

Rb rubidium.

RBI or **rbi** [,ɑr bi 'aɪ] *n., pl.* **RBIs, RBI's,** or **RBI.** *Baseball.* run batted in.

R.C. **1** ROMAN CATHOLIC. **2** RED CROSS.

rcd. received.

RCMP or **R.C.M.P.** ROYAL CANADIAN MOUNTED POLICE.

r–col•our•ing ['ɑr ,kʌlərɪŋ] *n. Phonetics.* the peculiar quality given to vowels preceding the sound [r] by the fact that the tongue is already retroflexed in anticipation of the [r].

rcpt receipt.

rd. **1** road. **2** rod(s). **3** round.

Rd. Road.

R.D. *U.S.* Rural Delivery (in postal addresses).

RDA recommended daily allowance (used in reference to vitamins and other nutrients).

r–dropping ['ɑr ,drɒpɪŋ] *adj. Phonetics.* characterized by not pronouncing the [r] after a vowel in English, as in some dialects in the United States and most of England.

re[1] [rei] *n. Music.* **1** the second tone of an eight-tone major scale. **2** the tone D of the scale of C major. See DO[2] for picture. ⟨See GAMUT⟩
☛ *Hom.* RAY [rei].

re[2] [ri] *prep.* with reference to; in the matter or case of; about; concerning. ⟨for L *in re* in the matter of⟩

re– *prefix.* **1** again; once more: *reappear, rebuild, reheat, reopen, re-enter.* **2** anew; again but in a completely different way: *redesign, rearrange, restructure.* **3** back: *recall, repay, replace.* ⟨< L⟩
☛ *Usage.* Most words beginning with **re-** are not hyphenated: *rearm, refine, remit.* However, a hyphen is often used if the letter following the **re-** is also *e*, as in *re-entry, re-establish*, and to distinguish words that have the same spelling but different morphology: *re-ally.* In addition, a hyphen is always used to distinguish a word in which **re-** means 'again' from another word that would otherwise have the same spelling: *recover* 'get back, get better', *re-cover* 'cover again'; *reform* 'make better, improve', *re-form* 'make or shape again'.

Re rhenium.

reach [ritʃ] *v., n.* —*v.* **1** get to; come to; arrive at: *to reach the top of a hill, the end of a book, an agreement, etc.* **2** stretch; stretch out: *to reach out one's hand.* **3** extend in space, time, operation, effect, influence, etc. (to): *farther than the eye can reach. The power of Rome reached to the ends of the known world. Radio reaches millions.* **4** get in touch with by anything extended, cast, etc.: *They lowered the anchor until they reached bottom.* **5** succeed in making a stretch of a certain length with the hand, etc.: *I cannot reach to the top of the wall.* **6** make a stretch in a certain direction: *The man reached for his dictionary. She reached toward the light.* **7** get at; influence: *Most people can be reached by flattery.* **8** contact; establish communication with: *I phoned twice last night but couldn't reach you. You can reach me at the following address.* **9** amount (to); be equal to; add up (to): *The cost of the war reached billions. Fatalities have reached into the thousands.* **10** *Informal.* venture to make a claim, joke, etc., with too little foundation: *I may be reaching here, but I think it's the only clinic of its kind in North America. What a bad pun—he's really reaching tonight!* **11** *Informal.* take or pass with the hand: *Please reach me the sugar.* **12** *Nautical.* sail on a course with the wind forward of the beam. **13** deliver (a blow, kick, etc.).
—*n.* **1** a stretching out; reaching: *By a long reach, the drowning man grasped the rope.* **2** the extent or distance of reaching: *out of one's reach.* **3** range; power; capacity: *the reach of the mind.* **4** a continuous stretch or extent: *a reach of woodland.* **5** a part of a river between bends. **6** a part of a canal between locks. **7** *Nautical.* the distance sailed on one tack. ⟨OE *rǣcan*⟩
—'reach•er, *n.*
☛ *Usage.* See note at COME.

reach–me–down ['ritʃ mi ˌdaʊn] *n., adj. Informal.* HAND-ME-DOWN.

re•act [ri'ækt] *v.* **1** act back; have an effect on the one that is acting: *Unkindness often reacts on the unkind person.* **2** act in response (*used with* **to**): *Dogs react to kindness by showing affection.* **3** act unfavourably or in opposition to something or somebody (*used with* **against**): *Some people react against fads.* **4 a** act chemically; undergo a reaction: *Acids react on metals. Baking soda reacts with vinegar.* **b** be affected by such a reaction: *Many people react badly to penicillin.* **5** return to a previous state, level, etc.

re–act [ˌri 'ækt] *v.* act or perform over again.

re•act•ance [ri'æktəns] *n. Electricity.* that part of the impedance of an alternating-current circuit which is due to inductance or capacitance or both. It is expressed in ohms.

re•ac•tant [ri'æktənt] *n. Chemistry.* any substance participating in or undergoing a chemical reaction.

re•ac•tion [ri'ækʃən] *n.* **1** a response to some event or force: *Our reaction to a joke is to laugh. The announcement of the new government budget brought an immediate reaction in the stock market.* **2** a response to an idea, plan, action, etc., indicating attitude or feeling: *What was her reaction to the idea?* **3 a** the occurrence of a condition directly opposed to a previous one: *We lived in a state of euphoria for several days before the reaction set in.* **b** an action, policy, statement, etc., usually extreme, made to oppose, counteract, or compensate for another: *Her authoritarian style is a reaction to her own parents' permissiveness.* **4** *Mechanics.* the equal but opposite force exerted by a body when it is subjected to any force from another body. **5** a tendency toward a previous political or economic policy or system. **6** *Chemistry.* **a** the interaction of two or more chemical elements or compounds involving the formation of different chemical bonds to produce different substances. The reaction between nitrogen and hydrogen produces ammonia. **b** a process in which the nucleus of an atom is transformed by interaction with another nucleus or a particle. **c** the state that results from such an interaction or process. **7** the response of the body to a drug, stimulus, or treatment, especially an adverse response.
—re'ac•tion•al, *adj.*

re•ac•tion•ar•y [ri'ækʃəˌnɛri] *adj., n., pl.*. **-ar•ies.** —*adj.* having to do with, marked by, or favouring REACTION (defs. 3b, 5), especially in politics, economics, etc.
—*n.* a person who favours reaction.

reaction engine *Rocketry. Aeronautics.* an engine that produces thrust in reaction to the momentum from the ejection of a stream of hot gases.

re•ac•tion•ist [ri'ækʃənɪst] *adj., n.* reactionary.

reaction time *Psychology.* the time between a stimulus and the response it elicits.

re–ac•ti•vate [ri 'æktɪˌveit] *v.* **-vated, -vating.** make or become active or effective again.

re•ac•tive [ri'æktɪv] *adj.* **1** of or having to do with reaction. **2** tending to react. **3** *Electricity.* of or having to do with reactance. **—re'ac•tive•ly,** *adv.* **—ˌre•ac'tiv•i•ty** or **re'ac•tive•ness,** *n.*

re•ac•tor [ri'æktər] *n.* **1** *Electricity.* a device, such as a coil, having low resistance and high inductance, used to introduce reactance into an alternating-current circuit. **2** a person or animal that reacts, especially one that reacts positively to a medical test for a disease, allergy, etc. **3** NUCLEAR REACTOR.

read[1] [rid] *v.* **read** [rɛd], **read•ing;** *n.* —*v.* **1** distinguish and understand the meaning of (symbols such as those used in writing or printing): *to read a book. The blind read Braille with their fingers.* **2** learn from writing or printing: *We read of heroes of other days.* **3** speak (printed or written words); say aloud (the words one sees or touches): *Read this story to me.* **4** watch and interpret the movements of (the lips of someone talking). **5** to know (a language) well enough to understand things written in it. **6** show by letters, figures, signs, etc.: *The thermometer reads 20°.* **7** give as the word or words in a particular passage: *For 'fail', a misprint, read 'fall'.* **8** *Esp. Brit.* study: *to read law.* **9** get or give the significance of; understand; interpret: *to read a person's mind. He read her angry look and hurriedly left the room. A prophet reads the future. Farmers read the sky.* **10** *Informal.* understand (a person) clearly: *I don't want this to happen again, do you read me?* **11** introduce (something not expressed or directly indicated) by one's manner of understanding or interpreting: *to read a hostile intent into a friendly letter.* **12** produce a certain impression when read; mean; be in effect when read: *This does not read like a child's composition.* **13** be worded in a certain way: *This line reads differently in the first edition.* **14** admit of being read or interpreted: *A rule that reads two different ways.* **15** bring or put by reading: *He reads himself to sleep.* **16** proofread. **17** give (a lecture or a lesson) as a reprimand. **18** *Computer technology.* copy (data) from (a source of input or storage device) by electronic means: *The salesclerk used a bar-code scanner to read the product code.*
read between the lines, discover a meaning or implication not stated outright in something.
read out, a read aloud: *She read out her answer to the class.* **b** *Computer technology.* produce a readout of.
read out of, expel from (a political party, etc.) by publicly reading an announcement to this effect.
read the water, a *Cdn.* scan the water from one's boat or canoe for signs of danger such as shoals, rapids, and snags. **b** when fishing, scan the water from the shore or from a boat, seeking a good place to cast a fly or a lure.
read up (on), acquire information (about) by reading; research by reading.
—*n.* **1** a spell of reading. **2** a piece of reading matter considered in terms of the pleasure it gives: *That novel is a good read.* ⟨OE *rǣdan* guess, read, counsel⟩
☛ *Hom.* REED.

read[2] [rɛd] *adj., v.* —*adj.* having knowledge gained by reading; informed (*usually used in combination*): *a well-read man.*
—*v.* pt. and pp. of READ[1].
☛ *Hom.* RED, REDD.

read•a•ble ['ridəbəl] *adj.* **1** interesting or enjoyable to read: *Her novels are very readable.* **2** legible: *readable handwriting.* **—ˌread•a'bil•i•ty** or **'read•a•ble•ness,** *n.* **—'read•a•bly,** *adv.*

re–ad•dress [ˌri ə'drɛs] *v.* **1** put a new address on: *to re-address a letter.* **2** deal with again in speech or writing: *to re-address a question.* **3** talk to again: *The keynote speaker will re-address the conference on the last day.* **4** apply (oneself) anew.

In each of the words below, **re-** *means* again *or* anew; *the pronunciation of the main part of each word is not changed.*

ˌre•ab'sorb
ˌre•ab'sorp•tion
ˌre•ac'cent
ˌre•ac'cept
ˌre•ac'cep•tance
ˌre•ac'claim
ˌre•ac'com•mo,date
ˌre•ac,com•mo'da•tion
ˌre•ac'cred•it
ˌre•ac'cuse
ˌre•ac'cus•tom
ˌre•ac'quaint
ˌre•ac'quaint•ance
ˌre•ac'quire
ˌre•ac•qui'si•tion
re•a'dapt
ˌre•ad•ap'ta•tion
re•'add

read•er ['ridər] *n.* **1** a person who reads something or reads in a certain way: *She is an avid science fiction reader. They are both poor readers. He is a palm reader.* **2 a** a book for learning and practising reading. **b** a collection of short works by a given author, on a given theme, or from a given period: *a reader in English metaphysical poetry.* **3** a person employed to read manuscripts and estimate their fitness for publication. **4** proofreader. **5** a person who reads or recites to entertain an audience. **6** a lay person appointed to read the Scripture passages or prayers aloud in a church service. Also, **lay reader.** **7** an employee who reads and records the totals on a meter, as for hydro, gas, or water consumption. **8** *Computer technology.* an electronic device that copies data from a source of input (punched card, bar code, etc.). **9** *Esp. Brit.* a senior instructor in certain universities. **10** an assistant who grades and corrects examinations, reads papers, etc. for a professor.

read•er•ship ['ridər,ʃɪp] *n.* **1** the reading public or audience of a particular publication or author, or the number of people it includes. **2** *Esp. Brit.* the position of a READER (def. 9).

read•i•ly ['rɛdəli] *adv.* **1** without reluctance; willingly or promptly: *She answered our questions readily. He doesn't readily accept advice.* **2** without difficulty; easily: *The parts fitted together readily.*

read•i•ness ['rɛdinɪs] *n.* **1** the state of being ready; preparedness. **2** quickness; promptness. **3** ease; facility. **4** willingness.

read•ing ['ridɪŋ] *n., v. —n.* **1** the act or process of getting the meaning of written or printed words. **2** a speaking out loud of written or printed words; a public recital. **3** the study of books, etc. **4** written or printed matter read or to be read: *There's good reading in this magazine.* **5** (*adjl.*) used in or for reading: *reading glasses, a reading room.* **6** the information shown by some letters, figures, or signs on a gauge or the scale of an instrument: *The reading on the thermometer was 38°.* **7** the interpreting of symbols, designs, plans, etc. **8** the form of a given word or passage in a particular edition of a book: *No two editions have the same reading for that passage.* **9** an interpretation: *Each actor gave the lines a different reading.* **10** the extent to which one has read; literary knowledge. **11** one of the three stages in the passage of a bill by a legislative assembly. The bill must be presented and voted on at each reading.
—v. ppr. of READ[1].

reading desk any desk or stand supporting reading material or at which a person reads, especially publicly.

reading frame *Genetics.* one of three ways of reading a DNA or RNA sequence in terms of triplets of bases. An **open reading frame** is a sequence of bases that contains no STOP CODONS and hence is potentially a gene.

reading room a special room for reading in a library, club, department of a university, etc.

read–on•ly memory ['rid 'ounli] *Computer technology.* computer memory whose contents can be retrieved but not modified. *Abbrev.*: ROM

read•out ['rid,ʌut] *n. Computer technology.* **1** information displayed by an electronic device (computer, calculator, etc.) on a screen or printed out on paper. **2** the process of retrieving and displaying such information: *With this program you get a much faster readout.*

read/write head ['rid 'rəit] HEAD (def. 32).

read•y ['rɛdi] *adj.* **read•i•er, read•i•est;** *n., v.* **read•ied, read•y•ing.** *—adj.* **1** prepared for immediate action or use; prepared: *Dinner is ready. The soldiers are ready for battle.* **2** willing: *The knights were ready to die for their lords.* **3** quick; prompt: *a ready answer; ready action.* **4** heartily or enthusiastically offered: *a ready welcome, ready assistance.* **5** quick in thought or action; dexterous: *a ready wit.* **6** apt; likely; liable: *She is too ready to find fault.* **7** immediately available: *ready money.*
make ready, prepare.
—n.
at the ready, ready for action: *The soldiers walked down the road with their guns at the ready.*
the ready, *Informal.* cash; money at hand.
—v. make ready; prepare. ⟨OE *rǣde* ready⟩
☛ *Syn. adj.* **3, 5. Ready,** PROMPT = quick to understand, observe, or act in response. **Ready,** chiefly describing a person's actions or words, or his or her mind, hands, instrument, etc. as the source of those actions or words, suggests preparedness to act or respond without reluctance or hesitation and with skill or ease: *With ready fingers the medic dressed the wound.* **Prompt,** referring either to the person or to what is done, emphasizes being quick to act without delay when the occasion demands or a request is made: *She is prompt to help students.*

read•y–made ['rɛdi 'meid] *adj.* **1** of clothes, made beforehand in standard sizes; not made to order. **2** not original; commonplace: *a magazine article filled with ready-made ideas.* **3** already established and available: *The postal strike provided him with a ready-made excuse for not writing.*

read•y–mix ['rɛdi ,mɪks] *or* ['mɪks] *adj.* ready to cook or use after adding liquid and, sometimes, other ingredients: *ready-mix muffins, ready-mix concrete.*

read•y–to–wear ['rɛdi tə 'wɛr] *adj., n. —adj.* ready-made.
—n. ready-made clothing; clothing manufactured in a range of standard sizes.

read•y–wit•ted ['rɛdi 'wɪtɪd] *adj.* bright; perceptive; having a quick mind.

re•a•gent [ri'eidʒənt] *n.* **1** a person, force, etc. that reacts. **2** *Chemistry.* **a** a substance that takes part in a reaction. Reagents are widely used in medicine, photography, and industry. **b** something that, when added to a substance, causes a reaction that aids in determining the composition of the substance.

re•al[1] ['riəl] *or* [ril] *adj.* **1** existing as a fact; not imagined or made up; objective; actual; true: *a real experience, the real reason.* **2** genuine: *a real diamond.* **3** *Law.* of or having to do with immovable property. Lands and houses are called real property. **4** *Mathematics.* of numbers, either rational or irrational, not imaginary. **5** *Optics.* of or having to do with an optical image formed by the actual convergence of light rays, as by a lens or mirror. **6** *Economics.* measured by reference to useful goods rather than money: *In a period of rising prices, real incomes fall if money incomes remain steady.*
for real, *Slang.* in fact; true or truly.
in real life, in reality; actually: *He plays a gangster in the TV series, but in real life he's a very gentle man.* ⟨< LL *realis* < L *res* matter⟩ **—'re•al•ness,** *n.*
☛ *Hom.* REEL [ril]; RIAL ['riəl].
☛ *Syn.* **1. Real,** ACTUAL, TRUE = existing as a fact. **Real** means that what is described is in fact what it seems, is thought, or is said to be, not pretended, imaginary, or made up: *Give your real name.* **Actual** means that what it describes has in reality happened or come into existence, and is not merely capable of happening or existing only in theory: *Name an actual case of bravery.* **True** means 'in agreement with what is real or actual, not false': *Tell the true story.*
☛ *Usage.* **Real.** In formal and most written or spoken English, **real** is used only as an adjective: *The excursion was a real pleasure for all of us.* In non-standard, dialect, and rare informal use, it is also an adverb meaning 'really' or 'very': *It was real kind of you to come.*

re•al[2] ['riəl]; *Spanish,* [re'al] *n., pl.* **re•als** or *(Spanish)* **re•a•les** [re'ales]. **1** a former unit of money of Spain and its possessions. **2** a silver coin worth one real. ⟨< Sp. < L *regalis* regal. Doublet of REGAL, ROYAL, RIAL.⟩
☛ *Hom.* RIAL.

re•al[3] [rei'ɑl] *n., pl.* **reis. 1** a former unit of money of Portugal or Brazil. **2** a coin worth one real. ⟨< Pg., ult. < L *regalis* regal⟩

real estate a piece of land, together with the buildings, fences, trees, water, and minerals that belong with it.

real estate agent a person dealing in REAL ESTATE.

re•al•gar [ri'ælgər] *n.* arsenic disulphide, As_2S_2, an orange-red monoclinic mineral used as a pigment, in fireworks, and as an ore of arsenic. ⟨ME < Med.L < Arabic *rahj al-ghar* dust of the mine⟩

re•al•i•a [ri'eiliə] *or* [ri'æliə] *n.pl.* **1** *Philosophy.* real things as opposed to ideas or abstractions. **2** *Education.* everyday objects used in teaching to demonstrate aspects of real life.

In each of the words below, **re-** *means* again *or* anew; *the pronunciation of the main part of each word is not changed.*

,re-ad'just	**,re-ad'mit**	**,re-a'dop•tion**	**,re-af•fir'ma•tion**
,re-ad'just•ment	**,re-ad'mit•tance**	**,re-af'fil•i,ate**	**,re-a'lign**
,re-ad'mis•sion	**,re-a'dopt**	**,re-af'firm**	**,re-a'lign•ment**

real income the actual purchasing power of money income.

re•al•ism ['riə,lɪzəm] *n.* **1** practical tendency: *His realism caused him to dislike fanciful schemes.* **2** a style in literature and art characterized by trying to picture nature, life, people, etc. objectively and factually. **3** *Philosophy.* **a** the doctrine that material objects have a real existence independent of our consciousness of them. **b** the doctrine that general ideas have a real existence independent of the mind.

re•al•ist ['riəlɪst] *n.* **1** a person interested in what is real and practical rather than what is imaginary or theoretical. **2** a writer or artist who tries to represent nature, life, people, etc. objectively and factually. **3** a person who believes in realism.

re•al•is•tic [,riə'lɪstɪk] *adj.* **1** like the real thing; lifelike. **2** of or having to do with realism in literature or art. **3** seeing things as they really are; practical. **4** of or having to do with realists or realism. **—,re•al'is•ti•cal•ly,** *adv.*

re•al•i•ty [ri'ælɪti] *n., pl.* **-ties. 1** the quality or state of being real: *He was convinced of the reality of what he had seen.* **2** the quality, especially in art, of resembling nature or being true to life: *the reality of a description. The dialogue lacks reality.* **3** a real thing, fact, or event: *the terrible realities of war. Her dream became a reality.* **4** actual existence; the true state of affairs: *They said her writing was just an attempt to escape from reality.*
in reality, really; actually; in fact: *We thought he was serious, but in reality he was joking.*

re•al•i•za•tion [,riəlɪ'zeiʃən] *or* [,riəlaɪ'zeiʃən] *n.* **1** the action of realizing or the state of being realized: *The explorers had a full realization of the dangers they might face. For years they saved, waiting for the realization of their hopes. The realization of all their property provided enough cash for a year-long world tour.*
2 something that is realized: *The farm was the realization of all her dreams.*

re•al•ize ['riə,laɪz] *v.* **-ized, -iz•ing. 1** understand clearly; be fully aware of: *They realize how hard you worked.* **2** make real; bring into actual existence: *Her uncle's present made it possible for her to realize her dream of going to college.* **3** cause to seem real.
4 change (property) into money: *Before going to England to live, he realized all his property in Canada.* **5** obtain as a return or profit: *They realized $10 000 from their investment.* **6** bring as a return or profit.

re•al•ly ['riəli] *or* ['rili] *adv., interj., —adv.* **1** actually; in fact: *things as they really are. She really didn't know who it was.*
2 without question; truly: *a really magnificent house.* **3** *Informal.* very; very much: *We'll have to really work for an hour, then we can lay off a bit. See what happens if you go really fast.*
—interj. an expression of surprise, disbelief, or disapproval: *Really! I don't believe it!*

realm [rɛlm] *n.* **1** kingdom. **2** range; domain: *the realm of science. Such an occurrence is outside the realm of possibility.* ⟨ME < OF *reialme* < *reial* regal < L *regalis.* See REGAL.⟩

real number *Mathematics.* a member of the set of numbers which includes all the RATIONAL NUMBERS (e.g., 3/4, 0.777…, -4/1) and all the IRRATIONAL NUMBERS (e.g., pi, square root of 2, e).

Re•al•po•li•tik [rei'ɑl,pɒlə,tik]; *German* [ʀe'al,pɔli,tik] *n.* foreign or domestic policy based on power and expediency rather than ideals and carried out without regard for world opinion or moral implications.

real property land and buildings, as distinct from personal property.

real–time ['riəl 'taɪm] *or* [,taɪm] *adj. Computer technology.* of or having to do with a system of computing in which the computer continuously obtains data from a source, processes it, and applies the results to the control of some other process going on simultaneously.

real time *Computer technology.* a real-time system or mode of computer operation or any other system characterized by the nearly simultaneous occurring and recording of events.

real•tor ['riəltər] *or* ['riəl,tɔr] *n.* **1** a member of an organization of people engaged in the business of buying and selling real estate. **2** the organization itself: *They are one of Canada's largest realtors, with 8000 agents nationwide.*

re•al•ty ['riəlti] *n.* REAL ESTATE. ⟨< *real*[1] (def. 3) + *-ty*[2]⟩

ream[1] [rim] *n.* **1** a quantity of sheets of paper of the same size and quality, usually 500, but sometimes 480 or 516; 20 quires.
2 Usually, **reams,** *pl. Informal.* a very large quantity: *She took reams of notes. Abbrev.:* rm. ⟨ME < OF *rayme* < Sp. < Arabic *rizmah* bundle⟩

ream[2] [rim] *v.* **1** enlarge or shape (a hole, the bore of a gun, etc.). **2** remove with a reamer. **3** clean out (a tobacco pipe) with a reamer. **4** extract juice from (citrus fruit) with a reamer.
ream out, *Slang.* scold at length; reprimand severely: *The teacher reamed out the class for their inattention.* ⟨origin uncertain; perhaps akin to OE *rȳman* enlarge < *rūm* room⟩

ream•er ['rimər] *n.* **1** a tool for enlarging or shaping a hole.
2 a utensil for squeezing the juice out of oranges, lemons, etc.
3 a tool for clearing out a tobacco pipe.

reap [rip] *v.* **1** cut (grain). **2** gather (a crop). **3** cut grain or gather a crop from: *to reap fields.* **4** get as a return or reward: *Kind acts often reap happy smiles.* **5** get a return: *Sow generously, reap abundantly.* ⟨OE *repan*⟩

reap•er ['ripər] *n.* **1** a person who or machine that cuts grain or gathers a crop. **2** a person who reaps. **3 the (Grim) Reaper,** the personification of death, often depicted as a hooded figure carrying a scythe.

rear[1] [rir] *n., adj. —n.* **1** the back part; the part opposite the front; back: *the rear of the house.* **2** the space or position at the back: *She moved toward the rear.* **3** Often, **rear end,** *Slang.* buttocks. **4** the last part of an army, fleet, etc.; the part farthest from the battlefront.
at or **in the rear of,** behind.
bring up the rear, come or be last: *We filed through the woods, with me bringing up the rear.*
—adj. located at or in the back. ⟨var. of *arrear*⟩

rear[2] [rir] *v.* **1** make grow; help to grow; raise, breed, or bring up: *He was reared in the city. She rears livestock.* **2** set up; build: *to rear a temple.* **3** raise; lift up: *to rear one's head.* **4** especially of a horse, rise on the hind legs; rise (*sometimes used with* **up**): *The horse reared as the fire engine dashed past.* **5** extend to a great height: *Mountain peaks reared up behind the valley.* ⟨OE *rǣran* raise, causative of *rīsan* rise⟩

rear–ad•mi•ral ['rir 'ædmərəl] *n.* **1** *Canadian Forces.* in Maritime Command, the equivalent of a major-general. See chart of ranks in the Appendix. **2** a naval officer of similar rank in other countries. *Abbrev.:* RAdm, R.Adm., or R.A.

rear–end ['rir 'ɛnd] *v.* hit (another vehicle) from behind.

rear guard that part of an army that protects the rear.

re•arm [ri'ɑrm] *v.* especially of a nation or a military force, arm again with new or better weapons.

re•ar•ma•ment [ri'ɑrməmənt] *n.* a rearming or being rearmed.

rear•most ['rir,moust] *adj.* farthest in the rear; last.

re•ar•range [,riə'reindʒ] *v.* **-ranged, -rang•ing. 1** arrange in a new or different way: *to rearrange furniture.* **2** arrange again.
—,re•ar'range•ment, *n.* **—,re•ar'rang•er,** *n.*

rear•view mirror ['rir,vju] a mirror on an automobile, etc., attached so as to give a view of the area to the rear.

rear•ward ['rirwərd] *adv. or adj.* toward or in the rear.

rea•son ['rizən] *n., v. —n.* **1** a cause or motive for an action, feeling, etc.; grounds: *I have my own reasons for doing this.* **2** a justification; explanation: *What is your reason for doing such poor work?* **3** the ability or power to think and draw conclusions:

In each of the words below, **re-** *means* again *or* anew; *the pronunciation of the main part of each word is not changed.*

,re•al•lo'ca•tion
,re•al'lot
,re•al'ly
re-'al•ter
,re•al•ter'a•tion
,re-'an•a,lyse
,re•a'nal•y•sis
re-'an•i,mate
,re•an•i'ma•tion
,re•ap'pear
,re•ap'pear•ance
,re•ap•pli'ca•tion
,re•ap'ply
,re•ap'point
,re•ap'point•ment
,re•ap'por•tion
,re•ap'por•tion•ment
,re•ap'prais•al
re-'ar•gue
,re•ar'rest
,re•as'cend
,re•as'cent

Reason separates humans from the lower primates. **4** right thinking; good sense. **5** sanity: *Have you lost your reason?*
beyond all reason, completely unreasonable or unreasonably.
bring to reason, cause to be reasonable.
by reason of, on account of; because of.
in or **within reason,** within reasonable and sensible limits.
stand to reason, be reasonable and sensible: *It stands to reason that she would resent your insults.*
with reason, with justification; properly.
—*v.* **1** think; think (about) logically; analyse: *Human beings can reason.* **2** conclude, infer, or deduce (that something is the case) from the relevant facts or premises. **3** discuss; argue in a rational way: *You just can't reason with him.* **4** urge or bring (someone *into* or *out of* some course of action) by rational argument.
reason away, get rid of by reasoning.
reason out, a think through and come to a conclusion; think out. **b** arrive at (a solution, etc.) by reasoning. ⟨ME < OF *raison* < L *ratio.* Doublet of RATIO, RATION.⟩ **—'rea•son•er,** *n.* **—'rea•son•less,** *adj.* **—'rea•son•less•ly,** *adv.*

☛ *Syn. n.* **1. Reason,** CAUSE, MOTIVE = the ground or occasion for an event, action, etc. **Reason** applies to the grounds or occasion that explains something that has happened, or one given as explanation, which may or may not be the true cause or motive: *The reason she went to the city was to attend university.* **Cause** applies to a person, thing, incident, or condition that directly brings about an action or happening: *The cause of death was given as poisoning.* **Motive** applies to the feeling or desire that makes a person do something: *Love for his children was his only motive.*

☛ *Usage.* **The reason is, the reason was,** etc. should be followed by **that,** not by **because.** Instead of *My reason for being late is because my car would not start,* say: *My reason for being late is that my car would not start.* Or avoid the word **reason** and say: *I was late because my car would not start.*

rea•son•a•ble ['rizənəbəl] *adj.* **1** according to reason; not absurd: *a reasonable explanation, a reasonable theory.* **2** fair or moderate; not extreme: *a reasonable request, a reasonable price.* **3** not high in price; inexpensive: *I expected the dress to be expensive, but it was really very reasonable.* **4** ready to listen to reason; sensible: *She's a reasonable person. Be reasonable; it can't possibly work that way.* **5** having the ability to reason. **—'rea•son•a•ble•ness,** *n.* **—'rea•son•a•bly,** *adv.*

☛ *Syn.* **1. Reasonable,** RATIONAL = according to reason. **Reasonable,** describing people or their actions, words, plans, or procedures, emphasizes showing good judgment and being governed by reason in deciding and choosing: *He took a reasonable view of the dispute and offered a solution that was fair, sensible, and practical.* **Rational** emphasizes having or showing the power to think logically and to draw conclusions that guide in doing or saying what is wise, sensible, or reasonable: *Her approach to the problem was rational.*

rea•soned ['rizənd] *adj., v.* —*adj.* justified rationally; supported by clear reasoning: *Give a reasoned defence of your decision.*
—*v.* pt. and pp. of REASON.

rea•son•ing ['rizənɪŋ] *n., v.* —*n.* **1** the process of drawing conclusions from facts. **2** reasons, arguments, etc. resulting from or used in this process.
—*v.* ppr. of REASON.

re–as•sem•ble [ˌri ə'sɛmbəl] *v.* **-bled, -bling. 1** come or bring together again. **2** assemble something that has been taken apart: *We reassembled the old clock piece by piece.*

re•as•sur•ance [ˌriə'ʃʊrəns] *n.* **1** a reassuring or being reassured. **2** *Brit.* reinsurance. **3** something that reassures.

re•as•sure [ˌriə'ʃʊr] *v.* **-sured, -sur•ing. 1** restore to confidence: *The captain's confidence during the storm reassured the passengers.* **2** assure again or anew. **3** *Brit.* insure again. **—ˌre•as'sur•ing•ly,** *adv.*

Ré•au•mur ['reiə,mjʊr]; *French,* [ʀeo'myʀ] *adj.* of, based on, or according to a scale for measuring temperature, known as the Réaumur scale, in which the freezing point of water is 0° and the boiling point is 80°. ⟨< René de *Réaumur* (1683-1757), a French physicist⟩

Reb [rɛb] *n.* Mister; used with the given name, or sometimes, the family name, of a Jewish man as a title of respect. ⟨< Yiddish < *rebe* < Hebrew *rabi* master, lord⟩

re•bar•ba•tive [rɪ'bɑrbətɪv] *adj.* causing aversion; forbidding. ⟨< F *rébarbatif* < MF *rebarber* resist, face (an enemy) < *barbe* beard⟩

re•bate¹ *n.* ['ribeit]; *v.* ['ribeit] *or* [ri'beit] *n., v.* **-bat•ed, -bat•ing.** —*n.* the return of part of the money paid; partial refund; discount.
—*v.* **1** give (an amount or proportion) as a rebate: *They will rebate $10 of the purchase price.* **2** deduct a portion from (a total payable): *Your bill has been rebated by 10 percent.* ⟨ME < OF *rabattre* beat down < *re-* back + *abattre* abate < *a-* (< L *ad-*) + *battre* beat < L *batuere*⟩

re•bate² ['ribeit] *or* ['ræbɪt] *n., v.* rabbet.
☛ *Hom.* RABBIT [ræbɪt].

reb•be ['rɛbə] *n.* **1** a teacher in a Jewish school. **2** a highly respected spiritual leader, especially a Hasid. **3** a title of respect for either of these. ⟨< Hebrew *rabi* master, teacher⟩

reb•bet•zin ['rɛbɪtsɪn] *n.* a rabbi's wife. ⟨< Yiddish⟩

A rebec

re•bec or **re•beck** ['ribɛk] *n.* a three-stringed musical instrument, resembling a violin, used in the Middle Ages. ⟨< F *rebec,* var. of OF *rebebe,* ult. < Arabic *rabāb*⟩

reb•el *n.* ['rɛbəl]; *v.* [rɪ'bɛl] *n., v.* **re•belled, re•bel•ling.** —*n.* **1** a person who opposes or takes up arms against his or her own government or ruler. **2** a person who resists authority or control: *She always was a rebel; her family never understood her.* **3** (*adjl.*) of, having to do with, or made up of, or being a rebel or rebels: *a rebel stronghold, a rebel army, a rebel student faction.*
—*v.* **1** use force or arms to oppose one's own government or an authority: *The people rebelled when the new tax was imposed. The troops rebelled against their commander.* **2** resist authority or control: *He rebelled against his parents.* **3** feel or express a great dislike: *We rebelled at the thought of having to stay home all weekend.* ⟨ME < OF < L *rebellare,* ult. < *re-* again + *bellum* war. Doublet of REVEL.⟩

re•bel•lion [rɪ'bɛljən] *n.* **1** organized resistance against one's own government or another authority; revolt. **2** a stance or attitude in opposition to some generally accepted convention or code of behaviour. ⟨< L *rebellio, -onis* < *rebellis* rebel < *rebellare.* See REBEL.⟩
☛ *Syn.* See note at REVOLT.

re•bel•lious [rɪ'bɛljəs] *adj.* **1** defying authority; acting like a rebel. **2** hard to manage; hard to treat. **—re'bel•lious•ly,** *adv.* **—re'bel•lious•ness,** *n.*

re•bind [ri'baɪnd] *v.* **-bound, -bind•ing.** bind again or anew.

re•birth [ri'bɜrθ] *or* ['ri,bɜrθ] *n.* **1** a being born again; reincarnation. **2** a new spiritual life; spiritual renewal. **3** revival; reawakening: *the rebirth of nationalism, the rebirth of hope.*

re•born [ri'bɔrn] *adj.* born again, renewed, or revived.

re•bound¹ *v.* [ri'baʊnd]; *n.* ['ri,baʊnd] *v., n.* —*v.* **1** spring or cause to spring back; bounce back. **2** resound or cause to resound; echo. **3** make a vigorous recovery, as from illness or depression: *Her courage rebounded.*
—*n.* **1** a springing back or resounding. **2** *Basketball.* a ball that bounds off the backboard when a scoring attempt has been missed.
on the rebound, a after a bounce off the wall, floor, etc. **b** (while) recovering from the failure of a relationship or from some other unhappy experience. ⟨ME < OF *rebondir* < *re-* back

In each of the words below, **re-** *means* again *or* anew; *the pronunciation of the main part of each word is not changed.*

ˌre-as'sert
ˌre-as'ser•tion
ˌre-as'sess
ˌre-as'sess•ment
ˌre-as'sign
ˌre-as'sign•ment
ˌre-as'sim•i,late
ˌre-as'so•ci,ate
ˌre-as'sume
ˌre-as'sump•tion
ˌre-at'tach
ˌre-at'tach•ment
ˌre-at'tempt
re-'au•dit
ˌre-au'then•ti,cate
re'au•thor,ize
ˌre-a'wak•en
re'bap•tism
ˌre•bap'tize
re'beau•ti,fy
re'bid
re'bind
re'boil

(< L) + *bondir* bound, resound, ? < VL *bombitire* < L *bombus* booming sound < Gk. *bombos*⟩

re•bound[2] [ri'baʊnd] *v.* pt. and pp. of REBIND.

re•bo•zo [rɪ'bouzou]; *Spanish* [re'boθo] *n.* a long covering for the head and shoulders, worn by Latin American women.

re•broad•cast [ri'brɒd,kæst] *v.* **-cast** or **-cast•ed, -cast•ing;** *n.* —*v.* **1** broadcast again at a later time or date. **2** relay (a television or radio program) as it is being received from another station.
—*n.* **1** the act of rebroadcasting. **2** a relayed or repeated television or radio broadcast.

re•buff [rɪ'bʌf] *n., v.* —*n.* **1** a blunt or sudden rejection, as of a person who makes advances, offers help or sympathy, makes a request, etc.; snub. **2** any check or setback.
—*v.* give a rebuff to. ⟨< F < Ital. *ribuffo*⟩

re•build [ri'bɪld] *v.* **-built, -build•ing. 1** build again or anew; restore. **2** repair or renovate extensively, especially after dismantling or disassembling, usually using new parts or materials: *rebuild a kitchen, rebuild a carburetor.*

re•built [ri'bɪlt] *v.* pt. and pp. of REBUILD.

re•buke [rɪ'bjuk] *v.* **-buked, -buk•ing;** *n.* —*v.* speak disapprovingly to; reprove.
—*n.* an expression of disapproval; scolding. ⟨ME < ONF *rebuker*; cf. OF *rebuchier* < *re-* back + *buchier* strike⟩ **—re'buk•er,** *n.* **—re'buk•ing•ly,** *adv.*
☛ *Syn. v.* See note at REPROVE.

re•bus ['ribəs] *n.* a puzzle in which a word or phrase is represented by pictures, letters, or signs suggesting the original sounds. A picture of a cat on a log is a rebus for *catalogue.* ⟨< L *rebus* by means of objects⟩

re•but [rɪ'bʌt] *v.* **-but•ted, -but•ting.** contradict or oppose by formal argument (the evidence presented by the other side); try to disprove (something): *Each team in the debate was given two minutes to rebut the other's arguments.* ⟨ME < OF *reboter* < *re-* back + *boter* butt[3] < Gmc.⟩

re•but•tal [rɪ'bʌtəl] *n.* **1** the act of rebutting. **2** a formal argument that contradicts or opposes.

re•but•ter [rɪ'bʌtər] *n.* a person who uses formal argument to contradict or oppose.

rec [rɛk] *n. Informal.* recreation.
☛ *Hom.* WRECK.

rec. 1 receipt. **2** recipe. **3** record; recorded; recorder; recording.

re•cal•ci•trant [rɪ'kælsətrənt] *adj., n.* —*adj.* **1** resisting authority or control; disobedient. **2** hard to manage or deal with.
—*n.* one who resists authority or control or is disobedient. ⟨< L *recalcitrans, -antis,* ppr. of *recalcitrare* kick back, ult. < *re-* back + *calx, calcis* heel⟩ **—re'cal•ci•trance** or **re'cal•ci•tran•cy,** *n.*

re•ca•lesce [,rikə'lɛs] *v.* **-lesced, -lesc•ing.** *Metallurgy.* of iron cooling from white heat, grow spontaneously hot again due to a heat-releasing change in crystal structure at a certain temperature. ⟨< L *recalescere* grow hot again⟩ **—,re•ca'les•cent,** *adj.* **—,re•ca'les•cence,** *n.*

re•call *v.* [rɪ'kɒl]; *n.* ['ri,kɒl] *or* [rɪ'kɒl] *v., n.* —*v.* **1** call back to mind; remember. **2** call back; order back; ask for the return of, especially a defective product for repair or refund: *The manufacturer recalled all cars of that model in order to correct the exhaust system. The ambassador was recalled.* **3** bring back: *recalled to life.* **4** take back; withdraw: *The order has been given and cannot be recalled.* **5** bring (a person, the attention, etc.) back to the matter at hand: *Lost in reverie, he finally recalled himself by an act of will.*
—*n.* **1 a** a recalling to mind. **b** ability to recall; memory: *He reads well as far as actual decoding goes, but his recall is poor.* **2** a calling back; ordering back. **3** a signal used in calling back troops, ships, etc. **4** a taking back; revocation; annulment. **5** the removal of a public official from office by the vote of the people: *There is no longer provision for recall in Canada.*
☛ *Syn. v.* **1.** See note at REMEMBER.

re•cant [rɪ'kænt] *v.* **1** take back formally or publicly; withdraw or renounce (a statement, opinion, purpose, etc.). **2** renounce an opinion or allegiance: *Though he was tortured to make him change his religion, the prisoner would not recant.* ⟨< L *recantare,* ult. < *re-* back + *canere* sing⟩

re•can•ta•tion [,rikæn'teiʃən] *n.* the act or action of recanting.

re•cap[1] *v.* [ri'kæp]; *n.* ['ri,kæp] *v.* **-capped, -cap•ping;** *n.* —*v.* **1** put a strip of rubber or similar material on (a worn surface of an automobile tire), by using heat and pressure to make a firm union. **2** put a cap or lid on again: *to recap a bottle of ginger ale.*
—*n.* a tire repaired in this manner.

re•cap[2] *v.* ['ri,kæp] *or* [ri'kæp]; *n.* ['ri,kæp] *v.* **-capped, -cap•ping;** *n. Informal.* —*v.* recapitulate.
—*n.* recapitulation: *a recap of the news.*

re•ca•pit•u•late [,rikə'pɪtʃə,leit] *v.* **-lat•ed, -lat•ing.** repeat or recite the main points of; tell briefly; sum up. ⟨< L *recapitulare* < *re-* again + *capitulum* chapter, section, dim. of *caput* head⟩

re•ca•pit•u•la•tion [,rikə,pɪtʃə'leiʃən] *n.* **1** a brief statement of the main points; summary. **2** *Music.* a repetition, usually in a later movement or section, of the initial theme of a composition. **—,re•ca'pit•u•la•tive,** *adj.* **—,re•ca'pit•u•la,to•ry** [,rikə'pɪtʃələ,tɔri], *adj.*

re•cap•ture [ri'kæptʃər] *v.* **-tured, -tur•ing;** *n.* —*v.* **1** capture or take again. **2** bring back; recall: *The picture album recaptured the days of the horse and buggy.*
—*n.* **1** a taking or being taken again. **2** something recaptured.

re•cast *v.* [ri'kæst]; *n.* ['ri,kæst] *v.* **-cast, -cast•ing;** *n.* —*v.* **1** cast again or anew; cast differently from before: *recast a bell, recast a vote. She was recast as the heroine in the film version.* **2** make over; remodel: *recast a sentence, recast the entire format.*
—*n.* **1** an act of recasting: *The director called for a recast.* **2** something produced by recasting: *The recast had a minute crack in it.*

recd. or **rec'd** received.

re•cede[1] [rɪ'sid] *v.* **-ced•ed, -ced•ing. 1** move back, down, or away; become more distant. **2** slope backward: *He has a chin that recedes.* **3** withdraw: *He receded from the agreement.* ⟨< L *recedere* < *re-* back + *cedere* go⟩

re•cede[2] [ri'sid] *v.* yield (something) to a former possessor; cede back.

re•ceipt [rɪ'sit] *n., v.* —*n.* **1** a written statement that money, a package, a letter, etc. has been received. **2** the act or fact of receiving or being received: *The goods will be sent on receipt of payment. She wrote to acknowledge receipt of the package.* **3** Usually, **receipts,** *pl.* money, etc. received: *The expenses were greater than the receipts.* **4** *Archaic.* recipe.
—*v.* **1** write on or stamp (a bill, etc.) to indicate that something has been received or paid for: *She asked them to receipt the bill.* **2** write or issue a receipt for (merchandise, services, etc., that have been paid for) ⟨ME *receite* < AF (OF *recoite*) < L *recepta,* fem. pp. of *recipere* receive. See RECEIVE.⟩

re•ceiv•a•ble [rɪ'sivəbəl] *adj.* **1** fit for acceptance, especially as payment: *Gold is receivable all over the world.* **2** (*used after the noun*) on which payment is to be received. *Bills receivable* is the opposite of *bills payable.* **3** able to be received. **4** (*noml.*) **receivables,** *pl.* bills or accounts receivable.

re•ceive [rɪ'siv] *v.* **-ceived, -ceiv•ing. 1** take (something offered or sent); take into one's hands or possession: *to receive gifts.* **2** have (something) bestowed, conferred, etc.: *to receive a name.* **3** be given; get: *to receive a letter from home.* **4** take; support; bear; hold: *The boat received a heavy load.* **5** take or let into the mind: *to receive new ideas.* **6** accept as true or valid: *a theory widely received.* **7** react to in a given way: *Her idea was badly received by the rest of us.* **8** agree to listen to: *to receive confession.* **9** experience; suffer; endure: *to receive a blow.* **10** let into one's house, society, etc.; welcome: *to receive strangers. The people of the neighbourhood were glad to receive the new couple.* **11** admit to a state or condition: *to receive a person into the Christian faith.* **12** be at home to friends and visitors: *She receives on Tuesdays.* **13** *Sports.* **a** catch or return (a serve, pass, ball, puck, etc.). **b** play a position in which this is one's main task. **14** *Radio and television.* change electromagnetic waves into sound or picture signals.
be on the receiving end, *Informal.* be subject to some kind of action, frequently unpleasant: *We were lucky to be on the receiving*

In each of the words below, **re-** *means* again *or* anew; *the pronunciation of the main part of each word is not changed.*

re'bur•i•al	**re'but•ton**	**,re•cal•cu'la•tion**	**,re•cap•i•tal•i'za•tion**	**re'cat•a,logue**
re'bur•y	**re'cal•cu,late**	**re'cal•i,brate**	**re'cap•i•tal,ize**	

end of her generosity. He was on the receiving end of their bad temper. ⟨ME *receve* < ONF *receivre* < L *recipere* < *re-* back + *cipere, capere* take⟩

☛ *Syn.* **1. Receive,** ACCEPT = take what is given, offered, or delivered. **Receive** carries no suggestion of positive action or of activity of the mind or will on the part of the receiver and means nothing more than to take to oneself or take in what is given or given out: *She received a prize.* **Accept** always suggests being willing to take what is offered, or giving one's consent: *She received a gift from him, but refused to accept it.*

re•ceived [rɪ'sivd] *adj., v. —adj.* accepted as standard; handed down as right: *Received wisdom has it that oysters are an aphrodisiac.*
—v. pt. and pp. of RECEIVE.

Received Pronunciation the pronunciation of English typical of educated upper middle class speakers of S England, held by some to be a standard of proper speech. *Abbrev.*: R.P.

re•ceiv•er [rɪ'sivər] *n.* **1** generally, anyone or anything that receives. **2** the part of a telephone that receives electrical impulses and converts them into sound. **3** a device in a radio, or television set that converts electromagnetic waves into sound or picture signals. **4** *Law.* one appointed to take charge of the property of bankrupts, or to care for property under litigation. **5** a person appointed to collect or be the treasurer of funds in a business, organization, etc. **6** *Sports.* **a** the player or side whose turn it is to RECEIVE (def. 14). **b** *Football.* the player intended to receive a forward pass. **7** a person who knowingly receives stolen goods or harbours offenders.

re•ceiv•er•ship [rɪ'sivər,ʃɪp] *n.* **1** the position of a RECEIVER (def. 4). **2** the condition of being in the control of a RECEIVER (def. 4): *The company did not do well and is now in receivership.*

receiving blanket a small, lightweight blanket for wrapping a newborn baby.

receiving line a group of people, usually the hosts and the guests of honour, who stand in a row at wedding receptions or other formal occasions in order to welcome each guest individually.

receiving set RECEIVER (defs. 2, 3).

re•cen•cy ['risənsi] *n.* the fact or condition of being recent.

re•cen•sion [rɪ'sɛnʃən] *n.* **1** the process of critical revision of a text based on examination of the text itself and its sources. **2** the revised text. ⟨< L *recensio* < *recensere* revise⟩

re•cent ['risənt] *adj., n. —adj.* **1** that has happened or been done not long ago: *a recent quarrel, a recent cold spell.* **2** made, begun, or originated not long ago; new: *an information pamphlet for recent parents. That result contradicts their most recent hypothesis.* **3** of or designating a time or period comparatively near to the present: *recent history, the most recent ice age.*
4 Recent, of, having to do with, or designating the most recent geological epoch (including the present time) beginning at the end of the glacial period, forming the last half of the Quaternary, or the rocks or plant and animal life characteristic of this period. See geological time chart in the Appendix.
—n. the Recent geological epoch or its rock series. ⟨< L *recens, -entis*⟩ **—'re•cent•ness,** *n.*

re•cent•ly ['risəntli] *adv.* lately; not long ago.

re•cep•ta•cle [rɪ'sɛptəkəl] *n.* **1** any container or place used to put things in to keep them conveniently. Bags, baskets, and vaults are all receptacles. **2** a wall socket for an electrical plug. **3** *Botany.* **a** the base of the flower to which all the parts of the flower are attached. See FLOWER for picture. **b** the structure bearing the reproductive organs or spores. ⟨< L *receptaculum,* ult. < *recipere* receive. See RECEIVE.⟩

re•cep•tion [rɪ'sɛpʃən] *n.* **1** the act of receiving: *calm reception of bad news.* **2** the fact of being received: *We were given a warm reception.* **3** a social gathering to receive and welcome people. **4** the quality of the sound in a radio or of the sound and picture signals in a television set. ⟨< L *receptio, -onis* < *recipere.* See RECEIVE.⟩

re•cep•tion•ist [rɪ'sɛpʃənɪst] *n.* a person employed in an office to welcome visitors, direct them, give out information, etc.

reception room a hall or room in a hotel that can be reserved for large parties, receptions, banquets, etc.

re•cep•tive [rɪ'sɛptɪv] *adj.* **1** able, quick, or willing to receive ideas, suggestions, or impressions, etc.: *a receptive mind.* **2** having to do with reception or receptors. **—re'cep•tive•ly,** *adv.* **—re'cep•tive•ness,** *n.*

re•cep•tiv•i•ty [,risɛp'tɪvɪti] *n.* the ability or readiness to receive.

re•cep•tor [rɪ'sɛptər] *n. Physiology.* **1** a cell or group of cells sensitive to stimuli; a sense organ. **2** part of a cell or tissue that reacts with certain molecules, with antibodies, hormones, etc. ⟨< L *receptor* receiver⟩

re•cess *n.* [rɪ'sɛs] *or (esp. def. 2)* ['risɛs]; *v.* [rɪ'sɛs] *n., v. —n.* **1** a time during which work, classes, or any other proceeding temporarily stops: *There will be a short recess before the next meeting. The children may have a snack during recess.* **2 a** a part in a wall or other surface set back from the rest; alcove; niche. **b** *Anatomy.* a small hollow or indented place in any surface. **3** an inner place or part; quiet, secluded place: *the recesses of a cave, the recesses of one's secret thoughts.*
—v. **1** stop or cause to stop for a break: *The convention recesses until afternoon. The judge recessed the court until the following day.* **2** put in an alcove or niche; set back. **3** make an alcove or niche in. ⟨< L *recessus* a retreat < *recedere* recede. See RECEDE[1].⟩

re•ces•sion[1] [rɪ'sɛʃən] *n.* **1** a going or moving backward in time or space; a receding. **2** a procession exiting from a formal gathering, church service, etc. **3** a backward slope. **4** a withdrawal. **5** a period of temporary business decline, shorter and less extreme than a depression. ⟨< L *recessio, -onis* < *recedere* recede. See RECEDE[1].⟩ **—re'ces•sion,ar•y,** *adj.*

re•ces•sion[2] [rɪ'sɛʃən] *n.* a ceding back to a former owner. ⟨< *re-* + *cession*⟩

re•ces•sion•al [rɪ'sɛʃənəl] *n., adj. —n.* a hymn or other piece of music sung or played while the clergy and the choir leave at the end of a church service.
—adj. **1** of or having to do with recession or a recession. **2** being a hymn, etc. that serves as a recessional.

re•ces•sive [rɪ'sɛsɪv] *adj., n. —adj.* **1** tending to go back; receding. **2** *Genetics.* of or designating a gene or trait that is expressed only in homozygotes, or, for X-linked genes, in hemizygotes. Compare DOMINANT. **—re'ces•sive•ly,** *adj.* **—re'ces•sive•ness,** *n.*
—n. Genetics. a recessive gene or trait.

recessive inheritance *Genetics.* the pattern of inheritance of traits determined by recessive genes. In **autosomal recessive inheritance,** the gene is on an autosome; parents are usually unaffected carriers, and affected individuals receive the recessive gene from each parent. The risk that a child of two carriers will be affected is 25 percent, and usually relatives other than siblings of affected individuals are at low risk. In **X-linked recessive inheritance,** the gene is on the X chromosome. A son of a carrier mother has a 50 percent risk of being affected, and a daughter of a carrier has a 50 percent risk of being a carrier herself. An affected male passes on the gene to all his daughters, who are carriers, but to none of his sons.

re•charge *v.* [ri'tʃɑrdʒ]; *n.* ['ri,tʃɑrdʒ]; *v.* **-charged, -charg•ing;** *n. —v.* to charge again.
—n. **1** the act of charging again. **2** that with which something is charged again.

ré•chauf•fé [,reiʃou'fei]; *French,* [Reʃo'fe] *n.* **1** a dish consisting of reheated leftovers. **2** any thing or idea that is outmoded but has been reworked or rehashed and brought back into service. ⟨< F, pp. of *réchauffer* heat again < *ré* again + *chauffer* heat⟩

re•cher•ché [rəʃɛr'ʃei] *or* [rə'ʃɛrʃei]; *French,* [RəʃɛR'ʃe] *adj.* **1** sought out or devised with care; rare; choice. **2 a** too studied; far-fetched: *That metaphor is a bit recherché.* **b** refined or elegant, especially excessively so; affected or precious: *His poetry is apt to be too recherché for the general taste.* ⟨< F *recherché* sought after < *re-* again + *chercher* search⟩

re•cid•i•vism [rɪ'sɪdɪ,vɪzəm] *n.* a tendency to chronic relapse into crime or antisocial behaviour. ⟨< L *recidivus* < *recidere* fall back < L *re-* back + *cadere* fall⟩

re•cid•i•vist [rɪ'sɪdɪvɪst] *n., adj. —n.* a habitual criminal.
—adj. of or having to do with recidivism or recidivists.
—re,cid•i'vis•tic, *adj.* **—re'cid•i•vous,** *adj.*

In each of the words below, **re-** *means* again *or* anew; *the pronunciation of the main part of each word is not changed.*

re'cer•ti,fy
re'chal•lenge
re'chan•nel
re'charge
re'chart
re'char•ter
re'check
re'chew
re'chris•ten

rec•i•pe ['rɛsəpi] *n.* **1** a set of directions for preparing something to eat or drink. **2** a set of directions for preparing anything by combining various ingredients: *a recipe for making soap.* **3** a means of reaching some state or condition: *a recipe for happiness.* ⟨< L *recipe* take!, imperative of *recipere* take, receive. See RECEIVE.⟩

re•cip•i•ent [rɪ'sɪpiənt] *n., adj.* —*n.* a person who or thing that receives something: *The recipients of the prizes had their names printed in the paper.*
—*adj.* receiving or willing to receive. ⟨< L *recipiens, -entis,* ppr. of *recipere.* See RECEIVE.⟩

re•cip•ro•cal [rɪ'sɪprəkəl] *adj., n.* —*adj.* **1** done or given in return or exchange: *a reciprocal gift.* **2** existing on both sides; mutual: *reciprocal friendship.* **3** *Mathematics.* inversely proportional; inverse; of reciprocals or their relations.
4 *Grammar.* expressing mutual action or relation. In *The two children like each other, each other* is a reciprocal pronoun.
—*n.* **1** *Mathematics.* a number so related to another that when multiplied together they give 1. The reciprocal of 3 is $\frac{1}{3}$, and the reciprocal of $\frac{1}{3}$ is 3. **2** something that is reciprocal. ⟨< L *reciprocus* returning⟩ **—re,cip•ro'cal•i•ty,** *n.*

re•cip•ro•cal•ly [rɪ'sɪprəkli] *adv.* in a reciprocal way; each to the other; mutually.

reciprocal translocation See TRANSLOCATION.

re•cip•ro•cate [rɪ'sɪprɪ,keit] *v.* **-cat•ed, -cat•ing. 1** give, do, feel, or show in return: *She loves me, and I reciprocate her love.* **2** give or do something in return: *They invited us to dinner, so we must reciprocate.* **3** move or cause to move with an alternating backward and forward motion: *a reciprocating valve.* ⟨< L *reciprocare* < *reciprocus* returning⟩ **—re,cip•ro'ca•tion,** *n.* **—re'cip•ro,ca•tor,** *n.* **—re'cip•ro•ca,to•ry,** *adj.*

reciprocating engine any engine in which the back-and-forth motion of a piston is converted into a circular motion of the crankshaft by means of a connecting rod. Most internal-combustion engines are of this type.

rec•i•proc•i•ty [,rɛsə'prɒsɪti] *n.* **1** a reciprocal state; mutual action, influence, or dependence. **2** a mutual exchange, especially an exchange of special privileges in regard to trade between two countries, institutions, etc.

re•cit•al [rɪ'səitəl] *n.* **1** the act of reciting; a telling of facts in detail: *Her recital of her experiences in the hospital bored her hearers.* **2** a story; account. **3** a program of music or dance given by a single performer or several individual performers, or by a small ensemble. **4** a public performance given by a number of music or dance pupils to show their skill. **—re'cit•al•ist,** *n.*

re•ci•tan•do [,reitʃi'tɑndou] *or* [,rɛsɪ'tɑndou] *adv. Music.* after the manner of a RECITATIVE[2]. ⟨< Ital.⟩

rec•i•ta•tion [,rɛsə'teiʃən] *n.* **1** a reciting; a telling of facts in detail. **2** a reciting of a prepared lesson by pupils before a teacher. **3** a repetition of something from memory, especially before an audience. **4** a piece repeated from memory. ⟨< L *recitatio, -onis* < *recitare.* See RECITE.⟩

rec•i•ta•tive[1] ['rɛsɪ,teitɪv] *or* [rə'səitətɪv] *adj.* of or having to do with recital; reciting: *a recitative account of the event.*

rec•i•ta•tive[2] [,rɛsɪtə'tiv] *n., adj.* —*n. Music.* **1** a style halfway between speaking and singing. Operas often contain passages of recitative, especially before an aria. **2** a passage, part, or composition in this style.
—*adj.* written or performed as a recitative; like a recitative in character. ⟨< Ital. *recitativo*⟩

re•cite [rɪ'səit] *v.* **-cit•ed, -cit•ing. 1** tell in detail: *He recited the day's adventures.* **2** mention in order; enumerate: *They recited a long list of grievances.* **3** repeat (a poem, etc.) before an audience. **4** repeat or answer questions (about): *to recite a lesson.* ⟨< L *recitare* < *re-* again + *citare* appeal to⟩ **—re'cit•er,** *n.*

reck [rɛk] *v. Archaic.* **1** care; heed. **2** be important or interesting; matter. ⟨OE *reccan*⟩
☛ *Hom.* WRECK.

reck•less ['rɛklɪs] *adj.* rash; heedless; careless: *Reckless of consequences, the boy played truant. Reckless driving causes many automobile accidents.* ⟨OE *recceléas*⟩ **—'reck•less•ly,** *adv.* **—'reck•less•ness,** *n.*
☛ *Syn.* See note at RASH[1].

reck•on ['rɛkən] *v.* **1** find the number or value of; count: *Reckon the cost before you decide.* **2** consider; judge; account: *She is reckoned the best player in the league.* **3** *Informal.* think; suppose: *I reckon that's the truth.* **4** depend; rely: *You can reckon on our help.* **5** settle accounts. **6** calculate; compute; do arithmetic.
reckon on, count on, take into account: *He didn't reckon on breaking his leg when he decided to try skiing.*
reckon up, count up: *Before you buy that new car, you had better reckon up all the hidden costs.*
reckon with, take into account; face: *We are going to have to reckon with higher prices for food.*
to be reckoned with, worthy of serious thought; important: *She is a writer to be reckoned with.* ⟨OE (*ge*)*recenian*⟩ **—'reck•on•er,** *n.*

reck•on•ing ['rɛkənɪŋ] *n., v.* —*n.* **1 a** the act or an instance of computing; a count or calculation: *By this reckoning, we still have 63 km to go.* **b** a calculated guess; estimation: *We should be there in around ten minutes, by my reckoning.* **2** the settlement of an account, or the giving of rewards or penalties for any action. **3** a bill, especially at an inn or tavern. **4** Usually, **dead reckoning.** *Nautical.* **a** the calculation of the position of a ship. **b** the position calculated.
—*v.* ppr. of RECKON.
day of reckoning, a time when one must account for or be punished for one's actions: *There will be a day of reckoning for your foolish behaviour.*

re•claim [rɪ'kleim] *v., n.* —*v.* **1** make available for cultivation, etc.: *to reclaim a swamp.* **2** rescue or bring back from wrong conduct, vice, etc.; reform. **3** recover from discarded or waste products: *to reclaim tin from cans.* **4** demand or obtain the return of: *The library sent a notice reclaiming the book.*
—*n.* the act or possibility of reclaiming. ⟨ME < OF *réclamer* < L *reclamare* cry out against < *re-* back + *clamare* cry out⟩ **—re'claim•a•ble,** *adj.* **—re'claim•er,** *n.* **—re'claim•ant,** *n.*
☛ *Syn.* **1.** See note at RECOVER.

re–claim [ri 'kleim] *v.* claim back or again: *She had trouble re-claiming the money.*

re•claimed lake [rɪ'kleimd] *Cdn.* a lake that has been restocked with trout following a drop in the number of species in it.

rec•la•ma•tion [,rɛklə'meiʃən] *n.* a reclaiming or being reclaimed: *the reclamation of deserts by irrigation.*

rec•li•nate ['rɛklɪnɪt] *or* ['rɛklɪ,neit] *adj. Botany.* of a leaf or stem, bending backward or downward so that the top part is on the ground.

re•cline [rɪ'klaɪn] *v.* **-clined, -clin•ing. 1** lean back or lie down: *to recline on a couch.* **2** lay (something) back or down: *He reclined his head on the pillow.* ⟨< L *reclinare* < *re-* back + *-clinare* lean⟩

re•clin•er [rɪ'klaɪnər] *n.* **1** a person or thing that reclines. **2** a type of armchair with a movable back and seat that can be adjusted by body motion or by a lever.

rec•luse *n.* ['rɛklus] *or* [rɪ'klus]; *adj.* [rɪ'klus] *n., adj.* —*n.* a person who lives shut up or withdrawn from the world.
—*adj.* shut up or apart from the world. ⟨ME < OF < L *reclusus* shut up, pp. of *recludere* < *re-* back + *claudere* shut⟩ **—re'clu•sion** [rɪ'kluʒən], *n.* **—re'clu•sive,** *adj.*
☛ *Syn. n.* **Recluse,** HERMIT = a person who lives apart from the rest of the world. A **recluse** withdraws for any of a variety of reasons, including a desire for complete privacy, or a feeling of alienation from society. The term **hermit** usually refers to someone who has withdrawn in order to concentrate on spiritual things or to lead a lifestyle based on values so radical as to be incompatible with general society.

rec•og•ni•tion [,rɛkəg'nɪʃən] *n.* **1** a knowing again; a recognizing; being recognized: *By a good disguise, he escaped recognition.* **2** acknowledgment; an admission that something is the case: *We insisted on complete recognition of our rights.* **3** notice; specifically, a greeting or other sign acknowledging someone's presence. **4** favourable notice; appreciation: *The actor soon won recognition from the public.* **5** formal approval or

In each of the words below, **re-** *means* again *or* anew; *the pronunciation of the main part of each word is not changed.*

re'cir•cle | **,re•clas•si•fi'ca•tion** | **re'clothe** | **re'co•di,fy**
re'cir•cu,late | **re'clas•si,fy** | **re'code**

sanction, as with diplomatic recognition of the existence of a state. ⟨< L *recognitio, -onis*⟩

re•cog•ni•zance [rɪ'kɒgnəzəns] *n. Law.* **1** a bond binding a person to perform some particular act, such as appearing in court on a particular day or keeping the peace. If no surety in the form of money or property is required, a person is said to be released on his or her own recognizance. **2** the sum of money to be forfeited if the required act is not performed. ⟨ME *reconissaunce, recognisance* < OF *reconuissance.* See RECOGNIZE.⟩

rec•og•nize ['rɛkəg,naɪz] *v.* **-nized, -niz•ing. 1** know as a person or thing already familiar to one: *I could scarcely recognize my old friend.* **2** identify: *to recognize a person from a description.* **3** know the meaning or significance of: *She recognized his qualities at once and appointed him chief advisor.* **4** acknowledge acquaintance with; greet: *to recognize a person on the street.* **5** acknowledge; accept; admit: *He recognized his duty to defend his country.* **6** take notice of: *People who wish to speak in a public meeting should stand up and wait till the chairperson recognizes them.* **7** show appreciation of. **8** acknowledge and agree to deal with: *For some years certain nations did not recognize the new government.* ⟨ME < OF *reconoistre* < L *recognoscere*, ult. < *re-* again + *com-* (intensive) + (*g*)*noscere* learn. Doublet of RECONNOITRE.⟩ **—'rec•og,niz•er,** *n.* **—'rec•og,niz•a•ble,** *adj.* **—'rec•og,niz•a•bly,** *adv.* **—,rec•og,niz•a'bil•i•ty,** *n.*

re•coil *v.* [rɪ'kɔɪl]; *n.* ['rikɔɪl] *or* [rɪ'kɔɪl] *v., n.* *—v.* **1** draw back; shrink back: *Most people would recoil at seeing a snake in their path.* **2** spring back: *The gun recoiled after I fired.* **3** react; backfire: *Revenge often recoils on the avenger.*
—n. **1** the act or action of drawing or shrinking back. **2** the distance or force with which a gun, spring, etc. springs back. ⟨ME < OF *reculer*, ult. < L *re-* back + *culus* rump⟩

rec•ol•lect [,rɛkə'lɛkt] *v.* call (something) back to mind; remember: *Did she? I don't recollect. He couldn't quite recollect the details.* ⟨from the same source as *re-collect*, but distinguished in meaning and pronunciation⟩
☛ *Syn.* See note at REMEMBER.

re–col•lect [,ri kə'lɛkt] *v.* **1** collect again. **2** recover control of (oneself). ⟨originally < L *recollectus*, pp. of *recolligere* < *re-* again + *colligere* collect, but later taken as < *re-* + *collect*, and pronounced accordingly⟩

rec•ol•lec•tion [,rɛkə'lɛkʃən] *n.* **1** the act or power of recalling to mind. **2** memory; remembrance. **3** something remembered.
☛ *Syn.* **1.** See note at MEMORY.

re•com•bi•nant [ri'kɒmbənənt] *adj., n. Genetics. —adj.* showing genetic recombination: *recombinant DNA.*
—n. an organism showing genetic recombination.

recombinant DNA *Genetics.* **1** DNA fragments from different organisms artificially linked together. **2** the research field making use of this; genes are incorporated into the DNA of bacteria or other appropriate organisms and replicated with the DNA of the host, thus becoming available in large quantity for study.

re•com•bi•na•tion [,rikɒmbə'neiʃən] *or* [ri,kɒmbə'neiʃən] *n.* **1** *Genetics.* the formation of new combinations of genes in a zygote that are different from the gene combinations of either parent, occurring especially as a result of the interchange of paired genes during meiosis. Recombination is an important natural means of producing variation in species and can also be performed artificially in the laboratory. **2** an act or result of combining again.

recombination frequency *Genetics.* the frequency of recombination between two gene loci, used as a measure of the distance between these loci on the chromosome.

rec•om•mend [,rɛkə'mɛnd] *v.* **1** speak in favour of; suggest favourably. **2** advise. **3** make pleasing or attractive: *The position of the cottage recommends it as a summer home.* **4** hand over for safekeeping: *In my absence, I recommend my children to the care of their aunt.* ⟨< Med.L *recommendare* < L *re-* again + *commendare* commend⟩ **—,rec•om'mend•er,** *n.*

rec•om•men•da•tion [,rɛkəmɛn'deiʃən] *n.* **1** the act of recommending. **2** something that speaks in favour of a person or thing or that expresses praise: *She got a very good recommendation from her former boss.* **3** something advised or recommended. *The doctor's recommendation was that the child stay in bed for a few days.*

rec•om•men•da•to•ry [,rɛkə'mɛndə,tɔri] *adj.* serving to speak in favour of, praise, or advise; recommending.

re•com•mit [,rikə'mɪt] *v.* **-mit•ted, -mit•ting. 1** commit again. **2** refer again to a committee.

re•com•mit•ment [,rikə'mɪtmənt] *n.* a recommitting or being recommitted.

re•com•mit•tal [,rikə'mɪtəl] *n.* recommitment.

rec•om•pense ['rɛkəm,pɛns] *v.* **-pensed, -pens•ing;** *n.*
—v. **1** pay (a person); pay back; reward: *They were well recompensed for their efforts.* **2** make a fair return for (an action, anything lost, damage done, hurt received, etc.): *The loss of property must be duly recompensed.*
—n. **1** a payment or reward: *She asked for fair recompense for the work she had done.* **2** a return for anything lost, damaged, etc.; amends: *He demanded recompense for the broken window.* ⟨< LL *recompensare*, ult. < L *re-* back + *com-* with, against + *pendere* weigh out in payment⟩

rec•on•cile ['rɛkən,saɪl] *v.* **-ciled, -cil•ing. 1** make or become friends again: *Those two still have not reconciled. After our long enmity, we were reconciled.* **2** settle (a quarrel, disagreement, etc.). **3** make agree; bring into harmony: *It is impossible to reconcile his story with the facts.* **4** make satisfied or content with something: *It is hard to reconcile oneself to being sick for a long time.* ⟨< L *reconciliare*, ult. < *re-* back + *concilium* bond of union⟩ **—'rec•on,cil•a•ble,** *adj.* **—'rec•on,cil•er,** *n.*

rec•on•cile•ment ['rɛkən,saɪlmənt] *or* [,rɛkən'saɪlmənt] *n.* reconciliation.

rec•on•cil•i•a•tion [,rɛkən,sɪli'eiʃən] *n.* a reconciling or being reconciled: *the reconciliation of opposite points of view. They had hopes of a reconciliation between the brothers.*

rec•on•cil•i•a•to•ry [,rɛkən'sɪliə,tɔri] *adj.* tending to reconcile.

rec•on•dite ['rɛkən,dəit] *or* [rɪ'kɒndəit] *adj.* **1** hard to understand; profound; abstruse. **2** little known; obscure; esoteric. ⟨< L *reconditus*, pp. of *recondere* store away, ult. < *re-* back + *com-* up + *dare* put⟩ **—'rec•on,dite•ly,** *adv.* **—'rec•on,dite•ness,** *n.*

re•con•di•tion [,rikən'dɪʃən] *v.* restore to a good or satisfactory condition by repairing or replacing parts, etc.: *The motor has been completely reconditioned.*

re•con•nais•sance [rɪ'kɒnəsəns] *n.* an examination or survey, especially for military purposes. ⟨< F *reconnaissance* (MF *reconoissance*)⟩

rec•on•noi•tre [,rɛkə'nɔɪtər] *or* [,rikə'nɔɪtər] *v.* **-tred, -tring. 1** approach and examine or observe in order to learn something; make a survey of (the enemy, the enemy's strength or position, a region, etc.) in order to gain information for military purposes. **2** approach a place and make a first survey of it: *It seemed wise to reconnoitre before entering the town.* Also, **reconnoiter.** ⟨< F *reconnoître*, earlier form of *reconnaître* (< OF *reconoistre*). Doublet of RECOGNIZE.⟩ **—,rec•on'noi•trer,** *n.*

re•con•sid•er [,rikən'sɪdər] *v.* consider again with a view to changing or reversing a position or decision: *The assembly voted to reconsider the bill. They have said they won't go, but we're hoping they will reconsider.* **—,re•con,sid•er'a•tion,** *n.*

re•con•sti•tute [ri'kɒnstə,tjut] *or* [ri'kɒnstə,tut] *v.* **-tut•ed, -tut•ing.** constitute anew; especially, restore (a condensed or dehydrated substance) to its original liquid state by adding water: *to reconstitute orange juice.* **—re,con•sti'tu•tion,** *n.*

In each of the words below, **re-** *means* again *or* anew; *the pronunciation of the main part of each word is not changed.*

,re•col•o•ni'za•tion	**,re•com'bine**	**,re•con'cep•tion**	**,re•con•fir'ma•tion**	**re'con•se,crate**
re'col•o,nize	**,re•com'mence**	**,re•con'cep•tu•al,ize**	**,re•con'nect**	**,re•con•se'cra•tion**
re'col•our	**,re•com'mence•ment**	**,re•con•den'sa•tion**	**,re•con'nec•tion**	**,re•con'sign**
re'comb	**,re•com'mis•sion**	**,re•con'dense**	**re'con•quer**	**,re•con'sol•i,date**
,re•com•bi'na•tion	**,re•com'pute**	**,re•con'firm**	**re'con•quest**	

re•con•struct [ˌrikən'strʌkt] *v.* **1** construct again; rebuild; make over. **2** try to discover (a sequence of events) by organizing in the mind all available information: *When the police reconstructed the crime, they realized who the murderer must be.* **3** build or rebuild, from artifacts or other available evidence, a model or duplicate of (something that existed previously): *Upper Canada Village is a reconstructed pioneer community.*

re•con•struc•tion [ˌrikən'strʌkʃən] *n.* **1** the act of reconstructing or being reconstructed. **2** the thing reconstructed.

re•con•struc•tive [ˌrikən'strʌktɪv] *adj.* having to do with or involved in reconstruction: *Their reconstructive efforts were hampered by lack of money.*

re•cord *v.* [rɪ'kɔrd]; *n.* ['rɛkərd] *or* ['rɛkɔrd] *v., n.* —*v.* **1** put or show in some permanent form; preserve for remembrance: *History is recorded in books. Fossils record the development of life forms.* **2** reproduce accurately in written or graphic form for future use: *Listen to the speaker and record what she says. The machine records the patient's heart rhythms.* **3** put on a phonograph disc, on magnetic tape, or on compact disc. **4** measure and tell; indicate; register: *The thermometer records temperatures.* **5** record something: *Do not enter the studio when we are recording.* **6** admit of being recorded: *Her voice does not record well.*
—*n.* **1** the permanent form or artifact of any event, speech, etc. **2** *Law.* **a** an official written account for future reference: *The secretary kept a record of what was done at the meeting.* **b** an authoritative copy of an official document: *a record of a deed.* **3** a thin, flat disc with narrow spiral grooves on its surface that reproduces sounds when played on a record player, or phonograph. **4** the known facts about what a person, team, animal, ship, etc. has done: *She has a fine record at school.* **5** a criminal record: *They say he has a record.* **6** a remarkable performance or event, going beyond others of the same kind, especially the best achievement in a sport: *to hold the record for the high jump.* **7** (*adjl.*) unequalled; greater, higher, better, etc. than ever before: *a record wheat crop.* **8** *Computer technology.* a set of information fields treated as a unit in a database. **9** a recording or being recorded: *What happened is a matter of record.*
break a record, improve on an unequalled standard previously set in some athletic event, etc.
go on record, state one's views publicly.
off the record, not intending or intended to be preserved or quoted: *The Prime Minister was speaking off the record.*
on record, written down, printed, or otherwise made available: *The facts of the murder are now on record.*
set the record straight, correct an erroneous view of what was said or done. ⟨ME < OF *recorder* < L *recordari* remember, ult. < *re-* back + *cor, cordis* heart, mind⟩

record changer a device on a record player that enables several records to be played one after the other automatically.

record club a business organization that regularly supplies selected phonograph records to its subscribers.

A recorder

re•cord•er [rɪ'kɔrdər] *n.* **1** a person who records, especially one whose work is making and keeping written accounts. **2** an apparatus or machine that records. **3** TAPE RECORDER. **4** a barrister or solicitor appointed as judge of a crown court in a city or borough. **5** a musical wind instrument resembling a flute but having the mouthpiece on the end rather than on the side.

re•cord•ing [rɪ'kɔrdɪŋ] *n., v., adj.* —*n.* **1** a sound record made on disc or tape. **2** the act of transcribing any sound or combination of sounds.
—*v.* ppr. of RECORD.
—*adj.* that records: *famous recording artist, recording studio.*

record player an instrument for playing back the sounds recorded on records, or discs, especially a small, portable one. It consists basically of a turntable, a needle (or stylus) that follows the grooves in the record, a pickup arm that converts the vibrations of the needle back into sound, and an amplifier and loudspeaker to make the sounds audible. Also called **phonograph.**

re•count [rɪ'kaʊnt] *v.* tell in detail; give an account of; narrate: *He recounted all the happenings of the day.* ⟨ME < ONF *reconter* < *re-* again + *conter* relate, count[1]⟩

re–count *v.* [ri 'kaʊnt]; *n.* ['ri ˌkaʊnt] *v., n.* —*v.* count again. —*n.* a second count, as of votes.

re•coup [rɪ'kup] *v.* **1** make up for; regain: *He recouped his losses.* **2** repay. **3** *Law.* deduct or withhold (part of an amount due) by virtue of some rightful claim. ⟨< F *recouper* < *re-* back + *couper* cut⟩

re•course ['rikɔrs] *or* [rɪ'kɔrs] *n.* **1** the act of turning to a person, organization, course of action, etc. when in need of help or protection (*usually in* **have recourse to**): *to have recourse to weapons. We had recourse to a doctor who lived nearby.* **2** a person, organization, course of action, etc. turned to for help or protection: *The child's recourse was always her mother.* **3** *Commerce.* the right to collect payment from the maker or endorser of a cheque or similar negotiable instrument. ⟨ME < OF < L *recursus* retreat, ult. < *re-* back + *currere* run⟩

re•cov•er [rɪ'kʌvər] *v.* **1** get back (something lost, taken away, or stolen). **2** make up for (something lost or damaged): *recover lost time.* **3** come back to life, health, one's senses, or normal condition: *He recovered quickly from his surgery.* **4** get (oneself) back to the proper position or condition; check (oneself): *He started to fall but recovered himself. She was about to make a rude comment but recovered herself just in time.* **5** *Law.* **a** obtain by judgment in a court. **b** obtain judgment in one's favour in a court. **6** *Sports.* **a** take back control or possession of (a ball, puck, etc.). **b** return to competitive strength after falling far behind. **7** rescue; deliver. **8** regain in usable form; reclaim. Many useful substances are now recovered from materials that used to be thrown away. ⟨ME < OF < L *recuperare.* Doublet of RECUPERATE.⟩ **—re'cov•er•er,** *n.*
☛ *Syn.* **1. Recover,** RECLAIM, RETRIEVE = get or bring something back. **Recover** = get something back again in one's possession after losing it: *He recovered the stolen furs.* **Reclaim** = bring back into usable or useful condition from a lost state: *Part of her farm is reclaimed swamp.* **Retrieve** = recover by effort or search: *The rescuers retrieved the victims of the mine disaster.*

re–cov•er [ri 'kʌvər] *v.* cover again or anew; especially, provide (a piece of upholstered furniture) with a new covering.

re•cov•er•y [rɪ'kʌvəri] *n., pl.* **-er•ies. 1** the act of recovering. **2** a coming back to health or normal condition. **3** the getting back of something that was lost, taken away, or stolen. **4** a return to a proper or original position or condition: *After her surgery, she made a quick recovery.* **5** *Law.* the obtaining of some property or right by the judgment of a law court. **6** the act of locating and repossessing a missile, nose cone, etc. after a flight in space. **7** the extraction, in usable form, of valuable material from waste.

recovery room in a hospital, a room in which patients are placed immediately after surgery, in order to recover from the effects of the anesthetic.

rec•re•an•cy ['rɛkriənsi] *n.* **1** cowardice. **2** unfaithfulness or treason.

rec•re•ant ['rɛkriənt] *adj., n.* —*adj.* **1** cowardly. **2** disloyal or traitorous.
—*n.* **1** a coward. **2** a traitor. ⟨ME < OF *recreant* confessing oneself beaten, ult. < L *re-* back + *credere* believe⟩
—'rec•re•ant•ly, *adv.*

rec•re•ate ['rɛkri,eit] *v.* **-at•ed, -at•ing. 1** refresh with games, pastimes, exercises, etc. **2** take recreation. ⟨ult. < L *recreare* restore < *re-* again + *creare* create⟩

re–cre•ate [ˌri kri'eit] *v.* **-at•ed, -at•ing.** create anew. **—ˌre-cre'a•tion,** *n.* **—ˌre-cre'a•tive,** *adj.*

rec•re•a•tion [ˌrɛkri'eiʃən] *n.* **1** a refreshing of the body and spirit through play or amusement. **2** a form of play or amusement that serves this purpose: *Her favourite recreation is tennis.* **—ˌrec•re'a•tion•al,** *adj.*

rec•re•a•tion•al vehicle [ˌrɛkri'eiʃənəl] any type of vehicle

In each of the words below, **re-** *means* again *or* anew; *the pronunciation of the main part of each word is not changed.*

ˌre•con'sult **ˌre•con'tam•i,nate** **ˌre•con'vene** **re'cook** **re'cop•y**

(such as a camper, trailer, etc.) fitted out as temporary living quarters and used for recreational purposes such as camping, travelling, etc. *Abbrev.*: RV

recreation room 1 in a hotel, apartment building, community centre, etc., a room for playing games, lounging, dancing, and other informal activities. 2 in a private home, a family room. Also, **rec room.**

rec•re•a•tive ['rɛkri,eitɪv] *adj.* refreshing; restoring.

re•crim•i•nate [rɪ'krɪmə,neit] *v.* **-nat•ed, -nat•ing.** accuse (someone) in return: *Tom said Harry had lied, and Harry recriminated by saying Tom had manipulated him.* ⟨< Med.L *recriminare*, ult. < L *re-* back + *crimen* charge⟩

re•crim•i•na•tion [rɪ,krɪmə'neiʃən] *n.* an accusing in return; counter accusation.

re•crim•i•na•tive [rɪ'krɪmənətɪv] *or* [rɪ'krɪmə,neitɪv] *adj.* recriminatory.

re•crim•i•na•to•ry [rɪ'krɪmənə,tɔri] *adj.* of or involving recrimination.

rec room [rɛk] *Informal.* RECREATION ROOM (def. 2).

re•cru•desce [,rikru'dɛs] *v.* **-desced, -desc•ing.** become active again or break out afresh; flare up again.

re•cru•des•cence [,rikru'dɛsəns] *n.* breaking out afresh after a period of being inactive or dormant; renewed activity: *In the last few years there has been a recrudescence of TB.* ⟨< L *recrudescere*, ult. < *re-* again + *crudus* raw⟩

re•cru•des•cent [,rikru'dɛsənt] *adj.* breaking out again.

re•cruit [rɪ'krut] *n., v.* —*n.* 1 a newly enlisted member of the armed forces. 2 a new member of any group or class.
—*v.* 1 a persuade (people) to join one of the armed forces. b strengthen or supply (armed forces) with new personnel. 2 acquire or attract (new members, employees, students, etc.) 3 engage in seeking out talented people with a view to hiring or enrolling them: *She recruits for IBM.* 4 enlist; engage: *She recruited the support of her mother in her appeal for renovations to the basement.* 5 renew (health, strength, or spirits). 6 get a new supply of; replenish. ⟨< F *recruter* < *recrue* recruit(ing), new growth < *recrû*, pp. of *recroître* < *re-* again (< L *re-*) + *croître* grow < L *crescere*⟩ **—re'cruit•er,** *n.*
—re'cruit•ment, *n.*

rect. 1 receipt. 2 rector; rectory.

rec•tal ['rɛktəl] *adj.* of or having to do with the rectum. **—'rec•tal•ly,** *adv.*

rec•tan•gle ['rɛk,tæŋgəl] *n.* 1 a right-angled parallelogram that is not square; an oblong. 2 any quadrilateral with four right angles. Squares and oblongs are rectangles. See QUADRILATERAL for picture. ⟨< F < LL *rectangulum* < L *rectus* right + *angulus* angle⟩

rec•tan•gu•lar [rɛk'tæŋgjələr] *adj.* 1 shaped like a rectangle. 2 of a solid or building, having a base shaped like a rectangle: *a rectangular tower.* 3 having one or more right angles. 4 placed at right angles. **—rec'tan•gu•lar•ly,** *adv.* **—rec,tan•gu'lar•i•ty** [rɛk,tæŋgjə'lɛrɪti], *n.*

rectangular coordinates *Mathematics.* coordinates whose axes meet at right angles, as in Cartesian geometry. Also, **Cartesian coordinates.**

rec•ti•fi•er ['rɛktə,faɪər] *n.* 1 a person who or thing that makes right, corrects, adjusts, etc. 2 *Electricity.* a device for changing alternating current into direct current.

rec•ti•fy ['rɛktə,faɪ] *v.* **-fied, -fy•ing.** 1 make right; put right; adjust; remedy: *The storekeeper admitted his mistake and was willing to rectify it.* 2 *Electricity.* change (an alternating current) into a direct current. 3 make a calculated adjustment to, in movement, balance, etc. 4 *Mathematics.* determine the length of (a curve). 5 purify; refine: *to rectify a liquor by distilling it several times.* ⟨< LL *rectificare* < L *rectus* right + *facere* make⟩ **—'rec•ti,fi•able,** *adj.* **—,rec•ti•fi'ca•tion,** *n.*

rec•ti•lin•e•ar [,rɛktə'lɪniər] *adj.* 1 in, moving in, or forming a straight line. 2 bounded or formed by straight lines. 3 characterized by straight lines. Also, **rectilineal.** ⟨< L *rectus* straight + E *linear*⟩ **—,rec•ti'lin•e•ar•ly,** *adv.*

rec•ti•tude ['rɛktə,tjud] *or* ['rɛktə,tud] *n.* 1 upright conduct or character; honesty; righteousness. 2 correctness, especially of judgment, procedure, etc. ⟨< LL *rectitudo* < L *rectus* straight⟩

rec•to ['rɛktou] *n., pl.* **-tos.** *Printing.* 1 the front of a sheet of printed paper; the side that is to be read first. 2 the right-hand page of an open book. Compare VERSO.

rec•tor ['rɛktər] *n.* 1 *Anglican Church.* a member of the clergy in charge of a parish. 2 *Roman Catholic Church.* a priest in charge of a college or a religious house or, sometimes, who directs other priests with whom he shares a parish ministry. 3 the head or principal of certain schools, colleges, or universities. ⟨< L *rector* ruler < *regere* to rule⟩ **—rec'tor•i•al,** *adj.*

rec•tor•ate ['rɛktərɪt] *n.* the position, rank, or term of a rector.

rec•to•ry ['rɛktəri] *n., pl.* **-ries.** the residence of a rector or pastor.

rec•trix ['rɛktrɪks] *n., pl.* **rec•tri•ces** ['rɛktrə,siz] *or* [rɛk'traisiz]. *Ornithology.* any of a bird's large tail feathers, which help direct its flight.

rec•tum ['rɛktəm] *n., pl.* **-tums** or **-ta** [-tə] the lowest part of the large intestine. See ALIMENTARY CANAL for picture. ⟨< NL *rectum*, for L *intestinum rectum* straight intestine⟩

rec•tus ['rɛktəs] *n., pl.* **-ti** [-taɪ] *or* [-ti]. *Anatomy.* any of several straight muscles, as in the thigh, abdomen, etc.

re•cum•ben•cy [rɪ'kʌmbənsi] *n.* a reclining or supine position or condition.

re•cum•bent [rɪ'kʌmbənt] *adj.* 1 lying down, reclining, or leaning. 2 inactive or idle; resting. ⟨< L *recumbens, -entis*, ppr. of *recumbere* recline⟩ **—re'cum•bent•ly,** *adv.*

re•cu•per•ate [rɪ'kupə,reit] *or* [rɪ'kjupə,reit] *v.* **-at•ed, -at•ing.** 1 get back to a former state or condition, especially, to recover from sickness or exhaustion: *She is at home, recuperating from surgery.* 2 get back; regain: *to recuperate one's health. He worked hard to recuperate his losses after the fire.* ⟨< L *recuperare* recover. Doublet of RECOVER.⟩

re•cu•per•a•tion [rɪ,kupə'reiʃən] *or* [rɪ,kjupə'reiʃən] *n.* a recuperating from sickness, exhaustion, loss, etc.

re•cu•per•a•tive [rɪ'kupərətɪv] *or* [rɪ'kupə,reitɪv], [rɪ'kjupərətɪv] *or* [rɪ'kjupə,reitɪv] *adj.* 1 of or having to do with recuperation from sickness or loss: *She has remarkable recuperative powers.* 2 aiding recuperation; helping to restore health, strength, etc.

re•cur [rɪ'kɜr] *v.* **-curred, -cur•ring.** 1 come up again; occur again; be repeated: *A leap year recurs every four years.* 2 return in thought or speech: *Old memories constantly recurred to him. He recurred to the matter of cost.* 3 have recourse (*to*): *She recurred to the disability clause and got the requirement waived.* ⟨< L *recurrere* < *re-* back + *currere* run⟩

re•cur•rence [rɪ'kɜrəns] *n.* an act or instance of recurring: *More care in the future will prevent recurrence of the mistake.*

recurrence risk *Genetics.* the probability that a given genetic condition will recur in a subsequent birth.

re•cur•rent [rɪ'kɜrənt] *adj.* 1 recurring; occurring again and again; repeated: *recurrent attacks of hay fever.* 2 *Anatomy.* of certain nerves and blood vessels, turned back so as to run in the opposite direction. ⟨< L *recurrens, -entis*, ppr. of *recurrere.* See RECUR.⟩ **—re'cur•rent•ly,** *adv.*

recurring decimal See REPEATING DECIMAL.

re•curve [ri'kɜrv] *v.* **-curved, -curv•ing.** curve back; bend back.

rec•u•san•cy ['rɛkjəzənsi] *or* [rɪ'kjuzənsi] *n.* the act or state of being recusant.

rec•u•sant ['rɛkjəzənt] *or* [rɪ'kjuzənt] *n., adj.* —*n.* 1 a person who refuses to submit to an established authority. 2 formerly, in England, a Roman Catholic who refused to attend the services of the Church of England.
—*adj.* of or like a recusant; refusing to submit. ⟨< L *recusans, -antis*, ppr. of *recusare* refuse, ult. < *re-* back + *causa* cause⟩

re•cy•cle [ri'saikəl] **re•cy•cled, re•cy•cling.** 1 reprocess waste material so that it can be used again: *Old cars can be recycled and the steel used again.* 2 use over again, sometimes with minimal alteration: *They recycle egg trays on their farm, as one tray will last several uses before it deteriorates.* 3 adapt to a

In each of the words below, **re-** *means* again *or* anew; *the pronunciation of the main part of each word is not changed.*

re'cross **re'crown** **re'crys•tal,ize** **re'cut**

new use without changing the essential form: *The old stables were recycled as studio apartments.*

re•cyc•ling [ri'saiklɪŋ] *n., v.* —*n.* the reprocessing of waste material so that it can be used again, or any other method of reusing something.
—*v.* ppr. of RECYCLE.

red [rɛd] *n., adj.* **red•der, red•dest.** —*n.* **1** the colour of blood, glowing coals, rubies, etc.; the colour of the visible spectrum having the longest light waves, at the end opposite to violet. **2** a red pigment or dye. **3 a** a red cloth or clothing. **b** red wine. **c** *Slang.* a capsule of secobarbital, usually coloured red. **d** any other red or reddish person, animal, or thing. **4** *Cdn.* sockeye. **5** Usually, **Red**, a radical socialist; a revolutionary. Communists are often referred to as Reds. **6** *Cdn.* a Liberal.
in the red, operating at a loss; in debt: *We'll be in the red soon if we don't cut down our expenses.*
see red, *Informal.* become very angry: *She sees red as soon as you mention the new by-law.*
—*adj.* **1** of or having the colour of blood, etc.; being like it; suggesting it: *red ink, red hair, a red fox.* **2** sore; inflamed; bloodshot: *red eyes.* **3** blushing. **4** red-hot. **5** Usually, **Red,** radically socialist or communist; revolutionary. **5** *Cdn.* of or having to do with Liberals. ⟨OE *rēad*⟩ —**'red•ly,** *adv.*
—**'red•ness,** *n.*
☛ *Hom.* READ², REDD.

red– form of **re-** in some cases before vowels, as in *redeem.*

re•dact [rɪ'dækt] *v.* **1** put in suitable form for publication; revise; edit. **2** draft; draw up (a proclamation, edict, etc.); compose. ⟨ME *redacten* < L *redactus*, pp. of *redigere* bring back (into order)⟩

re•dac•tion [rɪ'dækʃən] *n.* **1** the preparation of (usually, another person's) writings for publication; revising; editing. **2** the form or version of a work as prepared by revision or editing. ⟨< L *redactio, -onis* < *redactus*, pp. of *redigere* reduce < *red-* back + *agere* bring⟩

red alder a tree (*Alnus rubra*) native to SW British Columbia and growing into a conical shape. Its leaves are oval, with a rusty underside, and the fruit is winged. Its pale brown wood often turns reddish after cutting and is used for fine furniture and veneers; it is also an excellent firewood.

red alert 1 *Military or Civil Defence.* **a** the final stage of alert, when an attack by an enemy is expected at any moment. **b** the alarm sounded to effect this alert. **2** a signal or warning of imminent danger or the development of a critical situation.

red algae a marine alga, phylum Rhodophyta, forming red, purple, or brownish masses in the depths of the ocean.

re•dan [rɪ'dæn] *n.* a fortification with two walls forming an angle that points outward. ⟨< F *redan* a double notching, ult. < L *re-* again + *dens* tooth⟩

Red Angus a subpopulation of the ABERDEEN ANGUS, but having a reddish coat.

red ash *Cdn.* a tree (*Fraxinus pennsylvanica*) native to SW Ontario and the southern prairies, along river banks. It has long leaves with seven oval leaflets, and bears winged seeds. Its wood is hard and is used for tool handles and furniture.

red•bel•ly dace ['rɛd,bɛli] *Cdn.* a fish of the minnow family (*Chrosomus eos*) found in fresh water from Nova Scotia to the Peace River country. It grows to only 8 cm long and is olive or dark brown on the back, with (in the breeding male) red or silvery sides. It prefers shallow water, where it eats algae.

red–ber•ried elder ['rɛd ,bɛrid] *Cdn.* a tree (*Sambucus pubens*) native to southern British Columbia, having edible red berries instead of the usual blue ones. Wine can be made from the flowers.

red•bird ['rɛd,bɜrd] *n.* **1** the cardinal, *Cardinalis cardinalis.* **2** any of various birds with mainly red plumage, such as the SCARLET TANAGER.

red blood cell in the blood of vertebrates, one of the cells that carry oxygen to the tissues of the body. Red blood cells contain hemoglobin and give blood its red colour.

red–blood•ed ['rɛd 'blʌdɪd] *adj.* full of life and spirit; vigorous; lusty.

red–branched dogwood ['rɛd ,bræntʃt] a tree (*Cornus sanguinea*) having dark red leaves in fall and dark red branches in winter.

red•breast ['rɛd,brɛst] *n.* **1** the North American robin, *Turdus migratorious*, a type of varied thrush, or the European robin, *Erithacus rubecula*. Both have a red breast. **2** the knot, a large arctic sandpiper, *Calidris canutus*. **3** a freshwater sunfish, *Lepomis auritus*.

red•brick university ['rɛd,brɪk] *Esp. Brit.* **1** any university that is new or little known, especially one built since World War II. **2** any university that lacks prestige, especially by comparison with Oxford or Cambridge.

red•bud ['rɛd,bʌd] *n.* any of a genus (*Cercis*) of northern temperate shrubs and small trees of the pea family often cultivated for their small rosy-pink or purplish flowers, which appear before the leaves. There are two North American species, but only one (*C. canadensis*) extends into Canada, occurring in extreme southern Ontario. See also JUDAS TREE.

red•cap ['rɛd,kæp] *n.* a porter at a railway station, bus station, airport, etc., usually wearing a red cap as part of the uniform.

red carpet a carpet, traditionally red, laid out at formal receptions for royalty or other important persons.
roll out the red carpet (for), welcome (someone) royally and treat him or her with special consideration.

red–car•pet ['rɛd 'kɑrpət] *adj. Informal.* showing special courtesy: *They got the red-carpet treatment.*

red cedar 1 a small, cone-shaped juniper (*Juniperus virginiana*) found in southern Ontario and the eastern United States. Also called **red juniper, juniper. 2** WESTERN RED CEDAR. **3** the wood of either of these trees.

red cent *Informal.* the smallest amount of money; penny; something trivial: *I don't have a red cent on me. That thing is not worth a red cent.*

Red Chamber *Cdn.* **1** a name sometimes given to the Canadian Senate because of the colour of the rugs, draperies, etc. of the room in which the Senate meets. **2** the Senate Chamber itself.

red cherry PIN CHERRY.

Red Chevron *Cdn.* a Canadian veteran of World War I (1914-1918) who served at the Second Battle of Ypres.

red clover a clover (*Trifolium pratense*) native to Europe and Asia, having heads of fragrant, purplish red flowers. It is widely cultivated for forage and hay and also as a cover crop.

red•coat ['rɛd,kout] *n.* **1** formerly, a British soldier. **2** *Cdn.* a member of the RCMP.

red corpuscle RED BLOOD CELL.

Red Crescent a society in Muslim countries that parallels the RED CROSS; its emblem is a red crescent on a white background.

Red Cross 1 a group of societies in over 100 countries that work to relieve human suffering in time of war or peace. Co-operation among the national societies takes place through the League of Red Cross Societies. Major projects of the Canadian Red Cross, which is made up mostly of volunteers, are the free blood-transfusion service and the water safety program. The badge of most societies is a red cross on a white background. **2** a national society that is a branch of this organization: *the Canadian Red Cross.* **3 red cross, a** a red Greek cross on a white ground, the emblem of the Red Cross and a symbol of neutrality during war to mark hospitals, ambulances, etc. Also, **Geneva cross. b** the cross of Saint George, England's national emblem.

red cod *Cdn.* a reddish rock fish (*Sebastodes ruberrimus*) found in Pacific Coast waters; RED SNAPPER.

redd¹ [rɛd] *n.* a depression made on the bed of a river or stream by the female of salmon, trout, etc., for laying eggs in. ⟨origin uncertain⟩
☛ *Hom.* READ², RED.

redd² [rɛd] *v.* **redd** or **redd•ed, redd•ing.** *Informal or dialect.* tidy (*used with* **up**). ⟨< OE *hreddan* free, remove, apparently influenced by OE *geraedan* put in order⟩
☛ *Hom.* READ², RED.

red deer 1 a deer (*Cervus elaphus*) of Europe, Asia, and North Africa, about 120-135 cm tall at the shoulder, having a smooth, reddish coat, a buff-coloured patch on the rump, and a mane of dark, shaggy hair around the neck and shoulders. **2** the white-tailed deer of North America, especially in its reddish summer coat. **3** *Cdn.* formerly, the North American elk; wapiti.
☛ *Usage.* (def. 3). The name **red deer** was used for the elk by English explorers to western Canada, and many authorities today in fact consider the elk and European red deer to belong to the same species.

Red Delicious a type of sweet apple having a deep red skin.

red•den ['rɛdən] *v.* **1** make or become red: *The sky was just beginning to redden when we left home.* **2** blush: *She reddened with embarrassment.*

red•dish ['rɛdɪʃ] *adj.* somewhat red.

red dwarf *Astronomy.* a star of a faint reddish colour, about half the diameter of the sun and having a cooler surface.

re•deem [rɪ'dim] *v.* **1** buy back; regain by payment of some fee or price, or by labour: *The property was redeemed when the loan was paid back.* **2** pay off: *We redeemed the mortgage.* **3** convert (certificates, coupons, etc.) into cash or goods. **4** save the life or obtain the release of (someone) by paying a ransom. **5** carry out; make good; fulfill: *We redeem a promise by doing what we said we would.* **6** *Christianity.* of Christ, set (the human soul) free from the consequences of sin by his atoning sacrificial death; save from damnation. **7** make up for; balance: *A very good feature will sometimes redeem several bad ones.* **8** exonerate (oneself) by making amends. **9** reclaim (land). ⟨< L *redimere* < *red-* back + *emere* buy⟩

re•deem•a•ble [rɪ'diməbəl] *adj.* **1** capable of being redeemed. **2** that will be redeemed or paid: *bonds redeemable in ten years.*

re•deem•er [rɪ'dimər] *n.* **1** a person who redeems. **2 Redeemer,** *Christianity.* Jesus Christ.

red elm SLIPPERY ELM.

re•demp•tion [rɪ'dɛmpʃən] *n.* **1** the act or process, or an instance of redeeming: *redemption from sin, the redemption of a captive, the redemption of a loan.* **2** the state of being redeemed. ⟨< L *redemptio, -onis* < *redimere* redeem. See REDEEM. Doublet of RANSOM.⟩

re•demp•tive [rɪ'dɛmptɪv] *adj.* **1** serving to redeem. **2** of or concerning redemption.

re•demp•to•ry [rɪ'dɛmptəri] *adj.* redemptive.

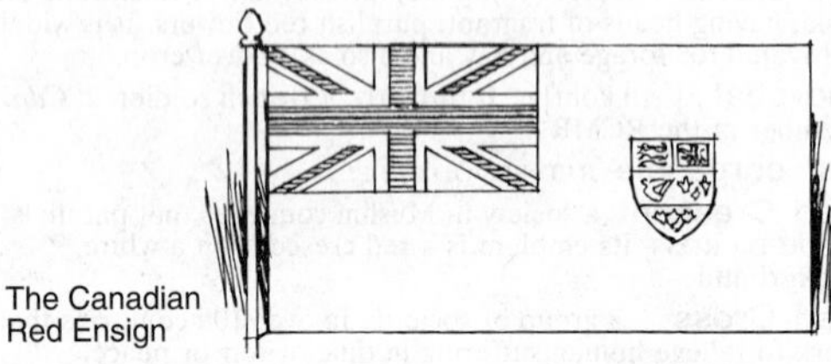
The Canadian Red Ensign

Red Ensign *Cdn.* **1** the distinctive Canadian flag until 1965, having a red ground with the arms of Canada on the fly and the Union Jack in the upper corner near the staff. It is based on the Red Ensign of the British Merchant Marine. Also called **Canadian Red Ensign. 2** the provincial flag of Ontario.

re•de•ploy [,ridɪ'plɔi] *v.* change the position of (troops) from one theatre of war to another. **—,re•de'ploy•ment,** *n.*

re•de•vel•op [,ridɪ'vɛləp] *n.* **1** develop again. **2** improve buildings or land. **3** *Photography.* put through a stronger developer a second time, to intensify the image. **—,re•de'vel•op•ment,** *n.*

red•eye ['rɛd,aɪ] *n.* **1** *Cdn. Slang.* **a** a drink made of beer and tomato juice. Also, **Calgary redeye. b** any cheap liquor, especially whisky. **2** ROCK BASS. **3** the red-eyed vireo (*Vireo olivaceous*), having a white stripe over the eye and a red iris.

red–eye ['rɛd ,aɪ] *n., adj.* *—n. Informal.* a commercial airline flight between two distant points, leaving late at night and arriving early in the morning.
—adj. Informal. of or being such a flight. ⟨< the red eyes of passengers suffering from lack of sleep⟩

redeye bass ROCK BASS.

Red Fife or **Fyfe (wheat)** [fəif] *Cdn.* the first variety of wheat to be produced in Canada, developed in the 1870s, near Peterborough, Ontario, by David Fife (?1804-1877).

red fir **1** any of several fir trees of the western U.S. that have reddish wood and bark. **2** the wood of any of these trees. **3** DOUGLAS FIR.

red fire a chemical that burns with a red light, used in fireworks, signals, etc.

red•fish ['rɛd,fɪʃ] *n.* **1** any of various reddish coloured marine food fishes (family Scorpaenidae) of the Atlantic coasts of North America and Europe. **2** *Cdn.* kokanee.

red flag **1** a symbol of rebellion, revolution, etc. **2** a sign of danger. **3** anything that stirs up anger.

A red fox

red fox **1** a fox (*Vulpes vulpes*) found throughout northern Europe, having mainly reddish brown fur. **2** the similar North American fox (*Vulpes fulva*). **3** the fur of either animal.

red giant *Astronomy.* a star in an intermediate stage of development, characterized by large volume and reddish colouring. Compare WHITE DWARF.

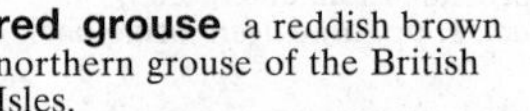

red grouse a reddish brown northern grouse of the British Isles.

red–hand•ed ['rɛd 'hændɪd] *adj.* **1** having hands red with blood. **2** in the very act of crime: *a man caught red-handed in robbery.* **—'red-'hand•ed•ly,** *adv.* **—'red-'hand•ed•ness,** *n.*

red hat **1** a cardinal's hat. **2** the position or rank of a cardinal.

red•head ['rɛd,hɛd] *n.* **1** a person having red hair: *All three of their children are redheads.* **2** a North American diving duck (*Aythya americana*), the male of which has a reddish brown head, blue bill, black breast, and grey back, sides, and wings. It closely resembles the canvasback but has a high, rounded forehead.

red•head•ed ['rɛd,hɛdɪd] *adj.* **1** having red hair. **2** having a red head.

redheaded woodpecker a North American woodpecker (*Melanerpes erythrocephalus*) having a black-and-white body and a red head and neck.

red herring **1** the common smoked herring. **2** something used to draw attention away from the real issue.

red hickory a variety of hickory tree (*Carya ovalis*) native to a small area of southern Ontario, having thick fruit husks splitting easily to the base; the kernel is sweet.

red hot *Informal.* HOT DOG.

red–hot ['rɛd 'hɒt] *adj.* **1** red with heat; very hot. **2** very enthusiastic; excited; violent. **3** fresh from the source.

red•in•gote ['rɛdɪŋ,gout] *n.* **1** a man's fitted, double-breasted coat with full skirts reaching below the knee, worn in the 18th and 19th centuries. **2** a woman's lightweight coat similar to this. ⟨< F < E *riding coat*⟩

red ink **1** a business loss or financial deficit. **2** the state of showing such a loss or deficit.

red•in•te•grate [rə'dɪntə,greit] *v.* **-grat•ed, -grat•ing. 1** make whole again; restore to a perfect state; renew; re-establish. **2** become whole again; be renewed. ⟨< L *redintegrare,* ult. < *red-* again + *integer* whole⟩ **—red,in•te'gra•tion,** *n.*

re•di•rect [,ridə'rɛkt] *or* [,ridaɪ'rɛkt] *v., adj.* *—v.* **1** direct again or anew: *to redirect a letter.* **2** give a new direction to: *to redirect the activities of an organization.*
—adj. U.S. Law. of or having to do with the re-examination of

In each of the words below, **re-** *means* again *or* anew; *the pronunciation of the main part of each word is not changed.*

re'dec•o,rate	**,re•def•i'ni•tion**	**,re•dem•on,stra•tion**	**re'di•al**	**,re•dis'cov•er**
,re•dec•o'ra•tion	**,re•de,lib•er'a•tion**	**,re•de'pos•it**	**,re•dif•fer'en•ti,ate**	**,re•dis'cov•er•y**
re'ded•i,cate	**,re•de'liv•er**	**,re•de'scribe**	**,re•di'gest**	**,re•dis'solve**
,re•ded•i'ca•tion	**,re•de'liv•er•y**	**,re•de'sign**	**,re•di'ges•tion**	**,re•dis'til**
,re•de'fine	**re'dem•on,strate**	**,re•de'ter•mine**	**re'dis•count**	**,re•dis•til'la•tion**

one's own witness after cross-examination by the lawyer for the other side. —ˌre•di'rec•tion, *n.*

re•dis•trib•ute [ˌridɪ'strɪbjut] *v.* **-uted, -ut•ing.** change the distribution of. —ˌ**re•dis'trib•u•tive,** *adj.*

re•dis•tri•bu•tion [ˌridɪstrə'bjuʃən] *n.* **1** a distribution made again or anew. **2** the revision, made every ten years, of the number of seats in the Canadian House of Commons to which each province is entitled on the basis of its population.

red flowering currant a shrub (*Ribes sanguineum*) growing to 2.5 m high and bearing pink to deep red flowers. It blooms in spring in open woods in western North America.

red•i•vi•vus [ˌrɛdə'vaɪvəs] *or* [ˌrɛdə'vivəs] *adj.* returned to life; reborn; revived: *Napoleon was a kind of Julius Caesar redivivus.* ⟨< LL, that lives again < L, renewed, renovated (*red-* + *vivus* alive)⟩

red juniper RED CEDAR (def. 1).

red lead red oxide of lead, used in paint, in making cement for pipes, and in making glass. *Formula*: Pb_3O_4

red–let•ter ['rɛd 'lɛtər] *adj.* **1** marked by red letters. **2** memorable; especially happy: *a red-letter day.* ⟨< the custom of printing important feast days and saints' days in red ink in the Church calendar⟩

red light 1 a red light as a traffic signal to stop: *He was fined for running a red light.* **2** *Informal.* any warning signal or instruction to stop, exercise caution, etc.

red–light ['rɛd 'ləit] *adj.* **1** of or having to do with a red light. **2** characterized by a concentration of brothels or other places of low repute: *a red-light district.*

red lily PINK ERYTHRONIUM.

red•line ['rɛd,laɪn] *v.* **-lined, -lining.** *n.* —*v.* **1** designate (an area in a city) as undesirable by outlining the area in red on a map. **2** refuse to do business with (establishments in such an area). **3** cancel or delete by drawing a red line through. **4** rev (an engine) too quickly so that the needle on the tachometer enters the red zone.
—*n. Hockey.* the centre line on a hockey rink, midway between the two bluelines: *"Centre ice" is halfway along the redline.*

redline² *Hockey.* the centre line on a hockey rink, midway between the two bluelines: *"Centre ice" is halfway along the redline.*

red maple a large tree (*Acer rubrum*) native to eastern Canada. Red flowers appear before the leaves.

red monkey flower PINK MONKEY FLOWER.

red mulberry a tree (*Morus rubra*) native to small areas of southern Ontario, having deciduous leaves; male and female flowers appear before the leaves, usually on the same tree. The wood is hard and durable, valued for building boats.

red mullet MULLET (def. 2).

re•do [ri'du] *v.* **-did, -done, -do•ing.** do again; do over.

red oak a tree (*Quercus rubra*) native to eastern Canada, having bristle-tipped lobes to the leaves and bearing large acorns. The wood is pink to reddish brown and is used for barrels to hold dry goods, and for flooring.

red•o•lent ['rɛdələnt] *adj.* **1** having a pleasant smell; fragrant. **2** smelling strongly; giving off an odour: *a kitchen redolent of fresh baking.* **3** suggestive (of thoughts or feelings): *Stonehenge is redolent of mystic power.* ⟨< L *redolens, -entis,* ppr. of *redolere* emit scent < *red-* back + *olere* to smell⟩ —**'red•o•lent•ly,** *adv.* —**'red•o•lence,** *n.*

red–osier dogwood ['rɛd 'ouʒər] *Cdn.* a North American shrub (*Cornus stolonifera*) common throughout Canada, having bright red twigs and branchlets, white flowers, and whitish fruit.

re•dou•ble [ri'dʌbəl] *v.* **-bled, -bling;** *n.* —*v.* **1** double again. **2** increase greatly; double: *When he saw land ahead, the swimmer redoubled his speed. The dough has redoubled in bulk already.* **3** repeat; echo; cause to echo: *The hills redoubled the sound of the horn.* **4** double back: *The fox redoubled on its trail to escape the hunters.* **5** *Bridge.* double one's opponent's double.
redouble one's efforts, try even harder.
—*n. Bridge.* the act of doubling one's opponent's double. ⟨< F *redoubler*⟩

re•doubt [rɪ'dʌut] *n.* a small fort standing alone. ⟨< F *redoute* < Ital. < VL *reductus* retreat < L *reducere.* See REDUCE.⟩

re•doubt•a•ble [rɪ'dʌutəbəl] *adj.* inspiring or worthy of fear, awe, or great respect; formidable: *a redoubtable warrior, a redoubtable opponent.* ⟨ME < OF *redoutable* < *redouter* dread < *re-* again + *douter* doubt < L *dubitare*⟩ —**re'doubt•a•bly,** *adv.*

re•dound [rɪ'daʊnd] *v.* come back with a (specified) result; contribute: *The number of scholarships we gained redound to the honour of our school.* ⟨ME < OF < L *redundare* overflow, ult. < *red-* back + *unda* wave⟩

re•dox ['ridɒks] *n.* OXIDATION-REDUCTION.

red–pen•cil ['rɛd 'pɛnsəl] *v.* **-cilled** or **-ciled, -cil•ling** or **-cil•ing.** delete or correct (writing) with or as if with a red pencil.

red pepper 1 a seasoning having a very strong, burning taste, made from the dried, ground fruit of a PEPPER (def. 5), or capsicum; cayenne. **2** a capsicum bearing pungent, red fruits used to make red pepper. **3** the fruit itself. **4** a mild, sweet red variety of the capsicum.

red pine a medium-tall pine (*Pinus resinosa*) of northeastern North America having long needles and egg-shaped cones without prickles. The wood of the red pine is used especially for poles, piles, and railway ties.

red•poll ['rɛd,poul] *n.* **1** any of several small finches (genus *Acanthis*) that breed in arctic and northern alpine regions, having greyish brown streaked plumage and a red or pinkish crown, especially the **common redpoll** (*A. flammea*). **2** a breed of cattle, originally from England, red in colour and hornless, used for either beef or dairy farming.

re•draft *v.* [ri'dræft]; *n.* ['ri,dræft] *v., n.* —*v.* draft again or anew.
—*n.* a second or later draft.

re•dress *v.* [rɪ'drɛs]; *n.* ['ridrɛs] *or* [rɪ'drɛs] *v., n.* —*v.* **1** set right; repair; remedy. **2** adjust evenly again. **3** balance: *The new budget will redress the old one.*
—*n.* a setting right; reparation; relief: *Any man deserves redress if he has been wronged.* ⟨< F *redresser* < *re-* again + *dresser* straighten, arrange⟩ —**re'dress•a•ble,** *adj.*

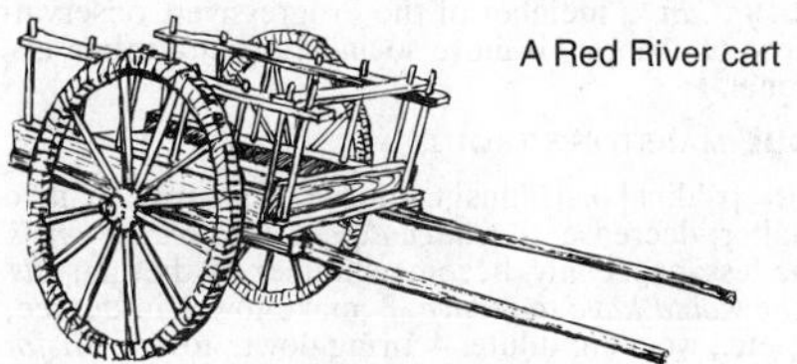
A Red River cart

Red River cart *Cdn.* formerly, a strong, two-wheeled cart made entirely of wood and pulled by oxen or horses. Red River carts were much used during pioneer days in the West.

Red River Rebellion *Cdn.* the uprising in 1869-1870 of mainly Métis settlers in the Red River region against the takeover of their territory by the government of Canada from the Hudson's Bay Company. The Métis' main objection was that it was done without consultation with the Red River settlers or assurance that their rights and way of life would be protected.

Red River Settlement *Cdn.* the colony that was founded on the Red River in Manitoba by Lord Selkirk in 1812. It was made up of Scottish and Irish settlers. Also, **Red River Colony.**

red salmon *Cdn.* sockeye.

red shift *Physics. Astronomy.* a displacement of the spectral lines of a celestial body toward the red end of the visual spectrum, caused by the Doppler effect. The existence of a red shift in the light emitted by stars of distant galaxies, which suggests that they are receding from our galaxy, is the main evidence for the theory of the expansion of the universe.

red–sid•ed bream ['rɛd ˌsaɪdəd] REDSIDE SHINER.

red•side shiner ['rɛd,saɪd] *Cdn.* a fish (*Richardsonius balteatus*) of the minnow family, found in British Columbian lakes. The redside shiner, which spawns from May to August, is

In each of the words below, **re-** *means* again *or* anew; *the pronunciation of the main part of each word is not changed.*

ˌre•di'vide **re'draw** **re'drill** **re'dry**

dark olive on the back and silvery on the sides and belly, and has a deep body which grows to a length of 15 cm.

red snapper 1 any of several reddish marine food fishes (genus *Lutjanus*). 2 any of several reddish fishes, especially the rockfish (*Sebastes ruberrimus*) of the E Pacific, a popular food fish.

red spring *Cdn. Pacific coast.* a red-fleshed variety of the spring salmon (*Onchorhyncus tshawytscha*).

red spruce 1 *Cdn.* a medium-sized spruce (*Picea rubens*) found mainly in the Maritimes and S Québec, having narrow, egg-shaped cones and shiny, yellowish green, often curved needles. Its young twigs used to be boiled as a cure for scurvy. 2 the soft, light wood of this tree.

red squirrel 1 a reddish brown North American squirrel (*Tamiasciurus hudsonicus*) found throughout Canada and the N United States, considerably smaller than the grey or black squirrel. 2 a reddish brown Eurasian squirrel (*Sciurus vulgaris*).

red•start ['rɛd,stɑrt] *n.* 1 any of a genus (*Phoenicurus*) of small European thrushes, especially *P. phoenicurus*, the male of which is grey with a brownish red breast and tail and a black throat, and the female brown. 2 any of a genus (*Setophaga*) of wood warblers, especially *S. ruticilla*, found throughout most of North America, the male of which has orange and black upper parts and white under parts. ⟨< *red* + *start* tail⟩

red tape strict and excessive attention to form and detail, especially in government business, causing delay and irritation. ⟨because official documents used to be tied with red tape⟩

red tide *Cdn.* 1 an area of sea water having a reddish coloration due to the presence of large numbers of micro-organisms (especially of genera *Gonyaulax* or *Gymnodinium*) that are constituents of plankton and that in large numbers are poisonous to many forms of marine life, and to humans if ingested through infected shellfish. 2 a population of such micro-organisms.

red•top ['rɛd,tɒp] *n.* any of various grasses (genus *Agrostis*) having panicles of tiny reddish-coloured flowers. Some redtops are important forage and pasture grasses.

Red Tory *Cdn.* a member of the Progressive Conservative party whose philosophy is more socialist-oriented than is conventional.

red trout MARSTON'S TROUT.

re•duce [rɪ'djus] *or* [rɪ'dus] *v.* **-duced, -duc•ing.** 1 make less; make smaller; decrease: *to reduce expenses, to reduce one's weight.* 2 become less; especially, become slimmer by dieting: *His doctor told him he would have to reduce.* 3 make lower in degree, intensity, etc.; weaken; dilute. 4 bring down; lower: *Misfortune reduced that poor woman to begging.* 5 bring to a certain state, form, or condition; change: *to reduce a verbal statement to writing. The teacher soon reduced the noisy class to order.* 6 conquer; subdue: *The army reduced the fort by a sudden attack.* 7 restore to its proper place or normal condition. A doctor can reduce a fracture or dislocation. 8 *Chemistry.* **a** combine with hydrogen. **b** remove oxygen from. **c** change (a compound) so that the valence of the positive element is lower. 9 *Mathematics.* simplify (an expression, formula, etc.). 10 smelt: *to reduce the ores of silver or copper.* 11 consume less: *Reduce, re-use, recycle are the watchwords of the environmental movement.* ⟨< L *reducere* < *re-* back + *ducere* bring⟩

re•duc•er [rɪ'djusər] *or* [rɪ'dusər] *n.* 1 one who or that which reduces. 2 *Plumbing.* a threaded cylindrical piece for connecting pipes of different sizes.

re•duc•i•ble [rɪ'djusəbəl] *or* [rɪ'dusəbəl] *adj.* that can be reduced: *4/8 is reducible to 1/2.*

re•duc•ing agent [rɪ'djusɪŋ] *or* [rɪ'dusɪŋ] *Chemistry.* any substance that reduces or removes the oxygen in a compound.

reducing glass a biconcave lens or mirror that produces a virtual image smaller than the object viewed through or in it.

re•duc•ti•o ad ab•sur•dum [rɪ'dʌktiou æd æb'sɜrdəm] *or* [rɪ'dʌkʃiou æd æb'sɜrdəm] *Latin.* a reduction to an absurdity; a method of proving something false by showing that the conclusions to which it leads are absurd.

re•duc•tion [rɪ'dʌkʃən] *n.* 1 a reducing or being reduced. 2 the amount by which a thing is reduced: *The reduction in cost was $5.* 3 a form of something produced by reducing; copy of something on a smaller scale. 4 *Chemistry.* a reaction in which each of the atoms affected gains one or more electrons. The atom or group of atoms that lose electrons become oxidized. 5 meiosis. ⟨< L *reductio, -onis* < *reducere.* See REDUCE.⟩ **—re'duc•tion•al,** *adj.*

re•duc•tion•ism [rɪ'dʌkʃə,nɪzəm] *n.* 1 the theory that any complex process or phenomenon, especially in psychology or biology, can be explained by reduction to the simplest physical mechanisms that operate during the process or phenomenon. 2 the practice of simplifying data, statements, or processes to the point of minimization or distortion. **—re'duc•tion•ist,** *n., adj.* **—re,duc•tion'is•tic,** *adj.*

re•duc•tive [rɪ'dʌktɪv] *adj.* 1 reducing or tending to reduce. 2 of or having to do with reduction or reductionism.

re•dun•dan•cy [rɪ'dʌndənsi] *n., pl.* **-cies.** 1 the state or quality of being redundant. 2 the unnecessary part or quantity of anything. 3 superfluous repetition, especially in words. 4 the presence of duplicate parts or systems in case of failure of the originals. 4 *Brit.* the state of being laid off or unemployed. Also, **redundance.**

re•dun•dant [rɪ'dʌndənt] *adj.* 1 extra; not needed. 2 that says the same thing again; using too many words for the same idea; wordy. In the sentence: *We two both had an apple each,* the expression *two both* is redundant. 3 duplicate; present as a backup in case of failure. 4 *Brit.* laid off or unemployed. ⟨< L *redundans, -antis,* ppr. of *redundare.* See REDOUND.⟩ **—re'dun•dant•ly,** *adv.*

re•du•pli•cate *v.* [rɪ'djuplə,keit] *or* [rɪ'duplə,keit]; *adj.* [rɪ'djupləkɪt] *or* [rɪ'dupləkɪt] *v.* **-cat•ed, -cat•ing;** *adj.* —*v.* 1 double; repeat. 2 *Linguistics.* form (new words) by repeating one or more syllables, sometimes with a change of vowel or consonant: *Examples: sing-song, fuddle-duddle.* 3 be or become doubled or repeated.
—*adj.* doubled or repeated. ⟨< L *reduplicare* < *re-* again + *duplicare* double < *duplex, duplicis* double⟩ **—re'du•pli•ca•tive,** *adj.*

re•du•pli•ca•tion [rɪ,djuplə'keiʃən] *or* [rɪ,duplə'keiʃən] *n.* 1 a reduplicating or being reduplicated; doubling; repetition. 2 something resulting from repeating; a duplicate; copy: *To the prisoner each day seemed a reduplication of the preceding day.* 3 *Linguistics.* **a** the process of reduplicating. **b** a word formed by reduplicating. **c** the added part in a word formed by reduplicating.

red•ware[1] ['rɛd,wɛr] *n.* a large, brown, edible seaweed of the kelp type (*Laminaria digitata*), commonly found off the N Atlantic coastlines. ⟨< *red* + *ware* < ME *war* seaweed⟩

red•ware[2] ['rɛd,wɛr] *n.* an early American unglazed earthenware pottery made from clay containing oxide. ⟨< *red* + *ware*[1]⟩

red willow *Cdn.* a shrub (*Cornus stolonifera*) with conspicuous red stems.

red•wing ['rɛd,wɪŋ] *n.* 1 a European thrush (*Turdus iliacus*) having mainly brown plumage with red on the underside of the wings and on the flanks. 2 RED-WINGED BLACKBIRD.

red–winged blackbird a North American blackbird (*Agelaius phoeniceus*), the male of which has black plumage with a bright red patch, edged on one side with yellow, on each wing.

red•wood ['rɛd,wʊd] *n.* 1 a giant coniferous tree (*Sequoia sempervirens*) native to the Pacific coast of North America from California to Oregon, highly valued for timber. The redwood is considered to be the tallest tree in the world, often more than 90 m tall, and also one of the longest-lived, some specimens being over 2000 years old. See also SEQUOIA, BIG TREE. 2 the brownish red, light wood of this tree. 3 any of various other trees having wood that is reddish or that yields a red dye; also, the wood of any of these trees.

ree•bok ['ribɒk] *n.* any of several varieties of deerlike South African antelope (*Pelea capriolus*), having curly, greyish fur and slender, sharp horns. Also, **rhebok.** ⟨< Afrikaans *ree* roe + *bok* buck⟩

re–echo [ri 'ɛkou] *v.* **-ech•oed, -ech•o•ing;** *n.* **-ech•oes.** —*v.*

In each of the words below, **re-** *means* again *or* anew; *the pronunciation of the main part of each word is not changed.*

re'dye

echo back.
—*n.* the echo of an echo.

reed [rid] *n., v.* —*n.* **1** any of various tall water or marsh grasses (especially genus *Phragmites*) having long, jointed, hollow stems. **2** a stalk or stalks of any of these grasses, especially as used for thatching, basketry, pens, etc. **3** something made from a reed or reeds, such as an arrow or a musical pipe. **4** *Music.* **a** a thin piece of wood, metal, cane, or plastic in a musical instrument that produces sound when vibrated by a current of air. **b** a wind instrument or organ pipe that produces sound by means of a reed or reeds; REED INSTRUMENT. **c** (*adjl.*) producing tones by means of reeds: *a reed organ.* **5** a device on a loom, consisting of vertical parallel wires, that serves to space the warp yarns evenly.
—*v.* **1** decorate with reeds. **2** thatch with or as if with reeds. ⟨OE *hrēod*⟩
☛ *Hom.* READ[1].

reed•bird ['rid,bɜrd] *n.* bobolink.

reed instrument a musical instrument that produces sound by means of a vibrating reed or reeds. Oboes, clarinets, and saxophones are reed instruments.

reed organ a musical keyboard instrument producing tones by means of small metal reeds. Two common forms are the **harmonium**, in which the air is forced outward through the reeds, and the **American organ**, in which the air is sucked inward.

reed pipe an organ pipe having a reed vibrated by air.

reed stop **1** a set of reed pipes in a pipe organ. **2** the knob that operates these pipes.

re–ed•u•cate [ri 'ɛdʒə,keit] *v.* **-cat•ed, -cat•ing. 1** educate again with the purpose of: **a** reforming or rehabilitating. **b** inculcating new attitudes or values. **c** indoctrinating with political theories or ideals. **d** preparing for a changed labour market. **2** try to bring (someone) back to normal functioning, as a stroke victim, etc. —**,re-ed'u'ca•tion,** *n.*

reed•y ['ridi] *adj.* **reed•i•er, reed•i•est. 1** full of reeds. **2** made of a reed or reeds. **3** like a reed or reeds. **4** sounding like a reed instrument: *a thin, reedy voice.* —**'reed•i•ness,** *n.*

reef[1] [rif] *n.* **1** a narrow ridge of rock, sand, or coral at or near the surface of the water: *The ship was wrecked on a hidden reef.* **2** a vein or lode in mining. ⟨< MDu., MLG *rif, ref* < ON *rif* rib. Cf. REEF[2].⟩

reef[2] [rif] *n., v. Nautical.* —*n.* **1** the part of a sail that can be rolled or folded up to reduce its size. **2** the area to which such a sail is reduced by reefing.
—*v.* **1** reduce the size of (a sail) by rolling or folding up a part of it. **2** reduce the length of (a topmast, bowsprit, etc.) by lowering, etc. ⟨ME *riff, refe* < Du. *reef, rif* < ON *rif* rib, reef. Cf. REEF[1].⟩

reef•er[1] ['rifər] *n.* **1** a person who reefs. **2** a short coat of thick cloth, worn especially by sailors and fishers. **3** a full-length, usually double-breasted, coat. ⟨< *reef*[2]⟩

reef•er[2] ['rifər] *n. Slang.* a cigarette containing marijuana. ⟨? < *reef*[2], since such cigarettes are rolled by hand⟩

reef•er[3] ['rifər] *n. Slang.* a refrigerated shipping container, railway car, truck trailer, or van. ⟨< *refrigerator*⟩

reef knot SQUARE KNOT. See KNOT for picture.

reek [rik] *n., v.* —*n.* **1** a strong, unpleasant smell. **2** smoke; steam; vapour.
—*v.* **1** send out vapour or a strong, unpleasant smell. **2** be wet with sweat or blood. **3** be filled with something unpleasant or offensive: *a government reeking with corruption.* **4** give out (an offensive quality) strongly or unmistakably (*usually used with* **of**):

His manner reeks of arrogance. **5** treat with or expose to smoke or fumes. ⟨OE *rēc*⟩
☛ *Hom.* WREAK.

reel[1] [ril] *n., v.* —*n.* **1** a frame turning on an axis, for winding thread, yarn, a fish line, rope, wire, etc. **2** a spool; roller. **3** something wound on a reel: *two reels of motion-picture film.* **4** the length of motion-picture film held by a reel.
off the reel, *Informal.* quickly and easily.
—*v.* **1** wind on a reel. **2** draw with a reel or by winding: *to reel in a fish.*
reel off, say, write, or make in a quick, easy way: *My grandfather can reel off stories by the hour.*
reel out, unwind or pull off a reel, as a fishing line. ⟨OE *hrēol*⟩
☛ *Hom.* REAL[1] [ril].

reel[2] [ril] *v., n.* —*v.* **1** sway, waver, fall back, or rock under a blow, shock, etc.: *Their first glimpse of the crash site made them reel back in horror. Our regiment reeled when the cavalry attacked it.* **2** cause to rock or sway. **3** be in a whirl; be dizzy. **4** stand or walk with swaying or staggering movements: *The drunk reeled across the room.*
—*n.* a reeling or staggering movement. ⟨special use of *reel*[1]⟩
☛ *Hom.* REAL[1] [ril].
☛ *Syn. v.* **1, 4. Reel,** STAGGER = stand or move unsteadily. **Reel** particularly suggests dizziness and unsteadiness, a swaying on one's feet and danger of toppling over at any moment: *Sick and faint, he reeled when he tried to cross the room.* **Stagger** particularly suggests being unable to keep one's balance, reeling to one side and the other or walking in a zigzag way: *The girl staggered in with the firewood.*

reel[3] [ril] *n.* **1** a lively Scottish dance, usually for four or eight dancers. **2** VIRGINIA REEL. **3** the music for either of these reels. ⟨special use of *reel*[2]⟩
☛ *Hom.* REAL[1] [ril].

reel–to–reel ['ril tə 'ril] *adj., n.* —*adj.* describing or pertaining to a type of tape recorder or film projector system using two separate reels on which the tape or film must be threaded to run from one to the other.
—*n.* a piece of equipment using this type of system.

re•en•force or **re–en•force** [ˌriɪn'fɔrs] *v.* **-forced, -forc•ing.** See REINFORCE.

re•en•force•ment or **re–en•force•ment** [ˌri ɪn'fɔrsmənt] *n.* See REINFORCEMENT.

re–en•try [ri 'ɛntri] *n., pl.* **-tries. 1** an entering again or returning, especially of a rocket or spacecraft into the earth's atmosphere after flight in outer space. **2** *Bridge. Whist.* a card that will enable one to take a trick, thus regaining the lead. Also, **re-entry card**.

reeve[1] [riv] *n.* **1** *Cdn.* in Ontario and some western provinces, the elected head of a rural municipal council; in Ontario, also the elected head of a village or township council. **2** *Brit.* formerly, bailiff; steward; overseer. ⟨OE *(ge)rēfa*⟩

reeve[2] [riv] *v.* **reeved** or **rove, reev•ing.** *Nautical.* **1** pass (a line) through a hole, ring, etc. **2** fasten by placing through or around something. ⟨? < Du. *reven* reef a sail⟩

reeve[3] [riv] *n.* the female of the RUFF[3].

reeve•ship ['riv,ʃɪp] *n. Cdn.* the office or position of a REEVE[1].

re–examine [ri ɪg'zæmən] *v.* **-mined, -min•ing. 1** examine again. **2** *Law.* question (a witness) again after cross-examination.

ref. **1** referee. **2** reference; referred. **3** reformation; reformed. **4** refund.

In each of the words below, **re-** *means* again *or* anew; *the pronunciation of the main part of each word is not changed.*

re-'ed•it
re-'ed•u,cate
,re-ed•u'ca•tion
,re-e'lect
,re-e'lec•tion
,re-em'bark
,re-em'bo•dy
,re-e'merge
,re-e'mer•gence
,re-e'mer•gent
re-'em•i,grate
re-'em•pha•sis
re-'em•pha,size
,re-em'ploy
,re-em'ploy•ment
,re-en'act
,re-en'act•ment
,re-en'dow
,re-en'gage
,re-en'gage•ment
,re-en'list
,re-en'list•ment
,re-en'slave
,re-en'slave•ment
re-'en•ter
re-'en•trance
,re-e'quip
,re-e'quip•ment
,re-e'rect
,re-e'rec•tion
,re-es'tab•lish
,re-es'tab•lish•ment
,re-e'val•u,ate
,re-e,val•u'a•tion
,re-e'vap•o,rate
,re-e,vap•o'ra•tion
,re-ex,am•i'na•tion
,re-ex'am•ine
re-'ex•ca,vate
,re-ex•ca'va•tion
,re-ex'change
,re-ex'hib•it
,re-ex•hi'bi•tion
,re-ex'pe•ri•ence
re-'ex•port
,re-ex•por'ta•tion
re'fab•ri,cate
re'fash•ion

re•face [ri'feis] *v.* **-faced, -fac•ing. 1** mend or repair the face or surface of (stone, walls, etc.) **2** replace the facing in (a garment).

re•fec•tion [rɪ'fɛkʃən] *n.* **1** refreshment by food or drink. **2** a meal; repast. ⟨< L *refectio, -onis* < *reficere.* See REFECTORY.⟩

re•fec•to•ry [rɪ'fɛktəri] *n., pl.* **-ries.** a room for meals, especially in a monastery, convent, or school. ⟨< LL *refectorium,* ult. < L *reficere* refresh < *re-* again + *facere* make⟩

re•fer [rɪ'fɜr] *v.* **-ferred, -fer•ring. 1** direct attention; make mention; allude (*to* something): *The article often refers to the cultural differences between East and West.* **2** relate; apply: *The rule refers only to special cases.* **3** send or direct for information, help, or action: *We referred her to the boss.* **4** turn for information or help: *Writers often refer to a dictionary.* **5** hand over; submit: *Let's refer the dispute to the umpire.* **6** consider as belonging or due; assign: *Many people refer their failures to bad luck instead of to poor work.* ⟨< L *referre* < *re-* back + *ferre* take⟩

☛ *Syn.* **1. Refer,** ALLUDE = speak of something in a way to turn attention to it. **Refer** = make direct and specific mention. **Allude** = mention incidentally or call attention indirectly: *She never referred to the incident in her writing, but often alluded to it in conversation.*

ref•er•ee [ˌrɛfə'ri] *n., v.* **-eed, -ee•ing.** *–n.* **1** a judge of play in certain games and sports including hockey, football, and boxing. **2** a person to whom something is referred for decision or settlement.
–v. act as referee; act as referee in.

ref•er•ence ['rɛfərəns] *n., adj., v.* *–n.* **-enced, -enc•ing. 1** a referring or being referred. **2** a word, statement, etc. directing attention: *This history contains many references to larger works.* **3** a statement, book, etc. to which attention is directed: *You will find that reference on page 16.* **4** something used for information or help: *A dictionary is a book of reference.* **5** a person who can give information about another person's character or ability. **6** the information given, usually in writing: *The boy had excellent references from people for whom he had worked.* **7** relation; respect; regard: *This test is to be taken by all pupils without reference to age or grade.* **8** *Linguistics.* the relation of a term to what it stands for.
in or **with reference to,** about; concerning.
make reference to, mention.
–adj. used for information or help: *a reference library.*
–v. **1** provide with references. **2** refer to.

ref•er•en•dum [ˌrɛfə'rɛndəm] *n., pl.* **-dums** or **-da** [-də]. **1** the process of submitting a law already passed by the law-making body to a direct vote of the citizens for approval or rejection. British Columbia and Alberta have provision for referendums. Compare PLEBISCITE. **2** the submitting of any matter to a direct vote: *In the 1992 referendum, the Charlottetown Accord was defeated.* ⟨< L *referendum* that which must be referred < *referre.* See REFER.⟩

ref•er•ent ['rɛfərənt] *n., adj.* *–n.* **1** an idea, person, or thing referred to. **2** *Linguistics.* the idea, thing, act, etc. that a term stands for.
–adj. containing a reference; referring.

ref•er•en•tial [ˌrɛfə'rɛnʃəl] *adj.* **1** making reference. **2** containing a reference. **3** used as a reference.

re•fer•ral [rɪ'fɜrəl] *n.* **1** a referring or directing to a specific person, place, or group. **2** the person thus referred.

re•fill *v.* [ri'fɪl]; *n.* ['riˌfɪl] *v., n.* *–v.* fill again.
–n. a material, supply, etc. to replace something that has been used up: *a coffee refill.* **–re'fill•a•ble,** *adj.*

re•fine [rɪ'faɪn] *v.* **-fined, -fin•ing. 1** make free from impurities. Sugar, oil, and metals are refined before being used. **2** make or become fine, polished, or cultivated. **3** make or become pure. **4** make or become finer, more elegant. **5** change or remove by polishing, purifying, etc. **6** make very fine, subtle, or exact.
refine on or **upon, a** improve. **b** excel. ⟨< *re-* + *fine* make fine⟩ **–re'fin•er,** *n.*

re•fined [rɪ'faɪnd] *adj., v.* *–adj.* **1** freed from impurities: *refined sugar.* **2** freed or free from grossness, coarseness, crudeness, vulgarity, etc. **3** having or showing cultivated feeling, taste, manners, etc.; polished: *a refined voice, refined manners.* **4** fine; subtle: *refined distinctions.* **5** minutely precise: *refined measurements.*
–v. pt. and pp. of REFINE.

re•fine•ment [rɪ'faɪnmənt] *n.* **1** fineness of feeling, taste, manners, or language. **2** the act or result of refining: *Gasoline is produced by the refinement of petroleum.* **3** an improvement. **4** a fine point; subtle distinction. **5** an improved, higher, or extreme form of something.

re•fin•er•y [rɪ'faɪnəri] *n., pl.* **-er•ies.** a building and machinery for purifying metal, sugar, petroleum, etc.

re•fin•ish [ri'fɪnɪʃ] *v.* give a new surface to (furniture, etc.).

re•fit *v.* [ri'fɪt]; *n.* ['rifɪt] *v.* **-fit•ted, -fit•ting;** *n.* *–v.* **1** fit, prepare, or equip for use again: *to refit an old ship.* **2** get fresh supplies (for).
–n. a fitting, preparing, or equipping for use again: *The ship went to the dry dock for a refit.*

re•flate [ri'fleit] *v.* **-flat•ed, -flat•ing.** *Economics.* cause the reflation of: *to reflate a depressed economy.* ⟨back formation < *reflation*⟩

re•fla•tion [ri'fleiʃən] *n.* *Economics.* an increase in the supply of money and credit following a period of deflation, for the purpose of stimulating the economy and increasing employment. ⟨*re-* + (*in*)*flation*⟩

re•flect [rɪ'flɛkt] *v.* **1** turn back or throw back (light, heat, sound, etc.): *The sidewalks reflect heat on a hot day.* **2** give back an image; give back a likeness or image of: *A mirror reflects your image.* **3** be returned or thrown back, as light from a smooth, shiny surface: *It's just the light reflecting off the water.* **4** reproduce or show like a mirror: *The newspaper reflected the owner's opinions.* **5** think; think carefully: *Take time to reflect before making major changes in your life.* **6** cast blame, reproach, or discredit: *Bad behaviour reflects on home training.* **7** serve to cast or bring: *A brave act reflects credit on the person who performs it.* ⟨< L *reflectere* < *re-* back + *flectere* bend⟩

☛ *Syn.* **5.** See note at THINK.

reflecting telescope a type of optical telescope in which the light rays entering it are brought to a focus by means of a concave mirror. Compare REFRACTING TELESCOPE.

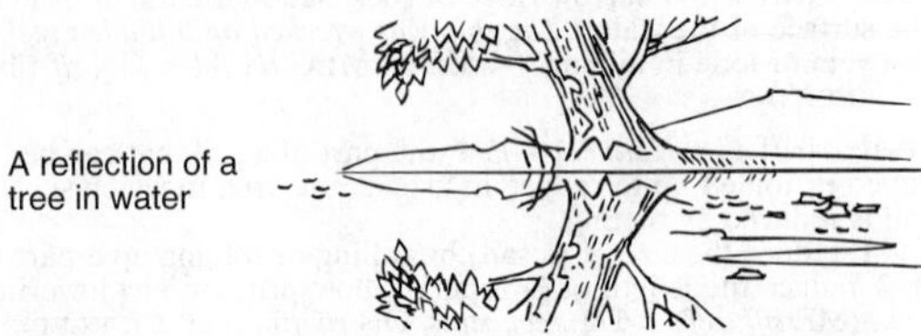
A reflection of a tree in water

re•flec•tion [rɪ'flɛkʃən] *n.* **1** a reflecting or being reflected. **2** something reflected. **3** a likeness; image: *You can see your reflection in a mirror.* **4** thinking; careful thinking: *On reflection, the plan seemed too dangerous.* **5** an idea or remark resulting from careful thinking. **6** a remark, action, etc. that casts blame or discredit. **7** blame; discredit. **8** See ANGLE OF REFLECTION.

re•flec•tive [rɪ'flɛktɪv] *adj.* **1** reflecting: *the reflective surface of polished metal.* **2** thoughtful: *a reflective look.* **–re'flec•tive•ly,** *adv.* **–re'flec•tive•ness,** *n.*

re•flec•tor [rɪ'flɛktər] *n.* **1** *Physics.* any thing, surface, or device that reflects light, heat, sound, etc., especially a piece of glass or metal, usually concave, for reflecting light in a required direction. **2** REFLECTING TELESCOPE. **3** *Physics.* material, such as graphite or heavy water, surrounding the core of a nuclear reactor and preventing, by reflection, the escape of neutrons.

re•flex *adj., n.* ['riflɛks]; *v.* [rɪ'flɛks] *adj., n., v.* *–adj.* **1** *Physiology.* not voluntary; coming as a direct response to a stimulation of some sensory nerve cells. Sneezing is a reflex act. **2** occurring in reaction or response. **3** bent or turned back. **4** *Geometry.* of an angle, more than 180° and less than 360°.
–n. **1** *Physiology.* an automatic action in direct response to a stimulation of certain nerve cells. Sneezing and shivering are reflexes. **2** something reflected; an image; reflection: *A law should be a reflex of the will of the people.*

In each of the words below, **re-** *means* again *or* anew; *the pronunciation of the main part of each word is not changed.*

re'fas•ten	**re'file**	**re'fil•ter**
re'fig•ure	**re'film**	**re'fi•nance**

—v. bend back; turn back. ⟨< L *reflexus,* pp. of *reflectere.* See REFLECT.⟩

reflex arc *Physiology.* the nerve path followed by impulses in a reflex action.

reflex camera a camera in which the image is reflected by a mirror or passed through a prism onto a ground glass plate in order to focus the lens.

re•flex•ive [rɪ'flɛksɪv] *adj., n. Grammar. —adj.* **1** having to do with a grammatical relationship in which an action turns back on the subject, and that the subject and object therefore have the same referent. **2** taking part in such a relationship: *reflexive verb.* *—n.* a reflexive verb or pronoun. *Example: In* The boy hurt himself, hurt *and* himself *are reflexives.* **—re'flex•ive•ly,** *adv.* **—,re•flex'iv•i•ty,** *n.*
☛ *Usage.* See note at SELF.

reflexive pronoun a pronoun, the object of a verb or preposition, which refers back to the subject of the sentence: *Examples: I cut* myself. *Give* yourself *ten minutes to do this exercise. They made a name for* themselves.
☛ *Usage.* See note at SELF.

reflexive verb a verb whose subject and object refer to the same person or thing.

ref•lu•ent ['rɛfluənt] *adj.* flowing back; ebbing. ⟨< L *refluens, -entis,* ppr. of *refluere* flow back < *re-* back + *fluere* flow⟩ **—'ref•lu•ence,** *n.*

re•flux ['ri,flʌks] *n.* **1** the ebb of a tide. **2** a flowing back; ebb. ⟨< *re-* + *flux*⟩

re•for•est [ri'fɔrɪst] *v.* replant (a previously logged or burnt over area) with trees.

re•for•est•a•tion [,rifɔrɪ'steiʃən] *n.* a replanting or being replanted with trees.

re•form [rɪ'fɔrm] *v., n. —v.* **1** make better in behaviour, attitudes, etc.: *Prisons should try to reform criminals instead of just punishing them.* **2** improve by removing faults or abuses: *to reform a city administration.* **3** correct one's own faults; improve one's behaviour: *The boy promised to reform if given another chance.* **4** *Chemistry.* to heat under pressure in order to crack and refine (petroleum, etc.).
—n. **1** an improvement, especially one made by removing faults or abuses; a change to improve conditions: *The new government put through many reforms.* **2** a change to a better standard of behaviour, morals, etc.; reformation. ⟨< L *reformare,* ult. < *re-* again + *forma* form⟩ **—re'form•a•ble,** *adj.*

Re•form [rɪ'fɔrm] *adj.* **1** of or having to do with the liberal branch of Judaism, as contrasted with the Orthodox and Conservative branches: *a Reform congregation.* **2** *Cdn.* of or having to do with the REFORM PARTY: *the Reform platform.*

re–form [ri 'fɔrm] *v.* **1** form again. **2** take a new shape. **3** give a new shape to.

ref•or•ma•tion [,rɛfər'meiʃən] *n.* **1** a reforming or being reformed; change for the better; improvement. **2 Reformation,** the 16th-century religious movement in Europe that began with the aim of reform in the Roman Catholic Church and ended with the establishment of certain Protestant churches. **—,ref•or'ma•tion•al,** *adj.*

re•form•a•tive [rɪ'fɔrmətɪv] *adj.* tending toward or inducing reform.

re•form•a•to•ry [rɪ'fɔrmə,tɔri] *adj., n., pl.* **-ries.** *—adj.* serving to reform; intended to reform.
—n. an institution for reforming young offenders against the law; a prison for juveniles.

re•formed [rɪ'fɔrmd] *adj., v.* **1** improved or changed for the better, especially as regards behaviour and ethical attitudes. **2 Reformed,** of or designating the Protestant churches, especially the Calvinist as distinct from the Lutheran. Compare EVANGELICAL.
—v. pt. and pp. of REFORM.

re•form•er [rɪ'fɔrmər] *n.* **1** a person who reforms, or tries to reform, some state of affairs, custom, etc.; a supporter of reforms. **2 Reformer, a** any leader of the Protestant Reformation. **b** *Cdn.* formerly, in Upper and Lower Canada, a member of a political group advocating a greater measure of responsible government. See REFORM PARTY (def. 1).

re•form•ism [rɪ'fɔrmɪzəm] *n.* a policy or doctrine advocating reform, especially political, social, or religious reform.

re•form•ist [rɪ'fɔrmɪst] *n., adj. —n.* a person who favours or supports reformism.
—adj. of or having to do with reformists or reformism.

Reform Party *Cdn.* **1** formerly, the party that opposed Tory rule in Upper Canada and the Maritimes in the 19th century, advocating a greater measure of responsible government and other reforms. Joseph Howe was a prominent leader of this party, one of the antecedents of the present LIBERAL PARTY. **2** a right-wing political party organized in Alberta in 1987 by Preston Manning, in opposition to the policies of the then ruling Progressive Conservatives in the federal government.

reform school reformatory.

re•fract [rɪ'frækt] *v.* **1** bend (a ray) from a straight course. Water refracts light. See ANGLE OF REFRACTION. **2** determine the degree of refraction of (an eye or lens). ⟨< L *refractus,* pp. of *refringere* break up < *re-* back + *frangere* break⟩

refracting telescope a type of optical telescope in which the light rays entering it are brought to a focus by a lens or set of lenses. Compare REFLECTING TELESCOPE.

The refraction of light rays entering the water makes the straw appear to be broken at the water line.

re•frac•tion [rɪ'frækʃən] *n.* **1** *Physics.* **a** the bending of a ray of light when it travels from one medium to another at an oblique angle, due to a slight change in the velocity of the light. When a ray of light crosses the boundary from air into water, the higher density of the water causes the wavelength to become shorter and the ray to turn slightly toward the perpendicular. See also ANGLE OF REFRACTION. **b** the bending or turning of any other wave, such as sound, when it passes from one medium into another of different density. **2** *Optics.* **a** the ability of the eye to refract light, permitting the formation of an image on the retina. **b** the determination of the condition of an eye with respect to this ability. **3** *Astronomy.* the apparent change in the position of a heavenly body in the sky, due to the refraction of light rays from it as they enter the earth's atmosphere.

re•frac•tive [rɪ'fræktɪv] *adj.* **1** having power to refract. **2** having to do with or caused by refraction. **—re'fract•ive•ly,** *adv.* **—re'fract•ive•ness,** *n.*

refractive index *Optics.* a measure of the extent to which a given medium refracts light; the ratio of the velocities of light in two given media. The **absolute refractive index,** which is the ratio of the speed of light in a vacuum to that in a given medium, is always greater than 1.

re•frac•tor [rɪ'fræktər] *n.* **1** anything that refracts. **2** REFRACTING TELESCOPE.

re•frac•to•ry [rɪ'fræktəri] *adj., n. —adj.* **1** hard to manage; stubborn; obstinate: *Mules are refractory.* **2** not yielding readily to treatment: *She had a refractory cough.* **3** hard to melt, reduce, or work: *Some ores are more refractory than others.*
—n. **1** an ore, cement, ceramic material, or similar substance that is hard to melt, reduce, or work. **2** a brick made of refractory material, used for lining furnaces, etc. **—re'frac•to•ri•ly,** *adv.* **—re'frac•to•ri•ness,** *n.*

re•frain[1] [rɪ'frein] *v.* hold oneself back: *Refrain from crime.* ⟨ME < OF < L *refrenare* < *re-* back + *frenum* bridle⟩
☛ *Syn.* **Refrain,** ABSTAIN = keep oneself from (doing) something. **Refrain** emphasizes checking an impulse, and means voluntarily not doing something one would like to do: *He politely refrained from saying what he thought of her hat.* **Abstain** emphasizes holding oneself back by force of will, and means deliberately and habitually doing without

In each of the words below, **re-** *means* again *or* anew; *the pronunciation of the main part of each word is not changed.*

re'fo•cus	**re'for•mu,late**	**re'for•ti,fy**
re'fold	**,re•for•mu'la•tion**	**re'frac•ture**

something one believes harmful or wrong, especially certain pleasures: *She is abstaining from alcohol.*

re•frain² [rɪ'frein] *n.* **1** a phrase or verse repeated regularly in a song or poem; chorus. **2** the music for a refrain. ⟨ME *refreyne* < OF *refrain*, ult. < VL *refrangere* break off, for L *refringere.* See REFRACT.⟩

re•fran•gi•bil•i•ty [rɪ,frændʒə'bɪlɪti] *n.* **1** the property of being refrangible. **2** the amount of refraction (of light rays, etc.) that is possible.

re•fran•gi•ble [rɪ'frændʒəbəl] *adj.* capable of being refracted: *Rays of light are refrangible.* ⟨< *re-* + L *frangere* to break⟩ **—re'fran•gi•ble•ness,** *n.*

re•fresh [rɪ'frɛʃ] *v.* make fresh or vigorous again; renew: *He refreshed his memory by a glance at the book. She refreshed herself with a cup of tea.* ⟨ME < OF *refrescher* < *re-* again + *fresche* fresh < Gmc.⟩ **—re'fresh•er,** *n.*

re•fresh•er course [rɪ'frɛʃər] a course taken to bring one's knowledge up to date.

re•fresh•ing [rɪ'frɛʃɪŋ] *adj., v. —adj.* **1** that makes fresh or vigorous again: *a refreshing drink.* **2** welcome as a pleasing change: *Your change in attitude is most refreshing.*
—v. ppr. of REFRESH. **—re'fresh•ing•ly,** *adv.*

re•fresh•ment [rɪ'frɛʃmənt] *n.* **1** a refreshing or being refreshed. **2** anything that refreshes. **3** Usually, **refreshments,** *pl.* food or drink: *to serve refreshments at a party.*

re•fried beans ['ri,fraɪd] a Mexican dish consisting of beans cooked in water and then fried and eaten with a main dish, such as a burrito. ⟨< Sp. *frijoles refritos*⟩

re•frig•er•ant [rɪ'frɪdʒərənt] *adj., n. —adj.* **1** refrigerating; cooling. **2** reducing bodily heat or fever.
—n. something that cools, etc. Ice is a refrigerant.

re•frig•er•ate [rɪ'frɪdʒə,reit] *v.* **-at•ed, -at•ing. 1** make or keep cold or cool. **2** preserve by keeping cold or cool. ⟨< L *refrigerare,* ult. < *re-* again + *frigus, -goris* cold⟩

re•frig•er•a•tion [rɪ,frɪdʒə'reiʃən] *n.* the act or process of cooling or keeping cold.

re•frig•er•a•tor [rɪ'frɪdʒə,reitər] *n.* an appliance, closet, or room equipped for keeping things, especially food and drink, cold.

re•fu•el [ri'fjuəl] *v.* **-elled** or **-eled, -el•ling** or **-el•ing. 1** supply with fuel again. **2** take on a fresh supply of fuel: *The transatlantic plane stopped at Gander to refuel.*

ref•uge ['rɛfjudʒ] *n.* **1** shelter or protection from danger, trouble, etc.; safety; security: *The cat took refuge from the angry dog in a tree.* **2** any person, thing, or action providing or seeming to provide safety, security, or comfort: *A deserted farmhouse was their refuge from the storm.* ⟨ME < OF < L *refugium* < *re-* back + *fugere* flee⟩

ref•u•gee [,rɛfjə'dʒi] *or* ['rɛfjə,dʒi] *n.* a person who flees for refuge or safety, especially to a foreign country, in time of persecution, war, etc. ⟨< F *réfugié*⟩

re•ful•gent [rɪ'fʌldʒənt] *adj.* shining brightly; radiant; splendid: *a refulgent sunrise.* ⟨< L *refulgens, -entis,* ppr. of *refulgere* < *re-* back + *fulgere* shine⟩ **—re'ful•gence,** *n.* **—re'ful•gent•ly,** *adv.*

re•fund¹ *v.* [rɪ'fʌnd]; *n.* ['rifʌnd] *v., n. —v.* pay back: *If these shoes do not wear well, the shop will refund your money.*
—n. **1** the return of money paid. **2** the money paid back. ⟨< L *refundere* < *re-* back + *fundere* pour⟩ **—re'fund•a•ble,** *adj.* **—re'fund•er,** *n.*

re•fund² [ri'fʌnd] *v.* **1** fund (an undertaking) for a second or further time. **2** *Finance.* change (a debt, loan, etc.) into a new form. ⟨< *re-* + *fund*⟩

re•fur•bish [ri'fɜrbɪʃ] *v.* polish up again; do up anew; brighten; renovate or restore. **—re'fur•bish•ment,** *n.*

re•fus•al [rɪ'fjuzəl] *n.* **1** the act of refusing: *Their refusal to play the game provoked the others.* **2** the right to refuse or take a thing before it is offered to others: *Give me the refusal of the car till tomorrow.* **3** *Equitation.* the act of a horse in refusing to jump a fence: *She had four faults and a refusal in the first round.*

re•fuse¹ [rɪ'fjuz] *v.* **-fused, -fus•ing. 1** decline to accept; reject: *to refuse an offer.* **2** deny (a request, demand, invitation); decline to give or grant: *to refuse admittance.* **3** decline (to do something): *to refuse to discuss the question.* **4** decline to accept or consent: *She is free to refuse.* **5** *Equitation.* of a horse, stop short at (a barrier) and decline to jump: *Big Ben seldom refused.* ⟨ME < OF *refuser* < L *refuses,* pp. of *refundere.* See REFUND¹.⟩

☛ *Syn.* **1. Refuse,** DECLINE, REJECT = not accept something offered. **Refuse** is the blunt term, implying a direct and sometimes an ungracious denial: *He refused to go with me.* **Decline** is more polite, implying a reluctant rather than a direct denial: *She declined my invitation.* **Reject** is more emphatic than **refuse,** implying a very positive and brusque denial: *He rejected my friendly advice.*

ref•use² ['rɛfjus] *or* ['rɛfjuz] *n., adj. —n.* useless stuff; waste; rubbish.
—adj. **1** rejected as worthless or of little value; discarded. **2** pertaining to waste or rubbish: *All garbage should be placed in the refuse bins.* ⟨ME, probably < OF *refus,* pp. of *refuser.* See REFUSE¹.⟩

re•fuse•nik [rɪ'fjuznɪk] *n.* formerly, a citizen of the Soviet Union, usually Jewish, who was refused permission to emigrate. Also, **refusnik.**

ref•u•ta•tion [,rɛfjə'teiʃən] *n.* **1** disproof of a claim, opinion, or argument. **2** something that refutes an argument, claim, or opinion, as a counterargument, counterclaim, etc.

re•fute [rɪ'fjut] *v.* **-fut•ed, -fut•ing.** prove (a claim, opinion, or argument) to be false or incorrect. ⟨< L *refutare* < OL *re-* back + *futare* cause to fall⟩ **—re'fut•er,** *n.* **—re'fut•a•ble,** *adj.* **—re'fut•a•bly,** *adv.*

☛ *Usage.* See note at CONFUTE.

reg [rɛg] *n. Informal.* regulation: *dress regs.* ⟨clipped form of *regulation*⟩

reg. **1** register; registered. **2** registrar; registry. **3** regular; regularly. **4** region. **5** regiment. **6** regulation.

re•gain [rɪ'gein] *v.* **1** get back; recover: *to regain health.* **2** get back to; reach again: *to regain the shore.*

re•gal ['rigəl] *adj.* **1** belonging to a monarch; royal: *Opening Parliament is a regal prerogative.* **2** like a king or queen; fit for a monarch; stately; splendid; magnificent. ⟨ME < L *regalis* < *rex, regis* king. Doublet of ROYAL, REAL², RIAL.⟩ **—'re•gal•ly,** *adv.*

☛ *Syn.* **1.** See note at ROYAL.

re•gale¹ [rɪ'geil] *v.* **-galed, -gal•ing. 1** entertain agreeably; delight with something pleasing: *The old sailor regaled the children with sea stories.* **2** entertain with a choice repast; feast. ⟨< F *régaler,* ult. < MDu. *wale* wealth⟩ **—re'gale•ment,** *n.* **—re'gal•er,** *n.*

re•gale² [rɪ'geil] *n. Cdn.* formerly: **1** an extra ration, especially of liquor, given to the employees of a fur company for a festive occasion such as Christmas. **2** a party, celebration, etc. held on such an occasion. **3** a ration of liquor given to boatmen at the start or finish of an arduous journey. ⟨< Cdn.F < MF *régale* pleasure, festivity⟩

re•ga•li•a [rɪ'geiliə] *or* [rɪ'geiljə] *n.pl.* **1** the emblems of royalty. Crowns, sceptres, etc. are regalia. **2** the emblems or decorations of any society, order, academic degree, etc. **3** finery, especially fine clothes: *in party regalia.* ⟨< L *regalia* royal things, neut. pl. of *regalis.* See REGAL.⟩

re•gal•i•ty [ri'gælɪti] *n., pl.* **-ties. 1** royalty; sovereignty; kingship. **2** a right or privilege having to do with a monarch. **3** a kingdom. **4** regal quality.

re•gard [rɪ'gɑrd] *v., n. —v.* **1** consider; think of: *She is regarded as the best doctor in town.* **2** show thought or consideration for; care for; respect: *They always regard their parents' wishes.* **3** heed: *No one regarded her screams.* **4** look at; look closely at; watch: *The teacher regarded me sternly.* **5** hold in affection; think highly of.
as regards, as for; concerning; relating to: *As regards money, I have enough.*
—n. **1** consideration; thought; care: *Have regard for the feelings of others.* **2** a look; steady look. **3** esteem; favour; good opinion. **4 regards,** *pl.* good wishes; an expression of esteem: *My regards to your mother.* **5** a point; particular matter: *in this regard.*
in or **with regard to,** about; concerning; relating to.
without regard to, not considering. ⟨< F *regarder* < *re-* back + *garder* guard⟩

☛ *Syn. n.* **1.** See note at RESPECT.

In each of the words below, **re-** *means* again *or* anew; *the pronunciation of the main part of each word is not changed.*

re'frame	**re'fresh•en**	**re'fur•nish**
re'freeze	**re'fry**	**re'gal•va,nize**

re•gard•ant [rɪ'gɑrdənt] *adj. Heraldry.* of a beast, looking backward, the head in profile: *a stag regardant.*

re•gard•ful [rɪ'gɑrdfəl] *adj.* **1** heedful; observant; mindful. **2** considerate; respectful. **—re'gard•ful•ly,** *adv.*

re•gard•ing [rɪ'gɑrdɪŋ] *prep., v. —prep.* with regard to; concerning; about: *a prophecy regarding the future.*
—v. ppr. of REGARD.

re•gard•less [rɪ'gɑrdlɪs] *adj., adv. —adj.* taking or showing no heed; careless.
—adv. Informal. in spite of what happens: *We plan to leave on Monday, and we will leave then, regardless.*
regardless of, despite; without regard for. **—re'gard•less•ly,** *adv.* **—re'gard•less•ness,** *n.*

☛ *Usage.* The form **irregardless** is not logical since it literally means 'not regardless'. As a result, it is generally considered to be non-standard and should be avoided in both speech and writing.

re•gat•ta [rɪ'gætə] *or* [rɪ'gɑtə] *n.* **1** a boat race. **2** a series of boat races: *the annual regatta of the yacht club.* ⟨< dial. Ital.⟩

re•gen•cy ['ridʒənsi] *n., pl.* **-cies. 1** the position, office, or function of a regent or group of regents: *The Queen Mother held the regency until the young king came of age.* **2** a body of regents. **3** a government consisting of regents. **4** a state or territory controlled by a regent or regents. **5** the time during which there is a regency. **6 Regency, a** in Great Britain, the period from 1811 to 1820 during which George, Prince of Wales, acted as regent for King George III. **b** *Architecture and design.* a style characterized by graceful, elegant lines, developed in England during the Regency. **c** in France, the period from 1715 to 1723 during which Philip, Duke of Orleans, acted as regent for King Louis XV. **d** the form of architecture and design characteristic of this period.

re•gen•er•a•cy [rɪ'dʒɛnərəsi] *n.* a regenerate state.

re•gen•er•ate *v.* [rɪ'dʒɛnə,reit]; *adj.* [rɪ'dʒɛnərɪt] *v.* **-at•ed, -at•ing;** *adj. —v.* **1** give a new and better spiritual life to. **2** improve the moral condition of; put new life and spirit into. **3** reform. **4** grow again; form (new tissue, a new part, etc.) to replace what is lost: *The mother's liver regenerated the lobe she had donated to her young child.* **5** *Physics. Chemistry.* **a** cause (a substance) to return intermittently to its original state or condition. **b** be so returned. **6** *Electronics.* amplify by transferring a portion of the power from the output to the input.
—adj. **1** born again spiritually. **2** made over in better form; formed anew morally. ⟨< L *regenerare* make over ult. < *re-* again + *genus, -neris* birth⟩ **—re'gen•er•a•ble,** *adj.* **—re,gen•er'a•tion,** *n.* **—re'gen•er,a•tor,** *n.*

re•gen•er•a•tive [rɪ'dʒɛnərətɪv] *adj.* **1** of or having to do with regeneration. **2** tending to regenerate. **—re'gen•er•a•tive•ly,** *adv.*

re•gent ['ridʒənt] *n., adj. —n.* **1** a person who rules in the name of a sick or absent sovereign or a sovereign who is not yet grown up: *The regent ruled for seven years until the boy king came of age.* **2** a member of a governing board. Many universities have boards of regents.
—adj. acting as a regent (*used after a noun*): *a princess regent.* ⟨< L *regens, -entis,* ppr. of *regere* rule⟩ **—'re•gent•ship,** *n.*

reg•gae ['rɛgei] *n.* a style of music that developed in Jamaica in the mid 1970s, a blend of calypso and rock rhythms in 4/4 time, with accented second and last beats. ⟨< Jamaican E; ? ult. < *rege* ragged⟩

reg•i•cide ['rɛdʒə,saɪd] *n.* **1** the crime of killing a monarch. **2** a person who commits regicide. ⟨< L *regi-,* stem of *rex* king + E *-cide*[1]⟩ **—,reg•i'cid•al,** *adj.*

re•gime or **ré•gime** [rɪ'ʒim]; *French,* [ʀe'ʒim] *n.* **1** a system of government or rule: *a communist regime.* **2** a particular ruling government. **3** a period of time in which a person or administration is in power: *the Trudeau regime.* **4** a prevailing system; a pattern of attitudes, behaviour, etc. **5** a regular system of living; regimen: *Monastic orders follow a strict regime.* ⟨< F < L *regimen.* Doublet of REGIMEN.⟩

reg•i•men ['rɛdʒəmən] *n.* **1** *Medicine.* a set of rules or habits of diet, exercise, or manner of living intended to improve health, reduce weight, etc. **2** the act of governing; government; rule. **3** *Grammar.* the influence of one word in determining the case or mood of another; GOVERNMENT (def. 6). ⟨< L *regimen* < *regere* rule. Doublet of REGIME.⟩

reg•i•ment *n.* ['rɛdʒəmənt]; *v.* ['rɛdʒə,mɛnt] *n., v. —n.* **1** in the army, a unit consisting of several companies or troops or batteries of soldiers organized into one large group consisting of at least two battalions, and commanded by a colonel. There are several regiments in a brigade or a division. **2** a large number: *a whole regiment of school children.*
—v. **1** form into a regiment or organized group. **2** assign to a regiment or group. **3** treat in a strict or uniform manner: *A totalitarian state regiments its citizens.* ⟨< LL *regimentum* rule < L *regere* to rule⟩

reg•i•men•tal [,rɛdʒə'mɛntəl] *adj., n. —adj.* of a regiment; having to do with a regiment: *regimental colours.*
—n. **regimentals,** *pl.* military uniform of a specific regiment. **—,reg•i'men•tal•ly,** *adv.*

reg•i•men•ta•tion [,rɛdʒəmɛn'teiʃən] *n.* **1** a formation into organized or uniform groups. **2** a making uniform by rigid structure and discipline. **3** a subjection to control. In time of war there may be regimentation of people's work, play, food, and clothing.

re•gi•na [rə'dʒinə] *or* [rə'dʒaɪnə] *n.* **1** queen. **2 Regina,** the official title of a reigning queen (*placed after the name*): *Victoria Regina, Elizabeth II Regina.*

re•gion ['ridʒən] *n.* **1** any large part of the earth's surface, especially one characterized by certain flora and fauna: *the region of the equator.* **2** a place; space; area: *an unhealthful region.* **3** a part of the body: *the region of the heart.* **4** a sphere; domain: *the region of art, the region of the imagination.* **5** *Cdn.* in Ontario, a geographical division for purposes of government, having wider powers than those of a county. Regions were established in 1973 in some parts of the province by combining counties and townships to provide for more effective planning. ⟨< L *regio, -onis* direction < *regere* direct⟩

re•gion•al ['ridʒənəl] *adj.* of or in a particular region, as opposed to a smaller area: *a regional storm.* **—'re•gion•al•ly,** *adv.*

re•gion•al•ism ['ridʒənə,lɪzəm] *n.* **1** concern with and loyalty to one's own geographical region within a country, rather than the country as a whole; regional patriotism. **2** in art and literature, emphasis on and reflection of the peculiar characteristics of a particular locale or region. **3** a linguistic feature or custom, etc. that is characteristic of a particular geographical region. **4** the division of a country, etc. into partially autonomous administrative areas called regions.

re•gion•al•ist ['ridʒənəlɪst] *n., adj. —n.* a person who favours or advocates regionalism.
—adj. of or having to do with regionalism or regionalists. **—,re•gion•al'is•tic,** *adj.*

ré•gis•seur [,reiʒi'sɜr]; *French,* [ʀeʒi'sœʀ] *n. Esp. ballet.* one responsible for staging a work; director. ⟨< F⟩

reg•is•ter ['rɛdʒɪstər] *n., v. —n.* **1** a list; record: *A register of attendance is kept in our school.* **2** a book in which a list or record is kept: *a hotel register.* **3** anything that records: *At the end of the day, the cash register tape should tally with the actual money taken in.* **4** *Computer technology.* a high-speed storage area in the central processing unit. **5** a registration or registry. **6** a registrar. **7** an opening in a wall or floor with a grid or other arrangement to regulate the amount of cooled or heated air that passes through. **8** *Music.* **a** part of the range of a voice or musical instrument, all the tones having the same quality or being formed in a similar manner: *Her upper register sounds a little forced.* **b** the set of pipes connected to an organ stop. **c** the organ stop itself. **9** *Printing.* the exact fit or correspondence of lines, columns, colours, etc. **10** *Linguistics.* the vocabulary, pronunciation, etc. belonging to a given level of usage such as formal, informal, slang, etc.
—v. **1** write in a list or record: *to register the names of the new members.* **2** have one's name written in a list or record; enrol: *You must register if you want to attend the conference.* **3 a** indicate; record: *The thermometer registers 28°.* **b** cause to be indicated or recorded: *She had a fever registering 39°.* **4** show (surprise, joy, anger, etc.) by the expression on one's face or by actions. **5** be understood: *I made an attempt to bring him up to date, but the information didn't even register.* **6** comprehend: *She seemed unable to register the fact that her home had been destroyed.* **7** arrange to

In each of the words below, **re-** *means* again *or* anew; *the pronunciation of the main part of each word is not changed.*

re'gath•er **re'gauge** **re'gild**

have (a letter, parcel, etc.) sent by REGISTERED MAIL. **8** *Printing.* **a** make (lines, columns, colours, etc.) fit or correspond exactly. **b** fit or correspond exactly. ⟨ME < Med.L *registrum* < L *regestrum*, neut. pp. of *regerere* record < *re-* back + *gerere* carry⟩

reg•is•tered ['rɛdʒɪstərd] *adj., v. —adj.* **1** legally certified by the government or a board: *a registered patent, a registered trademark.* **2** of cattle, horses, dogs, cats, etc., recorded with the appropriate official breeding association: *registered Holsteins.* **3** *Commerce.* of bonds, etc., having the owner's name officially listed with the issuing corporation and inscribed on the face of the bond, stock certificate, etc.
—v. pt. and pp. of REGISTER.

registered mail a postal service that provides proof that a letter or parcel has been sent and delivered and also guarantees compensation if the mail is not delivered.

reg•is•tra•ble ['rɛdʒɪstrəbəl] *adj.* that can be registered.

reg•is•trant ['rɛdʒɪstrənt] *n.* a person who registers or has registered: *a registrant for a trademark, registrants for a conference.*

reg•is•trar ['rɛdʒɪ,strar] *n.* **1** an official who keeps a register; an official recorder. **2** in some universities, colleges, etc., the officer in charge of admissions, examinations, and general regulations. **3** an official of a bank or trust company who certifies and registers securities for a corporation and ensures that the shares issued do not exceed the number authorized. ⟨< Med.L *registrarius*⟩

reg•is•tra•tion [,rɛdʒɪ'streiʃən] *n.* **1** the act of registering. **2** an entry in a register: *I can find no registration for you on that date.* **3** the number of people registered: *The conference registration exceeded all our expectations.* **4** a document certifying an act of registering. **5** *Music.* the selection of organ or harpsichord registers for playing a particular composition.

reg•is•try ['rɛdʒɪstri] *n., pl.* **-tries. 1** a registering; registration. **2** a place where a register is kept; an office of registration. **3** a book in which a list or record is kept. **4** a customs document declaring the nationality of a ship.

reg•nant ['rɛgnənt] *adj.* **1** ruling (*usually placed after the noun*): *the Queen regnant.* **2** exercising sway or influence; predominant. **3** prevalent; widespread. ⟨< L *regnans, -antis,* ppr. of *regnare* rule < *regnum* kingdom⟩

re•gress *v.* [rɪ'grɛs]; *n.* ['rigrɛs] *v., n. —v.* **1** go back; move in a backward direction. **2** return or cause to return to an earlier or less advanced state: *The hypnotist regressed his subject to childhood.*
—n. a going back; movement backward, or a return to a previous state. ⟨< L *regressus,* pp. of *regredi* < *re-* back + *gradi* go⟩
—re'gres•sor, *n.*

re•gres•sion [rɪ'grɛʃən] *n.* **1** the act of going back; backward movement. **2** *Psychology.* a way of trying to escape difficult problems by casting off responsibility and assuming other characteristics of childhood. **3** *Biology.* the reversion of offspring toward a more general condition. **4** *Statistics.* an analytic technique for determining the relationship between a dependent variable and an independent variable.

re•gret [rɪ'grɛt] *v.* **-gret•ted, -gret•ting;** *n. —v.* **1** feel sorrow or remorse about. **2** feel sorry; mourn.
—n. **1** the feeling of being sorry; sorrow or remorse. **2** a sense of loss. **3 regrets,** *pl.* a polite reply declining an invitation. ⟨ME < OF *regreter* < Gmc.; cf. ON *gráta* weep⟩ **—re'gret•ter,** *n.*
☛ *Syn. n.* **1. Regret,** REMORSE = a feeling of sorrow for a fault or wrongdoing. **Regret** suggests a troubled mind and a feeling of being dissatisfied and sorry about something one has or has not done: *With regret he remembered his forgotten promise.* **Remorse** suggests the mental torment of a gnawing conscience and deep sorrow for a wrong that can never be undone: *The boy was filled with remorse for the worry he had caused his mother.*

re•gret•ful [rɪ'grɛtfəl] *adj.* feeling or expressing regret. **—re'gret•ful•ly,** *adv.* **—re'gret•ful•ness,** *n.*

re•gret•ta•ble [rɪ'grɛtəbəl] *adj.* that should be or is regretted: *a regrettable incident.* **—re'gret•ta•bly,** *adv.*

re•grind [ri'graɪnd] *v.* **-ground, -grind•ing.** grind, as a lens, to a new prescription.

re•group [ri'grup] *v.* **1** form into a new arrangement or grouping: *to regroup military forces. You can regroup two bags of six oranges each to make three bags of four oranges each.* **2** *Mathematics.* in subtraction, decrease the digit in one column of the minuend by 1 in order to increase the value in the column on the right by 10: *To subtract 8 from 64, regroup 64 as 5 tens and 14 ones.* **3** *Informal.* reorganize in order to make a fresh start.

Regt. 1 regiment. **2** regent.

reg•u•lar ['rɛgjələr] *adj., n. —adj.* **1** fixed by custom or habit; usual; normal: *Six o'clock was her regular hour of rising.* **2** required by or following some rule or principle; according to rule: *A period is the regular ending for a sentence.* **3** coming, acting, or done again and again at the same time: *Saturday is a regular holiday.* **4** steady; habitual: *A regular customer is one who shops frequently at the same store.* **5** even in size, spacing, or speed; well-balanced: *regular features, regular teeth.* **6** symmetrical. **7** *Mathematics.* having all its angles equal and all its sides equal: *a regular triangle.* **8** *Botany.* having all the same parts of a flower alike in shape and size. **9** orderly; methodical; of fixed habits: *lead a regular life.* **10** properly fitted or trained: *The maid did the cooking while the regular cook was sick.* **11** *Grammar.* of a noun, verb, etc., changing according to the usual pattern of the language to show tense, number, person, etc.: *a regular verb.* **12** *Informal.* thorough; complete: *a regular bore.* **13** *Informal.* fine; agreeable; all right: *He's a regular fellow.* **14** permanently organized: *The regular army is under the direct control of the federal government.* **15** of or belonging to the permanent armed forces of a country: *Regular troops can be posted anywhere at any time.* **16** belonging to a religious order bound by certain rules. The regular clergy live in religious communities. **17** having bowel movements at consistent intervals; not constipated: *Our fibre cereal will keep you regular.*
—n. **1** a full-time member of a group: *The fire department was made up of regulars and volunteers.* **2** a person who makes the armed forces a full-time career. **3** a person belonging to a religious order bound by certain rules. **4** a regular customer, contributor, etc.: *He is a regular at this restaurant.* **5** *Sports.* a player on the regular team. ⟨ME < OF < L *regularis* < *regula.* See RULE.⟩ **—,reg•u'lar•i•ty,** *n.* **—'reg•u•lar•ly,** *adv.*
☛ *Syn. adj.* **4.** See note at STEADY.

reg•u•lar•ize ['rɛgjələ,raɪz] *v.* **-ized, -iz•ing.** make regular.

Regular Officer Training Plan a fully subsidized plan of up to five years' university study leading to a baccalaureate degree while training for a career as a regular officer in the Canadian Armed Forces. *Abbrev.:* ROTP or R.O.T.P.

reg•u•late ['rɛgjə,leit] *v.* **-lat•ed, -lat•ing. 1** control by rule, principle, or system: *Good schools regulate the behaviour of students.* **2** put in condition to work properly. **3** keep at some standard: *This instrument regulates the temperature of the room.* ⟨< LL *regulare* < L *regula.* See RULE.⟩ **—'reg•u•la•tive** or **'reg•u•la,to•ry** ['rɛgjələ,tɔri], *adj.* **—'reg•u•la•tive•ly,** *adv.*

reg•u•la•tion [,rɛgjə'leiʃən] *n., adj. —n.* **1** control by rule, principle, or system. **2** a rule; law: *traffic regulations.*
—adj. **1** according to or required by a regulation; standard: *Soldiers wear a regulation uniform.* **2** *Informal.* usual; ordinary.

reg•u•la•tor ['rɛgjə,leitər] *n.* **1** a person who or thing that regulates. **2** a device in a clock or watch to make it go faster or slower. **3** a very accurate clock used as a standard of time.

Reg•u•lus ['rɛgjələs] *n. Astronomy.* the brightest star in the constellation Leo.

re•gur•gi•tate [ri'gɜrdʒə,teit] *v.* **-tat•ed, -tat•ing. 1** of liquids, gases, partly digested foods, etc., rush, surge, or flow back. **2** bring (partly digested food) back from the stomach to the mouth: *Some birds regurgitate food to feed their young.* ⟨< Med.L *regurgitare,* ult. < L *re-* back + *gurges, -gitis* whirlpool⟩ **—re,gur•gi'ta•tion,** *n.*

re•ha•bil•i•tate [,rihə'bɪlə,teit] *or* [,riə'bɪlə,teit] *v.* **-tat•ed, -tat•ing. 1** restore to a good condition; make over in a new form: *The old house is to be rehabilitated.* **2** restore to former standing, rank, rights, privileges, reputation, etc.: *The former criminal completely rehabilitated himself and was trusted and respected by all.* **3** restore to a normal state of physical or mental

In each of the words below, **re-** *means* again *or* anew; *the pronunciation of the main part of each word is not changed.*

re'glaze **re'glue** **re'graft** **re'grow** **re'growth**

health and activity by treatment, therapy, etc. ⟨< Med.L *rehabilitare*, ult. < L *re-* again + *habilis* fit⟩
—ˌre•haˌbil•i'ta•tion, *n.* **—ˌre•ha'bil•iˌta•tive,** *adj.*

re•hash *v.* [ri'hæʃ]; *n.* ['rihæʃ] *v., n.* *—v.* deal with again; work up (old material) into a new form: *The question had been rehashed again and again.*
—n. **1** the act of rehashing. **2** something old put into a different form: *That composition is simply a rehash of an article in the encyclopedia.*

re•hears•al [rɪ'hɜrsəl] *n.* **1** the act of rehearsing. **2** a performance beforehand for practice or drill. **3** a detailed telling; report: *They embarked on a rehearsal of all their problems.*
in rehearsal, in the process of being prepared for performance.

re•hearse [rɪ'hɜrs] *v.* **-hearsed, -hears•ing. 1** practise (a play, part, etc.) for a public performance. **2** drill or train (a person, etc.) by repetition. **3** tell in detail; repeat: *The child rehearsed all the happenings of the day from beginning to end.* ⟨ME < OF *rehercier* < *re-* again + *hercier* harrow, ult. < L *hirpex, hirpicis* rake⟩

Reich [rəik]; *German,* [RAIX] empire, a term applied to the Holy Roman Empire, 962-1806 **(First Reich)**; the German Empire, 1871-1918 **(Second Reich)**; and Germany under Adolf Hitler, 1933-1945 **(Third Reich)**.

reichs•mark ['rəiksˌmɑrk]; *German,* ['RAIXSˌmaRk] *n.* **-marks** or **-mark.** the basic unit of money of Germany from 1924 to 1948. ⟨< G⟩

Reichs•tag ['rəiksˌtɑg]; *German,* ['RAIXS'tak] *n.* the former elective legislative assembly of the German Empire and Republic. It was established in 1871 but, under Hitler, gradually lost its powers.

re•i•fi•ca•tion [ˌriəfə'keiʃən] *n.* the act, process, or result of reifying.

re•i•fy ['riəˌfaɪ] *v.* **-fied, -fy•ing.** think of or treat (an abstract concept or idea, or a person) as a material thing.

reign [rein] *n., v.* *—n.* **1** the period of power of a ruler: *Queen Victoria's reign lasted sixty-four years.* **2** the royal power; rule: *The reign of a wise ruler benefits a country.* **3** existence everywhere; prevalence.
—v. **1** be a ruler: *A king reigns over his kingdom.* **2** exist everywhere; prevail: *Silence reigned on the lake, except for the sound of our paddles in the water.* ⟨ME < OF < L *regnum* < *regere* rule⟩
☛ *Hom.* RAIN, REIN.

Reign of Terror in France, a period of the Revolution from about March, 1793, to July, 1794, during which thousands of people were executed.

re•im•burse [ˌriɪm'bɜrs] *v.* **-bursed, -burs•ing.** pay back: *His employer reimbursed him for his travelling expenses.* ⟨< *re-* + obs. *imburse* < Med.L *imbursare* < L *in-* into + LL *bursa* purse; patterned on F *rembourser*⟩ **—ˌre•im'burse•ment,** *n.*

re•im•port *v.* [ˌriɪm'pɔrt]; *n.* [ri'ɪmpɔrt] *v., n.* *—v.* import something previously exported: *Raw materials are sometimes exported from Canada and later reimported in the form of manufactured goods.*
—n. reimportation.

re•im•por•ta•tion [ˌriɪmpɔr'teiʃən] *n.* **1** an importing of something previously exported. **2** the thing reimported.

rein [rein] *n., v.* *—n.* **1** a long, narrow strap or line fastened to the bit of a bridle, used to guide and control an animal, especially a horse. See HARNESS for picture. **2 reins,** *pl.* a means of control and direction: *to seize the reins of government.*
draw rein, a tighten the reins: *She drew rein as she approached the gate.* **b** slow down; stop.
give rein to, let move or act freely, without guidance or control: *to give rein to one's feelings.*
keep on a short or **tight rein,** keep under close supervision and control: *Some people work better when kept on a short rein.*
take the reins, take control.
—v. **1** check or pull with reins. **2** guide and control: *Rein your tongue.*
rein in or **up,** stop or cause to stop or go slower: *Rein in before your horse tramples the flowers!* ⟨ME < OF *rene,* ult. < L *retinere* hold back. See RETAIN.⟩
☛ *Hom.* RAIN, REIGN.

re•in•car•nate *v.* [ˌriɪn'kɑrneit]; *n.* [ˌriɪn'kɑrnɪt] *v.* **-nat•ed, -nat•ing;** *adj.* *—v.* give a new body to (a soul).
—adj. appearing to be a new incarnation or embodiment of someone else (*used after a noun*): *She is her grandmother reincarnate.*

re•in•car•na•tion [ˌriɪnkɑr'neiʃən] *n.* **1** a rebirth of the soul in a new body. **2** a new incarnation or embodiment.

rein•deer ['reinˌdir] *n., pl.* **-deer. 1** a large deer (*Rangifer tarandus*) of arctic and subarctic regions, both sexes of which have large, branching antlers. Reindeer have been domesticated since early times in N Europe and Asia. **2** *Cdn., esp. North.* caribou. ⟨ME < ON *hreindýri* < *hreinn* reindeer + *dýr* animal⟩

reindeer moss a grey, tufted, and branched lichen (*Cladonia rangiferina*) found in arctic and subarctic regions and providing the major food for reindeer and musk-oxen and also sometimes used for human food. Also called **caribou moss** in Canada.

re•in•force [ˌriɪn'fɔrs] *v.* **-forced, -forc•ing. 1** strengthen with new force or materials: *to reinforce an army or a fleet, to reinforce a garment with an extra thickness of cloth, to reinforce a wall or a bridge.* **2** strengthen: *to reinforce an argument, a plea, an effect, etc.* **3** *Psychology.* strengthen the probability of (a response to a stimulus) by giving a reward or removing a painful stimulus. Also, **reenforce** or **re-enforce.** ⟨< *re-* + *enforce*⟩

reinforced concrete concrete with steel embedded in it to make the structure stronger.

re•in•force•ment [ˌriɪn'fɔrsmənt] *n.* **1** the act of reinforcing or being reinforced. **2** something that reinforces. **3** *Psychology.* any procedure that increases the probability of a given response to a stimulus. **4 reinforcements,** *pl.* extra personnel and equipment, especially troops, warships, military aircraft, etc. Also, **reenforcement** or **re-enforcement.**

re•in•state [ˌriɪn'steit] *v.* **-stat•ed, -stat•ing.** restore to a former position or condition; establish again.
—ˌre•in'state•ment, *n.*

re•in•sur•ance [ˌriɪn'ʃʊrəns] *n.* **1** renewed insurance. **2** the transfer of insurance from one person to another.

re•in•sure [ˌriɪn'ʃʊr] *v.* insure again; insure under a contract by which a first insurer relieves himself or herself of the risk and transfers it to another insurer.

re•in•te•grate [ri'ɪntəˌgreit] *v.* **-grat•ed, -grat•ing. 1** make whole again; restore to a perfect state; renew or re-establish. **2** become whole again; be renewed. **—reˌin•te'gra•tion,** *n.*

re•in•ter•pret [ˌriɪn'tɜrprɪt] *v.* interpret again, especially in a new and different way.

reis [reis] *n.* pl. of REAL³. ⟨< Pg.⟩

re•is•sue [ri'ɪʃu] *v.* **-sued, -su•ing;** *n.* *—v.* **1** issue again: Snow White *has been reissued several times.* **2** come forth again: *The groundhog reissued from its burrow.*
—n. **1** something issued again, as a recording or book. **2** an

In each of the words below, re- *means* again *or* anew; *the pronunciation of the main part of each word is not changed.*

re'han•dle	**ˌre•im•po'si•tion**	**ˌre•in•fes'ta•tion**	**ˌre•in'stall**	**ˌre•in'vent**
re'hard•en	**ˌre•im'preg•nate**	**ˌre•in'flame**	**ˌre•in•stal'la•tion**	**ˌre•in'vest**
re'har•ness	**ˌre•im'pris•on**	**ˌre•in'flate**	**re-'in•teˌgrate**	**ˌre•in'ves•tiˌgate**
re'hear	**ˌre•im'pris•on•ment**	**ˌre•in'form**	**ˌre•in•te'gra•tion**	**ˌre•inˌves•ti'ga•tion**
re'heat	**ˌre•in'cor•poˌrate**	**ˌre•in'hab•it**	**ˌre•in'ter**	**ˌre•in'vest•ment**
re'hem	**ˌre•inˌcor•po'ra•tion**	**ˌre•in'oc•uˌlate**	**ˌre•in'ter•ment**	**ˌre•in'vig•orˌate**
re'hire	**ˌre•in'cur**	**ˌre•in'scribe**	**ˌre•in'ter•pret**	**ˌre•in'vite**
re'hos•pi•taˌlize	**ˌre•in'duce**	**ˌre•in'sert**	**ˌre•inˌter•pre'ta•tion**	**ˌre•in'voke**
re'house	**ˌre•in'duc•tion**	**ˌre•in'ser•tion**	**ˌre•in'ter•roˌgate**	**re-'is•sue**
ˌre•ig'nite	**ˌre•in'fect**	**ˌre•in'spect**	**ˌre•inˌter•ro'ga•tion**	
ˌre•im'plant	**ˌre•in'fec•tion**	**ˌre•in'spec•tion**	**ˌre•in•tro'duce**	
ˌre•im'pose	**ˌre•in'fest**	**ˌre•in'spire**	**ˌre•in•tro'duc•tion**	

official reprint after the original issue has been stopped: *a reissue of a commemorative stamp.*

re•it•er•ate [ri'ɪtə,reit] *v.* **-at•ed, -at•ing.** say or do several times; repeat (an action, demand, etc.) again and again: *The boy did not move, though the teacher reiterated her command.* ⟨< L *reiterare*, ult. < *re-* again + *iterum* again⟩ **—re,it•er'a•tion,** *n.*
☛ *Syn.* See note at REPEAT.

re•ject *v.* [rɪ'dʒɛkt]; *n.* ['ridʒɛkt] *v., n.* —*v.* **1** refuse to take, use, believe, consider, grant, etc.: *He rejected our help. She tried to join the army but was rejected.* **2** throw away as useless or unsatisfactory: *Reject all apples with soft spots.* **3** vomit. **4** refuse to accept; rebuff; deny affection to: *He rejected her children.* **5** *Medicine.* of a human or other animal, fail to accept (a transplanted organ or a graft) because of an immunological reaction: *The percentage of transplants that are rejected is much lower than it used to be.*
—*n.* a rejected person or thing: *The rejects were sold at a lower price.* ⟨< L *rejectus*, pp. of *reicere*. *rejicere* < *re-* back + *jacere* throw⟩ **—re'ject•er,** *n.*
☛ *Syn. v.* **1.** See note at REFUSE[1].

re•jec•tion [rɪ'dʒɛkʃən] *n.* **1** the act of rejecting or the state of being rejected. **2** the thing rejected. **3** *Biology.* an immune response against grafted or transplanted tissue that prevents the survival of the graft or transplant.

rejection slip a notification of rejection from a publisher to the author of a manuscript submitted for publication.

re•joice [rɪ'dʒɔɪs] *v.* **-joiced, -joic•ing. 1** be glad; be filled with joy. **2** make glad; fill with joy. ⟨ME < OF *rejoïss-*, a stem of *rejoïr*, ult. < L *re-* again + *gaudere* be glad⟩ **—re'joic•er,** *n.*

re•joic•ing [rɪ'dʒɔɪsɪŋ] *n., v.* —*n.* the feeling or expression of joy.
—*v.* ppr. of REJOICE.

re•join[1] [rɪ'dʒɔɪn] *v.* **1** join again; unite (people or things) again: *After leaving the armed forces for a year, she rejoined. The doctor rejoined the severed nerve.* **2** enter the company of (somebody) again: *After conferring briefly in private, the executive rejoined the members.* ⟨< *re-* + *join*⟩

re•join[2] [rɪ'dʒɔɪn] *v.* **1** answer; reply: *"Not on your life," he rejoined.* **2** answer a plaintiff's reply to the defendant's plea. ⟨< F *rejoindre* < *re-* back + *joindre* join⟩

re•join•der [rɪ'dʒɔɪndər] *n.* an answer to a reply; response. ⟨< F *rejoindre*, infin. used as n.⟩

re•ju•ve•nate [rɪ'dʒuvə,neit] *v.* **-nat•ed, -nat•ing. 1** make young or vigorous again; give new or youthful qualities to: *Your holiday seems to have rejuvenated you.* **2** restore a youthful appearance; revive. ⟨< *re-* < L *juvenis* young⟩
—re,ju•ve'na•tion, *n.* **—re'ju•ve,na•tor,** *n.*

rel. 1 relative; relatively; relating. **2** religion.

re–laid [ri 'leid] *v.* pt. and pp. of RE-LAY.

re•lapse *v.* [rɪ'læps]; *n.* ['rilæps] *v.* **-lapsed, -laps•ing;** *n.* —*v.* fall or slip back into a former state, way of acting, etc.: *After one cry of surprise, she relapsed into silence.*
—*n.* a falling or slipping back into a former state, way of acting, etc.: *He seemed to be getting over his illness but had a relapse.* ⟨< L *relapsus*, pp. of *relabi* < *re-* back + *labi* slip⟩

re•late [rɪ'leit] *v.* **-lat•ed, -lat•ing. 1** give an account of; tell: *The traveller related her adventures.* **2** connect in thought or meaning: Better *and* best *are related to* good. **3** have reference; be connected in any way: *We are interested in what relates to ourselves.* **4** establish or show sympathetic feeling toward a person or thing: *I find it hard to relate to punk rock.* ⟨< L *relatus*, pp. of *referre* < *re-* back + *ferre* bring⟩

re•lat•ed [rɪ'leitɪd] *adj., v.* —*adj.* **1** associated: *Those two ideas are related.* **2** told or narrated: *The tales related by my grandfather were often hilarious.* **3** *Music.* of tones or chords, melodically or harmonically closely connected; belonging to a melodic or harmonic series. **4** belonging to the same family; connected by a common origin: *English and Dutch are closely related languages. Are the two of you related?*
—*v.* pt. and pp. of RELATE. **—re'lat•ed•ness,** *n.*

re•la•tion [rɪ'leiʃən] *n.* **1** a connection in thought or meaning: *Your answer has no relation to the question.* **2** a connection or dealings between persons, groups, countries, etc.: *The relation of mother and child is the closest in the world.* **3 relations,** *pl.* dealings; affairs: *Our firm has business relations with her firm.* **4** a person who belongs to the same family as another, such as father, brother, aunt, etc.; relative. **5** the act or an instance of telling; account. **6** *Mathematics.* a property, as of equality or inequality, by which an ordered pair of quantities, expressions, etc. is associated.
in or **with relation to, a** in connection with: *Viewed in relation to current educational trends, the board chairperson's offhand remarks take on great importance.* **b** in comparison or proportion to: *Spending has gone up incredibly in relation to per capita income.* ⟨< L *relatio, -onis* < *relatus.* See RELATE.⟩

re•la•tion•al [rɪ'leiʃənəl] *adj.* **1** that relates. **2** having to do with relations. **3** specifying or indicating a relation.

re•la•tion•ship [rɪ'leiʃən,ʃɪp] *n.* **1** a connection or a particular instance of a connection; often, specifically, dealings between two persons or parties. **2** the condition of being related.

rel•a•tive ['rɛlətɪv] *n., adj.* —*n.* **1** a person who belongs to the same family as another, such as father, brother, aunt, etc. **2** RELATIVE PRONOUN.
—*adj.* **1** related or compared to each other: *Before ordering our dinner, we considered the relative merits of fried chicken and roast beef.* **2** depending for meaning on a relation to something else: *East is a relative term; for example, Regina is east of Vancouver but west of Toronto.* **3** *Grammar.* **a** designating a pronoun or pronominal adverb introducing a subordinate clause and having an antecedent in the main clause. **b** designating the clause introduced in this way, which gives more information about that antecedent. *Example: In* The man who wanted it is gone, who *is a relative pronoun, and* who wanted it *is a relative clause.*
relative to, a about; concerning: *a letter relative to my proposal.* **b** in proportion to: *He is strong relative to his size. This subject is little understood relative to its importance.* ⟨ME < LL *relativus* < L *relatus.* See RELATE.⟩ **—'rel•a•tiv,ize,** *v.*

relative clause an adjective clause introduced by a relative pronoun, **that, which,** or **who,** or a relative adverb, **where, when, why.** *Examples: The ball* that had been lost *was found by the caddy. Mike's plane,* which was lost in the storm, *landed safely in a field. They asked for a student* who would volunteer to play Santa Claus. *That is the place* where she lived. See also RESTRICTIVE CLAUSE.

relative pronoun the relative pronouns are **that, which (of which, whose)** and **who (whose, whom).** They introduce relative clauses and refer to an antecedent in the main clause. *Examples: A man* who *was there gave us the details. Our team,* which *scored first, had the advantage.* **Who** refers to people; **which,** to animals or things; and **that,** to animals or things, and, less often, to people.

relative density *Physics.* the ratio of the density of any substance to the density of a particular substance used as a standard. For solids and liquids, the standard is water; for gases, it is air.

relative humidity the ratio between the amount of water vapour actually present in the air and the amount it would take to saturate the air at the same temperature, expressed as a percentage. At 15°C, if the air contains 10 grams of water vapour per cubic metre, its relative humidity is about 80 percent; at 30°C with the same amount of water vapour, the air has a relative humidity of about 33 percent, because warmer air can hold more water vapour. Compare ABSOLUTE HUMIDITY.

rel•a•tive•ly ['rɛlətɪvli] *adv.* in a relative manner; in relation to something else; comparatively: *a relatively small difference.*

rel•a•tiv•ism ['rɛlətɪ,vɪzəm] *n. Philosophy.* any theory of knowledge or ethics which holds that all judgments or criteria of value are relative, varying with individuals, circumstances, cultures, etc. **—'rel•a•tiv•ist,** *n.* **—,rel•a•tiv'ist•ic,** *adj.*

rel•a•tiv•i•ty [,rɛlə'tɪvɪti] *n.* **1** the state or quality of being relative. **2** *Physics.* the character of being relative rather than absolute, as ascribed to motion or velocity. **3** *Physics.* a theory formulated by Albert Einstein in the equation $E = mc^2$ (energy = mass × the square of the speed of light). The **special theory of relativity** is based on the hypothesis that the speed of light is the same when measured by two observers even though one observer is moving at a constant velocity with respect to the other. The **general theory of relativity** is an extension of the special theory to relate the measurements of observers who are accelerated with respect to each other. Essentially, **a** there can be no speed

In each of the words below, **re-** *means* again *or* anew; *the pronunciation of the main part of each word is not changed.*

re'judge	re'kin•dle	re'knit	re'la•bel

greater than that of light in a vacuum, and there is no observable absolute motion, only relative motion. **b** matter and energy are equivalent. **c** time is relative.

re•la•tor [rɪ'leitər] *n.* a person who relates or narrates. ⟨< L⟩

re•lax [rɪ'læks] *v.* **1** loosen up; make or become less stiff or firm: *Relax your muscles to rest them.* **2** make or become less strict or severe; lessen in force: *Discipline is relaxed on the last day of school.* **3** relieve or be relieved from work or effort; give or take recreation or amusement: *Take a vacation and relax.* **4** weaken: *Don't relax your efforts because the examinations are over.* ⟨ME < L *relaxare,* ult. < *re-* back + *laxus* loose. Doublet of RELEASE.⟩ **—re'lax•er,** *n.* **—re'lax•ed•ly** [-'læksɪdli], *adv.*

re•lax•ant [rɪ'læksənt] *n., adj.* *—n.* a substance that relaxes, especially a drug used to relax muscles.
—adj. of, having to do with, or producing relaxation.

re•lax•a•tion [ˌrilæk'seiʃən] *n.* **1** a loosening: *the relaxation of the muscles.* **2** a lessening of strictness, severity, force, etc.: *the relaxation of discipline.* **3** a relief from work or effort; recreation; amusement. **4** the state or condition of being relaxed.

re•lay *n.* ['rilei]; *v.* [rɪ'lei] *or* ['rilei] *n., v.* *—n.* **1** a fresh supply: *New relays of men were sent to the battle front.* **2 a** RELAY RACE. **b** one part of a relay race. **c relays,** a sports meet, or a part of a meet, at which relay races are run. **3** *Sports.* the act of passing on a ball, puck, etc. from one player to another. **4** *Electricity.* an electromagnetic device in which a weak current controls a stronger current. A relay is used in transmitting telegraph or telephone messages over long distances. **5** *Machinery.* a device that extends or reinforces the action or effect of an apparatus. **6 a** one of several persons or groups taking on a job, mission, etc. in turn. **b** a system of working, sending messages, etc. by the use of several people or groups acting in turn.
—v. **1** take and carry farther: *Couriers will relay your message.* **2** *Electricity.* control, operate, or transmit by an electrical relay. **3** receive and then pass to another: *to relay a phone message, to relay a thrown ball.* ⟨ME < OF *relai* reserve pack of hounds, etc., ult. < *re-* back + *laier* leave < Gmc.⟩

re–lay [ri 'lei] *v.* **-laid, -lay•ing.** lay again: *We had to re-lay several of the floor tiles.*

re•lay race ['rilei] a race in which each member of a team runs, swims, etc. only a certain part of the distance and is relieved by a teammate when the turn is completed.

re•lease [rɪ'lis] *v.* **-leased, -leas•ing;** *n.* *—v.* **1** set free, let go, or relieve from confinement, tension, duty, pressure, penalty, etc.: *The prisoner was released. The nurse is released from duty at seven o'clock.* **2** give up (legal right, claim, etc.); make over to another (property, etc.) **3** permit to be published, shown, sold, etc.
—n. **1** a letting go; setting free. **2** freedom; relief from emotional stress or tension. **3** a device for releasing a part or parts of a mechanism. **4** *Law.* **a** the legal surrender of right, estate, etc. to another. **b** a document that accomplishes this. **5** an authorization for publication, exhibition, sale, etc. **6** an article, statement, film, recording, etc. made available for distribution. ⟨ME < OF *relaissier* < L *relaxare.* Doublet of RELAX.⟩ **—re'leas•er,** *n.*

☛ *Syn. v.* **1. Release,** FREE = set loose from something that holds back or keeps confined. **Release** emphasizes relaxing the hold on the person or thing: *He released the brakes of the truck.* **Free** emphasizes giving freedom by removing or unfastening whatever is holding: *She freed the bird from the cage.*

re–lease [ri 'lis] *v.* **-leased, -leas•ing.** lease again: *They have re-leased their apartment for another five years.*

rel•e•gate ['rɛləˌgeit] *v.* **-gat•ed, -gat•ing. 1** send away, usually to a lower position or condition. **2** send into exile; banish. **3** hand over (a matter, task, etc.). **4** assign or refer to a particular class, kind, order, etc. ⟨< L *relegare* < *re-* back + *legare* despatch < *legatus* having a commission < *lex, legis* law⟩ **—ˌrel•e'ga•tion,** *n.*

re•lent [rɪ'lɛnt] *v.* become less harsh, strict, or stubborn; be more tender, merciful, or yielding: *The headmaster relented and allowed Saturday leaves.* ⟨ult. < L *re-* again + *lentus* slow⟩

re•lent•less [rɪ'lɛntlɪs] *adj.* **1** without pity; unyielding; harsh: *The storm raged with relentless fury.* **2** persistent; determined: *Her relentless work finally paid off.* **—re'lent•less•ly,** *adv.*

rel•e•vant ['rɛləvənt] *adj.* bearing upon or connected with the matter in hand; to the point: *relevant questions.* ⟨< L *relevans, -antis* refreshing, ppr. of *relevare,* ult. < *re-* back + *levis* light⟩ **—'rel•e•vance** or **'rel•e•van•cy,** *adj.* **—'rel•e•vant•ly,** *adv.*

☛ *Syn.* See note at PERTINENT.

re•li•a•ble [rɪ'laɪəbəl] *adj.* worthy of trust; that can be depended on: *reliable sources of news.* **—reˌli•a'bil•i•ty** or **re'li•a•ble•ness,** *n.* **—re'li•a•bly,** *adv.*

☛ *Syn.* **Reliable,** TRUSTWORTHY = worthy of being depended on or trusted. **Reliable** suggests that the person or thing it describes can safely be believed or trusted, and counted on to do or be what is expected, wanted, or needed: *I have always found this to be a reliable brand of canned goods.* **Trustworthy,** usually describing people, suggests that they are fully deserving of complete confidence in their truthfulness, honesty, good judgment, justice, etc.: *She is a trustworthy news commentator.*

re•li•ance [rɪ'laɪəns] *n.* **1** trust; dependence: *A child has reliance on his mother.* **2** confidence: *I have every reliance on their judgment.*

re•li•ant [rɪ'laɪənt] *adj.* **1** relying; trusting or depending. **2** confident. **3** self-reliant.

rel•ic ['rɛlɪk] *n.* **1** a thing, custom, etc. that remains from the past: *This ruined bridge is a relic of pioneer days.* **2** something belonging to a holy person, kept as a sacred memorial: *That church is said to house a relic of the True Cross.* **3** an object having interest because of its age or its associations with the past; keepsake; souvenir. **4 relics,** *pl.* remains; ruins. **5** *Linguistics.* an otherwise archaic form still used in a particular speech area. *Example*: gotten *in North America.* ⟨ME < OF *relique* < L *reliquiae,* pl., remains⟩

rel•ict ['rɛlɪkt] *n.* **1** *Archaic.* a widow. **2** *Ecology.* a plant or animal surviving from an earlier period in an environment no longer typical for it. **3** *Geology.* a physical feature, mineral, etc. remaining after the rest has wasted away or been altered. ⟨< Med.L *relicta,* originally fem. pp. of L *relinquere.* See RELINQUISH.⟩

Reliefs (def. 9). The picture on the left is a detail from an ancient Greek sculpture in high relief; the picture on the right is a detail from an ancient Indic sculpture in low relief.

re•lief [rɪ'lif] *n.* **1** the lessening of, or freeing from, a pain, burden, difficulty, etc. **2** something that lessens or frees from pain, burden, difficulty, etc.; aid; help. **3** help, in the form of money, clothes, or food, given to poor people. **4** something that makes a pleasing change or lessens strain. **5** a release from a post of duty, often by the coming of a substitute: *This nurse is on duty from seven in the morning until seven at night, with only two hours' relief.* **6** a change of persons on duty. **7** a person or persons relieving others from duty: *The sentry was waiting for his relief.* **8** *Sculpture, painting, etc.* the projection of figures and designs from a flat surface. **9** a figure or design standing out from the surface from which it is cut, shaped, or stamped: *The panel was decorated with a relief of leaves and flowers.* **10** the appearance of standing out given to a drawing or painting by use of shadow, shading, colour, or line. **11 a** differences in height between the summits and lowlands of a region. **b** these differences as shown by various means on a map. **12** strong, clear manner of presentation; distinctness.
in relief, standing out from a surface, or from other ideas or considerations.
on relief, receiving money to live on from public funds. ⟨ME < AF *relef* < *relever.* See RELIEVE.⟩

relief map a map that shows the different heights of a surface by using shading, colours, etc., or solid materials such as clay.

In each of the words below, **re-** *means* again *or* anew; *the pronunciation of the main part of each word is not changed.*

re'laund•er | **re'learn** | **re'let** | **re'li•cense**

re•lieve [rɪ'liv] *v.* **-lieved, -liev•ing. 1** make less; make easier; reduce the pain or trouble of: *These pills will relieve a headache.* **2** set free: *Your coming relieves me of the bother of writing a long letter.* **3** rid: *May I relieve you of that used paper plate and cup?* **4** bring aid to; help: *Soldiers were sent to relieve the fort.* **5** give variety or a pleasing change to: *The plain black dress was relieved by a white collar.* **6** free (a person on duty) by taking his or her place. **7** make stand out more clearly. ⟨ME < OF *relever* < L *relevare* lighten. See RELEVANT.⟩ **—re'liev•er,** *n.*

re•lie•vo [rɪ'livou] *or* [rəl'jɛvou] *n., pl.* **-vos.** *Sculpture, painting, etc.* relief. ⟨< Ital. *rilievo*⟩

re•li•gion [rɪ'lɪdʒən] *n.* **1** belief in or worship of God or gods. **2** a particular system of religious belief and worship: *the Christian religion, the Islamic religion.* **3** a matter of zeal and conscience: *She makes a religion of keeping her house neat.*
get religion, *Informal.* undergo a change of lifestyle, often sudden, from non-belief to the acquisition of a system of beliefs. ⟨< L *religio, -onis* respect for what is sacred, probably originally, care (for worship and traditions) < *relegere* go through again < *re-* again + *legere* read⟩

re•li•gion•ism [rɪ'lɪdʒə,nɪzəm] *n.* excessive religious zeal.

re•li•gi•os•i•ty [rɪ,lɪdʒi'ɒsəti] *n.* an affectation of religious feelings.

re•li•gious [rɪ'lɪdʒəs] *adj., n., pl.* **re•li•gious.** *—adj.* **1** of religion; connected with religion. **2** much interested in religion; devoted to the worship of God or gods. **3 a** belonging to an order of monks, nuns, friars, etc. **b** of or connected with such an order. **4** strict; very careful: *We paid religious attention to the doctor's orders.*
—n. **1** a monk, nun, friar, etc.; member of a religious order. **2** such persons collectively. ⟨ME < OF < L *religiosus* < *religio.* See RELIGION.⟩ **—re'li•gious•ly,** *adv.* **—re'li•gious•ness,** *n.*

re•lin•quish [rɪ'lɪŋkwɪʃ] *v.* give up; let go: *The small dog relinquished its bone to the big dog. She has relinquished all hope of going to Europe this year.* ⟨ME < OF *relinquiss-*, a stem of *relinquir* < L *relinquere* < *re-* behind + *linquere* leave⟩
—re'lin•quish•er, *n.* **—re'lin•quish•ment,** *n.*

rel•i•quar•y ['rɛlə,kwɛri] *n., pl.* **-quar•ies.** a small box or other receptacle for a relic or relics. ⟨< MF *reliquaire* < *relique.* See RELIC.⟩

rel•ish ['rɛlɪʃ] *n., v. —n.* **1** a pleasant taste; a good or distinctive flavour: *Hunger gives relish to simple food.* **2** something to add flavour to food. Olives and pickles are relishes. **3** a kind of pickle made of chopped cucumbers, etc. **4** a slight dash (of something): *a relish of cloves in the sauce.* **5** a liking; appetite; enjoyment: *The hungry boy ate with great relish. The teacher has no relish for John's jokes.*
—v. **1** like; enjoy: *A cat relishes cream. She did not relish the prospect of staying after school.* **2** taste or have an agreeable flavour (*of*). ⟨earlier *reles* < OF *reles* remainder < *relesser, relaissier.* See RELEASE.⟩

re•live [ri'lɪv] *v.* **-lived, -living.** experience (an event, etc.) again, especially in one's imagination.

rel•le•no [rə'jeinou] *or* [rəl'jeinou] *adj., n. Mexican cookery. —adj.* filled with cheese: *chilis rellenos.*
—n. a chili relleno. ⟨< Am. Sp.⟩

re•luc•tance [rɪ'lʌktəns] *n.* **1** a reluctant feeling or quality; unwillingness. **2** slowness in action because of unwillingness. **3** *Electricity.* the resistance to magnetic flux offered by a magnetic circuit, equal to the ratio of the force causing the magnetic flux to the magnetic flux itself.

re•luc•tan•cy [rɪ'lʌktənsi] *n.* reluctance.

re•luc•tant [rɪ'lʌktənt] *adj.* **1** unwilling; showing unwillingness: *reluctant approval.* **2** slow to act because unwilling: *He was very reluctant to give his money away.* ⟨< L *reluctans, -antis* struggling against, ppr. of *reluctari,* ult. < *re-* back + *lucta* wrestling⟩ **—re'luc•tant•ly,** *adv.*
☛ *Syn.* **1. Reluctant,** LOATH = unwilling to do something. **Reluctant** suggests struggling against doing something one finds disagreeable or unpleasant, disapproves of, is afraid of, etc.: *He was reluctant to leave her, but he had no choice.* **Loath** suggests unwillingness because one feels the thing to be done is extremely disagreeable or hateful: *His parents were loath to believe their son would steal.*

re•ly [rɪ'laɪ] *v.* **-lied, -ly•ing.** depend; trust (*usually with* **on** *or* **upon**): *Rely on your own efforts.* ⟨ME < OF *relier* < L *religare* bind fast < *re-* back + *ligare* blind⟩
☛ *Syn.* **Rely,** DEPEND = have confidence in someone or something. **Rely** means count on, or put one's trust in, someone or something one has reason to believe will never fail to do what is expected or wanted: *He relies on his parents' advice.* **Depend** suggests confidently taking it for granted, with or without reason, that a person or thing will give the help or support expected or needed, because one is either unable or unwilling to do for oneself: *She depends on her friends to make her decisions.*

rem [rɛm] *n.* the unit for measuring the harm caused by radiation on human tissue. It is equal to the effect of one roentgen of X rays. ⟨< *r*oentgen + *e*quivalent + *m*an⟩

REM [rɛm] RAPID EYE MOVEMENT.

re•main [rɪ'mein] *v., n. —v.* **1** continue in a place; stay: *We remained at the lake till September.* **2** continue to be: *The town remains the same year after year.* **3** be left: *A few apples remain on the trees.*
—n. **remains,** *pl.* **a** what is left. **b** a dead body. **c** a writer's works not yet published at the time of his or her death. **d** things left from the past, such as a building, a monument, or parts of an animal or plant: *the remains of an ancient civilization, fossil remains.* ⟨ME < OF *remanoir* < L *remanere* < *re-* back + *manere* stay⟩
☛ *Syn. v.* **1, 2.** See note at STAY[1].

re•main•der [rɪ'meindər] *n., v. —n.* **1** the part left over; the rest: *After studying for an hour, she spent the remainder of the afternoon in play.* **2** *Arithmetic.* **a** a number left over after subtracting one number from another. *Example: In 9 – 2, the* remainder *is 7.* **b** a number left over after dividing one number by another. *Example: In 14 ÷ 3, the quotient is 4 with a* remainder *of 2.* **3** a copy or a number of copies of a book left in the publisher's hands after sales have dropped considerably or ceased, which the publisher sells at greatly reduced prices.
—v. sell (a book or books) as a remainder. ⟨ME < OF *remaindre,* infin. used as n.⟩

re•make *v.* [ri'meik]; *n.* ['ri,meik] *v.* **-made, -mak•ing;** *n.*
—v. make (something) again or anew.
—n. **1** the act of making again: *I had to do a remake of the pattern.* **2** the thing remade, as a film: *We watched the remake of* Stagecoach *last night.*

re•mand [rɪ'mænd] *v., n. —v.* **1** send back. **2** *Law.* **a** send back (a prisoner or an accused person) into custody. **b** send back (a case) to the court it came from for further action there.
—n. the act of remanding. ⟨ME < LL *remandare* < L *re-* back + *mandare* order⟩

re•mark [rɪ'mɑrk] *v., n. —v.* **1** say; speak; comment. **2** observe; notice.
—n. **1** something said in a few words; a short statement. **2** the act of noticing; observation. ⟨< F *remarquer* < *re-* again + *marquer* mark⟩

re•mark•a•ble [rɪ'mɑrkəbəl] *adj.* worthy of notice; unusual. **—re'mark•a•ble•ness,** *n.* **—re'mark•a•bly,** *adv.*

re•match *n.* ['ri,mætʃ]; *v.* [ri'mætʃ] *n., v. —n.* a second match between the same contestants.
—v. reschedule a match between the same contestants.

re•me•di•a•ble [rɪ'midiəbəl] *adj.* that can be remedied or cured. **—re'me•di•a•bly,** *adv.*

re•me•di•al [rɪ'midiəl] *adj.* **1** intended as a remedy or cure; curing; helping. **2** *Education.* of or having to do with a special course of study designed to improve a student's skills or knowledge in a given area: *remedial math, remedial English.* ⟨< LL *remedialis* < L *remedium.* See REMEDY.⟩ **—re'me•di•al•ly,** *adv.*

re•me•di•a•tion [rɪ,midi'eiʃən] *n.* **1** the correction of something defective. **2** *Education.* the process of overcoming or correcting learning disabilities or deficiencies.

rem•e•di•less ['rɛmədilɪs] *adj.* without remedy; incurable; irreparable.

In each of the words below, **re-** *means* again *or* anew; *the pronunciation of the main part of each word is not changed.*

re'light	**re'loan**	**re'made**	**re'mar•riage**	**re'meas•ure•ment**
re'line	**,re•lo'cate**	**re'make**	**re'mar•ry**	
re'list	**,re•lo'ca•tion**	**,re•man•u'fac•ture**	**re'mas•ter**	
re'load	**re'lock**	**re'map**	**re'meas•ure**	

rem•e•dy [ˈrɛmədi] *n., pl.* **-dies;** *v.* **-died, -dy•ing.** *—n.* **1** anything used to cure or relieve illness: *Aspirin and mustard plaster are two old cold remedies.* **2** anything intended to put right something bad or wrong: *The free movie was a remedy for the children's bad spirits.* **3** *Law.* legal redress; the legal means by which a right is enforced or a wrong redressed.
—v. put right; make right; cure. ⟨ME *remedie* < AF < L *remedium, remederi* < *re-* again + *mederi* heal⟩
☛ *Syn. v.* See note at CURE.

re•mem•ber [rɪˈmɛmbər] *v.* **1** have (something) come into the mind again; call to mind; recall. **2** recall something. **3** keep in mind; take care not to forget. **4** have memory: *Dogs remember.* **5** make a gift to; reward; tip: *Grandfather remembered us all in his will.* **6** mention (a person) as sending friendly greetings; recall to the mind of another: *Remember me to your mother when you see her.* **7** have compassionate regard for; meditate or pray about; honour the memory of: *Let us remember those who gave their lives for our freedom. We should remember the poor in our city. Please remember me on Friday when I go in for brain surgery.* ⟨ME < OF *remembrer* < L *rememorari*, ult. < *re-* again + *memor* mindful of⟩
☛ *Syn.* **1. Remember,** RECALL, RECOLLECT = think of something again by an act of memory. **Remember** emphasizes having something once known or experienced come back into one's mind, sometimes by a conscious effort but often through no act of will: *Do you remember that?* **Recall** emphasizes being able to remember, consciously calling back: *Yes, I recall the incident.* **Recollect,** more formal, particularly suggests a thinking process requiring a conscious or special effort to recall something that has been forgotten: *Now I recollect what he said.*

re•mem•brance [rɪˈmɛmbrəns] *n.* **1** the power to remember; memory. **2** the act of remembering or a state of being remembered. **3** a keepsake; any thing or action that makes one remember a person, place, or event; souvenir. **4 remembrances,** *pl.* greetings.

Remembrance Day *Cdn.* November 11, the day set aside to honour the memory of those in Canada killed in World Wars I and II, and in subsequent wars in which Canada has been involved.

re•mem•branc•er [rɪˈmɛmbrənsər] *n.* a person or thing that reminds one; reminder.

re•mind [rɪˈmaɪnd] *v.* make (one) think (*of* something); cause to remember.

re•mind•er [rɪˈmaɪndər] *n.* a thing or person that helps one remember: *I use string around my finger as a reminder.*

re•mind•ful [rɪˈmaɪndfəl] *adj.* **1** reviving a memory; reminiscent. **2** retaining a memory of something; remembering.

rem•i•nisce [ˌrɛməˈnɪs] *v.* **-nisced, -nisc•ing.** talk or think about past experiences or events. ⟨< a *reminiscence*⟩

rem•i•nis•cence [ˌrɛməˈnɪsəns] *n.* **1** a remembering; recalling past happenings, etc. **2** Often, **reminiscences,** *pl.* an account of something remembered; recollection: *reminiscences of the war.* **3** something that makes one remember or think of something else. **4** a memory or mental impression recollected; something remembered. **5** the quality of being reminiscent. ⟨< L *reminiscentia*, ult. < *reminisci* remember < *re-* again + *men-* think⟩

rem•i•nis•cent [ˌrɛməˈnɪsənt] *adj.* **1** recalling past events, etc.: *reminiscent talk.* **2** awakening memories of something else; suggestive: *a manner reminiscent of a statelier age.* **—ˌrem•iˈnis•cent•ly,** *adv.*

re•mise [rɪˈmaɪz] *v.* **-mised, -mis•ing.** *Law.* give up a claim to; surrender by deed.

re•miss [rɪˈmɪs] *adj.* careless; slack; neglectful; negligent: *A police officer who fails to report a crime is remiss in her duty.* ⟨< L *remissus*, pp. of *remittere* < *re-* back + *mittere* let go⟩ **—reˈmiss•ness,** *n.*

re•mis•si•ble [rɪˈmɪsəbəl] *adj.* that can be remitted. **—re,mis•siˈbil•i•ty,** *n.*

re•mis•sion [rɪˈmɪʃən] *n.* **1** a letting off (from debt, punishment, etc.): *The bankrupt sought remission of his debts.* **2** pardon; forgiveness: *Remission of sins is promised to those who repent.* **3** a lessening or apparent disappearance (of pain, force, labour, etc.). **4** a cessation, temporary or permanent, of a disease: *Her cancer is in remission.* **—reˈmis•sive,** *adj.*

re•mit [rɪˈmɪt] *v.* **-mit•ted, -mit•ting. 1** send money to a person or place: *Enclosed is our bill; please remit.* **2** send (money due): *Please remit payment.* **3** refrain from carrying out; refrain from exacting; cancel: *The queen remitted the prisoner's sentence.* **4** pardon; forgive: *power to remit sins.* **5** make less; decrease: *After we had rowed the boat into calm water, we remitted our efforts.* **6** become less or stop. **7** *Law.* send back (a case) to a lower court for further action. **8** defer. ⟨ME < L *remittere* send back, let go. See REMISS.⟩ **—reˈmit•ta•ble,** *adj.* **—reˈmit•ter,** *n.*

re•mit•tal [rɪˈmɪtəl] *n.* remission.

re•mit•tance [rɪˈmɪtəns] *n.* **1** the act of sending money to someone at a distance. **2** the money that is sent.

remittance man *Cdn.* formerly, a man who lived abroad on money sent from his relatives at home, often to ensure that he did not return to the Old Country to become an embarrassment to the family.

re•mit•tent [rɪˈmɪtənt] *adj.* lessening for a time; lessening at intervals: *a remittent fever.* **—reˈmit•tent•ly,** *adv.*

rem•nant [ˈrɛmnənt] *n.* **1** a remaining or leftover part or quantity, often small. **2** a piece of cloth, ribbon, lace, etc., left after the rest has been used or sold: *She bought a silk remnant at the sale.* ⟨ME < OF *remenant*, ppr. of *remenoir* remain < L *remanere.* See REMAIN.⟩

re•mod•el [riˈmɒdəl] *v.* **-elled** or **-eled, -el•ling** or **-el•ing. 1** model again. **2** make over; change or alter: *The old barn was remodelled into a house.*

re•mon•e•tize [riˈmɒnə,taɪz] *or* [riˈmʌnə,taɪz] *v.* **-tized, -tiz•ing.** restore to use as legal tender: *to remonetize silver.* **—reˌmon•e•tiˈza•tion,** *n.*

re•mon•strance [rɪˈmɒnstrəns] *n.* a protest; complaint in speech or writing. ⟨< Med.L *remonstrantia* < *remonstrare.* See REMONSTRATE.⟩

re•mon•strant [rɪˈmɒnstrənt] *adj., n. —adj.* remonstrating; protesting.
—n. a person who remonstrates.

re•mon•strate [rɪˈmɒnstreit] *or* [ˈrɛmən,streit] *v.* **-strat•ed, -strat•ing. 1** speak, reason, or plead in complaint or protest: *The supervisor remonstrated with the worker about his slackness.* **2** present arguments in protest or complaint. ⟨< Med.L *remonstrare* point out, ult. < L *re-* back + *monstrum* sign⟩ **—reˈmon•stra•tor,** *n.* **—ˌre•monˈstra•tion,** *n.* **—reˈmon•stra•tive,** *adj.* **—reˈmon•stra•tive•ly,** *adv.*

rem•o•ra [ˈrɛmərə] *or* [rəˈmɔrə] *n.* any of a family (Echeneidae) of fishes of warm seas having the front dorsal fin modified into a flat sucking disk on the head, by means of which they attach themselves to larger fish or to ships, rocks, etc. ⟨< L *remora* hindrance < *re-* re- + *mora* delay; from the idea that these fish delayed ships. 16c. See MORATORIUM.⟩

re•morse [rɪˈmɔrs] *n.* deep, painful regret for having done wrong: *Because he felt remorse for his crime, the thief confessed.* ⟨< L *remorsus* tormented, ult. < *re-* back + *mordere* bite⟩
☛ *Syn.* See note at REGRET.

re•morse•ful [rɪˈmɔrsfəl] *adj.* feeling or expressing remorse. **—reˈmorse•ful•ly,** *adv.* **—reˈmorse•ful•ness,** *n.*

re•morse•less [rɪˈmɔrslɪs] *adj.* without remorse; pitiless; cruel. **—reˈmorse•less•ly,** *adv.* **—reˈmorse•less•ness,** *n.*

re•mote [rɪˈmout] *adj.* **-mot•er, -mot•est;** *n. —adj.* **1** far away from a given place or time: *Dinosaurs lived in remote ages.* **2** out of the way; secluded: *a remote village.* **3** distantly related or connected: *a remote relative.* **4** slight; faint: *I haven't the remotest idea what you mean.* **5** aloof; distant in manner: *Her attitude toward the visitor was somewhat remote.* **6** not immediate or direct. **7** *Computer technology.* of or by means of a terminal located at some distance from the computer and requiring a communication line: *All of us who use the university computers have to do so in remote mode.* **8** operated by or used for REMOTE CONTROL: *a remote switch.*
—n. REMOTE CONTROL. ⟨ME < L *remotus*, pp. of *removere* remove. See REMOVE.⟩ **—reˈmote•ly,** *adv.* **—reˈmote•ness,** *n.*
☛ *Syn.* **1.** See note at DISTANT.

remote control **1** control from a distance, usually by electrical impulses or radio signals. **2** the device used to control

In each of the words below, **re-** *means* again *or* anew; *the pronunciation of the main part of each word is not changed.*

reˈmelt	**reˈmo•bi,lize**	**reˈmod•i,fy**	**reˈmould**
reˈmix	**ˌre•mod•i•fiˈca•tion**	**reˈmort•gage**	

the operation of a television set, VCR, slide projector, garage door opener, etc. **—re'mote-con'trol,** *adj.*

re•mount *v.* [ri'maʊnt]; *n.* ['rimaʊnt] *or* [ri'maʊnt] *v., n.* *—v.* **1** mount again. **2** furnish with fresh horses.
—n. a fresh horse, or a supply of fresh horses, for use in place of others.

re•mov•al [rɪ'muvəl] *n.* **1** a removing; a taking away: *We paid ten dollars for garbage removal.* **2** a change of place: *The store announces its removal to larger quarters.* **3** a dismissal from an office or position.

re•move [rɪ'muv] *v.* **-moved, -mov•ing;** *n.* *—v.* **1** move from a place or position; take off; take away: *Remove your hat.* **2** get rid of; put an end to: *to remove all doubt.* **3** kill. **4** dismiss from an office or position: *to remove an official for taking bribes.* **5** go away; move oneself to another place.
—n. **1** a moving away. **2** a step or degree of distance: *His cruelty was only one remove from crime.* **3** the distance by which one thing is separated from another: *at a far remove from the centre of business.* ⟨ME < OF < L *removere* < *re-* back + *movere* move⟩ **—re'mov•a•ble,** *adj.* **—re'mov•er,** *n.*

re•moved [rɪ'muvd] *adj., v.* *—adj.* **1** distant; remote. **2** separated by one or more steps or degrees of relationship: *She is my first cousin once removed.*
—v. pt. and pp. of REMOVE.

re•mu•ner•ate [rɪ'mjunə,reit] *v.* **-at•ed, -at•ing.** pay for work, services, trouble, etc.; reward. ⟨< L *remunerare,* ult. < *re-* back + *munus* gift⟩ **—re,mu•ner'a•tion,** *n.*
☛ *Syn.* See note at PAY[1].

re•mu•ner•a•tive [rɪ'mjunərətɪv] *or* [rɪ'mjunə,reitɪv] *adj.* paying; profitable. **—re'mu•ner•a•tive•ly,** *adv.*

Re•mus ['rimәs] *n. Roman mythology.* the twin brother of Romulus. See ROMULUS.

ren•ais•sance ['rɛnə,sɑns] *or* [,rɛnə'sɑns] *n., adj.* *—n.* **1** a revival; new birth. **2 the Renaissance, a** the great revival of art, literature, and classical learning in Europe during the 14th, 15th, and 16th centuries. **b** the period of time when this revival occurred. **c** in art, architecture, etc., a style developed in this period and characterized by the simplicity, elegance, and proportion of classical Greek and Roman models. **3** any similar revival of the arts.
—adj. **Renaissance,** of, pertaining to, or characteristic of the Renaissance. ⟨< F *renaissance* < *renaître* be born again, ult. < L *renasci.* See RENASCENT.⟩
☛ *Usage.* **Renaissance.** The word is capitalized when it refers to the period of history: *art of the Renaissance.* It is not capitalized when it refers to a revival: *a renaissance of interest in old-time melodramas.*

Renaissance man or **woman** someone who has acquired extensive knowledge of or proficiency in a wide range of fields.

re•nal ['rinəl] *adj.* **1** of or having to do with the kidneys. **2** near the kidney: *the renal arteries.* See KIDNEY for picture. ⟨< L *renalis* < *ren* kidney⟩

re•name [ri'neim] *v.* **-named, -nam•ing.** give a new name to; name again.

re•nas•cence [rɪ'næsəns] *or* [rɪ'neisəns] *n.* **1** a revival; new birth; renewal. **2** a being renascent. **3 the Renascence,** the Renaissance.

re•nas•cent [rɪ'næsənt] *or* [rɪ'neisənt] *adj.* being born again; reviving; springing again into being or vigour. ⟨< L *renascens, -entis,* ppr. of *renasci* < *re-* again + *nasci* be born⟩

ren•coun•ter [rɛn'kaʊntər] *n., v. Rare.* *—n.* **1** a hostile meeting; conflict; battle; duel. **2** a chance meeting.
—v. encounter casually. ⟨< F *rencontre* < *rencontrer* meet < re- again + *encontrer* encounter⟩

rend [rɛnd] *v.* **rent, rend•ing.** *Archaic or poetic.* **1** pull apart violently; tear: *Wolves will rend a lamb.* **2** split: *Lightning rent the tree.* **3** disturb violently: *Her mind was rent by doubt.* **4** remove with force or violence: *He rent the sword from the knight's hand.* ⟨OE *rendan*⟩ **—'rend•er,** *n.*

ren•der ['rɛndər] *v.* **1** cause to become; make: *An accident has rendered her helpless.* **2** give; do (for): *He rendered us a great service by his help.* **3** offer for consideration, approval, payment, etc.; hand in; report: *The treasurer rendered an account of all the money spent.* **4** make a statement of: *The jury will render their verdict soon.* **5** give in return: *Render thanks for kindness.* **6** pay as due: *The conquered rendered tribute to the conqueror.* **7 a** bring out the meaning of; represent. **b** perform or act; play or sing (music): *The actor rendered the part of Hamlet well. The pianist rendered the difficult passage with a light touch.* **8** change from one language to another; translate: *For homework, the class had to render a passage of Cicero from Latin into English.* **9** give up; surrender. **10** melt (fat, etc.); clarify or extract by melting. Fat from pigs is rendered into lard. ⟨ME < OF *rendre* < VL *rendere,* alteration of L *reddere* give as due, pay < *re-* as due + *dare* give; influenced by L *prendere* take⟩ **—'ren•der•a•ble,** *adj.* **—'ren•der•er,** *n.*

ren•der•ing ['rɛndərɪŋ] *n., v.* *—n.* **1** an interpretation in music or painting: *Her rendering of Beethoven is quite remarkable.* **2** a translation. **3** a representation in perspective drawing of a building, monument, interior, etc., giving the architect's or planner's vision of the furnished product.
—v. ppr. of RENDER.

ren•dez•vous ['rɒndei,vu]; *French,* [Rɑ̃de'vu] *n., pl.* **-vous** [-,vuz], *v.* **-voused** [-,vud], **-vous•ing** [-,vuɪŋ] *—n.* **1** an appointment or engagement to meet at a fixed place or time; a meeting by agreement. **2** a usual or habitual meeting place; gathering place: *The family had two favourite rendezvous, the library and the garden.* **3** a place agreed on for a meeting at a certain time, especially of ships, troops, or aircraft.
—v. **1** meet or come together at a rendezvous. **2** bring together at a rendezvous. ⟨< F *rendezvous* < *rendez-vous* betake yourself!⟩

ren•di•tion [rɛn'dɪʃən] *n.* **1** the act of rendering. **2** a performance of a dramatic part, musical composition, etc. **3** translation. ⟨< MF *rendition* < OF *rendre.* See RENDER.⟩

ren•e•gade ['rɛnə,geid] *n.* **1** a deserter from a religious faith, a political party, etc.; traitor. **2** an outlaw. **3** (*adjl.*) deserting; disloyal; like a traitor. ⟨< Sp. *renegado* < Med.L *renegatus,* pp. of *renegare* deny. See RENEGE.⟩

re•nege [rɪ'nɛg], [rɪ'neig], *or* [rɪ'nɪg] *v.* **-neged, -neg•ing;** *n.* *—v.* **1** *Card games.* fail to play a card of the suit that is led, although you have one. It is against the rules to renege. **2** *Informal.* back out; fail to keep a promise.
—n. Card games. a failure to follow suit when able to do so. ⟨< Med.L *renegare* < L *re-* back + *negare* deny⟩ **—re'neg•er,** *n.*

re•new [rɪ'nju] *or* [rɪ'nu] *v.* **1** make new again; make like new; restore. **2** make spiritually new. **3** begin again; get again; say, do, or give again: *to renew an attack, one's youth, one's vows, one's efforts.* **4** replace by new material or a new thing of the same sort; fill again. **5** give or get for a new period: *We renewed the lease for another year.* **6** renew a lease, note, etc. **7** become new again; regain strength or freshness. **—re'new•a•ble,** *adj.* **—re'new•er,** *n.*
☛ *Syn.* **1. Renew,** RESTORE, RENOVATE = put back in a new or former condition. **Renew** = put back in a condition like new something that has lost its freshness, force, or vigour. *She renewed the finish on the table.* **Restore** = put back in its original, former, or normal condition something that has been damaged, worn out, partly ruined, etc.: *That old pioneer fort has been restored.* **Renovate** = put in good condition or make like new by cleaning, repairing, redecorating, altering, etc.: *The store was renovated.*

re•new•al [rɪ'njuəl] *or* [rɪ'nuəl] *n.* **1** a renewing or being renewed. **2** something renewed, such as a magazine subscription.

re•new•ed•ly [rɪ'njuɪdli] *or* [rɪ'nuɪdli] *adv.* anew.

ren•i•form ['rɛnə,fɔrm] *or* ['rinə,fɔrm] *adj.* suggesting a kidney in shape or outline: *The marsh marigold has reniform leaves.* See LEAF for picture. ⟨< L *ren, renis* kidney + E *form*⟩

re•nin ['rinɪn] *n. Biochemistry.* a protolytic enzyme found in the kidneys, that causes hypertension when released into the bloodstream.

ren•net ['rɛnɪt] *n.* **1** the lining of the abomasum, usually of a calf. **2** an extract of this containing rennin, used for making cheese and junket. ⟨ME *rennet* < *renne(n)* run, OE *rinnan*⟩

ren•nin ['rɛnən] *n. Biochemistry.* an enzyme in the gastric juice that coagulates or curdles milk. ⟨< *rennet*⟩

re•nounce [rɪ'naʊns] *v.* **-nounced, -nounc•ing. 1** give up entirely, especially by making a formal declaration: *She renounced her claim to the money.* **2** cast off; refuse to recognize as one's own: *He renounced his wicked son.* **3** *Card games.* play a

In each of the words below, **re-** *means* again *or* anew; *the pronunciation of the main part of each word is not changed.*

re'mul•ti,ply **re'nom•i,nate** **,re•nom•i'na•tion** **,re•no•ti•fi'ca•tion** **re'no•ti,fy**

card of a different suit from that led. ⟨ME < OF *renoncer* < L *renuntiare,* ult. < *re-* back + *nuntius* message⟩
—re'nounce•ment, *n.*

ren•o•vate ['rɛnə,veit] *v.* **-vat•ed, -vat•ing.** make new again; make like new; restore to good condition; remodel: *to renovate a garment or a house.* ⟨< L *renovare,* ult. < *re-* again + *novus* new⟩
—'ren•o,va•tor, *n.*
☛ *Syn.* See note at RENEW.

ren•o•va•tion [,rɛnə'veiʃən] *n.* **1** a restoration to good condition; renewal or remodelling. **2 renovations,** *pl.* things done, or changes made, to accomplish this.

re•nown [rɪ'naʊn] *n.* the condition of being widely known; fame. ⟨ME < AF *renoun,* ult. < L *re-* repeatedly + *nomen* name⟩

re•nowned [rɪ'naʊnd] *adj.* famous.
☛ *Syn.* See note at FAMOUS.

rent[1] [rɛnt] *n., v.* *—n.* **1** a payment, especially when made regularly, for the right to occupy or use another's land, buildings, goods, etc. **2** *Economics.* what is paid for the use of natural resources.
for rent, available in return for rent paid: *That vacant apartment is for rent.*
—v. **1** pay at regular times for the use of (property): *We rent a house from Mr. Jokati.* **2** receive regular pay for the use of (property) (*often with* **out**): *She rents several other houses.* **3** be leased or let for rent: *This house rents for $1550 a month.* ⟨ME < OF *rente,* ult. < L *reddere* render. See RENDER.⟩ **—'rent•a•ble,** *adj.*
—'rent•er, *n.*

rent[2] [rɛnt] *n., adj., v.* *—n.* a torn place; tear; split.
—adj. torn; split.
—v. pt. and pp. of REND. ⟨originally v., var. of *rend*⟩

rent•al ['rɛntəl] *n., adj.* *—n.* **1** an amount received or paid as rent: *The monthly rental of her house is $1500.* **2** something rented or able to be rented. **3** the act of renting.
—adj. **1** of or in rent. **2** that rents or is rented: *a rental car.* ⟨< AF⟩

rent•als•man ['rɛntəlzmən] *n., pl.* **-men.** *Cdn.* in some provinces, an independent quasi-judicial official whose work is to resolve tenancy disputes. Also, **rent review officer.**

ren•tier [rɒn'tjei]; *French,* [Rɑ̃'tje] *n.* a person whose principal income is in the form of rent, dividends, interest, etc. ⟨< F < *rente* revenue + *-ier* -er[2]⟩

re•nun•ci•ate [rɪ'nʌnsi,eit] *v.* **-at•ed, -at•ing.** give up formally; renounce; disclaim.

re•nun•ci•a•tion [rɪ,nʌnsi'eiʃən] *n.* **1** a giving up of a right, title, possession, etc.; a renouncing. **2** a spoken or written declaration of this. ⟨< L *renuntiatio, -onis* < *renuntiare.* See RENOUNCE.⟩

re•o•pen [ri'oupən] *v.* **1** open again. **2** bring up again for discussion: *The matter is settled and cannot be reopened.*

re•or•der [ri'ɔrdər] *v., n.* *—v.* **1** put in order again; rearrange. **2** give a second or repeated order for goods; order again.
—n. a second or repeated order for goods.

re•or•gan•i•za•tion [ri,ɔrgənɪ'zeiʃən] *or* [ri,ɔrgənaɪ'zeiʃən] *n.* the act of reorganizing or the state of being reorganized.

re•or•gan•ize [ri'ɔrgə,naɪz] *v.* **-ized, -iz•ing. 1** organize anew; form again; arrange in a new way: *Classes will be reorganized after the first four weeks.* **2** form a new company to operate (a business in the hands of a receiver). **—re'or•gan,iz•er,** *n.*

rep[1] [rɛp] *n.* a heavy, ribbed fabric of wool, silk, cotton, etc. Also, **repp.** ⟨< F *reps* < E *ribs*⟩

rep[2] [rɛp] *n.* representative: *The company has hired several new sales reps.* ⟨clipped form⟩

rep[3] [rɛp] *n. Informal.* repertory (theatre): *She's playing in rep these days.* ⟨clipped form⟩

rep. **1** report; reported; reporter. **2** representative.

Rep. **1** Representative. **2** Republican; Republic.

re•pack•age [ri'pækɪdʒ] *v.* **-aged, -ag•ing. 1** package again in a better or more attractive form. **2** package (a bulk commodity) for sale under one's own label: *Many stores repackage products like detergents, candies,* etc.

re•paid [rɪ'peid] *v.* pt. and pp. of REPAY.

re•pair[1] [rɪ'pɛr] *v., n.* *—v.* **1** put in good condition again; mend; restore: *He repairs shoes.* **2** make up for; remedy; set right: *How can I repair the harm done?*
—n. **1** the act or work of repairing: *The repair of the school building was undertaken during the summer.* **2** an instance or piece of repairing: *The repair to the roof was badly done; it still leaks.* **3** a condition fit to be used: *Keeping highways in repair is a provincial responsibility.* **4** a condition with regard to the need for repairs: *The house was in bad repair.* ⟨ME < L *reparare* < *re-* again + *parare* prepare⟩ **—re'pair•er,** *n.*
☛ *Syn. v.* **1.** See note at MEND.

re•pair[2] [rɪ'pɛr] *v. Formal.* go (to a place): *After dinner we repaired to the balcony. Half of Victoria repairs to California in January.* ⟨ME < OF *repairer* < LL *repatriare* return to one's own country. Doublet of REPATRIATE.⟩

re•pair•a•ble [rɪ'pɛrəbəl] *adj.* capable of being repaired: *Is this old sofa repairable?*
☛ *Syn.* See note at REPARABLE.

re•pair•man [rɪ'pɛr,mæn] *or* [rɪ'pɛrmən] *n., pl.* **-men.** a man whose work is repairing machines, etc.

rep•a•ra•ble ['rɛpərəbəl] *adj.* that can be repaired or remedied. ⟨< L *reparabilis* < *reparare.* See REPAIR[1].⟩
—'rep•a•ra•bly, *adv.*
☛ *Syn.* **Reparable,** REPAIRABLE = capable of being repaired, remedied. **Repairable** is more often used with physical objects like shoes, furniture, etc. *These shoes are not repairable; I'll have to buy a new pair.* **Reparable** refers more to things like reputations, relations between people, etc.: *The business partners do not believe the rift between them is reparable.*

rep•a•ra•tion [,rɛpə'reiʃən] *n.* **1** a giving of satisfaction or compensation for wrong or injury done. **2** a compensation for wrong or injury: *How can we make reparation for the damage done to your reputation?* **3** Usually, **reparations,** *pl.* compensation demanded from a defeated enemy for the devastation of territory during war. **4** a repairing or being repaired; restoration to good condition. ⟨< LL *reparatio, -onis* < *reparare.* See REPAIR[1].⟩

rep•ar•tee [,rɛpər'ti] *or* [,rɛpɑr'ti] *n.* **1** a witty reply or replies. **2** talk characterized by clever and witty replies. **3** cleverness and wit in making replies. ⟨< F *repartie* < *repartir* reply, ult. < L *re-* back + *pars, partis* part⟩

re•pass [ri'pæs] *v.* **1** pass back. **2** pass again.

re•past [rɪ'pæst] *n.* **1** a meal; food. **2** a taking of food; eating: *a brief repast.* ⟨ME < OF *repast,* ult. < L *re-* again + *pascere* feed⟩

re•pa•tri•ate *v.* [ri'peitri,eit] *or* [ri'pætri,eit]; *n.* [ri'peitriɪt] *or* [ri'pætriɪt] *v.* **-at•ed, -at•ing;** *n.* *—v.* send back or restore to one's own country: *After peace was declared, refugees and prisoners of war were repatriated.*
—n. a person who is sent back to his or her own country. ⟨< LL *repatriare,* ult. < L *re-* back + *patria* native land. Doublet of REPAIR[2].⟩

re•pa•tri•a•tion [ri,peitri'eiʃən] *or* [ri,pætri'eiʃən] *n.* **1** the act or an instance of repatriating. **2 Repatriation,** *Cdn.* the return of the Statute of Westminster from the United Kingdom to Canada as the Canadian Constitution in 1982.

re•pay [rɪ'pei] *v.* **-paid, -pay•ing. 1** pay back; give back: *He repaid the money he had borrowed.* **2** make return for: *No thanks can repay such kindness.* **3** make return to; reward: *The boy's success repaid the teacher for her efforts.* **4** act similarly in return for: *to repay a visit.* ⟨< MF *repaier* < *re-* back (< L) + *paier* pay < L *pacare* pacify < *pax, pacis* peace⟩ **—re'pay•a•ble,** *adj.*
—re'pay•ment, *n.*

re•peal [rɪ'pil] *v., n.* *—v.* take back; withdraw; do away with: *A law may be repealed by act of Parliament.*
—n. the act of repealing; withdrawal; abolition: *She voted for the*

In each of the words below, **re-** *means* again *or* anew; *the pronunciation of the main part of each word is not changed.*

re'num•ber	**,re•oc'cur**	**,re•op'pose**	**re'pack**	**re'pave**
,re•ob'serve	**,re•oc'cur•rence**	**,re•or'dain**	**re'pack•age**	
,re•oc•cu'pa•tion	**re-'of•fer**	**re-'o•ri•ent**	**re'paint**	
re-'oc•cu,py	**re-'oil**	**,re-o•ri•en'ta•tion**	**re'pa•per**	

repeal of that law. ⟨ME < AF *repeler*, alteration of OF *rapeler* < *re-* back + *apeler* call < L *ad-* up + *pellare* call⟩

re•peat [rɪ'pit] *v., n.* —*v.* **1** do or make again; undergo again: *to repeat an error.* **2** say again: *to repeat a word for emphasis.* **3** say over; recite: *to repeat a poem from memory.* **4** say after another says: *Repeat the oath after me.* **5** tell to another or others: *I promised not to repeat the secret.* **6** recur (*usually reflexive*): *History repeats itself.* **7** be tasted again by belching: *Those onions have been repeating on me all evening.*
repeat oneself, say what one has already said.
—*n.* **1** the act of repeating. **2** a thing repeated: *We saw the repeat on television.* **3** *Music.* **a** a passage to be repeated. **b** a sign indicating this, usually a vertical arrangement of dots. Coming after a double bar line, it indicates the beginning of the passage to be repeated; before a double bar line, it indicates the end of the passage. ⟨< L *repetere* attack again < *re-* again + *petere* aim at⟩

☛ *Syn. v.* **1, 2. Repeat,** REITERATE = do or say again. **Repeat** is the common word meaning 'say, do, make, or perform something over again, once or many times': *The Glee Club will repeat the program next week.* **Reiterate,** more formal, means 'repeat again and again something said or a statement, objection, accusation, etc. made': *For months we reiterated our requests for better bus service.*

re•peat•a•ble [rɪ'pitəbəl] *adj.* **1** that can be repeated. **2** fit or decent enough to be repeated: *His jokes were not repeatable in mixed company.* **—re,peat•a'bil•i•ty,** *n.*

re•peat•ed [rɪ'pitɪd] *adj., v.* —*adj.* said, done, made, or happening a number of times: *repeated offers, repeated calls for help.*
—*v.* pt. and pp. of REPEAT.

re•peat•ed•ly [rɪ'pitɪdli] *adv.* again and again; more than once.

re•peat•er [rɪ'pitər] *n.* **1** REPEATING RIFLE. **2** a watch or clock that, if a spring is pressed, strikes again the hour it struck last. **3** a student who takes a course again or fails to pass on to the next grade. **4** *Informal.* a person who is repeatedly sent to a prison or reformatory; habitual criminal. **5 a** a device that amplifies voice sounds in telephonic communication. **b** a similar device for amplifying and relaying radio, telegraph, and radar signals. **6** any person or thing that repeats.

repeating decimal *Mathematics.* a decimal in which there is an indefinite repetition of the same figure or series of figures. *Examples*: .3333+, .2323+, 1.43666+

repeating rifle a rifle that fires several shots without being reloaded.

re•pel [rɪ'pɛl] *v.* **-pelled, -pel•ling. 1** force back; drive back; drive away: *They repelled the enemy.* **2** keep off or out; fail to mix with: *Oil and water repel each other. This tent repels moisture.* **3** ward off, as with a chemical substance or sound: *Mosquitoes are said to be repelled by very high-pitched tones.* **4** *Physics.* force apart or away by some inherent force. Particles with similar electric charges repel each other. **5** be displeasing (to); cause disgust (in). **6** reject. ⟨ME < L *repellere* < *re-* back + *pellere* drive⟩

re•pel•lent [rɪ'pɛlənt] *adj., n.* —*adj.* **1** unattractive; disagreeable. **2** repelling; driving back. **3** proof to a certain extent against some substance, etc.: *a water-repellent fabric.*
—*n.* something that repels, especially a substance or device used to keep away insects, such as mosquitoes or black flies.

re•pent [rɪ'pɛnt] *v.* **1** feel sorrow or remorse for one's sins or errors, to the extent of rejecting one's former behaviour and changing one's ways. **2** feel remorse for; regret: *to repent one's choice.* ⟨ME < OF *repentir*, ult. < L *re-* repeatedly + *paenitere* cause to regret⟩ **—re'pent•er,** *n.*

re•pent•ance [rɪ'pɛntəns] *n.* **1** sorrow for doing wrong. **2** sorrow; regret. **3** the rejection of one's old attitudes and actions in favour of new ones.

re•pent•ant [rɪ'pɛntənt] *adj.* repenting; feeling or showing repentance or regret; sorry for wrongdoing. ⟨< OF *repentant*, ppr. of *repentir.* See REPENT.⟩ **—re'pent•ant•ly,** *adv.*

re•per•cus•sion [,ripər'kʌʃən] *n.* **1** an indirect influence or reaction from an event. **2** a sound flung back; echo. **3** a springing back; rebound; recoil. ⟨< L *repercussio, -onis*, ult. < *re-* back + *per-* thoroughly + *quatere* beat⟩

rep•er•toire ['rɛpər,twɑr] *n.* **1** the list of plays, operas, parts, pieces, etc. that a company, an actor, a musician, or a singer is prepared to perform. **2** the entire set of skills or techniques that an individual has: *For a two-year-old, his repertoire of cute tricks is quite amazing.* ⟨< F < LL *repertorium.* Doublet of REPERTORY.⟩

rep•er•to•ry ['rɛpər,tɔri] *n., pl.* **-ries. 1** a catalogue or list of things; repertoire. **2** a store or stock of things ready for use. **3** storehouse. **4** the production system of a REPERTORY THEATRE: *The company is performing three plays in repertory.* ⟨< LL *repertorium* inventory, ult. < *reperire* find, get < *re-* again + *parere* get. Doublet of REPERTOIRE.⟩

repertory theatre 1 a theatre in which a company of actors, singers, or dancers present a repertoire of productions for a season. **2** a theatre in which one company presents a different production at regular intervals, such as every week, every two weeks, or every month.

re•pe•tend ['rɛpɪ,tɛnd] *or* [,rɛpɪ'tɛnd] *n.* **1** *Mathematics.* that part of a repeating decimal that is repeated indefinitely. In 1.46333, 3 is the repetend. **2** *Prosody.* a word, phrase, or larger element repeated, sometimes with variation, throughout a poem. **3** *Music.* a figure or phrase that is repeated throughout a composition.

rep•e•ti•tion [,rɛpə'tɪʃən] *n.* **1** the act of repeating; a doing or saying again: *Repetition helps learning. Any repetition of the offence will be punished.* **2** the thing repeated. ⟨< L *repetitio, -onis* < *repetere.* See REPEAT.⟩

rep•e•ti•tious [,rɛpə'tɪʃəs] *adj.* full of repetitions; repeating in a tiresome way. **—,rep•e'ti•tious•ly,** *adv.* **—,rep•e'ti•tious•ness,** *n.*

re•pet•i•tive [rɪ'pɛtətɪv] *adj.* of or characterized by repetition. **—re'pet•i•tive•ly,** *adv.* **—re'pet•i•tive•ness,** *n.*

re•phrase [ri'freiz] *v.* **-phrased, -phras•ing.** phrase again; phrase in a new or different way: *to rephrase a speech, to rephrase a melody.*

re•pine [rɪ'paɪn] *v.* **-pined, -pin•ing.** be discontented; fret; complain. ⟨< *re-* + *pine*[2]⟩

re•place [rɪ'pleis] *v.* **-placed, -plac•ing. 1** fill or take the place of. **2** get another in place of. **3** put back; put in place again; restore; pay back. **—re'place•a•ble,** *adj.* **—re'plac•er,** *n.*

☛ *Syn.* **1. Replace,** SUPERSEDE, SUPPLANT = take the place of another. **Replace** means take or fill as substitute or successor the place formerly held by another: *When one of the players on the team was hurt, another replaced her.* **Supersede,** chiefly used of things, especially suggests causing what is replaced to be put aside as out-of-date, no longer useful, etc.: *Buses have superseded streetcars.* **Supplant** when used of a person especially suggests forcing him or her out and taking over his or her place by scheming or treachery: *The dictator supplanted the president.*

re•place•ment [rɪ'pleismənt] *n.* **1** the act of replacing or the state of being replaced. **2** something or someone that replaces. **3** a person who takes the place of another, such as a member of the armed forces assigned to a particular unit to fill a vacancy.

re•play *v.* [ri'plei]; *n.* ['ri,plei] *v., n.* —*v.* play (a match, etc.) again.
—*n.* **1** a match thus played. **2** a repeated, often slow-motion, showing of part of a television sportscast, or of any sequence on film or videotape. **3** a repeat of any series of actions or events.

re•plen•ish [rɪ'plɛnɪʃ] *v.* fill again; provide a new supply for: *Her wardrobe needs replenishing. Please replenish the fire.* ⟨ME < OF *repleniss-*, a stem of *replenir*, ult. < L *re-* again + *plenus* full⟩ **—re'plen•ish•er,** *n.*

re•plen•ish•ment [rɪ'plɛnɪʃmənt] *n.* **1** a replenishing or being replenished. **2** a fresh supply.

re•plete [rɪ'plit] *adj., n.* —*adj.* **1** abundantly supplied; filled. **2** gorged with food and drink.
—*n. Entomology.* a type of worker ant serving as a repository of stored honeylike substance for later use by the entire colony of ants. ⟨ME < L *repletus*, pp. of *replere* < OF *re-* again + *plere* fill⟩

re•ple•tion [rɪ'pliʃən] *n.* fullness; excessive fullness.

re•plev•in [rɪ'plɛvɪn] *n., v. Law.* —*n.* **1** the recovery by a person of goods allegedly taken from him or her upon his or her giving security that the case shall be tried in court and the goods returned if he or she is defeated. **2** the writ by which the goods are thus recovered.

In each of the words below, **re-** *means* again *or* anew; *the pronunciation of the main part of each word is not changed.*

re'peo•ple	**re'pho•to,graph**	**re'plan**	**re'plate**
,re-pe'ti•tion	**re'pin**	**re'plant**	

—*v.* recover (goods) by replevin. ⟨ME < AF *replevine,* ult. < OF *re-* again + *plevir* pledge⟩

re•ple•vy [rɪ'plɛvi] *v.* **-vied, -vy•ing;** *n., pl.* **-plev•ies.** *Law.* —*v.* recover (possessions or goods) by replevin.
—*n.* the repossession of goods or chattels by a writ of replevin. ⟨ME < MF *replevir* to bail out⟩ **—re'plev•i•a•ble** or **re'plev•i•sa•ble,** *adj.*

rep•li•ca ['rɛpləkə] *n.* a copy; reproduction: *The artist made a replica of her portrait.* ⟨< Ital. *replica* < *replicare* reproduce < L *replicare* unroll. See REPLY.⟩

rep•li•cate *v.* ['rɛplə,keit]; *adj., n.* ['rɛpləkɪt] *v.* **-cat•ed, -cat•ing;** *adj., n.* —*v.* **1** duplicate or repeat as exactly as possible: *to replicate an experiment.* **2** fold or bend (something) back on itself.
—*adj. Botany.* folded back on itself: *a replicate leaf.*
—*n.* any of several identical experiments, procedures, etc.
—'rep•li•ca•ble, *adj.* **—'rep•li,ca•tive,** *adj.*

rep•li•ca•tion [,rɛplə'keiʃən] *n.* **1** the act or process of duplicating or repeating: *the replication of an experiment, the replication of a document.* **2** a copy; reproduction. **3** a reply, especially a rejoinder to an answer. **4** *Law.* REPLY (def. 2).

re•ply [rɪ'plaɪ] *v.* **-plied, -ply•ing;** *n., pl.* **-plies.** —*v.* **1** answer by words or action; answer: *Has he replied to your letter? The rebels replied with a burst of gunfire.* **2** give as an answer: *She replied, "I have no intention of going."* **3** *Law.* answer the defendant's plea.
—*n.* **1** a response or answer. **2** *Law.* the plaintiff's reply to a defendant's plea or counterclaim. ⟨ME < OF *replier* < L *replicare* unroll < *re-* back + *plicare* fold⟩
☛ *Syn. v.* See note at ANSWER.

re•po ['ripou] *n.* repossession. ⟨clipped form⟩

re•port [rɪ'pɔrt] *n., v.* —*n.* **1** an account or statement of facts: *a news report.* **2** an account officially expressed, generally in writing: *an annual report.* **3** the sound of a shot or an explosion. **4** common talk; rumour: *Report has it that our neighbours are leaving town.* **5** reputation.
—*v.* **1** make a report of; announce. **2** give a formal account of; state officially. **3** take down in writing; write an account of. **4** make a report. **5** act as reporter. **6** be answerable or subordinate to: *The supervisor reports directly to the manager.* **7** present; present oneself: *Report for duty at 9 a.m.* **8** announce as a wrongdoer; denounce: *to report someone to the police.* ⟨ME < OF *report* < *reporter* < L *reportare* < *re-* back + *portare* carry⟩

re•port•a•ble [rɪ'pɔrtəbəl] *adj.* **1** capable of being reported. **2** worth reporting; newsworthy: *a reportable news story.*

re•port•age [,rɛpɔr'tɑʒ] *or* [rɪ'pɔrtɪdʒ] *n.* **1** the act or process of reporting news or other factual information, especially in a journalistic style. **2** something reported in a journalistic style, such as a news story or other factual account.

report card a report sent at regular intervals by a school to parents or guardians, showing the quality of a student's work.

re•port•ed•ly [rɪ'pɔrtɪdli] *adv.* according to reports or rumours: *Several firms are reportedly interested in the new design.*

re•port•er [rɪ'pɔrtər] *n.* **1** a person who reports. **2** a person who gathers news for a newspaper, radio station, etc. **3** a person authorized to write the official reports of law cases.

rep•or•to•ri•al [,rɛpər'tɔriəl] *adj.* of or having to do with reporters or reporting. **—,rep•or'to•ri•al•ly,** *adv.*

re•pose[1] [rɪ'pouz] *n., v.* **-posed, -pos•ing.** —*n.* **1** rest or sleep: *Do not disturb her repose.* **2** quietness; ease: *He has repose of manner.* **3** peace; calmness.
—*v.* **1** lie at rest: *The cat reposed upon the cushion.* **2** lie dead: *His body reposed in the funeral home for two days before he was buried.* **3** rest from work or toil; take a rest. **4** be supported. **5** depend; rely (*on*). ⟨< F *repos* < *reposer* < LL *repausare* cause to rest < *re-* again + *pausare* pause⟩ **—re'pose•ful,** *adj.*

re•pose[2] [rɪ'pouz] *v.* **-posed, -pos•ing.** put; place (confidence, trust, faith, etc.) in a person or thing: *We repose complete confidence in his honesty.* ⟨< L *repositus,* pp. of *reponere* < *re-* back + *ponere* place; modelled on verbs ending in *-pose*⟩

re•pos•it [rɪ'pɒzɪt] *v.* put or place for storage or safekeeping: *The will was reposited with the lawyer.* ⟨< L *repositus.* See REPOSE[2].⟩

re•po•si•tion [,ripə'zɪʃən] *v.* position again or differently: *People reposition themselves for personal advantage.*

re•pos•i•to•ry [rɪ'pɒzɪ,tɔri] *n., pl.* **-ries. 1** a place or container where things are stored or kept: *The box was the repository for old magazines.* **2** a person to whom something is confided or entrusted. **3** a person or thing regarded as a source or storehouse. ⟨< L *repositorium* < *reponere* replace. See REPOSE[2].⟩

re•pos•sess [,ripə'zɛs] *v.* possess again; get possession of again, especially from a purchaser who has defaulted on payments: *His car was repossessed after he missed three payments.*

re•pos•ses•sion [,ripə'zɛʃən] *n.* **1** the act of repossessing. **2** that which is repossessed: *I got a good deal on this car because it was a repossession.*

re•pous•sé [rəpu'sei] *adj., n.* —*adj.* **1** of a design, raised in relief by hammering on the reverse side. A repoussé design can be made on thin metal. **2** ornamented or made in this manner.
—*n.* repoussé work. ⟨< F *repoussé* < *re-* back + *pousser* push⟩

repp [rɛp] *n.* See REP[1].

repr. 1 reprinted; reprint. **2** represent; represented; representing.

rep•re•hend [,rɛprɪ'hɛnd] *v.* reprove; rebuke; blame; find fault with; censure. ⟨ME < L *reprehendere,* originally, pull back < *re-* back + *prehendere* grasp⟩

rep•re•hen•si•ble [,rɛprɪ'hɛnsəbəl] *adj.* deserving reproof, rebuke, or blame. **—,rep•re'hen•si•bly,** *adv.* **—,rep•re,hen•si'bil•i•ty,** *n.*

rep•re•hen•sion [,rɛprɪ'hɛnʃən] *n.* reproof; rebuke; blame. ⟨< L *reprehensio, -onis* < *reprehendere.* See REPREHEND.⟩ **—,rep•re'hen•sive,** *adj.* **—,rep•re'hen•sive•ly,** *adv.*

rep•re•sent [,rɛprɪ'zɛnt] *v.* **1** stand for; be a sign or symbol of; indicate: *The stars on this map represent the cities.* **2** act in place of; speak and act for: *People are elected to represent us in the government.* **3** act the part of: *Each child will represent an animal at the party.* **4** show in a picture, statue, carving, etc.; give a likeness of; portray: *This painting represents the Fathers of Confederation.* **5** be a type of; be an example of: *A log represents a very simple kind of boat.* **6** describe; set forth: *She represented the plan as safe.* **7** bring before the mind; make one think of: *His fears represented the undertaking as impossible.* ⟨< L *repraesentare* < *re-* back + *praesentare* present[2]⟩

rep•re•sen•ta•tion [,rɛprɪzɛn'teiʃən] *n.* **1** the act of representing. **2** the condition or fact of being represented: *Taxation without representation is tyranny.* **3** representatives considered as a group. **4** a likeness; picture; model. **5** symbol; sign. **6** a performance of a play; presentation. **7** the process of forming mental images or ideas. **8** a protest; complaint. **9** an account; statement: *false representations.*

rep•re•sen•ta•tion•al [,rɛprɪzɛn'teiʃənəl] *adj.* **1** *Fine Arts.* of or having to do with a style that attempts to portray people, things, etc. as they are. **2** of or having to do with representation. **—,rep•re•sen'ta•tion•al•ly,** *adv.*

rep•re•sen•ta•tion•al•ism [,rɛprɪzɛn'teiʃənə,lɪzəm] *n.* **1** *Philosophy.* the theory that external objects are apprehended in the mind only through ideas or sense data. Compare PRESENTATIONISM. **2** *Fine Arts.* the theory and practice of depicting objects in a recognizable form, especially as they would appear to the human eye.

rep•re•sent•a•tive [,rɛprɪ'zɛntətɪv] *n., adj.* —*n.* **1** a person appointed or elected to act or speak for others: *She is the club's representative at the convention.* **2 Representative,** in the United States, a member of the House of Representatives. **3** a typical example; type: *The tiger is a representative of the cat family.* **4** salesperson: *our sales representatives.*
—*adj.* **1** having its citizens represented by chosen, usually elected, persons: *a representative government.* **2** representing: *Images representative of animals were made by the children.* **3** serving as an example of; typical: *Oak, birch, and maple are representative North American hardwoods.*
—,rep•re'sent•a•tive•ly, *adv.*

re•press [rɪ'prɛs] *v.* **1** prevent from acting; check: *She repressed her desire to laugh.* **2** keep down; put down: *The dictator repressed the revolt.* **3** *Psychoanalysis.* reject (a painful or undesirable memory or impulse) from the conscious mind. ⟨< L

In each of the words below, **re-** *means* again *or* anew; *the pronunciation of the main part of each word is not changed.*

re'pol•ish	**re-'pose**	**,re-pre'sent**
re'pop•u,late	**re'pot**	

repressus, pp. of *reprimere* < *re-* back + *premere* press⟩ **—re'press•er,** *n.* **—re'press•i•ble,** *adj.*

re–press [ri 'prɛs] *v.* **1** press again. **2** make copies of (a recording, etc.) from the original master.

re•pres•sion [rɪ'prɛʃən] *n.* **1** the act of repressing or the state of being repressed. **2** *Psychoanalysis.* **a** a defence mechanism by which unacceptable or painful impulses, emotions, or memories are put out of the conscious mind, their energy or effect remaining (according to Freudian theory) in the unconscious, where they influence personality and behaviour. **b** the thing so repressed.

re•pres•sive [rɪ'prɛsɪv] *adj.* tending to repress; having power to repress. **—re'pres•sive•ly,** *adv.* **—re'pres•sive•ness,** *n.*

re•prieve [rɪ'priv] *v.* **-prieved, -priev•ing;** *n.* *—v.* **1** delay the execution of (a person condemned to death). **2** give relief from any hardship or trouble.
—n. **1 a** a delay in carrying out a punishment, especially of the death penalty. **b** the order authorizing such a delay. **2** a temporary relief from any hardship or trouble. ⟨earlier *repry* < F *repris,* pp. of *reprendre* take back < L *reprehendere* (see REPREHEND); influenced by ME *repreve,* var. of *reprove* in sense of 'retest'⟩

rep•ri•mand ['rɛprə,mænd] *n., v.* *—n.* a severe or formal reproof.
—v. reprove severely or formally. ⟨< F *réprimande* < *réprimer* repress < L *reprimere.* See REPRESS.⟩

re•print *v.* [ri'prɪnt]; *n.* ['riprɪnt] *v., n.* *—v.* print again; print a new impression of.
—n. **1 a** the act of reprinting. **b** the new impression so produced. **c** offprint. **2** *Philately.* a stamp printed from the original plate after the issue has been discontinued.

re•pris•al [rɪ'praɪzəl] *n.* **1** any measure, economic or military, taken in retaliation by one nation against another. **2** any act of retaliation by one person against another. ⟨ME *reprisail* < OF *reprisaille.* See REPRISE.⟩

re•prise [rə'priz] *n., v.* **-prised, -pris•ing.** *—n. Music.* a repetition or return to a previous theme or subject.
—v. Music. present a reprise of (a song, theme, etc.) ⟨ME < MF, a taking back < OF, n. use of fem. pp. of *reprendre* take back < L reprehendere. See REPREHEND.⟩

re•proach [rɪ'proutʃ] *n., v.* *—n.* **1** blame. **2** disgrace. **3** any object or source of blame, censure, or disapproval. **4** an expression of blame, censure, or disapproval: *Her reproaches were hard to take, especially when she was not blameless either.*
—v. **1** blame; rebuke; criticize: *We reproached them for their lack of punctuality.* **2** disgrace. ⟨< F *reproche* < *reprocher* < VL *repropriare* lay at the door of, ult. < L *re-* again + *prope* near⟩
☛ *Syn. v.* **1.** See note at BLAME.

re•proach•ful [rɪ'proutʃfəl] *adj.* full of reproach; expressing reproach. **—re'proach•ful•ly,** *adv.* **—re'proach•ful•ness,** *n.*

re•proach•less [rɪ'proutʃlɪs] *adj.* without reproach; irreproachable.

rep•ro•bate *v.* ['rɛprə,beit]; *n., adj.* ['rɛprə,beit] *or* ['rɛprəbɪt] *n., adj., v.* **-bat•ed, -bat•ing.** *—n.* an unprincipled scoundrel.
—adj. morally abandoned; unprincipled: *reprobate acts.*
—v. disapprove; condemn; censure. ⟨< LL *reprobatus,* pp. of *reprobare* reprove < L *re-* dis- + *probare* approve < *probus* good. Doublet of REPROVE.⟩

rep•ro•ba•tion [,rɛprə'beiʃən] *n.* **1** disapproval; condemnation; censure. **2** a reprobate or condemnable state.

re•pro•duce [,riprə'djus] *or* [,riprə'dus] *v.* **-duced, -duc•ing.** **1** produce again: *A recording reproduces sound.* **2** make a copy of: *to reproduce a memo on a photocopier.* **3** produce offspring: *Most plants reproduce by seeds.* **—,re•pro'duc•er,** *n.* **—,re•pro'duc•i•ble,** *adj.*

re•pro•duc•tion [,riprə'dʌkʃən] *n.* **1** a reproducing or being reproduced. **2** a copy. **3** the process by which offspring are produced.

re•pro•duc•tive [,riprə'dʌktɪv] *adj.* **1** that reproduces. **2** for or concerned with reproduction.
new reproductive technologies, procedures such as in vitro fertilization, embryo transfer, and surrogate motherhood, developed to increase the probability of reproduction.
—,re•pro'duc•tive•ly, *adv.* **—,re•pro'duc•tive•ness,** *n.*

re•prog•ra•phy [rɪ'prɒgrəfi] *n.* the act of reproducing or the right to reproduce copyright material: *Cancopy is the Canadian collective in charge of reprography.* ⟨< *repro*duction + photo*graphy*⟩

re•proof [rɪ'pruf] *n.* words of blame or disapproval; blame. ⟨ME < OF *reprove* < *reprover*; influenced in form by *proof.* See REPROVE.⟩

re•prov•a•ble [rɪ'pruvəbəl] *adj.* deserving reproof.

re•prov•al [rɪ'pruvəl] *n.* a reproving or reproof.

re•prove [rɪ'pruv] *v.* **-proved, -prov•ing.** find fault with; express disapproval to (an offender): *Reprove the boy for teasing the cat.* ⟨ME < OF *reprover* < LL *reprobare.* Doublet of REPROBATE.⟩ **—re'prov•er,** *n.* **—re'prov•ing•ly,** *adv.*
☛ *Syn.* **Reprove,** REBUKE = criticize or scold someone for a fault. **Reprove** suggests expressing disapproval or blame directly to the person at fault, usually with the purpose or hope of correcting the fault: *The principal reproved the students who had been smoking in the locker room.* **Rebuke** means reprove sharply and sternly, with authority and often in public: *The sergeant rebuked the patrol officers who had been neglecting their duty.*

rep•tile ['rɛptaɪl] *n., adj.* *—n.* any of a class (Reptilia) of cold-blooded animals that breathe by means of lungs, have a body covered by horny scales, and, unlike amphibians, do not undergo metamorphosis. Present-day reptiles include crocodiles, alligators, lizards, snakes, and turtles; extinct reptiles include the dinosaurs.
—adj. reptilian. ⟨ME < LL *reptile,* originally neut. adj. < L *repere* crawl⟩

rep•til•i•an [rɛp'tɪliən] *adj., n.* *—adj.* **1** of, having to do with, or characteristic of reptiles. **2** mean, contemptible, or grovelling.
—n. reptile.

re•pub•lic [rɪ'pʌblɪk] *n.* **1** a nation or state in which the citizens elect representatives to manage the government, the head of which is usually a president rather than a monarch. **2** the type of government of such a nation or state. **3** any of various communist states, such as a constituent unit of the former Soviet Union, the former Yugoslavia, or China. **4** any community composed of peers: *the republic of authors and scholars.* ⟨< L *res publica* public interest, state⟩

re•pub•li•can [rɪ'pʌblɪkən] *adj., n.* *—adj.* **1** of a republic; like that of a republic. **2** favouring a republic. **3 Republican,** *U.S.* of or having to do with the REPUBLICAN PARTY.
—n. **1** a person who favours a republic. **2 Republican,** *U.S.* a member of the Republican Party.

re•pub•li•can•ism [rɪ'pʌblɪkə,nɪzəm] *n.* **1** republican government. **2** republican principles; adherence to republican principles. **3 Republicanism,** *U.S.* the principles or policies of the REPUBLICAN PARTY.

Republican Party in the United States, one of the two main political parties, the other being the Democratic Party.

re•pub•li•ca•tion [,ripʌblə'keiʃən] *n.* **1** the act of publishing anew. **2** a book, etc., published again.

re•pu•di•ate [rɪ'pjudi,eit] *v.* **-at•ed, -at•ing.** **1** refuse to accept; reject: *to repudiate a doctrine.* **2** refuse to acknowledge or pay: *to repudiate a debt.* **3** cast off; disown: *to repudiate a son.* ⟨< L *repudiare* < *repudium* divorce, probably originally, a spurning < *re-* back, away + *pod-* kick (related to *pes, pedis* foot)⟩ **—re'pu•di,a•tor,** *n.*

re•pu•di•a•tion [rɪ,pjudi'eiʃən] *n.* the act of repudiating; fact or condition of being rejected or unacknowledged.

re•pug•nance [rɪ'pʌgnəns] *n.* strong dislike, distaste, or aversion. Also, **repugnancy.**

re•pug•nant [rɪ'pʌgnənt] *adj.* **1** distasteful; disagreeable; offensive: *Work is repugnant to lazy people.* **2** objecting; averse. **3** contrary; opposed: *Segregation is repugnant to our idea of equality.* ⟨ME < L *repugnans, -antis,* ppr. of *repugnare* resist < *re-* back + *pugnare* fight⟩ **—re'pug•nant•ly,** *adv.*

re•pulse [rɪ'pʌls] *v.* **-pulsed, -puls•ing;** *n.* *—v.* **1** drive back; repel. **2** refuse to accept; reject: *She coldly repulsed his offer.* **3** disgust; repel: *The sight of the garbage dump repulsed him.*
—n. **1** a driving back; being driven back: *After the second repulse,*

In each of the words below, **re-** *means* again *or* anew; *the pronunciation of the main part of each word is not changed.*

re'price	**re'pro•gram**	**re-'prove**	**re'pub•lish**
re'pro•cess	**re'pros•e,cute**	**,re•pub•li'ca•tion**	

the enemy surrendered. 2 a refusal; rejection. ⟨< L *repulsus*, pp. of *repellere* repel. See REPEL.⟩

re•pul•sion [rɪˈpʌlʃən] *n.* 1 a strong dislike or aversion. 2 a repulse; a repelling or being repelled. 3 *Physics.* the force by which bodies of like electrical charge or magnetic polarity are repelled from each other.

re•pul•sive [rɪˈpʌlsɪv] *adj.* 1 causing strong dislike or aversion: *Snakes are repulsive to some people.* 2 tending to drive back or repel. **—reˈpul•sive•ly,** *adv.* **—reˈpul•sive•ness,** *n.*

rep•u•ta•ble [ˈrɛpjətəbəl] *adj.* having a good reputation; well thought of; in good repute. **—ˈrep•u•ta•bly,** *adv.*

rep•u•ta•tion [ˌrɛpjəˈteiʃən] *n.* 1 what people think and say the character of a person or thing is; character in the opinion of others: *She had the reputation of being very bright.* 2 a good name; high standing in the opinion of others: *The scandal ruined his reputation.* 3 fame: *She has an international reputation.*

re•pute [rɪˈpjut] *n., v.* **-put•ed, -put•ing.** *—n.* 1 reputation. 2 a good reputation.
—v. suppose (to be, have, do, etc.); consider generally: *He is reputed to be the richest man in the city.* ⟨< L *reputare* < *re-* over + *putare* think⟩

re•put•ed [rɪˈpjutɪd] *adj., v. —adj.* accounted or generally supposed to be such: *the reputed author of a book.*
—v. pt. and pp. of REPUTE. **—reˈput•ed•ly,** *adv.*

re•quest [rɪˈkwɛst] *v., n. —v.* 1 ask for; ask as a favour: *He requested a loan from the bank.* 2 ask: *He requested her to go with him.*
—n. 1 the act of asking: *She did it at our request.* 2 what is asked for: *He granted my request.* 3 the state of being asked for or sought after: *She is such a good dancer that she is in great request.*
by request, in response to a request. ⟨ME < OF *requester* < *requeste* < VL *requaesita* < *requaerere.* See REQUIRE.⟩
—reˈquest•er or **reˈquest•or,** *n.*
☛ *Syn. v.* **1.** See note at ASK.

Req•ui•em or **req•ui•em** [ˈrɛkwiəm] *or* [ˈrikwiəm] *n.* 1 *Roman Catholic Church.* a a Mass or similar religious service sung for the dead. b the music for such a service. c a musical composition of similar theme and style. 2 any hymn or other composition for the dead. ⟨< L *requiem*, accus. of *requies* rest; the first word of the Mass for the dead⟩

re•qui•es•cat in pa•ce [ˌrɛkwiˈɛskɑt ɪn ˈpɑtʃei]; *pl.* **requiescant in pace.** *Latin.* "May he (or she) rest in peace," a wish or prayer for the dead. *Abbrev.:* R.I.P. ⟨< L *requiescat* may he (or she) rest, ult. < *re-* again + *quies* rest; *in pace* in peace < *pax, pacis* peace⟩

re•quire [rɪˈkwaɪr] *v.* **-quired, -quir•ing.** 1 have need for; need; want: *The government requires more money.* 2 command; order; demand: *The rules require us all to be present.* ⟨ME < OF < L *requirere*, combining form of *requaerere* (< *re-* again + *quaerere* ask)⟩
☛ *Syn.* **2.** See note at DEMAND.

re•quire•ment [rɪˈkwaɪrmənt] *n.* 1 a need; something needed: *Patience is a requirement in teaching.* 2 a demand; something demanded: *She has fulfilled all requirements for graduation.*

req•ui•site [ˈrɛkwəzɪt] *adj., n. —adj.* required by circumstances; needed; necessary: *the qualities requisite for a leader, the number of votes requisite for election.*
—n. the thing needed: *Food and air are requisites for life.* ⟨ME < L *requisitus*, pp. of *requirere.* See REQUIRE.⟩ **—ˈreq•ui•site•ly,** *adv.* **—ˈreq•ui•site•ness,** *n.*

req•ui•si•tion [ˌrɛkwəˈzɪʃən] *n., v. —n.* 1 the act of requiring. 2 a demand made, especially a formal written demand: *the requisition of supplies for troops.* 3 the state of being required for use or called into service: *The car was in constant requisition for errands.* 4 an essential condition; requirement.
—v. 1 demand or take by authority: *to requisition supplies or labour.* 2 make demands of: *The army requisitioned the village for food.*

re•quit•al [rɪˈkwəitəl] *n.* 1 an act of repayment or return. 2 a repayment; payment; return: *What requital can we make for his kindness to us?*

re•quite [rɪˈkwəit] *v.* **-quit•ed, -quit•ing.** 1 pay back; make return for: *People of a high moral sense will requite evil with good.* 2 reward: *The knight requited the boy for his warning.* ⟨< *re-* + *quite*, var. of *quit*⟩

rere•dos [ˈrirdɒs], [ˈririrdɒs], *or* [ˈrɛrɪdɒs] *n.* a screen or a decorated part of the wall behind the altar of a church. ⟨ME < AF **reredos*, ult. < *rere* rear¹ + *dos* back < L *dossus*, var. of *dorsum*⟩

re•route [riˈrut] *or* [riˈrʌut] *v.* **-rout•ed, -rout•ing.** send by a new or different route.

re•run *v.* [riˈrʌn]; *n.* [ˈriˌrʌn] *v.* **-ran, -run•ning;** *n. —v.* run again.
—n. 1 a running again. 2 a television program or a film that is shown again.

res [rɛs], [rɛz], [reis], [riz], *or* [reiz] *Law.* 1 a thing or object. 2 a matter, case, or action. ⟨< L⟩

re•sale [ˈriˌseil] *or* [riˈseil] *n.* 1 the act of selling again or to a third party. 2 a selling at retail: *The store has a 20 percent markup over the wholesale price for resale.* 3 (*adjl.*) of or for resale: *The problem with domestic cars is their low resale value.*
—reˈsale•a•ble, *adj.*

re•scind [rɪˈsɪnd] *v.* deprive of force; repeal; cancel: *to rescind a law.* ⟨< L *rescindere* < *re-* back + *scindere* cut⟩

re•scis•sion [rɪˈsɪʒən] *n.* the act of rescinding. ⟨< LL *rescissio, -onis* < L *rescindere.* See RESCIND.⟩

re•script [ˈriskrɪpt] *n.* 1 a written answer to a question or petition, as from the Pope. 2 an edict; decree; an official announcement. 3 a rewriting. 4 something rewritten. ⟨< L *rescriptum*, originally neut. pp. of *rescribere* write in reply < *re-* back + *scribere* write⟩

res•cue [ˈrɛskju] *v.* **-cued, -cu•ing;** *n. —v.* 1 save from danger, capture, harm, etc.; free; deliver. 2 *Law.* take (a person) forcibly or unlawfully from a jail, the police, etc.; take (property) unlawfully from legal custody.
—n. 1 the act of saving or freeing from danger, capture, harm, etc. 2 *Law.* the forcible or unlawful taking of a person or thing from the care of the law. ⟨ME < OF *rescoure*, ult. < L *re-* back + *ex* out + *quatere* shake⟩ **—ˈres•cu•er,** *n.*
☛ *Syn. v.* **1. Rescue,** DELIVER = save or free from danger, harm, or restraint. **Rescue** suggests saving, by quick and forceful action, a person from immediate or threatened danger or harm, such as death, injury, attack, capture, confinement, etc.: *Searchers rescued the boys lost in the mountains.* **Deliver** suggests setting someone free from something holding him or her in captivity or under its power or control, such as prison, slavery, oppression, suffering, temptation, evil, etc.: *Advancing troops delivered the prisoners from their suffering.*

re•search [rɪˈsɜrtʃ] *or* [ˈrisɜrtʃ] *n., v. —n.* a careful hunting for facts or truth; inquiry; investigation: *Medical research has done much to lessen disease. The current researches into AIDS prevention and treatment are showing promise.*
—v. 1 carry out research. 2 inquire into (something) thoroughly; investigate. ⟨< MF *recerche* < *re-* again + *cerche* search⟩

re•search•er [rɪˈsɜrtʃər] *or* [ˈrisɜrtʃər] *n.* a person who carries out research, especially one whose work it is; investigator.

research library an academic library that holds materials useful to researchers.

re•seat [riˈsit] *v.* 1 seat again: *The audience was reseated after the singing of the national anthem.* 2 provide with a new seat or seats.

re•seau [reiˈzou] *or* [rəˈzou] *n.* 1 a lace network. 2 *Astronomy.* a network of lines on a glass plate, used in a telescope to produce similar lines on photographs of the stars. 3 *Meteorology.* a system of weather stations under the same control.
4 *Photography.* a screen with tiny coloured filters, used in colour photography. ⟨< F, network⟩

re•sect [rɪˈsɛkt] *v.* do a resection of (an organ, part, etc.).

re•sec•tion [rɪˈsɛkʃən] *n.* the removal of an organ, bone, part, etc., by surgery.

In each of the words below, **re-** *means* again *or* anew; *the pronunciation of the main part of each word is not changed.*

reˈpur•chase	**reˈquick•en**	**ˌre•reg•isˈtra•tion**	**reˈsad•dle**	**reˈscreen**
ˌre•pur•i•fiˈca•tion	**reˈread**	**ˌre•reˈlease**	**reˈsay**	**reˈseal**
reˈpur•iˌfy	**ˌre•reˈcord**	**ˌre•reˈvise**	**reˈsched•ule**	
reˈqual•iˌfy	**reˈreg•is•ter**	**reˈroll**	**reˈscore**	

re•se•da [rɪ'sidə] *or* ['rɛzɪdə] *n., adj. —n.* a greyish green: *Reseda is one of my favourite colours.*
—adj. greyish green, like the colour of the mignonette: *We painted the den reseda green. She bought a reseda-coloured lamp to match the new chair.*

re•sem•blance [rɪ'zɛmbləns] *n.* **1** the fact or state of similarity or likeness. **2** a degree or kind of likeness: *Fraternal twins often show great resemblance to each other.* **3** a likeness of something; something that resembles. ⟨< AF⟩
☛ *Syn.* **Resemblance,** SIMILARITY = likeness to another or between two persons or things. **Resemblance** emphasizes looking alike or having some of the same external features or superficial qualities: *There is some resemblance between the accounts of the fire, but all the important details are different.* **Similarity** especially suggests being of the same kind or nature, having some of the same essential qualities and usually a strong resemblance: *The similarity between the two reports suggests that one person wrote both.*

re•sem•ble [rɪ'zɛmbəl] *v.* **-bled, -bling.** be like; be similar to; have likeness to in form, figure, or qualities. ⟨ME < OF *resembler,* ult. < L *re-* again + *similis* similar⟩ **—re'sem•bler,** *n.*

re•sent [rɪ'zɛnt] *v.* feel injured and angry at; feel indignation at: *Our cat seems to resent having anyone sit in its chair.* ⟨< F *ressentir,* ult. < L *re-* back + *sentire* feel⟩ **—re'sent•er,** *n.*

re•sent•ful [rɪ'zɛntfəl] *adj.* feeling resentment; injured and angry; showing resentment. **—re'sent•ful•ly,** *adv.*
—re'sent•ful•ness, *n.*

re•sent•ment [rɪ'zɛntmənt] *n.* the feeling that one has at being wronged or insulted; indignation.

re•ser•pine [rɪ'sɜrpin], [rɪ'sɜrpən], ['rɛsərpɪn], *or* ['rɛsər,pin] *n.* a drug extracted from the roots of a SE Asian shrub of the dogbane family (*Rauwolfia serpentina*), used to lower blood pressure and as a sedative and tranquillizer. *Formula*: $C_{33}H_{40}N_2O_9$

res•er•va•tion [,rɛzər'veiʃən] *n.* **1** a keeping back; hiding in part. **2** a limiting condition; something not expressed: *The committee accepted the plan with reservations plainly stated. She outwardly approved of the plan with the mental reservation that she would change it to suit herself.* **3** an arrangement to keep a thing for a person; securing of accommodations, etc. We make reservations in advance for rooms at a hotel, seats at a theatre or on an airliner, etc. **4** something reserved. **5** in Canada, the provision made for the withholding of royal assent to a bill, federal or provincial, until it has been re-examined. **6** *U.S.* land set apart, usually by treaty, for the exclusive use of Native American peoples.

re•serve [rɪ'zɜrv] *v.* **-served, -serv•ing;** *n. —v.* **1** keep or hold back; retain: *to reserve the right to withdraw an offer after a certain time, to reserve criticism.* **2** set apart or save for future use. **3** set aside or have set aside for the use of a particular person or persons: *to reserve a table for two.*
—n. **1** something kept back or set aside for future use or contingency: *a reserve of strength, a small cash reserve.* **2** *Finance.* capital or assets that can be turned into cash quickly to meet liabilities, contingencies, etc. **3** Often, **reserves,** *pl.* **a** a part of a military force kept ready to help the main force in battle. **b** a part of the armed forces of a nation that in peace time is not on full-time, active duty. **4** a tract of public land set apart by the government for a specific purpose, especially for the preservation of wild animals and plants; preserve. **5** *Cdn.* a tract of land set apart, usually by treaty, for the exclusive use of First Nations peoples. **6** a person kept available to act as a substitute: *He is a reserve for the basketball team.* **7** the act of reserving. **8** the fact or condition of being reserved: *We still have a bit of cash in reserve.* **9** (*adjl.*) kept in reserve; being a reserve. **10** restraint, formality, or coolness of manner; avoidance of familiarity; silence or reticence. **11** an exception or qualification to the acceptance of some idea, belief, etc. ⟨ME < OF < L *reservare* < *re-* back + *servare* keep⟩ **—re'serv•er,** *n.*

reserve army the militia: *Members of the reserve army are not full-time soldiers.*

reserve bank 1 any of the 12 principal banks of the U.S. Federal Reserve system, especially the Federal Reserve Bank. **2** any bank authorized by a government to hold the reserves of other banks.

re•served [rɪ'zɜrvd] *adj., v. —adj.* **1** kept in reserve; kept by special arrangement: *reserved seats.* **2** set apart. **3** self-restrained in action or speech. **4** disposed to keep to oneself.
—v. pt. and pp. of RESERVE. **—re'serv•ed•ness,** *n.*

re•serv•ed•ly [rɪ'zɜrvɪdli] *adv.* in a reserved manner.

Reserve Entry Training Plan a program whereby students attend Canadian Forces Military Colleges at their own expense but are offered summer employment with the military. Graduates must serve five years as reserve officers. *Abbrev.*: RETP or R.E.T.P.

re•serv•ist [rɪ'zɜrvɪst] *n.* a member of the reserve army.

res•er•voir ['rɛzər,vwɑr] *or* ['rɛzər,vɔr] *n.* **1** a place where water is collected and stored for use: *This reservoir supplies the entire city.* **2** anything to hold a liquid: *A fountain pen has an ink reservoir.* **3** a place where anything is collected and stored: *Her mind is a reservoir of facts.* **4** a great supply. ⟨< F *réservoir* < *réserver* reserve⟩

re•set *v.* [ri'sɛt]; *n.* ['ri,sɛt] *v.* **-set, -set•ting;** *n. —v.* set again: *The gems were reset in gold. Pierre's broken arm had to be reset.*
—n. **1** the act of resetting. **2** the thing reset. **3** a plant that is replanted. **4** a device by which something is reset: *If your computer crashes, hit the reset. Where's the reset on this machine?*

res gestae ['reis 'dʒɛsti], ['dʒɛstei], *or* ['dʒɛstaɪ]
1 achievements; deeds; things done. **2** *Law.* statements, actions, etc., incidental to the principal fact of a matter under litigation, but so closely connected to it that they are admissible as evidence.

resh [reiʃ] *n.* the twenty-second letter of the Hebrew alphabet. See table of alphabets in the Appendix.

re•shape [ri'ʃeip] *v.* **-shaped, -shap•ing.** shape anew; form into a new or different shape.

re•side [rɪ'zaɪd] *v.* **-sid•ed, -sid•ing. 1** live *(in or at)* for a long time; dwell. **2** be *(in)*; exist *(in)*: *Her charm resides in her happy smile.* ⟨< L *residere* < *re-* back + *sedere* sit, settle⟩ **—re'sid•er,** *n.*

res•i•dence ['rɛzɪdəns] *n.* **1** a place where a person lives; house; home. **2** the act of residing; living; dwelling. **3** a period of residing in a place. **4** the fact of living or doing business in a place for the performance of certain duties, to comply with certain regulations, or to qualify for certain rights and privileges: *a writer in residence. They have not been in residence long enough to apply for citizenship.* **5** a building in which students, nurses, etc. live.
in residence, a living in a place: *The owner of the house is not in residence.* **b** living in an insitution while on duty or doing active work there: *a doctor in residence.*

res•i•den•cy ['rɛzɪdənsi] *n., pl.* **-cies. 1** RESIDENCE (def. 3, 4). **2 a** a period of advanced training as a specialist after graduation with a medical degree. **b** a doctor's position or training during this period. **3** the official residence of a governor general, ambassador, or any diplomatic officer. **4** formerly, the official residence in India of a representative of the Governor General at a native court.

res•i•dent ['rɛzɪdənt] *n., adj. —n.* **1** a person living in a place, not a visitor. **2** a physician during residency, especially one who has completed internship. **3** an official sent to live in a foreign land to represent his or her country. **4** formerly, a representative of the British Governor General of India at a native court. **5** a bird or animal that is not migratory. **6** a person living or doing business in a place in order to comply with certain regulations, or qualify for certain rights or privileges.
—adj. **1** staying; dwelling in a place. A resident owner lives on his or her property. **2** living in a place while on duty or doing active work. **3** not migratory: *English sparrows are resident birds.* **4** of qualities, present; intrinsic; inherent. **5** of a person, living or doing business in a place in order to comply with certain regulations, or to qualify for certain rights or privileges. ⟨ME < L *residens, -entis,* ppr. of *residere.* See RESIDE.⟩

res•i•den•tial [,rɛzɪ'dɛnʃəl] *adj.* **1** of, having to do with, or allocated or zoned for homes or residences: *They live in a good residential district.* **2** designating a school that provides living accommodation for students. **3** used as a residence: *a residential*

In each of the words below, **re-** *means* again *or* anew; *the pronunciation of the main part of each word is not changed.*

re'seed	**re'send**	**re'set•tle•ment**	**re'ship•ment**
re'seg•re,gate	**re'sen•tence**	**re'sew**	**re'shoot**
,re•seg•re'ga•tion	**re-'serve**	**re'sharp•en**	**re'show**
re'sell	**re'set•tle**	**re'ship**	**re'shuf•fle**

hotel. **4** of or having to do with residence: *a residential qualification for schoolteachers.*

residential school *Cdn. North.* especially formerly, a boarding school operated or subsidized by the federal government to accommodate students, particularly First Nations and Inuit students, attending classes at a considerable distance from their homes.

res•i•den•ti•ary [ˌrɛzɪˈdɛnʃəri] *or* [ˌrɛzɪˈdɛnʃiˌɛri] *adj., n., pl.* **-ar•ies.** *—adj.* **1** residing; resident. **2** obliged to be in official residence.
—n. **1** a resident. **2** a minister or priest attached to an official residence.

re•sid•u•al [rɪˈzɪdʒuəl] *adj., n. —adj.* **1** of or forming a residue; remaining; left over. **2** *Geology.* resulting from the weathering of rock: *residual clay soil, a residual deposit.*
—n. **1** the amount left over; remainder. **2** a fee paid to a performer or writer for each rerun of a radio or television broadcast, etc. **3** *Mathematics.* **a** the difference between a given value of a variable and the average of its possible values. **b** the difference between a theoretical value and its observed value.

re•sid•u•ar•y [rəˈzɪdʒuˌɛri] *adj.* **1 a** entitled to the remainder of an estate. **b** specifying how the residue of an estate should be disposed of. **2** pertaining to or characteristic of a residue or remainder.

res•i•due [ˈrɛzəˌdju] *or* [ˈrɛzəˌdu] *n.* **1** what remains after a part is taken; remainder: *The syrup had dried up, leaving a sticky residue.* **2** *Law.* the part of a testator's estate that is left after all debts, charges, and particular devises and bequests have been satisfied: *Mr. Benzarti's will directed that the residue of his property should go to his son.* **3** *Chemistry.* **a** an atom or group of atoms considered as a radical or part of a molecule. **b** residuum. ⟨< F < L *residuum*, neut. adj., left over. Doublet of RESIDUUM.⟩

re•sid•u•um [rɪˈzɪdʒuəm] *n., pl.* **-sid•u•a** [-ˈzɪdʒuə]. *Chemistry.* what is left at the end of any process such as evaporation, filtration, etc. ⟨< L. Doublet of RESIDUE.⟩

re•sign [rɪˈzaɪn] *v.* **1** take oneself out of a job, position, etc.; leave; depart (*often used with* **from**): *He resigned in a fit of rage. She has resigned from the club.* **2** give up: *She resigned her seat in Parliament.* **3** give in or yield, often unwillingly, but without complaint (*used with a reflexive pronoun*): *He had to resign himself to a week in bed when he hurt his back.* ⟨ME < OF < L *resignare* unseal, ult. < *re-* back + *signum* seal⟩
☛ *Usage.* **Resign** is often followed by **from,** though sometimes the object follows without the **from:** *She resigned from the editorship of the magazine* or *She resigned the editorship of the magazine.*

res•ig•na•tion [ˌrɛzɪgˈneiʃən] *n.* **1** the act of resigning. **2** a written statement giving notice that one resigns. **3** patient acceptance; quiet submission: *He bore the pain with resignation.*

re•signed [rɪˈzaɪnd] *adj., v. —adj.* showing or feeling resignation; accepting, often unwillingly; submissive: *resigned to an unhappy fate.*
—v. pt. and pp. of RESIGN.

re•sign•ed•ly [rɪˈzaɪnɪdli] *adv.* in a resigned manner; with resignation.

re•sil•i•ence [rɪˈzɪljəns] *or* [rɪˈzɪliəns] *n.* **1** the power of springing back; elasticity; a resilient quality or nature: *Rubber has resilience.* **2** buoyancy; the ability to regain one's good cheer quickly after a setback. Also, **resiliency.**

re•sil•i•ent [rɪˈzɪljənt] *or* [rɪˈzɪliənt] *adj.* **1** springing back; returning to the original form or position after being bent, compressed, or stretched: *resilient steel, resilient turf.* **2** buoyant; recovering quickly from trouble: *a resilient child.* ⟨< L *resiliens, -entis,* ppr. of *resilire* rebound < *re-* back + *salire* jump⟩ **—re'sil•i•ent•ly,** *adv.*

res•in [ˈrɛzən] *n., v. —n.* **1** a sticky, yellow or brown substance that flows from certain plants and trees, especially the pine and fir. It is used in medicine and varnish. The harder portion of resin remaining after heating is called **rosin.** **2** any similar substance that is made synthetically. Artificial resins are used in the manufacture of plastics.
—v. rub, coat, or treat with resin. ⟨< L *resina*⟩

res•in•if•er•ous [ˌrɛzəˈnɪfərəs] *adj.* of trees, yielding resin.

res•in•ous [ˈrɛzənəs] *adj.* **1** of resin. **2** like resin; containing resin; full of resin.

re•sist [rɪˈzɪst] *v., n. —v.* **1** act against (something); strive against; oppose: *The Celts resisted the Anglo-Saxons for as long as they could.* **2** act against something; oppose something: *Do not resist.* **3** strive successfully against; keep from: *I could not resist laughing.* **4** withstand the action or effect of: *A healthy body resists disease. The window resisted her efforts to open it.*
—n. a resistant substance applied for protection. ⟨< L *resistere* < *re-* back + *sistere* make a stand⟩ **—re'sist•er,** *n.*
☛ *Syn.* **1.** See note at OPPOSE.

re•sist•ance [rɪˈzɪstəns] *n.* **1** the act of resisting: *The bank clerk made no resistance to the robbers.* **2** the power to resist: *She has little resistance to germs and so is often ill.* **3** a thing or act that resists; an opposing force; opposition. An airplane can overcome the resistance of the air and go in the desired direction, while a balloon simply drifts. **4** *Electricity.* **a** the property of a conductor that opposes the passage of a current and changes electric energy into heat. The elements of electric stoves have high resistance. Copper has a low resistance. **b** a conductor, coil, etc. that offers resistance. **5** Usually, **Resistance,** people in a country occupied or controlled by another country who secretly organize and fight for their freedom: *the French Resistance in World War II.*

resistance coil *Electricity.* a coil or wire made of metal that has a high resistance, used especially for measuring resistance, reducing voltage or amperage, and producing heat.

re•sist•ant [rɪˈzɪstənt] *adj., n. —adj.* resisting.
—n. someone or something that resists.

re•sist•i•ble [rɪˈzɪstəbəl] *adj.* capable of being resisted. **—re,sist•i'bil•i•ty,** *n.*

re•sist•ive [rɪˈzɪstɪv] *adj.* able or inclined to resist.

re•sist•i•vi•ty [ˌrizɪsˈtɪvɪti] *n.* **1** the property or power of resistance. **2** *Electricity.* SPECIFIC RESISTANCE.

re•sist•less [rɪˈzɪstlɪs] *adj.* **1** that cannot be resisted: *A resistless impulse made him wander over the earth.* **2** not resisting.

re•sis•tor [rɪˈzɪstər] *n. Electricity.* a conducting body or device used in an electric circuit, etc. because of its resistance.

re•sole [riˈsoul] *v.* **-soled, -sol•ing.** put a new sole on (a shoe, etc.).

re•sol•u•ble[1] [rɪˈzɒljəbəl] *adj.* capable of being resolved.

re•sol•u•ble[2] [riˈsɒljəbəl] *adj.* able to be dissolved again.

res•o•lute [ˈrɛzəˌlut] *adj.* **1** determined; firm: *He was resolute in his attempt to climb to the top of the mountain.* **2** bold: *A soldier must be resolute in battle.* **3** indicating firmness, boldness, etc.: *a resolute air.* ⟨< L *resolutus*, pp. of *resolvere* resolve. See RESOLVE.⟩ **—'res•o,lute•ly,** *adv.*

res•o•lu•tion [ˌrɛzəˈluʃən] *n.* **1** something decided on; a thing determined: *She made a resolution to get up early.* **2** the quality or power of holding firmly to a purpose; determination. **3** a formal expression of opinion, especially as agreed upon by a group: *The club passed a resolution thanking the consultant for her help.* **4** the act or an instance of determining or solving: *the resolution of a problem.* **5** the act or process of breaking or separating into parts. **6** *Medicine.* a return to a normal condition, especially the subsiding of inflammation, as in a lung. **7** *Music.* **a** the progression of a chord from dissonance to consonance. **b** the chord to which the dissonant chord passes. **8** the power of a telescope, etc. to produce distinct images of closely adjacent objects or sources of light. **9** that section of a novel or play in which the plot is explained or resolved. **10** *Computer technology.* a measure of the clarity of the pictures or characters that a computer monitor or printer is able to produce from a matrix of dots: *The resolution of the monitor is 640 by 480 pixels.*

re•solve [rɪˈzɒlv] *v.* **-solved, -solv•ing;** *n. —v.* **1** make up one's mind firmly; determine: *He resolved to do better work in the future.* **2** express (a decision) formally, especially by vote: *It was resolved by the committee that the project be dropped.* **3** separate into parts or elements: *to resolve a chemical compound.* **4** answer and explain so as to clear away, dispel, or remove (doubt, etc.): *Her letter resolved all our doubts.* **5** solve; make a decision concerning: *to resolve a problem.* **6** change; separate into constituent parts; break up: *The assembly resolved itself into committees.* **7** be resolved or changed, as by breaking up or

In each of the words below, **re-** *means* again *or* anew; *the pronunciation of the main part of each word is not changed.*

re'sil•ver **re'sit•u,ate** **re'smooth** **re'soak** **re-'solve**

analysis. **8** *Medicine.* cause (inflammation) to subside. **9** *Music.* **a** follow (a dissonant tone or chord) by another to produce consonance. **b** of a dissonant tone or chord, progress to consonance. **10** *Optics.* make distinguishable or visible the separate adjacent parts of, as by means of a telescope: *to resolve a cluster of stars with a high-powered telescope.* **11** cause (a person) to make up his or her mind: *The experience resolved her never to lie again.*
—n. **1** something determined: *a resolve to do better.* **2** firmness in carrying out a purpose; determination. ⟨< L *resolvere* < *re-* un- + *solvere* loosen⟩ **—re'solv•a•ble,** *adj.* **—re'solv•er,** *n.*
☛ *Syn. v.* **1.** See note at DECIDE.

re•solved [rɪ'zɒlvd] *adj., v. —adj.* determined; resolute.
—v. pt. and pp. of RESOLVE.

re•solv•ed•ly [rɪ'zɒlvɪdli] *adv.* in a determined manner; with resolution.

res•o•nance ['rɛzənəns] *n.* **1** a resounding quality; a being resonant: *the resonance of an organ.* **2** *Physics.* a reinforcing and prolonging of sound by reflection or by vibration of other objects. The sounding board of a piano gives it resonance. **3** *Electricity.* the condition of a circuit adjusted to allow the greatest flow of current at a certain frequency. A radio set must be in resonance to receive music or speech from a radio station. **4** *Physics.* an elementary particle that is a very short-lived excited state of a stable particle. **5** *Chemistry.* the molecular property of having more than one structure.

res•o•nant ['rɛzənənt] *adj.* **1** resounding; continuing to sound; echoing: *a resonant tone.* **2** tending to increase or prolong sound: *a guitar has a resonant body.* **3** of or in resonance. **4** full of or intensified by resonance: *a resonant voice.* ⟨< L *resonans, -antis,* ppr. of *resonare,* ult. < *re-* back + *sonus* sound⟩ **—'res•o•nant•ly,** *adv.*

res•o•nate ['rɛzə,neit] *v.* **-nat•ed, -nat•ing. 1** resound; exhibit resonance. **2** cause to resound. **3** act as a resonator. **4** communicate (something) in a profound or powerful way (*used with* **with**): *Her poems resonate with longing.* ⟨< L *resonatus, resonare.* Doublet of RESOUND.⟩

res•o•na•tor ['rɛzə,neitər] *n.* **1** something that produces resonance; an appliance for increasing sound by resonance. **2** a device for detecting electromagnetic radiation, as radio broadcasting waves. **3** *Electronics.* a system or apparatus that can be put into oscillation by oscillations in another system. ⟨< NL⟩

re•sorb [rɪ'sɔrb] *or* [rɪ'zɔrb] *v.* absorb again.

res•or•cin [rɛ'zɔrsən] *n.* resorcinol. ⟨< *res(in)* + *orcin,* a chemical compound (< NL *orcina*)⟩

res•or•cin•ol [rɛ'zɔrsə,nɒl] *or* [rɛ'zɔrsə,noul] *n. Chemistry. Pharmacy.* a colourless crystalline substance that is used in medicine as an antiseptic, and in making dyes, drugs, etc. *Formula:* $C_6H_4(OH)_2$ ⟨< *resorcin* + *-ol*⟩

re•sorp•tion [rɪ'sɔrpʃən] *or* [rɪ'zɔrpʃən] *n.* the action or process of resorbing.

re•sort [rɪ'zɔrt] *v., n. —v.* **1** go; go often: *Many people resort to the beaches in hot weather.* **2** turn for help or use as a tool, means, or strategy: *to resort to violence.*
—n. **1** an assembling; a going to often, as a place or person: *A park is a place of popular resort in good weather.* **2** a place people go to, usually for relaxation or recreation: *There are many summer resorts in the mountains.* **3** the act of turning for help or using as a tool, means, or strategy: *The resort to force is a poor substitute for persuasion.* **4** a person or thing turned to for help or used as a tool, means, or strategy. ⟨ME < OF *resortir* < *re-* back + *sortir* go out⟩

re•sound [rɪ'zaʊnd] *v.* **1** give back sound; echo: *The hills resounded when he shouted.* **2** give back (sound); echo (sound). **3** sound loudly: *Radios resound from every house.* **4** be filled (with sound): *The room resounded with the children's shouts.* **5** repeat loudly: *to resound a hero's praise.* **6** be much talked about. ⟨ME *resounen* < MF *resoner* < L *resonare* < *re-* back + *sonare* sound. Doublet of RESONATE.⟩

re•sound•ing [rɪ'zaʊndɪŋ] *adj., v. —adj.* **1** reverberating; echoing: *The cabinet fell over with a resounding crash.* **2** loud or high-sounding: *a resounding speech.* **3** impressively thorough or complete: *a resounding victory.*
—v. ppr. of RESOUND. **—re'sound•ing•ly,** *adv.*

re•source [rɪ'zɔrs], ['rizɔrs], *or* [rɪ'sɔrs] *n.* **1** any supply that will meet a need: *We have resources of money, of quick wit, and of strength.* **2 resources,** *pl.* the actual and potential wealth of a person, business, or country; NATURAL RESOURCES. **3** any means of getting success or getting out of trouble: *Climbing a tree is a cat's resource when chased by a dog.* **4** skill in meeting difficulties, getting out of trouble, etc. **5** mental capability or strength: *inner resources.* ⟨< F *resource,* ult. < L *re-* again + *surgere* rise⟩

re•source•ful [rɪ'zɔrsfəl] *or* [rɪ'sɔrsfəl] *adj.* good at thinking of ways to do things; quick-witted; not easily doubted or frustrated. **—re'source•ful•ly,** *adv.* **—re'source•ful•ness,** *n.*

resp. 1 respectively. **2** respondent.

re•spect [rɪ'spɛkt] *n., v. —n.* **1** honour; esteem: *Children should show respect to those who are older and wiser.* **2** consideration; regard: *Show respect for other people's property.* **3** the condition or state of being honoured or esteemed: *She is held in respect by her peers.* **4 respects,** *pl.* expressions of respect; regards. **5** a point; matter; detail: *The plan is unwise in many respects.* **6** relation; reference.
in respect of, with reference or comparison to.
in respect that, because of the fact that; since.
with respect to, with relation, reference, or regard to (something): *We must plan with respect to the future of this organization.*
—v. **1** feel or show honour or esteem for: *We respect an honest person.* **2** show consideration for: *Respect the ideas and feelings of others.* **3** relate to; refer to; be connected with. ⟨< L *respectus* < *respicere* look back, have regard for < *re-* back + *specere* look⟩ **—re'spect•er,** *n.*
☛ *Syn. n. v,* **2. Respect,** REGARD = consideration, felt or shown, for someone or something of recognized worth or value. **Respect** emphasizes recognizing or judging the worth or value of someone or something and paying the consideration or honour due: *A soldier may feel respect for an officer he dislikes.* **Regard** emphasizes seeing that a person or thing is entitled to consideration, appreciation, or admiration, and usually suggests a kindly, friendly, or sympathetic feeling: *A person who reads another's mail has no regard for other people's privacy.*

re•spect•a•ble [rɪ'spɛktəbəl] *adj.* **1** worthy of respect; having a good reputation: *Respectable citizens obey the laws.* **2** having fair social standing; honest and decent; conforming to social norms: *His parents were poor but respectable people.* **3** fairly good; moderate in size or quality: *Sean's record in his career was respectable but not brilliant.* **4** good enough to use; fit to be seen. **—re,spect•a'bil•i•ty,** *n.* **—re'spect•a•bly,** *adv.*

re•spect•ful [rɪ'spɛktfəl] *adj.* showing respect; polite. **—re'spect•ful•ly,** *adv.* **—re'spect•ful•ness,** *n.*

re•spect•ing [rɪ'spɛktɪŋ] *prep., v. —prep.* regarding; about; concerning: *A discussion arose respecting the merits of different automobiles.*
—v. ppr. of RESPECT.

re•spec•tive [rɪ'spɛktɪv] *adj.* belonging to each; particular; individual: *The wrestlers returned to their respective corners.*

re•spec•tive•ly [rɪ'spɛktɪvli] *adv.* as regards each one in his or her turn or in the order mentioned: *McGregor, Kozinski, and Lee are 27, 43, and 35 years old respectively.*

re•spell [ri'spɛl] *v.* spell again or in a different way; especially, spell in a phonetic alphabet or the writing system of another language. **—re'spell•ing,** *n.*

res•pi•ra•tion [,rɛspə'reiʃən] *n.* **1** the act of inhaling and exhaling; breathing. **2** *Biology.* the processes by which an animal, plant, or living cell secures oxygen from the air or water, distributes it, combines it with substances in the tissues, and gives off carbon dioxide.

res•pi•ra•tor ['rɛspə,reitər] *n.* **1** a device worn over the nose and mouth to prevent inhaling harmful substances. **2** a device used to help a person breathe, or to give artificial respiration.

res•pi•ra•to•ry ['rɛspərə,tɔri] *or* [rɪ'spaɪrə,tɔri] *adj.* having to do with or used for breathing. The lungs are respiratory organs.

respiratory system the system of organs by which oxygen is taken into the body and exchanged with carbon dioxide, which is released; in mammals, the respiratory organs are the nasal passages, the pharynx, trachea, bronchi, and lungs.

In each of the words below, **re-** *means* again *or* anew; *the pronunciation of the main part of each word is not changed.*

re-'sort **re-'sound** **re'sow** **re'spec•i,fy**

re•spire [rɪ'spaɪr] *v.* **-spired, -spir•ing.** inhale and exhale; breathe. ⟨< L *respirare* < *re-* regularly + *spirare* breathe⟩

res•pite ['rɛspɪt] *n., v.* **-pit•ed, -pit•ing.** —*n.* **1** a time of relief and rest; lull: *A thick cloud brought a respite from the glare of the sun.* **2** a putting off; delay, especially in carrying out a sentence of death; reprieve.
—*v.* **1** give a respite to. **2** postpone; delay. ⟨ME < OF < VL *respectus* delay < LL *respectus* expectation < L *respectare* wait for. Related to RESPECT.⟩

re•splend•ent [rɪ'splɛndənt] *adj.* very bright; shining; splendid: *The queen was resplendent with jewels.* ⟨ME < L *resplendens, -entis,* ppr. of *resplendere* glitter < *re-* back + *splendere* shine⟩ **—re'splend•ence** or **re'splend•en•cy,** *n.* **—re'splend•ent•ly,** *adv.*

re•spond [rɪ'spɒnd] *v.* **1** answer; reply. **2** act in answer; react: *A dog responds to kind treatment by loving its master.* **3** react positively or favourably. ⟨ME < OF < L *respondere* < *re-* in return + *spondere* promise⟩
☛ *Syn.* **1.** See note at ANSWER.

re•spond•ent [rɪ'spɒndənt] *adj., n.* —*adj.* answering; responding.
—*n.* **1** a person who responds. **2** *Law.* a defendant, especially in a divorce case.

re•spond•er [rɪ'spɒndər] *n.* **1** a person who or thing that responds. **2** *Electronics.* **a** a device that indicates reception of a signal; TRANSPONDER. **b** the part of a transponder that transmits the reply.

re•sponse [rɪ'spɒns] *n.* **1** an answer by word or act. **2** a set of words said or sung by the congregation or choir in a religious service, in answer to the minister or priest. **3** *Psychology. Physiology.* any activity or behaviour resulting from stimulation; a reaction. **4** *Bridge.* a bid made in reply to a partner's previous bid, taking into account the cards held in the bidder's own hand. ⟨< L *responsum,* originally neut. pp. of *respondere* respond. See RESPOND.⟩

response time *Computer technology.* the elapsed time between a user's entering a request or command to a computer system, and the computer's providing the result: *The mainframe computer's response time worsened as more users logged on.*

re•spon•si•bil•i•ty [rɪ,spɒnsə'bɪlɪti] *n., pl.* **-ties. 1** a being responsible: *A small child does not feel much responsibility.* **2** something for which one is responsible: *Keeping house and caring for the children are his responsibilities.* **3** the ability to pay debts or discharge obligations.

re•spon•si•ble [rɪ'spɒnsəbəl] *adj.* **1** obliged or expected to account *(for): Each pupil is responsible for the care of the books given him or her. The government is responsible to the people for its proper conduct of the country's affairs.* **2** deserving credit or blame: *The bad weather is responsible for the small attendance.* **3** trustworthy; reliable: *A responsible person should take care of the money.* **4** involving obligation or duties: *The Prime Minister holds a very responsible position.* **5** able to tell right from wrong; able to think and act reasonably: *Babies are not responsible.* **6** able to pay debts or discharge obligations: *Grandmother is no longer financially responsible.* **—re'spon•si•ble•ness,** *n.* **—re'spon•si•bly,** *adv.*

responsible government 1 a form of government in which a cabinet, selected from the members of an elected legislature, acts as the executive, making decisions for which it is then held collectively responsible and accountable to the legislature. **2 Responsible Government,** this system of government as it existed in Canada from 1848-1867.

re•spon•sive [rɪ'spɒnsɪv] *adj.* **1** making answer; responding: *a responsive glance.* **2** easily moved; responding readily: *having a responsive nature, being responsive to kindness.* **3** using or containing RESPONSES (def. 2). **—re'spon•sive•ly,** *adv.* **—re'spon•sive•ness,** *n.*

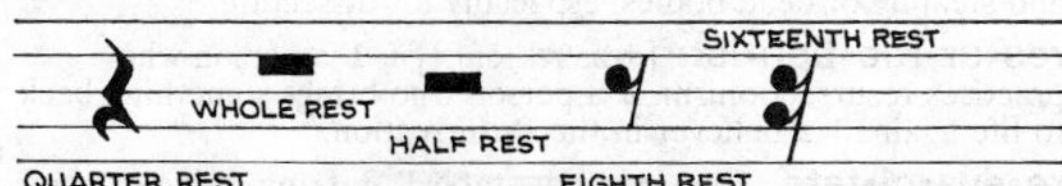

Musical rests (def. 7). A whole rest has the same duration as a whole note, a half rest the same as a half note, and so on.

rest¹ [rɛst] *n., v.* —*n.* **1** sleep; repose: *a good night's rest.* **2** ease after work or effort; freedom from activity: *Allow an hour for rest.* **3** freedom from anything that tires, troubles, disturbs, or pains; respite; peace of mind: *The medicine gave the sick man a short rest from pain.* **4** the absence of motion: *The driver brought the car to rest.* **5** a support: *a rest for a billiard cue.* **6** a place of rest: *sailors' rest.* **7** *Music.* **a** a measured period of silence. **b** a mark used in a musical score to indicate a period of silence of specific duration. **8** *Reading, prosody.* a pause. **9** death; the grave.
at rest, a asleep. **b** not moving: *The lake was at rest.* **c** free from pain, trouble, etc.: *The injured woman is now at rest.* **d** dead.
lay to rest, a bury: *Lay his bones to rest.* **b** deal with finally.
—*v.* **1** be still; sleep: *Lie down and rest.* **2** be free from work, trouble, pain, etc.: *He was able to rest during his holidays.* **3** stop moving; cause to stop moving: *The ball rested at the bottom of the hill.* **4** give rest to; refresh by rest: *Stop and rest your horse.* **5** lie, recline, sit, lean, etc., for rest or ease: *She spent the whole day resting in a chair.* **6** be supported: *The ladder rests against the wall.* **7** fix or be fixed: *Our eyes rested on the open book.* **8** be at ease: *Don't let her rest until she promises to visit us.* **9** become inactive; let remain inactive: *Let the matter rest. Rest the matter there.* **10** place for support; lay; lean: *to rest one's head in one's hands.* **11** rely (*on*); trust (*in*); depend; be based: *Our hope rests on you.* **12** cause to rely or depend; base; be imposed as a burden or responsibility: *We rest our hope on you.* **13** be found; be present: *In a democracy, government rests with the people.* **14** be dead; lie in the grave or at a funeral home. **15** *Law.* end voluntarily the introduction of evidence in (a case): *The lawyer rested his case.* **16** of agricultural land, be or leave unused for crops, especially in order to restore fertility. ⟨OE *restan*⟩
☛ *Hom.* WREST.

rest² [rɛst] *n., v.* —*n.* what is left; those that are left: *The rest of the crowd dispersed without incident.*
—*v.* continue to be: *You may rest assured that I will keep my promise.* ⟨< F *reste,* ult. < L *restare* be left < *re-* back + *stare* stand⟩
☛ *Hom.* WREST.
☛ *Usage. n.* **Rest** in this sense is always used with the definite article (*the*), and although always singular in form, uses the plural verb when it refers to more than one person or thing: *I ate half the leftover stew; the rest is in the freezer. We are leaving the meeting early, but the rest are staying for the reception.*

re•state [ri'steit] *v.* **-stat•ed, -stat•ing. 1** state again or anew. **2** state in a new way. **—re'state•ment,** *n.*

res•tau•rant ['rɛstə,rɒnt] *n.* a place to buy and eat a meal. ⟨< F *restaurant,* originally ppr. or *restaurer* restore⟩

res•tau•ra•teur [,rɛstərə'tɜr] *n.* the owner or manager of a restaurant. ⟨< F < ML *restaurator* one who restores⟩

rest cure *Medicine.* a treatment for mental or nervous disorders, consisting of rest and seclusion, a healthful diet, massage, etc.

rest•ful ['rɛstfəl] *adj.* **1** full of rest; giving rest. **2** quiet; peaceful. **—'rest•ful•ly,** *adv.* **—'rest•ful•ness,** *n.*

rest home an institution for the care of convalescents or the elderly.

rest•ing ['rɛstɪŋ] *adj., v.* —*adj.* **1** in a state of rest; inactive. **2** *Biology.* dormant, especially of spores or seeds. **3** *Cytology.* of a cell or cell nucleus, not dividing. **4** *Theatre and film.* of an actor, not currently appearing in a production.
—*v.* ppr. of REST.

res•ti•tu•tion [,rɛstə'tjuʃən] *or* [,rɛstə'tuʃən] *n.* **1** the giving back of what has been lost or taken away. **2** the act of making good any loss, damage, or injury: *It is only fair that those who do the damage should make restitution.* **3** a return to an original state. **4** what is given in compensation for loss, damage, or injury. ⟨< L *restitutio, -onis,* ult. < *re-* again + *statuere* set up⟩

res•tive ['rɛstɪv] adj. **1** restless; uneasy. **2** hard to manage. **3** refusing to go ahead; balky. ⟨ME < OF *restif* motionless < *rester* < L *restare.* See REST².⟩ **—'res•tive•ly,** *adv.* **—'res•tive•ness,** *n.*

rest•less ['rɛstlɪs] *adj.* **1** unable to rest; uneasy: *The dog seemed restless, as if he sensed some danger.* **2** without rest or sleep; not restful: *The sick child passed a restless night.* **3** rarely

In each of the words below, **re-** *means* again *or* anew; *the pronunciation of the main part of each word is not changed.*

re'spray	**re'sta•bi,lize**	**re'staff**	**re'stamp**	**re'ste•ri,lize**
re'sprin•kle	**re'stack**	**re'stage**	**re'start**	**re'stitch**

or never still or quiet; always moving: *You're very restless tonight.* **—'rest•less•ly,** *adv.* **—'rest•less•ness,** *n.*

re•stock [ri'stɒk] *v.* supply with a new stock; replenish.

res•to•ra•tion [,rɛstə'reiʃən] *n.* **1** the act of restoring or the condition of being restored: *the restoration of health, the restoration of a monarch.* **2** something restored. **3 Restoration,** in England: **a** the re-establishment of the monarchy in 1660 under Charles II. **b** the period from 1660 to 1688 during which Charles II and James II reigned.

re•stor•a•tive [rɪ'stɔrətɪv] *adj., n.* *—adj.* **1** capable of restoring; tending to restore health or strength. **2** of or pertaining to restoration.
—n. **a** something that restores health and strength. **b** something that revives an unconscious person.

re•store [rɪ'stɔr] *v.* **-stored, -stor•ing. 1** bring back; establish again: *to restore order.* **2** bring back to a former condition or to a normal condition: *The old house has been restored.* **3** give back; put back: *The thief was forced to restore the money to its owner.* **4** put (someone) back in a former place, office, rank, etc. ⟨ME < OF < L *restaurare*⟩ **—re'stor•er,** *n.*
☛ *Syn.* **2.** See note at RENEW.

re•strain [rɪ'strein] *v.* **1** hold back; keep down; keep in check; keep within limits: *She could not restrain her curiosity.* **2** keep in prison; confine. ⟨ME < OF *restreindre, restraindre* < L *restringere* restrict. See RESTRICT.⟩ **—re'strain•a•ble,** *adj.* **—re'strain•er,** *n.*
☛ *Syn.* **1.** See note at CHECK.

re•strain•ed•ly [rɪ'streinɪdli] *adv.* in a restrained manner; with restraint.

re•straint [rɪ'streint] *n.* **1** a restraining or being restrained. **2** a means of restraining: *A horse's bridle and a child's car seat are restraints.* **3** control of natural feeling or desire; reserve, moderation, or discipline: *We wish our MPs would show more fiscal restraint.* ⟨ME < OF *restraint(e)* < *restraindre.* See RESTRAIN.⟩

restraint of trade *Business.* the limitation or prevention of free competition.

re•strict [rɪ'strɪkt] *v.* **1** keep within limits; confine: *Our club membership is restricted to twelve.* **2** put limitations on: *to restrict the meaning of a word.* ⟨< L *restrictus*, pp. of *restringere* < *re-* back + *stringere* draw tight⟩

re•strict•ed [rɪ'strɪktɪd] *adj., v.* *—adj.* **1** limited or confined; kept within limits: *She is on a very restricted diet, and can have no sweets. Visitors are restricted to a small area of the gardens.* **2** having restrictions or limiting rules: *Factories may not be built in this restricted residential section.* **3** referring to the lowest category of classified documents: *She is allowed to see only files marked 'Restricted'.* **4** limited to members of a specified group: *This club is restricted to lawyers.* **5** of movies, limited to viewers over a specified age.
—v. pt. and pp. of RESTRICT.

re•stric•tion [rɪ'strɪkʃən] *n.* **1** something that restricts; a limiting condition or rule: *The restrictions on the use of the new gymnasium are these: no hard-soled boots or shoes; no fighting; no damaging of property.* **2** a restricting or being restricted: *This part is open to the public without restriction.*

restriction enzyme *Genetics.* an enzyme derived from bacteria that has the ability to cut DNA into fragments at specific sites, widely used in molecular genetics for DNA analysis.

restriction fragment length polymorphism *Genetics.* a polymorphic difference in DNA sequence between individuals that can be identified by cutting the DNA sequences with restriction enzymes, used in GENE MAPPING. *Abbrev.*: RFLP

re•stric•tive [rɪ'strɪktɪv] *adj.* restricting; limiting: *Some laws are prohibitive; some are only restrictive.* **—re'stric•tive•ly,** *adv.*

restrictive clause *Grammar.* an adjectival clause that is an essential and inseparable part of the sentence in which it appears.
☛ *Usage.* A **restrictive clause** restricts the noun it modifies in that it identifies or defines the member of the class of things being referred to and is for this reason an inseparable part of the noun construction; such clauses are never set off by commas, nor is there any perceptible pause before or after them in speech. *Example*: The man *who came to dinner* stayed for a month. A **non-restrictive clause** contains nothing more than descriptive detail and for this reason is merely a clause inserted into the main construction; such clauses must be set off from the main clause by commas and there is a perceptible pause, sometimes accompanied by a change in voice pitch, before and after them in speech. *Example*: The principal of the high school, *who is a most interesting man*, came to our house for dinner last evening.

re•string [ri'strɪŋ] *v.* **-strung, -string•ing.** put a new string or new strings on: *to restring a racket.*

rest room a public washroom, or toilet, as in a theatre or service station. Also, **restroom.**

re•struct•ure [ri'strʌktʃər] *v.* **-ured, -ur•ing. 1** alter, change, or restore the structure of: *His broken jaw was successfully restructured.* **2** plan or provide for a fundamental change in the organization of: *The new government will restructure several ministries.*

re•sult [rɪ'zʌlt] *n., v.* *—n.* **1** that which happens as the outcome of something: *The result of the fall was a broken leg.* **2 results,** *pl.* a good or useful outcome: *We want results, not talk.* **3** *Mathematics.* a quantity, value, etc., obtained by calculation. **4** an outcome; a score or grade; the record of such: *The result of the game was Edmonton 3, Calgary 0. The exam results will be posted tomorrow.*
—v. **1** be a result; follow as a consequence: *Sickness often results from eating too much.* **2** have as a result; end (*used with* **in**): *Eating too much often results in sickness.* ⟨< L *resultare* rebound, ult. < *re-* back + *salire* spring⟩
☛ *Syn. n.* **1.** See note at EFFECT.

re•sult•ant [rɪ'zʌltənt] *adj., n.* *—adj.* **1** resulting. **2** being an effect of two or more agents acting together.
—n. **1** a result. **2** *Physics. Mathematics.* any force that has the same effect as two or more forces acting together.
—re'sult•ant•ly, *adv.*

re•sume [rɪ'zum] *or* [rɪ'zjum] *v.* **-sumed, -sum•ing. 1** begin again; go on: *Resume reading where we left off.* **2** get or take again: *Those standing may resume their seats.* ⟨< L *resumere* < *re-* again + *sumere* take up⟩ **—re'sum•a•ble,** *adj.* **—re'sum•er,** *n.*

rés•u•mé ['rɛzə,mei] *French,* [ʀezy'me] *n.* **1** a short account of a person's education, employment history, etc., prepared for submission with a job application. **2** any summary, as of events, etc. ⟨< F *résumé*, originally pp. of *résumer* resume⟩

re•sump•tion [rɪ'zʌmpʃən] *n.* the act of resuming: *the resumption of duties after absence.* ⟨ME < LL *resumptio, -onis* < L *resumere.* See RESUME.⟩

re•sur•face [ri'sɜrfɪs] *v.* **-faced, -fac•ing. 1** provide with a new or different surface. **2** reappear: *She resurfaced in Vancouver under another name.* **3** reappear at the surface: *Helga resurfaced 30 seconds later, gasping for breath.*

re•surge [rɪ'sɜrdʒ] *v.* **-surged, -surg•ing.** rise again. ⟨< L *resurgere* < *re-* again + *surgere* rise⟩

re•sur•gence [rɪ'sɜrdʒəns] *n.* a rising again; revival: *a resurgence of energy.* **—re'sur•gent,** *adj.*

res•ur•rect [,rɛzə'rɛkt] *v.* **1** raise from the dead; bring back to life. **2** bring back to sight or into use: *resurrect an old custom.* ⟨< *resurrection*⟩

res•ur•rec•tion [,rɛzə'rɛkʃən] *n.* **1** a coming to life again; rising from the dead. **2 Resurrection,** *Christianity.* **a** the rising of Christ after His death and burial. **b** the rising of all the dead on Judgment Day. **3** the state of being alive again after death. **4** a restoration from decay, disuse, etc. ⟨< L *resurrectio, -onis,* ult. < *re-* again + *surgere* rise⟩

res•ur•rec•tion•ism [,rɛzə'rɛkʃə,nɪzəm] *n.* the exhumation and stealing of dead bodies, especially for dissection.

res•ur•rec•tion•ist [,rɛzə'rɛkʃənɪst] *n.* **1** a person who practises resurrectionism. **2** a person who brings something back to life again. **3** a believer in the Resurrection.

re•sus•ci•tate [rɪ'sʌsə,teit] *v.* **-tat•ed, -tat•ing.** bring or come back to life or consciousness; revive. ⟨< L *resuscitare,* ult. < *re-* again + *sub-* up + *citare* rouse < *ciere* stir up⟩
—re,sus•ci'ta•tion, *n.* **—re'sus•ci,ta•tive,** *adj.*

In each of the words below, **re-** *means* again *or* anew; *the pronunciation of the main part of each word is not changed.*

re'straight•en	**re'stud•y**	**,re•sub'mit**	**,re•sup'ply**
re-'strain	**re'stuff**	**,re•sub'scribe**	**re'sur•vey**
re'struc•ture	**re'style**	**re'sum•mon**	

re•sus•ci•ta•tor [rɪ'sʌsə,teitər] *n.* **1** an apparatus for forcing air or oxygen into the lungs of a person who has stopped breathing, in order to revive him or her. **2** a person who resuscitates.

ret [rɛt] *v.* **ret•ted, ret•ting.** expose (flax, hemp, etc.) to moisture or soak in water, in order to soften by partial rotting. ⟨< MDu. *reten*⟩

ret. **1** retain. **2** retired. **3** return.

re•tail *n., adj., adv., v. 1 and 2* ['riteil]; *v. 3* [rɪ'teil] *n., adj., v., adv. —n.* the sale of goods in small quantities directly to the final consumer: *Most stores sell at retail.* Compare WHOLESALE.
—adj. of, having to do with, or engaged in selling goods in small quantities: *the retail trade, a retail merchant. The prices in retail stores are always far higher than the wholesaler charges.*
—v. **1** sell in small quantities. **2** be sold in small quantities: *a dress retailing at $150.00.* **3** tell over again: *She retails everything she hears about her acquaintances.*
—adv. from a retail merchant or dealer: *He has to buy his supplies retail.* ⟨ME < OF *retail* scrap, ult. < *re-* back + *taillier* cut, ult. < L *talea* rod⟩

re•tail•er ['riteilər] *n.* a retail merchant or dealer.

re•tain [rɪ'tein] *v.* **1** continue to have or hold; keep: *She retained control of the business until she died. Porcelain retains heat longer than metal does.* **2** hold or keep in a fixed condition or state: *"Retain that pose as long as you can," the artist told her model.* **3** keep in mind; remember. **4** employ by payment of a fee: *He retained the best lawyer in the city.* ⟨ME < OF < L *retinere* < *re-* back + *tenere* hold⟩ **—re'tain•ment,** *n.*
☛ *Syn.* **1.** See note at KEEP.

re•tain•er[1] [rɪ'teinər] *n.* **1** a person or attendant, especially one who serves a person of rank or one who is a long-time family servant. **2** a device that holds in place or holds back a part of a machine. **3** a device that keeps teeth in place after orthodontic treatment. ⟨< *retain*⟩

re•tain•er[2] [rɪ'teinər] *n.* **1** a fee paid to secure services: *This lawyer receives a retainer before she begins work on a case.* **2** the fact of retaining or being retained in someone's service.
on retainer, retained for a fee: *Many businesses keep a lawyer on retainer.* ⟨< F *retenir*, n. use of infin. *retenir* retain⟩

retaining wall a wall built to hold back or confine a bank of earth, loose stones, etc.

re•take *v.* [ri'teik]; *n.* ['ri,teik] *v.* **-took, -tak•en, -tak•ing;** *n.*
—v. **1** take again: *The director wants the camera operator to retake that last scene.* **2** take back.
—n. **1** the act or process of rephotographing: *a retake of a scene in a motion picture.* **2** the film scene, etc. rephotographed or to be rephotographed.

re•tal•i•ate [rɪ'tæli,eit] *v.* **-at•ed, -at•ing.** repay one injury, etc. with another; return like for like: *If we insult them, they will retaliate.* ⟨< L *retaliare* < *re-* in return + *tal-* pay; influenced by *talis* such⟩ **—re'tal•i•a•tive** or **re'tal•i•a,to•ry,** *adj.*

re•tal•i•a•tion [rɪ,tæli'eiʃən] *n.* **1** the repaying of a wrong, injury, etc. with another; return of like for like. **2** the thing done to retaliate.

re•tard [rɪ'tɑrd] *v.* **1** make slow; delay the progress of; keep back; hinder: *Bad nutrition retarded her growth.* **2** be delayed or held back. ⟨< L *retardare*, ult. < *re-* back + *tardus* slow⟩
—re'tard•er, *n.*

re•tard•ant [rɪ'tɑrdənt] *n., adj. —n.* something, often a chemical, that slows up or delays an effect or an action.
—adj. holding back; tending to delay or make slower.

re•tar•da•tion [,ritɑr'deiʃən] *n.* **1** the act or an instance of retarding. **2** the extent to which something is retarded. **3** a significant, or noticeable, limitation or slowness of intellectual and social development. **4** something that retards; hindrance.

re•tard•ed [rɪ'tɑrdɪd] *adj., v. —adj.* **1** held back; hindered. **2** noticeably limited or slow in intellectual and social development.
—v. pt. and pp. of RETARD.

re•tard•er [rɪ'tɑrdər] *n.* **1** a person or thing that retards. **2** *Chemistry.* a substance used to delay a chemical reaction.

retch [rɛtʃ] *v.* make efforts to vomit; make movements like those of vomiting. ⟨OE *hrǣcan* clear the throat⟩
☛ *Hom.* WRETCH.

ret'd **1** returned. **2** retired.

rete ['riti] *n., pl.* **re•tia** ['ritiə] *or* ['riʃə]. **1** *Anatomy.* a network, as of fibres, blood vessels, or nerves. **2** a pierced plate on an astrolabe.

re•ten•tion [rɪ'tɛnʃən] *n.* **1** the fact of retaining or being retained. **2** the power to retain. **3** the ability to remember: *I was surprised by her retention; she remembered the names of all 13 people she had been introduced to that evening.* ⟨< L *retentio, -onis* < *retinere* retain. See RETAIN.⟩

re•ten•tion•ist [rɪ'tɛnʃə,nɪst] *n.* a person who supports the retention of a policy or practice, especially capital punishment.

re•ten•tive [rɪ'tɛntɪv] *adj.* **1** able to hold or keep. **2** able to remember. **—re'ten•tive•ly,** *adv.* **—re'ten•tive•ness,** *n.*

re•ten•tiv•i•ty [,ritɛn'tɪvɪti] *n.* **1** the power to retain; retentiveness. **2** *Physics.* the power of retaining magnetization after the magnetizing force has ceased to operate.

re•think [ri'θɪŋk] *v.* **-thought, -think•ing.** think over again, especially with a view to changing one's ideas, tactics, etc.: *We will have to rethink our energy strategy.*

re•ti•a•ri•us [,riʃi'ɛriəs] *n., pl.* **-rii** [-ri,aɪ] *or* [-ri,i]. *Roman antiquity.* a gladiator armed with a net for casting over his opponent, and a trident. ⟨< L *rete* net⟩

ret•i•cent ['rɛtəsənt] *adj.* disposed to keep silent or say little; not speaking freely; reserved in speech. ⟨< L *reticens, -entis*, ppr. of *reticere* keep silent < *re-* back + *tacere* be silent⟩
—'ret•i•cence, *n.* **—'ret•i•cent•ly,** *adv.*
☛ *Syn.* See note at SILENT.

re•tic•u•lar [rɪ'tɪkjələr] *adj.* **1** netlike. **2** intricate; entangled.

re•tic•u•late *adj.* [rɪ'tɪkjəlɪt] *or* [rɪ'tɪkjə,leit]; *v.* [rɪ'tɪkjə,leit] *adj., v.* **-lat•ed, -lat•ing.** *—adj.* netlike; covered with a network. Reticulate leaves have the veins arranged like the threads of a net. The lines on the surface of a ripe canteloupe are reticulate.
—v. **1** cover or mark with a network. **2** form a network.

re•tic•u•la•tion [rɪ,tɪkjə'leiʃən] *n.* **1** a reticulated formation, arrangement, or appearance; network. **2** one of the meshes of a network. ⟨< L *reticulatio, -onis*, ult. < *reticulum*, dim. of *rete* net⟩

ret•i•cule ['rɛtɪ,kjul] *n. Archaic.* a woman's small purse or handbag. ⟨< F < L *reticulum*, dim. of *rete* net. Doublet of RETICULUM.⟩

re•tic•u•lum [rɪ'tɪkjələm] *n., pl.* **-la** [-lə]. **1** a network; any reticulated system or structure. **2** *Zoology.* the second stomach of cud-chewing mammals. **3 Reticulum,** *Astronomy.* the Net, a southern constellation between Dorado and Horologium. ⟨< L. Doublet of RETICULE.⟩

re•ti•form ['ritə,fɔrm] *or* ['rɛtə,fɔrm] *adj.* netlike; reticular.

ret•i•na ['rɛtənə] *n., pl.* **-nas, -nae** [-,ni] *or* [-,naɪ]. *Anatomy.* a membrane at the back of the eyeball, composed of layers of nervous tissue and containing light-sensitive rods and cones. This membrane receives images and passes them on to the optic nerve. See EYE for picture. ⟨< Med.L *retina* < L *retinacula*, pl., band, reins < *retinere* retain. See RETAIN.⟩ **—'ret•i•nal,** *adj.*

ret•i•ni•tis [,rɛtə'naitɪs] *n. Pathology.* inflammation of the retina.

ret•i•no•blas•to•ma [,rɛtɪnoublæ'stoumə] *n. Genetics.* a form of cancer of the eye, occurring in young children, which may be inherited as an autosomal dominant trait. ⟨< *retina* + Gk. *blastos* sprout + E *-oma*⟩

re•ti•nol ['rɛtə,nɒl] *n.* **1** VITAMIN A. **2** *Chemistry.* a yellowish oil distilled from resin, and used in printing inks and solvents, and as a solvent and antiseptic. *Formula:* $C_{32}H_{16}$ ⟨< Gk. *rhetin(e)* resin + English *-ol*⟩

ret•i•no•scope ['rɛtənə,skoup] *n. Opthalmology.* an instrument used in retinoscopy.

ret•i•nos•co•py [,rɛtə'nɒskəpi] *n. Opthalmology.* an examination of the retina aimed at determining the refraction of the eye.

ret•i•nue ['rɛtə,nju] *n.* a group of attendants or retainers; a following: *The king's retinue accompanied him on the journey.*

In each of the words below, **re-** *means* again *or* anew; *the pronunciation of the main part of each word is not changed.*

re'swal•low	**re'tape**	**re'tell**	**re'thread**
re'syn•the,size	**re'teach**	**re'test**	**re'tie**
re'tab•u,late	**re'tel•e,vise**	**re'tes•ti,fy**	

⟨ME < OF *retenue*, originally fem. pp. of *retenir* retain < L *retinere.* See RETAIN.⟩

re•tire [rɪ'taɪr] *v.* **-tired, -tir•ing. 1** give up an office, occupation, etc.: *The teacher expects to retire at 65.* **2** remove from an office, occupation, etc.: *Government employees are usually retired at age 65.* **3** go away, especially to be quiet or alone: *She retired to her studio to finish her sculpting.* **4** withdraw; draw back; send back: *The government retires worn or torn bills from use.* **5** go back; retreat: *The enemy retired before the advance of our troops.* **6** go to bed: *We retire early.* **7** take up and pay off (bonds, loans, etc.). **8** *Baseball and cricket.* put out (a batter, side, etc.). ⟨< F *retirer* < *re-* back + *tirer* draw⟩

☛ *Syn.* **3.** See note at DEPART.

re•tired [rɪ'taɪrd] *adj., v. —adj.* **1** withdrawn from one's profession or occupation: *a retired sea captain.* **2** reserved; retiring: *a shy, retired nature.* **3** secluded; shut off; hidden: *a retired spot.* **4** for or given to persons in retirement.
—v. pt. and pp. of RETIRE.

re•tir•ee [rətaɪ'ri] *or* [rə'taɪri] *n.* a person who has retired from his or her occupation or profession. Also, **retirant**.

re•tire•ment [rɪ'taɪrmənt] *n.* **1** the act of retiring or the state of being retired, especially from an occupation or profession. **2** the age at which a person normally retires from work: *Several people in our department will reach retirement within the next year.* **3** (*adj.*) of, having to do with, or designed for people who are retired: *a retirement village.* **4** seclusion or privacy: *They live in retirement, neither making nor receiving visits.* **5** a secluded or private place.

re•tir•ing [rɪ'taɪrɪŋ] *adj., v. —adj.* shrinking from society or publicity; reserved; shy: *a retiring nature.*
—v. ppr. of RETIRE. **—re'tir•ing•ly,** *adv.*

re•took [ri'tʊk] *v.* pt. of RETAKE.

re•tool [ri'tul] *v.* **1** adapt or replace the tools of (a factory), usually in order to make a different product. **2** reorganize for the purpose of updating.

re•tort[1] [rɪ'tɔrt] *v., n. —v.* **1** reply quickly or sharply. **2** return in kind; turn (something) back on its originator: *to retort insult for insult or blow for blow.*
—n. **1** a sharp or witty reply. **2** the act of making such a reply. ⟨< L *retortus*, pp. of *retorquere* throw back < *re-* back + *torquere* twist⟩

re•tort[2] [rɪ'tɔrt] *n.* a container in a laboratory used for distilling or decomposing substances by means of heat. ⟨< Med.L *retorta*, originally fem. pp. of L *retorquere.* See RETORT[1].⟩

re•touch *v.* [ri'tʌtʃ]; *n.* ['ri,tʌtʃ] *v., n. —v.* **1** improve (a painting or photographic negative, etc.) by making slight changes. **2** tint or bleach (new growth of hair) to match previously dyed growth: *He had his roots retouched.*
—n. **1** the act of retouching: *The photo needs a retouch.* **2** a detail changed during retouching: *The retouch eliminates all the shadows.* **3** the thing retouched.

RETP or **R.E.T.P.** RESERVE ENTRY TRAINING PLAN.

re•trace [rɪ'treis] *v.* **-traced, -trac•ing.** go back over: *We retraced our steps to where we started.* ⟨< F *retracer* < *re-* back + *tracer* trace⟩ **—re'trace•a•ble,** *adj.*

re–trace [ri 'treis] *v.* **-traced, -trac•ing.** trace over again: *Re-trace these drawings.* ⟨< *re-* + *trace*⟩

re•tract [rɪ'trækt] *v.* **1** draw back or in: *Cats can retract their claws.* **2** withdraw; take back: *to retract an offer, to retract an opinion.* ⟨< L *retractare*, ult. < *re-* back + *trahere* draw⟩ **—re'tract•a•ble,** *adj.*

re•trac•ta•tion [,ritræk'teiʃən] *n.* a retracting of a promise, statement, etc.

re•trac•tile [rɪ'træktaɪl] *or* [rɪ'træktəl] *adj.* capable of retracting or being retracted, as the head of a turtle or the claws of a cat.

re•trac•tion [rɪ'trækʃən] *n.* **1** a drawing or being drawn back or in. **2** a taking back; withdrawal of a promise, statement, etc. **3** retractile power.

re•trac•tive [rɪ'træktɪv] *adj.* tending or serving to retract.

re•trac•tor [rɪ'træktər] *n.* **1** a person or thing that draws back something. **2** *Anatomy.* a muscle that retracts an organ, protruded part, etc. **3** a surgical instrument or device for drawing and holding back an organ or part.

re•tral ['ritrəl] *adj.* at or toward the back; posterior.

re•tread *v.* [ri'trɛd]; *n.* ['ri,trɛd] *v.* **-tread•ed, -tread•ing;** *n.*
—v. put a new tread on.
—n. **1** a retreaded tire. **2** *Slang.* a person, especially military, who returns to active work after retirement.

re•treat [rɪ'trit] *v., n. —v.* go back; move back; withdraw: *Seeing the big dog, the burglar retreated rapidly.*
—n. **1** the act of going back or withdrawing: *The army's retreat was orderly.* **2** a signal for retreat: *The drums beat a retreat.* **3** a signal on a bugle or drum, given in the army at sunset. **4 a** a safe, quiet place; place of rest or refuge. **b** retirement to such a place. **5 a** a period of withdrawal from regular life, singly or in a group, devoted to prayer, meditation, and other religious exercises. **b** a period of withdrawal from the regular working venue, usually as a group, devoted to building relationships and, often, to intensive discussion and consideration of major problems, with the goal of coming up with answers.
beat a retreat, run away; retreat: *We dropped the apples and beat a hasty retreat when the farmer shouted at us.* ⟨ME < OF *retraite*, orig. pp. of *retraire* < L *retrahere* retract < *re-* back + *trahere* draw. Related to RETRACT.⟩

re•trench [rɪ'trɛntʃ] *v.* **1** cut down; reduce (expenses, etc.). **2** reduce expenses: *In hard times, we must retrench.* ⟨< MF *retrencher* < *re-* back + *trencher* cut⟩

re•trench•ment [rɪ'trɛntʃmənt] *n.* **1** a reduction of expenses. **2** a cutting down; cutting off.

ret•ri•bu•tion [,rɛtrə'bjuʃən] *n.* **1** a deserved punishment; return for evil done, or sometimes, for good done. **2** the act of punishing or, sometimes, rewarding. ⟨< L *retributio, -onis*, ult. < *re-* back + *tribuere* assign⟩

re•trib•u•tive [rɪ'trɪbjətɪv] *adj.* paying back, especially bringing or inflicting punishment in return for some evil, wrong, etc. **—re'trib•u•tive•ly,** *adv.*

re•trib•u•to•ry [rɪ'trɪbjə,tɔri] *adj.* retributive.

re•triev•al [rɪ'trivəl] *n.* the act of retrieving.

re•trieve [rɪ'triv] *v.* **-trieved, -triev•ing;** *n. —v.* **1** get or fetch again; recover: *to retrieve a lost wallet.* **2** bring back to a former or better condition; restore: *to retrieve one's fortunes.* **3** make good; make amends for; repair: *to retrieve a mistake, to retrieve a loss or defeat.* **4** find and bring back (killed or wounded game): *Some dogs can never be trained to retrieve.* **5** *Computer technology.* access (data) from storage for display, as on a monitor.
—n. the act of retrieving: *The spaniel made a good retrieve.* ⟨ME < OF *retreuv-*, a stem of *retrouver* < *re-* again + *trouver* find⟩
—re'triev•a•ble, *adj.*

☛ *Syn.* **1.** See note at RECOVER.

re•triev•er [rɪ'trivər] *n.* **1** any of several breeds of medium-sized to large dog often trained to retrieve game from land or water. See also LABRADOR RETRIEVER, GOLDEN RETRIEVER. **2** any person or thing that retrieves.

ret•ro[1] ['rɛtrou] *n.* RETRO-ROCKET. ⟨clipped form⟩

ret•ro[2] ['rɛtrou] *adj.* **1** returning to something of an earlier time, as clothing, literature, etc. **2** retroactive: *retro pay, retro leave.* ⟨clipped form⟩

retro– *prefix.* backward; back; behind: *retrogress, retro-rocket.* ⟨< L *retro-* < *retro*, adv.⟩

ret•ro•ac•tive [,rɛtrou'æktɪv] *adj.* acting back; having an effect on what is past. A retroactive law applies to events that occurred before the law was passed. **—,ret•ro'ac•tive•ly,** *adv.* **—,ret•ro•ac'tiv•i•ty,** *n.*

ret•ro•cede[1] [,rɛtrə'sid] *v.* **-ced•ed, -ced•ing.** go back; recede. ⟨< L *retrocedere* < *retro-* backward + *cedere* go⟩

ret•ro•cede[2] [,rɛtrə'sid] *v.* **-ced•ed, -ced•ing.** cede back (territory, etc.). ⟨< *retro-* + *cede*⟩

ret•ro•choir ['rɛtrə,kwaɪr] *n.* the area of a church behind the choir or the main altar.

ret•ro•fire ['rɛtrou,faɪr] *v.* **-fired, -fir•ing;** *n. —v.* **1** ignite (a retro-rocket). **2** of a retro-rocket, become ignited.
—n. the firing of a retro-rocket.

In each of the words below, **re-** *means* again *or* anew; *the pronunciation of the main part of each word is not changed.*

re'ti•tle	**,re•trans'fer**	**,re•trans'la•tion**	**,re•trans'mit**
re'train	**,re'trans•late**	**,re•trans'mis•sion**	**re'tri•al**

ret•ro•fit ['rɛtrou,fɪt] *v.* **-fit•ted, -fit•ting;** *n.* *—v.* make adaptations to (an existing structure, such as a building, an airplane, a motor vehicle, etc.) using new equipment, in order to improve it: *to retrofit an old house with insulation.*
—n. **1** the act of retrofitting. **2** something that has been retrofitted.

ret•ro•flex ['rɛtrə,flɛks] *adj., v.* *—adj.* **1** bent backward. **2** *Phonetics.* made by raising the tip of the tongue and bending it backward. The vowel in *hurt* is retroflex.
—v. Phonetics. pronounce with the tip of the tongue raised and bent backward. ⟨< L *retroflexus,* pp. of *retroflectere* < *retro-* back + *flectere* bend⟩

ret•ro•flex•ion [,rɛtrə'flɛkʃən] *n.* **1** a bending or being bent backward. **2** *Phonetics.* retroflex pronunciation. Also, **retroflection.**

ret•ro•grade ['rɛtrə,greid] *adj., v.* **-grad•ed, -grad•ing.**
—adj. **1** moving backward; retreating. **2** becoming worse: *Eliminating that staff position was definitely a retrograde move.* **3** *Music.* proceeding from the last note to the first.
—v. **1** move or go backward. **2** fall back toward a worse condition; grow worse; decline. ⟨< L *retrogradus* < *retrogradi,* ult. < *retro-* backward + *gradi* go⟩

retrograde amnesia a loss of memory of events that happened before a specific point in time, usually the time of trauma that caused the amnesia.

ret•ro•gress [,rɛtrə'grɛs] *or* ['rɛtrə,grɛs] *v.* **1** move backward; go back. **2** become worse. **3** go back into an earlier, simpler state. ⟨< L *retrogressus,* pp. of *retrogradi.* See RETROGRADE.⟩

ret•ro•gres•sion [,rɛtrə'grɛʃən] *n.* **1** a backward movement. **2** a becoming worse; a falling off; decline. **3** deterioration; the passing from a more complex to a simpler state or structure.

ret•ro•gres•sive [,rɛtrə'grɛsɪv] *adj.* **1** moving backward. **2** becoming worse. **—,ret•ro'gres•sive•ly,** *adv.*

re•tro–rock ['rɛtrou ,rɒk] *n.* a style of popular music characterized by nostalgic themes and styles.

ret•ro–rock•et ['rɛtrou ,rɒkɪt] *n.* a rocket that fires in a direction opposite to that of the motion of a spacecraft or satellite, thus acting as a brake. Also, **retrorocket.**

ret•ro•spect ['rɛtrə,spɛkt] *n., v.* *—n.* a survey of past time, events, etc.; a thinking about the past.
in retrospect, when looking back.
—v. think of (something past) (*sometimes with* **to**). ⟨ult. < L *retrospectus* < *retro-* back + *specere* look⟩

ret•ro•spec•tion [,rɛtrə'spɛkʃən] *n.* the act or an instance of looking back on things past; a survey of past events or experiences.

ret•ro•spec•tive [,rɛtrə'spɛktɪv] *adj., n.* *—adj.* **1** looking back on things past; surveying past events or experiences. **2** applying to the past; retroactive.
—n. an art exhibition reviewing the work of an artist or group of artists over a number of years. **—,ret•ro'spec•tive•ly,** *adv.*

re•trous•sé [rətru'sei] *or* [rə'trusei] *adj.* turned up: *a retroussé nose.* ⟨< F⟩

ret•ro•vi•rus ['rɛtrə,vaɪrəs] *n.* any of a family (Retroviridae) of single-stranded RNA viruses including those that cause AIDS or are implicated in certain cancers, such as leukemia.

ret•si•na [rɛt'sinə] *or* ['rɛtsɪnə] *n.* a resin-flavoured Greek wine. ⟨< Mod.Gk. *resina* < Ital. *resina* < L *rēsīna* resin⟩

ret•ting ['rɛtɪŋ] *n., v.* *—n.* the process of wetting flax, hemp, etc., and allowing it to decay until the fibres can be easily separated from the woody parts of the stalks.
—v. ppr. of RET.

re•turn [rɪ'tɜrn] *v., n., adj.* *—v.* **1** go back; come back: *My brother will return this summer.* **2** bring, give, send, hit, put, or pay back: *Return that book to the library.* **3** go back in discourse: *Let us return to the last speaker's analysis.* **4** repay with something similar: *If you can do that for me, I'll return your effort one day.* **5** yield; produce: *The concert returned about $150 over expenses.* **6** report or announce officially: *The jury returned a verdict of guilty.* **7** reply: *"No!" he returned crossly.* **8** elect to a lawmaking body: *All but one of the incumbents were returned to office.* **9** *Card games.* **a** lead (the suit led by one's partner). **b** follow (the suit led by one's partner).
—n. **1** a going or coming back; a happening again. **2** something returned. **3** a bringing, giving, sending, or putting back: *a poor return for kindness.* **4** Often, **returns,** *pl.* a profit; an amount received. **5** a report; account: *election returns, income tax return.* **6** a reply. **7** *Sports.* **a** the act of sending a ball back. **b** the ball so returned. **c** *Football.* the runback of a ball received on a kick or an interception. **8** *Computer technology.* a computer operation to start a new line. A HARD RETURN also starts a new paragraph.
in return, as a return: *They let us use their garden, and in return we give them some of the produce.*
—adj. **1** of or having to do with a return: *a return ticket.* **2** sent, given, done, etc. in return: *a return game.* **3** repeated: *a return engagement.* **4** causing or allowing the return of some part of a device to its normal or starting position: *a return spring, a return valve.* ⟨ME < OF *retourner* < *re-* back + *tourner* turn⟩

re•turn•a•ble [rɪ'tɜrnəbəl] *adj.* **1** that can be returned. **2** meant or required to be returned.

returned man *Cdn.* a war veteran. Also, **returned soldier.**

re•turn•ee [rɪtɜr'ni] *or* [rɪ'tɜrni] *n.* a person who has returned, especially one who has returned to his or her own country after capture in a war or service abroad.

returning officer in Canada, the official who is responsible for the entire election procedure in a particular constituency, from preparing the voters' list and the ballots to proclaiming the winning candidate. In federal elections, returning officers are appointed by the Governor General in Council.

return trip **1** a trip to a place and back again; a round trip. **2** the trip back from a place: *On the way there we stopped at a motel, but we made the return trip in one day.*

re•tuse [rɪ'tjus] *or* [rɪ'tus] *adj. Botany.* especially of leaves or flower petals, having a rounded apex with a small notch in the middle. ⟨< L *retusus,* pp. of *retundere* blunt, beat back < *re-* back + *tundere* beat⟩

re•u•ni•fi•ca•tion [ri,junəfə'keiʃən] *n.* **1** the act or process of reunifying. **2** the state of being reunified.

re•u•ni•fy [ri'junə,faɪ] *v.* **-fied, -fy•ing.** restore unity to; bring back together again.

re•un•ion [ri'junjən] **1** a coming together again: *the reunion of parted friends.* **2** a social gathering of persons who have been separated or who have interests in common: *We have a family reunion every summer.*

re•u•nite [,riju'nəit] *v.* **-nit•ed, -nit•ing.** **1** bring together again: *Mother and child were reunited after years of separation.* **2** come together again.

rev [rɛv] *n., v.* **revved, rev•ving.** *Informal.*
—n. a revolution (of an engine or motor).
—v. increase the speed of (an engine or motor). ⟨clipped form of *revolution*⟩

rev. **1** revenue. **2** reverse. **3** review. **4** revised; revision. **5** revolution.

Rev. Reverend.

re•val•ue [ri'vælju] *v.* **-val•ued, -val•u•ing.** value again or anew. **—,re,val•u'a•tion,** *n.*

re•vamp *v.* [ri'væmp]; *n.* ['rivæmp] *v., n.* *—v.* **1** patch up; repair. **2** redesign; make over; overhaul completely.
—n. a revamping.

re•veal [rɪ'vil] *v.* **1** make known something hidden, secret, or mysterious: *Never reveal my secret.* **2** display; show: *Her smile revealed her even teeth.* ⟨ME < L *revelare,* ult. < *re-* back + *velum* veil⟩ **—re'veal•er,** *n.*

☛ *Syn.* **1. Reveal,** DISCLOSE = make known something hidden or secret. **Reveal** has a basic sense of uncovering or unveiling, and suggests making known something that has been hidden or screened: *At the new school she revealed an aptitude for science.* **Disclose** also has a basic sense of uncovering, but emphasizes making known something that has deliberately been kept secret: *They disclosed that they had been married for a month.*

rev•eil•le ['rɛvəli], [rə'væli], *or* [rə'vɛli] *n.* **1** a signal on a

In each of the words below, **re-** *means* again *or* anew; *the pronunciation of the main part of each word is not changed.*

re'try	**re'twist**	**re-use**	**re-'ut•ter**	**re'var•nish**
re'tune	**re'type**	**,re-u•ti•li'za•tion**	**re'vac•ci,nate**	
re'turf	**,re-up'hol•ster**	**re-'u•ti,lize**	**,re•vac•ci'na•tion**	

bugle or drum to waken military personnel in the morning: *The sound of the reveille reverberated throughout the camp.* **2** the time when this signal is sounded. ⟨< F *réveillez(-vous)* awaken!, ult. < L *re-* again + *ex-* up + *vigil* awake⟩

rev•el ['rɛvəl] *v.* **-elled** or **-eled, -el•ling** or **-el•ing;** *n.* —*v.* **1** take great pleasure *(in)*: *The children revel in country life.* **2** make merry: *The party-goers revelled till the small hours of the morning.*
—*n.* a noisy good time; merrymaking. ⟨ME < OF *reveler* be disorderly, make merry < L *rebellare.* Doublet of REBEL.⟩
—'rev•el•ler or **'rev•el•er,** *n.*

rev•e•la•tion [,rɛvə'leiʃən] *n.* **1** the act of making known: *The revelation of the thieves' hiding place by one of their own number caused their capture.* **2** the thing made known: *Her true nature was a revelation to me.* **3** *Theology.* God's disclosure of himself and of his will to his creatures. ⟨ME < LL *revelatio, -onis* < *revelare* reveal. See REVEAL.⟩

rev•e•la•tor•y ['rɛvələ,tɔri] *adj.* **1** making known; revealing. **2** concerning religious revelation.

rev•el•ry ['rɛvəlri] *n., pl.* **-ries.** boisterous revelling or festivity; wild merrymaking.

rev•e•nant ['rɛvənənt] *or* [,rɛvə'nɑ̃]; *French,* [Rəv'nɑ̃] *n.* **1** a person who returns after a long absence. **2** a person who returns after death; ghost. ⟨< F *revenant* ghost < *revenir* to come back⟩

re•venge [rɪ'vɛndʒ] *n., v.* **-venged, -veng•ing.** —*n.* **1** harm done in return for a wrong; vengeance; returning evil for evil: *a blow struck in revenge.* **2** a desire for vengeance: *She said nothing but there was revenge in her heart.* **3** a chance to win in a return game after losing a game.
—*v.* **1** do harm in return for: *His family vowed to revenge his death.* **2** take vengeance on behalf of (someone or oneself): *He vowed to revenge himself on them for the betrayal.*
be revenged, get revenge: *He swore to be revenged on his brother's murderers.* ⟨ME < MF *revenge* < OF *revengier,* ult. < L *re-* back + *vindicare* avenge < *vindex, -icis* defender⟩
☛ *Syn. v.* **1. Revenge,** AVENGE = inflict punishment in return for. **Revenge** suggests getting even with someone else, often in a mean or savage way: *The gangsters revenged the murder of one of their gang.* **Avenge** suggests more the morally righteous equalizing of wrongs: *We avenged the insult to our family.*

re•venge•ful [rɪ'vɛndʒfəl] *adj.* feeling or showing a strong desire for revenge. **—re'venge•ful•ly,** *adv.* **—re'venge•ful•ness,** *n.*

rev•e•nue ['rɛvə,nju] *n.* **1** money coming in; income: *The government gets revenue from taxes.* **2** the section of the government that collects taxes and duties. **2** a particular item of income. **3** a source of income. ⟨< F *revenue,* originally fem. pp. of *revenir* < L *re-* back + *venire* come⟩

Revenue Canada the government tax-collecting agency.

revenue stamp a stamp to show that money has been paid to the government as a tax on something.

re•ver•ber•ant [rɪ'vɜrbərənt] *adj.* reverberating.

re•ver•ber•ate [rɪ'vɜrbə,reit] *v.* **-at•ed, -at•ing. 1** echo back: *Her voice reverberates from the high ceiling.* **2** cast or be cast back; reflect (light or heat). **3** subject to reflected heat in a reverberatory furnace. ⟨< L *reverberare* beat back, ult. < *re-* back + *verber* a blow⟩

re•ver•ber•a•tion [rɪ,vɜrbə'reiʃən] *n.* **1** an echoing back of sound; echo. **2** a reflection of light or heat. **3** that which is reverberated. **4** *Physics.* multiple reflection of sound waves within a closed space so that the sound persists after the source has stopped or been stopped.

re•ver•ber•a•to•ry [rɪ'vɜrbərə,tɔri] *adj., n.* —*adj.* **1** characterized by or produced by reverberations; deflected. **2** characterizing a furnace, kiln, etc., in which heat is deflected downward from the roof.
—*n.* any such device employing reverberation.

re•vere [rɪ'vir] *v.* **-vered, -ver•ing.** love and respect deeply; honour greatly; show reverence for. ⟨< L *revereri* < *re-* back + *vereri* stand in awe of, fear⟩
☛ *Syn.* **Revere,** REVERENCE = feel deep respect and honour for someone or something. **Revere** means to regard with deep respect mixed with love someone of very noble character or something associated with such a person: *People revered the great philosopher.* **Reverence** means to regard with deep respect mixed with wonder, awe, and love something, such as a tradition, law, or object (seldom a person), considered as almost sacred and not to be violated, injured, or profaned: *We reverence the memory of our heroes.*

rev•er•ence ['rɛvərəns] *n., v.* **-enced, -enc•ing.** —*n.* **1** a feeling of deep respect, mixed with wonder, awe, and love. **2** a deep bow. **3 Reverence,** usually with *Your* or *His,* a title used in speaking of or to a Roman Catholic priest.
—*v.* regard with reverence. ⟨ME < L *reverentia* < *reverens.* See REVERENT.⟩
☛ *Syn. v.* See note at REVERE.

rev•er•end ['rɛvərənd] *adj., n.* —*adj.* worthy of great respect. —*n.* **1 Reverend,** a title for a member of the clergy. **2** *Informal.* a member of the clergy. ⟨ME < L *reverendus* be respected < *revereri.* See REVERE.⟩
☛ *Usage.* **Reverend,** usually preceded by **the,** is normally followed by the person's first name or initials: *the Reverend Helen Shaw, the Reverend H. Shaw.* However, it is acceptable to say *the Reverend Ms. Shaw,* but not *the Reverend Shaw.* The abbreviation (**Rev.**) is used in newspapers and in more-or-less informal writing: *the Reverend Helen Shaw, Rev. H. Shaw.*

rev•er•ent ['rɛvərənt] *adj.* feeling reverence; showing reverence. ⟨ME < L *reverens, -entis,* ppr. of *revereri* revere. See REVERE.⟩ **—'rev•er•ent•ly,** *adv.*

rev•er•en•tial [,rɛvə'rɛnʃəl] *adj.* reverent. **—,rev•er'en•tial•ly,** *adv.*

rev•er•ie ['rɛvəri] *n.* **1** the act of thinking dreamy thoughts; dreamy thinking of pleasant things: *He loved to indulge in reveries about the future.* **2** the condition of being lost in dreamy thoughts. **3** a fantastic idea; ridiculous fancy. **4** *Music.* a composition suggesting a dreamy or musing mood. Also, **revery.** ⟨< F *rêverie* < *rêver* to dream⟩

re•vers [rə'vir] *or* [rə'vɛr] *n., pl.* **re•vers** [rə'virz] *or* [rə'vɛrz]. **1** a part of the front of a garment, especially a coat lapel, that is turned back to show the facing or lining. **2** the facing used. ⟨< F *revers* reverse⟩

re•ver•sal [rɪ'vɜrsəl] *n.* a change to the opposite; a reversing or being reversed.

re•verse [rɪ'vɜrs] *n., adj., v.* **-versed, -vers•ing.** —*n.* **1** the opposite or contrary: *She did the reverse of what I ordered.* **2 a** the gear or gears that reverse the movement of machinery. **b** the position of the control that moves such a gear or gears. **3** movement in an opposite direction; a backward or contrary movement. **4** a change to bad fortune; check; defeat: *He used to be rich, but he met with reverses.* **5** the back or rear of anything. **6** the side of the coin, medal, etc. that does not have the principal design (opposed to OBVERSE).
—*adj.* **1** turned backward; opposite or contrary in position or direction: *the reverse side of a phonograph record.* **2** acting in a manner opposite or contrary to that which is usual. **3** causing an opposite or backward movement.
—*v.* **1** turn the other way; turn inside out; turn upside down. **2** *Dancing.* turn in a direction opposite to the one in which one has been moving. **3** change to the opposite; repeal. **4** cause (something) to move backward or turn upside down. **5** shift into reverse gear.
reverse the charges, make a collect telephone call. ⟨ME < L *reversus,* pp. of *revertere* turn around. See REVERT.⟩
—re'vers•er, *n.*
☛ *Syn. v.* **1. Reverse,** INVERT = turn something the other way. **Reverse** is the more general in application, meaning 'to turn to the other side or in an opposite position, direction, order, etc.': *In this climate one needs a coat that can be reversed when it begins to rain.* **Invert** means to turn upside down, or turn back to front, as in word order: *Invert the subject and the auxiliary to ask a question.*

re•verse•ly [rɪ'vɜrsli] *adv.* **1** in a reverse position, direction, or order. **2** on the other hand; on the contrary.

reverse video *Computer technology.* an attribute of a field on a computer screen involving the interchange of the screen's foreground and background colours, usually for purposes of highlighting the field.

re•vers•i•bil•i•ty [rɪ,vɜrsə'bɪləti] *n.* the fact or quality of being reversible.

re•vers•i•ble [rɪ'vɜrsəbəl] *adj., n.* —*adj.* **1** that can be reversed; that can reverse. **2** of a fabric, finished on both sides so that either can be used as the outer side.

In each of the words below, **re-** *means* again *or* anew; *the pronunciation of the main part of each word is not changed.*

,re•ver•i•fi'ca•tion **re'ver•i,fy**

—n. a garment made so that either side may be worn exposed. **—re'vers•i•bly,** *adv.*

re•ver•sion [rɪ'vɜrʒən] *or* [rɪ'vɜrʃən] *n.* **1** a return to a former condition, practice, belief, etc.; return. **2** the act of turning (something) or being turned the reverse way. **3** *Law.* **a** the right to possess a certain property under certain conditions. **b** the return of property to the grantor or his or her heirs. **c** an estate or property so returned. **4** *Biology.* **a** a return to certain characteristics that have not been present for two or more generations. **b** an organism showing such characteristics. **5** the granting of a prize or award to the person next in line for it when the first winner cannot accept it: *She won the Grade 10 physics prize by reversion.* ⟨ME < L *reversio, -onis* < *revertere* turn around. See REVERT.⟩

re•ver•sion•al [rɪ'vɜrʒənəl] *or* [rɪ'vɜrʃənəl] *adj.* of, having to do with, or involving a reversion.

re•ver•sion•ar•y [rɪ'vɜrʒə,nɛri] *or* [rɪ'vɜrʃə,nɛri] *adj.* reversional.

re•vert [rɪ'vɜrt] *v.* **1** go back; return: **a** to a previous owner or the heirs: *If a man dies without heirs, his property reverts to the government.* **b** to a previous practice, state, or belief: *After many years as a Buddhist, she reverted to Islam.* **2** *Biology.* return to certain characteristics that have not been present for two or more generations. ⟨ME < OF < L *revertere* < *re-* back + *vertere* turn⟩

rev•er•y ['rɛvəri] *n., pl.* **-er•ies.** See REVERIE.

re•vet [rɪ'vɛt] *v.* **re•vet•ted, re•vet•ting.** face (a wall, embankment, etc.) with masonry or other material. ⟨< F *revêtir* clothe, ult. < L *re-* again + *vestis* garment⟩

re•vet•ment [rɪ'vɛtmənt] *n.* **1** a retaining wall. **2** an ornamental facing of marble, tile, etc. on a common masonry wall. ⟨< F *revêtement*⟩

re•view [rɪ'vju] *v., n.* *—v.* **1** study again; look at again: *He reviewed the scene of the crime.* **2** look back on: *Before falling asleep, Helen reviewed the day's happenings.* **3** survey mentally; present a survey in speech or writing. **3** examine or re-examine with a view to evaluating; look over with care: *A superior court may review decisions of a lower court.* **4** inspect formally: *The Admiral reviewed the fleet.* **5** examine to give an account or critique of: *Mr. Lebrun reviews books for a living.* **6** review books, etc.

—n. **1** a studying again. **2** a looking back on; a survey. **3** a re-examination, especially for purposes of evaluation. **4** an examination; inspection. **5** a critical account of a published work or of a performance of a movie, play, concert, etc., giving its merits and faults. **6** a magazine containing articles on subjects of current interest, including accounts of books, etc.: *a law review, a film review.* **7** revue. ⟨< F *revue,* originally fem. pp. of *revoir* see again, ult. < L *re-* again + *videre* see⟩

☛ *Hom.* REVUE.

☛ *Syn. n.* **5. Review,** CRITICISM = an article or account criticizing a book, play, art exhibit, etc. **Review** applies particularly to an account giving some idea of what the book or play, etc. is about, its good and bad points, and the reviewer's critical or personal opinion: *That magazine contains good reviews of the new movies.* **Criticism** applies particularly to a scholarly article or essay giving a critical judgment based on deep and thorough study and definite critical standards of what is good and bad in books, music, pictures, etc.: *an anthology of recent Shakespeare criticism.*

re•view•er [rɪ'vjuər] *n.* **1** a person who reviews. **2** a person who writes articles discussing books, plays, etc.

reviewing stand a raised platform for those reviewing a formal parade of troops, a flypast, etc.

re•vile [rɪ'vaɪl] *v.* **-viled, -vil•ing.** call bad names; abuse with words: *The affluent homeowner reviled the tramp ambling past his front gate.* ⟨ME < OF *reviler* despise < *re-* again + *vil* vile < L *vilis* cheap⟩ **—re'vil•er,** *n.*

re•vile•ment [rɪ'vaɪlmənt] *n.* **1** the act of reviling. **2** reviling speech.

re•vise [rɪ'vaɪz] *v.* **-vised, -vis•ing;** *n.* *—v.* **1** read carefully and correct or improve; look over and change: *She has revised the poem she wrote.* **2** change; alter: *to revise one's opinion.*

—n. **1** the process of revising. **2** a revised form or version. **3** *Printing.* a proof sheet printed after corrections have been made. ⟨< F *reviser,* ult. < L *re-* again + *videre* see⟩ **—re'vis•er,** *n.*

Revised Standard Version an American Protestant revision of the AUTHORIZED VERSION of the Bible. The Revised Standard Version of the New Testament was published in 1946 and the complete Bible in 1952. *Abbrev.:* RSV or R.S.V.

Revised Version the revised form of the AUTHORIZED VERSION of the Bible. The Revised Version of the New Testament was published in 1881 and the Old Testament in 1885. *Abbrev.:* RV or R.V.

re•vi•sion [rɪ'vɪʒən] *n.* **1** the act or work of revising. **2** a revised form: *a revision of a book.*

re•vi•sion•ism [rɪ'vɪʒə,nɪzəm] *n.* the proposals, practices, or beliefs of revisionists.

re•vi•sion•ist [rɪ'vɪʒə,nɪst] *n.* **1** one who supports or favours revision. **2** a reviser, especially one of those responsible for the Revised Version of the Bible. **3** a communist who believes that the doctrines of Marxism may be interpreted flexibly and revised in the light of national circumstances. **4** one who reinterprets history in order to provide an account that fits with and rationalizes a change in ideology, often sacrificing intellectual honesty to do so.

re•vi•so•ry [rɪ'vaɪzəri] *adj.* of or having to do with revision.

re•viv•al [rɪ'vaɪvəl] *n.* **1** a bringing or coming back to life or consciousness. **2** a restoration to vigour or health. **3** a bringing or coming back to style, use, activity, etc.: *the revival of a play of years ago.* **4** an awakening or increase of religious faith. **5** special services or efforts made to awaken or increase religious faith.

re•viv•al•ism [rɪ'vaɪvə,lɪzəm] *n.* **1** the form of religious activity characteristic of revivals. **2** a desire to revive the ways and institutions of the past.

re•viv•al•ist [rɪ'vaɪvəlɪst] *n.* **1** a person, especially a member of the clergy, who holds special services to awaken religious faith. **2** a person who revives old customs, styles in art, etc.

Revival of Learning, Letters, or **Literature** the Renaissance, especially in its relation to letters and literature.

re•vive [rɪ'vaɪv] *v.* **-vived, -viv•ing. 1** bring back or come back to life or consciousness: *to revive a half-drowned person.* **2** bring or come back to a fresh, lively condition: *Flowers revive in water.* **3** become or make operational, valid, or effective again. **4** give energy and strength to; restore: *Hot coffee revived the cold, tired woman.* **5** bring back or come back to notice, use, fashion, memory, activity, etc.: *An old play is sometimes revived on the stage.* **6** return (someone) to a state of religious or spiritual fervour. ⟨< L *revivere* < *re-* again + *vivere* live⟩ **—re'viv•er,** *n.*

re•viv•i•fy [rɪ'vɪvə,faɪ] *v.* **-fied, -fy•ing. 1** restore to life; give new life to. **2** revive. **—re,viv•i•fi'ca•tion,** *n.* **—re'viv•i,fi•er,** *n.*

rev•o•ca•ble ['rɛvəkəbəl] *adj.* that can be repealed, cancelled, or withdrawn. **—,rev•o•ca'bil•i•ty** or **'rev•o•ca•ble•ness,** *n.* **—'rev•o•ca•bly,** *adv.*

rev•o•ca•tion [,rɛvə'keiʃən] *n.* a repeal; cancellation; withdrawal: *the revocation of a law.*

rev•o•ca•to•ry ['rɛvəkə,tɔri] *adj.* revoking; recalling; repealing.

re•voice [ri'vɔɪs] *v.* **-voiced, -voic•ing. 1** voice again or in reply; echo. **2** restore or readjust to a proper tone: *to revoice an organ pipe.*

re•voke [rɪ'vouk] *v.* **-voked, -vok•ing;** *n.* *—v.* **1** take back; repeal; cancel; withdraw: *The government revoked the bill before it was voted on.* **2** *Card games.* fail to follow suit when one can and should; renege.

—n. *Card games.* a failure to follow suit when one can and should. ⟨ME < OF < L *revocare* < *re-* back + *vocare* call⟩

re•volt [rɪ'voult] *n., v.* *—n.* the act or state of rebelling: *The town is in revolt.*

—v. **1** turn away from and fight against a leader; rise against the government or other authority: *The people revolted against the dictator.* **2** turn away with disgust: *to revolt at a bad smell.* **3** cause to feel disgust. ⟨< F < Ital. *rivolta,* ult. < L *revolvere* revolve. See REVOLVE.⟩ **—re'volt•er,** *n.*

☛ *Syn. n.* **Revolt,** INSURRECTION, REBELLION = a rising up in active resistance against authority. **Revolt** emphasizes casting off allegiance and refusing to accept existing conditions or control: *The revolt of the French mob that stormed the Bastille developed into revolution.* **Insurrection** suggests an armed uprising of a group or section against established authority, often to seize control for their own class or party: *The leader of*

In each of the words below, **re-** *means* again *or* anew; *the pronunciation of the main part of each word is not changed.*

re'vict•ual	**re'vis•it**	**,re•vi•tal•i'za•tion**
re'vin•di,cate	**re'vis•u•a,lize**	**re'vi•tal,ize**

the insurrection became a dictator. **Rebellion** applies to open armed resistance organized to force the government to do something or to overthrow it: *What started as a rebellion became a civil war.*

re•volt•ing [rɪ'voultɪŋ] *adj., v. —adj.* disgusting; repulsive. —*v.* ppr. of REVOLT. **—re'volt•ing•ly,** *adv.*

rev•o•lu•tion [ˌrɛvə'luʃən] *n.* **1** a complete, often violent, overthrow of an established government or political system: *The 1917 revolution ended the monarchy in Russia.* **2** a complete change: *Plastics have brought about a revolution in industry.* **3** a movement of an object in a circle or curve around another object or around some point: *The revolution of the earth around the sun causes the seasons.* **4** the act or fact of turning around a centre or axis; rotation: *The revolution of the earth on its axis causes day and night.* **5** a single complete turn around a centre: *The wheel of the motor turns at a rate of more than one thousand revolutions a minute.* **6** the time or distance of one revolution. **7** a complete cycle or series of events: *The revolution of the four seasons fills a year.* ⟨ME < OF < L *revolutio, -onis* < *revolvere* revolve. See REVOLVE.⟩

rev•o•lu•tion•ar•y [ˌrɛvə'luʃəˌnɛri] *adj., n., pl.* **-ar•ies.** —*adj.* **1** of or involving a REVOLUTION (defs. 1 and 2). **2** bringing or causing great changes. **3** rotating; revolving. —*n.* a revolutionist.

Revolutionary War in the United States, the war from 1775 to 1783 by which the thirteen American colonies won independence from Britain. Also called the **American Revolution.**

rev•o•lu•tion•ist [ˌrɛvə'luʃənɪst] *n.* a person who advocates, or takes part in, a revolution.

rev•o•lu•tion•ize [ˌrɛvə'luʃəˌnaɪz] *v.* **-ized, -iz•ing.** change completely; produce a very great change in: *Mechanization revolutionized farm life.*

re•volve [rɪ'vɒlv] *v.* **-volved, -volv•ing. 1** move in a circle; move in a curve around a point: *The moon revolves around the earth.* **2** turn around a centre or axis; rotate: *The wheels of a moving car revolve.* **3** cause to move in this way. **4** turn over in the mind; consider from many points of view: *He wishes to revolve the problem before giving an answer.* **5** move in a complete cycle or series of events: *The seasons revolve.* **6** focus on or be oriented toward something regarded as a centre: *My concerns revolve around cost.* **7** be reflected upon (in the mind). ⟨ME < L *revolvere* < *re-* back + *volvere* roll⟩ **—re'volv•a•ble,** *adj.*

☛ *Syn.* **1.** See note at TURN.

re•volv•er [rɪ'vɒlvər] *n.* **1** a pistol with a revolving cylinder in which the cartridges are contained, enabling it to be fired several times without reloading. See FIREARM for picture. **2** a person or thing that revolves.

re•vue [rɪ'vju] *n.* a theatrical entertainment including singing, dancing, etc., usually having as a theme parodies of recent plays, humorous treatments of happenings and fads of the past or current year, etc. ⟨< F. See REVIEW.⟩

☛ *Hom.* REVIEW.

re•vul•sion [rɪ'vʌlʃən] *n.* **1** a strong feeling of disgust or distaste: *The stench of rotting vegetables filled us with revulsion.* **2** a sudden, violent change of feeling: *He suddenly felt a revulsion from the long solitude.* **3** a drawing or being drawn back and away, especially suddenly or violently. ⟨< L *revulsio, -onis,* ult. < *re-* back + *vellere* tear away⟩

Rev. Ver. REVISED VERSION.

re•ward [rɪ'wɔrd] *n., v. —n.* **1** a return made for something good that has been done. **2** a money payment given or offered for capture of criminals, the return of lost property, etc. —*v.* **1** give a reward to. **2** give a reward for. ⟨ME < ONF *reward* < *rewarder,* dial. var. of *regarder* < *re-* back + *garder* guard. See REGARD.⟩

re•ward•ing [rɪ'wɔrdɪŋ] *adj., v. —adj.* **1** worthwhile; beneficial; giving a sense of satisfaction: *Helping others can be most rewarding.* **2** offering material or financial gain: *You will find this a rewarding investment.* —*v.* ppr. of REWARD.

re•wire [ri'waɪr] *v.* **-wired, -wir•ing. 1** put new wires on or in. **2** telegraph again.

re•word [ri'wɜrd] *v.* change the wording of; express differently.

re•work [ri'wɜrk] *v.* work anew; revise or reprocess.

re•write *v.* [ri'rəit], *n.* ['rirəit] *v.* **-wrote, -writ•ten, -writ•ing;** *n.* —*v.* **1** write again; write in a different form; revise. **2** write (a news story) from material supplied in a form that cannot be used as copy. —*n.* something rewritten, especially for publication.

Rex [rɛks] *n.* **1** the official title of a reigning king: *George VI Rex.* **2** a breed of domestic cat having short kinky fur, usually silver-grey. Also, **Cornish Rex.** ⟨< L, king⟩

Reyn•ard ['rɛnərd] *or* ['reinɑrd] *n.* **1** a fox that is the main character in a group of medieval fables about animals. **2 reynard,** any fox. ⟨ME < OF *Renart, Renard* < Gmc.⟩

Rf rutherfordium.

RF, R.F., or **r.f. 1** RADIO FREQUENCY. **2** *Baseball.* right fielder.

rg or **RG** *Football.* right guard.

r.h. 1 right hand. **2** relative humidity.

Rh 1 RH FACTOR. **2** rhodium.

R.H. 1 ROYAL HIGHNESS. **2** Royal Highlanders.

rhab•do•man•cy ['ræbdəˌmænsi] *n.* the art or skill of divination by use of a rod or wand, especially for the purpose of discovering underground springs, oil, ore, etc.; divining; dowsing. ⟨< Gk. *rhábdos* rod + *manteiā* divination⟩

Rhad•a•man•thine [ˌrædə'mænθɪn] *or* [ˌrædə'mænθaɪn] *adj.* **1** of or having to do with Rhadamanthus. **2** incorruptibly and sternly just.

Rhad•a•man•thus [ˌrædə'mænθəs] *n. Greek mythology.* a son of Zeus and brother of King Minos of Crete. Because he was such a just man during his life, he was made one of the three judges in Hades after his death.

Rhaeto–Romance [ˌritou rou'mæns] *n., adj. —n.* a group of Romance languages spoken in southeastern Switzerland, the Tyrol, and northern Italy, and including the Romansch dialects, Ladino, Tyrolese, and Friulian. —*adj.* of or having to do with Rhaeto-Romance. ⟨< L *Rhaetus* of Rhaetia, an Alpine province + *Romance*⟩

rhap•sod•ic [ræp'sɒdɪk] *adj.* of, having to do with, or characteristic of rhapsody; extravagantly enthusiastic; ecstatic. Also, **rhapsodical. —rhap'sod•i•cal•ly,** *adv.*

rhap•so•dist ['ræpsədɪst] *n.* **1** a person who talks or writes with extravagant enthusiasm. **2** a writer or reciter of rhapsodies.

rhap•so•dize ['ræpsəˌdaɪz] *v.* **-dized, -diz•ing. 1** talk or write with extravagant enthusiasm. **2** write or recite rhapsodies. **3** recite as a rhapsody.

rhap•so•dy ['ræpsədi] *n., pl.* **-dies. 1** an utterance or writing marked by extravagant enthusiasm: *She went into rhapsodies over the garden.* **2** *Music.* an instrumental composition following no regular form: *Liszt's Hungarian rhapsodies.* **3** an epic poem, or a part of such a poem, suitable for recitation at one time. ⟨< L < Gk. *rhapsōidia* verse-composition, ult. < *rhaptein* to switch⟩

Rh blood group system *Biochemistry.* a human blood group system important in blood transfusion and pregnancy. Blood is classified as either Rh+ (Rhesus positive) or Rh– (Rhesus negative). See RHESUS BABY. ⟨< *Rhesus* factor⟩

rhe•a ['riə] *n.* **1** either of two species constituting a family (Rheidae) of large, flightless birds of South America, resembling ostriches but smaller and having three toes instead of two and a completely feathered head and neck. This family of birds constitutes the order Rheiformes. **2** *Astronomy.* **Rhea,** one of the moons of Saturn. ⟨< L < Gk., after the goddess *Rhea*⟩

rhe•bok ['ribɒk] See REEBOK.

Rhein•gold ['raɪnˌgould]; *German,* ['Raɪnˌgɔlt] *n. German and Norse mythology.* a magic hoard of gold owned by the Nibelungs and later by Siegfried. Also, **Rhinegold.**

Rhen•ish ['rɛnɪʃ] *adj., n. —adj.* of the river Rhine or the regions near it. —*n.* RHINE WINE. ⟨< L *Rhenus* Rhine⟩

In each of the words below, **re-** *means* again *or* anew; *the pronunciation of the main part of each word is not changed.*

re'vote
re'wake
re'wak•en
re'warm
re'wash
re'wa•ter
re'wax
re'weave
re'weigh
re'weld
re'win
re'wind
re'word
re'work
re'wrap

rhe•ni•um ['riniəm] *n. Chemistry.* a rare, hard, greyish metallic chemical element that has chemical properties similar to those of manganese. *Symbol*: Re; *at.no.* 75; *at.mass* 186.2. ⟨< L *Rhenus* Rhine⟩

rhe•ol•o•gy [ri'ɒlədʒi] *n.* the study of the flow and deformation of matter, including elasticity, plasticity, and viscosity. ⟨< Gk. *rheos* flowing < *rheein* flow + E *-logy*⟩ **—,rhe•o'log•i•cal,** *adj.* **—rhe'ol•o•gist,** *n.*

rhe•om•e•ter [ri'ɒmətər] *n.* an instrument for measuring the flow of liquids, especially blood. ⟨< Gk. *rheos* flowing < *rheein* flow + E *-meter*⟩ **—,rheo'met•ric** [,riə'mɛtrɪk], *adj.* **—rhe'om•e•try,** *n.*

rhe•o•stat ['riə,stæt] *n. Electricity.* an instrument for regulating the strength of an electric current by introducing different amounts of resistance into the circuit. ⟨< Gk. *rheos* current + *statos* standing still⟩ **—,rhe•o'stat•ic,** *adj.*

Rhe•sus baby ['risəs] an infant having Rh+ blood, born of a mother with Rh– blood who has previously borne an Rh+ infant and thus developed antibodies to fetal Rh+ blood. These antibodies attack the red blood cells of the subsequent fetus.

Rhesus factor RH FACTOR.

rhesus monkey a small monkey (*Macaca mulatta*) of S Asia much used in biological and medical research. The rhesus monkey is a macaque. ⟨from a character in the *Iliad*⟩

rhet•o•ric ['rɛtərɪk] *n.* **1** the art or skill of using words effectively in speaking or writing. **2** a book about this art. **3** language used to persuade or influence others: *The crowd was impressed by the speaker's rhetoric.* **4** mere display in language. ⟨ME < L < Gk. *rhētorikē (technē)* art of an orator < *rhētōr* orator⟩

rhe•tor•i•cal [rɪ'tɔrɪkəl] *adj.* **1** of or having to do with rhetoric. **2** using rhetoric. **3** intended especially for display; artificial. **4** oratorical. **—rhe'tor•i•cal•ly,** *adv.*

rhetorical question a question asked only for effect, not for information, and not expecting an answer.

rhet•o•ri•cian [,rɛtə'rɪʃən] *n.* **1** a person skilled in rhetoric. **2** a person given to display in language. **3** a teacher of rhetoric.

rheum [rum] *n.* **1** a watery discharge, such as mucus, tears, or saliva. **2** a cold; catarrh. ⟨ME < OF < L < Gk. *rheuma* a flowing < *rheein* flow⟩
☛ *Hom.* ROOM [rum].

rheu•mat•ic [ru'mætɪk] *adj., n. Pathology.* —*adj.* **1** of rheumatism. **2** having rheumatism; liable to have rheumatism. **3** causing rheumatism. **4** caused by rheumatism.
—*n.* **1** a person who has rheumatism. **2 rheumatics,** *pl. Informal.* rheumatism. ⟨ME < L < Gk. *rheumatikos* < *rheuma.* See RHEUM.⟩

rheumatic disease *Pathology.* any of a group of diseases of the connective tissues having non-specific causes, including gout, rheumatic fever, and rheumatoid arthritis.

rheumatic fever *Pathology.* an acute disease occurring usually in children, characterized by fever, swelling, pain in the joints, and inflammation of the heart. It is usually associated with a previous streptococcal infection.

rheu•mat•ic•ky [ru'mætɪki] *adj.* **1** having rheumatism: *On wet days, my mother is very rheumaticky.* **2** afflicted with rheumatism: *My rheumaticky knee is bad today.*

rheu•ma•tism ['rumə,tɪzəm] *n. Pathology.* any of various painful conditions of the joints, muscles, or connective tissue, characterized by inflammation, stiffness, etc. Bursitis and arthritis are forms of rheumatism. ⟨< L < Gk. *rheumatismos*, ult. < *rheuma* rheum. See RHEUM.⟩

rheu•ma•toid ['rumə,tɔɪd] *adj.* **1** resembling or affected by rheumatism: *rheumatoid arthritis.* **2** having rheumatism. **—,rheu•ma'toi•dal•ly,** *adv.*

rheumatoid arthritis *Pathology.* a persistent disease that produces very painful swelling and inflammation of the joints and is often progressively crippling.

rheu•ma•tol•o•gy [,rumə'tɒlədʒi] *n. Medicine.* the study and treatment of rheumatic diseases.

rheum•y ['rumi] *adj.* **-i•er, -i•est. 1** full of rheum. **2** causing rheum; damp and cold.
☛ *Hom.* ROOMIE, ROOMY.

Rh factor *Biochemistry.* a substance, actually a group of antigens, often found in the blood of human beings and the higher mammals. Blood containing this substance **(Rh positive)** does not combine favourably with blood lacking it **(Rh negative).** Also formerly called **Rhesus factor.** ⟨because first discovered in the blood of the rhesus monkey⟩

Rh immune globulin *Immunology.* a preparation of concentrated antibody given intramuscularly to some Rh negative women during and after pregnancy with an Rh positive fetus. *Abbrev.*: RhiG

rhi•nal ['raɪnəl] *adj.* of or having to do with the nose; nasal. ⟨< Gk. *rhis, rhinos* nose⟩

Rh incompatibility differences in Rh blood group of donor and recipient of a blood transfusion, or between a mother and fetus. Rh antibodies formed by an Rh negative person can cause destruction of Rh positive red cells.

Rhine [raɪn] *n.* a major river in Europe, flowing through Switzerland, Germany, and the Netherlands, into the North Sea.

Rhine•gold ['raɪn,gould] See RHEINGOLD.

Rhineland ['raɪnlænd] *or* ['raɪnlənd] *n.* Germany west of the Rhine.

rhi•nen•ceph•a•lon [,raɪnɛn'sɛfə,lɒn] *n. Anatomy.* the part of the cerebrum containing the olfactory structures that receive sensory information from the olfactory nerves.

rhine•stone ['raɪn,stoun] *n.* an imitation diamond, made of glass or paste. ⟨translation of F *caillou du Rhin*⟩

Rhine wine [raɪn] **1** a wine produced in the valley of the Rhine. Most Rhine wines are white wines. **2** any of a variety of light, still, dry white wines produced elsewhere, especially in California and the Okanagan Valley of British Columbia.

rhi•ni•tis [raɪ'naɪtɪs] *n. Pathology.* inflammation of the nose or its mucous membrane. ⟨< NL < Gk. *rhis, rhinos* nose + *itis*⟩

rhi•no ['raɪnou] *n., pl.* **-nos.** rhinoceros.

rhino– *combining form.* nose. ⟨< Gk. *rhis, rhinos* nose⟩

rhi•noc•er•os [raɪ'nɒsərəs] *n., pl.* **-os•es** or (*esp. collectively*) **-os.** any of a small family (Rhinocerotidae) of large, plant-eating mammals of Africa and Asia having very thick, hairless skin, a massive body, short, thick legs with three-toed feet, and one or two large horns growing upright on the snout. All types of rhinoceros are now endangered. ⟨ME < L < Gk. *rhinokerōs*, ult. < *rhis* nose + *keras* horn⟩

A rhinoceros

rhinoceros beetle any of several medium-sized to very large tropical scarabaeid beetles, especially of the genus *Dynastes*, so called because of the presence of a hornlike projection on the head.

rhi•no•la•ryn•gol•o•gy [,raɪnou,lærɪŋ'gɒlədʒi] *n. Medicine.* the study and treatment of diseases of the nose and throat.

rhi•nol•o•gist [raɪ'nɒlədʒɪst] *n.* a physician specializing in rhinology.

rhi•nol•o•gy [raɪ'nɒlədʒi] *n.* the branch of medicine that deals with the nose and its diseases.

rhi•no•plas•ty ['raɪnə,plæsti] *n.* plastic surgery involving the nose. ⟨< *rhino-* + Gk. *-plastia* < *plassein* form⟩

rhi•nor•rhea [,raɪnə'riə] *n. Medicine.* an excessive mucous discharge from the nose. ⟨< *rhino-* + Gk. *-rrhoia* < *rheein* flow⟩

rhi•no•scope ['raɪnə,skoup] *n. Medicine.* an instrument for examining the nasal passages.

rhi•no•tra•che•i•tis ['raɪnou,treiki'əitɪs] *n. Pathology.* inflammation of the nose and trachea.

rhi•zo•car•pous [,raɪzou'kɑrpəs] *adj. Botany.* of perennial plants, having the root perennial but the stem annual, as perennial herbs.

rhi•zo•gen•ic [,raɪzou'dʒɛnɪk] *adj. Botany.* producing roots. Also, **rhizogenous** [raɪ'zɒdʒənəs] or **rhizogenetic.**

rhi•zoid ['raɪzɔɪd] *adj., n.* —*adj.* rootlike.
—*n.* one of the rootlike filaments in mosses, etc., by which the plant is attached to the substratum. ⟨< Gk. *rhiza* root + *eidos* form⟩ **—rhi'zoi•dal,** *adj.*

rhi•zome ['raɪzoum] *n. Botany.* a rootlike stem lying along or under the ground, that usually produces roots below and shoots from the upper surface; rootstock. ⟨< Gk. *rhizōma*, ult. < *rhiza* root⟩ **—rhi'zom•a•tous** [-'zɒmətəs] *or* [-'zoumətəs], *adj.*

rhi•zo•morph•ous [,raɪzou'mɔrfəs] *adj. Botany.* shaped like a root; rootlike.

rhi•zo•pod ['raɪzə,pɒd] *n.* any of a subclass (Rhizopoda) of protozoans, including the amoebas, that form temporary projections of protoplasm for moving about and taking in food. ⟨< NL *rhizopoda*, pl. < Gk. *rhiza* root + *pous, podos* foot⟩

rhi•zot•o•my [raɪ'zɒtəmi] *n., pl.* **-mies.** *Surgery.* the cutting or section of the spinal nerve roots, especially the posterior roots, in order to eliminate pain.

Rh negative lacking certain antigens in the blood, and incompatible with Rh positive blood.

rho [rou] *n.* the seventeenth letter of the Greek alphabet (Ρ, ρ). ☛ *Hom.* ROE, ROW.

rho•da•mine ['roudə,min] *or* ['roudəmɪn] *n. Chemistry.* **1** a red dye obtained from the condensation of phthalic anhydride with an alkyl aminophenol. **2** any of various related dyes, ranging in colour from red to pink. ⟨< Gk. *rhodo-* red + E *amine*⟩

Rhode Island [roud] a northeastern state of the United States. One of the 13 original states, it is the smallest state in the U.S.

Rhode Island Red [roud] a breed of American chicken that has reddish feathers and a black tail, and lays brown eggs.

Rho•de•sian man [rou'diʒən] an early type of human (*Homo rhodesiensis*, also classified as *Homo sapiens rhodesiensis*) of late Pleistocene times in Africa, characterized by long limb bones and a large face with prominent brow ridges. ⟨< Northern *Rhodesia*, former name of Zambia, in Africa⟩

Rhodesian ridge•back ['rɪdʒ,bæk] a breed of large African hunting dog having a short coat with a ridge of hair growing forward along the backbone, now used mainly as a guard dog.

Rhodes Scholar [roudz] a holder of any of a number of scholarships awarded annually to students from certain Commonwealth countries and the United States for study at Oxford University in England. ⟨< Cecil *Rhodes* (1853-1902), a British colonial statesman who provided for these scholarships in his will⟩

rho•dic ['roudɪk] *adj. Chemistry.* of or containing rhodium, especially when tetravalent.

rho•di•um ['roudiəm] *n. Chemistry.* a greyish white metallic element, forming salts that give rose-coloured solutions. It is similar to aluminum. *Symbol*: Rh; *at.no.* 45; *at.mass* 102.91 ⟨< Gk. *rhodon* rose⟩

rho•do•den•dron [,roudə'dɛndrən] *n.* **1** any of a very large genus (*Rhododendron*) of shrubs and small trees of the heath family, found mainly in the cooler regions of the northern hemisphere and the mountains of S Asia, having showy, bell-shaped or funnel-shaped flowers, and evergreen or deciduous leaves. Some rhododendrons are widely cultivated as garden plants. **2** the flower of any of these plants. ⟨< NL < Gk. *rhododendron* < *rhodon* rose + *dendron* tree⟩

rho•do•lite ['roudə,ləit] *n.* a pink or violet variety of garnet used as a gemstone. ⟨< Gk. *rhodo-* rose; rose-red + *-lite*⟩

rho•do•nite ['roudə,nəit] *n.* a reddish, translucent mineral consisting mainly of manganese silicate, that occurs in metamorphic rocks and is often used as an ornamental stone. *Formula*: $MnSiO_3$ ⟨< G *Rhodonit* < Gk. *rhodon* rose; rose-red + G *-it* -ite⟩

rho•dor•a [rou'dɔrə] *n.* any of a genus (*Rhododendron canadensis*) of shrubs of the heath family native to eastern Canada and New England, having pink or red flowers that appear before or with the leaves. It blooms in spring in damp places in eastern North America. ⟨< NL *Rhodora*, the former genus name⟩

rhomb [rɒm] *or* [rɒmb] *n.* rhombus.

rhom•bic ['rɒmbɪk] *adj.* **1** having the form of a rhombus. **2** having a rhombus as base or cross section. **3** bounded by rhombuses. **4** *Chemistry.* having to do with a system of crystallization characterized by three unequal axes intersecting at right angles.

rhom•bo•he•dron [,rɒmbə'hidrən] *n.* **1** a solid bounded by six rhombic planes. **2** a six-sided prism, each face being a rhombus.

rhom•boid ['rɒmbɔɪd] *n., adj.* *–n.* a parallelogram with only the opposite sides equal. See QUADRILATERAL for picture. *–adj.* shaped like a rhombus or rhomboid. Also (adj.), **rhomboidal.** ⟨< LL < Gk. *rhomboeidēs*⟩

rhom•bus ['rɒmbəs] *n., pl.* **-bus•es, -bi** [-baɪ] *or* [-bi]. **1** a parallelogram with equal sides that is not a square. See QUADRILATERAL for picture. **2** as a special case, an equilateral parallelogram including a square. **3** rhombohedron. ⟨< L < Gk. *rhombos*⟩

rhon•chus ['rɒŋkəs] *n., pl.* **-chi** [-kaɪ] *or* [-ki]. a coarse rattling or whistling sound resembling a snore, caused by an obstruction in the bronchial passages. ⟨< L *rhoncus* a snoring, croaking, perhaps related to Gk. *rhenchos* < *rhenchein* to snore⟩

rho•tic ['routɪk] *adj., n. Linguistics.* *–adj.* **1** describing a dialect of English in which the [r] is pronounced in syllable-final or preconsonantal position, as in *car* [kɑr] or *cart* [kɑrt]. Standard Canadian English is rhotic; standard British English is non-rhotic. **2** of or being an r-like sound. *–n.* a rhotic sound.

Rh positive having certain antigens present in the blood, incompatible with Rh negative blood.

rhu•barb ['rubɑrb] *n.* **1** any of several plants (genus *Rheum*) of the buckwheat family, especially a common garden plant (*R. rhaponticum*) having large, heart-shaped leaves and long, thick, red-and-green, juicy leafstalks with an acid taste that are used for pies, preserves, etc. The leaves of the rhubarb are poisonous. **2** the leafstalks of garden rhubarb. **3** the dried rhizomes and roots of any of several Asian rhubarbs, used as a laxative. **4** *Slang.* a heated dispute. ⟨ME < OF < Med.L *rheubarbarum*, ult. < Gk. *rhēon barbaron* foreign rhubarb⟩

rhumb [rʌm] *or* [rʌmb] *n. Nautical.* any of the 32 points of the compass. ⟨ult. (< F, Sp., or Pg.) < L *rhombus* < Gk. *rhombos* rhombus⟩

rhum•ba ['rʌmbə] *or* ['rʊmbə] *n., v.* **-baed, -ba•ing.** See RUMBA.

rhyme [raɪm] *v.* **rhymed, rhym•ing;** *n.* *–v.* **1** sound alike in the last part. *Examples*: Long *and* song *rhyme.* Go to bed *rhymes with* sleepyhead. **2** put or make into rhyme: *to rhyme a translation.* **3** make rhymes: *She enjoys rhyming.* **4** use (a word) with another that rhymes with it: *to rhyme* love *with* dove.
–n. **1** an agreement in the final sounds of words or lines. **2** a word or line having the same last sounds as another: Cat *is a rhyme for* mat. **3** verses or poetry with some of the lines ending in similar sounds.
without rhyme or reason, having no system or sense. Also, **rime.** ⟨ME < OF *rime* < L < Gk. *rhythmos* rhythm. Doublet of RHYTHM.⟩ **–'rhym•er,** *n.*
☛ *Hom.* RIME[2].

rhyme scheme the pattern of end rhymes used in a poem, and usually indicated by letters; for example, *abba abba cde cde* and *abab cdcd efef gg* are both rhyme schemes for the sonnet.

rhyme•ster ['raɪmstər] *n.* a maker of rather poor rhymes or verse. Also, **rimester.**

rhyming slang **1** a form of slang in which a rhyming word is substituted for the intended word, as in *apples and pears* for *stairs.* It is common in Cockney dialect. **2** a reduction in the rhyme by chopping off the rhyming word, as, *apples = stairs.*

rhythm ['rɪðəm] *n.* **1** a feature of movement involving a regular repetition of a beat, accent, stress, rise and fall, etc.: *the rhythm of dancing, skating, swimming, the rhythm of the tides, the rhythm of one's heartbeat.* **2** the repetition of an accent; arrangement of beats in a line of poetry: *The rhythms of "Twinkle, twinkle, little star" and "O Canada" are different.* **3** a grouping by accents or beats: *triple rhythm.* **4** *Music.* the pattern of movement produced by the combination of accent, metre, and tempo. **5** a patterned repetition of formal elements such as timing, emphasis, etc., in a work of art or literature; the effect produced by this patterning. **6** *Biology.* a pattern of involuntary behaviour, action, etc. occurring regularly and periodically. **7** any sequence of regularly recurring events: *visual rhythm.* ⟨< L < Gk. *rhythmos* < *rheein* flow. Doublet of RHYME.⟩

rhythm and blues a style of music that developed in black urban areas of the SW United States in the 1930s and that was basically blues sung, often shouted, to the accompaniment of large bands with saxophones, guitars, etc. and strong rhythm sections.

rhyth•mic ['rɪðmɪk] *adj.* having rhythm; of or having to do with rhythm. Also, **rhythmical. –'rhyth•mi•cal•ly,** *adv.*

rhythm method a form of birth control involving abstention from sexual intercourse during the estimated period of ovulation.

rhyt•i•dec•to•my [,rɪtə'dɛktəmi] *n., pl.* **-mies.** facelift. ⟨< Gk. *rhytis* wrinkle + E *-ectomy*⟩

R.I. **1** Queen and Empress (for L *Regina et Imperatrix*). **2** King and Emperor (for L *Rex et Imperator*).

ri•a ['riə] *n.* an inlet of the sea that was originally a river valley and which increases in depth toward the sea. ⟨< Sp.⟩

ri•al ['riəl] *n.* **1** the basic unit of money in Iran, divided into 100 dinars. **2** the basic unit of money in Oman, divided into 1000 baisas. **3** the basic unit of money in Saudi Arabia, divided into 100 halalas. See table of money in the Appendix. **4** the basic unit of money in Yemen divided into 100 fils. **5** a coin or note worth one rial. Also, **riyal.** ⟨< Persian < Arabic *riyal* < Sp. *real* < L *regalis* regal. Doublet of REAL², REGAL, ROYAL⟩
☛ *Hom.* REAL [riəl].

Ri•al•to [ri'ɒltou] *n.* **1** in Venice: **a** a former business district. **b** a famous bridge that crosses the Grand Canal. **2 rialto,** *Business.* a place of exchange; marketplace.

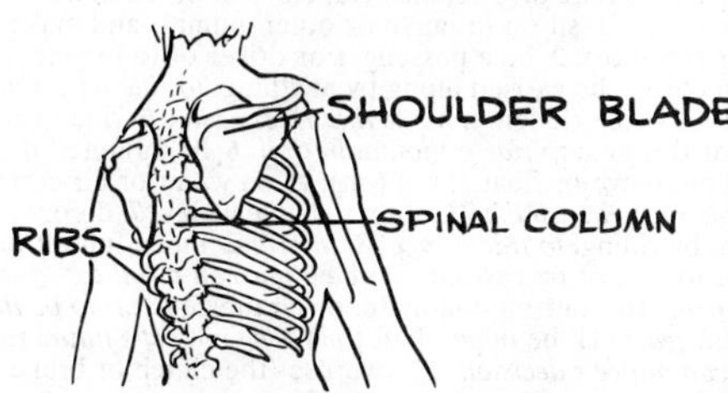

rib¹ [rɪb] *n., v.* **ribbed, rib•bing.** *—n.* **1** one of the curved bones extending from the backbone and enclosing the upper part of the body. See COLLARBONE for another picture. **2** one of a number of similar pieces forming a frame. An umbrella has ribs. **3** a thick vein of a leaf. **4** a ridge in a knitted or woven fabric. **5 a** a cut of meat containing a rib: *a rib of beef.* See BEEF and VEAL for pictures. **b ribs,** *pl.* spareribs. **6** *Architecture.* **a** one of the arches forming the supports for a vault. **b** a long, curved part of an arch.
tickle the ribs, cause laughter, as a joke.
—v. **1** furnish or strengthen with ribs. **2** mark with riblike ridges. ⟨ME *rible* < OE *rib* ult. < IE *rebh-* to arch, roof over⟩

rib² [rɪb] *n., v.* **ribbed, rib•bing.** *—n. Informal.* **a** a joke. **b** a teasing or mocking; a satire on or a parody of something.
—v. Informal. tease. ⟨clipping of *rib-tickler*⟩

rib•ald ['rɪbəld] *adj.* offensive in speech; coarsely mocking; irreverent; indecent; obscene. ⟨ME < OF *ribauld* < *riber* to be wanton < Gmc.⟩ **—'rib•ald•ly,** *adv.*

rib•ald•ry ['rɪbəldri] *n.* ribald language.

rib•and ['rɪbənd] *n. Archaic.* ribbon.

rib•band ['rɪb,bænd] *or* ['rɪbənd] *n. Shipbuilding.* a flexible strip of wood or metal running fore and aft across a ship's ribs to keep them in place until the outer plating or planking is put on. ⟨< *rib* + *band*⟩

ribbed [rɪbd] *adj., v. —adj.* having ribs or ridges.
—v. pt. and pp. of RIB.

rib•bing¹ ['rɪbɪŋ] *n., v. —n.* **1** ribs collectively. **2** a group or arrangement of ribs (See RIB¹, defs. 2, 4). **3** *Knitting.* an effect produced by knitting alternately plain and purl stitches, thus giving elasticity to the finished fabric.
—v. ppr. of RIB¹.

rib•bing² ['rɪbɪŋ] *n., v. —n. Informal.* teasing.
—v. ppr. of RIB².

rib•bon ['rɪbən] *n., v. —n.* **1 a** material in strips or bands. **b** a strip or band of silk, satin, velvet, etc. **2** anything like such a strip: *a typewriter ribbon.* **3 ribbons,** *pl.* torn pieces; shreds: *Her dress was torn to ribbons by the thorns and briars she had come through.* **4** a small badge of cloth worn as a sign of membership in an order, a decoration for bravery, prize for winning a contest, etc.: *the ribbon of the Victoria Cross.* **5** *Informal.* one of the reins for driving a horse.
—v. **1 a** decorate with ribbons. **b** mark with ribbons. **2** separate into shreds like ribbons. ⟨ME < OF *riban* < Gmc.⟩
—'rib•bon,like, *adj.*

ribbon development the building of houses, shops, and industrial buildings along a road.

ribbon farm a long, narrow holding of land fronting on a river, such as the farms of old Québec along the St. Lawrence River and those in the RED RIVER SETTLEMENT.

ribbon strip *Carpentry.* a thin horizontal board attached to studding to help support the ends of the joists.

ribbon worm any of a phylum (Nemertea, also called Rhynchocoela) of slender, unsegmented marine worms able to contract and stretch to an extreme length, sometimes over 25 m.

rib cage the cagelike structure formed by the ribs, enclosing the lungs, heart, etc.

rib eye a steak cut from the outer side of the ribs of beef.

ri•bo•fla•vin ['raɪbou,fleivən] *n. Biochemistry.* a constituent of the vitamin B complex, present in liver, eggs, milk, spinach, etc.; lactoflavin. It is sometimes called vitamin B_2 or G. ⟨< *ribose* + L *flavus* yellow⟩

ri•bo•nu•cle•ic acid [,raɪbounju'kliɪk] *or* [,raɪbounu'kliɪk] *Biochemistry.* a single-stranded molecule, transcribed from DNA, containing the sugar ribose instead of deoxyribose, and the bases adenine, guanine, uracil (replacing the thymine of DNA) and cytosine. One form carries genetic information from the nuclear DNA. *Abbrev.*: RNA

ri•bose ['raɪbous] *n. Chemistry.* a type of sugar made up of five carbon atoms to the molecule, instead of the six that make up glucose. *Formula*: $C_5H_{10}O_5$ ⟨< alteration of E *arabinose* (sugar), prepared from gum *arabic*⟩

ri•bo•so•mal RNA [,raɪbə'souməl] ribonucleic acid that is found in the ribosomes.

ri•bo•some ['raɪbə,soum] *n. Biology.* an organelle occurring in large numbers in the cytoplasm of a cell, concerned with the manufacture of protein.

rib–tick•ler ['rɪb ,tɪklər] *n. Informal.* a joke or funny story.

rice [rəis] *n., v.* **riced, ric•ing.** *—n.* **1** an annual cereal grass (*Oryza sativa*) cultivated throughout the world, from tropical to warm temperate regions, for its starchy, edible seeds. **2** the oblong seeds, or grain, of this plant, a major staple food.
—v. reduce (cooked potatoes, etc.) to a form resembling cooked rice, as by forcing through a sieve or ricer. ⟨ME < OF < Ital. *riso,* ult. < Gk. *oryza* < Iranian⟩

rice paper **1** a thin paper made from the straw of rice. **2** an edible paper made from the pith of the rice-paper plant.

rice–pa•per plant ['rəis ,peipər] a shrubby tree (*Tetraparax papyriferous*) of the ginseng family. The pith is used to make rice paper. Also, **rice-paper tree.**

ric•er ['rəisər] *n.* a utensil for ricing cooked potatoes, etc., by pressing them through small holes.

rich [rɪtʃ] *adj., n. —adj.* **1** having much money or property: *a rich man.* **2** well supplied; abounding: *Canada is rich in nickel and oil.* **3** abundant: *a rich supply.* **4** producing or yielding abundantly; fertile: *rich soil, a rich mine.* **5** valuable; having great worth: *a rich harvest.* **6** costly; elegant; luxurious; elaborate: *a rich dress, rich clothes.* **7** having many desirable elements or qualities. **8** of foods, made with much fat, egg, flavouring, etc. **9** of colours, sounds, smells, etc., deep; full; vivid: *a rich red, a rich tone.* **10** of wine, etc., strong and finely flavoured: *a rich, mellow sherry.* **11** of a fuel mixture, containing a high proportion of fuel to air. **12** *Informal.* very amusing, ridiculous.
—n. **the rich,** *pl.* rich people. ⟨OE *rice* < Gmc. < Celtic⟩
—'rich•ly, *adv.* **—'rich•ness,** *n.*
☛ *Syn. adj.* **1. Rich,** WEALTHY = having much money or property. **Rich** = having more than enough money, possessions, or resources for all normal needs and desires: *They own the mill in our town and are considered rich.* **Wealthy** = very rich, having a great store of money, property, and valuable possessions or resources: *Wealthy people are often patrons of the arts.*

rich•es ['rɪtʃɪz] *n.pl.* wealth; abundance of valuable things; much money, land, goods, etc. ⟨ME < OF *richesse,* taken as plural of *riche* rich < Gmc.⟩

Rich•ter scale ['rɪktər] a scale, ranging from 1 to 10, for measuring the intensity of an earthquake in terms of the vibrations produced at its centre. Each whole number on the scale, beginning with 1, represents a magnitude 10 times greater than the preceding one. An earthquake of magnitude 1 can be detected only by instruments; a magnitude of 7 indicates a major earthquake: *The most powerful earthquakes so far recorded registered 8.9 on the Richter scale.* ⟨after Charles F. Richter, American seismologist, (1900-1985)⟩

ri•cin ['rəisɪn] *or* ['rɪsɪn] *n. Chemistry.* a poisonous white powder isolated from the extremely toxic protein found in the bean of the castor-oil plant. ⟨< NL *ricinus* < L, the castor-oil plant⟩

ri•ci•no•le•ic acid [,rəisɪnə'liɪk] *or* [,rɪsɪnə'liɪk] *Chemistry.* a fatty acid found in castor oil and used to make soap, etc. *Formula*: $C_{18}H_{34}O_3$

ri•ci•no•lein [,rəisɪ'nouliɪn] *or* [,rɪsɪ'nouliɪn] *n. Chemistry.* the main constituent of castor oil, the glyceride of ricinoleic acid. *Formula*: $C_{57}H_{104}O_9$

rick¹ [rɪk] *n., v.* –*n.* **1** a stack of hay, straw, etc., especially one covered or thatched so that the rain will run off it. **2** *Esp. U.S.* a stack of cordwood or logs cut to even lengths and piled like a cord but not so wide.
–*v.* form into a rick or ricks. ⟨OE *hrēac*⟩
☛ *Hom.* WRICK.

rick² [rɪk] *n., v.* See WRICK.

rick•ets ['rɪkɪts] *n. Pathology.* a disease of childhood caused by lack of vitamin D or calcium, resulting in softening and, sometimes, bending of the bones; rachitis. ⟨apparently alteration of *rachitis*, influenced by *wrick* wrench, strain⟩

rick•ett•si•a [rɪ'kɛtsiə] *n., pl.* **-si•as** or **-si•ae** [-si,i]. any of a family (Rickettsiaceae, especially genus *Rickettsia*) of parasitic micro-organisms intermediate between bacteria and viruses, which usually live in lice, fleas, ticks, and other arthropods, and cause diseases such as typhus in human beings. ⟨after Howard T. *Ricketts* (1871-1910), U.S. pathologist. 20c.⟩

rick•et•y ['rɪkəti] *adj.* **1** liable to fall or break down; shaky: *a rickety old chair.* **2** having rickets; suffering from rickets. **3** feeble in the joints. **–'rick•et•i•ness,** *n.*

rick•ey ['rɪki] *n.* **1** a drink made of sugar, lime, carbonated water, and gin or some other alcoholic liquor. **2** a similar, non-alcoholic drink.

rick•rack ['rɪk,ræk] *n.* a flat, narrow, zigzag braid used for trimming. ⟨? reduplication of *rack¹*⟩

rick•shaw or **rick•sha** ['rɪkʃɒ] *n.* a small, two-wheeled hooded carriage, usually for one passenger, pulled by a cyclist, the carriage taking the place of the bicycle's rear wheel. Rickshaws were originally used in Japan and pulled by one or two men on foot. ⟨short for *jinrikishaw* < Jap. *jinrikisha* < *jin* person + *riki* power + *sha* vehicle⟩

ric•o•chet ['rɪkə,ʃei] *or* [,rɪkə'ʃei] *n., v.* **-cheted** [-'ʃeid], **-chet•ing** [-'ʃeiŋ]. –*n.* the skipping or rebounding of a projectile, such as a bullet, after striking a surface at an angle: *the ricochet of a bullet from a post, the ricochet of a flat stone on the water.*
–*v.* of a projectile, skip on or rebound from a surface: *The bullet ricocheted off the wall and shattered the vase on the table opposite.* ⟨< F⟩

ri•cot•ta [rɪ'kɒtə]; *Italian,* [ri'kɔtta] *n.* a mild Italian cheese, often used in making lasagna.

ric•tus ['rɪktəs] *n., pl.* **rictus** or **rictuses. 1** the width or gape of an open mouth or beak. **2** a fixed, gaping grimace or grin. ⟨< NL < L *rictus* open mouth, pp. of *ringi* open the mouth, gape. 18c.⟩ **–'ric•tal,** *adj.*

rid¹ [rɪd] *v.* **rid** or **rid•ded, rid•ding.** make free (from some troublesome thing): *What will rid a house of rats?*
be rid of, be freed from.
get rid of, a get free from: *I can't get rid of this cold.* **b** do away with: *Poison will get rid of the rats in the barn.* ⟨OE *(ge)ryddan* clear land⟩ **–'rid•der,** *n.*

rid² [rɪd] *v. Archaic or dialect.* a pt. and a pp. of RIDE.

rid•a•ble ['raɪdəbəl] *adj.* **1** able to be ridden: *Stallions are not as ridable as mares.* **2** able to be ridden over, through, or across: *The recent floods have made this route less ridable than before.*

rid•dance ['rɪdəns] *n.* **1** a clearing away or out; removal. **2** deliverance or relief from something.
good riddance, an expression of relief that something or somebody has been removed.

rid•den ['rɪdən] *v.* a pp. of RIDE.

–rid•den ['rɪdən] *combining form.* obsessed; overwhelmed by; full of; burdened with: *guilt-ridden, fear-ridden.*

rid•dle¹ ['rɪdəl] *n., v.* **-dled, -dling.** –*n.* **1** a puzzling or misleading question, statement, or problem, usually amusing and often involving a play on words. *Example*: *Q.*: *When is a door not a door? A.*: *When it is ajar.* **2** a person or thing that is hard to understand, explain, etc.: *Her disappearance remains a riddle.*
–*v.* **1** speak in riddles. **2** solve or explain (a riddle or question). ⟨OE *rǣdels* < *rǣdan* guess, explain; ME *redels* taken as pl.⟩

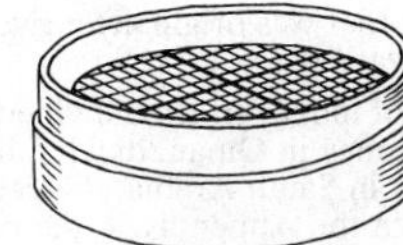
A garden riddle

rid•dle² ['rɪdəl] *v.* **-dled, -dling;** *n.* –*v.* **1** make many holes in: *The door of the fort was riddled with bullets.* **2** sift: *to riddle gravel.* **3** find fault with; criticize with verbal attacks; refute or disprove. **4** affect completely; permeate (*with* something undesirable): *a government riddled with corruption.*
–*n.* a coarse sieve. ⟨OE *hriddel* sieve⟩

ride [raɪd] *v.* **rode** or (*Archaic*) **rid, rid•den** or (*Archaic*) **rid, rid•ing;** *n.* –*v.* **1** sit on (a horse or other animal) and make use of it for transport. **2** be a passenger or driver of (a bicycle, roller coaster, etc.) **3** be carried along by anything: *to ride on a train.* **4** admit of being ridden: *a horse that rides easily.* **5** ride over, along, or through: *to ride a mountain trail.* **6** be mounted on; be carried on; move or float along (on), as on water or air currents: *The eagle rides the winds. The ship rode the waves.* **7** do or perform by riding: *to ride a race.* **8** *Informal.* make fun of; tease. **9** cause to ride or be carried: *to ride a man on a rail as punishment.* **10** control, dominate, or tyrannize over: *to be ridden by foolish fears.* **11** be dependent (*on*): *The project's future rides on the committee's decision.* **12** overuse (the clutch or brake in a vehicle) by treating it as a footrest. **13** overlap or rest on.
let ride, leave undisturbed or inactive: *Let the matter ride until the next meeting.*
ride down, a knock down. **b** overcome. **c** overtake by riding. **d** exhaust by riding.
ride high, enjoy success; do very well.
ride out, a withstand (a gale, etc.) without damage. **b** endure successfully.
ride up, slide up out of place: *That coat rides up at the back.*
–*n.* **1** a trip on the back of a horse, in a carriage, car, train, boat, etc.: *Let's go for a ride.* **2** a path, road, etc., made for riding: *They built a ride through the middle of the park.* **3** a mechanical amusement, such as a merry-go-round, Ferris wheel, etc.: *To a child, the rides are the best part of the fair.* **4** a turn on a merry-go-round, Ferris wheel, roller coaster, etc.: *Line up for the next ride.* **5** a chance or arrangement for transportation: *Do you need a ride to Saskatoon?*
take for a ride, *Slang.* **a** cheat. **b** murder. ⟨OE *rīdan*⟩
☛ *Syn. n.* **1. Ride,** DRIVE = a trip by some means of transportation. **Ride** emphasizes being carried along in or by something, as on horseback, in a boat, train, bus, etc., or in a car if one is going nowhere in particular or is strictly a passenger: *Let's go for a ride in my new car.* **Drive** emphasizes causing to move in a particular direction, and applies only to a trip in a horse-drawn or motor vehicle that one controls or operates or helps to direct: *Let's take a drive into the country.*

Ri•deau Hall ['ridou] *or* [ri'dou] the official residence of the Governor General of Canada, situated in Ottawa.

rid•er ['raɪdər] *n.* **1** a person who rides: *The Calgary Stampede is famous for its riders.* **2** anything added to a record, document, legislative bill, or statement after it was considered to be completed. **3** any object, device, or part mounted so that it straddles another piece. **–'rid•er•less,** *adj.*

rid•er•ship ['raɪdər,ʃɪp] *n.* **1** the passengers customarily using a particular system of transportation. **2** the total number of these passengers: *What is the ridership of the Skytrain?*

ridge [rɪdʒ] *n., v.* **ridged, ridg•ing.** –*n.* **1** any raised, narrow strip: *the ridges on corduroy cloth, the ridges in ploughed ground.* **2** the line where two sloping surfaces meet: *the ridge of a roof.* **3** a long, narrow chain of hills or mountains. **4** the long and narrow upper part of something: *the ridge of an animal's back.* **5** a long, narrow area of high barometric pressure.
–*v.* **1** form or make into ridges. **2** cover or mark with ridges. ⟨OE *hrycg*⟩ **–'ridg•y,** *adj.*

ridge•pole ['rɪdʒ,poul] *n.* the horizontal timber or pole along the top of a roof or tent. See FRAME for picture.

rid•i•cule ['rɪdə,kjul] *v.* **-culed, -cul•ing;** *n.* –*v.* laugh at; make fun of.
–*n.* laughter in mockery; words or actions that make fun of somebody or something. ⟨< F < L *ridiculum,* neut. of *ridiculus* ridiculous. See RIDICULOUS.⟩
☛ *Syn. v.* **Ridicule,** DERIDE, MOCK = make fun of someone or something and cause him or her or it to be laughed at. **Ridicule** emphasizes making fun of people or things, in either a merely thoughtless or an unkind way, with the intention of making them seem little and unimportant: *This boy ridicules his sisters' friends.* **Deride** emphasizes laughing in contempt and holding up to scorn: *Some people deride patriotic rallies and parades.* **Mock** means to ridicule by imitating scornfully: *The impudent girls mocked the teacher.*

ri•dic•u•lous [rɪ'dɪkjələs] *adj.* deserving ridicule; absurd; laughable. ⟨< L *ridiculus* < *ridere* laugh⟩ **—ri'dic•u•lous•ly,** *adv.* **—ri'dic•u•lous•ness,** *n.*

☛ *Syn.* **Ridiculous,** ABSURD, PREPOSTEROUS = not sensible or reasonable. **Ridiculous** emphasizes the laughable effect produced by something out of keeping with good sense: *Her attempts to be the life of the party were ridiculous.* **Absurd** emphasizes the contrast with what is true or sensible: *His belief that he was too clever to be caught in his wrongdoing was absurd.* **Preposterous** adds to **absurd** the idea of being unacceptable or perverse, as well as the notion of completely beyond belief: *The bandit made the preposterous suggestion that he would drop his gun if the police officer first dropped hers.*

rid•ing[1] ['raɪdɪŋ] *n.* **1** *Cdn.* a political division represented by a Member of Parliament or a Member of the Legislative Assembly; constituency. **2** *Brit.* formerly, one of the administrative divisions of the county of Yorkshire: *the West Riding.* ⟨ME *thriding* < ON *thrithjungr* one third; the *th-* was lost as a result of the previous *-t* or *-th* in the compounds *East Thriding, North Thriding, West Thriding*⟩

rid•ing[2] ['raɪdɪŋ] *n., adj., v.* *—n.* the act of one that rides.
—adj. **1** used for or in the act of riding: *riding boots, a riding crop.* **2** made to be operated by a rider: *a riding mower.*
—v. ppr. of RIDE.

riding boot a high boot worn by horseback riders.

riding crop a short whip with a loop on one end instead of a lash.

riding habit a type of dress or suit of clothes worn by horseback riders.

ri•el [ri'ɛl] *n.* the basic unit of money in Kampuchea, divided into 100 su. See table of money in the Appendix. ⟨origin unknown⟩

Riel Rebellions [ri'ɛl] *Cdn.* the RED RIVER REBELLION and the NORTHWEST REBELLION. ⟨after Louis David *Riel* (1844-1885), leader of the Métis, later hanged⟩

Ries•ling ['rizlɪŋ] *n.* **1** a fragrant dry or sweet white wine. **2** the grape from which this wine is made. **3** the vine bearing this grape, grown in Europe, the interior of British Columbia, and California.

Rif, the [rɪf] a mountainous region in N Morocco, along the Mediterranean coast.

rife [rəif] *adj.* **1** happening often; common; numerous; widespread. **2** well supplied; full; abounding: *The land was rife with rumours of war.* ⟨OE *rīfe*⟩

riff [rɪf] *n., v. Jazz music.* *—n.* a continuously repeated instrumental phrase, supporting a solo improvisation or forming the basis of a tune.
—v. play a riff or riffs. ⟨prob. shortened and altered form of *refrain*. 20c.⟩

Riff [rɪf] *n., pl.* **Riffs, Riff,** or **Riff•i** **['rɪfi]** a member of a Berber people of the Rif.

Riff•i•an ['rɪfiən] *adj., n.* *—adj.* of or having to do with the Riffs or the region they live in.
—n. a Riff.

rif•fle ['rɪfəl] *v.* **-fled, -fling;** *n.* *—v.* **1** leaf or flip through (a stack of paper, the pages of a book, etc.) quickly by sliding the thumb along the edges, so that the pages are momentarily separated. **2** shuffle cards, holding half the deck in each hand, by bending the edges slightly so that the two divisions slide into each other. **3** cause water to run in riffles. **4** form or become a riffle; flow over or through a riffle.
—n. **1** the act of shuffling cards by riffling. **2 a** a shoal or other object in a stream causing a ripple or a stretch of choppy water. **b** the ripple itself; a shallow rapid. **3** *Placer mining.* **a** a device consisting of slats or bars set diagonally into the bottom of a sluice box to catch the gold particles in gravel, water, etc. **b** any of these slats or bars individually. ⟨? variant of *ripple* or *ruffle*[1]⟩

riff•raff ['rɪf,ræf] *n., adj.* *—n.* **1** worthless people. **2** trash.
—adj. worthless. ⟨ME < OF *rif et raf* every scrap < *rifler* rifle[2] + *raffler* carry off⟩

ri•fle[1] ['rəifəl] *n., v.* **-fled, -fling.** *—n.* **1** a gun having spiral grooves in its barrel to spin the bullet as it is fired. See FIREARM for picture. **2** such a gun that is fired from the shoulder.
3 Rifles, *pl.* certain military units armed with rifles: *the Queen's Own Rifles.*
—v. **1** cut spiral grooves in (a gun). **2** propel at great speed as by throwing or hitting with a bat, racket, etc. ⟨ult. < F *rifler* scratch, groove, *rifle*[2]⟩

ri•fle[2] ['rəifəl] *v.* **-fled, -fling. 1** search and rob; ransack and rob. **2** steal; take away. **3** strip bare: *The boys rifled the apple tree.* ⟨ME < OF *rifler* < Gmc.⟩ **—'ri•fler,** *n.*

ri•fle•man ['rəifəlmən] *n., pl.* **-men. 1** a soldier armed with a rifle. **2** a man who uses a rifle.

rifle pit a pit or short trench that shelters riflemen firing at an enemy.

rifle range 1 a place for practice in shooting with a rifle: *The competition was held on the rifle range.* **2** the distance that a rifle will shoot a bullet: *The deer was beyond rifle range of the hunters.*

ri•fling ['rəiflɪŋ] *n., v.* *—n.* **1** the act or process of cutting spiral grooves in a gun barrel. **2** the system of spiral grooves in a rifle.
—v. ppr. of RIFLE.

rift [rɪft] *n., v.* *—n.* **1** a gap, split, or break: *a rift in the clouds.* **2** a breach in relations between individuals, groups, or nations; estrangement. **3** *Geology.* a fault, usually one along which movement was lateral.
—v. break or cause to break open or split.

rig[1] [rɪg] *v.* **rigged, rig•ging;** *n.* *—v.* **1** *Nautical.* **a** equip (a ship) with masts, sails, ropes, etc. **b** move (a shroud, boom, stay, etc.) to its proper place. **2** equip (used with **out**): *to rig out a football team.* **3** *Informal.* clothe; dress (usually used with **out** or **up**): *On Halloween the children rig themselves up in funny clothes.* **4** get ready for use. **5** put together in a hurry or by using odds and ends (*often used with* **up**): *The girls rigged up a tent, using a rope and a blanket.*
—n. **1** *Nautical.* the arrangement of masts, sails, ropes, etc. on a ship. A schooner has a fore-and-aft rig; that is, the sails are set lengthwise on the ship. **2** *Informal.* clothing or costume, especially when unusual, showy, etc.: *John's rig consisted of a silk hat and overalls.* **3** an outfit; equipment. **4 a** the machinery or installation used for locating and extracting petroleum or natural gas from the earth: *a drill rig, an oil rig.* **b** *Informal.* any seemingly complicated machine. **5** *Informal.* **a** any combination trucking unit, as a tractor trailer, a truck with a horse trailer, etc. **b** a wagon, with its horse or horses. **c** *Informal.* a large tractor-trailer, or just its tractor: *My uncle drives a rig for a living.* ⟨ME < Scand.; cf. Danish *rigge*⟩

rig[2] [rɪg] *n., v.* **rigged, rig•ging.** *—n. Brit.* a trick, prank, or swindle.
—v. **1** arrange dishonestly for one's own advantage: *to rig a race.* **2** arrange unfavourably. ⟨origin uncertain; ? < RIG[1]⟩

rig•a•ma•role ['rɪgəmə,roul] *n.* rigmarole.

Ri•gel ['raɪdʒəl] *or* ['raɪgəl] *n. Astronomy.* a first magnitude star, the brightest in the constellation Orion at most times of the year. See BETELGEUSE. ⟨< Arabic *rijl* foot, so called from its position in the left foot of Orion⟩

rig•ger ['rɪgər] *n.* **1** a person who rigs. **2** a person who rigs ships, or works with hoisting tackle, etc. **3** *Informal.* a person who manipulates something fraudulently.

☛ *Hom.* RIGOUR.

rig•ging ['rɪgɪŋ] *n., v.* *—n.* **1** the ropes, chains, etc. on a ship, used to support and work the masts, yards, sails, etc. **2** tackle; equipment.
—v. ppr. of RIG.

right [rəit] *adj., adv., n., v.* *—adj.* **1** good; just; lawful: *He did the right thing when he told the truth.* **2** correct; true: *the right answer.* **3 a** proper; fitting: *She always managed to say the right thing at the right time.* **b** reputable; approved by society: *the right clubs.* **4** favourable: *If the weather is right, we'll go.* **5** physically or mentally healthy; normal: *My head doesn't feel right.* **6** meant to be seen; most important: *the right side of cloth.* **7 a** of the side that is turned to the east when the main side faces north; opposite left: *You have a right hand and a left hand. The right bank of a river is the one to the right as one faces downstream.* **b** toward this side: *a right turn.* **c** to the right side of the person facing a given object: *It's on the right side of my desk.* **8** Often, **Right,** *Politics.* of, having to do with, supporting, or belonging to the most conservative element; rightist. **9** straight: *a right line.* **10** of, forming, or containing a 90° angle: *a right angle, a right cone.* **11** *Archaic.* rightful; real: *the right owner.*
—adv. **1** in a way that is good, just, or lawful: *He acted right when he told the truth.* **2** correctly; truly: *She guessed right.* **3** properly; well: *It's faster to do a job right the first time.* **4** favourably: *turn out right.* **5** into a good or suitable condition: *Put things right.* **6** on or to the right hand: *Turn right.* **7** exactly; just; precisely: *Put it right here.* **8** very (*used in some titles*): *Right Honourable.* **9** toward the political right: *I see her politics are shifting further right all the time.* **10** *Archaic or informal.* extremely: *I am right glad to see you.* **11** in a straight line; directly: *Look me right in the eye.* **12** completely: *His hat was knocked right off.* **13** yes; very well: *"Come at once," his mother called. "Right," he replied.*
right away, at once; immediately: *She promised to do it right away.*
right now, immediately; at the present time: *Stop that right now! They're playing in the yard right now.*

right off, at once; immediately.
—n. **1** that which is right: *Do right, not wrong.* **2** a just claim, title, or privilege: *the right to vote, copyright.* **3** fair treatment; justice. **4** the right side or hand: *Turn to your right. The school is on the right.* **5** a blow struck with the right hand: *He was knocked out with a right to the jaw.* **6 the Right** or **the right,** *Politics.* **a** a group or party generally supporting capitalism and private enterprise and opposed to socialism, government regulation of business, etc. **b** a group or party that tends to oppose political and social change; advocates or supporters of conservatism or reaction. **c** especially in some European legislatures, the members occupying the seats to the right of the presiding officer by virtue of their conservative or reactionary views. **7** *Business.* **a** the privilege of subscribing for a stock or bond. **b** a certificate granting such a privilege.
by rights or **by right,** rightly; properly; correctly.
in the right, on the right side of a conflict.
to rights, *Informal.* in or into proper condition, order, etc.: *It took us three hours to set the house to rights after the children's party.*
—v. **1** make correct: *to right errors.* **2** do justice to: *to right the oppressed.* **3** get or put into proper position: *The ship righted as the wave passed.* ⟨OE *riht*⟩ **—'right•er,** *n.* **—'right•ly,** *adv.* **—'right•ness,** *n.*
☛ *Hom.* RITE, WRIGHT, WRITE.

right about-face ['rəit ə,bʌut 'feis] **1** a turn in the opposite direction. **2** a complete reversal of one's views, behaviour, etc. Also, **right about, right about-turn.**

right angle an angle of 90°. See ANGLE for picture.

right–an•gled ['rəit 'æŋgəld] *adj.* containing a right angle or right angles; rectangular. Also, **right-angle.**

right brain that portion of the cortex that lies on the right side of the corpus callosum. It controls movement on the left side of the body, and is also mostly responsible for some non-verbal and non-linear thinking.

right•eous ['rəitʃəs] *adj.* **1** doing right; virtuous; behaving justly. **2** morally right or justifiable: *righteous indignation.* ⟨OE *rihtwīs* < *riht* right + *wīs* way, manner⟩ **—'right•eous•ly,** *adv.*

right•eous•ness ['rəitʃəsnɪs] *n.* upright conduct; virtue; the state or condition of being right and just.

right face a turn to the right.

right•ful ['rəitfəl] *adj.* **1** according to law; by rights: *the rightful owner of this dog.* **2** just and right; proper. **—'right•ful•ly,** *adv.* **—'right•ful•ness,** *n.*

right–hand ['rəit 'hænd] *adj.* **1** on or to the right. **2** of, for, or with the right hand. **3** most helpful or useful: *one's right-hand man.*

right–hand•ed ['rəit 'hændɪd] *adj., adv. —adj.* **1** using the right hand more easily and readily than the left: *The majority of humans are right-handed.* **2** done with the right hand: *a right-handed stroke.* **3** made to be used with the right hand: *Most scissors are right-handed.* **4** turning from left to right: *a right-handed screw.*
—adv. with the right hand: *She plays tennis right-handed and golf left-handed.* **—'right-'hand•ed•ly,** *adv.* **—'right-'hand•ed•ness,** *n.* **—'right-'hand•er,** *n.*

Right Honourable a title given to all members of the Privy Council of the United Kingdom. The prime minister of Canada has this title. *Abbrev.:* Rt. Hon.

right•ist ['rəitɪst] *n., adj. —n. Politics.* **1** a person who supports or favours conservative or reactionary policies. **2** a member of a conservative or reactionary organization.
—adj. having conservative or reactionary ideas. **—'right•ism,** *n.*

right–mind•ed ['rəit 'maɪndɪd] *adj.* having proper or moral opinions or principles. **—'right-'mind•ed•ly,** *adv.* **—'right-'mind•ed•ness,** *n.*

right of search the privilege of a nation at war to stop and search neutral vessels on the high seas for contraband, the finding of which renders the ship liable to seizure.

right of way **1** the right to go first; precedence over all others. **2** the right to pass over property belonging to someone else. **3** a route that may lawfully be used for this. **4** a strip of land on which a road, railway, power line, etc. is built.

right–siz•ing ['rəit ,saɪzɪŋ] *n.* the reduction of a company to its optimum size for profit.

right stuff, the *Informal.* certain qualities of character which lead to success, such as confidence, dependability, and courage.

right–to–life ['rəit tə 'ləif] *adj.* opposing abortion and euthanasia.

right triangle a triangle, one of whose angles is a right angle.

right•ward ['rəitwərd] *adj.* **1** on or toward the right. **2** situated on or pointing toward the right.

right whale **1** a large, thickset, black baleen whale (*Balaena glacialis*) of the northern hemisphere, having a large head, a thick lower lip that curves upward in a high bow on each side, and a very thick layer of blubber. It is an endangered species. **2** any other whale of the same family (Balaenidae). Right whales lack the throat grooves of other baleen whales. ⟨probably from the fact that these whales are large and slow-moving and therefore 'right' for hunting in the early days of whaling with sailing ships and hand harpoons⟩

right wing **1** the more conservative or reactionary faction of an assembly, group, or party. **2** *Hockey, lacrosse, etc.* **a** the playing position to the right of centre on a forward line. **b** the player in this position. **—'right-'wing,** *adj.* **—'right-'wing•er,** *n.*

right•y ['rəiti] *n., pl.* **-ies.** *Informal.* a right-handed person.

rig•id ['rɪdʒɪd] *adj.* **1** stiff; firm; not bending: *a rigid support.* **2** strict; not changing: *Our club has few rigid rules.* **3** severely exact; rigorous: *a rigid examination.* ⟨< L *rigidus* < *rigere* be stiff⟩ **—'rig•id•ly,** *adv.* **—ri'gid•i•ty** or **'rig•id•ness,** *n.*
☛ *Syn.* **1.** See note at STIFF. **2, 3.** See note at STRICT.

rig•ma•role ['rɪgmə,roul] *n.* **1** a fussy or complicated procedure. **2** meaningless or incoherent talk. ⟨earlier *ragman roll* < *ragman* list, catalogue (origin uncertain) + *roll*⟩

rig•or ['rɪgər] *n.* See RIGOUR.

rig•or mor•tis ['rɪgər 'mɔrtɪs] the stiffening of the muscles after death. ⟨< L *rigor mortis* stiffness of death⟩

rig•o•ro•so [,rɪgə'rousou] *adj. Music.* in exact rhythm; in strict timing. ⟨< Ital.⟩

rig•or•ous ['rɪgərəs] *adj.* **1** very demanding; strict: *the rigorous discipline in the army.* **2** harsh; severe: *a rigorous climate.* **3** thoroughly logical and scientific; exact: *the rigorous methods of science.* **—'rig•or•ous•ly,** *adv.*
☛ *Syn.* **1.** See note at STRICT.

rig•our or **rig•or** ['rɪgər] *n.* **1** strictness; severity. **2** harshness: *the rigour of a long, cold winter.* **3** logical exactness: *the rigour of scientific method.* **4** stiffness; rigidity, especially in body tissues or organs. **5** a shivering accompanied by a feeling of chilliness, often preceding a fever. ⟨ME < OF < L *rigor* < *rigere* be stiff⟩
☛ *Hom.* RIGGER.

Rig–Ve•da [,rɪg 'veidə] *or* [,rɪg 'vidə] *n.* the oldest and most important of the ancient sacred writings of Hinduism, consisting of approximately 1000 hymns dating from about 1500 B.C.

Riks•dag ['rɪks,dag] *n.* the Swedish houses of parliament.

rile [raɪl] *v.* **riled, ril•ing. 1** make angry or irritated. **2** ROIL (defs. 1-3). ⟨var. of *roil*⟩

rill[1] [rɪl] *n.* a tiny stream; little brook. ⟨Cf. Du. *ril* groove, furrow⟩

rill[2] [rɪl] *n. Astronomy.* any of a number of long, narrow valleys or trenches seen on the surface of the moon. ⟨< G *rille* furrow. See RILL[1].⟩

rim [rɪm] *n., v.* **rimmed, rim•ming.** *—n.* **1** an edge, border, or margin on or around anything: *the rim of a wheel, the rim of a cup.* **2 rims,** *pl.* the frames of eyeglasses. **3** of a wheel, **a** the outer circle attached to the hub by spokes. **b** the circular flange attaching an automobile wheel to the tire mounted on it.
—v. **1** form or put a rim around: *The well was rimmed with grass.* **2** decorate the edge of: *cups and saucers rimmed with gold.* **3 a** roll around the rim of: *The roulette ball rimmed the wheel.* **b** *Golf.* of the ball, roll around the rim and not fall in. ⟨OE *rima*⟩ **—'rim•less,** *adj.*

rime[1] [raɪm] *v.* **rimed, rim•ing.** *n.* See RHYME.

rime[2] [raɪm] *n., v.* **rimed, rim•ing.** *—n.* white frost; hoarfrost. *—v.* cover with rime. ⟨OE *hrīm*⟩
☛ *Hom.* RHYME.

rime•ster ['raɪmstər] *n.* See RHYMESTER.

rim•fire ['rɪm,faɪr] *adj.* **1** of or having to do with a type of cartridge having the primer set in a rim on the base. **2** of a firearm, designed to fire such cartridges.

rim•rock ['rɪm,rɒk] *n. Cdn., esp. West.* **1** an outcropping or ridge of rock, especially one that once formed the bank of a stream. **2** the crest of a range of hills or mountains.

rim•y ['raɪmi] *adj.* **rim•i•er, rim•i•est.** covered with rime or hoarfrost; frosty.

rind [raɪnd] *n.* the hard or firm outer covering (of oranges, melons, cheeses, etc.). The bark of a tree or plant may be called the rind. ⟨OE⟩

rin•der•pest ['rɪndər,pɛst] *n.* an acute and usually fatal infectious disease of cattle, sheep, etc., caused by a virus. ⟨< G < *Rinder* cattle + *Pest* pestilence⟩

ring[1] [rɪŋ] *n., v.* **ringed, ring•ing.** *—n.* **1** a circle. **2** a thin circle of metal or other material: *a napkin ring, rings on her fingers.* **3** persons or things arranged in a circle. **4** the outer edge or border of a coin, plate, wheel, or anything round and flat. **5** an enclosed space for races, games, circus performances, showing livestock, etc. The ring for a prize fight is square. **6** prize fighting: *His ambition was success in the ring.* **7** a competition; rivalry; contest: *in the ring for election to the House.* **8** a group of people combined for a selfish or bad purpose: *A ring of crooks controlled the smuggling operation.* **9 a** a cut all the way round a branch or the trunk of a tree. **b** the strip of bark thus formed. **10** ANNUAL RING.
run rings around, *Informal.* do much better than; outclass or surpass with ease.
—v. **1** put a ring around; enclose; form a circle around: *willows ringing a pond.* **2** *Sports.* toss a horseshoe, ring, etc. around (a certain mark or post). **3** provide with a ring. **4** put a ring in the nose of (an animal). **5** form into a ring or rings. **6** cut away the bark in a ring around (a tree or branch): *If you ring a birch tree, it will probably die.* **7** surround so as to prevent escape: *The wolves ringed the injured moose.* ⟨OE *hring*⟩ **—'ring•less,** *adj.*
☛ *Hom.* WRING.

ring[2] [rɪŋ] *v.* **rang, rung, ring•ing;** *n. —v.* **1** give forth a clear resounding sound, as a bell does: *Their laughter rang out.* **2** cause to give forth such a sound: *Ring the bell.* **3** cause (a bell or buzzer) to sound: *I had to ring twice before anyone came.* **4** make (a sound) by ringing: *The bells rang a joyous peal.* **5** have a given characteristic sound or quality. **6** call to church, prayers, etc. by ringing bells. **7** announce or proclaim by ringing; usher; conduct: *Ring out the old year; ring in the new.* **8** proclaim or repeat loudly everywhere: *to ring a person's praises.* **9** give back sound; echo or resound: *The mountains rang with the roll of thunder.* **10** be filled with report or talk: *The town rang with the news of the Canadian team's victory.* **11** sound: *Her words rang true.* **12** have a sensation as of sounds of bells: *My ears are ringing.* **13** *Esp. Brit.* call on the telephone (*often used with* **up**): *I'll ring you when I get home.* **14** summon by means of a bell or buzzer (*used with* **for**): *to ring for the steward.* **15** record (a specified amount) on a cash register (*used with* **up**): *The cashier rang up $15.50 instead of $155.00.*
ring a bell, be familiar: *That name doesn't ring a bell.*
ring off, *Esp. Brit.* end a telephone call; hang up the receiver.
ring up/down the curtain, a make a signal for a theatre curtain to be raised or lowered. **b** indicate the beginning or end of an action, event, etc.
—n. **1** the act of ringing. **2** the sound of a bell or buzzer: *I didn't hear the ring.* **3** a peal or set of bells, each with a different tone, as in a church tower or for hand-ringing. **4** a sound like that of a bell: *the ring of steel on steel.* **5** a characteristic sound or quality: *the ring of truth.* **6** a call on the telephone: *Give me a ring tonight.* ⟨OE *hringan*⟩ **—'ring•ing•ly,** *adv.*
☛ *Hom.* WRING.

ring•bolt ['rɪŋ,boult] *n.* a bolt with a ring fitted in its head.

ring•bone ['rɪŋ,boun] *n.* a morbid bony growth on the pastern bone of a horse, frequently causing lameness.

ring chromosome *Genetics.* an abnormal chromosome in which both telomeres have been deleted and the two broken ends have joined to form a ring.

ringed [rɪŋd] *adj.* **1** having or wearing a ring or rings: *heavily ringed fingers.* **2** marked or decorated with a ring or rings: *a ringed border.* **3** surrounded by a ring or rings: *The lake was ringed with evergreens.* **4** formed of or with rings; ringlike: *a ringed design.*

ringed perch YELLOW PERCH.

ringed seal a small earless seal (*Phoca hispida*) found in arctic and subarctic waters around the world, having a mainly brown or black coat with irregular cream-coloured rings. The ringed seal is the cornerstone of the traditional economy of the coastal Inuit, supplying them with food, clothing, blubber for lamps, and bone for tools.

ring•er[1] ['rɪŋər] *n.* **1** a person or thing that encircles, surrounds with a ring, etc. **2** a quoit, horseshoe, etc., thrown so as to fall over a peg. ⟨< *ring*[1]⟩
☛ *Hom.* WRINGER.

ring•er[2] ['rɪŋər] *n.* **1** a person or thing that rings; device for ringing a bell. **2** *Slang.* a horse, athlete, examination candidate, etc., entered in a competition or examination under false identification as a substitute for one of lesser ability. **3** *Slang.* a person or thing very much like another.
be a (dead) ringer for, be almost exactly like. ⟨< *ring*[2]⟩
☛ *Hom.* WRINGER.

ring•ette [rɪŋ'ɛt] *n.* an ice game similar to hockey, played on skates by two teams of six persons each, using straight sticks to try to shoot a rubber ring into the opposing team's goal.

ring finger the finger next to the little finger of either hand, where an engagement and/or wedding ring is customarily worn.

ring•git ['rɪŋgɪt] *n.* **1** the basic unit of money in Malaysia, divided into 100 sen. See table of money in the Appendix. **2** the basic unit of money in Brunei, divided into 100 cents. **3** a coin or note worth one ringgit. ⟨< Malay⟩

ring•lead•er ['rɪŋ,lidər] *n.* a person who leads others, especially in opposition to authority or law. ⟨< the phrase *to lead the ring* to be first⟩

ring•let ['rɪŋlɪt] *n.* **1** a long curl: *She wears her hair in ringlets.* **2** a little ring: *Drops of rain made ringlets in the pond.*
—'ring•let•ed, *adj.*

ring•mas•ter ['rɪŋ,mæstər] *n.* a man in charge of the performances in the ring of a circus.

ring–neck ['rɪŋ ,nɛk] *n.* **1** a type of green snake that has a yellow ring round its neck. **2** (*adjl.*) of an animal, having a distinctive coloured band around the neck: *ring-neck duck, ring-neck pheasant, ring-neck snake.* Also (def. 2), **ring-necked.**

Ring of the Nibelungs *Germanic mythology.* the magic ring made from the Rheingold by dwarf Alberich, leader of the Nibelungs.

ring ouzel a large European thrush (*Turdus torquatus*), the male having blackish plumage with a white crescent on the upper part of the breast.

ring•side ['rɪŋ,saɪd] *n.* **1** the area just outside the ring at a circus, prize fight, etc. **2** a place affording a close view. **3** (*adjl.*) at the ringside: *a ringside seat.*

ring•toss ['rɪŋ,tɒs] *n.* a game in which rings, usually made of braided rope, are tossed so as to land encircling an upright peg or stake.

ring•worm ['rɪŋ,wɜrm] *n. Pathology.* a contagious skin disease caused by fungi and characterized by ring-shaped patches.

rink [rɪŋk] *n.* **1** a sheet of ice for skating or playing hockey. **2** a smooth floor for roller skating. **3 a** a sheet of ice for curling. **b** a curling team of four players. **4** a section of a lawn-bowling green suitable for a match. **5** a building in which there is a rink; arena. ⟨< Scottish < OF *renc* course, rank[1] < Gmc.⟩

rink house *Cdn.* a small heated cabin near an outdoor rink, used by persons putting on or taking off ice skates.

rink rat *Cdn. Informal.* **1** a young person who helps with the chores around a hockey rink, often in return for free skating, free admission to hockey games, etc. **2** a young person who frequents a hockey rink for no particular purpose.

rinse [rɪns] *v.* **rinsed, rins•ing;** *n. —v.* **1** cleanse by washing lightly, especially by allowing water, etc. to run through, over, etc. (*often used with* **out**): *He rinsed his coffee cup under the tap. I rinse my mouth out after eating.* **2** remove (dirt, etc.) by rinsing: *to rinse the sand out of a swimsuit.* **3** give (laundry, dishes, etc.) a final washing in clear water to remove soap or detergent: *Rinse the dishes under hot water before you dry them.* **4** treat (hair) with a rinse: *She rinsed her hair with beer to give it body.*
—n. **1** the act or process of rinsing: *Give your sweater a good rinse in soft water.* **2** the liquid used in rinsing: *A lemon rinse is good for blond hair.* **3** a preparation to add temporary lustre or colour to the hair: *Some older women use a blue rinse on their white hair.* ⟨ME < OF *reincier*, ult. < L *recens* fresh⟩

ri•ot ['raɪət] *n., v. —n.* **1** a wild, violent public disturbance; disorder caused by an unruly crowd or mob: *We were afraid the demonstration would turn into a riot.* **2** any violent disorder or confusion. **3** a loud outburst: *to break out in a riot of laughter.* **4** loose living; wild revelling, or an instance of this: *His whole life is one long riot.* **5** a bright display: *The garden was a riot of colour.* **6** *Informal.* a very amusing person or performance: *She was a riot at the party.*
read the riot act, a give orders for disturbance to cease. **b** reprimand severely.
run riot, a act without restraint. **b** of plants, grow wildly or luxuriantly: *The weeds have run riot in our garden.* **c** run wild.
—v. **1** move in a wild, disorderly way: *The cowboys rioted into town.* **2** revel: *The Mardi Gras crowds rioted in the streets.* **3** take part in a violent public disturbance. **4** spend (money or time)

wastefully in loose living (*usually with* **away**): *They rioted away their inheritance in no time.* ⟨ME < OF *riote* dispute, ult. < L *rugire* roar⟩ **—'ri•ot•er,** *n.*

ri•ot•ous ['raɪətəs] *adj.* **1** taking part in a riot: *The riotous crowd was dispersed.* **2** of an act, having the characteristics of a riot or public disturbance. **3** boisterous; disorderly: *He was expelled from school for riotous conduct. Sounds of riotous glee came from the yard.* **4** debauched; dissolute. **5** of plant growth, luxuriant or profuse. **—'ri•ot•ous•ly,** *adv.* **—'ri•ot•ous•ness,** *n.*

rip[1] [rɪp] *v.* **ripped, rip•ping;** *n.* *—v.* **1** cut roughly; tear apart; tear off: *Rip the cover off this box.* **2** become torn apart: *The sheet will rip if you pull on it like that.* **3** cut or pull out the stitches of (a seam). **4** saw (wood) along the grain, as opposed to across the grain. **5** *Informal.* move fast or violently. **6** *Informal.* utter violently (*used with* **out**): *He ripped out an angry oath.*
rip into, *Informal.* attack violently.
rip off, *Slang.* **a** take advantage of; exploit or cheat. **b** steal.
—n. **1** a torn place. **2** a seam that has come unstitched in a garment. **3** an act of tearing. ⟨ME *rippe(n)*⟩
☛ *Syn. v.* **1.** See note at TEAR[2].

rip[2] [rɪp] *n.* **1** a stretch of rough water made by cross currents meeting. **2** a swift current made by the tide. ⟨? special use of *rip*[1] or clipping of *ripple*⟩

rip[3] [rɪp] *n. Informal.* **1** a worthless or dissolute person. **2** a worthless worn-out horse. **3** anything of little or no value: *I don't give a rip what she says.* ⟨? alteration of *rep*, short for *reprobate*⟩

R.I.P. REQUIESCAT IN PACE.

ri•par•i•an [rə'pɛriən] *or* [raɪ'pɛriən] *adj.* of or on the bank of a river, a lake, etc.: *riparian rights, riparian property.* ⟨< L *riparius* < *ripa* riverbank⟩

riparian right the right of a person living on a river to use of its water, for fishing or irrigation.

rip cord a cord that, when pulled, opens a parachute.

ripe [rəip] *adj.* **rip•er, rip•est.** **1** full-grown and ready to be gathered and eaten: *ripe fruit.* **2** resembling ripe fruit in ruddiness and fullness. **3** fully developed; mature: *a ripe cheese, ripe in knowledge.* **4** ready to break or be lanced: *a ripe boil.* **5** ready: *ripe for mischief.* **6** of time, far enough along. **7** advanced (in years): of *ripe years.* **8** bawdy: *a ripe joke.* ⟨OE *rīpe*⟩ **—'ripe•ly,** *adv.* **—'ripe•ness,** *n.*

rip•en ['rəipən] *v.* **1** become ripe. **2** make ripe.

rip–off ['rɪp ˌɒf] *n. Slang.* **1** the act or an instance of exploiting or cheating. **2** something that is grossly overpriced: *The exhibition midway was a big rip-off this year.* **3** the act or an instance of stealing.

ri•poste [rə'poust] *n., v.* **-post•ed, -post•ing.** *—n.* **1** *Fencing.* a quick thrust given after parrying a lunge. **2** a quick, sharp reply or return.
—v. make a riposte; reply; retaliate. ⟨< F < Ital. *risposta* reply, ult. < L *respondere* respond. See RESPOND.⟩

rip•per ['rɪpər] *n.* **1** one who or that which rips. **2** a tool for ripping.

rip•ping ['rɪpɪŋ] *adj. Brit. Slang.* fine; splendid.

rip•ple ['rɪpəl] *n., v.* **-pled, -pling.** *—n.* **1** a very little wave: *Throw a stone into still water and watch the ripples spread in rings.* **2** anything that seems like a little wave: *ripples in cardboard.* **3** a sound that reminds one of little waves: *a ripple of laughter in the crowd.* **4** RIFFLE (def. 2). **5** ice cream with ripplelike streaks of flavoured syrup: *butterscotch ripple.*
—v. **1** make a sound like rippling water. **2** form or have little waves. **3** flow with little waves on the surface. **4** make little waves on: *A breeze rippled the quiet waters.* ⟨origin uncertain⟩
☛ *Syn. n.* **1.** See note at WAVE.

ripple effect the spreading, in stages and with gradually diminishing force, of the results of an event.

rip•ply ['rɪpli] *or* ['rɪpəli] *adj.* characterized by ripples; rippling.

rip•rap ['rɪpˌræp] *n., v.* **-rapped, -rap•ping.** *—n.* **1** a wall or foundation of broken stones thrown together irregularly. **2** the broken stones so used.
—v. build or strengthen with loose, broken stones. ⟨varied reduplication of *rap*[1]⟩

rip•roar•ing ['rɪpˌrɔrɪŋ] *adj. Slang.* hilarious; uproarious.

rip•saw ['rɪpˌsɒ] *n.* a saw for cutting wood along the grain, not across the grain. ⟨< *rip*[1] + *saw*[1]⟩

rip•snort•ing ['rɪpˌsnɔrtɪŋ] *adj. Slang.* exciting, intense, or wild: *a ripsnorting party.* **—'ripˌsnort•er,** *n.*

rip•tide ['rɪpˌtaɪd] *n.* a strong current of churning water caused by one strong tide or current meeting another.

Rip Van Win•kle [ˌrɪp væn 'wɪŋkəl] **1** the hero of a story (1819) by Washington Irving. Rip falls asleep and wakes 20 years later to find everything changed. **2** someone who is ignorant of present-day conditions.

rise [raɪz] *v.* **rose, ris•en** ['rɪzən], **ris•ing;** *n.* *—v.* **1** get up from a lying, sitting, or kneeling position: *to rise from a chair.* **2** get up from sleep or rest: *to rise at dawn.* **3** go up; come up; ascend: *The kite rises in the air. The flood waters rose a metre.* **4** extend upward: *The tower rises to a height of 30 m.* **5** of fish, swim up to the surface of the water to get bait, surface food, etc.: *The trout are rising.* **6** slope upward: *Hills rise in the distance.* **7** go higher; increase: *Prices are rising.* **8** advance to a higher level of action, thought, feeling, expression, rank, position, etc.: *He rose from errand boy to president.* **9** become louder or of higher pitch: *Their angry voices rose.* **10** appear above the horizon: *The sun rises in the morning.* **11** start; begin; have a source (*used with* **from**): *The river rises from a spring. Quarrels often rise from trifles.* **12** come into being or action: *The wind rose rapidly.* **13** be built up, erected, or constructed: *Houses are rising on the edge of the town.* **14** become more animated or more cheerful: *Her spirits rose.* **15** revolt; rebel: *The slaves rose against their masters.* **16** grow larger and lighter: *Yeast makes dough rise.* **17** come to life again: *to rise from the dead.* **18** end a meeting or session; adjourn: *The House rose for the summer.* **19** be able to cope or deal with; respond adequately (*used with* **to**): *They rose to the occasion.*
—n. **1** an upward movement; ascent: *the rise of a balloon.* **2** the coming of a fish to the surface of the water to feed, seize bait, etc. **3** an upward slope: *The rise of that hill is gradual.* **4** a piece of rising or high ground; hill. **5** the vertical height of a step, slope, arch, etc. **6** an increase. **7** an advance in rank, power, etc. **8** an increase in loudness or in pitch. **9** a coming above the horizon. **10** an origin; beginning; start: *the rise of a river, the rise of a storm, the rise of a new problem.*
get a rise out of (someone), get an expected reaction, as of anger, protest, or incredulity, from (someone) by means of a calculated question, comment, etc.
give rise to, start; begin; cause; bring about: *The circumstances of his disappearance gave rise to the fear that he might have been kidnapped.* ⟨OE *rīsan*⟩
☛ *Usage.* **Rise.** *v.* **1, 2.** In referring to people, **arise** is formal and poetic; **rise** is rather formal; **get up**, the most frequent, is general and informal.

ris•en ['rɪzən] *v.* pp. of RISE.

ris•er ['raɪzər] *n.* **1** a person or thing that rises: *an early riser.* **2** the vertical part of a step: *The risers on this staircase are unusually deep.* **3 risers,** *pl.* a series of steplike benches, similar to bleachers but smaller and usually portable: *The choir filed onto the risers and stood ready to sing.*

ris•i•bil•i•ty [ˌrɪzə'bɪlɪti] *n., pl.* **-ties.** **1** an ability or inclination to laugh. **2** Often, **risibilities,** *pl.* desire to laugh; sense of humour.

ris•i•ble ['rɪzəbəl] *adj.* **1** able or inclined to laugh. **2** of laughter; used in laughter. **3** causing laughter; amusing; funny. ⟨< LL *risibilis*, ult. < L *ridere* laugh⟩

ris•ing ['raɪzɪŋ] *n., adj., v.* *—n.* **1** the act of a person or thing that rises. **2** something that rises. **3** a rebellion; revolt.
—adj. **1** that rises. **2** growing up: *the rising generation.*
—v. ppr. of RISE.

risk [rɪsk] *n., v.* *—n.* **1** a chance of harm or loss; danger. **2** *Insurance.* **a** a person or thing described with reference to the chance of loss from insuring him, her, or it. **b** an insurance obligation or possible loss. **c** the amount of possible loss. **3** a person or thing that cannot be relied on.
at risk, a in danger or jeopardy. **b** held financially responsible; under legal obligation.
run a risk or **take a risk,** expose oneself to the chance of harm or loss.
—v. **1** expose to the chance of harm or loss: *A soldier risks his life.* **2** take the risk of: *They risked getting wet.* ⟨< F *risque* < Ital. *risco* < *risciare* dare, originally, skirt cliffs in sailing < Gk. *rhiza* base, root⟩

risk capital capital not covered by collateral and invested in the hope of profit but at the risk of loss. Also called **venture capital.**

risk•y ['rɪski] *adj.* **risk•i•er, risk•i•est.** **1** full of risk; dangerous. **2** somewhat improper; risqué. **—'risk•i•ly,** *adv.* **—'risk•i•ness,** *n.*

ri•sot•to [rɪ'zɒtou]; *Italian,* [ri'sɔtto] *n.* an Italian dish consisting of rice browned in oil and cooked in chicken broth, usually flavoured with cheese and spices. ⟨< Ital.⟩

ris•qué [rɪ'skei] *adj.* suggestive of indecency; somewhat improper: *a risqué scene in a play.* ⟨< F *risqué,* pp. of *risquer* to risk⟩

ris•sole ['rɪsoul] *or* [rɪ'soul]; *French,* [ʀi'sɔl] *n.* a ball or cake of meat or fish mixed or coated with bread crumbs, egg, etc., and fried. ⟨< F⟩

rit. or **ritard.** ritardando.

ri•tar•dan•do [,ritɑr'dɑndou] *adj., adv., n. Music.* —*adj.* becoming gradually slower.
—*adv.* gradually more slowly. *Abbrev.:* rit. or ritard.
—*n.* **1** a gradual decrease in tempo. **2** a ritardando passage. ⟨< Ital. *ritardando* < *ritardare* retard⟩

rite [rəit] *n.* **1** a solemn ceremony: *Secret societies have their special rites.* **2** a particular form or system of ceremonies performed according to customary or prescribed rules or modes of behaviour. **3** any of the various versions of Christian liturgy, especially those pertaining to the Eucharist: *the roman rite.* **4** a division of Christian churches according to the form of liturgy used: *The Greek Orthodox Church is included in the Eastern Rite.* ⟨< L *ritus*⟩
☛ *Hom.* RIGHT, WRIGHT, WRITE.
☛ *Syn.* **1.** See note at CEREMONY.

rite of passage **1** *Anthropology.* one of a number of ceremonies marking the transition of an individual from one status or stage of life to another, such as the onset of puberty, marriage, entry into a clan, etc. **2** any special act or event in a person's life regarded as having great significance.

rit•u•al ['rɪtʃuəl] *n., adj.* —*n.* **1** a form or system of rites. The rites accompanying birth, marriage, and death are parts of the ritual of most cultures. **2** a book containing rites or ceremonies. **3** the carrying out of rites. **4** any set or formal procedure, act, etc., that is followed consistently.
—*adj.* of or having to do with rites; done as a rite: *a ritual dance.* ⟨< L *ritualis* < *ritus* rite⟩

rit•u•al•ism ['rɪtʃuə,lɪzəm] *n.* **1 a** a fondness for ritual. **b** insistence upon ritual for its own sake. **2** the study of ritual practices or religious rites.

rit•u•al•ist ['rɪtʃuəlɪst] *n.* **1** a person who practises or advocates observance of ritual. **2** a person who studies or knows much about ritual practices or religious rites.

rit•u•al•is•tic [,rɪtʃuə'lɪstɪk] *adj.* **1** having to do with ritual or ritualism. **2** fond of ritual. —**,rit•u•al'is•ti•cal•ly,** *adv.*

rit•u•al•ize ['rɪtʃuə,laɪz] *v.* **-ized, -iz•ing. 1** make a ritual of. **2** practise or promote ritualism (in).

rit•u•al•ly ['rɪtʃuəli] *adv.* with or according to a ritual or as part of a ritual: *Masks are used ritually by many peoples.*

ritz•y ['rɪtsi] *adj.* **ritz•i•er, ritz•i•est.** *Slang.* elegant or luxurious; posh: *a ritzy nightclub.* ⟨after the *Ritz* hotels established by Swiss hotelier César *Ritz* (1850-1918)⟩

riv. river.

ri•val ['raɪvəl] *n., adj., v.* **-valled** or **-valed, -val•ling** or **-val•ing.** —*n.* **1** a person who wants and tries to get the same thing as another; one who tries to equal or do better than another; competitor. **2** a thing that will bear comparison with something else; equal; match: *Her beauty has no rival.*
—*adj.* wanting the same thing as another; competing: *The rival store tried to get the other's trade.*
—*v.* **1** try to equal or outdo: *The stores rival each other in beautiful window displays.* **2** equal; match: *The sunset rivalled the sunrise in beauty.* ⟨< L *rivalis* using the same stream < *rivus* stream⟩

ri•val•ry ['raɪvəlri] *n., pl.* **-ries.** the action, position, or relation of a rival or rivals; competition: *There is rivalry among business firms for trade.*

rive [raɪv] *v.* **rived, rived** or **riv•en, riv•ing. 1** tear apart; split; cleave. **2** distress or cause pain to (the heart, spirit, etc.). ⟨ME < ON *rifa*⟩

riv•en ['rɪvən] *adj., v.* —*adj.* torn apart; split.
—*v.* a pp. of RIVE.

riv•er¹ ['rɪvər] *n.* **1** a large natural stream of water that flows into a lake, ocean, etc. **2** any abundant stream or flow: *rivers of blood.*
sell down the river, betray; mislead; abuse the trust of.
up the river, *Slang.* **a** to prison: *He was sent up the river for 30 years.* **b** in prison: *After three years up the river, she was paroled.* ⟨ME < OF *rivere* < L *riparius* of a riverbank < *ripa* bank⟩

riv•er² ['raɪvər] *n.* a person who or thing that rives. ⟨< *rive*⟩

river basin land that is drained by a river and its tributaries.

river bass SMALLMOUTH BASS.

river beauty BROAD-LEAVED WILLOW HERB.

riv•er•bed ['rɪvər,bɛd] *n.* the channel along which a river flows or used to flow.

river•boat ['rɪvər,bout] *n.* a boat, often flat-bottomed, suitable for use on rivers.

river darter a fish (*Imostoma shumardi*) living on the bottom of streams in eastern Canada. It spawns in spring.

river drive *Cdn. Logging.* the process or practice of floating logs downstream at high water.

river–driver *Cdn. Logging.* one who takes part in the process of floating or driving logs in a river drive.

riv•er•head ['rɪvər,hɛd] *n.* the source of a river.

river horse hippopotamus.

riv•er•ine ['rɪvə,raɪn], [,rɪvə'rin], *or* ['rɪvərɪn] *adj.* **1** of or having to do with a river. **2** located on or living near a river: *a riverine town.*

river lot **1** a lot fronting on a river. **2** *Cdn.* RIBBON FARM.

riv•er•side ['rɪvər,saɪd] *n.* **1** the bank of a river. **2** (*adjl.*) on the bank of a river: *The riverside path is much used.*

riv•et ['rɪvɪt] *n., v.* **riv•et•ed** or **riv•et•ing.** —*n.* a metal bolt having a head at one end, the other end made to be hammered flat once it is in position.
—*v.* **1** fasten with a rivet or rivets. **2** flatten the end (of a bolt) so as to form a head. **3** fasten or fix firmly: *Their eyes were riveted on the speaker.* ⟨ME < OF *rivet* < *river* fix < VL *ripare* come to shore < L *ripa* bank⟩ —**'riv•et•er,** *n.*

Riv•i•er•a [,rɪvi'ɛrə] *n.* a section of France and Italy along the Mediterranean Sea, famous as a resort area.

riv•u•let ['rɪvjəlɪt] *n.* a very small stream. ⟨< Ital. *rivoletto,* ult. < L *rivus* stream⟩

ri•yal [ri'ɑl] *n.* **1** the basic unit of money in Yemen, divided into 100 fils. See table of money in the Appendix. **2** the basic currency unit of Qatar, divided into 100 dirhem. **3** a note or coin worth one riyal. Also, **rial.** ⟨< Arabic *riyal* < Sp. *real*⟩

rm. **1** room. **2** ream.

R.M. **1** RURAL MUNICIPALITY. **2** Royal Marines.

R.M.C. ROYAL MILITARY COLLEGE.

Rn radon.

RN or **R.N.** **1** registered nurse. **2** Royal Navy.

RNA RIBONUCLEIC ACID.

R.N.W.M.P. ROYAL NORTH WEST MOUNTED POLICE.

roach¹ [routʃ] *n.* **1** cockroach. **2** *Slang.* the butt of a marijuana cigarette.

roach² [routʃ] *n., pl.* **roach** or **roach•es. 1** a European freshwater fish (esp. *Rutilus rutilus*) related to the carp. **2** any of various similar fishes, such as the North American sunfish. ⟨ME < OF *roche*⟩

roach³ [routʃ] *v., n.* —*v.* **1** trim the top of (a horse's mane, etc.) so that the part that is left stands upright. **2** brush (someone's hair) away from the forehead so that it flows up and over into an arch or high curve.
—*n.* hair, a nap, etc. that has been trimmed short. ⟨origin uncertain⟩

roach back any high curved back, especially of a horse or dog.

road [roud] *n.* **1** a highway between places; way made for trucks or automobiles to travel on: *The road from here to the city is being paved.* **2** a way, route, or course: *Our road went through the woods. He was soon on the road to ruin.* **3** railway. **4** Also, **roads,** *Nautical.* a place near the shore where ships can ride at anchor. **5** roadbed.
hold the road, drive or travel on a road easily, smoothly, and safely.
on the road, a travelling, especially as a sales representative. **b** of a theatre company, etc., on tour.
take to the road, a go on the road; begin to travel. **b** formerly, become a highwayman. ⟨OE *rād* a riding, journey< *rīdan* ride⟩

road agent *Esp. U.S.* formerly, a highwayman.

road allowance *Cdn.* land reserved by the government as public property to be used for roads. The land set aside includes the road and a certain amount of land on either side of it.

road•bed ['roud,bɛd] *n.* the foundation of a road or of a railway.

road•block ['roud,blɒk] *n.* **1** a road barricade set up by police: **a** to prevent wanted persons from escaping: *A roadblock* *was set up to stop the car thief.* **b** to check vehicles and drivers for infractions of the highway code: *The police have set up roadblocks to catch drunken drivers.* **2** an obstacle placed across a road. **3** any obstacle to progress.

road hockey a form of hockey played without skates and with a ball instead of a puck, on a hard surface such as a road or street.

road hog *Informal.* a driver who obstructs traffic by driving in the middle of the road, refusing to let other vehicles pass.

road•house ['roud,hʌus] *n.* a restaurant in the country where people can stop for refreshments and, sometimes, entertainment.

road•kill ['roud,kɪl] *n.* the body of an animal killed by a vehicle and left on the road or highway.

road metal broken stone, cinders, etc. used for roads and roadbeds.

road roller a machine or vehicle used in building or repairing roads, having large, smooth, heavy rollers for levelling and compressing road surfaces.

road•run•ner ['roud,rʌnər] a long-tailed bird (genus *Geococcyx*) of the deserts of the SW United States, that is related to the cuckoo. It usually runs instead of flying.

road show a play, opera, ballet, etc. that travels from city to city. Also, **roadshow**.

road•side ['roud,saɪd] *n.* **1** the side of a road. **2** (*adjl.*) beside a road: *a roadside inn.*

road•stead ['roud,stɛd] *n. Nautical.* ROAD (def. 4).

road•ster ['roudstər] *n.* **1** an open automobile of the 1920s and 1930s, especially a sporty style seating two or four passengers. **2** a horse for riding or driving on roads.

road test 1 the test of a car or other vehicle under normal operating conditions in order to discover its roadworthiness. **2** the practical part of a test for a driver's licence. **—'road-,test,** *v.*

road•way ['roud,wei] *n.* **1** a road. **2** the part of a road used by vehicles.

road•wor•thy ['roud,wɜrði] *adj.* of vehicles, fit for use on the road. **—'road,wor•thi•ness,** *n.*

roam [roum] *v., n.* —*v.* **1** go about with no special plan or aim; wander: *to roam through the fields.* **2** wander over: *They roamed the world in search of freedom.*
—*n.* a walk or trip with no special aim; wandering. **—'roam•er,** *n.*

☛ *Syn. v.* **1. Roam,** ROVE, RAMBLE = wander. **Roam** suggests going about here and there as one pleases over a wide area, with no special plan or aim: *The photographer roamed about the world.* **Rove** usually adds the suggestion of a definite purpose, though not of a settled destination: *Submarines roved the ocean.* **Ramble** particularly suggests straying from a regular path or plan and wandering about aimlessly for one's own pleasure: *We rambled through the shopping district.*

roan [roun] *adj., n.* —*adj.* **1** of an animal, yellowish brown or reddish brown sprinkled with grey or white. **2** made of or bound in leather of this colour.
—*n.* **1** an animal of this colour, especially a horse. **2** a soft, flexible leather made from sheepskin, used in bookbinding, often treated so as to resemble morocco. **3** a roan colour. ⟨< F < Sp. *roano,* probably < Gmc.⟩

roar [rɔr] *v., n.* —*v.* **1** make a loud, deep sound; make a loud noise: *The lion roared.* **2** utter loudly: *to roar out an order.* **3** make or put by roaring: *The crowd roared itself hoarse.* **4** laugh loudly. **5** move with a roar: *The train roared past us.*
—*n.* a loud, deep, sustained sound; loud noise. ⟨OE *rārian*⟩ **—'roar•er,** *n.*

roar•ing ['rɔrɪŋ] *adj., n., adv., v.* —*adj.* **1** emitting roars; bellowing. **2** riotous; noisy; boisterous. **3** successful; booming: *a roaring business.*
—*n.* **1** the act of one that roars. **2** a loud, full, sustained sound. **3** a disease of horses, characterized by loud breathing.
—*adv.* to such an extent that one is perceived to roar: *roaring mad.*
—*v.* ppr. of ROAR. **—'roar•ing•ly,** *adv.*

roaring forties the rough, stormy region in the North Atlantic Ocean that lies between 40° and 50° latitude.

roaring twenties the decade of the 1920s ⟨referring to the post World War I energy and buoyancy⟩

roast [roust] *v., n., adj.* —*v.* **1** cook (meat, etc.) by dry heat; cook in an oven, before or over an open fire, or in embers; bake. **2** dry or brown by heating: *to roast coffee beans.* **3** *Metallurgy.* heat (ore, etc.) in hot air in order to oxidize it or remove impurities. **4** make or become very hot. **5** be baked. **6** *Informal.* **a** make fun of; ridicule in public. **b** reprove; criticize severely.
—*n.* **1** a piece of roasted meat; a piece of meat to be roasted. **2** an informal outdoor meal, at which some food is cooked over an open fire: *a wiener roast.* **3** a special dinner for a well-known public figure who is ridiculed by the other guests. **4** the act of roasting or being roasted.
—*adj.* roasted: *roast beef.* ⟨ME < OF *rostir* < Gmc.⟩ **—'roast•ing,** *adj.*

roast•er ['roustər] *n.* **1** a pan or oven used in roasting. **2** a chicken, young pig, etc. fit to be roasted. **3** a person who or thing that roasts.

rob [rɒb] *v.* **robbed, rob•bing. 1** take away from by force or threats; steal from: *He was robbed of all his money. Bandits robbed the bank.* **2** steal (something from someone): *They said they would not rob again.* **3** take away some characteristic from; keep from having or doing: *The disease has robbed him of his strength.*
rob Peter to pay Paul, take something away from one to pay, satisfy, or advance another. ⟨ME < OF *rober* < Gmc.⟩

rob•ber ['rɒbər] *n.* a person who robs.
☛ *Syn.* See note at THIEF.

rob•ber•y ['rɒbəri] *n., pl.* **-ber•ies.** an act of robbing; theft. ⟨ME < OF *roberie* < *rober.* See ROB.⟩

robe [roub] *n., v.* **robed, rob•ing.** —*n.* **1** a long, loose outer garment. **2** a garment that shows rank, office, etc.: *a judge's robe, the king's robes of state.* **3** a covering or wrap: *He had a robe over his lap.* **4** *Cdn.* formerly, the dressed skin of a buffalo or other animal, used especially for protection against moisture and cold. **5** a bathrobe or dressing gown.
—*v.* put a robe on; dress. ⟨ME < OF *robe,* originally, plunder, booty⟩

rob•in ['rɒbən] *n.* **1** a large North American thrush (*Turdus migratorius*) having greyish brown upper parts and a brick-red breast and abdomen. **2** a small Eurasian thrush (*Erithacus rubecula*), the well-known **robin redbreast** of Britain, the male of which has a brownish back, orange-red throat and breast, and greyish abdomen. ⟨ME < OF *Robin,* dim. of Robert⟩

A robin

Robin Good•fel•low ['gʊd,fɛlou] Puck, a mischievous fairy of English folklore.

Robin Hood 1 *English legend.* the brave, chivalrous leader of an outlaw band living in Sherwood Forest, who robbed the rich to help the poor in the 12th century. **2** a person who helps the poor by acting illegally against wealthy people or institutions.

robin run the first run of maple syrup. Compare BUD RUN and FROG RUN.

rob•in's–egg blue ['rɒbɪnz ,ɛg] greenish blue.

ro•bot ['roubɒt] *or* ['roubət] *n.* **1** a machine in the shape of a human; a mechanical device that does some of the work of human beings. **2** a person who acts or works in a dull, mechanical way. ⟨invented by Karel Capek (1890-1938), a Czech writer, for his play, *R.U.R.*; suggested by Czech *robota* work, *robotnik* serf⟩ **—ro'bot•ic,** *adj.* **—'ro•bot,ism,** *n.* **—ro'bot•i•cal•ly,** *adv.*

robot bomb a jet-propelled winged missile having a warhead and automatic pilot.

ro•bot•ics [rou'bɒtɪks] *or* [rə'bɒtɪks] *n.* the development and use of robots to perform tasks normally done by people.

ro•bust [rou'bʌst] *or* ['roubʌst] *adj.* **1** strong and healthy; sturdy: *a robust person, a robust mind.* **2** suited to or requiring bodily strength: *robust exercises.* **3** rough; rude. **4** having a rich, full flavour, as coffee or wine. ⟨< L *robustus,* originally, oaken < *robur* oak⟩ **—ro'bust•ly,** *adv.* **—ro'bust•ness,** *n.*
☛ *Syn.* **1.** See note at STRONG.

ro•bus•tious [rou'bʌstʃəs] *adj. Archaic or humorous.* **1** rough; rude; boisterous. **2** robust; strong; stout.

roc [rɒk] *n. Arabian legend.* a bird of enormous size and strength. ⟨< Arabic *rokh, rukhkh* < Persian⟩

Ro•chelle salt [rou'ʃɛl] *Chemistry. Pharmacy.* a colourless or white crystalline compound, potassium sodium tartrate, used to silver mirrors, or as a laxative, and in baking powder. *Formula:* $KNaC_4H_4O_6 \cdot 4H_2O$ ⟨< La *Rochelle,* a city in France⟩

roch•et ['rɒtʃɪt] *n.* a vestment of linen or lawn resembling a surplice, worn by bishops and abbots of the Roman Catholic and Anglican churches. ⟨ME < OF *rochet*, ult. < Gmc.⟩

rock¹ [rɒk] *n.* **1** a large mass of stone. **2** any piece of stone individually or collectively; a stone of any size. **3** *Geology.* **a** the mass of mineral matter of which the earth's crust is made up. **b** a particular layer or kind of such matter. **4** something firm like a rock; support; defence. **5** anything that suggests or acts as a rock. **6** a curling stone. **7** ROCK CANDY. **8** *Slang.* a precious stone, especially a diamond. **9 rocks,** *pl. Slang.* money.
on the rocks, a wrecked; ruined. **b** *Informal.* bankrupt. **c** of alcoholic drinks, with ice but without water or mixes: *whisky on the rocks.* ⟨ME < OF *roque* < VL *rocca*⟩

rock² ['rɒk] *v., n.* —*v.* **1** move backward and forward, or from side to side; sway. **2** move or shake violently: *The earthquake rocked the houses.* **3** move powerfully with emotion; be shaken by emotion; upset or be upset: *The family was rocked by the news.* **4** put (to sleep, rest, etc.) with swaying movements.
rock the boat, *Informal.* make trouble; especially, disturb or upset a stable situation.
—*n.* **1** a rocking movement. **2** a kind of lively popular music with a heavy, regular beat, usually played with electronically amplified instruments. Rock often has elements of jazz or country and folk music. **3** (*adjl.*) of, having to do with, or being this type of music. ⟨OE *roccian*⟩
☛ *Syn. v.* **1.** See note at SWING.

rock•a•bil•ly ['rɒkə,bɪli] *n.* a type of popular music combining features of both rock-and-roll and hillbilly music.

rock–and–roll ['rɒk ən 'roul] *n.* **1** a style of popular music with a heavy beat, an early form of rock music. **2** a lively style of dancing to such music, characterized by improvisation and exaggerated movements. Also, **rock'n'roll.**

rock bass [bæs] a freshwater game fish (*Ambloplitis rupestris*) of the sunfish family, found in eastern North America.

rock bottom the very bottom; the lowest level.
hit rock bottom, reach the lowest level of one's life.

rock–bot•tom ['rɒk 'bɒtəm] *adj.* at the lowest possible level: *rock-bottom prices.*

rock–bound ['rɒk ,baʊnd] *adj.* surrounded by rocks; rocky. Also, **rockbound.**

rock burst a violent falling in of rocks from the walls of a mine.

rock candy sugar in the form of large, hard crystals.

rock cod **1** any of many fishes found in a rocky habitat. **2** any fish of the genus *Sebastes*, found in North Pacific and Atlantic waters.

Rock Cornish a chicken that is a cross between a Cornish chicken and a white Plymouth Rock. Rock Cornish chickens are usually killed young and eaten as broilers. Also called **Rock Cornish game hen.**

rock crystal a colourless, transparent variety of quartz, often used for jewellery, ornaments, etc.

rock elm a large tree (*Ulmus thomasii*) native to southern Ontario, having shiny dark green leaves and hairy, oval, winged fruit. Its wood, which is very hard, is used for piano frames and hockey sticks.

rock•er¹ ['rɒkər] *n.* **1** one of the curved pieces on which a cradle, rocking chair, etc. rocks. **2** ROCKING CHAIR. **3** a CRADLE (def. 6) used in placer mining.
off (one's) **rocker,** *Slang.* mad; crazy.

rock•er² ['rɒkər] *n.* **1** a ROCK² (*n.* def. 2) singer or musician. **2** a fan of rock music.

rocker arm *Machinery.* a rocking or oscillating arm or lever attached to a rockshaft, used in machinery such as automotive engines.

rocker panel one of the body panels below the passenger compartment or the doors of a vehicle.

rock•er•y ['rɒkəri] *n., pl.* **rock•er•ies.** an ornamental garden, or part of a garden, consisting of an arrangement of rocks and earth for growing plants and flowers; a rock garden. Rockeries are often built on sloping ground.

rock•et¹ ['rɒkɪt] *n., v.* —*n.* **1** a projectile consisting of a tube open at one end and filled with some substance that burns rapidly, creating expanding gases that propel the tube and whatever is attached to it at great speed. Rockets are used for fireworks and signalling, for propelling missiles, and for carrying satellites into outer space. **2** a spacecraft, missile, etc. propelled by such a projectile.
—*v.* **1** go like a rocket; rise or move extremely fast. **2** fly straight up rapidly. **3** put into orbit with a rocket. ⟨(? < F) < Ital. *rochetta*, probably dim. of *rocca* distaff (from the similarity in shape) < Gmc.⟩

rock•et² ['rɒkɪt] *n.* **1** any of various plants of the mustard family (genus *Hesperis*), having fragrant white, pink, or purple flowers, especially the **sea rocket. 2** a European plant of the mustard family, grown as a salad green. Also called **rocket salad.** ⟨< F *roquette* < Ital. *ruchetta*, dim of *ruca* < L *eruca* a herb⟩

rock•et•eer [,rɒkə'tir] *n.* **1** a person who works with or pilots rockets. **2** a rocket expert.

rock•et•ry ['rɒkɪtri] *n.* the designing and firing of rockets, missiles, etc.

rock•fish ['rɒk,fɪʃ] *n.* STRIPED BASS.

rock garden rockery.

rock•hound ['rɒk,haʊnd] *n. Informal.* a person who collects rocks as a hobby.

Rock•ies ['rɒkiz] *n.pl.* ROCKY MOUNTAINS.

rocking chair a chair mounted on rockers, or on springs, so that it can rock back and forth.

rocking horse a toy horse on rockers, for children to ride.

rock'n'roll ['rɒk ən 'roul] *n.* ROCK-AND-ROLL.

rock ptarmigan a brown-and-white chubby Arctic partridgelike fowl (*Lagopus rupestris*) of the Barren Grounds, that turns white in winter. Also, **rock grouse, rock partridge.**

rock rabbit **1** pika. **2** hyrax.

rock–ribbed ['rɒk ,rɪbd] *adj.* **1** having ridges of rock. **2** unyielding.

rock salt common salt as it occurs in the earth in large crystals.

rock•shaft ['rɒk,ʃæft] *n. Machinery.* a machine shaft designed so as to rock back and forth or oscillate on its journals rather than revolving, such as the shaft that operates the valves of a machine, or the shaft of a pendulum.

rock tripe *Cdn.* any of various grey or brown lichens (especially of genus *Umbilicaria*) that grow attached to rocks; they are edible when cooked and are often used as emergency food by northern travellers, etc.

rock•weed ['rɒk,wid] *n.* any of various coarse seaweeds growing on rocks near the shore.

rock wool a fibrous, wool-like material made by blowing a jet of steam or air through molten slag or rock. It is used especially for insulation and packing.

rock•y¹ ['rɒki] *adj.* **rock•i•er, rock•i•est. 1** full of rocks: *a rocky shore.* **2** made of rock. **3** like rock; hard; firm. **4** steadfast; firm. **5** unfeeling; hard in nature. ⟨< *rock¹*⟩

rock•y² ['rɒki] *adj.* **rock•i•er, rock•i•est. 1** likely to rock; shaky; unsteady: *That table is a bit rocky; put a piece of wood under the short leg.* **2** uncertain; filled with hazards or obstacles: *New businesses face a rocky future this year.* **3** *Informal.* sickish; weak; dizzy. ⟨< *rock²*⟩ **—'rock•i•ly,** *adv.* **—'rock•i•ness,** *n.*

Rocky Mountain goat MOUNTAIN GOAT.

Rocky Mountain juniper a small, bushy juniper (*Juniperus scopularum*) found in southern Alberta and British Columbia, and in the W United States.

Rocky Mountain maple DOUGLAS MAPLE.

Rocky Mountains a range of mountains lying in Alberta and British Columbia, and the western United States.

Rocky Mountain sheep bighorn.

Rocky Mountain spotted fever *Pathology.* an acute infectious disease caused by rickettsia and characterized by fever, joint and muscle pain, and a rash. It was first discovered in the Rocky Mountains but is now more widespread. Also called **Rocky Mountain fever.**

Rocky Mountain whitefish a freshwater fish (*Prosopium williamsoni*) found in Canada from the western slope of the Rockies to the Pacific. It weighs up to 1.5 kg and has a large dorsal fin.

Rocky Mountain white pine LIMBER PINE.

ro•co•co [rə'koukou] *n., adj.* —*n.* **1** *Architecture and design.* a style developed in France in the first half of the 18th century, marked by elaborate ornamentation. **2** *Literature.* a style of florid, ornamental writing. **3** *Music.* a style characterized by graceful, gay ornamentations.
—*adj.* of or having to do with rococo. ⟨< F *rococo*, ? < *rocaille* shellwork < *roc* rock⟩

rod [rɒd] *n.* **1** a thin, straight, cylindrical bar of any hard substance such as metal or wood, plastic or glass. See STEAM ENGINE for picture. **2** a thin, straight stick, either growing or cut off. **3** anything resembling a rod in shape. **4** a stick used to beat or punish. **5** punishment. **6** a long, light pole. **7** a long, springy, tapered piece of wood, metal, plastic, etc., to which a reel may be attached, used for fishing. **8** a non-metric unit for measuring length, equal to 5½ yards (about 5.03 metres). **9** a non-metric unit of square measure, equal to 30.5 square yards (25.29 square metres). **10** a stick used to measure with. **11** *Slang.* pistol. **12** a branch of a family or tribe: *the rod of Jesse.* **13** a staff or wand carried as a symbol of one's position. **14** power; authority; tyranny. **15** DIVINING ROD. **16** *Anatomy.* one of the microscopic sense organs in the retina of the eye that are sensitive to dim light. **17** *Bacteriology.* a cylindrical or rod-shaped bacterium; bacillus.
spare the rod and spoil the child, fail to punish, resulting in a spoilt child. ⟨OE *rodd*⟩

rode [roud] *v.* pt. of RIDE.

ro•dent ['roudənt] *n.* **1** any of an order (Rodentia) of relatively small gnawing mammals having a single pair of continually growing incisors in both the upper and lower jaws. The order includes beavers, squirrels, rats, and mice. **2** (*adjl.*) of or like a rodent. ⟨< L *rodens, -entis,* ppr. of *rodere* gnaw⟩

ro•de•o ['roudiou] *or* [rou'deiou] *n., pl.* **-de•os. 1** a contest or exhibition of skill in roping cattle, riding horses, etc. **2** *Esp. U.S.* the driving together of cattle; roundup. ⟨< Sp. *rodeo* < *rodear* go around⟩

rod•o•mon•tade [,rɒdəmən'teid] *or* [,rɒdəmən'tɑd] *n., adj., v.* **-tad•ed, -tad•ing.** —*n.* vain boasting; bragging.
—*adj.* bragging; boastful.
—*v.* brag; boast. ⟨< F < Ital. *rodomontata* < *Rodomonte,* a braggart king in a work of Lodovico Ariosto (1474-1533), an Italian poet < dial. *rodare* roll away (ult. < L *rota* wheel) + *monte* mountain < L *mons, montis*⟩

roe[1] [rou] *n.* **1** fish eggs. **2** the spawn of certain crustaceans. ⟨ME *rowe*⟩
☛ *Hom.* RHO, ROW.

roe[2] [rou] *n.* ROE DEER.
☛ *Hom.* RHO, ROW.

roe•buck ['rou,bʌk] *n.* a male roe deer. ⟨ME *robucke*⟩

roe deer a small deer (*Capreolus capreolus*) of Europe and Asia, having forked antlers. ⟨OE *rā*⟩

roent•gen ['rɛntgən] *or* ['rɛntjən], ['rʌntgən] *or* ['rʌntjən] *n.* the unit for measuring the effect of X rays or gamma rays. It is the quantity of radiation required to produce one electrostatic unit of electrical charge in one cubic centimetre of dry air under normal temperature and pressure. ⟨after Wilhelm Konrad *Roentgen* (1845-1923), a German physicist, who discovered X rays⟩

Roentgen ray X RAY.

ro•ga•tion [rou'geiʃən] *n.* **1** Usually, **rogations,** *pl. Christianity.* a solemn prayer or supplication, especially as chanted on the three days (Rogation Days) before Ascension Day. **2** in ancient Rome: **a** the proposal of a law by consuls or tribunes to be approved by the people. **b** a law so proposed. ⟨< L *rogatio, -onis* < *rogare* ask⟩

rog•a•tor•y ['rɒgə,tɔri] *adj.* questioning or asking questions, as in legal investigations: *a rogatory commission.*

rog•er ['rɒdʒər] *interj. Informal.* message received and understood; O.K. ⟨< the signaller's word for the letter *r,* for 'received'⟩

rogue [roug] *n., v.* **rogued, ro•guing.** —*n.* **1** a tricky or dishonest person; rascal. **2** a mischievous person. **3** an animal with a savage nature that lives apart from the herd: *rogue elephant.* **4** *Biology.* an individual, usually a plant, that varies from the standard.
—*v.* **1** eliminate defective plants from. **2** cheat. **3** be a rogue; act like a rogue. ⟨? short for earlier *roger* beggar⟩

ro•guer•y ['rougəri] *n., pl.* **-guer•ies. 1** the conduct of rogues; dishonest trickery. **2** playful mischief.

rogues' gallery a collection of photographs of known criminals and suspects, kept by the police for identification purposes.

ro•guish ['rougɪʃ] *adj.* **1** dishonest; rascally; having to do with or like rogues. **2** playfully mischievous. —**'ro•guish•ly,** *adv.* —**'ro•guish•ness,** *n.*

roil [rɔɪl] *v.* **1** make (a liquid) cloudy or muddy by stirring up sediment. **2** agitate or disturb. **3** especially of a liquid, be agitated or turbulent. **4** RILE (def. 1). ⟨< F *rouiller* rust, earlier, make muddy < OF *rouil* mud, rust, ult. < L *robigo* rust⟩

rois•ter ['rɔɪstər] *v.* be boisterous; revel noisily; swagger. ⟨< MF *ruistre* rude, ult. < L *rus* the country⟩ —**'rois•ter•er,** *n.* —**'rois•ter•ous,** *adj.*

role or **rôle** [roul] *n.* **1** a performer's part in a play, opera, etc.: *the leading role.* **2** a part played in real life: *He played an important role in the development of art in Canada.* ⟨< F *rôle* the roll (of paper, etc.) on which a part is written⟩
☛ *Hom.* ROLL.
☛ *Spelling.* **Role, rôle.** The spelling with the circumflex is still preferred by some people, especially in formal usage.

role model someone regarded by others as an inspiration for younger or less experienced people to imitate.

role–play ['roul ,plei] *v.* act as oneself or another in an imaginary situation for therapeutic or other purposes: *to role-play an interview. Young children do a lot of spontaneous role-playing.*

roll [roul] *v., n.* —*v.* **1** move or cause to move along by turning over and over: *A ball rolls. Roll the ball to me.* **2** wrap or become wrapped around on itself or on some other thing: *Roll the string into a ball.* **3** move or be moved on wheels: *The car rolled along. The baby rolled the toy truck across the floor.* **4** move smoothly; sweep along: *Waves roll in on the beach. The years roll on.* **5** turn around; revolve on an axis: *to roll an airplane.* **6** of a heavenly body, etc., perform a periodical revolution in an orbit. **7** move from side to side: *The ship rolled in the waves. The dancer rolled her hips in time to the drumbeat.* **8** turn over, or over and over: *The horse rolled in the dust. The police rolled the victim onto her back.* **9** walk with a swaying gait. **10** rise and fall again and again: *rolling country.* **11** *Archaic.* travel; wander; roam. **12** make flat or smooth with a roller; spread out with a rolling pin, etc. **13** put ink, paint, etc. on with a roller. **14** make deep, loud sounds: *Thunder rolls.* **15** beat (a drum) with rapid continuous strokes. **16** utter with full, flowing sound: *The organ rolled out the stirring music.* **17** utter with a trill: *to roll one's r's.* **18** *Informal.* have more than enough (*only in progressive tenses*): *be rolling in money.* **19 a** cast (dice). **b** turn up (a number) on a die: *to roll a five.* **20** *Slang.* rob (a person who is drunk or helpless), especially by turning him or her over to search through his or her pockets. **21** of eyes, move or turn from side to side and up and down. **22** move or turn (the eyes) from side to side and up and down. **23** make (a cigarette) by placing tobacco on a rectangle of paper and winding it into a cylindrical shape: *Cowboys roll their own.*
roll around, occur at regular intervals, especially as part of a cycle: *The annual exam panic has rolled around again.*
roll back, a cause (prices, wages, etc.) to return to a lower level. **b** *Informal.* set back; cause to fall behind.
roll in, *Informal.* **a** be surrounded by or luxuriate in large amounts of: *They appear to be rolling in money.* **b** arrive in large numbers: *The pledges rolled in, to the delight of the fundraisers.*
roll one's blanket or **bundle,** *Logging. Slang.* quit the job.
roll up, a increase; pile up or become piled up. **b** wrap up by turning over and over: *Cleopatra had herself rolled up in a rug.*
—*n.* **1** something rolled up; a cylinder formed by rolling (often forming a definite measure): *rolls of paper.* **2** a more or less rounded, cylindrical, or rolled-up mass. **3** continued motion up and down, or from side to side. **4** a rapid continuous beating on a drum. **5** a deep, loud sound: *the roll of thunder.* **6** a single revolution or act of rolling. **7** a motion like that of waves; undulation. **8** a roller, especially a revolving wheel-like tool used by bookbinders. **9** a record; list; list of names: *Call the roll.* **10 a** a small piece of dough which is cut, shaped, and often doubled or rolled over and then baked: *a dinner roll.* **b** a cake rolled up after being spread with something: *jelly roll.* **11** *Slang.* paper money rolled up. **12** *Slang.* money; funds. **13** a part which is rolled or turned over: *the roll in a hem.* **14** a rich or rhythmical flow of words: *the roll of a verse.* **15** a rolling gait; swagger: *walk with a roll.* **16** undulation on the surface of something; the feature of having such undulations.
a roll in the hay, *Slang.* an occasion of sexual intercourse.
on a roll, *Informal.* be in a period of good luck, having everything go right: *She's really on a roll; all her business deals have paid off lately.*
strike (someone) **off the rolls,** expel from membership. ⟨ME < OF *roller,* ult. < L *rota* wheel⟩
☛ *Hom.* ROLE.
☛ *Syn. n.* **9.** See note at LIST[1].

roll•a•way ['roulə,wei] *adj., n.* —*adj.* referring to anything on rollers or wheels designed for easy moving and storage when not in use: *a rollaway cot.*
—*n.* a folding bed having rollers so that it can be easily stored.

roll bar a strong steel bar in the shape of an inverted U that sits over and across the interior compartment of a vehicle, to prevent crushing and reduce injuries to the driver and passengers if the vehicle rolls over.

roll call 1 the calling of a list of names, as of soldiers, pupils, etc., to find out who are present. 2 the time of day for such a calling.

rolled oats hulled, steamed oats that have been pressed flat between rollers.

roll•er ['roulər] *n.* **1** anything that rolls; a cylinder on which something is rolled along or rolled up. **2** a cylinder of metal, stone, wood, etc., used for smoothing, pressing, crushing, etc. **3** a covered cylinder used for applying paint, ink, etc. **4** a long rolled bandage. **5** a long, swelling wave. **6** a person who rolls something. **7** a variety of canary that has a trilling voice. **8** a variety of tumbler pigeon. **9** *Cdn. Logging.* a logger who piles logs on a skidway.

roller bearing *Machinery.* a bearing in which the shaft turns on rollers to lessen friction.

Rol•ler•blades ['roulər,bleidz] *Trademark.* a brand of inline skates.

roller coaster a railway built for amusement, on which small open cars roll up and down steep inclines, round sharp corners, etc. at high speed.

roller skate one of a pair of skates equipped with small wheels, two at the front and two at the back, used on floors, roads, sidewalks, etc.

roll•er–skate ['roulər ˌskeit] *v.* **-skat•ed, -skat•ing.** move on roller skates. **—roller skater.**

rol•lick ['rɒlɪk] *v.* frolic; be merry; enjoy oneself in a free, hearty way. ⟨origin uncertain⟩

rol•lick•ing ['rɒlɪkɪŋ] *adj.* frolicking; jolly; lively. **—'rol•lick•ing•ly,** *adv.*

rol•lick•some ['rɒlɪksəm] *adj.* rollicking.

roll•ing ['roulɪŋ] *n., adj., v.* *—n.* the action, motion, or sound of anything that rolls or is being rolled: *the rolling of a ball, the rolling of thunder.*
—adj. that rolls: *Rolling land rises and falls in gentle slopes. A person with a rolling gait sways from side to side. A rolling collar turns back or folds over.*
—v. ppr. of ROLL.

rolling mill 1 a factory where metal is rolled into sheets and bars. 2 a machine for rolling metal.

rolling pin a cylinder of solid wood, porcelain, marble, etc., for rolling out dough.

rolling stock 1 the locomotives and cars of a railway. 2 all the trucks of a trucking company, etc.

roll•mop ['roul,mɒp] *n.* a fillet of herring rolled, often around a pickle, and marinated in brine to be served as an appetizer. ⟨< G *Rollmops* < *rollen* roll + *Mops* pug dog⟩

roll–top ['roul ˌtɒp] *adj., n.* *—adj.* having a top that rolls back: *a roll-top desk.*
—n. a roll-top desk.

ro•ly–po•ly ['rouli 'pouli] *adj., n., pl.* **-lies.** *—adj.* short and plump: *a roly-poly child.*
—n. **1** a short, plump person or animal. **2** *Brit.* a pudding made of jam or fruit spread on a rich dough, rolled up and cooked. ⟨apparently < *roll*⟩

Rom or **rom** [rɒm] *n.* a Gypsy man or boy. ⟨< Romany (the language of Gypsies), a married man⟩

ROM READ-ONLY MEMORY.

rom. *Printing.* roman (type).

Rom. 1 Roman. 2 Romania; Romanian. 3 Romance.

Ro•ma•ic [rou'meiɪk] *n., adj.* *—n.* the everyday spoken language of modern Greece.
—adj. of or having to do with this language. ⟨< Gk. *Rhōmaikos* Roman (of the Eastern Empire)⟩

ro•maine [rou'mein] *n.* a variety of lettuce (*Lactuca sativa longifolia*) having long green leaves with crinkly edges, joined loosely at the base. ⟨< F *romaine,* fem. adj., Roman⟩

ro•man [ʀoˈmɑ̃] *n. French.* **1** any novel. **2** a romantic novel. **3** a metrical romance of medieval French literature.

Ro•man ['roumən] *n., adj.* *—n.* **1** a native or inhabitant of ancient or modern Rome. **2 roman,** roman print or type. **3** the characters of the Roman alphabet: *The same Chinese name may have several different spellings in Roman.*
—adj. **1** of or having to do with ancient or modern Rome or its people. **2** of or having to do with the Roman Catholic Church. **3** *Architecture.* of or having to do with a style developed by the ancient Romans, characterized by massive walls and pillars, rounded arches and vaults, domes, and pediments. **4 roman,** of or designating an upright style of type, the one most commonly used in printing. The capital letters of roman type are modelled on those used in ancient Roman inscriptions. Compare ITALIC. **5** of or using the characters of the Roman alphabet: *The etymologies in this dictionary use Roman transliterations of words that come from languages using other scripts.* ⟨OE < L *Romanus* < *Roma* Rome⟩

roman à clef [ʀomɑ̃na'kle] *pl.* **ro•mans à clef** [ʀomɑ̃za'kle] *French.* a novel featuring real people or events slightly disguised, as with fictitious names.

Roman alphabet the alphabet used by the Romans to write Latin; our present alphabet derived from this with the additions of J, U, and W. Also, **Latin alphabet.**

Roman candle a kind of firework consisting of a tube that shoots out sparks and balls of fire.

Roman Catholic 1 a member of the Catholic Church that follows the Latin or Roman rite, as distinguished from the Eastern rites and that acknowledges the Pope as its head. 2 of or having to do with Roman Catholics or Roman Catholicism.

Roman Catholicism the doctrines, faith, practices, and system of government of the Roman Catholic Church.

ro•mance *n.* [rou'mæns] *or* ['roumæns]; *v.* [rou'mæns] *n., v.* **-manced, -manc•ing.** *—n.* **1** a love story. **2 a** a medieval story or poem telling of heroes and strange and exciting adventures. **b** any story of adventure, especially when set in a remote time or place, or involving heroes, strange happenings, etc. **3** the literary genre comprising any of these types of story. **4** a quality or aura of real events or conditions that suggests such stories, characterized by excitement, noble deeds, etc.: *the romance of an explorer's life.* **5** an interest in or inclination for adventure, mystery, love, etc. **6** a love affair. **7** a false or extravagant account. **8** *Music.* a short, lyrical composition.
—v. **1** make up extravagant or romantic stories. **2** think or talk in a romantic way. **3** exaggerate or lie. **4** make love to; court or woo romantically. ⟨ME < OF *romanz,* ult. < VL *romanice* in a Romance language < L *Romanus* Roman < *Roma* Rome⟩

Ro•mance [rou'mæns] *or* ['roumæns] *adj., n.* *—adj.* of or having to do with languages that developed from Latin, the language of the Romans. French, Italian, Spanish, Portuguese, Romanian, Catalan, Romansch, and Provençal are Romance languages.
—n. this group of languages.

Romance languages those languages descended from Latin, as Italian, Spanish, Portuguese, Romanian, Catalan, French, and Provençal.

ro•manc•er [rou'mænsər] *n.* **1** one who romances or makes up romances.

Roman Empire the empire of ancient Rome that lasted from 27 B.C. to A.D. 395, when it was divided into the **Eastern Roman Empire** and the **Western Roman Empire.**

Ro•man•esque [ˌroumə'nɛsk] *n., adj.* *—n. Architecture.* a style characterized by massiveness and round arches and vaults, developed in Europe during the early Middle Ages, between the periods of Roman and Gothic architecture.
—adj. of, in, or having to do with this style of architecture.

Ro•ma•nia [rou'meinjə] *n.* a country in SE Europe, bordering on the Black Sea. Also, **Rumania, Roumania.**

Ro•ma•ni•an [rou'meinjən] *or* [rou'meiniən] *n., adj.* *—n.* **1** a native or inhabitant of Romania. **2** the Romance language of the Romanians.
—adj. of or having to do with Romania, its people, or their language. Also, **Rumanian, Roumanian.**

Ro•man•ic [rou'mænɪk] *adj.* **1** Romance. **2** Roman. ⟨< L *Romanicus*⟩

Ro•man•ist ['roumənɪst] *n.* a student of Roman law, institutions, etc.

Ro•man•ize ['roumə,naɪz] *v.* **-ized, -iz•ing. 1** make or become Roman in character. **2** make or become Roman Catholic. **3** write or print in or convert to Roman characters. **—ˌRo•man•i'za•tion,** *n.*

Roman law the laws of the ancient Romans. Roman law is the basis of civil law in many countries.

Roman nose a nose having a prominent bridge.

Roman numerals the system of numerals used by the

ancient Romans. The values of the numerals are added together, except when a numeral is followed by another of greater value, in which case the smaller one is subtracted from the larger one. *Examples*: XI = 10 + 1 = 11; IX = 10 – 1 = 9; XIX = 10 + (10 – 1) = 19.

Ro•ma•no [rou'mɑnou] *n.* a hard Italian cheese similar to Parmesan, but somewhat sharper. 〈< Ital.〉

Ro•ma•nov or **Ro•ma•noff** ['roumə,nɒf] *or* [rou'mɑnɒf] *n.* the royal family of Russia from 1613 to 1917.

Roman rite the system of ceremonies used in the Roman Catholic Church in celebrating the Mass and administering the sacraments.

Ro•mansch or **Ro•mansh** [rou'mɑnʃ] *n.* See RHAETO-ROMANCE.

Roman shade a window shade that draws up into a series of concertinalike folds when raised.

ro•man•tic [rou'mæntɪk] *adj., n.* —*adj.* **1** characteristic of romances or romance; appealing to fancy and the imagination: *romantic tales of love and war.* **2** having ideas or feelings suited to romance: *a romantic teenager.* **3** suited to a romance: *What a romantic forest! Fairies might live here!* **4** fond of making up fanciful stories. **5** Often, **Romantic. a** of or having to do with art, music, and literature appealing to the emotions and the imagination in subject and style; not classical: *The novel* Jane Eyre *and Chopin's music are romantic.* Romantic writing usually tells about the unusual and adventurous aspects of life and uses complete freedom of form and expression. **b** of or having to do with romanticists or romanticism. **6** unrealistic or quixotic.
—*n.* **1** a romantic person. **2 Romantic,** an artist of the Romantic period; romanticist. 〈< F *romantique* < earlier *romant* a romance, var. of OF *romanz.* See ROMANCE.〉 **—ro'man•ti•cal•ly,** *adv.*

ro•man•ti•cism [rou'mæntə,sɪzəm] *n.* **1** a romantic spirit or tendency. **2** a style or movement in literature and art that prevailed in W Europe in the late 18th and early 19th centuries, characterized by a highly imaginative and emotional treatment of life, nature, and the supernatural. **3** *Music.* a style characterized by melodic inventiveness and rich harmonies.

ro•man•ti•cist [rou'mæntəsɪst] *n.* a follower of romanticism in literature, art, or music. Scott and Wordsworth were romanticists.

ro•man•ti•cize [rou'mæntə,saɪz] *v.* **-cized, -ciz•ing. 1** make romantic; give a romantic character to. **2** be romantic; act, talk, or write in a romantic manner. **—ro,man•ti•ci'za•tion,** *n.*

Romantic Movement the tendency toward romanticism in the literature, art, and music of the late 18th and early 19th centuries.

Rom•a•ny ['rɒməni] *n., pl.* **-nies;** *adj.* —*n.* **1** Gypsy. **2** the Indic language of the Gypsies.
—*adj.* belonging or having to do with the Gypsies or their language. 〈< Romany *Romani,* fem. and pl. of *Romano,* adj. < *Rom* gypsy, man, husband〉

Rom. Cath. ROMAN CATHOLIC.

Rome [roum] *n.* **1** the Roman Catholic Church. **2** the governing authority of the Roman Catholic Church: *The marriage was annulled by Rome.*

Rome (Beauty) a crisp variety of winter apple.

Ro•me•o ['roumi,ou] *n.* **1** the hero of Shakespeare's tragedy *Romeo and Juliet,* who killed himself for love. **2** any romantic male lover.

romp [rɒmp] *v., n.* —*v.* **1** play in a lively, boisterous way; rush and tumble in play. **2 a** run or go quickly and easily. **b** win easily.
—*n.* **1** a boisterous, lively play or frolic: *A pillow fight is a romp.* **2** *Archaic.* tomboy. **3** a swift but effortless victory in which all the others are left behind, as in racing: *to win in a romp.* 〈ult. var. of *ramp,* v.〉 **—'romp•er,** *n.*

romp•ers ['rɒmpərz] *n.pl.* a loose one-piece garment, worn by young children and consisting of a blouselike top and short, elasticized legs.

Rom•u•lus ['rɒmjələs] *n. Roman legend.* the founder and first king of Rome. As children, he and his brother Remus were nursed by a wolf. Romulus slew Remus for leaping derisively over the walls of his new city of Rome.

ron•deau ['rɒndou] *or* [rɒn'dou] *n., pl.* **ron•deaux** ['rɒndouz] *or* [rɒn'douz]. a short poem with thirteen (or ten) lines on two rhymes. The opening words are used in two places as an unrhymed refrain. The poem "In Flanders Fields" is a rondeau. 〈< MF *rondeau,* var. of *rondel* < OF *rondel.* Doublet of RONDEL.〉

ron•del ['rɒndəl] *or* [rɒn'dɛl] *n.* a short poem, usually with fourteen lines and two rhymes. The initial couplet is repeated in the middle and at the end. 〈ME < OF *rondel,* originally dim. of *rond* round < L *rotundus.* Doublet of RONDEAU.〉

ron•do ['rɒndou] *n., pl.* **-dos.** *Music.* a composition or movement having one principal theme to which return is made after the introduction of each subordinate theme. 〈< Ital. < F *rondeau* rondeau〉

rood [rud] *n.* **1** *Archaic.* the cross on which Christ died. **2** a representation of the cross; crucifix. 〈OE *rōd*〉
☛ *Hom.* RUDE.

rood beam a beam, usually surmounted by a rood, frequently the head of a rood screen, separating the nave from the choir and chancel of a church.

rood screen an elaborately carved screen, usually surmounted by a rood, separating the nave from the choir and chancel of a church.

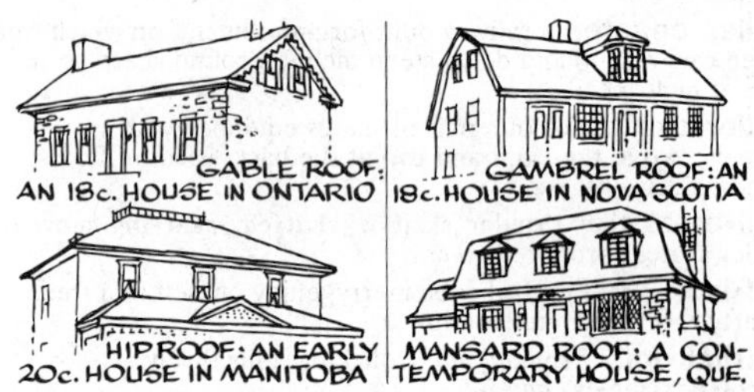

roof [ruf] *n., pl.* **roofs** or **rooves;** *v.* **1** the outermost top covering of a building. **2** something that in form or position resembles the roof of a building: *the roof of a cave, the roof of a car, the roof of the mouth.* **3** a house; home.
go through the roof or **hit the roof,** lose one's temper violently.
raise the roof, *Informal.* make a disturbance; create an uproar.
—*v.* **1** provide or cover with or as if with a roof. **2** work as a roofer. 〈OE *hrōf*〉

roof•er ['rufər] *n.* a person who makes or repairs roofs.

roof garden 1 a garden on the flat roof of a building. **2** a roof or top storey of a building, ornamented with plants, etc., and used for a restaurant, theatre, etc.

roof•ing ['rufɪŋ] *n., v.* —*n.* **1** material used for roofs. Shingles are a common roofing for houses. **2** the act of putting a roof on a building.
—*v.* ppr. of ROOF.

roof•less ['ruflɪs] *adj.* **1** having no roof. **2** having no home or shelter.

roof•top ['ruf,tɒp] *n.* the roof of a building, especially the outer surface.

roof•tree ['ruf,tri] *n.* the horizontal timber along the top of the roof.

rook[1] [rʊk] *n., v.* —*n.* **1** a common European bird (*Corvus frugilegus*) closely related to the North American crow. **2** *Slang.* a person who cheats at cards, dice, etc.
—*v. Slang.* cheat. 〈OE *hrōc*〉

rook[2] [rʊk] *n. Chess.* one of the pieces with which the game is played, also called a castle because of its top in the shape of a battlement. 〈ME < OF *roc,* ult. < Persian *rukh*〉

rook•er•y ['rʊkəri] *n., pl.* **-er•ies. 1** a breeding place of rooks; a colony of rooks. **2** a breeding place or colony where other birds or animals are crowded together: *a rookery of seals.* **3** a crowded, dirty, and poor tenement house or group of such houses.

rook•ie ['rʊki] *n. Informal.* a beginner, such as a recruit or a new player on a team. 〈? alteration of *recruit*〉

room [rum] *or* [rʊm] *n., v.* —*n.* **1** a part of a house, or other building, with walls separating it from the rest of the building of which it is a part. **2 rooms,** *pl.* lodgings. **3** the people in a room: *This room is awfully quiet all of a sudden.* **4** the space occupied by, or available for, something: *There is little room to move in a crowd.* **5** scope or opportunity: *room for improvement, room for advancement.*
—*v.* **1** rent a room; lodge: *The two women roomed together.* **2** provide with a room. 〈OE *rūm*〉
☛ *Hom.* RHEUM [rum].

room•er ['rumər] *n.* a person who lives in a rented room or rooms in another's house.
☛ *Hom.* RUMOUR.

room•ette [ru'mɛt] *n.* a small, private, single bedroom on some railway cars.

room•ful ['rum,fʊl] *or* ['rʊm,fʊl] *n., pl.* **-fuls. 1** enough to fill a room. **2** the people or things in a room.

room•ie ['rumi] *n. Informal.* room-mate.
☛ *Hom.* RHEUMY, ROOMY.

rooming house a house with rooms to rent.

room–mate ['rum ,meit] *n.* a person who shares a room or apartment with another or others.

room service in a hotel, lodge, etc., a special service by which one may order food or drink to be brought to one's room.

room•y ['rumi] *adj.* **room•i•er, room•i•est.** having plenty of space; large; spacious. **—'room•i•ness,** *n.* **—'room•i•ly,** *adv.*
☛ *Hom.* RHEUMY, ROOMIE.

roost [rust] *n., v.* *—n.* **1** a bar, pole, or perch on which birds rest or sleep. **2** a place for birds to roost in. **3** a place to rest or stay: *a robber's roost in the mountains.*
come home to roost, have unforeseen and unfavourable consequences for the originator; boomerang: *The stories he spread came home to roost when everyone thought they were about him.*
rule the roost, *Informal.* be in charge; have control.
—v. **1** sit or sleep on a roost: *roosting birds.* **2** settle down, as for the night. ⟨OE *hrōst*⟩

roost•er ['rustər] *n.* a male domesticated fowl; cock.

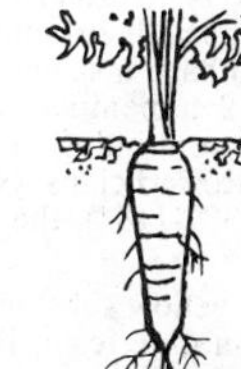
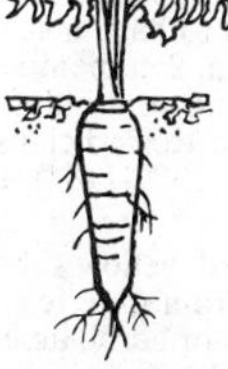

The two main types of root (fibrous roots and taproots) are shown at the left. The specialized aerial roots of an orchid are shown above.

root[1] [rut] *n., v.* *—n.* **1** the part of a plant that grows downward, usually into the ground, to hold the plant in place, absorb water and mineral foods from the soil, and often to store food material. **2** any underground part of a plant. **3** something like a root in shape, position, use, etc.: *the root of a tooth, the roots of the hair.* **4** a thing from which other things grow and develop; cause; source: *What is the root of her success?* **5** the essential part; core or base: *to get to the root of a matter.* **6 roots,** *pl.* ancestors or antecedents; one's heritage: *searching for one's roots.* **7 roots,** *pl.* a sense of belonging to a particular place or community or of having a certain heritage: *a person without roots.* **8** *Mathematics.* **a** the quantity that produces another quantity when multiplied by itself a certain number of times. 2 is the square root of 4 and the cube root of 8 ($2 \times 2 = 4$, $2 \times 2 \times 2 = 8$). **b** the quantity that satisfies an equation when substituted for an unknown quantity. In the equation $x^2 + 2x - 3 = 0$, 1 and –3 are the roots. **9** *Grammar.* a word or word element from which others are derived. *Example:* Room *is the root of* roominess, roomer, room-mate, *and* roomy. **10** *Music.* the fundamental tone of a chord.
take root, a send out roots and begin to grow. **b** become firmly established.
—v. **1** send out roots and begin to grow; become fixed in the ground: *Some plants root more quickly than others.* **2** fix firmly: *She was rooted to the spot by surprise.* **3** become firmly established.
root out or **up, a** uproot: *Careful, or you'll root up my pansies.* **b** get rid of completely: *to root out corruption in government.* ⟨OE *rōt* < ON *rót;* akin to L *radix*⟩ **—'root,like,** *adj.* **—'root•er,** *n.*
☛ *Hom.* ROUT[2] [rut], ROUTE [rut].

root[2] [rut] *v.* **1** dig with the snout: *Pigs like to root in gardens.* **2** poke; pry; search. ⟨OE *wrōtan*⟩ **—'root•er,** *n.*
☛ *Hom.* ROUTE [rut].

root[3] [rut] *v. Informal.* enthusiastically cheer or support a contestant, etc. ⟨probably < earlier *rout* shout, roar < ON *rauta*⟩ **—'root•er,** *n.*
☛ *Hom.* ROUT[2] [rut], ROUTE [rut].

root beer a soft drink flavoured with the juice of the roots of certain plants such as sarsaparilla and sassafras.

root canal 1 the central passage in the root of a tooth, containing blood vessels and nerves. **2** treatment for an infected or damaged root canal.

root cellar part of a house or barn below ground level, used for storing root vegetables such as carrots by keeping them cool in summer and preventing them from freezing in winter.

root crop a crop grown for its large, edible, underground parts. Beets, turnips, and parsnips are examples of root crops grown in Canada.

root hair a hairlike outgrowth from a root that absorbs water and dissolved minerals from the soil.

root•less ['rutlɪs] *adj.* having no roots: *a rootless transient.* **—'root•less•ness,** *n.* **—'root•less•ly,** *adv.*

root•let ['rutlɪt] *n.* a little root; a small branch of a root.

root•stock ['rut,stɒk] *n.* **1** rhizome. **2** a plant with another plant grafted on top.

root•worm ['rut,wɜrm] *n.* any of various insect larvae or worms that feed on plant roots.

rooves [ruvz] *n.* a pl. of ROOF.

rope [roup] *n., v.* **roped, rop•ing.** *—n.* **1** a strong, thick line or cord made by twisting smaller cords together. **2** lasso. **3** a number of things twisted or strung together: *a rope of pearls, a rope of onions.* **4** a cord or noose for hanging a person. **5** death by being hanged. **6** a sticky, stringy mass: *Molasses candy forms a rope.* **7** the cords defining the perimeter of a boxing ring or other competition area.
give (someone) **rope,** *Informal.* let a person act freely.
know the ropes, a know the various ropes of a ship. **b** *Informal.* know the procedures involved in a business or activity.
the end of (one's) **rope,** the end of one's resources, endurance, etc.
—v. **1** tie, bind, or fasten with a rope. **2** enclose or mark off with a rope. **3** catch (a horse, calf, etc.) with a lasso. **4** form a sticky, stringy mass: *Cook the syrup until it ropes when you lift it with a spoon.*
rope in or **into,** *Slang.* get or lead (someone) into some activity by trickery or persuasion: *The students roped us into hosting this potluck dinner.* ⟨OE *rāp*⟩

rope•danc•er ['roup,dænsər] *n.* a person who dances, walks, etc. on a rope stretched high above the floor or ground.

rope•walk ['roup,wɒk] *n.* a place where ropes are made. A ropewalk is usually a long, low shed or a long, level piece of ground.

rope•walk•er ['roup,wɒkər] *n.* a person who walks on a rope stretched high above the floor or ground. **—'rope,walk•ing,** *n.*

rope•way ['roup,wei] *n.* an aerial cable along which passengers or freight may be carried.

rop•y ['roupi] *adj.* **rop•i•er, rop•i•est. 1** forming sticky threads; stringy. **2** like a rope or ropes. **—'rop•i•ly,** *adv.* **—'rop•i•ness,** *n.*

roque [rouk] *n.* a form of croquet played on a hard court and modified from ordinary croquet so as to demand greater skill. ⟨abstracted from *croquet*⟩

Roque•fort ['roukfərt] *n.* a strongly flavoured French cheese made of goats' milk and veined with mould. ⟨made in caves at *Roquefort,* a town in S France⟩

ror•qual ['rɔrkwəl] *n.* any of a genus (*Balaenoptera*) of baleen whales of the same family (Balaenopteridae) as the humpback, having a long, streamlined body with a small dorsal fin and numerous grooves or furrows running along the throat to the belly; especially, *B. physalus,* found in almost all oceans and also called **fin whale** or **finback.** See also BLUE WHALE. ⟨< F < Norwegian *röyrkval,* literally, red whale⟩

Ror•schach test ['rɔrʃɑk] a psychological test that indicates personality traits, based on the subject's interpretation of ten different ink-blot designs. ⟨after Hermann *Rorschach* (1884-1922), a Swiss psychiatrist⟩

ro•sa•ceous [rou'zeiʃəs] *adj.* **1** belonging to the rose family. **2** like a rose. **3** rose-coloured. ⟨< L *rosaceus* < *rosa* rose[1]⟩

ro•sa•ri•an [rou'zɛriən] *n.* a person who develops or cultivates roses; a rose-grower.

ro•sa•ry ['rouzəri] *n., pl.* **-ries. 1** a string of beads for keeping count in saying a series of prayers. **2** a series of prayers said with this. **3** a rose garden; rose bed. ⟨< Med.L *rosarium* < L *rosarium* rose garden, ult. < *rosa* rose[1]⟩

rose[1] [rouz] *n., adj., v.* **rosed, ros•ing.** *—n.* **1** any of a genus (*Rosa*) of shrubs of the northern hemisphere, having compound leaves, showy flowers, and, usually, prickly stems. There are many cultivated species and varieties of rose. Wild roses have flowers with five petals. **2** the flower of any of these shrubs. **3** (*adjl.*) designating a large family (Rosaceae) of herbs, shrubs, and trees, found especially in temperate regions, that includes some of the most important fruit-bearing and ornamental shrubs and trees. Raspberries, strawberries, cherries, plums, peaches, hawthorns, brambles, and roses belong to the rose family. **4** any one of a number of similar or related plants. **5** a medium to dark, slightly purplish pink. **6** something shaped like a rose or suggesting a rose, such as a rosette, compass card, the sprinkling nozzle of a watering can, or a gem cut with faceted top and flat base. **7** a woman of great beauty, loveliness, or excellence.

Roses

come up roses, go or turn out extremely well.
under the rose, in secret; privately.
—adj. **1** of the colour rose. **2** of, containing, or having to do with a rose or roses: *rose bush, rose bowl.*
—v. make rosy. ⟨OE < L *rosa*⟩ **—'rose,like,** *adj.*

rose[2] [rouz] *v.* pt. of RISE.

ro•sé [rou'zei] *n.* a still or sparkling, light, pink table wine produced from red wine grapes by removing the skins during the early stages of fermentation. ⟨< F⟩

ro•se•ate ['rouziit] *or* ['rouzi,eit] *adj.* **1** rose-coloured; rosy. **2** cheerful; optimistic.

rose•bay ['rouz,bei] *n.* **1** oleander. **2** rhododendron.

rose•bud ['rouz,bʌd] *n.* the bud of a rose.

rose•bush ['rouz,bʊʃ] *n.* a shrub that bears roses; a rose plant.

rose–col•oured or **rose–col•ored** ['rouz ,kʌlərd] *adj.* **1** pinkish red. **2** bright; cheerful; optimistic.
rose-coloured glasses, an optimistic, but usually unfounded, view of a situation or of life in general.

rose fever *Pathology.* an allergic reaction similar to hay fever, believed to be caused by rose pollen.

rose geranium a geranium (*Pelargonium graveolens*) having small pink flowers and rose-scented, lobed leaves. The oil of the leaves of some varieties of rose geranium is used in perfumes as a substitute for attar of roses.

rose mallow 1 any of several species of hibiscus having large red, pink, or white flowers, especially *Hibiscus moscheutos*, native to marshy areas of E North America, from which many cultivated varieties have been derived. **2** hollyhock.

rose•mar•y ['rouz,mɛri] *n., pl.* **-mar•ies.** a European evergreen shrub (*Rosemarinus officinalis*) widely cultivated for its fragrant, greyish green leaves which are used as a flavouring and which yield an essential oil used in perfumes. Rosemary is a traditional symbol of remembrance. ⟨ME < L *ros maris*, literally, dew of the sea; by folk etymology associated with *rose* and *Mary*⟩

rose of Sharon 1 a shrub or small tree (*Hibiscus syriacus*) of the mallow family native to Asia, commonly cultivated for its large, bell-shaped, usually rose, purple, or white flowers. **2** a Eurasian shrub (*Hypericum calycinum*) closely related to the St.-John's-worts, cultivated for its large yellow flowers. **3** a plant of the Old Testament, thought to be the autumn crocus. Also called **Aaron's beard.**

rose oil a fragrant liquid distilled from roses, used in flavouring and perfumes. It can be yellow, green, or red.

ro•se•o•la [rou'ziələ] *or* [,rouzi'oulə] *n. Pathology.* **1** rubella. **2** any rose-coloured rash.

rose po•go•nia [pə'gounjə] an orchid (*Pogonia ophioglossoides*) having a fragrant, drooping pink flower. It blooms in summer in wet places in eastern North America.

Ro•set•ta stone [rou'zɛtə] a slab of black basalt found in 1799 near the mouth of the Nile, dated about 200 B.C. A decree carved on it in two kinds of ancient Egyptian writing (hieroglyphic and demotic) and in Greek provided the most important key to the understanding of Egyptian hieroglyphics. It is now in the British Museum in London, England. ⟨< *Rosetta* (< Arabic *Rashid*), a town near one of the mouths of the Nile⟩

ro•sette [rou'zɛt] *n.* **1** an ornament, object, or arrangement shaped like a rose. **2** such an ornament made of ribbon, given as a prize at a livestock show, horse show, dog show, etc. **3** *Architecture*. a carved or moulded rosette used as an ornament. Also, **rosace. 4** *Botany*. a circular cluster of leaves, petals, etc. ⟨< F *rosette*, dim. of *rose* rose[1]⟩

rose water water containing oil of roses, used as a perfume, cosmetic, and in cooking.

rose window a circular window, usually of stained glass, especially one with a pattern radiating from a centre.

rose•wood ['rouz,wʊd] *n.* **1** the hard, dark reddish wood of any of various tropical trees (especially of genus *Dalbergia*) of the pea family valued for fine furniture, panelling, etc. **2** any of the trees having such wood.

Rosh Ha•sha•nah or **Ha•sha•na** ['rɒʃ] *or* [rouʃhə'ʃɑnə]; *Hebrew*, ['ʀoʃ hɑʃɑ'nɑ] the Jewish New Year, falling usually in late September or early October. ⟨< Hebrew, lit., beginning of the year⟩

ro•shi ['rouʃi] *n.* in Zen Buddhism, a term of respect for a wise teacher, the head of a monastery, or the chief priest of a temple.

Ro•si•cru•cian [,rouzə'kruʃən] *or* [,rɒzə'kruʃən] *n., adj. —n.* **1** a member of a secret society, especially prominent in the 17th and 18th centuries, that claimed to have a special and secret knowledge of nature and religion. **2** a member of any of various similar societies founded later and continuing to this day.
—adj. of or having to do with the Rosicrucians. ⟨< Latinized version of Christian *Rosenkreuz* (1387-1484), the name of the supposed founder of the order⟩

ros•in ['rɒzən] *n., v. —n.* a hard, yellow substance that remains when turpentine is evaporated from pine resin. Rosin is rubbed on violin bows and on the shoes of acrobats, ballet dancers, boxers, etc. to keep them from slipping.
—v. cover or rub with rosin. ⟨ME var. of *resin*⟩

Ros•i•nan•te [,rɒzə'nænti] *or* [,rouzə'nantei] *n.* **1** in Cervantes' *Don Quixote*, the hero's thin and worn-out horse. **2** any very poor, thin, or worn-out horse.

Ross's goose ['rɒsiz] *Cdn.* a smallish white goose (*Chen rossii*) with black primary feathers, that breeds in the far north. ⟨< Bernard R. *Ross* (d. 1874), a Hudson's Bay Company factor⟩

ros•ter ['rɒstər] *n.* **1** a list of people's names and the duties assigned to them. **2** any list. ⟨< Du. *rooster*⟩

ros•tral ['rɒstrəl] *adj.* of or having to do with a rostrum.

ros•trum ['rɒstrəm] *n., pl.* **-trums, -tra** [-trə]. **1** a platform or stage for public speaking. **2** the beak of an ancient war galley, used for ramming enemy ships. **3** *Biology.* a beaklike part. ⟨< L *rostrum* beak < *rodere* gnaw; with reference to the speakers' platform in the Roman forum, which was decorated with the beaks of captured war galleys⟩

ros•y ['rouzi] *adj.* **ros•i•er, ros•i•est. 1** like a rose; rose red; pinkish red. **2** made of, decorated with, or like roses. **3** bright; cheerful: *a rosy future.* **—'ros•i•ness,** *n.* **—'ros•i•ly,** *adv.*

ro•sy–cheeked ['rouzi ,tʃikt] **1** having a healthy flush to the face. **2** of a child, chubby and attractive.

rosy twisted stalk a wildflower (*Streptopus roseus*) having drooping pink flowers followed by red berries thought to be laxative. It blooms in spring in woods in eastern North America.

rot [rɒt] *v.* **rot•ted, rot•ting;** *n., interj. —v.* **1** decay; spoil. **2** cause to decay. **3** disintegrate; weaken; fall (*off* or *away*) because of decay. **3** moisten or soak (flax, etc.) in order to soften; ret. **4** lose or cause to lose vigour; degenerate.
—n. **1 a** the process of rotting; decay. **b** the state of being rotten or decayed; rottenness. **2** rotten matter. **3** a liver disease of animals, especially of sheep, caused by a liver fluke and marked by anemia, weakness, and swollen jaws. **4** any of various diseases of plants marked by decay and caused by bacteria or fungi, as **crown rot. 5** *Slang.* nonsense; rubbish.
—interj. an exclamation expressing annoyance, contempt, disagreement, or disgust. ⟨OE *rotian*⟩
☛ *Hom.* WROUGHT.
☛ *Syn. v.* **1.** See note at DECAY.

ro•ta ['routə] *n.* **1** a roster. **2** a round of sporting events, as in golf. **3** *Roman Catholic Church.* an ecclesiastical court. The **Sacred Roman Rota,** in Rome, is an ecclesiastical court of final appeal.

Ro•tar•i•an [rou'tɛriən] *n., adj.* *–n.* a member of a Rotary Club.
–adj. of, belonging, or having to do with Rotary Clubs.
–Ro'tar•i•an,ism, *n.*

ro•ta•ry ['routəri] *adj., n., pl.* **-ries.** *–adj.* **1** turning on an axis like a top or a wheel; rotating. **2** having parts that rotate. **3** of an airplane engine, having radially arranged cylinders that revolve around a common fixed crankshaft. **4** *Cdn. Education.* of or operating under the ROTARY SYSTEM.
–n. **1** a TRAFFIC CIRCLE. **2** *Cdn. Education.* ROTARY SYSTEM. **3** a machine or engine, as a steam turbine, in which torque is directly produced without reciprocating parts. ⟨< Med.L *rotarius* < L *rota* wheel⟩

Rotary Club an association of business and professional people formed with the purpose of serving their community. Rotary Clubs form an international organization founded in Chicago in 1905.

rotary press a printing press having the type or plates mounted on a cylinder that rotates against, and prints on, a continuous sheet from a roll of newsprint paper.

rotary system *Cdn. Education.* a method of operation in schools, under which students move to different rooms (and specialist teachers) for different subjects.

ro•ta•ry–wing aircraft ['routəri 'wɪŋ] an aircraft such as a helicopter, supported in the air by an airfoil or rotors rotating around a vertical axis.

ro•tate ['routeit] *or* [rou'teit] *v.* **-tat•ed, -tat•ing. 1** move or cause to move around a centre or axis; turn in a circle; revolve. Wheels, tops, and the earth rotate. **2** change in a regular order; take turns or cause to take turns: *Farmers rotate crops.* ⟨< L *rotare* < *rota* wheel⟩
☛ *Syn.* **1.** See note at TURN.

ro•ta•tion [rou'teiʃən] *n.* **1** the act or process of moving around a centre or axis; a turning in a circle or revolving: *The earth's rotation causes night and day.* **2** a regular ordered change. **3** a system of such changes; taking turns in regular succession: *The job of classroom roll call is done in rotation.* **4** *Pool.* a version of the game in which the balls are played in rotation by number. **5** one complete turn of a body around its axis. **–ro'ta•tion•al,** *adj.*

rotation of crops *Agriculture.* the varying of the crops grown in the same field to keep the soil from losing its fertility.

ro•ta•tor ['routeitər] *or* [rou'teitər] *n.* **1** a person who or thing that rotates. **2** *Physiology.* a muscle that turns a part of the body. ⟨< L⟩

ro•ta•to•ry ['routə,tɔri] *adj.* **1** rotating; rotary. **2** causing rotation. **3** passing or following from one to another in a regular order.

rote [rout] *n.* a set, routine way of doing things.
by rote, by memory, without thought of the meaning: *to learn a lesson by rote.* ⟨ME; origin uncertain⟩

ro•te•none ['routə,noun] *n. Chemistry.* a white, crystalline, water-insoluble organic compound obtained from various plant roots, used as an insecticide and fish poison but harmless to mammals or birds. *Formula:* $C_{23}H_{22}O_6$ ⟨< Japanese *roten* derris + E *-one*⟩

rot•gut ['rɒt,gʌt] *n. Slang.* raw, cheap, and inferior alcoholic liquor.

rot•hole ['rɒt,houl] *n. Cdn.* a soft place in the ice over a lake, river, etc.

ro•ti•fer ['routəfər] *n.* any of a phylum (Rotifera) of minute or microscopic, multicellular, aquatic invertebrates having at one end of the body a disk with one or more rings of cilia. Some authorities classify the rotifers as a class within the phylum Aschelminthes, which also includes the nematodes. ⟨< NL *Rotifera*, pl. < *rota* wheel + *ferre* carry⟩

ro•tis•se•rie [rou'tɪsəri] *n.* **1** a rotating spit used in an oven under a broiler, or over an open fire, for roasting meat or fowl. **2** a portable oven containing such a device. **3** a shop or restaurant where meats or poultry cooked on a rotisserie are sold. ⟨< F *rotisserie* < *rôtir* to roast⟩

ro•to ['routou] *n.* rotogravure. ⟨by clipping⟩

ro•to•gra•vure [,routəgrə'vjʊr] *or* [,routə'greivjər] *n.* **1** a process of printing from an engraved copper cylinder on which the pictures, letters, etc. have been depressed instead of raised. **2** a print or section of a newspaper made by this process. ⟨< L *rota* wheel + E *gravure*⟩

ro•tor ['routər] *n.* **1** the rotating part of a machine or apparatus. See GYROSCOPE for picture. **2** a system of rotating blades by which a helicopter is enabled to fly. See HELICOPTER for picture. ⟨shortened form of *rotator*⟩

ro•to–thresh ['routou,θrɛʃ] *n., v. Cdn.* *–n.* Usually, **roto-thresh combine,** a rotary combine invented by the Streich Brothers of Clandeboye, Manitoba in the 1950s, which separates chaff from grain by means of a blast of air through a rotating drum. **2** thresh using a roto-thresh combine.

ro•to•till•er ['routou,tilər] *n.* a tool with motorized rotary blades for breaking up the soil. **–'ro•to,till,** *v.*

ROTP or **R.O.T.P.** REGULAR OFFICER TRAINING PLAN.

rot•ten ['rɒtən] *adj.* **1** decayed; spoiled: *a rotten egg.* **2** foul; bad-smelling: *rotten air.* **3** not in good condition; unsound; weak: *rotten boards.* **4** corrupt; dishonest. **5** *Slang.* bad; nasty. ⟨ME < ON *rotinn*⟩ **–'rot•ten•ly,** *adv.* **–'rot•ten•ness,** *n.*

rotten borough 1 in England before 1832, a borough that had only a few voters, but kept the privilege of sending a member to Parliament. **2** an electoral district having an insufficient number of voters to justify the representation it has.

rotten ice *Cdn.* ice which has become honeycombed in the course of melting and is in an advanced stage of decomposition.

rot•ter ['rɒtər] *n. Esp. Brit.* a thoroughly despicable person.

Rott•weil•er ['rɒtwailər] *n.* any of a German breed of large, powerful dogs having a short tail and a short, coarse coat of black hair with tan markings. ⟨< *Rottweil*, a town in SW Germany where these dogs were bred for herding⟩

A Rottweiler

ro•tund [rou'tʌnd] *adj.* **1** round; plump. **2** sounding rich and full; full-toned: *a rotund voice.* ⟨< L *rotundus*, ult. < *rota* wheel. Doublet of ROUND.⟩ **–ro'tund•ly,** *adv.*

A rotunda (def. 1) in the Renaissance style in Rome

ro•tun•da [rou'tʌndə] *n.* **1** a circular building or part of a building, especially one with a dome. **2** a large, circular room with a high ceiling. **3** *Cdn.* a large room or area with a high ceiling, such as the lobby of a hotel or the concourse of a railway station. ⟨< L *rotunda*, fem. of *rotundus.* See ROTUND.⟩

ro•tun•di•ty [rou'tʌndəti] *n., pl.* **-ties. 1** roundness; plumpness. **2** something round. **3** rounded fullness of tone.

rou•ble ['rubəl] *n.* See RUBLE.

rou•é [ru'ei] *or* ['ruei] *n.* a dissipated man; rake. ⟨< F *roué*, originally pp. of *rouer* break on the wheel < *roue* wheel < L *rota*; first applied to an 18c. group of profligates⟩

rouge [ruʒ] *n., v.* **rouged, roug•ing.** *–n.* **1** a red or reddish powder, paste, or liquid for colouring the cheeks or lips. **2** a red powder, chiefly ferric oxide, used for polishing metal, jewels, etc. Also called **jeweller's rouge. 3** *Cdn. Football.* **a** a play in which the team receiving a punt behind its own goal line is unable or unwilling to carry the ball back into the field of play, thus conceding a point to the opposition. **b** the single point conceded on such a play.
–v. **1** colour with rouge. **2** *Cdn. Football.* **a** score a rouge. **b** tackle (a defending player) in the end zone so as to score a

rouge: *Jones rouged Smith on the last play.* ⟨< F, red; football term, extended use of a British rugby term of obscure origin⟩

rouge et noir ['ruʒ ei 'nwɑr] a gambling game played with cards on a table marked in red and black in diamond shapes upon which the players place their cards. ⟨< F *rouge et noir* red and black⟩

rough [rʌf] *adj., n., v., adv. —adj.* **1** not smooth; not level; not even: *rough boards, a rough road.* **2** overgrown or rocky: *a rough path.* **3** without polish or fine finish: *rough diamonds.* **4** without luxury and ease: *a rough life in camp.* **5** without culture: *a rough man.* **6** not soft to the touch: *rough skin on my heel.* **7** not completed or perfected; done as a first try; without details: *a rough drawing, a rough idea.* **8** coarse and tangled: *a dog with a rough coat of hair.* **9** likely to hurt others; harsh; rude; not gentle: *rough manners.* **10** disorderly; riotous: *a rough crowd.*
11 *Informal.* unpleasant; hard; severe: *She was in for a rough time.* **12** requiring merely strength rather than intelligence or skill: *rough work.* **13** stormy: *rough weather.* **14** violently disturbed or agitated: *a rough sea.* **15** harsh, sharp, or dry to the taste: *rough wines.* **16** harsh to the ear: *a rough voice.*
17 *Phonetics.* pronounced with much breath; aspirated.
rough diamond, a good or true-hearted person with a gruff manner.
—n. **1** a coarse, violent person. **2** rough ground. **3** a rough thing or condition. **4** *Golf.* a part of a golf course adjacent to the fairway where there is long grass, etc.
in the rough, not polished or refined; coarse; crude.
—v. **1** make rough; roughen. **2** become rough. **3** treat roughly (*usually used with* **up**): *to rough someone up.* **4** *Sports.* illegally check, tackle, etc. (an opposing player) with unnecessary roughness. **5** shape or sketch roughly: *to rough out a plan, to rough in the outlines of a face for a drawing.*
rough in, prepare the basis of: *to rough in the plumbing.*
rough it, live without comforts and conveniences: *She spent last summer roughing it in a remote camp in the B.C. Rockies.*
—adv. in a rough manner; roughly: *Those boys play too rough for me.* ⟨OE *rūh*⟩ **—'rough•ness,** *n.*
☛ *Hom.* RUFF.

rough•age ['rʌfɪdʒ] *n.* **1** rough or coarse material. **2** the parts or kinds of food with a high fibre content which stimulate the movement of food and waste products through the intestines. Bran, fruit skins, and certain fruits are roughage.

rough–and–read•y ['rʌf ən 'rɛdi] *adj.* **1** rough and crude, but good enough for the purpose; crude but effective. **2** showing rough vigour rather than refinement.

rough–and–tum•ble ['rʌf ən 'tʌmbəl] *adj., n. —adj.* showing confusion and violence; with little regard for rules; unrestrainedly vigorous; boisterous.
—n. a fight or competition of this nature.

rough•cast ['rʌf,kæst] *n., v.* **-cast, -cast•ing.** *—n.* **1** a coarse plaster for outside surfaces such as the walls of buildings.
2 rough form.
—v. **1** cover or coat with coarse plaster. **2** make, shape, or prepare in a rough form: *to roughcast a story.*

rough–dry ['rʌf ,draɪ] *v.* **-dried, -dry•ing.** dry (clothes) after washing, without smoothing or ironing them.

rough•en ['rʌfən] *v.* **1** make rough. **2** become rough.

rough fish a fish that has no commercial value and is also not valued as a sport fish.

rough–hew ['rʌf 'hju] *v.* **-hewed, -hewed** or **-hewn, -hew•ing.**
1 hew (timber, stone, etc.) without smoothing or finishing.
2 shape crudely; give crude form to: *rough-hewn manners.*

rough•house *n.* ['rʌf,hʌus]; *v.* ['rʌf,haʊz] *n., v.* **-housed, -hous•ing.** *Slang. —n.* boisterous play; rowdy conduct; disorderly behaviour.
—v. **1** act in a boisterous, disorderly way. **2** disturb by such conduct.

rough•ing ['rʌfɪŋ] *n., v. —n. Sports.* the illegal act or practice of checking, tackling, etc. an opposing player with unnecessary roughness: *a penalty for roughing.*
—v. ppr. of ROUGH.

rough•leaf dogwood ['rʌf,lif] a small tree (*Cornus drummondii*) having leaves that are rough on top and have occasional stiff hairs. It has white fruits and greyish twigs.

rough•ly ['rʌfli] *adv.* **1** in a rough manner. **2** approximately.

rough•neck ['rʌf,nɛk] *n.* **1** *Informal.* a rough, coarse, bad-mannered person; a rowdy. **2** *Slang.* a member of an oil-drilling crew.

rough•rid•er ['rʌf,raɪdər] *n.* **1** a person used to tough, hard riding. **2** a person who breaks and rides rough, wild horses.

rough•shod ['rʌf,ʃɒd] *adj.* having horseshoes equipped with sharp caulks to prevent slipping.
ride roughshod over, domineer; show no consideration for; treat roughly.

rou•lade [ru'lɑd] *n.* **1** *Music.* a rapid succession of tones sung to a single syllable. **2** a slice of meat rolled about a filling of minced meat and cooked. ⟨< F *roulade* < *rouler* roll⟩

rou•lette [ru'lɛt] *n., v.* **-let•ted, -let•ting.** *—n.* **1** a gambling game in which a wheel is spun and players bet on where it will stop. **2** a small wheel with sharp teeth for making lines of marks, dots, or perforations.
—v. make such marks on with a roulette. ⟨< F *roulette*, ult. < *roue* < L *rota* wheel⟩

Rou•ma•nia [ru'meinjə] *or* [ru'meiniə] *n.* Romania.

Rou•ma•ni•an [ru'meinjən] *or* [ru'meiniən] *adj., n.* Romanian.

round [raʊnd] *adj., n., v., adv., prep. —adj.* **1** shaped like: **a** a ball, **b** a ring, **c** a cylinder, or the like; having a circular or curved outline or surface. **2** plump: *Her figure was short and round.*
3 making or requiring a circular movement: *The waltz is a round dance.* **4** full; complete: *a round dozen.* **5** large: *a good round sum of money.* **6** *Mathematics.* being an integer, not a fraction: *25 is a round number.* **7** general; approximate; to the nearest unit, ten, hundred, etc.: *The cost of the whole trip should be $500 in round figures. 3974 in round numbers would be 4000.* **8** plainly expressed; plain-spoken; frank: *The boy's father scolded him in good round terms.* **9** with a full tone: *a mellow, round voice.*
10 vigorous; brisk: *a round trot.* **11** *Phonetics.* rounded.
—n. **1** anything shaped like a ball, circle, cylinder, etc. The rungs of a ladder are sometimes called rounds. **2** a fixed course ending where it begins: *The watchman makes his rounds of the building every hour.* **3** a movement in a circle or about an axis: *the earth's yearly round.* **4** a series (of duties, events, etc.); routine: *a round of pleasures, a round of duties.* **5** the distance between any limits; range; circuit: *the round of human knowledge.* **6** a section of a game or sport: *a round in a boxing match, a round of cards.* **7** the firing of a single discharge from a number or group of rifles, guns, etc. at the same time. **8** the bullets, powder, etc. for such a shot. **9** a single bullet, artillery shell, etc. **10** a single serving of something, usually a drink, to each member of the group: *It's my round; you can pay for the next round.* **11** an act that a number of people do together: *a round of applause, a round of cheers.* **12** a dance in which the dancers move in a circle; ROUND DANCE.
13 *Music.* a short song, sung by several persons or groups beginning one after the other: *"Three Blind Mice" is a round.*
14 rounds, the ringing of a set of bells from the highest tone through the major scale to the lowest tone. **15** a form of sculpture in which the figures are apart from any background.
16 a cut of beef just above the hind leg. See BEEF for picture.
in the round, a in a form of sculpture in which the figures are apart from any background. **b** in the open or in real life; showing all sides or aspects. **c** *Theatre.* with the audience sitting all the way around a central area.
make or **go the rounds** or **round, a** go about from place to place in a certain course or through a certain area. **b** be passed, told, shown, etc. by many people from one to another.
—v. **1** make or become round: *The carpenter rounded the corners of the table.* **2** go wholly or partly around: *They rounded the island. The ship rounded Cape Horn. The car rounded the corner.*
3 turn around; wheel about: *The bear rounded and faced the hunters.* **4** *Phonetics.* utter (a vowel) with a circular opening of the lips: *The rounded vowels in English include* [ou] *and* [u].
round in, *Nautical.* haul in.
round off, a make or become round. **b** finish; complete: *round off a meal with a light dessert.* **c** generalize a number by expressing it in the nearest unit, ten, hundred, etc.: *The total was 361, but she rounded it off to 350. Please round the answer off to two decimal places.*
round on, a turn on to attack, or as if to attack. **b** reprimand.
round out, a give or acquire a rounder contour. **b** complete: *to round out a paragraph, to round out a career.*
round to, *Nautical.* come head up to the wind.
round up, a draw or drive together. **b** collect; muster: *Round up the usual suspects.*
—adv. **1** in a circle; with a whirling motion: *Wheels go round.*
2 on all sides; in every direction: *The travellers were compassed round by dangers.* **3** in circumference: *The pumpkin measures 105 cm round.* **4** by a longer road or way: *We went round by the candy store on our way home.* **5** from one to another: *A report is going round that the stores will close.* **6** through a recurring interval of time: *Summer will soon come round again.* **7** here and

there: *I am just looking round.* **8** for all: *There is just enough cake to go round.*
round and about, in various places.
—prep. **1** on all sides of: *Bullets whistled round him, but he was not hit.* **2** so as to encircle or surround: *They built a fence round the yard.* **3** so as to make a turn to the other side of: *She walked round the corner.* **4** to all or various parts of: *We took our cousins round the town.* **5** about; around: *Stand still and look round you.* **6** here and there in: *There are boxes for mail all round the city.*
get or **come round** (someone), **a** outwit (someone). **b** wheedle (someone). ⟨ME < OF *roont* (fem. *roonde*) < L *rotundus.* Doublet of ROTUND.⟩ **—'round•ness,** *n.*

☛ *Usage. adv., prep.* **Round,** AROUND. In Canadian usage **round** and **around** are often used interchangeably, with a definite tendency to use **around,** especially in speech, written dialogue, and technical writing. **Round** has a slightly more literary or poetic flavour. When heard in quick speech (usually after a word with a final vowel) it is the aphesis of **around.**

round•a•bout ['raʊndə,bʌut] *adj., n. —adj.* indirect: *a roundabout route. I heard about it in a roundabout way.*
—n. **1** an indirect way, course, or speech. **2** *Brit.* MERRY-GO-ROUND. **3** *Esp. Brit.* a TRAFFIC CIRCLE.

round dance **1** a dance performed by couples and characterized by circular or revolving movements. **2** a dance performed by dancers in a circle.

round•ed ['raʊndɪd] *adj., v. —adj.* **1** made round. **2** well-balanced; diversified; complete; developed in regard to tastes, opinions, abilities, etc. (*often compounded with* **well-**): *a rounded education, a well-rounded person.* **3** *Phonetics.* pronounced with the lips forming an O-shaped opening, as the vowel in *mood.*
—v. pt. and pp. of ROUND.

roun•del ['raʊndəl] *n.* **1** a small round ornament, window, panel, tablet, etc. **2** rondel. **3** rondeau. ⟨ME < OF *rondel.* See RONDEL.⟩

roun•de•lay ['raʊndə,lei] *n.* **1** a song in which a phrase or a line is repeated again and again. **2** a dance in which the dancers move in a circle. ⟨< MF *rondelet,* dim. of *rondel* (see RONDEL); influenced by *lay*[4]⟩

Round•head ['raʊnd,hɛd] *n.* in England, a supporter of Oliver Cromwell during the civil wars from 1642 to 1651. The Roundheads wore their hair cut short in contrast to the long curls of their opponents, the Cavaliers.

round•head•ed ['raʊnd,hɛdɪd] *adj.* **1** of a person, having a rounded head; brachycephalic. **2** of a screw, having a semispherical head. **3** of a window, having a semicircular top.

round•house ['raʊnd,hʌus] *n.* **1** a circular building for storing or repairing locomotives, built about a turntable. **2** *Nautical.* a cabin on the after part of a ship's quarterdeck. **3** *Informal.* **a** a punch or blow delivered with a wide swing. **b** (*adjl.*) of or designating such a punch or style of punching: *taking a roundhouse swing.* **4** *Baseball.* a widely curved pitch.

round•ish ['raʊndɪʃ] *adj.* somewhat round.

round•leaf dogwood ['raʊnd,lif] a small tree (*Cornus rugosa*) having almost round leaves with a white, woolly underside. It has blue fruits and greenish red twigs.

round lot the unit or quantity, or a multiple of this, in which commodities or securities are usually sold, as for example 100 shares of stock or $1000.00 worth of bonds.

round•ly ['raʊndli] *adv.* **1** in a round manner or form. **2** plainly, severely, or fully: *He was roundly scolded for getting in so late.*

round number **1** a whole number without a fraction. **2** a number in even tens, hundreds, thousands, etc. 3874 in round numbers would be 3900 or 4000.

round robin **1** a petition, protest, etc., with the signatures written in a circle so that it is impossible to tell who signed first. **2** any petition. **3** a letter, notice, etc. circulated to each member of a group in turn, who signs it and passes it on, often with additional comments. **4** *Sports.* a system of scheduling a number of games, in which every competing player or team is matched with every other one.

round–shoul•dered ['raʊnd ,ʃouldərd] *adj.* having the shoulders bent forward.

round steak a cut of beef just above the hind leg.

round table **1** a group of persons assembled for an informal discussion, etc. **2 Round Table, a** the table around which King Arthur and his knights sat. **b** King Arthur and his knights.

round–the–clock ['raʊnd ðə 'klɒk] *adj.* taking place through all 24 hours of the day: *This retirement home provides round-the-clock care.*

round trip a journey to a specific destination and back.

round•up ['raʊnd,ʌp] *n.* **1 a** the act of driving or bringing cattle or horses together from long distances. **b** the people and horses that take part in such a drive. **2** a gathering together of people or things: *a roundup of criminals, a roundup of late news, a roundup of old friends.*

round whitefish a fish (*Prosopium cylindraceum*) of the whitefish family, found in fresh water in eastern Canada.

round•wood ['raʊnd,wʊd] *n.* timber that is used in the round without being squared or cut into lumber, such as logs, poles, and pulpwood.

round•worm ['raʊnd,wɜrm] *n.* nematode.

roup[1] [rup] *n.* either of two diseases of poultry characterized by hoarseness and a discharge of mucus from the eyes, nostrils, and throat. One form of roup is contagious and is often fatal. ⟨origin uncertain⟩ **—'roup•y,** *adj.*

roup[2] [rup] *n.* hoarseness or huskiness. ⟨probably imitative⟩

rouse [raʊz] *v.* **roused, rous•ing;** *n. —v.* **1** arouse; wake up: *I was roused by the telephone.* **2** stir up; excite: *She was roused to anger by the insult.* **3** cause (game) to start from cover.
—n. **1** the act of rousing. **2** a signal for rousing or for action. ⟨origin uncertain⟩ **—'rous•er,** *n.*

rous•ing ['raʊzɪŋ] *adj., v. —adj.* **1** able to rouse or stir; lively; brisk: *a rousing speech, a rousing response.* **2** *Informal.* extraordinary; exceptional: *a rousing falsehood.*
—v. ppr. of ROUSE. **—'rous•ing•ly,** *adv.*

roust•a•bout ['rʌustə,bʌut] *n. Informal.* an unskilled labourer on wharves, ships, ranches, circuses, etc. ⟨< *roust* move, stir + *about*⟩

rout[1] [rʌut] *n., v. —n.* **1** the flight in disorder of a defeated army: *The enemy's retreat soon became a rout.* **2** a complete defeat. **3** *Archaic.* a crowd; band. **4** a group of followers. **5** a noisy, disorderly crowd; mob; rabble. **6** a riot; disturbance. **7** *Archaic.* a large evening party.
—v. **1** put to flight: *Our soldiers routed the enemy.* **2** defeat completely: *The home team routed the visitors with a score of ten to one.* ⟨ME < OF *route* detachment, ult. < L *rumpere* break⟩
☛ *Hom.* ROUTE [rʌut].

rout[2] [rʌut] *or* [rut] *v.* **1** dig *(out);* get by searching. **2** put *(out);* force *(out): The farmer routed his sons out of bed at five o'clock.* **3** dig with the snout, as pigs do. **4** poke; search; rummage. **5** hollow out or gouge with or as with a ROUTER. ⟨var. of *root*[2]⟩
☛ *Hom.* ROUTE [rʌut].
☛ *Hom.* ROOT, ROUTE [rut].

route [rut] *or* [rʌut] *n., v.* **rout•ed, rout•ing.** *—n.* **1** a way to go; road. **2** a fixed, regular course or area assigned to a person making deliveries, sales, etc.: *a newspaper route, a milk route.*
—v. **1** arrange the route for. **2** send by a certain route. ⟨ME < OF < L *rupta (via)* (a way) opened up, (a passage) forced < *rumpere* break⟩
☛ *Hom.* ROOT, ROUT[2] [rut].
☛ *Hom.* ROUT [rʌut].
☛ *Pronun.* **Route.** The pronunciation [rut] is the preferred form in Canada but [rʌut] is in common use, especially with reference to newspaper and delivery routes.

rout•er ['rʌutər] *n.* a tool or machine for cutting grooves in or hollowing out wood or metal.

rou•tine [ru'tin] *n., adj. —n.* **1** a fixed, regular method of doing things; habitual doing of the same things in the same way: *Getting up and going to bed are parts of your daily routine.* **2** an act or skit that is part of some entertainment. **3** a choreographed series of movements in dance, figure skating, gymnastics, etc. **4** *Computer technology.* a set of instructions for a specific operation.
—adj. **1** using routine: *routine methods, a routine operation.* **2** average or ordinary; run-of-the-mill: *a routine show with routine performances.* ⟨< F *routine* < *route* route⟩ **—rou'tine•ly,** *adv.* **—rou'tin•ize,** *v.* **—rou'tin•ism,** *n.*

rove[1] [rouv] *v.* **roved, rov•ing.** wander; wander about; roam: *She loved to rove over the fields and woods.* ⟨origin uncertain⟩
☛ *Syn.* See note at ROAM.

rove[2] [rouv] *v.* a pt. and a pp. of REEVE[2].

rov•er[1] ['rouvər] *n.* **1** a wanderer or roamer. **2** *Lacrosse.* a player who holds no special position but who may rove over the entire field. **3 Rover,** a member, aged 17 to 23, of the Scouts. ⟨< *rove*[1]⟩

rov•er[2] ['rouvər] *n.* **1** a pirate. **2** a pirate ship. ⟨< MDu. *rover* < *roven* rob⟩

row[1] [rou] *n.* **1** a line of people or things: *a row of potatoes.* **2** a street with a line of buildings on either side, all of a similar kind: *Cannery Row.*
hard row to hoe, a difficult thing to do. ⟨OE *rāw*⟩
☛ *Hom.* RHO, ROE.

row[2] [rou] *v., n.* —*v.* **1** move a boat by means of oars: *Row to the island.* **2** move (a boat, etc.) by the use of oars: *We had to row the dinghy.* **3** carry in a rowboat: *We were rowed to the shore.* **4** perform (a race, etc.) by rowing: *Cambridge rows against Oxford every year.* **5** row against in a race. **6** of a boat, use, require or be equipped with (a certain number of oars): *This shell rows four.*
—*n.* **1** the act of using oars. **2** a trip in a rowboat or a spell of rowing: *Let's go out for a row.* ⟨OE *rōwan*⟩ —**'row•er,** *n.*
☛ *Hom.* RHO, ROE.

row[3] [raʊ] *n., v.* —*n.* **1** a noisy quarrel; disturbance; clamour. **2** *Informal.* a squabble.
—*v.* **1** *Informal.* quarrel noisily; make noise. **2** *Informal.* scold. ⟨origin uncertain⟩

row•an ['rouən] *or* ['raʊən] *n.* **1** a mountain ash, especially the European mountain ash (*Sorbus aucuparia*). **2** either of two American mountain ashes (*Sorbus americana* or *S. sambucifolia*). **3** the fruit of any rowan. ⟨< Scand.; cf. Norwegian *raun*⟩

row•boat ['rou,bout] *n.* a small boat moved by oars.

row•dy ['raʊdi] *n., pl.* **-dies;** *adj.* **-di•er, -di•est.** —*n.* a rough, disorderly, quarrelsome person.
—*adj.* rough; disorderly; quarrelsome. ⟨probably < *row[3]*⟩
—**'row•di•ly,** *adv.* —**'row•di•ness,** *n.*

row•dy•ish ['raʊdiɪʃ] *adj.* like a rowdy; rough and disorderly; quarrelsome.

row•dy•ism ['raʊdi,ɪzəm] *n.* disorderly, quarrelsome conduct; rough, noisy behaviour: *rowdyism at Halloween.*

row•el ['raʊəl] *n., v.* **-elled** or **-eled, -el•ling** or **-el•ing.** —*n.* **1** a small wheel having sharp points, attached to the end of a spur. See SPUR for picture. **2** *Veterinary Medicine.* a piece of silk or leather inserted under the skin of an animal, especially a horse, to cause or promote drainage of pus or fluid from an infection.
—*v.* **1** use a rowel on. **2** urge on, using a rowel. ⟨ME < OF *roel,* ult. < L *rota* wheel⟩

row house [rou] one of several houses built together in a row and constituting one building.

rowing machine an exercise machine consisting of a sliding seat, two handles like oars, and a place to brace the feet, in which one can perform the movements of rowing, thus exercising the arms and abdomen.

row•lock ['rou,lɒk] *n.* oarlock.

roy•al ['rɔɪəl] *adj., n.* —*adj.* **1** of or having to do with kings and queens: *the royal family.* **2** belonging to a king or queen: *royal power.* **3** having or denoting the rank of a king or queen. **4** Usually, **Royal, a** serving a queen or king: *the Royal Household.* **b** in the armed services of the United Kingdom or the Commonwealth: *the Royal Navy.* **c** patronized by the royal family: *the Royal Society of Canada.* **5** from or by a king or queen: *a royal command.* **6** of a monarchy or its government. **7** appropriate for a king or queen; splendid: *a royal welcome.* **8** like a king or queen; noble; majestic: *She entered with royal dignity.* **9** fine; excellent; supreme. **10** ROYAL BLUE.
—*n.* **1** Sometimes, **Royal,** any member of a royal family. **2** *Nautical.* a small mast or sail set above the topgallant. **3** *Printing.* **a** a large size of paper for printing (20 × 25 inches, 51 × 64 cm). **b** a large size of paper for writing (19 × 24 inches, 48 × 61 cm). ⟨ME < OF *roial* < L *regalis.* Doublet of REAL[2], REGAL, RIAL.⟩ —**'roy•al•ly,** *adv.*
☛ *Syn. adj.* **1, 2, 7, 8. Royal,** REGAL, KINGLY = of or belonging to a monarch or monarchs. **Royal** is the most general in application, describing people or things associated with or belonging to a king or queen: *Sherwood Forest is a royal forest.* **Regal** emphasizes the majesty and stateliness or pomp and magnificence of the office, but is now used chiefly of people or things showing these qualities: *The general has a regal bearing.* **Kingly** emphasizes the personal character, actions, purposes, or feelings of or worthy of a king: *Tempering justice with mercy is a kingly virtue.*

royal assent the signature of the Queen or her representative giving approval to a bill that has been passed by Parliament or by a legislative assembly. A bill does not become law until royal assent has been given.

royal blue a rich, bright blue of full tone.

Royal Canadian Legion a Canadian organization of former military personnel, especially war veterans, and nowadays also the families of such personnel. It sponsors numerous community services and undertakes welfare work for veterans and their families.

Royal Canadian Mounted Police the federal police force of Canada since 1920; formerly the Royal North West Mounted Police. The Royal Canadian Mounted Police also act as provincial police in most Canadian provinces except Ontario and Québec. *Abbrev.:* RCMP or R.C.M.P.

royal commission *Cdn.* **1** any investigation by a person or persons commissioned by the Crown to inquire into some matter on behalf of the federal or a provincial government and to make a report recommending appropriate action. **2** the person or persons so commissioned.

royal flush *Poker.* a straight flush consisting of the Ace, King, Queen, Jack, and ten of one suit.

Royal Highness **1** United Kingdom in the Commonwealth: **a** prior to 1917, a title designating and used in addressing a brother, sister, child, grandchild, aunt, or uncle belonging to the male line of the British royal family. **b** since 1917, a title designating and used in addressing a child or grandchild of the sovereign. **c** any person to whom the Crown gives this title. **2** in other countries, a member of a royal family.

roy•al•ism ['rɔɪə,lɪzəm] *n.* adherence to a monarch or a monarchy.

roy•al•ist ['rɔɪəlɪst] *n., adj.* —*n.* **1** a supporter of a king or of a royal government. **2 Royalist, a** in England, a supporter of Charles I during the civil wars from 1642 to 1651. **b** in the United States, a supporter of George III during the Revolution; loyalist. **c** in France, Spain, etc., a supporter of the monarchy.
—*adj.* of or having to do with royalism or royalists.

royal jelly a viscous and highly nutritious substance secreted from the pharyngeal glands of young worker honey bees, fed to all larvae during their first few days of life, and afterward only to those larvae selected to be queens.

Royal Military College the oldest of the three Canadian military colleges, located at Kingston, Ontario. The other two, Royal Roads in Victoria, B.C. and Collège Militaire Royal in St. Jean, Québec, were disbanded in 1995.

Royal North West Mounted Police the earlier (1905-1920) name for the Royal Canadian Mounted Police.

royal palm any of several palm trees (genus *Roystonea*), especially a tropical American species (*R. regia*) having a tall, whitish trunk and pinnate leaves, widely cultivated for ornament.

royal poinciana a tropical tree (*Delonix regia*) of the pea family having wide-spreading limbs forming an umbrella-shaped crown and bearing large clusters of brilliant scarlet or orange flowers. It is a native of Madagascar but is widely cultivated throughout the tropics.

Royal Roads until 1995, one of Canada's three military colleges, located in Victoria, B.C. and being a degree-granting institution in its own right.

roy•al•ty ['rɔɪəlti] *n., pl.* **-ties. 1** a royal person; royal persons. Kings, queens, princes, and princesses are royalty. **2** the rank or dignity of a king or queen; royal power. **3** royal quality; nobility. **4** a royal right or privilege. **5** a royal right over a natural resource, etc., granted by a sovereign to a person or corporation. **6** a share of the receipts or profits paid to an owner of a patent or copyright; payment for the use of any of various rights. ⟨ME < OF *roialte* < *roial.* See ROYAL.⟩

R.P. RECEIVED PRONUNCIATION.

rpm or **r.p.m.** revolutions per minute.

rps or **r.p.s.** revolutions per second.

R.R. **1** RURAL ROUTE. **2** railroad. **3** Right Reverend. **4** ROYAL ROADS.

RRSP Registered Retirement Savings Plan.

RSV or **R.S.V.** REVISED STANDARD VERSION.

R.S.V.P. or **r.s.v.p.** please reply (for F *répondez s'il vous plaît*).

rt. right.

Rt.Hon. RIGHT HONOURABLE.

Rt.Rev. Right Reverend.

Ru ruthenium.

rub [rʌb] *v.* **rubbed, rub•bing;** *n.* —*v.* **1** move (one thing) back and forth (against another); move (two things) together, often as a means of warming or cleaning them: *Rub your cold hands to warm them.* **2** move one's hands or an object over the surface of; push and press along the surface of: *The nurse rubbed my back.* **3** press along the surface of, in moving; chafe or grate: *That door rubs against the floor. The back of this shoe rubs on my heel.*

4 apply or spread (polish, a mixture, etc.) on or over something, using pressure or friction. 5 make or bring to some condition by rubbing: *to rub silver bright, to rub one's hands dry.* 6 remove or be removed by rubbing (*usually with* **off** *or* **out**): *The spot won't rub off. He rubbed the skin off his hand when he fell.* 7 make an image of (an engraved or textured surface) by rubbing charcoal, graphite, etc. over a piece of paper placed on top of the surface: *Children like to rub coins. Many tourists rub the memorial brasses in old English churches.* 8 admit of rubbing.
rub along, *Brit. Informal.* keep going with difficulty: *Money is scarce, but we'll rub along.*
rub down, rub the body of; massage.
rub it in, *Informal.* keep on mentioning something humiliating.
rub off on, a cling to; become part of; take hold of. **b** *Informal.* of abstract qualities, become part of or take hold of someone's behaviour or character: *Some of her charitable nature has rubbed off on her associates.*
rub out, a erase; be erased: *to rub out a mistake.* **b** *Slang.* kill: *He was rubbed out by another gangster.*
rub the right way, please; pacify.
rub the wrong way, annoy; irritate.
—n. 1 the act of rubbing. 2 something, as a remark or act, that rubs or hurts the feelings: *He didn't like her mean rub at his slowness.* 3 a spot or area roughened by rubbing: *There's a rub on the elbow of my sweater.* 4 a difficulty: *The rub came when both girls wanted to sit with the driver.* ⟨ME *rubbe(n)*⟩

rub•a•boo or **rub•ba•boo** ['rʌbə,bu] *n. Cdn.* a soup made by boiling pemmican in water with flour and other ingredients. ⟨< Cdn.F *rababou* < Algonquian⟩

ru•ba•to [ru'bɑtou] *adj., n., adv. Music. —adj.* having some notes arbitrarily lengthened or shortened and others correspondingly altered.
—n. 1 a rubato passage or phrase. 2 the rubato execution or performance of a passage or phrase.
—adv. in a rubato manner. ⟨< Ital. (*tempo*) *rubato* stolen (time), pp. of *rubare* steal < Gmc.⟩

rub•ber[1] ['rʌbər] *n.* 1 an elastic substance obtained from the milky juice (latex) of various tropical plants, especially the rubber tree. It is airtight, water resistant, and does not conduct electricity. 2 SYNTHETIC RUBBER. 3 a waterproof overshoe. 4 an eraser: *Some pencils have a rubber on one end.* 5 any of various other things made of rubber or a similar substance. 6 a person who or thing that rubs. 7 (*adjl.*) made of rubber: *a rubber tire.* 8 *Slang.* a hockey puck. ⟨< *rub*⟩ **—'rub•ber,like,** *adj.*

rub•ber[2] ['rʌbər] *n. Card games, especially bridge or whist.* 1 a series of three or five games to be won by a majority. 2 the deciding game in such a series. ⟨origin uncertain⟩

rubber band a circular strip of rubber, used to hold things together.

rubber boa a small BOA (def. 1) in S British Columbia.

rubber cement a quick-drying adhesive consisting of rubber in a solvent.

rubber cheque *Slang.* a cheque that BOUNCES (*v.* 6).

rub•ber–chick•en circuit ['rʌbər 'tʃɪkən] *Cdn.* the tour made by an after-dinner speaker, the dinners being noted for tough chicken as the main course.

rubber ice *Cdn.* especially in the North, thin, flexible ice on the surface of seas, lakes, etc. Also, **rubbery ice.**

rub•ber•ize ['rʌbə,raɪz] *v.* **-ized, -iz•ing.** cover or treat with rubber.

rub•ber•neck ['rʌbər,nɛk] *n., v. Slang. —n.* a person who stares and gapes, especially a tourist or sightseer.
—v. stare; gape.

rubber plant 1 a tropical Asian plant (*Ficus elastica*) of the mulberry family, having large, thick, glossy leaves. The rubber plant becomes a tall tree in its native environment but is cultivated in dwarf form as a house plant in North America and Europe. 2 any of various plants that yield rubber. Compare RUBBER TREE.

rubber stamp 1 a stamp made of rubber, used with ink for printing dates, signatures, etc. 2 *Informal.* a person or group that approves or endorses something without thought or without power to refuse.

rub•ber–stamp ['rʌbər 'stæmp] *v.* 1 print or sign with a rubber stamp. 2 *Informal.* approve or endorse (a policy, bill, etc.) without thought or without power to refuse.

rubber tree a widely cultivated, tropical American tree (*Hevea brasiliensis*) of the spurge family that yields a latex that is the main commercial source of rubber. Compare RUBBER PLANT.

rub•ber•y ['rʌbəri] *adj.* like rubber; elastic; tough.

rub•bing ['rʌbɪŋ] *n., v. —n.* an image of an engraved or textured surface, such as a brass inscription or rock carving, made by rubbing charcoal, graphite, etc. over a piece of paper placed on top of the surface.
—v. ppr. of RUB.

rub•bish ['rʌbɪʃ] *n.* 1 worthless or useless stuff; waste; trash. 2 silly words and thoughts; nonsense. ⟨ME *robys*⟩

rub•ble ['rʌbəl] *n.* 1 rough, broken stones, bricks, etc., especially from collapsed or demolished buildings. 2 masonry made of this. ⟨ME *robel*; origin uncertain⟩

rub•by ['rʌbi] *n., pl.* **-bies.** *Cdn. Slang.* 1 rubbing alcohol used as a drink, especially when flavoured with cheap wine or rum. 2 a person who drinks rubbing alcohol, etc., often flavoured with cheap wine or rum, hence, an alcoholic, especially a derelict. ⟨< *rubb(ing alcohol)* + *y*[1]⟩

rub•by•dub ['rʌbi,dʌb] *n. Cdn. Slang.* RUBBY (def. 2). ⟨< *rubby* + *dub* a stupid, clumsy person⟩

rub•down ['rʌb,daʊn] *n.* a rubbing of the body; massage.

ru•be•fa•cient [,rubə'feiʃənt] *adj., n. —adj.* producing redness or irritation, especially of the skin: *a rubefacient ointment.*
—n. Medicine. a rubefacient medication or substance, such as a mustard plaster. ⟨< L *rubefaciens, -facientis,* pp. of *rubefacere* < *rubeus* red + *facere* make⟩

ru•be•fac•tion [,rubə'fækʃən] *n.* 1 the process or act of causing redness, as with a rubefacient. 2 redness of the skin caused by a rubefacient.

Rube Gold•berg ['rub 'gouldbərg] 1 having a fantastically elaborate and wildly inventive appearance. 2 designating anything laboriously complicated and contrived, intended to perform an apparently simple function. ⟨< *Reube*n L. *Goldberg* (1883-1970), an American cartoonist who specialized in ludicrously complicated contrivances⟩

ru•bel•la [ru'bɛlə] *n. Pathology.* a mild, contagious viral infection characterized by a low fever, headache, mild respiratory congestion, and a fine red rash; German measles. It is dangerous to women in the early stages of pregnancy as it may cause serious damage to the fetus.

ru•be•o•la [ru'biələ] *or* [,rubi'oulə] *n. Pathology.* measles. It is commonly called **red measles** to differentiate it from **German measles.** ⟨< NL *rubeola,* dim. of *rubeus* red⟩

Ru•bi•con ['rubə,kɒn] *n.* a point, decision, etc. from which one cannot turn back.
cross or **pass the Rubicon,** make an important and irrevocable decision. ⟨< *Rubicon,* a small river in E Italy, in ancient times forming part of the boundary between the Roman republic and its provinces. By crossing the Rubicon into the republic in 49 B.C., Julius Caesar broke the law forbidding a general to lead his troops out of the province in which he was stationed, and so committed himself to the civil war that ended with him as master of Rome.⟩

ru•bi•cund ['rubə,kʌnd] *adj.* reddish; ruddy. ⟨< L *rubicundus* < *rubere* be red⟩ **—,ru•bi'cun•di•ty,** *n.*

ru•bid•i•um [ru'bɪdiəm] *n. Chemistry.* a silver-white metallic chemical element resembling potassium. *Symbol*: Rb; *at.no.* 37; *at.mass* 85.47. ⟨< NL < L *rubidus* red < *rubere* be red (with reference to the two red lines in its spectrum)⟩

ru•ble ['rubəl] *n.* 1 the basic unit of money in Russia, divided into 100 kopeks. See table of money in the Appendix. 2 the basic unit of money in Tajikistan, divided into 100 kapeiks. 3 a coin or note worth one ruble. Also, **rouble.**

ru•bric ['rubrɪk] *n.* 1 a title or heading of a chapter, a law, etc., written or printed in red or in special lettering. 2 a direction for conducting religious services, inserted in a prayer book, ritual, etc. 3 any heading, rule, or guide. ⟨< L *rubrica* red colouring matter < *ruber* red⟩

ru•bri•cal ['rubrɪkəl] *adj.* 1 red; marked with red; printed or written in special lettering. 2 of, having to do with, or according to religious rubrics. **—'ru•bri•cal•ly,** *adv.*

ru•bri•cate ['rubrə,keit] *v.* **-cat•ed, -cat•ing.** 1 mark or colour with red. 2 furnish with rubrics. 3 regulate by rubrics.

ru•by ['rubi] *n., pl.* **-bies;** *adj. —n.* 1 a clear, hard, red precious stone that is a variety of corundum. 2 a piece of this stone, or a gem made from it. 3 a deep, glowing red or something having this colour.
—adj. deep, glowing red: *ruby lips, ruby wine.* ⟨ME < OF *rubi,* ult. (Cf. Med.L *rubinus*) < L *rubeus* red⟩ **—'ru•by,like,** *adj.*

ruby-throat•ed hummingbird ['rubi ,θroutɪd] a small hummingbird (*Archilochus colubris*) found in E North America, having a green back and head and, in the male, a red throat.

ruche [ruʃ] *n.* a pleated piece or fill of lace, ribbon, net, etc., used as trimming for women's dresses, blouses, etc. (< F *ruche*, originally, beehive)

ruch•ing ['ruʃɪŋ] *n.* **1** a trimming made of ruches. **2** fabric used to make ruches.

ruck[1] [rʌk] *n.* a crowd; the great mass of common or inferior people or things. (ME *ruke* heap, stack < Scand.; cf. Norwegian dial. *ruka*)

ruck[2] [rʌk] *v.* crease; wrinkle (*often with* **up**): *Your skirt's all rucked up at the back.*

ruc•kle ['rʌkəl] **-kled, -kling.** RUCK[2].

ruck•sack ['rʌk,sæk] *or* ['rʊk,sæk] *n.* knapsack. (< G *Rucksack*, literally, back sack)

ruck•us ['rʌkəs] *n. Slang.* a noisy disturbance or uproar; row. (? blend of *ruction* and *rumpus*)

ruc•tion ['rʌkʃən] *n. Informal.* a disturbance; quarrel; row. (? alteration of *insurrection*)

rud•der ['rʌdər] *n.* **1** a hinged, flat piece of wood or metal that projects into the water at the rear end of a boat or ship, by which the vessel is steered. The rudder is controlled by a tiller, wheel, or other apparatus. **2** a similar piece on an aircraft hinged vertically to the rear of the fin and used for right and left steering. See AIRPLANE for picture. **3** a person or thing that guides or steers. (OE *rōthor*) **—'rud•der•less,** *adj.* **—'rud•der,like,** *adj.*

rud•dy ['rʌdi] *adj.* **-di•er, -di•est;** *adv. —adj.* **1** red or reddish: *a ruddy glow.* **2** rosy and glowing, as with good health: *After skiing all afternoon the girls had ruddy cheeks.* **3** *Slang.* BLOODY (def. 6).
—adv. Slang. bloody. (OE *rudig*) **—'rud•di•ly,** *adv.* **—'rud•di•ness,** *n.*

ruddy duck a small, freshwater duck (*Oxyura jamaicensis*) that ranges from Canada south to the West Indies and Colombia. In breeding season the male has mainly reddish brown plumage with a black head, white cheeks, and blue bill.

rude [rud] *adj.* **rud•er, rud•est. 1** impolite; not courteous: *It is rude to stare at people.* **2** roughly made or done; without finish or polish; coarse; crude: *rude tools, a rude cabin.* **3** rough in manner or behaviour; violent; harsh: *Rude hands seized the child and threw him into the car.* **4** harsh to the ear; unmusical. **5** not having learned much; uncivilized; rather wild; barbarous. **6** belonging to the poor or to uncultured people; simple; without luxury or elegance. **7** not fully or properly developed. **8** robust; sturdy; vigorous: *rude health, rude strength.* (< L *rudis*) **—'rude•ly,** *adv.* **—'rude•ness,** *n.*
☛ *Hom.* ROOD.

ru•di•ment ['rudəmənt] *n.* **1** Usually, **rudiments,** *pl.* a part to be learned first; beginning: *the rudiments of grammar.* **2** something in an early stage of development. **3** *Biology.* **a** an organ or part incompletely developed in size or structure: *the rudiments of wings on a baby chick.* **b** an organ or part, such as the appendix, that does not develop completely and has no function. (< L *rudimentum* < *rudis* rude)

ru•di•men•ta•ry [,rudə'mɛntəri] *adj.* **1** to be learned or studied first; elementary. **2** in an early stage of development; undeveloped. **—,ru•di'men•ta•ri•ly,** *adv.*
☛ *Syn.* **1.** See note at ELEMENTARY.

rue[1] [ru] *v.* **rued, ru•ing. 1** be sorry for; regret (something). **2** *Archaic.* feel sorrow. (OE *hrēowan*)

rue[2] [ru] *n.* **1** any of a genus (*Ruta*) of aromatic Eurasian plants, especially *R. graveolens*, having small yellow flowers and strong-smelling evergreen leaves that yield a bitter oil formerly used in medicine. **2** (*adjl.*) designating the family (Rutaceae) of shrubs, trees, and herbs that includes rue as well as the citrus trees and the kumquats. (ME < OF < L *ruta*, ? < Gk. *rhytē*)

rue•ful ['rufəl] *adj.* **1** sorrowful; unhappy; mournful: *a rueful expression.* **2** causing sorrow or pity: *a rueful sight.* **3** feeling or expressing regret or shame. **—'rue•ful•ly,** *adv.* **—'rue•ful•ness,** *n.*

ruff[1] [rʌf] *n.* **1** a deep frill, stiff enough to stand out, worn around the neck by men and women in the 16th century. An Elizabethan ruff is still worn as part of the clerical habit of Danish Lutheran clergy. **2** a collar of specially marked feathers or hairs on the neck of a bird or animal. (? back formation from *ruffle*[1]) **—'ruff,like,** *adj.*
☛ *Hom.* ROUGH.

ruff[2] [rʌf] *v., n. Card games. —v.* trump.
—n. the act of trumping. (< MF *roffle* < OF *roffle, fonfle*; cf. Ital. *ronfa* a card game)
☛ *Hom.* ROUGH.

ruff[3] [rʌf] *n.* a shore bird (*Philomachus pugnax*) having a bill as long as the head, a ruff of feathers on the neck, and two ear tufts. Plumage, usually dull, includes a dark stripe down the back and tail. It visits Canada from Eurasia.
☛ *Hom.* ROUGH.

ruffed [rʌft] *adj., v. —adj.* having a ruff.
—v. pt. and pp. of RUFF[2].

ruffed grouse *Cdn.* a partridgelike game bird (*Bonasa umbellus*) occurring in many subspecies across Canada, having a small crest, a black or reddish brown ruff on either side of the neck, a fanlike tail, and barred and mottled brown plumage.

A ruffed grouse

ruf•fian ['rʌfjən] *or* ['rʌfiən] *n., adj. —n.* a rough, brutal, or cruel person.
—adj. rough; brutal; cruel. (< MF)

ruf•fian•ism ['rʌfjə,nɪzəm] *or* ['rʌfiə,nɪzəm] *n.* brutal conduct; ruffianly conduct or character.

ruf•fian•ly ['rʌfjənli] *or* ['rʌfiənli] *adj.* like a ruffian; violent; lawless.

ruf•fle[1] ['rʌfəl] *v.* **-fled, -fling;** *n. —v.* **1** make rough or uneven; wrinkle: *A breeze ruffled the lake.* **2** of a bird, when angry or frightened, make (feathers) stand erect: *The hen ruffled its feathers at the sight of the dog.* **3** gather into a ruffle. **4** trim with ruffles. **5** disturb; annoy: *Nothing can ruffle her calm temper.* **6** become ruffled. **7** shuffle (playing cards).
—n. **1** a roughness or unevenness in some surface; wrinkling. **2** a strip of cloth, ribbon, or lace gathered or pleated along one edge or along the middle and attached along this gathered or pleated line to a garment, curtain, etc. for decoration. **3** a disturbance; annoyance. **4** disorder; confusion. (ME; origin uncertain)

ruf•fle[2] ['rʌfəl] *n., v.* **-fled, -fling.** *—n.* a low, steady beat of a drum.
—v. beat (a drum) in this way. (? imitative)

ru•fi•yaa [ru'fija] *n.* the main unit of money in Maldives, divided into 100 laris. See table of money in the Appendix.

ru•fous ['rufəs] *adj.* reddish or reddish brown. (< L *rufus*)

rug [rʌg] *n.* **1** a heavy fabric floor covering. **2** a thick, warm cloth used as covering: *He wrapped his woollen rug around him.* **3** *Slang.* artificial turf. **4** *Slang.* a toupee. (< Scand.; cf. Norwegian dial. *rugga* coarse covering) **—'rug,like,** *adj.*

rug•by ['rʌgbi] *n.* **1** rugger. **2** *Cdn.* a game played by teams of twelve players who carry, pass, or kick an oval ball toward the opposing team's goal; Canadian football. (< *Rugby*, a famous school for boys in Rugby, England)
☛ *Usage.* **Rugby,** RUGGER, SOCCER. Though still heard in Canada, the term **rugby** (or **rugby football**) is being displaced by the American term **football.** As such, it is distinct from **rugger,** played with 15 players a side, and **soccer,** played with 11 players of whom only the goalie can play the ball with his or her hands.

rug•ged ['rʌgɪd] *adj.* **1** rough; wrinkled; uneven: *rugged ground.* **2** strong; vigorous; sturdy: *The pioneers were rugged people.* **3** strong and irregular: *rugged features.* **4** harsh; stern; severe: *rugged times.* **5** rude; unpolished; unrefined: *rugged manners.* **6** stormy: *rugged weather.* **7** rough or harsh to the ear. (< Scand.; cf. Swedish *rugga* roughen. See RUG.) **—'rug•ged•ly,** *adv.* **—'rug•ged•ness,** *n.*

rug•ger ['rʌgər] *n.* a game played by teams of fifteen players who kick or pass an oval ball toward the opposing team's goal. Also, **rugby football.** (< *rugby*)
☛ *Usage.* See note at RUGBY.

ru•gose ['rugous] *or* [ru'gous] *adj.* wrinkled; ridged; corrugated. (< L *rugosus* wrinkled) **—ru'gos•i•ty** [ru'gɒsəti], *n.*

ru•in ['ruən] *n., v. —n.* **1** a building, wall, etc. that has fallen to pieces: *That ruin was once a famous castle.* **2 ruins,** *pl.* that which is left after destruction, decay, or downfall, especially of a

building, wall, etc. that has fallen to pieces: *the ruins of an ancient city.* **3** very great damage; destruction; overthrow; decay: *The duke's enemies planned his ruin.* **4** a condition of destruction, decay, or downfall: *The house had gone to ruin and neglect.* **5** the cause of destruction, decay, or downfall; the downfall or undoing of a person: *Drink was his ruin.* **6** bankruptcy.
—v. **1** bring to ruin; destroy; spoil. **2** be destroyed; come to ruin. **3** make bankrupt. ⟨ME < OF < L *ruina* < *ruere* collapse⟩
☛ *Syn. n.* **2, 3, 4. Ruin,** DESTRUCTION = very great damage or complete loss. **Ruin** emphasizes falling to pieces or falling down, and applies to damage that impairs or ends the soundness, value, or beauty of something, especially a building, wall, etc., whether caused by decay or by a destructive force: *Proper care protects property from ruin.* **Destruction** emphasizes breaking to pieces or tearing down, and applies to damage caused by a wrecking or injuring force: *The storm caused widespread destruction.*
—v. **1.** See note at SPOIL.

ru•in•a•tion [ˌruəˈneiʃən] *n.* ruin; destruction; downfall.

ru•in•ous [ˈruənəs] *adj.* **1** bringing ruin; causing destruction. **2** fallen into ruins; ruined: *a building in ruinous condition.* **—ˈru•in•ous•ly,** *adv.*

rule [rul] *n., v.* **ruled, rul•ing.** *—n.* **1** a statement of what to do and not to do; a law; principle governing conduct, action, arrangement, etc.: *Obey the rules of the game.* **2** *Law.* an order by a court, based upon a principle of law. **3** a set of rules; code. A religious order lives under a certain rule. **4** control; government: *In a democracy the people have the rule.* **5** a period of power of a ruler; reign: *The B.N.A. Act was passed during the rule of Queen Victoria.* **6** a regular method; what usually happens or is done; what is usually true: *Fair weather is the rule in summer.* **7** RULER (def. 2). **8** *Printing.* a thin, type-high strip of metal, for printing a line or lines.
as a rule, usually.
work to rule. See WORK.
—v. **1** make a rule; decide. **2** make a formal decision: *The judge ruled against them.* **3** exercise the highest authority (*over*); control; govern; direct. **4** prevail; be current: *Prices of wheat and corn ruled high all year.* **5** mark with straight lines. **6** mark off with a ruler or other straight edge.
rule out, a eliminate or exclude: *The police ruled out foul play in the woman's death.* **b** stroke out (something written). ⟨ME < OF *riule* < L *regula* straight stick < *regere* guide. Doublet of RAIL¹.⟩ **—ˈrul•a•ble,** *adj.*
☛ *Syn. v.* **3. Rule,** GOVERN = direct or control by the exercise of authority or power. **Rule** emphasizes having complete control over others through supreme or absolute power, both to make laws or give commands and to force obedience: *He tries to rule his family as a dictator rules a nation.* **Govern** emphasizes directing and keeping under control by the active use of authority or power, usually for the good of the thing, person, or nation governed: *Parents govern their children until they develop the power to govern themselves.*

rule of three *Mathematics.* the method of finding the fourth term in a proportion when three terms are given.

rule of thumb **1** a rule based on experience or practice rather than on scientific knowledge. **2** a rough, practical method of procedure.

rul•er [ˈrulər] *n.* **1** a person who rules; monarch; sovereign; dictator. **2** a straight strip of wood, metal, etc., marked in units, such as centimetres, used in drawing lines or in measuring.

rul•ing [ˈrulɪŋ] *n., adj., v.* *—n.* **1** a decision of a judge or court or a government body. **2** ruled lines.
—adj. **1** that rules; governing; controlling. **2** predominating; prevalent.
—v. ppr. of RULE.

rum¹ [rʌm] *n.* **1** an alcoholic liquor made from sugar cane, molasses, etc. **2** any alcoholic liquor. ⟨short for obs. *rumbullion* rum; origin uncertain⟩

rum² [rʌm] *adj. Esp. Brit. Slang.* **1** odd; strange. **2** out of the ordinary, possibly dangerous. ⟨origin uncertain⟩

Ru•ma•ni•an [ruˈmeinjən] *or* [ruˈmeiniən] *n., adj.* Romanian.

rum•ba [ˈrʌmbə] *or* [ˈrʊmbə] *n., v.* **-baed, -ba•ing.** *—n.* **1** a dance that originated among the black people of Cuba, having a complex, syncopated rhythm in 2/4 or 4/4 time. **2** music for this dance.
—v. dance a rumba. Also, **rhumba.** ⟨< Sp. *rumba,* probably of African origin⟩

rum•ble [ˈrʌmbəl] *v.* **-bled, -bling;** *n.* *—v.* **1** make a deep, heavy, continuous sound. **2** move or cause to move with such a sound. **3** utter with such a sound.
—n. **1** a deep, heavy, continuous sound: *We hear the far-off rumble of thunder.* **2** *Slang.* a teenage gang fight. **3** the rear part of an automobile or carriage containing an extra seat or a place for baggage. See also RUMBLE SEAT. ⟨ME *romble(n),* ? ult. imitative⟩

rumble seat in certain old-fashioned types of automobile, an extra, open seat behind and outside the cab, recessed and covered with a hinged panel that forms the back of the seat when open.

rum•bling [ˈrʌmblɪŋ] *n., v.* *—n.* **1** early signs of dissatisfaction; rumour: *There were rumblings of the general strike earlier in the year.* **2** a deep, loud sound: *What's that rumbling in the basement?*
—v. ppr. of RUMBLE.

ru•men [ˈrumən] *n., pl.* **ru•mi•na** [ˈrumənə]. **1** the first stomach of an animal that chews the cud. **2** the cud of such an animal. ⟨< L *rumen* gullet⟩

ru•mi•nant [ˈrumənənt] *n., adj.* *—n.* an animal that chews the cud. Cows, sheep, and camels are ruminants.
—adj. **1** belonging to the group of ruminants. **2** meditative; reflective. ⟨< L *ruminans, -antis,* ppr. of *ruminare* chew cud < *rumen* gullet⟩

ru•mi•nate [ˈruməˌneit] *v.* **-nat•ed, -nat•ing. 1** chew (food) for a second time; chew the cud: *A cow ruminates its food.* **2** ponder; meditate: *She ruminated on the strange events of the past week.* ⟨< L *ruminare* chew the cud < *rumen* gullet⟩ **—ˈru•mi,nat•ing•ly,** *adv.* **—ˈru•mi,na•tor,** *n.* **—,ru•miˈna•tion,** *n.*

ru•mi•na•tive [ˈrumənətɪv] *or* [ˈruməˌneitɪv] *adj.* meditative; inclined to ruminate. **—ˈru•mi•na•tive•ly,** *adv.*

rum•mage [ˈrʌmɪdʒ] *v.* **-maged, -mag•ing;** *n.* *—v.* **1** search thoroughly by moving things about in a place or container: *I rummaged in my drawer for a pair of gloves.* **2** pull from among other things; bring to light (*often used with* **out** *or* **up**).
—n. **1** a rummaging search. **2** odds and ends: *a rummage sale.* ⟨< MF *arrumage* < *arrumer* stow cargo < **rum,* var. of *run* the hold of a ship < Gmc.⟩ **—ˈrum•mag•er,** *n.*
☛ *Syn. v.* **1.** See note at SEARCH.

rummage sale a sale of odds and ends, old clothing, etc., usually held to raise money for charity.

rum•my¹ [ˈrʌmi] *n.* a card game in which points are scored by assembling sets of three or four cards of the same rank or sequences of three or more cards of the same suit. ⟨origin uncertain⟩

rum•my² [ˈrʌmi] *n., pl.* **-mies;** *adj.* **-mi•er, -mi•est.** *—n. Slang.* drunkard.
—adj. like rum in taste or smell. ⟨< *rum*¹ + *-y*¹⟩

rum•my³ [ˈrʌmi] *adj.* **-mi•er, -mi•est.** *Esp. Brit. Slang.* odd; strange; queer. ⟨< *rum*² + *-y*¹⟩

ru•mour or **ru•mor** [ˈrumər] *n., v.* *—n.* **1** a story or statement talked of as news without any proof that it is true. **2** vague, general talk: *Rumour has it that Pierre will marry Indira.*
—v. tell or spread by rumour. ⟨ME < OF < L⟩
☛ *Hom.* ROOMER.

rump [rʌmp] *n.* **1** the hind part of the body of an animal, where the legs join the back. See HORSE for picture. **2** a cut of meat from this part. See BEEF and VEAL for pictures. **3** the corresponding part of the human body; buttocks. **4** an unimportant or inferior part; remnant, especially of a political party. ⟨ME < Scand.; cf. Danish *rumpe*⟩

rum•ple [ˈrʌmpəl] *v.* **-pled, -pling;** *n.* *—v.* crumple; crush; wrinkle: *This dress rumples easily.*
—n. a wrinkle; crease. ⟨Cf. MDu. *rompel*⟩

rum•pus [ˈrʌmpəs] *n. Informal.* a noisy disturbance or uproar; row. ⟨origin uncertain⟩

rumpus room RECREATION ROOM.

rum•run•ner [ˈrʌm,rʌnər] *n.* a person who or ship that smuggles alcoholic liquor into a country.

run [rʌn] *v.* **ran, run, run•ning;** *n.* *—v.* **1** move the legs and feet so that for a split second in each step, both feet are off the ground; go faster than walking: *A horse can run faster than a man.* **2** go hurriedly; hasten: *Run for help.* **3** flee: *Run for your life.* **4** cause to run; cause to move: *to run a horse.* **5 a** perform by, or as by, running: *to run errands.* **b** carry or take by, or as by, running: *Can you run this book over to the library for me?* **6** go; move; keep going; cause to move or to keep going, especially on a regular schedule: *This train runs to Calgary.* **7** creep; trail; climb: *Vines run along the sides of the road.* **8** go along (a way, path, etc.): *to run the course until the end.* **9** pursue; chase (game, etc.): *to run a fox.* **10** pass or cause to pass quickly: *A thought ran through my mind. Time runs on.* **11** trace; draw: *Run that report back to its source. She ran a series of lines across the page.* **12** stretch; extend: *Shelves run along the walls.* **13** range: *Her courses this term run from art history to applied chemistry.* **14** drive; force; thrust: *He ran a splinter into his hand.* **15** flow or cause to flow; flow with: *The streets ran oil after an oil truck overturned. Don't run the water needlessly.* **16** discharge fluid, mucus, or pus: *a running sore. My nose is running.* **17** get; become: *Never run into debt. The well ran dry.* **18** have a typical specified quality, form, size, price, etc.: *These potatoes run large. These jeans run $50 a pair.* **19 a** of colour, spread: *The colour ran when the dress was washed.* **b** of a dyed article, have its colour spread: *My red blouse ran.* **20** continue; last: *a lease to run two years.* **21** have currency or be current: *The story runs that school will close early today.* **22** have legal force. **23** take part in (a race or contest). **24 a** be a candidate for election: *She ran for the Tories in the last election.* **b** put up as a candidate: *All the parties are running more women this time.* **25** enter (a horse, etc.) in a race. **26** finish in a certain position in a race or competition: *Northern Dancer seldom ran lower than third.* **27** expose oneself to: *to run a risk.* **28** move or cause to move easily, freely, or smoothly: *A rope runs in a pulley.* **29** keep operating or cause to keep operating: *to run a machine.* **30** be worded: *How does the first verse run?* **31** be published or publish: *The newspapers didn't run the story about the moose in the middle of town.* **32** be shown or performed again and again: Anne of Green Gables *has run at the Charlottetown Festival for years.* **33** conduct; maintain; manage: *to run a business.* **34** go about, proceed, or grow without restraint: *Children were allowed to run about the streets.* **35** drop or cause to drop stitches; ravel: *I've just run my pantyhose.* **36** get past or through: *Enemy ships tried to run the blockade.* **37** smuggle: *to run rum.* **38** have (an advertisement, etc.) published in a newspaper: *She ran an ad in the evening paper.* **39** soften; become liquid; melt: *The wax ran when the candles were lit.* **40** shape by melting: *to run bullets through a mould.* **41** pass to or from the sea; migrate, as for spawning: *The salmon are running.* **42** return often to the mind: *That tune has been running in my head.* **43** *Computer technology.* **a** execute (a computer program): *She ran the accounts receivable program.* **b** of a computer program, carry out its processing: *The accounts payable program ran last night.* **44** make an unbroken sequence of (shots, strokes, etc.) in billiards, pool, etc.

run across, meet by chance.

run a fever, have a body temperature higher than normal.

run after, seek the attention or company of (someone), especially aggressively.

run away, a escape; flee. **b** desert one's home, family, etc. permanently.

run away with, a elope with: *She ran away with her lover.* **b** steal; abscond with; carry off. **c** win by doing far better than others. **d** cause to go out of control: *Her generosity ran away with her.*

run down, a cease to go; stop working. **b** pursue till caught or killed; hunt down. **c** knock down by running against or by riding or driving. **d** speak disparagingly against. **e** decline or reduce in vigour or health; fall off, diminish, or decrease; deteriorate. **f** *Baseball.* put (a base runner) out after trapping him or her between bases.

run down (or **over**) **to,** make a quick visit to.

run for it, run for safety.

run in, a pay a short visit: *We'll just run in for a minute.* **b** *Informal.* arrest and put in jail: *He was run in for drunken driving.*

run into, a meet by chance. **b** crash into; collide with.

run off, a drain or flow away. **b** drive away or off. **c** print; duplicate: *I ran off 100 copies of this form.* **d** run away; flee: *He ran off when he heard the police sirens.*

run off at the mouth, talk too much, especially about confidential information.

run on, a continue indefinitely, especially in speech. **b** add at the end of text. **c** continue text on the same line.

run out, come to an end; become exhausted.

run out (of), use up; have no more: *I can't bake a cake because I've run out of sugar. Have you any red balloons? No, we ran out.*

run over, a ride or drive over: *The car ran over some glass.* **b** overflow: *Coffee ran over into the saucer.* **c** exceed a limit. **d** go through quickly: *Please run over these figures to check my addition.*

run through, a consume or spend rapidly or recklessly: *The spendthrift ran through his inheritance in a year.* **b** pierce. **c** review; rehearse: *The teacher ran through the homework assignment a second time.*

run up, *Informal.* **a** make quickly: *Do you like this dress? I just ran it up.* **b** collect; accumulate: *Don't run up a big bill.*

—*n.* **1** the act of running: *He made a run to the corner and back.* **2** a running pace: *to set out at a run.* **3 a** a spell or period of causing (a machine, etc.) to operate. **b** the amount of anything produced in such a period: *During a run of eight hours the factory produced a run of 100 cars.* **4 a** a spell of causing something liquid to run or flow. **b** the amount that runs: *the run of sap from maple trees.* **5** a trip, especially a journey over a certain route: *The ship reached port after a six-week run.* **6** a quick visit: *We'll just take a run over to Vancouver.* **7** *Baseball or cricket.* the unit of score: *Our team scored four runs in the last inning.* **8** a period; a continuous spell or course; continuous extent: *a run of bad luck.* **9** a succession of performances: *This play has had a two-year run.* **10** an unbroken sequence of scoring plays in snooker, etc. **11** an onward movement; progress; course; trend: *the run of events.* **12** a continuous series or succession of something; succession of demands: *a run on the bank to draw out money.* **13** *Music.* a rapid succession of tones. **14** the usual kind: *the common run of humankind.* **15** freedom to go over or through, or to use: *The guests were given the run of the house.* **16** a flow or rush of water; small stream. **17** a number of fish moving together, especially a periodic movement to spawning grounds: *a run of salmon.* **18** *Cdn.* a period of abundance of animals. **19** a track, pipe, or trough, etc.: *a ski run.* **20** a stretch or enclosed space for animals: *a dog run.* **21** a place where stitches have slipped out or become undone: *a run in a stocking.* **22** a landing of smuggled goods. **23** *Nautical.* the extreme after part of the immersed part of a ship. **24** an act of smuggling: *a rum run.* **25 the runs,** *pl. Slang.* diarrhea.

a run for (one's) **money, a** strong competition. **b** satisfaction for one's efforts.

in the long (or **short**) **run,** over the long (or short) term.

on the run, a hurrying: *The butcher had so many orders that he was on the run all day.* **b** in retreat or rout: *Victory is ours; the enemy is on the run.* ⟨ME *rinne, renne,* ? < *runnon,* pp. of OE *rinnan* run⟩

run•a•bout ['rʌnə,bʌut] *n.* **1** a light automobile or carriage with a single seat. **2** a small motorboat. **3** a person who runs about from place to place.

run•a•round ['rʌnə,raʊnd] *n.* **1** *Slang.* a series of excuses, evasions, useless referrals, or deceptions: *They gave him the runaround.* **2** *Printing.* type set narrower than the full width of a column or page, to permit the insertion of an illustration, etc.

run•a•way ['rʌnə,wei] *n.* **1** a person or animal that runs away. **2** a horse, vehicle, etc. that runs out of control. **3** (*adjl.*) being a runaway: *a runaway horse.* **4** the act or an instance of running away or being out of control. **5** (*adjl.*) resulting from a running away, or done by runaways: *a runaway marriage.* **6** (*adjl.*) easily won or accomplished: *a runaway victory.* **7** (*adjl.*) of prices or inflation, rising quickly and uncontrollably.

run•ci•ble spoon ['rʌnsəbəl] any table utensil having the characteristics of both a fork and a spoon, especially an hors-d'oeuvres server shaped like a fork having two broad tines and one sharp, curved one. ⟨coined by Edward Lear in *The Owl and the Pussycat*⟩

run•ci•nate ['rʌnsənɪt] *or* ['rʌnsə,neit] *adj. Botany.* of a leaf, having large lobes or teeth pointing toward the base: *Dandelion leaves are runcinate.* See LEAF for picture. ⟨< L *runcina* plane (but taken as 'saw') < Gk. *rhykanē*; influenced by L *runcare* clear (of thorns, etc.)⟩

run•down ['rʌn,daʊn] *n.* **1** a brief account; summary: *Give me a rundown on what happened.* **2** *Baseball.* the act of putting a base runner out after trapping him or her between bases.

run–down ['rʌn 'daʊn] *adj.* **1** tired; sick. **2** falling to pieces; partly ruined: *a run-down building.* **3** that has stopped going or working.

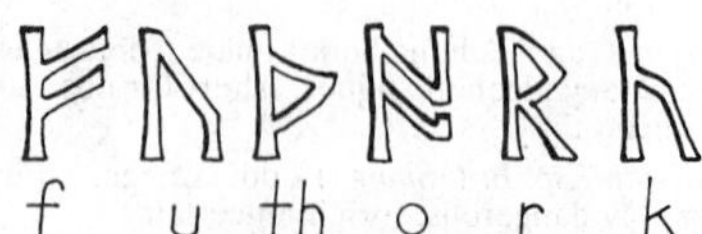

The first six letters of the English runic alphabet

rune [run] *n.* **1** any letter of an ancient Germanic or Turkic alphabet. **2** a mark that looks like a rune and has some mysterious, magic meaning. **3** a poem or other composition with magic meaning, which can be used to cast a spell. **4** an old Finnish or Scandinavian poem or song. ⟨< ON *rún*⟩

rung[1] [rʌŋ] pp. of RING[2].

rung[2] [rʌŋ] *n.* **1** a rod or bar used as a step of a ladder. **2** a crosspiece set between the legs of a chair or as part of the back or arm of a chair. **3** a spoke of a wheel. **4** a bar of wood resembling a spoke in shape and use. ⟨OE *hrung*⟩

ru•nic ['runɪk] *adj.* consisting of runes; written in runes; marked with runes; like a rune. ⟨< *rune* + *-ic*⟩

runic alphabet an alphabet used by the ancient Germanic peoples, loosely based on the Greco-Roman alphabet, for carving on wood or stone.

run–in ['rʌn ˌɪn] *n. Informal.* a sharp disagreement; an argument or quarrel: *I had a run-in with the director this morning.*

run•let ['rʌnlɪt] *n.* a small stream.

run•nel ['rʌnəl] *n.* a small stream or brook. ⟨OE *ryne* < *rinnan* run⟩

run•ner ['rʌnər] *n.* **1** a person who or animal that runs. **2** messenger: *a runner for a bank.* **3** a person who runs or works a machine, etc. **4** either of the narrow pieces on which a sleigh or sled slides. **5** the blade of a skate. **6** RUNNING SHOE. **7** a long, narrow strip: *We have a runner of carpet in our hall, and runners of linen and lace on our dressers.* **8** a smuggler; a person who or ship that tries to evade somebody. **9** a slender stem that grows along the ground and takes root, thus producing new plants. Strawberry plants spread by runners. **10 a** something on which something else runs or moves, such as a roller or caster. **b** the groove in which this runs.

run•ner–up ['rʌnər 'ʌp] *n.* the person, player, or team that takes second place in a contest.

run•ning ['rʌnɪŋ] *n., adj., v.* —*n.* **1** the act of a person who or thing that runs. **2** a flow of liquid; a discharge. **3** management or care: *the running of a business.* **4** operation: *the running of a machine.* **5** footing on a track: *The running is soft and wet today.*
be in the running, have a chance to win.
be out of the running, have no chance to win.
—*adj.* **1** cursive: *a running hand, running handwriting.* **2** discharging matter: *a running sore.* **3** flowing: *running water.* **4** liquid. **5** going or carried on continuously and concurrently: *a running commentary.* **6** current: *the running month.* **7** repeated continuously: *a running pattern.* **8** following in succession: *for three nights running.* **9** prevalent. **10** moving or proceeding quickly, easily, or smoothly. **11** slipping or sliding easily: *a running knot or noose.* **12** of plants, creeping or climbing. **13** that is measured in a straight line. **14** of the normal run of a train, bus, etc.: *the running time between towns.* **15** performed with or during a run: *a running leap.*
—*v.* ppr. of RUN.

running board a metal step beneath the doors of early automobiles, to make it easier for passengers to get in and out of the automobile.

running foot a short title printed at the bottom of each page, or each left- or right-hand page of a book, etc.

running gear **1** the wheels and axles of an automobile, locomotive, or other vehicle. **2** the clothing worn by runners, such as shorts, sweatsuit, running shoes, etc.

running head a heading printed at the top of each page, or each left- or right-hand page of a book, etc.

running knot a knot made to slip along the rope or cord around which it is tied; slip-knot.

running lights **1** lights required by law to be displayed on an aircraft or vessel between the times of sunset and sunrise. **2** lights on a vehicle that go on automatically if the vehicle is running.

running mate *Esp. U.S.* a candidate running jointly with another, but for a less important office, such as a candidate for vice-president.

running noose a noose with a running knot.

running shoe *Cdn.* a light casual shoe with a cloth, leather, or synthetic upper and pliable rubber sole with treads, used for sports or for general casual wear.

running stitch a series of short, even stitches all taken with one passage of the needle.

run•ny ['rʌni] *adj.* **1** having a tendency to flow: *The pie filling is a bit runny.* **2** of the nose, continuously discharging mucus.

run–off ['rʌn ˌɒf] *n.* **1** something that runs off. **2** the running off of water during a spring thaw or after a heavy rain. **3** a final, deciding race or contest.

run–of–the–mill ['rʌn əv ðə 'mɪl] *adj.* average or commonplace; ordinary: *a run-of-the-mill design.*

run–on ['rʌn ˌɒn] *adj., n.* —*adj.* **1** *Printing.* **a** continued to the end, without a break. **b** of or having to do with copy to be set immediately after the preceding material, without any paragraph break or other indentation. **2** *Poetry.* continuing to the next line without punctuation. **3** *Grammar.* of a sentence, having too many clauses put loosely together, without proper punctuation or transitional material.
—*n.* **1** *Printing.* run-on material. **2** a RUN-ON ENTRY in a dictionary.

run–on entry ['rʌn ˌɒn] in a dictionary, a derived word that is not defined but is shown at the end of the entry for the word from which it is formed. *Rurally* may be found as a run-on entry under *rural.*

runt [rʌnt] *n.* an animal, person, or plant that is smaller than the usual size. ⟨origin uncertain⟩

runt•y ['rʌnti] *adj.* **runt•i•er, runt•i•est.** stunted; dwarfish.

run•way ['rʌn,wei] *n.* **1** a strip having a level surface on which aircraft land and take off. **2** a ramp for other vehicles, such as that at a boat launching site. **3** *Cdn.* the channel or bed of a watercourse. **4** a channel, track, groove, trough, etc., along which something moves, slides, flows, etc. **5** the beaten track of deer or other animals. **6** an enclosed place for animals to run in; RUN (def. 20). **7** a long tongue of stage extending into the audience, commonly used for fashion shows.

ru•pee [ru'pi] *or* ['rupi] *n.* **1** the basic unit of money in India and Pakistan, divided into 100 paise (India) or paisas (Pakistan). **2** the basic unit of money in Mauritius, Seychelles, and Sri Lanka, divided into 100 cents. **3** the basic unit of money in Nepal, divided into 100 pice. See table of money in the Appendix. **4** a coin or note worth one rupee. ⟨< Hind. *rupiyah* < Skt. *rupya* wrought silver⟩

Ru•pert's Land ['rupərts] the name given to the territories granted to the Hudson's Bay Company by Charles II in 1670. Rupert's Land included all the land watered by rivers flowing into Hudson Bay. ⟨< Prince *Rupert,* who was the first governor of the Hudson's Bay Company⟩

ru•pi•ah [ru'piə] *n.* **1** the basic unit of money in Indonesia, divided into 100 sen. See table of money in the Appendix. **2** a note worth one rupiah. ⟨< Indonesian < Hind. *rupiyah.* See RUPEE.⟩

rup•ture ['rʌptʃər] *n., v.* **-tured, -tur•ing.** —*n.* **1** the tearing apart of body tissue: *the rupture of a muscle or blood vessel.* **2** a hernia. **3** a breaking off of friendly relations; especially, a break between nations that threatens to lead to war. **4** any breaking apart or break of relations: *the rupture of a marriage.*
—*v.* **1** burst or break: *A heart muscle has ruptured. He ruptured his spleen.* **2** have a hernia. **3** suffer or cause to suffer a breaking apart of friendly relations: *Their friendship has ruptured. She ruptured the family peace.* ⟨< L *ruptura* < *rumpere* burst⟩

ru•ral ['rʊrəl] *adj.* **1** in, of, having to do with, or like the country or the people who live in the country: *a rural upbringing, a rural riding.* **2** of or having to do with agriculture: *the rural economy.* ⟨< L *ruralis* < *rus, ruris* country⟩ —**'ru•ral•ly,** *adv.* —**'ru•ral•ist,** *n.* —**'ru•ral,ism,** *n.*

☛ *Syn.* **1. Rural,** RUSTIC, PASTORAL = of, relating to, or characteristic of the country. **Rural** expresses an objective attitude toward the country and country life as distinguished from towns and cities and city life, but is sometimes used to suggest pleasant country scenes: *Rural life is healthful and quiet.* **Rustic** suggests simplicity, lack of refinement, or roughness and clumsiness, especially in appearance, manners, etc.: *The cottage has a rustic charm.* **Pastoral** has poetic associations, suggesting shepherds, grazing flocks, green pastures, and a simple, peaceful life: *She paints pastoral pictures.*

rural dean *Esp. Brit.* a priest of the highest rank below an archdeacon in a district outside the cathedral city. He or she acts as the local deputy of a bishop or archdeacon.

rural municipality *Cdn.* in certain provinces, a municipal district in a rural area, administered by an elected reeve and council. *Abbrev.:* R.M.

rural route **1** a postal service by which mail is delivered by car or truck to the mailboxes of individual farms or country residences or businesses from a local post office. **2** any one route or circuit in this service: *There are four rural routes from this post office. Abbrev.:* R.R.

ruse [ruz] *or* [rus] *n.* a trick; stratagem. ⟨< F *ruse* < *ruser* dodge⟩

☛ *Syn.* See note at STRATAGEM.

rush[1] [rʌʃ] *v., n., adj.* —*v.* **1** move with speed or force: *We rushed along.* **2** attack with much speed and force; overcome by sudden attack: *They rushed the enemy.* **3** come, go, pass, act, etc. with speed or haste: *He rushes into things without knowing anything about them.* **4** send, push, force, do, perform, etc. with speed or haste: *Rush this order, please.* **5** urge to hurry: *Don't rush me.* **6** *Informal.* lavish much and frequent attention on: *He rushed the girl all summer.* **7** *Informal.* attempt to persuade to join a fraternity or sorority. **8** advance (a football) by running.
—*n.* **1** the act of rushing: *the rush of the flood.* **2** busy haste; hurry: *the rush of city life.* **3** a great or sudden effort of many people to go somewhere or get something: *the Christmas rush.*

Few people got rich in the Klondike gold rush. **4** an eager demand; pressure: *A sudden rush of business kept everyone working hard.* **5** a rapid attack in force. **6** *Football.* an attempt to carry the ball through the opposing line. **7** *Informal.* the lavishing of much attention, as in courting. **8 rushes,** *pl.* the first prints of film shot for a movie. **9** *Informal.* the onset of euphoria, with or without drugs; high.
with a rush, suddenly; quickly.
–adj. **1** requiring haste: *A rush order must be filled at once.* **2** done in: *a rush job.* ⟨originally, force out of place by violent impact; cf. OE *hrȳsc* a blow⟩ **–'rush•er,** *n.*
☛ *Syn. n.* **1, 2.** See note at HURRY.

rush² [rʌʃ] *n.* **1** any of a genus (*Juncus*) of marsh plants having round, pithy stems, grasslike leaves, and clusters of tiny, greenish or brownish flowers. The stems of some rushes are widely used for chair bottoms, mats, baskets, etc. The pith of the stems was also formerly used for wicks in candles. **2** (*adjl.*) designating the family (Juncaceae) of perennial, flowering marsh plants that includes these rushes, found in temperate and cold regions, and having slender leaves that are either grasslike or round and clusters of small flowers. **3** any of various other flowering marsh plants, especially of the sedge family, having round stems or hollow, stemlike leaves often used to make chair bottoms, mats, etc. **4** the stem or hollow leaf of a rush, used for baskets, etc. **5** (*adjl.*) made of or with rushes. **6** *Archaic.* something of little or no value: *not worth a rush.* ⟨OE *rysc*⟩ **–'rush,like,** *adj.*

rush hour the time of day when traffic is heaviest or when trains, buses, etc. are most crowded. **–'rush-,hour,** *adj.*

rush seat a seat for a stage show, sports event, etc., that is sold on the day of the performance or event.

rush•y ['rʌʃi] *adj.* **rush•i•er, rush•i•est. 1** abounding in or covered with rushes. **2** made of rushes.

rus in ur•be ['rʌs ɪn 'ɜrbi] *or* ['rʊs ɪn 'ʊrbei] *Latin.* the country in the city.

rusk [rʌsk] *n.* **1** a piece of bread or cake toasted in the oven. **2** a kind of light, crisp, sweet biscuit. ⟨< Sp., Pg. *rosca* roll⟩

Rus•sell fence ['rʌsəl] *Trademark.* a fence having pairs of crossed posts set in post-holes, the top rail set in the crotch, and other rails hung on wire loops. ⟨named for its inventor⟩

rus•set ['rʌsɪt] *adj., n. –adj.* reddish or yellowish brown.
–n. **1** a reddish or yellowish brown. **2** a coarse, russet-coloured cloth. Peasants used to make and wear russet. **3** a kind of apple having a rough, brownish skin. ⟨ME < OF *rousset,* ult. < L *russus* red⟩

Rus•sia ['rʌʃə] *n.* a very large country in E Europe and W Asia, properly called the Russian Federation.

rus•sia ['rʌʃə] *n.* RUSSIA LEATHER.

Russia leather a fine, smooth leather, usually dyed dark red, made from skins treated with birchbark oil. Russia leather is used especially for bookbinding.

Rus•sian ['rʌʃən] *n., adj. –n.* **1** a native or inhabitant of Russia; especially, a member of the dominant Slavic people of Russia. **2** a person descended from these people. **3** the Slavic language of the Russians.
–adj. of or having to do with Russia, its people, or their language.

Russian Church a branch of the Eastern Orthodox Church, until 1918 the national church of Russia.

Rus•sian•ize ['rʌʃə,naɪz] *v.* **-ized, -iz•ing.** make or become Russian in customs, language, etc. **–,Rus•sian•i'za•tion,** *n.*

Russian olive a tree or ornamental shrub (*Elaeagnus angustifolia*) which is sometimes mistaken for a willow, having silvery scales on its leaves and twigs.

Russian Revolution the revolution in which Russian workers, sailors, and soldiers, led by Lenin, overthrew the government of the Czar in 1917 and established the Soviet Union.

Russian roulette 1 a deadly game in which each player in turn spins the cylinder of a revolver which has been loaded with only one bullet, points the muzzle at his or her head, and pulls the trigger. **2** any potentially deadly or destructive activity.

Russian thistle a common annual weed (*Salsola pestifer,* also classified as *S. kali* var. *tenuifolia*) of the goosefoot family, introduced to North America from Europe and Asia, having very narrow leaves ending in a sharp point and tiny flowers that grow from the leaf axils. When the plant is mature, the leaves become very stiff and prickly and the nearly ball-shaped plant breaks off at ground level and is rolled by the wind, scattering its seed as it goes.

Russian wolfhound borzoi.

rust [rʌst] *n., v., adj. –n.* **1** the reddish brown or orange coating that forms on iron or steel when exposed to air or moisture. **2 a** any film, stain, or coating on any other metal due to oxidization, etc. **b** any oxidization resembling rust. **3** a harmful growth, habit, influence, or agency. **4** a plant disease or fungus that spots leaves and stems. **5** a reddish brown or orange.
–v. **1** become covered with rust. **2** cause to rust: *Rain rusted the old shovel kept outside.* **3** allow to degenerate by not using. **4** degenerate by not being used: *Don't let your mind rust during vacation.* **5** have or cause to have the disease or fungus rust.
–adj. reddish brown or orange. ⟨OE *rust,* var. of *rūst*⟩

rust•buc•ket ['rʌst,bʌkət] *n. Slang.* **1** a leaky boat or ship. **2** a rusting car or one that is prone to rust.

rus•tic ['rʌstɪk] *adj., n. –adj.* **1** belonging to or suitable for the country; rural: *rustic furnishings.* **2** simple; plain: *His rustic speech and ways made him uncomfortable in the city school.* **3** rough; awkward. **4** made of branches with the bark still on them: *rustic arches in a garden.*
–n. a country person or one regarded as being from the country because he or she is awkward, boorish, etc. ⟨< L *rusticus* < *rus* country⟩ **–'rus•ti•cal•ly,** *adv.*
☛ *Syn. adj.* **1.** See note at RURAL.

rus•ti•cate ['rʌstə,keit] *v.* **-cat•ed, -cat•ing. 1** go to or live in the country. **2** send to the country. **3** countrify. ⟨< L *rusticari* < *rusticus* rustic. See RUSTIC.⟩

rus•ti•ca•tion [,rʌstə'keiʃən] *n.* **1** the act of rusticating or the state of being rusticated. **2** residence in the country.

rus•tic•i•ty [rʌ'stɪsəti] *n., pl.* **-ties. 1** a rustic quality, characteristic, or peculiarity. **2** rural life.

rust•i•ly ['rʌstəli] *adv.* in such a manner as to suggest rustiness.

rus•tle ['rʌsəl] *v.* **-tled, -tling,** *n. –v.* **1** make a succession of light, soft sounds, as of things gently rubbing together: *leaves rustling in the breeze.* **2** move or stir (something) so that it makes such a sound: *We could hear her rustling papers in the next room.* **3** *Informal.* steal (cattle, etc.). **4** *Informal.* act, do, or get with energy or speed: *We'll have to rustle if we want to finish in time.*
rustle up, *Informal.* **a** gather; find. **b** get ready; prepare: *The cook rustled up some food.*
–n. a light, soft sound of things gently rubbing together, such as leaves make when moved by the wind. ⟨OE *hrūxlian* make noise⟩

rus•tler ['rʌslər] *n.* **1** *Informal.* a cattle thief. **2** an active, energetic person. **3** a person who or thing that rustles.

rust•less ['rʌstlɪs] *adj.* **1** free from rust. **2** rustproof.

rust•proof ['rʌst,pruf] *adj., v. –adj.* resisting rust.
–v. treat with a preparation that resists rust.

rust•y ['rʌsti] *adj.* **rust•i•er, rust•i•est. 1** covered with rust; rusted: *a rusty knife.* **2** made by rust. **3** coloured like rust. **4** stiff or not moving quietly because of rust. **5** faded: *a rusty black.* **6** weakened or deficient from lack of use or practice: *My mother says her biology is rusty.* **–'rust•i•ness,** *n.*

rut¹ [rʌt] *n., v.* **rut•ted, rut•ting.** *–n.* **1** a track made in the ground, especially by a wheel. **2** a channel or groove in which something runs. **3** a fixed or established way of acting, especially a dull routine: *She decided to change jobs because she felt she was getting into a rut.*
–v. make a rut or ruts in: *The road to the cottage was deeply rutted.* ⟨? var. of *route*⟩

rut² [rʌt] *n., v.* **rut•ted, rut•ting.** *–n.* **1** the sexual excitement of deer, goats, sheep, etc., occurring at regular intervals. **2** the period during which this excitement lasts.
–v. be in rut. ⟨ME < OF *ruit* < L *rugitus* bellowing < *rugire* bellow⟩

ru•ta•ba•ga ['rutə,beigə] *or* [,rutə'beigə] *n.* a turnip (*Brassica napobrassica*) with a very large yellowish root. ⟨< Swedish (dial.) *rotabagge,* literally, root bag⟩

Ruth [ruθ] *n.* a woman who is devoted to her mother-in-law. ⟨in the Bible, a Moabite woman who left her own people to go to Bethlehem with her mother-in-law, Naomi, to whom she was devoted. Her story is told in the Book of Ruth.⟩

Ru•the•ni•an [ru'θinjən] *or* [ru'θiniən] *n.* **1** *Cdn.* formerly, any of the many Slavic immigrants, particularly Ukrainians, coming to Canada from central Europe in the late 1800s and early 1900s. **2** a member of a group of Ukrainians living in W Ukraine and E Slovakia. **3** the dialect of Ukrainian spoken by these people. ⟨< *Ruthenia,* a former province in E Czechoslovakia⟩

ru•the•ni•um [ru'θiniəm] *n. Chemistry.* a hard, brittle, greyish metallic element of the platinum group. *Symbol*: Ru; *at.no.* 44; *at.mass* 101.07. ⟨< NL, named after *Ruthenia* because it was discovered in the Urals⟩

ruth•er•for•di•um [ˌrʌðər'fɔrdiəm] *n. Chemistry.* a very unstable, artificially created, radioactive element. *Symbol*: Rf; *at.no.* 104; *at.mass* 257; *half-life* approx. 70 seconds. Also called **kurchatovium.** ⟨after Ernest *Rutherford* (1871-1973), the British physicist, who discovered the atomic nucleus⟩
☛ *Usage.* No name has yet been officially adopted internationally for element 104. Scientists in Russia and the United States both claim priority in synthesizing this element. **Rutherfordium** is the name proposed by the U.S. group and **kurchatovium** the one proposed by the Russian group.

ruth•less ['ruθlɪs] *adj.* having no pity; showing no mercy; cruel. **—'ruth•less•ly,** *adv.* **—'ruth•less•ness,** *n.*

ru•ti•lant ['rutələnt] *adj.* glowing with golden light.

ru•ti•lat•ed ['rutəˌleitɪd] *adj. Mineralogy.* containing rutile in the form of long, thin spars.

ru•tile ['rutaɪl] *or* ['rutil] *n.* a lustrous, reddish brown or black, crystalline form of titanium dioxide, widely occurring in igneous and metamorphic rocks. It is an important ore of titanium. *Formula*: TiO_2 ⟨< F < G *Rutil* < L *rutilus* reddish⟩

rut•ty ['rʌti] *adj.* **-ti•er, -ti•est.** full of ruts. **—'rut•ti•ness,** *n.*

RV **1** RECREATIONAL VEHICLE. **2** re-entry vehicle.

RV or **R.V.** REVISED VERSION.

Rwan•da [rə'wandə] *n.* a country in E central Africa.

Rx or **rx** **1** in medical prescriptions, take (for L *recipe*). **2** tens of rupees.

-ry *noun-forming suffix.* **1** the occupation or work of a ——: *dentistry, chemistry.* **2** the act of a ——: *mimicry.* **3** the quality, state, or condition of a ——: *rivalry.* **4** a group of ——s, considered collectively: *peasantry.* ⟨short form of *-ery*⟩

Ry. railway.

rye [raɪ] *n.* **1** a cereal grass (*Secale cereale*) widely grown in northern Europe and northern North America for grain and straw. **2** the seeds, or grain, of this plant, used for bread or for fodder. **3** flour made from this grain. **4** bread made from rye flour: *He ordered a corned beef on rye.* **5** whisky made from rye. **6** *Cdn.* a blended whisky made from rye and other grains; Canadian whisky. ⟨OE *ryge*⟩
☛ *Hom.* WRY.

rye–grass ['raɪ ˌgræs] *n.* any of several grasses (genus *Lolium*) native to Europe and Northern Africa, widely cultivated as a pasture grass in western Europe, Britain, New Zealand, and along the Atlantic and Pacific coasts of North America.

rye whisky whisky made from rye.

Ss *Ss*

s or S [ɛs] *n., pl.* **s's** or **S's. 1** the nineteenth letter of the English alphabet. **2** any speech sound represented by this letter. **3** a person or thing identified as *s*, especially the nineteenth in a series. **4** something shaped like the letter S. **5** (*adjl.*) of or being an S or s. **6** a printed or written representation of this letter. **7** any device, such as a printer's type, a lever, or a key on a keyboard, that produces an s or S.

's[1] an abbreviation of *is, has*, or *does*, added to the preceding pronoun or noun. *Examples*: *He's here. She's given the books away. What's that mean?*

's[2] an abbreviation of *us*, used with *let. Example*: *Let's go.*

–s[1] *suffix.* **1** used to form the plural of most nouns, as in *hats, boys, dogs, houses, monkeys, taxis, handfuls.* **2** used to form certain adverbs. *Examples*: always *and* mornings *in* You will always find him home mornings. ⟨OE *-as*⟩

–s[2] *suffix.* used to form the third person singular of verbs in the present indicative, as in *tells, drives, loses.* ⟨OE *-es*⟩

–'s a suffix used to form the possessive case of singular nouns and also of plural nouns not ending in *s*, as in *boy's, dog's, child's, women's, children's.* ⟨OE *-(e)s*⟩

s. 1 shilling(s). **2** son(s). **3** second(s). **4** singular. **5** series. **6** society. **7** south. **8** southern.

S 1 south; southern. **2** sulphur. **3** the sea element of the Canadian Forces.

S. 1 south; southern. **2** Saint. **3** School. **4** Saturday. **5** Sunday. **6** September. **7** Section. **8** Sea. **9** Senate. **10** Signor. **11** Society.

S.A. 1 SOUTH AMERICA. **2** SOUTH AFRICA. **3** South Australia. **4** SALVATION ARMY.

Sab•bat ['sæbət] *n.* a meeting of witches and sorcerers, held four times a year, and characterized by orgiastic ritual, nude dancing, etc. ⟨special usage of *Sabbath*⟩

Sab•ba•tar•i•an [ˌsæbə'tɛriən] *n., adj. –n.* **1** a Christian who observes Saturday as the Sabbath. **2** a Christian who favours a very strict observance of the Sabbath.
–adj. **1** of or having to do with the Sabbath or its observance. **2** concerning the practices and beliefs of Sabbatarians.

Sab•ba•tar•i•an•ism [ˌsæbə'tɛriəˌnɪzəm] *n.* **1** the observance of Saturday as the Sabbath. **2** very strict observance of the Sabbath.

Sab•bath ['sæbəθ] *n.* **1** the seventh day of the week, Saturday, observed as a day of rest and worship by Jews and members of some Christian denominations. **2** Sunday, observed as a day of rest and worship by most Christians. **3** (*adjl.*) of or belonging to the Sabbath. **4** any day set aside for prayer: *Friday is the Muslim Sabbath.* **5 sabbath,** any day or period of rest. ⟨< L < Gk. *sabbaton* < Hebrew *shabbāth* < *shābath* to rest⟩

Sabbath school a meeting of children and Seventh-Day Adventist religious teachers, held on a Saturday.

sab•bat•i•cal [sə'bætɪkəl] *adj., n. –adj.* **1** of, having to do with, or suitable for the Sabbath: *sabbatical laws.* **2** of or having to do with sabbatical leave. Also, **sabbatic.**
–n. **1** SABBATICAL LEAVE. **2** a regularly recurring time of rest. ⟨< Gk. *sabbatikos* < *sabbaton.* See SABBATH.⟩

sabbatical leave a leave of absence for a year or half year given to teachers, usually in a university and especially once in seven years, for study and travel.

sa•ber ['seibər] See SABRE.

Sa•bine ['seibaɪn] *or* ['sæbaɪn] *n., adj. –n.* **1** a member of an ancient people in central Italy who were conquered by the Romans in the 3rd century B.C. **2** the Italic language of the Sabines.
–adj. of or having to do with the Sabines or their language. ⟨< L *Sabinus*⟩

Sabine's gull a small Arctic gull (*Xema sabinii*) having a forked tail, grey head, and black collar. ⟨after Sir Edward *Sabine* (d. 1883), British explorer⟩

sa•ble ['seibəl] *n., adj. –n.* **1** a small flesh-eating mammal (*Martes zibellina*) of the forests of N Asia, closely related to the martens, having glossy, dark brown or black fur. **2** the fur of the sable, one of the most costly furs. **3** any of various related animals, such as the North American marten, or their fur. **4** (*adjl.*) made of the fur of a sable. **5** the colour of sable fur, usually a dark blackish brown.
–adj. **1** of the colour of sable. **2** *Poetic.* black or very dark: *sable garments of mourning.* **3** *Heraldry.* black, indicated in engraving by close cross-hatching. ⟨ME < OF *sable*, ult. < Slavic⟩

sable antelope a large South African antelope (*Hippotragus niger*) with large scimitar-shaped horns and, in the male, a black coat. It is an endangered species.

sa•ble•fish ['seibəlˌfɪʃ] *n., pl.* **-fish** or **-fish•es.** blackcod.

sa•bot [sə'bou] *or* ['sæbou]; *French*, [sa'bo] *n.* **1** a shoe hollowed out of a single piece of wood, worn by peasants in France, Belgium, etc. **2** a coarse leather shoe having a thick wooden sole. ⟨< F *sabot* < OF *çabot*, alteration of *çavate* old shoe < Arabic *sabbāt*; influenced by OF *bote* boot⟩

sab•o•tage ['sæbəˌtɑʒ] *n., v.* **-taged, -tag•ing.** *–n.* **1** the destruction of machinery or tools, a hindering of a manufacturing process, waste of materials, etc., by workers as a threat or act of protest against an employer. **2** damage or destruction by civilians or enemy agents to interfere with a military operation or war effort. Sabotage may be carried out by civilians against conquerors of their country or by enemy agents or by sympathizers within a country at war. **3** any destruction or damage intended to hinder or hurt.
–v. commit sabotage on or against; damage or destroy deliberately: *The group was accused of trying to sabotage the negotiations for a new labour contract.* ⟨< F *sabotage* < *saboter* bungle, walk noisily < *sabot.* See SABOT.⟩

sab•o•teur [ˌsæbə'tɜr] *n.* a person who commits sabotage. ⟨< F⟩

sa•bra ['sɑbrə] *n.* a person born in Israel; native Israeli. ⟨< Hebrew *sābrāh* cactus, thought of as being tough and prickly outside but soft inside⟩

sa•bre ['seibər] *n., v.* **-bred, -bring.** *–n.* **1** a heavy, curved sword having a sharp point and cutting edge. See SWORD for picture. **2** a light sword used in fencing or duelling, having a tapering, flexible blade with a full cutting edge along one side. A sabre is heavier than a foil.
–v. strike, wound, or kill with a sabre. Also, **saber.** ⟨< F *sabre*, alteration of *sable*, ult. < Hungarian *szablya* < *szabni* cut⟩

sa•bre–rat•tling ['seibər ˌrætlɪŋ] *n.* a show of military strength in order to intimidate.

sabre saw a hand-held power saw for light work, having a narrow blade that moves back and forth at high speed.

sabre–toothed ['seibər ˌtuθt] *adj.* having long, curved upper canine teeth often extending below the lower jaw.

A sabre-toothed tiger, about 175 cm long excluding the tail. Its fangs were about 20 cm long.

sabre–toothed tiger any of a number of extinct tigerlike mammals of the cat family having very long, curved upper canine teeth.

sac [sæk] *n.* a baglike part in an animal or plant, often containing liquids: *the sac of a honeybee.* ⟨< F < L *saccus* sack[1]. See SACK[1].⟩ **–'sacˌlike,** *adj.*
☛ *Hom.* SACK, SACQUE.

Sac [sæk] *or* [sɒk] *n.* Sauk.
☛ *Hom.* SACK, SACQUE [sæk].

SAC *U.S.* Strategic Air Command.

sac•cade [sæ'kɑd] *n.* **1** *Equitation.* the act of reining in a horse quickly with one strong pull on the reins. **2** *Ophthalmology.* a series of quick little movements of the eyes from one point to another, as in reading. ⟨< F *saccade* jerk, jolt⟩

sac•cha•ride ['sækəˌraɪd] *or* ['sækərɪd] *n. Chemistry.* **1** an organic compound containing sugar. **2** any of the carbohydrates; a monosaccharide. **3** an ester of sucrose.

sac•cha•rin ['sækərɪn] *n. Chemistry.* a very sweet substance obtained from coal tar, used as a calorie-free substitute for sugar. Saccharin is very much sweeter than cane sugar. *Formula:* $C_7H_5NO_3S$

sac•cha•rine ['sækərɪn], ['sækə,rin], *or* ['sækə,raɪn] *adj.* **1** of, like, or containing sugar: *a saccharine taste.* **2** too sweet. **3** unpleasantly friendly or agreeable; ingratiating: *a saccharine smile.* ⟨< Med.L *saccharum* sugar < Gk. *sakcharon* ult. < Skt. *çarkarā*, originally, gravel, grit⟩ **—'sac•cha•rine•ly,** *adv.* **—,sac•cha'rin•i•ty,** *n.*

sac•er•do•tal [,sæsər'doutəl] *adj.* of priests or the priesthood; priestly. ⟨< L *sacerdotalis* < *sacerdos, -otis* priest < *sacra* rites + verb stem *dot-* put, set < *dare* give⟩

sac•er•do•tal•ism [,sæsər'doutə,lɪzəm] *n.* **1** the character, system, or practices of the priesthood. **2** a religious doctrine that emphasizes the necessity of having priests as mediators between God and people. **3** excessive respect for or belief in the authority and power of priests. **—,sac•er'do•tal•ist,** *n.*

sa•chem ['seitʃəm] *n.* **1** among Algonquian peoples, a hereditary ruler or chief, especially the chief of a confederacy of tribes. **2** any North American leader or chief of the First Nations. ⟨< Algonquian. Related to SAGAMORE.⟩

Sa•cher torte ['sɑkər]; *German,* ['zaxər] a chocolate cake filled and glazed with apricot preserves and chocolate icing, and often served with whipped cream. Also, **Sachertorte.**

sa•chet [sæ'ʃei] *n.* **1** a small bag or pad containing perfumed powder, used especially for scenting linens and clothes. **2** the powder in such a bag or pad. **3** a small packet of shampoo, etc. ⟨< F *sachet,* dim. of *sac* sack[1]⟩
☛ *Hom.* SASHAY.

sack[1] [sæk] *n., v.* *—n.* **1** a large bag, usually made of coarse cloth, commonly used for holding grain, flour, potatoes, or coal. **2** the amount that a sack can hold. **3** a sack and its contents. **4** *U.S.* any bag or its contents: *a sack of candy.* **5** Also, **sacque. a** a woman's loose-fitting dress. **b** a short, loose-fitting jacket. See SACK COAT. **6** *Slang.* bed: *He was still in the sack at 10.30 a.m.* **7 the sack,** *Informal.* dismissal from a job, etc.: *He got the sack for always coming to work late.*
hit the sack, *Slang.* go to bed: *I'm about ready to hit the sack.*
—v. **1** put into a sack or sacks. **2** *Informal.* discharge from employment; fire. ⟨OE *sacc* < L *saccus* < Gk. *sakkos* < Hebrew *saq*⟩
☛ *Hom.* SAC, SACQUE.
☛ *Syn. n.* **1.** See note at BAG.

sack[2] [sæk] *v., n.* *—v.* plunder or pillage: *The invaders sacked the town.*
—n. the plundering of a captured city. ⟨< F *sac* < Ital. *sacco* < VL *saccare* take by force < Gmc.; influenced by L *saccus* sack[1]⟩ **—'sack•er,** *n.*
☛ *Hom.* SAC, SACQUE.

sack[3] [sæk] *n.* a dry sherry or other strong, light-coloured wine. ⟨< F *(vin) sec* dry (wine) < L *siccus*⟩
☛ *Hom.* SAC, SACQUE.

sack•but ['sæk,bʌt] *n.* **1** a musical wind instrument of the Middle Ages, the ancestor of the trombone. **2** an ancient harplike stringed instrument mentioned in the Bible. ⟨< F by folk etymology from *saquebute* < *saquer* pull + *bouter* push⟩

sack•cloth ['sæk,klɒθ] *n.* **1** coarse cloth for making sacks. **2** a garment of such cloth worn as a sign of mourning or penance.

sack coat a loose-fitting jacket or suit coat having a straight-cut back.

sack•ful ['sæk,fʊl] *n., pl.* **-fuls. 1** enough to fill a sack. **2** *Informal.* a very large amount of anything.

sack•ing ['sækɪŋ] *n., v.* *—n.* coarse cloth, such as burlap, for making sacks, etc.
—v. ppr. of SACK[1] and SACK[2].

sacque [sæk] *n.* See SACK[1] (def. 5). ⟨var. of *sack*[1]⟩
☛ *Hom.* SAC, SACK.

sa•cral[1] ['seikrəl] *or* ['sækrəl] *adj.* of or having to do with religious ceremonies or observances.

sa•cral[2] ['seikrəl] *or* ['sækrəl] *adj. Anatomy.* of or near the sacrum. See SPINAL COLUMN for picture.

sac•ra•ment ['sækrəmənt] *n.* **1** in some Christian churches, any of certain formal religious ceremonies, such as baptism, established or recognized by Jesus, considered especially sacred. **2** Often, **Sacrament,** the Eucharist or the elements of the Eucharist; the consecrated bread and wine or the bread alone. **3** something sacred; a sacred sign, token, or symbol. **4** a solemn promise; oath. ⟨< L *sacramentum,* ult. < *sacer* holy⟩

sac•ra•men•tal [,sækrə'mɛntəl] *adj., n.* *—adj.* **1** of, having to do with, or being a sacrament: *sacramental wine.* **2** especially sacred.
—n. Roman Catholic Church. a ceremony similar to, but not included among, the sacraments. The use of holy water is a sacramental. **—,sac•ra'men•tal•ly,** *adv.* **—,sac•ra•men'tal•i•ty,** *n.*

sac•ra•men•tal•ism [,sækrə'mɛntə,lɪzəm] *n.* **1** belief in the efficacy and necessity of the sacraments as a means to salvation and the state of grace. **2** belief in or emphasis on the importance of sacred rites and objects.

sa•cred ['seikrɪd] *adj.* **1** belonging to or dedicated to God or a god; set apart for worship: *the sacred altar, a sacred grove.* **2** coming from God; worthy of religious reverence; holy: *the sacred Scriptures.* **3** connected with religion; religious: *sacred music.* **4** worthy of the highest respect: *the sacred memory of a dead hero.* **5** dedicated to some person, object, or purpose: *This monument is sacred to the memory of the Unknown Soldier.* **6** that must not be violated or disregarded: *sacred oaths.* ⟨originally pp. of ME *sacre(n)* sanctify < L *sacrare* < *sacer* holy⟩ **—'sa•cred•ly,** *adv.* **—'sa•cred•ness,** *n.*

Sacred College *Roman Catholic Church.* the College of Cardinals.

sacred cow a person or thing so highly regarded as to be beyond criticism. ⟨an allusion to the traditional Hindu veneration of the cow⟩

sac•ri•fice ['sækrə,fəis] *n., v.* **-ficed, -fic•ing.** *—n.* **1** the act of offering to a god. **2** the thing offered: *The ancient Hebrews killed animals on the altars as sacrifices to God.* **3** the act or an instance of giving up or destroying one valued thing for the sake of something else considered more valuable or important: *the sacrifice of one's life for an ideal, the sacrifice of an ideal for commercial gain.* **4** the thing given up or destroyed. **5** a loss from selling something below its value: *He will sell his house at a sacrifice because he needs the money.* **6** *Baseball.* a bunt or fly that helps a runner to advance although the batter is put out.
—v. **1** give or offer to a god. **2** give up, suffer the loss of, or injure or destroy something valuable or important for a particular belief or purpose: *to sacrifice one's life for another person, to sacrifice business for pleasure. We decided to sacrifice part of the garden for a patio.* **3** offer or make a sacrifice. **4** sell at a loss. **5** *Baseball.* help (a runner) to advance by a SACRIFICE (def. 6). ⟨ME < OF < L *sacrificium,* ult. < *sacra* rites + *facere* perform⟩ **—'sac•ri,fic•er,** *n.*

sac•ri•fi•cial [,sækrə'fɪʃəl] *adj.* of, having to do with, involving, or being a sacrifice. **—,sac•ri'fi•cial•ly,** *adv.*

sac•ri•lege ['sækrəlɪdʒ] *n.* an intentional injury to anything sacred; disrespectful treatment of anyone or anything sacred: *Robbing the church is considered a sacrilege.* ⟨ME < OF < L *sacrilegium* temple robbery < *sacrum* sacred object + *legere* pick up⟩

sac•ri•le•gious [,sækrə'lɪdʒəs] *adj.* **1** injurious or insulting to sacred persons or things; involving sacrilege. **2** guilty of sacrilege. **—,sac•ri'le•gious•ly,** *adv.*

sac•ris•tan ['sækrɪstən] *n.* the person in charge of the sacred vessels, vestments, etc., of a Christian church. Also, **sexton.** ⟨ME < Med.L *sacristanus,* ult. < L *sacer* holy. Doublet of SEXTON.⟩

sac•ris•ty ['sækrɪsti] *n., pl.* **-ties.** the place where the sacred vessels, robes, etc., of a Christian church are kept. ⟨< Med.L *sacristia,* ult. < L *sacer* holy⟩

sac•ro•il•i•ac [,sækrou'ɪli,æk] *adj., n. Anatomy.* *—adj.* of, having to do with, or designating the part of the body where the sacrum and ileum meet.
—n. the joint or part of the body where the sacrum and ileum meet.

sac•ro•sanct ['sækrə,sæŋkt] *adj.* **1** most holy or sacred; not to be violated. **2** *Informal.* very much revered; not to be scorned or laughed at: *That old car of hers is sacrosanct to her.* ⟨< L *sacrosanctus,* ult. < *sacer* sacred + *sancire* consecrate⟩

sac•ro•sanc•ti•ty [,sækrou'sæŋktəti] *n.* the fact or state of being sacrosanct; an especial sacredness.

sa•crum ['seikrəm] *or* ['sækrəm] *n., pl.* **-cra** [-krə] or **-crums.** *Anatomy.* the triangular bone at the lower end of the spine, formed by the joining of several vertebrae and serving as the back of the pelvis. See PELVIS and SPINAL COLUMN for pictures. ⟨< L *(os) sacrum* sacred (bone)⟩

sad [sæd] *adj.* **sad•der, sad•dest. 1** feeling or expressing sorrow or grief: *a sad look, a sad child.* **2** characterized by sorrow or grief: *a sad life, a sad occasion.* **3** causing sorrow or grief; distressing: *a sad disappointment.* **4** dark or dull in colour; not cheerful-looking: *He always dressed in sad greys and browns.* **5** *Informal.* shocking; hopeless; pitiable: *This is a sad mess.* ⟨OE *sæd* sated⟩ **—'sad•ly,** *adv.*

☛ *Syn.* **1. Sad,** DEJECTED, DEPRESSED = unhappy and low in spirits. **Sad,** the general word, meaning 'not glad, cheerful, or happy', particularly suggests feeling sorrowful or mournful, but not the cause or degree of the feeling: *Moonlight makes her sad.* **Dejected** suggests casting down of the spirits by some disappointing, discouraging, or frustrating happening or situation: *He is dejected over her leaving.* **Depressed** suggests sinking into a low-spirited, discouraged, or gloomy state as the result of an experience or physical, mental, or other condition: *He is depressed by his failure.*

SAD SEASONAL AFFECTIVE DISORDER.

sad•den ['sædən] *v.* make or become sad: *It saddened him to think that he might never see them again.*

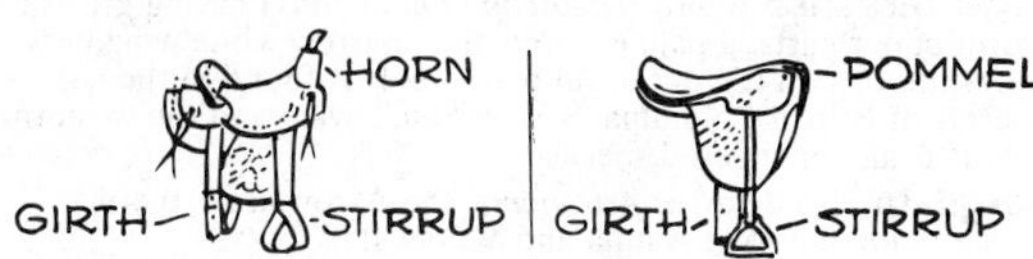

A western saddle An English saddle

sad•dle ['sædəl] *n., v.* **-dled, -dling.** *—n.* **1** a seat, usually padded and leather-covered, for a rider on an animal such as a horse. **2** a seat for a rider on a bicycle, etc. **3** the part of a harness that holds the shafts, or to which a checkrein is attached. See HARNESS for picture. **4** a coloured marking on the back of an animal: *a white dog with a black saddle and black ears.* **5** the part of any animal's back which could bear a saddle. **6** anything shaped or used like a saddle. **7** a ridge between two mountain peaks. **8** a cut of meat consisting of the upper back portion of an animal, including both loins: *a saddle of venison.*
in the saddle, *Informal.* in a position of control.
—v. **1** put a saddle on. **2** burden: *She is saddled with a big house that she does not need or want.* **3** put (something) as a burden (*on*): *They saddled the hardest part of the job on me.* ⟨OE *sadol*⟩

sad•dle•back ['sædəl,bæk] *n.* **1** anything that has a low, concave curve in the back, resembling a saddle. **2** an animal having a marking on its back that resembles a saddle.

sad•dle–backed ['sædəl ,bækt] *adj.* **1** having a low, concave curve in the back, resembling the shape of a saddle, as some horses. **2** *Topography.* having a depression or hollow between two peaks.

sad•dle•bag ['sædəl,bæg] *n.* **1** one of a pair of bags laid over an animal's back behind the saddle. **2** a similar bag hanging over the rear wheel of a bicycle or motorcycle.

sad•dle•bow ['sædəl,bou] *n.* the raised front part of a saddle, having the shape of a curved arch, or bow.

sad•dle•cloth ['sædəl,klɒθ] *n.* a cloth put between an animal's back and the saddle.

saddle horse **1** a horse specially trained and used for riding. **2** the **American saddle horse,** a breed of medium-sized, dark-coloured horse, specially developed for its easy gait, and used as a show horse.

sad•dler ['sædlər] *n.* a person who makes or sells saddles and harness.

sad•dler•y ['sædləri] *n., pl.* **-dler•ies. 1** the work of a saddler. **2** the shop of a saddler. **3** saddles, harness, and other equipment for horses; tack.

saddle shoe a white lace-up shoe, having a saddle of a contrasting colour, usually black, brown, or navy blue.

saddle soap a soap, usually mainly Castile combined with neat's-foot oil, used for cleaning and preserving any leather articles.

saddle stitch a spaced running stitch, often decorative, placed along the edge of a fabric or leather.

sad•dle•tree ['sædəl,tri] *n.* the frame of a saddle.

Sad•du•cee ['sædʒə,si] *or* ['sædjə,si] *n.* a member of a Jewish sect (approximately 1st century B.C. to 1st century A.D.) that accepted the Mosaic law but rejected the oral laws and traditions as well as a belief in an afterlife and the coming of a Messiah. ⟨OE *sadducēas*, pl. < LL < LGk. *Saddoukaios* < Hebrew *Tsaddūq* Zadok, a Hebrew high priest in the time of David⟩

sade ['sɑdə] *n.* the twentieth letter of the Hebrew alphabet. See table of alphabets in the Appendix.

sa•dhu ['sɑdu] *n.* a Hindu holy man. ⟨< Skt. *sadhu* straight⟩

sad•i•ron ['sæd,aɪərn] *n.* a heavy, solid flatiron that is pointed at both ends, used for ironing clothes. ⟨< *sad*, in obs. or dial. sense of 'firm, solid' + *iron*⟩

sad•ism ['sædɪzəm] *or* ['seidɪzəm] *n. Psychiatry.* **1** delight in cruelty; getting pleasure from inflicting physical or mental pain on another person or on an animal. **2** a form of sexual perversion in which sexual gratification is obtained by inflicting pain on one's partner. Compare MASOCHISM. ⟨< F; from Marquis Donatien de *Sade* (1740-1814), who wrote of this condition⟩

sad•ist ['sædɪst] *or* ['seidɪst] *n.* one who practises sadism.

sa•dis•tic [sə'dɪstɪk] *adj.* of, having to do with, or showing sadism: *a sadistic streak, a sadistic act.* **—sa'dis•ti•cal•ly,** *adv.*

sad•ness ['sædnɪs] *n.* sorrow; grief.

sad•o•mas•o•chism [,sædou'mæsə,kɪzəm] *or* [,seidou'mæsə,kɪzəm] *n.* the combination of sadism and masochism in a single personality or in a relationship between persons.

sad•o•mas•o•chist [,sædou'mæsəkɪst] *or* [,seidou'mæsəkɪst] *n.* a person who is given to sadomasochism.

sad•o•mas•o•chis•tic [,sædou,mæsə'kɪstɪk] *or* [,seidou,mæsə'kɪstɪk] *adj.* of, having to do with, or exhibiting sadomasochism: *a sadomasochistic relationship.*

SAE **1** self-addressed envelope. **2** stamped addressed envelope.

sa•fa•ri [sə'fɑri] *n., pl.* **-ris;** *adj. —n.* **1** a journey or hunting expedition, especially in E Africa. **2** any long trip or expedition. *—adj.* of or having to do with a style of clothing similar to that worn on safari, especially, designating a belted jacket with a full skirt and pairs of large pockets above and below the belt: *a safari jacket*. ⟨< Arabic⟩

safe [seif] *adj.* **saf•er, saf•est;** *n. —adj.* **1** free from harm or danger; providing freedom from harm or danger: *Keep money in a safe place.* **2** not harmed: *He returned from war safe and sound.* **3** out of danger; secure: *We feel safe with the dog in the house.* **4** put beyond power of doing harm: *a criminal safe in prison.* **5** cautious; careful; risk-free: *a safe guess, a safe move.* **6** that can be depended on: *a safe guide.* **7** *Baseball.* (of a batter or base runner) reaching a base or home plate without being out.
—n. **1** a box or place that can be locked, used for keeping things safe; especially, a heavy steel or iron chest or room for money, jewels, documents, etc. **2** any container for keeping food: *a meat safe.* **3** *Slang.* a condom. ⟨ME < OF *sauf* < L *salvus*⟩ **—'safe•ly,** *adv.* **—'safe•ness,** *n.*

☛ *Syn. adj.* **1. Safe,** SECURE = free from danger. Although often used interchangeably, **safe** emphasizes being not exposed to danger, harm, or risk: *The children are safe in their own yard.* **Secure** emphasizes being protected or guarded against loss, attack, injury, or other anticipated or feared danger or harm: *Children feel secure with their parents.*

safe–con•duct or **safe conduct** ['seif 'kɒndʌkt] *n.* **1** the privilege of passing safely through a region, especially in time of war. **2** a paper granting this privilege. **3** the act of escorting safely.

safe•crack•er ['seif,krækər] *n.* a thief who specializes in safecracking.

safe•crack•ing ['seif,krækɪŋ] *n.* the act or practice of breaking open safes and stealing the contents.

safe–de•pos•it box ['seif dɪ'pɒzɪt] *Esp. U.S.* SAFETY DEPOSIT BOX.

safe•guard ['seif,gɑrd] *v., n. —v.* **1** keep safe; guard against hurt or danger; protect: *Pure food laws safeguard our health.* **2** guard; convoy.
—n. **1** a protection; defence: *Keeping clean is a safeguard against disease.* **2** a guard; convoy. ⟨ME < OF *sauvegarde* < *sauve*, fem. of *sauf* safe (< L *salvus*) + *garde* guard < Gmc.⟩

safe house a house or apartment in a building whose innocuous appearance makes it a safe and convenient locale for intelligence organizations to hold meetings, safeguard agents, etc.

safe•keep•ing ['seif'kipɪŋ] *n.* keeping safe; protection; care.

safe sex sexual intercourse using a condom and other precautions to guard against pregnancy and STDs, such as AIDS.

safe•ty ['seifti] *n., pl.* **-ties. 1** the quality or state of being safe; freedom from harm or danger: *They did not stop running until they had reached safety.* **2** a device on a firearm, machine, etc., designed to prevent injury through accidental or careless operation. **3** (*adjl.*) designed to give extra safety; designed to protect against harm through accident or misuse: *a safety lamp, safety glass, a safety belt.* **4** *Football.* SAFETY TOUCH. **5** *Slang.* a condom.

safety belt **1** SEAT BELT. **2** a strap used by window cleaners, loggers, linemen, etc. to prevent falling.

safety deposit box a box in the vault of a bank, etc., for the storage of valuables such as original documents, bonds, jewellery, etc.

safety glass glass that resists shattering, made of two or more layers of glass joined together by a layer of transparent plastic.

safety island a marked area or a platform built in the middle of a thoroughfare for the convenience of pedestrians boarding and getting off buses, streetcars, etc.

safety lamp **1** a miner's lamp in which the flame is kept from setting fire to explosive gases by a piece of wire gauze. **2** an electric lamp similarly protected.

safety match a match that will ignite only when struck on a specially prepared surface.

safety pin a pin bent back on itself to form a spring, and having a guard that covers the point in order to prevent injury or accidental unfastening.

safety razor a razor having a replaceable blade that is protected and angled to reduce the risk of cutting the skin.

safety touch *Cdn. Football.* the act of putting a ball down behind one's own goal line after a teammate has made it go there, thus conceding two points to the opposing team.

safety valve **1** a valve in a steam boiler, etc., that opens and lets steam or fluid escape when the pressure becomes too great. **2** something that helps a person get rid of anger, nervousness, etc. in a harmless way: *She uses aerobics as a safety valve to relieve stress.*

saf•flow•er ['sæ,flaʊər] *n.* **1** an annual herb (*Carthamus tinctorius*) of the composite family having large red or orange flower heads yielding a red dye or a medicinal drug, and seeds that are rich in oil. **2** a red dye prepared from the flower heads. ⟨< *saf(fron)* + *flower*⟩

safflower oil an edible oil obtained from safflower seeds.

saf•fron ['sæfrən] *n., adj.* —*n.* **1** a purple-flowered autumn crocus (*Crocus sativus*) native to the Old World. **2** the dried orange-coloured stigmas of this crocus, used to flavour and colour rice, candy, drinks, etc. **3** a medium orange or orange yellow. Also, **saffron yellow.**
—*adj.* medium orange or orange yellow. ⟨< F *safran,* ult. < Arabic *za'faran*⟩

sag [sæg] *v.* **sagged, sag•ging;** *n.* —*v.* **1** sink under weight or pressure; bend down in the middle. **2** hang down unevenly: *Your dress sags in the back.* **3** become less firm or elastic; yield through weakness, weariness, or lack of effort; droop; sink: *The exhausted hikers sagged to the ground.* **4** decline in sales or price. **5** of a ship, drift from its course.
—*n.* **1** the act, state, or degree of sagging. **2** the place where anything sags. ⟨Cf. Du. *zakken* sink⟩

sa•ga ['sɑgə] *or* ['sægə] *n.* **1** a type of prose story of heroic deeds written in Old Norse in the Middle Ages. **2** any extended story of adventure or heroic deeds. **3** *Informal.* a sequence of many events spanning a relatively long period and thought of as long or complicated (*sometimes used facetiously*): *She delights in the ongoing saga of her cousin's marital problems.* ⟨< Scand. Akin to SAW³.⟩

sa•ga•cious [sə'geiʃəs] *adj.* **1** wise in a keen, practical, far-sighted way; shrewd. **2** resulting from or showing wisdom or sagacity. ⟨< L *sagax, acis*⟩ **—sa'ga•cious•ly,** *adv.* **—sa'ga•cious•ness,** *n.*
☛ *Syn.* **1.** See note at SHREWD.

sa•gac•i•ty [sə'gæsɪti] *n., pl.* **-ties.** keen, sound judgment; mental acuteness; shrewdness.

sag•a•more ['sægə,mɔr] *n.* **1** among Algonquian peoples, an elected ruler or chief of a tribe, especially one subordinate to a sachem. **2** sachem. ⟨earlier *sagamo* < Algonquian. Related to SACHEM.⟩

sage¹ [seidʒ] *adj.* **sag•er, sag•est;** *n.* —*adj.* **1** wise: *a sage adviser.* **2** showing wisdom or good judgment: *a sage reply.* **3** *Archaic or poetic.* solemn-faced.
—*n.* a very wise person. ⟨ME < OF *sage,* ult. < L *sapere* be wise⟩ **—'sage•ly,** *adv.* **—'sage•ness,** *n.*
☛ *Syn. adj.* **1, 2.** See note at WISE¹.

sage² [seidʒ] *n.* **1** any of a genus (*Salvia*) of plants of the mint family; especially, **scarlet sage** (*S. splendens*), grown for its brilliant red flowers, and **garden sage** (*S. officinalis*), grown for its aromatic leaves. **2** the dried leaves of the garden sage, used mainly as a seasoning for meats and vegetables. **3** sagebrush. ⟨ME < OF *sauge* < L *salvia.* Doublet of SALVIA.⟩

sage•brush ['seidʒ,brʌʃ] *n.* any of several shrubs (genus *Artemisia*) of the composite family native to the dry plains of W North America. Common sagebrush (*A. tridentata*) has greyish green leaves and smells like sage.

sage grouse a very large grouse (*Centrocercus urophasianus*) common on the plains of W North America. In common with other members of the grouse family, the males perform an elaborate courtship dance.

sage hen **1** SAGE GROUSE. **2** a female sage grouse.

sage thrasher a bird (*Oreoscoptes montanus*) having greyish brown upper parts, a pale eyebrow line, narrow white wing bars, and white tips on the outer tail feathers. It is found in the interior of British Columbia, SW Saskatchewan, and the western U.S. It is an endangered species.

Sa•git•ta [sə'dʒɪtə] *n. Astronomy.* the Arrow, a northern constellation between Aquila and Vulpecula.

sag•it•tal ['sædʒɪtəl] *adj.* **1** *Anatomy.* **a** of or having to do with the suture between the two parietal bones of the skull. **b** of a venous canal within the skull parallel to this suture. **c** of or in the longitudinal median plane of this suture, thought of as dividing the body into right and left halves. **2** resembling an arrow or arrowhead. ⟨< L *sagitta* arrow⟩

Sag•it•tar•i•an [,sædʒə'tɛriən] *n. Astrology.* a person born under the sign of Sagittarius.

Sag•it•tar•i•us [,sædʒə'tɛriəs] *n.* **1** *Astronomy.* the Archer, a southern constellation thought of as having the shape of a centaur drawing a bow. **2** *Astrology.* **a** the ninth sign of the zodiac. The sun enters Sagittarius about November 23. See ZODIAC for picture. **b** a person born under this sign. ⟨< L *Sagittarius,* literally, the Archer < *sagitta* arrow⟩

sag•it•tate ['sædʒə,teit] *adj.* especially of a leaf, shaped like an arrowhead. See LEAF for picture. ⟨< NL *sagittatus* < L *sagitta* arrow⟩

sa•go ['seigou] *n., pl.* **-goes.** a powdered or granulated starch prepared from the pith of a sago palm, used in making puddings and as a stiffening agent for textiles. ⟨< Malay *sagu*⟩

sago palm **1** any of various tropical Asian palms (especially of genera *Metroxylon* and *Arenga*) that yield the starch sago. **2** any of several cycads that yield sago, especially *Cycas revoluta,* also cultivated as a conservatory plant.

Sa•gue•nay ['sægə,nei] *or* [,sægə'nei] *n.* **1** a river in central Québec, running 200 km south from Lac St. Jean to the St. Lawrence River. **2** the area from 48°N to 51°N in Québec, from the St. Lawrence River to the heights of land constituting the watershed between Hudson Bay and the St. Lawrence River.

Sa•hap•tian [sə'hæpʃən] *n.* a language family of the First Nations, consisting of Sahaptin and Nez Percé. ⟨< Interior Salish *s'aptnx* Nez Percé⟩

Sa•hap•tin [sə'hæptɪn] *n.* **1** a people of the First Nations living in Washington, Oregon, and Idaho. **2** the language of these people.

Sa•har•an [sə'hærən], [sə'hɛrən], *or* [sə'hɑrən] *adj., n.* —*adj.* of or having to do with the Sahara, a desert in N Africa, or its inhabitants.
—*n.* a native or inhabitant of the Sahara Desert.

sa•hib ['sɑb] *or* ['sɑhɪb], ['sɑib] *or* ['sɑhib] *n.* sir; master (*used as a title of respect by Indians in colonial India when speaking to or of a European man*). ⟨< Hind. < Arabic *çāḥib* lord⟩

said [sɛd] *v., adj.* —*v.* pt. and pp. of SAY.
—*adj.* named or mentioned before: *the said witness.*

sail [seil] *n., pl.* **sails** or (def. 3) **sail;** *v.* —*n.* **1** a piece of cloth spread to the wind to make a vessel move through the water. **2** the sails of a ship collectively. **3** a ship: *a fleet numbering thirty sail.* **4** something like a sail, such as the part of an arm of a windmill that catches the wind. **5** a trip on a boat with sails: *Let's go for a sail.*
in sail, in a ship with sails.
make sail, *Nautical.* **a** spread out the sails of a ship. **b** begin a trip by water.
set sail, begin a trip by water.
take in sail, a lower or lessen the sails of a ship. **b** *Informal.* lessen one's hopes, ambitions, etc.
under sail, moving with the sails spread out.
—*v.* **1** travel on water by the action of wind on sails. **2** travel on a ship of any kind: *She is sailing to Europe on the Queen Elizabeth*

II. **3** move smoothly and majestically like a ship with sails: *The hawk sailed by. Mrs. Grand sailed into the room.* **4** to sail upon, over, or through: *to sail the seas.* **5** manage or navigate (a ship or boat): *They sailed the yacht right around the Island. The girls are learning to sail.* **6** begin a trip by water: *We sail at 2 p.m.* **7** move swiftly: *The football sailed over the goal post. He sailed right through the red light.*
sail into, *Slang.* **a** attack; beat. **b** criticize; scold. ⟨OE *segl*⟩
☛ *Hom.* SALE.

sail•board ['seil,bɔrd] *n.* a long, narrow board, usually of plastic, with provision for a sail, used in sailboarding.

sail•board•ing ['seil,bɔrdɪŋ] *n.* windsurfing.

sail•boat ['seil,bout] *n.* a boat that is moved by a sail or sails. See SLOOP for picture.

sail•cloth ['seil,klɒθ] *n.* **1** canvas or other material used for making sails. **2** a similar material used in making clothes, curtains, etc.

sail•er ['seilər] *n.* a ship described in terms of its sailing power: *the best sailer in the fleet, a fast sailer.*
☛ *Hom.* SAILOR.

sail•fish ['seil,fɪʃ] *n., pl.* **-fish** or **-fishes.** any of a genus (*Istiophorus*) of large blue-and-silver fishes of the open sea, found in tropical and temperate waters, having an elongated, spearlike upper jaw and a large, high, sail-like dorsal fin. Sailfish belong to the same family (Istiophoridae) as the marlins.

sail•ing ['seilɪŋ] *n., adj., v.* —*n.* **1** the act of a person or thing that sails. **2** the art or sport of navigating a sailboat.
—*adj.* of or having to do with ships or shipping.
—*v.* ppr. of SAIL.

sail•or ['seilər] *n.* **1** a member of the crew of a ship or boat, especially one who is not an officer. **2** a person serving in the navy, especially one below the rank of petty officer. **3** a person whose hobby or pastime is sailing: *She's a keen sailor.* **4** any person who travels by water, especially with reference to his or her liability to seasickness: *I'm a bad sailor.* **5** SAILOR HAT. **6** SAILOR SUIT. **7** SAILOR COLLAR. **—'sail•or,like,** *adj.*
☛ *Hom.* SAILER.

sailor collar a large, flat collar resembling the collar of a traditional sailor's blouse, having squared corners at the back and tapering to a point at the bottom of a V neck at the front.

sailor hat a flat-crowned hat with a wide brim slightly turned up all around.

sail•or•ly ['seilərli] *adj.* like or suitable for a sailor.

sailor suit a child's suit resembling the traditional middy blouse and pants worn by sailors. Sailor suits are usually navy blue trimmed with white, or vice versa.

sail•past ['seil,pæst] *n.* a procession of boats whose captains salute the commodore of a yacht club, or a dignitary in whose honour the event is held.

sail•plane ['seil,plein] *n., v.* **-planed, -plan•ing.** —*n.* a light glider that can stay aloft for a long time supported by air currents.
—*v.* fly such a glider.

saint [seint] *n., v., adj.* —*n.* **1** a very holy person. **2** a person who has died and gone to heaven. **3** *Roman Catholic Church.* a person who has been canonized. **4** a person who is very humble, patient, etc., like a saint. **5** angel. **6 Saint,** Mormon. **7** (*adjl.*) **Saint,** holy or sacred (*used as a title before the name of a canonized person or an archangel*): *Saint Francis, St. Hilda. Abbrev.*: St. or S.; *pl.* Sts. or SS. **8** according to the New Testament, any Christian.
—*v.* **1** make a saint of; canonize. **2** call or consider a saint.
—*adj.* holy; sacred. ⟨ME < OF < L *sanctus* consecrated⟩
—'saint,like, *adj.*
☛ *Usage.* **Saint.** Entries commonly written in the abbreviated form, such as *St. Elmo's fire* and *St.-John's-wort,* will be found in their alphabetical places after **St.**

Saint Ag•nes' Eve ['ægnɪs] the night of January 20, when a maiden was supposed to see a vision of her future husband if she performed certain ceremonies.

Saint An•drew's cross ['ændruz] See ST. ANDREW'S CROSS.

Saint An•tho•ny's cross ['ænθəniz] *or* ['æntəniz] a tau or T-shaped cross.

Saint Anthony's fire *Pathology.* See ST. ANTHONY'S FIRE.

Saint Ber•nard [bər'nɑrd] a breed of big, powerful working dog, often tan and white, having a large head. These intelligent dogs were first bred by the monks of the St. Bernard hospice in the Alps to rescue travellers lost in the snow.

A Saint Bernard dog

saint•ed ['seintɪd] *adj., v.* —*adj.* **1** declared to be a saint. **2** thought of as a saint; gone to heaven. **3** sacred; very holy. **4** saintly: *my sainted mother.*
—*v.* pt. and pp. of SAINT.

Saint Geor•ge's Day ['dʒɔrdʒɪz] April 23rd, celebrated in honour of the patron saint of England.

saint•hood ['seint,hʊd] *n.* **1** the character or status of a saint. **2** saints as a group.

Saint–Jean Bap•tiste Society [sɛ̃ʒɑ̃ba'tist] *Cdn.* an organization in the Province of Québec that is dedicated to the preservation and fostering of French culture in Canada. St. Jean Baptiste Day (June 24) is a holiday in Québec. ⟨< *Saint Jean Baptiste* St. John the Baptist, patron saint of Québec⟩

Saint Kitts and Ne•vis ['kɪts ən 'nɛvɪs] an island country in the West Indies.

Saint Lu•cia ['luʃə] *or* ['lusiə] an island country in the West Indies.

saint•ly ['seintli] *adj.* **-li•er, -li•est.** like a saint; very holy or very good. **—'saint•li•ness,** *n.*

Saint Mar•tin's summer ['mɑrtənz] *Brit.* a spell of warm weather in late fall; Indian summer. ⟨so called because it occurs around St. Martin's feast day, November 11th⟩

Saint Nicholas **1** the patron saint of Russia and Greece, and of children, sailors, travellers, etc. Nicholas was a bishop in Asia Minor in the 4th century A.D. **2** SANTA CLAUS.

Saint Pat•rick's Day ['pætrɪks] March 17th, the feast of St. Patrick, celebrated by the Irish (and now by others) in honour of the patron saint of Ireland.

saint•ship ['seintʃɪp] *n.* sainthood.

Saint Valentine's Day February 14th, the feast of St. Valentine, a martyr of the 3rd century A.D., now a day to send cards and gifts to one's lover, friends, schoolmates, etc.

Saint Vin•cent ['vɪnsənt] an island country in the West Indies, properly called **Saint Vincent and the Grenadines.**

Saint Vi•tus's dance ['vəitəsɪz] See ST. VITUS'S DANCE.

saith [sɛθ] *v. Archaic.* 3rd pers. sing., present tense, of SAY. *She saith* means *she says.*

saj•ja•da [sə'dʒɑdə] *n.* in Islam, the prayer rug upon which worshippers kneel and bow during daily prayers. ⟨< Arabic⟩

sake¹ [seik] *n.* **1** benefit; account; interest: *Don't go to any trouble just for my sake. For your own sake, drive carefully.* **2** purpose; aim: *He moved to the country for the sake of peace and quiet. For the sake of argument, let us suppose that the Tories win the election.*
for goodness' (or **Pete's, heaven's, gosh,** etc.) **sake** or **sakes,** *Informal.* an exclamation of impatience, annoyance, surprise, etc.
for old times' sake, in memory of former days. ⟨OE *sacu* cause at law⟩

sa•ke² ['sɑki] *or* ['sæki] *n.* a Japanese fermented alcoholic drink made from rice. Also, **saki.** ⟨< Japanese⟩

sal [sæl] *n. Pharmacology.* SALT (def. 2): *sal volatile.* ⟨< L⟩

sa•laam [sə'lɑm] *n., v.* —*n.* **1** a salutation or greeting used especially among Muslims. The full form is **salaam aleikum.** **2** a very low bow, made with the palm of the right hand placed on the forehead. **3** any ceremonial or respectful greeting or bow.
—*v.* **1** greet with a salaam. **2** make a salaam. ⟨< Arabic *salām* peace⟩

sal•a•ble ['seiləbəl] *adj.* See SALEABLE. **—,sal•a'bil•i•ty,** *n.*

sa•la•cious [sə'leiʃəs] *adj.* **1** lustful; lecherous. **2** of writings, pictures, etc., erotic or lewd; tending to arouse sexual desire. ⟨< L *salax, -acis*⟩ **—sa'la•cious•ly,** *adj.* **—sa'la•cious•ness,** *n.*

sa•lac•i•ty [sə'læsəti] *n.* a salacious quality.

sal•ad ['sæləd] *n.* **1** raw, leafy, green vegetables, such as lettuce, spinach, endive, etc., often mixed with other raw vegetables such as tomatoes, celery, sweet peppers, mushrooms, etc., and served with a dressing. **2** a similar cold dish made with cooked meat, fish, vegetables, eggs, potatoes, or fruits, etc., served with a dressing. **3** any leafy, green vegetable eaten raw, especially lettuce. ⟨ME < OF < Provençal *salada*, ult. < L *sal* salt⟩

salad bar a selection of salad items, arranged as a buffet, from which the customer can choose.

salad days days of youthful inexperience.

salad dressing a sauce for use in or on a salad.

salad greens leafy green vegetables, such as lettuce or watercress, eaten raw in a salad.

sa•lal [sə'læl] *n. Cdn.* **1** a small evergreen shrub (*Gaultheria shallon*) native to the Pacific coast, having glossy leaves, showy white flowers, and edible, purplish berries. Salal is closely related to wintergreen. **2** the berry of this shrub. ⟨< Chinook Jargon *(klkwu)-shala*⟩

A spotted salamander—about 15 cm long including the tail

sal•a•man•der ['sælə,mændər] *n.* **1** any of an order (Urodela, also called Caudata) of tailed amphibians resembling lizards but having moist, scaleless skin and often weak or rudimentary legs, and having an aquatic larval stage during which they breathe by gills; especially, any of several species of the family Salamandridae, such as the European **fire salamander** (*Salamandra salamandra*). **2** *Mythology and legend.* a reptile able to live in fire. **3** in the ancient Greek theory of the four elements, the spirit that inhabited fire. **4** any of various items used in connection with fire, such as: **a** a poker. **b** a portable stove or oven. **c** a metal plate with a handle, heated so as to brown pastry or casseroles. ⟨ME < OF < L < Gk. *salamandra*⟩

sa•la•mi [sə'lɑmi] *n.* a highly seasoned sausage of pork and beef or beef alone, often flavoured with garlic. Salami may be eaten dried or fresh. ⟨< Ital. *salami*, pl. of *salame*, ult. < L *sal* salt⟩

sal ammoniac AMMONIUM CHLORIDE.

sal•a•ried ['sælərid] *adj.* **1** receiving a salary. **2** of a position, giving a salary.

sal•a•ry ['sæləri] *n., pl.* **-ries.** fixed pay for regular work, usually paid every two weeks or monthly. ⟨ME < AF < L *salarium* soldier's allowance for salt < *sal* salt⟩

☛ *Syn.* **Salary,** WAGE = fixed amount paid for regular work. **Salary** is used more for professional and office work, and for pay spoken of as covering a longer period of time: *The young engineer was paid a salary of $40 000.* **Wage** is used more for manual and physical work, and for pay spoken of as covering an hour, day, or week: *The minimum wage was fixed at $7.50 an hour.*

sa•lat [sə'lɑt] *n.* in Islam, ritual prayer offered five times daily to Allah. ⟨< Arabic⟩

sal•chow ['sɑlkaʊ] *n. Figure skating.* a jump that includes a full turn in mid-air. ⟨< Ulrich *Salchow*, a Swedish skating champion⟩

sale [seil] *n.* **1** the act of selling; exchange of goods or services for money or, sometimes, other material compensation: *Did he make the sale? That was the last sale of the day.* **2 sales,** *pl.* the amount sold; gross receipts: *Today's sales were larger than yesterday's.* **3** the chance to sell; demand; market. **4** a selling at lower prices than usual: *This store is having a sale on suits.* **5** auction. **6 sales,** the work involved in selling (*used with a singular verb*): *Her first job was in sales.*
for sale, to be sold; available for buying: *There are several nice houses for sale in this area.*
on sale, a offered at a reduced price: *All the winter boots are on sale now.* **b** for sale: *Tickets for the concert will be on sale here on Monday.* ⟨OE *sala*⟩

☛ *Hom.* SAIL.

sale•a•ble ['seiləbəl] *adj.* easily sold; fit to be sold. **—,sale•a'bil•i•ty,** *n.*

sal•e•ra•tus [,sælə'reitəs] *n.* sodium bicarbonate or potassium bicarbonate used as a leavening agent in cooking. ⟨var. of L *sal aeratus* airy salt⟩

sales•clerk ['seilz,klɜrk] *n.* a person whose work is selling goods in a store.

sales•man ['seilzmən] *n., pl.* **-men. 1** a man whose work is selling goods in a store; salesclerk. **2** a sales representative.

sales•man•ship ['seilzmən,ʃɪp] *n.* the skill or technique of selling.

sales•peo•ple ['seilz,pipəl] *n.pl.* salespersons.

sales•per•son ['seilz,pɜrsən] *n.* **1** a salesclerk. **2** a sales representative.

sales representative a person employed as representative of a company to sell its goods or services in a certain territory.

sales•room ['seilz,rum] *or* ['seilz,rʊm] *n.* a room where things are sold or shown for sale.

sales talk 1 argument intended to persuade someone to buy something. **2** any argument intended to persuade.

sales tax a tax on the amount received for articles sold, collected from the consumer at the time of purchase.

sales•wom•an ['seilz,wʊmən] *n., pl.* **-wom•en** [-,wɪmɪn]. **1** a woman whose work is selling goods in a store; salesclerk. **2** a sales representative.

sal•i•cin ['sæləsɪn] *n. Pharmacology.* a bitter, white crystalline compound of glucose, obtained from the bark of various willows and poplars. It is used in medicine as a tonic and to reduce fever. *Formula*: $C_{13}H_{18}O_7$ ⟨< F *salicine* < L *salix, salicis* willow⟩

Sal•ic law ['sælɪk] *or* ['seilɪk] formerly, **1** the code of laws of the Franks and other Germanic tribes, especially the provision that prevented women from inheriting land. **2** in France and Spain, a law excluding females from succession to the crown. ⟨< Med.L *Salicus* < LL *Salii* the Salian Franks, a tribe of Franks who dwelt in the regions of the Rhine near the North Sea⟩

sa•lic•y•late [sə'lɪsəlɪt] *or* [sə'lɪsə,leit], [,sælə'sɪlɪt] *or* [,sælə'sɪleit] *n. Chemistry.* a salt or ester of salicylic acid.

sal•i•cyl•ic [,sælə'sɪlɪk] *adj. Chemistry.* of or having to do with salicin.

salicylic acid *Chemistry. Pharmacology.* a white, crystalline compound used as a mild antiseptic and preservative, and as a medicine for rheumatism, gout, etc. Aspirin is a common preparation of salicylic acid. *Formula*: $C_7H_6O_3$ ⟨< *salicin*⟩

sa•li•ence ['seiliəns] *or* ['seiljəns] *n.* **1** the quality or state of being salient. **2** a striking part or feature. Also, **saliency.**

sa•li•ent ['seiliənt] *or* ['seiljənt] *adj., n.* —*adj.* **1** standing out; easily seen or noticed; prominent; striking: *the salient features in a landscape, the salient points in a speech.* **2** pointing outward; projecting: *a salient angle.* **3** *Heraldry.* standing with forepaws raised as if jumping (*used after the noun*): *a lion salient.*
—*n.* **1** a salient angle or part. **2** the part of a fort or line of trenches that projects toward the enemy. ⟨< L *saliens, -entis*, ppr. of *salire* leap⟩ **—'sa•li•ent•ly,** *adv.*

sa•li•en•tian [,seili'ɛnʃiən] *adj.* of or having to do with the superorder Salientia, consisting of the frogs and toads and some extinct species.

sa•lif•er•ous [sə'lɪfərəs] *adj.* containing or producing salt.

sa•line ['seilaɪn] *or* ['seilin] *adj., n.* —*adj.* **1** of salt; like salt; salty. **2** containing common salt or any other salts.
—*n.* **1** a salt spring, well, lick, or marsh. **2** a substance containing common salt or any other salts. ⟨< L *sal* salt⟩

sa•lin•i•ty [sə'lɪnəti] *n.* saltiness; saline quality.

Salis•bur•y steak ['sɒlzbəri] chopped beef shaped before cooking into a patty about twice the size of a hamburger, usually served with a gravy.

Sa•lish ['seilɪʃ] *n., adj.* —*n.* **1** a member of a people of the First Nations of British Columbia and the NW United States. A division is made between the **Coast Salish** and the **Interior Salish,** and in the U.S., the **Straits Salish. 2** any of the group of related languages spoken by the Salish.
—*adj.* of or having to do with the Salish: *the Salish people.*

Sa•lish•an ['seilɪʃən] *adj., n.* —*adj.* of or having to do with the Salish First Nations peoples or their languages.
—*n.* Salish.

sa•li•va [sə'laɪvə] *n.* the liquid that the salivary glands secrete into the mouth to keep it moist, aid in chewing, and start digestion. ⟨< L⟩

sal•i•var•y ['sælə,vɛri] *adj.* of or producing saliva.

salivary gland *Anatomy.* any of various glands that secrete saliva into the mouth. The salivary glands of human beings and most other vertebrates are digestive glands that secrete saliva containing enzymes, salts, albumin, etc.

sal•i•vate ['sælə,veit] *v.* **-vat•ed, -vat•ing. 1** secrete saliva, especially an excessive amount. **2** produce an excessive flow of saliva in. ⟨< L *salivare* < *saliva* saliva⟩

sal•i•va•tion [ˌsælə'veiʃən] *n.* **1** the secretion of saliva. **2** an abnormally large flow of saliva.

sal•let ['sælɪt] *n.* a light, rounded medieval helmet, with or without a visor. ⟨< F < Ital. < L *caelata*, fem. pp. of *caelare* chisel < *caelum* chisel⟩

sal•low[1] ['sælou] *adj., v. —adj.* of or having a pallid, yellowish complexion: *a sallow face. He still looks sallow after his illness.*
—v. make or become yellow. ⟨OE *salo*⟩ **—'sal•low•ness,** *n.*

sal•low[2] ['sælou] *n.* **1** willow. **2** a willow twig. ⟨OE *sealh*⟩

sal•low•ish ['sælouɪʃ] *adj.* somewhat sallow.

sal•ly ['sæli] *n., pl.* **-lies;** *v.* **-lied, -ly•ing.** *—n.* **1** a sudden attack on an enemy made from a defensive position; sortie. **2** a sudden rushing forth. **3** a going forth; trip; excursion. **4** a sudden start into activity. **5** an outburst. **6** a witty remark.
—v. (*used with* **out** *or* **forth**) **1** go suddenly from a defensive position to attack an enemy. **2** rush forth suddenly. **3** set out briskly. **4** go on an excursion or trip. **5** of things, issue forth. ⟨< F *saillie*, ult. < L *salire* leap⟩

Sal•ly Ann ['sæli 'æn] *Informal.* SALVATION ARMY.

Sal•ly Lunn ['sæli 'lʌn] a slightly sweetened tea cake, served hot with butter. ⟨after *Sally Lunn*, a woman who sold such cakes in Bath, England, at the end of the 18c.⟩

sal•ma•gun•di [ˌsælmə'gʌndi] *n.* **1** a dish of chopped meat, anchovies, eggs, onions, oil, etc. **2** any mixture or medley of things, qualities, etc. ⟨< F *salmigondis*, ult. < Ital. *salami conditi* pickled sausages⟩

sal•mi ['sælmi] *n.* a highly seasoned stew, especially of game. ⟨< F *salmi*, short for *salmigondis* salmagundi⟩

salm•on ['sæmən] *n., pl.* **-on** or **-ons;** *adj. —n.* **1** any of various saltwater and freshwater fishes (family Salmonidae) that are highly prized as food and game fish, especially the Atlantic salmon or any species of Pacific salmon. **2** a yellowish pink.
—adj. having the colour yellowish pink. ⟨ME *samon* < OF < L *salmo, -onis*, probably 'leaper' < *salire* leap⟩

sal•mon•ber•ry ['sæmən,bɛri] *n., pl.* **-ries. 1** a showy shrub (*Rubus spectabilis*) of the Pacific coast having red flowers and edible, salmon-coloured, raspberrylike fruit. **2** the fruit of the salmonberry.

sal•mo•nel•la [ˌsælmə'nɛlə] *or* [ˌsæmə'nɛlə] *n., pl.* **-lae** [-laɪ] *or* [-li] or **las.** *Bacteriology.* any of various bacteria causing food poisoning, typhoid, and other infectious diseases. ⟨< NL *Salmonella*, the genus name < Daniel E. *Salmon* (1850-1914), American pathologist⟩

sal•mon•el•lo•sis [ˌsælmənɛ'lousɪs] *n. Pathology.* a type of food poisoning caused by eating food contaminated with salmonella, characterized by the sudden onset of fever, vomiting, diarrhea, and intestinal pain.

sal•mo•nid ['sælmənɪd] *adj., n. —adj.* belonging to the family Salmonidae.
—n. a salmonid fish, such as a salmon, char, trout, or whitefish.

salm•o•noid ['sæmə,nɔɪd] *or* ['sælmə,nɔɪd] *adj., n. —adj.* of or belonging to a suborder (Salmonidea) of fishes including the salmon and trout.
—n. a salmonoid fish.

salmon pink yellowish pink.

salmon trout LAKE TROUT.

sa•lon [sə'lɒn] *or* ['sælɒn]; *French,* [sa'lɔ̃] *n., pl.* **-lons. 1** a large room for receiving or entertaining guests. **2** an assembly of guests in such a room. **3** a gathering of artists, writers, and other interested people in the home of a prominent person. **4** a place used to exhibit works of art. **5** an exhibition of works of art. **6** a business establishment that provides services such as hairdressing and manicuring. ⟨< F < Ital. *salone* < *sala* hall < Gmc.⟩

sa•loon [sə'lun] *n.* **1** a place where alcoholic drinks are sold and drunk; bar. **2** a large room for general or public use: *Concerts are often held in the saloon of a ship. The ship's passengers ate in the dining saloon.* **3** *Brit.* sedan. Also, **saloon car.** ⟨< F *salon* salon. See SALON.⟩

sa•loon•keep•er [sə'lun,kipər] *n.* a person who keeps a SALOON (def. 1).

sal•pi•glos•sis [ˌsælpə'glɒsɪs] *n.* any of a genus (*Salpiglossis*) of herbs of the nightshade family native to Chile, having brilliantly coloured, funnel-shaped flowers. ⟨< NL *Salpiglossis*, the genus name < Gk. *salpinx, -pingos* trumpet + *glossa* tongue, referring to the shape of the stigma⟩

sal•si•fy ['sælsəfi] *or* ['sælsə,faɪ] *n.* **1** a European biennial plant of the composite family having a long, fleshy, edible root. **2** the root of this plant, eaten as a vegetable. Salsify has an oysterlike flavour. ⟨< F *salsifis* < Ital. *sassefrica* < L *saxifraga.* Doublet of SAXIFRAGE.⟩

sal soda WASHING SODA; crystallized sodium carbonate.

salt [sɒlt] *n., adj., v. —n.* **1** a white crystalline compound found in the earth and in sea water; sodium chloride. Salt is used to season and preserve food. **2** a usually crystalline chemical compound derived from an acid by replacing the hydrogen wholly or partly by a metal or an electropositive radical. Baking soda is a salt. **3** that which gives liveliness, piquancy, or pungency to anything. **4** SALTCELLAR. **5** *Informal.* sailor. **6 salts,** *pl.* **a** a salt prepared for use as a laxative: *Epsom salts, Rochelle salts.* **b** SMELLING SALTS. **c** scented salt for softening bath water.
above or **below the salt,** in a superior or inferior position.
eat (someone's) **salt,** be someone's guest.
salt of the earth, a person, or people, considered to be especially fine, noble, etc.
with a grain of salt, with some reservation or allowance: *The police officer took their story with a grain of salt.*
worth (one's) **salt,** worth one's support, wages, etc.
—adj. **1** containing salt: *salt water.* **2** tasting or smelling like salt; suggesting the sea. **3** overflowed with or growing in salt water: *salt marshes, salt grasses.* **4** cured or preserved with salt: *salt pork.* **5** sharp; pungent; to the point; lively: *salt speech.*
—v. **1** mix or sprinkle with salt. **2** cure or preserve with salt. **3** provide or feed with salt: *to salt cattle.* **4** make interesting; season: *conversation salted with wit.* **5** *Chemistry.* **a** treat with any salt. **b** add a salt to (a solution) in order to precipitate a dissolved substance.
salt a mine, put ore, gold dust, etc., into a mine to create a false impression of value.
salt away or **down, a** pack with salt to preserve: *The fish were salted down in a barrel.* **b** *Informal.* store away: *The miser salted a lot of money away.* ⟨OE *sealt*⟩

SALT Strategic Arms Limitation Talks.

sal•ta•rel•lo [ˌsɒltə'rɛlou] *n.* **1** a lively Italian dance for one or two people. **2** the music for a saltarello. ⟨< Ital. *saltare* leap⟩

salt•box ['sɒlt,bɒks] *n.* **1** a box for holding salt. **2** a style of architecture, especially of a house, having two storeys in the front and one in the back, with an asymmetrical gable roof.

salt•bush ['sɒlt,bʊʃ] *n.* any of several plants or shrubs of the goosefoot family (genus *Atriplex*), often found growing in alkaline or saline soil.

salt•cel•lar ['sɒlt,sɛlər] *n.* a shaker or small dish for holding salt, used on the table. ⟨ME *saltsaler* < *salt*, n. + obs. *saler* saltcellar < OF *salier*, masc., *saliere*, fem. < L *salarius*, adj. of salt < *sal* salt⟩

salt chuck *Cdn.* on the west coast and in the Northwest, the sea; saltwater, including all inlets, bays, and canals affected by tidewater. ⟨< E *salt* + Chinook Jargon *chuck* water⟩

salt•chuck•er ['sɒlt,tʃʌkər] *n.* a saltwater fisherman.

Sal•teaux ['sæltou] *or* ['sɒltou] *n., pl.* **Sal•teaux;** *adj. —n.* a member of an Algonquian people, a western branch of the Ojibwa.
—adj. of or having to do with the Salteaux.

salt•ed ['sɒltɪd] *adj., v.* **1** seasoned, cured, or preserved with salt. **2** experienced; hardened.
—v. pt. and pp. of SALT.

salt•er ['sɒltər] *n.* **1** a person who makes or sells salt. **2** a person who salts meat, fish, etc. **3** *Cdn.* a vehicle that spreads salt on snowy or icy roads.

salt grass *Cdn., esp. Pacific coast.* any of a genus (*Distichlis*) of North American grasses that grow in saline or alkaline soils, especially *D. spicata* and *D. stricta*.

salt•ie or **sal•ty** ['sɒlti] *n. Informal.* a saltwater vessel, especially a freighter sailing the Great Lakes.

salt•ine [sɒl'tin] *n.* a thin, crisp, salted cracker.

sal•tire ['sɒltaɪr], ['sæltaɪr], *or* ['sɒltir] *n. Heraldry.* a diagonal cross, the arms running from upper left to lower right, and from upper right to lower left; ST. ANDREW'S CROSS; crisscross. ⟨ME *sawtire* < OF *saultoir* X-shaped hurdle < *saulter* jump < L *saltare*⟩

salt lick 1 a place where common salt occurs naturally on the surface of the ground and where animals go to lick it up. **2** a block of salt placed in a pasture for cattle, etc. to lick.

salt•pe•tre [ˌsɒlt'pitər] *n.* **1** a mineral used in making gunpowder, in explosives, etc.; potassium nitrate; nitre. **2** a kind of fertilizer; sodium nitrate. Also, **saltpeter.** ⟨ME < OF *salpetre* < Med.L *sal petrae* salt of rock < Gk. *petra* rock⟩

salt pork fatty pork that has been cured in salt.

salt rheum *Informal.* a skin eruption; eczema.

salt–ris•ing bread ['sɒlt ˌraɪzɪŋ] bread made from a fermenting dough of salted milk, cornmeal, flour, sugar, and soda, and held over as a STARTER (def. 6) from a previous baking. See also SOURDOUGH.

salt•shak•er ['sɒltˌʃeikər] *n.* a container for salt, having a perforated top for sprinkling the salt.

salt•wa•ter ['sɒltˌwɒtər] *adj.* **1** of, containing, or having to do with salt water or the sea: *a saltwater solution, saltwater fishing.* **2** living or found in the sea: *saltwater fish.*

salt•works ['sɒltˌwɜrks] *n.* a place or building where salt is made.

salt•wort ['sɒltˌwɜrt] *n.* **1** any of several plants (genus *Salsola*) of the goosefoot family found on seashores and in salt marshes, especially a European species (*S. kali*), also occurring on the E coast of North America. See also RUSSIAN THISTLE. **2** glasswort.

salt•y ['sɒlti] *adj.* **salt•i•er, salt•i•est. 1** containing or tasting of salt: *Sweat and tears are salty. The soup is too salty.* **2** to the point; witty and a bit improper: *a salty remark.* **3** suggesting the sea or nautical life: *a salty breeze.* **—'salt•i•ly,** *adv.* **—'salt•i•ness,** *n.*

sa•lu•bri•ous [sə'lubriəs] *adj.* healthful. ⟨< L *salubris* < *salus* good health⟩ **—sa'lu•bri•ous•ly,** *adv.* **—sa'lu•bri•ous•ness,** *n.*

sa•lu•bri•ty [sə'lubrɪti] *n.* healthfulness.

sa•lu•ki [sə'luki] *n.* a breed of sporting dog, similar in build to a greyhound but taller, having short, silky hair, and fringed ears and tail. It is probably the oldest known breed of dog, familiar to ancient Egyptians, Arabs, and Hebrews. ⟨< Arabic *salugi,* of *Satuq,* an ancient city of Arabia⟩

sal•u•tar•y ['sæljəˌtɛri] *adj.* **1** beneficial: *The teacher gave the girl salutary advice.* **2** good for the health; wholesome: *Walking is a salutary exercise.* ⟨< L *salutaris* < *salus, salutis* good health⟩

sal•u•ta•tion [ˌsæljə'teiʃən] *n.* **1** a greeting; saluting: *The man raised his hat in salutation.* **2** something uttered, written, or done to salute. Most letters begin with a salutation, such as "Dear Sir" or "My Dear Mrs. Rainwater."

sa•lu•ta•to•ry [sə'lutəˌtɔri] *adj.* expressing greeting; welcoming: *The chair opened the proceedings with salutatory remarks.*

sa•lute [sə'lut] *v.* **-lut•ed, -lut•ing;** *n.* *—v.* **1** honour in a formal manner by raising the hand to the head, by firing guns, by dipping flags, etc.: *The soldier saluted the officer.* **2** meet with kind words, cheers, a bow, a kiss, etc.; greet. **3** make a bow, gesture, etc. to. **4** come to; meet: *Shouts of welcome saluted their ears.* **5** make a salute. **6** express praise, respect, or commendation (of or for).
—n. **1** the act of saluting; a sign of welcome, farewell, or honour. **2** the position of the hand, gun, etc., in saluting. **3** an event or ceremony held to honour or congratulate someone, or to remember or commend something. ⟨ME < L *salutare* greet < *salus, salutis* good health⟩ **—sa'lut•er,** *n.*

Sal•va•do•ran [ˌsælvə'dɔrən] *n., adj.* *—n.* a native or inhabitant of El Salvador.
—adj. of or having to do with El Salvador or its people. Also, **Salvadorian.**

sal•vage ['sælvɪdʒ] *n., v.* **-vaged, -vag•ing.** *—n.* **1** the act or process of rescuing a ship or its cargo from wreck, capture, etc. **2** payment made or due for such saving or rescuing. **3** the property saved or rescued. **4** the act of saving or rescuing anything from wreckage, destruction, etc. **5** anything saved or rescued for use, such as scrap metal, wood, etc.: *They used mostly salvage to build their cabin.* **6** the saving or rescuing of one's reputation, dignity, etc.
—v. **1** save or rescue from wreckage, destruction, etc.: *We salvaged quite a few parts from the engine of the old car.* **2** save or rescue (pride, etc.) from harm or ruin: *to salvage one's dignity.* ⟨< F *salvage,* ult. < L *salvus* safe⟩ **—'sal•vag•er,** *n.*

sal•va•tion [sæl'veiʃən] *n.* **1** a saving or being saved. **2** a person or thing that saves: *Christians believe that Christ is the salvation of the world.* **3** a saving of the soul; deliverance from sin and from punishment for sin. ⟨ME < OF < LL *salvatio, -onis,* ult. < L *salvus* safe⟩

Salvation Army an international organization with a quasi-military structure, whose mandate is to spread the Christian religion and to help the poor and unfortunate, founded in England in 1865 by William Booth (1829-1912).

salve[1] [sæv], [sɑv], *or* [sɒv] *n., v.* **salved, salv•ing.** *—n.* **1** a smooth medicinal ointment to put on wounds and sores to soothe or heal them. **2** something soothing; balm: *The kind words were a salve to her hurt feelings.*
—v. **1** put salve on. **2** soothe; smooth over: *He salved his conscience by the thought that his lie harmed no one.* ⟨OE *sealf*⟩

salve[2] [sælv] *v.* **salved, salv•ing.** save from loss or destruction; salvage. ⟨back formation from *salvage*⟩

sal•ver ['sælvər] *n.* a tray, especially a silver one for serving drinks, for presenting letters or visiting cards, etc. ⟨< F < Sp. *salva,* originally, foretasting, ult. < L *salvus* safe⟩
☛ *Hom.* SALVOR.

sal•vi•a ['sælviə] *n.* any of a large genus (*Salvia*) of herbs and shrubs of the mint family, especially a popular garden plant (*S. splendens*), also called **scarlet sage,** having showy spikes of scarlet flowers. Garden sage is also a salvia. ⟨< L *salvia,* probably < *salvus* healthy; with reference to its supposed healing properties. Doublet of SAGE[2].⟩

sal•vif•ic [sæl'vɪfɪk] *adj.* giving salvation or redemption.

sal•vo ['sælvou] *n., pl.* **-vos** or **-voes. 1** the discharge of several guns at the same time, as a broadside or as a salute. **2** a load of bombs or missiles released at the same time from an aircraft. **3** a round of cheers or applause. ⟨< Ital. *salva,* ult. < L *salve* hail!, be in good health!⟩

sal vo•la•ti•le [ˌsæl və'lætɪli] **1** an aromatic solution of ammonium carbonate and alcohol, used to relieve faintness, etc. **2** ammonium carbonate. *Formula*: NH_4CO_3 ⟨< NL *sal volatile* volatile salt. 17c.⟩

sal•vor ['sælvər] *n.* a person who salvages or takes part in salvaging a vessel or its cargo.
☛ *Hom.* SALVER.

sa•ma•dhi [sə'mɑdi] *n. Hinduism. Buddhism.* the highest degree of meditation. ⟨< Skt.⟩

sa•maj [sə'mɑdʒ] *n. Hinduism.* **1** a religious association or society. **2** any assembly of Hindu worshippers: *"Hindu Prarthana Samaj" is the name of Toronto's oldest Hindu temple.* ⟨< Hind.⟩

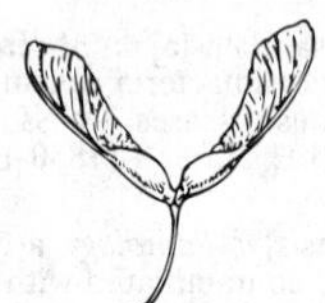

A samara of a maple

sam•a•ra ['sæmərə] *or* [sə'mɛrə] *n.* any dry fruit that has a winglike extension and does not split open when ripe. The fruit of the maple tree is a double samara with one seed in each half. See FRUIT for picture. ⟨< L *samara* elm seed⟩

Sa•mar•i•tan [sə'mærətən] *or* [sə'mɛrətən] *n., adj.* *—n.* **1** a native or inhabitant of Samaria, a district in the northern part of ancient Palestine. **2** See GOOD SAMARITAN.
—adj. of or having to do with Samaria or its people.

sa•mar•i•um [sə'mɛriəm] *n. Chemistry.* a rare, lustrous, grey metallic element used especially in alloys that form permanent magnets. *Symbol*: Sm; *at.no.* 62; *at.mass* 150.4. ⟨< *samar(skite),* a mineral < G *Samarskit,* after Col. *Samarski,* a Russian⟩

sam•ba ['sɑmbə] *or* ['sæmbə] *n., v.* **-baed, -ba•ing.** *—n.* **1** a Brazilian dance of African origin, having a syncopated rhythm in double time. **2** the music for this dance.
—v. dance the samba. ⟨< Pg.⟩

Sam Browne belt ['sæm 'braʊn] a leather belt having a supporting piece passing over the right shoulder, worn by army officers, etc. ⟨after Sir *Samuel* J. *Browne,* a British army officer (1824-1901)⟩

sam•bu•ca [sæm'bjukə] *or* [sæm'bukə] *n.* an ancient Greek musical instrument with strings. ⟨< L < Gk. *sambyke*⟩

same [seim] *adj., pron.* *—adj.* **1** not another; identical: *We came back the same way we went.* **2** just alike; not different: *Look, you and Sandy are wearing the same dress!* **3** unchanged: *He is the same kind old man.* **4** just spoken of; aforesaid: *The girls were talking about an eccentric person. This same man wore his hair very long and was always dressed in white.*
—pron. the same person or thing.
all the same, notwithstanding; nevertheless.
just the same, a in the same manner. **b** nevertheless.

the same, in the same manner: Sea *and* see *are pronounced the same.* ⟨OE⟩

☛ *Syn. adj.* **1, 2. Same,** IDENTICAL means not different from another or each other. Both may mean that what is described is not another person or thing but the one already mentioned or otherwise suggested: *That is the same (*or *identical) man I saw yesterday.* When describing two or more people or things, **same** means alike, of one kind, appearance, size, or quality, etc.: *He always has the same lunch.* **Identical** means absolutely alike, agreeing exactly in every detail: *Their cars are identical.*

☛ *Usage.* **Same** must always be preceded by a definite determiner (*the, this, that,* etc.).

samekh ['sæmɛk] *n.* the sixteenth letter of the Hebrew alphabet. See table of alphabets in the Appendix.

same•ness ['seimnɪs] *n.* **1** the state of being the same; an exact likeness; identity or uniformity. **2** a lack of variety; tiresomeness; monotony.

S.Amer. SOUTH AMERICA; SOUTH AMERICAN.

sam•gha ['sɑŋə] *n. Jainism.* the worldwide 'four-fold' congregation consisting of monks, nuns, and laymen.

Sa•mi ['sɑmi] *n.* a Lapplander.

Sa•mi•an ['seimiən] *n., adj.* —*n.* a native or inhabitant of Samos, a Greek island in the Aegean Sea.
—*adj.* of or having to do with Samos or its people. ⟨< Gk. *Samios* of Samos⟩

sam•i•sen ['sæmɪ,sɛn] *n.* a Japanese musical instrument resembling a banjo, having three strings and played with a large, elongated plectrum. ⟨< Japanese < Chinese *san hsien*⟩

sam•ite ['sæmɔit] *or* ['seimɔit] *n.* a heavy, rich silk fabric, sometimes interwoven with gold, worn in the Middle Ages. ⟨ME < OF < Med.Gk. *hexamiton* < Gk. *hex* six + *mitos* thread⟩

Sa•moa [sə'mouə] *n.* a country of islands in the South Pacific.

Sa•mo•an [sə'mouən] *n., adj.* —*n.* **1** a native or inhabitant of Samoa. **2** the Polynesian language of the Samoans.
—*adj.* of or having to do with Samoa, its people, or their language.

sa•mo•sa [sə'mousə] *n.* an East Indian deep-fried dish consisting of spicy meat or vegetables in pastry. ⟨< Hind.)

sam•o•var ['sæmə,vɑr] *or* [,sæmə'vɑr] *n.* a metal urn with a tap, used for heating water for tea. ⟨< Russian *samovar,* literally, self-boiler⟩

Sam•o•yed [,sɑmə'jɛd] *or* [sə'mɔɪɪd] *n., adj.* —*n.* **1** a member of a Uralic-speaking people living in northern Siberia. **2** any of a subgroup of languages spoken by the Samoyeds. **3** a Siberian breed of large work dog, having a long-haired, white or cream-coloured coat, and used in arctic regions to guard reindeer herds and to pull sleds.
—*adj.* of or having to do with the Samoyed people or languages, or with the breed of dog. ⟨< Russian *samoed,* prob. < Lapp *Sāme-Ǟednàma* of Lapland⟩

sam•pan ['sæmpæn] *n.* a type of small boat sculled by one or more oars at the stern, usually having a single sail and a cabin made of mats. Sampans are used in the rivers and coastal waters of China, SE Asia, and Japan. ⟨< Chinese < Pg.; origin uncertain⟩

sam•phire ['sæmfaɪr] *n.* **1** a plant (*Crithmum maritimum*) of the parsley family found on rocky coasts of Europe, having fleshy divided leaves. **2** glasswort. ⟨earlier *sampere* < F *(herbe de) Saint Pierre* (herb of) St. Peter⟩

sam•ple ['sæmpəl] *n., v.* **-pled, -pling.** —*n.* **1** a part or single item taken to represent a larger whole or a group; a part or item shown or presented as evidence of what the rest is like: *The display samples are not for sale. We sent a sample of the soil to the university for testing.* **2** (*adjl.*) serving as a sample: *a sample copy.*
—*v.* take a sample of, especially in order to test quality, etc.: *We sampled the cake and found it very good.* ⟨var. of *essample,* var. of *example*⟩

☛ *Syn. n.* See note at EXAMPLE.

sam•pler ['sæmplər] *n.* **1** a person who samples. **2** a piece of cloth embroidered with letters of the alphabet, verses, etc. in various stitches to show skill in needlework. **3** a book, kit, etc. providing a collection of samples. ⟨< OF *essamplaire* < LL *exemplarium* < L *exemplum* example⟩

sam•pling ['sæmplɪŋ] *n., v.* —*n.* **1** a small part or number selected for the purpose of testing or analysing. **2** the act or process of selecting this part or number.
—*v.* ppr. of SAMPLE.

sam•sa•ra [səm'sɑrə] *n.* **1** *Hinduism.* the ongoing cycle of death and rebirth in the world. **2** *Buddhism.* the coming into being as a mortal human. ⟨< Skt., a running together⟩

Sam•son ['sæmsən] *n.* **1** in the Bible, a judge of Israel who had very great strength. He confided to Delilah that his strength was in his hair, and she cut it off while he slept, so that his enemies, the Philistines, could overcome him. **2** any man of unusually great strength. ⟨< LL < ecclesiastical Gk. *Sampson* < Hebrew *shimshon* like the sun⟩

Samson fox *Cdn.* a red fox lacking guard hairs, giving its fur a burnt appearance. ⟨< *Samson,* the Israelite judge who destroyed the Philistines' grain by letting loose foxes with torches tied to their tails⟩

sam•u•rai ['sæmə,raɪ] *n., pl.* **-rai. 1** in feudal Japan, the military class, consisting of the retainers of the great nobles. **2** a member of this class. **3** in later English use, a Japanese army officer or other military person. ⟨< Japanese⟩

san [sæn] *n. Informal.* sanatorium, especially one for the treatment of tuberculosis: *She spent six months in the san.*

–san a Japanese title of respect, used after a name.

San An•dre•as fault [ən'dreiəs] *Geology.* a fault line in rock running from Southern California to Alaska, along which earthquakes often occur. ⟨after *San Andreas* Lake in San Mateo County⟩

san•a•tive ['sænətɪv] *adj.* healing; having power to cure. ⟨ME < LL *sanativus,* ult. < L *sanus* healthy⟩

san•a•to•ri•um [,sænə'tɔriəm] *n., pl.* **-ri•ums** or **-ri•a** [-riə]. **1** an establishment for the treatment of the sick, especially persons with long-term or chronic diseases, such as tuberculosis. **2** a health resort. ⟨< NL *sanatorium,* neut. of LL *sanatorius* health-giving, ult. < L *sanus* healthy⟩

san•be•ni•to [,sænbə'nitou] *n.* **1** a yellow penitential garment with a red St. Andrew's Cross on both the front and the back, worn by a confessed heretic under trial by the Inquisition. **2** a black garment ornamented with flames, devils, etc., worn by a condemned heretic at an AUTO-DA-FÉ. ⟨< Sp. *San Benito* St. Benedict, from its resemblance to the cloak, or scapular, he introduced⟩

San•cho Pan•za ['sæntʃou 'pænzə]; *Spanish,* ['santʃɔ 'panθa] the squire to Don Quixote whose credulity and simplicity combined with down-to-earth common sense act as a foil to the Don's idealism.

sanc•ti•fi•ca•tion [,sæŋktəfə'keiʃən] *n.* a sanctifying or being sanctified; consecration; purification from sin.

sanc•ti•fied ['sæŋktə,faɪd] *adj., v.* —*adj.* **1** consecrated. **2** sanctimonious.
—*v.* pt. and pp. of SANCTIFY.

sanc•ti•fy ['sæŋktə,faɪ] *v.* **-fied, -fy•ing. 1** make holy: *A life of sacrifice had sanctified her.* **2** set apart as sacred; observe as holy: *"Lord, sanctify this our offering to Thy use."* **3** make free from sin. **4** justify; make right. **5** make into a source of spiritual blessing. ⟨ME < OF < L *sanctificare* < *sanctus* holy + *facere* make⟩ —**'sanc•ti,fi•er,** *n.*

sanc•ti•mo•ni•ous [,sæŋktə'mouniəs] *adj.* making a show of holiness; putting on airs of sanctity; pretending to be pious. —**,sanc•ti'mo•ni•ous•ly,** *adv.* —**,sanc•ti'mo•ni•ous•ness,** *n.*

sanc•ti•mo•ny ['sæŋktə,mouni] *n.* a show of holiness; airs of sanctity; hypocrisy in religious matters. ⟨< L *sanctimonia* < *sanctus* holy⟩

sanc•tion ['sæŋkʃən] *n., v.* —*n.* **1** permission with authority; approval: *We have the sanction of the law to play ball in this park.* **2** a solemn ratification. **3 a** a provision of a law enacting a penalty for disobedience to it or a reward for obedience. **b** the penalty or reward. **4** an action by several nations toward another, such as a blockade, economic restrictions, etc., intended to force it to obey international law. **5** a consideration that leads one to obey a rule of conduct. **6** a binding force.
—*v.* **1** authorize; approve; allow: *Her conscience does not sanction stealing.* **2** ratify. ⟨< L *sanctio, -onis* < *sancire* ordain⟩ —**'sanc•tion•er,** *n.*

☛ *Syn. v.* **1.** See note at APPROVE.

sanc•ti•ty ['sæŋktəti] *n., pl.* **-ties. 1** holiness; saintliness; godliness. **2** the fact or quality of being inviolable or sacred; a being hallowed: *the sanctity of a church, the sanctity of the home.* **3 sanctities,** *pl.* **a** sacred obligations, feelings, etc. **b** objects possessing sanctity. ⟨< L *sanctitas* < *sanctus* holy⟩

sanc•tu•ar•y ['sæŋktʃu,ɛri] *n., pl.* **-ar•ies. 1** any sacred place. Churches, mosques, synagogues, temples, and other houses of worship are sanctuaries. **2** the part of a Christian church: **a** around the altar. **b** where the congregation meets for worship. **3** a place of refuge or protection for birds and animals, where hunting and trapping are prohibited by law. **4** a refuge or protection: *The lost travellers found sanctuary in a deserted hut.*

5 the temple at Jerusalem. 6 the sacred place where the Ark of the Covenant was kept in the temple at Jerusalem. ⟨ME < OF < L *sanctuarium*, ult. < *sanctus* holy⟩

sanc•tum ['sæŋktəm] *n., pl.* **-tums** or (*rare*) **-ta** [-tə]. **1** a sacred place. **2** a private room or office where a person can be undisturbed. ⟨< L *sanctum*, originally neut. adj., holy⟩

sanc•tum sanc•to•rum ['sæŋktəm sæŋk'tɔrəm] **1** *Latin.* holy of holies. **2** an especially private place.

Sanc•tus ['sæŋktəs] *or* ['sʌŋktʊs] *n.* **1** a hymn beginning "Sanctus, Sanctus, Sanctus" in Latin and "Holy, holy, holy" in English, ending the preface of the Mass or Eucharistic service. **2** the musical setting of this. ⟨< L *sanctus*, holy; first word of this hymn⟩

sand [sænd] *n., v., adj.* —*n.* **1** tiny grains of worn-down or disintegrated rock finer than gravel but coarser than silt: *Sand is found along seashores and in deserts.* **2 sands,** *pl.* a tract or region composed mainly of sand: *the sands of the desert.* **3 sands,** *pl.* the sand in an hourglass thought of as moments or particles of time. **4** *Slang.* courage; pluck; grit. **5** a very light greyish brown.
—*v.* **1** sprinkle with sand: *to sand an icy walk.* **2** fill up or cover with sand. **3** clean, smooth, or polish by rubbing with an abrasive such as sandpaper. **4** mix with sand, especially to adulterate.
—*adj.* very light greyish brown. ⟨OE⟩ —**'sand,like,** *adj.*

san•dal ['sændəl] *n.* a kind of open shoe consisting of a sole kept on the foot by means of any of various arrangements of straps over the toes or instep and often around the heel and ankle. See SHOE for picture. ⟨ME < L < Gk. *sandalion*⟩

san•dalled or **san•daled** ['sændəld] *adj.* wearing sandals.

san•dal•wood ['sændəl,wʊd] *n.* **1** the fragrant, hard, light-coloured heartwood of any of several evergreen trees (genus *Santalum*) of S Asia, especially **white sandalwood** (*S. album*), used in cabinetwork and for ornamental carved objects such as boxes and fans, and also burned as incense. **2** a tree that yields this wood. The sandalwood is partially parasitic on the roots of other trees. **3** any of various other, similar trees or their wood. ⟨< *sandal* (< Med.L *sandalum*, ult. < Skt. *çandana*) + *wood*⟩

sand•bag ['sænd,bæg] *n., v.* **-bagged, -bag•ging.** —*n.* **1** a bag filled with sand. Sandbags are used to form temporary dams, protective walls for trenches used in battle, and as ballast on balloons. **2** a small bag of sand used as a club.
—*v.* **1** furnish with sandbags. **2** hit or stun with, or as if with, a sandbag. **3** thwart (something); cause (something) to fail.

sand•bank ['sænd,bæŋk] *n.* a ridge of sand.

sand bar a ridge of sand in a river or along a shore, formed by the action of tides or currents.

sand•blast ['sænd,blæst] *n., v.* —*n.* **1** a blast of air or steam containing sand, used to clean, grind, cut, or decorate hard surfaces such as glass, stone, or metal. **2** the apparatus used to apply such a blast. A sandblast is often used in cleaning the outside of buildings.
—*v.* use a sandblast on.

sand•box ['sænd,bɒks] *n.* a box for holding sand, especially for children to play in.

sand–cast ['sænd ˌkæst] *v.* **-cast, -cast•ing.** produce (a cast) by pouring metal, plaster, wax, etc. into a sand mould.

sand cat a desert cat (*Felis margarita*) somewhat bigger than the domestic cat but smaller than the great cats, having furry padding between the toes to prevent it from sinking in the sand. It lives in the Sahara and in deserts of southwest Asia, and is an endangered species.

sand cherry **1** any of several North American shrubs (genus *Prunus*) of the rose family, especially common in the Prairie Provinces. **2** the edible, purplish or black berry of any of these shrubs.

sand dab any of several small, edible flatfish, especially the flounders (genus *Citharichthys*) of the Pacific coast of North America.

sand dollar any of various flat, thin-edged, disk-shaped marine invertebrates (order Clypeasteroida) found in shallow, sandy-bottomed, coastal waters. Sand dollars are flat sea urchins. ⟨from their resemblance to a silver dollar⟩

sand•er ['sændər] *n.* **1** *Cdn.* a truck having a device for spreading sand on icy roads. **2** the device itself. **3** a tool or machine for cleaning, smoothing, or polishing by means of sandpaper or some similar material. **4** any person or thing that sands.

sand•er•ling ['sændərlɪŋ] *n.* a small, common sandpiper (*Calidris alba*) with grey and white plumage, usually found inhabiting sandy beaches. ⟨< *sand* + *-erling* < OE *yrthling* kind of bird, ploughman⟩

sand flea **1** any of various tiny terrestrial crustaceans (order Amphipoda, especially family Talidridae) that hop like fleas, found in the sand of seashores. **2** chigoe.

sand fly **1** any of various small two-winged flies (genus *Phlebotomus*), the females of which have mouthparts adapted for sucking blood. Sand flies sometimes transmit diseases. **2** any of various other small two-winged flies.

sand•glass ['sænd,glæs] *n.* hourglass.

san•dhi ['sʌndi], ['sændi], *or* ['sɑndi] *n. Linguistics.* a change in the sound of a morpheme or morphemes in a given phonetic context, as in *gonna* for *going to*. ⟨< Skt. *samdhi* joining⟩

sand•hill crane ['sænd,hɪl] a crane (*Grus canadensis*) of central and eastern North America, mainly bluish grey with a bare reddish patch on the forehead and upper face. The sandhill crane resembles the great blue heron.

Sand Hills *Cdn.* a region in southeastern Alberta, long sacred to the Plains First Nations, and often a euphemism for death: *Aunt Martha? She went to the Sand Hills five years ago.*

sand•hog ['sænd,hɒg] *n.* a person who works under compressed air in underground or underwater construction, as in a caisson or tunnel.

sand•man ['sænd,mæn] *or* ['sændmən] *n. Folklore.* an imaginary man who makes children sleepy by sprinkling sand in their eyes.

sand•pa•per ['sænd,peipər] *n., v.* —*n.* a strong paper with a layer of sand or some other rough material glued to it, used for smoothing, cleaning, or polishing.
—*v.* smooth, clean, or polish with sandpaper.

sand•pip•er ['sænd,pəipər] *n.* **1** any of numerous small or medium-sized shore birds (especially of genera *Actitus* and *Erolia*) having slender legs and long toes, a long, slender bill, and spotted or streaked, brownish or greyish plumage. **2** (*adjl.*) designating the worldwide family (Scolopacidae) of shore birds that includes the sandpipers, curlews, snipes, and woodcocks.

A sandpiper

sand•spit ['sænd,spɪt] *n.* a stretch of low, sandy land jutting out into water.

sand•stone ['sænd,stoun] *n.* a kind of sedimentary rock consisting of grains of sand held together by a natural cementing material.

sand•storm ['sænd,stɔrm] *n.* a storm of wind that carries clouds of sand.

sand trap *Golf.* a pit or depression filled with sand, usually located near the green to serve as a hazard on a golf course.

sand•wich ['sænwɪtʃ] *or* ['sænwɪdʒ] *n., v.* —*n.* **1** two or more slices of bread with meat, jelly, cheese, or some other filling between them. **2** something formed by similar arrangement: *an ice-cream sandwich.* **3** *Cdn. Hockey. Slang.* a defensive play in which an attacking player is bodychecked simultaneously by two opponents, often defencemen.
—*v.* put or squeeze (*between*): *When he went to get his car, he found it sandwiched between two trucks.* ⟨after John Montagu, the fourth Earl of *Sandwich* (1718-1792)⟩

sandwich board a pair of signboards, usually hinged at the top, designed to be hung from a person's shoulders with one board in front and the other behind, and used for advertising or picketing.

sandwich man **1** a person carrying a sandwich board. **2** a maker or seller of sandwiches.

sand•wort ['sænd,wɜrt] *n.* any of a genus (*Arenaria*) of herbs of the pink family that grow in low tufts or mats in sandy soil and have many very small, white or purplish flowers.

sand•y ['sændi] *adj.* **sand•i•er, sand•i•est.** **1** containing, consisting of, or covered with sand: *Most of the shore is rocky, but there is a sandy beach.* **2** of the colour of sand: *sandy hair.* **3** like sand in texture, etc. —**'sand•i•ness,** *n.*

sane [sein] *adj.* **san•er, san•est.** **1** having a healthy mind; especially, in law, able to make rational judgments and to appreciate the effects of one's actions. **2** showing good sense; reasonable or sensible: *a sane foreign policy.* **3** regulated by

reason; rational. ⟨< L *sanus* healthy⟩ **—'sane•ly,** *adv.* **—'sane•ness,** *n.*
☛ *Hom.* SEINE.

sang [sæŋ] *v.* pt. of SING.

San•gat ['sʌŋgət] *n. Sikhism.* a congregation, community, or assembly of worshippers: *The Sangat assembles each Sunday for worship.*

sang–froid [sɑ̃'fʀwa] *n. French.* coolness of mind; calmness; composure. ⟨literally, cold blood⟩

san•gha ['sʌŋgə] *n.* **1** *Buddhism.* the entire worldwide community of ordained monks and nuns. **2** *Buddhism, Jainism.* any religious community or monastic order. ⟨< Skt. *sangha*⟩

san•gui•nar•i•a [,sæŋgwə'nɛriə] *n.* **1** bloodroot. **2** a drug derived from the bloodroot, used as a stimulant, emetic, etc. ⟨< NL⟩

san•gui•nar•y ['sæŋgwə,nɛri] *adj.* **1** with much blood or bloodshed; bloody: *a sanguinary battle.* **2** delighting in bloodshed; bloodthirsty. ⟨< L *sanguinarius* < *sanguis, sanguinis* blood⟩ **—'san•gui,nar•i•ness,** *n.* **—'san•gui,nar•i•ly,** *adv.*

san•guine ['sæŋgwɪn] *adj.* **1** cheerful and hopeful; optimistic; confident: *a sanguine disposition. They were sanguine of success.* **2** having a healthy, red colour; ruddy: *a sanguine complexion.* **3** in the physiology of the Middle Ages, having a temperament in which blood predominates over other humours; having an active circulation, ruddy complexion, and a cheerful and ardent disposition. **4** *Archaic.* sanguinary. ⟨ME < OF < L *sanguineus* < *sanguis, sanguinis* blood⟩ **—'san•guine•ly,** *adv.* **—'san•guine•ness,** *n.*

san•guin•e•ous [sæŋ'gwɪniəs] *adj.* **1** of or like blood; bloody. **2** blood-red. **3** bloodthirsty. **4** SANGUINE (def. 1).

san•guiv•or•ous [sæŋ'gwɪvərəs] *adj.* feeding on blood, as some bats and insects. ⟨< L *sanguis* blood + E *-vorous*⟩

San•he•drin [sæn'hidrən], [sæn'hɛdrən], *or* ['sænədrɪn] *n.* the supreme council and highest religious and legal authority of the ancient Jewish nation. ⟨< Late Hebrew < Gk. *synedrion* council, literally, sitting together < *syn-* together + *hedra* seat⟩

san•i•tar•i•an [,sænə'tɛriən] *n., adj.* —*n.* a person familiar with, or engaged in, sanitary work.
—*adj.* sanitary.

san•i•tar•i•um [,sænə'tɛriəm] *n., pl.* **-i•ums** or **-i•a** [-iə]. sanatorium. ⟨< NL < L *sanitas* health < *sanus* healthy⟩

san•i•tar•y ['sænə,tɛri] *adj.* **1** of or having to do with health and the conditions that affect health: *She works for the sanitary division of the public works.* **2** free from dirt or anything bad for health: *The top of the picnic table was not very sanitary.* ⟨< F *sanitaire*, ult. < L *sanus* healthy⟩ **—'san•i,tar•i•ly,** *adv.* **—'san•i,tar•i•ness,** *n.*

sanitary napkin or **pad** a disposable absorbent pad worn on the outside of the body to absorb the discharge from menstruation.

san•i•ta•tion [,sænə'teiʃən] *n.* the working out and practical application of sanitary measures, such as disposal of garbage and government inspection of food.

san•i•tize ['sænə,taɪz] *v.* **-tized, -tiz•ing. 1** make sanitary by cleaning, sterilizing, etc.: *The lining of these shoes has been sanitized.* **2** make (something) less offensive, by freeing it from anything objectionable, incriminating, or offensive.

san•i•ty ['sænəti] *n.* **1** soundness of mind; especially, in law, the ability to make rational judgments and appreciate the effects of one's actions. **2** soundness of judgment; sensibleness; reasonableness. ⟨< L *sanitas* < *sanus* healthy⟩

sank [sæŋk] *v.* pt. of SINK.

San Ma•ri•no [,sæn mə'rinou] a country in central Italy, in the Appenines near the Adriatic Sea. It is the world's smallest republic.

san•nya•si [sʌn'jɑsi] *n. Hinduism.* **1** a mendicant and homeless Hindu holy man. **2** a disciple of certain gurus. ⟨< Hind., one who casts away⟩

sans [sænz]; *French,* [sɑ̃] *prep.* without: *"sans teeth, sans eyes, sans taste, sans everything."* ⟨ME < OF *sanz*, ult. < L *sine* without, prob. influenced by L *absentia* (abl.) in the absence (of)⟩

sans–cu•lotte [,sænzkjʊ'lɒt]; *French,* [sɑ̃ky'lɔt] *n.* **1** formerly, in France, a contemptuous term for a republican of the poorer classes, adopted by the revolutionaries of the French Revolution as a designation of honour. **2** any extreme republican or revolutionary. ⟨< F *sans-culotte* without knee breeches⟩

San•sei ['sæn,sei] *or* ['sæn'sei] *n., pl.* **-sei** or **-seis.** a native-born Canadian or United States citizen whose grandparents were Japanese immigrants; an offspring of Nisei parents. ⟨< Japanese *san* third + *sei* generation⟩

San•skrit ['sænskrɪt] *n.* the ancient literary language of India. ⟨< Skt. *samskrta* prepared, cultivated (applied to the literary language as contrasted with the vernacular language). Cf. PRAKRIT.⟩

sans pa•reil [sɑ̃pa'ʀɛj] *French.* without equal.

sans–ser•if ['sænz 'sɛrɪf] *or* ['sæns 'sɛrɪf] *n., adj.* —*n. Printing.* any style of type having no serifs.
—*adj.* of or having to do with this type: *Entry words in this dictionary are printed in a sans-serif type.*

sans sou•ci [sɑ̃su'si] *French.* without care or worry.

San•ta *n.* ['sæntə]; *adj.* ['sæntə] *or* ['sʌntə] *n., adj.* —*n.* SANTA CLAUS.
—*adj. Spanish and Italian.* SAINT (def. 7) (*feminine form*): *Santa Maria.*

Santa Claus ['sæntə ,klɒz] Saint Nicholas, the saint of Christmas giving; according to the modern conception, a jolly old man with a white beard, dressed in a fur-trimmed red suit. ⟨< Du. dial. *Sante Klaas* Saint Nicholas⟩

Santa Ger•tru•dis ['sæntə gər'trudɪs] *n.* a hardy American breed of cattle, developed from shorthorn and Brahman stock to withstand extreme temperatures, especially heat. ⟨< a section of the King Ranch in Texas⟩

san•tim [sæn'tim] *n., pl.* **san•tims** or **san•ti•mi** [sæn'timi] a unit of currency in Latvia, equal to 1/100 of a lat. See table of money in the Appendix.

São To•me e Prin•ci•pe ['sɑ̃ʊ tou'mei ei 'prɪnsɪpi] an island country off the west coast of Africa.

sap¹ [sæp] *n.* **1** the liquid that circulates through a plant as blood does in animals. Rising sap carries water and salt from the roots; sap travelling downward carries sugar, gums, resins, etc. **2** any body fluid essential to life or health. **3** vital spirit; health and vigour: *the sap of youth.* **4** *Slang.* a silly, stupid person; fool. ⟨OE *sæp*⟩ **—'sap•less,** *adj.*

sap² [sæp] *v.* **sapped, sap•ping;** *n.* —*v.* **1** weaken or use up; undermine: *The extreme heat sapped their strength.* **2** dig under or wear away the foundation of: *The walls of the boathouse had been sapped by the waves.* **3** dig protected trenches. **4** approach (the enemy's position) by means of such trenches. **5** make a tunnel under.
—*n.* **1** the making of trenches to approach a besieged place or an enemy's position. **2** a trench protected by the earth dug up; a trench dug to approach the enemy's position. ⟨< MF *sappe*, n., < *sapper*, v. < Ital. *zappare* < *zappa* spade, hoe⟩

sa•pi ['sɑpi] *n. Cdn., esp. Northwest.* a fish, a subspecies of the Arctic char (*Salvelinus alpinus malma*); DOLLY VARDEN.

sap•id ['sæpɪd] *adj.* **1** having a flavour or taste. **2** pleasing to the taste; savoury. **3** agreeable, interesting, or engaging to the mind. ⟨< L *sapidus* < *sapere* to taste⟩ **—sa'pid•i•ty,** *n.*

sa•pi•ent ['seipiənt] *or* ['sæpiənt] *adj.* having or displaying great wisdom, good judgment, or sagacity. ⟨< L *sapiens, -entis*, ppr. of *sapere* be wise⟩ **—'sa•pi•ence** or **'sa•pi•en•cy,** *n.* **—'sa•pi•ent•ly,** *adv.*

sap•ling ['sæplɪŋ] *n.* **1** a young tree. **2** a young person.

sap•o•dil•la [,sæpə'dɪlə] *n.* **1** a large evergreen tree (*Achras zapota*) of tropical America, the latex of which yields chicle. **2** the large, edible fruit of this tree, having a rough, brown skin and yellowish pulp that tastes somewhat like that of a pear. **3** (*adjl.*) designating a family of tropical plants, most of which are trees, including the sapodilla and numerous other trees of economic importance as sources of latex. ⟨< Sp. *zapotilla*, ult. < Nahuatl⟩

sap•o•na•ceous [,sæpə'neiʃəs] *adj.* soapy; like soap: *Some cheeses have a saponaceous texture.* ⟨< Med.L *saponaceus* < L *sapo, saponis* soap⟩

sa•pon•i•fy [sə'pɒnə,faɪ] *v.* **-fied, -fy•ing.** *Chemistry.* **1** make (a fat or oil) into soap by treating it with an alkali. **2** be saponified; become soap. **3** decompose (an ester of an acid) into an alcohol and a salt of the acid. ⟨< NL *saponificare* < L *sapo, saponis* soap + *facere* make⟩ **—sa,pon•i•fi'ca•tion,** *n.* **—sa'pon•i,fi•er,** *n.* **—sa'pon•i,fi•a•ble,** *adj.*

sap•o•nin ['sæpənɪn] *n.* any of various glucose derivatives found in certain plants, that form a lather with water and are used in detergents and as foaming and emulsifying agents. ⟨< F *saponine* < L *sapo, sapon-* soap. 19c.⟩

sap•o•nite ['sæpə,nəit] *n.* a hydrated silicate of magnesium and aluminum that occurs in amorphous masses in veins and cavities of metamorphic rocks such as serpentine. It is a soft mineral with a soapy feel. ⟨< Swedish *saponit* < L *sapo, saponis* soap. 19c.⟩

sap•per ['sæpər] *n.* a soldier employed in the construction of trenches, fortifications, etc., especially in reference to (in Canada) the regiment of the Royal Canadian Engineers and (in the United Kingdom) the Royal Engineers. ⟨< *sap*[2]⟩

Sap•phic ['sæfɪk] *adj., n.* —*adj.* **1** of or having to do with Sappho, a Greek lyric poetess of Lesbos, an island in the Aegean Sea, who lived about 600 B.C. **2** having to do with certain poetic metres, or a stanza form, used by or named after Sappho. **3** of or having to do with female homosexuality.
—*n.* a Sapphic stanza or strophe.

sap•phire ['sæfaɪr] *n., adj.* —*n.* **1** a precious stone, a variety of corundum of any colour other than red, especially blue. **2** a gem made from this stone. **3** a bright blue, the colour usually associated with the gem.
—*adj.* bright blue. ⟨ME < OF < L < Gk. *sappheiros* < Semitic; cf. Hebrew *sappīr* < Skt. *çani-priya* dear to the planet Saturn⟩

sap•phi•rine ['sæfə,rin], ['sæfə,raɪn], *or* ['sæfərɪn] *adj., n.* —*adj.* **1** of or like sapphire, especially in colour. **2** made of sapphire.
—*n.* **1** a pale blue or greenish silicate of aluminum and magnesium. **2** a blue type of spinel. ⟨< late ME *saphyryn* < OF < Gk. *sappheirinos* like lapis lazuli⟩

sap•py ['sæpi] *adj.* **-pi•er, -pi•est. 1** full of sap. **2** *Slang.* silly; foolish. **—'sap•pi•ly,** *adv.* **—'sap•pi•ness,** *n.*

sap•ro•gen•ic [,sæprə'dʒɛnɪk] *adj.* producing or formed by putrefaction or decay. ⟨< Gk. *sapros* rotten + *-genic*⟩

sap•ro•lite ['sæprə,ləit] *n. Geology.* soft, decomposed rock lying in its original place. ⟨< Gk. *sapros* rotten + E *-lite*⟩

sap•ro•phyte ['sæprə,fəit] *n.* an organism that lives on decaying organic matter; especially, a plant, such as any of several species of fungi. ⟨< Gk. *sapros* rotten + E *-phyte*⟩

sap•ro•phyt•ic [,sæprə'fɪtɪk] *adj.* of or like a saprophyte; living on dead organic matter. **—,sap•ro'phyt•i•cal•ly,** *adv.*

sap•sa•go ['sæpsə,gou] *or* [sæp'seigou] *n.* a hard, greenish, skim-milk cheese of Swiss origin, flavoured and coloured with sweet clover. ⟨alteration of G *Schabziger* < *schaben* to grate + dialect *Ziger* a kind of cheese⟩

sap•suck•er ['sæp,sʌkər] *n.* either of two North American woodpeckers (*Sphyrapicus varius* or *S. thyroideus*) that drill holes in trees to feed on sap and insects.

sap weather *Cdn.* spring weather, with cold nights and warm days, that in sugar maples makes the sap run ready for collecting. Also, **sugar weather**.

sap•wood ['sæp,wʊd] *n.* the sap-carrying tissue between the bark and the heartwood of most trees. The sapwood is softer and usually lighter in colour than the heartwood.

sar•a•band ['særə,bænd] *or* ['sɛrə,bænd] *n.* **1** a slow and stately Spanish dance. **2** the music for this dance. ⟨< F < Sp. *zarabanda*⟩

Sar•a•cen ['særəsən] *or* ['sɛrəsən] *n.* **1** a member of any of the nomadic tribes of Syria and the neighbouring borders of the Roman Empire. **2** later, any Arab. **3** in the Middle Ages, especially during the Crusades, a Muslim, either Arab or Turkish.
—*adj.* of or having to do with the Saracens.

Sar•a•cen•ic [,særə'sɛnɪk] *or* [,sɛrə'sɛnɪk] *adj.* of or having to do with the Saracens.

sar•casm ['sɑrkæzəm] *n.* **1** a sneering or cutting remark; an ironic taunt. **2** the act of making such remarks to a person to hurt his or her feelings; bitter irony: *Her sarcasm was obvious when she called the frightened boy a hero.* ⟨< LL < Gk. *sarkasmos* < *sarkazein* sneer, strip off flesh < *sarx, sarkos* flesh⟩
☛ *Usage.* See note at IRONY.

sar•cas•tic [sɑr'kæstɪk] *adj.* **1** characterized by sarcasm: *a sarcastic remark.* **2** using or tending to use sarcasm: *He gets sarcastic when his feelings are hurt.* **—sar'cas•ti•cal•ly,** *adv.*

Sar•cee ['sɑrsi] *n., pl.* **-cee** or **-cees;** *adj.* —*n.* **1** a member of a people of the First Nations formerly living in the region of the upper Athabasca River in Alberta, now living mainly near Calgary. **2** the Athapascan language of the Sarcee.
—*adj.* of or having to do with the Sarcee or their language.

sarce•net ['sɑrsnɛt] *or* ['sɑrsə,nɛt] *n.* a soft, thin silk fabric. Also, **sarsenet.** ⟨ME < AF *sarzinett,* dim. of *Sarzin* Saracen⟩

sar•coid•o•sis [,sɑrkɔɪ'dousɪs] *n. Pathology.* a chronic disease of unknown origin, characterized by lesions or granulomatous tubercles in or on the lymph nodes, skin, eyes, lungs, bones, etc. ⟨< Gk. *sarkoeides* fleshy (< *sarx, sarkos* flesh) + E *-osis*⟩

sar•co•ma [sɑr'koumə] *n., pl.* **-mas** or **-ma•ta** [-mətə]. *Pathology.* a cancerous tumour that develops in connective tissue, bone, or muscle. ⟨< NL < Gk. *sarkōma,* ult. < *sarx, sarkos* flesh⟩

sar•coph•a•gus [sɑr'kɒfəgəs] *n., pl.* **-gi** [-dʒaɪ] *or* [-dʒi] or **-gus•es.** a stone coffin, especially one ornamented with sculpture or inscriptions. ⟨< L < Gk. *sarkophagos,* originally, flesh-eating (stone) < *sarx, sarkos* flesh + *phagein* eat⟩

sar•cous ['sɑrkəs] *adj.* consisting of or referring to flesh or skeletal muscle. ⟨< Gk. *sarx, sarkos* flesh⟩

sard [sɑrd] *n.* **1** a deep brownish red variety of chalcedony. Sard is traditionally classified as a variety of carnelian. **2** a gem made from this stone. ⟨< L *sarda*; cf. Gk. *sardios (lithos)* stone from Sardis in Lydia⟩

sar•dine [sɑr'din] *n., pl.* **-dines** or (*esp. collectively*) **-dine. 1** any of various food fishes (especially of genera *Sardina, Sardinops,* or *Sardinella*) of the herring family. Some species of small or young sardines are commonly preserved and canned in water, tomato sauce, or oil. **2** such a fish or any of various other small, herringlike fishes when preserved and canned in water, tomato sauce, or oil.
packed like sardines, very crowded. ⟨ME < OF < Ital. < L *sardina* < *sarda* sardine < Gk., perhaps < *Sardō* Sardinia⟩

Sar•din•i•an [sɑr'dɪniən] *n., adj.* —*n.* **1** a native or inhabitant of Sardinia, a large island off the SW coast of Italy. **2** the Romance language of the Sardinians.
—*adj.* of or having to do with Sardinia, its people, or their language.

sar•don•ic [sɑr'dɒnɪk] *adj.* bitterly mocking or cynical and disdainful: *She listened to their naïve proposal with a sardonic smile.* ⟨< F < L < Gk. *sardonios,* a Sardinian plant that supposedly produced hysterical convulsions when eaten⟩ **—sar'don•i•cal•ly,** *adv.*

sar•don•yx [sɑr'dɒnɪks] *or* ['sɑrdənɪks] *n.* **1** a variety of onyx containing layers of sard and chalcedony, usually white. **2** a piece of this stone, or a gem, often a cameo, made from it. ⟨ME < L < Gk. *sardonyx,* probably < *sardios* sard + *onyx* onyx⟩

sar•gas•so [sɑr'gæsou] *n., pl.* **-sos.** gulfweed. Also, **sargassum**. ⟨< Pg. *sargasso* < *sarga,* a type of grape⟩

A sari

sa•ri ['sɑri] *n., pl.* **-ris.** a garment worn by women especially in India, Pakistan, and neighbouring countries, consisting of a long piece of light fabric, usually cotton or silk, draped around the body so that one end forms a long skirt and the other end hangs loosely over the shoulder or is draped over the head. ⟨< Hind.⟩

sa•rong [sə'rɒŋ] *n.* **1** a rectangular piece of cloth, usually a brightly coloured printed material, worn as a skirt by men and women in the Malay Archipelago, Sri Lanka, and some parts of India. **2** a fabric used to make this garment. ⟨< Malay *sārung*⟩

sar•sa•pa•ril•la [,sæspə'rɪlə] *or* [,sɑrsəpə'rɪlə] *n.* **1** any of several tropical American prickly climbing plants (genus *Smilax*) of the lily family. **2** the dried roots of any of these plants, formerly used for medicinal purposes, from which an extract is prepared that is used in flavouring various carbonated drinks, such as root beer. **3** a carbonated drink flavoured with sarsaparilla or something like it. **4** any of various plants resembling sarsaparilla, especially the North American **wild sarsaparilla** (*Aralia nudicaulis*) of the ginseng family. ⟨< Sp. < *zarza* bramble + *parrilla,* dim. of *parra* vine⟩

sarse•net ['sɑrsnɛt] See SARCENET.

Sar•si ['sɑrsi] See SARCEE.

sar•to•ri•al [sɑr'tɔriəl] *adj.* of tailors, tailoring, or tailored clothes: *Her clothes were a sartorial triumph.* ⟨< L *sartorius* of a tailor, ult. < *sarcire* patch⟩ **—sar'to•ri•al•ly,** *adv.*

SASE self-addressed stamped envelope.

sash[1] [sæʃ] *n.* a long, broad strip of cloth or ribbon, worn as an ornament around the waist or over one shoulder. ⟨earlier *shash* < Arabic *shāsh* turban⟩

sash[2] [sæʃ] *n., v. —n.* **1** the frame which holds the glass in a window or door. **2** the frame together with its pane or panes of glass, usually forming a movable part of a window: *She raised the sash to let in the spring air.*
—v. furnish with a sash or sashes. ⟨altered *chassis,* taken as pl.⟩

sa•shay [sæ'ʃei] *v., n. Informal. —v.* **1** move or walk casually in a bold or swaggering manner: *He sashayed up to the front door as if he owned the place.* **2** perform a chassé, usually in square dancing.
—n. an excursion or trip. ⟨alteration of *chassé* a gliding dance step < F⟩
☛ *Hom.* SACHET [sæ'ʃei].

sa•shi•mi [sæ'ʃimi] *n.pl.* very thin slices of raw fish, used as food in Japan. ⟨< Japanese *sashi* (< *sasu* pierce) + *mi* meat⟩

Sask. Saskatchewan.

Sas•katch•e•wan [sə'skætʃə,wɒn] *or* [sə'skætʃəwən] *n.* **1** a province of central Canada, between Alberta on the west and Manitoba on the east. **2** a river rising in Alberta and flowing east across Saskatchewan to Lake Winnipeg in Manitoba. ⟨< Cree⟩

Sas•katch•e•wan•i•an [sə,skætʃə'wɒniən] *n., adj. —n.* a native or long-term resident of Saskatchewan. Also, **Saskatchewaner.**
—adj. of or having to do with Saskatchewan.

sas•ka•toon [,sæskə'tun] *n. Cdn.* **1** a North American shrub (*Amelanchier alnifolia*) of the rose family found from western Ontario to the Yukon and south to Colorado, having tiny white flowers that bloom in May and edible purple berries. **2** the sweet, juicy berry of this shrub. Saskatoons are harvested wild in western Canada and used especially in pies and preserves. ⟨< Algonquian (Cree) *misaskwatomin* < *misaskwat* tree of many branches + *min* fruit⟩

Sas•quatch ['sɑskwɒtʃ] *or* ['sæskwɒtʃ] *n. Cdn.* a wild hairy creature of subhuman appearance, supposed to inhabit certain northwestern mountain regions. ⟨< Salish *seśxac*⟩

sass [sæs] *n., v. Informal. —n.* back talk; impudence or cheekiness.
—v. be saucy to; be impudent or cheeky. ⟨var. of *sauce*⟩

sas•sa•fras ['sæsə,fræs] *n.* **1** an aromatic, North American tree (*Sassafras albidum*) of the laurel family, having small clusters of yellow flowers and bluish black berries. **2** the aromatic dried bark of its root, used in medicine, as a flavouring in candy, soft drinks, etc. ⟨< Sp. *sasafras*⟩

Sas•se•nach ['sæsə,næk] *or* ['sæsə,næx] *n. Scottish and Irish.* **1** Englishman. **2** the English people as a whole. ⟨< Irish *sasenach* Saxon < ML *Saxonicus.* Related to SAXON.⟩

sas•sy ['sæsi] *adj.* **-si•er, -si•est.** *Dialect.* saucy.

sa•stru•gi [sæ'strugi] *n.pl., sing.* -**ga** [-gə] *Cdn., esp. North.* ridges of hard-packed snow, formed by the wind and often attaining a height of more than one metre. Also, **zastrugi.** ⟨< Russian⟩

sat [sæt] *v.* pt. and pp. of SIT.

SAT SCHOLASTIC APTITUDE TEST.

Sat. Saturday.

Sa•tan ['seitən] *n.* Lucifer; the Devil. ⟨OE < LL < Gk. < Hebrew *sātān* enemy, plotter < *sātan* plot against⟩

sa•tang [sæ'tæŋ] *or* [sɑ'tæŋ] *n., pl.* **-tang.** a unit of money in Thailand, equal to 1/100 of a baht. See table of money in the Appendix. ⟨< Thai *satān*⟩

sa•tan•ic [sə'tænɪk] *or* [sei'tænɪk] *adj.* **1** of or having to do with Satan: *satanic magic.* **2** showing extreme viciousness or cruelty; very wicked: *a satanic act of revenge.* **—sa'tan•i•cal•ly,** *adv.*

Sa•tan•ism ['seitə,nɪzəm] *n.* **1** devil worship, especially a French cult of the 1890s that professed worship of Satan, often characterized by blasphemous perversions of Christian rites. **2** the beliefs or rites of devil worship. **3** wickedness; a malicious or diabolical disposition. **—'Sa•tan•ist,** *adj., n.* **—,Sa•tan'is•tic,** *adj.*

satch•el ['sætʃəl] *n.* a small bag, often having a shoulder strap, for carrying books, clothes, etc. ⟨ME < OF < L *saccellus,* double dim. of *saccus* sack[1]. See SACK[1].⟩

sate [seit] *v.* **sat•ed, sat•ing. 1** satisfy fully (any appetite or desire). **2** supply with more than enough, so as to disgust or weary. ⟨alteration of *sade* (OE *sadian* glut; cf. SAD) under influence of L *satiare* satiate. See SATIATE.⟩
☛ *Syn.* **2.** See note at SATIATE.

sa•teen [sæ'tin] *n.* a fabric, usually cotton, woven in a satin weave and having a smooth, lustrous face. ⟨var. of *satin*⟩

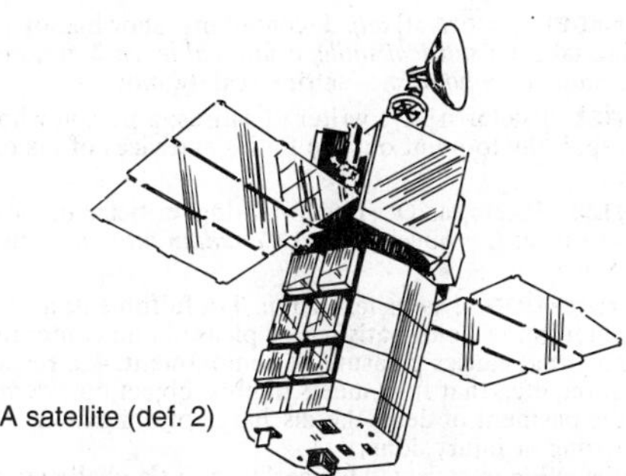
A satellite (def. 2)

sat•el•lite ['sætə,ləit] *n.* **1** *Astronomy.* a small planet that revolves around a larger planet, especially around one of the nine major planets of the solar system. **2** a machine-made object or vehicle sent into an orbit around the earth or other heavenly body. **3** a follower or attendant upon a person of importance. **4** a servile follower. **5** a country that is nominally independent but actually controlled by a more powerful country. **6** a town or city situated near a large city and partially dependent on it. **7** (*adjl.*) of, having to do with, or being a satellite: *a satellite nation.* ⟨< L *satelles, -itis* attendant⟩

sa•tem ['sɑtəm] *or* ['seitəm] *adj. Linguistics.* of or having to do with the language groups in which Indo-European [k] became palatal instead of remaining velar. The satem language group includes Indo-Iranian, Armenian, Albanian, Baltic, and Slavic. Compare CENTUM. ⟨< Avestan, hundred, because the intial [s] of this word is an example of the palatalization of the Indo-European stop⟩

sa•ti [sʌti] *n., pl.* **-tis.** suttee.

sa•tia•ble ['seiʃəbəl] *adj.* that can be satiated. **—,sa•ti•a'bil•i•ty** or **'sa•ti•a•ble•ness,** *n.*

sa•ti•ate *v.* ['seiʃi,eit]; *adj.* ['seiʃiɪt] *v.* **-at•ed, -at•ing;** *adj. —v.* **1** feed fully; satisfy fully. **2** weary or disgust with too much.
—adj. satiated; sated. ⟨< L *satiare* < *satis* enough⟩ **—,sa•ti'a•tion,** *n.*
☛ *Syn. v.* **2. Satiate,** SATE, SURFEIT = fill with more than enough to satisfy. **Satiate** chiefly means 'feed, literally or figuratively, a person, mind, etc., too much', to the point where something that did please or was wanted no longer gives pleasure: *Children who are given every toy they see become satiated.* **Sate** usually means 'satisfy a desire or appetite' so fully that it dies: *Will nothing sate his lust for power?* **Surfeit** emphasizes excess, overeating or oversupplying to the point of making sick or disgusted: *He surfeited them with candy and sodas.*

sa•ti•e•ty [sə'taɪəti] *n.* the feeling of having had too much; disgust or weariness caused by excess; a satiated condition. ⟨< F < L *satietas* < *satis* enough⟩

sat•in ['sætən] *n.* **1** a soft fabric, usually of silk or rayon, woven in a satin weave, having a smooth, lustrous face and a dull back. See WEAVE for picture. **2** a smoothness or glossiness like that of satin: *the satin of the silver bowl.* **3** (*adjl.*) of or like satin: *a satin dress, a satin finish on a silver bowl.* ⟨ME < OF < Arabic *zaitūnī*⟩

satin stitch an embroidery stitch using long stitches placed closely together, producing a solid surface resembling the smooth finish of satin. See EMBROIDERY for picture.

satin weave a weave in which the crosswise threads alternately cross over a number of lengthwise threads and under a single thread, producing a soft, luxurious fabric with a smooth, glossy surface. See WEAVE for picture.

sat•in•wood ['sætən,wʊd] *n.* **1** an East Indian tree (*Chloroxylon swietenia*) of the mahogany family (or, according to some authorities, the rue family) having hard, yellowish brown wood with a satiny lustre. **2** the wood of this tree, used for fine furniture, farm tools, etc.

sat•in•y ['sætəni] *adj.* like satin in smoothness and gloss.

sat•ire ['sætaɪr] *n.* **1** a literary genre characterized by the use of irony to attack a vice or foolishness. **2** a literary work in this genre. Jonathan Swift's *Gulliver's Travels* is a satire. **3** the use of irony, often biting or bitter, to attack vice or foolishness. ⟨< L *satira*, var. of *(lanx) satura* mixed (dish) < *satur* full⟩
☛ *Usage.* See note at IRONY.

sa•tir•ic [sə'tɪrɪk] *adj.* **1** of or having to do with satire: *satiric verse.* **2** satirical.

sa•tir•i•cal [sə'tɪrɪkəl] *adj.* **1** containing, showing, or reflecting satire: *a satirical smile, a satirical letter.* **2** fond of using satire: *a satirical columnist.* **—sa'tir•i•cal•ly,** *adv.*

sat•i•rist ['sætərɪst] *n.* a writer of satires; a person who uses satire, especially to point out the follies and vices of his or her own times.

sat•i•rize ['sætə,raɪz] *v.* **-rized, -riz•ing.** criticize or ridicule by means of satire: *Her novel satirizes Canadian attitudes toward the United States.*

sat•is•fac•tion [,sætɪs'fækʃən] *n.* **1** a fulfilment; a satisfying. **2** the condition of being satisfied or pleased and contented. **3** anything that causes pleasure or contentment. **4** a response, information, etc., that fully meets doubts, objections, demands, etc. **5** the payment of debt; the discharge of obligation; a making up for wrong or injury done.
give satisfaction, a satisfy. **b** formerly, accept a challenge to a duel from a person one has wronged. ⟨ME < OF < L *satisfactio, -onis* < *satisfacere.* See SATISFY.⟩

sat•is•fac•to•ry [,sætɪs'fæktəri] *adj.* satisfying; good enough to satisfy. **—,sat•is'fac•to•ri•ly,** *adv.* **—,sat•is'fac•to•ri•ness,** *n.*

sat•is•fy ['sætɪs,faɪ] *v.* **-fied, -fy•ing. 1** give enough to; fulfil (desires, hopes, demands, etc.); put an end to (needs, wants, etc.): *He satisfied his hunger with a sandwich and milk.* **2** fully meet (an objection, doubt, demand, etc.). **3** make contented; please: *Are you satisfied now?* **4** give satisfaction. **5** pay; make right: *After the accident he satisfied all claims for the damage he had caused.* **6** set free from doubt; convince: *She was satisfied that it was an accident.* **7** make up for a wrong or injury. ⟨ME < OF < L *satisfacere* < *satis* enough + *facere* do⟩
—'sat•is,fi•a•ble, *adj.* **—'sat•is,fi•er,** *n.* **—'sat•is,fy•ing•ly,** *adv.*
☛ *Syn.* **1, 3. Satisfy,** CONTENT[2] = meet, wholly or partly, a person's desires and wants. **Satisfy** suggests giving enough to fulfil a person's desires, hopes, needs, etc.: *The little mongrel satisfied the boy's desire for a dog.* **Content** suggests giving enough to please a person and keep him from feeling deprived: *A letter from her once a week contented him.*

sa•to•ri [sə'tɔri] *n.* in Zen Buddhism, the state of enlightenment, especially as attained through sudden flashes of intuition. ⟨< Japanese *sato* awake⟩

sa•trap ['seitræp] *or* ['sætrəp] *n.* **1** a ruler, often a tyrant, who is subordinate to a higher ruler. **2** in ancient Persia, a governor of a province. ⟨ME < L < Gk. *satrapēs* < OPersian *kshathra-pāwan* guardian of the realm⟩

sa•trap•y ['seitrəpi] *or* ['sætrəpi] *n., pl.* **-trap•ies.** the province, position, or authority of a satrap.

Sat•su•ma [sæt'sumə] *n.* **1** a type of thin, porcelain pottery. **2** a type of orange, originally grown in Japan, but now in the southern U.S. ⟨name of a Japanese province⟩

sat•u•ra•ble ['sætʃərəbəl] *adj.* that can be saturated. **—,sat•u•ra'bil•i•ty,** *n.*

sat•u•rate ['sætʃə,reit] *v.* **-rat•ed, -rat•ing. 1** fill completely with moisture; soak: *Saturate the peat moss with water before planting the bulbs in it.* **2** fill or imbue: *a ceremony saturated with tradition.* **3** *Military.* overwhelm with heavy bombing or shelling. **4** cause (a substance, air, vapour, etc.) to absorb or unite with the greatest possible amount of another substance: *to saturate air with water vapour.* ⟨< L *saturare* glut < *satur* full⟩
—'sat•u,ra•tor or **'sat•u,rat•er,** *n.*

sat•u•rat•ed ['sætʃə,reitɪd] *adj.* **1** thoroughly wet. **2 a** of a solution, containing the maximum amount of dissolved substance that can normally be dissolved at a given temperature and pressure. **b** of an organic compound, containing no double or triple bonds and thus not able to unite directly with other compounds or elements. **3** of a colour, containing little or no white; pure and rich.

sat•u•ra•tion [,sætʃə'reiʃən] *n.* **1** the act or process of saturating. **2** the state or condition of being saturated. **3** the degree of a colour's chromatic purity. The less white a colour contains, the greater its saturation.

saturation point 1 the point at which a substance can absorb no more of another substance. **2** the stage beyond which no more can be accepted, endured, etc. **3** a point at which a market is supplied with as much of a particular commodity as it can absorb.

Sat•ur•day ['sætər,dei] *or* ['sætərdi] *n.* the seventh day of the week, following Friday. ⟨OE *Sæterdæg, Sætern(es)dæg,* partial translation of L *Saturni dies* day of Saturn (the planet)⟩

Sat•urn ['sætərn] *n.* **1** *Roman mythology.* the god of agriculture, ruler of the world until overthrown by his son Jupiter, and corresponding to the Greek god Cronus. **2** *Astronomy.* the second largest planet in the solar system, the sixth in distance from the sun. The planet has at least ten satellites and is surrounded by seven thin concentric rings composed of particles that may be chunks of ice. ⟨< L *Saturnus,* associated by the Romans with *satio* sowing, ult. < *serere* to sow⟩

Sat•ur•na•li•a [,sætər'neiliə] *or* [,sætər'neiljə] *n.pl.* **1** the ancient Roman festival of Saturn, celebrated in December with much feasting and merrymaking. **2 saturnalia,** a period of unrestrained revelry and licence (*used with a singular or plural verb*). ⟨< L⟩

Sat•ur•na•li•an [,sætər'neiliən] *or* [,sætər'neiljən] *adj.* **1** of or having to do with the ancient Roman festival of Saturn. **2 saturnalian,** riotously merry; revelling without restraint.

Sa•tur•ni•an [sə'tɜrniən] *adj.* **1** of or having to do with the god Saturn, whose reign is referred to as the 'golden age'. **2** prosperous, happy, or peaceful. **3** of or having to do with the planet Saturn.

sat•ur•ni•id [sə'tɜrniɪd] *n.* any of certain large, brightly coloured, hairy-bodied moths of the family Saturniidae.

sat•ur•nine ['sætər,naɪn] *adj.* gloomy, grave, or taciturn: *a saturnine disposition.* ⟨< *Saturn;* those born under the planet's sign are supposed to be morose⟩ **—'sat•ur,nine•ly,** *adv.*

sat•ya•gra•ha ['sʌtjə,grʌhə] *or* [sət'jɑgrəhə] *n.* in India, the policy and philosophy inaugurated in 1919 by Mahatma Gandhi, emphasizing the use of non-co-operation and passive resistance to achieve social reform. ⟨< Skt. *satya* truth + *agraha* persistence⟩

sat•yr ['sætər] *or* ['seitər] *n.* **1** *Greek mythology.* any of a class of minor woodland gods who were companions of Bacchus and indulged in merrymaking and lechery. In early Greek art they were pictured as men with the ears and tail of a horse. In later Roman art they became partially assimilated with the Roman fauns, and were represented as having the ears, tail, horns, and legs of a goat. **2** a lecherous man. **3** a man with satyriasis. **4** any of numerous usually brownish butterflies (family Satyridae) often having eyelike spots on the wings. ⟨ME < L < Gk. *satyros*⟩

sat•yr•i•a•sis [,sætə'raɪəsɪs] *n.* a pathological condition in men, marked by an uncontrollable desire for sexual intercourse.

sauce [sɒs] *n., v.* **sauced, sauc•ing.** *—n.* **1** something, usually a thick liquid, served with food to enhance the flavour. Mint sauce is eaten with lamb, and many different sauces with desserts. **2** fruit stewed to a smooth, thick consistency: *cranberry sauce, applesauce.* **3** something that adds interest or relish. **4** *Informal.* sauciness. **5 the sauce.** *Slang.* alcoholic liquor.
—v. **1** prepare with sauce; season. **2** give interest or flavour to. **3** *Informal.* be saucy to. ⟨ME < OF < L *salsa,* fem. adj., salted, ult. < *sal, salis* salt⟩

sauce–boat ['sɒs ,bout] *n.* a kind of low jug or pitcher used for serving gravy, sauces, etc. Also called **gravy boat.**

sauce•box ['sɒs,bɒks] *n. Informal.* an impertinent person, especially a child.

sauce•pan ['sɒs,pæn] *n.* a deep cooking utensil of metal, glass, ceramic, etc., usually having a lid, and a long handle at the side, and used for cooking on top of the stove.

sau•cer ['sɒsər] *n.* **1** a shallow dish to set a cup on. **2** any small, round, shallow dish, such as a dish put under a flowerpot to catch excess water. **3** something round and shallow like a saucer. ⟨ME *saucer* sauce dish < OF *saucier* < *sauce.* See SAUCE.⟩ **—'sau•cer,like,** *adj.*

sau•ci•er [sou'sjei]; *French,* [so'sje] *n.* a chef or chef's assistant who specializes in making sauces.

sau•ci•ness ['sɒsinəs] *n.* behaviour lacking in respect: *That child's sauciness is verging on rudeness.*

sau•cy ['sɒsi] *adj.* **-ci•er, -ci•est. 1** showing lack of respect; rude. **2** pert; smart: *a saucy hat.* ⟨< *sauce*⟩ **—'sau•ci•ly,** *adv.*
☛ *Syn.* **1.** See note at IMPERTINENT.

Sau•di ['saʊdi] *adj., n. —adj.* characteristic of or having to do with Saudi Arabia or its inhabitants.
—n. a native or inhabitant of Saudi Arabia. ⟨clipped form of *Saudi Arabia*⟩

Saudi Arabia ['saʊdi ə'reibiə] a large country between the Red Sea and the Persian Gulf. See LEBANON for map.

sauer•kraut ['saʊr,krʌut] *n.* cabbage cut fine, salted, and allowed to ferment; cabbage pickled in brine. ⟨< G *Sauerkraut* < *sauer* sour + *Kraut* cabbage⟩

sau•ger ['sɒgər] *n.* a North American freshwater fish of the perch family (*Stizostedion canadense*) that is a popular food and game fish. It is closely related to the walleye. ⟨origin uncertain; ? < North American Indian⟩

Sauk [sɒk] *n., pl.* **Sauks** or **Sauk. 1** a member of an American Indian people formerly living in the Fox River valley in Wisconsin. **2** a dialect of Fox spoken by the Sauks. Also, **Sac.**

sault [su] *n. Cdn.* a waterfall or rapids (*now used mainly in place names*): *Sault Ste. Marie.* ⟨obs. spelling of F *saut* leap, jump, falls < L *saltus* < *salire* to leap⟩
☛ *Hom.* SOU, SUE.

sau•na ['sɒnə] *or* ['saʊnə] *n.* **1** a relatively dry hot bath using dry heat to cause perspiration as well as some steam produced by applying small amounts of water to hot stones. This is usually followed by a plunge in cold water and/or a mild beating of the skin with birch switches. **2** a house or other structure used for such baths. ⟨< Finnish⟩

saun•ter ['sɒntər] *v., n. –v.* walk along slowly and quietly; stroll: *saunter through the park.*
–n. **1** a leisurely or careless gait. **2** a stroll. ⟨origin uncertain⟩ **–'saun•ter•er,** *n.*

sau•ri•an ['sɔriən] *n., adj. –n.* **1** any of a suborder (Sauria) of reptiles commonly known as lizards. Geckos, horned toads, chameleons, etc., are saurians. **2** any of various reptiles resembling the lizards, such as the crocodiles.
–adj. of, designating, or like lizards. ⟨< NL *sauria,* pl. < Gk. *sauros* lizard⟩

-saurus *combining form.* lizard; dinosaur: *brontosaurus.* ⟨< NL < Gk. *sauros* lizard⟩

sau•ry ['sɔri] *n., pl.* **-ries** or **-ry.** any of a family (Scomberesocidae) of long, slender fishes found in tropical and temperate seas, having a pointed, beaklike snout. ⟨< NL < Gk. *sauros* lizard⟩
☛ *Hom.* SORRY.

sau•sage ['sɒsɪdʒ] *n.* chopped pork, beef, or other meats, seasoned and stuffed into a thin casing or skin. ⟨ME < ONF *saussiche* < LL *salsicia,* ult. < L *sal, salis* salt⟩

sau•té [sou'tei] *adj., v.* **-téed, -té•ing.** *n. –adj.* fried quickly in a little fat, over a high heat.
–v. fry quickly in a little fat.
–n. a dish of food prepared in this way. ⟨< F *sauté,* pp. of *sauter* jump < L *saltare* hop, frequentative of *salire* leap⟩

sau•terne [sou'tɜrn] *n.* **1** a French white table wine. **2** any wine of the same type. ⟨< *Sauternes,* a district in S France, where the grapes are grown⟩

sauve qui peut [sovki'pø] *French.* a general rout; hasty flight. ⟨literally, let (everyone) save (himself) who can⟩

sav•age ['sævɪdʒ] *adj., n., v.* **-aged, -ag•ing.** *–adj.* **1** of animals, not tamed or under human control; wild and fierce: *savage beasts of the jungle.* **2** of geographical features, wild and rugged: *savage mountain scenery.* **3** ferocious or brutal: *a savage attack by a mugger.* **4** enraged; furiously angry.
–n. **1** a fierce, brutal, or cruel person. **2** a crude or boorish person.
–v. attack fiercely or brutally: *The child was savaged by a dog.* ⟨ME < OF *sauvage* < LL *salvaticus,* ult. < L *silva* forest⟩ **–'sav•age•ly,** *adv.* **–'sav•age•ness,** *n.*
☛ *Syn. adj.* **1, 3.** See note at FIERCE.

sav•age•ry ['sævɪdʒri] *n., pl.* **-ries. 1** the quality or condition of being ferocious or brutal: *The savagery of their attack took the enemy by surprise.* **2** an act of cruelty or brutality.

sa•van•na or **sa•van•nah** [sə'vænə] *n.* **1** a treeless plain. **2** a region of tropical or subtropical grassland having a scattering of trees. **3** especially in the Maritimes, a swamp or tract of peat bog; muskeg. ⟨< earlier Sp. *zavana* < Arawakan⟩

sa•vant [sə'vɑnt] *or* ['sævənt] *n.* a widely respected person of learning. ⟨< earlier F ppr. of *savoir* know < L *sapere* be wise⟩

save[1] [seiv] *v.* **saved, sav•ing;** *n. –v.* **1** make (someone or something) safe from harm, danger, loss, etc.; rescue: *to save a drowning woman.* **2** keep safe from harm, danger, hurt, loss, etc.; protect (something): *to save one's honour.* **3** lay (something) aside; store up: *She saves pieces of string.* **4** keep from spending or wasting (something): *Save your strength.* **5** avoid expense or waste: *She saves in every way she can.* **6** prevent; make (something) less: *to save work, to save trouble, to save expense.* **7** treat (something) carefully to lessen wear, weariness, etc.: *Large print saves one's eyes.* **8** set (someone) free from sin and its consequences. **9** *Computer technology.* copy (a program or data) onto auxiliary storage, so that if the program or data currently in main memory is lost, a copy will still be available: *Before proceeding to type the next section, the legal secretary saved the first section of the contract he was typing into the word-processing system.*
–n. the act of saving, especially by preventing an opponent from scoring: *The Leafs' goalie made a great save.* ⟨ME < OF < LL *salvare* < L *salvus* safe⟩ **–'sav•er,** *n.*

save[2] [seiv] *prep., conj. –prep.* except; but: *She works every day of the week save Sunday.*
–conj. Archaic. unless. ⟨var. of *safe,* in sense of 'not being involved'⟩

sav•in ['sævən] *n.* **1** a shrubby Eurasian juniper (*Juniperus sabina*) having dark foliage that yields an oil formerly used in medicine. **2** this oil. **3** any of several related shrubs. Also, **savine.** ⟨ult. < L *sabina,* originally adj., Sabine⟩

sav•ing ['seivɪŋ] *adj., n., prep., conj., v. –adj.* **1** that saves. **2** tending to save up money; avoiding waste; economical. **3** making or stating a reservation (about something): *a saving clause.*
–n. **1** an act or way of saving money, time, etc.: *It will be a saving to take this shortcut.* **2** Often, **savings** (*sing. in function*), the amount saved: *a savings of 10%.* **3 savings,** *pl.* money saved.
–prep. **1** save; except. **2** with all due respect to or for.
–conj. except.
–v. ppr. of SAVE.

savings account a deposit account in a bank, trust company, or credit union on which interest is paid.

sav•iour or **sav•ior** ['seivjər] *n.* **1** a person who saves or rescues. **2 the Saviour,** *Christianity.* Jesus Christ. ⟨ME < OF < LL *salvator* < *salvare.* See SAVE[1].⟩
☛ *Spelling.* See note at -OR.

sa•voir–faire ['sævwɑr 'fɛr]; *French,* [savwaʀ'fɛʀ] *n.* the knowledge of just the right thing to do or say, especially in social situations. ⟨< F *savoir-faire,* literally, knowing how to act⟩

sa•voir–vi•vre ['sævwɑr 'vivrə]; *French,* [savwaʀ'vivʀ] *n.* knowledge of the world and of the ways or usages of polite society; good breeding. ⟨< F *savoir-vivre,* literally, knowing how to live⟩

sa•vor•y ['seivəri] *n., pl.* **-vor•ies.** any of a genus (*Satureia*) of fragrant herbs of the mint family, used for seasoning food; especially, **summer savory.** ⟨ME *saverey,* ult. < L *satureia*⟩
☛ *Hom.* SAVOURY.

sa•vour or **sa•vor** ['seivər] *n., v. –n.* **1** a taste or smell; flavour: *The soup has a savour of onion.* **2** a distinctive quality; noticeable trace: *There is a savour of conceit in everything he says.*
–v. **1** taste or smell (*of*): *That sauce savours of lemon.* **2** perceive or appreciate by taste or smell: *He savoured the soup with pleasure.* **3** enjoy (something) fully: *The child savoured the attention lavished on her by her grandparents.* **4** give flavour to; season. **5** have the quality or nature (*of*): *a request that savours of a command.* ⟨ME < OF < L *sapor*⟩ **–'sa•vour•er** or **'sa•vor•er,** *n.* **–'sa•vour•less** or **'sa•vor•less,** *adj.*

sa•vour•y or **sa•vor•y** ['seivəri] *adj.* **-vour•i•er** or **-vor•i•er, -vour•i•est** or **-vor•i•est;** *n., pl.* **-vour•ies** or **-vor•ies.**
–adj. **1** pleasing in taste or smell, especially because of the seasoning: *The savoury smell of roasting turkey greeted us as we entered the house.* **2** having a salt or piquant flavour and not a sweet one: *There were both sweet and savoury relishes on the table.* **3** morally acceptable: *Her reputation was not particularly savoury.*
–n. a small portion of highly seasoned food served at the beginning or end of a dinner to stimulate the appetite or digestion. ⟨ME < OF *savoure,* ult. < L *sapor* taste⟩ **–'sa•vour•i•ness** or **'sa•vor•i•ness,** *n.*
☛ *Hom.* SAVORY.

sa•voy [sə'vɔɪ] *n.* See SAVOY CABBAGE.

Sa•voy [sə'vɔɪ] *n.* the French noble family that ruled Italy from 1861 to 1946.

Sa•voy•ard [sə'vɔɪɑrd] *or* [,sævɔɪ'ɑrd]; *French,* [savwa'jaʀ] *n., adj. –n.* **1** a native or inhabitant of Savoy, a region in E France. **2** an actor, producer, or warm admirer of Gilbert and Sullivan's operas, many of which were first produced at the Savoy Theatre in London, England.
–adj. **1** of Savoy or its people. **2** of or having to do with the Savoy Theatre in London.

Savoy cabbage a type of cabbage having a compact head and wrinkled leaves. ⟨< *Savoie* Savoy, a region in E France⟩

sav•vy ['sævi] *v.* **-vied, -vy•ing;** *n., adj. Slang.* —*v.* know; understand.
—*n.* understanding; intelligence; sense.
—*adj.* shrewd; knowing; skilful. ⟨< Sp. or Pg. *sabe* (you) know, both ult. < L *sapere* be wise. 18c.⟩

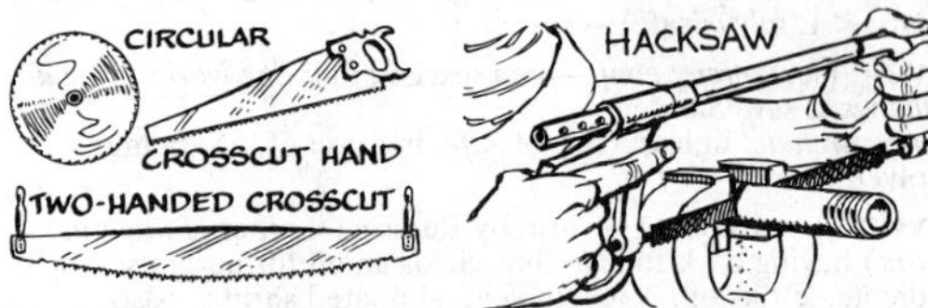

Saws. The circular saw (upper left) is mounted in a frame and turned by a motor. The other three are used by hand.

saw[1] [sɒ] *n., v.* **sawed, sawed** or **sawn, saw•ing.** —*n.* **1** a tool for cutting hard material such as wood or metal, consisting of a blade or disk with sharp teeth on the edge, especially such a tool operated by hand. **2** a device or machine that includes such a tool.
—*v.* **1** cut with a saw. **2** make with a saw. **3** use a saw. **4** be sawed: *Pine saws more easily than oak.* **5** cut as if with a saw; move (through) as if sawing. ⟨OE *sagu*⟩ —**'saw•er,** *n.*

saw[2] [sɒ] *v.* pt. of SEE[1].

saw[3] [sɒ] *n.* a wise saying; proverb: *"A stitch in time saves nine" is a familiar saw.* ⟨OE *sagu.* Related to SAY.⟩

saw•buck ['sɒ,bʌk] *n.* **1** sawhorse. **2** *Slang.* a ten-dollar bill (from the X (Roman numeral for ten) formed by the legs of the sawhorse, with a pun on *buck*). ⟨< Du. *zaagbok*⟩

saw•dust ['sɒ,dʌst] *n.* the particles of wood produced in sawing.

sawed–off ['sɒd 'ɒf] **1** designating a shotgun with the end of the barrel cut off. **2** *Slang.* of less than average height; short.

saw•fish ['sɒ,fɪʃ] *n., pl.* **-fish** or **-fish•es.** any of a family (Pristidae) of sharklike rays found in warm coastal waters, having an elongated, bladelike snout with strong teeth along the edges on both sides.

saw•fly ['sɒ,flaɪ] *n., pl.* **-flies.** any of a superfamily (Tenthredinoidea) of insects belonging to the same order as ants, bees, and wasps, the adult female having a sawlike part on its egg-laying organ which it uses to cut slits in plants, depositing its eggs in these openings. Adult sawflies can be distinguished from bees and wasps by their thick bodies.

saw•horse ['sɒ,hɔrs] *n.* a frame on which wood is placed for sawing.

saw•log ['sɒ,lɒg] *n. Cdn.* a log suitable for processing in a sawmill.

saw•mill ['sɒ,mɪl] *n.* **1** a place where timber is sawed into planks, boards, etc. by power-driven machines. **2** a large machine for sawing.

sawmill burner a conical furnace for burning sawdust at a sawmill.

sawn [sɒn] *v.* a pp. of SAW[1].

saw–off ['sɒ ,ɒf] *n. Cdn. Slang.* **1** *Politics.* **a** an arrangement between two parties by which one agrees not to enter a candidate in one riding if the other agrees not to enter a candidate in a different riding. **b** an arrangement by which one party agrees after an election to drop charges of corruption against another if the second party will make a similar agreement. **2** the repayment of a debt; any act of compensation. **3** any arrangement by which one concession is balanced against another. **4** *Sports and games.* a tie.

saw–whet owl ['sɒ ,wɛt] a small North American owl (*Aegolius acadicus*) having dark brown plumage on the head, back, and wings, and white on the breast and abdomen, and having a characteristic rasping, metallic call.

saw•yer ['sɔɪjər] *or* ['sɒjər] *n.* a person whose work is sawing timber. ⟨< *saw*[1] + *-yer,* as in *lawyer*⟩

sax [sæks] *n. Informal.* saxophone.

sax•a•tile ['sæksə,taɪl] *or* ['sæksətɪl] *adj. Biology.* living or growing on or among rocks. Also, **saxicolous** [sæks'ɪkələs]. ⟨< L *saxatilis* frequenting rocks < *saxum* rock⟩

sax•horn ['sæks,hɔrn] *n.* any of a family of trumpetlike, valved brass instruments ranging from soprano to bass, used especially in military-style brass bands. ⟨after Adolphe *Sax* (1814-1894) the inventor⟩

sax•i•frage ['sæksəfrɪdʒ], ['sæksə,frædʒ], *or* ['sæksə,freidʒ] *n.* **1** any of various low-growing plants (family Saxifragaceae, especially genus *Saxifraga*) having clusters of white, pink, yellow, or purple flowers and thick, fleshy leaves that often grow in rosettes from the base of the plant. Some species are cultivated for rock gardens. **2** (*adjl.*) designating the family (Saxifragaceae) of mostly perennial herbs that includes the saxifrages and, in some classifications, gooseberries, currants, and mock oranges. ⟨ME < LL *saxifraga,* ult. < *saxum* rock + *frangere* break. Doublet of SALSIFY.⟩

sax•ist ['sæksɪst] *n. Informal.* saxophonist.

sax•i•tox•in [,sæksɪ'tɒksɪn] *n.* a powerful poison causing partial paralysis, resulting from ingesting shellfish that have fed on the dinoflagellate *Gonyoulax catanella,* the causative agent of RED TIDE.

Sax•on ['sæksən] *n., adj.* —*n.* **1** a member of an ancient Germanic people of NW Germany. They invaded and conquered Britain in the 5th and 6th centuries A.D., settling in western and southern England. **2** the language of the Saxons. **3** Anglo-Saxon. **4** a native of Saxony, a region in eastern Germany. **5** the modern Low German dialect of Saxony.
—*adj.* **1** of or having to do with the early Saxons or their language. **2** Anglo-Saxon. **3** English. **4** of or having to do with Saxony. ⟨< L *Saxo,* pl. *Saxones* < Gmc.⟩

sax•o•ny ['sæksəni] *n.* **1** a kind of fine wool. **2** a twisted knitting yarn made from this wool. **3** a fabric made from this.

sax•o•phone ['sæksə,foun] *n.* any of a group of musical wind instruments ranging from soprano to bass, having a curved metal body, keys for the fingers, and a single-reed mouthpiece. ⟨See SAXHORN⟩ —**,sax•o'phon•ic** [,sæksə'fɒnɪk], *adj.*

A saxophone

sax•o•phon•ist ['sæksə,founɪst] *n.* a person who plays the saxophone, especially a skilled player.

sax•tu•ba ['sæks,tjubə] *or* ['sæks,tubə] *n.* a bass saxhorn. ⟨< *sax(horn)* + *tuba*⟩

say [sei] *v.* **said, say•ing;** *n.* —*v.* **1** speak; utter; pronounce: *What did you say? She says that word quite oddly.* **2** put into words; express; declare: *Say what you think.* **3** recite; repeat: *Say your prayers.* **4** suppose; take as an estimate: *You can learn in, say, ten lessons.* **5** arrive at an opinion: *It is hard to say which dress is prettier.* **6** read: *It says here, 'Shake well'. What does the thermometer say this morning?*
go without saying, be extremely obvious: *It goes without saying that he will be furious when he gets the bill.*
that is to say, that is; in other words.
to say nothing of, without mentioning: *The hotel itself cost a lot, to say nothing of the meals.*
—*n.* **1** what a person says or has to say. **2** the chance to say something: *I have had my say.* **3** the power or authority to speak, decide, or exert influence: *Who has the say in this matter?* ⟨OE *secgan*⟩ —**'say•er,** *n.*

say•est ['seiɪst] *v. Archaic.* 2nd pers. sing., present tense, of SAY. *Thou sayest* means *you* (sing.) *say.*

say•ing ['seiɪŋ] *n., v.* —*n.* something said, especially a wise statement that is often repeated: *I remember a saying of my mother's. "Haste makes waste" is a saying.*
—*v.* ppr. of SAY.

says [sɛz] *v.* 3rd pers. sing., present tense, of SAY.

say–so ['sei ,sou] *n. Informal.* **1** an unsupported statement: *Don't do it just on his say-so; he might not know what he's talking about.* **2** authority or power to decide; say: *She has no say-so in the matter.*

sayst [seist] *v. Archaic.* sayest.

say•yid or **sa•yid** ['sɑjɪd] *or* ['seiɪd] *n.* an Islamic title of respect, given to some descendants of Mohammed.

sb. substantive.

Sb antimony (for L *stibium*).

sc. 1 scene. 2 science. 3 scilicet.

s.c. SMALL CAPITALS.

Sc 1 scandium. 2 STRATO-CUMULUS.

Sc. Scottish; Scotland.

SC *Cdn.* STAR OF COURAGE.

S.C. 1 SOCIAL CREDIT (PARTY). 2 SUPREME COURT. 3 SECURITY COUNCIL.

scab [skæb] *n., v.* **scabbed, scab•bing.** *—n.* **1** the crust that forms over a sore or wound during healing. **2** a skin disease in animals, especially sheep. **3** any of several fungous diseases of plants, usually producing dark, crustlike spots. **4** any of the spots caused by that plant disease. **5** *Slang.* a worker who will not join a trade union or who takes a striker's place. **6** *Slang.* a rascal; scoundrel.
—v. **1** become covered with a scab (*usually used with* **over**). **2** *Slang.* act or work as a scab. ⟨< Scand.; cf. Danish *skab*⟩

scab•bard ['skæbərd] *n.* **1** a sheath or case for the blade of a sword, dagger, etc. See SWORD for picture. **2** *Cdn.* SKATE-GUARD. ⟨ME < AF *escaubers*, pl. < Gmc.⟩

scab•by ['skæbi] *adj.* **-bi•er, -bi•est. 1** covered with or consisting of scabs: *scabby skin.* **2** having SCAB (def. 2). **3** *Informal.* low; mean: *a scabby trick.* **—'scab•bi•ly,** *adv.* **—'scab•bi•ness,** *n.*

scab•by–nosed wavey ['skæbi ˌnouzd] *Cdn. North.* Ross's goose, a smallish goose that breeds in the Far North.

sca•bies ['skeibiz] *or* ['skeibiiz] *n. Pathology.* a contagious skin infection caused by a mite (*Sarcoptes scabiei*), the female of which burrows beneath the outer layer of skin, laying its eggs there, and producing a skin eruption that is intensely itchy; the itch. ⟨< L *scabies* itch < *scabere* scratch⟩

sca•bi•o•sa [ˌskeibi'ousə] *n.* SCABIOUS[2] (def. 1).

sca•bi•ous[1] ['skeibiəs] *adj.* **1** of, having to do with, or like scabies. **2** having scabs. ⟨< L *scabiosus* mangy, rough < *scabies.* See SCABIES.⟩

sca•bi•ous[2] ['skeibiəs] *n.* **1** any of a genus (*Scabiosa*) of annual and perennial Mediterranean plants of the teasel family having dense, dome-shaped heads of various colours, especially the cultivated **sweet scabious. 2** any of various related plants, especially of genus *Krautia.* ⟨< ML *scabiosa (herba)* (herb) for scabies, originally adj. fem. of *scabiosus* scabious < L *scabies.* See SCABIES.⟩

scab•land ['skæbˌlænd] *n.* a region stripped of topsoil by floods, characterized by low, rocky hills.

scab rock 1 an area of scabland. **2** the bare rock at the surface of scabland.

sca•brous ['skeibrəs] *or* ['skæbrəs] *adj.* **1** rough with very small points or projections. **2** full of difficulties; harsh. **3** hard to treat with decency; indelicate. ⟨< LL *scabrosus* < L *scaber* scaly⟩

scads [skædz] *n.pl. Slang.* a large quantity. ⟨origin uncertain⟩

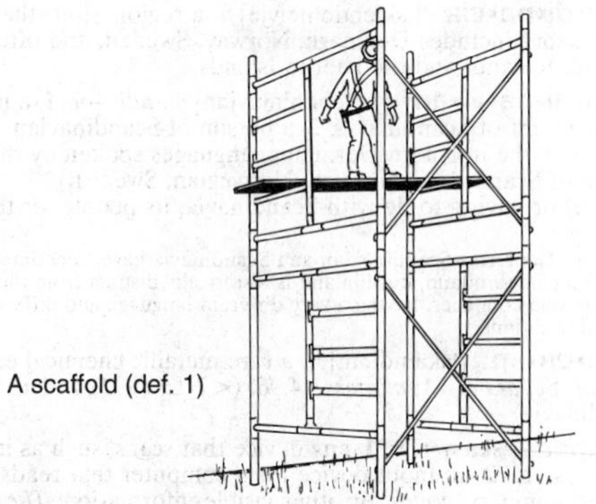

A scaffold (def. 1)

scaf•fold ['skæfəld] *n., v. —n.* **1** a temporary structure for holding workers, such as construction workers or window washers, when working at a height above the ground or floor during the construction, repair, etc., of a building. **2** a raised platform used as a base for a gallows or guillotine. **3** any raised framework or platform.
—v. furnish or support with a scaffold. ⟨ME < var. of OF *eschaffault*, from same source as *catafalque*⟩

scaf•fold•ing ['skæfəldɪŋ] *n., v. —n.* **1** a scaffold or system of scaffolds. **2** materials for building scaffolds.
—v. ppr. of SCAFFOLD.

scal•age ['skeilɪdʒ] *n.* **1** a percentage assessed for deduction in weight or price, to allow for shrinkage, leakage, etc. **2** an estimate of the amount of lumber in a log being scaled. (See SCALE[3], *v.* def. 4.)

scal•ar ['skeilər] *adj., n. —adj.* **1** able to be represented on a scale or line; having magnitude but no direction, such as temperature. **2** in, on, or having to do with scales.
—n. Mathematics. Physics. a quantity having magnitude only. Compare VECTOR.

sca•lar•i•form [skə'lærəˌfɔrm] *or* [skə'lɛrəˌfɔrm] *adj.* ladderlike, especially in having crosswise markings or ridges resembling the rungs of a ladder.

scalar product *Mathematics.* a scalar equal to the product of the lengths of two vectors and the cosine of the angle between them.

scal•a•wag ['skæləˌwæg] *n. Informal.* a good-for-nothing person; scamp; rascal. Also, **scallywag.** ⟨origin uncertain⟩

scald[1] [skɒld] *v., n. —v.* **1** burn with or as if with hot liquid or steam. **2** pour boiling liquid over; use boiling liquid on: *Flowerpots should be scalded before using.* **3** heat or be heated almost to boiling, but not quite.
—n. a burn caused by hot liquid or steam: *The scald on her hand came from lifting a pot cover carelessly.* ⟨< dial. OF *escalder* < LL *excaldare* < L *ex-* very + *calidus* hot⟩

scald[2] [skɒld] *or* [skɑld] *n.* See SKALD.

scale[1] [skeil] *n., v.* **scaled, scal•ing.** *—n.* **1 a** one of the thin, flat, hard plates forming the outer covering of some fishes, snakes, and lizards. **b** a similar thin plate on the legs of birds or on the wings of certain insects. **2** a thin layer or piece like a scale: *Scales of skin peeled off after she had scarlet fever.* **3** tartar coating that forms on teeth. **4** the oxide coating that forms on the inside of a boiler, kettle, etc. **5** SCALE LEAF. **6** SCALE INSECT. **7** *Metallurgy.* a flaky film of oxide, especially iron oxide, that forms on metals when they are heated or rusty.
—v. **1** remove scale or scales from. **2** come off in thin pieces or a thin layer: *The paint is starting to scale.* **3** remove in thin layers. **4** cover with scale or scales. **5** become coated with scale. ⟨ME < OF *escale* < Gmc.⟩ **—'scale•less,** *adj.* **—'scaleˌlike,** *adj.*

scale[2] [skeil] *n., v.* **scaled, scal•ing.** *—n.* **1** either of the two dishes or pans of a balance. **2** Usually, **scales,** *pl.* **a** a balance. **b** any instrument for weighing. **3 Scales,** *pl. Astronomy. Astrology.* Libra.
tip the scales at, have as one's mass; weigh: *She tips the scales at 65 kg.*
tip or **turn the scale** or **scales,** be the deciding factor; decide: *His year of experience tipped the scales in his favour and he got the job.*
—v. **1** have as one's mass; weigh: *He scales 80 kg.* **2** weigh on scales: *The produce is scaled and packaged on the premises.* ⟨ME < ON *skál* bowl. Akin to SHALE, SHELL.⟩

scale[3] [skeil] *n., v.* **scaled, scal•ing.** *—n.* **1** a series of steps or degrees; scheme of graded amounts: *The scale of wages in this factory ranges from $250 to $400 a day.* **2** a series of marks made along a line at regular distances, for use in measuring: *A thermometer has a scale.* **3** an instrument marked in this way, used for measuring, etc. **4 a** the size of a plan, map, drawing, or model compared with what it represents: *a map drawn to a scale of 1 cm for each 10 km.* **b** a line on a map showing this comparison. **5** relative size or extent: *to entertain on a large scale.* **6** a system of numbering. The decimal scale counts by tens, as in cents, dimes, dollars. **7** *Music.* a specific series of tones ascending or descending in pitch, or the prescribed system of intervals according to which they are arranged.
—v. **1** climb: *They scaled the wall by ladders.* **2** reduce or increase by a certain proportion (*used with* **down** or **up**): *All prices were scaled down 10 percent.* **3** make according to a scale. **4** *Cdn.* measure (logs) in order to estimate the volume of lumber in board feet. ⟨ME < L *scala* ladder, ult. < *scandere* climb⟩ **—'scal•a•ble,** *adj.*

scale insect any of numerous small plant-eating insects constituting several families within the order Homoptera, the wingless females of which typically secrete a protective scale around themselves and their eggs.

scale leaf a modified plant leaf that covers a dormant bud in winter and falls away when growth begins again.

scale model a model of a building, ship, etc., which uses a set of small measurements to represent larger ones: *The architect* *showed a scale model of the new arena, with one centimetre representing one metre.*

sca•lene [skei'lin] *or* ['skeilin] *adj.* **1** of a triangle, having three unequal sides. See TRIANGLE for picture. **2** of a cone or cylinder, having its axis not perpendicular to the base. ⟨< LL < Gk. *skalēnos* limping, uneven⟩

scal•er ['skeilər] *n.* **1** one that scales. **2** *Cdn.* a person employed to SCALE[3] (def. 4) timber. **3** SCALING CIRCUIT.

scaling circuit *Electronics.* an electronic circuit designed to put out a single pulse after a certain specified number of input pulses, thus measuring large numbers of pulses with greater facility.

scaling ladder a ladder for climbing high walls.

scal•lion ['skæljən] *n.* **1** a kind of onion that does not form a large bulb. Also called **green onion. 2** a shallot. **3** a leek. ⟨ME < AF *scal(o)un* < L *(caepa) Ascalonia* (onion) from Ascalon, in Palestine⟩

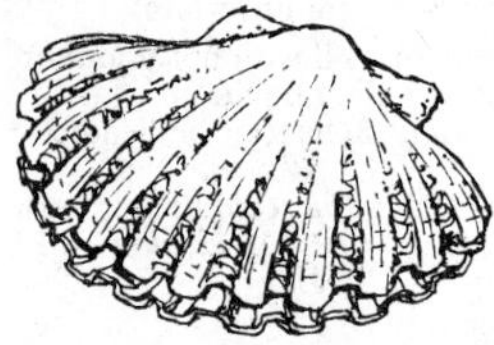

A Eurasian scallop
(Pecten jacobaeus)

A collar with
a scalloped edge

scal•lop ['skæləp] *or* ['skɒləp] *n., v.* —*n.* **1** any of a family (Pectinidae) of bivalve molluscs resembling clams but having a fan-shaped shell with ridges that form a wavy edge around the shell. **2** the large, edible adductor muscle of certain species of scallop. **3** a single valve of the shell of a scallop. Scallops are often used as dishes for baking or serving food. Pilgrims returning from Palestine formerly wore scallops as the sign of their pilgrimage. **4** one of a series of curves forming an edge, especially on cloth.
—*v.* **1** *Cooking.* bake with sauce, bread crumbs, etc., in a scallop shell or other low dish; escallop: *to scallop oysters.* **2** decorate or finish (an edge, as of cloth) with a series of scallops: *to scallop the hem of a tablecloth.* Sometimes, **scollop.** ⟨ME < OF *escalope* shell < Gmc.⟩

scallop dragger or **scalloper** ['skæləpər] *Cdn. Maritimes.* a fishing vessel equipped to drag for scallops.

scal•ly•wag ['skælɪ,wæg] *n.* scalawag.

sca•lop•pi•ne [,skælə'pini] *or* [,skɑlə'pini] *n., pl.* **scaloppini.** an Italian dish consisting of a thin slice of meat cooked with wine: *veal scaloppine.*

scalp [skælp] *n., v.* —*n.* **1** the skin on the top and back of the head, usually covered with hair. **2** a part of this skin from the crown of the head with the hair attached, taken from a conquered enemy and kept as a token of victory. The taking of scalps was formerly practised among certain First Nations and European peoples. **3** *Informal.* any trophy or token of victory.
—*v.* **1** cut or tear the scalp from. **2** *Informal.* **a** buy and sell (stocks, etc.) to make small, quick profits. **b** buy (tickets to theatre productions, games, etc.) and resell at greatly increased prices, usually just before the performance or game. ⟨ME < Scand.; cf. ON *skálpr* sheath⟩ —**'scalp•er,** *n.* —**'scalp•less,** *adj.*

scal•pel ['skælpəl] *n.* a small, sharp, straight knife used in surgery and dissections. ⟨< L *scalpellum,* dim. of *scalprum* knife < *scalpere* carve⟩

scalp lock 1 *Cdn.* See SCALP (*n.* def. 2). **2** a long lock or a tuft of hair left on the top of the shorn head of some First Nations men.

scal•y ['skeili] *adj.* **scal•i•er, scal•i•est. 1** having scales like a fish. **2** covered or encrusted with a layer of something like scales: *This iron pipe is scaly with rust.* **3** like or suggesting scales. **4** peeling or shedding in flakes or scales. **5** infested with scale insects. **6** *Slang.* contemptible, stingy, or shabby: *a scaly lot of ruffians.* —**'scal•i•ness,** *n.*

scaly anteater pangolin.

scam [skæm] *n., v.* **scammed, scam•ming.** —*n.* any fraud or swindle, especially a confidence game, intended to make a quick profit.
—*v.* defraud or cheat by means of a scam: *Elderly people are often scammed by fraudulent home repair companies.*

scamp[1] [skæmp] *n.* **1** a rascal; rogue; worthless person. **2** a mischievous person, especially a child. ⟨< dial. *scamp* roam, probably < *scamper*⟩

scamp[2] [skæmp] *v.* do (work, etc.) in a hasty, careless manner. ⟨prob. < ON *skammr* short⟩

scam•per ['skæmpər] *v., n.* —*v.* **1** run or move away quickly. **2** run about playfully.
—*n.* playful running about: *Let the dog out for a scamper.* ⟨ult. < OF *escamper* run away, ult. < L *ex-* out of + *campus* field⟩

scam•pi ['skæmpi] *or* ['skɑmpi] *n.pl.* large shrimps or prawns, especially when used in Italian dishes. ⟨< Ital., pl. of *scampo* prawn⟩

scan [skæn] *v.* **scanned, scan•ning;** *n.* —*v.* **1** look at closely; examine with care: *His mother scanned his face to see if he was telling the truth.* **2** *Informal.* glance at; look over hastily: *She took a few minutes to scan the newspaper headlines.* **3** find or test (the metre of a poem) by marking the lines off into feet. *Example:* Tíger! | Tíger! | búrning | bríght | Ín the | fórests | óf the | níght. | **4** read or recite (poetry) so as to emphasize the metre. **5** fit a particular metrical pattern: *Your poem is good, but this line does not scan.* **6** *Electronics.* pass a rapidly moving beam of light over (a scene, picture, etc.) in order to sense and transmit or reproduce an image of it, as for television or input to a computer. **7** read or interpret (data such as bar codes, magnetic strips on credit cards, etc.) using an electronic scanner. **8** search (an area) with radar. **9** *Medicine.* examine (any biologically active tissue, especially an internal body part) using some form of imaging such as ultrasound or tomography.
—*n.* **1** the act or process or an instance of scanning. **2** the product of scanning or the thing scanned: *to look at scans for a software demo, a CAT scan.* ⟨ME < LL *scandere* scan verses < L *scandere* climb⟩ —**'scan•na•ble,** *adj.*

scan•dal ['skændəl] *n.* **1** a shameful action, condition, or event that brings disgrace or offends public opinion: *It was a scandal for the city official to take tax money for her own use.* **2** damage to someone's reputation; disgrace. **3** public talk about a person that will hurt his or her reputation; malicious gossip. ⟨ME < ONF < L < Gk. *skandalon* trap. Doublet of SLANDER.⟩

scan•dal•ize ['skændə,laɪz] *v.* **-ized, -iz•ing.** offend by doing something thought to be wrong or improper; shock. —**,scan•dal•i'za•tion,** *n.*

scan•dal•mon•ger ['skændəl,mʌŋgər] *or* ['skændəl,mɒŋgər] *n.* a person who spreads scandal or malicious gossip.

scan•dal•ous ['skændələs] *adj.* **1** bringing disgrace; shameful; shocking: *scandalous behaviour.* **2** consisting of or spreading scandal or slander; slandering: *a scandalous piece of gossip.* —**'scan•dal•ous•ly,** *adv.*

scandal sheet a newspaper or periodical that features sensational stories and malicious gossip.

Scan•di•na•via [,skændə'neivjə] *n.* a region of northern Europe that includes Denmark, Norway, Sweden, and often Finland, Iceland, and the Faeroe Islands.

Scan•di•na•vi•an [,skændə'neivjən] *n., adj.* —*n.* **1** a native or inhabitant of Scandinavia. **2** a person of Scandinavian descent. **3** the northern Germanic languages spoken by the people of Scandinavia (Danish, Norwegian, Swedish).
—*adj.* of or having to do with Scandinavia, its people, or their languages.

☛ *Usage.* The terms **Scandinavian** and **Scandinavia** have sometimes been used to include Finland, but Finland is historically distinct from the Scandinavian countries, having a very different language and different cultural traditions.

scan•di•um ['skændiəm] *n.* a rare metallic chemical element. *Symbol:* Sc; *at.no.* 21; *at.mass* 44.96. ⟨< NL < L *Scandia* Scandinavia⟩

scanner ['skænər] *n.* **1** any device that scans, such as in a radar system. **2** an input device for a computer that reads printed numbers, codes, or other visible information: *The cashier rang up my purchase using a scanner to read the price on the label.*

scan•sion ['skænʃən] *n.* the analysis of the metre of poetry or a particular poem, using certain symbols for different levels of stress or tonic accent. ⟨< L *scansio, -onis* < *scandere* scan⟩

scant [skænt] *adj., v., adv.* —*adj.* **1** not enough in size, amount, or quantity: *making do with scant provisions.* **2** scarcely full or complete; not coming quite up to a particular measure: *He takes a scant teaspoon of sugar in his tea. You have a scant hour in*

which to pack. **3** having an inadequate supply (*usually used with* **of**): *scant of breath.*
—v. make scant; limit or cut down; stint: *Don't scant the butter if you want a rich cake.*
—adv. Dialect. scarcely; barely; hardly. ⟨ME < ON *skamt*, neut. adj., short⟩

scant•ling ['skæntlɪŋ] *n.* **1** a small beam or piece of timber, especially one used as an upright piece in the frame of a building. **2** the dimensions of stone or timber used in building: *timber of small scantling.* **3** the set of standard dimensions of parts of a structure, especially a ship: *The two ships were built to the same scantling.* ⟨var. of ME *scantilon* < OF *escantillon*, ult. probably < LL *cantus* corner < Gk. *kanthos* corner of the eye⟩

scant•y ['skænti] *adj.* **scant•i•er, scant•i•est. 1** not enough: *His scanty clothing did not keep out the cold.* **2** barely enough; meagre: *a scanty harvest.* **3** lacking in space. ⟨< *scant*, adj.⟩ **—'scant•i•ly,** *adv.* **—'scant•i•ness,** *n.*
☛ *Syn.* **Scanty,** SPARSE, MEAGRE = less than is needed or normal. **Scanty** emphasizes falling short of the amount or measure necessary to satisfy a need or come up to a standard: *The scanty rainfall is causing a water shortage.* **Sparse** emphasizes a thin scattering of what there is, particularly of numbers or units: *He carefully combs his sparse hair.* **Meagre** suggests a lack of something necessary for fullness, completeness, richness, body, strength, etc.: *His meagre soil produces meagre crops.*

scape[1] [skeip] *n., v.* **scaped, scap•ing.** See 'SCAPE.

scape[2] [skeip] *n.* **1** *Botany.* a leafless flower stalk rising from the ground, such as that of the dandelion. **2** something like a stalk, such as the shaft of a feather or of a column. ⟨< L *scapus* stalk; cf. dial. Gk. *skapos* branch⟩

'scape [skeip] *n., v.* **'scaped, 'scap•ing.** *Archaic.* escape. ⟨ME *scapen*, aphetic form of *escapen*⟩

scape•goat ['skeip,gout] *n., v. —n.* **1** a person or thing made to bear the blame for the mistakes or sins of others. **2** in the Old Testament, a goat on which the sins of the people were laid symbolically by the ancient Jewish high priests on the Day of Atonement. The goat was then driven into the wilderness.
—v. make a scapegoat of. ⟨< *'scape* + *goat*⟩

scape•grace ['skeip,greis] *n.* a reckless, good-for-nothing person; scamp.

s.caps SMALL CAPITALS.

scap•u•la ['skæpjələ] *n., pl.* **-lae** [-,li] *or* [-,laɪ] or **-las.** *Anatomy.* a SHOULDER BLADE. ⟨< LL⟩

scap•u•lar ['skæpjələr] *adj., n. —adj.* of the shoulder or shoulder blade.
—n. **1** *Roman Catholic Church.* a loose, sleeveless garment hanging from the shoulders, worn by certain religious orders. **2** a symbol of devotion or association with a religious order, consisting of two small pieces of cloth joined by shoulder pieces and worn to hang down over the chest and back. **3** a bird's feather growing where the wing joins the body, or near there. **4** *Anatomy.* scapula. ⟨ME < LL, ult. < L *scapulae* shoulders⟩

scar[1] [skɑr] *n., v.* **scarred, scar•ring.** *—n.* **1** the mark left by a healed cut, wound, burn, or sore. **2** any disfiguring mark or blemish resulting from injury or use. **3** any mark like this. A fallen leaf leaves a scar where it separated from the stem. **4** a lasting effect from grief, etc.: *War leaves deep scars on the minds of those who endure it.*
—v. **1** of a wound, etc., form a scar; heal over. **2** make a scar on: *The door was badly scarred by the fire.* ⟨ME < OF *escare* < L < Gk. *eschara* scab, hearth⟩ **—'scar•less,** *adj.*

scar[2] [skɑr] *n.* **1** a steep, rocky place on the side of a mountain; precipice; cliff. **2** a low rock in the sea. Also, **scaur.** ⟨ME < ON *sker* reef⟩

scar•ab ['skærəb] *or* ['skɛrəb] *n.* **1** a large black beetle (*Scarabaeus sacer*) regarded as sacred by the ancient Egyptians. **2** an image of this beetle, used in ancient Egypt as a charm, ornament, etc. **3** any highly coloured beetle of the same family (Scarabaeidae), including June bugs, dung beetles, and the cockchafer. ⟨< MF < L *scarabaeus* < Gk.⟩

scar•a•bae•id [,skærə'biɪd] *or* [,skɛrə'biɪd] *n., adj. —n.* any member of the Scarabaeidae, the family to which scarabs, dung beetles, June beetles, etc. belong.
—adj. of or having to do with the Scarabaeidae.

scar•a•bae•us [,skærə'biəs] *or* [,skɛrə'biəs] *n., pl.* **-bae•us•es** or **-bae•i** [-'biaɪ]. scarab.

scar•a•mouch or **scar•a•mouche** ['skærə,muʃ] *or* ['skɛrə,muʃ], ['skærə,mʌutʃ] *or* ['skɛrə,mʌutʃ] *n.* **1** braggart. **2** rascal. **3 Scaramouch,** a stock character in traditional Italian comedy. ⟨< F < Ital. *scaramuccia* skirmish⟩

scarce [skɛrs] *adj.* **scarc•er, scarc•est;** *adv. —adj.* hard to get; rare: *Good cooks are scarce.*
make (oneself) **scarce,** *Informal.* **a** go away. **b** stay away.

scarce as hen's teeth, *Informal.* very scarce.
—adv. scarcely. ⟨ME < ONF *escars* < VL *excarpsus*, ult. < L *ex-* out + *carpere* pluck⟩ **—'scarce•ness,** *n.*
☛ *Syn. adj.* **1.** See note at RARE[1].

scarce•ly ['skɛrsli] *adv.* **1** only just; barely; hardly: *scarcely old enough for school. We could scarcely see through the fog.* **2** very probably not: *I will scarcely pay that much.* **3** decidedly not: *She can scarcely have said that.*
☛ *Syn.* **1.** See note at HARDLY.
☛ *Usage.* See note at HARDLY.

scar•ci•ty ['skɛrsəti] *n., pl.* **-ties.** too small a supply; lack; rarity.

scare [skɛr] *v.* **scared, scar•ing;** *n. —v.* **1** make or become frightened: *The dog's barking scared the children. She doesn't scare easily.* **2** drive (*off* or *away*) by frightening: *The watchdog scared away the robbers by barking.*
scare up, *Informal.* get or get together quickly: *We made camp and then tried to scare up some food.*
—n. **1** a fright: *I got a real scare when the lights went out.* **2** a state of alarm or panic: *There was a polio scare last summer. The flight was delayed because of a bomb scare.* ⟨ME < ON *skirra* < *skjarr* timid⟩
☛ *Syn. v.* **1.** See note at FRIGHTEN.

scare•crow ['skɛr,krou] *n.* **1** an object, usually a figure of a man dressed in old clothes, set in a field to frighten birds away from crops. **2** a person who is thin and gaunt or who dresses like a scarecrow. **3** anything that fools people into being frightened.

scared [skɛrd] *adj., v. —adj.* filled with fear; afraid.
—v. pt. and pp. of SCARE.

scare•dy–cat ['skɛrdi ,kæt] *n. Informal.* a person who frightens easily and unreasonably.

scare•mon•ger ['skɛr,mʌŋgər] *or* ['skɛr,mɒngər] *n.* one who spreads unfounded rumours; alarmist.

scarf[1] [skɑrf] *n., pl.* **scarves** or (rarely) **scarfs. 1** a square, triangular, or long, narrow strip of cloth worn about the neck, shoulders, head, or waist. **2** a long strip of cloth used as a decorative cover for a dresser, table, etc.; runner. **3** a sash worn across the chest to indicate membership in some ceremonial order. ⟨probably < dial. OF *escarpe* < Gmc.⟩

scarf[2] [skɑrf] *n., pl.* **scarfs;** *v. —n.* **1** a joint made by cutting away part of the ends of beams, etc., so that they overlap and fit tightly together without increasing the overall thickness. See JOINT for picture. **2** an end cut in this way. **3** *Whaling.* a cut made along the body of a whale in preparation for removing the blubber.
—v. **1** join by a scarf. **2** cut a scarf on (a piece of wood). **3** *Whaling.* cut scarfs and remove the blubber from the body of (a whale). ⟨ME < Scand.; cf. Swedish *skarv*⟩

scarf[3] [skɑrf] *v. Slang.* eat in large quantities. ⟨origin uncertain⟩

scarf•pin ['skɑrf,pɪn] *n.* an ornamental pin worn in a scarf or necktie.

scarf•skin ['skɑrf,skɪn] *n.* the outer layer of skin; epidermis.

scar•i•fi•ca•tion [,skærəfə'keiʃən] *or* [,skɛrəfə'keiʃən] *n.* **1** the act or an instance of scarifying. **2** a scratch or scratches made by scarifying.

scar•i•fy ['skærə,faɪ] *or* ['skɛrə,faɪ] *v.* **-fied, -fy•ing. 1** make scratches or cuts in the surface of (the skin, etc.), as for vaccination. **2** criticize severely; hurt the feelings of. **3** loosen (soil) without turning it over. **4** break up (a road surface) prior to repaving. ⟨< LL < L *scarifare* < Gk. *skariphasthai* scratch < *skariphos* stylus⟩ **—'scar•i,fi•er,** *n.*

scar•la•ti•na [,skɑrlə'tinə] *n. Pathology.* a mild form of SCARLET FEVER. ⟨< NL < Ital. *scarlattina*, fem. of *scarlattino*, dim. of *scarlatto* scarlet⟩

scar•let ['skɑrlɪt] *n., adj. —n.* **1** a light, brilliant red with a slight tinge of orange. **2** cloth or clothing having this colour: *The Mounties look impressive in their scarlets.*
—adj. of the colour scarlet. ⟨ME < OF *escarlate*, ? ult. < Persian *saqirlat* rich cloth⟩

scarlet fever an acute contagious disease characterized by a scarlet rash, sore throat, and fever.

scarlet pimpernel See PIMPERNEL.

scarlet runner a tropical American perennial climbing bean plant (*Phaseolus multiflorus*, also called *P. coccineus*) having large scarlet flowers and long green pods. The scarlet runner is widely grown as an annual plant in temperate climates, both for ornament and for its edible pods and seeds.

scarlet sage a popular garden plant (*Salvia splendens*) having spikes of scarlet flowers.

scarlet tanager a tanager (*Piranga olivacea*) of central and E North America, the adult male having a bright red body with black wings and tail in spring and summer, the red changing to olive green in fall and winter. The female is mainly olive green and pale yellow in colour.

scarp [skɑrp] *n., v. —n.* **1** a steep slope. **2** the inner slope or side of a ditch surrounding a fortification.
—v. make into a steep slope; slope steeply. ⟨< Ital. *scarpa* < Gmc.⟩

scarp•er ['skɑrpər] *v. Esp. Brit.* run off or depart suddenly, especially if leaving unpaid bills behind.

scarves [skɑrvz] *n.* a pl. of SCARF.

scar•y ['skɛri] *adj.* **scar•i•er, scar•i•est.** *Informal.* **1** causing fright or alarm: *a scary movie.* **2** easily frightened.
☛ *Hom.* SKERRY.

scat[1] [skæt] *interj., v.* **scat•ted, scat•ting.** *Informal. —interj.* an impatient exclamation used especially to drive away an animal.
—v. beat it; get away quickly: *She told the boys to scat.* ⟨< *scatter*⟩
☛ *Hom.* SKAT [skæt].

scat[2] [skæt] *n., v.* **scat•ted, scat•ting.** *Music. —n.* **1** jazz singing, often in a very high register, with nonsense syllables instead of words. In scat, the voice is used as a musical instrument. **2** (*adjl.*) of or having to do with this type of singing.
—v. sing scat. ⟨perhaps imitative⟩
☛ *Hom.* SKAT [skæt].

scat[3] [skæt] *n.* a wild animal's feces. ⟨< Gk. *skor, skatos*⟩
☛ *Hom.* SKAT [skæt].

scathe [skeið] *v.* **scathed, scath•ing;** *n. —v.* **1** blast or sear with invective; wither with satire. **2** injure or destroy by fire, lightning, etc.; scar; scorch. **3** *Archaic.* injure; damage.
—n. **1** hurt; harm. **2** *Archaic.* a matter for sorrow or regret. ⟨ME < ON *skathi* injury⟩

scathe•less ['skeiðlɪs] *adj.* without harm; unhurt.

scath•ing ['skeiðɪŋ] *adj.* extremely severe or damaging to a person's self-esteem: *scathing criticism.* **—'scath•ing•ly,** *adv.*

sca•tol•o•gy [skə'tɒlədʒi] *n.* **1** the study of excrement, used in paleontology, for medical diagnosis, etc. **2** abnormal interest in excrement, excretory functions, etc. **3** obscene literature. ⟨< Gk. *skōr, skatos* excrement + E *-logy*⟩ **—ˌscat•o'log•i•cal,** *adj.*

scat•ter ['skætər] *v., n. —v.* **1** throw here and there; sprinkle: *to scatter ashes on an icy sidewalk.* **2** cover by scattering: *The path was scattered with leaves.* **3** separate and drive off in different directions: *The police scattered the mob.* **4** separate and go in different directions: *The hens scattered.* **5** *Physics.* reflect or refract (a beam of radiation) irregularly and in all directions.
—n. **1** the act or fact of scattering. **2** something that is scattered. **3** a small number occurring or distributed irregularly or here and there: *a scatter of houses in the valley.* ⟨ME; probably var. of SHATTER⟩ **—'scat•ter•er,** *n.*
☛ *Syn. v.* **3. Scatter,** DISPEL, DISPERSE = separate and drive away. **Scatter** means to separate and drive off in different directions a group or mass of people or objects: *The wind scattered my papers.* **Dispel** applies only to things that cannot be touched, such as clouds and feelings, and means 'drive away as if by scattering in the air': *The wind dispelled the fog.* **Disperse** means the same as **scatter,** but is more formal and may suggest even spreading in every direction: *Storms dispersed the convoy.*

scat•ter•brain ['skætərˌbrein] *n.* a thoughtless, frivolous person.

scat•ter•brained ['skætərˌbreind] *adj.* thoughtless; frivolous; not able to think steadily.

scat•tered ['skætərd] *adj., v. —adj.* not occurring together or in great numbers; few and far apart: *scattered instances of violence. We heard scattered shouts in the distance.*
—v. pt. and pp. of SCATTER.

scat•ter•gun ['skætərˌgʌn] *n.* **1** shotgun loaded with multiple shot, as birdshot. **2** (*adjl.*) suggesting the effect of a load of shot from a scattergun: *a scattergun blast of 67 different policy proposals.*

scat•ter•ing ['skætərɪŋ] *n., adj., v. —n.* **1** a small number or quantity occurring or situated at irregular intervals: *a scattering of cheers, a scattering of villages.* **2** the act of one that scatters.
—adj. widely separated; occurring here and there.
—v. ppr. of SCATTER.

scatter rug a small, loose rug, often placed for effect.

scat•ty ['skæti] *adj.* **-ti•er, -ti•est.** *Brit. Informal.* scatterbrained.

scaup [skɒp] *n.* either of two diving ducks (*Aythya affinis* or *A. marila*), the adult male having black-and-white plumage and the female brownish plumage. Both species of scaup are found in Canada. ⟨*scaup,* var. of dial. *scalp,* a bank providing a bed for shellfish⟩

scaur [skɔr] *n. Brit.* SCAR[2].
☛ *Hom.* SCORE.

scav•enge ['skævəndʒ] *v.* **-enged, -eng•ing. 1 a** clean streets and waterways by collecting garbage, rubbish, etc. **b** pick over, feed on, use, or sell garbage, rubbish, etc. **2** salvage (something usable) from discarded materials, rubbish, etc.: *to scavenge usable wood scraps.* **3** of an animal, feed on garbage or other dead or decaying matter. **4** expel (exhaust gas) from the cylinder of an internal combustion engine. **5** chemically remove (impurities) from molten metal. ⟨back formation < *scavenger*⟩

scav•en•ger ['skævəndʒər] *n.* **1** an animal that feeds on dead animals or other decaying matter. Vultures and jackals are scavengers. **2** a person who cleans streets, taking away dirt and rubbish. **3** a person who searches through discarded material for something of value. ⟨alteration of *scavager,* literally, inspector < *scavage* toll < OF *scawager* < *escauwer* inspect < Flemish *scauwen*⟩

sce•nar•i•o [sɪ'nɛriou] *or* [sɪ'nɑriou] *n., pl.* **-nar•i•os. 1 a** an outline of a film, giving the main facts about the scenes, persons, and acting. **b** a movie script. **2** an outline of any play, opera, etc. **3** an outline of a course of action or sequence of events, proposed as a possible outcome of a real or imagined situation: *In our revolution scenario, the rebels are bound to be defeated within a week.* ⟨< Ital. *scenario,* ult. < L *scena* scene. See SCENE.⟩

sce•nar•ist [sɪ'nɛrɪst] *or* [sɪ'nɑrɪst] *n.* a person who writes scenarios.

scene [sin] *n.* **1** the time, place, circumstances, etc., of a play or story: *The scene of the novel is Québec City in the year 1759.* **2** the place where anything is carried on or takes place: *the scene of an accident, the scene of my childhood.* **3** the painted screens, hangings, etc., used on a stage to represent places: *The scene represents a city street.* **4** a formal division of an act of a play, having continuity of action taking place in a single location: *The king comes to the castle in Act I, Scene 2.* **5** a particular incident of a play or film: *the trial scene in* The Merchant of Venice. **6** an action, incident, situation, etc., occurring in reality or represented in literature or art: *He has painted a series of pictures called "Scenes of My Boyhood."* **7** a view; picture: *The white sailboats on the blue water made a pretty scene.* **8** a show of strong feeling in front of others; exhibition; display: *The child kicked and screamed and made such a scene that his mother was ashamed of him.* **9** *Informal.* sphere of activity; the context or environment in which an activity takes place: *Last night's party was a bad scene.*
behind the scenes, a out of sight of the audience. **b** privately; secretly, not publicly: *A lot of planning for the Festival was done behind the scenes.*
come on the scene, join an activity or group.
make the scene, *Slang.* appear at a particular place; engage in a particular activity. ⟨< F *scène* < L *scena* < Gk. *skēnē,* originally, tent, where actors changed costumes⟩
☛ *Hom.* SEEN, SIN[2].
☛ *Syn.* **7.** See note at VIEW.

scen•er•y ['sinəri] *n., pl.* **-er•ies. 1** *Theatre.* the painted hangings, fittings, etc. used to represent places. **2** the general appearance of the natural features of a place: *mountain scenery.*

sce•nic ['sinɪk] *or* ['sɛnɪk] *adj.* **1** of or having to do with natural scenery; having much fine scenery: *The scenic splendours of Lake Louise are famous.* **2** belonging to the stage of a theatre; of or having to do with stage effects: *The production of the musical comedy was a scenic triumph.* **3** *Art.* representing an action, incident, situation, etc.

scenic dome a transparent dome at the top of a railway car, designed for better viewing of the passing scenery.

sce•nog•ra•phy [sɪ'nɒgrəfi] *n.* **1** the representing of objects according to the rules of perspective. **2** scene painting.

scent [sɛnt] *n., v. —n.* **1** a smell, especially an agreeable one: *the scent of new-mown hay, the scent of roses.* **2** the sense of smell; ability to detect smells: *Bloodhounds have a keen scent.* **3** a smell left in passing, enabling hunters and their hounds to track an animal: *The dogs followed the fox by its scent.* **4** any means by which a person or thing can be traced: *The police picked up the thief's scent again where he had stopped for gas.* **5** perfume.
—v. **1** become aware of through smell: *The dog immediately scented the rabbit and dashed off after it.* **2** hunt by using the

sense of smell: *The dog scented about till it found the trail.* **3** use the sense of smell on: *to scent the air for signs of rain.* **4** apply perfume to: *She scented her handkerchief. This tobacco has been scented.* **5** fill with odour: *Lilacs scented the air.* **6** get or have a suspicion or inkling of: *They scented trouble and left quickly.* ⟨ME < OF *sentir* smell < L *sentire* feel⟩ **—'scent•ed,** *adj.*
☛ *Hom.* CENT.
☛ *Syn. n.* See note at SMELL.

scent•less ['sɛntlɪs] *adj.* having no smell.

scep•ter ['sɛptər] *n., v.* See SCEPTRE.

scep•tered ['sɛptərd] *adj., v.* See SCEPTRED.

scep•tic or **skep•tic** ['skɛptɪk] *n.* **1 a** a person who questions the truth of a particular theory or supposed fact; doubter. **b** loosely, a person who habitually doubts everything except what he or she has experienced first-hand. **2** *Philosophy.* a person who doubts or questions the possibility or certainty of human knowledge of anything. **3** a person who doubts the truth of religious doctrines. ⟨< L < Gk. *skeptikos* reflective < *skeptesthai* reflect⟩

scep•ti•cal or **skep•ti•cal** ['skɛptɪkəl] *adj.* having to do with, characteristic of, or marked by scepticism: *They showed him all their data, but he remained sceptical about the plan.*
—'scep•ti•cal•ly or **'skep•ti•cal•ly,** *adv.*

scep•ti•cism or **skep•ti•cism** ['skɛptə,sɪzəm] *n.* **1** a sceptical attitude; a general tendency to doubt or have doubts about a particular idea or thing. **2** doubt or unbelief with regard to religion. **3** *Philosophy.* the doctrine that nothing can be certainly known.

scep•tre ['sɛptər] *n., v.* **-tred, -tring.** *—n.* **1** the rod or staff carried by a ruler as a symbol of royal power or authority. **2** royal or imperial power or authority.
—v. **1** furnish with a sceptre. **2** invest with regal authority. Also, **scepter.** ⟨ME < OF < L < Gk. *skēptron* staff⟩

scep•tred ['sɛptərd] *adj., v. —adj.* **1** furnished with or bearing a sceptre. **2** invested with regal authority; regal.
—v. pt. and pp. of SCEPTRE. Also, **sceptered.**

sch. school.

Scha•den•freu•de ['ʃadən,fʀɔɪdə] *n. German.* pleasure taken in the misfortunes and unhappiness of another. ⟨< G < *Schaden* harm + *Freude* joy⟩

sched•ule ['skɛdʒuəl] *or* ['ʃɛdʒuəl], *n., v.* **-uled, -ul•ing.** *—n.* **1** a written or printed statement of details; list. A railway timetable is a schedule of the coming and going of trains. **2** the time or times fixed for doing something, arrival at a place, etc.: *The bus was an hour behind schedule.* **3** a listing of the games to be played by the teams in the league.
—v. **1** make a schedule of; enter in a schedule. **2** plan or arrange (something) for a definite time or date: *The convention has been scheduled for early fall.* ⟨ME < OF < LL *schedula,* dim. of L *scheda, schida* sheet of papyrus < Gk. *schidē* split piece of wood⟩

schef•fler•a [ʃə'flirə] *or* [ʃə'flɛrə] *n.* any of a genus (*Schefflera*) of tropical and subtropical plants of the ginseng family, some of which are grown as house plants in temperate regions.

Sche•her•a•za•de [ʃə,hɛrə'zɑdə] *or* [ʃə,hɛrə'zɑd] *n.* in the *Arabian Nights,* the narrator of the tales, a young bride of the murderous Sultan, who saves her own life by keeping the Sultan interested in her stories.

sche•ma ['skimə] *n., pl.* **sche•ma•ta** ['skimətə] *or* [skɪ'mætə] **1** an outline, synopsis, plan, or scheme. **2** *Kantian philosophy.* the general idea or concept common to all members of a class. **3** *Psychology.* a view of reality organizing one's experience and knowledge. ⟨< L < Gk. *schēma, -atos* figure, appearance⟩

sche•mat•ic [ski'mætɪk] *or* [skɪ'mætɪk] *adj.* having to do with or having the nature of a diagram, plan, or scheme; diagrammatic. **—sche'mat•i•cal•ly,** *adv.*

sche•ma•tize ['skimə,taɪz] *v.* **-tized, -tiz•ing.** reduce to or represent as a formula or scheme: *to schematize the metre of a poem.* **—,sche•ma•ti'za•tion,** *n.*

scheme [skim] *n., v.* **schemed, schem•ing.** *—n.* **1** a program of action; plan: *She has a scheme for extracting gold from sea water.* **2** a plot: *a scheme to cheat the government.* **3** a system of connected things, parts, thoughts, etc.; design: *The colour scheme of the room is blue and gold.* **4** a diagram, outline, or table.
—v. plan or plot: *Those people were scheming to bring the jewels into the country without paying duty.* ⟨< L < Gk. *schēma, -atos* figure, appearance⟩ **—'schem•er,** *n.*
☛ *Syn. v.* See note at PLOT.

schem•ing ['skimɪŋ] *adj., v. —adj.* given to forming sly or tricky schemes; deceitful and crafty.
—v. ppr. of SCHEME. **—'schem•ing•ly,** *adv.*

scher•zan•do [skɛr'tsɑndou] *adj., adv., n. Music. —adj.* playful; sportive.
—adv. playfully; sportively.
—n. a playful movement or passage; composition to be played or sung in this manner. ⟨< Ital. *scherzando* < *scherzare* to play, sport < *scherzo.* See SCHERZO.⟩

scher•zo ['skɛrtsou] *n., pl.* **-zos** or **-zi** [-tsi]. *Music.* a light and playful composition or part of a sonata, concerto, or symphony. ⟨< Ital. < G *Scherz* joke⟩

Schick test [ʃɪk] *Medicine.* a test to determine susceptibility to or immunity from diphtheria, made by injecting a dilute diphtheria toxin under the skin. If the skin becomes inflamed as a result, the person is not immune to the disease. ⟨after Dr. Béla *Schick* of Vienna (born 1877)⟩

schil•ling ['ʃɪlɪŋ] *n.* **1** the basic unit of money in Austria, divided into 100 groschen. See table of money in the Appendix. **2** a coin worth one schilling. ⟨< G⟩

schip•per•ke ['skɪpərki] *n.* a Belgian breed of small, sturdy, black watchdog having erect ears and the tail completely docked. ⟨< Du *schipperke,* dim. of *schipper* skipper, since originally used on boats as a watchdog⟩

schism ['sɪzəm], ['skɪzəm], *or* ['ʃɪzəm] *n.* **1** the division or separation of a group into opposing factions. **2** a division within or separation from an established church, caused by some difference of opinion on faith or discipline. **3** the offence of promoting or causing such a division or separation. **4** a faction formed by schism. **5** discord; strife. ⟨ME < OF < LL < Gk. *schisma* < *schizein* split⟩

schis•mat•ic [sɪz'mætɪk], [skɪz'mætɪk], *or* [ʃɪz'mætɪk] *adj., n.*
—adj. **1** causing or likely to cause schism. **2** inclined toward, or guilty of, schism.
—n. a person who tries to cause a schism or takes part in one.

schis•mat•i•cal [sɪz'mætɪkəl], [skɪz'mætɪkəl], *or* [ʃɪz'mætɪkəl] *adj.* schismatic.

schist [ʃɪst] *n.* a crystalline metamorphic rock that splits easily into layers. ⟨< F < L < Gk. *schistos* cleft < *schizein* split⟩

schist•ose ['ʃɪstous] *adj.* of or like schist; having the structure of schist. Also, **schistous** ['ʃɪstəs].

schis•to•some ['ʃɪstə,soum] *or* ['skɪstə,soum] *n.* any of a genus (*Schistosoma*) of blood flukes, some of which cause bilharzia in people.

schis•to•so•mi•a•sis [,ʃɪstəsə'maɪəsəs] *or* [,skɪstəsou'maɪəsɪs] *n. Pathology.* bilharzia.

schizo– *combining form.* divided; split: *schizocarp.* ⟨< Gk. *schizein* split⟩

schiz•o•carp ['skɪtsə,kɑrp] *or* ['skɪzə,kɑrp] *n. Botany.* a dry compound fruit that splits when ripe into two or more closed parts containing one seed each. ⟨< *schizo-* + Gk. *karpos* fruit⟩
—,schiz•o'carp•ous or **,schiz•o'carp•ic,** *adj.*

schiz•o•gen•e•sis [,skɪtsə'dʒɛnəsɪs] *or* [,skɪzə'dʒɛnəsɪs] *n.* reproduction by fission.

schiz•oid ['skɪtsɔɪd] *adj., n. —adj.* **1** characterized by, tending toward, or resulting from schizophrenia: *schizoid tendencies. He's a bit schizoid.* **2** *Psychology. Psychiatry.* of or having to do with a personality disorder marked by withdrawal, passivity, introversion, etc.
—n. a schizoid person.

schiz•o•phre•ni•a [,skɪtsə'friniə] *n. Psychiatry.* a severe mental disorder of unknown origin, characterized by dissociation from reality accompanied by delusions and hallucinations, possible intellectual deterioration, bizarre behaviour, and social isolation. Formerly known as **dementia praecox.** ⟨< NL < Gk. *schizein* split + *phrēn* mind⟩

schiz•o•phren•ic [,skɪtsə'frɛnɪk] *or* [,skɪtsə'frinɪk] *adj., n.*
—adj. of or having to do with schizophrenia.
—n. a person with schizophrenia.

schle•miel [ʃlə'mil] *n. Slang.* a gullible, inept person; a bungler or fool. Also, **schlemihl.** ⟨< Yiddish < Hebrew *Shelumiel,* a biblical character⟩

schlep or **schlepp** [ʃlɛp] *v.* **schlepped, schlep•ping;** *n. Slang. —v.* **1** haul or lug (something): *I don't want to schlep the suitcase all over town.* **2** traipse; drag oneself: *I spent the afternoon schlepping all over town in search of a decent bookstore.*
—n. **1** a stupid or ineffectual person. **2** a difficult or tiresome undertaking, journey, etc.: *It was a long schlep.* Also, **shlep** or **shlepp.** ⟨< Yiddish < MHG *sleppen* drag, haul⟩

schlock [ʃlɒk] *n., adj. Slang.* —*n.* something that is shoddy or inferior.
—*adj.* shoddy or inferior: *a schlock movie.* Also, **schlocky.** ⟨< Yiddish *shlak* cheap merchandise, prob. < MHG *slag, slak* a blow⟩

schmaltz or **schmalz** [ʃmɑlts] *or* [ʃmɒlts] *n. Slang.* extreme sentimentalism, especially in music, literature, or art. ⟨< G *Schmaltz* melted fat⟩

schmaltz•y or **schmalz•y** [ˈʃmɑltsi] *or* [ˈʃmɒltsi] *adj. Slang.* of or having to do with schmaltz; overly sentimental.

schmear [ʃmir] *n. Slang.* **1** an activity, plan, etc., along with all its features. **2** a bribe.
the whole schmear, everything involved. ⟨< Yiddish *shmirn* to smear, grease < MHG *smirwen*⟩

schmo or **schmoe** [ʃmou] *n. Slang.* a foolish or unsophisticated person. Also, **shmo.** ⟨< Yiddish⟩

schmooze [ʃmuz] *n., v.* **schmoozed, schmooz•ing.** *Slang.* —*n.* idle chat, especially as an ingratiating overture; gossip.
—*v.* gossip; converse in an idle manner. ⟨< Yiddish *shmues* chat, rumour, gossip < Hebrew *shemua* rumour, news⟩

schmoz•zle [ˈʃmɒzəl] *n. Slang.* a messy or complicated business. ⟨< Yiddish⟩

schmuck [ʃmʌk] *n. Slang.* an obnoxious, contemptible, or foolish person. ⟨< Yiddish *shmok* penis⟩

schnapps or **schnaps** [ʃnɑps] *or* [ʃnʌps] *n.* **1** Hollands. **2** any of various distilled liquors. ⟨< G⟩

schnau•zer [ˈʃnʌutsər] *or* [ˈʃnaʊzər] *n.* any of three breeds of terrier originally developed in Germany, having a short, wiry coat, small ears, bushy eyebrows, and a beard. The three breeds are the **standard schnauzer, giant schnauzer,** and **miniature schnauzer.** ⟨< G *Schnauzer* < *Schnauze* snout⟩

schnit•zel [ˈʃnɪtsəl] *n.* a breaded and seasoned veal or pork cutlet. ⟨< G⟩

schnook [ʃnʊk] *n. Slang.* a dull or stupid person; an easy target. Also, **shnook.** ⟨origin unknown⟩

schnoz•zle [ˈʃnɒzəl] *n. Slang.* nose. Also, **schnoz.** ⟨ult. < Yiddish⟩

schol•ar [ˈskɒlər] *n.* **1** a learned person; a person having much knowledge. **2** a specialist in some academic field: *a classics scholar.* **3** a pupil at school; learner. **4** a student who is given money by some institution to allow him or her to continue studying; the holder of a scholarship: *a Rhodes scholar.* ⟨ME < AF < LL *scholaris* < L *schola* school. See SCHOOL[1].⟩
☛ *Syn.* See note at STUDENT.

schol•ar•ly [ˈskɒlərli] *adj., adv.* —*adj.* **1** of, like, or fit for a scholar: *scholarly habits.* **2** having much knowledge; learned. **3** fond of learning; studious. **4** thorough and orderly in presenting or treating a subject: *a scholarly book.*
—*adv.* in a scholarly manner. —**ˈschol•ar•li•ness,** *n.*

schol•ar•ship [ˈskɒlər,ʃɪp] *n.* **1** the possession of knowledge gained by study; quality of learning and knowledge: *The painstakingly thorough treatment of events showed the excellence of the historian's scholarship.* **2** a grant of money or other aid to help a student continue his or her studies, awarded on the basis of academic achievement. **3** a fund to provide this money.

scho•las•tic [skəˈlæstɪk] *adj., n.* —*adj.* **1** of schools, scholars, or education; academic: *scholastic achievements or methods; scholastic life.* **2** of or like scholasticism.
—*n.* **1** Often, **Scholastic.** a person who favours scholasticism. **2** in the Middle Ages, a theologian and philosopher. ⟨< L < Gk. *scholastikos,* ult. < *scholē* school[1]⟩ —**schoˈlas•ti•cal•ly,** *adv.*

Scholastic Aptitude Test a standardized university entrance examination consisting of multiple-choice questions designed to test verbal, mathematical, and written English skills.

scho•las•ti•cism [skəˈlæstə,sɪzəm] *n.* **1** in the Middle Ages, a system of theological and philosophical teaching based chiefly on the authority of the church fathers and of Aristotle, and characterized by a formal method of discussion. **2** an adherence to traditional doctrines and methods.

scho•li•a [ˈskouliə] *n.* pl. of SCHOLIUM.

scho•li•ast [ˈskouli,æst] *n.* an ancient or medieval grammarian who wrote comments upon the classics; one who made scholia. ⟨< LL < Gk. *scholiastēs*⟩

scho•li•um [ˈskouliəm] *n., pl.* **-li•a** [-liə]. **1** an annotation by an ancient or medieval grammarian upon a passage in the Greek or Latin classics. **2** a note added by way of illustration or amplification. ⟨< Med.L < Gk. *scholion,* dim. of *scholē* discussion⟩

school[1] [skul] *n., v.* —*n.* **1** a place for teaching and learning. **2** the physical plant of any institution of learning. **3** instruction in school; education received at school: *Most children start school when they are about five years old.* **4** a regular course of meetings of teachers and pupils for instruction. **5** a session of such a course. **6** those who are taught and their teachers. **7** any place, situation, experience, etc., as a source of instruction or training: *the school of adversity.* **8** a group of people holding the same beliefs, working or living in the same style, etc.: *the Dutch school of painting, a gentleman of the old school.* **9 a** a particular department or faculty in a university. **b** the room, rooms, buildings, or group of buildings set apart for it: *a school of dentistry.* **10** a place of training or discipline. **11** (*adjl.*) of or having to do with a school or schools.
—*v.* **1** educate in a school; teach. **2** train; discipline: *School yourself to control your temper.* ⟨OE *scōl* < L *schola* < Gk. *scholē,* originally, leisure⟩

school[2] [skul] *n., v.* —*n.* a large group of the same kind of fish or water animals swimming together.
—*v.* swim together in a school. ⟨ME < MDu. *schole* a crowd. Akin to SHOAL[2].⟩

school age **1** the age at which a child begins to go to school. **2** the years during which going to school is compulsory or customary.

school board *Cdn.* a group of people, usually elected, who manage the public elementary and secondary schools in a designated area; a board of education.

school•book [ˈskul,bʊk] *n.* a book for study in schools.

school•boy [ˈskul,bɔɪ] *n.* a boy attending school.

school•child [ˈskul,tʃaɪld] *n., pl.* **-child•ren.** a child who goes to school.

school crossing–guard *Cdn.* a person employed to shepherd children across busy streets on their way to and from school.

school day **1** any day on which classes are held: *Saturday is not a regular school day.* **2** the number of hours of instruction on such a day: *The normal school day is about five hours long.*

school district *Cdn., esp. West.* an area designated as a unit for the local administration of public schools.

school•fel•low [ˈskul,fɛlou] *n.* a companion at school.

school•girl [ˈskul,gɜrl] *n.* a girl attending school.

school guard **1** a member of a SCHOOL PATROL. **2** SCHOOL CROSSING-GUARD.

school•house [ˈskul,hʌus] *n.* a small building used as a school, especially in a village.

school•ing [ˈskulɪŋ] *n., v.* —*n.* **1** instruction in school; education received at school. **2** the cost of instruction.
—*v.* ppr. of SCHOOL.

school•ma'am [ˈskul,mæm] *or* [ˈskulmɑm] *n. Informal.* schoolmarm.

school•man [ˈskulmən] *n., pl.* **-men. 1** Usually, **Schoolman,** a teacher of philosophy and theology in a medieval European university; scholastic. **2** a teacher or scholar.

school•marm [ˈskul,mɑrm] *n. Informal.* **1** a female schoolteacher, especially in a rural or village school. **2** a very strict conservative teacher or similar person of either sex. **3** *Cdn. Slang. Logging.* a forked tree. Also, **schoolmarm tree.**

school•mas•ter [ˈskul,mæstər] *n. Old-fashioned.* **1** a man who teaches in or manages a school. **2** any person or thing that teaches or disciplines.

school•mate [ˈskul,meit] *n.* a companion at school.

school•mis•tress [ˈskul,mɪstrɪs] *n. Old-fashioned.* a woman who teaches in or manages a school.

school patrol an organized group of older schoolchildren who escort younger ones across busy streets.

school•room [ˈskul,rum] *or* [ˈskul,rʊm] *n.* a room in which pupils are taught.

school•teach•er [ˈskul,titʃər] *n.* a person who teaches in a school.

school trustee an elected member of a school board or board of education.

school•work [ˈskul,wɜrk] *n.* material or lessons worked on in class or at home.

school•yard [ˈskul,jɑrd] *n.* a piece of ground around or near a school, used for play, games, etc.

school year that part of the year during which school is in session.

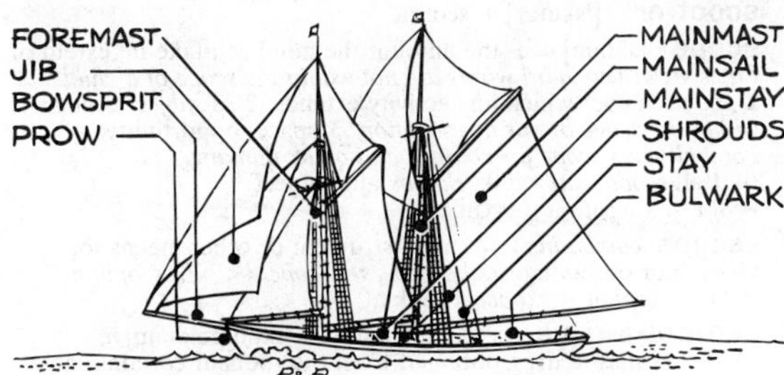

The *Bluenose*, a famous Canadian schooner

schoon•er ['skunər] *n.* **1** *Nautical.* a ship with two or more masts and fore-and-aft sails. **2** *Informal.* a large glass for beer. **3** PRAIRIE SCHOONER. ⟨< *scoon* skim, probably < Scand.⟩

schoon•er–rigged ['skunər ˌrɪgd] *adj.* having fore-and-aft sails, like a schooner.

schot•tische ['ʃɒtɪʃ] *or* [ʃɒ'tiʃ] *n.* **1** a dance in 2/4 time, resembling the polka. **2** the music for such a dance. ⟨< G *Schottische*, literally, Scottish⟩

schuss [ʃʊs] *n., v. Skiing. —n.* **1** a straight, downhill run at high speed. **2** a straight, downhill course for making such a run. *—v.* make such a run. ⟨< G⟩

schwa [ʃwɑ] *or* [ʃwɒ] *n.* **1** an unstressed vowel sound such as that of the *a* in *about*, the *u* in *circus*, or the *o* in *lemon*; neutral vowel. **2** the symbol (ə) used to represent this sound. ⟨< G < Hebrew *sh'wa*⟩

sci. **1** science. **2** scientific.

sci•at•ic [saɪ'ætɪk] *adj.* **1** *Anatomy.* of, having to do with, or in the region of the hip. **2** of, having to do with, or caused by sciatica. ⟨< Med.L *sciaticus*, alteration of L *ischiadicus* < Gk. < *ischion* hip joint⟩

sci•at•i•ca [saɪ'ætɪkə] *n. Pathology.* pain along the path of the sciatic nerve and its branches; neuralgia of the hips and legs. ⟨< Med.L *sciatica*, fem. of *sciaticus.* See SCIATIC.⟩

sciatic nerve the largest nerve in the human body, beginning in the pelvis and running down along the back of the thigh.

sci•ence ['saɪəns] *n.* **1** knowledge of general facts, laws, and relationships that is obtained through systematic observation and experiment, especially as applied to the physical world and the phenomena associated with it: *new discoveries in science, natural science.* **2** a branch of such knowledge. Biology and chemistry are sciences. **3** any branch of knowledge arranged in an orderly system and considered as an object of study: *Economics is a social science.* **4** a technique, skill, etc. that can be studied in a systematic way: *the science of boxing. Photography is both an art and a science.* ⟨ME < OF < L *scientia* knowledge < *scire* know⟩

science fiction a type of fiction, usually futuristic, based on actual or fanciful elements of science or technology.

sci•en•tial [saɪ'ɛnʃəl] *adj.* **1** having knowledge. **2** of or having to do with knowledge or science.

sci•en•tif•ic [ˌsaɪən'tɪfɪk] *adj.* **1** using the facts and laws of science: *a scientific method, a scientific farmer.* **2** of or having to do with science; used in science: *scientific books, scientific instruments.* **3** systematic or accurate in method, training, etc., as in an exact science. ⟨< LL *scientificus* < *scientia* knowledge + *facere* make⟩ **—ˌsci•en'tif•i•cal•ly,** *adv.*

scientific method the principles and procedures of scientific investigation, including: (1) the recognition and description of a particular problem, (2) the collection of data related to this problem, through observation and experimentation, (3) the interpretation of the data and formulation of a hypothesis to describe the event, law, or relationship discovered, and (4) the testing of the hypothesis by more observation and experimentation.

sci•en•tist ['saɪəntɪst] *n.* **1** a person who is trained in science, especially a natural science, and whose work is scientific investigation. **2 Scientist,** CHRISTIAN SCIENTIST.

sci–fi ['saɪ 'faɪ] *Informal.* **1** SCIENCE FICTION. **2** (*adjl.*) of, having to do with, or designating science fiction: *sci-fi fans. She has a huge sci-fi collection.*

scil•i•cet ['sɪləˌsɛt] *adv.* to wit; namely. ⟨< L *scilicet* < *scire* know + *licet* it is allowed⟩

scil•la ['sɪlə] *n.* any of a genus (*Scilla*) of bulbous herbs of the lily family having narrow leaves and small bell-shaped flowers. Also called **squill.**
☛ *Hom.* SCYLLA.

scim•i•tar ['sɪmətər] *or* ['sɪməˌtɑr] *n.* a short, curved sword having a cutting edge on the convex side, formerly used especially by Arabs and Turks. See SWORD for picture. ⟨< Ital. *scimitarra*⟩

scin•til•la [sɪn'tɪlə] *n.* a spark or trace: *There is not a scintilla of evidence against her.* ⟨< L *scintilla* spark. Doublet of TINSEL.⟩

scin•til•late ['sɪntəˌleit] *v.* **-lat•ed, -lat•ing. 1** sparkle; flash: *The snow scintillates like diamonds in the sun.* **2** be brilliant in conversation; be witty. **3** emit (sparks or flashes of light). ⟨< L *scintillare* < *scintilla* spark⟩ **—'scin•til,lat•ing•ly,** *adv.*

scin•til•la•tion [ˌsɪntə'leiʃən] *n.* **1** a sparkling; flashing. **2** a spark; flash. **3** a brilliant display of wit. **4** *Astronomy.* what is perceived as the twinkling of stars, due to changes in the density of the atmosphere.

scintillation counter an instrument that measures radiation by the scintillations produced by ionization. Also called **scintillometer** [ˌsɪntə'lɒmətər].

sci•o•lism ['saɪəˌlɪzəm] *n.* superficial knowledge. ⟨< LL *sciolus* knowing little, ult. < *scire* know⟩

sci•o•list ['saɪəlɪst] *n.* a person who pretends to have more knowledge than he or she really has. **—ˌsci•o'list•ic,** *adj.*

sci•on ['saɪən] *n.* **1** a bud or branch cut for grafting or planting. Also, **cion. 2** descendant. ⟨ME < OF *cion*, probably ult. < L *secare* to cut⟩

sci•roc•co [ʃə'rɒkou] *n.* See SIROCCO.

scis•sile ['sɪsaɪl] *adj.* able to be divided or cut smoothly. ⟨< L *scissilus* < *scissus*, pp. of *scindere* to cut⟩

scis•sion ['sɪʒən] *or* ['sɪʃən] *n.* the act of cutting, dividing, or splitting; separation. ⟨ME < LL *scissio, -onis* < *scindere* split⟩

scis•sor ['sɪzər] *v.* **1** cut with scissors. **2** move (arms or legs) with a scissorlike motion.

scis•sors ['sɪzərz] *n.* **1** a tool or instrument for cutting that has two sharp blades so fastened that their edges slide against each other (*usually used with a plural verb*). **2** *Gymnastics.* a forward and backward movement of the legs suggesting the action of scissors (*used with a singular or plural verb*). **3** *Wrestling.* a hold in which the opponent's body or head is held with the legs (*used with a singular verb*). ⟨ME < OF *cisoires*, pl., < LL *cisorium*, sing., tool for cutting, ult. < L *caedere* cut; confused with *scindere* cleave, split⟩ **—'scis•sor,like,** *adj.*

sci•u•rid [saɪ'jʊrɪd] *n.* any of the rodents belonging to the family Sciuridae, such as squirrels, marmots, and chipmunks. **—sci'u•roid** or **sci'u•rine,** *adj.*

scler•a ['sklɛrə] *or* ['sklirə] *n. Anatomy.* the tough, fibrous, white outer membrane covering all of the eyeball except the part covered by the cornea. See EYE for picture. ⟨< NL < Gk. *skleros* hard⟩

scle•ri•tis [sklə'rəitɪs] *n. Pathology.* inflammation of the sclera.

scle•ro•der•ma [ˌsklɛrə'dɜrmə] *or* [ˌsklirə'dɜrmə] *n.* **1** *Pathology.* an abnormal hardening and thickening of the skin, caused by fibrous tissue growth. **2** a disease involving hardening and rigidity of connective tissue anywhere in the body.

scle•ro•der•ma•tous [ˌsklɛrə'dɜrmətəs] *or* [ˌsklirə'dɜrmətəs] *adj.* **1** *Zoology.* covered with a hard tissue, as scales. **2** of or having to do with scleroderma.

scle•rom•e•ter [sklə'rɒmətər] *n.* an instrument for measuring the hardness of a substance, especially a mineral.

scle•ro•pro•tein [ˌsklɛrə'proutin] *or* [ˌsklirə'proutin] *n. Biochemistry.* any of several insoluble animal proteins.

scle•ro•sis [sklə'rousɪs] *n., pl.* **-ses** [-siz]. **1** *Pathology.* **a** a hardening of a tissue or part of the body by an increase of connective tissue or the like at the expense of more active tissue. **b** a disease characterized by such hardening, as in the arteries. **2** *Botany.* a hardening of a tissue or cell wall of a plant by thickening or the formation of wood.

scle•ro•the•ra•py [ˌsklɛrou'θɛrəpi] *or* [ˌsklirou'θɛrəpi] *n. Medicine.* a treatment for varicose or ruptured esophageal veins, in which the veins are injected with a hardening solution. It may be used cosmetically to treat spider veins.

scle•rot•ic [sklə'rɒtɪk] *adj., n. —adj.* **1** having to do with or

being the sclera. **2** of, having to do with, or affected with sclerosis.
—n. sclera. ⟨< NL *scleroticus* < Gk. *sklēros* hard⟩

scoff[1] [skɒf] *v., n.* *—v.* make fun to show one does not believe something; mock; deride (*used with* **at**).
—n. **1** mocking words or acts. **2** something ridiculed or mocked. ⟨ME < Scand.; cf. Danish *skuffe* deceive⟩ **—'scoff•er,** *n.* **—'scoff•ing•ly,** *adv.*

☛ *Syn. v.* **Scoff,** JEER, SNEER = show scorn or contempt for someone or something by mocking or biting words or by laughter. **Scoff** emphasizes speaking in an insultingly contemptuous or mocking way about something others respect or believe in: *She scoffs at religion.* **Jeer** implies a louder and coarser or more sarcastic way of making fun and, particularly, suggests mocking laughter: *The mob jeered when the speaker got up to talk.* **Sneer** emphasizes an insultingly contemptuous facial expression or tone of voice, or a slighting and hinting way of speaking: *He sneers at everything sentimental.*

scoff[2] [skɒf] *v., n. Slang.* *—v.* **1** eat, especially greedily. **2** pilfer: *Who scoffed my pencil sharpener?*
—n. food; a meal. ⟨variant of dialect *scaff* food⟩

scold [skould] *v., n.* *—v.* **1** find fault with and criticize severely or angrily; rebuke with severe or angry words: *His mother scolded him for tearing his jacket.* **2** find fault; talk angrily: *He's always scolding.*
—n. a person who makes a habit of scolding. ⟨ME, probably < ON *skáld* poet, in sense of 'lampooner'⟩ **—'scold•er,** *n.*

☛ *Syn. v.* **1. Scold,** UPBRAID, CHIDE = find fault with someone. **Scold** particularly suggests cross and impatient, often loud and insistent, finding fault or expressing disapproval in angry or abusive words, not always with good reason: *That woman is always scolding the children in our neighbourhood.* **Upbraid,** more formal, always suggests a definite fault or offence, and emphasizes angrily and sharply or severely blaming and trying to shame: *He upbraided them for tormenting animals.* **Chide** usually suggests milder words of disapproval, or blame intended to correct: *He chided her for carelessness.*

sco•li•o•sis [ˌskouli'ousɪs] *n. Pathology.* lateral curvature of the backbone. ⟨< Gk., a bending⟩

scol•lop ['skɒləp] *n. or v.* scallop.

sconce[1] [skɒns] *n.* a bracket projecting from a wall, used to hold a candle or other light. ⟨ME < Med.L *sconsa,* ult. < L *abscondere* hide⟩

sconce[2] [skɒns] *n.* **1** a small detached fort or bulwark. **2** a hut; shed; screen or shelter of some sort. ⟨< Du. *schans* fortress, originally, wickerwork < G. *Schanze* originally, bundle of wood⟩

sconce[3] [skɒns] *n.* **1** the head, especially the top of the head. **2** brains; good sense; wit. ⟨origin uncertain⟩

scone [skɒn] *or* [skoun] *n.* a TEA BISCUIT, especially a large one. ⟨probably < MDu. *schoon(brot)* fine (bread)⟩

scoop [skup] *n., v.* *—n.* **1** a tool like a small shovel, having a short handle and a deeply concave blade for dipping out or shovelling up things. **2** a small kitchen utensil for ice cream, mashed potatoes, etc., having a deep, rounded bowl and a horizontal handle. **3** the part of a dredge, shovel, etc. that holds coal, sand, etc. **4** the amount taken up at one time by a scoop. **5** a place or thing hollowed out. **6** the action or process of scooping. **7** *Slang.* **a** the publishing of a piece of news before a rival newspaper does. **b** the piece of news as published. **8** *Informal.* the latest information, especially if confidential: *So, what's the scoop on Tom and Linda?* **9** *Cdn.* a trough made from a small split and hollowed log, usually pine or basswood, and used for a type of roofing.
—v. **1** take up or out with a scoop, or as a scoop does. **2** hollow out; dig out; make by scooping: *The children scooped holes in the sand.* **3** *Slang.* publish a piece of news before (a rival newspaper). **4** *Cdn.* hollow out (scoops) with an adze or axe. **5** *Cdn.* roof with scoops. ⟨partly < MDu. *schoepe* bucket, partly < MDu. *schoppe* shovel⟩

scoop•ful ['skupˌfʊl] *n., pl.* **-fuls.** as much as a scoop can hold.

scoop roof *Cdn.* a roof made of scoops. Also, **log-trough roof.**

scoot [skut] *v., n.* *—v.* **1** *Informal.* go quickly; dart: *She scooted out the side door just as I came in the front.* **2** *Informal.* a mild form of SCRAM: *Scoot, out of my way!*
—n. **1** *Informal.* the act of scooting. **2** *Cdn.* a strong-hulled, flat-bottomed boat, driven by an aircraft propeller on an engine mounted toward the stern, designed for travelling on water, through slob ice, or over ice or snow. ⟨probably < Scand.; cf. ON *skióta* shoot⟩

scoot•er[1] ['skutər] *n., v.* *—n.* **1** a child's vehicle consisting of a long footboard with a wheel at the front and the back, steered by raised handlebars and moved by pushing against the ground with one foot. **2** MOTOR SCOOTER. **3** a sailboat with runners, for use on either water or ice.
—v. go or travel by scooter. ⟨< *scoot*⟩

scoot•er[2] ['skutər] *n.* scoter.

scope [skoup] *n.* **1** the amount the mind can take in; extent of one's view: *Very hard words are not within the scope of a child.* **2** the area over which any activity extends: *This subject is not within the scope of our investigation.* **3** space; opportunity: *Football gives scope for courage and quick thinking.*
⟨< Ital. *scopo,* ult. < Gk. *skopos* aim, object⟩
☛ *Syn.* **1.** See note at RANGE.

-scope *combining form.* an instrument or other means for viewing or observing: *stethoscope, telescope.* ⟨< NL *-scopium* < Gk. *-skopion* < *skopeein* look at⟩

sco•pol•a•mine [skou'pɒləˌmin] *or* [skou'pɒləmɪn] *n. Pharmaceutics.* a drug obtained from the roots of certain plants of the nightshade family, used as a sedative or truth serum or, with morphine, to relieve pain. *Formula:* $C_{17}H_{21}NO_4$ ⟨< NL *Scopolia,* a genus of plants (named after Giacomo A. *Scopoli* (1723-1788), an Italian naturalist) + E *amine*⟩

scor•bu•tic [skɔr'bjutɪk] *adj. Pathology.* **1** having to do with or of the nature of scurvy. **2** affected with scurvy. ⟨< NL *scorbuticus* < *scorbutus* scurvy < F *scorbut* < Gmc.⟩

scorch [skɔrtʃ] *v., n.* *—v.* **1** burn slightly; burn on the outside: *The cake tastes scorched. The maid scorched the shirt in ironing it.* **2** parch with intense heat; dry up; wither: *grass scorched by the sun.* **3** criticize with harsh or sarcastic words. **4** *Informal.* drive or ride very fast: *She scorched along the empty road.*
—n. **1** a slight burn. **2** on plants, the browning and withering of leaves caused by excessive heat, some types of fungus, etc. ⟨ME; cf. *skorken* < ON *skorpna* dry up⟩
☛ *Syn. v.* **1.** See note at BURN.

scorched–earth policy ['skɔrtʃt 'ɜrθ] a military policy of destroying all crops, buildings, etc., in the course of a retreat, so as to leave nothing useful for the enemy.

scorch•er ['skɔrtʃər] *n.* **1** *Informal.* a very hot day. **2** *Informal.* a person who drives or rides very fast. **3** a scathing criticism. **4** a person who or thing that scorches.

score [skɔr] *n., v.* **scored, scor•ing.** *—n.* **1 a** the points made in a game, contest, examination, etc. **b** the record of points made: *The score was 9 to 2 in our favour.* **2** an amount owed; debt; account: *He paid his score at the inn.* **3** a group or set of twenty; twenty. **4 scores,** *pl.* a large number, but less than hundreds: *Scores died in the epidemic.* **5** a written or printed piece of music arranged for different instruments or voices: *the score of a musical comedy.* **6** a cut; scratch; stroke; mark; line: *The slave's back showed scores made by the whip.* **7** the act of making or winning a point; a successful stroke, rejoinder, etc. **8** an account; reason; ground: *Don't worry on that score.* **9 the score,** *Informal.* the truth about anything or things in general; the facts: *The new man doesn't know the score yet.*
on the score of, because of; on account of.
pay off or **settle a score,** get even for an injury or wrong.
—v. **1 a** *Game, contest, etc.* make as total points. **b** keep a record of (the number of points made in a game, contest, etc.). **c** be counted as in the score. **d** make as an addition to the score; gain; win; make (a run, hit, etc.): *She scored five runs for our team.* **2** keep a record of as an amount owed; mark; set down: *The innkeeper scored on a slate the number of drinks each person had.* **3** achieve a success; succeed. **4 a** *Music.* arrange (a composition) for different instruments or voices. **b** write out (music) in score. **5** cut; scratch; mark with a line: *Mistakes are scored in red ink.* **6** *Informal.* blame or scold severely. **7** make a partial cut in: *Score the cardboard with a knife before bending.* **8** *Slang.* succeed in seducing someone: *Did you score? Yes, with Linda.* ⟨OE < ON *skor* notch⟩ **—'score•less,** *adj.* **—'scor•er,** *n.*
☛ *Hom.* SCAUR.

score•board ['skɔrˌbɔrd] *n. Sports.* a large board for posting the score and, sometimes, other details of a game or other sporting event.

score•card ['skɔrˌkɑrd] *n. Sports.* **1** a card bearing the names of players and other information relevant to an athletic event. **2** a card for keeping the score of a game, match, etc. Also, **score card.**

score•keep•er ['skɔrˌkipər] *n. Sports.* the person who officially keeps a record of the score at a sporting event.

sco•ri•a ['skɔriə] *n., pl.* **-ri•ae** [-riˌi] *or* [-riˌaɪ]. **1** refuse left from ore after the metal has been melted out; slag. **2** solidified lava having a great many cavities, like a very coarse pumice. ⟨< L < Gk. *skōria* < *skōr* dung⟩

sco•ri•a•ceous [ˌskɔri'eiʃəs] *adj.* like or consisting of scoria.

sco•ri•fy ['skɔrə,faɪ] *v.* **-fied, -fy•ing. 1** separate gold or silver from (ore) by fusion with lead. **2** reduce by scorifying. **—,sco•ri•fi'ca•tion,** *n.* **—'sco•ri,fi•er,** *n.*

scorn [skɔrn] *v., n.* *—v.* **1** look down upon; think of as mean or low; despise: *She scorned their attempts at reconciliation. He scorns his critics as being out-of-date and incompetent.* **2** reject or refuse as low or wrong: *The judge scorned to take a bribe.*
—n. **1** a feeling that a person, animal, or act is mean or low; contempt: *We feel scorn for a traitor.* **2** an object of such a feeling. **3** an expression of derision or contempt in speech or by action. ⟨ME < OF *escarnir* < Gmc.⟩ **—'scorn•er,** *n.*
☛ *Syn. n.* **1. Scorn,** CONTEMPT, DISDAIN = a feeling that a person or thing is mean, low, or worthless. **Scorn,** which expresses the strongest feeling, adds to this basic meaning the idea of disgust mixed with anger, sometimes shown by unkind and bitter laughter: *We feel scorn for a person who avoids responsibilities.* **Contempt** adds to the basic meaning the idea of disgust mixed with strong disapproval: *We feel contempt for a coward.* **Disdain** adds the idea of feeling oneself above anything mean or low and rejecting it: *We feel disdain for a person who cheats.*

scorn•ful ['skɔrnfəl] *adj.* showing contempt; mocking; full of scorn. **—'scorn•ful•ly,** *adv.* **—'scorn•ful•ness,** *n.*

Scor•pi•o ['skɔrpjou] *or* ['skɔrpi,ou] *n.* **1** *Astronomy.* a constellation in the Milky Way, thought of as having the shape of a scorpion. Also, **Scorpius. 2** *Astrology.* **a** the eighth sign of the zodiac. The sun enters Scorpio about October 23. See ZODIAC for picture. **b** a person born under this sign. ⟨< L *scorpio* scorpion⟩

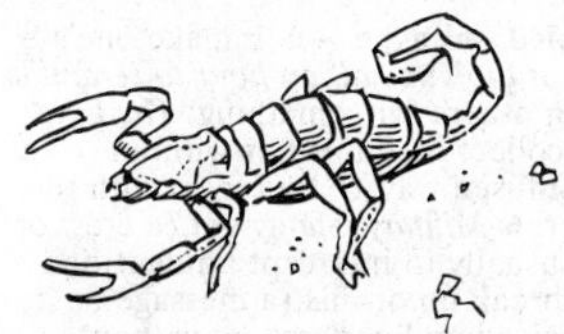
A scorpion—the different species range in size from 1.3 to 18 cm long

scor•pi•on ['skɔrpjən] *or* ['skɔrpiən] *n.* **1** any of an order (Scorpionida) of arachnids having six pairs of appendages, the first two pairs adapted for grasping and tearing apart prey and the others used for walking, and having a segmented abdomen that tapers to form a tail with a poisonous stinger at the tip. **2** in the Bible, a whip or scourge, probably studded with metal points. **3 Scorpion,** *Astronomy. Astrology.* Scorpio. ⟨< L *scorpio, -onis,* ult. < Gk. *skorpios*⟩

Scor•pi•us ['skɔrpiəs] *n.* SCORPIO (def. 1).

scot [skɒt] *n.* formerly, a tax or levy assessed or paid. Compare SCOT-FREE. ⟨ME < ON *skit.* Related to SHOT[1].⟩

Scot [skɒt] *n.* **1** a native or inhabitant of Scotland, a division of the United Kingdom. **2** a person of Scottish descent. **3** a member of a Celtic tribe of N Ireland that migrated to N Great Britain in the 5th and 6th centuries. ⟨OE *Scottas,* pl., Irishmen, Scotsmen < LL *Scottus* Irishman⟩
☛ *Usage.* **Scot,** SCOTCH, SCOTS. **Scot** refers to the people, the natives of Scotland or their descendants, as do **Scotsman** and **Scotswoman**. The related adjective is **Scots** or **Scottish**. **Scotch**, except in reference to whisky, is considered derogatory, although it is used adjectivally in set phrases like **Scotch egg** and **Scotch pine**.

Scot. Scotland; Scottish; Scotch.

scotch [skɒtʃ] *v.* **1** wound so as to cripple or make temporarily harmless: *to scotch a snake without killing it.* **2** stamp out; stifle; crush: *to scotch a rumour.* **3** cut; score; gash. ⟨ME; origin uncertain⟩

Scotch [skɒtʃ] *n., adj.* *—n.* **1** SCOTCH WHISKY. **2** Scottish.
—adj. Scottish.
☛ *Usage.* See note at SCOT.

Scotch broom the broom (*Cytisus scoparius*), an invasive weed on Vancouver Island and sporadically on the B.C. mainland.

Scotch broth a thick soup containing mutton, vegetables, and oats or barley.

Scotch egg a hard-boiled egg covered in sausage meat, breaded and deep-fried. It is often eaten cold with salad.

Scotch fir SCOTS PINE.

Scotch grain a pebbled finish used on heavy leather, as for desk tops, men's shoes, etc.

Scotch–I•rish ['skɒtʃ 'aɪrɪʃ] *adj., n.* *—adj.* **1** of, having to do with, or designating the population of Ulster that is descended from Scottish settlers. **2** of, having to do with, or designating the descendants of those members of this group who emigrated from Ulster to North America in the early 19th century. **3** of both Scottish and Irish descent.
—n. a person of both Scottish and Irish descent.

Scotch•man ['skɒtʃmən] *n., pl.* **-men.** Scot.

Scotch mist 1 a drizzly mixture of fog and rain. **2** a drink made of Scotch whisky and crushed ice.

Scotch pine SCOTS PINE.

Scotch tape *Trademark.* a transparent, self-sealing, adhesive plastic tape for patching, sealing, etc.

Scotch terrier SCOTTISH TERRIER.

Scotch verdict in certain criminal cases in Scottish law, a verdict of 'not proven' rather than 'not guilty'.

Scotch whisky a whisky made in Scotland, distilled from barley malt.

Scotch woodcock a dish made of toast spread with anchovy paste, topped with scrambled egg.

sco•ter ['skoutər] *n.* any of a small genus (*Melanitta*) of diving ducks found along the northern coasts and large lakes and rivers of North America and Europe, the adult male having mostly black plumage, the female mostly brown. ⟨? < dial. *scote,* var. of *scoot*⟩

scot–free ['skɒt 'fri] *adj. or adv.* completely free from injury, punishment, penalty, etc.: *His partner was convicted of fraud but he got off scot-free.* Compare SCOT.

Sco•tia ['skouʃə] *n. Poetic.* Scotland. ⟨< Med.L⟩

Scot•land ['skɒtlənd] *n.* a division of the United Kingdom taking in the northern part of Great Britain and the adjacent islands.

Scotland Yard 1 in England, the headquarters of the London Metropolitan Police, properly called **New Scotland Yard. 2** the London Police, especially the Criminal Investigation Department. ⟨< the building in which the London police headquarters was formerly located, in Great Scotland Yard, the site of the former London residence of the kings of Scotland⟩

sco•to•ma [skə'toumə] *n., pl.* **-ma•ta** [-mətə]. *Pathology.* loss of vision or a dark area in the visual field; blind spot. ⟨< LL < Gk. *skotoma* < *skotos* dark⟩

Scots [skɒts] *n., adj.* *—n.* any of the dialects of English spoken in Scotland.
—adj. of, having to do with, or characteristic of Scotland, its people, their English dialects, or their Gaelic language.
☛ *Usage.* See note at SCOT.

Scots fir SCOTS PINE.

Scots–Gael•ic ['skɒts 'geilɪk] *or* ['gɑlɪk] *n.* the Celtic language of the Scottish Highlanders.

Scots•man ['skɒtsmən] *n., pl.* **-men.** a man who is a native or inhabitant of Scotland; a Scot.

Scots pine 1 a pine (*Pinus sylvestris*) native to N Europe and Asia but now widely planted in Canada, having spreading branches and short, twisted, bluish green needles. **2** the hard, yellowish wood of this tree, valuable for timber. Also called **Scotch pine, Scotch fir, Scots fir.**

Scots•wom•an ['skɒts,wʊmən] *n., pl.* **-wom•en** [-,wɪmɪn]. a woman who is a native or inhabitant of Scotland; a female Scot.

Scot•ti•cism ['skɒtə,sɪzəm] *n.* a word, expression, pronunciation, etc. that is characteristic of Scottish English.

Scot•tie or **Scot•ty** ['skɒti] *n. Informal.* SCOTTISH TERRIER.

Scot•tish ['skɒtɪʃ] *adj., n.* *—adj.* of, having to do with, or characteristic of Scotland, its people, or their English dialects or Gaelic language; Scots.
—n. **1 the Scottish,** *pl.* **a** the people of Scotland. **b** people of Scottish descent. **2** Scots.

Scottish deerhound deerhound.

Scottish Gaelic SCOTS-GAELIC.

Scottish rite one of the two advanced ceremonial divisions of Freemasonry leading to the 33rd degree. Compare YORK RITE.

Scottish terrier an old Scottish breed of short-legged terrier having rough, wiry hair and pointed, standing ears.

scoun•drel ['skaʊndrəl] *n.* a mean or wicked person; a person without principles; villain. ⟨? < OF *escondre* hide, abscond < L *ex-* from + *condere* hide⟩ **—'scoun•drel•ly,** *adj.*

scour[1] [skaʊr] *v., n.* *—v.* **1** clean or polish by vigorous rubbing: *Scour the frying pan with cleanser.* **2** remove by vigorous rubbing.

3 remove dirt and grease from (raw wool) by washing. 4 clear of dirt, weeds, etc.: *We scoured the pond to make it swimmable.* 5 dig or dig out by the action of running water: *The stream had scoured a channel.* 6 a get rid of as if by cleaning: *She tried to scour the memory from her brain.* b clear out as if by cleaning: *Scour your mind clear of every base thought.*
—*n.* 1 the act of scouring. 2 the place scoured, as in a stream bed. 3 **scours,** diarrhea in cattle. ⟨prob. < MDu. < OF *escurer,* ult. < L *ex-* completely + *cura* care⟩ **—'scour•er,** *n.*

scour² [skaʊr] *v.* 1 move quickly over: *People scoured the country round about for the lost child.* 2 look into every part of; search: *scour one's memory for a forgotten date.* 3 go swiftly in search or pursuit. ⟨ME, probably < OF *escourre* run forth, ult. < L *ex-* out + *currere* run⟩

scourge [skɜrdʒ] *n., v.* **scourged, scourg•ing.** *—n.* 1 a whip. 2 any means of punishment. 3 some thing or person that causes great trouble or misfortune, as a plague, war, etc.
—v. 1 whip severely; flog. 2 punish severely. 3 put great hardship or suffering on; afflict or oppress. ⟨ME < AF *escorge,* ult. < L *ex-* out + *corrigia* whip⟩

scour•ings ['skaʊrɪŋz] *n.pl.* 1 dirt or other material removed by scouring or cleaning. 2 the lowest level or class of society; rabble: *the scourings of the slums.*

scouse [skʌus] *n.* 1 a sailor's stew, made with meat and hardtack. Also, **lobscouse.** 2 **Scouse,** Liverpudlian.

scout¹ [skʌut] *n., v.* *—n.* 1 a person sent to find out what the enemy is doing. A scout usually wears a uniform; a spy does not. 2 a warship, aircraft, etc. used to find out what the enemy is doing. 3 a person sent out to get information, especially about one's opponents, competitors, etc. 4 a person who looks for promising recruits for a film studio, sports team, etc. 5 the act of scouting. 6 **Scout,** a member of the Scouts organization. 7 *Slang.* a fellow; person: *Kim's a good scout.* 8 *Cdn.* a person employed to search out promising mineral properties and to check on the activities of competitors.
—v. 1 act as a scout. 2 hunt around to find something: *Go and scout for firewood.* 3 observe or examine to get information. ⟨ME < OF *escoute* act of listening, listener < *escouter* listen < L *auscultare*⟩

A Scout (def. 6)

scout² [skʌut] *v.* 1 refuse to believe in; reject with scorn: *She scouted the idea of a dog with two tails.* 2 scoff. ⟨< Scand.; cf. ON *skúta* taunt⟩

scout car 1 a police car that patrols streets and roads, maintaining contact with the station by radio telephone. 2 a lightly armoured military reconnaissance vehicle. 3 a wide-tracked vehicle designed for use on northern muskeg.

Scout•er ['skʌutər] *n.* an adult working directly with a group of Scouts, Cubs, or Beavers.

Scout•ing ['skʌutɪŋ] *n.* the activities, programs, or principles of the Scouts.

Scout•mas•ter ['skʌut,mæstər] *n.* TROOP SCOUTER.

Scouts Canada a non-political, non-denominational, co-educational organization for boys and girls, young men and young women. Its aim is to help them to learn co-operation, leadership, and self-reliance, to acquire knowledge and appreciation of the outdoors, and to develop physically and spiritually. Scouts Canada has five programs for different ages: Beavers, Cubs, Scouts, Venturers, and Rovers.

scow [skaʊ] *n.* a large, flat-bottomed boat used especially to carry bulk freight, such as sand or coal, and usually either towed by a tug or pushed with a pole, like a raft. ⟨< Du. *schouw*⟩

scow–house ['skaʊ ,hʌus] *n. Cdn. Pacific coast.* a dwelling built on floats at the shore, and usually constructed so that it can be towed from one mooring to another. Also, **floathouse.**

scowl [skaʊl] *v., n.* *—v.* 1 draw the eyebrows down and together and tighten the mouth, especially as an expression of anger or sullenness; frown: *She scowled at us and asked what we were doing there.* 2 express with a scowl: *He scowled his displeasure.*
—n. an angry or sullen look. ⟨ME *skoul;* akin to Danish *skule* cast down the eyes⟩ **—'scowl•er,** *n.*
☛ *Syn. v.* 1. See note at FROWN.

scrab•ble ['skræbəl] *v.* **-bled, -bling;** *n.* *—v.* 1 scratch or scrape about with hands, claws, etc.; scramble. 2 struggle or scramble feverishly, desperately, etc.: *scrabble for scraps of food, scrabble for a living.* 3 scrawl; scribble.
—n. 1 a scraping; scramble. 2 **Scrabble,** *Trademark.* a game played with small wooden or plastic squares with different letters on them, arranged to form words somewhat as in a crossword puzzle. ⟨< Du. *schrabbelen,* frequentative of *schrabben* scratch⟩

scrag [skræg] *n., v.* **scragged, scrag•ging.** *—n.* 1 a skinny or scrawny person or animal. 2 a lean, bony cut of meat, especially the lean end of a neck of mutton or veal. 3 *Slang.* the neck.
—v. 1 *Slang.* put to death by hanging or garrotting. 2 *Slang.* wring the neck of. ⟨< Scand.; cf. dial. Swedish *skragge* old and torn thing⟩

scrag•gly ['skrægli] *adj.* **-gli•er, -gli•est.** rough, irregular, or ragged: *a scraggly garden. The child's hair was scraggly and matted.*

scrag•gy ['skrægi] *adj.* **-gi•er, -gi•est.** 1 lean; thin. 2 scraggly. **—'scrag•gi•ly,** *adv.* **—'scrag•gi•ness,** *n.*

scram [skræm] *v.* **scrammed, scram•ming.** *Slang.* go away: *Scram! You're in the way here. She told the kids to scram.* ⟨short for *scramble*⟩

scram•ble ['skræmbəl] *v.* **-bled, -bling;** *n.* *—v.* 1 make one's way by climbing; crawling, etc.: *It took us half an hour to scramble up the rocky hill.* 2 struggle with others for something: *The boys scrambled to get the football.* 3 collect in a hurry or without method. 4 mix together in a confused way. 5 fry (eggs) with the whites and yolks mixed together. 6 *Military. Slang.* get (a crew or aircraft) into the air hurriedly, usually to intercept unidentified planes. 7 *Telecommunications.* break up or mix (a message or signal), so that it cannot be received and understood without special equipment. 8 make one's way in a hurried, ungraceful, or disorganized fashion: *As soon as she heard the ring, she scrambled to answer the door.*
—n. 1 a climb or walk over rough ground. 2 a struggle to possess: *the scramble for wealth.* 3 any disorderly struggle or activity. 4 *Military. Slang.* the act or process of scrambling. 5 a disorderly rush. ⟨var. of *scrabble*⟩ **—'scram•bler,** *n.*

scrap¹ [skræp] *n., v.* **scrapped, scrap•ping.** *—n.* 1 a small discarded or leftover piece of food: *The cook gave the scraps to the dog.* 2 a small detached or separated bit or piece: *scraps of paper, fabric scraps.* 3 a bit of something written, printed, etc.: *She read out scraps from the letter.* 4 material or articles discarded as useless and fit only to be broken down, melted, etc. and reprocessed: *a yard full of iron scrap.* 5 (*adjl.*) in the form of scrap or scraps: *She buys scrap metal.* 6 **scraps,** *pl.* cracklings.
—v. 1 throw aside as worn out or useless: *They decided to scrap their old chesterfield.* 2 condemn or abandon as useless, not worth the effort, etc.: *The missile project was scrapped.* ⟨ME < ON *scrap* < *scrapa* scrape⟩

scrap² [skræp] *n., v.* **scrapped, scrap•ping.** *Informal.* *—n.* a fight or quarrel.
—v. have a scrap; fight or quarrel. ⟨var. of *scrape*⟩ **—'scrap•per,** *n.*

scrap•book ['skræp,bʊk] *n.* a book in which pictures or clippings are pasted and kept.

scrape [skreip] *v.* **scraped, scrap•ing;** *n.* *—v.* 1 rub with something sharp or rough; make smooth or clean thus: *Scrape your muddy shoes with this old knife.* 2 remove by rubbing with or against something sharp or rough: *The man scraped some paint off the table when he pushed it through the doorway.* 3 scratch or graze by rubbing against something rough: *She fell and scraped her knee on the sidewalk.* 4 rub with a harsh sound; rub harshly: *Don't scrape your feet on the floor. The branch of the tree scraped against the window.* 5 give a harsh sound; grate. 6 dig: *The child scraped a hole in the sand.* 7 collect (goods or money) with difficulty or a little at a time: *Kee has scraped together enough money for his first year at university.* 8 draw one foot back along the ground in making a bow.
bow and scrape. See BOW¹.
scrape acquaintance, take the trouble to get acquainted.
scrape along, through, or **by,** barely get through; manage with difficulty: *That family can just scrape by but never asks for charity. She scraped through the examination.*
—n. 1 the act of scraping. 2 a scraped place. 3 a harsh, grating sound: *the scrape of the bow of a violin.* 4 a position hard to get out of; difficulty. ⟨ME < ON *skrapa*⟩

scrap•er ['skreipər] *n.* 1 one who or that which scrapes. 2 an instrument or tool for scraping: *We removed the loose paint with a scraper.*

scrap•ing ['skreipɪŋ] *n., v.* *—n.* **1** the act of a person who or thing that scrapes. **2** the sound produced by this: *We could hear the scraping of the shovel against the sidewalk.* **3** Usually, **scrapings,** *pl.* that which is scraped off, together, or up: *Put the scrapings into this box.*
—v. ppr. of SCRAPE.

scrap iron or **metal** broken or waste pieces of old iron or other metal collected for reworking.

scrap•per ['skræpər] *n. Informal.* a person who or animal that fights readily or effectively, especially a small one: *The way she took on that bully showed that she was a scrapper.*

scrap•ple ['skræpəl] *n.* scraps of pork boiled with corn meal, made into cakes, sliced, and fried. ⟨< *scrap¹*⟩

scrap•py¹ ['skræpi] *adj.* **-pi•er, -pi•est.** made up of odds and ends; fragmentary; disconnected. ⟨< *scrap¹*⟩ **—'scrap•pi•ly,** *adv.* **—'scrap•pi•ness,** *n.*

scrap•py² ['skræpi] *adj.* **-pi•er, -pi•est.** *Informal.* fond of fighting. ⟨< *scrap²*⟩ **—'scrap•pi•ly,** *adv.* **—'scrap•pi•ness,** *n.*

scratch [skrætʃ] *v., n., adj.* *—v.* **1** break the surface of, mark, or cut slightly with something sharp or rough: *Your shoes have scratched the chair.* **2** tear or dig into with the nails or claws: *The cat scratched her.* **3** rub or scrape to relieve itching: *He scratched his head.* **4** rub or scrape with a harsh noise: *He scratched his fingernail along the chalkboard.* **5** scribble. **6** strike out; draw a line through; cancel. **7** withdraw from a race or contest: *The horse was scratched because of an injury.* **8** gather by effort; scrape. **9** manage with difficulty (*used with* **by** *or* **along**). **10** *Billiards.* make a shot that incurs a penalty.
scratch the surface, do something in a superficial way.
—n. **1** the act of scratching. **2** a very slight cut on the skin. **3** the sound of scratching: *the scratch of a pen.* **4** a mark made by scratching or scribbling. **5** the starting place of a race or contest. **6** *Slang.* money. **7** *Billiards.* a shot that incurs a penalty, especially when the cue ball is pocketed instead of hitting the object ball.
from scratch, a with no advantages; from the beginning: *He lost his notes and so had to start his project again from scratch.* **b** in cooking, from unprepared materials; without a mix: *I love chocolate cake made from scratch.*
up to scratch, up to standard; in good condition; of acceptable quality.
—adj. **1** made up from whatever is on hand: *a scratch meal, a scratch football team.* **2** done by or dependent on chance: *a scratch shot.* ⟨ME *scracche* < ME *scratten, cracche*; cognate with MDu. *cratsen*⟩

Scratch [skrætʃ] *n.* Old Scratch; Satan; the Devil. ⟨ME *skratte* probably < ON *skratti* monster, sorcerer; related to OHG *scraz* goblin, wood-demon⟩

scratch hit *Baseball.* a poorly hit ball that is credited as a base hit.

scratch pad a pad of paper used for rough work or casual writing.

scratch paper paper used for rough work or casual writing.

scratch test *Medicine.* a medical test for suspected allergies, in which the skin is scratched or punctured and an allergen applied to the scratch by rubbing; resulting redness indicates an allergy.

scratch•y ['skrætʃi] *adj.* **scratch•i•er, scratch•i•est. 1** that scratches or scrapes: *a scratchy rosebush.* **2** giving a prickly feeling; irritating to the skin: *This woollen dress is scratchy.* **3** making a scratching noise: *a scratchy pen.* **4** consisting of or made with scratches: *a scratchy drawing.* **5** irritable; peevish. **—'scratch•i•ly,** *adv.* **—'scratch•i•ness,** *n.*

scrawl [skrɒl] *v., n.* *—v.* write or draw poorly, carelessly, or hastily: *She scrawled a note on the back of an envelope.*
—n. **1** poor, careless, or hasty handwriting: *I could hardly read the doctor's scrawl.* **2** something scrawled, such as a hastily or badly written letter or note. ⟨? < obs. *scrawl* spread the arms, gesticulate (of uncertain origin); possible blend of *sprawl* and *crawl* or of *scratch* and *sprawl*⟩ **—'scrawl•er,** *n.*

scraw•ny ['skrɒni] *adj.* **-ni•er, -ni•est. 1** *Informal.* excessively lean, thin, or skinny: *Turkeys have scrawny necks.* **2** of plants or trees, of stunted growth. ⟨< Scand.; cf. dial. Norwegian *skran*⟩ **—'scraw•ni•ness,** *n.*

scream [skrim] *v., n.* *—v.* **1** give voice to a loud, sharp, piercing cry, usually from fright, anger, or sudden pain. **2** produce a loud, shrill, harsh noise: *The siren screamed.* **3** utter or speak very shrilly or loudly: *"That's wet paint!" she screamed. We had to scream to hear each other above the music.* **4** laugh loudly or uncontrollably: *The audience screamed at the clown's antics.* **5** produce an extremely startling effect: *"War declared!" the headlines screamed.*
—n. **1** a loud, sharp, piercing cry. **2** a loud, shrill, harsh noise. **3** *Informal.* something or somebody extremely funny. ⟨ME; ? < ON *skræma* scare⟩
☛ *Syn. v.* **1. Scream,** SHRIEK = make a loud, sharp, piercing sound. **Scream** means to give out suddenly a loud, high-pitched, piercing cry expressing fear, pain, or almost hysterical anger or joy: *She screamed when she saw the child fall.* **Shriek** suggests a more high-pitched, wild, hair-raising and back-tingling cry, expressing extreme terror, horror, agony, or uncontrolled rage or laughter: *The prisoner shrieked when he was tortured.*

scream•er ['skrimər] *n.* **1** a person who or thing that screams. **2** any of three species making up a family (Anhimidae) of large South American marsh birds having a plump body with mainly grey or black plumage, spurs on the front edge of the wings, and a very loud, trumpeting call. The closest relatives of the screamers are ducks, geese, and swans. **3** a large and sensational headline.

scream•ing ['skrimɪŋ] *adj., v.* *—adj.* **1** that screams. **2** evoking screams of laughter: *a screaming farce.* **3** startling: *screaming headlines, screaming colours.*
—v. ppr. of SCREAM.

scream•ing•ly ['skrimɪŋli] *adv.* to an extreme degree, so as to make one wish to scream: *screamingly funny.*

screaming mee•mies ['mimiz] extreme nervous feeling; hysteria. ⟨used of the sound of German shells in WWI⟩

scree [skri] *n.* a steep slope of loose, fragmented rock lying below a cliff or bluff. ⟨< ON *skritha* glide⟩

screech¹ [skritʃ] *v. or n.* scream; shriek. ⟨ME *scritch,* imitative⟩ **—'screech•er,** *n.*

screech² [skritʃ] *n. Cdn. esp. Nfld. Slang.* **1** a potent dark rum. **2** any cheap, potent liquor or wine. ⟨ult. < Scottish dial. *screigh* whisky, influenced by *screech¹*⟩

screech owl **1** any of several small New World owls (genus *Otus*) having hornlike tufts of feathers on the head. Screech owls have a mournful, wailing, whistling call. **2** *Esp. Brit.* any owl that screeches, as distinguished from one that hoots.

A screech owl

screech•y ['skritʃi] *adj.* **screech•i•er, screech•i•est.** screeching.

screed [skrid] *n.* **1** a long speech or piece of writing. **2** a strip of plaster (or wood) of the proper thickness, applied to the wall as a guide in plastering. ⟨ME var. of OE *scrēade* shred⟩

screen [skrin] *n., v.* *—n.* **1** a covered frame that hides, protects, or separates. **2** a framed device consisting of wire or a synthetic substitute woven together with small openings in between the strands: *We have screens at our windows to keep out flies.* **3** an ornamental partition. **4** anything like a screen: *A screen of trees hides our house from the road.* **5** a flat, usually white specially prepared surface on which a slide or film is projected. **6** films collectively or the film industry: *a star of stage and screen.* **7** the surface of an electronic display device (LCD, cathode-ray tube, etc.) on which the image appears: *a television screen, a radar screen.* **8** a sieve for sifting sand, gravel, coal, seed, etc. **9** a body of soldiers detached toward the enemy to protect an army. **10** an escort of destroyers, etc. to protect battleships, aircraft carriers, etc., especially against submarine attack. **11** *Photo-engraving.* a transparent plate with fine lines that cross at right angles, used to produce the minute dots in a half-tone. **12** *Computer technology.* **a** a computer monitor or terminal. **b** the set of information displayed on a computer monitor or terminal at one time: *The screen currently displayed on this monitor is the patient's medical history.*
—v. **1** shelter, protect, or hide with, or as with, a screen: *She screened her face from the fire with a fan. The mother tried to screen her guilty son.* **2** show (a film) on a screen. **3** photograph with a movie camera. **4** adapt (a story, etc.) for reproduction as a film. **5** be suitable for reproducing on a film screen. **6** sift with a screen. **7** examine carefully to test quality, suitability, etc.: *Applicants for this job must be carefully screened.* **8** print with a

screen or by the silk-screen process. **9** of a story, etc. be reproduced or be suitable for reproducing as a film: *This story should screen well.* ⟨ME < OF *escren* < Gmc.⟩ **—'screen•a•ble,** *adj.* **—'screen•er,** *n.* **—'screen,like,** *adj.*

screen dump *Computer technology.* a computer-generated copy of the contents of a computer screen, usually printed.

screen•ing ['skriniŋ] *n., v.* *—n.* **1** a fine wire or synthetic mesh for making screens, filters, etc. **2** **screenings,** *pl.* the matter separated out by sifting through a sieve or screen. **3** the act of one who screens.
—v. ppr. of SCREEN.

screen•play ['skrin,plei] *n.* a story or play written for production as a film, including description of characters and scenes, dialogue, etc.

screen saver *Computer technology.* a pattern that appears on the screen whenever there is a pause in input, to save wear and tear on the screen.

screen test a filmed audition to discover whether the person being auditioned suits the medium or could play a specific part.

screen–test ['skrin ,tɛst] *v.* **1** give a screen test to. **2** undergo a screen test.

screw [skru] *n., v.* *—n.* **1** a fastening device like a nail but having a ridge twisting evenly around its length, and a slot or recess in the head: *Turn the screw to the right to tighten it.* **2** a simple machine consisting of a spiral ridge around a cylinder that acts to exert pressure in any of various ways. Certain kinds of jacks use a screw as the means for exerting the force to raise an object. **3** a part into which this cylinder fits and advances. **4** something that resembles a screw. **5** a spiral or screwing motion. **6** *Informal.* a very stingy person; miser. **7** SCREW PROPELLER. **8** *Slang.* a guard in a prison.
have a screw loose, *Slang.* be crazy or eccentric.
put the screws on, *Informal.* use pressure or force to get something.
—v. **1** turn as one turns a screw; twist; put (*on* or *together*) or take (*off* or *apart*) in this way: *Screw the lid on the jar.* **2** turn like a screw; be fitted for being put together or taken apart by a screw or screws. **3** twist or contort. **4** fasten or tighten with a screw or screws. **5** force, press, or stretch tight by using screws. **6** *Informal.* **a** force to do something; **b** force people to tell or to give up: *They managed to screw the truth out of him.* **7** gather for an effort (used with **up**): *She finally screwed up enough courage to dive.* **8** *Slang.* swindle; take unfair advantage of.
screw around, *Slang.* **a** spend time wastefully. **b** engage in promiscuous sexual intercourse.
screw up, *Slang.* make a mess of; botch; bungle. ⟨ME < OF *escroue* nut, screw < VL *scroba* < L *scrobis* ditch, vulva, influenced by L *scrofa* a sow⟩

screw•ball ['skru,bɒl] *n., adj.* *—n.* **1** *Slang.* an eccentric or crazy person. **2** *Baseball.* a pitch thrown with a break or spin opposite to that of a curve.
—adj. Slang. eccentric or crazy: *screwball comedy. That was a screwball thing to do.*

screw•driv•er ['skru,draivər] *n.* **1** a tool for putting in or taking out screws by turning them. **2** an alcoholic drink consisting of vodka mixed with orange juice.

screw eye a screw with a loop as the head.

screw jack jackscrew.

screw propeller a device consisting of a revolving hub with radiating, slightly twisted blades, used for propelling a steamship, aircraft, etc.

screw thread the spiral ridge of a screw.

screw•y ['skrui] *adj.* **-i•er, -i•est.** *Slang.* crazy or eccentric. **—'screw•i•ness,** *n.*

scrib•ble ['skrɪbəl] *v.* **-bled, -bling;** *n.* *—v.* **1** write or draw carelessly or hastily. **2** make meaningless marks. **3** compose hurriedly, paying no attention to style or form.
—n. **1** something scribbled. **2** handwriting which is difficult to read: *I can't read your scribble.* ⟨ME < Med.L *scribillare*, ult. < L *scribere* write⟩

scrib•bler ['skrɪblər] *n.* **1** a person who scribbles. **2** *Cdn.* a pad of paper or a book in which to make notes, do rough work, etc. **3** an author of little or no importance.

scribe [skraib] *n., v.* **scribed, scrib•ing.** *—n.* **1** a person who copies manuscript, especially in ancient or medieval times. **2** a member of the class of professional interpreters of the Jewish law. **3** a writer; author. **4** a public clerk or secretary. **5** scriber.
—v. mark or cut with something sharp. ⟨ME < L *scriba* < *scribere* write⟩ **—'scrib•al,** *adj.*

scrib•er ['skraibər] *n.* a tool for marking on wood, metal, etc. Also, **scribe.**

scrim [skrɪm] *n.* **1** lightweight, loosely woven cotton or linen fabric having a mesh weave, used for curtains. **2** *Theatre.* a hanging of similar material, used as a backdrop or as a semi-transparent curtain, depending on whether it is lit from the front or the back. ⟨origin uncertain⟩

scrim•mage ['skrɪmɪdʒ] *n., v.* **-maged, -mag•ing.** *—n.* **1** a rough fight or struggle. **2** *Football.* a play that takes place after the two teams are lined up and the ball is snapped back. **3** *Rugby, rugger.* scrummage.
—v. **1** take part in a rough fight or struggle. **2** *Football.* take part in a scrimmage. ⟨ult. var. of *skirmish*⟩

scrimp [skrɪmp] *v.* **1** be very economical; stint; skimp: *They had to scrimp for several years to save enough for a good down payment on a house.* **2** make too small, short, or scant; be very sparing of (*used with* **on**): *to scrimp on food.* **3** treat stingily or very economically. ⟨probably < ON *skrimpa* shrivel⟩

scrimp•y ['skrɪmpi] *adj.* **scrimp•i•er, scrimp•i•est.** too small; too little; scanty; meagre. **—'scrimp•i•ly,** *adv.* **—'scrimp•i•ness,** *n.*

scrim•shaw ['skrɪm,ʃɒ] *n., v.* *—n.* **1** the art or practice of drawing on or carving pieces of whalebone or ivory, as traditionally done by sailors in their leisure time. **2** an article produced in this way. **3** such articles collectively.
—v. produce scrimshaw (from). ⟨origin uncertain⟩

scrip[1] [skrɪp] *n.* **1** a certificate, coupon, voucher, etc. establishing the bearer's right to something. **2** *Cdn.* a certificate issued to the Métis after the Riel Rebellions, as compensation for lands. A **land-scrip** entitled the holder to 240 acres of land; a **money-scrip** entitled the holder to a choice between $240 cash and 240 acres of land. **3** a short piece of writing, such as a certificate or schedule. ⟨var. of *script*⟩

scrip[2] [skrɪp] *n. Archaic.* a small bag or wallet. ⟨ME < OF *escrepe* < Gmc.⟩

scrip•sit ['skrɪpsɪt] *v. Latin.* (he or she) wrote (it); notation placed after the writer's name on a manuscript, etc.

script [skrɪpt] *n., v.* *—n.* **1** the style of forming written letters, figures, signs, etc.; handwriting: *German script.* **2** *Printing.* a style of type that looks like handwriting. **3** the written text of a play, an actor's part, a radio or television broadcast, a film, etc. **4** *Cdn.* SCRIP[1] (def. 2).
—v. Informal. write a script for (a radio or television show, play, film, etc.). ⟨< L *scriptum*, originally neut. pp. of *scribere* write⟩

scrip•to•ri•um [skrɪp'tɔriəm] *n., pl.* **-ri•ums** or **-ri•a** [-riə]. a writing room, especially a room in a medieval monastery set apart for writing or copying manuscripts. ⟨< Med.L *scriptorium*, ult. < L *scribere* write⟩

scrip•tur•al or **Scrip•tur•al** ['skrɪptʃərəl] *adj.* of, according to, contained in, or based on the Scriptures. **—'scrip•tur•al•ly,** *adv.*

Scrip•ture ['skrɪptʃər] *n.* **1** sometimes, **the Scriptures** or **the Holy Scriptures,** *pl.* the Bible. **2** **scripture,** any sacred, authoritative, or inviolable writing. ⟨ME < L *scriptura* a writing < *scribere* write⟩

script•writ•er ['skrɪpt,rəitər] *n.* a person who writes scripts for films or radio or television programs.

scrive•ner ['skrɪvnər] *n. Archaic.* **1** a public writer of letters or documents for others; scribe or clerk. **2** a notary. ⟨ME < obs. *scrivein* < OF *escrivein*, ult. < L *scribere* write⟩

scrod [skrɒd] *n.* a young cod or haddock, especially one split for cooking. ⟨< MDu. *schrode* piece cut off⟩

scrof•u•la ['skrɒfjələ] *n. Pathology.* tuberculosis of the lymph nodes, especially in the neck, and sometimes of the bones and joint surfaces, characterized by swelling and formation of pus. ⟨< Med.L *scrofula*, sing. < L *scrofulae*, pl. < *scrofa* a sow; ? from fanciful comparison of glandular swellings to little pigs⟩

scrof•u•lous ['skrɒfjələs] *adj.* **1** of, having to do with, or affected with scrofula. **2** resembling scrofula. **3** of literature, etc., morally degenerate. **—'scrof•u•lous•ly,** *adv.* **—'scrof•u•lous•ness,** *n.*

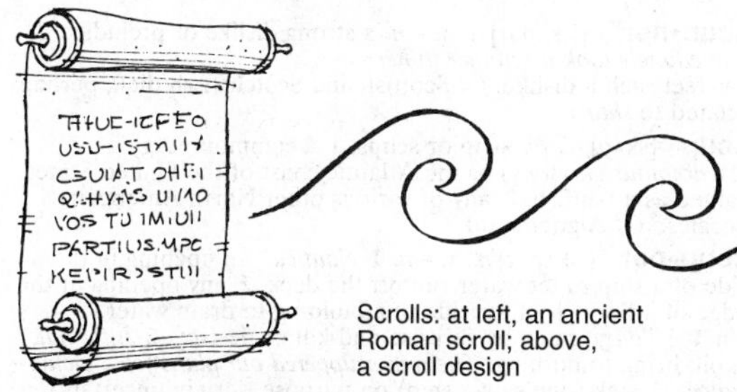
Scrolls: at left, an ancient Roman scroll; above, a scroll design

scroll [skroul] *n., v.* *—n.* **1** a roll of parchment or paper, especially one with writing on it. **2** a list of names, events, etc.; roll; schedule: *to be entered in the scrolls of history.* **3** an ornament resembling a partly unrolled sheet of paper in cross-section, or having a spiral or coiled form. **4** the curved head of a violin, etc.
—v. Computer technology. **a** move the lines of writing on the screen of a computer's video display up or down, to allow room for new lines to be added. **b** view (records, a document, etc.) successively in this way (*used with through*). ⟨alteration of *scrow* (influenced by roll), ult. < OF *escroe* scrap < Gmc.⟩
—'scroll-ˌlike, *adj.*

scroll bar *Computer technology.* a narrow horizontal or vertical rectangle on a screen, whose contents are used to indicate the direction to scroll in or a specific location in the data to move to directly, and often also to indicate the current location.

scroll saw a very narrow saw for cutting thin wood in curved or ornamental patterns.

scroll•work ['skroulˌwɜrk] *n.* decorative work characterized by scrolls, especially such work done in wood with a scroll saw.

Scrooge [skrudʒ] *n.* any mean or stingy person. ⟨in Dickens' story *A Christmas Carol*, an embittered old miser⟩

scro•tum ['skroutəm] *n., pl.* **-ta** [-tə] or **-tums.** *Anatomy.* in most male mammals, the pouch of skin that contains the testicles. ⟨< L⟩ **—'scro•tal,** *adj.*

scrounge [skraʊndʒ] *v.* **scrounged, scroung•ing.** *Informal.* **1** find or collect by hunting around: *They're out scrounging kindling for the fire.* **2** get by begging; mooch; cadge: *She was always scrounging cigarettes.* **3** take without permission; pilfer: *to scrounge bricks from a construction site.* **4** look around for something; forage: *She scrounged around in the drawer, looking for a pencil.* ⟨< dial. *scrunge* steal⟩ **—'scroung•er,** *n.*

scrub¹ [skrʌb] *v.* **scrubbed, scrub•bing;** *n.* *—v.* **1** wash or clean by rubbing hard with a brush or cloth: *to scrub the kitchen floor.* **2** remove or try to remove (dirt, a spot, etc.) by rubbing with a brush or cloth. **3** rub hard in cleaning: *She had to scrub to get the ink off.* **4** wash the hands and arms before performing a surgical operation (*usually used with* **up**). **5** *Informal.* **a** get rid of; wipe out. **b** call off, especially at the last minute: *The launching was scrubbed.* **6** remove impurities from (a gas or vapour): *to scrub the air emissions of a lead smelter.*
—n. the act or an instance of scrubbing. ⟨? < MDu. *schrubben*⟩
—'scrub•ba•ble, *adj.*

scrub² [skrʌb] *n., adj.* *—n.* **1 a** an area of low, stunted trees or shrubs. **b** any single low, stunted tree or shrub. **2** any person, animal, or thing that is undersized, inferior, or of little significance: *He is a little scrub of a man.* **3** *Sports.* a player not on the regular team.
—adj. **1** small; inferior. A scrub ball team is made up of inferior, substitute, or untrained players. **2** of or for players not on the regular team. ⟨ME; var. of *schrobbe*, OE *scrybb* brushwood. See SHRUB¹.⟩

scrub•ber ['skrʌbər] *n.* **1** an apparatus for purifying a gas or vapour. **2** any person who or thing that scrubs.

scrub•by ['skrʌbi] *adj.* **-bi•er, -bi•est. 1** low; stunted; small; undersized or insignificant: *scrubby trees.* **2** covered with scrub: *scrubby land.* **3** shabby; mean. **—'scrub•bi•ness,** *n.*

scrub pine *Cdn.* a popular name for any of various small or scrubby pines of the genus *Pinus*, such as the **jack pine** or **whitebark pine**.

scrub•wo•man ['skrʌbˌwʊmən] *n., pl.* **-wo•men** [-wɪmɪn]. a woman hired to clean a house or place of business; cleaning woman; charwoman.

scruff [skrʌf] *n.* the back of the neck or the skin at the back of the neck: *She picked up the kitten by the scruff of the neck.* ⟨possibly < ON *skrufr* tuft of hair, by metathesis from *skurfr* < *skufr*⟩

scruf•fy ['skrʌfi] *adj.* **-fi•er, -fi•est.** unkempt, slovenly, or shabby: *That scruffy little kid is John's sister.* **—'scruf•fi•ly,** *adv.* **—'scruf•fi•ness,** *n.*

scrum•mage ['skrʌmɪdʒ] *n. Rugby, rugger.* a formation in which the forwards of each side bend down and lock together in two or three ranks, each side pushing against the other when the ball is placed in the middle. Also, **scrum.** ⟨var. of *scrimmage*⟩

scrump•tious ['skrʌmpʃəs] *adj. Informal.* splendid, especially to the taste; delicious; first-rate: *a scrumptious meal.* ⟨? alteration of *sumptuous*⟩ **—'scrump•tious•ly,** *adv.* **—'scrump•tious•ness,** *n.*

scrunch [skrʌntʃ] *v., n.* *—v.* **1** crunch, crush, or crumple: *He scrunched the paper into a tiny ball.* **2** hunch or squeeze: *We scrunched down behind the fence and waited.* **3** move with or make a scrunching sound: *They scrunched over the snow.*
—n. the act or sound of scrunching. ⟨imitative⟩

scru•ple ['skrupəl] *n., v.* **-pled, -pling.** *—n.* **1** a feeling of uneasiness which keeps a person from doing something that might be morally or ethically wrong: *He had scruples about accepting the free tickets.* **2** a feeling of doubt about what one ought to do: *No scruple ever holds her back from prompt action.* **3** moral integrity: *a man of scruple.* **4** a unit for measuring mass, traditionally used by druggists, equal to 20 grains (about 1.3 g): *Three scruples make one dram.* **5** a very small amount.
—v. **1** hesitate or be unwilling (to do something one feels may be wrong): *A dishonest man does not scruple to deceive others.* **2** have scruples. ⟨< MF < L *scrupulus* a feeling of uneasiness, originally dim. of *scrupus* sharp stone; figuratively, uneasiness, anxiety⟩ **—'scru•ple•less,** *adj.*

scru•pu•lous ['skrupjələs] *adj.* **1** having or showing a strict regard for what is right; having moral integrity: *He was scrupulous in his dealings with customers.* **2** very careful or exact; painstaking: *scrupulous attention to detail. She worked out the plan with scrupulous care.* **—'scru•pu•lous•ly,** *adv.* **—'scru•pu•lous•ness** or **ˌscru•pu'los•i•ty,** *n.*

☛ *Syn.* **2. Scrupulous,** PUNCTILIOUS = very careful and exact. **Scrupulous** emphasizes attending thoroughly to details and being very careful to follow strictly and exactly what one knows is right or true: *She takes scrupulous care of the children's health.* **Punctilious,** a formal word, emphasizes paying special and scrupulously exact, often excessive, attention to fine points of laws, rules, and requirements for conduct, behaviour, or performance of duties: *He is punctilious about returning borrowed books.*

scru•ti•neer [ˌskrutə'nir] *n., v.* *—n. Chiefly Cdn. and Brit.* **1** a person who represents the interests of a particular candidate or party at a polling station on election day in order to ensure that the voting procedure and counting of ballots are properly carried out. **2** in any organization or institution, an official examiner of votes at any election or other procedure requiring a vote.
—v. act as a scrutineer. ⟨< *scrutin(y)* + *-eer*⟩

scru•ti•nize ['skrutəˌnaɪz] *v.* **-nized, -niz•ing.** examine closely; inspect carefully: *The jeweller scrutinized the diamond for flaws.* **—'scru•tiˌniz•er,** *n.* **—'scru•tiˌniz•ing•ly,** *adv.*

scru•ti•ny ['skrutəni] *n., pl.* **-nies. 1** a close examination; careful inspection: *Her work looks all right at first glance, but it will never bear scrutiny.* **2** a searching look at something; searching gaze. **3** an official examination of the votes cast at an election. ⟨ME < LL *scrutinium* < L *scrutari* ransack⟩

scu•ba ['skubə] *n.* a portable apparatus used for breathing while swimming underwater or diving. ⟨< *s*elf-*c*ontained *u*nderwater *b*reathing *a*pparatus⟩

scu•ba–dive ['skubə ˌdaɪv] *v.* **-dived** or **-dove, -div•ing.** swim and explore underwater using scuba equipment.

scuba diver a person who uses scuba gear to breathe while swimming under water or diving.

scud [skʌd] *v.* **scud•ded, scud•ding;** *n.* *—v.* run or move swiftly: *Clouds scudded across the sky, driven by the high wind.*
—n. **1** the action of scudding. **2** clouds or spray driven by the wind. ⟨possibly < OE *scudan* hurry⟩

scuff [skʌf] *v., n.* *—v.* **1** walk without lifting the feet; SHUFFLE (def. 1). **2** wear or injure the surface of by hard use: *to scuff one's shoes. Stop scuffing the carpet!* **3** become worn or rubbed: *That carpet is scuffing in front of your chair.*
—n. **1** the act of scuffing. **2** the sound made by scuffing. **3** a slipper having a toe piece but no covering for the heel. **4** a worn or rubbed place: *He touched up the scuffs with polish.* ⟨var. of *scuffle*⟩

scuf•fle ['skʌfəl] *v.* **-fled, -fling;** *n.* *—v.* **1** struggle or fight in a rough, confused manner, but not violently: *The children scuffled for first place in the lineup.* **2** SHUFFLE (def. 1).
—n. **1** a confused, rough struggle or fight. **2** a shuffling or the sound of shuffling. ⟨< Scand.; cf. Swedish *skuffa* push⟩
—'scuf•fler, *n.*

scuffle hoe a hoe with a flat blade, used for weeding.

scull [skʌl] *n., v.* *—n.* **1** an oar worked from side to side over the stern of a boat to propel it forward. **2** one of a pair of oars used, one on each side, by a single rower. **3** the act of propelling by sculls. **4** a light racing boat for one or more rowers using sculls; sculler.
—v. propel (a boat) by a scull or by sculls. ⟨ME; origin unknown⟩
☛ *Hom.* SKULL.

scull•er ['skʌlər] *n.* **1** a person who sculls. **2** a boat propelled by sculling.

scul•ler•y ['skʌləri] *n., pl.* **-ler•ies.** *Esp. Brit.* a small room where the dirty, rough work of a kitchen is done. ⟨ME < OF *escuelerie,* ult. < L *scutella,* dim. of *scutra* platter⟩

scul•lion ['skʌljən] *n. Archaic.* **1** a servant who does the dirty, rough work in a kitchen. **2** a low, contemptible person. ⟨ME < OF *escouillon* swab, cloth < *escouve* broom < L *scopa*⟩

sculp [skʌlp] *v., n. Cdn., esp. Nfld.* *—v.* remove the skin and adhering blubber from (a seal).
—n. the skin of a seal with its adhering blubber after it has been removed from the dead animal. ⟨var. of *scalp*⟩

scul•pin ['skʌlpɪn] *n.* any of a family (Cottidae) of scaleless or partially scaled, chiefly marine fishes having a large, spiny head. ⟨? alteration of *scorpene* < L *scorpaena* < Gk. *skorpaina,* kind of fish < *skorpios* scorpion⟩

sculpt [skʌlpt] *v.* carve; sculpture: *to sculpt a statue.* ⟨back-formed < *sculptor*⟩

sculp•tor ['skʌlptər] *n.* **1** a person who makes figures by carving, modelling, casting, etc.; an artist in sculpture. Sculptors work in marble, wood, bronze, etc. **2 Sculptor,** *Astronomy.* a southern constellation containing the south galactic pole, located between Phoenix and Cetus. ⟨< L *sculptor,* late var. of *scalptor* < *scalpere* carve⟩

sculp•tur•al ['skʌlptʃərəl] *adj.* of, having to do with, or like sculpture: *The fine use of light and shadow gave the painting a sculptural quality.* **—'sculp•tur•al•ly,** *adv.*

sculp•ture ['skʌlptʃər] *n., v.* **-tured, -tur•ing.** *—n.* **1** the art or process of carving, modelling, or welding hard or plastic substances into figures. Sculpture includes carving statues from stone or wood, casting in bronze, working in metal, and modelling in clay, soap, plastics, or wax. **2** sculptured work; a piece of such work.
—v. **1** carve, model, or weld into a three-dimensional work of art. **2** change or shape by erosion: *The snowbanks had been sculptured into strange shapes by the wind.* **3** decorate with sculpture. ⟨ME < L *sculptura,* late var. of *scalptura* < *scalpere* carve⟩

sculp•tured ['skʌlptʃərd] *adj., v.* *—adj.* **1** carved, moulded, cast, etc., in sculpture. **2** covered or ornamented with sculpture.
—v. pt. and pp. of SCULPTURE.

sculp•tur•esque [,skʌlptʃə'rɛsk] *adj.* like a sculpture in shapeliness, graceful contours, etc.

scum [skʌm] *n., v.* **scummed, scum•ming.** *—n.* **1** a surface film or layer formed when certain liquids are boiled or metals melted: *The scum had to be skimmed from the top of the boiling maple syrup.* **2** the layer of algae or other matter that forms on the top of still water. **3** low, worthless people; rabble.
—v. **1** form scum or become covered with scum. **2** remove scum from; skim. ⟨ME < MDu. *schuum*⟩

scum•ble ['skʌmbəl] *v.* **-bled, -bling;** *n.* *—v.* **1 a** soften (the outlines or colour of a painting) by retouching with a thin coat of opaque colour applied with a dry brush. **b** soften (the outlines of a drawing) by rubbing. **2** make by this process.
—n. **1** the effect so produced. **2** the act of scumbling.

scum•my ['skʌmi] *adj.* **-mi•er, -mi•est. 1** consisting of or covered with scum. **2** low; worthless.

scun•ner[1] ['skʌnər] *n. Cdn. Nfld.* the assistant to the master of the watch on a boat. ⟨< *scun,* var. of *scan*⟩

scun•ner[2] ['skʌnər] *n., v.* *—n.* a strong dislike or prejudice: *I immediately took a scunner to her.*
—v. feel such a dislike. ⟨< Scottish and Scotch-Irish dial., perhaps related to *shun*⟩

scup [skʌp] *n., pl.* **scup** or **scups. 1** a common porgy (*Stenotomus chrysops*) of the Atlantic coast of the United States, valued as a panfish. **2** any of various other North American porgies. ⟨< Algonquian⟩

scup•per ['skʌpər] *n., v.* *—n.* **1** *Nautical.* an opening in the side of a ship to let water run off the deck. **2** any opening at the edge of a floor, roof, or side of a building to drain water.
—v. **1** *Military.* catch by surprise and kill or destroy. **2** *Informal.* spoil; bring to nothing: *The rain scuppered our plans for a picnic supper.* **3** sink (one's own ship) on purpose. ⟨origin uncertain⟩

scurf [skɜrf] *n.* **1** small scales of dead skin; dandruff. **2** any scaly matter on a surface. ⟨ME < Scand.; cf. Icelandic *skurfa*⟩

scurf•y ['skɜrfi] *adj.* **scurf•i•er, scurf•i•est.** of, like, or covered with scurf. **—'scurf•i•ness,** *n.*

scur•ril•i•ty [skə'rɪləti] *n., pl.* **-ties. 1** the quality or act of using coarse or indecent language. **2** indecent or abusive language. **3** an indecent or coarse remark.

scur•ri•lous ['skɜrələs] *adj.* **1** using coarse or indecent language; foulmouthed: *a scurrilous rabblerouser.* **2** containing obscenities and abuse: *a scurrilous political pamphlet, a scurrilous attack.* ⟨< L *scurrilis* < *scurra* buffoon⟩ **—'scur•ri•lous•ly,** *adv.* **—'scur•ri•lous•ness,** *n.*

scur•ry ['skɜri] *v.* **-ried, -ry•ing;** *n., pl.* **-ries.** *—v.* run quickly; hurry: *We could hear the mice scurrying about in the walls.*
—n. **1** a hasty running; hurrying. **2** a short-distance race. ⟨? < *hurry-scurry,* varied reduplication of *hurry*⟩

S–curve ['ɛs ,kɜrv] *n.* a curve in the shape of the letter S.

scur•vy ['skɜrvi] *n., adj.* **-vi•er, -vi•est.** *—n. Pathology.* a disease caused by lack of vitamin C, characterized by swollen and bleeding gums, livid spots on the skin, and prostration. Scurvy used to be common among sailors when they had little to eat except bread and salt meat.
—adj. low; mean; contemptible: *a scurvy fellow, a scurvy trick.* ⟨< *scurf*⟩ **—'scur•vi•ly,** *adv.* **—'scur•vi•ness,** *n.*

scurvy grass *Cdn.* a herb (*Cochlearia officinalis*) of the mustard family, common in northern regions and formerly used in treating scurvy.

scut[1] [skʌt] *n.* a short tail, especially that of a rabbit or deer. ⟨< LME *scut* hare, probably < ON *skutr* stern, back end⟩

scut[2] [skʌt] *n.* a worthless or despicable person. ⟨of uncertain origin; possibly < Scots *scoot,* ME *scoute*⟩

scu•ta ['skjutə] *n.* pl. of SCUTUM.

scu•tage ['skjutɪdʒ] *n.* in the feudal system, a payment given to a lord by a fee-holder in lieu of military service.

scu•tate ['skjuteit] *adj.* **1** *Zoology.* having shieldlike plates or large scales of bone, shell, etc. **2** *Botany.* round. Nasturtiums have scutate leaves. ⟨< L *scutatus* having a shield < *scutum* shield⟩

scutch [skʌtʃ] *v., n.* *—v.* separate (flax or cotton fibre) from woody parts by beating; make (fibre) ready for use by beating.
—n. scutcher. ⟨probably < MF *escoucher* (F *écoucher*) to beat flax < VL *excuticare* to remove skin, peel < L *ex* out + *cutis* skin⟩

scutch•eon ['skʌtʃən] *n.* escutcheon.

scutch•er ['skʌtʃər] *n.* an implement for scutching.

scute [skjut] *n.* SCUTUM (def. 1).

scu•tel•la [skju'tɛlə] *n.* pl. of SCUTELLUM.

scu•tel•late [skju'tɛlɪt] *or* [skju'tɛleit], ['skjutəlɪt] *or* ['skjutə,leit] *adj. Biology.* **1** having scutella. **2** formed into a scutellum.

scu•tel•la•tion [,skjutə'leiʃən] *n.* **1** a whole covering of small plates or scales. **2** an arrangement of plates or scales.

scu•tel•lum [skju'tɛləm] *n., pl.* **-tel•la** [skju'tɛlə]. *Zoology. Botany.* a small plate, scale, or other shieldlike part. ⟨< NL *scutellum,* dim. of L *scutum* shield⟩

scut•tle[1] ['skʌtəl] *n.* a kind of bucket for holding or carrying coal. ⟨< L *scutella* platter⟩

scut•tle[2] ['skʌtəl] *v.* **-tled, -tling;** *n.* scamper; scurry. ⟨var. of *scuddle,* frequentative of *scud*⟩ **—'scut•tler,** *n.*

scut•tle[3] ['skʌtəl] *n., v.* **-tled, -tling.** *—n.* **1** a small opening with a lid or cover, especially in the deck or side of a ship. **2** the lid or cover for any such opening.
—v. **1** cut a hole or holes through the bottom or sides of (a ship) to sink it. **2** cut a hole or holes in the deck of (a ship) to salvage the cargo. **3** ruin or destroy (an undertaking, hope, etc.): *The*

minister's premature statement to the press scuttled the conference. **4** abandon or withdraw from; SCRAP[1] (*v.* def. 2). ⟨? < F < Sp. *escotilla* hatchway⟩

scut•tle•butt ['skʌtəl,bʌt] *n.* **1** *Nautical.* a drinking fountain or a cask containing drinking water on a ship. **2** *Slang.* rumour, gossip, and stories not based on fact.

scu•tum ['skjutəm] *n., pl.* **-ta** [-tə]. **1** a shieldlike part of bone, shell, etc., as on the body of certain reptiles or insects. **2** a long, oblong wooden shield used by Roman infantry. **3 Scutum,** Astronomy. the Shield, a southern constellation between Sagittarius and Aquila. ⟨< L *scutum* shield⟩

scuz•zy ['skʌzi] *adj.* **-zi•er, -zi•est.** *Slang.* grungy or sleazy. ⟨origin uncertain⟩

Scyl•la ['sɪlə] *n.* **1** a dangerous rock opposite the whirlpool Charybdis, at the extreme southwestern tip of Italy. **2** *Classical mythology.* a monster with six heads and twelve arms that lived on this rock and snatched sailors from ships.
between Scylla and Charybdis, between two equally dangerous alternatives, of which the avoiding of one means being faced with the other.
☛ *Hom.* SCILLA.

scy•pho•zo•an [,səifə'zouən] *n.* any jellyfish of the class Scyphozoa, having no velum. ⟨< NL < Gk. *skyphos* cup + *zoon* animal⟩

scy•phus ['səifəs] *n., pl.* **scy•phi** ['səifaɪ]. **1** a type of drinking cup from ancient Greece, having a flat base and two handles. **2** a part shaped like a cup, as in a flower. ⟨< L < Gk. *skyphos* cup⟩

A scythe

scythe [saɪð] *n., v.* **scythed, scyth•ing.** *—n.* an implement used for cutting grass, grain, etc., consisting of a long, slightly curved blade set at an angle on the end of a long handle.
—v. cut with a scythe. ⟨OE *sīthe*; spelling infl. by L *scindere* cut⟩

Scyth•i•an ['sɪθiən] *n., adj. —n.* **1** a native or inhabitant of Scythia, an ancient region in SE Europe. **2** the extinct Iranian language of the Scythians.
—adj. of or having to do with Scythia, its people, or their language.

s.d. **1** without naming a date (for L *sine die*). **2** several dates.

SD **1** *Statistics.* STANDARD DEVIATION. **2** the intelligence and counter-espionage section of the Nazi SS (for G *Sicherheitsdienst*).

S.D. SCHOOL DISTRICT.

Se selenium.

SE or **S.E.** southeast; southeasterly; southeastern.

sea [si] *n.* **1** the great body of salt water that covers almost three fourths of the earth's surface; the ocean. **2** any large body of salt water, smaller than an ocean, partly or wholly enclosed by land: *the North Sea, the Mediterranean Sea.* Also called **inland sea. 3** a large lake of fresh water. **4** a large, heavy wave: *A high sea swept away the ship's masts.* **5** the swell of the ocean: *a rough sea, a calm sea.* **6** an overwhelming amount or vast expanse: *a sea of trouble, a sea of faces.* **7** (*adjl.*) of, pertaining to, or for use at sea: *a sea chest.* **8** *Astronomy.* MARE[2].
at sea, a out on the sea. **b** *Informal.* puzzled; confused: *His complicated explanation left me even more at sea about the problem.*
follow the sea, be a sailor.
go to sea, a become a sailor. **b** begin a voyage.
put to sea, begin a voyage. ⟨OE *sǣ*⟩
☛ *Hom.* C, SEE, SI.

sea anchor *Nautical.* a device, such as a large canvas funnel or bag, dragged in the water to slow a vessel, keep it from drifting, or keep it heading into the wind.

sea anemone any of numerous flowerlike, often bright-coloured polyps (order Actiniaria) found especially in warm seas, having a fleshy, cylinder-shaped body with a mouth opening at the upper end and surrounded by many tentacles.

sea bag a large canvas bag, tubular in shape and closed with a drawstring, in which sailors carry their gear.

sea bass any of various marine fishes belonging to the same family (Serranidae) as the groupers and jewfish, found especially along the Atlantic coast of North America and including some important food and game fishes, such as the **black sea bass** (*Centropristes striatus*).

sea•bed ['si,bɛd] *n.* the bed or bottom of the sea.

sea bird any bird that spends most of its time on or near the open sea. Gulls, cormorants, murres, and puffins are sea birds.

sea biscuit hardtack.

sea•board ['si,bɔrd] *n., adj. —n.* the land near the sea; seacoast; seashore: *the Atlantic seaboard.*
—adj. bordering on the sea.

sea bread hardtack; SHIP BISCUIT.

sea bream any of various marine fishes (family Sparidae) found especially in warm eastern Atlantic and Mediterranean waters, such as the **red sea bream** (*Pagellus centrodontus*), highly valued as a food fish. Fishes of this family found along the western Atlantic coasts are usually known as **porgies.**

sea breeze a breeze blowing from the sea toward the land.

sea butterfly any of a subclass (Opisthobranchia) of mostly very small marine gastropods, having a pair of winglike lobes that are used for swimming.

sea cadet a person under military age who is undertaking basic naval training in an organization subsidized by the sea elements of the armed forces.

sea captain **1** the master of a seagoing vessel. **2** one who commands a merchant ship.

sea change **1** a major transformation, often for the better. **2** a change or alteration brought about by the sea.

sea•coast ['si,koust] *n.* land along the sea.

sea•cock ['si,kɒk] *n. Nautical.* any cock or valve on a ship that opens through the hull to the sea.

sea cow **1** a manatee, dugong, or any similar mammal living in the sea. **2** a walrus.

sea cucumber any of a class (Holothuroidea) of marine invertebrates found in all oceans, having a long, flexible, cylindrical body.

sea dog **1** a sailor having long experience at sea. **2** any of various seals.

sea eagle any of various large, fish-eating eagles, such as the **bald eagle.**

sea element *Cdn.* the branch of the Canadian Forces having to do with ships of war and their officers and personnel, formerly known as the Royal Canadian Navy.

sea elephant ELEPHANT SEAL.

sea•far•er ['si,fɛrər] *n.* a traveller on the sea, especially a sailor.

sea•far•ing ['si,fɛrɪŋ] *adj., n. —adj.* going, travelling, or working on the sea: *He had been a seafaring man all his life.*
—n. **1** the calling or profession of a sailor. **2** the act or fact of travelling by sea.

sea–flea ['si ,fli] *n.* a tiny, one-person speedboat driven by a powerful motor and used especially for racing, so called because it skims the surface of the water.

sea foam **1** foam on the sea. **2** meerschaum.

sea•food ['si,fud] *n.* **1** edible saltwater fish and shellfish. **2** loosely, food made from or consisting of any fish, including those from freshwater sources.

sea•fowl ['si,faʊl] *n., pl.* **-fowls** or (*esp. collectively*) **-fowl.** any bird that lives on or near the sea.

sea•front ['si,frʌnt] *n.* that part of a town or built up area that is situated on the edge of and faces the sea; waterfront.

sea•girt ['si,gɜrt] *adj. Poetic.* surrounded by the sea.

sea•go•ing ['si,gouɪŋ] *adj.* **1** going by sea; seafaring. **2** fit for going to sea.

sea green light bluish green. **—'sea-,green,** *adj.*

sea gull any of various large gulls, especially the **herring gull.**

sea horse 1 any of a number of small marine fishes (family Syngnathidae) found in warm seas, having rings of scales around the body, a forward-curled, prehensile tail, and a horselike head set at an angle to the body. Sea horses swim in an upright position. 2 *Archaic.* a walrus. 3 a mythical sea creature having the foreparts of a horse and the hind parts of a fish. Sea horses were the steeds of the sea gods.

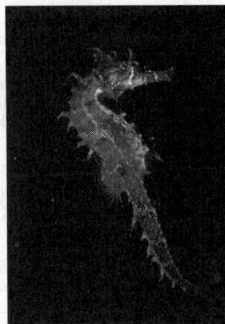

A sea horse

sea ice *Cdn.* masses of ice in the sea; ice formed from frozen salt water.

sea–island cotton 1 a fine grade of long-staple cotton (*Gossypium barbadense*), originally grown on the Sea Islands off the SE coast of the U.S., and now mainly in the West Indies. 2 fabric made from this cotton.

sea king a Scandinavian pirate chief of the Middle Ages. ⟨translation of Old Icelandic *sǣkonungr*⟩

seal[1] [sil] *n., v.* —*n.* 1 a design stamped on a piece of wax, etc. to show ownership or authenticity, or a paper circle, mark, etc. representing it. The official seal is attached to important government papers. 2 a stamp for marking things with such a design: *a seal with one's initials on it.* 3 a piece of wax, paper, metal, etc. on which the design is stamped. 4 **a** something that fastens or closes something tightly. **b** a state, fact, or instance of closing or being closed tightly: *Use weatherstripping to ensure a good seal.* 5 something that secures; a pledge: *under seal of secrecy.* 6 something that settles or determines: *the seal of authority.* 7 a mark; sign. 8 a special kind of sticker, often shaped like a postage stamp and issued by various charitable organizations: *Christmas seals, Easter seals.* 9 a small quantity of water left in a trap to prevent the escape of foul air from a sewer or drain. **10 the seals,** the symbols of public office.
set (one's) **seal to, a** put one's seal on. **b** approve.
—*v.* 1 mark (a document) with a seal; make binding or certify by affixing a seal: *The treaty was signed and sealed by both governments.* 2 stamp as an evidence of standard measure or quality or legal size: *to seal weights and measures.* 3 close tightly; shut; fasten: *Seal the letter before mailing it. He sealed the jars of fruit. Her promise sealed her lips.* 4 close up the cracks of: *They sealed the log cabin with clay.* 5 fix firmly. 6 settle; determine; decide beyond recall: *The judge's word sealed the prisoner's fate.* 7 give a sign that (something) is true: *to seal a promise with a kiss. They sealed their bargain by shaking hands.* 8 apply sealer to (a porous surface) before painting it. ⟨ME < AF *seal,* ult. < L *sigillum,* dim. of *signum* sign⟩ **—'seal•a•ble,** *adj.*
☛ *Hom.* CEIL.

seal[2] [sil] *n., pl.* **seals** or **seal** (for 1); *v.* —*n.* 1 any of numerous carnivorous aquatic mammals comprising two families (Phocidae and Otariidae) of pinnipeds found especially in cold seas, having a streamlined, fur-covered body, limbs modified into flippers, and a thick layer of fat, or blubber, under the skin, that provides insulation, acts as a food reserve, and makes the animals more buoyant. See also HAIR SEAL, EARED SEAL. 2 the pelt of a seal, especially a fur seal; sealskin. 3 leather made from the skin of a seal. 4 another fur or synthetic substitute that resembles sealskin.
—*v.* hunt seals. ⟨OE *seolh*⟩ **—'seal-,like,** *adj.*
☛ *Hom.* CEIL.

A seal

seal•ant ['silənt] *n.* a substance used for sealing, especially any of various substances used for waterproofing wood, joints in a pipe, etc.

sea lavender any of several perennial plants (genus *Limonium*) found in temperate coastal regions, having dense spikes of small white, pink, or mauve flowers.

sea lawyer *Slang.* 1 *Nautical.* a sailor given to arguing and questioning commands, regulations, etc. 2 anyone given to arguing, etc.

sea legs *Informal.* the ability to balance or walk steadily on a rolling or pitching ship; a lack of seasickness.
get (one's) **sea legs,** *Informal.* become accustomed to the motion of a ship, especially after an initial period of seasickness.

seal•er[1] ['silər] *n.* 1 something that seals, especially a substance applied to a porous surface such as wood to prevent paint or varnish from soaking in. 2 a glass jar that can be sealed, usually one holding about a litre or half a litre, used for home preserving of food. 3 an official appointed to examine and test weights and measures. ⟨< *seal*[1]⟩

seal•er[2] ['silər] *n.* 1 a person who hunts seals. 2 a ship used for hunting seals. ⟨< *seal*[2]⟩

seal•er•y ['siləri] *n., pl.* **-er•ies.** 1 the act or trade of hunting for seals. 2 a place where seals are hunted. Also, **seal fishery.**

sea lettuce any seaweed of the genus *Ulva,* having edible, leaflike blades and frequently used raw as garden fertilizer.

sea level the level of the surface of the sea, especially when halfway between mean high and low water. Mountains, plains, ocean beds, etc. are measured in metres above or below sea level. See PLATEAU for picture.

sea lily any of numerous crinoids that, in the adult stage, are attached to the sea bottom by a long stalk. Some sea lilies may grow to a length of 60 cm.

sealing wax a substance used for sealing letters, etc., consisting of a mixture of resin, shellac, turpentine, and pigment that is hard at normal temperatures but becomes soft when heated.

sea lion any of several large eared seals of the Pacific Ocean, having small external ears and a coat of short, coarse hair that lacks a distinct undercoat. The **northern sea lion** (*Eumetopias jubata*) is found in the coastal waters off British Columbia.

seal ring a finger ring engraved with a design so that it can be used as a seal. Also, **signet ring.**

seal•skin ['sil,skɪn] *n.* 1 the pelt or fur of a fur seal, prepared for use. 2 a garment made of this fur.

Sea•ly•ham ['siliəm] *or* ['sili,hæm] *n.* a breed of small terrier originally developed in Wales, having short legs, a rough, shaggy coat, and a square jaw. Also, **Sealyham terrier.** ⟨< *Sealyham,* a Welsh estate where the breed was originated⟩

Sealyhams

seam [sim] *n., v.* —*n.* 1 the join formed when two pieces of cloth, canvas, leather, etc. are sewn together. 2 the row of stiches at this join. 3 any join where edges come together: *The seams of the boat must be filled in if they leak. The seams of the carpet hardly show.* 4 any mark or line like a seam. 5 *Geology.* a layer; stratum: *a seam of coal.*

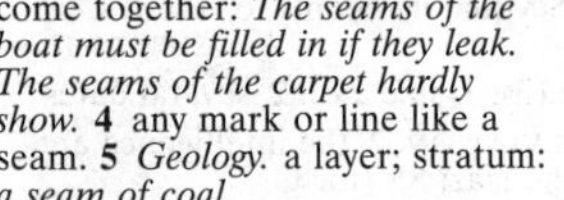

—*v.* 1 join by sewing or as if by sewing. 2 mark with lines or wrinkles: *Years of exposure to the harsh climate had seamed her face.* 3 develop cracks or fissures. ⟨OE *sēam*⟩ **—'seam•less,** *adj.*
☛ *Hom.* SEEM.

sea•man ['simən] *n., pl.* **-men.** 1 a sailor, especially one who sails the ocean. 2 a sailor who is not an officer.
☛ *Hom.* SEMEN.

sea•man•like ['simən,ləik] *adj.* like or fit for a good seaman; having or showing seamanship.

sea•man•ship ['simən,ʃɪp] *n.* skill in handling and navigating a ship.

sea•mark ['si,mɑrk] *n.* 1 a lighthouse, beacon, or other landmark visible from the sea, used as a guide for a ship's course. 2 a line on the shore that shows the limit of the tide.

seam•er ['simər] *n.* 1 a person who or thing that seams. 2 a machine that joins two pieces of metal.

sea mew a sea gull, especially *Larus canus;* MEW[2].

sea mile a nautical mile (about 1.85 km).

sea monster 1 a huge fish, cetacean, or the like. 2 a fabulous marine animal of terrifying proportions and shape.

sea•mount ['si,maʊnt] *n.* a submarine mountain that rises from the ocean floor but does not reach the surface of the water.

seam•stress ['simstrɪs] *n.* a woman who sews, especially one whose occupation is sewing. Also, **sempstress.**

seam•y ['simi] *adj.* **seam•i•er, seam•i•est.** 1 least attractive or pleasant; sordid or squalid: *the seamy side of life.* **2** showing seams; especially, showing the rough edges of the seams on the inside of a garment, etc. **—'seam•i•ness,** *n.*

sé•ance ['seiɑns]; *French* [se'ɑ̃s] *n.* **1** a meeting of people trying to communicate with spirits of the dead by the help of a medium. **2** formerly, any session or meeting. ⟨< F *séance* < *seoir* sit < L *sedere*⟩

sea nettle any large jellyfish that stings.

sea otter a large marine otter (*Enhydra lutris*) of N Pacific coastal waters having large, flipperlike hind feet and a thick, reddish brown or dark brown coat. It was hunted almost to extinction for its fur, and is now a rare and protected species.

sea•plane ['si,plein] *n.* an airplane that can take off from and come down on water.

sea•port ['si,pɔrt] *n.* **1** a port or harbour on the seacoast. **2** a city or town with a harbour that ships can reach from the sea.

sea power **1** naval strength: *The United States possesses great sea power.* **2** a nation having great naval strength: *Canada is not one of the world's major sea powers.* Compare AIR POWER.

sea purse the horny case or pouch produced by certain species of fish, such as some sharks, to protect their eggs and anchor them to rocks, weeds, etc.

sea•quake ['si,kweik] *n.* a submarine earthquake.

sear [sir] *v., n., adj.* *—v.* **1** burn or char the surface of: *The hot iron seared his flesh.* **2** make hard or unfeeling: *Years of cruelty had seared her heart.* **3** dry up; wither. **4** become dry, burned, or hard.
—n. a mark made by searing.
—adj. Archaic. See SERE. ⟨OE *sēarian*, v. < *sēar*, adj.⟩
☛ *Hom.* CERE, SEER, SERE.
☛ *Syn. v.* **1.** See note at BURN.

search [sɜrtʃ] *v., n.* *—v.* **1** try to find by looking; seek; look (*for*): *We searched all day for the lost cat.* **2** look through; go over carefully; examine, especially for something lost or concealed: *The police searched the prisoner to see if he had a gun.* **3** look through (writings, records, etc.) in order to discover if certain things are there: *to search land titles.* **4** examine by probing: *The doctor searched the wound for the bullet.* **5** look carefully at: *She searched his face for clues as to what he was thinking.* **6** *Computer technology.* examine (data) in a computer in order to find items meeting certain criteria. **7** *Archaic.* pierce or penetrate.
search out, a look for. **b** find by searching.
—n. the act of searching; examination.
in search of, trying to find; looking for: *They went in search of buried treasure.* ⟨ME < OF *cerchier*, ult. < L *circus* circle⟩
—'search•a•ble, *adj.* **—'search•er,** *n.*
☛ *Syn. v.* **2. Search,** EXPLORE, RUMMAGE = look through a place or thing for something. **Search** = look carefully through something, trying to find what is there, or hunting for something lost or hidden: *The police searched the woods for the murderer.* **Explore** = go into a region, field of interest, etc. to discover the facts about it, its nature, condition, quality, etc.: *Geologists explored the newly discovered mineral deposit.* **Rummage** = search thoroughly a ship, house, trunk, etc. by moving or looking among the contents: *She rummaged through the drawers looking for a map.*

search•ing ['sɜrtʃɪŋ] *adj., v.* *—adj.* **1** examining carefully; thorough: *a searching gaze or look, a searching examination.* **2** piercing; penetrating: *a searching wind.*
—v. ppr. of SEARCH. **—'search•ing•ly,** *adv.*

search•light ['sɜrtʃ,ləit] *n.* **1** a device that can throw a bright, far-reaching beam of light in any direction desired. **2** the beam of light thus thrown.

search–mas•ter ['sɜrtʃ ,mæstər] *n.* the person in charge of a search-and-rescue operation.

search warrant a legal document authorizing the search of a house or building for stolen or contraband goods, persons wanted by the police, etc.

sea robber a pirate.

sea robin any of a family (Triglidae) of bottom-living marine fishes having a bony, armoured head and fan-shaped pectoral fins, with a few elongated rays that are used as feelers and for walking along the bottom of the sea. Some sea robins, such as the **northern sea robin** (*Prionotus carolinus*) of the North American Atlantic coast, can produce sounds with the muscular vibration of their swim bladders.

sea room space at sea free from obstruction, in which a ship can easily sail, tack, turn around, etc.

sea rover **1** a pirate. **2** a pirate ship.

sea–run ['si ,rʌn] *adj.* of a fish, returning to its freshwater birthplace to spawn after having lived in the sea for a period of time; anadromous.

sea salt salt obtained from seawater, sold in health food stores as an alternative to iodized salt.

sea•scape ['si,skeip] *n.* **1** a picture, often a painting, showing scenery on the sea. **2** a view of scenery on the sea. ⟨modelled on *landscape*⟩

Sea Scout a member of the Scouts, aged 11 to 14, belonging to a program that emphasizes activities involving boats, boating, swimming, rescue work, and the lore of the sea.

sea serpent **1** a huge snakelike sea monster often reported as having been seen in the sea, but never proven to exist. **2** SEA SNAKE.

sea•shell ['si,ʃɛl] *n.* the shell of any sea mollusc, such as an oyster, conch, abalone, etc.

sea•shore ['si,ʃɔr] *n.* **1** the land along the sea; the beach at the seaside. **2** *Law.* that part of the shore lying between the high-water and low-water marks; foreshore.

sea•sick ['si,sɪk] *adj.* suffering from seasickness.

sea•sick•ness ['si,sɪknɪs] *n.* **1** nausea and dizziness caused by the pitching and rolling of a ship at sea. **2** *Informal.* nausea and dizziness caused by any similar motion, as when travelling in a motor vehicle or aircraft or swinging in a hammock; MOTION SICKNESS.

sea•side ['si,saɪd] *n.* **1** the land along the sea; seacoast; seashore. **2** (*adjl.*) beside the sea: *a seaside inn.*

sea slug any of various marine gastropods of the suborder Nudibranchia, having fringelike projections on a highly coloured body. Also, **nudibranch.**

sea snake any of a family (Hydrophidae) of poisonous aquatic snakes having a laterally compressed, rudderlike tail, found in tropical seas, especially in the Indian and W Pacific Oceans.

sea•son [si'zən] *n., v.* *—n.* **1** one of the four periods of the year; spring, summer, autumn, or winter. **2** a period of the year with reference to the particular conditions of weather, temperature, etc., that characterize it: *monsoon season.* **3** any period of time marked by something special: *the Christmas season, the harvest season.* **4** the time when something is occurring, active, at its best, or in fashion, or when a place is most frequented: *the baseball season.* **5** any period or time: *a season of rest, the season of one's youth.* **6** a suitable or fit time.
for a season, for a time.
in good season, early enough.
in season, a at the right or proper time. **b** in the time or condition for hunting, etc. **c** early enough. **d** of foodstuffs, available according to the time of year. **e** of an animal, in heat.
in season and out of season, at all times.
out of season, not in season.
—v. **1** improve the flavour of by adding salt, herbs, or spices, etc.: *season soup with salt.* **2** give interest or character to: *season conversation with wit.* **3** make fit for use by a period of keeping or treatment: *Wood is seasoned for building by drying and hardening it.* **4** become fit for use. **5** accustom; make used: *Soldiers are seasoned to battle by experience in war.* **6** make less extreme; temper: *Season justice with mercy.* **7** make (an athlete, actor, etc.) competent through experience of actual working conditions. ⟨ME < OF *seson* < L *satio, -onis* a sowing, ult. < *serere* sow⟩ **—'sea•son•er,** *n.*
☛ *Usage.* **Seasons.** The names **spring, summer, fall, autumn,** and **winter** are not capitalized.

sea•son•a•ble ['sizənəbəl] *adj.* **1** suitable to the season: *Hot weather is seasonable in July.* **2** coming at the right or proper time: *The second expedition brought seasonable aid to the people who had survived the first.* **—'sea•son•a•ble•ness,** *n.*
—'sea•son•a•bly, *adv.*
☛ *Usage.* **Seasonable,** SEASONAL, while both relating to a time or season, are properly differentiated in use. **Seasonable** indicates appropriateness to a time of year, or timeliness, as in *Snow is seasonable during the winter in most parts of Canada.* **Seasonal** refers to things related to or controlled by the changing seasons: *Working as a store Santa Claus is seasonal employment.*

sea•son•al ['sizənəl] *adj.* **1** of, having to do with, or occurring in a particular season: *seasonal variations in the weather, seasonal rains.* **2** depending on or affected by the season: *seasonal unemployment, a seasonal worker.*
—'sea•son•al•ly, *adv.*

seasonal affective disorder a form of depression which occurs at regular times in the year, such as in the winter or in the spring and fall. *Abbrev.:* SAD

sea•son•ing ['sizənɪŋ] *n., v.* *—n.* **1** something that is added to

food to give extra flavour. Salt, pepper, spices, and herbs are used as seasonings. 2 anything that adds interest or character: *conversation with a seasoning of wit.*
—v. ppr. of SEASON.

season ticket a ticket that gives its holder the right to attend a series of games or entertainments, or to make unlimited trips on a railway, bus, etc. for a stated period of time.

sea squirt any of a class (Ascidiacea) of minute invertebrates found in all seas from near the shore down to the greatest depths, characterized by a saclike body having openings through which water passes. Most sea squirts are free-swimming as larvae, but sedentary as adults.

sea star a starfish.

seat[1] [sit] *n., v.* *—n.* **1** something to sit on. **2** a place to sit. **3** a place in which one has the right to sit: *We have reserved seats in the first balcony.* **4** a right to sit as a member of a legislature, city council, stock exchange, etc: *The Conservatives lost almost all their seats in the last election.* **5** that part of a chair, bench, stool, etc. on which one sits. **6** that part of the body on which one sits, or the clothing covering it. **7** a manner of sitting on horseback. **8** that on which anything rests; base.
by the seat of (one's) **pants,** in an unsystematic or intuitive way.
take a seat, sit down.
—v. **1 a** set or place on a seat: *to seat a person on a chair.* **b** assist in finding or settling in a seat. **2** have seats for (a specified number): *That stadium seats thirty thousand people.* **3** provide with a particular seat or seats. **4** put a seat on.
be seated, a sit down. **b** be sitting. **c** be situated. ⟨ME < ON *sǽti*⟩
☛ *Hom.* CETE.

seat[2] [sit] *n., v.* *—n.* **1** an established place or centre: *A university is a seat of learning. The seat of our government is in Ottawa.* **2** the throne of a king, etc.; the authority or dignity of a king, etc. **3** a residence; home: *The family seat of the Percys is in Northumberland.* **4** location; situation; site: *the seat of a disease.* **5** the organ or part of the body thought of as the centre of some faculty, power, or quality: *In Western culture, the heart is the seat of the emotions.*
—v. fix in a particular or proper place; settle; locate: *The bottom knob of piece A should be firmly seated in the depression in the top of piece B before the mechanism is engaged.* ⟨OE *sǣte*⟩
☛ *Hom.* CETE.

seat belt a belt or arrangement of straps in an automobile or aircraft, designed to hold an occupant in the seat in case of a crash, jolt, bump, etc.

seat•ing ['sitɪŋ] *n., v.* *—n.* **1** upholstery for covering seats. **2 a** the arrangement of seats for a dinner party, in a theatre, etc. **b** the seats themselves. **3** a base on which something rests or in which it is fixed: *the seating of a valve.* **4** the act of one that seats.
—v. ppr. of SEAT.

SEATO Southeast Asia Treaty Organization.

seat–of–the–pants ['sit əv ðə 'pænts] *adj. Cdn. Informal.* **1** done in an intuitive or unsystematic way. **2** done without the aid of instruments: *a seat-of-the-pants landing.*

sea trout 1 any of various trouts or chars that spend part of their lives in the sea. **2** any of several weakfishes, especially *Cynoscion nebulosus*, which is also called **spotted sea trout. 3** *Cdn. Atlantic Provinces.* a variety of trout that spawns in freshwater rivers. **4** *Cdn. Pacific coast.* steelhead.

sea unicorn *Cdn.* the narwhal (*Monodon monoceros*).

sea urchin any of a class (Echinoidea) of marine invertebrates typically having a spherical or slightly flattened body with a rigid outer shell of fused plates bearing rows of movable spines.

sea wall a strong wall or embankment made to prevent the waves from wearing away the shore, to act as a breakwater, etc.

sea•ward ['siwərd] *adv., adj., n.* *—adv. or adj.* **1** toward the sea: *Our house faces seaward.* **2** of a wind, blowing from the sea: *a seaward breeze. The wind is blowing seaward.*
—n. the direction toward the sea: *The island lies one kilometre to seaward.* Also (*adv.*), **seawards.**

sea•wa•ter ['si,wɒtər] *n.* the salt water in the ocean.

sea•way ['si,wei] *n.* **1** a way or route over the ocean. **2** the progress of a ship through the waves. **3** a rough sea. **4** an inland waterway that connects with the open sea and is deep enough to permit ocean shipping: *the St. Lawrence Seaway.*

sea•weed ['si,wid] *n.* **1** any plant or plants growing in the sea, especially a sea alga such as kelp. **2** a similar plant in fresh water; properly, **freshwater seaweed.**

sea wind a wind blowing from the sea toward the land.

sea•wor•thy ['si,wɜrði] *adj.* fit for sailing on the sea; able to withstand storms at sea. **—'sea,wor•thi•ness,** *n.*

sea wrack material cast ashore by the sea, especially seaweed.

se•ba•ceous [sɪ'beiʃəs] *adj.* **1** *Physiology.* of, having to do with, or being fat; fatty. **2** producing sebum: *sebaceous glands.* See EPIDERMIS for picture. ⟨< L *sebaceus* < *sebum* grease⟩

se•bac•ic acid [sɪ'bæsɪk] *or* [sɪ'beisɪk] *Chemistry.* a white, crystalline acid obtained by the distillation of oleic acid. It is used in the production of certain plasticizers, polyester rubbers, alkyd resins, etc. *Formula*: $C_{10}H_{18}O_4$ ⟨< L *sebaceus* < *sebum* grease⟩

se•ba•go [sɪ'beigou] *n.* ouananiche. ⟨< Lake *Sebago*, Maine⟩

seb•or•rhe•a or **seb•or•rhoe•a** [,sɛbə'riə] *n. Pathology.* an abnormally great discharge of sebum from the sebaceous glands, resulting in excessively oily, crusty, or scaly skin. ⟨< *sebum* + Gk. *-rrhoia* < *rheein* flow⟩

se•bum ['sibəm] *n. Physiology.* the oily substance produced by the sebaceous glands to lubricate the skin and hair. ⟨< L, grease⟩

sec[1] [sɛk] *adj.* of wine, especially champagne, dry. ⟨< F⟩

sec[2] *Mathematics.* secant.

sec. 1 secretary. **2 a** second(s) (unit of time). **b** second(s) (unit of angular measure). **3** section(s). **4** secant. **5** according to (for L *secundum*). **6** secondary. **7** sector.

se•cant ['sikənt] *or* ['sikænt] *n., adj.* *—n.* **1** *Geometry.* a line that intersects a curve at two or more points. **2** *Trigonometry.* **a** a straight line drawn from the centre of a circle through one extremity of an arc to the tangent from the other extremity of the same arc. **b** the ratio of the length of this line to the length of the radius of the circle. **c** the ratio of the length of the hypotenuse of a right-angled triangle to the length of the side adjacent to an acute angle. See SINE[1] for picture.
—adj. intersecting. ⟨< L *secans*, *-antis*, ppr. of *secare* cut⟩

Secateurs

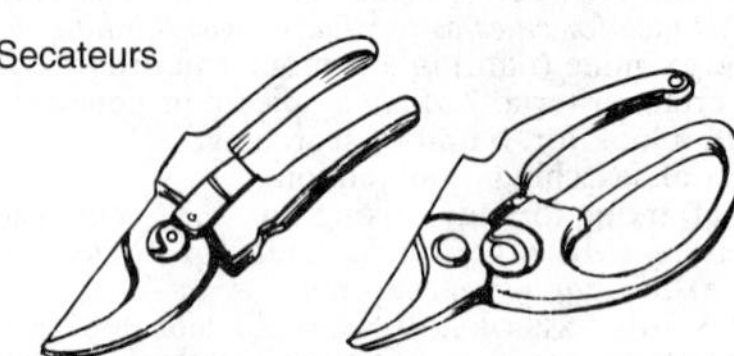

se•ca•teurs ['sɛkə,tɜrz] *or* [,sɛkə'tɜrz] *n.pl.* one-handed pruning shears or clippers. ⟨< F < L *secare* cut⟩

sec•co ['sɛkou]; *Italian*, ['sɛkkɔ] *n., adj.* *—n.* the technique of painting on dry plaster, using colours mixed with water.
—adj. pertaining to this technique; dry. ⟨ < Ital. *secco* dry < L *siccus*⟩

se•cede [sɪ'sid] *v.* **-ced•ed, -ced•ing.** withdraw formally from an organization, especially a church or a political federation. ⟨< L *secedere* < *se-* apart + *cedere* go⟩ **—se'ced•er,** *n.*

se•ces•sion [sɪ'sɛʃən] *n.* a formal withdrawing from an organization, especially a church or a political federation. ⟨< L *secessio*, *-onis* < *secedere.* See SECEDE.⟩ **—se'ces•sion•al,** *adj.*

se•ces•sion•ism [sɪ'sɛʃə,nɪzəm] *n.* the principles or policy of those in favour of secession. **—se'ces•sion•ist,** *n., adj.*

se•clude [sɪ'klud] *v.* **-clud•ed, -clud•ing.** shut off or keep apart from others; isolate: *He has secluded himself and no longer accepts visitors.* ⟨< L *secludere* < *se-* apart + *claudere* shut⟩

se•clud•ed [sɪ'kludɪd] *adj., v.* *—adj.* shut off from others; undisturbed.
—v. pt. and pp. of SECLUDE.

se•clu•sion [sɪ'kluʒən] *n.* **1** a keeping apart or being shut off from others; retirement: *She lives in seclusion, apart from her friends.* **2** a secluded place. ⟨< Med.L *seclusio*, *-onis* < L *secludere.* See SECLUDE.⟩

se•clu•sive [sɪ'klusɪv] *adj.* **1** fond of seclusion. **2** tending to seclude. **—se'clu•sive•ly,** *adv.* **—se'clu•sive•ness,** *n.*

se•co•bar•bit•al [,sɛkou'bɑrbə,tɒl] *n.* a barbiturate drug, used as a sedative. *Formula*: $C_{12}H_{18}N_2O_3$

sec•ond[1] ['sɛkənd]; for *v.* def. 3 [sə'kɒnd] *adj., adv., n., v.* *—adj.* **1** next after the 1st; 2nd: *the second seat from the front.* **2** next below the first in rank, authority, etc.: *the second officer*

on a ship. **3** another; other: *Napoleon has been called a second Caesar.* **4** *Music.* being or having to do with a part subordinate to and usually lower than the first in an ensemble composition: *second soprano.*
at second hand. See HAND.
—adv. **1** in the second group, division, rank, etc.; secondly. **2** in the second place: *to run second.*
—n. **1** a person who or thing that is second. **2 seconds,** *pl.* articles below first quality or having some defect. **3** a person who supports or aids another; backer: *The prize fighter had a second.* **4** *Music.* **a** the second, usually lower, part in a composition for ensemble performance. **b** a voice or instrument rendering such a part. **c** a tone on the next degree from a given tone. **d** the interval between the two. **e** the harmonic combination of such tones. **f** the second note in a scale. **5** a forward gear or speed of a motor vehicle having a ratio to the engine speed between that of first and third. **6** Often, **seconds,** *pl.* a second helping of food: *Anyone for seconds?*
—v. **1 a** support; back up: *to second another person's idea. I second Dr. Hemmings.* **b** attend; assist (a boxer or duellist). **2** in parliamentary procedure, express approval or support of (a motion): *One member made a motion and another seconded it.* **3** assign (a person, especially a member of the armed forces, or a teacher) temporarily to some office outside his or her regular appointment: *Professor Lee has been seconded to the Ministry of Education.* ⟨ME < OF < L *secundus* < *sequi* follow⟩
—'sec•ond•er, *n.*

sec•ond² ['sɛkənd] *n.* **1** an SI unit for measuring time. There are sixty seconds in one minute, sixty minutes in one hour, and twenty-four hours in one day. The second is one of the seven base units in the SI. *Symbol*: s **2** any short period of time: *I'll be with you in a second.* **3** a unit used with the SI for measuring plane angles. There are sixty seconds in one minute and sixty minutes in one degree. *Symbol*: ″
this second, now. ⟨ME < OF < Med.L *secunda* (*minuta*) second (minute), i.e., the result of the second division of the hour into sixty parts⟩

Second Advent SECOND COMING.

sec•ond•ar•y ['sɛkən,dɛri] *adj., n., pl.* **-ar•ies.** *—adj.* **1** next after the first in order, place, time, etc. **2** not main or chief; having less importance. **3** not original; derived. **4** *Electricity.* being or having to do with a coil or circuit in which a current is produced by induction. **5** *Chemistry.* **a** involving the substitution of two atoms or groups. **b** of a carbon atom, attached to two other atoms in a ring. **6** *Geology.* produced from another mineral by decay, alteration, etc. **7** *Linguistics.* **a** made by adding an affix to a base that is already a word. **b** designating a form or process that developed relatively recently from an earlier process.
—n. **1** a person or thing that is secondary, second in importance, or subordinate. **2** SECONDARY STRESS. **3** *Electricity.* a coil or circuit in which a current is produced by induction.
—'sec•ond,ar•i•ly, *adv.*

secondary accent SECONDARY STRESS.

secondary colour a colour produced by mixing two or more primary colours. Compare PRIMARY COLOUR.

secondary feather a feather used in flying, situated on the second segment of a bird's wing.

secondary school a school attended after elementary or junior high school; a high school or collegiate institute.

secondary sex characteristic any of the physical manifestations that distinguish male from female but are not required for reproduction, such as distribution of body fat, female breasts, change of voice pitch in adolescent males, differences in muscularity, etc.

secondary stress *Linguistics.* **1** a stress accent that is weaker than the strongest stress in a word (primary stress), but stronger than weak stress. The second syllable of *ab,bre•vi'a•tion* has a secondary stress. **2** a mark, such as (,), used to show where this stress falls. **3** the second strongest of the four degrees of phonemic stress.

second childhood a period or state of mental decline associated with old age; dotage.

second class 1 a class ranking next below the first or highest. **2** the grade of travel accommodation next below the best. **3** an inferior grade or quality. **4** a mail classification that includes newspapers and periodicals sent to subscribers. **5** with second-class accommodation: *to travel second class.* **2** by second-class mail. **—'sec•ond-'class,** *adj.*

Second Coming *Christianity.* the return of Christ to earth as king and judge at the end of the world.

second cousin the child of one's parent's first cousin.

second fiddle 1 the part played by the second violin(s) in an orchestra or string group. **2** *Informal.* a person in a secondary role or subsidiary position.
play second fiddle, be in a secondary position in comparison to someone else.

second growth 1 a crop of grass or hay that comes up after the first crop has been cut; aftergrass. **2** a new growth of trees in an area where virgin forest has been cut or burned. **3** any new growth in an area that has been cleared of vegetation.

sec•ond–guess ['sɛkənd 'gɛs] *v. Informal.* solve a problem, criticize, etc., by using hindsight.

second hand an extra hand on a clock or watch, pointing to the seconds.

sec•ond–hand ['sɛkənd 'hænd] *adj.* **1** not original; obtained from another: *second-hand information.* **2** not new; used already by someone else: *second-hand clothes.* **3** dealing in used goods: *a second-hand bookshop.*

second lieutenant the lowest-ranking commissioned officer in the armed forces. See chart of ranks in the Appendix. *Abbrev.*: 2Lt. or 2Lt

sec•ond•ly ['sɛkəndli] *adv.* in the second place.

second mortgage additional funding lent on the security of property such as a house. It has second claim on the property, the first mortgage having the prior claim.

second nature a habit, quality, skill, etc. that a person has acquired and had for so long that it seems to be almost a part of his or her nature.

second person *Grammar.* the form of a pronoun or verb used to indicate the person spoken to. *You* and *your* are used for the second person, both singular and plural.

sec•ond–rate ['sɛkənd 'reit] *adj.* of inferior quality or value; mediocre: *a second-rate diamond, a second-rate author.*
—'sec•ond-'rat•er, *n.*

second sight the power to see distant objects or future events; clairvoyance.

second thoughts reservations or change of mind about a previous decision, course of action, etc.

second wind 1 a recovery or renewal of breath and energy following the initial feeling of exhaustion during an effort, as in running a race. **2** any recovery or renewal of energy: *The rise in steel production faltered in early spring and then got its second wind.*

se•cre•cy ['sikrəsi] *n., pl.* **-cies. 1** the condition of being secret. **2** the condition of being kept secret. **3** the act or habit of keeping things secret: *They relied on her secrecy.* ⟨< *secret*, adj.⟩

se•cret ['sikrɪt] *adj., n. —adj.* **1** kept from the knowledge of others: *a secret marriage.* **2** keeping to oneself what one knows: *Be as secret as the grave.* **3** known only to a few: *a secret society.* **4** kept from sight; hidden: *a secret drawer.* **5** retired; secluded: *a secret place.* **6** working or acting in secret: *a secret agent, secret police.* **7** very hard to understand or discover.
—n. **1** something undisclosed or hidden; a mystery. **2** something known only to a few. **3** a hidden or little-known explanation; key: *The secret to this delicious sauce is a dab of horseradish.*
in secret, in private; not openly. ⟨< F *secret* < L *secretus*, pp. of *secernere* set apart < *se-* apart + *cernere* separate. Doublet of SECRETE.⟩ **—'se•cret•ly,** *adv.*

☛ *Syn. adj.* **1. Secret,** COVERT, CLANDESTINE = done, made, or carried on without the knowledge of others. **Secret** is the general word describing something hidden or kept from sight or knowledge: *They have secret plans.* **Covert,** formal, suggests being done or kept under cover, and describes looks, meanings, or actions that are disguised or not open: *A hint is a covert suggestion.* **Clandestine,** formal, describes something underhand or with an unlawful or wicked purpose: *He feared someone would learn of his clandestine trips.*

secret agent an agent of a government intelligence service.

sec•re•tar•i•al [,sɛkrə'tɛriəl] *adj.* of a secretary; having to do with a secretary: *He learned to do word processing and other secretarial work.*

sec•re•tar•i•at [,sɛkrə'tɛriɪt] *n.* **1** the office or position of secretary, especially of a secretary or secretary-general as the administrative head of an organization. **2** the administrative unit controlled by a secretary or secretary-general: *the United Nations Secretariat.* **3** a group of secretaries. **4** a place where a secretary or secretary-general transacts business. ⟨< F *secrétariat*⟩

sec•re•tar•y ['sɛkrə,tɛri] *n., pl.* **-tar•ies. 1** someone who writes letters, keeps records, etc. for a person, company, club, etc.: *Our club has a secretary who keeps the minutes of the meeting.* **2** in some countries, a person who administers a department of the government: *Secretary of State.* **3** a diplomatic agent, usually of lower rank in an embassy or legation, often designated as first secretary, second secretary, etc. **4** a writing desk with a set of drawers, and often having shelves for books. ⟨ME < LL *secretarius* confidential officer < L *secretum,* n., secret, originally pp., neut. of *secretus.* See SECRET.⟩

secretary bird a large, long-legged African bird of prey (*Sagittarius serpentarius*) that feeds mainly on reptiles, so called because its crest suggests pens stuck over the ear.

A secretary bird

sec•re•tar•y–gen•er•al ['sɛkrə,tɛri 'dʒɛnərəl] *n., pl.* **sec•re•tar•ies-gen•er•al.** the chief or senior secretary; the administrator or head of a secretariat: *the Secretary-General of the United Nations.*

se•crete [sɪ'krit] *v.* **-cret•ed, -cret•ing. 1** produce and release: *Glands in the mouth secrete saliva.* **2** keep secret; hide. ⟨< L *secretus.* Doublet of SECRET.⟩ **—se'cre•tor,** *n.*

se•cre•tion [sɪ'kriʃən] *n.* **1** a substance that is secreted by some part of an animal or plant. Bile is a secretion of the liver. **2** the producing and releasing of such a substance. **3** the act of concealing; hiding.

se•cre•tive ['sikrətɪv] *or* [sɪ'kritɪv] *for 1;* [sɪ'kritɪv] *for 2. adj.* **1** having the habit of secrecy; not frank and open. **2** causing or aiding secretion. **—'se•cre•tive•ly,** *adv.* **—'se•cre•tive•ness,** *n.*

se•cre•to•ry [sɪ'kritəri] *adj., n., pl.* **-ries.** *—adj.* secreting; of or causing secretion.
—n. an organ of the body that secretes.

secret police in a dictatorship or similar regime, a special government police force that operates covertly to control and suppress activities considered subversive.

secret service the branch of a government that makes clandestine investigations, and whose members are sworn to secrecy about their activities.

secret society 1 an association of which some ceremonies and activities are known only to members. **2** an organization to promote some cause by secret methods, its members being sworn to observe secrecy.

sect [sɛkt] *n.* **1** a group of people having similar principles, beliefs, or opinions, especially religious; denomination. **2** a group of people forming part of a larger religious body but differing from some of the larger body's beliefs or customs: *Anglo-Catholics are a sect of the Anglican Church.* ⟨< L *secta* party, school, probably < *sectari* keep following, intensive of *sequi* follow⟩

sect. section; sectional.

sec•tar•i•an [sɛk'tɛriən] *adj., n. —adj.* **1** of or having to do with a sect. **2** characteristic of one sect only; strongly prejudiced in favour of a certain sect. **3** narrow-minded or limited, especially regarding religious views.
—n. **1** a devoted member of a sect, especially a narrow-minded or strongly prejudiced member. **2** a member of a religious group separated from an established church.

sec•tar•i•an•ism [sɛk'tɛriə,nɪzəm] *n.* the spirit or tendencies of sectarians; adherence or too great devotion to a particular sect.

sec•ta•ry ['sɛktəri] *n., pl.* **-ries.** a member of a particular sect, especially a member of a religious group separated from an established church. ⟨< Med.L *sectarius* < L *secta.* See SECT.⟩

sec•tile ['sɛktaɪl] *or* ['sɛktɪl] *adj.* capable of being cut smoothly by a knife. ⟨< F < L *sectilis* < *secare* cut⟩

sec•tion ['sɛkʃən] *n., v. —n.* **1** a part; division; slice: *Divide the cake into sections. His section of the family estate was larger than his sister's.* **2** a division of a book, etc.: *Chapter X has seven sections.* **3** a region; part of a country, city, etc.: *The city has a business section and a residential section.* **4** a division of a company, office, or other organization. **5** a military formation that is smaller than a platoon and is usually commanded by a corporal. **6** the act of cutting, especially as part of a surgical procedure: *Caesarian section.* **7** a view of a thing as it would appear if cut straight through; CROSS SECTION. **8** a district or tract of land one mile square; 260 ha (about 640 acres): *She farms two sections near Regina.* **9** one of the parts of something that is built of a number of similar parts: *the sections of a wall unit.* **10** a thin slice of a tissue, mineral, etc. cut off for microscopic examination. **11** a part of a railway line kept up by one group of workers. **12** a part of a sleeping car containing an upper and a lower berth. **13** one of two or more trains operating on the same schedule. **14** *Bookbinding.* a number of sheets folded together to form a unit. **15** a division of an orchestra, band, or choir: *the string section, the alto section.*
—v. cut or divide into sections: *to section an orange.*
section off, partition: *This area of the classroom has been sectioned off as a lab.* ⟨< L *sectio, -onis* < *secare* cut⟩

sec•tion•al ['sɛkʃənəl] *adj.* **1** having to do with a particular section; local. **2** made of sections: *a sectional bookcase.* **—'sec•tion•al•ly,** *adv.*

sec•tion•al•ism ['sɛkʃənə,lɪzəm] *n.* excessive regard for sectional interests; sectional prejudice or hatred. **—'sec•tion•al•ist,** *n., adj.*

sec•tion•al•ize ['sɛkʃənə,laɪz] *v.* **-ized, -iz•ing. 1** make sectional. **2** divide into sections. **—,sec•tion•al•i'za•tion,** *n.*

section gang a crew of workers assigned to look after a section of railway track.

section hand a worker in a SECTION GANG.

section line *Cdn., esp. West.* **1** the survey line setting off a section. **2** a road running along the survey line separating sections.

sec•tor ['sɛktər] *n.* **1** *Geometry.* the part of a circle between two radii and the included arc. See CIRCLE for picture. **2** *Military.* a clearly defined area that a given unit protects or covers with fire; the part of a front held by a unit. **3** an instrument consisting of two rulers connected by a joint. A sector is used in measuring or drawing angles. **4** *Computer technology.* a segment of a track on a computer disk usually capable of storing a fixed amount of data. ⟨< LL < L *sector* cutter < *secare* cut⟩

sec•u•lar ['sɛkjələr] *adj., n. —adj.* **1** worldly; not religious or sacred: *secular music, a secular education.* **2** living in the world; not belonging to a religious order: *the secular clergy, a secular priest.* **3** secularistic; of secularism. **4** occurring once in an age; lasting for an age or century. **5** lasting through long ages; going on from age to age.
—n. a secular priest. ⟨< L *saecularis* < *saeculum* age, world⟩ **—'sec•u•lar•ly,** *adv.*

secular humanism humanism that embraces secularism.

sec•u•lar•ism ['sɛkjələ,rɪzəm] *n.* **1** rejection of religion in favour of an attitude and lifestyle of worldliness. **2** opposition to the introduction of religion into public schools or any other public sphere.

sec•u•lar•ist ['sɛkjələrɪst] *n.* a believer in secularism. **—,sec•u•lar'ist•ic,** *adj.*

sec•u•lar•i•ty [,sɛkjə'lærɪti] *or* [,sɛkjə'lɛrɪti] *n.* a secular spirit or quality; worldliness.

sec•u•lar•ize ['sɛkjələ,raɪz] *v.* **-ized, -iz•ing. 1** make secular or worldly; separate from religious connection or influence: *to secularize the schools.* **2** transfer (property) from the possession of the church to that of the government. **3** release (someone) by authority from religious vows. **—,sec•u•lar•i'za•tion,** *n.* **—'sec•u•lar,iz•er,** *n.*

se•cure [sɪ'kjʊr] *adj., v.* **-cured, -cur•ing.** *—adj.* **1** safe against loss, attack, escape, etc.: *to keep a prisoner secure within a dungeon. This is a secure hiding place. Land in a growing city is a secure investment.* **2** sure; certain; that can be counted on: *We know in advance that our victory is secure.* **3** free from care or fear: *She hoped for a secure old age.* **4** firmly fastened; not likely to give way: *The boards of this bridge do not look secure.*
—v. **1** make safe; protect: *Every loan was secured by bonds or mortgages.* **2** make oneself safe; be safe: *We must secure against the dangers of the coming storm.* **3** make (something) sure or certain. **4** make firm or fast: *Secure the locks on the windows.* **5** get; obtain: *Secure your tickets early. We secured their permission.* **6** tie up; restrain. ⟨< L *securus* < *se-* free from + *cura* care. Doublet of SURE.⟩ **—se'cur•a•ble,** *adj.* **—se'cur•er,** *n.* **—se'cure•ly,** *adv.* **—se'cure•ness,** *n.*
☛ *Syn. adj.* See note at SAFE.

se•cu•ri•ty [sɪ'kjʊrɪti] *n., pl.* **-ties. 1** freedom from danger, care, or fear; a feeling or the condition of being safe. **2** certainty. **3** procedures to ensure defence against illegal entry, sabotage, etc. or against escape from prison. **4** something that secures or makes safe: *My watchdog is a security against burglars.* **5** personnel responsible for safety: *Advise security of any unusual happenings on the premises.* **6 securities,** *pl.* bonds, stocks, etc.:

These railway securities can be sold for $5000. **7** something given as a guarantee that a person will be able to pay back a loan or fulfil some duty, promise, etc. A life-insurance policy may serve as security for a loan. **8** a person who agrees to be responsible for another.

Security Council in the United Nations, a permanent body whose function is to maintain world peace. It has five permanent members—France, the United Kingdom, the People's Republic of China, Russia, and the United States—and ten non-permanent members.

se•dan [sɪ'dæn] *n.* **1** a closed automobile seating four or more people. **2** SEDAN CHAIR. ⟨poss. < Ital. dial. *sedente* sitting < L *sedere* to sit⟩

sedan chair an enclosed chair carried on poles by two people.

se•date [sɪ'deit] *adj., v.* **-dat•ed, -dat•ing.** *—adj.* **1** quiet; calm; serious: *He is a very sedate child and would rather read than play.* **2** decorous or dignified.
—v. make calm, as with a drug: *The grieving widow had to be sedated.* ⟨< L *sedatus,* pp. of *sedare* calm⟩ **—se'date•ly,** *adv.* **—se'date•ness,** *n.*

se•da•tion [sɪ'deiʃən] *n.* **1** the producing of a relaxed state by means of a sedative; treatment with sedatives. **2** a relaxed or painless state produced or as if produced by a sedative.

sed•a•tive ['sɛdətɪv] *n., adj. —n.* **1** a medication that lessens pain or excitement. **2** anything soothing or calming.
—adj. **1** lessening pain or excitement. **2** soothing; calming.

sed•en•tar•y ['sɛdən,tɛri] *adj.* **1** used to sitting still much of the time: *Sedentary people get little physical exercise.* **2** that keeps one sitting still much of the time: *Bookkeeping is a sedentary occupation.* **3** moving little and rarely; fixed to one spot. **4** not migratory: *Pigeons are sedentary birds.* ⟨< L *sedentarius,* ult. < *sedere* sit⟩ **—'sed•en,tar•i•ly,** *adv.* **—'sed•en,tar•i•ness,** *n.*

Se•der ['seidər] *n., pl.* **Se•ders** or **Se•dar•im** [sə'dɑrɪm]. the religious rites and feast held in Jewish homes on the first two nights of Passover. ⟨< Hebrew⟩

sedge [sɛdʒ] *n.* any of a large family (Cyperaceae) of grasslike plants that grow in marshes, bogs, and shallow water, having solid, often triangular stems, long, narrow leaves, and spikelets of tiny, petalless flowers; especially, any of the genus *Carex.* ⟨OE *secg*⟩

sedged [sɛdʒd] *adj.* **1** made of sedge. **2** abounding in or bordered with sedge.

sedg•y ['sɛdʒi] *adj.* **-i•er, -i•est. 1** sedged: *a sedgy brook.* **2** of or like sedge.

sed•i•ment ['sɛdəmənt] *n.* **1** any matter that settles to the bottom of a liquid; dregs. **2** *Geology.* earth, stones, etc. deposited by water, wind, or ice: *Each year the Nile overflows and deposits sediment on the land.* ⟨< F < L *sedimentum* < *sedere* settle⟩

sed•i•men•tal [,sɛdə'mɛntəl] *adj.* sedimentary.

sed•i•men•ta•ry [,sɛdə'mɛntəri] *adj.* **1** of or having to do with sediment. **2** *Geology.* designating rock that is made up of sediment, fragments of older rock, or organic materials. Shale is a kind of sedimentary rock. **—,sed•i•men'tar•i•ly,** *adv.*

sed•i•men•ta•tion [,sɛdəmɛn'teiʃən] *n.* a depositing of sediment.

se•di•tion [sɪ'dɪʃən] *n.* speech or action causing discontent or rebellion against the government; incitement to discontent or rebellion. ⟨ME < L *seditio, -onis* < *sed-,* var. of *se-* apart + *ire* go⟩ **—se'di•tion•ist,** *n.*

se•di•tion•ar•y [sɪ'dɪʃə,nɛri] *adj., n., pl.* **-ar•ies.** *—adj.* having to do with or involving sedition.
—n. one guilty of sedition.

se•di•tious [sɪ'dɪʃəs] *adj.* **1** stirring up discontent or rebellion. **2** taking part in sedition; guilty of sedition. **3** having to do with sedition. **—se'di•tious•ly,** *adv.* **—se'di•tious•ness,** *n.*

se•duce [sɪ'djus] *or* [sɪ'dus] *v.* **-duced, -duc•ing. 1** persuade or entice (a person to whom one is not married) to engage in sexual intercourse. **2** lead away from virtue or right action or thought; tempt into wrongdoing. **3** attract or lure. **4** win over; beguile; entice. ⟨< L *seducere* < *se-* aside + *ducere* lead⟩ **—se'duc•er,** *n.*

se•duce•ment [sɪ'djusmənt] *or* [sɪ'dusmənt] *n.* seduction.

se•duc•i•ble [sɪ'djusəbəl] *or* [sɪ'dusəbəl] *adj.* that can be seduced.

se•duc•tion [sɪ'dʌkʃən] *n.* **1** the act of seducing; the fact or condition of being seduced. **2** something that seduces; temptation; attraction. ⟨< L *seductio, -onis* < *seducere.* See SEDUCE.⟩

se•duc•tive [sɪ'dʌktɪv] *adj.* **1** alluring; captivating; charming. **2** tending to seduce. **—se'duc•tive•ly,** *adv.* **—se'duc•tive•ness,** *n.*

se•duct•ress [sɪ'dʌktrɪs] *n.* temptress; a woman who seduces, especially for sexual purposes.

se•du•li•ty [sɪ'djulɪti] *or* [sɪ'dulɪti] *n.* the quality of being sedulous; diligent application or care.

sed•u•lous ['sɛdʒələs] *adj.* hard-working; diligent; painstaking. ⟨< L *sedulus* < *se dolo* without deception⟩ **—'sed•u•lous•ly,** *adv.* **—'sed•u•lous•ness,** *n.*

se•dum ['sidəm] *n.* any of a genus (*Sedum*) of plants of the same family as the houseleeks, having fleshy leaves and clusters of white, pink, or yellow flowers. Some sedums are cultivated as garden flowers. ⟨< L *sedum* houseleek⟩

see¹ [si] *v.* **saw, seen, see•ing. 1** perceive with the eyes; look at: *See that black cloud.* **2** use the eyes to see things: *Can you see under water?* **3** have the power of sight: *The blind do not see.* **4** perceive with the mind; understand: *I see what you mean.* **5** find out; learn: *I will see what needs to be done.* **6** take care; make sure: *See that you lock the back door.* **7** think of; consider: *They saw her as the answer to all their problems.* **8** have knowledge or experience of; undergo: *That coat has seen hard wear.* **9** attend; escort; go with: *to see someone home.* **10** meet; have a talk with: *The professor wishes to see you alone.* **11** call on: *I went to see a friend.* **12** receive a visit from: *He is too ill to see anyone.* **13** visit; attend: *We saw the Canadian National Exhibition.* **14** visualize or imagine: *She could see herself standing on the platform to receive the gold medal in the upcoming Olympics.* **15** accept as a possibility: *I can't see spending $100 on a hotel room when we can stay with the Saunders for nothing.* **16** date on a regular basis: *Are you still seeing that guy you met at camp?* **17** reflect: *Let's see now, where should we hang this picture?* **18** *Poker, etc.* meet (a bet) by staking an equal sum.
see after, take care of.
see fit (to), consider it right (to): *Go if you see fit to do so.*
see into, understand the real character or hidden purpose of.
see off, go with to the starting place of a journey.
see (one's) **way (clear) to,** consider the possibility of doing something.
see out, go through with; finish.
see red, *Slang.* become angry.
see through, a understand the real character or hidden purpose of. **b** go through with; finish. **c** watch over or help through a difficulty: *His friends saw him through his financial difficulties.*
see to, look after; take care of. ⟨OE *sēon*⟩
☛ *Hom.* C, SEA.
☛ *Syn.* **1. See,** PERCEIVE, OBSERVE = become aware of something through sight. **See,** the general word, means 'be conscious of what is before the eyes', with or without trying: *We saw someone standing in the doorway.* **Perceive,** the formal substitute for **see,** emphasizes using the mind as well as the eyes and consciously noticing or recognizing what is seen: *We perceived the figure to be your mother.* **Observe** suggests directing the attention as well as the eyes to what is seen: *We observed a change in her.*

see² [si] *n.* **1** the position or authority of a bishop. **2** the district under a bishop's authority; diocese; bishopric. ⟨ME < OF *sie* < L *sedes* abode; OF form infl. by *siet* sits < L *sedet*⟩
☛ *Hom.* C, SEA, SI.

seed [sid] *n., pl.* **seeds** or **seed;** *adj., v. —n.* **1** the thing from which a flower, vegetable, or other plant grows; a small, grainlike fruit: *Farmers often save part of a crop for the seeds.* **2** a bulb, sprout, or any part of a plant from which a new plant will grow. **3** seeds collectively. **4** the source or beginning of anything: *seeds of trouble.* **5** children; descendants: *The Jews are the seed of Isaac.* **6** semen; sperm. **7** a minute bubble arising in glass during fusion. **8** a player of high ranking in a tennis tournament.
go to seed, a come to the time of yielding seeds: *Dandelions' heads turn white when they go to seed.* **b** come to the end of vigour, usefulness, prosperity, etc.: *After the mines closed, the town went to seed.*
—adj. of or containing seeds; used for seeds.
—v. **1** sow with seeds; scatter seeds over: *The farmer seeded her field with corn.* **2** sow (seeds). **3** produce seeds; shed seeds. **4** remove the seeds from: *He seeded the grapes for the salad.* **5** *Sports.* **a** schedule (tournament players or teams) so that the best ones will not meet each other in the early matches. **b** rank (a player) in relation to other contestants: *the top-seeded contestant.* **6** scatter Dry Ice or other chemicals into (clouds) from an airplane in an effort to produce rain artificially. ⟨OE *sǣd*⟩ **—'seed•less,** *adj.* **—'seed,like,** *adj.*
☛ *Hom.* CEDE.

seed•bed ['sid,bɛd] *n.* **1** soil that is specially prepared for nurturing plants from seed. 2 any place conducive to growth and development; breeding ground.

seed capsule SEED VESSEL.

seed•case ['sid,keis] *n.* any pod, capsule, or other dry, hollow fruit that contains seeds.

seed coat the outer layer protecting the seed from damage and water loss.

seed•er ['sidər] *n.* **1** one who or that which seeds. **2** a machine or device for planting seeds. **3** a machine or device for removing seeds.
☛ *Hom.* CEDAR.

seed leaf *Botany.* the embryo leaf in the seed of a plant; cotyledon.

seed•ling ['sidlɪŋ] *n., adj.* —*n.* **1** a young plant grown from a seed. **2** a young tree less than 1 m high.
—*adj.* **1** developed or raised from seed. **2** like a small seed; existing in a rudimentary state.

seed money money provided for the initial stages of financing a new business, research project, etc., often with a view to attracting further funding.

seed pearl a very small pearl.

seed plant any plant that bears seeds. Most seed plants have flowers and produce seeds in fruits; some, such as the pines, form seeds on cones.

seeds•man ['sidzmən] *n., pl.* **-men. 1** a sower of seed. **2** a dealer in seed.

seed tree a tree providing seed for natural reproduction.

seed vessel *Botany.* any pod, capsule, or other hollow fruit that contains seeds; pericarp.

seed•y ['sidi] *adj.* **seed•i•er, seed•i•est. 1** full of seeds. **2** gone to seed. **3** *Informal.* shabby; no longer fresh or new: *seedy clothes.* **4** *Informal.* being or looking unwell or run down. **—'seed•i•ly,** *adv.* **—'seed•i•ness,** *n.*

see•ing ['siɪŋ] *n., adj., conj., v.* —*n.* **1** vision; the sense of sight. **2** the act of someone using the eyes to see.
—*adj.* not blind.
—*conj.* in view of the fact; considering: *Seeing that coaxing won't work, we'll have to try something else.*
—*v.* ppr. of SEE.

Seeing Eye an organization that breeds and trains dogs as guides for blind people.

seek [sik] *v.* **sought, seek•ing. 1** try to find; look for: *We are seeking a new home.* **2** hunt; search: *to seek for something lost.* **3** try to get; pursue; work for or toward: *Friends sought her advice.* **4** try; attempt: *He seeks to make peace with his enemies.* **5** go to: *Being sleepy, he sought his bed.* ⟨OE *sēcan*⟩ **—'seek•er,** *n.*

seem [sim] *v.* **1** appear; appear to be: *He seemed a very old man.* **2** appear to oneself: *I still seem to hear the music.* **3** appear to exist: *There seems no need to wait longer.* **4** appear to be true or to be the case (that): *This, it seems, is your idea of cleaning a room.* ⟨ME < ON *sæma* < *sæmr* seemly⟩
☛ *Hom.* SEAM.
☛ *Syn.* **1. Seem,** APPEAR = give the impression or have the outward look of being something that (it) may or may not be in fact or reality. Although the two words are often used interchangeably, **seem** particularly suggests showing signs or giving other indications that point to a conclusion and serve as the basis of an opinion arrived at: *She seems to be sick. His efforts seem in vain.* **Appear** particularly suggests the way the thing looks on the surface or is seen or perceived by the observer: *He does appear pale, but to me he appears able to work.*

seem•ing ['simɪŋ] *adj., n., v.* —*adj.* apparent; that appears to be: *a seeming advantage.*
—*n.* appearance: *It was worse in its seeming than in reality.*
—*v.* ppr. of SEEM. **—'seem•ing•ly,** *adv.*

seem•ly ['simli] *adj.* **-li•er, -li•est;** *adv.* —*adj.* **1** suitable or proper: *She thought the young couple's behaviour was not seemly.* **2** having a pleasing appearance.
—*adv.* properly; becomingly; fittingly. ⟨ME < ON *sæmiligr*⟩ **—'seem•li•ness,** *n.*
☛ *Syn.* See note at FITTING.

seen [sin] *v.* pp. of SEE[1].
☛ *Hom.* SCENE, SIN[2].

seep [sip] *v., n.* —*v.* ooze; trickle; leak: *Water seeps through sand.* —*n.* **1** a place where an underground liquid, like water or oil, has oozed through the surface and formed a small pool or spring. **2** seepage. ⟨apparently < MDu. *sipen*; akin to OE *sipian* to leak⟩

seep•age ['sipɪdʒ] *n.* **1** a seeping; slow leakage. **2** moisture or liquid that seeps: *a centimetre of seepage in the basement.*

seep•er ['sipər] *n.* a pit for collecting water that seeps into cellars, etc.; sump.

seer [sir] *n.* a person who foretells future events; prophet.
☛ *Hom.* CERE, SEAR, SERE.

seer•suck•er ['sir,sʌkər] *n.* a thin, crinkled cotton, linen, etc. fabric, frequently patterned in a narrow stripe or pastel plaid. ⟨< Hind. < Persian *shir o shakkar*, literally, milk and sugar⟩

see•saw ['si,sɒ] *n., v., adj.* —*n.* **1** teeter-totter. **2** continuous motion up and down or back and forth: *the seesaw of a pitching ship.*
—*v.* **1** teeter-totter. **2** move continuously up and down or back and forth.
—*adj.* moving up and down, or back and forth, or ahead and behind: *a seesaw score.* ⟨varied reduplication of *saw*[1]⟩

seethe [sið] *v.* **seethed, seeth•ing;** *n.* —*v.* **1** bubble and foam: *Water seethed under the falls.* **2** be excited or disturbed almost to the point of open anger. **3** soak; steep. **4** *Archaic.* boil.
—*n.* **1** the act or state of seething. **2** an agitated or excited state. ⟨OE *sēothan* boil⟩
☛ *Syn. v.* **2.** See note at BOIL[1].

see–through ['si ,θru] *adj.* especially of fabric or a garment, sheer or transparent: *a see-through blouse.*

seg•ment ['sɛgmənt] *n., v.* —*n.* **1** a part cut, marked, or broken off; division; section: *Some oranges are easily pulled apart into segments.* **2** *Geometry.* **a** a part of a circle, sphere, etc. cut off by a line or plane: *A segment of a circle is an area that is bounded or cut off by a chord.* See CIRCLE for picture. **b** any of the finite sections of a divided line. **3** *Biology.* one of a series of parts having a more or less similar structure: *a segment of a tapeworm.* **4** *Computer technology.* **a** a portion of data. **b** a section of a program that is independently loadable and executable. **5** *Linguistics.* a phone, regarded as a part of a larger unit of speech.
—*v.* divide into segments. ⟨< L *segmentum* < *secare* cut⟩

seg•men•tal [sɛg'mɛntəl] *adj.* **1** composed of segments. **2** of or having to do with segments. **3** having the form of a segment of a circle. **—seg'men•tal•ly,** *adv.*

seg•men•tar•y ['sɛgmən,tɛri] *adj.* segmental.

seg•men•ta•tion [,sɛgmən'teiʃən] *n.* **1** a division into segments. **2** *Biology.* the growth and division of a cell into two, four, eight cells, and so on.

seg•re•gate *v.* ['sɛgrə,geit]; *adj.* ['sɛgrəgɪt] *or* ['sɛgrə,geit] *v.* **-gat•ed, -gat•ing;** *adj.* —*v.* **1** separate from others; set apart; isolate: *To protect the other patients, the doctor segregated the child with mumps.* **2** separate from the rest and collect in one place. **3** separate or keep apart (one racial group) from another or from the rest of society, especially in schools, separate public facilities, etc.
—*adj.* segregated. ⟨< L *segregare* < *se-* apart from + *grex, gregis* herd⟩

seg•re•gat•ed ['sɛgrə,geitɪd] *adj., v.* —*adj.* **1** separated from others; kept apart; isolated. **2** restricted to one racial, ethnic, etc. group: *a segregated neighbourhood.* **3** maintaining separate facilities on the basis of race, etc.: *segregated schools.*
—*v.* pt. and pp. of SEGREGATE.

seg•re•ga•tion [,sɛgrə'geiʃən] *n.* **1** a separation from others; setting apart; isolation. **2** the separation of one racial group from another or from the rest of society, especially in schools, theatres, etc. **3** a thing separated or set apart; an isolated part, group, etc. **4** *Genetics.* See MENDEL'S LAWS.

seg•re•ga•tion•ist [,sɛgrə'geiʃənɪst] *n., adj.* —*n.* a person who believes in the keeping apart of one race from another in housing, schools, etc.
—*adj.* of or favouring segregation.

seg•re•ga•tive ['sɛgrə,geitɪv] *adj.* **1** tending to segregate. **2** *Rare.* keeping apart from others; unsociable.

se•gue ['sɛgwei] *v.* **-gued, -gue•ing;** *n.* —*v.* **1** *Music.* go on immediately to the next part or section without a break. **2** *Music.* perform as the preceding section. **3** make a smooth and uninterrupted transition from one thing to another.
—*n.* a smooth and uninterrupted transition. ⟨< Ital., (there) follows, 3rd person sing. pres. indic. of *seguire* < L *sequī* follow⟩

seiche [seiʃ] *n.* a periodic rising and falling of the level of water in a lake, usually attributed to local changes in atmospheric pressure. ⟨< Swiss French⟩

Seid•litz powder ['sɛdlɪts] a mild laxative consisting of two powders, one tartaric acid and the other a mixture of sodium bicarbonate and Rochelle salt. These are dissolved separately, and the solutions are mixed and drunk while effervescing. ⟨after *Seidlitz*, a village in Bohemia⟩

seif [səif] *n.* a long, crescent-shaped dune stretching in the direction of the wind that caused it. ⟨< Arabic *saif* sword, from its shape⟩

sei•gneur or **seign•ior** [sɪ'njɜr]; *French,* [sɛ'njœʀ] *n.* formerly: **1** *Cdn.* in French Canada, a person granted a seigneury; landowner. **2** a feudal lord or landowner. A **grand seigneur** was a person of high rank. ⟨< F *seigneur* < OF *seignor* < *accus.* of L *senior.* See SENIOR. Doublet of SIEUR.⟩

sei•gneu•ri•al [sɪ'njɜriəl] *adj.* of or having to do with a seigneur. Also, **seigniorial.**

sei•gneur•y or **seign•ior•y** ['sɛnjəri] *n., pl.* **sei•gneur•ies** or **seign•ior•ies.** formerly: **1** *Cdn.* in French Canada, a tract of land or an estate originally granted to an individual by the King of France. **2** the power or authority of a seigneur. **3** a feudal lord's domain. **4** a group of lords. ⟨ME < OF *seignorie* < *seignor.* See SEIGNEUR.⟩

seign•ior•age ['sɛnjərɪdʒ] *n.* **1** formerly, something claimed by a sovereign or superior as a prerogative. **2** a charge for coining gold or silver.

sei•gnio•ri•al [sɪ'njɔriəl] *adj.* See SEIGNEURIAL.

seine [sein] *n., v.* **seined, sein•ing.** *–n.* a fishing net that hangs straight down in the water. A seine has floats at the upper edge and sinkers at the lower.
–v. fish or catch with a seine: *to seine for herring.* ⟨OE *segne* < L *sagena* < Gk. *sagēnē*⟩
☛ *Hom.* SANE.

sein•er ['seinər] *n.* **1** a fishing boat equipped with a seine. **2** a person who fishes using a seine.

seishe [seiʃ] *n.* See SEICHE.

seism ['saɪzəm] *n.* an earthquake. ⟨< Gk. *seismos* earthquake < *seiein* shake⟩

seis•mic ['saɪzmɪk] *or* ['səismɪk] *adj.* **1** of or having to do with shocks or tremors in the earth caused by earthquakes, explosions, etc.: *seismic waves.* **2** of or having to do with earthquakes: *seismic safety.* **3** having to do with or involved in the study of earth shocks or tremors: *seismic crews, a seismic survey.* **4** likely to undergo earthquakes: *Vancouver Island is a seismic area.* **–'seis•mi•cal•ly,** *adv.*

seis•mic•i•ty [saɪz'mɪsɪti] *or* [səis'mɪsɪti] *n.* the extent to which an area is subject to earthquake activity, taking into account frequency, intensity, duration, and distribution.

seismo– *combining form.* earthquake: *seismograph.* ⟨< Gk. *seismos*⟩

seis•mo•gram ['saɪzmə,græm] *or* ['səismə,græm] *n.* a record of an earthquake obtained by a seismograph.

seis•mo•graph ['saɪzmə,græf] *or* ['səismə,græf] *n.* an instrument for recording the direction, intensity, and duration of earthquakes. **–seis'mog•ra•pher,** *n.*

seis•mo•graph•ic [,saɪzmə'græfɪk] *or* [,səismə'græfɪk] *adj.* **1** of a seismograph. **2** of seismography.

seis•mog•ra•phy [saɪz'mɒgrəfi] *or* [səis'mɒgrəfi] *n.* **1** the art of using the seismograph in recording earthquakes. **2** the branch of seismology dealing especially with the mapping and description of earthquakes.

seis•mol•o•gist [saɪz'mɒlədʒɪst] *or* [səis'mɒlədʒɪst] *n.* a person who is trained in seismology, especially one whose work it is.

seis•mol•o•gy [saɪz'mɒlədʒi] *or* [səis'mɒlədʒi] *n.* the study of earthquakes and other movements of the earth's crust. **–,seis•mo'log•i•cal,** *adj.* **–,seis•mo'log•i•cal•ly,** *adv.*

seis•mom•e•ter [saɪz'mɒmətər] *or* [səis'mɒmətər] *n.* seismograph.

seis•mo•scope ['saɪzmə,skoup] *or* ['səismə,skoup] *n.* an instrument that records the occurrence and time of an earthquake but gives no futher information.

sei whale [sei] *or* [saɪ] a small, grey or bluish rorqual (*Balaenopterus borealis*) found in most oceans. ⟨< Norwegian *sei* coalfish; they are often seen together⟩

seize [siz] *v.* **seized, seiz•ing. 1** take hold of suddenly; clutch; grasp: *When she lost her balance, she seized his arm.* **2** grasp with the mind: *to seize an idea, the point, etc.* **3** take possession of by force: *The soldiers seized the city.* **4** take into custody; arrest. **5** take possession of or come upon suddenly: *A fever seized her.* **6** take possession of by legal authority: *The customs officer seized the tourist's shotgun.* **7** *Law.* put in possession of; possess (*usually in the passive*). **8** bind; lash; make fast: *to seize one rope to another.* **9** of a moving part of an engine or other mechanism, get stuck or jammed (*often used with* **up**): *The valve has seized up.* **seize on** or **upon, a** take hold of suddenly. **b** make use of or adopt (an idea, etc.) eagerly. ⟨ME < OF *seisir,* ult. < Gmc.⟩
☛ *Syn.* **1. Seize,** GRASP, CLUTCH[1] = take hold of something. **Seize** emphasizes taking hold suddenly and with force: *The dog seized the sausages.* **Grasp** emphasizes seizing and holding firmly with the fingers, claws, or talons closed around the object so as not to lose it: *The eagle grasped the rat.* **Clutch** suggests grasping eagerly, sometimes greedily, and tightly as in a clenched fist: *The child clutched her toy.*

sei•zin ['sizɪn] *n. Law.* a type of possession or right of possession characteristic of freehold estates.

seiz•ing ['sizɪŋ] *n., v. –n.* **1** a binding, lashing, or fastening together with several turns of small rope, cord, etc. **2** a fastening made in this way. **3** a small rope, cord, etc. used for making such fastenings.
–v. ppr. of SEIZE.

sei•zure ['siʒər] *n.* **1** the act of seizing. **2** the condition of being seized. **3** a short period of unconsciousness which occurs suddenly and is accompanied by a general, more or less violent, contraction of the muscles. **4** any sudden onset of disease: *heart seizure.*

Se•ka•ni [sɛ'kɑni] *n., pl.* **Se•ka•ni;** *adj. –n.* **1** a member of a First Nations people living in northern British Columbia. **2** the Athapaskan language spoken by these people.
–adj. of or having to do with these people, their language or culture.

se•la•chi•an [sɪ'leikiən] *n., adj. –n.* any member of the group Selachii, comprising sharks, skates, and rays.
–adj. belonging to the Selachii. ⟨< Gk. *selachos* shark⟩

se•lah ['silə] *n.* a Hebrew word occurring frequently at the end of a verse in the Psalms and Habakkuk in the Bible, thought to be a direction to musicians.

sel•dom ['sɛldəm] *adv.* rarely; not often: *She is seldom ill.* ⟨OE *seldum*⟩

se•lect [sɪ'lɛkt] *v., adj. –v.* choose; pick out: *Select the book you want.*
–adj. **1** picked as best; chosen specially: *A few select officials were admitted to the conference.* **2** choice; superior: *That store carries a select line of merchandise.* **3** careful in choosing; particular as to friends, company, etc.: *He belongs to a very select club.* ⟨< L *selectus,* pp. of *seligere* < *se-* apart + *legere* choose⟩ **–se'lect•a•ble,** *adj.* **–se'lect•ly,** *adv.* **–se'lect•ness,** *n.*

se•lec•tion [sɪ'lɛkʃən] *n.* **1** the act or process of selecting or the state of being selected: *the selection of a coat.* **2** one or more persons or things that have been selected: *My dessert selection was an apple strudel.* **3** a range of things from which one may select: *The shop offered a very good selection of children's books.* **4** *Biology.* the natural or artificial process by which certain animals or plants survive and are perpetuated while others are not.

se•lec•tive [sɪ'lɛktɪv] *adj.* **1** selecting, especially carefully; having the power to select. **2** having to do with selection. **3** *Electronics.* responding to oscillations of a certain frequency only. When a selective radio is tuned to one station, those on other wavelengths are excluded. **–se'lec•tive•ly,** *adv.* **–se'lec•tive•ness,** *n.*

se•lec•tiv•i•ty [sɪlɛk'tɪvɪti] *or* [,silɛk'tɪvɪti] *n.* **1** the quality or degree of being selective. **2** *Electronics.* the property of a circuit, instrument, etc. by virtue of which it responds to electric oscillations of a particular frequency; especially, the ability of a radio receiving set to receive certain frequencies or waves to the exclusion of others.

se•lec•tor [sɪ'lɛktər] *n.* **1** a person who selects. **2** a mechanical or electrical device that selects.

Se•le•ne [sɪ'lini] *n. Greek mythology.* the goddess of the moon. ⟨< Gk. *Selene* the moon⟩

se•le•nic acid [sɪ'linɪk] *or* [sɪ'lɛnɪk] *Chemistry.* a colourless, water-soluble crystalline acid which is strong, corrosive and similar to sulphuric acid in action. *Formula:* H_2SeO_4

sel•e•nite ['sɛlə,nəit] *or* [sə'linəit] *n.* a variety of gypsum, found in transparent crystals and foliated masses. ⟨< L < Gk. *selēnitēs (lithos)* (stone) of the moon < *selēnē* moon; its brightness was supposed to vary with the moon⟩

se•le•ni•um [sɪ'liniəm] *n. Chemistry.* a non-metallic chemical element resembling sulphur in chemical properties. Because its electrical resistance varies with the amount of light, selenium is used in photo-electric cells. *Symbol:* Se; *at.no.* 34; *at.mass* 78.96. ⟨< NL < Gk. *selēnē* moon⟩

sel•e•nog•ra•phy [ˌsɛlə'nɒgrəfi] *n.* the branch of astronomy dealing with the study of the moon's surface.

sel•e•nol•o•gy [ˌsɛlə'nɒlədʒi] *n.* the branch of astronomy dealing with the moon in general, especially the nature and origin of its physical features.

se•le•nous acid [sə'linəs] *or* ['sɛlənəs] *Chemistry.* a poisonous, water-soluble crystalline powder used as a reagent. *Formula*: H_2SeO_3

self [sɛlf] *n., pl.* **selves;** *adj., pron., pl.* **selves.** *–n.* **1** one's own person: *his very self.* **2** one's own welfare, interests, etc.: *A selfish person puts self first.* **3** the nature, character, etc. of a person or thing: *She does not seem like her former self.*
–adj. being the same throughout; all of one kind, quality, colour, material, etc.
–pron. Informal. myself; himself; herself; yourself: *a cheque made payable to self.* ⟨OE⟩
☛ *Usage.* **Self** as a suffix forms the reflexive and intensive pronouns: **myself, yourself, himself, herself, itself, oneself, ourselves, yourselves, themselves.** These are used as reflexive objects (*I couldn't help myself*) or for emphasis (*I can do that myself*).

self– *prefix.* **1** of or over oneself, etc.: *self-conscious, self-control.* **2** by or in oneself or itself, etc.: *self-inflicted, self-evident.* **3** to or for oneself, etc.: *self-addressed, self-respect.* **4** automatic; automatically: *self-starter, self-closing.* **5** of the same fabric as the main part: *self-collared.* ⟨< *self*⟩

self–a•base•ment [ˌsɛlf ə'beismənt] *n.* a humbling or humiliation of oneself.

self–ab•hor•rence [ˌsɛlf əb'hɔrəns] *n.* loathing of or disgust at oneself.

self–ab•ne•ga•tion ['sɛlf ˌæbnə'geiʃən] *n.* self-denial.

self–ab•sorp•tion [ˌsɛlf əb'zɔrpʃən] *or* [əb'sɔrpʃən] *n.* **1** absorption in one's own thoughts, affairs, etc. **2** *Physics.* absorption of radiation by the radiating substance. **–ˌself-ab'sorbed,** *adj.*

self–ab•use [ˌsɛlf ə'bjus] *n.* **1** blame or reproach of oneself. **2** misuse of one's talents or skills. **3** abuse of one's physical condition. **4** masturbation.

self–act•ing [ˌsɛlf 'æktɪŋ] *adj.* working by itself: *a self-acting machine.*

self–ad•dressed [ˌsɛlf ə'drɛst] *adj.* addressed to oneself: *a self-addressed envelope.*

self–a•nal•y•sis [ˌsɛlf ə'næləsɪs] *n.* the use of psychoanalytic techniques to analyse one's own personality without the help of a trained practitioner.

self–as•ser•tion [ˌsɛlf ə'sɜrʃən] *n.* an insistence on the legitimacy of one's desires, opinions, claims, etc.

self–as•ser•tive [ˌsɛlf ə'sɜrtɪv] *adj.* insisting on the legitimacy of one's own desires, claims, opinions, etc.; asking due recognition for oneself. **–ˌself-as'ser•tive•ly,** *adv.*

self–as•sur•ance [ˌsɛlf ə'ʃʊrəns] *n.* self-confidence.

self–as•sured [ˌsɛlf ə'ʃʊrd] *adj.* self-confident; sure of oneself. **–ˌself-as'sur•ed•ness** [ˌsɛlf ə'ʃʊrɪdnɪs], *n.*

self–cen•tred [ˌsɛlf 'sɛntərd] *adj.* **1** occupied with one's own interests and affairs. **2** selfish. **3** being a fixed point around which other things move. **–ˌself-'cen•tred•ly,** *adv.* **–ˌself-'cen•tred•ness,** *n.*

self–col•oured or **self–col•ored** [ˌsɛlf 'kʌlərd] *adj.* **1** of one uniform colour. **2** of the natural colour of an object.

self–com•mand [ˌsɛlf kə'mænd] *n.* control of oneself.

self–com•mun•ion [ˌsɛlf kə'mjunjən] *n.* communion with oneself.

self–com•pla•cent [ˌsɛlf kəm'pleisənt] *adj.* pleased with oneself; self-satisfied. **–ˌself-com'pla•cence** or **ˌself-com'pla•cen•cy,** *n.* **–ˌself-com'pla•cent•ly,** *adv.*

self–com•posed [ˌsɛlf kəm'pouzd] *adj.* being composed; showing composure; calm.

self–con•ceit [ˌsɛlf kən'sit] *n.* vanity; too much pride in oneself or one's ability; an inflated opinion of one's own worth.

self–con•cept [ˌsɛlf 'kɒnsɛpt] *n.* one's idea of one's own basic character and nature.

self–con•fessed [ˌsɛlf kən'fɛst] *adj.* being something or having some characteristic by one's own admission: *a self-confessed spy, a self-confessed glutton.*

self–con•fi•dence [ˌsɛlf 'kɒnfədəns] *n.* belief in one's own ability, power, judgment, etc.; confidence in oneself.

self–con•fi•dent [ˌsɛlf 'kɒnfədənt] *adj.* believing in one's own ability, power, judgment, etc. **–ˌself-'con•fi•dent•ly,** *adv.*

self–con•scious [ˌsɛlf 'kɒnʃəs] *adj.* **1** conscious of how one is appearing to others; embarrassed, especially by the presence of other people and their attitude toward one; shy. **2** conscious of one's own existence, feelings, thoughts, etc.: *Human beings are self-conscious.* **–ˌself-'con•scious•ly,** *adv.* **–ˌself-'con•scious•ness,** *n.*

self–con•se•quence [ˌsɛlf 'kɒnsəkwəns] *n.* a sense of one's own importance.

self–con•sist•ent [ˌsɛlf kən'sɪstənt] *adj.* consistent with oneself or itself; having its parts or elements in agreement. **–ˌself-con'sist•ent•ly,** *adv.*

self–con•tained [ˌsɛlf kən'teind] *adj.* **1** saying little; reserved; self-controlled. **2** containing in oneself or itself all that is necessary; independent of what is external. **3** having all its working parts contained in one case, cover, or framework: *A watch is self-contained.* **4** of an apartment, etc., having all facilities (bathroom, kitchen, etc.) within itself, and having a private entrance.

self–con•tent [ˌsɛlf kən'tɛnt] *n.* happiness with one's lot and performance in life; complacency.

self–con•tent•ed [ˌsɛlf kən'tɛntɪd] *adj.* complacent; self-satisfied.

self–con•tra•dic•tion ['sɛlf ˌkɒntrə'dɪkʃən] *n.* **1** a contradiction of oneself or itself. **2** a statement containing elements that are contradictory.

self–con•tra•dic•to•ry ['sɛlf ˌkɒntrə'dɪktəri] *adj.* contradicting oneself or itself. **–'self-ˌcon•tra'dic•to•ri•ly,** *adv.*

self–con•trol [ˌsɛlf kən'troul] *n.* the ability to control one's own actions, feelings, etc. **–ˌself-con'trolled,** *adj.*

self–crit•i•cism [ˌsɛlf 'krɪtəˌsɪzəm] *n.* criticism of oneself.

self–de•cep•tion [ˌsɛlf dɪ'sɛpʃən] *n.* the act or an instance of deceiving oneself as to one's true motives, feelings, etc. Also, **self-deceit.**

self–de•cep•tive [ˌsɛlf dɪ'sɛptɪv] *adj.* deceiving oneself, especially as to one's true feelings. **–ˌself-de'cep•tive•ly,** *adv.*

self–de•feat•ing [ˌsɛlf dɪ'fitɪŋ] *adj.* thwarting its or one's own purposes or intentions because of built-in inconsistencies.

self–de•fence [ˌsɛlf dɪ'fɛns] *n.* **1** defence of one's own person, property, reputation, etc. **2** any physical skill by which one can defend one's own person, as boxing or any of the martial arts. **3** *Law.* the right to defend oneself and one's property against violence. Also, **self-defense.**

self–de•ni•al [ˌsɛlf dɪ'naɪəl] *n.* a sacrifice of one's own desires and interests; the act of going without things one wants.

self–de•ny•ing [ˌsɛlf dɪ'naɪɪŋ] *adj.* unselfish; sacrificing one's own wishes and interests.

self–de•struct [ˌsɛlf dɪ'strʌkt] *v. Informal.* of a mechanism, machine, etc., automatically destroy itself: *The tape-recorder will self-destruct if it is tampered with.*

self–de•struct•ing [ˌsɛlf dɪ'strʌktɪŋ] *adj., v. –adj.* designed to destroy itself by disintegrating automatically on a pre-set signal. *–v.* ppr. of SELF-DESTRUCT.

self–de•struc•tion [ˌsɛlf dɪ'strʌkʃən] *n.* **1** destruction or ruin of oneself or itself. **2** suicide.

self–de•ter•mi•na•tion [ˌsɛlf dɪˌtɜrmə'neiʃən] *n.* **1** direction from within only, without influence or force from without. **2** the deciding by the people of a nation what form of government they are to have, without reference to the wishes of any other nation. **–ˌself-de'ter•mined,** *adj.* **–ˌself-de'ter•min•ing,** *adj.*

self–de•vo•tion [ˌsɛlf dɪ'vouʃən] *n.* self-sacrifice; devotion of oneself to others or to a cause.

self–dis•ci•pline [ˌsɛlf 'dɪsəplɪn] *n.* the ability to control and train oneself; the act of so doing.

self–dis•cov•er•y [ˌsɛlf dɪ'skʌvəri] *n.* the act or process of discovering one's own real nature, character, etc.; the achievement of self-knowledge.

self–dump•er [ˌsɛlf 'dʌmpər] *n. Cdn. Logging.* a huge barge that has the mechanism to dump its load of logs automatically into the water when it arrives at its destination.

self–ed•u•cat•ed [ˌsɛlf 'ɛdʒəˌkeitɪd] *adj.* self-taught; educated by one's own efforts. **–ˌself-ˌed•u'ca•tion,** *n.*

self–ef•face•ment [ˌsɛlf ɪ'feismənt] *n.* the act or habit of modestly keeping oneself in the background. **–ˌself-ef'fac•ing,** *adj.*

self–em•ployed [ˌsɛlf əm'plɔɪd] *adj.* not employed by others;

working for oneself: *Doctors, lawyers, and farmers are usually self-employed.* **—,self-em'ploy•ment,** *n.*

self–es•teem [,sɛlf ə'stim] *n.* a good opinion of oneself; self-respect.

self–ev•i•dent [,sɛlf 'ɛvədənt] *adj.* evident by itself; needing no proof. **—,self-'ev•i•dent•ly,** *adv.*

self–ex•am•i•na•tion [,sɛlf əg,zæmə'neiʃən] *n.* examination into one's own state, conduct, motives, etc.

self–ex•ist•ent [,sɛlf əg'zɪstənt] *adj.* existing independently of any other cause; having an independent existence. **—,self-ex'is•tence,** *n.*

self–ex•plan•a•to•ry [,sɛlf ək'splænə,tɔri] *adj.* explaining itself; that needs no explanation; obvious.

self–ex•pres•sion [,sɛlf ək'sprɛʃən] *n.* an expression of one's personality, especially through music, writing, painting, etc.

self–fer•til•i•za•tion [,sɛlf ,fɜrtələ'zeiʃən] *or* [-,fɜrtəlaɪ'zeiʃən] *n.* **1** *Botany.* fertilization of the ovum of a plant by pollen from a gamete of the same flower. **2** *Zoology.* in hermaphroditic animals, fertilization of the ovum by sperm from the same individual.

self–fill•ing [,sɛlf 'fɪlɪŋ] *adj.* that can fill itself.

self–ful•fil•ling [,sɛlf fʊl'fɪlɪŋ] *adj.* **1** causing self-fulfilment. **2** coming about or happening as a result of having been expected or prophesied.

self–ful•fil•ment or **–ful•fill•ment** [,sɛlf fʊl'fɪlmənt] *n.* the act or process of fulfilling one's ambitions, desires, etc. through one's own efforts.

self–gov•erned [,sɛlf 'gʌvərnd] *adj.* having self-government.

self–gov•ern•ing [,sɛlf 'gʌvərnɪŋ] *adj.* that governs itself.

self–gov•ern•ment [,sɛlf 'gʌvərmənt] *or* ['gʌvərnmənt] *n.* **1** government of a group by its own members: *self-government through elected representatives.* **2** self-control.

self–heal ['sɛlf ,hil] *n.* a low-growing European herb (*Prunella vulgaris*) of the mint family, having blue or purple flowers, and formerly believed to possess healing powers. Also, **selfheal.**

self–help [,sɛlf 'hɛlp] *n.* the act of providing for or helping oneself; getting along without assistance from others.

self–help group a mutual aid organization of people sharing a similar problem.

self•hood ['sɛlf,hʊd] *n.* **1** personality; individuality; the state of being an individual. **2** selfishness; self-centredness.

self–im•age [,sɛlf 'ɪmədʒ] *n.* one's opinion or general idea of oneself, especially in relation to others.

self–im•por•tance [,sɛlf ɪm'pɔrtəns] *n.* a having or showing too high an opinion of one's own importance; conceit; behaviour showing conceit.

self–im•por•tant [,sɛlf ɪm'pɔrtənt] *adj.* having or showing too high an opinion of one's own importance; conceited. **—,self-im'por•tant•ly,** *adv.*

self–im•posed [,sɛlf ɪm'pouzd] *adj.* of an action or condition, imposed on oneself by oneself.

self–im•prove•ment [,sɛlf ɪm'pruvmənt] *n.* the improvement of one's character, mind, etc. by one's own efforts.

self–in•duced [,sɛlf ɪn'djust] *or* [ɪn'dust] *adj.* **1** induced by itself; induced by oneself. **2** *Electricity.* produced by self-induction.

self–in•duc•tion [,sɛlf ɪn'dʌkʃən] *n.* *Electricity.* the inducing of electromotive force in a circuit by a varying current in that circuit.

self–in•dul•gence [,sɛlf ɪn'dʌldʒəns] *n.* the gratification of one's own desires, passions, etc. with too little regard for the welfare of others.

self–in•dul•gent [,sɛlf ɪn'dʌldʒənt] *adj.* characterized by self-indulgence. **—,self-in'dul•gent•ly,** *adv.*

self–in•flict•ed [,sɛlf ɪn'flɪktɪd] *adj.* inflicted on oneself by oneself.

self–in•ter•est [,sɛlf 'ɪntrɪst] *n.* **1** an interest in one's own welfare with too little care for the welfare of others; selfishness. **2** personal advantage.

self•ish ['sɛlfɪʃ] *adj.* **1** caring too much for oneself; caring too little for others: *A selfish person puts his or her own interests first.* **2** showing care solely or chiefly for oneself: *selfish motives.* **—'self•ish•ly,** *adv.* **—'self•ish•ness,** *n.*

self–knowl•edge [,sɛlf 'nɒlɪdʒ] *n.* knowledge of one's own character, ability, etc.

self•less ['sɛlflɪs] *adj.* having no regard or thought for self; unselfish. **—'self•less•ly,** *adv.* **—'self•less•ness,** *n.*

self–love ['sɛlf 'lʌv] *n.* **1** love of oneself; selfishness; conceit. **2** proper regard for oneself.

self–made ['sɛlf 'meid] *adj.* **1** made by oneself. **2** successful through one's own efforts: *A self-made woman is one who has succeeded in business, etc., without the usual formal training or education.*

self–mov•ing [,sɛlf 'muvɪŋ] *adj.* that can move by itself.

self–o•pin•ion•at•ed [,sɛlf ə'pɪnjə,neitɪd] *adj.* obstinately holding to one's own views or opinions.

self–or•dained [,sɛlf ɔr'deind] *adj.* SELF-FULFILLING (def. 2).

self–per•pet•u•at•ing [,sɛlf pər'pɛtʃu,eitɪŋ] *adj.* that can be continued or renewed indefinitely without outside action or influence: *a self-perpetuating oligarchy.*

self–pit•y [,sɛlf 'pɪti] *n.* pity for oneself and one's problems.

self–pol•li•na•tion [,sɛlf ,pɒlə'neiʃən] *n.* the transfer of pollen from a stamen to a pistil of the same flower or to the pistil of a different flower on the same plant.

self–pos•sessed [,sɛlf pə'zɛst] *adj.* having or showing control of one's feelings and acts; not excited, embarrassed, or confused; calm.

self–pos•ses•sion [,sɛlf pə'zɛʃən] *n.* the control of one's feelings and actions; composure; calmness.

self–praise [,sɛlf 'preiz] *n.* praise of oneself; boasting.

self–pres•er•va•tion [,sɛlf ,prɛzər'veiʃən] *n.* **1** the preservation of oneself from harm or destruction. **2** this is a basic instinct of all animal life forms.

self–pro•nounc•ing [,sɛlf prə'naʊnsɪŋ] *adj.* of dictionaries, etc. showing pronunciation by having diacritics or accents added to the spelling rather than using a phonemic transcription.

self–pro•pelled [,sɛlf prə'pɛld] *adj.* propelled by an engine, motor, etc., within itself: *a self-propelled missile.*

self–re•cord•ing [,sɛlf rɪ'kɔrdɪŋ] *adj.* that makes a record of its own operations; recording automatically.

self–re•gard [,sɛlf rɪ'gɑrd] *n.* **1** concern or consideration for oneself and one's own interests. **2** SELF-RESPECT.

self–reg•is•ter•ing [,sɛlf 'rɛdʒɪstərɪŋ] *adj.* registering automatically.

self–reg•u•lat•ing [,sɛlf 'rɛgjə,leitɪŋ] *adj.* regulating oneself or itself. **—,self-,reg•u'la•tion,** *n.*

self–re•li•ance [,sɛlf rɪ'laɪəns] *n.* a reliance on one's own acts, abilities, etc. **—,self-re'li•ant,** *adj.* **—,self-re'li•ant•ly,** *adv.*

self–re•proach [,sɛlf rɪ'proutʃ] *n.* blame directed at oneself by one's own conscience. **—,self-re'proach•ful,** *adj.*

self–re•spect [,sɛlf rɪ'spɛkt] *n.* respect for oneself; proper pride.

self–re•spect•ing [,sɛlf rɪ'spɛktɪŋ] *adj.* having self-respect; properly proud.

self–re•straint [,sɛlf rɪ'streint] *n.* self-control. **—,self-re'strained,** *adj.*

self–re•veal•ing [,sɛlf rɪ'vilɪŋ] *adj.* expressing or disclosing one's most private thoughts and feelings, usually inadvertently.

self–right•eous [,sɛlf 'raɪtʃəs] *adj.* thinking that one is more moral than others; thinking that one is very good and pleasing to God. **—,self-'right•eous•ly,** *adv.* **—,self-'right•eous•ness,** *n.*

self–ris•ing flour [,sɛlf 'raɪzɪŋ] flour with salt and leavening added before packaging.

self–rule [,sɛlf 'rul] *n.* SELF-GOVERNMENT.

self–sac•ri•fice [,sɛlf 'sækrə,fəis] *n.* the sacrifice of one's own interests and desires for one's duty, another's welfare, etc.

self–sac•ri•fic•ing [,sɛlf 'sækrə,fəisɪŋ] *adj.* unselfish; giving up things for someone else.

self•same ['sɛlf,seim] *adj.* the very same: *We study the selfsame books that you do.* ⟨< *self*, adj. + *same*⟩

self–sat•is•fac•tion ['sɛlf ,sætɪs'fækʃən] *n.* satisfaction with oneself; complacence.

self–sat•is•fied [,sɛlf 'sætɪs,faɪd] *adj.* pleased with oneself; complacent.

self–seek•er ['sɛlf 'sikər] *n.* a person who seeks his or her own interests too much.

self–seek•ing [,sɛlf 'sikɪŋ] *adj., n.* *—adj.* selfish. *—n.* selfishness.

self–serve ['sɛlf 'sɜrv] *adj.* SELF-SERVICE.

self–serv•ice [ˌsɛlf 'sɜrvɪs] *n., adj.* *—n.* the serving of oneself in a restaurant, store, gas station, etc.
—adj. designed to be used by the customer without the aid of an attendant, operator, etc.

self–serving [ˌsɛlf 'sɜrvɪŋ] *adj.* **1** preoccupied with one's own interests, especially if selfish or self-centred. **2** serving to further one's own interests.

self–start•er [ˌsɛlf 'stɑrtər] *n.* **1** an electric motor or other device used to start an engine automatically. **2** *Informal.* a person who has initiative: *Wanted: a proven self-starter for unusual sales opportunities.*

self–styled ['sɛlf 'staɪld] *adj.* so called by oneself: *a self-styled leader whom no one follows.*

self–suf•fi•cien•cy [ˌsɛlf sə'fɪʃənsi] *n.* **1** the ability to supply one's own needs. **2** *Archaic.* conceit; self-assurance.

self–suf•fi•cient [ˌsɛlf sə'fɪʃənt] *adj.* **1** asking and needing no help; independent. **2** *Archaic.* having too much confidence in one's own resources, powers, etc.; conceited.
—ˌself-suf'fi•cient•ly, *adv.*

self–suf•fic•ing [ˌsɛlf sə'fəisɪŋ] *adj.* sufficing in or for oneself or itself; self-sufficient.

self–sup•port [ˌsɛlf sə'pɔrt] *n.* unaided support of oneself.

self–sup•port•ing [ˌsɛlf sə'pɔrtɪŋ] *adj.* earning one's expenses; getting along without help.

self–sus•tain•ing [ˌsɛlf sə'steinɪŋ] *adj.* **1** self-supporting. **2** capable of going on once started; self-perpetuating.

self–taught ['sɛlf 'tɒt] *adj.* taught by oneself without aid from others.

self–will [ˌsɛlf 'wɪl] *n.* insistence on having one's own way.

self–willed [ˌsɛlf 'wɪld] *adj.* insisting on having one's own way; objecting to doing what others ask or command.

self–wind•ing [ˌsɛlf 'waɪndɪŋ] *adj.* that is wound automatically.

sell [sɛl] *v.* **sold, sell•ing;** *n.* *—v.* **1** exchange for money or other payment: *sell a house.* **2** deal in; keep for sale: *The butcher sells meat.* **3** do the work of a salesperson. **4** be on sale; be sold: *This model sells for $95.* **5** give up; betray: *The traitor sold his country for money.* **6** be or cause to be accepted, approved, or adopted: *to sell an idea to the public. That plan will never sell.* **7** *Slang.* cheat; trick; hoax.
sell off, dispose of by sale.
sell on, a inspire with the desire to buy or possess something: *She has sold me on a convertible as opposed to a sedan.*
b *Informal.* show or convince of the value, truth, etc. of something: *For a time he was sold on folk music.*
sell out, a sell all that one has of; get rid of by selling.
b *Informal.* betray, especially by a secret bargain. **c** compromise one's integrity: *to sell out to political pressure.*
sell short, a sell (securities) that one does not yet own.
b undervalue; underestimate.
sell up, *Brit.* sell off.
—n. **1** *Slang.* a cheat; trick; hoax. **2** the act or a method of selling: *a soft sell.* ⟨OE *sellan*⟩
☛ *Hom.* CELL.

sell•er ['sɛlər] *n.* **1** a person who sells. **2** a thing considered with reference to its sale: *This book is a bestseller.*
☛ *Hom.* CELLAR.

seller's market an economic situation in which the seller has the advantage because goods are scarce and prices tend to be high. Compare BUYER'S MARKET.

sell–out ['sɛl ˌʌut] *n.* **1** *Informal.* a selling out of something or someone. **2** *Informal.* a performance of a play, sports event, etc. for which all seats are sold.

selt•zer ['sɛltsər] *n.* **1** a bubbling mineral water containing salt, sodium, calcium, and magnesium carbonates. **2** a flavoured drink of similar composition. ⟨< G *Selterser* < *Selters,* Germany, where it is found⟩

sel•vage or **sel•vedge** ['sɛlvɪdʒ] *n.* **1** the edge of a fabric finished off to prevent ravelling. **2** the border or edge of cloth, paper, etc., especially if surplus. **3** the margin of plain paper around a sheet of stamps. ⟨< *self* + *edge;* because it serves itself as an edge⟩

selves [sɛlvz] *n.* pl. of SELF: *She had two selves—a friendly self and a shy self.*

Sem. 1 Seminary. **2** Semitic.

se•man•tic [sə'mæntɪk] *adj.* **1** having to do with meaning. **2** having to do with semantics. **—se'man•ti•cal•ly,** *adv.*

se•man•ti•cist [sə'mæntəˌsɪst] *n.* a person trained in semantics, especially one whose work it is.

se•man•tics [sə'mæntɪks] *n.* (*used with a singular verb*) **1** the scientific study of the meanings, and the development of meanings, of words. **2** the branch of semiotics dealing with the relation between signs and what they denote. **3** the relation between words, signs, or symbols and their connotations, or the exploitation of this to mislead. ⟨< LL *semanticus* < Gk. *sēmantikos* having meaning, ult. < *sēma* sign⟩

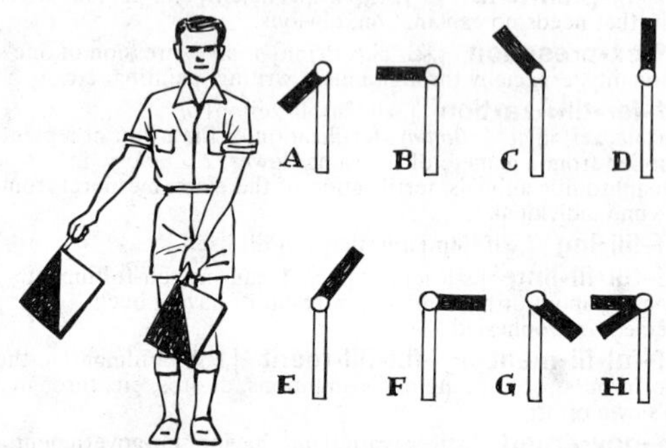

Semaphore: the arm positions for the first eight letters of the alphabet are shown at right. The man at left is giving the signal for the letter A.

sem•a•phore ['sɛməˌfɔr] *n., v.* **-phored, -phor•ing.** *—n.* **1** an apparatus for signalling; upright post or structure with movable arms, an arrangement of lanterns, flags, etc. used in railway signalling. **2** a system of signals for sending messages by using different positions of the arms or flags, or by using other mechanical devices: *Many Scouts and Guides learn semaphore.*
—v. signal by semaphore. ⟨< Gk. *sēma* signal + *-phoros* carrying⟩

se•ma•si•ol•o•gy [sɪˌmeizɪ'ɒlədʒi] *n.* SEMANTICS (defs. 1, 2).

sem•blance ['sɛmbləns] *n.* **1** the outward appearance: *Her story had the semblance of truth, but was really false.* **2** likeness: *These clouds have the semblance of a huge head.* ⟨ME < OF *semblance* < *sembler* seem, ult. < L *similis* similar⟩

sem•eme ['simim] *or* ['sɛmim] *n. Linguistics.* **1** the meaning of a morpheme. **2** a basic unit of meaning. ⟨coined in 1933 by Leonard Bloomfield (1887-1949), American linguist < Gk. *sema* sign⟩

se•men ['simən] *n.* the thick, whitish fluid produced by the reproductive organs of male mammals and containing the male reproductive cells, or sperm. ⟨< L *semen* seed⟩
☛ *Hom.* SEAMAN.

se•mes•ter [sə'mɛstər] *n.* **1** a half of a school year. **2** a period of six months. **3** loosely, one of any number of school terms. ⟨< G < L *semestris* semi-annual, ult. < *sex* six + *mensis* month⟩

se•mi ['sɛmi] *n.* **1** semitrailer. **2** Usually, **semis,** *pl.* the semifinal round of a competition.

semi– *prefix.* **1** half: *semicircle* = *half circle.* **2** partly; incompletely: *semicivilized* = *partly civilized.* **3** twice in the specified time period: *semi-annually* = *every half year, or twice a year.* ⟨< L⟩
☛ *Usage.* **Semi-** usually is hyphenated before root words beginning with a vowel and before proper nouns and proper adjectives: *semi-annual, semi-invalid, semi-Christian.* In other cases a hyphen is optional, though one's own usage should be consistent.
☛ *Pronun.* See note at ANTI-.

sem•i–an•nu•al [ˌsɛmi 'ænjuəl] *adj., n.* *—adj.* **1** occurring every half year. **2** lasting a half year: *a semi-annual plant.*
—n. something that occurs or appears twice a year.

sem•i–an•nu•al•ly [ˌsɛmi 'ænjuəli] *adv.* twice a year.

sem•i–ar•id [ˌsɛmi 'ærɪd] *or* ['ɛrɪd] *adj.* having very little rainfall.

sem•i–au•to•mat•ic [ˌsɛmi ˌɒtə'mætɪk] *n., adj.* *—n.* a semi-automatic firearm.
—adj. **1** of machinery, partly automatic and partly run by hand. **2** of a firearm, using the ejective power of the shell to automatically reload the gun, but requiring a trigger pull to fire.

sem•i–au•ton•o•mous [ˌsɛmi ɒ'tɒnəməs] *adj.* self-governing with regard to internal affairs, but under the guidance of a controlling government, organization, etc. for external relations.

sem•i•breve ['sɛmiˌbriv] *n. Brit. Music.* the longest note in common use; a whole note.

sem•i•cir•cle ['sɛmiˌsɜrkəl] *n.* half a circle: *We sat in a semicircle around the fire.*

sem•i•cir•cu•lar [ˌsɛmi'sɜrkjələr] *adj.* having the form of half a circle.

semicircular canal *Anatomy.* any of three curved, tubelike canals in the inner part of the ear that help us keep our balance.

sem•i•civ•i•lized [ˌsɛmi'sɪvəˌlaɪzd] *adj.* partly civilized.

sem•i•co•lon ['sɛmiˌkoulən] *n.* a mark of punctuation (;) that shows a separation less marked than that shown by a period but more so than that shown by a comma.

sem•i•con•duct•or [ˌsɛmikən'dʌktər] *n. Electricity.* any of a group of solids, such as silicon and germanium, that are poor conductors of electricity at low temperatures, but good conductors at high temperatures.

sem•i•con•scious [ˌsɛmi'kɒnʃəs] *adj.* half-conscious; not fully conscious. **—ˌsem•i'con•scious•ly,** *adj.* **—ˌsem•i'con•scious•ness,** *n.*

sem•i•dai•ly [ˌsɛmi'deili] *adv.* twice a day.

sem•i•dark•ness [ˌsɛmi'dɑrknəs] *n.* partial darkness.

sem•i•de•tached [ˌsɛmidɪ'tætʃt] *adj.* partly detached, used especially of either of two houses joined by a common wall but separated from other buildings.

sem•i•de•vel•oped [ˌsɛmidɪ'vɛləpt] *adj.* not fully developed.

sem•i•di•am•e•ter [ˌsɛmidaɪ'æmətər] *n.* **1** half a diameter; a radius. **2** *Astronomy.* half the diameter of a celestial body with a visible disk; its radius.

sem•i•di•ur•nal [ˌsɛmidaɪ'ɜrnəl] *adj.* **1** occurring every 12 hours or twice each day. **2** lasting or taking half a day.

sem•i•di•vine [ˌsɛmidə'vaɪn] *adj.* partly divine.

sem•i•fi•nal or **sem•i–fi•nal** [ˌsɛmi'faɪnəl] *or* ['sɛmiˌfaɪnəl] *n., adj. —n.* one of the two rounds, matches, etc. that settles who will play in the final one, which follows. *—adj.* designating or having to do with such a round, match, game, etc.: *a semifinal score.*

semi•fi•nal•ist [ˌsɛmi'faɪnəlɪst] *n.* one who has qualified for the semifinal round of a competition.

sem•i•flu•id [ˌsɛmi'fluɪd] *adj., n. —adj.* imperfectly fluid; extremely viscous.
—n. a substance neither solid nor liquid; one that flows but is very thick: *A soft-boiled egg yolk is a semifluid.*

sem•i•for•mal [ˌsɛmi'fɔrməl] *adj., n. —adj.* designed for or designating a somewhat formal social occasion: *a semiformal gown, a semiformal dinner party.*
—n. a semiformal gown.

sem•i•liquid [ˌsɛmi'lɪkwɪd] *adj. or n.* semifluid.

sem•i•lu•nar [ˌsɛmi'lunər] *adj.* shaped like a half moon.

sem•i•month•ly [ˌsɛmi'mʌnθli] *adj., adv., n., pl.* **-lies.** *—adj.* occurring or appearing twice a month.
—adv. twice a month.
—n. **1** something that occurs or appears twice a month. **2** a magazine or paper published twice a month.

sem•i•nal ['sɛmənəl] *adj.* **1** of or having to do with semen or seed. **2** containing semen or seed. **3** having to do with reproduction. **4** like seed; having the possibility of future development: *seminal ideas.* ⟨ME < L *seminalis* < *semen* seed⟩

sem•i•nar ['sɛməˌnɑr] *n.* **1** a group of college or university students doing research under direction. **2** a course of study or work for such a group. **3** a meeting of such a group. **4** a specialized conference or short, intensive course of study. ⟨< G < L *seminarium* plant nursery, hotbed < *semen* seed. Doublet of SEMINARY.⟩

sem•i•nar•i•an [ˌsɛmə'nɛriən] *n.* a student at a seminary, especially one training to be a member of the clergy.

sem•i•nar•y ['sɛməˌnɛri] *n., pl.* **-nar•ies. 1** a school or college for training students to be priests, ministers, rabbis, etc. **2** a school, especially one beyond high school. **3** an academy or boarding school, especially one for young women. **4** a place for instruction, training, or development. ⟨< L *seminarium.* Doublet of SEMINAR.⟩

sem•i•na•tion [ˌsɛmə'neiʃən] *n.* sowing; propagation; dissemination.

sem•i•nif•er•ous [ˌsɛmə'nɪfərəs] *adj.* **1** bearing or producing seed. **2** conveying or containing semen.

sem•i•niv•or•ous [ˌsɛmə'nɪvərəs] *adj.* seed-eating, as some birds.

Sem•i•nole ['sɛməˌnoul] *n.* **1** a member of a Native American people now living in Florida and Oklahoma. **2** the Creek language of these people.

sem•i•of•fi•cial [ˌsɛmiə'fɪʃəl] *adj.* partly official; having some degree of authority.

se•mi•ol•o•gy [ˌsimi'ɒlədʒi] *or* [ˌsɛmi'ɒlədʒi] *n.* the study of signs used as signals, as in semaphore and in traffic control.

se•mi•ot•ics [ˌsimi'ɒtɪks] *or* [ˌsɛmɪ'ɒtɪks] *n.* (*used with a singular verb*) **1** semantics. **2** the study of signs in a linguistic system, their meaning, their relationships, and their effect on behaviour.

sem•i–o•vip•ar•ous [ˌsɛmi ou'vɪpərəs] *adj.* bearing live young in a state of incomplete development, as the marsupials.

sem•i•per•me•a•ble [ˌsɛmi'pɜrmiəbəl] *adj.* partly permeable; able to be penetrated or passed through by some substances but not by others.

sem•i•pre•cious [ˌsɛmi'prɛʃəs] *adj.* of gemstones, having less commercial value than precious stones. Amethysts and garnets are semiprecious stones; diamonds and rubies are precious stones.

sem•i–pri•vate [ˌsɛmi 'praɪvət] *adj.* of a hospital room, designed to accommodate two patients.

sem•i•qua•ver ['sɛmiˌkweivər] *n. Brit. Music.* a sixteenth note.

Se•mir•a•mis [sə'mirəmɪs] *n.* a legendary Assyrian queen who lived about 800 B.C. The alleged founder of Babylon, she was noted for her beauty and wisdom.

sem•i•skilled [ˌsɛmi'skɪld] *adj.* partly skilled; engaged in manual work requiring some, but relatively little, training.

sem•i•sol•id [ˌsɛmi'sɒlɪd] *adj., n. —adj.* partly solid.
—n. a partly solid substance.

sem•i•sweet ['sɛmiˌswit] *adj.* somewhat sweet; containing a small amount of sugar or other sweetener: *semisweet chocolate.*

Sem•ite ['sɛmɔit] *or* ['simɔit] *n.* **1** a member of any people speaking a Semitic language as their native tongue: *Jews and Arabs are Semites.* **2** a descendant of Shem. **3** loosely, any Jewish person.

Se•mit•ic [sə'mɪtɪk] *adj., n. —adj.* of or having to do with the Semites or their languages.
—n. a group of languages including Hebrew, Arabic, Aramaic, Phoenician, and Assyrian.

Sem•i•tism ['sɛməˌtɪzəm] *n.* **1** Semitic character, especially the ways, ideas, influence, etc. of the Jews. **2** a Semitic word or idiom.

sem•i•tone ['sɛmiˌtoun] *n. Music.* the smallest interval of the modern scale; a half tone; half step. **—ˌsem•i'ton•al•ly,** *adv.*

sem•i•trail•er ['sɛmiˌtreilər] *n.* a large trailer used for carrying freight, having wheels at the back but supported in front by the truck tractor to which it is hitched.

sem•i•trop•i•cal [ˌsɛmi'trɒpɪkəl] *adj.* halfway between tropical and temperate: *Mexico is a semitropical country.*

sem•i•vow•el ['sɛmiˌvouəl] *n.* **1** *Phonetics.* a gliding sound that is pronounced like a vowel but cannot by itself form a syllable. **2** a letter or character representing such a sound. *W* and *y* are semivowels in *win* and *yet* respectively.

sem•i•week•ly [ˌsɛmi'wikli] *adj., adv., n., pl.* **-lies.** *—adj.* occurring or appearing twice a week.
—adv. twice a week.
—n. **1** something that occurs or appears twice a week. **2** a magazine or paper published twice a week.

sem•i•year•ly [ˌsɛmi'jirli] *adj., adv., n., pl.* **-lies.** *—adj.* occurring or appearing twice a year; SEMI-ANNUAL (def. 1).
—adv. twice a year.
—n. something that occurs or appears twice a year.

sem•o•li•na [ˌsɛmə'linə] *n.* the coarsely ground hard parts of wheat remaining after the fine flour has been sifted through, used in making puddings, macaroni, etc. ⟨< Ital. *semolino,* ult. < L *simila* fine flour⟩

sem•per ['sɛmpər] *adv. Latin.* always.

sem•per•vi•vum [ˌsɛmpərˈvaɪvəm] *n.* any of various succulent plants of the houseleek (genus *Sempervivum*), having thick, fleshy leaves and small yellow, pink, or red flowers; similar to the SEDUM, to which they are related. They are commonly known as **hens and chickens**. ⟨< L *semper* always + *vivus* living⟩

sem•pi•ter•nal [ˌsɛmpɪˈtɜrnəl] *adj.* everlasting; eternal. ⟨ME < LL *sempiternalis*, ult. < L *semper* forever⟩

sem•pli•ce [ˈsɛmplɪˌtʃei] *adv. Music.* simply; with simplicity. ⟨< Ital., simply⟩

sem•pre [ˈsɛmprei] *adv. Music.* always the same. ⟨< Ital. < L *semper* always⟩

semp•stress [ˈsɛmstrɪs] *or* [ˈsɛmpstrɪs] *n.* seamstress.

sen [sɛn] *n., pl.* **sen. 1** a unit of money in Indonesia equal to 1/100 of a rupiah. See table of money in the Appendix. **2** a unit of money in Malaysia, equal to 1/100 of a ringgit. **3** a unit of money in Japan, equal to 1/100 of a yen. **4** a coin worth one sen. ⟨< Japanese⟩

Sen. 1 Senate; Senator. **2** Senior.

sen•ate [ˈsɛnɪt] *n.* **1** a governing or lawmaking assembly: *the senate of a university.* **2** the upper and smaller branch of an assembly or parliament that makes laws. **3 Senate,** the upper and smaller branch of a specific parliament or legislature. The Canadian Senate, which consists of 104 members, is made up of appointed representatives from each province. ⟨ME < OF < L *senatus* < *senex* old man⟩
☛ *Hom.* SENNIGHT, SENNIT [ˈsɛnɪt].

Senate Chamber the chamber in the Parliament buildings where the Senate of Canada convenes. Also, **Red Chamber**.

sen•a•tor [ˈsɛnətər] *n.* a member of a senate. ⟨< L⟩

sen•a•to•ri•al [ˌsɛnəˈtɔriəl] *adj.* **1** of or befitting a senator or senators. **2** consisting of senators. **3** entitled to elect a senator: *a senatorial district.*

sen•a•tor•ship [ˈsɛnətərˌʃɪp] *n.* the position, duties, etc. of a senator.

send [sɛnd] *v.* **sent, send•ing. 1** cause or direct to go from one place to another: *to send a child on an errand.* **2** cause or enable (a person) to do something, go somewhere, etc. for a period of time: *They sent all their children to university.* **3** refer (a reader) to some author, authority, etc.: *to send a reader to the dictionary.* **4** cause to be carried: *to send a letter.* **5** cause to come, occur, be, etc.; become: *It was enough to send a person crazy. Send help at once. The earthquake sent destruction to the village.* **6** despatch a message or messenger: *Send for a doctor.* **7** drive; impel; throw: *She sent the ball into the rough.* **8** put forth; emit: *The volcano sent clouds of smoke into the air.* **9** *Electricity.* **a** transmit (radio signals, etc.). **b** transmit (a current, electromagnetic wave, etc.) by means of pulsation. **10** *Slang.* excite greatly or inspire.
send around, cause to circulate: *Have you seen the memo that the manager sent around?*
send (away) for, mail a request for.
send packing, send away or force to leave quickly: *When I caught the employee stealing, I sent him packing.*
send up, a *Informal.* send to prison: *The prisoner was sent up for life for the murder.* **b** make fun of, especially by parody. **c** release upward; cause to rise. ⟨OE *sendan*⟩
—ˈsend•er, *n.*

sen•dal [ˈsɛndəl] *n.* **1** a silk fabric used during the Middle Ages. **2** a garment made of it. ⟨ME < OF *cendal*, ult. < Gk. *sindon* fine cloth⟩

send–off [ˈsɛnd ˌɒf] *n.* **1** a friendly demonstration in honour of a person setting out on a journey, course, career, etc. **2** *Informal.* a start given to a person or thing.

send•up [ˈsɛndˌʌp] *n.* a spoof; a takeoff, especially by means of parody.

se•ne [ˈseinei] *n.* a unit of currency in Western Samoa, equal to 1/100 of a tala. See table of money in the Appendix.

Sen•e•ca [ˈsɛnəkə] *n., pl.* **Seneca** or **Senecas;** *adj.* —*n.* **1** a member of a Native American people living mainly in New York State. The Seneca belonged to the Iroquois Confederacy. **2** the Iroquoian language of the Seneca.
—*adj.* of or having to do with the Seneca or their language.

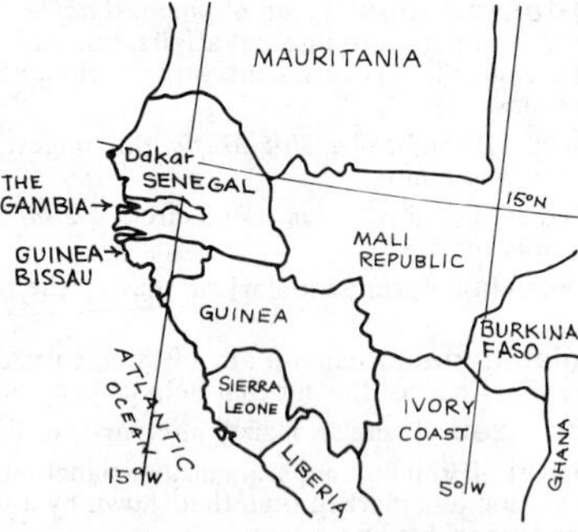

Sen•e•gal [ˈsɛnəˌgɒl] *n.* a republic in W Africa.

Sen•e•gal•ese [ˌsɛnəgəˈliz] *n., pl.* **-ese;** *adj.* —*n.* a native or inhabitant of Senegal.
—*adj.* of or having to do with Senegal or its people.

se•nes•cent [səˈnɛsənt] *adj.* growing old; beginning to show old age. ⟨< L *senescens, -entis*, ppr. of *senescere* grow old, ult. < *senex* old⟩ **—seˈnes•cence,** *n.*

sen•es•chal [ˈsɛnəʃəl] *n.* in the Middle Ages, a steward in charge of a royal palace, nobleman's estate, etc. Seneschals often had the powers of judges or generals. ⟨ME < OF < Gmc.; cf. OHG *senescalh* (*sene-* old + *scalh* servant)⟩

se•nile [ˈsinaɪl] *or* [ˈsɛnaɪl] *adj.* **1** of, having to do with, or characteristic of old age. **2** having to do with, characteristic of, or showing the mental confusion, memory loss, etc. often associated with old age. **3** *Geology.* having reached an advanced stage of erosion; made flat or level by the action of water, wind, etc.: *a senile valley.* ⟨< L *senilis* < *senex* old⟩ **—ˈse•nile•ly,** *adv.*

se•nil•i•ty [səˈnɪləti] *n.* the quality or state of being senile.

sen•ior [ˈsinjər] *adj., n.* —*adj.* **1** older or elderly: *a senior citizen.* **2** the older; designating a father whose son has the same given name: *John Parker, Senior.* **3** higher in rank or longer in service: *Ms. Jones is the senior member of the firm of Jones and Desqui.* **4** *Esp. U.S.* of or having to do with a graduating class.
—*n.* **1** an older person. **2** SENIOR CITIZEN: *Admission is $8, students and seniors $5.* **3** a person of higher rank or longer service. **4** *Esp. U.S.* a member of the graduating class of a high school or college.
be (someone's) **senior,** be older than someone. ⟨< L *senior*, comparative of *senex* old. Doublet of SIRE.⟩

senior citizen any member of the community who is aged 65 or over, or beyond the normal retirement age.

senior government *Cdn.* a provincial government or the federal government, or both, as opposed to a municipal government.

sen•ior•i•ty [sɪˈnjɔrəti] *n., pl.* **-ties. 1** superiority in age or standing; the state or fact of being older: *Harry felt that two years' seniority gave him the right to advise his sister.* **2** priority or precedence in office or service: *A captain has seniority over a lieutenant.*

senior public school a school for grades 6 to 8.

se•ni•ti [ˈsɛnəti] *n., pl.* **seniti.** a unit of money of Tonga, equal to 1/100 of a pa'anga.

sen•na [ˈsɛnə] *n.* **1** any of various cassias, especially either of two species (*Cassia angustifolia* and *C. acutifolia*) used in medicine. **2** the dried leaves or roots of a senna, used as a laxative. ⟨< NL < Arabic *sana*⟩

sen•night [ˈsɛnəit] *or* [ˈsɛnɪt] *n. Archaic.* seven nights and days; a week. ⟨OE *seofon nihta* seven nights⟩
☛ *Hom.* SENNIT, SENATE [ˈsɛnɪt].

sen•nit [ˈsɛnɪt] *n.* **1** a kind of flat, braided cordage used on shipboard, formed by plaiting strands of rope yarn or other fibre. **2** braided straw or grass used to make hats. **3** a braid or plait. ⟨origin uncertain⟩
☛ *Hom.* SENNIGHT, SENATE [ˈsɛnɪt].

sen•sate [ˈsɛnseit] *adj.* **1** perceived through the senses of sight, hearing, touch, taste, or smell. **2** being able to perceive through the physical senses.

sen•sa•tion [sɛnˈseiʃən] *n.* **1** the action of the senses; power to see, hear, feel, taste, smell, etc.: *A dead body is without sensation.* **2** a feeling: *Ice gives a sensation of coldness; sugar, of sweetness.* **3** a state of strong or excited feeling: *The announcement of war caused a sensation throughout the country.* **4** the cause of such feeling: *The first manned orbit of the earth*

was a great sensation. **5** a vague or generalized feeling not attributable to any specific cause. ⟨< LL *sensatio, -onis,* ult. < L *sensus.* See SENSE.⟩
☛ *Syn.* **1.** See note at SENSE.

sen•sa•tion•al [sɛn'seiʃənəl] *adj.* **1** arousing strong or excited feeling: *The first landing on the moon was a sensational event.* **2** trying to arouse strong or excited feeling: *a sensational newspaper story.* **3** of the senses; having to do with sensation. **4** of, based on, or adhering to sensationalism in philosophy. **5** *Informal.* extremely good: *a sensational performance.* **—sen'sa•tion•al•ly,** *adv.*

sen•sa•tion•al•ism [sɛn'seiʃənə,lɪzəm] *n.* **1** sensational methods; sensational writing, language, etc. **2** *Philosophy.* the theory or doctrine that all ideas are derived solely through sensation.

sen•sa•tion•al•ist [sɛn'seiʃənəlɪst] *n.* **1** a sensational writer, speaker, etc.; one who tries to make a sensation. **2** a believer in philosophical sensationalism. **—sen,sa•tion•al'ist•ic,** *adj.*

sense [sɛns] *n., v.* **sensed, sens•ing.** *—n.* **1** one of the special functions or mechanisms of the body by which humans and animals perceive the world around them and become aware of changes within themselves. Sight, hearing, touch, taste, and smell are the five senses. **2** a sensation felt through one of these senses: *a sense of pain.* **3** the ability to perceive. **4** a mental feeling: *The extra lock on the door gave him a sense of security.* **5** the faculties of the mind or soul, compared or contrasted with the bodily senses: *moral sense.* **6** an understanding; appreciation; the ability to judge things: *a sense of direction, a sense of beauty. Everyone thinks she has a sense of humour.* **7** Usually, **senses,** *pl.* normal, sound condition of mind. **8** judgment; intelligence: *He had the good sense to keep out of foolish quarrels. Common sense could have prevented the accident.* **9** a meaning: *He was a gentleman in every sense of the word.* **10** discourse that has a satisfactory or intelligible meaning: *to speak or write sense.* **11** the general opinion: *The sense of the assembly was clear even before the vote.* **12** purpose; point; usefulness: *What's the sense of slaving to earn so much money if you've no time left to spend it?*
in a sense, in some respects; to some degree.
make sense, have a meaning; be understandable or reasonable: Cow cat bless Monday *does not make sense.*
—v. **1** be aware; feel: *She sensed that he was tired.* **2** *Informal.* understand. ⟨ME < L *sensus* < *sentire* perceive⟩
☛ *Syn. n.* **1, 2. Sense,** SENSATION, SENSIBILITY = the power or act of feeling or perceiving. **Sense** applies especially to the power of the mind to respond to a stimulus or influence outside itself, but implies awareness or full consciousness of something existing rather than bodily reaction: *She has a sense of well-being.* **Sensation** applies to physical feeling, particularly the response to stimulation of a bodily organ like the eyes or nerves: *He has no sensation in his feet.* **Sensibility** applies to the capacity for feeling or perceiving physically or, especially, emotionally: *She has no sensibility for pain.* **10.** See note at MEANING.
☛ *Hom.* CENSE.

sense•less ['sɛnslɪs] *adj.* **1** unconscious: *A blow on the head knocked her senseless.* **2** foolish; stupid. **3** meaningless: *senseless words.* **—'sense•less•ly,** *adv.* **—'sense•less•ness,** *n.*

sense organ the eye, ear, or other part of the body by which a person or an animal receives sensations of colours, sounds, smells, etc.

sen•si•bil•i•ty [,sɛnsə'bɪləti] *n., pl.* **-ties. 1** the ability to feel or perceive: *Some drugs lessen a person's sensibility.* **2** fineness of feeling: *He has an unusual sensibility for colours.* **3** Usually, **sensibilities,** *pl.* sensitive feelings. **4** a tendency to feel hurt or be offended too easily. **5** awareness; consciousness.
☛ *Syn.* **1.** See note at SENSE.

sen•si•ble ['sɛnsəbəl] *adj.* **1** having or showing good judgment; wise. **2** aware; conscious: *I am sensible of your kindness.* **3** that can be noticed: *a sensible reduction in expenses.* **4** that can be perceived by the senses. **5** sensitive. ⟨ME < LL *sensibilis,* ult. < L *sentire* feel⟩ **—'sen•si•bly,** *adv.*
☛ *Syn.* **1. Sensible,** PRACTICAL = having or showing good sense. **Sensible** emphasizes having and using common sense and good judgment in acting and speaking, and particularly suggests natural intelligence: *She is too sensible to do anything foolish.* **Practical** emphasizes using common sense in everyday affairs, and particularly suggests being given to action rather than thought or imagination and being concerned with the usefulness, application, and results of knowledge, principles, and methods: *He is a practical man and does not understand dreamers and scientists.*

sen•si•tive ['sɛnsətɪv] *adj.* **1** receiving impressions readily: *The eye is sensitive to light.* **2** easily affected or influenced: *The mercury in the thermometer is sensitive to changes in temperature.* **3 a** easily offended or hurt emotionally: *He's a sensitive soul.* **b** empathetic; appreciating the feelings of others. **4** of or connected with the senses or with sensation. **5** extremely perceptive intellectually or aesthetically. **6** *Medicine.* unusually susceptible, as to a serum. **7** *Biology.* able to respond to stimulation by various external agents, as light, gravity, etc. **8** involving classified documents, etc. ⟨ME < Med.L *sensitivus* < L *sensus.* See SENSE.⟩ **—'sen•si•tive•ly,** *adv.* **—,sen•si'tiv•i•ty** or **,sen•si•tive•ness,** *n.*
☛ *Syn.* **2. Sensitive,** SUSCEPTIBLE = easily affected or influenced. **Sensitive** particularly suggests having, by nature or because of a physical or emotional condition, an especially keen or delicate capacity for feeling (physical or mental) or for responding or reacting to an external action, force, or influence: *Sensitive people are quickly touched by something beautiful or sad.* **Susceptible** particularly suggests having a nature, character, or makeup that makes a person or thing unable to resist an influence and thus be easily acted on: *Susceptible people are easily tricked.*

sensitive plant 1 either of two tropical American mimosas (*Mimosa pudica* and *M. sensitiva*) cultivated as house and greenhouse plants in temperate regions for their foliage, which folds up and droops when touched. **2** any of various other plants showing sensitiveness to touch.

sen•si•tize ['sɛnsə,taɪz] *v.* **-tized, -tiz•ing. 1** make sensitive. Camera films have been sensitized to light. **2** *Medicine.* make unusually sensitive to a protein or other substance by repeated injections. **—'sen•si,tiz•er,** *n.* **—,sen•si•ti'za•tion,** *n.*

sen•si•tom•e•ter [,sɛnsə'tɒmətər] *n.* a device measuring photographic sensitivity to light.

sen•sor ['sɛnsər] *n.* a device for receiving and transmitting a physical stimulus such as heat, light, or pressure: *Sensors were applied to the astronaut's body to record her pulse, temperature, etc.*
☛ *Hom.* CENSER, CENSOR.

sen•so•ri•al [sɛn'sɔriəl] *adj.* sensory.

sen•so•ri•um [sɛn'sɔriəm] *n., pl.* **-ri•ums** or **-ri•a** [-riə]. **1** the supposed seat of sensation in the brain. **2** *Physiology.* the whole sensory apparatus of the body. ⟨< LL *sensorium,* ult. < L *sentire* feel⟩

sen•so•ry ['sɛnsəri] *adj.* **1** of or having to do with sensation: *sensory organs.* **2** *Physiology.* of nerves, ganglia, etc., conveying an impulse from the sense organs to a nerve centre.

sen•su•al ['sɛnʃuəl] *adj.* **1** having to do with the bodily senses rather than with the mind or soul: *sensual pleasures.* **2** caring too much for the pleasures of the senses. **3** lacking in moral restraints; lustful; lewd. **4** arousing or exciting the senses. **5** of or having to do with the senses or sensation. ⟨ME < LL *sensualis* < L *sensus.* See SENSE.⟩ **—'sen•su•al•ly,** *adv.*
☛ *Syn.* **1, 2. Sensual,** SENSUOUS = of or concerned with the senses. **Sensual** describes things that give pleasurable satisfaction to the bodily senses and appetites and applies to people who indulge their desires and feelings for pure physical pleasure, often suggesting baseness or excess: *A glutton derives sensual pleasure from eating.* **Sensuous,** usually favourable, describes people highly sensitive to beauty and the pleasure of the senses and feelings, and applies to things that give pleasure through the senses: *She derives sensuous delight from old music.*

sen•su•al•ism ['sɛnʃuə,lɪzəm] *n.* sensuality.

sen•su•al•ist ['sɛnʃuəlɪst] *n.* a person who indulges too much in the pleasures of the senses: *Gluttons and drunkards are sensualists.* **—,sen•su•al'ist•ic,** *adj.*

sen•su•al•i•ty [,sɛnʃu'æləti] *n., pl.* **-ties. 1** a sensual nature. **2** an excessive indulgence in the pleasures of the senses. **3** lewdness.

sen•su•al•ize ['sɛnʃuə,laɪz] *v.* **-ized, -iz•ing.** make sensual. **—,sen•su•al•i'za•tion,** *n.*

sen•su•ous ['sɛnʃuəs] *adj.* **1** of or derived from the senses; having an effect on the senses; perceived by the senses: *the sensuous thrill of a warm bath, a sensuous love of colour.* **2** enjoying the pleasures of the senses. **—'sen•su•ous•ly,** *adv.* **—'sen•su•ous•ness,** *n.*
☛ *Syn.* **1, 2.** See note at SENSUAL.

sent[1] [sɛnt] *v.* pt. and pp. of SEND.

sent[2] [sɛnt] *n., pl.* **sen•ti. 1** a unit of money in Estonia, equal to 1/100 of a kroon. See table of money in the Appendix. **2** a unit of money in Somalia, equal to 1/100 of a shilin. **3** a unit of money in Tanzania, equal to 1/100 of a shiling.

sen•te ['sɛntei] *n., pl.* **li•sen•te** [li'sɛntei] a unit of money in Lesotho, equal to 1/100 of a lati. See table of money in the Appendix.

sen•tence ['sɛntəns] *n., v.* **-tenced, -tenc•ing.** *—n.* **1** *Grammar.* a word or group of words making a grammatically complete statement, question, request, command, or exclamation. A sentence usually consists of a subject plus a predicate with a finite verb. **2** *Mathematics.* a group of symbols that expresses a complete idea or a requirement. *Examples:* $4 + 2 = 6$ (a **closed sentence** expressing a complete idea); $x + 2 = 6$ (an **open sentence** expressing a requirement). **3** *Law.* **a** a decision by a

judge on the punishment of a criminal. **b** the punishment itself. **4** *Archaic.* a short, wise saying; proverb.
—*v.* pronounce punishment on: *The judge sentenced the thief to five years in prison.* ⟨< F < L *sententia*, originally, opinion < *sentire* feel⟩ —**'sen•tenc•er,** *n.*

sen•ten•tial [sɛn'tɛnʃəl] *adj.* **1** having to do with or of the nature of a judicial sentence. **2** having to do with a grammatical sentence. —**sen'ten•tial•ly,** *adv.*

sen•ten•tious [sɛn'tɛnʃəs] *adj.* **1** full of meaning; saying much in few words. **2** speaking as if one were a judge settling a question. **3** inclined to make wise sayings; abounding in proverbs. ⟨ME < OF < Med.L *sententiosus* < *sententia.* See SENTENCE.⟩ —**sen'ten•tious•ly,** *adv.* —**sen'ten•tious•ness,** *n.*

sen•ti ['sɛnti] *n.* pl. of SENT[2].

sen•tience ['sɛnʃəns] *or* ['sɛnʃiəns] *n.* a capacity for feeling: *Some people believe in the sentience of flowers.*

sen•tient ['sɛnʃənt] *or* ['sɛnʃiənt] *adj., n.* —*adj.* that can feel; having feeling: *a sentient being.*
—*n.* one who or that which feels. ⟨< L *sentiens, -entis*, ppr. of *sentire* feel⟩ —**'sen•tient•ly,** *adv.*

sen•ti•ment ['sɛntəmənt] *n.* **1** a mixture of thought and feeling. Admiration, patriotism, and loyalty are sentiments. **2** feeling, especially refined or tender feeling; emotional sensitivity. **3** a thought or saying that expresses feeling. **4** a mental attitude; personal opinion. **5** SENTIMENTALITY (defs. 2, 3). ⟨ME < OF < Med.L *sentimentum* < L *sentire* feel⟩

☛ *Syn.* **2. Sentiment,** SENTIMENTALITY = refined or tender feeling, or a quality or characteristic showing or produced by such feeling. **Sentiment,** usually used in a good sense, suggests genuine, sincere, and refined, delicate, or tender feeling: *Anniversaries and birthdays are times for sentiment.* **Sentimentality** suggests affected or false, excessive or exaggerated feeling, sickening tenderness, or weakly emotional show, and therefore is used unfavourably or contemptuously: *Sentimentality toward criminals is as dangerous as it is disgusting.*

sen•ti•men•tal [,sɛntə'mɛntəl] *adj.* **1** having or showing much tender feeling: *sentimental poetry.* **2** likely to act from feelings rather than from logical thinking. **3** of sentiment; dependent on sentiment: *She values her mother's gift for sentimental reasons.* **4** having or showing too much sentiment. —**,sen•ti'men•tal•ly,** *adv.*

sen•ti•men•tal•ism [,sɛntə'mɛntə,lɪzəm] *n.* sentimentality.

sen•ti•men•tal•ist [,sɛntə'mɛntəlɪst] *n.* **1** a sentimental person. **2** one who indulges in sentimentality.

sen•ti•men•tal•i•ty [,sɛntəmən'tæləti] *n., pl.* **-ties. 1** a tendency to be influenced by sentiment rather than reason. **2** an excessive indulgence in sentiment. **3** a feeling expressed too openly or sentimentally.

☛ *Syn.* **2.** See note at SENTIMENT.

sen•ti•men•tal•ize [,sɛntə'mɛntə,laɪz] *v.* **-ized, -iz•ing. 1** indulge in sentiment; affect sentiment. **2** make sentimental. **3** be sentimental about. —**,sen•ti,men•tal•i'za•tion,** *n.*

sen•ti•mo [sɛn'timou] *n.* a unit of money in the Philippines, equal to $^1/_{100}$ of a piso. See table of money in the Appendix.

sen•ti•nel ['sɛntənəl] *n., v.* **-nelled** or **-neled, -nel•ling** or **-nel•ing.** —*n.* a person or animal stationed to keep watch and guard against surprise attack.
stand sentinel, act as a sentinel; keep watch.
—*v.* **1** stand guard over; watch as a sentinel. **2** furnish with or as if with a sentinel or sentinels. **3** post as a sentinel. ⟨< F < Ital. *sentinella* < LL *sentinare* avoid danger wisely < L *sentire* feel⟩

sen•try ['sɛntri] *n., pl.* **-tries.** a person, especially a soldier, stationed at a place to keep watch and guard against surprise attacks, etc.
stand sentry, watch; guard: *We stood sentry over the sleepers.* ⟨? abbreviation of *sentrinel*, var. of *sentinel*⟩

A sentry box

sentry box a small roofed structure for sheltering a sentry.

sep. **1** sepal(s). **2** separate.

Sep. **1** September. **2** Septuagint.

se•pal ['sipəl] *n. Botany.* one of the leaflike divisions of the calyx, or outer covering, of a flower. In a carnation, the sepals make a green cup at the base of the flower. In a tulip, the sepals are coloured like the petals. See FLOWER for picture. ⟨< NL *sepalum*, short for L *separatum petalum* separate petal, coined by H.J. de Necker in 1790⟩

sep•a•ra•ble ['sɛpərəbəl] *adj.* that can be separated. —**,sep•a•ra'bil•i•ty** or **'sep•a•ra•ble•ness,** *n.* —**'sep•a•ra•bly,** *adv.*

sep•a•rate *v.* ['sɛpə,reit]; *adj., n.* ['sɛprɪt] *or* ['sɛpərɪt] *v.* **-rat•ed, -rat•ing;** *adj., n.* —*v.* **1** be between; keep apart; divide: *The Atlantic Ocean separates North America from Europe.* **2** take apart; part; disjoin: *to separate church and state.* **3** live apart or cause to live apart. A husband and wife may be separated by agreement or by order of a court. **4** divide into parts, individuals, or groups; divide or part (a mass, compound, whole) into elements, classes, etc.: *to separate a tangle of string.* **5** of a mass, group, or compound, draw, come, or go apart; become disconnected or disunited; part company; withdraw (from): *After classes the students separated in all directions. The rope separated under the strain.* **6** put apart; take away: *Separate your books from mine.* **7** put out (a joint): *a separated shoulder.*
—*adj.* apart from others; distinct; not joined; individual; single: *separate clubs. These are two separate questions. Our teeth are separate from each other.*
—*n.* **1** something separate. **2** Usually, **separates,** *pl.* single items of clothing, as a skirt, shirt, etc., that can be mixed and matched with a variety of other such items. ⟨< L *separare* < *se-* apart + *parare* get⟩ —**'sep•a•rate•ly,** *adv.*

☛ *Syn. v.* **2. Separate,** DIVIDE = part or put apart two or more people, things, or elements. **Separate** emphasizes parting or causing to be apart people or things that have been together, whether or not actually connected or united: *We have decided to separate the twins for the summer.* **Divide** emphasizes separating, breaking up, cutting, etc. a mass, body, or whole into individuals, parts, or sections: *The instructor divides the class for field trips.*

separate school **1** *Cdn.* a school for children belonging to the Catholic or non-Catholic religious minority in a particular district, operated by a school board elected by the minority ratepayers, and financed by taxes imposed on them by the board as well as by grants from the provincial Department of Education. It is under the jurisdiction of the Department of Education and follows the same basic curriculum as that laid down for public schools. **2** a Roman Catholic parochial school.

separate school board *Cdn.* a board, usually elected, of trustees responsible for the separate schools in a given area.

separate school district *Cdn.* the area within which a separate school board operates.

sep•a•ra•tion [,sɛpə'reiʃən] *n.* **1** the act of separating; dividing; taking apart. **2** the condition of being separated. **3** the line or point where things separate: *They soon came to the separation of the path into two tracks.* **4** *Law.* the living apart of husband and wife by agreement or by order of a court.

sep•a•ra•tism ['sɛprə,tɪzəm] *or* ['sɛpərə,tɪzəm] *n.* **1** a principle or policy for separation, secession, or segregation. **2** *Cdn.* advocacy or support of the withdrawal of a province from Confederation.

sep•a•ra•tist ['sɛprətɪst] *or* ['sɛpərətɪst] *n., adj.* —*n.* **1** an advocate or supporter of separatism. **2** *Cdn.* an advocate or supporter of the withdrawal of a province from Confederation.
—*adj. Cdn.* consisting of or pertaining to separatism or separatists.

sep•a•ra•tive ['sɛprətɪv], ['sɛpərətɪv], *or* ['sɛpə,reitɪv] *adj.* tending to separate; causing separation.

sep•a•ra•tor ['sɛpə,reitər] *n.* **1** a person who or thing that separates, especially a machine for separating cream from milk, wheat from chaff or dirt, etc. **2** an orthodontic device inserted between closely spaced teeth to prevent them from overlapping. ⟨< L⟩

Se•phar•dic [sɪ'fɑrdɪk] *adj.* of, having to do with, or descended from the Sephardim.

Se•phar•dim [sɪ'fɑrdɪm] *n.pl., sing.* **-di** [-di]. Spanish or Portuguese Jews and their descendants, as distinguished from the Ashkenazim of central and eastern Europe.

se•pi•a ['sipiə] *n., adj.* —*n.* **1** a brown paint or ink prepared from the inky fluid of cuttlefish. **2** a dark brown. **3** a drawing, photograph, etc. in tones of brown.
—*adj.* **1** dark brown. **2** done in sepia: *a sepia print.* ⟨< L < Gk.⟩

se•poy ['sipɔɪ] *n.* formerly, a native of India who was a soldier in the British army in India. ⟨< Pg. < Hind. < Persian *sipāhī* soldier < *sipāh* army⟩

sep•sis ['sɛpsɪs] *n. Pathology.* a toxic condition resulting from the absorption of any of various pus-forming bacteria or their toxins into the blood or tissues from a wound, etc. Blood poisoning, or septicemia, is a type of sepsis. ⟨< NL < Gk. *sēpsis* putrefaction < *sēpein* rot⟩

sept [sɛpt] *n.* **1** a subdivision or branch of a clan, especially in Scotland and Ireland. **2** *Anthropology.* any group believing itself to be descended from a common ancestor. ⟨possibly < L *septum* paddock, enclosure⟩

Sept. 1 September. 2 Septuagint.

sep•ta•gon ['sɛptə,gɒn] *n.* a closed plane figure having seven interior angles and seven sides.

sep•tal ['sɛptəl] *adj. Biology.* of or having to do with a septum.

Sep•tem•ber [sɛp'tɛmbər] *n.* the ninth month. September has 30 days. ⟨< L *September* < *septem* seven; from the order of the Roman calendar⟩

sep•te•nar•y ['sɛptə,nɛri], [sɛp'tɛnəri], *or* [sɛp'tinəri] *adj., n., pl.* **-nar•ies.** *—adj.* **1** forming a group of seven. **2** septennial. *—n.* **1** the number seven. **2** a group or set of seven things. **3** a period of seven years. **4** *Prosody.* a line of verse having seven metrical feet. ⟨< L *septenarius* seven-year period < *septum* seven + *annus* year⟩

sep•ten•ni•al [sɛp'tɛniəl] *adj.* **1** lasting seven years. **2** occurring every seven years. ⟨< L *septennium* seven-year period < *septem* seven + *annus* year⟩ **—sep'ten•ni•al•ly,** *adv.*

sep•tet or **sep•tette** [sɛp'tɛt] *n.* **1** *Music.* **a** a composition for seven voices or instruments. **b** seven singers or players. **2** any group of seven. ⟨< G < L *septem* seven; modelled after *duet*⟩

sep•tic ['sɛptɪk] *adj., n. Pathology. —adj.* **1** causing infection or putrefaction. **2** caused by infection or putrefaction. *—n.* a substance that causes or promotes sepsis. ⟨< L < Gk. *sēptikos* < *sēpein* rot⟩

sep•ti•ce•mi•a or **sep•ti•cae•mi•a** [,sɛptə'simiə] *n. Pathology.* a disease caused by the presence of micro-organisms and their toxins in the bloodstream; blood poisoning. ⟨< NL < Gk. *sēptikos* septic (ult. < *sēpein* rot) + *haima* blood⟩ **—,sep•ti'ce•mic** or **,sep•ti'cae•mic,** *adj.*

septic tank a tank in which sewage is acted on by bacteria.

sep•til•lion [sɛp'tɪljən] *n., adj. —n.* **1** in Canada, the United States, and France, 1 followed by 24 zeros. **2** in the United Kingdom, 1 followed by 42 zeros. *—adj.* equalling one septillion in number. ⟨< F *septillion* (< L *septem* seven), modelled after *million* million⟩

sep•tu•a•ge•nar•i•an [,sɛptʃuədʒə'nɛriən], [,sɛptjuədʒə'nɛriən], *or* [,sɛptuədʒə'nɛriən] *adj., n. —adj.* of the age of 70 years, or between 70 and 80 years old. *—n.* a person who is 70 or between 70 and 80 years old. ⟨< L *septuagenarius,* ult. < *septuaginta* seventy⟩

sep•tu•ag•e•nar•y [,sɛptʃu'ædʒə,nɛri], [,sɛptju'ædʒə,nɛri], *or* [,sɛptu'ædʒə,nɛri] *adj., n., pl.* **-nar•ies.** septuagenarian.

Sep•tu•a•ges•i•ma [,sɛptʃuə'dʒɛsəmə], [,sɛptjuə'dʒɛsəmə], *or* [,sɛptuə'dʒɛsəmə] *n.* the third Sunday before Lent. ⟨< L *septuagesima,* literally, seventieth⟩

Sep•tu•a•gint ['sɛptʃuə,dʒɪnt], ['sɛptjuə,dʒɪnt], *or* ['sɛptuə,dʒɪnt] *n.* the Greek translation of the Old Testament that was made before the time of Christ. ⟨< L *septuaginta* seventy; because it was supposed to have been done in seventy days by seventy scholars who were brought to Alexandria by Ptolemy II of Egypt⟩

sep•tum ['sɛptəm] *n., pl.* **-ta** [-tə]. a dividing wall; partition: *There is a septum of bone and cartilage between the nostrils. The inside of a green pepper is divided into chambers by septa.* ⟨< L *saeptum* a fence < *saepire* hedge in⟩

sep•tu•ple [sɛp'tjupəl] *or* [sɛp'tupəl], [sɛp'tʌpəl] *or* ['sɛptəpəl] *adj., v.* **-pled, -pling;** *n. —adj.* **1** seven times as great; sevenfold. **2** made up of seven parts; sevenfold. *—v.* make or become seven times as great. *—n.* the product of multiplying something seven times. ⟨< LL *septuplus* < L *septem* seven + *-plus* -fold⟩

sep•ul•cher ['sɛpəlkər] See SEPULCHRE.

se•pul•chral [sə'pʌlkrəl] *adj.* **1** of sepulchres or tombs. **2** of burial: *sepulchral ceremonies.* **3** deep and gloomy; dismal; suggesting a tomb.

sep•ul•chre ['sɛpəlkər] *n., v.* **-chred, -chring.** *—n.* a place of burial; tomb. *—v.* bury (a dead body) in a sepulchre. Also, **sepulcher.** ⟨ME < OF < L *sepulcrum* < *sepelire* bury⟩

sep•ul•ture ['sɛpəltʃər] *n. Archaic.* **1** burial. **2** a place of burial; sepulchre. ⟨ME < OF < L *sepultura* < *sepelire* bury⟩

seq. 1 sequel. 2 the following (for L *sequens*).

se•quel ['sikwəl] *n.* **1** that which follows; a continuation. **2** something that follows as a result of some earlier happening; result. **3** a complete story continuing an earlier one about the same people. ⟨ME < L *sequela* < *sequi* follow⟩

se•que•la [sɪ'kwɛlə] *n., pl.* **-lae** [-li] *or* [-laɪ]. **1** anything following or resulting. **2** *Pathology.* a disease or morbid condition that is the result of a previous disease. ⟨< L. See SEQUEL.⟩

se•quence ['sikwəns] *n., v.* **-quenced, -quenc•ing.** *—n.* **1** the coming of one thing after another; succession; order of succession: *Arrange the names in alphabetical sequence.* **2** a connected series: *a sequence of lessons on one subject.* **3** something that follows; result: *Crime has its sequence of misery.* **4** *Card games.* a set of three or more cards of the same suit following one after another in order of value. **5 a** part of a motion picture consisting of an episode without breaks. **b** any group of scenes of a motion picture taken as a unit. **6** *Music.* a series of melodic or harmonic phrases repeated three or more times at successive pitches upward or downward. *—v.* **1** arrange in a sequence. **2** *Biology.* determine the order of bases in (a sample of DNA). ⟨ME < LL *sequentia,* ult. < L *sequi* follow⟩

☛ *Syn.* **2.** See note at SERIES.

se•quent ['sikwənt] *adj., n. —adj.* **1** following; subsequent. **2** following in order; consecutive. **3** following as a result; consequent. *—n.* that which follows; result; consequence. ⟨< L *sequens, -entis,* ppr. of *sequi* follow⟩

se•quen•tial [sɪ'kwɛnʃəl] *adj.* **1** sequent. **2** forming a sequence or connected series; characterized by a regular sequence of parts. **—se'quen•tial•ly,** *adv.*

sequential access *Computer technology.* a method of access to any item of data (in a computer storage device) that requires all preceding data to be accessed first. **—se'quen•tial-'ac•cess,** *adj.*

se•ques•ter [sɪ'kwɛstər] *v.* **1** remove or withdraw from public use or from public view: *The shy old lady sequestered herself from all strangers. The jury was sequestered during the trial.* **2** *Law.* take away (property) for a time from an owner until a debt is paid or some claim is satisfied. **3** seize by authority; take and keep: *The soldiers sequestered food from the people they conquered.* ⟨ME < LL *sequestrare* < *sequester* trustee, mediator < *sequi* follow⟩

se•ques•trate [sɪ'kwɛstreit] *v.* **-trat•ed, -trat•ing.** **1** SEQUESTER (defs. 2, 3). **2** *Archaic.* SEQUESTER (def. 1). **—se'ques,tra•tor,** *n.*

se•ques•tra•tion [,sikwɛ'streiʃən] *or* [səkwɛ'streiʃən] *n.* **1** *Law.* **a** the seizing and holding of property until legal claims are satisfied. **b** a writ authorizing this. **2** a forcible or authorized seizure; confiscation. **3** a separation or withdrawal from others; seclusion.

se•quin ['sikwɪn] *n.* **1** a small spangle used to ornament dresses, scarves, etc. **2** any of various former Italian gold coins. ⟨< F < Ital. *zecchino* < *zecca* mint < Arabic *sikka* a stamp⟩ **—'se•quinned** or **'se•quined,** *adj.*

se•quoi•a [sɪ'kwɔɪə] *n.* either of two giant, very long-lived, coniferous evergreen trees, the **redwood** and the **big tree,** found in the coastal regions of the SW United States. Each is the only living member of its genus, and both belong to the same family (Taxodiaceae) as the bald cypress. See also BIG TREE, REDWOOD. ⟨< NL *sequoia* < *Sequoya* (Cherokee *Sikwayi*) (1770?-1843), an Indian who invented the Cherokee system of writing⟩

A sequoia

se•ra ['sirə] *n.* a pl. of SERUM.

se•rac [sə'ræk]; *French,* [sɛ'ʀak] *n.* a large block or pinnaclelike mass of ice on a glacier, formed by the intersection of crevasses. ⟨< Swiss F *sérac,* a kind of white cheese⟩

se•ragl•io [sə'ræljou] *n., pl.* **-ragl•ios.** **1** the women's quarters of a Muslim house or palace; harem. **2** in Turkey, a palace.

⟨< Ital. *serraglio*, ult. < L *serare* lock up; influenced by Turkish *serāī* palace⟩

se•ra•pe [sə'rɑpi] *n.* a shawl or blanket, often having bright colours, worn as a cape or cloak by Indians in Spanish-American countries. ⟨< Mexican Sp. *serape* or *sarape*⟩

ser•aph ['sɛrəf] *n., pl.* **-aphs** or **-a•phim.** one of the highest of the nine orders of angels. ⟨< *seraphim*, pl., < LL < Hebrew⟩

se•raph•ic [sə'ræfɪk] *adj.* **1** of seraphs. **2** like a seraph; angelic. **—se'raph•i•cal•ly,** *adv.*

ser•a•phim ['sɛrə,fɪm] *n.* a pl. of SERAPH.

Se•ra•pis [sə'reipɪs] *n. Egyptian mythology.* a god of the lower world, the dead Apis.

Serb [sɜrb] *n., adj. —n.* **1** a native or inhabitant of Serbia. **2** Serbian.
—adj. Serbian. ⟨< *Serbian*⟩

Ser•bia ['sɜrbiə] *n.* a country in E Europe, part of the former Yugoslavia, lying to the north of Greece and west of Bulgaria.

Ser•bi•an ['sɜrbiən] *n., adj. —n.* **1** the Slavic language spoken by the Serbs, very closely related to Croatian. See SERBO-CROATIAN. **2** a Serb.
—adj. of or having to do with Serbia, its people, or their language.

Ser•bo–Cro•a•tian ['sɜrbou krou'eiʃən] *n., adj. —n.* the Slavic language of the Serbs and Croats, consisting of Serbian, written with the Cyrillic alphabet, and Croatian, written with the Latin alphabet, with slight dialectal differences.
—adj. of or having to do with this language or the people who speak it.

sere [sir] *adj.* dried up; withered. ⟨var. of *sear*⟩
☛ *Hom.* SEAR, SEER.

ser•e•nade [,sɛrə'neid] *n., v.* **-nad•ed, -nad•ing.** *—n.* **1** music played or sung outdoors at night, especially by a lover under his lady's window. **2** a piece of music suitable for such a performance. **3** an instrumental composition having several movements. **4** *Informal.* any piece of music sung or played.
—v. **1** sing or play a serenade to. **2** sing or play a serenade. ⟨< F < Ital. *serenata*, ult. < L *serenus* serene⟩ **—,ser•e'nad•er,** *n.*

ser•en•dip•i•tous [,sɛrən'dɪpətəs] *adj.* possessing, or characterized or accomplished by serendipity: *serendipitous inspiration.* **—,ser•en'dip•i•tous•ly,** *adv.*

ser•en•dip•ity [,sɛrən'dɪpəti] *n.* the faculty of accidentally making fortunate discoveries; happening upon things, information, etc. by chance. ⟨coined by Horace Walpole in 1754, from *Serendip* in the title of the Persian fairy tale *The Three Princes of Serendip*, whose heroes make many fortunate discoveries accidentally⟩

se•rene [sə'rin] *adj.* **1** peaceful; calm: *a serene smile.* **2** clear; bright; not cloudy: *a serene sky.* **3 Serene,** part of some royal titles: *Her Serene Highness, Princess Grace of Monaco.* ⟨< L *serenus*⟩ **—se'rene•ly,** *adv.*
☛ *Syn.* **1.** See note at PEACEFUL.

se•ren•i•ty [sə'rɛnəti] *n., pl.* **-ties. 1** quiet peace; calmness. **2** clearness; brightness (of the sky).

serf [sɜrf] *n.* **1** especially in medieval Europe, a person who worked on a feudal estate and passed with the land from one owner to another. **2** a person treated almost like a slave; a person who is mistreated, underpaid, etc. ⟨< F < L *servus* slave⟩ **—'serf,like,** *adj.*
☛ *Hom.* SURF.

serf•dom ['sɜrfdəm] *n.* **1** the condition of a serf. **2** the custom of having serfs. Serfdom existed all over Europe in the Middle Ages and lasted in Russia till the middle of the 19th century.

serge [sɜrdʒ] *n., v.* **serged, serg•ing.** *—n.* a twilled woollen or silk cloth having a diagonal surface rib.
—v. finish (a seam or edge) using overcast stitches. ⟨ME < OF *serge*, ult. < L *serica (vestis)* silken (garment) < Gk. *sērikē* < *Sēres* the Chinese. Cf. SILK.⟩
☛ *Hom.* SURGE.

ser•gean•cy ['sɑrdʒənsi] *n., pl.* **-cies.** the position, rank, or duties of a sergeant.

ser•geant ['sɑrdʒənt] *n.* **1** *Canadian Forces.* a non-commissioned officer ranking next above a master corporal and below a warrant officer. See table of ranks in the Appendix. **2** a non-commissioned officer of similar rank in the armed forces of other countries. **3** a police officer, senior to a constable and below an inspector. **4** SERGEANT AT ARMS. *Abbrev.*: Sgt. or Sgt ⟨ME < OF *sergent* < L *serviens, -entis*, ppr. of *servire* serve⟩

sergeant at arms or **ser•geant–at–arms** ['sɑrdʒənt ət 'ɑrmz] *n., pl.* **ser•geants at arms** or **ser•geants-at-arms.** an officer who keeps order in a legislature, law court, etc.

ser•geant–ma•jor ['sɑrdʒənt 'meidʒər] *n.* in the army, a non-commissioned officer who is senior to a staff sergeant and junior to a warrant officer. *Abbrev.*: S.M.

serg•er ['sɜrdʒər] *n.* a special sewing machine for use with knit fabrics. It serges all seams, using thread from four bobbins.

Sergt. Sergeant.

se•ri•al ['siriəl] *n., adj. —n.* a story presented one part at a time in a magazine, on radio or television, etc.
—adj. **1** published, broadcast, or televised one part at a time: *a serial publication, a serial story.* **2** of, having to do with, or arranged in a series: *books arranged in serial order.* **3** of or concerning a serial: *serial rights to a book.* **4** *Music.* based on transformations of a fixed arrangement of the twelve tones of the chromatic scale; twelve-tone. ⟨< NL *serialis* < L *series.* See SERIES.⟩ **—'se•ri•al•ly,** *adv.*
☛ *Hom.* CEREAL.

se•ri•al•ism ['siriə,lɪzəm] *n. Music.* the twelve-tone technique.

se•ri•al•ize ['siriə,laɪz] *v.* **-ized, -iz•ing.** present in the form of a serial: *a novel serialized in a magazine.* **—,se•ri•al•i'za•tion,** *n.*

serial killer a person who murders more than two people.

serial number an individual number given to a person, article, etc., as a means of easy identification.

serial port *Computer technology.* a PORT[2] (def. 6b) which delivers the bits of a data byte serially, one after the other, rather than synchronously, as in a **parallel port.**

se•ri•ate ['siriɪt] *or* ['siri,eit] *adj.* arranged or occurring in one or more series. **—'se•ri•ate•ly,** *adv.*

se•ri•a•tim [,siri'eitɪm] *or* [,sɛri'eitɪm] *adv.* in a series; one after another. ⟨< Med.L⟩

se•ri•cin ['sɛrəsɪn] *n.* a gelatinous, amorphous substance holding the two gossamer strands of a raw silk fibre together. ⟨< L *sericum* silk + E *-in*⟩

ser•i•cul•ture ['sɛrə,kʌltʃər] *n.* the raising and care of silkworms for the production of raw silk. ⟨< F *séri(ci)culture* < L *sericum* silk + *cultura* culture⟩

se•ries ['siriz] *n., pl.* **-ries. 1** a number of things, usually similar, occurring or placed one after the other in a row: *A series of rooms opened off the long hall. A series of rainy days spoiled their vacation.* **2** coins, stamps, etc. of a particular issue, ruler, country, etc. **3** written or artistic works that are produced one after another, usually having a common subject or purpose, and often by a single author, artist, or composer. **4** *Electricity.* a type of end-to-end interconnection of the components in a circuit such that the same current flows through them all. **5** *Mathematics.* the indicated sum of a finite or infinite sequence of numbers. *Examples*: *1+2+3+4+5 (finite)*; *5+9+13+17+... (infinite)*. ⟨< L *series* < *serere* join⟩
☛ *Syn.* **1. Series,** SEQUENCE, SUCCESSION = a number of things, events, etc. arranged or coming one after another in some order. **Series** applies to a number of similar things with the same purpose or relation to each other: *She gave a series of lectures on Mexico.* **Sequence** implies a closer or unbroken connection in thought, between cause and effect, in numerical or alphabetical order, etc.: *The lecturer reviewed the sequence of events leading to peace.* **Succession** emphasizes following in order of time, sometimes place, usually without interruption: *a succession of colds.*
☛ *Usage.* **Series.** Commas are used between the members of a series of three or more short items, although usage is divided over the insertion of a comma before the last item of the series. Since this comma is sometimes needed to avoid confusion, it is better to use it all the time: *He forgot to pack his toothbrush, comb, and shaving equipment.*

se•ries–wound ['siriz ,waʊnd] *adj. Electricity.* wound so that the field magnet coils are connected in series with the armature and carry the same current.

ser•if ['sɛrɪf] *n. Printing.* a thin or smaller line used to finish off a main stroke of a letter, as at the top and bottom of M in this font. ⟨? < Du. *schreef* stroke, line < *schrijven* write < L *scribere*⟩

ser•i•graph ['sɛrə,græf] *n.* an original colour print produced by a silk-screen process. ⟨< L *seri(cum)* silk + E *-graph*⟩ **—se'rig•ra•pher** [sə'rɪgrəfər], *n.* **—se'rig•ra•phy,** *n.*

se•ri•o–com•ic [,siriou 'kɒmɪk] *adj.* partly serious and partly comic. **—,se•ri•o-'com•i•cal•ly,** *adv.*

se•ri•ous ['siriəs] *adj.* **1** thoughtful; grave: *a serious face.* **2** in earnest; not joking; sincere: *She was serious about the subject. His remarks were dead serious, though the audience took them lightly.* **3** needing thought; important: *Choice of one's life work is a serious matter.* **4** treating weighty or important subjects: *a serious film.* **5** important because it may do much harm; dangerous: *The*

badly injured child was in serious condition. ⟨< LL *seriosus* < L *serius* earnest⟩ **—'se•ri•ous•ly,** *adv.* **—'se•ri•ous•ness,** *n.*
☛ *Hom.* CEREUS.
☛ *Syn.* **1.** See note at GRAVE².

ser•mon ['sɜrmən] *n.* **1** a public talk on religion or something connected with religion. Ministers preach sermons in church. **2** a serious talk, often long and tiresome, about morals, conduct, duty, etc.: *After the guests left, the boy got a sermon on table manners from his mother.* ⟨ME < OF < L *sermo, -onis* a talk, originally, a stringing together of words < *serere* join⟩

ser•mon•ette [ˌsɜrmə'nɛt] *n.* **1** a brief sermon. **2** a short, often scolding, lecture.

ser•mon•ize ['sɜrməˌnaɪz] *v.* **-ized, -iz•ing. 1** give a sermon; preach. **2** preach or talk seriously to; lecture. **—'ser•monˌiz•er,** *n.*

Sermon on the Mount Christ's sermon to His disciples, containing the main principles of Christianity.

se•ro– *prefix.* having to do with serum: *serology.* Also, especially before a vowel, **ser-**.

se•ro•log•i•cal [ˌsirə'lɒdʒəkəl] *adj.* of or having to do with serology. **—ˌse•ro'log•i•cal•ly,** *adv.*

se•rol•o•gist [sɪ'rɒlədʒɪst] *n.* a person trained in serology, especially one whose work it is.

se•rol•o•gy [sɪ'rɒlədʒi] *n.* **1** the study of the use of serums in curing or preventing disease. **2** the testing of blood serum: *All the serology is done at our main lab.* ⟨< *sero-* (< L *serum* whey) + *-logy*⟩

ser•o•to•nin [ˌsɛrə'tounɪn] *n. Biochemistry.* a neurotransmitter that is synthesized from tryptophan in the hypothalamus region of the brain. It can produce muscle contraction and an increase in body temperature, and is associated with the regulation of emotion, sleep, memory, etc. *Formula*: $C_{10}H_{12}N_2O$ ⟨< *sero-* (< L *serum* whey) + *ton(ic)* + *-in*⟩

se•rous ['sirəs] *adj.* **1** of serum; having to do with serum. **2** like serum; watery. Tears are drops of a serous fluid. ⟨< L *serosus* < *serum* whey⟩

serous membrane *Anatomy. Zoology.* any of the thin, membranous linings, such as the peritoneum or pericardium, of various body cavities.

se•row ['sɛrou] *n.* a goat antelope (genus *Capricornus*) of east Asia, having a dark coat and sometimes a mane. ⟨< Lepcha, a Tibeto-Burman language of the N Indian subcontinent⟩

ser•pent ['sɜrpənt] *n.* **1** a snake, especially a large snake. **2** a sly, treacherous person. **3 the Serpent,** the Devil; Satan. **4** *Music.* an early wooden wind instrument, coiled like a snake and having a coarse, bass tone. ⟨< L *serpens, -entis,* orig. ppr. of *serpere* creep⟩

ser•pent•a•ri•um [ˌsɜrpən'tɛriəm] *n.* a place where snakes are kept in captivity, usually as an exhibit.

ser•pen•tine ['sɜrpənˌtaɪn] *or* ['sɜrpənˌtin] *adj., n. —adj.* **1** of or like a serpent. **2** winding; twisting: *the serpentine course of a creek.* **3** cunning; sly; treacherous: *a serpentine suggestion.*
—n. **1** a mineral consisting chiefly of a hydrous silicate of magnesium, usually green, and sometimes spotted like a serpent's skin. *Formula*: $Mg_3Si_2O_5(OH)_4$ **2** in figure skating, a school figure consisting of two figure eights sharing one loop. **3** any of various other things having a coiled or twisted shape. ⟨< LL *serpentinus* < L *serpens, -entis* serpent⟩

ser•rate *adj.* ['sɛrɪt] *or* ['sɛreit]; *v.* [sə'reit] *or* ['sɛreit] *adj., v.* **-rat•ed, -rat•ing.** *—adj.* **1** of a leaf, having a margin with sawlike notches angled toward the tip. See LEAF for picture. **2** having a notched edge; serrated.
—v. notch like a saw; make serrations in or on. ⟨< L *serratus* < *serra* a saw⟩

ser•rat•ed [sə'reitɪd] *or* ['sɛreitɪd] *adj.* having a notched edge; toothed.

ser•ra•tion [sə'reiʃən] *or* [sɛ'reiʃən] *n.* **1** a serrated edge or formation. **2** one of its series of notches. **3** the fact or condition of being serrate. Also, **serrature** ['sɛrətʃər].

ser•ried ['sɛrid] *adj.* crowded closely together. ⟨< F *serré,* pp. of *serrer* press close⟩

ser•ru•late ['sɛrəlɪt] *or* ['sɛrjəlɪt], ['sɛrəˌleit] *or* ['sɛrjəˌleit] *adj.* very finely notched: *a serrulate leaf.* ⟨< NL *serrulatus* < L *serrula,* dim. of *serra* a saw⟩

ser•ru•la•tion [ˌsɛrə'leiʃən] *or* [ˌsɛrjə'leiʃən] *n.* **1** something that is serrulate in form. **2** one notch in a serrulate edge. **3** a very fine serration.

se•rum ['sirəm] *n., pl.* **se•rums** or **se•ra** ['sirə]. **1** the clear, pale yellow, watery part of the blood that separates from the clot when blood coagulates. **2** a liquid used to prevent or cure a disease, usually obtained from the blood of an animal that has been made immune to the disease. Diphtheria antitoxin is a serum. **3** any watery animal liquid, such as lymph. **4** whey. ⟨< L *serum* whey⟩

serum albumin 1 *Biochemistry.* the chief protein of blood plasma, synthesized in the liver and important in controlling osmotic pressure and the transportation of metabolic products. **2** the commercial form of this product, used in the preparation of some foodstuffs and in the treatment of shock.

ser•val ['sɜrvəl] *n.* a medium-sized wildcat (*Felis serval*) of the African bush having long legs, large ears, and a tawny coat with black spots and stripes. ⟨< NL < Pg. *(lobo) cerval* lynx, ult. < L *cervus* stag⟩

A serval

serv•ant ['sɜrvənt] *n.* **1** a person employed in a household. **2** a person employed by another, especially a government. Police officers and firefighters are public servants. **3** a person devoted to any service: *Priests are the servants of their God.* **4** *Cdn.* formerly, an employee of the Hudson's Bay Company, specifically one other than an officer holding a commission from the Company. ⟨ME < OF *servant,* ppr. of *servir* serve. See SERVE.⟩
—'serv•ant•less, *adj.*

serve [sɜrv] *v.* **served, serv•ing;** *n. —v.* **1** give service to; work for or in; obey or honour. *An employee serves an employer.* **2** give service; work; perform official duties: *He served as butler. She served three years in the armed forces.* **3** wait on at table; bring food or drink to: *An old waiter served us.* **4** put (food or drink) on the table; prepare or present (food) in a given way (*sometimes with* **up**): *The waiter served the first course. He always serves vegetables with some kind of sauce.* **5** furnish or supply (*with* something): *The dairy serves us with milk. The soldiers were served with a round of ammunition.* **6** help; aid: *Let me know if I can serve you in any way.* **7** be useful, favourable, or suitable; be what is needed; be of use: *Boxes served as seats. The ship will sail when the wind and tide serve.* **8** be useful for; fulfil; satisfy the need of: *This will serve my purpose. One batch will serve 20. This park serves a large community.* **9** treat: *The prisoner was poorly served.* **10** pass; spend: *The thief served a term in prison.* **11** *Law.* **a** deliver (an order from a court, etc.). **b** present (someone) with an order from a court, etc.: *She was served with a notice to appear in court.* **12** act as a server at (Mass). **13** *Tennis, badminton, etc.* put (the ball or shuttlecock) in play by hitting. **14** wait on (customers) in a store: *Are you being served?* **15** *Nautical.* bind or wind (a rope, etc.) with fine cord or wire to strengthen or protect it. **16** of a male animal, especially a stud, copulate with (a female).
serve (someone) **right,** be just what someone deserves: *The punishment served her right.*
—n. Tennis, badminton, etc. **1** the act or way of serving a ball or shuttlecock. **2** a player's turn to serve. ⟨ME < OF *servir* < L *servire* < *servus* slave⟩

serv•er ['sɜrvər] *n.* **1** a person who serves. **2** a tray for dishes. **3** any of various pieces of tableware for serving food: *a cake or pie server.* **4** *Roman Catholic or High Anglican Church.* a person who assists the priest at Mass or Eucharist; acolyte. **5** *Computer technology.* a computer (or a component) that provides a service (data storage, printing, etc.) to other computers connected to the same network: *The print server allowed all of the network users to share the laser printer.*

serv•ice ['sɜrvɪs] *n., adj., v.* **-iced, -ic•ing.** *—n.* **1** a helpful act or acts; aid; conduct that is useful to others: *He performed many services for his country.* **2** supply; arrangements for supplying something useful or necessary: *The bus service was good.* **3** occupation or employment as a servant: *go into service.* **4** work done for others; performance of duties; work: *Mrs. Brown no longer needs the services of a doctor.* **5** repairs or maintenance of merchandise, such as appliances, provided to the consumer by the retailer or manufacturer. **6** advantage; benefit; use: *This coat has given me great service. Every available truck was pressed into service.* **7** a department of government or public employment, or persons engaged in it: *the civil service.* **8** duty in the navy, army, air force, etc.: *active service.* **9** **a** a religious meeting, ritual, or ceremony: *We attend church services twice a week.* **b** the music or liturgy for such a meeting or ceremony: *They wrote their own wedding service.* **10** regard; respect; devotion; obedience. **11** the manner of serving food; the food served. **12** a set of dishes, etc.: *a silver tea service.* **13** *Law.* the serving of a process or writ upon a person. **14** *Tennis, squash, badminton, etc.* **a** the act or manner of serving the ball or shuttlecock. **b** a player's turn to serve. **15** *Nautical.* a fine cord or wire wound about a rope, etc. to strengthen or protect it. **16** **services,** *pl.* **a** work done in the service of others; helpful labour, as opposed to production, manufacturing, construction work, etc.: *goods and services.* **b** arrangements or installations for public use, such as electricity, water supply, and sewers. **17** **the service** or **the services,** the navy, army, or air force. **18** in breeding animals, the act of putting a male with a female for mating.

at (someone's) **service,** ready to do, or be used for, whatever someone wants.

in service, **a** in working order; functioning: *We'll call you as soon as the line is in service again. Is their telephone in service?* **b** performing the duties of a servant.

of service, helpful; useful.

out of service, not in working order; not functioning: *This elevator is out of service.*

—adj. **1** used by or assisting household servants, tradespeople, etc.: *a service door, service pantry.* **2** belonging to a branch of the armed forces, especially on regular active duty: *a service cap, a service uniform.* **3** providing maintenance or repairs: *Take the broken toaster to the service department.* **4** supplying a service to the public, as opposed to goods: *This decade has seen a surge in service industries.*

—v. **1** make fit for service; keep fit for service: *The mechanic serviced our automobile.* **2** provide with a service or with services: *Two trains serviced the town.* **3** SERVE (def. 16). ⟨ME < OF < L *servitium* < *servus* slave⟩

serv•ice•a•ble ['sɜrvɪsəbəl] *adj.* **1** useful for a long time; able to stand much use. **2** capable of giving good service; useful. **3** *Archaic.* willing to be useful. **—,serv•ice•a'bil•i•ty** or **'serv•ice•a•ble•ness,** *n.* **—'serv•ice•a•bly,** *adv.*

serv•ice•ber•ry ['sɜrvɪs,bɛri] *n., adj.* *—n.* **1** any of several North American shrubs or small trees (genus *Amelanchier*) of the rose family having showy white flowers and sweet, purplish, edible berries. Also called **shadbush.** See also SASKATOON. **2** the fruit of any of these plants.

—adj. of or made with the berries of these plants: *serviceberry jam, serviceberry pie.*

service cap a uniform cap having a round, flat top and a visor, worn by most armed services in the world.

service centre **1** a stopping area adjoining an expressway, consisting of a service station, restaurant, toilet facilities, etc. **2** *Cdn.* a town or city serving as a shopping and distribution centre for the surrounding region: *In summer our small town is the service centre for a large resort area.*

service club **1** an organization, such as the Rotary or the IODE, formed to promote the welfare of its community and to further the interests of its members. **2** a recreation centre for military personnel.

service elevator an elevator used to carry goods, servants, or tradespeople, not for the use of the general public.

service line in various sports, such as tennis, volleyball, etc., the line from behind which a ball must be served or beyond which a served ball may not go.

serv•ice•man ['sɜrvɪs,mæn] *or* ['sɜrvɪsmən] *n., pl.* **-men.** **1** a male member of the armed forces. **2** a man whose job is to maintain and repair machines, appliances, etc.

service road **1** ACCESS ROAD. **2** a road, generally parallelling an expressway, to carry local traffic and to provide access to adjoining property.

services college *Cdn.* formerly, one of three military institutions of higher learning (the Royal Military College of Canada, le Collège Militaire de Saint-Jean, and Royal Roads) where military cadets could take university degrees in Arts, Science, and Engineering. Royal Roads and le Collège Militaire de Saint-Jean were disbanded in 1995.

service station **1** a place for supplying automobiles with gasoline, oil, water, repairs, etc. **2** a place where repairs, parts, adjustments, etc. can be obtained for mechanical or electrical devices.

service tree either of two varieties of the European mountain ash, *Sorbus domestica* or *S. torminalis*, having white flowers and small round edible fruits.

service vote *Cdn.* in an election, the votes of members of the armed forces who are on duty away from their home ridings. These votes are tallied separately and reported some time after the general count of votes.

serv•ice•wom•an ['sɜrvɪs,wʊmən] *n., pl.* **serv•ice•wom•en** [-wɪmɪn]. a female member of the armed forces.

ser•vi•ette [,sɜrvi'ɛt] *n.* a paper NAPKIN (def. 1). ⟨< F *serviette* < *servir* serve⟩

ser•vile ['sɜrvaɪl] *or* ['sɜrvɪl] *adj.* **1** fawning or submissive: *servile flattery.* **2** of or having to do with slaves: *a servile revolt, servile work.* **3** fit for a slave. **4** yielding through fear, lack of spirit, etc.: *An honest judge cannot be servile to public opinion.* ⟨ME < L *servilis* < *servus* slave⟩ **—'ser•vile•ly,** *adv.* **—ser'vil•i•ty** [sər'vɪləti] or **'ser•vile•ness,** *n.*

serv•ing ['sɜrvɪŋ] *n., v., adj.* *—n.* the portion of food served to a person at one time; a helping.

—v. ppr. of SERVE.

—adj. used for the service of food at table: *a serving spoon, serving bowls.*

ser•vi•tude ['sɜrvɪ,tjud] *or* ['sɜrvɪ,tud] *n.* **1** slavery; bondage. **2** forced labour as a punishment: *The criminal was sentenced to five years' servitude.* **3** *Law.* **a** the condition of property subject to a right of enjoyment possessed by some person other than its owner, or attaching to some other property. **b** such a right of enjoyment. ⟨ME < OF < L *servitudo* < *servus* slave⟩

ser•vo ['sɜrvou] *n., adj.* *—n.* **1** servomechanism. **2** servomotor.

—adj. of or involving a servomechanism.

ser•vo•mech•an•ism [,sɜrvou'mɛkə,nɪzəm] *n.* an electronic control system in which some type of control mechanism, such as hydraulic or pneumatic, etc. is activated by a low-energy signal that brings about the desired amount of control.

ser•vo•mo•tor ['sɜrvou,moutər] *n.* the motor of a servomechanism.

ses•a•me ['sɛsəmi] *n.* **1** a tropical annual plant (*Sesamum indicum*) widely cultivated for its small, oval, oily seeds. **2** the seeds of this plant, used to flavour bread, etc. and also as a source of oil. **3** See OPEN SESAME. ⟨< Gk. < Semitic⟩

ses•qui– *prefix.* one and a half: *sesquicentennial.* ⟨< L⟩

ses•qui•cen•ten•ni•al [,sɛskwɪsɛn'tɛnjəl] *n., adj.* *—n.* a 150th anniversary or its celebration.

—adj. having to do with, or marking the completion of, a period of a century and a half. ⟨< L *sesqui-* one and a half + E *centennial*⟩

ses•qui•ox•ide [,sɛskwi'ɒksaɪd] *n.* *Chemistry.* an oxide containing three atoms or equivalents of oxygen and two of another element.

ses•qui•pe•da•li•an [,sɛskwɪpə'deiliən] *adj., n.* *—adj.* **1** of a word, very long; containing many syllables. **2** using long words. **3** one and a half feet in length (almost half a metre).

—n. a very long word. ⟨< L *sesquipedalis* half a yard long < *sesqui* one and a half + *pes, pedis* foot⟩ **—,ses•qui•pe'da•li•an,ism,** *n.*

ses•sile ['sɛsaɪl] *or* ['sɛsɪl] *adj.* **1** *Botany.* attached by a base instead of by a stem, as a leaf having no petiole or a flower having no peduncle or pedicel. **2** *Zoology.* sedentary; fixed to one spot; not able to move around, as barnacles and sponges. ⟨< L *sessilis* sitting < *sedere* sit⟩

ses•sion ['sɛʃən] *n.* **1** a sitting or meeting of a court, council, legislature, etc.: *a session of Parliament.* **2** a series of such sittings. **3** the term or period of such sittings: *This year's session of Parliament was unusually long.* **4** a period of meetings, classes, etc.: *Our school has two sessions, one in the morning and one in the afternoon. She attended the university during the summer session.* **5** any meeting: *a heated session with the head of the department.* **6** a stretch of any kind of activity: *The boy had a little crying session but he's cheered up now.* **7** the minister and elders of a Presbyterian church.

in session, meeting: *The teachers were in session all Saturday morning.* ⟨ME < L *sessio, -onis* < *sedere* sit⟩

☛ *Hom.* CESSION.

ses•sion•al ['sɛʃənəl] *adj.* **1** of a session; having to do with sessions. **2** occurring every session.

sessional indemnity *Cdn.* in certain provinces of Canada, the remuneration paid each session to a Member of the Legislative Assembly.

ses•terce ['sɛstɜrs] *n.* an ancient Roman coin of small value. ⟨< L *sestertius*, originally, adj., two and a half < *semis* half unit (< *semi-* half + *as* unit) + *tertius* third⟩

ses•ter•tium [sə'stɜrʃəm] *n., pl.* **-tia** [-ʃə]. an ancient Roman unit of money equal to a thousand sesterces. ⟨gen. pl. of *sestertius*, masc., erroneously formed as a neut. nom. sing., short for *milia sestertium* thousands of sesterces⟩

ses•tet [sɛs'tɛt] *n.* **1** *Music.* sextet. **2** *Prosody.* **a** the last six lines of Italian or Petrarchan sonnets. **b** any six-line poem or stanza. ⟨< Ital. *sestetto*, ult. < L *sex* six⟩

set [sɛt] *v.* **set, set•ting;** *adj., n.* —*v.* **1** put in some place; put; place: *Set the box on its end.* **2 a** put in the right place, position, or condition: *to set a broken bone.* **b** arrange (the hair) when damp to make it take a certain position. **3** adjust according to a standard: *to set a clock.* **4** put in some condition or relation: *A spark set the woods on fire. The slaves were set free.* **5** put (a price, etc.); fix at a certain amount or rate: *The jeweller set the value of the watch at $500.* **6** put (a body part) in a given position: *set one's hand to the plough. Never set foot in my house again.* **7** post, appoint, or station for the purpose of performing some duty: *to set a detective on a case.* **8** fix; arrange; appoint: *to set a time limit for taking an examination.* **9** provide for others to follow: *to set a good example.* **10** put in a fixed, rigid, or settled state: *to set one's jaw, set one's mind against something.* **11** congeal or cause to congeal; jell: *Jelly sets as it cools.* **12** put in a frame or other thing that holds: *to set a diamond in gold.* **13** decorate with gems attached by a metal mounting: *a bracelet set with diamonds.* **14** of the sun or moon, go down; sink: *The sun sets in the west.* **15 a** put (a hen) to sit on eggs to hatch them. **b** place (eggs) under a hen to be hatched. **16** plant or transplant (a seedling, shoot, etc.). **17** of a dog, indicate the position of game by standing stiffly and pointing with the nose. **18** hang or fit in a particular manner: *That coat sets well.* **19** have a direction; tend: *The current sets to the south.* **20** begin to move. **21** bring (an instrument or tool) into contact with (something else), implying an expected result: *set a match to tinder, set pen to paper.* **22** begin to apply; begin to apply oneself: *Have you set to work?* **23** form fruit in the blossom. **24** *Music.* arrange (music) for certain voices or instruments: *The song has been set for flute and guitar.* **25** *Printing.* put (type) in the order required. **26 a** make (the colour of fabrics, etc.) fast. **b** of the colour of fabric, become fast: *The colour will set after the first wash.*
set about, start work upon; begin: *Set about your washing.*
set against, a make unfriendly toward. **b** balance with. **c** compare or contrast with.
set apart, reserve.
set aside, a put to one side. **b** put by for later use. **c** discard, dismiss, or leave out; reject; annul.
set back, a stop; hinder; delay: *The job was set back because of the accident.* **b** *Informal.* cost (a person) a specified amount: *The new car set her back $20 000.* **c** put (the hands of a clock or watch) to an earlier time, especially back to standard time after daylight saving.
set bread, mix batter or dough and leave it to rise.
set down, a deposit; put down: *set down a suitcase.* **b** put down in writing or printing. **c** consider due; ascribe: *Your failure in the test can be set down to too much haste.* **d** land (a plane).
set forth, a make known; express; declare. **b** start out: *We set forth on our trip.*
set (great) store by, value highly.
set in, a begin. **b** blow or flow toward the shore. **c** incorporate (a part) into a whole, as a sleeve into a garment, a paragraph into a text, etc.
set off, a cause to explode. **b** start to go: *set off for home.* **c** emphasize or enhance by contrast: *The green shirt set off his red hair.* **d** balance; compensate: *Her losses were set off by some gains.* **e** mark off; separate from the others: *One sentence was set off from the rest by quotation marks.* **f** make (something) start or sound: *Press this button to set off the timer.*
set on or **set upon, a** attack: *The dog set on the old man.* **b** urge to attack.
set (one's) heart on, be very eager to have or do.
set out, a start to go. **b** spread out to show, sell, or use. **c** plant. **d** plan; intend (to do something). **e** mark out; define.
set straight, a correct the crooked position of. **b** correct a wrong impression, opinion, etc. of.
set to, a begin: *Set to work.* **b** begin fighting or arguing: *The two boys set to.*
set to music, a compose music to fit (words). **b** fit (words) to an existing piece of music: *The same hymn has been set to three different tunes.*
set up, a build. **b** begin; start. **c** put up high; raise in place, position, power, pride, etc. **d** claim; pretend. **e** make ready; prepare; arrange. **f** establish. **g** put in an upright position. **h** fund, fit out, etc. for some undertaking: *They set him up in the textile business.* **i** arrange a situation so as to incriminate or make vulnerable; subject to a set-up.
set (oneself) up for, a claim or pretend to be. **b** act in such a way as to incur or invite.
—*adj.* **1** fixed or appointed beforehand; established: *a set time, set rules.* **2** fixed; rigid: *a set smile. She has set opinions.* **3** firm; hard; congealed: *Is the pudding set yet?* **4** resolved; determined: *He is set on going today.*
all set, all ready to start, go, etc.
dead set on (or **against**) **something,** absolutely determined (not) to do or allow something.
get set, a get ready. **b** poise oneself to begin a race.
set in (one's) **ways,** of stubbornly fixed habits; obstinate.
—*n.* **1** a number of things or persons belonging together: *a set of dishes.* **2** *Mathematics.* a specified collection of elements, especially a collection having some feature or features in common: *the set of all right triangles, the set of even integers.* **3** a device for receiving or sending by radio, television, telephone, telegraph, etc. **4 a** the complete scenery for a play, act, scene, etc. **b** the physical setting for a scene in a motion picture, television show, etc. **5** the way a thing is put or placed; form; shape: *Her jaw had a stubborn set.* **6** the way in which anything fits: *the set of a coat.* **7 a** a direction; tendency; course; drift: *The set of opinion was toward building a new bridge.* **b** the direction in which a current flows or a wind blows. **8** a warp; bend; displacement: *a set to the right.* **9** a slip, bulb, or shoot for planting. **10** a young fruit just formed from a blossom. **11** the act or manner of setting. **12** *Tennis.* a group of six or more games. To win a set, one side must win at least six games, and two more than the other side. **13** a snare or trap. **14** *Printing.* the width of a piece of type. **15** *Square dancing.* **a** a group of four couples. **b** the figures of a square dance. **c** a series of dance pieces played or danced one after the other. **16** the pointing of a dog, such as a setter, in the presence of game. **17 a** a lotion or spray used to fix a hairstyle in place. **b** a hairstyle that has been set. **18** a fishing net, floats, weights, etc., in place and ready to be or being towed. ⟨OE *settan*⟩
☛ *Syn. v.* **1.** See note at PUT.
☛ *Usage.* **Set,** SIT. People and things *sit* (pt., *sat*) or they are *set* (pt., *set*), meaning 'placed': *I like to sit in a hotel lobby. That book has sat on the shelf for a long time. The waiter set the soup down with a flourish. The post was set 1 m into the ground.*

Set [sɛt] *n.* the ancient Egyptian god of evil, represented as having an animal's head with a pointed snout. Also, **Seth.**

se•ta ['sitə] *n., pl.* **se•tae** [-ti] *or* [-taɪ]. *Zoology. Botany.* any slender, stiff, bristlelike structure. Earthworms have two pairs of setae in each segment. ⟨< L *saeta*⟩

se•ta•ceous [sɪ'teiʃəs] *adj.* **1** furnished with or having bristles. **2** bristle-shaped; like a bristle or bristles. ⟨< NL *setaceus*⟩ **—se'ta•ceous•ly,** *adv.*

set•back ['sɛt,bæk] *n.* **1** a check to progress; reverse. **2** *Architecture.* **a** a steplike setting back of the upper storeys of a tall building in order to give better light and air in the street. **b** an upper or lower part of a wall, set back to form a shelf or niche respectively.

se•tif•er•ous [sə'tɪfərəs] *adj.* having bristles; bristly.

se•tig•er•ous [sə'tɪdʒərəs] *adj.* having bristles.

set–in ['sɛt 'ɪn] *adj.* of part of a garment, made separately and affixed to another part: *set-in sleeves.*

set–off ['sɛt ,ɒf] *n.* **1** a setting off on a trip; a start; departure. **2** a thing used to set off or adorn; ornament; decoration. **3** something that counterbalances or makes up for something else; a compensation; offset. **4** a settlement of a debt by means of a claim in the debtor's favour. **5** a claim so used.

se•tose ['sitous] *or* [sɪ'tous] *adj.* setaceous.

set piece 1 a piece of literature, music, etc. which is an impressive example of a conventional form. **2** *Theatre.* a piece of a stage set.

set point *Tennis.* the point that, if won, enables the player (and his or her partner, in doubles) to win the set.

set•screw ['sɛt,skru] *n.* **1** a machine screw used to fasten gears, pulleys, etc. to a shaft. **2** any screw that is turned to adjust, set, or regulate something.

set square a flat, right-angled piece of wood or metal that enables the user to draw straight lines and right angles accurately. It is used by carpenters, drafters, etc.

set•tee [sɛ'ti] *n.* a sofa with a back and, usually, arms. ⟨< *set*⟩

set•ter ['sɛtər] *n.* **1** any of several breeds of hunting dog usually trained to locate game and indicate its presence by pointing. Setters were originally trained to crouch when they had located game. **2** a person or thing that sets or arranges things: *a setter of type, a setter of jewels.*

set theory the branch of mathematics dealing with the relations between SETS (def. *n.* 2).

set•ting ['sɛtɪŋ] *n., v.* —*n.* **1** a frame or other thing in which something is set. The mounting of a jewel is its setting. **2** *Theatre.* the scenery of a play; a set. **3** the place, time, etc. of a play or story. **4** the surroundings; background: *a scenic mountain setting.* **5** the music composed to go with a story, poem, etc. **6** the eggs that a hen sits on for hatching. **7** the act of one that sets. **8** the dishes or cutlery required to set one place at a table. **9** the position of a dial or selector that has been set: *I left the radio at the right setting for our favourite station.* **10** social context; environment; milieu: *You couldn't use this kind of discipline technique in a classroom setting.* **11** *Cdn. Logging.* the whole of an area logged from a single SPAR TREE.
—*v.* ppr. of SET.

set•tle[1] ['sɛtəl] *v.* **-tled, -tling. 1 a** determine; decide; agree (on): *Have you settled on a time for leaving?* **b** end or resolve (a dispute); deal with (a problematic person or thing) finally. **2** put or be put in order; arrange: *I must settle all my affairs before going away for the winter.* **3** pay; arrange payment: *to settle a bill.* **4** take up residence (in a new country or place): *to settle in Manitoba.* **5** establish colonies or communities in: *The French settled Québec.* **6** set or be set in a fairly permanent position, place, or way of life: *She is settled in her new job.* **7** establish (someone else) as a resident: *New immigrants were settled by the government in less populated areas.* **8** put or come to rest in a particular place; put in or come to a definite condition: *His cold settled in his lungs.* **9** arrange in or come to a desired or comfortable position: *The cat settled itself in the chair.* **10** make or become quiet: *A vacation will settle your nerves.* **11** go down; sink: *The end of that wall has settled 5 cm.* **12** of liquid, make or become clear: *A beaten egg or cold water will settle coffee.* **13** of dregs, sink or cause to sink to the bottom. **14** make or become firm and compact: *to settle the contents of a barrel.*
settle down, a live a more regular life. **b** direct steady effort or attention: *to settle down to studying.* **c** calm down; become quiet.
settle for, accept (something) in place of one's real preference or desire.
settle (something) **on** or **upon** (someone), give (property, etc.) to by law.
settle up, pay a bill or bills; make payment.
settle with, a pay a debt to. **b** come to an agreement with. **c** get revenge on. ⟨OE *setlan* < *setl* settle[2]⟩
☛ *Syn.* **1.** See note at FIX.

set•tle[2] ['sɛtəl] *n.* a long wooden seat with arms and a high back, and often having a boxlike base that can be used as a storage chest. ⟨OE *setl*⟩

set•tle•ment ['sɛtəlmənt] *n.* **1** the act of settling or the state of being settled. **2** establishment in life; stability; permanence. **3** a deciding; determining: *the settlement of a date.* **4** a putting in order; arrangement. **5** a payment: *Settlement of all claims against the firm will be made shortly.* **6** the settling of persons in a new region: *The settlement of the British along the Atlantic coast of North America gave England claim to that section.* **7** a region settled in this way: *England had many settlements along the Atlantic coast.* **8** a group of buildings or community and the people living there: *The explorers spent the night in a First Nations settlement.* **9** a place in a poor, neglected neighbourhood where work for its improvement is carried on. Also, **settlement house. 10** the settling of property upon someone: *She received $200 000 by a marriage settlement.* **11** the amount so given. **12** a gradual sinking or subsidence of a structure, etc.

settlement officer *n. Cdn.* a government official with the Department of Immigration, who advises newly-arrived immigrants and directs them to their place of settlement.

set•tler ['sɛtlər] *n.* a person who settles, especially in a new region.

set•tlings ['sɛtlɪŋz] *n.pl.* sediment.

set–to ['sɛt ˌtu] *n., pl.* **-tos.** *Informal.* a fight; dispute.

set–up ['sɛt ˌʌp] *n.* **1** an arrangement of apparatus, machinery, etc. **2** any physical arrangement, plan of action, etc. **3** the arrangement of an organization. **4** *Slang.* **a** a contest or match where the outcome is assured. **b** anything that is very easy to do or whose outcome is readily predictable. **c** a contestant whose defeat is expected in such a match. **5** an arranging of circumstances so as to incriminate someone, trick him or her into a given action, or otherwise make him or her vulnerable. **6** one's manner of holding the head and body; carriage; bearing. **7** the materials, such as a glass, and the fixings, such as soda water, ice, etc., for mixing an alcoholic drink. Also, **setup**.

sev•en ['sɛvən] *n., adj.* —*n.* **1** one more than six; 7: *Ten minus three equals seven.* **2** the numeral 7: *This 7 looks like a 1.* **3** the seventh in a set or series; especially, a playing card having seven spots: *She led with a seven of spades.* **4** a set or series of seven persons or things: *He arranged the cards in sevens.*
—*adj.* **1** one more than six; 7: *They stayed seven days.* **2** being seventh in a set or series (*used mainly after the noun*): *Lesson Seven was boring.* ⟨OE *seofon*⟩

sev•en•fold ['sɛvən,fould] *adv., adj.* —*adv.* **1** seven times as much or as many. **2** seven times as much or as often; in the proportion of seven to one.
—*adj.* **1** seven times as much or as many. **2** having seven parts.

Seven Hills the hills on and about which Rome was built.

seven seas all the seas and oceans of the world, traditionally believed to be the Arctic, Antarctic, North Atlantic, South Atlantic, North Pacific, South Pacific, and Indian Oceans: *to sail the seven seas.*

sev•en•teen ['sɛvən'tin] *n., adj.* —*n.* **1** seven more than ten; 17: *Seventeen plus three is twenty.* **2** the numeral 17: *I think it's a 17, not an 11.* **3** the seventeenth in a set or series. **4** a set or series of seventeen persons or things.
—*adj.* **1** seven more than ten; 17: *It costs about seventeen dollars.* **2** being seventeenth in a set or series (*used after the noun*): *Chapter Seventeen looks interesting.* ⟨OE *seofontēne*⟩

sev•en•teenth ['sɛvən'tinθ] *adj. or n.* **1** next after the sixteenth; last in a series of 17; 17th. **2** one, or being one, of 17 equal parts.

sev•enth ['sɛvənθ] *adj., n.* —*adj.* **1** next after the sixth; last in a series of 7; 7th. **2** being one of 7 equal parts.
—*n.* **1** the next after the sixth; the last in a series of 7. **2** one of 7 equal parts. **3** *Music.* **a** the tone six degrees above the tonic in a diatonic scale. **b** the interval between any two tones in a diatonic scale that are six degrees apart. **c** the combination of two such tones. **d** the chord consisting of the tonic, third, fifth, and seventh tones of a diatonic scale.

Seventh Day Adventist a member of a Christian group that believes that the second coming of Christ is near at hand. Seventh Day Adventists keep the sabbath on Saturday, the seventh day.

seventh heaven *Esp. Islam.* **1** the outermost or highest of seven heavens surrounding the earth, where Allah and his angels reside. **2** the highest place or condition of joy and happiness.

sev•enth•ly ['sɛvənθli] *adv.* in the seventh place.

sev•en•ti•eth ['sɛvəntiɪθ] *adj. or n.* **1** next after the sixty-ninth; last in a series of 70; 70th. **2** one, or being one, of 70 equal parts.

sev•en•ty ['sɛvənti] *n., pl.* **-ties;** *adj.* —*n.* **1** seven times ten; 70. **2 seventies,** *pl.* the years from seventy through seventy-nine, especially of a century or of a person's life: *He was still skiing regularly well into his seventies.*
—*adj.* being seven times ten; 70. ⟨OE *seofontig*⟩

Seven Wonders of the World the seven structures of the ancient world considered by ancient and medieval scholars to be most remarkable. They are the Egyptian Pyramids, the Mausoleum at Halicarnassus, the Temple of Artemis (Diana) at Ephesus, the walls and hanging gardens of Babylon, the Colossus of Rhodes, the statue of Zeus by Phidias at Olympia, and the Pharos (lighthouse) at Alexandria.

Seven Years' War a war fought between Britain and France and their allies (1756-1763) in Europe, North America, India, etc. In Canada, the French were defeated by the British in 1759, making Canada a British colony. In North America, the war was known also as the **French and Indian War.**

sev•er ['sɛvər] *v.* **1** cut apart; cut off: *to sever a rope. The axe severed his head from his body.* **2** part; divide; separate: *The church was severed into two factions. The rope severed and the swing fell down.* **3** break off: *The two countries severed relations.* ⟨ME < OF *sevrer,* ult. < L *separare* separate. See SEPARATE.⟩

sev•er•a•ble ['sɛvərəbəl] *adj.* **1** able to be severed. **2** *Law.* separable or capable of being treated as separate from the whole, as the terms of a contract. —**ˌsev•er•a'bil•i•ty,** *n.*

sev•er•al ['sɛvrəl] *or* ['sɛvərəl] *adj., pron.* —*adj.* **1** being more than two or three but not many; some; a few: *to gain several kilograms.* **2** individual; different: *The boys went their several ways, each on his own business.* **3** considered separately; single: *the several steps in the process of making paper.*
—*pron.* more than two or three but not many; some; a few:

Several have given their consent. ⟨ME < AF *several*, ult. < L *separ* distinct < *separare* separate. See SEPARATE.⟩

sev•er•al•ly ['sɛvrəli] *or* ['sɛvərəli] *adv.* **1** separately; singly; individually: *Consider these points, first severally and then collectively.* **2** respectively. **3** *Archaic.* apart from others; independently.

sev•er•al•ty ['sɛvrəlti] *or* ['sɛvərəlti] *n., pl.* **-ties. 1** the state of being separate or distinct. **2** *Law.* **a** of an estate, land, etc., the condition of being held or owned by separate or individual rights. **b** the estate or land so held.

sev•er•ance ['sɛvərəns] *n.* **1** a severing or being severed; separation; division: *the severance of diplomatic relations between two countries.* **2** *Law.* a division of land into parts for building.

severance pay additional pay, based on seniority, granted to employees that are laid off from a business, company, etc.

se•vere [sə'vir] *adj.* **-ver•er, -ver•est. 1** very strict; stern; harsh: *The judge imposed a severe sentence on the criminal.* **2** serious; grave: *a severe illness.* **3** very plain or simple; without ornament: *Her severe dress made her look old.* **4** sharp; violent: *a severe criticism, a severe storm.* **5** difficult: *a series of severe tests.* **6** rigidly exact, accurate, or methodical: *severe reasoning.* ⟨< L *severus*⟩ **—se'vere•ly,** *adv.* **—se'vere•ness,** *n.*

se•ver•i•ty [sə'vɛrɪti] *n., pl.* **-ties. 1** strictness; sternness; harshness. **2** violence; sharpness: *the severity of storms, pain, disease, grief, etc.* **3** simplicity of style or taste; plainness. **4** seriousness. **5** accuracy; exactness. **6** something severe.

se•viche [sə'vitʃei] *or* [sə'viʃ] *n.* See CEVICHE.

Sè•vres ['sɛvrə] *n.* **1** a choice and costly kind of porcelain. **2** something made of this porcelain. ⟨< *Sèvres*, a town in N France, where this porcelain is made⟩

sew [sou] *v.* **sewed, sewn** or **sewed, sew•ing. 1** work with needle and thread: *Can you sew?* **2** make with needle and thread: *He sewed a pair of pants.* **3** fasten with stitches: *sew a patch onto a garment.*
sew up, a close with stitches: *The doctor sewed up the wound.* **b** *Informal.* assure the outcome of. **c** *Informal.* acquire monopoly or sole control of. **d** complete or conclude successfully. ⟨OE *seowian*⟩
☛ *Hom.* SO, SOH, SOW[1].

sew•age ['suɪdʒ] *n.* the waste that passes through sewers.

sew•er[1] ['suər] *n.* a pipe or channel to carry off waste water and refuse. Sewers are usually underground. ⟨ME < OF *sewiere* sluice from a pond, ult. < L *ex* by + *aqua* water⟩

sew•er[2] ['souər] *n.* a person or thing that sews. ⟨< *sew*⟩

sew•er[3] ['suər] *n.* in medieval England, a head servant in charge of arranging the table and serving the meals. ⟨ME < AF *asseour*, literally, seater, ult. < L *ad-* by + *sedere* sit⟩

sew•er•age ['suərɪdʒ] *n.* **1** the removal of waste matter by sewers. **2** a system of sewers. **3** sewage.

sew•ing ['souɪŋ] *n., adj., v. —n.* **1** work done with a needle and thread. **2** something to be sewn.
—adj. for sewing: *a sewing room.*
—v. ppr. of SEW.

sewing circle a group of people, especially women, who meet regularly to sew for their church, for charity, etc.

sewing machine a machine for sewing or stitching cloth.

sewn [soun] *v.* a pp. of SEW.

sex [sɛks] *n., v. —n.* **1 a** either of the two categories, male and female, into which human beings, animals, and plants are divided according to their function in the reproductive process. **b** all the characteristics which distinguish males and females. **c** all the members of either category, collectively. **2** the fact or condition of being male or female: *without regard to age or sex. Sex is not a feature of inanimate objects.* **3** sexual attraction between people: *Sex makes the world go round.* **4** behaviour motivated by such attraction. **5** SEXUAL INTERCOURSE. **6** the genitals. **7** (*adjl.*) of or having to do with sex: *sex education.*
—v. **1** determine the sex of (young chickens, kittens, puppies, etc.). **2** make sexually more interesting or appealing (*usually used with* **up**): *You could put a slit in the side of the skirt to sex it up.* **3** excite or arouse sexually (*usually used with* **up**). ⟨< L *sexus*⟩

sex•a•ge•nar•i•an [,sɛksədʒə'nɛriən] *adj., n. —adj.* of the age of 60 years, or between 60 and 70 years old.
—n. a person aged 60, or between 60 and 70. ⟨< L *sexagenarius*, ult. < *sexaginta* sixty⟩

sex•ag•e•nar•y [sɛk'sædʒə,nɛri] *adj., n., pl.* **-nar•ies.** *—adj.* **1** of or having to do with the number 60; composed of or going by sixties. **2** sexagenarian.
—n. a sexagenarian.

Sex•a•ges•i•ma [,sɛksə'dʒɛsəmə] *n.* in the Christian calendar, the second Sunday before Lent. ⟨< L *sexagesima*, literally, sixtieth⟩

sex•a•ges•i•mal [,sɛksə'dʒɛsəməl] *adj., n. —adj.* having to do with or based upon the number 60. A sexagesimal fraction is one whose denominator is 60 or a power of 60.
—n. a sexagesimal fraction.

sex appeal sexual attractiveness.

sex chromosome *Genetics.* a chromosome (X or Y) in most animals and some plants, different in shape and function from the other chromosomes, that determines an individual's sex.

sex chromatin *Biology.* a deeply staining mass of chromatin seen in interphase cells of female mammals, representing an inactive X chromosome.

sex determination the mechanism by which the sex of an organism is determined. In mammals, the sex of the embryo depends on whether the ovum, which contains an X chromosome, is fertilized by a sperm which carries an X chromosome (producing a female) or a Y chromosome (producing a male).

sexed [sɛkst] *adj., v. —adj.* **1** having sexual characteristics. **2** having (a given) appetite for sex: *over-sexed.*
—v. pt. and pp of SEX.
☛ *Hom.* SEXT.

sex•en•ni•al [sɛk'sɛniəl] *adj., n. —adj.* **1** occurring every six years. **2** of or lasting for six years.
—n. the sixth anniversary. **—sex'en•ni•al•ly,** *adv.*

sex hormone *Biochemistry.* any steroid hormone, such as estrogen, testosterone, etc. that can influence the development of or have an effect on the reproductive system or the secondary sex characteristics.

sex•ism ['sɛksɪzəm] *n.* prejudice or discrimination against a person or group of persons on the basis of their sex.

sex•ist ['sɛksɪst] *adj., n. —adj.* characterized by prejudice or discrimination on the basis of sex: *a sexist attitude or remark.*
—n. a person who has such an attitude.

sex•less ['sɛkslɪs] *adj.* **1** lacking sexual characteristics; neuter. **2** lacking interest in sex.

sex–limited ['sɛks ,lɪmɪtɪd] *adj. Genetics.* referring to a trait that is expressed in one sex only.

sex–linked ['sɛks ,lɪŋkt] *adj. Genetics.* of inherited characters, determined by genes carried on a sex chromosome.

sex•ol•o•gy [sɛk'sɒlədʒi] *n.* the systematic study of the sexual behaviour of humans. **—sex'ol•o•gist,** *n.*

sex ratio *Sociology.* the ratio of the sexes in a given population. At birth, the ratio is approximately 105 males to every 100 females, or 1.05.

sex symbol a person who is famous for his or her sex appeal.

sext [sekst] *n.* **1** the fourth of the seven canonical hours set aside for Christian prayer and meditation. **2** the office or service for this hour. ⟨< L *sexta (hora)* sixth (hour) < *sex* six; because it originally came at the sixth hour of the day (noon)⟩
☛ *Hom.* SEXED.

sex•tan ['sɛkstən] *n., adj. —n.* a fever or ague characterized by paroxysms that recur every sixth day.
—adj. **1** of such a fever or ague. **2** recurring every sixth day. ⟨< NL *sextana (febris* fever*)* < L *sex* six⟩
☛ *Hom.* SEXTON.

Sex•tans ['sɛkstənz] *n. Astronomy.* an equatorial constellation between Hydra and Leo.

sex•tant ['sɛkstənt] *n.* **1** an astronomical instrument used by navigators, surveyors, etc. for measuring the angular distance between two objects. Sextants are used at sea to measure the altitude of the sun, a star, etc. in order to determine the latitude and longitude. Compare QUADRANT. **2** one sixth of a circle. ⟨< L *sextans, -antis* a sixth < *sex* six⟩

sex•tet or **sex•tette** [sɛks'tɛt] *n.* **1** *Music.* **a** a composition for six voices or instruments. **b** six singers or players. **2** any group of six. ⟨alteration of *sestet*, after L *sex* six⟩

sex•til•lion [sɛks'tɪljən] *n.* **1** in Canada, the United States, and France, 1 followed by 21 zeros. **2** in the United Kingdom, 1 followed by 36 zeros. ⟨< F *sextillion* (< L *sextus* sixth), modelled after *million* million⟩

sex•ton ['sɛkstən] *n.* **1** a person employed as caretaker of a church and its adjacent property. A sexton's duties sometimes include ringing the church bell for services, etc. and digging

graves. 2 an administrative official in a synagogue. ⟨ME < OF *secrestein* < Med.L *sacristanus* sacristan. Doublet of SACRISTAN.⟩
☛ *Hom.* SEXTAN.

sex•tu•ple [sɛks'tjupəl] *or* [sɛks'tupəl], [sɛks'tʌpəl] *or* ['sɛkstəpəl] *adj., n., v.* **-pled, -pling.** *—adj.* **1** consisting of six parts; sixfold. **2** six times as great. **3** *Music.* characterized by six beats to the measure.
—n. a number or amount six times as great as another.
—v. make or become six times as great. ⟨< L *sextus* sixth; modelled after *quadruple*⟩

sex•tu•plet [sɛks'tʌplɪt], [sɛks'tjuplɪt], [sɛks'tuplɪt], *or* ['sɛkstəplɪt] *n.* **1** one of six children, animals, etc. born of the same mother at the same time. **2** a group of six things. ⟨< *sextuple*, modelled after *triplet*⟩

sex•u•al ['sɛkʃuəl] *adj.* **1** of or having to do with sex or the sexes: *sexual distinctions.* **2** of or having to do with relations between the sexes: *sexual conflict, sexual morality.* **3** *Biology.* having or involving sex: *sexual reproduction.* ⟨< LL *sexualis* < L *sexus* sex⟩ **—'sex•u•al•ly,** *adv.*

sexual harassment unwelcome sexual advances, sexual comments, etc. directed toward someone by a fellow employee, an employer, or a superior, especially if compliance constitutes a form of blackmail.

sexual intercourse **1** a joining of the sexual organs of a male and a female human being, usually with the transfer of semen from the male to the female. **2** any act involving the sex organs of male or female.

sex•u•al•i•ty [,sɛkʃu'ælәti] *n.* **1** sexual character; possession of sex. **2** attention to sexual matters; sexual drive.

sex•y ['sɛksi] *adj.* **sex•i•er, sex•i•est.** *Informal.* **1** sexually provocative or stimulating: *a sexy dress, sexy beauties.* **2** especially concerned with sex: *a sexy novel.* **—'sex•i•ly,** *adv.* **—'sex•i•ness,** *n.*

Sey•chelles [sei'ʃɛl] *or* [sei'ʃɛlz] *n.pl.* a large group of islands in the Indian Ocean, north of Madagascar, formerly a British colony, now an independent member of the Commonwealth.

sf or **SF** SCIENCE FICTION.

sf. sforzando.

sfer•ics ['sfɛrɪks] *n.pl.* See SPHERICS[2].

sfor•zan•do [sfɔr'tsɑndou] *adj., adv., n. Music. —adj.* with special, usually sudden, emphasis.
—adv. in a sforzando manner.
—n. a tone or chord performed in this way. *Abbrev.*: sf. or sfz. ⟨< Ital. *sforzando* forcing⟩

sfz. sforzando.

s.g. SPECIFIC GRAVITY.

Sgt. or **Sgt** sergeant.

Sgt.Maj. sergeant-major.

sh [ʃ] *interj.* used to urge silence.

Shab•bat [ʃɑ'bɑt] *n. Judaism.* Sabbath. Also, **Shabbos** ['ʃɑbəs].

shab•by ['ʃæbi] *adj.* **-bi•er, -bi•est. 1** much worn: *His old suit looks shabby.* **2** wearing old or much worn clothes. **3** poor or neglected; run-down: *a shabby old house.* **4** not generous; mean; unfair: *It is shabby not to speak to an old friend just because she is poor.*
not too shabby, an expression of approval: *She's getting $2000 a month—that's not too shabby!* ⟨< dial. *shab* scab, OE *sceabb*⟩ **—'shab•bi•ly,** *adv.* **—'shab•bi•ness,** *n.*

shack [ʃæk] *n., v. —n.* **1** a roughly built hut or cabin: *The girls made a shack in the backyard.* **2** a house in bad condition.
—v.
shack up, *Slang.* live with a person of the opposite sex in a common-law union. ⟨? < Mexican Sp. *jacal* wooden hut < Nahuatl *xacalli*⟩

shack•le ['ʃækəl] *n., v.* **-led, -ling.** *—n.* **1** a metal band fastened around the ankle or wrist of a prisoner, slave, etc. Shackles are usually fastened to each other, the wall, floor, etc. by chains. **2** the link fastening together the two rings for the ankles and wrists of a prisoner. **3** anything that prevents freedom of action, thought, etc. **4** something for fastening or coupling. **5 shackles,** *pl.* fetters; chains.
—v. **1** put shackles on. **2** restrain; hamper. **3** fasten or couple with a shackle. ⟨OE *sceacel*⟩ **—'shack•ler,** *n.*

shack•town ['ʃæk,taʊn] *n.* a residential area consisting of roughly built huts or cabins; a collection of shacks.

shad [ʃæd] *n., pl.* **shad** or **shads.** any of several saltwater fishes (genus *Alosa*) of the herring family that ascend rivers in the spring to spawn. The American shad (*A. sapidissima*) of the North Atlantic coast is a valuable food fish. ⟨OE *sceadd*⟩

shad•ber•ry ['ʃæd,bɛri] *n., pl.* **-ries.** *Cdn., esp. Maritimes.* **1** the fruit of the shadbush. **2** shadbush; serviceberry. ⟨? because the bush flowers at the season when shad appear in Atlantic rivers⟩

shad•blos•som ['ʃæd,blɒsəm] *n.* shadbush.

shad•bush ['ʃæd,bʊʃ] *n. Cdn., esp. Maritimes.* serviceberry.

Shaddock

shad•dock ['ʃædək] *n.* **1** a SE Asian citrus tree (*Citrus grandis*, also called *C. maxima*) bearing very large, usually pear-shaped, edible, yellow fruit with a tart flavour. **2** the fruit of this tree. ⟨after Captain *Shaddock*, its first western cultivator⟩

shade [ʃeid] *n., v.* **shad•ed, shad•ing.** *—n.* **1** a partly dark place, not in the sunshine. **2** a slight darkness or coolness afforded by something that cuts off light: *the shade of a tree.* **3** a place or condition of comparative obscurity. **4 the shades, a** darkness of evening or night. **b** Hades. **c** the spirits of the dead. **5** something that shuts out, diminishes, or screens the light, as a blind: *Pull down the shades of the windows.* **6** lightness or darkness of colour; difference of hue: *silks in all shades of blue.* **7** the dark part of a picture. **8** a very small difference, amount, or degree: *a shade too long.* **9** a darkening look, feeling, etc.; shadow; cloud: *A shade of doubt troubled her.* **10 a** a ghost; spirit: *the shades of departed heroes.* **b** anything unreal or insubstantial. **11 shades,** *pl. Slang.* sunglasses.
in or **into the shade, a** out of the light. **b** in or into a condition of being unknown or unnoticed.
shades of (something or someone)! reminiscent of (an event or a prominent person from the past): *Shades of the Depression! Shades of Margaret Thatcher!*
—v. **1 a** screen the light of. **b** screen from light; darken. **2** obscure. **3** make dim or gloomy. **4** show small differences; change little by little: *This scarf shades from deep rose to pale pink.* **5** lessen slightly: *Can't you shade the price for me?* **6** in drawing and painting, mark with various degrees of darkness to show gradation of light or colour: *The artist shaded the picture of the ball to make it look more real.* ⟨OE *sceadu*⟩ **—'shade•less,** *adj.*
☛ *Syn. n.* **6.** See note at COLOUR.

shad–fly ['ʃæd ,flaɪ] *n. Cdn. Maritimes.* any of various winged insects that appear in the spring, especially the mayfly.

shad•ing ['ʃeidɪŋ] *n., v. —n.* **1** a covering from the light. **2** the use of black or colour to give the effect of shade in a picture. **3** a slight or gradual variation of colour, character, etc.
—v. ppr. of SHADE.

shad•ow ['ʃædou] *n., v. —n.* **1** the dark image cast by some person, animal, or thing intercepting or cutting off light. **2** shade; darkness; partial shade. **3 the shadows,** darkness after sunset. **4** the dark part of a place or picture. **5** a little bit; small degree; slight suggestion: *There's not a shadow of a doubt about her guilt.* **6** ghost. **7** a faint image or likeness: *You look worn to a shadow. A short growth of beard is a shadow.* **8 a** a reflected image. **b** a prophetic or prefiguring image. **9** protection; shelter. **10** a person who follows another closely and secretly. **11** a constant companion; follower. **12 a** sadness; gloom. **b** the cause of such emotion. **13** obscurity. **14** a gloomy or troubled look or expression. **15** something insubstantial or unreal.
under or **in the shadow of,** very near to.
—v. **1** protect from light; shade: *The grass is shadowed by huge oaks.* **2** cast a shadow on. **3** represent faintly (*often used with* **forth**). **4** follow closely and secretly. **5** make sad or gloomy. **6** represent in a prophetic way. ⟨from oblique case forms of OE *sceadu* shade⟩ **—'shad•ow•er,** *n.* **—'shad•ow•less,** *adj.* **—'shad•ow,like,** *adj.*

shad•ow•box [ˈʃædouˌbɒks] *v.* engage in shadowboxing.

shadow box 1 a boxlike frame, having artificial lighting and a glass front, in which an arrangement of small objects, a painting, piece of stained glass, etc. may be attractively presented. 2 a device to shade a surface on which a film is to be projected in daylight.

shad•ow•box•ing [ˈʃædouˌbɒksɪŋ] *n., v. —n.* **1** boxing before a mirror or with an imaginary opponent for exercise or training. **2** engaging in cautious preliminaries before taking positive action in an argument, struggle, campaign, etc.
—v. ppr. of SHADOWBOX.

shadow cabinet the senior, policy-making members of an opposition or minority party in a legislature, each of whom is assigned as critic to the corresponding member of the real cabinet.

shad•ow•graph [ˈʃædouˌgræf] *n.* **1** a picture produced by throwing a shadow on a lighted screen. **2** radiograph.

shad•ow•y [ˈʃædoui] *adj.* **1** having much shadow or shade; shady. **2** like a shadow; dim, faint, or slight: *He saw a shadowy outline on the window curtain.* **3** not real; ghostly.
—ˈshad•ow•i•ly, *adv.* **—ˈshad•ow•i•ness,** *n.*

shad•y [ˈʃeidi] *adj.* **shad•i•er, shad•i•est. 1** in the shade; shaded. **2** giving shade. **3** *Informal.* of doubtful honesty, character, etc.: *He has engaged in rather shady occupations.*
on the shady side of, older than; beyond the age of: *on the shady side of thirty.* **—ˈshad•i•ly,** *adv.* **—ˈshad•i•ness,** *n.*

shaft [ʃæft] *n., v. —n.* **1** in a machine, a cylindrical bar that rotates or supports rotating parts. **2** a deep passage sunk in the earth. The entrance to a mine is called a shaft. **3** a well-like or tunnel-like passage; a long, narrow space: *an elevator shaft, an air shaft.* **4** the long, slender stem of an arrow, spear, lance, etc. **5** an arrow, spear, lance, etc. **6** any long, slender object, part, or construction, as the midsection of the long bones, the stem of a candelabrum, an obelisk, etc. **7** something aimed at a person as one might aim an arrow or spear: *shafts of ridicule.* **8** a ray or beam of light. **9** a wooden pole by means of which a horse is harnessed to a carriage, etc. **10** a column. **11** the main part of a column. See COLUMN for picture. **12** a flagpole. **13** the long, straight handle of a hammer, axe, golf club, etc. **14** a stem; stalk. **15** the rib of a feather.
—v. Slang. cheat; exploit; deal unfairly with (someone).
get the shaft, *Slang.* be cheated or unfairly dealt with.
give (someone) **the shaft,** *Slang.* cheat; deal unfairly with (someone). ⟨OE *sceaft*⟩ **—ˈshaftˌlike,** *adj.*

shag [ʃæg] *n., v.* **shagged, shag•ging.** *—n.* **1** a mass or growth of long, rough, matted hair, wool, etc. **2** a long, rough, matted nap or fibre. **3** cloth, a rug, etc. having a long, rough nap. **4** coarsely shredded tobacco. **5** a cormorant.
—v. make shaggy. ⟨OE *sceacga*⟩

shag•a•nap•pi [ˈʃægəˌnæpi] *n.* **1** thongs, straps, lines, or cords made from rawhide. **2** an Indian pony; cayuse. ⟨< Algonquian⟩

shag•bark [ˈʃægˌbɑrk] *n.* **1** a North American hickory (*Carya ovata*) having rough, loose, grey bark and large, sweet-tasting, edible nuts. Also called **shagbark hickory. 2** the nut of this tree. Shagbarks have fairly thin shells and are considered the best hickory nuts. **3** the wood of this tree.

shagged [ʃægd] *adj., v. —adj. Slang. Esp. Brit.* extremely tired; worn out; exhausted (*often with* **out**).
—v. pt. and pp. of SHAG.

shag•gy [ˈʃægi] *adj.* **-gi•er, -gi•est. 1** covered with a thick, rough mass of hair, wool, etc.: *a shaggy dog.* **2** long, thick, and rough: *shaggy eyebrows.* **3** having a long, rough nap; of coarse texture. **4** rough, coarse, or unkempt: *The dog had shaggy hair.* ⟨< *shag*⟩ **—ˈshag•gi•ly,** *adv.* **—ˈshag•gi•ness,** *n.*

shag•gy–dog story [ˈʃægi ˈdɒg] a joke in which the humour depends on a long recital of trivial incidents building up to an absurd and unexpected ending. ⟨from an original story of this type about a shaggy dog⟩

shag•gy•mane [ˈʃægiˌmein] *n.* an edible inky-cap mushroom (*coprinus comatus*) having a shaggy pileus of yellowish scales.

sha•green [ʃəˈgrin] *n.* **1** a kind of untanned leather with a granular surface, made from the skin of the horse, ass, seal, and other animals. **2** the rough skin of dogfish or certain other sharks, used for cleaning and polishing. ⟨< F *chagrin* < Turkish *saghri* rump of a horse, leather from this⟩

Shah [ʃɑ] *n.* formerly, a title of an Iranian male ruler. ⟨< Persian⟩

Shai•tan [ʃəiˈtɑn] *n. Islam.* Satan. ⟨< Arabic⟩

shake [ʃeik] *v.* **shook, shak•en, shak•ing;** *n., adj.*
—v. **1** move quickly backward and forward, up and down, or from side to side: *to shake a rug. The fence was shaking in the wind.* **2** bring, throw, force, rouse, scatter, etc. by or as if by such movement: *to shake snow off one's clothes.* **3** be shaken: *Sand shakes off easily.* **4** clasp (hands) in greeting, congratulating, etc. another: *to shake hands.* **5** tremble: *She is shaking with cold.* **6** make tremble: *The explosion shook the town.* **7** totter; waver: *Her courage began to shake.* **8** cause to totter or waver; make less firm: *to shake the very foundations of society. His lie shook my faith in his honesty.* **9** agitate or upset: *We were badly shaken by the news.* **10** trill. **11** *Informal.* get rid of (*often used with* **off**): *Can't you shake him? I can't seem to shake off this cold.* **12** mix (dice) before throwing.
shake down, a bring or throw down by shaking. **b** cause to settle by shaking. **c** bring into working order. **d** *Slang.* get money from dishonestly.
shake up, a shake hard. **b** stir up. **c** jar in body or nerves. **d** subject to a shake-up.
—n. **1** the act or fact of shaking: *a shake of the head.* **2** *Informal.* earthquake. **3** a drink made by shaking the ingredients together: *a milk shake.* **4** *Slang.* a moment: *I'll be there in two shakes.* **5** *Music.* a rapid alternation of a note with a tone above or below it; a trill. **6 the shakes,** *pl.* a fit of shaking or trembling. **7** a crack in a growing tree; fissure. **8** a long unplaned shingle or board, usually hand split, used for roofing and siding: *a barn roofed with cedar shakes.* **9** *Informal.* manner of treatment; deal: *All she wants is a fair shake.*
no great shakes, *Informal.* not unusual, extraordinary, or important.
—adj. of or having to do with roofing shakes: *a shake roof, shake siding, a shake mill.* ⟨OE *sceacan*⟩ **—ˈshak•a•ble** or **ˈshake•a•ble,** *adj.*
☛ *Hom.* SHEIK [ʃeik].
☛ *Syn. v.* **5. Shake,** TREMBLE, QUIVER[1] = move with unsteady, irregular, rapid, and repeated movements from side to side or up and down. **Shake,** the general word, suggests a rapid, irregular, more or less violent, or abrupt motion: *She shook with laughter.* **Tremble,** used chiefly of people or animals, suggests uncontrollable, continued shaking with quick, short movements, caused by fear, strong feeling, cold, etc.: *In his excitement his hands trembled.* **Quiver** suggests a slight trembling or vibrating motion: *The dog's nostrils quivered at the scent.*

shake•down [ˈʃeikˌdaʊn] *n.* **1** a makeshift bed: *We made a shakedown of straw and blankets on the floor.* **2** the process of shaking down. **3** a bringing into proper condition or working order by practice: *The warship was given a shakedown by a trial voyage.* **4** *Slang.* an exaction of money, etc., especially as in various forms of graft or blackmail. **5** a thorough search.

shak•en [ˈʃeikən] *v.* pp. of SHAKE.

shak•er [ˈʃeikər] *n.* **1** a person who shakes something. **2** a machine or utensil used in shaking: *a cocktail shaker.* **3** a container having a perforated top, used for dispensing small amounts of pepper, salt, etc. **4 Shaker,** a member of an American religious sect, so called from body movements that formed part of their worship. Shakers owned all their property in common and advocated a strict, simple lifestyle.

Shake•spear•e•an or **Shake•spear•i•an** [ʃeikˈspiriən] *adj., n. —adj.* of, having to do with, or suggestive of William Shakespeare (1564-1616) or his works.
—n. a specialist in the study of the works of Shakespeare.

Shakespearean sonnet the sonnet form perfected by William Shakespeare, consisting of three quatrains of alternating rhyme (abab cdcd efef) and a final rhyming couplet (gg). It is also known as the **English sonnet.**

Shake•spear•i•an [ʃeikˈspiriən] *adj. or n.* Shakespearean.

shake–up [ˈʃeik ˌʌp] *n. Informal.* a sudden and complete change; drastic rearrangement of policy, personnel, etc.: *a shake-up in the government.*

shaking palsy PARKINSON'S DISEASE.

shak•o [ˈʃækou] *n., pl.* **shak•os.** a high, stiff military hat with a plume or other ornament. See HAT for picture. ⟨< Hungarian *csákó* peaked (cap) < G *Zacke* point, spike⟩

Shak•ti [ˈʃʌkti] *n. Hinduism.* **1** one of the three great classical divinities, the mother goddess who stands for nature in all its aspects, the main object of worship among Hindus in northeastern India. **2** the wife of a god, especially Shiva.
—ˈShak•tism, *n.*

shak•y [ˈʃeiki] *adj.* **shak•i•er, shak•i•est. 1** shaking; tremulous; nervous or unsteady: *a shaky voice.* **2** liable to break down; weak: *a shaky porch.* **3** not to be depended on; not reliable: *a shaky business firm, a shaky knowledge of art.*
—ˈshak•i•ly, *adv.* **—ˈshak•i•ness,** *n.*

shale [ʃeil] *n.* a fine-grained sedimentary rock formed from clay that has been subjected to great pressure. Shale splits easily into thin layers. It is also, by a process of distillation, the source of a mineral oil used for fuel. ⟨OE *scealu* shell. Akin to SCALE[2], SHELL.⟩

shall [ʃæl]; *unstressed,* [ʃəl] *v., pt.* **should,** *pres. sing.* or *pl.* **shall.** an auxiliary verb used: **1** in questions to ask what one is to do: *Shall we go? Shall I wait?* **2** in statements, especially with the second and third persons, to show obligation or express a command: *You shall pay attention.* **3** in statements to indicate simple future time: *I shall go tomorrow if I cannot make it today.* ⟨OE *sceal*⟩
☛ *Usage.* See note at WILL[1].

shal•loon [ʃæ'lun] *n.* a light, twilled woollen cloth, used chiefly for linings. ⟨< F *chalon* < *Chalons-sur-Marne,* a city in NE France⟩

shal•lop ['ʃæləp] *n. Archaic.* a small, light, open boat propelled by sail or oars. ⟨< F *chaloupe* < Du. *sloepe.* Doublet of SLOOP.⟩

shal•lot [ʃə'lɒt] *n.* **1** a small perennial herb (*Alium ascalonicum*) related to and resembling the onion, but having a bulb composed of sections or cloves. **2** a bulb or clove of this plant, used for seasoning. It is stronger in flavour than an onion, but milder than garlic. ⟨ult. < F *eschalotte,* alteration of OF *eschaloigne* scallion < L *(caepa) Ascalonia* (onion) from Ascalon, in Palestine⟩

shal•low ['ʃælou] *adj., n., v.* —*adj.* **1** not deep: *shallow water, a shallow dish, shallow breathing.* **2** lacking depth of thought, knowledge, feeling, etc.: *a shallow mind.*
—*n.* Usually, **shallows,** *pl.* a shallow place: *The children splashed in the shallows of the pond.*
—*v.* make or become less deep. ⟨ME *shalowe,* related to OE *sceald,* adj., shallow⟩ **—'shal•low•ly,** *adv.* **—'shal•low•ness,** *n.*

sha•lom [ʃɑ'loum] *n., interj.* peace; traditional Jewish greeting or farewell. ⟨< Mod.Hebrew⟩

shalt [ʃælt] *v. Archaic.* 2nd pers. sing., present tense, of SHALL. *Thou shalt* means *You* (sing.) *shall.*

shal•y ['ʃeili] *adj.* **-i•er, -i•est.** of, like, or containing shale.

sham [ʃæm] *n., adj., v.* **shammed, sham•ming.** —*n.* **1** a pretence; fraud. **2** a counterfeit; imitation. **3** a person who is a fraud. **4** a cover or the like used to give a thing a different outward appearance: *a pillow sham.*
—*adj.* pretended; feigned; being an imitation: *The soldiers fought a sham battle for practice.*
—*v.* **1** pretend; feign: *He shammed sickness so he wouldn't have to work.* **2** create a false imitation of. ⟨originally dial. var. of *shame*⟩ **—'sham•mer,** *n.*

sha•man ['ʃeimən], ['ʃɑmən], *or* ['ʃæmən] *n.* a medicine man or woman; a priest believed to have the power to influence spirits for good or evil. ⟨< Russian *shaman* < Tungus *saman* < Pali *samana* < Sanskrit *sramana* Buddhist monk; (literally) self-tormentor < *sramati* he tires⟩

sha•man•ism ['ʃeimə,nɪzəm], ['ʃɑmə,nɪzəm], *or* ['ʃæmə,nɪzəm] *n.* **1** a religion of the Ural-Altaic peoples of N Asia and Europe, characterized by belief in spirits, demons, and gods that can be influenced only by the shamans. **2** any of various similar religions, as among some First Nations or Inuit peoples. **—'sha•man•ist,** *n.* **—,sha•man'is•tic,** *adj.*

sha•mas ['ʃɑməs] *n., pl.* **sha•mos•im** [ʃɑ'mɒsɪm]. *Judaism.* **1** caretaker of a synagogue. **2** the candle from which the other candles of the menorah are lit for Hanukkah. ⟨See SHAMUS⟩

sham•a•teur ['ʃæmətʃər], ['ʃæmə'tʃɜr], *or* [ʃæmə'tɛr] *n. Slang. Sports.* a player who is classed as an amateur but is paid as if he or she were professional. ⟨blend of *sham* and *amateur*⟩

sham•a•teur•ism ['ʃæmətʃə,rɪzəm], [,ʃæmə'tʃɜrɪzəm], *or* [ʃæmə'tɜrɪzəm] *n. Slang. Sports.* **1** the practice of using shamateurs. **2** the fact or condition of being a shamateur.

sham•ble ['ʃæmbəl] *v.* **-bled, -bling;** *n.* —*v.* walk awkwardly, unsteadily, or lazily: *The tired, sick man shambled to his bed.*
—*n.* a shambling walk. ⟨probably ult. special use of *shamble,* sing. of *shambles;* with reference to the straddling legs of a bench⟩

sham•bles ['ʃæmbəlz] *n.pl. or sing.* **1** slaughterhouse. **2** a place of butchery or of great bloodshed. **3** *Informal.* confusion; mess; general disorder: *The room was a shambles.* ⟨OE *sc(e)amel* < L *scamellum,* dim. of *scamnum* bench; originally, a table on which meat is sold⟩

shame [ʃeim] *n., v.* **shamed, sham•ing.** —*n.* **1** a painful feeling of having done something wrong, improper, or silly: *to blush with shame.* **2** a disgrace; dishonour. **3** a fact to be sorry about: *It is a shame to be so wasteful.* **4** a person or thing to be ashamed of; cause of disgrace. **5** a sense of what is decent or proper.
for shame! you should be ashamed!
put to shame, a disgrace; make ashamed. **b** surpass; make dim by comparison: *Her careful work put the rest of us to shame.*
shame on (someone)! (someone) should be ashamed: *Shame on you for being so hard on that poor child!*
—*v.* **1** cause to feel shame. **2** drive or force by shame. **3** bring disgrace upon. ⟨OE *sceamu*⟩

shame•faced ['ʃeim,feɪst] *adj.* **1** bashful; shy. **2** showing shame and embarrassment. ⟨originally < *shamefast* (OE *sc(e)amfœst,* apparently, fixed in shame), taken as from *shame,* n. + *face*⟩ **—'shame,fac•ed•ly** [-,feisɪdli], *adv.*
—'shame,fac•ed•ness, *n.*

shame•ful ['ʃeimfəl] *adj.* causing or deserving shame; bringing disgrace; scandalous. **—'shame•ful•ly,** *adv.*
—'shame•ful•ness, *n.*

shame•less ['ʃeimlɪs] *adj.* having no sense of what is decent or proper. **—'shame•less•ly,** *adv.* **—'shame•less•ness,** *n.*

sham•my ['ʃæmi] *n., pl.* **-mies;** *v.,* **-mied, -my•ing.** —*n.* **1** CHAMOIS (def. 2). **2** (*adjl.*) made of chamois.
—*v.* polish with a chamois.

sham•poo [ʃæm'pu] *v.* **-pooed, -poo•ing;** *n.* —*v.* **1** wash the hair or scalp of (a person). **2** wash (a rug, etc.) with a soapy preparation. **3** *Archaic.* massage.
—*n.* **1** a preparation used for shampooing. **2** a washing of the hair, the scalp, a rug, etc. with such a preparation. **3** *Archaic.* massage. ⟨< Hind. *chhāmpo,* literally, press!⟩ **—sham'poo•er,** *n.*

sham•rock ['ʃæm,rɒk] *n.* **1** any of various plants having leaves composed of three rounded leaflets, such as wood sorrel or any of several clovers. The shamrock, the national emblem of Ireland and an international symbol of St. Patrick's Day, is said to have been chosen by St. Patrick to symbolize the Trinity, but the identity of the actual species has never been established. **2** a leaf of any of these plants, or a symbolic depiction or representation of such a leaf. ⟨< Irish *seamróg,* dim. of *seamair* clover⟩

sha•mus ['ʃeiməs] *or* ['ʃɑməs] *n. Slang.* a detective, especially a private detective. ⟨< Yiddish *shames* sexton, caretaker < Hebrew *shammash;* ? infl. by Irish *Séamas* James⟩

shan•dy ['ʃændi] *n.* a drink made by mixing beer and a soft drink, usually ginger ale or ginger beer. ⟨origin uncertain⟩

shang•hai [ʃæŋ'haɪ] *or* ['ʃæŋhaɪ] *v.* **-haied, -hai•ing. 1** make unconscious by drugs, liquor, etc. and put on a ship to serve as a sailor. **2** bring by trickery or force. ⟨with reference to the practice of securing sailors by kidnapping or other violent and illegal means for long voyages, often to *Shanghai,* China⟩

Shang•hai [ʃæŋ'haɪ] *n.* one of a long-legged breed of domestic fowls. ⟨< *Shanghai,* a seaport in China⟩

Shan•gri–La [,ʃæŋgrɪ 'lɑ] *n.* an imaginary, idyllic earthly paradise. ⟨an inaccessible land in *Lost Horizon,* a novel by James Hilton (1900-1954), an English author⟩

shank [ʃæŋk] *n., v.* —*n.* **1** *Anatomy.* in humans, the part of the leg between the knee and the ankle. **2** the corresponding part in animals, or a cut of meat from it. See BEEF, LAMB, and VEAL for pictures. **3** the whole leg. **4** any part like a leg, stem, or shaft. The shank of a fish-hook is the straight part between the hook and the loop. See ANCHOR for picture. **5** *Printing.* the body of a piece of type. **6** the narrow part of a shoe, connecting the broad part of the sole with the heel. **7** a rigid loop on the back of some buttons **(shank buttons)** by which they are sewn to a garment. **8** the latter end or part of anything.
go or **ride (on, by,** etc.) **shank's mare,** go on foot rather than ride; walk: *It was a lovely evening, so we rode shank's mare to the party.*
—*v. Golf.* strike (the ball) with the heel of a club. ⟨OE *sceanca*⟩

shan't [ʃænt] *v.* shall not.

shan•tung [ʃæn'tʌŋ] *or* ['ʃæntʌŋ] *n.* **1** a heavy pongee, a kind of soft silk. **2** a similar fabric of cotton, rayon, etc. ⟨< *Shantung,* a province in NE China⟩

shan•ty[1] ['ʃænti] *n., pl.* **-ties.** *Cdn.* **1** a roughly built hut or cabin. **2** the log-built living quarters of a gang of loggers. ⟨< Cdn.F *chantier* loggers' headquarters < F *chantier* timber yard, dock < L *cantherius* framework, beast of burden; perhaps also from or influenced by Irish *sean tig* hut⟩

shan•ty² [ˈʃænti] *n., pl.* **-ties.** a song sung by sailors in rhythm with the motions made during their work. Also, **chantey, chanty.** ⟨var. of *chantey* < F *chanter* sing⟩

shan•ty•man [ˈʃænti,mæn] *or* [ˈʃæntimən] *n., pl.* **-men.** *Cdn.* formerly, someone living and working in a logging camp; a logger.

shan•ty•town [ˈʃænti,taʊn] *n.* an area of a city where people live in small, dilapidated houses or shacks. ⟨< *shanty*¹⟩

shape [ʃeip] *n., v.* **shaped, shap•ing.** *—n.* **1** the outward contour or outline; the form of a person or thing; figure: *the shape of a triangle. All circles have the same shape; rectangles have different shapes.* **2** an assumed appearance: *A witch was supposed to take the shape of a cat or a bat.* **3** something seen, or thought to be seen, though having no definite or describable form: *A white shape stood at her bedside.* **4** condition, especially good condition: *He exercises to keep in shape. Am I ever out of shape!* **5** a definite form; proper arrangement; order: *Take time to get your thoughts into shape.* **6** a kind; sort: *dangers of every shape.* **7** mould; pattern. **8** something shaped; jelly, pudding, etc. shaped into a mould.
take shape, have or take on a definite form.
—v. **1** form into a shape: *The child shapes clay into balls.* **2** *Esp. Brit.* take shape; assume form: *Her plan is shaping well.* **3** adapt in form: *That hat is shaped to your head.* **4** give definite form or character to: *events that shape people's lives.* **5** direct; plan; devise; aim: *to shape one's course in life.* **6** express in words: *to shape a question.*
shape up, a take on a certain form or appearance; develop. **b** show a certain tendency. **c** develop as desired. **d** behave as required; do what one is supposed to do: *You'd better shape up or you'll be fired.* ⟨OE *(ge)sceap,* n. *sceapen,* v., pp. of *sceppan* create⟩ **—ˈshap•er,** *n.*
☛ *Syn. n.* **1.** See note at FORM.

SHAPE [ʃeip] Supreme Headquarters Allied Powers Europe.

shape•less [ˈʃeiplɪs] *adj.* **1** without definite shape. **2** having an unattractive shape. **—ˈshape•less•ly,** *adv.* **—ˈshape•less•ness,** *n.*

shape•ly [ˈʃeipli] *adj.* **-li•er, -li•est.** especially of the female figure, having a pleasing shape; well-formed. **—ˈshape•li•ness,** *n.*

shape–up [ˈʃeip ,ʌp] *n. Informal.* a system of hiring shorehands or other labourers whereby they line up each workday to be selected for work.

shard [ʃɑrd] *n.* **1** a broken piece; fragment. **2** a piece of broken earthenware or pottery. **3** *Zoology.* a hard case or covering, such as that on a beetle's wing. Also (*for defs. 1 and 2*), **sherd.** ⟨OE *sceard*⟩

share¹ [ʃɛr] *n., v.* **shared, shar•ing.** *—n.* **1** a part belonging to one individual; portion; part: *Do your share of the work.* **2** a part of anything owned in common with others: *One of the owners offered to sell her share in the boat.* **3** each of the parts into which the ownership of a company or corporation is divided: *The ownership of this company is divided into several million shares.*
go shares, share something.
on shares, sharing in the risks and profits.
—v. **1 a** use together; enjoy together; have in common: *The sisters share a room.* **b** let another join in using: *I shared my book with another student.* **2** divide into parts, giving each a part: *The child shared his candy with his sister.* **3** share one's things: *Toddlers must know what possession is before they can learn to share.* **4** have a share; take part: *Everyone shared in making the picnic a success.* **5** *Informal.* tell; communicate (one's ideas, etc.): *In his travelogue Mr. Yin shared his impressions of Ireland.* ⟨OE *scearu* division⟩ **—ˈshar•er,** *n.* **—ˈshare•a•ble** or **ˈshar•a•ble,** *adj.*
☛ *Syn. v.* **1. Share,** PARTICIPATE, PARTAKE = use, enjoy, or have something in common with another. **Share** means either to give or take a part, and emphasizes the idea of common possession, enjoyment, use, etc.: *He shares a room with his brother.* **Participate,** more formal, followed by **in,** means 'take part together with others in an idea, feeling, or action': *She participated in the discussion.* **Partake,** now formal and usually followed by **of,** means 'take a share of food, pleasure, qualities, etc.': *They partook of our meal.*

share² [ʃɛr] *n.* ploughshare. ⟨OE *scear*⟩

share•crop [ˈʃɛr,krɒp] *v.* **-cropped, -crop•ping.** farm (land) or raise (a crop) as a sharecropper.

share•crop•per [ˈʃɛr,krɒpər] *n.* a person who farms land for the owner in return for part of the crops.

share•hold•er [ˈʃɛr,houldər] *n.* a person owning shares of stock.

share•ware [ˈʃɛr,wɛr] *n. Computer technology.* computer software that is copyrighted but is distributed free of charge to potential users, usually with a request that a fee be remitted if the user continues to use the software.

shark¹ [ʃɑrk] *n.* any of an order (Selachii) of cartilaginous fishes having a torpedo-shaped body, a tough, grey or whitish hide covered with tiny tubercles, two dorsal fins, and five to seven gill slits on either side of the head. Most sharks are marine fishes, and most are carnivorous. See also BASKING SHARK, DOGFISH, WHITE SHARK. ⟨origin uncertain⟩ **—ˈshark,like,** *adj.*

A dogfish shark

shark² [ʃɑrk] *n.* **1** a dishonest person who preys on others: *a loan shark.* **2** *Slang.* a person usually good at something; an expert: *a shark at mathematics.* ⟨< G *Schork,* var. of *Schurke* scoundrel⟩

shark•skin [ˈʃɑrk,skɪn] *n.* **1** cloth made from fine threads of wool, rayon, or cotton, used in suits. **2** the skin of a shark, or leather made from it. **3** a woven fabric having a pebbled pattern.

shark•suck•er [ˈʃɑrk,sʌkər] *n.* remora.

sharp [ʃɑrp] *adj., adv., n., v. —adj.* **1** having a thin cutting edge or a fine point: *a sharp knife, a sharp pencil.* **2** relatively pointed; not rounded: *a sharp nose, a sharp corner on a box.* **3** with a sudden extreme change of direction: *a sharp turn. From the field there is a sharp drop down to the river.* **4** very cold: *sharp weather, a sharp morning.* **5** severe; biting: *sharp words.* **6** causing a sensation like a cut or pinprick; affecting the senses or emotions keenly: *a sharp taste, a sharp noise, a sharp pain.* **7** clear; distinct: *the sharp contrast between black and white.* **8** quick; brisk: *a sharp walk or run.* **9** fierce; violent: *a sharp struggle.* **10** keen; eager: *a sharp desire, a sharp appetite.* **11** being aware of things quickly: *a sharp eye, sharp ears.* **12** watchful; wide-awake: *a sharp watch.* **13** quick in mind; clever: *a sharp child.* **14** shrewd; artful; almost dishonest: *sharp practice. She is sharp at a bargain.* **15** high in pitch; shrill. **16** *Music.* **a** above the true pitch. **b** raised a half step in pitch: *F sharp.* **c** of a key, having sharps in the signature. **17** *Slang.* attractive; striking in looks, value, etc.: *a sharp car. The manager's new suit looks sharp.*
—adv. **1** promptly, exactly: *Come at one o'clock sharp.* **2** in a sharp manner; in an alert manner; keenly: *Look sharp!* **3** suddenly: *to pull a horse up sharp.* **4** above true pitch: *to sing sharp.* **5** at a sharp angle: *Turn sharp at the corner.*
—n. **1** *Music.* **a** a tone one half step, or half note, above a given tone. **b** the sign (♯) that stands for such a tone. **2** a swindler; sharper. **3** *Informal.* expert. **4 sharps,** *pl.* the hard part of wheat requiring a second grinding. **5** an extremely fine-tipped sewing needle.
—v. Music. make or sound sharp. ⟨OE *scearp*⟩ **—ˈsharp•ly,** *adv.* **—ˈsharp•ness,** *n.*
☛ *Syn. adj.* **13. Sharp,** KEEN¹, ACUTE, used figuratively to describe a person or the mind, means 'quickly aware or penetrating'. **Sharp** emphasizes being well suited to cutting or piercing through things, and suggests cleverness, shrewdness, or quickness to see and take advantage, sometimes dishonestly: *She is a sharp lawyer.* **Keen** emphasizes being shaped to slash through things, and suggests clear-sightedness, vigour, and quickness of perception and thinking: *He has a keen mind.* **Acute,** literally meaning 'coming to a sharp point', suggests penetrating perception, insight, or understanding: *He is an acute interpreter of current events.*

sharp–eared [ˈʃɑrp ,ird] *adj.* having an acute sense of hearing.

sharp•en [ˈʃɑrpən] *v.* **1** make sharp: *to sharpen a pencil. Sharpen your wits.* **2** become sharp: *His voice sharpened as he became angry.* **—ˈsharp•en•er,** *n.*

sharp•er [ˈʃɑrpər] *n.* **1** a swindler; cheat. **2** a gambler who makes a living by cheating at cards, etc.

sharp–eyed [ˈʃɑrp ,aɪd] *adj.* **1** having keen sight: *a sharp-eyed person.* **2** watchful; very observant; vigilant.

sharp•ie [ˈʃɑrpi] *n.* **1** a long, flat-bottomed boat having one or two masts, each rigged with a triangular sail. **2** a cunning or devious person.

sharp–shinned hawk [ˈʃɑrp ,ʃɪnd] a North American hawk (*Accipiter striatus*) having a barred rust-and-white breast, charcoal back, short, rounded wings, and a long tail. It feeds mostly on small birds. Also, **sharpshin.**

sharp•shoot•er [ˈʃɑrp,ʃutər] *n.* a person who shoots very well, especially with a rifle. **—ˈsharp,shoot•ing,** *n., adj.*

sharp–sight•ed [ˈʃɑrp ˈsəitɪd] *adj.* **1** having sharp sight. **2** sharp-witted. **—ˈsharp-ˈsight•ed•ly,** *adv.* **—ˈsharp-ˈsight•ed•ness,** *n.*

sharp–tailed grouse ['ʃɑrp ˌteild] a medium-sized grouse (*Pedioecetes phasianellus*) of central and W North America, so called because of its short, pointed tail. Also, **sharptail.**

sharp–tongued ['ʃɑrp ˌtʌŋd] *adj.* harsh, critical, or sarcastic in speech.

sharp–wit•ted ['ʃɑrp 'wɪtɪd] *adj.* having or showing a quick, keen mind. **—'sharp-'wit•ted•ly,** *adv.* **—'sharp-'wit•ted•ness,** *n.*

shash•lik ['ʃɑʃlɪk] *n.* kebabs, especially with mutton for the meat. ⟨< Russian *shashlyk* < Turkish *shish* skewer⟩

Shas•ta daisy ['ʃæstə] a chrysanthemum (*Chrysanthemum maximum*) widely cultivated in numerous varieties for its large, daisylike, white flowers. ⟨< Mount *Shasta* in N California⟩

shat•ter ['ʃætər] *v., n. —v.* **1** break into pieces: *A stone shattered the window. The glass shattered.* **2** disturb greatly; destroy: *The great mental strain shattered his mind. Her hopes were shattered.*
—n. **shatters,** *pl.* fragments. ⟨ME *schater(en)*; probably var. of *scatter*⟩ **—'shat•ter•er,** *n.* **—'shat•ter•ing•ly,** *adv.*
☛ *Syn. v.* **1.** See note at BREAK.

shat•ter•proof ['ʃætər,pruf] *adj.* that can break without shattering.

shave [ʃeiv] *v.* **shaved, shaved** or **shav•en, shav•ing;** *n. —v.* **1** remove hair with a razor; cut hair from (a person, the scalp, face, legs, etc.) with a razor. **2** cut off (hair) with a razor. **3** cut (off) in thin slices; cut thin slices from. **4** cut very close. **5** come very close to; graze: *The car shaved the corner.* **6** *Informal.* reduce (a price, etc.) slightly; deduct (a small amount) from a price.
—n. **1** the cutting off of hair with a razor. **2** a tool for shaving, scraping, removing thin slices, etc. **3** a shaving; thin slice.
a close shave, a narrow miss or escape: *The shot missed her, but it was a close shave.* ⟨OE *sceafan*⟩

shave•ling ['ʃeivlɪŋ] *n.* a youth.

shav•en ['ʃeivən] *adj., v. —adj.* **1** shaved. **2** closely cut. **3** tonsured.
—v. a pp. of SHAVE.

shav•er ['ʃeivər] *n.* **1** a person who shaves. **2** an instrument for shaving. **3** *Informal.* a youngster; a small boy.

Sha•vi•an ['ʃeiviən] *adj., n. —adj.* of, having to do with, or characteristic of George Bernard Shaw (1856-1950), an Irish dramatist and critic.
—n. a devoted admirer of Shaw or his works.

shav•ing ['ʃeivɪŋ] *n., v., adj. —n.* **1** Often, **shavings,** *pl.* a very thin piece or slice. Shavings of wood are cut off by a plane. **2** the act or process of cutting hair from the face, chin, legs, etc. with a razor.
—v. ppr. of SHAVE.
—adj. used for shaving: *shaving cream.*

Sha•vu•ot [ʃə'vuout] *or* [ˌʃɑvu'out] *n. Judaism.* a holiday commemorating the giving of the law at Mount Sinai; originally, a spring harvest celebration. It is observed on the sixth and seventh days of Sivan and is sometimes called the Feast of Weeks or Pentecost. ⟨< Hebrew < *shavua* week < *sheva* seven⟩

shawl [ʃɒl] *n.* a square or oblong piece of cloth to be worn about the shoulders or head. ⟨< Persian⟩

shawl collar a broad or rolled collar tapering down across the chest to the side of the waist, as on a bathrobe.

shawm [ʃɒm] *n.* a medieval musical instrument resembling an oboe. ⟨ME < OF *chalemie*, var. of *chalemel*, ult. < L < Gk. *kalamos* reed⟩

Shaw•nee [ʃɒ'ni] *n., pl.* **-nee** or **-nees. 1** a member of a Native American people formerly living in Tennessee and South Carolina, now in Oklahoma. **2** the Algonquian language of the Shawnee.

shay [ʃei] *n. Informal.* a chaise, a light carriage with two wheels and one seat. ⟨< *chaise*, taken as pl.⟩

she [ʃi] *pron., subj.* **she,** *obj.* **her,** *poss.* **hers,** *pl. subj.* **they,** *pl. obj.* **them,** *pl. poss.* **theirs;** *n., pl.* **she's.** *—pron.* **1** the girl, woman, or female animal already referred to and identified. **2** anything personified as feminine and already referred to and identified.
—n. any girl, woman, or female animal, or thing personified as feminine: *Is it a he or a she? In poetic English, all countries are she's.* ⟨probably OE demonstrative pronoun *sīo, sēo, sīe*⟩
☛ *Hom.* SHEA.

shea [ʃi] *n.* a W African tree (*Butyrospermum parkii*) whose nutlike seeds contain a thick fat used for cooking and soapmaking. ⟨< Mandingo *si*⟩
☛ *Hom.* SHE.

sheaf [ʃif] *n., pl.* **sheaves;** *v. —n.* **1** a bundle of cut grain bound in the middle for drying, loading, and stacking. **2** a bundle of like things laid or otherwise kept together lengthwise: *a sheaf of arrows.* **3** any bundle or lot of things: *a sheaf of notes.*
—v. SHEAVE[1]. ⟨OE *scēaf*⟩

shear [ʃir] *v.* **sheared** or *(archaic)* **shore, sheared** or **shorn, shear•ing;** *n. —v.* **1** cut with or as if with shears or scissors. **2** cut the wool or fleece from: *The farmer sheared her sheep.* **3** cut close; cut off; trim. **4** to strip or deprive as if by cutting: *The assembly had been shorn of its legislative powers.* **5** break or be broken by a force causing two parts or pieces to slide on each other in opposite directions: *Too much pressure on the handles of the scissors sheared off the rivet holding the blades together.*
—n. **1** the act or process of shearing (*often used to define a sheep's age*): *a ewe of two shears.* **2** that which is taken off by shearing. **3** one blade of a pair of shears. **4** SHEARS (defs. 1, 2). **5 a** a force causing two parts or pieces to slide on each other in opposite directions. **b** the strain or damage caused by such a force. ⟨OE *sceran*⟩ **—'shear•er,** *n.*
☛ *Hom.* SHEER.

shear•ling ['ʃirlɪŋ] *n.* **1** a sheep, usually a yearling, that has been shorn only once. **2** the hide of any newly-shorn sheep, tanned with the wool on.

shears [ʃirz] *n.pl. or sing.* **1** large scissors. **2** any cutting instrument resembling scissors. **3** an apparatus for hoisting heavy weights, consisting of two or more poles fastened together at the top to support a block and tackle; sheerlegs. ⟨OE *scēar*⟩

shear•wa•ter ['ʃir,wɒtər] *n.* any of various oceanic birds (family Procellariidae) belonging to the same order as petrels and albatrosses, having long, narrow, pointed wings, a hooked bill, and mainly dark plumage, and having the habit of skimming the surface of the water in flight. ⟨< *shear*, v. + *water*, n.⟩

shear zone *Geology.* a belt of rock crushed and metamorphosed by compression.

sheath [ʃiθ] *n., pl.* **sheaths** [ʃiðz]; *v. —n.* **1** a case or covering for the blade of a sword, knife, etc. **2** any similar covering, especially on an animal or plant. **3** a woman's dress, having a fitted bodice and straight skirt, usually worn unbelted.
—v. sheathe. ⟨OE *scēath*⟩

sheathe [ʃið] *v.* **sheathed, sheath•ing. 1** put (a sword, etc.) into a sheath. **2** enclose in a case or covering: *a mummy sheathed in linen, doors sheathed in metal.* **3** retract (the claws).

sheath•ing ['ʃiðɪŋ] *n., v. —n.* a casing; covering. The first covering of boards on the frame of a house is sheathing.
—v. ppr. of SHEATHE.

sheath knife a knife carried in a sheath.

sheave[1] [ʃiv] *v.* **sheaved, sheav•ing.** gather and tie into a sheaf or sheaves. ⟨< *sheaf*⟩

sheave[2] [ʃiv] *or* [ʃɪv] *n.* a wheel with a grooved rim; the wheel of a pulley. ⟨var. of *shive*, ME *schive*⟩

she•bang [ʃə'bæŋ] *n. Slang.* **1** an outfit; concern, especially in **the whole shebang. 2** an affair; event. **3** shed; hut. ⟨origin uncertain⟩

She•bat [ʃə'bɑt] *or* [ʃə'vɑt] *n.* in the Hebrew calendar, the eleventh month of the ecclesiastical year, and the fifth month of the civil year.

she•been [ʃɪ'bin] *n. Irish dialect.* a place where liquor is sold without a licence. ⟨< Irish *síbín*⟩

shed[1] [ʃɛd] *n.* **1** a small building used for shelter, storage, etc., usually having only one storey: *a tool shed.* **2** a large, sturdy structure with a roof and three sides, for storing and repairing machinery, shearing sheep, etc. ⟨OE *sced* shelter⟩

shed[2] [ʃɛd] *v.* **shed, shed•ding. 1** cause or allow (tears, blood, etc.) to flow: *He shed his enemy's blood. The girl shed tears.* **2** throw off; cast aside or lose by a natural process: *A snake sheds its skin.* **3** throw off or lose a covering, hair, etc.: *Our cat sheds a lot.* **4** repel; not allow to penetrate: *An umbrella sheds water.* **5** scatter abroad; give forth: *The sun sheds light.* **6** get rid of (something unwanted): *I'm trying to shed some weight.* **7** decrease (the load on a power line) by temporarily disconnecting users.
shed blood, destroy life; kill.
shed (one's) **blood** or (one's) **own blood,** sacrifice one's life. ⟨OE *scēadan*⟩

she'd [ʃid]; *unstressed,* [ʃɪd] **1** she had. **2** she would.

shed•der ['ʃɛdər] *n.* **1** a person or thing that sheds. **2** a crab or lobster beginning to shed its shell.

sheen [ʃin] *n.* soft brightness; lustre: *Satin and polished silver have a sheen.* ⟨OE *scēne* bright⟩
☛ *Hom.* SHIN[2].

sheen•y [ˈʃini] *adj.* **-i•er, -i•est** bright; lustrous.

sheep [ʃip] *n., pl.* **sheep. 1** any of a genus (*Ovis*) of hoofed cud-chewing bovid mammals (related to goats, cattle, etc.) native to mountainous regions of North America and Europe, especially one species (*O. aries*) raised in many breeds for its wool, meat, and hide. See also DALL SHEEP, AOUDAD. **2** a person who is weak, timid, or easily led.
make or **cast sheep's eyes at,** look at in a yearning, loving way.
separate the sheep from the goats, distinguish the better, superior, etc. people from the rest. ⟨OE *scēap*⟩ **—ˈsheep,like,** *adj.*

sheep•ber•ry [ˈʃip,bɛri] *n.* a North American viburnum (*viburnum lentago*) having white flowers and dark blue berries.

sheep•cote [ˈʃip,kout] *n.* a covered enclosure for sheep.

sheep–dip [ˈʃip ˌdɪp] *n.* **1** a liquid disinfectant and insecticide in which sheep are immersed to destroy parasites, etc. in their fleece. **2** a trough, etc. filled with such a substance.

sheep•dog [ˈʃip,dɒg] *n.* **1** a dog trained to watch or herd sheep. **2** See OLD ENGLISH SHEEPDOG and SHETLAND SHEEPDOG.

sheep•fold [ˈʃip,fould] *n.* a pen or enclosure for sheep.

sheep•herd•er [ˈʃip,hɜrdər] *n.* a person who watches and tends large numbers of sheep while they are grazing on the unfenced land. **—ˈsheep,herd•ing,** *n.*

sheep•hook [ˈʃip,hʊk] *n.* a shepherd's staff.

sheep•ish [ˈʃipɪʃ] *adj.* **1** awkwardly bashful or embarrassed: *a sheepish smile.* **2** like a sheep; timid; weak; stupid. **—ˈsheep•ish•ly,** *adv.* **—ˈsheep•ish•ness,** *n.*

sheep•man [ˈʃip,mæn] *or* [ˈʃipmən] *n., pl.* **-men. 1** a person who owns and raises sheep. **2** sheepherder.

sheep range a tract of land on which sheep are pastured. Also, **sheep ranch, sheep-run** (*esp. Australia*), **sheepwalk** (*esp. Brit.*).

sheep•shank [ˈʃip,ʃæŋk] *n.* a kind of knot, hitch, or bend made in a rope to shorten it temporarily. See KNOT for picture.

sheeps•head [ˈʃips,hɛd] *n.* **1** a food fish (*Archosargus probatocephalus*) of the Atlantic coast of the U.S., related to the porgies and sea breams. **2** various other similar fishes, especially the **freshwater drum** (*Aplodinotus grunniens*) of the Great Lakes and the **red wrasse** (*Semicossyphus pulcher*) of the SW coast of the U.S.

sheep•shear•ing [ˈʃip,ʃirɪŋ] *n.* **1** the act of shearing sheep. **2** the season when sheep are typically sheared. **3** a festival held at this time.

sheep•skin [ˈʃip,skɪn] *n.* **1** the skin of a sheep, especially with the wool on it. **2** leather or parchment made from the skin of a sheep. **3** *Informal.* diploma. **4** (*adjl.*) made of sheepskin: *a sheepskin rug.*

sheep sorrel a perennial herb (*Rumex acetosella*) of the northern hemisphere, having sour-tasting, narrow leaves, usually lobed at the base, and small, reddish flowers.

sheep•walk [ˈʃip,wɒk] *n. Esp. Brit.* SHEEP RANGE.

sheer[1] [ʃir] *adj., adv., n.* —*adj.* **1** very thin; almost transparent: *a sheer white dress.* **2** unmixed with anything else; complete: *sheer weariness, sheer determination.* **3** straight up and down; steep: *From the top of the wall there was a sheer drop of 50 m to the water below.*
—*adv.* **1** completely; quite: *He found himself sheer in the middle of the fight.* **2** vertical; very steeply.
—*n.* **1** a garment of nearly transparent material. **2** the material itself. ⟨OE *scīr* bright; probably from ON *skærr* bright⟩
—ˈsheer•ness, *n.*
☛ *Hom.* SHEAR.

sheer[2] [ʃir] *v., n.* —*v.* turn or cause to turn sharply from a course; turn aside; swerve or cause to swerve.
—*n.* **1** an abrupt change of course. **2** the upward curve of a ship's deck from the middle toward each end. **3** the position in which a ship at anchor is placed to keep it clear of the anchor. ⟨var. of *shear*, v., in the sense of 'part'⟩
☛ *Hom.* SHEAR.

sheer•legs SHEARS (def. 3).

sheer•ly [ˈʃirli] *adv.* absolutely; thoroughly; quite.

sheet[1] [ʃit] *n., v.* —*n.* **1** a large piece of cloth, usually cotton or partly cotton, used to sleep on or under. **2** a broad, thin piece of anything: *a sheet of glass.* **3** a single piece of paper. **4** *Printing.* a large piece of paper comprising several pages of print and forming, when folded, a signature to be bound into a book. **5** a flat pan, with or without a raised edge, for baking: *a cookie sheet.* **6** newspaper. **7** a broad, flat surface: *a sheet of water.* **8** the ice surface on which a game of curling is played. **9** a sail. **10** *Geology.* a relatively broad, thin layer or deposit of igneous or sedimentary rock. **11** *Philately.* the large block of stamps printed by one impression of a plate.
—*v.* furnish or cover with a sheet. ⟨OE *scēte*⟩ **—ˈsheet,like,** *adj.*

sheet[2] [ʃit] *n., v.* —*n. Nautical.* **1** a rope that controls the angle at which a sail is set. **2 sheets,** *pl.* the space at the bow or stern of an open boat.
three sheets to the wind, *Slang.* drunk.
—*v.*
sheet home, *Nautical.* stretch (a square sail) as flat as possible by pulling hard on the sheets fastened to it. ⟨OE *scēata*⟩

sheet anchor 1 *Nautical.* a large anchor used only in emergencies. **2** the chief support or source of security. ⟨origin uncertain⟩

sheet bend a kind of knot to fasten two ropes together. See KNOT for picture.

sheet•ing [ˈʃitɪŋ] *n., v.* —*n.* **1** cloth of cotton, linen, nylon, etc. for bed sheets. **2** a lining or covering of timber or metal, used to protect a surface. **3** the process of lining or covering with sheets, or of forming into sheets.
—*v.* ppr. of SHEET.

sheet iron iron in sheets or thin plates.

sheet lightning lightning in broad flashes.

sheet metal metal in thin pieces or plates.

sheet music music printed on unbound sheets of paper.

Shef•field plate [ˈʃɛfild] an especially durable silver plate made by rolling out sheets of copper and silver fused together. ⟨< *Sheffield*, a city in England⟩

sheik or **sheikh** [ʃik] *or* [ʃeik] *n.* **1** an Arab chief or head of a family, village, or tribe. **2** a Muslim religious leader. **3** a title of respect used by Muslims. **4** *Slang.* a man supposed to be irresistibly fascinating to women; a great lover. ⟨< Arabic *shaikh*, originally, old man⟩
☛ *Hom.* CHIC [ʃik], SHAKE [ʃeik].

sheik•dom or **sheikh•dom** [ˈʃikdəm] *or* [ˈʃeikdəm] *n.* the territory ruled by a sheik.

shei•la [ˈʃilə] *Australia and New Zealand. Slang.* a girl or young woman. ⟨< *Sheila*, feminine name⟩

shek•el [ˈʃɛkəl] *n.* **1** a unit for measuring mass, used by the ancient Babylonians, Phoenicians, and Hebrews, equal to about 14 g. **2** a silver or gold coin of the ancient Hebrews weighing one shekel. **3** the basic unit of money in Israel, divided into 10 agorot. See table of money in the Appendix. **4 shekels,** *pl. Slang.* money or riches. Also (def. 3), **shequel.** ⟨< Hebrew⟩

shel•drake [ˈʃɛl,dreik] *n., pl.* **-drakes** or (*esp. collectively*) **-drake. 1** shelduck. **2** merganser. ⟨< obs. *sheld* variegated + *drake*⟩

A shelduck, about 60 cm long

shel•duck [ˈʃɛl,dʌk] *n.* any of several Old World ducks (tribe Tadornini), somewhat gooselike in appearance and having a short bill and typically brightly coloured plumage, such as the black-and-white **common shelduck** (*Tadorna tadorna*) of Europe.

shelf [ʃɛlf] *n., pl.* **shelves. 1** a thin, flat piece of wood, or other material, fastened to a wall or frame to hold things, such as books, dishes, etc. **2** the objects on a shelf, or their quantity: *shelves of linen. Tidy your shelves, please.* **3** anything like a shelf, such as a ledge or layer of rock.
on the shelf, put aside as no longer useful or desirable. ⟨probably < LG *schelf*⟩ **—ˈshelf,like,** *adj.*

shelf ice See ICE SHELF.

shelf life the length of time a perishable product can stay on a store shelf before it is considered unfit for sale or consumption: *What is the shelf life of these cartons of milk?*

shell [ʃɛl] *n., v.* —*n.* **1** a hard outside covering of an animal. Oysters, turtles, and beetles all have shells. **2** the hard outside covering of a nut, seed, fruit, etc. **3** the hard outside covering of

an egg. **4** the outer part or appearance; outward show: *Going to church is the mere shell of religion.* **5** any framework or outside covering of a structure. **6** a long, narrow racing boat of light wood, rowed by a crew using long oars. **7** a hollow case of pastry or the lower crust of a pie. **8** a cartridge used in a rifle or shotgun. **9** a metal projectile filled with explosives that is fired by artillery and explodes on impact. **10** a cartridgelike firework that explodes in the air. **11** *Physics.* **a** an orbit of electrons about the nucleus of an atom in which the electrons all have approximately the same amount of energy. **b** a group of nucleons, all having approximately the same energy. **12** a woman's sleeveless and usually collarless top or blouse.
come out of (one's) **shell,** stop being shy or reserved; join in conversation, etc. with others.
retire into (one's) **shell,** become shy and reserved; refuse to join in conversation, etc. with others.
—*v.* **1** take out of a shell: *to shell peas.* **2** fall or come out of the shell. **3** come away or fall off as an outer covering does. **4** separate (the grains of corn or wheat) from a cob or ear: *to shell corn.* **5** bombard by artillery fire: *The enemy shelled the town.* **6** seek and gather seashells: *to go shelling.*
shell out, a *Informal.* hand over (money); pay up: *He shelled out $15 for the roses.* **b** give out candy at Halloween: *Are you shelling out tonight?* ⟨OE *sciell.* Akin to SCALE[2], SHALE.⟩ **—'shell-,like,** *adj.*

she'll [ʃil]; *unstressed,* [ʃɪl] she will.

shel•lac [ʃə'læk] *n., v.* **-lacked, -lack•ing.** *—n.* **1** purified lac (a resin), used for making varnishes, leather polishes, etc. **2** a varnish for wood or metal, consisting of shellac dissolved in alcohol.
—*v.* **1** coat or treat with shellac. **2** *Informal.* defeat completely. ⟨< *shell* + *lac*[1], translation of F *laque en écailles* lac in thin plates⟩

shell•bark ['ʃɛl,bɑrk] *n.* shagbark.

shell•er ['ʃɛlər] *n.* **1** a person who shells something. **2** a tool or machine used in shelling.

shell•fire ['ʃɛl,faɪr] *n.* bombardment by explosive shells or projectiles.

shell•fish ['ʃɛl,fɪʃ] *n., pl.* **-fish** or **-fish•es.** any aquatic invertebrate animal having a shell, especially edible molluscs or crustaceans, such as oysters, clams, crabs, and lobsters. ⟨OE *scilfisc*⟩

shell game **1** the game of betting which of three rapidly manipulated cups or nutshells conceals a small object, which may or may not actually be hidden under any of them. **2** *Informal.* a swindle. Also (def. 1), **thimble rig.**

shell ice *Cdn. North.* a formation of ice remaining as a shell, after the water over which it was formed has receded.

shell•proof ['ʃɛl,pruf] *adj.* secure against shells, bombs, etc.

shell shock *Psychiatry.* any of the many types of nervous or mental disorders formerly thought to result from prolonged exposure to exploding shells, bombs, etc., but now attributed to the accumulated emotional and psychological strain of warfare.

shell•shocked ['ʃɛl,ʃɒkt] *adj.* **1** suffering from shell shock. **2** *Informal.* extremely surprised or shocked.

shell•y ['ʃɛli] *adj.* **shell•i•er, shell•i•est. 1** abounding in shells. **2** consisting of a shell or shells.

shel•ter ['ʃɛltər] *n., v. —n.* **1** something that covers or protects from weather, danger, or attack: *Trees serve as a shelter from the sun.* **2** protection; refuge: *We took shelter from the storm in a barn.*
—*v.* **1** protect; shield; hide: *shelter runaway slaves.* **2** find shelter; take shelter: *The sheep sheltered from the hot sun in the shade of the haystack.* ⟨? < ME *sheltrum* < OE *scildtruma* a guard < *scild* shield + *truma* a band of men⟩ **—'shel•ter•er,** *n.* **—'shel•ter•ing•ly,** *adv.* **—'shel•ter•less,** *adj.*

shel•ter•belt ['ʃɛltər,bɛlt] *n.* a barrier of trees or shrubs that functions as protection against the wind and rain and serves to lessen erosion.

shelter tent a small tent, usually made of pieces of waterproof cloth, called **shelter halves,** that fasten together.

shel•tie or **shel•ty** ['ʃɛlti] *n.* **1** SHETLAND SHEEPDOG. **2** SHETLAND PONY. ⟨< Orkney dialect *sjalti* < ON *Hjalti* Shetlander⟩

shelve [ʃɛlv] *v.* **shelved, shelv•ing. 1** place on a shelf: *to shelve books.* **2** furnish with a shelf or shelves. **3** set aside or postpone: *to shelve an issue.* **4** cause (a person) to retire from active service or employment. **5** of ground, etc., slope gradually. ⟨ult. < *shelf*⟩

shelves [ʃɛlvz] *n.* pl. of SHELF.

shelv•ing ['ʃɛlvɪŋ] *n., v. —n.* **1** wood, metal, etc. for shelves. **2** shelves collectively.
—*v.* ppr. of SHELVE.

She•ma [ʃə'mɑ] *n. Judaism.* the declaration of the fundamentals of Jewish belief, especially the unity of God. ⟨< Hebrew *shma yisroel* "Hear, O Israel," the first words⟩

Shem•ite ['ʃɛmɔit] *n.* Semite. ⟨< *Shem,* the oldest of Noah's three sons in the Bible⟩

she•nan•i•gan [ʃə'nænəgən] *n. Informal.* Usually, **shenanigans,** *pl.* mischief or trickery. ⟨origin uncertain⟩

shent [ʃɛnt] *adj. Archaic.* **1** shamed. **2** blamed; scolded. **3** defeated. **4** ruined. **5** damaged. ⟨pp. of *shend* revile, OE *scendan*⟩

She•ol ['ʃioul] *or* ['ʃiɒl] *n.* **1** a Hebrew name for the abode of the dead. **2 sheol,** *Informal.* hell. ⟨< Hebrew⟩

shep•herd ['ʃɛpərd] *n., v. —n.* **1** a person who takes care of sheep. **2** sheepherder. **3** a person who cares for and protects. **4** a spiritual guide; pastor. **5 the Good Shepherd,** Jesus Christ.
—*v.* **1** take care of. **2** guide; direct: *The teacher shepherded the children safely out of the burning building.* ⟨OE *scēaphierde* < *scēap* sheep + *hierde* herder < *heord* a herd⟩

shepherd dog See SHEEPDOG.

shep•herd•ess ['ʃɛpərdɪs] *n. Poetic.* a woman or girl who takes care of sheep.

shepherd's pie a dish consisting of cubed or ground beef or lamb mixed with gravy and topped with mashed potatoes.

shep•herd's purse a common, weedy plant (*Capsella bursa pastoris*) of the mustard family having tiny white flowers and flattened, triangular pods.

shequ•el ['ʃɛkəl] See SHEKEL (def. 3).

Sher•a•ton ['ʃɛrətən] *adj., n. —adj.* of, like, or having to do with a light, graceful style of furniture characterized by straight lines and little ornamentation.
—*n.* **1** this style of furniture. **2** a piece of furniture in this style. ⟨< Thomas *Sheraton* (1751-1806), an English maker and designer of furniture⟩

sher•bet ['ʃɜrbət] *n.* **1** a frozen dessert made of fruit juice, sugar, water, gelatin, and sometimes milk or egg white. **2** *Brit.* a cold drink made of water, sugar, and fruit juice or flavouring. **3** a stemmed glass with a wide bowl, used for serving desserts. ⟨< Turkish, Persian < Arabic *sharibah* to drink⟩

sherd [ʃɜrd] *n.* See SHARD.

she•rif [ʃə'rif] *n.* **1** a descendant of Mohammed through his daughter Fatima. **2** an Arab prince or ruler, especially the chief magistrate of Mecca or, formerly, the sovereign of Morocco. Also, **shereef.** ⟨< Arabic *sharif* exalted⟩

sher•iff ['ʃɛrɪf] *n.* **1** in Canada, an official whose job is to enforce certain court orders, such as evicting persons for failure to pay rent and escorting convicted persons to prison. **2** in the United States, the most important law enforcing officer of a county. **3** in England and Wales, the chief executive officer of a county or shire, nominally responsible for the administration of justice, the conduct of parliamentary elections, etc. ⟨OE *scīrgerēfa* < *scīr* shire + *gerēfa* reeve[1]⟩

sheriff's sale *Cdn.* a sale of property or goods conducted by a sheriff, following a court order for seizure and sale to satisfy a judgment.

Sher•pa ['ʃɜrpə] *n.* **1** a member of a Himalayan people living on both sides of the Tibet-Nepal border, famous as mountain climbers and guides. **2** the Sino-Tibetan language of this people.

sher•ry ['ʃɛri] *n., pl.* **-ries. 1** a strong Spanish wine fortified with brandy and ranging in flavour from very dry to sweet. It varies in colour from pale yellow to brown. **2** any similar wine. ⟨earlier *sherris* (taken as pl.) wine from *Jeres,* a Spanish town⟩

Sher•wood Forest ['ʃɜr,wʊd] a royal forest near Nottingham in England, where Robin Hood is said to have lived.

she's [ʃiz]; *unstressed* [ʃɪz] **1** she is. **2** she has.

Shet•land ['ʃɛtlənd] *n.* **1** SHETLAND PONY. **2** SHETLAND SHEEPDOG. **3 a** SHETLAND WOOL. **b** a knitted fabric or garment (usually a sweater) made of this wool. ⟨< *Shetland* Islands, a group of British islands northeast of Scotland⟩

Shetland pony a small, sturdy, rough-coated pony, originally from the Shetland Islands.

Shetland sheep a breed of sheep from Shetland, noted for its fine wool.

Shetland sheepdog a breed of small dog that looks like a miniature collie, originally bred in the Shetland Islands for herding sheep.

Shetland wool a fine, hairy, strong worsted, spun from the wool of Shetland sheep and widely used in knitting shawls, sweaters, etc.

shew [ʃou] *n. or v.* **shewed, shewn, shew•ing.** *Archaic.* show.

shew•bread ['ʃou,brɛd] *n. Judaism.* the unleavened bread placed near the altar every Sabbath by the ancient Jewish priests as an offering to God. Also, **showbread.**

SHF or **shf** SUPERHIGH FREQUENCY.

Shi•ah ['ʃiə] *n.* **1** one of the two major branches of the Islamic religion. **2** Shiite. Compare SUNNI.

shi•at•su [ʃi'ɑtsu] *n.* massage therapy making use of acupressure. ⟨< Japanese⟩

shib•bo•leth ['ʃɪbəlɪθ] *or* ['ʃɪbə,lɛθ] *n.* **1** any peculiarity of speech, habit, or custom considered distinctive of a particular group, class, etc. **2** any test word, password, watchword, or pet phrase of a political party, a class, sect, etc. ⟨< Hebrew *shibbōleth* stream; used as a password by the Gileadites to distinguish the fleeing Ephraimites, because they could not pronounce [ʃ]⟩

shied [ʃaɪd] *v.* pt. and a pp. of SHY.

shield [ʃild] *n., v.* —*n.* **1** a piece of armour carried on the arm to protect the body in battle. **2** any person or thing that protects: *She held up a newspaper as a shield against the sun.* **3** something shaped like a shield. **4** a covering for moving parts of machinery. **5** *Electricity.* the insulation on electric wiring. **6 a** any substance, such as lead or water, to protect against exposure to radiation, especially in nuclear reactors. **b** a barrier built out of one of these substances. **7 a** a framework pushed ahead in a tunnel to prevent the earth from caving in while the tunnel is being lined. **b** a movable framework protecting a miner at his or her work. **8** a steel screen or plate attached to a cannon, howitzer, etc. to protect the crew, mechanism, etc. **9 a** a police officer's badge. **b** an escutcheon; coat of arms. **10** a piece of fabric, often rubberized, worn inside a dress or other garment at the armpit. **11** *Zoology.* a protective plate covering a part, as a scute, carapace, or plastron. **12 a** *Geology.* a slightly convex formation of Precambrian rock covering a large area. **b the Shield,** *Cdn.* CANADIAN SHIELD.
—*v.* **1** be a shield to; protect; defend. **2** serve as a shield. ⟨OE *sceld*⟩

shift [ʃɪft] *v., n.* —*v.* **1** change from one place, position, person, sound, etc. to another; change: *The wind has shifted to the southeast. She shifted the heavy bag from one hand to the other.* **2** be rather dishonest; scheme. **3** get rid of. **4** change the position of (the gears of an automobile). **5** change from lower to upper case, or from upper to lower, using the **shift key** on a typewriter or computer keyboard.
shift for oneself, manage to get along on one's own.
—*n.* **1** a change of direction, position, attitude, etc.: *a shift of the wind, a shift in policy.* **2** a group of workers who work during the same period of time: *The night shift comes on at 11 o'clock.* **3** the time during which such a group works: *I usually work the day shift.* **4** a way of getting on; scheme; trick: *The lazy boy tried every shift to avoid doing his work.* **5** gearshift. **6 a** a woman's chemise. **b** a woman's casual dress having straight, loose-fitting lines. **7** *Football.* a change in the arrangement of the players before a ball is put into play. **8** *Geology.* a slight fault or dislocation in a seam or stratum. **9** *Linguistics.* a sound change that affects the phonetic and phonemic system of a language or language group.
make shift, a manage to get along. **b** manage with effort or difficulty. **c** do as well as one can. ⟨OE *sciftan* arrange⟩
—**'shift•er,** *n.*

shift•less ['ʃɪftlɪs] *adj.* lazy; inefficient. —**'shift•less•ly,** *adv.* —**'shift•less•ness,** *n.*

shift•y ['ʃɪfti] *adj.* **shift•i•er, shift•i•est. 1** tricky; sly; not straightforward. **2** resourceful. **3** *Sports.* fast and tricky in playing style. —**'shift•i•ly,** *adv.* —**'shift•i•ness,** *n.*

shi•gel•la [ʃɪ'gɛlə] *n., pl.* **-las** or **-lae** [-li] *or* [-laɪ]. *Bacteriology.* a gram-negative bacillus (genus *Shigella*). Some species of shigella cause dysentery. ⟨< K. *Shiga*, Japanese bacteriologist (1870-1957)⟩

Shih Tzu ['ʃi 'dzu] a breed of toy dog from China having long, silky fur covering short legs in a skirtlike fashion, and a curved plumelike tail. ⟨< Mandarin, lion⟩

Shi•ite ['ʃiəit] *n., adj.* —*n.* a member of the Shiah branch of Islam.
—*adj.* of, being, or having to do with a Shiite or Shiites.

shil•in ['ʃɪlɪn] *n.* the basic unit of money in Somalia, divided into 100 senti. See table of money in the Appendix.

shi•lin•gi [ʃɪ'lɪŋi] *n.* the basic unit of money in Tanzania, divided into 100 senti. See table of money in the Appendix.

shill [ʃɪl] *n., v. Slang.* —*n.* a person who acts as a decoy or confederate of a barker, peddler, or gambler in order to influence bystanders to bid, buy, bet, etc.
—*v.* work as a shill; act as a decoy or lure. ⟨origin unknown⟩

shil•le•lagh or **shil•la•lah** [ʃə'leili] *or* [ʃə'leilə] *n. Irish.* a stick to hit with; cudgel. ⟨< *Shillelagh*, a village in the Irish Republic⟩

shil•ling ['ʃɪlɪŋ] *n.* **1** a former unit of money in the United Kingdom, equal to 1/20 of a pound. **2** the basic unit of money in Kenya and Uganda, divided into 100 cents. See table of money in the Appendix. **3** a coin or note worth one shilling. ⟨OE *scilling*⟩

shil•ly–shal•ly ['ʃɪli ,ʃæli] *adj., v.* **-lied, -ly•ing;** *n.* —*adj.* vacillating; wavering; hesitating; undecided.
—*v.* be undecided; vacillate; hesitate.
—*n.* an inability to decide; hesitation. ⟨varied reduplication of *shall I?*⟩

shi•ly ['ʃaɪli] *adv.* See SHYLY.

shim [ʃɪm] *n., v.* **shimmed, shim•ming.** —*n.* a thin strip of metal or wood used to fill up space, make something level, etc.
—*v.* put a shim or shims in. ⟨origin uncertain⟩

shim•mer ['ʃɪmər] *v., n.* —*v.* **1** gleam faintly: *The satin shimmers.* **2** appear as a wavering image reflected in heat waves or on rippling water.
—*n.* a faint gleam or shine. ⟨OE *scimrian*⟩ —**'shim•mer•ing•ly,** *adv.*

shim•mer•y ['ʃɪməri] *adj.* shimmering; gleaming softly.

shim•my ['ʃɪmi] *n., pl.* **-mies;** *v.* **-mied, -my•ing.** —*n.* **1** a ragtime dance characterized by shaking of the hips and shoulders. **2** an unusual shaking or vibration, especially of the front wheels of a car, truck, etc. **3** a chemise.
—*v.* **1** dance the shimmy. **2** shake; vibrate. ⟨var. of *chemise* (taken as pl.)⟩

shin[1] [ʃɪn] *n., v.* **shinned, shin•ning.** —*n.* **1** the front part of the leg from the knee to the ankle. See LEG for picture. **2** in beef cattle, the lower part of the foreleg.
—*v.* climb up or down a rope, pole, etc. by gripping alternately with the hands and feet: *to shin up a tree.* ⟨OE *scinu*⟩

shin[2] [ʃin] *n.* the twenty-third letter of the Hebrew alphabet. See table of alphabets in the Appendix.
☛ *Hom.* SHEEN.

shin•bone ['ʃɪn,boun] *n.* the front bone of the leg below the knee; tibia.

shin•dig ['ʃɪn,dɪg] *n. Informal.* a merry or noisy dance, party, etc. ⟨? variant of *shindy*, suggesting a dig, or blow, on the shin⟩

shin•dy ['ʃɪndi] *n., pl.* **-dies.** *Slang.* **1** a disturbance; rumpus. **2** a shindig. ⟨origin uncertain⟩

shine [ʃaɪn] *v.* **shone** or (*esp. for def.* 3) **shined, shin•ing;** *n.* —*v.* **1** send out light; be bright with light; reflect light; glow: *The sun shines.* **2** do very well; be brilliant; excel: *Mary shines in French.* **3** make bright; polish: *shine shoes.* **4** cause to shine: *shine a light.*
shine up to, *Slang.* try to please and get the friendship of.
—*n.* **1** light; brightness; radiance. **2** a lustre; polish; gloss, as of silk. **3** fair weather; sunshine: *rain or shine.* **4** polish put on shoes. **5** *Slang.* a trick; prank.
take a shine to, *Informal.* become fond of; like. ⟨OE *scīnan*⟩

shin•er ['ʃaɪnər] *n.* **1** any of numerous small freshwater cyprinid fishes (especially genus *Notropis*) of North America. **2** *Slang.* BLACK EYE. **3** a person or thing that shines.

shin•gle[1] ['ʃɪŋgəl] *n., v.* **-gled, -gling.** —*n.* **1** a thin piece of wood, etc. used for roofing, etc. Shingles are laid in overlapping rows with the thicker ends exposed. **2** *Informal.* a small signboard, especially for a doctor's or lawyer's office. **3** a woman's short haircut.
hang out (one's) **shingle,** *Informal.* of lawyers, doctors, and dentists, establish a professional practice; open an office.
—*v.* **1** cover with shingles: *to shingle a roof.* **2** cut (the hair) short. ⟨var. of earlier *shindle* < L *scindula*⟩

shin•gle[2] ['ʃɪŋgəl] *n.* **1** loose stones or pebbles such as lie on the seashore; coarse gravel. **2** a beach or other place covered with such pebbles. ⟨origin uncertain; cf. Norwegian *singling* small, round pebble⟩

shin•gles ['ʃɪŋgəlz] *n. sing. or pl. Pathology.* a viral disease that causes painful irritation of a group of nerves and an outbreak of itching spots or blisters. ⟨ME < Med.L *cingulus*, var. of L *cingulum* girdle < *cingere* gird⟩

shin•gly ['ʃɪŋgli] *adj.* consisting of or covered with small, loose stones or pebbles.

shin•guard ['ʃɪn,gɑrd] *n.* a protective pad worn on the shins, as in various sports.

shin•ing ['ʃaɪnɪŋ] *adj., v.* —*adj.* **1** that shines; bright. **2** brilliant; outstanding.
—*v.* ppr. of SHINE. —**'shin•ing•ly,** *adv.*

shin•ny[1] ['ʃɪni] *n., pl.* **-nies;** *v.* **-nied, -ny•ing.** *Cdn.* —*n.* **1** a simple kind of hockey, played on the ice with skates, or without skates on the street or in a field; road hockey. **2** the stick used in this game. **3** *Slang.* the game of ice hockey.
—*v.* play shinny. Also, **shinney.** ⟨< Scottish dial. *shinny* or *shinty*⟩

shin•ny[2] ['ʃɪni] *v.* **-nied, -ny•ing.** *Informal.* shin; climb: *to shinny up a tree.*

shin•plas•ter ['ʃɪn,plæstər] *n.* **1** *Cdn. Informal.* formerly, a banknote worth 25 cents, issued in 1870, 1900, and 1923. **2** a piece of paper currency of any of various small denominations, issued privately or by a government; especially, such a note devalued by inflation or poor security.

shin splints a painful strain of the lower leg muscles, which often occurs after prolonged running. Also, **shinsplints.**

Shin•to ['ʃɪntou] *n., adj.* —*n.* **1** the main religion of Japan, primarily a system of nature worship and ancestor worship, in which the Emperor is traditionally revered as divine. **2** an adherent of this religion.
—*adj.* of or having to do with Shinto. ⟨< Japanese < Chinese *shin tao* way of the gods⟩

Shin•to•ism ['ʃɪntou,ɪzəm] *n.* the Shinto religion.
—**'Shin•to•ist,** *n.* —**,Shin•to'ist•ic,** *adj.*

shin•y ['ʃaɪni] *adj.* **shin•i•er, shin•i•est. 1** shining; bright: *a shiny new nickel.* **2** worn to a glossy smoothness: *a coat shiny from hard wear.* —**'shin•i•ness,** *n.*

ship [ʃɪp] *n., v.* **shipped, ship•ping.** —*n.* **1** any large vessel for travel on water, such as a steamship, frigate, or galley. **2** a large sailing vessel, especially one with three or more masts. **3** an airship, airplane, spacecraft, etc. **4** the officers and crew of a vessel.
about ship! *Nautical.* turn the ship around! put the ship on the other tack!
jump ship, a desert one's ship. **b** leave an organization, etc. to avoid a difficult situation.
when (someone's) **ship comes in** or **home,** when someone's fortune is made; when one has money.
—*v.* **1** put, take, or receive on board a ship. **2** go on board a ship. **3** travel on a ship; sail. **4** send or carry from one place to another by a ship, train, truck, etc.: *Did he ship it by express?* **5** engage for service on a ship: *to ship a new crew.* **6** take a job on a ship: *He shipped as cook.* **7** take in (water) over the side, as a vessel does when the waves break over it. **8** fix (something) in a ship or boat in its proper place for use: *to ship a rudder.*
ship out (or **off**), **a** go to sea. **b** send out by ship. **c** dismiss; send away. **d** leave. ⟨OE *scip*⟩ —**'ship•pa•ble,** *adj.*

–ship *suffix.* **1** the office, position, or occupation of ——: *authorship, kingship.* **2** the quality, state, or condition of being ——: *kinship, partnership.* **3** the act, acts, power, or skill of ——: *leadership, workmanship.* **4** the relation between ——s: *comradeship.* **5** one with the rank or status of —— (*used, usually with a possessive, to form a term of address*): *your ladyship.* **6** the members, collectively, of the class of ——: *readership.* ⟨OE *-scipe*⟩

ship biscuit a kind of hard biscuit formerly used on shipboard; hardtack. Also, **ship's biscuit.**

ship•board ['ʃɪp,bɔrd] *n., adj.* —*n.*
on shipboard, on or inside a ship.
—*adj.* occurring, found, etc. on a ship: *a shipboard romance.*

ship bread SHIP BISCUIT; hardtack. Also, **ship's bread.**

ship•break•er ['ʃɪp,breikər] *n.* a person who breaks up or contracts to break up ships no longer seaworthy.
—**'ship,break•ing,** *n.*

ship•build•er ['ʃɪp,bɪldər] *n.* a person who designs or constructs ships.

ship•build•ing ['ʃɪp,bɪldɪŋ] *n.* **1** the designing or building of ships. **2** the art of building ships. **3** (*adjl.*) of or used in shipbuilding; having to do with shipbuilding.

ship canal a canal wide and deep enough for ships.

ship chandler a dealer in ship supplies, such as cordage, canvas, etc.

ship•lap ['ʃɪp,læp] *n. Carpentry.* **1** a flush, overlapping joint between boards, formed by cutting corresponding rabbets in the adjoining edges and lapping the boards to the depth of the rabbets. **2** boards thus rabbeted.

ship•load ['ʃɪp,loud] *n.* **1** a full load for a ship. **2** the load or cargo carried by a ship.

ship•man ['ʃɪpmən] *n., pl.* **-men. 1** *Archaic.* sailor. **2** the master of a ship.

ship•mas•ter ['ʃɪp,mæstər] *n.* a master, commander, or captain of a ship.

ship•mate ['ʃɪp,meit] *n.* **1** a fellow sailor on a ship. **2** a person who sails on the same ship; fellow passenger.

ship•ment ['ʃɪpmənt] *n.* **1** the act of shipping goods. **2** goods sent at one time to a person, firm, etc.

ship money formerly, in England, a tax to provide money for the building and maintenance of naval ships, levied at various times until it was abolished in 1641.

ship of the desert a camel.

ship of the line formerly, a sailing warship carrying 74 or more guns, corresponding to the modern battleship.

ship•own•er ['ʃɪp,ounər] *n.* a person who owns a ship or ships.

ship•per ['ʃɪpər] *n.* a person or company that ships goods.

ship•ping ['ʃɪpɪŋ] *n., v.* **1** the act or business of sending goods by water, rail, etc. **2** ships collectively; the ships of a nation, city, or business. **3** their total tonnage.
—*v.* ppr. of SHIP.

shipping clerk a person whose work is to see to the packing and shipment of goods.

shipping room a room in a business house, factory, etc., from which goods are sent.

ship–rigged ['ʃɪp ,rɪgd] *adj. Nautical.* rigged with square sails on all three masts.

ship•shape ['ʃɪp,ʃeip] *adj., adv.* —*adj.* in good order; trim.
—*adv.* in a trim, neat manner.

ship's husband a person who has general care of a ship in port, overseeing supplies, repairs, entering and clearing procedures, etc.

ship's papers the documents required by international law to be carried on board a merchant ship and produced on demand.

ship•way ['ʃɪp,wei] *n.* **1** the sloping structure on which a ship is built and then launched. **2** a SHIP CANAL.

ship•worm ['ʃɪp,wɜrm] *n.* any of various marine bivalve molluscs (family Teredinidae) having a long, wormlike body and a small shell adapted for boring into wood. Shipworms can do great damage to wooden piers, ships, etc.

ship•wreck ['ʃɪp,rɛk] *n., v.* —*n.* **1** the destruction or loss of a ship. **2** a wrecked ship. **3** destruction; ruin: *The shipwreck of his plans discouraged him.*
—*v.* cause to suffer shipwreck.

ship•wright ['ʃɪp,rəit] *n.* a person who builds or repairs ships.

ship•yard ['ʃɪp,jɑrd] *n.* a place near the water where ships are built or repaired.

shire [ʃaɪr] *n.* one of the counties into which England is divided. ⟨OE *scīr*⟩

Shire [ʃaɪr] *n.* SHIRE HORSE.

shire horse any of the largest breed of draft horses having very hairy legs, said to be descended from the war horses of the Middle Ages. ⟨< the *Shires,* midland counties of England where they are chiefly raised⟩

shire•town ['ʃaɪr,taun] *n. Cdn. Maritimes.* a COUNTY SEAT.

shirk [ʃɜrk] *v., n.* —*v.* avoid or get out of doing (work, duty, etc.).
—*n.* a person who shirks or does not do his or her share. ⟨< G *Schurke* rascal⟩ —**'shirk•er,** *n.*

shirr [ʃɜr] *v., n.* —*v.* **1** draw up or gather (cloth) on parallel threads. **2** bake (eggs) in a shallow dish with butter, etc.
—*n.* Also, **shirring.** a shirred arrangement of cloth, etc. ⟨origin unknown⟩

shirt [ʃɜrt] *n.* **1** a garment for the upper part of the body, made of a light material such as cotton, a cotton blend, or silk, and typically having a collar, sleeves, a front opening with buttons, and a tail that is tucked into the pants. **2** an upper garment in any of various other styles. **3** an undergarment for the upper part of the body; undershirt.
in (one's) **shirt sleeves,** without a coat or jacket on.

keep (one's) **shirt on,** *Slang.* stay calm; keep one's temper.
lose (one's) **shirt,** *Slang.* lose everything one owns. ⟨ME *schirte,* OE *scyrte.* Cf. SKIRT.⟩ **—'shirt•less,** *adj.*

shirt•band ['ʃɜrt,bænd] *n.* the neckband or other band of a shirt.

shirt•dress ['ʃɜrt,drɛs] *n.* a tailored dress with a bodice similar to a shirt.

shirt•ing ['ʃɜrtɪŋ] *n.* cloth for shirts.

shirt–sleeve ['ʃɜrt ,sliv] *adj.* **1** appropriate for dressing without a coat or jacket: *This is shirt-sleeve weather.*
2 characterized by informality: *shirt-sleeve diplomacy.*

shirt–tail ['ʃɜrt ,teil] *n.* **1** the part of a shirt extending below the waist, usually worn tucked into the pants or skirt. **2** (*adjl.*) distantly related: *a shirt-tail cousin.*

shirt•waist ['ʃɜrt,weist] *n.* the bodice of a shirtdress.

shish ke•bab ['ʃɪʃ kə,bɑb] cubes of lamb, beef, or other meat, marinated and cooked with mushrooms, tomatoes, onions, etc. on a skewer or spit. Also, **shish kabob.** ⟨< Armenian *shish kabab*⟩

shiv [ʃɪv] *n. Slang.* a knife or razor, especially when used as an offensive weapon. A switchblade is a kind of shiv. ⟨perhaps < earlier *chive* file, knife < Romany⟩

shiv•a or **shi•vah** ['ʃɪvə] *n. Judaism.* a period of seven days' mourning for a dead relative. ⟨< Hebrew *shib'ah* seven⟩

Shi•va ['ʃivə] *n. Hinduism.* one of the three great classical divinities, the creator and destroyer, a remote, austere god who remains in a state of constant meditation, worshipped as the highest god by many Hindus. Also, **Siva.**

shiv•a•ree [,ʃɪvə'ri] *n., v.* **-reed, -ree•ing.** *—n.* **1** a celebration held to do honour to a newly married couple; charivari. **2** a noisy serenade for a newly married couple, often performed in a spirit of mockery. **3** any noisy celebration.
—v. serenade (a newly married couple) in this manner. ⟨var. of *charivari*⟩

shiv•er[1] ['ʃɪvər] *v., n. —v.* shake with cold, fear, etc.
—n. **1** a shaking from cold, fear, etc. **2 the shivers,** a fit of such shaking. ⟨ME *schiveren;* origin uncertain⟩ **—'shiv•er•er,** *n.*
☛ *Syn. v.* **1. Shiver,** SHUDDER, QUAKE = shake or tremble. **Shiver,** used chiefly of people and animals, suggests a quivering of the flesh: *The child crept shivering into bed.* **Shudder** especially suggests sudden sharp shivering of the whole body in horror or extreme disgust: *She shuddered at the ghastly sight.* **Quake** suggests violent trembling with fear or cold, or shaking and rocking from a violent disturbance: *The house quaked on its foundations.*

shiv•er[2] ['ʃɪvər] *v., n. —v.* break into small pieces: *He shivered the mirror with a hammer.*
—n. a small piece; splinter. ⟨origin uncertain⟩

shiv•er•y ['ʃɪvəri] *adj.* **1** quivering from cold, fear, etc.; shivering. **2** inclined to shiver from cold. **3** chilly. **4** causing shivers.

shlep or **shlepp** [ʃlɛp] *v.* **shlepped, shlep•ping.** See SCHLEP.

shmo [ʃmou] *n.* See SCHMO.

shnook [ʃnʊk] *n.* See SCHNOOK.

shoal[1] [ʃoul] *n., adj., v. —n.* **1** a place in a sea, lake, or stream where the water is shallow. **2** a sandbank or sand bar that makes the water shallow: *The ship was wrecked on the shoals.*
—adj. shallow.
—v. **1** become shallow. **2** of a ship, sail into a shallower area of (water). ⟨OE *sceald* shallow⟩

shoal[2] [ʃoul] *n., v. —n.* a large number; crowd: *a shoal of fish.*
—v. form into a shoal; crowd together. ⟨OE *scolu*⟩

shoal•y ['ʃouli] *adj.* full of shoals or shallow places.

shoat [ʃout] *n.* a young pig able to feed itself. Also, **shote.** ⟨origin uncertain⟩

shock[1] [ʃɒk] *n., v. —n.* **1** the impact of colliding objects or forces. **2** the effect of this; a sudden, violent shake, blow or crash: *the shock of an earthquake. The two trains collided with a terrible shock.* **3** a sudden and violent emotional or mental disturbance: *She reeled with shock at the bad news.* **4** something that causes such a disturbance. *His death was a great shock to his family.* **5** *Pathology.* a condition of physical collapse or depression, together with a sudden drop in blood pressure, often resulting in unconsciousness. Shock may set in after a severe injury, great loss of blood, or a sudden emotional disturbance. **6** a sudden stimulation of the nerves and muscles produced by an electric current passing through the body. **7** SHOCK ABSORBER (def. 2).
—v. **1** strike or cause to strike together violently. **2** cause to feel surprise, horror, or disgust: *That child's bad language shocks everyone.* **3** give an electric shock to. **4** cause to suffer shock. **5** be shocked, horrified, etc.: *He shocks too easily.* ⟨probably < F *choc,* n., *choquer,* v.⟩ **—'shock•er,** *n.* **—,shock•a'bil•i•ty,** *n.* **—'shock•a•ble,** *adj.*

shock[2] [ʃɒk] *n. or v.* stook. ⟨ME < MLG or MDu. *schok*⟩ **—'shock•er,** *n.*

shock[3] [ʃɒk] *n.* a thick, bushy mass: *She has a shock of red hair.* ⟨? < *shock*[2]⟩

shock absorber 1 anything that absorbs or lessens shocks. **2** a device used on automobiles to absorb or lessen the shocks caused by rough roads. **3** a similar device on the landing gear of aircraft.

shock–head•ed ['ʃɒk ,hɛdɪd] *adj.* having a thick, bushy mass of hair.

shock•ing ['ʃɒkɪŋ] *adj., v. —adj.* **1** causing intense and painful surprise: *shocking news.* **2** offensive; disgusting; revolting: *a shocking sight.* **3** *Informal.* very bad: *shocking manners.*
—v. ppr. of SHOCK. **—'shock•ing•ly,** *adv.*

shocking pink very bright pink.

shock•proof ['ʃɒk,pruf] *adj.* **1** able to endure or resist shock. **2** protected against electric shock.

shock therapy ELECTRO-CONVULSIVE THERAPY.

shock treatment 1 ELECTRO-CONVULSIVE THERAPY. **2** any act intended to shock.

shock troops troops chosen and specially trained for making attacks.

shock wave 1 a disturbance of the atmosphere created by the movement of an aircraft, rocket, etc. at a velocity greater than that of sound. **2** a similar effect caused by an explosion.

shod [ʃɒd] *v.* pt. and pp. of SHOE.

shod•dy ['ʃɒdi] *n., pl.* **-dies;** *adj.* **-di•er, -di•est.** *—n.* **1** an inferior kind of wool made of woollen waste, old rags, yarn, etc. **2** cloth made of woollen waste. **3** anything inferior made to look like what is better.
—adj. **1** made of woollen waste. **2** of poor quality: *shoddy construction.* **3** pretending to be, or made to appear, better than it is: *a shoddy necklace.* **4** mean; shabby: *shoddy treatment, a shoddy trick.* ⟨origin uncertain⟩ **—'shod•di•ly,** *adv.* **—'shod•di•ness,** *n.*

Some current shoe styles

shoe [ʃu] *n., v.* **shod, shoe•ing.** *—n.* **1** an outer covering for a person's foot, usually consisting of a firm or thick sole and separate heel and a thinner, flexible upper part of leather, cloth, or a synthetic material resembling leather. **2** anything like a shoe in shape or use, such as a base into which something fits for support. **3** a horseshoe. **4** a ferrule; metal band, etc. to protect the end of a staff, pole, etc. **5** BRAKE SHOE. **6** the outer case of an automobile tire. **7** a sliding plate or contact by which an electric car takes current from the third rail. **8** *Cdn.* a snowshoe. **9** the strip of metal on the underside of a sled runner. Also, **shoeing.**
fill (someone's) **shoes,** take someone's place.
(if) the shoe fits (wear it), (if or since) a given statement applies to the case in question (take it to heart).
in (someone's) **shoes,** in someone's place, situation, or circumstances. *I wouldn't like to be in the murderer's shoes right now.*
the shoe is on the other foot, the situation is reversed.
wait for the other shoe to drop. See DROP.
where the shoe pinches, where the real trouble or difficulty lies.

—*v.* **1** furnish with a shoe or shoes: *A blacksmith shoes horses.* **2** protect or arm at the point; edge or face with metal: *a stick shod with steel.* **3** *Cdn.* travel by snowshoe. ⟨OE *scōh*⟩ **—'sho•er,** *n.* **—'shoe•less,** *adj.*
☛ *Hom.* SHOO.

shoe•bill ['ʃu,bɪl] *n.* a large cranelike bird (*Balaeniceps rex*) of central Africa, having a broad, flat bill.

shoe•black ['ʃu,blæk] *n.* a person who cleans and polishes shoes to earn money.

shoe•horn ['ʃu,hɔrn] *n., v.* —*n.* a curved piece of metal, horn, etc. inserted at the heel of a shoe to make it slip on easily.
—*v. Informal.* force into a tight space.

shoe•lace ['ʃu,leis] *n.* a cord, braid, or leather strip for fastening a shoe.

shoe•mak•er ['ʃu,meikər] *n.* a person who makes or repairs shoes. **—'shoe•mak•ing,** *n.*

shoe•pack or **shoe•pac** ['ʃu,pæk] *n. Cdn.* **1** a variety of moccasin used especially for snowshoeing, having uppers of thick, oiled leather that extend above the ankle and, often, a stiff sole. Also called **Canadian shoe** or **larrigan. 2** a kind of manufactured boot modelled after this moccasin, often with a rubber sole. ⟨by folk etymology < Lenape (Delaware) *shipak* moccasin⟩

shoe•shine ['ʃu,ʃaɪn] *n.* **1** the shining or polishing of shoes. **2** the polished look of shined shoes. **3** shoeblack.

shoe•string ['ʃu,strɪŋ] *n., adj.* —*n.* **1** a shoelace. **2** a very small amount of money used to start or carry on a business, travel expedition, etc.: *The firm is paying its way, but it is operating on a shoestring. "See Europe on a shoestring!"*
—*adj.* **1** very long and thin like a shoestring: *shoestring fries.* **2** of or using a small amount, especially of money: *a shoestring budget.*

shoe tree a device with a shaped front for keeping a shoe in shape when it is not being worn.

sho•far ['ʃoufar], ['ʃoufɑr], *or* [ʃou'fɑr] *n., pl.* **sho•fars** or **sho•froth** ['ʃoufrout] *or* [ʃou'frout]. *Judaism.* a musical wind instrument made from a ram's horn, sounded in the synagogue as part of the ritual marking Rosh Hashanah and Yom Kippur. The use of the shofar dates back to the time of the ancient Hebrews. Also, **shophar.** ⟨< Hebrew *shōphār* ram's horn⟩

sho•gun ['ʃou,gʌn], ['ʃougən], *or* ['ʃou,gun] *n.* the former hereditary commander in chief of the Japanese army. The shoguns were the real rulers of Japan for hundreds of years until 1867. ⟨< Japanese < Chinese *chiang chun* army leader⟩

sho•gun•ate ['ʃougənɪt] *or* ['ʃougə,neit] *n.* **1** the position, rank, or rule of a shogun. **2** government by shoguns.

sho•lom [ʃɑ'loum] *n., interj.* See SHALOM.

shone [ʃɒn] *v.* a pt. and pp. of SHINE.

shoo [ʃu] *interj., v.* **shooed, shoo•ing.** —*interj.* an exclamation used to scare away hens, birds, etc.
—*v.* **1** scare or drive away: *Shoo those flies away from the sugar.* **2** exclaim or call "shoo."
☛ *Hom.* SHOE.

shoo•fly pie ['ʃu,flaɪ] a one-crust pie with a very sweet filling of molasses and brown sugar.

shoo–in ['ʃu ,ɪn] *n. Informal.* **1** a candidate, team, etc. who is regarded as certain to win; sure winner. **2** an election, contest, etc. considered easy to win.

shook[1] [ʃʊk] *n.* **1** a set of pieces, cut and ready to assemble, that are used in making boxes, barrels, articles of furniture, etc. **2** a stook or shock of sheaves of grain. ⟨origin uncertain⟩

shook[2] [ʃʊk] *v.* pt. of SHAKE.

shoon [ʃun] *n. Archaic.* a pl. of SHOE.

shoot [ʃut] *v.* **shot, shoot•ing;** *n., interj.* —*v.* **1** hit, wound, or kill with a bullet, arrow, etc.: *to shoot a rabbit.* **2** send with force or speed at or as if at a target: *to shoot an arrow. She shot question after question at us.* **3** fire or use (a weapon such as a gun, bow, catapult, etc.) **4** of a gun, etc., send a bullet: *This gun shoots straight.* **5** kill game in or on: *to shoot a farm.* **6** *Informal.* terrorize, destroy, or wreck by shooting (*used with* **up**): *to shoot up a town.* **7 a** move suddenly and swiftly: *A car shot by us. Flames shot up from the burning house. Pain shot up her arm. He shot back the bolt.* **b** cast forth or out with violence: *a volcano shooting lava; a dragon shooting fire.* **8** pass quickly along, through, or over (rapids, a waterfall, etc.): *to shoot Niagara Falls in a barrel.* **9** grow quickly by or as if by putting out shoots; grow bigger or taller quickly (*used with* **up, forth,** *etc.*): *The grain is really shooting up in the warm weather. He shot up 5 cm last summer.* **10 a** take (a picture) with a camera; photograph. **b** start the cameras in photographing a movie scene. **11** project sharply: *a cape that shoots out into the sea.* **12** dump; empty out. **13** vary with some different colour, quality, feature, etc.: *The dress was shot with threads of gold. Her speech was shot with humorous asides.* **14** measure the altitude of: *to shoot the sun.* **15** *Games, sports.* **a** send or propel (a ball, marble, puck, etc.) toward an objective. **b** cast or toss (the dice) in craps. **16** play (craps, pool, casual basketball, etc.). **17** make or get by shooting: *to shoot holes in a wall, to shoot twenty points.* **18** open, loosen, remove, etc. by setting off a charge of an explosive: *to shoot an oil well.* **19** *Informal.* spend uselessly; waste: *The whole day was shot.* **20** *Informal.* give an injection to. **21** *Slang.* take (an illegal drug) by injection (*often used intransitively with* **up**): *to shoot up. He shoots heroin.*
shoot at or **for,** *Informal.* aim at; aspire to.
shoot down, a kill or bring down by shooting: *He was shot down in cold blood. They shot down two enemy aircraft.* **b** reject or criticize harshly.
shoot (straight) from the hip, *Informal.* **a** speak frankly. **b** speak without much forethought.
shoot off (one's) **mouth.** *Slang.* speak arrogantly, impudently, or indiscreetly.
—*n.* **1** an act or round of shooting. **2** shooting practice. **3** a trip, party, or contest for shooting. **4 a** the act of sprouting or growing. **b** a new part growing out; young bud or stem. **5** a sloping trough for conveying coal, grain, water, etc. to a lower level; chute.
—*interj. Informal.* **1** a mild exclamation of disappointment, annoyance, etc. **2** go ahead and say what you want: *"Can I make a comment?" "By all means; shoot!"* ⟨OE *scēotan*⟩ **—'shoot•er,** *n.*
☛ *Hom.* CHUTE.

shooting gallery 1 a long room or deep booth fitted with targets for practice in shooting. **2** *Slang.* a place where drug addicts can inject themselves with narcotic drugs.

shooting iron *Informal.* a firearm or gun, especially a pistol or rifle.

shooting star 1 a meteor resembling a star seen falling or darting through the sky. **2** any of a genus (*Dodecatheon*) of plants of the primrose family found especially in W North America, having clusters of rose, purple, or white flowers whose petals and sepals turn backward.

shooting stick a type of walking stick, pointed at one end and having a large handle that unfolds into a seat at the other, used by spectators at outdoor sporting events.

shoot•out or **shoot–out** ['ʃut,ʌut] *n.* **1** a decisive gun battle: *a shootout between rebels and militia.* **2** any desperate and decisive contest, quarrel, or argument.

shop [ʃɒp] *n., v.* **shopped, shop•ping.** —*n.* **1** a place where things are sold; store, especially a small, specialized one. **2** a place where things are made or repaired: *She works in a carpenter's shop.* **3** a place where a certain kind of work is done: *a barber shop.* **4** a specialty area in a department store: *This store has a very chic young men's shop.* **5** INDUSTRIAL ARTS.
set up shop, start work or business.
shut up shop, stop work or business temporarily or permanently.
talk shop, talk about one's work or profession.
—*v.* **1** visit stores to look at or buy things. **2** frequent (sales, a given store, etc.) as a customer: *Are you going to shop the January sales? Shop Wensley's for value!*
shop around, a go from store to store to compare prices, quality, selection, etc. before deciding on a purchase. **b** investigate possibilities in search of a better method, idea, employer, etc. ⟨OE *sceoppa*⟩

shop assistant *n.* a person who works in a shop or store.

sho•phar ['ʃoufər], ['ʃoufɑr], *or* [ʃou'fɑr] *n.* See SHOFAR.

shop•keep•er ['ʃɒp,kipər] *n.* a person who carries on business in a shop or store.

shop•lift•ing ['ʃɒp,lɪftɪŋ] *n.* the act of stealing goods from a store while pretending to be a customer. **—'shop,lift,** *v.* **—'shop,lift•er,** *n.*

shop•man ['ʃɒpmən] *n., pl.* **-men.** a shopkeeper.

shop•per ['ʃɒpər] *n.* **1** a person who visits stores to look at or buy things. **2** a person hired to buy goods at retail for another, especially one hired by a retail store to buy items of merchandise from competitive stores in order to determine how similar items offered by it compare in price and quality.

shop•ping ['ʃɒpɪŋ] *n., v.* —*n.* the buying of groceries, clothes, etc.: *He does his shopping on Wednesdays and Saturdays.*
go shopping, go to the store or stores in order to buy groceries, clothes, etc.
—*v.* ppr. of SHOP.

shopping centre 1 a concentration of retail stores, restaurants, cinema, and various other consumer services, usually in a suburban residential district, built as a unit and having ample parking, spacious walks, etc. 2 the street or streets of a town where the main stores and shops are concentrated. 3 a town, city, etc. serving as a retail and distribution centre for the surrounding region.

shopping mall SHOPPING CENTRE (def. 1).

shopping plaza *Cdn.* a SHOPPING CENTRE (def. 1), especially a small one in which the stores open only to the outdoors.

shop steward a union worker elected by fellow workers to represent them in dealings with management and to maintain union rules.

shop•talk ['ʃɒp,tɒk] *n.* **1** the specialized language or vocabulary of a specific occupation or field of work; JARGON (def. 3). **2** the discussion of business or professional matters, especially outside office hours.

☛ *Usage.* **Shoptalk** (def. 1) is a less formal term for JARGON (def. 3) and refers to a private or restricted aspect of language. It is appropriate to use shoptalk when writing for and about people in a particular walk of life. In speaking or writing for a wider audience, shoptalk can be useful for the sake of realism if its meaning is explained or clear from the context. Otherwise, it should be avoided.

shop•worn ['ʃɒp,wɔrn] *adj.* **1** soiled as a result of being displayed or handled in a store. **2** no longer new, interesting, or appealing: *shopworn slogans, shopworn ideas.*

Sho•ran or **sho•ran** ['ʃɔr,æn] *n.* an electronic navigating system for aircraft and guided missiles. Signals are sent from the craft to two transponders on the ground, from whose responding signals the exact position of the craft may be determined. ⟨< *short range navigation*⟩

shore¹ [ʃɔr] *n.* **1** the land at the very edge of a sea, lake, etc. **2** the land near a sea, lake, etc.: *There is good farmland on the western shore of the island.* **3 shores,** *pl.* land: *foreign shores.* **4** *Law.* the land between high-water and low-water marks.
in shore, in or on the water, near or nearer to the shore.
off shore, in or on the water, not far from the shore. ⟨ME *schore,* OE *scora,* cf. MLG or MDu. *schore*⟩

shore² [ʃɔr] *n., v.* **shored, shor•ing.** —*n.* a prop placed against or beneath something to support it.
—*v.* prop (*up*) or support with shores. ⟨ME; ? < MDu. *schore* prop⟩ —**'shor•er,** *n.*

shore³ [ʃɔr] *v. Archaic.* a pt. of SHEAR.

shore bird any of various birds, such as sandpipers and plovers, that live mostly on the shores of oceans and lakes.

shore•hand ['ʃɔr,hænd] *n.* a person whose work is loading and unloading ships, etc.

shore ice *Cdn., esp. Northern.* sea ice that is anchored to the shore and extends seaward in a great shelf.

shore leave *Navy.* **1** permission given to officers or crew to go ashore. **2** the time spent ashore.

shore•less ['ʃɔrlɪs] *adj.* **1** having no shore. **2** boundless.

shore•line ['ʃɔr,laɪn] *n.* the line where shore and water meet.

shore pine a form of the lodgepole pine found along the Pacific coast.

shore•ward ['ʃɔrwərd] *adv. or adj.* toward the shore.

shor•ing ['ʃɔrɪŋ] *n., v.* —*n.* the shores or props for supporting a building, ship, etc.
—*v.* ppr. of SHORE².

shorn [ʃɔrn] *v., adj.* —*v.* a pp. of SHEAR.
—*adj.* **1** sheared. **2** deprived.

short [ʃɔrt] *adj., adv., n., v.* —*adj.* **1** not long; of small extent from end to end: *a short distance, a short time, a short street.* **2** not long for its kind: *a short tail.* **3** not tall: *a short man, short grass.* **4** not coming up to the right amount, measure, standard, etc.: *The cashier is short in her accounts.* **5** not being or having enough; scanty: *The prisoners were kept on a short allowance of food.* **6 a** brief, concise; condensed. **b** so brief as to be rude: *She was so short with me that I felt hurt.* **7** *Phonetics.* **a** of vowels or syllables, occupying a relatively short time in utterance. **b** popularly, being one of the English vowels in *fat, net, pin, not, up.* **8** breaking or crumbling easily. Pastry is made short with lard or butter. **9** of memory, forgetting things relatively quickly. **10** of a person's temper, easily lost. **11** not possessing at the time of sale the stocks or commodities that one sells. **12** denoting or having to do with such sales of stocks or commodities. **13** depending for profit on a decline in prices.
in short order, promptly; quickly.
make short work of, deal with quickly.
run short, a not have enough. **b** not be enough.
short and sweet, pleasantly brief.
short for, as an abbreviation of.
short of, a not up to; less than; except: *Nothing short of your best work will satisfy me.* **b** not having enough of: *I'm short of money just now.* **c** before reaching, doing, etc; away from: *We were a mile short of home. They finished just short of midnight.* **d** apart from (some extreme measure): *Short of expelling him, there's not much we can do.*
the short end of the stick, unfair treatment; less than one's due.
—*adv.* **1** so as to be or make short. **2** abruptly; suddenly: *The horse stopped short.* **3** briefly.
bring up short, a check or halt suddenly. **b** rebuke sharply.
cut short, bring to an end suddenly.
fall short (of), a fail to reach a goal or standard. **b** be insufficient.
sell short, a sell without possessing at the time the stocks, etc. that are being sold: *It is risky to sell short.* **b** short-change; fail to give what is due: *By spending so much time at the office he is selling his family short.*
—*n.* **1** something short. **2** SHORT CIRCUIT. **3** a person who has sold short; a sale made by selling short; stock sold short. **4** any short film, as a cartoon, newsreel, etc., especially one shown on the same program with a full-length, or feature, film. **5** *Baseball.* shortstop: *to play short.* **6 shorts,** *pl.* **a** short pants that reach no lower than the knees. **b** short underpants worn by men or boys. **c** the mixture of bran and coarse meal left over after milling.
for short, as an abbreviation.
in short, a briefly. **b** in summary.
—*v.* **1** *Electricity.* short-circuit (*often used with* **out**). **2** give less than what is due or required; short-change: *We were shorted on pencils when the supplies arrived.* ⟨OE *sceort*⟩ —**'short•ness,** *n.*

☛ *Syn. adj.* **1. Short,** BRIEF = of small extent. **Short** may describe either space or time, but when describing time it often suggests cutting or stopping short before finishing: *Because he was late, he could take only a short walk today.* **Brief** almost always describes time and means 'coming to an end quickly', and therefore, when applied to speeches or writing, is more likely to suggest leaving out unimportant or unnecessary details than cutting off the end: *A brief essay is short but to the point.*

short•age ['ʃɔrtɪdʒ] *n.* **1** too small an amount; a lack: *There is a shortage of grain because of poor crops.* **2** the amount by which something is deficient.

short•bread ['ʃɔrt,brɛd] *n.* a type of cookie that is rich in butter and crumbles easily.

short•cake ['ʃɔrt,keik] *n.* **1** a type of cake made of rich biscuit dough with shortening. **2** a sweet cake filled or spread with fruit. **3** shortbread.

short–change ['ʃɔrt 'tʃeindʒ] *v.* **-changed, -chang•ing.** *Informal.* **1** give less than the right change to. **2** cheat; give less than is due. —**'short-'chang•er,** *n.*

short circuit *Electricity.* **1** an electrical circuit, formed accidentally or intentionally, that bypasses the main circuit. An accidental short circuit, in which worn or faulty wires touch each other, may blow a fuse or cause a fire. **2** the resulting disruption of the main circuit.

short–cir•cuit ['ʃɔrt 'sɜrkɪt] *v.* **1** develop or bring about a short circuit (in). **2** get around or avoid; bypass: *to short-circuit the usual administrative procedure.* **3** frustrate or hinder: *to short-circuit a plan.*

short•com•ing ['ʃɔrt,kʌmɪŋ] *n.* a fault; defect.

short•cut ['ʃɔrt,kʌt] *n., v.* **-cut, -cut•ting.** —*n.* **1** a quicker or less distant route: *We took a shortcut through the field.* **2** a method, procedure, etc. that is simpler or quicker than the standard one: *to take shortcuts in cooking.*
—*v.* use or take a shortcut.

short–day ['ʃɔrt ,dei] *adj. Botany.* requiring short periods of light and long periods of darkness.

short division *Mathematics.* division using a divisor containing only one digit, and in which the steps of the process are not written down in full.

short•en ['ʃɔrtən] *v.* **1** make shorter; cut off. **2** become shorter. **3** make rich with butter, lard, etc. **4** take in (sail). —**'short•en•er,** *n.*

☛ *Syn.* **1. Shorten,** CURTAIL, ABBREVIATE = make shorter. **Shorten** is the general word, meaning 'reduce the length or extent of something': *The new highway shortens the trip.* **Curtail,** more formal, means 'cut something short by taking away or cutting off a part', and particularly suggests causing loss or incompleteness: *Bad news made him curtail his trip.* **Abbreviate,** used chiefly of words and phrases, means 'shorten by leaving out syllables, letters, or sounds', sometimes by using initial letters or substitutions: *Abbreviate* kilogram *to* kg *after numerals.*

short•en•ing ['ʃɔrtnɪŋ] *n.* fat, sometimes specifically vegetable fat as distinguished from butter or lard, used in pastries, cakes, etc.

short•fall [ˈʃɔrt,fɒl] *n.* **1** the act or an instance of falling short; failure to meet a need or reach a goal: *The chair of the fund-raising campaign has predicted a shortfall.* **2** the amount of such a failure; deficiency.

short fuse *Informal.* a short temper.

shorthair [ˈʃɔrt,hɛr] *n.* any domestic cat of a breed characterized by short hair.

short•hand [ˈʃɔrt,hænd] *n.* **1** a method of rapid writing which uses symbols or a combination of letters and symbols to represent sounds. **2** writing in such symbols. **3** (*adjl.*) using or written in shorthand: *a shorthand note.*

short–hand•ed [ˈʃɔrt ˈhændɪd] *adj.* **1** not having enough workers or helpers. **2** *Hockey, etc.* playing without the services of one or more players as a result of penalties or injuries. **—ˈshort-ˈhand•ed•ness,** *n.*

short•horn [ˈʃɔrt,hɔrn] *n.* a breed of cattle, originally from England, having short horns, raised for both beef and milk.

short•ish [ˈʃɔrtɪʃ] *adj.* rather short.

short list a list of the most likely applicants, nominees, recommended items, etc., taken from a longer list by some screening or judging process, and from which a final choice will be made.

short–list [ˈʃɔrt ˈlɪst] *or* [ˈʃɔrt ˌlɪst] *v.* place on a SHORT LIST.

short–lived [ˈʃɔrt ˈlɪvd] *or* [ˈlaɪvd] *adj.* living only a short time; lasting only a short time: *Unfortunately the truce was short-lived and war broke out again.*

short•ly [ˈʃɔrtli] *adv.* **1** in a short time; before long; soon. **2** in a few words; briefly. **3** briefly and rudely.

short order in a restaurant, snack bar, etc., a food or dish that can be prepared and served quickly.

short–or•der [ˈʃɔrt ˌɔrdər] *adj.* in a restaurant, etc., having to do with the cooking of foods that require little time to prepare: *a short-order cook.*

short–range [ˈʃɔrt ˈreindʒ] *adj.* **1** of a gun, missile, etc., effective over a limited distance. **2** not reaching or looking far ahead: *short-range plans.*

short shrift **1** little mercy, respite, or delay. **2** not enough care or attention: *He had so many extra-curricular activities that his schoolwork got short shrift.*

short–shrift [ˈʃɔrt ˈʃrɪft] *v.* give SHORT SHRIFT to.

short–sight•ed [ˈʃɔrt ˈsəitɪd] *adj.* **1** near-sighted; not able to see far. **2 a** lacking in foresight; not prudent. **b** characterized by or proceeding from lack of foresight: *a short-sighted strategy.* **—ˈshort-ˈsight•ed•ly,** *adv.* **—ˈshort-ˈsight•ed•ness,** *n.*

short–staffed [ˈʃɔrt ˈstæft] *adj.* not having enough staff; short of the regular or necessary number of people.

short•stop [ˈʃɔrt,stɒp] *n. Baseball.* **1** a player stationed between second base and third base. **2** the area that he or she covers.

short story a prose story with a full plot, but much shorter than a novel.

short subject SHORT (*n.* def. 4).

short–tailed weasel [ˈʃɔrt ˌteild] ERMINE (def. 1).

short–tem•pered [ˈʃɔrt ˈtɛmpərd] *adj.* easily made angry; quick-tempered.

short–term [ˈʃɔrt ˈtɜrm] *adj.* **1** lasting or intended for a short period of time: *our short-term plans.* **2** falling due, earned, etc. in a short time: *a short-term loan, short-term gains.*

short–term memory memory for recent events. Compare LONG-TERM MEMORY.

short ton 2000 pounds avoirdupois (about 0.9 tonnes).

short–waist•ed [ˈʃɔrt ˌweistɪd] *adj.* having a high waistline; short from neck to waistline.

short wave *Electricity.* a high-frequency radio wave having a wavelength of 60 m or less.

short–wave [ˈʃɔrt ˌweiv] *adj., v.* **-waved, -wav•ing.** transmit by short waves: *The prime minister's speech was short-waved overseas.* *—adj.* of or having to do with short wave: *a short-wave broadcast, a short-wave radio.*

short–weight *v.* [ˈʃɔrt ˈweit]; *n.* [ˈʃɔrt ˌweit] *v., n.* *—v.* give less than the weight charged for: *We were short-weighted 30 kg on that shipment.* *—n.* the act or amount of this: *The short-weight on that shipment was 30 kg.*

short–wind•ed [ˈʃɔrt ˈwɪndɪd] *adj.* **1** getting out of breath too quickly; having difficulty in breathing. **2** of writing or speech, so brief as to be unsatisfying: *a short-winded explanation.*

short•y or **short•ie** [ˈʃɔrti] *n., pl.* **-ies.** *Informal.* a relatively short thing or person: *Your last visit was a real shortie.*

Sho•sho•ne [ʃouˈʃouni] *n., pl.* **-ne** or **-nes.** **1** a member of a Native American people scattered over the W U.S. **2** their language.

Sho•sho•ne•an [ʃouˈʃouniən] *or* [ˌʃouʃəˈniən] *n., adj.* *—n.* a group of Native American languages of the United States that includes Comanche, Hopi, Shoshone, etc. *—adj.* of, designating, or having to do with this group of languages.

shot¹ [ʃɒt] *n., v.* **shot•ted, shot•ting.** *—n.* **1** the discharge of a gun or cannon: *She heard two shots.* **2** the act of shooting. **3** small pellets of lead or steel that make up the charge of a shotgun cartridge. **4** a single ball of lead for a gun or cannon. **5** an attempt to hit by shooting: *That was a good shot.* **6** *Sports.* a stroke or an attempt to score. **7** the distance a weapon can shoot; range: *They were within rifle shot of the fort.* **8** a person who shoots, with reference to his or her method, skill, etc.: *She is a good shot.* **9** *Informal.* an injection, as of a vaccine or drug: *a polio shot.* **10** a sharp or critical remark. **11** an attempt; try: *I'm not very good at puzzles, but I'll take a shot at it.* **12** a bet or guess. **13** *Track and field.* a heavy metal ball that is put (or thrown) for distance. **14** *Photography.* a snapshot. **15** a single sequence of a motion picture taken with one camera without a break. **16** *Informal.* a single drink of alcoholic liquor. **17** *Informal.* a dose. **18** *Mining.* a blast. **19** an amount to be paid: *She offered to pay the shot.*
call the shots, *Informal.* be in a position of control.
like a shot, very quickly; suddenly; eagerly.
long shot, an attempt at something difficult.
not by a long shot, not at all.
put the shot, *Track and field.* cast the ball in the shot-put event.
shot in the arm, *Informal.* something that stimulates or revives; an incentive; spur.
shot in the dark, a wild guess.
—v. load or weight with shot. ⟨OE *sceot*. Related to SCOT.⟩

shot² [ʃɒt] *v., adj.* *—v.* pt. and pp. of SHOOT. *—adj.* **1** of a fabric, woven so as to show changing colours; iridescent: *shot taffeta, blue silk shot with gold.* **2** streaked with a contrasting colour: *black hair shot with grey.* **3** permeated or infused (*often used with* **through**): *a clever speech shot through with humour.* **4** *Informal.* worn out, ruined, used up, etc.: *This old dictionary is just about shot. He said his nerves were shot.*

shote [ʃout] *n.* See SHOAT.

shot•gun [ˈʃɒt,gʌn] *n.* **1** a large firearm having a long barrel with a smooth bore and firing cartridges filled with shot. **2** (*adjl.*) of, having to do with, or produced by a shotgun: *a shotgun blast.* **3** (*adjl.*) involving compulsion. **4** (*adjl.*) covering a broad field; indiscriminate or haphazard: *a shotgun approach to criticism.*
ride shotgun, accompany as an armed guard, originally on a stagecoach but now in an armoured vehicle, etc.

shotgun marriage or **wedding** *Informal.* a marriage or wedding enforced or arranged on account of pregnancy.

shot hole **1** a hole drilled in rock, etc. into which explosives are placed for blasting. **2** a hole bored by an insect in timber or wood. **3** a disease of plants, caused by infection or injury, which makes the leaves look as if hit by shotgun pellets.

shot–put [ˈʃɒt ˌpʊt] *n.* **1** *Track and field.* an athletic event or contest in which contestants send a heavy metal ball (the shot) as far as possible with one overhand throw from the shoulder. **2** one such act of throwing the shot. **—ˈshot-ˌput•ter,** *n.*

shot rock or **shot–rock** [ˈʃɒt ˌrɒk] *n.* **1** *Curling.* the stone nearest the centre of the target; the stone that counts toward the score. **2** pieces of loose rock that are the result of blasting.

shot•smith [ˈʃɒt,smɪθ] *n. Cdn. Curling.* a skilled curler; one who consistently succeeds at difficult shots.

should [ʃʊd]; *unstressed,* [ʃəd] *v.* **1** a word used: **a** to express obligation or duty: *I really should do my homework before I go out.* **b** to express a state of affairs that is desirable or to be recommended: *Everyone should learn to swim.* **c** to suggest that the speaker is uncertain about a thing or unwilling to believe something: *I don't see why you should think that. It's strange that they should be so late.* **d** to express a condition in the future (*often inverted with the subject*): *Should we have any trouble, we'll call you.* **e** to express a probability or expectation: *She should be there by now.* **2** pt. of SHALL (def. 3): *I hoped I should see you.* ⟨OE *sceolde*⟩

shoul•der ['ʃouldər] *n., v.* —*n.* **1** the part of the body to which an arm of a human being, a foreleg of an animal, or a wing of a bird is attached. **2** the part of a garment covering this.
3 shoulders, *pl.* the two shoulders and the upper part of the back. **4** a cut of meat including the upper foreleg and adjacent parts. See LAMB, PORK, and VEAL for pictures. **5** a shoulderlike part or projection: *She grasped the shoulder of the rock.* **6** the edge of a road or highway, often unpaved: *Do not drive on the shoulder.* **7** *Printing.* the flat surface on a piece of type extending beyond the base of the letter. **8** the angle between the face and flank of a bastion in a fortification.
cry on (someone's) **shoulder,** tell (someone) one's problems in hopes that he or she will sympathize.
give (someone) **the cold shoulder,** snub or intentionally ignore.
put (one's) **shoulder to the wheel,** make a great effort.
shoulder to shoulder, a side by side; together. **b** with united effort.
straight from the shoulder, frankly; directly.
—*v.* **1** take upon or support with the shoulder or shoulders: *shoulder a tray.* **2** bear (a burden, blame, etc.); assume (responsibility, expense, etc.). **3** push with the shoulders: *He shouldered his way through the crowd.*
shoulder arms, *Military.* **a** hold a rifle almost upright with the barrel resting in the hollow of the shoulder and the butt in the hand. **b** the command to do this. **c** the position so assumed. ⟨OE *sculdor*⟩ —**'shoul•der,like,** *adj.*

shoulder bag a purse or tote bag with a long strap by which it can be hung from the shoulder.

shoulder belt a safety belt, as in a car, that passes diagonally over the chest and one shoulder.

shoulder blade the flat triangular bone in the upper back behind either shoulder; scapula. See RIB and COLLARBONE for pictures.

shoulder knot 1 a knot of ribbon or lace worn on the shoulder. **2** a braided cord decoration fastened to the shoulders of some military dress uniforms.

shoulder strap 1 a strap worn over the shoulder to hold a garment up. **2** a strap attached to something, by which to carry it over the shoulder.

should•n't ['ʃʊdənt] *v.* should not.

shouldst [ʃʊdst] *v. Archaic.* 2nd pers. sing. of SHOULD. *Thou shouldst* means *you* (sing.) *should.*

shout [ʃʌut] *v., n.* —*v.* **1** call or cry loudly and vigorously.
2 talk or laugh very loudly. **3** express by a shout or shouts: *The crowd shouted its approval.*
shout (someone) **down,** silence someone by very loud talk.
—*n.* **1** a loud, vigorous call or cry. **2** a loud outburst of laughter.
give (someone) **a shout,** call or telephone someone: *Give me a shout when you're ready.* ⟨ME *schoute*; ? ult. var. of *scout*[2]⟩
—**'shout•er,** *n.*

shove [ʃʌv] *v.* **shoved, shov•ing;** *n.* —*v.* **1** push; move forward or along by the application of force from behind. **2** push roughly or rudely; jostle.
shove off, a push away from the shore; row away. **b** *Slang.* leave; start.
—*n.* push. ⟨OE *scūfan*⟩ —**'shov•er,** *n.*
☛ *Syn. v.* **1.** See note at PUSH.

shov•el ['ʃʌvəl] *n., v.* **-elled** or **-eled, -el•ling** or **-el•ing.**
—*n.* **1** a tool with a longish handle and broad, concave blade, used to lift and throw loose matter: *a coal shovel.* **2 a** a part of a machine having a similar use. **b** the whole machine. **3** a shovelful. **4** SHOVEL HAT.
—*v.* **1** lift and throw with a shovel. **2** make with a shovel: *They shovelled a path through the snow.* **3** work with a shovel. **4** gather up, as if with a shovel, crudely or in large quantities: *The hungry man greedily shovelled the food into his mouth.* ⟨OE *scofl*⟩

shov•el•board ['ʃʌvəl,bɔrd] *n.* See SHUFFLEBOARD.

shov•el•er ['ʃʌvələr] *n.* See SHOVELLER.

shov•el•ful ['ʃʌvəl,fʊl] *n., pl.* **-fuls.** as much as a shovel holds.

shovel hat a hat having a broad brim turned up at the sides and projecting with shovel-like curves in front and behind. Some clergymen formerly wore shovel hats.

shov•el•head ['ʃʌvəl,hɛd] *n.* a shark (*Sphyrna tiburo*) similar to but smaller than the hammerhead, having a head shaped like the blade of a shovel.

shov•el•ler or **shov•el•er** ['ʃʌvələr] *n.* **1** a duck (*Anas clypeata*, also classified as *Spatula clypeata*) of ponds and marshes of the northern hemisphere, having a large, broad bill, and the male having a green head, white breast, and chestnut body. **2** a person who or thing that shovels.

show [ʃou] *v.* **showed, shown** or **showed, show•ing;** *n.* —*v.* **1** give (someone) the chance to see or look at (something): *She showed us her new coat.* **2** reveal; manifest; disclose: *His gift showed how generous he was.* **3** be in sight; appear; be seen: *Joy showed in her face.* **4** point out: *A child showed us the way to town.* **5** direct; guide: *Show him out.* **6** make clear or explain (to) by demonstration: *Show them how to use the stove.* **7** of something preferably concealed, be noticeable or visible: *Your slip is showing. The stain hardly shows.* **8** prove: *She showed that it was true.* **9** grant; give: *to show mercy, to show favour.* **10** display; lay open to view or examination by interested parties. **11** have a given effect when so displayed: *A newly painted house shows better.* **12** of a list, instrument, etc., indicate: *a watch showing twelve o'clock.* **13** enter (an animal, etc.) in a show for competition. **14** be obviously pregnant: *She's just starting to show.*
15 *Informal.* be present as arranged or expected: *Her date didn't show, so she went alone.* **16** *Sports.* **a** finish among the first three in a race. **b** finish third in a race or competition, especially in a horse race. Compare WIN (def. 1), PLACE (def. 8b).
17 a *Informal.* appear in or present a theatrical performance: *We are showing at the Centennial Hall.* **b** of such a performance or a film, be running or playing: *What's showing at the local cinema?*
show off, make a boastful or proud display (of); act or talk so as to try to attract attention, inspire envy or admiration, etc.: *That boy is always showing off. She showed off her new ring.*
show up, a expose. **b** stand out: *She is very tall and shows up in any crowd.* **c** *Informal.* put in an appearance: *The prime minister showed up at the first concert.* **d** *Informal.* surpass so greatly as to make obvious the inferiority of.
—*n.* **1** a display: *The jewels made a fine show.* **2** a display for effect. **3** any kind of public exhibition or display: *a horse show.*
4 a showing: *The club voted by a show of hands.* **5** an appearance: *There is some show of truth in his excuse.* **6** a false appearance: *He hid his treachery by a show of friendship.* **7** a trace; indication: *a show of oil in a region.* **8** *Informal.* an entertainment, such as a stage play or movie: *a vaudeville show.*
9 *Informal.* a movie theatre. **10** an object of scorn; something odd; queer sight: *Don't make a show of yourself.* **11** *Informal.* a chance; opportunity. **12** *Sports.* third place in a race or competition, especially in a horse race. **13** *Medicine.* the bloody discharge at the onset of childbirth.
for show, for effect; to attract attention: *Some houses are furnished for show, not comfort.*
get the show on the road, *Slang.* get started; get things underway.
good show! well done!
run the show, be in charge.
steal the show, take attention away from the main participant, especially by a superior performance. ⟨OE *scēawian* look at⟩
☛ *Syn. n.* **1. Show,** DISPLAY = a public exhibiting. **Show** suggests something exposed to sight or put forward unconsciously, by oversight, or intentionally for others to look at: *That was a disgraceful show of temper.* **Display** suggests something spread out or unfolded to be seen clearly, or arranged so as to call attention to its fineness, beauty, strength, or other qualities: *That florist has the most beautiful displays in the city.*

show and tell in primary school, a time for students to pass around and talk about something they have brought.

show bill a poster, placard, etc. advertising a show.

show•biz ['ʃou,bɪz] *n. Slang.* SHOW BUSINESS.

show•boat ['ʃou,bout] *n., v.* —*n.* **1** a steamboat with a theatre for plays. Showboats carry their own actors and make frequent stops to give performances. **2** *Informal.* a showoff.
—*v. Informal.* show off.

show•bread ['ʃou,brɛd] *n.* See SHEWBREAD.

show business all the occupations and businesses that make up the entertainment industry, including theatre, film, television, and radio. —**'show-,bus•i•ness,** *adjl.*

show•case ['ʃou,keis] *n., v.* **-cased, -cas•ing.** —*n.* **1** a glass case to display and protect articles in stores, museums, etc.
2 anything that displays: *Québec City is a showcase of Canadian history.*
—*v.* display advantageously.

show•down ['ʃou,daʊn] *n.* **1** a forced disclosure of facts, purposes, methods, etc. in order to bring matters to a head or to a definite conclusion. **2** *Card games.* the displaying of the hands of the players at the end of a round.

show•er ['ʃaʊər] *n., v.* —*n.* **1** a brief fall of rain. **2** anything like a fall of rain: *a shower of hail, a shower of tears, a shower of sparks from an engine.* **3** a giving in abundance: *a shower of advice, a shower of good wishes.* **4** a party for giving presents to a woman or couple about to be married, or on some other special occasion. **5 a** a bath in which water is sprayed over the body from above in small jets. **b** the apparatus or enclosure for this.

—*v.* **1** rain for a short time. **2** wet with a shower; spray; sprinkle. **3** have a shower bath. **4** come or fall in a shower. **5** send in a shower; pour down: *They showered gifts upon her. The tree showered blossoms on the lawn.* **6** give something to (someone) in abundance: *They showered the proud parents with compliments.* ⟨OE *scur*⟩

shower bath SHOWER (def. 4).

show•er•y [ˈʃaʊəri] *adj.* **1** raining in showers. **2** having many showers. **3** like a shower.

show•girl [ˈʃou,gɜrl] *n.* CHORUS GIRL.

show•ing [ˈʃouɪŋ] *n.* **1** the act of putting upon display, demonstrating, or presenting to view. **2** an exhibition or display. **3** a presentation or appearance.

show•jump•ing [ˈʃou,dʒʌmpɪŋ] *n.* demonstration, at a public event, of competitive skill in riding a horse and making it jump over obstacles. **—ˈshow,jump•er,** *n.*

show•man [ˈʃoumən] *n., pl.* **-men. 1** a person who manages a show. **2** a person skilled in presenting things in a dramatic and exciting way.

show•man•ship [ˈʃoumən,ʃɪp] *n.* **1** the management of shows. **2** skill in managing shows or in publicity.

shown [ʃoun] *v.* a pp. of SHOW.

show–off [ˈʃou ,ɒf] *n.* **1** *Informal.* a person who shows off. **2** a showing off.

show•piece [ˈʃou,pis] *n.* **1** an item in an exhibition. **2** anything displayed as an outstanding example of its kind.

show•place [ˈʃou,pleis] *n.* any place considered worth exhibiting because of its superior beauty, interest, etc.

show•room [ˈʃou,rum] *or* [ˈʃou,rʊm] *n.* a room used for the display of goods or merchandise.

show window a window in the front of a store, where things are shown for sale.

show•y [ˈʃoui] *adj.* **show•i•er, show•i•est. 1** making a display; striking; conspicuous: *A peony is a showy flower.* **2** too bright and gaudy to be in good taste; ostentatious. **—ˈshow•i•ly,** *adv.* **—ˈshow•i•ness,** *n.*

shrank [ʃræŋk] *v.* pt. of SHRINK.

shrap•nel [ˈʃræpnəl] *n.* **1** a shell filled with fragments of metal and powder, set to explode in the air. **2** the fragments scattered by such a shell. ⟨after the inventor, Henry *Shrapnel* (1761-1842), a British army officer⟩

shred [ʃrɛd] *n., v.* **shred•ded** or **shred, shred•ding.** —*n.* **1** a very small piece torn off or cut off; a very narrow strip; scrap: *The wind tore the sail to shreds.* **2** a particle; fragment; bit: *There's not a shred of evidence that he took the money.*
—*v.* **1** tear or cut into small pieces. **2** be reduced to shreds: *Don't wash that in the machine; it'll shred.* ⟨OE *scrēade*⟩

shred•der [ˈʃrɛdər] *n.* **1** a machine for destroying sensitive documents by tearing them into shreds. **2** a machine that shreds scraps, vegetables, etc. **3** any person who or thing that shreds.

shrew [ʃru] *n.* **1** any of a family (Soricidae) of small, mouselike mammals found almost throughout the world, having a long, pointed snout, short, velvety fur, and tiny, beadlike eyes. Shrews are extremely active and often ferocious, attacking animals larger than themselves, such as mice. **2** a bad-tempered and quarrelsome person. ⟨OE *scrēawa*⟩

shrewd [ʃrud] *adj.* **1** having or showing a keen, practical mind; astute and penetrating: *a shrewd observer, a shrewd comment.* **2** *Archaic.* sharp or biting: *a shrewd wind.* **3** *Archaic.* spiteful or mischievous. ⟨earlier *shrewed,* < *shrew,* v., in sense of 'scold'⟩ **—ˈshrewd•ly,** *adv.* **—ˈshrewd•ness,** *n.*

☛ *Syn.* **1. Shrewd,** SAGACIOUS, ASTUTE = having a sharp or keen mind and good judgment, especially in practical affairs. **Shrewd** emphasizes sharpness and an ability to see below the surface of things, and suggests natural cleverness in practical affairs or, sometimes, craftiness: *He is a shrewd businessman.* **Sagacious** emphasizes a keen or penetrating understanding of practical affairs and an ability to arrive at wise decisions: *The company director was a sagacious woman.* **Astute** adds to **shrewd** the idea of having unusual power to see through and understand things and of being hard to fool: *She is an astute diplomat.*

shrew•ish [ˈʃruɪʃ] *adj.* scolding; bad-tempered. **—ˈshrew•ish•ly,** *adv.* **—ˈshrew•ish•ness,** *n.*

shrew•mouse [ˈʃru,mʌus] *n., pl.* **-mice.** SHREW (def. 1).

shriek [ʃrik] *n., v.* —*n.* **1** a loud, sharp, shrill sound: *We heard the shriek of the engine's whistle.* **2** a loud, shrill laugh or cry.
—*v.* **1** make such a sound. **2** utter loudly and shrilly. ⟨< ON *skrækja*⟩

☛ *Syn. v.* **1.** See note at SCREAM.

shriev•al•ty [ˈʃrivəlti] *n., pl.* **-ties.** the office, term of office, or jurisdiction of a sheriff.

shrieve [ʃriv] *n. Archaic.* sheriff. ⟨var. of *sheriff*⟩

shrift [ʃrɪft] *n. Archaic.* **1** confession to a priest, followed by the imposing of penance and the granting of absolution. **2** the act of shriving. ⟨OE *scrift* < L *scriptus* written⟩

shrike [ʃrəik] *n.* any of a family (Laniidae) of mainly Old World songbirds having a strong, hooked bill and feeding on insects, small birds, and mammals, which they often impale on thorns, barbed wire, etc. Two species of shrike are found in Canada. ⟨OE *scrīc*⟩

shrill [ʃrɪl] *adj., v., n., adv.* —*adj.* **1** having a high pitch; high and sharp in sound; piercing: *Crickets make shrill noises.* **2** full of shrill sounds. **3** offensively insistent: *shrill protests.*
—*v.* **1** make a shrill sound. **2** utter shrilly.
—*n.* a shrill sound.
—*adv.* with a shrill sound. ⟨ME *shrille*⟩ **—ˈshrill•ness,** *n.* **—ˈshril•ly,** *adv.*

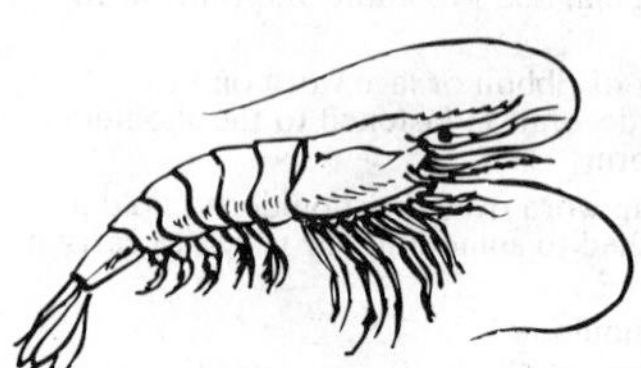
A shrimp—the different species range in size from 2.5 to 20 cm long

shrimp [ʃrɪmp] *n., pl.* **shrimp** or **shrimps;** *v.* —*n.* **1** any of a suborder (Natantia) of mostly marine decapod crustaceans having a relatively slender, laterally compressed body encased in a thin, semitransparent shell, well-developed swimmerets on the abdomen, a fanlike tail, and long antennae; especially, any of the smaller members of this group (genera *Crangon, Peneus,* etc.), usually from four to eight centimetres long. Compare PRAWN. **2** any of various other shrimplike crustaceans. **3** a small, weak, or insignificant person.
—*v.* fish for shrimp. ⟨ME *shrimpe;* cf. MHG *schrimpen* shrink up⟩ **—ˈshrimp,like,** *adj.*

shrine [ʃrain] *n., v.* **shrined, shrin•ing.** —*n.* **1** a case, box, etc. holding a holy object. **2** the tomb of a saint, etc. **3** a place of worship: *a wayside shrine.* **4** a place or object considered as sacred because of its memories, history, etc.
—*v.* enclose in a shrine or something like a shrine. ⟨OE *scrīn* < L *scrinium* case⟩

shrink [ʃrɪŋk] *v.* **shrank, shrunk** or **shrunk•en, shrink•ing;** *n.*
—*v.* **1** draw back: *The dog shrank from the whip. A shy person shrinks from making new acquaintances.* **2** become smaller: *The wool sweater shrank when it was washed.* **3** make smaller; cause to contract: *Hot water shrinks wool.*
—*n.* **1** the act or process of shrinking. **2** *Slang.* a psychiatrist. ⟨OE *scrincan*⟩ **—ˈshrink•a•ble,** *adj.* **—ˈshrink•er,** *n.*

☛ *Syn. v.* **1. Shrink,** FLINCH = draw back from something painful, unpleasant, etc. **Shrink** suggests instinctive drawing back physically or mentally, by or as if by contracting or drawing away some part of the body in fear, horror, or sensitiveness, from something anticipated as painful or disagreeable: *He shrank from admitting his guilt.* **Flinch** suggests drawing back or turning away in spite of one's desire or determination not to, in reaction to physical or any other kind of pain: *She could bear torture without flinching.*

☛ *Usage.* See note at SHRUNK.

shrink•age [ˈʃrɪŋkɪdʒ] *n.* **1** the fact or process of shrinking. **2** the amount or degree of shrinking: *a shrinkage of two centimetres in the length of a sleeve.* **3** the difference between the weight of livestock at the time of shipping and its finished weight after hanging, bleeding, cutting, etc. **4** an amount of inventory lost that cannot be accounted for.

shrinking violet a very shy person.

shrink–wrap ['ʃrɪŋk ˌræp] *v.* **-wrapped, -wrap•ping;** *n.* —*v.* wrap (merchandise) tightly in a thin, clear plastic film that shrinks closely around the contours of the article as it is sealed.
—*n.* such wrapping.

shrive [ʃraɪv] *v.* **shrove** or **shrived, shriv•en** or **shrived, shriv•ing.** *Archaic.* **1** hear the confession of, impose penance on, and grant absolution to. **2** make confession. **3** hear confessions.
shrive oneself, confess to a Christian priest and do penance. ⟨OE *scrīfan* < L *scribere* write⟩

shriv•el ['ʃrɪvəl] *v.* **-elled** or **-eled, -el•ling** or **-el•ing. 1** dry up; wither; shrink and wrinkle: *The hot sunshine shrivelled the grass.* **2** waste away; become useless. **3** make helpless or useless. ⟨origin unknown⟩

shriv•en ['ʃrɪvən] *v.* a pp. of SHRIVE.

shroud [ʃraʊd] *n., v.* —*n.* **1** a cloth or garment in which a dead person is wrapped for burial. **2** something that covers, conceals, or veils: *The fog was a shroud over the city.* **3** *Nautical.* one of a set of supporting ropes running from a masthead to the side of a ship. See SCHOONER for picture. **4** on a parachute, any of the suspension lines running from the canopy to the harness.
—*v.* **1** wrap for burial. **2** cover; conceal; veil: *The earth is shrouded in darkness.* ⟨OE *scrūd*⟩

shroud–laid ['ʃraʊd ˌleid] *adj.* of a rope, consisting of four strands twisted to the right around a core.

shrove [ʃrouv] *v.* a pt. of SHRIVE.

Shrove•tide ['ʃrouvˌtaɪd] *n.* in the Christian calendar, the three days, **Shrove Sunday, Shrove Monday,** and **Shrove Tuesday,** before Ash Wednesday, the first day of Lent. Shrovetide is a time for confession, absolution, rejoicing, and feasting.

shrub[1] [ʃrʌb] *n.* a woody plant smaller than a tree, usually with many separate stems starting from or near the ground; bush. ⟨OE *scrybb* brush⟩ —**'shrub,like,** *adj.*

shrub[2] [ʃrʌb] *n.* **1** a drink made from fruit juice, sugar, and, usually, rum or brandy. **2** a drink of fruit juice and water. ⟨< Arabic *shurb* drink⟩

shrub•ber•y ['ʃrʌbəri] *n., pl.* **-ber•ies. 1** shrubs collectively. **2** a place planted with shrubs.

shrub•by ['ʃrʌbi] *adj.* **-bi•er, -bi•est. 1** like a shrub or shrubs. **2** covered with shrubs. **3** consisting of shrubs.
—**'shrub•bi•ness,** *n.*

shrug [ʃrʌg] *v.* **shrugged, shrug•ging;** *n.* —*v.* raise (the shoulders) as an expression of dislike, doubt, indifference, impatience, etc.
shrug off, dismiss lightly; minimize.
—*n.* **1** a raising of the shoulders in this way. **2** a short jacket ending at or above the waistline. ⟨ME *schrugge(n)* shiver; origin uncertain⟩

shrunk [ʃrʌŋk] *v.* a pp. and a pt. of SHRINK.
☛ *Usage.* **Shrunk, shrunken.** The preferred past participle is **shrunk:** *The shirt has shrunk.* The form **shrunken,** the original past participle, is generally used as the adjective, especially before nouns: *a shrunken face.*

shrunk•en ['ʃrʌŋkən] *adj., v.* —*adj.* grown smaller; shrivelled.
—*v.* a pp. of SHRINK.
☛ *Usage.* See note at SHRUNK.

shru•ti ['ʃrʊti] *n.* the collective term for all sacred Hindu scriptures. ⟨< Skt.⟩

shtetl ['ʃtɛtəl] *n.* **1** formerly, a Jewish village community in E Europe. **2** a Pennsylvania Dutch village community. ⟨ult. < dim. of MHG *stat,* city⟩

shtick [ʃtɪk] *n.* **1** a comic routine or scene on stage. **2** an act or gimmick to get attention. **3** a distinguishing characteristic or ability. ⟨< Yiddish *shtik* prank, piece < MHG *stück*⟩

shuck [ʃʌk] *n., v.* —*n.* **1** a husk; pod. **2** an oyster or clam shell.
—*v.* **1** remove the shucks from. **2** *Informal.* take or throw off (clothing, etc.): *He shucked his jacket at the door.* ⟨origin uncertain⟩ —**'shuck•er,** *n.*

shucks [ʃʌks] *interj. Informal.* an exclamation of disgust, regret, impatience, embarrassment, etc.

shud•der ['ʃʌdər] *v., n.* —*v.* tremble with horror, fear, cold, etc.: *She shudders at the sight of a snake.*
—*n.* a trembling; quivering. ⟨ME *shodder(en),* frequentative of OE *scūdan* shake⟩ —**'shud•der•ing•ly,** *adv.* —**'shud•der•y,** *adj.*
☛ *Syn. v.* See note at SHIVER[1].

shuf•fle ['ʃʌfəl] *v.* **-fled, -fling;** *n.* —*v.* **1** walk without lifting the feet: *The sick man shuffles feebly along.* **2** scrape or drag (the feet). **3** dance with a shuffle. **4** mix (cards, etc.) so as to change the order. **5** push about; thrust or throw with clumsy haste: *He shuffled on his clothes and ran out of the house.* **6** move this way and that: *shuffle a stack of papers.* **7** act or answer, put or get, etc. in a tricky or evasive way.
shuffle off, get rid of, often specifically in an evasive way: *She shuffled off the responsibility for the arrangements.*
—*n.* **1** a scraping or dragging movement of the feet. **2** a dance with a shuffle. **3** a shuffling of cards. **4** the right or turn to shuffle (cards). **5** a movement this way and that. **6** a trick; unfair act; evasion: *Through some legal shuffle he secured a new trial.*
lose (something) **in the shuffle,** overlook, lose, etc. (something) in the bustle or confusion of the moment. ⟨? < LG *schuffeln.* Akin to SHOVE.⟩ —**'shuf•fler,** *n.*

shuf•fle•board ['ʃʌfəlˌbɔrd] *n.* **1** a game played by pushing large wooden or iron disks along a surface to certain spots. **2** the marked surface on which the game is played. Also, **shovelboard.**

shul [ʃul] *n., pl.* **shuln** [ʃuln]. synagogue. ⟨< Yiddish, lit., school < MHG *schuol*⟩

shun [ʃʌn] *v.* **shunned, shun•ning.** keep away from; avoid. ⟨OE *scunian*⟩ —**'shun•ner,** *n.*

shun•pike ['ʃʌnˌpaik] *n. Slang.* a quiet by-road, used by motorists to avoid major highways. ⟨< *shun* + *(turn)pike;* originally, in the United States, a road used to avoid paying tolls on a turnpike⟩ —**'shun,pik•er,** *n.*

shun•pik•ing ['ʃʌnˌpəikɪŋ] *n.* the practice of using quiet by-roads for motoring, rather than fast major highways.

shunt [ʃʌnt] *v., n.* —*v.* **1** move out of the way; turn aside. **2** sidetrack; put aside; get rid of. **3 a** switch (a train) from one track to another. **b** switch (anything) to another route or place. **4** *Electricity.* **a** carry (a part of a current) by means of a shunt. **b** of a current, be so carried. **5** furnish or divert with a shunt.
—*n.* **1** a turning aside; shift. **2** a railway switch. **3** *Electricity.* a wire or other conductor joining two points in a circuit and forming a path through which a part of the current will pass. **4** *Medicine.* a channel, either synthetic or surgically reconstructed, through which bodily fluids may be diverted. ⟨ME *schunt* shy[1] (*v.*); ? < *shun*⟩ —**'shunt•er,** *n.*

shush [ʃʌʃ] *v., interj.* —*v.* tell or cause to become silent; silence (someone); hush (*often used with* **up**).
—*interj.* quiet! hush!

Shu•swap ['ʃuswɒp] *n., pl.* **Shu•swap** or **Shu•swaps;** *adj.* —*n.* **1** a First Nations people of the southern interior of British Columbia. **2** their Salishan language.
—*adj.* of or having to do with this people or their language or culture.

shut [ʃʌt] *v.* **shut, shut•ting;** *adj.* —*v.* **1 a** close (a receptacle or opening) by pushing or pulling a lid, door, or other such part into place: *to shut a box, to shut a window.* **b** put (such a part) over an opening: *Shut the lid.* **2** close (the eyes, a knife, a book, etc.) by bringing parts together. **3** close or lock the doors and windows of (*often used with* **up**): *After Thanksgiving we shut our cottage up for the winter.* **4** become shut; be closed: *The door doesn't shut properly.* **5** enclose or exclude; keep from going out or coming in (*used with* **in, out,** etc.): *She was shut in prison. They shut the cat out.* **6** cease operation (of) permanently or temporarily: *The office shuts at 5. They shut the store early today.*
shut down, a close by lowering. **b** close (a factory, etc.) for a time; stop work. **c** of fog, darkness, etc., settle down so as to cover or envelop. **d** *Informal.* put a stop or check on.
shut off, a prevent the flow or passage of or through: *They had to shut off the electricity for two hours for repairs. They've shut off the main line.* **b** isolate or separate from others: *We were shut off from the world in our cozy cottage.*
shut out, *Sports.* defeat (a team) without allowing it to score.
shut up, a confine (in a place). **b** *Informal.* stop or cause to stop talking.
—*adj.* closed; fastened up; enclosed. ⟨OE *scyttan* bolt up⟩

shut•down ['ʃʌtˌdaʊn] *n.* a shutting down; a closing of a factory, etc. for a time.

shut–eye ['ʃʌt ˌaɪ] *n. Slang.* sleep.

shut–in ['ʃʌt ˌɪn] *adj., n.* —*adj.* confined indoors, especially by sickness or weakness.
—*n.* a person who is kept from going out by sickness, weakness, etc.

shut–off ['ʃʌt ˌɒf] *n.* **1** something, such as a valve, switch, etc., that stops the flow or movement of something. **2** the act of stopping a flow or movement.

shut–out ['ʃʌt ˌʌut] *n.* **1** *Sports.* **a** the defeat of a team without allowing it to score. **b** the game in which this occurs. **c** *Hockey.* the credit given to a goalie for achieving such a victory for his or her team. **2** a lockout.

shut•ter ['ʃʌtər] *n., v.* —*n.* **1** a movable cover for a window.

2 a movable cover, slide, etc. for closing an opening. The device that opens and closes in front of the film or plate in a camera is a shutter. **3** a person or thing that shuts.
—*v.* put a shutter or shutters on or over. ⟨< *shut*⟩

shut•ter•bug ['ʃʌtər,bʌg] *n. Slang.* a photography enthusiast.

shut•tle ['ʃʌtəl] *n., v.* **-tled, -tling.** —*n.* **1** a device used in weaving for carrying the weft between the warp threads, from one side of the web to the other. **2** a similar device on which thread is wound for tatting, etc. **3** a device on a sewing machine that carries the lower thread back and forth to loop with the upper thread in making a stitch. **4** any of various other devices or things that go back and forth. **5** a bus, train, aircraft, etc. that runs back and forth regularly over a short distance. **6** the route travelled by such a vehicle, or the service or system of operating it. **7** (*adjl.*) of, involving, or designating such a vehicle or route: *a shuttle bus, a shuttle service.* **8** SPACE SHUTTLE. **9** a shuttlecock.
—*v.* **1** move quickly to and fro. **2** of ships, aircraft, buses, etc., carry (passengers) between two points: *This bus shuttles between Toronto and Hamilton.* ⟨OE *scutel* a dart < *scēotan* shoot⟩

shut•tle•cock ['ʃʌtəl,kɒk] *n.* **1** a cone-shaped ring of feathers or light plastic with a cork or similar base, used in the game of badminton; commonly called a **bird**. **2** a cork with feathers stuck in one end, which is hit back and forth by a small racket in the game of BATTLEDORE AND SHUTTLECOCK.

shy[1] [ʃaɪ] *adj.* **shy•er** or **shi•er, shy•est** or **shi•est;** *v.* **shied, shy•ing;** *n., pl.* **shies.** —*adj.* **1** uncomfortable in company; bashful: *Helga is shy and dislikes parties.* **2** easily frightened away; timid: *A deer is a shy animal.* **3** cautious; wary. **4** of plants or animals, not very productive.
fight shy of, keep away from; avoid.
shy of, *Informal.* **a** having too little; lacking: *We are shy of butter. The team is shy of a goalkeeper.* **b** less than; short of: *The arrow fell just shy of the mark.*
—*v.* **1** start back or aside suddenly: *The horse shied at the newspaper blowing along the ground.* **2** SHRINK (def. 1).
—*n.* a sudden start to one side. ⟨OE *scēoh*⟩ —**'shy•ness,** *n.*
☛ *Syn. adj.* **1. Shy,** BASHFUL = uncomfortable in the presence or company of others. **Shy** suggests a lack of self-confidence that makes a person shrink from making friends or going up to others, and is shown by a reserved or timid manner: *People who appear snobbish are often really shy.* **Bashful** suggests shrinking by nature from being noticed, shown by awkward and embarrassed behaviour in the presence of strangers: *The boy was too bashful to ask her to dance.*

shy[2] [ʃaɪ] *v.* **shied, shy•ing;** *n., pl.* **shies.** —*v.* throw; attempt: *The girl shied a stone at the tree.*
—*n.* **1** a throw; fling. **2** *Informal.* a verbal attack; sarcastic or taunting remark. **3** *Informal.* a try; attempt. ⟨origin uncertain⟩

Shy•lock ['ʃaɪ,lɒk] *n.* **1** in Shakespeare's *The Merchant of Venice*, a relentless and vengeful moneylender. **2** any person who lends money at exorbitant interest rates and insists on prompt payment.

shy•ly ['ʃaɪli] *adv.* in a shy or timid manner.

shy•ster ['ʃəistər] *n. Informal.* a lawyer or other person who uses improper or questionable methods in his or her business or profession. ⟨origin uncertain⟩

si [si] *n. Music.* ti. ⟨See GAMUT⟩
☛ *Hom.* C, SEA, SEE.

Si silicon.

SI Système international d'unités (International System of Units), the system adopted by Canada as the official system of measurement. See METRIC SYSTEM.

si•al ['saɪəl] *n.* the upper layer of the earth's continental crust, composed of comparatively light rocks, such as granite, that are rich in silica and aluminum. ⟨< *si*licon + *al*uminum. 20c.⟩

si•al•ic [saɪ'ælɪk] *adj.* of, having to do with, or being sial.

Si•a•mese [,saɪə'miz] *n., pl.* **-mese;** *adj.* —*n.* **1** Thai. **2** a breed of cat having a lithe, sinuous body and short hair, always dark at the ears, feet, and tail. **3 a** a pipe coupling in the shape of a Y for joining two pipes or hoses to a single pipe. **b** a low, outdoor water outlet in a wall, having two openings for fire hoses.
—*adj.* **1** Thai. **2** of or being such a dual coupling or outlet. ⟨< *Siam*, the former name of Thailand⟩

Siamese twins twins joined together at birth, now usually called **conjoined twins.** ⟨< Eng and Chan (1811-1874), twin boys born in Siam (now Thailand), joined together at the chest⟩

sib [sɪb] *adj., n.* —*adj.* related by blood; closely related; akin.
—*n.* **1** a kinsman or relative. **2** one's kin. **3** a brother or sister. **4** *Anthropology.* a group having a common unilineal descent. ⟨OE *sibb*⟩

Si•be•ri•an [saɪ'biriən] *n., adj.* —*n.* a native or inhabitant of Siberia, a part of Russia extending across northern Asia.
—*adj.* of or having to do with Siberia or its people.

Siberian husky a breed of medium-sized working dog originally developed in Siberia, having a brush tail and a thick coat of black, tan, or grey with white markings. It is much used in the North.

sib•i•lant ['sɪbələnt] *adj., n.* —*adj.* **1** hissing. **2** *Phonetics.* articulated with a hissing sound.
—*n. Phonetics.* a hissing sound or a letter or symbol representing it. The sounds represented by [s], [z], [ʃ], and [ʒ] are sibilants. ⟨< L *sibilans, -antis*, ppr. of *sibilare* hiss⟩ —**'sib•i•lance** or **'sib•i•lan•cy,** *n.*

sib•i•late ['sɪbə,leit] *v.* **-lat•ed, -lat•ing. 1** utter a hissing sound. **2** *Phonetics.* pronounce with a hissing sound. ⟨< L *sibilare* hiss⟩ —**,sib•i'la•tion,** *n.*

sib•ling ['sɪblɪŋ] *n.* a brother or sister. ⟨< *sib* + *-ling*⟩

sib•yl ['sɪbəl] *n.* **1** in ancient times, any of several prophetesses that the Greeks and Romans consulted about the future. **2** a prophetess; fortuneteller; witch. ⟨< L < Gk. *sibylla*⟩

sib•yl•line ['sɪbə,laɪn], ['sɪbə,lin], *or* ['sɪbəlɪn] *adj.* **1** of or like a sibyl; prophetic; mysterious. **2** said or written by a sibyl.

Sibylline Books a collection of prophecies and advice, venerated and consulted by the ancient Romans.

sic[1] [sɪk] *adv. Latin.* so; thus.
☛ *Usage.* **Sic** is used, usually in square brackets, to emphasize that a strange or incorrect word or form in a quoted passage is recorded just as it is in the original: *The picture caption read "Victoria, capitol [sic] of British Columbia."*
☛ *Hom.* SICK.

sic[2] [sɪk] *v.* **sicked, sick•ing. 1** set upon or attack. **2** incite to set upon or attack (*used with* **on**). Also, **sick.** ⟨var. of *seek*⟩
☛ *Hom.* SICK.

sic•ca•tive ['sɪkətɪv] *adj., n.* —*adj.* drying.
—*n.* a drying substance, especially a drier used in painting. ⟨< LL *siccativus* < L *siccare* make dry < *siccus* dry⟩

Si•cil•ian [sə'sɪljən] *n., adj.* —*n.* **1** a native or inhabitant of Sicily. **2** a dialect of Italian spoken in Sicily.
—*adj.* of or having to do with Sicily, its people, or their dialect.

Sic•i•ly ['sɪsəli] an island in the Mediterranean near the SW tip of Italy, to which it belongs along with other nearby smaller islands.

sick[1] [sɪk] *adj.* **1** in poor health; having some disease; ill. **2** of or for a sick person; connected with sickness. **3** showing sickness: *a sick look.* **4** (*noml.*) **the sick,** people who are sick. **5** feeling nausea; inclined to vomit: *sick to the stomach.* **6** weary or disgusted (*usually followed by* **of**): *She is sick of school. I'm sick of hearing that same old excuse.* **7** deeply affected with sorrow or longing: *sick at heart.* **8** mentally, morally, or emotionally disturbed or abnormal. **9** not in the proper condition. **10** pale; wan. **11** morbid; sadistic; cruel: *a sick joke, sick humour.* ⟨OE *sēoc*⟩
be sick, *Informal.* vomit.
☛ *Hom.* SIC.
☛ *Syn.* **1. Sick** and ILL (def. 1) have the same meaning. **Ill** is used in more formal contexts. In British use, **ill** is the general word and **sick** means simply 'nauseated' or 'sick to the stomach'.

sick[2] [sɪk] *v.* See SIC[2].

sick bay 1 a place used as a hospital on a ship. **2** a room or rooms set apart for the care of the sick or injured, especially in a school, etc.

sick•bed ['sɪk,bɛd] *n.* the bed of a sick person.

sick building syndrome illness due to poor ventilation or other environmental conditions in a building, especially a large office building.

sick day one day of SICK LEAVE.

sick•en ['sɪkən] *v.* **1** become sick: *The bird sickened when kept in the cage.* **2** make sick: *The sight of blood sickened her.*

sick•en•ing ['sɪkənɪŋ] *adj., v.* —*adj.* **1** making sick; causing nausea, faintness, disgust, or loathing. **2** becoming sick.
—*v.* ppr. of SICKEN. —**'sick•en•ing•ly,** *adv.*

sick headache a headache with nausea; migraine.

sick•ish ['sɪkɪʃ] *adj.* **1** somewhat sick. **2** somewhat sickening. —**'sick•ish•ly,** *adv.* —**'sick•ish•ness,** *n.*

A sickle

sick•le ['sɪkəl] *n., v.* **-led, -ling.** *—n.* a tool consisting of a short, curved blade on a short handle, used for cutting grass, etc. *—v.* mow or cut with a sickle. ⟨OE *sicol* < L *secula*; related to *secare* cut⟩

sick leave time off from work, usually with pay, allowed for illness or injury.

sickle cell anemia *Pathology.* a hereditary anemia affecting primarily African-Americans, in which large numbers of red blood cells become sickle-shaped due to a defective form of hemoglobin.

sick•ly ['sɪkli] *adj.* **-li•er, -li•est;** *adv. —adj.* **1** often sick; not strong; not healthy. **2** of or having to do with sickness: *His skin is a sickly yellow.* **3** causing sickness: *That place has a sickly climate.* **4** faint; weak; pale. **5** weak; mawkish: *sickly sentimentality.* *—adv.* in a sick manner. **—'sick•li•ness,** *n.*

sick•ness ['sɪknɪs] *n.* **1** the condition of being sick. **2** a particular illness; disease. **3** nausea; vomiting.

sick parade in the armed forces, the appearance of persons requiring medical attention before the medical officer or his or her staff.

sick pay wages paid to an employee on SICK LEAVE.

sick•room ['sɪk,rum] *or* ['sɪk,rʊm] *n.* a room set aside for a person or persons who are ill.

side [saɪd] *n., adj., v.* **sid•ed, sid•ing.** *—n.* **1** a surface or line bounding a thing: *the sides of a square.* **2** one of the surfaces of an object that is not the front, back, top, or bottom: *There is a door at the side of the house.* **3** either of the two surfaces of paper, cloth, etc.: *Write only on one side of the paper.* **4** a particular surface: *the outer and inner sides of a hollow ball, the side of the moon turned toward the earth.* **5** either the right or the left part of a thing; either part or region beyond a central line: *the east side of a city, our side of the street, turn to one side.* **6** either the right or the left part of the body of a person or an animal: *a pain in one's side.* **7** the space immediately next to a person or thing: *Put this table on the left side of the bookcase. She ran to her father's side.* **8** the slope of a hill or bank. **9** a bank or shore of a river. **10** an aspect or view of someone or something: *the better side of one's nature, the bright side of a difficulty.* **11** a group of persons opposed to another group: *Both sides are ready for the battle.* **12** a team. **13** the position, course, attitude, or part of one person or party against another: *It is pleasant to be on the winning side of a dispute.* **14** a part of a family; line of descent: *The man is British on his mother's side.* **15** *Informal.* an order of food to complement a main dish: *a side of fries.* **16** *Billiards. Brit.* a spinning motion given a ball by hitting it quickly on the side; ENGLISH (def. 4). **17** *Esp. Brit. Slang.* pretentious airs. **18** *Cdn. Lumbering.* an area in a logging camp constituting a separate operation on its own spur of track, with many of its own facilities.
by (someone's) **side,** near someone: *He wanted his family by his side.*
on the side, *Informal,* **a** in addition to one's ordinary duties, etc. **b** as a complement to a main dish: *a hamburger with fries on the side.*
on the —— side, tending to be ——: *on the strict side. This rhubarb is on the tart side.*
side by side, a beside one another. **b** equally: *Hourly earnings of our employees rank side by side with those in similar industries.* **c** co-operatively; as companions: *We will be working side by side with you in your new role as director.*
split (one's) **sides,** laugh very hard.
take sides, place oneself with one person or group against another.
—adj. **1** at one side; on one side: *the side aisles of a theatre.* **2** from one side: *a side view.* **3** toward one side: *a side glance.* **4** less important: *a side issue.* **5** constituting a separate order to complement a main dish: *a side salad.*
—v. **1** take the part of; favour one among opposing or differing groups or persons (*used with* **with**): *The sisters always side with each other.* **2** put siding on (a house, etc.). ⟨OE *side*⟩

side arms weapons, such as a sword, revolver, bayonet, etc., carried at the side or on a belt.

side•band ['saɪd,bænd] *n. Radio.* the band of frequencies above or below the carrier frequency, produced by the modulation of the carrier wave.

side•bar ['saɪd,bɑr] *n.* a very brief article printed next to a main one, enlarging upon some aspect of the main article.

side•board ['saɪd,bɔrd] *n.* **1** a piece of dining-room furniture having drawers and shelves for holding silver and linen, and space on top for dishes. **2** an additional and removable board placed on the side of a truck, wagon, etc. to form or to increase the height of a side.

side boards *Hockey.* the fence surrounding the playing surface; BOARDS (def. 3b). Also, **sideboards.**

side•burns ['saɪd,bɜrnz] *n.pl.* facial hair growing down in front of the ears, especially when the chin is shaved. ⟨alteration of *burnsides,* from Ambrose E. *Burnside* (1824-1881), an American general who wore thick side whiskers⟩

side•car ['saɪd,kɑr] *n.* **1** a small, one-wheeled car for a passenger, baggage, etc. attached to the side of a motorcycle. **2** a cocktail made with Cointreau, brandy, and lemon juice in approximately equal parts.

side chair a straight-backed chair without arms, often part of a dining room suite.

side channel a small offshoot of a river, sometimes running for some distance before rejoining the main stream, sometimes coming to a dead end, and usually shallow, narrow, and sluggish.

-sided *adjective-forming suffix.* having —— sides: *three-sided.*

side dish a dish served in addition to the main dish of a course.

side effect an incidental consequence of a course of action, treatment, etc., especially an undesirable reaction to a drug.

side•hill ['saɪd,hɪl] *n.* hillside.

side•kick ['saɪd,kɪk] *n. Slang.* a partner or assistant; a close or constant companion.

side•light **1** light coming from the side. **2** a piece of incidental information about a subject. **3** either of two lights carried by a moving ship at night, a red one on the port side and a green one on the starboard side. **4** a window or other opening for light in the side of a building, ship, etc. **5** a window at the side of a door or of another window.

side•line ['saɪd,laɪn] *n., v.* **-lined, -lin•ing.** *—n.* **1** a line at the side of something. **2** *Football, etc.* a line that marks the limit of play on the side of the field. **3** Often, **sidelines,** *pl.* the space just outside these lines: *They watched the game from the sidelines.* **4 a** a line of goods, trade, etc. that is additional, auxiliary, and secondary to the primary one. **b** any enterprise, business, etc. carried on apart from that in which one is chiefly or officially employed.
on the sidelines, a in the space along the sidelines of a playing field. **b** inactive; not taking an active part in a game, enterprise, etc. **c** actively involved but not in a prominent or central role.
—v. put on the sidelines; make inactive: *to sideline a player for fighting.*

side•long ['saɪd,lɒŋ] *adj. or adv.* **1** to one side; toward the side. **2** from the side; indirect(ly) or oblique(ly): *a sidelong glance.*

side•man ['saɪd,mæn] *or* ['saɪdmən] *n., pl.* **-men.** an instrumentalist in a jazz group or dance band other than the leader or a soloist.

side•piece ['saɪd,pis] *n.* a piece forming a side or part of a side, or fixed by the side, of something.

si•de•re•al [saɪ'diriəl] *adj.* **1** of or having to do with the stars. **2** *Astronomy.* measured with reference to the stars. A **sidereal year** is about twenty minutes longer than a solar year. ⟨< L *sidereus* astral < *sidus, sideris* star⟩ **—si'de•re•al•ly,** *adv.*

sidereal day *Astronomy.* the time interval between two passages of the vernal EQUINOX (def. 2) over the celestial meridian, or a single full rotation of the earth; about four minutes shorter than a solar day.

sidereal month *Astronomy.* the time it takes for the moon to make one full revolution around the earth in relation to a fixed star; on average, 27.32 solar days.

sid•er•ite ['sɪdə,rəit] *n.* **1** an iron ore composed of iron carbonate. Siderite occurs in various forms and colours.

Formula: $FeCO_3$. **2** a meteorite consisting mainly of iron. ⟨< L < Gk. *sidērītēs* < *sidēros* iron⟩

side•road ['saɪd,roud] *n. Cdn.* in Ontario, a road built along the side line of a concession, connecting concession roads and usually running east-west.

side road **1** a secondary road, often unpaved, leading to a main road or highway. **2** *Cdn.* See SIDEROAD.

sid•er•o•sis [,sɪdə'rousɪs] *n. Pathology.* a lung disease resulting from the inhalation of iron or other metal particles. ⟨< Gk. *sideros* iron + E *-osis*⟩

side•sad•dle ['saɪd,sædəl] *n., adv.* —*n.* a woman's saddle so made that both of the rider's legs are on the same side of the horse.
—*adv.* on or as if on a sidesaddle.

side•show ['saɪd,ʃou] *n.* **1** a small show in connection with a principal one: *the sideshows of a circus.* **2** any minor proceeding or affair connected with a more important one.

side•slip ['saɪd,slɪp] *n., v.* **-slipped, -slip•ping.** —*n.* **1** a slip or skid to one side. **2** the slipping to one side of an aircraft.
—*v.* slip or cause to slip or skid to one side.

sides•man ['saɪdzmən] *n., pl.* **-men.** *Anglican Church.* an assistant to a churchwarden, who shows people to their seats, helps take up the offering, etc. in services.

side•split•ting ['saɪd,splɪtɪŋ] *adj.* extremely or uproariously funny.

side step **1** a step or stepping to one side. **2** a step at the side of a ship, vehicle, etc.

side•step ['saɪd,stɛp] *v.* **-stepped, -step•ping.** **1** step aside. **2** avoid by or as if by stepping aside; evade: *She never sidestepped a responsibility.* **—'side,step•per,** *n.*

side street a less important street than a main road; a street leading off a main road.

side•stroke ['saɪd,strouk] *n. Swimming.* a stroke executed while lying on one's side in the water, the arms moving in a fashion similar to the breast stroke and the legs in a scissor kick.

side•swipe ['saɪd,swəip] *v.* **-swiped, -swip•ing;** *n.* —*v.* hit with a sweeping blow or strike along the side: *The drunk driver sideswiped a parked car.*
—*n.* a sweeping blow or strike along the side.

side•track ['saɪd,træk] *n., v.* —*n.* **1** a railway siding. **2** a turning or being turned aside: *Stick to the business at hand and avoid sidetracks.*
—*v.* **1** switch (a train, etc.) to a siding. **2** put aside; turn or be turned aside: *The teacher refused to be sidetracked by questions on other subjects.*

side trip a short, extra trip not included in the main itinerary of a journey or voyage.

side•walk ['saɪd,wɒk] *n.* a place to walk at the side of a street, usually paved.

side•ward ['saɪdwərd] *adj. or adv.* toward one side. Also (*adv.*), **sidewards.**

side•way ['saɪd,wei] *adv., adj., n.* —*adv. or adj.* sideways.
—*n.* **1** a side street, not a main road; byway. **2** a sidewalk.

side•ways ['saɪd,weiz] *adv. or adj.* **1** toward one side: *to walk sideways.* **2** from one side: *a sideways glimpse.* **3** with one side toward the front or toward the observer: *to stand sideways, to place a book sideways on a shelf.*

side–wheel ['saɪd ,wil] *adj.* of or designating a steamboat having a paddle wheel on each side. **—'side-,wheel•er,** *n.*

side whisker **1** a hair growing long on the side of the face. **2 side whiskers,** *pl.* the whiskers that grow on the cheek or side of the face.

side•wind•er ['saɪd,waɪndər] *n.* **1 a** a small rattlesnake (*Crotalus cerastes*) of the desert regions of the U.S., having a hornlike protuberance over each eye and moving over loose sand by forming sideways loops. **b** any Old World snake that moves in this fashion. **2** *Informal.* a heavy punch delivered with a sidewise swipe of the arm.

side•wise ['saɪd,waɪz] *adv. or adj.* sideways.

sid•ing ['saɪdɪŋ] *n., v.* —*n.* **1** a short railway track to which cars can be switched from a main track. **2** the boards forming the sides of a wooden building. **3** any of various styles of weatherproof facing on houses, etc., usually consisting of overlapping lengths of vinyl or aluminum, shingles, etc. **4** *Cdn.* a place in the country along a secondary railway line, having a grain elevator with a residence for the agent and, sometimes, a few other houses, stores, etc.
—*v.* ppr. of SIDE.

si•dle ['saɪdəl] *v.* **-dled, -dling;** *n.* —*v.* move sideways, especially shyly or stealthily: *The little boy shyly sidled up to the visitor. She sidled her chair closer to mine, hoping to be noticed.*
—*n.* a movement sideways. ⟨< *sideling* sidelong⟩

SIDS SUDDEN INFANT DEATH SYNDROME.

siege [sidʒ] *n., v.* **sieged, sieg•ing.** —*n.* **1** the surrounding of a fortified place by an army trying to capture it; a besieging or being besieged. **2** any long or persistent effort to overcome resistance; any long-continued attack: *a siege of illness.*
lay siege to, a besiege. **b** attempt to win or get by long and persistent effort.
—*v.* besiege. ⟨ME < OF siege, ult. < L *sedere* sit⟩

☛ *Syn. n.* **1. Siege,** BLOCKADE = a military operation to cut off normal communications and supplies of a place. **Siege,** chiefly a land operation, means surrounding a city or fortified place, cutting off all movement to and from it, and usually assaulting it: *The British had barely laid siege to Detroit in 1812 when it surrendered.* **Blockade** applies to an operation, chiefly but not always naval, to close a harbour, coast, or city and cut off its supplies by controlling ship movements or other transportation to and from it, but does not suggest attacking it: *The airlift defeated the blockade of Berlin.*

Sieg•fried ['sigfrid] *or* ['zikfrid]; *German,* ['zikfʀit] *n. Germanic legend.* a hero who killed a dragon and bathed in its blood to make himself invulnerable. He won the treasure of the Nibelungs.

sie•mens ['simənz] *n.* an SI unit for measuring electrical conductance. One siemens is the conductance between two points of a conductor when a current of one ampere produces one volt of electromotive force. *Symbol:* S ⟨after W. von *Siemens* (1823–1883), English engineer born in Germany⟩

si•en•na [si'ɛnə] *n.* **1** a yellowish brown colouring matter **(raw sienna)** made from earth containing iron. **2** a reddish brown colouring matter **(burnt sienna)** made by roasting earth containing iron. **3** a yellowish brown or reddish brown. ⟨short for Ital. *terra di Sien(n)a* earth of Siena, a city in Italy⟩

si•er•ra [si'ɛrə] *n.* **1** a chain of hills or mountains with jagged peaks. **2** any of various marine fishes of the genus *Scomboromorus,* especially *S. sierra,* found in the Pacific Ocean off SW North America and prized as a sport and food fish. ⟨< Sp. *sierra,* literally, a saw < L *serra*⟩

Si•er•ra Le•one [si'ɛrə li'oun] *or* [li'ouni] an independent republic on the coast of W Africa, a member of the British Commonwealth. See map at SENEGAL.

si•es•ta [si'ɛstə] *n.* a nap or rest taken at noon or in the afternoon. ⟨< Sp. < L *sexta (hora)* sixth (hour), noon⟩

sieur [sjœʀ] *n. French.* formerly, a title of respect for a man; Sir. ⟨< F < VL *seiorem* < L *seniorem,* accus. of *senior* senior. Doublet of SEIGNEUR.⟩

sieve [sɪv] *n., v.* **sieved, siev•ing.** —*n.* a utensil having holes that let liquids and fine particles, but not large pieces, pass through: *Shaking flour through a sieve removes lumps.*
—*v.* put through a sieve. ⟨OE *sife*⟩ **—'sieve,like,** *adj.*

si•fa•ka [sə'fɑkə] *n.* any lemur of the genus *Propithecus,* having black-and-white soft fur and a long tail. ⟨< Malagasy⟩

sif•fleur [sɪ'flɜr] *n. Cdn.* HOARY MARMOT. ⟨< Cdn.F, literally, whistler⟩

sift [sɪft] *v.* **1** separate larger particles from smaller ones by shaking in a sieve: *Sift the bread crumbs and put the larger pieces in a separate pile.* **2** sprinkle through a sieve: *Sift sugar onto the top of the cake.* **3** use a sieve. **4** fall through, or as if through, a sieve: *The snow sifted softly down.* **5** examine very carefully: *The jury sifted the evidence to decide if the woman was guilty.* **6** distinguish; tell apart and separate: *sift truth from falsehood.* ⟨OE *siftan* < *sife* sieve⟩ **—'sift•er,** *n.*

sigh [saɪ] *v., n.* —*v.* **1** draw in and let out a very long, deep, loud breath because one is sad, tired, relieved, etc. **2** say or express with a sigh. **3** make a sound like a sigh: *The wind sighed in the treetops.* **4** wish very much; long: *He sighed for home and friends.* **5** lament with sighing: *to sigh over one's unhappy fate.* **6** spend or pass in sighing: *sighing the hours away.*
—*n.* the act or sound of sighing. ⟨ME *sighe(n),* ult. < OE *sīcan*⟩ **—'sigh•er,** *n.* **—'sigh•ing•ly,** *adv.*

sight [səit] *n., v.* —*n.* **1** the power of seeing; vision: *Birds have better sight than dogs.* **2** the act or fact of seeing; a look: *love at first sight.* **3** the range or field of vision: *Land was in sight.* **4** the thing seen; view: *The vase of flowers was a pretty sight.* **5** something worth seeing: *see the sights of the city.* **6** *Informal.* something that looks bad, ridiculous, or odd: *Her clothes were a sight.* **7** a device on a gun, surveying instrument, etc. used in

taking aim or observing. **8** an observation taken with a telescope or other instrument; aim taken with a gun, etc. **9** a way of looking or thinking; regard: *The old doll was precious in the child's sight.* **10** *Informal.* a great deal: *That's a sight more money than I can afford.* **11** (*adjl.*) read, interpreted, performed, etc. at sight: *a sight balance. Our Latin test included a sight passage to be translated.*
a sight for sore eyes, a welcome or pleasant sight.
at sight, as soon as seen or presented: *She reads music at sight.*
catch sight of, see: *I caught sight of her.*
in sight of, where one can see or be seen by: *We live in sight of the school.*
know by sight, know sufficiently to recognize when seen: *I've never met him but I know him by sight.*
lower (one's) **sights,** reduce one's ambition.
on sight, as soon as seen or presented; at sight.
out of sight, a out of the field of vision. **b** out of reach; unreasonably high. **c** *Slang.* excellent.
out of sight of, where one cannot see or be seen by: *out of sight of land, out of sight of the neighbours.*
set (one's) **sights on,** aim for; try to attain.
sight unseen, without seeing beforehand: *She bought the radio sight unseen.*
–*v.* **1** see: *At last Columbus sighted land.* **2** take a sight or observation (of). **3** aim (a weapon) by means of sights. **4** aim at by using sights; target. **5** adjust the sight of (a gun, etc.). **6** provide with sights. ⟨OE *(ge)siht*⟩
☛ *Hom.* CITE, SITE.

sight draft a written order from one bank to another, requiring a certain amount of money to be paid on demand.

sight•ed ['səitɪd] *adj., v.* –*adj.* **1** having the sense of sight; able to see. **2** (*used in compounds*) having sight of a given kind: *shortsighted.*
–*v.* pt. and pp. of SIGHT.

sight•less ['səitlɪs] *adj.* **1** blind. **2** *Poetic.* invisible. **–'sight•less•ly,** *adv.* **–'sight•less•ness,** *n.*

sight•ly ['səitli] *adj.* **-li•er, -li•est. 1** pleasing to the sight. **2** affording a fine view. **–'sight•li•ness,** *n.*

sight•read ['səit,rid] *v.* **sight•read, sight•read•ing.** play an instrument or sing by reading (music not previously seen). **–'sight,read•ing,** *n.*

sight•see ['səit,si] *v.* go around to see objects or places of interest. **–'sight,se•er,** *n.*

sight•see•ing ['səit,siɪŋ] *n., adj., v.* –*n.* the act of going around to see objects or places of interest.
–*adj.* engaged in this act or designed for it: *a band of sightseeing Americans; a sightseeing tour.*
–*v.* ppr. of SIGHTSEE.

sig•ma ['sɪgmə] *n.* **1** the eighteenth letter of the Greek alphabet. Σ, σ, or, when final, ς = English S, s. **2** something shaped like an S. **3** something shaped like a C (the uncial form of sigma).

sig•mate ['sɪgmeit] *adj.* shaped like a sigma.

sig•moid ['sɪgmɔɪd] *adj., n.* –*adj.* **1** having a double curve like the letter S. **2** having a single curve like the letter C. **3** of or having to do with the SIGMOID FLEXURE.
–*n.* SIGMOID FLEXURE. ⟨< Gk. *sigmoeidēs* < *sigma* sigma + *eidos* form⟩

sigmoid flexure 1 *Anatomy.* the S-shaped curve of the large intestine between the descending colon and the rectum. **2** *Zoology.* any S-shaped curve in a structure.

sig•moid•o•scope [sɪg'mɔɪdə,skoup] *n. Medicine.* a tubelike instrument with a light, for examining the rectum, colon, and sigmoid flexure.

sign [saɪn] *n., v.* –*n.* **1 a** any mark used to mean, represent, or point out something. **b** *Mathematics.* a mark or symbol used to indicate an operation to be performed on a quantity or number, a relation of quantities or numbers, etc. The four signs of the arithmetic operations are addition (+), subtraction (–), multiplication (×), division (÷). The sign (=) means 'equals'. The signs (+) and (–) in algebra and higher mathematics define positive and negative numbers. **c** *Music.* a flat, sharp, or other symbol used in notation to give directions, indicate tonality, etc. **2** a motion or gesture used to mean, represent, or point out something: *A nod is a sign of agreement. We talked to the man by signs since we knew no Japanese.* **3 a** a conventionalized SIGN LANGUAGE for the deaf. **b** one of the gestures of this language. **4** an inscribed board, space, etc., serving for advertisement, information, etc.: *The sign reads, "Keep off the grass."* **5** an indication; trace; evidence: *signs of life. The hunter found signs of deer.* **6** an indication of a coming event: *The robin is a sign of spring.* **7** an omen, portent, or miracle; a supernatural manifestation. **8** *Astrology.* any of the twelve divisions of the zodiac: *What is your sign? Mine is Gemini.*
–*v.* **1** attach one's name (to) in order to show authority, agreement, obligation, etc.; write one's name (on): *Sign on the dotted line. Sign this letter.* **2** write as a signature: *Sign your initials here. He signed his full name.* **3** hire by a written agreement: *to sign a new player.* **4** accept employment or some other obligation by a written agreement: *They signed for three years.* **5** give a sign to; signal: *to sign someone to enter.* **6** communicate by gesture: *to sign assent.* **7** communicate by means of SIGN LANGUAGE. **8** mark with a sign.
sign away, give (something) up or away by signing.
sign in, indicate, by signing a register, etc., that one is present.
sign off, a in radio and television, stop broadcasting. **b** *Informal.* bring (a letter, speech, lecture, etc.) to a close. **c** log off a computer.
sign on, a sign up. **b** log onto a computer.
sign up, a accept a job by putting one's name to an agreement. **b** hire in this way. **c** enlist in the armed services. **d** indicate an intention to participate in anything by writing one's name.
sign out, a indicate, by signing a register, etc., that one will not be present. **b** borrow (a book, equipment, etc.) by signing some record.
sign over, transfer by signing one's name. ⟨ME < OF < L *signum*⟩ **–'sign•a•ble,** *adj.* **–'sign•er,** *n.* **–'sign,like,** *adj.*
☛ *Hom.* SINE[1], SYNE.
☛ *Syn. n.* **5.** See note at MARK[1]. **6, 7. Sign,** OMEN = an indication of something about to happen. **Sign** applies to something perceived as evidence or an indication of something else: *Those big black clouds are signs of a storm. She interpreted the unsettling dream as a sign that she should not accept the position.* **Omen** applies to a thing or event that is seen, particularly from a religious or superstitious point of view, as extraordinary or of supernatural origin and as a promise of something good or bad to come: *He believed the blackbird's call was an omen of death.*

sig•nal ['sɪgnəl] *n., adj., v.* **-nalled** or **-naled, -nal•ling** or **-nal•ing.** –*n.* **1 a** a sign, token, etc. that gives information or notice of something: *A flashing red light is a warning signal.* **b** the device that produces such a sign or token: *Both rear signals were broken in the accident.* **2** a sign agreed upon or understood as the occasion of concerted action: *to give the signal to advance.* **3** anything that produces a response or action: *The defeat of the government was the signal for a mass uprising.* **4** *Radio, television, etc.* **a** a wave, current, impulse, etc. serving to convey sounds and images. **b** a sound or image so conveyed. **5** *Bridge, etc.* a bid or play designed to give information to one's partner. **6 signals,** *pl. Football.* **a** the numbers called by an offensive back, usually the quarterback, designating a particular play. **b** the numbers called by a member of the defensive team to direct the positions of the players. **7 signals,** *pl.* SIGNAL CORPS. **8** (*adjl.*) used as a signal or in signalling: *a signal flag or fire.*
–*adj.* remarkable; striking; notable; having the effect of a sign: *a signal success, a signal advance.*
–*v.* **1** make a signal or signals (to): *He signalled the car to stop by raising his hand.* **2** make known by a signal or signals: *A bell signals the end of a class period.* ⟨< F *signal*, ult. < L *signum* sign⟩ **–'sig•nal•ly,** *adv.*

signal corps a unit of the armed forces in charge of communications. Also, **signals.**

sig•nal•ize ['sɪgnə,laɪz] *v.* **-ized, -iz•ing. 1** make stand out; make notable: *The present century has been signalized by many great inventions.* **2** point out; mention specially; draw attention to. **3 a** make signals to; communicate with by signal. **b** announce by a signal or signals. **–,sig•nal•i'za•tion,** *n.*

sig•nal•ler or **sig•nal•er** ['sɪgnələr] *n.* **1** a soldier in the infantry, artillery, etc. who looks after communications within the regiment. **2** a signalman. **3** a person who or thing that signals.

sig•nal•ling or **sig•nal•ing** ['sɪgnəlɪŋ] *n., v.* –*n.* the act of using, making, or controlling signals.
–*v.* ppr. of SIGNAL.

sig•nal•man ['sɪgnəlmən] *or* ['sɪgnəl,mæn] *n., pl.* **-men. 1** a railway employee in charge of the signals. **2** a person who sends or receives signals, as in the armed forces.

sig•na•to•ry ['sɪgnə,tɔri] *n., pl.* **-ries;** *adj.* –*n.* **1** a signer of a document. **2** a nation, corporation, etc. on whose behalf one or more persons sign a document: The signatories to the agreement were *the United Kingdom, France, and Russia.*
–*adj.* signing: *signatory delegates.*

sig•na•ture ['sɪgnətʃər] *n.* **1** a person's name, written by that person in his or her characteristic style. **2** such a writing of one's name. **3** *Music.* the sign printed at the beginning of a staff to show the key and time of a piece of music. 4 *Printing.* **a** a sheet folded into pages, forming a section of a book. **b** a letter or number printed at the bottom of the first page of such a sheet, telling how it is to be folded. 5 a tune, song, or slogan, used to identify a radio or television program; theme song. Also, **signature tune.** 6 any distinctive feature, characteristic, etc.: *Garotting with a telephone cord was the murderer's signature.* 6 *Pharmacy.* that part of a prescription that gives the directions to be marked on the container of the medicine. ⟨< LL *signatura*, ult. < L *signum* sign⟩

sign•board ['saɪn,bɔrd] *n.* a board having a sign, notice, advertisement, inscription, etc. on it.

Signed English a language for the deaf using signs from AMERICAN SIGN LANGUAGE but based on English syntax, incorporating additional signs for function words such as *for* and *to* and grammatical suffixes such as *-ing* and *-ed*. It is generally the system taught in schools for the deaf.

sig•net ['sɪgnɪt] *n.* 1 a small seal: *The order was sealed with the king's signet.* 2 the impression made by it. ⟨ME < OF *signet*, ult. < L *signum* seal⟩

signet ring SEAL RING.

sig•nif•i•cance [sɪg'nɪfəkəns] *n.* 1 importance; consequence: *The chairperson wanted to see him on a matter of significance.* 2 meaning: *Do you understand the significance of this picture?* 3 expressiveness; significant quality: *the significance of her smile.*

sig•nif•i•cant [sɪg'nɪfəkənt] *adj.* 1 full of meaning; important; of consequence: *July 1, 1867, is a significant date for Canadians.* 2 having a meaning; expressive: *Smiles are significant of pleasure.* 3 having or expressing a hidden or special meaning: *A significant nod from his friend warned him to stop talking.* 4 *Statistics.* being or having to do with a deviation from the predicted result that is too great to be attributable to chance. ⟨< L *significans, -antis*, ppr. of *significare* signify. See SIGNIFY.⟩
—sig'nif•i•cant•ly, *adv.*
☛ *Syn.* 2, 3. See note at EXPRESSIVE.

sig•ni•fi•ca•tion [,sɪgnəfə'keiʃən] *n.* 1 the meaning or sense of something. 2 the act or process of signifying.

sig•nif•i•ca•tive [sɪg'nɪfəkətɪv] *or* [sɪg'nɪfə,keitɪv] *adj.* 1 serving to signify; having a meaning. 2 significant or suggestive.

sig•ni•fy ['sɪgnə,faɪ] *v.* **-fied, -fy•ing.** 1 be a sign of; mean: *"Oh!" signifies surprise.* 2 make known by signs, words, or actions: *He signified his consent with a nod.* 3 have importance; be of consequence; matter: *What a fool says does not signify.* ⟨ME < OF < L *significare* < *signum* sign + *facere* make⟩
—'sig•ni,fi•a•ble, *adj.* **—'sig•ni,fi•er,** *n.*

sign language 1 communication in which movements and positions of the hands and fingers stand for words, ideas, etc. 2 a conventionalized system used for such communication especially by and with the deaf, as SIGNED ENGLISH, AMERICAN SIGN LANGUAGE, or the sign language of the Plains people of the First Nations.

sign manual *pl.* **signs manual.** 1 a person's signature, especially that of a sovereign or magistrate on an official document. 2 a distinctively individual sign, stamp, or quality.

sign of the cross *Christianity.* a hand gesture indicating the shape of a cross, made by a priest in blessing or by any person as an act of reverence.

sign of the zodiac SIGN (*n.* def. 8).

si•gno•ry ['sinjəri] *n., pl.* **-ries.** See SEIGNEURY. ⟨ME < OF *signorie*, var. of *seignorie* (see SEIGNEURY); influenced by Ital. *signoria*⟩

sign•post ['saɪn,poust] *n.* 1 a post having a sign, notice, or direction on it; guidepost. 2 anything that marks, points, guides, or from which bearings may be taken, conclusions drawn, etc.

Sikh [sik] *n., adj. —n.* a member of a religious sect, founded in N India in the early 16th century as an offshoot of Hinduism. It has adopted from Islam the belief in one God, and has retained from Hinduism the belief in Karma and reincarnation while rejecting the caste system and the worship of images.
—adj. of or having to do with the Sikhs or their religion. ⟨< Hind. *sikh* disciple⟩

Sikh•ism ['sikɪzəm] *n.* the beliefs and doctrines of the Sikhs.

si•lage ['saɪlɪdʒ] *n.* green fodder for farm animals, preserved and stored in a silo; ensilage. ⟨< *ensilage*, after *silo*⟩

si•lence ['saɪləns] *n., v.* **-lenced, -lenc•ing;** *interj. —n.* 1 the absence of sound or noise; stillness. 2 a state of keeping still; not talking. 3 **a** an omission of mention or notice in a narrative. **b** the omission or refusal to write, communicate, or reply (about something); secrecy: *Silence in matters of public interest is intolerable in a free society.* 4 oblivion; the state of being not spoken of: *events consigned henceforth to silence.*
in silence, without saying anything: *They finished their work in silence.*
—v. 1 stop the speech or noise of; make silent; quiet: *They asked him to silence the noisy children.* 2 make silent on a certain topic by persuasion, restraint, force, etc.: *Her strong arguments soon silenced the opposition. The new government attempted to silence the press.* 3 stop (enemy guns, etc.) from firing by destroying or disabling with return fire.
—interj. be silent! ⟨ME < OF < L *silentium*, ult. < *silere* be silent⟩

si•lenc•er ['saɪlənsər] *n.* 1 a person who or thing that silences. 2 *Brit.* a muffler on an internal-combustion engine. 3 a device for deadening the sound of a firearm.

si•lent ['saɪlənt] *adj.* 1 quiet; still; noiseless: *a silent house, the silent hills.* 2 not speaking; saying little or nothing: *You're very silent today.* 3 not spoken; not said out loud: *a silent prayer, silent disapproval.* 4 of a letter in a word, not pronounced in speech. The *l* in *folk* and the *b* in *lamb* are silent. 5 not active; taking no open or active part. A **silent partner** shares in financing but not in managing a business. 6 omitting mention of something, as in a narrative: *The book is silent on the question of motive for his actions.* 7 designating a motion picture without spoken dialogue: *The first movies were silent.* 8 of a heart attack, occurring without perceptible symptoms. ⟨< L *silens, -entis*, ppr. of *silere* be silent⟩
—'si•lent•ly, *adv.* **—'si•lent•ness,** *n.*
☛ *Syn.* 2. **Silent,** TACITURN, RETICENT = saying little or nothing. **Silent** especially means 'not talkative', characteristically speaking only when necessary, or saying very little, but also means saying nothing on some particular occasion for some special reason: *He is a silent, thoughtful boy.* **Taciturn** means 'not fond of talking', being by nature inclined to be silent and avoid conversation: *She is a taciturn woman who dislikes parties.* **Reticent** means 'not saying all one knows, disposed to keep silent', especially about private affairs: *She is reticent about her early life.*

Si•le•nus [saɪ'linəs] *n. Greek mythology.* 1 the foster father and companion of Dionysus and leader of the satyrs. He is represented as a short, stout, drunken old man. 2 **silenus,** a woodland deity similar to a satyr.

si•le•sia [saɪ'liʒə] *or* [sə'liʒə], [saɪ'liʃə] *or* [sə'liʃə] *n.* a fine, light, smooth cotton cloth used for lining. ⟨< *Silesia*, a region in central Europe where it was originally made⟩

Si•le•sian [saɪ'liʒən] *or* [sə'liʒən], [saɪ'liʃən] *or* [sə'liʃən] *n., adj. —n.* a native or inhabitant of Silesia, a region in central Europe, now divided between Germany, Czechoslovakia, and Poland.
—adj. of or having to do with Silesia.

si•lex ['saɪlɛks] *n.* 1 silica. 2 a strong, heat-resistant glass that is mostly quartz. ⟨< L *silex* flint⟩

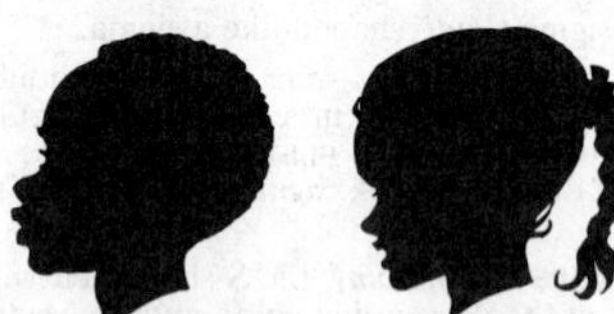

Silhouettes of children's heads

sil•hou•ette [,sɪlu'ɛt] *or* ['sɪlu,ɛt] *n., v.* **-et•ted, -et•ting.** *—n.* 1 an outline portrait cut out of black paper or filled in with some single colour. 2 a dark image outlined against a lighter background. 3 the contour of a garment, figure, etc.: *Her dress has the new, slim silhouette.*
in silhouette, shown in outline, or in black against a white background.
—v. show as a silhouette: *The mountain was silhouetted against the sky.* ⟨after Etienne de *Silhouette* (1709-1767), a French minister of finance⟩

sil•i•ca ['sɪləkə] *n.* a compound that occurs in crystalline form, as in quartz, and in non-crystalline form, as in opal, and that also forms the main ingredient of sand. *Formula*: SiO_2 Also called **silicon dioxide.** ⟨< NL < L *silex, -licis* flint⟩

silica gel a non-crystalline form of silica resembling sand, but having many fine pores that make it highly absorbent. Silica gel is used as a drying and deodorizing agent in air conditioners, etc.

sil•i•cate ['sɪləkɪt] *or* ['sɪlə,keit] *n. Chemistry.* any of many insoluble compounds of silicon, oxygen, and a metal or metals that make up the largest class of minerals. Silicates are found widely in rocks of the earth and are used in building materials such as glass, bricks, and cement.

si•li•ceous or **si•li•cious** [sə'lɪʃəs] *adj.* **1** of, having to do with, containing, or resembling silica or a silicate. **2** thriving in soil that is rich in silica. ⟨< L *siliceus* of flint < *silex, -licis* flint⟩

si•lic•ic [sə'lɪsɪk] *adj. Chemistry.* of, having to do with, or derived from silica or silicon.

sil•i•cide ['sɪlɪ,saɪd] *n. Chemistry.* a compound of two elements, one of which is silicon.

sil•i•cif•er•ous [,sɪlɪ'sɪfərəs] *adj.* containing, producing, or combined with silica. ⟨< E *silica* + *-ferous*⟩

si•lic•i•fy [sə'lɪsə,faɪ] *v.* **-fied, -fy•ing. 1** convert into or impregnate with silica. **2** become silica or be impregnated with it. **—si,lic•i•fi'ca•tion,** *n.*

sil•i•con ['sɪlɪ,kɒn] *or* ['sɪlɪkən] *n.* a non-metallic element that occurs naturally only in compounds and is the most abundant element, next to oxygen, in the earth's crust. Silicon combines with oxygen to form silica. *Symbol*: Si; *at.no.* 14; *at.mass* 28.09. ⟨< *silica*⟩

silicon carbide *Chemistry.* a hard, insoluble, blue-black crystalline compound produced by heating carbon with sand in an electric furnace. It is used as an abrasive and as an electrical resistor.

silicon dioxide See SILICA.

sil•i•cone ['sɪlə,koun] *n. Chemistry.* any of a large group of organic silicon compounds that are water-resistant and are good insulators for heat, cold, or electricity. Silicones are used to make lubricants, synthetic rubber, waterproof polishes, etc.

silicone rubber a synthetic rubber made from certain silicones, having great tensile strength and elasticity over a wide range of temperatures.

Silicon Valley an area in the Santa Clara valley region southeast of San Francisco where many of the leading high-technology design and manufacturing companies in the micro-electronics field are located. ⟨< the silicon wafers used in semiconductor devices⟩

sil•i•co•sis [,sɪlə'kousɪs] *n. Pathology.* a disease of the lungs caused by continually breathing air filled with dust from quartz or silicates. ⟨< *silic-* flint, silica (< L *silex, -licis* flint) + *-osis* diseased condition⟩

silk [sɪlk] *n., v.* **1** a fine, soft, tough protein fibre produced by silkworms for their cocoons and used to make textiles. **2** any of various similar fibres produced by other insect larvae, usually for cocoons. **3** thread, yarn, or cloth made from the silk produced by silkworms. **4** silklike fibre, thread, or cloth made artificially. **5** a garment of silk or silklike cloth, such as the gown worn by a King's or Queen's Counsel. **6** anything like silk in softness, lustre, etc.: *corn silk.* **7 silks,** *pl.* the blouse and cap worn by a jockey or harness race driver, the colours of which identify the owner of the horse. **8** (*adjl.*) of, like, or having to do with silk: *silk thread, a silk finish.* **9** parachute.
hit the silk, *Slang.* bail out from a plane using a parachute.
take silk, become a King's or Queen's Counsel.
—v. of corn, develop silk. ⟨OE *sioloc* < *Slavic* < Gk. *sērikos* < *Sēres* the Chinese⟩ **—'silk,like,** *adj.*

silk cotton kapok.

silk–cot•ton tree ['sɪlk ,kɒtən] any of various large, spiny tropical trees of the genus *Ceiba* whose seeds are covered with silk cotton, especially *C. pentandra*, from which kapok is obtained.

silk•en ['sɪlkən] *adj.* **1** made of silk: *a silken dress.* **2** like silk; smooth, soft, and glossy: *silken hair.* **3** of a voice, manner, etc., smoothly agreeable and polite, especially when suggesting insincerity or an ulterior motive: *He spoke in silken tones.* **4** clothed in silk: *silken legs.*

silk hat TOP HAT.

silk–screen ['sɪlk ,skrin] *n., v. —n.* **1** a method of colour printing in which a screen of silk or similar material is prepared as a stencil and the colouring matter is forced through the mesh in all the areas of the design to be printed. **2** a print produced by this process. **3** (*adjl.*) having to do with or produced by this process.
—v. produce (a print) by means of silk-screen.

silk–stock•ing ['sɪlk 'stɒkɪŋ] *adj., n. —adj.* **1** dressing fashionably and elegantly; especially, formerly, wearing silk stockings. **2** of or for aristocratic or wealthy people: *He caters to the silk-stocking trade.*
—n. a wealthy or aristocratic person.

Silk Train *Cdn.* formerly, a CPR train carrying Japanese silk from the West Coast to the eastern centres.

silk•worm ['sɪlk,wɜrm] *n.* **1** the hairless, yellowish larva of an Asiatic moth (*Bombyx mori*) that produces the silk used for textiles. The silkworm feeds mainly on mulberry leaves. **2** any of various other moth caterpillars that spin cocoons of silk. ⟨OE *seolcwyrm*⟩

silk•y ['sɪlki] *adj.* **silk•i•er, silk•i•est. 1** of or like silk, or covered with a silklike substance; smooth, soft, glossy, etc.: *Some cats have silky fur.* **2** of a voice, manner, etc., smooth and extremely polite, especially so as to suggest insincerity or an ulterior motive: *a silky voice describing the features of a new luxury-model car.* **—'silk•i•ly,** *adv.* **—'silk•i•ness,** *n.*

sill [sɪl] *n.* **1** a horizontal piece of wood, block of stone, etc. that forms the bottom of a window or door frame. See FRAME for picture. **2** a large beam on which the wall of a house, etc. rests. **3** *Geology.* a mass or sheet of igneous rock that has come between layers of other rock while molten and has solidified there. ⟨OE *syll*⟩

sil•la•bub ['sɪlə,bʌb] *n.* See SYLLABUB.

sil•li•ness ['sɪlinɪs] *n.* **1** foolishness; being silly. **2** a silly act, thing, etc.

sil•ly ['sɪli] *adj.* **-li•er, -li•est;** *n., pl.* **-lies.** *—adj.* **1** without sense or reason; foolish; inane. **2** half-witted. **3** *Archaic.* simple; innocent; harmless. **4** *Informal.* stunned; dazed: *to knock someone silly.* **5** trivial; frivolous: *I'm tired of their silly little disagreements.*
—n. Informal. a silly person: *You two are a pair of sillies!* ⟨OE *sælig* happy < *sæl* happiness⟩
☛ *Syn.* **1.** See note at FOOLISH.

si•lo ['saɪlou] *n., pl.* **-los;** *v.* **-loes, -loed, -lo•ing.** *—n.* **1** an airtight building or pit in which green fodder for farm animals is stored. **2** a vertical underground shaft in which missiles, nuclear rockets, etc. are housed ready for launching.
—v. put or store in a silo. ⟨< Sp. < L < Gk. *siros* graincellar⟩

silt [sɪlt] *n., v. —n.* very fine earth, sand, etc. carried by moving water and deposited as sediment: *The river mouth is being choked up with silt.*
—v. make or become choked or filled with silt or mud. ⟨ME; cf. Danish, Norwegian (dial.) *sylt* salt marsh. Akin to SALT.⟩
—sil'ta•tion, *n.*

silt•stone ['sɪlt,stoun] *n.* a kind of fine-grained sedimentary rock formed from silt that has been subjected to great pressure.

silt•y ['sɪlti] *adj.* **silt•i•er, silt•i•est.** of, like, or full of silt.

Si•lu•ri•an [sə'lʊriən] *or* [saɪ'lʊriən] *adj., n. Geology. —adj.* of or having to do with an early Paleozoic period or the rocks formed during it. The earliest vertebrates appeared toward the end of the Silurian period. See geological time chart in the Appendix.
—n. **1** an early period of the Paleozoic era, beginning approximately 375 million years ago. **2** the rocks formed during this period. ⟨< L *Silures*, an ancient people of SE Wales where rock of this period occurs abundantly⟩

sil•va ['sɪlvə] *n., pl.* **-vas** or **-vae** [-vi] *or* [-vaɪ]. **1** the forest trees of a particular region or time. **2** a treatise on forest trees, or a descriptive list or catalogue of trees. Also, **sylva.** ⟨< L *silva* forest⟩

sil•van ['sɪlvən] *adj.* See SYLVAN.

sil•ver ['sɪlvər] *n., adj., v. —n.* **1** *Chemistry.* a white, metallic element that is a precious metal. It takes a high polish, it can be moulded, stretched, hammered, or drawn thin without breaking, and it is the best conductor of heat and electricity. Silver is used for jewellery, cutlery, dishes, coins, etc. *Symbol*: Ag; *at.no.* 47; *at.mass* 107.87. **2** coins, especially those made of silver or having a silvery colour: *Do you have any silver?* **3** cutlery, dishes, etc. made of or plated with silver; silverware: *I spent half an hour polishing the silver.* **4** any cutlery. **5** the colour of silver. **6** something having the colour of silver. **7** a soft, lustrous, light grey or white: *The dull grey of her hair had turned to a lovely silver.* **8** SILVER MEDAL. **9** *Photography.* any of the silver halides used in film developing, etc., as silver iodide, silver bromide, or silver chloride.
—adj. **1** made of, plated with, or containing silver: *a silver spoon, silver thread.* **2** of, having to do with, or resembling silver: *a silver sheen, the silver standard. The back of a mirror has a silver coating.* **3** having the colour of silver: *silver buttons, silver shoes.* **4** of a soft, lustrous, light grey or white colour: *silver hair.* **5** having a light, clear, ringing sound. **6** eloquent: *a silver tongue.* **7** designating the 25th anniversary of an event: *a silver jubilee.*

—v. **1** cover or coat with silver or something like silver: *to silver a spoon, to silver a mirror.* **2** give a sheen to, like that of silver: *Moonlight silvered the lake.* **3** make or become white or very light grey: *Her hair had silvered since he had last seen her.* ⟨OE *siolfor*⟩

Silver Age **1** *Classical mythology.* the second age of humankind, inferior to the Golden Age. **2 silver age,** a period following, and inferior to, a period of brilliance.

sil•ver•ber•ry ['sɪlvər,bɛri] *n. Cdn.* WOLF WILLOW.

silver birch **1** a Eurasian birch (*Betula pendula*) having silvery white bark and drooping branches, widely cultivated as an ornamental tree. Also called **weeping birch. 2** any of various other birches having white bark.

silver bromide *Chemistry.* a yellowish, crystalline compound, not soluble in water and usually in the form of a powder, that darkens on exposure to light. It is used chiefly in photographic emulsions. *Formula*: AgBr

silver chloride *Chemistry.* a white, crystalline compound that darkens on exposure to light, used in photography, infrared spectrography, and the manufacture of medical silver preparations. *Formula*: AgCl

sil•ver•fish ['sɪlvər,fɪʃ] *n., pl.* **-fish** or **-fish•es. 1** a quick-moving, wingless insect (*Lepisma saccharina*), a species of bristletail having a body covered with silver scales, often found in buildings, where it feeds on food scraps and on sized papers and fabrics. **2** a silvery variety of goldfish. **3** any of various silver-coloured fishes, such as the tarpon.

silver fox **1** a colour phase of the red fox of North America, in which the fur is black but tipped with white. **2** the fur of this fox.

silver frost *Cdn., esp. Maritimes.* SILVER THAW.

silver gilt **1** silver that has been gilded or given a wash resembling gilt. **2** a thin decorative coating of silver leaf, silver plate, or an imitation of these. **—'sil•ver-,gilt,** *adj.*

silver iodide *Chemistry.* a pale yellow, powdery compound that darkens on exposure to light, used in photography and medicine and to seed clouds in artificial rainmaking. *Formula*: AgI

sil•ver•jar ['sɪlvər,dʒɑr] *n. Cdn.* **1** a young RINGED SEAL. **2** its fur.

silver leaf silver beaten into very thin sheets.

silver lining the brighter side of a gloomy or unfortunate situation.

silver maple a maple (*Acer saccharinum*) found especially in southern central and eastern Canada, having deeply lobed leaves that are light green above and silvery underneath. The silver maple is a popular shade and ornamental tree.

silver medal a medal, made of silver or being silver in colour, awarded to the person or team finishing in second place in a competition.

sil•vern ['sɪlvərn] *adj. Archaic.* of or like silver.

silver nitrate *Chemistry. Pharmacy.* a white, crystalline salt obtained by treating silver with nitric acid, used in medicine as an antiseptic, in photography, dyeing, etc. *Formula*: $AgNO_3$

silver paper paper covered or coated on one side with a metallic layer resembling silver. Silver paper is used as decoration in greeting cards, as a wrapping for chocolate bars, etc.

silver plate **1** dishes, cutlery, etc. made of silver or of copper, etc. plated with silver. **2** a plating of silver.

sil•ver–plate ['sɪlvər 'pleit] *v.* **-plat•ed, -plat•ing.** coat (another metal or a metal object) with silver, especially by electroplating: *This cutlery has been silver-plated.*

sil•ver•point ['sɪlvər,pɔɪnt] *n.* **1** a technique of drawing on specially prepared paper using a silver-tipped stylus. **2** a drawing produced in this way.

silver screen **1** a screen with a silverlike coating on which motion pictures are shown. **2** films collectively.

sil•ver•side ['sɪlvər,saɪd] *n.* any of a family (Atherinidae) of mostly small marine and freshwater fishes having a silver stripe along each side of the body. Also called **silversides.**

sil•ver•smith ['sɪlvər,smɪθ] *n.* an artist or artisan who makes and repairs articles of silver.

silver standard a monetary standard in which silver of a specified weight and fineness is the definition of the basic unit of currency.

silver thaw *Cdn.* **1** a storm of quick-freezing rain. **2** the glitter ice found after such a rain, encrusting trees, rocks, and other surfaces.

sil•ver•tip ['sɪlvər,tɪp] *n. Cdn.* a colour phase of the grizzly bear found in the Rocky Mountain region, in which the pelage is dark brown with the long hairs of the back and shoulders tipped with white.

sil•ver–tongued ['sɪlvər ,tʌŋd] *adj.* persuasive; eloquent: *a silver-tongued politician.*

sil•ver•ware ['sɪlvər,wɛr] *n.* **1** articles, especially cutlery or dishes, made of or plated with silver. **2** loosely, cutlery of any metal.

silver wedding the 25th anniversary of a wedding.

sil•ver•y ['sɪlvəri] *adj.* **1** having a lustre or sheen like that of silver: *silvery moonbeams, a silvery gown.* **2** having a soft, clear resonance; melodious: *silvery laughter, a silvery voice.* **3** containing or consisting of silver. **—'sil•ver•i•ness,** *n.*

sil•vics ['sɪlvɪks] *n.pl.* (*used with a singular verb*) the scientific study of forests and forest ecology. It combines forestry, zoology, and soil science. ⟨< *silva*⟩

sil•vi•cul•ture ['sɪlvə,kʌltʃər] *n.* the branch of forestry dealing with the cultivation and care of forests. Also, **sylviculture.** ⟨< F < L *silva* forest + *cultura* culture⟩ **—,sil•vi'cul•tur•al,** *adj.* **—,sil•vi'cul•tur•ist,** *n.*

sim•i•an ['sɪmiən] *adj., n. —adj.* of, having to do with, or like apes or monkeys.
—n. an ape or monkey. ⟨< L *simia* ape, apparently < Gk. (name) *Simias* < *simos* snub-nosed⟩

sim•i•lar ['sɪmələr] *adj.* **1** having characteristics in common; much the same as; like or alike: *A creek and a brook are similar. Your desk is similar to mine.* **2** *Geometry.* of figures, having the same shape but not necessarily the same size: *similar triangles.* ⟨< F *similaire* < L *similis* like⟩ **—'sim•i•lar•ly,** *adv.*

sim•i•lar•i•ty [,sɪmə'lærəti] *or* [,sɪmə'lɛrəti] *n., pl.* **-ties. 1** the state of being similar; a likeness; resemblance: *Their similarity is uncanny.* **2** some feature or point in which things are similar: *There are several similarities between the two models.*
☛ *Syn.* See note at RESEMBLANCE.

sim•i•le ['sɪməli] *n.* a figure of speech that expresses a comparison between two unlike things, usually introduced by *like* or *as. Examples*: *a face like marble. He had a mind as sharp as a tack. She could run like the wind.* Compare METAPHOR. ⟨< L *simile*, neut. adj., like⟩
☛ *Usage.* See note at METAPHOR.

si•mil•i•tude [sə'mɪlə,tjud] *or* [sə'mɪlə,tud] *n.* **1** a similarity or likeness: *similitude of structure.* **2** *Archaic.* a parable, allegory, or simile. **3** *Archaic.* a counterpart or image. ⟨< L *similitudo* < *similis* like⟩

Sim•men•tal ['zɪmən,tal] *n.* any of a breed of large cattle originally from Switzerland, having a white face and a red-and-white body, and used for beef and milk and, sometimes, as a draft animal. ⟨< *Simmental*, a valley in Switzerland⟩

sim•mer ['sɪmər] *v., n. —v.* **1 a** keep or stay at or just below the boiling point: *The stew should be simmered for two hours.* **b** cook in a simmering liquid: *Simmer the chicken pieces in the seasoned sauce.* **2** be on the point of bursting or breaking out; be in an inner turmoil: *The student simmered with indignation, but said nothing.*
simmer down, a calm down; cool down: *She told the excited child to simmer down.* **b** reduce (a liquid) by simmering it.
—n. the state of simmering; a degree of heat at or just below the boiling point: *Keep the sauce at a simmer.* ⟨earlier *simper*; ? imitative⟩
☛ *Syn. v.* **2.** See note at BOIL[1].

si•mo•ni•ac [sɪ'mouni,æk] *n.* one who engages in simony.

si•mo•ni•a•cal [,saɪmə'naɪəkəl] *or* [,sɪmə'naɪəkəl] *adj.* **1** guilty of simony. **2** of, having to do with, or involving simony. **—,si•mo'ni•a•cal•ly,** *adv.*

Si•mon Le•gree ['saɪmən lə'gri] a severe or too-demanding employer, officer, overseer, etc. ⟨< *Simon Legree*, a brutal slave dealer in the novel *Uncle Tom's Cabin* by Harriet Beecher Stowe⟩

si•mon–pure ['saɪmən 'pjʊr] *adj. Informal.* **1** real; genuine; authentic and unadulterated: *simon-pure maple sugar.* **2** morally incorruptible: *He's not as simon-pure as he pretends.* ⟨< *Simon Pure*, the name of a Quaker in Mrs. Centlivre's comedy *A Bold Stroke for a Wife* (1717), whose identity is questioned but proved genuine⟩

si•mo•ny ['saɪməni] *or* ['sɪməni] *n.* the buying or selling of ecclesiastical positions or promotions, pardons, etc. ⟨< LL *simonia*, from *Simon* Magus, a biblical Samaritan magician, who tried to buy the power of conferring the Holy Spirit⟩

si•moom [sɪ'mum] *n.* a hot, dry, suffocating, usually sand-laden, wind or whirlwind of the deserts of the Arabian peninsula and N Africa, occurring mainly in spring and summer. ⟨< Arabic *semūm*⟩

si•moon [sɪ'mun] *n.* simoom.

simp [sɪmp] *n. Slang.* a simpleton; fool. ⟨< *simpleton*⟩

sim•pa•ti•co [sɪm'pætɪ,kou] *or* [sɪm'pɑtɪ,kou] *adj.* congenial; agreeable; like-minded. ⟨< Ital. *simpatico* < L *sympathia* sympathy⟩

sim•per ['sɪmpər] *v., n.* —*v.* **1** smile in a silly, affected way. **2** express by a simper; say with a simper.
—*n.* a silly, affected smile. ⟨Cf. G *zimper(lich)* affected, coy⟩

sim•per•ing ['sɪmpərɪŋ] *adj., v.* —*adj.* silly and affected: *I can't stand simpering compliments.* **—'sim•per•ing•ly,** *adv.*
—*v.* ppr. of SIMPER.

sim•ple ['sɪmpəl] *adj.* **-pler, -plest;** *n.* —*adj.* **1** easy to do or understand: *a simple problem, simple language.* **2** not divided into parts; single; not compound. An oak leaf is a simple leaf. *John called his dog* is a simple sentence. **3** having few parts; not complex; not involved; elementary: *a simple one-celled animal.* **4** with nothing added; bare; mere: *My answer is the simple truth.* **5** without ornament; not rich or showy; plain: *simple clothes.* **6** natural; not affected; not showing off: *He has a pleasant, simple manner.* **7** honest; sincere: *a simple heart.* **8** not subtle; not sophisticated; innocent; artless: *a simple child.* **9** common; ordinary: *a simple citizen.* **10** humble: *Her parents were simple people.* **11** dull; stupid; weak in mind. **12** insignificant; requiring little attention: *Why are you making such a fuss, it's just a simple scratch.* **13** *Botany.* originating from a single pistil or carpel. **14** *Music.* of time or metre, having only two, three, or four beats per measure.
—*n.* **1** a foolish, stupid person. **2** something simple. **3** *Archaic.* **a** a herb or other plant used in medicine. **b** the medicine made from it. ⟨ME < OF < L *simplex*⟩ **—'sim•ple•ness,** *n.*
☛ *Syn. adj.* **1.** See note at EASY.

simple closed curve *Geometry.* a closed plane curve that does not cross itself.

simple equation *Mathematics.* LINEAR EQUATION.

simple fraction COMMON FRACTION.

simple fracture a clean fracture in which the broken ends of the bone do not pierce the skin. Compare COMPOUND FRACTURE.

sim•ple–heart•ed ['sɪmpəl 'hɑrtɪd] *adj.* having or showing a simple, unaffected, sincere nature.

simple interest interest paid only on the principal of a loan, etc. Compare COMPOUND INTEREST.

simple machine any of several elementary devices for transmitting a force or changing its direction in order to overcome a resistance and lessen work. Usually considered as the six basic types are the **lever, pulley, wheel and axle, inclined plane, screw,** and **wedge.**

sim•ple–mind•ed ['sɪmpəl 'maɪndɪd] *adj.* **1** natural and inexperienced; artless; unsophisticated: *a simple-minded approach to a complex problem.* **2** foolish or feeble-minded. **3** mentally retarded. **—'sim•ple-'mind•ed•ly,** *adv.* **—'sim•ple-'mind•ed•ness,** *n.*

simple sentence *Grammar.* a sentence consisting of one main clause. *Examples: The whistle blew. We got back yesterday.*

sim•ple•ton ['sɪmpəltən] *n.* a silly person; fool. ⟨< *simple*⟩

sim•plex ['sɪmplɛks] *adj., n.* —*adj.* **1** simple; not compound or complex. **2** permitting transmission of signals in one direction only, as in a telegraphic system, computer circuit, etc. Compare DUPLEX (def. 2), DIPLEX. **3** *Genetics.* referring to a family in which there is only a single case of a specific genetic trait.
—*n. Geometry.* the simplest figure possible in Euclidean space of a specified dimension; in one dimension, a line, in two dimensions, a triangle, etc.

sim•plic•i•ty [sɪm'plɪsəti] *n., pl.* **-ties. 1** the state or quality of being simple in form or structure; freedom from complexity: *the simplicity of a design. They appreciated the simplicity of the directions he had given them.* **2** absence of luxury, ornamentation, etc.; plainness: *simplicity of dress, the simplicity of a lifestyle.* **3** absence of show or pretence; sincerity or naturalness: *The old woman answered all their questions with simplicity.* **4** lack of shrewdness; ignorance or dullness: *His simplicity made him easy to fool.* ⟨< L *simplicitas* < *simplex*, *-icis* simple⟩

sim•pli•fi•ca•tion [,sɪmpləfə'keiʃən] *n.* **1** the act or process of simplifying: *Simplification of the plan will take some time.* **2** something that has been simplified: *This is a simplification of an earlier model.*

sim•pli•fy ['sɪmplə,faɪ] *v.* **-fied, -fy•ing.** make simple or simpler; make plainer, easier, or more streamlined: *to simplify a design. The plot of your story is a little confusing, and should be simplified.* ⟨< F *simplifier* < Med.L *simplificare* < L *simplus* simple + *facere* make⟩ **—'sim•pli,fi•er,** *n.*

sim•plism ['sɪmplɪzəm] *n.* the habit of resorting to false or undue simplicity. **—'sim•plist,** *n.*

sim•plis•tic [sɪm'plɪstɪk] *adj.* **1** simplified to such an extent as to be misleading; given a false simplicity by ignoring some important aspects: *Her interpretation of the issue of international disarmament is biassed and simplistic.* **2** given to oversimplification: *I find him too simplistic.* **—sim'plis•ti•cal•ly,** *adv.*

sim•ply ['sɪmpli] *adv.* **1** in a simple manner: *to dress simply. She explained the procedure simply and clearly. You are talking as simply as an idiot.* **2** merely; only: *The baby did not simply cry, he yelled. He thinks of his car simply as a means of transportation.* **3** really; absolutely: *simply perfect.*

sim•u•la•crum [,sɪmjə'leikrəm] *n., pl.* **-cra** [-krə] *or* **-crums. 1** a faint, shadowy, or unreal likeness; mere semblance: *The dictator permitted only a simulacrum of democracy.* **2** an image. ⟨< L *simulacrum*, ult. < *similis* like⟩

sim•u•late ['sɪmjə,leit] *v.* **-lat•ed, -lat•ing;** *adj.* —*v.* **1** pretend; feign: *Anne simulated interest to please her friend.* **2** act like; look like; imitate: *Certain insects simulate leaves.* **3** manufacture or be an imitation of: *to simulate pearls. This drink simulates fruit juice.* **4** reproduce or imitate the conditions of for training, experimentation, etc.: *to simulate flight in training pilots.* **5** generate a model or virtual version of, using a computer.
—*adj. Archaic.* simulated. ⟨< L *simulare* < *similis* like⟩
—'sim•u,la•tor, *n.*

sim•u•la•tion [,sɪmjə'leiʃən] *n.* **1** the act of simulating something. **2** a simulated event, product, display, etc.

sim•u•la•tive ['sɪmjələtɪv] *or* ['sɪmjə,leitɪv] *adj.* simulating.

si•mul•cast ['saɪməl,kæst] *or* ['sɪməl,kæst] *v.* **-cast** *or* **-cast•ed, -cast•ing;** *n.* —*v.* broadcast a program over radio and television at the same time or over more than one radio or television station at the same time: *CBC FM Radio and Television will simulcast the concert live from the civic auditorium.*
—*n.* a broadcast made in this way. ⟨< *simul(taneous)* + *(broad)cast*⟩

si•mul•ta•ne•ous [,saɪməl'teiniəs] *or* [,sɪməl'teiniəs] *adj.* existing, done, or happening at the same time: *The two simultaneous shots sounded like one.* ⟨< Med.L *simultaneus* simulated; confused in sense with L *simul* at the same time⟩ **—,si•mul'ta•ne•ous•ly,** *adv.* **—,si•mul'ta•ne•ous•ness** or **,si•mul•ta'ne•i•ty** [-tə'niəti] *or* [-tə'neiəti], *n.*

simultaneous equations *Algebra.* two or more equations whose variables have the same values in each equation and are equal in number to the number of equations.

sin[1] [sɪn] *n., v.* **sinned, sin•ning.** —*n.* **1 a** a breaking of the law of God. **b** the state or condition resulting from this. **2** any act regarded as immoral or bad; wrongdoing: *It's a sin to waste food.*
—*v.* **1** break the law of God. **2** do wrong. ⟨OE *synn*⟩

sin[2] [sin] *n.* **1** the twenty-fourth letter of the Hebrew alphabet. **2** the twelfth letter of the Arabic alphabet. See table of alphabets in the Appendix. ⟨< Hebrew⟩
☛ *Hom.* SEEN, SCENE.

sin[3] *Mathematics.* SINE[1].

SIN [sɪn] *Cdn.* SOCIAL INSURANCE NUMBER.

Sin•bad ['sɪnbæd] *n.* in the *Arabian Nights*, a sailor who had seven extraordinary voyages.

sin bin *Cdn. Slang. Hockey.* PENALTY BOX.

since [sɪns] *prep., conj., adv.* —*prep.* **1** from (a past time) continuously till now: *The package has been ready since noon.* **2** at any time between (some past time or event) and the present: *We have not seen her since Saturday.*
—*conj.* **1** in the course of the period following the time when: *He has written home only once since he left us.* **2** continuously or counting from the time when: *Charles has worked hard since he left school. It is five years since we moved.* **3** because: *Since you feel tired, you should rest.*
—*adv.* **1** from then till now: *She got sick last Saturday and has been in bed ever since.* **2** at some time between a particular past time and the present: *At first she refused but she has since*

accepted. **3** before now; ago: *I heard that old joke long since.* ⟨ME *sinnes, sithenes* < OE *siththan* then, later < *sith* late⟩
☛ *Syn. conj.* See note at BECAUSE.

sin•cere [sɪn'sir] *adj.* **-cer•er, -cer•est.** free from pretence or deceit; genuine in feeling; honest and straightforward: *a sincere expression of sympathy, a sincere person.* ⟨< L *sincerus*⟩ **—sin'cere•ly,** *adv.* **—sin'cer•i•ty** [-'sɛrəti] or **sin'cere•ness,** *n.*

sin•ci•put ['sɪnsɪ,pʌt] *n., pl.* **sin•ci•puts** or **sin•cip•i•ta** [sɪn'sɪpɪtə]. *Anatomy.* the upper front part of the skull. ⟨< L < *semi* half + *caput* head⟩ **—sin'cip•i•tal,** *adj.*

Sind•bad ['sɪnbæd] *n.* See SINBAD.

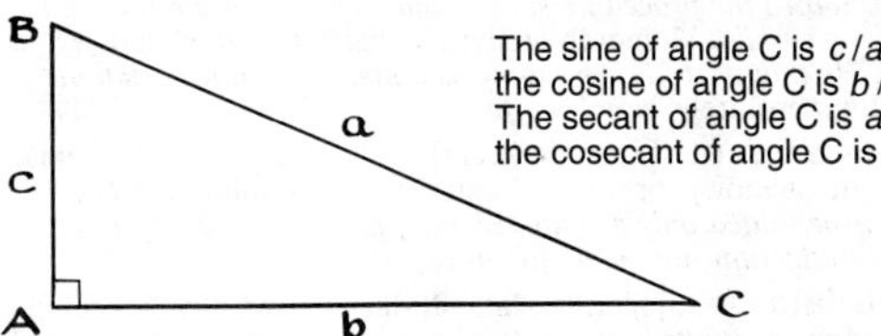
Triangle ABC is a right triangle of which A is the right angle and a is the hypotenuse.
B
C
A
a
b
C
The sine of angle C is c/a and the cosine of angle C is b/a. The secant of angle C is a/b and the cosecant of angle C is a/c.

sine¹ [saɪn] *n. Trigonometry.* **1** in a right triangle, the ratio of the length of the side opposite an acute angle to the length of the hypotenuse. In the diagram, the sine of angle C = c/a (or AB/BC); the sine of angle B = b/a (or AC/BC). **2** in a circle, the ratio of the line forming a right angle with the radius that passes through one end of an arc, to the radius passing through the other end of the arc. ⟨< L *sinus* bend, bosom < Med.L translation of Arabic *jaib* sine, bosom⟩
☛ *Hom.* SIGN, SYNE.

si•ne² ['sɪni] *or* ['saɪni] *prep. Latin.* without.

si•ne•cure ['saɪnə,kjʊr] *or* ['sɪnə,kjʊr] *n.* **1** an extremely easy job; a position requiring little or no work and usually paying well. **2** an ecclesiastical benefice without parish duties. ⟨< Med.L *(beneficium) sine cura* (benefice) without care (of souls)⟩ **—'si•ne•cure,ship,** *n.* **—'si•ne,cur•ist,** *n.*

sine curve [saɪn] *Mathematics.* a curve whose equation is $y = \sin x$. Also called **sinusoid.**

si•ne di•e ['sɪni 'diei] *or* ['saɪni 'daɪi] *Latin.* without a day fixed for future action: *The committee adjourned sine die.* ⟨literally, without day⟩

si•ne qua non ['sɪni kwɑ 'noun] *or* ['saɪni kwei 'nɒn] something essential; an indispensable condition or thing: *It was a sine qua non that all parties concerned should be included in the negotiations.* ⟨< LL *sine qua non* without which not⟩

sin•ew ['sɪnju] *n.* **1** a tough, strong band or cord that joins muscle to bone; tendon. **2** strength; energy: *moral sinew.* **3** Usually, **sinews,** *pl.* a means of strength or power; mainstay: *Guns are the sinews of war.*
—v. strengthen by furnishing with sinews. ⟨OE *sionu*⟩

sine wave [saɪn] *Physics.* a periodic oscillation having a SINE CURVE as its wave form.

sin•ew•y ['sɪnjui] *adj.* **1** strong and muscular: *The blacksmith had broad shoulders and sinewy arms.* **2** vigorous; forcible: *sinewy arguments, sinewy prose.* **3** of meat, having many or large sinews; tough; stringy. **—'sin•ew•i•ness,** *n.*

sin•fo•ni•a [,sɪnfə'niə]; *Italian,* [,sinfɔ'nia] *n., pl.* **-ni•e** [-'niei]. *Music.* **1** a symphony. **2** an orchestral overture, especially to an 18th century Italian opera. ⟨< Ital.⟩

sin•fo•niet•ta [,sɪnfən'jɛtə]; *Italian,* [,sinfɔ'njetta] *n.* **1** a short instrumental piece modelled on the symphony. **2** a small orchestra, usually consisting chiefly or entirely of strings. ⟨< Ital. *sinfonietta* < dim. of *sinfonia* symphony⟩

sin•ful ['sɪnfəl] *adj.* characterized by sin or having a tendency to sin. **—'sin•ful•ly,** *adv.* **—'sin•ful•ness,** *n.*

sing [sɪŋ] *v.* **sang** or (*archaic*) **sung, sung, sing•ing;** *n. —v.* **1** make music with the voice: *She often sings on television.* **2** utter musically: *He seemed almost to sing his lines from the play.* **3** chant; intone: *The priest sings Mass.* **4** make pleasant musical sounds: *Birds sing.* **5** bring something into a given state by singing: *Sing the baby to sleep.* **6** tell in song or poetry: *Homer sang of Troy.* **7** tell of in song or poetry: *They sang the deeds of heroes.* **8** proclaim: *sing a person's praises.* **9** make a ringing, whistling, humming, or buzzing sound: *The teakettle sang.* **10** have the sensation of a ringing, buzzing, or humming sound: *A bad cold made her ears sing.* **11** admit of being sung: *This arrangement of the song sings more easily than that one.* **12** exult; be full of joy: *His heart sang at the sound of her step.* **13** *Slang.* reveal; inform; tell all.
sing out, call loudly; shout.
—n. **1** a singing, ringing, or whistling sound: *the sing of a bullet in flight.* **2 a** a time or round of singing, especially in a group: *to have a good sing.* **b** a social function where people gather to sing: *There is a carol sing over at the city hall at 9 p.m. tonight.* ⟨OE *singan*⟩ **—'sing•a•ble,** *adj.*

sing. singular.

Sing•a•pore ['sɪŋə,pɔr] an independent republic, member of the British Commonwealth, on an island off the S tip of the Malay Peninsula and adjacent islets. Its capital city has the same name. **—,Sing•a'por•e•an,** *adj.*

singe [sɪndʒ] *v.* **singed, singe•ing;** *n. —v.* **1** burn a little; scorch: *He got too close to the fire and singed his eyebrows.* **2** expose (the carcass of a chicken, etc.) to flame for a very short while to burn off down, fuzz, etc. **3** burn the ends of (hair) after a haircut. **4** remove the nap from (cloth) by burning during manufacture.
singe (one's) **wings,** be slightly harmed, especially by some risky venture.
—n. **1** the act of singeing. **2** a slight burn resulting from this. ⟨OE *sengan*⟩

sing•er ['sɪŋər] *n.* **1** a person who sings, especially one who sings well or whose profession is singing: *She's an opera singer.* **2** a bird having a varied and musical call: *Our canary is a fine singer.*

Sin•gha•lese [,sɪŋgə'liz] *n. or adj.* See SINHALESE.

singing house *Cdn.* in Inuit culture, a special building where communal singing and dancing take place.

sin•gle ['sɪŋgəl] *adj., n., v.* **-gled, -gling.** *—adj.* **1** one and no more; only one: *Please give me a single piece of paper.* **2** regarded as distinct from others in the same class; particular: *open every single day of the year.* **3** for only one; individual: *The sisters share one room with two single beds in it.* **4** without others; alone: *He came to the party single.* **5 a** not married: *a single man.* **b** of unmarried people: *the single lifestyle.* **6** having only one on each side: *The knights engaged in single combat.* **7** of a flower, having only one set of petals. There are both single and double varieties of roses. **8** not double; not multiple: *single houses.* **9** sincere; honest; genuine: *She showed single devotion to her religion.*
—n. **1** a single thing or person. **2** *Baseball.* **a** a hit that allows a runner on base to advance by one base only. **b** a hit that allows the batter to reach first base only. **3** *Cricket.* a hit for which one run is scored. **4** a game for two people only. **5** *Football.* a single point scored by kicking into or beyond the end zone; rouge. **6 singles,** *pl.* a game played with only one person on each side. **7** (*adjl.*) **singles,** for single people looking for social companions: *a singles club.*
—v. **1** pick (one) from among others (*used with* **out**): *The teacher singled Imelda out for praise.* **2** *Baseball.* **a** make a hit that allows (a runner on base) to advance by one base only. **b** make a hit that allows the batter to reach first base. ⟨ME < OF < L *singulus*⟩
☛ *Syn. adj.* **1. Single,** SOLE¹, ONLY = one alone. **Single** emphasizes the idea of one and no more: *She buys a single new dress each year.* **Sole** adds the idea of being by itself, the single one (or group) that there is or that is to be considered: *My sole purpose is to help you.* **Only,** often a less emphatic substitute for **sole,** emphasizes the idea of being by itself, without others of its kind: *He is an only child.* Unlike **single,** both **sole** and **only** can sometimes be used with plural nouns: *the sole survivors, our only friends.*

single–acting ['sɪŋgəl 'æktɪŋ] *adj.* of an engine, pump, etc., having pistons that act in one direction only.

single bed a bed wide enough for one person: *The hotel room had two single beds.*

sin•gle–breast•ed ['sɪŋgəl ,brɛstɪd] *adj.* of a coat, jacket, etc., overlapping across the breast just enough to fasten with only one button or row of buttons.

single entry a simple style of bookkeeping in which amounts received and those paid out are recorded on one account only. Compare DOUBLE ENTRY.

single file 1 a line of persons or things arranged one behind another. **2** in a line, one behind the other: *We walked single file along the narrow path.*

sin•gle–foot ['sɪŋgəl ,fʊt] *n., v. —n.* the gait of a horse in which one foot is put down at a time; RACK³.
—v. of a horse, go at a single-foot.

single–gene disorder ['sɪŋgəl 'dʒin] *Genetics.* a genetic defect due to mutation in a single gene or gene pair.

sin•gle–hand•ed ['sɪŋgəl 'hændɪd] *adj., adv.* —*adj.* **1** without help from others; working alone: *a single-handed effort.* **2** using or requiring only one hand: *a single-handed sword.*
—*adv.* **1** without help: *She built all the cupboards single-handed.* **2** with only one hand: *It is pretty hard to tie a knot single-handed.* —**'sin•gle-'hand•ed•ly,** *adv.* —**'sin•gle-'hand•ed•ness,** *n.*

sin•gle–heart•ed ['sɪŋgəl 'hɑrtɪd] *adj.* having or showing sincerity of heart or purpose. —**'sin•gle-'heart•ed•ly,** *adv.* —**'sin•gle-'heart•ed•ness,** *n.*

sin•gle–mind•ed ['sɪŋgəl 'maɪndɪd] *adj.* **1** having or showing sincerity and devotion to one purpose or aim. **2** sincere and guileless. —**'sin•gle-'mind•ed•ly,** *adv.* —**'sin•gle-'mind•ed•ness,** *n.*

sin•gle•ness ['sɪŋgəlnɪs] *n.* the state or quality of being single: *singleness of purpose. After years of singleness she decided to get married.*

sin•gle–space ['sɪŋgəl ˌspeis] *v.* **-spaced, -spac•ing;** *adv.* —*v.* write, type, or key with no blank lines between lines of print: *Quotations set off within an essay should always be single-spaced.*
—*adv.* with no blank lines between lines of print: *Always key quotations single-space.*

sin•gle•stick ['sɪŋgəlˌstɪk] *n.* formerly: **1** a stick with a handguard, used instead of a sword in fencing. **2** the art of fencing with such a stick.

sin•glet ['sɪŋglɪt] *n.* a kind of sleeveless undershirt or jersey worn by men.

sin•gle•ton ['sɪŋgəltən] *n.* **1** something occurring singly or apart from others; especially, a child or animal born alone, without a twin. **2** a playing card that is the only one of a suit in a person's hand. **3** *Hockey, etc.* a single point.

sin•gle–track ['sɪŋgəl 'træk] *adj.* **1** of a railway, etc., having only a single track. **2** *Informal.* preoccupied or able to deal with only one thing at a time; one-track.

sin•gle•tree ['sɪŋgəlˌtri] *n.* the swinging bar of a carriage or wagon, to which the traces are fastened. Also, **swingletree.**

sin•gly ['sɪŋgli] *adv.* **1** as a single person or thing; separately: *Misfortunes never come singly.* **2** one by one; one at a time in sequence: *Let us consider each point singly.* **3** by one's own efforts; without help; single-handed.

sing•song ['sɪŋˌsɒŋ] *n., adj., v.* —*n.* **1** a monotonous, up-and-down rhythm. **2** a monotonous tone or sound in speaking. **3** a monotonous or jingling verse. **4** a gathering for singing.
—*adj.* monotonous in rhythm: *a singsong recitation of the multiplication table.*
—*v.* recite or speak in a singsong way.

sin•gu•lar ['sɪŋgjələr] *adj., n.* —*adj.* **1** extraordinary; unusual: *"Treasure Island" is a story of singular interest to children.* **2** strange; queer; peculiar: *The detectives were greatly puzzled by the singular nature of the crime.* **3** being the only one of its kind: *an event singular in history.* **4** *Grammar.* signifying or denoting reference to only one person, thing, instance, etc. *Dog* is singular; *dogs* is plural. **5** *Logic.* individual or separate; particular as opposed to general.
—*n. Grammar.* **1** the singular form of a word. **2** a word or construction in the singular. **3** the category itself to which such words, forms, etc. belong: *Some languages mark neither singular nor plural.* ⟨< L *singularis* < *singulus* single⟩ —**'sin•gu•lar•ly,** *adv.*

sin•gu•lar•i•ty [ˌsɪŋgjə'lærɪti] *or* [ˌsɪŋgjə'lɛrɪti] *n., pl.* **-ties.** **1** peculiarity; oddness; strangeness; unusualness: *The singularity of the stranger's appearance attracted much attention.* **2** something singular; a peculiar trait or feature; oddity: *One of the giraffe's singularities is the length of its neck.*

sin•gu•lar•ize ['sɪŋgjələˌraɪz] *v.* **-ized, -iz•ing.** **1** make singular. **2** *Grammar.* put into the singular: *Singularize all the nouns and verbs in this sentence.*

Sin•ha•la ['sɪnhələ] *or* ['sɪnələ] *n.* the Indic language of the Sinhalese, which is the official language of Sri Lanka.

Sin•ha•lese [ˌsɪnhə'liz] *or* [ˌsɪnə'liz] *n., pl.* **-lese;** *adj.* —*n.* **1** a member of a people who make up the majority of the population of Sri Lanka. **2** Sinhala.
—*adj.* of or having to do with the Sinhalese or their language. ⟨< Skt. *Sinhala* Sri Lanka + E *-ese*⟩

sin•is•ter ['sɪnɪstər] *adj.* **1** showing or suggesting ill will or evil; wicked or malignant: *a sinister look, a sinister plan, a sinister motive.* **2** giving a warning of bad fortune or trouble; ominous: *a sinister sky, sinister rumblings of rebellion.* **3** extremely unfortunate; disastrous: *She met a sinister fate.* **4** of or on the left. **5** *Heraldry.* of or on the left-hand side of a shield, etc. from the point of view of the person bearing it; on the right of a person viewing it. ⟨< OF *sinistre* or L *sinister* on or to the left; in foretelling the future, the left side was considered by the Romans to be unlucky or ill-fated⟩ —**'sin•is•ter•ly,** *adv.* —**'sin•is•ter•ness,** *n.*

sin•is•tral ['sɪnɪstrəl] *adj.* **1** of or having to do with the left side; left; left-handed. **2** of a spiral shell, having the whorl rising clockwise from the opening at bottom left toward the apex. —**'sin•is•tral•ly,** *adv.* —**ˌsin•is'tral•i•ty** [ˌsɪnɪ'strælətі], *n.*

Si•nit•ic [sɪ'nɪtɪk] *or* [saɪ'nɪtɪk] *n., adj.* —*n.* the branch of the Sino-Tibetan family of languages that comprises all the various dialects and languages for which the model is standard literary Chinese.
—*adj.* of or having to do with the Chinese people, language or culture.

sink [sɪŋk] *v.* **sank** or **sunk, sunk, sink•ing;** *n.* —*v.* **1** go down; fall slowly; go lower and lower: *The sun is sinking. He sank to the floor in a faint.* **2** make go down; make fall: *Lack of rain sank the water level of the lake.* **3** go or cause to go beneath the surface (of water, quicksand, etc.): *The ship is sinking. The submarine sank two ships.* **4** drop gradually in overall height, surface level, etc. over time or space: *The lake sinks yearly. Between here and Sutton the land sinks to nearly sea level.* **5** become lower or weaker: *The wind has sunk.* **6** make lower; reduce: *She sank her voice to a whisper.* **7** pass gradually (into a state of sleep, silence, oblivion, etc.). **8** go or cause to go deeply: *Let the lesson sink into your mind.* **9** make by digging or drilling: *The workers are sinking a well.* **10** set into a hole dug or drilled: *to sink a pipe.* **11** insert or fasten into a hollow space, etc.: *a stone sunk into the wall.* **12** become worse: *Her spirits sank.* **13** come nearer and nearer to death: *Come quickly, your mother is sinking fast.* **14** stoop (to a base action or moral condition); lower oneself in character. **15** defeat or demoralize. **16** invest (money), especially unprofitably. **17** keep quiet about; conceal: *to sink evidence.* **18** fall in; become hollow: *The sick man's cheeks have sunk.* **19** *Basketball.* **a** put (the ball) through the hoop. **b** score (a point) in this way. **20** *Golf.* **a** hit (the ball) into a hole. **b** score by doing so with (a stroke).
sink in, be properly understood and assimilated: *I've told him three times, but it doesn't seem to have sunk in.*
—*n.* **1** a shallow basin or tub with a drainpipe. **2** a drain; sewer. **3** a place where dirty water or any filth collects. **4** a place of vice or corruption. **5** a low-lying area in land where waters collect, or where they disappear by sinking downward or by evaporation. **6** a depression in land caused by the collapse or dissolution of the structures or materials beneath it. ⟨OE *sincan*⟩ —**'sink•a•ble,** *adj.*
☛ *Hom.* SYNC.

sink•age ['sɪŋkɪdʒ] *n.* the act or amount of sinking.

sink•er ['sɪŋkər] *n.* **1** a person or thing that sinks. **2** a lead weight for sinking a line or net for fishing. **3** *U.S. Slang.* a doughnut. **4** *Baseball.* a ball pitched so as to curve sharply downward just before reaching the plate.

sink•hole ['sɪŋkˌhoul] *n.* **1** the hole in a sink, etc. for waste to pass through. **2** a hollow or cavity in limestone, etc. through which surface water drains into an underground passage or cavern. **3** *Cdn.* **a** MUSKEG (def. 1). **b** a small depression in the prairie, usually with alkaline springs beneath it and so having no herbage. **4** SINK (def. 6). **5** SINK (defs. 3, 5). **6** SINK (def. 4).

sinking fund a fund set up by a government, corporation, etc. to offset a borrowing. Certain sums of money are regularly set aside to accumulate at interest so that when the debt, such as a debenture, matures, there will be enough money to pay it off.

sin•less ['sɪnlɪs] *adj.* without sin; free from sin. —**'sin•less•ly,** *adv.* —**'sin•less•ness,** *n.*

sin•ner ['sɪnər] *n.* a person who sins or does wrong.

Sinn Fein ['ʃɪn 'fein] a political organization in Ireland, founded about 1905, for the complete political separation of Ireland from Britain. ⟨< Irish *Sinn Féin* we ourselves⟩ —**Sinn Feiner.**

Sino– **1** Often **sino-**, Chinese: *sinology.* **2** Chinese and ——: *Sino-Japanese = Chinese and Japanese.*

si•nol•o•gist or **Si•nol•o•gist** [saɪ'nɒlədʒɪst] *or* [sɪ'nɒlədʒɪst] *n.* a person versed in sinology, especially one whose work it is.

si•no•logue or **Si•no•logue** ['saɪnəˌlɒg] *or* ['sɪnəˌlɒg] *n.* sinologist.

si•nol•o•gy or **Si•nol•o•gy** [saɪ'nɒlədʒi] *or* [sɪ'nɒlədʒi] *n.* the study of Chinese literature, art, culture, etc. —**ˌsi•no'log•i•cal,** *adj.*

Si•no–Ti•bet•an ['saɪnou tə'bɛtən] *n.* a family of languages that includes Burmese, Thai, and Tibetan, as well as most of the languages of China.

sin•ter ['sɪntər] *n., v.* —*n.* **1** a crust or deposit of silica or calcium carbonate formed on rocks, etc. by the evaporation of mineral springs, geysers, etc. **2** *Metallurgy.* a conglomerate of materials fused by sintering.
—*v. Metallurgy.* **1** fuse (various materials) to form larger masses by the combined action of heat and pressure. **2** undergo this process. ⟨< G *Sinter* dross, slag⟩

sin•u•ate *adj.* ['sɪnjuɪt] *or* ['sɪnju,eit]; *v.* ['sɪnju,eit] *adj., v.* **-at•ed, -at•ing.** —*adj.* **1** winding; sinuous; wavy. **2** *Botany.* especially of leaves, having a wavy margin, with deep indentations. See LEAF for picture.
—*v.* follow a sinuous course; bend this way and that. ⟨< L *sinuatus*, pp. of *sinuare* bend, wind < *sinus* a curve⟩ **—'sin•u•ate•ly,** *adv.* **—,sin•u'a•tion,** *n.*

sin•u•os•i•ty [,sɪnju'ɒsəti] *n., pl.* **-ties. 1** a sinuous form or character; the quality or state of being sinuous. **2** something that is sinuous; a curve or bend.

sin•u•ous ['sɪnjuəs] *adj.* **1** having many curves or turns; winding: *The motion of a snake is sinuous.* **2** indirect; devious. **3** morally crooked. ⟨< L *sinuosus* < *sinus* curve⟩ **—'sin•u•ous•ly,** *adv.* **—'sin•u•ous•ness,** *n.*

si•nus ['saɪnəs] *n.* **1** *Anatomy.* **a** a cavity or hollow in the body, especially one of the cavities in the bones of the skull that connect with the nose. **b** a large channel for venous blood. **2** *Pathology.* a long, narrow channel leading from an abscess and serving for the discharge of pus. **3** *Botany.* a curve or indentation between the lobes of a leaf. **4 a** any curved hollow or cavity. **b** any curve or bend. ⟨< L, curve⟩

si•nus•i•tis [,saɪnə'saitɪs] *n. Pathology.* the inflammation of a sinus of the skull.

si•nus•oid ['saɪnə,sɔɪd] *n. Mathematics.* SINE CURVE. **—,si•nus'oid•al,** *adj.*

Si•on ['saɪən] *n.* Zion.

Siou•an ['suən] *n., adj.* —*n.* **1** a stock or family of languages spoken by peoples of the First Nations of central and eastern North America. **2** a member of any of the peoples speaking one of these languages, including the Assiniboines and the Dakota.
—*adj.* of, having to do with, or designating these peoples or their languages.

Sioux [su] *n., pl.* **Sioux** [su] *or* [suz] *or adj.* **1** Dakota. **2** Siouan.

sip [sɪp] *v.* **sipped, sip•ping;** *n.* —*v.* drink little by little: *She sipped her tea.*
—*n.* a very small drink: *He took a sip.* ⟨OE *sypian* take in moisture⟩
☛ *Syn. v.* See note at DRINK.

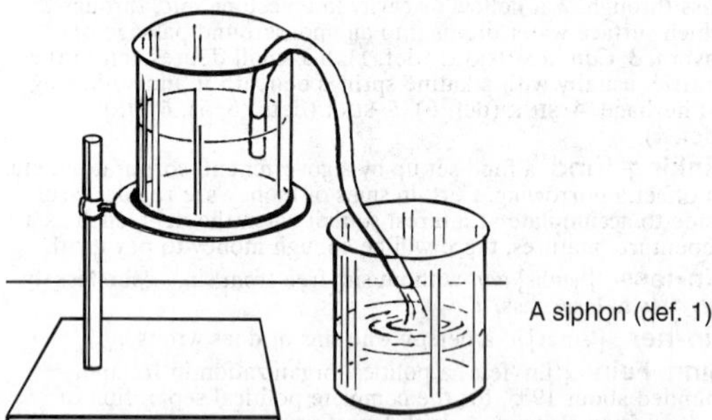

A siphon (def. 1)

si•phon ['səifən] *n., v.* —*n.* **1** a bent tube through which liquid can be drawn over the edge of one container into another at a lower level by air pressure. **2** a bottle for soda water, having a tube through which the liquid is forced out by the pressure of the gas in the bottle. **3** a tube-shaped organ of some shellfish for drawing in and expelling water, etc.
—*v.* **1** draw off by means of a siphon or pass through a siphon: *She siphoned water from the rain barrel onto the garden.* **2** flow through a siphon; be so drawn off. **3** draw off as if with a siphon. Also, **syphon.** ⟨< L < Gk. *siphōn* pipe⟩

si•phon•age ['səifənɪdʒ] *n.* the act, object, or amount of siphoning.

si•phon•al ['səifənəl] *adj.* of or having to do with a siphon.

siphon bottle SIPHON (*n.* def. 2).

sip•pet ['sɪpɪt] *n.* **1** a bit or fragment of anything. **2** a small piece of bread, toast, etc. for dipping in a sauce, gravy, etc.; sop. **3** a crouton. ⟨prob. dim. of *sop*⟩

sir [sɜr]; *unstressed,* [sər] *n.* **1** sometimes (*especially in letter saluations*), **Sir,** a respectful or formal term of address used to a man (*used only alone, never with a name*): *Excuse me, sir.* **2 Sir,** the title used before the given name or full name of a knight or baronet: *Sir Wilfrid Laurier.* **3** *Archaic.* a term of respect used before a man's given name or the title of his office or profession: *sir priest, sir knight.* ⟨var. of *sire*⟩
☛ *Usage.* **Sir** (def. 2) is usually used with a person's given name plus his surname or with a given name alone, but not with the surname only. Thus *Sir Winston Churchill* might have been addressed or referred to as *Sir Winston*, but not *Sir Churchill.*

sir•dar ['sɜrdɑr] *or* [sər'dɑr] *n.* **1** a leader or military commander in India, Pakistan, and Afghanistan. **2** formerly, the British commander of the Egyptian army. ⟨< Hind. *sardar* chief < Persian⟩

sire [saɪr] *n., v.* **sired, sir•ing.** —*n.* **1** *Poetic or archaic.* a father or male ancestor. **2** the male parent of an animal, especially a domestic animal: *The sire of Danger, a great racehorse, was Lightning.* **3** *Archaic.* a respectful form of address for a king or a great noble: *"I'm killed, Sire!" said the messenger to King Richard.*
—*v.* be the father of; beget (*used especially for male domestic animals*): *Lightning sired Danger.* ⟨ME < OF < VL *seior* < L *senior*, nom., older. Doublet of SENIOR.⟩

si•ren ['saɪrən] *n.* **1** a device that produces a loud, penetrating sound, used as a warning of the approach of an ambulance, police vehicle, etc. or as a warning of an air raid. **2** *Greek mythology.* one of a group of human or partly human female creatures who by their sweet, enchanting singing lured sailors to destruction upon the rocks where the sirens lived. **3** a dangerously seductive woman; temptress. **4** (*adjl.*) of a siren or like that of a siren; enchanting. **5** any of a family (Sirenidae) of eel-like salamanders having permanent gills and no posterior limbs. ⟨ME < OF < L < Gk. *seirēn*⟩ **—'si•ren,like,** *adj.*

si•re•ni•an [saɪ'riniən] *n.* SEA COW.

si•ren•ic [saɪ'rɛnɪk] *adj.* sirenlike; seductive; alluring.

Sir•i•us ['siriəs] *n. Astronomy.* the brightest (fixed) star in the sky; the Dog Star. ⟨< L < Gk. *Seirios*⟩

sir•loin ['sɜrlɔɪn] *n.* a choice cut of beef from the part of the loin in front of the rump. See BEEF and VEAL for pictures. ⟨obs. *surloin* < var. of OF *surlonge* < *sur* over (< L *super*) + *longe* loin, ult. < L *lumbus*⟩

si•roc•co [sə'rɒkou] *n., pl.* **-cos. 1** a hot, dry, southerly wind of N Africa that often picks up moisture as it crosses the Mediterranean, reaching Sicily and S Italy as a hot, oppressively humid wind. **2** any hot oppressive wind. Also, **scirocco** [ʃə'rɒkou]. ⟨< F < Ital. < Arabic *shărūq* < *shărq* east⟩

sir•rah ['sɜrə] *n. Archaic.* fellow, used as a term of address to men and boys when speaking contemptuously, angrily, impatiently, etc. ⟨var. of *sir*⟩

sir•ree [sə'ri] *interj. Informal.* a word used after *yes* or *no* to add emphasis: *Yes, sirree, that was one awful storm!* ⟨< *sir*⟩

Sir Rog•er de Cov•er•ley [sər 'rɒdʒər də 'kʌvərli] an old-fashioned country dance, similiar to the Virginia reel. ⟨name of a country squire in essays in *The Spectator* (1711–1714) by British writers J. Addison and Sir Richard Steele⟩

sir•up ['sirəp] *or* ['sɜrəp] *n.* See SYRUP.

sir•up•y ['sirəpi] *or* ['sɜrəpi] *adj.* See SYRUPY.

sis [sɪs] *n. Informal.* sister. ⟨clipped form⟩

sis•al ['sɪsəl] *or* ['səisəl] *n.* **1** a strong white fibre, used for making rope, twine, etc. **2** a West Indian plant (*Agave sisalana*) of the amaryllis family from whose leaves this fibre is prepared. Also called **sisal hemp.** ⟨< *Sisal*, a town in Yucatán, Mexico⟩

sis•ka•wet ['sɪskə,wɛt] *n. Cdn.* a variety of lake trout (*Salvelinus namaycush siscowet*) found mainly in Lake Superior. Also, **siscowet.** ⟨< Cdn.F *sisquoette* < Algonkian Ojibwa *pemitewiskawet* that which has oily flesh⟩

sis•kin ['sɪskən] *n.* a yellowish green Eurasian finch (*Carduelis spinus*). See also PINE SISKIN.

sis•si•fied ['sɪsə,faɪd] *adj. Informal.* effeminate or cowardly.

sis•sy ['sɪsi] *n., adj. Informal.* —*n.* a cowardly or weak person. —*adj.* of, like, or for a sissy. **—'sis•sy•ish,** *adj.* ⟨*sis* + *-y*[2]⟩

sis•ter ['sɪstər] *n.* **1** a woman or girl having the same parents as another person; a woman or girl thought of in her relationship to other children of her parents. **2** HALF SISTER. **3** a sister-in-law. **4** a stepsister. **5** a foster sister. **6** a quality or thing thought of as female that resembles or is closely connected with another. **7** a woman closely associated with another, such as a fellow member of a club, church, etc. **8** an intimate female friend, regarded as a sister. **9** a member of a religious order of women; nun: *Sisters of Charity.* **10** *Informal.* a familiar term of address for any woman or girl. **11** *Esp. Brit.* a senior nurse or head nurse in a hospital. **12** (*adj.*) related as if by sisterhood: *sister ships.* ⟨ME < ON *systir*; cf. OE *sweoster*⟩ **—'sis•ter•less,** *adj.*

sister chromatid *Genetics.* one of the pair of chromatids seen in a chromosome of a dividing cell.

sis•ter•hood ['sɪstər,hʊd] *n.* **1** the state of being a sister. **2** a spiritual bond, like that between sisters; a sisterly relationship: *A feeling of sisterhood had developed between them over the years.* **3** an association or society of women with some common aim, characteristic, set of beliefs, etc.: *a sisterhood of nuns.*

sis•ter–in–law ['sɪstər ɪn 'lɒ] *n., pl.* **sis•ters-in-law. 1** the sister of one's husband or wife. **2** the wife of one's brother. **3** the wife of one's brother-in-law.

sis•ter•ly ['sɪstərli] *adj.* of, having to do with, or like a sister: *sisterly advice.* **—'sis•ter•li•ness,** *n.*

Sis•tine ['sɪstin] *adj.* **1** of or having to do with any of the five popes named Sixtus. **2** of or having to do with the Sistine Chapel, the chapel of the Pope in the Vatican, decorated with frescoes by Michelangelo and other great artists. ⟨< Ital. *sistino*⟩

sis•trum ['sɪstrəm] *n., pl.* **-trums** or **-tra** [-trə]. a metal percussion instrument consisting of a frame with rings that rattle when shaken, used especially in ancient Egypt, in the worship of Isis. ⟨ME < L < Gk. *seistron* < *seiein* shake⟩

Sis•y•phe•an [,sɪsə'fiən] *adj.* **1** of or having to do with Sisyphus. **2** futile, laborious, and unending.

Sis•y•phus ['sɪsəfəs] *n. Greek legend.* a king of Corinth condemned in Hades for his misdeeds and punished by eternally having to roll a large stone up a steep hill, from which it always rolled down again.

sit [sɪt] *v.* **sat, sit•ting. 1 a** rest on the buttocks, with the weight off the feet: *She sat in a chair.* **b** of a four-legged animal, rest on the haunches with the front legs unbent. **2** seat; cause to sit: *The woman sat the little boy down hard.* **3** bear oneself on; sit on: *He sat his horse well.* **4** be in a certain place or position: *The clock has sat on that shelf for years.* **5** have a seat in an assembly, etc.; be a member of a council: *to sit in Parliament.* **6** hold a session: *The court sits next month.* **7** place oneself as required. **8** be in a state of rest; remain inactive. **9** lie; press or weigh: *Care sat heavy on her brow.* **10** perch: *birds sitting on a rail.* **11** baby-sit. **12** cover eggs so that they will hatch; brood. **13** fit: *Her coat sits well.* **14** write (an examination). **15** of wind, blow from a given direction (*used with* **in**): *The wind is sitting in the east.*
sit back, a relax, with the back supported, in a chair. **b** be complacently inactive when action is required.
sit down, a take a seat. **b** put (oneself or another) in a sitting position.
sit in, take part in a sit-in.
sit in (on), a take part in (a game, conference, etc.) **b** attend as an observer: *to sit in on a session at the legislature.*
sit on or **upon, a** sit in judgment or council on. **b** have a seat on (a jury, commission, etc.). **c** *Informal.* think about; consider over a period of time. **d** *Informal.* check, rebuke, or snub. **e** delay or prevent action on or use of.
sit on one's hands, do nothing when there is action to be taken.
sit out, a remain seated during (a dance). **b** stay through; wait through: *to sit out a storm. They sat out the performance although the singing was poor.* **c** stay later than (another).
sit up, a raise the body to a sitting position. **b** keep such a position. **c** cause to take such a position. **d** stay up instead of going to bed. **e** *Informal.* start up in surprise. **f** of four-legged animals, rest on the haunches and hold the front legs in the air in front of the chest.
sit well with, be approved by or acceptable to: *The whole idea does not sit very well with her.* ⟨OE *sittan*⟩
☛ *Usage.* See note at SET.

si•tar [sɪ'tɑr] *n.* a lutelike instrument having a very long neck and a varying number of strings. The sitar was developed in India. ⟨< Hind. *sitār*, lit. three-stringed < Persian *Si* three + *tār* string⟩

sit•com ['sɪt,kɒm] *n. Informal.* SITUATION COMEDY.

sit–down ['sɪt ,daʊn] *adj.* **1** of a strike, being one in which employees stop working but stay in their place of employment until an agreement is reached. **2** of a meal, eaten at a table.

site [səit] *n., v.* **sit•ed, sit•ing.** *—n.* **1** the ground on which a structure or group of structures is, was, or will be located: *the site of the new civic centre.* **2** a piece of land regarded in terms of its suitability for a given purpose: *a good shopping mall site. This would be a poor site for a housing development.* **3** the location or scene of something: *a company site. They visited the site of the Battle of Queenston Heights.* **4** *Computer technology.* a file or group of linked files that can be accessed at a certain address on the WORLD WIDE WEB.
—v. choose a position for; locate; place: *They sited the new building on a hill.* ⟨< L *situs*⟩
☛ *Hom.* CITE, SIGHT.

sith [sɪθ] *adv., prep., or conj. Archaic.* since. ⟨OE *sīth* after⟩

sit–in ['sɪt ,ɪn] *n.* a form of protest in which a group of people occupy a public place and remain seated there for a long time.

Sit•ka deer ['sɪtkə] a smaller subspecies (*Odocoileus Lemionus sitkensis*) of the BLACKTAILED DEER. ⟨< *Sitka*, a town in Alaska⟩

Sit•ka spruce 1 a very tall spruce (*Picea sitchensis*) found along the Pacific coast of North America, having stiff, very sharp, yellowish green needles and long, cylinder-shaped cones. The sitka spruce is the largest of the spruces, usually between 38 and 50 m high. **2** the light, soft wood of this tree.

si•tol•o•gy [səi'tɒlədʒi] *n.* the science of food or diet; dietetics. ⟨< Gk. *sitos* food + E *-logy*⟩
☛ *Hom.* CYTOLOGY.

sit•ter ['sɪtər] *n.* **1** baby-sitter. **2** any person or thing that sits, especially a brooding hen.

sit•ting ['sɪtɪŋ] *n., v., adj. —n.* **1** the act of one that sits. **2** a single time of remaining seated; one uninterrupted occasion of sitting: *The portrait took five sittings. She read eight chapters at one sitting.* **3** a meeting or session of a legislature, court, etc. **4 a** the number of eggs on which a bird sits. **b** a period of brooding on eggs. **5** one or two or more consecutive fixed times for serving a particular meal, when all cannot be served at once, as on a train, ship, etc.: *the second sitting for dinner.*
—v. ppr. of SIT.
—adj. seated.

sitting duck *Informal.* an easy target or mark.

sitting room a room furnished with comfortable chairs, chesterfields, etc.; parlour.

sit•u•ate ['sɪtʃu,eit] *v.* **-at•ed, -at•ing;** *adj. —v.* put in a certain place; locate.
—adj. Archaic. situated. ⟨< LL *situatus*, pp. of *situare* < L *situs* location⟩

sit•u•at•ed ['sɪtʃu,eitɪd] *adj., v. —adj.* **1** having a location or site of a given kind or quality or in a given place: *Montréal is well situated.* **2** having a certain financial or social position: *The doctor was quite well situated.*
—v. pt. and pp. of SITUATE.

sit•u•a•tion [,sɪtʃu'eiʃən] *n.* **1** circumstances: *Act reasonably in all situations.* **2** site; location; place: *Our house has a beautiful situation on a hill.* **3** a place to work; job. **4** a critical state of affairs.
☛ *Syn.* **3.** See note at POSITION.

sit•u•a•tion•al [,sɪtʃu'eiʃənəl] *adj.* **1** of or having to do with situations. **2** determined by the situation: *situational ethics.*

situation comedy a radio or television comedy series consisting of unconnected, usually weekly episodes featuring the same cast of characters in each episode.

sit–up ['sɪt ,ʌp] *n.* a conditioning exercise that consists of raising the body from a lying to a sitting position without using the hands for support.

si•tus ['səitəs] *n., pl.* **-tus.** a position, situation, or location, especially the proper or original position, as of a part of the body or organ. ⟨< L⟩

sitz bath [sɪts] *or* [zɪts] **1** a small tub or basin for bathing in a sitting position, so that only the buttocks and hips are immersed. **2** a bath so taken, especially as part of a medical treatment. ⟨< G *Sitzbad* < *Sitz* seat + *Bad* bath⟩

sitz•mark ['sɪts,mɑrk] *or* ['zɪts,mɑrk] *n.* a hole or furrow in the snow made by a skier who has fallen backwards. ⟨< G *Sitzmarke* < *Sitz* a sitting, seat + *Marke* sign⟩

Si•va ['sivə] *or* ['ʃivə] *n. Hinduism.* See SHIVA. ⟨< Skt.⟩

Si•van [si'vɑn] *or* ['sɪvən] *n.* in the Hebrew calendar, the third month of the ecclesiastical year, and the ninth month of the civil year, corresponding roughly to late May and early June.

six [sɪks] *n., adj.* *—n.* **1** one more than five. **2** the numeral 6: *Is that supposed to be a 6 or a 9?* **3** the sixth in a set or series; especially, a playing card or side of a die having six spots: *If you throw a six, you get another turn.* **4** one of the sections into which a pack of Wolf Cubs or Brownies is divided. **5** any set or series of six persons or things: *He arranged the ten chips as a six and a four.*
at sixes and sevens, a in disorder or confusion. **b** in dispute or disagreement.
—adj. **1** being one more than five. **2** being sixth in a set or series (*used mainly after the noun*): *I'm bogged down in Chapter Six.* ⟨OE *siex* six⟩

six–eight ['sɪks 'eit] *adj. Music.* indicating or having six eighth notes in a bar or measure, the first and fourth of which are accented: *a piece in six-eight time.*

six•er ['sɪksər] *n.* the leader of a six of Wolf Cubs or Brownies.

six•fold ['sɪks,fould] *adj., adv.* *—adj.* **1** six times as much or as many. **2** having six parts.
—adv. six times as much or as many.

six–gun ['sɪks ,gʌn] *n.* a six-shooter.

Six Nations a federation of Iroquois First Nations peoples called the **Five Nations** until the Tuscarora tribe joined in about 1722. The other peoples are the Mohawk, Oneida, Onondaga, Cayuga, and Seneca.

six–pack ['sɪks ,pæk] *n.* **1** six bottles or cans of a soft drink or beer, packaged and sold as a unit. **2** a package of six of the same or similar things sold as a unit, such as plant seedlings, batteries, etc.: *a six-pack of batteries.*

six•pence ['sɪkspəns] *n.* formerly, **1** a sum of six British pennies. **2** a British coin having a value of six pennies under the old system of pounds, shillings, and pence. It has not been minted since 1970.

six•pen•ny ['sɪks,pɛni] *or* ['sɪkspəni] *adj.* **1** of little worth; cheap. **2** designating a kind of nail about 5 cm long, once costing six pennies per 100.

six–shoot•er ['sɪks ,ʃutər] *n.* a revolver that can fire six shots without being reloaded.

six•teen ['sɪks'tin] *n., adj.* *—n.* **1** six more than ten; 16: *I got sixteen out of twenty.* **2** the numeral 16: *Is that a 91 or a 16?* **3** the sixteenth in a set or series. **4** a set or series of sixteen persons or things.
—adj. **1** being six more than ten. **2** being sixteenth in a set or series of sixteen persons or things. ⟨OE *sixtēne*⟩

six•teenth ['sɪks'tinθ] *adj. or n.* **1** next after the fifteenth; last in a series of 16; 16th. **2** one, or being one of, 16 equal parts.

sixteenth note *Music.* a note one sixteenth of the time value of a whole note. See NOTE for picture.

sixteenth rest *Music.* a rest lasting one sixteenth as long as a whole rest, or as long as a sixteenth note. See REST¹ for picture.

sixth [sɪksθ] *n., adj.* *—n.* **1** the next after the fifth; the last in a series of six; 6th. **2** one of six equal parts. **3** *Music.* **a** in a diatonic scale, the tone five degrees above the tonic; the 6th tone. **b** a tone five degrees above any other tone. **c** the interval between two such tones. **d** a chord containing tones at such an interval.
—adj. being the sixth or a sixth.

sixth•ly ['sɪksθli] *adv.* in the sixth place.

sixth sense a power of perception beyond the five senses; intuition.

six•ti•eth ['sɪkstiɪθ] *adj. or n.* **1** next after the fifty-ninth; last in a series of 60; 60th. **2** one, or being one, of 60 equal parts.

six•ty ['sɪksti] *n., pl.* **-ties;** *adj.* *—n.* **1** six times ten; 60. **2 sixties,** *pl.* the years from sixty through sixty-nine, especially of a century or of a person's life: *Rock music became popular in the sixties.*
—adj. being six times ten. ⟨OE *siextig, sixtig*⟩

six•ty•fold ['sɪksti,fould] *adj. or adv.* sixty times as much or as many.

sixty–fourth note ['sɪksti 'fɔrθ] *Music.* a note having the time value of one sixty-fourth of a whole note. See NOTE for picture.

sixty–fourth rest *Music.* a rest lasting one sixty-fourth of a whole rest, or as long as a sixty-fourth note.

siz•a•ble ['saɪzəbəl] *adj.* fairly large. Also, **sizeable.** **—'siz•a•bly,** *adv.* **—'siz•a•ble•ness,** *n.*

size¹ [saɪz] *n., v.* **sized, siz•ing.** *—n.* **1** the amount of surface or space a thing takes up; dimensions. **2** an extent; amount; magnitude: *the size of an industry.* **3** one of a series of measures: *Her shoes are size 10. The size of card I want is 7 cm × 12 cm.* **4** *Informal.* the actual condition; true description. **5** (*adjl.*) sized (*used only in compounds*): *She cut the meat into bite-size pieces.*
of a size, of the same size.
—v. **1** arrange according to size or in sizes. **2** make of certain size.
size up, *Informal.* **a** form an opinion of; estimate. **b** come up to some size or grade. ⟨ult. var. of *assize,* in sense of 'to set a standard of weights and measures'⟩
☛ *Syn. n.* **1, 2. Size,** VOLUME, BULK = the measure of something. **Size** applies particularly to the dimensions (length, width, and height or depth) of something, but also to the extent of surface occupied or the number of individuals included: *What is the size of your herd?* **Volume** is used of something measured by the cubic metres, etc. it occupies, especially something that rolls or flows: *The volume of water confined by the new dam is tremendous.* **Bulk** refers to size or quantity measured in three dimensions, and often suggests largeness: *Let the dough double in bulk.*

size² [saɪz] *n., v.* **sized, siz•ing.** *—n.* a sticky preparation made from materials like glue, starch, or resin, and used as a glaze or filler for cloth, paper, plaster, leather, etc.
—v. coat or treat with size. ⟨< F *assise* a sitting, fixing, layer⟩

size•a•ble ['saɪzəbəl] *adj.* See SIZABLE.

sized [saɪzd] *adj., v.* *—adj.* **1** having a specified size or bulk (*used in compounds*): *giant-sized.* **2** ranked or arranged according to size.
—v. pt. and pp. of SIZE.

siz•ing ['saɪzɪŋ] *n., v.* *—n.* **1** SIZE². **2** the process of treating with size.
—v. ppr. of SIZE.

siz•zle ['sɪzəl] *v.* **-zled, -zling;** *n.* *—v.* **1** make a hissing sound, as fat does when it is frying or burning. **2** be very hot: *The pavement sizzled in the 40° sun.* **3** be full of barely restrained emotion; show or evoke such emotion: *sizzling with resentment. This thriller absolutely sizzles with suspense.*
—n. a hissing sound. ⟨imitative⟩ **—'siz•zler,** *n.*

S.J. SOCIETY OF JESUS.

SJAA or **S.J.A.A.** St. John Ambulance Association.

SJAB or **S.J.A.B.** St. John Ambulance Brigade.

sjam•bok ['ʃæmbɒk] *or* ['ʃæmbʌk] *n., v.* *—n.* in South Africa, a heavy whip, usually made from the hide of a rhinoceros.
—v. beat or flog with such a whip. ⟨< Afrikaans < Malay *cambuk* whip < Hind. *cabuk*⟩

SK Saskatchewan (*used esp. in computerized address systems*).

skald [skɒld] *or* [skɑld] *n.* an ancient Scandinavian poet and singer. Also, **scald.** ⟨< ON *skáld.* Cf. SCOLD.⟩ **—'skald•ic,** *adj.*

skat [skæt] *or* [skɑt] *n.* a card game for three players. ⟨< G < Ital. *scarto* discard, n.⟩
☛ *Hom.* SCAT [skæt].

skate¹ [skeit] *n., v.* **skat•ed, skat•ing.** *—n.* **1** a boot with a metal blade, or runner, attached to the sole, designed for gliding over ice. **2** the runner itself, together with its frame, especially when forming a separate part that is attached to a shoe or boot by means of clamps, straps, etc. **3** ROLLER SKATE. **4** INLINE SKATE.
—v. glide or move along on or as if on skates. ⟨< Du. *schaats* < OF *escache* stilt < Gmc.⟩ **—'skat•er,** *n.*

skate² [skeit] *n., pl.* **skate** or **skates.** any of a family (Rajidae) of large, bottom-dwelling, egg-laying rays found in tropical and temperate seas, having very broad fins, giving them a diamond shape from above, and, in some species, having weak electric organs in the tail. ⟨ME < ON *skata*⟩

skate•board ['skeit,bɔrd] *n., v.* *—n.* a small, narrow board of wood or plastic, usually about 45-50 cm long, shaped somewhat like a surfboard but equipped with a pair of roller-skate wheels at each end, and used for coasting along streets, sidewalks, etc.
—v. ride on a skateboard. **—'skate,board•er,** *n.*

skate•board•ing ['skeit,bɔrdɪŋ] *n., v.* *—n.* the act or practice of using a skateboard for sport.
—v. ppr. of SKATEBOARD.

skate–guard ['skeit ,gɑrd] *n.* a long piece of hard plastic with a groove in it, used as a protective covering for the blade of an ice skate.

skating rink **1** a smooth sheet of ice for skating. **2** a smooth floor for roller skating or inline skating.

skean or **skene** [skin] *n.* a dagger formerly used in Ireland and Scotland. ⟨< Irish *scian,* Scots Gaelic *sgian*⟩

ske•dad•dle [skɪ'dædəl] *v., n.* *—v.* **-dled, -dling.** *Informal.* run away; scatter in flight.

—n. an act of skedaddling; a rushed and scattered flight. ⟨origin uncertain⟩

skeet [skit] *n. Trapshooting.* a type of target practice using clay pigeons that are released into the air so as to imitate the flight of birds. Also, **skeet shooting.** ⟨ult. < ON *skjóta* to shoot⟩

skeet•er ['skitər] *n. Informal.* **1** mosquito. **2** a small sailboat used on ice; an iceboat.

skeg [skɛg] *n.* **1** *Nautical.* a projection, often an extension of the keel, supporting the rudderpost. **2** a fin on the bottom of a surfboard toward the rear. ⟨< Du. *schegge* < ON *skegg* beard, projection⟩

skein [skein] *n.* **1** a loosely coiled bundle of yarn or thread, or of something similar. **2** a confused tangle. **3** a flock of geese in flight. ⟨ME < OF *escaigne*; ult. origin uncertain⟩

skel•e•tal ['skɛlətəl] *adj.* of, having to do with, attached to, or forming a skeleton.

skel•e•ton ['skɛlətən] *n.* **1** *Anatomy. Zoology.* the framework of bones and cartilage of a vertebrate animal that supports the soft tissues and protects the internal organs. **2** a very thin person or animal: *He was just a skeleton after his long illness.* **3** the basic framework or structure of something: *The steel skeleton of an office tower, the skeleton of a story.* **4** the greatly deteriorated remains of anything. **5** (*adjl.*) of, like, or having the characteristics of a skeleton; basic or essential; constituting a minimum: *A skeleton crew remained on board while the ship was at the dock.*
skeleton at the feast, a person or thing casting gloom on a joyful occasion.
skeleton in the closet, something shameful that is kept secret, as in a family. ⟨< NL *sceleton* < Gk. *skeleton*, neut, adj., dried up⟩
—'skel•e•ton,like, *adj.*

skel•e•ton•ize ['skɛlətə,naɪz] *v.* **-ized, -iz•ing. 1** make a skeleton of. **2** outline; sketch out; draft in outline: *a skeletonized report.* **3** greatly reduce the numbers of.

skeleton key a key made to open many locks.

skelp[1] [skɛlp] *n., v. Scottish. —n.* a slapping or smacking noise; spank.
—v. **1** spank; slap. **2** move quickly; hurry. ⟨probably imitative⟩

skelp[2] [skɛlp] *n.* a strip of iron or steel used in the making of pipes or tubes. ⟨origin unknown⟩

skep•tic ['skɛptɪk] *n. or adj.* See SCEPTIC.

skep•ti•cal ['skɛptɪkəl] *adj.* See SCEPTICAL.

skep•ti•cism ['skɛptə,sɪzəm] *n.* See SCEPTICISM.

sker•ry ['skɛri] *n., pl.* **-ries.** *Esp. Scottish.* a small, rocky island or reef. ⟨< Orkney dialect < ON *sker* reef. See SCAR[2].⟩
☛ *Hom.* SCARY.

sketch [skɛtʃ] *n., v. —n.* **1** a rough, quickly done drawing, painting, or design. **2** an outline; plan. **3** a short, light description, story, play, etc.: *a vaudeville sketch.* Sunshine Sketches of a Little Town *is a collection of short stories by Stephen Leacock.*
—v. **1** make a sketch or sketches: *We spent the afternoon sketching.* **2** make a sketch of; draw or describe roughly. ⟨< Du. *schets* < Ital. *schizzo* < L < Gk. *schedios* impromptu, ult. < *schesthai* be near⟩ **—'sketch•er,** *n.*

sketch•book ['skɛtʃ,bʊk] *n.* a book of or for rough, quick drawings.

sketch•y ['skɛtʃi] *adj.* **sketch•i•er, sketch•i•est. 1** like a sketch; having or giving only outlines or main features. **2** incomplete; slight; imperfect: *a sketchy meal.* **—'sketch•i•ly,** *adv.* **—'sketch•i•ness,** *n.*

skew [skju] *adj., n., v. —adj.* **1** twisted to one side; slanting. **2** having a part that deviates from a straight line, right angle, etc. **3** unsymmetrical or unbalanced. **4** *Mathematics.* lying in different planes, not intersecting and not parallel.
—n. a slant; twist; something that is skew.
—v. **1** slant; twist. **2** give a slanting form, position, or direction to. **3** turn aside; swerve. **4** represent unfairly; distort. ⟨ME < ONF *eskiuer* shy away from, eschew < Gmc.⟩

skew•back ['skju,bæk] *n.* **1** a sloping surface against which the end of an arch rests. **2** a stone, course of masonry, or the like, with such a surface.

skew•bald ['skju,bɒld] *adj., n. —adj.* especially of horses, having patches of white and any other colour except black, usually brown.
—n. a horse, pony, or other animal of this coloration.

skew•er ['skjuər] *n., v. —n.* **1** a long pin of wood or metal stuck through a cut of meat to hold it together while it is cooking, or on which to thread pieces of meat, vegetable, etc. in order to broil them. **2** something shaped or used like a long pin.
—v. **1** fasten with a skewer or skewers. **2** pierce with or as if with a skewer. ⟨earlier *skiver*; origin uncertain⟩

skew•ness ['skjunəs] *n.* **1** the fact or quality of being skew. **2** *Statistics.* **a** of a distribution, lack of symmetry. **b** a measure of such asymmetry.

ski [ski] *n., pl.* **skis;** *v.* **skied, ski•ing.** *—n.* **1** one of a pair of long pieces of wood, metal, plastic, etc. that can be fastened to boots to enable a person to glide over snow. **2** a skilike device fastened to the undercarriage of an aircraft and used in place of wheels for landing on snow, mud, sand, etc. **3** WATER SKI.
—v. **1** glide over the snow on skis. **2** water-ski. ⟨< Norwegian⟩
—'ski•a•ble, *adj.* **—'ski•er,** *n.*

ski boot a boot made specially to fit on a ski.

skid [skɪd] *v.* **skid•ded, skid•ding;** *n. —v.* **1** slip or slide out of control, while moving: *The car skidded on the slippery road.* **2** prevent from going around by means of a skid. **3** slide along without going around, as a wheel does when held by a skid. **4** slide on a skid or skids. **5** cause to slide or slip. **6** *Lumbering.* slide or drag (logs) down a prepared slide or along a SKID TRAIL or SKID ROAD (def. 1).
—n. **1** a slip or slide sideways out of control: *His car went into a skid.* **2** a piece of wood or metal used to prevent a wheel from going around by pressing on the rim. **3** a piece of timber or a runner on which something heavy may slide. **4** a frame on which heavy articles may be piled for moving to another position, often by lifting with a crane. **5** a runner on the bottom of an airplane to enable the airplane to slide along the ground when landing.
hit the skids, *Slang.* suffer a serious decline or failure.
on the skids, *Slang.* headed for dismissal, failure, or other disaster.
put the skids under, *Slang.* cause the failure or decline of.
⟨? < Scand.; cf. O Frisian *skīd* stick of wood⟩

Ski–Doo [skɪ'du] *or* ['skidu] *n. Trademark.* a type of snowmobile.

skid road **1** *Cdn. Lumbering.* formerly, a road of greased skids, over which logs were dragged by teams of mules, oxen, or horses. **2** SKID ROW.

skid row a run-down district of cheap hotels and bars, used as a hangout by vagrants, petty criminals, etc. ⟨< *skid road,* an area of town used by loggers⟩

skid trail *Lumbering.* a trail cut through the bush for dragging or hauling logs from the cutting area.

skies [skaɪz] *n., v. —n.* pl. of SKY.
—v. 3rd pers. sing.; present tense, of SKY.

skiff [skɪf] *n.* **1** a small, light rowboat with a rounded bottom and flat stern. **2** a small, light boat with a centreboard and a single sail. ⟨< F < Ital. *schifo* < Gmc.⟩

ski•jor•ing [ski'dʒɔrɪŋ] *or* ['skidʒɔrɪŋ]; *Norwegian,* [ʃi'jørɪŋ] *n.* a sport in which a person on skis is pulled along by a horse or vehicle. ⟨< Norwegian *skikjøring* < *ski* ski + *kjøring* driving⟩
—'ski,jor•er, *n.*

ski jump **1** a jump made by a person on skis. **2** a place for making such a jump.

skil•fish ['skɪlfɪʃ] *n., pl.* **-fish** or **-fish•es.** blackcod. ⟨< Haida *sqil* fish⟩

skil•ful or **skill•ful** ['skɪlfəl] *adj.* **1** having skill; expert. **2** showing skill. **—'skil•ful•ness** or **'skill•ful•ness,** *n.*

skil•ful•ly or **skill•ful•ly** ['skɪlfəli] *adv.* with skill; expertly.

ski lift a mechanism for transporting skiers to the top of a slope, usually by means of a chair running on a suspended cable.

skill [skɪl] *n.* **1** ability gained by practice or knowledge; expertness: *It takes skill to tune a piano.* **2** an ability or technique that can be learned: *One must master the basic language skills.* **3** an art or craft that is learned through training or experience: *the skill of carpentry.* ⟨ME < ON *skil* distinction⟩

skilled [skɪld] *adj.* **1** having skill; trained; experienced: *a skilled worker.* **2** showing skill; requiring skill: *Bricklaying is skilled labour.*
☛ *Syn.* **1.** See note at EXPERT.

skil•let ['skɪlɪt] *n.* **1** a shallow pan with a long handle, used for frying; frying pan. **2** *Brit.* a long-handled cooking pot or kettle, often having legs. ⟨ME *skelet*; origin uncertain⟩

skill•ful ['skɪlfəl] *adj.* See SKILFUL.

skill•ful•ly ['skɪlfəli] *adv.* See SKILFULLY.

skim [skɪm] *v.* **skimmed, skim•ming;** *n. —v.* **1** remove from the surface of a liquid: *to skim the cream from the milk.* **2** take

something from the surface of: *She skims the milk to get cream.* **3** move lightly over: *The pebble I threw skimmed the little waves. The skaters skimmed the ice.* **4** glide along: *The swallows were skimming by.* **5** send skimming; skip: *You can skim a flat stone over the water.* **6** read rapidly or superficially; read with omissions, especially in order to get the general sense or purpose: *It took me an hour to skim the book.* **7** cover or become covered with a thin layer of ice, scum, etc. (*sometimes used with* **over**). **8** *Slang.* avoid paying tax on (income, especially illicit income) by concealing it.
—*n.* **1** that which is skimmed off. **2** the act of skimming. **3** a thin film on a liquid. **4** SKIM MILK. ⟨ME < OF *escumer* < *escume* scum < Gmc.⟩

skim•mer ['skɪmər] *n.* **1** a person or thing that skims; especially a long-handled, shallow ladle with small holes, used in skimming liquids. **2** any of several sea birds (genus *Rhynchops*) that skim along the surface of water to get food. **3** a straw hat with a flat crown and wide brim.

skim milk milk from which the cream has been removed.

skim•mings ['skɪmɪŋz] *n.pl.* **1** anything skimmed from a liquid. **2** *Placer Mining.* fine gold deposited in the gravel and on the banks of a river; it is brought down in a freshet and washed out again in the next high water.

ski•mo•bile ['skimə,bil] *n.* a vehicle resembling a small automobile but running on tracks, designed for carrying skiers to the top of a slope.

skimp [skɪmp] *v.* **1** supply in too small an amount: *Don't skimp the butter in making a cake.* **2** be very saving or economical: *She had to skimp to send her daughter to university.* **3** do imperfectly. ⟨? alteration of *scrimp*⟩

skimp•y ['skɪmpi] *adj.* **skimp•i•er, skimp•i•est. 1** scanty; not enough. **2** too saving or economical. **—'skimp•i•ly,** *adv.* **—'skimp•i•ness,** *n.*

skin [skɪn] *n., v.* **skinned, skin•ning.** —*n.* **1** the outer layer of tissue of a human or animal body, especially when relatively soft and flexible. **2** the skin of a fur-bearing or hairy animal, together with its covering of fur or hair; hide or pelt. **3 a** any outer or surface layer, as the rind of a fruit, a sausage casing, etc. **b** SKIM (*n.* 3). **4** a container made of skin for holding liquids. **5** the outer covering of a structure such as an aircraft or ship. **6** *Slang.* a swindler. **7** *Slang.* a skinflint. **8 skins,** *pl. Slang.* drums. **9** (*adjl.*) *Informal.* pornographic: *skin magazines.*
by the skin of (one's) **teeth,** *Informal.* very narrowly; barely.
get under (someone's) **skin,** *Informal.* annoy or irritate someone.
have a thick (or **thin**) **skin,** be very insensitive (or sensitive) to criticism.
in or **with a whole skin,** safe and sound.
no skin off (one's) **nose** (or **back**), of no interest or concern to one.
save (one's) **skin,** *Informal.* escape without harm.
—*v.* **1** take the skin off: *Jack skinned his knees when he fell. The hunter skinned the deer.* **2** strip, scrape, or peel off like skin: *The fall skinned the paint on her new bicycle.* **3** shed skin. **4** cover or become (*sometimes with* **over**) covered with skin. **5** *Slang.* swindle (someone) of money, etc.; cheat. **6** *Slang.* slip away (*often with* **out**).
skin alive, *Slang.* **a** torture; flay. **b** scold severely. **c** defeat completely.
skin by (or **through**), *Informal.* just barely pass or succeed. ⟨ME < ON *skinn*⟩

☛ *Syn. n.* **2. Skin,** HIDE[2], PELT = the outer covering of the body of an animal. **Skin** is the general word applying to this covering of a person or animal: *The skin of a calf makes soft leather.* **Hide** applies especially to the tough skin of a large animal, raw or tanned: *The hide of cows is tough.* **Pelt** applies especially to the skin of a fur- or wool-bearing animal before dressing or tanning: *Trappers sell pelts of foxes; stores sell dressed skins.*

skin–deep ['skɪn 'dip] *adj.* **1** of a wound, etc., no deeper than the skin. **2** of an emotion, impression, quality, etc., not deep or lasting in effect; of no real significance: *Beauty is only skin-deep.*

skin diver a person engaged in skin diving. Also, **skindiver.**

skin diving swimming under water, using a face mask and flippers, usually with a snorkel or scuba gear, and, in cold water, a rubber or rubberized suit to protect the body against the cold. **—'skin-,dive,** *v.*

skin flick *Slang.* a film exploiting nudity and explicit sex.

skin•flint ['skɪn,flɪnt] *n.* a mean, stingy person.

skin•ful ['skɪn,fʊl] *n., pl.* **-fuls. 1** as much as a skin container can hold. **2** *Informal.* as much as the stomach can hold; especially, as much wine, liquor, etc. as a person can take.

skin game *Informal.* a game or action in which the outcome is rigged; swindle.

skin graft *Surgical.* a piece of skin taken from another part of the body or another person to replace skin that has been burned or otherwise damaged or destroyed.

skin grafting *Surgical.* the action or process of making a skin graft; the surgical transplanting of skin.

skin•head ['skɪn,hɛd] *n.* **1** a bald person. **2** a member of a group of youths, originally in England in the 1960s, characterized by shaven or cropped heads, who engage in rowdyism. **3** a member of any of various similar groups now also in Europe and North America, many of whom support neo-Nazi principles. **4** a neo-Nazi.

skink [skɪŋk] *n.* any of a family (Scinidae) of mostly small lizards having a long, round body with small, smooth scales, and short limbs or no limbs at all. ⟨< L < Gk. *skinkos*⟩

skin•less ['skɪnlɪs] *adj.* without a skin or casing: *skinless weiners.*

skin•ner ['skɪnər] *n.* **1** a person who removes the skin from an animal. **2** a person who prepares or deals in skins or furs. **3** a person who drives draft animals, especially mules.

skin•ny ['skɪni] *adj.* **-ni•er, -ni•est. 1** having too little flesh; too thin or lean: *She was always skinny as a child, but usually healthy.* **2** like skin. **3** skimpy; insufficient. **—'skin•ni•ness,** *n.*

skin•ny–dip ['skɪni ,dɪp] *v.* **-dipped, -dip•ping;** *n.* —*v. Informal.* swim in the nude.
—*n.* a nude swim. **—skinny dipper. —skinny dipping.**

skin test a test in which a substance is introduced under the skin or into an abraded area in order to detect a disease or allergy.

skin–tight ['skɪn ,tʌit] *adj.* of clothes, fitting very closely.

skip[1] [skɪp] *v.* **skipped, skip•ping;** *n.* —*v.* **1** leap lightly; spring; jump: *Lambs skipped in the fields.* **2** leap lightly over (rope) as a game: *The children skipped all through recess.* **3** move along by stepping and hopping first with one foot, then with the other. **4** send bounding along a surface: *Children like to skip stones on the lake.* **5** go bounding along a surface. **6** pass over; fail to notice; omit: *Answer the questions in order without skipping.* **7** change quickly from one task, pleasure, subject, etc. to another. **8** *Informal.* leave in a hurry: *He skipped town to avoid meeting his enemies.* **9** be promoted past (the next regular grade) in school. **10** *Informal.* stay away from a session of: *to skip classes.*
—*n.* **1** a light spring, jump, or leap. **2** a gait, especially of children, in which hops and steps are alternated. **3** the act of passing over or omitting. **4** something that is omitted. ⟨ME < Scand.; cf. MSwedish *skuppa*⟩

skip[2] [skɪp] *n., v.* **skipped, skip•ping.** —*n.* **1** *Informal.* the captain of a boat or ship; skipper. **2** *Sports.* the captain of a curling team or a lawn bowling team.
—*v.* serve as skip of (a curling or lawn bowling team). ⟨clipped form of *skipper*⟩

skip[3] [skɪp] *n.* **1** *Mining or quarrying.* a huge bucket or cage in which heavy loads of workers or materials may be raised or lowered to and from ground level. **2** *Theatre.* a basket of theatrical costumes. ⟨earlier *skep* < OE *sceppe* < ON *skeppa* bushel basket⟩

skip•jack ['skɪp,dʒæk] *n., pl.* **skip•jacks.** any of various fishes that leap out of the water or play on the surface of the water, such as any of several tunas.

ski patrol a group of expert skiers who patrol ski slopes helping skiers who are in trouble, making sure skiers obey the rules of the area, etc.

ski plane an airplane equipped with runners or skis for taking off from or landing on snow.

ski pole either of a pair of light poles used in skiing for balance and forward propulsion, having a leather strap and hand grip at one end and a pointed metal tip at the other with a disk just above the tip to keep the pole from sinking into the snow.

skip•per[1] ['skɪpər] *n., v.* —*n.* **1** the captain of a ship, especially of a small trading or fishing boat. **2** any captain or leader.
—*v.* be the skipper of (a crew or boat). ⟨ME < MDu. *schipper* < *schip* ship⟩

skip•per[2] ['skɪpər] *n.* **1** any of a large family (Hesperiidae) of small, butterflylike insects belonging to the same order as butterflies and moths, having a heavy body and threadlike antennae with a hook at the end. **2** any of various skipping insects. **3** saury. **4** any person or thing that skips. ⟨< *skip*⟩

skipping rope a length of rope, often having a handle at each end, used to SKIP[1] (def. 2) with. The rope is swung over and under the jumper, who leaps over it whenever it reaches his or her feet.

skip tracer *Informal.* a strong-arm debt collector for a loan company.

skirl [skɜrl] *v., n.* —*v.* **1** of bagpipes, sound loudly and shrilly. **2** play a bagpipe.
—*n.* the sound of a bagpipe. ⟨probably < Scand.; cf. dial. Norwegian *skrylla*⟩

skir•mish ['skɜrmɪʃ] *n., v.* —*n.* **1** a minor fight in wartime between small groups of soldiers, ships, aircraft, etc. **2** a minor conflict, argument, contest, etc.
—*v.* take part in a skirmish. ⟨ME < Scand.; < OF *eskirmiss-* a stem of *eskirmir*, originally, ward off < Gmc.⟩

skir•mish•er ['skɜrmɪʃər] *n.* a person who engages in a skirmish, especially one of a group of soldiers sent out in advance of an army to clear the way for the main attack or to prevent a surprise attack by the enemy, etc.

skirt [skɜrt] *n.* **1** a women's and girls' garment for the lower body that hangs freely from the waist and may be wide or narrow, long or short: *She wore a skirt and blouse.* **2** the free-hanging part of a dress, jumper, cassock, etc. that extends from the waist down. **3** a cloth facing or hanging that resembles a skirt: *a dressing table with a skirt.* **4** a border; edge. **5** the fringe of a group of people, or the rim or outer edge of an area. **6** one of the flaps hanging from the sides of a saddle.
—*v.* **1** extend along or form a border or edge around: *The road skirts the lake.* **2** pass along the border or edge of: *The girls skirted the forest because they did not want to go through it.* **3** avoid or evade: *to skirt an issue.* ⟨ME *skirte* < ON *skyrta* shirt⟩

skirt•ing ['skɜrtɪŋ] *n., v.* —*n.* cloth for making skirts.
—*v.* ppr. of SKIRT.

ski slope a hill used for skiing.

skit [skɪt] *n.* a short dramatic sketch that contains humour or satire. ⟨< Scand.; cf. ON *skyti* shooter⟩

ski tow a motorized conveyor for towing skiers to the top of a slope on their skis, usually consisting of an endless moving rope or cable which the skiers hang onto.

skit•ter ['skɪtər] *v.* **1** move lightly or quickly; skim or skip along a surface. **2** *Fishing.* draw (a lure) over the surface of the water with a skipping motion.

skit•tish ['skɪtɪʃ] *adj.* **1** apt to start, jump, or run; easily frightened: *a skittish horse.* **2** fickle; changeable. **3** coy.
—'skit•tish•ly, *adv.* **—'skit•tish•ness,** *n.*

skit•tle ['skɪtəl] *n.* **1 skittles,** *pl.* a British game in which the players try to knock down nine wooden pins by rolling or throwing wooden disks or balls at them. **2** one of the pins used in this game.
beer and skittles, pure amusement; fun and games: *Life isn't all beer and skittles.* ⟨< Scand.; cf. Danish *skyttel* shuttle⟩

skiv•vies ['skɪviz] *n.pl. Slang.* underwear: *Don't come in, I'm in my skivvies.*

skoal [skoul] *interj.* a drinking toast meaning "To your health!" or "Cheers!" ⟨< ON *skál* bowl⟩

skoo•kum ['skukəm] *or* ['skʊkəm] *adj., n. Cdn. West Coast and Northwest.* —*adj.* powerful, big, or brave: *a skookum bacon-and-egg breakfast.*
—*n.* an evil genius or spirit. ⟨< Chinook Jargon⟩

skookum chuck *Cdn. West Coast and Northwest.* **1** a swift current; white water; rapids. **2** tidal rapids.

Skt. Sanskrit.

sku•a ['skjuə] *n.* **1** a gull-like bird (*Catharacta skua*) resembling and related to the jaegers, but larger and more robust and without the elongated central tail feathers of the jaegers. The breeding range of the skua includes both the arctic and antarctic regions. Also called **great skua. 2** *Esp. Brit.* any bird of the family Stercorariidae, including the jaegers. ⟨< Faroese *skūgvur* < ON *skúfr*⟩

skul•dug•ger•y or **skull•dug•ger•y** [skʌl'dʌgəri] *n. Informal.* trickery; dishonesty. ⟨origin uncertain⟩

skulk [skʌlk] *v., n.* —*v.* **1** move in a stealthy, furtive manner; slink: *The burglar skulked around the house, looking for an easy way in.* **2** sneak away or keep out of sight to avoid danger, work, etc.: *He skulked at home to avoid facing the bully.*
—*n.* a person who skulks. ⟨ME < Scand.; cf. Danish *skolke*⟩
—'skulk•er, *n.* **—'skulk•ing•ly,** *adv.*
☛ *Syn. v.* See note at LURK.

skull [skʌl] *n.* **1** the bones of the head; the part of the skeleton of a vertebrate animal that encloses and protects the brain and organs of sight, hearing, and smell. **2** the head, thought of as the seat of intelligence: *It's impossible to get anything into his thick skull.*
out of (one's) **skull,** *Informal.* **a** crazy. **b** (*as a complement to* **bored**) completely; utterly: *The political debates bored us out of our skulls.* ⟨ME *scolle*; cf. dial. Norwegian *skul* shell⟩
☛ *Hom.* SCULL.

skull and crossbones a picture of a human skull above two crossed bones, often used on pirates' flags as a symbol of death, and now often used on the labels of poisonous substances, etc.

skull•cap ['skʌl,kæp] *n.* **1** a close-fitting cap with no brim. **2** any plant of the genus *Scutellaria* of mints, having a calyx shaped like a helmet.

skunk [skʌŋk] *n., v.* —*n.* **1** any of various small, black-and-white New World mammals of the weasel family noted for their ability to defend themselves by ejecting an extremely bad-smelling, oily liquid from a pair of anal glands. The commonest and best-known species is *Mephitis mephitis*, also called the **striped skunk**, having a white patch on the top of the head that continues along the back as a single or double band of white, often extending to the long, bushy tail. **2** the fur of a skunk. **3** *Informal.* a despicable person.
—*v. Slang.* hold scoreless; defeat utterly. ⟨< Algonquian⟩

A skunk

skunk cabbage 1 a low-growing, perennial swamp herb (*Symplocarpus foetidus*) of the arum family found in E North America, having large, broad leaves and a purplish-spotted spathe, and giving off a strong, offensive odour when bruised. **2** a similar and related plant (*Lysichitum americanum*) of W North America.

sky [skaɪ] *n., pl.* **skies;** *v.* **skied** or **skyed, sky•ing.** —*n.* **1** the space high above the earth, appearing as a great arch or dome covering the world; the region of the clouds or the upper air; the heavens: *a blue sky, a cloudy sky. A vapour trail stretched across the sky.* **2** heaven. **3** climate or weather: *warm tropical skies.*
out of a clear (**blue**) **sky,** suddenly; unexpectedly.
praise (someone or something) **to the skies,** praise very highly or extravagantly: *The review praised the director of the film to the skies.*
—*v.* hit, throw, or raise high into the air. ⟨ME *ski(es)* cloud(s) < ON *sky*⟩

sky blue 1 a light, clear blue. **2** Usually **Sky Blue,** *Cdn.* formerly, an officer of the Hudson's Bay Company, so called because of the colour of the uniform. **—'sky-'blue,** *adj.*

sky•cap ['skaɪ,kæp] *n.* a porter at an airport. ⟨modelled on *redcap*⟩

sky•div•er ['skaɪ,daɪvər] *n.* a person who engages in sky-diving.

sky•div•ing ['skaɪ,daɪvɪŋ] *n.* the sport of jumping from an airplane at a moderate height and making certain manoeuvres while falling free before opening one's parachute. **—'sky,dive,** *v.*

Skye terrier or **Skye** [skaɪ] *n.* a breed of small terrier originally developed in Scotland, having short legs, a long body, and long, shaggy hair. ⟨< the Isle of *Skye* near Scotland⟩

A Skye terrier

sky•ey ['skaɪi] *adj.* of or like the sky.

sky–high ['skaɪ 'haɪ] *adv. or adj.* **1** to a great height; high up in the air: *to throw something sky-high.* **2** to a high degree or level: *Prices have gone sky-high in the last month.* **3** excessive: *sky-high prices.*
blow sky-high, blow to pieces: *The warehouse was blown sky-high.*

sky•jack ['skaɪ,dʒæk] *v.* take over (an aircraft) by force, causing it to be flown to a place other than its destination. ⟨blend of *sky* + *hijack*⟩ **—'sky,jack•er,** *n.* **—'sky,jack•ing,** *n.*

sky•lark ['skaɪ,lɑrk] *n., v.* —*n.* an Old World lark (*Alauda arvensis*) having inconspicuous, brown-streaked plumage, and famous for the beautiful song of the male, produced while the

bird is soaring at great heights. The skylark was introduced into southern British Columbia and has become established there.
—*v.* frolic or play pranks.

sky•light ['skaɪ,ləit] *n.* a window in a roof.

sky•line ['skaɪ,laɪn] *n.* **1** the line at which earth and sky seem to meet; horizon. **2** the outline of buildings, mountains, trees, etc. as seen against the sky, from a distance: *The skyline of Vancouver is spectacular.* **3** *Logging.* part of the rigging of a spar tree.

sky lobby **1** a lobby for a high building. **2** a lobby on an upper floor.

sky pilot *Slang.* a member of the clergy, especially a chaplain.

sky•rock•et ['skaɪ,rɒkɪt] *n., v.* —*n.* a firework that can be shot high into the air, where it bursts in a shower of sparks and stars; rocket.
—*v.* rise or increase suddenly and quickly, like a skyrocket: *Prices were skyrocketing. The actor had skyrocketed to fame with her first movie.*

sky•sail ['skaɪ,seil] *or* ['skaɪsəl] *n. Nautical.* in a square-rigged ship, a light sail set at the top of the mast above the royal.

sky•scrap•er ['skaɪ,skreipər] *n.* an extremely tall building.

sky•walk ['skaɪ,wɒk] *n.* SKYWAY (def. 3).

sky•ward ['skaɪwərd] *adv. or adj.* toward the sky.

sky•wards ['skaɪwərdz] *adv.* skyward.

sky•way ['skaɪ,wei] *n.* **1** a route used by aircraft; an air lane. **2** a stretch of elevated highway. **3** a covered walkway between upper storeys of two buildings or towers.

sky•writ•ing ['skaɪ,rəitɪŋ] *n.* **1** the tracing of words, etc. against the sky from an airplane by means of smoke or some similar substance. **2** the letters, words, etc. so traced.
—'sky,write, *v.* **—'sky,writ•er,** *n.*

S.L. or **S/L** SQUADRON LEADER.

slab [slæb] *n., v.* **slabbed, slab•bing.** —*n.* **1** a broad, flat, thick piece (of stone, wood, meat, etc.): *This sidewalk is made of slabs of stone. The hungry boy ate a slab of cheese as big as his hand.* **2** the piece of wood cut from the outside of a log in squaring it. **3** *Baseball. Slang.* the place where the pitcher stands to deliver the ball.
—*v.* **1** make into slabs. **2** cut the outside pieces from (a log). **3** lay or cover with slabs. ⟨ME *slabbe;* origin uncertain⟩

slab•ber ['slæbər] *v., n.* slobber.

slack[1] [slæk] *adj., n., v., adv.* —*adj.* **1** not tight or firm; loose: *The rope hung slack.* **2** careless: *He is a slack housekeeper.* **3** slow: *The horse was moving at a slack pace.* **4** not active; not brisk; dull: *Business is slack at this season.* **5** lax; morally spineless.
—*n.* **1** the part that hangs loose: *She pulled in the slack of the rope.* **2** a dull season; quiet period. **3** a stopping of a strong flow of the tide or a current of water.
take up the slack, take up the extra load caused by loss of workers, lost time, increased demand, etc.
—*v.* **1** make slack; let up on. **2** be or become slack; let up. **3** slake (lime).
slack off, a loosen. **b** lessen one's efforts.
slack up, slow down; go more slowly.
—*adv.* in a slack manner. ⟨OE *slæc*⟩ **—'slack•ly,** *adv.*
—'slack•ness, *n.*

slack[2] [slæk] *n.* dirt, coal dust, and small pieces of coal left after coal has been screened. ⟨ME *slac;* cf. G *Schlacke*⟩

slack•en ['slækən] *v.* **1** make or become slower; slow down: *Don't slacken now; we're almost finished. The work slackened as the temperature climbed.* **2** make or become less active, vigorous, brisk, intense, forceful, etc.: *Her business slackens in winter. The heavy rain should slacken soon.* **3** make or become looser: *Slacken the rope. The rope slackened as the boat neared the pier.*

slack•er ['slækər] *n. Informal.* a person who shirks work or evades his or her duty.

slack–jawed ['slæk ,dʒɒd] *adj.* having a loose-hanging jaw or a partly open mouth, often as an indication of surprise or confusion.

slacks [slæks] *n.pl.* pants designed for casual wear by either men or women.

slack water the time between tides when the water does not move either way.

slag [slæg] *n., v.* **slagged, slag•ging.** —*n.* **1** the rough, hard, waste left after metal is separated from ore by melting. See BLAST FURNACE for picture. **2** a light, spongy lava.
—*v.* form slag; change into slag. ⟨< MLG *slagge*⟩

slag•gy ['slægi] *adj.* of, like, or having to do with slag.

slain [slein] *v.* pp. of SLAY.

slake [sleik] *v.* **slaked, slak•ing. 1** satisfy (thirst, desire for revenge, wrath, etc.). **2** put out (a fire). **3 a** cause the disintegration of (lime) by treatment with water. See SLAKED LIME. **b** of lime, be changed thus. **4** *Rare.* make or become less active, vigorous, intense, etc. ⟨OE *slacian* < *slæc* slack⟩

slaked lime a soft, white crystalline powder, $Ca(OH)_2$, obtained when lime is treated with water, and used in mortars, plasters, and cements; calcium hydroxide.

sla•lom ['slɑləm] *or* ['slæləm] *n., v.* —*n.* **1** *Skiing.* a zigzag downhill race on a course set between a series of posts. **2** any race over a similar course, such as in a car or on a motorcycle.
—*v.* ski on such a course. ⟨< Norwegian⟩

slam[1] [slæm] *v.* **slammed, slam•ming;** *n.* —*v.* **1** shut with force and noise; close with a bang: *She slammed the window down. The door slammed.* **2** throw, push, hit, or move with force and noise. **3** *Informal.* criticize harshly.
—*n.* **1** a violent and noisy closing, striking, etc.; bang: *John threw his books down with a slam.* **2** *Informal.* a harsh criticism.
⟨? < Scand.; cf. Icel. and dial. Norwegian *slamra* slam⟩

slam[2] [slæm] *n.* **1** *Bridge.* the winning of 12 (a **little** or **small slam**) or all 13 (a **grand slam**) tricks. **2** in certain other card games, the winning of all the tricks in one hand. ⟨origin uncertain⟩

slam–bang ['slæm 'bæŋ] *adv. Informal.* **1** with noisy violence. **2** quickly and carelessly; slap-bang.

slam•mer ['slæmər] *n. Slang.* Usually, **the slammer,** jail or prison. ⟨< SLAM[1]⟩

slan•der ['slændər] *n., v.* —*n. Law.* **1** the act or practice of making false oral statements meant to do harm to the reputation of another. Slander is a crime in Canada. **2** such a statement. Compare LIBEL.
—*v.* speak or spread slander against. ⟨ME < OF *esclandre* scandal < L *scandalum.* Doublet of SCANDAL.⟩ **—'slan•der•er,** *n.*

slan•der•ous ['slændərəs] *adj.* spreading or containing slander: *a slanderous remark.* **—'slan•der•ous•ly,** *adv.*

slang [slæŋ] *n., v.* —*n.* **1** vocabulary and usage that differ from the standard, consisting mainly of new, usually colourful, humorous, or vigorous words or phrases, or such meanings for existing words or phrases. Slang is often adopted by a particular group of people to set themselves apart from others; it often passes quickly out of use because it depends on novelty for much of its effect. Slang that is useful and appropriate often passes into standard usage, for example, the word *jazz.* **2** jargon; shoptalk: *In the slang of the Canadian fur trade, stealing furs from a warehouse was called* indoor trapping.
—*v.* attack with abusive language; rail at; scold. ⟨origin uncertain⟩
☛ *Usage.* Slang is not usually considered acceptable in formal speech or writing, and should be avoided even in informal situations when one is communicating with people outside one's own group. See also the notes at STANDARD and INFORMAL.

slang•y ['slæŋi] *adj.* **slang•i•er, slang•i•est.** using or containing much slang: *The writing is too slangy for an essay.*
—'slang•i•ly, *adv.* **—'slang•i•ness,** *n.*

slank [slæŋk] *v. Archaic.* a pt. of SLINK[1].

slant [slænt] *v., n.* —*v.* **1** slope: *Most handwriting slants to the right.* **2** interpret or present from a particular angle to appeal to a particular group or interest: *a magazine slanted toward the teenage audience.* **3** distort on purpose to give a certain impression; falsify: *The newspaper slanted the story by leaving out some of the facts.*
—*n.* **1** a slanting or oblique direction or position; a slope: *The greenhouse roof has a sharp slant.* **2** (*adjl.*) sloping: *a slant roof.* **3** a peculiar or personal attitude or viewpoint: *Her reminiscences provide us with an interesting slant on the political scene of the sixties.* ⟨var. of ME *slent* to slant < Scand.; cf. Norwegian *slenta*⟩
—'slant•ing•ly, *adv.*
☛ *Syn. v.* **1.** See note at SLOPE.

slant•ing ['slæntɪŋ] *adj., v.* —*adj.* sloping.
—*v.* ppr. of SLANT. **—'slant•ing•ly,** *adv.*

slant•ways ['slænt,weiz] *adv.* slantwise.

slant•wise ['slænt,waɪz] *adv., adj.* —*adv.* in a slanting manner; obliquely.
—*adj.* slanting; oblique.

slap [slæp] *n., v.* **slapped, slap•ping;** *adv.* —*n.* **1** a blow with the open hand or with something flat. **2** the sharp sound of a slap or something similar. **3** sharp words of blame; a direct insult or rebuff.

—v. **1** strike with the open hand or with something flat. **2** put, dash, or cast with force and a sharp sound: *She slapped the book down on the table.* **3** beat or hit with a slapping sound: *waves slapping against the dock.*
slap down, scold sharply.
—adv. Informal. **1** straight; directly: *The thief ran slap into a police officer.* **2** suddenly. ⟨< LG *slappe*⟩

slap–bang ['slæp 'bæŋ] *adv., adj. —adv.* **1** speedily; immediately. **2** thoughtlessly; in a headlong manner.
—adj. headlong; thoughtless; slapdash.

slap•dash ['slæp,dæʃ] *adv., adj., n. —adv. Informal.* hastily and carelessly.
—adj. hasty and careless.
—n. hasty, careless action, methods, or work.

slap•hap•py ['slæp,hæpi] *adj. Informal.* **1** in a giddy, giggly, or exaggeratedly silly mood; recklessly carefree. **2** punch-drunk.

slap•shot ['slæp,ʃɒt] *n. Cdn. Hockey.* a fast, not always accurate, shot made with a powerful swinging stroke.

slap•stick ['slæp,stɪk] *n., adj. —n.* **1** two long, narrow boards fastened so as to slap together loudly when a clown, actor, etc. hits somebody with them. **2** comedy full of broad humour and rough play.
—adj. characterized by broad humour and rough play: *a slapstick comedy.*

slap–up ['slæp ,ʌp] *adj. Informal.* **1** of best quality: *a slap-up performance.* **2** elegant; extravagant: *The State Dinner was a slap-up affair.*

slash [slæʃ] *v., n. —v.* **1** cut with a sweeping stroke of a sword, knife, etc.; gash: *He slashed the bark off the tree with his knife.* **2** make a slashing stroke. **3** cut or slit to let a different cloth or colour show through. **4** whip severely; lash. **5** criticize sharply, severely, or unkindly. **6** cut down severely; reduce a great deal: *Her salary was slashed when business became bad.* **7** cut out parts of (a book, etc.); change greatly (a book, etc.). **8** clear (land) of trees and brush.
—n. **1** the oblique sign; a virgule (/). **2** a sweeping, slashing stroke: *the slash of a sword, the slash of the rain.* **3** a cut or wound made by such a stroke; gash. **4** a sharp cutting down; great reduction: *a slash in prices.* **5** an ornamental slit in a garment that lets a different cloth or colour show through. **6** an open space in a forest, usually littered with chips, broken branches, etc. **7** a litter of chips, broken branches, etc. left in a forest by wind and storm. **8** the debris left after a logging operation. ⟨ME *slasche(n)*; cf. OF *esclachier* break⟩ **—'slash•er,** *n.*

slash fire *Cdn.* a fire in SLASH (*n.* def. 7), usually deliberately set and carefully controlled, to tidy up the area and encourage future growth.

slash•ing ['slæʃɪŋ] *adj., n., v. —adj.* **1** violent; severe: *slashing rain.* **2** impetuous; dashing.
—n. **1** a tract of land prepared for clearing. **2** *Hockey. Lacrosse.* the act of striking or swinging at an opposing player with a stick. The action incurs a penalty.
—v. ppr. of SLASH.

slash pocket a pocket set slantwise or lengthwise into a garment, often with the opening in a side seam.

slat [slæt] *n., v.* **slat•ted, slat•ting.** *—n.* a long, thin, narrow piece of wood or metal.
—v. provide or build with slats. ⟨ME < OF *esclat* split piece < Gmc.⟩

slate[1] [sleit] *n., v.* **slat•ed, slat•ing;** *adj. —n.* **1** a fine-grained, bluish grey rock formed from the compression of layers of shale or clay that splits easily into thin, smooth layers. Slate is used to cover roofs. **2** a thin piece of slate or material like slate, especially one used for writing on, or as a roofing tile: *Children used to do their schoolwork on slates they carried with them.* **3** a dark bluish grey. Also, **slate blue. 4 a** a list of candidates, officers, etc. to be considered for appointment, nomination, etc. **b** a list of activities; agenda: *What's on your slate for this evening?*
a clean slate, a record not marked by mistakes, dishonour, etc.: *She is entering public office with a clean slate.*
—v. **1** cover with slate. **2** list as a candidate, scheduled activity, etc.: *He is slated for the office of club president. The farewell party is slated for Friday at 4 p.m.*
—adj. dark bluish grey. ⟨ME < OF *esclate,* var. of *esclat* slat < Gmc.⟩ **—'slate,like,** *adj.*

slate[2] [sleit] *v.* **sla•ted, sla•ting. 1** beat violently. **2** criticize severely. ⟨? var. of *slat[2]*⟩

slat•er ['sleitər] *n.* **1** a person who covers roofs, etc. with slates. **2** WOOD LOUSE.

slath•er ['slæðər] *n., v. Informal. —n.* **slathers,** a great quantity: *slathers of bacon and eggs.*
—v. spread thickly or lavishly. ⟨origin unknown⟩

slat•tern ['slætərn] *n.* **1** a woman who is dirty, careless, or untidy in her dress, her ways, her housekeeping, etc. **2** a loose woman; slut. ⟨< Brit. dial. *slatter* slop; origin uncertain; cf. LG *slattje* slattern⟩

slat•tern•ly ['slætərnli] *adj.* **1** slovenly; untidy. **2** typical of a slattern. **—'slat•tern•li•ness,** *n.*

slat•y ['sleiti] *adj.* **slat•i•er, slat•i•est. 1** of or containing slate. **2** slate-coloured.

slaugh•ter ['slɒtər] *n., v. —n.* **1** the killing of an animal or animals for food; butchering. **2** brutal killing; much or needless killing.
—v. **1** butcher. **2** kill brutally; massacre. **3** *Informal.* defeat by a wide margin. ⟨ME < Scand.; cf. ON *slátr* butcher-meat < *slá* slay⟩ **—'slaugh•ter•er,** *n.*

slaugh•ter•house ['slɒtər,hʌus] *n.* a place where animals are killed for food; abattoir.

slaugh•ter•ous ['slɒtərəs] *adj.* murderous; destructive.

Slav [slæv] *or* [slɑv] *n., adj. —n.* a member of any of a group of E European peoples who speak Slavic languages, such as Russians, Poles, Czechs, Slovaks, and Bulgarians.
—adj. Slavic. ⟨< Med.L *Slavus, Sclavus.* See SLAVE.⟩

Slav. Slavic; Slavonic; Slavonian.

slave [sleiv] *n., v.* **slaved, slav•ing.** *—n.* **1** a person who is the property of another. Slaves used to be bought and sold like cattle. **2** a person who is controlled or ruled by some desire, habit, or influence: *A drunkard is a slave to drink.* **3** a person who works like a slave. **4** an ant that is captured and forced to work for other ants. **5 a** an electronic device that receives and relays radio signals transmitted by a master control, as in loran navigation. **b** a mechanical or electric device for manipulating objects by remote control. **6** (*adjl.*) of or done by slaves: *built by slave labour.*
—v. **1** work like a slave. **2** trade in slaves. ⟨ME < OF < Med.L *Sclavus* Slav (captive) < LGk. *Sklabos,* ult. < Slavic *slovo.* See SLOVENE.⟩ **—'slave,like,** *adj.*

Slave [sleiv] *n., pl.* **Slaves** or **Slave;** *adj. —n.* **1** a member of a people of the First Nations in the Northwest Territories living between the Rockies and Great Slave Lake. **2** the Athapascan language of the Slaves.
—adj. of or having to do with the Slaves or their language. Also, **Slavey.** ⟨translation of Cree *awokanak* slaves⟩

slave driver 1 a person who supervises slaves at work. **2** an employer, supervisor, etc. who is excessively harsh or demanding.

slave•hold•er ['sleiv,houldər] *n.* an owner of slaves.

slave•hold•ing ['sleiv,houldɪŋ] *adj., n. —adj.* owning slaves.
—n. the owning of slaves.

slav•er[1] ['sleivər] *n.* **1** a dealer in slaves. **2** a ship used in the slave trade. ⟨< *slave*⟩

slav•er[2] ['slævər] *v., n. —v.* **1** let saliva run from the mouth; drool. **2** cover or wet with saliva.
—n. saliva running from the mouth. ⟨ME < Scand.; cf. Icel. *slafra.* Related to SLOBBER.⟩

slav•er•y ['sleivəri] *n.* **1** the condition of being a slave. Many Africans were captured by Europeans and sold into slavery in America. **2** the custom of owning slaves: *They fought against slavery.* **3** a condition like that of a slave: *slavery to the dictates of fashion.* **4** hard work like that of a slave: *She said the job was pure slavery.*

slave trade traffic in slaves; the buying and selling of slaves for profit.

Slav•ey ['sleivi] *n., adj.* Slave.

Slav•ic ['slævɪk] *or* ['slɑvɪk] *adj., n. —adj.* of or having to do with the Slavs or their languages.
—n. the branch of the Indo-European family of languages that includes Bulgarian, Czech, Polish, Russian, Serbo-Croatian, Slovak, Ukrainian, etc.

slav•ish ['sleivɪʃ] *adj.* **1** of or having to do with a slave or slaves. **2** like or characteristic of a slave; weakly submissive and servile: *a slavish personality, a slavish follower.* **3** lacking originality and independence: *a slavish translation of the original, slavish reliance on a pattern.* **—'slav•ish•ly,** *adv.* **—'slav•ish•ness,** *n.*

Sla•vo•ni•an [slə'vouniən] *adj., n. —adj.* **1** of or having to do with Slavonia, a region in Croatia, or its people. **2** *Archaic.*

Slavic.
—*n.* **1** a native or inhabitant of Slavonia. **2** *Archaic.* Slavic.

Sla•von•ic [slə'vɒnɪk] *adj. or n.* Slavic.

slaw [slɒ] *n.* coleslaw. ⟨< Du. *sla*, contraction of *salade* salad⟩

slay [slei] *v.* **slew** or **slayed** (for 2), **slain, slay•ing. 1** kill with violence, especially in battle: *Many soldiers were slain on that hill.* **2** *Slang.* amuse greatly: *That comedian just slays me.* ⟨OE *slēan*⟩ **—'slay•er,** *n.*
☛ *Hom.* SLEIGH.
☛ *Syn.* **1.** See note at KILL.

sleave [sliv] *v.* **sleaved, sleav•ing;** *n.* —*v.* divide or separate into smaller threads.
—*n.* **1** a small silk thread made by separating a thicker thread. **2** any tangled mass. ⟨OE *slǣfan*, as in *tōslǣfan* divide⟩
☛ *Hom.* SLEEVE.

sleaze [sliz] *n. Informal.* **1** a sleazy person. **2** something sleazy, as reading or viewing material, behaviour, etc. **3** sleazy quality; sleaziness. ⟨< *sleazy*⟩

slea•zy ['slizi] *adj.* **-zi•er, -zi•est. 1** flimsy and poor: *sleazy cloth.* **2** *Informal.* shoddy, squalid, disreputable, or low: *a sleazy, run-down hotel.* ⟨origin uncertain⟩ **—'slea•zi•ly,** *adv.* **—'slea•zi•ness,** *n.*

sled [slɛd] *n., v.* **sled•ded, sled•ding.** —*n.* **1** a small, low vehicle having runners instead of wheels, used especially for carrying loads over ice and snow. Before the snowmobile, the common means of winter transportation in the North was a sled pulled by a team of dogs. **2** a child's plaything consisting of a flat surface on runners, for sliding down hills on snow. **3** stoneboat.
—*v.* ride or carry on a sled. ⟨< MDu. *sledde*⟩

sled•ding ['slɛdɪŋ] *n., v.* —*n.* **1** the act of riding or coasting on a sled. **2** the condition of the snow or ice as a surface for a sled: *The new snow made for good sledding.* **3** conditions in general, as they affect progress or advance toward a goal; progress: *He found it tough sledding at first because everything was strange to him.*
—*v.* ppr. of SLED.

sled dog a dog trained and used to draw a sled, especially in the Arctic.

sledge[1] [slɛdʒ] *n., v.* **sledged, sledg•ing.** —*n.* **1** a low, heavy vehicle mounted on runners, used for carrying loads, and drawn over snow or ice or dragged over the ground by draft animals. **2** *Esp. Brit.* a sled or sleigh.
—*v.* ride or carry on a sledge. ⟨< MDu. *sleedse*⟩

sledge[2] [slɛdʒ] *n., v.* **sledged, sledg•ing.** —*n.* a sledgehammer.
—*v.* strike with or as if with a sledgehammer. ⟨OE *slecg*⟩

sledge•ham•mer ['slɛdʒ,hæmər] *n., v.* —*n.* **1** a large, heavy hammer, usually swung with both hands. **2** (*adjl.*) powerful or crushing: *sledgehammer sarcasm.*
—*v.* hit with, or as if with, a sledgehammer.

sleek [slik] *adj., v.* —*adj.* **1** smooth and glossy; looking highly polished: *sleek hair.* **2** having a well-groomed, well-fed appearance: *a sleek cat. She was looking very sleek and healthy after her holiday.* **3** too smooth in speech, manners, etc.; slick. **4** trim and elegant: *a sleek ship.*
—*v.* make smooth and glossy: *He sleeked down his hair.* ⟨var. of *slick*⟩ **—'sleek•ly,** *adv.* **—'sleek•ness,** *n.*

sleep [slip] *v.* **slept, sleep•ing;** *n.* —*v.* **1** rest the body and mind; be without ordinary consciousness. **2** be in a condition like sleep: *The seeds sleep in the ground all winter.* **3** spend or pass in sleeping (*usually used with* **away** *or* **out**): *to sleep the morning away.* **4** provide with or offer sleeping accommodation for: *a hotel that sleeps 500 people.* **5** fail to pay attention.
sleep around, *Slang.* have sexual intercourse with a number of different people.
sleep in, a remain in bed later than usual: *We always sleep in on a Sunday morning.* **b** sleep late or oversleep: *He was late because he slept in.* **c** live at one's place of work: *The maid slept in.*
sleep like a log, sleep soundly or heavily.
sleep off, get rid of by sleeping: *She was sleeping off a headache.*
sleep on, put off deciding on, in order to consider further: *He said he would sleep on the idea.*
sleep over, spend the night at another person's home.
sleep with, have sexual intercourse with.
—*n.* **1** a condition in which body and mind are very inactive, occurring naturally and regularly in all animals. **2** a period spent in sleeping. **3** a state or condition like sleep. **4** in plants, a sleeplike state similar to that of animals, characterized by closing petals, leaves, etc.; nyctitropism. **5** mucus that is sometimes secreted by the eyes during sleep, and that collects and hardens especially in the inner corners of the eyes.
in (one's) **sleep, a** while sleeping. **b** completely effortlessly.
last sleep, death.
put to sleep, a put (an animal, especially a pet) to death humanely: *We had to put our dog to sleep because it was old and sick.* **b** cause to sleep. ⟨OE *slǣpan*⟩ **—'sleep•like,** *adj.*

sleep•er ['slipər] *n.* **1** a person or animal that sleeps: *They made their way silently past the sleepers. She's a sound sleeper.* **2** a railway sleeping car. **3** a horizontal beam, especially one on or near the ground, that supports a structure. **4** *Esp. Brit.* a tie to support a railway track. **5** someone or something that is unexpectedly successful, especially a book, play, or motion picture that is an unexpected hit or winner: *Her first play was the sleeper of the season.* **6** a small, plain gold ring worn instead of an earring in a newly pierced ear lobe to prevent the hole from growing closed. **7** a one-piece garment for infants, extending down from the neck and covering the feet.

sleeping bag a zippered bag for sleeping in, usually waterproof and warmly lined, used especially when camping.

sleeping car a railway car with berths or small rooms for passengers to sleep in.

sleeping partner a partner who takes no active part in managing the business; a silent partner.

sleeping pill a pill or capsule containing a drug that causes sleep.

sleeping sickness *Pathology.* **1** an infectious and generally fatal disease common in tropical Africa, caused by the bite of the tsetse fly (*Glossina palpalis*), characterized by fever, weakness, and lethargy. **2** a viral infection of the brain characterized by apathy, impairment of vision, and extreme muscle weakness. Also called (def. 2) **epidemic encephalitis.**

sleeping tablet SLEEPING PILL.

sleep•less ['sliplɪs] *adj.* **1** not able to sleep. **2** not providing or producing sleep: *sleepless nights.* **3** continually active or watchful: *a sleepless sentry, a sleepless memory.* **—'sleep•less•ly,** *adv.* **—'sleep•less•ness,** *n.*

sleep•o•ver ['slip,ouvər] *n.* a party for children where guests spend the night at the host's home.

sleep•walk ['slip,wɒk] *v.* walk about while asleep. **—'sleep,walk•er,** *n.* **—'sleep,walk•ing,** *n.*

sleep•y ['slipi] *adj.* **sleep•i•er, sleep•i•est. 1** ready to go to sleep; inclined to sleep. **2** not active; quiet. **3** inducing sleep; soporific: *a warm, sleepy day.* **4** lethargic; of or showing sleepiness: *a sleepy smile.* **—'sleep•i•ly,** *adv.* **—'sleep•i•ness,** *n.*
☛ *Syn.* **Sleepy,** DROWSY = ready or inclined to sleep. **Sleepy** is the general word describing people or things, particularly suggesting being ready to fall asleep or having a tendency to sleep: *She never gets enough rest and is always sleepy.* **Drowsy** particularly suggests being heavy or dull with sleepiness: *After lying in the sun, he became drowsy.*

sleep•y•head ['slipi,hɛd] *n.* a person who is sleepy or not paying attention: *He's such a sleepyhead in the morning!*

sleet [slit] *n., v.* —*n.* **1** precipitation in the form of transparent or translucent pellets of ice smaller than 5 mm. **2** partly frozen rain, often mixed with snow. **3** a mixture of snow and rain. **4** a fall or shower of sleet.
—*v.* be the case that sleet is falling (*used with the subject* **it**): *It began to sleet.* ⟨ME *slete*⟩

sleet•y ['sliti] *adj.* **sleet•i•er, sleet•i•est.** of, like, or characterized by sleet. **—'sleet•i•ness,** *n.*

sleeve [sliv] *n., v.* **sleeved, sleev•ing.** —*n.* **1** the tubelike part of a garment that extends from the shoulder and covers the arm or part of the arm. **2** a tube or tubelike machine part enclosing a rod or another tube. See TURNBUCKLE for picture. **3** a paper or plastic cover for a phonograph record.
have up (one's) **sleeve,** have in reserve, concealed but ready for use when needed: *She had one more trick up her sleeve.*
laugh in or **up** (one's) **sleeve.** See LAUGH.
—*v.* provide with a sleeve or sleeves. ⟨OE *slīefe*⟩ **—'sleeve,like,** *adj.* **—'sleeve•less,** *adj.*
☛ *Hom.* SLEAVE.

sleeved [slivd] *adj.* having sleeves of a specified kind (*used especially in compounds*): *a long-sleeved shirt.*

Sleighs: at the right, a cutter; at the left, a children's sleigh

sleigh [slei] *n., v.* —*n.* **1** a light carriage mounted on runners, used for carrying persons over snow or ice, and usually drawn by a horse or horses. A cutter is a kind of sleigh. **2** SLED (def. 2).
—*v.* travel or ride in a sleigh. ⟨< Du. *slee*, var. of *slede* sled⟩
☛ *Hom.* SLAY.

sleigh–bells ['slei ˌbɛlz] *n.pl. Cdn.* a number of small bell-like metal balls attached to a sleigh or to the harness of the animal pulling it.

sleigh•ing ['sleiɪŋ] *n., v.* —*n.* **1** riding in a sleigh. **2** the conditions for sleighing: *The warm rain spoiled the sleighing.*
—*v.* ppr. of SLEIGH.

sleight [sləit] *n.* **1** skill; dexterity. **2** a clever trick. ⟨ME < ON *slǽgth* < *slǽgr* sly. See SLY.⟩
☛ *Hom.* SLIGHT.

sleight of hand **1** skill and quickness in moving the hands, as in juggling or conjuring tricks. **2** a display of skill and quickness with the hands; a trick or juggling act requiring such skill.

slen•der ['slɛndər] *adj.* **1** gracefully narrow and slight of frame; slim: *a tall, slender girl, a slender hand.* **2** long and thin; not wide or big around in proportion to length or height: *a slender sapling. A pencil is a slender piece of wood.* **3** scanty; meagre; not adequate: *a slender meal, a slender income, a slender hope.* ⟨ME *slendre, sclendre*; origin uncertain⟩ **—'slen•der•ly,** *adv.* **—'slen•der•ness,** *n.*
☛ *Syn.* **1. Slender,** SLIM = thin, not big around. **Slender,** describing a person or thing and meaning tall or long and thin, suggests good proportions, gracefulness, and beauty: *Many girls want to be slender. The legs of those chairs are slender.* **Slim** emphasizes lack of flesh and lightness of frame or build: *He is a slim boy who may fill out as he becomes older.*

slen•der•ize ['slɛndəˌraɪz] *v.* **-ized, -iz•ing. 1** make slender. **2** cause to look slender or less stout: *a slenderizing dress.*

slept [slɛpt] *v.* pt. and pp. of SLEEP.

sleuth [sluθ] *n., v.* —*n. Informal.* detective.
—*v.* be or act like a detective. ⟨clipping from *sleuthhound*⟩

sleuth•hound ['sluθˌhaʊnd] *n.* **1** a bloodhound. **2** *Informal.* a detective. ⟨ME < ON *sloth* trail + E *hound*⟩

slew[1] [slu] *v.* pt. of SLAY.
☛ *Hom.* SLOUGH[1], SLUE [slu].

slew[2] [slu] *v., n.* —*v.* **1** turn or swing on a pivot or as if on a pivot: *He slewed around in his seat to get a better look. We slewed the telescope around to the east.* **2** skid or turn sharply: *The car slewed around the curve. She slewed the car to the right to avoid the dog.*
—*n.* **1** a turn, twist, or skid. **2** the position into which something has slewed or been slewed. Also, **slue.** ⟨origin uncertain⟩
☛ *Hom.* SLOUGH[1], SLUE [slu].

slew[3] [slu] *n.* See SLOUGH[1].
☛ *Hom.* SLOUGH[1], SLUE [slu].

slew[4] [slu] *n. Informal.* a lot; a large number or amount: *There were a whole slew of people waiting at the stage door.* Also, **slue.** ⟨< Irish Gaelic *sluagh* host, crowd⟩
☛ *Hom.* SLOUGH[1], SLUE [slu].

slice [sləis] *n., v.* **sliced, slic•ing.** —*n.* **1** a thin, flat, broad piece cut from something, especially food: *a slice of bread, meat, or cake.* **2** a knife or spatula with a thin, broad blade. **3** a part; share: *She wanted a slice of the profits.* **4** *Sports.* **a** a hit made so that the ball curves away in the direction corresponding to the side from which it was hit. **b** a ball so hit. Compare HOOK (def. 9).
slice of life, a realistic portrayal or view of everyday life.
—*v.* **1** cut into slices: *He sliced the loaf of bread.* **2** cut off as a slice: *I sliced a piece of the meatloaf for myself.* **3** cut or pass through like a knife: *A bullet sliced the air by her head. The plough sliced through the earth.* **4** *Sports.* hit (a ball) so that it curves away in the direction corresponding to the side from which it was hit. Compare HOOK (def. 10).
any way (or **no matter how**) **you slice it,** no matter how you look at it. ⟨ME < OF *esclice* thin chip < Gmc.⟩

slic•er ['sləisər] *n.* a person or thing that slices, especially a mechanical device for slicing food: *a meat slicer.*

slick [slɪk] *adj., v., n., adv.* —*adj.* **1** sleek; smooth: *slick hair.* **2** slippery; greasy: *a road slick with ice or mud.* **3** *Informal.* clever; ingenious. **4** smooth in speech, manners, etc., especially in a tricky or deceitful way. **5** *Informal.* of or like that of a smooth, tricky person; cunningly made up: *a slick excuse.* **6** *Informal.* showing technical skill but lacking true artistry or depth. **7** *Slang.* fine, stylish, etc.: *a slick sports car.*
—*v.* make sleek or smooth.
—*n.* **1** a smooth patch or surface, especially a patch of oil, etc. on water or a paved road. **2** *Informal.* a magazine printed on heavy, glossy paper. **3 a** a tool used for scraping and smoothing leather. **b** a trowel for smoothing the top of a mould in casting metals.
—*adv.* in a slick manner; slickly. ⟨ME *slike*, adj. OE *slician* make smooth⟩ **—'slick•ly,** *adv.* **—'slick•ness,** *n.*

slick•en•side ['slɪkənˌsaɪd] *n. Geology.* a more or less smooth and polished rock surface produced by friction, pressure, or cleavage, usually along a fault plane.

slick•er ['slɪkər] *n.* **1** a long, loose, waterproof coat, usually made of oilskin. **2** *Slang.* a sly, tricky person.

slick–lick•er ['slɪk ˌlɪkər] *n.* a device for removing large oil slicks from water, consisting basically of a large conveyor belt covered with absorbent material like towelling that soaks up the oil.

slid [slɪd] *v.* pt. and pp. of SLIDE.

slide [slaɪd] *v.* **slid, slid•ing;** *n.* —*v.* **1** move smoothly over a surface: *The bureau drawers slide in and out.* **2** move easily or quietly or secretly: *The thief slid behind the curtains.* **3** pass without heeding or being heeded. **4** pass by degrees; slip: *She has slid into bad habits.* **5** pass or put quietly or secretly: *He slid a gun into his pocket.* **6** slip in an uncontrolled manner: *The car slid into the ditch.* **7** *Music.* pass or progress from tone to tone without perceptible step or break. **8** *Baseball.* throw the body, usually feet first, along the ground in running to a base, so as to avoid being tagged, to break up a double play, etc.
let slide, neglect; not bother about: *He has been letting his business slide lately.*
—*n.* **1** the act of sliding: *The children each took a slide in turn.* **2 a** an inclined CHUTE[1] (def. 1) on which children can play. **b** any smooth surface for sliding on. **3** a track, rail, etc. on which something slides. **4** something that works by sliding. **5** *Music.* the U-shaped tube of a brass instrument such as a trombone that is pushed in or out to change the pitch of the tones. **6 a** a mass of earth, snow, etc. sliding down. **b** the sliding down of such a mass. **7** a small, thin sheet of glass on which objects are placed for microscopic examination. **8** a small transparent photograph made of glass or film. Slides are put in a projector and shown on a screen. **9** *Music.* **a** rapid ascending or descending series of three or more notes, composed of grace notes which ornament the last or principal note. **b** a passing from tone to tone without perceptible step or break. **10** *Baseball.* a throwing of the body, usually feet first, along the ground in running to a base, so as to avoid being tagged, to break up a double play, etc. ⟨OE *slīdan*⟩ **—'slid•er,** *n.*
☛ *Syn. v.* **1. Slide,** SLIP[1], GLIDE = move along smoothly, especially over a surface. **Slide** emphasizes continuous contact with a smooth or slippery surface: *The boat slid down the bank into the water.* **Slip** emphasizes the smoothness or slipperiness of the surface or absence of any hindrance, and suggests sliding suddenly without intention: *One of the climbers slipped on the rocks.* **Glide** emphasizes continuous, smooth, even, easy movement, not necessarily along a surface: *The swans glide gracefully on the lake.*

slide fastener zipper.

slide projector a device for projecting the image on a slide onto a screen or wall. The slides are housed in a carousel, which moves forward one slide when the control is pressed.

slide rule a ruler that has a sliding middle strip, marked with logarithmic scales, used by engineers, physicists, etc. for making rapid calculations.

slid•ing ['slaɪdɪŋ] *adj., v.* —*adj.* **1** adjusted relative to some variable. **2** moving or operating on a track or groove: *a sliding door.*
—*v.* ppr. of SLIDE.

sliding scale a scale or standard, as for wages, tariffs, or fees, that is adjusted to fit certain conditions or situations. Wages based on a sliding scale are adjusted according to the cost of living.

slight [sləit] *adj., v., n.* —*adj.* **1** not much; not important; small;

not intense: *I have a slight headache.* **2** not big around; slender: *She is a slight girl.* **3** frail; flimsy: *a slight excuse.*
—v. treat as of little value; pay too little attention to; neglect: *He felt slighted because he was not asked to the party.*
—n. slighting treatment; an act showing neglect or lack of respect. ⟨OE *-sliht* level, as in *earthslihtes* level with the ground⟩
—'slight•ness, *n.*
☛ *Hom.* SLEIGHT.
☛ *Syn. v.* **Slight,** OVERLOOK, NEGLECT = pay too little or no attention to someone or something needing or deserving it. **Slight** emphasizes intentionally treating a person, thing, work, or duty as of too little importance to deserve consideration or attention: *He slights his cousins because they are poor.* **Overlook** emphasizes unintentionally failing to see something needing attention, because of other concerns, haste, carelessness, etc.: *She overlooked the telephone bill.* **Neglect** emphasizes failing to give enough or deserved attention or care to a person, duty, etc.: *He neglects his teeth.*

slight•ing ['sləitɪŋ] *adj., v. —adj.* that detracts; contemptuous; disrespectful: *a slighting remark.*
—v. ppr. of SLIGHT. **—'slight•ing•ly,** *adv.*

slight•ly ['sləitli] *adv.* **1** to a slight degree; somewhat; a little: *I knew him slightly.* **2** slenderly: *She's very slightly built.*

sli•ly ['slaɪli] See SLYLY.

slim [slɪm] *adj.* **slim•mer, slim•mest;** *v.* **slimmed, slim•ming.** *—adj.* **1** slender; gracefully thin: *a slim girl, a slim waist.* **2** small or scanty; slight: *There is a slim chance that he will get the letter in time. Her chances of escape were slim.*
—v. make or become slender or more slender: *He is trying to slim down. A girdle is designed to slim the figure.* ⟨< Du. *slim* bad⟩
—'slim•ly, *adv.* **—'slim•ness,** *n.*
☛ *Syn.* **1.** See note at SLENDER.

slime [slaɪm] *n., v.* **slimed, slim•ing.** *—n.* **1** a soft, slippery, sticky mud or something like it. **2** a slippery, sticky substance given off by snails, slugs, fish, etc. **3** disgusting filth.
—v. **1** cover or smear with, or as with, slime. **2** clear (skins, fish, etc.) of slimy matter by scraping. **3** *Slang.* defame in a despicable way. ⟨OE *slīm*⟩

slim•y ['slaɪmi] *adj.* **slim•i•er, slim•i•est. 1** covered with slime. **2** of or like slime. **3** disgusting; vile; filthy. **4** using sly or crafty flattery, insinuation, etc.; base; treacherous; dishonourable.
— 'slim•i•ly, *adv.* **—'slim•i•ness,** *n.*

sling [slɪŋ] *n., v.* **slung, sling•ing.** *—n.* **1** a strip of leather with a string fastened to each end, for throwing stones by first whirling them around in the air and then releasing them; slingshot. **2** a throw; the act or an instance of slinging. **3** a hanging loop of cloth fastened around the neck to support an injured arm or hand. **4** a loop of rope, band, chain, etc. by which heavy objects are lifted, carried, or held: *The men lowered the boxes into the cellar by a sling. Rifles have slings.* **5** a type of women's shoe having an open heel secured by a strap.
—v. **1** throw with a sling. **2** throw; cast; hurl; fling. **3** raise, lower, etc. with a sling. **4** hang in a sling; hang so as to swing loosely: *The soldier's gun was slung over her shoulder.* **5** *Slang.* mix; serve: *to sling hash.* ⟨ME, perhaps < ON *slyngva*⟩

sling•er ['slɪŋər] *n.* **1** a fighter armed with a sling. **2** a worker in charge of slings used in hoisting, etc. **3** a person who slings.

sling•shot ['slɪŋ,ʃɒt] *n.* **1** a Y-shaped stick with a band of rubber between its prongs, used to shoot pebbles, etc.; catapult. **2** SLING (def. 1).

slink¹ [slɪŋk] *v.* **slunk** or *(archaic)* **slank, slunk, slink•ing.** move in a sneaking, guilty manner; sneak: *After stealing the meat, the dog slunk away.* ⟨OE *slincan*⟩ **—'slink•ing•ly,** *adv.*

slink² [slɪŋk] *v.* **slinked** or **slunk, slink•ing;** *n., adj. —v.* of animals, give birth to prematurely.
—n. any animal born prematurely.
—adj. born prematurely. ⟨< *slink¹*⟩

slink•y ['slɪŋki] *adj.* **-i•er, -i•est. 1** furtive; sneaking. **2** of clothing, tight-fitting in an alluring, graceful way: *a slinky gown.*
—'slink•i•ly, *adv.* **—'slink•i•ness,** *n.*

slip¹ [slɪp] *v.* **slipped** or *(archaic)* **slipt, slip•ping;** *n. —v.* **1** go or move smoothly, quietly, easily, or quickly: *She slipped out of the room. Time slips by. The ship slipped through the waves. The drawer slips into place.* **2** slide; move out of place: *The knife slipped and cut him.* **3** slide suddenly without wanting to: *She slipped on the icy sidewalk.* **4** cause to slip; put, pass, or draw smoothly, quietly, or secretly: *He slipped back the bolt. She slipped the ring from her finger. Slip the note into Mary's hand.* **5** put on or take off (something) easily or quickly: *Slip on your coat. Slip off your shoes.* **6** pass without notice; pass through neglect; escape: *Don't let this opportunity slip.* **7** get loose from; get away from; escape from: *The dog has slipped its collar. Your name has slipped my mind.* **8** let go; release: *She slipped the hound. The ship has slipped anchor and is off.* **9** move gradually into some state, habit, attitude, etc. **10** make a mistake or error. **11** fall off; decline; deteriorate: *New car sales have slipped.*
let slip, tell or say without meaning to: *She let the secret slip in a careless moment. He let slip that she was pregnant.*
slip one over on, *Informal.* get the advantage of by trickery.
slip up, *Informal.* make a mistake or error.
—n. **1** the act or fact of slipping. **2** something that covers and can be slipped on or off; covering: *Pillows are covered by slips.* **3** a dress-length or skirt-length undergarment of nylon, silk, etc. worn by women and girls. **4** a mistake; error: *a slip in grammar. That remark was a slip of the tongue.* **5** a space for ships between wharves or in a dock. **6** an inclined platform alongside the water, on which ships are built, repaired, or landed. **7** a leash for a dog. **8** *Cricket.* **a** the position of a player behind and to the side of the wicketkeeper. **b** the player in this position.
give (someone) **the slip,** *Informal.* escape from or get away from someone: *She gave her creditors the slip.*
slip of the tongue, a remark made by mistake. ⟨probably < MLG *slippen*⟩
☛ *Syn. v.* **1-3.** See note at SLIDE.

slip² [slɪp] *n., v.* **slipped, slip•ping.** *—n.* **1** a small stem or shoot cut from a plant, used to grow a new plant, either by rooting in water or earth or by grafting; a cutting; scion. **2** a long, narrow strip of paper, cloth, etc.: *a sales slip.* **3** a young, slender person: *He is just a slip of a boy.*
—v. take a stem or shoot from (a plant) to grow a new plant. ⟨probably < MDu. or MLG *slippen* cut⟩

slip•case ['slɪp,keis] *n.* a box for a book or set of books, open on one side to display the spine(s).

slip•cov•er ['slɪp,kʌvər] *n.* **1** a removable, fitted cloth cover for a chair, chesterfield, etc. **2** a dust jacket for a book.

slip–knot ['slɪp ,nɒt] *n.* **1** a knot made to slip along the rope or cord around which it is made. **2** a knot that can be undone by a pull. See KNOT for picture. Also, **slipknot.**

slip noose a noose made with a slip-knot.

slip–on ['slɪp ,ɒn] *adj., n. —adj.* **1** that can be put on or taken off easily or quickly, as a slipper or shoe with no fastenings. **2** that must be put on or taken off over the head.
—n. a slip-on glove, blouse, sweater, etc.

slip•page ['slɪpɪdʒ] *n.* **1** the act or fact of slipping. **2** *Machinery.* the loss in time, distance, or amount between a standard and what is achieved, between theoretical and actual speed, power, output, etc.

slip•per ['slɪpər] *n., v. —n.* a light, soft, casual shoe that is easily slipped on and off the foot, worn indoors.
—v. strike with a slipper, as a punishment. **—'slip•per•less,** *adj.*

slip•pered ['slɪpərd] *adj.* wearing slippers.

slip•per•y ['slɪpəri] *adj.* **-per•i•er, -per•i•est. 1** causing or likely to cause sliding and slipping because of smoothness, greasiness, etc.: *Wet or icy streets are slippery. A waxed floor is slippery.* **2** slipping away easily; hard to hold firmly: *Wet soap is slippery.* **3** difficult to handle or pin down: *a slippery situation, a slippery concept.* **4** not to be depended on; tricky or deceitful: *a slippery character.* ⟨< obs. *slipper* slippery, OE *slipor*⟩
—'slip•per•i•ly, *adv.* **—'slip•per•i•ness,** *n.*

slippery elm 1 an elm (*Ulmus rubra*) of E North America having an inner bark that becomes slimy or slippery when moistened. **2** the inner bark of this tree.

slip•shod ['slɪp,ʃɒd] *adj.* **1** careless in dress, habits, speech, etc.; untidy; slovenly. **2** carelessly done: *slipshod work, a slipshod performance.* **3** shuffling: *a slipshod gait.* **4** wearing shoes worn down at the heel.

slip•stitch ['slɪp,stɪtʃ] *n., v. —n.* **1** an almost invisible kind of stitch used for sewing folded edges, such as hems, made by alternately taking a stitch inside the folded edge and a very tiny stitch in the body of the article being sewn. **2** a pattern stitch in knitting and crochet.
—v. sew, knit, or crochet with slipstitches.

slip•stream ['slɪp,strim] *n.* **1** a backward-moving stream of air created beside a rapidly moving object, such as an aircraft or a motor vehicle. **2** the area of decreased air pressure immediately behind such a moving object.

slipt [slɪpt] *v. Archaic.* a pt. of SLIP¹.

slip–up ['slɪp ,ʌp] *n.* **1** *Informal.* a mistake; error. **2** an unfortunate accident.

slip•way ['slɪp,wei] *n.* **1** in a shipyard, the area sloping down to the water, on which the WAYS (def. 16) are located.

2 *Whaling.* on a factory ship, a ramp for hauling the carcasses on board.

slit [slɪt] *v.* **slit, slit•ting;** *n.* —*v.* **1** make a long, straight cut in; cut open: *He used a paper knife to slit the envelope open.* **2** cut lengthwise into strips: *to slit leather into thongs.*
—*n.* a straight, narrow cut or opening: *the slit in a letter box, a slit for a buttonhole. Her eyes were just slits.* ⟨ME *slitte(n)*⟩
—'slit•ter, *n.*

slith•er ['slɪðər] *v., n.* —*v.* **1** slide unsteadily down or along a loose or gravelly surface: *We slithered down the embankment to the road.* **2** move or go with a gliding or sliding motion: *The snake slithered away into the grass.* **3** walk by sliding the feet. **4** make (something) slide.
—*n.* a slithering movement. ⟨OE *slidrian*⟩ **—'slith•e•ry,** *adj.*

slit skirt a narrow skirt having a slit, or vent, in the lower part of the seam at one or both sides or at the front or back, for ease in walking and sitting.

slit trench a narrow trench constructed in a battle zone, especially during World War I, to hold one or more soldiers and protect them from direct attack, shell fragments, etc.

sliv•er ['slɪvər] *n., v.* —*n.* **1** a long, thin, sharp piece that has been split off, broken off, or cut off; splinter: *a sliver of wood, a sliver of glass.* **2** a very narrow slice: *Give me just a sliver of pie.* **3** a loose fibre of wool, cotton, etc. obtained by carding or combing.
—*v.* split or break into slivers. ⟨ult. < OE *slīfan* split⟩

sliv•o•vitz ['slɪvəvɪts], ['slivəvɪts], *or* ['ʃlɪvəvɪts] *n.* a usually colourless plum brandy made especially in E Europe. ⟨< Serbo-Croatian *šljivovica* < *šljiva* plum⟩

slob [slɒb] *n.* **1** *Slang.* an untidy or boorish person. **2** *Cdn.* SLOB ICE. **3** *Irish.* mud. ⟨probably < Irish *slab,* var. of *slaba* mud < Gmc.⟩

slob•ber ['slɒbər] *v., n.* —*v.* **1** let liquid run out from the mouth; drool: *The dog slobbered all over my skirt.* **2** wet or smear with saliva, etc. **3** speak in a silly, sentimental way.
—*n.* **1** saliva or other liquid running out from the mouth. **2** silly, sentimental talk or emotion. ⟨probably ult. < Du. *slobberen*⟩

slob•ber•y ['slɒbəri] *adj.* **1** slobbering. **2** disagreeably wet; sloppy. **—'slob•ber•i•ness,** *n.*

slob ice *Cdn.* a mass of densely packed chunks of heavy, sludgy ice, especially sea ice.

sloe [slou] *n.* **1** the blue-black, tart, plumlike fruit of the blackthorn (*Prunus spinosa*). **2** the blackthorn shrub itself. **3** any of several wild plums of the genus *Prunus.* ⟨OE *slāh*⟩
☛ *Hom.* SLOW.

sloe–eyed ['slou ,aɪd] *adj.* **1** having very dark eyes. **2** having oval eyes.

sloe gin a liqueur made of gin and flavoured with sloes.

slog [slɒg] *v.* **slogged, slog•ging;** *n. Informal.* —*v.* **1** plod heavily: *We slogged through the snow to the cabin.* **2** work hard and steadily: *She slogged away at the assignment.* **3** hit hard.
—*n.* **1** a spell of hard, steady, or plodding work: *a half-hour's slog through muskeg.* **2** a hard blow. ⟨var. of *slug*²⟩

slo•gan ['slougən] *n.* **1** a word or phrase used by a business, club, political party, etc. to advertise its purpose; motto: *'Service with a smile' was the store's slogan.* **2** a war cry. ⟨< Scots Gaelic *sluagh-ghairm* < *sluagh* army + *gairm* cry⟩

A sloop

sloop [slup] *n.* **1** a sailboat having one mast, a mainsail, a jib, and sometimes other sails. **2** *Logging.* a single sleigh used for hauling logs. **3** *Cdn. British Columbia.* a hayrack mounted on runners. ⟨< Du. *sloep,* earlier *sloepe.* Doublet of SHALLOP.⟩

slooping voyage *Cdn.* a local trip around Hudson Bay on a sailing craft operated by Inuit.

sloop of war formerly: **1** a small warship having guns on the upper deck only. **2** a sailing ship mounted with 10-32 guns.

slop¹ [slɒp] *v.* **slopped, slop•ping;** *n.* —*v.* **1** spill liquid upon; spill; splash. **2** splash through mud, slush, or water.
slop over, a overflow; spill over the edge of a container when it is tilted or bumped. **b** *Slang.* show too much feeling, enthusiasm, etc.
slop through, *Slang.* do carelessly.
—*n.* **1** liquid spilled or splashed about. **2** *Slang.* food that is badly cooked or unappetizing. **3** *Slang.* mawkishness; mawkish talk or writing: *How can you listen to that slop?* **4** Often, **slops,** *pl.* **a** partially liquid kitchen waste. On a farm, slops are often fed to pigs, etc. **b** any liquid or partially liquid waste. **5** a thin liquid mud or slush. **6** weak liquid food, such as gruel. **7** *Slang.* a sloppy person. ⟨ME *sloppe* a mud hole; origin uncertain⟩

slop² [slɒp] *n.* Usually, **slops,** *pl.* **1** cheap ready-made clothing. **2** clothes, bedding, etc. supplied to sailors on a ship. **3** *Archaic.* wide, baggy breeches. ⟨OE *slop,* as in *oferslop* overgarment⟩

slope [sloup] *v.* **sloped, slop•ing;** *n.* —*v.* **1** lie at an angle or slant; be inclined up or down: *a sloping roof. The land slopes toward the sea.* **2** cause to slant: *He sloped the ground so that rainwater would run away from the basement wall.*
—*n.* **1** any line, surface, land, etc. that goes up or down at an angle: *If you roll a ball up a slope, it will roll down again.* **2** the amount of slope. **3** land draining into a certain ocean. ⟨OE *-slopen,* pp. of *-slūpan* slip⟩ **—'slop•ing•ly,** *adv.*
☛ *Syn. v.* **1. Slope,** SLANT = go off at an angle from a straight line or level surface. **Slope** is used chiefly of a surface that goes up or down from a level, usually gradually unless sharpness, steepness, etc. is stated: *The fields slope up to the foothills.* **Slant** is the general word and means 'turn or go off noticeably in any degree up, down, or to one side from a line straight up and down or across': *That picture slants to the left.*

slop•py ['slɒpi] *adj.* **-pi•er, -pi•est. 1** very wet; slushy: *sloppy ground, sloppy weather.* **2** splashed or soiled with liquid: *a sloppy table.* **3** *Informal.* careless; slovenly: *to do sloppy work, to use sloppy English.* **4** *Informal.* weak; silly: *sloppy sentiment.* **5** loose or baggy; ill-fitting: *sloppy clothes.* **—slop•pi•ly,** *adv.*
—'slop•pi•ness, *n.*

sloppy Joe a dish consisting of ground beef cooked with tomato sauce and spices, served in a bun.

slop•shop ['slɒp,ʃɒp] *n.* a store where cheap ready-made clothing is sold. ⟨< *slop*²⟩

slosh [slɒʃ] *n., v.* —*n.* **1** SLUSH (defs. 1, 2). **2** *Informal.* a watery or weak drink. **3** the sound of liquid splashing around.
—*v.* **1** splash in slush, mud, or water. **2** go about idly. **3** of liquid, splash around: *The soapy water sloshed on the floor when he shoved the pail. She could hear the soup sloshing in the vacuum bottle.* ⟨? blend of *slop* and *slush*⟩

sloshed [slɒʃt] *v., adj.* —*v.* pt. and pp. of SLOSH.
—*adj. Slang.* drunk.

slot¹ [slɒt] *n., v.* **slot•ted, slot•ting.** —*n.* **1** a small, narrow opening or groove: *Vending machines have coin slots. We have a letter slot in our front door.* **2** a place or position in a series or scheme: *The new comedy series has a good time slot.* **3** *Hockey.* **the slot,** the area two or three paces in front of the goal crease. An offensive forward tries to occupy the slot so as to be in a good position to score when the puck is passed to him or her. **4** *Informal.* SLOT MACHINE. **5** *Computer technology.* a receptacle in a computer into which an expansion card may be inserted.
—*v.* **1** make a slot or slots in. **2** place in a series or scheme: *The new show will be slotted after the six o'clock news.* ⟨ME < OF *esclot* the hollow between the breasts⟩

slot² [slɒt] *n.* a track or trail left by an animal, especially a deer. ⟨< OF *esclot* hoof print, probably < ON *slóth* trail. Akin to SLEUTH.⟩

sloth [slɒθ] *or* [slouθ] *n.* **1** unwillingness to work or exert oneself; laziness; indolence: *His sloth keeps him from engaging in sports.* **2** any of several slow-moving edentate mammals (family Bradypodidae) of Central and South America that dwell in trees, hanging upside down by all four feet from tree branches and feeding on leaves and fruits. ⟨< *slow*⟩

A sloth (def. 2)

sloth bear a long-haired bear (*Melursus ursinus*) of S India and Sri Lanka, having a long, flexible snout adapted for feeding on termites.

sloth•ful ['slɒθfəl] *or* ['slouθfəl] *adj.* unwilling to work or exert oneself; lazy; idle. **—'sloth•ful•ly,** *adv.* **—'sloth•ful•ness,** *n.*

slot machine a coin-operated machine, especially a gambling machine in which one pulls a handle to try to match up a series of symbols.

slouch [slʌutʃ] *v., n.* *—v.* **1** stand, sit, walk, or move in an awkward, drooping manner: *The weary man slouched along.* **2** droop or bend downward.
—n. **1** a bending forward of head and shoulders; an awkward, drooping way of standing, sitting, or walking. **2** a drooping or bending downward of the brim of a hat, etc. **3** an awkward, slovenly, or inefficient person. ⟨origin uncertain⟩

slouch hat a soft hat, usually with a broad brim that bends down easily.

slouch•y ['slʌutʃi] *adj.* **slouch•i•er, slouch•i•est.** not erect in posture or gait; slouching: *a slouchy walk.*

slough[1] [slu] *for 1–4; usually* [slaʊ] *for 5 n.* **1** *Cdn. West.* a body of fresh water formed by rain or melted snow. **2** a soft, deep, muddy place; mud hole. **3** a backwater or side channel of a stream. **4** on the Pacific coast, a shallow or marshy inlet of the sea. **5** a state of hopeless discouragement or degradation. Also, **slew, slue.** ⟨OE *slōh*⟩
☛ *Hom.* SLEW, SLUE [slu].

slough[2] [slʌf] *n., v.* *—n.* **1** the outer layer of a snake's skin, periodically cast off by the snake. **2** a layer of dead skin or tissue that drops or falls off as a wound, sore, etc. heals. **3** anything that has been shed or cast off: *the slough of outmoded ideas, the slough of grief.*
—v. **1** drop off; throw off; shed: *The snake sloughed its skin.* **2** shed skin or other outer part. **3** be shed or cast; drop or fall: *A scab sloughs off when new skin takes its place.* **4** cast off as undesirable, tiresome, bothersome, etc. (*usually used with* **off**): *to slough off a heavy backpack. He sloughed off his depression and started anew.* **5** *Card games.* discard (a losing card). Also, **sluff.** ⟨ME *slugh(e), slouh* < Gmc.; cf. G *Schlauch* skin, bag⟩

slough of despond [slaʊ] *or* [slu] a state of hopeless dejection; deep despondency. ⟨< *Slough of Despond,* an obstacle in John Bunyan's *Pilgrim's Progress,* 17c.⟩

slough•y[1] ['slui] *or* ['slaʊi] *adj.* **slough•i•er, slough•i•est.** soft and muddy; full of soft, deep mud. ⟨< *slough[1]*⟩

slough•y[2] ['slʌfi] *adj.* of dead skin; covered with dead skin. ⟨< *slough[2]*⟩

Slo•vak ['slouvæk] *n., adj.* *—n.* **1** a member of a Slavic people living mainly in Slovakia. **2** the Slavic language of the Slovaks.
—adj. of or having to do with Slovakia, the Slovaks, or their language. ⟨< Czech *Slovák,* originally, Slav⟩

Slo•vak•ia [slə'vækiə] *n.* a country in eastern Europe, forming the eastern half of the former Czechoslovakia, bordered by Poland, Austria, Romania, and the Czech Republic.

Slo•vak•i•an [slə'vækiən] *adj. or n.* Slovak.

slov•en[1] ['slʌvən] *n., adj.* *—n.* a person who is untidy, dirty, or careless in dress, appearance, habits, work, etc.
—adj. slovenly. ⟨? ult. < Flemish *sloef* dirty, Du. *slof* careless⟩

slov•en[2] ['slʌvən] *n. Cdn.* in the Atlantic Provinces, a long, low wagon having a high driver's box; dray. ⟨origin uncertain⟩

Slo•vene ['slouvin] *n., adj.* *—n.* **1** a member of a Slavic group of people living in Slovenia. The Slovenes are closely related to the Croats, Serbians, and other southern Slavs. **2** their language.
—adj. of or having to do with Slovenia, its people, or their language; Slovenian. ⟨< G < OSlavic *Slověne,* literally, speaker < *slovo* word; distinguished from Germans who were called 'mutes'⟩

Slo•ve•nia [slə'viniə] *or* [slə'vinjə] *n.* a country in eastern Europe, formerly a constituent republic of Yugoslavia, located between Austria and Croatia.

Slo•ve•ni•an [slə'viniən] *or* [slə'vinjən] *adj. or n.* Slovene.

slov•en•ly ['slʌvənli] *adj.* **-li•er, -li•est;** *adv.* *—adj.* untidy, dirty, or careless in dress, appearance, habits, work, etc.
—adv. in a slovenly manner: *He dresses very slovenly.*
—'slov•en•li•ness, *n.*

slow [slou] *adj., v., adv.* *—adj.* **1 a** taking a long time; taking longer than usual; not quick: *a slow journey, slow movements.* **b** moving at a low speed; not fast: *a slow current, slow traffic.* **2** behind time; running at less than proper speed: *Mail delivery is slow today.* **3** obtuse; stupid; of low mental ability. **4** indicating time earlier than the correct time: *a slow clock.* **5** causing a low or lower rate of speed: *slow ground, a slow track.* **6** burning or heating slowly or gently: *a slow flame.* **7** dull; not interesting: *a slow party.* **8** not brisk; slack: *Business is slow.* **9** behind the times; not smart or up-to-date: *a slow town.* **10** of time, passing slowly or heavily. **11** *Photography.* requiring longer exposure because of either low film sensitivity or smaller lens opening.
—v. **1** make slow or slower; reduce the speed of: *to slow down a car.* **2** become slow; go slower (*often used with* **up** or **down**): *Slow up when you drive through a town.*
—adv. in a slow manner. ⟨OE *slāw*⟩ **—'slow•ly,** *adv.* **—'slow•ness,** *n.*
☛ *Hom.* SLOE.
☛ *Syn. adj.* **1. Slow,** LEISURELY, DELIBERATE = taking a long time to do something or to happen. **Slow,** the general term, suggests taking longer than usual or necessary: *We took the slow train.* **Leisurely** suggests slowness because of having plenty of time: *I like leisurely meals.* **Deliberate,** describing people or their acts, suggests slowness due to care, thought, or self-control: *Her speech is deliberate.*
☛ *Usage.* **Slow** and **slowly** are both used as adverbs. In most written English **slowly** is preferred, except in road signs (such as *go slow, drive slow*). There is a distinction between *The buses are running slow* (late) and *This bus is going slowly.*

slow–cook•er ['slou ˌkʊkər] *n.* an electric cooking pot, usually of metal with a crockery liner, with a tight-fitting lid, used for cooking main dishes (meats, poultry, vegetables, etc.) over a period of several hours at low temperatures.

slow•down ['slou,daʊn] *n.* a slowing down: *There has been a slowdown in housing construction lately. The employees' protest took the form of a work slowdown.*

slow ice *Hockey.* **1** ice covered with ice particles skinned off the surface by the players' skates, the effect being to impede movement and slow down the game. **2** ice not frozen as hard as it should be because of defective freezing equipment or too high temperatures, as in late spring.

slow match a fuse that burns very slowly, used for setting fire to gunpowder, dynamite, etc.

slow motion **1** action at less than normal speed. **2** film or videotape showing action at less than its actual speed.
—'slow-'mo•tion, *adj.*

slow•poke ['slou,pouk] *n. Informal.* a person who moves, works, or acts very slowly.

slow time standard time, as opposed to daylight saving time, which is often called **fast time:** *We go back on slow time in fall.*

slow–wit•ted ['slou 'wɪtɪd] *adj.* slow at thinking; dull; stupid.
—'slow-'wit•ted•ly, *adv.* **—'slow-'wit•ted•ness,** *n.*

slow•worm ['slou,wɜrm] *n.* a blindworm.

sloyd [slɔɪd] *n.* a system of manual training by means of graded courses in woodworking, etc., originating in Sweden. Also, **sloid, slojd.** ⟨< Swedish *slöjd* skill⟩

SLt. or **S.Lt.** sub-lieutenant.

slub [slʌb] *v.* **slubbed, slub•bing;** *n.* *—v.* twist (wool, yarn, etc.) slightly before spinning.
—n. **1** a slightly twisted piece of cotton, silk, or wool. **2** an uneven lump in a strand of yarn. ⟨Cf. MDu. *slubbe*⟩

slub yarn yarn, usually for knitting or crocheting, that has uneven lumps as part of the design.

sludge [slʌdʒ] *n.* **1** soft mud; mire. **2** a soft, thick, muddy mixture, deposit, sediment, etc., such as that produced in sewage treatment processes. **3** small pieces of newly formed sea ice. ⟨origin uncertain⟩

sludg•y ['slʌdʒi] *adj.* **sludg•i•er, sludg•i•est.** like or containing sludge.

slue[1] [slu] *v.* **slued, slu•ing;** *n.* See SLEW[2].
☛ *Hom.* SLEW, SLOUGH[1] [slu].

slue[2] [slu] *n.* SLOUGH[1].
☛ *Hom.* SLEW.

slue[3] [slu] *n.* See SLEW[4].
☛ *Hom.* SLEW, SLOUGH[1] [slu].

sluff [slʌf] *v.* SLOUGH[2] (def. 5).

slug[1] [slʌg] *n., v.* **slugged, slug•ging.** **1** any of various mainly terrestrial gastropod molluscs resembling snails but having no shell or only a rudimentary shell. **2** any of various other invertebrates having a soft, slimy body, such as the caterpillars of certain moths. **3** *Informal.* a slow-moving person, animal, or vehicle. **4** a bullet. **5** a roughly shaped, roundish lump of metal. **6** a small disk, such as one used illegally instead of a coin in a coin-operated machine. **7** *Printing.* **a** a strip of metal used to space lines of type. A slug is thicker than a printer's lead. **b** a line of type cast in one piece by a linotype machine. **c** a brief headline to indicate the subject of the material.
—v. put in a SLUG (def. 7a) to space (lines of type). ⟨ME *slugg* sluggard, ? < Scand.; cf. dial. Swedish *slogga* be sluggish⟩

slug² [slʌg] *v.* **slugged, slug•ging;** *n.* —*v. Informal.* hit hard with the fist, a bat, or a blunt weapon.
—*n.* **1** *Informal.* a hard blow. **2** *Slang.* a drink; shot: *a slug of whisky.* ⟨origin uncertain⟩ —**'slug•ger,** *n.*

slug•a•bed ['slʌgə,bɛd] *n.* a lazy person staying in bed long after the normal getting-up time. ⟨ME *slug* be slothful + BED⟩

slug•gard ['slʌgərd] *n., adj.* —*n.* a person who is habitually lazy and idle.
—*adj.* lazy; idle. ⟨ME < *slug* be slothful + *-ard,* personal suffix with derogatory sense, as in *drunkard.* See SLUG¹.⟩
—**'slug•gard•ly,** *adv.*

slug•ger ['slʌgər] *n.* a person who hits hard, or slugs, especially: **a** a boxer or prize fighter. **b** a baseball player who is a hard hitter, especially one with many extra-base hits to his or her credit.

slug•gish ['slʌgɪʃ] *adj.* **1** slow; lacking energy or vigour: *a sluggish mind.* **2** very slow in movement, growth, or flow: *a sluggish river, sluggish blood circulation. The economy has been sluggish for the past few months.* **3** lazy or idle. ⟨< *slug¹*⟩
—**'slug•gish•ly,** *adv.* —**'slug•gish•ness,** *n.*

sluice [slus] *n., v.* **sluiced, sluic•ing.** —*n.* **1** a structure having a gate for holding back or controlling the water of a canal, river, or lake. **2** a gate that holds back or controls the flow of water. When the water behind a dam gets too high, the sluices are opened. **3** the water held back or controlled by such a gate. **4** something that controls the flow or passage of anything: *War opens the sluices of hatred and bloodshed.* **5** a long, sloping trough through which water flows, used to wash gold from sand, dirt, or gravel. **6** a channel for carrying off overflow or surplus water.
—*v.* **1** let out or draw off (water) by opening a sluice. **2** flow or pour in a stream; rush: *Water sluiced down the channel.* **3** flush or cleanse with a rush of water; pour or throw water over. **4** *Placer mining.* wash (gold) from sand, dirt, or gravel in a sluice. **5** send (logs, etc.) along a channel of water. ⟨ME < OF *escluse,* ult. < L *ex-* out + *claudere* shut⟩

sluice–box ['slus ,bɒks] *n. Placer mining.* formerly, a long sluice fitted with riffles, in which gold was separated from gravel, muck, etc.

sluice gate a gate to control the flow of water in a sluice.

slum¹ [slʌm] *n., v.* **slummed, slum•ming.** —*n.* Often, **slums,** *pl.* a district or area in a city characterized by overpopulation, poor housing and sanitation, and social problems.
—*v.* visit slums or other places considered inferior to one's usual surroundings, especially out of curiosity or for amusement. ⟨origin uncertain⟩ —**'slum•mer,** *n.*

slum² [slʌm] *n. Cdn. Placer mining.* thick, slippery mud, or gumbo, found in the creek valleys of the interior of British Columbia. ⟨shortening of *slumgullion*⟩

slum•ber ['slʌmbər] *v., n.* —*v.* **1** sleep, especially in a peaceful manner. **2** pass in sleep: *to slumber away the morning hours.* **3** be inactive, dormant, or negligent: *The volcano had slumbered for years. The incident awakened her slumbering conscience.*
—*n.* **1** Sometimes, **slumbers,** *pl.* sleep: *The child was deep in slumber. His slumbers were interrupted by the sound of a siren.* **2** an inactive, dormant, or negligent state or condition. ⟨ult. < OE *slūma,* n.⟩ —**'slum•ber•er,** *n.*

slum•ber•ous ['slʌmbərəs] *adj.* **1** sleepy; heavy with drowsiness: *slumberous eyelids.* **2** causing or inducing sleep. **3** characterized by or suggestive of a state of sleep or inactivity: *the slumberous calm of a summer evening.* —**'slum•ber•ous•ly,** *adv.* —**'slum•ber•ous•ness,** *n.*

slum•brous ['slʌmbrəs] *adj. Poetic.* slumberous.
—**'slum•brous•ly,** *adv.* —**'slum•brous•ness,** *n.*

slum•gul•lion [slʌm'gʌljən] *n.* **1** *Cdn.* a kind of stew made with whatever is available. **2** the detritus left after whale carcasses have been processed. **3** a deposit of red-coloured mud in mining sluices. ⟨a fanciful coinage for something viscid and thick like mud⟩

slum•lord ['slʌm,lɔrd] *n. Informal.* an absentee owner of slum property, especially one who charges exorbitant rent.

slum•my ['slʌmi] *adj.* of, having to do with, or like a slum.

slump [slʌmp] *v., n.* —*v.* **1** drop or fall suddenly and heavily: *He slumped to the floor in a dead faint.* **2** have or assume a drooping posture: *The bored students slumped in their seats, waiting for the bell.* **3** go into a marked decline: *Business has slumped.*
—*n.* **1** a sudden physical collapse. **2** a great or sudden decline in prices, activity, etc. **3** a long period during which a person is not working or performing as well as usual: *The team's pitcher is in a slump and they have lost several games in a row.* **4** a slouching, bent position or manner of walking. ⟨? imitative⟩

slung [slʌŋ] *v.* pt. and pp. of SLING.

slung shot a piece of metal, stone, etc. fastened to a short strap, chain, etc., used as a weapon.

slunk [slʌŋk] *v.* a pt. and a pp. of SLINK.

slur [slɜr] *v.* **slurred, slur•ring;** *n.* —*v.* **1** pass lightly over; go through hurriedly or in a careless way. **2** speak or write (sounds, letters, etc.) so indistinctly that they run into each other. **3** *Music.* **a** sing or play (two or more tones of different pitch) without a break; run together in a smooth, connected manner. **b** mark with a slur. **4** harm the reputation of; insult; slight.
—*n.* **1** a slurred pronunciation, sound, etc. **2** *Music.* **a** a slurring of tones. **b** a curved mark (⌒) (‿) indicating this. **c** the notes so marked. **3** an insulting or slighting remark. **4** a blot or stain (upon reputation): *Malicious rumour left a slur on his good name.* ⟨ME *slor* mud⟩

slur ice *Cdn. Maritimes.* a thin mixture of mushy ice and water, found especially near shore. ⟨probably < Brit. dial. *slur* thin, washy mud⟩

slurp [slɜrp] *v., n. Informal.* —*v.* eat or drink noisily or with a sucking sound.
—*n.* a slurping sound. ⟨< Du. *slurpen* lap⟩

slur•ry ['slɜri] *n., pl.* **-ries;** *v.* **-ried, -ry•ing.** —*n.* a thin mixture of water and an insoluble substance such as cement, mud, or clay.
—*v.* make into a slurry. ⟨Related to SLUR⟩

slush [slʌʃ] *n.* **1** partly melted snow; snow and water mixed. **2** soft mud. **3** *Informal.* silly, sentimental talk, writing, etc. **4** grease. ⟨origin uncertain⟩

slush fund **1** money set aside for special projects. **2** money collected or set aside for dishonest purposes, such as bribery or improper political or business lobbying.

slush hole *Cdn., esp. North.* a patch of rotten ice on the surface of a lake or river.

slush•y ['slʌʃi] *adj.* **slush•i•er, slush•i•est. 1** covered with slush; having much slush: *a slushy sidewalk.* **2** made up of or like slush: *slushy snow.* —**'slush•i•ness,** *n.*

slut [slʌt] *n.* **1** a woman of loose morals. **2** a slovenly, untidy woman; slattern. **3** *Archaic.* a bold or saucy girl. ⟨ME *slutte, slotte;* origin uncertain⟩

slut•tish ['slʌtɪʃ] *adj.* having to do with, like, or characteristic of a slut. —**'slut•tish•ly,** *adv.* —**'slut•tish•ness,** *n.*

sly [slaɪ] *adj.* **sly•er** or **sli•er, sly•est** or **sli•est;** *n.*
—*adj.* **1** clever in deceiving or tricking: *The sly cat stole the meat while the cook's back was turned.* **2** not straightforward or open; cleverly underhanded; crafty: *His sly questions were intended to get them to reveal more than they realized. They had developed a sly scheme for taking over control of the organization.* **3** playfully mischievous or knowing: *a sly wink.*
—*n.*
on the sly, in a way meant to avoid notice; secretly: *They got their information on the sly.* ⟨ME *slēgh* skilful < ON *slœgr,* originally, able to strike < *slá* slay⟩ — **'sly•ness,** *n.*

☛ *Syn. adj.* **1, 2. Sly,** CUNNING = having or showing an ability to get what one wants by secret or indirect means. **Sly** emphasizes lack of frankness and straightforwardness, and suggests stealthy actions or secrecy and deceit in dealing with others: *That sly girl managed to get her best friend's job.* **Cunning** emphasizes an instinctive cleverness in getting the better of others by tricks or schemes, unfair dealing, or cheating: *They were cunning enough to get complete control of the company.*

sly•boots ['slaɪ,buts] *n.* a person who is attractively cunning or mischievous.

sly•ly ['slaɪli] *adv.* in a sly manner. Also, **slily.**

Sm samarium.

S.M. Sergeant-Major.

S/M or **s/m** sadomasochism.

smack¹ [smæk] *n., v.* —*n.* **1** a slight taste or flavour: *The sauce had a smack of nutmeg.* **2** a trace; suggestion: *The old sailor still had a smack of the sea about him.* **3** *Slang.* heroin.
—*v.* have a smack: *The Irishman's speech smacked of the Old Country.* ⟨OE *smæcc*⟩

smack² [smæk] *v., n., adv.* —*v.* **1** open (the lips) quickly so as to make a sharp sound. **2** kiss loudly. **3** slap. **4** crack (a whip, etc.). **5** make a sharp, slapping sound.
—*n.* **1** a sharp sound made by opening the lips quickly. **2** a loud kiss. **3** a slap or crack. **4** the sound of any kind of smacking.

smack down, *Informal.* put (someone) in his or her place.
—adv. **1** *Informal.* suddenly and sharply; with or as if with a smack. **2** exactly: *He dropped a bit of ketchup smack in the middle of his white shirt.* ⟨ult. imitative⟩

smack³ [smæk] *n.* **1** a small sailboat with one mast. **2** a similar fishing boat with a well for keeping fish alive. ⟨probably < Du. *smak*⟩

smack•er [ˈsmækər] *n.* **1** one who or that which smacks. **2** *Informal.* a resounding kiss; smack. **3** *Slang.* a dollar.

smack•ing [ˈsmækɪŋ] *adj., v.* *—adj.* **1** lively, brisk, or strong. **2** making a quick, sharp sound: *a smacking kiss, a smacking blow.*
—v. ppr. of SMACK.

small [smɒl] *adj., adv., n.* *—adj.* **1** not large; little; not large as compared with other things of the same kind: *a small house.* **2** not great in amount, degree, extent, duration, value, strength, etc.: *a small dose, small hope of success. The cent is our smallest coin.* **3** young: *small children.* **4** not important: *a small matter.* **5** not prominent; of low social position; humble; poor: *People great and small mourned Laurier's death.* **6** having little land, capital, etc.: *a small farmer, a small dealer.* **7** gentle; soft; low: *a small voice, a small crumbling sound.* **8** mean: *A man with a small nature is not generous.* **9** of letters, lower-case; not capital.
feel small, be ashamed or humiliated.
—adv. **1** into small pieces. **2** in low tones.
sing small, change to a humble tone or manner.
—n. **1** something that is small; a small, slender, or narrow part or thing: *the small of the back.* **2 smalls,** *pl. Esp. Brit. Informal.* small articles of clothing, especially underwear. ⟨OE *smæl*⟩
—ˈsmall•ness, *n.*
☛ *Syn. adj.* **1.** See note at LITTLE.

small arms weapons easily carried by a person and held in the hand or hands while being fired: *Rifles and revolvers are classed as small arms.*

small beer **1** weak beer. **2** *Slang.* people or matters of little or no consequence.

small capital a type of capital letter about the same height as a lower case x in the same type size and face. Small capitals are often used for acronyms or abbreviations in printed materials. Small capitals are used in this dictionary for cross-references. *Examples*: A.D. 1066, UNICEF Christmas cards. *Abbrev.*: s.c.

small change **1** coins of small value, such as nickels, dimes, etc. **2** anything small and unimportant.

small circle a circle on a sphere, its plane not passing through the centre of the sphere.

small claims court a court with limited jurisdiction for dealing in an informal and inexpensive way with civil cases involving small claims for breach of contract or debt.

small fry **1** small or young fish. **2** babies or children; small or young creatures. **3** unimportant people or things.

small game wild animals and birds, such as rabbits, grouse, quail, etc., hunted as game, but smaller than BIG GAME.

small hours the early hours of the morning, from midnight to 3 or 4 a.m.

small intestine the long, narrow part of the intestine where most of the absorption of digested food takes place, extending from the stomach to the large intestine. In adults the small intestine is more than 6 m long. See ALIMENTARY CANAL for picture.

small•ish [ˈsmɒlɪʃ] *adj.* somewhat small.

small letter a lower-case letter, not a capital.

small–mind•ed [ˈsmɒl ˌmaɪndɪd] *adj.* petty or mean.
—ˈsmall-ˈmind•ed•ly, *adv.* **—ˈsmall-ˈmind•ed•ness,** *n.*

small–mouth bass [ˈsmɒlˌmʌuθ] a North American freshwater fish (*Micropterus dolomieu*) with yellowish green colouring and having the lower jaw extending up to the eye.

small potatoes *Informal.* an unimportant person or thing or group of persons or things: *The last deal was just small potatoes, compared with what she's planning now.*

small•pox [ˈsmɒlˌpɒks] *n. Pathology.* an acute, contagious viral disease characterized by fever and blisterlike eruptions on the skin that usually leave permanent pitlike scars, called pockmarks. It was thought to have been eradicated by about 1980, but isolated cases have recently been discovered in remote parts of the world.

small–scale [ˈsmɒl ˌskeil] *adj.* **1** small in operation or scope; limited: *She runs a small-scale import business.* **2** of a map, etc., drawn to a small scale, not permitting much detail.

small screen television. **—ˈsmall-ˌscreen,** *adj.*

small talk light, informal conversation; chit-chat.

small–time [ˈsmɒl ˌtaɪm] *adj. Slang.* minor, petty, or insignificant: *a small-time crook. His business ventures are strictly small-time.*

small–town [ˈsmɒl ˈtaʊn] *adj.* **1** of or coming from a small town. **2** narrow; provincial: *small-town bigotry.*

smalt [smɒlt] *n.* **1** powdered, deep blue glass, obtained from potash, silica, and cobalt oxide, and used as a pigment. **2** the pigment so prepared. **3** the deep blue colour of this pigment. ⟨< F < Ital. *smalto* < Gmc. Related to SMELT.⟩

smarm [smɑrm] *v. Esp. Brit. Informal.* act in a toadying or obsequiously flattering way. ⟨var. of dial. *smalm* plaster down⟩

smarm•y [ˈsmɑrmi] *adj.* **-i•er, -i•est.** *Informal.* obsequiously flattering; toadying. **—ˈsmarm•i•ness,** *n.*

smart [smɑrt] *v., n., adj., adv.* *—v.* **1** feel sharp pain: *Her eyes smarted.* **2** cause sharp pain: *The cut smarts.* **3** feel acute distress or irritation: *He smarted from the scolding.* **4** suffer: *She will smart for this.*
—n. **1** a sharp pain or feeling of resentment: *He still felt the smart of her brusque rejection.* **2 smarts,** *pl.* astuteness; cleverness.
—adj. **1** sharp; severe: *She gave the horse a smart blow.* **2** keen; active; lively: *They walked at a smart pace.* **3** clever; bright: *a smart child.* **4** fresh and neat; in good order: *He looked smart in his uniform.* **5** stylish; fashionable. **6** *Informal or dialect.* fairly large; considerable. **7** witty, humorous, or clever in an annoying way: *a smart remark, a smart reply.* **8** incorporating some degree of artificial intelligence.
—adv. in a smart manner. ⟨OE *smeortan,* v., *smeart,* adj.⟩
—ˈsmart•ly, *adv.* **—ˈsmart•ness,** *n.*

smart al•eck or **al•ec** [ˈælɪk] an obnoxious person who tries to show, especially by flippant retorts, that he or she is cleverer than others. **—ˈsmart-ˌa•leck•y, ˈsmart-ˌa•leck** or **ˈsmart-ˌa•lec,** *adj.*

smart•ass [ˈsmɑrtˌæs] *n., adj. Slang.* *—n.* smart aleck.
—adj. like or characteristic of a smartass; smart-alecky. Also (*adj.*) **smartassed.**

smart•en [ˈsmɑrtən] *v.* **1** improve in appearance; brighten. **2** make or become brisker or more alert.
smarten up, come to one's senses; reflect soberly on one's conduct and change it.

smart•weed [ˈsmɑrtˌwid] *n.* any of several weedy plants (genus *Polygonum*) of the buckwheat family typically having lance-shaped leaves and erect or drooping spikes of tiny greenish, pink, or white flowers, and some of which have a stinging, acid taste and a juice irritating to the skin.

smash [smæʃ] *v., n., adv.* *—v.* **1** break into pieces with violence and noise: *to smash a window.* **2** destroy; shatter; ruin; crush; defeat: *to smash an argument, to smash an attack.* **3** be broken to pieces: *The dishes smashed on the floor.* **4** become ruined. **5** rush violently; crash: *The car smashed into a tree.* **6** *Tennis, badminton, etc.* hit (a ball) with a hard, fast overhand stroke. **7** hit with a hard blow.
—n. **1** the act or an instance of smashing: *The two cars collided with a terrific smash.* **2** the sound of a smash: *We heard the smash of broken glass but couldn't see anything.* **3** (*adjl.*) *Informal.* being an instant sensation: *from her new smash album.* **4** a crushing defeat; disaster. **5** a business failure; bankruptcy. **6** *Tennis, badminton, etc.* a hard, fast overhand stroke. **7** a hard blow. **8** a drink made of water, mint, sugar, and brandy or other alcoholic liquor. **9** *Informal.* SMASH HIT.
come or **go to smash,** *Informal.* **a** smash into broken pieces. **b** go to ruin: *Our plans for a European vacation this fall have gone to smash.*
—adv. with a smash: *I drove smash into the fence.* ⟨a blend of *smack²* and *mash*⟩ **—ˈsmash•a•ble,** *adj.* **—ˈsmash•er,** *n.*
☛ *Syn. v.* **1.** See note at BREAK.

smashed [smæʃt] *v., adj.* *—v.* pt. and pp. of SMASH.
—adj. Slang. very drunk or high on drugs.

smash hit a very successful play, film, recording, etc.

smash•ing [ˈsmæʃɪŋ] *v., adj.* *—v.* ppr. of SMASH.
—adj. Esp. Brit. Informal. fine; excellent; splendid.

smash–up [ˈsmæʃ ˌʌp] *n.* **1** a bad collision of motor vehicles. **2** *Informal.* complete collapse or failure; ruin: *the smash-up of a business empire.*

smat•ter [ˈsmætər] *v., n.* *—v. Rare.* **1** speak (a language, words, etc.) with only superficial knowledge (of it or them). **2** dabble in.
—n. smattering. ⟨Cf. Swedish *smattra* rattle⟩

smat•ter•ing [ˈsmætərɪŋ] *n., v.* *—n.* **1** a slight or superficial knowledge of a language or a subject: *He has a smattering of Italian that he picked up on a visit to Italy last summer.* **2** a low

number or amount: *The class is mostly women with a smattering of men.*
—*v.* ppr. of SMATTER.

smear [smir] *v., n.* **1** cover or stain with anything sticky, greasy, or dirty: *Her fingers were smeared with jam.* **2** rub or spread (oil, grease, paint, etc.). **3** blur or make a streak across (a drawing, writing, etc.): *The corner of the painting was smeared a bit while it was still wet.* **4** receive a mark or stain; be smeared: *Wet paint smears easily.* **5** harm the reputation of; slander: *She attempted to smear her opponent by suggesting that he had accepted bribes while in office.* **6** *Slang.* defeat overwhelmingly.
—*n.* **1** a mark or stain left by smearing. **2** a small amount of something, such as blood, spread on a slide for examination with a microscope. **3 a** a charge or accusation, usually without any basis, against a person, group, etc. **b** the act of harming or trying to harm another's reputation: *The smear was unsuccessful.* **4** (*adjl.*) of or characterized by such charges or accusations: *a smear campaign.* ⟨OE *smerian, smirian* < *smeoru* grease⟩

smear•case ['smir,keis] *n.* cream cheese or cottage cheese. ⟨< G *Schmierkäse* < *schmieren* to spread + *Käse* cheese⟩

smear•y ['smiri] *adj.* **smear•i•er, smear•i•est. 1** smeared. **2** tending to smear. —**'smear•i•ness,** *n.*

smeg•ma ['smɛgmə] *n.* sebum, especially as secreted under the foreskin. ⟨< L < Gk., detergent < *smekhein* wash⟩

smell [smɛl] *v.* **smelled** or **smelt, smell•ing;** *n.* —*v.* **1** perceive with the olfactory nerves in the nose: *I smell smoke in the air.* **2** detect or recognize smells. **3** sniff (at) in order to detect an odour: *Smell the meat to see if it's off. She picked up a rose and smelled it.* **4** give out a smell. **5** have or give out a bad smell. **6** detect a trace or suggestion of: *We smelled trouble.* **7** have a suggestion or trace (*usually used with* **of**): *The plan smells of trickery.*
smell out, track (something) down by or as if by smelling; detect; investigate: *The dog will smell out a thief.*
smell up, *Informal.* cause to have a bad smell: *That garbage is smelling up the whole house.*
—*n.* **1** an act of smelling; sniff. **2** the sense of smelling: *Smell is keener in dogs than in people.* **3** the quality in a thing that affects the sense of smell: *the smell of burning cloth.* **4** a trace; suggestion. ⟨ME *smelle*(*n*); origin uncertain⟩ — **'smell•er,** *n.*
☛ *Syn. n.* **3. Smell,** ODOUR, SCENT = the property or quality of a thing that affects the sense organs of the nose. **Smell** is the general word, used especially when the effect on the sense organs is emphasized, but often suggests that the effect is unpleasant: *She never got used to the farmyard smells.* **Odour** is often interchanged with **smell,** but is more neutral and applies particularly to the distinctive or specific smell itself as belonging to and coming from what is smelled: *I find the odour of hay especially pleasing.* **Scent** also emphasizes the distinctive or specific smell, but is usually used when the effect is pleasant: *He loves the scent of roses.*

smelling salts a form of ammonia that, when inhaled, helps to relieve faintness, headaches, etc.

smell•y ['smɛli] *adj.* **smell•i•er, smell•i•est.** giving off a strong, unpleasant odour. —**'smell•i•ness,** *n.*

smelt[1] [smɛlt] *v.* **1** melt (ore) in order to get the metal out of it. **2** obtain (metal) from ore by melting. **3** refine (impure metal) by melting. ⟨< MDu. or MLG *smelten.* Related to SMALT.⟩

smelt[2] [smɛlt] *n., pl.* **smelt** or **smelts. 1** any of various small, edible fishes (family Osmeridae) having a long, slender, silvery body and two dorsal fins. The **rainbow smelt** (*Osmerus mordax*), found in the Great Lakes and along northern and arctic coasts, is a commercially important food fish. **2** (*adjl.*) designating the family (Osmeridae) that includes the smelts and the oolichan and caplin. ⟨OE⟩

smelt[3] [smɛlt] *v.* a pt. and a pp. of SMELL.

smelt•er ['smɛltər] *n.* **1** a person whose work or business is smelting ores or metals. **2** an establishment or plant where smelting is done.

smid•gen or **smid•gin** ['smɪdʒən] *n. Informal.* a tiny piece or small amount; mite: *I'll have toast with just a smidgen of butter.* Also, **smidgeon.** ⟨origin uncertain⟩

smi•lax ['smaɪlæks] *n.* **1** any of a genus (*Smilax*) of woody or herbaceous, often prickly, vines found in warm and tropical regions, having clusters of yellowish green or white flowers and bluish black or red berries. **2** a twining plant (*Asparagus asparagoides*) of the lily family having shiny, bright green, flattened, leaflike stems. It is often cultivated by florists. ⟨< L < Gk.⟩

smile [smaɪl] *v.* **smiled, smil•ing;** *n.* —*v.* **1** look pleased or amused; show pleasure, favour, kindness, amusement, etc. by an upward curve of the mouth. **2** look pleasantly or agreeably; look with favour. **3** bring, put, drive, etc. by smiling: *Smile your tears away.* **4** give (a smile): *The child smiled a sunny smile.* **5** express by a smile: *He smiled consent.* **6** show scorn, disdain, etc. by a curve of the mouth: *She smiled bitterly.*
—*n.* **1** the act of smiling. **2** the facial expression resulting from the act of smiling: *She made a smile on the clown she had drawn.* **3** a favouring look or regard; a pleasant look or aspect. ⟨ME *smile(n)*⟩ —**'smil•er,** *n.* —**'smil•ing•ly,** *adv.*

smirch [smɜrtʃ] *v., n.* —*v.* **1** make dirty; soil or stain with soot, dirt, dust, etc. **2** bring dishonour or disgrace on; sully: *to smirch one's reputation.*
—*n.* **1** a dirty mark; a smear or stain. **2** dishonour or disgrace. ⟨ME *smorch*; ? < OF *esmorcher* torture, ult. < L *ex-* (intensive) + LL *mordicare* bite⟩

smirk [smɜrk] *v., n.* —*v.* smile in a knowing, self-satisfied way. —*n.* a knowing or self-satisfied smile. ⟨OE *smearcian* smile⟩

smite [sməit] *v.* **smote, smit•ten** or **smote, smit•ing. 1** *Archaic or poetic.* strike or hit hard: *The hero smote the giant with his sword.* **2** have a sudden, strong effect on: *The thief's conscience smote him.* **3** *Archaic or poetic.* come with force (*upon*): *The waves smote upon the shore. The sound of a blacksmith's hammer smote upon their ears.* **4** *Archaic or poetic.* strike down; punish severely, or destroy. ⟨OE *smītan*⟩
—**'smit•er,** *n.*

smith [smɪθ] *n.* **1** a person who makes or shapes things out of metal (*used mainly in compounds*): *a goldsmith, a tinsmith.* **2** a blacksmith. ⟨OE⟩

smith•er•eens [,smɪðə'rinz] *n.pl. Informal.* small pieces; bits: *The plate was smashed to smithereens.* Also, **smithers.** ⟨apparently from Irish *smidirín* fragments⟩

smith•son•ite ['smɪθsə,nəit] *n.* zinc ore in the form of zinc carbonate. *Formula*: $ZnCO_3$ ⟨after James *Smithson* (1765-1829), the British scientist who distinguished it from calamine⟩

smith•y ['smɪθi] *or* ['smɪði] *n., pl.* **smith•ies.** the workshop of a smith, especially a blacksmith. ⟨ME *smithi* < ON *smithja*⟩

smit•ten ['smɪtən] *adj., v.* —*adj.* **1** hard hit; struck: *sudden sparks from smitten steel.* **2** suddenly and strongly affected: *smitten with terror.* **3** *Informal.* very much in love: *He's really smitten.* **4** *Informal.* favourably impressed: *They were quite smitten with her new proposal.*
—*v.* a pp. of SMITE.

smock [smɒk] *n., v.* —*n.* a loose, coatlike outer garment, usually of cotton, worn to protect clothing.
—*v.* **1** ornament with smocking: *The little girl's dress was smocked from the neckline to the waist.* **2** clothe in a smock. ⟨OE *smocc*⟩ —**'smock,like,** *adj.*

smock•ing ['smɒkɪŋ] *n., v.* —*n.* decorative stitching used on clothing, made by gathering material closely with rows of stitches in a honeycomb pattern.
—*v.* ppr. of SMOCK.

smog [smɒg] *n.* **1** a combination in the air of smoke or other chemical fumes and fog. **2** polluted air from any source hanging low in the atmosphere and perceptible to the eye or nose. ⟨a blend of *smoke* and *fog*⟩ —**'smog•gy,** *adj.*

smoke [smouk] *n., v.* **smoked, smok•ing.** —*n.* **1** the visible mixture of gases and particles of carbon that rises when anything burns; a cloud from anything burning. **2** something resembling this. **3** *Physics. Chemistry.* gas or a gaseous medium containing a suspension of solid particles. **4** something unsubstantial, quickly passing, or without result. **5** that which is smoked; a cigar, cigarette, pipe, etc. **6** the act or period of smoking tobacco.
go up in smoke, be unsuccessful; fail to materialize, as a plan or dream.
—*v.* **1** give off smoke, steam, etc. excessively or undesirably: *The fireplace smokes.* **2 a** draw the smoke from (a pipe, cigar, or cigarette) into the mouth and, usually, the lungs and puff it out again. **b** smoke tobacco as a matter of habit. **3** preserve or flavour (meat, fish, etc.) by exposing to smoke. **4** drive (out or away) by smoke, or as if by smoke. **5** use smoke to stupefy (flying insects). **6** make, bring, pass, etc. by smoking. **7** colour, darken, or stain with smoke. **8** *Archaic.* find out; suspect; detect.
smoke out, a drive out with smoke. **b** find out and make known. ⟨OE *smoca*⟩

smoke bomb a kind of bomb containing chemicals that give out dense smoke when the bomb bursts.

smoke detector a device, installed in a dwelling or place of business, that emits a piercing noise as a warning that excessive smoke or heat has been detected in the area.

smoke drift a cloud of smoke seen at a distance and indicating a forest fire.

smoke•house ['smouk,hʌus] *n.* an outbuilding where meat or fish is treated with smoke to preserve and flavour it.

smoke•jump•er ['smouk,dʒʌmpər] *n.* a person trained and equipped to fight forest fires who is parachuted into an area where there is a fire.

smoke•less ['smouklɪs] *adj.* having or producing no smoke: *Anthracite coal burns with an almost smokeless flame.*

smokeless powder a substitute for ordinary gunpowder that gives off little or no smoke when it explodes.

smok•er ['smoukər] *n.* **1** a person who smokes tobacco. **2** a railway car or compartment where smoking is permitted. **3** an informal gathering for smoking, card-playing, and other entertainment.

smoke screen **1** a mass of thick smoke used to hide a ship, aircraft, etc. from the enemy. **2** anything used to hide or obscure a plan, project, etc.: *a smoke screen of false information.*

smoke•stack ['smouk,stæk] *n.* **1** a tall chimney. **2** a pipe that discharges smoke, etc.: *the smokestack of a boat.*

smoke tree either of two small trees (genus *Cotinus*) of the cashew family having large, feathery clusters of tiny flowers that from a distance look like puffs of smoke. One species (*C. americanus*) is native to North America; the other (*C. coggygria*) is Eurasian.

smoking gun *Informal.* any proof of wrongdoing.

smok•y ['smouki] *adj.* **smok•i•er, smok•i•est. 1** giving off much smoke: *a smoky fire.* **2** full of smoke. **3** darkened or stained with smoke. **4** like smoke or suggesting smoke: *a smoky grey, a smoky taste.* **—'smok•i•ly,** *adv.* **—'smok•i•ness,** *n.*

smol•der ['smouldər] *v., n.* See SMOULDER.

smolt [smoult] *n.* a young salmon or sea trout, usually two or three years old, that has turned silvery in colour and is preparing to migrate from a stream or lake to the sea or from a stream to a large lake. Compare PARR. ⟨ME. Probably akin to SMELT[2].⟩

smooch [smutʃ] *v., n. Slang. —v.* kiss or pet.
—n. a kiss. **—'smooch•y,** *adj.*

smooth [smuð] *adj., v., adv., n. —adj.* **1** having an even surface, like glass, silk, or still water; flat; level: *smooth stones.* **2** free from turbulence or roughness: *smooth sailing, a smooth flight.* **3** without lumps: *smooth sauce.* **4** without hair: *a smooth face.* **5** without trouble or difficulty; easy: *a smooth course of affairs.* **6** calm; serene: *a smooth temper.* **7** polished; pleasant; polite, especially with an ulterior motive or insincerely: *That salesman is a smooth talker.* **8** not harsh in sound or taste: *smooth verses, smooth wine.* **9** having an easy, frictionless movement.
—v. **1** make smooth or smoother: *Smooth this dress with a hot iron. She smoothed out the ball of crushed paper and read it.* **2** become even and flat: *The wrinkles in the plastic tablecloth had smoothed out in the warm sunshine.* **3** make easy.
smooth away, get rid of (troubles, difficulties, etc.).
smooth down, calm; soothe.
smooth over, make (something) seem less wrong, unpleasant, or noticeable: *The teacher tried to smooth over the argument between the two girls.*
—adv. in a smooth manner.
—n. **1** the act of smoothing. **2** a smooth part or place. ⟨OE *smōth*⟩ **—'smooth•er,** *n.* **—'smooth•ly,** *adv.* **—'smooth•ness,** *n.*

smooth•bore ['smuð,bɔr] *adj., n. —adj.* of a gun, having no grooves on the inside of the barrel; not rifled.
—n. a gun having a barrel with a smooth bore.

smooth•faced ['smuð,feist] *adj.* **1** having a smooth face; beardless or clean-shaven: *a smoothfaced youth.* **2** having a smooth surface: *smoothfaced brick.* **3** having the appearance of being agreeable and sincere: *a smoothfaced hypocrite.*

smooth•ie or **smooth•y** ['smuði] *n., pl.* **smooth•ies.** *Slang.* a smooth, persuasive, often insincere person.

smooth muscle the unstriated, contractile, involuntary muscles occurring in various internal organs such as the bowel, stomach, and uterus, but not in the heart.

smooth–spo•ken ['smuð 'spoukən] *adj.* speaking easily and pleasantly; polished in speech.

smooth–tongued ['smuð 'tʌŋd] *adj.* speaking smoothly and agreeably; suave and plausible: *a smooth-tongued liar.*

smor•gas•bord ['smɔrgəs,bɔrd] *n.* **1** a buffet meal, featuring a large variety of meats, salads, etc. **2** a restaurant that serves this sort of meal. ⟨< Swedish *smörgåasbord* hors d'oeuvres < *smörgås* open sandwich + *bord* table⟩

smote [smout] *v.* a pt. of SMITE.

smoth•er ['smʌðər] *v., n. —v.* **1** make unable to get air; kill by depriving of air: *The murderer smothered his victim with a pillow.* **2** be unable to breathe freely; suffocate: *We almost smothered in that stuffy room.* **3** cover thickly: *In the fall the grass is smothered with leaves.* **4** deaden or put out by covering thickly: *The fire is smothered by ashes.* **5** keep back; check; suppress: *She smothered a sharp reply.* **6** hamper or oppress by too much affection, overprotection, advice, etc. **7** cook in a covered pot or baking dish: *to smother chicken, to smother cabbage.*
—n. **1** a cloud of dust, smoke, spray, etc. **2** anything that smothers. **3** the condition of being smothered. ⟨ME *smorther*, n., based on OE *smorian* suffocate⟩ **—'smoth•er•er,** *n.*

smoth•er•y ['smʌðəri] *adj.* tending to smother; full of dust, smoke, spray, etc.

smoul•der or **smol•der** ['smouldər] *v., n. —v.* **1** burn and smoke without flame: *The fire smouldered most of the night.* **2** exist or continue in a suppressed condition: *The people's discontent smouldered for years before it broke out into open rebellion.* **3** show suppressed feeling: *The woman's eyes smouldered with anger.*
—n. **1** a slow, smoky burning without flame. **2** a state of smouldering. ⟨ME *smolderen*; akin to Du. *smeulen*⟩

smudge [smʌdʒ] *n., v.* **smudged, smudg•ing.** *—n.* **1** a dirty mark; smear. **2** a smoky fire made to drive away insects or to protect plants from frost. **3** *Cdn.* SMUDGE POT.
—v. **1** mark with dirty streaks; smear: *The child's drawing was smudged.* **2** use a SMUDGE (def. 2) or smudges on or in, especially in an orchard. ⟨origin uncertain⟩

smudge pot *Cdn.* a can, pail, etc. often with a perforated bottom, used to build a SMUDGE (def. 2).

smudg•y ['smʌdʒi] *adj.* **smudg•i•er, smudg•i•est.** smudged; marked with smudges. **—'smudg•i•ly,** *adv.* **—'smudg•i•ness,** *n.*

smug [smʌg] *adj.* **smug•ger, smug•gest. 1** too pleased with one's own goodness, cleverness, respectability, etc.; self-satisfied; complacent: *Nothing disturbs the smug beliefs of some narrow-minded people.* **2** *Archaic.* sleek; neat; trim. ⟨originally, neat, spruce; probably < Du. or LG *smuk* spruce, adj.⟩ **—'smug•ly,** *adv.* **—'smug•ness,** *n.*

smug•gle ['smʌgəl] *v.* **-gled, -gling. 1** secretly take (things) into or out of a country which are prohibited by law or on which one has not paid the required duty: *to smuggle heroin, to smuggle watches.* **2** bring, take, put, etc. secretly: *Rob tried to smuggle his puppy into the house.* ⟨< LG *smuggeln*⟩ **—'smug•gler,** *n.*

smut [smʌt] *n., v.* **smut•ted, smut•ting.** *—n.* **1** soot, dirt, etc. **2** a place soiled with smut. **3** indecent or obscene talk, writing, or pictures. **4** any of various plant diseases caused by fungi of the order Ustilaginales, affecting mainly cereal grasses and characterized by the formation of sooty masses of spores on the affected plant parts. **5** any fungus causing such a disease.
—v. **1** soil or be soiled with smut. **2** affect (a plant or crop) with smut. **3** of a plant or crop, become affected with smut. ⟨OE *smitte*; influenced by *smudge, smutch*⟩

smut•ty ['smʌti] *adj.* **-ti•er, -ti•est. 1** soiled with smut, soot, etc.; dirty. **2** indecent or obscene. **3** of a plant, affected with smut. **—'smut•ti•ness,** *n.*

Sn tin (for L *stannum*).

snack [snæk] *n., v. —n.* a light meal: *She eats a snack before going to bed.*
—v. eat a snack. ⟨< MLG *snakken*⟩
snack on, eat as a snack.

snack bar a counter where light meals, coffee, etc. are served.

snaf•fle[1] ['snæfəl] *n., v.* **-fled, -fling.** *—n.* a slender, jointed bit used on a bridle.
—v. control or manage by a snaffle. ⟨? < Gmc.; cf. Du. *snavel* beak, mouth⟩

snaf•fle[2] ['snæfəl] *v.* **-fled, -fling.** *Informal.* pilfer; steal. ⟨origin uncertain⟩

sna•fu [snæ'fu] *adj., n., v.* **-fued, -fu•ing.** *Slang. —adj.* being in a characteristic state of confusion and disorder.
—n. confusion; chaos.
—v. put into disorder and confusion. ⟨from the initial letters of '*s*ituation *n*ormal—*a*ll *f*ouled *u*p'⟩

snag [snæg] *n., v.* **snagged, snag•ging.** *—n.* **1** a tree or branch held fast in a river or lake. Snags are dangerous to boats. **2** any sharp or rough projecting point, such as the broken end of a branch. **3** the stump of a tooth; a projecting tooth. **4** a hidden or unexpected obstacle: *He had to drop his plans because of a snag.* **5** a pulled or broken thread in fabric.
—v. **1** hinder. **2** run or catch on a snag. **3** clear of snags. **4** tear or pull (fabric) so as to make a snag. **5** acquire: get hold of: *How*

did you snag that job? ⟨? < Scand.; cf. dial. Norwegian *snage* point of land⟩

snag•gle•tooth [ˈsnægəl,tuθ] *n., pl.* **-teeth.** a tooth that grows apart from or beyond the others.

snag•gle–toothed [ˈsnægəl ˌtuθt] *adj.* having uneven, broken, or projecting teeth.

snag•gy [ˈsnægi] *adj.* **-gi•er, -gi•est. 1** having snags: *a snaggy tree, a snaggy river.* **2** projecting sharply or roughly.

A tree snail found in Florida—about 25 mm long

snail [sneil] *n.* **1** any gastropod mollusc having an external, spirally coiled shell, especially those species that live on land or in fresh water. **2** a lazy or slow-moving person or animal. ⟨OE *snegel*⟩ **—ˈsnail-,like,** *adj.*

snail–paced [ˈsneil ˌpeist] *adj.* moving at a very slow speed.

snake [sneik] *n., v.* **snaked, snak•ing.** *—n.* **1** any of a large suborder (Serpentes, also called Ophidia) of reptiles having an extremely elongated, scaly-skinned body, no legs, no movable eyelids, and no external ears, and moving by means of undulations of the body. Snakes and lizards constitute the order Squamata. **2** a sly, treacherous person. **3** a long, flexible metal rod used to clear drainpipes of obstructions.
snake in the grass, a person who seems to be a friend but is actually faithless; a secret enemy.
—v. **1** move, wind, or curve like a snake. **2** *Informal.* drag; haul. **3** *Informal.* jerk. ⟨OE *snaca*⟩ **—ˈsnake,like,** *adj.*

snake•bird [ˈsneik,bɜrd] *n.* any of a genus (*Anhinga*, constituting the family Anhingidae) of large aquatic birds found in tropical and warm temperate regions, having a long, straight, pointed bill, a long, slender neck, and a long, broad tail. Snakebirds belong to the same order as pelicans and cormorants.

snake•bite [ˈsneik,bəit] *n.* **1** the bite of a snake, especially a poisonous one. **2** the condition resulting from the bite of a poisonous snake.

snake charmer a person who entertains an audience by demonstrating an apparent power to hypnotize, or charm, poisonous snakes.

snake dance 1 an informal single-file procession of people who join hands or hold the waist of the person in front, and dance in a weaving path through buildings, streets, etc., especially as part of a celebration. **2** a ceremonial dance among certain peoples in which snakes are handled, invoked, etc. The Hopi people of the SW United States have a traditional snake dance.

snake fence a fence made of horizontal tiers of wooden rails laid zigzag so that their ends overlap at an angle.

snake oil any liquid presented as a cure-all or tonic but having no true medicinal properties.

snake pit 1 a pit filled with snakes. **2** a place of utter confusion and distress; especially, a psychiatric hospital that is overcrowded and where patients are not properly cared for.

snake•root [ˈsneik,rut] *n.* **1** any of various plants whose roots have at some time been used as a remedy for snakebite. Two North American species are **black snakeroot** (*Sanicula marilandica*) and **white snakeroot** (*Eupatorium urticaefolium*). **2** the root of either of these plants.

snake•skin [ˈsneik,skɪn] *n.* **1** the skin of a snake. **2** a leather made from it.

snak•y [ˈsneiki] *adj.* **snak•i•er, snak•i•est. 1** of or like a snake or snakes. **2** curving, turning, or twisting, suggesting the movements of a snake: *a snaky path up the hillside.* **3** having many snakes. **4** sly; venomous; treacherous. **—ˈsnak•i•ly,** *adv.* **—ˈsnak•i•ness,** *n.*

snap [snæp] *v.* **snapped, snap•ping;** *n. —v.* **1** make or cause to make a sudden, sharp sound: *This wood snaps as it burns. She snapped her fingers in time to the music.* **2** move, shut, fasten, etc. with a snap: *He snapped the lid shut. The latch snapped into place.* **3** break suddenly with a sharp sound: *The violin string snapped.* **4** become suddenly unable to endure a strain: *Her nerves snapped.* **5** make a sudden, quick bite or snatch in the direction of (*often used with* **at** or **up**): *The dog snapped at the child's hand. The dog snapped up the meat.* **6** seize eagerly (*used with* **at**): *He snapped at the chance to go to Europe.* **7** speak sharply or impatiently: *"Silence!" snapped the captain. Don't snap at him; he doesn't understand what you want.* **8** move quickly and sharply: *The soldiers snapped to attention.* **9** of the eyes, seem to flash or spark: *Her eyes snapped with anger.* **10** *Photography.* take a snapshot of. **11** *Football.* pass (the ball) between the legs to start play.
snap back, make a quick recovery.
snap out of it, *Slang.* change one's (negative) attitude, habit, etc., especially suddenly.
snap (someone's) **head off,** display sudden anger or irritation at someone.
snap up, take, accept, believe, or buy eagerly.
—n. **1** a sudden, sharp breaking of something hard or brittle: *the snap of a branch.* **2** the quick, sharp sound of a snap: *The box shut with a snap. The blade broke with a snap.* **3** a quick, sudden bite or snatch. **4** quick, sharp speech. **5** *Informal.* the quality or condition of being energetic, lively, and alert. **6** (*adjl.*) made or done quickly or unexpectedly: *A snap judgment is often wrong. The government called a snap election.* **7** DOME FASTENER: *The jacket closes with snaps.* **8** a snapping of the fingers. **9** a thin, crisp cookie: *a gingersnap, lemon snaps.* **10** *Informal.* a snapshot. **11** *Informal.* a snapdragon. **12** *Slang.* **a** a very easy job, piece of work, etc.: *The exam was a snap.* **b** a person easy to persuade or deal with. **13** *Slang.* (*adjl.*) very easy: *a snap assignment.* **14** *Football.* **a** the act of passing the ball between the legs by the centre at the start of play. **b** the player in the middle of the line of scrimmage; the centre.
a cold snap, a short spell of cold weather.
not a snap, not at all. ⟨< MDu. or MLG *snappen*⟩

snap•drag•on [ˈsnæp,drægən] *n.* **1** any of several plants (genus *Antirrhinum*) of the figwort family having showy, two-lipped, white, yellow, red, pink, or purple flowers. Most garden snapdragons are varieties of *A. majus*, native to the Mediterranean. **2** an old game in which people try to snatch raisins from burning brandy.

snap fastener DOME FASTENER.

snap•per [ˈsnæpər] *n.* **1** any of a family (Lutjanidae) of mostly large marine fishes found in warm and tropical waters, including some important food fishes. **2** SNAPPING TURTLE. **3** a person who or thing that snaps.

snapping beetle CLICK BEETLE.

snapping turtle any of a family (Chelydridae, comprising two species) of large, edible, freshwater turtles of North and Central America having powerful, hooked jaws. The **common snapping turtle** (*Chelydra serpentina*) is found from Canada south to Central America.

snap•pish [ˈsnæpɪʃ] *adj.* **1** quick and sharp in speech or manner; curt and irritable: *She's very snappish today.* **2** apt to bite or snap. **—ˈsnap•pish•ly,** *adv.* **—ˈsnap•pish•ness,** *n.*

snap•py [ˈsnæpi] *adj.* **-pi•er, -pi•est. 1** *Informal.* brisk and vigorous: *We went at a snappy pace.* **2** *Informal.* sharply chilly: *a snappy fall day.* **3** *Informal.* smart; stylish: *a snappy sports jacket. He's a snappy dresser.* **4** snappish.
make it snappy, *Informal.* be quick about it; hurry: *We're waiting, so make it snappy with your phone call.* **—ˈsnap•pi•ly,** *adv.* **—ˈsnap•pi•ness,** *n.*

snap•shot [ˈsnæp,ʃɒt] *n.* **1** an informal photograph, such as one taken by an amateur photographer with a hand-held camera, often without regard to artistic or creative effects. **2** a shot from a firearm, taken quickly without proper aim.

snap shot *Cdn. Hockey.* a quick, expert wrist shot aimed at the goal.

snare¹ [snɛr] *n., v.* **snared, snar•ing.** *—n.* **1** a noose for catching small animals and birds. **2** something that acts as a temptation and by which one is entangled; trap: *It is easy to be caught in the snare of popularity.*
—v. catch in a snare. ⟨ME < ON *snara*⟩ **—ˈsnar•er,** *n.*
☛ *Syn. n.* **1.** See note at TRAP¹.

snare² [snɛr] *n.* one of the twisted gut or rawhide strings or spiralled lengths of wire stretched across the bottom of a SNARE DRUM. ⟨probably < MDu. or MLG⟩

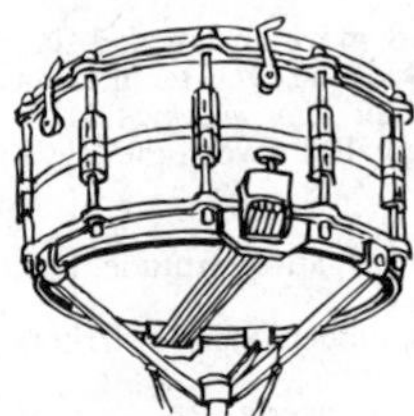
A snare drum, showing the snares on the bottom

snare drum a small drum having lengths of wire, gut, or rawhide stretched across the bottom to make a rattling sound when the drum is struck.

snark•y ['snɑrki] *adj.* **-i•er, -i•est.** *Slang.* showing annoyance in a sarcastic and snappish way: *He made some snarky comments about the way the meeting was conducted.* **—'snark•i•ly,** *adv.* **—'snark•i•ness,** *n.* ⟨< Du., Low G *snorken* to snore⟩

snarl[1] [snɑrl] *v., n.* *—v.* **1** of a dog, etc., growl while baring and snapping the teeth: *The dog snarled at the stranger.* **2** speak harshly in a sharp, menacing tone. **3** say or express with a snarl: *to snarl a threat.*
—n. the act or sound of snarling. ⟨earlier *snar;* cf. MDu. or MLG *snarren* rattle⟩ **—'snarl•er,** *n.* **—'snarl•ing•ly,** *adv.* **—'snarl•y,** *adj.*

snarl[2] [snɑrl] *n., v.* *—n.* **1** a tangle, especially of hair, thread, yarn, etc.: *She combed the snarls out of her hair.* **2** confusion and disorder: *His legal affairs were in a snarl.*
—v. **1** tangle or become tangled. **2** complicate or confuse: *Traffic soon became snarled when the traffic lights broke down.* ⟨< *snare*[1]⟩ **—'snarl•y,** *adj.*

snatch [snætʃ] *v., n.* *—v.* **1** seize suddenly; grasp hastily: *She snatched her jacket and ran.* **2** take suddenly (*used with* **off, away,** etc.): *He snatched off his hat and bowed.* **3** save or attain narrowly or by quick action: *They snatched victory from what seemed to be sure defeat.* **4** *Slang.* kidnap or steal: *to snatch a purse, to snatch the child.* **5** *Weightlifting.* lift (a weight) with a snatch (*n.* 5).
snatch at, a try to seize or grasp: *He snatched at the railing to keep himself from falling.* **b** eagerly take advantage of: *She snatched at the chance to travel.*
—n. **1** the act of snatching: *The girl made a snatch at the ball.* **2** a short time: *He had a snatch of sleep sitting in his chair.* **3** a small amount; bit; scrap: *to hear snatches of conversation.* **4** *Slang.* the act of kidnapping or stealing. **5** *Weightlifting.* a lift in which the weight is raised from the floor to an overhead position in a single quick movement. ⟨Cf. MDu. *snakken*⟩ **—'snatch•er,** *n.*

snatch•y ['snætʃi] *adj.* **-i•er, -i•est.** done or occurring in snatches; disconnected; irregular. **—'snatch•i•ly,** *adv.* **—'snatch•i•ness,** *n.*

snath [snæθ] *n.* the long wooden handle of a scythe. ⟨var. of *snead,* OE *snǣd*⟩

snathe [sneið] *n.* See SNATH.

snaz•zy ['snæzi] *adj.* **-i•er, -i•est.** *Slang.* attractive in a showy and stylish way: *a snazzy new car, a snazzy outfit.* ⟨? blend of *snappy* and *jazzy*⟩ **—'snaz•zi•ly,** *adv.* **—'snaz•zi•ness,** *n.*

sneak [snik] *v.* **sneaked** or (*informal*) **snuck, sneak•ing;** *n.* *—v.* **1** move in a stealthy, sly way: *The man sneaked about the barn watching for a chance to steal the dog.* **2** get, put, pass, etc. in a stealthy, sly way. **3** *Informal.* steal. **4** act in a mean, contemptible, cowardly way.
sneak out of, avoid by slyness.
—n. **1** the act of sneaking. **2** a person who sneaks; a sneaking, cowardly, contemptible person. **3** someone who betrays his or her friends. **4** (*adjl.*) stealthy; underhand; sneaking: *a sneak thief, a sneak attack.* **5** *Informal.* SNEAKER (def. 1): *He arrived in sneaks and sweats.* ⟨Cf. OE *snīcan*⟩

sneak•er ['snikər] *n.* **1** a light shoe with a cloth or soft leather upper and pliable rubber sole, used for sports like tennis, badminton, etc. or for general casual wear. **2** a person that sneaks; a sneak.

sneak•ing ['snikɪŋ] *adj., v.* *—adj.* **1** that one cannot justify or does not like to confess: *I have a sneaking suspicion that she doesn't know what she's talking about. He had a sneaking admiration for his adventuresome but irresponsible brother.* **2** mean and underhand; furtive and cowardly: *sneaking treachery, a sneaking manner.*
—v. ppr. of SNEAK. **—'sneak•ing•ly,** *adv.*

sneak preview a special single showing of a new film prior to regular distribution in order to test audience reaction.

sneak thief a person who takes advantage of open doors, windows, or other easy opportunities to steal.

sneak•y ['sniki] *adj.* **sneak•i•er, sneak•i•est.** sly, mean, or underhand. **—'sneak•i•ness,** *n.* **—'sneak•i•ly,** *adv.*

sneer [snir] *v., n.* *—v.* **1** smile, laugh, speak, etc. in such a way as to show contempt or scorn: *They sneered at his attempts to curry favour with the boss. She sneers at any expression of sentiment.* **2** say or express with scorn or contempt: *"Bah!" he sneered with a curl of his lip.*
—n. a look or words expressing scorn or contempt. ⟨ME *snere(n)*⟩ **—'sneer•er,** *n.* **—'sneer•ing•ly,** *adv.*
☛ *Syn. v.* **1.** See note at SCOFF[1].

sneeze [sniz] *v.* **sneezed, sneez•ing;** *n.* *—v.* expel air suddenly and violently through the nose and mouth by an involuntary spasm, due to an irritation of the lining of the nose.
not to be sneezed at, *Informal.* not to be disregarded, despised, or made light of: *A saving of ten dollars is not to be sneezed at.*
—n. a sudden, violent expelling of air through the nose and mouth. ⟨ME *snese(n),* var. of earlier *fnese(n),* OE *fnēosan*⟩ **—'sneez•er,** *n.*

snell [snɛl] *n.* a short piece of gut, etc. by which a fish-hook is fastened to a longer line. ⟨? < Du. *snel;* cf. G *schnellen* snap⟩

snick[1] [snɪk] *v., n.* *—v.* **1** cut slightly; snip or nick. **2** *Cricket.* give (a ball) a light, glancing blow.
—n. **1** a small cut; a nick. **2** *Cricket.* **a** a light, glancing blow given to the ball by the batsman. **b** the ball so hit. ⟨?; cf. Scottish *sneck* cut off, OIcel. *snikka* whittle⟩

snick[2] [snɪk] *v., n.* *—v.* make or cause to make a clicking sound.
—n. a slight, sharp sound; click. ⟨imitative⟩

snick•er ['snɪkər] *n., v.* *—n.* a half-suppressed and usually disrespectful laugh; sly or silly laugh; giggle.
—v. laugh in this way. ⟨imitative⟩

snick•er•snee ['snɪkər,sni] *n.* a heavy knife or short sword. ⟨< earlier *snick or snee,* alteration of *stick or snee* < Du. *steken* to thrust + *snijen* to cut⟩

snide [snaɪd] *adj., n.* *—adj.* **1** spitefully or slyly sarcastic: *When he did not get the part in the play, he started making snide remarks about the director.* **2** mean or cheap: *a snide trick.* **3** *Brit.* counterfeit; false; bogus: *a snide gem.*
—n. Brit. counterfeit jewellery. ⟨? < Du. or G; cf. G *schneidend* cutting, sarcastic⟩ **—'snide•ly,** *adv.* **—'snide•ness,** *n.*

snies [snaɪz] *n.* a pl. of SNY.

sniff [snɪf] *v., n.* *—v.* **1** draw air through the nose in short, quick breaths that can be heard. **2** smell with sniffs: *The dog sniffed suspiciously at the stranger.* **3** try the smell of: *to sniff a new perfume.* **4** inhale (the fumes of): *to sniff glue. He sniffed the steam to clear his head.* **5** show contempt by or as if by sniffing: *to sniff at an inexpensive gift.* **6** suspect; detect: *The police sniffed a plot and broke up the meeting.*
sniff out, smell out.
—n. the act or sound of sniffing: *a loud sniff.* ⟨ME. Akin to SNIVEL, SNUFF.⟩

snif•fle ['snɪfəl] *v.* **-fled, -fling;** *n.* *—v.* **1** sniff again and again: *The child stopped crying, but kept on sniffling.* **2** breathe audibly through a partly clogged nose.
—n. **1** the act or sound of sniffling. **2 the sniffles,** a head cold marked by a runny nose and sniffling. **—'snif•fler,** *n.* **—'snif•fly,** *adj.*

sniff•y ['snɪfi] *adj.* **sniff•i•er, sniff•i•est.** *Informal.* **1** inclined to sniff. **2** contemptuous; scornful; disdainful. Also, **sniffish.** **—'snif•fi•ly,** *adv.* **—'snif•fi•ness,** *n.*

snif•ter ['snɪftər] *n.* **1** a pear-shaped glass having a short stem and used especially for brandy, the narrow top serving to retain the aroma of the liquor. **2** a small drink of liquor. ⟨< dial. *snift* sniff⟩

snig•ger ['snɪgər] *n., v.* snicker.

snig•gle ['snɪgəl] *v.* **-gled, -gling.** try to catch (eels) by jiggling a baited hook in or near their holes.

snip [snɪp] *v.* **snipped, snip•ping;** *n.* *—v.* cut with a small, quick stroke or series of strokes with scissors: *He snipped the thread.*
—n. **1** the act of snipping: *With a few snips she cut out a paper doll.* **2** the sound made by the act of snipping. **3** a small piece cut off: *Pick up the snips of cloth and thread from the floor.* **4** any small piece; bit; fragment. **5** *Informal.* **a** a small or unimportant person. **b** a cheeky, impertinent person. **6 snips,** *pl.* hand shears for cutting metal. ⟨< Du. or LG *snippen*⟩ **—'snip•per,** *n.*

snipe [snəip] *n., pl.* **snipe** or **snipes;** *v.* **sniped, snip•ing.** *—n.* **1** any of several shore birds of the sandpiper family found in

most parts of the world, having a long bill used in digging for worms in the mud, eyes set far back in the head, short legs with long toes, and a very short tail. Only one species (*Capella gallinago*) is found in North America. Snipe are important game birds in Europe. **2** a shot from a concealed place.
—v. **1** hunt snipe. **2** shoot at, as a sniper does.
snipe at, attack suddenly or unexpectedly, especially by words. ⟨ME < ON *-snípe*, originally, snapping bird⟩

snip•er ['snəipər] *n.* a person who shoots from a concealed place at one enemy or target at a time, as a hunter shoots at game.

snip•pet ['snɪpɪt] *n.* **1** a small piece snipped off; bit; scrap; fragment: *snippets of information.* **2** *Informal.* a small or unimportant person.

snip•py ['snɪpi] *adj.* **-pi•er, -pi•est. 1** *Informal.* sharp; curt. **2** *Informal.* haughty; disdainful. **3** made up of scraps or fragments. **—'snip•pi•ness,** *n.* **—'snip•pi•ly,** *adv.*

snit [snɪt] *n. Informal.* a state of agitation, especially of peevish annoyance.

snitch[1] [snɪtʃ] *v. Slang.* snatch; steal. ⟨origin unknown⟩
—'snitch•er, *n.*

snitch[2] [snɪtʃ] *v., n. Slang. —v.* be an informer; tell tales.
—n. an informer. ⟨originally, nose; origin uncertain⟩
—'snitch•er, *n.*

sniv•el ['snɪvəl] *v.* **-elled** or **-eled, -el•ling** or **-el•ing;** *n.*
—v. **1** cry with sniffling. **2** put on a show of grief; whine. **3** run at the nose; sniffle.
—n. **1** pretended grief or crying; whining. **2** a running from the nose; sniffling. ⟨ME < OE **snyflan* < *snofl* mucus⟩ **—'sniv•el•ler** or **'sniv•el•er,** *n.*

snob [snɒb] *n.* **1** a person who cares too much for rank, wealth, and position, being too anxious to please or imitate people above him or her and too ready to ignore those below him or her. **2** a person who is contemptuous of the popular taste in some field, and is attracted to esoteric or learned things for their own sake: *a literary snob, a musical snob.* ⟨origin uncertain⟩
—'snob•by, *adj.*

snob•ber•y ['snɒbəri] *n., pl.* **-ber•ies.** snobbishness.

snob•bish ['snɒbɪʃ] *adj.* of, being, or like a snob.
—'snob•bish•ly, *adv.* **—'snob•bish•ness** or **'snob•bism,** *n.*

snood [snud] *n., v. —n.* **1** a pouch, often of net, for loosely holding a woman's long hair at the nape of the neck. It is tied on or attached with hairpins, etc. **2** a headband or ribbon formerly worn around the hair by young unmarried women in Scotland.
—v. confine or bind (the hair) with a snood. ⟨OE *snōd*⟩

snook•er ['snʊkər] *n., v. —n.* a type of pool played with 15 red balls and 6 other balls of different colours. Compare POOL[2] (def. 1).
—v. **1** leave (one's opponent) a shot in which he or she cannot aim directly at the object ball but must reach it off the cushion. **2** place (someone) in a difficult or frustrating situation; thwart. **3** dupe; outwit. ⟨origin unknown. 19c.⟩

snoop [snup] *v., n. Informal. —v.* go about in a sneaking, prying way; prowl; pry.
—n. a person who snoops. ⟨< Du. *snoepen* eat in secret⟩
—'snoop•er, *n.* **—'snoop•y,** *adj.*

snoose [snus] *n.* a kind of snuff, prepared damp and in grated form, used for chewing. Also, **Copenhagen snuff.** ⟨< Danish, Swedish, etc. *snus*, shortening of *snutstobak* < *snusa, snuse* sniff + *tobak* tobacco⟩

snoot [snut] *n. Slang.* **1** the nose. **2** the face. ⟨originally a Scottish var. of *snout*⟩

snoot•y ['snuti] *adj.* **snoot•i•er, snoot•i•est.** *Informal.* snobbish; conceited. **—'snoot•i•ly,** *adv.* **—'snoot•i•ness,** *n.*

snooze [snuz] *v.* **snoozed, snooz•ing;** *n. Informal. —v.* take a nap; sleep; doze.
—n. a nap; doze. ⟨origin uncertain⟩

snore [snɔr] *v.* **snored, snor•ing;** *n. —v.* **1** breathe during sleep with a harsh, rough sound. **2** pass in snoring: *The lazy man snored away the afternoon.*
—n. the sound made in snoring. ⟨ME *snore(n)*, ? imitative⟩
—'snor•er, *n.*

snor•kel ['snɔrkəl] *n., v.* **-kelled** or **-keled, -kel•ling** or **-kel•ing.** *—n.* **1** a shaft for taking in air and discharging gases that allows submarines to remain submerged for a long time. See SUBMARINE for picture. **2** a curved tube held in the mouth which enables swimmers to breathe just below the surface of water.
—v. swim or stay underwater, using a snorkel to breathe. ⟨< LG slang *snorkel* nose < MLG **snorkeln*, frequentative of *snorken* snore; because the snorkel is the 'nose' of the submarine and its intake valve makes a snoring sound⟩

snort [snɔrt] *v., n. —v.* **1** force the breath violently through the nose with a loud, harsh sound: *The horse snorted.* **2** make a sound like this: *The engine snorted.* **3** show contempt, defiance, anger, etc. by snorting. **4** say or express with a snort: *"Indeed!" snorted my aunt.* **5** *Slang.* ingest (a narcotic drug in powdered form, especially cocaine) into the system by sniffing it up into the nasal passages.
—n. **1** the act or sound of snorting. **2** *Slang.* a small, quick drink, especially of liquor taken neat. ⟨< *snore*⟩ **—'snort•er,** *n.*

snot [snɒt] *n.* **1** *Vulgar.* mucus from the nose. **2** *Slang.* a flippant and disrespectful person. ⟨OE *gesnot*⟩

snot•ty ['snɒti] *adj.* **-ti•er, -ti•est;** *n., pl.* **-ties.** *—adj.* **1** *Vulgar.* dirty with snot. **2** *Slang.* mean or contemptible. **3** *Slang.* insolent or arrogant.
—n. Brit. Slang. a midshipman.

snout [snʌut] *n.* **1** the projecting part of an animal's head that contains the nose, mouth, and jaws. Pigs, dogs, and crocodiles have snouts. **2** anything like an animal's snout. **3** *Informal.* a person's nose, especially a large or ugly one. ⟨ME *snoute*; akin to G *Schnauze*⟩

snout beetle WEEVIL (def. 1).

snow [snou] *n., v. —n.* **1** water vapour frozen into crystals in the upper atmosphere and falling to earth in the form of individual crystals or large flakes consisting of many crystals together. **2** a continuous fall of snow. **3** *Poetic.* pure whiteness. **4** something resembling or suggesting snow. **5** *Slang.* cocaine or heroin. **6** *Cdn.* SNOW APPLE. **7** a pattern of dots on a television screen caused by atmospheric interference with the signals. **8** *Informal.* SNOW TIRE.
—v. **1** be the case that snow or something like it is falling (*used with the subject* **it**): *It has been snowing since last night.* **2** fall or scatter like snow: *The apple trees were snowing blossoms in the garden.* **3** cover, block up, shut in, etc. with snow or as if with snow (*used with* **in, up, under,** *etc., and usually used in the passive*): *The town was snowed in for a week after the blizzard. She is snowed under with work. The car was completely snowed under.* **4** *Slang.* deceive, mislead, or charm by glib or elaborate talk. ⟨OE *snāw*⟩

snow angel a shaped depression resembling a traditional angel figure, made by lying down in soft snow and moving the outstretched arms and legs over the surface of the snow to form the shape of wings and gown.

snow apple *Cdn.* a fine eating apple having crisp, white flesh and a deep red skin.

snow•ball ['snou,bɒl] *n., v. —n.* **1** a rounded mass of snow that has been pressed or rolled together, often used for throwing in play. **2** any of several cultivated viburnums, especially a sterile variety of *V. opulus*, having large, showy, spherical clusters of white flowers.
—v. **1** throw snowballs (at). **2** increase, expand, or accumulate at an accelerating rate; cause to increase very fast: *Demands for an independent investigation are snowballing.*

snow•bank ['snou,bæŋk] *n.* a large mass or drift of snow.

snow•ber•ry ['snou,bɛri] *n., pl.* **-ries. 1** any of several shrubs (genus *Symphoricarpos*) of the honeysuckle family having white berries, especially a small, pink-flowered, North American species (*S. albus*). **2** any of various other shrubs having white berries. **3** the berry of any of these shrubs.

snow•bird ['snou,bɜrd] *n. Cdn.* **1** SNOW BUNTING. **2** a junco. **3** a tourist, especially a Canadian, who escapes the northern winter by travelling to the warm south and returning home in late spring.

snow–blind ['snou ,blaɪnd] *adj.* suffering from snow blindness. Compare ICE-BLIND.

snow blindness *Cdn.* a painful inflammation of the eyes, caused by overexposure to the glare of sunlight on wide expanses of snow or ice, and resulting in temporary partial or complete blindness.

snow•blink ['snou,blɪŋk] *n.* the glare caused by the reflection of the sun's rays off snow.

snow•blow•er ['snou,blouər] *n. Cdn.* a machine that clears snow by drawing it in by means of a large fan and blowing it out in another direction.

snow boot a waterproof boot, usually well-lined, for use in snow.

snow•bound ['snou,baʊnd] *adj.* shut in by snow; snowed in.

snow bunting *Cdn.* a small songbird (*Plectrophenax nivalis*) of the same family as grosbeaks, goldfinches, and sparrows that breeds in the Arctic and winters in northern temperate regions, having mostly white plumage with back and wings black in breeding season and mainly rusty brown in winter. The snow bunting is a common sight in most of southern Canada in winter; in the Arctic, it is a harbinger of spring.

snow–capped ['snou ,kæpt] *adj.* topped with snow: *snow-capped mountains.*

snow cruising *Cdn.* driving or riding on a motorized snow vehicle, often as recreation.

snow devil a whirling column of snow sucked up in a vortex by the wind.

snow•drift ['snou,drɪft] *n.* **1** a mass or bank of snow piled up by the wind. **2** snow driven before the wind.

snow•drop ['snou,drɒp] *n.* any of a genus (*Galanthus*) of spring-blooming, bulbous Eurasian herbs of the amaryllis family, especially *G. nivalis*, having drooping, white, bell-shaped flowers.

snow•fall ['snou,fɒl] *n.* **1** a fall of snow. **2** the amount of snow falling within a certain time and area: *The snowfall at Banff in that one storm was 30 cm.*

snow fence *Cdn.* a lath and wire fence erected in winter alongside roads, etc. to prevent snow from drifting.

snow fencing *Cdn.* **1** the material of which snow fences are made. **2** SNOW FENCE.

snow•field ['snou,fild] *n.* a large expanse of snow.

snow•flake ['snou,fleik] *n.* a single feathery crystal, or flake, of snow.

snow goose *Cdn.* a wild goose (*Chen caerulescens*) that breeds in the Arctic, the adult typically white with black wing tips and having a pinkish bill with a blackish patch on each side and reddish legs and feet. Some ornithologists, especially in Europe, classify the snow goose as *Anser caerulescens.* See also BLUE GOOSE.

snow•house ['snou,hʌus] *n.* **1** an igloo. **2** formerly, among the Inuit, a building of snow blocks intended for communal gatherings. **3** a crude hut, cave, or fort made out of snow as a form of play.

snow job *Slang.* an intensive effort to persuade or deceive by flattering, glib, or elaborate talk.

snow knife *Cdn.* a knife about 35 cm long, having a broad, curved blade and used chiefly for cutting snow blocks for igloos.

snow leopard a large mammal (*Panthera uncia*) of the cat family found in the mountains of central Asia, having a long, thick, greyish coat marked with dark spots arranged in rosettes. It is closely related to the leopard.

snow lily *Cdn.* GLACIER LILY.

snow line a height on mountains, etc. above which there is snow all year round.

snow•man ['snou,mæn] *n., pl.* **-men.** a mass of snow made into a figure shaped somewhat like a man.

snow•melt ['snou,mɛlt] *n.* liquid resulting from the melting of snow.

snow melter *Cdn. Prairies.* a metal trough placed on bricks; it is filled with snow and a fire is built under it to provide drinking water for livestock in the winter.

snow•mo•bile ['snoumə,bil] *n., v.* **-biled, -bil•ing.** *Cdn. —n.* **1** a small, open motor vehicle for travelling over snow and ice, equipped with skis at the front, by which it is steered, and having a caterpillar track beneath the body. Snowmobiles are used as a means of transportation, especially in the North, and also for sport. **2** a large, closed-in vehicle similar to this, but having two tracks and designed to carry a number of persons, goods, etc.; bombardier. **3** (*adjl.*) designed for wear when snowmobiling: *a snowmobile suit, snowmobile boots.*
—v. travel by snowmobile; ride or drive a snowmobile.
—'snow•mo,bil•er, *n.* **—'snow•mo,bil•ing,** *n., adj.*

snow–on–the–mountain ['snou ən ðə 'maʊntən] a plant of the spurge family (Euphorbia marginata) widely cultivated in North America, having white-margined upper leaves and small but showy white bracts.

snowpack ['snou,pæk] *n.* the snow accumulating over an area during the winter and melting in the spring, often relied upon to provide water during the rest of the year for reservoirs, dams, etc.: *If we don't get more of a snowpack, there'll be a water shortage next summer.*

snow•pants ['snou,pænts] *n.* warm, heavily lined, often waterproof pants, usually with a bib and shoulder straps, worn in very cold or snowy weather over regular pants, especially as part of a two-piece snowsuit.

snow pea a variety of pea (*Pisum sativum macrocarpon*) whose pods are flat, sweet, and crisp, containing very tiny seeds. The pods are used whole, frequently in stir-fry or other Chinese dishes.

snow•plough or **snow•plow** ['snou,plaʊ] *n., v. —n.* **1** a machine for clearing away snow from streets, railway tracks, etc. by means of a large blade that pushes the snow as the machine moves forward. **2** a skiing manoeuvre used for stopping, in which the tips of the skis are pointed toward each other and the inside edges dug into the snow.
—v. to stop, using this manoeuvre.

snow•shed ['snou,ʃɛd] *n.* a long shed built over a railway track or a highway to protect it from snowslides.

snow•shine ['snou,ʃaɪn] *n.* snowblink.

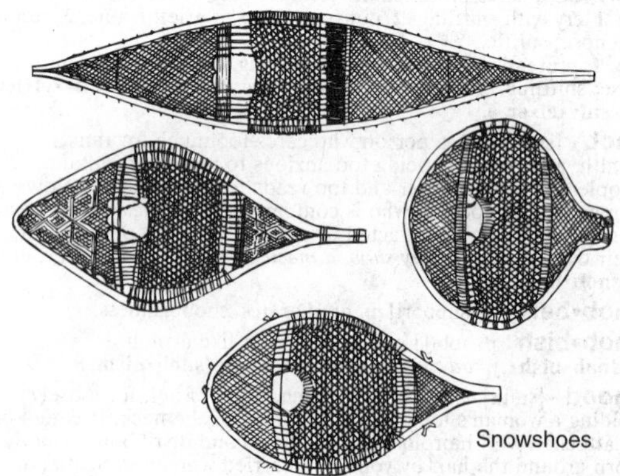
Snowshoes

snow•shoe ['snou,ʃu] *n., v.* **-shoed, -shoe•ing.** *—n.* **1** a light wooden frame with a network of leather strips stretched across it. Trappers in the far North wear snowshoes on their feet to keep from sinking in deep, soft snow. **2** *Cdn.* SNOWSHOE HARE.
—v. walk or travel on snowshoes. **—'snow,sho•er,** *n.*

snowshoe hare *Cdn.* a medium-sized hare (*Lepus americanus*) common throughout the forested regions of N North America, having grizzled brown fur in summer which, throughout most of the animal's range, turns to white in winter, and having very large, broad hind feet which in winter are very heavily furred, giving the animal its common name. Also called **snowshoe rabbit, varying hare.**

snow shovel a shovel having a large, square or rectangular blade curved from top to bottom, for clearing snow.

snow•slide ['snou,slaɪd] *n.* **1** the sliding down of a mass of snow on a steep slope. **2** the mass of snow that slides.

snow snake **1** a North American Indian game in which a wooden stick is slid as far as possible along a smooth patch of ice or snow, or along a furrow in snow. **2** the stick used in this game. Also, **snowsnake**.

snow•storm ['snou,stɔrm] *n.* a storm with falling snow.

snow•suit ['snou,sut] *n.* a warm, heavily lined or padded one- or two-piece outer garment, usually with a hood, worn in very cold or snowy weather, especially by children.

snow thrower a snowblower.

snow tire a tire for motor vehicles, having a deeply cut tread to provide extra traction when driving in snow or mud.

snow–white ['snou 'wəit] *adj.* white as snow.

snow•y ['snoui] *adj.* **snow•i•er, snow•i•est. 1** with falling snow: *a snowy day, snowy weather.* **2** covered with snow. **3** like snow; white as snow: *She has snowy hair.* **4** having a blurred and dotted pattern: *The TV picture is snowy.* **—snow'i•ly,** *adv.*
—'snow•i•ness, *n.*

snowy owl a large owl (*Nyctea nyctea*) ranging from the Arctic to the northern U.S. in winter, having mainly white plumage with some brown spots or bars (more in the female), yellow eyes, and feathered toes. The female is bigger than the male.

A snowy owl

snub [snʌb] *v.* **snubbed, snub•bing;** *n.* *—v.* **1** treat coldly or with contempt. **2** check or stop (a rope or cable) running out by winding it around a post or other object. **3** check or stop the motion of (a boat, horse, etc.) in this way.
—n. **1** cold or contemptuous treatment; a rebuff or slight. **2** a sudden check or stop. ⟨ME < ON *snubba* reprove⟩

snub•ber [ˈsnʌbər] *n.* **1** a person that snubs. **2** a device for snubbing a rope, cable, etc. **3** an early type of shock absorber for automobiles.

snub•by [ˈsnʌbi] *adj.* **-bi•er, -bi•est. 1** of a nose, short and turned up at the end. **2** inclined to snub people; snooty.

snub nose a short, turned-up nose.

snub–nosed [ˈsnʌb ˌnouzd] *adj.* **1** having a short, turned-up nose. **2** of a handgun, having a short barrel.

snuck [snʌk] *v. Informal.* a pt. and a pp. of SNEAK.
☛ *Usage.* Though it is widely used, especially in such phrases as **snuck in** and **snuck up on,** this form is generally regarded as nonstandard in formal or written English.

snuff[1] [snʌf] *v., n.* *—v.* **1** draw in through the nose; draw up into the nose: *He snuffs up salt-and-water mist to cure a cold.* **2** sniff; smell (*at*): *The dog snuffed at the track of the fox.* **3** take powdered tobacco into the nose by snuffing; use snuff.
—n. **1** an act or the sound of snuffing. **2** powdered tobacco that is snuffed into the nose, rubbed on the gum, or placed between gums and cheek.
up to snuff, *Informal.* in perfect order or condition; as good as expected. ⟨< MDu. *snuffen* sniff⟩

snuff[2] [snʌf] *v., n., adj.* *—v.* **1** cut or pinch off (the burned wick of a candle). **2** put out (a candle); extinguish. **3** *Slang.* murder; put to death.
snuff out, a put out; extinguish. **b** put an end to suddenly and completely: *to snuff out all hope of freedom.*
—n. the burned part of a candlewick.
—adj. denoting a type of pornographic film showing sexual activity ending in murder of one partner by the other. ⟨ME; origin uncertain; cf. G *Schnuppe,* n.⟩

snuff•box [ˈsnʌfˌbɒks] *n.* a small, often ornamented box for holding snuff, carried on the person in a pocket, or used as a knick-knack.

snuf•fer [ˈsnʌfər] *n.* **1** a device for extinguishing a candle, consisting of a small, cone-shaped metal cup, usually at the end of a handle, that is inverted over the flame. **2 snuffers,** *pl.* an instrument like a pair of scissors for trimming the wick of a burning candle or extinguishing the candle.

snuf•fle [ˈsnʌfəl] *v.* **-fled, -fling;** *n.* *—v.* **1** breathe noisily through a partly clogged nose. **2** smell; sniff. **3** speak, sing, utter, etc. through the nose or with a nasal tone.
—n. **1** the act or sound of snuffling. **2** the nasal tone of voice of a person who snuffles. **3 the snuffles,** *Informal.* **a** a fit of snuffling; stuffed-up condition of the nose, caused by a cold, hay fever, etc. **b** a respiratory disease of animals. ⟨ult. < *snuff[1]* or its source⟩ **—ˈsnuf•fler,** *n.* **—ˈsnuf•fly,** *adj.*

snuff•y [ˈsnʌfi] *adj.* **snuff•i•er, snuff•i•est. 1** like snuff. **2** soiled or stained with snuff. **3** having the habit of using snuff. **4** having, or affected by, a partly clogged nose. **5** disagreeable; cross. **—ˈsnuff•i•ly,** *adv.* **—ˈsnuff•i•ness,** *n.*

snug [snʌg] *adj.* **snug•ger, snug•gest;** *v.* **snugged, snug•ging.**
—adj. **1** comfortable; warm; sheltered: *The cat has found a snug corner behind the stove.* **2** neat; trim; compact: *The cabins on the boat are snug.* **3** well-built; seaworthy: *a snug ship.* **4** fitting closely: *That coat is a little too snug.* **5** small but sufficient: *A snug income enables him to live in comfort.* **6** hidden; concealed: *He lay snug until the searchers passed by.*
—v. make snug. ⟨Cf. Swedish *snygg* neat, trim⟩ **—ˈsnug•ly,** *adv.* **—ˈsnug•ness,** *n.*
☛ *Syn. adj.* **1. Snug,** COSY = comfortable. **Snug** emphasizes the comfort and security of a small space, warm and sheltered from the weather, or of a quiet and peaceful life, protected from disturbance or excitement: *The children were snug in their beds.* **Cosy** emphasizes warmth, shelter, and ease, often affection or friendliness, making for comfort and contentment: *She was sitting in a cosy corner by the fire.*

snug•ger•y [ˈsnʌgəri] *n., pl.* **-ger•ies.** a snug place, position, room, etc.

snug•gies [ˈsnʌgiz] *n.pl.* women's warm underwear, reaching to just above the knee.

snug•gle [ˈsnʌgəl] *v.* **-gled, -gling. 1** lie or press closely for warmth or comfort or from affection; nestle; cuddle. **2** hold or draw close. ⟨< *snug*⟩ **—ˈsnug•gly,** *adj.*

snye or **sny** [snaɪ] *n., pl.* **snyes** or **snies.** *Cdn. Ontario.* **1** a side channel of a stream, especially one that bypasses a falls or rapids. **2** *Logging.* such a channel used as a route for rafts and booms of timber. ⟨< Cdn.F *chenail;* cf. F *chenal* channel⟩

so[1] [sou] *adv., adj., conj., interj., pron.* *—adv.* **1** in this way; in that way; in the same way; as shown: *Hold your pen so.* **2** as described or stated: *He was always active and is still very much so.* **3** to this degree; to that degree: *Do not walk so fast.* **4** to a certain unspecified maximum degree: *I can only be so patient. She will take just so much and no more.* **5** to such a degree; to the same degree (*as*): *He was not so cold as she was.* **6** very: *You are so kind.* **7** very much: *My head aches so.* **8** likewise; also: *She likes dogs; so does he.* **9** indeed (*always stressed; used emphatically or in contradiction of a negative*): *She was so insistent! I did so clean my room!*
and so forth or **and so on,** et cetera; and other things of the same sort.
just so, *Informal.* exactly correct(ly) and in order: *She insists on everything being just so.*
or so, more or less: *It cost a dollar or so.*
so as, so that (*with an infinitive for defs. a & b*).
so much for, a that is enough said or done about: *So much for my opinion; now let's hear yours.* **b** it is clear that (something) has completely failed to live up to expectations: *So much for their 'sale to end all sales!'*
so that, a with the result that. **b** with the purpose that. **c** provided that; as long as: *I don't care how much it costs, just so that I know it's done right.*
so what? why should anyone care about that?
—adj. true (*used only predicatively*): *Is that really so, or are you making it up? Just saying it over and over won't make it so.*
—conj. **1** with the result or effect that: *The snow had drifted so it resembled a giant lying on its back.* **2** with the purpose or intention that: *I did the work so he would not need to. Go away so I can rest.* **3** and for this or that reason; and therefore: *The dog was hungry, so we fed it.*
—interj. **1** well! I see! **2** (*interrogatively*) what now? what does it matter?
—pron. **1** approximately that: *a kilogram or so.* **2** the same: *When she left, he did so too.* **3** whatever has been or is going to be said; this; that: *He was lazy and I told him so.* ⟨OE *swā*⟩
☛ *Hom.* SEW, SOH, SOW[1].

so[2] [sou] *n. Music.* a syllable used for the fifth tone of an eight-tone scale; SOL[1]. ⟨See GAMUT⟩
☛ *Hom.* SEW, SOW[1].

so or **s.o.** *Baseball.* strikeout(s).

So. South; Southern.

soak [souk] *v., n.* *—v.* **1** make very wet; wet through. **2** remain or let remain in water or other liquid until wet through. **3** remain in a bath, etc. for relaxation or therapy. **4** be absorbed (*often with* **in**): *Water will soak into the earth. Just let that idea soak in for a while.* **5** absorb or suck (*used with* **up**): *A sponge will soak up water. We soaked up the sunshine. She would read for hours, soaking up knowledge.* **6** immerse or engross (oneself) in some pursuit. *She's soaking herself in Eastern mysticism.* **7** *Slang.* drink heavily. **8** *Slang.* punish severely; strike hard. **9** *Slang.* make pay (too much); charge or tax (heavily): *The new tax system really soaks the middle class. He soaked me $80 for a watch that doesn't even keep time!*
—n. **1** the act or process of soaking. **2** the state of being soaked. **3** the liquid in which anything is soaked. **4** *Slang.* a heavy drinker. ⟨OE *socian*⟩ **—ˈsoak•age,** *n.*
☛ *Syn. v.* **1.** See note at WET.

so–and–so [ˈsou ən ˌsou] *n., pl.* **-sos. 1** a person or thing not named. **2** *Informal.* an unpleasant or distasteful person.

soap [soup] *n., v.* *—n.* **1** a lathering substance used with water for washing, usually made of a fat and caustic soda or potash. **2** *Slang.* money, especially money as used for bribery. **3** *Informal.* SOAP OPERA.
no soap, *Slang.* **a** no; that is an unacceptable proposal. **b** no results; nothing accomplished.
—v. rub with soap. ⟨OE *sāpe*⟩ **—ˈsoap•less,** *adj.*

soap•bark ['soup,bɑrk] *n.* **1** any of various New World trees (genera *Quillaja* and *Pithecellobium*) whose inner bark contains saponin. **2** the bark of any of these trees.

soap•ber•ry ['soup,bɛri] *n., pl.* **-ries. 1** any of a genus (*Sapindus*) of mainly tropical woody plants or trees bearing fruit that is used as a soap substitute. **2** the fruit or nut of a soapberry. **3** (*adjl.*) designating a family (Sapindaceae) of mainly tropical woody plants, shrubs, and trees, including the soapberries, litchi, etc. **4** *Cdn.* a low shrub (*Shepherdia canadensis*) of the oleaster family having translucent orange-red fruit in small clusters, found throughout Canada and the N United States.

soap•box ['soup,bɒks] *n., v.* *—n.* **1** a box, especially of wood, in which soap is packed. **2** an empty box used as a temporary platform by agitators or other speakers addressing gatherings in the open air. **3** a position, forum, etc. exploited as an opportunity to make opinionated or impassioned addresses to the public: *The Letters page is not a soapbox for fanatics.* **4** (*adjl.*) of or for such addresses or the people who make them: *soapbox rhetoric.*
—v. **1** address an audience in the open air in an informal and emotional manner. **2** pontificate on a subject in the manner of such speakers.

soap bubble a bubble made with soapy water.

soap•o•lal•lie ['soupə,læli] *n. Cdn.* **1** a drink or dessert made from the soapberry. **2** soapberry. Also, **soopolallie.** ⟨< Chinook Jargon *soap* soap + *olallie* berry⟩

soap opera a radio or television drama presented in serial form, usually featuring emotional situations involving human relationships.

soap•stone ['soup,stoun] *n.* a heavy, soft stone that feels somewhat like soap; steatite: *Carvings by the Inuit are often made of soapstone.*

soap•suds ['soup,sʌdz] *n.pl.* bubbles and foam made with soap and water.

soap•wort ['soup,wɜrt] *n.* a tall European perennial herb (*Saponaria officinalis*) of the pink family, having clusters of fragrant pink or white flowers and leaves containing a lathering juice formerly used as a soap substitute.

soap•y ['soupi] *adj.* **soap•i•er, soap•i•est. 1** covered with soap or soapsuds: *soapy hands.* **2** containing soap: *soapy water.* **3** like soap; smooth and slippery or greasy: *Soapstone feels soapy.* **4** melodramatic; reminiscent of a soap opera. **5** unpleasantly suave or smooth-spoken. **—'soap•i•ly,** *adv.* **—'soap•i•ness,** *n.*

soar [sɔr] *v.* **1** fly at a great height; fly upward: *The eagle soared without flapping its wings.* **2** of prices, sales, etc., rise or increase rapidly and to an extreme level: *During the tourist season, hotel rates soared.* **3** rise beyond what is common and ordinary; aspire: *His ambition soared to the throne.* **4** *Poetic.* reach in soaring: *soar the heights.* **5** fly or move through the air by means of rising air currents: *A glider can soar for a great distance.* ⟨ME < OF *essorer*, ult. < L *ex-* out + *aura* breeze < Gk.⟩
☛ *Hom.* SORE.

Soave [sou'ɑvei] *or* ['swɑvei] *n.* a dry white Italian wine. ⟨a town in northern Italy⟩

sob [sɒb] *v.* **sobbed, sob•bing;** *n.* *—v.* **1** cry or sigh with short, quick breaths. **2** put, send, etc. by sobbing: *She sobbed herself to sleep.* **3** make a sound like a sob: *The wind sobbed.* **4** say or express with sobs: *He sobbed out his story.*
—n. **1** the catching of a short, quick breath because of grief, etc. **2** the sound of this. ⟨ME *sobbe(n)*, perhaps ult. imitative⟩

so•ber ['soubər] *adj., v.* *—adj.* **1** not drunk. **2** temperate; moderate: *The Puritans led sober, hard-working lives.* **3** quiet; serious; solemn: *a sober expression.* **4** calm; sensible: *The judge's sober opinion was not influenced by prejudice or strong feeling.* **5** free from exaggeration: *sober facts.* **6** quiet in colour: *dressed in sober grey.*
—v. make or become sober: *The experience of being lost in the bush sobered her.*
sober up (or **down** or **off**), **a** recover or cause to recover from too much alcoholic drink. **b** make or become serious, quiet, or solemn. ⟨ME < OF < L *sobrius*⟩ **—'so•ber•ly,** *adv.* **—'so•ber•ness,** *n.*
☛ *Syn. adj.* **3.** See note at GRAVE[2].

so•ber–mind•ed ['soubər ,maɪndɪd] *adj.* having or showing a sober mind; self-controlled; sensible. **—'so•ber-'mind•ed•ly,** *adv.* **—'so•ber-'mind•ed•ness,** *n.*

so•ber•sid•ed ['soubər,saɪdɪd] *adj.* of a serious or earnest disposition.

so•ber•sides ['soubər,saɪdz] *n., pl.* **-sides.** a serious or earnest person.

so•bri•e•ty [sə'braɪəti] *n., pl.* **-ties. 1** soberness. **2** temperance in the use of alcoholic liquors. **3** moderation. **4** quietness; seriousness. ⟨< L *sobrietas*⟩

so•bri•quet ['soubrə,kei], [,soubrə'kei], *or* ['soubrə,kɛt] *n.* a nickname. Also, **soubriquet.** ⟨< F⟩

sob sister *Informal.* a person who writes or tells a SOB STORY.

sob story *Informal.* a story that is excessively pathetic or sentimental, especially one calculated to arouse pity.

Soc. 1 Society. **2** Socialist.

soc•age or **soc•cage** ['sɒkɪdʒ] *n.* formerly, in England, feudal tenure of land under which the tenant paid a definite rent or did a definite amount of work, but gave no military service to his lord. ⟨ME < AF *socage* < *soc* < Med.L *soca* < OE *sōcn* seeking, inquiry, jurisdiction⟩

so–called ['sou 'kɒld] *adj.* **1** called thus. **2** called thus improperly or incorrectly: *Her so-called friend dislikes her.*

soc•cer ['sɒkər] *n.* a game played between two teams of eleven players each, using a round ball. In soccer, only the goalkeeper may touch the ball with hands and arms. Also called **association football.** ⟨< *as*soc., abbreviation of *association (football)*; for the ending cf. *rugger* for *rugby*⟩
☛ *Usage.* See note at RUGBY.

so•cia•bil•i•ty [,souʃə'bɪləti] *n., pl.* **-ties. 1** the quality of being sociable; degree to which one is sociable. **2** the act or an instance of being sociable.

so•cia•ble ['souʃəbəl] *adj., n.* *—adj.* **1** liking company; friendly: *The Smiths are a sociable family and entertain a great deal.* **2** marked by conversation and companionship: *We had a sociable afternoon together.*
—n. Esp. U.S. an informal social gathering; a social. ⟨< L *sociabilis* < *sociare* associate < *socius.* See SOCIAL.⟩
—'so•cia•bly, *adv.* **—'so•cia•ble•ness,** *n.*
☛ *Syn. adj.* **1.** See note at SOCIAL.

so•cial ['souʃəl] *adj., n.* *—adj.* **1** of or dealing with human beings in their relations to each other; having to do with the life of human beings in a community: *social problems. History and geography are social sciences.* **2** living, or liking to live, with others: *Human beings are social creatures.* **3** for companionship or friendliness; having to do with companionship or friendliness: *a social club.* **4** liking company; participating in many group events: *She is a social person.* **5** connected with fashionable society: *a social leader.* **6** of animals, living together in organized communities. Ants and bees are social insects.
—n. Cdn. an informal social gathering or party, often for the purpose of raising funds for a church or a charitable organization. ⟨< L *socialis* < *socius* companion, originally adj., sharing in⟩
☛ *Syn. adj.* **4. Social,** SOCIABLE = pertaining to, characterized by, or inclined to companionship and friendliness. **Social** suggests being in the habit of mingling with others at events intended for this purpose: *They are a very social couple and entertain often.* **Sociable** describes one's nature or disposition, and means being at ease in company and being inclined to seek and enjoy companionship and friendly relations even with strangers: *He is a likable, sociable person.*

social assistance *Cdn.* benefits paid through SOCIAL INSURANCE programs.

social climber a person who actively tries to gain admission to a group that has a higher social standing.

social contract or **compact** in the republican idealist theory of various 18th century political philosophers, especially Rousseau, the consent of the governed to give up certain personal liberties in exchange for protection, on which all government depends.

Social Credit Party a Canadian political party, founded in Alberta in the 1930s. Its traditional, essentially right-wing policies are based on certain economic theories originally developed by Major C.H. Douglas (1878-1952).

Social Credit Rally a Canadian political party formed in 1962 from the Québec wing of the Social Credit Party. ⟨translation of F *Ralliement des Créditistes*⟩

social disease any disease communicated by sexual intercourse; venereal disease.

social insurance benefits, such as old-age pension, family allowance, unemployment insurance, etc., provided by a government.

Social Insurance Number *Cdn.* a nine-digit number by which the federal government identifies an individual for purposes of income tax, unemployment insurance, old-age pension, etc. *Abbrev.*: SIN

so•cial•ism ['souʃə,lɪzəm] *n.* **1** a political and economic theory or system in which the means of production and distribution are owned, managed, or controlled by a central, democratically elected authority; in Marxist doctrine, the stage between capitalism and communism in the evolution of a society. Compare CAPITALISM, COMMUNISM. **2** any political movement whose goal is to set up this system.

so•cial•ist ['souʃəlɪst] *n., adj. —n.* a person who favours and supports socialism.
—adj. socialistic: *a socialist government.*

so•cial•is•tic [,souʃə'lɪstɪk] *adj.* **1** of or having to do with socialism or socialists. **2** advocating or supporting socialism. **—,so•cial'is•ti•cal•ly,** *adv.*

so•cial•ite ['souʃə,lait] *n.* a person who is prominent in fashionable society.

so•ci•al•i•ty [,souʃi'æləti] *n., pl.* **-ties. 1** social activity; social intercourse. **2** social nature or tendencies: *The congregating of people in cities and towns shows sociality.*

so•cial•ize ['souʃə,laɪz] *v.* **-ized, -iz•ing. 1** make social; make fit for living with others. **2** adapt to community needs. **3** engage in social interchange or activity: *During her spares she liked to socialize with other students in the lounge.* **4** establish or regulate in accordance with socialism. **—,so•cial•i'za•tion,** *n.*

socialized medicine the provision of medical care and hospital services for all classes of society, especially through government subsidy and administration.

so•cial•ly ['souʃəli] *adv.* **1** in a social way or manner; in relation to other people. **2** as a member of society or of a social group: *He is an able man, but socially he is a failure.*

social register a list of people who are prominent in fashionable society.

social science the systematic study of people, their activities, and their customs in relationship to others. Anthropology, sociology, economics, and political science are social sciences. **—social scientist.**

social security *Esp. U.S.* SOCIAL INSURANCE.

social service SOCIAL WORK.

social studies a course of study in elementary schools that includes elements of history, geography, sociology, civics, economics, etc.

social work work directed toward the betterment of social conditions in a community. Social work includes such services as medical clinics, aid for the aged and disabled, counselling for families, and recreational activities.

social worker a trained professional employed by a community or government to do social work.

so•ci•e•tal [sə'saɪətəl] *adj.* of or having to do with human society. **—so'ci•e•tal•ly,** *adv.*

so•ci•e•ty [sə'saɪəti] *n., pl.* **-ties. 1 a** all the people of a particular place and time who have developed organized cultural and social patterns and institutions: *Drug-control laws are passed for the good of society.* **b** a particular form of such organization: *Urban society is a relatively recent phenomenon. Magic plays an important part in some preliterate societies.* **2** people thought of as a group because of common economic position, similar interests, etc.: *in cultivated society.* **3** the fashionable or privileged people in a community: *a leader of society.* **4** (*adjl.*) of, for, or characteristic of the fashionable or privileged people: *a society ball, a society page in a magazine.* **5** a group of persons joined together for a common purpose or by a common interest. A club, a fraternity, a lodge, or an association may be called a society. **6** company; companionship: *I enjoy his society.* **7** *Ecology.* **a** an interdependent community of organisms. **b** a natural group of plants of a single species forming a community within a larger ecological community. ⟨< L *societas* < *socius* companion⟩

Society of Friends a Christian sect founded by George Fox in England in 1650. See QUAKER.

Society of Jesus a Roman Catholic religious order for men, founded by Saint Ignatius Loyola in 1534. Its members are called Jesuits. *Abbrev.*: S.J.

socio– *combining form.* with reference to society, sociology, or social concerns: *sociobiology, sociocultural.* ⟨combining form of L *socius* companion⟩

so•ci•o–e•co•nom•ic [,souʃou ,ɛkə'nɒmɪk] *or* [,souʃou ,ikə'nɒmɪk], [,sousiou ,ɛkə'nɒmɪk] *or* [,sousiou ,ikə'nɒmɪk] *adj.* of or having to do with social and economic matters: *a socio-economic study on poverty in big cities.*

so•ci•o•lin•guis•tics [,souʃoulɪŋ'gwɪstɪks] *or* [,sosioulɪŋ'gwɪstɪks] *n.* the branch of linguistics that deals with the study of language in a speech community, the social and cultural factors affecting language use and language choice, and the effects that languages in contact have on one another. **—,so•ci•o•lin'guis•tic,** *adj.* **—,so•ci•o'lin•guist,** *n.*

so•ci•o•log•i•cal [,sousiə'lɒdʒɪkəl] *or* [,souʃə'lɒdʒɪkəl] *adj.* **1** of or having to do with the structure of human society or problems relating to it: *The care of the poor is a sociological problem.* **2** of sociology. **—so•ci•o'log•i•cal•ly,** *adv.*

so•ci•ol•o•gist [,sousi'ɒlədʒɪst] *or* [,souʃi'ɒlədʒɪst] *n.* a student of human society and its problems; a person skilled in sociology.

so•ci•ol•o•gy [,sousi'ɒlədʒi] *or* [,souʃi'ɒlədʒi] *n.* the systematic study of the structure, origin, and development of human society and community life; the science of social facts. Sociology deals with social conditions, such as crime, power, or poverty, and with social institutions, such as marriage or the church. ⟨< L *socius* companion + E *-logy*⟩

so•ci•om•e•try [,sousi'ɒmətri] *or* [,souʃi'ɒmətri] *n.* **1** the study, using quantitative techniques, of the social relationships among members of a group. **2** the techniques and tests used in such a study. **—,so•ci•o'met•ric,** *adj.*

so•ci•o•path ['souʃə,pæθ] *or* ['sousiə,pæθ] *n.* a person in whom psychopathic personality leads to a lack of social or moral responsibility. **—,so•ci•o'path•ic,** *adj.*

sock[1] [sɒk] *n., v. —n.* **1** a cloth foot covering, usually knitted, worn inside a shoe and extending above the ankle, sometimes to the knee. **2** a light shoe worn by actors in ancient Greek and Roman comedy. **3** the theatrical art of comedy; comic drama. Compare BUSKIN (def. 3). **4** windsock.
—v.
sock away, *Informal.* save up (money).
sock in, *Informal.* close (an airfield) to takeoffs and landings by aircraft because of bad weather (*usually used in the passive*). ⟨< L *soccus*⟩

sock[2] [sɒk] *v., n., adv. Slang. —v.* strike or hit hard.
—n. a hard blow.
—adv. squarely; directly. ⟨origin uncertain⟩

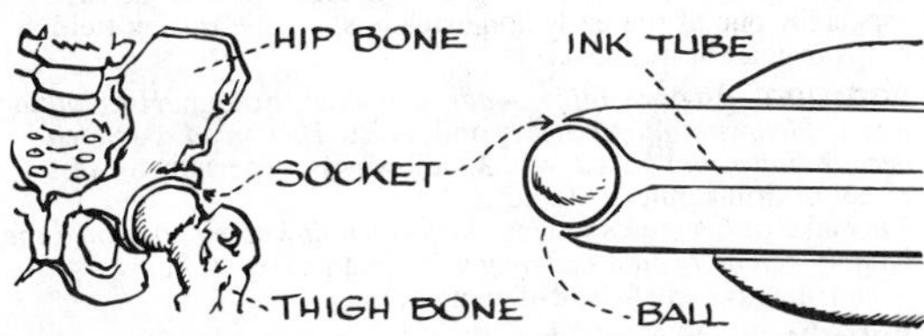

The hip joint, a ball-and-socket joint

The ball and socket forming the tip of a ballpoint pen

sock•et ['sɒkɪt] *n., v. —n.* **1** a hollow part or piece for receiving and holding something. A candlestick has a socket in which to set a candle. Eyes and hips are set in sockets. An electric light has a socket into which the bulb is screwed. **2** *Electricity.* a connecting place for electric wires and plugs.
—v. **1** provide with a socket. **2** insert into a socket. ⟨ME < AF *soket* < *soc* ploughshare < Celtic⟩

sock•eye ['sɒk,aɪ] *n., pl.* **sock•eye** or **sock•eyes.** *Cdn.* a small Pacific salmon (*Oncorhynchus nerka*) found along the coasts of British Columbia and Alaska, greenish blue and metallic green in colour and having red, oily flesh highly valued for its flavour. The male sockeye changes colour to a bright red, and the female to dark red, in spawning season. Also, **sockeye salmon.** ⟨< Salish *suk-kegh* red fish, altered by folk etymology⟩

so•cle ['sɒkəl] *or* ['soukəl] *n. Architecture.* a plinth; a block or platform to support a statue, column, wall, etc. ⟨< L *socculus* little shoe⟩

So•crat•ic [sə'krætɪk] *adj.* of or having to do with Socrates (469-399 B.C.), a famous Athenian philosopher, his philosophy, followers, etc.

Socratic irony a method of forcing an opponent to make statements exposing the weakness of his or her position, by feigning ignorance in discussion.

Socratic method the use of a series of questions to lead pupils to think, to make opponents contradict themselves, etc.

So•cred ['sou,krɛd] *n. Cdn. Informal.* **1** the SOCIAL CREDIT PARTY. **2** a member of this party.

sod [sɒd] *n., v.* **sod•ded, sod•ding.** *–n.* **1** ground covered with grass. **2** a piece or layer of ground containing the grass and its roots.
under the sod, dead and buried.
–v. cover with sods. ⟨< MDu. or MLG *sode*⟩ **–'sod•less,** *adj.*

so•da ['soudə] *n.* **1** any of several substances containing sodium, such as sodium carbonate, sodium bicarbonate, caustic soda (NaOH), or sodium oxide (Na_2O). Soda is used in the manufacture of soap and glass. Washing soda (sal soda) is used in cleaning. Baking soda is used in cooking and as a medicine. **2** SODA WATER. **3** soda water flavoured with fruit juice or syrup, and often containing ice cream. **4** *U.S.* SOFT DRINK; POP[1] (def. 3). ⟨< Med.L⟩ **–'so•dic,** *adj.*

soda ash *Chemistry.* partly purified sodium carbonate.

soda biscuit *Esp. Brit.* SODA CRACKER.

soda cracker a simple, light, thin cracker made with little or no sugar or shortening, often sprinkled with salt before baking.

soda fountain **1** an apparatus for holding soda water, syrups, ice, etc., having taps for drawing off the liquids. **2** a counter with places for holding soda water, flavoured syrups, ice cream, etc. **3** a store having such a counter.

soda jerk or **jerk•er** ['dʒɛrkər] *Informal.* a person who serves at a soda fountain.

soda lime a granular white mixture of calcium hydroxide and sodium hydroxide or potassium hydroxide, used as a reagent and to absorb moisture and acid gases, as in gas masks or oxygen therapy.

so•da•lite ['soudə,ləit] *n.* an opaque silicate of sodium and aluminum with chlorine, found in igneous rock and often blue in colour. *Formula*: $Na_4Al_3Si_3O_{12}Cl$

so•dal•i•ty [sou'dæləti] *n., pl.* **-ties. 1** fellowship; friendship. **2** an association, society, or fraternity. **3** *Roman Catholic Church.* a lay society having religious or charitable purposes. ⟨< L *sodalitas* < *sodalis* sociable⟩

soda water water charged with carbon dioxide to make it bubble and fizz, often used as a mixer in an alcoholic drink with scotch, rye, etc.

sod•bust•er ['sɒd,bʌstər] *n. Cdn. Slang.* a prairie farmer, especially one of the early homesteaders, or one raising field crops instead of livestock.

sod•den ['sɒdən] *adj., v. –adj.* **1** soaked through: *His clothing was sodden with rain.* **2** heavy and moist: *This bread is sodden because it was not baked well.* **3** dull-witted, especially as an effect of drunkenness; stupid.
–v. make or become sodden: *The sudden downpour soddened the laundry before it could be brought in.* ⟨old pp. of *seethe*⟩
–'sod•den•ly, *adv.* **–'sod•den•ness,** *n.*

sod•dy ['sɒdi] *n., pl.* **-dies.** *West.* **1** a dwelling consisting of an excavation, often in the bank of a coulee, with a roof of sods. **2** a dwelling having walls of sods and a canvas or sod roof supported by wooden rafters. Also, **sod house, hut,** or **shack.**

so•di•um ['soudiəm] *n.* a soft, silver-white metallic element which reacts violently with water and occurs in nature only in compounds. Salt and soda contain sodium. *Symbol*: Na; *at.no.* 11; *at.mass* 22.99. ⟨< *soda*⟩

sodium benzoate *Chemistry. Pharmacy.* a white, water-soluble powder used chiefly as a food preservative and as an antiseptic. Also called BENZOATE OF SODA. *Formula*: $NaC_7H_5O_2$

sodium bicarbonate *Chemistry. Pharmacy.* a powdery white salt used in cooking, medicine, etc.; baking soda; bicarbonate of soda. *Formula*: $NaHCO_3$

sodium carbonate *Chemistry.* a salt that occurs in a powdery white form and in a hydrated crystalline form; washing soda. It is used for softening water, making soap and glass, neutralizing acids, etc. *Formula*: Na_2CO_3

sodium chloride *Chemistry.* common salt. *Formula*: NaCl

sodium cyanide *Chemistry.* a poisonous substance, composed of fine white crystals, used in the CYANIDE PROCESS for extracting gold and silver from ores, in fumigating, etc. *Formula*: NaCN

sodium fluoride *Chemistry.* a crystalline salt, poisonous in large quantities, used as an insecticide and disinfectant and as a preventive of tooth decay. *Formula*: NaF

sodium hydroxide *Chemistry.* a white solid that is a strong, corrosive alkali; caustic soda. *Formula*: NaOH

sodium hypochlorite *Chemistry.* a crystalline salt, used as an insecticide, a disinfectant, in household bleaches, etc. *Formula*: NaOCl

sodium iodide *Chemistry.* a white, odourless salt, used for the treatment of nervous disorders, in animal fodder, in photography, etc. *Formula*: NaI

sodium nitrate *Chemistry.* a colourless crystalline substance used in making fertilizers, explosives, etc.; Chile saltpetre. *Formula*: $NaNO_3$

sodium nitrite *Chemistry.* a white or yellowish salt made by heating sodium nitrate, used especially in the manufacture of dyes and as a meat preservative. *Formula*: $NaNO_2$

sodium oxide *Chemistry.* an oxide of sodium, especially Na_2O, that reacts with water to form sodium hydroxide.

Sodium Pen•to•thal ['pɛntə,θɒl] *Pharmacy. Trademark.* a barbiturate used as an anesthetic. *Formula*: $C_{11}H_{17}N_2O_2SNa$

sodium phosphate *Chemistry.* any sodium salt of phosphoric acid, especially **monosodium phosphate** (NaH_2PO_4), **disodium phosphate** (Na_2HPO_4), or **trisodium phosphate** (Na_3PO_4), all three of which are widely used in industrial chemical processes.

sodium pro•pi•o•nate [prə'paiə,neit] *Chemistry.* a clear, odourless crystalline compound, $C_3H_5O_2Na$, a common food preservative.

sodium sulphate *Chemistry.* one of two white, crystalline salts of sodium, especially Na_2SO, used in a variety of manufacturing processes such as the production of detergents, wood pulp, dyes, and glass.

so•di•um–va•pour lamp ['soudiəm 'veipər] an electric lamp used in streetlights, producing a yellow-orange light by means of an electric current passing through a tube of neon and sodium vapour.

Sod•om ['sɒdəm] *n.* any extremely wicked or corrupt place. ⟨after the city in the Bible that was destroyed by fire from heaven because of its wickedness⟩

sod•om•ite ['sɒdə,məit] *n.* **1** a person who practises sodomy. **2 Sodomite,** a native or inhabitant of Sodom.

sod•om•ize ['sɒdə,maɪz] *v.* **-ized, -iz•ing.** subject to sodomy.

sod•o•my ['sɒdəmi] *n.* sexual relations regarded as abnormal, especially between two males or between a human being and an animal. ⟨ME < OF *sodomie* < LL < *Sodom*⟩

sod shack SOD HOUSE.

sod turning ['sɒd ,tɜrnɪŋ] *n.* the breaking of ground for digging the foundations of a building, often accompanied by a ceremony.

-soever *suffix.* no matter ——; ——ever: *whosoever, whatsoever, whensoever, wheresoever, howsoever.*

so•fa ['soufə] *n.* a long, upholstered seat or couch having a back and arms; chesterfield. ⟨< F < Arabic *ṣuffah*⟩

sofa bed a couch or chesterfield that opens out into a bed.

so•far ['soufɑr] *n.* a system for determining the source of a sound under water using triangulation. ⟨< *so*und *f*ixing *a*nd *r*anging⟩

sof•fit ['sɒfɪt] *n. Architecture.* the under surface or face of an architrave, arch, eave, cornice, etc. See ARCH for picture. ⟨< Ital. *soffitto*, ult. < L *sub-* under + *figere* fix⟩

soft [sɒft] *adj., adv., n., interj. –adj.* **1** not hard; yielding readily to touch or pressure: *a soft pillow.* **2** not hard compared with other things of the same kind: *Pine wood is soft. Copper and lead are softer than steel.* **3** not sharp or distinctly contrasting; gentle and graceful: *soft shadows, soft outlines.* **4** fine in texture; not rough or coarse; smooth: *soft skin.* **5** not loud: *a soft voice.* **6** quietly pleasant; mild; not harsh: *soft breezes.* **7** not glaring or bright: *soft light.* **8** gentle; kind; tender: *a soft heart.* **9** weak; lacking in fortitude, stamina, self-discipline, etc.: *The army had become soft from idleness and luxury.* **10** silly. **11** *Phonetics.* of the letters *c* and *g* in English, representing fricatives or affricates, as in *city* and *gem*, rather than stops, as in *corn* and *get.* Compare HARD (def. 13). **12** *Informal.* easy; easy-going, especially excessively or inappropriately so: *a soft job, a soft person.* **13** of water, comparatively free from certain mineral salts that prevent soap from lathering. **14** of a drug, considered not seriously addictive or harmful to health. Marijuana is regarded by some as a soft drug. Compare HARD (def. 14). **15** of currency, not supported by gold or silver or not easily convertible into other

currencies, and therefore likely to fluctuate or depreciate in value. Compare HARD (def. 15). **16** of the stock market, etc., tending toward declining prices; unstable. **17** of X rays, not very powerful or penetrating. **18** of pornography, not very explicit. Also (def. 18), **soft-core.**
soft on, a lenient toward. **b** fond of or infatuated with.
—adv. softly; quietly; gently.
—n. that which is soft; a soft part.
—interj. Archaic. hush! stop! ⟨OE *sōfte*⟩ **—'soft•ly,** *adv.* **—'soft•ness,** *n.*

soft•ball ['sɒft,bɒl] *n.* **1** a modified kind of baseball game that uses a larger and softer ball. **2** the ball used in that game.

soft–boiled ['sɒft ,bɔɪld] *adj.* of eggs, boiled only for about three minutes so that the yolk is still soft.

soft•bound ['sɒft,baʊnd] *adj., n. —adj.* of a book or edition, having covers of thin cardboard, heavy paper, or a similar flexible material and usually sold more cheaply than a hardbound book; paperback; softcover.
—n. a book or edition bound in this way.

soft coal BITUMINOUS COAL.

soft copy *Computer technology.* computer data that is not printed out but remains on the disk.

soft•cov•er ['sɒft,kʌvər] *adj. or n.* softbound.

soft drink a carbonated drink that is non-alcoholic, such as ginger ale, cola, etc.

soft•en ['sɒfən] *v.* **1** make softer: *Hand lotion softens the skin. Too much luxury had softened him.* **2** become softer: *Soap softens in water. Her heart softened when she heard of their desperate plight.* **3** lessen the resistance of (an opponent) through preliminary action. **4** decrease; decline. **—'soft•en•er,** *n.*

softening of the brain *Pathology.* deterioration of cerebral tissue resulting in loss of mental faculties.

soft–finned ['sɒft ,fɪnd] *adj.* of fish, having fins whose membrane is supported by soft rays; opposed to SPINY-FINNED.

soft goods clothing, textiles, etc.; DRY GOODS.

soft–head•ed ['sɒft ,hɛdɪd] *adj. Informal.* silly; stupid; foolish. **—'soft-'head•ed•ly,** *adv.* **—'soft-'head•ed•ness,** *n.*

soft–heart•ed ['sɒft 'hɑrtɪd] *adj.* gentle; kind; tender. **—'soft-'heart•ed•ly,** *adv.* **—'soft-'heart•ed•ness,** *n.*

soft•ie ['sɒfti] *n.* See SOFTY.

soft landing the landing of a spacecraft at relatively low speed and without damage or injury.

soft palate the fleshy back part of the roof of the mouth; the velum.

soft pedal on a piano or other instrument, a pedal used to reduce volume or resonance.

soft–ped•al ['sɒft 'pɛdəl] *v.* **-alled** or **-aled, -al•ling** or **-al•ing. 1** use a pedal on (a piano, organ, etc.) to soften musical tones. **2** make quieter, less noticeable, or less strong. **3** *Informal.* make less noticeable; de-emphasize: *You'd better soft-pedal some of what happened on the trip when your mother's around.*

soft return *Computer technology.* a RETURN (def. 8) inserted by the program and not by the user. Compare HARD RETURN.

soft sell *Informal.* a sales approach that uses indirect persuasive tactics rather than pushy, aggressive ones. Compare HARD SELL. **—'soft-'sell,** *adj.*

soft–shell ['sɒft ,ʃɛl] *adj., n. —adj.* **1** characterized by a relatively soft shell. **2** having a temporarily soft shell following recent moulting.
—n. an animal having such a shell.

soft–shell clam any of several marine clams (genus *Mya*) having a thin, crumbly shell, especially an edible species (*M. arenaria*) of the Atlantic coasts of North America and Europe.

soft–shell crab 1 an edible crab (*Collinectis sapidus*), mainly blue in colour, of the Atlantic coast of North America, especially from Delaware to Texas. **2** any crab whose shell is soft due to recent moulting.

soft shoe 1 tap dancing done in soft-soled shoes, without taps. **2** a dance in the soft-shoe style: *Fred Astaire did a wonderful soft shoe.* **3** the style of shoe used for this.

soft–shoe ['sɒft ,ʃu] *v.* **-shoed, -shoe•ing;** *adj. —v. Informal.* dance SOFT SHOE.
—adj. denoting a type of show dancing like tap dancing but without the metal taps on the dancer's shoes.

soft shoulder an unpaved strip at the side of a road, for emergency stopping, etc.

soft soap 1 a liquid or partly liquid soap. **2** *Informal.* flattery.

soft–soap ['sɒft 'soup] *v.* **1** apply soft soap to. **2** use soft soap in washing. **3** *Informal.* flatter. **—'soft-'soap•er,** *n.*

soft–spo•ken ['sɒft 'spoukən] *adj.* **1** speaking with a soft voice: *a soft-spoken man.* **2** spoken softly: *soft-spoken words.*

soft spot 1 a feeling of tenderness or affection: *She still had a soft spot in her heart for her first boyfriend.* **2** a vulnerable spot or point: *a soft spot in an otherwise strong argument.*

soft touch *Informal.* a person who lends or gives money, etc. easily.

soft•ware ['sɒft,wɛr] *n. Computer technology.* the standard programming procedures and specific programs associated with a computer system. Compare HARDWARE (def. 3).

soft wheat a wheat that has a high starch and low gluten content, used to make pastry flour, etc.

soft•wood ['sɒft,wʊd] *n.* **1** wood that is easily cut. **2** a tree that has needles or does not have broad leaves. Pines and firs are softwoods; oaks and maples are hardwoods. **3** the wood of such a tree.

soft•y ['sɒfti] *n., pl.* **soft•ies.** *Informal.* **1** a soft, silly, or weak person. **2** one who is easily imposed upon. Also, **softie.**

sog•gy ['sɒgi] *adj.* **-gi•er, -gi•est. 1** thoroughly wet; soaked: *a soggy washcloth.* **2** damp and heavy: *soggy bread.* ⟨< dial. *sog* bog, swamp < Scand.; cf. ON *soggr* damp⟩ **—'sog•gi•ly,** *adv.* **—'sog•gi•ness,** *n.*

soh [sou] *n. Music.* sol.
☛ *Hom.* SEW, SO[1], SOW[1].

soi–di•sant [swadi'zɑ̃] *adj. French.* **1** calling oneself thus; self-styled. **2** so-called; pretended.

soi•gné [swa'njei] *adj., fem.* **soignée.** *French.* **1** well-groomed; elegant. **2** carefully maintained or arranged.

soil[1] [sɔɪl] *n.* **1** ground; earth; dirt: *A farmer tills the soil.* **2** specifically, the diggable top layer of earth in which plants will grow or can be grown. **3** something thought of as a place for growth. **4** territory; country. **5 the soil,** agriculture as a way of life or livelihood: *Her family had been people of the soil for generations.* ⟨ME < AF < L *solium* seat, influenced by L *solum* soil⟩

soil[2] [sɔɪl] *v., n. —v.* **1** make dirty: *He soiled his clean clothes.* **2** become dirty: *White shirts soil easily.* **3** spot; stain: *The splashing paint soiled the wall.* **4** disgrace; dishonour: *His actions have soiled the family name.* **5** corrupt morally.
—n. **1** a spot; stain. **2** sewage or manure. ⟨ME < OF *soillier,* ult. < L *suile* pigsty < *sus* pig⟩

soil[3] [sɔɪl] *v.* feed (cattle, horses, etc.) with fresh green fodder, especially as a purgative. ⟨? < OF *saoler* < L *satullare* fill with food⟩

soi•rée or **soi•ree** [swa'rei] *n.* an evening party or social gathering. ⟨< F *soirée* < *soir* evening⟩

so•journ *v.* ['soudʒɜrn] *or* [sou'dʒɜrn]; *n.* ['soudʒɜrn] *v., n. —v.* stay for a time: *The Israelites sojourned in the land of Egypt.*
—n. a brief stay. ⟨ME < OF *sojorner,* ult. < L *sub* under + *diurnus* of the day⟩ **—'so•journ•er,** *n.*

sol[1] [soul] *n. Music.* **1** the fifth tone of an eight-tone major scale. **2** the tone G. See DO[2] for picture. ⟨See GAMUT⟩
☛ *Hom.* SOLE, SOUL.

sol[2] [soul] *or* [sɒl] *n.* **1** the basic unit of money in Peru, divided into 100 centimos. See table of money in the Appendix. **2** a coin worth one sol. ⟨< Sp.⟩
☛ *Hom.* SOLE, SOUL.

sol[3] [sɒl] *or* [soul] *n. Physical chemistry.* a suspension of a colloid in a liquid. ⟨shortened form of hydro*sol*⟩
☛ *Hom.* SOLE, SOUL.

sol. solution; soluble.

Sol [sɒl] *n.* **1** *Roman mythology.* the god of the sun, corresponding to the Greek god Helios. **2** the sun.

Sol. Solicitor.

sol•ace ['sɒlɪs] *n., v.* **-aced, -ac•ing.** *—n.* comfort or relief, or a source of this: *She found solace from her troubles in music.*
—v. comfort; relieve: *He solaced himself with a book.* ⟨ME < OF < L *solacium* < *solari* console⟩ **—'sol•ac•er,** *n.*

so•lar ['soulər] *adj.* **1** of the sun: *a solar eclipse.* **2** having to do with the sun: *solar research.* **3** coming from the sun: *solar heat.* **4** measured or determined by the earth's motion in relation to the sun. A solar year is about 365¼ days long. **5** working by means of the sun's light or heat. A solar battery traps sunlight and converts it into electrical energy. **6** *Astrology.* subject to the sun's influence. ⟨ME < L *solaris* < *sol* sun⟩

solar cell *Electricity.* a small device for converting sunlight into electrical energy. It consists of thin wafers of a semiconductor, such as silicon, to which traces of certain other substances have been added. Sunlight striking the semiconductor produces charges which flow from the cell as an electric current.

solar collector a device, such as a glass-covered metal pan or plate that has been painted dull black, used to trap heat from sunlight. Solar collectors are used together with a storage device and a distribution system to provide heating for buildings, etc.

solar constant the average amount of solar energy received per unit area by the earth, 1388 w/m^2.

solar cooker an oven using direct solar energy.

solar day the period of time from when the sun is at the meridian at any place on earth until the next time it reaches the same meridian.

solar eclipse See ECLIPSE (def. 1).

solar energy energy derived from the sun's radiation as a source of electrical power.

solar flare *Astronomy.* an eruption of gases on the sun, usually associated with sunspots, which produces ultraviolet radiation and causes ionization in the earth's upper atmosphere.

solar house a house designed to obtain part or all of its space and water heating directly from the sun by means of solar collectors, large windows facing the winter sun, etc.

so•lar•i•um [sə'lɛriəm] *n., pl.* **-lar•i•ums** or **-lar•i•a** [-'lɛriə]. a glass-enclosed room, porch, etc. where people can lie or sit in the sun. ⟨< L *solarium* < *sol* sun⟩

so•lar•ize ['soulə,raɪz] *v.* **-ized, -iz•ing. 1** expose to the sun's rays, either as a form of treatment, or, if done to excess, with injurious effect. **2** *Photography.* subject to, or undergo, long exposure during development in order to achieve certain special effects in tone, etc.

solar panel a panel, on a satellite, roof, etc., that collects solar radiation so the energy can be used to generate electricity or heat.

solar plexus 1 *Anatomy.* the network of nerves situated at the upper part of the abdomen, behind the stomach and in front of the aorta. **2** *Informal.* the pit of the stomach.

solar prominence *Astronomy.* a large cloud of luminous solar gases such as hydrogen, calcium, or sodium, arching above the sun's chromosphere and occasionally flaring outward; especially numerous in the areas above sunspots.

solar system the sun and all the planets, satellites, comets, etc. that are within its gravitational field.

solar wind the continuous flow of charged particles from the sun into space.

solar year the period of time required for the earth to make one revolution around the sun, which equals about 365¼ days.

sold [sould] *v.* pt. and pp. of SELL.

sol•der ['sɒdər] *n., v.* —*n.* **1** a metal or alloy that can be melted and used for joining or mending metal surfaces, parts, etc. **2** anything that unites firmly or joins closely.
—*v.* **1** fasten, mend, or join (things) with solder. **2** unite or be united firmly; join or be joined closely. **3** mend; repair; patch. ⟨ME < OF *soldure,* ult. < L *solidus* solid⟩ **—'sol•der•a•ble,** *adj.* **—'sol•der•er,** *n.* **—'sol•der•less,** *adj.*

sol•der•ing iron ['sɒdərɪŋ] an electrical tool with a pointed or wedge-shaped bit that is heated in order to melt and apply solder.

sol•dier ['souldʒər] *n., v.* —*n.* **1** a person who serves in an army. **2** a private or a non-commissioned officer. **3** a person having skill or experience in war. **4** a person who serves in any cause: *soldiers of Christ.* **5** in colonies of certain ants or termites, an individual having a large head and powerful jaws, adapted for defending the colony.
—*v.* **1** act or serve as a soldier. **2** *Informal.* shirk work, especially on pretence of illness.
soldier on, carry on in spite of great difficulty: *Her debilitating illness made her job more and more difficult, but she soldiered on.* ⟨ME < OF *soldier* < *soulde* pay < L *solidus,* a Roman coin⟩

sol•dier•ly ['souldʒərli] *adj.* like or suitable for a soldier. **—'sol•dier•li•ness,** *n.*

soldier of fortune 1 a person serving or ready to serve as a soldier under any government for money, adventure, or pleasure; military adventurer. **2** any person in pursuit of adventure.

sol•dier•y ['souldʒəri] *n., pl.* **-dier•ies. 1** soldiers collectively. **2** a body of soldiers. **3** military training or knowledge.

sole¹ [soul] *adj.* **1** one and only; single: *the sole heir.* **2** only: *We three were the sole survivors.* **3** of or for only one person or group and not others; exclusive: *the sole right of use.* **4** done, etc. alone: *a sole undertaking.* **5** *Law.* unmarried. ⟨ME < OF < L *solus*⟩
☛ *Hom.* SOL [soul], SOUL.
☛ *Syn.* **1, 2.** See note at SINGLE.

sole² [soul] *n., v.* **soled, sol•ing.** —*n.* **1** the bottom or under surface of the foot. **2** bottom of a shoe, slipper, boot, etc. **3** a piece of leather, rubber, etc. cut to fit the bottom of a shoe, slipper, boot, etc. **4** the undersurface; under part; bottom.
—*v.* put a sole on. ⟨ME < OF *sole,* ult. < L *solea* < *solum* bottom, ground⟩
☛ *Hom.* SOL [soul], SOUL.

sole³ [soul] *n., pl.* **sole** or **soles. 1** any of a family (Soleidae) of flatfishes including some species highly valued as food fishes, such as the **European sole** (*Solea solea*), also called **Dover sole. 2** any of various similar flatfishes belonging to other families. ⟨ME < MF < L *solea,* originally, sole²⟩
☛ *Hom.* SOL [soul], SOUL.

sol•e•cism ['sɒlə,sɪzəm] *n.* **1** a violation of the grammatical or other accepted usages of a language; a mistake in using words. *I done it* is a solecism. **2** a mistake in social behaviour; breach of good manners or etiquette. ⟨< L < Gk. *soloikismos,* supposedly < *Soloi,* a Greek colony in Cilicia, an ancient region in Asia Minor⟩ **—'sol•e•cist,** *n.* **—,sol•e'cis•tic** or **,sol•e'cis•ti•cal,** *adj.* **—,sol•e'cis•ti•cal•ly,** *adv.*

sole•ly ['soulli] *adv.* **1** as the only one or ones; alone: *You will be solely responsible.* **2** only; purely; entirely: *He does it solely for convenience.*

sol•emn ['sɒləm] *adj.* **1** serious; grave; earnest: *a solemn face.* **2** evoking serious or grave thoughts: *The organ played solemn music.* **3** done with form and ceremony; strictly observed, in accord with ritual and tradition. **4** connected with religion; sacred. ⟨ME < OF < L *sollemnis*⟩ **—'sol•emn•ly,** *adv.* **—'sol•emn•ness,** *n.*

so•lem•ni•fy [sə'lɛmnə,faɪ] *v.* **-fied, -fy•ing.** make solemn.

so•lem•ni•ty [sə'lɛmnəti] *n., pl.* **-ties. 1** a solemn quality; seriousness; impressiveness. **2** Often, **solemnities,** *pl.* a solemn, formal ceremony: *The solemnities were concluded with a prayer by the college chaplain.*

sol•em•nize ['sɒləm,naɪz] *v.* **-nized, -niz•ing. 1** observe with ceremonies: *Christian churches solemnize the resurrection of Christ at Easter.* **2** hold or perform (a ceremony or service): *The marriage was solemnized in the cathedral.* **3** make serious or grave. **—,sol•em•ni'za•tion,** *n.*

so•le•noid ['soulə,nɔɪd] *or* ['sɒlə,nɔɪd] *n. Electricity.* a spiral or cylindrical coil of wire that acts like a magnet when a current passes through it. ⟨< F < Gk. *sōlēn* pipe⟩ **—,so•le'noid•al,** *adj.*

sol–fa ['soul ,fɑ] *n., v.* **-faed** [-fɑd], **-fa•ing.** *Music.*
—*n.* **1 a** TONIC SOL-FA. **b** the syllables used in tonic sol-fa, representing the tones of any scale: do, re, mi, fa, so(l), la, ti, do. **2** (*adjl.*) of or having to do with tonic sol-fa: *sol-fa notation, sol-fa syllables.*
—*v.* use the sol-fa syllables in singing. ⟨< Ital. *solfa* < *sol* + *fa.* See GAMUT.⟩

sol•fa•ta•ra [,soulfə'tɑrə] *n.* an opening in a volcano, venting only gases and mist. ⟨< Ital. < *solfo* sulphur < L *sulfur*⟩

sol•feg•gio [sɒl'fɛdʒou] *or* [sɒl'fɛdʒi,ou] *n., pl.* **-gios. 1** a sol-fa exercise. **2** TONIC SOL-FA. ⟨< Ital. *solfeggio* < *solfa*⟩

so•lic•it [sə'lɪsət] *v.* **1** ask (a person) earnestly; ask for or try to get (something): *The tailor sent around cards soliciting trade.* **2** make appeals or requests: *to solicit for contributions.* **3** influence (someone) to do wrong; tempt; entice: *To solicit a judge means to offer her bribes.* **4** accost (a person) with offers of sex for money. ⟨ME < L *sollicitare* < *sollicitus.* See SOLICITOUS.⟩ **—so'lic•i•tant,** *n.*
☛ *Syn.* **1.** See note at ASK.

so•lic•i•ta•tion [sə,lɪsə'teiʃən] *n.* **1** an earnest request; entreaty. **2** an urging to do wrong; temptation; enticement.

so•lic•i•tor [sə'lɪsətər] *n.* **1** a person who entreats or requests. **2** a person who seeks trade or business. **3** a lawyer, especially one who does not plead in court. In the United Kingdom, a solicitor prepares a case and a barrister pleads it. In Canada, the same person may be both solicitor and barrister. **4** a lawyer for a town, city, etc.

solicitor general *pl.* **solicitors general. 1** in Canada: **a** the federal cabinet minister having primary responsibility for law enforcement and correctional services, including the RCMP and the Canadian Penitentiary Service. **b** in Alberta, the cabinet minister responsible for correctional services. **c** in Ontario, the cabinet minister responsible for the police. Compare ATTORNEY GENERAL. **2** a law officer ranking next below an attorney general. Also, **solicitor-general,** *pl.* **solicitors-general.**

so•lic•i•tous [sə'lɪsətəs] *adj.* **1** showing care or concern; anxious; concerned: *Parents are solicitous for their children's progress.* **2** desirous; eager: *solicitous to please.* ⟨< L *sollicitus* < OL *sollus* all + *citus* stirred up, pp. of *ciere* arouse⟩ **—so'lic•i•tous•ly,** *adv.* **—so'lic•i•tous•ness,** *n.*

so•lic•i•tude [sə'lɪsə,tjud] *or* [sə'lɪsə,tud] *n.* **1** anxious care; anxiety; concern. **2** a cause of this.
☛ *Syn.* See note at CARE.

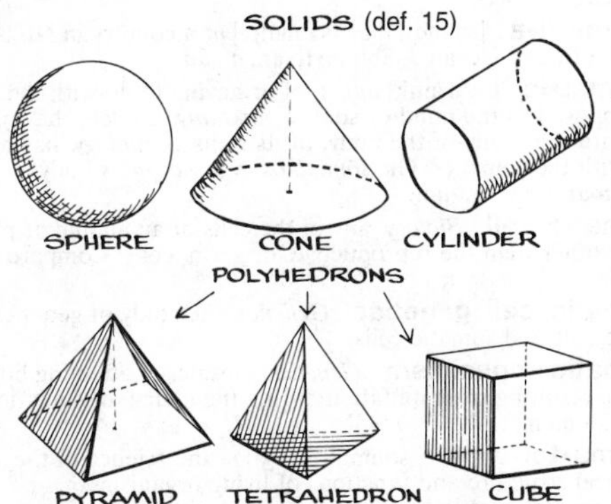

sol•id ['sɒlɪd] *adj., n.* *—adj.* **1** not a liquid or a gas: *Water becomes solid when it freezes.* **2** not hollow: *A bar of iron is solid; a pipe is hollow.* **3** hard; firm: *They were glad to leave the boat and put their feet on solid ground.* **4** strongly made or put together: *This is not a very solid table.* **5** alike throughout; of a single colour, substance, etc. throughout: *The cloth is a solid blue. This is a solid gold brooch.* **6** firmly united: *The country was solid for peace.* **7** serious; not superficial or trifling: *a background of solid study.* **8** genuine; real: *solid comfort.* **9** that can be depended on: *He is a solid citizen.* **10** having or showing good judgment; sound; sensible; intelligent: *a solid book by a solid thinker.* **11** financially sound or strong: *a solid business.* **12** whole or entire and in succession: *I waited three solid hours.* **13** undivided; continuous: *a solid row of houses.* **14** *Printing.* having the lines of type not separated by leads; having few open spaces. **15** *Mathematics.* **a** having length, breadth, and thickness: *A cylinder is a solid figure.* **b** of or having to do with three-dimensional figures: *solid geometry, a solid angle.* **16** written without a hyphen. *Earthworm* is a solid compound. **17** *Informal.* on a friendly, favourable, or advantageous footing: *to get in solid with one's employer.* **18** thorough; downright; vigorous; substantial: *a good, solid blow.* **19** *Slang.* very good, but not spectacular or particularly creative: *a solid performance.*
—n. **1** a substance that is not a liquid or a gas. **2** a body that has length, breadth, and thickness. A cube is a solid. ⟨ME, ult. < L *solidus*⟩ **—'sol•id•ly,** *adv.* **—'sol•id•ness,** *n.*
☛ *Syn. adj.* 3. See note at FIRM[1].

sol•i•dar•i•ty [,sɒlə'dærɪti] *or* [,sɒlə'dɛrɪti] *n., pl.* **-ties.** unity or fellowship arising from common responsibilities and interests. ⟨< F *solidarité*⟩

solid geometry the branch of mathematics that deals with objects having the three dimensions of length, breadth, and thickness.

so•lid•i•fy [sə'lɪdə,faɪ] *v.* **-fied, -fy•ing. 1** make or become solid; harden: *Extreme cold will solidify water. Jelly solidifies as it gets cold.* **2** make or become firmly united, sound, or strong. **3** make or become crystallized. **—so,lid•i•fi'ca•tion,** *n.*

so•lid•i•ty [sə'lɪdəti] *n., pl.* **-ties.** the state or quality of being solid; firmness; soundness or stability; density.

sol•id–state ['sɒlɪd 'steit] *adj. Electronics.* **1** of or having to do with the study of the properties of solid materials, especially of their molecular structure, the movement of their electrons, etc. The transistor was developed as a result of research in solid-state physics. **2** utilizing the electrical, magnetic, etc. properties of solid materials, especially semiconductor materials: *a solid-state radio receiver.*

sol•i•dus ['sɒlədəs] *n., pl.* **-di** [-,daɪ] *or* [-,di]. **1** a Roman gold coin introduced by Constantine, later called a bezant. **2** a sloping line (/) used as a dividing line in writing dates (20/7/82), fractions (2/3), etc. and to indicate alternative words (and/or), ratios (km/h), etc. Also called **slash** or **virgule.** ⟨< L *solidus,* short for *solidus (nummus)* solid (coin)⟩

sol•i•fluc•tion or **sol•i•flux•ion** [,soulə'flʌkʃən] *or* [,sɒlə'flʌkʃən] *n. Geology.* the movement of soil and rock waste caused by weather. ⟨< L *solum* ground, earth + E *fluxion*⟩

so•lil•o•quize [sə'lɪlə,kwaɪz] *v.* **-quized, -quiz•ing. 1** talk to oneself. **2** speak a soliloquy; utter in a soliloquy. **—so'lil•o•quist** [sə'lɪləkwɪst], *n.* **—so'lil•o,quiz•er,** *n.*

so•lil•o•quy [sə'lɪləkwi] *n., pl.* **-quies. 1** the act of talking to oneself. **2** a speech made by an actor to himself or herself when alone on the stage. A soliloquy may be used to impart knowledge to the audience, to reveal a character's true motives, etc. ⟨< LL *soliloquium* < L *solus* alone + *loqui* speak⟩

sol•ip•sism ['sɒlɪp,sɪzəm] *n. Philosophy.* **1** the theory that the only thing the self can know is its own existence and experiences. **2** the theory that the only reality is the self. ⟨< L *solus* alone + *ipse* self + E *-ism*⟩

sol•ip•sist ['sɒlɪpsɪst] *n., adj.* *—n.* a person who follows or believes in solipsism.
—adj. solipsistic.

sol•ip•sis•tic [,sɒlɪp'sɪstɪk] *adj.* of or having to do with solipsism or solipsists.

sol•i•taire ['sɒlə,tɛr] *or* [,sɒlə'tɛr] *n.* **1** any of various card games played by one person. **2** a diamond or other gem set by itself. ⟨< F < L *solitarius.* Doublet of SOLITARY.⟩

sol•i•tar•y ['sɒlə,tɛri] *adj., n., pl.* **-tar•ies.**
—adj. **1** alone; single; only: *A solitary rider was seen in the distance.* **2** without companions; away from people; lonely: *He leads a solitary life in his hut in the mountains. The house is in a solitary spot many kilometres from a town.* **3** done without companions: *She returned to her solitary pursuits.* **4 a** *Zoology.* living alone or in pairs, rather than in colonies: *the solitary bee.* **b** *Botany.* growing separately; not forming clusters: *a solitary stipule.*
—n. **1** a person living alone, away from people. **2** *Informal.* SOLITARY CONFINEMENT: *The prisoner was put in solitary.* ⟨ME < L *solitarius,* ult. < *solus* alone. Doublet of SOLITAIRE.⟩
—'sol•i,tar•i•ly, *adv.* **—'sol•i,tar•i•ness,** *n.*

solitary confinement the keeping of a prisoner in complete isolation from others, often as a penalty for misbehaviour while in prison.

sol•i•tude ['sɒlə,tjud] *or* ['sɒlə,tud] *n.* **1** the condition of being alone: *He likes company and hates solitude.* **2** a lonely place. **3** loneliness. ⟨< L *solitudo* < *solus* alone⟩
☛ *Syn.* **1. Solitude,** ISOLATION = a state of being alone. **Solitude,** applying to a state of being either where there are no other people for company or uninvolved (either voluntarily or involuntarily) with those around, emphasizes aloneness, the fact or feeling of being entirely by oneself, without companions: *The prospector lived in solitude in the desert. After visiting her mob of relatives for three weeks, she looked forward to the solitude of her own home.* **Isolation** emphasizes being separated or cut off from others or standing apart from the rest of the world, and when used of people usually has a somewhat negative connotation: *A single mountain peak rose in splendid isolation. People working in the Far North are often paid extra to compensate for the isolation.*

sol•mi•za•tion [,sɒlmə'zeiʃən] *n. Music.* the system of singing the syllables *do, re, mi, fa, sol, la, ti, do* to the tones of the eight-tone scale; sol-fa. ⟨< F *solmisation,* ult. < *sol* + *mi.* See GAMUT.⟩

so•lo ['soulou] *n., pl.* **-los;** *adj., adv., v.* **-loed, -lo•ing.** *—n.* **1** a piece of music arranged for one voice or instrument. **2** anything done without a partner, companion, instructor, etc.
—adj. **1** arranged for and performed by one voice or instrument: *a solo part.* **2** performing or acting alone: *a solo violin, a solo pilot.* **3** done without a partner, companion, instructor, etc.; performed alone: *a solo flight, a solo dance.*
—adv. by oneself; without a helper or companion: *to fly solo.*
—v. perform a solo. ⟨< Ital. *solo* alone < L *solus*⟩

so•lo•ist ['soulouɪst] *n.* a person who performs a solo.

Sol•o•mon ['sɒləmən] *n.* any man of great wisdom. ⟨in the Bible, a king of Israel and son of David, famous for his wisdom and for the great temple which he had built in Jerusalem⟩

Solomon Gun•dy ['gʌndi] *Cdn.* salted herring marinaded in vinegar, with pickling spices and onions. ⟨by folk etymology < *salmagundi*, possibly influenced by a nursery rhyme about Solomon Grundy⟩

Solomon Islands a country of islands in the SW Pacific Ocean.

Solomon's seal 1 the Star of David, especially as a medieval mystical symbol. See STAR OF DAVID for picture. 2 any of several perennial plants (genus *Polygonatum*) of the lily family having greenish or white flowers and a white underground stem marked with prominent, seal-like leaf scars.

So•lon ['soulən] *or* ['soulɒn] *n.* **1** a wise man; sage. **2** *Informal.* a member of a legislature. ⟨< *Solon* (638?-558? B.C.), a wise Athenian lawgiver⟩

so long *Informal.* goodbye; farewell. ⟨by folk etymology from Arabic *salaam*⟩

sol•stice ['sɒlstɪs] *or* ['soulstɪs] *n.* **1** either of the two times in the year when the sun is at its greatest distance from the celestial equator. In the Northern Hemisphere, June 21 or 22, the **summer solstice,** is the longest day of the year and December 21 or 22, the **winter solstice,** is the shortest. **2** either of the two points reached by the sun at these times. **3** a turning or culminating point; furthest limit; crisis. ⟨ME < OF < L *solstitium*, ult. < *sol* sun + *sistere* stand still⟩

sol•sti•tial [sɒl'stɪʃəl] *or* [soul'stɪʃəl] *adj.* having to do with a solstice.

sol•u•bil•i•ty [,sɒljə'bɪləti] *n., pl.* **-ties. 1** the quality (of certain substances) of dissolving or being dissolved easily: *the solubility of sugar in water.* **2** a measure of this quality or property, expressed as the amount of the substance in question that can be dissolved in a given solvent under certain conditions of temperature and pressure. **3** the quality of being solvable or explainable, as problems, questions, etc.

sol•u•bi•lize ['sɒljəbə,laɪz] *v.* **-lized, -liz•ing.** make or become soluble or more soluble, as by treatment with some other substance. **—,sol•u•bi•li'za•tion,** *n.*

sol•u•ble ['sɒljəbəl] *adj.* **1** that can be dissolved or made into liquid: *Salt is soluble in water.* **2** that can be solved: *soluble puzzles.* ⟨< L *solubilis* < *solvere* dissolve⟩ **—'sol•u•bly,** *adv.*

soluble glass WATER GLASS (def. 2).

sol•ute ['sɒljut] *or* ['soulut] *n.* a solid, gas, etc. dissolved in a liquid to make a solution: *Salt is a solute in sea water.* ⟨< L *solutus*, pp. of *solvere* dissolve, loosen⟩

so•lu•tion [sə'luʃən] *n.* **1** the solving of a problem: *The solution of the problem required many hours.* **2** an explanation or answer: *The police are seeking a solution to the crime.* **3** *Mathematics.* the set of values that satisfy a given equation. **4** the process of dissolving; changing of a solid or gas to a liquid by treatment with a liquid. **5** a liquid or mixture formed by dissolving. **6** a separating into parts; a breaking up. **7** the condition of being dissolved: *Sugar and salt can be held in solution in water.* ⟨ME < OF < L *solutio, -onis* a loosing < *solvere* loosen⟩

solution set SOLUTION (def. 3).

So•lu•tre•an [sə'lutriən] *adj.* denoting or having to do with an Upper Paleolithic culture of Europe, characterized by the making of fine, narrow, leaf-shaped flint blades. ⟨< *Solutré*, village in France where remains were found⟩

solv•a•ble ['sɒlvəbəl] *adj.* **1** capable of being solved. **2** capable of being dissolved. **—,solv•a'bil•i•ty,** *n.*

solv•ate ['sɒlveit] *v.* **-at•ed, -at•ing;** *n. Chemistry.* —*v.* **1** cause the molecules or ions of (a solvent and solute) to combine. **2** be so combined.
—*n.* the resulting complex. **—solv'a•tion,** *n.*

Sol•vay process ['sɒlvei] an industrial manufacturing process in which sodium chloride (salt) is treated with carbon dioxide and ammonia to produce sodium carbonate (soda). ⟨< Ernest *Solvay* (1838-1922), the Belgian chemist who originated it⟩

solve [sɒlv] *v.* **solved, solv•ing.** find the answer to; clear up; explain: *The mystery was never solved. He has solved all the problems in the lesson.* ⟨ME < L *solvere* loosen⟩ **—'solv•er,** *n.*

sol•ven•cy ['sɒlvənsi] *n.* the ability to pay all one owes.

sol•vent ['sɒlvənt] *adj., n.* —*adj.* **1** able to pay all that one owes: *A bankrupt firm is not solvent.* **2** especially of a liquid, able to dissolve another substance.
—*n.* **1** a substance, usually a liquid, that can dissolve other substances: *Water is a solvent of sugar and salt.* **2** a thing that solves. ⟨< L *solvens, -entis*, ppr. of *solvere* loosen, pay⟩

som [sɒm] *n.* the basic unit of currency in Kirghizia and Uzbekistan, divided into 100 tyyn. See table of money in the Appendix.

so•ma[1] ['soumə] *n., pl.* **so•ma•ta** ['soumətə] or **so•mas.** *Biology.* all the tissues and organs of an animal or plant except the germ cells; body. ⟨< NL < Gk. *sōma* body⟩

so•ma[2] ['soumə] *n.* **1** an intoxicating or hallucinogenic drink prepared from the juice of a plant, used in ancient Vedic rituals. **2** the plant from whose juice this drink was prepared, variously identified as a species of milkweed or a mushroom. ⟨< Skt.⟩

So•ma•li [sə'mɑli] *n., pl.* **-li** or **-lis;** *adj.* —*n.* **1** a member of a people inhabiting Somalia. The Somalis are apparently of mixed African and Mediterranean descent. **2** the Afro-Asiatic language of the Somalis.
—*adj.* of or having to do with Somalia, the Somalis, or their language.

So•ma•li•a [sə'mɑliə] *or* [sə'mɑljə] *n.* a country in NE Africa on the Indian Ocean. **—So'ma•li•an,** *n., adj.*

so•mat•ic [sə'mætɪk] *adj.* **1** of or having to do with the body, as opposed to the mind or soul. **2** *Anatomy. Zoology.* having to do with the cavity of the body, or its walls. **3** *Biology.* having to do with the soma. ⟨< Gk. *sōmatikos* < *sōma, -atos* body⟩ **—so'mat•i•cal•ly,** *adv.*

somatic cell *Biology.* any of the cells of an animal or plant body other than the reproductive, or germ, cells. Compare GERM CELL.

somatic cell genetics *Genetics.* the study of genetics using cultured somatic cells.

somatic mosaicism *Genetics.* mosaicism affecting body parts, resulting from mutation during the course of somatic development.

so•ma•tol•o•gy [,soumə'tɒlədʒi] *n.* the science of the physical structure and functions of living organisms. **—,so•ma•to'log•i•cal,** *adj.* **—,so•ma'tol•o•gist,** *n.*

so•ma•to•plasm ['soumətə,plæzəm] *or* [sə'mætə,plæzəm] *n.* *Biology.* **1** the protoplasm of a somatic cell. **2** somatic cells collectively as opposed to germ cells. **—,so•ma•to'plas•tic,** *adj.*

so•ma•to•type [sə'mætə,taip] *or* ['soumətə,taip] *n.* body type; physique.

som•bre ['sɒmbər] *adj.* **1** dark; gloomy: *A cloudy winter day is sombre.* **2** melancholy; dismal: *His losses made him very sombre.* **3** serious; sober, grave, or solemn. Also, **somber.** ⟨< F *sombre*, probably ult. < L *sub-* under + *umbra* shade⟩ **—'som•bre•ly,** *adv.* **—'som•bre•ness,** *n.*

som•brer•o [sɒm'brɛrou] *n., pl.* **-brer•os.** a broad-brimmed hat with a high crown worn especially in Mexico and the SW United States. See HAT for picture. ⟨< Sp. *sombrero*, ult. < L *sub-* under + *umbra* shade⟩

some [sʌm]; *unstressed*, [səm] *adj., pron., adv.* —*adj.* **1** certain, but not known or not named: *Some people sleep more than others.* **2** a number of: *She left the city some years ago.* **3** a quantity of: *Drink some milk.* **4** a; any: *Ask some waiter to come here.* **5** *Informal.* remarkably big, good, poor, etc.: *That was some storm!*
—*pron.* **1** certain unnamed persons or things: *Some think so.* **2** a certain number or quantity: *I ate some and threw the rest away.*
and then some, *Informal.* and a good deal more than that, too.
—*adv.* **1** *Informal.* to some degree or extent; somewhat: *She likes playing tennis some.* **2** *Informal.* to a great degree or extent: *That's going some!* **3** approximately (a given number of): *Some twenty people saw it.* ⟨OE *sum*⟩
☛ *Hom.* SUM.

-some[1] *suffix.* **1** tending to ——: *frolicsome, meddlesome.* **2** causing ——: *awesome, troublesome.* **3** tending to be ——: *lonesome.* ⟨OE *-sum*⟩

-some[2] *suffix.* a group of —— (*used with numerals*): *twosome, foursome.* ⟨< *some*⟩

-some[3] *combining form. Biology.* a body or part of one, especially of a cell: *chromosome.* ⟨< Gk. *soma* body⟩

some•bod•y ['sʌm,bʌdi], ['sʌm,bɒdi], *or* ['sʌmbədi] *pron., n., pl.* **-bod•ies.** —*pron.* a person not known or named; some person; someone.
—*n.* a person of importance: *She acts as if she were somebody since she won the prize.*

some•day ['sʌm,dei] *adv.* at some future time.

some•how ['sʌm,haʊ] *adv.* in a way not known or not stated; in one way or another: *I'll finish this work somehow.*
somehow or other, in one way or another.

some•one ['sʌm,wʌn] *or* ['sʌmwən] *pron.* some person; somebody.

some•place ['sʌm,pleis] *adv.* in or to some place; somewhere.

som•er•sault ['sʌmər,sɒlt] *n., v.* —*n.* a complete roll of the body, forward or backward, bringing the feet over the head.
—*v.* roll in this way. Also, **summersault.** ⟨ME *sombresault* < Provençal *sobresaut*, ult. < L *supra* over + *saltus* jump⟩

som•er•set ['sʌmər,sɛt] *n., v.* somersault.

some•thing ['sʌmθɪŋ] *n., adv.* —*n.* **1** some thing; a particular thing not named or not known: *I've got something important to tell you. She has something on her mind.* **2** a certain amount or quantity; part; little: *Something of doubt remains.* **3** a thing or person of some value or importance: *He thinks he's something.* **4** a thing or person that is to a certain extent an example of what is named: *She was something of a violinist.*
—*adv.* somewhat; to some extent or degree: *He is something like his father.*

some•time ['sʌm,taɪm] *adv., adj.* —*adv.* **1** at one time or another in the future: *Come over sometime.* **2** at an indefinite point of time: *It happened sometime last March.*
—*adj.* **1** former: *a sometime pupil of the school.* **2** being or doing so, happening, etc. only at times: *She is a sometime churchgoer.*

some•times ['sʌm,taɪmz] *adv.* now and then; at times: *He comes to visit sometimes.*

some•way ['sʌm,wei] *adv.* in some way.

some•what ['sʌm,wʌt] *or* ['sʌmwət] *adv., n.* —*adv.* to some extent or degree; slightly: *somewhat round.*
—*n.* some part or amount; a bit: *It was somewhat of a struggle. Somewhat of the fun is lost when you hear a joke the second time.*

some•where ['sʌm,wɛr] *adv., n.* —*adv.* **1** in or to some place; in or to one place or another: *He lives somewhere in the neighbourhood.* **2** at some point along a continuum or in a series: *It happened somewhere in the last century. She must be somewhere in her fifties. That colour is somewhere between blue and green.*
get somewhere, *Informal.* make headway; be successful.
—*n.* some indefinite place: *a ticket to somewhere.*

so•mite ['soumɑit] *n.* **1** *Zoology.* any one of the series of like body segments in such animals as worms, lobsters, etc. **2** *Embryology.* any of the segments of mesoderm in a vertebrate embryo which later become muscle and bone. ⟨< *soma*[1] + *-ite*⟩ **—'somi•tal** ['soumɪtəl] or **so'mit•ic** [sou'mɪtɪk], *adj.*

som•me•lier [,sʌməl'jei]; *French,* [sɔmə'lje] *n., pl.* **-liers** [-'jeiz]; *French,* [-'je]. wine steward; one in a restaurant, etc. whose job it is to select and serve the wines. ⟨< F < MF, originally, one in charge of pack animals < *somier* pack horse < LL *sagmarius* < *sagma* pack saddle⟩

som•nam•bu•lant [sɒm'næmbjələnt] *adj., n.* —*adj.* sleepwalking or having the habit of sleepwalking.
—*n.* somnambulist.

som•nam•bu•late [sɒm'næmbjə,leit] *v.* **-lat•ed, -lat•ing.** walk about while asleep; sleepwalk. **—som,nam•bu'la•tion,** *n.* **—som'nam•bu,la•tor,** *n.*

som•nam•bu•lism [sɒm'næmbjə,lɪzəm] *n.* sleepwalking. ⟨< L *somnus* sleep + *ambulare* walk⟩

som•nam•bu•list [sɒm'næmbjəlɪst] *n.* a sleepwalker. **—som,nam•bu'lis•tic,** *adj.* **—som,nam•bu'lis•ti•cal•ly,** *adv.*

som•nif•er•ous [sɒm'nɪfərəs] *adj.* **1** causing sleep, as drugs, influences, etc. **2** sleepy. ⟨< L *somnifer* < *somnus* sleep + *ferre* bring⟩ **—som'nif•er•ous•ly,** *adv.*

som•no•lence ['sɒmnələns] *n.* **1** sleepiness; drowsiness. **2** the quality of causing sleepiness. Also, **somnolency.**

som•no•lent ['sɒmnələnt] *adj.* **1** sleepy; drowsy. **2** causing sleepiness. ⟨< L *somnolentus* < *somnus* sleep⟩ **—'som•no•lent•ly,** *adv.*

Som•nus ['sɒmnəs] *n. Roman mythology.* the god of sleep.

son [sʌn] *n.* **1** a boy or man spoken of in relation to either or both of his parents. **2** a man or boy regarded as, or in the legal position of, a son. **3** a male descendant. **4** a son-in-law. **5** a boy or man attached to a country, a cause, etc. as a child is to its parents: *sons of liberty.* **6** anything thought of as a son in relation to its origin. **7** a term of address to a boy or man from an older person, priest, etc. **8 the Son,** *Christianity.* Jesus Christ. ⟨OE *sunu*⟩ **—'son•less,** *adj.*
☛ *Hom.* SUN.

so•nance ['sounəns] *n.* a sonant quality or state.

so•nant ['sounənt] *adj., n.* —*adj.* **1** of sound; having sound; sounding. **2** *Phonetics.* pronounced with the vocal cords vibrating; voiced.
—*n. Phonetics.* **1** a sound pronounced with the vocal cords vibrating; a voiced sound. [z] and [v] are sonants; [s] and [f] are not. **2** a sonorant, especially one forming the nucleus of a syllable, as (in some systems of notation) [l] in riddle ['rɪdl]. ⟨< L *sonans, -antis,* ppr. of *sonare* to sound < *sonus,* a sound⟩

so•nar ['sounɑr] *n.* a device using the reflection of underwater sound waves for navigation, range finding, detecting submerged objects, etc. ⟨< *so*und *na*vigation and *r*anging⟩

so•na•ta [sə'nɑtə] *n. Music.* an instrumental composition for one or two instruments, having, in its traditional form, three or four movements in contrasted rhythms but related keys: *a piano sonata.* ⟨< Ital. *sonata,* literally, sounded (on an instrument, as distinguished from sung), ult. < L *sonus* sound⟩

sonata form a musical form used especially for the first movement of a sonata, symphony, concerto, etc. The sonata form usually has three main divisions, exposition, development, and recapitulation, often followed by a coda.

son•a•ti•na [,sɒnə'tinə] *n. Music.* a short or simplified sonata. ⟨< Ital. *sonatina,* dim. of *sonata* sonata⟩

sonde [sɒnd] *n.* any of various types of probe, such as a rocket, balloon, or radiosonde, used for observing and measuring atmospheric phenomena. ⟨< F, plumbline⟩

sone [soun] *n.* a unit of loudness, the equivalent of one kilohertz at forty decibels over the auditory threshold.

son et lumière [sõely'mjɛʀ] *French.* **1** a method of presenting a historical spectacle either outdoors at night or in a large darkened arena or auditorium, using special lighting techniques, sound effects, music, and narration. **2** a spectacle of this kind. Also, **sound-and-light show.** ⟨< F, sound and light⟩

song [sɒŋ] *n.* **1** something to sing; a short poem set to music. **2 a** poetry: *fame celebrated in song.* **b** a poem that has a lyrical quality: *a song of childhood.* **3 a** a piece of music for, or as if for, a poem that is to be sung. **b** *Informal.* any piece of music. **4** the act or practice of singing: *The canary burst into song.* **5** any sound like singing: *the cricket's song, the song of the teakettle, the song of the brook.*
for a song, very cheaply: *I bought the bike for a song at an auction.*
song and dance, *Informal.* **a** an explanation or account, not necessarily true, and often intended to impress or deceive. **b** fuss; disturbance; turmoil: *He made a great song and dance about having to do the job.* ⟨OE *sang*⟩ **—'song,like,** *adj.*

song•bird ['sɒŋ,bɜrd] *n.* **1** a bird that sings. **2** a passerine bird, especially any species of the suborder Oscines, having vocal organs specialized for producing varied and, in many cases, melodic calls.

song cycle a series of songs, usually by the same lyricist and composer, unified by theme and form.

song•fest ['sɒŋ,fɛst] *n.* a social event featuring singing, including group singing.

song•less ['sɒŋlɪs] *adj.* **1** not able to sing, as a bird. **2** not characterized by or giving rise to singing; joyless; bleak.

song sparrow a small North American sparrow (*Melospiza melodia*) having black, brown, and white plumage and noted for its pleasing song.

song•ster ['sɒŋstər] *n.* **1** *Informal.* **a** a singer. **b** a writer of songs or poems. **2** a songbird. ⟨OE *sangestre*⟩

song•stress ['sɒŋstrɪs] *n. Informal.* **a** a woman singer. **b** a woman writer of songs or poems.

song thrush a common Old World thrush (*Turdus philomelos*) that is noted for its singing, having plumage that is brown above and white below, with a spotted breast. Also called **mavis.**

song•writ•er ['sɒŋ,rəitər] *n.* a composer of music or lyrics or both, especially one who composes pop songs.

son•ic ['sɒnɪk] *adj.* **1** of, having to do with, or using sound waves. **2** of or having to do with the speed of sound in air (331 m/s at 0°C). ⟨< L *sonus* sound⟩ **—'son•i•cal•ly,** *adv.*

sonic barrier the sudden increase in aerodynamic resistance experienced by an aircraft when it approaches the speed of sound (331 m/s or about 1192 km/h at 0°C).

sonic boom the sound, like that of an explosion, of the shock wave formed in front of an aircraft travelling above the speed of sound.

sonic depth finder sonar.

sonic mine a container holding an explosive charge that is put under water and exploded by propeller vibrations; acoustic mine.

so•nif•er•ous [sə'nɪfərəs] *adj.* carrying or producing sound. ⟨< L *sonus* sound + E *-ferous*⟩

son–in–law ['sʌn ɪn ˌlɒ] *n., pl.* **sons-in-law.** the husband of one's daughter.

son•net ['sɒnɪt] *n.* a poem having 14 lines, usually in iambic pentameter, and a certain arrangement of rhymes. Shakespearean and Petrarchan sonnets differ in the arrangement of the rhymes. ⟨< F < Ital. < Provençal *sonet*, ult. < L *sonus* sound⟩

son•net•eer [ˌsɒnə'tir] *n., v.* *—n.* a writer of sonnets.
—v. write sonnets.

son•ny ['sʌni] *n., pl.* **-nies.** *Informal.* a word used in speaking to a young boy: *Say, sonny, can you tell me how to get to the city hall from here?*
☛ *Hom.* SUNNY.

so•no•buoy ['sounəˌbɔɪ] *or* ['sounəˌbui] *n. Navigation.* a buoy equipped with devices for detecting underwater sounds and transmitting them by radio. ⟨< L *sonus* sound + E *buoy*⟩

Son of God *Christianity.* Jesus Christ as the incarnation of the second person of the Trinity.

Son of Man *Christianity.* Jesus Christ, especially as the promised Messiah.

so•no•gram ['sounəˌgræm] *or* ['sɒnəˌgræm] *n.* **1** *Medicine.* the visual image produced by reflected sound waves using ultrasound equipment: a diagnostic tool. **2** *Physics.* a graphic representation of sound patterns. ⟨< L *sonus* sound + E *-gram*⟩

so•no•graph ['sounəˌgræf] *or* ['sɒnəˌgræf] *n.* a machine that produces sonograms. ⟨< L *sonus* sound + E *-graph*⟩
—so'nog•ra•phy [sə'nɒgrəfi], *n.*

so•nog•ra•pher [sə'nɒgrəfər] *n.* a technician who makes use of a sonograph.

so•nom•e•ter [sə'nɒmətər] *n.* **1** an instrument used in measuring the pitch of musical tones or for experimenting with vibrating strings. **2** an instrument used for testing a person's hearing. ⟨< L *sonus* sound + E *-meter*⟩

son•o•rant ['sɒnərənt], ['sounərənt], *or* [sə'nɔrənt] *n., adj. Phonetics.* *—n.* **1** a sound that is less sonorous than a vowel but more so than an obstruent, and that may occur as a syllabic nucleus, such as [l], [r], and the nasals. **2** a sound produced by relatively unobstructed air passage, such as a vowel, semivowel, liquid, or nasal.
—adj. pertaining to or having the characteristics of a sonorant.

so•nor•i•ty [sə'nɔrəti] *n., pl.* **-ties.** the state or quality of being sonorous.

son•o•rous ['sɒnərəs], ['sounərəs], *or* [sə'nɔrəs] *adj.* **1** giving out or having a deep, loud sound. **2** of sound, full and rich. **3** having an impressive sound; high-sounding: *sonorous phrases, a sonorous style.* **4** *Phonetics.* having a certain degree of resonance or vocalic quality. Vowels are more sonorous than sonorants; sonorants are more sonorous than obstruents. ⟨< L *sonorus*, ult. < *sonor* sound⟩ **—'son•o•rous•ly,** *adv.* **—'son•o•rous•ness,** *n.*

son•ship ['sʌnʃɪp] *n.* the fact or state of being a son.

Sons of Freedom *Cdn.* an extreme sect of Doukhobors located, for the most part, in British Columbia and engaging in such forms of antigovernment protest as arson, disrobing, and bombing. Also called **Community Doukhobors, Freedomites.**

soon [sun] *adv.* **1** in a short time; before long: *I will see you again soon.* **2** before the usual or expected time; early: *Why have you come so soon?* **3** promptly; quickly: *As soon as I hear, I will let you know.* **4** readily; willingly: *The brave soldier would as soon die as yield to the enemy.*
had sooner, would more readily; prefer to.
sooner or later, ultimately; eventually. ⟨OE *sōna* at once⟩
☛ *Usage.* **No sooner than.** After **no sooner** the connective used is **than,** not **when:** *The fly had no sooner hit the water than* (not *when*) *a huge trout snapped at it.*

soot [sʊt] *n., v.* *—n.* a black substance, mostly carbon, in the smoke from burning coal, wood, oil, etc. Soot makes smoke dark and collects on the inside of chimneys.
—v. cover or blacken with soot. ⟨OE *sōt*⟩ **—'soot•less,** *adj.*

sooth [suθ] *n., adj. Archaic.* *—n.* truth.
—adj. true. ⟨OE *sōth*⟩

soothe [suð] *v.* **soothed, sooth•ing. 1** quiet; calm; comfort: *The mother soothed the crying child.* **2** make (pain, grief, etc.) less painful; relieve; ease. ⟨OE *sōthian*⟩ **—'sooth•ing•ly,** *adv.*

sooth•er ['suðər] *n.* **1** a person who or thing that soothes. **2** a baby's pacifier.

sooth•fast ['suθˌfæst] *adj. Archaic.* **1** truthful; loyal. **2** true; based on truth.

sooth•ly ['suθli] *adv. Archaic.* truly; in truth.

sooth•say ['suθˌsei] *v.* **-said** [-ˌsɛd], **-say•ing.** foretell the future; make predictions; prophesy.

sooth•say•er ['suθˌseiər] *n.* a person who claims to foretell the future; person who makes prophecies. ⟨< *sooth* + *sayer*⟩

sooth•say•ing ['suθˌseiɪŋ] *n., v.* *—n.* **1** the foretelling of future events. **2** a prediction or prophecy.
—v. ppr. of SOOTHSAY.

soot•y ['sʊti] *adj.* **soot•i•er, soot•i•est. 1** covered or blackened with soot. **2** dark brown or black; dark-coloured. **—'soot•i•ly,** *adv.* **—'soot•i•ness,** *n.*

sop [sɒp] *n., v.* **sopped, sop•ping.** *—n.* **1** a piece of food dipped or soaked in milk, broth, etc. **2** something given to appease or quiet; bribe. **3** a person or thing that is thoroughly soaked.
—v. **1** dip or soak. **2** take up (water, etc.); wipe; mop: *Please sop up that water with a cloth.* **3** be drenched. **4** soak thoroughly; drench. **5** of a liquid, soak in or through: *The water sopped through the carpet.* ⟨OE *sopp*⟩

sop. soprano.

SOP Standard Operating Procedure; Standing Operating Procedure. Also, **S.O.P.**

soph•ic ['sɒfɪk] *adj.* of, having to do with, or teaching wisdom. ⟨< Gk. *sophikos* < *sophos* wise, clever⟩

soph•ism ['sɒfɪzəm] *n.* a clever but misleading or specious argument; an argument based on false or unsound reasoning. ⟨ME < OF < L < Gk. *sophisma*, ult. < *sophos* clever⟩

soph•ist ['sɒfɪst] *n.* **1** Usually, **Sophist,** one of a group of professional teachers of ancient Greece who gave instruction in rhetoric, grammar, science, the nature of virtue, the history of society, and other teachings designed especially to promote success in public life. The Sophists were accused of not really seeking the truth, but being only interested in success in debate, even at the expense of honesty. **2** a person who reasons cleverly but falsely. **3** in early use, a philosopher or sage.

so•phis•tic [sə'fɪstɪk] *adj.* **1** clever but misleading; based on false or unsound reasoning. **2** using clever but misleading arguments; reasoning falsely or unsoundly. **3** characteristic of or pertaining to sophists or sophistry. **—so'phis•ti•cal•ly,** *adv.*

so•phis•ti•cal [sə'fɪstəkəl] sophistic.

so•phis•ti•cate *v.* [sə'fɪstəˌkeit]; *n.* [sə'fɪstəkɪt] *or* [sə'fɪstəˌkeit] *v.* **-cat•ed, -cat•ing;** *n.* *—v.* **1** make experienced in worldly ways; cause to lose one's natural simplicity and frankness. **2** mislead (a person) or corrupt (an argument, etc.) by using sophistry. **3** of instruments, devices, etc., make more complex and refined. **4** argue using sophistry; quibble: *tiresome letters to the editor sophisticating on a variety of topics.*
—n. a sophisticated person. ⟨ME < Med.L *sopohisticare* < L < Gk. *sophistikos* sophistical, ult. < *sophos* clever⟩

so•phis•ti•cat•ed [sə'fɪstəˌkeitɪd] *adj., v.* *—adj.* **1** refined, cultured, and experienced in worldly ways: *a sophisticated writer.* **2** appealing to sophisticated people: *a sophisticated novel, a sophisticated little restaurant.* **3** lacking natural simplicity, frankness, etc.; too refined, worldly-wise, etc. **4** of mechanical or electronic devices, complex and advanced in design: *sophisticated missiles.*
—v. pt. and pp. of SOPHISTICATE. **—so'phis•ti,cat•ed•ly,** *adv.*

so•phis•ti•ca•tion [səˌfɪstə'keiʃən] *n.* **1** the act, process, or result of sophisticating. **2** the quality or state of being sophisticated. **3** a sophisticated feature.

soph•ist•ry ['sɒfɪstri] *n., pl.* **-ries. 1** unsound reasoning; the act or practice of using faulty argument. **2** a clever but superficial and misleading argument.

soph•o•more ['sɒfəˌmɔr] *n., adj. U.S.* *—n.* a student in the second year of college or high school.
—adj. of or having to do with second-year college or high-school students. ⟨earlier *sophomer*, originally, taking part in dialectic exercises < *sophom*, var. of *sophism*⟩

soph•o•mor•ic [ˌsɒfə'mɔrɪk] *adj.* conceited and pretentious but crude and ignorant. **—ˌsoph•o'mor•i•cal•ly,** *adv.*

sop•o•rif•er•ous [ˌsɒpə'rɪfərəs] *or* [ˌsoupə'rɪfərəs] *adj.* bringing sleep; soporific. ⟨< L *soporifer* < *sopor* deep sleep + *ferre* bring⟩

sop•o•rif•ic [ˌsɒpə'rɪfɪk] *or* [ˌsoupə'rɪfɪk] *adj., n.* *—adj.* **1** causing or tending to cause sleep. **2** sleepy; drowsy.
—n. something that causes sleep, as a drug or medicine. ⟨< L *sopor* deep sleep + *facere* make⟩ **—ˌsop•o'rif•i•cal•ly,** *adj.*

sop•ping ['sɒpɪŋ] *adj.* soaked; drenched.

sop•py ['sɒpi] *adj.* **-pi•er, -pi•est. 1** soaked; very wet: *soppy ground, soppy weather.* **2** *Informal.* weakly sentimental. **—'sop•pi•ness,** *n.*

so•pra•ni•no [,souprə'ninou] *or* [,sɒprə'ninou] *adj., n. —adj.* of or being a musical instrument that is smaller and higher-pitched than the soprano: *a sopranino recorder.*
—n. such an instrument. ⟨< Ital., dim. of *soprano*⟩

so•pran•o [sə'prænou] *or* [sə'prɑnou] *n., pl.* **-pran•os.** *Music.* **1** the highest singing voice for women, girls, or boys, the normal range being from middle C to approximately an octave and a half to two octaves higher. **2** a singer who has such a voice. **3** the part sung by a soprano. Soprano is the highest part in standard four-part harmony for male and female voices. **4** an instrument having the highest range in a family of musical instruments. **5** (*adjl.*) having to do with, having the range of, or designed for a soprano. **6** a high-pitched voice. ⟨< Ital. *soprano* < *sopra* above < L *supra*⟩

so•ra ['sɔrə] *n.* a small short-billed rail (*Porzana carolina*) common to marshy areas of North America. ⟨origin unknown⟩

Sorb [sɔrb] *n.* a member of a Slavic people mainly confined to an area of eastern Germany south of Berlin. Also called **Wend. —'Sor•bi•an,** *adj.*

sor•bet ['sɔrbət] *or* [sɔr'bei] *n.* sherbet.

sor•bi•tol ['sɔrbə,tɒl] *n. Biochemistry.* a sweet, white, water-soluble crystalline powder, found in cherries, plums, many berries, and seaweed, and used in the manufacture of artificial sweeteners, synthetic resins, varnishes, etc., and as a moistener in creams and lotions. *Formula*: $C_6H_8(OH)_6$ ⟨< *sorb* (< F *sorbe* < L *sorbus*) other name for service tree + *-itol*⟩

Sor•bonne [sɔr'bʌn] *or* [sɔr'bɒn]; *French,* [sɔʀ'bɔn] *n.* the seat of the faculties of letters and science of the University of Paris.

sor•cer•er ['sɔrsərər] *n.* a person who practises magic with the aid of evil spirits; black magician; wizard or witch.

sor•cer•y ['sɔrsəri] *n., pl.* **-cer•ies.** magic performed with the aid of evil spirits; witchcraft. ⟨ME < OF *sorcerie,* ult. < L *sors* lot⟩ **—'sor•cer•ous,** *adj.*

sor•did ['sɔrdɪd] *adj.* **1** dirty; filthy: *The poor family lived in a sordid hut.* **2** low; base; contemptible. **3** caring too much for money; meanly selfish; greedy. ⟨< L *sordidus* dirty < *sordere* be dirty < *sordes* dirt⟩ **—'sor•did•ly,** *adv.* **—'sor•did•ness,** *n.*

sore [sɔr] *adj.* **sor•er, sor•est;** *n., adv. —adj.* **1** painful; aching; tender; smarting: *a sore throat, a sore finger.* **2** of a person or animal, feeling physical pain: *She was sore from the long hike the previous day.* **3** sad; distressed: *The suffering of the refugees made her heart sore.* **4** easily angered or offended; irritable; touchy. **5** *Informal.* offended; angered; vexed: *He is sore at missing the game.* **6** causing pain, misery, anger, or offence; vexing: *Their defeat is a sore subject with the members of the team.* **7** severe; distressing: *Your going away is a sore grief to us.*
—n. **1** a painful place on the body where the skin or flesh is broken or bruised. **2** a cause of pain, sorrow, offence, etc.
—adv. Archaic. greatly; very much: *They were sore afraid.* ⟨OE *sār*⟩ **—'sore•ly,** *adv.* **—'sore•ness,** *n.*
☛ *Hom.* SOAR.

sore•head ['sɔr,hɛd] *n. Informal.* a person who is easily angered or offended.

sor•ghum ['sɔrgəm] *n.* **1** any of an Old World genus (*Sorghum*) of annual and perennial cereal grasses, especially a cornlike African species (*S. vulgare*) widely cultivated in many varieties as a cereal crop, as a source of edible oil, starch, and syrup, and for fodder. **2** syrup made from the juice of cultivated sorghum. ⟨< NL < Ital. < L *syricum* Syrian⟩

so•ror•i•ty [sə'rɔrəti] *n., pl.* **-ties. 1** sisterhood. **2** a club or society of women or girls. There are student sororities in many North American universities. Compare FRATERNITY. ⟨probably < Med.L *sororitas* < L *soror* sister⟩

so•ro•sis [sə'rousɪs] *n. Botany.* a multiple fruit, as a pineapple or a mulberry, formed by the consolidation of many flowers and seed vessels. ⟨< NL < Gk. *soros* heap⟩

sorp•tion ['sɔrpʃən] *n. Physical chemistry.* the binding of one substance by another by any means, such as absorption, adsorption, etc. ⟨by back formation⟩

sor•rel[1] ['sɔrəl] *adj., n. —adj.* reddish brown.
—n. **1** a reddish brown. **2** a reddish brown horse. ⟨ME < OF *sorel* < *sor* yellowish brown⟩

sor•rel[2] ['sɔrəl] *n.* **1** any of several plants (genus *Rumex*) of the buckwheat family, especially *R. acetosa,* found throughout temperate North America and Eurasia, having sour-tasting, arrow-shaped leaves that are used as a vegetable or as salad greens or as a flavouring in sauces and soups. **2** WOOD SORREL. ⟨ME < OF *surele* < *sur* sour < Gmc.⟩

sor•row ['sɔrou] *n., v. —n.* **1** grief; sadness; regret. **2** a cause of grief, sadness, or regret; trouble; suffering; misfortune: *Her sorrows have aged her.* **3** mourning; the outward expression of grief, sadness, or regret.
—v. feel or show grief, sadness, or regret. ⟨OE *sorg*⟩
—'sor•row•er, *n.* **—'sor•row•less,** *adj.*
☛ *Syn. n.* **1. Sorrow,** GRIEF, DISTRESS = mental suffering caused by loss or trouble. **Sorrow** suggests deep sadness or mental pain caused by the loss of someone or something dear or the experiencing or doing of something bad or wrong: *The dope addict became a criminal and brought great sorrow to his mother.* **Grief** emphasizes deeply or keenly felt sorrow or very painful regret: *Her grief when he died was unbearable.* **Distress** particularly suggests the strain or pressure of pain (physical or mental), grief, fear, anxiety, etc. caused by any trouble: *War causes widespread distress.*

sor•row•ful ['sɔroufəl] *adj.* **1** full of sorrow; feeling sorrow; sad. **2** showing sorrow. **3** causing sorrow. **—'sor•row•ful•ly,** *adv.* **—'sor•row•ful•ness,** *n.*

sor•ry ['sɔri] *adj.* **-ri•er, -ri•est;** *interj. —adj.* **1** feeling pity, regret, sympathy, etc.; sad: *I am sorry that you are sick.* **2** wretched; poor; pitiful: *The homeless family was a sorry sight.* **3** worthless; useless; so inferior as to be contemptible: *That's a sorry excuse. What a sorry piece of work!*
be sorry, ask pardon, as in making an apology.
—interj. **a** I am sorry; pardon me. **b** I regret I cannot do, give, etc. what you ask. **c** (*with interrogative intonation*) pardon? What did you say? ⟨OE *sārig* < *sār* sore⟩ **—'sor•ri•ly,** *adv.* **—'sor•ri•ness,** *n.*
☛ *Hom.* SAURY.

sort [sɔrt] *n., v. —n.* **1** a kind; class: *What sort of work does he do?* **2** a character; quality; nature. **3** a person or thing of a certain kind or quality: *He is a good sort.* **4** the act or process, or an instance, of sorting something: *to do an alphabetical sort on a list.* **5** Usually, **sorts,** *pl. Printing.* **a** any of the characters of a font of type. **b** rarely used characters of a specific font. **6** *Archaic.* a way; fashion; manner: *It was their custom to act in this sort.*
of a sort or **of sorts, a** of one kind or another. **b** of a poor or mediocre quality.
out of sorts, a ill, cross, or uncomfortable. **b** *Printing.* lacking a particular character in a font of type.
sort of, *Informal.* **a** somewhat; rather: *I'm sort of scared.* **b** more or less; as it were; in a way: *I didn't work at this poem, it just sort of came to me.*
—v. **1** arrange by kinds or classes; arrange in order: *Sort these cards according to their colours.* **2** find and separate from others (*used with* **out**): *The farmer sorted out the best apples for eating.* **3** *Archaic.* agree; accord.
sort out, a find and separate from others. **b** *Informal.* resolve or get to the bottom of; make sense of: *They were able to sort out their problems. You listen to him and see if you can sort out what he wants.* ⟨ME < OF *sorte,* ult. < L *sors, sortis,* originally, lot⟩
—'sort•a•ble, *adj.* **—'sort•er,** *n.*
☛ *Syn. n.* **1.** See note at KIND[2].
☛ *Usage.* See note at KIND[2].

sor•tie ['sɔrti] *n.* **1** a sudden attack by troops from a defensive position. **2** a single round trip of a military aircraft against an enemy. ⟨< F *sortie* < *sortir* go out⟩

sor•ti•lege ['sɔrtəlɪdʒ] *n.* **1** a drawing of lots for the purpose of divination or sorcery. **2** black magic; sorcery.

so•rus ['sɔrəs] *n., pl.* **so•ri** [-raɪ] *or* [-ri]. *Botany.* any of the dotlike clusters of spores on the back of the frond of a fern. ⟨< NL < Gk. *sōros* heap⟩

S O S ['ɛs,ou'ɛs] **1** a signal of distress consisting of the letters *s o s* of the Morse code (. . . ——— . . .), used in wireless telegraphy. **2** *Informal.* any urgent call for help.
☛ *Usage.* **SOS** is a code signal only; it is not an abbreviation.

so–so ['sou ,sou] *or* ['sou 'sou] *adj., adv. —adj.* neither very good nor very bad.
—adv. passably; indifferently; tolerably.

sos•te•nu•to [,sɒstə'nutou] *adj., adv., n., pl.* **-tos.** *Music.*
—adj. **1** sustained; prolonged; held. **2** played or sung at a slower but steady tempo; andante.
—adv. in a sostenuto manner.
—n. a sostenuto note, movement, or passage; composition to be played or sung in this manner. ⟨< Ital. *sostenuto,* pp. of *sostenere* sustain < L *sustinere.* See SUSTAIN.⟩

sot [sɒt] *n.* drunkard. ⟨OE < Med.L *sottus*⟩ **—'sot•tish,** *adj.*

so•te•ri•ol•o•gy [sə,tiri'ɒlədʒi] *n.* the branch of theology that deals with how salvation is accomplished. ⟨< Gk. *soteria* salvation < *soter* saviour⟩

So•thic ['souθɪk] *or* ['sɒθɪk] *adj.* **1** of or having to do with

Sirius, the Dog Star, or its rising. **2** of or having to do with an ancient Egyptian method of measuring time, based on the rising of this star. A **Sothic year** was 365.25 days; a **Sothic cycle** was 1460 such years. ⟨< Gk. *Sothiakos* < *Sothis* the Dog Star⟩

sot•to vo•ce ['sɒtou 'voutʃi]; *Italian*, ['sɔtto 'vɔtʃe] **1** in a low tone. **2** aside; privately. ⟨< Ital., below (normal) voice⟩

sou [su] *n.* **1** a former French coin, worth 5 centimes or 1/20 of a franc. **2** anything of little value. ⟨< F *sou* ult. < L *solidus*, a Roman coin⟩
☛ *Hom.* SAULT, SUE.

sou•brette [su'brɛt] *n.* **1** a maidservant or lady's maid in a play or opera, especially one displaying coquetry, pertness, and a spirit of intrigue; a lively or pert young woman character. **2** an actress or singer taking such a part. ⟨< F < Provençal *soubreto* coy < *soubrar* set aside, L *superare* be above⟩

sou•bri•quet ['subrə,kei], [,subrə'kei], *or* ['subrə,kɛt] *n.* See SOBRIQUET.

souf•fle ['sufəl] *n. Pathology.* a blowing or murmuring sound on breathing, heard through a stethoscope.

souf•flé [su'flei] *or* ['suflei] *n., adj., v.* **souf•fléed, souf•flé•ing.**
–n. a frothy baked dish, usually made light by adding stiffly beaten egg whites: *cheese soufflé.*
–adj. Also, **souffléed.** puffed up by beating or cooking: *soufflé potatoes.*
–v. make (food) puffed up or light by beating, cooking, adding stiffly beaten egg whites, etc.: *to soufflé potatoes.* ⟨< F *soufflé*, originally pp. of *souffler* puff up⟩

sough [saʊ] *or* [sʌf] *v., n.* *–v.* make a rustling or murmuring sound: *The pines soughed when the wind blew.*
–n. a rustling or murmuring sound. ⟨OE *swōgan*⟩
☛ *Hom.* SOW[2] [saʊ].

sought [sɒt] *v.* pt. and pp. of SEEK.

sought–after ['sɒt ,æftər] *adj.* desirable; much in demand.

souk [suk] *n.* a Middle Eastern open-air marketplace. Also, **suk, sukh, suq.**

soul [soul] *n., adj.* *–n.* **1 a** the spiritual part of a person, regarded as the source of thought, feeling, and action, and considered as distinct from the body. Many religions believe that the soul and the body are separated in death and that the soul lives forever. **b** the spiritual, moral, or emotional nature of human beings as opposed to the physical nature. **2 a** energy of mind or feelings; spirit: *She puts her whole soul into her work.* **b** a quality showing such energy or spirit, warmth: *Her music is technically sophisticated but has no soul.* **3** a cause of inspiration and energy: *Florence Nightingale was the soul of the movement to reform nursing.* **4** the essential part: *Brevity is the soul of wit.* **5** a person: *Don't tell a soul.* **6** an embodiment: *He is the soul of honour.* **7** the spirit of a dead person. **8** among North American Blacks, a consciousness of and sense of pride in their African heritage. **9** SOUL MUSIC.
upon my soul! an exclamation of surprise, wonder, etc.
–adj. of, having to do with, or reflecting the cultural heritage of American Blacks. ⟨OE *sāwol*⟩
☛ *Hom.* SOL [soul], SOLE.

soul catcher *Cdn. Pacific coast.* an instrument consisting of a carved bone tube, traditionally used by medicine men of the Haida, Tlingit, and Tsimshian to capture the wandering souls of the sick and return them to their bodies.

soul food food popular in the S U.S., having its origin in traditional Black American cookery and including such items as chitterlings, collard greens, cornbread, ham hocks, and yams.

soul•ful ['soulfəl] *adj.* **1** full of feeling; deeply emotional. **2** expressing or suggesting a deep feeling. **–'soul•ful•ly,** *adv.* **–'soul•ful•ness,** *n.*

soul•less ['soullɪs] *adj.* having no soul; without spirit or noble feelings. **–'soul•less•ly,** *adv.* **–'soul•less•ness,** *n.*

soul music a style of rhythm and blues developed by Black Americans in the late 1950s, incorporating elements of gospel music along with emotionally intense lyrics and vocals.

soul–search•ing ['soul ,sɜrtʃɪŋ] *n.* a deep and honest effort, especially during a crisis, to evaluate one's own motives, beliefs, etc. so as to assess one's conduct and attitudes.

sound[1] [saʊnd] *n., v.* *–n.* **1** what is or can be heard; auditory sensation. **2** the vibrations causing this sensation. Sound travels in waves. **3** a noise, note, tone, etc. whose quality indicates its source or nature: *the sound of fighting.* **4** the distance within which a noise may be heard: *within sound.* **5** *Phonetics.* one of the simplest elements composing speech: *a vowel sound.* **6** the effect produced on the mind by what is heard: *a warning sound, a queer sound.* **7** sounds as recorded for or transmitted by television, radio, or film, or their quality or volume; sound track: *Many TV commercials appear silly when you turn off the sound. I couldn't really enjoy the movie because of the poor sound.* **8** mere noise without meaning.
–v. **1** make a sound or noise: *The trumpet sounds for battle. The wind sounds like an animal howling.* **2** seem to the hearer: *That excuse sounds odd.* **3** pronounce: *Sound each syllable.* **4** be pronounced: *'Rough' and 'ruff' sound alike.* **5** be heard as a sound; issue or pass as sound; be mentioned. **6** be filled with sound. **7** cause to sound: *to sound a minor chord on the piano.* **8** order or direct by a sound: *to sound a retreat.* **9** indicate or signal; make known; announce: *The trumpets sounded the call to arms. The grandfather clock was just sounding midnight.* **10** proclaim; cause to resound: *to sound someone's praises.* **11** test by noting sounds: *to sound a person's lungs.*
sound off, *Informal.* **a** speak loudly and volubly, especially to give an opinion or complain. **b** speak in a boastful or offensive way.
sound out, read (an unfamiliar or difficult word) one letter or syllable at a time. ⟨ME *sounen* < OF *son*, n., *soner*, v. (< L *sonare*), < L *sonus*⟩ **–'sound•a•ble,** *adj.*

sound[2] [saʊnd] *adj., adv.* *–adj.* **1** free from injury, decay, or defect: *a sound ship, sound fruit.* **2** free from disease; healthy: *a sound body and mind.* **3** strong; safe; secure: *a sound business firm.* **4** solid: *sound rock.* **5** correct; right; reasonable; reliable: *sound advice.* **6** without any legal defect: *a sound title.* **7** having orthodox or conventional ideas: *politically sound.* **8** thorough; hearty: *a sound whipping, a sound sleep.* **9** free from moral decay or fault; morally stalwart.
–adv. deeply; thoroughly: *sound asleep.* ⟨ME *sund*, OE *(ge)sund*⟩ **–'sound•ly,** *adv.* **–'sound•ness,** *n.*
☛ *Syn. adj.* **5.** See note at VALID.

sound[3] [saʊnd] *v., n.* *–v.* **1** measure the depth of (water) by letting down a weight fastened to the end of a line. **2** measure (depth) by this method. **3** examine or test (the ocean floor, etc.) by a line arranged to bring up a sample. **4** inquire into the feelings, inclination, etc. of (a person): *to sound someone on his or her political views.* **5** examine; probe; investigate. **6** go toward the bottom; dive: *The whale sounded.* **7** examine with a sound.
sound out, a inquire into a person's feelings, opinions, etc.; examine indirectly: *John sounded her out on the project, but she didn't seem interested.* **b** find out by such means: *He tried to sound out whether they really liked his paintings or not.*
–n. Medicine. a long, slender instrument used by doctors in examining body cavities. ⟨ME < OF *sonder*, probably < Gmc. source of *sound[4]*⟩ **–'sound•a•ble,** *adj.*

sound[4] [saʊnd] *n.* **1** a narrow passage of water joining two larger bodies of water or separating an island and the mainland: *Queen Charlotte Sound.* **2** an arm of the sea: *Howe Sound.* **3** the air bladder of a fish. ⟨OE *sund* swimming; partly < ON *sund* strait⟩

sound barrier SONIC BARRIER.

sound bite a short clip on a news program, featuring a brief statement or part of one by a politician, reporter, celebrity, etc., especially a recorded one inserted into many broadcasts or one that is often quoted.

sound•board ['saʊnd,bɔrd] *n.* **1** a thin, resonant piece of wood forming part of a musical instrument, as in a violin or piano, to increase the fullness of its tone. **2** SOUNDING BOARD (def. 2).

sound effects noises, as of rain, traffic, crowds, doorbells, etc., called for in the script of a play or motion picture.

sound•er[1] ['saʊndər] *n.* **1** a person who or thing that makes a sound. **2** *Telegraphy.* an electromagnetic receiving instrument that converts a telegraphic message into sound. ⟨< *sound[1]*⟩

sound•er[2] ['saʊndər] *n.* a person who or thing that measures the depth of something, as water. ⟨< *sound[3]*⟩

sound•ing[1] ['saʊndɪŋ] *adj., v.* *–adj.* **1** giving forth sound, especially resonant or sonorous sound: *sounding brass.* **2** pompous; bombastic: *sounding rhetoric.*
–v. ppr. of SOUND[1]. ⟨< *sound[1]*⟩

sound•ing[2] ['saʊndɪŋ] *n., v.* *–n.* **1** the act of measuring the depth of water or examining the bottom by letting down a weight fastened to the end of a line. **2** the data obtained in this way. **3** a penetration and examination of the atmosphere or of outer space for scientific observation. **4** investigation; examination: *take a sounding of public opinion.* **5** *Medicine.* examination with a sound or probe. **6 soundings,** *pl.* **a** the depths of water found by a line and weight. **b** a place where the water is shallow enough for a sounding line to touch bottom.
–v. ppr. of SOUND[3]. ⟨< *sound[3]*⟩

sounding board 1 SOUNDBOARD (def. 1). 2 a structure used to direct sound toward an audience. 3 a means of bringing opinions, etc. out into the open. 4 a person or group to whom one can tentatively communicate one's ideas to get critical input or to test reactions.

sounding line a line having a weight fastened to the end, used to measure the depth of water.

sound•less[1] ['saʊndlɪs] *adj.* without sound; making no sound. ⟨< *sound*[1]⟩ **—'sound•less•ly,** *adv.* **—'sound•less•ness,** *n.*

sound•less[2] ['saʊndlɪs] *adj.* immeasurably deep; bottomless: *a soundless mystery, soundless love.* ⟨< *sound*[3]⟩ **—'sound•less•ly,** *adv.* **—'sound•less•ness,** *n.*

sound•proof ['saʊnd,pruf] *adj., v. —adj.* not letting sound pass through.
—v. make soundproof.

sound track 1 a recording of the sounds of words, music, etc., made along one edge of a motion-picture film. 2 the auditory effect of this: *That video has a lousy sound track.* 3 a separate recording of it, or of its musical portions only, on a cassette, CD, etc.: *After seeing a great movie she always wants to buy the sound track.* Also, **soundtrack.**

sound truck a truck or van equipped with loudspeakers, etc. for making public announcements in the streets.

sound waves the progressive vibrations by which sounds are transmitted.

soup [sup] *n., v. —n.* 1 a liquid food made by boiling meat, vegetables, fish, etc. 2 *Informal.* a heavy, wet fog or cloud formation: *The pilot relied heavily on instruments to fly through the thick soup.* 3 *Slang.* power; horsepower.
in the soup, *Informal.* in difficulties; in trouble.
—v.
soup up, *Slang.* increase the power, capacity, or efficiency of: *to soup up an engine.* ⟨< F *soupe* < Gmc.⟩

soup•çon [sup'sɔ̃] *n. French.* a slight trace or flavour; very small amount. ⟨< F *soupçon* suspicion⟩

soup kitchen a place that serves food free or at a very low charge to poor or unemployed people or to victims of a flood, fire, or other disaster.

soup•spoon ['sup,spun] *n.* a spoon with a large round bowl, bigger than a teaspoon or dessert spoon, for eating soup.

soup•y ['supi] *adj.* **soup•i•er, soup•i•est.** 1 like soup, especially **a** dense and opaque: *a pool of stagnant, soupy water; soupy fog.* **b** runny: *This jelly is soupy.* 2 maudlin; overly sentimental.

sour [saʊr] *adj., v., n., adv. —adj.* 1 having the basic taste sensation produced by acids; sharp and biting: *Lemon juice is sour. Most green fruit is sour.* 2 fermented; spoiled. Sour milk is healthful, but most foods are not good to eat when they have become sour. 3 having a fermented or rank smell.
4 disagreeable; bad-tempered; peevish: *a sour old man.*
5 showing or expressing bad temper or peevishness: *a sour face.*
6 unusually acid: *sour soil.* 7 cold and wet; damp: *sour weather.*
be or **go sour on, a** be or become resentful toward. **b** be or become disenchanted or disillusioned with.
go sour, fall below usual standards of excellence or interest; fall off.
—v. 1 make or become sour; turn sour. 2 make or become peevish, bad-tempered, or disagreeable. 3 fall below usual standards of excellence or interest.
sour on, take or cause to take a dislike for.
—n. 1 something sour. 2 a sour alcoholic drink, such as whisky and lemon juice: *a whisky sour.*
—adv. in a sour manner. ⟨OE *sūr*⟩ **—'sour•ly,** *adv.* **—'sour•ness,** *n.*
☛ *Syn. adj.* **4, 5. Sour,** TART[1], ACID used figuratively to describe a person's looks, disposition, words, manner of expression, etc. mean 'resembling vinegar or lemons in harshness or sharpness'. **Sour** emphasizes harsh, forbidding, or irritable qualities, and suggests bad temper or a disagreeable mood, surly rudeness, grouchiness, or sullenness: *That janitor has a sour disposition.* **Tart** emphasizes sharp and stinging qualities: *His tart answer made her cry.* **Acid** emphasizes biting, sarcastic, severely critical qualities: *I read an acid comment on the political situation.*

source [sɔrs] *n., v.* **sourced, sourc•ing.** *—n.* 1 a beginning of a brook or river; fountain; spring. 2 a place from which anything comes or is obtained. 3 a person, book, statement, etc. that supplies information.
—v. 1 contract a supplier, professional, or manufacturer in order to obtain (parts, materials, services, etc.) 2 find or determine the source of (information, etc.) ⟨ME < OF *sourse,* ult. < L *surgere* rise, surge⟩

source•book ['sɔrs,bʊk] *n.* an anthology of writings used as basic resource material in studying something: *a sourcebook in medieval history including excerpts from many Renaissance documents.*

source code *Computer technology.* code written directly by a programmer, as opposed to code generated by a computer: *She altered her source code in order to fix a bug in the program.*

source language 1 the language of origin of a text to be translated. 2 *Computer technology.* the computer language (e.g., COBOL) in which software is originally written. 3 *Linguistics.* the language from which borrowings into another language are taken. 4 a speaker's mother tongue as the source of characteristic forms of interference in the production of utterances in the second language.

sour cherry 1 a common variety of cherry tree (*Prunus cerasus*) whose sour fruits are much used in preserves, pies, etc. 2 the fruit.

sour cream a sour-tasting dairy product with a thick, smooth consistency, made from milk solids, bacterial culture, etc. It is used as a condiment and in cooking.

sour•dough ['saʊr,doʊ] *n. Cdn.* 1 dough containing active yeast, saved from one baking for the next. Prospectors and pioneers used sourdough for making bread to avoid the need for fresh yeast. 2 (*adjl.*) made with sourdough: *sourdough bread.* 3 a prospector or pioneer in northwestern Canada or Alaska. 4 any old resident, experienced hand, etc.; person who is not a tenderfoot. 5 a native or inhabitant of Yukon Territory.

sour grapes contempt for something because one cannot have it or do it oneself. ⟨< Aesop's fable of the fox and the grapes⟩

sour•puss ['saʊr,pʊs] *n. Informal.* a person who looks or is gloomy, grumpy, or ill-tempered, especially habitually.

sour•sop ['saʊr,sɒp] *n.* 1 a small, tropical American evergreen tree (*Annona muricata*) of the custard-apple family having leaves with a spicy smell and large, spiny fruit with tart, edible flesh. 2 the fruit of this tree.

sou•sa•phone ['suzə,foʊn] *n.* a type of tuba that encircles the player's body and has a wide movable bell; used in brass bands. ⟨< John Philip *Sousa,* American composer and bandmaster (1854-1932), its inventor⟩

sous–chef ['su ,ʃɛf] *n.* the person next in rank to the head chef in a kitchen; chef's assistant. ⟨< F *sous* under, subordinate + *chef* head⟩

souse [sʌus] *v.* **soused, sous•ing;** *n. —v.* 1 plunge into liquid; drench; soak in a liquid. 2 soak in vinegar, brine, etc.; pickle. 3 *Slang.* make or become drunk.
—n. 1 a plunging into a liquid; drenching. 2 liquid used for pickling. 3 something soaked or kept in pickle, especially the head, ears, and feet of a pig. 4 *Slang.* drunkard. ⟨ME; ult. < OF *sous* pickled pork, ult. < Gmc. **sult-,* **salt-* salt⟩

sou•tache [su'tæʃ] *or* ['sutæʃ] *n.* a narrow braid used for trimming. ⟨< F < Hungarian *sujtás* trimming⟩

sou•tane [su'tɑn] *or* [su'tæn] *n.* a cassock. ⟨< F < Ital. *sottana,* ult. < L *sub* under⟩

south [sʌuθ] *n., adj., adv. —n.* 1 the direction to the right as one faces the rising sun; direction opposite to north, or the cardinal compass point corresponding to this direction. 2 Also, **South,** the part of the earth or of any country, etc. toward the south.
—adj. 1 toward the south. 2 from the south. 3 in the south.
4 South, designating the southern part of a geographical area having a proper name: *South America, South Europe.*
—adv. 1 in or toward the south: *The journey south took two days. Oranges grow down south.* 2 **south of,** farther south than: *They live south of London.*
south of the border, *Cdn.* in or to the United States. ⟨OE *sūth*⟩

South Africa a country, member of the Commonwealth, on the southern tip of Africa.

South African *n., adj. —n.* a native or inhabitant of South Africa.
—adj. of or having to do with South Africa or its people.

South African Dutch 1 the Boers or Afrikaners.
2 Afrikaans.

South America a continent in the southern half of the Western Hemisphere, bounded by the Atlantic and Pacific Oceans.

South American *n., adj. —n.* a native or inhabitant of the continent of South America.
—adj. of or having to do with South America or its people.

south•bound ['sʌuθ,baʊnd] *adj.* going toward the south.

South Ca•ro•li•na [,kærə'laɪnə] *or* [,kɛrə'laɪnə] a southern state of the United States, south of North Carolina.

South Da•ko•ta [də'koutə] a northerly state of the United States, south of North Dakota.

South•down ['sʌuθ,daʊn] *n.* an English breed of small, hornless sheep raised for mutton. ⟨< *South Downs,* the area in S England where this breed originated⟩

south•east [,sʌuθ'ist] *n., adj., adv. —n.* **1** the direction or compass point halfway between south and east. **2** a place that is in the southeast part or direction.
—adj. or adv. of, at, in, to, toward, or from the southeast: *the southeast corner of the house, to walk southeast.*

south•east•er [,sʌuθ'istər] *n.* a wind or storm from the southeast.

south•east•er•ly [,sʌuθ'istərli] *adj., adv., n., pl.* **-lies.** *—adj. or adv.* **1** toward the southeast. **2** from the southeast.
—n. a wind from the southeast.

south•east•ern [,sʌuθ'istərn] *adj.* of, at, in, to, toward, or from the southeast.

south•east•ward [,sʌuθ'istwərd] *adv., adj., n. —adv. or adj.* toward the southeast.
—n. southeast.

south•east•ward•ly [,sʌuθ'istwərdli] *adj., adv. —adj.* **1** toward the southeast. **2** of winds, from the southeast.
—adv. toward the southeast.

south•east•wards [,sʌuθ'istwərdz] *adv.* southeastward.

south•er ['saʊðər] *or* ['sʌuθər] *n.* a wind or storm from the south.

south•er•ly ['sʌðərli] *adj., adv., n., pl.* **-lies.** *—adj. or adv.* **1** toward the south. **2** from the south.
—n. a wind that blows from the south.

south•ern ['sʌðərn] *adj.* **1** toward the south: *a southern view.* **2** from the south: *a southern breeze.* **3** of or in the south or the southern part of the country. **4 Southern,** of, in, or having to do with the South. ⟨OE *sūtherne*⟩

Southern blotting *Genetics.* a technique, devised by Ed Southern, for transfer of DNA fragments that have been separated by electrophoresis to a nitrocellulose filter, enabling the detection of specific fragments by radioactive probes. The end result is a **Southern blot**.

Southern Cross *Astronomy.* a southern constellation of four bright stars in the form of a cross, used in finding the direction south.

South•ern•er ['sʌðərnər] *n.* **1** a native or inhabitant of the southern United States. **2 southerner,** a native or inhabitant of the southern region of a specified country or area.

southern hemisphere the half of the earth between the Equator and the South Pole.

southern lights AURORA AUSTRALIS.

south•ern•ly ['sʌðərnli] *adj.* southerly.

south•ern•most ['sʌðərn,moust] *adj.* farthest south.

south•ing [saʊðɪŋ] *or* ['sʌuθɪŋ] *n.* **1** a movement toward the south. **2** a distance due south, specifically, such a distance covered by water.

South Ko•rea [kə'riə] *n.* a country forming the southern part of the Korean Peninsula, properly called the Republic of Korea.

south•land ['sʌuθlənd] *or* ['sʌuθ,lænd] *n.* land in the south; the southern part of a country.

south•most ['sʌuθ,moust] *adj.* farthest south.

south•paw ['sʌuθ,pɒ] *n., adj. Slang. —n.* **1** a left-handed baseball pitcher. **2** any left-handed person.
—adj. left-handed.

South Pole the southern end of the earth's axis.

South Sea Islander a native or inhabitant of the **South Sea Islands**, islands in the S Pacific Ocean.

South Shore *Cdn.* **1** in Québec, the southern shore of the St. Lawrence River and the Gulf of St. Lawrence. **2** in Nova Scotia, the southeastern shore of the peninsula, roughly from Halifax to Yarmouth and some distance in.

south–south•east ['sʌuθ,sʌuθ'ist] *n., adj., adv. —n.* the direction or compass point midway between south and southeast.
—adj. or adv. in, toward, or from this direction.

south–south•west ['sʌuθ,sʌuθ'wɛst] *n., adj., adv. —n.* the direction or compass point midway between south and southwest.
—adj. or adv. in, toward, or from this direction.

south•ward ['sʌuθwərd] *adv., adj., n. —adv. or adj.* toward the south; south.
—n. a southward part, direction, or point.

south•ward•ly ['sʌuθwərdli] *adj., adv. —adj.* **1** toward the south. **2** of winds, coming from the south.
—adv. toward the south.

south•wards ['sʌuθwərdz] *adv.* southward.

south•west [,sʌuθ'wɛst] *n., adj., adv. —n.* **1** the direction halfway between south and west. **2** a place that is in the southwest part or direction.
—adj. or adv. of, at, in, to, toward, or from the southwest.

south•west•er [,sʌuθ'wɛstər] *or* [,saʊ'wɛstər] *n.* **1** a wind or storm from the southwest. **2** a waterproof hat having a broad brim at the back to protect the neck, worn especially by seamen. See HAT for picture. **3** an oilskin slicker worn especially by seamen and fishers in rough weather.

south•west•er•ly [,sʌuθ'wɛstərli] *adj., adv., n., pl.* **-lies.** *—adj. or adv.* toward or from the southwest.
—n. a wind from the southwest.

south•west•ern [,sʌuθ'wɛstərn] *adj.* of, at, in, to, toward, or from the southwest.

south•west•ward [,sʌuθ'wɛstwərd] *adv., adj., n. —adv. or adj.* toward the southwest.
—n. southwest.

south•west•ward•ly [,sʌuθ'wɛstwərdli] *adj., adv. —adj.* **1** toward the southwest. **2** of winds, from the southwest.
—adv. toward the southwest.

south•west•wards [,sʌuθ'wɛstwərdz] *adv.* southwestward.

sou•ve•nir [,suvə'nir] *or* ['suvə,nir] *n.* something to remind one of a place, person, or occasion; a keepsake. ⟨< F *souvenir,* originally infinitive, < L *subvenire* come to mind < *sub-* up + *venire* come⟩

souv•la•ki [suv'lɑki] *or* [suf'lɑki] *n.* a Greek dish consisting of lamb or pork cooked over an open flame on a skewer and served with tahini and Greek salad. ⟨< Mod.Gk. *soubla* skewer⟩

sou'west•er [,saʊ'wɛstər] *n.* southwester.

sov•er•eign ['sɒvrən] *or* ['sʌvrən] *n., adj. —n.* **1** a king or queen; a supreme ruler; monarch. **2** a person, group, or nation having supreme control or dominion; ruler; governor; lord; master: *sovereign of the seas.* **3** a former British gold coin, worth one pound.
—adj. **1** having the rank or power of a sovereign. **2** greatest in rank or power: *a sovereign court.* **3** independent of the control of other governments. **4** above all others; supreme; greatest: *Character is of sovereign importance.* **5** excellent or powerful: *a sovereign cure for colds.* ⟨ME < OF *soverain,* ult. < L *super* over⟩ **—'sov•er•eign•ly,** *adv.*

sov•er•eign•ty ['sɒvrənti] *or* ['sʌvrənti] *n., pl.* **-ties.** **1** supreme power or authority. **2** freedom from outside control; independence in exercising power or authority: *Countries that are satellites lack full sovereignty.* **3** a state, territory, community, etc. that is independent or sovereign. **4** rank, power, or jurisdiction of a sovereign.

sovereignty association *Cdn.* a policy proposed in the late 1970s by the Québec government, under which the province would become an independent state but would remain associated with Canada. Also, **sovereignty-association**.

so•vi•et ['souviɪt] *n., adj. —n.* **1** Often, **Soviet,** formerly in the Soviet Union and now in Russia and Uzbekistan: **a** either of two elected assemblies **(village soviets, town soviets). b** any of the higher elected assemblies. The highest assembly of all is the **Supreme Soviet. 2 Soviets,** *pl.,* the administration or the people of the former Soviet Union. **3** any council like a Russian soviet.
—adj. **1** of or having to do with soviets. **2 Soviet,** of or having to do with the former Soviet Union. ⟨< Russian *soviet* council⟩

so•vi•et•ism ['souviɪ,tɪzəm] *n.* **1** a system of government by means of soviets. **2** communism.

so•vi•et•ize ['souviɪ,taɪz] *v.* **-ized, -iz•ing.** bring under a soviet type of government; change to a soviet government.
—,so•vi•et•i'za•tion, *n.*

So•vi•et•ol•o•gy [,souviɪ'tɒlədʒi] *n.* the study of the political and economic systems of the former Soviet Union.
—,So•vi•et'ol•o•gist, *n.*

sov•ran ['sɒvrən] *n., adj. Poetic.* sovereign.

sow¹ [sou] *v.* **sowed, sown** or **sowed, sow•ing. 1** plant (seed or a crop): *It was time to begin sowing. They sowed more oats than*

wheat. **2** plant seed in: *to sow a field with rye.* **3** introduce or implant; spread or disseminate: *to sow discontent.* ⟨OE *sāwan*⟩ **—'sow•er,** *n.*
☛ *Hom.* SEW, SO, SOH.

sow² [saʊ] *n.* **1** a fully grown female pig. **2** the adult female of some other mammals, especially the bear. **3** *Metallurgy.* **a** a large mass of metal that has solidified in the common channel or sluice that conveys the molten metal from the blast furnace to the casting moulds. **b** the channel itself. ⟨OE *sugu* or *sū*⟩
☛ *Hom.* SOUGH [saʊ].

sow bug [saʊ] WOOD LOUSE.

sown [soun] *v.* a pp. of SOW¹.

sow thistle [saʊ] any composite plant of the genus *Sonchus*, having yellow flowers and thistlelike leaves; generally considered a weed.

soy [sɔɪ] *n.* **1** SOY SAUCE. **2** soybean. ⟨< Japanese, short for *shoyu* < Chinese *shi-yu* < *shi*, a type of bean + *yu* oil⟩

soy•a ['sɔɪə] *n.* soy.

soya bean soybean.

soy•bean ['sɔɪ,bin] *n.* **1** an annual bean (*Glycine max*) native to E Asia, widely cultivated for its protein-rich seeds and for forage and soil improvement. **2** the seed of this plant, used for food and livestock feed and yielding an oil used as a cooking oil and for making margarine, etc. as well as for resins, paints, chemicals, etc.

soy sauce any of several thin, dark brown sauces made from soybeans fermented in brine and used as a flavouring, especially in Chinese and Japanese cooking.

soz•zled ['sɒzəld] *adj. Informal.* drunk.

sp. **1** special. **2** specific. **3** species. **4** spelling. **5** spirits.

s.p. *Law.* without issue; childless. ⟨< L *sine prole*⟩

spa [spɑ] *n.* **1** a mineral spring. **2** a place where there is a mineral spring, especially a health resort at such a place. **3** any fashionable resort. **4** a fitness centre; a place where people can work out, take saunas, have massages, etc. **5** a whirlpool bath accommodating several people seated on a ledge around the inside. ⟨< *Spa*, a resort city in Belgium⟩

space [speis] *n., v.* **spaced, spac•ing.** *—n.* **1** the unlimited room or expanse extending in all directions and in which all material things exist: *The earth moves through space.* **2** the extent of area or volume: *We have plenty of space in this house.* **3** the unoccupied area or expanse between, over, around, and within material things. **4** a limited place or area: *a parking space.* **5** OUTER SPACE. **6** (*adjl.*) of outer space; of or for travel in outer space. **7** a given distance; a stretch: *The road is bad for the space of 10 km.* **8** a given length of time: *He has not seen his brother for the space of ten years.* **9** *Archaic.* an interval of time; a while. **10** a time in which to do something; opportunity. **11** accommodations on a train, etc. **12** a part of a surface; a blank between words, etc.: *Fill in the spaces as directed.* **13** **a** the extent or room (in a periodical, book, letter, etc.) available for, or occupied by, written or printed matter. **b** *Advertising.* the part of a page or number of lines in a periodical, newspaper, etc., or broadcast time on radio or television, available or used for advertising. **14** *Printing.* **a** one of the blank types used to separate words, etc. **b** the area left blank by such a piece of type or by other mechanical means. **15** *Music.* one of the intervals between the lines of a staff. **16** *Informal.* freedom and opportunity to pursue one's own interests independently and without interference.
—v. **1** fix the space or spaces of; divide into spaces. **2** separate by spaces: *Space your words evenly when you write.*
space out, arrange (items, or elements of a whole) with more space or time in between: *Space out the title so it will extend to both margins. If you space the interviews out a little, you won't feel so rushed.* ⟨ME < OF *espace* < L *spatium*⟩

space age the current period of history, thought of as being marked by the first efforts of human beings to explore and conquer outer space. It is usually considered to date from the launching of Sputnik I by the then Soviet Union on Oct. 4, 1957.

space bar **1** a horizontal bar at the bottom of a typewriter keyboard, used to leave a blank space in type by advancing the carriage without producing a character. **2** a similar bar at the bottom of a computer keyboard used to enter a blank space and move the cursor one character width to the right or, in conjunction with other keys or commands, to carry out some function in a program.

space capsule an unmanned spacecraft.

space•craft ['speis,kræft] *n., pl.* **space•craft.** any manned or unmanned vehicle designed for flight in outer space.

spaced–out ['speist 'ʌut] *adj. Slang.* **1** acting in a dazed or stupefied manner, as if or because of being under the influence of a narcotic. **2** out of touch with the real world. Also, **spaced.**

space heater a small electric or gas-powered unit used to heat a limited or enclosed area, as a room or part thereof.

space•less ['speislɪs] *adj.* **1** independent of space; infinite. **2** occupying no space.

space•man ['speis,mæn] *or* ['speismən] *n., pl.* **-men.** **1** a male astronaut. **2** any man, especially a scientist, concerned with space flight.

space medicine a branch of aviation medicine concerned with the effects on the human body of travel in outer space.

space•port ['speis,pɔrt] *n.* a centre for the assembly, testing, and launching of spacecraft.

spac•er ['speisər] *n.* **1** a device for spacing words, etc. as in a typesetting machine. **2** an instrument by which to reverse a telegraphic current to increase the speed of transmission.

space•ship ['speis,ʃɪp] *n.* spacecraft.

space shuttle a manned spacecraft used more than once to go from earth to a space station. It resembles an airplane, consisting of a reusable orbiter, two reusable rocket boosters, and an expendable tank of liquid propellants.

space station an artificial earth satellite to be used as an observatory or as a launching site for space ships.

space•suit ['speis,sut] an airtight suit designed to protect astronauts from radiation, heat, lack of oxygen, etc., the condition of the earth's atmosphere being maintained within the suit. Also, **space suit.**

space telescope a telescope equipped with a camera, made to orbit the earth and relay astronomical information.

space–time continuum ['speis 'taɪm] **1** the four-dimensional continuum, having three spatial co-ordinates and one temporal, in which all physical entities and events may be located. **2** the physical reality existing within this continuum.

space•walk ['speis,wɒk] *n., v.* *—n.* the action, task, or mission performed by an astronaut in outer space while outside the craft. *—v.* perform such a task: *She is looking forward to spacewalking on her next mission.*

space•ward ['speiswərd] *adj. or adv.* toward outer space.

space writer a writer for a newspaper, magazine, etc. who is paid according to the space filled by his or her copy.

spa•cial ['speiʃəl] *adj.* See SPATIAL.

spac•ing ['speisɪŋ] *n., v.* *—n.* **1** the fixing or arranging of spaces. **2** the manner in which spaces are arranged: *uneven spacing.* **3** space or spaces in printing or other work.
—v. ppr. of SPACE.

spa•cious ['speiʃəs] *adj.* **1** having or affording much space or room; large; roomy: *The rooms of the palace were spacious.* **2** of great extent or area; extensive; vast. **3** broad in scope or range; not limited or narrow; expansive: *a spacious mind.* ⟨< L *spatiosus* < *spatium* space⟩ **—'spa•cious•ly,** *adv.* **—'spa•cious•ness,** *n.*

spac•y or **spac•ey** ['speisi] *Slang.* **-i•er, -i•est.** spaced-out.

spade¹ [speid] *n., v.* **spad•ed, spad•ing.** *—n.* **1** a tool for digging, having a relatively flat blade which can be pressed into the ground with the foot, and a long handle with a grip or crosspiece at the top. **2** any implement resembling a spade.
call a spade a spade, call a thing by its real name; speak plainly and frankly.
—v. **1** dig with a spade. **2** cut, remove, or dig up with a spade or similar instrument. ⟨OE *spadu*; akin to L *spatha.* See SPADE².⟩ **—'spade,like,** *adj.*

spade² [speid] *n.* **1** a black figure (♠) used on playing cards. **2** a playing card bearing such figures. **3** **spades,** *pl.* the suit of playing cards bearing such figures, usually the highest ranking suit in card games.
in spades, *Informal.* to an extreme degree; very emphatically. ⟨< Ital. *spada* < L *spatha* < Gk. *spathē* sword, broad blade⟩

spade•fish ['speid,fɪʃ] *n.* any of a family (Ephippidae) of spiny-finned, flat, percoid food fishes found off the American Atlantic coast.

spade•ful ['speidfəl] *n., pl.* **-fuls.** the amount that can be dug out with or carried on a spade.

spade•work ['speid,wərk] *n.* preliminary or preparatory work on which further work is to be based, as data-gathering, especially when regarded as difficult or tedious.

A jack-in-the-pulpit (left) and a calla lily (right)

spa•dix ['speidɪks] *n., pl.* **spa•dix•es** or **spa•di•ces** ['speidə,siz] *or* [spei'daisiz]. *Botany.* a spike composed of minute flowers on a fleshy stem. A spadix is usually enclosed in a petal-like leaf called a spathe, as in the jack-in-the-pulpit and the calla lily. ⟨< L < Gk. *spadix* palm branch⟩

spaet•zle or **spät•zle** ['ʃpɛtslə] *n.pl.* a German dumpling or handmade noodles produced by pressing an egg dough through a colander and boiling the result in stock. ⟨< G dial.⟩

spa•ghet•ti [spə'gɛti] *n.* **1** long, slender sticks made of pasta, soft when cooked: *Spaghetti is thinner than macaroni.* **2** *Electricity.* an insulating cloth or plastic tube used for covering bare wire or holding a group of insulated wires together. ⟨< Ital. *spaghetti*, pl. dim. of *spago* cord⟩

spa•ghet•ti•ni [,spægɛ'tini] *n.* pasta in strands thinner than spaghetti but not as thin as vermicelli. ⟨< Ital. dim. of *spaghetti*⟩

spaghetti squash a large squash (*Cucurbita pepo*), the flesh of which tends to separate into strands when cooked.

Spain [spein] *n.* a country in southern Europe sharing the Iberian peninsula with Portugal.

spake [speik] *v. Archaic.* a pt. of SPEAK.

spall [spɒl] *n., v.* —*n.* a chip, splinter, or small piece of stone or ore.
—*v.* **1** break up roughly, split, or chip (ore), especially to prepare it for sorting. **2** chip off, especially at the edges. A stone may spall under pressure. ⟨ME *spalle*⟩

spall•a•tion [spɒ'leiʃən] *n. Physics.* a nuclear reaction in which a nucleus breaks up under bombardment and ejects particles or photons.

Sp.Am. Spanish American.

span[1] [spæn] *n., v.* **spanned, span•ning.** —*n.* **1** the distance between two supports: *The arch had a span of 15 m.* **2** the part between two supports: *The bridge crossed the river in three spans.* **3** a space of time, as the period of life of a person. **4** the full extent: *the span of a bridge, the span of memory.* **5** wingspan. **6** a unit for measuring length based on the distance between the tip of the thumb and the tip of the little finger of a spread-out hand; about 18 to 23 cm.
—*v.* **1** measure by the hand spread out: *This post can be spanned by one's two hands.* **2** encircle or encompass (the waist, wrist, etc.) with the hand or hands. **3** extend over: *A bridge spanned the river.* **4** provide with something that extends over or across: *to span a river with a bridge.* ⟨OE *spann*⟩

span[2] [spæn] *n.* a pair of horses, mules, etc. harnessed and driven together. ⟨< Du. or LG *span* < *spannen* stretch, yoke⟩

span[3] [spæn] *v. Archaic.* a pt. of SPIN.

span•dex ['spændɛks] *n. Chemistry.* a very light, synthetic elastic fibre composed of a long-chain polymer of polyurethane, used especially in swimsuits and women's undergarments. ⟨anagram of *expands*⟩

span•drel ['spændrəl] *n. Architecture.* **1** the triangular space between the curve of an arch and the rectangular moulding or framework enclosing the arch. **2** the space between the curves of two adjacent arches and the moulding above them. See ARCH for picture. Also, **spandril.** ⟨ME *spandrell* < AF *spaundre* ? < OF *espander* expand⟩

spang [spæŋ] *adv. Informal.* directly, with a smack; exactly on the mark. ⟨perhaps < dial. *spang* a jerk, smack⟩

span•gle ['spæŋgəl] *n., v.* **-gled, -gling.** —*n.* **1** a small piece of glittering metal, plastic, etc. used for decoration: *The dress was covered with spangles.* **2** any small, bright bit.
—*v.* **1** decorate with spangles. **2** sprinkle with, or as if with, small, bright bits: *The sky is spangled with stars.* **3** glitter. ⟨dim. of earlier *spang*, probably < MDu. *spange* brooch⟩ —**'span•gly,** *adj.*

Span•iard ['spænjərd] *n.* a native or inhabitant of Spain.

span•iel ['spænjəl] *n.* **1** any of several breeds of dog, usually of small or medium size, having long, silky hair and drooping ears. **2** a person who yields too easily to others. ⟨ME < OF *espagneul*, originally, Spanish < L *Hispania* Spain⟩

Span•ish ['spænɪʃ] *n., adj.* —*n.* **1 the Spanish,** *pl.* the people of Spain. **2** the Romance language of Spain and most countries of South America.
—*adj.* of or having to do with Spain, Spaniards, or Spanish.

Span•ish–A•mer•i•can ['spænɪʃ ə'mɛrəkən] *adj., n.* —*adj.* **1** of or having to do with Spain and America, or with Spain and the United States. **2** of, having to do with, or designating **Spanish America,** the parts of America where Spanish is the prevailing language.
—*n.* **Spanish American,** a native or inhabitant of a Spanish-American country, especially a person of Spanish descent.

Spanish Armada the great fleet sent by Philip II of Spain to attack England in 1588, defeated by the English under the command of Sir Francis Drake.

Spanish bayonet any of several yuccas, especially a treelike species (*Yucca aloifolia*) having stiff, spearlike, spine-tipped leaves, and clusters of white flowers.

Spanish fly **1** a bright green blister beetle (*Lytta vesicatoria*) of S Europe. Also called **cantharis. 2** a powder made from the crushed wing covers of these beetles, used in medicine as a counterirritant, diuretic, and aphrodisiac.

Spanish Inquisition **1** the body of men appointed during the Renaissance by the Roman Catholic Church to suppress heresy in Spain. It was put under state control at the end of the 15th century and was very active during the 16th century. **2** the activities of this body of men.

Spanish Main formerly, **1** the mainland of America adjacent to the Caribbean Sea, especially between the mouth of the Orinoco River and the Isthmus of Panama. **2** in later use, the Caribbean Sea.

Spanish moss a greyish green air plant (*Tillandsia usneoides*) of the pineapple family found in tropical and warm temperate America, and growing as very long, beardlike masses hanging from trees.

Spanish omelette an omelette containing chopped onion, tomato, and green pepper.

Spanish onion a large, mild, juicy onion often eaten raw in sandwiches, hamburgers, salads, etc.

Spanish rice rice cooked with chopped onions, tomato, and green pepper.

spank[1] [spæŋk] *v., n.* —*v.* strike, usually on the buttocks, with the open hand, especially as a punishment for a child.
—*n.* such a blow. ⟨imitative⟩ —**'spank•er,** *n.*

spank[2] [spæŋk] *v. Informal.* go quickly and vigorously; move at a speedy rate. ⟨probably back formation from *spanking[2]*⟩

spank•er ['spæŋkər] *n.* **1 a** a fore-and-aft sail on the mast nearest the stern of a square-rigged vessel. **b** a similar sail on a schooner-rigged vessel having three or more masts. **2** *Informal.* a fast horse. **3** *Informal.* anything fine, large, unusual for its kind, etc. ⟨apparently < *spanking[2]* or *spank[2]* move fast⟩

spank•ing[1] ['spæŋkɪŋ] *n., v.* —*n.* a slap or series of slaps with the open hand, especially on the buttocks, as a punishment for children.
—*v.* ppr. of SPANK[1].

spank•ing[2] ['spæŋkɪŋ] *adj., adv., v.* —*adj.* brisk; lively; vigorous: *a spanking breeze, a spanking team of horses.*
—*adv. Informal.* extremely; thoroughly: *a spanking good time, spanking clean.*
(brand) spanking new, *Informal.* completely new.
—*v.* ppr. of SPANK[2]. ⟨Cf. Danish *spanke* strut⟩

span•less ['spænlɪs] *adj.* that cannot be spanned.

span•ner ['spænər] *n.* **1** any thing or person that spans. **2** *Esp. Brit.* a tool for holding and turning a nut, bolt, etc.; wrench.
put or **throw a spanner in the works,** create difficulty.

spar[1] [spɑr] *n., v.* **sparred, spar•ring.** —*n.* **1** a stout pole used to support or extend the sails of a ship; mast, yard, boom, etc. of a ship. **2** the main beam of an airplane wing. **3** a large pole or boom used as part of a crane or derrick.
—*v.* provide (a ship) with spars. ⟨ME *sparre*, akin to OE *spere* spear; cf. ON *sparri*, MDu. *sparre*⟩

spar[2] [spɑr] *v.* **sparred, spar•ring;** *n.* —*v.* **1** box with feinting movements or light blows, as when training. **2** dispute or wrangle. **3** of a gamecock, fight with the feet or spurs.

—*n.* **1** a sparring movement. **2** a boxing match. **3** a dispute. ⟨< MF *esparer* kick < Ital. *sparare* fling < *s-*, intensive (< L *ex-*) + *parare* parry⟩

spar³ [spɑr] *n.* a shiny, crystalline mineral that splits into flakes easily. ⟨OE *spær-*; cf. *spæren* gypsum⟩ **—'spar,like,** *adj.*

spar deck *Nautical.* the upper deck extending from one end of a ship to the other.

spare [spɛr] *v.* **spared, spar•ing;** *adj.* **spar•er, spar•est;** *n.* —*v.* **1** show mercy to; refrain from harming or destroying: *He spared his enemy.* **2** show consideration for; save from labour, pain, etc.: *We walked uphill to spare the horse.* **3** get along without; do without: *Father couldn't spare the car, so Iris had to walk.* **4** make (a person, etc.) free from (something); relieve or exempt (a person, etc.) from (something): *She did the work to spare you the trouble.* **5** use in small quantities or not at all; be saving of: *We spared no expense.* **6** have free or available for use: *Can you spare the time? I have no money to spare.*
(enough and) to spare, more than enough; plenty.
not spare oneself, do one's utmost.
—*adj.* **1** free for other use: *spare time.* **2** extra; in reserve: *a spare tire.* **3** thin; lean: *The speaker was a tall, spare man.* **4** small in quantity; meagre; scanty: *a spare diet.*
—*n.* **1** an extra or duplicate person or thing: *We have five tires, including a spare.* **2** *Bowling.* **a** the knocking down of all the pins with two rolls of a ball. **b** the score made in this way. ⟨OE *sparian*⟩ **—'spare•ly,** *adv.* **—'spare•ness,** *n.* **—'spar•er,** *n.*

spare•rib ['spɛr,rɪb] *n.* a rib of meat, especially pork, having less meat than the ribs near the loins. See PORK for picture. ⟨transposition of *ribspare* < MLG *ribbespēr* rib cut⟩

spar•ing ['spɛrɪŋ] *adj., v.* —*adj.* **1** that spares. **2** avoiding waste; economical; frugal: *a sparing use of sugar. He is very sparing of his time.*
—*v.* ppr. of SPARE. **—'spar•ing•ly,** *adv.* **—'spar•ing•ness,** *n.*

spark [spɑrk] *n., v.* —*n.* **1** a tiny particle of flame or burning material: *The burning wood threw off sparks.* **2** *Electricity.* **a** a flash given off when electricity jumps across an open space. An electric spark explodes the gas in the engine of an automobile. **b** the discharge occurring at the same time. **3** a flash; gleam: *a spark of light.* **4** the smallest amount: *I haven't a spark of interest in the plan.* **5** life or vitality. **6** a glittering bit. **7 sparks,** *pl.* (*with singular verb*) or **Sparks** (*as term of address*). *Slang.* the radio operator of a ship.
—*v.* **1** flash; gleam. **2** send out small bits of fire; produce sparks. **3** operate properly in forming sparks, as the ignition in an internal-combustion engine. **4** stir to activity; stimulate: *to spark a revolt, to spark sales, ideas, etc.* ⟨OE *spearca*⟩ **—'spark•less,** *adj.* **—'spark•less•ly,** *adv.* **—'spark,like,** *adj.*

spark chamber *Physics.* a device for detecting charged or ionizing elementary particles, consisting of a set of oppositely charged metal plates separated by an inert gas, so that the passage of a charged particle ionizes the gas and causes a spark between the plates.

spark coil *Electricity.* an induction coil for producing sparks.

spark gap *Electricity.* the space between two electrodes, in which sparks occur.

spar•kle ['spɑrkəl] *v.* **-kled, -kling;** *n.* —*v.* **1** send out little sparks: *The fireworks sparkled.* **2** shine; glitter; flash; gleam: *The diamonds sparkled.* **3** be brilliant; be lively: *Her wit sparkles.* **4** bubble: *Ginger ale sparkles.* **5** cause to sparkle.
—*n.* **1** a little spark. **2** a shine; glitter; flash; gleam: *I like the sparkle of her eyes.* **3** brilliance; liveliness: *We admired the sparkle of his wit.* ⟨< *spark¹*⟩
☛ *Syn. n.* **2.** See note at FLASH.

spar•kler ['spɑrklər] *n.* **1** a person or thing that sparkles. **2** a hand-held firework, in the form of a specially coated metal stick, that sends out profuse showers of little sparks. **3** *Informal.* a sparkling gem, especially a diamond.

spark plug **1** a device in the cylinder of a gasoline engine by which the mixture of gasoline and air is exploded by an electric spark. See CYLINDER for picture. **2** *Informal.* a person who gives energy or enthusiasm to others.

spar•ring partner ['spɑrɪŋ] **1** a boxer or any person who spars with a professional boxer as a form of practice or training. **2** a person with whom one habitually engages in friendly debate for mutual stimulation, refining one's ideas, etc.

spar•row ['spærou] *or* ['spɛrou] *n.* **1** any of a genus (*Passer*) of small, dull-coloured weaverbirds, especially the English sparrow. See ENGLISH SPARROW. **2** any of various North American finches or other similar related birds having brown and grey streaked plumage. See CHIPPING SPARROW, SONG SPARROW. ⟨OE *spearwa*⟩

sparrow hawk **1** a small North American falcon (*Falco sparverius*) having mainly reddish brown upper parts and white or buff under parts, spotted and barred with black, and feeding on large insects, such as grasshoppers and caterpillars, and on mice and some small birds. **2** any of several small hawks, especially an Old World species (*Accipiter nisus*) that feeds exclusively on small birds, especially sparrows.

spar•ry ['spɑri] *adj.* resembling or containing mineral spar.

sparse [spɑrs] *adj.* **spars•er, spars•est. 1** thinly scattered; occurring here and there: *a sparse population, sparse hair.* **2** scanty; meagre. ⟨< L *sparsus,* pp. of *spargere* scatter⟩ **—'sparse•ly,** *adv.* **—'sparse•ness** or **'spar•si•ty,** *n.*
☛ *Syn.* See note at SCANTY.

Spar•tan ['spɑrtən] *n., adj.* —*n.* **1** a native or inhabitant of Sparta, a city in ancient Greece. The Spartans were noted for their simplicity of life, severity, courage, and brevity of speech. **2** a person who is courageous, self-denying, disciplined, etc.
—*adj.* **1** of or having to do with Sparta or its people. **2** like that of the Spartans: *Spartan courage, Spartan endurance.* **3** characterized by sternness, frugality, simplicity, self-discipline, etc.: *a Spartan upbringing.*

Spar•tan•ism ['spɑrtə,nɪzəm] *n.* **1** the beliefs and methods of ancient Sparta. **2** any discipline, method, etc. like that of the ancient Spartans.

spar tree *Lumbering.* part of an arrangement for facilitating the hauling of logs, consisting of a tall tree trimmed of its top and branches, strengthened with guy ropes, and rigged with a heavy cable on pulleys which is also attached to stumps at various points within a radius of several hundred metres. A machine moves the cable, to which logs are hooked by one end at some distance from the ground, dragging them from the cutting area to the yard to be piled.

spasm ['spæzəm] *n.* **1** a sudden, involuntary contraction of a muscle or muscles. **2** any sudden, brief fit or spell of unusual energy or activity: *a spasm of temper, a spasm of industry.* ⟨< L < Gk. *spasmos* < *spaein* draw up, tear away⟩

spas•mod•ic [spæz'mɒdɪk] *adj.* **1** having to do with spasms; resembling a spasm: *a spasmodic cough.* **2** sudden and violent, but brief; occurring very irregularly or in bursts. **3** disjointed; choppy: *a spasmodic style, spasmodic writing.* ⟨< Med.L *spasmodicus* < Gk. *spasmōdēs* < *spasmos.* See SPASM.⟩ **—spas'mod•i•cal•ly,** *adv.*

spas•tic ['spæstɪk] *adj. Pathology.* **1** caused by a spasm or spasms. **2** of, having to do with, or characterized by spasms. **3** having or related to spastic paralysis. ⟨< L < Gk. *spastikos* < *spaein* draw up⟩

spastic paralysis *Pathology.* a condition, symptomatic of cerebral palsy, in which the muscles are in a continuous state of contraction and the reflexes of tendons are greatly increased, resulting in immobility of the affected body parts.

spat¹ [spæt] *n., v.* **spat•ted, spat•ting.** —*n.* a slight quarrel. —*v.* have a slight quarrel. ⟨? imitative⟩

spat² [spæt] *v.* a pt. and a pp. of SPIT¹.

spat³ [spæt] *n.* a short, usually cloth gaiter covering the ankle and instep, worn by men especially in the late 19th and early 20th centuries and also by women in the early 20th century. ⟨short for *spatterdash*⟩

spat⁴ [spæt] *n., v.* **spat•ted, spat•ting.** —*n.* the spawn of oysters; young oyster.
—*v.* of oysters, spawn. ⟨origin uncertain. Perhaps related to SPIT¹.⟩

spate [speit] *n.* **1** a flood; downpour. **2** a sudden outburst: *a spate of words, a spate of advertising.* ⟨ME; related to OE *spātan* spit⟩

spa•tha•ceous [spə'θeiʃəs] *n.* of, like, or having a spathe. Also, **spathose** ['speiθous].

spathe [speið] *n. Botany.* a large bract or pair of bracts that enclose a flower cluster. The calla lily has a white spathe around a yellow flower cluster. See SPADIX for picture. ⟨< Gk. *spathē* palm branch, oar blade⟩ **—spathed,** *adj.*

spath•ic ['spæθɪk] *adj. Mineralogy.* of or like spar; especially, chipping or flaking easily like spar. Also, **spathose** ['spæθous]. ⟨< G *spath* < MHG *spat* spar⟩

spa•tial ['speiʃəl] *adj.* **1** of or having to do with space. **2** existing in space. **3** occupying or taking up space. ⟨< L *spatium* space⟩ —**,spa•ti'al•i•ty** [,speiʃi'ælɪti], *n.*

spa•tial•ly ['speiʃəli] *adv.* in spatial respects; so far as space is concerned; in space.

spa•tio–tem•po•ral ['speiʃou 'tɛmpərəl] *adj.* **1** of or existing or occurring in both space and time. **2** referring to the SPACE-TIME CONTINUUM. Also, **spatiotemporal.** ⟨< L *spatium* space + E *temporal*⟩ —**'spa•tio-'tem•po•ral•ly,** *adv.*

spat•ter ['spætər] *v., n.* —*v.* **1** scatter or dash in drops or particles: *to spatter mud.* **2** fall in drops or particles: *Rain spatters on the sidewalk.* **3** strike in a shower; strike in a number of places: *Bullets spattered the wall.* **4** splash or spot with mud, paint, etc. **5** stain with slander, disgrace, etc.
—*n.* **1** a spattering: *a spatter of hail.* **2** the sound of spattering. **3** a splash or spot. ⟨Cf. Du. or LG *spatten* splash; akin to Flemish *spatteren* spatter⟩

spat•ter•dash ['spætər,dæʃ] *n.* a high leather legging worn especially in the 18th century as protection from mud when riding, etc.

spat•ter•dock ['spætər,dɒk] *n.* any of several water lilies (genus *Nuphar*), especially a common, yellow species (*N. advenum*) of E North America. ⟨< obs. *splatterdock* < *splatter* + *dock*[4]⟩

spat•u•la ['spætʃələ] *n.* a tool with a broad, flat, flexible blade, used in cooking and baking, for mixing drugs, for spreading paints, etc. ⟨< L *spatula,* dim. of *spatha* flat blade < Gk. *spathē*⟩

spat•u•late ['spætʃəlɪt] *or* ['spætʃə,leit] *adj.* **1** shaped like a spatula; rounded somewhat like a spoon. **2** *Botany.* having a broad, rounded end and a narrow base: *a spatulate leaf.* **3** wide at the tips: *spatulate fingers.*

spav•in ['spævən] *n.* a disease of horses in which a bony swelling forms at the hock, causing lameness. ⟨ME < OF *espavain,* probably < Gmc.⟩ —**'spav•ined,** *adj.*

spawn [spɒn] *n., v.* —*n.* **1** the eggs of fish, frogs, shellfish, etc. **2** young fish, frogs, etc. when newly hatched from such eggs. **3** (*used especially of something or someone undesirable*) **a** offspring, especially a large number of offspring. **b** a product; result. **4** the mass of white, threadlike fibres from which fungi grow; mycelium, especially as prepared for growing mushrooms.
—*v.* **1** of fish, etc., produce or deposit (eggs): *Salmon spawn in the rivers of British Columbia.* **2** give birth to; bring forth (*usually something undesirable*) in great quantity: *The comedian spent ten minutes spawning poor jokes.* ⟨ME < OF *espandre* < L *expandere* spread out. Doublet of EXPAND.⟩ —**'spawn•er,** *n.*

spay [spei] *v.* remove the ovaries, or in some cases the ovaries and uterus, of (a female animal). ⟨ME < AF *espeir,* ult. < OF *espee* sword < L *spatha.* See SPADE[2].⟩

SPCA or **S.P.C.A.** Society for the Prevention of Cruelty to Animals.

speak [spik] *v.* **spoke** or (*archaic*) **spake, spok•en** or (*archaic*) **spoke, speak•ing. 1** say words; talk: *A cat cannot speak. Speak distinctly.* **2** converse or consult: *They spoke together for over an hour.* **3** say; utter: *She didn't speak a word the whole time we were there.* **4** give a speech or lecture: *Who is going to speak at the forum? She spoke to them about law reform.* **5** tell; express; make known: *Speak the truth.* **6** use or know how to use in speaking, as a language: *I couldn't understand what they said because they were speaking Gaelic. Do you speak Swedish?* **7** express (an idea, feeling, etc.); communicate: *Their eyes spoke. His expression spoke deep sorrow.* **8** make a plea, request, application, reservation, etc. (*used with* **for**): *to speak for seats ahead of time.* **9** serve as spokesperson; represent (*used with* **for**): *She spoke for us all.* **10** make a statement or mention (*used with* **of, about,** *etc.*): *They spoke of renovating their house.* **11** give forth a characteristic sound: *The cannon spoke.* **12** be an indication or evidence: *His clothing speaks of wealth. It was an unselfish action that spoke well for her.* **13** of dogs, bark when told: *Speak for the biscuit, Dusty!* **14** *Archaic.* show to be; characterize as: *His conduct speaks him honourable.*
so to speak, to speak in such a manner.
speak for itself, be self-evident or self-explanatory.
speak out or **up, a** speak loudly and clearly. **b** speak freely and without restraint: *They were all too frightened to speak out.*
speak volumes. See VOLUME.
speak well for, be evidence for or in favour of.
to speak of, of any significance (*used with negatives and interrogatives*): *I have no complaints to speak of.* ⟨OE *specan*⟩

☛ *Syn.* **Speak,** TALK = say or use words. **Speak,** somewhat more formal, emphasizes the uttering of clear and distinct speech sounds and the saying of words, and usually suggests that there is a definite hearer or audience and that the sounds and words are logically or grammatically connected: *Professor Randolph will speak on nuclear energy.* **Talk** emphasizes using words interactively, in conversation, but often suggests more or less meaningless continued speaking, or the basic facility of uttering words, whether in connected discourse or not: *Some people are always talking. Ashley was already talking at 15 months of age.* Also, **speak** may take a direct object; **talk** does so only in very informal usage or in certain fixed expressions: *Do you speak French? Don't speak a word. Don't talk nonsense!*

speak•eas•y ['spik,izi] *n., pl.* **-eas•ies.** *Esp. U.S. Slang.* during the era of prohibition, a place where alcoholic liquors were sold contrary to law.

speak•er ['spikər] *n.* **1** a person who speaks, especially one who speaks before an audience: *Our next speaker is Professor Chapman.* **2** a person who speaks on behalf of others; spokesman or spokeswoman. **3 Speaker,** a person who presides over an assembly: *the Speaker of the House of Commons.* **4** loudspeaker.

Speaker of the House 1 in Canada and the United Kingdom, the presiding officer of the House of Commons. **2** in the United States, the presiding officer of the House of Representatives.

speak•er•phone ['spikər,foun] *n.* **1** a telephone equipped with microphone and loudspeaker, so that no handpiece is needed and more than one person can participate in the call. **2** a special function on a telephone activating or deactivating this equipment: *When the conversation became more intimate, he switched off the speakerphone.*

speak•er•ship ['spikər,ʃɪp] *n.* the position of presiding officer.

speak•ing ['spikɪŋ] *n., adj., v.* —*n.* the act, utterance, or discourse of a person who speaks.
—*adj.* **1** that speaks or seems to speak; giving information as if by speech; expressive: *a speaking example of a thing, speaking eyes.* **2** used in, suited to, or involving speech: *a speaking part in a play.* **3** permitting conversation: *on speaking terms, a speaking acquaintance with a person, within speaking distance.* **4** lifelike: *a speaking likeness.*
—*v.* ppr. of SPEAK.

speaking in tongues a phenomenon reported in the New Testament and still today, in which a person in a religious ecstasy utters sounds which may or may not be those of another language unknown to the speaker and which are believed to be inspired by God; glossolalia.

speaking tube a device used to convey the voice over a limited distance, as within a house or ship.

spear[1] [spir] *n., v.* —*n.* **1** a weapon having a long shaft and a sharp-pointed head. **2** an instrument having a similar form but forked at one end, used especially for catching fish.
—*v.* **1** pierce with a spear: *to spear a fish.* **2** pierce or stab with anything sharp. **3** *Hockey.* check (an opponent) illegally by stabbing with the point of the stick blade. **4** *Football.* block (an opponent) with the helmet instead of with the body. ⟨OE *spere*⟩ —**'spear•er,** *n.*

spear[2] [spir] *n., v.* —*n.* a sprout or shoot of a plant: *a spear of grass.*
—*v.* sprout or shoot into a long stem. ⟨var. of *spire*[1]; influenced by *spear*[1]⟩

spear grass *Cdn.* any of a number of grasses of the genus *Stipa* having lance-shaped leaves and sharp-pointed, bearded fruits capable of piercing skin or flesh.

spear•head ['spir,hɛd] *n., v.* —*n.* **1** the sharp-pointed striking end of a spear. **2** the part, person, or group that comes first in an attack, undertaking, etc.: *She was the spearhead of the project to make the park here.*
—*v.* go first in (an attack, undertaking, etc.): *Tanks spearheaded the army's advance.*

spear•man ['spirmən] *n., pl.* **-men.** a soldier armed with a spear.

spear•mint ['spir,mɪnt] *n.* a European mint (*Mentha spicata*) widely cultivated for its aromatic leaves, which yield an oil used for flavouring. ⟨< *spear*[1] + *mint*[1]; from the shape of the inflorescence⟩

spear side the paternal side or branch of a family. Compare DISTAFF SIDE.

spec [spɛk] *n. Informal.* **1** Usually, **specs,** *pl.* specifications. **2 specs,** *pl.* spectacles, eyeglasses. **3** SPECULATION (defs. 3, 4).
on spec, in the hope but with no assurance of making a profit.

spec. 1 special. **2** specification. **3** speculation.

spe•cial [spɛʃəl] *adj., n. —adj.* **1** of a particular kind; different from others: *This desk has a special lock.* **2** not general; individual. **3** more than ordinary; unusual; exceptional: *Today's topic is of special interest.* **4** held in unusually high regard; valued in an exceptional way: *a special friend, a special favourite.* **5** for a particular person, thing, purpose, etc.: *The railway ran special trains on holidays. Send the letter by a special messenger.*
—n. **1** a special train, car, bus, etc. **2** any special person or thing. **3** a special edition of a newspaper. **4** in a store, restaurant, etc., a product that is specially featured; bargain: *a weekend special.* **5** a specially produced television show, not one of the regular daily or weekly programs. **6** *Cdn.* SPECIAL CONSTABLE. ⟨ME < L *specialis* < *species* appearance. Doublet of ESPECIAL.⟩
☛ *Syn. adj.* **Special,** PARTICULAR = not general, but belonging or relating to one person, thing, or group, as distinguished from others. **Special** emphasizes the idea of qualities making one different from others of its kind, or other kinds, and giving it a character, nature, use, etc. of its own: *Babies need special food.* **Particular** emphasizes the idea of pertaining to one considered as an individual, apart from all others of the same kind or covered by a general statement: *These synonym studies give both the general and particular meanings of words.*

special constable *Cdn.* a person sworn in for special duty as a police constable, especially with the RCMP.

special delivery the delivery of a letter or package by a special messenger rather than by the regular letter carrier. Special delivery mail is handled faster than regular mail.

special effects *Film. Television.* complex visual and sound effects beyond the normal range of photography and recording, such as thunder and lightning, distortions of sight or sound, shape or size changes, etc.

spe•cial•ism ['spɛʃə,lɪzəm] *n.* devotion or restriction to one particular branch of study, business, etc.

spe•cial•ist ['spɛʃəlɪst] *n.* a person who devotes or restricts himself or herself to one particular branch of study, business, etc.: *Dr. White is a specialist in diseases of the nose and throat.*

spe•ci•al•i•ty [,spɛʃi'æləti] *n., pl.* **-ties. 1** the state of being special; specialness. **2** a special quality or characteristic; the distinctive characteristic or feature of a thing. **3** a special point; particular; detail. **4** *Brit.* a special pursuit, branch, product, etc.; specialty.

spe•cial•ize ['spɛʃə,laɪz] *v.* **-ized, -iz•ing. 1** pursue some special branch of study, work, etc.: *Many students specialize in engineering.* **2** adapt to special conditions; give special form, use, duty, etc. to; limit. **3** develop in a special way; take on a special form, use, etc. **4** mention specially; specify. **5** go into particulars. **—,spe•cial•i'za•tion,** *n.*

spe•cial•ly ['spɛʃəli] *adv.* in a special manner or degree or for a special purpose; particularly.
☛ *Usage.* See note at ESPECIALLY.

spe•cial•ty ['spɛʃəlti] *n., pl.* **-ties. 1** a special field of study; special line of work, profession, trade, etc.: *Repairing watches is his specialty.* **2** a product, article, etc. to which special attention is given: *This store makes a specialty of children's clothes.* **3** a special or particular characteristic; peculiarity. **4** a special point or item; particular; detail. **5** *Law.* a sealed contract or deed. **6** *(adjl.)* of stores or shops or their goods, specialized; appealing or catering to a certain type of clientele. ⟨ME < OF *(e)specialte* < L *specialitas* < *specialis.* See SPECIAL.⟩

spe•ci•a•tion [,spiʃi'eiʃən] *or* [,spisi'eiʃən] *n. Biology.* the coming into existence of new species in the course of evolution, generally as a result of ecological or physical factors, such as isolation, that prevent previously interbreeding populations from continuing to do so. **—'spe•ci,ate,** *v.*

spe•cie ['spiʃi] *n.* money in the form of coins; metal money. Loonies are specie.
in specie, a in coin. **b** in kind. ⟨< L *(in) specie,* abl. of *species* kind⟩

spe•cies ['spiʃiz] *or* ['spisiz] *n., pl.* **-cies. 1** *Biology.* the narrowest major category in the classification of plants and animals; the major subdivision of a genus or subgenus. See classification chart in the Appendix. **2** kind or sort: *a species of advertisement.* **3** *Roman Catholic or Eastern Orthodox Church.* **a** the consecrated bread and wine of the Eucharist. **b** their natural physical form and properties unchanged by consecration. **4** *Logic.* a class of objects or individuals having certain characteristics in common and included with other similar classes in a larger grouping or genus. **5 the species,** the human race. ⟨< L *species* appearance, sort, form. Doublet of SPICE.⟩

specif. specifically.

spe•cif•ic [spə'sɪfɪk] *adj., n. —adj.* **1** definite; precise; particular: *There was no specific reason for the quarrel.* **2** of a particular or special kind; serving a particular purpose. **3** characteristic; peculiar or distinguishing: *A scaly skin is a specific feature of snakes.* **4** curing some particular disease. **5** produced by some special cause. **6** *Biology.* of or having to do with a species. **7** *Physics.* being that of a given substance or object relative to a fixed standard or unit. **8** (*often used in compounds*) uniquely applicable to or determined by: *gender-specific, culture-specific. Genius is not specific to race.*
—n. **1** any particular statement, quality, fact, detail, etc. **2** *Medicine.* a cure for some particular disease: *Quinine is a specific for malaria.* ⟨< LL *specificus* constituting a species < L *species* sort + *facere* make⟩ **—spe'cif•i•cal•ly,** *adv.* **—spe'cif•ic•ness,** *n.*

spec•i•fi•ca•tion [,spɛsəfə'keiʃən] *n.* **1** the act of specifying; a definite mention: *Mary made careful specification of the kinds of cake and candy for her party.* **2** Usually, **specifications,** *pl.* a detailed written description of the dimensions, materials, performance standards, etc. for a building, road, computer, boat, etc.: *The repairs had not been done according to specifications.* **3** something specified; a particular item, article, etc. **4** *Patent law.* a detailed statement of particulars.

specific duty a customs duty on a specified article or quantity of articles, regardless of its market value.

specific gravity RELATIVE DENSITY. *Abbrev.:* s.g. or sp.gr.

specific heat *Physics.* **1** a number that expresses the ratio of the quantity of heat needed to raise the temperature of a given substance one Celsius degree to that needed to raise the temperature of an equal mass of water one degree: *The specific heat of aluminum is about 0.2.* **2** SPECIFIC HEAT CAPACITY.

specific heat capacity *Physics.* the quantity of heat needed to raise the temperature of one unit of a substance one Celsius degree.

specific impulse *Rocketry.* a measure of the efficiency of a rocket engine. It is the thrust delivered in a given time per unit weight of propellant expended.

spec•i•fic•i•ty [,spɛsə'fɪsəti] *n.* the condition or quality of being specific.

specific resistance *Electricity.* the electrical resistance between two opposite surfaces of a one-centimetre cube of a given substance; resistivity.

spec•i•fy ['spɛsə,faɪ] *v.* **-fied, -fy•ing. 1** mention or name definitely; state or describe in detail: *Did you specify any particular time for us to call?* **2** include in the specifications: *The contractor would have used cement blocks, but bricks were specified.* **3** stipulate or provide explicitly as a condition. ⟨ME < OF < LL *specificare* < *specificus.* See SPECIFIC.⟩ **—,spec•i'fi•a•ble,** *adj.* **—'spec•i,fi•er,** *n.*

spec•i•men ['spɛsəmən] *n., adj. —n.* **1** one of a group or class taken to show what the others are like; a single part, thing, etc. regarded as an example of its kind: *The statue was a fine specimen of Greek sculpture.* **2** *Informal.* a human being; person: *The professor was an odd specimen.* **3** *Medicine.* a sample of some bodily excretion for laboratory analysis.
—adj. that is a specimen. ⟨< L *specimen* < *specere* view⟩

spe•ci•os•i•ty [,spiʃi'ɒsəti] *n., pl.* **-ties. 1** the quality of being specious. **2** a specious act, appearance, remark, etc.

spe•cious ['spiʃəs] *adj.* **1** seeming desirable, reasonable, or probable, but not really so; apparently good or right, but without real merit: *The teacher saw through John's specious excuse.* **2** making a good outward appearance in order to deceive: *His dishonest actions showed him to be nothing but a specious hypocrite.* ⟨< L *speciosus* < *species* appearance⟩ **—'spe•cious•ly,** *adv.* **—'spe•cious•ness,** *n.*

speck [spɛk] *n., v. —n.* **1** a small spot; stain: *Can you clean the specks off this wallpaper?* **2** a tiny bit; particle: *I have a speck in my eye. She hasn't a speck of decency.*
—v. mark with specks: *This fruit is badly specked.* ⟨OE *specca*⟩

speck•le ['spɛkəl] *n., v.* **-led, -ling.** *—n.* a small spot or mark: *This hen is grey with white speckles.*
—v. mark with speckles.

speckled char or **trout** BROOK TROUT.

spec•ta•cle ['spɛktəkəl] *n.* **1** something to look at; sight: *The children at play among the flowers made a charming spectacle.* **2** a public show or display: *The big parade was a fine spectacle.* **3** a person or thing set before the public view as an object of curiosity, contempt, wonder, or admiration. **4 spectacles,** *pl.* **a** a pair of glasses to help a person's sight or to protect the eyes. **b** a means or medium through which anything is viewed or regarded; point of view.

make a spectacle of oneself, behave foolishly or crudely in public. ⟨ME < L *spectaculum*, ult. < *specere* view⟩

spec•ta•cled ['spɛktəkəld] *adj.* **1** provided with or wearing spectacles. **2** having a marking resembling spectacles: *a spectacled snake.*

spec•tac•u•lar [spɛk'tækjələr] *adj., n.* —*adj.* **1** making a great display: *The television program included a spectacular scene of a storm.* **2** having to do with a spectacle or show.
—*n.* a spectacular event or show: *a TV spectacular.*

spec•tac•u•lar•ly [spɛk'tækjələrli] *adv.* **1** in a spectacular manner or degree. **2** as a spectacle.

spec•ta•tor ['spɛkteitər] *or* [spɛk'teitər] *n.* a person who watches without taking part; onlooker: *Thousands of spectators lined the streets, waiting for the parade to come by.* ⟨< L *spectator* < *spectare* watch < *specere* view⟩

spectator sport a sport that attracts many spectators who do not practise the sport themselves: *Hockey and football are spectator sports.*

spec•ter ['spɛktər] *n.* See SPECTRE.

spec•tra ['spɛktrə] *n.* a pl. of SPECTRUM.

spec•tral ['spɛktrəl] *adj.* **1** of or like a spectre; ghostly: *He saw the spectral form of the headless horseman.* **2** of or produced by the spectrum: *spectral colours.* **3** *Physics.* having to do with one wavelength of radiation. **—spec'tral•i•ty** [spɛk'trælɪti], *n.* **—'spec•tral•ly,** *adv.* **—'spec•tral•ness,** *n.*

spec•tre ['spɛktər] *n.* **1** ghost. **2** something causing terror or dread. Also, **specter.** ⟨< L *spectrum* appearance. See SPECTRUM.⟩
☛ *Syn.* **1.** See note at GHOST.

spectro– *combining form.* of or having to do with a spectrum or spectral analysis: *spectroscope.*

spec•tro•gram ['spɛktrə,græm] *n.* a photographic record of a spectrum.

spec•tro•graph ['spɛktrə,græf] *n.* an instrument that produces a spectrogram. **—,spec•tro'graph•ic,** *adj.* **—,spec•tro'graph•i•cal•ly,** *adv.*

spec•tro•he•li•o•gram [,spɛktrə'hiliə,græm] *n.* a photograph of the sun in the light of only one wavelength, such as that of hydrogen or calcium (red and violet respectively).

spec•tro•he•li•o•graph [,spɛktrə'hiliə,græf] *n.* an instrument for obtaining a spectroheliogram by filtering light.

spec•trom•e•ter [spɛk'trɒmətər] *n. Optics.* an instrument for measuring wavelengths in spectra. **—,spec•tro'met•ric** [,spɛktrə'mɛtrɪk], *adj.* **—spec'trom•e•try,** *n.*

spec•tro•scope ['spɛktrə,skoup] *n. Optics.* an instrument for obtaining and examining the spectrum of radiation from any source by the passage of rays through a prism or a grating. **—,spec•tro'scop•ic** [,spɛktrə'skɒpɪk], *adj.* **—,spec•tro'scop•i•cal•ly,** *adv.*

spec•tros•co•py [spɛk'trɒskəpi] *n.* **1** the science that deals with the examination and analysis of spectra and with the use of the spectroscope. **—spec'tros•co•pist,** *n.*

spec•trum ['spɛktrəm] *n., pl.* **-tra** [-trə] or **-trums. 1 a** the band of colours formed when a beam of light is broken up by being passed through a prism or by some other means. A rainbow has all the colours of the spectrum: red, orange, yellow, green, blue, indigo, and violet. **b** the band of colours formed when any radiant energy is broken up. The ends of such a spectrum are not visible to the eye, but are studied by photography, heat effects, etc. **c** an image displaying any kind of radiation or motion as a distribution of waves or particles in an orderly arrangement by frequency, intensity, wavelength charge, etc. **2** *Radio.* the frequency range between 10 kilohertz and 300 000 megahertz. **3** range; scope; compass; scale or continuum: *the spectrum of political thought.* **4** Also, **ocular spectrum.** an afterimage. ⟨< L *spectrum* appearance < *specere* view⟩

spec•u•la ['spɛkjələ] *n.* a pl. of SPECULUM.

spec•u•lar ['spɛkjələr] *adj.* **1** of or like a mirror; reflecting. **2** having to do with a speculum. ⟨< L *specularis* < *speculum* mirror. See SPECULUM.⟩ **—'spec•u•lar•ly,** *adv.*

spec•u•late ['spɛkjə,leit] *v.* **-lat•ed, -lat•ing. 1** reflect; theorize: *The philosopher speculated about time and space.* **2** guess; conjecture: *She refused to speculate about the possible winner.* **3** buy or sell stocks, real estate, etc. when there is a large risk, with the hope of making a profit from future price changes. **4** take part or invest in a risky enterprise in the hope of making large gains. ⟨< L *speculari* < *specula* watchtower < *specere* look⟩

spec•u•la•tion [,spɛkjə'leiʃən] *n.* **1** thought; hypothesis: *Former speculations about electricity were often unscientific.* **2** a guessing; conjecture. **3** the act of buying or selling where there is a risk, with the hope of making a profit from future price changes: *His speculations in stocks made him poor.* **4** a taking part in any risky enterprise in the hope of making great gains.

spec•u•la•tive ['spɛkjələtɪv] *or* ['spɛkjə,leitɪv] *adj.* **1** thoughtful; reflective. **2** theoretical rather than practical. **3** conjectural; hypothetical. **4** risky. **5** of or involving speculation in land, stocks, etc. **—'spec•u•la•tive•ly,** *adv.* **—'spec•u•la•tive•ness,** *n.*

spec•u•la•tor ['spɛkjə,leitər] *n.* **1** a person who speculates, usually in business. **2** a person who buys tickets for shows, games, etc. in advance, hoping to sell them later at a higher price. ⟨< L *speculator* explorer, spy⟩

spec•u•lum ['spɛkjələm] *n., pl.* **-la** [-lə] or **-lums. 1** a mirror of polished metal, especially of a highly reflective alloy of copper and tin. A reflecting telescope contains a speculum. **2** *Surgery.* an instrument for enlarging an opening in order to examine a cavity. **3** *Zoology.* a brightly coloured patch on the wing of a duck, distinguishing its species. ⟨< L *speculum* mirror < *specere* view⟩

sped [spɛd] *v.* a pt. and a pp. of SPEED.

speech [spitʃ] *n.* **1** the act of speaking; talk. **2** the power of speaking; ability to speak: *Animals lack speech.* **3** a manner of speaking: *The sailor's speech showed that he was a Newfoundlander.* **4** what is said; the words spoken: *We made the usual farewell speeches.* **5** a public address. **6** a number of lines spoken by an actor in a single sequence. **7** a particular language or dialect: *His native speech was French.* **8** the study and practice of spoken language: *to take a course in speech.* ⟨OE *spǣc*⟩
☛ *Syn.* **5. Speech,** ADDRESS, ORATION = a talk made to an audience. **Speech** is the general word applying to a prepared or unprepared, formal or informal talk made for some purpose: *Most after-dinner speeches are interesting.* **Address** suggests a prepared formal speech, usually of some importance or given on an important occasion: *Who gave your commencement address?* **Oration** applies to a formal address on a special occasion, and particularly suggests artistic style, dignity, and eloquence: *a funeral oration.*

speech community *Linguistics.* any group of people sharing the same language or dialect.

Speech from the Throne in countries of the Commonwealth acknowledging the British monarch as the head of state, a statement of government policy for the coming year read in the opening session of Parliament by the British monarch or his or her representative.

speech•i•fy ['spitʃə,faɪ] *v.* **-fied, -fy•ing.** *Humorous or contemptuous.* make a speech or speeches. **—'speech•i,fi•er,** *n.*

speech•less ['spitʃlɪs] *adj.* **1** temporarily unable to speak, as from overwhelming emotion: *George was speechless with anger.* **2** not having the faculty of speech. **3** silent: *A frown was her speechless reply.* **4** so as to make or be temporarily unable to speak: *to knock someone speechless.* **—'speech•less•ly,** *adv.* **—speech•less•ness,** *n.*
☛ *Syn.* **1, 2.** See note at DUMB.

speech•writ•er ['spitʃ,rəitər] *n.* someone employed to compose speeches for a public figure, such as a politician.

speed [spid] *n., v.* **sped** or **speed•ed, speed•ing.** —*n.* **1** swiftness or rapidity of movement. **2** a rate of movement or action; velocity: *a speed of 100 km/h. The boys ran at full speed.* **3** an arrangement of gears to give a certain rate of movement: *a ten-speed bike. Most cars with manual transmissions have five forward speeds.* **4** *Photography.* **a** a measure of the sensitivity (of a film or paper) to light, expressed by low numbers for slow film and higher numbers for fast film. **b** the length of time a shutter is open to expose the film. **c** the maximum effective opening of a lens, aperture, indicated by an F NUMBER. **5** *Informal.* one's preference, level of ability or interest, etc.: *Using the computer strictly for word-processing is about my speed.* **6** *Slang.* any of various amphetamines used as mood-elevating drugs, especially methamphetamine. **7** *Archaic.* good luck; success.
at speed, quickly.
up to speed, operating at the normal, expected, or prescribed rate or level: *He is recovering, but he's not quite up to speed yet. It will take a while to get the new company up to speed.*
—*v.* **1** go quickly: *The boat sped over the water.* **2** make go quickly: *to speed a horse.* **3** send quickly: *to speed a message.* **4** go faster than is safe or lawful: *The driver of the car was caught speeding near the school zone.* **5** help forward; promote: *to speed an undertaking.* **6** design or set (a machine) to function at a given speed. **7** *Archaic.* succeed; have (good or bad) fortune. **8** *Archaic.* give success to: *God speed you.*
speed up, go or cause to go more quickly; increase in speed. ⟨OE *spēd*⟩
☛ *Syn. n.* **1.** See note at HURRY.

speed•boat ['spid,bout] *n.* a motorboat built to go at high speeds.

speed bump in parking lots, laneways, etc., a ridge across the pavement to deter drivers from going too fast.

speed•er ['spidər] *n.* **1** a person or thing that goes at a fast pace, especially a motorist who indulges in speeding. **2** *Cdn.* a small trolley powered by a gasoline engine, used on railway tracks by maintenance crews. **3** *Cdn. Lumbering.* a small track car used especially for carrying supervisors, company officials, and supplies on a logging railway.

speed•ing ['spidɪŋ] *n., v.* *—n.* the act of driving faster than the legal speed limit.
—v. ppr. of SPEED.

speed limit the top speed at which vehicles are legally allowed to travel on a particular road.

speed•om•e•ter [spə'dɒmətər] *or* [spɪ'dɒmətər] *n.* an instrument to indicate the speed of an automobile or other vehicle.

speed•read•ing ['spid,ridɪŋ] *n.* the technique of reading much faster than normal, with comprehension and memory.
—'speed,read, *v.*

speed skate an ice skate made specially for speed skating.

speed skating the sport of competing with others to see who can skate fastest on ice. **—'speed-,skate,** *v.* **—speed skater.**

speed•ster ['spidstər] *n.* **1** a person who travels at high speed. **2** a fast car; sports car.

speed trap a section of road or highway where police set up a means, usually hidden, of catching persons who are speeding.

speed–up ['spid ,ʌp] *n.* an increase in speed or production rate, especially as imposed on a workforce with no corresponding increase in pay: *a speed-up in manufacturing.*

speed•way ['spid,wei] *n.* a road or track for fast driving or for car or motorcycle races.

speed•well ['spid,wɛl] *n.* any of a genus (*Veronica*) of annual and perennial plants found chiefly in north temperate regions. Some speedwells are cultivated in gardens for their blue, pink, or white flowers.

speed•y ['spidi] *adj.* **speed•i•er, speed•i•est.** fast; rapid; quick; swift; prompt: *speedy workers, a speedy change, speedy progress, a speedy decision.* **—'speed•i•ly,** *adv.* **—'speed•i•ness,** *n.*

speiss [spəis] *n. Metallurgy.* a by-product of the smelting process of ores such as copper, iron, and nickel which contain arsenic or antimony; a mixture of metallic arsenides or antimonides. ⟨< G *Speise* food, amalgam⟩
☛ *Hom.* SPICE.

spe•le•ol•o•gist [,spili'ɒlədʒɪst] *n.* a person trained in speleology, especially one whose work it is.

spe•le•ol•o•gy [,spili'ɒlədʒi] *n.* the scientific study of caves, including the geology, flora and fauna, etc. ⟨< L *spelaeum* cave < Gk. *spēlaion* + *-logy*⟩ **—,spe•le•o'log•i•cal,** *adj.*

spell[1] [spɛl] *v.* **spelled** or **spelt, spell•ing. 1** write or say the letters of (a word) in order. **2** write words with the correct letters in the correct order: *She cannot spell well.* **3** make up or form (a word): *C-a-t spells cat.* **4** mean: *Delay spells danger.*
spell out, a write out in full: *All numerals under 100 should be spelled out.* **b** read with difficulty, as by sounding out each letter. **c** explain very clearly and definitively; make explicit: *She can't read between the lines; you have to spell everything out for her.* ⟨ME < OF *espeller* < Gmc.⟩

spell[2] [spɛl] *n.* **1** a word or set of words having magic power. **2** fascination; charm.
cast a spell on, put under or as if under the influence of magic power; fascinate; charm completely.
under a spell, controlled by a spell; spellbound: *The explorer's story held the children under a spell.* ⟨OE *spell* story⟩

spell[3] [spɛl] *n., v.* **spelled, spell•ing.** *—n.* **1** a period of work or duty: *The sailor's spell at the wheel was four hours.* **2** a period or time of anything: *a spell of coughing, a spell of hot weather.* **3** the relief of one person by another in doing something. **4** *Informal.* an attack or fit of illness or nervous excitement. **5** *Informal.* a brief period: *to rest for a spell.*
—v. **1** *Informal.* work in place of (another) for a while (*sometimes used with* **off**): *to spell another person at rowing a boat.* **2** give a time of rest to. ⟨OE *spelian*, v.⟩

spell•bind ['spɛl,baɪnd] *v.* **-bound, -bind•ing.** make spellbound; fascinate; enchant.

spell•bind•er ['spɛl,baɪndər] *n.* a speaker or writer who can hold his or her audience spellbound.

spell•bound ['spɛl,baʊnd] *adj., v.* *—adj.* too interested to move; fascinated; enchanted.
—v. pt. and pp. of SPELLBIND. ⟨< *spell*[2] + *bound*[1]⟩

spell check an execution of a SPELL CHECKER; the process of checking spelling using a spell checker: *Run a spell check on this before printing it.*

spell checker *Computer technology.* a component of a computer software package that attempts to verify whether individual words typed into the computer are spelled correctly: *The word-processing system's spell checker was used to scan the memorandum for errors.* Also called **spelling checker.**

spell•er ['spɛlər] *n.* **1** a person who spells words in a specified manner: *I'm a poor speller.* **2** a book for teaching spelling.

spell•ing ['spɛlɪŋ] *n., v.* *—n.* **1** the writing or saying of the letters of words in order. **2** the way a word is spelled: *Many English words have more than one spelling.* **3 a** the way words in general (in a given language) are spelled; conventional patterns of orthography. **b** the study of this.
—v. ppr. of SPELL.

spelling bee a spelling contest in which players are eliminated for making errors, until only one person, the winner, is left.

spelling pronunciation a usually nonstandard pronunciation of a word by a person who has only seen it written, based on or influenced by the spelling. The pronunciation of *gunwale* as ['gʌn,weil] instead of ['gʌnəl] is a spelling pronunciation.

spelt[1] [spɛlt] *v.* a pt. and a pp. of SPELL[1].

spelt[2] [spɛlt] *n.* an old species of wheat (*Triticum spelta*) no longer much cultivated. ⟨< LL *spelta*⟩

spel•ter ['spɛltər] *n.* zinc, usually in the form of small bars. ⟨origin uncertain; cf. LG *spialter*⟩

spe•lunk•er [spɪ'lʌŋkər] *n.* a person who studies and explores caves as a hobby. ⟨< L *spelunca* cave < Gk. *spēlaion* + E *-er*[2]⟩
—spe'lunk•ing, *n.*

spen•cer[1] ['spɛnsər] *n.* a short, fitted or semifitted jacket for men or women, worn in the late 18th and early 19th centuries. ⟨after George John *Spencer*, the second Earl Spencer (1758-1834)⟩

spen•cer[2] ['spɛnsər] *n. Nautical.* a trysail on a square-rigged vessel. ⟨origin uncertain⟩

Spen•ce•ri•an [spɛn'siriən] *adj.* of or having to do with Herbert Spencer (1820-1903), an English philosopher, or his philosophy, the main tenets of which were social evolution and laissez faire.

spend [spɛnd] *v.* **spent, spend•ing. 1** pay out: *She spent ten dollars today.* **2** pay out money: *Earn before you spend.* **3** use; use up; give out; expend or put forth: *Don't spend any more energy on that job.* **4** pass (time, etc.): *to spend a day at the beach.* **5** wear out; exhaust: *The storm has spent its force.* **6** waste; squander: *He spent his fortune on horse racing.* **7** lose (something, such as one's life), as for a cause. ⟨OE *-spendan* (as in *forspendan* use up) < L *expendere.* Doublet of EXPEND.⟩ **—'spend•er,** *n.*
☛ *Syn.* **Spend,** EXPEND, DISBURSE = pay out (money, time, effort, etc.) **Spend** is the common word, meaning 'pay out (money, or other resources) for some thing or purpose': *He spends all he earns.* **Expend,** more formal, emphasizes the idea of using up by spending sums or amounts, commonly large, that reduce or exhaust a fund: *She expends her energy on parties.* **Disburse,** formal and exclusively financial, means 'pay out (money) from a fund for expenses': *The treasurer reports what he disburses.*

spending money pocket money; money usually carried on the person, for incidental personal expenses.

spend•thrift ['spɛnd,θrɪft] *n., adj.* *—n.* a person who wastes money.
—adj. extravagant with money; wasteful.

Spen•se•ri•an [spɛn'siriən] *adj.* of, having to do with, or characteristic of Edmund Spenser (1552?-1599), an English poet, or his work.

Spenserian stanza the stanza used by Edmund Spenser in his *Faerie Queene,* consisting of eight iambic pentameter lines and a final alexandrine, with three rhymes arranged thus: ababbcbcc.

spent [spɛnt] *v., adj.* —*v.* pt. and pp. of SPEND.
—*adj.* **1** used up: *Her energy was soon spent.* **2** worn out; tired: *a spent swimmer, a spent horse.*

sperm¹ [spɜrm] *n.* **1** the mature male reproductive cell produced by almost all animals and plants that reproduce sexually; a male gamete. The sperm of mammals are very tiny and consist of a head that contains the genes and a thin tail by which they propel themselves inside the female reproductive tract. **2** semen. ⟨ME < LL < Gk. *sperma* seed < *speirein* sow¹⟩

sperm² [spɜrm] *n.* **1** spermaceti. **2** SPERM WHALE. **3** SPERM OIL. ⟨short for *spermaceti,* etc.⟩

sper•ma•cet•i [ˌspɜrməˈsɛti] *or* [ˌspɜrməˈsiti] *n.* a whitish, waxy substance obtained from the oil in the head of the sperm whale and used in making fine candles, ointments, cosmetics, etc. ⟨< Med.L *sperma ceti* sperm of a whale < LL *sperma* sperm, seed < Gk., and L *cetus* large sea animal < Gk. *kētos*⟩

sper•ma•go•ni•um [ˌspɜrməˈgouniəm] *n., pl.* **-ni•a** [-niə]. in certain fungi and lichens, a reproductive structure producing sperm cells. ⟨< NL < LL *sperma* sperm + NL *-gonium* reproductive cell or cell-producing structure (< Gk. *gonos* procreation, semen, offspring)⟩

sper•ma•ry [ˈspɜrməri] *n., pl.* **-ries.** an organ in which human or animal sperm are developed; male gonad or testis. ⟨< NL *spermarium* < LL *sperma* sperm⟩

sper•mat•ic [spərˈmætɪk] *adj.* **1** of or having to do with sperm; seminal; generative. **2** having to do with a spermary.

spermatic cord *Anatomy.* a cord suspending the testis within the scrotum and passing into the abdominal cavity. It contains blood vessels, the vas deferens, lymph ducts, and nerves.

sper•ma•to•cyte [ˈspɜrmətəˌsəit] *or* [spərˈmætəˌsəit] *n.* **1** *Botany.* a germ cell from which a male gamete develops. **2** *Zoology.* an immature male sex cell after the first stage of division from a spermatogonium. ⟨< NL *spermato-* (combining form < Gk. *sperma, spermatos*) sperm + *-cyte*⟩

sper•ma•to•gen•e•sis [ˌspɜrmətəˈdʒɛnəsɪs] *or* [spərˌmætəˈdʒɛnəsɪs] *n. Biology.* the whole process of production and development of spermatozoa. **—ˌsperma•to•geˈnet•ic,** *adj.*

sper•ma•to•go•ni•um [ˌspɜrmətəˈgouniəm] *or* [spərˌmætəˈgouniəm] *n., pl.* **-ni•a** [-niə]. *Zoology.* a male germ cell at a very early stage before division. ⟨< NL *spermato-* (see SPERMATOCYTE) + *-gonium.* See SPERMAGONIUM.⟩ **—ˌsperma•toˈgo•ni•al,** *adj.*

sper•ma•to•phyte [ˈspɜrmətəˌfəit] *or* [spərˈmætəˌfəit] *n.* any plant that reproduces by means of seeds, including the **angiosperms** (flowering plants) and the **gymnosperms** (conifers, etc.). Spermatophytes make up a major plant group which in earlier classification systems constitute a division, or phylum (Spermatophyta), of the plant kingdom. ⟨< Gk. *sperma, -atos* seed + E *-phyte*⟩ **—ˌsperma•toˈphyt•ic** [-ˈfɪtɪk], *adj.*

sper•ma•to•zo•on [ˌspɜrmətəˈzouən] *or* [spərˌmætəˈzouən] *n., pl.* **-zo•a** [-ˈzouə]. a sperm of an animal. ⟨< Gk. *sperma, -atos* seed + *zōion* animal⟩ **—ˌsper•ma•toˈzo•al, ˌsper•ma•toˈzo•an,** or **ˌsper•ma•toˈzo•ic,** *adj.*

sperm bank a storage facility for frozen sperm that may be used for artificial insemination.

sperm•i•cide [ˈspɜrmɪˌsaɪd] *n.* an agent or substance capable of killing sperm. **—ˌsperm•iˈcid•al,** *adj.*

sperm oil a light yellow oil from the sperm whale, used for lubricating.

sperm whale a large toothed whale (*Physeter catodon,* constituting the family Physeteridae) having a very large, blunt-nosed head which has a cavity containing spermaceti. Sperm whales have long been hunted for spermaceti and also for ambergris and sperm oil.

sper•ry•lite [ˈspɛrəˌləit] *n.* a whitish, crystalline mineral, a compound of platinum and arsenic. *Formula*: $PtAs_2$ ⟨< F.L. *Sperry,* the Canadian chemist who discovered it⟩

spes•sar•tite [ˈspɛsərˌtəit] *n.* a deep red variety of garnet used as a gemstone, containing aluminum and manganese. ⟨< F < *Spessart* name of a mountain range in Germany⟩

spew [spju] *v., n.* —*v.* **1** vomit: *The dog spewed on the rug.* **2** cast forth; throw out: *The volcano was spewing lava. He spewed out a stream of insults.* **3** be cast or thrown out or forth; gush: *The words spewed from her mouth in an angry torrent.*
—*n.* that which is spewed out. Also, **spue.** ⟨OE *spīwan*⟩ **—ˈspew•er,** *n.*

sp.gr. SPECIFIC GRAVITY.

sphag•num [ˈsfægnəm] *n.* **1** any of the mosses of the genus *Sphagnum,* found growing in bogs; peat moss. **2** such moss packed in bulk and used for fertilizing, potting, transplanting, etc. ⟨< NL < Gk. *sphagnos,* a kind of moss⟩ **—ˈsphag•nous,** *adj.*

sphal•er•ite [ˈsfæləˌrəit] *or* [ˈsfeiləˌrəit] *n.* a native zinc sulphide, found in both crystalline and massive forms; blende. *Formula*: ZnS ⟨< Gk. *sphaleros* deceptive, slippery < *sphallen* overthrow, baffle + E *-ite¹*⟩

sphe•noid [ˈsfinɔɪd] *adj., n.* —*adj.* **1** wedge-shaped. **2** *Anatomy.* of or having to do with a compound bone of the base of the skull.
—*n. Anatomy.* this bone. ⟨< NL < Gk. *sphenoeidēs* < *sphēn* wedge + *eidos* form⟩ **—spheˈnoi•dal,** *adj.*

spher•al [ˈsfirəl] *adj.* **1** of or like a sphere; spherical. **2** symmetrical.

sphere [sfir] *n., v.* **sphered, spher•ing.** —*n.* **1** *Geometry.* a round solid figure bounded by a surface that is at all points equally distant from the centre. See SOLID for picture. **2** an object approximately like this in form; ball; globe. **3** the place or field in which a person or thing exists, acts, works, etc.: *His sphere is advertising. People used to say that woman's sphere was the home.* **4** a range; extent; region: *the United Kingdom's sphere of influence.* **5** any of the stars or planets. The earth, sun, and moon are spheres. **6** *Astronomy.* CELESTIAL SPHERE. **7** in ancient astronomy, any one of a series of hypothetical transparent, concentric globes, one inside another, in which the stars and planets were supposed to be set. Revolution of the spheres was believed to cause the apparent motion of the heavenly bodies. **8** *Poetic.* the heavens; the sky viewed as a sphere by an observer on the ground.
—*v. Poetic.* form into a sphere or enclose in a sphere. ⟨< L < Gk. *sphaira*⟩

spher•i•cal [ˈsfɛrɪkəl] *or* [ˈsfirɪkəl] *adj.* **1** shaped like a sphere. **2** of or having to do with a sphere or spheres. **3** *Geometry.* **a** of an angle, formed by the intersection of two GREAT CIRCLES on a sphere. **b** of a closed figure, formed on the surface of a sphere and bounded by the arcs of three or more great circles: *a spherical polygon, a spherical triangle.* **c** dealing with such figures: *spherical geometry, spherical trigonometry.*

spherical aberration the distortional effect produced by a spherical lens or mirror.

spherical coordinates *Mathematics.* the set of three coordinates that locate a point in three-dimensional space. They are: the length of the point's radius vector; the angle of this vector and one axis; and the angle made by the plane of the vector with another, perpendicular axis.

spher•i•cal•ly [ˈsfɛrɪkli] *or* [ˈsfirɪkli] *adv.* **1** in the form of a sphere, or of part of a sphere. **2** so as to be spherical.

sphe•ric•i•ty [sfɪˈrɪsɪti] *n., pl.* **-ties.** spherical form; roundness.

spher•ics¹ [ˈsfɛrɪks] *n.* (*used with a singular verb*) spherical geometry or trigonometry. ⟨< LL *sphericus* < Gk. *sphairikos.* See SPHERE.⟩

spher•ics² or **sfer•ics** [ˈsfɛrɪks] *n.* **1** (*used with a singular verb*) a branch of meteorology in which electronic devices are used to study weather forecasting and atmospheric conditions. **2** these devices. **3** atmospherics. ⟨short for *atmospherics*⟩

sphe•roid [ˈsfirɔɪd] *n.* a body shaped somewhat like a sphere. **—spheˈroi•dal,** *adj.*

sphe•rom•e•ter [sfɪˈrɒmətər] *n.* an instrument used for finding the radius of a sphere and for measuring the curvature of a spherical surface.

spher•ule [ˈsfɛrul] *or* [ˈsfɛrjul], [ˈsfirul] *or* [ˈsfirjul] *n.* a small sphere or spherical body. **—ˈspher•u•lar** [ˈsfɛrjələr], *adj.*

sphinc•ter [ˈsfɪŋktər] *n. Anatomy.* a ringlike muscle that surrounds an opening or passage of the body, and can contract to close it. ⟨< LL < Gk. *sphinktēr* < *sphingein* squeeze⟩ **—ˈsphinc•ter•al,** *adj.*

sphin•gid [ˈsfɪndʒɪd] *n.* HAWK MOTH. ⟨< *Sphingidae* taxonomic family name < *sphinx*⟩

sphinx [sfɪŋks] *n., pl.* **sphinx•es.** **1** a statue of a lion's body with the head of a man, ram, or hawk. **2 Sphinx, a** *Greek mythology.* a monster with the head and breasts of a woman, the body of a lion, and wings. The Sphinx at Thebes proposed a riddle to every passer-by and killed those unable to guess the answer. **b** the immense sphinx by the Pyramids at Giza, near Cairo in Egypt. **3** a puzzling or mysterious person. **4** HAWK MOTH. ⟨< L < Gk.⟩ **—'sphinx,like,** *adj.*

The Sphinx

sphinx moth HAWK MOTH.

sp.ht. SPECIFIC HEAT.

sphyg•mic ['sfɪgmɪk] *adj. Physiology. Medicine.* of or having to do with the pulse.

sphygmo– *combining form.* the pulse; pulsation: *sphygmograph.* ⟨< Gk. *sphygmos* throbbing, heartbeat < *sphyzein* throb, beat⟩

sphyg•mo•gram ['sfɪgmə,græm] *n.* a diagram of the pulse beats as recorded by a sphygmograph.

sphyg•mo•graph ['sfɪgmə,græf] *n.* an instrument that records the rate, strength, etc. of the pulse. ⟨< Gk. *sphygmos* pulse + E *-graph*⟩ **—,sphyg•mo'graph•ic,** *adj.* **—sphyg'mog•ra•phy** [sfɪg'mɒgrəfi], *n.*

sphyg•moid ['sfɪgmɔɪd] *adj. Physiology. Medicine.* resembling the pulse; pulselike.

sphyg•mo•ma•nom•e•ter [,sfɪgmoumə'nɒmətər] *n. Medicine.* an instrument for measuring blood pressure, especially in an artery. ⟨< *sphygmo-* + Gk. *manos* at intervals + E *-meter*⟩ **—,sphyg•mo,man•o'met•ric** [,sfɪgmou,mænə'mɛtrɪk], *adj.* **—,sphyg•mo•ma'nom•e•try,** *n.*

spi•ca ['spəikə] *n., pl.* **spi•cae** ['spəisi]. **1** *Botany.* a spike. **2** *Surgery.* a spiral bandage wrapped with reversed turns, as a figure eight. **3 Spica,** *Astronomy.* a very bright star in the northern constellation Virgo. ⟨< L *spica* ear of grain⟩

spi•cate ['spəikeit] *adj.* **1** *Botany.* **a** having spikes. **b** arranged in spikes. **2** *Zoology.* having the form of a spike; pointed. ⟨< L *spicatus,* pp. of *spicare* furnish with spikes < *spica* spike[2]⟩

spic•ca•to [spɪ'kɑtou] *n., adj., adv. Music.* —*n.* a way of playing a stringed instrument so that the bow bounces lightly on the strings.
—*adj.* played or to be played in this manner.
—*adv.* in this manner. ⟨< Ital., pp. of *spiccare* detach⟩

spice [spəis] *n., v.* **spiced, spic•ing.** —*n.* **1** any of various seasonings obtained from plants and used to flavour food. Pepper, cinnamon, cloves, ginger, and nutmeg are common spices. **2** such substances considered collectively or as a material. **3** a spicy, fragrant odour. **4 a** character or interest: *A few good metaphors added spice to the narrative.* **b** something that adds character or interest. **5** a slight touch or trace: *a spice of wickedness.*
—*v.* **1** put spice in; season. **2** add flavour or interest to (*sometimes used with* **up**). ⟨ME < OF *espice,* ult. < L *species* sort. Doublet of SPECIES.⟩
☛ *Hom.* SPEISS.

spice•ber•ry ['spəis,bɛri] *n., pl.* **-ries.** the creeping wintergreen (*Gaultheria procumbens*) of E Canada.

spice•bush ['spəis,bʊʃ] *n.* **1** an aromatic shrub (*Lindera benzoin*) of the laurel family, having small yellow flowers in dense clusters followed by yellow or red pungent, edible berries, native to E North America. **2** Carolina allspice, a hardy shrub of the genus *Calycanthus* of the laurel family, having scented brownish flowers. **3** any other shrub of either genus.

spic•er•y ['spəisəri] *n., pl.* **-er•ies. 1** spices; a collection of spices. **2** a spicy flavour or fragrance.

spick–and–span ['spɪk ən 'spæn] *adj.* **1** neat and clean; spruce or smart: *a spick-and-span room, apron, or uniform.* **2** fresh; new. ⟨short for *spick-and-span-new* < *spick,* var. of *spike[1]* + *span-new* (< ON *spán-nýr* < *spánn* chip + *nýr* new)⟩

spic•u•late ['spɪkjəlɪt] *or* ['spɪkjə,leit] *adj.* **1** having spicules; consisting of spicules. **2** having the form of a spicule. Also, **spicular.**

spic•ule ['spɪkjul] *n.* **1** a small, slender, sharp-pointed piece, usually bony or crystalline. **2** *Zoology.* one of the small, slender, calcareous or siliceous bodies that form the skeleton of a sponge. **3** *Botany.* a small spike of flowers; spikelet. **4** a small SOLAR PROMINENCE. ⟨< L *spiculum,* dim. of *spicum,* var. of *spica* ear of grain⟩

spic•y ['spəisi] *adj.* **spic•i•er, spic•i•est. 1** flavoured with spice. **2** having a taste or smell like that of spice: *spicy apples.* **3** lively; keen: *spicy conversation.* **4** somewhat improper: *Some of his stories were a bit spicy.* **5** producing spices; abounding with spices. **—'spic•i•ly,** *adv.* **—'spic•i•ness,** *n.*

spi•der ['spəidər] *n.* **1** any of an order (Araneida, also called Araneae) of arachnids found throughout the world, having an unsegmented body with two main divisions, four pairs of walking legs, and organs for producing silk which is used for making nests, webs to catch prey, or cocoons for their eggs. **2** any of various implements, tools, or machine parts having radiating arms, spokes, etc. **3** a cast-iron frying pan of a type originally made with long metal legs to stand over an open fire. ⟨OE *spīthra* < *spinnan* spin⟩ **—'spi•der,like,** *adj.*

spider crab any crab of the family Majidae, having a pear-shaped body and long, thin legs.

spider monkey any of a genus (Ateles) of monkeys having long, thin limbs and a long, prehensile tail.

spider plant a plant of Africa (*Chlorophytum comosum*), having narrow leaves often streaked with white, and sending out stolons from which new plants are generated. It is a common house plant.

spider web a web spun by a spider.

spi•der•wort ['spəidər,wɜrt] *n.* **1** any of a genus (*Tradescantia*) of perennial plants having somewhat grasslike leaves and clusters of purple, blue, or white flowers. The **wandering Jew** is a spiderwort. **2** (*adjl.*) designating a family (Commelinaceae) of mainly tropical plants that includes the spiderworts, all having jointed and often branching stems with parallel-veined leaves.

spi•der•y ['spəidəri] *adj.* **1** long and thin like a spider's legs. **2** suggesting a spider's web: *spidery handwriting.* **3** full of, or infested with, spiders. **4** resembling or behaving like a spider.

spie•gel•ei•sen ['spigə,laɪzən] *n.* a type of pig iron having a high manganese content. ⟨< G *Spiegel* mirror + *Eisen* iron⟩

spiel[1] [spil] *or* [ʃpil] *n., v. Slang.* —*n.* talk; speech; harangue, especially of a glib, repetitive, noisy nature.
—*v.* make or give such a speech; deliver a spiel.
spiel off, *Slang.* recite rapidly from memory: *The waiter spieled off the entire dessert menu without a hitch.* ⟨< G *spielen* play⟩

spiel[2] or **'spiel** [spil] *n. Cdn. Curling.* bonspiel.

spiel•er[1] ['spilər] *or* ['ʃpilər] *n. Slang.* a person who spiels, especially one who exaggerates and has a lot to say. ⟨< *spiel[1]*⟩

spiel•er[2] or **'spiel•er** ['spilər] *n. Cdn. Curling.* a person who takes part in a bonspiel. ⟨< *spiel[2]*⟩

spiff [spɪf] *v. Slang.* make spiffy or spiffier (*used with* **up**): *She came down all spiffed up for the party.*

spiff•y ['spɪfi] *adj.* **spiff•i•er, spiff•i•est.** *Slang.* smart; neat; trim. ⟨< dial. E *spiff* dandified (person)⟩ **—'spiff•i•ly,** *adv.* **—'spiff•i•ness,** *n.*

spig•ot ['spɪgət] *n.* **1** a valve for controlling the flow of water or other liquid from a pipe, tank, barrel, etc. **2** a tap or faucet. **3** a peg or plug used to stop the small hole of a cask, barrel, etc.; bung. **4** a plain end of a section of pipe, inserted into the widened socket end of the next section to form a joint. ⟨ME; ? via OF < base of *spike*⟩

spike[1] [spəik] *n., v.* **spiked, spik•ing.** —*n.* **1** a large, strong nail. **2** a sharp-pointed object or part, especially one made of metal: *a fence with spikes at the top.* **3** SPIKE HEEL. **4** one of a set of metal projections on the sole and sometimes the heel of a shoe to improve traction. **5 spikes,** *pl.* a pair of shoes having these. **6** a young deer's unbranched antler. **7** (*adjl.*) having such an antler: *a spike buck.* **8** on any of various kinds of charts, the graphic representation of a sudden peak, as of temperature, brain waves, etc. **9** *Volleyball.* the action of spiking the ball.
—*v.* **1** fasten with spikes: *The men spiked the rails to the ties when laying the track.* **2** provide or equip with spikes: *Runners wear spiked shoes to keep from slipping.* **3** pierce or injure with a spike. **4** make (a cannon) useless by driving a spike into the touchhole. **5** put an end or stop to; make useless; block: *to spike an attempt.* **6** *Slang.* add liquor to (a drink, etc.). **7** *Slang.* make stronger, more effective, more stimulating, etc. by adding special elements. **8** style (hair) into spikes using gel. **9** *Volleyball.* hit (the ball) very sharply straight down into the opposing team's court from a position close to the net. **10** illegally drive spikes into (living trees) as a form of environmental protest against their being cut

for timber: *The demonstrators spiked six trees before the police arrived.*
spike (someone's) **guns,** obstruct or defeat (someone). ⟨ME < Scand. < L *spica*; cf. Swedish *spik* nail⟩ **—'spik•er,** *n.* **—'spike,like,** *adj.*

spike² [spəik] *n.* **1** an ear of grain. **2** a long, pointed flower cluster. See INFLORESCENCE for picture. ⟨ME < L *spica*⟩

spike heel a high, thin heel on a woman's dress shoe.

spike•let ['spəiklɪt] *n.* a small or secondary spike, especially one of the small spikes that make up a spike, or head, of grain or grass. Each spikelet of wheat may produce one or more kernels.

spike•nard ['spəik,nɑrd] *or* ['spəiknərd] *n.* **1** a sweet-smelling ointment used in ancient times. **2** a fragrant East Indian plant (*Nardostachys jatamansi*) of the valerian family from which this ointment was probably obtained. **3** a perennial herb (*Aralia racemosa*) of the ginseng family native to North America. ⟨ME < Med.L *spica nardi* ear of nard⟩

spik•y ['spəiki] *adj.* **1** having spikes; set with sharp, projecting points. **2** having the shape of a spike or a series of spikes: *spiky hair.* **—'spi•ki•ness,** *n.*

spile [spaɪl] *n., v.* **spiled, spil•ing.** *—n.* **1** a peg or plug of wood used to stop the small hole of a cask or barrel. **2** a spout for drawing off sap from sugar maple trees. **3** a heavy stake or beam driven into the ground as a support.
—v. **1** stop up (a hole) with a plug. **2** furnish with a spout. **3** furnish, strengthen, or support with stakes or piles. ⟨< MDu. or MLG *spile,* splinter, peg⟩

spill¹ [spɪl] *v.* **spilled** or **spilt, spill•ing;** *n. —v.* **1** let (liquid or any matter in loose pieces) run or fall, especially accidentally: *to spill milk or salt.* **2** fall or flow out: *Water spilled from the pail.* **3** scatter. **4** shed (blood). **5** *Informal.* cause to fall from a horse, car, boat, etc. **6** *Nautical.* let the wind out of (a sail). **7** *Slang.* make known; tell.
spill over, a overflow. **b** spread; have an effect or influence beyond the intended bounds.
spill the beans. See BEAN.
—n. **1** spilling. **2** the quantity spilled. **3** spillway. **4** *Informal.* a fall. ⟨OE *spillan*⟩ **—'spill•er,** *n.*

spill² [spɪl] *n.* **1** a splinter. **2** a piece of wood or paper used to light candles, etc. **3** a disposable container in the form of a paper cone. **4** SPILE (def. 1). **5** a small pin or rod of metal, on which something turns. ⟨? ult. var. of *spile*⟩

spill•age ['spɪlɪdʒ] *n.* **1** a spilling of liquid, food, etc. **2** that which is spilled; the quantity spilled.

spil•li•kin ['spɪləkɪn] *n.* **1** a jackstraw. **2 spillikins,** the game of jackstraws (*used with a singular verb*). ⟨< *spill²*⟩

spill•o•ver ['spɪl,ouvər] *n.* **1** excess; an amount that has spilled over or overflowed. **2** the act of spilling over or overflowing. **3** an effect or influence going beyond intended bounds. **4** (*adjl.*) going beyond intended bounds: *a spillover effect.*

spill•way ['spɪl,wei] *n.* a channel or passage for the escape of surplus water from a dam, river, etc.

spilt [spɪlt] *v.* a pt. and a pp. of SPILL¹.

spin [spɪn] *v.* **spun** or *(archaic)* **span, spun, spin•ning;** *n.*
—v. **1** turn or make turn rapidly: *The wheel spins round. The boy spins his top.* **2** specifically of the wheels of a vehicle, turn rapidly without traction, as on an icy surface. **3** feel as if one were whirling around; feel dizzy: *My head is spinning.* **4** draw out and twist (cotton, flax, wool, etc.) into thread. **5** make (thread, yarn etc.) by drawing out and twisting cotton, wool, flax, etc. **6** make (a thread, web, cocoon, etc.) by giving out from the body sticky material that hardens into thread. A spider spins a web. **7** make (glass, gold, etc.) into thread. **8** run, ride, drive, etc. rapidly. **9** invent; make up; tell: *The old sailor used to spin yarns about adventures at sea.* **10** cause water to be drained from wet clothes, etc. in the drum of a washing machine by rotation at high speed. **11** of an aircraft, fall in a spin. **12** shape on a lathe or wheel: *spin an earthenware vase.*
spin out, make long and slow; draw out; prolong: *Try not to spin out your story.*
—n. **1** the action of spinning. **2** a ride, run, or drive, especially a short one: *Get your bicycle and come for a spin with me.* **3** a rapid turning around of an aircraft as it falls. **4** *Informal.* a biassed or slanted interpretation of statements, facts, events, etc. **5** *Physics.* **a** the rotation of an elementary particle about its axis, producing a **spin energy** which is expressed as a quantum number value. Spin is a property by which particles may be differentiated. **b** a quantum number representing this energy. It may be integral (0, 1, or 2) or half integral. Electrons have a spin of ½. **c** total or intrinsic angular momentum of an elementary particle. ⟨OE *spinnan*⟩

spi•na bi•fi•da ['spaɪnə 'bɪfədə] *Pathology.* a congenital defect in which the spinal column, or part of it, is imperfectly closed, exposing the spinal cord and meninges.

spin•ach ['spɪnɪtʃ] *n.* **1** a plant (*Spinacia oleracea*) of the goosefoot family cultivated for its large, dark green, edible leaves. **2** its leaves, eaten cooked as a vegetable or raw in salads. ⟨< OF *(e)spinache* < Med.L < Sp. *espinaca* < Arabic⟩

spi•nal ['spaɪnəl] *adj., n. —adj.* **1** of, having to do with, or located near the backbone. **2** of, having to do with, or affecting the SPINAL CORD. **3** resembling a spine in form or function: *a spinal ridge or hill.*
—n. Medicine. an anesthetic for the lower part of the body. ⟨< LL *spinalis* < L *spina.* See SPINE.⟩ **—'spi•nal•ly,** *adv.*

spinal canal the cavity formed by the arches of the vertebrae, through which the SPINAL CORD travels.

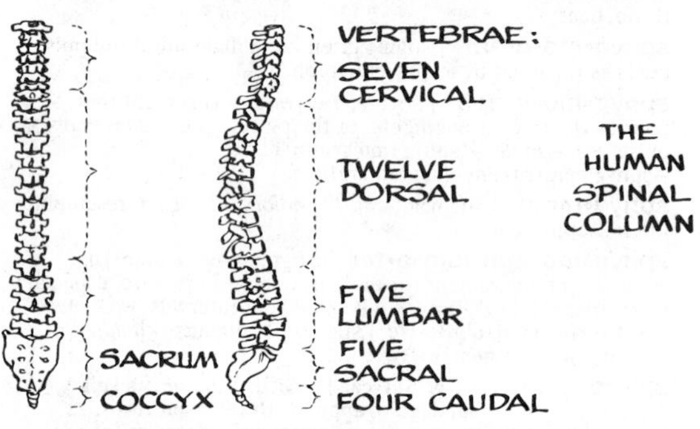

spinal column in human beings and other vertebrates, the series of small bones along the middle of the back, that encloses and protects the spinal cord and provides support for the body. The many bones of the spinal column, called vertebrae, are held together by muscles and tendons that allow movement in different directions. See RIB for picture.

spinal cord the thick, whitish cord of nerve tissue that extends from the brain down through most of the backbone and from which nerves to various parts of the body branch off. See BRAIN for picture.

spin•dle ['spɪndəl] *n., v.* **-dled, -dling.** *—n.* **1** a rod or pin used in spinning to twist, wind, and hold thread. See SPINNING WHEEL for picture. **2** a unit for measuring the length of yarn, equal to 13 825 m for cotton and 13 167 m for linen. **3** any rod or pin that turns around, or on which something turns. Axles and shafts are spindles. **4** one of the turned or more or less cylindrical supporting parts of a balustrade or stair rail, or in the back of some chairs. **5** *Biology.* a spindle-shaped bundle of fibres that form during the process of cell division, along which the chromosomes move to opposite ends of the parent cell. **6** a vertical metal spike mounted on a base, set on a desk, table, etc., on which papers are transfixed pending permanent filing. **7** a vertical shaftlike marker put on submerged hazards as a warning to navigators.
—v. **1** especially of a shoot, stem, or plant, grow tall and thin. **2** file (papers) temporarily on a spindle. ⟨OE *spinel*; related to *spinnan* spin⟩

spindle file SPINDLE (*n.,* def. 6).

spindle horn FOREST GOAT.

spin•dle–leg•ged ['spɪndəl ,lɛgd] *or* [,lɛgɪd] *adj.* having long, thin legs.

spin•dle•legs ['spɪndəl,lɛgz] *n.pl.* **1** long, thin legs. **2** *Informal.* a person with long, thin legs (*used with a singular verb*): *Spindlelegs, as the boys call John, is a good basketball player.*

spin•dle•shanked ['spɪndəl,ʃæŋkt] *adj.* spindle-legged.

spin•dle•shanks ['spɪndəl,ʃæŋks] *n.pl.* spindlelegs.

spindle side DISTAFF SIDE.

spindle tree any small tree of the genus *Euonymus,* especially *E. europaeus,* whose hard wood was much used for spindles.

spin•dling ['spɪndlɪŋ] *adj., v. —adj.* spindly.
—v. ppr. of SPINDLE.

spin•dly ['spɪndli] *adj.* **-dli•er, -dli•est.** very long and slender; too tall and thin.

spin doctor *Informal.* a person whose function is to provide and publicize a suitable SPIN (def. 4) on statements, events, etc. on behalf of a government, politician, etc.

spin•drift ['spɪn,drɪft] *n.* spray blown or dashed up from the waves. Also, **spoondrift.** ⟨var. of *spoondrift*⟩

spine [spaɪn] *n.* **1** SPINAL COLUMN; backbone. **2** something that looks like a backbone, such as a ridge of land, or functions as a main support. **3** *Botany.* a stiff, sharp-pointed growth of woody tissue on a plant such as a cactus or hawthorn. **4** *Zoology.* a stiff, sharp-pointed projection on an animal body, such as any of the quills on a porcupine's tail or any of the rigid rays of a fish's fin. **5** the back portion of a book where the pages are held together, or the part of the cover over this. **6** courage, determination, etc., as that by which a person is supported in the face of danger or adversity: *Threats merely stiffened his spine.* ⟨< L *spina*, originally, thorn⟩ **—'spine,like,** *adj.*

spined [spaɪnd] *adj.* having a spine or spines.

spi•nel [spɪ'nɛl] *or* ['spɪnəl] *n.* a crystalline mineral, consisting chiefly of oxides of magnesium and aluminum, that occurs in various colours. Transparent spinel is used for jewellery. ⟨< F < Ital. *spinella*, ult. < L *spina* thorn⟩

spine•less ['spaɪnlɪs] *adj.* **1** without spines or sharp-pointed processes: *a spineless cactus.* **2** having no backbone: *All insects are spineless.* **3** having a weak spine; limp. **4** without moral force, resolution, or courage; weak-willed; feeble. **—'spine•less•ly,** *adv.* **—'spine•less•ness,** *n.*

spin•et ['spɪnɪt] *or* [spɪ'nɛt] *n.* **1** formerly, a musical keyboard instrument like a small harpsichord. **2** a compact upright piano. **3** a small electronic organ. ⟨< F < Ital. *spinetta*, probably named after Giovanni *Spinetti*, an Italian inventor⟩

spin•i•fex ['spɪnɪ,fɛks] *n.* **1** any of a genus (*Spinifex*) of Australian grasses having sharp-pointed leaves and spiny seeds, often planted on sand dunes because their long underground stems anchor the sand. **2** any of various similar Australian grasses, especially of genus *Triodia.* ⟨< NL < L *spina* thorn + *facere* to make⟩

spin•na•ker ['spɪnəkər] *n. Nautical.* a large, triangular sail carried by yachts on the side opposite the mainsail when running before the wind. ⟨supposedly from *Sphinx*, a yacht on which first used, perhaps influenced by *spanker*⟩

spin•ner ['spɪnər] *n.* **1 a** a fly, real or artificial, for trout-fishing. **b** a fishing lure with fluttering or revolving blades, or any one of these blades. **2** a domed fairing that covers the hub of an aircraft's propeller and revolves with it. **3** any person, animal, or thing that spins.

spin•ner•et [,spɪnə'rɛt] *or* ['spɪnə,rɛt] *n.* **1** the organ by which spiders, silkworms, etc. spin their threads. **2** a perforated device for manufacturing synthetic fibres. Also (def. 2), **spinnerette**. ⟨dim. of *spinner*⟩

spin•ney ['spɪni] *n., pl.* **-neys.** *Esp. Brit.* a thicket; a small wood and its undergrowth, especially one preserved for sheltering game birds. ⟨< OF *espinnei*, ult. < L *spina* thorn⟩

spinning jenny an early type of spinning machine having more than one spindle, whereby one person could spin a number of threads at the same time.

A spinning wheel. The large wheel causes the smaller one to turn, and this revolves the horizontal spindle, twisting the thread and winding it up at the same time.

spinning wheel an apparatus for spinning cotton, flax, wool, etc. into thread or yarn, consisting of a large wheel, operated by hand or foot, and a single spindle.

spin•off ['spɪn,ɒf] *n.* a by-product or fringe benefit of an operation, activity, product, etc. Also, **spin-off.**

spi•nose ['spaɪnous] *or* [spaɪ'nous] *adj.* full of spines or thorns; spiny. ⟨< L *spinosus* < *spina* thorn⟩ **—spi'nos•i•ty** [spaɪ'nɒsəti], *n.*

spi•nous ['spaɪnəs] *adj.* **1** resembling a spine or thorn; spinelike. **2** having spines; spinose.

Spi•no•zism [spɪ'nouzɪzəm] *n.* the philosophy of Baruch Spinoza (1632-1677), who taught that God or Nature is the sole infinite reality, of whose infinite attributes human beings can only know thought and extension. **—Spi'no•zist,** *n.*

spin•ster ['spɪnstər] *n.* **1** any woman who has never been married (*used especially in legal documents*). **2** an elderly or middle-aged woman who has never married. **3** *Archaic.* a woman whose occupation is spinning. ⟨ME *spinster* < *spin* + *-ster*⟩ **—'spin•ster•ish,** *adj.* **—'spin•ster•ly,** *adj.* **—'spin•ster,hood,** *n.*

spin•tha•ri•scope [spɪn'θærə,skoup] *or* [spɪn'θɛrə,skoup] *n.* a device that displays on a fluorescent screen the scintillations caused by alpha rays striking it from a radioactive substance. ⟨< Gk. *spintharis* spark + E *-scope*⟩

spi•nule ['spaɪnjul] *or* ['spɪnjul] *n. Zoology. Botany.* a small, sharp-pointed spine. **—'spi•nu,lose,** *adj.*

spin•y ['spaɪni] *adj.* **spin•i•er, spin•i•est. 1** covered with spines; having spines; thorny: *a spiny cactus, a spiny porcupine.* **2** spinelike. **3** difficult; troublesome: *a spiny problem. The manager is being unusually spiny today.* **—'spin•i•ness,** *n.*

spiny anteater echidna.

spiny dogfish any of various small sharks belonging to the order Squaliformes, family Squalidae, having one sharp spiny process in front of each dorsal fin, especially *Squalus acanthias* of North Atlantic coastal waters and *Squalus suckleyi* of the Pacific coast of North America.

spin•y–finned ['spaɪni ,fɪnd] of fish, having fins with stiff spines supporting the membrane; opposed to SOFT-FINNED.

spiny lobster any of the family Palinuridae of large edible crustaceans, distinguished from the true lobster by the absence of pincers and the presence of a spiny shell.

spi•ra•cle ['spirəkəl] *or* ['spaɪrəkəl] *n.* **1** a small body opening in certain animals, used for respiration. Rays and sharks have spiracles on the top of the head, through which they take in water for their gills. Insects and spiders breathe through a series of spiracles on the side of the body. The blowhole of a whale is a spiracle. **2** a vent or air hole, such as an opening in the ground through which underground vapours are given off. ⟨< L *spiraculum* < *spirare* breathe⟩ **—spi'rac•u•lar** [spɪ'rækjələr], *adj.*

spi•rae•a [spaɪ'riə] *n.* See SPIREA.

spi•ral ['spaɪrəl] *n., adj., v.* **-ralled** or **-raled, -rall•ing** or **-ral•ing.** *—n.* **1** *Geometry.* **a** a plane curve formed by a point moving around a fixed central point in a continuously increasing or decreasing arc. **b** helix. **2** an object having the form of a spiral, such as a watch spring. **3** a single coil of a spiral. **4** a flight or course in the form of a spiral. **5** a constant increasing or decreasing, especially of two or more interdependent quantities: *an inflationary spiral.*
—adj. having the form or shape of a spiral: *a spiral spring, the spiral stripes on a barber pole.*
—v. **1** move or cause to move in a spiral: *The flaming airplane spiralled to earth. The wind spiralled the fallen leaves in the yard.* **2** form (into) a spiral. **3** increase or decrease in a spiral. ⟨< Med.L *spiralis* < L *spira* a coil < Gk. *speira*⟩ **—'spi•ral•ly,** *adv.*

spiral galaxy *Astronomy.* a cluster of stars in the apparent form of a spiral.

spiral nebula SPIRAL GALAXY.

spi•rant ['spaɪrənt] *n. Phonetics.* a consonant uttered with audible friction through a partially blocked cavity, such as [s], [θ], or [v]; fricative. ⟨< L *spirans*, *-antis*, ppr. of *spirare* breathe⟩

spire[1] [spaɪr] *n., v.* **spired, spir•ing.** *—n.* **1** the top part of a tower or steeple that narrows to a point. **2** anything tapered and pointed, as for example the spike or top part of a plant, a narrow mountain peak, etc.: *The sunset shone on the rocky spires of the mountains.*
—v. **1** extend upward like a spire. **2** furnish with a spire. ⟨OE *spir*⟩ **—'spire,like,** *adj.*

spire[2] [spaɪr] *n.* **1** a coil; spiral. **2** a single twist of a coil or spiral. **3** *Zoology.* the upper part of a spiral shell, as of that of a gastropod. ⟨< L < Gk. *speira* coil⟩

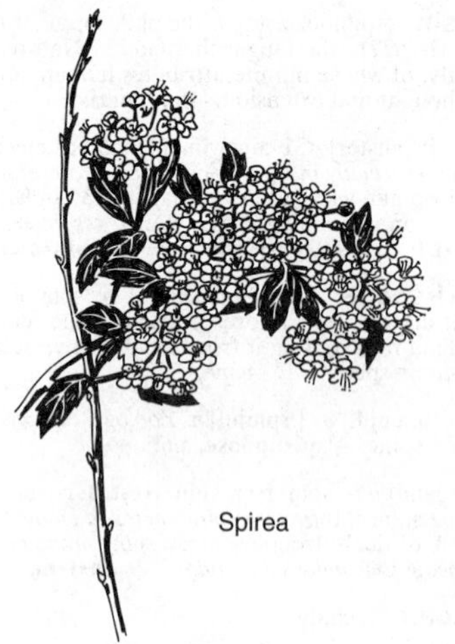

Spirea

spi•re•a or **spi•rae•a** [spaɪ'riə] *n.* any of a genus (*Spiraea*) of shrubs and herbs of the rose family, including many varieties and hybrids cultivated for their showy clusters of small white, pink, or red flowers. ⟨< L < Gk. *speiraia,* apparently < *speira* coil. 17c.⟩

spi•ril•lum [spaɪ'rɪləm] *n., pl.* **-ril•la** [-'rɪlə]. **1** any of a genus (*Spirillum*) of rigid, spiral-shaped, gram-negative bacteria. **2** any similarly shaped micro-organism. See BACILLI for picture. ⟨< NL *spirillum* < L *spira* spire[2] < Gk. *speira*⟩

spir•it ['spɪrɪt] *n., v. —n.* **1** the immaterial part of a human being; the soul: *Many religions teach that at death the spirit leaves the body.* **2** the moral, religious, or emotional nature of human beings or a human being. **3 a** the impersonal life force or life principle of the universe. **b** life, will, thought, or consciousness in general, as distinct from matter in general. **4** a supernatural being, such as a god, a ghost, or a fairy. **5** (*adjl.*) having to do with spirits, spiritualism, spiritualistic phenomena, etc. **6 the Spirit, a** God. **b** *Christianity.* the Holy Spirit, the third Person of the Trinity. **7** Often, **spirits,** *pl.* a state of mind; disposition; temper: *She is in good spirits.* **8** a person; personality: *Montcalm was a noble spirit.* **9** an influence that stirs up and rouses: *A spirit of reform marked the 19th century.* **10** characteristic attitude; prevailing quality: *the spirit of the age.* **11 spirits,** *pl.* liveliness; cheerfulness. **12** courage; vigour; liveliness: *That racehorse has spirit.* **13** enthusiasm and loyalty. **14** the real meaning or intent: *The spirit of a law is more important than its words.* **15** Often, **spirits,** *pl.* **a** a solution in alcohol: *spirits of camphor, spirit of ammonia.* **b** an alcoholic drink made by distilling the juice of certain fruits, grains, roots, etc.; liquor: *He drinks beer but no spirits.* **c** *Chemistry.* any liquid product of distillation, such as turpentine. **16** (*adjl.*) using alcohol as fuel: *a spirit lamp.*
out of spirits, sad; gloomy.
—v. **1** carry (*away* or *off*) secretly: *The child has been spirited away.* **2** conjure (up). ⟨< L *spiritus,* originally, breath < *spirare* breathe. Doublet of ESPRIT, SPRITE.⟩

spir•it•ed ['spɪrɪtɪd] *adj.* full of energy and spirit; lively; dashing: *a spirited racehorse.* **—'spir•it•ed•ly,** *adv.* **—'spir•it•ed•ness,** *n.*

spirit gum a gum solution, often gum arabic in ether, used to attach false hair to the head, face, hands, etc., by actors or those wishing to disguise themselves.

spir•it•ism ['spɪrɪ,tɪzəm] *n.* spiritualism.

spir•it•less ['spɪrɪtlɪs] *adj.* without spirit or courage; depressed. **—'spir•it•less•ly,** *adv.* **—'spir•it•less•ness,** *n.*

spirit level an instrument used to find out whether a surface is level. When the bubble of air in the glass tube of a spirit level laid on a surface is exactly at the middle of the tube, the surface is level.

spir•i•to•so [,spɪrə'tousou] *adj., adv. Music. —adj.* spirited; lively.
—adv. with spirit; in a lively manner. ⟨< Ital.⟩

spirits of wine ALCOHOL (def. 1).

spir•i•tu•al ['spɪrɪtʃuəl] *or* ['spɪrɪtʃəl] *adj., n. —adj.* **1** of or having to do with the spirit as distinct from corporeal or material things: *our spiritual nature.* **2** having to do with the intellect, the mind, or the spirit. **3** sacred; religious: *spiritual songs.* **4** of the church, as opposed to secular institutions: *spiritual authority.* **5** of or having to do with spirits; supernatural. **6** of, having to do with, or involving SPIRITUALISM (def. 2). **7** devoted to or very interested in spiritual things. **8** *Christianity.* yielded to the Holy Spirit.
—n. a deeply emotional religious song or hymn with a jazz rhythm. Spirituals developed from the folk music of the black people in the S United States. **—'spir•i•tu•al•ly,** *adv.*

spir•i•tu•al•ism ['spɪrɪtʃuə,lɪzəm] *or* ['spɪrɪtʃə,lɪzəm] *n.* **1** the belief that spirits of the dead communicate with the living, especially through persons called mediums. **2** emphasis or insistence on the spiritual; the doctrine that spirit alone is real.

spir•i•tu•al•ist ['spɪrɪtʃuəlɪst] *or* ['spɪrɪtʃəlɪst] *n.* a person who believes in or practises spiritualism.

spir•i•tu•al•is•tic [,spɪrɪtʃuə'lɪstɪk] *or* [,spɪrɪtʃə'lɪstɪk] *adj.* of or having to do with spiritualism or spiritualists.
—,spir•i,tu•al'is•ti•cal•ly, *adv.*

spir•i•tu•al•i•ty [,spɪrɪtʃu'æləti] *n., pl.* **-ties. 1** a devotion to spiritual things; spiritual quality. **2** something belonging in ecclesiastical law to the church, a member of the clergy, or religion. **3** incorporeal existence.

spir•i•tu•al•ize ['spɪrɪtʃuə,laɪz] *or* ['spɪrɪtʃə,laɪz] *v.* **-ized, -iz•ing. 1** make spiritual. **2** interpret or analyse so as to give a spiritual sense to. **—,spir•i•tu•al•i'za•tion,** *n.*

spir•i•tu•el [,spɪrɪtʃu'ɛl]; *French,* [spiʀity'ɛl] *adj., fem.* **spir•i•tu•elle.** showing a refined mind or wit. ⟨< F *spirituel,* ult. < L *spiritus.* See SPIRIT.⟩

spir•i•tu•ous ['spɪrɪtʃuəs] *adj.* **1** containing alcohol: *spirituous liquors.* **2** distilled, not fermented.
—,spir•i•tu'os•i•ty [,spɪrɪtʃu'ɒsəti], *n.*

spiro–[1] *prefix.* respiration: *spirograph.* ⟨combining form of L *spirare* breathe⟩

spiro–[2] *prefix.* spirals; coils: *spiroid.* ⟨combining form of L *spira* < Gk. *speira* coil⟩

spi•ro•chete ['spaɪrə,kit] *n. Bacteriology.* any of an order (Spirochaetales) of flexible, spiral-shaped bacteria, including the species that causes syphilis. Also, **spirochaete.** ⟨< NL < Gk. *speira* coil + *chaitē* hair⟩

spi•ro•graph ['spaɪrə,græf] *n.* an instrument for recording respiratory movements.

spi•ro•gy•ra [,spaɪrə'dʒaɪrə] *n. Botany.* any of several algae that grow in scumlike masses in freshwater ponds or tanks. ⟨< NL < Gk. *speira* coil + *gyros* circle⟩

spi•roid ['spaɪrɔɪd] *adj.* spiral in form; shaped like a screw.

spi•rom•e•ter [spaɪ'rɒmətər] *n.* an instrument for measuring the capacity of the lungs, by the amount of air that can be breathed out after the lungs have been filled as full as possible. ⟨< L *spirare* breathe + E *-meter*⟩ **—,spi•ro'met•ric** [,spaɪrə'mɛtrɪk], *adj.* **—spi'rom•e•try,** *n.*

spirt [spɜrt] *v., n.* See SPURT.

spir•y ['spaɪri] *adj.* **-i•er,, -i•est. 1** having the form of a spire; tapering. **2** having many spires.

spit[1] [spɪt] *v.* **spat** or **spit, spit•ting;** *n. —v.* **1** eject saliva from the mouth. **2** eject from the mouth, as sunflower seeds, etc. (*often with* **out**). **3** throw out: *The gun spits fire.* **4** express hatred or contempt by or as if by spitting (*at, on,* etc.) a person or thing. **5** make a hissing noise: *The cat spits when angry.* **6** sputter. **7** rain or snow slightly. **8** utter viciously or scornfully (*used with* **out**): *He spat out the threat that they would be sorry.*
spit up, regurgitate: *The baby spat up the milk. The baby must be getting teeth; she's been spitting up a lot.*
—n. **1** the liquid produced in the mouth; saliva. **2** the noise or act of spitting. **3** a frothy or spitlike secretion given off by some insects. **4** a light rain or snow.
the spit of, *Informal.* just like. ⟨OE *spittan*⟩ **—'spit•ter,** *n.*

spit[2] [spɪt] *n., v.* **spit•ted, spit•ting.** *—n.* **1** a sharp-pointed, slender rod or bar on which meat is roasted, usually turned so that the meat is cooked evenly. **2** a narrow point of land running into the water.
—v. **1** run a spit through; put on a spit. **2** pierce; stab. ⟨OE *spitu*⟩

spit and image *Informal.* See SPITTING IMAGE.

spit and polish *Informal.* a high standard of cleanliness or neatness. ⟨from the soldier's practice of using spit in polishing boots, etc.⟩

spit•ball ['spɪt,bɒl] *n.* **1** a small ball of chewed-up paper, used as a missile. **2** *Baseball.* a curve, now illegal, resulting from the pitcher's moistening one side of the ball with saliva.

spit•bug ['spɪt,bʌg] *n.* any insect of the family Cercopidae, whose larvae create white foam on plants.

spit curl *Informal.* a small wisp of hair that is dampened, curled, and pressed against the cheek, temple, etc.

spite [spəit] *n., v.* **spit•ed, spit•ing.** *—n.* ill will; a grudge.
in spite of, not prevented by; notwithstanding: *We decided to go in spite of the rain.*
—v. show ill will toward; annoy: *He left his yard dirty to spite the people who lived next door.* ⟨shortened from ME *despit* despite⟩
—'spite•less, *adj.*
☛ *Syn. n.* **1. Spite,** MALICE, GRUDGE = ill will against another. **Spite** suggests envy or a mean disposition, and applies to active ill will shown by doing mean, petty things to hurt or annoy: *She ruined his flowers out of spite.* **Malice** emphasizes actual wish or intention to injure, and suggests hatred or, especially, a disposition that delights in doing harm or seeing others hurt: *Gossips are motivated by malice.* **Grudge** suggests wishing to get even for real or imagined injury, and applies to ill will nursed over a long time: *He bears grudges.*

spite•ful ['spəitfəl] *adj.* full of ill will; eager to annoy; behaving with ill will and malice. **—'spite•ful•ly,** *adv.* **—'spite•ful•ness,** *n.*

spit•fire ['spɪt,faɪr] *n.* **1** a person, especially a woman or girl, who has a quick and fiery temper. **2** something that sends forth fire, such as a cannon or some kinds of fireworks.

spitting image *Informal.* exact or perfect likeness: *In that dress she looked the spitting image of her grandmother.* Also, **spit and image.** ⟨altered from *spit*[1] *and image*⟩

spit•tle ['spɪtəl] *n.* saliva; SPIT[1]. ⟨< *spit*[1]⟩

spit•toon [spɪ'tun] *n.* a receptacle or container for spitting into, often having a funnel-shaped top; cuspidor.

spitz [spɪts] *n.* any of various types of small dog having long, thick hair, erect ears, a pointed muzzle, and a tail curling over the back; especially a white variety of Pomeranian, the smallest of all the spitz breeds. ⟨< G *spitz* pointed⟩

spiv [spɪv] *n. Brit. Slang.* a person who avoids honest work and makes a living by dubious, usually illegal, means, especially by buying and selling goods on the black market. ⟨prob. a dial. var. of *spiff* dandified person. 20c.⟩

splake [spleik] *n., pl.* **splake** or **splakes.** *Cdn.* a fertile hybrid game fish, produced by fertilizing lake trout eggs with sperm from brook (or speckled) trout. ⟨*sp(eckled)* + *lake* trout⟩

splanch•nic ['splæŋknɪk] *adj.* relating to the viscera: *the splanchnic nerve.* ⟨< Gk. *splanchnon* gut⟩

splash [splæʃ] *v., n. —v.* **1** cause (water, mud, etc.) to fly about. **2** dash liquid about: *The baby likes to splash in his tub.* **3** cause to scatter a liquid about: *She splashed the oars as she rowed.* **4** fall in scattered masses or drops: *The waves splashed on the beach.* **5** dash water, mud, etc., on so as to wet, spatter, or soil. **6** fall, move, or go with a splash or splashes: *She splashed across the brook.* **7** mark with spots or patches. **8** display (a picture or story) prominently in a newspaper or magazine: *The scandal was splashed all over the front page.*
—n. **1** the action or sound of splashing: *The splash of the wave knocked him over. The boat upset with a loud splash.* **2** a spot of liquid splashed on something. **3** an amount of splashed liquid. **4** a spot; patch: *The dog is white with brown splashes.*
make a splash, *Informal.* attract attention; cause excitement.
⟨alteration of *plash,* n., OE *plæsc* puddle⟩

splash•down ['splæʃ,daʊn] *n.* the landing of a capsule or other spacecraft in the ocean after re-entry.

splash•er ['splæʃər] *n.* **1** one who or that which splashes. **2** something that protects from splashes.

splash•y ['splæʃi] *adj.* **splash•i•er, splash•i•est. 1** making a splash or splashes. **2** full of irregular spots or streaks. **3** *Informal.* attracting attention; causing excitement.

splat[1] [splæt] *n.* a broad, flat piece of wood, especially such a piece forming the central upright part of the back of a chair. ⟨origin uncertain; ? < ME *splat* to split open; cut up⟩

splat[2] [splæt] *v.* **splat•ted, splat•ting;** *n., adv. —v.* make a sharp slapping or splashing sound: *The heavy rain splatted against the window.*
—n. such a sound.
—adv. making such a sound: *He threw the tomato splat against the wall. It went splat on the ground.*

splat•ter ['splætər] *v. or n.* splash; spatter. ⟨blend of *spatter* and *splash*⟩

splay [splei] *v., adj., n. —v.* **1** spread; flare. **2** make slanting.
—adj. **1** wide and flat. **2** awkward and clumsy. **3** slanted outward.
—n. **1** a spread; flare. **2** a slanting surface; surface that makes an oblique angle with another. ⟨< *display*⟩

splay•foot ['splei,fʊt] *n., pl.* **-feet.** a broad, flat foot, especially one turned outward.

splay–foot•ed ['splei ,fʊtɪd] *adj.* **1** having splayfeet. **2** awkward; clumsy.

spleen [splin] *n.* **1** a vascular ductless organ located at the left of the stomach in mammals and serving to store blood, destroy worn-out red blood cells, form lymphocytes, filter bacteria, etc. It was formerly believed to be the seat of certain emotions, especially low spirits, bad temper, and spite. **2** a similar organ in other vertebrates. **3** ill humour, especially when mingled with spite: *to vent one's spleen on others.* **4** *Archaic.* melancholy. ⟨ME < L < Gk. *splēn*⟩

splen•dent ['splɛndənt] *adj.* shining; gleaming; brilliant; splendid. ⟨ME < L *splendens, -entis,* ppr. of *splendere* be bright⟩

splen•did ['splɛndɪd] *adj.* **1 a** brilliant; glorious: *a splendid sunset, splendid jewels.* **b** magnificent; grand: *a splendid palace, a splendid victory.* **2** very good; fine; excellent: *a splendid chance.* ⟨< L *splendidus* < *splendere* be bright⟩ **—'splen•did•ly,** *adv.* **—'splen•did•ness,** *n.*
☛ *Syn.* **1.** See note at MAGNIFICENT.

splen•dif•er•ous [splɛn'dɪfərəs] *adj. Informal.* splendid; magnificent. ⟨< Med.L *splendifer,* for LL *splendorifer* (< L *splendor, -oris* splendour + *ferre* to bear) + E *-ous*⟩
—splen'dif•er•ous•ly, *adv.* **—splen'dif•er•ous•ness,** *n.*

splen•dour or **splen•dor** ['splɛndər] *n.* **1** great brightness; brilliant light. **2** a magnificent show; pomp; glory. ⟨ME < L *splendour* < *splendere* be bright⟩ **—'splen•dor•ous** or **'splen•drous,** *adj.*

sple•nec•to•my [splə'nɛktəmi] *n.* surgical removal of the spleen.

sple•net•ic [splə'nɛtɪk] *adj., n. —adj.* **1** having to do with the spleen. **2** bad-tempered; irritable; peevish.
—n. a person who is splenetic in disposition. ⟨< LL *spleneticus* < Gk. *splēnitis* disease of the spleen < *splēn* spleen⟩
—sple'net•i•cal•ly, *adv.*

splen•ic ['splɛnɪk] *or* ['splinɪk] *adj.* of or having to do with the spleen. ⟨< L < Gk. *splēnikos* < *splēn* spleen⟩

splice [spləis] *v.* **spliced, splic•ing;** *n. —v.* **1** join together (ropes, wire, yarn, etc.) by weaving together ends that have been untwisted. A splice is usually fastened by bolting or binding. **2** join together (two pieces of timber) by overlapping. **3** join together (film, tape, etc.) by cementing to a third piece that overlaps the two cut ends. **4** *Slang.* marry.
—n. **1** a joining of ropes, timbers, tapes, etc. by splicing. **2** a joint made in such a way. **3** *Slang.* a marriage; wedding. ⟨< MDu. *splissen*⟩ **—'splic•er,** *n.*

spline [splaɪn] *n., v.* **splined, splin•ing.** *—n.* **1** a long, narrow, relatively thin strip of wood or metal; slat. **2** a long, flexible strip of wood or the like used in drawing curves. **3** a flat, rectangular piece or key fitting into a groove or slot between parts of a machine, etc. **4** the groove for such a piece.
—v. fit with a spline. ⟨origin uncertain⟩

splint [splɪnt] *n., v. —n.* **1** a rigid arrangement of wood, metal, plaster, etc. to hold a broken or dislocated bone in place until it is put in a cast or, sometimes, until it heals. **2** a thin strip of wood, such as is used in making baskets. **3** a thin metal strip or plate. Old armour often had overlapping splints to protect the elbow, knee, etc. and allow easy movement. **4** a hard, bony growth on the SPLINT BONE of a horse, mule, etc.
—v. **1** secure, hold in position, or support by means of a splint or splints. **2** support as if with splints. ⟨< MDu. or MLG *splinte*⟩

splint bone one of the two smaller bones on either side of the cannon bone of a horse, etc.

splin•ter [splin'tər] *n., v. —n.* **1** a thin, sharp piece of wood, bone, glass, etc.: *He got a splinter in his hand. The mirror broke into splinters.* **2** a SPLINTER GROUP.
—v. split or break into splinters. ⟨< MDu.⟩

splinter group or **party** a body formed by a small dissenting group that has broken away from a political party, religious organization, etc.

splin•ter•y ['splɪntəri] *adj.* **1** apt to splinter: *splintery wood.* **2** of or like a splinter. **3** rough and jagged, as if from splintering. **4** full of splinters.

split [splɪt] *v.* **split, split•ting;** *n., adj. —v.* **1** break or cut from end to end, or in layers. **2** separate into parts; divide: *The huge tree split when it was struck by lightning. They split the cost of the dinner between them.* **3** divide into different groups, factions, parties, etc. **4** *Chemistry.* **a** divide (a molecule) into two or more

individual atoms. **b** divide (an atomic nucleus) into two portions of approximately equal mass by forcing the absorption of a neutron. **5** issue a certain number of new shares of (stock) for each share currently held. **6** *Slang.* leave; depart: *Let's split.*
split hairs. See HAIR.
split off, remove, separate, or be separated by splitting.
split (one's) **vote, ticket**, or **ballot,** *Esp. U.S.* vote for candidates of different political parties.
split up, a divide into parts. **b** end a lasting relationship: *They split up after five years together.* **c** go off in different directions.
—*n.* **1** the act or process of splitting. **2** a narrow break, gap, or tear caused by splitting. **3** a breach or division created in a group. **4** a faction formed in this way. **5** *Slang.* a portion or share, especially of loot. **6** a confection consisting of fruit, such as a banana, split lengthwise and topped with ice cream, whipped cream, nuts, etc. **7** *Informal.* a bottle of mineral water, champagne, etc. half the usual size. **8** *Informal.* a drink of liquor half the usual size. **9** Often, **splits,** *pl.* an exercise in which one lowers oneself to the floor with the legs stretched out in opposite directions. **10** a single thickness of leather resulting from horizontal splitting. **11** a flexible wooden strip used for making baskets.
—*adj.* divided or separated from end to end. ⟨< MDu. *splitten*⟩
—'split•ter, *n.*

split decision *Boxing.* a decision of a bout on whose outcome the referee and the judges did not unanimously agree.

split infinitive *Grammar.* an infinitive having an adverb between *to* and the verb. *Example*: *He wants to never work, but to always play.*

☛ *Usage.* **Split infinitive.** Although split infinitives are not necessarily wrong, awkward ones should be avoided. Awkward: *After a while I was able to, although not very accurately, distinguish the good customers from the sulky ones.* Improved: *After a while I was able to distinguish, though not very accurately, the good customers from the sulky ones.*

split–lev•el ['splɪt 'lɛvəl] *adj., n.* —*adj.* referring to a type of dwelling divided so that each floor level is about half a storey higher or lower than the one beside it, with a short flight of stairs leading between levels.
—*n.* a house or building so constructed.

split personality *Psychology.* a personality characterized by two seemingly independent, contradictory patterns of behaviour.

split second 1 a very small part of a second. **2** an imperceptible length of time: *I'll be finished in a split second.*

split–sec•ond ['splɪt 'sɛkənd] *adj.* **1** extremely quick; happening in a flash; instantaneous: *a split-second decision.* **2** accurate to the fraction of a second: *split-second timing.*

split shift a period of work divided into two periods such that the interval between them is greater than the normal meal or refreshment break.

split•ting ['splɪtɪŋ] *adj., v.* —*adj.* **1** that splits. **2** very painful; aching severely: *a splitting headache. My head is splitting.*
—*v.* ppr. of SPLIT.

splodge [splɒdʒ] *n., v.* splotch.

splotch [splɒtʃ] *n., v.* —*n.* a large, irregular spot; splash.
—*v.* **1** make splotches: *Be careful of that pen; it splotches.* **2** splash so as to leave splotches: *The carpet was splotched with paint.* ⟨? blend of *spot* and *blotch*⟩

splotch•y ['splɒtʃi] *adj.* **-i•er, -i•est.** marked with splotches.

splurge [splɜrdʒ] *n., v.* **splurged, splurg•ing.** *Informal.* —*n.* **1** a showing off; an ostentatious display. **2** a lavish or extravagant expenditure: *They made a big splurge for their daughter's wedding.* **3** an instance of extravagant self-indulgence.
—*v.* **1** show off. **2** spend money extravagantly. **3** indulge oneself extravagantly: *After dieting for two weeks, he splurged and had two pieces of pecan pie.*

splut•ter ['splʌtər] *v., n.* —*v.* **1** talk in a hasty, confused way, especially when excited: *She spluttered an explanation of her mistake.* **2** make spitting or popping noises; sputter: *The baked apples are spluttering in the oven.*
—*n.* the act or sound of spluttering. ⟨? var. of *sputter*⟩
—'splut•ter•er, *n.*

Spode or **spode** [spoud] *n. Trademark.* a type of fine pottery or porcelain. ⟨after Josiah *Spode* (1754-1827), a famous potter of Staffordshire, England⟩

spod•u•mene ['spɒdʒə,min] *n.* a yellow or light green mineral, lithium aluminum silicate, a semiprecious stone. *Formula*: $LiAl(SiO_3)_2$

spoil [spɔɪl] *v.* **spoiled** or **spoilt, spoil•ing;** *n.* —*v.* **1** damage; make unfit for use; destroy: *He spoils a dozen pieces of paper in the process of writing a letter.* **2** especially of perishable food, be damaged; become bad or unfit for use: *The fruit spoiled because I kept it too long.* **3** damage the character or disposition of, especially by being too indulgent, permissive, etc.: *That child is being spoiled by too much attention.* **4** mar; detract from the quality, pleasure, etc., of: *She spoiled the surprise by giving too many broad hints.* **5** *Archaic.* despoil, plunder, rob, or pillage: *The Romans spoiled the Egyptians.*
be spoiling for, *Informal.* be longing for (a fight, etc.).
—*n.* **1** Often, **spoils,** *pl.* **a** plunder taken in time of war; things won: *The soldiers carried the spoils back to their own land.* **b** any goods, property, etc. seized by force or similar means after a struggle. **2** an object of plundering; prey. **3 spoils,** *pl. U.S.* government offices and positions regarded as being at the disposal of the successful political party. **4** waste removed in excavating, mining, etc.: *The spoil removed from the mine was used in road building.* ⟨ME < OF *espoillier*, ult. < L *spolium* booty, spoil⟩

☛ *Syn. v.* **1. Spoil,** RUIN = damage beyond repair or recovery. **Spoil** emphasizes damage that so reduces or weakens the value, strength, beauty, usefulness, etc. of something as to make the thing useless or bring it to nothing: *Her friend's unkind comments spoiled her pleasure in her new dress.* **Ruin** emphasizes bringing to an end the value, soundness, beauty, usefulness, health and happiness, etc. of someone or something through a destructive force or irretrievable loss: *He ruined his eyes by reading in a poor light.*

spoil•age ['spɔɪlɪdʒ] *n.* **1** something spoiled, or the amount of it: *We allow for 2 percent spoilage in our shipments.* **2** the decay of food by the action of bacteria. **3** a spoiling or being spoiled.

spoil•er ['spɔɪlər] *n.* **1** a person who or thing that spoils. **2** a person who takes spoils. **3** a competitor or candidate who is unlikely to win but who does well enough to affect the other participants' results. **4 a** a device intended to interrupt airflow and increase drag around an aerodynamic surface such as the wing of an aircraft, to reduce lift in a descent. **b** a similar device, often in the form of a transverse fin or blade, on a moving vehicle such as a sports car.

spoils•man ['spɔɪlzmən] *n., pl.* **-men.** *U.S.* **1** a person who receives a share, or seeks such a share, of political spoils; one who supports a party for this purpose. **2** one who supports the SPOILS SYSTEM.

spoil•sport ['spɔɪl,spɔrt] *n.* a person who spoils or prevents the fun of others.

spoils system *U.S.* the system or practice in which public offices with their salaries and advantages are at the disposal of the victorious political party for its own purposes and in its own (rather than the public) interest.

spoilt [spɔɪlt] *v.* a pt. and a pp. of SPOIL.

spoke[1] [spouk] *v.* **1** a pt. of SPEAK. **2** *Archaic.* a pp. of SPEAK.

spoke[2] [spouk] *n., v.* **spoked, spok•ing.** —*n.* **1** one of the bars running from the centre of a wheel to the rim. **2** a rung of a ladder. **3** one of the radial grips protruding from the outer edge of a ship's wheel.
put a spoke in (someone's) **wheel,** stop or hinder someone from doing something.
—*v.* provide with spokes. ⟨OE *spāca*⟩

spo•ken ['spoukən] *v., adj.* —*v.* a pp. of SPEAK.
—*adj.* **1** expressed with the mouth; uttered; told: *the spoken word.* **2** (*in compounds*) speaking in a certain way: *a soft-spoken man.*

spoke•shave ['spouk,ʃeiv] *n.* a cutting tool having a blade with a handle at each end, originally used for shaping spokes, but now for dressing any curved or rounded surface.

spokes•man ['spouksmən] *n., pl.* **-men.** a man who speaks for another or others.

spokes•per•son ['spouks,pɜrsən] *n.* a person who speaks for another or others: *Ms. Chung was the spokesperson for the factory workers.*

spokes•wom•an ['spouks,wʊmən] *n., pl.* **-wom•en** [-,wɪmən]. a woman who speaks for another or others.

spo•li•ate ['spouli,eit] *v.* **-at•ed, -at•ing.** rob; plunder; despoil. ⟨< L *spoliatus*, ult. < *spolium* booty⟩

spo•li•a•tion [,spouli'eiʃən] *n.* **1** a plundering; robbery. **2** any act of spoiling or damaging. **3** the plundering of neutrals at sea in time of war. **4** *Law.* the act of destroying a document, or of tampering with it so as to destroy its value as evidence. ⟨ME < L *spoliatio, -onis*, ult. < *spolium* booty⟩

spon•da•ic [spɒn'deiɪk] *adj. Prosody.* of or having to do with a spondee; constituting a spondee; consisting of or characterized by a spondee or spondees.

spon•dee ['spɒndi] *n. Prosody.* a foot or measure consisting of two long or accented syllables. The spondee is used to vary other metres. *Example*: Só stróde | hé báck | slów to | the wóund | ed Kíng. ⟨ME < L < Gk. *spondeios* < *spondē* libation; originally used in songs accompanying libations⟩

sponge [spʌndʒ] *n., v.* **sponged, spong•ing.** *—n.* **1** any of a phylum (Porifera) of aquatic multicellular invertebrate animals, usually living in colonies permanently attached to rocks in the sea, and certain species of which have a fibrous, porous, elastic internal skeleton. **2** a piece of the skeleton of such sponges, which readily absorbs water and is used for bathing, scrubbing, etc. **3** a product resembling this skeletal material, made of rubber or cellulose, etc. **4** something like a sponge, such as a gauze pad used in surgery. **5** the act of wiping or rubbing with a sponge: *Just give that floor a sponge, will you? I think I'll just have a quick sponge instead of a shower.* **6** a mop for cleaning the bore of a cannon. **7** yeast dough, especially before kneading. **8** a light, porous, steamed or baked pudding. **9** SPONGE CAKE. **10** *Informal.* SPONGER (def. 4). **11** *Informal.* a person who drinks heavily. **12** *Metallurgy.* a porous mass of a metal such as platinum, obtained by reduction at a temperature lower than the melting point. **13** a person who absorbs much or is regarded as capable of absorbing much: *Children are sponges for knowledge.*
throw or **toss in the sponge** or **throw up the sponge,** give up; admit defeat.
—v. **1** wipe or rub with a wet sponge; make clean or damp in this way. **2** remove or wipe (away or off) with a sponge: *Sponge the mud spots off the car.* **3** absorb. **4** rub or wipe (out) as if with a sponge; remove all traces of; obliterate; efface. **5** gather sponges. **6** *Informal.* live or profit at the expense of another (*used with* **on** *or* **off**): *That lazy man won't work; he just sponges on his family.* ⟨< L < Gk. *spongia*⟩ **—'sponge,like,** *adj.*

sponge bath a washing of the body with a wet sponge or cloth without getting into water.

sponge cake a light, spongy cake made with eggs, sugar, flour, etc. but no shortening.

spong•er ['spʌndʒər] *n.* **1** a person who sponges. **2** a machine for sponging cloth. **3** a person or vessel engaged in gathering sponges. **4** *Informal.* a person who gets by at the expense of others.

sponge rubber a light rubber resembling a sponge but firmer than foam rubber, produced by whipping air into latex or bubbling carbon dioxide through it, used for padding, gaskets, rubber balls, etc.

spon•gy ['spʌndʒi] *adj.* **-gi•er, -gi•est. 1** like a sponge; soft, light, and full of holes: *spongy moss, spongy dough.* **2** absorbent. **3** of or pertaining to a sponge. **—'spon•gi•ness,** *n.*

spon•son ['spɒnsən] *n.* **1** a part projecting from the side of a ship or boat, used for support or protection. **2** a projection from the side of a ship or tank, used to support a gun or to enable it to be trained fore or aft; gun platform. **3** an air-filled section on either side of a seaplane, canoe, etc. to steady it. ⟨? shortening and alteration of *expansion*⟩

spon•sor ['spɒnsər] *n., v. —n.* **1** a person or group that supports or is responsible for a person or thing: *the sponsor of a proposed law, the sponsor of a student applying for a scholarship. I will serve as her sponsor for admission to our club.* **2** a person who takes vows for an infant at baptism; a godfather or godmother. **3** a company, store, or organization that pays the cost of a radio or television program for purposes of advertising, public relations, etc. **4** a person who pledges or gives a certain amount of financial assistance to an organization, or to someone entering a sporting event for charity.
—v. act as sponsor for. ⟨< L < *spondere* give assurance⟩
—'spon•sor,ship, *n.*

spon•so•ri•al [spɒn'sɔriəl] *adj.* of or having to do with a sponsor.

spon•ta•ne•i•ty [,spɒntə'niəti] *or* [,spɒntə'neiəti] *n., pl.* **-ties. 1** the state, quality, or fact of being spontaneous. **2** a spontaneous action, movement, etc.

spon•ta•ne•ous [spɒn'teiniəs] *adj.* **1** caused by natural impulse or desire; not forced or compelled; not planned beforehand: *Both sides burst into spontaneous cheers at the skilful play.* **2** happening without external cause or help; caused entirely by inner forces: *The eruption of a volcano is spontaneous.* **3** growing or produced naturally; not planted, cultivated, etc. ⟨< LL *spontaneus* < L *sponte* of one's own accord⟩
—spon'ta•ne•ous•ly, *adv.* **—spon'ta•ne•ous•ness,** *n.*
☛ *Syn.* **1.** See note at VOLUNTARY.

spontaneous abortion MISCARRIAGE (def. 2).

spontaneous combustion the bursting into flame of a substance as a result of the heat produced by chemical action within the substance itself.

spoof [spuf] *n., v. Slang. —n.* **1** a trick or hoax. **2** a light satirical parody; takeoff.
—v. **1** play tricks on (someone); fool (someone). **2** make a light satirical parody on. ⟨coined by Arthur Roberts (1852-1933), a British comedian⟩ **—'spoof•er,** *n.*

spook [spuk] *n., v. —n. Informal.* **1** a ghost; spectre. **2** anyone appearing ghastly or spectral. **3** a secret agent; spy; member of a government or other official intelligence agency.
—v. **1** startle or scare (a person or animal). **2** become startled or scared: *Our cat spooks every time the phone rings.* ⟨< Du.⟩

spook•y ['spuki] *adj.* **spook•i•er, spook•i•est.** *Informal.* **1** like or suggesting spooks; weird; eerie. **2** especially of horses, easily spooked; jumpy; skittish.

spool [spul] *n., v. —n.* **1** a cylinder of plastic, wood, or metal, often hollow, and having a flared rim at either end to prevent the thread, etc. from slipping off, on which thread, wire, etc. is wound. **2** something like a spool in shape or use.
—v. **1** wind on a spool. **2** *Computer technology.* transfer (output, such as a print job) to a peripheral via a spooler. ⟨< MDu. *spoele*⟩

spool•er ['spulər] *n. Computer technology.* a piece of system hardware or software for buffering output from a computer to a peripheral, such as a printer, in such a way as to free the main application to continue with other tasks.

spoon [spun] *n., v. —n.* **1** a utensil consisting of a small, shallow bowl at the end of a handle, used to take up or stir food or drink. **2** something shaped like a spoon. **3** *Golf.* a kind of club having a wooden head; formerly, a number 3 wood. **4** a shiny, curved lure having hooks attached for catching fish. Also (def. 4), **spoon bait.**
born with a silver spoon in one's mouth, born lucky or rich.
—v. **1** take up in a spoon. **2** hollow out or form in the shape of the bowl of a spoon. **3** *Slang.* kiss and caress amorously, especially in a way considered foolish or sentimental. **4** troll for or catch (fish) with a spoon. **5** *Sports.* hit (a ball) upward in a weak and scooping manner. ⟨OE *spōn* chip, shaving⟩
—'spoon,like, *adj.*

spoon•bill ['spun,bɪl] *n.* **1** any of a small subfamily (Plataleinae, of the family Threskiornithidae) of tropical and subtropical wading birds having long legs and a long bill with a broad, horizontally flattened tip, as the **roseate spoonbill. 2** any other bird having a similar bill, such as the shoveller duck.

spoon•drift ['spun,drɪft] *n.* See SPINDRIFT. ⟨< *spoon* sail before the wind (of uncertain origin) + *drift*⟩

spoon•er•ism ['spunə,rɪzəm] *n.* an unintentional, often humorous, transposing of the first letters or sounds of successive words. *Example*: kinkering kongs *for* conquering kings. ⟨after Rev. William A. *Spooner* (1844-1930), of New College, Oxford, who was famous for such mistakes⟩

spoon–feed ['spun ,fid] *v.* **-fed, -feed•ing. 1** feed with a spoon. **2** spoil; coddle; overprotect: *Industry is being spoon-fed with government grants.* **3** teach or give instructions in such a way as to stifle independent thought or creativity.

spoon•ful ['spun,fʊl] *n., pl.* **-fuls.** as much as a spoon can hold.

spoon•y ['spuni] *adj.* **spoon•i•er, spoon•i•est;** *n., pl.* **spoonies.** *Informal. —adj.* sentimentally amorous; demonstratively fond.
—n. **1** a sentimental or overfond lover. **2** a simpleton.
—'spoon•i•ly, *adv.* **—'spoon•i•ness,** *n.*

spoor [spur] *n., v. —n.* the trail of a wild animal; track.
—v. track by or follow a spoor. ⟨< Afrikaans *spoor* < MDu.; cf. OE *spor* footprint⟩

spo•rad•ic [spə'rædɪk] *adj.* **1** appearing or happening at irregular intervals in time: *sporadic outbursts.* **2** being or occurring apart from others; isolated. **3** appearing in scattered instances: *sporadic cases of scarlet fever.* Also, **sporadical.** ⟨< Med.L < Gk. *sporadikos* scattered, ult. < *spora* a sowing⟩
—spo'rad•i•cal•ly, *adv.*

spo•ran•gi•um [spə'rændʒiəm] *n., pl.* **-gi•a** [-dʒiə]. *Botany.* a receptacle in which asexual spores are produced; spore case. The little brown spots sometimes seen on the underside of ferns are sporangia. ⟨< NL < Gk. *spora* seed + *angeion* vessel⟩
—spo'ran•gi•al, *adj.*

spore [spɔr] *n., v.* **spored, spor•ing.** *—n.* **1** *Biology.* a single cell, produced either asexually or by the union of gametes, that

becomes free and is capable of developing into a new plant or animal. Ferns produce spores. **2** a germ or seed.
–v. produce spores. ⟨< NL < Gk. *spora* seed⟩

sporo– *prefix.* spore: *sporangium.*

spo•ro•phyl or **spo•ro•phyll** ['spɔrə,fɪl] *n. Botany.* any leaf that bears spores or spore cases. ⟨< Gk. *spora* seed + *phyllon* leaf⟩

spo•ro•phyte ['spɔrə,fəit] *n.* the spore-producing form or generation of a plant that reproduces by alternation of generations. It develops from the union of gametes and is the dominant form of higher plants. Compare GAMETOPHYTE. ⟨< Gk. *spora* seed + E *-phyte*⟩ **–,spo•ro'phyt•ic** [,spɔrə'fɪtɪk], *adj.*

spor•ran ['spɔrən] *n.* in Scottish Highland dress, a large purse, commonly of fur or leather, hanging from the belt in front. See KILT for picture. ⟨< Scots Gaelic *sporan*⟩

sport [spɔrt] *n., v. –n.* **1** a game, contest, or other pastime requiring some skill and a certain amount of physical exertion. Baseball and fishing are outdoor sports; bowling and basketball are indoor sports. **2** amusement or recreation: *That was great sport.* **3** (*adjl.*) of or suitable for sports. **4** playful joking; fun: *to say a thing in sport.* **5** ridicule. **6** the object of a joke; plaything: *His hat blew off and became the sport of the wind.* **7** a sports enthusiast. **8** *Informal.* a person who behaves in a sportsmanlike manner; good fellow: *Be a sport.* **9** *Informal.* a gambler. **10** *Slang.* a flashy or showy person. **11** *Biology.* an animal or plant that varies suddenly or in a marked manner from the normal type, as a stem of white flowers on a pink petunia plant.
make sport of, make fun of; laugh at; ridicule: *Don't make sport of his mistakes.*
–v. **1** amuse oneself; play: *Lambs sport in the fields.* **2** jest, often at the expense or discomfort of another. **3** *Informal.* display; wear: *to sport a new hat.* **4** *Biology.* become or produce a sport. ⟨ult. short for *disport*⟩
☛ *Syn. n.* **1.** See note at PLAY.

sport•ful ['spɔrtfəl] *adj.* playful. **–'sport•ful•ly,** *adv.*

sport•ing ['spɔrtɪŋ] *adj., v. –adj.* **1** of, interested in, or engaging in sports. **2** sportsmanlike: *Letting the little boy throw first was a sporting gesture.* **3** willing to take a chance. **4** *Informal.* involving risk; uncertain. **5** interested in sporting events involving betting.
–v. ppr. of SPORT. **–'sport•ing•ly,** *adv.*

spor•tive ['spɔrtɪv] *adj.* playful; merry: *The old dog seemed as sportive as the puppy.* **–'spor•tive•ly,** *adv.* **–'spor•tive•ness,** *n.*

sports [spɔrts] *adj.* **1** of sports; suitable for sports: *a sports outfit.* **2** especially of a man's garment, not intended for wear with or as part of a suit; casual: *a sports jacket, sports shirt.*

sports car **1** any low, fast, two-seater car, usually one having an open top. **2** any car appealing to driving enthusiasts and designed for high speeds and manoeuvrability.

sports•cast ['spɔrts,kæst] *n.* a radio or television broadcast of a sports event or of news or discussion of sports events. **–'sports,cast•er,** *n.*

sports•man ['spɔrtsmən] *n., pl.* **-men. 1** a man who takes part in sports, especially hunting, fishing, or racing. **2** one who likes or follows sports. **3** a person who plays fair and is generous to his or her opponents. **4** a person who is willing to take a chance.

sports•man•like ['spɔrtsmən,ləik] *adj.* like or befitting a sportsman; fair and honourable. Also, **sportsmanly.**

sports•man•ship ['spɔrtsmən,ʃɪp] *n.* **1** the qualities or conduct of a sportsman; fair play and generosity to one's opponents. **2** ability in sports.

sports•plex ['spɔrts,plɛks] *n.* a multipurpose recreational site providing facilities for a number of indoor and outdoor sports, such as swimming, tennis, and skating, at the same time.

sports•wear ['spɔrts,wɛr] *n.* clothing designed for casual wear or recreation.

sports•wom•an ['spɔrts,wʊmən] *n., pl.* **-wom•en** [-,wɪmən]. a woman who takes part in sports.

sports•writ•er ['spɔrts,rəitər] *n.* a newspaper or magazine writer who reports sporting events.

sport•y ['spɔrti] *adj.* **sport•i•er, sport•i•est.** *Informal.* **1** sportsmanlike; sporting. **2** of clothing, showy or flashy. **3** dashing in dress, appearance, manners, etc. **–'sport•i•ly,** *adv.* **–'sport•i•ness,** *n.*

spor•u•late ['spɔrjə,leit] *v.* **-lat•ed, -lat•ing.** *Biology.* produce spores. **–,spor•u'la•tion,** *n.*

spor•ule ['spɔrjul] *n. Biology.* a small spore, especially a spore of certain fungi.

spot [spɒt] *n., v.* **spot•ted, spot•ting;** *adj. –n.* **1** a small discolouring or disfiguring mark made by a foreign substance; stain; speck: *a spot of ink on the paper.* **2** a stain or blemish on one's character or reputation; moral defect; fault; flaw: *Her character is without spot.* **3** a small part of a surface differing in some way from the rest, as in colour, material, or finish: *His tie is blue with white spots.* **4** a place: *From this spot you can see the ocean.* **5** *Esp. Brit. Informal.* a small amount; a little bit: *a spot of lunch.* **6** *Informal.* a position or place with reference to: **a** employment. **b** radio or television scheduling, etc. **7** *Informal.* a spotlight. **8** (*adjl.*) on hand; ready: *a spot answer.* **9** *Botany.* a plant disease; leaf spot. **10 a** a figure or dot on a playing card, domino, or die to show its kind and value. **b** a card, etc. bearing a given number of these: *I had a seven spot of each suit.* **11** a piece of paper money of a given value: *Do you have a five spot? I don't want to break my fifty spot.*
hit the high spots of, *Informal.* deal with the salient points of.
hit the spot, *Informal.* especially of food or drink, be just right; be satisfactory.
in a spot, in a difficult situation.
in spots, a in one spot, part, place, point, etc. and another: *Their argument was weak in spots.* **b** at times; by snatches.
on the spot, a at the very place. **b** at once. **c** in trouble or difficulty: *She put me on the spot by resigning so suddenly.* **d** in a position where an immediate response is expected of one.
–v. **1** make spots (on): *to spot a dress. This pen spots; I'll have to throw it out.* **2** become spotted; have spots: *This silk will spot.* **3** stain, sully, or tarnish (character, reputation, etc.): *He spotted his reputation by lying repeatedly.* **4** place in a certain spot; scatter in various spots: *Lookouts were spotted all along the coast.* **5** *Informal.* pick out; find out; recognize: *The teacher spotted every mistake.* **6** tag for future action; locate: *to spot the enemy.* **7** watch and report (plays) in sports. **8** give to an opponent as an advantage or handicap. **9** act as a SPOTTER (defs. 3-6, 8).
–adj. conducted at random: *a spot check.* ⟨ME, perhaps < G; cf. MDu. *spotte,* ON *spotti*⟩

spot announcement a brief advertisement or announcement made between radio or television programs or at some point during a program.

spot cash money paid just as soon as goods are delivered or work is done.

spot check **1** a brief, rough sampling. **2** a check made without warning. **–'spot-,check,** *v.*

spot fire **1** JUMP FIRE. **2** *Cdn.* an isolated forest fire, limited to a relatively small area.

spot•less ['spɒtlɪs] *adj.* without a spot or blemish, either physical or moral. **–'spot•less•ly,** *adv.* **–'spot•less•ness,** *n.*

spot•light ['spɒt,ləit] *n., v.* **-light•ed** or **-lit, -light•ing.** *–n.* **1** a strong light thrown upon a particular place or person. **2** a lamp that gives such a light: *a spotlight in a theatre.* **3** anything that focusses attention on a person or thing; public notice.
–v. **1** light up with a spotlight or spotlights. **2** call attention to; give public notice to.

spot•ted ['spɒtɪd] *adj., v. –adj.* **1** stained with spots: *a spotted wall.* **2** marked with spots: *a spotted dog.* **3** sullied: *a spotted reputation.*
–v. pt. and pp. of SPOT.

spotted adder MILK SNAKE.

spotted alder *Cdn.* SWAMP ALDER.

spotted fever *Pathology.* any of various fevers causing spots on the skin, especially cerebrospinal fever or typhus fever.

spotted owl a rather rare owl (*Strix occidentalis*) of the western coastal area of North America and inland to the Rocky Mountains, having dark brown plumage with heavily barred and spotted underparts, a puffy round head, and dark eyes.

spot•ter ['spɒtər] *n.* **1** a person who makes or removes spots. **2** a device for making or removing spots. **3** a person who observes a wide area of enemy terrain in order to locate, and direct artillery fire against, any of various targets. **4** a civilian who watches for enemy aircraft over a city, town, etc. **5** a person employed to keep watch on employees, customers, etc. for evidence of dishonesty or other misconduct. **6** any person, aircraft, device, etc. that looks, watches, or observes for some specialized purpose or detail. **7** a machine that automatically sets up the pins in a bowling alley. **8** *Sports.* **a** a person who assists a sportscaster by identifying the players. **b** an assistant to a football coach, reporting plays from a position in the stands. **c** a person stationed close to a performing gymnast for the purpose of guarding against injury.

spot•ty ['spɒti] *adj.* **-ti•er, -ti•est. 1** having spots; spotted. **2** not of uniform quality; irregular: *His work was spotty.* **—'spot•ti•ly,** *adv.* **—'spot•ti•ness,** *n.*

spous•al ['spaʊzəl] *n., adj. —n. Archaic.* Usually, **spousals,** *pl.* the ceremony of marriage.
—adj. of or having to do with a spouse or marriage. ⟨ME *spousaille* < MF *espousailles*⟩ **—'spous•al•ly,** *adv.*

spouse [spʌus] *n., pl.* **spous•es** ['spʌusɪz] *or* ['spaʊzɪz] a husband or wife. ⟨ME < OF < L *sponsus, sponsa,* pp. of *spondere* bind oneself⟩

spout [spʌut] *v., n. —v.* **1** throw out (a liquid) in a stream or spray: *A whale spouts water when it breathes.* **2** flow out with force: *Water spouted from a break in the pipe.* **3** *Informal.* speak or utter in loud tones with affected emotion, or rapidly and volubly: *The old-fashioned actor spouted his lines. She's always spouting proverbs.*
—n. **1** a stream or jet. **2** a pipe for carrying off water: *Rain runs down a spout from our roof to the ground.* **3** a tube or lip by which liquid is poured from a vessel. A teakettle, a coffee pot, and a syrup jug have spouts. **4** a trough or chute for carrying non-liquid substances such as grain, flour, and coal. **5** a column of spray thrown into the air by a whale in breathing.
up the spout, *Slang.* ruined; done for. ⟨Cf. MDu. *spouten*⟩ **—'spout•er,** *n.* **—'spout•less,** *adj.* **—'spout,like,** *adj.*

S.P.Q.R. the Senate and the People of Rome (for L *Senatus Populusque Romanus*).

sprad•dle ['sprædəl] *v.* **-dled, -dling. 1** spread or stretch (the legs) apart; straddle. **2** sprawl. ⟨probably a blend of *sprawl* and *straddle*⟩

sprain [sprein] *v., n. —v.* injure (a joint or muscle) by a sudden twist or wrench: *He sprained his ankle.*
—n. an injury caused by a sudden twist or wrench. ⟨origin uncertain⟩

sprang [spræŋ] *v.* a pt. of SPRING.

sprat [spræt] *n.* **1** a small food fish (*Clupea sprattus*) of the herring family that is common along the Atlantic coasts of Europe. **2** any of various small or young fishes related to the sprat. ⟨OE *sprott*⟩

sprawl [sprɒl] *v., n. —v.* **1** lie or sit with the limbs spread out, especially ungracefully: *The people sprawled on the beach in their bathing suits.* **2** crawl or move awkwardly. **3** spread out or develop in an irregular and straggling way: *sprawling suburbs. Her handwriting sprawled across the page.* **4** cause to sprawl.
—n. the act or position of sprawling. ⟨OE *sprēawlian*⟩

spray[1] [sprei] *n., v. —n.* **1** liquid going through the air in small drops: *We were wet with the sea spray.* **2** something like this: *A spray of bullets hit the target.* **3** an instrument that sends a liquid out as spray. **4** the jet of mist, etc., shot out by such a device. **5** any of a number of products that are dispensed from a container in a mist: *hair spray.*
—v. **1 a** dispense, direct, or apply (a liquid) in a mist or small drops: *Spray this paint on the far wall.* **b** be so dispensed, etc. **2** scatter spray on or over: *We spray apple trees to keep the fruit free of disease.* **3** direct numerous small missiles, etc. upon: *The soldiers sprayed the enemy with bullets.* **4** direct (something that dispenses spray): *Spray the hose over here.* ⟨? < MDu. *sprayen*⟩ **—'spray•er,** *n.*

spray[2] [sprei] *n.* **1** a small branch or piece of some plant with its leaves, flowers, or fruit: *a spray of lilacs, a spray of ivy, a spray of berries.* **2** a floral arrangement or an ornament like this. ⟨ME; cf. Danish *sprag*⟩

spray gun device used to spray paint, insecticide, or other liquids.

spread [sprɛd] *v.* **spread, spread•ing;** *n., adj. —v.* **1** cover or cause to cover a large or larger area; stretch out; unfold; open: *to spread rugs on the floor, to spread one's arms, a fan that spreads when shaken.* **2** cause (a job or other activity) to be continued over a period of time: *He spread his reading assignment over several days.* **3** move further apart: *The rails of the track have spread.* **4** hammer out flat: *She spread the end of the rivet with a hammer.* **5** lie or cause to lie; extend: *Fields of corn spread out before us.* **6** make or become widely or generally prevalent; be or cause to be propagated or disseminated: *to spread a religion. He spread the news. The sickness spread rapidly.* **7** cover with a thin layer: *She spread each slice with butter.* **8** put as a thin layer: *He spread jam on his bread.* **9** be put as a thin layer: *This paint spreads evenly.* **10** set (a table) for a meal. **11** put (food) on a table.
spread (oneself) **thin,** take on too many projects at one time, so that either the work or one's health suffers.
spread (one's) **wings, a** exercise one's independence. **b** develop one's abilities.
—n. **1** the act of spreading: *Doctors fight the spread of disease.* **2** the width; extent; amount of or capacity for spreading: *the spread of a bird's wings, the spread of elastic.* **3** a stretch; expanse. **4** the difference between the highest and lowest numbers of a set, as test scores, market prices, etc. **5** Also called **point spread,** in betting, the number of points by which one team is supposed to beat the other. **6** a cloth covering for a bed or table. **7** *Informal.* the food put on the table; feast. **8** something for spreading on bread, crackers, etc., such as butter or jam. **9** the area of land owned by a rancher. **10** a piece of advertising, a news story, etc. occupying a large number of adjoining columns: *The advertisement was a three-column spread.* **11** two facing pages of a newspaper, magazine, etc. viewed as a single unit in make-up.
—adj. stretched out; expanded; extended. ⟨OE *sprǣdan*⟩ **—'spread•er,** *n.*

spread–ea•gle ['sprɛd ,igəl] *adj., v.* **-gled, -gling.** *—adj.* **1** having the form of an eagle with wings spread out. **2** offensively pro-U.S.
—v. stretch out all the limbs of; cause to lie with arms and legs outstretched.

spread•sheet ['sprɛd,ʃit] *n.* **1** *Computer technology.* a computer method of making calculations in rows and columns, allowing for manipulation, retrieval, and adjustment based on newly entered data. **2** *Accounting.* a worksheet arranged in columns, allowing for easy analysis of related entries on a single sheet.

spree [spri] *n.* **1** a lively frolic; a jolly time. **2** a period during which a person drinks alcoholic liquor to excess; bout of drinking. **3** a period of intense activity. ⟨origin uncertain⟩

sprig [sprɪg] *n., v.* **sprigged, sprig•ging.** *—n.* **1** a shoot, twig, or small branch: *He wore a sprig of heather in his buttonhole.* **2** an ornament or design shaped like a sprig. **3** a scion or offspring of some person, class, institution, etc. **4** a young man; stripling. **5** a small, headless nail.
—v. **1** decorate (pottery, fabrics, etc.) with designs representing sprigs. **2** strip a sprig or sprigs from (a plant, tree, etc.). **3** fasten with sprigs or brads. ⟨ME *sprigge*⟩ **—'sprig•gy,** *adj.*

spright•ly ['sprəitli] *adj.* **-li•er, -li•est.** lively and quick. ⟨< *spright,* var. of *sprite*⟩ **—'spright•li•ness,** *n.*

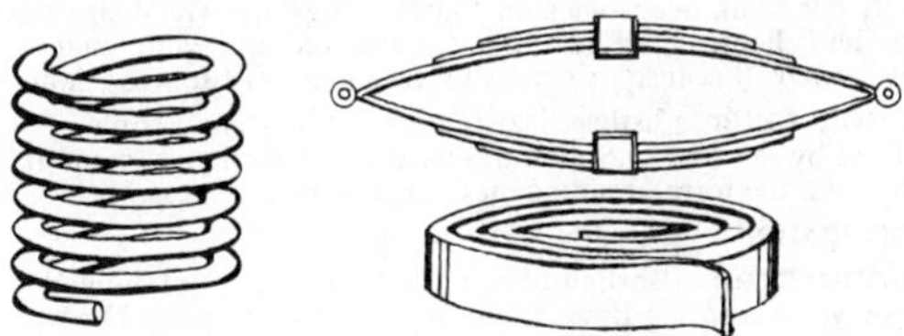

Three different types of metal springs

spring [sprɪŋ] *v.* **sprang** or **sprung, sprung, spring•ing;** *n., adj. —v.* **1** move or rise rapidly or suddenly; leap; jump: *The boy sprang to his feet.* **2** fly back or away as if by elastic force: *The door sprang shut.* **3** arise, appear, etc., suddenly and spontaneously: *When I say* lullaby, *what springs to mind?* **4** cause to spring; cause to act by a spring: *spring a trap.* **5** be flexible, resilient, or elastic; be able to spring: *This branch springs enough to use as a snare.* **6** come from some source; arise; grow (*often with* **up**): *Plants sprang up from the seeds we planted.* **7** derive by birth or parentage; be descended; be the issue of: *to spring from Loyalist stock.* **8** begin to move, act, grow, etc. suddenly; burst forth: *Sparks sprang from the fire. Towns sprang up where oil was discovered.* **9** bring out, produce, reveal, or make suddenly: *to spring a surprise on someone.* **10** *Informal.* pay (*for*): *Who's going to spring for a pizza?* **11** crack, split, warp, bend, strain, or break: *Frost had sprung the rock wall. The road has sprung in several places because of frost.* **12** force to open, slip into place, etc. by or as if by bending: *The burglar was able to spring the lock quite easily.* **13** rouse (partridges, etc.) from cover. **14** *Slang.* secure the release of (a person) from prison by bail or otherwise.
spring a leak, crack and begin to let water through.
spring a mine, cause the gunpowder or other explosive in a mine to explode.
—n. **1** leap or jump: *a spring over the fence.* **2** an elastic device regulating motion or cushioning impact, that returns to its original shape after being pulled or held out of shape: *Beds have wire springs. Many clocks have no spring.* **3** elastic quality: *The old*

man's knees have lost their spring. **4** a flying back from a forced position. **5** the season after winter (in North America, March, April, May) when plants begin to grow. **6** the season between winter and summer; in the northern hemisphere, the three months between the vernal equinox (approximately March 21st) and the summer solstice (approximately June 21st). **7** a small stream of water flowing naturally from the earth. **8** a source; origin; cause. **9** the first and freshest period: *the spring of life.* **10** a crack, bend, strain, or break. **11** SPRING SALMON.
—adj. **1** having a spring or springs. **2** of, having to do with, typical of, or suitable for the season of spring. Spring wheat is wheat sown in spring. **3** from a spring. Spring water often contains healthful minerals. ⟨OE *springan*⟩ **—'spring,like,** *adj.*

spring beauty any of a genus (*Claytonia*) of perennial plants of the purslane family having succulent leaves and white or pinkish, star-shaped flowers that bloom in spring.

spring•board ['sprɪŋ,bɔrd] *n.* **1** a flexible board used to give added spring in diving, jumping, or vaulting. **2** anything that gives one a good start toward a goal or purpose: *Hard work was her springboard to success.*

spring•bok ['sprɪŋ,bɒk] *n., pl.* **-boks** or (*esp. collectively*) **-bok.** a small, graceful antelope (*Antidorcas marsupialis*) of semi-arid regions of southern Africa, known for its habit of suddenly leaping straight up into the air when alarmed, and for its ability to run with high, springing bounds. ⟨< Afrikaans *springbok* springing buck < Du. *springen* leap + *bok* antelope⟩

spring chicken **1** a young chicken used for frying or broiling. **2** *Slang.* a young person: *She's no spring chicken.*

springe [sprɪndʒ] *n., v.* **springed, spring•ing.** *—n.* a snare for catching small game, consisting of a loop of rope or wire attached to a bent-over branch or sapling, and held so that the movement of the animal in the trap releases the loop and the animal is snared and lifted into the air.
—v. catch in a springe. ⟨OE *sprengan* cause to spring⟩

spring•er ['sprɪŋər] *n.* **1** a person or thing that springs. **2** *Architecture.* the part of the structure immediately above the point where the vertical support of an arch ends and the curve begins. See ARCH[1] for picture. **3** SPRINGER SPANIEL. **4** springbok.

springer spaniel either of two breeds of large spaniel often trained as bird dogs. The **English springer spaniel** has a wavy white coat with liver, black, or tan markings; the **Welsh springer spaniel** is lighter in build and has a dark red and white coat, never wavy. ⟨because originally used to SPRING (def. 13) game⟩

spring fever a listless, lazy feeling felt by some people, caused by the first sudden warm weather of spring. In some it may take the form of abundant energy or restlessness.

spring•halt ['sprɪŋ,hɒlt] *n.* stringhalt.

spring•head ['sprɪŋ,hɛd] *n.* **1** the source or fountainhead from which a spring flows. **2** the source of something: *The springhead of her anger lay in his intransigence.*

spring lock a lock that fastens automatically by a spring.

spring roll an oriental appetizer similar to an EGG ROLL, but often smaller, more cylindrical, and with more finely ground contents and crisper pastry.

spring salmon *Cdn.* the largest Pacific salmon (*Oncorhynchus tshawytscha*), found from California to Alaska, mainly dark greenish blue and silver in colour and having red, white, or, sometimes, pink flesh. Spring salmon are highly valued as food fish.

spring•tail ['sprɪŋ,teil] *n.* any of an order (Collembola) of small, primitive, wingless insects found throughout the world, having a forked, tail-like appendage which they use for leaping.

spring•tide ['sprɪŋ,taɪd] *n. Archaic or poetic.* springtime.

spring tide **1** the greatest difference between the high and low tides, occurring either at or just after a new or a full moon. **2** any great flood, swell, or rush.

spring•time ['sprɪŋ,taɪm] *n.* **1** the season of spring. **2** the first or earliest period: *the springtime of life.*

spring•y ['sprɪŋi] *adj.* **spring•i•er, spring•i•est. 1** yielding; flexible; elastic. **2** jaunty; lively; full of bounce: *a springy personality.* **3** having many springs of water. **4** spongy with moisture, as soil in the area of a subterranean spring or springs. **—'spring•i•ly,** *adv.* **—'spring•i•ness,** *n.*

sprin•kle ['sprɪŋkəl] *v.* **-kled, -kling;** *n.* *—v.* **1** scatter in drops or tiny bits. **2** scatter (something) in drops or tiny bits: *He sprinkled sand on the icy sidewalk.* **3** spray or cover with small drops or bits: *to sprinkle flowers with water.* **4** dot or vary with something scattered here and there. **5** rain a little.
—n. **1** the act of sprinkling. **2** a sprinkling; small quantity. **3** a light rain. ⟨ME *sprenklen* or *sprinklen*; cf. Du. *sprenkelen*⟩

sprin•kler ['sprɪŋklər] *n.* **1** a device used to water lawns. **2** a device attached to the ceiling of a building from which water is sprayed in the event of a fire.

sprin•kling ['sprɪŋklɪŋ] *n., v.* *—n.* a small number or amount scattered here and there: *We had a sprinkling of rain early this morning before the sun came out.*
—v. ppr. of SPRINKLE.

sprint [sprɪnt] *v., n.* *—v.* run at top speed, especially for a short distance.
—n. **1** a short race or dash at full speed. **2** a short burst of any intense activity. ⟨ME *sprente(n)*⟩ **—'sprint•er,** *n.*

sprit [sprɪt] *n.* a small pole that supports and stretches a sail. ⟨OE *sprēot*⟩

sprite [sprəit] *n.* **1** an elf; fairy; goblin. **2** a human with spritelike qualities. ⟨ME < OF *esprit* spirit < L *spiritus.* Doublet of ESPRIT, SPIRIT.⟩ **—'sprite,like,** *adj.*

sprit•sail ['sprɪt,seil] *or* ['sprɪtsəl] *n.* a sail supported and stretched by a sprit.

spritz [sprɪts] *or* ['ʃprɪtz] *v., n.* *—v.* squirt or spray (something) in sudden bursts: *She spritzed her hair with water to revive the curl.*
—n. any of various kinds of hair-care products that are applied by spritzing. ⟨< G *spritzen* squirt⟩

sprit•zer ['sprɪtsər] *or* ['ʃprɪtzər] *n.* a long drink made of chilled white wine and club soda.

sprock•et ['sprɒkɪt] *n.* **1** one of a set of projections on the rim of a wheel, arranged so as to fit into the links of a chain. The sprockets keep the chain from slipping. **2** Also, **sprocket wheel,** a wheel made with sprockets. ⟨origin uncertain⟩

sprout [sprʌut] *v., n.* **1** begin to grow; shoot forth: *Seeds sprout. Buds sprout in the spring.* **2** cause to grow: *The rain has sprouted the corn.* **3** develop rapidly: *She's sprouting like a weed.* **4** *Informal.* remove sprouts from: *He sprouted the potatoes twice every winter.*
—n. **1** a small shoot or bud. **2** a small child. **3 sprouts,** *pl.* BRUSSELS SPROUTS. **4 sprouts,** *pl.* the first stalks of germinating beans, eaten as a vegetable: *bean sprouts, alfalfa sprouts.* ⟨OE *-sprūtan*, as in *āsprūtan*⟩

spruce[1] [sprus] *n.* **1** any of a genus (*Picea*) of evergreen tree of the pine family found throughout the northern areas of the world, having hanging cones and short, needlelike leaves growing singly along the stems. There are five species of spruce native to Canada. **2** the wood of any of these trees. ⟨ME *Spruce*, var. of *Pruce* Prussia, perhaps because the trees first came from there⟩

spruce[2] [sprus] *adj.* **spruc•er, spruc•est;** *v.* **spruced, spruc•ing.** *—adj.* neat; trim: *John looked very spruce in his new suit.*
—v. make spruce or make oneself spruce (*usually used with* **up**): *The new slipcovers spruce up the living room. She spruced up before going in for the interview.* ⟨? < *Spruce leather* a superior type of leather formerly imported from Prussia and popular in the 16c. See SPRUCE[1].⟩ **—'spruce•ly,** *adv.* **—'spruce•ness,** *n.*

spruce beer a fermented drink made with an extract of spruce twigs and sugar (or molasses) boiled together.

spruce budworm a moth (*Choristoneura fumiferana*) whose larva feeds on the young needles of spruce and fir and is one of the most serious periodic pests of these trees in Canada and the N United States.

spruce fir *Cdn.* any of a number of fir trees, especially the balsam.

spruce grouse BUSH PARTRIDGE.

spruce hen the female of the spruce grouse or spruce partridge.

spruce partridge *Cdn.* a grouse (*Canachites canadensis*), dark grey barred with black, found in swampy woods.

spruce tea *Cdn.* an infusion of tender young spruce shoots, used to prevent scurvy.

sprue[1] [spru] *n. Pathology.* a chronic disease, found mainly in the tropics, caused by malabsorption of food nutrients by the small intestine, and characterized by anemia, diarrhea, and ulceration of the digestive tract. ⟨< Du. *spruw*⟩

sprue[2] [spru] *n.* **1** an opening through which molten metal or plastic is poured into a mould. **2** the waste metal left in this channel. ⟨origin uncertain⟩

sprung [sprʌŋ] *v.* a pt. and pp. of SPRING.

sprung rhythm a poetic rhythm based on the natural

rhythms of English prose, comprising an irregular number of feet, each with a stressed syllable and any number of unstressed syllables, including none. ⟨coined by the English poet Gerard Manley Hopkins (1844-1889)⟩

spry [spraɪ] *adj.* **spry•er, spry•est.** especially of an elderly person, active; lively; nimble: *The spry old lady travelled everywhere.* ⟨? < Scand.; cf. Swedish *sprugg* active⟩ **—'spry•ly,** *adv.* **—'spry•ness,** *n.*

spt. seaport.

spud [spʌd] *n., v.* **spud•ded, spud•ding.** *—n.* **1** a tool with a narrow blade, for digging up or cutting the roots of weeds. **2** a tool resembling a chisel, for removing bark. **3** *Informal.* a potato. *—v.* **1** dig up or remove with a spud. **2** make a hole as the first stage in drilling (an oil well) (*often used with* **in**): *The new well was spudded in two weeks ago.* ⟨Cf. Danish *spyd* spear⟩

Spud Island *Cdn. Slang.* Prince Edward Island.

Spud Islander *Cdn. Slang.* a Prince Edward Islander.

spue [spju] *v.* **spued, spu•ing.** See SPEW.

spume [spjum] *n., v.* **spumed, spum•ing.** *—n. or v.* foam; froth. ⟨< L *spuma*⟩

spu•mes•cent [spju'mɛsənt] *adj.* **1** frothy; foamy; like foam. **2** frothing; foaming. **—spu'mes•cence,** *n.*

spu•mo•ne [spə'mouni]; *Italian,* [spu'mɔne] *n.* a type of Italian ice cream, usually containing fruit, nuts, etc. Also, **spumoni.** ⟨< Ital.⟩

spum•y ['spjumi] *adj.* **spum•i•er, spum•i•est.** covered with, consisting of, or resembling spume; foamy; frothy.

spun [spʌn] *v.* a pt. and pp. of SPIN.

spun glass glass fibre, made by spinning liquid glass into threads.

spunk [spʌŋk] *n.* **1** *Informal.* courage; pluck; spirit; mettle. **2** a spark. **3** tinder or punk.
get (one's) **spunk up,** *Informal.* show courage, pluck, or spirit.
⟨< Irish or Scots Gaelic *sponnc* < L *spongia* sponge < Gk.⟩

spunk•y ['spʌŋki] *adj.* **spunk•i•er, spunk•i•est.** *Informal.* especially of relatively small or weak people or animals, courageous; plucky; spirited. **—'spunk•i•ly,** *adv.* **—'spunk•i•ness,** *n.*

spun rayon a yarn made from rayon threads. When woven, spun rayon often resembles linen cloth.

spun silk silk waste or floss spun into yarn.

spun sugar CANDY FLOSS.

spur [spɜr] *n., v.* **spurred, spur•ring.** *—n.* **1** a pricking device worn on a rider's heel for urging a horse on. **2** anything that urges on: *Ambition was the spur that made him work.* **3** something like a spur. Many types of cockbirds have spurs on their legs. **4** an abnormal outgrowth of bone, usually on a joint. **5** a ridge projecting from or subordinate to the main body of a mountain or mountain range. **6** any short branch: *a spur of a railway.* **7** CLIMBING IRON. **8** *Botany.* a narrow, hollow projection formed at the base of a sepal or petal, as in the larkspur or the violet, often containing nectar.
on the spur of the moment, on a sudden impulse; without previous thought or preparation.
win (one's) **spurs,** make a reputation for oneself; attain distinction.
—v. **1** prick with spurs. **2** urge one's horse on with spurs. **3** go or ride quickly. **4** strike or wound with a spur or spurs. **5** urge on: *Pride spurred the boy to fight.* **6** provide with a spur or spurs.
spur on, encourage. ⟨OE *spura*⟩

spurge [spɜrdʒ] *n.* **1** any of a large genus (*Euphorbia*) of plants having a bitter, milky juice and clusters of small flowers. Some species and varieties of spurge are grown as garden flowers. The poinsettia is a spurge. **2** (*adjl.*) designating a family (Euphorbiaceae) of plants found in most temperate and tropical regions that includes spurge, croton, rubber, and cassava. Most plants of the spurge family have milky juice. ⟨ME < OF *espurge,* ult. < L *ex* out + *purgare* purge⟩

spur gear **1** SPUR WHEEL. **2** gearing using such wheels.

spu•ri•ous ['spjʊriəs] *adj.* **1** not coming from the right source; not genuine; false; sham: *a spurious document.* **2** *Botany.* of two or more parts of plants, superficially resembling each other but differing in form and structure. **3** illegitimate. ⟨< L *spurius*⟩ **—'spu•ri•ous•ly,** *adv.* **—'spu•ri•ous•ness,** *n.*

spurn [spɜrn] *v., n.* *—v.* **1** refuse with scorn; scorn: *The judge spurned the bribe.* **2** resist with scorn: *They spurned restraint.* **3** strike with the foot; kick away.
—n. **1** disdainful rejection; contemptuous treatment. **2** a kick. ⟨OE *spurnan*⟩

spurred [spɜrd] *adj., v.* *—adj.* having spurs or a spur.
—v. pt. and pp. of SPUR.

spur•ri•er ['spɜriər] *n.* a maker of spurs.

spurt [spɜrt] *v., n.* *—v.* **1** flow suddenly in a stream or jet; gush out; squirt: *Blood spurted from the wound.* **2** cause to gush out. **3** put forth great energy for a short time; show great activity for a short time: *The runners spurted near the end of the race.*
—n. **1** a sudden rushing forth; jet: *Spurts of flame broke out all over the building.* **2** a great increase of effort or activity for a short time. **3** a sudden outburst of feeling, etc. **4** a sudden rise in prices, improvement in business, etc. Also, **spirt.** ⟨var. of *sprit,* OE *spryttan*⟩

spur track a branch railway track connected with the main track at one end only.

spur wheel a wheel with teeth projecting sideways from the rim, parallel to the axis; the simplest form of gearwheel or cogwheel. Also, **spur gear.**

sput•nik ['spʌtnɪk] *or* ['spʊtnɪk] *n.* any of a series of earth satellites put into orbit by the former Soviet Union. Sputnik I, launched in 1957, was the first artificial satellite to orbit the earth. ⟨< Russian *sputnik* companion, satellite⟩

sput•ter ['spʌtər] *v., n.* *—v.* **1** make spitting or popping noises: *fat sputtering in the frying pan. The firecrackers sputtered.* **2** throw out (drops of saliva, bits of food, etc.) in excitement or in talking too fast. **3** say (words or sounds) in haste and confusion.
—n. **1** confused talk. **2** a sputtering; sputtering noise. ⟨probably echoic; cf. Du. *sputtern*⟩ **—'sput•ter•er,** *n.*

spu•tum ['spjutəm] *n., pl.* **-ta** [-tə]. **1** saliva; spit. **2** what is coughed up from the lungs and spat out. ⟨< L⟩

spy [spaɪ] *n., pl.* **spies;** *v.* **spied, spy•ing.** *—n.* **1** a person who keeps secret watch on the actions of others, especially of an enemy or a competitor. **2** a person paid by a government to gather secret information about the government plans, military strength, etc. of another country.
—v. **1** keep secret watch, especially for a hostile purpose (*usually used with* **on**): *They had two men spying on the house.* **2** be a spy; engage in espionage: *The punishment for spying in wartime is death.* **3** catch sight of; see: *They spied a car in the distance.* **4** find out or try to find out by careful observation; search (*often used with* **out**): *to spy out all the happenings in the neighbourhood.* ⟨ME < OF *espie,* n., *espier,* v.< Gmc.⟩

spy•glass ['spaɪ,glæs] *n.* a small, hand-held refracting telescope.

spy•mas•ter ['spaɪ,mæstər] *n.* a person who directs the activities of, and acts as a clearing agent for, a SPY RING.

spy ring an organized group of spies.

sq. **1** square. **2** the following (for L *sequens*). **3** sequence. **4** squadron.

sq. ft. square foot (or feet).

sq. in. square inch(es).

sq. m. square metre(s).

sq. mi. square mile(s).

sqq. the following ones (for L *sequentia*).

squab [skwɒb] *n., adj.* *—n.* **1** a very young bird, especially a young pigeon. **2** a short, stout person. **3** a thick, soft cushion. **4** a sofa; couch.
—adj. **1** newly hatched. **2** short and stout. ⟨Cf. dial. Swedish *sqvabb* loose or fat flesh, dial. Norwegian *skvabb* soft wet mass⟩

squab•ble ['skwɒbəl] *n., v.* **-bled, -bling.** *—n.* a petty, noisy quarrel: *children's squabbles.*
—v. take part in a petty, noisy quarrel. ⟨? imitative⟩
—'squab•bler, *n.*

squab•by ['skwɒbi] *adj.* **-bi•er, -bi•est.** short and stout; squat.

squad [skwɒd] *n.* **1** the smallest unit of military personnel, grouped especially for drill, inspection, or work. **2** *U.S.* the smallest tactical unit in the United States army. **3** any small group of persons working together. ⟨< F < Ital. *squadra* square⟩

squad car SCOUT CAR.

squad•ron ['skwɒdrən] *n.* **1** a part of a naval fleet used for special service. **2** a cavalry unit consisting of two or more troops, together with headquarters and supporting units. **3** an air-force unit larger than a flight and smaller than a group. **4** any group. ⟨< Ital. *squadrone* < *squadra* square⟩

squadron leader **1** the leader of a squadron of cavalry, tanks, or airplanes. **2** an air-force officer ranking next above a flight lieutenant and below a wing commander. *Abbrev.*: S.L. or S/L

squal•id ['skwɒlɪd] *adj.* **1** filthy, degraded, and wretched, especially as the result of poverty or neglect. **2** sordid. ⟨< L *squalidus* < *squalere* be filthy⟩ **—'squal•id•ness** or **squa'lid•i•ty,** *n.* **—'squal•id•ly,** *adv.*

squall[1] [skwɒl] *n.* **1** a sudden, violent gust of wind, often with rain, snow, or sleet. **2** *Informal.* a spell of trouble. ⟨Cf. Swedish *skval-regn* sudden downpour of rain⟩

squall[2] [skwɒl] *v., n.* *—v.* cry out loudly; scream violently: *The baby squalled.*
—n. a loud, harsh cry: *The parrot's squall was heard all over the house.* ⟨< Scand.; cf. ON *skvala* cry out⟩ **—'squall•er,** *n.*

squall jacket windbreaker.

squal•ly[1] ['skwɒli] *adj.* **squal•li•er, squal•li•est. 1** disturbed by sudden and violent gusts of wind: *squally weather.* **2** blowing in squalls. **3** *Informal.* threatening; troublesome.

squal•ly[2] ['skwɒli] *adj.* **-li•er, -li•est.** of an infant, given to frequent sudden fits of angry crying: *a squally baby.* ⟨< *squall*[2] + *-ly*[2]⟩

squal•or ['skwɒlər] *n.* the quality or state of being squalid; misery and dirt. ⟨< L⟩

squa•ma ['skweimə] *n., pl.* **-mae** [-mi] *or* [-maɪ]. *Biology.* a scale or scalelike part: *a squama of bone.* ⟨< L⟩

squa•mate ['skweimeit] *adj.* having scales; covered with scales.

squa•ma•tion [skwei'meiʃən] *or* [skwə'meiʃən] *n.* **1** the condition or state of being squamate. **2** the external arrangement of squamae or scales.

Squa•mish ['skwɒmɪʃ] *n.* **1** a First Nations people of the southwest coast of British Columbia. **2** the Salishan language spoken by these people. Also, **Squawmish. 3 squamish,** a squally storm apparently originating in the area to the northwest of the Lower Mainland area of British Columbia.

squa•mose ['skweimous] *adj.* squamous.

squa•mous ['skweiməs] *adj.* furnished with, covered with, or formed of scales; characterized by the development of scales; scalelike. ⟨< L *squamosus*⟩

squam•u•lose ['skwæmjə,lous] *or* ['skweimjə,lous] *adj.* covered or furnished with small or tiny scales.

squan•der ['skwɒndər] *v.* spend foolishly; waste: *He squandered his money in gambling.* ⟨origin uncertain⟩ **—'squan•der•er,** *n.*

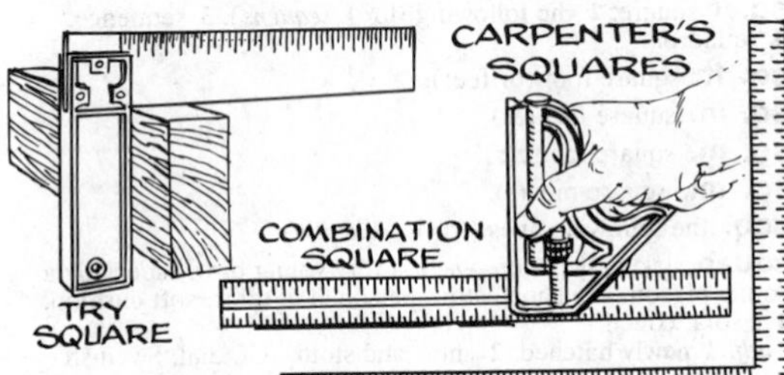

square [skwɛr] *n., adj.* **squar•er, squar•est;** *v.* **squared, squar•ing;** *adv.* *—n.* **1** a plane figure with four equal sides and four right angles. See QUADRILATERAL for picture. **2** anything of or near this shape or having one face in this shape. **3** a marked rectangular space on a game board, as a chessboard, checkerboard, etc. **4** a space in a city or town bounded by streets on four sides: *This square is filled with stores.* **5** one side, or the distance along one side of such a space; block. **6** an open space in a city or town bounded by streets on four sides, often planted with grass, trees, etc. **7** any similar open space, such as the meeting of streets. **8** the buildings surrounding such a place. **9** PARADE SQUARE. **10** an instrument having two straight edges that meet to form a right angle, used in carpentry, etc. for drawing and testing right angles. **11** *Mathematics.* the product obtained when a number is multiplied by itself. The square of 4 is 16. **12** *Slang.* a person who is not in tune with the latest fashions in popular entertainment, culture, etc. **13** formerly, a body of troops drawn up in square formation. **14** Often, **squares,** *pl. Cdn. Slang.* SQUARE MEAL.

back to square one, back to the beginning or the starting point.

on the square, a at right angles. **b** *Informal.* just(ly); fair(ly); honest(ly).

out of square, a not at right angles; out of order; incorrect or incorrectly. **b** not in agreement or accord.

—adj. **1** having four equal sides and four right angles. **2** cubical or nearly so. **3** having one square face in cross section. **4** of a specified length on each side of a square: *a room five metres square.* **5** of measure, expressed using such units: *Prices of flooring are usually given in terms of square metres.* **6** having breadth more nearly equal to length or height than is usual; angular: *a square jaw.* **7** forming or having a right angle: *a square corner.* **8** straight; level; even. **9** leaving no balance; even: *make accounts square.* **10** just; fair; honest: *a square deal.* **11** straightforward; direct: *a square refusal.* **12** *Informal.* satisfying: *a square meal.* **13** *Mathematics.* of or being the product of a number multiplied by itself. **14** solid and strong. **15** *Slang.* not up to date; old-fashioned.

—v. **1** make square; make rectangular; make cubical. **2** mark out in squares. **3** bring to the form of a right angle. **4** make straight, level, or even: *to square a picture on the wall.* **5** adjust; settle: *Let us square our accounts.* **6** agree or cause to agree; conform: *His acts do not square with his promises. I can't square his story with hers.* **7** regulate. **8** *Mathematics.* **a** find the equivalent of (a figure) in square measure. **b** multiply (a number) by itself. **9** *Sports.* bring (the score of a game or contest) to equality; tie: *to square the score with a touchdown in the third quarter.* **10** *Slang.* win over, conciliate, or secure the silence or consent of, especially by bribery; bribe.

square away, a of a ship, set the sails so that it will stay before the wind. **b** tidy; put in order. **c** take care of (a matter); settle.

square off, *Informal.* put oneself in a position of defence or attack.

square (oneself), *Informal.* **a** make up for something one has said or done. **b** get even.

square the circle, a find a square equal in area to a circle. **b** attempt something impossible.

square up, a settle accounts. **b** take up a fighting stance; get ready to fight. **c** square (defs. 2-6).

—adv. **1** *Informal.* fairly or honestly. **2** so as to be square; in square or rectangular form; at right angles. ⟨ME < OF *esquar*(r)*e*, ult. < L *ex* out + *quadrus* square⟩ **—'square•ly,** *adv.*

square dance a dance performed by four or more couples arranged in some set form, especially in a square. The quadrille and Virginia reel are square dances.

square–dance ['skwɛr ,dæns] *v.* **-danced, -danc•ing.** take part in a square dance. **—'square-,danc•er,** *n.*

square deal *Informal.* fair and honest treatment.

square flipper *Cdn.* BEARDED SEAL.

square knot a knot firmly joining two loose ends of rope or cord; reef knot. Each end is formed into a loop which both encloses and passes through the other. See KNOT for picture.

square meal a substantial or satisfying meal.

square measure a unit or system of units for measuring area. The hectare is a square measure.

square–rigged ['skwɛr ,rɪgd] *adj. Nautical.* having the principal sails set at right angles across the masts.

square–rig•ger ['skwɛr ,rɪgər] *n. Nautical.* a square-rigged ship.

square root *Mathematics.* a number that produces a given number when multiplied by itself. If the given number is 16, the square root is 4.

square sail *Nautical.* a four-sided sail set beneath a horizontal yard positioned athwart the keel.

square shooter *Informal.* a fair and honest person.

square•tail ['skwɛr,teil] *n. Cdn.* **1** BROOK TROUT. **2** PRAIRIE CHICKEN (defs. 1 and 2).

square timber *Cdn.* formerly, squared logs such as those rafted to the Québec timber coves for shipment.

square–toed ['skwɛr ,toud] *adj.* having a broad, square toe: *a square-toed boot.*

squar•ish ['skwɛrɪʃ] *adj.* nearly square; having breadth more nearly equal to length or height than is usual.

squar•rose ['skwærous], ['skwɛrous], *or* [skwə'rous] *adj. Biology.* having a rough, scaly, or ragged surface. ⟨< L *squarrosus* scabbed⟩

squash[1] [skwɒʃ] *v., n.* *—v.* **1** press until soft or flat; crush; be crushed in this way: *The boy squashed the bug. Carry the cream puffs carefully, for they squash easily.* **2** make a squashing sound;

move with a squashing sound: *We heard her squash through the mud and slush.* **3** put an end to; stop by force: *The police squashed the riot.* **4** *Informal.* silence with a crushing argument, reply, etc. **5** crowd; squeeze.
—n. **1** something squashed; a crushed mass. **2** a squashing; a squashing sound. **3** a game resembling handball and tennis, played in a walled court with rackets and a rubber ball. **4** a similar game played with a larger racket resembling a tennis racket; squash tennis. **5** *Esp. Brit.* a drink made from concentrate, containing crushed fruit: *lemon squash.* ⟨< OF *esquasser*, ult. < L *ex* out + *quassare*, intensive of *quatere* shake⟩ **—'squash•er,** *n.*

squash² [skwɒʃ] *n., pl.* **squash** or **squash•es. 1** the edible fruit of *Cucurbita maxima* and certain bushy varieties of *C. pepo* of the gourd family, having a greatly variable shape, size, and colour. **2** a plant that produces such fruits. See also SUMMER SQUASH, WINTER SQUASH. ⟨< Algonquian⟩

squash bug a dark brown or black North American bug (*Anasa tristis* of family Coreidae) that is a pest of squash, pumpkin, and related plants.

squash•y ['skwɒʃi] *adj.* **squash•i•er, squash•i•est. 1** easily squashed: *squashy cream puffs.* **2** soft and wet: *squashy ground.* **3** having a crushed appearance. ⟨< *squash¹*⟩ **—'squash•i•ly,** *adv.* **—'squash•i•ness,** *n.*

squat [skwɒt] *v.* **squat•ted** or **squat, squat•ting;** *adj., n.* *—v.* **1** crouch on the heels. **2** cower or crouch close to the ground. **3** sit on the ground or floor with the legs drawn up closely beneath or in front of the body. **4** settle on another's land or in another's property without title or right. **5** settle on public land to acquire ownership of it under government regulation.
—adj. **1** crouching: *We saw a squat figure in front of the fire.* **2** short and thick; low and broad: *The burglar was a squat, dark man. I like that squat teapot.*
—n. the act of squatting; squatting posture. ⟨ME < OF *esquatir* crush, ult. < L *ex-* out + *coactus* forced, pp. of *cogere* < *co-* together + *agere* drive⟩

squat–shack ['skwɒt ʃæk] *n. Cdn.* the shack of a squatter.

squat•ter ['skwɒtər] *n.* **1** a person who settles on another's land or in another's property without right. **2** a person who settles on public land to acquire ownership of it. **3** a person, animal, etc. that crouches or squats.

squat•ty ['skwɒti] *adj.* **-ti•er, -ti•est.** SQUAT (*adj.* 2)

squaw•ber•ry ['skwɒ,bɛri] *n. Cdn.* **1** a kind of blueberry, *accinium stamineum.* **2** bearberry. **3** partridgeberry. ⟨< Algonquian element + E *berry*⟩

squaw•fish ['skwɒ,fɪʃ] *n., pl.* **-fish** or **-fishes.** any of a genus (*Ptychocheilus*) of relatively large cyprinid fishes found in the rivers and lakes of W North America, especially the **northern squawfish** (*P. oregonensis*) of British Columbia, the Peace River region, and the NW United States. ⟨See SQUAWBERRY⟩

squawk [skwɒk] *v., n.* *—v.* **1** make a loud, harsh sound: *Chickens and ducks squawk when frightened.* **2** utter harshly and loudly. **3** *Slang.* complain loudly.
—n. **1** a loud, harsh sound. **2** *Slang.* a loud complaint. ⟨imitative⟩ **—'squawk•er,** *n.*

squawk box *Slang.* a loudspeaker of a public address system.

squaw winter *Cdn.* in the North, an early spell of winter weather, often coming before an Indian summer. ⟨See SQUAWBERRY⟩

squeak [skwik] *v., n.* *—v.* **1** make a short, sharp, shrill sound: *A mouse squeaks.* **2** cause to squeak. **3** utter with a squeak. **4** *Slang.* turn informer; squeal.
squeak through or **by,** *Informal.* pass (something, such as a test) with difficulty and by a narrow margin.
—n. **1** a short, sharp, shrill sound. **2** *Informal.* an act of getting by or through with difficulty; escape: *a narrow squeak.* ⟨ME; probably echoic; cf. Swedish *sqväka* croak⟩

squeak•er ['skwikər] *n.* **1** *Informal.* a game, fight, or other contest won by a narrow margin. **2** someone or something that squeaks.

squeak•y ['skwiki] *adj.* **squeak•i•er, squeak•i•est.** squeaking. **—'squeak•i•ly,** *adv.* **—'squeak•i•ness,** *n.*

squeak•y–clean ['skwiki 'klin] *adj. Informal.* **1** very clean. **2** morally pure, wholesome, etc. (*often ironic*).

squeal [skwil] *v., n.* *—v.* **1** make a long, sharp, shrill cry: *A pig squeals when it is hurt.* **2** utter sharply and shrilly. **3** *Slang.* turn informer. **4** *Informal.* complain loudly; squawk.
—n. **1** a long, sharp, shrill cry. **2** *Informal.* an act of informing against another. **3** *Informal.* an act of complaining loudly. ⟨imitative⟩ **—'squeal•er,** *n.*

squeam•ish ['skwimɪʃ] *adj.* **1** too proper, modest, etc.; easily shocked. **2** too particular; too scrupulous. **3** slightly sick at one's stomach; sickish. **4** easily turned sick. ⟨var. of earlier *squeamous* < AF *escoymous*⟩ **—'squeam•ish•ly,** *adv.* **—'squeam•ish•ness,** *n.*

squee•gee ['skwidʒi] *n., v.* **-geed, -gee•ing.** *—n.* **1** an implement consisting of a handle at right angles to a sponge with a rubber blade on one side, for sweeping water from wet decks, scraping water off windows after washing, cleaning a floor, etc. **2** any of various similar devices. **3** *Photography.* a device with a roller for pressing water from prints, etc.
—v. sweep, scrape, or press with a squeegee. ⟨? < *squeege*, var. of *squeeze*⟩

squeeze [skwiz] *v.* **squeezed, squeez•ing;** *n.* *—v.* **1** press hard, especially from both sides: *Don't squeeze the kitten; you will hurt it.* **2** hug: *She squeezed her child.* **3** force (something) into or out of by pressing: *I can't squeeze another thing into my trunk. Squeeze the juice out of three lemons and add to the sauce.* **4** burden; oppress: *Heavy taxes squeezed the people.* **5** get by pressure, force, or effort: *The dictator squeezed money from the people.* **6** *Informal.* put pressure on or try to influence (a person or persons) to do something, especially pay money. **7** yield to pressure: *Sponges squeeze easily.* **8** force a way: *He squeezed through the crowd.* **9** press (the hand) in friendship or affection. **10** *Bridge.* compel (an opponent) to discard or unguard a valuable card.
—n. **1** the act or an instance of squeezing: *a squeeze of the hand.* **2** a hug. **3** a crush; crowd. **4** a small quantity or amount squeezed out. **5** something made by pressing; cast; impression. **6** *Informal.* a situation from which escape is difficult. **7** *Informal.* pressure used to extort a favour, money, etc. **8** SQUEEZE PLAY. **9** *Business.* pressure resulting from shortages. **10** *Slang.* girlfriend or lover: *my main squeeze.*
tight squeeze, *Informal.* a difficult situation. ⟨ult. < OE *cwӯsan*⟩ **—'squeez•er,** *n.*

squeeze play **1** *Baseball.* a play executed when a runner on third base starts for home as soon as the pitcher begins to pitch. **2** *Bridge.* a play or series of plays in which the holder of a card that may win a trick is compelled to discard it or to unguard another possible winner. **3** *Informal.* an attempt to force somebody into a difficult situation or to make him or her act against his or her wishes.

squelch [skwɛltʃ] *v., n.* *—v.* **1** cause to be silent; crush: *She squelched him with a look of contempt.* **2** strike or press on with crushing force. **3** walk in mud, water, wet shoes, etc., making a splashing or sucking sound. **4** make the sound of one doing so.
—n. **1** a crushing retort. **2** a splashing or sucking sound made by walking in mud, water, wet shoes, etc. ⟨earlier *quelch*, blend of *quell* and *crush*⟩ **—'squelch•er,** *n.*

squib [skwɪb] *n., v.* **squibbed, squib•bing.** *—n.* **1** a short, witty attack in speech or writing; sharp sarcasm. **2** a brief item in a newspaper used mainly to fill space. **3** a small firework that burns with a hissing noise and finally explodes. **4** a broken firecracker. **5** *Informal.* a short written assignment, usually a report or critique.
—v. **1** say, write, or publish a squib or squibs. **2** assail or attack with squibs; lampoon. **3** set off or fire a squib. **4** go off in the manner of a squib. ⟨origin uncertain⟩

squid [skwɪd] *n., pl.* **squid** or **squids;** *v.* **squid•ded, squid•ding.** *—n.* any of various ten-armed marine cephalopod molluscs (genera *Loligo, Omnastrephes, Architeuthis,* etc.), having an elongated body, a pair of triangular tail fins, and a mouth surrounded by ten sucker-bearing arms, two of which are long tentacles used to capture prey.
—v. fish for squid or with a squid as bait. ⟨< *squit*, dial. var. of *squirt*⟩

squid•jig•ger ['skwɪd,dʒɪgər] *n. Cdn., esp. Nfld.*: **1** a device for catching squid, made of several hooks so joined that their points form a compact circle which is pulled or jerked through the water. **2** a person who so fishes for squid. **—'squid,jig•ging,** *n.*

squif•fy ['skwɪfi] *adj. Slang.* drunk; intoxicated. Also, **squiffed** [skwɪft]. ⟨origin uncertain⟩

squig•gle ['skwɪgəl] *n., v.* **-gled, -gling.** *—n.* a twist, curve, curlicue, or wriggle.
—v. **1** make with crooked or twisted strokes; scribble; scrawl. **2** writhe; squirm; wriggle. ⟨blend of *squirm* and *wiggle*⟩

squill [skwɪl] *n.* **1** a Mediterranean plant (*Urginea maritima*) of the lily family having spikes of small white flowers and a bulb that is used in medicine. Also, **sea squill. 2** scilla, especially any of several species cultivated in rock gardens, etc. for their spring-blooming, usually blue, flowers. ⟨< L *squilla*, var. of *scilla* < Gk. *skilla*⟩

squil•la ['skwɪlə] *n.* stomatopod.

squint [skwɪnt] *v., n., adj.* —*v.* **1** look or peer with the eyes partly closed: *He squinted at the sign.* **2** have a squint: *She used to squint before she got glasses.* **3** look sideways or askance. **4** cause (an eye) to squint. **5** incline; tend.
—*n.* **1** a tendency to look with the eyes partly closed. **2** *Ophthalmology.* cross-eye; strabismus. **3** the act or an instance of squinting. **4** inclination; tendency. **5** *Informal.* a brief, casual look: *Take a squint at this.*
—*adj.* **1** looking sideways or askance. **2** of the eyes, having a squint. ⟨< *asquint*, of uncertain origin⟩ —**'squint•er,** *n.*

squint–eyed ['skwɪnt ˌaɪd] *adj.* **1** having a squint; cross-eyed. **2** disapproving; malicious; prejudiced.

squint•ing ['skwɪntɪŋ] *adj., v.* —*adj.* **1** that squints. **2** *Grammar.* concerning structural ambiguity of a modifier that can be interpreted as part of either the preceding or following structure. *Example*: often *in* visiting relatives often can be a nuisance.
—*v.* ppr. of SQUINT.

squire [skwaɪr] *n., v.* **squired, squir•ing.** —*n.* **1** in England, a country gentleman; especially, the chief landowner in a district. **2** formerly, a young man of noble family who attended a knight till he himself was made a knight. **3** an attendant. **4** a woman's escort.
—*v.* **1** formerly, attend as squire. **2** escort (a woman). ⟨ult. var. of *esquire*⟩ —**'squire,like,** *adj.*

squire•ar•chy ['skwaɪrɑrki] *n., pl.* **-chies. 1** the landed gentry as a socio-economic class. **2** a society or system in which the landed gentry hold most of the power.

squirm [skwɜrm] *v., n.* —*v.* **1** wriggle; writhe; twist: *The restless boy squirmed in his chair.* **2** show great embarrassment, annoyance, confusion, etc.
—*n.* a wriggle; writhe; twist. ⟨? imitative⟩

squirm•y ['skwɜrmi] *adj.* **squirm•i•er, squirm•i•est.** squirming; wriggling.

squir•rel ['skwɜrəl] *or* [skwɜrl] *n., v.* **squir•relled** or **squir•reled, squir•rel•ling** or **squir•rel•ing.** —*n.* **1** any of numerous small, quick-moving, arboreal rodents (genera *Sciurus* and *Tamiascurus* of family Sciuridae) having a long, bushy tail and feeding mainly on nuts and seeds. See also GREY SQUIRREL, RED SQUIRREL. **2** any other rodent of the family Sciuridae, especially a **flying squirrel** or a **ground squirrel**. **3** the fur of a squirrel.
—*v.* store or hide for future use (*usually used with* **away**): *He had vast supplies of paper squirrelled away in the closet.* ⟨ME < AF *esquirel* < L *sciurus* < Gk. *skiouros* < *skia* shadow + *oura* tail⟩

squir•rel•ly ['skwɜrəli] *or* ['skwɜrli] *adj. Slang.* **1** crazy. **2** mentally unbalanced, especially as a result of long isolation in the bush; BUSHED (def. 2).

squirt [skwɜrt] *v., n.* —*v.* **1** force out (liquid) through a narrow opening: *squirt water through a tube.* **2** come out in a jet or stream: *Water squirted from a hose.* **3** wet or soak by shooting liquid in a jet or stream: *The elephant squirted me with its trunk.*
—*n.* **1** the act of squirting. **2** a jet of liquid, etc. **3** a small pump, syringe, or other device for squirting a liquid. **4** *Informal.* an insignificant person who is impudent or self-assertive. **5** a young child. ⟨ME; probably echoic; cf. LG *swirtjen*, alteration of earlier *swirt* young or small < LG or Du. *swirtjen*⟩ —**'squirt•er,** *n.*

squirt gun WATER PISTOL.

squish [skwɪʃ] *v., n.* —*v.* **1** make a soft splashing sound when walking in mud, water, etc. **2** *Informal.* squash; squeeze.
—*n.* **1** a squishing sound. **2** the act of squeezing briefly: *Give this little button a squish, and you'll get an eyeful of water.* ⟨imitative alteration of *squash*⟩ —**'squish•y,** *adj.*

sq. yd. square yard(s).

Sr strontium.

Sr. **1** Senior. **2** Sir. **3** Sister.

Sri Lan•ka [ʃri 'lʌŋkə] *or* [ˌsri 'lʌŋkə] an island country in the Indian Ocean, southeast of India, formerly called Ceylon.

S.R.O. standing room only.

SS¹ ['ɛs'ɛs] *n.* formerly, a select military unit in the Nazi Party whose members served as Hitler's bodyguard, concentration camp guards, security police, etc. ⟨< G, short for *Schutzstaffel*⟩

SS² **1** steamship. **2** *Typing.* single space.

SS. Saints.

S.S. **1** steamship. **2** SUNDAY SCHOOL. **3** Secretary of State. **4** SEPARATE SCHOOL. **5** SECONDARY SCHOOL. **6** school section. **7** STAFF SERGEANT.

SSE or **S.S.E.** south-southeast.

SST supersonic transport.

SSW or **S.S.W.** south-southwest.

st. **1** street. **2** stet. **3** stone (weight). **4** stanza. **5** statute. **6** stitch. **7** strophe.

St. **1** Street. **2** Saint. **3** Strait.

sta. station; stationary.

stab [stæb] *v.* **stabbed, stab•bing;** *n.* —*v.* **1** pierce or wound with a pointed weapon. **2** thrust (a pointed weapon); aim a blow. **3** penetrate suddenly and sharply; pierce. **4** wound sharply or deeply in the feelings: *The mother was stabbed to the heart by her son's thoughtlessness.*
stab in the back, attempt to injure in a sly, treacherous manner; slander.
—*n.* **1** a thrust or blow made with a pointed weapon; any thrust. **2** a wound made by stabbing. **3** an injury to the feelings. **4** *Informal.* an attempt. **5** a sudden, sharp feeling of pain, either physical or mental.
have or **make a stab at,** try; attempt. ⟨ult. related to *stub*⟩ —**'stab•ber,** *n.*

Sta•bat Ma•ter ['stɑbɑt 'mɑtər] *or* ['steibæt 'meitər] *Roman Catholic Church.* **1** a celebrated 13th century Latin hymn concerning the Virgin Mary at the Cross. **2** a musical setting of this hymn. **3** any of certain other Latin hymns beginning with the same words. **4** a musical setting of any of these hymns. ⟨< L *Stabat Mater dolorosa* "the Mother was standing full of grief," the first three words of the hymn⟩

sta•bile *adj.* ['steibaɪl] *or* ['steibəl]; *n.* ['steibil] *or* ['steibaɪl] *adj., n.* —*adj.* **1** *Medicine.* **a** retaining its chemical structure and effectiveness at ordinary temperatures. **b** of or having to do with the method of electrotherapy in which one electrode is kept stationary over the part to be treated. **2** stable; fixed.
—*n. Art.* a stationary, abstract sculpture made of cut or shaped metal, wood, etc.

sta•bil•i•ty [stə'bɪləti] *n., pl.* **-ties. 1** the condition of being fixed in position; firmness. **2** permanence. **3** steadfastness of character, purpose, etc. **4** the tendency of an object to return to its original position. **5** *Chemistry, nuclear physics.* the property of being stable.

sta•bi•lize ['steibəˌlaɪz] *v.* **-lized, -liz•ing. 1** make stable or firm. **2** become stable. **3** prevent changes in; hold steady: *stabilize prices.* **4** keep (a ship, aircraft, spacecraft, etc.) steady by special construction or automatic devices. —**ˌsta•bi•li'za•tion,** *n.*

sta•bi•liz•er ['steibəˌlaɪzər] *n.* **1** a person or thing that makes something stable. **2** a device for keeping a ship, aircraft, spacecraft, etc. steady. **3** a substance added to foods, chemical substances, compounds, etc., to prevent deterioration and prolong stability.

sta•ble¹ ['steibəl] *n., v.* **-bled, -bling.** —*n.* **1** a building, fitted with stalls, rack and manger, etc., in which horses are kept. **2** a barn, shed, or other building in which any domestic animals, such as cattle, goats, etc. are kept. **3** a group of animals housed in such a building. **4** Often, **stables,** *pl.* the buildings and grounds where racehorses are quartered and trained. **5** a group of racehorses belonging to one owner. **6** the persons caring for such a group. **7** *Informal.* a group of athletes, artists, writers, etc. who work under the same management.
—*v.* **1** put or keep (horses or other livestock) in a stable. **2** lodge (horses or other livestock) in a stable. ⟨ME < OF < L *stabulum*⟩

sta•ble² ['steibəl] *adj.* **1** not likely to move, fall apart, or change; firm; steady. **2** lasting without change; permanent. **3** able to return to its original position. **4** *Chemistry.* of a compound, not easily decomposed. **5** reliable; trustworthy; mentally constant. **6** *Nuclear physics.* not subject to radioactive decay. ⟨ME < AF < L *stabilis*⟩ —**'sta•bly,** *adv.*

sta•ble•boy ['steibəlˌbɔɪ] *n.* a boy who works in a stable.

sta•ble•girl ['steibəlˌgɜrl] *n.* a girl who works in a stable.

sta•ble•mate ['steibəlˌmeit] *n.* **1** any of a number of horses sharing a stable. **2** one of a number of horses owned by the same person or syndicate. **3** *Informal.* one of a number of persons belonging to the same company, organization, etc.

stab•ling ['steiblɪŋ] *n., v.* —*n.* **1** the act or fact of providing room or space in a stable, for horses or other farm or draft animals. **2** a stable or stable buildings collectively, or their capacity.
—*v.* ppr. of STABLE¹.

stab•lish ['stæblɪʃ] *v. Archaic.* establish.

stacc. staccato.

stac•ca•to [stə'kɑtou] *adj., adv., n.* —*adj.* **1** *Music.* **a** of a note, short, distinctly separate from the notes on either side. **b** of a passage, played so that each note is short and detached. **2** disconnected; abrupt: *staccato speech.*
—*adv.* in a staccato manner.
—*n.* **1** *Music.* a staccato passage or composition; a piece to be played or sung staccato. **2** a disconnected, abrupt quality or manner. *Abbrev.*: stacc. ⟨< Ital. *staccato*, literally, detached⟩

stack [stæk] *n., v.* —*n.* **1** a large, round or conical pile of hay, straw, etc. arranged for storage in the open air. **2** an orderly pile of anything: *a stack of wood, a stack of coins.* **3** a number of rifles arranged to form a cone or pyramid. **4** Often, **stacks,** *pl. Informal.* a large quantity or amount: *stacks of work.* **5** a number of chimney flues or pipes forming a single structure. **6** a chimney or ship's funnel. **7** Usually, **stacks,** *pl.* **a** compactly arranged bookshelves for the storage of large numbers of books, as in a library. **b** the part of a library in which the main collection of books is shelved. **8** *Brit.* a unit for measuring a quantity of firewood, equal to about 3.06 m^3. **9** an arrangement of aircraft circling an airport at different altitudes, waiting for clearance to land.
blow (one's) **stack,** *Slang.* lose one's temper.
—*v.* **1** pile or arrange in a stack: *to stack hay or firewood. We stacked the books on the floor.* **2** load with something: *The table was stacked with records.* **3** arrange (a deck of playing cards, etc.) secretly in order to cheat. **4** assign (aircraft approaching an airport) to circling patterns at different altitudes above the airport to wait for clearance to land. **5** assign (telephone calls) to positions in the order received, to await a free line. **6** *Computer technology.* assign (computer commands or programs) to positions in the order entered, to await execution.
stack the cards or **deck,** *Informal.* secretly and unfairly arrange circumstances beforehand.
stack up, a *Informal.* measure up. **b** add up; seem plausible: *His story doesn't stack up.* **c** compare: *How does this software stack up against the competition?* ⟨ME < ON *stakkr*⟩
—'stack•er, *n.*

Stad•a•co•na [ˌstædə'kounə] *n.* the name of the Iroquois village on the site of the present city of Québec when it was visited by Jacques Cartier in 1535.

stade [steid] *n.* STADIUM (def. 2).

stad•hold•er ['stædˌhouldər] *n.* **1** the chief magistrate of the former republic of the United Provinces of the Netherlands. **2** formerly, the viceroy or governor of a province in the Netherlands. Also, **stadtholder.** ⟨< Du. *stadhouder* < *stad* place, city + *houder* holder⟩

sta•di•a[1] ['steidiə] *n.* an instrument for measuring distances or heights by means of angles. A surveyor's transit is one kind of stadia. ⟨? ult. < *stadium*, or its source⟩

sta•di•a[2] ['steidiə] *n.* a pl. of STADIUM.

sta•di•um ['steidiəm] *n., pl.* **-di•ums** or **-di•a. 1** an oval or U-shaped structure with rows of seats around a large, open space, used for games, concerts, etc. **2** an ancient Greek running track for foot races, with rows of seats along each side and at one end. The stadium at Athens was about 185 m long. **3** *Biology.* a stage in the development of an animal or plant organism. ⟨< L < Gk. *stadion*, ancient Greek measure of length, equal at Athens to about 185 m⟩

stadt•hold•er ['stætˌhouldər] *n.* stadholder.

staff [stæf] *n., pl.* **staves** or **staffs** *for 1, 2, and 6,* **staffs** *for 3 & 4; v.* —*n.* **1** a stick, pole, or rod used as a support, as an emblem of office, as a weapon, etc.: *The flag hangs on a staff.* **2** something that supports or sustains: *Bread is called the staff of life.* **3** a group attending a chief officer, such as a prime minister, premier, mayor, or other executive person; a group of assistants working with their chief as a unit. **4** *Military.* a group of officers that assists a commanding officer in planning and supervisory operations. **5** (*adjl.*) pertaining to or for the use of a staff: *Where are the staff washrooms?* **6** *Music.* the five lines and four spaces between them on which the notes, rests, etc. are written.
—*v.* provide with officers or employees. ⟨OE *stæf*⟩

staf•fer ['stæfər] *n.* a member of a staff, as of a newspaper, government department, etc.

staff officer a military officer who assists in planning and supervising operations.

Staf•ford•shire Terrier ['stæfərdʃər] a member of either of two breeds, the **American Staffordshire Terrier,** or **pit bull terrier,** and the **Staffordshire Bull Terrier,** both developed in the 19th century by crossing terriers with bulldogs. They are characterized by short hair, a broad skull, and a stocky, muscular build that gives the dogs great strength for their size.

staff sergeant 1 in the army and air force, a non-commissioned officer junior to a warrant officer. **2** in the Royal Canadian Mounted Police, a non-commissioned officer senior to a sergeant and junior to a sergeant major. *Abbrev.*: S.S.

stag [stæg] *n., adj., adv., v.* —*n.* **stagged, stag•ging. 1** an adult male deer, especially the male of the European red deer. **2** a male hog or bull castrated as an adult. **2** *Informal.* **a** a man who goes to a dance, party, etc. without a female partner. **b** a dinner party, etc. attended by men only.
—*adj. Informal.* for or attended by men only: *a stag dinner.*
—*adv. Informal.* unaccompanied by a person of the opposite sex: *He went stag to the party.*
—*v.* attend a social event without an escort of the opposite sex. ⟨OE *stagga*⟩

stag beetle any of a family (Lucanidae) of beetles, the males of which have antlerlike mandibles.

stage [steidʒ] *n., v.* **staged, stag•ing.** —*n.* **1** one step or degree in a process; period of development. An insect passes through several stages before it is full-grown. **2 a** the raised platform in a theatre or any area where the actors perform. **b** the entire working area of a theatre or performance locale. **3** the theatre; the drama; an actor's profession: *Shakespeare wrote for the stage.* **4** the scene of action: *Queenston Heights was the stage of a famous battle.* **5** a section of a rocket or missile having its own motor and fuel, that drops off after serving its purpose. **6** *Archaic,* a stagecoach. **7** a place of rest on a journey; a regular stopping place. **8** the part of a journey between two places of rest; the distance between stops. **9** a platform; flooring. **10** a scaffold. **11** any platform raised high or built off the ground for the safe drying of fish, meat, etc. **12** *Geology.* a subdivision of stratified rocks laid down during a single geological age.
by or **in easy stages,** a little at a time; slowly; often stopping: *We made the long journey in easy stages.*
on the stage, as an actor.
—*v.* **1** put on a stage; arrange for performance: *The play was excellently staged.* **2** be suited to the theatre: *That scene will not stage well.* **3 a** arrange to have an effect; plan and carry out: *The angry people staged a riot.* **b** fake; contrive; put on or do for effect only: *They don't really disagree; the whole argument was staged.* **4** *Archaic.* travel by stagecoach. **5** carry out or do by stages: *staged disarmament.* **6** design to burn out and detach from a rocket or missile: *to stage a motor or a fuel tank.* **7** place on a stage for drying. **8** *Esp. military.* establish a position or base as a stop in a planned movement or operation. ⟨ME < OF *estage*, ult. < L *stare* stand⟩ **—'stageˌlike,** *adj.*

stage•coach ['steidʒˌkoutʃ] *n.* a large, four-wheeled, horse-drawn coach formerly used for carrying passengers, mail, and parcels over a regular route.

stage•craft ['steidʒˌkræft] *n.* **1** skill in, or the art of, writing, adapting, or presenting plays. **2** skill in the techniques of staging plays, such as scenery, lighting, etc.

stage direction 1 an instruction written into the script or added by the director, indicating the arrangement of the stage and how the actors move, speak, etc. **2** the technique and skill practised by a stage director.

stage director 1 a stage manager, especially a chief or executive stage manager. **2** *Esp. U.S.* a director.

stage door an outside door of a theatre leading to the dressing rooms, stage, etc., used by actors, stagehands, etc.

stage fright a nervous fear experienced when appearing before an audience.

stage•hand ['steidʒˌhænd] *n.* a person whose work is moving scenery, arranging lights, etc. in a theatre.

stage–man•age ['steidʒ ˌmænɪdʒ] *v.* **-aged, -ag•ing. 1** act as stage manager for (a theatrical production). **2** arrange, direct, or present for a particular effect, especially from behind the scenes: *A few revolutionaries had stage-managed the whole crisis.*

stage manager *Theatre.* the person responsible for the arrangement of the stage, including the placing and changing of scenery, props, etc. and for the proper running of each performance.

stag•er ['steidʒər] *n.* **1** a person of long experience. **2** formerly, a horse used for drawing a stagecoach.

stage–struck ['steidʒ ˌstrʌk] *adj.* extremely interested in acting and the theatre; wanting very much to become an actor.

stage whisper 1 a loud whisper on a stage, meant for the audience to hear. **2** a whisper meant to be heard by others than the person addressed.

stag•ey ['steidʒi] *adj.* See STAGY.

stag•fla•tion [stæg'fleiʃən] *n.* a state of continuing inflation combined with rising unemployment and lack of economic growth. ⟨< *stag(nation)* + *(in)flation*⟩

stag•ger ['stægər] *v., n.* —*v.* **1** sway or reel (from weakness, a heavy load, or drunkenness). **2** cause to sway or reel: *The blow staggered him for a moment.* **3** become unsteady; waver. **4** hesitate. **5** cause to hesitate or become confused. **6** confuse or astonish greatly: *We were staggered by the news of the air disaster.* **7** make helpless. **8** arrange in a zigzag or shifted pattern or way: *The rows of seats in the theatre were staggered so that each person could see past the one in front.* **9** schedule at intervals, often to prevent congestion or confusion: *The school was so crowded that classes had to be staggered. Vacations were staggered so that only one person was away at a time.*
—*n.* **1** the act or an instance of staggering. **2** a staggered arrangement. **3 staggers,** a disease of the central nervous system that affects horses and some other domestic animals and is characterized by a staggering or swaying gait (*used with a singular verb*). Also called **blind staggers.** ⟨ult. < ON *stakra* frequentative of *stacka* push, stagger⟩ —**'stag•ger•er,** *n.* —**'stag•ger•ing•ly,** *adv.*
☛ *Syn. v.* **1.** See note at REEL[2].

A staghound

stag•hound ['stæg,haʊnd] *n.* a breed of hounds resembling the foxhound but larger, formerly used for hunting deer, etc.

stag•ing ['steidʒɪŋ] *n., v.* —*n.* **1** a temporary platform or structure of posts and boards for support, as in building; scaffolding. **2** the act or process of putting a play on the stage. **3** a travelling by stages or by stagecoach. **4** the business of running stagecoaches.
—*v.* ppr. of STAGE.

staging area **1** *Military.* an area where troops are assembled and readied for movement to a theatre of operations: *London was the main staging area for southern Ontario in World War II.* **2** any area used as an assembly point for things or persons prior to movement together to another location: *A staging area for the Commonwealth Games athletes was created out of a former parking lot and its adjacent areas.*

stag jacket *Cdn.* a short, warm jacket, originally made of mackinaw cloth, tight at the waist and roomy in the shoulders.

stag•nan•cy ['stægnənsi] *n.* a stagnant condition.

stag•nant ['stægnənt] *adj.* **1** not running or flowing: *stagnant air, stagnant water.* **2** foul from standing still: *a stagnant pool of water.* **3** not active; sluggish; dull. ⟨< L *stagnans, -antis,* ppr. of *stagnare.* See STAGNATE.⟩ —**'stag•nant•ly,** *adv.*

stag•nate ['stægneit] *v.* **-nat•ed, -nat•ing. 1** be stagnant; become stagnant. **2** make stagnant. ⟨< L *stagnare* < *stagnum* standing water⟩

stag•na•tion [stæg'neiʃən] *n.* a becoming or making stagnant; stagnant condition.

stag shirt *Cdn.* a shirt of heavy woollen cloth, similar in design to a STAG JACKET.

stag•y ['steidʒi] *adj.* **stag•i•er, stag•i•est. 1** of or having to do with the stage. **2** suggestive of the stage; theatrical. **3** artificial; pompous; affected. —**'stag•i•ly,** *adv.* —**'stag•i•ness,** *n.*

staid [steid] *adj., v.* —*adj.* having a settled, quiet character; sober; sedate.
—*v. Archaic.* a pt. and a pp. of STAY[1]. ⟨originally pp. of *stay[1]* in sense of 'restrain'⟩ —**'staid•ly,** *adv.* —**'staid•ness,** *n.*

stain [stein] *n., v.* —*n.* **1** a discoloration; soil; spot. **2** a natural spot or patch of colour different from the main colour, as on an animal. **3** a cause of reproach, infamy, or disgrace; a moral blemish; stigma: *a stain on one's character or reputation.* **4** a liquid dye used to colour or darken wood, fabric, etc. **5** a dye or pigment used to make transparent or very small structures visible, or to differentiate tissue elements by colouring, for microscopic study.
—*v.* **1** discolour; spot or cause to discolour or spot: *Grape juice stains. The tablecloth is stained where food has been spilled.* **2** take, or receive, a stain; admit of staining. **3** bring reproach or disgrace on (a person's reputation, honour, etc.); blemish; soil. **4** corrupt morally; taint with guilt or vice; defile. **5** colour with dye, pigment, etc.: *to stain a microscopic specimen.* ⟨earlier *distain* < OF *desteindre* take out the colour, ult. < L *dis-* off + *tingere* dye⟩ —**'stain•a•ble,** *adj.* —**'stain•er,** *n.*

stained glass **1** glass coloured by metallic oxides, used in church windows, etc. **2** a window or windows made of many pieces of stained glass, usually arranged to represent figures, scenes, etc. and joined together by grooved strips of lead.

stained–glass ['steind 'glæs] *adj.* **1** of or having to do with stained glass: *stained-glass windows, a stained-glass designer.* **2** *Informal.* having or revealing a superficial or oversentimental attitude to religion; sanctimonious: *stained-glass piety.*

stain•less ['steinlɪs] *adj., n.* —*adj.* **1** without stain; spotless. **2** that will not stain or rust. **3** formed from STAINLESS STEEL.
—*n.* stainless steel cutlery: *Many young people nowadays prefer stainless to silver for their tableware. You should not put stainless and silver in the same basket in the dishwasher.* —**'stain•less•ly,** *adv.* —**stain'less•ness,** *n.*

stainless steel steel containing chromium, nickel, or some other metal that makes it resistant to rust and corrosion.

stair [stɛr] *n.* **1** one of a series of steps for going from one level or floor to another. **2** Usually, **stairs,** *pl.* a set of such steps; stairway: *the top of the stairs.* ⟨OE *stǣger*⟩ —**'stair•less,** *adj.*
☛ *Hom.* STARE.

stair•case ['stɛr,keis] *n.* a flight of stairs with its framework; stairs.

stair•way ['stɛr,wei] *n.* a flight or flights of steps; stairs.

stair•well ['stɛr,wɛl] *n.* a vertical space or shaft containing a staircase.

stake [steik] *n., v.* **staked, stak•ing.** —*n.* **1** a stick or post pointed at one end for driving into the ground. **2** formerly, the post to which one was tied for execution by burning: *Joan of Arc was accused of heresy by the English and burned at the stake.* **3** Often, **stakes,** *pl.* **a** something that is risked for gain or loss: *They played for high stakes.* **b** the prize in a race or contest: *The stakes were divided among three winners.* **4** an interest or share in something, especially a commercial undertaking. **5** *Informal.* GRUBSTAKE (def. 3).
at stake, to be won or lost; risked: *His honour is at stake.*
pull up stakes, *Informal.* move away: *After seven years of drought, they finally pulled up stakes and left the farm.*
—*v.* **1** fasten to a stake or with a stake. **2** *Cdn.* **a** *Mining.* mark with stakes; mark the boundaries of: *The miner staked his claim.* **b** *Lumbering.* lay claim to (a timber berth) by marking out its boundaries with stakes prior to registering the claim. **3** risk (money or something valuable) on the result of a game or on any chance. **4** risk the loss of; hazard. **5** *Informal.* grubstake. **6** *Informal.* assist (a person) with money or other resources (*used with* **to**): *I'll stake you to a dinner if you'll come.*
stake out, put or keep under police surveillance. ⟨OE *staca*⟩
stake (out) a claim. See CLAIM. —**'stak•er,** *n.*
☛ *Hom.* STEAK.

stake driver a bittern (*Botaurus lentiginosus*), so called from its deep, hollow cry, suggesting the sound of a stake being pounded into mud.

stake•hold•er ['steik,houldər] *n.* **1** the person who takes care of what is bet and pays it to the winner. **2** a person or group having an interest, or stake, in an undertaking, community, etc. with respect to a particular issue.

stake–out ['steik,ʌut] *n. Informal.* **1** surveillance by police of a building or area where criminal activity is expected or where a criminal suspect is believed to be: *She and her partner are on a stake-out this week.* **2** the place from which the surveillance is carried out. Also, **stakeout.**

stak•ey ['steiki] *adj. Cdn. Slang.* with money available; having money to spend.

sta•lac•ti•form [stə'læktə,fɔrm] *adj.* shaped like a stalactite.

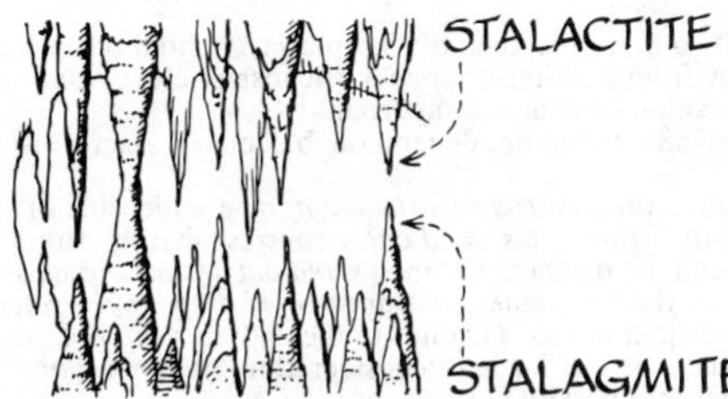

sta•lac•tite [stə'læktəit] *or* ['stæløk,təit] *n.* an icicle-shaped mass of calcium carbonate hanging from the roof of a limestone cave, formed by dripping water. Compare STALAGMITE. ⟨< NL *stalactites* < Gk. *stalaktos* dripping < *stalassein* trickle⟩ **—,stal•ac'tit•ic** [,stælək'tɪtɪk], *adj.*

sta•lag ['stæləg]; *German,* ['ʃta,lak] *n.* a German camp for prisoners of war. ⟨< G *Stalag* < *Sta(mm)lag(er)* base camp⟩

sta•lag•mite [stə'lægməit] *or* ['stæləg,məit] *n.* a cone-shaped mass of calcium carbonate formed on the floor of a limestone cave by water dripping from the roof. Compare STALACTITE. ⟨< NL *stalagmites* < Gk. *stalagmos* a drop < *stalassein* trickle⟩ **—,stal•ag'mit•ic** [,stæləg'mɪtɪk], *adj.*

stale¹ [steil] *adj.* **stal•er, stal•est;** *v.* **staled, stal•ing.** *—adj.* **1** not fresh: *stale bread.* **2** of a carbonated beverage, beer, etc., having lost its effervescence; flat. **3** no longer new or interesting: *a stale joke.* **4** out of condition as a result of overtraining or excessive exertion over a period of time: *The horse has gone stale from too much running.* **5** temporarily lacking in vigour, nimbleness, etc., especially as a result of underactivity. **6** *Law.* especially of a claim, having lost legal effectiveness or force through being left dormant for an unreasonable length of time.
—v. **1** make stale. **2** become stale. ⟨ME; origin uncertain; cf. MDu. *stel* stale⟩ **—'stale•ly,** *adv.* **—'stale•ness,** *n.*

stale² [steil] *v.* **staled, stal•ing;** *n. —v.* of horses and cattle, urinate.
—n. the urine of horses and cattle. ⟨origin uncertain; cf. OF *estaler,* Du. and MHG *stallen*⟩

stale•mate ['steil,meit] *n., v.* **-mat•ed, -mat•ing.** *—n.* **1** *Chess.* the position of the pieces when no move can be made without putting the king in check. **2** any position in which no action can be taken; a complete standstill.
—v. **1** put in a position in which no action can be taken; bring to a complete standstill. **2** *Chess.* subject to a stalemate. ⟨ME *stale* stalemate (probably < AF *estale* standstill < Gmc.) + *mate* < *checkmate*⟩

Sta•lin•ism ['stælə,nɪzəm] *or* ['stɑlə,nɪzəm] *n.* the theory or system of Communism practised under Joseph Stalin (1879-1953), chief minister of the Soviet Union from 1924 to 1953, especially as characterized by coercion and severe oppression of opposition.

Sta•lin•ist ['stælənɪst] *or* ['stɑlənɪst] *n., adj. —n.* a follower or believer in Stalinism.
—adj. of, having to do with, or characteristic of Stalinism.

stalk¹ [stɒk] *n.* **1** the stem or main axis of a plant. **2** any slender, supporting or connected part of a plant. A flower or leaf blade may have a stalk. **3** any similar part of an animal. The eyes of a crayfish are on stalks. **4** any slender upright support. ⟨ME *stalke;* ? dim. of OE *stalu* wooden upright, related to OE *stela* stalk, support⟩ **—'stalk•less,** *adj.*
☛ *Hom.* STOCK.

stalk² [stɒk] *v., n. —v.* **1** approach or pursue stealthily and with hostile intent: *The hunters stalked the lion.* **2** spread silently and steadily (through): *Disease stalked through the land.* **3** walk haughtily or angrily: *She stalked from the room in a huff.* **4** harass or terrorize by persistent following, threatening, telephoning, loitering near the home or workplace of, etc.
—n. **1** a haughty gait. **2** an act of stalking. ⟨OE *-stealcian,* as in *bestealcian* steal along⟩ **—'stalk•er,** *n.*
☛ *Hom.* STOCK.

stalk•ing–horse ['stɒkɪŋ ,hɔrs] *n.* **1** a horse or figure of a horse, behind which a hunter conceals himself or herself in stalking game. **2** anything or anyone used to hide intended plans or acts; a pretext or RED HERRING (def. 2).

stall¹ [stɒl] *n., v. —n.* **1** a place in a stable for one animal. **2 a** a small, enclosed compartment used for a specific purpose: *a shower stall, a milking stall.* **b** a marked-off space for an individual, as in a parking garage. **3** a small place in a larger building, designated for selling or trading. **4** an enclosed seat in the choir or chancel of a church. **5** one of the sheaths for the fingers in a glove. **6** any of various other sheaths, receptacles, cubicles, compartments, etc. **7 stalls,** *pl. Brit.* **a** the orchestra seats in a theatre. **b** the people sitting there. **8** an act or instance of stalling (*v.* 3-6).
—v. **1** live in a stall, stable, kennel, etc. **2** put or keep in a stall. **3** come or bring to a standstill, usually against one's wish: *He stalled the engine of his automobile.* **4** come to a stop because of too heavy a load or too little fuel. **5** stick or cause to stick fast in mud, snow, etc. **6** of an aircraft, lose so much speed that it cannot be controlled. ⟨OE *steall*⟩ **—'stall-,like,** *adj.*

stall² [stɒl] *n., v. Informal. —n.* a pretext to prevent action, the accomplishment of a purpose, etc.
—v. **1** pretend; be evasive; use pretexts: *You have been stalling long enough.* **2** put (someone or something) off in this way; delay: *The process has been stalled for a long time.* ⟨< AF *estal* decoy < Gmc.; cf. OHG *stal* place, stall. Akin to STALL¹.⟩

stal•lion ['stæljən] *n.* an uncastrated male horse, especially one kept for breeding purposes. ⟨ME < OF *estalon* < Gmc.⟩

stall shower a small boothlike enclosure in which one may take a shower bath.

stal•wart ['stɒlwərt] *adj., n. —adj.* **1** strongly built. **2** strong and brave. **3** firm; steadfast: *a stalwart friend.*
—n. **1** a stalwart person. **2** a loyal supporter. ⟨OE *stǣlwierthe* serviceable < *stathol* position + *wierthe* worthy⟩ **—'stal•wart•ly,** *adv.* **—'stal•wart•ness,** *n.*

sta•men ['steimən] *n., pl.* **sta•mens** or **stam•i•na** ['stæmənə]. *Botany.* the male reproductive organ of a flower, consisting of a threadlike stem called a filament and an anther. The anther of the stamen produces pollen grains that become sperm. See FLOWER for picture. ⟨< L *stamen* warp, thread⟩

stam•i•na¹ ['stæmənə] *n.* enduring strength or energy: *A long-distance runner needs stamina.* ⟨< L *stamina* threads (of life, spun by the Fates)⟩

stam•i•na² ['stæmənə] a plural of STAMEN.

stam•i•nate ['stæmənɪt] *or* ['stæmə,neit] *adj. Botany.* **1** having stamens but no pistils. **2** having a stamen or stamens; producing stamens.

stam•i•nif•er•ous [,stæmə'nɪfərəs] *adj. Botany.* STAMINATE (def. 2).

stam•i•node ['stæmə,noud] *n. Botany.* a sterile or abortive stamen.

stam•mer ['stæmər] *v., n. —v.* **1** repeat the same sound in an effort to speak; hesitate in speaking: *She stammers whenever she is nervous.* **2** utter in this manner: *to stammer an excuse.*
—n. a stammering; stuttering: *John has a nervous stammer.* ⟨OE *stamerian*⟩ **—'stam•mer•er,** *n.* **—'stam•mer•ing•ly,** *adv.*
☛ *Syn. v.* **1. Stammer,** STUTTER = speak in a stumbling or jerky way or by repeating the same sound. Although they are often used interchangeably, **stammer** usually suggests a plainly seen, painful effort to form and give voice to sounds and words, and speaking with breaks or silences in or between words, especially when extremely embarrassed or through fear or emotional disturbance. **Stutter** more often suggests a habit of repeating rapidly or jerkily the same sound, especially initial consonants such as [s], [p], etc.

stamp [stæmp] *v., n. —v.* **1** bring down (one's foot) with force: *to stamp on a spider, to stamp one's foot in anger.* **2** fix firmly or deeply: *His words were stamped on my mind.* **3** remove by force from one's feet: *to stamp the earth off one's boots on coming in from the fields.* **4** walk heavily or noisily in anger: *She stamped out of the room in a huff.* **5** pound; crush; trample; tread with the feet: *She stamped out the fire.* **6** mark with an instrument that cuts, shapes, or impresses a design. **7** impress, mark, or cut out (a design, characters, words, etc.) on something, especially to indicate genuineness, quality, inspection, etc. **8** impress with an official stamp or mark: *to stamp a deed.* **9** show or consider to be of a certain quality or character; consign to a certain category, outlook, etc., as though by stamping: *Certain experiences stamp you for life. Once she had been in prison she felt she was permanently stamped as a convict. His speech stamps him as an educated man.* **10** stick a stamp or stamps on.
stamp out, a put out by stamping. **b** put an end to by force.
—n. **1 a** a small piece of paper with a gummed back, put on letters, papers, parcels, etc. to show that the required postage has been paid. **b** a similar piece of paper used for any of various purposes: *a trading stamp.* **2** the act of stamping. **3** a mark printed by a machine to show that postage has been, or will be, paid. **4** a heavy metal piece used to crush or pound rock, etc. **5** a mill or machine that crushes rock, etc. **6** an instrument that cuts, shapes, or impresses a design on (paper, wax, metal, etc.); a thing that puts a mark on. **7** the mark made with such an instrument. **8** an official mark or seal certifying quality,

genuineness, validity, etc. **9** impression; marks: *Her face bore the stamp of suffering.* **10** kind; type: *Men of his stamp are rare.* ⟨ME *stampe(n)*⟩ **—'stamp•er,** *n.*

stam•pede [stæm'pid] *n., v.* **-ped•ed, -ped•ing.** *—n.* **1** a sudden scattering or headlong flight of a frightened herd of cattle or horses. **2** any headlong flight of a large group: *the stampede of a panic-stricken crowd from a burning building.* **3** a general rush: *a stampede to newly discovered gold fields.* **4** *Cdn.* a rodeo, often accompanied by other amusements usually found at a fair: *the Calgary stampede.*
—v. **1** scatter or flee in a stampede. **2** make a general rush. **3** cause to stampede. ⟨< Mexican Sp. *estampida* (in Sp. *estampida* uproar) < *estampar* stamp, ult. < Gmc.⟩
—stam'ped•er, *n.*

stamp hinge a very small, folded piece of thin adhesive paper for securing a postage stamp to the page of a stamp album.

stamping ground or **grounds** *Informal.* a favourite or much-frequented place: *He was happy to return to his old stamping ground.*

stamp pad a pad soaked with ink for use with a rubber or metal stamp.

stance [stæns] *n.* **1** *Golf, etc.* the position of the feet of a player when making a stroke. **2** manner of standing; posture: *an erect stance.* **3** an attitude or mental position taken with respect to something: *Their stance with regard to immigration was hardening day by day.* ⟨< OF *estance,* ult. < L *stare* stand⟩

stanch[1] [stɒntʃ] *v.* See STAUNCH[1]. **—'stanch•er,** *n.*

stanch[2] [stɒntʃ] *adj.* See STAUNCH[2]. **—'stanch•ly,** *adv.* **—'stanch•ness,** *n.*

stan•chion ['stænʃən] *n., v. —n.* **1** an upright bar, post, or rod used as a support. **2** a device for loosely restraining cattle in a stall, consisting of a pair of upright metal bars that are set into a supporting framework and fastened about the animal's neck.
—v. **1** provide, strengthen, or support with a stanchion or stanchions. **2** confine (a cow) by a stanchion. ⟨< OF *estanchon,* ult. < L *stare* stand⟩

stand [stænd] *v.* **stood, stand•ing;** *n. —v.* **1** be upright on one's feet: *Don't stand if you are tired, but sit down.* **2** have specified height when upright: *He stands 180 cm in his socks.* **3** rise to one's feet: *He stood when she entered the room.* **4** be set upright; be placed; be located: *The box stands over there.* **5** set upright or in an indicated position, condition, etc.: *Stand the box here.* **6** be in a certain place, rank, scale, etc.: *She stood first in her class for service to the school.* **7** take or keep a certain position: *"Stand back!" called the police officer to the crowd.* **8** take and maintain a way of thinking or acting; abide (by): *to stand for fair play, stand on one's rights.* **9** be in a stated or given condition: *She stands innocent of any wrong. The poor man stands in need of food and clothing.* **10** be unchanged; hold good; remain the same: *The rule against lateness will stand.* **11** stay in place; last: *The old house has stood for a hundred years.* **12** gather and stay: *Tears stood in her eyes.* **13** bear; tolerate: *I can't stand that song!* **14** be submitted to (a trial, test, ordeal, etc.); undergo: *Stand a rigid examination.* **15** withstand: *cloth that will stand wear.* **16** *Informal.* bear the expense of: *to stand dinner for someone. I'll stand you a trip to Hawaii for your birthday.* **17** *Nautical.* take and hold a specified course: *The ship stood out to sea.* **18** of a dog, point. **19** stop moving; halt; stop: *"Stand!" cried the sentry.* **20** become or remain still or motionless; not move or be operated: *The pumps were allowed to stand.* **21** of plants, grow erect: *corn standing in the fields.* **22** of an account, score, etc., show a (specified) position of the parties concerned: *The score stands in his favour.* **23** of a domestic male animal, be available for breeding, usually for a fee. **24** be a candidate; make oneself available (*for*): *She is planning to stand for Parliament in the next election.*
stand a chance, have a chance.
stand behind, support; vouch for; guarantee.
stand by, a be near. **b** side with; help; support: *to stand by a friend.* **c** keep; maintain: *He always stands by his promises.* **d** be or get ready for use, action, etc.: *The radio operator was ordered to stand by.* **e** be a passive onlooker.
stand down, step off or retire for a time from a place or post.
stand easy, stand completely at ease.
stand for, a represent; mean. **b** be on the side of; take the part of; uphold: *Our school stands for fair play.* **c** *Informal.* put up with: *The teacher said she would not stand for talking during class.* **d** sail or steer toward.
stand in, *Informal.* **a** be associated or friendly; be on good terms. **b** serve as a substitute for somebody.
stand off, a *Informal.* keep off; keep away. **b** hold oneself aloof, especially from an offer or appeal, friendship, etc. **c** *Nautical.* take a position or course away from.
stand on, a be based on; depend on. **b** demand; assert; insist on; claim.
stand out, a project: *His ears stood out.* **b** be noticeable or prominent: *Certain facts stand out.* **c** contrast sharply with a background; be distinct: *The trees stand out against the sunset.* **d** refuse to yield: *to stand out against popular opinion.* **e** refuse to come in or join others. **f** endure to the end: *to stand out the war.*
stand over, a be left for later consideration, treatment, or settlement. **b** supervise closely.
stand to, serve at one's post.
stand up, a get to one's feet; rise: *She stood up and began to speak.* **b** endure; last: *That fabric won't stand up under hard wear.* **c** *Informal.* break a date with; fail to meet: *He has never forgiven her for standing him up.*
stand up for, take the part of; defend; support: *to stand up for a friend.*
stand up to, defy or face boldly: *The young boy stood up to the bully.*
stand up with, *Informal.* act as best man, bridesmaid, etc. to.
—n. **1** the act of standing. **2** a halt; stop. **3** a stop for defence, resistance, etc.: *We made a last stand against the enemy.* **4** a halt on a theatrical tour to give a performance: *a one-night stand.* **5** a town where such a halt is made. **6** a place where a person stands; position. **7 stands,** *pl.* a raised place where people can sit or stand: *We had seats in the stands for the opening ceremonies.* **8** a moral position with regard to other persons, a question, etc.: *to take a new political stand.* **9** a station for a row of vehicles available for hire: *a stand for taxis.* **10** the place where a witness stands or sits to testify in court. **11** something to put things on or in: *Leave your wet umbrella in the stand in the hall.* **12** a stall, booth, table, etc. for a small business: *a newspaper stand.* **13** a standing growth of plants, such as trees or a crop: *a fine stand of timber, a stand of wheat.* ⟨OE *standan*⟩
☛ *Syn. v.* **13.** See note at BEAR[1].

stand–a•lone ['stænd ə,loun] *adj., n. Computer technology.*
—adj. **1** able to perform its functions without other hardware or software.
—n. a unit or program having this characteristic.

stand•ard ['stændərd] *n., adj. —n.* **1** anything taken as a basis of comparison; model: *Your work is not up to standard.* **2** a rule, test, or requirement. **3** an authorized weight or measure. **4** a commodity serving as a basis of value in a monetary system: *the gold standard.* **5** the legally prescribed proportion of metal and alloy to be used in coins. **6** the lowest level or grade of excellence of produce, a product, etc. **7** a flag or emblem: *The dragon was the standard of China.* **8** an upright support: *The floor lamp has a long standard.* **9** *Horticulture.* a tree or shrub grafted or trained so as to have one tall, straight stem. **10** the largest of the four basic sizes of automobile. Compare SUBCOMPACT, COMPACT, and INTERMEDIATE. **11** a piece of popular or light classical music included in the permanent repertoire of a variety of types of musical groups, because of its enduring qualities.
—adj. **1** of the accepted or normal size, amount, power, quality, etc.: *the standard rate of pay, a standard gauge.* **2** used as a standard; according to rule. **3** having recognized excellence or authority: *Scott and Dickens are standard authors.* **4** of a usable or serviceable grade or quality; not of good or fine quality: *standard quality sheets.* **5** *Linguistics.* designating or characterized by the vocabulary, pronunciation, syntax, etc. accepted by the majority of educated native speakers as appropriate for almost any situation. **6** of a tree or shrub, grafted or trained so as to have one tall, straight stem: *Standard rose bushes.* ⟨ME < OF *estandart* < Gmc.⟩
☛ *Syn. n.* **1. Standard,** CRITERION = something used to measure or judge a person or thing. **Standard** applies to a rule, principle, ideal, pattern, or measure generally accepted for use as a basis of comparison in determining the quality, value, quantity, social, moral, or intellectual level, etc. of something: *That school has high standards of teaching.* **Criterion** means a feature or condition used as a test in judging the true nature, goodness, or worth of a person, thing, or accomplishment: *Popularity is not everybody's criterion of a good motion picture.*
☛ *Usage.* **Standard English** is the kind of English that educated people use in public and accept as appropriate for almost any situation. It includes **formal** and **informal** levels of language, but not **slang.** Standard Canadian English differs somewhat from standard American or British English. See also the note at INFORMAL.

standard atmosphere a unit for measuring atmospheric pressure, equal to the mean pressure at sea level at a temperature of 15°C. One standard atmosphere is about 101.3 kilopascals. *Symbol*: atm

stand•ard•bear•er ['stændərd,bɛrər] *n.* **1** an officer or soldier who carries a flag or standard. **2** a person who carries a banner in a procession. **3** a conspicuous leader of a movement, political party, etc.

stand•ard–bred or **stand•ard•bred** ['stændərd ˌbrɛd] *adj., n.* —*adj.* **1** of horses, poultry, etc., bred to meet set standards of excellence for a breed, species, etc. **2** of a horse, bred for drawing light vehicles or for use in harness races.
—*n.* a breed of horses noted as trotters and pacers and much used in harness racing.

standard deviation *Statistics.* a measure of variability in a frequency distribution, equal to the square root of the mean of the squares of the deviation from the arithmetic mean of the distribution.

standard gauge *Railway.* **1** a width of 145.3 cm between the parallel rails of a railway track. **2** a railway constructed to this gauge. **3** a railway car or engine built to run on tracks of this gauge. **—'stan•dard-'gauge,** *adj.*

stand•ard•i•za•tion [ˌstændərdə'zeiʃən] *or* [ˌstændərdaɪ'zeiʃən] *n.* a standardizing or being standardized.

stand•ard•ize ['stændərˌdaɪz] *v.* **-ized, -iz•ing. 1** make standard in size, shape, weight, quality, strength, etc.: *Many of the parts of an automobile engine are standardized to fit a number of different makes.* **2** regulate by a standard. **3** test by a standard.

standard lamp a household lamp on a pole fixed in a base on the floor and tall enough to provide light for someone sitting on a chair or chesterfield.

standard of living the way of living that a person or community considers necessary to provide enough material things for comfort, happiness, etc.

Standard Time the time officially adopted for a region or country, based on the distance from Greenwich, England. The world is divided into 24 standard time zones. Compare DAYLIGHT-SAVING TIME.

stand•by ['stændˌbaɪ] *n., pl.* **-bys,** *adj.* —*n.* **1** a person or thing that can be relied upon; chief support; ready resource. **2** a ship kept in readiness for emergencies. **3** an order or signal for a boat to stand by. **4** any person or thing held in reserve. **5** a person waiting to board an aircraft, bus, etc. if space becomes available. **6** (*advl.*) on standby: *to fly standby.*
on standby, a waiting to act as a standby. **b** waiting for a chance to board a plane, ship, etc.
—*adj.* referring to something or someone acting as a standby: *a standby passenger.*

stand•ee [stæn'di] *n.* a person who has to stand in a theatre, bus, etc. because of lack of seats.

stand–in ['stænd ˌɪn] *n.* **1** a person whose work is to occupy the place of an actor while the lights, cameras, etc. are being arranged. **2** a person or thing that takes the place of another; substitute: *He acted as a stand-in for his boss at the meeting.*

stand•ing ['stændɪŋ] *n., adj., v.* —*n.* **1** position; reputation: *citizens of good standing.* **2** length of service, experience, residence, etc., especially as determining position, wages, etc.: *Her standing in the company entitled her to two months' vacation.* **3** duration: *a feud of long standing between two families.* **4** the act or position of one that stands.
—*adj.* **1** straight up; erect: *a standing position, standing timber.* **2** done from or in an erect position: *a standing jump, a standing ovation.* **3** permanent, fixed, or long-term; always operative or ready: *a standing invitation, a standing army, a standing order.* **4** not flowing; stagnant: *standing water.* **5** *Printing.* of type, set and stored for later printings. **6** that stands, as opposed to hanging: *a standing lamp.*
—*v.* ppr. of STAND.

standing room **1** space to stand in. **2** space to stand in after all the seats are taken.

standing wave *Physics.* a wave resulting from the interference between a transmitted and a reflected wave, whose amplitude is constant at each point on its axis, with zero amplitude at the nodes and maximum amplitude at the antinodes.

stand–off ['stænd ˌɒf] *n., adj.* —*n.* **1** a standing off or apart; reserve; aloofness. **2** a tie or draw in a game or conflict.
—*adj.* standing off or apart; reserved; aloof.

stand–off•ish ['stænd 'ɒfɪʃ] *adj.* reserved; aloof.

stand–out ['stænd ˌʌut] *n. Informal.* a thing or person that is outstanding in appearance or performance.

stand•pat ['stændˌpæt] *adj. Informal.* standing firm for things as they are; opposing any change. **—'stand'pat•ter,** *n.*

stand•pipe ['stændˌpəip] *n.* **1** a large vertical pipe or tower to hold water and maintain water pressure at a desired level. **2** a water pipe connected to the water supply of a building, used to supply the internal fire hoses.

stand•point ['stændˌpɔɪnt] *n.* a point of view; mental attitude.

St. An•drew's cross ['ændruz] a diagonal cross; specifically, a white crisscross on a dark blue background. See CROSS for picture.

stand•still ['stændˌstɪl] *n.* a complete stop; halt; pause.

stand–up ['stænd ˌʌp] *adj.* **1** having an erect or upright position: *a stand-up collar.* **2** done or taken in a standing position: *a stand-up lunch.* **3** made for or to allow a standing position: *a stand-up lunch counter.* **4** of or designating a comedian who performs alone, standing and talking to the audience.

stan•hope ['stænhoup] *or* ['stænəp] *n.* a kind of light, open, one-seated, horse-drawn carriage with two or four wheels. ⟨after Fitzroy *Stanhope* (1787-1864), a British clergyman⟩

stank [stæŋk] *v.* a pt. of STINK.

Stan•ley Cup ['stænli] **1** the cup presented annually to the winning team in a special end-of-season competition between National Hockey League clubs. **2** the competition, or playoffs, for this trophy. ⟨< Sir Frederick Arthur *Stanley*, 16th Earl of Derby (1841-1908), Governor General of Canada, 1888-1893⟩

stan•na•ry ['stænəri] *n., pl.* **-ries. 1** a place where tin is mined or smelted. **2** in the United Kingdom, **a** a tin mining area. **b** an area in Cornwall and Devon where tin is mined. ⟨< Med.L *stannaria* < LL *stannum* tin⟩

stan•nic ['stænɪk] *adj.* **1** of or having to do with tin. **2** containing tin with a valence of four. ⟨< LL *stannum* tin⟩

stan•nite ['stænəit] *n.* a black or grey tetravalent sulphide of tin, copper, and iron. *Formula*: CU_2FeSnS_4

stan•nous ['stænəs] *adj. Chemistry.* **1** of or having to do with tin. **2** containing tin with a valence of two.

stannous chloride *Chemistry.* a crystalline compound of tin dissolved with hydrochloric acid, used to silver mirrors and to galvanize tin, as a reducing agent for some chemicals, etc. *Formula*: $SnCl_2$

St. An•tho•ny's fire ['ænθəniz] *or* ['æntəniz] *Pathology.* any of various inflammations of the skin, such as erysipelas.

stan•za ['stænzə] *n.* **1** *Prosody.* a group of lines of poetry, commonly four or more, arranged according to a fixed plan. **2** *Sports.* any period of time in, or division of, a game, as an inning in baseball or a quarter in football. ⟨< Ital. *stanza*, originally stopping place, ult. < L *stare* stand⟩

stan•za•ic [stæn'zeiɪk] *adj. Prosody.* of, having to do with, or designating verse composed in stanzas.

sta•pes ['steipiz] *n., pl.* **sta•pes** or **sta•pe•dez** [stə'pidiz]. *Anatomy.* the stirrup bone, the innermost of the three small bones in the middle ear. See EAR¹ for picture. ⟨< Med.L *stapes* stirrup⟩ **—sta'pe•di•al** [stə'pidiəl], *adj.*

staph•y•lo•coc•cal [ˌstæfələ'kɒkəl] *adj. Bacteriology.* **1** of or having to do with staphylococcus. **2** caused by staphylococcus. Also, **staphylococcic** [ˌstæfələ'kɒksɪk].

staph•y•lo•coc•cus [ˌstæfələ'kɒkəs] *n., pl.* **-coc•ci** [-'kɒkaɪ] *or* [-'kɒksaɪ]. *Bacteriology.* any of a genus (*Staphylococcus*) of round or oval, gram-positive bacteria, occurring in irregular clusters and also singly or in pairs, and including many species that are pathogenic. ⟨< NL *Staphylococcus*, the genus name < Gk. *staphylē* bunch of grapes + *kokkos* grain⟩

sta•ple¹ ['steipəl] *n., v.* **-pled, -pling.** —*n.* **1** a U-shaped piece of metal with pointed ends. Staples are driven into doors, wood, etc. to hold hooks, pins, or bolts. **2** a similar device for fastening papers, etc. together, being a small piece of thin wire in the form of a square, short-armed U, the ends of which are driven through the layers of material and clinched on the other side.
—*v.* fasten with a staple or staples. ⟨OE *stapol* post⟩

sta•ple² ['steipəl] *n., adj., v.* **-pled, -pling.** —*n.* **1** the most important or principal raw material or commodity grown or manufactured in a place: *Wheat is the staple in Saskatchewan.* **2** any major article of trade. **3** a chief element or material. **4** a raw material. **5** a fibre of cotton, wool, etc. **6** a short fibre that must be spun to form a yarn. **7** *Archaic.* the principal market of a place; the chief centre of trade. **8** a necessary food item that is used regularly or as a basic part of the diet: *I'm going to stock up on staples; they're having a big sale at the bulk food store.*
—*adj.* **1** most important; principal: *The weather is a staple subject of conversation.* **2** established in commerce: *a staple trade.* **3** regularly produced in large quantities for the market.

–*v.* sort according to fibre: *to staple wool.* ⟨ME < OF *estaple* mart < Gmc.⟩

sta•pler¹ ['steiplər] *n.* **1** a device used for fastening papers, etc. together by means of wire staples. **2** a hand- or electric-powered tool used to drive heavy staples into wood, plaster, etc. Also, **staple gun.** ⟨< *staple¹*⟩

sta•pler² ['steiplər] *n.* a person who sorts and grades fibres of wool, cotton, etc. ⟨< *staple²*⟩

star [stɑr] *n., v.* **starred, star•ring.** –*n.* **1** any of the heavenly bodies, especially one that is not the moon, a planet, a comet, or a meteor, appearing as bright points in the sky at night. **2** *Astrology.* a planet or constellation of the zodiac, considered as influencing people and events. **3** a conventional plane figure having five points, or sometimes six, like these: ☆✡ **4** something having or suggesting this shape, used as a mark of excellence, designation of rank, badge of honour, etc. **5** an asterisk (*). **6** a person of brilliant qualities: *an athletic star.* **7** a person who is famous in some art, profession, etc., especially one who plays the lead in a performance: *a film star.* **8** (*adjl.*) chief; best; leading; excellent: *the star player on a football team.* **9** fate; fortune.
see stars, *Informal.* see flashes of light as a result of a hard blow on the head.
thank (one's) **(lucky) stars,** be thankful for one's good luck.
–*v.* **1** mark or ornament with stars: *Leslie's card was starred for perfect attendance.* **2** mark with an asterisk. **3** single out for special notice or recommendation. **4** be prominent; be a leading performer; excel: *She has starred in many movies.* **5** present as a star. ⟨OE *steorra*⟩

star•board ['stɑrbərd] *or* ['stɑr,bɔrd] *n., adj., v.* –*n.* the right side of a ship or aircraft, facing forward.
–*adj.* of or on the right side of a ship or aircraft.
–*v.* turn (the helm) to the right. ⟨OE *stēorbord* the side from which a vessel was steered < *stēor* steering paddle + *bord* side (of a ship)⟩

starch [stɑrtʃ] *n., v.* –*n.* **1** a tasteless, odourless, white carbohydrate found in many vegetables, including potatoes, and cereal crops, such as wheat, rice, and corn. **2** a preparation of this substance used to stiffen clothes, curtains, etc. **3** a similar preparation produced artificially. **4 starches,** *pl.* foods containing much starch. **5** a stiff, formal manner; stiffness. **6** *Informal.* vigour; energy.
take the starch out of, *Informal.* cause to lose courage, confidence, or determination.
–*v.* stiffen (clothes, curtains, etc.) with starch. ⟨OE *stercan* make rigid (in *stercedferhth* stouthearted) < *stearc* stiff, strong⟩

Star Chamber or **star chamber** **1** formerly, in England, an arbitrary, secret court that existed by statute and became notorious for its harsh methods of trial. It was established in 1487 and abolished in 1641. **2** any similar court, committee, or group.

starch•y ['stɑrtʃi] *adj.* **starch•i•er, starch•i•est. 1** like starch; containing starch. **2** stiffened with starch. **3** stiff in manner; formal. **–'starch•i•ness,** *n.* **–'starch•i•ly,** *adv.*

star–crossed ['stɑr ,krɒst] *adj.* ill-fated; doomed to failure and unhappiness: *star-crossed lovers.*

star•dom ['stɑrdəm] *n.* **1** the condition or fact of being a star actor or performer. **2** star actors or performers as a group.

star•dust ['stɑr,dʌst] **1** masses of stars that look so small as to suggest particles of dust. **2** particles of matter falling from space to the earth. **3** *Informal.* glamour; happy enchantment.

stare [stɛr] *v.* **stared, star•ing;** *n.* –*v.* **1** look long and directly with the eyes wide open, usually from wonder, surprise, stupidity, curiosity, or mere rudeness. **2** bring to a named condition by staring: *stare someone into confusion.* **3** gaze at. **4** be very striking or glaring: *His eyes stared with anger.* **5** stand up roughly: *When animals are ill, their fur stares.*
stare down or **stare out of countenance,** confuse or embarrass by staring.
stare (someone) **in the face, a** be very evident; force itself on the notice of: *His spelling mistake was staring him in the face.* **b** very likely or certain to happen soon.
stare (someone) **up and down,** gaze at or survey (someone) from head to foot.
–*n.* a long and direct look with the eyes wide open. ⟨OE *starian*⟩ **–'star•er,** *n.*
☛ *Hom.* STAIR.
☛ *Syn. v.* **1.** See note at GAZE.

star•fish ['stɑr,fɪʃ] *n., pl.* **-fish** or **-fish•es.** any of a class (Asteroidea) of marine invertebrate animals having a flattened, fleshy, spiny body with five or more arms radiating from a central disk.

star•flow•er ['stɑr,flaʊər] *n.* **1** any of several low-growing perennial plants (genus *Trientalis*) of the primrose family having a whorl of leaves at the top of the stem and small, white, star-shaped flowers. **2** STAR-OF-BETHLEHEM.

star•gaze ['stɑr,geiz] *v.* **-gazed, -gaz•ing. 1** gaze at the stars. **2** be absent-minded; daydream. **–'star,gaz•er,** *n.*

star•ing ['stɛrɪŋ] *adj., v.* –*adj.* **1** very conspicuous; too bright; glaring: *a staring mistake.* **2** gazing with a stare; wide open: *staring eyes.*
–*v.* ppr. of STARE.

stark [stɑrk] *adj., adv.* –*adj.* **1** bare; barren; desolate: *a stark landscape.* **2** stiff: *The dog lay stark in death.* **3** downright; complete: *That fool is talking stark nonsense.* **4** grim; harsh; stern: *stark reality.* **5** *Archaic.* strong; sturdy.
–*adv.* **1** entirely; completely: *stark crazy, stark naked.* **2** in a stark manner. ⟨OE *stearc* stiff, strong⟩ **–'stark•ly,** *adv.* **–'stark•ness,** *n.*

stark•ers ['stɑrkərz] *adj.* **1** *Esp. Brit. Slang.* stark naked (*used only after the noun modified*). **2** *Slang.* crazy.

stark naked *adj.* (**stark-naked** *before a noun*) completely naked. ⟨ME *sternaked* (stert altered after *stark*), lit. tail-naked; *stert* < OE *steort* tail⟩

star•less ['stɑrlɪs] *adj.* without stars; without starlight.

star•let ['stɑrlɪt] *n.* **1** a young actress or singer being trained for leading roles in film or television. **2** a little star.

star•light ['stɑr,ləit] *n., adj.* –*n.* light from the stars.
–*adj.* **1** of or pertaining to starlight. **2** starlit.

star•like ['stɑr,ləik] *adj.* **1** shaped like a star. **2** shining like a star.

star•ling ['stɑrlɪŋ] *n.* any of a family (Sturnidae) of Old World songbirds, especially a common dark brown or glossy black, short-tailed bird (*Sturnus vulgaris*) that is native to Europe but has become naturalized in North America, Australia, and New Zealand, and is often considered a pest. ⟨OE *stærling*⟩

star•lit ['stɑr,lɪt] *adj.* lighted by the stars: *a starlit night.*

star–of–Beth•le•hem ['stɑr əv 'bɛθlə,hɛm] *or* ['bɛθliəm] *n.* any of several bulbous herbs (genus *Ornithogalum*) of the lily family, especially (*O. umbellatum*), having narrow leaves and clusters of white, star-shaped flowers. ⟨< the star that heralded Christ's birth⟩

Star of Courage *Cdn.* a decoration awarded for an act of outstanding courage. It is one of a series of three Canadian bravery decorations, the other two being the CROSS OF VALOUR (the highest award) and the MEDAL OF BRAVERY. *Abbrev.*: SC

Star of David

Star of David a six-pointed star or hexagram formed by two superimposed, often interlaced, equilateral triangles. It is an ancient decorative motif and mystical symbol which figured as a Christian symbol in the Middle Ages. From about the 17th century it became a symbol of Judaism and is featured on the flag of Israel. Also called **Magen David.** See also SOLOMON'S SEAL.

starred [stɑrd] *adj., v.* –*adj.* **1** decorated with stars. **2** marked with a star or stars. **3** presented as a star actor or performer. **4** influenced by the stars or by fate.
–*v.* pt. and pp. of STAR.

star•ry ['stɑri] *adj.* **-ri•er, -ri•est. 1** lighted by stars; containing many stars: *a starry sky.* **2** shining like stars: *starry eyes.* **3** like a star in shape. **4** of or having to do with stars. **5** consisting of stars. **–'star•ri•ly,** *adv.* **–'star•ri•ness,** *n.*

star•ry–eyed ['stɑri ,aɪd] *adj.* tending to be too optimistic or idealistic; romantically naïve.

Stars and Stripes the flag of the United States.

star sapphire **1** a sapphire which reflects light in the shape of a brilliant star as a result of its crystalline structure. **2** a gem made from such a stone.

star–stud•ded ['stɑr ,stʌdɪd] *adj.* filled or covered with stars:

a star-studded sky. They are planning a new production of the play, with a star-studded cast.

start [stɑrt] *v., n.* —*v.* **1** get in motion; set out; begin a journey: *The train started on time.* **2** begin: *to start a book. The meeting started at 8 o'clock.* **3** set moving, going, acting, etc.; cause to set out; cause to begin: *to start an automobile, to start a fire.* **4** give a sudden, involuntary jerk or twitch; move suddenly: *She started in surprise.* **5** come, rise, or spring out suddenly: *Tears started from his eyes.* **6** burst or stick out: *eyes seeming to start from their sockets.* **7** rouse (game): *to start a rabbit.* **8** become loose. **9** open (a container) and begin using its contents: *Will you start that bottle of wine, please?* **10** enter (someone or something) or be entered in a race or other contest.
start in or **start out,** begin to do something.
start off, begin a journey or race.
start up, a rise suddenly; spring up. **b** come suddenly into being or notice. **c** begin or cause (an engine) to begin operating. **d** begin (an activity): *to start up a new operation. A new drama club has just started up at school.*
to start with, in the first place; first of all: *Not only did she lose more money than they did, she was poorer to start with. To start with, you can clear up this huge mess.*
—*n.* **1** the beginning of a movement, action, process of development or construction, etc.: *to make an early start. We were all there at the start. There has been a decrease in housing starts.* **2** a setting in motion; signal to start. **3** a sudden movement; jerk. **4** a surprise; fright. **5** a beginning ahead of others; advantage: *He got the start of his rivals.* **6** a chance of starting a career, etc.: *Her father gave her a start.* **7** a spurt of activity: *to work by fits and starts.* **8** the place, line, etc. where a race begins; the starting point of a race, hike, etc. ⟨var. of OE *styrtan* leap up⟩
☛ *Syn. v.* **2, 3.** See note at BEGIN.

start•er ['stɑrtər] *n.* **1** a person or thing that starts. **2** a person who gives the signal for starting. **3** an electric motor used to start an internal-combustion engine. **4** a special kind of food for baby animals. **5** the first in a series of things. **6** a chemical agent or bacterial culture used to start a reaction, especially in the formation of acid in making cheese, vinegar, sourdough, etc. **7** a person with initiative, motivation, and an innovative spirit.
for starters, a *Slang.* first of all; to begin with. **b** *Informal.* as a first course or hors d'oeuvres: *Shall we have escargots for starters?*

starting blocks adjustable blocks against which a runner places his or her feet, as an aid to a fast start in a race.

starting point a place of starting; beginning.

star•tle ['stɑrtəl] *v.* **-tled, -tling;** *n.* —*v.* **1** frighten suddenly; surprise: *to startle someone.* **2** move suddenly in fear or surprise: *The horse startled when the gun went off.* **3** cause to make a sudden movement: *The hunters startled the deer.*
—*n.* a sudden shock of surprise or fright. ⟨OE *steartlian* struggle⟩

star•tling ['stɑrtlɪŋ] *adj., v.* —*adj.* surprising; frightening.
—*v.* ppr. of STARTLE. —**'star•tling•ly,** *adv.*

star•va•tion [stɑr'veiʃən] *n.* **1** the condition of suffering from extreme hunger; being starved. **2** death from lack of food. **3** (*adjl.*) of or pertaining to a minimum of food and drink required to sustain life: *starvation rations, a starvation diet.*

starve [stɑrv] *v.* **starved, starv•ing. 1** die because of hunger. **2** suffer severely because of hunger. **3** weaken or kill with hunger. **4** force or subdue by lack of food: *They starved the enemy into surrendering.* **5** *Informal.* feel hungry (*only in progressive tenses*): *I'm starving. What's for dinner?* **6** have a strong desire or craving (*for*); need. **7** weaken or destroy, or be destroyed, by lack of something needed.
starve down or **out,** force or subdue by lack of food.
starve for, suffer from lack of; long for; crave: *to starve for news. That child is starving for affection.* ⟨OE *steorfan* die⟩

starve•ling ['stɑrvlɪŋ] *adj., n.* —*adj.* starving; hungry.
—*n.* a person or animal that is suffering from lack of food.

stash [stæʃ] *v., n. Informal.* —*v.* hide or put away for safekeeping or future use.
—*n.* **1** a place where something is hidden away or stored. **2** something hidden away or stored: *a small stash of money.* ⟨origin uncertain⟩

sta•sis ['steisɪs] *or* ['stæsɪs] *n., pl.* **-ses** [-siz]. **1** *Pathology.* a slowing or stopping of the normal flow of circulating blood or other fluid in the body, as intestinal wastes encountering a blockage. **2** a state of balance or motionlessness. ⟨< NL *stasis* < Gk. *stasis* a standing < *sta-*, a root of *histanai* stand⟩

stat. **1** statute. **2** statuary; statue. **3** *Medicine. Informal.* immediately.

state [steit] *n., v.* **stat•ed, stat•ing.** —*n.* **1** the condition of a person or thing; form: *He is in a state of poor health. Ice is water in a solid state.* **2** a particular condition of mind or feeling: *a state of uncertainty, a state of excitement.* **3** a person's position in life; rank: *a humble state.* **4** ceremonious and luxurious style; pomp and dignity: *living in state.* **5** (*adjl.*) of or for very formal and ceremonious occasions: *state robes.* **6** NATION (def. 1). **7** Also, **State,** one of several organized political groups of people that together form a nation: *The state of Alaska is one of the United States.* **8** the territory of a state. **9** the civil government; the highest civil authority: *affairs of state.* **10** (*adjl.*) of or having to do with civil government or authority: *state control.*
in or **into a state,** *Informal.* in or into a very agitated or excited condition.
lie in state, of the body of a monarch, political leader, etc., lie in an open coffin for public view before burial.
—*v.* **1** tell in speech or writing; express; say: *to state one's views.* **2** settle; fix. ⟨< L *status* condition, position < *stare* stand; common in L phrase *status rei publicae* condition of the republic. Doublet of ESTATE.⟩ —**'stat•a•ble,** *adj.*
☛ *Syn. n.* **1. State,** CONDITION = the form or way in which something exists, especially as affected by circumstances. **State** is the general word, sometimes used in a very general way without reference to anything concrete, more often referring to the circumstances in which a person or thing exists or to his, her, or its nature or form at a certain time: *The state of the world today should interest every serious person.* **Condition** applies to a particular state thought of especially as produced by circumstances or other causes: *The condition of the patient is critical.*

state•craft ['steit,kræft] *n.* **1** statesmanship. **2** crafty statesmanship.

stat•ed ['steitɪd] *adj., v.* —*adj.* **1** said; told. **2** fixed; settled.
—*v.* pt. and pp. of STATE. —**'stat•ed•ly,** *adv.*

state•hood ['steit,hʌd] *n.* the condition of being a state.

state•house ['steit,hʌus] *n. U.S.* the building in which the legislature of a state meets; the capitol of a state.

state•less ['steitlɪs] *adj.* **1** without nationality; without citizenship in any country. **2** without states or boundaries: *a stateless world.*

state•ly ['steitli] *adj.* **-li•er, -li•est.** dignified; imposing; grand; majestic. —**'state•li•ness,** *n.*
☛ *Syn.* See note at GRAND.

state•ment ['steitmənt] *n.* **1** the act of stating; the manner of stating something. **2** something stated; report. **3** *Commerce.* a summary of an account, showing credits, debits, and balance. **4** a sentence that states something or makes an assertion; declarative sentence.

state of the art the most up-to-date and sophisticated stage of a technology or art. —**'state-of-the-'art,** *adj.*

state•room ['steit,rum] *or* ['steit,rʊm] *n.* a private room on a ship or, formerly, on a railway passenger train.

States, the [steits] *n.pl.* the UNITED STATES OF AMERICA. ⟨ellipsis from full name⟩

state's evidence *U.S.* **1** evidence brought forward by the government in a criminal case. **2** testimony given in court by a criminal against his or her associates in a crime.
turn state's evidence, testify in court against one's associates in a crime. Compare QUEEN'S EVIDENCE.

States–Gen•er•al ['steits 'dʒɛnərəl] *n.* **1** in France, the legislative body before 1789, consisting of representatives of the three estates, the clergy, the nobility, and the middle class; Estates-General. **2** in the Netherlands, the lawmaking body made up of two houses.

states•man ['steitsmən] *n., pl.* **-men.** a man skilled in the management of public or national affairs. —**'states•man,like,** *adj.*
☛ *Syn.* See note at POLITICIAN.

states•man•ly ['steitsmənli] *adj.* like, worthy of, or befitting a statesman.

states•man•ship ['steitsmən,ʃɪp] *n.* the qualities of a statesman; skill in the management or direction of public or national affairs.

state socialism a form of socialism in which government control, management, or ownership is used to improve social conditions.

states of matter the forms in which all substances can exist: solid, liquid, or gas.

states•wom•an ['steits,wʊmən] *n., pl.* **-wom•en** [-,wɪmən]. a woman skilled in the management of public or national affairs.

stat•ic ['stætɪk] *adj., n.* —*adj.* **1** at rest; standing still: *Civilization does not remain static, but changes constantly.* **2** having to do with bodies at rest or with forces that balance each other. **3** acting by weight without producing motion: *static*

pressure. **4** *Electricity.* having to do with stationary charges that balance each other. **5** of or having to do with atmospheric electricity that interferes with radio reception.
–n. **1** atmospheric electricity. **2** interference, especially with radio signals, due to such electricity. **3** *Slang.* a negative reaction; FLAK (def. 3): *She got a lot of static for what she said on television.* ⟨< Gk. *statikos* causing to stand, ult. < *stēnai* stand⟩ **–'stat•i•cal•ly,** *adv.*

static cling the clinging of things to each other, especially clothing, due to STATIC ELECTRICITY.

stat•i•ce ['stætisi] *or* ['stætɪs] *n.* any of the various annual or perennial plants of the genus *Limonium*, having large, leathery, basal leaves and clusters of small, delicate flowers on a leafless stem. The flowers retain their colour when dried, thus giving the plant its common name of **everlasting**. Also called **sea lavender**.

static electricity *Electricity.* the electricity contained in or produced by charged bodies. Static electricity can be produced by rubbing a glass rod with a silk cloth.

stat•ics ['stætɪks] *n.* (*used with a singular verb*) the branch of mechanics that deals with the study of bodies at rest and the action of forces that balance each other to produce equilibrium.

sta•tion ['steiʃən] *n., v.* *–n.* **1** a place to stand in; a place that a person, army unit, or naval fleet is appointed to occupy in the performance of some duty; an assigned post: *The police officer took her station at the corner.* **2** a building or place used for a definite purpose: *a police station, a postal station, a weather station.* **3** the place or equipment for sending out or receiving programs, messages, etc. by radio or television. **4** a stopping place on a regular train or bus route, where passengers wait, buy tickets, etc.: *a railway station.* **5** a military camp or establishment. **6** social position; rank. **7** *Australian.* a ranch or large farm. **8** the native environment of a given plant or animal. **9** *Cdn. Nfld.* temporary quarters established on shore during fishing season.
–v. **1** give a position or place to; place: *He stationed himself just outside the hotel.* **2** post or assign to a military camp or establishment. ⟨< L *statio, -onis* < *stare* stand⟩

station agent a person in charge of a railway station.

sta•tion•ar•y ['steiʃə,nɛri] *adj.* **1** having a fixed station or place; not movable: *A factory engine is stationary.* **2** standing still; not moving. **3** not changing in size, number, activity, etc.: *The population of this town has been stationary for ten years at about 5000 people.* ⟨< L *stationarius* < *statio.* See STATION.⟩
☛ *Hom.* STATIONERY.
☛ *Usage.* Do not confuse **stationary** and STATIONERY. Stationary, with an **a** in the second last syllable, is an adjective. **Stationery**, meaning 'writing material', is a noun.

stationary front *Meteorology.* a front between warm and cold air masses that is still or moving at a speed of less than 8 km/h.

sta•tion•er[1] ['steiʃənər] *n.* a person who sells paper, pens, pencils, inks, etc. ⟨< Med.L *stationarius* shopkeeper, originally, stationary, as distinct from a roving peddler⟩

sta•tion•er[2] ['steiʃənər] *n. Cdn. Nfld.* a migratory fisher who establishes temporary quarters on shore.

sta•tion•er•y ['steiʃə,nɛri] *n.* material for writing; paper, cards, and envelopes.
☛ *Hom.* STATIONARY.
☛ *Usage.* See note at STATIONARY.

station house a building used as a station, especially a police or fire station.

sta•tion•mas•ter ['steiʃən,mæstər] *n.* the person in charge of a railway station.

Stations of the Cross *Roman Catholic Church.* **1** fourteen scenes from the Passion of Christ, usually painted or sculpted and ranged around the walls of a church. **2** the prayers, devotions, etc. performed in sequence at these stations.

station wagon a closed automobile that can serve both as a passenger car and as a light truck, having a large, windowed cargo compartment in the rear, usually opened and closed by means of a tailgate.

stat•ism ['steitɪzəm] *n.* **1** a highly centralized governmental control of the economy, information media, etc. of a state or nation. **2** advocacy of the sovereignty of a state, especially of a republic.

stat•ist[1] ['stætɪst] *n.* a statistician.

stat•ist[2] ['steitɪst] *n.* one advocating statism.

sta•tis•tic [stə'tɪstɪk] *adj., n.* *–adj.* statistical.
–n. an item, element, etc. in a set of STATISTICS (def. 1).

sta•tis•ti•cal [stə'tɪstɪkəl] *adj.* of or having to do with statistics; consisting of or based on statistics.

sta•tis•ti•cal•ly [stə'tɪstɪkli] *adv.* in a statistical manner; according to statistics.

stat•is•ti•cian [,stætə'stɪʃən] *n.* a person trained in the science of statistics, especially one whose work it is.

sta•tis•tics [stə'tɪstɪks] *n.pl.* **1** numerical facts about people, the weather, business conditions, etc., collected and classified systematically. **2** the science of collecting, classifying, analysing, and interpreting such facts in order to show their significance (*used with a singular verb*). ⟨ult. < G < NL *statisticus* political, ult. < L *status* state. See STATE.⟩

Statistics Canada *Cdn.* a government body which issues statistics on many subjects, mostly obtained through the census.

sta•tor ['steitər] *n. Electricity.* a stationary unit that encloses rotating parts of a turbine, electric generator or motor, etc. ⟨< NL < L *stator* sustainer < *sistere* cause to stand < *stare* to stand⟩

stat•o•scope ['stætə,skoup] *n.* **1** a form of aneroid barometer for registering very small variations in atmospheric pressure. **2** an instrument for detecting a small rise or fall of an aircraft. ⟨< Gk. *statos* standing still + E *-scope*⟩

stats [stæts] *n.pl. Informal.* statistics.

Stats•Can ['stæts'kæn] *n.* STATISTICS CANADA.

stat•u•ar•y ['stætʃu,ɛri] *n., pl.* **-ar•ies;** *adj.* *–n.* **1** statues collectively. **2** the art of making statues. **3** a sculptor.
–adj. of or for statues: *statuary marble.*

stat•ue ['stætʃu] *n.* an image of a person or animal, or an abstract form, carved in stone, wood, etc., cast in bronze, iron, plaster, etc., or modelled. ⟨< F < L *statua*, ult. < *stare* stand⟩

stat•u•esque [,stætʃu'ɛsk] *adj.* like a statue in dignity, formal grace, or classic beauty. **–,stat•u'esque•ness,** *n.*

stat•u•ette [,stætʃu'ɛt] *n.* a small statue. ⟨< F *statuette*, dim. of *statue* statue⟩

stat•ure ['stætʃər] *n.* **1** height: *A man 185 cm tall is above average stature.* **2** development; physical growth, or mental or moral maturity. **3** reputation or distinction: *He is a man of great stature in his profession.* ⟨ME < OF < L *statura* < *stare* stand⟩

sta•tus ['stætəs] *or* ['steitəs] *n.* **1** condition; state: *Diplomats are interested in the status of world affairs.* **2** one's social or professional standing; position; high rank; prestige: *her status as a doctor.* **3** legal position. ⟨< L *status* < *stare* stand⟩

status quo [kwou] **1** the way things are; the existing state of affairs. **2** STATUS QUO ANTE. ⟨< L *status quo* the state in which⟩

status quo an•te ['ænti] *Latin.* the way in which things were previously.

status symbol something which is supposed to indicate high social rank or status, as certain material positions, membership in certain clubs, or the pursuit of certain recreational activities.

stat•u•ta•ble ['stætʃətəbəl] *adj.* statutory. **–'stat•u•ta•bly,** *adv.*

stat•ute ['stætʃut] *n.* **1** a law enacted by a legislative body. **2** a law; decree; a formally established rule. **3** *International Law.* an instrument annexed or subsidiary to an international agreement, especially a treaty. ⟨< OF *estatut*, ult. < L *statuere* establish, ult. < *stare* stand⟩
☛ *Syn.* **1.** See note at LAW.

statute book a collection or record of statutes.

statute law written law; law expressed or stated by statutes.

statute mile a unit for measuring distance on land, equal to 5280 feet (about 1.61 km).

statute of limitations *Law.* any statute that specifies a certain period of time after which legal action cannot be brought or offences punished.

Statute of Westminster an act of the British Parliament, passed in 1931, by which Canada and other dominions were granted the authority to make their own laws.

stat•u•to•ry ['stætʃə'tɔri] *adj.* **1** having to do with a statute. **2** fixed by statute. **3** punishable by statute: *statutory rape.* **–'stat•u,to•ri•ly,** *adv.*

statutory holiday a public holiday, fixed by statute, on which government and business offices, schools, courts, etc. are closed. In Canada these include Christmas Day, Boxing Day, New Year's Day, Good Friday, Victoria Day, Canada Day, Labour Day, and Thanksgiving Day.

statutory rape the crime of a man or boy having sexual intercourse with a girl below the age of consent.

staunch[1] [stɒntʃ] *v.* **1** stop (a flow of blood), etc. **2** stop the flow of blood from (a wound). **3** cease flowing. Also, **stanch.** ⟨ME < OF *estanchier* < VL *extanicare* press together, literally, un-thin < L *ex-* un- + Celtic *tan-* thin⟩ **—'staunch•er,** *n.*

staunch[2] [stɒntʃ] *adj.* **1** firm; strong. **2** loyal; steadfast. **3** watertight: *a staunch boat.* Also, **stanch.** ⟨ME < OF *estanche,* fem. < *estanchier.* See STAUNCH[1].⟩ **—'staunch•ly,** *adv.* **—'staunch•ness,** *n.*

stave [steiv] *n., v.* **staved** or **stove, stav•ing.** *—n.* **1** one of the curved pieces of wood that form the sides of a barrel, tub, etc. **2** a stick or staff. **3** a rung of a ladder. **4** *Prosody.* a verse or stanza of a poem, song, etc. **5** *Music.* STAFF (def. 6).
—v. **1** smash a hole in (a barrel, boat, etc.) (*used with* **in**). **2** become smashed or broken in. **3** furnish with staves.
stave off, put off; keep back; delay or prevent: *The lost campers ate birds' eggs to stave off starvation.* ⟨< *staves,* pl. of *staff*⟩
☛ *Usage.* **Staved, stove.** The variant past tense and past participle **stove** is used chiefly with reference to the breaking of boats and the like: *The waves stove* (or *staved) the boat in,* but *He staved off his creditors.*

staves [steivz] *n.* **1** a pl. of STAFF. **2** pl. of STAVE.

stay[1] [stei] *v.* **stayed** or (*archaic*) **staid, staying;** *n. —v.* **1** continue to be as indicated; remain: *to stay clean. Stay here till I call you.* **2** live for a while; dwell: *She is staying with her aunt while her mother is ill.* **3** stop; halt: *We have no time to stay.* **4** pause; wait: *Time and tide stay for no man.* **5** wait for; await. **6** put an end to for a while; satisfy (hunger, appetite, etc.). **7** put off; hold back; delay; restrain; check: *The chief stayed judgment till she could hear both sides.* **8** endure to the end of: *unable to stay a race.* **9** keep up or keep even (with someone), as in a contest or race, a discussion, etc.: *Now, stay with me while I go through these points.*
stay put, remain in the same place or condition; remain stationary, fixed, or established: *Stay put till I get there. This label won't stay put.*
—n. **1** a staying; a stop; time spent: *a pleasant stay in the country.* **2** a check; restraint: *a stay on one's activity.* **3** *Law.* a delay in carrying out the order of a court: *The judge granted the condemned man a stay for an appeal.* **4** *Informal.* staying power; endurance. ⟨< OF *ester* stand < L *stare*⟩ **—'stay•er,** *n.*
☛ *Syn. v.* **1. Stay,** REMAIN = continue in some (stated) place, position, state, condition, relation, action, etc. Both verbs essentially emphasize the idea of keeping on in the same place or state without leaving or stopping. **Stay** emphasizes the idea of keeping on in the present or in some specified place, state, condition, etc. without leaving or stopping: *She decided to stay in school another year.* **Remain,** often used interchangeably with **stay,** but the more formal of the two, emphasizes keeping on in the same place or state, without changing in condition, quality, or form: *This room remains cool all summer.*

stay[2] [stei] *n., v.* **stayed, stay•ing.** *—n.* **1** a support; prop; brace. **2** a spiritual or moral support. **3** a thin, flat strip of plastic, bone, etc. used to stiffen a corselet, corset, brassiere, shirt collar, etc. **4 stays,** *pl.* formerly, a corset.
—v. **1** support; prop; hold up. **2** strengthen or secure mentally or spiritually; fix or cause to rest in dependence or reliance. ⟨probably ult. < OF *estayer* < Gmc.⟩ **—'stay•er,** *n.*

stay[3] [stei] *n., v.* **stayed, stay•ing.** *—n.* a strong rope, chain, or wire attached to something to steady it: *The mast of a ship is held in place by stays.* See SCHOONER for picture.
in stays, of a ship, in the act of changing from one tack to another.
—v. **1** support or secure with or as if with stays. **2** of a ship, change to the other tack. **3** put (a ship) on the other tack. ⟨OE *stæg*⟩

stay–at–home ['stei ət ˌhoum] *n., adj. —n.* a person who prefers to stay home rather than go out or travel for fun and recreation.
—adj. of or characteristic of someone who prefers to stay at home rather than go out, travel, etc.

staying power the ability to endure: *He doesn't work very fast, but he has great staying power.*

stay•sail ['stei,seil] *or* ['steisəl] *n. Nautical.* a sail fastened on a stay or rope.

stay•stitch ['stei,stɪtʃ] *v.* make fairly large stitches along (the edge of a cut piece of cloth) to prevent it from ravelling or stretching out of shape as a result of being handled.

stbd. starboard.

St. Bernard SAINT BERNARD.

STD sexually transmitted disease.

Ste. Sainte.

stead [stɛd] *n.* a place, specifically of a person or thing filled by some substitute: *The sales manager could not come, but sent her assistant in her stead.*
stand (someone) **in good stead,** be of advantage or service to someone. ⟨OE *stede*⟩

stead•fast ['stɛd,fæst] *or* ['stɛdfəst] *adj.* **1** loyal; unwavering. **2** firmly fixed; not moving or changing. Also, **stedfast.** ⟨OE *stedefæst* < *stede* place + *fæst* fast[1], firm⟩ **—'stead,fast•ly,** *adv.* **—'stead,fast•ness,** *n.*

stead•y ['stɛdi] *adj.* **stead•i•er, stead•i•est;** *v.* **stead•ied, stead•y•ing;** *interj., adv., n., pl.* **stead•ies.** *—adj.* **1** changing little; uniform; regular: *steady progress, a steady customer.* **2** firmly fixed; firm; not swaying or shaking: *to hold a ladder steady.* **3** not easily excited; calm: *steady nerves.* **4** resolute; steadfast: *a steady friendship.* **5** having good habits; reliable: *a steady young man.* **6** of a ship, keeping nearly upright in a heavy sea. **7** *Informal.* being one's regular girlfriend or boyfriend: *Mary was his steady girl.*
—v. **1** make steady; keep steady. **2** become steady.
—interj. **1** be calm! don't get excited! **2** *Nautical.* hold the helm as it is! keep on course!
—adv.
go steady, a *Informal.* date one person or each other only. **b** go carefully.
—n. Informal. a regular girlfriend or boyfriend; a person who is being courted regularly by the same person. ⟨< *stead*⟩ **—'stead•i•ly,** *adv.* **—'stead•i•ness,** *n.*
☛ *Syn. adj.* **1. Steady,** REGULAR = constant or uniform in acting, doing, moving, happening. **Steady** particularly suggests uninterrupted or unchanging movement, action, progress, or direction: *He has been unable to find steady work.* **Regular** emphasizes following a fixed, usual, or uniform procedure, practice, program, or pattern: *She is a regular subscriber to several magazines.*

stead•y–state ['stɛdi 'steit] *adj.* maintaining the same basic condition; unchanging in quality, structure, behaviour, etc.: *a steady-state current.*

steady–state theory *Astronomy.* the theory that the universe has now the same basic form as always, matter being continuously created to replace that which is naturally destroyed. Compare BIG BANG THEORY.

steak [steik] *n.* **1** a thick slice of meat from a beef carcass, usually broiled or fried; beef steak. **2** a similar slice of other meat or of fish for broiling or frying: *ham steak, salmon steak.* **3** ground meat shaped and cooked somewhat like a steak: *hamburger steak.* ⟨ME < ON *steik*⟩
☛ *Hom.* STAKE.

steak knife a table knife having a very sharp serrated blade, specially designed for cutting meat that may be tough.

steak tartare raw beefsteak ground up and mixed with seasoning and raw egg.

steal [stil] *v.* **stole, sto•len, steal•ing;** *n. —v.* **1** take (something) that does not belong to one; take dishonestly: *to steal money.* **2** take, get, or do secretly or without permission: *to steal a look at someone.* **3** take, get, or win by art, charm, or gradual means: *She steals all hearts.* **4** move secretly or quietly: *She stole out of the house.* **5** move slowly or gently: *The years steal by.* **6** *Baseball.* of a runner, advance a base without the help of a hit or error.
steal the scene or **show,** dominate a performance, especially as a supporting actor.
—n. **1** *Informal.* the act of stealing. **2** *Informal.* the thing stolen. **3** *Informal.* something obtained very cheaply or very easily: *At that price the car is a steal.* **4** *Informal.* a dishonest or unethical transaction at a great profit. **5** *Baseball.* a safe advance from one base to another by stealing. ⟨OE *stelan*⟩ **—'steal•er,** *n.*
☛ *Hom.* STEEL.
☛ *Syn. v.* **1. Steal,** PILFER, FILCH = take dishonestly or wrongfully and secretly something belonging to someone else. **Steal** is the general and most common word: *Thieves stole the silver.* **Pilfer,** more formal, means 'steal and carry away in small amounts': *In many supermarkets hidden guards watch for people who pilfer food.* **Filch** particularly suggests stealthy or furtive pilfering, usually of objects of little value: *The teenagers filched some candy from the counter.*

stealth [stɛlθ] *n.* secret or sly action: *He obtained the letter by stealth, taking it while his sister's back was turned.* ⟨< *steal*⟩

stealth•y ['stɛlθi] *adj.* **stealth•i•er, stealth•i•est.** done or acting in a secret manner; secret; sly: *a stealthy walk, stealthy robbers.* **—'stealth•i•ly,** *adv.* **—'stealth•i•ness,** *n.*

steam [stim] *n., v. —n.* **1** the invisible vapour or gas into which water is changed when it is heated to the boiling point. Compare WATER VAPOUR. **2** the white cloud or mist formed when the invisible vapour from boiling water condenses as it cools. **3 a** the vapour from boiling water, kept under pressure to generate mechanical power and for heating and cooking: *Engines powered*

by steam were formerly used to run threshing machines, tractors, etc. **b** the power thus generated. **4** *Informal.* power or energy.
full steam ahead, with all possible power or energy: *They went full steam ahead as soon as they got final approval.*
let or **blow off steam,** *Informal.* **a** get rid of excess energy: *He took the kids to the playground so they could let off steam.* **b** relieve one's feelings of anger, frustration, etc.: *Wait till we get home before you let off steam.*
run out of steam, *Informal.* lose power, energy, or effectiveness.
—*v.* **1** give off steam: *The soup was steaming. Their mitts were steaming on the radiator.* **2** become covered with steam (*usually used with* **up**): *The windshield had steamed up inside the car.* **3** rise as vapour: *Mist was steaming off the lake.* **4** expose to the action of steam; prepare, treat, etc. with steam: *to steam oneself for a cold, to steam a pudding, to steam a letter open.* **5** move or travel by the power of steam: *The ship steamed away.* **6** move quickly, as if powered by steam: *She really steams along on her bike.* **7** *Informal.* be angry; fume (*only in progressive tenses*): *She was steaming by the time he got there, half an hour late.*
steamed up, *Informal.* **a** angry, fuming: *He gets all steamed up about nothing.* **b** full of energy and enthusiasm: *She's steamed up now about her science project.* ⟨OE *stēam*⟩ **—'steam,like,** *adj.*

steam bath a kind of bath taken by sitting or standing in a steam-filled room or chamber.

steam•boat ['stim,bout] *n.* a boat propelled by a STEAM ENGINE.

steam boiler a boiler in which water is heated to make steam.

steam chest or **box** a chamber through which the steam of an engine passes from the boiler to the cylinder.

steamed [stimd] *adj., v.* —*adj.* **1** *Informal.* angry. **2** cooked, etc. by steam.
—*v.* pt. and pp. of STEAM.

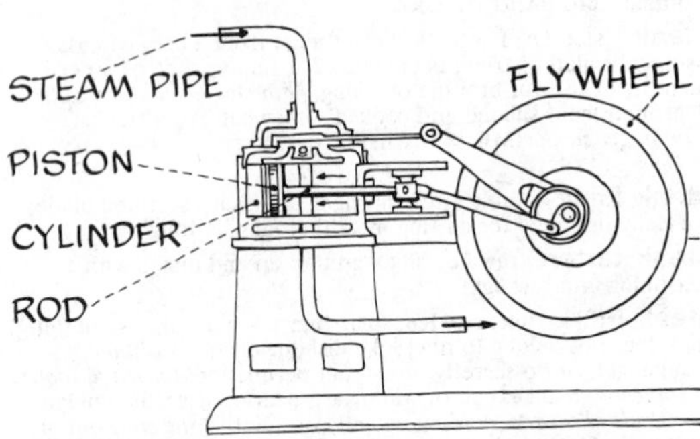

A steam engine. The pressure of the steam forced into the cylinder pushes the piston back and forth. This causes the rod to turn a shaft that passes on motion to wheels or other parts. The weight of the heavy flywheel attached to the shaft keeps the shaft turning evenly.

steam engine **1** an engine operated by steam, typically one in which a sliding piston in a cylinder is moved by the expansive action of steam generated in a boiler. **2** a steam locomotive.

steam•er ['stimər] *n.* **1** a steamboat; steamship. **2** an engine run by steam. **3** a container in which something is steamed or kept warm. **4** a soft-shelled clam.

steamer chair an outdoor folding chair, usually made of wood and canvas and having a leg rest, such as is found on the sun deck of a passenger ship; deck chair.

steamer rug a blanket, especially one used to keep a person warm in a chair on the deck of a ship.

steam fitter a person who installs and repairs steam pipes, radiators, boilers, etc. **—steam fitting.**

steam heat heat given off by steam in radiators and pipes.

steam iron an electric iron in which water is heated to produce steam that is released through holes in the undersurface to dampen cloth while pressing it.

steam–roll•er ['stim ,roulər] *n., v.* —*n.* **1** a road roller, especially one powered by steam. **2** an overpowering force used to crush opposition. **3** (*adj.*) designating or using a relentlessly overpowering force.
—*v.* **1** override by crushing power or force; crush: *to steam-roller all opposition.* **2** force by this means: *to steam-roller a bill through Parliament.* **3** make level, smooth, etc. with a steam-roller. **4** use steam-roller methods; advance with overwhelming force.

steam•ship ['stim,ʃɪp] *n.* a ship propelled by a steam engine.

steam shovel a machine for digging, formerly always operated by steam, but now by an internal-combustion engine.

steam•tight ['stim,tɔit] *adj.* impervious to steam: *a steamtight valve.*

steam turbine a turbine moved by steam.

steam•y ['stimi] *adj.* **steam•i•er, steam•i•est. 1** of steam; like steam; rising in steam. **2** full of steam; giving off steam. **3** *Slang.* having to do with sexual activity: *steamy confessions, a steamy romance.* **—'steam•i•ly,** *adv.* **—'steam•i•ness,** *n.*

ste•ap•sin [sti'æpsən] *n. Biochemistry.* an enzyme in the pancreatic juice that converts fats into more easily digested fatty acids and glycerin. ⟨blend of *stea(rin)* and *(pe)psin*⟩

ste•a•rate ['stiə,reit] *or* ['stireit] *n. Chemistry.* a salt of STEARIC ACID.

ste•ar•ic [sti'ærɪk], [sti'ɛrɪk], *or* ['stirɪk] *adj.* having to do with stearin, suet, or fat. ⟨< F *stéarique* < Gk. *stear* fat⟩

stearic acid *Chemistry.* a solid, white substance obtained from certain fats and used in making candles. *Formula*: $C_{18}H_{36}O_2$

ste•a•rin ['stiərɪn] *or* ['stirɪn] *n.* **1** *Chemistry.* a colourless, odourless substance, glyceryl stearate, that is the chief constituent of many animal and vegetable fats, used in making soaps, adhesives, etc. *Formula*: $(C_{18}H_{35}O_{23})C_3H_5$ **2** a mixture of fatty acids used for making candles, solid alcohol, etc. ⟨< F *stéarine* < Gk. *stear* fat⟩

ste•a•rine ['stiərɪn] *or* ['stiə,rin], ['stirɪn] *or* ['stirin] *n.* stearin.

ste•a•tite ['stiə,tɔit] *n.* a rock composed of impure talc; soapstone. ⟨< L *steatitis* < Gk. *stear, -atos* fat⟩

ste•a•tit•ic [,stiə'tɪtɪk] *adj.* like or composed of soapstone.

ste•a•to•pyg•ia [,stiətou'pɪdʒiə] *or* [,stiətou'paɪdʒiə] *n.* a heavy or excessive deposit of fat on the buttocks. ⟨< Gk. *steatos* tallow + *pyge* buttocks⟩

ste•a•to•sis [,stiə'tousɪs] *n. Pathology.* **1** fatty degeneration. **2** any disease of the sebaceous glands. ⟨< NL < Gk. *stear, -atos* fat + NL *-osis* -osis⟩

sted•fast ['stɛd,fæst] *or* ['stɛdfəst] *adj.* See STEADFAST. **—'sted,fast•ly,** *adv.* **—'sted,fast•ness,** *n.*

steed [stid] *n. Poetic.* a horse, especially a high-spirited riding horse. ⟨OE *stēda*⟩

steel [stil] *n., v.* —*n.* **1** an alloy of iron and carbon that is very hard, strong, and tough. Other metals, such as nickel or manganese, may be added to the basic alloy for specific purposes. **2** something made from steel, such as: **a** a sword. **b** a piece of steel for making sparks. **c** a rod of steel for sharpening knives. **d** a narrow strip of steel in a corset. **e** the heavy, specially shaped piece of metal used to depress the strings of a STEEL GUITAR. **3** (*adj.*) made of steel. **4** steel-like hardness or strength: *nerves of steel.* **5** (*adj.*) resembling steel in hardness, colour, etc. **6** *Cdn.* **a** a railway track: *Steel has been laid for 200 km north.* **b** the railway line: *They arranged to meet at steel.* **7 steels,** *pl.* shares in steel-producing firms. **8** a STEEL GUITAR.
—*v.* **1** point, edge, or cover with steel. **2** make hard or strong like steel: *He tried to steel his heart against the sufferings of the poor.* ⟨OE *stēle*⟩ **—'steel•less,** *adj.* **—'steel-,like,** *adj.*
☛ *Hom.* STEAL.

steel band a band composed of steel drums, common in the West Indies.

steel blue a lustrous dark blue, like the colour of tempered steel. **—'steel-'blue,** *adj.*

steel drum a tuned percussion instrument originating in Trinidad, made from an oil drum by cutting off one end and part of the sides and shaping the other end into sections (called notes), each tuned to a specific note. Steel drums may be tuned for a soprano, tenor, or bass range.

steel engraving **1** the process or art of engraving on a steel-coated copper plate. **2** the plate so produced.

steel guitar an electric guitar held on the lap, played by picking with one hand while pressing and sliding a STEEL (def. 2e) along the strings with the other hand to change the pitch.

steel•head or **steel•head trout** ['stil,hɛd] *n., pl.* **-head** or **-heads.** *Cdn.* a fish (*Salmo gardnerii*) of the Pacific coast which spawns in fresh water after spending two or three years at sea. See also RAINBOW TROUT and KAMLOOPS TROUT.

steel mill a place where steel is made.

steel wool fine steel threads or shavings in a pad, etc., used for cleaning or polishing.

steel•work ['stil,wɜrk] *n.* a part or the whole of an article or structure made from steel.

steel•work•er ['stil,wɜrkər] *n.* a person who works in a place where steel is made.

steel•works ['stil,wɜrks] *n.pl. or sing.* a place where steel is made.

steel•y ['stili] *adj.* **steel•i•er, steel•i•est. 1** made of steel. **2** like steel in colour, strength, or hardness. **—'steel•i•ness,** *n.*
☛ *Hom.* STELE.

steel•yard ['stil,jɑrd] *or* ['stiljərd] *n.* a portable balance for weighing, having a horizontal bar on a pivot with a movable weight at the longer arm and, at the end of the shorter arm, a hook for holding the object to be weighed. It is designed to be suspended from a hook or from the user's hand. ⟨< *steel* + *yard²*, in the sense of 'rod'⟩

steen•bok ['stin,bɒk] *or* ['stein,bɒk] *n.* STEINBOK (def. 1). ⟨< Afrikaans *stenbok* < *steen* stone + *bok* buck⟩

steep¹ [stip] *adj., n.* *—adj.* **1** having a sharp slope; almost straight up and down: *The hill is steep.* **2** *Informal.* unreasonable: *a steep price.* **3** of a story, etc., exaggerated; incredible.
—n. a steep slope. ⟨OE *stēap*⟩ **—'steep•ly,** *adv.* **—'steep•ness,** *n.*
☛ *Syn. adj.* **1. Steep,** ABRUPT, PRECIPITOUS = having a slope almost straight up and down. **Steep** suggests having a very sharp slope that is hard to go up: *I do not like to drive up a steep hill.* **Abrupt** is used especially of an extremely steep slope that is sudden or unexpected: *After they passed the huge stump, the path made an abrupt descent to a little clearing.* **Precipitous** suggests something as abrupt and straight up and down as a precipice: *The climbers will attempt to scale the precipitous eastern slope of the peak.*

steep² [stip] *v., n.* *—v.* **1** soak (something), especially so as to soften, cleanse, or extract an essence. **2** undergo such soaking: *Let the tea steep for five minutes.* **3** make thoroughly wet; saturate or immerse: *a sword steeped in blood.* **4** imbue; permeate (*usually used in the passive*): *ruins steeped in gloom, a mind steeped in hatred.*
—n. **1** the process of steeping or the state of being steeped. **2** the liquid or bath in which something is steeped. ⟨probably < OE *stēap* bowl⟩ **—'steep•er,** *n.*

stee•ple ['stipəl] *n.* **1** a high tower rising above the roof of a church, etc., and usually having a spire at the top. **2** such a tower, together with the spire or other structure surmounting it. ⟨OE *stēpel* < *stēap* steep⟩ **—'stee•ple,like,** *adj.*

stee•ple•bush ['stipəl,bʊʃ] *n.* hardhack, a shrub (*Spirren tomentosa*) that has pink, purple, or white flowers in steeple-shaped clusters.

stee•ple•chase ['stipəl,tʃeis] *n., v.* **-chased, -chas•ing.** *—n.* **1** a horse race over a course having ditches, hedges, and other obstacles. **2** a foot race over a similar course or across country.
—v. ride or run in a steeplechase. ⟨from the courses being originally sight-marked by the steeples of village churches, the race being run across country from one to the next⟩
—'stee•ple,chas•er, *n.*

stee•ple•jack ['stipəl,dʒæk] *n.* a person who climbs steeples, tall chimneys, etc. to paint, make repairs, etc.

steer¹ [stir] *v., n.* *—v.* **1** guide the course of: *to steer a ship, a sled, an automobile, or an airplane.* **2** guide; lead; conduct; pilot: *to steer a person through a crowd.* **3** set and follow: *He steered a course for home.* **4** be guided: *This car steers easily.* **5** guide a ship, car, bicycle, etc.: *The pilot steered for the harbour. The cabbie steered toward the curb.* **6** direct one's way or course.
steer clear of, keep away from; avoid.
—n. Slang. an idea or a suggested course of action. ⟨OE *stēoran*⟩
—'steer•er, *n.*
☛ *Hom.* STERE.

steer² [stir] *n.* a full-grown, castrated male of cattle, less than four years old. Steers are usually raised for their meat. Compare OX.
☛ *Hom.* STERE.

steer•age ['stirɪdʒ] *n.* **1** the part of a passenger ship occupied by passengers travelling at the cheapest rate. **2** the act of steering. **3** the manner in which a ship is affected by the helm.

steer•age•way ['stirɪdʒ,wei] *n.* the amount of forward motion a ship must have before it can be steered.

steering committee a committee struck to consider order of business, priorities, management of operations, etc.

steering gear the apparatus for steering an automobile, ship, etc.

steering wheel the wheel that is turned to steer an automobile, ship, etc.

steers•man ['stirzmən] *n., pl.* **-men.** a person who steers a ship.

steeve [stiv] *v.* **steeved, steev•ing;** *n.* *—v.* stow cargo, usually by means of a derrick or spar.
—n. the derrick or spar so used. ⟨ME < OF *estiver* or Sp. *estivar* < L *stipare* compress, pack tight⟩

steg•o•sau•rus [,stɛgə'sɔrəs] *n., pl.* **-ri** [-raɪ] *or* [-ri]. any of a genus (*Stegosaurus*) of large, plant-eating dinosaurs of the late Jurassic period having two rows of large, triangular, bony plates along the back. ⟨< NL < Gk. *stegos* roof + *sauros* lizard⟩

stein [staɪn] *n.* **1** a beer mug. **2** the amount it holds, approximately half a litre. ⟨< G *Stein* stone⟩

stein•bok ['staɪn,bɒk] *n.* **1** a small, reddish brown African antelope (*Raphicerus campestris*), the male of which has small, straight horns. **2** an ibex native to the Alps. ⟨See STEENBOK⟩

ste•la ['stilə] *or* ['stɛlə] *n., pl.* **ste•lae** [-li] *or* [-laɪ]. stele.

ste•le ['stili] *n., pl.* **-lae** [-li] *or* [-laɪ] or **-les. 1** an upright slab or pillar of stone bearing an inscription, sculptural design, etc., **2** a prepared surface on the face of a building, a rock, etc., bearing an inscription or the like. **3** *Botany.* the central axial cylinder of vascular tissue in the roots and stems of plants. ⟨< Gk.⟩
☛ *Hom.* STEELY.

stel•lar ['stɛlər] *adj.* **1** of or having to do with the stars; of a star; like a star. **2** chief: *a stellar role.* **3** of or having to do with a star performer; outstanding. ⟨< L *stellaris* < *stella* star⟩

stel•late ['stɛlɪt] *or* ['stɛleit] *adj.* spreading out like the points of a star; star-shaped. ⟨< L *stellatus* < *stella* star⟩ **—'stel•late•ly,** *adv.*

Stel•ler's jay ['stɛlərz] a large, crested jay (*Cyanocitta stelleri*) of W North America, having dark blue and black plumage. ⟨< Georg Wilhelm *Steller* (1709-1745), a German naturalist⟩

Steller's sea cow a huge, extinct sea mammal of the N Pacific Ocean, belonging to the same order as the dugong and manatee. It was discovered in the mid 18th century and within 30 years was hunted to extinction. ⟨See STELLER'S JAY⟩

stel•li•form ['stɛlə,fɔrm] *adj.* star-shaped.

stel•lu•lar ['stɛljələr] *adj.* **1** set with small stars. **2** shaped like small stars. **3** brilliant; outstanding.

St. El•mo's fire ['ɛlmouz] a fiery light caused by a discharge of atmospheric electricity, often seen on masts, towers, etc.

St. Elmo's light ST. ELMO'S FIRE.

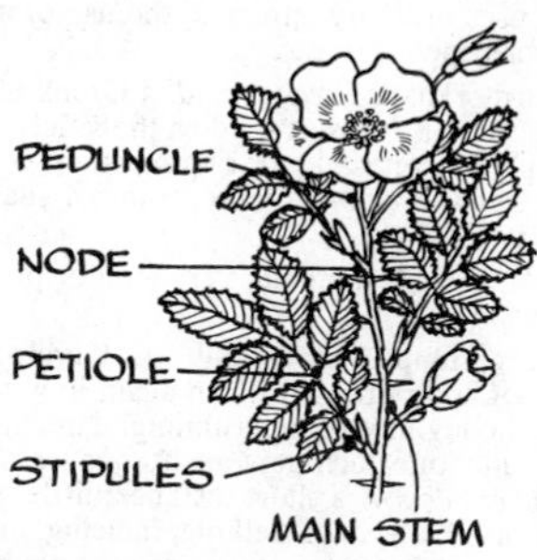

stem¹ [stɛm] *n., v.* **stemmed, stem•ming.** *—n.* **1** the main part of a plant, usually above the ground, that develops buds and shoots. See FLOWER for picture. **2** the part of a flower, a fruit, or a leaf that joins it to the plant or tree; petiole or pedicel. **3** anything like or suggesting the stem of a plant: *the stem of a goblet, the stem of a pipe, etc.* **4** the line of descent of a family. **5** *Grammar.* the part of a word to which endings are added and inside which changes are made. *Run* is the stem of *running, runner, ran,* etc. **6** the upright timber or metal piece at the bow or front end of a boat, to which the ship's sides are joined.
from stem to stern, a from one end of the ship to the other. **b** along the full length of anything.
—v. **1** remove the stem from (a leaf, fruit, etc.). **2** grow out;

develop; come from: *The difficulty stems from her failure to plan properly.* ⟨OE *stemn*⟩ **–'stem,like,** *adj.*

stem[2] [stɛm] *v.* **stemmed, stem•ming. 1** stop; check; dam up. **2** make progress against: *stem the swift current.* ⟨< ON *stemma*⟩

stem cell *Genetics.* an uncommitted cell that can differentiate into any of several cell types.

stem•less ['stɛmlɪs] *adj.* having no stem; having no visible stem.

stemmed [stɛmd] *adj., v.* *–adj.* **1** having a stem. **2** having the stem removed.
–v. pt. and pp. of STEM.

stem•mer ['stɛmər] *n.* a person or thing that removes stems from leaves, fruit, etc.

stem•ware ['stɛm,wɛr] *n.* goblets or drinking glasses having stems, used for wine, liqueurs, etc.

stem•wind•ing ['stɛm,waɪndɪŋ] *adj.* of a watch, winding by turning a knob on the stem.

stench [stɛntʃ] *n.* a very bad smell; stink. ⟨OE *stenc*; related to *stincan* smell⟩

sten•cil ['stɛnsəl] *n., v.* **-cilled** or **-ciled, -cil•ling** or **-cil•ing.**
–n. **1** a thin sheet of metal, paper, etc. having letters or designs cut through it. **2** the letters or designs made by tracing or filling in the cutouts.
–v. mark, paint, or make with a stencil: *The curtains have a stencilled border.* ⟨ult. < OF *estanceler* ornament with colours, ult. < L *scintilla* spark⟩

sten•o ['stɛnou] *n., pl.* **-os.** *Informal.* stenographer.

sten•o•graph ['stɛnə,græf] *n., v.* *–n.* **1** a character used in shorthand. **2** any of various keyboard instruments, resembling a typewriter, used for writing in shorthand.
–v. write in shorthand.

ste•nog•ra•pher [stə'nɒgrəfər] *n.* a person whose chief work is taking dictation and transcribing it on a typewriter, etc.

sten•o•graph•ic [,stɛnə'græfɪk] *adj.* **1** of, having to do with, or produced by stenography. **2** of style, concise.
–,sten•o'graph•i•cal•ly, *adv.*

ste•nog•ra•phy [stə'nɒgrəfi] *n.* shorthand or the act of using it. ⟨< Gk. *stenos* narrow + E *-graphy*⟩

ste•no•sis [stə'nousɪs] *n., pl.* **-ses** [-siz]. *Pathology.* an abnormal narrowing or constriction of a canal or passage in the body, especially a constriction of a heart valve. ⟨< Gk. *stenos* narrow + E *-osis*⟩

ste•not•ic [stə'nɒtɪk] *adj.* of or having to do with stenosis.

Sten•o•type ['stɛnə,taɪp] *n.* **1** *Trademark.* a kind of typewriter used in stenotypy. **2 stenotype,** a letter or group of letters used for a sound, word, or phrase in stenotypy. ⟨< Gk. *stenos* narrow + E *type*⟩

sten•o•typ•y ['stɛnə,taɪpi] *or* [stə'nɒtəpi] *n.* **1** a form of shorthand that uses ordinary letters. **2** the use of a Stenotype machine to record speeches, etc.

Sten•tor ['stɛntɔr] *n.* **1** *Greek legend.* a Greek herald in the Trojan War, whose voice was as loud as the voices of fifty men. **2 stentor,** any person with a loud, ringing voice. **3 stentor,** any member of the genus *Stentor* of large, trumpet-shaped, heterotrichous protozoans.

sten•to•ri•an [stɛn'tɔriən] *adj.* very loud or powerful in sound. ⟨< *Stentor*⟩

step [stɛp] *n., v.* **stepped, step•ping.** *–n.* **1** a movement made by lifting the foot and putting it down again in a new position; one motion of the leg in walking, running, dancing, etc. **2** the distance covered by one such movement: *She was three steps away when he called her back.* **3** a short distance; little way: *The school is only a step away.* **4** a way of walking, dancing, marching, etc.: *a slow step.* **5** a sequence of steps taken in a particular manner and forming a unit or pattern of a particular dance: *a cha-cha step.* **6** a place for the foot in going up or coming down. A stair or a rung of a ladder is a step. **7** the sound made by putting the foot down: *We thought we heard steps in the next room.* **8** a footprint: *steps in the mud.* **9** an action: *taking steps to reduce absenteeism.* **10** a degree in a series; a grade in rank. **11** *Music.* **a** a degree of the staff or the scale. **b** the interval between two successive degrees of the scale. **12** a part like a step; support, frame, etc. for holding the end of something upright: *the step of a mast.*
in step, a keeping one's pace uniform with that of another or others or in time with music. **b** making one's actions or ideas agree with those of another person or persons; in agreement.
keep step, move, think, or act in step.
out of step, a not keeping pace with others or in time to music. **b** not in harmony or accord.
step by step, little by little; slowly; in stages.
take steps, adopt, put into effect, or carry out measures considered to be necessary, desirable, etc.: *Steps have already been taken to deal with the emergency.*
watch (one's) **step, a** step carefully. **b** be careful.
–v. **1** move the legs as in walking, running, dancing, etc.: *Step lively!* **2** perform the steps of (a dance). **3** walk a short distance: *Step this way.* **4** put the foot down: *to step on a worm.* **5 a** make or arrange like a flight of steps. **b** arrange (tests, etc.) in a series of grades of difficulty. **6** set (a mast); fix or place in a support. **7** *Informal.* go fast: *They were really stepping along.*
step down, a come down. **b** abdicate or resign from an office or position: *She stepped down from the presidency.* **c** decrease: *to step down the rate of flow in a pipeline.*
step in, a come in. **b** intervene.
step off, measure by taking steps: *Step off the distance from the door to the window.*
step on it, *Informal.* go faster; hurry up.
step out, *Informal.* **a** go out for entertainment. **b** leave a room or building very briefly: *She's just stepped out for a few minutes.*
step up, a go up; approach. **b** make go higher, faster, etc.; increase: *to step up production.* ⟨OE *steppan*⟩
☛ *Hom.* STEPPE.

step– *prefix.* related by the remarriage of a parent, not by blood: *stepmother, stepsister.* ⟨OE *stēop-*⟩

step•broth•er ['stɛp,brʌðər] *n.* a stepfather's or stepmother's son by a former marriage.

step•child ['stɛp,tʃaɪld] *n., pl.* **-chil•dren.** a child of one's husband or wife by a former marriage.

step•dame ['stɛp,deim] *n. Archaic.* stepmother.

step•daugh•ter ['stɛp,dɒtər] *n.* a daughter of one's husband or wife by a former marriage.

step–down ['stɛp ,daʊn] *adj.* **1** serving or causing to decrease gradually. **2** *Electricity.* especially of a transformer, lowering the voltage of a current.

step•fa•ther ['stɛp,fɒðər] *n.* a man who has married one's mother after the death or divorce of one's natural father.

steph•a•no•tis [,stɛfə'noutɪs] *n.* any climbing plant of the genus *Stephanotis* of the milkweed family, especially *S. floribundus,* a woody vine cultivated for its waxy, white, sweet-scented flowers often used in bridal wreaths and bouquets. ⟨< NL < Gk., fit for a crown < *stephanos* crown⟩

step–in ['stɛp ,ɪn] *adj., n.* *–adj.* of garments, shoes, etc., put on by being stepped into.
–n. such a garment or shoe.

step•lad•der ['stɛp,lædər] *n.* a portable ladder consisting of narrow flat steps fixed in a hinged, free-standing supporting frame.

step•moth•er ['stɛp,mʌðər] *n.* a woman who has married one's father after the death or divorce of one's natural mother.

step–out well ['stɛp ,ʌut] a gas or oil well dug near the site of another that has already been proved productive, giving further proof of reserves in the area.

step•par•ent ['stɛp,pɛrənt] *n.* a stepfather or stepmother.

steppe [stɛp] *n.* **1** one of the vast, treeless plains in SE Europe and in Asia. **2** a vast, treeless plain. ⟨< Russian *step'*⟩
☛ *Hom.* STEP.

step•per ['stɛpər] *n.* a person or animal that steps, especially in a particular manner: *a high stepper.*

step•ping–stone ['stɛpɪŋ ,stoun] *n.* **1** a stone or one of a line of stones in shallow water, a marshy place, etc. used in crossing. **2** a stone for use in mounting or ascending. **3** anything serving as a means of advancing or rising.

step•sis•ter ['stɛp,sɪstər] *n.* a stepfather's or stepmother's daughter by a former marriage.

step•son ['stɛp,sʌn] *n.* a son of one's husband or wife by a former marriage.

step–up ['stɛp ,ʌp] *adj., n.* *–adj.* **1** serving or causing to increase gradually. **2** *Electricity.* especially of a transformer, increasing the voltage of a current.
–n. an increase: *a step-up in production.*

step•wise ['stɛp,waɪz] *adv.* in a step or steps.

–ster *suffix. Often facetious.* **1** one that ——s: *fibster.* **2** one that makes ——: *maltster, rhymester.* **3** one that is ——: *youngster.* **4** special meanings: *gangster, roadster, teamster.* ⟨OE *-estre, -istre*⟩

ster. sterling.

ste•ra•di•an [stə'reidiən] *n.* an SI unit for measuring solid angles, equal to the angle from the centre of a sphere which cuts off an area on the surface of the sphere equal to the square of the radius. The steradian is used mostly in mathematics; it is one of the two supplementary units in the SI. See RADIAN for picture. *Symbol*: sr

stere [stir] *n.* a unit of volume equal to one cubic metre, sometimes used for measuring stacked timber. ⟨< F < Gk. *stereos* solid⟩
☛ *Hom.* STEER.

ster•e•o ['stɛri,ou] *or* ['stiri,ou] *n., adj.* —*n.* **1** stereophonic reproduction. **2** a set or apparatus for stereophonic reproduction. **3** *Informal.* a radio, record player, or tape-recorder equipped with a stereophonic system. **4** any stereophonic system or its use, as in a film or television program. **5** stereotype.
—*adj.* **1** stereophonic. **2** produced for use with stereophonic equipment.

stereo– *combining form.* solid or three-dimensional: *stereoscope.* ⟨< Gk. *stereos* solid⟩

ster•e•o•bate ['stɛriə,beit] *or* ['stiriə,beit] *n.* a solid mass of masonry, visible above ground, as the foundation of a building. ⟨< F *stéréobate* < L *stereobata* < Gk. *stereobates* < *stereo* solid + *baino* walk⟩

ster•e•o•chem•is•try [,stɛriə'kɛmɪstri] *or* [,stiriə'kɛmɪstri] *n.* the branch of chemistry dealing with the three-dimensional spatial arrangement of the atoms that make up molecules.

ster•e•om•e•try [,stɛri'ɒmətri] *or* [,stiri'ɒmətri] *n.* the determination of the size and shape of solid bodies.

ster•e•o•phon•ic [,stɛriə'fɒnɪk] *or* [,stiriə'fɒnɪk] *adj.* in sound reproduction, of or produced by the use of two or more microphones, recording channels, loudspeakers, etc. in order to give a three-dimensional effect. **—,ster•e•o'phon•i•cal•ly,** *adv.* **—,ster•e'oph•o•ny,** *n.*

ster•e•op•ti•con [,stɛri'ɒptəkən] *or* [,stiri'ɒptəkən] *n.* a slide projector having a powerful light that projects two images at once, throwing three-dimensional pictures upon a screen. ⟨< NL < Gk. *stereos* solid + *optikos* relating to vision⟩

ster•e•o•scope ['stɛriə,skoup] *or* ['stiriə,skoup] *n.* an instrument through which two pictures of the same object or scene are viewed, one by each eye. The picture thus viewed appears to have three dimensions. **—,ster•e•o'scop•ic,** *adj.* **—,ster•e•o'scop•i•cal•ly,** *adv.* **—,ster•e'os•co•py,** *n.*

ster•e•o•type ['stɛriə,təip] *or* ['stiriə,təip] *n., v.* **-typed, -typ•ing.** —*n.* **1** *Printing.* **a** a one-piece plate of type metal cast from a mould made from a surface of composed type. **b** the method or process of making such plates. **2** something that has a fixed form, as if cast from a mould; especially, a kind of oversimplified mental picture shared by many people in a group: *He fits the stereotype of the insecure bully.* **3** a person or group that represents such a mental picture: *The novel's hero is a stereotype of the ambitious young man.*
—*v.* **1** *Printing.* **a** make a stereotype of. **b** print from stereotypes. **2** have or show a mental stereotype of. **—'ster•e•o,typ•er,** *n.*

ster•e•o•typed ['stɛriə,təipt] *or* ['stiriə,təipt] *adj., v.* —*adj.* **1** printed from a stereotype. **2** not original or individual; too conventional and rigid.
—*v.* pt. and pp. of STEREOTYPE.

ster•e•o•typ•ic [,stɛriə'tɪpɪk] *or* [,stiriə'tɪpɪk] *adj.* stereotypical.

ster•e•o•typ•i•cal [,stɛriə'tɪpɪkəl] *or* [,stiriə'tɪpɪkəl] *adj.* of, having to do with, or representing a mental stereotype.

ster•e•o•typ•y ['stɛriə,təipi] *or* ['stiriə,təipi] *n.* **1** the process of making stereotype plates. **2** printing from stereotype plates. **3** an abnormality consisting of repeating a certain action, as in some phases of schizophrenia.

ster•ic ['stɛrɪk] *or* ['stɪrɪk] *adj. Chemistry.* concerning or relating to the arrangement of atoms in a molecule. ⟨< *stereo-* + *-ic*⟩

steric hindrance *Chemistry.* the prevention or inhibition of a chemical reaction because of the obstruction of reacting atoms in a molecule.

ster•ile ['stɛraɪl] *or* ['stɛrɪl] *adj.* **1** free from living micro-organisms, especially potentially harmful ones: *sterile surgical instruments.* **2** of animals or plants, failing or not able to reproduce; barren. **3** not producing crops or vegetation: *sterile land, sterile seed.* **4** *Botany.* **a** of a plant, not bearing fruit or spores. **b** of a flower, producing only stamens, or producing neither stamens nor pistils. **5** not producing results: *sterile hopes.* **6** not evoking any feeling, warmth, etc.; lifeless or dull. ⟨< L *sterilis*⟩ **—'ster•ile•ly,** *adv.*

ste•ril•i•ty [stə'rɪləti] *n.* a sterile condition or character.

ster•i•li•za•tion [,stɛrələ'zeiʃən] *or* [,stɛrəlaɪ'zeiʃən] *n.* a sterilizing or being sterilized: *the sterilization of dishes by boiling them.*

ster•i•lize ['stɛrə,laɪz] *v.* **-lized, -liz•ing. 1** make free from living germs: *The water had to be sterilized by boiling to make it fit to drink.* **2** permanently deprive of fertility by removing or disabling reproductive organs. **3** make unproductive, unprofitable, or useless. **—'ster•i,liz•er,** *n.*

ster•ling ['stɜrlɪŋ] *n., adj.* —*n.* **1** British money, especially the pound as the standard British monetary unit in international trade: *to pay in sterling.* **2** sterling silver or things made of it.
—*adj.* **1** of or payable in British money. **2** designating a silver alloy of a standard quality, that is not less than 92.5 percent pure silver, the remaining 7.5 percent usually being copper. **3** made of sterling silver. **4** of dependable excellence: *a sterling character.* ⟨probably ult. < OE *steorra* star (as on certain early Norman coins)⟩

sterling area or **bloc** a group of countries having currencies tied to the British pound sterling and holding reserves mainly in British sterling.

stern[1] [stɜrn] *adj.* **1** severe; strict; harsh: *a stern master, a stern frown.* **2** hard; not yielding; firm: *stern necessity.* **3** grim: *stern mountains.* ⟨OE *stirne*⟩ **—'stern•ly,** *adv.* **—'stern•ness,** *n.*

stern[2] [stɜrn] *n.* the rear of a ship or boat. ⟨probably < ON *stjórn* steering⟩

ster•na ['stɜrnə] *n.* a pl. of STERNUM.

ster•nal ['stɜrnəl] *adj.* of or having to do with the breastbone or sternum. ⟨< NL *sternalis*⟩

stern chase *Nautical.* a chase in which the pursuing ship follows in the wake of the other.

stern chaser a gun in the stern of a ship for protection against an enemy ship following in its wake.

stern•most ['stɜrn,moust] *adj. Nautical.* **1** nearest the stern. **2** farthest in the rear.

stern•post ['stɜrn,poust] *n. Nautical.* the principal piece of timber or iron in the stern of a ship. Its lower end is fastened to the keel, and it usually supports the rudder.

stern sheets *Nautical.* the space at the stern of an open boat.

ster•num ['stɜrnəm] *n., pl.* **-na** [-nə] or **-nums.** *Anatomy. Zoology.* breastbone. ⟨< NL < Gk. *sternon* chest⟩

ster•nu•ta•tion [,stɜrnjə'teiʃən] *n.* the act of sneezing. ⟨< L *sternutatio, -onis* < *sternutare* sneeze, frequentative of *sternuere* sneeze⟩

ster•nu•ta•tive [stər'njutətɪv] *or* [stər'nutətɪv] *adj.* causing sneezing. Also, **sternutatory** [-,tɔri].

ster•nu•ta•tor ['stɜrnjə,teitər] *n.* any substance, especially a gas, that incapacitates its victims by causing severe respiratory irritation.

stern•ward ['stɜrnwərd] *adv. or adj.* toward the stern; astern.

stern•wards ['stɜrnwərdz] *adv.* sternward.

stern•way ['stɜrn,wei] *n. Nautical.* the backward movement of a ship.

stern–wheel•er ['stɜrn ,wilər] *n.* a steamboat driven or appearing to be driven by a paddle wheel at the stern or rear.

ster•oid ['stɛrɔɪd] *or* ['stirɔɪd] *n. Biochemistry.* any of a large group of organic compounds, including the sterols, the bile acids, and the sex hormones, distributed widely in living plant and animal cells. ⟨< *ster(ol)* + *-oid*⟩

ster•ol ['stɛrɒl] *or* ['stirɒl] *n. Biochemistry.* any of various complex organic alcohols distributed widely in living plant and animal cells. ⟨contraction of *cholesterol*⟩

ster•to•rous ['stɜrtərəs] *adj.* making a heavy snoring sound: *stertorous breathing.* ⟨< NL *stertor* snoring < L *stertere* snore⟩ **—'ster•to•rous•ness,** *n.* **—'ster•to•rous•ly,** *adv.*

stet [stɛt] *n., v.* **stet•ted, stet•ting.** —*n.* 'let it stand', a direction on printer's proof, a manuscript, etc. to retain cancelled matter (usually accompanied by a row of dots under or beside the matter).
—*v.* mark for retention. ⟨< L *stet* let it stand⟩

steth•o•scope ['stɛθə,skoup] *n. Medicine.* an instrument used by doctors for listening to sounds in the lungs, heart, etc. ⟨< Gk. *stēthos* chest + E *-scope*⟩ **—ste'thos•co•py** [stɛ'θɒskəpi], *n.*

steth•o•scop•ic [ˌstɛθəˈskɒpɪk] *adj.* **1** having to do with the stethoscope or its use. **2** made or obtained by the stethoscope. **—ˌsteth•oˈscop•i•cal•ly,** *adv.*

ste•ve•dore [ˈstivəˌdɔr] *n., v.* **-dored, -dor•ing.** *—n.* a person who loads and unloads ships.
—v. load or unload (a vessel or cargo). ⟨< Sp. *estivador,* ult. < L *stipare* pack down. See STEEVE.⟩

stew [stju] *or* [stu] *v., n. —v.* **1** cook by slow boiling or simmering. **2** *Informal.* worry; fret. **3** be overcome by heat, overcrowding, humidity, etc.; swelter.
stew in (one's) **own juice,** suffer the consequence of one's actions.
—n. **1** a dish, usually consisting of meat, vegetables, etc., cooked by slow boiling or simmering: *beef stew.* **2** any food cooked in this way. **3** *Informal.* a state of worry; fret. ⟨ME < OF *estuver* < VL *extufare* < L *ex-* out + Gk. *typhos* vapour⟩

stew•ard [ˈstjuərd] *or* [ˈstuərd] *n.* **1** a person who looks after the needs of persons in a club or on a ship, train, aircraft, etc., especially one in charge of food and table service. **2** a person who manages another's property: *She is the steward of that great estate.* **3** a person responsible for the careful management of any kind of resources or property. **4** a person appointed to manage a dinner, ball, show, etc. **5** SHOP STEWARD. ⟨OE *stigweard* < *stig* hall + *weard* keeper, ward⟩

stew•ard•ship [ˈstjuərdˌʃɪp] *or* [ˈstuərdˌʃɪp] *n.* **1** the position, duties, and responsibilities of a steward. **2** management for others, using the skills and abilities of a steward.

stewed [stjud] *or* [stud] *adj., v. —adj.* **1** prepared for eating by stewing. **2** *Slang.* intoxicated; inebriated; drunk.
—v. pt. and pp. of STEW.

stew•pan [ˈstjuˌpæn] *or* [ˈstuˌpæn] *n.* a pan for stewing.

stg sterling.

stge storage.

St. George's cross [ˈdʒɔrdʒəz] a red, upright cross on a white background, one of the three crosses that make up the Union Flag of Great Britain and Northern Ireland (Union Jack).

sthen•ic [ˈsθɛnɪk] *adj.* **1** having to do with vigour or nervous energy. **2** *Medicine.* accompanied by an unhealthy increase in vital processes, such as circulation and respiration. ⟨< NL *sthenicus* < Gk. *sthenos* strength⟩

stib•i•um [ˈstɪbiəm] *n.* antimony. ⟨< L < Gk. *stibi* < Egyptian⟩

stich [stɪk] *n.* a line of poetry; verse: *a Biblical stich.* ⟨< Gk. *stichos* line < *steichein* march in a line⟩
☛ *Hom.* STICK.

stich•ic [ˈstɪkɪk] *adj.* **1** of, having to do with, or based on a single line or lines of verse as opposed to a stanza or stanzas. **2** designating verse composed in lines that are metrically the same.

stick¹ [stɪk] *n., v.* **sticked, stick•ing.** *—n.* **1** a long, thin piece of wood, especially a small branch or twig: *The lawn was littered with sticks and leaves blown down during the storm.* **2** such a piece of wood shaped for a special use: *a walking stick, a hockey stick.* **3** something like a stick in shape; a long, slender piece of anything: *a stick of candy, a stick of celery, a licorice stick.* **4** *Informal.* a stiff, awkward, or stupid person. **5** a lever used to work certain main controls of an airplane; the stickshift of a motor vehicle. **6** *Nautical.* a mast or yard. **7** *Informal.* a portion of alcoholic liquor added to a drink. **8** *Printing.* **a** a small metal tray in which type is set by hand. **b** the amount of type so set. **9 the sticks,** *pl. Informal.* any place distant from urban areas; back country.
on the stick, alert and efficient.
shake a stick at, *Informal.* notice (*used with negatives*): *There was not enough snow to shake a stick at.*
—v. furnish with a stick or sticks to support or prop. ⟨OE *sticca*⟩
☛ *Hom.* STICH.

stick² [stɪk] *v.* **stuck, stick•ing;** *n. —v.* **1** pierce with a pointed instrument; thrust (a point) into; stab. **2** kill by stabbing or piercing. **3** fasten by thrusting the point or end into or through something: *He stuck a flower in his buttonhole.* **4** *Informal.* put in a place or position: *Stick it in the drawer.* **5** thrust or be thrust; extend (from, out, through, up, etc.): *Don't stick your head out of the car window. His arms stuck out of his coat sleeves.* **6** fasten; attach by means of some adhesive: *Stick a stamp on the letter.* **7** become fixed or fastened: *These labels won't stick to my canning jars.* **8** set pointed things into the surface of: *to stick a ham with cloves.* **9** ornament with things attached by an adhesive of some sort: *Her school locker was stuck all over with photos of her favourite rock stars.* **10** keep close: *The boy stuck to his mother's heels.* **11** come to or be at a standstill: *Our car stuck in the mud.* **12** bring to a stop: *Our work was stuck by the breakdown of the machinery.* **13** *Informal.* make sticky with something: *Oh, Mom, he's got the knife handle all stuck up with jam!* **14** keep on; hold fast: *to stick to a task, to stick to one's friends when they are in trouble.* **15** *Informal.* puzzle. **16** be puzzled; hesitate; have scruples. **17** *Slang.* **a** impose upon; cheat. **b** leave (a person) with, especially something to pay. **18** *Informal.* stand or put up with; tolerate: *I won't stick her insults much longer.* **19** become embedded, entangled, jammed, seized up, etc.: *The steering has stuck.*
stick around, *Informal.* stay or wait nearby.
stick at, hesitate or stop for: *She sticks at nothing to get her own way.*
stick by or **to,** remain resolutely faithful or attached to; refuse to desert: *He sticks by his friends when they are in trouble.*
stick in (one's) **craw** or **throat,** be very hard for one to do or take.
stick it out, *Informal.* put up with unpleasant conditions, circumstances, etc.; endure: *Try to stick it out for a few more days.*
stick it to (someone), *Slang.* make (someone) suffer.
stick out like a sore thumb, be conspicuous.
stick (something) **out,** *Informal.* put up with until the end.
stick together, keep or cling together; stay united; support each other or one another.
stick to (one's) **ribs,** of food, be satisfying or filling.
stick up, *Slang.* hold up; rob.
stick up for, *Informal.* support; defend.
—n. **1** a thrust. **2** a sticky condition. **3** a standstill; stop. ⟨OE *stician*⟩
☛ *Syn. v.* **6, 7, 10. Stick,** ADHERE = cling or become firmly or closely attached to another or each other. **Stick,** the common and general word, particularly suggests being fastened together or to another person or thing by or as if by something gummy: *Flies stick to flypaper.* **Adhere,** a more formal word sometimes used as a dignified substitute for **stick,** means cling fast or remain firmly attached to someone or something, by itself or of its own accord: *Adhesive tape does not adhere well to her skin.*
☛ *Hom.* STICH.

stick•boy [ˈstɪkˌbɔɪ] *n. Cdn.* **1** *Hockey.* the person who looks after the hockey sticks used by a team. **2** *Football.* one of two people responsible for moving the measuring sticks in a game.

stick country *Cdn. B.C. and Northwest.* the wooded country of the interior. ⟨< Chinook Jargon *stik* wood, tree; forest⟩

Stick country *Cdn. B.C. and Northwest.* the wooded country of the STICK INDIANS.

stick•er [ˈstɪkər] *n.* **1** a person who or thing that sticks. **2** a gummed or self-adhesive label or small decorative picture for sticking to something. **3** a burr; thorn. **4** *Informal.* a puzzle.

stick figure **1** a simple figure of a person or animal drawn with straight lines except for a circle representing the head. **2** an inadequately developed character in a novel, play, etc.

stick•han•dle [ˈstɪkˌhændəl] *v.* **-dled, -dling.** *Cdn.* **1** *Hockey.* manoeuvre (the puck) by deft handling of the stick, especially to avoid opposing checkers. **2** manoeuvre skilfully, especially in difficult circumstances: *to stickhandle a proposal through various government committees.* **—ˈstickˌhan•dler,** *n.* **—ˈstickˌhan•dling,** *n.*

sticking point **1** the place where a thing stops and holds. **2** any factor that prevents the solution of a problem: *When the contract was being reviewed, the sticking point was shorter hours.*

Stick Indian *Cdn. B.C. and Northwest.* a First Nations person from the bush country of the interior, originally so-called by the natives of the Pacific Coast. ⟨Chinook Jargon *stik* wood, bush, forest, thus forest dwellers as opposed to people of the coast⟩

stick insect any of a family (Phasmidae) of chiefly tropical, plant-eating insects having a very long, twiglike body and long, thin legs. Most stick insects are wingless.

stick–in–the–mud [ˈstɪk ɪn ðə ˌmʌd] *n. Informal.* **1** a person who prefers the old to the new; a conservative; a fogey. **2** a person who lacks initiative or resourcefulness.

stick•le [ˈstɪkəl] *v.* **-led, -ling. 1** make objections about trifles; insist stubbornly. **2** feel difficulties about trifles; have objections; scruple. ⟨probably ult. < OE *stihtan* arrange⟩

stick•le•back [ˈstɪkəlˌbæk] *n., pl.* **-back** or **-backs.** any of a family (Gasterosteidae) of small, scaleless fishes found in fresh and salt waters in northern regions, having a row of sharp spines on the back. The male builds an elaborate nest for the eggs. ⟨ME *styklylbak* < OE *sticel* prick, sting + *bæc* back⟩

stick•ler [ˈstɪklər] *n.* **1** a person who contends stubbornly or insists on trifles (*used with* **for**): *She is a stickler for accuracy.*

2 something that puzzles. ⟨Obs. *stickle* be an umpire < ME *stightlen* control, frequentative of *stight(i)an* set in order⟩

stick•man ['stɪk,mæn] *n., pl.* **-men.** *Slang.* **1** a croupier at a casino or gambling house. **2** *Sports.* a person who handles a stick or bat.

stick•pin ['stɪk,pɪn] *n.* a straight pin worn for ornament or to hold a necktie in place.

stick•shift ['stɪk,ʃɪft] *n.* **1** a gearshift lever that sticks upward from the floor of a motor vehicle. **2** manual transmission.

stick–up ['stɪk ,ʌp] *n. Slang.* a holdup; robbery.

stick•work ['stɪk,wɜrk] *n.* skilful use of a stick, especially in hockey.

stick•y ['stɪki] *adj.* **stick•i•er, stick•i•est. 1** that sticks: *sticky goo.* **2** that makes things stick; covered with adhesive matter: *sticky flypaper.* **3** *Informal.* unpleasantly humid: *sticky weather.* **4** *Informal.* puzzling; difficult: *a sticky problem.* **5** *Slang.* unpleasant; extremely disagreeable: *a sticky situation.*
sticky end, a painful death.
sticky fingers, *Informal.* a tendency to steal.
sticky wicket, a *Cricket.* a WICKET (def. 5b) made damp by rain, causing the ball to bounce awkwardly. **b** *Informal.* an awkward, difficult, or dangerous situation. **—'stick•i•ly,** *adv.* **—'stick•i•ness,** *n.*

sties [staɪz] *n.* pl. of STY.

stiff [stɪf] *adj., n., v.* —*adj.* **1** not easily bent: *a stiff collar.* **2** hard to move: *stiff hinges.* **3** not able to move easily: *She was stiff and sore after running in the marathon.* **4** drawn tight; tense: *a stiff cord.* **5** not fluid; firm: *stiff jelly.* **6** dense; compact: *stiff soil.* **7** not easy or natural in manner; formal: *a stiff style of writing. He gave a stiff bow.* **8** lacking grace of line, form, or arrangement: *stiff geometrical designs.* **9** resolute; steadfast; unyielding: *a stiff resistance.* **10** strong and steady in motion: *a stiff breeze.* **11** difficult to deal with; hard: *a stiff examination.* **12** harsh or severe: *a stiff penalty.* **13** strong: *a stiff drink.* **14** *Informal.* more than seems suitable: *a stiff price.* **15** of words, forcefully delivered: *a stiff lecture.*
—*n. Slang.* **1** a dead body; corpse. **2** a drunken person. **3** a man; fellow: *He hired a couple of stiffs to do the job for him.* **4** a tramp or hobo. **5** a very formal, priggish, or dull person. **6** a stingy person, especially one who does not tip enough or at all.
—*v.* cheat; rob, especially by not paying or tipping as due: *He stiffed me.* ⟨OE *stīf*⟩ **—'stiff•ly,** *adv.* **—'stiff•ness,** *n.*
☛ *Syn. adj.* **1. Stiff,** RIGID = not easily bent or capable of being bent or turned without breaking. **Stiff,** the general word, describes anything so firm or solid that it does not bend easily or cannot be bent without injury: *Library books need stiff covers.* **Rigid** describes something so stiff and hard that it will not bend at all and cannot be bent without breaking: *The bodies of animals become rigid after death.*

stiff•en ['stɪfən] *v.* **1** make stiff: *You can stiffen that collar with starch.* **2** become stiff: *The jelly will stiffen as it cools. Pat stiffened with anger.* **—'stiff•en•er,** *n.*

stiff•en•ing ['stɪfənɪŋ] *n., v.* —*n.* **1** a making or becoming stiff. **2** something used to stiffen.
—*v.* ppr. of STIFFEN.

stiff–necked ['stɪf ,nɛkt] *adj.* **1** having a stiff neck. **2** stubborn; obstinate.

sti•fle¹ ['stəifəl] *v.* **-fled, -fling. 1** stop the breath of; smother: *The smoke stifled the firemen.* **2** be unable to breathe freely: *I am stifling in this close room.* **3** keep back; suppress; stop: *to stifle a cry, to stifle a yawn, to stifle business activity, to stifle a rebellion.* **4** hamper or constrain by overprotection, possessiveness, overinvolvement, etc. **5** be stifled. ⟨ME *stuffle(n), stiffle(n)* < *stuffe(n)* stuff, stifle; influenced by ON *stífla* dam up⟩

sti•fle² ['stəifəl] *n.* the joint above the hock in a horse or dog, corresponding to the knee in a human.

sti•fling ['stəiflɪŋ] *adj., v.* —*adj.* closely oppressive; suffocatingly stuffy.
—*v.* ppr. of STIFLE.

stig•ma ['stɪgmə] *n., pl.* **stig•mas** or **stig•ma•ta** ['stɪgmətə], [stɪg'mætə], *or* [stɪg'mɑtə]. **1** a mark of disgrace; a stain or reproach on one's reputation. **2** a distinguishing mark or sign. **3** a small spot or mark; a spot in the skin that bleeds or turns red. **4** a small mark, scar, etc., on the skin of an animal or the surface of a plant, as an eyespot on a butterfly's wing. **5** *Pathology.* a visible mark symptomatic of a disease. **6** *Botany.* the part of the pistil of a plant that receives the pollen. See FLOWER for picture. **7** **stigmata,** *pl.* marks or wounds like the five wounds on the crucified body of Christ, said to appear supernaturally on the bodies of certain devout persons. **8** *Archaic.* a special mark burned on a slave or criminal. ⟨< L < Gk., scar, brand < *stizein* prick, tattoo⟩

stig•ma•ta ['stɪgmətə], [stɪg'mætə], *or* [stɪg'mɑtə] *n.* a pl. of STIGMA.

stig•mat•ic [stɪg'mætɪk] *adj., n.* —*adj.* of or having to do with a stigma; like that of a stigma; marked by a stigma.
—*n.* a person bearing marks suggesting the wounds of Christ. Also, **stigmatist.**

stig•ma•tism ['stɪgmə,tɪzəm] *n.* **1** the absence of astigmatism. **2** a condition in which the person has the stigmata of Christ.

stig•ma•tize ['stɪgmə,taɪz] *v.* **-tized, -tiz•ing. 1** set some mark of disgrace upon; reproach. **2** brand. **3** produce stigmas on. **—,stig•ma•ti'za•tion,** *n.* **—'stig•ma,tiz•er,** *n.*

stil•bene ['stɪl,bin] *n. Chemistry.* a colourless crystalline hydrocarbon used in making dyes. *Formula*: $C_{14}H_{12}$

stil•bes•trol [stɪl'bɛstrɒl] *n. Pharmacy.* a synthetic estrogen derived from stilbene; diethylstilbestrol. *Formula*: $C_{18}H_{20}O_2$

stile¹ [staɪl] *n.* **1** a step or steps for getting over a fence or wall. **2** a turnstile. ⟨OE *stigel*; related to *stīgan* climb⟩
☛ *Hom.* STYLE.

stile² [staɪl] *n.* a vertical piece in a door, panelled wall, etc. ⟨prob. < Du. *stijl* pillar, doorpost⟩
☛ *Hom.* STYLE.

sti•let•to [stɪ'lɛtou] *n., pl.* **-tos** or **-toes. 1** a dagger with a narrow blade tapering to a sharp point. **2** a small, sharp-pointed instrument for making eyelet holes in embroidery. **3** STILETTO HEEL. ⟨< Ital. *stiletto,* ult. < L *stilus* pointed instrument⟩

stiletto heel SPIKE HEEL.

still¹ [stɪl] *adj., v., n., adv.* —*adj.* **1** remaining in the same position or at rest; motionless; stationary: *stand, sit, or lie still.* **2** quiet; tranquil; undisturbed: *The lake is still now.* **3** soft; low; subdued: *a still, small voice.* **4** not bubbling: *still wine.* **5** silent; soundless. **6** *Photography.* **a** of a photograph, consisting of a single frame. **b** of a camera, photography, etc., producing or having to do with still photographs.
—*v.* **1** make calm or quiet: *to still a crying child.* **2** become calm or quiet. **3** relieve or allay: *to still someone's fears.*
—*n.* **1** *Poetic.* silence: *the still of the night.* **2** *Photography.* a photograph taken with a still camera. **3** an individual picture, or frame, from a film, especially one made into a poster for promotion.
—*adv.* **1** at or up to some time in the present, past, or future: *She came yesterday and she is still here. The matter is still unsettled. It will still be here.* **2** even; yet: *still more, still worse.* **3** nevertheless: *Proof was given, but they still doubted. He is dull; still, he tries hard.* **4** without moving; quietly. **5** *Archaic or poetic.* steadily; constantly; always. ⟨OE *stille*⟩
☛ *Syn. adj.* **1, 2, 5.** See note at QUIET.

still² [stɪl] *n.* **1** an apparatus for distilling liquids, especially alcoholic liquors. **2** a place where alcoholic liquors are distilled; distillery. ⟨short form of *distil*⟩

still•birth ['stɪl,bɜrθ] *n.* **1** the birth of a dead fetus. **2** a fetus, weighing at least 500 g, born dead.

still•born ['stɪl,bɔrn] *adj.* **1** dead when born. **2** **a** destined never to be realized: *stillborn hopes.* **b** that fails right from the beginning: *a stillborn book or play.*

still hunt a quiet or secret pursuit; an instance of STILL HUNTING.

still–hunt ['stɪl ,hʌnt] *v. Cdn.* engage in STILL HUNTING.

still hunting tracking down and creeping up on game through deep, soft snow or in an otherwise noiseless manner. **—still hunter.**

still life *pl.* **still lifes. 1** inanimate objects, such as fruit, flowers, furniture, pottery, etc., shown in a picture. **2** a picture showing such things.

still–life ['stɪl 'ləif] *adj.* of or having to do with still life: *a still-life painting.*

still•ness ['stɪlnɪs] *n.* **1** quiet; silence. **2** the absence of motion; calm.

stil•ly *adj.* ['stɪli]; *adv.* ['stɪlli] *adj.* **-li•er, -li•est;** *adv.* —*adj. Poetic.* quiet; still; calm: *the stilly night.*
—*adv.* calmly; quietly.

stilt [stɪlt] *n.* **1** one of a pair of poles to stand on and hold while walking, each with a support for the foot at some distance above the ground. **2** a long post or pole used to support a house, shed, etc. above the water. **3** any of various shore birds of warm regions belonging to the same family (Recurvirostridae) as avocets, such as the **black-necked stilt,** having a long, straight bill and very long, thin legs. ⟨ME *stilte*⟩ **—'stilt,like,** *adj.*

stilt•ed ['stıltıd] *adj.* **1** stiffly dignified or formal: *stilted conversation.* **2** awkward; not flowing well. **3** raised above the ordinary level. **—'stilt•ed•ly,** *adv.* **—'stilt•ed•ness,** *n.*

Stil•ton cheese ['stıltən] a rich, white cheese veined with mould when well ripened. ⟨< *Stilton,* a village in Huntingdonshire, England, where it was first made⟩

stim•u•lant ['stımjələnt] *n., adj. —n.* **1** a food, drug, medicine, etc. that temporarily increases the activity of some part of the body. Tea and coffee are stimulants and alcohol is popularly supposed to be. **2** something that spurs one on or stirs one up; a motive, influence, etc. that rouses one to action: *Hope is a stimulant.*
—adj. stimulating. ⟨< L *stimulans, -antis,* ppr. of *stimulare.* See STIMULATE.⟩

stim•u•late ['stımjə,leit] *v.* **-lat•ed, -lat•ing. 1** spur on; stir up; rouse to action: *Praise stimulated her to work hard.* **2** *Physiology. Medicine.* increase temporarily the functional activity of (a nerve, organ, or other part of the body). **3** excite with alcoholic liquor; intoxicate. **4** act as a stimulant or a stimulus. ⟨< L *stimulare* < *stimulus* goad⟩ **—'stim•u,la•tor** or **'stim•u,lat•er,** *n.* **—,stim•u'la•tion,** *n.*

stim•u•la•tive ['stımjələtıv] *or* ['stımjə,leitıv] *adj., n. —adj.* tending to stimulate; stimulating.
—n. something that stimulates; a stimulus.

stim•u•lus ['stımjələs] *n., pl.* **-li** [-,laı] *or* [-,li]. **1** something that stirs to action or effort: *Ambition is a great stimulus.* **2** *Physiology. Psychology.* something that excites some part of the body to activity. ⟨< L *stimulus,* originally, goad⟩

sting [stıŋ] *v.* **stung, sting•ing;** *n. —v.* **1** prick with a sharp-pointed organ: *Bees, wasps, and hornets sting.* **2** feel or cause to feel sharp emotional pain: *She was stung by the mockings of the other children. He was still stinging from her insult.* **3** cause a feeling like that of a sting: *Mustard stings.* **4** of certain plants, etc., produce irritation, rash, or inflammation in (a person's skin) by contact. **5** affect with a tingling pain, burning sensation, sharp hurt, etc.: *stung by a spark.* **6** drive or stir up as if by a sting: *Their ridicule stung her into making a sharp reply.* **7** *Slang.* impose upon; charge too much.
—n. **1** the wound caused by stinging: *Put ointment on the sting to take away the pain.* **2** stinger. **3** a sharp pain: *The ball team felt the sting of defeat.* **4** something that causes sharp pain. **5** something that drives or urges sharply. **6** a stinging quality; capacity to sting or hurt. **7** *Slang.* a means of catching swindlers, confidence tricksters, etc., as used by law officers and other authorities, where the authorities masquerade as buyers or sellers. ⟨OE *stingan*⟩ **—'sting•ing•ly,** *adv.* **—'sting•less,** *adj.*

sting•a•ree ['stıŋə,ri] *or* [,stıŋə'ri] *n.* stingray. ⟨alteration of *stingray*⟩

sting•er ['stıŋər] *n.* **1** the sharp part of an insect or animal that pricks or wounds and often poisons. **2** anything that stings. **3** *Informal.* a stinging blow, remark, etc.

sting•ray ['stıŋ,rei] *n.* any of a family (Dasyatidae) of rays having winglike fins that give them a round or diamond-shaped outline and having a long, thin, whiplike tail with one or more poisonous spines near the base of the tail that can inflict a very painful wound which is sometimes fatal to human beings. Stingrays bear live young.

stin•gy ['stındʒi] *adj.* **-gi•er, -gi•est. 1** mean about spending, lending, or giving; not generous: *He tried to save money without being stingy.* **2** scanty; meagre. ⟨Related to STING⟩ **—'stin•gi•ly,** *adv.* **—'stin•gi•ness,** *n.*

stink [stıŋk] *n., v.* **stank** or **stunk, stunk, stink•ing.**
—n. **1** a bad smell. **2** *Slang.* a great deal of complaint or criticism: *There was a stink about the new dates for exams. She's sure to raise a stink about the shoddiness of the work.*
—v. **1** have a bad smell. **2** cause to have a very bad smell (*usually used with* **up**): *That fish is stinking up the whole house.* **3 a** have a very bad reputation; be in great disfavour. **b** savour offensively (*of*): *His remark stinks of treason.* **4** *Informal.* be of poor quality or unattractive in some way: *Her novel stank. That idea stinks.*
stink out, drive out with stinking smoke or fumes. ⟨OE *stincan* to smell⟩ **—'stin•ky,** *adj.*

stink•bug ['stıŋk,bʌg] *n.* any of various plant-eating, heteropterous bugs having a disagreeable odour, especially any of the family Pentatomidae.

stink•er ['stıŋkər] *n.* **1** a person or thing that has an offensive smell. **2** *Slang.* a low, mean, contemptible person. **3** *Slang.* something unpleasant or contemptible.

stink•ing ['stıŋkıŋ] *adj., adv., v. —adj.* **1** foul-smelling. **2** extremely disagreeable or objectionable.
—adv. excessively; objectionably: *stinking rich.*
—v. ppr. of STINK. **—'stink•ing•ly,** *adv.*

stin•ko ['stıŋkou] *adj. Slang.* drunk.

stink•weed ['stıŋk,wid] *n.* **1** a Eurasian annual herb (*Thlaspi arvense*) of the mustard family that has become naturalized as a common weed in North America, having white flowers and irregularly toothed leaves that give off a disagreeable odour when crushed. **2** any of various other plants having a disagreeable odour.

stint [stınt] *v., n. —v.* **1** keep on short allowance; be saving or careful in using or spending; limit: *The parents stinted themselves of food to give it to their children.* **2** be saving; get along on very little. **3** *Archaic.* stop.
—n. **1** limit; limitation: *That generous woman gives without stint.* **2** an amount or share set aside. **3 a** a task assigned: *Washing the breakfast dishes was his daily stint.* **b** a period spent in some activity: *She refreshed herself with a short stint of piano-playing before returning to her chores.* **4** *Archaic.* a stop. ⟨OE *styntan* blunt⟩ **—'stint•er,** *n.* **—'stint•ing•ly,** *adv.*

stipe [stəip] *n.* **1** *Botany.* a stalk; stem: *the stipe of a mushroom, the stipe of a fern.* **2** *Zoology.* a stalk or stalklike part. ⟨< F < L *stipes* trunk⟩

sti•pel ['stəipəl] *n. Botany.* a secondary stipule situated at the base of a leaflet of a compound leaf. ⟨< NL *stipella,* dim. of L *stipula.* See STIPULE.⟩ **—'sti'pel•late** [stəi'pɛlıt] *or* [stəi'pɛleit], *adj.*

sti•pend ['stəipɛnd] *n.* **1** in some professions, fixed or regular pay; salary: *A magistrate receives a stipend.* **2** a regular allowance paid under the terms of a scholarship. ⟨< L *stipendium* < *stips* wages, originally, coin + *pendere* weigh out⟩

sti•pen•di•ar•y [stəi'pɛndi,ɛri] *adj., n., pl.* **-ar•ies.** *—adj.* **1** receiving a stipend. **2** paid for by a stipend. **3** of or having to do with a stipend. **4** performing services for regular pay.
—n. a person who receives a stipend; a salaried member of the clergy, judiciary, etc.

stip•ple ['stıpəl] *v.* **-pled, -pling;** *n. —v.* **1** paint, draw, or engrave in dots. **2** produce a stippled effect on.
—n. **1** the method of painting, drawing, or engraving by stippling. **2** the effect produced by this method. **3** stippled work. ⟨< Du. *stippelen*⟩ **—'stip•pler,** *n.*

stip•u•lar ['stıpjələr] *adj. Botany.* **1** of or having to do with stipules. **2** stipulelike; having stipules.

stip•u•late[1] ['stıpjə,leit] *v.* **-lat•ed, -lat•ing.** specify; state definitely; demand as a condition of agreement: *She stipulated that she should receive a month's vacation every year if she took the job.* ⟨< L *stipulari* stipulate⟩ **—'stip•u,la•tor,** *n.* **—,stip•u'la•tion,** *n.*

stip•u•late[2] ['stıpjəlıt] *or* ['stıpjə,leit] *adj. Botany.* having stipules. ⟨< *stipule*⟩

stip•ule ['stıpjul] *n. Botany.* one of a pair of little leaflike parts at the base of a leaf stem. See STEM[1] for picture. ⟨< L *stipula* stem; related to *stipes* trunk. Doublet of STUBBLE.⟩

stir[1] [stɜr] *v.* **stirred, stir•ring;** *n. —v.* **1** move or cause to move about: *No one was stirring in the house. The wind stirred the leaves.* **2** mix by moving around with a spoon, fork, stick, etc.: *to stir sugar into one's coffee, to stir batter.* **3** be mixed with a spoon, etc.: *This dough stirs hard.* **4** set going; affect strongly; excite: *Luc was stirred by the premier's impassioned plea for unity.* **5** become active, much affected, or excited: *The countryside was stirring with new life.*
stir oneself, move briskly; bestir oneself.
stir up, a rouse to action, activity, or emotion; excite; stimulate. **b** instigate; provoke; induce: *to stir up a mutiny.*
—n. **1** a movement. **2** a state of motion, activity, briskness, bustle, excitement, etc. **3** a public disturbance, tumult, or revolt. **4** the act of stirring. **5** a jog; poke. ⟨OE *styrian*⟩ **—'stir•rer,** *n.*

☛ *Syn. n.* **2. Stir,** BUSTLE[1], ADO = excitement or excited activity. **Stir** particularly suggests a disturbance, especially where there has been quiet, or a great deal of excitement: *There was a stir in the courtroom.* **Bustle** suggests noisy, excited, energetic activity: *All the week before the class picnic, studying gave way to the bustle of preparations.* **Ado** suggests much needless or pointless busyness and fuss, especially over something not worth it: *They made much ado about a comfortable bed for the kitten.*

stir[2] [stɜr] *n. Slang.* prison. ⟨origin uncertain⟩

stir–cra•zy ['stɜr ,kreizi] *adj. Slang.* mentally disturbed on account of long imprisonment or confinement, or from subjection to endless, restricted routines.

stir–fry ['stɜr ,fraı] *v.* **-fried, -fry•ing;** *n. —v.* cook (small pieces

of meat, vegetables, etc.) by frying briefly in a wok with oil, while stirring constantly.
n. a dish made in this way.

stirps [stɜrps] *n., pl.* **stir•pes** ['stɜrpiz]. **1** stock; family. **2** *Law.* the person from whom a family is descended. ⟨< L *stirps,* originally, stem⟩

stir•ring ['stɜrɪŋ] *adj., v.* —*adj.* **1** moving; active; lively: *stirring times.* **2** rousing; moving; exciting: *a stirring speech.*
—*v.* ppr. of STIR[1]. —**'stir•ring•ly,** *adv.*

stir•rup ['stɜrəp] *or* ['stirəp] *n.* **1** one of a pair of foot supports that hang from a saddle. See SADDLE for picture. **2** a piece resembling a stirrup used as a support or clamp. **3** STIRRUP BONE. ⟨OE *stigrāp* < *stige* climbing + *rāp* rope⟩

stirrup bone the stapes of the ear. See EAR[1] for picture.

stirrup cup **1** a cup of wine or other liquor offered to a rider mounted for departure. **2** any farewell drink.

stirrup leather or **strap** the strap that connects a stirrup to the saddle.

stirrup pump a hand-operated pump with a stirrup-shaped foot rest, used for extinguishing small fires.

stitch [stɪtʃ] *n., v.* —*n.* **1** in sewing, embroidering, etc., a movement of a threaded needle through the cloth and back out again. **2** *Surgery.* a similar movement through skin, etc. **3** in knitting, crocheting, etc., a single turn or twist of yarn around a knitting needle or crochet hook. **4** the loop of thread, etc. made by a stitch: *The doctor will take the stitches out of the wound tomorrow.* **5** a particular method of making stitches: *a buttonhole stitch.* **6** a small piece of cloth or clothing. **7** *Informal.* the smallest bit: *The lazy boy wouldn't do a stitch of work.* **8** a sudden, sharp pain: *a stitch in the side.*
in stitches, laughing uncontrollably: *Her anecdotes had us in stitches.*
—*v.* **1 a** make stitches in; fasten with stiches. **b** decorate with stitches. **2** sew. ⟨OE *stice* puncture⟩ —**'stitch•er,** *n.*

stitch•e•ry ['stɪtʃəri] *n.,pl.* **-ries. 1** the art or pastime of doing ornamental needlework, such as embroidery, crewelwork, or needlepoint. **2** a piece of ornamental needlework.

stitch•ing ['stɪtʃɪŋ] *n., v.* —*n.* **1** the act or work of one who stitches. **2** stitches collectively.
—*v.* ppr. of STITCH.

sti•ver ['staɪvər] *n.* **1** a former unit of money in the Netherlands, equal to 1/20 of a guilder. **2** a coin worth one stiver. **3** something having little value. ⟨< Du. *stuiver*⟩

St. James Street [dʒeimz] *Cdn.* **1** in Montréal, a street on which are located the city's principal banking firms. **2** the financial or moneyed interests of Montréal.

St.–John's–wort [ˌsənt 'dʒɒnz ˌwɜrt] *n.* any of numerous shrubs or perennial herbs (genus *Hypericum*) of temperate regions, including some that are cultivated as garden flowers. See also ROSE OF SHARON (def. 2).

sto•a ['stouə] *n., pl.* **sto•ae** [-i] *or* [-aɪ] or **sto•as. 1** *Greek architecture.* a portico, usually detached and of considerable length, used as a promenade or meeting place. **2 the Stoa,** the Porch, a public walk at Athens, where Zeno, the philosopher who founded Stoicism, taught. ⟨< Gk.⟩

stoat [stout] *n.* **1** ERMINE (def. 1). **2** any weasel having a black-tipped tail, especially in its brown summer coat. ⟨ME *stote;* origin uncertain⟩

sto•chast•ic [stə'kæstɪk] *adj.* **1** having to do with chance; governed by the laws of probability. **2** *Mathematics.* of a mathematical process, characterized by a sequence of random variables. **3** random. —**sto'chas•ti•cal•ly,** *adv.*

stock [stɒk] *n., v.* —*n.* **1** a supply or store of goods, materials, equipment, etc. regularly kept on hand for sale or for use as needed; inventory: *a large stock of information. The store has already received most of its spring stock. We keep a stock of canned foods at the cottage in case of emergency.* **2** (*adjl.*) kept regularly in stock and available: *stock sizes.* **3** cattle or other farm animals; livestock: *purebred Jersey stock.* **4** *Botany.* rhizome. **5** (*adjl.*) for livestock or for the raising of livestock: *a stock farm.* **6** (*adjl.*) in common use; commonplace or trite: *a stock response. The weather is a stock topic of conversation.* **7** *Finance.* **a** the capital of a company or corporation, divided into portions or shares of uniform amount which are represented by transferable certificates. The holder of one of these is considered a part owner, rather than a creditor, of the company. The profits of a company are divided among the owners of stock. **b** shares in the ownership of an incorporated business. The holder of stock in a company owns a part of that company in proportion to the amount of stock he or she holds. **c** (*adjl.*) of, having to do with, or dealing with stock or stocks: *a stock exchange, a stock broker.* **8** a group having a common origin; family or race: *She is of Spanish stock.* **9** *Linguistics.* a family of related languages. **10** an original ancestor of a family, tribe, or race, breed or plant variety. **11** a part used as a support or handle; a part or framework to which other parts are attached: *the wooden stock of a rifle, the stock of a whip.* **12 stocks,** *pl.* **a** a wooden frame having holes for the feet and, sometimes, for the hands and head, into which people were formerly locked in public as a punishment for minor offences. **b** a frame of timbers on which a ship rests during construction. **c** a frame which holds horses still for shoeing. **13** *Cards.* the draw pile. **14** raw material used to manufacture something: *All the cabinetmaker's wood was kiln-dried stock.* **15** a particular kind of paper: *The advertisement was printed on heavy stock.* **16** liquid in which meat or fish has been cooked, used as a base for soups, sauces, etc.: *chicken stock.* **17** a stiff band of cloth worn around the neck by men, especially in the 19th century: *A stock is still worn as part of a formal riding habit for both men and women.* **18** *Theatre.* **a** the repertoire of plays produced by a company at a single theatre. **b** a STOCK COMPANY, or such companies and their activities as a category or type of theatrical production (*used without an article*): *She is playing in summer stock.* **19** a STOCK CAR. **20** the trunk of a tree or the main stem of a plant. **21** a stump. **22** *Archaic.* a person or thing that is stupid or lifeless: *"You stocks and stones!"* **23** *Horticulture.* **a** a tree or plant that furnishes cuttings for grafting. **b** the stem into which a graft is inserted. **24** the crosspiece of an anchor. See ANCHOR for picture. **25** any of a genus (*Matthiola*) of plants of the mustard family having flowers that are usually fragrant.
in stock, available for sale or use; on hand.
on the stocks, being built, as a ship.
out of stock, sold out or used up; not immediately available for sale or use.
set stock by, value: *to set great stock by a remedy.*
take stock, a find out how much stock there is on hand. **b** make an assessment or examination: *We decided to stop and take stock of our situation before continuing with the scheme.*
take stock in, a *Informal.* take an interest in; consider important; trust: *I take no stock in his promise.* **b** take shares in (a company).
—*v.* **1** supply or furnish: *to stock a lake with fish, to stock a farm. Our camp is well stocked for the week.* **2** put stock out onto (shelves); fill or cover with merchandise: *The shelves are well stocked with canned goods.* **3** keep regularly for use or sale: *Our corner store stocks school supplies.* **4** fasten to or provide with a stock. **5** of a plant, send out shoots.
stock up, lay in a supply (*used with* **on**): *to stock up on firewood for the winter. We're getting low on breakfast cereal; better stock up.*
⟨OE *stocc*⟩
☛ *Hom.* STALK.

stock•ade [stɒ'keid] *n., v.* **-ad•ed, -ad•ing.** —*n.* **1** an enclosure for defence made of large, strong upright posts placed closely together in the ground: *A heavy stockade protected the trading post from attack.* **2** a fort, camp, etc. surrounded by a stockade. **3** a pen or other enclosed space made with upright posts, stakes, etc. **4** an enclosure for military prisoners.
—*v.* protect, fortify, or surround with a stockade. ⟨< F *estacade,* ult. < Provençal *estaca* stake < Gmc.⟩

stock•bro•ker ['stɒkˌbroukər] *n.* a person who buys and sells stocks and bonds for customers.

stock•bro•ker•age ['stɒkˌbroukərɪdʒ] *n.* the business of a stockbroker. Also, **stockbroking.**

stock car **1** a railway freight car for livestock. **2** an automobile of a standard make that has been altered in various ways for use in racing.

stock company **1** *Finance.* a company whose capital is divided into shares. **2** *Theatre.* a company employed more or less permanently under the same management, usually at one theatre, to perform many different plays.

stock dove a wild pigeon (*Columba oenas*) of Europe.

stocker ['stɒkər] *n.* **1** one who or that which stocks. **2** a young, motherless or stray calf; dogie.

stock exchange **1** a place where stocks and bonds are bought and sold. **2** an association of brokers and dealers in stocks and bonds.

stock•fish ['stɒkˌfɪʃ] *n., pl.* **-fish** or **-fish•es.** fish preserved by splitting and drying in the air without salt.

stock•hold•er ['stɒkˌhouldər] *n.* an owner of stocks or shares in a company.

Stock•holm syndrome ['stɒkˌhoum] *or* ['stɒkˌhoulm] a

situation in which hostages come to identify with their captors and become sympathetic to them. ⟨named after an incident in Stockholm, Sweden, in 1973, in which a robber held bank employees captive⟩

stock•i•net [ˌstɒkə'nɛt] *n.* an elastic, machine-knitted fabric used for making underwear, etc. Also, **stockinette.** ⟨earlier, *stocking-net*⟩

stock•ing ['stɒkɪŋ] *n.* **1** a close-fitting, knitted covering of nylon, cotton, wool, etc. for the foot and leg. **2** a sock, especially a man's sock. **3** something suggesting a stocking, especially a patch of different colour on the leg of an animal.
in (one's) **stocking feet,** wearing socks or stockings but no shoes: *Don't run around in your stocking feet; the floor's too dirty. He's 188 cm tall in his stocking feet.* ⟨< *stock* stocking, OE *stocc*⟩ **—'stock•ing•less,** *adj.* **—'stock•inged,** *adj.*

stocking cap TUQUE (def. 1).

stock in trade **1** the stock of a dealer or company; goods kept for sale. **2** tools or other materials needed to carry on a trade or business. **3** any resources, practices, etc. that are characteristic of a particular person, group, or business: *The featured speaker's stock in trade is a slightly rumpled look and a charming smile that audiences love.* Also, **stock-in-trade.**

stock•job•ber ['stɒkˌdʒɒbər] *n.* **1** a stockbroker, especially one who deals in questionable stocks. **2** a stockbroker who buys and sells securities for other brokers but not for the public.

stock–keep•er ['stɒk ˌkipər] a person in charge of a stock of materials or goods in a warehouse, etc. The stock-keeper keeps an inventory of goods on hand, received, or shipped.

stock•man ['stɒkmən] *n., pl.* **-men.** **1** a man who owns or manages livestock. **2** STOCK-KEEPER.

stock market **1** a place where stocks and bonds are bought and sold; stock exchange. **2** the buying and selling in such a place. **3** the prices of stocks and bonds across a country: *The stock market is falling.*

stock•pile ['stɒkˌpaɪl] *n., v.* **-piled, -pil•ing.** *—n.* a supply of raw materials, manufactured items, etc. built up and held in reserve in case of a shortage or emergency: *a stockpile of weapons, a stockpile of canned goods.*
—v. collect or bring together such a reserve supply: *to stockpile nuclear weapons.*

stock•pot ['stɒkˌpɒt] *n.* a pot in which soup stock is prepared: *They keep all leftover bones for the stockpot.*

stock raising the raising of livestock. **—stock raiser.**

stock•room ['stɒkˌrum] *or* ['stɒkˌrʊm] *n.* **1** a room where stock is kept. **2** a room in a hotel, etc. where sales representatives can show their samples.

stock–still ['stɒk 'stɪl] *adj.* motionless: *She stood stock-still and listened.*

stock•tak•ing ['stɒkˌteikɪŋ] *n.* **1** the act of checking the supply of goods on hand: *The store will be closed two days for stocktaking.* **2** any review of one's position, qualifications, potential, etc.

stock•y ['stɒki] *adj.* **stock•i•er, stock•i•est.** having a solid, sturdy, somewhat thick form or build: *a stocky child, a stocky stem.* **—'stock•i•ly,** *adv.* **—'stock•i•ness,** *n.*

stock•yard ['stɒkˌjɑrd] *n.* a place with pens and sheds for cattle, sheep, hogs, and horses. Livestock is kept in a stockyard before being slaughtered or sent to market.

stodg•y ['stɒdʒi] *adj.* **stodg•i•er, stodg•i•est.** **1** dull or uninteresting; tediously commonplace; drab; plain: *a stodgy style of writing.* **2** very old-fashioned; out-of-date: *He's very stodgy and set in his ways.* **3** of food, heavy and indigestible. **4** heavily built and slow-moving: *A stodgy figure came lumbering through the fog.* ⟨< *stodge* stuff; origin unknown⟩ **—'stodg•i•ly,** *adv.* **—'stodg•i•ness,** *n.*

sto•gie or **sto•gy** ['stougi] *n., pl.* **-gies.** a long, slender, cheap cigar. ⟨< *Conestoga,* a town in Pennsylvania⟩

Sto•ic ['stouɪk] *n., adj. —n.* **1** a member of a school of philosophy founded by Zeno (336?-264? B.C.), a Greek philosopher. This school taught that virtue is the highest good and that human beings should be free from passion and unmoved by life's happenings. **2 stoic,** a person who remains calm, represses feelings, and is indifferent to pleasure and pain. *—adj.* **1** having to do with the philosophy of the Stoics, or with its followers. **2 stoic,** stoical. ⟨< L *stoicus* < Gk. *stoikos,* literally, pertaining to a stoa⟩

sto•i•cal ['stouɪkəl] *adj.* like a stoic; self-controlled; indifferent to pleasure and pain. **—'sto•i•cal•ly,** *adv.*

stoi•chi•om•e•try [ˌstɔɪki'ɒmətri] *n.* the branch of chemistry dealing with the quantitative relationships, proportions, etc. of elements in combination. ⟨< Gk. *stoikheion* element + E *-metry*⟩ **—ˌstoi•chi•o'met•ric,** *adj.*

Sto•i•cism ['stouəˌsɪzəm] *n.* **1** the philosophy of the Stoics. **2 stoicism,** patient endurance; indifference to pleasure and pain.

stoke [stouk] *v.* **stoked, stok•ing.** **1** stir up and feed fuel to: *to stoke a fire in a fireplace, to stoke a furnace.* **2** tend (a boiler, furnace, etc.)
stoke up, a put fuel on (a fire) or in (a furnace). **b** *Informal.* give or feed in abundance, in order to renew energy, make able to act, etc.; fill *(with).* **c** *Informal.* eat heartily. ⟨< *stoker*⟩

stoke•hold ['stoukˌhould] *n.* **1** the place in a steamship where the furnaces, boilers, etc. are. **2** STOKEHOLE (def. 2).

stoke•hole ['stoukˌhoul] *n.* **1** the hole through which fuel is put into a furnace. **2** the space in front of a boiler or furnace of a ship from which the fires are tended. **3** STOKEHOLD (def. 1).

stok•er ['stoukər] *n.* **1** a person who tends the fires of a furnace or boiler, especially on a steamship. **2** a mechanical device for tending and feeding a furnace. ⟨< Du. *stoker* < *stoken* stoke⟩

STOL [stɒl], [stoul], *or* ['ɛsˌtɒl] an aircraft that can take off and land on a short runway. ⟨*s*hort *t*akeoff and *l*anding⟩

stole¹ [stoul] *v.* pt. of STEAL.

stole² [stoul] *n.* **1** a long, narrow strip of silk or other material worn around the neck by a minister or priest during certain religious functions. **2** a woman's long, wide scarf or wrap worn around the shoulders with the ends hanging down in front: *a mink stole, a knitted stole.* **3** a long, loose robe worn by women in ancient Rome. ⟨OE < L < Gk. *stolē* robe⟩

sto•len ['stoulən] *v.* pp. of STEAL.

stol•id ['stɒlɪd] *adj.* having or showing no emotion; hard to arouse; not excitable: *stolid opposition to new ideas. Her stolid presence was a comfort during the uproar.* ⟨< L *stolidus* immovable⟩ **—sto'lid•i•ty** [stə'lɪdəti] or **'stol•id•ness,** *n.* **—'stol•id•ly,** *adv.*

stol•len ['ʃtɔlən] *German. n.* a festive German bread containing nuts and fruit. ⟨literally, post, because of its shape⟩

STOLONS

sto•lon ['stoulən] *n.* **1** *Botany.* a slender horizontal branch, growing from the base of a plant, that takes root at the tip and produces a new plant; runner. Strawberry plants have stolons. **2** *Zoology.* a stemlike growth, as in certain polyps, that produces buds from which new individuals grow. ⟨< L *stolo, -onis* a shoot⟩

sto•ma ['stoumə] *n., pl.* **sto•ma•ta** ['stoumətə] *or* ['stɒmətə] or **sto•mas.** **1** *Botany.* one of the very tiny openings in the surface of a leaf, etc. through which water vapour and gases pass in and out. **2** *Zoology.* a small, mouthlike opening in lower animals. **3** a permanent artificial opening between a cavity or canal of the body and the surface or between two cavities or canals. ⟨< NL < Gk. *stoma, -atos* mouth⟩

stom•ach ['stʌmək] *n., v. —n.* **1** *Anatomy, zoology.* a large internal organ, the part of the alimentary canal in which the first stage of digestion takes place. Food passes into the stomach from the esophagus and from the stomach into the intestines. See ALIMENTARY CANAL and LIVER for pictures. **2** *Zoology.* in ruminant animals, a similar section of the alimentary canal, or all such sections considered as a whole. **3** a cavity in an invertebrate animal having a similar function. **4** the lower part of the front of the body; abdomen: belly: *My stomach aches. He was hit in the stomach.* **5** desire for food; appetite: *no stomach for dinner.* **6** any tolerance or liking: *I had no stomach for a fight. She's got no stomach for that kind of behaviour.*
—v. **1** eat or keep in one's stomach: *She can't stomach spinach.* **2** put up with; bear; endure: *He won't stomach arrogance.* ⟨ME < OF < L < Gk. *stomachos* < *stoma* mouth⟩

stom•ach•ache ['stʌmək,eik] *n.* a steady pain in the abdomen.

stom•ach•er ['stʌməkər] *n.* a stiff, often elaborately decorated panel laced over the front of a tight-fitting bodice. Stomachers were worn by both men and women in the 15th and 16th centuries, and in the 17th and 18th centuries by women only, usually under the bodice.

sto•mach•ic [stə'mækɪk] *adj., n. —adj.* **1** of or having to do with the stomach. **2** beneficial to the stomach, digestion, or appetite.
—n. a medicine for the stomach. **—sto'mach•i•cal•ly,** *adv.*

stomach pump *Medicine.* a type of suction pump introduced into the stomach by a flexible tube inserted into the esophagus through the mouth or nose, in order to remove the contents of the stomach, as in the case of poisoning or internal bleeding.

sto•ma•ta ['stoumətə] *or* ['stɒmətə] *n.* a pl. of STOMA.

sto•mat•al ['stoumətəl] *or* ['stɒmətəl] *adj.* **1** of or having to do with a stoma. **2** having a stoma or stomata; stomate.

sto•mate ['stoumeit] *adj., n. —adj.* having stomata or a stoma.
—n. a stoma.

sto•mat•ic [stə'mætɪk] *adj.* **1** of or having to do with the mouth. **2** STOMATAL (def. 2).

sto•ma•ti•tis [,stoumə'təitɪs] *or* [,stɒmə'təitɪs] *n. Pathology.* any of various types of inflammation of the mouth. ⟨< NL *stomatis* < Gk. *stoma, -atos* mouth + NL *-itis*⟩

sto•ma•to•pod ['stoumətə,pɒd] *or* [stə'mætə,pɒd] *n.* any crustacean of the order Stomatopoda.

sto•mat•ous ['stoumətəs] *or* ['stɒmətəs] *adj.* stomatal.

stomp [stɒmp] *v., n. —v.* tread heavily or stamp with the foot or feet. *He stomped angrily out of the room.*
—n. **1** the act of stomping. **2** a popular dance of the 1930s, marked by lively music and stamping of the feet. **3** the jazz music for such a dance. ⟨var. of *stamp*⟩

–stomy *combining form.* a surgical procedure in which an artificial opening is made in some part: *colostomy.* ⟨< Gk. *-stomia* < *stoma* mouth⟩

stone [stoun] *n., pl.* **stones** or (for def. 9) **stone;** *v.* **stoned, ston•ing. 1** a hard mineral matter that is not metal; rock. Stone is much used in building. **2** a small piece of rock. **3** a piece of rock of definite size, shape, etc. used for a particular purpose, such as a tombstone, millstone, etc.: *Her grave is marked by a fine stone.* **4** (*adjl.*) having to do with or made of stone: *a stone wall.* **5** a gem; jewel. **6** *Medicine.* a stonelike concretion, usually of mineral salts or cholesterol, which sometimes forms in the kidneys or gall bladder, causing sickness and pain; CALCULUS (def. 2). **7** the single seed, usually covered by a hard shell, found inside such fruits as peaches, plums, cherries, and avocados; a pit. **8** CURLING STONE. **9** *Brit.* a unit of mass equal to about 6.34 kg (14 lb.): *He weighed more than fourteen stone.* **10** (*adjl.*) made of stoneware: *a stone bottle.*
cast the first stone, be the first to criticize.
leave no stone unturned, do everything that can be done.
—v. **1** put stone on; pave, build, line, etc. with stone. **2** rub with or on a stone. **3** throw stones at; drive out or kill by throwing stones: *Adulterous women used to be stoned out of the community.* **4** take stones or seeds out of: *to stone cherries or plums.* ⟨OE *stān*⟩ **—'stone,like,** *adj.*

Stone Age the earliest known period of any human culture, characterized by the use of tools and weapons made of stone. The Stone Age is usually divided into the Paleolithic (early Stone Age), Mesolithic (Middle Stone Age), and Neolithic (Late or New Stone Age) periods.

stone–blind ['stoun 'blaɪnd] *adj.* totally blind.

stone•boat ['stoun,bout] *n.* a low kind of sled, often having runners made of logs, used for transporting stones taken from fields and for other heavy hauling.

stone–broke ['stoun 'brouk] *adj. Slang.* not having any money at all.

stone bruise a bruise caused by a stone, especially one on the sole of the foot.

stone–cold ['stoun 'kould] *adj., adv. —adj.* cold as stone; completely cold: *By the time she got back, his soup was stone-cold.*
—adv. absolutely; quite; completely: *He claimed he was stone-cold sober.*

stone•crop ['stoun,krɒp] *n.* any of various sedums found in rocky places, having yellow, red, or white flowers. ⟨OE *stāncrop*⟩

stone•cut•ter ['stoun,kʌtər] *n.* **1** a person who cuts or carves stone. **2** a machine for cutting or dressing stone.

stoned [stound] *adj., v. —adj.* **1** having the stones, or pits, removed: *stoned peaches.* **2** *Slang.* high on, or stupefied with, drugs or alcohol.
—v. pt. and pp. of STONE.

stone–dead ['stoun 'dɛd] *adj.* completely dead; lifeless.

stone–deaf ['stoun 'dɛf] *adj.* totally deaf.

stone•fly ['stoun,flaɪ] *n.* any of several soft-bodied primitive aquatic insects of the order Plecoptera, a food source for game fish, which makes them (or flies modelled on them) popular bait for sport fishing.

stone fruit any fruit that has a layer of pulp outside a hard shell containing a seed; any drupe. Peaches, cherries, olives, etc. are stone fruits.

stone–ground ['stoun ,graʊnd] *adj.* of whole-grain flour, made by grinding the whole kernels of grain between millstones, instead of processing the grain to separate the bran from the pulp and then adding bran again after grinding.

stone marten 1 a marten (*Martes foina*) of Europe and Asia that has a patch of white fur on the throat and breast. **2** the fur of this animal.

stone•ma•son ['stoun,meisən] *n.* a person who cuts stone or builds walls, etc. of stone.

stone•ma•son•ry ['stoun,meisənri] *n.* **1 a** the act of building or paving with stone: *She does stonemasonry as well as carpentry.* **b** the result of this act: *That's a nice piece of stonemasonry.* **2** the art or craft of building in stone: *Stonemasonry is a dying skill.*

Stone sheep *Cdn.* a dark brown or black subspecies of the Dall sheep, *Ovis canadensis stonei*, found in the mountains of N British Columbia and adjacent parts of the Yukon. Also, **Stone's sheep.** ⟨after A. J. *Stone*, U.S. sportsman and naturalist⟩

stone's throw a short distance: *The park is only a stone's throw from our house.*

stone•wall ['stoun,wɒl] *v.* **1** meet (questions, probes, etc.) with complete lack of co-operation or response; engage in obstructive or delaying tactics: *to stonewall an official inquiry. The legislation took months to go through because the government kept stonewalling.* **2** *Cricket.* of a batsman, play a defensive game by continually blocking the ball rather than batting for runs. **—'stone,wal•ler,** *n.* **—'stone,wal•ling,** *n., adj.*

stone•ware ['stoun,wɛr] *n.* **1** a hard, non-porous, opaque pottery fired at a temperature that is higher than that for earthenware, but lower than that for porcelain. Compare EARTHENWARE, PORCELAIN. **2** articles made of stoneware. **3** (*adjl.*) made of stoneware.

stone•work ['stoun,wɜrk] *n.* **1** work done in stone. **2** the part of a building made of stone. **3 stoneworks,** pl. (*used with a singular verb*) a place for the cutting and dressing of stone, used for masonry, monuments, etc.

stone•work•er ['stoun,wɜrkər] *n.* a person who shapes or cuts stone for use in buildings, sculpture, etc.; stonecutter.

Ston•ey ['stouni] *n., pl.* **Ston•ey, Ston•eys,** or **Ston•ies.** Assiniboine. Also, **Stony.**

ston•y ['stouni] *adj.* **ston•i•er, ston•i•est. 1** having many stones: *The beach is stony.* **2** hard like stone. **3 a** fixed or expressionless: *a stony stare.* **b** cold and unfeeling: *a stony heart.* **c** of fear, grief, etc., petrifying, stupefying. **—'ston•i•ly,** *adv.* **—'ston•i•ness,** *n.*

Ston•y ['stouni] *n., pl.* **Ston•y** or **Ston•ies.** See STONEY.

ston•y–heart•ed ['stouni 'hɑrtɪd] *adj.* pitiless and unfeeling; cold-hearted; cruel.

stood [stʊd] *v.* pt. and pp. of STAND.

stooge [studʒ] *n., v.* **stooged, stoog•ing.** *Informal. —n.* **1** a person on the stage who asks questions of a comedian and is the butt of the comedian's jokes. **2** a person who follows and flatters another; hanger-on.
—v. be or act as a stooge (*for*). ⟨origin uncertain⟩

stook [stuk] *or* [stʊk] *n., v. —n.* an upright arrangement of sheaves, intended to speed up drying in the field.
—v. build (hay) into such arrangements of sheaves. ⟨ME *stouke*; cf. MLG *stuke* pile of sheaves, bundle⟩ **—'stook•er,** *n.*

stook•ing ['stukɪŋ] *or* ['stʊkɪŋ] *n., v. —n. Cdn.* the practice or skill of setting sheaves of grain up in stooks.
—v. ppr. of STOOK.

stook threshing the practice of threshing in the field from the stooks rather than first hauling the sheaves to the barn.

stool [stul] *n., v.* —*n.* **1** a separate seat for one person, having three or four legs or a central pedestal and having no back or arms. **2 a** a low bench used to rest the feet on or to kneel on; footstool. **b** a low bench used to give one added height; step-stool: *She stands on a stool to reach the top shelf.* **3** a seat to be used as a toilet. **4** waste matter from the bowels. **5** the stump or root of a plant from which shoots grow. **6** a cluster of shoots growing from such a base. **7** a bird used as a decoy, tied to a pole, perch, or stool. **8** STOOL PIGEON.
—*v.* **1** send out shoots. **2** turn informer; be or act as a stool pigeon. ⟨OE *stōl*⟩ **—'stool-ˌlike,** *adj.*

stool pigeon **1** a pigeon used to lead other pigeons into a trap. **2** *Slang.* a spy for the police or other intelligence-gathering agency; informer. Also, **stoolie.** ⟨probably from the former practice of tying the decoy bird to a STOOL (defs. 5, 6)⟩

stoop[1] [stup] *v., n.* —*v.* **1** bend forward and downward: *to stoop over a desk.* **2** carry (the head and shoulders) bent forward. **3** descend from a superior rank or position; condescend: *She would never stoop to speak to the workers.* **4** lower oneself morally; demean oneself: *He stooped to cheating his customers in trying to save his business.* **5** swoop down like a hawk attacking prey. **6 a** *Archaic.* submit; yield. **b** subdue; humble (oneself).
—*n.* **1** an act of bending forward and downward. **2** a forward and downward bend of the head and shoulders, especially when habitual: *She walks with a noticeable stoop.* **3** a lowering of oneself; condescension or a demeaning of oneself. **4** the descent of a hawk, etc. on its prey. ⟨OE *stūpian*⟩ **—'stoop•er,** *n.*
☛ *Hom.* STOUP, STUPE.

stoop[2] [stup] *n.* a small porch or platform at the entrance of a house. ⟨< Du. *stoep*⟩
☛ *Hom.* STOUP, STUPE.

stop [stɒp] *v.* **stopped** or (*archaic*) **stopt, stop•ping;** *n.* —*v.* **1** keep from moving, acting, doing, functioning, etc.: *to stop a clock, to stop a speaker. I couldn't stop her making a fool of herself.* **2** cut off; withhold: *to stop supplies.* **3** put an end to; terminate: *to stop a noise, to stop work.* **4** interrupt a journey for a short rest or visit: *to stop at a hotel.* **5** leave off moving, acting, doing, being, etc.; cease: *All work stopped. Stop making so much fuss!* **6** close by filling; fill holes in; close: *to stop a hole, a leak, or a wound.* **7** close (a vessel) with a cork, plug, or the like: *to stop a bottle.* **8** block; obstruct: *A fallen tree stopped traffic.* **9** check (a blow, stroke, etc.); parry; ward off. **10** *Boxing.* defeat by a knockout. **11** *Sports.* defeat: *to stop an opposing team.* **12** *Music.* **a** close (a finger hole, etc.) in order to produce a particular note from a wind instrument. **b** press down (a string of a violin, etc.) in order to alter the pitch of tone produced. **13** instruct a bank not to honour (a cheque, bill, etc.) when presented: *to stop a cheque.*
stop at nothing, have no moral scruples.
stop down, *Photography.* reduce the aperture of the lens.
stop in, by, or **off,** *Informal.* stop for a short stay on the way to somewhere else.
stop over, a make a short stay. **b** make a STOPOVER (def. 1).
—*n.* **1** a stay or staying; a halt: *We made a stop for lunch.* **2** a being stopped. **3** the place where a stop is made. **4** anything that stops; an obstacle; a plug. **5** any piece or device that serves to check or control movement or action in a mechanism. **6** any of several punctuation marks: *A period is a full stop.* **7** a word used in telegrams, cables, etc. instead of a period. **8** *Music.* **a** the closing of a finger hole or aperture in the tube of a wind instrument, or the act of pressing with the finger on a string of a violin, etc. so as to alter the pitch of its tone. **b** a key or other device used for this purpose. **c** in organs, a graduated set of pipes of the same kind, or the knob or handle that controls them. **9** *Photography.* the aperture of a lens, or the f number indicating this. **10** *Phonetics.* **a** a sudden, complete stopping of the breath stream, usually followed by its sudden release. **b** a consonant made in this way.
pull out all the stops, do something in the biggest way possible; exert maximum effort.
put a stop to, stop; end: *We put a stop to his tricks.* ⟨OE *stoppian,* ult. < L *stuppa* tow < Gk. *styppē*⟩
☛ *Syn. v.* **1-3, 8, 9. Stop,** ARREST, CHECK = keep (someone or something) from continuing an action, movement, progress, etc. **Stop** is the general word, and means 'bring an advance or movement to an end': *She stopped the car.* **Arrest** emphasizes stopping and firmly holding back progress, development, or action that is already advancing: *Jonathan's tuberculosis was arrested early.* **Check** suggests stopping or arresting suddenly, sharply, or with force, sometimes only temporarily: *An awning over the sidewalk checked her fall and saved her life.*
☛ *Syn. v.* **5. Stop,** CEASE, PAUSE = leave off. **Stop,** the general word, means 'leave off', particularly doing, acting, moving, or going ahead: *The train stopped. She stopped breathing.* **Cease** is more formal and literary, but also means 'come to an end', and therefore is used of things that were existing or lasting, or to emphasize that action or movement has stopped permanently: *All life has ceased. She has ceased to breathe.* **Pause** means 'stop for a time', but suggests going on again. It cannot be followed immediately by a gerundive form. *He paused in his work to tie his shoe* and not *He paused working to tie his shoe.*

stop•cock ['stɒp,kɒk] *n.* a cock or valve for regulating the flow of a gas or liquid in a pipe, etc.

stop codon *Genetics.* one of the three codons that do not code for a specific amino acid but signal for termination of synthesis of an amino acid chain.

stope [stoup] *n., v.* **stoped, stop•ing.** —*n.* a steplike excavation formed in a mine as ore is extracted in successive layers.
—*v.* mine by cutting stopes. ⟨? < LG *stope*⟩

stop•gap ['stɒp,gæp] *n.* **1** anything that fills the place of something lacking; a temporary substitute. **2** (*adjl.*) serving as a stopgap: *stopgap legislation.*

stop•light ['stɒp,lɔit] *n.* **1** a traffic light or signal. **2** one of a set of lights on the rear end of any automotive vehicle, indicating that the brakes are set or being set.

stop•log ['stɒp,lɒg] *n.* a block of wood or concrete used to control an outlet in a dam.

stop•off ['stɒp,ɒf] *n. Informal.* stopover.

stop order an order to a broker to buy or sell commodities, stocks, etc. whenever the market reaches a set price.

stop•o•ver ['stɒp,ouvər] *n.* **1** a stopping over in the course of a journey, especially with the privilege of proceeding later on the ticket originally issued for the journey. **2** a place where such a stop is made: *Our first stopover was Regina.*

stop•page ['stɒpɪdʒ] *n.* **1** a stopping or being stopped. **2** something causing a blockage or obstruction.

stop•per ['stɒpər] *n., v.* —*n.* **1** a plug or cork for closing a bottle, tube, etc. **2** a person who or thing that brings (something) to a halt or causes (something) to stop functioning; a check.
—*v.* close or fit with a stopper: *to stopper a flask.*

stop•ple ['stɒpəl] *n., v.* **-pled, -pling.** —*n.* a stopper for a bottle, etc.
—*v.* close or fit with a stopper. ⟨ME *stoppel*⟩

stop street a side street from which vehicles may not enter a main street without first stopping. Compare THROUGH STREET.

stopt [stɒpt] *v. Archaic.* a pt. and a pp. of STOP.

stop•watch ['stɒp,wɒtʃ] *n.* a watch having a hand that can be stopped or started at any instant. A stopwatch indicates fractions of a second and is used for timing races and contests.

stor•age ['stɔrɪdʒ] *n.* **1** the act or condition of being stored. **2** *Computer technology.* memory of data on a tape or disk. **3** a place or space for storing: *She has put her furniture in storage. This house has very little storage.* **4** the cost of storing. **5** *Electricity.* the production, by electric energy, of chemical reactions that can be reversed to produce electricity, especially that occurring in and exemplified by the charging of a STORAGE BATTERY.

storage battery *Electricity.* a device for producing electric current, consisting of a group of electrochemical cells that can be recharged; BATTERY (def. 2).

store [stɔr] *n., v.* **stored, stor•ing.** —*n.* **1** a place where goods are kept for sale. **2 a** a thing or things laid up for use; supply; stock. **b stores,** *pl.* supplies or provisions of needed articles: *All the uniforms are kept in the quartermaster's stores.* **3** *Esp. Brit.* a place where supplies are kept for future use; storehouse. **4** (*adjl.*) not homemade; store-bought: *store bread.* **5** *Archaic.* quantity; abundance: *We wish them store of happy days.*
in store, a on hand; in reserve; saved for the future. **b** to be faced in the near future: *Had she known what lay in store for her, she would never have considered leaving her job.*
mind the store, *Informal.* look after or keep a check on things.
set, put, or **lay store by,** value; esteem: *She sets great store by her mother's opinion.*
—*v.* **1** supply or stock: *My brain is stored with trivia. The cupboards are stored with useless gadgets.* **2** put away for future use; lay up. **3** put in a warehouse or place used for preserving. **4** accommodate the storage of: *This cupboard will store blankets nicely.* **5** remain acceptable for use when stored in a given manner: *Cooked rice stores well in the refrigerator.* **6** *Computer technology.* enter and retain (data) in a computer memory unit. ⟨ME < OF *estorer* construct, restore, store < L *instaurare* restore, originally, establish < *in* upon + **staurus* pillar⟩ **—'stor•er,** *n.*

store–bought ['stɔr ,bɒt] *adj. Informal.* bought at a store instead of being homemade: *store-bought cookies, a store-bought dress.*

store•front ['stɔr,frʌnt] *n.* **1** the front of a store or shop: *All the storefronts were newly painted.* **2** (*adjl.*) of a business office, social service, etc., situated at street level in a business district and providing direct access for the public: *a storefront legal office.* **3** (*adjl.*) operating a storefront business or service: *a storefront lawyer.*

store•house ['stɔr,hʌus] *n.* **1** a building where things are stored; warehouse. **2** an abundant supply or source: *A library is a storehouse of information.*

store•keep•er ['stɔr,kipər] *n.* a person who has charge of a store or stores.

store meat *Cdn. North.* the kind of meat obtainable in a store as opposed to meat obtained by hunting.

store•room ['stɔr,rum] *or* ['stɔr,rʊm] *n.* a room where things are stored.

store teeth *Cdn. Informal.* false teeth; dentures.

store•wide ['stɔr,waɪd] *adj.* of or having to do with all or most of the departments in a STORE (def. 1): *storewide renovations*.

sto•rey ['stɔri] *n., pl.* **-reys** or **-ries. 1** a level or floor of a house or other building. **2** the set of rooms or apartments on one level or floor. **3** any tier or other horizontal division. Also, **story.** ⟨? ult. special use of *story* in the sense of 'a row of historical statues across a building front'⟩
☛ *Hom.* STORY.

sto•reyed ['stɔrid] *adj.* having storeys, especially of a specified number (*usually used in compounds*): *a two-storeyed house.* Also, **storied.**
☛ *Hom.* STORIED.

sto•ried ['stɔrid] *adj.* **1** celebrated in story or history: *the storied Klondike.* **2** ornamented with designs representing happenings in history or legend: *a storied tapestry.* **3** storeyed. ⟨< *story*[1]⟩
☛ *Hom.* STOREYED.

stork [stɔrk] *n.* **1** any of a family (Ciconiidae) of large, long-legged wading birds found mainly in warm parts of the Old World, having a long neck, a long, heavy bill, and, typically, white and black plumage. The Eurasian **white stork** (*Ciconia ciconia*), which often nests on rooftops, has long been a symbol of good fortune among the peoples of Europe; according to folklore it brings new babies into the home. **2 the stork,** *Informal.* the process or fact of childbirth: *It was a close race with the stork, but we reached the hospital in time.* ⟨OE storc⟩ **—'stork,like,** *adj.*

A stork

storm [stɔrm] *n., v.* *—n.* **1** a very strong wind, especially one with a velocity of about 100 to 120 km/h; windstorm. **2 a** a violent outbreak of rain with strong winds and, often, thunder and lightning: *The clouds threatened an approaching storm.* **b** a sandstorm. **c** any heavy and especially sudden fall of snow, sleet, hail, etc., together with a strong wind. **3** anything like a storm: *a storm of arrows.* **4** a violent outburst or disturbance: *a storm of tears, a storm of angry words.* **5** a violent attack: *The castle was taken by storm.* **6** a STORM WINDOW or STORM DOOR.
storm in a teacup, great excitement or commotion over something unimportant.
—v. **1** be a storm; be stormy: *It stormed for three days.* **2** be violent; rage. **3** speak loudly and angrily. **4** rush violently: *to storm out of the room.* **5** attack violently: *The troops stormed the city.* ⟨OE⟩

storm•bound ['stɔrm,baʊnd] *adj.* isolated, cut off or confined by a storm or storms.

storm cellar a cellar for shelter during cyclones, tornadoes, etc.

storm centre or **center 1** the moving centre of a cyclone, where the pressure is lowest and the wind is comparatively calm. **2** any centre of trouble, tumult, etc.

storm door an extra door fixed outside a regular door as protection against cold, wind, etc. in winter.

storm petrel STORMY PETREL (def. 1).

storm•proof ['stɔrm,pruf] *adj., v.* *—adj.* **1** not liable to damage from storms. **2** providing protection from storms.
—v. treat (something) so that it is not affected by storms.

Storm's stork [stɔrmz] a stork (*Ciconia stormi*) found in lowland forests in SE Asia, standing 85 cm tall and weighing 1.5-2 kg. It is an endangered species.

storm trooper 1 a member of the Nazi private army formed by Adolf Hitler around 1923 and disbanded in 1934. **2** an extremely brutal or vicious individual, especially one with some authority over others.

storm window an extra window fixed on the outside of a regular window as protection against cold, wind, etc. in winter.

storm•y ['stɔrmi] *adj.* **storm•i•er, storm•i•est. 1** having storms; likely to have storms; troubled by storms. **2** rough and disturbed; violent: *They had stormy quarrels.* **—'storm•i•ly,** *adv.* **—'storm•i•ness,** *n.*

stormy petrel 1 any of several small, black-and-white petrels, sea birds whose presence is supposed to give warning of a storm; especially, a petrel (*Hydrobates pelagicus*) of the N Atlantic and Mediterranean. **2** anyone believed likely to cause trouble or to indicate trouble.

Stor•ting or **Stor•thing** ['stɔr,tɪŋ] *n.* the national parliament of Norway. ⟨< Norwegian *storting*, earlier *storthing* < *stor* great + *thing* assembly⟩

sto•ry[1] ['stɔri] *n., pl.* **-ries;** *v.* **-ried, -ry•ing.** *—n.* **1** an account of some happening or group of happenings: *Tell us the story of your life.* **2 a** such an account, either true or made up, intended to interest the reader or hearer; a tale. **b** SHORT STORY. **3** an amusing anecdote; a joke, especially an unusually long one. **4** *Informal.* a falsehood. **5** stories as a branch of literature: *a character famous in story.* **6** the plot of a play, novel, etc. **7** a newspaper article, or material for such an article. **8** a radio or television report. **9** an unsubstantiated report; rumour. **10** *Archaic.* history: *well-read in story.*
another or **a different story,** a completely different matter or thing.
cut or **make a long story short,** get to the point of a narrative.
the same old story, the same tedious routine or excuse.
—v. Archaic. tell the history or story of. ⟨ME < AF *estorie* < L < Gk. *historia* history. Doublet of HISTORY.⟩ **—'sto•ry•less,** *adj.*
☛ *Syn. n.* **1-3. Story,** ANECDOTE, TALE = a spoken or written account of some happening or happenings. **Story** applies to any such account, true or made up, long or short, in prose or verse, intended to interest another: *I like stories about science.* **Anecdote** applies to a brief story about a single actual incident, usually funny or with an interesting point, often in the life of a famous person: *He knows many anecdotes about life at sea.* **Tale** applies to a longer story told as if giving true facts about some happening or situation but usually made up or exaggerated: *She reads tales of frontier days.*
☛ *Hom.* STOREY.

sto•ry[2] ['stɔri] *n., pl.* **-ries.** See STOREY.

sto•ry•board ['stɔri,bɔrd] *n.* a large board or series of panels on which are arranged a sequence of outlines or sketches showing the progressive changes occurring throughout a film, as for a movie, television production, video, etc.

sto•ry•book ['stɔri,bʊk] *n.* **1** a book containing one or more stories or tales, especially for children. **2** (*adjl.*) of or like that of a storybook; romantic: *a storybook hero, a storybook ending.*

sto•ry•tell•ing ['stɔri,tɛlɪŋ] *n. or adj. Informal.* **1** telling stories. **2** telling falsehoods; lying. **'sto•ry,tell•er,** *n.*

sto•tin•ka [stə'tɪŋkə] *n., pl.* **-ki** [-ki]. a unit of money in Bulgaria, equal to 1/100 of a lev. ⟨< Bulgarian⟩

stoup [stup] *n.* **1** a drinking vessel of varying size, such as a cup, flagon, or tankard. **2** the amount it holds. **3** a basin for holy water at the entrance of a church. ⟨< ON *staup*⟩
☛ *Hom.* STOOP.

stout [stʌut] *adj., n.* *—adj.* **1** bulky; somewhat fat: *He's getting stout.* **2** strong or thick; solid; substantial: *a stout ship, a stout walking stick. The fort has stout walls.* **3** brave; bold: *She has a stout heart.* **4** not yielding; stubborn; determined: *stout resistance.* **5** characterized by endurance or staying power: *a stout horse, a stout engine.* **6** sized to fit a large person.
—n. **1** a strong, dark brown beer brewed with roasted malt. **2** a stout person. **3 a** a piece of clothing sized to fit a large person. **b** the size of such a piece of clothing. ⟨ME < OF *estout* strong < Gmc. root *stolt-* proud < L *stultus* foolish⟩ **—'stout•ly,** *adv.* **—'stout•ness,** *n.*
☛ *Syn. adj.* **1.** See note at FAT.

stout–heart•ed ['stʌut ,hartɪd] *adj.* brave; bold; courageous. **—'stout-'heart•ed•ly,** *adv.* **—'stout-'heart•ed•ness,** *n.*

stove[1] [stouv] *n.* **1** an apparatus for cooking and heating, using electricity or burning a fuel such as gas, oil, or wood. **2** a kiln or a similar heating device or chamber. ⟨OE *stofa* warm bathing room < VL *stufa* < *extufare* sweat out, ult. < L *ex-* out + Gk. *typhos* vapour. Related to STEW.⟩

stove² [stouv] *v.* a pt. and a pp. of STAVE.
☛ *Usage.* See note at STAVE.

stove•pipe ['stouv,pəip] *n.* **1** a sheet metal pipe of large diameter connected to a fuel-burning stove, used to carry smoke and gases from the stove to a chimney. **2** *Informal.* a tall silk hat. Also, **stovepipe hat.**

stow [stou] *v.* **1** pack; store: *The cargo was stowed in the ship's hold. Just stow your things in that cupboard.* **2** pack things closely in; fill by packing: *They stowed the little cabin with supplies for the trip.* **3** *Slang.* stop: *Stow the chatter!*
stow away, hide on a ship, aircraft, etc. to avoid paying the fare or to escape. ⟨ult. < OE *stōw* place⟩ **—'stow•er,** *n.*

stow•age ['stouɪdʒ] *n.* **1** a stowing or being stowed: *The stowage of all their equipment took them two hours.* **2** a room or place for stowing: *The boat has stowage fore and aft.* **3** capacity for stowing: *Our boat has stowage for a three-day cruise.* **4** what is stowed. **5** the charge for stowing something.

stow•a•way ['stouə,wei] *n.* a person who hides on a ship, aircraft, etc. to get a free passage or to escape.

STP standard temperature and pressure.

St. Pat•rick's Cross ['pætrɪks] a red diagonal cross on a white background; one of the three crosses that make up the Union Flag of Great Britain and Northern Ireland (Union Jack).

str. **1** steamer. **2** strait.

stra•bis•mus [strə'bɪzməs] *n. Ophthalmology.* a disorder of vision due to the turning of one eye or both eyes from the normal position so that both cannot be directed at the same point or object at the same time; squint; cross-eye. ⟨< NL < Gk. *strabismos,* ult. < *strabos* squint-eyed⟩ **—stra'bis•mic** or **stra'bis•mal,** *adj.*

Strad [stræd] *n.* Stradivarius.

strad•dle ['strædəl] *v.* **-dled, -dling;** *n.* —*v.* **1** sit or stand with one's legs on either side of (something): *He straddled the chair. She stood straddling the row of lettuce as she hoed.* **2** be or lie across (something): *A footbridge straddled the brook. A pair of glasses straddled her nose.* **3** spread or be spread apart: *His legs straddled as he floundered through the snow.* **4** avoid committing oneself on (an issue); favour or appear to favour both sides: *She is still straddling the question, but will soon have to decide one way or the other.*
—*n.* **1** the act of straddling or the position of a person who straddles. **2** the distance covered in straddling. ⟨< var. of dial. *striddle,* frequentative of *stride*⟩ **—'strad•dler,** *n.*

Strad•i•var•i•us [,strædə'vɛriəs] *n.* a violin, viola, or cello made by Antonio Stradivari (1644-1737), a violin-maker of Cremona, Italy, or by members of his family. These instruments are famous for their exquisite tone. Often shortened to **Strad.**

strafe [streif] *v.* **strafed, straf•ing.** bombard or shell heavily; especially, rake enemy ground positions with machine-gun fire from low-flying aircraft. ⟨from a German slogan of World War I, *Gott strafe England!* May God punish England!⟩ **—'straf•er,** *n.*

strag•gle ['strægəl] *v.* **-gled, -gling. 1** wander in a scattered fashion: *Cows straggled along the lane.* **2** stray from or lag behind the rest. **3** spread in an irregular, rambling manner: *Vines straggled over the old wall.* ⟨blend of *stray* and *draggle*⟩ **—'strag•gler,** *n.*

strag•gly ['strægli] *adj.* **1** spread out in an irregular, rambling way; straggling. **2** of hair, beard, etc., long, loose or limp, and messy.

straight [streit] *adj., adv., n.* —*adj.* **1** without a bend or curve; direct: *a straight line, a straight path.* **2 a** frank; honest; upright; outspoken: *straight conduct.* **b** right; correct: *straight thinking.* **3** in proper order or condition: *Keep your accounts straight.* **4** continuous: *in straight succession.* **5** thoroughgoing or unreserved: *a straight Tory.* **6** unmodified; undiluted: *a straight comedy, straight whisky.* **7** *Informal.* reliable: *a straight tip.* **8** *Poker.* made up of a sequence of five cards: *a straight flush.* **9** serious rather than comic; natural rather than eccentric: *a straight part in a play.* **10** *Slang.* **a** conventional in behaviour, dress, views, etc. **b** free of alcohol and drugs. **c** not engaging in criminal behaviour. **11** *Slang.* heterosexual.
set straight. See SET.
the straight and narrow (path), ethically correct principles of action: *Following the straight and narrow should keep you out of trouble.*
—*adv.* **1** in a straight line: *Walk straight.* **2** directly: *She headed straight home.* **3** in an erect position; upright: *Stand up straight.* **4** frankly; honestly; uprightly: *Live straight.* **5** continuously: *Drive straight on.* **6** without delay. **7** without qualification or modification of any kind.
straight away or **off,** at once.
straight out, *Informal.* frankly; explicity.
straight up, (of alcoholic drinks) without ice.
—*n.* **1** the condition of being straight; straight form, position, or line. **2** a straight part, as of a racecourse. **3** *Poker.* a sequence of five cards. **4** *Slang.* a person who is conventional. **5** *Slang.* a heterosexual person. ⟨OE *streht,* pp. of *streccan* stretch⟩ **—'straight•ly,** *adv.* **—'straight•ness,** *n.*
☛ *Hom.* STRAIT.

straight angle an angle of 180°.

straight–arm ['streit ,ɑrm] *v., n.* —*v.* **1** force or push one's way as if with a stiff arm. **2** *Football.* prevent (an opponent) from making a tackle by holding one's arm straight in front or straight to the side.
—*n.* the act of straight-arming.
straight arrow. *Informal.* a person of high integrity.

straight•a•way ['streitə,wei] *n., adj., adv.* —*n.* a straight course; especially, the straight part of a closed race course or a straight stretch of highway: *They were now on a straightaway, making excellent time.*
—*adj.* having, taking, or keeping to a straight course.
—*adv.* as quickly as possible; at once; immediately: *The captain read the letter and burned it straightaway.* Also, **straightway.**

straight chain *Chemistry.* an open chain of atoms, usually carbon, having no side or branching chains.

straight chair a usually unupholstered chair with a vertical back, straight or no arms, and straight legs.

straight•edge ['streit,ɛdʒ] *n.* **1** a strip of wood or metal having one edge accurately straight, used in obtaining or testing straight lines and level surfaces. **2** RULER (def. 2).

straight•en ['streitən] *v.* **1** make straight or become straight: *Straighten your shoulders.* **2** put in the proper order or condition (*usually used with* **up** *or* **out**): *He straightened up his room. We have to straighten out our accounts to see how much we owe.* **3** *Informal.* make or become better in behaviour, etc.; reform (*usually used with* **out** *or* **up**): *Her parents have tried to straighten her out but she still keeps getting into trouble.* **—'straight•en•er,** *n.*
☛ *Hom.* STRAITEN.

straight face an expressionless face, especially one showing no trace of amusement: *He kept a straight face through the whole ridiculous story.* **—'straight-,faced,** *adj.*

straight flush *Poker.* a sequence of five cards of the same suit, ranking higher than four of a kind.

straight•for•ward [,streit'fɔrwərd] *adj.* **1** honest; frank: *a straightforward person, a straightforward answer.* **2** without complications; clear-cut and precise: *The plan was straightforward.* **3** going straight ahead; direct. **—,straight'for•ward•ly,** *adv.* **—,straight'for•ward•ness,** *n.*

straight•for•wards [,streit'fɔrwərdz] *adv.* straightforward.

straight man an actor who feeds lines to another actor who then provides the comic punch lines.

straight–out ['streit 'ʌut] *adj. Informal.* out-and-out; complete; thorough.

strain¹ [strein] *v., n.* —*v.* **1** draw tight; stretch: *The weight strained the rope.* **2** pull hard: *The dog strained at its leash.* **3** stretch more than one should: *She strained the truth in telling the story.* **4** use to the utmost: *He strained his eyes to see.* **5** injure or be injured by too much effort or by stretching, pressing, or twisting: *The runner strained her heart.* **6** change the shape of (something) or otherwise deform it by submitting it to mechanical stress. **7** make a very great effort. **8** press or pour through a material or device that allows only liquid to pass through it: *Consommé is a soup that has been strained.* **9** remove by filtering: *We strained out all the bits of eggshell.* **10** drip through. **11** press closely; squeeze; hug.
—*n.* **1** a force or weight that stretches. **2 a** too much muscular or physical effort. **b** an injury caused by too much effort or by stretching. **3** deformation resulting from mechanical stress. **4** any severe, trying, or wearing pressure: *the strain of worry.* **5** the effect of such pressure on the body or mind. ⟨ME < OF < L *stringere* draw tight⟩

strain² [strein] *n.* **1** a line of descent; race; stock: *The Irish strain in him explains his sense of humour.* **2** a group of animals or plants that form a part of a breed, race, or variety. **3** an inherited quality: *There is a strain of musical talent in her family.* **4** a trace or streak: *That horse has a mean strain.* **5** Often, strains, *pl.* a part of a piece of music; melody; song. **6** a manner or style of doing or speaking: *She wrote in a playful strain.* ⟨var. of OE *strēon* gain, begetting⟩

strained [streind] *adj., v.* *—adj.* **1** produced by effort; forced; not natural; not relaxed; characterized by forced behaviour: *a strained laugh. Their first meeting after the quarrel was strained.* **2** dangerously tense; near open conflict: *strained relations between the two nations.*
—v. pt. and pp. of STRAIN.

strain•er ['streinər] *n.* a utensil or device for straining, filtering, or sifting: *A filter, a sieve, and a colander are strainers.*

strait [streit] *n., adj.* *—n.* **1** a narrow channel connecting two larger bodies of water. **2 straits,** *pl.* difficulty; need; distress. *—adj. Archaic.* **1** narrow; limited; confining. **2** strict: *The nun took strait vows.* ⟨ME < OF *estreit* < L *strictus* drawn tight. Doublet of STRICT.⟩ **—'strait•ly,** *adv.* **—'strait•ness,** *n.*
☛ *Hom.* STRAIGHT.

strait•en ['streitən] *v.* **1** restrict or limit in range, scope, or amount: *a mind straitened by prejudice.* **2** *Archaic.* make or become narrow.
in straitened circumstances, needing money badly.
☛ *Hom.* STRAIGHTEN.

strait•jack•et ['streit,dʒækɪt] *n., v.* *—n.* **1** a strong, tight garment used to bind the arms in keeping a violent person from harming himself or herself or others. **2** anything that hampers or confines: *a legal straitjacket. She felt that the school system should break out of the straitjacket of tradition.*
—v. confine in or as if in a straitjacket.

strait–laced ['streit 'leist] *adj.* very strict in matters of conduct; prudish.

strake [streik] *n. Nautical.* a single breadth of planks or metal plates along the side of a ship from the bow to the stern. ⟨Related to STRETCH⟩

stra•mo•ni•um [strə'mouniəm] *n.* **1** a drug prepared from the dried leaves of jimsonweed or another plant of the same genus, used especially in the treatment of asthma. **2** jimsonweed. ⟨< NL⟩

strand[1] [strænd] *v., n.* *—v.* **1** leave in a helpless position: *He was stranded a thousand kilometres from home with no money.* **2** run aground; drive on the shore: *The ship was stranded on the rocks.*
—n. Poetic. a shore; land bordering a sea, lake, or river. ⟨OE⟩

strand[2] [strænd] *n., v.* *—n.* **1** one of the threads, strings, or wires that are twisted together to make a rope or cable: *This is a rope of three strands.* **2** a fibre, hair, etc. **3** a string of beads, pearls, etc.
—v. **1** form (a rope, yarn, etc.) by twisting strands together. **2** destroy (a rope, yarn, etc.) by breaking strands. ⟨ME < OF *estran* < Gmc.⟩

strange [streindʒ] *adj.* **strang•er, strang•est. 1** unusual; queer; peculiar: *It was a strange accident: he was unhurt, but the driver was killed. She had the strangest laugh. It's strange that you didn't get the book, because I left it right on your desk.* **2** not known, seen, or heard of before; unfamiliar: *strange faces, a strange language. The procedure was entirely strange to her.* **3** unaccustomed; inexperienced (*used with* **to**): *She made the mistake because she is still strange to the job.* **4** *Archaic.* foreign; alien: *travelling in strange lands.* **5** *Physics.* of or being an elementary particle having an as yet incompletely identified property (**strangeness**) conserved in strong interactions (see STRONG FORCE) and used to explain certain characteristics of radioactive decay. A **strange particle** has a quantum number other than zero.
feel strange, feel out of place; feel awkward: *He still feels strange in his brother-in-law's home.*
make strange, of a baby or small child, show fear or distress at the presence of someone unknown or not very well known: *She hardly ever makes strange.* ⟨ME < OF *estrange* < L *extraneus* foreign. Doublet of EXTRANEOUS.⟩ **—'strange•ly,** *adv.* **—'strange•ness,** *n.*
☛ *Syn. adj.* **1. Strange,** ODD, PECULIAR = unusual or out of the ordinary. **Strange** always suggests the idea of something unfamiliar and outside the usual, ordinary, expected, or natural order: *A strange quiet pervaded the city.* **Odd** suggests a strangeness that is puzzling, or a quality different from the normal or regular: *That is an odd colour.* **Peculiar** particularly suggests a quality or character so individual as to be uncommon and seem strange or odd: *Raising frogs is a peculiar way to make a living.*

stran•ger ['streindʒər] *n.* **1** a person not known, seen, or heard of before: *She is a stranger to me.* **2** a person new to a place; one who is not yet well acquainted with a place or its inhabitants, etc.; newcomer: *He is a stranger in this area.* **3** a person or thing that is unaccustomed to or not at home in

something; one that has no experience of something (*used with* **to**): *She is no stranger to hard work.* **4** a person from another country; foreigner or alien. **5** *Archaic.* a visitor; guest. **6** *Law.* an outsider who is not privy (*to* a contract, etc.).

stran•gle ['stræŋgəl] *v.* **-gled, -gling. 1** kill by squeezing the throat to stop the breath: *The infant Hercules strangled a snake with each hand.* **2** suffocate; choke: *His high collar seemed to be strangling him. She almost strangled on a piece of meat that caught in her throat.* **3** choke down; suppress; keep back; repress; stifle: *to strangle an impulse to laugh. Their efforts at reform were strangled by the bureaucracy.* ⟨ME < OF *estrangler* < L *strangulare* < Gk. *strangalaein,* ult. < *strangos* twisted. Doublet of STRANGULATE.⟩ **—'stran•gler,** *n.*

stran•gle•hold ['stræŋgəl,hould] *n.* **1** *Wrestling.* an illegal hold by which an opponent is choked. **2** a controlling or dominant position that chokes opposition, freedom of movement, etc.; an unshakable or deadly grip: *One company had a stranglehold on the market.*

stran•gles ['stræŋgəlz] *n. Veterinary pathology.* a streptococcal infection of the respiratory tract in horses, caused by the bacterium *Streptococcus equi,* characterized by inflammation of the mucous membranes of the upper air passages and abscesses in the submaxillary and other lymph nodes: equine distemper.

stran•gu•late ['stræŋgjə,leit] *v.* **-lat•ed, -lat•ing. 1** *Pathology. Surgery.* make or become compressed or constricted so as to stop circulation. **2** strangle; choke. ⟨< LL *strangulare.* Doublet of STRANGLE.⟩

stran•gu•la•tion [,stræŋgjə'leiʃən] *n.* **1** the act of strangling or the state of being strangled. **2** the state of strangulating or being strangulated.

strap [stræp] *n., v.* **strapped, strap•ping.** *—n.* **1** a narrow strip of leather, cloth, or other material that bends easily and is used to hold, fasten, or secure something: *She wore a sun dress with narrow shoulder straps. The box was strengthened by straps of steel.* **2** a narrow strip of leather to sharpen razors on; strop. **3** a looped band suspended from an overhead bar in a bus, train, etc. for standing passengers to hold on to. **4** a piece of solid but flexible leather, formerly used as an instrument of corporal punishment in schools.
—v. **1** fasten with a strap. **2** punish by beating with a strap. **3** sharpen on a strap or strop. **4** bind or support (an injured limb, etc.) with an adhesive or elastic bandage. ⟨var. of *strop*⟩

strap•hang•er ['stræp,hæŋər] *n. Informal.* a passenger in a crowded streetcar, subway train, bus, etc. who stands, holding on to a strap or bar for support.

strap•less ['stræplɪs] *adj.* having no shoulder straps; leaving the shoulders and arms completely bare: *a strapless evening gown.*

strapped [stræpt] *adj., v.* *—adj.* **1** without money; having no ready cash: *I'm strapped, so I won't be able to go to the movie after all.* **2** suffering from a shortage of anything (*used with* **for**): *Sorry we can't stay; we're really strapped for time.*
—v. pt. and pp. of STRAP.

strap•per ['stræpər] *n.* **1** a person who or thing that straps. **2** *Informal.* a tall, robust person.

strap•ping ['stræpɪŋ] *adj., n., v.* *—adj. Informal.* tall, strong, and healthy: *a fine, strapping girl.*
—n. a beating with a strap as punishment.
—v. ppr. of STRAP.

stra•ta ['strætə] *or* ['streitə] *n.* a pl. of STRATUM.

strat•a•gem ['strætədʒəm] *n.* **1** a scheme or trick for deceiving and outwitting the enemy in war. **2** any clever scheme or trick designed to achieve a goal: *He got the position by an unusual stratagem.* **3** skill in using such schemes or tricks: *The plan requires stratagem to be effective.* ⟨< F < L < Gk. *stratēgēma,* ult. < *stratēgos* general. See STRATEGY.⟩
☛ *Syn.* **Stratagem,** ARTIFICE, RUSE = a scheme or device to trick or mislead others. **Stratagem** applies to a plan to gain one's own ends or to defeat those of others by skilful deception: *The general planned a stratagem to trap the enemy.* **Artifice** applies to clever tricks or devices, sometimes mechanical, to gain one's ends by misleading, and usually deceiving, others: *Filmmakers often employ artifice to get realistic effects.* **Ruse** applies to a trick or device to gain one's ends indirectly by deceiving others about one's real purpose: *His supposed appointment was simply a ruse to leave early.*

stra•te•gic [strə'tidʒɪk] *adj.* **1** of, having to do with, or based on strategy: *a strategic retreat, a strategic move. The booth was in a strategic location, just inside the entrance to the fairgrounds.* **2** important in or necessary to strategy: *Each element of the armed forces is a strategic link in our national defence. She went over the strategic points again at the end of her talk.* **3** having to do with or designating materials essential for warfare. 4 specially trained or made for destroying enemy bases, industry, or communications behind the lines of battle: *a strategic bomber.* Also, **strategical.** **—stra'te•gi•cal•ly,** *adv.*

stra•te•gics [strə'tidʒɪks] *n.* STRATEGY (def. 1).

strat•e•gist ['strætədʒɪst] *n.* a person skilled in strategy.

strat•e•gy ['strætədʒi] *n., pl.* **-gies. 1** the science and art of war; the overall planning and directing of the military operations of a nation or group of nations at war with another, including political and economic decisions affecting the nation or nations as a whole. **2** a plan based on this. **3** any skilful plan: *She needed a strategy to gain time until she was ready to move.* **4** the skilful planning and management of something: *Strategy is important in an election campaign.* ⟨< Gk. *stratēgia* < *stratēgos* general < *stratos* army + *agein* lead⟩

strath•spey [,stræθ'spei] *or* ['stræθ,spei] *n.* **1** a lively Scottish dance resembling a slow reel. **2** the music for this dance. ⟨< *Strath Spey*, a district in Scotland⟩

strat•i•fi•ca•tion [,strætəfə'keiʃən] *n.* **1** the act or process of arranging in layers or strata; an instance or the state of being arranged in layers or strata. **2** an arrangement in layers or strata. **3** *Geology.* **a** the formation of strata; deposition or occurrence in strata. **b** a stratum.

strat•i•fy ['strætə,faɪ] *v.* **-fied, -fy•ing.** arrange, form, or deposit in layers or strata. ⟨< Med.L *stratificare* < L *stratum* (see STRATUM) + *facere* make⟩

stra•tig•ra•pher [strə'tɪgrəfər] *n.* a person trained in stratigraphy, especially one whose work it is.

stra•tig•ra•phy [strə'tɪgrəfi] *n.* **1** the branch of geology that deals with the origin, composition, and arrangement of the strata of a region, country, etc. **2** the order and arrangement of strata. ⟨< *stratum* covering, layer + E *-graphy*⟩ **—,strat•i'graph•ic** [,strætə'græfɪk], *adj.* **—,strat•i'graph•i•cal•ly,** *adv.*

stra•toc•ra•cy [strə'tɒkrəsi] *n.* government by the military. **—,strat•o'crat•ic** [,strætə'krætɪk], *adj.* **—'strat•o,crat,** *n.*

stra•to–cu•mu•lus [,streitou'kjumjələs] *or* [,strætou'kjumjələs] *n.* a low, often extensive cloud layer consisting of rounded masses or rolls showing dark patches on the underside where the masses are thickest. ⟨< L *stratus* a spreading out + E *cumulus*⟩

strat•o•sphere ['strætə,sfir] *n.* the region of the earth's atmosphere just above the troposphere, characterized by a concentration of ozone, chiefly horizontal winds, and temperatures that increase with altitude. It extends to a height of about 50 km, where the mesosphere begins. ⟨< L *stratus* a spreading out + E *sphere*⟩ **—,strat•o'spher•ic** [-'sfɛrɪk], *adj.*

Strata of rock

stra•tum ['strætəm] *or* ['streitəm] *n., pl.* **stra•ta** ['strætə] *or* ['streitə] or **stra•tums. 1** a horizontal layer of material, especially one of several parallel layers placed one upon another. **2** *Geology.* a layer of sedimentary rock or earth, usually one of a series of distinct, more or less horizontal, layers in the earth's crust, representing continuous periods of deposition. **3** a similar distinct horizontal region or section of the sea or atmosphere. **4** *Biology.* a single layer of tissue or cells. **5** *Sociology.* a socio-economic level of society, comprising persons of similar education, culture, etc.: *Professional people, such as doctors and lawyers, represent one stratum of society.* ⟨< NL < L *stratum*, neut. pp. of *sternere* spread out⟩

stra•tus ['streitəs] *or* ['strætəs] *n., pl.* **-ti** [-taɪ] *or* [-ti]. a very low, sheetlike layer of grey cloud like fog, from which rain may fall as drizzle. ⟨< L *stratus* a spreading out < *sternere* spread⟩

straw [strɒ] *n.* **1** the stalks or stems of grain after drying and threshing. Straw is used for bedding for horses and cows, for making hats, and for many other purposes. **2** a pale yellow colour, similar to that of straw. **3** a single stem or stalk, especially of a grass. **4** (*adjl.*) made of straw: *a straw hat.* **5** a slender tube made of waxed paper, plastic, etc., used for sucking up drinks. **6** a bit; trifle: *He doesn't care a straw.* **7** STRAW MAN (def. 3). **8** (*adjl.*) of little value or consequence; worthless.
grasp or **catch at a straw** or **at straws,** try anything in desperation.
straw in the wind, something taken as an indication of a trend. ⟨OE *strēaw*⟩

straw•ber•ry ['strɒ,bɛri] *n., pl.* **-ries. 1** the small, juicy, edible, red fruit of any of several plants (genus *Fragaria*) of the rose family. A strawberry is not a fruit in the botanical sense; the juicy part is an enlarged flower receptacle and the actual fruits are the tiny, seedlike achenes on its surface. **2** a plant that produces strawberries. There are many varieties of cultivated strawberry. ⟨OE *strēa(w)berige, strēowberige* straw + berry; reason for the name is unknown⟩

strawberry blond or **blonde 1** reddish blond. **2** a person with reddish blond hair.
☛ *Spelling.* See note at BLOND.

strawberry mark a small, reddish birthmark.

strawberry roan 1 reddish roan. **2** a reddish roan horse.

strawberry tea *Cdn.* a social gathering at which tea and strawberries are served, the purpose being to raise money for charitable work.

straw•board ['strɒ,bɔrd] *n.* coarse cardboard made of straw pulp, used for boxes, packing, etc.

straw boss *Informal.* a supervisor with little authority.

straw•flow•er ['strɒ,flaʊər] *n.* an Australian annual herb (*Helichrysum bracteatum*) of the composite family, widely grown for its yellow, orange, red, or white papery flowers which can be dried for use in permanent bouquets.

straw–hat ['strɒ 'hæt] *adj.* of or concerning plays, musical shows, etc. performed in resort and suburban areas during the summer: *straw-hat theatre.* ⟨from the wearing of straw hats in summer⟩

straw man 1 a scarecrow. **2** a weak opposing argument or view put forward by a speaker or writer for the purpose of attacking and easily overcoming it. **3** a token candidate or opponent who is put in for appearances by one party or side, but who does not expect to win. **4** a person used as a front for someone else's real intentions or activities.

straw vote an unofficial poll or vote taken to find out how a group of people feel about a particular candidate or issue.

straw•y ['strɒi] *adj.* **1** of, containing, or resembling straw. **2** strewn or thatched with straw.

stray [strei] *v., n., adj.* *—v.* **1** lose one's way or get separated from a group. **2** move or wander aimlessly or without conscious control: *Her eyes strayed around the room as she listened.* **3** turn from the right course; go wrong. **4** digress; not pay attention; not concentrate.
—n. **1** a person or thing that has strayed, such as a domestic animal wandering at large: *Our dog is a stray that we picked up a year ago.* **2** Usually, **strays,** *pl.* electromagnetic waves that interfere with radio reception; static.
—adj. **1** wandering or lost: *a stray cat.* **2** occurring here and there or now and then; scattered or isolated: *We could hear stray snatches of song from across the lake. There were a few stray huts along the beach.* **3** unwanted or wasted: *stray magnetic fields.* ⟨ME < OF *estraier*, originally adj. < VL *stratarius* roaming the streets < LL (*via*) *strata.* See STREET.⟩ **—'stray•er,** *n.*
☛ *Syn. v.* **1.** See note at WANDER.

streak [strik] *n., v.* *—n.* **1** a long, thin mark or line of a different colour or texture: *He has a streak of dirt on his face. We saw a streak of lightning.* **2** layer; stratum; vein of ore: *Side bacon has streaks of fat and streaks of lean.* **3** a vein; strain; element: *She has a streak of humour, though she looks very serious.* **4** *Informal.* a brief period; spell: *a streak of luck.* **5** *Mineralogy.* a line of coloured powder, often differing from the colour of the mineral in mass, left by scratching a mineral or rubbing it over a hard white surface called a **streak plate.** This line is often an important feature of identification.
like a streak, *Informal.* very fast; at full speed: *The dog heard the whistle and was off like a streak.*
talk a blue streak. See BLUE STREAK.
—v. **1** make streaks in or on: *hair streaked by the sun.* **2** become streaked. **3** *Informal.* move very fast; go at full speed. **4** *Informal.* run naked through a crowd or in a public place. ⟨OE *strica*⟩ **—'streak•er,** *n.*

streak•y ['striki] *adj.* **streak•i•er, streak•i•est. 1** marked with streaks; streaked: *The wall is streaky where the paint did not cover properly.* **2** occurring in streaks: *streaky clouds near the horizon. The colour is streaky and faded.* **3** varying or uneven in quality, character, activity, etc.: *a streaky performance.* **—'streak•i•ly,** *adv.* **—'streak•i•ness,** *n.*

stream [strim] *n., v.* *—n.* **1** a body of flowing water in a channel or bed, especially a narrow river or a brook. **2** any flow or current of water or other liquid. **3** a steady flow or current, like that of a liquid: *a stream of light, a stream of fresh air.* **4** a continuous series or succession: *a stream of words, a stream of cars.* **5** a prevailing drift, trend, or flow. **6** *Education.* a single grouping of students within a grade, having similar abilities and/or educational goals.

on stream, in or into production: *The refinery went bankrupt only a few months after it had gone on stream.*

—v. **1** move in a stream: *The sunlight streamed in the window. Tears streamed from his eyes. Soldiers streamed out of the fort.* **2** give off or produce a stream: *Her eyes streamed with tears.* **3** be very wet; drip or run with water, etc.: *streaming windows, a streaming umbrella.* **4** extend or float at full length: *The flag streamed in the wind. Her long hair streamed out behind her as she ran.* **5** discharge or cause to send forth: *The damaged car streamed gasoline onto the pavement.* **6** *Education.* separate (students) into classes or sections according to their academic abilities or educational interests. ⟨OE *strēam*⟩ **—'stream,like,** *adj.*

☛ *Syn. n.* **1. Stream,** CURRENT = a flow of liquid or something fluid. **Stream** emphasizes the idea of a continuous flow, as of water in a river or from a spring or tap: *Because of the lack of rain, many streams dried up.* **Current** emphasizes the strong or rapid, onward movement in a certain direction, and applies particularly to the more swiftly moving part of a stream, ocean, body of air, etc.: *He let his boat drift with the current.* *—v.* **1.** See note at FLOW.

stream•er ['strimər] *n.* **1** any long, narrow, flowing or floating thing: *Streamers of ribbon hung from her hat. Streamers of light are in the northern sky.* **2** a long, narrow flag. **3** a newspaper headline that runs all the way across the page.

Stream•ers ['strimərz] *n. Cdn.* the northern lights; AURORA BOREALIS.

stream•flow ['strim,flou] *n.* the velocity and volume of water flowing at a given time in a channel or stream.

stream•let ['strimlɪt] *n.* a small stream.

stream•line ['strim,laɪn] *n., v.* **-lined, -lin•ing.** *—n.* **1** the path of a particle of a fluid past a solid body in a smooth flow. **2** a shape, or contour, designed to offer as little resistance as possible for motion through air or water.

—v. **1** give such a contour to; design or construct with a streamline: *They began to streamline cars in the 1930s.* **2** bring up to date; modernize: *to streamline the curriculum.* **3** organize to make simpler or more efficient: *to streamline a procedure.*

stream•lined ['strim,laɪnd] *adj., v.* *—adj.* **1** having a contour designed to offer as little resistance as possible for motion through air or water: *The first streamlined car was the 1933 Chrysler.* **2** organized and efficient: *a streamlined program.* **3** without extra bulk, etc.: *a streamlined figure.*

—v. pt. and pp. of STREAMLINE.

stream of consciousness *Psychology.* an individual's mental processes or experiences considered as flowing in an unbroken stream.

stream–of–con•scious•ness ['strim əv 'kɒnʃəsnɪs] *adj.* of or having to do with a style of narrative writing such that the narrator's or character's thoughts and perceptions are recorded in random form, ostensibly as they occur, without regard to sequence or structure.

street [strit] *n.* **1** a public road in a small or large community, usually having sidewalks and buildings along the sides. **2** the part of such a road for automobiles, trucks, etc.: *Don't play in the street.* **3** people who live in the buildings on a street: *The whole street was against the new by-law.* **4** (*adjl.*) of, on, or near the street: *The camera department is on the street level of the store.* **5** (*adjl.*) of clothing, suitable for everyday wear in public: *She changed into her street clothes before leaving the hospital.* **6 the street,** an environment or way of life associated with a part of a city characterized by poverty, crime, prostitution, etc., where survival depends on toughness, scepticism, and self-reliance. **7** (*adjl.*) of, having to do with, or characteristic of such an environment or way of life: *a street kid, street language.*

on or **in the street, a** homeless: *You'll be out in the street if you don't pay your rent soon.* **b** without a job: *He was on the street for three months before he found another job.*

the man in the street, the typical person; the average person. ⟨OE *strǣt* < LL *(via) strata* paved (road), pp. of L *sternere* lay out⟩ **—'street,like,** *adj.*

street Arab STREET URCHIN.

street•car ['strit,kɑr] *n.* a large electrically powered vehicle that runs on rails on city streets and is used for public transportation.

street•light ['strit,ləit] *n.* a powerful light, usually mounted on a pole, that is one of a series of such lights used to provide illumination for the streets of a town or city.

street people **1** people who live mainly in and around the streets of a city, such as vagrants, alienated young people, and the homeless. **2** people of a ghetto or crowded neighbourhood who gather in or frequent the streets of their area.

street smarts the ability, learned by living on the streets, to survive in almost any circumstances, especially in an environment of poverty, danger, and neglect.

street urchin a homeless child who wanders about the streets. Also, **street Arab.**

street•walk•er ['strit,wɒkər] *n.* a prostitute who solicits on the streets.

street•wise ['strit,waɪz] *adj. Informal.* knowledgeable in the ways of the STREET (def. 6); shrewd, sceptical, etc.

strength [strɛŋθ], [strɛŋkθ], *or* [strɛnθ] *n.* **1** the capacity to exert or produce force; power or vigour: *Hercules was a man of great strength.* **2** the capacity to resist force or strain: *the strength of a rope, the strength of a wall. He doesn't have enough strength of mind to stick to a diet.* **3** the capacity to resist attack: *the strength of a fort, the strength of an argument.* **4** the number of effective soldiers, warships, team members, etc.; power measured in numbers: *Our team was not at full strength for the game.* **5** intensity; potency: *the strength of a beverage, the strength of a sound.* **6** a person or thing that gives strength or firmness; support: *He said his children were his strength when his wife died.* **7** the existence of a firm or rising level of stock or commodity prices on an exchange, etc.

on the strength of, relying or depending on; with the support or help of: *We hired the woman on the strength of your recommendation.* ⟨OE *strengthu* < *strang* strong⟩

☛ *Syn.* **1.** See note at POWER.

strength•en ['strɛŋθən], ['strɛŋkθən], *or* ['strɛnθən] *v.* make or become stronger. **—'strength•en•er,** *n.*

stren•u•ous ['strɛnjuəs] *adj.* **1** requiring or marked by much energy or effort: *Squash is a strenuous game. We had a strenuous day moving into the new house.* **2** full of energy; persistently active and vigorous: *strenuous efforts, strenuous opposition.* ⟨< L *strenuus*⟩ **—'stren•u•ous•ly,** *adv.* **—'stren•u•ous•ness,** *n.*

☛ *Syn.* **1, 2.** See note at VIGOROUS.

strep [strɛp] *n. Informal.* **1** streptococcus. **2** STREP THROAT.

strep throat *Informal.* a streptococcal infection characterized by a sore and inflamed throat and, often, fever.

strep•to•coc•cus [,strɛptə'kɒkəs] *n., pl.* **-coc•ci** [-'kɒksaɪ]. *Bacteriology.* any of a group of spherical bacteria that multiply by dividing in only one direction, usually forming chains. Many serious infections and diseases are caused by streptococci. ⟨< NL < Gk. *streptos* curved + *kokkos* grain⟩ **—,strep•to'coc•cal,** *adj.*

strep•to•my•cin [,strɛptə'məisən] *n. Pharmacy.* a powerful antibiotic drug similar to penicillin, effective against tuberculosis, typhoid fever, and certain other bacterial infections. *Formula:* $C_{21}H_{39}N_7O_{12}$ ⟨< Gk. *streptos* curved + *mykēs* fungus⟩

stress [strɛs] *n., v.* *—n.* **1 a** constraining force; physical, mental, or emotional pressure or strain: *under the stress of hunger, the stresses of urban living.* **b** the situation or condition causing such strain. **2** a state or condition resulting from such pressure or strain: *suffering from stress.* **3** *Physics.* **a** a force exerted when one body or body part pushes against, pulls, or twists another body or body part: *Stresses must be carefully balanced in building a bridge.* **b** the intensity of such a force per unit area. It is usually measured in pascals. **c** deformation or strain caused by such a force. **d** the internal opposing resistance when an elastic body reacts to such a force. **4** emphasis or special importance given to something: *The course lays stress on basic computational skills.* **5** emphasis placed on a syllable of a word or a word in an utterance, making it louder or more forceful than the ones surrounding it. In a polysyllabic English word there is always at least one main stress (**primary stress**); there may also be one or more that are somewhat weaker (**secondary stress**). In the word *farmer* the stress is on the first syllable; the second syllable has no stress. In the word *institutionalize* the first and last syllables have secondary stresses and the third syllable has the primary stress. **6** a mark written or printed to show which syllable or syllables of a word are uttered more loudly or forcefully than the surrounding ones. In this dictionary ' is a primary stress and , is a secondary stress; both are placed before the syllable concerned. *Examples:* 'leg•en,da•ry, ,in•sti'tu•tion•al,ize, ,ne•o'clas•si•cist,

'six'teen. 7 *Prosody.* **a** emphasis or prominence given to a syllable or word as part of a metrical pattern. **b** a syllable given such emphasis. 8 *Music.* accent.
—*v.* 1 give emphasis or importance to: *to stress safety on the job.* 2 pronounce with stress: Accept *is stressed on the second syllable.* 3 place under stress. ⟨partly < *distress,* partly < OF *estrece* narrowness, oppression, ult. < L *strictus,* pp. of *stringere* draw tight⟩

stretch [strɛtʃ] *v., n.* —*v.* 1 draw out or be drawn out; extend or be extended to full length: *The blow stretched him out on the ground. She stretched luxuriously in the sunshine.* 2 continue over a distance; extend from one place to another; fill space; spread: *The forest stretches for miles.* 3 extend one's body or limbs. 4 straighten out. 5 reach out; hold out: *He stretched out his hand for the money.* 6 draw out to greater or too great size; draw out of the original shape or proportion: *Stretch the shoe a little.* 7 become longer or wider without breaking: *Rubber stretches.* 8 draw tight; strain: *She stretched the violin string until it broke.* 9 make great effort. 10 cause to make a great or maximum effort, often resulting in greater ability. 11 extend beyond proper limits: *He stretched the law to suit his purpose.* 12 *Informal.* exaggerate: *to stretch the truth.*
—*n.* 1 an unbroken length; extent: *A stretch of sand hills lay between the road and the ocean.* 2 a continuous length of time. 3 *Slang.* a term of imprisonment. 4 *Racing.* one of the two straight sides of a course, especially the part between the last turn and the finish line. Also, **home stretch.** 5 the action of stretching or the state of being stretched. 6 a capacity for stretching: *a textile fabric with stretch.* 7 (*adjl.*) capable of being stretched; elastic: *a stretch fabric for swimsuits, a stretch wig.* ⟨OE *streccan*⟩ —**'stretch•y,** *adj.*

stretch•er ['strɛtʃər] *n.* 1 a frame or other device for stretching something: *a glove stretcher.* 2 a frame having a canvas or similar covering and either wheels or carrying handles on which to move the sick, wounded, or dead. 3 *Masonry.* a brick or stone laid horizontally with its length along the length of a wall. Compare HEADER (def. 3). 4 *Carpentry.* a piece extending between two other pieces of a framework in order to brace or support them, as the legs of a chair.

stretcher–bearer ['strɛtʃər ˌbɛrər] *n.* a person who helps to carry an injured person on a STRETCHER (def. 2), especially on the battlefield or at the scene of a disaster.

stretcher case a person who has to be carried on a stretcher because of serious injury or illness: *Several bus passengers were hurt in the accident, but there were no stretcher cases.*

stretch•out ['strɛtʃˌʌut] *n.* 1 a practice of labour management in a company or industry whereby workers are required to do extra work without extra compensation. 2 an extension of the time schedule for meeting a production quota.

strew [stru] *v.* **strewed, strewn** or **strewed, strew•ing.** 1 scatter; sprinkle: *The pages were strewn all over the floor. He strewed shredded coconut on the cake.* 2 cover with something scattered or sprinkled: *The bed was strewn with dirty clothes.* 3 be scattered over; be sprinkled over: *Litter strewed the lawn.* ⟨OE *strēowian*⟩

strewn [strun] *n.* a pp. of STREW.

stri•a ['straɪə] *n., pl.* **-ae** [-i] *or* [-aɪ]. 1 a slight furrow or channel. 2 a linear marking; a narrow stripe or streak, as of colour or texture, especially one of a number in parallel arrangement: *the striae of the voluntary muscles.* 3 *Architecture.* a fillet between the flutes of columns, etc. 4 *Geology. Mineralogy.* one of the parallel lines on the face of a glaciated surface or a crystal. ⟨< L⟩

stri•at•ed ['straɪeitɪd] *adj.* striped, streaked, or furrowed: *the striated plumage of a bird, a striated muscle.* ⟨< L *striatus,* pp. of *striare* furrow, channel < *stria* furrow, channel⟩

stri•a•tion [straɪ'eiʃən] *n.* 1 a striated condition or appearance. 2 a stria; one of a number of parallel striae.

strick•en ['strɪkən] *adj., v.* —*adj.* affected or overwhelmed by disease, trouble, sorrow, etc.: *a stricken conscience. Help was rushed to the fire-stricken city.*
stricken in years, old.
—*v.* a pp. of STRIKE.

strick•le ['strɪkəl] *n., v.* **-led, -ling.** —*n.* 1 a stick for levelling the contents of a filled container. 2 a tool for sharpening a blade.
—*v.* use a strickle on. ⟨ME *strikile* < OE *stricel* < *strican.* See STRIKE.⟩

strict [strɪkt] *adj.* 1 enforcing a rule or set of rules with great care: *The teacher was strict but not unfair.* 2 requiring complete obedience: *They were under strict orders not to leave the barracks.* 3 exact; precise: *a strict translation. He wasn't trespassing in the strict sense of the word.* 4 complete; absolute: *It was told to him in strict confidence. She lives in strict seclusion.* 5 very careful in following a standard or principle: *a strict Muslim.* 6 *Archaic.* close; tight. ⟨< L *strictus,* pp. of *stringere* bind tight. Doublet of STRAIT.⟩ —**'strict•ly,** *adv.* —**'strict•ness,** *n.*

☛ *Syn.* **1, 2. Strict,** RIGID, RIGOROUS = severe and unyielding or stern. **Strict** emphasizes showing or demanding a very careful and close following of a rule, standard, or requirement: *Our supervisor is strict and insists that we follow instructions.* **Rigid** emphasizes being firm and unyielding, not changing or relaxing for anyone or under any conditions: *He maintains a rigid working schedule.* **Rigorous** emphasizes the severity or sternness of the demands made, conditions imposed, etc.: *We believe in rigorous enforcement of the laws.*

stric•ture ['strɪktʃər] *n.* 1 an unfavourable criticism; critical remark. 2 an abnormal narrowing of some duct or tube of the body. 3 something that binds or limits; a restriction. ⟨< L *strictura* < *stringere* bind tight⟩

strid•den ['strɪdən] *v.* pp. of STRIDE.

stride [straɪd] *v.* **strode, strid•den, strid•ing;** *n.* —*v.* 1 walk with long steps (along or through): *She was striding too fast for me. He strode the streets all morning.* 2 pass with one long step: *He strode over the brook.* 3 *Archaic or poetic.* bestride or straddle.
—*n.* 1 a long step: *With two strides he was at the door.* 2 the distance covered by such a step. 3 a striding gait: *The child could not keep up with her father's stride.* 4 of a quadruped, one complete progressive movement finished when the legs return to their original relative positions; the distance so covered: *The distance between the next pair of jumps on this equestrian course is four strides.* 5 **strides,** *pl.* progress at an unexpectedly good rate: *She has made great strides on this project.*
hit (one's) **stride,** reach one's normal speed or level of efficiency: *By the second day of working together they had hit their stride and were making good progress.*
take in stride or **in** (one's) **stride,** do or handle without difficulty or hesitation; cope with easily: *She took the defeat in stride. The award came as a surprise, but she took it in her stride.* ⟨OE *strīdan*⟩ —**'strid•er,** *n.*

☛ *Syn. v.* **1.** See note at WALK.

stri•dent ['straɪdənt] *adj.* 1 making or having a harsh sound; grating or shrill: *a strident voice, the strident sound of a power saw.* 2 commanding attention in an unpleasant, irritating way: *strident colours. They agreed with his argument, but they didn't like the strident tone of the letter.* ⟨< L *stridens, -entis,* ppr. of *stridere* sound harshly⟩ —**'stri•dence** or **'stri•den•cy,** *adj.* —**'stri•dent•ly,** *adv.*

strid•u•lant ['strɪdʒələnt] *adj.* stridulating. Also, **stridulous.**

strid•u•late ['strɪdʒəˌleit] *v.* **-lat•ed, -lat•ing.** produce a shrill, grating sound, as a cricket or katydid does, by rubbing together certain parts of the body. ⟨< NL *stridulare* < L *stridulus* producing a harsh or grating sound < *stridere* sound harshly⟩ —**ˌstrid•u'la•tion,** *n.* —**'strid•u•laˌto•ry** ['strɪdʒələˌtɔri], *adj.*

strife [strəif] *n.* 1 the act or fact of quarrelling or fighting; bitter or violent conflict: *The relationship between the siblings had always been full of strife.* 2 a struggle or contest between rivals. ⟨ME < OF *estrif* < Gmc.⟩

strig•il ['strɪdʒəl] *n.* in ancient Greece and Rome, a scraper for the skin, used after physical exercise, a bath, etc. ⟨< L *strigilis;* related to *stringere* draw tight, strip off, scrape⟩

strike [strəik] *v.* **struck, struck** or **strick•en, strik•ing;** *n.* —*v.* 1 hit (someone or something); deal a blow to: *to strike a person in anger.* 2 deal; give: *to strike a blow in self-defence.* 3 make by stamping; printing, etc.: *to strike a medal.* 4 set or be set on fire by hitting or rubbing: *to strike a match.* 5 affect the mind or feeling of; impress: *The plan strikes me as silly.* 6 cause to impact forcefully (with something): *She struck the cymbals. They struck their hands together.* 7 sound; signal or indicate by sounding: *The clock strikes twelve times at noon. The clock struck midnight.* 8 overcome, as by death, disease, suffering, fear, etc.: *They were struck with terror.* 9 make an attack: *The enemy will strike at dawn.* 10 occur to: *An amusing thought struck her.* 11 find or come upon (ore, oil, water, etc.). 12 refuse to work at a factory, business, etc. in order to get better pay or achieve other demands: *The coal miners struck.* 13 cross; rub: *Strike out the last word. Strike his name off the list.* 14 take, put, etc. by a blow: *Strike off his head.* 15 proceed or advance, especially in a new direction or at a different speed: *We struck into a gallop. We walked along the road 1 km, then struck out across the fields.* 16 assume: *She struck an attitude.* 17 penetrate: *The roots of oaks strike deep. Her comments strike to the heart of the manner.* 18 get by figuring: *Strike an average.* 19 enter upon; make; decide: *The employer and the workers have struck an agreement.* 20 lower or take down (a sail, flag, tent, etc.). 21 strickle; make level with

the top edge of a measure. **22** of a snake, etc., wound or try to wound with fangs, claws, or sting. **23** of fish, take hold of the bait: *The fish are striking well today.* **24** hook (a fish that has taken the bait) by jerking the line sharply. **25** collide with suddenly and forcefully: *The car struck a fence.* **26** fall on; touch; reach; catch: *The sun struck his eyes.* **27** come across; come upon; find: *to strike an amusing book.* **28** *Theatre.* remove (a scene) from the stage; remove the scenery, etc. of (a play). **29** take down (a tent or tents); break (camp).
strike a balance, a find the difference between the credit and debit sides of an account. **b** adopt a moderate course between two extremes.
strike home, a make an effective thrust or stroke with a weapon or tool. **b** make a strong impression: *The words of warning struck home.*
strike it rich, *Informal.* **a** find rich ore, oil, etc. **b** have a sudden or unexpected great success.
strike out, a cross out; rub out. **b** *Baseball.* fail to hit three times: *The batter struck out.* **c** *Baseball.* cause to fail to hit three times: *The pitcher struck out six players.* **d** fail. **e** *Swimming.* use arms and legs to move forward. **f** aim a blow from the shoulder. **g** make a start by personal effort or enterprise.
strike up, a begin or cause to begin: *The two boys struck up a friendship. Strike up the band!* **b** begin to play, sing, or sound: *to strike up a song.*
—n. **1** the act or fact of finding rich ore in mining, oil in drilling, etc.; sudden success. **2** a general quitting of work in order to force an employer or employers to agree to the workers' demands for higher wages, shorter hours, etc. **3** the act of striking. **4** *Baseball.* **a** the failure of the batter to make a proper hit. **b** a pitched ball that passes above the plate at a height between the level of the batter's shoulders and that of his or her knees. **5** *Bowling.* **a** an upsetting of all the pins with the first ball bowled. **b** the score so made. **6** a number of coins made at one time. **7** a taking hold of the bait. **8** a sudden jerk on the line by a fisher in order to hook the fish that has taken the bait. **9** a metal piece in a doorjamb, into which the latch of a lock fits when the door closes. Also, **strike plate. 10** an attack.
on strike, having stopped work to get more pay, shorter hours, etc.: *The workers voted to go on strike.* ⟨OE *strican* rub, stroke⟩

strike–bound ['strəik ˌbaʊnd] *adj.* immobilized by a labour strike.

strike•break•er ['strəikˌbreikər] *n.* a person actively involved in trying to break up a strike, especially one hired to replace a striking employee.

strike•break•ing ['strəikˌbreikɪŋ] *n.* forceful measures taken to break up a strike.

strike•out ['strəikˌʌut] *n. Baseball.* **1** an out made by a pitcher throwing three strikes against the batter. **2** the act of striking out. *Abbrev.*: so or s.o.

strike plate STRIKE (def. *n.* 9).

strik•er ['strəikər] *n.* **1** a person who or thing that strikes. **2** a worker who is on strike. **3** *Soccer.* the main attacking forward of a team. **4** a hammer or clapper in a clock that strikes the hour or rings an alarm.

strike zone *Baseball.* the area above home plate through which the ball must be pitched for the umpire to call a strike. It extends from the batter's knees to the top of the lettering on his or her uniform.

strik•ing ['strəikɪŋ] *adj., v. —adj.* **1** attracting attention because of some unusual quality; remarkable: *a striking use of colour, a striking dress.* **2** that strikes or is on strike: *The striking workers have rejected the latest offer.*
—v. ppr. of STRIKE. **—'strik•ing•ly,** *adv.* **—'strik•ing•ness,** *n.*

Strine [straɪn] *n.* Australian English. ⟨< *Australian* as pronounced by Australians; coined by A. Morrison⟩

string [strɪŋ] *n., v.* **strung, strung** or *(rare)* **stringed, string•ing.**
—n. **1** fine cord or thick thread consisting of twisted fibres. **2** a piece of this. **3** a series of objects threaded or hung on a string: *a string of pearls, a string of fish.* **4** a length of wire, catgut, or nylon for a musical instrument or sports racket: *the strings of a violin, the strings of a tennis racket.* **5 strings,** *pl. Music.* **a** violins, cellos, and other stringed instruments collectively. **b** the section of an orchestra composed of stringed instruments. **6** anything used for tying: *apron strings.* **7** a cordlike part of a plant, especially the tough fibre connecting the two halves of the pod of a STRING BEAN. **8** a series or sequence of like things in a line or as if in a line: *a string of cars, a string of victories.* **9** *Informal.* a condition; proviso: *an offer with strings attached to it.* **10** the racehorses belonging to a particular stable or owner. **11** a group of persons or things under the same ownership or management: *a string of restaurants.* **12** a squad of contestants or players grouped according to ability, as **first string** (the best), **second string,** etc. **13 a** STRINGER (def. 7). **b** stringcourse. **14** *Computer technology. Linguistics.* any sequence of characters, words, etc. treated as a unit.
have or **keep** (someone) **on a string,** dominate or control someone completely.
have two strings to (one's) **bow,** have more than one way of doing or getting something.
pull strings, use one's influence, especially secretly: *There were more qualified applicants, but he got the job because she pulled some strings for him.*
pull the strings, direct the actions of others, often secretly: *He is supposed to be retired, but he still pulls the strings on all the company's big deals.*
—v. **1** thread or hang on a string: *to string beads.* **2** furnish with a string or strings: *to string a violin, to string a bow. She had her tennis racket strung.* **3** tie or hang with a string or rope: *We dry herbs by stringing them from the rafters in the barn.* **4** extend or stretch from one point to another: *to string a cable.* **5** tune the strings of (an instrument). **6** remove the stringy fibres from: *We sat there stringing beans.* **7** form into a string or strings. **8** move, lie, or arrange in a line or series. **9** *Slang.* fool or deceive (*often used with* **along**): *Are you stringing me?*
string along, *Informal.* **a** go along; follow: *He asked if he could string along with them.* **b** agree or accept: *stringing along with the majority opinion.* **c** deceive; keep up the hopes of by giving encouragement, making false promises, etc.
string (someone) **a line,** *Informal.* deceive or try to deceive with words.
string out, prolong; stretch; extend: *The program was strung out too long.*
string up, *Informal.* kill by hanging: *The horse thief was caught and strung up from the nearest tree.* ⟨OE *streng*⟩ **—'string•less,** *adj.* **—'stringˌlike,** *adj.*

string bass DOUBLE BASS.

string bean 1 a green bean or wax bean, especially a variety having stringlike fibres connecting the two halves of the pod. **2** *Informal.* a tall, very thin person.

string•board ['strɪŋˌbɔrd] *n.* the board or facing that covers the ends of the steps in a staircase.

string bog *Cdn.* a series or chain of small sinkholes or patches of muskeg, as distinguished from a large swamp or bog.

string•course ['strɪŋˌkɔrs] *n. Architecture.* a horizontal band running around a structure, usually raised and decorated.

stringed instrument a musical instrument having strings, played by striking, by plucking, or with a bow. The violin, piano, harp, and guitar are stringed instruments.

strin•gent ['strɪndʒənt] *adj.* **1** strict; severe: *stringent laws.* **2** lacking ready money; tight: *a stringent market for loans.* **3** convincing; forcible: *stringent arguments.* ⟨< L *stringens, -entis,* ppr. of *stringere* bind tight⟩ **—'strin•gen•cy,** *n.* **—'strin•gent•ly,** *adv.*

string•er ['strɪŋər] *n.* **1** a person who or thing that strings. **2 a** a long, horizontal supporting timber in a building. **b** a stringpiece. **3** a part-time or local correspondent for a newspaper or magazine. **4** a newspaper correspondent paid on the basis of linage. **5** a member of a team ranked according to ability; person ranked according to ability: *a first-stringer.* **6** a heavy, horizontal timber or girder supporting the ties of a railroad trestle or bridge or the flooring of a wooden bridge. **7** a stringboard. **8** *Geology.* a narrow vein of a mineral. **9** the long, light reinforcement of an airplane fuselage, a rocket, etc. **10** *Fishing.* **a** a long, stout cord or wire that can be passed through the gills of fish that have been caught. **b** *Cdn.* a chain along which a number of snap hooks are spaced, used for stringing caught fish, each being attached through a gill to one of the hooks. **11** *Cdn.* a log or timber set across a stream to serve as a footbridge.

string•halt ['strɪŋˌhɒlt] *n.* a lame condition of one or both hind legs of a horse, caused by spasms of the muscles that make the legs jerk when the horse walks. Also, **springhalt.**

string•piece ['strɪŋˌpis] *n.* a long, horizontal beam used to strengthen or connect parts of a framework.

string quartet 1 a quartet of performers on stringed instruments. **2** the instruments themselves, usually consisting of two violins, a viola, and a cello. **3** a composition for string quartet.

string tie a short, narrow necktie.

string•y ['strɪŋi] *adj.* **string•i•er, string•i•est. 1** like, containing, or consisting of fibres or strings: *tough, stringy meat.*

Her hair was long and stringy. **2** forming strings: *a stringy syrup.* **3** lean and sinewy; wiry: *a boy of about sixteen, tall and stringy.* **—'string•i•ness,** *n.*

strip¹ [strɪp] *v., n.* —*v.* **stripped** or *(rare)* **stript, strip•ping.** **1** remove the clothing, covering, or outer layer from: *to strip a bed, to strip a baby for a bath, to strip a banana, to strip a table for refinishing.* **2** undress: *He stripped down to his shorts.* **3** perform a striptease. **4** tear or pull off; remove: *to strip wallpaper from a wall, to strip the fruit from a tree.* **5** make bare; clear out or empty: *to strip a house of its furniture, to strip a forest of its timber.* **6** take away the titles, rights, etc. of. **7** deprive of or rob: *to be stripped of one's pride.* **8** break or damage the thread or teeth of (a gear, screw, etc.). **9** milk (a cow) thoroughly. **10** dismantle or disassemble (a machine, gun, etc.) for cleaning, repairing, etc.
—*n.* the act or an instance of undressing or of performing a striptease. ⟨OE *-strīepan,* as in *bestrīepan* plunder⟩

strip² [strɪp] *n.* **1** a long, narrow, flat piece of some material: *a strip of metal, a strip of paper. She tore the cloth into strips for a bandage. The bark came off in strips.* **2** a long, narrow tract of land, forest, etc. **3** an airstrip. **4** a COMIC STRIP. **5** *Philately.* three or more stamps attached in a vertical or horizontal row. ⟨probably < MLG *strippe* strap⟩

strip cropping or **planting** the planting of alternate rows of crops having strong and weak root systems, done along the contours of a slope to lessen soil erosion.

stripe¹ [strəip] *n., v.* **striped, strip•ing.** —*n.* **1** a long, narrow band of different colour or texture: *A tiger has black stripes. The wallpaper is white with green stripes.* **2** fabric, wallpaper, etc. having a pattern of parallel bands: *She used a stripe for the slipcovers.* **3 stripes,** *pl.* a number or combination of strips of braid on the sleeve of a uniform to show rank, length of service, etc. **4** a sort; type: *people of a different stripe.*
—*v.* mark with stripes. ⟨< MDu.⟩

stripe² [strəip] *n.* a stroke or lash with a whip. ⟨probably a special use of *stripe¹*⟩

striped [strəipt] *adj., v.*—*adj.* having stripes; marked with stripes.
—*v.* pt. and pp. of STRIPE¹.

striped bass a game and food fish (*Morone saxatilis*) of coastal North America, of a silvery colour with black stripes along the side. Also, **striper.**

strip•ling ['strɪplɪŋ] *n.* an adolescent boy; youth. ⟨< *strip²* + *-ling*⟩

strip mine a mine operated by digging out layers of earth on the surface to expose the ore. **—strip mining.**

stripped–down ['strɪpt 'daʊn] *adj.* reduced to essentials.

strip•per ['strɪpər] *n.* **1** a person who or thing that strips. **2** an oil well producing several hours daily and requiring time to rebuild pressure before the oil flows again. **3** a striptease dancer.

strip poker a type of poker in which the loser of each hand must take off a piece of clothing.

stript [strɪpt] *v.* a pt. and a pp. of STRIP¹.

strip•tease ['strɪp,tiz] *n.* **1** an entertainment in which a performer slowly undresses before an audience, to the accompaniment of music. **2** *(adjl.)* of, having to do with, or featuring striptease: *a striptease act, a striptease club.* **—'strip,teas•er,** *n.*

strive [straɪv] *v.* **strove** or **strived, striv•en, striv•ing. 1** try hard; make a great effort: *to strive for self-control.* **2** fight or contend; vie: *The swimmer strove against the tide. The wrestlers strove with each other.* ⟨ME < OF *estriver* < Gmc.⟩

striv•en ['strɪvən] *v.* pp. of STRIVE.

strobe [stroub] *n.* **1** STROBE LIGHT. **2** stroboscope.

strobe light an apparatus for producing very brief, brilliant flashes of light, either by means of a neon- or xenon-filled tube in which rapid electric discharges produce flashes of light or by means of a steady, intense light with a rotating, perforated disk in front of it or a rotating, perforated globe around the whole light, casting the beams in all directions. Strobe lights are used in photography, theatre, discothèques, etc. ⟨short for *stroboscope*⟩

stro•bi•la [strou'baɪlə] *n., pl.* **-lae** [-li] *or* [-laɪ] *Zoology.* **1** the main body of a tapeworm, excluding the head and neck. **2** the chain of segments of the larval, attached stage of scyphozoan jellyfish, each segment giving rise to a free-swimming form by transverse budding. ⟨< Mod.L < Gk. *strobile* plug of lint shaped like a pine cone⟩

stro•bile ['strɒbaɪl] *or* ['stroubəl] *n. Botany.* any seed-producing cone, such as a pine cone, or a compact mass of scalelike leaves that produce spores, such as the cone of the club moss. ⟨< LL < Gk. *strobilos* pine cone < *strobos* a whirling around⟩

stro•bo•scope ['stroubə,skoup] *n.* **1** an instrument for studying periodic motion by the illumination of a moving body in flashes or at intervals. **2** STROBE LIGHT. ⟨< G *Stroboskop* < Gk. *strobos* a whirling + G *-skop,* equivalent to E *-scope*⟩ **—,stro•bo'scop•ic** [,stroubə'skɒpɪk], *adj.*

strode [stroud] *v.* pt. of STRIDE.

stro•ga•noff ['strougə,nɒf] *or* ['strɒgə,nɒf] *adj.* denoting a dish of meat cooked with sour cream, onions, mushrooms, and spices (*used after a noun*): *beef stroganoff.* ⟨prob. eponymic; identity uncertain⟩

stroke¹ [strouk] *n., v.* **stroked, strok•ing.** —*n.* **1** an act of striking; blow: *The house was hit by a stroke of lightning.* **2** a sound made by striking: *We arrived on the stroke of three.* **3** a piece of luck, fortune, etc.: *a stroke of bad luck.* **4** *Mechanics.* **a** a single complete movement to be made again and again, especially of a moving part or parts, in one direction and, sometimes, back again in the other. **b** the distance travelled by this part. **5** *Tennis, golf, etc.* the hitting of a ball. **6** a throb or pulsing, as of the heart. **7** a movement or mark made by a pen, pencil, brush, etc.: *He writes with a heavy down stroke.* **8** a vigorous attempt to attain some object: *a bold stroke for freedom.* **9** a feat or achievement: *a stroke of genius.* **10** an effective or noteworthy touch in any art form, especially literature. **11** an act, piece, or amount of work, etc.: *a stroke of work.* **12** *Pathology.* **a** a sudden injury to the brain caused by the rupture or blockage of a blood vessel, resulting in a sudden inability to feel or move, with partial or complete loss of consciousness. **b** a sudden attack of any of various illnesses (*used only in compounds*): *heatstroke, sunstroke.* **13** a sudden action like a blow in its effect, as in causing pain, injury, or death: *a stroke of fate, the stroke of death.* **14** *Swimming.* **a** one of a series of propelling movements, involving the pull of one arm (or both together) with one or more kicks. **b** a style or method of swimming: *She has mastered the butterfly stroke.* **15** *Rowing.* **a** a single pull of the oar. **b** the style or rate of pulling the oars: *She rows with a strong stroke.* **c** STROKE OAR (def. 2).
keep stroke, make strokes at the same time.
—*v.* **1** act as the stroke of (a rowing crew): *Who stroked the Vancouver crew?* **2** mark with a stroke or strokes, especially in order to cancel. ⟨Related to STRIKE or its source⟩ **—'strok•er,** *n.*
☛ *Syn. n.* **1.** See note at BLOW¹.

stroke² [strouk] *v.* **stroked, strok•ing;** *n.* —*v.* **1** move the hand gently over: *She stroked the kitten.* **2** flatter, praise, etc. to approve or to persuade.
stroke the wrong way, a stroke (an animal) in the direction contrary to that in which the fur naturally lies. **b** ruffle or irritate (a person), especially by going counter to his or her wishes.
—*n.* **1** a stroking movement. **2 strokes,** *pl.* flattery or praise, usually with the intent to show approval or to persuade. ⟨OE *strācian*⟩

stroke oar 1 the oar nearest the stern of the boat. **2 a** the rower who pulls this oar, setting the time of the stroke for the other rowers. **b** the position of this rower.

stroll [stroul] *v., n.* —*v.* **1** take a quiet walk for pleasure; walk. **2** wander from place to place. **3** stroll along or through: *Every evening they strolled the path by the river.*
—*n.* a leisurely walk. ⟨origin uncertain⟩

stroll•er ['stroulər] *n.* **1** a kind of light carriage for wheeling a young child, in which the child can sit upright. **2** a person who strolls: *The park was filled with strollers.* **3** a wanderer, especially an actor who goes from place to place in search of work.

stro•mat•o•lite [strou'mætə,ləit] *n. Geology.* a laminated, calcareous fossil structure built primarily in the Precambrian period by marine algae, having a rounded or columnar shape. These formations are still being produced, and serve as evidence for dating early life forms. ⟨< Gk. *stroma* cover + E *-lite*⟩ **—,stro•mat•o'lit•ic** [strou,mætə'lɪtɪk], *adj.*

strong [strɒŋ] *adj., adv.* —*adj.* **1** having much force or power of any kind, physical, moral, political, etc.: *a strong wind, strong muscles, a strong nation.* **2** able to last, endure, resist, etc.: *a strong fort, a strong rope.* **3** healthy; thriving; robust. **4** not easily influenced, changed, etc.; firm: *a strong will.* **5** able, skilled, or talented in a particular field. **6** of great force or effectiveness: *strong arguments.* **7** having a certain number: *The group numbered 100 strong.* **8** having a particular quality or property in high degree: *a strong poison, a strong acid, strong tea.* **9** containing much alcohol: *a strong drink.* **10** having much

flavour or odour: *strong seasoning, strong perfume.* **11** having an unpleasant taste or smell: *strong butter.* **12** intense: *a strong light.* **13** arousing, expressing, or characterized by powerful emotion: *strong words, a strong dislike.* **14** of stocks or the stock market, steady or advancing toward higher prices. **15** *Grammar.* of or designating a verb or class of verbs inflected by a vowel change within the stem of the word. *Examples*: *find, found; give, gave, given; sing, sang, sung.* **16** of a syllable or beat, stressed or accented.
—*adv.* in a strong manner: *They're still going strong.* ⟨OE *strang*⟩
—**'strong•ly,** *adv.*

☛ *Syn. adj.* **1, 2. Strong,** STURDY, ROBUST = having or showing much power, force, or vigour. **Strong** is the general word, describing people, animals, plants, or things, and especially suggesting great power or force in acting, resisting, or enduring: *Loggers need strong backs and arms.* **Sturdy** suggests unyielding power or strength coming from good, solid construction: *Children need sturdy clothes.* **Robust** emphasizes healthy vigour of mind or body and a toughness of muscle or spirit: *Sports make children robust.*

strong–arm ['strɒŋ ˌɑrm] *adj., v. Informal.* —*adj.* having or using force or violence: *strong-arm tactics.*
—*v.* use force or violence on: *to strong-arm someone into submission.*

strong•box ['strɒŋˌbɒks] *n.* a strongly made box for holding valuables.

strong breeze *Meteorology.* a wind with a speed between 39 and 49 km/h. See chart of Beaufort scale in the Appendix.

strong drink alcoholic drink; liquor.

strong force or **interaction** *Physics.* the interaction between elementary particles that holds the nucleus of an atom together. Compare WEAK FORCE.

strong gale *Meteorology.* a wind with a speed between 75 and 88 km/h. See chart of Beaufort scale in the Appendix.

strong•hold ['strɒŋˌhould] *n.* **1** a fort or fortress. **2** a secure place or centre: *a stronghold of freedom. The city is the stronghold of the Liberal party in the province.*

strong•man ['strɒŋˌmæn] *n., pl.* **-men. 1** a muscular man who performs feats of strength in a carnival, circus, etc. **2** a leader who obtains power by force and suppression; dictator.

strong–mind•ed ['strɒŋ 'maɪndɪd] *adj.* **1** having a strong mind; mentally vigorous. **2** determined; strong-willed; stubborn. —**'strong-'mind•ed•ly,** *adv.* —**'strong-'mind•ed•ness,** *n.*

strong•room ['strɒŋˌrum] *or* [strɒŋˌrʊm] *n.* a specially built room, usually burglar- and fireproof, in which valuables are placed for safekeeping.

strong woods *Cdn.* forest; big trees; heavy woods. ⟨translation of F *bois fort(s)*⟩

stron•tia ['strɒnʃə], ['strɒntʃə], ['strɒntjə], *or* ['strɒntiə] *n. Chemistry.* **1** a greyish white amorphous powder resembling lime. Also, **strontium oxide.** *Formula*: SrO **2** STRONTIUM HYDROXIDE.

stron•tian ['strɒnʃən], ['strɒntʃən], ['strɒntjə], *or* ['strɒntiən] *n.* strontium, especially in compounds.

stron•tium ['strɒnʃəm], ['strɒntʃəm], ['strɒntjəm], *or* ['strɒntiəm] *n. Chemistry.* a soft, silvery white, metallic element which occurs only in combination with other elements. Strontium is used in making alloys and in fireworks and signal flares. *Symbol*: Sr; *at.no.* 38; *at.mass* 87.62. ⟨< NL *strontium* < *Strontian*, a parish in Scotland, the site of the lead mines where strontium was first discovered⟩

strontium hydroxide *Chemistry.* **1** a white powder, slightly soluble in water, used chiefly to refine beet sugar. *Formula*: $Sr(OH)_2$ **2** STRONTIA (def. 1).

strontium 90 *Chemistry.* a radioactive isotope of strontium that occurs in the fallout from nuclear explosions. Strontium 90 is dangerous because it is absorbed by bones and tissues and may replace the calcium in the body.

strop [strɒp] *n., v.* **stropped, strop•ping.** —*n.* STRAP (defs. 1, 2).
—*v.* sharpen on a strop. ⟨ME; ult. < L *stroppus* band < Gk. *strophos*⟩

stro•phe ['stroufi] *n.* **1 a** the part of an ancient Greek ode sung by the chorus when moving from right to left. **b** such movement of the chorus. Compare ANTISTROPHE. **2** a series of lines forming a division of a poem and having metrical structure which is repeated in a second group of lines (the antistrophe), especially in ancient Greek choral and lyric poetry. **3** any of two or more metrically corresponding series of lines forming divisions of a lyric poem; stanza. ⟨< Gk. *strophē*, originally, a turning (i.e., a section sung by the chorus while turning)⟩
—**'stroph•ic** ['strɒfɪk] *or* ['stroufɪk], *adj.*

stroud [straʊd] *n. Cdn.* **1** a heavy woollen cloth popular in the

North as material for blankets, leggings, capotes, etc. **2** a garment or blanket made of this material. ⟨< *Stroud*, England, where it was first made⟩

strove [strouv] *v.* a pt. of STRIVE.

struck [strʌk] *v., adj.* —*v.* pt. and a pp. of STRIKE.
—*adj.* closed or affected in some way by a strike of workers: *The newspaper plant has been struck for a week.*

struc•tur•al ['strʌktʃərəl] *adj.* **1** of or having to do with building. **Structural steel** is steel made into beams, girders, etc. **2** of or having to do with structure or structures: *the structural differences between the two organizations.* **3** of or proceeding from STRUCTURAL LINGUISTICS: *structural grammar.* **4** *Biology.* of or having to do with the organic structure of an animal or plant; morphological. **5** *Geology.* having to do with the structure of rock, the earth's crust, etc. **6** *Chemistry.* of or showing the placement or manner of attachment of the atoms that make up a particular molecule. —**'struc•tur•al•ly,** *adv.*

struc•tur•al•ism ['strʌktʃərəˌlɪzəm] *n.* any theory or study that tends to emphasize structure more than function, especially in psychology, linguistics, etc. —**'struc•tur•al•ist,** *n., adj.*

structural linguistics a branch of linguistic study in which languages are analysed and described in terms of their structural elements and the patterns in which these elements combine, with little or no regard to meaning or to underlying forms.

structural protein *Biochemistry.* a protein that plays a structural rather than enzymatic function in the body.

struc•ture ['strʌktʃər] *n., v.* **-tured, -tur•ing.** —*n.* **1** a building; something built. **2** anything composed of parts arranged together: *The human body is a wonderful structure.* **3** the manner of building; the way parts are put together; construction: *The structure of the apartment building was excellent.* **4** the arrangement or interrelation of parts, elements, etc. forming something, especially as it determines its special character or nature: *the structure of a molecule, the structure of a sentence, a complex economic structure.*
—*v.* **1** make into a structure; build; fabricate. **2** organize; put together in a systematic way. **3** make structured. ⟨< L *structura* < *struere* arrange⟩

☛ *Syn.* **1.** See note at BUILDING.

struc•tured ['strʌktʃərd] *adj., v.* —*adj.* regimented; systematized; formalized: *Some students thrive in a highly structured classroom environment.*
—*v.* pt. and pp. of STRUCTURE.

stru•del ['strudəl]; *German,* ['ʃtʀudəl] *n.* a pastry made of very thin dough rolled up around a filling, usually of some fruit, such as apples, cherries, etc., and baked. ⟨< G⟩

strug•gle ['strʌgəl] *v.* **-gled, -gling;** *n.* —*v.* **1** move one's arms and legs about violently in an effort to get free: *The child struggled to get down from her mother's lap.* **2** make strong efforts against an opponent or against difficulties; try hard: *For years she had to struggle to make a living. He struggled to control his anger. He struggled mightily to overcome the stronger man, but to no avail.* **3** move or make one's way with great effort: *She struggled through the hedge. The old man struggled to his feet.*
—*n.* **1** great effort or hard work: *It was always a struggle for her to express herself.* **2** fighting; conflict: *In the 16th century England and Spain were engaged in a struggle for control of the seas.* ⟨ME *strugle(n)*, *strogele(n)*; origin uncertain⟩ —**'strug•gler,** *n.*

strum [strʌm] *v.* **strummed, strum•ming;** *n.* —*v.* **1** play by brushing the fingers across the strings (of): *to strum a guitar. We heard her strumming on her banjo.* **2** produce (music) in this way: *to strum a tune.*
—*n.* the act or an instance or the sound of strumming: *the strum of a banjo.* ⟨? imitative⟩ —**'strum•mer,** *n.*

stru•ma ['strumə] *n., pl.* **-mae** [-mi] *or* [-maɪ]. **1 a** scrofula. **b** goitre. **2** *Botany.* a cushionlike swelling on an organ. ⟨< NL < L⟩

strum•pet ['strʌmpɪt] *n. Archaic.* a prostitute. ⟨ME; origin uncertain⟩

strung [strʌŋ] *v.* pt. and a pp. of STRING.

strung out *Slang.* **1** weakened, etc. in body or mind by addiction to a drug. **2** suffering the effects of severe mental strain due to any cause.

strut¹ [strʌt] *v.* **strut•ted, strut•ting;** *n.* —*v.* walk in a stiff, erect manner, suggesting vanity or self-importance: *He strutted about the room in his new jacket.*
strut (one's) **stuff,** *Informal.* show off one's capabilities or skills.

—*n.* a strutting walk. ⟨ME *stroute,* OE *strūtian* stand out stiffly. Akin to STRUT[2].⟩ **—'strut•ter,** *n.*

☛ *Syn. v.* **Strut,** SWAGGER = walk or hold oneself with an air of importance. **Strut** emphasizes putting on an air of dignity by sticking the chest out and holding the head and body stiffly and proudly, to show how important one is: *The little boy put on his father's medals and strutted around the room.* **Swagger** emphasizes showing off how much better one is than others by striding boldly, rudely, or insultingly, and often suggests contempt for others, especially those in positions of authority: *After being put on probation again, the girls swaggered out of the courtroom.*

strut[2] [strʌt] *n., v.* **strut•ted, strut•ting.** —*n.* a supporting bar fitted into a framework, designed to resist longitudinal pressure; brace.
—*v.* brace or support by a strut or struts. ⟨?< LG *strutt* stiff⟩

stru•thi•ous ['struθiəs] *adj.* designating, resembling, or related to the ostrich or other ratite birds. ⟨< L *struthio* < LGk. *strouthion* < Gk. *strouthos* sparrow; cf. Gk. *strouthos ho megas* ostrich, literally, big bird⟩

strych•nine ['strɪknin], ['strɪknɪn], *or* ['strɪknaɪn] *n. Pharmacy.* a bitter, poisonous compound consisting of colourless crystals obtained from nux vomica and related plants. Strychnine is used in small doses as a stimulant for the central nervous system. *Formula*: $C_{21}H_{22}N_2O_2$ ⟨< F < L < Gk. *strychnos* nightshade⟩

Stu•art ['stjuərt] *or* ['stuərt] *n.* **1** the royal family that ruled Scotland from 1371 to 1603 and England and Scotland from 1603 to 1649 and from 1660 to 1714. **2** a member of this family.

stub [stʌb] *n., v.* **stubbed, stub•bing.** —*n.* **1** a short piece that is left: *the stub of a pencil, a cigarette stub.* **2** the short piece of a ticket or of each leaf in a chequebook, etc. kept as a record: *a cheque stub.* **3** something short and blunt; especially, something cut short or stunted in growth: *a stub of a tail.* **4** the cut or broken end of a tree or plant still in the ground; STUMP (def. 1).
—*v.* **1** strike (one's toe) against something. **2** clear (land) of tree stumps. **3** dig up by the roots. **4** put out (a cigarette or cigar) by crushing the burning end in an ashtray, etc. (*often used with* **out**). ⟨OE⟩

stub•ble ['stʌbəl] *n.* **1** the lower ends of stalks of grain that are left in the ground after the grain is cut. **2** any short, rough growth like this, especially a very short growth of beard. ⟨ME < OF *stuble* < LL *stupula*, var. of L *stipula* stem. Doublet of STIPULE.⟩

stub•ble–jump•er ['stʌbəl ˌdʒʌmpər] *n. Cdn. Slang.* a prairie farmer.

stub•bly ['stʌbli] *adj.* **1** covered with stubble. **2** resembling stubble; bristly: *a stubbly mustache.*

stub•born ['stʌbərn] *adj.* **1** obstinate; fixed or unyielding in purpose or opinion; pigheaded: *He's just too stubborn to admit he was wrong.* **2** determined; dogged; resolute: *a stubborn fight for freedom, stubborn courage.* **3** hard to deal with or manage: *a stubborn cough. Facts are stubborn things; they can't be changed.* ⟨probably ult. < *stub*⟩ **—'stub•born•ly,** *adv.* **—'stub•born•ness,** *n.*

☛ *Syn.* **1.** See note at OBSTINATE.

stub•by ['stʌbi] *adj.* **-bi•er, -bi•est. 1** short and thick or short and blunt, like a STUB (def. 3): *stubby fingers, a stubby pencil.* **2** short, dense, and stiff: *a stubby beard.* **3** having many stubs or stumps. **—'stub•bi•ly,** *adv.* **—'stub•bi•ness,** *n.*

stuc•co ['stʌkou] *n.* **-coes, -cos;** *v.* **-coed, -co•ing.** —*n.* **1** a hard, rough, strong material usually made of cement, sand, and a small amount of lime, used as a covering for the outer walls of buildings. **2** a fine plaster used for moulding into architectural decorations. **3** stuccowork.
—*v.* cover or decorate with stucco. ⟨< Ital. < Gmc.; cf. OHG *stukki* crust⟩

stuc•co•work ['stʌkou,wɜrk] *n.* work done in stucco.

stuck [stʌk] *v.* pt. and pp. of STICK[2].

stuck–up ['stʌk 'ʌp] *adj. Informal.* too proud; conceited; haughty.

stud[1] [stʌd] *n., v.* **stud•ded, stud•ding.** —*n.* **1** a head of a nail, a knob, etc. sticking out from a surface: *The belt was ornamented with silver studs.* **2** a kind of small button used to fasten the collar or front of a man's shirt. **3** one of a row of upright posts, usually wooden, which form part of the frame to which boards or laths are nailed in making a wall of a building. See FRAME for picture. **4** a projecting pin on a machine. **5** a crosspiece put in each link of a chain cable to strengthen it. **6** a small, buttonlike simple earring for a pierced ear, that sits snug against the earlobe and does not dangle below it.
—*v.* **1** set with studs or something like studs: *He plans to stud the sword hilt with jewels.* **2** be set or scattered over: *Little islands stud the harbour.* **3** set like studs; scatter at intervals: *Stooks of wheat were studded over the field.* **4** provide with studs. ⟨OE *studu*⟩

stud[2] [stʌd] *n.* **1** a male animal, especially a stallion, kept for breeding. **2** a group of horses or, sometimes, other animals, kept mainly for breeding. **3** a place where such animals are kept. **4** (*adjl.*) of, having to do with, or kept as a stud: *a stud farm.* **5** *Slang.* a virile man, especially one who is sexually promiscuous. **6** STUD POKER.
at stud, of a male animal, available for breeding. ⟨OE *stōd*⟩

stud•book ['stʌd,bʊk] *n.* a book giving the pedigrees of thoroughbred horses.

stud•ding ['stʌdɪŋ] *n., v.* —*n.* **1** the studs forming the framework of a wall. **2** lumber for studs.
—*v.* ppr. of STUD[1].

stud•ding•sail ['stʌdɪŋ,seil] *or* ['stʌnsəl] *n. Nautical.* a light sail set at the side of a square sail. ⟨origin unknown⟩

stu•dent ['stjudənt] *or* ['studənt] *n.* **1** a person who is studying in a school, college, or university. **2** a person who studies; one who investigates or observes systematically: *a student of human nature.* ⟨< L *studens, -entis*, ppr. of *studere*, originally, be eager⟩

☛ *Syn.* **Student,** PUPIL, SCHOLAR = a person who is studying or being taught. **Student,** emphasizing the idea of studying, applies to anyone who loves to study or studies a subject, but especially to someone attending a high school, college, or university: *Several high-school students were there.* **Pupil,** emphasizing personal supervision by a teacher, applies especially to a child in an elementary school or to someone studying personally with a teacher: *She was the pupil of a famous opera singer.* **Scholar** now applies chiefly to a learned person who is an authority in some field or to a student who has a scholarship: *She is a distinguished medieval scholar.*

student body all the students at a school, etc. collectively.

student teacher a student in the faculty of education at a college or university, who is engaged in practice teaching under supervision at the elementary or secondary level as a requirement for his or her degree.

stud•horse ['stʌd,hɔrs] *n.* a stallion kept for breeding.

stud•ied ['stʌdid] *adj., v.* —*adj.* **1** produced or marked by deliberate effort or design; intentional: *studied politeness. What she said to me was studied insult.* **2** prepared or planned carefully and thoughtfully: *a studied essay.*
—*v.* pt. and pp. of STUDY. **—'stud•ied•ly,** *adv.* **—'stud•ied•ness,** *n.*

☛ *Syn. adj.* See note at ELABORATE.

stu•di•o ['stjudiou] *or* ['studiou] *n., pl.* **-di•os. 1 a** the workroom of a painter, sculptor, photographer, etc. **b** a room in which a music teacher, dramatic coach, etc. gives lessons. **2** a place where films or recordings are made. **3** a place from which a radio or television program is broadcast. **4** STUDIO APARTMENT. ⟨< Ital. < L *studium* study, enthusiasm. Doublet of ÉTUDE, STUDY.⟩

studio apartment a small apartment or flat, usually consisting of one main room, a bathroom, and sometimes a kitchenette. Also, **bachelor apartment, bachelorette.**

studio couch a couch, usually without a back or arms, that can be converted into a bed.

stu•di•ous ['stjudiəs] *or* ['studiəs] *adj.* **1** fond of study: *She's very studious.* **2** thoughtful and painstaking; deliberate and anxiously careful: *He made a studious effort to please his customers.* **—'stu•di•ous•ly,** *adv.* **—'stu•di•ous•ness,** *n.*

stud poker a type of poker in which one or more cards are dealt face down on the first round and the rest are either dealt face up or alternating rounds of cards are dealt face up and face down. Betting is done on each round of open cards. ⟨shortening of *studhorse poker*⟩

stud•y ['stʌdi] *n., pl.* **stud•ies;** *v.* **stud•ied, stud•y•ing.** —*n.* **1** the effort to learn by reading or thinking. **2** a careful examination; investigation; a paper presenting the results of such an examination or investigation. **3** a subject studied; branch of learning; something investigated or to be investigated. **4** a room for study, reading, writing, etc. **5** a literary or artistic work that deals in careful detail with one particular subject. **6** a sketch for a picture, story, etc. **7** *Music.* a composition designed primarily for practice in a particular technical problem; a concert version of this, often of great difficulty and brilliance. **8** an earnest effort, or the object of endeavour or effort: *Her constant study is to please her parents.* **9 studies,** a person's work as a student: *to return to one's studies after a vacation.*
a brown study, deep thought; reverie: *She's in a brown study.*
a quick study, someone, such as an actor, who learns material by heart quickly.
—*v.* **1** try to learn or gain knowledge (about) by means of books, observation, or experiment: *to study history. He studies most of the*

time. **2** examine carefully: *We studied the map to find the shortest road home.* **3** consider with care; think (out); plan: *The prisoner studied ways to escape.* **4** give care and effort to; try hard: *The grocer studies to please her customers.* **5** memorize or try to memorize: *to study one's part in a play.* **6** read or reread (a book, notes, etc.) carefully and intently with the purpose of mastering the contents, as for a test. **7** be a student; attend a college or university: *She's studying to be a doctor.* ⟨ME < AF < L *studium*, originally, eagerness. Doublet of ÉTUDE, STUDIO.⟩
☛ *Syn. v.* **3.** See note at CONSIDER.

stuff [stʌf] *n., v. —n.* **1** what a thing is made of; material. **2** a woollen fabric. **3** a thing or things; substance: *The doctor applied some kind of stuff to the burn.* **4** goods; belongings: *He was told to move his stuff out of the room.* **5** silly writing, talk, or thoughts; nonsense. **6** inward qualities; character: *He's got the right stuff to make a success of it.* **7** *Slang.* an illicit drug. **8** trade; skill; basic ability; special ability: *She really knows her stuff in the classroom. Watch her do her stuff on that horse.*
strut one's stuff. See STRUT[1].
that's the stuff! *Informal.* an expression of encouragement.
—v. **1** pack full; fill. **2** stop or block (*often used with* **up**): *My nose is stuffed by a cold.* **3** fill the skin of (a dead animal) to make it look as it did when alive. **4** fill (a chicken, turkey, etc.) with seasoned bread crumbs, etc. in preparation for cooking. **5** force; push; thrust: *He stuffed his clothes into the drawer.* **6** eat or cause to eat too much. ⟨ME < OF *estoffe*, ? ult. < L *stuppa* tow[2], oakum < Gk. *stypē*⟩

stuffed shirt *Informal.* a pompous, conceited person, especially one who is old-fashioned or conservative.

stuff•ing ['stʌfɪŋ] *n., v. —n.* **1** any soft material used to fill or stuff cushions, upholstered furniture, toys, etc. **2** seasoned bread crumbs, etc. for stuffing a chicken, turkey, etc. for cooking. **3** the act of someone or something that stuffs.
knock the stuffing out of, defeat.
—v. ppr. of STUFF.

stuff•y ['stʌfi] *adj.* **stuff•i•er, stuff•i•est. 1** lacking fresh air: *a stuffy room.* **2** lacking freshness or interest; dull: *a stuffy conversation.* **3** stopped up: *I've got a stuffy nose from hay fever.* **4** prim and proper, narrow-minded; boring, stodgy: *Don't be so stuffy; it was only a harmless joke.* **5** angry or sulky. **—'stuff•i•ly,** *adv.* **—'stuff•i•ness,** *n.*

stul•ti•fy ['stʌltə,faɪ] *v.* **-fied, -fy•ing. 1** cause to appear foolish or absurd; reduce to foolishness or absurdity. **2 a** make futile. **b** make passive or weak by requiring absolute obedience or conformity or by excessive routine, lack of stimulation, etc.: *the stultifying atmosphere of a prison or of a dictatorship.* **3** *Law.* claim the insanity and consequent lack of legal responsibility of (oneself or someone else). ⟨< LL *stultificare* < L *stultus* foolish + *facere* make⟩ **—,stul•ti•fi'ca•tion,** *n.* **—'stul•ti,fi•er,** *n.*

stum•ble ['stʌmbəl] *v.* **-bled, -bling;** *n. —v.* **1** trip by striking the foot against something: *She stumbled, but did not fall.* **2** walk unsteadily, tripping often: *The tired hikers stumbled along.* **3** speak or act in a hesitating, faltering way: *The frightened boy stumbled through his recitation.* **4** make a mistake; do wrong. **5** come (*on, upon, across,* etc.) by accident or chance: *While in the country, she stumbled upon some fine antiques.* **6** *Archaic.* cause to stumble or pause.
—n. the act or an instance of stumbling. ⟨ME, rel. to Norwegian *stumla*, with euphonic *b*⟩ **—'stum•bler,** *n.* **—'stum•bling•ly,** *adv.*

stum•bling–block ['stʌmblɪŋ ,blɒk] *n.* an obstacle or hindrance; something that causes difficulty or slows down progress: *Procrastination is a main stumbling-block to success.*

stump [stʌmp] *n., v. —n.* **1** the lower end of a tree trunk left after the tree has fallen or been cut down. **2** anything left after the main or important part has worn down or been removed: *The dog wagged its stump of a tail. By the end of the lecture, her piece of chalk was reduced to a stump.* **3** a person with a short, thick build. **4** a place where a political speech is made. **5** a heavy step. **6** the sound made by stiff walking or heavy steps. **7** a wooden leg. **8** Usually, **stumps,** *pl. Informal.* legs. **9** *Fine arts.* a tight roll of paper or other material pointed at the ends and used to soften pencil marks in drawing. **10** *Cricket.* one of the three upright sticks of a wicket.
on the stump, *Cdn.* of timber, not yet logged.
up a stump, *Informal.* unable to act, answer, etc.; impotent; baffled.
—v. **1** remove stumps from (land). **2** reduce to a stump; cut off or wear down. **3** go about or travel through (an area), making speeches: *All the candidates are out stumping the riding this week.* **4** walk in a heavy, clumsy way. **5** *Informal.* make unable to answer, do, etc: *The first question was easy but the second one stumped him.* **6** *Fine arts.* modify or soften (a crayon or pencil drawing or rendering) using a STUMP (*n.* def. 9). **7** *Cricket.* put (a batsman) out by knocking down the bails while he or she is out of his or her ground. ⟨Cf. MLG *stump*⟩ **—'stump•er,** *n.* **—'stump,like,** *adj.*

stump•age ['stʌmpɪdʒ] *n. Cdn.* **1** a price paid for the right to cut standing timber. **2** a tax or royalty paid to the government on each tree taken out of a timber berth. **3** the right to cut standing timber. **4** standing trees, viewed as an asset; the amount of standing timber available for cutting.

stump fence *Cdn.* a fence constructed of pine roots turned on edge and laid in a line, all facing in one direction.

stump speaker a person who makes political speeches from a platform, etc. **—stump speech.**

stump•y ['stʌmpi] *adj.* **stump•i•er, stump•i•est. 1** short and thick. **2** having many stumps. **—'stump•i•ly,** *adv.* **—'stump•i•ness,** *n.*

stun [stʌn] *v.* **stunned, stun•ning;** *n. —v.* **1** make senseless; knock unconscious: *He was stunned by the fall.* **2** bewilder; shock; overwhelm: *She was stunned by the news of her friend's death.*
—n. **1 a** the act of stunning or dazing. **b** the condition of being stunned. **2** a thing that stuns; stunner. ⟨OE *stunian* crash, resound; influenced by OF *estoner* resound, stun, ult. < L *ex-* + *tonare* thunder⟩

stung [stʌŋ] *v.* pt. and pp. of STING.

stunk [stʌŋk] *v.* a pt. and pp. of STINK.

stun•ner ['stʌnər] *n.* **1** a person, thing, or blow that makes senseless, shocks, or bewilders. **2** *Informal.* a very striking or attractive person or thing.

stun•ning ['stʌnɪŋ] *adj., v. —adj.* **1** that stuns: *a stunning blow.* **2** very attractive or good-looking; strikingly pretty: *a stunning model, a stunning new hat.* **3** excellent or delightful; first-rate; splendid: *a stunning performance.*
—v. ppr. of STUN. **—'stun•ning•ly,** *adv.*

stun•sail ['stʌnsəl] *n.* studdingsail.

stunt[1] [stʌnt] *v., n. —v.* check or hinder in growth or development: *Lack of proper food stunts a plant.*
—n. a check in growth or development. ⟨ME, OE *stunt* stupid, foolish⟩

stunt[2] [stʌnt] *n., v. Informal. —n.* a feat or act intended to thrill an audience or to attract attention; an act showing boldness or skill: *Circus riders perform stunts on horseback.*
—v. perform such feats. ⟨probably a var. of *stint* task⟩

stunt•man ['stʌnt,mæn] *or* ['stʌntmən] *n., pl.* **-men.** *Film, TV.* a man who substitutes for an actor in scenes involving dangerous manoeuvres.

stunt•wom•an ['stʌnt,wʊmən] *n., pl.* **-wom•en** [-,wɪmən] *Film, TV.* a woman who substitutes for an actor in scenes involving dangerous manoeuvres.

stu•pa ['stupə] *n.* a large, dome-shaped mound erected as a shrine by Buddhists. ⟨< Skt. *stupa* heap⟩

stupe [stjup] *or* [stup] *n.* a small, hot, wet cloth or compress of soft material used in dressing a wound, to stimulate circulation, etc. ⟨ME < L *stupa* coarse flax < Gk. *stypē*⟩
☛ *Hom.* STOOP, STOUP [stup].

stu•pe•fa•cient [,stjupə'feiʃənt] *or* [,stupə'feiʃənt] *adj., n.* *—adj.* stupefying.
—n. a drug or agent that produces stupor. ⟨< L *stupefaciens, -entis,* ppr. of *stupefacere.* See STUPEFY.⟩

stu•pe•fac•tion [,stjupə'fækʃən] *or* [,stupə'fækʃən] *n.* **1** the act of stupefying or a state of being stupefied. **2** utter astonishment or total bewilderment.

stu•pe•fy ['stjupə,faɪ] *or* ['stupə,faɪ] *v.* **-fied, -fy•ing. 1** make dazed, dull, or senseless: *stupefied by a drug.* **2** overwhelm with shock or amazement; astound: *They were stupefied by the calamity.* ⟨< L *stupefacere* < *stupere* be amazed + *facere* make⟩ **—'stu•pe,fi•er,** *n.*

stu•pen•dous [stju'pɛndəs] *or* [stu'pɛndəs] *adj.* **1** amazing; marvellous: *Niagara Falls is a stupendous sight.* **2** unusually large or great: *a stupendous meal, a stupendous structure.* ⟨< L *stupendus* < *stupere* be amazed⟩ **—stu'pen•dous•ly,** *adv.* **—stu'pen•dous•ness,** *n.*

stu•pid ['stjupɪd] *or* ['stupɪd] *adj., n. —adj.* **1** not intelligent; dull: *a stupid person.* **2** not interesting: *a stupid book.* **3** showing lack of intelligence or good sense: *That was a stupid thing to do.* **4** dazed: *He was still stupid from the effect of the sedative.*
—n. Informal. a stupid person. ⟨< L *stupidus* < *stupere* be dazed⟩ **—'stu•pid•ly,** *adv.* **—'stu•pid•ness,** *n.*
☛ *Syn. adj.* **1. Stupid,** DULL = having or showing little intelligence. **Stupid,** describing people or what they say or do, particularly suggests

being by nature lacking in good sense or ordinary intelligence: *Running away from an accident is stupid.* **Dull** particularly suggests a mind slow in understanding and lacking in sharpness and alertness, either by nature or because of overwork, poor health, etc., and needing to be stirred up and made more lively: *The mind becomes dull if the body gets no exercise.*

stu•pid•i•ty [stju'pɪdəti] *or* [stu'pɪdəti] *n., pl.* **-ties. 1** the quality or state of being stupid. **2** a stupid act, idea, etc.

stu•por ['stjupər] *or* ['stupər] *n.* **1** loss or lessening of the power to feel or think: *The man lay in a stupor, unable to tell what had happened to him.* **2** mental or moral numbness; torpor. ⟨< L < *stupere* be dazed⟩ **—'stu•por•ous,** *adj.*

stur•dy ['stɜrdi] *adj.* **-di•er, -di•est. 1** strong; stout; solidly built: *sturdy legs. What we need for the baby is a good sturdy playpen.* **2** not yielding; firm: *sturdy resistance, sturdy defenders.* ⟨ME < OF *esturdi* violent, originally, dazed⟩ **—'stur•di•ly,** *adv.* **—'stur•di•ness,** *n.*

☛ *Syn.* **1.** See note at STRONG.

stur•geon ['stɜrdʒən] *n., pl.* **-geon** or **-geons.** any of a family (Acipenseridae) of sharklike, bony fishes found in north temperate waters, having a heavy, almost cylindrical body with several longitudinal rows of bony plates, and a small mouth on the underside of the head. Sturgeon are valued as a source of caviar and isinglass. ⟨ME < AF *esturgeon,* ult. < Gmc.⟩

Sturm and Drang ['ʃtʊʀm ʊnt 'dʀaŋ] *German.* a German romantic movement of the latter half of the 18th century, characterized by an emphasis on individual perception and sensibility, opposition to rationalism and the establishment, and in some cases extreme nationalism. ⟨< G, literally, storm and stress; from the title of a play by F.M. von Klinger (1752-1831)⟩

stut•ter ['stʌtər] *v., n. —v.* **1** repeat the same sound in an effort to speak. *Example*: *C-c-c-can't they go?* **2** say, speak, or sound with a stutter: *to stutter a reply.*
—n. the act or habit of stuttering. ⟨< dial. *stut*; cf. Du. *stotteren*⟩ **—'stut•ter•er,** *n.* **—'stut•ter•ing•ly,** *adv.*

☛ *Syn. v.* See note at STAMMER.

St. Vi•tus's dance ['vəitəsɪz] *Pathology.* chorea.

sty[1] [staɪ] *n., pl.* **sties. 1** a pen for pigs. **2** any filthy place. ⟨OE *stig*⟩

sty[2] or **stye** [staɪ] *n., pl.* **sties** or **styes.** *Ophthalmology.* a small, inflamed swelling on the edge of the eyelid, resembling a small boil. ⟨probably < ME *styanye* (taken to mean 'sty on eye'), ult. < OE *stīgend* rising + *ēage* eye⟩

Styg•i•an ['stɪdʒiən] *adj.* **1** of or having to do with the river Styx or the lower world. **2** dark; gloomy. **3** of an oath, completely binding; inviolable like the oath by the Styx, which the gods themselves feared to break. Also, **stygian.** ⟨< L *Stygius* < Gk. *Stygios* < *Styx, Stygos* Styx⟩

style [staɪl] *n., v.* **styled, styl•ing.** *—n.* **1 a** fashion: *dressed in the latest styles.* **b** a fashionable garment: *Shop here for the latest styles at the best prices.* **2** a manner; method; way, especially of expression in the arts: *the Gothic style of architecture.* **3** a way of writing or speaking. **4** a fashionable, elegant, or admirable way or manner: *She dresses in style.* **5** excellence, originality, or character in artistic or literary work. **6** an official name; title: *Salute him with the style of King.* **7** STYLUS (def. 1). **8** something like this in shape or use, such as a mapping pen. **9** a pointer on a dial, chart, etc. **10** *Botany.* the stemlike part of the pistil of a flower containing the stigma at its top. See FLOWER for picture. **11** the rules of spelling, punctuation, etc. used by a particular printer, publisher, etc.
—v. **1** give a distinctive design or manner to; design, fashion, or arrange: *dresses styled in Paris. She uses a blow dryer to style her hair.* **2** name; call: *Joan of Arc was styled the Maid of Orléans.* **3** make the spelling, punctuation, etc. of (something) conform to specific conventions, such as those used by a particular publisher, etc. ⟨ME < OF < L *stilus,* originally, pointed writing instrument; influenced in modern spelling by Gk. *stylos* column. Doublet of STYLUS.⟩ **—'style•less,** *adj.*

☛ *Hom.* STILE.

☛ *Syn. n.* **1.** See note at FASHION.

style•book ['staɪl,bʊk] *n.* **1** a book containing rules of punctuation, capitalization, etc., used by printers, editors, etc. **2** a book showing fashions in dress, etc.

styl•et ['staɪlɪt] *n.* **1 a** STILETTO (def. 1). **b** any similar slender, pointed weapon. **2** *Medicine.* **a** PROBE (def. 3). **b** a slender wire inserted into a soft catheter or cannula to clear it or make it rigid.

styl•i•form ['staɪlə,fɔrm] *adj.* in the shape of a STYLUS (def. 1).

styl•ish ['staɪlɪʃ] *adj.* fashionable; smart: *a stylish new coat.* **—'styl•ish•ly,** *adv.* **—'styl•ish•ness,** *n.*

styl•ist ['staɪlɪst] *n.* **1** a person, especially a writer, who has or aims at a good style or whose work is characterized by a particular style: *Her editorials read well because she is a stylist.* **2 a** a person who designs or advises concerning fashionable interior decoration, clothes, etc. **b** hairstylist.

sty•lis•tic [staɪ'lɪstɪk] *adj.* of or having to do with style. **—sty'lis•ti•cal•ly,** *adv.*

sty•list•ics [staɪ'lɪstɪks] *n.pl.* (*used with a singular verb*) **1** the study, analysis, and description of the distinctive features of word choice, syntactic construction, etc. that make up the style of a particular author or literary group. **2** a similar study of a given language or languages.

styl•ize ['staɪlaɪz] *v.* **-ized, -iz•ing.** make or design according to a conventional or standard style or pattern rather than according to nature: *Our new bedroom wallpaper has tiny stylized tulips.* **—,styl•i'za•tion,** *n.* **—'styl•iz•er,** *n.*

styloid process ['staɪlɔɪd] *Anatomy.* a long, slender projection or process of a bone, particularly that from the base of the temporal bone.

sty•lus ['staɪləs] *n.* **1** a pointed instrument used in ancient times for writing on wax or clay tablets. **2** a needlelike device of jewel, steel, etc. attached to the cartridge on the pickup arm of a phonograph, and which rests in the groove of a record, transmitting the vibration to the cartridge; needle. **3** a similar device used for cutting the grooves on the original disc when recording music, etc. **4** a pointed instrument used for marking, engraving, or writing, as on a mimeograph stencil, the drum of an oscillograph, etc. ⟨< L *stilus.* Doublet of STYLE.⟩

sty•mie ['staɪmi] *n., v.* **-mied, -mie•ing.** *—n.* **1** *Golf.* a situation on a putting green in which an opponent's ball is directly between the player's ball and the hole. **2** a situation in which one is blocked or frustrated.
—v. **1** *Golf.* hinder with a stymie. **2** block completely: *He was stymied by the last question on the exam and gave up on it.* ⟨? < Scots *stymie* a person having poor eyesight⟩

styp•sis ['stɪpsɪs] *n.* the application or use of a styptic.

styp•tic ['stɪptɪk] *adj., n. —adj.* able to stop or check bleeding; astringent.
—n. something that stops or checks bleeding by contracting the tissue. Alum is a common styptic. ⟨< L < Gk. *styptikos* < *styphein* constrict⟩

styptic pencil a pencil-shaped stick of alum or other styptic substance, used on slight wounds to stop bleeding.

sty•rene ['staɪrin] *n.* an aromatic liquid hydrocarbon used mainly in making synthetic rubber and plastics. *Formula*: C_8H_8 ⟨< L *styrax* an aromatic resin < Gk.⟩

Sty•ro•foam ['staɪrə,foum] *n. Trademark.* a kind of lightweight, firm polystyrene plastic used for insulation, packaging, etc.

Styx [stɪks] *n. Greek mythology.* a river in the lower world. The souls of the dead were ferried across it into Hades. ⟨< L < Gk. *Styx* (related to *stygeein* hate)⟩

su [su] *n.* a unit of money in Kampuchea equal to 1/100th of a riel. See table of money in the Appendix.

sua•sion ['sweiʒən] *n. Rare.* persuasion: *Moral suasion is an appeal to one's sense of what is right.* ⟨ME < L *suasio, -onis* < *suadere* persuade⟩

sua•sive ['sweisɪv] *adj. Rare.* persuasive. **—'sua•sive•ly,** *adv.* **—'sua•sive•ness,** *n.*

suave [swɑv] *adj.* smoothly agreeable or polite. ⟨< F < L *suavis* agreeable⟩ **—'suave•ly,** *adv.* **—'suave•ness,** *n.*

sua•vi•ty ['swɑvəti] *n., pl.* **-ties. 1** a smoothly agreeable quality of behaviour; smooth politeness. **2** a smooth remark, act, etc.

sub [sʌb] *n., adj., v.* **subbed, sub•bing.** *Informal. —n. or adj.* **1** substitute. **2** submarine. **3** subordinate.
—v. act as a substitute.

sub– *prefix.* **1** under; below: *subway, submarine.* **2** further or again: *subdivide, sublease.* **3** near; bordering upon: *subarctic.* **4** nearly; almost: *subarid.* **5** secondary, subordinate, or assistant: *substation, subhead.* **6** resulting from further division; a subordinate portion of: *subcommittee, subspecies.* **7** *Chemistry.* **a** having only a small or less than usual amount of: *suboxide.* **b** a basic compound of: *subcarbonate.* **8** in a comparatively small degree or proportion; somewhat: *subacid.* Also, **suc-** before *c*; **suf-** before *f*; **sug-** before *g*; **sum-** in some cases before *m*; **sup-** before *p*; **sur-** before *r*; **sus-** in some cases before *c, p, t.* ⟨< L *sub,* prep.⟩

sub. 1 substitute. 2 subscription. 3 suburban; suburbs. 4 subaltern.

sub•ac•id [sʌb'æsɪd] *adj.* moderately acid. Oranges are a subacid fruit. **—ˌsub•a'cid•i•ty,** *n.* **—sub'ac•id•ly,** *adv.*

sub•a•cute [ˌsʌbə'kjut] *adj.* 1 not quite acute; moderately acute: *a subacute angle.* 2 *Medicine.* of a disease, between chronic and acute.

sub•a•gent ['sʌbˌeidʒənt] *n.* a person employed as the agent of an agent; a subordinate or deputy agent.

sub•al•pine [sʌb'ælpaɪn] *or* [sʌb'ælpɪn] *adj.* 1 of or referring to the regions at the foot of the Alps. 2 *Botany.* growing on a mountain below the tree line but above the foothills.

sub•al•tern [sʌb'ɒltərn] *or, esp. for n. 1,* ['sʌbəlˌtɜrn] *adj., n.* *—adj.* 1 lower in rank or status. 2 *Logic.* of a proposition, particular in relation to a given universal proposition.
—n. 1 *Esp. Brit.* a lieutenant, especially a second lieutenant. 2 someone in a subordinate position or of lower rank. ⟨< LL *subalternus* < L *sub-* under + *alternus* alternate⟩

sub•an•tarc•tic [ˌsʌbænt'ɑrktɪk] *or* [ˌsʌbænt'ɑrtɪk] *adj., n.* *—adj.* of, having to do with, or like the region just north of the Antarctic Circle.
—n. the region just north of the Antarctic Circle.

sub•a•quat•ic [ˌsʌbə'kwɒtɪk] *or* [ˌsʌbə'kwætɪk] *adj.* somewhat or partly aquatic: *subaquatic plants.*

sub•a•que•ous [sʌb'ækwiəs] *or* [sʌb'eikwiəs] *adj.* 1 under water; suitable for use under water. 2 formed under water. 3 living under water.

sub•arc•tic [sʌb'ɑrktɪk] *or* [sʌb'ɑrtɪk] *adj., n.* *—adj.* of, having to do with, or like the region just south of the Arctic Circle.
—n. the region just south of the Arctic Circle.

sub•ar•id [sʌb'ærɪd] *or* [sʌb'ɛrɪd] *adj.* moderately arid.

sub•a•tom•ic [ˌsʌbə'tɒmɪk] *adj. Physics.* having to do with the inside of the atom or with particles smaller than atoms.

sub–base•ment ['sʌb ˌbeismənt] *n.* a storey below the main basement of a building.

sub•ce•les•tial [ˌsʌbsə'lɛstʃəl] *adj.* beneath the heavens; earthly; terrestrial.

sub•cel•lar ['sʌbˌsɛlər] *n.* a cellar beneath another cellar.

sub•class ['sʌbˌklæs] *n.* 1 *Biology.* a secondary category in the classification of plants and animals that is a grouping within a class and includes one or more orders. 2 a primary division within a class. 3 *Esp. Mathematics.* a subset.

sub•cla•vi•an [sʌb'kleiviən] *adj., n. Anatomy.* *—adj.* 1 located or running under the clavicle or collarbone, as some arteries and veins. 2 of or having to do with those blood vessels.
—n. a subclavian artery; subclavian vein.

sub•cli•ni•cal [sʌb'klɪnɪkəl] *adj. Medicine.* of a disease, in the early or less serious stages; showing no clinical symptoms.

sub•com•mit•tee ['sʌbkəˌmɪti] *n.* a small committee chosen from a larger general committee for some special duty.

sub•com•pact [sʌb'kɒmpækt] *or* ['sʌbˌkɒmpækt] *n.* the smallest of the four basic sizes of automobile. Compare COMPACT[1], INTERMEDIATE, and STANDARD.

sub•con•scious [sʌb'kɒnʃəs] *adj.* 1 existing in the mind and affecting thoughts, attitudes, or behaviour but not consciously felt: *a subconscious motive, subconscious inhibitions.* 2 not completely conscious or aware: *In his subconscious state, he thought he heard a knocking sound.* 3 (*noml.*) **the subconscious,** thoughts, feelings, etc. existing in the mind but not consciously recognized. **—sub'con•scious•ly,** *adv.*

sub•con•scious•ness [sʌb'kɒnʃəsnɪs] *n.* 1 the quality or state of being not completely conscious. 2 the subconscious.

sub•con•ti•nent [sʌb'kɒntənənt] *or* ['sʌbˌkɒntənənt] *n.* 1 a very large land mass that is smaller than the land masses usually called continents. Greenland is a subcontinent. 2 a large section of a continent that has considerable geographical or political independence: *the Indian subcontinent.* **—ˌsubˌcon•ti'nen•tal,** *adj.*

sub•con•tract *n.* ['sʌbˌkɒntrækt]; *v.* [sʌb'kɒntrækt] *or* [ˌsʌbkən'trækt] *n., v.* *—n.* 1 a contract under a previous contract; contract for carrying out a previous contract or a part of it: *The contractor for the new school building gave my father the subcontract to install the plumbing.*
—v. make a subcontract: *The plumbing for the new school was subcontracted to a local firm.*

sub•con•trac•tor [sʌb'kɒntræktər], ['sʌbˌkɒntræktər], ['sʌbkənˌtræktər], *or* [ˌsʌbkən'træktər] *n.* a person or company that contracts to carry out part or all of a contract made by someone else.

sub•cost•al [sʌb'kɒstəl] *adj., n.* *—adj.* located beneath the ribs.
—n. a muscle lying in this area.

sub•cul•ture ['sʌbˌkʌltʃər] *n.* 1 **a** an element or cultural group within a larger culture, but distinguished from it by features of belief, custom, conduct, background, etc.: *The academic community is a subculture.* **b** the beliefs, customs, values, etc. of such a group. 2 *Bacteriology.* a culture of bacteria, etc. derived from another culture.

sub•cu•ta•ne•ous [ˌsʌbkju'teiniəs] *adj.* 1 under the skin. 2 living under the skin. 3 placed or performed under the skin. **—ˌsub•cu'ta•ne•ous•ly,** *adv.*

sub•dea•con [sʌb'dikən] *or* ['sʌbˌdikən] *n.* a member of the clergy next below a deacon in rank. **—sub'dea•con•ate** or **ˌsub•di'ac•on•ate,** *n.*

sub•di•vide ['sʌbdəˌvaɪd] *v.* **-vid•ed, -vid•ing.** 1 divide again; divide into smaller parts. 2 divide (land) into lots for houses, buildings, etc.: *A developer bought the farm and subdivided it into building lots.* **—'sub•diˌvid•er,** *n.*

sub•di•vi•sion ['sʌbdəˌvɪʒən] *n.* 1 a division into smaller parts. 2 a part of a part. 3 a tract of land divided into building lots. 4 the houses, community, etc. established on such a tract.

sub•dom•i•nant [sʌb'dɒmənənt] *n., adj.* *—n.* 1 *Music.* the fourth tone of a diatonic scale; the tone next below the dominant. 2 anything that is subdominant.
—adj. 1 *Music.* of or having to do with this fourth tone. 2 not completely dominant.

sub•duc•tion [səb'dʌkʃən] *n.* 1 the process by which something is pulled down; the act or action of pulling or being pulled. 2 *Geology.* the result of the collision of two of the earth's crustal plates, one sinking beneath or being overridden by the other.

sub•due [səb'dju] *or* [səb'du] *v.* **-dued, -du•ing.** 1 conquer: *The Spaniards subdued the Indian peoples of South America.* 2 keep down; hold back; suppress: *to subdue a desire to laugh.* 3 tone down; soften or reduce: *They pulled down the blinds to subdue the light.* 4 alleviate: *to subdue a fever.* 5 bring under control mentally by coercion, intimidation, or training. 6 bring (wilderness) under cultivation. ⟨ME *sodewe* < OF *soduire* deceive < L *subducere* draw away < *sub-* from under + *ducere* lead; influenced in meaning by L *subdere* subdue < *sub-* under + *dare* put⟩ **—sub'du•a•ble,** *adj.* **—sub'du•er,** *n.*

sub•dued [səb'djud] *or* [səb'dud] *adj., v.* *—adj.* 1 lacking in intensity or strength: *subdued colours.* 2 quietened down; less spirited or lively than usual: *He was quiet and subdued all afternoon.*
—v. pt. and pp. of SUBDUE.

sub•en•try ['sʌbˌɛntri] *n.* an entry listed under a main entry: *In this dictionary, idioms are included as subentries under the entry word.*

su•be•re•ous [sə'biriəs] *adj.* corky; like cork. ⟨< L *subereus* < *suber* cork⟩

sub•fam•i•ly ['sʌbˌfæməli] *n., pl.* **-lies.** 1 *Biology.* a secondary category in the classification of plants and animals that is a grouping within a family and includes one or more genera. 2 *Linguistics.* a group of languages within a language family.

sub•freez•ing ['sʌb'frizɪŋ] *adj.* 1 below the freezing point of water (0° Celsius, 32° Fahrenheit). 2 below the specific freezing point of a specific liquid.

sub•fusc or **sub•fusk** ['sʌbˌfʌsk] *or* [sʌb'fʌsk] *adj., n.* *—adj.* 1 darkish; dull in colour: *subfusc woods at twilight.* 2 not distinctive; monotonous; drab: *rows of subfusc city houses.*
—n. Brit. especially at the universities of Oxford and Cambridge, dark clothing and academic gowns worn when writing examinations and for other official occasions. ⟨< L *subfuscus* < *sub-* under + *fuscus* dark⟩

sub•ge•nus ['sʌbˌdʒinəs] *n., pl.* **sub•gen•er•a** ['sʌbˌdʒɛnərə] or **sub•ge•nus•es.** *Biology.* a secondary category in the classification of plants and animals that is a grouping within a genus and includes one or more species.

sub•group ['sʌbˌgrup] *n.* a subordinate group; a division of a group.

sub•head ['sʌbˌhɛd] *n.* 1 the title, or heading, of a subdivision of an article, chapter, etc. 2 a subordinate title, headline, etc.: *Newspaper articles often have a subhead above or below the headline.* 3 the person ranked immediately below the head of an educational institution or of a department.

sub•head•ing ['sʌb,hɛdɪŋ] *n.* SUBHEAD (defs. 1 & 2).

sub•hu•man [sʌb'hjumən] *adj.* **1** below the human race or type; less than human. **2** almost human: *subhuman primates.*

su•bi•to ['subi,tou] *adv. Music.* suddenly; quickly; abruptly. ⟨< Ital.⟩

subj. **1** subject; subjective; subjectively. **2** subjunctive.

sub•ja•cent [sʌb'dʒeisənt] *adj.* **1** situated below; underlying. **2** being in a lower situation, though not directly beneath. ⟨< L *subjacens, -entis,* ppr. of *subjacere* < *sub-* below + *jacere* lie⟩ **—sub'ja•cen•cy,** *n.*

sub•ject *n., adj.* ['sʌbdʒɛkt] *or* ['sʌbdʒɪkt]; *v.* [səb'dʒɛkt] *n., adj., v. —n.* **1** something thought about, discussed, etc. **2** something learned or taught; a course of study, field of learning, etc.: *English, history, mathematics, and biology are required subjects in this school.* **3** a person under the power, control, or influence of another: *the Queen's subjects.* **4** a person or thing that undergoes or experiences something. **5** an underlying motive, reason, or grounds: *a subject for complaint.* **6** *Grammar.* the word or group of words in a sentence about which something is said in the predicate. In the sentence *His little brother went to find him, His little brother* is the subject; in *Their travellers' cheques were stolen, Their travellers' cheques* is the subject. **7 a** the theme of a book, poem, or other literary work. **b** a figure, scene, object, incident, etc. chosen by an artist for representation. **c** *Music.* the theme or melody on which a composition or movement is based. **8** *Philosophy.* **a** the substance of anything as opposed to its qualities. **b** mind or self as opposed to everything outside the mind. **9** *Logic.* **a** that term of a proposition of which the other term is affirmed or denied. *Example*: In a proposition such that X is Y/not Y, X is the subject and Y is the predicate: *All flesh* (X) *is grass* (Y). **b** the actual thing or person represented by this term.
—adj. under some power or influence: *A colony is a subject nation.*
subject to, a under the power or influence of: *We are subject to our country's laws.* **b** likely to have: *Many children are subject to colds.* **c** depending on; on the condition of: *I bought the car subject to your approval.*
—v. **1** bring under some power or influence: *Rome subjected all Italy to her rule.* **2** cause to undergo or experience something: *The savages subjected their captives to torture.* **3** lay open or expose; make liable *(to): Credulity subjects one to impositions.* ⟨ME < OF < L *subjectus,* pp. of *subjicere, subicere* place under < *sub-* under + *jacere* throw⟩

☛ *Syn. n.* **1. Subject,** TOPIC = the main thing or idea thought, talked, or written about, as in a conversation, lecture, essay, book. **Subject** is the general word: *He tried to change the subject. Juvenile delinquency is a broad subject.* **Topic** often applies to a subject having to do with a current event or problem, but particularly means a limited and definitely stated subject that is, or is to be, discussed in a lecture, essay, etc. or some part of it: *"The plan for a recreation centre" is today's topic.*

sub•jec•tion [səb'dʒɛkʃən] *n.* **1** the act of bringing under some power or influence: *The new dictator's first concern was the subjection of the rebel forces.* **2** the condition of being under some power or influence: *They lived in subjection to an old aunt.*

sub•jec•tive [səb'dʒɛktɪv] *adj., n. —adj.* **1** originating or existing in the mind; belonging to the person thinking rather than to the object thought of: *Ideas and opinions are subjective; facts are objective.* **2** dealing with the thoughts and feelings of the speaker, writer, painter, etc.; personal: *a subjective poem.* Compare OBJECTIVE (def. 2). **3** *Philosophy.* **a** of or relating to reality as perceived by the mind, as distinct from reality as independent of the mind. **b** influenced by an individual's state of mind: *a subjective perception or apprehension.* **c** having to do with the substance of anything, as opposed to its qualities and attributes. **4** *Grammar.* of, having to do with, or being the grammatical form of an English pronoun that shows that it is the subject of a sentence. There are six English pronouns with special subjective forms: *I, we, he, she, they,* and *who.* Compare OBJECTIVE (def. 3).
—n. Grammar. **1** the category consisting of subjective forms. The English subjective corresponds roughly to the nominative case in German and Latin. **2** a word or construction in the subjective form. *I* and *who* are subjectives. **—sub'jec•tive•ly,** *adv.* **—sub'jec•tive•ness,** *n.*

sub•ject•iv•ism [səb'dʒɛktə,vɪzəm] *n.* **1** *Epistemology.* the doctrine that all knowledge is subjective, that is, limited to the self's experience, and therefore cannot be objective or transcendant. **2** *Ethics.* any of a number of theories holding that moral and ethical judgments are reflections of personal or community feelings and emotions. **3** any philosophical theory holding that personal experience and conviction are most important. **4** subjectivity. **—sub'ject•iv•ist,** *n., adj.* **—sub,ject•iv'ist•ic,** *adj.*

sub•jec•tiv•i•ty [,sʌbdʒɛk'tɪvəti] *n.* the quality or condition of being subjective: *The subjectivity of his account of the war makes it unreliable as a source of information.*

subject matter the thing or things discussed or considered in a book, speech, debate, etc.

sub•join [səb'dʒɔɪn] *v.* **1** add at the end; append. **2** place in immediate juxtaposition to something else. ⟨< MF *subjoindre* < L *subjungere* < *sub-* under + *jungere* join⟩ **—sub'join•der,** *n.*

sub ju•di•ce [sʌb 'dʒudəsi] before a judge or court; under judicial consideration. ⟨< L⟩

sub•ju•gate ['sʌbdʒə,geit] *v.* **-gat•ed, -gat•ing. 1** subdue; conquer. **2** bring under complete control; make subservient or submissive. ⟨ME < LL *subjugare* < *sub-* under + *jugum* yoke⟩ **—'sub•ju,ga•tor,** *n.* **—,sub•ju'ga•tion,** *n.*

sub•junc•tive [səb'dʒʌŋktɪv] *n., adj. Grammar. —n.* **1** a set of verb forms used to express a state or act as possible, conditional, desirable, doubtful, or hypothetical rather than as fact. The subjunctive is a mood and is independent of tense. It is not used much in modern English, normally being replaced by other constructions. Compare INDICATIVE, IMPERATIVE. **2** a verb form in the subjunctive. In *God bless the Queen! Come what may, we will see it through,* and *If I were you I'd try again,* the verb forms *bless, come,* and *were* are subjunctives.
—adj. of, having to do with, or designating the subjunctive. ⟨< LL *subjunctivus,* ult. < L *sub-* under + *jungere* join⟩

sub•king•dom ['sʌb,kɪŋdəm] *n. Biology.* a secondary category in the classification of plants and animals that is a grouping within a kingdom and includes one or more phyla.

sub•lease *n.* ['sʌb,lis]; *v.* [sʌb'lis] *or* ['sʌb,lis] *n., v.* **-leased, -leas•ing.** *—n.* a lease of all or part of some property given by the person who rents the property himself or herself from the owner.
—v. grant or take a sublease of. **—,sub•les'see,** *n.* **—sub'les•sor,** *n.*

sub•let *v.* [sʌb'lɛt] *or* ['sʌb,lɛt]; *n.* ['sʌb,lɛt] *v.* **-let, -let•ting;** *n. —v.* **1** rent to another (some property that has been rented to oneself): *She sublet her apartment while she was away last summer.* **2** give part of (a contract) to another; subcontract: *The contractor for the whole building sublet the contract for the plumbing.* **3** take or hold a sublease of.
—n. an apartment, etc. that has been obtained by or is available for subletting.

sub–lieu•ten•ant [,sʌblɛf'tɛnənt]; *esp. U.S.,* [,sʌblu'tɛnənt] *n.* **1** *Canadian Forces.* in Maritime Command, the equivalent of a lieutenant. See chart of ranks in the Appendix. **2** a naval officer of similar rank in other countries. *Abbrev.*: SLt., S.Lt., or Sub.Lt.

sub•li•mate *v.* ['sʌblə,meit]; *adj., n.* ['sʌbləmɪt] *or* ['sʌblə,meit] *v.* **-mat•ed, -mat•ing;** *adj., n. —v.* **1** *Psychology.* change the natural expression of (an impulse or desire) into one considered more socially or personally acceptable: *to sublimate one's aggressiveness.* **2** *Chemistry.* **a** sublime (a solid substance); extract by subliming. **b** refine or purify. **3** make nobler or purer.
—adj. sublimated.
—n. a substance produced by the process of subliming. Frost and snow are sublimates; they form directly from water vapour in the air. ⟨< L *sublimare,* originally, raise < *sublimis* lofty⟩

sub•li•ma•tion [,sʌblə'meiʃən] *n.* **1** the act or process of sublimating or subliming. **2** the resulting product or state.

sub•lime [sə'blaɪm] *adj., v.* **-limed, -lim•ing.** *—adj.* **1** noble; majestic; lofty or exalted: *the sublime Dante, the sublime beauty of the Rocky Mountains.* **2** *(noml.)* **the sublime,** that which is lofty, noble, exalted, etc. **3** perfect; supreme: *She carried on with sublime indifference to what people might say.*
—v. **1** *Chemistry.* **a** subject (a solid substance) to the action of heat to produce a vapour which may then be condensed to a solid again. Some substances can be purified by subliming them. **b** pass directly from a solid state to a vapour and back again. Some substances that will sublime are arsenic, camphor, and Dry Ice. **2** make higher or nobler; make sublime. ⟨ME < OF, ult. < L *sublimis,* originally, sloping up < *sub-* up + *limen* lintel⟩ **—sub'lime•ly,** *adv.* **—sub'lime•ness,** *n.*

sub•lim•i•nal [sə'blɪmənəl] *adj.* **1** *Psychology.* existing or acting below the threshhold of conscious awareness: *the subliminal self. The committee protested against the use of subliminal advertising on television.* **2** too weak or small to be felt or noticed. ⟨< *sub-* + L *limen, liminis* threshold⟩ **—sub'lim•i•nal•ly,** *adv.*

sub•lim•i•ty [sə'blɪməti] *n., pl.* **-ties. 1** the quality or state of being sublime; lofty excellence or grandeur. **2** something sublime.

sub•lin•gual [sʌb'lɪŋgwəl] *or* [sʌb'lɪŋgjuəl] *adj., n. Anatomy. —adj.* located beneath or on the underside of the tongue.
—n. a sublingual gland, artery, etc.

Sub.Lt. sub-lieutenant.

sub•lu•nar [sʌb'lunər] *adj.* sublunary.

sub•lu•nar•y [sʌb'lunəri] *or* ['sʌblə,nɛri] *adj.* **1** situated beneath the moon or between the earth and the moon. **2** of or like the earth. ⟨< NL *sublunaris,* ult. < L *sub-* under + *luna* moon⟩

sub•ma•chine gun [,sʌbmə'ʃin] a lightweight automatic or semi-automatic gun, designed to be fired from the shoulder or hip.

sub•mar•gin•al [sʌb'mardʒənəl] *adj.* **1** *Biology.* near the margin of an organ or part. **2** below a required minimum standard: *submarginal living conditions.* **3** of land, etc., not productive enough to be worth cultivating, developing, etc.

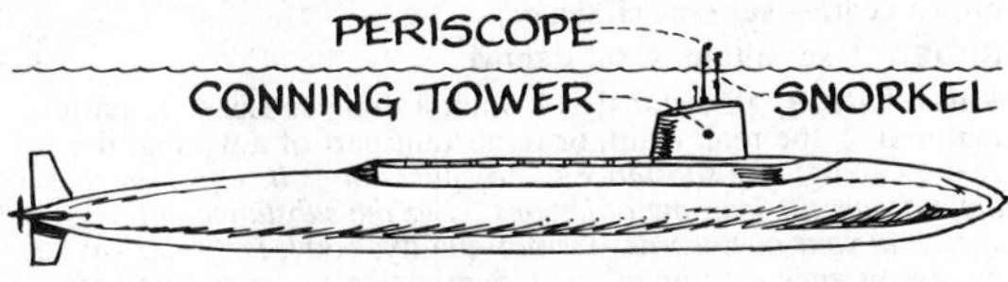

A submarine

sub•ma•rine *n., v.* ['sʌbmə,rin] *or* [,sʌbmə'rin]; *adj.* [,sʌbmə'rin] *n., v.* **-rined, -rin•ing;** *adj. —n.* **1** a boat that can operate under water, used in warfare for discharging torpedoes, etc. **2** a large sandwich consisting of a long roll that is split lengthwise and filled with a variety of cold meats, cheese, tomatoes, onions, coleslaw, etc.
—v. attack or sink by a submarine.
—adj. **1** of or carried out by a submarine or submarines: *submarine tactics, submarine warfare.* **2** placed, growing, or used below the surface of the sea: *submarine plants.*

submarine chaser a small (30-60 m), fast patrol vessel, designed and equipped for use in antisubmarine operations.

sub•mar•i•ner [sʌb'mærənər] *or* [sʌb'mɛrənər], ['sʌbmə,rinər] *or* [,sʌbmə'rinər] *n.* a member of the crew of a submarine.

sub•max•il•la [,sʌb'mæksələ] *n., pl.* **-lae** [-,li] *or* [-,laɪ] or **-las.** *Anatomy. Zoology.* the lower jaw or jawbone.

sub•max•il•lar•y [,sʌb'mæksə,lɛri] *adj., n., pl.* **-lar•ies.**
—adj. **1** of, having to do with, or situated under the lower jaw. **2** of or having to do with either of the salivary glands situated beneath the lower jaw, one on either side.
—n. a submaxillary part, especially the lower jawbone.

sub•me•di•ant [sʌb'midiənt] *n. Music.* the sixth tone of the diatonic scale.

sub•merge [səb'mɜrdʒ] *v.* **-merged, -merg•ing. 1** put under water; cover with water or other liquid: *A big wave submerged us. At high tide this path is submerged.* **2** cover; bury: *His talent was submerged by his shyness.* **3** sink under water; go below the surface. **4** sink out of sight. ⟨< L *submergere* < *sub-* under + *mergere* plunge⟩ **—sub'mer•gence,** *n.*

sub•merse [səb'mɜrs] *v.* **-mersed, -mers•ing.** submerge. ⟨< L *submersus,* pp. of *submergere.* See SUBMERGE.⟩

sub•mersed [səb'mɜrst] *adj., v. —adj.* **1** submerged. **2** *Botany.* growing under water.
—v. pt. and pp. of SUBMERSE.

sub•mers•i•ble [səb'mɜrsəbəl] *adj., n. —adj.* that can be submerged: *a submersible pump.*
—n. a ship or craft that can operate under water for research, exploration, etc.

sub•mer•sion [səb'mɜrʒən] *or* [səb'mɜrʃən] *n.* submergence.

sub•mi•cro•scop•ic [,sʌb,məikrə'skɒpɪk] *adj.* too small to be seen through an ordinary microscope; visible only by means of an electron microscope.

sub•mis•sion [səb'mɪʃən] *n.* **1** the act of submitting; a yielding to the power, control, or authority of another. **2** a state of extreme obedience or humility: *an attitude of submission. The servant bowed in submission.* **3** a referring or being referred to the consideration or judgment of another or others. **4** a petition; a formal request. **5** a report; something submitted for consideration. **6** *Law.* an agreement by both parties to submit a dispute to arbitration and to abide by the decision made. ⟨ME < L *submissio, -onis* < *submittere.* See SUBMIT.⟩

sub•mis•sive [səb'mɪsɪv] *adj.* yielding to the power, control, or authority of another; obedient; humble. **—sub'mis•sive•ly,** *adv.* **—sub'mis•sive•ness,** *n.*

sub•mit [səb'mɪt] *v.* **-mit•ted, -mit•ting. 1** yield to the power, control, or authority of another or others; surrender; yield: *The thief submitted to arrest by the police. I will not submit my child to such treatment.* **2** refer to the consideration or judgment of another or others: *The secretary submitted a report of the last meeting. She submitted a bid on the contract for the new shopping centre.* **3** offer as an opinion; respectfully propose or affirm: *We submit that the proposed expansion of the airport is unnecessary.* ⟨ME < L *submittere* < *sub-* under + *mittere* let go⟩
☛ *Syn.* **1.** See note at YIELD.

sub•mul•ti•ple [sʌb'mʌltəpəl] *n.* a number or quantity contained exactly within another number or quantity. The millimetre is a submultiple of the metre.

sub•nor•mal [sʌb'nɔrməl] *adj.* **1** lower or smaller than normal: *subnormal temperatures.* **2** below normal, especially in mental ability. **—sub'nor•mal•ly,** *adv.*

sub•or•bit•al [sʌb'ɔrbɪtəl] *adj.* **1** not in or going into a complete orbit: *The new space capsule was tested in a suborbital flight.* **2** *Anatomy.* situated below the orbit of the eye: *the suborbital nerve.*

sub•or•der ['sʌb,ɔrdər] *n. Biology.* a secondary category in the classification of plants and animals that is a grouping within an order and includes one or more families. **—sub'or•din•al,** *adj.*

sub•or•di•nate *adj., n.* [sə'bɔrdənɪt]; *v.* [sə'bɔrdə,neit] *adj., n., v.* **-nat•ed, -nat•ing.** *—adj.* **1** inferior in rank: *In the armed forces, lieutenants are subordinate to captains.* **2** inferior in importance; secondary: *a subordinate argument, a subordinate issue.* **3** under the control or influence of something else. **4** *Grammar.* of, having to do with, or designating a clause that depends for its complete sense on a main clause. A subordinate clause functions as an adjective, adverb, or noun in a complex sentence.
—n. a subordinate person or thing.
—v. make subordinate: *The host politely subordinated his wishes to those of his guests.* ⟨< Med.L *subordinatus,* pp. of *subordinare,* ult. < L *sub-* under + *ordo, ordinis* order⟩ **—sub'or•di•nate•ly,** *adv.*

sub•or•di•na•tion [sə,bɔrdə'neiʃən] *n.* **1** the act of subordinating or the quality or state of being subordinate. **2** a subordinate position or importance. **3** a submission to authority; willingness to obey; obedience.

sub•orn [sə'bɔrn] *v.* **1** *Law.* persuade by bribery or other means to do something illegal, especially to give false testimony in court: *A friend of the accused was charged with suborning a witness.* **2** obtain by bribery or other means: *to suborn perjury.* ⟨< L *subornare* < *sub-* secretly + *ornare* equip⟩ **—,sub•or'na•tion,** *n.* **—sub'orn•er,** *n.*

sub•phy•lum ['sʌb,faɪləm] *n. Biology.* a secondary category in the classification of plants and animals that is a grouping within a phylum and includes one or more classes.

sub•plot ['sʌb,plɒt] *n.* a subordinate plot within the main plot of a novel, film, play, etc.

sub•poe•na [sə'pinə] *or* [səb'pinə] *n., v.* **-naed, -na•ing.** *Law.*
—n. a written order, or summons, requiring a person to be present in court for a specified purpose at a specified time. Also (*esp. U.S.*), **subpena.**
—v. summon with a subpoena. ⟨< NL *sub poena* under penalty⟩

sub•po•lar [sʌb'poulər] *adj.* **1** subarctic. **2** subantarctic.

sub•ro•gate ['sʌbrə,geit] *v.* **-gated, -gat•ing.** *Law.* substitute (one person or thing) for another in respect of a right or claim. ⟨< L *subrogare* < *sub-* in place of + *rogare* ask⟩

sub•ro•ga•tion [,sʌbrə'geiʃən] *n. Law.* the substitution of one person or thing for another, especially the substitution of one party for another as creditor, with the transference of all the rights and duties of the original creditor.

sub ro•sa [sʌb 'rouzə] in strict confidence; privately. ⟨< *sub rosa* under the rose; the rose was an ancient symbol of secrecy⟩

sub•rout•ine ['sʌbru,tin] *n. Computer technology.* an instruction sequence in a computer program that can be prewritten and used or referred to as often as needed.

sub•scribe [səb'skraɪb] *v.* **-scribed, -scrib•ing. 1** promise to give or pay (a sum of money): *She subscribed $75 to the hospital* *fund.* **2** arrange and pay to receive a periodical or a service regularly for a given length of time (*used with* **to**): *He subscribes to several magazines.* **3** write (one's name) at the end of a document, etc.; sign one's name. **4** write one's name at the end of; show one's consent or approval by signing: *Thousands of citizens subscribed the petition.* **5** give one's consent or approval; agree: *She will not subscribe to anything unfair.* **6** agree with or be in favour of. **7** write (a number or other notation) slightly below and to the right of a word, number, formula, etc.; make subscript: *Subscribe the numbers so that the formula reads H_2SO_4.* ⟨ME < L *subscribere* < *sub-* under + *scribere* write⟩ **—sub'scrib•er,** *n.*

sub•script ['sʌb,skrɪpt] *n., adj.* *—n.* a small number, letter, etc. written immediately below or below and to one side of another number, letter, etc. *Example*: *In* H_2SO_4 *the* 2 *and the* 4 *are subscripts.*
—adj. written underneath or low on the line: *a subscript number.* ⟨< L *subscriptus*, pp. of *subscribere.* See SUBSCRIBE.⟩

sub•scrip•tion [səb'skrɪpʃən] *n.* **1** a subscribing. **2** a sum of money subscribed: *His subscription to the Fresh Air Fund was $25. We are raising subscriptions for a new arena.* **3** something obtained by subscribing, especially a magazine, etc. or a service paid for in advance for a specific period of time: *Your symphony subscription expires after the next concert.* **4** something written at the end of a thing; a signature. **5** a signing, as of one's name on a document. **6** consent or approval, usually in writing.

sub•sec•tion ['sʌb,sɛkʃən] *n.* a part of a section.

sub•se•quence¹ ['sʌbsəkwəns] *n.* **1** the quality or state of following or coming after. **2** an event or circumstance that follows or comes later.

sub•se•quence² ['sʌb,sikwəns] *n. Mathematics.* a sequence within a sequence.

sub•se•quent ['sʌbsəkwənt] *adj.* coming after; following; later: *Subsequent events proved him right. That problem is dealt with in a subsequent chapter. The package arrived on the day subsequent to her call.* ⟨< L *subsequens, -entis*, ppr. of *subsequi* < *sub-* up + *sequi* follow⟩ **—'sub•se•quent•ly,** *adv.*

sub•serve [səb'sɜrv] *v.* **-served, -serv•ing.** be of use or service in helping along (a purpose, action, etc.); promote: *Chewing food well subserves digestion.* ⟨< L *subservire* < *sub-* under + *servire* serve⟩

sub•ser•vi•ent [səb'sɜrviənt] *adj.* **1** tamely submissive; slavishly polite and obedient; servile. **2** useful as a means to help a purpose or end; serviceable. **3** serving in a subordinate role. ⟨< L *subserviens, -entis*, ppr. of *subservire* < *sub-* under + *servire* serve⟩ **—sub'ser•vi•ence** or **sub'ser•vi•en•cy,** *n.* **—sub'ser•vi•ent•ly,** *adv.*

sub•set ['sʌb,sɛt] *n. Mathematics. Logic.* a set whose members are also members of another set or series: *The set of dogs is a subset of the set of mammals.*

sub•side [səb'saɪd] *v.* **-sid•ed, -sid•ing. 1** sink to a lower level: *After the rain stopped, the flood waters subsided.* **2** grow less; die down; become less active or intense: *The storm finally subsided.* **3** fall to the bottom; settle. ⟨< L *subsidere* < *sub-* down + *sidere* settle⟩ **—sub'sid•ence** [səb'saɪdəns] *or* ['sʌbsədəns], *n.*

sub•sid•i•ar•y [səb'sɪdiəri], [səb'sɪdʒəri], *or* [səb'sɪdi,ɛri] *adj., n., pl..* **-ar•ies.** *—adj.* **1** useful to assist or support; auxiliary; supplementary. **2** subordinate; secondary. **3** of, having to do with, or maintained by a subsidy.
—n. **1** a thing or person that assists or supplements. **2** a company having over half of its stock owned or controlled by another company: *The bus line was a subsidiary of the railway.* **3** *Music.* a secondary or subordinate theme or subject. ⟨< L *subsidiarius* < *subsidium* reserve troops⟩

sub•si•dize ['sʌbsə,daɪz] *v.* **-dized, -diz•ing. 1** aid or assist with a grant of money: *The government subsidizes shipping lines and airlines that carry mail.* **2** buy the aid or assistance of with a grant of money. **—'sub•si,diz•er,** *n.* **—,sub•si•di'za•tion,** *n.*

sub•si•dy ['sʌbsədi] *n., pl.* **-dies.** a grant or contribution of money, especially one made by a government. ⟨< L *subsidium* aid, reserve troops⟩

sub•sist [səb'sɪst] *v.* **1** stay alive; live: *While the hikers were stranded they subsisted on berries.* **2** continue to be; exist: *Many superstitions still subsist.* **3** *Philosophy.* be possible to conceive of logically and to make true statements about; having timeless or abstract existence. **4** have as its ground or source (*used with* **in**). ⟨< L *subsistere* < *sub-* up to + *sistere* stand⟩

sub•sist•ence [səb'sɪstəns] *n.* **1** existence; continuance. **2** the state or fact of staying alive; living. **3** a means of staying alive; livelihood, especially a minimal or marginal one: *The sea provides a subsistence for fishers.* **4** *Philosophy.* the quality of having abstract existence as a logical concept. **5** (*adj.*) characterized by no surplus for trade; yielding the minimum necessary for survival: *a subsistence economy, subsistence farming.*

sub•soil ['sʌb,sɔɪl] *n.* the layer of earth that lies just under the surface soil.

sub•son•ic [sʌb'sɒnɪk] *adj.* **1** having to do with or designed for use at a speed less than that of sound. **2** designating or pertaining to a speed less than that of sound at the same height above sea level. **3** referring to a wave frequency lower than those audible to the normal human ear.

sub•space ['sʌb,speis] *n.* **1** a space within a larger space: *The used book store occupies a subspace in the Student Union Building.* **2** *Mathematics.* a non-empty subset of a set of vectors.

sub•spe•cies ['sʌb,spiʃiz] *or* ['sʌb,spisiz] *n., pl.* **-cies.** a geographical grouping within an animal or plant species based on inherited biological differences. Subspecies often develop when groups of a particular species have been isolated from each other for many generations. The grizzly is a subspecies of the brown bear. **—,sub•spe'cif•ic,** *adj.*

subst. 1 substitute. **2** substantive.

sub•stance ['sʌbstəns] *n.* **1** what a thing consists of; matter; material. **2** the real, main, or important part of anything; the real meaning: *The substance of an education is its effect on your life, not just the learning of lessons. Give the substance of the speech in your own words.* **3** solid quality; body: *Pea soup has more substance than bouillon.* **4** depth; significant content: *Her writing is superficial and lacks substance.* **5** wealth; property. **6** a particular kind of matter: *The little pond is covered with a green substance.* **7** *Philosophy.* **a** one of certain things said to underly all phenomena, and in which accidents or attributes inhere. **b** something that subsists by itself; a separate or distinct thing.
in substance, a essentially; mainly. **b** really; actually. ⟨ME < OF < *substantia* < *substare* stand firm < *sub-* up to + *stare* stand⟩

☛ *Syn.* **1. Substance,** MATTER, MATERIAL = what a thing consists or is made of. **Substance** suggests 'what a thing consists of', as apart from the form in which it exists, and applies both to things existing in the physical world and to those given actual form only in the mind: *The substance of the plan is good.* **Matter** applies to substance that occupies space and that physical objects consist of: *Matter may be gaseous, liquid, or solid.* **Material** applies particularly to matter from which something is made: *Wood is an important building material.*

sub•stan•dard [sʌb'stændərd] *adj.* **1** falling short of a minimum standard of quality: *The substandard sheets are being sold at very low prices.* **2** of language, differing from the standard usage of a group, especially by deviating from what is considered grammatical or acceptable by educated people: *Words like* ain't *and constructions like* them books *are considered substandard by many people.*

sub•stan•tial [səb'stænʃəl] *adj.* **1** real; actual: *People and things are substantial; dreams and ghosts are not.* **2** large; important; ample: *Maria has made a substantial improvement in health.* **3** strong; firm; solid: *The house is substantial enough to last a hundred years.* **4** in the main; in essentials: *The stories told by the two girls were in substantial agreement.* **5** well-to-do; wealthy. **6** of real or solid worth or value; weighty; sound: *substantial criticism, substantial evidence.* **7** *Philosophy.* of or being a substance; existing independently as a substance. ⟨ME < L *substantialis* < *substantia.* See SUBSTANCE.⟩
—sub'stan•tial•ly, *adv.* **—sub,stan•ti'al•i•ty** [sʌb,stænʃi'ælɪti] *or* **sub'stan•tial•ness,** *n.*

sub•stan•ti•ate [səb'stænʃi,eit] *v.* **-at•ed, -at•ing. 1** establish by evidence; prove: *to substantiate a rumour, a claim, a theory, etc.* **2** give concrete or substantial form to. **—sub,stan•ti'a•tion,** *n.*

sub•stan•ti•val [,sʌbstən'taɪvəl] *adj.* of, having to do with, or being a substantive. **—,sub•stan'ti•val•ly,** *adv.*

sub•stan•tive ['sʌbstəntɪv] *n., adj.* *—n. Grammar.* a noun or pronoun or an adjective, phrase, or clause used as a noun.
—adj. **1** *Grammar.* **a** used as a noun. **b** showing or expressing existence. The verb *be* is the substantive verb. **2** independent. **3** real; actual. **4** having a firm or solid basis. **5** significant or SUBSTANTIAL (def. 2) in amount. **6** relating to the practical, essential, or pertinent elements of a matter. ⟨ME < LL *substantivus*, ult. < *substare.* See SUBSTANCE.⟩
—'sub•stan•tive•ly, *adv.* **—'sub•stan•tive•ness,** *n.*

sub•sta•tion ['sʌb,steiʃən] *n.* a branch station; subordinate station: *Besides the main post office in our city, there are six substations.*

sub•sti•tute ['sʌbstɪ,tjut] *or* ['sʌbstɪ,tut] *n., v.* **-tut•ed, -tut•ing.** *—n.* **1** a person or thing used in or taking the place of another: *Margarine is a common substitute for butter. We were*

taught by a substitute today because our teacher was sick. **2** (*adjl.*) taking the place of or put in for another: *a substitute teacher.* **3** *Grammar.* any form, word, or construction replacing a word or phrase of the same syntactic function. In *If you must criticize, do so gently, do so* is a substitute for *criticize.*
—*v.* **1** put in the place of another: *We substituted brown sugar for molasses in these cookies.* **2** take the place of another (*used with* **for**): *She substituted for her father at the hearing.* ⟨ME < L *substitutus,* pp. of *substituere* < *sub-* instead + *statuere* establish⟩

sub•sti•tu•tion [ˌsʌbstɪˈtjuʃən] *or* [ˌsʌbstɪˈtuʃən] *n.* **1** the replacing of one person or thing by another. **2** something that functions as a replacement.

sub•sti•tu•tion•al [ˌsʌbstɪˈtjuʃənəl] *or* [ˌsʌbstɪˈtuʃənəl] *adj.* **1** having to do with or characterized by substitution. **2** acting or serving as a substitute. **—ˌsub•stiˈtu•tion•al•ly,** *adv.*

sub•sti•tu•tive [ˈsʌbstɪˌtjutɪv] *or* [ˈsʌbstɪˌtutɪv] *adj.* **1** having to do with or involving substitution. **2** serving as, or capable of serving as, a substitute.

sub•stra•ta [ˈsʌbˌstrætə] *or* [ˈsʌbˌstreitə] *n.* a pl. of SUBSTRATUM.

sub•strate [ˈsʌbstreit] *n., adj.* —*n.* **1** substratum. **2** *Biochemistry.* the substance upon which an enzyme operates. **3** *Electronics.* the supporting material on which an electronic circuit is formed or fabricated.
—*adj.* of or having to do with anything that is a substratum: *a substrate language.*

sub•stra•tum [ˈsʌbˌstrætəm] *or* [ˈsʌbˌstreitəm] *n., pl.* **-stra•ta** [-ˌstrætə] *or* [-streitə] or **-stra•tums.** **1** a layer lying under another. **2** a layer of earth lying just under the surface soil; subsoil. **3** a basis; foundation: *The story has a substratum of truth.* **4** *Biology.* the base or matter from which an organism develops. **5** *Linguistics.* a language, usually of a conquered or minority people, that has left traces in the language replacing or superseding it. In a pidgin language, part of the lexicon is always from the substratum. ⟨< NL *substratum,* neut. of L *substratus,* pp. of *substernere* < *sub-* under + *sternere* spread⟩

sub•struc•ture [ˈsʌbˌstrʌktʃər] *n.* a structure forming a foundation. Also, **substruction** [sʌbˈstrʌkʃən].
—subˈstruc•tur•al, *n.*

sub•sume [səbˈsum] *or* [səbˈsjum] *v.* **-sumed, -sum•ing.** incorporate (an idea, term, proposition, etc.) within a more general or comprehensive one; bring under a broader category or classification: *Your suggestion has been subsumed under point 4 of the committee's recommendations.* ⟨< NL *subsumere* < L *sub-* under + *sumere* assume⟩ **—subˈsump•tion** [-ˈsʌmpʃən], *n.*

sub•teen [ˈsʌbˌtin] *n. Informal.* **1** a boy or girl who is almost a teenager. **2** (*adjl.*) of or for subteens.

sub•tem•per•ate [sʌbˈtɛmpərɪt] *adj.* referring to or occurring in the colder parts of the Temperate Zone.

sub•ten•ant [ˈsʌbˌtɛnənt] *n.* a tenant of a tenant; one who rents land, a house, or the like, from a tenant.
—subˈten•an•cy, *n.*

sub•tend [səbˈtɛnd] *v.* **1** *Geometry.* **a** define by marking off the endpoints of: *A chord subtends an arc of a circle.* **b** of a line, arc, etc., be opposite to (an angle): *The hypotenuse subtends the right angle of a right-angled triangle. An arc of a circle subtends the central angle of the arc.* **2** *Botany.* underlie, usually so as to enclose or surround: *a flower subtended by a leafy bract.* ⟨< L *subtendere* < *sub-* under + *tendere* stretch⟩

sub•ter•fuge [ˈsʌbtərˌfjudʒ] *n.* a trick, excuse, or other deceptive expedient used to escape something unpleasant: *The student's headache was only a subterfuge to avoid taking the examination.* ⟨< LL *subterfugium,* ult. < L *subter-* from under + *fugere* flee⟩

sub•ter•ra•ne•an [ˌsʌbtəˈreiniən] *adj.* **1** underground: *A subterranean passage led from the castle to a cave.* **2** carried on secretly; hidden. ⟨< L *subterraneus* < *sub-* under + *terra* earth⟩

sub•ter•ra•ne•ous [ˌsʌbtəˈreiniəs] *adj.* subterranean.
—ˌsub•terˈra•ne•ous•ly, *adv.*

sub•text [ˈsʌbˌtɛkst] *n.* the underlying or implied meaning, especially with reference to literature and drama.

sub•tile [ˈsʌtəl] *or* [ˈsʌbtɪl] *adj. Archaic.* subtle. ⟨ME < OF *subtil,* learned borrowing < L *subtilis.* See SUBTLE.⟩
—ˈsub•tile•ly, *adv.* **—ˈsub•tile•ness,** *n.*

sub•til•i•ty or **sub•til•ty** [sʌbˈtɪlɪti] *or* [ˈsʌbtəlti] *n., pl.* **-ties.** *Archaic.* subtlety.

sub•ti•tle [ˈsʌbˌtəitəl] *n., v.* **-tled, -tling.** —*n.* **1** an additional or subordinate title of a book, article, etc. **2** a written piece of dialogue or description shown between the scenes of a silent film or as part of the scenes of a foreign-language film.
—*v.* **1** give a subtitle to. **2** provide subtitles for: *The German dialogue in many World War II films is subtitled in English.*

sub•tle [ˈsʌtəl] *adj.* **1** delicate; fine: *a subtle odour of perfume.* **2** faint; mysterious: *a subtle smile.* **3** **a** having a keen, quick mind; discerning; acute: *She is a subtle observer.* **b** demanding mental acuity: *subtle distinctions.* **4** sly; crafty; tricky: *a subtle scheme to get some money.* **5** skilful; clever; expert. **6** working unnoticeably or secretly; insidious: *a subtle poison or drug.* **7** of a gas, sparse; light. ⟨ME < OF *soutil* < L *subtilis,* originally, woven underneath⟩ **—ˈsub•tly,** *adv.* **—ˈsub•tle•ness,** *n.*

sub•tle•ty [ˈsʌtəlti] *n., pl.* **-ties.** **1** the quality or state of being subtle. **2** something subtle, especially a fine distinction: *He did not understand all the subtleties of the author's argument.*

sub•ton•ic [sʌbˈtɒnɪk] *n. Music.* the seventh tone of a scale; the tone next below the upper tonic; leading note.

sub•top•ic [ˈsʌbˌtɒpɪk] *n.* one of the secondary topics into which a main topic is divided.

sub•to•tal [ˈsʌbˌtoutəl] *n., v.* **-talled** or **-taled, -tal•ling** or **-tal•ing.** —*n.* the total of a group of figures that form part of a series of figures to be added.
—*v.* calculate a subtotal for (a set of figures).

sub•tract [səbˈtrækt] *v.* **1** *Mathematics.* take away (a number or quantity) from another number or quantity: *Subtract 2 from 10 and you have 8, but subtract 10 from 2 and you have –8.* **2** take away (a part) from a whole. ⟨< L *subtractus,* pp. of *subtrahere* < *sub-* from under + *trahere* draw⟩ **—subˈtract•er,** *n.*

☛ *Syn.* **1, 2. Subtract,** DEDUCT = take away. **Subtract** = to take away from a whole, but in present usage is almost never used except in its mathematical sense, commonly meaning 'to take away one number from another': *He subtracted 89 from 200.* **Deduct** = take away a quantity or amount from a total or whole: *He deducted the price of the cup I broke from the amount he owed me. She deducted 89 cents from $2.00.*

sub•trac•tion [səbˈtrækʃən] *n.* **1** the act or an instance of subtracting. **2** *Mathematics.* the process of finding the difference between two numbers or quantities. A simple subtraction is $10 - 2 = 8$.

sub•trac•tive [səbˈtræktɪv] *adj.* **1** tending or having power to subtract. **2** *Mathematics.* of a number or quantity, that is to be subtracted; having the minus sign (–).

sub•tra•hend [ˈsʌbtrəˌhɛnd] *n. Mathematics.* a number or quantity to be subtracted from another. In $10 - 2 = 8$, the subtrahend is 2. ⟨< L *subtrahendus* < *subtrahere.* See SUBTRACT.⟩

sub•trop•i•cal [sʌbˈtrɒpɪkəl] *adj.* **1** bordering on the tropics; nearly tropical. **2** pertaining to or having the nature of these regions. Also, **subtropic.**

sub•trop•ics [sʌbˈtrɒpɪks] *n.pl.* the region bordering on the tropics.

sub•urb [ˈsʌbərb] *n.* **1** a district, town, or village just outside or near a city or town. **2 the suburbs,** the residential section or sections on the outskirts of a city or town. ⟨ME < L *suburbium* < *sub-* below + *urbs* city⟩

sub•ur•ban [səˈbɜrbən] *adj., n.* —*adj.* **1** having to do with a suburb; in a suburb: *We have an excellent suburban train service.* **2** characteristic of a suburb or its inhabitants.
—*n.* suburbanite.

sub•ur•ban•ite [səˈbɜrbəˌnəit] *n.* a person who lives in a suburb.

sub•ur•bi•a [səˈbɜrbiə] *n.* **1** the suburbs of a city. **2** the residents of the suburbs, thought of as a distinct social class. **3** the values, attitudes, etc. thought to be characteristic of residents of the suburbs.

sub•ven•tion [səbˈvɛnʃən] *n.* **1** money granted to aid or support some cause, institution, or undertaking; subsidy. **2** **a** the providing of help, support, or relief. **b** an instance of this. ⟨ME < OF < LL *subventio, -onis* < L *subvenire* come to one's aid < *sub-* under + *venire* come⟩ **—subˈven•tion,a•ry,** *adj.*

sub•ver•sion [səbˈvɜrʒən] *or* [səbˈvɜrʃən] *n.* the act of subverting or being subverted; overthrow; especially, an attempt to overthrow a government by working against it secretly from within the country. ⟨ME < OF < LL *subversio, -onis* < L *subvertere.* See SUBVERT.⟩

sub•ver•sive [səbˈvɜrsɪv] *adj., n.* —*adj.* tending or designed to overthrow or destroy a government, institution, etc., especially from within: *a subversive scheme.*
—*n.* a person who seeks to overthrow or undermine a government, etc., especially from within. **—subˈver•sive•ly,** *adv.*

sub•vert [səbˈvɜrt] *v.* **1** ruin; overthrow; destroy: *Dictators subvert democracy.* **2** undermine the principles of; corrupt. ⟨ME

< OF < L *subvertere* < *sub-* up from under + *vertere* turn⟩
—sub'vert•er, *n.*

sub•way [ˈsʌb,wei] *n.* **1** an electric railway running for all or most of its length beneath the surface of the streets in a city. **2** an underground passage for pipes, etc. **3** *Brit.* an underpass, such as under a bridge. **4** *Esp. Brit.* a pedestrian underpass under the ground.

suc– *prefix.* the form of SUB- occurring before *c*, as in *succeed.*

suc•ceed [sək'sid] *v.* **1** turn out well; prosper: *His plans succeeded. Any able person who works hard can succeed.* **2** accomplish what is attempted or intended: *The attack succeeded beyond all expectations. After much discussion, Jill succeeded in convincing her father that she needed her own car.* **3** come next after; follow; take the place of: *Diefenbaker succeeded St. Laurent as Prime Minister of Canada.* **4** come into possession of an office, title, or property through right of birth, etc. (*used with* **to**): *The Prince of Wales succeeds to the throne of England.* ⟨ME < L *succedere* < *sub-* up (to) + *cedere* go⟩
—suc'ceed•er, *n.*
☛ *Syn.* **3.** See note at FOLLOW.

suc•cess [sək'sɛs] *n.* **1** a favourable result; a wished-for ending; good fortune. **2** the gaining of wealth, position, etc.: *He has had little success in life.* **3** a person or thing that succeeds. **4** result; outcome; fortune: *What success did you have in finding a new cook?* ⟨< L *successus* < *succedere.* See SUCCEED.⟩

suc•cess•ful [sək'sɛsfəl] *adj.* **1** having success; ending in success. **2** prosperous; fortunate. **—suc'cess•ful•ly,** *adv.*

suc•ces•sion [sək'sɛʃən] *n.* **1** a number of persons or things following one after the other; series: *a succession of capable leaders, a succession of misfortunes.* **2** the act or process of following one after the other. **3** the right of succeeding to an office, property, or rank: *There was a dispute about the rightful succession to the throne.* **4** the order of persons having such a right: *The monarch's eldest child is next in succession to the throne.* **5** *Ecology.* the slow, progressive replacement of one community of plants or animals by another until a climax community characteristic of a specific environment is reached.
in succession, one after another: *We visited our sick friend several days in succession.*
☛ *Syn.* **1.** See note at SERIES.

succession duty *Law.* a tax payable on the value of all property or interest acquired by inheritance. Also, **death duty.**

suc•ces•sive [sək'sɛsɪv] *adj.* **1** coming one after another; following in order; consecutive: *It rained for three successive days.* **2** concerning or referring to succession. **—suc'ces•sive•ly,** *adv.*
☛ *Syn.* **Successive,** CONSECUTIVE = following one after another without interruption or a break. **Successive** emphasizes the idea of coming one after another in order or without interruption: *She has worked on three successive Saturdays.* **Consecutive** emphasizes the closeness of the connection or the idea of following immediately or continuously: *She worked three consecutive days last week.*

suc•ces•sor [sək'sɛsər] *n.* a person or thing that comes next after another in a series; especially, a person who succeeds to an office, position, ownership of property, or title. ⟨< L⟩

suc•cinct [sək'sɪŋkt] *adj.* marked by clear, brief expression; concise: *She gave a succinct account of her meeting with the director.* ⟨ME < L *succinctus*, pp. of *succingere* tuck up clothes for action < *sub-* up + *cingere* gird⟩ **—suc'cinct•ly,** *adv.*
—suc'cinct•ness, *n.*

suc•cin•ic acid [sək'sɪnɪk] *Chemistry.* a colourless, crystalline, water-soluble dibasic acid, used in medicine and in the production of dyes, lacquers, and perfumes. *Formula*: $C_4H_6O_4$

suc•cor ['sʌkər] *n.* See SUCCOUR.

suc•co•ry ['sʌkəri] *n.* chicory.

suc•co•tash ['sʌkə,tæʃ] *n.* a dish made of cooked sweet corn and lima beans or green beans, often with cream, butter, and green onions. It was originally a North American Indian dish. ⟨< Algonquian⟩

Suc•coth ['sʊkəs], [sə'kous], *or* [su'kɒt]; *Hebrew*, [su'kɔt]. See SUKKOTH.

suc•cour or **suc•cor** ['sʌkər] *n., v.* —*n.* **1** help; aid; relief: *to give succour in time of need.* **2** a person or thing that gives help or aid.
—*v.* help or assist (a person or animal) in distress or need; relieve: *to succour the wounded.* ⟨ME < OF *sucurs*, ult. < L *succurrere* run to help < *sub-* up (to) + *currere* run⟩
☛ *Hom.* SUCKER.

suc•cu•bus ['sʌkjəbəs] *n., pl.* **-bi** [-baɪ]. **1** an evil spirit in female form, reputed to have sexual intercourse with men while they sleep. Compare INCUBUS. **2** a prostitute. ⟨ME < ML (by contamination from *incubus*) < LL *succuba* strumpet < L *succubare* to lie beneath < *sub* below + *cubare* to lie⟩

suc•cu•lent ['sʌkjələnt] *adj.* **1** juicy: *a succulent fruit.* **2** full of vigour and richness; not dull. **3** of a plant, having thick, fleshy tissues adapted for storing water, either in the stem, as cactuses, or in the leaves. Most succulents are native to desert or semi-arid regions.
—*n.* a succulent plant. ⟨< L *succulentus* < *succus* juice⟩
—'suc•cu•lence or **'suc•cu•len•cy,** *n.* **—'suc•cu•lent•ly,** *adv.*

suc•cumb [sə'kʌm] *v.* **1** give way to superior force, etc. or to overwhelming desire; yield (*usually with* **to**): *He succumbed to temptation and stole the money. After several days of fighting, the garrison succumbed.* **2** die or die of (*used with* **to**): *She succumbed to her injuries two days after being admitted to hospital.* ⟨ME < L *succumbere* < *sub-* down + *-cumbere* (< *cubare*) lie⟩

such [sʌtʃ] *adj., pron.* —*adj.* **1** of that kind; of the same kind or degree: *I have never seen such a sight.* **2** being as described to so great an extent: *She wore such thin clothes it is no wonder she caught cold.* **3** of the kind already spoken of or suggested: *The ladies took only tea and coffee and such drinks.* **4** so great, so bad, so good, etc.: *He is such a liar.* **5** whatever; whichever: *Make such repairs as you deem necessary. They bought only such luxuries as they could afford.*
such and such, a certain one or ones not named or identified; some; certain: *The bank was robbed in such and such a town by such and such persons.*
such as, a of the kind or degree that; of a given kind: *His behaviour was such as might be expected of a young child.* **b** of a similar or the same kind: *Inane letters such as this one should not appear in a respectable newspaper.* **c** for example: *members of the dog family, such as the wolf, fox, and jackal.*
such as it is or **was,** although of a questionable quality or barely adequate: *The food, such as it was, was plentiful.*
—*pron.* one or more persons or things of a given kind: *The box contains blankets and towels and such.*
as such, a as being what is indicated or implied: *A leader, as such, deserves respect.* **b** in or by itself; intrinsically considered: *Mere good looks, as such, will not take you far.* ⟨ME, OE *swylc, swelc* < *swa* so + *līc* like⟩

such•like ['sʌtʃ,ləik] *adj., pron.* —*adj.* of such kind; of a like kind.
—*pron.* persons or things of the same kind: *deceptions, disguises, and suchlike.* ⟨late ME⟩

suck [sʌk] *v., n.* —*v.* **1** draw into the mouth by using the lips and tongue to create a partial vacuum: *Lemonade can be sucked through a straw.* **2** draw something from with the mouth: *to suck oranges.* **3** draw milk from the breast, a teat, or a bottle. **4** draw by sucking: *He sucked at his pipe.* **5** take in; absorb: *Plants suck up moisture from the earth. A sponge sucks in water.* **6** draw in; swallow: *The whirlpool sucked down the boat.* **7** draw air instead of water: *The pump sucked noisily.* **8** hold in the mouth to draw on, moisten, or dissolve; lick: *The child sucked a lollipop.* **9** bring into a given condition by sucking: *The baby had sucked the bottle empty and was crying for more.* **10** *Slang.* be extremely unsatisfactory; be disgusting; be of poor quality: *This lecture sucks*
suck in, *Slang.* defraud; dupe.
suck up to, *Slang.* ingratiate oneself with.
—*n.* **1** the act of sucking. **2** a sucking force or sound. **3** something sucked, or its quantity; a sip or lick: *Let me have a suck at your lollipop.* ⟨OE *sūcan*⟩

suck•er ['sʌkər] *n., v.* —*n.* **1** an animal or thing that sucks. **2** any of a family (Catostomidae) of freshwater fishes found mainly in North America, having a soft, thick-lipped, toothless mouth, usually on the undersurface of the head. **3** in some animals, an organ for sucking or holding fast by a sucking force. **4** a tube or duct used to suck up some substance. **5** *Botany.* **a** a shoot growing from an underground stem or root. **b** an adventitious shoot from the trunk or a branch of a tree or plant. **6 a** the piston of a suction pump. **b** the valve of such a piston. **7** *Slang.* a person easily deceived or exploited. **8** a lump of hard candy; lollipop on a stick.
be a sucker for, *Slang.* have an inordinate weakness or predilection for (a specified thing).
—*v.* **1** remove suckers from (corn, tobacco, etc.). **2** form suckers. **3** *Slang.* treat as a fool or simpleton; deceive; dupe.
☛ *Hom.* SUCCOUR.

suck•er•fish ['sʌkər,fɪʃ] *n.* remora.

suck•le ['sʌkəl] *v.* **-led, -ling. 1** feed with milk from the breast, udder, etc.: *The cat suckles its kittens.* **2** suck at the breast, teat, etc. **3** nourish; bring up. ⟨< *suck*⟩

suck•ler ['sʌklər] *n.* **1** any animal that suckles its young; mammal. **2** suckling.

suck•ling ['sʌklɪŋ] *n.* a young animal or child that has not yet been weaned.

su•crase ['sukreis] *n. Biochemistry.* a digestive enzyme in certain plants and in animal intestines which changes sucrose into dextrose and fructose.

su•cre ['sukrei] *n.* **1** the basic unit of money in Ecuador, divided into 100 centavos. See table of money in the Appendix. **2** a coin worth one sucre. ⟨Antonio José de *Sucre* (1793-1830), a South American general and liberator⟩

su•crose ['sukrous] *n. Chemistry.* the sugar obtained from sugar cane, sugar beets, etc. *Formula*: $C_{12}H_{22}O_{11}$ ⟨< F *sucre* sugar + *-ose*[2]⟩

suc•tion ['sʌkʃən] *n.* **1** the production of a vacuum by removing all or part of the air in a space with the result that atmospheric pressure forces fluid or gas into the vacant space or causes surfaces to stick together: *Lemonade is drawn through a straw by suction.* **2** the force caused in this way. **3** the act or process of sucking. **4** (*adjl.*) causing a suction; working by suction: *a suction valve.* ⟨< L *suctio, -onis* < *sugere* suck⟩

suction cup a cuplike device of rubber, etc., designed to adhere to smooth surfaces by creating a vacuum when pressed against them and then released: *Toy arrows are often tipped with suction cups.*

suc•to•ri•al [sʌk'tɔriəl] *adj.* adapted for sucking or suction.

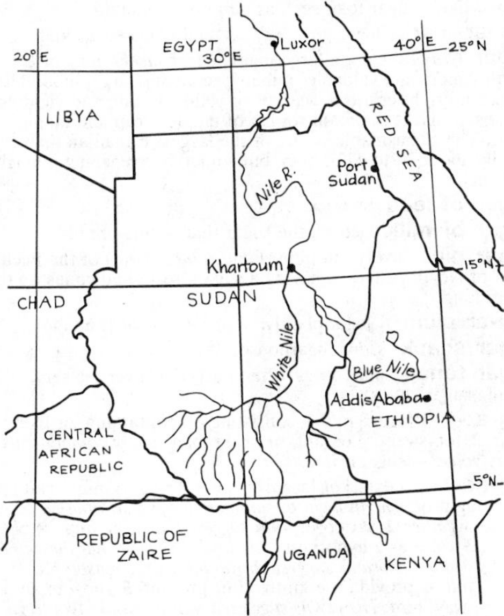

Su•dan [su'dæn] *n.* **1** a country in NE Africa. **2 the Sudan**, a semi-arid region in north central Africa south of the Sahara Desert, and reaching from the Atlantic to the Red Sea.

Su•da•nese [,sudə'niz] *n., pl.* **-nese;** *adj. —n.* a native or inhabitant of Sudan or of the Sudan.
—adj. of or having to do with Sudan, the Sudan, or the Sudanese.

Sudan grass a variety of sorghum widely grown for hay and fodder.

Su•dan•ic [su'dænɪk] *adj.* **1** of or having to do with the Sudan or its inhabitants. **2** of or being any of various languages belonging to either of two branches (Eastern Sudanic and Central Sudanic) of a subcategory of the Niger-Congo or Chari-Nile subfamily of languages. This includes most of the non-Hamitic and non-Bantu languages of northern and central Africa.

su•da•to•ri•um [,sudə'tɔriəm] *n., pl.* **-ri•a** [-riə]. a hot-air bath for inducing sweating. ⟨< L *sudatorium*, ult. < *sudor* sweat⟩

su•da•to•ry ['sudə,tɔri] *adj.* **1** sudorific. **2** having to do with a sudatorium.

sud•den ['sʌdən] *adj., n. —adj.* **1** not expected; found or come upon unexpectedly: *The army made a sudden attack on the fort. There was a sudden turn in the road.* **2** quick; rapid; abrupt: *The cat made a sudden jump at the mouse. The government made a sudden shift in foreign policy.*
—n.
all of a sudden, in a sudden manner: *All of a sudden he stopped and listened.* ⟨ME < AF *sodein* < L *subitaneus* < *subitus* sudden⟩ **—'sud•den•ly,** *adv.* **—'sud•den•ness,** *n.*

sudden death **1** instant or unexpected death. **2** *Sports.* an extra game played to break a tie, or an extra period of play for the same purpose, ending as soon as either side scores. **—'sud•den-'death,** *adj.*

sudden infant death syndrome death due to cessation of breathing in an apparently healthy infant, usually during sleep. The cause is unknown but may be related to a faulty respiration control mechanism or to chronic oxygen deficiency. Also, **crib death.** *Abbrev.*: SIDS

su•dor•if•er•ous [,sudə'rɪfərəs] *adj.* secreting sweat: *sudoriferous glands.*

su•dor•if•ic [,sudə'rɪfɪk] *adj., n. —adj.* causing or promoting sweat.
—n. a sudorific agent or remedy. ⟨< NL *sudorificus* < L *sudor* sweat + *facere* make⟩

suds [sʌdz] *n.pl., v. —n.* **1** soapy water. **2** the bubbles and foam on soapy water. **3** any froth or foam. **4** *Slang.* beer.
—v. **1** *Informal.* form suds: *This shampoo doesn't suds well.* **2** wash in suds: *Just suds the stockings and hang them to dry.* ⟨? < MDu. *sudse* bog⟩

sud•sy ['sʌdzi] *adj.* full of suds; frothy: *sudsy dishwater.*

sue [su] *v.* **sued, su•ing. 1** *Law.* **a** start a lawsuit against: *He sued the railway because his cow was killed by a train.* **b** take action: *to sue for damages.* **2** beg or ask (*for*); plead: *Messengers came suing for peace.* **3** *Archaic.* court; woo.
sue out, apply for and get (a writ, pardon, etc.) from a law court. ⟨ME < AF *suer*, ult. < L *sequi* follow⟩ **—'su•a•ble,** *adj.*
☛ *Hom.* SAULT, SOU.

suede or **suède** [sweid] *n.* **1** a kind of soft leather that has a velvety nap on one or both sides. **2** a kind of cloth with a short nap that looks and feels much like suede. Also, **suede cloth.** **3** (*adjl.*) made of suede. ⟨< F *(de) Suède* (from) Sweden⟩

su•et ['suɪt] *n.* the hard fat about the kidneys and loins of cattle or sheep. Suet is used in cooking and to make tallow. ⟨ME < AF **suet*, dim. of *sue*, OF *sieu* tallow < L *sebum*⟩

su•et•y ['suɪti] *adj.* **1** like suet. **2** containing suet.

suf– *prefix.* the form of SUB- occurring before *f*, as in *suffer* and *suffice.*

suf. or **suff.** suffix.

suf•fer ['sʌfər] *v.* **1** have pain, grief, injury, loss, etc.: *Sick people suffer.* **2** have, feel, or experience (pain, grief, harm, loss etc.): *His business suffered enormous losses during the war.* **4** allow; permit: *He stood politely and suffered his great-aunt to give him the usual peck on the cheek.* **5** bear with patiently; endure: *I will not suffer such insults.* ⟨ME < AF < L *sufferre* < *sub-* up + *ferre* bear⟩ **—'suf•fer•er,** *n.*

suf•fer•a•ble ['sʌfərəbəl] *or* ['sʌfrəbəl] *adj.* that can be endured or allowed. **—'suf•fer•a•bly,** *adv.*

suf•fer•ance ['sʌfərəns] *or* ['sʌfrəns] *n.* **1** permission or consent not actually given but only implied by a failure to object or prevent: *They managed to get their supplies through with the sufferance of the neutral country.* **2** the power to bear or endure; patient endurance.
on sufferance, allowed or tolerated, but not really wanted: *Our cousin came with us to the party on sufferance.*

suf•fer•ing ['sʌfərɪŋ] *or* ['sʌfrɪŋ] *n., v. —n.* pain, trouble, or distress.
—v. ppr. of SUFFER.

suf•fice [sə'fais] *v.* **-ficed, -fic•ing. 1** be enough; be sufficient: *The money will suffice for one year.* **2** satisfy; make content: *A small amount sufficed her.*
suffice it to say, it is enough if I say only (*that*): *Suffice it to say that he was very upset.* ⟨ME < OF < L *sufficere* < *sub-* up (to) + *facere* make⟩

suf•fi•cien•cy [sə'fɪʃənsi] *n., pl.* **-cies. 1** a sufficient amount; a large enough supply: *The ship had a sufficiency of provisions for a voyage of two months.* **2** the quality or state of being sufficient; adequacy: *They questioned the sufficiency of the preparations.*

suf•fi•cient [sə'fɪʃənt] *adj.* **1** as much or as good, strong, etc. as is needed; enough: *sufficient proof. His academic performance last semester was not sufficient to qualify for university entrance.*

2 *Logic.* of a condition, having a relationship with a second statement such that if the condition is fulfilled the second statement must be true. 3 *Archaic.* competent; able. ⟨ME < L *sufficiens, -entis,* ppr. of *sufficere.* See SUFFICE.⟩ **—suf'fi•cient•ly,** *adv.*

☛ *Syn.* **1.** See note at ENOUGH.

suf•fix *n.* ['sʌfɪks]; *v.* [sə'fɪks] *n., v.* *—n.* **1** *Grammar.* **a** a derivational ending put at the end of a word to form another word of different meaning or function, as in bad*ly*, good*ness*, spoon*ful*, amaze*ment*. Compare PREFIX. **b** an inflectional ending, as in talk*s*, talk*ed*, talk*ing*. **2** something added at the end of something else.
—v. add or attach as a suffix. ⟨< NL < L *suffixum,* neut. pp. of *suffigere* < *sub-* upon + *figere* fasten⟩ **—suf'fix•ion** or **,suf•fix'a•tion,** *n.*

suf•fix•al ['sʌfɪksəl] *adj.* having to do with or of the nature of a suffix.

suf•fo•cate ['sʌfə,keit] *v.* **-cat•ed, -cat•ing. 1** kill by stopping the breath or the supply of breathable air. **2** have or cause to have difficulty in breathing: *The smell of sulphur suffocated me. I was suffocating in that hot, smoky room.* **3** die for lack of air in the lungs: *The victims of the fire had not burned to death but had suffocated.* **4** be or cause to be unable to develop: *He longed to escape the suffocating environment of his home town.* ⟨< L *suffocare,* originally, narrow up < *sub-* up + *foces,* dial. var. of *fauces* throat, narrow entrance⟩ **—'suf•fo,cat•ing•ly,** *adv.* **—,suf•fo'ca•tion,** *n.* **—'suf•fo,ca•tive,** *adj.*

Suf•folk ['sʌfək] *n.* **1** any of an English breed of hornless sheep raised especially for meat. **2** any of an English breed of heavy-bodied, chestnut-coloured workhorses. ⟨< *Suffolk,* a county in England⟩

suf•fra•gan ['sʌfrəgən] *n.* **1** a bishop consecrated to assist another bishop. **2** (*adj.*) assisting or auxiliary to. **3** any bishop considered in relation to his or her archbishop. ⟨ME < OF *suffragan,* ult. < L *suffragium* suffrage. See SUFFRAGE.⟩

suf•frage ['sʌfrɪdʒ] *n.* **1** the right to vote; franchise: *Alberta granted suffrage to women in 1916.* **2** a vote, especially a vote in support of a person or a proposal. **3** a casting of votes. **4** a short prayer of supplication. ⟨ME < L *suffragium* supporting vote < *sub-* nearby + *frag-* applause (related to *fragor* din, crash, originally, a breaking)⟩

suf•fra•gette [,sʌfrə'dʒɛt] *n.* formerly, a militant female advocate of suffrage for women.

suf•fra•gist ['sʌfrədʒɪst] *n.* a person who favours giving suffrage to more people, especially to women. **—'suf•fra,gism,** *n.*

suf•fuse [sə'fjuz] *v.* **-fused, -fus•ing.** overspread or flood from within or below with colour, light, a fluid, etc.: *At twilight the sky was suffused with colour. Her eyes were suffused with tears.* ⟨< L *suffusus,* pp. of *suffundere* < *sub-* (up from) under + *fundere* pour⟩ **—suf'fu•sive,** *adj.*

suf•fu•sion [sə'fjuʒən] *n.* **1** a suffusing or being suffused. **2** that with which anything is overspread: *a suffusion of light or colour.*

Su•fi ['sufi] *n.* **1** any of the various sects of Islam which tend toward mysticism and asceticism. **2** a member of any of these sects. ⟨< Arabic, ascetic, literally, man of wool < *suf* wool⟩

Su•fism ['sufɪzəm] *n.* the system of mystical thought and ascetic practice of the Sufis.

sug– *prefix.* the form of SUB- occurring before *g*, as in *suggest.*

sug•ar ['ʃʊgər] *n., v.* *—n.* **1** a sweet crystalline substance consisting entirely or mainly of sucrose and obtained especially from sugar cane or sugar beets. Sugar is much used as a sweetener and preservative of foods and as a source of carbohydrate for the diet. **2** *Chemistry.* any of the class of carbohydrates to which this substance belongs. Glucose and levulose are sugars. **3** a sugar bowl, especially as forming a set with a cream jug. **4** sweet or honeyed words; flattery. **5** *Informal.* sweetheart; darling. **6** *Slang.* money. **7** *Cdn.* **a** MAPLE SUGAR. **b** SUGAR MAPLE.
—v. **1** mix or sprinkle with sugar; put sugar in or on: *She sugared her tea. We sugared the buns before baking them.* **2** form sugar; crystallize: *Honey sugars if kept too long.* **3** *Cdn.* make maple sugar by boiling maple syrup until it is thick enough to crystallize (*usually used with* **off**). **4** make more pleasant or agreeable: *He sugared his criticism of the team with some praise for the individual players.* ⟨ME < OF *sucre* < Med.L < Arabic *sukkar* < Persian < Skt. *sarkara,* originally, grit⟩ **—'su•gar•less,** *adj.*

sugar beet a variety of beet having a large white root with high sugar content, grown commercially for the sugar it yields.

sugar bush *Cdn.* a grove of SUGAR MAPLES.

sugar cabin *Cdn.* sugarhouse.

sugar cane a very tall, coarse, perennial grass (*Saccharum officinarum*) having a strong, jointed stem and flat leaves, widely cultivated in warm regions as a source of sugar.

sug•ar–coat ['ʃʊgər ,kout] *v.* **1** cover with sugar. **2** cause to seem more pleasant or agreeable.

sug•ar–coat•ing ['ʃʊgər ,koutɪŋ] *n., v.* *—n.* **1** a covering of sugar. **2** anything that makes something seem more pleasant or agreeable.
—v. ppr. of SUGAR-COAT.

sugar corn SWEET CORN.

sugar cube a cake of sugar in cube form.

sugar daddy *Cdn. Slang.* a wealthy, elderly or middle-aged man who lavishes gifts and money on a younger woman in return for her favours.

su•gar•house ['ʃʊgər,hʌus] *n. Cdn.* an outbuilding in which maple sap is boiled in large quantities to make maple syrup or maple sugar. Also, **sugar cabin, sugar hut, sugaring hut,** or **sugar shack.**

sugaring off *Cdn.* **1** the converting of maple syrup into sugar by boiling it until it crystallizes. **2** a gathering of friends and neighbours to assist in this process and enjoy a party afterward. Also, **sugaring-off party.**

sugar loaf 1 a cone-shaped mass of sugar. **2** something shaped like a sugar loaf, such as a hill or mountain.

sug•ar–loaf ['ʃʊgər ,louf] *adj.* shaped like a sugar loaf.

sugar maple *Cdn.* a large maple (*Acer saccharum*) of E North America, a valuable timber tree having large, lobed leaves that turn bright crimson, scarlet, or yellow in fall, and yielding a sweet sap that is the main source of maple syrup and maple sugar. The sugar maple is one of the largest Canadian maples, usually about 24 to 27 m high, but sometimes reaching a height of 35 m.

sugar of lead LEAD ACETATE.

sugar of milk lactose, the sugar that occurs in milk.

sugar pine a very tall pine (*Pinus lambertiana*) of the Pacific coast of North America, having a sugary resin and cones up to 50 cm long.

sug•ar•plum ['ʃʊgər,plʌm] *n.* a piece of candy; bonbon.

sugar shack *Cdn.* sugarhouse.

sugar tongs small tongs, often part of a silver tea service, for serving sugar cubes.

sug•ar•y ['ʃʊgəri] *adj.* **1** consisting of, containing, or like sugar. **2** too sweet, pleasant, or agreeable: *sugary compliments, a sugary voice.* **—'sug•ar•i•ness,** *n.*

sug•gest [sə'dʒɛst] *or* [səg'dʒɛst] *v.* **1** bring to mind; call up the thought of: *The thought of summer suggests swimming, tennis, and hot weather.* **2** propose: *John suggested a swim, and we all agreed.* **3** raise as a hypothesis: *My lord, I suggest that the witness is lying. Many historians suggest corruption as the reason for Rome's fall.* **4** provide the motive for; prompt. **5** show in an indirect way; hint: *His yawns suggested that he would like to go to bed.* ⟨< L *suggestus,* pp. of *suggerere* put under, supply, suggest < *sub-* up + *gerere* bring⟩ **—sug'gest•er,** *n.*

sug•gest•i•ble [sə'dʒɛstəbəl] *or* [səg'dʒɛstəbəl] *adj.* **1** easily influenced by suggestion. **2** that can be suggested. **—sug,gest•i'bil•i•ty,** *n.*

sug•ges•tion [sə'dʒɛstʃən] *or* [səg'dʒɛstʃən] *n.* **1** a suggesting: *The trip was made at his suggestion.* **2** the thing suggested: *The picnic was an excellent suggestion.* **3** the calling up of one idea by another because they are connected or associated in some way. **4** a very small amount; slight trace: *She spoke English with just a suggestion of an accent.* **5** *Psychology.* **a** the insinuation of an idea, belief, or impulse into the mind, especially a hypnotized person's mind, in the absence of normal critical thought, contrary ideas, etc. **b** the idea, belief, or impulse so insinuated.

sug•ges•tive [sə'dʒɛstɪv] *or* [səg'dʒɛstɪv] *adj.* **1** tending to suggest ideas, acts, or feelings: *A mild breeze is suggestive of spring.* **2** tending to suggest something improper or indecent; risqué: *a suggestive remark.* **—sug'ges•tive•ness,** *n.* **—sug'ges•tive•ly,** *adv.*

☛ *Syn.* **1.** See note at EXPRESSIVE.

su•i•cid•al [,suə'saɪdəl] *adj.* **1** having to do with suicide. **2** considering committing suicide: *He had been suicidal for some time.* **3** ruinous to one's own interests; disastrous to oneself: *It* *would be suicidal for a store to sell many things below cost.* **—ˌsu•i'cid•al•ly,** *adv.*

su•i•cide ['suəˌsaɪd] *n., v.* **-cid•ed, -cid•ing.** *—n.* **1** the killing of oneself on purpose. **2** the destruction of one's own interests or prospects. **3** a person who kills himself or herself on purpose. *—v. Informal.* commit suicide. ⟨< NL *suicidium* < L *sui* of oneself + *-cidium* act of killing⟩

su•i ge•ne•ris ['sui 'dʒɛnərɪs] *or* ['suaɪ] *Latin.* of his, her, its, or their peculiar kind; unique.

su•i ju•ris ['sui 'dʒʊrɪs] *or* ['suaɪ] *Law.* able to manage one's own affairs or assume legal responsibility, by virtue of being of legal age and sound mind. ⟨< L, of one's own right⟩

su•int ['suɪnt] *or* [swɪnt] *n.* a greasy substance occurring naturally in the fleece of sheep. ⟨< F *suer* sweat⟩

suit [sut] *n., v. —n.* **1** a set of clothes to be worn together: *A man's suit consists of a coat and pants and, often, a vest. The knight wore a suit of armour.* **2** *Law.* a case in a court; application to a court for justice: *He started a suit to collect damages for his injuries.* **3** *Card games.* one of the four sets of cards (spades, hearts, diamonds, and clubs) in a deck. **4** a request; asking. **5** a wooing; courting: *His suit was successful and she married him.*
bring suit (against), take legal action; sue.
follow suit, a *Card games.* play a card of the same suit as that first played. **b** follow the example of another.
—v. **1** provide with clothes. **2** make suitable; make fit: *to suit the punishment to the crime.* **3** be suitable for; agree with: *The Canadian climate suits apples and wheat, but not oranges or tea.* **4** be agreeable or convenient (to); please; satisfy: *Which date suits best? A light snack would suit me just fine.* **5** be becoming to: *That hat suits you.*
suit (oneself), do as one pleases.
suit up, dress in special clothing, as in an athletic uniform, for some special activity. ⟨ME < AF *siute* < VL *sequita* < L *sequi* follow. Doublet of SUITE.⟩

suit•a•ble ['sutəbəl] *adj.* right for the occasion, purpose, condition, etc.; fitting; appropriate: *The park gives the children a suitable playground.* **—ˌsuit•a'bil•i•ty,** *n.* **—'suit•a•ble•ness,** *n.* **—'suit•a•bly,** *adv.*
☛ *Syn.* See note at FIT[1].

suit•case ['sutˌkeis] *n.* a more or less rigid, flat, rectangular travelling case.

suit coat or **suit•coat** ['sutˌkout] *n.* the long-sleeved upper part, or jacket, of a suit.

suite [swit] *n.* **1** a set of connected rooms to be used as a unit by one person or group: *a suite in a hotel. She lives in a large suite above a store.* **2** a set of furniture that matches. **3** any set or series of like things. **4** *Music.* **a** an instrumental composition consisting of a series of connected movements: *suite for strings.* **b** a set of dance tunes, usually all in one key or in related keys. **5** a group of attendants: *The queen travelled with a suite of twelve.* ⟨< F < OF < VL *sequita.* Doublet of SUIT.⟩
☛ *Hom.* SWEET.

suit•ing ['sutɪŋ] *n., v. —n.* cloth for making suits.
—v. ppr. of SUIT.

suit•or ['sutər] *n.* **1** a man who is courting a woman. **2** *Law.* a person bringing a suit in a court. **3** anyone who sues or petitions.

suk or **sukh** [suk] *n.* See SOUK.

su•ki•ya•ki [ˌsuki'jɑki] *n.* a Japanese dish consisting mainly of fried meat, onions, and other vegetables. ⟨< Japanese⟩

Suk•koth or **Suk•kot** ['sʊkəs], [sə'kous], *or* [su'kɔt]; *Hebrew,* [su'kɔt] *n.* a Jewish festival extending for eight days from the 15th day of Tishri. It celebrates the harvest and commemorates the wandering of the Jews in the wilderness after the Exodus. Also, **Succoth, Feast of Booths,** or **Feast of Tabernacles.** ⟨< Hebrew, literally, booths⟩

sul•cate ['sʌlkeit] *adj.* marked with parallel grooves, as some plant stems.

sul•cus ['sʌlkəs] *n., pl.* **-ci** [-saɪ] *or* [-si] **1** a groove; furrow. **2** *Anatomy.* any of the furrows separating the cerebral convolutions. ⟨< L *sulcus* furrow⟩

sulf– See SULPH-.

sulk [sʌlk] *v., n. —v.* hold oneself aloof in a sullen manner; be sulky: *The child stood sulking in a corner.*
—n. **1** a fit of sulking; a sulky mood: *She was in a sulk because nothing was going her way.* **2 the sulks,** *pl.* ill humour shown by sulking: *He has the sulks.* ⟨< *sulky*⟩

sulk•y[1] ['sʌlki] *adj.* **sulk•i•er, sulk•i•est.** silent and bad-humoured because of resentment; sullen: *She became sulky when she could not have her own way.* ⟨Cf. OE *āsolcen* lazy⟩ **—'sulk•i•ly,** *adv.* **—'sulk•i•ness,** *n.*
☛ *Syn. adj.* See note at SULLEN.

sulk•y[2] ['sʌlki] *n., pl.* **-ies.** a very light, two-wheeled carriage for one person. ⟨? < *sulky*[1], possibly because the rider is alone⟩

sul•len ['sʌlən] *adj.* **1** silent because of bad humour or anger: *The sullen child refused to answer my question.* **2** showing bad humour or anger: *"I don't care," was his sullen reply.* **3** gloomy; dismal: *The sullen skies threatened rain.* ⟨ME < OF *solain,* ult. < L *solus* alone⟩ **—'sul•len•ly,** *adv.* **—'sul•len•ness,** *n.*
☛ *Syn.* **1. Sullen,** SULKY[1], GLUM = silent and bad-humoured or gloomy. **Sullen** suggests an ill-natured refusal to talk or be co-operative because of anger or bad humour or disposition: *It is disagreeable to have to sit at the breakfast table with a sullen person.* **Sulky** suggests moody or childish sullenness because of resentment or discontent: *Children sometimes become sulky when they are jealous.* **Glum** carries less suggestion of bad humour or bad temper, and emphasizes a dismal silence because of low spirits or some depressing condition or happening: *He is glum about world affairs.*

sul•ly ['sʌli] *v.* **-lied, -ly•ing;** *n., pl.* **-lies.** soil; stain; tarnish. ⟨OE *sōlian* < *sōl* dirty⟩

sulph– or **sulf–** *combining form.* of sulphur; containing sulphur: *sulphide.*

sul•pha or **sul•fa** ['sʌlfə] *adj. Pharmacy.* of or having to do with SULPHA DRUGS. ⟨< *sulphanilamide*⟩

sul•pha•di•a•zine or **sul•fa•di•a•zine** [ˌsʌlfə'daɪəˌzin] *or* [ˌsʌlfə'daɪəzɪn] *n. Pharmacy.* a sulpha drug used mainly in treating meningitis, pneumonia, and infections of the intestines.

sulpha drug or **sulfa drug** *Pharmacy.* any of a group of synthetic organic drugs, such as sulphanilamide or a drug derived from it, that are used in treating various infections or diseases caused by bacteria.

sul•pha•nil•a•mide or **sul•fa•nil•a•mide** [ˌsʌlfə'nɪləˌmaɪd] *or* [ˌsʌlfə'nɪləmɪd] *n. Pharmacy.* a white, crystalline, synthetic compound derived from coal tar, from which most sulpha drugs are derived. *Formula:* $C_6H_8N_2O_2S$ ⟨< *sulphanil(ic acid)* + *amide*⟩

sul•pha•nil•ic acid or **sul•fa•nil•ic acid** [ˌsʌlfə'nɪlɪk] *Chemistry.* a greyish white crystalline solid, slightly water-soluble, used mainly in the manufacture of dyes and drugs. *Formula:* $C_6H_7NO_3S$ ⟨< *sulph-* + *anil(ine)* + *-ic*⟩

sul•phate or **sul•fate** ['sʌlfeit] *n., v.* **-phat•ed, -phat•ing.** *Chemistry. —n.* a salt or ester of sulphuric acid.
—v. **1** treat with or change into a sulphate. **2** *Electricity.* develop or cause to develop a layer of lead sulphate (on the negative plates of a storage battery). **—sul'pha•tion** or **sul'fa•tion,** *n.*

sul•phide or **sul•fide** ['sʌlfaɪd] *n. Chemistry.* any compound of sulphur with another element or radical.

sul•phite or **sul•fite** ['sʌlfəit] *n. Chemistry.* a salt or ester of sulphurous acid.

sul•phon•a•mide or **sul•fon•a•mide** [sʌl'fɒnəˌmaɪd] *or* [sʌl'fɒnəmɪd], [ˌsʌlfə'næmaɪd] *or* [ˌsʌlfə'næmɪd] *n.* **1** *Pharmacy.* any of a group of sulpha drugs, derived from sulphanilimide, that check bacterial infection. **2** *Chemistry.* **a** any organic compound that contains the univalent radical $-SO_2NH_2$. **b** the radical itself. ⟨< *sulfonyl* + *-amide*⟩

sul•pho•nate or **sul•fo•nate** ['sʌlfəˌneit] *n., v.* **-nat•ed, -nat•ing.** *Chemistry. —n.* a salt or ester of sulphonic acid.
—v. convert into a sulphonate by treating with sulphuric acid.

sul•phone or **sul•fone** ['sʌlfoun] *n. Chemistry.* any organic compound containing the divalent group SO_2 in a chemical link with two alkyl groups. **—sul'phon•ic** or **sul'fon•ic** [sʌl'fɒnɪk], *adj.*

sul•pho•nyl or **sul•fo•nyl** ['sʌlfəˌnɪl] *n. Chemistry.* the divalent radical SO_2. ⟨< *sulphone* + *-yl*⟩

sul•phur or **sul•fur** ['sʌlfər] *n., v. —n.* **1** *Chemistry.* **a** a light yellow, non-metallic chemical element that burns with a blue flame and a stifling odour. Sulphur is used mainly in making gunpowder and matches, in vulcanizing rubber, and in treating skin diseases. Symbol: S; *at.no.* 16; *at.mass* 32.06. **b** (*adjl.*) containing sulphur. **2** any of various butterflies (family Pieridae) having yellow or orange wings with black borders. **3** a yellow with a greenish cast.
—v. treat with sulphur or a compound of sulphur. ⟨ME < L *sulphur* brimstone⟩

sul•phu•rate or **sul•fu•rate** ['sʌlfjəˌreit] *or* ['sʌlfəˌreit] *v.* **-rat•ed, -rat•ing.** combine, treat, or impregnate with sulphur, the fumes of burning sulphur, etc. **—ˌsul•phu'ra•tion** or **ˌsul•fu'ra•tion,** *n.*

sulphur dioxide or **sulfur dioxide** *Chemistry.* a heavy, colourless gas that has a sharp odour, used as a bleach, disinfectant, preservative, and refrigerant. *Formula:* SO_2

sul•phu•re•ous or **sul•fu•re•ous** [sʌl'fjʊriəs] *adj.* **1** of, containing, or like sulphur. **2** resembling sulphur in colour; greenish yellow.

sul•phu•ret or **sul•fu•ret** *n.* ['sʌlfjə,rɛt] *or* ['sʌlfə,rɛt]; *v.* [,sʌlfjə'rɛt] *or* [,sʌlfə'rɛt] *n., v.* **-ret•ted** or **-ret•ed, -ret•ting** or **-ret•ing.** *—n. Chemistry.* a sulphide.
—v. treat or combine with sulphur; sulphurize.

sul•phu•ret•ed or **sul•fu•ret•ed** [,sʌlfjə'rɛtɪd] *or* [,sʌlfə'rɛtɪd] *adj.* See SULPHURETTED.

sul•phu•ret•ted or **sul•fu•ret•ted** [,sʌlfjə'rɛtɪd] *or* [,sʌlfə'rɛtɪd] *adj.* **1** combined with sulphur. **2** containing sulphur or a compound of sulphur.

sul•phu•ric or **sul•fu•ric** [sʌl'fjʊrɪk] *adj. Chemistry.* **1** of or having to do with sulphur or SULPHURIC ACID. **2** containing sulphur, especially with a higher valence than sulphurous compounds.

sulphuric acid or **sulfuric acid** *Chemistry.* a heavy, colourless, oily, very strong acid; oil of vitriol. Sulphuric acid is used in making explosives, in refining petroleum, etc. *Formula:* H_2SO_4

sul•phu•rize or **sul•fu•rize** ['sʌlfjə,raɪz] *or* ['sʌlfə,raɪz] *v.* **-rized, -riz•ing. 1** combine or treat with sulphur or something containing sulphur. **2** fumigate using sulphur dioxide.

sul•phur•ous or **sul•fur•ous** ['sʌlfərəs] *or* ['sʌlfjərəs]; *in chemistry, also,* [sʌl'fjʊrəs] *adj.* **1** of or having to do with sulphur. **2** containing sulphur, especially with a lower valence than sulphuric compounds. **3** like sulphur, especially sulphur that is burning. **4** of or like the fires of hell; hellish. **5** violent, fiery, or scathing. **—'sul•phur•ous•ly** or **'sul•fur•ous•ly,** *adv.* **—'sul•phur•ous•ness** or **'sul•fur•ous•ness,** *n.*

sulphurous acid or **sulfurous acid** *Chemistry.* a weak, unstable, colourless acid known only in solution or in the form of its salts, used as a bleach, reducing agent, etc. *Formula:* H_2SO_3

sul•phur•y or **sul•fur•y** ['sʌlfəri] *adj.* of or like sulphur.

Sul•pi•cian [sʌl'pɪʃən] *n.* a priest of a Roman Catholic order founded in 1642 to conduct seminaries of theology. ⟨< F *sulpicien* < St. *Sulpice,* Paris, the founder's parish + *-en* -an⟩

sul•tan ['sʌltən] *n.* **1** the ruler of a Muslim country. Turkey was ruled by a sultan until 1922. **2** an absolute ruler. ⟨ult. < Arabic *sultān* ruler⟩

sul•tan•a [sʌl'tɑnə] *or* [sʌl'tænə] *n.* **1** the wife of a sultan. **2** the mother, sister, or daughter of a sultan. **3** a small, seedless raisin. **4** the small, seedless, pale yellow grape from which these raisins are prepared. Sultanas are also cultivated for wine. ⟨< Ital.⟩

sul•tan•ate ['sʌltənɪt] *or* ['sʌltə,neit] *n.* **1** the position, authority, or period of rule of a sultan. **2** the territory ruled over by a sultan.

sul•try ['sʌltri] *adj.* **-tri•er, -tri•est. 1** of weather or atmosphere, uncomfortably hot, humid, and close. **2** very hot; fiery: *the sultry sun.* **3** full of, arousing, or characterized by passion or sensuality: *a sultry glance, a sultry movie scene.* ⟨< obs. *sulter,* v.; akin to *swelter*⟩ **—'sul•tri•ly,** *adv.* **—'sul•tri•ness,** *n.*

sum [sʌm] *n., v.* **summed, sum•ming.** *—n.* **1** an amount of money: *He paid a huge sum for that bicycle.* **2** the number or quantity obtained by adding two or more numbers or quantities together. **3** *Esp. Brit.* a problem in arithmetic: *She's very good at sums.* **4** the whole or total amount: *Winning the prize seemed to her the sum of happiness.* **5** gist; net effect; general purport (of something said or written). **6** *Mathematics.* the limit of the first *n* terms of an infinite series as *n* approaches infinity.
in sum, a in a few words; briefly; in short. **b** to summarize.
—v. find the total of.
sum up, a express or tell briefly; summarize: *to sum up the main points of a lesson.* **b** collect or add up into a whole. **c** review the chief points of evidence to a jury before the jury retires to consider a verdict. **d** form or express an idea of the qualities or character of; size up. ⟨< L *summa,* originally fem. adj., highest⟩
☛ *Hom.* SOME.
☛ *Syn. n.* **2.** See note at NUMBER.

sum– *prefix.* the form of SUB- occurring in some cases before *m,* as in *summon.*

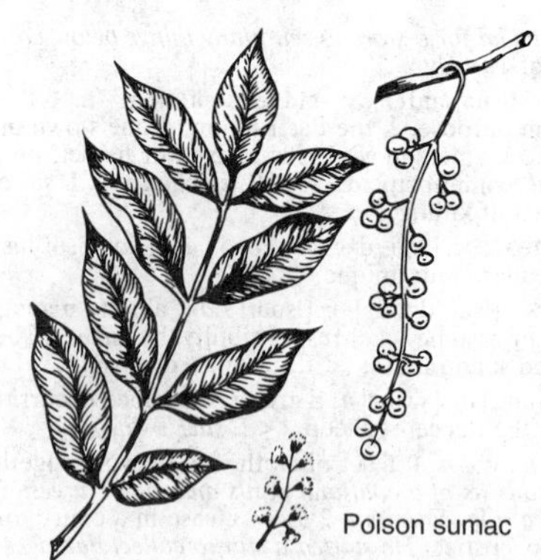

Poison sumac

su•mac ['ʃumæk] *or* ['sumæk] *n.* **1** any of a genus (*Rhus*) of trees, shrubs, and vines having compound leaves that turn a brilliant red in the fall. Some species, such as the poison sumac, have leaves that are poisonous to the touch. **2** a common sumac (*Rhus typhina*) also called **staghorn sumac,** having cone-shaped clusters of red fruit, native to eastern Canada and often planted as an ornamental tree. **3** the dried, powdered leaves and flowers of various sumacs, used in tanning and dyeing. Also, **sumach.** ⟨ME < OF < Arabic *summāq*⟩

Su•ma•tra [su'mɑtrə] *or* [su'mætrə] *n.* a large island in the western part of Indonesia, south of the Malay Peninsula.

Su•ma•tran [su'mɑtrən] *or* [su'mætrən] *n., adj. —n.* a native or inhabitant of Sumatra.
—adj. of or having to do with Sumatra or its people.

Su•me•ri•an [su'miriən] *or* [su'mɛriən] *n., adj. —n.* **1** a member of an ancient non-Semitic people who were the earliest known inhabitants of Sumer, a region in the valley of the Euphrates River. **2** the extinct language of the Sumerians, of no known relationship to any other language.
—adj. of or having to do with Sumer, the Sumerians, or their language.

su•mi ['sumi] *n.* **1** a Japanese form of art and calligraphy using sticks made of soot held together with glue and dipped in water. **2** this material used for writing and painting. ⟨< Japanese⟩

sum•ma ['sʊmə] *or* ['sʌmə] *n., pl.* **-mae** [-aɪ] *or* [-i] or **-mas.** a scholarly written summary of an area of study.

sum•ma cum lau•de ['sʊmə ,kʊm 'laʊdei] *or* ['sʌmə ,kʌm 'lɔdi] *Latin.* with the highest honour. ⟨< L⟩

sum•ma•ri•ly [sə'mɛrəli] *or* ['sʌmərəli] *adv.* in a summary manner; briefly or without delay.

sum•ma•ri•za•tion [,sʌmərə'zeiʃən] *or* [,sʌməraɪ'zeiʃən] *n.* **1** the act of summarizing. **2** a summary.

sum•ma•rize ['sʌmə,raɪz] *v.* **-rized, -riz•ing.** make or be a summary (of); express briefly: *The review summarized the plot of the novel.*

sum•ma•ry ['sʌməri] *n., pl.* **-ries;** *adj. —n.* a brief statement or account giving the main points: *The history book had a summary at the end of each chapter.*
—adj. **1** concise and comprehensive; brief. **2** direct and prompt; without delay or formality; often, too hasty or without time for due consideration: *a summary dismissal. The soldier took summary vengeance on his betrayers.* **3** of legal proceedings, carried out without the formalities or complexities of the usual process of law: *The summary dismissal of the case came as a surprise to everyone.* ⟨< L *summarium* < *summa* sum⟩
☛ *Hom.* SUMMERY.
☛ *Syn. n.* **Summary,** DIGEST = a brief presentation of facts or subject matter. **Summary** applies to a brief statement, in one's own words, giving only the main points of an article, chapter, book, speech, subject, proposed plan, etc.: *Give a summary of today's lesson.* **Digest,** applying particularly to a collection of materials in condensed form, sometimes applies to a shortened form of an article, etc., leaving out less important details but keeping the original order, emphasis, and words: *Some magazines contain digests of books.*

summary offence *Law.* a criminal offence that is less serious than an indictable offence. In Canada, a summary offence in most cases carries a maximum penalty of a $500 fine or six months' imprisonment, or both. Compare INDICTABLE OFFENCE. Also, **summary conviction offence.**

sum•ma•tion [sə'meiʃən] *n.* **1** the process of finding the sum or total; addition. **2** the total. **3** *Law.* the final charge of a judge to the jury before they consider the verdict.

sum•mer[1] ['sʌmər] *n., v.* —*n.* **1** the warmest season of the year; season of the year between spring and autumn. **2** a year of age: *a girl of seventeen summers.* **3** a period or stage of maturity or fulfilment; prime: *He was in the summer of his life.* **4** anything comparable to summer in its warmth, beauty, etc.: *the summer of her smile, the summer of your nearness.* **5** (*adjl.*) of or in summer: *the summer sun, summer holidays.* **6** (*adjl.*) fit for or used in summer: *summer clothes, a summer cottage.*
—*v.* **1** pass or spend the summer: *to summer at the seashore.* **2** keep or feed during the summer: *The cattle were summered on the mountain.* ⟨OE *sumor*⟩

sum•mer[2] ['sʌmər] *n.* any of various supporting beams or capstones. ⟨ME < of *somier* pack horse⟩

summer cottage a rustic house or cabin, usually built near a body of water or in a resort area and used for holidaying during summer. **—summer cottager.**

summer fallow land ploughed and left unseeded for a season or more in order to destroy weeds, improve the soil, etc.; fallow. **—'sum•mer-,fal•low,** *v.*

sum•mer•house ['sʌmər,hʌus] *n.* a small structure in a park or garden in which to sit in warm weather. Summerhouses often have no walls.

summer house a summer cottage; summer residence.

summer resort a place where people go for summer holidays.

sum•mer•sault ['sʌmər,sɒlt] *n., v.* See SOMERSAULT.

summer sausage a spicy smoked sausage, cured to varying degrees of hardness and dryness, that keeps well without refrigeration.

summer savory a European herb (*Satureja hortensis*) of the mint family widely grown for its leaves, which are used as a flavouring in cooking meats and vegetables.

summer school a school or university session held in summer, usually over a period of four to six weeks, offering a selection of regular courses, each compressed into daily classes of several hours. **—'sum•mer-,school,** *adjl.*

summer solstice *Astronomy.* **1** in the northern hemisphere, the time when the sun is farthest north from the equator, about June 21 or 22. **2** the point reached by the sun at this time.

summer squash **1** the fruit of any of several bushy varieties of a plant (*Cucurbita pepo*) of the gourd family, smaller than pumpkins and winter squashes and varying greatly in shape and colour. Summer squashes are used as a cooked vegetable in summer before they are fully ripe, when their skins are soft; they cannot be stored like winter squashes. **2** a plant that produces such fruits.

sum•mer•time ['sʌmər,taɪm] *n.* **1** the summer season; summer. **2** any period in which energy is greatest or talent most productive; prime: *in the summertime of life.*

sum•mer•y ['sʌməri] *adj.* of, like, or fit for summer: *a summery breeze. She wore a light, summery dress.*
☛ *Hom.* SUMMARY.

sum•mit ['sʌmɪt] *n.* **1** the highest point; top; peak: *the summit of a mountain.* **2** the highest degree or state: *The summit of her ambition was to be a foreign correspondent.* **3** *Informal.* a conference at the highest level. **4** (*adjl.*) of, having to do with, or being a discussion between heads of government: *a summit conference, summit meetings.*
at the summit, at the level of diplomacy involving heads of government; at the highest level. ⟨ME < OF *somete,* ult. < L *summus* highest⟩
☛ *Syn.* **1.** See note at TOP[1].

sum•mit•ry ['sʌmɪtri] *n.* **1** the use of summit meetings to conduct diplomatic negotiations; summit meetings collectively. **2** the art or skill of organizing, conducting, and negotiating at summit meetings.

sum•mon ['sʌmən] *v.* **1** call with authority or urgency; order to come; send for: *to summon citizens to defend their country. A telegram summoned Jill home.* **2** call together: *to summon an assembly.* **3** order or notify formally to appear in court, especially to answer a charge. **4** call upon: *to summon a fort to surrender.* **5** muster; gather or collect; rouse: *Jack summoned his courage and entered the deserted house.* ⟨< L *summonere* hint to < *sub-* secretly + *monere* warn⟩ **—'sum•mon•er,** *n.*
☛ *Syn.* **1.** See note at CALL.

sum•mons ['sʌmənz] *n., pl.* **-mons•es;** *v.* —*n.* **1** an urgent or authoritative call for the presence or attendance of a person. **2** *Law.* **a** an order or notice to a person from an authority to appear before a court or judge on or before a certain date, especially to answer as a defendant to a charge made against him or her. **b** the writ **(writ of summons)** by which such an order is made: *The police officer handed her a summons.* **3** something that summons; a message or signal to come or appear: *He heard the summons of his friend's car horn.*
—*v.* serve with a summons. ⟨ME < OF *somonse* < *somondre* summon, ult. < L *summonere.* See SUMMON.⟩

sum•mum bo•num ['sʊməm 'bounəm] *Latin.* the highest or chief good.

su•mo ['sumou] *n.* a stylized form of wrestling originating in Japan, in which each contestant tries to force his opponent out of the ring or make him touch the ground with any body part other than the sole of the foot, the contestants being tall and unusually heavy men. ⟨< Japanese *sumo* compete⟩

sump [sʌmp] *n.* **1** a pit or reservoir for collecting water, oil, sewage, etc. **2** a pool at the bottom of a mine, where water collects and from which it is pumped. ⟨ME < MDu. *somp* or MLG *sump* swamp⟩

sump pump a pump for removing collected water, sewage, etc. from a sump.

sump•ter ['sʌmptər] *n. Archaic.* a pack horse or mule. ⟨ME < OF *sommetier,* ult. < L *sagma, -atos* pack-saddle < Gk.⟩

sump•tu•ar•y ['sʌmptʃu,ɛri] *adj.* having to do with the regulating of expenses; especially, limiting personal expenditure on moral or religious grounds to prevent extravagance: *sumptuary laws.* ⟨< L *sumptuarius* < *sumptus* expense < *sumere* spend⟩

sump•tu•ous ['sʌmptʃuəs] *adj.* costly; magnificent; rich: *The ambassador gave a sumptuous banquet.* ⟨< L *sumptuosus* < *sumptus* expense < *sumere* spend⟩ **—'sump•tu•ous•ly,** *adv.* **—'sump•tu•ous•ness,** *n.*

sum total **1** the total amount added up. **2** the total result, everything included. **3** the net effect or purport.

sun [sʌn] *n., v.* **sunned, sun•ning.** —*n.* **1** the brightest heavenly body in the sky; the star around which the earth and planets revolve. The sun provides light, heat, and energy for the solar system. **2** the light and warmth of the sun: *to sit in the sun.* **3** any heavenly body made up of burning gas and having satellites. **4** something like the sun in brightness, splendour, or centrality; something that is a source of light, honour, glory, or prosperity, or that is a centre around which other things, people, etc. revolve. **5** a figure, image, ornament, etc. made to resemble the sun, as a heraldic bearing, usually charged with human features, or a kind of circular firework. **6** *Archaic.* a day. **7** *Archaic.* a year.
a place in the sun, a position in the public eye; a prominent position.
from sun to sun, from sunrise to sunset.
under the sun, on earth; in the world.
—*v.* **1** expose (oneself) to the sun's rays. **2** bronze, warm, or dry in the sunshine. ⟨OE *sunne*⟩
☛ *Hom.* SON.

Sun. Sunday.

sun•baked ['sʌn,beikt] *adj.* **1** baked by exposure to the sun: *sunbaked bricks.* **2** hardened, dried out, or cracked, etc. by too much sunlight: *sunbaked soil.*

sun•bath or **sun bath** ['sʌn,bæθ] *n.* an exposure of the body to sunshine or a sunlamp.

sun•bathe ['sʌn,beið] *v.* **-bathed, -bath•ing.** take a sunbath; bask in the sun. **—'sun,bath•er,** *n.*

sun•beam ['sʌn,bim] *n.* a ray of sunlight.

sun•bird ['sʌn,bərd] *n.* any of a family (Nectariniidae) of small, tropical Old World songbirds having a long, slender, downward-curving bill and a tube-shaped tongue adapted for feeding on nectar, the males having bright-coloured plumage.

sun•block ['sʌn,blɒk] *n.* **1** a powerful sunscreen that offers a high degree of protection against the sun by blocking out all or nearly all of the harmful ultraviolet rays. **2** any lotion, cream, etc. containing such a substance.

sun•bon•net ['sʌn,bɒnɪt] *n.* a large bonnet having a wide brim and a flap at the back that shade the face and neck.

sun•bow ['sʌn,bou] *n.* the spectrum of colours produced by sunlight shining through fine spray; a rainbow in the absence of rain.

sun•burn ['sʌn,bərn] *n., v.* **-burned** or **-burnt, -burn•ing.** —*n.* an inflammation of the skin caused by too much exposure to the rays of the sun or of a sunlamp.
—*v.* get or cause to get a sunburn: *Her skin sunburns very quickly.*

sun•burnt ['sʌn,bɜrnt] *v.* a pt. and a pp. of SUNBURN.

sun•burst ['sʌn,bɜrst] *n.* **1** the sun shining suddenly through a break in clouds. **2** a brooch with jewels arranged to look like the sun with its rays. **3** any such pattern or design.

sun•dae ['sʌndei] *or* ['sʌndi] *n.* a serving of ice cream with syrup, crushed fruits, nuts, etc. poured over it. ⟨probably < *Sunday*, originally the only day on which it was served⟩
☛ *Hom.* SUNDAY.

Sun•day ['sʌndei] *or* ['sʌndi] *n.* **1** the first day of the week, observed in Canada and many other countries as the general day of rest and relaxation. **2** *(adjl.)* of, having to do with, or taking place on Sunday: *Sunday Mass.* **3** *(adjl.)* associated with Sunday, especially as a special day or a day of leisure and recreation: *a Sunday painter, Sunday drivers, Sunday clothes.*
a month of Sundays, an indefinitely long time: *That wouldn't happen again in a month of Sundays.* ⟨OE *sunnandæg*, translation of L *dies solis* day of the sun⟩
☛ *Hom.* SUNDAE.

Sunday best *Informal.* best clothes.

Sun•days ['sʌndeiz] *or* ['sʌndiz] *adv.* every Sunday: *Sundays we get up late.*

Sunday school **1** a school held by a church on Sundays for teaching religion, especially to children. **2** its members.

sun•deck ['sʌn,dɛk] *n.* **1** a passenger ship's upper deck. **2** a balcony, terrace, or other area in or on a building, beside a swimming pool, etc., designed for lounging and sunbathing. Also, **sun deck**.

sun•der ['sʌndər] *v., n.* —*v.* break or cause to break apart; sever or separate.
—*n.*
in sunder, apart: *Lightning tore the tree in sunder.* ⟨OE *sundrian* < *sundor* apart⟩

sun•dew ['sʌn,dju] *or* ['sʌn,du] *n.* **1** any of a genus (*Drosera*) of insect-eating bog plants found throughout the world, having leaves covered with hairs with glands at the tips. The glands produce a sticky, glistening substance resembling dewdrops that attracts and captures insects. **2** *(adjl.)* designating a small family (Droseraceae) of insect-eating plants which includes the sundews and three other groups of plants. The **Venus's-flytrap** is a member of the sundew family.

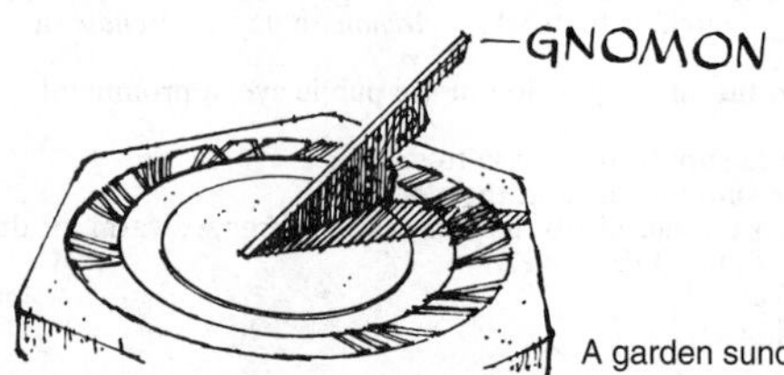

A garden sundial

sun•di•al ['sʌn,daɪəl] *or* ['sʌn,daɪl] *n.* an instrument for telling the time of day by the position of the shadow of a rod or pointer cast by the sun on a usually horizontal disk marked off in hours.

sun disk a winged disk with a serpent on each side, symbolic of the Egyptian sun god.

sun•dog ['sʌn,dɒg] *n.* **1** parhelion. **2** a small halo or incomplete rainbow near the horizon.

sun•down ['sʌn,daʊn] *n.* SUNSET (def. 3).

sun•dress ['sʌn,drɛs] *n.* a light dress for women or girls for hot weather, supported by narrow shoulder straps and exposing the shoulders and often the back.

sun–dried ['sʌn ,draɪd] *adj.* dried by exposure to the sun: *sun-dried apples.*

sun•dry ['sʌndri] *adj., pron., n.* —*adj.* several; various; miscellaneous: *From sundry hints, he guessed he was to be given a bicycle on his birthday.*
—*pron.*
all and sundry, everybody; one and all: *He sent out invitations to all and sundry to visit him in his new house.*
—*n.* **sundries,** *pl.* sundry things; miscellaneous items not named. ⟨OE *syndrig* separate < *sundor* apart⟩

sun•fast ['sʌn,fæst] *adj.* made to resist fading by sunlight: *sunfast colours.*

sun•fish ['sʌn,fɪʃ] *n., pl.* **-fish** or **-fish•es. 1** any of various small, North American freshwater fishes (family Centrarchidae, especially genus *Lepomis*) having a deep, compressed, usually brightly coloured body and a long dorsal fin. Some species are valued as food and game fish. **2** *(adjl.)* designating the family of freshwater fishes that comprises the sunfishes, basses, and crappies. **3** any of a family (Molidae) of large ocean fishes, especially one species (*Mola mola*) having a scaleless, silvery, compressed body that is about as deep as it is long, giving the fish a chopped-off look. Sunfish often rest on the surface of the water in the sun.

sun•flow•er ['sʌn,flaʊər] *n.* **1** a very tall annual plant (*Helianthus annuus*) of the composite family having large leaves and a very large, flat flower head surrounded by rays of long yellow petals. The sunflower is native to North and South America, but is widely cultivated throughout the world, especially for its seeds and the oil they yield. **2** any of a number of other annual or perennial plants of the same genus, such as the prairie sunflower (*H. petiolaris*).

sung [sʌŋ] *v.* **1** *Archaic.* a pt. of SING. **2** pp. of SING.

sun•glass•es ['sʌn,glæsɪz] *n.pl.* eyeglasses with tinted lenses designed to protect the eyes from direct sunlight or glare.

sun god a god who personifies the sun or is associated with it.

sunk [sʌŋk] *v., adj.* —*v.* **1** *Archaic.* pt. of SINK. **2** pp. of SINK.
—*adj. Informal.* doomed; ruined; done for: *If anyone finds out I told you this, I'm sunk.*

sunk•en ['sʌŋkən] *adj., v.* —*adj.* **1** that has been sunk: *a sunken ship.* **2** submerged: *a sunken rock.* **3** situated or constructed below the general level: *a sunken garden, a sunken living room.* **4** fallen in; hollow: *sunken eyes.*
—*v. Archaic.* a pp. of SINK.

sun•lamp ['sʌn,læmp] *n.* an electric lamp emitting ultraviolet rays, used for therapy or for producing an artificial suntan.

sun•less ['sʌnlɪs] *adj.* without sunlight; dark: *a sunless day, sunless caverns.*

sun•light ['sʌn,ləit] *n.* the light of the sun.

sun•lit ['sʌn,lɪt] *adj.* lighted by the sun.

Sun•na or **Sun•nah** ['sʊnə] *n.* the traditional part of Muslim law, attributed to Mohammed and preserved alongside the Koran. ⟨< Arabic *sunna* form, course, way⟩

Sun•ni ['sʊni] *n., pl.* **Sun•ni,** *adj.* —*n.* a member of one of the two great sects of Islam. The Sunni, who regard the historical line of the first four caliphs as the rightful succession to Mohammed, observe the Sunna. Compare SHIAH.
—*adj.* Sunnite. —**'Sun•nism,** *n.*

Sun•nite ['sʊnəit] *n., adj.* —*n.* Sunni.
—*adj.* of the Sunni or their religion.

sun•ny ['sʌni] *adj.* **-ni•er, -ni•est. 1** having much sunshine: *a sunny day.* **2** exposed to, lighted by, or warmed by the direct rays of the sun: *a sunny room.* **3** like the sun. **4** bright; cheerful; happy: *a sunny disposition.* —**'sun•ni•ly,** *adv.* —**'sun•ni•ness,** *n.*
☛ *Hom.* SONNY.

sunny side **1** the side of a house, street, etc. on which the sun shines or is shining. **2** the cheerful or optimistic aspect of something: *She usually looks at the sunny side of things.*
on the sunny side of, somewhat younger than (an age given in round numbers): *He's still on the sunny side of 50.*
sunny side up, of an egg, fried on one side only and with the yolk unbroken: *I like my eggs sunny side up.*

sun parlour or **parlor** sunroom.

sun porch a porch enclosed largely by glass or screen, designed to admit plenty of sunlight.

sun•proof ['sʌn,pruf] *adj.* impervious to or unaffected by the rays of the sun: *These sunproof curtains will not fade.*

sun•rise ['sʌn,raɪz] *n.* **1** the appearance of the sun above the horizon in the morning. **2** the often rosy colour of the sky that accompanies the sun's appearance. **3** the time of day when the sun rises; the beginning of day.

sunrise industry a new industry that is already flourishing and viewed as a gateway to prosperity, great opportunity, etc.

sun•roof ['sʌn,ruf] *or* ['sʌn,rʊf] *n.* **1** an automobile roof having a panel that can be opened to admit air and sunlight. **2** the panel that opens.

sun•room ['sʌn,rum] *or* ['sʌn,rʊm] *n.* a room with many windows to let in sunlight.

sun•screen ['sʌn,skrin] *n.* **1** a substance put on the skin to block ultraviolet rays and prevent sunburn. **2** a lotion, cream, etc. containing such a substance. **3** sunshade.

sun•set ['sʌn,sɛt] *n.* **1** the setting of the sun; the last appearance of the sun in the evening. **2** the often red, pink, etc.

colour of the sky accompanying the disappearance of the sun. **3** the time of day when the sun sets; the close of day. **4** any decline or close: *Old age is often thought of as the sunset of life.*

sunset law a law stipulating that certain government programs, etc. be automatically terminated after a given period unless reapproved by the legislature.

sun•shade ['sʌn,ʃeid] *n.* an umbrella, parasol, awning, blind, etc. used to provide protection from the sun.

sun•shine ['sʌn,ʃaɪn] *n.* **1** the shining of the sun; light or warmth of the sun; sunny weather. **2** a place lighted or warmed by the direct rays of the sun: *Let's sit in the sunshine.* **3 a** brightness; cheerfulness; happiness: *to bring sunshine into someone's life.* **b** a source of these.

sun•shin•y ['sʌn,ʃaɪni] *adj.* **-shin•i•er, -shin•i•est. 1** having much sunshine. **2** bright; cheerful; happy.

sun•spot ['sʌn,spɒt] *n.* one of the dark spots, caused by temporary cooling, that appear from time to time on the surface of the sun. Sunspots, usually visible only through a telescope, have a strong magnetic field.

sun•stroke ['sʌn,strouk] *n. Pathology.* a heatstroke caused by overexposure to direct sunlight. Sunstroke is serious because the body's sweating system has stopped functioning and can no longer cool the body.

sun•struck ['sʌn,strʌk] *adj.* affected with sunstroke.

sun•suit ['sʌn,sut] *n.* an abbreviated one-piece or two-piece garment worn by children in hot weather.

sun•tan ['sʌn,tæn] *n., adj. —n.* **1** a bronzed colouring of a person's skin resulting from exposure to the sun. **2** a light bronze or reddish brown.
—adj. light bronze or reddish brown.

sun•tanned ['sʌn,tænd] *adj.* having a suntan; browned by the sun: *suntanned vacationers.*

sun•up ['sʌn,ʌp] *n.* SUNRISE (def. 3). Also, **sun-up**.

sun•ward ['sʌnwərd] *adv. or adj.* toward the sun.

sun•wards ['sʌnwərdz] *adv.* sunward.

sup [sʌp] *v.* **supped, sup•ping.** eat the evening meal; take supper: *He supped alone on bread and milk.* ⟨ME < OF *soper.* See SUPPER.⟩

sup– *prefix.* the form of SUB- occurring before *p*, as in *suppress.*

sup. 1 supra. **2** superior. **3** superlative. **4** supply. **5** supplement; supplementary. **6** supreme.

su•per ['supər] *n., adj., adv. —n. Informal.* **1** SUPERNUMERARY (def. 2). Mobs on the stage are usually made up of supers. **2** a superintendent. **3** an item, product, etc. of top quality, extra large size, etc.: *Please fill my car with super.*
—adj. **1** *Slang.* excellent; wonderful: *a super movie.* **2** extreme or excessive: *This kind of super individualism is not healthy.*
—adv. Informal. extremely; excessively: *She is super polite.*

super– *prefix.* **1** over; above: *superimpose, superstructure.* **2** besides; extra: *superadd, supertax.* **3** to a greater than normal degree; to excess; exceedingly: *superabundant, supersensitive, supercharge.* **4** surpassing; beyond: *superman, supernatural.* **5** having a superior rank or position: *superintendent.* **6** larger, stronger, better, etc. than others: *supermall, superglue.* ⟨< L *super* over, above⟩

super. 1 superfine. **2** superintendent. **3** superior. **4** supernumerary.

su•per•a•ble ['supərəbəl] *adj.* capable of being overcome; surmountable. ⟨< L *superabilis* < *superare* overcome < *super* over⟩ **—,su•per•a'bil•i•ty,** *n.* **—'su•per•a•bly,** *adv.*

su•per•a•bound [,supərə'baʊnd] *v.* **1** be very abundant. **2** be too abundant.

su•per•a•bun•dant [,supərə'bʌndənt] *adj.* more than is needed; excessive. **—,su•per•a'bun•dance,** *n.* **—,su•per•a'bun•dant•ly,** *adv.*

su•per•add [,supər'æd] *v.* add besides; add further: *A toothache was superadded to her other troubles.* ⟨< L *superaddere* < *super-* besides + *addere* add⟩ **—,su•per•ad'di•tion,** *n.*

su•per•an•nu•ate [,supər'ænju,eit] *v.* **-at•ed, -at•ing. 1** cause to retire on a pension on reaching a certain age or owing to ill health. **2** make old-fashioned or out-of-date. ⟨earlier *superannate* < Med.L *superannatus* more than a year old < L *super annum* beyond a year; influenced in spelling by L *annuus* annual⟩

su•per•an•nu•at•ed [,supər'ænju,eitɪd] *adj., v. —adj.* **1** retired on a pension. **2** too old for work, service, etc. **3** old-fashioned; out-of-date.
—v. pt. and pp. of SUPERANNUATE.

su•per•an•nu•at•ion [,supər,ænju'eiʃən] *n.* **1** the process or the state of being superannuated. **2** a pension or allowance granted to a retired person.

su•perb [su'pɜrb] *adj.* **1** grand; stately; majestic; magnificent; splendid: *The mountain scenery in the Rockies is superb. The queen's jewels were superb.* **2** rich; elegant; sumptuous: *a superb dinner.* **3** very fine; first-rate; excellent: *The actor gave a superb performance.* ⟨< L *superbus* < *super-* above⟩ **—su'perb•ly,** *adv.* **—su'perb•ness,** *n.*
☛ *Syn.* **1.** See note at MAGNIFICENT.

su•per•cal•en•der ['supər,kæləndər] *n., v. —n.* a calender with multiple rollers, imparting a high gloss to paper.
—v. give (paper) a high gloss by pressing in a supercalender.

su•per•car•go ['supər,kɑrgou] *n., pl.* **-goes** or **-gos.** an officer on a merchant ship, who has charge of the cargo and the business affairs of the voyage. ⟨earlier *supracargo* < Sp. *sobrecargo*⟩

su•per•charge ['supər,tʃɑrdʒ] *v.* **-charged, -charg•ing. 1** charge with excessive vigour, emotion, etc.: *The atmosphere at the trial was supercharged with tension.* **2** augment the power or efficiency of (an engine, vehicle, etc.) by fitting it with a supercharger. **3** PRESSURIZE (def. 1).

su•per•charg•er ['supər,tʃɑrdʒər] *n.* in an internal-combustion engine, a blower, pump, compressor, etc. for forcing more of the mixture of air and gasoline vapour into the cylinders than the action of the pistons would draw. It is designed to increase the power or efficiency of an engine. A similar device is used to pressurize aircraft.

su•per•cil•i•ar•y [,supər'sɪliəri] *or* [,supər'sɪli,ɛri] *adj. Anatomy. Zoology.* of, having to do with, or near the eyebrow; over the eye. ⟨< NL *superciliaris* < L *supercilium* eyebrow < *super-* above + *cel-* cover⟩

su•per•cil•i•ous [,supər'sɪliəs] *adj.* showing scorn or indifference because of a feeling of superiority; haughty, proud, and contemptuous; disdainful: *supercilious politeness, a supercilious desk clerk.* ⟨< L *superciliosus* < *supercilium* eyebrow. See SUPERCILIARY.⟩ **—,su•per'cil•i•ous•ly,** *adv.*
☛ *Syn.* See note at PROUD.

su•per•class ['supər,klæs] *n. Biology.* a secondary category in the classification of plants and animals, including one or more classes within a phylum or division. It is usually a narrower classification than a subphylum.

su•per•com•pu•ter ['supərkəm,pjutər] *n.* a very large and complex computer which can perform many operations at the same time.

su•per•con•duc•tiv•i•ty [,supər,kɒndʌk'tɪvɪti] *n. Physics.* the property of being able to conduct electricity without resistance, found in lead and tin and some other metals at temperatures near absolute zero (–273.16°C). Also, **superconduction. —,su•per•con'duc•tive,** *adj.* **—,su•per•con'duc•tor,** *n.*

su•per•cool *v.* [,supər'kul]; *adj.* [,supər'kul] *or* ['supər,kul] *v., adj. —v.* **1** cool (a liquid) below its freezing point without causing it to crystallize or solidify. **2** undergo such cooling.
—adj. **1** unusually cool in temperature, especially as a setting on a climate control device, etc. **2** *Slang.* very hip; very sophisticated.

su•per•dom•i•nant [,supər'dɒmənənt] *n. Music.* the sixth tone in a scale; the tone next above the dominant.

su•per–du•per ['supər 'dupər] *adj. Informal.* extremely big, good, effective, etc. ⟨< *super* by reduplication⟩

su•per•e•go [,supər'igou] *n. Psychoanalysis.* the part of the psyche that represents conscience, enforcing moral standards learned by internalizing the behaviour of parents and other models.

su•per•em•i•nent [,supər'ɛmənənt] *adj.* of superior eminence, rank, or dignity; standing out or rising above others. **—,su•per'em•i•nent•ly,** *adv.* **—,su•per'em•i•nence,** *n.*

su•per•er•o•ga•tion [,supər,ɛrə'geiʃən] *n.* the doing of more than is required by duty. ⟨< LL *supererogatio, -onis* < L *super-* over + *erogare* pay out⟩

su•per•e•rog•a•to•ry [,supərə'rɒgə,tɔri] *adj.* **1** doing or being more than is required by duty: *a supererogatory act of assistance.* **2** unnecessary; superfluous: *a supererogatory explanation of what everyone had seen quite clearly.*

su•per•fam•i•ly ['supər,fæməli] *n. Biology.* a secondary category in the classification of plants and animals, including one or more families within an order. It is usually a narrower classification than a suborder.

su•per•fe•ta•tion [ˌsupərfi'teiʃən] *n.* the existence of two embryos or fetuses of different ages in the uterus due to the fertilization of a new ovum while a pregnancy is already in progress. ⟨< Med.L *superfetatio* < L *superfetare* < *super* + *fetare* impregnate < *fetus*⟩

su•per•fi•cial [ˌsupər'fɪʃəl] *adj.* **1** of, on, or affecting the surface: *superficial burns, superficial measurement.* **2** concerned with or understanding only what is on the surface; not thorough; shallow or casual: *a superficial person, a superficial reading.* **3** of or having to do with outward appearance only; general or external: *a superficial resemblance.* ⟨< L *superficialis* < *superficies* surface < *super-* above + *facies* form⟩ **—ˌsu•per'fi•cial•ly,** *adv.* **—ˌsu•per'fi•cial•ness,** *n.*

su•per•fi•ci•al•i•ty [ˌsupərˌfɪʃi'ælɪti] *n., pl.* **-ties. 1** the quality or state of being superficial. **2** something superficial.

su•per•fi•ci•es [ˌsupər'fɪʃiiz] *or* [ˌsupər'fɪʃiz] *n., pl.* **-fi•ci•es. 1** the surface or outside face of a thing. **2** the outward appearance of something, especially as contrasted with its inner nature. ⟨< L *superficies* upper side, surface < *super-* over + *facies* form⟩

su•per•fine ['supərˌfaɪn] *or* [ˌsupər'faɪn] *adj.* **1** very fine in texture or size; extra fine: *superfine cotton, superfine sugar.* **2** too refined or subtle: *superfine distinctions.* **3** of commercial goods, etc., very high in quality: *superfine china.* **—ˌsu•per'fine•ly,** *adv.* **—ˌsu•per'fine•ness,** *n.*

su•per•flu•id [ˌsupər'fluɪd] *or* ['supərˌfluɪd] *n., adj. —n.* a liquid, such as liquid helium, that has no viscosity when reduced to temperatures approaching absolute zero.
—adj. extraordinarily fluid; having superfluidity.
—ˌsu•per•flu'id•i•ty, *n.*

su•per•flu•i•ty [ˌsupər'fluəti] *n., pl.* **-ties. 1** the state or quality of being superfluous. **2** a greater amount than is needed; excess. **3** something not needed: *Luxuries are superfluities.*

su•per•flu•ous [su'pɜrfluəs] *adj.* **1** excess; beyond what is sufficient or necessary: *In writing telegrams omit superfluous words.* **2** uncalled for; irrelevant: *a superfluous remark.* ⟨< L *superfluus*, ult. < *super-* over + *fluere* flow⟩ **—su'per•flu•ous•ly,** *adv.* **—su'per•flu•ous•ness,** *n.*

su•per•gi•ant ['supərˌdʒaɪənt] *n. Astronomy.* a very large and brilliant star with a diameter greater than that of the sun, as Betelgeuse.

su•per•heat [ˌsupər'hit] *v.* **1** heat (a liquid) above its boiling point without producing vaporization. **2** heat (steam apart from water) above the point of saturation so that a reduction in temperature will not result in condensation. **3** overheat; heat very hot.

su•per•heat•er [ˌsupər'hitər] *n.* a device for superheating steam.

su•per•het•er•o•dyne [ˌsupər'hɛtərəˌdaɪn] *adj., n. Radio. —adj.* of or having to do with a kind of radio reception in which signals are received at a supersonic frequency and combined with locally produced oscillations of a lower supersonic frequency before being rectified and amplified.
—n. a superheterodyne radio receiving set.

su•per•high frequency ['supərˌhaɪ] *Radio.* any frequency between 3000 and 30 000 megahertz. *Abbrev.:* SHF or shf

su•per•high•way ['supərˌhaɪwei] *or* [ˌsupər'haɪˌwei] *n.* a high-speed expressway or freeway divided by a median and having two or more traffic lanes in each direction.

su•per•hu•man [ˌsupər'hjumən] *adj.* **1** above or beyond ordinary human power, experience, etc.: *By a superhuman effort, the hunter choked the leopard to death.* **2** above or beyond what is human: *Angels are superhuman beings.* **—ˌsu•per'hu•man•ly,** *adv.* **—ˌsu•per'hu•man•ness,** *n.*

su•per•im•pose [ˌsupərɪm'pouz] *v.* **-posed, -pos•ing. 1** put or lay on top of something else. **2** put or join (*onto* something else) as an additional, separate or discrete component.

su•per•im•po•si•tion [ˌsupərˌɪmpə'zɪʃən] *n.* a superimposing or being superimposed.

su•per•in•cum•bent [ˌsupərɪn'kʌmbənt] *adj.* **1** lying or resting and exerting pressure on something else: *a superincumbent stratum of rock.* **2** of pressure, exerted from above. **3** overhanging. **—ˌsu•per•in'cum•bence** or **ˌsu•per•in'cum•ben•cy,** *n.* **—ˌsu•per•in'cum•bent•ly,** *adv.*

su•per•in•duce [ˌsupərɪn'djus] *or* [ˌsupərɪn'dus] *v.* **-duced, -duc•ing.** bring in or develop as an addition. **—ˌsu•per•in'duc•tion,** *n.*

su•per•in•tend [ˌsupərɪn'tɛnd] *v.* oversee and direct (work or workers); act as a superintendent of; supervise. ⟨< LL *superintendere* < L *super-* above + *intendere* direct⟩

su•per•in•tend•ence [ˌsupərɪn'tɛndəns] *n.* guidance and direction; supervision.

su•per•in•tend•en•cy [ˌsupərɪn'tɛndənsi] *n., pl.* **-cies.** the position, authority, or work of a superintendent.

su•per•in•tend•ent [ˌsupərɪn'tɛndənt] *n., adj. —n.* **1** a person who oversees, directs, or manages: *a superintendent of schools, a superintendent of a factory.* **2** a police officer of high rank, below a commissioner or chief and above an inspector. **3** a person in charge of the maintenance of an apartment building, office building, etc. *Abbrev.:* Supt. or supt.
—adj. superintending.

su•pe•ri•or [sə'piriər] *adj., n. —adj.* **1** very good; excellent: *superior work in school.* **2** higher in quality; better; greater: *The last brand of coffee we tried was superior to this.* **3** higher in position, rank, importance, etc.: *a superior officer.* **4** above yielding or giving in (*to*): *superior to flattery.* **5** showing a feeling of being above others; proud: *superior airs, superior manners.* **6** higher in physical position or location; upper. **7** *Printing.* written above and beside a letter or symbol: *a superior number.* **8** *Botany.* growing above some other part or organ, as: **a** the ovary when situated above or free from the (inferior) calyx. **b** the calyx when adherent to the sides of the (inferior) ovary and thus seeming to rise from its top. **9** *Anatomy.* situated higher or above; closer to the head: *the superior vena cava.* **10** *Astronomy.* of a planet, farther than Earth is from the sun.
—n. **1** a person who is higher in rank or more accomplished than another: *A captain is a lieutenant's superior.* **2** the head of a monastery or convent. **3** *Printing.* a superior letter or figure; superscript. ⟨ME < OF < L *superior*, comparative of *superus*, adj., above < *super*, prep., above⟩ **—su'pe•ri•or•ly,** *adv.*

superior court a court of law having absolute jurisdiction to administer justice according to the law, as distinguished from courts of limited jurisdiction, such as county or district courts. Superior courts in Canada include the Supreme Court of Canada and the supreme courts of the provinces.

su•pe•ri•or•i•ty [səˌpiri'ɔrɪti] *n.* the quality or state of being superior: *He was convinced of the superiority of the new computer system over the old one.*

superiority complex a feeling of being superior to other people; an exaggerated feeling of self-importance.

su•per•ja•cent [ˌsupər'dʒeisənt] *adj.* lying just above or on top. ⟨< LL *superjacere* < *super-* over + *jacere* lie, be laid or thrown⟩

superl. superlative.

su•per•la•tive [sʊ'pɜrlətɪv] *adj., n. —adj.* **1** of the highest kind; above all others; supreme: *Terry Fox was a man of superlative courage.* **2** exaggerated; excessive; hyperbolic: *Such superlative praise could not be sincere.* **3** *Grammar.* of or expressing the highest degree of comparison of an adjective or adverb. *Fairest, best,* and *most slowly* are the superlative forms of *fair, good,* and *slowly.*
—n. **1** a person, thing, or degree above all others; supreme example; pinnacle. **2** *Grammar.* **a** the third or highest of three degrees of comparison of adjectives and adverbs. **b** the form or combination of words that shows this degree.
talk in superlatives, exaggerate. ⟨ME < MF < LL *superlativus*, ult. < *super-* beyond + *latus*, pp. *ferre* carry⟩ **—su'per•la•tive•ly,** *adv.* **—su'per•la•tive•ness,** *n.*

su•per•man ['supərˌmæn] *n., pl.* **-men. 1** a man having superhuman powers. **2** the ideal man as conceived by the German philosopher Friedrich W. Nietzsche (1844-1900), who would be above the weaknesses of ordinary humans and have superior physical and intellectual powers.

su•per•mar•ket ['supərˌmɑrkɪt] *n.* a large self-service store selling groceries and household articles.

su•per•nal [su'pɜrnəl] *adj.* **1** heavenly; divine. **2** of, coming from, or in the sky. **3** lofty. ⟨< L *supernus* < *super* above⟩ **—su'per•nal•ly,** *adv.*

su•per•na•tant [ˌsupər'neitənt] *adj.* floating above or on the surface, as oil on water.

su•per•na•tion•al [ˌsupər'næʃənəl] *adj.* above or independent of limitations imposed by national sovereignty; taking in or involving more than one nation: *Europe may one day become a supernational state.*

su•per•nat•u•ral [ˌsupər'nætʃərəl] *adj., n. —adj.* of, having to do with, or caused by some agency or force outside the known

laws of nature; especially, of, having to do with, or caused by God or a god or other spirit: *a supernatural event, supernatural powers.*
—*n.* **the supernatural,** supernatural agencies, influences, or phenomena. —ˌ**su•per'nat•u•ral•ly,** *adv.*

su•per•nat•u•ral•ism [ˌsupər'nætʃərəˌlɪzəm] *n.* **1** the quality or state of being supernatural. **2** a belief in supernatural force or agencies as producing effects in the universe.
—ˌ**su•per'nat•u•ral•ist,** *n.*

su•per•norm•al [ˌsupər'nɔrməl] *adj.* **1** above or beyond what is normal. **2** paranormal.

su•per•no•va [ˌsupər'nouvə] *n., pl.* **-vae** [-vi] *or* [-vaɪ] or **-vas.** *Astronomy.* a star that has exploded, becoming up to a hundred million times brighter than the sun for a few days and leaving behind a large, expanding shell of gases and debris (the **supernova remnant**), which may radiate light, radio waves, and X rays for hundreds or thousands of years.

su•per•nu•mer•ar•y [ˌsupər'njuməˌrɛri] *or* [ˌsupər'numəˌrɛri] *adj., n., pl.* **-ar•ies.** —*adj.* in excess of the usual or necessary number; extra.
—*n.* **1** an extra person or thing. **2** *Theatre.* a person who appears on the stage but has no lines to speak: *In addition to the regular actors, there were 20 supernumeraries for the mob scene.* ⟨< LL *supernumerarius* excessive in number < L phrase *super numerum* beyond the number⟩

su•per•or•der ['supərˌɔrdər] *n. Biology.* a secondary category in the classification of plants and animals, including one or more orders within a class. It is usually a narrower classification than a subclass.

su•per•or•di•nate [ˌsupər'ɔrdənɪt] *adj., n.* —*adj.* superior in rank.
—*n.* a person or thing that is superordinate.

su•per•phos•phate [ˌsupər'fɒsfeit] *n.* **1** an acid phosphate. **2** any of various fertilizing materials composed chiefly of soluble phosphates.

su•per•phys•i•cal [ˌsupər'fɪzɪkəl] *adj.* beyond what is physical or explainable by physical laws.

su•per•pose [ˌsupər'pouz] *v.* **-posed, -pos•ing. 1** *Geometry.* place (a figure) upon another so that the two coincide. **2** superimpose. ⟨< F *superposer* < *super-* above + *poser* (see POSE[1])⟩ —ˌ**su•per•po'si•tion,** *n.*

su•per•pow•er ['supərˌpaʊər] *n.* **1** an extremely powerful nation; especially, one of a very small number of nations that dominate the world and compete with each other for economic or political control of blocs of less powerful nations. **2** extensive or extraordinary power.

su•per•sat•u•rate [ˌsupər'sætʃəˌreit] *v.* **-rat•ed, -rat•ing.** add to beyond the ordinary saturation point; saturate abnormally. A **supersaturated solution** is one in which more of a substance is dissolved than the solvent will hold under normal conditions.

su•per•sat•u•ra•tion [ˌsupərˌsætʃə'reiʃən] *n.* **1** the act of supersaturating. **2** an unstable condition of a vapour or solution, in which the density of the vapour or dissolved substance is in excess of that which is normally in equilibrium.

su•per•scribe [ˌsupər'skraɪb] *or* ['supərˌskraɪb] *v.* **-scribed, -scrib•ing. 1** write (words, letters, one's name, etc.) at the top of, above, or on the outside of something: *Her name was superscribed on the document.* **2** write something at the top of or over: *to superscribe a document or a monument.* ⟨< LL < L *superscribere* write over (as a correction) < *super-* above + *scribere* write⟩

su•per•script ['supərˌskrɪpt] *adj., n.* —*adj.* written above.
—*n.* a number, letter, etc. written directly above or above and to one side of another letter, number, etc. *Example*: In $a^3 \times b^n$, the ^{3} and the ^{n} are superscripts. ⟨< LL *superscriptus*, pp. of *superscribere.* See SUPERSCRIBE.⟩

su•per•scrip•tion [ˌsupər'skrɪpʃən] *n.* **1** the act of writing above, on, or outside of something. **2** something written above or on the outside. **3** an address on a letter or parcel.

su•per•sede [ˌsupər'sid] *v.* **-sed•ed, -sed•ing. 1** cause to be set aside as obsolete or inferior; displace: *Electric lights had superseded gas lights in most homes by the 1920s.* **2** fill the place of; succeed: *Mrs. McKenzie has superseded Mr. Mossop as principal of the school.* **3** set aside or ignore in promotion; promote another over the head of. ⟨< L *supersedere* be superior to, refrain from < *super-* above + *sedere* sit⟩ —ˌ**su•per'sed•er,** *n.*
—ˌ**su•per'se•dure** [-'sidʒər] or ˌ**su•per'sed•ence,** *n.*
☛ *Syn.* **1, 2.** See note at REPLACE.

su•per•sen•si•tive [ˌsupər'sɛnsətɪv] *adj.* extremely or morbidly sensitive. —ˌ**su•per'sen•si•tive•ly,** *adv.*
--ˌ**su•per'sen•si•tive•ness** or ˌ**su•per**ˌ**sen•si'tiv•i•ty,** *n.*

su•per•ses•sion [ˌsupər'sɛʃən] *n.* the act of superseding or the state of being superseded; supercedure.

su•per•son•ic [ˌsupər'sɒnɪk] *adj.* **1** having a frequency above the human ear's audibility limit of about 20 kilohertz. **2** of, having to do with, or produced by waves or vibrations of such frequency. **3** of, having to do with, or being a speed greater than the speed of sound in air (about 1200 km/h at sea level). **4** capable of moving at a speed greater than the speed of sound: *supersonic aircraft.* —ˌ**su•per'son•i•cal•ly,** *adv.*

su•per•son•ics [ˌsupər'sɒnɪks] *n.pl.* (*used with a singular verb*) the systematic study of supersonic phenomena.

su•per•star ['supərˌstɑr] *n.* a person who is outstanding in his or her field; especially, a person outstanding in the field of sports or entertainment.

su•per•sti•tion [ˌsupər'stɪʃən] *n.* **1** an unreasoning and abject fear of what is unknown or mysterious. **2** a belief or practice founded on ignorant fear or mistaken reverence: *A common superstition considers it bad luck to sleep in a room numbered 13.* **3** a system of such beliefs. ⟨ME < OF < L *superstitio, -onis*, ? originally, a standing over, as in wonder or awe < *super-* above + *stare* stand⟩

su•per•sti•tious [ˌsupər'stɪʃəs] *adj.* having to do with, caused by, or showing superstition: *She was superstitious about the number 13.* —ˌ**su•per'sti•tious•ly,** *adv.* —ˌ**su•per'sti•tious•ness,** *n.*

su•per•stra•tum ['supərˌstrætəm] *or* ['supərˌstreitəm] *n., pl.* **-stra•ta** [-ˌstrætə] *or* [-ˌstreitə] or **-stra•tums. 1** a stratum lying over another. **2** *Linguistics.* traces, in a language, of the influence of the language of a conquering or dominant people, as of Norman French in English.

su•per•struc•ture ['supərˌstrʌktʃər] *n.* **1** all of a building above the foundation. **2** the parts of a ship above the main deck. **3** a structure built on something else. **4** a concept, etc. based on a more general or fundamental one.

su•per•tank•er ['supərˌtæŋkər] *n.* a very large tanker.

su•per•tax ['supərˌtæks] *n.* a tax in addition to an ordinary tax; surtax.

su•per•ton•ic [ˌsupər'tɒnɪk] *n. Music.* the second tone of a scale; the tone next above the tonic.

su•per•vene [ˌsupər'vin] *v.* **-vened, -ven•ing.** come as something additional or interrupting, especially if unusual. ⟨< L *supervenire* < *super-* upon + *venire* come⟩ —ˌ**su•per'ven•ient,** *adj.*
—ˌ**su•per'ven•tion** [ˌsupər'vɛnʃən], *n.*

su•per•vise ['supərˌvaɪz] *v.* **-vised, -vis•ing.** look after and direct (work or workers, a process, etc.); oversee; superintend; manage: *She supervised the planning of the year's activities.* ⟨< Med.L *supervisus* < L *super-* over + *videre* see⟩
—'**su•per**ˌ**vi•sor,** *n.*

su•per•vi•sion [ˌsupər'vɪʒən] *n.* the act, process, or occupation of supervising or the state of being supervised: *They built the boat under their father's supervision.*

su•per•vi•so•ry [ˌsupər'vaɪzəri] *adj.* of or having to do with supervision or a supervisor: *supervisory duties. She was employed in a supervisory capacity.*

su•pi•nate ['supɪˌneit] *v.* **-nat•ed, -nat•ing.** turn (the hand and wrist, or the foot) so that the palm or sole faces upward or forward. ⟨< L *supinare* lay backward < *supinus* supine⟩
—ˌ**su•pi'na•tion,** *n.*

su•pi•na•tor ['supəˌneitər] *n. Anatomy.* a muscle used in supination.

su•pine *adj.* ['supaɪn] *or* [su'paɪn]; *n.* ['supaɪn] *adj., n.* —*adj.* **1** lying on the back with the face upward: *The patient was placed in a supine position.* Compare PRONE. **2** morally or mentally inactive or passive; sluggish: *supine indifference.* **3** of the hand or foot, with the palm or sole facing out or up.
—*n. Latin grammar.* a verbal noun formed from the stem of the past participle. ⟨< L *supinus*⟩ —'**su•pine•ly,** *adv.*
—'**su•pine•ness,** *n.*

supp [sʌp] *n. Informal.* supplemental examination: *He has to write supps in order to pass his year.*

supp. or **suppl.** supplement; supplementary.

sup•per ['sʌpər] *n.* **1** the evening meal; the third main meal of the day: *We usually have supper at 6 o'clock.* **2** *Esp. Brit.* a light meal eaten late in the evening, as after going to the theatre. **3** the food served at either of these meals: *I enjoyed supper.* **4** an informal public social event that takes place in the evening,

featuring a meal and often held to raise money: *a church supper.* ⟨ME < OF *soper*, originally infinitive, to sup < Gmc.⟩
—'sup•per•less, *adj.*

sup•per•time ['sʌpər,taɪm] *n., adj. —n.* the time at which supper is served.
—adj. occurring at or during supper: *suppertime conversation.*

sup•plant [sə'plænt] *v.* **1** take the place of; displace or set aside: *Machinery has supplanted hand labour in the making of shoes.* **2** take the place of by unfair or treacherous means: *The rebels plotted to supplant the legal government.* ⟨ME < L *supplantare* trip up < *sub-* under + *planta* sole of the foot⟩
—,sup•plan'ta•tion, *n.*
☛ *Syn.* **1, 2.** See note at REPLACE.

sup•ple ['sʌpəl] *adj.* **-pler, -plest;** *v.* **-pled, -pling.**
—adj. **1** capable of being bent or folded without breaking or cracking: *a supple birch tree, supple leather.* **2** able to move and bend or twist easily and gracefully: *a supple dancer.* **3** readily adaptable to different ideas, circumstances, people, etc.; yielding: *a supple mind.* **4** servile or overly compliant, especially in an insincere way to advance one's own interest.
—v. make or become supple. ⟨ME < OF < L *supplex* submissive < *supplicare.* See SUPPLICATE.⟩ **—'sup•ple•ly,** *adv.*
—'sup•ple•ness, *n.*

sup•ple•ment *n.* ['sʌpləmənt]; *v.* ['sʌplə,mɛnt] *n., v. —n.*
1 something added to complete a thing, or to make it larger or better: *a diet supplement.* **2** a section added to a printed work to improve or complete it: *The newspaper has a supplement every Saturday.* **3** *Geometry.* SUPPLEMENTARY ANGLE.
—v. supply what is lacking in; add to; complete: *to supplement one's income.* ⟨< L *supplementum,* ult. < *sub-* up + *-plere* fill⟩
☛ *Syn. n.* **2. Supplement,** APPENDIX = something added to a book or paper to complete or improve it. **Supplement** applies to a section added later or printed separately to give completeness by bringing the information up to date, correcting mistakes, or presenting special features: *This world history has a supplement covering recent events.* **Appendix** applies to a section added at the end of a book to give extra information that is useful for reference but not necessary for completeness: *The appendix contains a list of currencies. —v.* See note at COMPLEMENT.

sup•ple•men•tal [,sʌplə'mɛntəl] *adj., n.*
—adj. supplementary.
—n. a SUPPLEMENTAL EXAMINATION. **—,sup•ple'men•tal•ly,** *adv.*

supplemental examination an examination held for students who have failed the regular examination.

sup•ple•men•ta•ry [,sʌplə'mɛntəri] *adj., n., pl.* **-ries.** *—adj.* added to supply what is lacking; additional: *The new members of the class received supplementary instruction.*
—n. a supplementary person or thing. **—,sup•ple•men'ta•ri•ly,** *adv.*

supplementary angle *Geometry.* either of two angles or arcs which together equal 180° (*usually used in the plural*). A 45° angle and a 135° angle are supplementary angles.

sup•ple•men•ta•tion [,sʌpləmən'teiʃən] *n.* **1** the act or process of supplementing. **2** an additional supplement.

sup•ple•tion [sə'pliʃən] *n.* **1** *Linguistics.* an inflectional allomorph that is completely different in form and origin from the base morpheme, as the whole present tense of the verb *to be, better* as the comparative of *good,* the plural *-ren* instead of *-s* in *children,* etc. **2** the process by which such a form arises.
⟨< Med.L *suppletio* < L *suppletus* < *supplere* supply⟩

sup•ple•tive [sə'plitɪv] *or* ['sʌplətɪv] *adj. Linguistics.* of, being, or having to do with a suppletion.

sup•pli•ant ['sʌpliənt] *adj., n. —adj.* **1** asking humbly and earnestly; entreating: *a suppliant petitioner.* **2** expressing supplication: *suppliant gestures. They raised suppliant hands.*
—n. a person who asks humbly and earnestly: *She knelt as a suppliant before the queen.* Also, **supplicant.** ⟨< F *suppliant,* ppr. of *supplier* < L *supplicare.* See SUPPLICATE.⟩ **—'sup•pli•ant•ly,** *adv.* **—'sup•pli•ance,** *n.*

sup•pli•cate ['sʌplə,keit] *v.* **-cat•ed, -cat•ing. 1** beg (a person) humbly and earnestly: *The mother supplicated the judge to spare her son.* **2** beg humbly for (something); seek by entreaty: *to supplicate a blessing.* **3** pray humbly. ⟨< L *supplicare* < *sub-* down + *plicare* bend⟩ **—'sup•pli,cat•ing•ly,** *adv.*
—'sup•pli,ca•tor, *n.*

sup•pli•ca•tion [,sʌplə'keiʃən] *n.* **1** the act of supplicating. **2** a humble and earnest request or prayer: *Their supplications were granted.*

sup•pli•ca•to•ry ['sʌpləkə,tɔri] *adj.* making or expressing supplication.

sup•ply¹ [sə'plaɪ] *v.* **-plied, -ply•ing;** *n., pl.* **-plies.**
—v. **1** furnish; provide: *The city supplies books for the children. This filtration plant supplies the whole city with water.* **2** make up for (a loss, lack, absence, etc.): *to supply a deficiency.* **3** satisfy (a want, need, etc.): *There was just enough to supply the demand.* **4** fill (a place, vacancy, pulpit, etc.) as a substitute.
—n. **1** a quantity ready for use; stock; store: *Our school gets its supply of paper from the city.* **2** the quantity of an article in the market available for purchase: *the supply of coffee.* **3 supplies,** *pl.* the food, equipment, etc. necessary for an army, expedition, or the like. **4** (*adjl.*) of or having to do with such supplies or their management: *supply routes, a supply officer.* **5** a person, such as a teacher or a member of the clergy, who supplies a vacancy as a substitute. **6** (*adjl.*) serving as a substitute: *a supply teacher.* **7** the act of supplying. **8** Often, **supplies,** *pl.* a sum of money provided by parliament, or a like body, to meet the expenses of government.
in (short, good, etc.) **supply,** available to a specified extent: *Apples are in short supply this year.*
on supply, serving or available to serve as a substitute. ⟨ME < OF < L *supplere* < *sub-* up + *-plere* fill⟩ **—sup'pli•er,** *n.*

sup•ply² ['sʌpli] *adv.* in a supple manner; supplely.

sup•ply–side [sə'plaɪ ,saɪd] *adj. Economics.* of or having to do with an economic theory holding that the reduction of taxes will generate greater productivity by making more money available for investment.

sup•port [sə'pɔrt] *v., n. —v.* **1** keep from falling; hold up: *Walls support the roof.* **2** be able to withstand (a given weight or strain) without collapsing. **3** give strength or courage to; keep up; help: *Hope supports us in trouble.* **4** provide for: *She supported her nephew while he was at university.* **5** supply funds or means for; bear the expense of: *to support the expenses of government.* **6** maintain, keep up, or keep going: *This city supports two orchestras.* **7** be in favour of; back; second: *He supports the Liberals. Do you support the deregulation of industry?* **8** help prove; bear out: *The facts support his claim.* **9** in military use, assist or protect (another unit) in combat: *Artillery fire supported the infantry attack.* **10** put up with; bear; endure: *She couldn't support life without friends.* **11** *Theatre.* **a** act with (a leading actor); assist; attend. **b** act (a part or character) with success.
—n. **1** the act of supporting or the condition of being supported; help; aid: *He needs the support of a scholarship.* **2** maintenance; means of livelihood: *the support of a family.* **3** a person or thing that supports; prop: *The neck is the support of the head. She has to wear a back support.* **4** *Military.* **a** assistance or protection given by one element or unit to another. **b** a unit that helps another in combat. Aircraft may be used as a support for infantry. **c** the part of any unit held back at the beginning of an attack as reserve. ⟨ME < OF < L *supportare* bring up < *sub-* up + *portare* carry⟩ **—sup'port•er,** *n.* **—sup'port•a•ble,** *adj.*
☛ *Syn. v.* **Support,** MAINTAIN, UPHOLD = hold up or keep up, literally or figuratively. **Support** suggests bearing the weight or strain, serving as a prop, or giving needed strength to prevent something or someone from falling or sinking: *Teammates supported the injured player.* **Maintain** suggests keeping up in a good state or condition by providing what is needed to prevent loss of strength, health, value, etc.: *Provincial governments maintain the highways. You cannot maintain a family on this income.* **Uphold** chiefly suggests giving aid or moral support to a person, cause, belief, etc.: *He upheld his brother's honour. —n.* **2.** See note at LIVING.

sup•port•er [sə'pɔrtər] *n.* **1** a person who or thing that supports. **2** a follower or backer. **3** *Heraldry.* either of two figures, human or animal, flanking the shield or escutcheon in a coat of arms.

support group a group of individuals affected by some disease, traumatic experience, etc. who meet regularly to support one another, exchange useful information, etc.

sup•port•ive [sə'pɔrtɪv] *adj.* offering or furnishing support: *supportive testimony, a supportive friend.* **—sup'port•ive•ly,** *adv.*
—sup'port•ive•ness, *n.*

sup•pose [sə'pouz] *v.* **-posed, -pos•ing. 1** consider as a possibility; assume for the sake of argument: *Suppose it doesn't work; what will we do then?* **2** think probable; believe: *I suppose she will come as usual. I suppose I'll be left with the dishes again.* **3** involve as necessary; imply; PRESUPPOSE (def. 2): *An invention supposes an inventor.* **4** presume the existence or presence of: *The author of the story supposes a race of intelligent beings living in another galaxy.* ⟨ME < OF *supposer* < *sub-* under + *poser* (see POSE¹)⟩ **—sup'pos•a•ble,** *adj.*

sup•posed *adj.* [sə'pouzd] *or* [sə'pouzɪd] *for def. 1;* [sə'poust] *for defs. 2-4; v.* [sə'pouzd] *adj., v. —adj.* **1** accepted as real or true, but mistakenly or without proof or evidence; believed or

imagined: *a supposed insult. We need to take a closer look at the supposed improvements in the postal system.* **2** designed or intended: *What is that supposed to mean?* **3** obliged or expected (*to*): *I was supposed to bring the cake, but I forgot.* **4** permitted; allowed (*to*) (*used only in the negative*): *You are not supposed to jump on the bed.*
—v. pt. and pp. of SUPPOSE. **—sup'pos•i•tive** [sə'pɒzətɪv], *adj.*

sup•pos•ed•ly [sə'pouzɪdli] *adv.* according to what is or was supposed: *He was supposedly sleeping but we discovered that he was out.*

sup•pos•ing [sə'pouzɪŋ] *conj., v. —conj.* in the event that; assuming that: *Supposing it rains, shall we go?*
—v. ppr. of SUPPOSE.

sup•po•si•tion [ˌsʌpə'zɪʃən] *n.* **1** the act of supposing. **2** something supposed; assumption: *He entered the campaign on the supposition that his friends would support him.* ⟨ME < OF < Med.L *suppositio, -onis,* ult. < L *sub-* under + *ponere* place⟩

sup•po•si•tion•al [ˌsʌpə'zɪʃənəl] *adj.* of or based on supposition; hypothetical; supposed. **—ˌsup•po'si•tion•al•ly,** *adv.*

sup•pos•i•ti•tious [səˌpɒzə'tɪʃəs] *adj.* **1** put in place of another with intent to defraud; counterfeit: *supposititious writings, a supposititious heir.* **2** hypothetical; supposed. Sometimes, **suppositious.** ⟨< L *supposititius,* ult. < *sub-* under + *ponere* place⟩ **—supˌpos•i'ti•tious•ly,** *adv.*

sup•pos•i•to•ry [sə'pɒzəˌtɔri] *n., pl.* **-ries.** a medicated preparation in the form of a cone or cylinder to be put into the rectum or other opening of the body, where it releases the medicine into the system by melting. ⟨< LL *suppositorium* (thing) placed underneath, ult. < L *sub-* under + *ponere* place⟩

sup•press [sə'prɛs] *v.* **1** put an end to; stop by force; put down: *The troops suppressed the rebellion by firing on the mob.* **2** keep in; hold back; check: *She suppressed a yawn.* **3** hide; refuse to make known: *The government was accused of suppressing important facts.* **4** stop or prohibit the publication or circulation of: *The book was suppressed because it contained libelous statements.* **5** hinder or restrain the secretion, process, or growth of: *to suppress bleeding. The Pill suppresses ovulation.* **6** *Electronics. Radio.* eliminate (unwanted frequencies, interference) from a signal. **7** *Psychiatry.* consciously prevent oneself from thinking about or expressing (an undesirable idea, impulse, etc.) ⟨ME < L *suppressus,* pp. of *supprimere* < *sub-* down + *premere* press⟩ **—sup'press•er** or **sup'pres•sor,** *n.* **—sup'press•i•ble,** *adj.* **—sup'pres•sive,** *adj.* **—sup'pres•sive•ly,** *adv.*

sup•pres•sant [sə'prɛsənt] *n.* a substance, especially a drug, that suppresses undesirable conditions, reflexes, etc.: *a cough suppressant.*

sup•pres•sion [sə'prɛʃən] *n.* **1** a suppressing or being suppressed: *the suppression of a revolt, the suppression of an impulse to cough, the suppression of facts.* **2** *Psychiatry.* a suppressed thought or feeling.

sup•pu•rate ['sʌpjəˌreit] *v.* **-rat•ed, -rat•ing.** form or discharge pus; fester. ⟨< L *suppurare* < *sub-* under + *pus* pus⟩

sup•pu•ra•tion [ˌsʌpjə'reiʃən] *n.* **1** the formation or discharge of pus. **2** pus.

sup•pu•ra•tive ['sʌpjərətɪv] *or* ['sʌpjəˌreitɪv] *adj., n. —adj.* **1** promoting suppuration. **2** suppurating.
—n. a medicine or application that promotes suppuration.

su•pra ['suprə] *adv.* **1** above. **2** in a book, manuscript, etc., before; previously. ⟨< L⟩

supra– *prefix.* above, over, beyond, or greater than: *suprarenal, supra-orbital.* ⟨< L⟩

su•pra•mo•lec•u•lar [ˌsuprəmə'lɛkjələr] *adj.* **1** of a level of structure or organization above that of the molecule. **2** composed of aggregates of molecules.

su•pra•na•tion•al [ˌsuprə'næʃənəl] *adj.* supernational.

su•pra–or•bit•al [ˌsuprə 'ɔrbɪtəl] *adj., n. —adj.* above the eye socket.
—n. a bone or scale thus located, as in some reptiles. Compare POSTORBITAL.

su•pra•re•nal [ˌsuprə'rinəl] *adj., n. Anatomy. —adj.* situated above or on the kidney; especially, adrenal.
—n. a suprarenal part, especially an adrenal gland. ⟨< *supra-* above + L *renes* kidneys⟩

su•pra•seg•men•tal [ˌsuprəsɛg'mɛntəl] *adj., n. Phonetics. —adj.* of, having to do with, or designating significant features that accompany a sequence of sounds, or segments, in an utterance, such as, in English, stress and pitch.
—n. such a feature.

su•prem•a•cist [sə'prɛməˌsɪst] *n.* one who believes in or advocates the innate superiority or supremacy of a certain group, especially a racial group.

su•prem•a•cy [sə'prɛməsi] *n.* **1** the quality or state of being supreme. **2** supreme authority or power.

su•preme [sə'prim] *adj., n. —adj.* **1** highest in rank or authority: *a supreme ruler.* **2** of or belonging to a person or thing that is supreme: *supreme authority.* **3** highest in degree or quality; greatest; utmost: *supreme disgust, supreme courage.* **4** ultimate; final: *To give one's life is to make the supreme sacrifice.*
—n. Cookery. **1** a rich sauce of stock, cream, and egg yolk. **2** a meat dish cooked and served in this sauce: *chicken supreme.* ⟨< L *supremus,* ult. < *super* above⟩ **—su'preme•ly,** *adv.*

Supreme Being God.

Supreme Court 1 in Canada: **a** the highest appeal court of Canada in civil and criminal matters. It consists of nine judges and hears appeals from the provincial courts of appeal and from the federal court dealing with matters of taxation, copyright, etc. **b** the highest appeal or trial court in some provinces. **2** a similar court in other countries.

Supt. or **supt.** superintendent.

suq [sʊk] *n.* See SOUK.

sur–[1] *prefix.* upon: over, or above: *surcharge, surcoat, surtax.*

sur–[2] *prefix.* the form of SUB- occurring before *r,* as in *surreptitious.*

sur. 1 surplus. **2** surcharge. **3** surname.

su•ra ['sʊrə] *n.* a major section or chapter of the Koran. ⟨Arabic, literally, enclosure⟩
☛ *Hom.* SURAH.

su•rah ['sʊrə] *n.* a soft, twilled silk, rayon, etc. ⟨< *Surat,* a city in W India⟩
☛ *Hom.* SURA.

su•ral ['sʊrəl] *adj. Anatomy.* of or having to do with the calf of the leg. ⟨< NL *suralis* < L *sura* calf of the leg⟩

sur•cease [sər'sis] *n., v. —n. Archaic or poetic.* end; cessation.
—v. cease. ⟨ME < OF *sursis,* pp. of *surseoir* refrain < L *supersedere.* See SUPERSEDE.⟩

sur•charge *n.* ['sɜrˌtʃɑrdʒ]; *v.* [sər'tʃɑrdʒ] *or* ['sɜrˌtʃɑrdʒ] *n., v.* **-charged, -charg•ing.** *—n.* **1** an extra charge: *The express company made a surcharge for delivering the trunk outside of the city limits.* **2** an overcharge. **3** an additional and usually excessive load, burden, or supply: *a surcharge of punishment.* **4** an additional mark printed on a postage stamp to change its value, date, etc. **5** a stamp bearing such a mark.
—v. **1** impose a surcharge on (a person, account, etc.) **2** impose a surcharge of (a given amount). **3** overload or overfill: *The widower's heart was surcharged with grief.* **4** print a surcharge on (a postage stamp). ⟨< F *surcharger* < *sur-* over (< L *super-*) + *charger* charge < L *carricare* to load < *carrus* load⟩

sur•cin•gle ['sɜrsɪŋgəl] *n.* **1** a strap or belt around a horse's body to keep a saddle, blanket, or pack in place. **2** a sash or belt on a cassock, as of a priest, etc. ⟨ME < OF *surcengle* < *sur-* over (< L *super-*) + *cengle* girdle < L *cingula* < *cingere* gird⟩

sur•coat ['sɜrˌkout] *n.* an outer coat or cloak, especially such a garment once worn by knights over their armour. ⟨ME < OF *surcote* < *sur-* over (< L *super-*) + *cote* coat < Gmc.⟩

sur•cu•lose ['sɜrkjəˌlous] *adj. Botany.* having or bearing suckers. ⟨< NL *surculosus* < L *surculus* little twig, sucker, dim. of *surus* twig, branch⟩

surd [sɜrd] *n., adj.* **1** *Phonetics.* a voiceless sound. **2** *Mathematics.* a quantity that cannot be expressed in whole numbers or fractions; an irrational number. *Example:* $\sqrt{2}$
—adj. **1** *Phonetics.* uttered without vibration of the vocal cords; unvoiced or voiceless. **2** *Mathematics.* that cannot be expressed in whole numbers or fractions; irrational. ⟨< L *surdus* unheard⟩

sure [ʃʊr] *or* [ʃɜr] *adj.* **sur•er, sur•est;** *adv., interj. —adj.* **1** free from doubt; certain; having ample reason for belief; confident; positive: *He is sure of success in the end. I am sure of her guilt.* **2** safe; reliable; foolproof: *a sure messenger, a sure remedy.* **3** never missing, slipping, etc.; unfailing; unerring: *sure aim, a sure touch.* **4** certain to be or to happen: *The army faced sure defeat. He is sure to win the prize.* **5** indubitable; unquestionably true: *a sure statement.* **6** *Archaic.* secure or safe.
be sure, be careful; do not fail: *Be sure to lock the door when you leave.*
for sure, *Informal.* **a** surely; certainly: *He's coming for sure.* **b** sure; certain: *That's for sure.*
make sure, a act so as to make something certain: *Make sure you*

don't lose this. **b** get sure knowledge: *Make sure of your facts before accusing me!*
sure enough, *Informal.* **a** certainly. **b** just as predicted or expected.
to be sure, a surely; certainly. **b** it must be acknowledged; admittedly.
–adv. Informal. surely; certainly.
–interj. certainly; yes indeed (*sometimes used ironically*). ⟨ME < OF *sur* < L *securus.* Doublet of SECURE.⟩ **–'sure•ness,** *n.*

☛ *Syn. adj.* **1. Sure,** CERTAIN, CONFIDENT = having no doubt about a person, fact, statement, action, etc. **Sure** emphasizes being free from doubt in one's own mind: *Police are sure he was murdered.* **Certain,** often interchangeable with **sure,** more definitely suggests positive reasons or proof to support one's trust or belief: *They have been certain since they uncovered new evidence.* **Confident** suggests a strong and unshakable belief: *They are confident they will solve the case soon.*

☛ *Usage.* **Sure** is primarily an adjective: *a sure footing. Are you sure?* As an adverb, **sure** is often used in informal speech instead of **surely** or as an equivalent of **certainly** or **yes:** *Sure, I'm coming. That sure is interesting.* In writing, this usage should be used only in dialogue or in very informal situations.

sure–fire ['ʃʊr ˌfaɪr] *adj. Informal.* that will not fail; certain: *a sure-fire formula.*

sure–foot•ed ['ʃʊr 'fʊtɪd] *adj.* not liable to stumble, slip, or fall. **–'sure-'foot•ed•ly,** *adv.* **–'sure-'foot•ed•ness,** *n.*

sure•ly ['ʃʊrli] *or* ['ʃɜrli] *adv.* **1** undoubtedly; certainly: *Half a loaf is surely better than none.* **2** really (*used to emphasize or intensify a statement*): *Surely you can't be serious!* **3** without mistake; without missing, slipping, etc.; firmly: *The goat leaped surely from rock to rock.* **4** steadily; with definite progress: *slowly but surely.* **5** yes indeed.

Sû•re•té [ʃʊrə'teɪ]; *French,* [syʀ'te] *n.* **1** *Cdn., Québec.* police. **2** in France, the criminal investigation section of the police department. ⟨< F⟩

sure thing *Informal.* **1** something sure to happen, succeed, etc. **2** yes! certainly!: *Can you open this jar for me? Sure thing!*

sur•e•ty ['ʃʊrəti] *n., pl.* **-ties. 1** security against loss, damage, or failure to do something: *An insurance company gives surety against loss by fire.* **2** a person who agrees to be legally responsible for another: *She was surety for her brother's appearance in court on the day set for the trial.* **3** *Archaic.* a sure thing; certainty.

sur•e•ty•ship ['ʃʊrətiˌʃɪp] *n. Law.* the obligation of a person to answer for the debt, fault, or conduct of another.

surf [sɜrf] *n.* **1** the waves or swell of the sea breaking on the shore or upon shoals, reefs, etc. **2** the deep pounding or thundering sound of this. **3** the foam accompanying this.
–v. **1** travel or ride on the crest of the waves, especially with a surfboard. **2** *Computer technology. Informal.* search for material of interest on the INTERNET or WORLD WIDE WEB. ⟨earlier *suff;* possibly var. of *sough*⟩ **–'surf•er,** *n.* **–'surf•y,** *adj.*
☛ *Hom.* SERF.

sur•face ['sɜrfɪs] *n., v.* **-faced, -fac•ing.** *–n.* **1** the outer side of anything: *the surface of a golf ball, the surface of a mountain.* **2** its area. **3** the top of the ground or soil, or of a body of water or other liquid: *The stone sank below the surface.* **4** any face or side of a thing: *A cube has six surfaces.* **5** that which has length and breadth but no thickness: *a plane surface in geometry.* **6** the outward appearance: *He seems rough, but you will find him very kind below the surface.* **7** (*adjl.*) of, on, or having to do with the surface or with external aspects only: *a surface view.* **8** (*adjl.*) functioning, carried out, etc. on land or sea, that is, on the earth's surface: *surface mail, surface travel.*
–v. **1** put a surface on; make smooth: *to surface a road.* **2** bring or come to the surface: *to surface a submarine. The submarine surfaced.* **3** be noticed, become known, etc. after hiding or being hidden: *The truth has surfaced at last. The fugitive surfaced two days later in Halifax.* ⟨< F *surface* < *sur-* above (< L *super-*) + *face* face, ult. < L *facies* form⟩ **–'sur•fac•er,** *n.*

sur•face–act•ive ['sɜrfɪs ˌæktɪv] *adj. Chemistry.* of a substance, lowering the surface tension of the liquid in which it is dissolved.

surface mail **1** mail transported by land and sea, rather than by air. **2** the system or service of sending mail in this way.

surface noise noise from the friction of the needle of a record player against the record.

surface structure *Linguistics.* in generative or transformational grammar, the structure of a sentence as it is actually uttered or written as opposed to its underlying mental representation. Compare DEEP STRUCTURE.

surface tension *Physics.* an elasticlike property of the surface of a liquid that makes it tend to contract, caused by the forces of attraction between the molecules of the liquid.

sur•fac•tant [sər'fæktənt] *n. Chemistry.* a surface-active agent ⟨*surf(ace)-act(ive) a(ge)nt*⟩

surf•board ['sɜrfˌbɔrd] *n., v. –n.* a more-or-less oblong board on which a person may stand or lie in order to ride on the crest of a wave as it comes in to the beach.
–v. engage in the sport of riding on a surfboard.

surf•boat ['sɜrfˌbout] *n.* a strong boat specially made for use in heavy surf.

surf duck a scoter; especially the SURF SCOTER.

sur•feit ['sɜrfɪt] *n., v. –n.* **1** a grossly excessive indulgence in something; too much; excess: *A surfeit of food makes one sick. A surfeit of advice annoys me.* **2** disgust or nausea caused by this; painful satiety. **3** an abnormal physical condition caused by gluttony, intemperance, etc.
–v. **1** feed or cause to take too much, so as to cause nausea or disgust. **2** take too much of something; indulge too much. ⟨ME < OF *surfait,* originally pp., overdone < *sur-* over (< L *super-*) + *faire* do < L *facere*⟩
☛ *Syn. v.* See note at SATIATE.

surf•ing ['sɜrfɪŋ] *n., v. –n.* the sport of using a surfboard to ride toward shore on the crest of a wave.
–v. ppr. of SURF.

surf scoter a large sea duck (*Melanitta perspicillata*) of North America, ranging from Alaska to southern California. The adult male is black with two white patches on its head.

surge [sɜrdʒ] *v.* **surged, surg•ing;** *n. –v.* **1** rise and fall in waves or billows: *the surging sea.* **2** move as a wave; roll, swell, or sweep forward: *A great wave surged over us. Joy surged through him when he saw her. The crowd surged out of the arena.* **3** of electric voltage or current, increase abruptly or oscillate violently.
–n. **1** the swelling and rolling of the sea. **2 a** a swelling, rolling, or sweeping forward like a wave: *A surge of anger swept over her.* **b** a wavelike mass or volume (of something) moving in this way. **3** a sudden increase; often, specifically, an increase in electric current: *a surge of power, a surge of adrenalin.* ⟨ult. (probably through OF *surgeon* a spring) < L *surgere* rise < *sub-* up + *regere* reach⟩
☛ *Hom.* SERGE.

sur•geon ['sɜrdʒən] *n.* a medical doctor who specializes in surgery. ⟨ME < AF *surgien,* OF *cirurgien* < *cirurgie.* See SURGERY. Doublet of CHIRURGEON.⟩

sur•geon•fish ['sɜrdʒənˌfɪʃ] *n.* any tropical fish of the genus *Acanthurus* having a compressed body and sharp movable spines on both sides of the tail.

sur•ger•y ['sɜrdʒəri] *n., pl.* **-ger•ies. 1 a** the treatment of disease, injury, etc. by using the hands or instruments to mend or remove an organ, tissue, or part, or to remove foreign matter in the body: *The fracture was a serious one that required surgery.* **b** an instance of such treatment: *Dr. Jameson will perform the surgery, which will take 45 minutes.* **2** the branch of medicine that deals with such treatment. **3** an operating room. **4** *Brit.* a doctor's or dentist's office. ⟨ME < OF *surgerie, cirurgerie* < *cirurgie* < L < Gk. *cheirourgia,* ult. < *cheir* hand + *ergon* work⟩

sur•gi•cal ['sɜrdʒɪkəl] *adj.* **1** of, having to do with, or characteristic of surgeons or surgery; *a surgical specialist, surgical precision.* **2** used in surgery: *surgical instruments.* **3** resulting from surgery: *surgical fever.* **–'sur•gi•cal•ly,** *adv.*

Su•ri•name ['sʊrɪˌnɑm] *or* ['sʊrɪˌnæm] a country in northern South America on the Atlantic Ocean, between French Guiana and Guyana.

sur•ly ['sɜrli] *adj.* **-li•er, -li•est.** bad-tempered and unfriendly; rude; gruff: *a surly answer.* ⟨ult. < *sir,* in sense of 'lord'⟩ **–'sur•li•ly,** *adv.* **–'sur•li•ness,** *n.*

sur•mise *v.* [sər'maɪz]; *n.* [sər'maɪz] *or* ['sɜrmaɪz] *v.* **-mised, -mis•ing;** *n. –v.* guess: *We surmised that the delay was caused by some accident.*
–n. **1** the formation of an idea with little or no evidence; a guessing: *His guilt was a matter of surmise; there was no proof.* **2** a guess. ⟨ME < OF *surmise* accusation, ult. < *sur-* upon (< L *super-*) + *mettre* put < L *mittere* send⟩
☛ *Syn. v.* See note at GUESS.

sur•mount [sər'maʊnt] *v.* **1** overcome: *She surmounted many difficulties.* **2** be at or on the top of: *The dish was piled with ice cream, nuts, and chocolate chunks, the whole surmounted by a cherry.* **3** go up and across; get up and over: *to surmount a hill.* **4** place something on top of; cap. ⟨ME < OF *surmonter* < *sur-* over (< L *super-*) + *monter* mount < L *mons, montis* mountain⟩ **–sur'mount•a•ble,** *adj.*

sur•name ['sɜr,neim] *n., v.* **-named, -nam•ing.** *—n.* **1** the name that members of a family have in common; family name; last name: *Kahn is the surname of Nathan Kahn.* **2** a name added to a person's real name: *William I of England had the surname "the Conqueror."*
—v. give an added name to; call by a surname: *Simon was surnamed Peter.* ⟨< F *surnom* < *sur-* over (< L *super-*) + *nom* name < L *nomen*; influenced by E *name*⟩

sur•pass [sər'pæs] *v.* **1** do or be better or greater or more than; be superior to: *The experience surpassed anything he had known before. She surpasses all the other team members in her ability to score.* **2** be too much or too great for; go beyond the range or capacity of: *The magnificence of the sight surpassed description.* ⟨< F *surpasser* < *sur-* beyond + *passer* pass⟩ **—sur'pass•a•ble,** *adj.* **—sur'pass•ing•ly,** *adv.*
☛ *Syn.* **1.** See note at EXCEL.

sur•plice ['sɜrplɪs] *n.* a loose white gown, less than floor-length and having very wide sleeves, worn in some Christian churches over the cassock by the clergy and choir members during a service. ⟨ME < AF *surpliz,* OF *surpelice* < *sur-* over (< L *super-*) + *pelice* fur garment, ult. < L *pellis* hide⟩ **—'sur•pliced,** *adj.*

sur•plus ['sɜrpləs] *or* ['sɜrplʌs] *n.* **1** an amount over and above what is needed; an extra quantity left over; excess. **2** *Accounting.* an excess of assets over liabilities. **3** (*adjl.*) that exceeds what is needed; forming a surplus: *The store's surplus stock was put on sale at the end of the season.* ⟨ME < OF *surplus* < *sur-* over (< L *super-*) + *plus* more < L *plus*⟩

sur•plus•age ['sɜrpləsɪdʒ] *n.* **1** that which is surplus; excess. **2** unnecessary words; irrelevant material.

surplus value *Economics.* the difference between the market value of a worker's product and the wages he or she is paid for producing it.

sur•prise [sər'praɪz] *or* [sə'praɪz] *n., v.* **-prised, -pris•ing.** *—n.* **1** a feeling caused by something unexpected. **2** something unexpected. **3** (*adjl.*) that is not expected; surprising: *a surprise party, a surprise visit.* **4** an instance of catching unprepared or coming upon suddenly; a sudden attack.
take by surprise, a catch unprepared; come on suddenly and unexpectedly. **b** astonish.
—v. **1** cause to feel surprised; astonish. **2** catch unprepared; come upon suddenly; attack suddenly: *The enemy surprised the fort.* **3** cause (a person, etc.) to act involuntarily, by doing, saying, being etc. something unexpected (*used with* **into**): *The news surprised her into tears.* **4** find or discover (something) by a sudden or unexpected question, attack, etc.; detect or elicit by surprise tactics: *to surprise the truth of the matter from someone.* **5** present (someone) unexpectedly (*with* a gift, etc.) ⟨ME < OF *surprise,* pp. fem. of *surprendre* < *sur-* over (< L *super-*) + *prendre* take < L *prehendere*⟩
☛ *Syn. v.* **1. Surprise,** ASTONISH, AMAZE = strike a person with a sudden feeling as of perplexity, confusion, or wonder. **Surprise,** the general word, suggests the sudden feeling caused by something unexpected or out of the ordinary: *His answer surprised her.* **Astonish** suggests the stronger feeling caused by something too extraordinary to be possible: *She astonished many people by graduating from university with honours after getting dismal grades in high school.* **Amaze** emphasizes the idea of bewildered wonder: *New scientific discoveries constantly amaze us.*

sur•pris•ing [sər'praɪzɪŋ] *or* [sə'praɪzɪŋ] *adj., v. —adj.* causing surprise: *a surprising recovery.*
—v. ppr. of SURPRISE. **—sur'pris•ing•ly,** *adv.*

sur•re•al [sə'riəl] *or* [sə'ril] *adj.* surrealistic.

sur•re•al•ism [sə'riə,lɪzəm] *or* [sə'rilɪzəm] *n.* a style in art and literature characterized by the attempt to portray the functioning of the subconscious mind, especially as in dreams, often by combining conventional and unconventional elements or by distorting the conventional. ⟨< F *surréalisme*⟩

sur•re•al•ist [sə'riəlɪst] *or* [sə'rilɪst] *n., adj. —n.* an artist or writer who uses surrealism.
—adj. of or having to do with surrealism or surrealists.

sur•re•al•is•tic [sə,riə'lɪstɪk] *or* [,sɜriə'lɪstɪk] *adj.* **1** of or having to do with surrealism or surrealists. **2** having a strange and unreal quality, like a surrealist painting: *a surrealistic experience.* **—sur,re•al'is•ti•cal•ly,** *adv.*

sur•ren•der [sə'rɛndər] *v., n. —v.* **1** give up control or possession of, especially under compulsion or demand from another or after a struggle; renounce: *to surrender a fort to an invader, to surrender an office. As the storm increased, the people on the raft surrendered all hope.* **2** give oneself up; stop resisting; give in to a demand for submission: *The captain had to surrender when the ammunition ran out.* **3** give in to an emotion, etc. (*used with a reflexive pronoun*): *to surrender oneself to grief.* **4** cancel (an insurance policy) in return for a cash sum.
—n. the act or an instance of surrendering. ⟨ME < AF *surrendre* < OF *sur-* over (< L *super-*) + *rendre* render < L *reddere* give as due, pay⟩

surrender value the value of an insurance policy in terms of the cash payable to the holder if the policy is cancelled, or surrendered.

sur•rep•ti•tious [,sɜrəp'tɪʃəs] *adj.* **1** done, made, or acquired secretly; secret and stealthy or unauthorized: *a surreptitious wink, a surreptitious gift.* **2** acting in a secret or stealthy way: *He was very surreptitious in his movements.* ⟨< L *surrepticius,* ult. < *sub-* secretly + *rapere* snatch⟩ **—,sur•rep'ti•tious•ly,** *adv.* **—,sur•rep'ti•tious•ness,** *n.*

sur•rey ['sɜri] *n., pl.* **-reys.** a light, four-wheeled, horse-drawn carriage having two seats for four persons and, usually, a flat top. ⟨< *Surrey,* a county in SE England⟩

sur•ro•gate ['sɜrəgɪt] *or* ['sɜrə,geit] *n.* **1** a person who acts for or takes the place of another; substitute or deputy. **2** (*adjl.*) of, having to do with, or acting as a surrogate: *surrogate parents, a surrogate pleasure.* ⟨< L *surrogatus,* pp. of *surrogare* substitute < *sub-* instead + *rogare* ask for⟩ **—'sur•ro•gate,ship,** *n.*

surrogate court *Cdn.* **1** a court of law that deals with wills and other matters relating to the estates of deceased persons. **2** *Nfld.* formerly, a court held by a magistrate appointed from among the captains at the fisheries.

surrogate mother a woman who undergoes artificial insemination and bears a child for another woman who is unable to do so. **—surrogate motherhood.**

sur•round [sə'raʊnd] *v., n. —v.* **1** come or be all around; shut in on all sides; enclose: *News reporters surrounded the minister as she emerged from the legislature. The little girl was surrounded by her toys. Police surrounded the house.* **2** extend around the outside or edge of: *A high fence surrounds the field. The inscription on the medal was surrounded by a design of flowers.* **3** be or form part of the environment of: *Love and goodwill surrounded him.* **4** cause to be surrounded by: *The invalid's family surrounded him with every comfort. The king surrounded himself with flatterers.*
—n. something that surrounds, such as a border or edging. ⟨ME < AF *surounder* surpass < LL *superundare* overflow < L *super-* over + *unda* wave; influenced in meaning by *round*⟩

sur•round•ings [sə'raʊndɪŋz] *n.pl.* surrounding things, conditions, etc.; environment.

sur•tax ['sɜr,tæks] *n., v. —n* an additional or extra tax: *A surtax was temporarily levied by the government on incomes above $60 000.*
—v. impose a surtax on. ⟨< F *surtaxe* < *sur-* over + *taxe* tax⟩

sur•tout [sər'tu] *or* [sər'tut] *n.* **1** a man's overcoat, common in the late 19th century; frock coat. **2** a hooded mantle for women. ⟨< F *surtout* < *sur-* over + *tout* all⟩

sur•veil•lance [sər'veiləns] *n.* **1** a watch kept over a person, place, thing, activity, etc.: *She has been under police surveillance for several weeks.* **2** supervision. ⟨< F *surveillance* < *sur-* over (< L *super-*) + *veiller* watch < L *vigilare*⟩

sur•vey *v.* [sər'vei]; *n.* ['sɜrvei] *v., n., pl.* **-veys.** *—v.* **1** look over; take a general view of: *She surveyed the scene before her. They surveyed the wreckage.* **2** examine or inspect the condition, situation, etc. of: *He surveyed the alternatives open to him and decided he had to act at once.* **3** determine the exact boundaries and contours of (an area of land) by measuring distances, angles, etc.: *The land is being surveyed for subdivision into building lots.* **4** survey land: *He spent the summer surveying for the town.*
—n. **1** a general or comprehensive study or view of something: *Her book includes a survey of 20th century Canadian poetry.* **2 a** an inspection or investigation of the condition, situation, etc. of something: *Our first survey of the house showed us that it needed a lot of repairs.* **b** specifically, an investigation of a social, political, etc. nature, carried out by means of oral or written questionnaires, interviews, etc.: *A recent survey shows that public opinion on the issue has changed.* **3** a written statement or description of the result of such an investigation or examination: *The government survey of food prices has just been published.* **4** the act or an instance of surveying land. **5** a map or plan produced by such a survey. **6** *Cdn.* **a** a tract of land divided into building lots; subdivision. **b** the houses or community built on such land. ⟨ME < AF *surveier,* ult. < L *super-* over + *videre* see⟩

sur•vey•ing [sər'veiɪŋ] *n., v. —n.* **1** the science or technique of measuring the boundaries and contours of particular areas on, above, or beneath the earth's surface by using the principles of geometry. **2** the act or business of making such measurements. —*v.* ppr. of SURVEY.

sur•vey•or [sər'veiər] *n.* a person who surveys, especially one whose work is making land surveys. **—sur'vey•or,ship,** *n.*

surveyor's measure a system for measuring land area, formerly used by surveyors. The basic unit was the chain, a unit of length equal to about 20 m, which was divided into 100 links each equal to about 20 cm.

sur•viv•al [sər'vaɪvəl] *n.* **1** the act or fact of surviving; a continuing to live, or exist: *He had little chance of survival when his food ran out.* **2** a person, thing, custom, belief, etc. that has lasted from an earlier time. **3** (*adjl.*) of, having to do with, or assisting survival: *survival techniques, a survival kit.*

sur•viv•al•ist [sər'vaɪvəlɪst] *n.* a person determined to survive at all costs, especially one who stores food, weapons, etc. against the prospect of catastrophe, either natural, as an earthquake, or artificial, as a nuclear war.

survival of the fittest *Biology.* the process or result of NATURAL SELECTION.

sur•vive [sər'vaɪv] *v.* **-vived, -viv•ing. 1** endure (extreme hardship or suffering, attack, disaster, etc.) without dying or being destroyed; remain (in spite of): *Several of the original buildings still survive. The roses did not survive the winter.* **2** live longer than; outlive: *He survived his wife by three years.* ⟨ME < AF *survivre* < *sur-* over (< L *super-*) + *vivre* live < L *vivere*⟩

sur•vi•vor [sər'vaɪvər] *n.* **1** a person who or thing that survives. **2** a person who is likely to survive almost anything by virtue of his or her determination, adaptability, wits, etc. **3** a joint owner who has rights to the whole property on the death of another owner. **—sur'vi•vor,ship,** *n.*

sus– *prefix.* the form of SUB- occurring in some cases before *c, p, t,* as in *susceptible, suspend, sustain.*

sus•cep•ti•bil•i•ty [sə,sɛptə'bɪləti] *n., pl.* **-ties. 1** the quality or state of being susceptible: *susceptibility to disease.* **2** *Physics.* the capacity of a substance to be magnetized, measured by the ratio of the magnetization to the magnetizing force. *Symbol*: k **3 susceptibilities,** *pl.* sensitive feelings.

sus•cep•ti•ble [sə'sɛptəbəl] *adj.* **1** open or liable to an influence, stimulus, etc.; readily affected (*used with* **to**): *He is susceptible to flattery. Children are susceptible to many diseases.* **2** sensitive and impressionable; easily influenced by feelings or emotions: *Tales of adventure appealed to her susceptible nature.*
susceptible of, capable of receiving or undergoing: *a statement not susceptible of proof. Oak is susceptible of a high polish.* ⟨< LL *susceptibilis,* ult. < L *sub-* up + *capere* take⟩
—sus'cep•ti•ble•ness, *n.* **—sus'cep•ti•bly,** *adv.*
☛ *Syn.* **2.** See note at SENSITIVE.

su•shi ['suʃi] *n.* a Japanese dish consisting of balls or cakes of cold cooked rice and raw fish or other garnish. ⟨< Japanese⟩

sus•lik ['sʌslɪk] *n.* a small Eurasian ground squirrel (*Citellus citellus*). ⟨< Russian⟩

sus•pect *v.* [sə'spɛkt]; *n., adj.* ['sʌspɛkt] *v., n., adj.* —*v.* **1** have an impression of the presence or existence of: *The old fox suspected danger and did not touch the trap.* **2** tend to believe to be guilty, false, bad, etc. without proof: *The police officer suspected him.* **3** feel no confidence in; doubt: *The judge suspected the truth of the thief's excuse.* **4** be suspicious: *I'm sure she suspects.* **5** be inclined to think or believe that: *I suspect he was just trying to be funny.*
—*n.* a person suspected: *The police have arrested two suspects.*
—*adj.* open to or viewed with suspicion; suspected or deserving to be suspected: *That version of the story is suspect.* ⟨ME < OF *suspect,* adj. (F *suspecter,* v.) < L *suspectus,* pp. of *suspicere* < *sub-* under + *specere* look⟩

sus•pend [sə'spɛnd] *v.* **1** hang from a support above so as to be free on all sides: *The lamp was suspended from the ceiling.* **2** hold or keep in place somewhere between the top and bottom, as solid particles in a fluid: *We saw the smoke suspended in the still air.* **3** stop for a while: *to suspend work on the project, to suspend hostilities.* **4** make temporarily inoperative: *to suspend a law.* **5** defer (sentence on a convicted person) under certain conditions. **6** remove or exclude for a while from some privilege or job as punishment for an offence: *to suspend a member of a team, to be suspended from school.* **7** delay or defer; put off: *to suspend judgment.* **8** *Music.* hold (a note) while the chord changes.
suspend (payment), declare inability to pay one's debts; fail in business; declare insolvency. ⟨ME < L *suspendere* < *sub-* up + *pendere* hang⟩

sus•pend•ed animation [sə'spɛndɪd] a temporary state resembling death, in which the vital bodily functions cease.

suspended sentence *Law.* a sentence given to a convicted person, that remains unenforced subject to the person's good behaviour for a certain length of time.

sus•pend•ers [sə'spɛndərz] *n.* **1** straps worn over the shoulders to hold up the pants; braces. **2** garters worn by men to hold up their socks. Also, **sock suspenders.**

sus•pense [sə'spɛns] *n.* **1** the condition of being uncertain about an outcome or decision, or a feeling of tension, anxiety, or excitement resulting from such uncertainty: *The detective story kept me in suspense until the very end. We all felt the suspense as we waited for the announcement of the winner.* **2** (*adjl.*) producing suspense, especially pleasant excitement: *a suspense novel.* ⟨ME < OF *(en) suspens* (in) abeyance, ult. < L *suspendere.* See SUSPEND.⟩ **—sus'pense•ful,** *adj.*

suspense account an account for the temporary entry of items to be permanently allocated at a later time.

sus•pen•sion [sə'spɛnʃən] *n.* **1** the act of suspending or the state or period of being suspended. **2** a support on which something is suspended. **3** an arrangement of springs, etc. for supporting the body of an automobile, railway car, etc. **4** *Chemistry.* a mixture in which very small particles of a solid remain suspended in a fluid without dissolving. **5** *Electricity.* a wire or filament for supporting the moving parts of various instruments. **6** the method or mechanism by which the pendulum or balance wheel is suspended in a clock or watch. **7** *Music.* **a** a prolonging of one or more tones of a chord into the following chord, usually producing a temporary discord. **b** the tone or tones so prolonged.

suspension bridge a bridge having its roadway hung on cables or chains between towers. See BRIDGE[1] for picture.

suspension points *Printing.* a series of dots, typically three for less than a sentence and four for a full sentence or more, inserted in a piece of text to indicate ellipsis.

sus•pen•sive [sə'spɛnsɪv] *adj.* **1** inclined to suspend judgment; undecided in mind. **2** having to do with or characterized by suspense, uncertainty, or apprehension. **3** having the effect of temporarily stopping something: *a suspensive veto.* **4** involving such suspension.
—sus'pen•sive•ly, *adv.*

sus•pen•so•ry [sə'spɛnsəri] *adj., n., pl.* **-ries.**
—*adj.* **1** supporting or suspending: *a suspensory muscle, the suspensory ligament of the eye.* **2** deferring; delaying.
—*n.* a muscle, ligament, bandage, etc. that holds up or supports a part of the body.

sus•pi•cion [sə'spɪʃən] *n.* **1** the act or an instance of suspecting: *His suspicion of the stranger turned out to be well founded.* **2** the feeling or state of mind of a person who suspects: *an atmosphere of suspicion.* **3** the idea or theory of a person who suspects: *He had a suspicion that the document was forged.* **4** the condition of being suspected: *She tried to protect herself by diverting suspicion to someone else.* **5** a slight trace; suggestion: *She speaks with just a suspicion of an accent.*
above suspicion, so honest, honourable, etc. as not to be suspected of wrongdoing: *They said their old servants were all above suspicion.*
on suspicion, because of being suspected: *He was arrested on suspicion of robbery.*
under suspicion, suspected; believed guilty but not proven to be so. ⟨ME < L *suspicio, -onis* < *suspicere.* See SUSPECT.⟩
☛ *Syn. n.* **1. Suspicion,** DISTRUST, DOUBT = lack of trust or confidence in someone. **Suspicion** suggests fearing, or believing without enough or any proof, that someone or something is guilty, wrong, false, etc.: *Suspicion points to him, but the evidence is circumstantial.* **Distrust** emphasizes lack of confidence or trust, especially in a person, and may suggest certainty of guilt, falseness, etc.: *Even her mother feels distrust toward her.* **Doubt** emphasizes lack of certainty, and suggests inability to commit oneself fully: *In spite of the good recommendations he had received from several people, she had some residual doubt about his character.*

sus•pi•cious [sə'spɪʃəs] *adj.* **1** causing one to suspect: *A man was seen loitering near the house in a suspicious manner. They left under suspicious circumstances.* **2** feeling suspicion; distrustful; suspecting: *It was the way he said it that made me suspicious.* **3** tending to suspect; prone to distrust: *She has a very suspicious nature. Our dog is suspicious of strangers.* **4** showing suspicion: *The dog gave a suspicious sniff at my leg.* **—sus'pi•cious•ly,** *adv.* **—sus'pi•cious•ness,** *n.*

sus•pi•ra•tion [,sʌspə'reiʃən] *n.* a long, deep sigh.

sus•pire [sə'spaɪr] *v.* **-pired, -pir•ing.** take a long, deep breath; sigh. ⟨< L *suspirare* < *sub-* up + *spirare* breathe⟩

sus•tain [sə'stein] *v.* **1** keep up; keep going. **2** supply with food, provisions, etc.: *to sustain an army.* **3** hold up; support:

Arches sustain the weight of the roof. Hope sustains him in his misery. **4** bear; endure: *The sea wall sustains the shock of the waves.* **5** suffer; experience: *to sustain a great loss.* **6** allow; admit; favour: *The court sustained his suit.* **7** agree with; confirm: *The facts sustain her theory.* ⟨ME < OF < L *sustinere* < *sub-* up + *tenere* hold⟩ **—sus'tain•a•ble,** *adj.* **—sus'tain•er,** *n.*

sustained yield in the management of forests, fisheries, etc., the maintenance of a steady yield by keeping annual growth or increase at least as high as annual output.

sustaining pedal the pedal on a piano that causes a note to be prolonged or carried over.

sustaining program or **programme** a radio or television program having no sponsor but maintained at the expense of a station or network.

sus•te•nance ['sʌstənəns] *n.* **1** a means of sustaining life; food or provisions: *He has gone for a week without sustenance.* **2** sustaining or being sustained; especially, a supplying or being supplied with food or provisions. ⟨ME < OF *sustenance* < *sustenir* sustain < L *sustinere.* See SUSTAIN.⟩

su•sur•rant [sə'sɜrənt] *adj.* of sounds, softly whispering, rustling, or murmuring: *the susurrant leaves.* ⟨< L *susurrans,* ppr. of *susurrare* to whisper⟩

su•sur•ra•tion [ˌsusə'reiʃən] *n.* a soft whispering, rustling, or murmuring sound: *the susurration of silk skirts.* Also, **susurrus** [sə'sɜrəs].

sut•ler ['sʌtlər] *n.* formerly, a person who followed an army and sold provisions, etc. to the soldiers. ⟨< earlier < Du. *soeteler* < *soetelen* ply a low trade⟩

sut•ra *n.* **1** *Hinduism.* **a** a Sanskrit saying based on any of the Vedic writings. **b** a collection of such sayings. **2** *Buddhism.* a narrative or dialogue from Buddhist scripture. ⟨< Skt., a thread⟩

sut•tee or **sa•ti** ['sʌti] *or* [sʌ'ti] *n.* **1** a Hindu widow who throws herself on the burning funeral pile of her husband and is burned with him. **2** the Hindu custom of a widow burning herself with the body of her husband. Suttee is now illegal in India, but persists. ⟨< Hind. < Skt. *satī* faithful wife⟩

su•ture ['sutʃər] *n., v.* **-tured, -tur•ing.** *—n.* **1** *Surgery.* the act or process of joining together the edges of a cut or wound by stitching. **2** a length of material, such as gut, thread, or wire, used in stitching wounds. **3** one of the stitches closing a wound. **4** a joining of parts by or as if by sewing, or the joint or line formed in this way. **5** *Anatomy.* the line where the edges of two bones fuse to form a rigid joint, as between the bones of the skull. **6** *Biology.* the line between adjoining parts, such as that along which clamshells join or pea pods split.
—v. join or unite by suture or as if by a suture. ⟨< L *sutura* < *suere* sew⟩ **—'su•tur•al,** *adj.*

su•ze•rain ['suzərɪn] *or* ['suzəˌrein] *n.* **1** a feudal lord. **2** a state or government exercising political control over the foreign affairs of a dependent state. ⟨< F *suzerain* < *sus* above (< L *sursum* upward), modelled on *souverain* sovereign⟩

su•ze•rain•ty ['suzərɪnti] *or* ['suzəˌreinti] *n., pl.* **-ties.** the position or authority of a suzerain.

s.v. under the following word or heading (for L *sub verbo* or *sub voce*).

svelte [svɛlt] *adj.* slender; lithe. ⟨< F < Ital. *svelto,* pp. < L *ex-* out + *vellere* pluck⟩

Sven•ga•li [svɛn'gɑli] *n.* someone who completely dominates another person, usually from sinister or selfish motives. ⟨so named after the evil hypnotist in George du Maurier's novel *Trilby* (1894)⟩

Sw. Swedish; Sweden.

SW, S.W. or **s.w.** southwest; southwestern.

swab [swɒb] *n., v.* **swabbed, swab•bing.** *—n.* **1** a mop for cleaning decks, floors, etc. **2** a bit of absorbent material usually attached to the end of a small stick, used for cleansing or removing material from, or applying medicine to, some part of the body. **3** a specimen taken with a swab for examination for bacteria, etc. **4** a sponge attached to a handle, used for cleaning the bore of a firearm. **5** *Slang.* a clumsy or contemptible person.
—v. **1** clean with or as if with a swab. **2** apply medication to with a swab: *to swab a person's throat.* Also, **swob.** ⟨< *swabber*⟩

swab•ber ['swɒbər] *n.* **1** a person who uses a swab. **2** SWAB (defs. 1, 2, 4). ⟨< Du. *zwabber* < *zwabben* swab⟩

Swa•bi•an ['swɑbiən] *or* ['sweibiən] *adj., n.* *—adj.* of or having to do with Swabia, a former duchy in SW Germany.
—n. a native or inhabitant of Swabia.

swacked [swækt] *adj. Slang.* **1** drunk. **2** exhausted: *I was completely swacked after walking the 15 km to the lake and back.*

swad•dle ['swɒdəl] *v.* **-dled, -dling;** *n.* *—v.* **1** wrap (a baby) with SWADDLING CLOTHES. **2** wrap tightly with bandages or thick layers of cloth; swathe.
—n. the cloth used for swaddling. ⟨OE *swæthel* band, bandage. Related to SWATHE[1].⟩

swad•dling clothes ['swɒdlɪŋ] **1** long, narrow strips of cloth formerly used for wrapping a newborn infant. **2** anything that restrains freedom of thought or action.

swag [swæg] *n., v.* **swagged, swag•ging.** *—n.* **1** *Slang.* things stolen; booty or spoils acquired dishonestly. **2** *Australian.* a bundle of personal belongings such as that carried by a tramp, a traveller in the bush, etc. **3** an ornamental festoon of flowers, leaves, ribbons, draperies, etc.
—v. **1** lurch or sag. **2** arrange in or adorn with ornamental festoons. ⟨special use of *swag,* v., sway, probably < Scand.; cf. dial. Norwegian *svagga* sway⟩

swage [sweidʒ] *n., v.* **swaged, swag•ing.** *—n.* **1** a tool for bending metal. **2** a die or stamp for giving a particular shape to metal by hammering, stamping, etc.
—v. bend or shape by using a swage. ⟨ME < OF *souage*⟩

swag•ger ['swægər] *v., n., adj.* *—v.* **1** walk with a bold, defiant, or superior air; strut about or show off in a vain or insolent way: *The bully swaggered into the schoolyard.* **2** boast or brag noisily. **3** influence or force by bluster; bluff.
—n. a swaggering way of walking or acting.
—adj. Informal. elegantly stylish: *swagger clothes.* ⟨< *swag*⟩ **—'swag•ger•er,** *n.* **—'swag•ger•ing•ly,** *adv.*
☛ *Syn. v.* **1.** See note at STRUT[1].

swagger stick a short, light stick or cane, formerly carried by military officers.

swag lamp an electric lamp suspended from the ceiling by means of two hooks a distance apart, and a chain that forms a SWAG (def. 3) between them.

swag•man ['swægmən] *n., pl.* **-men.** *Austral.* **1** a tramp; BUSHWHACKER (def. 1). **2** an itinerant worker. ⟨< Australian slang *swag* + *-man*⟩

Swa•hi•li [swɑ'hili] *or* [swə'hili] *n., pl.* **-li** or **-lis. 1** a member of a Bantu-speaking people of Zanzibar and the nearby African coast. **2** a Bantu language spoken originally in Zanzibar and the nearby coast of Africa, characterized by a large proportion of words of Arabic origin. Swahili is the common language of trade, the LINGUA FRANCA, in Tanzania, Kenya, Zaire, and Uganda. ⟨literally, people of the coast < Arabic *sawāhil,* pl. of *sāhil* coast⟩

swain [swein] *n. Archaic or poetic.* **1** a suitor; lover. **2** a young man who lives in the country. ⟨ME < ON *sveinn* boy⟩

swale [sweil] *n.* a low, wet piece of land; low place. ⟨ME, probably < Scand.; cf. ON *svalr* cool⟩

swal•low[1] ['swɒlou] *v., n.* *—v.* **1** pass (food, drink, etc.) from the mouth to the stomach by the action of muscles in the throat. **2** perform the act of swallowing: *It hurts when I swallow.* **3** *Informal.* believe (a statement, etc.) readily or gullibly: *She'll never swallow that story.* **4** accept meekly, without protest or resentment: *to swallow an affront.* **5** take back; retract: *She threatened to make him swallow his words.* **6** keep back; repress: *to swallow one's tears, to swallow resentment.* **7** engulf, absorb, or destroy, as if by swallowing (*usually used with* **up**): *Several small countries were swallowed up by the imperial forces. The waves swallowed the swimmer.* **8** pronounce or speak (words or sounds) indistinctly.
—n. **1** the act of swallowing. **2** the amount swallowed at one time. **3** *Rare.* gullet. ⟨OE *swelgan*⟩ **—'swal•low•er,** *n.*

swal•low[2] ['swɒlou] *n.* **1** any of a family (Hirundinidae) of small, swift-flying birds found in many parts of the world, having long, narrow, pointed wings, a long, more or less forked tail, and a short, broad bill that can open very wide to catch insects in flight. **2** various other similar but unrelated birds, such as the CHIMNEY SWIFT. ⟨OE *swealwe*⟩

swal•low•tail ['swɒlouˌteil] *n.* **1** a deeply forked tail, such as that of a swallow. **2** something shaped like or suggesting a swallowtail. **3** a SWALLOW-TAILED COAT. **4** any of various mostly brightly coloured butterflies (family Papilionidae) having a tail-like extension at the end of each hind wing. See also TIGER SWALLOWTAIL.

A swallowtail butterfly

swal•low–tailed ['swɒlou ˌteild] *adj.* having a tail or end that is deeply forked or extends into long, tapering points.

swallow–tailed coat tailcoat.

swallowtail snowshoe *Cdn.* a kind of snowshoe common among First Nations peoples of northeastern Canada, used for travel through deep, soft snow and underbrush. It comes to a point at the back.

swam [swæm] *v.* pt. of SWIM.

swa•mi ['swɑmi] *n., pl.* **-mis. 1** the title of a Hindu religious teacher. **2** learned person; teacher; pundit. ⟨< Hind. < Skt. *svāmin* master, lord, owner⟩

swamp [swɒmp] *n., v.* —*n.* **1** an area of wet land sometimes partially covered with water, especially such an area having trees and shrubs as well as grasses and sedges. **2** (*adjl.*) of, for use in, or found in swamps: *swamp grasses.*
—*v.* **1** cover or fill with water; flood or soak: *A huge wave swamped the boat. All our provisions were swamped.* **2** become filled with water and sink: *Our boat swamped in the storm.* **3** overwhelm as by a flood; make helpless with too much or too many of something: *swamped with work. The lottery winner was swamped with letters asking for money.* **4** *Cdn.* **a** cut (a road or trail) through bush country, especially for hauling lumber (*sometimes used with* **out**). **b** haul or skid (timber) along such a road or trail. **c** *Nfld.* build (a road or path) with a bedding of boughs for hauling loads of wood in winter.
swamp out, *Cdn. Informal.* clean out thoroughly, especially with soap and water and a mop or brush. ⟨?< MDu. *somp*; akin to MHG *sumpf*⟩

swamp alder 1 *Cdn.* the speckled alder, *Alnus rugosa*, common in wet areas from Saskatchewan to Nova Scotia. **2** a variety of this species, found in Canada only in Nova Scotia and growing also in the northeastern United States.

swamp buggy 1 a type of amphibious motor vehicle, usually equipped with four-wheel drive, oversized and deeply treaded tires, and a raised chassis, used for travelling in and around swampy areas. **2** *Cdn. North.* a tracked vehicle capable of pulling a heavy trailer over rough and boggy terrain.

swamp cat *Cdn.* a tracked vehicle for pulling a CAT-TRAIN.

swamp cypress BALD CYPRESS.

swamp elm *Cdn.* a common species of elm, *Ulmus Americana*, found from central Saskatchewan to the Maritimes.

swamp•er ['swɒmpər] *n.* **1** *Lumbering.* a logger employed in cutting roads and, often, in trimming branches from felled trees. **2** a general helper; especially, a truck driver's helper. **3** a person who lives or works in or around swamps.

swamp fever 1 malaria. **2** leptospirosis, a common disease of dogs. **3** EQUINE INFECTIOUS ANEMIA.

swamp•land ['swɒmpˌlænd] *n.* a tract of land covered with swamps.

swamp maple *Cdn.* the red maple, *Acer rubrum*, found in moist areas of Canada from Lake Superior eastward.

swamp rabbit *Cdn. North.* muskrat prepared as food.

swamp•y ['swɒmpi] *adj.* **swamp•i•er, swamp•i•est. 1** of, containing, or consisting of a swamp or swamps: *swampy meadowland.* **2** like a swamp; soft and wet: *The yard was swampy after the heavy rain.* **—'swamp•i•ness,** *n.*

Swampy Cree one of the two main divisions of Cree Indians, scattered in groups over the woodlands of northwestern Ontario. Also called **Woodland Cree.**

swan [swɒn] *n., v.* **swanned, swan•ning.** —*n.* **1** any of a small subfamily (Cygninae) of large, typically pure white, aquatic birds of the same family as ducks and geese, having webbed feet, a long, slender neck that is curved back in swimming but stretched out straight in flight, and a very long, convoluted windpipe that allows them to make a variety of far-reaching calls. Many authorities classify the North American species in a separate genus (*Olor*), but others place them in the genus *Cygnus*, together with all other species except the South American **coscoroba swan** (*Coscoroba coscoroba*). See also TRUMPETER SWAN, WHISTLING SWAN. **2** a poet or singer. Shakespeare is sometimes called the Swan of Avon. **3** a person of great beauty, purity, etc. **4 Swan,** *Astronomy.* the constellation Cygnus.
—*v. Informal.* move serenely or casually, with no hurry and often no particular purpose or destination: *She's been swanning around Europe for six months now.* ⟨OE⟩ **—'swan,like,** *adj.*

swan dive a graceful dive in which the legs are held straight from the toes to the hips, the back is arched, and the arms are spread like the wings of a gliding bird. The diver's arms come forward and together just before entering the water.

swang [swæŋ] *v. Archaic or dialect.* a pt. of SWING.

swank [swæŋk] *Slang. v., n.* —*v.* show off; swagger: *She was swanking around in her new outfit.*
—*n.* **1** swaggering behaviour, speech, etc. **2** style and dash; smartness; elegance. **3** (*adjl.*) swanky: *Their apartment is very swank.* ⟨Cf. OE *swancor* lithe⟩

swank•y ['swæŋki] *adj.* **swank•i•er, swank•i•est.** stylish and dashing; smart; elegant: *a swanky car.* **—'swank•i•ly,** *adv.* **—'swank•i•ness,** *n.*

swan•ner•y ['swɒnəri] *n., pl.* **-ner•ies.** a place where swans are bred and raised.

swan's–down ['swɒnz ˌdaʊn] *n.* **1** the soft down of a swan, used for trimming, powder puffs, etc. **2** a fine, thick, soft cloth made of a mixture of cotton or silk with wool. **3** a very soft, absorbent cotton flannel. Also, **swansdown.**

swan song 1 the song that a swan is said to sing just before it dies. **2** a person's farewell performance or final statement, composition, painting, etc.

swap [swɒp] *v.* **swapped, swap•ping;** *n. Informal.* —*v.* exchange; barter; trade.
—*n.* a trading; trade. Also, **swop.** ⟨ME *swappe* strike, strike the hands together; probably imitative; the modern meaning arose from the practice of 'striking hands' as a sign of agreement in bargaining⟩ **—'swap•per,** *n.*

sward [swɔrd] *n.* a grassy surface; turf. ⟨OE *sweard* skin⟩ **—'sward•ed,** *adj.*

sware [swɛr] *v. Archaic.* a pt. of SWEAR.

swarm[1] [swɔrm] *n., v.* —*n.* **1** a large group of honeybees, led by a queen bee, leaving a hive to start a new colony elsewhere. **2** a colony of bees settled together in a hive. **3** a large number of insects, birds, people, etc. clustered together and usually moving about: *a swarm of children, swarms of migrating birds.* **4** such a group, specifically, of teenagers, often armed with bats, sticks, etc. and seeking victims. **5** *Biology.* a group of free-swimming, single-celled organisms, especially zoospores.
—*v.* **1** of honeybees, fly off together to start a new colony. **2** fly or move about in great numbers; throng: *The mosquitoes swarmed about us.* **3** crowd or overrun; be crowded or overrun; teem: *Our camp swarmed with mosquitoes. Tourists swarmed the streets.* **4** especially of swarms of teenagers: **a** move around in a group, often with bad intentions. **b** attack (a victim) in a group with the purpose of taking clothes, money, etc. **5** *Biology.* of zoospores, etc., escape from the parent organism in a swarm, with characteristic movement. ⟨OE *swearm*: akin to L *susurrus* hum, Skt. *svara* voice⟩
☛ *Syn. n.* **3.** See note at CROWD.

swarm[2] [swɔrm] *v.* climb by shinning. ⟨origin uncertain⟩

swarth•y ['swɔrði] *or* ['swɔrθi] *adj.* **swarth•i•er, swarth•i•est.** having a dark skin. ⟨earlier *swarty* < *swart* dark + *-y*[1]⟩ **—'swarth•i•ly,** *adv.* **—'swarth•i•ness,** *n.*
☛ *Syn.* See note at DUSKY.

swash [swɒʃ] *v., n.* —*v.* **1** dash (water, etc.) about; splash. **2** move with a splashing, washing sound: *The water swashed against the boat.* **3** swagger.
—*n.* **1** a swashing action or sound: *the swash of waves against a boat.* **2** the act of swaggering. **3** a narrow channel of water cutting through a sandbank or between a sandbank and the shore. **4** the ground under water or over which water washes. ⟨probably imitative⟩

swash•buck•ler ['swɒʃˌbʌklər] *n.* a swaggering swordsman, bully, or boaster. ⟨< *swash* + *buckler*⟩

swash•buck•ling ['swɒʃˌbʌklɪŋ] *n. or adj.* swaggering; bullying; boasting.

swas•ti•ka ['swɒstɪkə] *or* [swɒ'stikə] *n.* an ancient symbol or ornament found in various cultures, consisting of a cross with equal arms whose ends are bent at right angles, all in the same direction. The Nazis adopted the swastika with the arms bent in a clockwise direction. ⟨< Skt. *svastika* < *svasti* luck < *su* well + *asti*, n., being < *as* be⟩

swat [swɒt] *v.* **swat•ted, swat•ting;** *n. Informal.* —*v.* hit with a smart or quick blow: *to swat a fly.*
—*n.* a smart or quick blow. ⟨originally var. of *squat*⟩ **—'swat•ter,** *n.*

swatch [swɒtʃ] *n.* **1** a sample of cloth or other similar material. **2** a small sample, bunch, patch, etc. of anything. ⟨origin uncertain⟩

swath [swɒθ] *n., v.* —*n.* **1** the space covered by a single cut of a scythe or by one cut of a mowing machine. **2** a row of grass,

grain, etc. cut by a scythe or mowing machine. **3** a long, wide strip or belt.
cut a (wide) swath, a make a destructive sweep: *The aggressive new company cut a swath through its competitors.* **b** make a forceful impression or intimidating display: *She cuts a wide swath in this town.*
—*v.* cut grain with a swather. ⟨OE *swæth* track, trace⟩

swathe¹ [swɒð] *or* [sweið] *v.* **swathed, swath•ing;** *n.* —*v.* **1** wrap up closely or completely: *swathed in a blanket.* **2** bind with bandages; bandage: *to swathe an injured arm.* **3** envelop or surround like a wrapping: *a mountaintop swathed in cloud.*
—*n.* a wrapping or bandage. ⟨OE *swathian*⟩

swathe² [swɒð] *or* [sweið] *n.* See SWATH.

swath•er [ˈswɒθər] *n.* a machine used for cutting grain that is not dry or that is mixed with weeds. ⟨< *swath*⟩

swat•ter [ˈswɒtər] *n.* **1** any person who or thing that swats. **2** a household article, consisting of a flexible piece of mesh on a long handle, for swatting flies, etc.

sway [swei] *v., n.* —*v.* **1** swing slowly back and forth or from side to side from a base or pivot: *The tower of dominoes swayed and fell. The trees swayed in the wind.* **2** move or bend slowly down or to one side, as if from weight or pressure: *He suddenly felt dizzy and swayed against the wall.* **3** cause to sway: *The wind sways the grass.* **4** change or influence in opinion, feeling, etc.: *Nothing could sway her after she made up her mind.* **5** be so changed or influenced: *Her ideas swayed with every new thing she read on the subject.* **6** *Archaic or poetic.* govern or rule.
—*n.* **1** a swaying: *the sway of a branch in the wind.* **2** a controlling influence or power: *under the sway of a violent emotion. The rebel leader held sway over a large territory.* ⟨ME < Scand.; akin to ON *sveigja*⟩
☛ *Syn. v.* **1.** See note at SWING.

sway•back [ˈswei,bæk] *n.* **1** an abnormally hollow or sagging back in horses, etc., especially as a result of strain or overwork. **2** an abnormal forward curve of the middle of the spine in human beings. **—ˈsway,backed,** *adj.*

Swa•zi [ˈswɒzi] *n., pl.* **Swa•zi** or **Swa•zis. 1** a member of the Nguni, a farming people of Swaziland and the Republic of South Africa. **2** the Bantu language spoken by them.

Swa•zi•land [ˈswɒzɪ,lænd] an independent kingdom in SE Africa, bordered on the east by Mozambique and on the north, west, and south by South Africa. It is a member of the British Commonwealth of Nations.

swear [swɛr] *v.* **swore** or (*archaic*) **sware, sworn, swear•ing. 1** use profane or obscene language; curse. **2** utter (an oath). **3** state emphatically or with strong conviction: *I swear I would never have made it if you hadn't come along just then.* **4** promise on oath or solemnly to observe or do something: *I swear to obey the rules of this club. A witness at a trial has to swear to tell the truth.* **5** declare, calling God or some other sacred or powerful thing or being to witness; testify or state under oath. **6** bind by an oath; require to promise: *Members of the club were sworn to secrecy.* **7** admit to office or service by administering an oath to: *to swear a witness.* **8** bring, set, take, etc. by swearing: *to swear a person's life away.*
swear by, a name as one's witness in taking an oath. **b** have great confidence in.
swear in, admit to office or service by causing to take an oath: *to swear in a jury.*
swear off, promise to give up: *to swear off smoking.*
swear out, get (a warrant for arrest) by taking an oath that a certain charge is true. ⟨OE *swerian*⟩ **—ˈswear•er,** *n.*
☛ *Syn.* **1.** See note at CURSE.

swear•word [ˈswɛr,wɜrd] *n.* a word or phrase used in cursing; a profane or obscene word or phrase.

sweat [swɛt] *n., v.* **sweat•ed** or **sweat, sweat•ing.**
—*n.* **1** moisture coming through the pores of the skin. **2** a fit or condition of sweating: *He was in a cold sweat from fear.* **3** *Informal.* a condition of anxiety, impatience, or anything that might make a person sweat: *We were all in a sweat over the big test we would get on Monday.* **4** moisture given out by something or gathered on its surface, as by condensation, etc.: *The water pipes were covered with sweat.* **5** an exuding of moisture from something, or the process of producing an exudation, as part of certain industrial processes, as tanning. **6** anything that causes sweat; hard work or strenuous exertion; labour. **7 sweats,** *pl. Informal.* clothes for working out, jogging, etc.; sweat suit.
by the sweat of (one's) **brow,** by one's own efforts and hard work.
no sweat, *Slang.* with no difficulty; easily.
old sweat, *Informal.* an old soldier.
—*v.* **1** give out moisture through the pores of the skin. **2** cause to sweat: *She sweated her horse by riding it too hard.* **3** give off or cause to give off moisture as part of processing; ferment: *to sweat hides or tobacco in preparing them for use.* **4** come or give out in drops; ooze. **5** give out (moisture); collect or gather (moisture) on the surface: *A pitcher of ice water sweats on a hot day.* **6** wet or stain with sweat. **7** get rid of by sweating or as if by sweating: *to sweat off excess weight, to sweat out a fever.* **8** cause to work hard and under adverse conditions: *That employer sweats her workers.* **9** *Informal.* work very hard. **10** suffer severely, especially as a penalty: *The prisoner sweated under the severe questioning.* **11** be annoyed or vexed; fume: *sweat over a delay.* **12** *Slang.* worry about; take great pains over: *Don't sweat this test; just give it your best shot.* **13** *Slang.* deprive of or cause to give up something, especially money; rob; fleece. **14** *Metallurgy.* **a** heat (solder) till it melts. **b** join (metal parts) by heating. **c** heat (metal) in order to remove an easily fusible constituent.
sweat blood, *Informal.* be subjected to great strain, as by overwork, extreme anxiety, etc.
sweat it out, *Informal.* wait anxiously for something to happen.
sweat out, *Informal.* struggle, wait, or suffer through (something): *to sweat out an exam. She sweated out the long, anxious night.* ⟨ME *swete,* n., v. < OE *swǣtan,* v.⟩
☛ *Syn. n.* **1. Sweat,** PERSPIRATION = moisture coming through the pores of the skin. **Sweat** is the direct native English word, used always when speaking of animals or things and often of people, especially when the moisture is flowing freely or is mixed with grime or blood: *Sweat streamed down the horse's flanks. After two hours of heavy gardening her blouse was soaked with sweat.* **Perspiration** is applicable only when speaking of human beings: *Tiny drops of perspiration formed at his temples.*

sweat•band [ˈswɛt,bænd] *n.* **1** a band, usually of leather, lining the inside edge of a hat or cap to protect it from sweat. **2** a cloth band tied around the head or wrist to absorb sweat.

sweat•box [ˈswɛt,bɒks] *n.* **1** a boxlike device used to sweat certain commodities before use or sale, as figs, hides, etc. **2** *Slang.* a very small cell in which a prisoner is confined as a special punishment.

sweat•er [ˈswɛtər] *n.* **1** a knitted or crocheted outer garment for the upper body, made of wool, acrylic, cotton, etc.; a pullover or cardigan. **2** a person who or thing that sweats: *a heavy sweater.* **3** (*adjl.*) of or for a sweater or sweaters: *a sweater pattern, sweater wool.* **4** (*adjl.*) styled like a sweater: *a sweater dress, a sweater coat.*

sweat gland a small gland, just under the skin, that secretes sweat. See EPIDERMIS for picture.

sweat•ing sickness [ˈswɛtɪŋ] a highly infectious fatal disease prevalent in 15th and 16th century Europe, characterized by fever and very heavy sweating.

sweat pants long, loose pants made of a warm, absorbent fabric such as fleece-lined cotton, and having a string-tied or elasticized waist and, often, knitted cuffs at the ankles, worn for warm-up exercises, or as all-purpose casual dress. Also, **sweatpants.**

sweat shirt a long-sleeved, usually collarless pullover, made of a warm, absorbent fabric such as fleece-lined cotton, worn for outdoor sports, warm-up exercises, or as all-purpose casual dress. Also, **sweatshirt.**

sweat•shop [ˈswɛt,ʃɒp] *n.* a place where workers are employed at low pay for long hours under adverse conditions.

sweat suit a suit consisting of a sweat shirt and sweat pants. Also, **sweatsuit.**

sweat top SWEAT SHIRT.

sweat•y [ˈswɛti] *adj.* **sweat•i•er, sweat•i•est. 1** sweating; covered with sweat. **2** causing sweat: *sweaty work, sweaty weather.* **3** of or like sweat: *a sweaty odour.* **—ˈsweat•i•ly,** *adv.* **—ˈsweat•i•ness,** *n.*

Swed. Sweden; Swedish.

Swede [swid] *n.* **1** a native or inhabitant of Sweden. **2** a person of Swedish descent. ⟨< MLG or MDu.⟩

Swe•den [ˈswidən] a country in northern Europe, the eastern part of the Scandinavian peninsula, flanked on the west and north by Norway.

Swe•den•bor•gi•an [,swidənˈbɔrdʒiən] *or* [,swidənˈbɔrgiən] *n., adj.* —*n.* a believer in the religious doctrines of Emanuel Swedenborg (1688-1772), a Swedish philosopher, scientist, and mystic claiming direct contact with the spiritual world; a member of Swedenborg's Church of the New Jerusalem.
—*adj.* having to do with Swedenborg, his doctrines, or his followers. **—,Swe•den'bor•gi•an,ism,** *n.*

Swede•saw [ˈswid,sɒ] *n. Cdn.* a handsaw having a bowlike tubular frame, the blade being kept taut by the tension of the bow. It is used for pruning trees, sawing pulpwood, etc.

⟨apparently < *Swedish saw*; cf. *Swedish fiddle* or *violin*, originally, loggers' slang for a large crosscut saw⟩

Swed•ish ['swidɪʃ] *n., adj.* —*n.* **1 the Swedish,** *pl.* the people of Sweden. **2** the North Germanic language of Sweden.
—*adj.* of or having to do with Sweden, its people, or their language.

sweep [swip] *v.* **swept, sweep•ing;** *n.* —*v.* **1** clean or clear with a broom, brush, etc.; use a broom or something similar to remove dirt (from): *Sweep the steps.* **2** move, drive, or take away with or as with a broom, brush, etc.: *She swept the snippings into a pile. He swept the fallen leaves and twigs off the path.* **3** remove with a sweeping motion; carry along: *A flood swept away the bridge. The wind sweeps the snow into drifts.* **4** touch or brush in passing; trail (upon): *Her dress sweeps the ground.* **5** pass or cause to pass over with a steady, smooth movement: *Her fingers swept the strings of the harp. His eye swept the sky, searching for signs of rain. She swept the flashlight beam to and fro over the backyard.* **6** range over; SCOUR[2]: *Enthusiasm for the candidate swept the country.* **7** move or pass swiftly, forcefully, etc.: *Pirates swept down on the town.* **8** move with purpose, grace, and dignity: *The lady swept out of the room.* **9** move or extend in a long course or curve: *The shore sweeps to the south for some distance.* **10** drag (a river, etc.) **11** rake with gunfire. **12** win (any contest or series of contests) overwhelmingly or in its entirety.
sweep under the carpet, try to hide or ignore (a problem).
—*n.* **1** the act of sweeping, clearing away, or removing: *He made a clean sweep of all his debts.* **2** a steady, driving motion or swift onward course of something: *The sweep of the wind kept the trees from growing tall.* **3** a smooth, flowing motion or line; dignified motion: *the sweep of verse.* **4** a long curve; bend: *the sweep of a road.* **5** a swinging or curving motion; a sweeping stroke or blow: *He cut the grass with strong sweeps of his scythe.* **6** a trailing or brushing (of low branches, long skirts, etc.) **7** a continuous extent; stretch: *The house looked upon a wide sweep of farming country.* **8** the reach; range; extent: *The mountain is beyond the sweep of your eye.* **9** a winning of all the games in a series, match, contest, etc.; complete victory. **10** an act of surveying, reconnoitring, attacking, etc. carried out over a definite area: *The bombers cleared the coast by aerial sweeps.* **11** a person who sweeps chimneys, streets, etc. **12** any implement for sweeping, such as a broom; sweeper. **13** a long oar. **14** *Electronics.* one passage of an electron beam over the fluorescent screen of a cathode-ray tube. **15** a blade or sail of a windmill. **16** a long pole which pivots on a high post and is used to raise or lower a bucket in a well. **17** Usually, **sweeps,** *pl.* a sweepstakes contest. ⟨ME *swepen* < OE *swapan.* Akin to SWOOP.⟩ —**'sweep•a•ble,** *adj.*

sweep•back ['swip,bæk] *n. Aeronautics.* **1** the shape of an airplane wing which slants back from the fuselage. **2** the angle which such a wing or other airfoil makes with the lateral axis of the airplane.

sweep–check ['swip ˌtʃɛk] *v. Hockey.* check (an opponent) by crouching while sweeping the ice surface in an arc with the stick so as to deflect the puck from the blade of the opponent's stick.
—**'sweep-ˌcheck•er,** *n.*

sweep check *Hockey.* an act or instance of sweep-checking.

sweep•er ['swipər] *n.* **1** a person who or thing that sweeps: *a carpet sweeper.* **2** *Cdn.* a tree that has been undermined by the current of a river or stream so that some of its leaves and branches hang down into the water, though its roots remain anchored to the bank. **3** *Curling.* either of the lead and second members of a curling rink.

sweep•ing ['swipɪŋ] *adj., n., v.* —*adj.* **1** passing or extending over a wide space: *a sweeping glance.* **2** having wide range; extensive; thoroughgoing: *sweeping reforms.* **3** not considering exceptions or limitations; indiscriminate: *a sweeping statement.* **4** extending in a long, curved line. **5** moving swiftly and smoothly or along a somewhat curved course. **6** complete or overwhelming: *a sweeping victory.*
—*n.* **1** the act or work of a person who or thing that sweeps: *The porch needs a good sweeping.* **2 sweepings,** *pl.* things that have been swept up; refuse: *Put the sweepings in that box.*
—*v.* ppr. of SWEEP. —**'sweep•ing•ly,** *adv.*

sweep–sec•ond hand ['swip 'sɛkənd] the hand on a clock or watch that indicates the passage of seconds; second hand.

sweep•stakes ['swip,steiks] *n.sing. or pl.* **1** a form of lottery for gambling on horse races, etc. Each person pays a specified sum to draw a ticket bearing the name of one of the competitors in a race or contest; the money paid in goes to the holder or holders of tickets on the winner of the race or contest. **2** the race or contest. **3** a race or contest in which the prize or prizes derive from a pooling of the stakes of the contestants, with or without additional contributions by the sponsor or sponsors of the contest. **4** a prize in any such race or contest. ⟨ME, *swepestake* literally a person who wins, or sweeps, all the stakes⟩

sweet [swit] *adj., n., adv.* —*adj.* **1** having a taste like sugar or honey. **2** pleasing to the sense of smell; fragrant, like roses, perfume, etc.: *The air was sweet with the scent of lilacs. Vanilla has a sweet smell.* **3** pleasing to the ear; harmonious: *sweet music.* **4** attractive, charming, kind, etc.: *She had a sweet smile. He's a sweet child. It's sweet of you to help.* **5** very pleasurable; gratifying or satisfying: *sweet praise, sweet dreams of success. Revenge is sweet.* **6** schmaltzy; cloyingly sentimental: *I hate those sweet verses in some greeting cards.* **7** fresh; not sour, fermented, or spoiled: *sweet cider. Is the milk still sweet?* **8** not salty: *sweet butter.* **9** of soil, not too acid. **10** dear; darling. **11** of a wine, not dry. **12** *Informal.* easily managed, handled, or dealt with: *a sweet ship.* **13** *Chemistry.* free from corrosive salt, sulphur, acid, etc. or unpleasant gases and odours. **14** *Music.* of or designating jazz characterized by a regular beat and straightforward melody, with little improvisation.
be sweet on, *Informal.* be in love with.
—*n.* **1** sweet taste; sweetness: *The tastebuds for sweet are concentrated in certain areas of the tongue.* **2** sweetheart; darling. **3 the sweet,** that which is sweet: *to take the bitter with the sweet.* **4 sweets,** *pl.* food, such as candy, cake, etc., containing a lot of sugar or other sweetening agent: *I like sweets.* **5 sweets,** *pl.* gratifying or delightful features or experiences: *the sweets of success.* **6** *Esp. Brit.* a piece of candy or a sweet dessert: *Would you like a sweet?*
—*adv.* in a sweet manner; sweetly. ⟨OE *swēte*⟩ —**'sweet•ly,** *adv.* —**'sweet•ness,** *n.*
☛ *Hom.* SUITE.

sweet alyssum a common, low-growing garden plant (*Lobularia maritima*) of the mustard family native to Europe, having clusters of small, white, or mauve flowers. Sweet alyssum is popular for flower borders, window boxes, etc.

sweet–and–sour ['swit ən 'saʊr] *adj.* of food, prepared with a thickened sauce containing sugar together with vinegar or lemon juice: *sweet-and-sour pork.*

sweet basil BASIL (def. 1).

sweet bay **1** LAUREL (def. 1). **2** a small tree (*Magnolia virginiana*) native to the SE United States, having fragrant, creamy white flowers.

sweet•bread ['swit,brɛd] *n.* the pancreas or thymus of a calf, lamb, etc., used as meat.

sweet•bri•er ['swit,braɪər] *n.* a wild rose (*Rosa rubiginosa*; also called *R. eglanteria*) native to Europe and Asia but now naturalized in E North America, having fragrant leaves and fragrant pink flowers. Also, **sweetbriar.**

sweet cic•e•ly ['sɪsəli] **1** any of various herbs of North America belonging to the umbel family, having aromatic roots, compound leaves, and small white flowers in clusters. **2** a European herb of the same family whose leaves taste like anise and were formerly much used in cooking.

sweet cider unfermented cider.

sweet clover any of a genus (*Melilotus*) of plants of the pea family, having small flowers and leaflets in groups of three. It is widely grown to improve the soil and for use as hay.

sweet corn any of several varieties of corn having kernels with a high sugar content, that are eaten as a vegetable when young and tender, in the milky stage. Sweet corn is the common table corn.

sweet•en ['switən] *v.* **1** make sweet. **2** become sweet. **3** make more pleasant or agreeable. **4** make (the stomach, soil, etc.) less acidic.
sweeten the pot, make an offer more agreeable, usually with more money.

sweet•en•er ['switənər] *n.* something that sweetens, especially an artificial substitute for sugar or honey, such as saccharin.

sweet•en•ing ['switənɪŋ] *n., v.* —*n.* something that sweetens.
—*v.* ppr. of SWEETEN.

sweet fern a North American shrub (*Comptonia asplenifolia*), also called *C. peregrina*) of the wax-myrtle family, having long, scented, fernlike leaves.

sweet flag a tall, perennial marsh plant (*Acorus calamus*) of the arum family, found in north temperate regions, having tiny flowers, long, sword-shaped leaves, and a thick, fragrant underground stem.

sweet gale a low-growing shrub (*Myrica gale*) of the wax-myrtle family, found along river banks and in marshy places in North America, Europe, and Asia. The wood and leaves of the sweet gale are fragrant when crushed.

sweet grass any of various sweet-smelling grasses, such as *Hierochloe odorata*, found throughout North America and Eurasia.

sweet gum **1** a tall shade and timber tree (*Liquidambar styraciflua*) of E North America having star-shaped leaves that turn scarlet or gold in the fall. The bark of the sweet gum yields a fragrant, pleasant-tasting liquid balsam, or gum, used in medicines and in making perfumes, etc. **2** the hard, fine-grained wood of this tree, highly valued for making fine furniture, mouldings, etc. **3** the gum or balsam yielded by this tree.

sweet•heart ['swit,hɑrt] *n.* **1** a loved one; lover. **2** darling. **3** *Informal.* a very charming, pleasant, or obliging person: *You'll give me a ride? What a sweetheart!*

sweetheart deal a contract arranged by union leaders and management, setting terms that are advantageous to management and detrimental to the interests of workers. Also, **sweetheart contract.**

sweetheart neckline a neckline for women's clothing that is low in front and scalloped in the shape of the top of a heart.

sweet•ie ['switi] *n. Informal.* sweetheart.

sweetie pie *Informal.* sweetheart.

sweet•ing ['switɪŋ] *n.* **1** a sweet apple. **2** *Archaic.* sweetheart.

sweet•ish ['switɪʃ] *adj.* somewhat sweet.

sweet marjoram a garden herb (*Majorana hortensis*, sometimes classified as *Origanum hortensis*) of the mint family, having aromatic leaves commonly used as a seasoning in cookery.

sweet•meat ['swit,mit] *n.* an article of food prepared with much sugar or honey; especially, candied or crystallized fruit or preserves.

sweet nothings trivial endearments exchanged by lovers.

sweet pea **1** an annual climbing plant (*Lathyrus odoratus*) of the pea family, native to Italy but long cultivated in many parts of the world, having fragrant flowers of many different colours. **2** the flower of this plant.

sweet pepper **1** the large, fleshy, green or red fruit of a PEPPER (def. 5), or capsicum, having a mild, somewhat sweet taste. It is eaten raw in salads or cooked as a vegetable. **2** a plant that bears this fruit.

sweet potato **1** a perennial tropical vine (*Ipomoea batatas*) of the morning-glory family, widely cultivated in tropical and warm temperate regions, having a large tuberous root that is used for food. **2** its sweet, starchy root, ranging in colour from white to orange inside and light brown to rose outside. Sweet potatoes are usually served as a cooked vegetable.

sweet–sop ['swit ,sɒp] *n.* **1** a small tropical American tree (*Annona squamosa*) of the custard-apple family, widely cultivated in tropical regions for its yellowish green, edible fruit. **2** the fruit of this tree, having soft, sweet, pale yellow pulp.

sweet spirit of nitre *Pharmacy.* a medicine used as a sedative, as a means of increasing sweating, etc.

sweet talk flattery.

sweet–talk ['swit ,tɒk] *v. Informal.* coax or flatter.

sweet–tem•pered ['swit 'tɛmpərd] *adj.* having or showing a gentle or pleasant nature; amiable.

sweet tooth a fondness or craving for sweet foods.

sweet wil•liam or **sweet Wil•liam** ['wɪljəm] a widely cultivated pink (*Dianthus barbatus*) having flat clusters of small, fragrant, showy flowers often spotted or banded in different colours.

swell [swɛl] *v.* **swelled, swelled** or **swol•len, swell•ing;** *n., adj.* —*v.* **1** grow or make larger in size, amount, degree, force, etc.: *Bread dough swells as it rises. The river is swollen by rain. His head is swollen where he bumped it. Savings may swell into a fortune. The sound swelled from a murmur to a roar.* **2** be larger or thicker in a particular place; stick out; cause to stick out: *A barrel swells in the middle.* **3** rise or cause to rise above the level: *Rounded hills swell gradually from the village plain.* **4** *Informal.* become or make proud or conceited.
—*n.* **1** the act of swelling; an increase in amount, degree, force, etc. **2** the conditon of being swollen. **3** a part that swells out. **4** a piece of higher ground; a rounded hill. **5** a long, unbroken wave or a series of such waves. **6** a swelling tone or sound. **7** *Music.* **a** a crescendo followed by a diminuendo. **b** the signs for this (< >). **8** a device in an organ, etc. to control the volume of sound. **9** *Informal. Esp. Brit.* a fashionable person.

—*adj.* **1** *Informal.* stylish; grand. **2** *Slang.* excellent; first-rate. ⟨OE *swellan*⟩
☛ *Syn. v.* **1.** See note at EXPAND.

swelled head pride; conceit; an exaggerated or unjustified appreciation of one's own worth: *Ever since she was made CEO, she's had a swelled head.*

swell•ing ['swɛlɪŋ] *n., v.* —*n.* **1** a swollen part: *There is a swelling on his head where he bumped it.* **2** the condition of being swollen; an increase in size.
—*v.* ppr. of SWELL.

swel•ter ['swɛltər] *v., n.* —*v.* **1** suffer from heat, as by sweating freely, feeling faint, etc. **2** cause to swelter; oppress with heat.
—*n.* a sweltering condition or atmosphere. ⟨frequentative of obs. *swelt*, OE *sweltan* die⟩ **—'swel•ter•ing•ly,** *adv.*

swel•ter•ing ['swɛltərɪŋ] *adj., v.* —*adj.* **1** extremely and unpleasantly hot: *a sweltering day.* **2** suffering from excessive heat: *The sweltering children were glad to leave the stuffy gym.*
—*v.* ppr. of SWELTER.

swept [swɛpt] *v.* pt. and pp. of SWEEP.

swept–back ['swɛpt ,bæk] *adj.* of the wings of an aircraft, slanting backward from the base to the tip.

swerve [swɜrv] *v.* **swerved, swerv•ing;** *n.* —*v.* turn aside sharply from a straight course or line: *The road swerves to the right here and goes around the lake. He swerved the car to avoid hitting the child.*
—*n.* the act or instance of turning aside sharply: *The swerve of the ball made it hard to hit.* ⟨OE *sweorfan* rub, file⟩

SWG standard wire gauge.

swift [swɪft] *adj., n.* —*adj.* **1** moving or able to move very fast: *a light, swift sailboat. She took the swiftest horse.* **2** coming or happening quickly: *a swift response.* **3** quick or prompt to act, etc.: *He is swift to repay a kindness.* **4** (*advl.*) in a swift manner; swiftly: *a swift-flowing river.*
—*n.* **1** any of a family (Apodidae) of small, mostly dull-coloured birds noted for their speed in flight, having long, narrow wings that, when closed, extend well past the tip of the tail. Swifts resemble swallows when in flight, but are not related to them. **2** any of various small North American lizards (genera *Sceloporus* and *Uta*) that run quickly. **3** *Cdn.* a small fox (*Vulpes velox hebes*) formerly common on the prairies. Also called **kit fox.** ⟨OE⟩ **—'swift•ness,** *n.* **—'swift•ly,** *adv.*

swift–foot•ed ['swɪft 'fʊtɪd] *adj.* able to run swiftly.

Swift–Tut•tle or **Swift–Tut•tle's comet** ['swɪft 'tʌtəlz] a comet expected to approach the earth in 2126.

swig [swɪg] *n., v.* **swigged, swig•ging.** *Informal.* —*n.* a big or hearty drink or swallow, especially of liquor.
—*v.* drink heartily or greedily. ⟨origin uncertain⟩ **—'swig•ger,** *n.*

swill [swɪl] *n., v.* —*n.* **1** kitchen scraps and other vegetable refuse, especially when partly liquid; garbage; slops. Swill is sometimes fed to pigs. **2** a deep drink, especially of liquor; swig.
—*v.* **1** drink greedily or in great quantity; guzzle. **2** feed with swill: *to swill the pigs.* **3** wash by flooding with water. ⟨OE *swilian*⟩

swim [swɪm] *v.* **swam, swum, swim•ming;** *n.* —*v.* **1** make oneself move in water by movements of the arms and legs, tail, or fins: *I'm learning to swim.* **2** cover or cross by swimming: *to swim a river. I swam four lengths of the pool.* **3** make (a person or animal) swim: *He swam his horse across the stream.* **4** use (a certain stroke) in swimming: *I can't swim the breast stroke any more.* **5** float in a liquid: *There were some bits of parsley swimming in the soup.* **6** **a** be covered or flooded with a liquid or, figuratively, anything: *a roast swimming in gravy, eyes swimming with tears. The floor was swimming with water. We are swimming in magazines these days; we should cancel a few subscriptions.* **b** have far too much room (*in* a garment): *swimming in an old suit coat of his father's.* **7** go smoothly; glide. **8** have a feeling of floating or reeling; be dizzy: *The heat and noise made my head swim.* **9** appear to spin or whirl: *Their faces swam before me.*
—*n.* **1** the act or a period of swimming: *We went for a swim.* **2** the distance covered or to be covered in swimming: *a 4-km swim.* **3** (*adjl.*) of, having to do with, or involving swimming: *a swim meet.*
in the swim, in the main current of activity in fashion, business, politics, etc.: *She's socially very active and likes to be in the swim.* ⟨OE *swimman*⟩ **—'swim•mer,** *n.*

swim bladder the air bladder of a fish.

swim•mer•et ['swɪmə,rɛt] *n. Zoology.* one of a number of abdominal limbs or appendages in many crustaceans, usually adapted for swimming and thus distinguished from other limbs adapted for walking or grasping. ⟨dim. of *swimmer*⟩

swim•ming ['swɪmɪŋ] *n., adj., v.* —*n.* **1** the practice, sport, or act of swimming: *Tom is an expert at both swimming and diving.* **2** a state of dizziness or giddiness; vertigo.
—*adj.* **1** that swims: *swimming scallops.* **2** of or for swimming or swimmers: *a swimming teacher, a swimming pool.* **3** filled with tears; watery: *swimming eyes.* **4** faint; dizzy: *a swimming sensation.*
—*v.* ppr. of SWIM.

swim•ming•ly ['swɪmɪŋli] *adv.* with great ease or success: *Everything went swimmingly at our party.*

swimming pool a large tank of concrete, plastic, etc., built into or on the ground for swimming or bathing in.

swim•suit ['swɪm,sut] *n.* a close-fitting garment worn for swimming or bathing; bathing suit.

swim•wear ['swɪm,wɛr] *n.* swimsuits, collectively.

swin•dle ['swɪndəl] *v.* **-dled, -dling;** *n.* —*v.* **1** take money or property from (someone) by deceit or fraud; cheat: *They said he had swindled them. She swindled them out of their savings.* **2** get (money or property) by deceit or fraud: *She had swindled $200 from him.*
—*n.* an act of swindling; a cheating or defrauding: *The whole deal was a swindle.* ⟨< *swindler*⟩

swin•dler ['swɪndlər] *n.* a person who cheats or defrauds. ⟨< G *Schwindler* < *schwindeln* be dizzy, act thoughtlessly, cheat⟩

swine [swaɪn] *n., pl.* **swine. 1** a pig; hog. **2** a coarse or beastly person. ⟨OE *swīn*⟩

swine•herd ['swaɪn,hɜrd] *n.* a person who tends swine.

swing [swɪŋ] *v.* **swung** or (*archaic*) **swang, swung, swing•ing;** *n.* —*v.* **1** move freely to and fro in an arc or circle from an upper or overhead support that remains still: *A pendulum swings. His arms swung as he walked. Monkeys swing through the trees.* **2** move on or as if on hinges or a pivot: *The screen door was swinging in the wind. The gate swung slowly shut. She swung around and confronted them.* **3** cause to swing: *to swing a golf club. He swung his arms.* **4** carry or transport something that is suspended: *The crane swung the cargo into the hold.* **5** move or cause to move with a sweeping motion: *I swung the suitcase up onto the rack. The car swung into the driveway.* **6** move or cause to move to and fro on a swing, in a hammock, etc.: *Several children were swinging in the playground. He was swinging his little sister.* **7** be suspended or hang freely: *The microphone swung from an overhead track.* **8** *Slang.* be put to death by hanging. **9** hang so as to swing; suspend: *We swung the hammock between two trees.* **10** *Informal.* manage successfully: *We didn't think she'd be able to swing the deal.* **11** move with a free, rhythmic motion: *The soldiers came swinging down the street.* **12** *Music.* play or sing (a melody) in the style of swing. **13** *Slang.* follow a lifestyle that emphasizes unrestrained enjoyment of the fashionable social pleasures: *He is quiet at work, but they say he swings after hours.* **14** *Slang.* of a place, occasion, etc., be lively, exciting, and unrestrained: *The party was swinging by the time I got there. The town really swings these days.* **15** travel or pass in a sweeping or curving course: *The highway goes straight as an arrow for 100 km and then swings up around the border of the national park.*
—*n.* **1** a swinging movement, stroke, or blow: *One swing of the axe split the log in two. He took a swing at me but missed.* **2** *Golf, etc.* the width or manner of a swing: *a wide swing. She has an excellent swing.* **3** a seat hung from ropes or chains, on which one may swing for pleasure. **4** a swinging gait, movement, or rhythm. **5** freedom of action. **6** the normal rhythm or sequence of activity: *to get into the swing of a new job.* **7** *Music.* a style of jazz that evolved in the 1930s, characterized by a smooth but lively rhythm with more syncopation than in ragtime. Swing was usually played by large bands. **8** (*adjl.*) of, having to do with, or playing music in this style: *a swing band.* **9** a trip around a country, region, etc.; tour: *a swing through the Maritimes.* **10** *Cdn.* in the North: **a** a train of sleighs or freight canoes, so called because they move, or swing, over a certain route in periodic trips. **b** a train of freight sleighs drawn by tractors; cat-train. **11** *Cdn.* a cowhand who rides out to the side of a herd to keep it from spreading.
in full swing, going on actively and completely; without restraint: *By ten the party was in full swing.*
take a swing at, aim a blow at. ⟨OE *swingan* beat⟩
☛ *Syn. v.* **1. Swing,** SWAY, ROCK[2] = move back and forth or from side to side. **Swing** applies to the movement of something attached at one side or the end or ends, and often but not always suggests a regular or rhythmical movement: *The lantern hanging overhead swung in the wind.* **Sway** suggests the unsteady swinging motion of something that bends or gives easily at any pressure: *The branches sway in the breeze.* **Rock** may suggest a gentle motion, but more often suggests the violent swaying of something shaken hard: *The house rocked in the storm.*

swing•er ['swɪŋər] *n.* **1** *Slang.* a person who follows a lifestyle that emphasizes unrestrained enjoyment of fashionable social pleasures: *A couple of swingers drove by in an expensive sports car.* **2** a person who or thing that swings.

swin•gle ['swɪŋgəl] *n., v.* **-gled, -gling.** —*n.* a wooden instrument shaped like a large knife, for beating flax or hemp and scraping from it the woody or coarse portions.
—*v.* clean (flax or hemp) by beating and scraping. ⟨OE *swingel* < *swingan* beat⟩

swin•gle•tree ['swɪŋgəl,tri] *n.* See SINGLETREE.

swing music jazz music, especially for dancing, in which the players improvise freely on the original melody.

swing riding *Cdn. Politics.* a marginal constituency; one in which the majority vote could go any way.

swing shift in factories, etc., the working hours between the day and night shifts, usually from 4 p.m. to midnight.

swin•ish ['swaɪnɪʃ] *adj.* of, characteristic of, or like swine; hoggish, beastly, or coarse: *swinish behaviour.* **—'swin•ish•ly,** *adv.* **—'swin•ish•ness,** *n.*

swipe [swəip] *n., v.* **swiped, swip•ing.** —*n. Informal.* a swift, sweeping stroke; hard blow: *She made two swipes at the golf ball without hitting it.*
take a swipe at, *Informal.* try to hit; aim a blow at: *He took a swipe at me, but I ducked.*
—*v.* **1** *Informal.* strike with a swift sweeping blow. **2** *Slang.* steal. ⟨Cf. OF *swipu* scourge⟩

swirl [swɜrl] *v., n.* —*v.* **1** move or drive along with a twisting motion; whirl: *dust swirling in the air, a stream swirling over rocks.* **2** have a twisting shape or pattern. **3** appear the way something does to a dizzy person: *The room swirled around her when she heard the news.*
—*n.* **1** a swirling movement or mass; eddy. **2** something having a twisting shape or pattern: *a swirl of whipped cream.* ⟨ME (Scottish); ? < Scand.; cf. Norwegian dial. *svirla* whirl⟩
—'swirl•er, *n.*

swish [swɪʃ] *v., n., adj.* —*v.* **1** move, pass, or swing with a light hissing or brushing sound: *The whip swished through the air.* **2** make such a sound: *Her long skirt swished as she danced across the floor.* **3** cause to swish: *He swished the stick through the branches. The horse swished its tail.*
—*n.* a swishing movement or sound: *the swish of little waves on the shore.*
—*adj. Esp. Brit. Slang.* smart; posh. ⟨? imitative⟩

Swiss [swɪs] *n., pl.* **Swiss;** *adj.* —*n.* **1** a native or inhabitant of Switzerland, a small country in W Europe. **2** a person of Swiss descent. **3 the Swiss,** *pl.* the people of Switzerland. **4** Usually, **swiss,** a fine, sheer, crisp, usually cotton fabric originally from Switzerland, often having a pattern of woven or flocked dots or figures. **5** SWISS CHEESE.
—*adj.* of or having to do with Switzerland or its people. ⟨< F *Suisse*⟩

Swiss chard a variety of white beet whose leaves and stalks are eaten as a vegetable.

Swiss cheese a firm, pale yellow or whitish cheese having a mild, slightly nutty flavour and many large holes that form as the cheese ripens. Also, **Swiss.**

Swiss Guards a body of soldiers who act as bodyguard to the Pope in the Vatican.

Swiss muslin a fine, sheer muslin ornamented with raised dots or figures.

Swiss steak a cut of steak prepared by pounding it with flour and seasonings, browning it, and then cooking it slowly in a sauce with onions and, sometimes, tomatoes, sweet peppers, etc.

switch [swɪtʃ] *n., v.* —*n.* **1** *Electricity.* a device for making or breaking a connection in an electric circuit. **2** a pair of movable rails by which a train can shift from one track to another. **3** a turn; change; shift: *a switch of votes to another candidate.* **4** a slender stick used in whipping. **5** a stroke; lash: *The big dog knocked a vase off the table with a switch of its tail.* **6** anything resembling a whip in appearance or use. **7** a long tress of hair, often artificial, bound at one end, used to add bulk or length to a woman's hair for some hairstyles. **8** an exchange; one thing given for another.
—*v.* **1** *Electricity.* **a** connect, disconnect, or change the path of (an electric circuit) by means of a switch. **b** start or stop the electric current to (an appliance, lamp, etc.) by operating a switch: *I switched on the radio. Don't forget to switch the light off.*

2 move (a train, railway car, etc.) or be moved from one track to another by means of a switch. **3** turn aside; change course or direction: *He was driving on the outside lane but suddenly switched.* **4** shift or divert (something): *She quickly switched the subject.* **5** exchange: *The children switched lunches.* **6** make an exchange: *You wash and I'll dry, and next time we'll switch.* **7** strike with a switch. **8** move or swing like a switch: *The horse was switching its tail.* ⟨probably < var. of LG *swutsche*⟩ **—'switch•er,** *n.* **—'switch,like,** *adj.*

switch•back ['swɪtʃ,bæk] *n., v.* *—n.* **1** a railway or road climbing a steep grade in a zigzag course. **2** *Brit.* ROLLER COASTER.
—v. take a zigzag course.

switch•blade ['swɪtʃ,bleid] *n.* a pocketknife whose blade springs open at the press of a button or knob.

switch•board ['swɪtʃ,bɔrd] *n. Electricity.* a panel containing the necessary switches, meters, etc. for opening, closing, combining, or controlling electric circuits. A telephone switchboard has plugs for connecting one line to another.

switch•gear ['swɪtʃ,gir] *n. Electricity.* an apparatus for operating switches in electrical circuits.

switch•man ['swɪtʃmən] *n., pl.* **-men.** a man in charge of one or more railway switches.

switch•o•ver ['swɪtʃ,ouvər] *n.* the act of changing over; a comprehensive or systematic turning to something new.

switch•yard ['swɪtʃ,jɑrd] *n.* a railway yard where cars are switched from one track to another, joined to make trains, etc.

Swit•zer•land ['swɪtsərlənd] *n.* a landlocked republic in west central Europe, bordered by France to the west and northwest, Germany to the northeast, Austria to the east, and Italy to the south.

swiv•el ['swɪvəl] *n., v.* **-elled** or **-eled, -el•ling** or **-el•ing.**
—n. **1** a fastening joining two parts so that one part may turn without moving the other. **2** SWIVEL GUN.
—v. **1** turn on a swivel or as if on a swivel: *She swivelled the chair around. He swivelled his eyes in our direction. The weathervane swivelled in the wind.* **2** fasten or support by a swivel. ⟨ult. < OE *swīfan* move⟩

swivel chair a chair that turns on a swivel in its base.

swivel gun a gun mounted on a swivel so that it can be turned in any direction.

swiv•et ['swɪvɪt] *n. Informal.* a state of nervous excitement or annoyance: *She always gets in a swivet before the dinner guests arrive.* ⟨origin unknown⟩

swiz•zle ['swɪzəl] *n., v.* **-zled, -zling.** *—n.* any of various alcoholic mixed drinks, especially one made with rum or other liquor, ice, bitters, and sugar.
—v. **1** stir with a SWIZZLE STICK. **2** drink (alcoholic liquor) habitually or excessively. ⟨apparently var. of earlier *switchel*; origin unknown⟩

swizzle stick a small stick of plastic, glass, etc. used to stir alcoholic drinks.

swob [swɒb] *n., v.* **swobbed, swob•bing.** See SWAB.
—'swob•ber, *n.*

swol•len ['swoulən] *adj., v.* *—adj.* swelled: *a swollen ankle.*
—v. a pp. of SWELL.

swoln [swouln] *adj. Archaic.* swollen.

swoon [swun] *v., n.* *—v.* **1** faint. **2** become ecstatic. **3** of sound, fade or die (away) gradually.
—n. a loss of consciousness: *He fell in a swoon.* ⟨ult. < OE *geswōgen* in a swoon⟩

swoop [swup] *v., n.* *—v.* **1** move with a rush; especially, make a sudden, swift attack (*usually used with* **down**): *The eagle swooped down on the mouse. The horsemen swooped down on the village and burned it.* **2** seize; snatch (*used with* **up**): *She swooped the puppy up in her arms.*
—n. the act or an instance of swooping.
at or **in one fell swoop,** all at once. ⟨ult. < OE *swāpan* sweep⟩
—'swoop•er, *n.*

swoosh [swuʃ] *v., n.* *—v.* move with or make a sound like a rush of liquid or air: *The car swooshed by.*
—n. the act or an instance of swooshing: *We heard a swoosh as the water rushed into the tank.*

swop [swɒp] *v.* **swopped, swop•ping;** *n.* See SWAP.
—'swop•per, *n.*

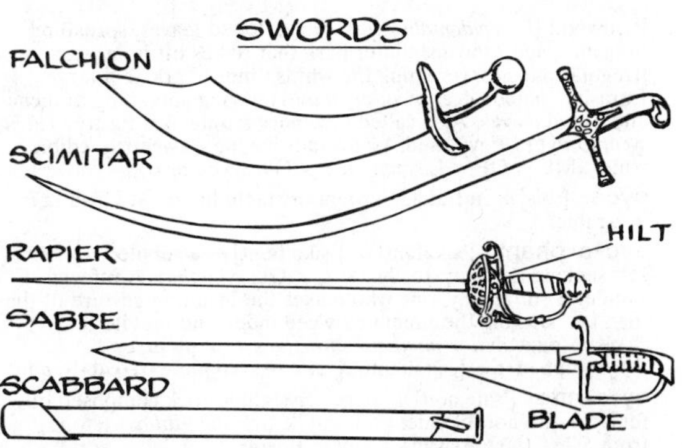

sword [sɔrd] *n.* **1** a hand weapon, usually metal, with a long sharp blade fixed in a handle or hilt. **2** something resembling a sword, such as the elongated upper jawbone of the swordfish. **3** a symbol of power, authority, or honour: *the sword of justice.* **4 the sword,** war or military power: *The pen is mightier than the sword. The conqueror ruled by the sword.* **5 the sword,** violence or warfare as a source of death or destruction: *to die by the sword.*
at sword's points, very unfriendly; ready to fight or quarrel.
cross swords, fight or quarrel: *I wouldn't want to cross swords with him; he's mean.*
draw the sword, begin a war.
put to the sword, kill, especially in war: *The captives were put to the sword.* ⟨OE *sweord*⟩ **—'sword,like,** *adj.*

sword dance any dance performed with swords or over swords laid on the ground. **—sword dancer.**

sword•fish ['sɔrd,fɪʃ] *n., pl.* **-fish** or **-fish•es.** a very large food and game fish (*Xiphias gladius*) found in tropical and temperate seas throughout the world, having a tall, scaleless back fin, a crescent-shaped tail fin, and a very long, flat, swordlike upper jawbone with which it slashes and pierces its prey. It is the only member of the family Xiphiidae, distantly related to the marlins and tunas.

sword grass any of various grasses or plants having swordlike leaves.

sword knot a looped strap, ribbon, etc. attached to the hilt of a sword, serving as a means of supporting it from the wrist or as an ornament.

Sword of Damocles See DAMOCLES.

sword•play ['sɔrd,plei] *n.* the action, practice, or art of wielding a sword, especially in fencing.

swords•man ['sɔrdzmən] *n., pl.* **-men. 1** a man skilled in using a sword. **2** a man using a sword.

swords•man•ship ['sɔrdzmən,ʃɪp] *n.* skill in using a sword.

sword•tail ['sɔrd,teil] *n.* any of several small, tropical freshwater fishes (genus *Xiphophorus*), especially a brightly coloured Central American species (*X. helleri*) having a long, swordlike extension on the tail fin. Swordtails are bred in many colours for keeping in aquariums.

swore [swɔr] *v.* a pt. of SWEAR.

sworn [swɔrn] *v., adj.* *—v.* pp. of SWEAR.
—adj. **1** having taken an oath; bound by an oath. **2** declared, promised, etc. with an oath.

swot [swɒt] *v.* **swot•ted, swot•ting;** *n. Brit. Slang.* *—v.* study very hard.
—n. **1** hard work, especially hard study at schoolwork. **2** a person who swots. ⟨apparently Scottish var. of *sweat*⟩ **—'swot•ter,** *n.*

swum [swʌm] *v.* pp. of SWIM.

swung [swʌŋ] *v.* a pt. and pp. of SWING.

sy– the form of SYN- before *s* plus a consonant, as in *system.*

syb•a•rite ['sɪbə,rəit] *n.* a person who cares very much for luxury and pleasure. ⟨< *Sybarite,* an inhabitant of *Sybaris,* an ancient Greek city in Italy known for its luxury⟩
—'syb•a•rit,ism, *n.*

syb•a•rit•ic [,sɪbə'rɪtɪk] *adj.* luxurious; voluptuous.
—,syb•a'rit•i•cal•ly, *adv.*

syc•a•more ['sɪkə,mɔr] *n.* **1** any of a genus (*Platanus*) of trees constituting the North American and Eurasian plane tree family (Platanaceae); especially, a large North American hardwood (*P. occidentalis*) with broad, lobed leaves, spreading branches, and brownish outer bark that flakes off in large, irregular patches, revealing the whitish inner bark. **2** a large Eurasian maple (*Acer pseudoplatanus*) having spreading branches and broad leaves. Also called **sycamore maple. 3** a fig tree (*Ficus sycamorus*) of Egypt and Asia Minor having a sweetish, edible fruit. ⟨ME < OF < L *sycomorus* < Gk. *sykomoros*⟩

syce [sɔis] *n.* in India, a groom or stable hand. ⟨< Urdu *sa'is* < Arabic⟩

syc•o•phant ['sɪkəfənt] *or* ['sɪkə'fænt] *n.* a servile, self-seeking flatterer; toady. ⟨< L < Gk. *sykophantēs* informer, slanderer (originally, one who makes the insulting gesture of the 'fig', i.e., sticking the thumb between index and middle finger) < *sykon* fig, vulva + *phainein* show⟩ **—'syc•o•phan•cy,** *n.* **—,syc•o'phan•tic** [,sɪkə'fæntɪk], *adj.* **—,syco'phan•ti•cal•ly,** *adv.*

sy•e•nite ['saɪə,nəit] *n.* a grey crystalline rock composed of feldspar and hornblende. ⟨< L < Gk. *Syēnitēs (lithos)* (stone) from *Syēnē* (now Aswan), a city in Egypt⟩

syl– the form of SYN- before *l*, as in *syllogism.*

syl. or **syll. 1** syllable. **2** syllabus.

syl•la•bar•y ['sɪlə,bɛri] *n., pl.* **-ies 1** a writing system for a given language, in which each symbol stands for a syllable, often a consonant plus a vowel. **2** a list of syllables.

syl•la•bi ['sɪləbaɪ] *n.* a plural of SYLLABUS.

syl•lab•ic [sɪ'læbɪk] *adj., n. —adj.* **1** of, having to do with, based on, or consisting of syllables. **2** of a nonvowel, forming a syllable or the nucleus of a syllable, as the second *l* in *little.* **3** pronounced syllable by syllable. **4** *Prosody.* designating verse based on the number of syllables in a line rather than on the arrangement of stresses or quantities.
—n. **1** a syllabic speech sound. **2** a written sign or character representing a syllable. **3 syllabics,** *pl.* syllabic verse.
—syl'lab•i•cal•ly, *adv.*

syl•lab•i•cate [sɪ'læbə,keit] *v.* **-cat•ed, -cat•ing.** form or divide into syllables; syllabify. **—syl,lab•i'ca•tion,** *n.*

syl•lab•i•fy [sɪ'læbə,faɪ] *v.* **-fied, -fy•ing.** syllabicate. **—syl,lab•i•fi'ca•tion,** *n.*

syl•la•bize ['sɪlə,baɪz] *v.* **-bized, -biz•ing. 1** form or divide into syllables. **2** utter with careful distinction of syllables.

syl•la•ble ['sɪləbəl] *n., v.* **-bled, -bling.** *—n.* **1** a word or part of a word spoken as a unit, usually consisting of a vowel sound alone or a vowel sound with one or more consonant sounds. *See* is a word of one syllable, consisting of a consonant sound [s] plus a vowel sound [i]. **2** in writing or printing, a letter or group of letters corresponding roughly to a syllable of spoken language. The syllables of entry words in this dictionary are separated by dots, as in **syl•la•ble.** A word that has to be broken at the end of a line is usually hyphenated between two syllables. **3** the slightest bit or detail of something: *She promised not to breathe a syllable of the secret to anyone.*
—v. pronounce or utter in or as if in syllables. ⟨ME < OF < L < Gk. *syllabē,* originally, a taking together < *syllambanein* < *syn-* together + *lambanein* take⟩

syl•la•bub ['sɪlə,bʌb] *n.* a dessert made of cream, eggs, and wine, usually sweetened and flavoured. Also, **sillabub.** ⟨origin uncertain⟩

syl•la•bus ['sɪləbəs] *n., pl.* **-bus•es** or **-bi** [-,baɪ] *or* [-,bi]. **1** a course of study. **2** a brief statement of the main points of a speech, a book, etc. ⟨< NL *syllabus,* erroneous reading of L and Gk. *sittyba* parchment label⟩

syl•lep•sis [sə'lɛpsɪs] *n., pl.* **-ses** [-siz]. *Grammar.* the use of a word with two others **a** in two different senses simultaneously. *Example*: *He* took *a bath and his things and left.* **b** only one of which agrees with it grammatically. *Example*: *Either you or it* goes. ⟨< Gk. < *syllambanein.* See SYLLABLE⟩ **—syl'lep•tic,** *adj.*

syl•lo•gism ['sɪlə,dʒɪzəm] *n.* **1** *Logic.* a form of argument or reasoning consisting of two statements, a general (the **major premise**) and a particular (the **minor premise**), and a conclusion drawn from them. *Example*: *All trees have roots; an oak is a tree; therefore, an oak has roots.* **2** a reasoning in this form; deduction from the general to the particular. **3** a specious or very subtle argument; a deviously crafty piece of reasoning. ⟨< L < Gk. *syllogismos,* originally, inference, ult. < *syn-* together + *logos* a reckoning⟩ **—,syl•lo'gis•tic,** *adj.* **—,syl•lo'gis•ti•cal•ly,** *adv.*

syl•lo•gize ['sɪlə,dʒaɪz] *v.* **-gized, -giz•ing. 1** argue or reason by syllogisms. **2** deduce by syllogism.

sylph [sɪlf] *n.* **1** a slender, graceful girl or woman. **2** in the ancient Greek theory of the four elements, the spirit that inhabited the air. ⟨< NL *sylphes,* pl.; a coinage of Paracelsus (1493?-1541), a Swiss alchemist and physician⟩ **—'sylph,like,** *adj.*

syl•va ['sɪlvə] *n.* See SILVA.

syl•van ['sɪlvən] *adj.* **1** of, having to do with, or characteristic of the woods. **2** living or situated in the woods: *a sylvan retreat.* Also, **silvan.** ⟨< L *silvanus* < *silva* forest⟩

syl•vat•ic [sɪl'vætɪk] *adj.* **1** of, belonging to, or found in woods; sylvan: *sylvatic animals.* **2** of or carried by insects or animals that are found in woods or forests: *sylvatic plague.*

syl•vi•cul•ture ['sɪlvə,kʌltʃər] *n.* See SILVICULTURE.

syl•vite ['sɪlvəit] *n.* a common mineral, potassium chloride, occurring in cubic crystals, an important source of potassium. *Formula*: Cl ⟨< NL (*sal digestivus*) *sylvii* digestive salt of *Sylvius* (probably after François de la Boe *Sylvius* (1614-1672), a Flemish anatomist) + E *-ite*[1]⟩

sym– *prefix.* the form of SYN- occurring before *b, m, p,* as in *symbol, symmetry, sympathy.*

sym. 1 symbol. **2** symmetrical. **3** symphony. **4** symptom.

sym•bi•o•sis [,sɪmbaɪ'ousɪs] *or* [,sɪmbi'ousɪs] *n.* **1** *Biology.* the association or living together of two unlike organisms in a relationship that benefits each of them. The lichen, which is composed of an alga and a fungus, is an example of symbiosis; the alga provides the food, and the fungus provides water and protection. **2** any relationship of mutual interdependence between two unlike things or people. ⟨< NL < Gk. *symbiōsis,* ult. < *syn-* together + *bios* life⟩ **—,sym•bi'ot•ic** [,sɪmbaɪ'ɒtɪk] *or* [,sɪmbi'ɒtɪk], *adj.* **—,sym•bi'ot•i•cal•ly,** *adv.*

sym•bol ['sɪmbəl] *n., v.* **-bolled** or **-boled, -bol•ling** or **-bol•ing.** *—n.* **1** something that or someone who stands for or represents something else, especially an idea, quality, condition, or other abstraction: *The lion is the symbol of courage; the lamb, of meekness; the olive branch, of peace; the cross, of Christianity. Terry Fox has become a symbol of courage and hope to millions of Canadians.* **2** a letter, figure, or sign conventionally used in writing or printing, standing for a process, object, quantity, relation, etc.: *The marks* +, –, ×, *and* ÷ *are symbols for add, subtract, multiply, and divide.*
—v. symbolize. ⟨< L < Gk. *symbolon* token, ult. < *syn-* together + *ballein* throw⟩
☛ *Hom.* CYMBAL.
☛ *Syn. n.* **1.** See note at EMBLEM.

sym•bol•ic [sɪm'bɒlɪk] *adj.* **1** used as a symbol: *The maple leaf is symbolic of Canada.* **2** of, expressed by, or using symbols: *Writing is a symbolic form of expression.* **—sym'bol•i•cal•ly,** *adv.*

symbolic logic a method in formal logic that uses a formalized language, or calculus, to represent terms and relationships, permitting a precision in the formulation and analysis of propositions that is not possible in ordinary language.

sym•bol•ism ['sɪmbə,lɪzəm] *n.* **1** the use of conventional or traditional signs, etc. to represent things, especially things that are abstract or invisible; representation by symbols. **2** a system of symbols: *The cross, the crown, the lamb, and the lily are parts of Christian symbolism. The rose, the shamrock, and the thistle are part of the heraldic symbolism of the British Isles.* **3** a symbolic meaning or character. **4** a movement in art and literature seeking to express ideas, feelings, or states of mind through the symbolic use of objects, shapes, words, etc.

sym•bol•ist ['sɪmbəlɪst] *n.* **1** a person who uses symbols or symbolism. **2** an artist or writer who makes much use of colours, sounds, etc. as symbols, especially as part of an artistic and literary movement. **3** a person who is skilled in the study or interpretation of symbols.

sym•bol•is•tic [,sɪmbə'lɪstɪk] *adj.* of symbolism or symbolists.

sym•bol•ize ['sɪmbə,laɪz] *v.* **-ized, -iz•ing. 1** be a symbol of; stand for; represent: *A dove symbolizes peace.* **2** represent or express by a symbol or symbols: *We symbolize the chemical composition of water by the formula H_2O.* **3** use symbols. **—'sym•bol,iz•er,** *n.* **—'sym•bo,li'za•tion,** *n.*

sym•bol•o•gy [sɪm'bɒlədʒi] *n.* **1** the science or study of symbols. **2** the use of symbols; symbolism. ⟨< NL *symbologia* < Gk. *symbolon* + NL *-logia* -logy. See SYMBOL.⟩

sym•met•ri•cal [sɪ'mɛtrɪkəl] *adj.* **1** having or showing symmetry: *a symmetrical design, a symmetrical curve. The tree on our front lawn has an almost symmetrical crown.* **2** *Botany.* of a flower: **a** having the same number of parts in each whorl. **b** divisible vertically into similar halves. **3** *Chemistry.* having a structural formula characterized by a regular repeated pattern. **4** *Logic. Mathematics.* of a proposition, equation, etc., so constituted that the truth or value is not changed by interchanging the terms. **5** *Pathology.* of a disease, affecting corresponding organs or parts at the same time, such as both arms or both lungs or both ears equally. Also, **symmetric.** **—sym'met•ri•cal•ly,** *adv.*

sym•me•trize ['sɪmə,traɪz] *v.* **-trized, -triz•ing.** reduce to symmetry; make symmetrical.

sym•me•try ['sɪmətri] *n., pl.* **-tries. 1** a regular, balanced arrangement on opposite sides of a line or plane, or around a centre or axis. **2** pleasing proportions between the parts of a whole; a well-balanced arrangement of parts; harmony. **3** *Botany.* agreement in number of parts along the cycles of organs that compose a flower. ⟨< L < Gk. *symmetria* < *syn-* together + *metron* measure⟩

sym•pa•thet•ic [,sɪmpə'θɛtɪk] *adj.* **1** having or showing kind feelings toward others; sympathizing. **2** inclined to agree or approve; favourably inclined: *They are sympathetic to our idea.* **3** enjoying the same things and getting along well together; congenial: *He enjoys the skating club because he finds most of the members sympathetic.* **4** *Anatomy. Physiology.* designating or referring to the part of the autonomic nervous system other than the cerebro-spinal part. **5** *Physics.* of or designating vibrations caused by vibrations of exactly the same period in a neighbouring body. **6** of a symptom, being agreeable: *That is not a particularly sympathetic idea.* **7** a response to some influence or disorder in another part of the body or in another person: *sympathetic toothache, sympathetic weight gain by husbands of pregnant women.* **—,sym•pa'thet•i•cal•ly,** *adv.*

sym•pa•thize ['sɪmpə,θaɪz] *v.* **-thized, -thiz•ing. 1** feel or show sympathy: *sympathize with a child who has hurt himself.* **2** share in or agree with a feeling or opinion: *My mother sympathizes with my plan to be a doctor.* **3** enjoy the same things and get along well together. **4** experience sympathetic symptoms. ⟨< F *sympathiser* < *sympathie* sympathy⟩ **—'sym•pa,thiz•ing•ly,** *adv.*

sym•pa•thiz•er ['sɪmpə,θaɪzər] *n.* a person who sympathizes; especially, a person who is favourably inclined toward a particular belief or person.

sym•path•o•lyt•ic [,sɪmpəθə'lɪtɪk] *adj.* having the effect of opposing or decreasing the physiological results in the sympathetic nervous system of certain drugs, treatments, etc. ⟨< *sympath(etic)* + *-lytic* (< Gk. *lytikos* loosing < *lysis* a loosing)⟩

sym•pa•thy ['sɪmpəθi] *n., pl.* **-thies. 1** a sharing of another's sorrow or trouble; a sharing, or ability to share: *We feel sympathy for a person who is ill. She has no sympathy whatsoever.* **2** an agreement in feeling; the condition or fact of having the same feeling: *The sympathy between the twins was so great that they always smiled or cried at the same things.* **3** agreement; approval; favour: *He is in sympathy with my plan.* **4 a** an affinity between certain things, whereby they are similarly or correspondingly affected by the same influence. **b** an action or response induced by such a relationship. ⟨< L < Gk. *sympatheia* < *syn-* together + *pathos* feeling⟩

☛ *Syn.* **1.** See note at PITY.

sym•pat•ric [sɪm'pætrɪk] *adj. Biology.* referring to closely related species capable of sharing the same geographical area without loss of identity due to interbreeding.

sym•pet•al•ous [sɪm'pɛtələs] *adj. Botany.* gamopetalous.

sym•phon•ic [sɪm'fɒnɪk] *adj.* **1** of, having to do with, or having the character of a symphony: *a symphonic composition.* **2** of or having to do with harmony of sounds; harmonious. **—sym'phon•i•cal•ly,** *adv.*

symphonic poem *Music.* a free-form composition for symphony orchestra, usually consisting of only one movement and usually descriptive or rhapsodic in character, often attempting to translate a literary or pictorial idea.

sym•pho•ni•ous [sɪm'founiəs] *adj.* harmonious. **—sym'pho•ni•ous•ly,** *adv.*

sym•pho•ny ['sɪmfəni] *n., pl.* **-nies. 1** a long and elaborate musical composition for a full orchestra. A symphony is usually in the form of a sonata, with three or four movements that are different in rhythm and speed but related in key. **2** SYMPHONY ORCHESTRA. **3** a concert given by a symphony orchestra: *We're going to the symphony tonight.* **4** anything characterized by harmonious composition, blending, etc., such as sounds or colours: *In autumn the woods are a symphony in red, brown, and yellow.* ⟨ME < OF < L < Gk. *symphōnia* harmony, concert, band < *syn-* together + *phōnē* voice, sound⟩

symphony orchestra a large orchestra for playing symphonies and similar works, made up of brass, woodwind, percussion, and stringed instruments.

sym•phy•sis ['sɪmfəsɪs] *n., pl.* **-ses** [-,siz]. **1** *Anatomy.* **a** a union of two bones or other parts originally separate, especially of two similar bones on opposite sides of the body, such as the pubic bones or the two halves of the lower jawbone. **b** the line of junction thus formed. **2** *Botany.* a fusion of parts of a plant that are normally separate. ⟨< Gk. *symphysis* growing together < *symphyein* to unite < *syn* together + *phyein* grow⟩

sym•po•si•um [sɪm'pouziəm] *or* [sɪm'pouʒəm] *n., pl.* **-si•ums** or **-si•a** [-ziə] *or* [-ʒə]. **1** a collection of the opinions of several persons on a subject: *This magazine contains a symposium on sports.* **2** a formal meeting at which several specialists give their views on a subject. **3** in ancient Greece, an after-dinner drinking party featuring stimulating intellectual conversation. ⟨< L < Gk. *symposion* < *syn-* together + *posis* drinking⟩

symp•tom ['sɪmptəm] *n.* **1** something that indicates the existence of something else; sign: *symptoms of discontent.* **2** *Pathology.* a noticeable change in the normal working of the body, that indicates or accompanies disease or injury: *The doctor made her diagnosis after studying the patient's symptoms.* ⟨< LL < Gk. *symptōma* a happening, ult. < *syn-* together + *piptein* fall⟩

symp•to•mat•ic [,sɪmptə'mætɪk] *adj.* **1** being a sign; indicative or characteristic: *Riots are symptomatic of political or social unrest.* **2** indicating or accompanying a disease, etc.: *The infection caused a symptomatic fever.* **3** having to do with or according to symptoms of disease, etc. **—,symp•to'mat•i•cal•ly,** *adv.*

symp•to•ma•tol•o•gy [,sɪmptəmə'tɒlədʒi] *n.* **1** the branch of medical science dealing with symptoms. **2** the collective symptoms of a patient or disease.

syn– *prefix.* with, jointly, or at the same time: *synchronous, synopsis, synthesis.* Also **sy-** before *s* plus a consonant; **syl-** before *l*; **sym-** before *b, m, p.* ⟨< Gk. *syn* with, together⟩

syn. synonym; synonymous; synonymy.

syn•a•gogue ['sɪnə,gɒg] *n.* **1** a building used by a Jewish congregation as a house of worship and religious instruction. **2** a Jewish congregation or assembly. **3** Judaism as a whole. ⟨ME < LL < Gk. *synagōgē*, literally, assembly, ult. < *syn-* together + *agein* bring⟩

syn•apse ['sɪnæps] *or* [sɪ'næps] *n. Physiology.* a place where a nerve impulse passes from one nerve cell to another. ⟨< Gk. *synapsis* conjunction < *syn-* together + *haptein* fasten⟩

syn•ap•sis [sɪ'næpsɪs] *n., pl.* **syn•ap•ses** [-siz]. *Genetics.* the pairing of homologous chromosomes during the first of the two meiotic divisions in germ cell formation.

sync [sɪŋk] *n., v.* **synced, sync•ing.** *Informal.* *–n.* synchronization, especially of sound and action or of speech and lip movement, as in television or films.
in sync, synchronized; compatible.
out of sync, not synchronized; not compatible: *His ideas are usually out of sync with mine.*
–v. synchronize.

☛ *Hom.* SINK.

syn•chro ['sɪŋkrou] *n. Informal.* SYNCHRONIZED SWIMMING.

synchro– *prefix.* synchronized; synchronous: *synchromesh, synchrotron.*

syn•chro•mesh ['sɪŋkrə,mɛʃ] *n.* in an automobile, a gear or system of gears constructed so as to mesh with a minimum of friction and noise when the driver shifts from one speed to another, by bringing both gears to the same speed of rotation before shifting. ⟨< *synchro(nous)* + *mesh*⟩

syn•chro•nal ['sɪŋkrənəl] *adj.* synchronous.

syn•chron•ic [sɪn'krɒnɪk] *or* [sɪŋ'krɒnɪk] *adj.* **1** concerned with a subject or with phenomena regarded from a single viewpoint in time, without reference to causes, antecedents, or changes: *synchronic linguistics.* Compare DIACHRONIC. **2** synchronous. **—syn'chron•i•cal•ly,** *adv.*

syn•chron•i•ci•ty [,sɪŋkrə'nɪsəti] *n.* **1** SYNCHRONISM (def. 1). **2** the occurrence at the same time of two apparently unrelated happenings that later are seen to be somehow connected, either symbolically or realistically.

syn•chro•nism ['sɪŋkrə,nɪzəm] *n.* **1** the quality or state of being concurrent. **2** a parallel arrangement of historical events or persons according to their dates.

syn•chro•nize ['sɪŋkrə,naɪz] *v.* **-nized, -niz•ing. 1** happen at the same time; be simultaneous; coincide (*with*). **2** make occur or operate at the same time or speed: *to synchronize all the clocks in the building, to synchronize the flash with the camera shutter, to synchronize the sound with the action in a motion picture.* **3** establish or show the correspondence of the dates of (events).

⟨< Gk. *synchronizein* < *synchronos* synchronous. See SYNCHRONOUS.⟩ **—'syn•chro,niz•er,** *n.* **—,syn•chro•ni'za•tion,** *n.*

synchronized swimming a competitive sport in which pairs or groups of swimmers perform identical dancelike or gymnastic movements in the water.

syn•chro•nous ['sɪŋkrənəs] *adj.* **1** occurring or existing at exactly the same time; simultaneous. **2** moving or taking place at the same rate and exactly together. **3** *Physics.* having coincident periods, or coincident periods and phases, as an alternating electric current. ⟨< LL < Gk. *synchronos* < *syn-* together + *chronos* time⟩ **—'syn•chro•nous•ly,** *adv.*

syn•chro•ny ['sɪŋkrəni] *n.* SYNCHRONISM (def. 1).

syn•chro•tron ['sɪŋkrə,trɒn] *n. Physics.* a type of accelerator that accelerates electrified particles by means of a varying magnetic field and an alternating high-frequency electric field. ⟨< *synchro(nous)* + *-tron* as in *electron*⟩

syn•cli•nal [sɪn'klaɪnəl], [sɪŋ'klaɪnəl], *or* ['sɪŋklɪnəl] *adj.* **1** sloping downward from opposite directions so as to form a trough or inverted arch. **2** of, having to do with, or containing a syncline.

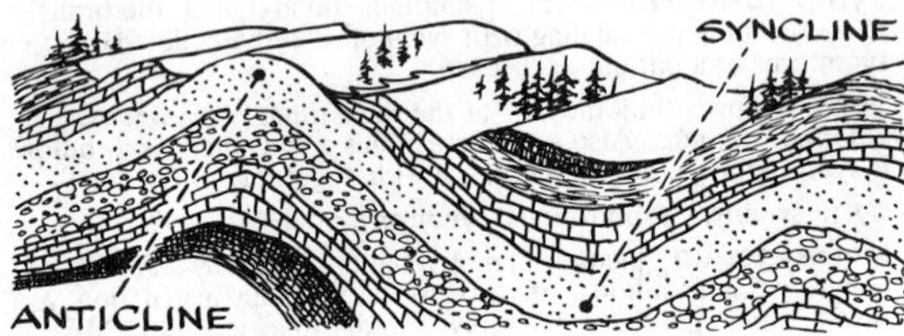

Layers of sedimentary rock forming a syncline and anticline

syn•cline ['sɪŋklaɪn] *n. Geology.* a downward fold, or trough, of stratified rock, in which the layers slope upward in opposite directions from the centre. Compare ANTICLINE. ⟨< Gk. *synklinein* lean, incline < *syn-* together + *klinein* bend⟩

syn•co•pate ['sɪŋkə,peit] *v.* **-pat•ed, -pat•ing. 1** *Music.* **a** change (a regular rhythm) by beginning a note on an unaccented beat and holding it into an accented one or beginning it midway through a beat and continuing it midway into the next one. **b** introduce such shifted accents into (a passage or piece of music). **2** *Linguistics.* shorten (a word) by syncope. ⟨< LL *syncopare* < *syncope.* See SYNCOPE.⟩

syn•co•pa•tion [,sɪŋkə'peiʃən] *n.* **1** *Music.* **a** the action or art of syncopating a musical rhythm or piece of music. Syncopation is much used in jazz. **b** a syncopated rhythm, piece of music, etc. **2** *Linguistics.* syncope.

syn•co•pe ['sɪŋkəpi] *n.* **1** *Linguistics.* a reduction in the number of syllables in a word by the loss or omission of a sound or sounds from the middle. *Example*: batt'ry *for* battery. **2** *Pathology.* a temporary loss of consciousness due to an inadequate supply of blood to the brain, caused by illness, extreme pain or emotion, etc.; fainting. ⟨< LL < Gk. *synkopē*, originally, a cutting off, ult. < *syn-* together + *koptein* cut⟩

syn•cre•tism ['sɪŋkrə,tɪzəm] *n.* **1** a tendency or effort to reconcile different or opposed religious or philosophical belief systems, or to absorb some of the tenets of one into the system of another. **2** *Linguistics.* **a** the merging, as by historical language change, of originally different inflectional categories into one. **b** the resulting sameness of forms. **3** the doctrines of George Calixtus (1586-1656), a Lutheran who aimed at uniting Protestant sects and, eventually, all Christendom. ⟨< NL < Gk. *synkrētismos* (< *synkrētizein* combine, ally, apparently originally as in a union or federation of Cretan communities < *Krēs, Krētos* Crete)⟩ **—syn'cret•ic** [sɪn'krɛtɪk] or **,syn•cre'tis•tic,** *adj.*

syn•cre•tize ['sɪŋkrə,taɪz] *v.* **-tized, -tiz•ing.** combine or attempt to combine (different or opposed systems, philosophical or religious belief systems, etc.) ⟨< NL *syncretizare* < Gk. *synkrētizein.* See SYNCRETISM.⟩

syn•dac•tyl [sɪn'dæktəl] *adj.* having two or more fingers or toes joined, as by webbing.

syn•dac•ty•ly [sɪn'dæktəli] *n. Medicine.* a congenital defect of the hand in which two or more fingers are completely or partially fused. There are several different forms, some of which are heritable.

syn•dic ['sɪndɪk] *n.* **1** *Brit.* a person who manages the business affairs of a university or other corporation. **2** a government official or chief magistrate. ⟨< LL *syndicus* < Gk. *syndikos* advocate < *syn-* together + *dikē* justice⟩

syn•di•cal•ism ['sɪndəkə,lɪzəm] *n.* a movement in industrial unions, aimed at unionizing all workers and taking control of industry and government by direct means such as a general strike.

syn•di•cal•ist ['sɪndəkəlɪst] *n.* a person who favours or supports syndicalism. **—,syn•di•cal'is•tic,** *adj.*

syn•di•cate *n.* ['sɪndəkɪt]; *v.* ['sɪndə,keit] *n., v.* **-cat•ed, -cat•ing.** *—n.* **1** a group of individuals or organizations who combine to carry out some undertaking, especially one requiring a large capital investment. **2** an agency that sells special articles, photographs, etc. to a large number of newspapers or magazines for publication at the same time. **3** a group of businesses, especially newspapers, under one management. **4** an association or combination of criminals controlling organized crime. *—v.* **1** combine into a syndicate. **2** manage by a syndicate. **3** publish or broadcast through a syndicate, as certain newspaper columns, television series, etc. ⟨< F *syndicat* < *syndic* < LL *syndicus.* See SYNDIC.⟩ **—,syn•di'ca•tion,** *n.*

syn•drome ['sɪndrəm] *or* ['sɪndroum] *n.* **1** *Pathology. Psychiatry.* a number of symptoms that taken together indicate the presence of a specific condition or disease. **2** a characteristic pattern of anomalies of several body parts, thought to be causally related. **3** any set of ideas, attitudes, or customs that together indicate a state of mind, pattern of behaviour, etc.: *the yuppie syndrome.* ⟨< NL < Gk. *syndromē*, literally, a running together < *syn-* with + *dromos* course, related to *dramein* run⟩

syne [saɪn] *adv., prep., or conj. Scottish.* since.
☛ *Hom.* SIGN, SINE[1].

syn•ec•do•che [sɪ'nɛkdəki] *n. Rhetoric.* a figure of speech by which a part is put for the whole, the special for the general, the material for the thing made from it, or vice versa. *Examples*: *a factory employing 500* hands (*persons*); *to eat of the* tree (*its fruit*); *a* Solomon (*wise man*); *a* marble (*a statue*) *on its pedestal.* ⟨< LL < Gk. *synekdochē*, ult. < *syn-* with + *ek-* out + *dechesthai* receive⟩ **—,syn•ec'doch•ic** [,sɪnɪk'dɒkɪk], *adj.*

syn•e•col•o•gy [,sɪnə'kɒlədʒi] *n.* a branch of ecology dealing with the development and distribution of ecosystems in relation to their natural habitat. Compare AUTECOLOGY.

syn•er•get•ic [,sɪnər'dʒɛtɪk] *adj.* working together; co-operative.

syn•er•gism ['sɪnər,dʒɪzəm] *n.* synergy. ⟨< NL *syn- ergismus* < Gk. *synergéin* work together. See SYNERGY.⟩ **—,syn•er'gist•ic,** *adj.*

syn•er•gy ['sɪnərdʒi] *n., pl.* **-ies.** the combined or co-operative action of two or more agents, groups, or parts, etc. that together increase each other's effectiveness: *the synergy of the muscles of the body.* ⟨< NL < Gk. *synergia* joint work < *synergéin* work together < *syn-* together + *ergon* work⟩ **—syn'er•gic,** *adj.*

syn•od ['sɪnəd] *n.* **1** an assembly called together under authority to discuss and decide church affairs; a church council. **2** a court of the Presbyterian Church ranking next above the presbytery. **3** an assembly; convention; council. ⟨< LL < Gk. *synodos* assembly, meeting < *syn-* together + *hodos* a going⟩ **—'syn•od•al,** *adj.*

syn•od•ic [sɪ'nɒdɪk] *adj.* SYNODICAL (def. 1).

syn•od•i•cal [sɪ'nɒdɪkəl] *adj.* **1** *Astronomy.* having to do with the conjunctions of the heavenly bodies. The synodical period of the moon is the time between one new moon and the next. **2** synodal.

syn•o•nym ['sɪnənɪm] *n.* **1** one of two or more words of a language having the same or nearly the same meaning. *St. Vitus's dance* and *chorea* are synonyms. *Sharp* is a synonym for one meaning of *keen; enthusiastic* is a synonym for another meaning of *keen.* Compare ANTONYM. **2** a word or expression generally accepted as another name for something or strongly associated with something: *Churchill's name has become a synonym for patriotic devotion to one's country.* **3** *Botany. Zoology.* a wrong or wrongly applied taxonomic name. ⟨ME < LL < Gk. *synōnymon*, originally adj., neut. of *synōnymos* synonymous. See SYNONYMOUS.⟩

syn•on•y•mous [sɪ'nɒnəməs] *adj.* being a synonym or synonyms. The words *velocity* and *speed* are synonymous. In parts of Canada, *spring* is synonymous with *flooding rivers.* ⟨< Med.L < Gk. *synōnymos* < *syn-* together + dial. *onyma* name⟩ **—syn'on•y•mous•ly,** *adv.*

syn•on•y•my [sɪ'nɒnəmi] *n., pl.* **-mies. 1** the quality or state of being synonymous. **2** the study of synonyms. **3** the use of synonyms together in discourse for emphasis or amplification. *Example*: *in any* shape *or* form. **4** a set, list, or system of synonyms.

syn•op•sis [sɪ'nɒpsɪs] *n., pl.* **-ses** [-siz]. a brief statement giving a general view of some subject, book, play, etc.; summary. ⟨< LL < Gk. *synopsis* < *syn-* together + *opsis* a view⟩

syn•op•size [sɪ'nɒpsaɪz] *v.* **-sized, -siz•ing.** make a synopsis of.

syn•op•tic [sɪ'nɒptɪk] *adj.* **1** giving a general view; summarizing. **2** Often, **Synoptic.** taking a common view. *Matthew*, *Mark*, and *Luke* are called the **Synoptic Gospels** because they are much alike in content, order, and statement. **—syn'op•ti•cal•ly,** *adv.*

syn•op•ti•cal [sɪ'nɒptɪkəl] *adj.* synoptic.

syn•os•to•sis [,sɪnɒ'stousɪs] *n. Anatomy.* a fusion of bones that are usually separate into a single bone. ⟨< *syn-* + Gk. *osteon* bone + E *-osis*⟩

syn•o•vi•a [sɪ'nouviə] *n. Physiology.* a lubricating liquid secreted by certain membranes, such as those of the joints. ⟨< NL *synovia*; coinage of Paracelsus (1493?-1541), a Swiss alchemist and physician⟩

syn•o•vi•al [sɪ'nouviəl] *adj.* consisting of, containing, or secreting synovia: *synovial fluid, a synovial membrane.*

syn•o•vi•tis [,sɪnə'vəitɪs] *n. Pathology.* inflammation of a synovial membrane.

syn•tac•tic [sɪn'tæktɪk] *adj.* of, having to do with, or according to the rules of syntax. **—syn'tac•ti•cal•ly,** *adv.*

syn•tac•ti•cal [sɪn'tæktəkəl] *adj.* syntactic.

syn•tac•tics [sɪn'tæktɪks] *n.* (*used with a singular verb*) the branch of semiotics dealing with the formal relations among signs and symbols as separate from their meanings or their users.

syn•tag•mat•ic [,sɪntæg'mætɪk] *adj.* syntactic.

syn•tax ['sɪntæks] *n.* **1** the arrangement of words to form sentences, clauses, or phrases; sentence structure. **2** the patterns of such arrangement in a given language. **3** the use or function of a word, phrase, or clause in a sentence. **4** *Computer technology.* the structure of a computer language and its rules. ⟨< LL < Gk. *syntaxis*, ult. < *syn-* together + *tassein* arrange⟩

syn•the•ses ['sɪnθə,siz] *n.* pl. of SYNTHESIS.

syn•the•sis ['sɪnθəsɪs] *n., pl.* **-ses** [-,siz]. **1** a combination of parts or elements into a whole. Compare ANALYSIS. **2** the combination produced in this way. **3** *Chemistry.* the formation of a compound by the chemical union of chemical elements, combination of simpler compounds, etc. Alcohol, ammonia, rubber, etc. can be artificially produced by synthesis.
3 *Philosophy and logic.* **a** the combination or unification of particular phenomena, observed or hypothesized, into a general body or abstract whole. **b** as used by the German philosopher Immanuel Kant (1724-1804), the action of the understanding in combining and unifying separate concepts or the isolated data of sensation into a cognizable whole. **c** deductive reasoning.
d the third and highest stage in the Hegelian dialectic, the combination of thesis and antithesis for a new, higher truth. ⟨< L < Gk. *synthesis* < *syn-* together + *tithenai* put⟩

syn•the•size ['sɪnθə,saɪz] *v.* **-sized, -siz•ing. 1** combine into a complex whole by synthesis. **2** *Chemistry.* form or produce by synthesis: *to synthesize rubber.* **—,syn•the•si'za•tion,** *n.*

syn•the•siz•er ['sɪnθə,saɪzər] *n.* **1** a person who or thing that synthesizes. **2** an electronic device that simulates and blends conventional and ultrasonic musical sounds.

syn•thet•ic [sɪn'θɛtɪk] *adj., n.* *—adj.* **1** having to do with synthesis: *synthetic chemistry.* **2** made by chemical synthesis: *synthetic rubies, synthetic silk.* **3** *Linguistics.* designating a language characterized by the use of affixes and inflectional endings rather than by the use of separate words, such as auxiliary verbs and prepositions, to express the same concepts. Latin is a synthetic language, while English is analytic. For example, the Latin *amabitur* expresses in one word the English sentence *He will be loved.* **4** not real or genuine; artificial: *synthetic affection.* **5** *Logic.* true by virtue of direct observation or established fact.
—n. a substance or material made by chemical synthesis. Synthetics are very common for clothing, etc. because they are easy to care for.
☛ *Syn. adj.* **2.** See note at ARTIFICIAL.

syn•thet•i•cal [sɪn'θɛtəkəl] *adj.* synthetic. **—syn'thet•i•cal•ly,** *adv.*

synthetic rubber any of numerous elastic substances resembling natural rubber, made from various chemicals, such as butadiene and styrene (for general-purpose synthetic rubber); ethylene, propylene, etc. (for polyurethane rubber); or oxygen and silicon (for silicone rubber).

syph•i•lis ['sɪfəlɪs] *n. Pathology.* a contagious venereal disease caused by a spirochete (*Trepenema pallidum*), characterized by a long progress in three main stages over many years and finally, if untreated, causing bones, muscles, and nerve tissue to degenerate. Syphilis is usually transmitted through sexual intercourse. It is not hereditary, but can be transmitted inside the uterus from mother to child. ⟨< NL *syphilis* < *Syphilus*, the hero of a Latin poem describing the disease, written in 1530 by Fracastoro, a physician and poet of Verona, Italy⟩

syph•i•lit•ic [,sɪfə'lɪtɪk] *adj., n.* *—adj.* **1** having to do with syphilis. **2** affected with syphilis.
—n. a person affected with syphilis.

sy•phon ['səifən] *n., v.* See SIPHON.

Syr•ia ['siriə] *n.* a republic in the NW part of the eastern end of the Mediterranean. See LEBANON for map.

Syr•i•ac ['siriæk] *n.* a dialect of Aramaic spoken in ancient Syria and surviving as a liturgical language used in a number of Eastern churches.

Syr•i•an ['siriən] *n., adj.* *—n.* **1** a native or inhabitant of Syria. **2** a native or inhabitant of ancient Syria, a region between the E Mediterranean coast and the desert of N Arabia.
—adj. of or having to do with modern or ancient Syria or its people.

sy•rin•ga [sə'rɪŋgə] *n.* **1** MOCK ORANGE. **2** LILAC (def. 1). ⟨< NL *syringa* < Gk. *syrinx*, *-ingos* shepherd's pipe⟩

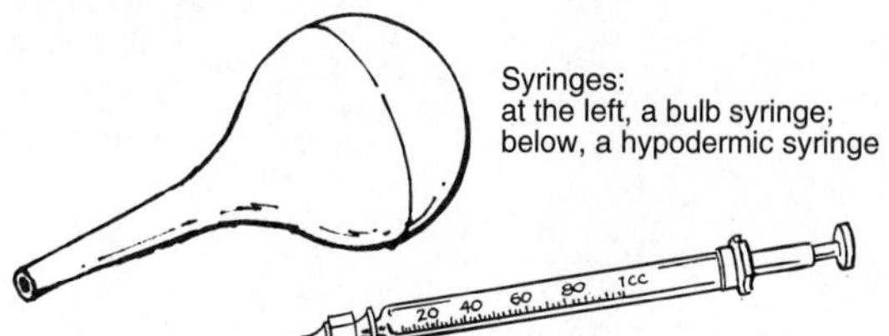

Syringes: at the left, a bulb syringe; below, a hypodermic syringe

sy•ringe [sə'rɪndʒ] *n., v.* **-ringed, -ring•ing.** *—n.* **1** a device consisting of a narrow tube with a nozzle at one end and a compressible rubber bulb at the other, for drawing in a quantity of fluid and then forcing it out in a stream. Syringes are used to clean wounds, inject fluids into body cavities, etc. **2** a similar device consisting of a hollow needle attached to a hollow barrel with a plunger, used for injecting medicine under the skin, withdrawing body fluids, etc; hypodermic syringe.
—v. clean, wash, inject, etc. by means of a syringe. ⟨< Gk. *syrinx*, *-ingos* pipe⟩

syr•inx ['sirɪŋks] *n., pl.* **sy•rin•ges** [sə'rɪndʒiz] or **syr•inx•es. 1** the vocal organ of birds, situated where the trachea divides into the right and left bronchi. **2** a panpipe. ⟨< L < Gk. *syrinx* shepherd's pipe⟩

syr•up ['sirəp] *or* ['sɜrəp] *n.* **1** a thick solution of sugar and water, usually combined with flavouring or medicine: *cough syrup.* **2** the condensed juice of a plant or fruit; especially, sugar cane juice that remains uncrystallized in the refining of sugar, or the juice condensed from the sap of the sugar maple. **3** *Informal.* excessive sweetness of style or manner. ⟨ME < OF *sirop* < Arabic *sharāb* drink⟩ **—'syr•up,like,** *adj.*

syr•up•y ['sirəpi] *or* ['sɜrəpi] *adj.* **1** of, like, or suggesting syrup in consistency or sweetness. **2** excessively sweet in style or manner; cloying.

sys•op ['sɪs,ɒp] *n. Computer technology. Informal.* SYSTEMS OPERATOR. ⟨< *sys*(*tems*) *op*(*erator*)⟩

sys•tem ['sɪstəm] *n.* **1** a set of things or parts forming a whole: *a mountain system, a railway system, a computer system.* **2** an ordered group of facts, principles, beliefs, practices, etc.: *a system of government, a system of education.* **3** *Astronomy.* **a** a theory or hypothesis of the relationship of the heavenly bodies by which their observed movements and phenomena are explained: *the Copernican system.* **b** a group of heavenly bodies forming a whole that follows certain natural laws. **4** a plan; scheme; method: *a system for betting.* **5** orderliness in getting things done. **6** *Biology.* **a** a set of organs or parts in an animal body of the same or similar structure, or subserving the same function: *the nervous system, the respiratory system.* **b** the animal body as an organized whole; the organism in terms of its vital processes or functions: *to take food into the system.* **7** the world; universe. **8** *Geology.* a major division of rocks including two or more series, formed during a geological period. **9** *Chemistry.* **a** an assemblage of substances which are in, or tend to approach, equilibrium. **b** a substance, or an assemblage of substances, considered as a separate entity for the purpose of restricted study. **10** *Music.* a set of staves linked by a brace. ⟨< LL < Gk. *systēma* < *syn-* together + *stēsai* cause to stand⟩ **—'sys•tem•less,** *adj.*

sys•tem•at•ic [ˌsɪstə'mætɪk] *adj.* **1** based on, involving, or forming a system: *a systematic investigation, a systematic classification.* **2** orderly and methodical: *She is a systematic worker.* **3** taxonomic. **—ˌsys•tem'at•i•cal•ly,** *adv.*

☛ *Syn.* **2.** See note at ORDERLY.

sys•tem•at•i•cal [ˌsɪstə'mætɪkəl] *adj.* systematic.

sys•tem•at•ics [ˌsɪstə'mætɪks] *n.* (*used with a singular verb*) taxonomy.

sys•tem•a•tize ['sɪstəməˌtaɪz] *v.* **-tized, -tiz•ing.** arrange according to a system; make into a system: *to systematize one's methods.* **—ˌsys•tem•a•ti'za•tion,** *n.* **—'sys•tem•aˌtiz•er,** *n.*

system board *Computer technology.* motherboard.

sys•tem•ic [sɪ'stɛmɪk] *adj., n.* *—adj.* **1** *Physiology. Pathology.* **a** of, having to do with, or affecting the body as a whole. **b** of or having to do with the general blood circulation, except for that supplied to the lungs through the pulmonary artery. **2** of an insecticide, fungicide, etc., entering the tissues of a plant and making the plant itself poisonous to pests. **3** of or having to do with a system: *The causes of poverty in our society are largely systemic.*
—n. a systemic pesticide.

sys•tem•ize ['sɪstəˌmaɪz] *v.* **-ized, -iz•ing.** systematize. **—ˌsys•tem•i'za•tion,** *n.*

systems analysis the process or profession of using various techniques to break down a system into its basic elements in order to understand the system and discover ways to improve it. Systems analysis is used for business organizations, information systems, etc.

systems analyst a person whose work is systems analysis.

systems operator a person in charge of an information or computer system.

sys•to•le ['sɪstəˌli] *or* ['sɪstəli] *n. Physiology.* the normal rhythmical contraction of the heart. Compare DIASTOLE. ⟨< NL < Gk. *systolē* contraction < *syn-* together + *stellein* wrap⟩ **—sys'tol•ic** [sɪ'stɒlɪk], *adj.*

systolic pressure the blood pressured when the heart is fully contracted. It is higher than DIATOLIC PRESSURE.

syz•y•gy ['sɪzədʒi] *n., pl.* **-gies.** *Astronomy.* either of the two points (opposition or conjunction) in the orbit of the moon or a planet when it lies approximately in a straight line with the earth and the sun. ⟨< LL *syzygia* < Gk. < *syzygos* yoked, paired < *syn-* together + *zygon* yoke⟩

Sze•chu•an ['sɛtʃwɒn] *or* ['sɛtʃuɒn] *adj.* of or having to do with a hot, spicy type of food from southern China. ⟨< *Szechuan,* a province in SW China⟩

Tt *Tt*

t or **T** [ti] *n., pl.* **t's** or **T's. 1** the twentieth letter of the English alphabet. **2** any speech sound represented by this letter. **3** a person or thing identified as *t*, especially the twentieth in a series. **4** something shaped like the letter T. **5** (*adj.*) of or being a T or t. **6** any device, such as a printer's type, a lever, or a key on a keyboard, that produces a t or T.
to a T, exactly; perfectly: *That suits me to a T.*
☛*Hom.* TE, TEA, TEE, TI.

t 1 tonne(s). **2** temperature (common, or Celsius). **3** time.

t. 1 teaspoon(s). **2** *Grammar.* tense. **3** *Grammar.* transitive. **4** ton(s). **5** territory. **6** tenor. **7** in the time of (for L *tempore*). **8** town. **9** township. **10** telephone. **11** terminal. **12** troy weight.

't a contracted form of *it* used before or after a verb. *Examples*: *'twas, make't.*

T 1 tritium. **2** temperature (thermodynamic). **3** torque. **4** period (one cycle of time). **5** tesla.

T. 1 territory. **2** Tuesday. **3** Testament. **4** tablespoon(s).

Ta tantalum.

TA or **T.A. 1** teaching assistant. **2** tutorial assistant.

tab [tæb] *n., v.* **tabbed, tab•bing.** *—n.* **1** a small flap, strap, loop, or projecting piece: *He wore a fur cap with tabs over the ears.* **2** a small projection or attached piece on a card or folder used as a filing aid. Tabs may be labelled, numbered, colour-coded, etc. **3** *Informal.* a bill or check; a statement of costs: *to pay the tab.* **4** *Informal.* TABULATOR (def. 2).
keep tabs, tab, or **a tab on,** *Informal.* keep track of; keep watch on: *She was asked to keep tabs on his little brother.*
pick up the tab, *Informal.* pay; assume the expense or bear the cost of anything.
—v. **1** put a tab on (something): *to tab index cards.* **2** name or mark; identify: *She was very quickly tabbed as a show-off.* ⟨origin uncertain⟩

ta•bac [ta'bak] *Cdn. French.* a strong, dark, homegrown tobacco formerly smoked by many French Canadians.

tab•a•nid ['tæbə,nɪd] *n.* any of the members of the family Tabanidae of bloodsucking flies, including the horseflies and deer flies. ⟨< L *tabanus* horsefly⟩

tab•ard ['tæbərd] *n.* **1** a short, loose coat worn by a herald, emblazoned with his sovereign's coat of arms. **2** a short surcoat or tunic worn over armour by a knight, having short sleeves and open sides, and emblazoned with the knight's coat of arms. **3** a coarse, loose outer garment formerly worn out of doors by the lower classes and also by monks and foot soldiers. **4** a similar modern garment, sleeveless or short-sleeved and often open at the sides. ⟨ME < OF *tabart*⟩

Ta•bas•co [tə'bæskou] *n. Trademark.* a peppery sauce, used on fish, meat, etc. and prepared from the fruit of a hot red pepper. ⟨< *Tabasco*, a state in Mexico⟩

tab•bou•leh [tə'buli] *or* [tə'bulə] *n.* a Middle Eastern dish consisting of bulgur wheat with very finely chopped parsley, tomatoes, mint and other herbs, with a dressing of olive oil and lemon juice. Also, **tabouli, tabuli.** ⟨< Arabic *tabbula*⟩

tab•by ['tæbi] *n., pl.* **-bies;** *adj.* *—n.* **1** a domestic cat having a grey or brownish coat with dark stripes. **2** any cat, especially a female. **3** silk taffeta with a watered or moiré finish.
—adj. **1** brown or grey with dark stripes. **2** made of or like silk taffeta with a watered or moiré finish. ⟨< F < Arabic *'attābiy* (def. 3), from a section of Baghdad where such cloth was first made⟩

tab•er•nac•le ['tæbər,nækəl] *n., v.* **-nac•led, -nac•ling.** **1 Tabernacle,** the covered wooden framework carried by the Israelites for use as a place of worship during their journey from Egypt to Palestine. **2** a Jewish temple. **3** a building used as a place of worship for a large group of people. **4** the human body thought of as the temporary dwelling of the soul. **5** *Archaic.* a temporary dwelling; tent. **6** a tomb, shrine, etc. with a canopy. **7** a small chest or cupboard in a church, often built into the altar, for keeping consecrated bread and wine.
—v. put or dwell in or as in a tabernacle. ⟨< L *tabernaculum* tent < *taberna* cabin⟩ **—,tab•er'nac•u•lar** [-'nækjələr], *adj.*

ta•bes ['teibiz] *n. Medicine.* atrophy caused by any disease, or the disease causing it. ⟨< L, a wasting away < *tabere* waste away⟩ **—ta'bes•cent** [tə'bɛsənt], *adj.* **—ta'bet•ic** [tə'bɛtɪk], *adj.*

tab key the key on a keyboard that activates the tabulator.

tab•la ['tʌblə] *n.* a musical instrument consisting of a pair of small, tuned hand drums. ⟨< Hind. or Urdu < Arabic *ṭabla* drum⟩

tab•la•ture ['tæblətʃər] *n.* a system of notation for guitar chords, with vertical lines representing the strings, horizontal lines representing the frets, and dots on the lines showing where the fingers should depress the strings. ⟨< F < L *tabulatus* tablet⟩

ta•ble ['teibəl] *n., v.* **-bled, -bling.** *—n.* **1** a piece of furniture or equipment having a smooth, flat top on legs. **2** the food put on a table to be eaten: *Mrs. Brown sets a good table.* **3** (*adj.*) for using or putting on a table: *table mats, a table lamp.* **4** (*adj.*) for serving at the table, as opposed to using in a recipe or for some industrial purpose: *table wine, table salt.* **5** the persons seated at a table. **6** a flat land surface; plateau. **7** *Architecture.* **a** a flat, vertical, usually rectangular surface forming a distinct feature in a wall. **b** a horizontal moulding, especially a cornice. **8** the flat surface of a jewel. **9** very condensed tabulated information; a list: *The table of contents is in the front of the book.* **10** a thin, flat piece of wood, stone, metal, etc.; a tablet: *The Ten Commandments were written on tables of stone.* **11** matter inscribed or written on tables.
at table, at a meal.
on the table, of a bill, motion, etc.: **a** before a committee, legislative body, etc. for discussion. **b** *U.S.* put off or shelved.
set or **lay the table,** arrange cutlery, dishes, etc. on the table for a meal.
turn the tables, reverse conditions or circumstances completely: *The enemy troops had advanced, but our sudden attack turned the tables on them.*
under the table, a secretly; covertly. **b** drunk and insensible.
—v. **1** put on a table. **2** make a list or condensed statement of; tabulate. **3** present (a motion, report, etc.) for consideration. **4** *Esp. U.S.* put off discussion of (a bill, motion, etc.); shelve. ⟨ME < OF < L *tabula* plank, tablet⟩

tab•leau [tæ'blou] *or* ['tæblou] *n., pl.* **-leaux** or **-leaus. 1** a striking scene; picture. **2** a representation of a picture, statue, scene, etc. by a person or group posing silently and motionlessly in appropriate costume. Also, **tableau vivant.** ⟨< F *tableau* picture, dim. of *table* table⟩

tableau vi•vant [vi'vɑ̃] TABLEAU (def. 2).

tab•leaux [tæ'blouz] *or* ['tæblouz] *n.* pl. of TABLEAU.

ta•ble•cloth ['teibəl,klɒθ] *n.* a cloth for covering a table.

ta•ble d'hôte ['tɑbəl 'dout] *or* ['tæbəl 'dout]; *French,* [tabl'dot] *pl.* **ta•bles d'hôte** ['tɑbəlz-] *or* ['tæbəlz-]; *French* [tabl-]. **1** in a restaurant, hotel, etc., a complete meal with specified courses, offered at a fixed price and, often, served at a set time. **2** (*adj.*) designating such a meal. Compare À LA CARTE. ⟨< F *table d'hôte*, literally, host's table⟩

ta•ble–hop•ping ['teibəl ,hɒpɪŋ] *n.* going from table to table in a club, restaurant, etc., in order to visit with friends. **—'table-,hop,** *v.*

table knife a knife, usually having a rounded tip, designed for use at the table, for cutting food on one's plate, etc.

ta•ble•land ['teibəl,lænd] *n.* a plateau that rises sharply from a lowland area or the sea.

table linen tablecloths, napkins, etc.

table salt refined salt, such as that used to season food at the table.

ta•ble•spoon ['teibəl,spun] *n.* **1** a spoon larger than a teaspoon or dessertspoon, used to serve vegetables, etc. **2** a standard unit of measurement in cookery, equal to three teaspoons, or about 15 mL. *Abbrev.*: T., tbs., or tbsp. **3** tablespoonful: *The recipe calls for a tablespoon of sugar.*

ta•ble•spoon•ful ['teibəl,spunfʊl] *n., pl.* **-fuls.** the amount that a tablespoon can hold.

tab•let ['tæblɪt] *n.* **1** a small, thin, flat slab of stone, wood, ivory, etc. used in ancient times to write or draw on, or in modern times for other specific purposes. **2** a number of sheets of writing paper fastened together at one edge; a pad of paper. **3** a small, flat surface with an inscription. **4** a small, flat piece of medicine, candy, etc.: *vitamin tablets.* ⟨< F *tablette* < *table* table⟩

table talk *Informal.* conversation at or as at meals.

table tennis an indoor game resembling tennis, played on a table with small wooden paddles and a very light, hollow, plastic ball. Also called **ping-pong.**

ta•ble•top ['teibəl,tɒp] *n.* **1** the top of a table: *The tabletop was scarred with cigarette burns.* **2** *(adjl.)* of a machine, instrument, or apparatus, designed to be used on a table; not having its own stand or support: *a tabletop loom.*

ta•ble•ware ['teibəl,wɛr] *n.* the dishes, cutlery, glassware, etc. used at meals.

table wine an ordinary red or white still wine for drinking with meals, usually containing between 9 and 15 percent alcohol.

tab•loid ['tæblɔɪd] *n.* **1** a newspaper, usually having a page that is half the ordinary size and that presents the news through pictures and short articles. **2** a newspaper of this size that exploits sensationalism by means of lurid headlines and heavy use of photographs, and whose sources are sometimes questionable. **3** *(adjl.)* condensed. ⟨< *tablet* + *-oid*⟩

ta•boo [tə'bu] *adj., v.* **-booed, -boo•ing;** *n., pl.* **-boos.** *—adj.* **1** forbidden by custom or tradition; banned: *Eating human flesh is taboo in most cultures.* **2** set apart as sacred, unclean, or cursed, and forbidden to general use. **3** of people, restricted by taboo.
—v. forbid; prohibit; ban.
—n. **1** a prohibition; ban. **2 a** the system or act of setting things apart as sacred, unclean, or cursed. **b** the fact or condition of being so placed. **c** the prohibition or interdict itself. Also, **tabu.** ⟨< Tongan (lang. of the Tonga Islands in the S Pacific) *tabu*⟩
☛ *Spelling.* **Taboo, tabu. Taboo** is more generally used than **tabu,** except in anthropology.

ta•bor ['teibər] *n.* a small drum, used especially in the Middle Ages to accompany a pipe or fife played by the same person. ⟨ME < OF *tabur,* of Oriental origin; cf. Persian *tabīrah* drum⟩

tab•o•ret or **tab•ou•ret** ['tæbə,rɛt] *or* [,tæbə'rɛt] *n.* **1** a stool. **2** a frame for embroidery. **3** a small, low stand or table. **4** *Archaic.* a small tabor. Also (def. 4), **taborin** or **tabourin.** ⟨< F *tabouret*⟩

ta•bou•li [tə'buli] *n.* See TABBOULEH.

ta•bu [tə'bu] *adj., v.* **-bued, -bu•ing;** *n., pl.* **-bus.** See TABOO.
☛ *Spelling.* See note at TABOO.

tab•u•lar ['tæbjələr] *adj.* **1** of, having to do with, or arranged in tables or lists; especially, written or printed in columns and rows. **2** flat like a table: *a tabular rock.* **3** ascertained or calculated through the use of a table or list. ⟨< L *tabularis* relating to a board or plate < *tabula* plank, tablet⟩
—'tab•u•lar•ly, *adv.*

tab•u•la ra•sa ['tæbjələ 'rɑsə] *or* ['rɑzə] *pl.* **tab•u•lae ra•sae** ['tæbjə,li 'rɑsi] *or* ['tæbjə,laɪ 'rɑsaɪ]. *Latin.* **1** in some philosophical thought, the human mind viewed as blank, as at birth, before any outside impressions are received. **2** a clean slate. ⟨literally, a scraped, or erased, slate⟩

tab•u•late *v.* ['tæbjə,leit]; *adj.* ['tæbjəlɪt] *or* ['tæbjə,leit] *v.* **-lat•ed, -lat•ing;** *adj.* *—v.* arrange (facts, figures, etc.) in tables or lists.
—adj. **1** having a flat surface. **2** of coral, consisting of thin, horizontal plates.

tab•u•la•tion [,tæbjə'leiʃən] *n.* an arrangement in tables or lists.

tab•u•la•tor ['tæbjə,leitər] *n.* **1** a person, machine, piece of software, etc. that tabulates. **2** a device or function key on a typewriter or computer for fixing paragraph and column indentions.

ta•bu•li [tə'buli] *n.* See TABBOULEH.

tac•a•ma•hac ['tækəmə,hæk] *n.* **1** a strong-smelling gum resin used in incenses, ointments, etc. **2** any of several trees yielding this gum, such as the balsam poplar. Also, **tacamahaca** [,tækəmə'hækə]. ⟨< Sp. *tacamahaca* < Nahuatl⟩

ta•cet ['teisɪt] *v. Music.* a command to be silent; a direction to the voice or instrument to be silent for the indicated number of bars. ⟨< L, is silent⟩

tach•isme or **tach•ism** ['tæʃɪzəm]; *French,* [ta'ʃism] *n.* a style of abstract painting based on the dribbling or splashing of paint on canvas to see what form it will take. ⟨< F *tachisme* < *tache* blot + *-isme* -ism⟩

tach•iste or **tach•ist** ['tæʃɪst]; *French,* [ta'ʃist] *adj., n.* *—adj.* using the technique of tachisme.
—n. a painter using this technique.

ta•chis•to•scope [tə'kɪstə,skoup] *n.* a piece of equipment, often used in psychological experiments and tests, that displays words or visual images of various kinds in succession, each for a fraction of a second. ⟨< Gk. *tachistos* (superlative of *tachys* swift) + E *-scope*⟩

ta•chom•e•ter [tə'kɒmətər] *n.* an instrument for measuring speed of rotation, especially that of the crankshaft of a motor vehicle engine. A tachometer measures engine rpm (revolutions per minute). ⟨< Gk. *tachos* speed + E *-meter*⟩ **—ta'chom•e•try,** *n.*

tachy– *combining form.* rapid; speed(y). ⟨< Gk. *tachys* swift⟩

tach•y•car•dia [,tækə'kɑrdiə] *n.* an abnormally or excessively rapid heartbeat. ⟨< Mod.L < Gk. *tachys* swift + *kardia* heart⟩

tach•y•graph ['tækə,græf] *n.* **1** a piece of tachygraphic writing. **2** a person capable of producing tachygraphy.

ta•chyg•ra•phy [tə'kɪgrəfi] *n.* **1** a type of shorthand or speed writing, especially the ancient Greek and Roman writing used for stenography. **2** the art of writing in this shorthand.
—,tach•y'graph•ic [,tækə'græfɪk], *adj.* **—ta'chyg•ra•pher,** *n.*

ta•chym•e•ter [tə'kɪmətər] *n.* a surveying instrument that rapidly measures distances, angles, and elevations.

tach•y•on ['tæki,ɒn] *n. Physics.* a hypothetical elementary particle that moves faster than light. ⟨< *tachy-* + *-on* (< *ion*) suffix for subatomic particle⟩

tac•it ['tæsɪt] *adj.* **1** unspoken; silent: *a tacit prayer.* **2** implied or understood without being openly expressed: *Their eating the food was a tacit confession that they liked it.* **3** *Law.* existing out of custom or from silent consent but not expressly stated. ⟨< L *tacitus,* pp. of *tacere* be silent⟩ **—'tac•it•ly,** *adv.* **—'tac•it•ness,** *n.*

tac•i•turn ['tæsə,tɜrn] *adj.* speaking very little; not fond of talking. ⟨< L *taciturnus* < *tacitus* tacit. See TACIT.⟩
—'tac•i,turn•ly, *adv.*
☛ *Syn.* See note at SILENT.

tac•i•tur•ni•ty [,tæsə'tɜrnəti] *n.* the habit of keeping silent; disinclination to talk much.

tack[1] [tæk] *n., v.* *—n.* **1** any of various types of very short, sharp nail with a flat head, used for fastening upholstery, carpets, etc. in place, pinning paper to a drawing board, notices on a bulletin board, etc. **2** a sewing stitch used as a temporary fastening. **3** stickiness; sticky condition or quality. **4** *Nautical.* **a** a zigzag course against the wind. **b** the movement of a boat or ship in relation to the direction of the wind. When on port tack, a ship has the wind on its left. **c** a zigzag movement; one of the movements in a zigzag course. **d** a rope to hold in place a corner of some sails. **e** the corner to which this is fastened. **5** a course of action or conduct: *To demand what she wanted was the wrong tack to take with her mother.*
—v. **1** fasten with tacks. **2** sew with temporary stitches or by other impermanent means. **3** attach; add, especially as an afterthought: *She tacked the postscript to the end of the letter. The whole paragraph reads as though it were tacked on; let's rewrite it.* **4** *Nautical.* **a** sail (a vessel) in a zigzag course against the wind. **b** change from one tack to another. **5** move along any zigzag route. **6** change one's attitude, conduct, or course of action. **7** use indirect methods. ⟨< dial. OF *taque* nail < Gmc.⟩
—'tack•er, *n.*

tack[2] [tæk] *n. Informal.* food, especially coarse or disagreeable food. ⟨origin unknown⟩

tack[3] [tæk] *n.* **1** equipment for saddle horses, such as bridles and saddles. **2** *(adjl.)* of or for such equipment: *a tack room, a tack box.* ⟨< *tackle*⟩

tack•le ['tækəl] *n., v.* **-led, -ling.** *—n.* **1** equipment; apparatus; gear. Fishing tackle means the rod, line, hooks, etc. **2** a set of ropes and pulleys for lifting, lowering, or moving heavy things. The sails of a ship are raised and moved by tackle. **3** the act of tackling. **4** *Football.* a player between the guard and the end on either side of the line.
—v. **1** try to deal with: *We all have our own problems to tackle.* **2** lay hold of; seize: *Sarah tackled the runner and pulled him to the ground.* **3** *Football.* seize and stop (an opponent having the ball) by bringing to the ground. **4** *Soccer.* obstruct (an opponent) in order to get the ball away from him or her. **5** fasten or attach by means of tackle. ⟨ME < MDu. or MLG *takel*⟩ **—'tack•ler,** *n.*

tack•y[1] ['tæki] *adj.* sticky. ⟨TACK[1] + -y[1]⟩ **—'tack•i•ness,** *n.*

tack•y[2] ['tæki] *adj.* **tack•i•er, tack•i•est.** *Informal.* **1** shabby or shoddy; of poor quality or appearance: *a row of tacky little houses.* **2** cheap and vulgar; in bad taste: *a tacky magazine, a tacky costume.* ⟨origin uncertain; cf. dial. G *tacklig* untidy⟩
—'tack•i•ly, *adv.* **—'tack•i•ness,** *n.*

ta•co ['tɑkou] *n., pl.* **tacos.** a Mexican food consisting of a tortilla folded around a filling of meat, cheese, beans, etc.

tac•o•nite ['tækə,nɔit] *n.* a kind of rock consisting of about 30 percent iron ore. ⟨< *Taconic* Mts. (Massachusetts and Vermont) + *-ite*⟩

tact [tækt] *n.* **1** a keen sense of the right or fitting thing to say or do so as to avoid hurting someone's feelings; sensitivity in dealing with people. **2** a sense of what is aesthetically tasteful or appropriate; discrimination. **3** the sense of touch. ⟨< L *tactus* sense of feeling < *tangere* touch⟩

tact•ful ['tæktfəl] *adj.* **1** having tact. **2** showing tact. **—'tact•ful•ly,** *adv.* **—'tact•ful•ness,** *n.*

tac•tic ['tæktɪk] *n., adj. —n.* a device or procedure for accomplishing a goal.
—adj. having to do with system, pattern, or arrangement. ⟨< NL *tacticus* < Gk. *taktikos* < *tassein.* See TACTICS.⟩

tac•ti•cal ['tæktəkəl] *adj.* **1** of or having to do with tactics; especially, having to do with the disposal of naval, ground, or air forces in action against an enemy. **2** organized for or used in action against enemy troops, rather than against enemy bases, industry, etc., behind the lines of battle: *a tactical bomber.* **3** having or showing cleverness and skill in planning or manoeuvring: *a tactical statesman.* **—'tac•ti•cal•ly,** *adv.*

tac•ti•cian [tæk'tɪʃən] *n.* a person skilled or trained in tactics.

tac•tics ['tæktɪks] *n.pl.* **1** the science and art of managing naval, ground, or air forces in active combat (*used with a singular verb*). **2** the operations themselves: *The generals' tactics were successful.* **3** any procedures or devices to gain advantage or success: *Those are dangerous tactics to use. When his coaxing failed, the little boy changed his tactics and began to cry.* ⟨< NL *tactica* < Gk. *taktikē (technē)* the art of arranging < *tassein* arrange⟩

tac•tile ['tæktaɪl] *or* ['tæktəl] *adj.* **1** of, having to do with, or using the sense of touch: *a tactile impression. The tongue is a tactile organ.* **2** that is or can be perceived by touch; tangible: *Heat and cold are tactile qualities.* ⟨< L *tactilis* < *tangere* touch⟩

tac•til•i•ty [tæk'tɪləti] *n.* the capability of being felt by touch.

tact•less ['tæktlɪs] *adj.* **1** without tact: *a tactless person.* **2** showing no tact: *a tactless reply.* **—'tact•less•ly,** *adv.* **—'tact•less•ness,** *n.*

tac•tu•al ['tæktʃuəl] *adj.* **1** of or having to do with the sense of touch; tactile. **2** arising from the sense of touch; giving sensations of touch. ⟨< L *tactus.* See TACT.⟩ **—'tac•tu•al•ly,** *adv.*

tad [tæd] *n. Informal.* **1** a young boy. **2** a small amount; bit: *Move the picture to the right just a tad.* ⟨origin uncertain; ? < *tadpole*⟩

tad•pole ['tæd,poul] *n.* the aquatic larva of a frog or toad, having a short, round body, gills, and a long tail with a fin along each side. As it matures, the external gills are lost and internal ones develop, the tail resorbs, and legs appear. ⟨ME *tad* toad + *pol* poll (head); apparently 'a toad that is all head'⟩

tae•di•um vi•tae ['tidiəm 'vitaɪ] *Latin.* ennui. ⟨lit., weariness of life⟩

tae kwon do ['taɪ 'kwɒn 'dou] a Korean martial art similar to karate but more aggressive, especially in its use of powerful, leaping kicks.

tael [teil] *n.* **1** any of various units of mass used in E Asia, varying in value from about 30 gm to 70 gm. **2** formerly, a Chinese unit of money equal to the value of silver weighing one tael. ⟨< Pg. < Malay *tahil* mass⟩
☛ *Hom.* TAIL, TALE.

ta'en [tein] *Poetic.* taken.

tae•nia ['tiniə] *n., pl.* **-ni•ae** [-ni,i] *or* [-ni,aɪ]. **1** *Architecture.* on a Doric entablature, the narrow part between the frieze and the architrave. **2** *Anatomy.* any structure or part with a flat, ribbonlike form. **3** *Zoology.* any tapeworm of genus *Taenia*, especially certain ones that are parasitic in humans. **4** in ancient Greece, a headband. ⟨< L < Gk. *tainia* ribbon⟩

taf•fe•ta ['tæfətə] *n.* **1** a stiff cloth of silk, rayon, nylon, etc. in a plain weave having a smooth, glossy surface on both sides. **2** (*adjl.*) similar to or made from taffeta: *a taffeta skirt.* ⟨ME < OF < Persian *taftah* silk or linen < *tāftan* shine⟩

taff•rail ['tæf,reil] *n.* **1** a rail around a ship's stern. **2** the upper part of the stern of a wooden ship. ⟨< Du. *tafereel* panel, dim. of *tafel* table⟩

taf•fy ['tæfi] *n.* **1** a kind of hard but chewy candy made of brown sugar or molasses boiled down, often with butter, and pulled to make it porous. **2** *Cdn.* maple-syrup candy, often made by pouring the syrup over snow so that it hardens in brittle sheets. **3** *Informal.* flattery. Also, **toffee, toffy.** ⟨var. of *toffee*⟩

Taf•fy ['tæfi] *n., pl.* **-fies.** *Slang.* Welshman. ⟨< Welsh pronunciation of *Dafydd* David⟩

taffy apple an apple stuck on a stick and dipped in hot taffy, which forms a thick glaze as it cools.

taffy pull *Cdn.* a social affair at which taffy is made from maple syrup or other syrups, as sugar-molasses.

tag[1] [tæg] *n., v.* **tagged, tag•ging.** *—n.* **1** a piece of card, paper, leather, cloth, etc. to be tied or fastened to something as a label or marker: *Each coat in the store has a tag with the price marked on it.* **2** a small hanging piece; a loosely attached piece; a loose end. **3** a tab or loop by which a coat is hung up or a boot pulled on. **4** a metal or plastic covering for the end of a shoelace. **5** a quotation, moral, etc. added at the end of a speech, story, etc., for ornament or effect. **6** a piece of cardboard, etc., sometimes with a piece of string attached, sold by charitable organizations, etc. to raise money. **7** the last line or lines of a song, play, actor's speech, etc. Also, TAG LINE. **8** *Fishing.* a small piece of bright material, such as tinsel, wrapped around the shank of the hook near the tail of an artificial fly. **9** *Informal.* a nickname. **10** TAG QUESTION (def. 2).
—v. **1** add for ornament or effect. **2** furnish with a tag or tags. **3** mark; label; identify: *to tag suitcases and trunks.* **4** accompany, by or as if by following or trailing behind (*usually used with* **along**): *children tagging along behind the parade. She sneaked out of the house because she didn't want her brother to tag along.* **5** sell tags: *She tagged for the Cancer Society.* **6** give an epithet, sobriquet, or nickname to. **7** end (a speech or story) with a tag. **8 a** put a parking ticket on (a vehicle). **b** charge (someone) with a traffic or parking violation. ⟨ME *tagge* ? < Scand.; cf. Swedish *tagg* bark, tooth, and Norwegian *tagge* tooth⟩

tag[2] [tæg] *n., v.* **tagged, tag•ging.** *—n.* **1** a children's game in which the player who is 'it' chases the others until he or she touches one. The one touched is then 'it' and must chase the others. **2** *Baseball.* the act of touching a base runner with the ball, or of touching a base with the foot or with the ball while holding the ball.
—v. **1** touch or tap with the hand. **2** *Baseball.* put out a base runner with a touch of the ball. ⟨probably an extended meaning or special use of *tag*[1]⟩

Ta•ga•log [tə'gɑləg] *n.* **1** a member of a Malay people living in the Philippines, especially Luzon. **2** the language of this people, the official language of the Philippines. It is related to Indonesian and to Malay.

tag day a day on which TAGS (def. 6) are sold on behalf of a charitable organization, etc.

tag end **1** a loosely hanging or attached bit or end. **2** the last part of something.

tag line **1** a punch line. **2** a slogan or catch phrase. **3** a last line or phrase in a play, speech, etc.

tag•meme ['tægmim] *n. Linguistics.* the smallest unit of grammatical analysis in tagmemics. ⟨< Gk. *tagm(a)* (< base of *tassein*) arrangement + *-eme.* Coined by L. Bloomfield, c.1933⟩

tag•me•mics [tæg'mimɪks] *n. Linguistics.* a theory of language and school of linguistics derived from American structuralism, which regards as the basic grammatical relationship the correlation between a grammatical function and the class of items able to appear in that function.
—tag'me•mic, *adj.*

tag question **1** a question formed by the addition of a short interrogative structure to a statement and usually raising the expectation of agreement or consent as an answer, as *can't you* in *You can do that, can't you?*; *is she* in *She isn't here yet, is she?* It is equivalent to *n'est-ce pas* in French and *nicht wahr* in German. **2** the interrogative phrase itself.

tag sale GARAGE SALE.

ta•hi•ni [tə'hini] *n.* sesame seed paste, much used in Middle Eastern cuisine. ⟨< Arabic < *tahin* flour < *tahana* grind⟩

Ta•hi•ti [tə'hiti] *n.* an island country in the S Pacific.

Ta•hi•ti•an [tə'hiʃən] *or* [tə'hitiən] *n., adj. —n.* **1** a native or inhabitant of Tahiti. **2** the Polynesian language of the Tahitians.
—adj. of or having to do with Tahiti, its people, or their language.

Tahl•tan ['tɑltæn] *n., adj. —n.* **1** a member of a First Nations people of NW British Columbia. **2** the Athapaskan language of this people.
—adj. of or having to do with the Tahltans.

Tahltan (bear) dog an extinct breed of small dog resembling a long-haired fox terrier, used by the Tahltan First Nations people to hunt bear, and for its wool-like hair.

Tai [taɪ] *n.* a group of languages spoken in southwest Asia, considered by some to be a separate language family, and by others to be a sub-branch of the Sino-Tibetan language family; the group includes Tai, Lao, and Shan. Also, **Thai.**

tai chi ['taɪ 'tʃi] *or* ['taɪ 'dʒi] a Chinese martial art also used as a cycle of postures and slow exercise movements said to be an aid to meditation and general well-being. Also, **tai chi chuan, t'ai chi, tai ji.** ⟨< Mandarin *tai ji quan* fist of the Great Ultimate⟩

tai•ga ['taɪgə] *n. Cdn.* BOREAL FOREST. ⟨< Russian⟩

tail¹ [teil] *n., v.* *—n.* **1** rearmost part of an animal's body, especially if it extends from the back in a thin, flexible piece. **2** something like an animal's tail: *the tail of a kite.* **3** the stern of an airplane, especially the stabilizing planes located there. **4** *Astronomy.* the luminous train extending from the head of a comet. **5** the hind part of anything; back; rear: *the tail of a cart.* **6** a part at the end of anything; conclusion: *toward the tail of his letter.* **7** (*adjl.*) at the tail, back, or rear. **8** (*adjl.*) coming from behind: *a strong tail wind.* **9** *Printing.* the bottom margin of a page. **10** *Informal.* a person who follows another to watch and report on his or her movements. **11 tails,** *pl.* **a** the reverse side of a coin. **b** *Informal.* tailcoat. **c** the long, tapering pieces at the back of a tailcoat. **d** formal dress for men. **12** a long braid or tress of hair. **13** retinue; train. **14** the bottom end of a pool, millrace, etc.; tailrace. **15** TAIL END.
at the tail of, following.
on (one's) **tail,** *Informal.* following one, especially very closely.
turn tail, run away from danger, trouble, etc.
with (one's) **tail between** (one's) **legs,** afraid; dejected; humiliated.
—v. **1** furnish with a tail. **2** form a tail. **3 a** remove or cut off a tail or end part from. **b** dock the tail of (a horse, dog, etc.). **4** follow close after; form the tail of. **5** *Slang.* follow closely and secretly, especially in order to watch or to prevent escaping. **6** occur less and less; gradually stop; diminish; subside; die away (*used with* **off** *or* **away**). **7** fall behind; lag; straggle. **8 a** join (one thing) to the end of another; fasten (timber) by an end. **b** of a brick, beam, etc., be secured in a wall at one end. ⟨OE *tægel*⟩
—'tail•less, *adj.* **—'tail-,like,** *adj.*
☛ *Hom.* TALE, TAEL.

tail² [teil] *n., adj. Law.* *—n.* **1** limitation on ownership, especially of an estate, to a person and his or her direct heirs. **2** the order of succession by these heirs.
—adj. limited in such a way (*always follows the noun*).
⟨ME *taile* < OF *taille* a cutting < *taillier* cut⟩

tail•board ['teil,bɔrd] *n.* a board at the back end of a vehicle such as a cart, wagon, or truck, that can be let down or removed when loading or unloading.

tail•bone ['teil,boun] *n.* coccyx.

tail•coat ['teil,kout] *n.* a man's formal coat cut away at the front and extending at the back in two long, tapering pieces, or tails.

tail end **1** the rear or bottom end: *the tail end of the parade.* **2** the concluding period; the last part: *the tail end of the school year.* **3** *Informal.* the buttocks.

tail•fan ['teil,fæn] *n.* the fan-shaped part at the rear end of a lobster or crayfish, used to propel the animal backward.

tail•gate ['teil,geit] *n., v.* **-gated, -gat•ing;** *adj.* *—n.* **1** a tailboard, especially on a truck or station wagon. **2** the lower gate of a canal lock.
—v. of a driver or a motor vehicle, follow (another vehicle) too closely.
—adj. conducted on or around a lowered tailgate: *a tailgate party, a tailgate picnic.*

tail•ing ['teilɪŋ] *n., v.* *—n.* **1** the part of a projecting stone or brick put in a wall. **2 tailings,** *pl.* leavings; remainders, especially waste matter left over after the mining or milling of ore.
—v. ppr. of TAIL.

tail–light ['teil ,lɔit] *n.* a light, usually red, at the back end of an automobile, wagon, train, etc. Also, **tail-lamp.**

tai•lor ['teilər] *n., v.* *—n.* a person whose business is making or repairing clothes.
—v. **1** make clothes, especially clothes that are cut and shaped to fit the body and that are finely finished. **2** make (clothes) by tailoring. **3** sew (a thing) so as to exactly fit something else, as a cover for a seat cushion, etc. **4** make or adjust to suit a particular need: *The standard house design can be tailored to suit the individual buyer.* **5** render (something) neat and trim: *an affluent suburb full of neatly-tailored lawns.* ⟨ME < AF *taillour,* ult. < L *taliare* cut < L *talea* rod, cutting⟩

tai•lor•bird ['teilər,bɜrd] *n.* any of a small genus (*Orthotomus*) of Old World warblers of tropical Asia that stitch the edges of large leaves together with plant fibres to form a support and camouflage for their nests.

tai•lored ['teilərd] *adj., v.* *—adj.* **1** made by a tailor. **2** having simple, shaped, and fitted lines; not loose, draped, frilly, etc.: *a tailored shirt or suit, a tailored bedspread.* Compare DRESSMAKER (*adj.*) **3** very trim and neat.
—v. pt. and pp. of TAILOR.

tai•lor•ing ['teilərɪŋ] *n., v.* *—n.* **1** the business or work of a tailor. **2** the workmanship or skill of a tailor: *expert tailoring.*
—v. ppr. of TAILOR.

tai•lor–made ['teilər 'meid] *adj., n.* *—adj.* **1** made by a tailor or as if by a tailor: *His suit was tailor-made.* **2** of women's clothes, simple, trim, and well-fitting; tailored. **3** made especially to suit a particular person, object, or purpose: *a tailor-made course of study.* **4** *Slang.* of cigarettes, factory-made rather than rolled by hand.
—n. Slang. a cigarette made in a factory rather than rolled by hand.

tailor's chalk a usually thin, flat piece of hard chalk or soapstone, used in sewing for making temporary guide marks on cloth.

tail•piece ['teil,pis] *n.* **1** a piece forming the end or added at the end. **2** *Printing.* a small decorative engraving placed at the end of a chapter, etc. **3** in a violin, etc., a triangular piece of ebony or other wood to which the lower ends of strings are fastened. **4** a short beam or rafter inserted in a wall and supported by a header.

tail•pipe **1** a pipe leading from the muffler to the rear of a motor vehicle, through which exhaust gases are discharged. **2** a corresponding pipe through which a jet engine is exhausted. See JET ENGINE for picture. Also, **tail pipe.**

tail•race ['teil,reis] *n.* **1** the part of a millrace below the wheel. **2** a channel for floating away refuse and residue from a mine.

tail•spin ['teil,spɪn] *n.* **1** a downward spin of an aircraft with the nose pointed down. **2** a state of panic or confusion: *The news threw the whole household into a tailspin.*

tail wind a wind blowing in the direction of the course of an aircraft, ship, etc.; a wind coming from behind: *We made very good time because we had a tail wind all the way.*

taint [teint] *n., v.* *—n.* **1** a spot or trace of infection, decay, or corruption. **2** a moral blemish; a trace of discredit or dishonour: *a taint of vice. There was no taint of self-interest in his transactions.*
—v. **1** give a taint to; infect, spoil, or contaminate: *tainted meat. Her reputation had been tainted by a questionable business deal.* **2** become tainted; become infected, spoiled, or corrupted: *Meat taints quickly if not kept cold.* ⟨ME; partly var. of *attaint,* partly < OF *teint,* pp. of *teindre* dye < L *tingere*⟩

tai•pan¹ [taɪ'pæn] *n.* in China, the owner and administrator of a foreign firm. ⟨< Chinese⟩

tai•pan² [taɪ'pæn] *n.* a large poisonous Australian snake of the cobra family, *Oxyuranus scutellatus.* ⟨< an aboriginal language of Australia⟩

Tai•wan [taɪ'wɑn] *n.* an island republic to the southeast of mainland China, properly called the Republic of China.

Tai•wan•ese [,taɪwɑ'niz] *n., adj.* *—n.* **1** a native or inhabitant of Taiwan. **2** the Chinese language of Taiwan.
—adj. of or pertaining to Taiwan.

Ta•jik ['tɑdʒɪk] *or* [tɑ'dʒɪk] *n.* **1** a member of an ethnic group living mainly in Tajikistan, but also in Afghanistan, Uzbekistan, and China. **2** Also, **Tajiki** [tɑ'dʒiki] *or* ['tɑdʒiki], the Indo-Iranian language of the Tajiks, related to Persian but frequently written in the Cyrillic alphabet.

Ta•ji•ki•stan [tæ'dʒikə,stæn] *n.* a country in central Asia.

ta•ka ['tɑkɑ] *n., pl.* **ta•ka.** the basic unit of money in Bangladesh. See table of money in the Appendix.

take [teik] *v.* **took, tak•en, tak•ing;** *n.* *—v.* **1** lay hold of; grasp: *He took her by the hand.* **2 a** seize; catch; capture: *to take a wild animal in a trap.* **b** come upon suddenly: *to be taken by surprise.* **c** apprehend (someone who is doing or has done something wrong): *He was taken by police at the scene of the crime.* **3** conquer: *The British took Québec in 1759.* **4** have the proper effect; catch hold; lay hold: *The fire has taken. The vaccination took.* **5** accept: *Take my advice. The man won't take a cent less for the car. The priest takes confessions at 10 a.m.* **6** get; receive; assume the ownership or possession of: *She took the gifts and opened them.* **7** derive (something) from a source: *The village takes its name from the river flowing through it.* **8** steal: *What did the thieves take?* **9 a** win: *He took first prize.* **b** receive (something bestowed, conferred, administered, etc.): *to take a degree in science, to take a vow.* **10** receive in an indicated manner; react to someone or something: *to take it all in good fun. Take it seriously.* **11** receive into the body; swallow; inhale; drink: *to take* *food, to take snuff.* **12** absorb: *Wool takes a dye well.* **13** stick to a surface; stick; adhere: *This ink doesn't take on glossy paper.* **14** have capacity for; admit: *The elevator only takes 10 people. The scale will take up to 100 kg.* **15** get; have: *to take a seat, to take comfort, to take shelter.* **16** use; make use of: *to take medicine, to take therapy.* **17 a** indulge in: *to take a rest, to take a vacation.* **b** expose oneself to for beneficial effect: *take the air.* **18** of fish, seize (the bait); bite. **19 a** submit to; put up with; go through: *to take hard punishment.* **b** tolerate; withstand: *I can only take so much pressure.* **20** study: *to take physiology.* **21** need; require: *It takes time and patience to learn how to drive an automobile.* **22** choose; select: *I'd take the green over the blue.* **23** remove: *Please take the waste basket away and empty it.* **24** remove by death or killing: *Pneumonia took him. She took her own life.* **25** remove something; detract: *Her paleness takes from her beauty.* **26** subtract: *If you take 2 from 7, you have 5.* **27** lead: *Where will this road take me?* **28** travel by means of: *to take the train, to take a scenic route.* **29** go with; escort: *Take her home.* **30** carry: *Take your lunch along.* **31** obtain by some special method: *to take a sighting, to take aim, to take a person's temperature. They took his fingerprints. Please take my photograph.* **32** deliver or perform (a given act) with a specified target: *to take a swipe at someone.* **33** form and hold in mind; feel: *to take a certain view. Josée takes pride in her schoolwork.* **34** make; do; put forth: *to take a stand, to take a decision.* **35** use up; occupy (time): *This could take all morning.* **36** of ice, to form or become thick enough to support people. **37 a** understand: *I take the meaning.* **b** understand in a given way; interpret: *How did you take his remark?* **38** suppose: *He took her to be a tourist.* **39** regard; consider: *Let us take an example.* **40** assume: *She took responsibility for the household.* **41** take charge of; lead; conduct: *Ms. Loewen took our class today. The rector has a funeral to take this afternoon.* **42** engage; hire; lease: *to take a house.* **43** write down; record: *to take dictation, to take a message on the phone.* **44** receive and pay for regularly: *to take a newspaper.* **45 a** photograph: *to take a scene of a movie. I'll take the two of you standing in front of the fountain.* **b** be photographed: *She takes poorly from the left side.* **46** execute (a song, scene of a play, etc.) in rehearsal: *Let's take it from the top. Take it again from the second verse.* **47** become affected by: *to take a cold.* **48** *Grammar.* be used with: *A plural noun takes a plural verb.* **49** please; attract; charm: *The song took our fancy.* **50** win favour: *Do you think the new play will take?* **51** go; resort; retire: *The deer took to the woods. She took to her bed.* **52** become: *He took sick.* **53** of something planted, begin to grow; strike root: *The petunias seem to have taken quite well.* **54** attempt to get over, through, around, etc.: *My horse took the fence easily. Don't take the corners so fast!* **55** *Informal.* **a** hit; strike: *The puck took him right in the thigh.* **b** be hit or struck by: *She took a stone in her left eye.* **56** *Baseball.* of a batter, let (a pitched ball) pass without swinging at it. **57** *Cricket.* **a** catch and put out. **b** capture (a wicket), especially by striking it with the ball. **58** apply: *I'm going to take the scissors to that thatch of hair one of these days.* **59** *Slang.* copulate with (a woman). **60** *Slang.* swindle; cheat.

take aback. See ABACK.

take after, a be like; resemble: *Kazimira takes after her mother.* **b** chase in order to try to seize or capture: *The dog took after the rabbit.* **c** follow the example of.

take against, take sides against; oppose.

take amiss, a misinterpret. **b** be offended at.

take back, a withdraw; retract. **b** remind of the past: *The letter took me back ten years.* **c** regain possession of.

take down, a write down (something said by another). **b** lower the price of. **c** lower. **d** take apart. **e** knock down. **f** abase; humiliate.

take five (or **ten**, etc.), take a break for the number of minutes indicated.

take for, suppose (especially erroneously) to be.

take in, a receive; admit: *to take in boarders.* **b** make smaller or narrower. **c** register mentally. **d** deceive; trick; cheat: *I was taken in by the strange boy's friendly manner; in fact, he wasn't friendly at all.* **e** include; comprise: *The Golden Horseshoe takes in all of Metro Toronto, Hamilton, and other cities around the western end of Lake Ontario.* **f** visit; attend: *to take in the sights, to take in a movie.*

take it, assume: *Do I take it you'll come?*

take it on the chin, *Informal.* undergo verbal or physical assault; suffer a series of misfortunes: *He's really been taking it on the chin lately—first he lost his job and then his wife died.*

take it or leave it, accept or reject it without modification.

take it out of, a *Informal.* exhaust; fatigue. **b** take something from (a person) in compensation; exact satisfaction from.

take (it) out on, *Informal.* relieve (one's anger or annoyance) by scolding or hurting (someone).

take it upon (oneself), assume the responsibility (to do): *They took it upon themselves to pay the debt.*

take kindly to, look favourably upon; be friendly toward.

take lying down, *Informal.* endure without a protest.

taken with, a affected or attacked by: *taken with a bad case of the flu.* **b** favourably impressed by: *I was quite taken with the new décor.*

take off, a leave the ground or water: *Three airplanes took off at the same time.* **b** *Informal.* give an amusing imitation of; mimic (*used with* **on**). **c** *Informal.* leave; rush away: *He took off at the first sign of trouble.* **d** remove (clothing). **e** *Informal.* start: *The week's celebrations take off on Friday night.* **f** spend (time) away from work, school, etc.: *She took a day off.* **g** subtract; deduct: *We'll take 20 percent off.* **h** be highly successful or well-received: *His new album has really taken off in the States.*

take on, a engage; hire. **b** undertake to deal with: *to take on an opponent.* **c** *Informal.* show great excitement, grief, etc. **d** acquire: *to take on the appearance of health.*

take (one's) **time,** not hurry.

take out, a remove; get rid of. **b** borrow (a book, etc.) from a library or similar collection. **c** apply for and obtain (a licence, patent, etc.). **d** escort; go on a date with. **e** destroy: *The bomb took out two munitions factories.*

take over, a take the ownership or control of. **b** adapt.

take (someone) **up on** (something), accept: *She took him up on his invitation to a champagne supper.*

take to, a form a liking for; become fond of: *She has really taken to skiing. They took to each other right away.* **b** develop a habit of: *She's taken to throwing a temper tantrum whenever she doesn't get her way.*

take to (one's) **heels,** run away; escape.

take up, a soak up; absorb: *A sponge takes up liquid.* **b** make smaller or shorter. **c** begin to do, play, study, etc.; undertake: *He took up piano lessons in the summer.* **d** pay off (a debt). **e** lift; pick up. **f** establish a homestead; settle on (land): *He took up land in Alberta.* **g** collect; gather together. **h** adopt (an idea, purpose, etc.); accept (a challenge). **i** secure the loose end of (a stitch). **j** reprove; rebuke: *to take someone up short.* **k** fill; occupy: *The description took up a whole page.*

take up the slack, a absorb the free play in any mechanical system, pull in the loose part of a rope, etc. **b** fill the gap, take over the workload, take care of the backlog, etc. left by someone.

take up with, *Informal.* begin to associate or be friendly with.

well taken, of a point, argument, etc. in a discussion, worth considering; astute; relevant.

–n. **1** the amount or number taken: *a great take of fish.* **2** the act of taking. **3** that which is taken. **4** *Slang.* receipts; profits: *the box-office take.* **5** the act of transplanting or grafting. **6** in films: **a** a scene or sequence photographed at one time. **b** the act or process of making a photograph or scene in a film. **7 a** the act or process of making a recording for a record, tape, etc. **b** the recording made. **c** a section of a performance recorded at one time. **8** anything that takes hold successfully or turns out right: *The tomato plants are all takes. Was your vaccination a take?*

on the take, *Slang.* taking or seeking bribes. ⟨OE < ON *taka*⟩ **–'tak•er,** *n.*

take–charge ['teik 'tʃɑrdʒ] *adj. Informal.* forceful; assertive; seemingly or actually ready and able to assume authority.

take–home pay ['teik ˌhoum] the balance remaining after taxes, insurance payments, etc. have been deducted from one's wages or salary.

tak•en ['teikən] *v.* pp. of TAKE.

take•off ['teikˌɒf] *n.* **1** *Informal.* a mocking but generally good-humoured imitation: *The highlight of the evening was his clever takeoff on the prime minister.* **2** the act of leaving the ground or other surface, as in jumping or flying: *The plane was on the runway and ready for takeoff.* **3** the place or point at which a person or thing leaves the ground, etc. **4** any starting point or act of starting out. Also, **take-off.**

take•out ['teikˌʌut] *adj., n.* *–adj.* **1** of or designating prepared food packaged in disposable containers and sold by a restaurant, etc. to be eaten away from the premises: *a takeout dinner.* **2** designating a restaurant, etc. that sells such food. **3** *Bridge.* designating a bid that releases a partner from a double or other bid.

–n. **1** *Curling.* a shot that hits an opposing stone so as to remove it from the house. **2** *Bridge.* a bid that releases a partner from a double or other bid. **3** any act of taking out. **4** food prepared in a restaurant to be eaten elsewhere: *Let's just eat takeout tonight.* Also, **take-out.**

take•o•ver ['teikˌouvər] *n.* **a** a taking over; seizure of ownership or control: *a takeover of a country by the army.*

b buy-out: *the takeover of one business enterprise by a larger one.* Also, **take-over**.

take-up ['teik ˌʌp] *n., adj.* —*n.* **1** the action of taking up, as by absorbing, gathering, reeling in, etc. **2** a device for taking in or tightening.
—*adj.* of or having to do with a device that takes in or tightens: *a take-up reel.*

tak•ing ['teikɪŋ] *adj., n., v.* —*adj.* attractive, charming, or winning: *a taking smile.*
—*n.* **1** the act of a person or thing that takes. **2** something that is taken, such as a catch of fish. **3 takings,** *pl.* money taken in; receipts.
—*v.* ppr. of TAKE. —**'tak•ing•ly,** *adv.*

ta•la[1] ['tɑlɑ] *n.* the major unit of currency of Western Samoa, equal to 100 sene. See table of money in the Appendix. ⟨< Samoan⟩

ta•la[2] ['tɑlə] *n.* any of the fixed rhythms in the traditional music of India, played on a drum or other percussion instrument. ⟨< Skt. *tala* slapping or clapping⟩

talc [tælk] *n.* **1** a soft, smooth, white, grey, or greenish mineral with a soapy feel, used in making talcum or face powder, lubricants, etc. Talc consists of hydrated magnesium silicate. *Formula*: $Mg_3Si_4O_{10}(OH)_2$ **2** TALCUM POWDER. Also, **talcum.** ⟨< Med.L *talcum* < Arabic *talq* < Persian *talk*⟩

talcum powder ['tælkəm] a powder made of purified white talc, often perfumed, for use on the face and body.

tale [teil] *n.* **1** a series of happenings or events related; recital or account: *They listened in shocked silence to his tale of the day's events.* **2** a story of true, legendary, or fictitious events, especially when imaginatively treated: *tales of dragons. The old sea captain told the children tales of his adventures.* **3** a malicious piece of gossip or scandal, either true or false: *She's always telling tales.* **4** a lie; untruth; *Come on now, children, don't tell tales.* **5** *Archaic.* a tally or total.
tell tales, spread gossip or scandal; tattle.
tell tales out of school, reveal confidential matters.
tell the tale, a show the true state of affairs; be revealing. **b** be effective; work. **c** *Esp. Brit. Slang.* tell a story intended to attract pity. ⟨OE *talu*⟩
☛ *Hom.* TAEL, TAIL.
☛ *Syn.* **1, 2.** See note at STORY[1].

tale•bear•er ['teil,bɛrər] *n.* a person who spreads gossip or scandal; telltale.

tale•bear•ing ['teil,bɛrɪŋ] *n., adj.* —*n.* the spreading of gossip or scandal.
—*adj.* that engages in spreading gossip or scandal.

tal•ent ['tælənt] *n.* **1** a special natural ability; ability: *a talent for music.* **2** general intelligence or ability: *a person of talent.* **3** a person or persons having talent: *They were looking for local talent.* **4** any of various units of mass or money used among the ancient Greeks, Romans, Assyrians, etc. ⟨ME < OF < L *talentum* (def. 4) < Gk. *talanton*⟩
☛ *Syn.* **1.** See note at ABILITY.

tal•ent•ed ['tæləntɪd] *adj.* having great natural ability; gifted: *a talented musician.*

talent scout a person who looks for and recruits people having talent in a particular field of activity, especially in the public entertainment field or professional sports.

talent show a show made up of separate performances of singing, dancing, etc. by amateurs looking for recognition as performers.

ta•ler ['tɑlər] *n.* See THALER.

ta•les ['teiliz] *or* ['tɑliz] *n.pl. Law.* **1** persons chosen to fill a vacancy on a jury caused by the absence or disqualification of any of the original jury members. **2** the writ that summons such persons to jury duty. ⟨< MF < Med.L *tales (de circumstantibus)* such (of the bystanders)⟩

tales•man ['teilzmən] *or* ['teilizmən] *n., pl.* **-men.** *Law.* a person chosen to fill a vacancy on a jury caused by the absence or disqualification of any of the original jury members.

tale•tell•er ['teil,tɛlər] *n.* **1** storyteller. **2** talebearer.

ta•li ['teilaɪ] *or* ['teili] *n.* pl. of TALUS.

tal•i•on ['tæliən] *n.* the principle of imposing punishment that corresponds in kind and in degree to the offence. ⟨ME *talioun* < MF *talion* < L *talio, talionis* < *talis* such⟩ —**,tal•i'on•ic** [,tæli'ɒnɪk], *adj.*

tal•i•pes ['tælə,piz] *n. Medicine.* clubfoot. ⟨< NL < L *talus* ankle + *pes* foot⟩

tal•i•pot ['tælə,pɒt] *n.* a tall palm tree (*Corypha umbraculifera*) of S India, Sri Lanka, and Myanmar, having large, fan-shaped leaves used for making fans and umbrellas, for covering houses, and in place of paper for writing. Also, **talipot palm.** ⟨< Sinhalese *talapata* < Skt. *tāla* fan palm + *pattra* leaf⟩

tal•is•man ['tælɪsmən] *or* ['tælɪzmən] *n., pl.* **-mans. 1** a stone, ring, etc. engraved with figures or characters supposed to have magic power; charm. **2** anything that acts as a charm. ⟨< F < Arabic < LGk. *telesma* < Gk. *telesma* initiation into the mysteries < *teleein* perform < *telos* completion⟩

tal•is•man•ic [,tælɪs'mænɪk] *or* [,tælɪz'mænɪk] *adj.* having to do with or serving as a talisman. —**,tal•is'man•i•cal•ly,** *adv.*

talk [tɒk] *v., n.* —*v.* **1** use words; speak; express oneself in words: *A child learns to talk.* **2** exchange words; converse: *The two ministers talked for an hour.* **3** use in speaking; utter: *to talk sense, to talk French.* **4** bring, put, drive, direct, help, etc. by talk: *to talk a person to sleep. If you don't know how to load the program, I'll talk you through it over the phone. They talked me around to their point of view.* **5** discuss: *to talk politics.* **6** consult; confer: *to talk with one's doctor.* **7** communicate: *to talk in sign language.* **8** *Informal.* speak of; bring (something particularly remarkable) into consideration: *I'm talking billions of dollars!* **9** make sounds that suggest speech: *The birds were talking loudly.* **10** disclose secrets: *We have ways to make you talk.* **11** gossip; spread rumours: *Someone was talking behind their backs.*
look who's talking, *Slang.* the person talking critically has no right to do so, as he or she is himself or herself guilty.
now you're talking, *Informal.* now you are saying what I want to hear.
talk around, discuss at length without coming to the point or to a conclusion.
talk at, speak to in such a way as to inhibit a response; preach to.
talk away, a spend (time) in talking; pass by talking. **b** remove or take away by talking: *I talked away my fears.*
talk back, *Informal.* answer rudely or disrespectfully.
talk big, *Slang.* talk boastfully; brag.
talk down, a silence by talking louder or longer. **b** speak condescendingly *(to).* **c** belittle; disparage: *He talks down his competitor's products.* **d** give (a pilot) radio instructions for landing because of instrument failure or poor visibility.
talk into, persuade (someone) into (doing something).
talk of or **about, a** mention; deal with in talk or writing: *In her article she talks about the national debt.* **b** consider with a view to doing: *They're talking of selling everything and moving to Australia.*
talk off (or **out of) the top of** (one's) **head,** *Informal.* utter one's immediate thoughts or ideas without consideration.
talk out, a resolve or try to resolve (a problem, etc.) by means of discussion. **b** in Parliament, discuss (a bill) until the time for adjournment and so prevent its being put to a vote.
talk out of, dissuade (someone) from (doing something): *We talked him out of trying to hitchhike home.*
talk over, a discuss; consider together. **b** persuade or convince by arguing: *She soon talked them over.* **c** talk out (def. **a**).
talk (someone's) **ear** (or **leg,** etc.) **off,** *Informal.* talk to (someone) at seemingly interminable length.
talk tall, *Slang.* exaggerate.
talk the hind leg off a donkey, talk constantly.
talk the talk, utter the prescribed opinion; say the desired or expected thing.
talk up, talk earnestly in favour of; campaign for.
you should talk, *Informal.* you are guilty of the very thing you are criticizing.
—*n.* **1** the use of words; spoken words; speech; conversation. **2** an informal speech. **3** a way of talking: *baby talk.* **4** a conference; council: *peace talks.* **5** gossip or rumour: *There is talk of a quarrel between them.* **6** a subject for talk or gossip: *She is the talk of the town.* **7** *Informal.* boastful or empty words: *Their threat was just talk.*
big talk, boastful talk; bragging.
have a talk with, admonish; advise. ⟨ME *talke(n)*, ult. related to *tell*⟩
☛ *Syn. v.* **1.** See note at SPEAK.

talk•a•thon ['tɒkə,θɒn] *n.* an extra-long public discussion or session of speech-making: *The city council's evening meeting turned into an all-night talkathon.*

talk•a•tive ['tɒkətɪv] *adj.* having the habit of talking a great deal; fond of talking. —**'talk•a•tive•ly,** *adv.* —**'talk•a•tive•ness,** *n.*
☛ *Syn.* **Talkative,** LOQUACIOUS = talking much. **Talkative,** the common word, emphasizes a fondness for talking and a tendency to talk a great deal: *He is a talkative old man who knows everybody in town.* **Loquacious,** a

formal word, adds the idea of talking smoothly and easily and suggests a steady stream of words: *The president of the club is a loquacious person.*

talk•er ['tɒkər] *n.* **1** a person who talks. **2** a talkative person.

talk•fest ['tɒk,fɛst] *n. Slang.* gabfest.

talk•ie ['tɒki] *n. Informal.* TALKING PICTURE.
☛ *Hom.* TALKY.

talking book the text of a book read on audio tape, for the visually or physically impaired.

talking head a person shown close-up on television, engaged only in speaking, especially pompously or tiresomely.

talking picture an early name for a film with synchronized sound.

talking point an important point in a discussion or argument; a point to be emphasized or that serves as a basis for discussion: *These facts may not prove our case but at least they are a talking point.*

talk•ing–to ['tɒkɪŋ ,tu] *n., pl.* **-tos.** *Informal.* a scolding.

talk show a radio or television show featuring interviews with well-known people or people who have some special interest or cause. The studio audience is usually encouraged to participate, and often listeners are invited to phone in. **—'talk-,show,** *adj.*

talk•y ['tɒki] *adj.* **1** talkative. **2** containing too much talk or dialogue: *a talky novel.* **—'talk•i•ness,** *n.*
☛ *Hom.* TALKIE.

tall [tɒl] *adj.* **1** of considerable height; high: *Mountains are tall.* **2** higher than the average or than surrounding things: *The trees in the valley were very tall. She is a tall woman.* **3** of a particular height: *He is 185 cm tall.* **4** *Informal.* **a** unreasonable or bordering on unreasonable: *That's a tall order.* **b** hard to believe; exaggerated: *a tall tale.* ⟨OE *(ge)tæl* prompt, active⟩
—'tall•ness, *n.*
☛ *Syn.* **1, 2.** See note at HIGH.

tall•ish ['tɒlɪʃ] *adj.* somewhat tall.

tal•lit or **tal•lith** [tɑ'lit] *or* ['tɑlɪs] *n.* PRAYER SHAWL. ⟨< Hebrew⟩

tal•low ['tælou] *n.* the hard, white, rendered fat of cattle and sheep, used mainly for making candles, soap, lubricants, etc. Tallow is produced by melting suet.
—v. smear or grease with tallow. ⟨ME *talgh*⟩

tal•low•y ['tæloui] *adj.* **1** like tallow; fat; greasy. **2** yellowish white; pale.

tall ship a large sailing ship of traditional design, such as a clipper, schooner, etc., usually used for training, exhibition, or publicity purposes.

tall story or **tale** *Informal.* an unlikely or exaggerated story.

tal•ly ['tæli] *n., pl.* **-lies;** *v.* **-lied, -ly•ing.** *—n.* **1** an account, reckoning or score: *the tally of a game.* **2** something on which a score or account is kept. **3** a specific number or a mark representing such a number, used as a unit in counting: *The ballots were counted in tallies of 20.* **4** a mark, label, or ticket used for identification or classification: *He checked the tallies on the crates.* **5** *Sports.* a scoring point; a run, goal, etc. **6** something corresponding to or duplicating something else, such as the counterfoil of a cheque. **7** correspondence or agreement. **8** formerly, **a** a stick of wood in which notches were cut to represent numbers and which was then split lengthwise so both parties of a transaction had a record of the amount involved. **b** a notch made in such a stick.
—v. **1** mark on a tally; count or add (*often with* **up**): *to tally a score.* **2** *Sports.* make scoring points; score: *We tallied seven goals in our last game. The other team didn't even tally.* **3** agree; correspond: *Your account tallies with mine. The two reports do not tally.* **4** provide with an identifying mark, label, or ticket. ⟨ME < AF *tallie*, ult. < L *talea* rod⟩

tal•ly•ho [,tæli'hou] *interj., n., pl.* **-hos;** *—interj.* the cry of a hunter to encourage the hounds when the fox is sighted.
—n. **1** a sounding of this cry by a hunter. **2** a coach drawn by two or four horses; four-in-hand. ⟨apparently alteration of F *taïaut*, OF *taho, tietau*⟩

tally sheet a sheet on which a record or score is kept, especially a record of votes.

tally stick TALLY (def. 8a).

Tal•mud ['tælməd] *or* ['tɑlmʊd] *n.* **1** the body of traditional Jewish civil and canonical law, made up of the Mishnah and the Gemara. **2** the Gemara as distinct from the Mishnah. ⟨< Hebrew *talmūd* instruction⟩

Tal•mud•ic [tæl'mʌdɪk] *or* [tɑl'mʊdɪk] *adj.* of or having to do with the Talmud.

Tal•mud•ist ['tælmədɪst] *or* ['tɑlmʊdɪst] *n.* **1** one of the writers or compilers of the Talmud. **2** a person who accepts the authority of the Talmud. **3** a person who knows much about the Talmud. **—'Tal•mud,ism,** *n.*

tal•on ['tælən] *n.* **1** a claw, especially of a bird of prey. **2** a human finger or hand resembling a claw in appearance or when thought of as grasping. **3** the part of the bolt of a lock against which the key presses. ⟨ME < OF *talon* heel, ult. < L *talus* ankle⟩ **—'tal•oned,** *adj.*

ta•lus[1] ['teiləs] *n., pl.* **-li** [-laɪ] *or* [-li]. the highest tarsal bone in the foot, situated just below the bottom ends of the lower leg bones and joined to them. The talus and the ends of the lower leg bones form the ANKLE (def. 3). See LEG for picture. ⟨< L⟩

ta•lus[2] ['teiləs] *n.* **1** a slope. **2** a sloping side or face of a wall, rampart, parapet, or other fortification. **3** *Geology.* a sloping mass of rocky fragments lying at the base of a cliff or the like. ⟨< F < L *talutium* a sign of the presence of a gold mine near the surface < Celtic⟩

tam [tæm] *n.* **1** tam-o'-shanter. **2** beret.

ta•ma•le [tə'mɑli] *n.* a Mexican food made of minced meat seasoned with red peppers, rolled in corn meal, wrapped in cornhusks, and roasted or steamed. ⟨< Am.Sp. < Nahuatl *tamalli*⟩

tam•a•rack ['tæmə,ræk] *n. Cdn.* **1** a small or medium-sized larch tree (*Larix laricina*) found mainly in muskeg and swamp areas throughout most of Canada. Tannin, used in tanning leather, can be extracted from the bark of the tamarack. **2** the wood of this tree. ⟨< Algonquian⟩

tamarack swamp or **muskeg** *Cdn.* a low-lying, wet tract of land where tamarack flourish.

tam•a•rind ['tæmə,rɪnd] *n.* **1** a tropical evergreen tree (*Tamarindus indica*) of the pea family native to E Africa, having hard yellowish wood, yellow flowers with reddish veins, and a datelike fruit with an acid pulp. **2** the fruit, used in foods, drinks, and medicine. ⟨ult. < Arabic *tamr-hindi* date of India⟩

tam•a•risk ['tæmə,rɪsk] *n.* any of a genus (*Tamarix*) of shrubs and small trees of warm and tropical regions having small, scalelike leaves and long, feathery clusters of tiny pink or white flowers, often grown as ornamentals or windbreaks along exposed seashores, on salt flats, and in deserts, where few other plants can flourish. ⟨ME < LL *tamariscus*, var. of L *tamarix*⟩

tam•bac ['tæmbæk] *n.* See TOMBAC.

tam•ba•la [tɑm'bɑlə] *n., pl.* **-la** or **-las** or **matambala** [,mɑtɑm'bɑlə]. a unit of money in Malawi, equal to 1/100 of a kwacha. See table of money in the Appendix. ⟨< Bantu⟩

tam•bour ['tæmbʊr] *or* [tæm'bʊr] *n., v.* *—n.* **1** a drum. **2** a pair of embroidery hoops; a circular frame for holding in place cloth to be embroidered. **3** embroidery done on this. **4** a flexible panel made of a number of wooden slats fastened to cloth, vinyl, etc. or interlocking with each other, used instead of a door or lid, in a piece of furniture such as a roll-top desk, a nightstand, or a wall unit.
—v. embroider on a tambour. ⟨< F, drum⟩

tam•bour•a [tæm'bʊrə] *n.* a musical instrument of India, resembling a lute but having no frets, used to produce a drone accompaniment. ⟨< Persian < Arabic *ṭanbūr*⟩

tam•bou•rin ['tæmbərɪn]; *French* [tɑ̃bu'ʀɛ̃] *n.* **1** a lively folk dance of Provence, France. **2** the music for such a dance. **3** a small, narrow drum used in Provence. ⟨< F, dim. of *tambour* drum⟩

A tambourine

tam•bou•rine [,tæmbə'rin] *n.* a small, shallow drum with one head and with jingling metal disks around the side, played by shaking, striking with the knuckles, or rubbing with the thumb. ⟨< F *tambourin*, dim. of *tambour* drum⟩ **—,tam•bou'rin•ist,** *n.*

tame [teim] *adj.* **tam•er, tam•est;** *v.* **tamed, tam•ing.** *—adj.* **1** of an animal, changed by humans from a wild state to a state of being able to be handled or managed in order to serve as a beast of burden, source of food or clothing, pet, etc. **2 a** gentle and easy to control; docile. **b** servile; broken in spirit. **3** without spirit; dull and lifeless: *a tame story, a tame election campaign.*
—v. **1** make or become tame, or domesticated: *to tame a horse. White rats tame easily.* **2** make submissive or docile: *Severe discipline had finally tamed her.* **3** tone down or mitigate: *He was told to tame his language.* **4** take away the ruggedness, dangerousness, challenging quality, etc. of: *to tame the wilderness, to tame the inner city.* ⟨OE *tam*⟩ **—'tame•a•ble** or **'tam•a•ble,** *adj.* **—'tame•ly,** *adv.* **—'tame•ness,** *n.* **—'tam•er,** *n.*

tame•less ['teimlɪs] *adj.* not tamed or not capable of being tamed.

Tam•il ['tʌməl], ['tɑməl], *or* ['tæməl] *n., adj.* *—n.* **1** a member of a people of mainly Dravidian ancestry living especially in S India and in Sri Lanka. **2** the Dravidian language of the Tamils.
—adj. of or having to do with the Tamils or their language.

Tam•muz ['tɑmuz] *n.* **1** in the Hebrew calendar, the fourth month of the ecclesiastical year and tenth month of the civil year. **2** *Babylonian mythology.* a god of agriculture, whose annual rebirth and return to the earth symbolized spring and its new growth. Also, **Thammuz.** ⟨< Hebrew⟩

tam–o'–shan•ter ['tæm ə 'ʃæntər] *n.* a type of peakless woollen cap originating in Scotland, having a tight headband, a flat, loose, round crown, and, frequently, a pompom. ⟨from the name of the hero in a poem by Scottish poet Robert Burns⟩

tamp [tæmp] *v.* **1** pack down firmly by a series of taps or blows. **2** in blasting, fill (the hole containing explosive) with dirt, etc. ⟨? < *tampion*⟩ **—'tam•per,** *n.*

tam•per ['tæmpər] *v.* **1** interfere with or alter in an improper way, so as to damage or weaken (*used with* **with**): *The lock had been tampered with but not broken. It was obvious that someone had tampered with the evidence.* **2** engage in secret illegal arrangements, such as bribery. ⟨ult., var. of *temper*⟩
—'tam•per•er, *n.*
☛ *Syn.* **1.** See note at MEDDLE.

tam•pi•on ['tæmpiən] *n.* **1** a wooden plug placed in the muzzle of a gun to keep out dampness and dust. **2** a plug for the top of an organ pipe. Also, **tompion.** ⟨< F *tampon*, ult. < *taper* plug < Gmc.⟩

tam•pon ['tæmpɒn] *n., v.* *—n.* a plug of cotton or other absorbent material inserted into a wound or body cavity to stop bleeding or to absorb blood, etc.
—v. plug with a tampon: *to tampon a wound.* ⟨< F. See TAMPION.⟩

tam•tam ['tʌmtʌm] *or* ['tæmtæm] *n.* **1** a gong with indefinite pitch. **2** tomtom. ⟨< Hind., any percussion instrument⟩

Tam•worth ['tæm,wɜrθ] *n. Cdn.* a type of boar which has been bred in Canada since the 19th century. ⟨town in Staffordshire, England, where it was originally bred⟩

tan [tæn] *v.* **tanned, tan•ning;** *n., adj.* *—v.* **1** make (hide) into leather by treating it with a solution containing tannin or a similar chemical agent to preserve it and keep it soft and flexible. **2** make (light skin) brown by exposure to the sun or a sunlamp: *He was deeply tanned after a summer spent out of doors.* **3** become tanned: *My sister tans more quickly than I do.* **4** *Informal.* spank or thrash in punishment (especially in **tan someone's hide**).
—n. **1** a medium or light, slightly reddish brown. **2** the brown colour acquired by light skin from exposure to the sun or a sunlamp. **3** the liquid used in tanning hides, or the active ingredient in it, such as tannin. **4** tanbark.
—adj. having the colour tan: *tan shoes.* ⟨< Med.L *tannare*⟩

tan or **tan.** tangent.

Tan•ach [tɑ'nɑx] *n. Judaism.* the three divisions of the Old Testament: the Law (Torah), the Prophets (Neviim) and the Hagiographa (Ketuvim) taken as a whole. ⟨vocalization of Hebrew root TNK, acronym of *Torah, Nabhiim, Kathūbhim*⟩

tan•a•ger ['tænədʒər] *n.* any of a family (Thraupidae) of small to medium-sized, mostly bright-coloured American songbirds found mainly in woodlands. Most tanagers are found only in the tropics, but three species, including the scarlet tanager, are regular summer visitors in Canada. ⟨< NL < Tupi *tangara*⟩

tan•bark ['tæn,bɑrk] *n.* **1** any bark rich in tannin, crushed or cut into small pieces and used in tanning hides. Used tanbark is often recycled as a covering for circus rings, racetracks, etc. **2** a surface, as a riding track or circus ring, covered with tanbark: *When her horse shied, she hit the tanbark with a thud.*

tan•dem ['tændəm] *adv., adj., n.* *—adv.* one behind the other: *to drive horses tandem.*
—adj. having animals, seats, parts, etc. arranged one behind the other.
—n. **1** a team of horses harnessed tandem. **2** a two-wheeled carriage drawn by horses harnessed tandem. **3** a bicycle with two seats and two sets of pedals, one behind the other. **4** a truck or other vehicle with two attached units, as a cab for pulling and a trailer to carry the load.
in tandem, a one ahead of the other; in tandem formation: *mounted in tandem.* **b** closely together; in partnership or co-operation: *working in tandem.* ⟨< L *tandem* at length < *tam* so⟩

tan•doo•ri [tɑn'duri] *adj.* of any of various East Indian dishes, cooked in a clay oven or **tandoor.** ⟨< Hind. *tandur* < Turkish < Arabic *tannur* portable oven⟩

tang[1] [tæŋ] *n., v.* *—n.* **1** a pleasantly strong and distinctive taste or flavour or smell: *the tang of blue cheese, the tang of sea air.* **2** a stimulating, distinctive or characteristic quality or property: *We need a slogan with more tang.* **3** a slight touch or suggestion; trace. **4** a long, slender projecting point, shank, or prong forming the part of a chisel, file, sword, knife, etc. that fits into the handle.
—v. **1** provide with a spike, flange, or other tang. **2** give a distinct taste or flavour to. ⟨ME < ON *tangi* point⟩ **—'tang•y,** *adj.*

tang[2] [tæŋ] *n., v.* *—n.* a sharp, ringing sound.
—v. **1** make a sharp, ringing sound. **2** cause to ring loudly. ⟨imitative⟩

Tang or **T'ang** [tæŋ] *n.* a Chinese dynasty, A.D. 618-906, a period during which China expanded and its art and science flourished.

Tan•gan•yi•kan [,tæŋgən'jikən] *n., adj.* *—n.* a native or inhabitant of Tanganyika, a former state in E Africa, now a part of the Republic of Tanzania.
—adj. of or having to do with Tanganyika or its people.

tan•ge•lo ['tændʒə,lou] *n.* a citrus fruit (*Citrus tangelo*) developed by crossing the grapefruit and the tangerine, now grown in several varieties. ⟨blend of *tangerine* + *pomelo*⟩

tan•gen•cy ['tændʒənsi] *n.* the quality or state of being tangent.

tan•gent ['tændʒənt] *adj., n.* *—adj.* **1** touching. **2** *Geometry.* touching at one point only and not intersecting. These circles are tangent:
—n. **1** a line, curve, or surface that is tangent to a curve or curved surface. **2** *Trigonometry.* in a right triangle, the ratio of the length of the side opposite an acute angle to the length of the side (not the hypotenuse) adjacent to the angle. **3** *Geometry.* the part of a line tangent to a curve from the point of tangency to the x axis. *Abbrev.:* tan or tan.
fly off or **go off on** (or **at**) **a tangent,** change suddenly from one course of action or thought to another. ⟨< L *tangens, -entis,* ppr. of *tangere* touch⟩

tan•gen•tial [tæn'dʒɛnʃəl] *adj.* **1** of, being, or having to do with a tangent. **2** in the direction of a tangent. **3** diverging; digressing. **4** only slightly connected. **—tan'gen•tial•ly,** *adv.*

tan•ge•rine [,tændʒə'rin] *or* ['tændʒə,rin] *n., adj.* *—n.* **1** any of several varieties of mandarin orange having a thin, reddish orange skin and easily separated segments. **2** a reddish orange colour.
—adj. having the colour tangerine. ⟨< F *Tanger* Tangiers, a seaport in Morocco⟩

tan•gi•ble ['tændʒəbəl] *adj., n.* *—adj.* **1** capable of being touched or felt by touch: *A chair is a tangible object.* **2** real; actual; definite: *tangible evidence.* **3** whose value can be accurately appraised: *Real estate is tangible property.*
—n. **tangibles,** *pl.* things whose value is easily appraised; material assets. ⟨< LL *tangibilis* < *tangere* touch⟩ **—'tan•gi•bly,** *adv.* **—'tan•gi•ble•ness,** *n.* **—,tan•gi'bil•i•ty,** *n.*

tan•gle ['tæŋgəl] *v.* **-gled, -gling;** *n.* *—v.* **1** twist and twine together in a confused mass. **2** become tangled: *Her hair tangles easily because it is fine and straight.* **3** involve in something that hampers or obstructs; snare or entrap (*often used with* **up**): *He has tangled himself in a complicated business deal.* **4** get into a fight or argument (*with*): *Don't tangle with her.*
—n. **1** a twisted or confused mass; a snarl or jumble: *a tangle of contradictory statements.* **2** a complicated, confused, or bewildered state or condition: *Her business affairs are in a*

dreadful tangle. My mind was in such a tangle I didn't hear a word he said. **3** a matted bit of hair. ⟨ME *tanglen* probably var. of *taglen* entangle < Scand.; cf. dial. Swedish *taggla* disorder⟩ **—'tan•gle•ment,** *n.* **—'tan•gler,** *n.*

tan•gled ['tæŋgəld] *adj., v. —adj.* **1** confused, disordered, or snarled: *a tangled pile of stockings, tangled hair.* **2** very involved or complicated: *a tangled web of lies, tangled relationships.*
—v. pt. and pp. of TANGLE.

tan•gly ['tæŋgli] *adj.* full of tangles; tangled.

tan•go ['tæŋgou] *n., pl.* **-gos;** *v.* **-goed, -go•ing.** *—n.* **1** a Latin American ballroom dance of African origin, in 2/4 or 4/4 time and characterized by dips and slow glides. **2** the music for this dance.
—v. dance the tango. ⟨< Sp.⟩

The tangram

tan•gram ['tæŋ,græm], ['tæn,græm], *or* ['tæŋgrəm] *n.* a Chinese puzzle consisting of a square cut into five triangles, a square, and a rhomboid, which can be combined so as to form a great variety of figures. ⟨? < Chinese *t'ang* Chinese + E *-gram*; cf. *anagram, cryptogram,* etc.⟩

tank [tæŋk] *n., v. —n.* **1** a large container for liquid or gas: *an oil tank.* **2** as much as a tank will hold; tankful: *They used up almost a tank of gas just driving around.* **3** an armoured, enclosed combat vehicle carrying machine guns and, usually, an artillery piece and moving on tracks. **4** *Esp. U.S.* a pool, small lake, or pond, especially one made as a swimming pool or reservoir.
—v. put or store in a tank.
tank up, a *Informal.* fill the tank of one's vehicle with fuel.
b *Slang.* drink much alcoholic liquor. ⟨? < Pg. *tanque* < L *stagnum* pool⟩

tan•ka ['tɑŋkə] *n.* an unrhymed Japanese verse form of 31 syllables over five lines, distributed as 5, 7, 5, 7, 7. ⟨< Japanese < Mandarin *duan* short + *ge* song⟩

tank•age ['tæŋkɪdʒ] *n.* **1** the capacity of a tank or tanks. **2** storage in tanks. **3** the price charged for storage in tanks. **4** the waste matter left over from the rendering of fat in slaughterhouse tanks, dried and ground and used as fertilizer or feed.

tank•ard ['tæŋkərd] *n.* a large, usually silver or pewter drinking mug with a handle and, often, a hinged cover. ⟨ME; cf. MF *tanquart,* MDu. *tanckaert*⟩

tank car a railway car with a tank for carrying liquids or gases.

tanked [tæŋkt] *adj., v. —adj. Slang.* drunk.
—v. pt. and pp. of TANK.

tank•er ['tæŋkər] *n.* a ship, aircraft, or truck having a tank or tanks for carrying oil, gasoline, or other liquid freight.

tank farm a tract of land containing many large tanks for the storing of oil.

tank farming hydroponics.

tank•ful ['tæŋkfʊl] *n., pl.* **-fuls.** as much as will fill a tank.

tank top a sleeveless, buttonless knit shirt with very low neck and back, worn in very hot weather, for athletics, or over a T-shirt.

tank truck a truck equipped with a large tank for carrying oil, gasoline, or other liquid freight.

tan•nate ['tæneit] *n.* a salt of tannic acid.

tan•ner ['tænər] *n.* a person whose work is tanning hides.

tan•ner•y ['tænəri] *n., pl.* **-ner•ies.** a place where hides are tanned.

tan•nic ['tænɪk] *adj.* **1** of or obtained from tanbark or tannin. **2** of red wine, tasting of tannin absorbed from the oak barrels in which the wine is aged.

tannic acid a form of tannin.

tan•nin ['tænən] *n.* an acid obtained from the bark or galls of oaks, etc. and from certain plants, used in tanning, dyeing, making ink, and in medicine. ⟨< F *tanin*⟩

tan•ning ['tænɪŋ] *n., v. —n.* **1** the process or art of converting hide or skins into leather. **2** a making brown, as by exposure to sun. **3** *Informal.* a severe spanking or thrashing.
—v. ppr. of TAN.

tanning parlour an establishment, or a part of a beauty salon, where clients may tan themselves by various methods, especially by sitting or lying on benches under sun lamps.

Ta•no•an ['tɑnouən] *n.* a family of Native American languages, including Kiowa and some of the languages of pueblos in New Mexico and Arizona.

tan•sy ['tænzi] *n., pl.* **-sies. 1** a coarse, strong-smelling, bitter-tasting perennial herb (*Tanacetum vulgare*) native to Europe, now common in North America, having large, toothed leaves and small, yellow flowers. Tansy was formerly much used as a food seasoning and medicine. **2** any of numerous other plants of the same genus. ⟨ME < OF < LL < Gk. *athanasia,* originally, immortality⟩

tan•ta•lite ['tæntə,ləit] *n.* a black, crystalline mineral, the principal ore of tantalum. *Formula*: $FeMn(TaNb)_2O_6$ ⟨< *tantalum* + *-ite*⟩

tan•ta•lize ['tæntə,laɪz] *v.* **-lized, -liz•ing.** torment or tease by keeping something desired in sight but out of reach, or by holding out hopes that are repeatedly disappointed. ⟨< Tantalus⟩ **—'tan•ta•li'za•tion,** *n.* **—'tan•ta,liz•er,** *n.*

tan•ta•liz•ing ['tæntə,laɪzɪŋ] *adj., v. —adj.* enticing; desirable, especially of something unobtainable or out of reach.
—v. ppr. of TANTALIZE. **—'tan•ta,liz•ing•ly,** *adv.*

tan•ta•lum ['tæntələm] *n.* a rare, hard, greyish metallic chemical element that is resistant to acids. It is used in alloys for making surgical instruments. *Symbol*: Ta; *at.no.* 73; *at.mass* 180.95. ⟨< *Tantalus*; because it will not absorb acid⟩ **—tan'tal•ic** [tæn'tælɪk], *adj.* **—'tan•ta•lous,** *adj.*

Tan•ta•lus ['tæntələs] *n.* **1** *Greek mythology.* a Greek king punished in Hades by having to stand up to his chin in water, under branches laden with fruit. Whenever he tried to eat or drink, the fruit or water withdrew from his reach. **2 tantalus,** an open rack containing decanters for wine or spirits, closed with a lock.

tan•ta•mount ['tæntə,maʊnt] *adj.* having the same force, effect, etc.; equivalent (*to*): *His silence when questioned was tantamount to an admission of guilt.* ⟨< AF *tant amunter* amount to as much < *tant* as much (< L *tantum*) + *amunter,* OF *amonter.* See AMOUNT.⟩
☛ *Syn.* See note at EQUAL.

tan•ta•ra [,tæntə'rɑ] *n.* **1** a blast of a trumpet or horn. **2** any similar sound. ⟨imitative⟩

tan•tiv•y [tæn'tɪvi] *n., adv. —n.* **1** a hunting cry. **2** a rapid or headlong movement; rush or gallop.
—adv. at full speed or gallop. ⟨imitative⟩

tan•to ['tɑntou]; *Italian,* ['tanto] *adv. Music.* so much or too much: *allegro ma non tanto.*

tan•tra or **Tan•tra** ['tʌntrə] *or* ['tɑntrə] *n.* any of a number of ancient writings underlying Hindu and Buddhist mysticism. ⟨< Skt.⟩ **—'tan•tric,** *adj.* **—'tan•trism,** *n.*

tan•trum ['tæntrəm] *n.* a violent, childish outburst of bad temper. ⟨origin uncertain⟩

Tan•za•nia [,tænzə'niə] *n.* a country in E Africa on the Indian Ocean.

Tan•za•ni•an [,tænzə'niən] *n., adj. —n.* a native or inhabitant of Tanzania.
—adj. of or having to do with Tanzania or its people.

Tao [daʊ] *n.* **1** in Taoism, 'the way', the eternal, transcendent, and mystical entity that is the supreme creative force. **2** the ultimate reality of the cosmos; the principle of harmony, orderliness, and integration. ⟨< Chinese *tao* the way⟩
☛ *Hom.* DHOW.

Tao•ism ['daʊɪzəm] *n.* **1 a** a 2500-year-old Chinese philosophy based on the teachings of Laotse (c. 500 B.C.) that conceives of nature as being ordered by the balance between positive and negative forces underlying the existence of all things. **b** the related belief in or adherence to a rational code of human behaviour emphasizing humility, simplicity, truthfulness, and selflessness. **2** a religion that was developed from this philosophy, with influence from Confucianism and Buddhism. Taoism is characterized by the worship of many gods and a belief in magic.

Tao•ist ['daʊɪst] *n., adj. —n.* a believer in Taoism.
—adj. of or having to do with Taoism or Taoists. **—Tao'is•tic,** *adj.*

Tao Te Ching [ˌdaʊ də ˈdʒɪŋ] *n.* an ancient text of philosophical speculation and mystical reflection, widely studied and revered in Taoism.

tap[1] [tæp] *v.* **tapped, tap•ping;** *n.* *—v.* **1** strike lightly and usually audibly: *to tap on a window.* **2** cause to strike in this way: *She tapped her foot on the floor.* **3** make, put, etc. by light, usually audible blows: *to tap a rhythm, to tap time, to tap the ashes out of a pipe.* **4** repair with a TAP (def. 3). **5** select or designate, especially for membership in a society or club. **6** tap-dance.
—n. **1** a light, audible blow: *There was a tap at the door.* **2** the sound of a light blow. **3** a piece of leather, etc. added to the sole or heel of a shoe to repair it. **4** a small steel plate on a shoe to reduce wear or to make a louder tap in tap-dancing.
5 tap-dancing. ⟨ME < OF *taper;* imitative⟩ **—'tap•per,** *n.*

tap[2] [tæp] *n., v.* **tapped, tap•ping.** *—n.* **1** a device for turning on and off the flow of fluid in a pipe. **2** a stopper or plug to close a hole in a cask containing liquid. **3** a certain kind or quality of liquor. **4** *Informal.* taproom. **5** a special spigot for inserting into a hole in a maple tree to draw off the sap. **6 a** an electrical connection on a coil somewhere other than at the end. **b** the place where an electrical connection is or can be made. **7** any long, tapering cylinder, especially a taproot. **8** a tool for cutting threads of internal screws, etc. **9** a wiretapping. **10** surgery to let out liquid: *spinal tap.*
on tap, a ready to be let out of a keg or barrel and served.
b ready for use; on hand.
—v. **1** make a hole in to let out liquid: *They tapped the sugar maples when the sap began to flow.* **2** draw the plug from: *to tap a cask.* **3** furnish with a tap. **4** let out (liquid) by piercing or by drawing a plug. **5** let out liquid from by surgery. **6** make (resources, reserves, etc.) accessible; make a connection with (*often used with* **into**); penetrate to; open up: *This highway taps a large district.* **7** use or draw on (*often used with* **into**). **8** make a connection with (a telephone line) in order to eavesdrop.
9 make an internal screw thread in. **10** *Slang.* ask (a person) for money, help, etc. ⟨OE *tæppa*⟩ **—'tap•per,** *n.*

ta•pa [ˈtɑpə] *n.* **1** an unwoven cloth of the Pacific islands, made by steeping and beating the inner bark of a mulberry tree. **2** this bark. ⟨< Polynesian⟩

tap dance a dance in which the steps are accented by loud taps of the toe or heel, performed wearing shoes having metal TAPS[1] (def. 4).

tap–dance [ˈtæp ˌdæns] *v.* **-danced, -danc•ing.** dance a tap dance. **—'tap-ˌdanc•er,** *n.*

tape [teip] *n., v.* **taped, tap•ing.** *—n.* **1** a long, narrow, woven strip of cotton, linen, etc. Tape is used to make loops and bind seams. **2** such a strip coated with a sticky substance to make it adhere to a surface: *adhesive tape, masking tape, electrical tape.* **3** a long, narrow strip of other material. Surveyors measure with a steel tape. Stock quotations are printed on paper tape: *ticker tape.* **4 a** magnetic audio recording tape. **b** a recording made on this tape. **5** videotape. **6** the strip, string, etc. stretched across a racetrack at the finish line.
—v. **1** fasten with tape; wrap with tape. **2** record on tape.
3 attach a tape or tapes to. **4** measure with a tape measure.
get (something or someone) **taped,** *Slang.* understand (something or someone): *I had some problems with this, but I think I've got it taped now. She hates her boss, but she's really got him taped.* ⟨ME *tape,* var. of *tappe,* OE *tæppe*⟩ **—'tape,like,** *adj.*

tape deck an apparatus for making and playing tape recordings, especially a separate component of a stereo system.

tape grass a freshwater plant (*Vallisneria spiralis*) of warm temperate regions having long, ribbonlike leaves that are entirely submerged. Also called **eelgrass, wild celery.**

tape•line [ˈteipˌlaɪn] *n.* TAPE MEASURE.

tape measure a long, narrow strip of flexible steel, cloth, paper, etc., marked off in millimetres, centimetres, feet, inches, etc., for measuring length or distance.

tap•er [ˈteipər] *v., n.* *—v.* **1** make or become gradually smaller toward one end: *The church spire tapers to a point.* **2** grow or cause to grow gradually less; diminish: *Their business tapered to nothing as people moved away.*
taper off, a gradually reduce; leave off or stop (something): *She thought she could taper off smoking rather than quit outright. He has been a heavy drinker but is trying to taper off.* **b** become less and less: *When he stood his ground, opposition eventually tapered off.*
—n. **1** a gradual lessening in thickness, diameter, or width toward one end: *pant legs with a slight taper.* **2** a gradual decrease of force, capacity, etc. **3** a figure that tapers to a point; a slender cone or pyramid; spire. **4** a slender candle. **5** a long wick coated with wax, used to light candles, lamps, etc. ⟨OE *tapor*⟩
—'ta•per•ing•ly, *adv.*
☛ *Hom.* TAPIR.

tape–re•cord [ˈteip rɪˌkɔrd] *v.* record on magnetic tape.

tape recorder *n.* a device for recording sound on magnetic tape and also playing back the recorded sound. In recording, the sound is converted into electric waves which magnetize the tape. When the recording is played back, the magnetic patterns on the tape create electric waves which are changed into sound and amplified.

tape recording **1** a tape on which a recording of sound, etc. has been made. **2** the reproduced or recorded sounds, etc. themselves: *She was listening to a rather poor tape recording of Handel's* Messiah.

tap•es•tried [ˈtæpəstrid] *adj.* **1** covered or decorated with a tapestry or tapestries: *tapestried walls.* **2** represented in tapestry. **3** intricately and richly interwoven, like a tapestry.

tap•es•try [ˈtæpəstri] *n., pl.* **-tries. 1 a** heavy, thick, handwoven fabric having designs or pictures woven into it, used to hang on walls, cover furniture, etc. **b** a picture or representation in such fabric: *a tapestry of Queen Victoria's coronation.* **2** a machine-made fabric woven to resemble this. ⟨ME < OF *tapisserie,* ult. < *tapis* < L < Gk. *tapētion,* dim. of *tapēs* carpet, covering⟩

tape•worm [ˈteipˌwɜrm] *n.* any of numerous flatworms (class Cestoda) that in the adult stage live as parasites in the intestines of human beings and other vertebrates.

tap•ing [ˈteipɪŋ] *n., v.* *—n.* **1** TAPE RECORDING. **2** a quantity of punched or magnetic tape, containing data for use in a computer, etc.
—v. ppr. of TAPE.

tap•i•o•ca [ˌtæpiˈoukə] *n.* **1** a starchy food in the form of white grains prepared from the root of the cassava plant. Tapioca is used especially for puddings and as a thickener for foods.
2 pudding, etc. made from tapioca. ⟨ult. < Tupi-Guarani *tipioca*⟩

ta•pir [ˈteipər] *n.* any of a genus (*Tapirus*) of heavy, thick-skinned, woodland mammals having four toes on the front feet and three on the hind feet, and a long, tapered, flexible snout. They belong to the same order (Perissodactyla) as horses and rhinoceroses. ⟨< Tupi *tapira*⟩
☛ *Hom.* TAPER.

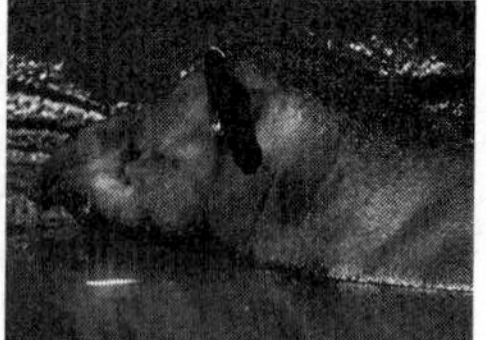

A tapir

tap•is [ˈtæpi] *or* [ˈtæpɪs] *n.*
1 *Archaic.* a carpet or tapestry.
2 *Cdn. North.* a blanket worn by sled dogs.
on the tapis, being given attention; under discussion. ⟨< F *tapis.* See TAPESTRY.⟩

tap•pet [ˈtæpɪt] *n.* a projecting machine part, cam, etc. that intermittently comes into contact with another part to which it communicates, or from which it receives, an intermittent motion. ⟨< *tap[1]*⟩

tap•room [ˈtæpˌrum] *or* [ˈtæpˌrʊm] *n.* a room where alcoholic liquor is sold; barroom.

tap•root [ˈtæpˌrut] *n.* the main root of certain plants, such as the dandelion or carrot, that grows straight downward with root hairs or rootlets branching out from it. See ROOT[1] for picture.

taps [tæps] *n.* (*usually used with a singular verb*) the last bugle call at night, serving as a signal that all lights in soldiers' quarters are to be put out. Taps is also played at military funerals and memorial services, especially in the United States. Compare LAST POST. ⟨prob. shortened from *taptoo,* an earlier form of *tattoo[1]*. See TATTOO[1].⟩

tap•ster [ˈtæpstər] *n.* a person who draws and serves liquor in a tavern or barroom. ⟨OE *tæppestre,* fem.⟩

tar[1] [tɑr] *n., v.* **tarred, tar•ring.** *—n.* **1** a thick, brown or black, sticky substance obtained by the distillation of wood or coal. **2** a similar, condensible substance found in the smoke from burning tobacco. **3** (*adjl.*) of or like tar; covered or impregnated with tar: *tar paper.*
—v. **1** cover or smear with tar: *a tarred roof.* **2** smear or besmirch as if with tar: *tarred by his own bad reputation.*
tar and feather, smear heated tar on and then cover with feathers as a punishment.
tarred with the same brush (or **stick**), having similar faults or defects.

tar with (a specified) **brush,** disgrace in a specified way; stigmatize. ⟨OE *teoru*⟩

tar[2] [tɑr] *n. Informal.* sailor. ⟨special use of *tar[1]* or short for *tarpaulin*⟩

ta•ra•did•dle or **tar•ra•did•dle** ['tærə,dɪdəl] *or* ['tɛrə,dɪdəl] *n. Informal.* **1** a petty lie; fib. **2** twaddle. ⟨origin uncertain⟩

tar•an•tel•la [,tærən'tɛlə] *or* [,tɛrən'tɛlə] *n.* **1** a rapid, whirling southern Italian dance in 6/8 time, usually performed by couples. **2** the music for this dance. ⟨< Ital. *tarantella* < *Taranto,* a city in S Italy; influenced by Ital. *tarantola* tarantula⟩

Tarantula: a bird spider, one of the world's largest spiders — body about 8 cm long

ta•ran•tu•la [tə'ræntʃʊlə] *n., pl.* **-las, -lae** [-,li] *or* [-,laɪ]. **1** a large, hairy, southern European wolf spider (*Lycosa tarentula*) whose bite is painful, but not serious. Its bite was formerly believed to cause an uncontrollable desire to dance. **2** any large hairy spider thought of as poisonous; especially any of a family (Theraphosidae) of spiders found in tropical America, Mexico, and the southern United States, some species reaching a body length of about 8 cm. The bite of some South American tarantulas can be dangerous but all the species found in the United States are harmless to human beings. ⟨< Med.L *tarantula,* ult. < L *Tarentum* Taranto. See TARANTELLA.⟩

tar•boosh [tɑr'buʃ] *n.* a close-fitting, brimless cap like a fez, worn by Muslim men either alone or as the inner part of a turban. ⟨< Arabic *tarbūsh*⟩

Tar•de•noi•si•an [,tɑrdə'nɔɪziən] *adj.* of or relating to a mesolithic culture using small flint instruments. ⟨< Fère-en-*Tardenois,* town in France where artifacts were discovered⟩

tar•di•grade ['tɑrdɪ,greid] *n.* any of a phylum (Tardigrada) of tiny aquatic invertebrates having a short segmented body and four pairs of segmented legs like those of arthropods, to which they are thought to be related. ⟨< F < L *tardigradus* slow-moving < *tardus* slow + *gradi* walk⟩

tar•dive dys•ki•ne•sia ['tɑrdɪv ,dɪskə'niʒə] a neuro-muscular disorder characterized by twitching or spasms of the face and caused by prolonged use of certain drugs including some tranquillizers and dopamine.

tar•dy ['tɑrdi] *adj.* **-di•er, -di•est. 1** after the proper or desired time; late: *a tardy attempt at reform.* **2** slow or sluggish: *tardy growth, a tardy pace.* ⟨< F *tardif,* ult. < L *tardus*⟩ **—'tar•di•ly,** *adv.* **—'tar•di•ness,** *n.*
☛ *Syn.* **1.** See note at LATE.

tare[1] [tɛr] *n.* **1** any of several vetches, especially the common vetch (*Vicia sativa*). Tare is grown for fodder and for enriching the soil. **2** the seed of a vetch. **3** in the Bible, an injurious weed, possibly the darnel. ⟨Cf. MDu. *tarwe* wheat⟩
☛ *Hom.* TEAR[2].

tare[2] [tɛr] *n., v.* **tared, tar•ing.** *—n.* **1** a deduction made from the gross mass of something in a container to allow for the mass of the container. **2** the amount of this.
—v. calculate the tare on. ⟨< F *tare,* ult. < Arabic *ṭarḥah* < *ṭaraḥa* reject⟩
☛ *Hom.* TEAR[2].

targe [tɑrdʒ] *n. Archaic.* a shield or buckler. ⟨ME < OF < Gmc.⟩

tar•get ['tɑrgɪt] *n., v. —n.* **1** a mark for shooting at. **2** something aimed at, as in a wartime operation: *The bomber's target was a bridge.* **3** a flat round object, usually marked with a series of concentric circles, the centre of which is to be aimed at in any kind of shooting practice or contest. **4** a goal or objective: *The target for the fund-raising drive was $10 000.* **5** an object of scorn or abuse: *Her absent-mindedness made her a target for their practical jokes.* **6** a shield, especially a small, round one; buckler. **7** the plate opposite the cathode in an X-ray tube, upon which the cathode rays impinge and produce X rays. **8** any substance, object, or surface bombarded by high-energy nuclear particles, electrons, etc., such as the plate in a television camera tube that receives the image from the screen plate. **9** a disk-shaped signal on a railway switch that shows whether the switch is open or closed.
on target, to the purpose; to the point; appropriate or valid: *Her criticism of the book was right on target.*
—v. **1** make into or put up as a target. **2** direct at a target. ⟨ME *targete,* dim. of *targe* < OF < Gmc.⟩

target date the expected date of completion of a project.

target language 1 the language into which a text or discourse is to be translated. **2** a language or a particular form of a language other than one's first, that one is in the process of learning: *Standard English is the target language of most ESL students.*

tar•iff ['tærɪf] *or* ['tɛrɪf] *n., v. —n.* **1** a list or schedule of duties or taxes imposed by a government on imports and, sometimes, exports. **2** any duty or tax in such a list or schedule: *There is a very high tariff on jewellery.* **3** a schedule of rates or prices of a business, etc.: *This hotel has the highest tariff in town.*
—v. **1** make subject to a tariff; set a tariff on. **2** list the tariff or tariffs on. **3** fix the price of in accordance with a tariff. ⟨< Ital. *tariffa* arithmetic < Arabic *tar'īf* information⟩

tar•la•tan ['tɑrlətən] *n.* a thin, sheer, usually heavily-sized muslin used for costumes and trimming, for stiffening garments, etc. ⟨< F *tarlatane*⟩

Tar•mac ['tɑrmæk] *n. Trademark.* a paving material consisting of crushed stone bound with coal tar. ⟨< *tar[1]* + *mac(adam)*⟩

tarn [tɑrn] *n.* a small mountain lake or pool. ⟨ME < ON *tjörn*⟩

tar•na•tion [tɑr'neiʃən] *interj. Informal.* a euphemism for damnation.

tar•nish ['tɑrnɪʃ] *v., n. —v.* **1** dull the lustre or brightness of; discolour: *The salt tarnished the silver saltshaker.* **2** lose lustre and brightness or become discoloured, especially through exposure to the air or certain chemical substances: *This silver does not tarnish.* **3** spoil; mar: *His involvement in that business deal has tarnished his reputation. Her fond memories of her father were tarnished by Roy's unpleasant disclosure.* **4** grow less appealing; become uninviting; pall; fade.
—n. **1** the condition of being tarnished or the film or coating characteristic of this condition: *We took the tarnish off with silver polish.* **2** any unattractiveness, especially mild disgrace; blot. ⟨< F *ternir* < *terne* dark, ? < Gmc.⟩

ta•ro ['tɑrou] *n., pl.* **-ros. 1** a tropical plant (*Colocasia esculenta*) of the same family as the jack-in-the-pulpit, grown in the Pacific islands for its edible starchy roots. **2** the root of the taro. ⟨< Polynesian⟩

tar•ot ['tærou] *or* ['tɛrou], ['tærət] *or* ['tɛrət] *n.* **1** a pack of 14th-century Italian playing cards, consisting of 78 cards including 22 trumps. **2** the 22 trump cards, often used by fortunetellers. **3 tarots,** the game played with these cards. ⟨< F < Ital. *tarocchi*⟩

tarp [tɑrp] *n. Informal.* tarpaulin.

tar paper heavy paper coated or impregnated with tar to make it waterproof, for use on roofs, outer walls, etc.

tar•pau•lin [tɑr'pɒlən] *n.* **1** a sheet of waterproofed canvas or other coarse strong cloth, used for protection against the weather. **2** a sailor's hat made of this or similar material. **3** *Archaic.* sailor; tar. ⟨< *tar[1]* + *pall* in sense of 'covering'⟩

Tar•pei•an Rock [tɑr'piən] in Rome, the rock on the Capitoline Hill from which persons convicted of treason were hurled. ⟨< *Tarpeia,* a legendary Roman maiden⟩

tar•pon ['tɑrpɒn] *n., pl.* **-pon** or **-pons.** a large, silver-coloured game fish (*Tarpon atlanticus*) found in the warmer parts of the Atlantic Ocean. ⟨origin uncertain⟩

tar•ra•did•dle ['tɑrə,dɪdəl] *or* ['tɛrə,dɪdəl] See TARADIDDLE.

tar•ra•gon ['tærəgən] *or* ['tɛrəgən] *n.* **1** a perennial Old World herb (*Artemesia dracunculus*) of the composite family widely cultivated for its aromatic leaves, which are used as seasoning in salads, sauces, etc. **2** the leaves of this plant. ⟨< OF *targon* < Med.L *tarcon* < Arabic *tarkhūn,* perhaps < Gk. *dragontion* adderwort⟩

tar•ry[1] ['tæri] *or* ['tɛri] *v.* **-ried, -ry•ing.** *Poetic or Archaic.* **1** stay or lodge for a time: *He tarried at the inn till he felt well again.* **2** delay in going or coming, or in doing; be tardy: *Why do you tarry so long?* **3** wait (for). ⟨OE *tergan* vex, irritate; meaning influenced by OF *targer* delay, ult. < L *tardare*⟩ **—'tar•ri•er,** *n.*
☛ *Hom.* TERRY ['tɛri].

tar•ry[2] ['tɑri] *adj.* **-ri•er, -ri•est.** of, like, or covered with tar: *a tarry smell.* ⟨< *tar[1]*⟩

tar•sal ['tɑrsəl] *adj., n.* *—adj.* of or having to do with the tarsus.
—n. a tarsal bone or cartilage.

tar sands *Cdn.* a deposit (especially the one in Alberta, known as the **Alberta tar sands**) of bitumen mixed with sand, clay, and various minerals, having the appearance and texture of asphalt paving, and found near the earth's surface or hundreds of metres deep. The bitumen in the tar sands can be processed into a lighter, liquid form which is called synthetic crude oil to distinguish it from the traditional petroleum occurring naturally in a liquid state.

tar•si•er ['tɑrsiər] *or* ['tɑrsi,ei] *n.* a small, nocturnal primate (family Tarsiidae, genus *Tarsius*) of Indonesia and the Philippines having a long, thin tail and large eyes. They are arboreal and feed mainly on insects and small lizards. ⟨< F *tarse* tarsus, because of the bone structure of their feet⟩

tar•sus ['tɑrsəs] *n., pl.* **-si** [-saɪ] *or* [-si]. **1** the group of bones between the lower leg bones and the metatarsal bones, forming the ankle and the back half of the foot. The tarsus contains seven bones, including the talus and the heel bone. See LEG for picture. **2** the corresponding part in the hind leg of a four-footed animal, forming the backward-bending joint between the lower thigh and the shank. **3** the shank of a bird's leg. **4** the last segment of an insect's leg. **5** the small plate of connective tissue in the eyelid. ⟨< NL < Gk. *tarsos* sole of the foot, originally, crate⟩

tart[1] [tɑrt] *adj.* **1** having a pleasantly sharp, sour taste: *a tart apple.* **2** having a sharp, cutting or caustic quality: *a tart reply.* ⟨OE *teart*⟩ **—'tart•ly,** *adv.* **—'tart•ness,** *n.*
☛ *Syn.* **2.** See note at SOUR.

tart[2] [tɑrt] *n., v.* *—n.* **1** a small shell of pastry filled with cooked fruit, jam, etc., serving one person. **2** *Slang.* prostitute.
—v. Informal. dress or decorate, especially in a cheap and gaudy way (*used with* **up**): *The resort was all tarted up for the tourist season.* ⟨ME < OF *tarte*⟩

tar•tan[1] ['tɑrtən] *n.* **1** a plaid pattern for cloth originating in Scotland and designed with the stripes in varying widths and colours to distinguish the different families, or clans: *The main colour in the Douglas tartan is green.* **2** a similar pattern designed as an official symbol of a group, etc.: *The colours of Canada's Maple Leaf tartan represent the colours of maple leaves in different seasons.* **3** cloth woven with such a pattern, especially woollen cloth in a twill weave: *I bought a length of tartan.* **4** a garment made of such cloth: *She wore her tartan.* **5** (*adjl.*) made of tartan: *a tartan skirt.* **6** (*adjl.*) of or like tartan: *a tartan design.* ⟨? < MF *tiretaine* linsey-woolsey⟩

tar•tan[2] ['tɑrtən] *n.* a single-masted vessel with a lateen sail and a jib, used in the Mediterranean. ⟨< F < Ital. *tartana*⟩

tar•tar ['tɑrtər] *n.* **1** an acid substance derived from grape juice that collects as a crustlike deposit on the inside of wine casks. Purified tartar is called cream of tartar. *Formula*: $KHC_4H_4O_6$ **2** a hard deposit on the teeth, consisting of proteins from saliva, calcium carbonate or other salts, and, usually, food particles; dental calculus. ⟨ME < OF *tartre* < Med.L < Med.Gk. *tartaron*⟩ **—'tar•tar•ous,** *adj.*

Tar•tar ['tɑrtər] *n.* **1** See TATAR. **2 tartar,** a violent-tempered or savage person.
catch a tartar, meet with or oppose a person who is unexpectedly stronger than oneself. ⟨ME < Med.L *Tartarus* < Persian *Tātār*, influenced in form by L *Tartarus* Hades⟩

tartar emetic a poisonous, white, crystalline tartrate of potassium and antimony, used in medicine to cause vomiting and sweating, as a mordant in dyeing, etc. *Formula*: $K(SbO)C_4H_4O_6 \cdot \frac{1}{2}H_2O$

tar•tar•ic [tɑr'tærɪk] *or* [tɑr'tɛrɪk] *adj.* of, having to do with, containing, or derived from tartar.

tartaric acid a colourless crystalline acid found in many plants, especially grapes. Tartaric acid is usually obtained commercially from tartar and is used in food and medicines, in photography, etc. *Formula*: $C_4H_6O_6$

tartar sauce a sauce made of mayonnaise with chopped pickles, olives, capers, etc., typically eaten with seafood.

Tar•ta•rus ['tɑrtərəs] *n. Greek mythology.* **1** the abyss below Hades, where Zeus hurled the Titans, who had rebelled against him. **2** a place of punishment in Hades for the spirits of the worst sinners. **3** Hades. ⟨< L < Gk. *Tartaros*⟩ **—Tar'tar•e•an** [tɑr'tɛriən], *adj.*

Tar•ta•ry ['tɑrtəri] *n.* See TATARY.

tart•let ['tɑrtlɪt] *n.* a small tart.

tar•trate ['tɑrtreit] *n.* a salt or ester of tartaric acid.

tar•trat•ed ['tɑrtreitɪd] *adj.* **1** containing or derived from tartar. **2** combined with tartaric acid. **3** formed into a tartrate.

tar•tra•zine ['tɑrtrə,zin] *n.* a yellow dye used in colouring food, cosmetics, drugs, etc., to which some sensitive individuals are allergic. Also called (*U.S.*) **yellow no. 5.** ⟨< *tartar* + *azo* + *-ine*⟩

tart•y ['tɑrti] *adj.* **tart•i•er, tart•i•est.** *Slang.* suggesting or like that of a prostitute: *That's a really tarty get-up.*

tas•bih [tæz'bi] *n.* a rosary, or prayer beads, used by some Muslims as a memory aid during prayers. ⟨< Arabic⟩

task [tæsk] *n., v.* *—n.* **1** work to be done; a piece of work that has been assigned or undertaken: *One of his tasks was to take the garbage out.* **2** something hard or unpleasant that has to be done: *She was left with the task of breaking the news to her mother.*
take to task, reprove: *The teacher took him to task for not studying harder.*
—v. **1** assign a task to: *They tasked her with the organization of the membership drive.* **2** put a strain on; burden; tax. ⟨ME < ONF *tasque*, var. of *tasche* < VL *tasca*, var. of *taxa* < Med.L *taxare.* See TAX.⟩ **—'task•er,** *n.*

task force a temporary group specially organized under one leader for a particular task: *A naval task force was sent to turn away the spy ship. The mayor set up a task force to study the effects of the proposed expressway.*

task•mas•ter ['tæsk,mæstər] *n.* a person who sets tasks for others to do; especially, one who is very demanding or severe.

Tas•ma•nia [tæz'meiniə] *or* [tæz'meinjə] an island state of Australia just south of Victoria.

Tas•ma•ni•an [tæz'meiniən] *or* [tæz'meinjən] *n., adj.* *—n.* a native or inhabitant of Tasmania.
—adj. of or having to do with Tasmania or its people.

Tasmanian devil a small, fierce, carnivorous marsupial (*Sarcophilus harrisi*) of Tasmania having a large head, black fur masked with white, and powerful jaws.

Tasmanian wolf or **tiger** a fierce, carnivorous marsupial (*Thylacinus cynocephalus*) of Tasmania, having brownish fur with darker dorsal stripes. It is probably extinct. Also called **thylacine.**

Tass or **TASS** [tæs] *n.* the official news agency of the former Soviet Union. ⟨< *T*(elegraphnoe) *A*(genstvo) *S*(ovetskogo) *S*(oyuza) Telegraph Agency of the Soviet Union⟩

tas•sel ['tæsəl] *n., v.* **-selled** or **-seled, -sell•ing** or **-sel•ing.** *—n.* **1** a hanging bunch of equal-sized lengths of yarn, cord, strung beads, etc. fastened together at the top and used to ornament curtains, etc. **2** something resembling a tassel, such as the group of flower spikelets at the top of the main stem of a corn plant.
—v. **1** put a tassel or tassels on; ornament with a tassel or tassels. **2** form or produce tassels, as corn does. **3** remove the tassels from (growing corn) to improve the crop. ⟨ME < OF *tassel*; ult. origin uncertain⟩

taste [teist] *n., v.* **tast•ed, tast•ing.** *—n.* **1** what is special about something to the sense organs of the mouth; flavour: *He has never liked the taste of green olives.* **2** the sensation produced in these organs: *Sweet, sour, salt, and bitter are four important tastes.* **3** the sense by which the flavour of things is perceived: *Her taste is unusually keen.* **4** a little bit; sample: *to take a taste of a cake.* **5** a liking: *Suit your own taste.* **6** the ability to perceive and enjoy what is beautiful and excellent. **7** a manner or style that shows such ability: *Their house is furnished in excellent taste.* **8** the prevailing typical style in an age, class, or country: *in the Moorish taste.* **9** any little exposure to or experience *(of): brief tastes of joy.* **10** a representative experience: *The snowstorm gave me a taste of northern winter.* **11** the act of tasting or the fact of being tasted.
a bad or **nasty taste in the mouth,** an unpleasant feeling or memory left by a negative experience.
in bad (or **good, poor,** etc.) **taste,** of a remark, action, etc., showing an inadequate (or good, etc.) sense of aesthetics, fitness to the occasion or propriety: *Her joke was in terribly poor taste.*

to (one's) **taste,** in harmony with one's preferences; to one's liking; pleasing: *That style of furniture is not to his taste.*
to taste, in the amount that suits one's palate: *Add salt and pepper to taste.*
–v. **1** try the flavour of (something) by taking a little into the mouth. **2** perceive by the sense of taste: *She tasted almond in the cake.* **3** have a particular flavour: *The soup tastes of onion. This pudding tastes a bit burnt.* **4** eat or drink a little bit (of): *to taste of the forbidden fruit. I was too sick to even taste dinner.* **5** experience; have (*sometimes used with* **of**): *to taste freedom, to taste of pleasure.* ⟨ME < OF *taster*, originally, feel⟩
–'tast•a•ble, *adj.*

☛ *Syn. n.* **1. Taste,** FLAVOUR = the property or quality of a thing that affects the sense organs of the mouth. **Taste** is the general and neutral word: *Mineral oil has no taste.* **Flavour** refers to characteristic taste, especially good taste, belonging to a thing, or a specially noticeable quality in the taste: *These berries have no flavour, but merely a sweet taste.*

taste bud any of certain small groups of cells, most of which are in the outer layer of the tongue, that are sense organs of taste.

taste•ful ['teistfəl] *adj.* **1** having or showing good taste: *tasteful furnishings.* **2** pleasing to the taste; tasty: *tasteful food.* **–'taste•ful•ly,** *adv.* **–'taste•ful•ness,** *n.*

taste•less ['teistlɪs] *adj.* **1** not appealing to the sense of taste; without flavour; bland: *The meat was dry and tasteless.* **2** having or showing a lack of sensitivity to beauty and artistic worth: *a tasteless choice of accessories.* **3** showing a lack of sensitivity to what is appropriate or proper: *She made a tasteless remark about his having gained weight.* **–'taste•less•ly,** *adv.* **–'taste•less•ness,** *n.*

tast•er ['teistər] *n.* **1** a person who tastes; especially, one whose work is testing the quality of tea, wine, etc. by tasting it. **2** a utensil or container used in tasting or sampling. **3** formerly, a person who took a bit of food or drink before it was touched by his master or employer as a precaution against poison.

tast•y ['teisti] *adj.* **tast•i•er, tast•i•est. 1** pleasing to the taste; appetizing; flavourful: *That cake is very tasty.* **2** *Rare.* tasteful. **–'tast•i•ly,** *adv.* **–'tast•i•ness,** *n.*

tat[1] [tæt] *v.* **tat•ted, tat•ting. 1** do tatting; work at tatting. **2** make by tatting: *to tat a lace edging.* ⟨? back formation from *tatting*⟩

tat[2] [tæt] See TIT FOR TAT.

ta–ta [tɑ'tɑ] *interj. Esp. Brit.* goodbye (*usually facetious in Canada*).

ta•ta•mi [tə'tɑmi] *n., pl.* **-mi** or **-mis.** a floor mat woven of straw, used especially in Japanese homes for sitting or lying on. ⟨< Japanese⟩

Ta•tar ['tɑtər] *n. or adj.* **1** a member of a Turkic people living mainly in southwestern Russia. **2** the Turkic language of the Tatars. **3** a member of any of various groups of Asian nomads of ancient and medieval times; especially, a Mongol people that formed part of the hordes of Genghis Khan. **4** (*adjl.*) of or having to do with the Tatars. Also, especially formerly, **Tartar**.

Ta•ta•ry ['tɑtəri] *n.* the kingdom of the Tartars in the late Middle Ages which, at its greatest, under Genghis Khan, extended from SW Russia east to the Pacific. Also, especially formerly, **Tartary**.

ta•ter ['teitər] *n. Dialect or facetious.* potato.

tat•ter ['tætər] *n., v.* *–n.* **1** a torn piece left hanging; shred: *After the storm the flag hung in tatters on the mast.* **2 tatters,** *pl.* torn or ragged clothing.
–v. tear or wear to pieces; make or become ragged. ⟨ult. < Scand.; cf. ON *tötturr* rag⟩

tat•ter•de•mal•ion [,tætərdɪ'meiljən] *or* [,tætərdɪ'mæljən] *n.* a person in tattered clothes; ragamuffin. ⟨< *tatter* + *-demalion*, of uncertain origin⟩

tat•tered ['tætərd] *adj., v.* *–adj.* **1** torn or ragged; in tatters: *a tattered dress.* **2** wearing torn or ragged clothes: *a tattered urchin.*
–v. pt. and pp. of TATTER.

tat•ter•sall ['tætər,sɒl] *n., adj.* *–n.* **1** a pattern of squares made by light crossbars on a background of a solid dark colour. **2** a fabric with this pattern.
–adj. made of such a fabric; having this pattern: *a tattersall jacket.* ⟨< *Tattersall's*, a London horse market; this was a popular pattern for horse blankets⟩

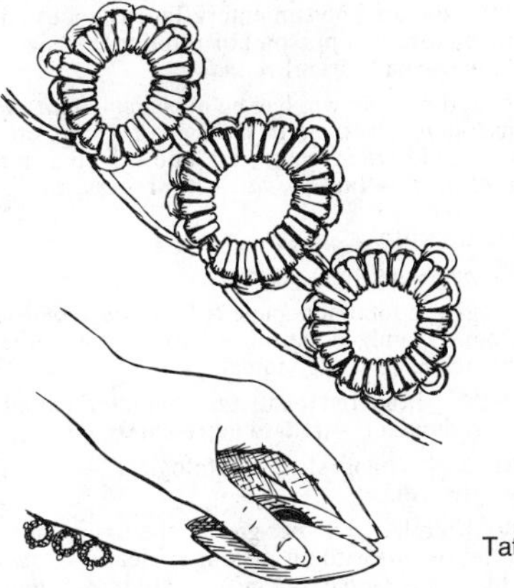
Tatting

tat•ting ['tætɪŋ] *n., v.* *–n.* **1** the act or process of making a delicate kind of lace by looping and knotting cotton or linen thread by hand, using a small shuttle. **2** the lace made in this way.
–v. ppr. of TAT. ⟨? < Brit. dial. *tat* tangle⟩

tat•tle ['tætəl] *v.* **-tled, -tling;** *n.* *–v.* **1** reveal secrets; tell tales. **2** betray; give away (*used with* **on**): *He tattled on his sister and she was punished.* **3** talk idly or foolishly; gossip. **4** say or reveal by tattling: *They tattled the story to the principal.*
–n. idle talk or gossip. ⟨Cf. MDu. *tatelen* stutter⟩ **–'tat•tler,** *n.*

tat•tle•tale ['tætəl,teil] *n.* a person who tells secrets, especially to get other people into trouble.

tat•too[1] [tæ'tu] *or* [tə'tu] *v.* **-tooed, -too•ing;** *n., pl.* **-toos.** *–v.* **1** mark (the skin), often permanently, with designs or patterns by pricking it and putting in colours. **2** mark (a design) on the skin in this way: *The sailor had a ship tattooed on his arm.*
–n. **1** a mark or design made by tattooing. **2** the act or practice of tattooing the skin. ⟨< Polynesian *tatau*⟩ **–tat'too•er,** *n.* **–tat'too•ist,** *n.*

tat•too[2] [tæ'tu] *or* [tə'tu] *n., pl.* **-toos;** *v.* **-tooed, -too•ing.** *–n.* **1** a signal on a bugle or drum calling soldiers to their quarters at night. **2** a series of raps, taps, etc.: *The hail beat a loud tattoo on the roof.* **3** a military display, especially music and parading by show units.
–v. tap continuously; drum: *tattooing with one's fingers on the table.* ⟨< Du. *taptoe* < *tap* tap of a barrel + *toe* pull to, shut⟩

tat•ty ['tæti] *n.* shabby or tacky: *a row of tatty little houses.* ⟨< Scottish dialect; cf. OE *tættec* a tatter⟩

tau [taʊ] *or* [tɒ] *n.* **1** the nineteenth letter (T, τ = English T, t) of the Greek alphabet. **2** TAU PARTICLE.
☛ *Hom.* TAU [tɒ].

tau cross a cross shaped like the Greek letter tau, sometimes having broadened ends. See CROSS for picture.

taught [tɒt] *v.* pt. and pp. of TEACH.
☛ *Hom.* TAUT, TOT.

tau lepton TAU PARTICLE.

taunt [tɒnt] *v., n.* *–v.* **1** tease or reproach in a scornful or insulting way; jeer at; mock: *At school she had been taunted about being poor. They taunted him with cowardice.* **2** get or drive by taunts: *They taunted him into taking the dare.*
–n. a scornful or insulting remark. ⟨obs. phrase *taunt (pour taunt)*, var. of F *tant pour tant* tit for tat⟩ **–'taunt•ing•ly,** *adv.*

tau particle an unstable charged lepton having a mass approximately 3500 times larger than the electron. Also, **tau lepton**.

taupe [toup] *n. or adj.* medium brownish grey. ⟨< F *taupe*, originally, mole < L *talpa*⟩
☛ *Hom.* TOPE.

tau•rine[1] ['tɒraɪn] *or* ['tɒrɪn] *adj.* **1** of or like a bull; bovine. **2** of or having to do with Taurus. ⟨< L *taurinus* < *taurus* bull⟩

tau•rine[2] ['tɒrin] *or* ['tɒrɪn] *n.* a neutral crystalline compound obtained from bile. *Formula*: $C_2H_7NO_3S_2$

tau•rom•a•chy [tɒ'rɒməki] *n.* bullfighting.

Tau•rus ['tɒrəs] *n.* **1** *Astronomy.* a northern constellation thought of as having the shape of a bull. **2** *Astrology.* **a** the second sign of the zodiac. The sun enters Taurus about April 20. See ZODIAC for picture. **b** a person born under this sign. ⟨< L *taurus* bull⟩ **—'Tau•re•an** ['tɔriən], *n., adj.*

taut [tɒt] *adj.* **1** tightly drawn; having no slack: *a taut rope.* **2** strained; tense: *taut nerves, a taut smile.* **3** of a ship, etc., efficiently run; in good order; neat, trim, and tidy. ⟨earlier *taught,* apparently var. of *tight*⟩ **—'taut•ly,** *adv.* **—'taut•ness,** *n.*
☛ *Hom.* TAUGHT, TOT.
☛ *Syn.* **1.** See note at TIGHT.

tauto– *combining form.* same: *tautomer.*

tau•tog ['tɒtɒg] *n.* a food and game fish (*Tautoga onitis*) of the wrasse family found mainly along the Atlantic coast of the United States; blackfish. ⟨< Algonquian⟩

tau•to•log•i•cal [,tɒtə'lɒdʒəkəl] *adj.* characterized by or using tautology; redundant. **—,tau•to'log•i•cal•ly,** *adv.*

tau•tol•o•gous [tɒ'tɒləgəs] *adj.* tautological. **—tau'tol•o•gous•ly,** *adv.*

tau•tol•o•gy [tɒ'tɒlədʒi] *n., pl.* **-gies. 1** the saying of a thing over again in other words without making it clearer or more forceful; redundancy. *Example:* the *modern* student of *today.* **2** an instance of this. **3** *Logic.* a statement that is necessarily true by virtue of its form. *Example: She is either present or not.* ⟨< LL < Gk. *tautologia,* ult. < *to auto* the same (thing) + *legein* say⟩

tau•to•mer ['tɒtəmər] *n.* a compound exhibiting tautomerism. ⟨< *tauto-* + Gk. *meros* part⟩

tau•tom•er•ism [tɒ'tɒmə,rɪzəm] *n. Chemistry.* the property of some organic compounds that enables them to be in a state of equilibrium between differing isomeric structures, and to react to form either. **—,tau•to'mer•ic** [,tɒtə'mɛrɪk], *adj.*

tau•to•nym ['tɒtə,nɪm] *n.* in scientific nomenclature, a name in which the components for genus and species are identical, as *Naja naja* for the cobra de capello, an Indian species of cobra. **—,tau•to'nym•ic** or **tau'ton•y•mous** [tɒ'tɒnəməs], *adj.* **—tau'ton•y•my** [tɒ'tɒnəmi], *n.*

tav [tɑv] *or* [tɒv], [tɑf] *or* [tɒf] *n.* the twenty-fifth letter of the Hebrew alphabet. See table of alphabets in the Appendix.

tav•ern ['tævərn] *n.* **1** a place where alcoholic drinks are sold and drunk. **2** *Archaic.* an inn. Hotels have taken the place of the old taverns. ⟨ME < OF < L *taberna,* originally, rude dwelling⟩

ta•ver•na [tə'vɜrnə] *n.* a small casual Greek restaurant. ⟨< Mod.Gk. *taberna* < L. See TAVERN.⟩

tav•ern•er ['tævərnər] *n.* the owner or proprietor of a tavern. ⟨ME < AF < OF *tavernier*⟩

taw [tɒ] *n.* **1** in the game of marbles, a large fancy marble used for shooting. **2** a game of marbles played with taws. **3** the line from which the players shoot their marbles. ⟨origin uncertain⟩

taw•dry ['tɒdri] *adj.* **-dri•er, -dri•est.** showy and cheap. ⟨ult. alteration of *St. Audrey,* from cheap laces sold at St. Audrey's fair in Ely, England⟩ **—'taw•dri•ly,** *adv.* **—'taw•dri•ness,** *n.*

taw•ny ['tɒni] *adj.* **-ni•er, -ni•est;** *n.* *—adj.* brownish yellow: *the tawny coat of a lion.*
—n. a brownish yellow. ⟨ME < OF *tanné,* pp. of *tanner* tan⟩ **—'taw•ni•ness,** *n.*

tax [tæks] *n., v.* *—n.* **1** money paid by people for the support of the government, for public works, etc.: *Taxes are paid to the federal, provincial, and municipal governments.* **2** a burden, duty, or demand that oppresses; strain: *Climbing stairs is a tax on a weak heart.*
—v. **1** put a tax on: *When the British taxed tea, the American colonists revolted.* **2** cause to pay a tax or taxes: *The voters complain that they are already taxed to the limit.* **3** lay a heavy burden on; be hard on: *Reading in poor light taxes the eyes.* **4** accuse or charge (*used with* **with**): *The office manager taxed Rob with having neglected his work.* **5** *Law.* examine and fix (the costs of a lawsuit, etc.). ⟨< Med.L *taxare* impose a tax < L *taxare* estimate, assess, charge < Gk. *taxai,* aorist infin. of *tassein* assign⟩ **—'tax•er,** *n.* **—'tax•less,** *adj.*

tax•a ['tæksə] *n.* pl. of TAXON.

tax•a•bil•i•ty [,tæksə'bɪləti] *n.* the state of being taxable.

tax•a•ble ['tæksəbəl] *adj.* liable to be taxed; subject to taxation: *Children's clothes are not taxable in some provinces.*

tax•a•tion [tæk'seiʃən] *n.* **1** the act of taxing: *Taxation is necessary to provide roads, schools, and police protection.* **2** the amount people pay for the support of the government; taxes.

tax–deductible ['tæks dɪ'dʌktəbəl] *adj.* allowed as a deduction from the gross when calculating income tax.

tax•eme ['tæksim] *n. Linguistics.* any minimal feature of a grammatical construction, such as word selection, word order, pitch, stress, etc. ⟨coined by U.S. linguist L. Bloomfield (1933) < Gk. *taxis* arrangement + *-eme* (< *phoneme*)⟩ **—tax'em•ic,** *adj.*

tax–ex•empt ['tæksɛg'zɛmpt] *adj.* **1** free from taxes; not taxed. **2** generating tax-free income.

tax–free ['tæks 'fri] *adj.* **1** not taxable. **2** of an economy, jurisdiction, etc., in which there are no taxes.

tax haven a foreign country or corporation where taxes are not imposed, used by residents or investors from another country to escape taxation: *Switzerland is used as a tax haven by many very wealthy people.*

tax•i ['tæksi] *n., pl.* **tax•is;** *v.* **tax•ied, tax•i•ing** or **tax•y•ing.** *—n.* an automobile driven for hire, usually having a meter for recording the fare.
—v. **1 a** ride in a taxi: *It's just as cheap to taxi to the airport as to take the shuttle bus.* **b** transport by taxi: *They taxied the parcel to us.* **2** of an aircraft, move across the ground or water under its own power: *An airplane taxis down the runway before takeoff and taxis to the terminal building after landing.* **3** cause an aircraft to move in this way: *The pilot taxied the plane out onto the Tarmac.* ⟨short for *taxicab*⟩

tax•i•cab ['tæksi,kæb] *n.* taxi. ⟨contraction of *taximeter cab.* See TAXIMETER.⟩

tax•i•der•mist ['tæksə,dɜrmɪst] *n.* a person trained in taxidermy, especially one whose work it is.

tax•i•der•my ['tæksə,dɜrmi] *n.* the art of preparing the skins of animals and stuffing and mounting them in lifelike form. ⟨< Gk. *taxis* arrangement (< *tassein* arrange) + *derma* skin⟩ **—,tax•i'der•mal** or **,tax•i'der•mic,** *adj.*

tax•i•me•ter ['tæksi,mitər] *n.* a device fitted to a hired vehicle for showing the fare as it accumulates. ⟨< F *taximètre* < *taxe* fare < *mètre* meter⟩

tax•is ['tæksɪs] *n., pl.* **-es** [-iz]. **1** *Biology.* movement of a free-moving organism in response to an external stimulus. The movement may be toward or away from the stimulus. **2** *Surgery.* the manipulation or replacement by hand of a displaced structure or organ without cutting tissue. ⟨< NL < Gk. *tassein* put in order, arrange⟩

taxi stand a place where taxis may park while waiting to be hired: *There's a taxi stand in front of the railway station.*

tax•i•way ['tæksi,wei] *n.* any of the paved, marked pathways by which airplanes taxi between a runway and a parking area, terminal, or hangar.

tax•on ['tæksɒn] *n., pl.* **taxa.** a taxonomic unit, such as a family or a genus.

tax•o•nom•ic [,tæksə'nɒmɪk] *adj.* of, based on, or having to do with taxonomy or a particular taxonomy. **—,tax•o'nom•i•cal•ly,** *adv.*

tax•on•o•mist [tæk'sɒnəmɪst] *n.* a person knowledgable about taxonomy.

tax•on•o•my [tæk'sɒnəmi] *n., pl.* **-mies. 1** the study, in any discipline, of the principles of scientific classification. **2** *Biology.* the classification of animals and plants according to natural relationships based on structure, patterns of change and variation, etc. The basic categories, from the most general to the most specific, are *kingdom, phylum* (or for plants, *division*), *class, order, family, genus,* and *species.* **3** any particular system of classification: *She tried to come up with a taxonomy of the personality types in her workplace.* ⟨< F *taxonomie* < Gk. *taxis* arrangement (< *tassein* arrange) + *-nomos* assigning⟩

tax•pay•er ['tæks,peiər] *n.* a person who pays a tax or taxes or is required by law to do so.

tax•pay•ing ['tæks,peiɪŋ] *adj.* paying a tax or taxes: *the taxpaying public.*

tax rate the rate of taxation on property, income, etc.

tax return the report of one's income, or the form on which it is made, to a government for purposes of taxation.

tax shelter any financial arrangement or investment that results in a reduction of taxes.

tax•us ['tæksəs] *n., pl.* **taxus.** yew.

Tay–Sachs disease ['tei 'sæks] a rare but fatal hereditary disease, occurring mainly in infants and young children of eastern European Jewish descent, caused by an enzyme deficiency. It is characterized by a red spot on the retina, gradual blindness, mental retardation, and paralysis. ⟨after W. *Tay*

(1843-1927), English physician, and B. *Sachs* (1858-1944), American neurologist⟩

taz•za ['tɑtsə] *n.* a wide, shallow cup having a foot. ⟨< Ital. < Arabic *tasa* shallow metal cup⟩

Tb terbium.

TB *Informal.* tuberculosis.

TBA, t.b.a., or **tba** to be announced.

T–bar ['ti ˌbɑr] *n.* a horizontal bar attached by a vertical bar to a cable in the air which tows skiers up a hill as they hold onto the bar.

T–bill TREASURY BILL.

T–bone ['ti ˌboun] *n.* a beefsteak taken from the middle part of the loin, containing a T-shaped bone and a bit of tenderloin. Also, **T-bone steak.**

tbs. or **tbsp.** tablespoon; tablespoons.

Tc technetium.

T cell the type of lymphocyte that recognizes foreign proteins and triggers mechanisms for their destruction.

TD or **td** *Football.* touchdown.

te [ti] *n.* See TI¹.
☛ *Hom.* T, TEA, TEE, TI.

Te tellurium.

tea [ti] *n.* **1** a dark brown or greenish drink made by pouring boiling water over the crushed, dried leaves of a tropical or subtropical Asian evergreen shrub (*Camellia sinensis*). **2** the dried and prepared leaves from which this drink is made. Most tea comes from China, Japan, and India. **3** the shrub itself. **4** any dried plant or part of a plant that resembles or is used as tea: *a tin of raspberry leaf tea.* **5** *Brit.* a meal in the late afternoon or early evening, at which tea is commonly served. **6** an afternoon reception at which tea is served. **7** a hot drink made from herbs, meat broth, etc.: *fruit tea, beef tea.*
another cup of tea, *Informal.* a very different sort of thing.
(one's) **cup of tea,** *Informal.* just what one likes. ⟨< dial. Chinese *t'e*⟩
☛ *Hom.* T, TE, TEE, TI.

tea bag a small, porous paper or gauze packet containing enough tea leaves for one or two cups of tea and used instead of loose leaves when brewing tea.

tea ball a hollow, perforated metal or china ball which is filled with tea leaves and put in hot water to make tea.

tea•ber•ry ['tiˌbɛri] *n.* wintergreen.

tea biscuit a small, cakelike baked good made with baking powder; scone.

tea caddy or **canister** a small can or tin-lined box for keeping tea fresh.

tea•cart ['tiˌkɑrt] *n.* TEA WAGON.

teach [titʃ] *v.* **taught, teach•ing. 1** show or explain how to do: *We taught our dog a new trick. His mother taught him to drive.* **2 a** help (someone) acquire (a skill, habit, character trait, etc.) by instruction, example, or both: *She taught us honesty.* **b** cause (someone) to learn, realize, acknowledge, or understand: *That experience taught me not to believe everything I hear. He taught her that no hero is perfect.* **3** give instruction to: *He taught my sister last year.* **4** give lessons in: *She teaches mathematics.* **5** give instruction; be a teacher by profession: *He taught for 40 years.* ⟨OE *tǣcan* show⟩
☛ *Syn.* **1, 2. Teach,** INSTRUCT = give or convey knowledge or information to someone. **Teach** emphasizes causing or enabling a person to learn something by giving information, explanation, and training, by showing how as well as what to learn, and by guiding the learner's studies: *Some children learn to read by themselves, but most need to be taught.* **Instruct** emphasizes providing, in a systematic way, the necessary information or knowledge about a subject: *He instructs classes in chemistry.*
☛ *Usage.* See note at LEARN.

teach•a•ble ['titʃəbəl] *adj.* **1** of a person, able and willing to be taught. **2** of a skill, habit, or body of information, capable of being passed on by a teacher: *This curriculum is very teachable. Some things are just not teachable and must be learned by experience.* **—ˌteach•a'bil•i•ty,** *n.* **—'teach•a•ble•ness,** *n.*

teach•er ['titʃər] *n.* a person who teaches, especially a trained professional teaching in a school or college.

teach•er•age ['titʃərədʒ] *n.* formerly, in rural areas and small towns, a house owned by a board of education for the use of the schoolteacher.

teach•ing ['titʃɪŋ] *n., v.* —*n.* **1** the work or profession of a teacher. **2** the act of one who teaches. **3** what is taught; doctrine or precept: *the teachings of Islam.*
—*v.* ppr. of TEACH.

teaching assistant a graduate student in a university or college, who teaches some classes on behalf of a professor.

tea cloth 1 *Brit.* TEA TOWEL. **2** a decorative cloth for a tea table.

tea cosy a hatlike insulated covering, often knitted or crocheted, for putting over a teapot to keep the tea hot. Also, **tea cozy.**

tea•cup ['tiˌkʌp] *n.* **1** a cup used with a saucer for drinking tea, coffee, etc. A teacup is usually smaller than a mug or a measuring cup. **2** as much as a teacup holds; teacupful.
storm in a teacup. See STORM.

tea•cup•ful ['tikʌpˌfʊl] *n., pl.* **-fuls.** as much as a teacup holds.

tea•house ['tiˌhʌus] *n., pl.* **-hous•es** [-ˌhaʊzɪz] a place where tea and other light refreshments are served. There are many teahouses in Japan and China.

teak [tik] *n.* **1** a tall East Indian tree (*Tectona grandis*) of the verbena family, one of the most valuable timber trees in the world. **2** the fragrant yellowish brown wood of this tree, used for building ships and bridges, making fine furniture, flooring and panelling, etc. Teak is valued mainly for its hardness and durability; beams of teak have lasted more than 1000 years. **3** (*adjl.*) made of this wood. ⟨< Pg. < Malayalam *tēkka*⟩

tea•ket•tle ['tiˌkɛtəl] *n.* a covered kettle with a spout and handle, used for boiling water to make tea, etc.

teak•wood ['tɪkˌwʊd] *n.* TEAK (defs, 2, 3).

teal [til] *n., pl.* **teal** or **teals. 1** any of several small freshwater ducks (genus *Anas*) of America, Europe, and Asia. The two commonest Canadian teals are the blue-winged teal (*A. discors*) and green-winged teal (*A. carolinensis*). **2** TEAL BLUE. ⟨ME *tele*; cf. Du. *taling, teling*⟩

teal blue a medium to dark greenish blue.

team [tim] *n., v.* —*n.* **1** a group of people forming one of the sides in a game or competition: *a debating team, a football team.* **2** a group of people working or acting together; crew: *He was on the clean-up team.* **3 a** two or more horses or other animals harnessed together to work. **b** the animals and vehicle together. **4** (*adjl.*) done or made by a team; having to do with a team: *a team effort. There is a real team spirit in the office.*
—*v.* **1** join together in a team (*usually used with* **up**): *We teamed up to clean the classroom after the party. She teamed stronger students with weaker ones.* **2** drive a team. **3** work, carry, haul, etc. with a team. ⟨OE *tēam*⟩
☛ *Hom.* TEEM.

team•mate ['timˌmeit] *n.* a fellow member of a team.

team•ster ['timstər] *n.* **1** a truck driver. **2** a person who drives a team of horses or other draft animals, especially as an occupation.

team teaching a system of teaching in which several teachers co-ordinate the instruction of a group of students. Team teaching may involve bringing together different subject areas or different aspects of one subject, or different teaching and learning styles. **—team teacher.**

team•work ['timˌwɜrk] *n.* the acting together of a number of people to make the work of the group successful and effective: *Football calls for teamwork.*

tea party TEA (def. 6).

tea•pot ['tiˌpɒt] *n.* a container with a handle and a spout, for making and serving tea.
tempest in a teapot. See TEMPEST.

tea•poy ['tiˌpɔɪ] *n.* **1** a small three-legged table or stand. **2** a small table that holds a tea service. ⟨< Hind. *tipai*, prob. alteration < Persian *si-paya* three-legged stand⟩

tear¹ [tir] *n., v.* —*n.* **1 tears,** *pl.* **a** salty liquid secreted by a gland in the eyelid that serves to lubricate and wash the eye and that overflows the eyelids, especially in weeping: *He had tears in his eyes. We laughed till the tears came.* **b** the act of weeping: *Tears will not help. She broke into tears. The baby is in tears.* **2** a drop of the liquid secreted by the eyes: *There was a tear on the baby's cheek.* **3** something suggesting a tear: *a tear of dew.* **4 tears,** *pl.* sorrow or grief: *this vale of tears.*
—*v.* of an eye or the eyes, fill with tears: *The bitter wind made her eyes tear.* ⟨OE *tēar*⟩
☛ *Hom.* TIER.

tear² [tɛr] *v.* **tore, torn, tear•ing;** *n.* —*v.* **1** pull apart by force: *to tear a box open.* **2** make by pulling apart: *She tore a hole in her dress.* **3** make a hole, rip, or injury in by a pull: *The nail tore her coat. She tore a ligament while running.* **4** pull hard; pull violently:

He tore down the enemy's flag. **5** cut badly; wound: *The jagged stone tore his skin.* **6** rend by conflict; divide: *The political party was torn by two factions. Her affections were torn between her family and her lover.* **7** remove by effort: *He could not tear himself from that spot.* **8** distress greatly; torment; make miserable: *She was torn by grief.* **9** become torn: *Lace tears easily.* **10** hurry; rush; dash: *Stop tearing through the house!*
tear at, make violent attempts to damage, tear, or remove with the hands: *He tore at the straps holding the box closed.*
tear down, a pull down; raze; destroy: *The city tore down a whole block of houses.* **b** bring about the wreck of; discredit; ruin: *She tried to tear down his reputation.*
tear into, a attack or criticize severely. **b** begin (an activity) with speed and gusto.
—n. **1** a torn place. **2** the act or process of tearing. **3** a hurry; rush; dash. **4** *Slang.* a spree. **5** a fit of violent anger. ⟨OE *teran*⟩
☛ *Hom.* TARE.
☛ *Syn. v.* **1. Tear,** RIP = pull apart by force something flexible or non-metallic, such as paper, cloth, skin, plant material, etc. **Tear** = pull apart or into pieces, often with some care or along a joint, whether intended for this purpose or not, but usually leaving rough or ragged edges: *He tore the coupon off the bottom of the flyer. Tear the lettuce into bite-sized pieces.* **Rip** = tear or cut roughly or quickly and forcefully, often accidentally: *She ripped a huge hole in her skirt. She ripped the accusing letter to shreds.*

tear bomb [tir] a bomb that sends forth TEAR GAS.

tear•drop ['tir,drɒp] *n.* **1** a single tear. **2** something shaped like a tear or a falling drop, especially a gem. **3** (*adjl.*) shaped like a tear or falling drop: *teardrop earrings.*

tear•ful ['tirfəl] *adj.* **1** flowing with or accompanied by tears: *a tearful face, a tearful goodbye.* **2** causing tears; sad. **—'tear•ful•ly,** *adv.* **—'tear•ful•ness,** *n.*

tear gas [tir] a gas that irritates the eyes, causing tears and temporary blindness, used especially in breaking up riots.

tear–gas ['tir ,gæs] *v.* **-gassed, -gas•sing.** use tear gas on; subdue with TEAR GAS.

tear•jerk•er ['tir,dʒɜrkər] *n. Informal.* a story, film, etc. calculated to play on the emotions (usually sadness) of the audience or reader.

tear•less ['tirlɪs] *adj.* **1** without tears; not crying. **2** incapable of weeping. **—'tear•less•ly,** *adv.* **—'tear•less•ness,** *n.*

tea•room ['ti,rum] *or* ['ti,rʊm] *n.* a room or shop where tea, coffee, and light meals are served.

tea rose **1** any of several varieties of cultivated hybrid rose typically having a scent resembling that of dried tea leaves. The original hybrid (*Rosa odorata*) from which they are derived no longer exists. See also HYBRID TEA ROSE. **2** a yellowish pink colour.

tear sheet [tɛr] a sheet or page torn out of a magazine or newspaper and distributed for a special purpose such as giving an advertiser proof of publication.

tear•y ['tiri] *adj.* **tear•i•er, tear•i•est.** tearful; crying. **—'tear•i•ly,** *adv.* **—'tear•i•ness,** *n.*

tease [tiz] *v.* **teased, teas•ing;** *n. —v.* **1** bother or annoy (someone) by means of jokes, questions, ridicule, etc.: *The other boys teased Jim about his curly hair.* **2** say something playfully without really meaning it: *I don't know when to believe you—you're always teasing.* **3** tantalize. **4** comb (hair) by holding it up and working the hairs back toward the scalp, giving it a frizzy or fluffy appearance. **5** comb out or card (wool, etc.) **6** raise a nap on (cloth). **7** gently pull apart (plant roots, tangled fibres, etc.). **8** arrive at (a meaning, solution, etc.) by long, careful, and concentrated thought, as if untangling something (*usually used with* **out**). **9** beg: *The child teases for every little thing that he sees.* *—n.* **1** a person or thing that teases. **2** the act of teasing or the state of being teased. ⟨OE *tǣsan*⟩ **—'teas•ing•ly,** *adv.*
☛ *Syn. v.* **1. Tease,** PLAGUE, PESTER = vex or torment by continuous or persistent annoyance. **Tease** emphasizes driving a person or animal to lose patience and flare up in irritation or anger, especially by unkind jokes or tricks: *The children teased the dog until it bit them.* **Plague** emphasizes the presence of someone or something thought of as a trial or affliction: *Her little brother plagues her.* **Pester** emphasizes continued repetition of nuisances, requests, or petty vexations: *He pesters his mother for candy.*

tea•sel ['tizəl] *n., v.* **-selled** or **-seled, -sel•ling** or **-sel•ing.** *—n.* **1** any of several Old World biennial plants (genus *Dipsacus*), especially **fuller's teasel** (*D. fullonum*), having prickly leaves and heads of small flowers with sharp, stiff, hooked bracts. **2** a dried flower head of teasel, especially fuller's teasel, formerly much used in the textile industry for raising a nap on woollen cloth. **3** a mechanical device used for the same purpose.
—v. raise a nap on (cloth) with teasels. Also, **teazel** or **teazle.** ⟨OE *tǣsel*⟩ **—'tea•sel•ler** or **'tea•sel•er,** *n.*

teas•er ['tizər] *n.* **1** a person or thing that teases. **2** *Informal.* an annoying problem; a puzzling task.

tea service a set of silver or other metal for serving tea or, sometimes, coffee, usually consisting of a teapot, hot water pot (which may be used as a coffee pot), cream jug, and sugar bowl.

tea set a set of china dishes for serving tea, etc., usually consisting of a teapot, sugar bowl, cream jug, teacups, saucers, and small plates.

tea•spoon ['ti,spun] *n.* **1** a spoon slightly smaller than a dessertspoon, commonly used to stir tea or coffee, eat desserts, etc. **2** a standard unit of measurement in cooking, equal to one third of a tablespoon, or about 5 mL. *Abbrev.:* t. or tsp. **3** teaspoonful: *I put in a teaspoon of salt.*

tea•spoon•ful ['tispun,fʊl] *n., pl.* **-fuls.** the amount that a teaspoon can hold. 1 teaspoonful = ⅓ tablespoonful.

teat [tit] *n.* **1** of female mammals, the nipple of a breast or udder, from which the young suck milk. **2** any similar small projection. ⟨ME < OF *tete* < Gmc.⟩

tea•time ['ti,taɪm] *n.* **1** the time tea is served. **2** *Brit.* late afternoon.

tea towel a towel for drying dishes that have been washed.

tea wagon a small table on wheels, used in serving tea, etc.

tea•zel or **tea•zle** ['tizəl] See TEASEL.

Te•bet or **Te•beth** [tei'veit] *or* ['teivəs] *n.* in the Hebrew calendar, the tenth month of the ecclesiastical year and the fourth month of the civil year.

tech [tɛk] *n. Informal.* **1** technical school or college. **2** technician: *a lab tech.*

tech. **1** technical; technician. **2** technological; technologist; technology.

te•chie ['tɛki] *n. Informal.* **1** a student in a technical course or school. **2** a skilled technician or person who is an avid user of high tech.

tech•ne•ti•um [tɛk'niʃəm] *or* [tɛk'niʃiəm] *n.* a silver-grey, artificially produced, radioactive metallic element. *Symbol:* Tc; *at.no.* 43; *at.mass* 98.91; *half-life* 2.6 million years. ⟨< Gk. *technētos* artificial < *technē* art, because this was the first artificial element⟩

tech•nic ['tɛknɪk] *n.* **1** technique. **2 technics,** *pl.* (*used with a singular or plural verb*). **a** technology. **b** the study, science, or principles of an art or the arts, especially when mechanical or industrial. **3 technics,** *pl.* technical details, points, terms, etc. ⟨< Gk. *technikos* < *technē* art, skill, craft⟩

tech•ni•cal ['tɛknəkəl] *adj.* **1** of or having to do with a mechanical or industrial art or with applied science: *a technical school, a technical expert. Technical training is needed for many jobs in industry.* **2** of or having to do with the special facts or characteristics of a science or art; specialized: Electrolysis, tarsus, *and* enzyme *are technical words.* **3** treating a subject in scientific detail; using highly specialized vocabulary: *The book gets very technical after the first chapter.* **4** strictly according to the rules or principles of a certain science, art, game, etc.: *a technical victory, a technical distinction.* **5** *Informal.* making unduly fine distinctions: *OK, OK, I was 90 seconds late; let's not get technical.* **6** of or having to do with technique: *Her singing shows technical skill but her voice is weak.* ⟨< *technic*⟩ **—'tech•ni•cal•ly,** *adv.* **—'tech•ni•cal•ness,** *n.*

tech•ni•cal•i•ty [,tɛknə'kæləti] *n., pl.* **-ties. 1** a technical matter, point, detail, term, etc.; especially one that only a specialist is likely to be aware of or to appreciate: *She was acquitted on a legal technicality.* **2** the quality or state of being technical: *The technicality of the article soon discouraged him.*

technical knockout *Boxing.* a knockout called by the referee when he considers a fighter, though not knocked out, to be too severely injured to continue the match. *Abbrev.:* TKO, T.K.O., t.k.o.

tech•ni•cian [tɛk'nɪʃən] *n.* **1** a person trained or skilled in the technical details of a subject: *an electrical technician, a laboratory technician.* **2** a person skilled in the technique of an art: *a superb technician at the keyboard.*

Tech•ni•col•or ['tɛknə,kʌlər] *n. Trademark.* a process for making films in colour, in which three single-colour films, made at the same time but each showing tones of a different primary colour, are combined into one full-colour print.

tech•ni•col•our or **tech•ni•col•or** ['tɛknə,kʌlər] *adj., n.* *—adj.* highly colourful; vivid.
—n. bright, vivid colours: *She was a vision in technicolour.*

(< *Technicolor*, trademark) —**'tech•ni,col•oured** or **tech•ni,col•ored,** *adj.*

tech•nique [tɛk'nik] *n.* **1** a method or way of performing the technical details of an art; technical skill: *The pianist's technique was brilliant, but his interpretation of the piece lacked warmth.* **2** a special method or system used to accomplish something: *a new technique for removing cataracts.* (< F)

techno– *combining form.* technique; technology. (< Gk. *techne* craft)

tech•noc•ra•cy [tɛk'nɒkrəsi] *n.* **1** a theory, popular in the early 1930s, of governmental, social, and industrial management according to the findings of scientists and engineers, administered by technologists. **2** a government in which this theory is applied. **3** a state governed by such a system. (< Gk. *technē* craft + *kratos* rule, power)

tech•no•crat ['tɛknə,kræt] *n.* **1** a person in favour of technocracy. **2** one of the leaders or functionaries in a technocracy. —**,tech•no'crat•ic,** *adj.*

tech•no•gra•phy [tɛk'nɒgrəfi] *n.* the description of arts and sciences in relation to their historical development and ethnic and geographical distribution. —**,tech•no'graph•i•cal,** *adj.*

tech•no•log•i•cal [,tɛknə'lɒdʒəkəl] *adj.* of, having to do with, or resulting from technology: *a technological age, technological advances, technological diseases.* Also, **technologic.** —**,tech•no'log•i•cal•ly,** *adv.*

tech•nol•o•gist [tɛk'nɒlədʒɪst] *n.* a person skilled in a branch of technology.

tech•nol•o•gy [tɛk'nɒlədʒi] *n.* **1** scientific knowledge applied to practical uses; applied science: *Engineering is a branch of technology.* **2** the system by which society is provided with the things needed to sustain life or desired for comfort. **3** technical language. **4** a process, method, invention, etc., arising from applied science and designed especially for dealing with a given task or problem: *We don't have the technology here for that kind of image-reproduction.* (< Gk. *technologia* systematic treatment < *technē* art + *-logos* treating of)

tech•y ['tɛtʃi] *adj.* **tech•i•er, tech•i•est.** See TETCHY.

tec•ton•ic [tɛk'tɒnɪk] *adj.* **1** of or having to do with the architecture or construction of a building; structural. **2** *Geology.* of or having to do with changes in the earth's crust, the forces that cause them, and the structures that result. (< LL *tectonicus* < Gk. *tektonikos* of building < *tektōn* carpenter) —**tec'ton•i•cal•ly,** *adv.*

tec•ton•ics [tɛk'tɒnɪks] *n.* **1** *Architecture.* the art or science of designing and constructing practical and beautiful buildings. **2** *Geology.* the study of the earth's crust.

tec•trix ['tɛktrɪks] *n., pl.* **-tri•ces** [-trə,siz]. COVERT (def. 3). (< NL, fem. of *tector* one that covers < *tectus* pp. of *tegere* cover)

ted [tɛd] *v.* **ted•ded, ted•ding.** spread out (hay) for drying. (ME < ON *tethja* spread manure)

ted•der ['tɛdər] *n.* a machine for stirring and spreading out hay to speed up drying.

ted•dy ['tɛdi] *n.* a woman's one-piece undergarment combining a chemise top with short underpants.

teddy bear a stuffed toy made to look somewhat like a bear cub. (Teddy, nickname of Pres. Theodore Roosevelt, d. 1919, known for his fondness for big-game hunting)

ted•dy–boy or **Ted•dy–boy** ['tɛdi ,bɔɪ] *n. Brit. Slang.* **1** in the 1950s and 1960s, a rebellious, often delinquent youth affecting the dress style of the reign of Edward VII. **2** an idle young ruffian; any well-dressed delinquent youth. (from the fancy clothes worn by such persons, cut in the style of Edward VII, nicknamed *Teddy*)

Te De•um [tei 'deiəm] *or* [ti 'diəm] **1** a hymn of praise and thanksgiving sung in some Christian churches at morning service and also on special occasions. **2** a musical setting for this hymn. **3** a thanksgiving service including this hymn. (< L *Te Deum (laudamus)* (We praise) thee, O God, the first words of the hymn)

te•di•ous ['tidiəs] *adj.* long, boring, and tiring: *a tedious lecture.* (ME < LL *taediosus* < L *taedium* tedium. See TEDIUM.) —**'te•di•ous•ly,** *adv.* —**'te•di•ous•ness,** *n.*
☛ *Syn.* See note at TIRESOME.

te•di•um ['tidiəm] *n.* **1** the quality or state of being tedious; tiresomeness; tediousness. **2** the state of being bored; boredom. (< L *taedium* < *taedet* it is wearisome)

tee¹ [ti] *n., v.* **teed, tee•ing.** —*n.* **1** *Curling.* the centre circle of the target toward which the stones are aimed; the centre of the house; button. **2** the target in various other games, such as quoits. **3** *Golf.* **a** an area from which a player makes the first stroke in playing a hole. **b** a little mound of sand or dirt or a short wooden or plastic peg on which a golf ball is placed when a player drives.
—*v. Golf.* place (the ball) in position for hitting it on, or as if on, a tee (*often used with* **up**).
tee off, a drive a golf ball from a tee. **b** begin; start. **c** *Slang.* make angry or annoyed: *The whole thing really teed me off.* (17c. *teaz*; origin uncertain)
☛ *Hom.* T, TE, TEA, TI.

tee² [ti] *n.* **1** the letter T. **2** something shaped like a T, especially a three-way joint, as with pipes. **3** a T-shirt.
☛ *Hom.* T, TE, TEA, TEE.

tee–hee ['ti 'hi] *interj., n., v.* **-heed, -hee•ing.** —*interj.* a word representing the sound of a tittering laugh.
—*n.* **1** the sound of a tittering laugh. **2** a titter; snicker; giggle.
—*v.* titter; snicker; giggle. (imitative)

tee line *Curling.* the line that runs through the centre of the house, parallel to the HOG LINE.

teem¹ [tim] *v.* **1** abound; swarm: *The swamp teemed with mosquitoes.* **2** be fertile, fruitful, or prolific. (OE *tēman* < *tēam* progeny)
☛ *Hom.* TEAM.

teem² [tim] *v.* pour; come down in torrents. (ME < ON *tœma* empty)
☛ *Hom.* TEAM.

teen [tin] *n., adj.* —*n.* **1 teens,** *pl.* of a century or a person's age, the years from thirteen to nineteen: *He was still in his teens when he got married. The songs in this book date from the teens and twenties.* **2** *Informal.* teenager: *a club for teens.*
—*adj. Informal.* teenage.

–teen *suffix.* forming the names of the cardinal numerals from 13 to 19. (ME *-tene* < OE *-tene* inflected form of *tien* ten)

teen•age ['tin,eidʒ] *adj.* of, for, being, or having to do with teenagers: *a teenage club, teenage boys.*

teen•aged or **teen–aged** ['tin,eidʒd] *adj.* being a teenager.

teen•ag•er ['tin,eidʒər] *n.* a person in his or her teens.

teen•sy ['tinsi] *adj.* **-si•er, -si•est.** *Informal.* tiny. Also, **teensy-weensy.**

tee•ny ['tini] *adj.* **-ni•er, -ni•est;** *n.* —*adj. Informal.* tiny; wee: *a teeny bit of sugar.*
—*n.* a tiny person or thing. Also (adj.), **teeny-weeny.**

tee•ny–bop•per ['tini ,bɒpər] *n.* **1** a pre-adolescent, especially a girl, who follows the latest fads in popular music, clothes, etc. **2** a pre-adolescent, especially a girl. Also, **teenybopper.**

tee•pee ['tipi] *n.* a cone-shaped tent used mainly by the First Nations people, consisting of a frame of poles spread out at the ground and joined at the top, covered with animal skins (originally buffalo hide), canvas, etc. Compare WIGWAM. Also, **tepee, tipi.** (< Dakota *tipi*)

tee shirt T-SHIRT.

tee•ter ['titər] *n., v.* —*n.* **1** a swaying movement; reeling. **2** a teeter-totter.
—*v.* **1** rock unsteadily; sway: *to teeter on stilts.* **2** balance on a teeter-totter. (var. of dial. *titter* totter, probably < ON *titra* shake)
☛ *Hom.* TITRE.

tee•ter–tot•ter ['titər ,tɒtər] *n., v.* —*n.* **1** a long plank balanced on a raised central support, used especially by children in a game in which they sit at opposite ends and move alternately up and down; seesaw. **2** the game of teeter-tottering.
—*v.* play by moving up and down on a teeter-totter: *We watched the children teeter-tottering in the playground.*

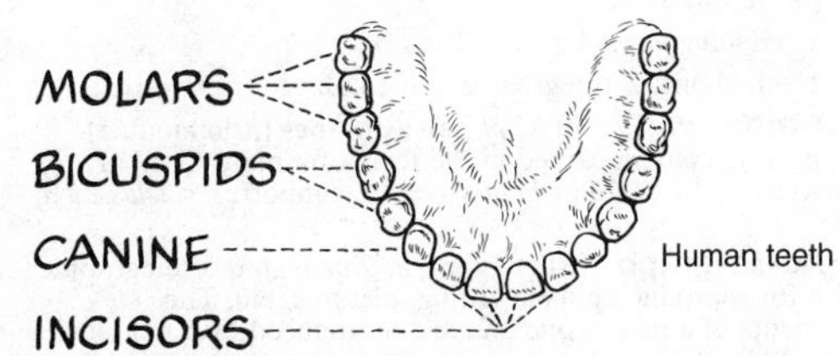

Human teeth

teeth [tiθ] *n.* pl. of TOOTH.

by the skin of (one's) **teeth,** very narrowly; barely: *He escaped by the skin of his teeth.*
cut (one's) **teeth on.** See CUT.
grit or **set** (one's) **teeth,** prepare to endure something without complaining.
in (someone's) **teeth,** to someone's face or openly.
in the teeth of, a straight against; in the face of: *She advanced in the teeth of the gale.* **b** in defiance of; in spite of.
lie through (one's) **teeth,** tell an outright or brazen falsehood.
put teeth in or **into,** put force into.
show (one's) **teeth,** show anger; threaten.
sink (or **get**) (one's) **teeth into,** have one's abilities fully engaged or occupied by.
throw in (someone's) **teeth, a** blame or reproach someone for: *He threw the lie in her teeth.* **b** utter (an insult, etc.) at someone viciously.
to the teeth, to the limit of what is possible; to the utmost: *She was armed to the teeth.*

teethe [tið] *v.* **teethed, teeth•ing.** cut one's first teeth; grow primary teeth: *The baby is teething.*

teeth•er ['tiðər] *n.* an object of hard rubber, plastic, etc. for babies to bite on when they are teething.

teeth•ing ['tiðɪŋ] *n., v.* *—n.* **1** the developing or cutting of teeth; dentition. **2** (*adjl.*) having to do with the process of cutting teeth: *a gel to relieve teething pain, a teething ring to chew on, teething biscuits.*
—v. ppr. of TEETHE.

tee•to•tal ['ti'toutəl] *adj.* **1** of, having to do with, or practising total abstinence from alcoholic liquor. **2** *Informal.* absolute, complete, or entire. ⟨< *total,* with initial letter repeated⟩ **—'tee'to•tal•ly,** *adv.*

tee•to•tal•er ['ti'toutələr] See TEETOTALLER.

tee•to•tal•ism ['ti'toutə,lɪzəm] *n.* the principle or practice of total abstinence from alcoholic liquor. **—'tee'to•tal•ist,** *n.*

tee•to•tal•ler or **tee•to•tal•er** ['ti'toutələr] *n.* a person who never drinks alcoholic liquor.

tee•to•tum ['ti'toutəm] *n.* **1** a four-sided top spun with fingers, each side being marked with letters to determine whether the spinner has won or lost. **2** any top spun with the fingers. ⟨< *totum* (< L *totum* all, the whole), with the initial letter repeated. The four sides of the top were marked T (*totum* all), A (*aufer* take), D (*depone* put), and N (*nihil* nothing).⟩

Tef•lon ['tɛflɒn] *n. Trademark.* a tough synthetic resin (polytetrafluoroethylene) used in making bearings, etc. and as a coating on the inside of cooking utensils, the bottom of steam irons, etc. to prevent sticking.

teg•men ['tɛgmən] *n., pl.* **-mi•na** [-mənə]. **1** *Zoology.* a forewing of a cockroach or related insect, made of a hard, leathery material. **2** *Botany.* the inner covering of a seed. **3** any other covering layer. ⟨< L < *tegere* cover⟩ **—'teg•mi•nal,** *adj.*

teg•u•lar ['tɛgjələr] *adj.* **1** having to do with or resembling a tile. **2** consisting of tiles. **3** arranged like tiles. ⟨< L *tegula* tile⟩ **—'teg•u•lar•ly,** *adv.*

teg•u•ment ['tɛgjəmənt] *n. Rare.* integument. ⟨< L *tegumentum* < *tegere* cover⟩ **—,teg•u'men•tal** or **,teg•u'men•ta•ry,** *adj.*

te•ja•no or **Te•ja•no** [tei'hɑnou] *n.* a style of music of the region around the Texas-Mexico border, characterized by complex rhythms and played on the accordion. ⟨< Am.Sp., Texan⟩

tek•tite ['tɛktəit] *n.* a small, rounded, glassy body thought to be produced by the impact of meteorites on the earth's surface. Tektites are found in large quantities in certain parts of the world, especially Australia. ⟨< Gk. *tēktos* molten + E *-ite*[1]⟩

tel [tɛl] *n.* See TELL[2].

tel– *combining form.* **1** TELE-. **2** TELO-.

tel. **1** telephone. **2** telegram. **3** telegraph.

tel•a•mon ['tɛlə,mɒn] *n., pl.* **tel•e•mo•nes** [,tɛlə'mouniz]. a supporting column carved in the form of a man. Compare CARYATID. ⟨< L < Gk. *telamōn* bearer, supporter < *telassai* to bear⟩

Tel•Au•to•graph [tɛl'ɒtə,græf] *n. Trademark.* a telegraphic device for reproducing handwriting, pictures, etc. The movements of a pen at one end are reproduced by a pen at the other end.

tele– or **tel–** *combining form.* **1** over, from, or to a long distance, as in *telegraph, telephone.* **2** of, in, or by television, as in *telecast.* ⟨< Gk. *tēle* far⟩

tel•e•cast ['tɛlə,kæst] *v.* **-cast** or **-cast•ed, -cast•ing;** *n.* *—v.* broadcast by television.
—n. a television program or broadcast. ⟨< *tele(vision)* + *(broad)cast*⟩ **—'tel•e,cast•er,** *n.*

tel•e•com ['tɛlə,kɒm] *n.* telecommunication.

tel•e•com•mu•ni•ca•tion [,tɛləkə,mjunə'keiʃən] *n.* **1** communication at a distance, especially by means of a system using electromagnetic impulses, as in telegraph, telephone, radio, television, or computer. **2** Usually, **telecommunications,** the science that deals with such communication (*used with a singular or plural verb*).

tel•e•com•mut•ing [,tɛləkə'mjutɪŋ] *n.* the practice of working at home or elsewhere outside one's place of employment, by means of a computer linked electronically to one's place of employment. **—,tel•e•com'mut•er,** *n.*

tel•e•con ['tɛlə,kɒn] *n.* **1** a device that flashes messages sent by teletype from long distances onto a screen, thus enabling groups in widely scattered places to hold conferences. **2** a conference held by means of a telecon. ⟨< *tele(type)* + *con(ference)*⟩

tel•e•con•fer•ence ['tɛlə,kɒnfərəns] *n.* a business meeting, educational workshop, etc., bringing together participants in various locations, using electronic means such as closed-circuit television, speakerphones, etc. **—'tel•e,con•fer•enc•ing,** *n.*

tel•e•course ['tɛlə,kɔrs] *n.* a televised academic course that may be taken for credit at a community college or university.

tel•e•du ['tɛlə,du] *n.* a badgerlike creature of SE Asia (*Mydous javanensis*) having brown fur with a white stripe on the back and spraying a foul-smelling secretion when attacked. ⟨< Javanese⟩

tel•e•film ['tɛlə,fɪlm] *n.* a film made for television.

tel•e•gen•ic [,tɛlə'dʒɛnɪk] *adj.* appearing attractive on television; suitable for televising. ⟨< *tele(vision)* + *(photo)genic*⟩

Tel•e•globe Canada ['tɛlə,gloub] a crown corporation providing international satellite services.

te•leg•o•ny [tə'lɛgəni] *n.* the alleged transmission of genetic traits from one sire to later offspring born of the same female to a different sire. ⟨< *tele-* + Gk. *gonia* begetting⟩ **—,tel•e'gon•ic** [,tɛlə'gɒnɪk], *adj.*

tel•e•gram ['tɛlə,græm] *n.* a message sent by telegraph.

tel•e•graph[1] ['tɛlə,græf] *n., v.* *—n.* an apparatus, system, or process for sending or receiving coded messages by electricity, especially over a wire.
—v. **1** send (a message) by telegraph: *They telegraphed the news of the escape.* **2** send a telegram to (someone): *She telegraphed us yesterday.* **3** send by means of an order made by telegraph: *to telegraph flowers.* **4** *Informal.* **a** in boxing, indicate unintentionally that one is about to punch. **b** give away (an intention) in advance.

tel•e•graph[2] ['tɛlə,græf] *v. Cdn. Informal.* especially in Québec, cast (a vote) illegally by impersonating another voter. ⟨< Cdn.F⟩

te•leg•ra•pher [tə'lɛgrəfər] *n.* a person whose work is sending and receiving messages by telegraph. Also, **telegraphist.**

tel•e•graph•ic [,tɛlə'græfɪk] *adj.* **1** of, having to do with, or transmitted by telegraph: *a telegraphic message.* **2** of prose style, clipped, concise, or elliptical. **—,tel•e'graph•i•cal•ly,** *adv.*

te•leg•ra•phy [tə'lɛgrəfi] *n.* the making or operating of telegraphs.

Tel•e•gu ['tɛlə,gu] *n.* See TELUGU.

tel•e•ki•ne•sis [,tɛləkə'nisɪs] *or* [,tɛləkaɪ'nisɪs] *n.* **1** the moving of an object by means of the power of thought alone, without physical contact. **2** the ability to bring about such movement.

tel•e•ki•net•ic [,tɛləkə'nɛtɪk] *or* [,tɛləkaɪ'nɛtɪk] *adj.* having to do with, characterized by, or caused by telekinesis.

tel•e•mark ['tɛlə,mɑrk] *n. Skiing.* a stop or turn made by advancing one ski and slowly turning its tip inward in front of the other one. ⟨< *Telemark,* a region in Norway⟩

tel•e•mar•ket•ing [,tɛlə'mɑrkətɪŋ] *n.* selling, advertising, or promoting goods or services over the telephone. **—,tel•e'mar•ket•er,** *n.*

te•lem•e•ter *n.* [tə'lɛmətər]; *v.* ['tɛlə,mitər] *n., v.* *—n.* **1** a device used in rockets, etc. for measuring heat, radiation, speed, etc. and transmitting the information, especially by radio, to a distant station where it is recorded. **2** RANGE FINDER.
—v. measure and transmit by telemeter.

tel•e•met•ric [ˌtɛlə'mɛtrɪk] *adj.* of or having to do with telemeters or telemetry. **—ˌtel•e'met•ri•cal•ly,** *adv.*

te•lem•e•try [tə'lɛmətri] *n.* **1** the use of telemeters for measuring and transmitting information. **2** the equipment used in this process: *The ground telemetry indicated that the retrorockets on the space capsule had been fitted.*

tel•en•ceph•a•lon [ˌtɛlɛn'sɛfəˌlɒn] *n.* the anterior section of the forebrain, comprising the cerebral hemispheres, olfactory lobes, etc. **—ˌtel•en•ce'phal•ic** [-sə'fælɪk], *adj.*

te•le•o•log•i•cal [ˌtiliə'lɒdʒəkəl] *or* [ˌtɛliə'lɒdʒəkəl] *adj.* **1** of or having to do with teleology. **2** relating to final causes. **3** having to do with design or purpose in nature.

te•le•ol•o•gy [ˌtili'ɒlədʒi] *or* [ˌtɛli'ɒlədʒi] *n. Philosophy.* **1** the study of final causes or of ultimate purposes. **2** a particular account of these in a given system of philosophy: *Kantian teleology.* **3 a** purpose or design as shown in nature, or the study of this. **b** the doctrine that all things in nature were made to fulfil a plan or design. **4 a** the fact or quality of being purposeful. **b** the doctrine that mechanisms alone cannot explain the facts of nature, and that purposes have causal power. ⟨< NL *teleologia* < Gk. *telos* end + *-logos* treating of⟩ **—ˌte•le'ol•o•gist,** *n.*

tel•e•ost ['tɛliˌɒst] *or* ['tiliˌɒst] *n.* any of the orders of bony fishes of the subclass Teleostei such as eels, plaice, or salmon, having a consolidated skeleton, a swim bladder, and thin cycloid scales.

tel•e•path ['tɛləˌpæθ] *n.* a person who is capable of telepathy.

tel•e•path•ic [ˌtɛlə'pæθɪk] *adj.* **1** of or having to do with telepathy. **2** accomplished by telepathy. **—ˌtel•e'path•i•cal•ly,** *adv.*

te•lep•a•thist [tə'lɛpəθɪst] *n.* **1** a student of or believer in telepathy. **2** a person who has telepathic power.

te•lep•a•thy [tə'lɛpəθi] *n.* the communication of one mind with another without using speech, hearing, sight, or any other sense used normally to communicate.

tel•e•phone ['tɛləˌfoun] *n., v.* **-phoned, -phon•ing.** *—n.* **1** a system or process for transmitting sound or speech over distances by converting it into electrical impulses that are sent through a wire or via a satellite. **2** the apparatus used for this process, consisting of a transmitter and a receiver, and a dialling or push-button mechanism for connecting the apparatus to other lines.
—v. **1** talk through a telephone; communicate by telephone: *Wait till he's finished telephoning.* **2** make a telephone call to: *Did you telephone her?* **3** send by telephone: *to telephone a message.* **—'tel•eˌphon•er,** *n.*

telephone book TELEPHONE DIRECTORY.

telephone booth a small enclosure in a public place, containing a telephone that is usually coin-operated.

telephone directory a book containing an alphabetical list of names of individuals or companies subscribing to the telephone system in a particular area, together with their telephone numbers and, often, their addresses.

tel•e•phon•ic [ˌtɛlə'fɒnɪk] *adj.* of, having to do with, or sent by telephone. **—ˌtel•e'phon•i•cal•ly,** *adv.*

te•leph•o•ny [tə'lɛfəni] *n.* the study of communication by telephone, or the making or operating of telephones.

tel•e•pho•to ['tɛləˌfoutou] *adj., n. —adj.* of or designating a system of lenses for a camera, designed to produce a large image of a distant object.
—n. **1** TELEPHOTO LENS. **2** a photograph taken with a camera having a telephoto lens. **3 Telephoto,** *Trademark.* **a** a device for sending photographs by telegraphy. **b** a picture sent in this way.

tel•e•pho•to•graph [ˌtɛlə'foutəˌgræf] *n., v. —n.* **1** a picture taken with a camera having a telephoto lens. **2** a picture sent by telegraphy.
—v. **1** take (a picture) with a camera having a telephoto lens. **2** send (a picture) by telegraphy.

tel•e•pho•to•graph•ic [ˌtɛləˌfoutə'græfɪk] *adj.* of, having to do with, or designating the process of telephotography.

tel•e•pho•tog•ra•phy [ˌtɛləfə'tɒgrəfi] *n.* **1** the method or process of photographing distant objects by using a camera with a telephoto lens. **2** the method or process of sending and reproducing pictures by telegraph by the conversion of light rays into electric signals which can then be sent over wire or radio channels and reconverted at the receiving end.

telephoto lens a lens for a camera that produces a large image of a distant object.

tel•e•port ['tɛləˌpɔrt] *v.* move (something) without touching it, by telekinesis.

tel•e•port•a•tion [ˌtɛləpɔr'teiʃən] *n.* **1** the movement of an object without touching it, as by telekinesis. **2** in theory, the transportation of a physical entity through space by its conversion into energy and reconversion into matter at its destination.

tel•e•print•er ['tɛləˌprɪntər] *n. Esp. Brit.* teletypewriter.

tel•e•pro•cess•ing [ˌtɛlə'prousɛsɪŋ] *or* [ˌtɛlə'prɒsɛsɪŋ] *n.* data processing by computer, with the data being conveyed over communication lines between terminals that may be quite distant from each other.

Tel•e•Promp•ter ['tɛləˌprɒmptər] *n. Trademark.* a device consisting of a moving band that gives a prepared speech line, read by speakers who are being televised. ⟨< *tele(vision) prompter*⟩

tel•e•ran ['tɛləˌræn] *n.* a system of air navigation by which radar mappings and other data are collected by ground stations and transmitted to aircraft by means of television. ⟨short for *Tele(vision) R(adar) A(ir) N(avigation)*⟩

Tel•e•sat Canada ['tɛləˌsæt] a corporation that provides domestic satellite service.

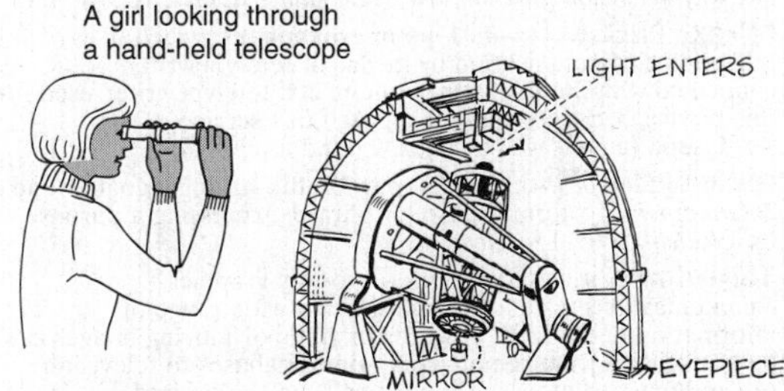

A large reflecting telescope in an observatory. A large concave mirror at the bottom reflects light from an object being studied to one or more flat mirrors and then to a magnifying lens called the eyepiece.

tel•e•scope ['tɛləˌskoup] *n., v.* **-scoped, -scop•ing.** *—n.* **1** an instrument for directly viewing distant objects, using lenses or mirrors or both to make the object appear nearer and larger. **2** RADIO TELESCOPE.
—v. **1** slide one part within the other like the sections of a hand telescope: *Built-in radio aerials are made so that they can be telescoped.* **2** force or be forced one into the other as in a collision: *When the two trains collided, the force of the crash telescoped the first few cars.* **3** shorten; condense. ⟨< NL *telescopium,* ult. < Gk. *tēle* far + *-skopion* instrument for observing < *skopeein* watch⟩

tel•e•scop•ic [ˌtɛlə'skɒpɪk] *adj.* **1** of or having to do with a telescope. **2** obtained or seen by means of a telescope: *a telescopic view of the moon.* **3** visible only through a telescope: *telescopic stars.* **4** far-seeing: *telescopic vision.* **5** making distant things look close and large. **6** consisting of parts that slide inside one another like the tubes of some telescopes: *a telescopic antenna.*

tel•e•scop•i•cal•ly [ˌtɛlə'skɒpɪkli] *adv.* **1** in a telescopic manner. **2** by a telescope.

te•les•co•py [tə'lɛskəpi] *n.* the design and use of telescopes.

tel•e•sis ['tɛləsɪs] *n. Sociology.* the purposeful application of natural forces or processes to achieve specific social ends. ⟨< Gk. *telesis* event < *telein* fulfil < *telos* end⟩

tel•es•the•sia [ˌtɛləs'θiʒə] *or* [ˌtɛləs'θiziə] *n.* extrasensory perception of remote objects or happenings. **—ˌtel•es'thet•ic** [-'θɛtɪk], *adj.*

tel•e•text ['tɛləˌtɛkst] *n.* **1** a method of superimposing printed words on a television picture. **2** the words so shown.

tel•e•thon ['tɛləˌθɒn] *n.* a television program or series of programs lasting a very long time and, usually, serving to solicit funds for a charitable cause. ⟨< *tele-* + *-thon* as in *marathon*⟩

tel•e•type ['tɛləˌtəip] *n., v.* **-typed, -typ•ing.** *—n.* **1** teletypewriter. **2 Teletype,** *Trademark.* a brand of teletypewriter. **3** the process or a system of communication by

means of a teletypewriter: *to transmit information by teletype.* **4** a message sent by teletypewriter.
—*v.* send (a message) by means of a teletypewriter.

tel•e•type•writ•er [ˌtɛlə'təipˌrəitər] *n.* a telegraphic transmitting and receiving device resembling a typewriter, that converts a message typed on it into electric impulses which are transmitted through a telephone system to another device like it which decodes and prints out the message.

tel•e•view ['tɛləˌvju] *v.* watch (a live event) by means of television. **—'tel•eˌview•er,** *n.*

tel•e•vise ['tɛləˌvaɪz] *v.* **-vised, -vis•ing.** pick up and transmit by television: *All the games are being televised.*

tel•e•vi•sion ['tɛləˌvɪʒən] *n.* **1** the process of transmitting the image of an object, scene, or event by radio or wire so that a person in some other place can see it at once. In television, waves of light from an object are changed into electric waves that are transmitted by radio or wire, and then changed back into waves of light that produce an image of the object on a screen. **2** the apparatus on which these pictures may be seen. **3 a** the business of television broadcasting; the television industry. **b** all the equipment, buildings, and activities related to this business or industry. **4** (*adjl.*) having to do with television in any way: *television program, television guide. Abbrev.*: TV or T.V.

tel•ex ['tɛlɛks] *n., v.* —*n.* **1** an international service for telegraphic communication by means of teletypewriters connected with the telephone system. **2** a teletypewriter used for this service. **3** a message sent through this service.
—*v.* **1** send (a message) by telex. **2** send a telex to.

te•lic ['tilɪk] *or* ['tɛlɪk] *adj.* **1** purposeful; having a goal or end. **2** *Grammar.* of a form, clause, or phrase, expressing a purpose. ⟨< Gk. *telikos* final < *telos* end⟩

Tel•i•don ['tɛləˌdɒn] *n. Cdn.* a two-way graphics communications system through which a wide range of information in the form of words or static or moving images can be transmitted from remote computer databases to television sets in homes or offices. The user calls up the desired information by means of a decoder or terminal in the form of a keyboard or a calculatorlike keypad.

tell[1] [tɛl] *v.* **told, tell•ing. 1** put in words; say or write: *Tell the truth.* **2** recount or narrate (a story, facts, etc.) in speech or writing. **3** give an account to; inform: *Tell us about it.* **4** make known; disclose: *Don't tell where the money is.* **5** relate something; give an account or description (*of*): *telling of all the places she had visited.* **6** act as a talebearer; reveal something secret or private: *Promise not to tell.* **7** recognize, know, or distinguish: *He couldn't tell which house it was. We could tell something was wrong.* **8** order or direct: *Tell him to stop!* **9** be evidence or an indication (*of*): *Her clenched hands told of her anger, though she said nothing.* **10** count (votes, etc.). **11** have effect or force: *Every blow told.*
all told, counting everyone or everything; altogether: *We'll be 15 people all told.*
do tell! *Informal.* Oh, really? Is that a fact? (*often sarcastic*).
I (can) tell you, yes indeed; I emphasize: *I tell you, he knows all about it.*
let me tell you, yes indeed; I emphasize.
tell apart, distinguish one from the other or others: *Nobody could tell the sisters apart.*
tell me about it, *Slang.* I have experienced exactly what you mean: *"This machine is such a pain to use." "Tell me about it! I wasted half an hour with it this morning!"*
tell me another one, *Slang.* that's hard to believe: *You made that table? Tell me another one!*
tell off, a count off; count off and detach for some special duty. **b** *Informal.* rebuke strongly; castigate: *His father told him off for staying out late.*
tell on, a inform on; tell tales about. **b** have a harmful effect on; break down: *The strain told on the man's health.*
tell (one's) **beads.** See BEAD.
tell time, know what time it is by the clock: *a child learning to tell time.*
you're telling me, *Slang.* I agree with you! ⟨OE *tellan*⟩

tell[2] [tɛl] *n. Archaeology.* especially in the Middle East, an artificial mound or hill covering successive stages of remains of an ancient settlement. Also, **tel.** ⟨< Arabic *tall* mound⟩

tell•a•ble ['tɛləbəl] *adj.* capable or worthy of being told.

tell•er ['tɛlər] *n.* **1** a person who tells a story. **2** a cashier in a bank. A teller in a bank takes in, gives out, and counts money. **3** a person appointed to count votes, etc.

tell•ing ['tɛlɪŋ] *adj., v.* —*adj.* **1** having a marked effect or great force; impressive or effective: *a telling blow.* **2** that tells or reveals much; significant: *She cast him a telling glance.*
—*v.* ppr. of TELL. **—'tell•ing•ly,** *adv.*

tell•tale ['tɛlˌteil] *n.* **1** a person who tells tales on others; tattletale; talebearer. **2** (*adjl.*) revealing thoughts, actions, etc. that are supposed to be secret: *telltale fingerprints, a telltale blush.* **3** any of various devices that indicate or record something: *A time clock is sometimes called a telltale.*

tel•lu•ri•an [tɛ'lʊriən] *n., adj.* —*n.* an inhabitant of the earth. —*adj.* of or inhabiting the earth. ⟨< L *tellus, telluris* earth⟩

tel•lu•ric[1] [tɛ'lʊrɪk] *adj.* concerning the earth as a planet; terrestrial. ⟨< L *tellus, telluris* earth⟩

tel•lu•ric[2] [tɛ'lʊrɪk] *adj. Chemistry.* derived from or containing tellurium, especially in its higher valences. ⟨< *tellurium*⟩

tel•lu•ride ['tɛljəˌraɪd] *or* ['tɛljərɪd] *n.* a compound of tellurium with an electropositive element or a radical.

tel•lu•rite ['tɛljəˌrəit] *n.* a salt or ester of tellurous acid.

tel•lu•ri•um [tɛ'lʊriəm] *n.* a rare, silver-white chemical element resembling sulphur in its chemical properties and usually occurring in nature combined with gold, silver, or other metals. *Symbol*: Te; *at.no.* 52; *at.mass* 127.60. ⟨< NL < L *tellus, -uris* earth⟩

tel•lu•rize ['tɛljəˌraɪz] *v.* **-rized, -riz•ing.** combine or treat with tellurium.

tel•lu•rom•e•ter [ˌtɛljə'rɒmətər] *n.* an electronic surveying instrument for measuring distance by timing a radio microwave from one point to another and back. ⟨< L *tellus, telluris* earth + E *-meter*⟩

tel•lu•rous ['tɛljərəs] *or* [tɛ'lʊrəs] *adj.* derived from or containing tellurium, especially in a low valence.

tel•ly ['tɛli] *n. Brit. Informal.* **1** television. **2 tellies,** *pl.* television programs.

telo– *combining form.* end. ⟨< Gk. *telos* end⟩

tel•o•mere ['tɛləˌmir] *n.* the end of an arm of a chromosome. ⟨< *telo-* + Gk. *meros* part⟩

tel•o•phase ['tɛləˌfeiz] *n.* the last stage of cell division, in which the chromosomes gradually resume their normal interphase state.

tel•pher ['tɛlfər] *n., v.* —*n.* a cable car for carrying loads, sometimes suspended from a separate car or truck running along the top of the cable.
—*v.* transport (loads) by means of such a car or cars. ⟨shortened from *telephore* < *tele-* + *-phore*⟩ **—'tel•pher•age,** *n.*

tel•son ['tɛlsən] *n.* the last segment, or a projecting part of it, in the body of a crustacean or an arachnid. ⟨< Gk. *telson* limit, boundary⟩ **—tel'son•ic** [tɛl'sɒnɪk], *adj.*

Tel•u•gu ['tɛləˌgu] *n., adj.* —*n.* **1** a Dravidian language, spoken in southeastern India. **2** a speaker of Telugu. **3** the script in which Telugu is written.
—*adj.* of or having to do with Telugu. Also, **Telegu.**

tem•er•ar•i•ous [ˌtɛmə'rɛriəs] *adj.* reckless; rash; bold. ⟨< L *temerarius* < *temere* heedlessly.⟩

te•mer•i•ty [tə'mɛrəti] *n.* reckless boldness; rashness. ⟨< L *temeritas* < *temere* heedlessly⟩

temp [tɛmp] *n. Informal.* temporary employee; someone hired to fill a temporary vacancy caused by illness, leave of absence, etc. or to deal with a temporary backlog. ⟨< *temporary*⟩

temp. 1 temperature. **2** temporary. **3** in the time of (for L *tempore*).

tem•per ['tɛmpər] *n., v.* —*n.* **1** a state of mind; disposition; condition: *She was in a good temper.* **2** an angry state of mind: *In her temper she broke a vase.* **3** a calm or controlled state of mind: *He became angry and lost his temper.* **4** a tendency to anger quickly or to fits of rage: *That young lady has quite a temper—watch out!* **5** the degree of hardness, toughness, etc. of a substance: *The temper of the clay was right for shaping.* **6** a substance added to something to modify its properties or qualities.
—*v.* **1** moderate; soften: *Temper justice with mercy.* **2** bring to a proper or desired condition of hardness, toughness, etc. by mixing or preparing. A painter tempers colours by mixing them with oil. Steel is tempered by heating it and working it till it has the proper degree of hardness and toughness. **3** *Music.* tune or adjust the pitch of (an instrument, a voice, etc.). ⟨OE *temprian* < L *temperare*, originally, observe due measure < *tempus, -poris* time, interval⟩

☛ *Syn. n.* **1.** See note at DISPOSITION.

tem•per•a ['tɛmpərə] *n. Painting.* **1** a method in which colours are mixed with white of egg or some similar substance instead of oil. **2** the paint used. **3** an opaque, powdered colouring matter with gum or glue binder, used dissolved in water for painting posters, for children's artwork, etc. Also called **poster colour** or **poster paint.** ⟨< Ital.⟩

tem•per•a•ment ['tɛmpərəmənt] *or* ['tɛmprəmənt] *n.* **1** an individual's usual way of thinking, feeling, and acting; natural disposition: *a person of shy temperament, the artistic temperament.* **2** great or extreme sensitivity, especially when characterized by irritability or an unwillingness to submit to ordinary rules and restraints: *Temperament is often attributed to actors and artists.* **3** in medieval physiology, the combination and proportions in an individual of the four cardinal humours, choleric, sanguine, phlegmatic, and melancholic. **4** *Music.* the adjustment of the intervals, as in tuning a piano, to produce twelve equally spaced semitones of the octave, so as to fit the instrument for use in all keys. ⟨< L *temperamentum* < *temperare.* See TEMPER.⟩
☛ *Syn.* **1.** See note at DISPOSITION.

tem•per•a•men•tal [,tɛmpərə'mɛntəl] *or* [,tɛmprə'mɛntəl] *adj.* **1** of, having to do with, or due to TEMPERAMENT (def. 1); constitutional: *Cats have a temperamental dislike for water.* **2** extremely sensitive and excitable or unpredictable in behaviour: *a temperamental actor. When he gets temperamental like that, it's impossible to reason with him.* **3** of machines, etc., erratic; unpredictable (*used facetiously*): *Good luck with that toaster oven; it's very temperamental.* **—,tem•per•a'men•tal•ly,** *adv.*

tem•per•ance ['tɛmpərəns] *or* ['tɛmprəns] *n.* **1** moderation in action, speech, habits, etc. **2** moderation in the use of alcoholic drinks. **3** the principle and practice of not using alcoholic drinks at all. ⟨ME < AF *temperaunce* < L *temperantia* < *temperare.* See TEMPER.⟩

tem•per•ate ['tɛmpərɪt] *or* ['tɛmprɪt] *adj.* **1** not very hot and not very cold: *a temperate climate, the temperate regions of the world.* **2** having to do with or found in regions with a moderate climate: *temperate plants.* **3** self-restrained; moderate: *They spoke in a calm, temperate manner.* **4** moderate in using alcoholic drinks; abstemious. ⟨< L *temperatus,* pp. of *temperare.* See TEMPER.⟩ **—'tem•per•ate•ly,** *adv.* **—'tem•per•ate•ness,** *n.*
☛ *Syn.* **3, 4.** See note at MODERATE.

Temperate Zone or **temperate zone** either of two regions comprising the middle latitudes north and south of the equator, between the tropics and the polar regions, forming part of a now obsolete classification system for world climate zones. See also **Frigid Zone, Torrid Zone.**

tem•per•a•ture ['tɛmpərətʃər] *or* ['tɛmprətʃər] *n.* **1** the degree of heat or cold measured on a scale. The temperature of freezing water is 0°C (32°F.). **2** the degree of heat contained in a living body. The normal temperature of the human body is about 37°C (98.6°F.). **3** a level of body heat that is above normal; fever: *He stayed home all day because he had a temperature.* **4** THERMODYNAMIC TEMPERATURE. ⟨< L *temperatura,* ult. < *tempus, -poris* time, season⟩

temperature gradient *Meteorology.* the rate of change of temperature relative to distance or altitude.

tem•pered ['tɛmpərd] *adj., v.* *—adj.* **1** softened; moderated. **2** having a particular disposition (*used in compounds*): *an even-tempered person.* **3** treated by tempering; brought to a desired condition of hardness and toughness: *a sword of tempered steel.* **4** *Music.* of a scale, interval, etc., tuned or adjusted in pitch according to equal temperament.
—v. pt. and pp. of TEMPER.

tem•pest ['tɛmpɪst] *n.* **1** a violent windstorm, usually accompanied by rain, hail, or snow. **2** a violent disturbance; uproar; tumult: *a tempest of cheers.*
tempest in a teapot, great excitement or commotion over something unimportant. ⟨ME < OF *tempest(e)* < var. of L *tempestas* < *tempus* time, season⟩

tem•pes•tu•ous [tɛm'pɛstʃuəs] *adj.* **1** stormy: *a tempestuous night.* **2** violent: *a tempestuous argument.* **—tem'pes•tu•ous•ly,** *adv.* **—tem'pes•tu•ous•ness,** *n.*

tem•pi ['tɛmpi] *n.* pl. of TEMPO.

Tem•plar ['tɛmplər] *n.* **1** in full, **Knight Templar** a member of a religious and military order founded among the Crusaders about 1118 to protect the Holy Sepulchre and pilgrims to the Holy Land. **2** Often, **templar,** *Brit.* a lawyer or law student having chambers in the Temple, London, an area which formerly belonged to the Templars. ⟨< Med.L *templarius* < L *templum* temple¹⟩

tem•plate ['tɛmplɪt] *or* ['tɛmpleit] *n.* **1** a thin piece of wood, metal, plastic, or cardboard used as a pattern in cutting an object or shape out of wood, metal, cloth, etc. **2** any pattern, model, or mould determining the form of a series of similar things. Some Semitic languages have verb templates consisting of three consonants: different vowels inserted between them form different tenses, aspects, etc. of the verb. **3** *Computer technology.* something used as a guide (for the use of keyboard keys, for creating a spreadsheet, for drawing flowchart symbols, etc.): *She built her own income-tax spreadsheet from the templates provided for the spreadsheet package.* **4** a stout, short piece of wood or stone placed horizontally under a beam or girder to distribute downward thrust, as over a doorway. **5** a wedge or block to support a ship's keel. Also, **templet.** ⟨< var. of *templet*; probably influenced by *plate*⟩

tem•ple¹ ['tɛmpəl] *n.* **1** a building used for religious services or worship. **2** specifically, **a** a synagogue. **b** a Mormon church. **3** Often, **Temple,** any of three such buildings built in succession by the Jews in ancient Jerusalem. **4** any place in which God is thought of as residing. **5** any large or impressive building having a particular function for some organization or for the public: *a Masonic temple. The courthouse is a temple of justice.* ⟨OE *temp(e)l* < L *templum*⟩

tem•ple² ['tɛmpəl] *n.* **1** the flattened part of the head on either side of the forehead. **2** either of the side supports of a pair of eyeglasses passing above and behind the ears. ⟨ME < OF *temple,* ult. < L *tempus*⟩

tem•ple³ ['tɛmpəl] *n.* a device in a loom for keeping the web stretched to the correct width during weaving. ⟨ME *temple* < MF, prob. < L *templus* small timber⟩

tem•plet ['tɛmplɪt] *n.* See TEMPLATE. ⟨< F *templet, templette,* dim. of *temple* temple³⟩

tem•po ['tɛmpou] *n., pl.* **-pos, -pi** [-pi]. **1** *Music.* **a** the time or rate of speed of a composition or passage: *The tempo of this piece is very fast. He didn't play it at the correct tempo.* **b** (*adjl.*) indicating a specific tempo: *a tempo mark.* **2** characteristic rate of activity or motion; pace: *the fast tempo of modern life.* ⟨< Ital. *tempo* time < L *tempus.* Doublet of TENSE².⟩

tem•po•ral¹ ['tɛmpərəl] *adj.* **1** of, having to do with, limited by or to, or designating time as opposed to eternity or as opposed to space. **2** of or having to do with secular things; worldly: *temporal concerns.* **3** *Grammar.* **a** expressing time, as an adverb or a clause. **b** of tense. ⟨ME < OF < L *temporalis* < *tempus, -poris* time⟩ **—'tem•po•ral•ly,** *adv.*

tem•po•ral² ['tɛmpərəl] *adj.* of or having to do with the temples of the head: *the temporal artery, the temporal bones.* ⟨ME < OF < L *temporalis* < *tempus, -poris* temple²⟩

tem•po•ral•i•ty [,tɛmpə'rælətі] *n., pl.* **-ties. 1** the quality or state of being temporal. **2** Usually, **temporalities,** *pl.* secular possessions of a church, especially revenues or properties.

tem•po•rar•y ['tɛmpə,rɛri] *adj., n.* *—adj.* lasting or used for a short time only; not permanent: *a temporary shelter, a temporary inconvenience.*
—n. a person employed for a short time: *They hired several temporaries last summer.* ⟨< L *temporarius* < *tempus, -poris* time⟩ **—,tem•po'rar•i•ly,** *adv.* **—'tem•po,rar•i•ness,** *n.*
☛ *Syn.* **Temporary,** TRANSIENT = lasting or staying only for a time. **Temporary** emphasizes existing or being used or in effect for a time, and describes either something meant only for the time being or something liable to come to an end at any time: *He has a temporary job. Our school is a temporary building.* **Transient** emphasizes quick passing, and describes something that stays or lasts only a short time: *His nervousness was transient, and passed when he began to speak.*

tem•po•ri•za•tion [,tɛmpərə'zeiʃən] *or* [,tɛmpəraɪ'zeiʃən] *n.* the act or practice of temporizing; a compromise.

tem•po•rize ['tɛmpə,raɪz] *v.* **-rized, -riz•ing. 1** evade immediate action or decision in order to gain time, avoid trouble, etc. **2** fit one's acts to the time or occasion. **3** make or discuss terms; negotiate, often only to gain time. ⟨< MF *temporiser,* ult. < L *tempus, -poris* time⟩ **—'tem•po,riz•er,** *n.*

tempt [tɛmpt] *v.* **1** make, or try to make (a person) do something wrong by promising pleasure or some advantage: *They tempted him to steal.* **2** appeal to strongly; be very attractive to: *sweets that tempt one's appetite.* **3** cause to feel strongly inclined (*usually used in the passive*): *After three failures he was tempted to quit.* **4** provoke or defy: *It would be tempting fate to take that old car on the road.* **5** *Archaic.* test: *God tempted Abraham by asking him to sacrifice his son.* ⟨< L *temptare* try⟩ **—'tempt•a•ble,** *adj.*

temp•ta•tion [tɛmp'teiʃən] *n.* **1** the act of tempting or the state of being tempted: *No temptation could make her false to her friend.* **2** something that tempts: *The money lying on the counter was a temptation to him.*

tempt•er ['tɛmptər] *n.* **1** a person who tempts. **2 the Tempter,** the Devil; Satan.

tempt•ress ['tɛmptrɪs] *n.* a woman who tempts or entices, especially for sexual purposes.

tem•pu•ra [tɛm'pʊrə] *or* ['tɛmpʊrə] *n.* a dish of shrimp, vegetables, etc. coated in a light batter and deep-fried. ⟨< Japanese⟩

tem•pus fu•git ['tɛmpəs 'fjudʒɪt] *or* ['fugɪt] *Latin.* time flies.

ten [tɛn] *n., adj. —n.* **1** one more than nine; 10. **2** the numeral 10: *That's a 10, not a 16.* **3** the tenth in a set or series; especially, a playing card having ten spots: *She played a ten of clubs.* **4** a ten-dollar bill. **5** a set or series of ten persons or things: *Bundle the ticket books into tens.*
—adj. **1** being one more than nine. **2** being tenth in a set or series (*used mainly after the noun*): *Chapter Ten will be discussed tomorrow.* ⟨OE *tīen, tēn*⟩

ten. tenor.

ten•a•ble ['tɛnəbəl] *adj.* capable of being held or defended: *a tenable position, a tenable theory.* ⟨< F *tenable* < *tenir* hold < L *tenere*⟩ **—,ten•a•bly,** *adv.* **—,ten•a'bil•i•ty** or **'ten•a•ble•ness,** *n.*

ten•ace ['tɛneɪs] *or* ['tɛnəs] *n. Bridge, Whist.* a sequence of two high cards in the same suit with the middle one missing, as the king and the jack.

te•na•cious [tə'neiʃəs] *adj.* **1** holding fast; not readily letting go: *a tenacious grip, the tenacious jaws of a bulldog. She is tenacious of her rights.* **2** stubborn or persistent; not readily giving up: *a tenacious salesperson, tenacious courage.* **3** especially good at remembering: *a tenacious memory.* **4** tending to stick or cling: *tenacious burrs.* **5** holding fast together; not easily pulled apart; tough: *a tenacious metal.* ⟨< L *tenax, -acis* < *tenere* hold⟩ **—te'na•cious•ly,** *adv.* **—te'na•cious•ness,** *n.*

te•nac•i•ty [tə'næsəti] *n.* the quality or state of being tenacious.

te•nac•u•lum [tə'nækjələm] *n., pl.* **-la** [-lə] a surgical instrument ending in a pointed hook, for raising and holding parts. ⟨< L, tool for holding < *tenere* hold⟩

ten•an•cy ['tɛnənsi] *n., pl.* **-cies. 1** the state of being a tenant; the act of occupying and paying rent for land or buildings. **2** the length of time a tenant occupies a property. **3** the period of holding an office or position: *a long tenancy as mayor.*

ten•ant ['tɛnənt] *n., v. —n.* **1** a person paying rent for the temporary use of the land or buildings of another person: *They have tenants on the second floor of their house.* **2** a person or thing that occupies: *Birds are tenants of the trees.*
—v. hold or occupy as a tenant; inhabit. ⟨< F *tenant,* originally ppr. of *tenir* hold < L *tenere*⟩ **—'ten•ant•less,** *adj.* **—'ten•ant•a•ble,** *adj.*

tenant elector *Cdn. B.C.* a person having the right to vote in municipal elections as a rent-paying resident (as opposed to a property owner).

tenant farmer a person who farms someone else's land, paying rent in cash or with a portion of the produce.

ten•ant•ry ['tɛnəntri] *n., pl.* **-ries. 1** all the tenants on an estate. **2** TENANCY (def. 1).

tench [tɛntʃ] *n., pl.* **tench** or **tench•es.** a European freshwater game fish (*Tinca tinca*) that is noted for the length of time it can live out of water. The tench is a cyprinid. ⟨ME < OF *tenche* < LL *tinca*⟩

Ten Commandments in the Bible, the ten rules for living and for worship that God gave to Moses on Mount Sinai.

tend[1] [tɛnd] *v.* **1** have an inclination or tendency: *She tends to use large canvases for her paintings. He tends to dress conservatively.* **2** move or extend; be directed: *The coastline tends to the south here.* **3** conduce; lead as a general rule: *Authoritarianism tends toward oppression of the individual.* ⟨ME < OF *tendre* < L *tendere* stretch, aim. Doublet of TENDER[2].⟩

tend[2] [tɛnd] *v.* **1** take care of; look after; attend to: *She tends shop for her father. A shepherd tends his flock.* **2** serve; wait upon. **3** *Nautical.* stand by and watch over (a line, anchor cable, etc.) to prevent fouling. **4** *Informal.* pay attention (*to*): *Just tend to your work and never mind what everyone else is doing.* ⟨< *attend*⟩

tend•ance ['tɛndəns] *n.* attention; care.

tend•en•cy ['tɛndənsi] *n., pl.* **-cies. 1** a natural disposition, inclination, or leaning toward a particular kind of action, behaviour, etc.: *a tendency to favour pastel colours, a tendency to reject new ideas without considering them. Wood has a tendency to swell if it gets wet.* **2** trend; general course of development: *The tendency in industry is toward more and more automation.* ⟨< Med.L *tendentia* < L *tendere.* See TEND[1].⟩
☛ *Syn.* **2.** See note at DIRECTION.

ten•den•tious [tɛn'dɛnʃəs] *adj.* having or promoting a particular aim or point of view, especially in an aggressive or deliberately distorted manner; biassed: *tendentious writings.* ⟨< Med.L *tendentia.* See TENDENCY.⟩ **—ten'den•tious•ly,** *adv.* **—ten'den•tious•ness,** *n.*

ten•der[1] ['tɛndər] *adj.* **1** not hard or tough; soft: *tender meat.* **2** not strong and hardy; delicate: *tender young grass.* **3** kind; affectionate; loving: *She spoke tender words to the child.* **4** not rough or crude; gentle: *With tender, loving hands, the father bathed his baby.* **5** young; immature: *at the tender age of two.* **6** sensitive; painful; sore: *a tender wound.* **7** feeling pain or grief easily; easily injured; vulnerable: *a tender conscience, tender pride. Her tender heart had been broken by this experience.* **8** considerate; careful: *He handles people in a tender manner.* **9** requiring careful or tactful handling: *a tender situation.* ⟨ME < OF *tendre* < L *tener*⟩ **—'ten•der•ly,** *adv.* **—'ten•der•ness,** *n.*

ten•der[2] ['tɛndər] *v., n. —v.* **1** offer formally: *We tendered our thanks.* **2** *Business.* make (an offer to buy, supply, etc.): *Several firms tendered for the contract.* **3** *Law.* offer (money, goods, etc.) in payment of a debt or other obligation.
—n. **1** a formal offer: *She refused his tender of marriage.* **2** the thing offered. Money that may be offered as payment for a debt is called legal tender. **3** *Business.* an offer to buy, supply, etc. **4** *Law.* an offer of money, goods, etc. in payment of a debt, etc. ⟨< OF *tendre* < L *tendere* extend. Doublet of TEND[1].⟩ **—'ten•der•er,** *n.*
☛ *Syn. v.* **1.** See note at OFFER.

tend•er[3] ['tɛndər] *n.* **1** a small boat carried or towed by a big one and used for landing passengers. **2** a small ship used for carrying supplies and passengers to and from larger ships, seaplanes, submarines, etc. **3** formerly, the car attached behind a steam locomotive and used for carrying coal, oil, water, etc. **4** a person or thing that tends another. ⟨< *tend*[2]⟩

ten•der•foot ['tɛndər,fʊt] *n., pl.* **-foots** or **-feet.** *Informal.* **1** a newcomer to the pioneer life of the West. **2** a person not used to rough living and hardships. **3** an inexperienced person; beginner. **4** a young person in the first stage of being a Scout or Girl Guide.

tender fruit in the food marketing and transportation industry, fruits, such as peaches, that are highly susceptible to bruising and so require a certain kind of handling or packaging.

ten•der–heart•ed ['tɛndər 'hɑrtɪd] *adj.* kindly; sympathetic. **—'ten•der-'heart•ed•ly,** *adv.* **—'ten•der-'heart•ed•ness,** *n.*

ten•der•ize ['tɛndə,raɪz] *v.* **-ized, -iz•ing.** make (meat) tender; soften by applying a tenderizer, pounding with a wooden mallet, etc. **—,ten•der•i'za•tion,** *n.*

ten•der•iz•er ['tɛndə,raɪzər] *n.* a substance containing enzymes or other softening ingredients, sprinkled on or rubbed into meat to tenderize it before cooking.

ten•der•loin ['tɛndər,lɔɪn] *n.* **1** a tender part of the loin of beef or pork, located on either side of the backbone. **2** a district of a city noted for its high level of vice, crime, and corruption. (Originally applied to an area of New York City, from the rich living supposed to be gained there by corrupt police officers.)

ten•di•ni•tis [,tɛndə'nəitɪs] *n.* inflammation of a tendon.

ten•di•nous ['tɛndənəs] *adj.* **1** of or like a tendon. **2** consisting of tendons. ⟨< F *tendineux* < *tendon* tendon < Med.L. See TENDON.⟩

ten•don ['tɛndən] *n.* a tough, strong band or cord of tissue that joins a muscle to a bone or some other part; sinew. ⟨< Med.L *tendo, -onis* < Gk. *tenōn*; influenced by L *tendere* stretch⟩

ten•dril ['tɛndrəl] *n.* **1** a threadlike part of a climbing plant that attaches itself to something and helps support the plant. **2** something resembling such a part of a plant: *tendrils of hair curling about a child's face.* ⟨< F *tendrillon,* ult. < L *tener* tender⟩

ten•e•brous ['tɛnəbrəs] *adj.* dark; gloomy; dim. ⟨< L *tenebrosus* < *tenebrae* darkness⟩

ten•e•ment ['tɛnəmənt] *n.* **1** a building, especially in a poor section of a city, divided into sets of rooms for separate families. **2** a part of a house or building occupied by a tenant as a separate dwelling. **3** any house or building to live in; a dwelling house. **4** *Law.* any land, buildings, etc. held from a superior by tenure. ⟨ME < OF *tenement,* ult. < L *tenere* hold⟩ **—,ten•e'men•tal** or **,ten•e'men•ta•ry,** *adj.*

tenement house TENEMENT (def. 1).

ten•et ['tɛnɪt] *n.* a doctrine, principle, belief, or opinion held as true. ⟨< L *tenet* he holds⟩

ten•fold ['tɛn,fould] *adj., adv. —adj.* **1** ten times as much or as many. **2** having ten aspects or parts.
—adv. ten times as much or as many.

ten–gal•lon hat ['tɛn 'gælən] a large, wide-brimmed hat, often worn by cowboys. ⟨< Sp. *galón* braid, cowboy hats being originally decorated with a number of braids; confused with *gallon*, as if in reference to the hat's size⟩

ten•ge ['tɛŋgei] *n.* the basic unit of money in Kazakhstan, divided into 100 cents. See table of money in the Appendix.

Ten•nes•see [,tɛnə'si] *n.* a southeastern state of the United States.

Tennessee walking horse one of a breed of saddle horses having a natural, easy walking gait. It is developed mainly from Morgan and Standardbred stock.

ten•nis ['tɛnɪs] *n.* **1** a game played on a special outdoor court or on the grass by two or four players who knock a ball back and forth over a net with a racket **(tennis racket). 2** COURT TENNIS. ⟨ME < AF *tenetz* hold!, ult. < L *tenere*⟩

tennis court a place prepared and marked out to play tennis on.

tennis elbow an inflammation of the synovial membrane or tendons of the elbow caused by strain due to repeated or excessive rotation of the forearm, as in swinging the racket in tennis.

tennis shoe RUNNING SHOE.

ten•on ['tɛnən] *n., v. —n.* the end of a piece of wood cut so as to fit into a hole (the mortise) in another piece and so form a joint. See JOINT for picture.
—v. **1** cut so as to form a tenon. **2** fit together with tenon and mortise. ⟨ME < OF, ult. < L *tenere* hold⟩

ten•or ['tɛnər] *n.* **1** the general tendency or direction; a settled course: *The calm tenor of her life has never been disturbed by excitement or trouble.* **2** the general meaning or drift: *I understand French well enough to get the tenor of her lecture.* **3** *Law.* **a** the exact words or intent and meaning of a document, etc. as distinguished from their effect. **b** an exact copy. **4** the highest ordinary, or natural, adult male singing voice, covering the range from D below middle C to C above middle C. Compare COUNTERTENOR. **5** a singer who has such a voice. **6** the part sung by a tenor. Tenor is the second lowest part in a standard four-part harmony for men's and women's voices. **7** an instrument having a range next above that of the bass in a family of musical instruments. **8** (*adjl.*) having to do with, having the range of, or designed for a tenor. **9** a high-pitched male speaking voice. **10** in change-ringing, the bell having the lowest tone in a peal. **11** the thing or idea described or represented figuratively in a metaphor. In *His life is measured out in coffee-spoons*, *His life* is the tenor. Compare VEHICLE. ⟨ME < OF < L *tenor*, originally, a holding on < *tenere* hold⟩

tenor clef a clef sign placing middle C on the second-highest line of the staff, used in notation for tenor instruments.

ten•o•rite [,tɛnə,rəit] *n.* a black mineral, copper oxide, occurring in the form of tiny scales in copper deposits and in volcanic areas. ⟨< G. *Tenore* (1780-1861), Italian botanist⟩

te•not•o•my [tə'nɒtəmi] *n., pl.* **-mies.** the surgical cutting of a tendon. ⟨< Gk. *tenon* tendon + NL *-tomia* < Gk. *tome* a cutting < *temnein* cut⟩

ten•pen•ny ['tɛn,pɛni] *or* ['tɛnpəni] *adj.* **1** *Brit.* worth or costing ten pennies. **2** designating a kind of large-sized nail, once costing ten pennies per hundred.

ten•pin ['tɛn,pɪn] *n.* **1 tenpins** (*used with a singular verb*), a bowling game similar to fivepins, but using a larger and heavier ball (about 70 cm in circumference) to knock over ten pins instead of five . **2** one of the pins used in this game. **3** (*adjl.*) designating this type of bowling or the ball or alley used for it: *In the States they have only tenpin bowling.*

ten•rec ['tɛnrɛk] *n.* any of a family (Tenrecidae) of small, insect-eating mammals resembling hedgehogs, especially the tailless tenrec *Tenrec ecaudatus* of Madagascar. ⟨< F < Malagasy *tandraka*⟩

tense¹ [tɛns] *adj.* **tens•er, tens•est;** *v.* **tensed, tens•ing.** *—adj.* **1** stretched tight; strained to stiffness: *a tense rope, a face tense with pain.* **2** strained; keyed up; uneasy or unable to relax: *tense feelings, tense nerves. We were all tense with anticipation.* **3** full of or marked by mental, emotional, or interpersonal tension: *a tense moment, a tense meeting.* **4** *Phonetics.* of vowels, articulated with relatively taut muscles of the tongue and jaw. [i] and [u] are tense vowels. Compare LAX.
—v. stretch tight; stiffen: *She tensed her muscles for the leap. He tensed immediately when he saw the Doberman.* ⟨< L *tensus*, pp. of *tendere* stretch⟩ **—'tense•ly,** *adv.* **—'tense•ness,** *n.*

tense² [tɛns] *n.* **1 a** a set of verb forms showing the time, duration, etc. of the action or state expressed by the verb. The simple past tense in English is used to express an action or state that is completed or ended. **b** the grammatical category to which such forms belong; the marking of verbs for time: *Some languages do not have tense.* **2** a form of a verb indicating a particular time, etc. of an action or state. The simple past tense of *go* is *went.* ⟨ME < OF *tens* time < L *tempus.* Doublet of TEMPO.⟩ **—'tense•less,** *adj.*

ten•si•ble ['tɛnsəbəl] *adj.* capable of being stretched. ⟨< Med.L *tensibilis* < L *tendere* stretch⟩ **—,ten•si'bil•i•ty,** *n.*

ten•sile ['tɛnsaɪl] *or* ['tɛnsəl] *adj.* **1** of or having to do with tension. **2** capable of being stretched; ductile. ⟨< NL *tensilis* < L *tendere* stretch⟩

tensile strength a measure of resistance to stress in the direction of length. It is expressed in the force per unit of area (of a cross-section) of the maximum load, pulling lengthwise, that can be applied to a material without it breaking: *Steel has great tensile strength.*

ten•sil•i•ty [tɛn'sɪləti] *n.* a tensile quality; ductility.

ten•sim•e•ter [tɛn'sɪmətər] *n.* an instrument that measures vapour pressure. ⟨< *tension* + *-meter*⟩

ten•si•om•e•ter [,tɛnsi'ɒmətər] *n.* an instrument for measuring tension or stress in a substance. ⟨< *tension* + *-meter*⟩

ten•sion ['tɛnʃən] *n.* **1** a stretching. **2** a stretched condition: *The tension of the spring is caused by the weight.* **3** mental, emotional, or interpersonal stress or strain: *political tension, family tensions. A mother feels tension when her baby is sick.* **4 a** a stress caused by the action of a pulling force. An elevator exerts tension on the cables supporting it. **b** the force or forces exerting such a pull. **5** a device to control the pull or strain on something. The tension in a sewing machine may be adjusted to keep the thread tight or loose. **6** the number of stitches per centimetre necessary to make a knitted or crocheted item work out to the desired size. **7** voltage: *high-tension wires.* **8** the pressure of a gas. **9** the equilibrium of opposing forces or elements, as in a work of literature or art. ⟨< LL *tensio, -onis* < L *tendere* stretch⟩

ten•sion•al ['tɛnʃənəl] *adj.* of or having to do with tension.

ten•si•ty ['tɛnsəti] *n.* a tense quality or state.

ten•sor ['tɛnsər] *or* ['tɛnsɔr] *n.* **1** *Physiology.* a muscle that stretches or tightens some part of the body. **2** *Mathematics.* a vector quantity, defined by a set of at least three components, that transforms linearly. ⟨< NL⟩

ten–strike ['tɛn ,strəik] *n.* **1** *Tenpins.* the stroke that knocks down all the pins. **2** *Informal.* any completely successful stroke or act.

tent¹ [tɛnt] *n., v. —n.* **1** a movable shelter, usually made of canvas or nylon and often supported by one or more poles and ropes or wires. **2** a tentlike device to regulate the temperature and humidity of the air in treating certain respiratory diseases.
—v. **1** camp out or live in a tent. **2** cover with or accommodate in a tent. ⟨ME < OF *tente*, ult. < L *tendere* stretch⟩ **—'tent,like,** *adj.*

tent² [tɛnt] *n., v., Medicine. —n.* a small, compact mass of gauze or lint inserted in a natural orifice or a wound to hold it open or dilate it.
—v. keep (a wound or natural orifice) open or dilated by the use of such a plug. ⟨ME *tente* < OF *tente* probe < *tenter* try, test⟩

ten•ta•cle ['tɛntəkəl] *n.* **1** a long, slender, flexible growth on the head or around the mouth of an animal, used to touch, hold, or move; feeler. **2** a sensitive, hairlike growth on a plant. **3** something that resembles a tentacle in its reach and grasp: *The tentacles of a dictator's power reach into every home.* ⟨< NL *tentaculum* < L *tentare* try. See TENTATIVE.⟩ **—'ten•ta•cled,** *adj.*

ten•tac•u•lar [tɛn'tækjələr] *adj.* of, forming, or resembling tentacles.

tent•age ['tɛntɪdʒ] *n.* **1** a supply or number of tents. **2** equipment for tents.

ten•ta•tive ['tɛntətɪv] *adj.* **1** done as a trial or experiment; experimental: *a tentative plan.* **2** not final; subject to revision; provisional: *a tentative schedule.* **3** hesitant; unsure; timid: *a tentative smile. She was enthusiastic, but he was rather tentative about the whole thing.* ⟨< Med.L *tentativus* < L *tentare* try out, intensive of *tendere* stretch, aim; associated in L with *temptare* feel out⟩ **—'ten•ta•tive•ly,** *adv.* **—'ten•ta•tive•ness,** *n.*

tent caterpillar the larva of any of various moths (family Lasiocampidae), especially *Malacosoma americanum,* that feeds on the leaves of deciduous trees. Tent caterpillars live in colonies in tentlike webs which they spin in the crotches of trees in early spring.

ten•ter ['tɛntər] *n., v.* *—n.* a framework on which cloth is stretched so that it may set or dry evenly without shrinking. *—v.* stretch (cloth) on a tenter. ⟨ult. < L *tentus,* pp. of *tendere* stretch⟩

ten•ter•hook ['tɛntər,hʊk] *n.* one of the hooks or bent nails that hold the cloth stretched on a tenter.
on tenterhooks, in painful suspense; anxious.

tenth [tɛnθ] *adj. or n.* **1** next after the 9th; last in a series of ten; 10th. **2** one, or being one, of 10 equal parts.

tenth•ly ['tɛnθli] *adv.* in the tenth place.

tent ring a ring of stones used to hold down a tent, such as a teepee or tupik, often remaining in position after the tent has been removed.

tent stitch PETIT POINT (def. 1).

tent trailer a small TRAILER (def. 2) of which the roof and part of the walls are made of canvas, folding down when not in use.

ten•u•i•ty [tə'njuəti] *or* [tə'nuəti] *n.* a rarefied condition; thinness; slightness.

ten•u•ous ['tɛnjuəs] *adj.* **1** thin; slender. **2** not dense; rarefied: *tenuous air.* **3** weakly founded; not firm or substantial: *As the agreement they have reached is very tenuous, we must be careful not to provoke either of them.* ⟨< L *tenuis* thin⟩ **—'ten•u•ous•ly,** *adv.* **—'ten•u•ous•ness,** *n.*

ten•ure ['tɛnjər] *n.* **1 a** a holding; possessing. **b** the right to hold or possess. **2** the length of time of holding or possessing: *The tenure of office of the president of our club is one year.* **3** the manner of holding land, buildings, etc. from a feudal lord or superior. **4** the conditions, terms, etc. on which anything is held or occupied. **5** permanent status in one's job, granted to a teacher, especially a university professor, after certain specified conditions of length of service, performance, etc. have been met. ⟨ME < OF *tenure,* ult. < L *tenere* hold⟩ **—'ten•ured,** *adj.*

ten•u•ri•al [tə'njuriəl] *adj.* having to do with tenure, especially of land.

te•nu•to [tɛ'nutou] *adj., n., pl.* **-ti** [-ti]. *Music.* *—adj.* of a note, held or to be held to its full time value.
—n. a note or chord so played. ⟨< Ital. *tenuto,* pp. of *tenere* hold < L⟩

te•o•cal•li [,tiou'kæli]; *Spanish,* [,teo'kaji] *n.* any of the temples of the ancient Aztecs, usually having a truncated pyramid for the base. ⟨< Nahuatl *teokalli* temple < *teotl* god + *kalli* house⟩

te•pee ['tipi] See TEEPEE.

teph•ra ['tɛfrə] *n.* solids cast forth from an erupting volcano, light enough to be carried on the wind. ⟨< Gk. *tephra* ashes⟩

tep•id ['tɛpɪd] *adj.* **1** slightly warm; lukewarm. **2** having or showing little enthusiasm: *a tepid welcome.* ⟨< L *tepidus*⟩ **—'tep•id•ly,** *adv.* **—te'pid•i•ty** or **'tep•id•ness,** *n.*

te•qui•la [tə'kilə] *n.* **1** a Mexican agave (*Agave tequilana*) from which mescal is made. **2** a strong alcoholic liquor made by redistilling mescal. ⟨< Am.E < Am.Sp. < *Tequila,* a town in Mexico⟩

ter– *prefix.* three; thrice: *tercentenary.* ⟨< L *ter* thrice⟩

ter. **1** territory; territorial. **2** terrace.

ter•a– *prefix.* trillion; 10^{12}: *terametre.* ⟨< Gk. *teras* monster⟩

ter•aph ['tɛrəf] *n., pl.* **ter•a•phim** ['tɛrə,fɪm]. a small image or object venerated as a household god by ancient Semitics. ⟨ME < LL *theraphim* < Gk. *theraphin* < Hebrew *terafim*⟩

ter•a•tism ['tɛrə,tɪzəm] *n.* a malformed animal or human fetus. **—'ter•a,toid,** *adj.*

ter•a•to– *combining form.* monstrosity; malformation. ⟨< Gk. *teras, teratos,* wonder, monster⟩

ter•a•to•gen ['tɛrətədʒən] *or* [tə'rætədʒən] an agent, such as a chemical, that produces or tends to produce fetal malformation. **—,ter•a•to'gen•ic** [-'dʒɛnɪk], *adj.*

ter•a•to•gen•e•sis [,tɛrətə'dʒɛnəsɪs] *n.* the production of fetal malformation.

ter•a•tol•o•gy [,tɛrə'tɒlədʒi] *n.* **1** *Biology.* the scientific study of malformations or gross abnormalities in animal or vegetable organisms. **2** the study of mythological or fantastic creatures. **—,ter•a•to'log•i•cal,** *adj.*

ter•a•to•ma [,tɛrə'toumə] *n. Pathology.* a tumour made up of heterogenous tissues, especially embryonic hair and teeth.

ter•bi•um ['tɜrbiəm] *n.* a rare metallic chemical element of the yttrium group. *Symbol*: Tb; *at.no.* 65; *at.mass* 158.93. ⟨< *terb-,* abstracted from *Ytterby,* a town in Sweden⟩

terce [tɜrs] *n.* TIERCE (def. 5).
☛ *Hom.* TERSE.

ter•cel ['tɜrsəl] *n.* a male falcon or goshawk, especially a male peregrine falcon as used in falconry. Compare FALCON (def. 2). Also, **tiercel.** ⟨ME < OF *tercel,* ult. < L *tertius* third⟩

ter•cen•te•nar•y [,tɜrsɛn'tɛnəri], [,tɜrsɛn'tinəri], *or* [tɜr'sɛntə,nɛri] *adj. or n., pl.* **-nar•ies.** tricentennial. ⟨< L *ter* three times + E *centenary*⟩

ter•cen•ten•ni•al [,tɜrsɛn'tɛniəl] *adj. or n.* tricentennial.

ter•cet ['tɜrsɪt] *or* [tɜr'sɛt] *n.* **1** a group of three lines rhyming together, or connected by rhyme with the adjacent group or groups of three lines. **2** *Music.* triplet. ⟨< F < Ital. *terzetto,* ult. < L *tertius* third⟩

ter•e•bene ['tɛrə,bin] *n. Pharmacology.* a mixture of terpenes prepared by mixing turpentine with sulphuric acid, used chiefly as an expectorant.

ter•e•binth ['tɛrə,bɪnθ] *n.* a small tree (*Pistacia terebinthus*) of the cashew family, of the Mediterranean area of Europe, yielding turpentine.

ter•e•bin•thine [,tɛrə'bɪnθɪn], [,tɛrə'bɪnθin], *or* [,tɛrə'bɪnθaɪn] *adj.* **1** pertaining to or resembling turpentine. **2** of or pertaining to the terebinth.

te•re•do [tə'ridou] *n., pl.* **-dos.** shipworm, especially any of the genus *Teredo.* ⟨< L < Gk. *terēdōn* < *tereein* bore⟩

te•rete [tə'rit] *or* ['tɛrit] *adj. Biology.* cylindrical. ⟨< L *teres* round, smooth⟩

ter•gi•ver•sate ['tɜrdʒəvər,seit] *v.* **-sat•ed, -sat•ing.** **1** change one's attitude or opinions with respect to a cause or subject; turn renegade. **2** shift or shuffle; be evasive. ⟨< L *tergiversatus,* ult. < *tergum* back + *vertere* turn⟩ **—'ter•gi•ver,sa•tor,** *n.* **—,ter•gi•ver'sa•tion,** *n.*

ter•i•ya•ki [,tɛri'jɑki] *or* [,tɛri'jæki] *n.* meat or fish, broiled or grilled after being marinated in specially seasoned soy sauce. ⟨< Japanese *teri* shine + *yaki* broil⟩

term [tɜrm] *n., v.* *—n.* **1** a word or phrase used in a recognized and definite sense in some particular subject, science, art, business, etc.: *medical terms, terms about radio.* **2** a word or expression: *an abstract term, a term of reproach.* **3** a set period of time; the length of time that a thing lasts: *a president's term of office.* **4** one of the long periods into which the school year may be divided: *the fall term.* **5** a date fixed for a payment, end of lease, etc. **6** the normal period between conception and birth, or the end of this period: *After two miscarriages, she finally carried the third baby to term.* **7** *Law.* one of the periods of time when certain courts are in session. **8** *Mathematics.* **a** one of the members in a proportion or ratio. **b** one or more numerals or symbols constituting a unit in an expression. Terms in an algebraic expression are always separated by + or –. The expressions x and xy each consist of one term; $xy + ab$ is an expression consisting of two terms. **9** *Logic.* **a** word or words that form the subject or predicate of a proposition. **b** one of the three elements forming the subjects and predicates in a syllogism. In the example at SYLLOGISM, the terms are *tree, oak,* and *have roots.* **10** *Archaic.* a boundary; end; limit. **11** **terms,** *pl.* **a** conditions: *the terms of a treaty.* **b** a way of speaking: *flattering terms.* **c** personal relations: *on good terms, on speaking terms.*
bring to terms, compel to agree, assent, or submit; force to come to terms.
come to terms, reach an agreement; become reconciled: *The quarrelling sisters finally came to terms. He finally came to terms with his own mortality.*
in terms of, a concerning; with regard to; from the standpoint of: *How's he doing in terms of financial stability?* **b** in the conceptual framework of: *It can't be understood in terms of pure science.*
terms of reference, the matters referred to a person, committee, etc. for study; instructions indicating the scope of an inquiry.
—v. name; call; describe as: *He might be termed handsome.* ⟨ME

< OF *terme* < L *terminus* end, boundary line. Doublet of TERMINUS.〉 **—'term•less,** *adj.*

ter•ma•gan•cy ['tɜrməgənsi] *n.* shrewishness.

ter•ma•gant ['tɜrməgənt] *n., adj. —n.* a violent, quarrelling, scolding woman.
—adj. violent; quarrelling; scolding. 〈ME < OF *Tervagan,* a fictitious Muslim deity〉 **—'ter•ma•gant•ly,** *adv.*

ter•mi•na•ble ['tɜrmənəbəl] *adj.* **1** able to be ended: *The contract was terminable by either party.* **2** coming to an end after a certain time: *a loan terminable in ten years.* **—,ter•mi•na'bil•i•ty** or **'ter•mi•na•ble•ness,** *n.* **—'ter•mi•na•bly,** *adv.*

ter•mi•nal ['tɜrmənəl] *adj., n. —adj.* **1** at the end; forming the end part. A terminal flower or bud is one growing at the end of a stem, branch, etc. **2** coming at the end: *a terminal examination.* **3** having to do with a term. **4** occurring at regular intervals or at the end of each term. **5** at the end of a railway, bus, or aircraft line: *a terminal station.* **6** having to do with the handling of freight at a terminal. **7** marking a boundary, limit, or end. **8 a** of a disease, incurable and fatal: *terminal cancer.* **b** of a patient, fatally ill.
—n. **1** the end; end part. **2** either end of a railway line, airline, shipping route, etc. where sheds, hangars, garages, offices, etc., and stations to handle freight and passengers are located; terminus: *Prince George is the terminal of the Pacific Great Eastern railway.* **3** a station for the transfer of passengers and cargo, or any of the buildings located there: *Pearson International Airport now has three terminals. We picked him up at the bus terminal.* **4** a device for making an electrical connection: *the terminals of a battery.* **5** an apparatus, such as a visual display unit, by which a user can give information to or receive information from a computer, communications system, etc. 〈< L *terminalis* < *terminus* end〉

ter•mi•nal•ly ['tɜrmənəli] *adv.* **1** at the end. **2** with respect to a termination. **3** with a terminal disease; fatally: *She is terminally ill.*

terminal velocity *Physics.* the highest unchanged velocity reached by a falling body when the force of the medium through which it is falling is equal in magnitude and opposite in direction to the force of gravity.

ter•mi•nate ['tɜrmə,neit] *v.* **-nat•ed, -nat•ing. 1** bring to an end; put an end to: *to terminate a partnership.* **2** come to an end or terminus: *His contract terminates soon. The Wilson bus terminates at the subway.* **3** occur at or form the end of; bound; limit. **4** fire or dismiss (a worker). **5** *Slang.* kill. 〈< L *terminare* < *terminus* end〉 **—'ter•mi,na•tor,** *n.*

ter•mi•na•tion [,tɜrmə'neiʃən] *n.* **1** an ending; end; outcome. **2** an end part. **3** the ending of a word; suffix. In *gladly,* the adverbial termination is *-ly.*

termination codon STOP CODON.

ter•mi•na•tive ['tɜrmənətɪv] *or* ['tɜrmə,neitɪv] *adj.* tending or serving to terminate.

ter•mi•na•tor ['tɜrmɪ,neitər] *n.* **1** a person or thing that terminates. **2** the line that divides the light and dark parts of a planet or moon.

ter•mi•no•log•i•cal [,tɜrmənə'lɒdʒəkəl] *adj.* of or having to do with terminology. **—,ter•mi•no'log•i•cal•ly,** *adv.*

ter•mi•nol•o•gy [,tɜrmə'nɒlədʒi] *n., pl.* **-gies. 1** the set of special words or terms used in a science, art, business, etc.: *medical terminology.* **2** the scientific or systematic study of terms. 〈< G *Terminologie* < Med.L *terminus* term + Gk. *-logos* treating of〉

term insurance life insurance that expires at the end of a specified period of time.

ter•mi•nus ['tɜrmənəs] *n., pl.* **-nus•es** or **-ni** [-,naɪ] *or* [-,ni]. **1** either end of a railway line, bus line, etc.; terminal. **2** a city or station at the end of a railway line, bus line, etc. **3** an ending place; final point; goal; end. **4** a stone, post, etc. marking a boundary or limit. 〈< L *terminus.* Doublet of TERM.〉

ter•mite ['tɜrməit] *n.* any of an order (Isoptera) of antlike, social insects, found chiefly in tropical regions, having a soft, pale-coloured body and a broad abdomen. Termites eat cellulose, the main constituent of wood, and can be very destructive if they invade buildings. 〈< NL *termes, -itis,* special use of L *termes* woodworm〉

term paper a major essay or report assigned for a term at an academic institution.

tern [tɜrn] *n.* any of a subfamily (Sterninae) of typically grey-and-white, aquatic birds related to and resembling gulls, but usually smaller and having a pointed bill and, usually, a deeply forked tail. 〈< Scand.; cf. Danish *terne*〉
☛ *Hom.* TURN.

Terns

ter•na•ry ['tɜrnəri] *adj.* **1** consisting of three; involving or based on three; triple. **2** third in order or rank. 〈< L *ternarius,* ult. < *ter* three times〉

ter•nate ['tɜrnɪt] *or* ['tɜrneit] *adj.* **1** consisting of three. **2** arranged in threes. **3** *Botany.* **a** consisting of three leaflets. **b** having leaves arranged in whorls of three.

terne•plate ['tɜrn,pleit] *n.* steel plate coated with an alloy of lead and tin. 〈< F *terne* dull + E *plate*〉

ter•pene ['tɜrpin] *n.* **1** any of a class of unsaturated monocyclic hydrocarbons of the general formula $C_{10}H_{16}$, found in the resins and essential oils of plants, especially conifers and oranges, and used in the production of perfumes, medicines, etc. **2** this class or any of its oxygenated derivatives. 〈< G *terpen* < *terp* turpentine + E *-ene*〉

Terp•sich•o•re [tərp'sɪkəri] *n. Greek mythology.* the Muse of dancing.

terp•si•cho•re•an [,tɜrpsəkə'riən] *or* [,tɜrpsə'kɔriən] *adj.* **1** having to do with dancing: *the terpsichorean art.* **2** pertaining to Terpsichore.

terr. 1 territory. **2** terrace.

ter•ra al•ba ['tɛrə 'ælbə] finely powdered gypsum or any of various other white mineral substances used in the manufacture of paints, ceramics, paper, etc. 〈< L, white earth〉

ter•race ['tɛrɪs] *n., v.* **-raced, -rac•ing.** *—n.* **1** a flat level of land like a large step, especially one of a series of such levels on a slope, made by humans for cultivation. **2** a geological formation similar to this. **3** a street along the side, bottom, or top of a slope. **4** a row of houses on such a street. **5** a paved outdoor space adjoining a house and often overlooking a lawn or garden, used for lounging, dining, etc. **6** the flat roof of a house, especially a house of Spanish or Oriental style.
—v. form into a terrace or terraces; furnish with terraces. 〈< OF *terrace,* ult. < L *terra* earth〉

ter•ra cot•ta ['tɛrə 'kɒtə] **1** a kind of hard, brownish red earthenware, used for vases, statuettes, decorations on buildings, etc. **2** a piece of this earthenware, or something made from it. **3** a dull brownish red. 〈< Ital. *terra cotta* < *terra* earth + *cotta* baked〉 **—'ter•ra-'cot•ta,** *adj.*

ter•ra fir•ma ['tɛrə 'fɜrmə] solid earth; dry land. 〈< L〉

ter•rain [tə'rein] *or* ['tɛrein] *n.* **1** land; a tract of land, especially considered as to its extent and natural features in relation to its use for some specific purpose. **2** terrane. 〈< F *terrain,* ult. < L *terra* land〉
☛ *Hom.* TERRANE.

ter•ra in•cog•ni•ta ['tɛrə ,ɪnkɒg'nitə] *or* [ɪn'kɒgnətə] *Latin.* unknown territory: *Anything other than English cuisine seemed to be terra incognita to the new chef.*

ter•rane [tə'rein] *or* ['tɛrein] *n. Geology.* **1** a rock formation or a series of formations. **2** an area where a particular formation or group of rocks is predominant. **3** terrain. 〈< *terrain*〉
☛ *Hom.* TERRAIN.

ter•ra•pin ['tɛrəpɪn] *n.* any of various small, edible turtles (family Emydidae) living in fresh or brackish water. See also DIAMONDBACK TERRAPIN. 〈< Algonquian〉

ter•rar•i•um [tə'rɛriəm] *n., pl.* **-i•ums,** or **-i•a** [-iə]. a glass or plastic enclosure in which plants or small land animals are kept. 〈< NL *terrarium* < L *terra* land〉

ter•raz•zo [tɛ'rɑtsou] *n.* a floor made of small pieces of marble embedded in cement. 〈< Ital. *terrazzo* terrace, balcony < *terra* earth〉

ter•rene [tɛ'rin], [tə'rin], *or* ['tɛrin] *adj.* TERRESTRIAL (defs. 1, 5).
☛ *Hom.* TERRINE [tɛ'rin], [tə'rin]; TUREEN [tə'rin].

ter•res•tri•al [tə'rɛstriəl] *adj., n. —adj.* **1** of the earth; having to do with the earth. **2** of land, not water or air: *Islands and continents make up the terrestrial parts of the earth.* **3** living on the ground, not in the air or water or in trees: *terrestrial animals.* **4** growing on land; growing in the ground: *terrestrial plants.*

5 worldly; earthly. 6 *Astronomy.* of a planet, similar in composition and size to the earth.
—n. an inhabitant of earth. ⟨ME < L *terrestris* < *terra* earth⟩
☛ *Syn. adj.* **5.** See note at EARTHLY.

terrestrial globe **1** the earth. **2** a sphere with the map of the earth on it.

terrestrial planet *Astronomy.* one of the four small, rocky, inner planets of the earth's solar system: Mercury, Venus, Earth, Mars. Also called **inner planet.**

ter•ret [ˈtɛrɪt] *n.* one of the round loops or rings on the saddle of a harness, through which the driving reins pass. ⟨var. of *toret* < OF *toret* < *tour* < L *tornus.* See TOUR.⟩

terre–verte [ˈtɛr ˌvɛrt] *n.* any of various soft green clays used as colouring matter in art. ⟨< F, literally, green earth⟩

ter•ri•ble [ˈtɛrəbəl] *adj.* **1** causing great fear; dreadful; awful: *a terrible roar.* **2** distressing; severe: *the terrible suffering caused by war.* **3** *Informal.* extremely bad, unpleasant, etc.: *She has a terrible temper.* ⟨< L *terribilis* < *terrere* terrify⟩
—'ter•ri•ble•ness, *n.*

ter•ri•bly [ˈtɛrəbli] *adv.* **1** *Informal.* extremely: *We were terribly afraid. I'm terribly sorry I stepped on your toe.* **2** in a terrible or fearsome manner: *The ogre frowned terribly.*

ter•ric•o•lous [tɛˈrɪkələs] *or* [təˈrɪkələs] *adj. Biology.* living on, in, or near the ground. ⟨< L *terricola* earth dweller (< *terra* earth + *colere* dwell, till) + E *-ous*⟩

ter•ri•er [ˈtɛriər] *n.* any of several breeds of dog, such as the Airedale, fox terrier, or Scotch terrier, having either a short-haired, smooth coat or a long-haired, rough coat. Terriers were formerly used to pursue burrowing animals. ⟨< F *terrier,* ult. < L *terra* earth⟩

ter•rif•ic [təˈrɪfɪk] *adj.* **1** causing great fear; terrifying. **2** *Informal.* very unusual; remarkable; extraordinary: *A terrific hot spell ruined many of the crops.* **3** *Slang.* very good; wonderful: *He is a terrific football player. The party was terrific.* ⟨< L *terrificus* < *terrere* terrify + *-ficus* making⟩ **—ter'rif•i•cal•ly,** *adv.*

ter•ri•fied [ˈtɛrəˌfaɪd] *adj., v. —adj.* filled with great fear; thoroughly frightened.
—v. pt. and pp. of TERRIFY.
☛ *Syn.* See note at AFRAID.

ter•ri•fy [ˈtɛrəˌfaɪ] *v.* **-fied, -fy•ing.** fill with great fear; frighten very much. ⟨< L *terrificare* < *terrere* terrify + *facere* make⟩
—'ter•ri,fy•ing•ly, *adv.*

ter•rine [tɛˈrin] *or* [təˈrin] *n.* **1** an earthenware or pottery dish or casserole, primarily intended for baking a pâté or similar combination of game, meat, vegetables, etc. **2** a pâté cooked in such a dish. ⟨< F. See TUREEN.⟩
☛ *Hom.* TERRENE [tɛˈrin], [təˈrin]; TUREEN [təˈrin].

ter•ri•to•ri•al [ˌtɛrəˈtɔriəl] *adj., n. —adj.* **1** of or having to do with territory: *Many wars have been fought for territorial gain.* **2** *Cdn.* **Territorial,** of or having to do with a Territory: *the Territorial Council.* **3** of or restricted to a particular territory or region. **4** Also, **Territorial,** *Brit.* organized for home defence. **5** *Ethology.* characterized by territoriality.
—n. **Territorial,** *Brit.* a soldier of a Territorial force.
—,ter•ri'to•ri•al•ly, *adv.*

Territorial Council **1** in Yukon Territory, an elected body consisting of seven members and responsible for local government. **2** the Council of the Northwest Territories.

ter•ri•to•ri•al•i•ty [ˌtɛrəˌtɔriˈæləti] *n.* **1** the status or condition of being territorial. **2** *Ethology.* the behaviour shown by an animal in defining and defending its territory. **3** the protection of a territory or a strong attachment to it.

ter•ri•to•ry [ˈtɛrəˌtɔri] *n., pl.* **-ries. 1** land: *Much territory in Africa is desert.* **2** a region; an area of land: *The company leased a large territory for oil explorations.* **3** land or waters under the rule or jurisdiction of a government or nation: *The British Empire included many territories. Most of Canadian territory is north of the 49th parallel.* **4 Territory, a** in Canada, a region having its own elected council and administered by a commissioner appointed by the federal government: *the Northwest Territories, Yukon Territory.* **b** a region having similar status in some other countries. **5** a region assigned to a sales representative or agent. **6** a domain or sphere of knowledge or activity: *the territory of biochemistry. Baby care used to be strictly female territory.* **7** *Ethology.* the area occupied and defended by an animal or animals, especially against intruders of the same species. ⟨ME < L *territorium* < *terra* land⟩

ter•ror [ˈtɛrər] *n.* **1** great fear. **2** a cause of great fear. **3** *Informal.* a person or thing that causes much trouble and unpleasantness. **4 the Terror,** REIGN OF TERROR. **5** violence or threats of violence as a means of organized intimidation or coercion; TERRORISM (def. 3). ⟨ME < OF < L *terror* < *terrere* terrify⟩

ter•ror•ism [ˈtɛrəˌrɪzəm] *n.* **1** the act of terrorizing; use of terror. **2** the condition of fear and submission produced in terrified people. **3** a method of opposing a government through the use of violence against civilians, taking of hostages, etc., to gain specific demands.

ter•ror•ist [ˈtɛrərɪst] *n.* **1** a person who uses or favours terrorism. **2** (*adjl.*) of, having to do with, or like terrorists: *a terrorist bomb, terrorist tactics.*

ter•ror•is•tic [ˌtɛrəˈrɪstɪk] *adj.* using or favouring methods that inspire terror.

ter•ror•i•za•tion [ˌtɛrərəˈzeiʃən] *or* [ˌtɛrəraɪˈzeiʃən] *n.* the act of terrorizing or the state of being terrorized; rule by terror.

ter•ror•ize [ˈtɛrəˌraɪz] *v.* **-ized, -iz•ing. 1** fill with terror. **2** rule or subdue by causing terror. **—'ter•ror,iz•er,** *n.*

ter•ror–strick•en [ˈtɛrər ˌstrɪkən] *adj.* terrified.

ter•ry [ˈtɛri] *n., pl.* **-ries. 1** a rough cloth made of uncut looped yarn, usually cotton. **2** the uncut loops: *This towel is so old all the terry is worn off, leaving only the weave.* Also (def. 1), **terry cloth.** ⟨? < F *tiré* drawn⟩
☛ *Hom.* TARRY.

terse [tɜrs] *adj.* **ters•er, ters•est. 1** brief and to the point: *a terse account of a voyage, a terse writer.* **2** abrupt or curt. ⟨< L *tersus,* pp. of *tergere* rub, polish⟩ **—'terse•ly,** *adv.*
—'terse•ness, *n.*
☛ *Hom.* TERCE.

ter•tian [ˈtɜrʃən] *n., adj. —n.* a fever or ague that reaches a peak every other day.
—adj. recurring every other day. ⟨ME < L *tertiana (febris* fever*)* < *tertius* third⟩

ter•ti•ar•y [ˈtɜrʃəri] *or* [ˈtɜrʃiˌɛri] *adj., n., pl.* **-ar•ies.** *—adj.* **1 Tertiary,** *Geology.* of or having to do with the Tertiary or the rocks formed during it. **2** of the third order, degree, rank, formation, etc.: *the tertiary feathers on a bird, a tertiary point in an argument, tertiary education.* **3** *Chemistry.* **a** third in order; formed by substitution of three atoms or groups. **b** designating or containing a carbon atom attached to three other carbon atoms in a ring or chain.
—n. **1 Tertiary,** *Geology.* **a** the third chief period of time in the formation of the earth's surface, beginning approximately 60 million years ago. During this period the great mountain systems, such as the Rockies, Alps, Himalayas, and Andes, appeared and rapid development of mammals occurred. See geological time chart in the Appendix. **b** the rocks formed during this period. **2** one of a bird's flight feathers. ⟨< L *tertiarius* < *tertius* third⟩

ter•ti•um quid [ˈtɜrʃiəm ˈkwɪd] *Latin.* something related in some way to two things, but distinct from both; something intermediate between two things. ⟨literally, third thing⟩

ter•va•lent [tərˈveilənt] *or* [ˈtɜrveilənt] *adj.* trivalent.

Ter•y•lene [ˈtɛrəˌlin] *n. Trademark.* a crease-resistant synthetic polyester fibre, much used for shirts, dresses, suits, etc. and often mixed with wool or other yarns.

ter•za ri•ma [ˈtɛrtsə ˈrimə] an Italian form of iambic verse consisting of ten-syllable or eleven-syllable lines arranged in tercets, the middle line of each tercet rhyming with the first and third lines of the following tercet. Shelley's *Ode to the West Wind* is in terza rima. ⟨< Ital. *terza rima* < *terza* third + *rima* rhyme⟩

TESL [ˈtɛsəl] teaching English as a second language.

tes•la [ˈtɛslə] *n.* an international unit of magnetic induction, equal to one weber per square metre. *Abbrev.:* T ⟨after Nikola *Tesla* (1856-1943), Croatian-born American scientist⟩

tes•sel•late *v.* [ˈtɛsəˌleit]; *adj.* [ˈtɛsəlɪt] *or* [ˈtɛsəˌleit] *v.* **-lat•ed, -lat•ing;** *adj. —v.* make of small squares or blocks, or in a checkered pattern.
—adj. made in small squares or blocks or in a checkered pattern. ⟨< L *tessellatus,* ult. < *tessera.* See TESSERA.⟩
—,tes•sel'la•tion, *n.*

tes•ser•a [ˈtɛsərə] *n., pl.* **tes•ser•ae** [-ˌi] *or* [-ˌaɪ]. **1** a small piece of marble, glass, etc. used in mosaic work. **2** a small square of bone, wood, etc. used in ancient times as a token, tally, ticket, die, etc. ⟨< L < Gk. *tessera* piece having four corners < *tessares* four⟩

tes•ser•act [ˈtɛsəˌrækt] *n.* the generalization of a cube to four dimensions. ⟨< Gk. *tesser(es)* four + *actis* ray⟩

tes•si•tu•ra [ˌtɛsɪˈturə] *n. Music.* the range within which most of the notes of a given vocal or instrumental part of a composition fall: *"The Queen of the Night" aria in* The Magic Flute *has an incredibly broad tessitura.* ⟨< Ital., texture⟩

test¹ [tɛst] *n., v. —n.* **1 a** an examination; trial of knowledge or skill: *People who want to drive an automobile must pass a test. The teacher gave the class a test in arithmetic.* **b** the set of questions or problems used to evaluate the knowledge or skills being examined. **2** any means of trial: *Trouble is a test of character.* **3** a criterion against which something may be judged; standard; touchstone. **4** *Chemistry.* **a** an examination of a substance to see what it is or what it contains. **b** a process or substance used in such an examination.
—v. **1** subject to a test; try out; examine: *to test water for bacteria. She tested the boy's honesty by leaving money on the table.* **2** give a test: *A doctor may not test for HIV without the patient's knowledge and consent.* **3** be revealed to be, as a result of a test: *She tested negative for TB.* **4** perform or score on tests: *These students test alarmingly low in math and science.* ⟨ME < OF *test* vessel used in assaying < L *testum* earthen vessel⟩ **—'test•a•ble,** *adj.*
☛ *Syn. n.* **1.** See note at TRIAL.

test² [tɛst] *n.* TESTA (def. 1).

test. **1** testamentary. **2** testator.

tes•ta ['tɛstə] *n., pl.* **-tae** [-ti] *or* [-taɪ]. **1** *Zoology.* a shell; the hard covering of certain animals. **2** *Botany.* the hard outside coat of a seed. ⟨< L *testa* earthen vessel⟩

tes•ta•ceous [tɛ'steiʃəs] *adj.* **1** of, having to do with, or like a shell. **2** having a hard, continuous outer covering or shell **3** brownish red or brownish yellow in colour.

tes•ta•cy ['tɛstəsi] *n.* **1** the leaving of a will at death. **2** the state of being testate.

tes•ta•ment ['tɛstəmənt] *n.* **1** written instructions telling what to do with a person's property after his or her death; a will. **2** a solemn agreement or covenant, especially between God and human beings. **3 Testament, a** a main division of the Christian Bible; the Old Testament or the New Testament. **b** *Informal.* New Testament. ⟨ME < L *testamentum,* ult. < *testis* witness⟩

tes•ta•men•ta•ry [,tɛstə'mɛntəri] *adj.* **1** of or having to do with a testament or will. **2** given, done, or appointed by a testament or will. **3** in a testament or will.

tes•tate ['tɛsteit] *adj., n. —adj.* having made and left a valid will.
—n. a person who has died leaving a will. ⟨< L *testatus,* pp. of *testari* make a will < *testis* witness⟩

tes•ta•tor ['tɛsteitər] *or* [tɛ'steitər] *n.* **1** a person who makes a will. **2** a person who has died leaving a valid will.

tes•ta•trix [tɛ'steitrɪks] *n., pl.* **-tri•ces** [-trə,siz]. **1** a woman who makes a will. **2** a woman who has died leaving a valid will.

test ban an agreement between nations to ban the testing of nuclear weapons.

test case *Law.* **1** a case whose outcome may set a precedent. **2** a legal action taken, often with the agreement of both parties, for the express purpose of determining the position of the law on some matter such as the constitutionality of a certain statute.

test–drive ['tɛst ,draɪv] *v.* **-drove, -driv•en, -driv•ing.** drive (a car or other vehicle) to try it out. **—'test-,driv•er,** *n.*

test•er¹ ['tɛstər] *n.* a person or thing that tests. ⟨< *test*⟩

tes•ter² ['tɛstər] *n.* a canopy over a four-poster bed or an altar. ⟨probably < OF *testre,* ult. < VL *testa* head < L *testa* earthen pot⟩

tes•tes ['tɛstiz] *n.* pl. of TESTIS.

test–fly ['tɛst ,flaɪ] *v.* **-flew, -flown, -fly•ing.** fly (an aircraft) to try it out.

tes•ti•cle ['tɛstəkəl] *n.* the male reproductive organ of most animals, which produces sperm. In most mammals, the testicles are contained in an external pouch called the scrotum. ⟨< L *testiculus,* dim. of *testis.* See TESTIS.⟩ **—tes'ti•cu•lar** [tɛ'stɪkjələr], *adj.*

tes•tic•u•late [tɛ'stɪkjʊlɪt] *or* [tɛ'stɪkjʊ,leit] *adj. Botany.* **1** shaped like a testis. **2** having tubers shaped like testicles, as some orchids.

tes•ti•fy ['tɛstə,faɪ] *v.* **-fied, -fy•ing. 1** give evidence (of); bear witness (*usually used with* **to**): *The excellence of Shakespeare's plays testifies to his genius. The firm testified their appreciation of her work by raising her pay.* **2** declare solemnly; affirm. **3** *Law.* declare or give evidence under oath before a judge, coroner, etc.: *The police testified that the speeding car had crashed into the truck. The witness was unwilling to testify.* ⟨ME < L *testificari* < *testis* witness + *facere* make⟩ **—'tes•ti,fi•er,** *n.*

tes•ti•mo•ni•al [,tɛstə'mouniəl] *n., adj. —n.* **1** a certificate of character, conduct, qualifications, value, etc.; recommendation: *The boy looking for a job has testimonials from his teachers and former employer. Advertisements for patent medicines often contain testimonials from people who have used them.* **2** something given or done to show esteem, admiration, gratitude, etc.: *The members of the church collected money for a testimonial to their retiring pastor.*
—adj. given or done as a testimonial.

tes•ti•mo•ny ['tɛstə,mouni] *or* ['tɛstɪməni] *n., pl.* **-nies. 1** a statement, especially one used for evidence or proof: *A witness gave testimony that Mrs. Doe was at home at 9 p.m.* **2** evidence: *The pupils presented their teacher with a watch in testimony of their respect and affection.* **3** an open declaration or profession of one's faith. **4** *Archaic.* the Ten Commandments. **5 testimonies,** *pl. Archaic.* the laws of God; the Scriptures. ⟨ME < L *testimonium* < *testis* witness⟩
☛ *Syn.* **1, 2.** See note at EVIDENCE.

tes•tis ['tɛstɪs] *n., pl.* **-tes.** testicle. ⟨< L *testis* witness (of virility)⟩

test–mar•ket ['tɛst ,mɑrkɪt] *v.* advertise and sell (a new product, service, etc.) experimentally and evaluate its success so as to make necessary changes.

tes•tos•ter•one [tɛ'stɒstə,roun] *n.* a male steroid hormone produced mainly by the testicles. It is also extracted from animal testicles or made synthetically for use in medicine. *Formula:* $C_{19}H_{28}O_2$ ⟨< *testes* + *sterol*⟩

test paper 1 a paper for recording one's answers in a written examination, or the paper on which the questions are printed. **2** specially prepared paper, such as litmus paper, for doing chemical tests.

test pattern a still picture or series of coloured stripes, etc. on a television screen, transmitted between normal broadcasting times to test the quality of the image for colour, resolution, position, etc.

test pilot a pilot employed to test new or experimental aircraft by subjecting them to greater than normal stress.

test tube a thin glass tube closed at one end, used in doing chemical tests.

test–tube baby or **test tube baby** ['tɛst ,tjub] *or* ['tɛst ,tub] a baby conceived by IN VITRO FERTILIZATION.

tes•tu•di•nal [tɛ'stjudɪnəl] *or* [tɛ'studinəl] *adj.* of, having to do with, or resembling a tortoise or the shell of a tortoise. ⟨See TESTUDO⟩

tes•tu•do [tɛ'stjudou] *or* [tɛ'studou] *n., pl.* **-di•nes** [-də,niz]. **1** in ancient Rome: **a** a movable shelter with a strong and usually fireproof arched roof, used for protection in siege operations. **b** a shelter formed by a body of troops overlapping their shields above their heads. **2** some other sheltering contrivance. ⟨< L *testudo,* literally, tortoise < *testa* shell⟩

tes•ty ['tɛsti] *adj.* **-ti•er, -ti•est.** easily irritated; impatient. ⟨ME < AF *testif* headstrong < OF *teste* head < L *testa* pot⟩ **—'tes•ti•ly,** *adv.* **—'tes•ti•ness,** *n.*

tet [tɛt] *or* [tɛs] *n.* the tenth letter of the Hebrew alphabet. See table of alphabets in the Appendix.

Tet [tɛt] the Vietnamese festival of the lunar New Year. ⟨< Vietnamese⟩

tet•a•nus ['tɛtənəs] *n.* **1** a disease caused by certain bacilli usually entering the body through wounds, characterized by violent spasms, stiffness of many muscles, and even death. Tetanus of the lower jaw is called lockjaw. **2** *Physiology.* a condition of prolonged contraction of a muscle, produced by a rapid succession of stimuli. ⟨ME < L < Gk. *tetanos* < *teinein* stretch⟩ **—te'tan•ic** [tɛ'tænɪk], *adj.*

tet•a•ny ['tɛtəni] *n. Medicine.* a type of disorder marked by muscular spasms. ⟨< F *tetanie*⟩

tetch•y ['tɛtʃi] *adj.* **tetch•i•er, tetch•i•est.** irritable; touchy. Also, **techy.** ⟨? < ME *teche, tache* fault < OF *teche* mark, quality⟩ **—'tetch•i•ly,** *adv.* **—'tetch•i•ness,** *n.*

tête–à–tête ['tɛt ə 'tɛt] *or* ['teit ə 'teit] *adv., adj., n. —adv.* of two people, together in private: *They dined tête-à-tête.*
—adj. of or for two people in private.
—n. **1** a private conversation between two people. **2** an S-shaped seat built so that two people can sit facing one another. ⟨< F *tête-à-tête* head to head⟩

tête–bêche ['tɛt 'bɛʃ] *adj. Philately.* referring to a pair of stamps printed so that one is upside down. ⟨< F *tête* head + *bêche* < *bêchevet* the head of one against the foot of the other⟩

teth or **tet** [tɛt] *or* [tɛs] *n.* See TET.

teth•er ['tɛðər] *n., v.* —*n.* a rope or chain for fastening an animal so that it can graze only within certain limits.
at the end of (one's) **tether,** *Informal.* at the end of one's resources or endurance: *After the class had gone wild for an hour, the teacher was at the end of his tether.*
—*v.* fasten with a tether. ⟨ME < ON *tjóthr*⟩

teth•er•ball ['tɛðər,bɒl] *n.* a game for two players in which they hit a ball hung by a rope from a pole, each trying to make the rope wind all the way around the pole in a direction opposite to the opponent's.

tet•ra ['tɛtrə] *n.* any of various colourful freshwater fishes of family Characidae, of tropical America, often kept in aquariums. ⟨< NL *tetragonopterus*, a former genus name < *tetragon* + *-pterous* (< Gk. *pteron* wing)⟩

tetra– *combining form.* four, as in *tetrahedron.* Also, before vowels, **tetr-**. ⟨< Gk. *tetra-*, combining form of *tessares* four⟩

tet•ra•bas•ic [,tɛtrə'beisɪk] *adj. Chemistry.* of or being an acid having four replaceable hydrogen atoms per molecule.

tet•ra•chlor•ide [,tɛtrə'klɔraɪd] *n.* a chloride having four atoms of chlorine per molecule.

tet•ra•chord ['tɛtrə,kɔrd] *n. Music.* a series of four notes in the diatonic scale, the first and last notes of the series being a perfect fourth apart; half an octave. ⟨< L < Gk. *tetrachordos* producing four tones < *tessares* four + *chordē* string⟩
—,tet•ra'chord•al, *adj.*

tet•ra•cy•cline [,tɛtrə'saiklin] *n.* an antibiotic derived from a soil bacterium (*Streptomyces viridifaciens*) or synthetically produced, effective against a wide variety of disease bacteria and viruses. *Formula*: $C_{22}H_{24}N_2O_8$ ⟨< *tetra-* + *cycl(ic)* + *-in*⟩

tet•rad ['tɛtræd] *n.* **1** a group or collection of four. **2** *Chemistry.* an atom, element, or radical with a valence of four. **3** *Biology.* a group of four cells formed within a diploid cell by meiosis. **4** *Genetics.* a group of four chromatids formed when a pair of chromosomes splits during meiosis. ⟨< Gk. *tetros, tetrados* a group of four⟩

tet•ra•eth•yl lead [,tɛtrə'ɛθəl] a colourless, poisonous liquid used as an antiknock in gasoline.

tet•ra•gon ['tɛtrə,gɒn] *n.* a plane figure having four angles and four sides; quadrangle; quadrilateral.

te•trag•o•nal [tɛ'trægənəl] *adj.* **1** pertaining to or having the shape of a tetragon; quadrangular. **2** having to do with a system of crystallization in which the three axes intersect at right angles, two of them being equal in length and the third either longer or shorter.

tet•ra•gram ['tɛtrə,græm] *n.* a word having four letters.

Tet•ra•gram•ma•ton [,tɛtrə'græmə,tɒn] *n.* the four Hebrew letters yod, he, vav, and he, together representing the name of God, usually transliterated as YHVH, and pronounced as *Yahweh*. Since the second or third century B.C., this name has been too sacred to be uttered aloud, and so *Adonai* (Lord) is substituted in speech.

tet•ra•he•dral [,tɛtrə'hidrəl] *or* [,tɛtrə'hɛdrəl] *adj.* **1** of, having to do with, or being a tetrahedron. **2** having four sides.
—,tet•ra'he•dral•ly, *adv.*

tet•ra•he•dron [,tɛtrə'hidrən] *or* [,tɛtrə'hɛdrən] *n., pl.* **-drons, -dra** [-drə]. a polyhedron having four faces. The most common tetrahedron is a pyramid whose base and three sides are equilateral triangles. See SOLID for picture. ⟨< LGk. *tetraedron* < Gk. *tessares* four + *hedra* seat, base⟩

te•tral•o•gy [tɛ'trælədʒi] *n., pl.* **-gies.** a series of four connected dramas, operas, etc., specifically, a series of three tragic and one satyric drama performed consecutively at the festival of Dionysus in ancient Athens. ⟨< Gk. *tetralogia* < *tessares* four + *logos* discourse⟩

te•tram•er•ous [tɛ'træmərəs] *adj. Biology.* consisting of four sections or parts, or arranged in sets of four. ⟨< Gk. *tetra-* four + *meros* part⟩

te•tram•e•ter [tɛ'træmətər] *adj., n.* —*adj.* consisting of four measures or feet.
—*n.* a line of verse having four measures or feet. *Example*: The stág | at éve | had drúnk | his fíll. ⟨< L < Gk. *tetrametron* < *tessares* four + *metron* measure⟩

tet•ra•ploid ['tɛtrə,plɔɪd] *adj. Biology.* having four times the basic or haploid number of chromosomes. ⟨< *tetra-* + *(ha)ploid*⟩

tet•ra•pod ['tɛtrə,pɒd] *n., adj.* —*n.* any four-limbed vertebrate animal, or one having had four-limbed ancestors, such as the whale or the snake.
—*adj.* having four limbs, or being descended from a four-limbed animal.

tet•rap•ter•ous [tɛ'træptərəs] *adj. Zoology.* having four wings or winglike appendages. ⟨< *tetra-* + Gk. *pteron* wing⟩

tet•ra•spore ['tɛtrə,spɔr] *n. Botany.* any asexual spore produced by meiosis in fours.

tet•rarch ['tɛtrɑrk] *or* ['titrɑrk] *n.* **1** in ancient Rome, the ruler of a part (originally a fourth part) of a province: *Herod the Tetrarch.* **2** any subordinate ruler. ⟨< L < Gk. *tetrarchēs* < *tessares* four + *archos* ruler⟩ **—tet'rarch•ic,** *adj.*

tet•rar•chy ['tɛtrɑrki] *or* ['titrɑrki] *n., pl.* **-chies. 1** the government or jurisdiction of a tetrarch. **2** the territory governed by a tetrarch. **3** government by four persons. **4** a set of four rulers. **5** a country divided into four governments. Also, **tetrarchate** [tɛ'trɑrkeit].

tet•ra•tom•ic [,tɛtrə'tɒmɪk] *adj.* of or being a molecule made up of four atoms or atom groups, or having four that are replaceable.

tet•ra•va•lent [,tɛtrə'veilənt] *or* [tɛ'trævələnt] *adj. Chemistry.* **1** having a valence of four. **2** having four valences. ⟨< *tetra-* + L *valens, -entis*, ppr. of *valere* be worth⟩

tet•raz•zi•ni [,tɛtrə'zini] *adj. Cuisine.* Sometimes, **Tetrazzini,** diced and mixed with noodles in a creamy mushroom sauce, sprinkled with parmesan cheese and browned in the oven. ⟨after Luisa *Tetrazzini*, Italian soprano (1871-1940)⟩

tet•rode ['tɛtroud] *n.* an electron tube with four electrodes, a cathode, an anode, a control grid, and a screen grid. ⟨< Gk. *tetra-* four + *hodos* way⟩

te•trox•ide [tɛ'trɒksaɪd] *n.* any oxide having four atoms of oxygen in each molecule. ⟨< *tetr-*, var. of *tetra-* + *oxide*⟩

tet•ter ['tɛtər] *n.* an itching skin disease. Eczema is a tetter. ⟨OE *teter*⟩

Teut. 1 Teutonic. **2** Teuton.

Teu•ton ['tjutən] *or* ['tutən] *n.* **1** a member of an ancient Germanic people of N Europe. **2** a member of any of the N European peoples speaking a Germanic language, especially a German. ⟨< L *Teutones, Teutoni*, pl.⟩

Teu•ton•ic [tju'tɒnɪk] *or* [tu'tɒnɪk] *adj., n.* —*adj.* **1** of or having to do with the ancient Teutons. **2** of, having to do with, or designating the Germanic languages or the people who speak them. **3** German.
—*n.* Germanic. **—Teu'ton•i•cal•ly,** *adv.* **—'Teu•ton,ism,** *n.*

Te•wa ['tiwə] *or* ['teiwə] **1** a member of any of seven Native American peoples living in New Mexico and Arizona. **2** the Tanoan language of these peoples.

Tex•as ['tɛksəs] *n.* a southern state of the United States.

Texas gate in the West, an opening in a fence, designed to let people and vehicles through but hinder cattle, horses, or deer, the surface being made of metal tubes, often revolving, or rails, bars, etc. laid crosswise.

Texas leaguer *Baseball.* a fly ball that falls in fair territory between converging fielders from the infield and the outfield.

Tex–Mex ['tɛks 'mɛks] *adj.* referring to a style of cuisine, music, etc. that combines Texan and Mexican elements. Also, **TexMex, tex-mex.**

text [tɛkst] *n.* **1** the main body of reading matter in a book, as distinct from headings, notes, appendices, illustrations, etc.: *This history contains 300 pages of text and about 50 pages of notes, explanations, and questions for study.* **2** the original words of a writer or public speaker: *Always quote the exact words of a text.* **3** the lyrics of a song or words of an oratorio, etc., as distinct from the music. **4** any one of the various wordings of a poem, play, etc.; version; edition. **5** language in use, regarded at its highest level of structure; discourse. **6** a short Biblical passage used as the subject of a sermon: *The minister preached on the text "Love thy neighbour as thyself."* **7** topic; subject. **8** textbook. ⟨ult. < L *textus*, originally, texture < *texere* weave⟩ **—'text•less,** *adj.*

text•book ['tɛkst,bʊk] *n., adj.* —*n.* a book used as a basis of instruction or as a standard reference in a particular course of study.
—*adj.* suitable as or conforming to a description in a textbook; typical; classic: *Her behaviour was a textbook example of how not to impress people.*

text edition a special edition of a book designed for school or college use, sometimes without a dust jacket. Compare TRADE EDITION.

text editor *Computer technology.* a program for manipulating large text files.

text hand large, neat handwriting, such as was formerly used to distinguish text from notes.

tex•tile ['tɛkstaɪl] *n., adj.* *—n.* **1** a woven or knit fabric. **2** material suitable for weaving.
—adj. **1** woven: *Linen is a textile material.* **2** suitable for weaving: *Cotton, silk, and wool are common textile materials.* **3** of or having to do with weaving: *the textile art.* **4** of or having something to do with the making, selling, etc. of textiles: *the textile business.* ⟨< L *textilis* < *texere* weave⟩

tex•tu•al ['tɛkstʃuəl] *adj.* **1** of or having to do with the text: *A misprint is a textual error.* **2** based on or conforming to a text.

textual criticism the analysis of a manuscript or printed text to correct the additions, errors, or omissions of copyists, printers, etc. in an attempt to establish the probable original text: *textual criticism of the Bible.*

tex•tu•al•ism ['tɛkstʃuə,lɪzəm] *n.* strict adherence to the actual letter of the text. **—'tex•tu•al•ist,** *n.*

tex•tu•al•ly ['tɛkstʃuəli] *adv.* in regard to the text.

tex•tur•al ['tɛkstʃərəl] *adj.* of texture; having to do with texture. **—'tex•tur•al•ly,** *adv.*

tex•ture ['tɛkstʃər] *n., v.* **-tured, -tur•ing.** *—n.* **1** the arrangement, thickness, and quality of threads in a woven fabric: *Burlap has a much coarser texture than linen.* **2** the arrangement of the parts of anything; structure; constitution; make-up: *the texture of society, of a piece of writing, of one's life. Sandstone and granite have very different textures.* **3** the consequent feel of something to the sense of touch. **4** *Painting, sculpture, etc.* the representation of the structure and minute moulding of a surface, as distinct from its colour. **5** the musical quality of combined voices, instruments, etc.: *the harsh texture of brass instruments.*
—v. give a particular texture to. ⟨< L *textura* < *texere* weave⟩

tex•tured ['tɛkstʃərd] *adj., v.* *—adj.* **1** having a certain texture. **2** bulky; looped: *textured wool.*
—v. pt. and pp. of TEXTURE.

t.g. *Biology.* TYPE GENUS.

TG *Linguistics.* TRANSFORMATIONAL GRAMMAR.

TGIF *Informal.* Thank God it's Friday.

T–group ['ti ,grup] *n.* a group of people organized under the leadership of a psychologist, etc. for the development of self awareness and sensitivity toward others through group interaction. ⟨< training group⟩

Th thorium.

Th. Thursday.

–th[1] *suffix.* used to form: **a** nouns of action, such as *birth* from *bear, growth* from *grow.* **b** abstract nouns of condition or quality, such as *depth* from *deep, width* from *wide.* ⟨ME *-th(e)* < OE *-thu, -tho,* cognate with L *-tus,* Gk. *-tos*⟩

–th[2] *suffix.* used in the formation of ordinal numbers from the cardinal numbers four and up (*fourth, thirteenth, seventy-fifth*) except those compounds ending in -one, -two, or -three (*forty-first, eighty-second, thirty-third*). ⟨ME *-the, -te* < OE *-(o)the, (o)tha,* cognate with L *-tus,* Gk. *-tos*⟩

–th[3] a postvocalic variant of -ETH, archaic third person singular, present tense: *doth* from *do* + *eth.*

Thai [taɪ] *n., adj.* *—n.* **1** a native or inhabitant of Thailand. **2** the official language of Thailand. **3** TAI.
—adj. of or having to do with Thailand, its people, or their language.

Thai•land ['taɪ,lænd] *n.* a country in SE Asia, formerly called Siam.

thal•a•men•ceph•a•lon [,θæləmɛn'sɛfə,lɒn] *n.* diencephalon. **—,thal•a•men•ce'phal•ic,** *adj.*

thal•a•mus ['θæləməs] *n., pl.* **-mi** [-,maɪ] *or* [-,mi]. **1** a part of the brain where a nerve emerges or appears to emerge. The **optic thalami** are two large, oblong masses of grey matter forming a part of the midbrain. **2** the receptacle or torus of a flower. ⟨< L *thalamus* inside room < Gk. *thalamos*⟩ **—tha'lam•ic** [θə'læmɪk], *adj.*

thal•as•se•mia [,θælə'simiə] *n.* an inherited form of chronic anemia, usually found among people of Mediterranean origin and marked by faulty synthesis of hemoglobin. ⟨< Gk. *thalassa* sea, in reference to the Mediterranean⟩

tha•las•sic [θə'læsɪk] *adj.* **1** of or having to do with the sea or seas, especially smaller bodies of water as opposed to the large oceans. **2** found, growing, or living in the sea; marine. ⟨< Gk. *thalassa* sea + E *-ic*⟩

tha•ler ['tɑlər] *n., pl.* **-ler.** a former German silver coin. Also, **taler.** ⟨< G *Taler,* earlier *Thaler.* Akin to DOLLAR.⟩

Tha•li•a [θə'laɪə] *or* ['θeiliə] *n. Greek mythology.* **1** the Muse of comedy and idyllic poetry. **2** one of the three Graces.

tha•lid•o•mide [θə'lɪdə,maɪd] *n.* a drug formerly used as a tranquillizer. Its use by pregnant women was found to cause malformation of their babies. *Formula*: $C_{13}H_{10}N_2O_4$
thalidomide baby, a malformed baby born to a woman who took thalidomide during pregnancy.

thal•lic ['θælɪk] *adj.* having to do with or containing thallium, especially when trivalent.

thal•li•um ['θæliəm] *n.* a rare metallic chemical element that is soft and malleable. Its spectrum is marked by a green band. *Symbol*: Tl; *at.no.* 81; *at.mass* 204.37. ⟨< NL < Gk. *thallos* green shoot⟩

thal•lo•phyte ['θælə,fəit] *n.* any of the group (Thallophyta) of lower plants having a relatively simple, undifferentiated body (called a thallus) without true stems, roots, or leaves. Modern classification systems using this grouping regard the Thallophyta as constituting a subkingdom that includes the algae, bacteria, and fungi. ⟨< Gk. *thallos* green shoot + E *-phyte*⟩
—,thal•lo'phyt•ic [-'fɪtɪk], *adj.*

thal•lous ['θæləs] *adj.* of a chemical compound, containing monovalent thallium.
☛ *Hom.* THALLUS.

thal•lus ['θæləs] *n., pl.* **thal•li** ['θælaɪ] *or* ['θæli] or **thal•lus•es.** a plant body lacking differentiation into true stems, roots, and leaves, characteristic of algae, fungi, and lichens. ⟨< NL < Gk. *thallos* green shoot⟩ **—'thal•loid,** *adj.*
☛ *Hom.* THALLOUS.

Tham•muz ['tɑmmuz] *n.* See TAMMUZ.

than [ðæn]; *unstressed,* [ðən] *conj., prep.* **1** in comparison with; compared to: *This train is faster than that one.* **2** except; besides; other than: *How else can we come than on foot?* **3** *Informal.* when (*used especially after clauses with inverted subject and verb introduced by* **scarcely, hardly,** etc., on the analogy of **no sooner...than**): *Hardly had we arrived than we were set to work.* ⟨OE⟩

☛ *Usage.* **Than** acts usually as a conjunction joining comparative adjectives and adverbs (as well as adverbs expressing a difference or exception, such as **rather, otherwise,** and **else**) with the second part of the comparison: *nicer than usual; otherwise than he did; more quickly than yesterday.* The part of speech, case, tense, etc. of the word following **than** depends on its function in the clause containing it, whether the clause itself is completely expressed or not. Compare: *Cindy likes Jane better* than *(she likes)* me. (comparing objects) *Cindy likes Jane better* than I *(do).* (comparing subjects) *I am taller* than he *(is).* (comparing subjects) In informal speech, however, in sentences such as the last, the objective case is often used even by educated speakers, making **than** into a preposition: *I am taller* than him. In a few special constructions **than** acts regularly as a preposition: *We can drive no further* than Montréal. *We read about Eisenstein,* than whom *there was no greater film director.*

than•a•tol•o•gy [,θænə'tɒlədʒi] *n.* the study of death and dying from the perspective of social sciences.
—,than•a'tol•o•gist, *n.*

Than•a•tos ['θænə,tɒs] *n.* **1** in early Greek mythology, the personification of death. **2** *Psychology.* the death instinct, especially when shown in violent aggression. ⟨< Gk. *thanatos* death⟩

thane [θein] *n.* **1** in Anglo-Saxon England, a man who ranked between an earl and an ordinary freeman. Thanes held lands of the king or lord and gave military service in return. **2** formerly, in Scotland, a baron or lord; chief of a clan. Also, **thegn.** ⟨OE *thegn*⟩ **—'than•age,** *n.*

thank [θæŋk] *v., n., interj.* *—v.* **1** tell (another) that one is pleased and grateful for something given or done; express gratitude to: *He thanked them for their hospitality.* **2** consider or hold responsible: *We can thank the previous committee for the financial mess we're in now. You have only yourself to thank if you run out of gas.*
thank goodness (or **heavens, God,** etc.), an expression of relief or satisfaction: *Thank goodness, they arrived safely.*
thank you, the standard courteous expression of appreciation: *"It's a lovely present. Thank you."*
—n. **thanks,** *pl.* **a** the act of thanking; an expression of gratitude: *to give thanks for a favour, to give thanks before a meal.* **b** a feeling of kindness and gratitude: *You have our heartful thanks.*
thanks to, owing to; because of: *Thanks to his efforts, we won the game. The fair was a disaster, thanks to the storm.*
—interj. **thanks,** *Informal.* thank you: *Thanks. I appreciate your help.* ⟨OE *thanc,* originally, thought⟩

thank•ful ['θæŋkfəl] *adj.* feeling or expressing thanks; grateful.
☛ *Syn.* See note at GRATEFUL.

thank•ful•ly ['θæŋkfəli] *adv.* **1** with thanks; gratefully. **2** (*as a sentence modifier*) fortunately: *She had an accident; thankfully, however, she was not hurt.*

thank•ful•ness ['θæŋkfəlnɪs] *n.* a thankful feeling; gratitude.

thank•less ['θæŋklɪs] *adj.* **1** not likely to be rewarded with thanks; not appreciated: *Giving advice is usually a thankless act.* **2** not feeling or expressing thanks; without a desire to do a favour in return: *The thankless woman did nothing for the neighbour who had helped her.* **—'thank•less•ly,** *adv.* **—'thank•less•ness,** *n.*

thanks•giv•ing ['θæŋks,gɪvɪŋ] *or* [,θæŋks'gɪvɪŋ] *n.* **1** a giving of thanks. **2** an expression of thanks: *They offered thanksgiving for the bountiful harvest.* **3 Thanksgiving,** Thanksgiving Day.

Thanksgiving Day **1** in Canada, the second Monday in October, a day set apart as a statutory holiday on which to give thanks for God's goodness and for the harvest. **2** in the United States, the fourth Thursday in November, a holiday observed for similar reasons.

thank–you ['θæŋk,ju] *n., adj.* *—n.* an expression of thanks: *She left without so much as a goodbye or a thank-you.*
—adj. expressing thanks: *a thank-you letter.*

that [ðæt]; *unstressed,* [ðət] *adj., pl.* **those;** *pron., pl.* (for def. 1) **those;** *conj., adv.* *—adj.* pointing out, indicating, or emphasizing some person, thing, idea, etc. already mentioned or understood, especially one some distance away in place or time or in the spoken or written context. *Do you know that boy over there? I will not allow that piano to be misused. What was that noise? She has that certain something.* When used with *this, that* refers to something far or farther away and *this* refers to something near. *That route is shorter than this one.*
—pron. **1** some person, thing, idea, etc. already mentioned or understood, often one that is to be emphasized or contrasted with another nearer in place or time: *That is a better drawing than this. That's the spirit! That's not fair. After that they went home. What was that?* **2** (*relative pron.*) which, who, or whom: *Is he the man that trains dogs? Have you read the book that I gave you?* **3** the one; the thing or person to be identified: *Those who have been there will understand. That which is good is beautiful. Our house is older than that of our neighbours.* **4 a** when; at or in which: *The year that we went to England, they had a terrible drought.* **b** *Informal.* where; at or in which: *For our honeymoon we went back to the place that we first met.*
at that, *Informal.* **a** with no more talk, work, etc.: *Let's just leave it at that.* **b** on reconsideration: *We may need more money at that.* **c** in fact; moreover: *She made it all by herself, and without a recipe at that.*
in that, in the respect or sense that: *His plan is superior in that it is more practical.*
that is, a namely; to be precise; to wit: *Only one person, that is, the principal herself, opposed the idea.* **b** in other words; what I mean to say is: *If you have other plans, that is, if you can't come, just say so.*
that's that, *Informal.* that is finished, settled, or decided: *We're not going, and that's that.*
—conj. **that** is used: **1** to introduce a noun clause and connect it with the preceding verb as its object: *I know that 6 and 4 are 10.* **2** to show purpose: *He ran fast that he might not be late.* **3** to show result: *He ran so fast that he was five minutes early.* **4** to show cause: *I wonder what happened, not that I care.* **5** to express a wish with some words understood: *Oh,* [how I wish] *that she were here!* **6** to show anger, surprise, awe, etc., with some words understood: [What a bitter surprise it is] *That one so fair should be so false!*
—adv. **1** to that extent or degree; so. *He cannot stay up that late.* **2** very (*used with negatives and often preceded by* **all**): *He's handsome, but not that bright.* ⟨OE *thæt*⟩
☛ *Usage.* **That** (pron., def. 2), **who, which. That** as a relative pronoun refers to persons or things, **who** to persons, **which** only to things: *The people who* (or *that*) *were in the auditorium listened to the speech in silence. She solved in five minutes a problem that* (or *which*) *I had struggled with for five hours.* **That** introduces only clauses that are restrictive; **which,** on the other hand, may also introduce clauses that are non-restrictive. Restrictive: *The book that she selected for her report was the longest in the list.* Non-restrictive: *The privilege of free speech, which we hold so dear, is now endangered.*

thatch [θætʃ] *n., v.* *—n.* **1** straw, rushes, palm leaves, etc., bound, matted, or loosely woven together and used as a roof or covering. **2** a roof or covering of thatch. **3** *Informal.* the hair covering the head. **4** the layer of decaying bits of grass, leaves, etc., at the base of growing vegetation: *Early in the spring, rake your lawn to clear the thatch and allow air, water, and fertilizer to penetrate more easily.*
—v. roof or cover with thatch. ⟨OE *thæc*⟩ **—'thatch•y,** *adj.* **—'thatch•er,** *n.*

thatch•ing ['θætʃɪŋ] *n., v.* *—n.* **1** THATCH (defs. 1, 2). **2** the art or activity of making thatch: *Thatching has almost become a lost art.*
—v. ppr. of THATCH.

that's [ðæts] **1** that is. **2** that has: *That's never stopped me.*

thau•ma•tol•o•gy [,θɒmə'tɒlədʒi] *n.* the study of miracles. ⟨< Gk. *thauma, thaumatos* miracle + E *-logy*⟩

thau•ma•turge ['θɒmə,tɜrdʒ] *n.* one who works miracles. ⟨< Gk. *thauma, thaumatos* miracle + *-orgos* working < *ergon* work⟩

thau•ma•tur•gy ['θɒmə,tɜrdʒi] *n.* the working of wonders or miracles; magic. **—,thau•ma'tur•gi•cal,** *adj.*

thaw [θɒ] *v., n.* *—v.* **1** melt (ice, snow, or anything frozen); make free from frost: *Thaw these chicken legs before frying them. Salt was put on the sidewalk to thaw the ice.* **2** become warm enough to melt ice, snow, etc.: *If the sun stays out, it will probably thaw today.* **3** become free of frost, ice, etc.: *The ground has begun to thaw. The pond thaws in April.* **4** warm up so as to lose stiffness, numbness, etc. from having been very cold for a long time (*often used with* **out**): *After their tramp through the biting wind they all sat by the fire to thaw.* **4** make or become less stiff and formal in manner; soften: *Our shyness thawed under her kindness.*
—n. **1** a thawing. **2** a period of weather above the freezing point (0°C); time of melting. ⟨OE *thawian*⟩ **—'thaw•er,** *n.*
☛ *Syn. v.* **1.** See note at MELT.

the[1] (*unstressed before a consonant,* [ðə]; *when stressed, and always before vowels,* [ði]) *definite article.* The word *the* shows that a certain one (or ones) is meant, already understood or identified, or about to be identified. Various special uses are: **1** to mark a noun as indicating something well-known or unique: *the prodigal son, the Alps, the hour of victory, the Duke of Wellington. Was that the moment to act?* **2** to mark a noun as indicating the best known or most important of its kind (*usually stressed*): *the* [ði] *place to dine.* **3** to mark a noun as being used generically: *to hang the head in shame, to wear the shirt tucked in. The dog is a quadruped.* **4** before adjectives used as nouns: *to visit the sick.* **5** distributively, to denote any one separately: *candy at five dollars the kilogram.* ⟨OE *sē* (nom. masc. art) that; influenced by forms in *th-* from other cases and genders, e.g., *thone, thære, thæm,* etc.⟩
☛ *Usage.* **The.** Repetition of the article before the various nouns of a series emphasizes their distinctness: The *colour,* the *fragrance, and the* patterns *of these flowers make them universal favourites.* Compare: The *colour, fragrance, and patterns of these flowers make them universal favourites.*

the[2] [ðə] *or* [ði] *adv.* The word *the* is used to modify an adjective or adverb in the comparative degree: **1** signifying 'in or by that', 'on that account', 'in some or any degree': *If you start now, you will be back the sooner.* **2** used correlatively, in one instance with relative force and in the other with demonstrative force, and signifying 'by how much…by so much', 'in what degree…in that degree': *the more the merrier, the sooner the better.* ⟨OE *thy̆*⟩

the•a•tre ['θiətər] *n.* **1** a place where plays and other stage performances are acted or where films are shown. **2** a place that looks like a theatre in its arrangement of seats: *the operating theatre of a hospital.* **3** a place where some action proceeds; scene of action: *France has too often been a theatre of war.* **4 a** plays; the writing and producing of plays; drama. **b** a play, situation, dialogue, etc. considered as to its effectiveness on the stage: *This scene is bad theatre.* **5** the community of people engaged in theatrical work: *What's she doing these days? Oh, she's been in the theatre for years.* **6** the study of acting, directing, stagecraft, etc., as a secondary or post-secondary academic subject: *She took her degree in theatre.* Sometimes, **theater.** ⟨ME < OF < L < Gk. *theatron,* ult. < *thea* view⟩

the•a•tre•go•er ['θiətər,gouər] *n.* one who goes to the theatre, especially one who goes frequently.

the•a•tre–in–the–round ['θiətər ɪn ðə 'raʊnd] *n.* **1** a theatre having the stage situated in the centre, surrounded with seats on all sides. **2** the presentation of plays in such theatres.

theatre of the absurd drama that represents absurd situations and rejects the usual dramatic structure and conventions in order to express the meaninglessness and alienation of human existence.

the•at•ri•cal [θi'ætrɪkəl] *adj., n.* *—adj.* **1** of or having to do with the theatre or actors: *theatrical performances, a theatrical*

company. **2 a** suggesting a theatre or acting. **b** for display or effect; artificial; histrionic; melodramatic; exaggerated: *He is always telling theatrical stories.* Also, **theatric.**
—n. **theatricals,** *pl.* theatrics. **—the'at•ri•cal•ly,** *adv.* **—the'at•ri•cal,ism,** *n.*
☛ *Syn. adj.* **2.** See note at DRAMATIC.

the•at•ri•cal•i•ty [θi,ætrə'kæləti] *n.* the quality of being theatrical.

the•at•rics [θi'ætrɪks] *n., pl.* **1** dramatic performances, especially as given by amateurs. **2** matters having to do with the stage and acting. **3** actions of a theatrical or artificial character.

The•ban ['θibən] *n., adj. —n.* a native or inhabitant of the city of Thebes in ancient Greece or the city of Thebes in ancient Egypt.
—adj. of or having to do with either city or its inhabitants.

the•be ['tɛbɛ] *n., pl.* **the•be. 1** a unit of currency of Botswana, equal to 1/100 of a pula. See money table in the Appendix. **2** a coin worth one thebe. ⟨< Bantu, literally, shield⟩

the•ca ['θikə] *n., pl.* **-cae** [-si] **1** *Biology.* a spore case or other enclosing organ or sac. **2** *Zoology, Anatomy.* a tough sheath or case enclosing an organ or organism. ⟨< NL < L < Gk. *theke* case⟩ **—'the•cal,** *adj.* **—'the•cate,** *adj.*

thee [ði] *pron. Archaic or poetic.* the objective form of THOU: *"Hail to thee, blithe Spirit!"* ⟨OE *thē*⟩
☛ *Usage.* See note at THOU.

theft [θɛft] *n.* **1** the act of stealing: *The woman was put in prison for theft.* **2** an instance of stealing: *The theft of the jewels caused much excitement.* ⟨OE *thēoft* < *thēof* thief⟩

thegn [θein] *n.* See THANE.

the•ine ['θiin] *or* ['θiən] *n.* caffeine. Also, **thein.** ⟨< NL *thea* tea + *-ine*[2]⟩

their [ðɛr]; *unstressed,* [ðər] *adj.* **1** a possessive form of THEY: of, belonging to, or made or done by them or themselves: *They did their best. They all raised their hands. That's their house.*
2 Their, a word used as part of any of certain formal titles when using the title to refer to the people holding it: *Their Majesties are resting.* ⟨ME < ON *their(r)a*⟩
☛ *Hom.* THERE, THEY'RE.
☛ *Usage.* **Their, theirs** are the possessive forms of **they. Their** is a determiner and is always followed by a noun: *This is their farm.* **Theirs** is a pronoun and stands alone: *This farm is theirs.*

theirs [ðɛrz] *pron.* a possessive form of THEY: that which belongs to them: *The painting isn't theirs, it's just rented.*
of theirs, belonging to or associated with them: *We're friends of theirs.*
☛ *Hom.* THERE'S.
☛ *Usage.* See note at THEIR.

the•ism ['θiɪzəm] *n.* **1 a** belief in one god rather than many; monotheism as opposed to polytheism or pantheism. **b** a belief in one God, the creator and ruler of the universe, supernaturally revealed to humankind, immanent, and knowable. Opposed to DEISM. **2** belief in a deity or deities; religious faith or conviction. ⟨< Gk. *theos* god⟩

the•ist ['θiɪst] *n.* a believer in theism.

the•is•tic [θi'ɪstɪk] *adj.* of or having to do with theism or theists. **—the'is•ti•cal•ly,** *adv.*

them [ðɛm]; *unstressed,* [ðəm] *pron.* the objective form of **they.** *The books were a gift, but I don't really like them.* ⟨ME *theim* < ON⟩

the•mat•ic [θi'mætɪk] *or* [θə'mætɪk] *adj.* **1** of or having to do with a theme or themes. **2** *Linguistics.* **a** of or having to do with a noun or noun phrase in a sentence, in its semantic relationships to the action or state expressed by the verb, usually considered from the standpoint of its interaction with syntactic structure: *thematic roles, thematic relations.* **b** of, being, or having to do with a vowel whose function is strictly morphological, joining a stem to an affix but itself adding no meaning.

theme [θim] *n.* **1** a topic; subject: *Patriotism was the speaker's theme.* **2** a short written composition. **3** a dominant, recurring and unifying idea or motif. **4** *Music.* **a** the principal melody in a composition. **b** a short melody repeated in different forms in an elaborate composition. **5 a** a melody used to identify a particular radio or television program; signature tune. **b** the main piece of music recurring throughout a film: *Can you play the theme from* Dr. Zhivago? ⟨ME < L < Gk. *thema,* literally, something set down⟩

theme park an amusement centre in which the buildings, landscaping, rides, etc., are designed around a central theme, such as fairytales, a past age, outer space, etc.

theme song THEME (def. 5).

them•selves [ðɛm'sɛlvz] *or* [ðəm'sɛlvz] *pron.* **1** a reflexive pronoun, the form of **they** used as an object when it refers to the same people as the subject: *They hurt themselves in climbing down.* **2** a form of **they** or **them** added for emphasis: *They did it themselves.* **3** their normal or usual selves: *They were ill and were not themselves.*

then [ðɛn] *adv., n., adj. —adv.* **1** at that time: *Prices were lower then.* **2** soon afterwards: *The noise stopped, and then began again.* **3** next in time or place: *First comes spring, then summer.* **4** at another time: *Now one student does best and then another.* **5** also; besides: *The dress seems too good to throw away, and then, it is very attractive.* **6** in that case; therefore: *If Erika broke the window, then she should pay for it.*
but then, but at the same time; but on the other hand.
then and there, at that time and place; at once and on the spot.
—n. that time: *By then we shall know the result.*
—adj. being at that time in the past; existing then: *the then prime minister.* ⟨OE *thænne*⟩

the•nar ['θinɑr] *n., adj. —n.* the palm of the hand or the part of it at the base of the thumb.
—adj. of this part of the hand. ⟨< NL < Gk.⟩

thence [θɛns] *or* [ðɛns] *adv. Literary or Archaic.* **1** from that place; from there: *A few kilometres thence was a river.* **2** for that reason; therefore: *You didn't work, thence no pay.* **3** from that time; from then: *a year thence.* ⟨ME *thennes* < OE *thanan(e)*⟩

thence•forth [,θɛns'fɔrθ] *or* [,ðɛns'fɔrθ] *adv.* from then on; from that time forward: *Women were given the same rights as men. Thenceforth they could vote.*

thence•for•ward [,θɛns'fɔrwərd] *or* [,ðɛns'fɔrwərd] *adv. Archaic.* thenceforth.

theo– *combining form.* God; a god or gods: *theology = study of God; theogony = study of the origin of the gods.* Also, before a vowel, **the-.** ⟨< Gk. *theos* god⟩

the•o•bro•mine [,θiou'broumin] *or* [,θiou'broumɪn] *n.* a bitter, crystalline, water-insoluble poisonous powder, a caffeinelike alkaloid found in tea and obtained from the beans and leaves of the cacao plant, used chiefly as a diuretic, stimulant, and vasodilator. ⟨< NL < Gk. *theos* god + *broma* food + E *-ine*⟩

the•o•cen•tric [,θiə'sɛntrɪk] *adj.* having God as the centre or focus of thought and feeling; God-centered.
—,the•o'cen•tri•cal•ly, *adv.* **—,the•o'cen•trism,** *n.*

the•oc•ra•cy [θi'ɒkrəsi] *n., pl.* **-cies. 1** a system of government in which God, or a god, is recognized as the supreme civil ruler and divine law is taken as the law of the state. **2** a system of government by priests. **3** a country governed by a theocracy. ⟨< Gk. *theokratia* < *theos* god + *kratos* rule⟩

the•o•crat ['θiə,kræt] *n.* **1** a ruler, or member of a governing body, in a theocracy. **2** a person who favours theocracy.

the•o•crat•ic [,θiə'krætɪk] *adj.* **1** of or having to do with theocracy. **2** having a theocracy. **—,the•o'crat•i•cal•ly,** *adv.*

the•od•o•lite [θi'ɒdə,ləit] *n.* a surveying instrument for measuring horizontal and vertical angles. ⟨< NL *theodelitus*; ult. origin unknown⟩ **—the,od•o'lit•ic** [-'lɪtɪk], *adj.*

the•og•o•ny [θi'ɒgəni] *n., pl.* **-nies. 1** the origin of the gods. **2** an account of this; genealogical account of the gods. ⟨< Gk. *theogonia* < *theos* god < *gonos* begetting, descent⟩
—,the•o'gon•ic [,θiə'gɒnɪk], *adj.*

the•o•lo•gian [,θiə'loudʒən] *n.* a person skilled or trained in theology.

the•o•log•i•cal [,θiə'lɒdʒəkəl] *adj.* **1** of or having to do with theology. A theological school trains people for the ministry. **2** referring to the nature and will of God. **—,the•o'log•i•cal•ly,** *adv.*

the•ol•o•gize [θi'ɒlə,dʒaɪz] *v.,* **-gized, -giz•ing. 1** treat as part of a system of theology. **2** engage in theological speculation.

the•ol•o•gy [θi'ɒlədʒi] *n., pl.* **-gies. 1** the study of the nature of God and of God's relations to humankind and the universe. **2** the study of religion and religious beliefs. **3** a system of religious beliefs. ⟨ME < OF *theologie,* < L < Gk. *theologia* < *theos* god + *-logos* treating of⟩

the•om•a•chy [θi'ɒməki] *n.* strife or warfare among or against the gods. ⟨< Gk. *theomakhia* < *theos* god + *makhe* battle⟩

the•oph•a•ny [θi'ɒfəni] *n.* the visible manifestation or appearance of God or of a god or gods to a person. ⟨< LL < Gk. *theophaneia* < *theos* god + *phainein* show⟩

the•or•bo [θi'ɔrbou] *n.* a form of lute used in the 17th century, having two parallel necks each with a set of strings. ⟨< F *théorbe* < Ital. *tiorba*, of uncertain origin⟩

the•o•rem ['θiərəm] *n.* **1** *Mathematics.* **a** a statement to be proved. **b** a statement of relations that can be expressed by an equation or formula. **2** any statement or rule that can be proved to be true. ⟨< L < Gk. *theōrēma* < *theōreein* consider. See THEORY.⟩ **—,the•o•re'mat•ic,** *adj.*

the•o•ret•i•cal [,θiə'rɛtəkəl] *adj.* **1** planned or worked out in the mind, not from experience; based on theory or speculation, not on fact; limited to theory or constituting theory. **2 a** dealing with theory only; not practical. **b** having knowledge as its end or object; concerned with knowledge only, not with accomplishing anything or producing anything; purely scientific. Also, **theoretic.**

the•o•ret•i•cal•ly [,θiə'rɛtɪkli] *adv.* in theory; according to theory; in a theoretical manner.

the•o•re•ti•cian [,θiərə'tɪʃən] *n.* a person who knows much about the theory of an art, science, etc.

the•o•rist ['θiərɪst] *n.* a person who forms theories.

the•o•rize ['θiə,raɪz] *v.* **-rized, -riz•ing.** form a theory or theories; speculate. **—'the•o,riz•er,** *n.* **—,the•o•ri'za•tion,** *n.*

the•o•ry ['θiəri] *or* ['θiri] *n., pl.* **-ries. 1** an explanation based on thought or speculation. **2** an explanation based on observation and reasoning: *the theory of evolution, Einstein's theory of relativity.* **3** the principles or methods of a science or art rather than its practice: *the theory of music.* **4** an idea or opinion about something. **5** speculative thought or fancy as opposed to fact or practice. **6** *Mathematics.* a set of theorems which constitute a connected, systematic view of some branch of mathematics: *the theory of probabilities.* ⟨< LL < Gk. *theōria* < *theōreein* consider < *theōros* spectator < *thea* a sight + *horaein* see⟩

☛ *Syn.* **1, 2. Theory,** HYPOTHESIS = an explanation based on observation and thought. **Theory** applies to a general principle explaining a large number of related facts, occurrences, or other phenomena in nature, mechanics, etc.: *Einstein's theory of relativity explains the motion of moving objects.* A theory is evaluated not by testing per se but by its simplicity and the number of different things it explains. **Hypothesis** applies to a proposed description of specific states or events based on a certain group of facts, admittedly unproved but accepted for the time being as probable or as an experimental guide: *The chemists tested their hypothesis in the lab but found that their results were not repeatable.*

theory of games GAME THEORY.

the•o•soph•i•cal [,θiə'sɒfəkəl] *adj.* of or having to do with theosophy. Also, **theosophic.**

the•os•o•phist [θi'ɒsəfɪst] *n.* a person who believes in theosophy.

the•os•o•phy [θi'ɒsəfi] *n.* a philosophy or religion that claims to have a special insight into the divine nature through spiritual self-development. Modern theosophy includes many of the teachings of Buddhism and Brahmanism. New Age is a form of theosophy. ⟨< Med.L < LGk. *theosophia*, ult. < Gk. *theos* god + *sophos* wise⟩

ther•a•peu•tic [,θɛrə'pjutɪk] *adj.* of or having to do with the treatment or curing of disease or the preservation of good health; curative. Also, **therapeutical.** ⟨< NL *therapeuticus*, ult. < Gk. *therapeuein* cure, treat < *theraps* attendant⟩ **—,ther•a'peu•ti•cal•ly,** *adv.*

ther•a•peu•tics [,θɛrə'pjutɪks] *n.* a branch of medicine that deals with the treating or curing of disease; therapy.

ther•a•peu•tist [,θɛrə'pjutɪst] *n.* a person who specializes in therapeutics.

ther•a•pist ['θɛrəpɪst] *n.* a person trained to administer therapy.

ther•a•py ['θɛrəpi] *n., pl.* **-pies.** the treatment of diseases or disorders after or instead of surgery (*often used in compounds*): *physiotherapy, hydrotherapy. These exercises are good therapy for your back.* ⟨< NL < Gk. *therapeia* < *therapeuein.* See THERAPEUTIC.⟩

Ther•a•va•da [,tɛrə'vɑdə] *n.* one of the major branches of Buddhism, the 'Southern School'. It emphasizes the humanity of Buddha. ⟨< Pali (sacred lang. of Buddhism, from Skt.), teaching of the elders⟩

Ther•a•va•din [,tɛrə'vɑdɪn] *n.* a follower of Theravada Buddhism.

there [ðɛr]; *unstressed,* [ðər] *adv., n., interj. —adv.* **1** in or at that place: *Sit there.* **2** to or into that place: *Go there at once.* **3** at that point in an action, speech, etc.: *You have done enough; you may stop there.* **4** in that matter, particular, or respect: *You are mistaken there.* **5** A meaningless *there* is used as a dummy subject in sentences where the real subject has been moved out of the usual slot: *There are three new houses on our street. Is there a drugstore near here?* **6** *There* is used with inversion of the verb and real subject to call attention to some person or thing: *There goes the bell. Just do this for me, there's a good girl.*
all there, *Informal.* **a** wide-awake; alert. **b** not crazy; sane.
—n. that place: *From there go on to Hamilton.*
—interj. There is used to express satisfaction, triumph, defiance, dismay, encouragement, comfort, etc.: *There, there, don't cry. I'll go if I want to, so there!* ⟨OE *thǣr*⟩

☛ *Usage.* **There** (*adv.* defs. 5, 6). When the real subject is singular, a singular verb is used after **there:** *There was much work to be done.* When the real subject is plural, a plural verb is usual: *There are many answers in the back of the book.*
☛ *Hom.* THEIR, THEY'RE.

there•a•bouts ['ðɛrə,bʌuts] *or* [,ðɛrə'bʌuts] *adv.* **1** near that place: *She's from Nova Scotia; Halifax, or thereabouts.* **2** near that time. **3** near that number, amount, etc. Also, **thereabout.**

there•af•ter [,ðɛr'æftər] *adv.* **1** after that; afterward. **2** *Archaic.* accordingly.

there•at [,ðɛr'æt] *adv.* **1** when that happened; at that time. **2** because of that; because of it. **3** at that place.

there•by [,ðɛr'baɪ] *adv.* **1** by means of that; in that way: *He wished to travel and thereby study the customs of other countries.* **2** in connection with that: *Calgary won the game, and thereby hangs a tale.* **3** near there.

there•for [,ðɛr'fɔr] *adv. Formal.* for that purpose; for that; for this; for it: *He promised to give a building for a hospital and as much land as should be necessary therefor.*

there•fore ['ðɛr,fɔr] *adv.* for that reason; as a result of that; consequently. ⟨ME *therfore* < *ther* there + *fore*, var. of *for* for⟩

☛ *Syn.* **Therefore,** CONSEQUENTLY=indicate a logical or causal relationship between ideas by connecting to one statement a group of words stating a conclusion or result. **Therefore** indicates formally and precisely that the second group of words states the necessary conclusion to be drawn from the first: *He was the only candidate; therefore, he was elected.* **Consequently,** also formal, indicates a reasonable conclusion, but may also be used to connect a statement of effect or result: *She is the popular candidate; consequently, she will be elected. I overslept and, consequently, was late.*

there•from [,ðɛr'frʌm] *adv.* from that; from this; from it.

there•in [,ðɛr'ɪn] *adv.* **1** in that place; in it. **2** in that matter; in that way; in that respect.

there•in•af•ter [,ðɛrɪn'æftər] *adv.* after (a given point) in that piece of text.

there•in•to [,ðɛr'ɪntu] *or* [,ðɛrɪn'tu] *adv.* **1** into that place; into it. **2** into that matter.

there'll [ðɛrl] **1** there will. **2** there shall.

there•of [,ðɛr'ʌv] *or* [,ðɛr'ɒv] *adv.* **1** of that; of it. **2** from it; from that source.

there•on [,ðɛr'ɒn] *adv.* **1** on that; on it. **2** immediately after that.

there's [ðɛrz] **1** there is. **2** there has: *There's been an accident.*
☛ *Hom.* THEIRS.

there•to [,ðɛr'tu] *adv. Formal.* **1** to that; to it: *The castle stands on a hill, and the road thereto is steep and rough.* **2** in addition to that; also.

there•to•fore [,ðɛrtə'fɔr] *or* ['ðɛrtə,fɔr] *adv. Formal.* before that time; until then.

there•un•der [,ðɛr'ʌndər] *adv.* **1** under that; under it. **2** under the authority of that; according to that.

there•un•to [,ðɛr'ʌntu] *or* [,ðɛrʌn'tu] *adv. Archaic.* to that; to it.

there•up•on [,ðɛrə'pɒn] *adv.* **1** immediately after that. **2** because of that; therefore. **3** on that; on it; on that subject.

there•with [,ðɛr'wɪθ] *or* [,ðɛr'wɪð] *adv. Formal.* **1** with that; with it. **2** immediately after that; then.

there•with•al ['ðɛrwɪ,ðɒl] *or* [,ðɛrwɪ'ðɒl] *adv.* **1** with that; with this; with it. **2** in addition to that; also.

the•ri•o•mor•phic [,θɛriou'mɔrfɪk] *adj.* thought of or represented as being in the form of an animal, as certain deities. Compare ANTHROPOMORPHIC. ⟨< Gk. *theriomorphos* < *therion* beast + *morphē* form⟩

therm [θɜrm] *n.* a unit of heat equalling 100 000 BTU. ⟨< Gk. *thermē* heat⟩

ther•mae [,θɜrmi] *n.pl.* **1** hot springs or baths. **2** the public baths and bathing establishments of ancient Rome.

ther•mal ['θɜrməl] *adj., n. —adj.* **1** of, having to do with,

caused by, or producing heat or warmth. **2** warm or hot: *thermal springs.* **3** designed to conserve heat or warmth: *thermal underwear.*
—n. a bubble, or column, of rising air currents that are warmer than the surrounding air. Thermals are used by gliders and by certain migratory birds to gain altitude. ⟨< Gk. *thermē* heat⟩
—'ther•mal•ly, *adv.*

thermal barrier the point of speed beyond which an aircraft is subjected to dangerously high temperatures as a result of friction with the atmosphere.

thermal pollution disruption of water ecosystems by allowing water heated as a by-product of certain industrial processes to flow into rivers and lakes and raise their temperature.

thermal printer *Computer technology.* a computer printer that produces images by applying heat to specially treated paper, causing it to discolour in the shape of the desired image.

thermal spring a natural spring whose water is warmer than the surrounding atmosphere; hot spring.

ther•mic ['θɜrmɪk] *adj.* of or having to do with heat; thermal. **—'ther•mi•cal•ly,** *adv.*

therm•i•on ['θɜrmaɪən] *or* ['θɜrmiən] *n. Physics.* an ion, either positive or negative, emitted by an incandescent material. **—,therm•i'on•ic** [,θɜrmi'ɒnɪk], *adj.*

therm•i•on•ics [,θɜrmi'ɒnɪks] *n.* the branch of physics that deals with the study and science of thermionic activity.

thermionic valve VACUUM TUBE.

ther•mis•tor [θər'mɪstər] *n.* a very small electronic resistor used to measure or regulate heat through changes in conductivity. ⟨blend of *therm(al)* and *(res)istor*⟩

thermo– or **therm–** *combining form.* heat, as in *thermodynamics.* ⟨< Gk. *thermē*⟩

ther•mo•ba•rom•e•ter [,θɜrmoubə'rɒmətər] *n.* an instrument that measures pressure by recording the change in the boiling point of a liquid. **—,ther•mo,ba•ro'met•ric** [-,bærə'mɛtrɪk], *adj.*

ther•mo•chem•is•try [,θɜrmou'kɛmɪstri] *n.* the branch of chemistry that studies the relation of heat to chemical change. **—,ther•mo'chem•i•cal,** *adj.*

ther•mo•cline ['θɜrmou,klaɪn] *n.* a layer of water below the surface layer in the ocean or a lake, characterized by a marked decrease in temperature with increase in depth (1°C per metre). ⟨< *thermo-* + *(in)cline*⟩

ther•mo•cou•ple ['θɜrmou,kʌpəl] *n.* the junction of a pair of dissimilar metallic conductors, such as copper and iron, maintained at different temperatures so as to generate a thermo-electric current that can be used to measure the temperature of a third substance at the point of junction. Also, **thermo-electric couple.**

ther•mo•dy•nam•ic [,θɜrmoudaɪ'næmɪk] *adj.* **1** of or having to do with thermodynamics. **2** using force due to heat or to the conversion of heat into mechanical energy. **—,ther•mo•dy'nam•ic•al•ly,** *adv.*

ther•mo•dy•nam•ics [,θɜrmoudaɪ'næmɪks] *n.* the branch of physics that deals with the relations between heat and mechanical energy or work.

thermodynamic temperature temperature considered as a basic physical quantity that is a measure of the thermal energy possessed by a body, expressed in kelvins. *Symbol:* *T* See also ABSOLUTE ZERO.

ther•mo–e•lec•tric [,θɜrmou ɪ'lɛktrɪk] *adj.* of or having to do with the relation between heat and electricity. Also, **thermo-electrical. —,ther•mo–e'lec•tri•cal•ly,** *adv.*

thermo–electric couple thermocouple.

ther•mo–e•lec•tric•i•ty [,θɜrmou ɪlɛk'trɪsəti] *or* [-,ilɛk'trɪsəti] *n.* **1** electricity produced directly by heat or temperature difference. **2** the branch of physics dealing with thermo-electric phenomena.

ther•mo•gen•e•sis [,θɜrmou'dʒɛnəsɪs] *n.* the production of heat, especially in an animal body by physiological processes. **—ther'mog•e•nous** [θɜr'mɒdʒənəs] or **,ther•mo•ge'net•ic,** *adj.*

ther•mo•gram ['θɜrmə,græm] *n.* **1** the record produced by a thermograph. **2** a photographic image produced by thermography.

ther•mo•graph ['θɜrmə,græf] *n.* a type of thermometer that includes a system for recording temperature variations over a period of time, or from one part of the body to another, on a graph. It is sometimes used to distinguish normal and abnormal tissue.

ther•mog•ra•phy [θər'mɒgrəfi] *n.* **1** the technique or process of producing a photographic image of an object by means of a camera that measures the heat emitted by it. Thermography is used in the diagnosis of cancerous tumours, etc. **2** a printing or writing process involving the use of heat, especially one that produces raised printing. **—ther'mog•ra•pher,** *n.* **—,ther•mo'graph•ic,** *adj.*

ther•mo•karst ['θɜrmou,kɑrst] *n. Cdn.* the melting of permafrost with a high ice content and the resultant collapse of the ground, producing deep gullies, trenches, or sinks. Thermokarst is often produced by the removal of insulating plant and soil cover. ⟨< *thermo-* + *karst*⟩

ther•mo•lu•mi•nes•cence [,θɜrmou,lumə'nɛsəns] *n.* the release of stored energy in the form of light when a substance is subjected to heat, used especially in the dating of ancient artifacts. **—,ther•mo,lu•mi'nes•cent,** *adj.*

ther•mo•ly•sis [θər'mɒləsɪs] *n.* **1** *Physiology.* dispersion of heat from the body. **2** *Chemistry.* dissociation of a compound by heat. **—,ther•mo'ly•tic** [,θɜrmə'lɪtɪk], *adj.*

ther•mo•mag•net•ic [,θɜrmoumæg'nɛtɪk] *adj.* of or having to do with the interrelation of heat and magnetism.

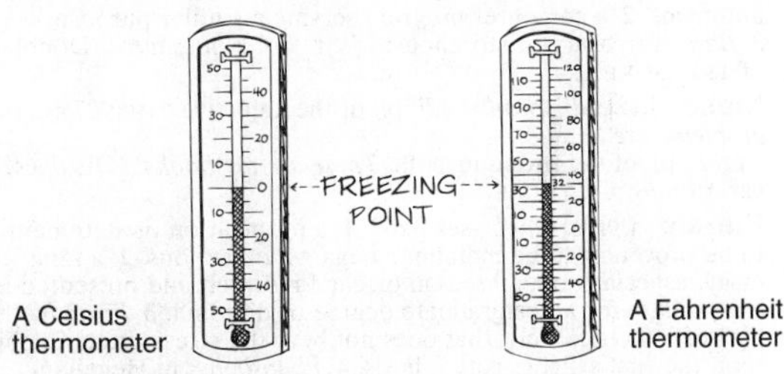

A Celsius thermometer

A Fahrenheit thermometer

ther•mom•e•ter [θər'mɒmətər] *n.* an instrument for measuring temperature, usually by means of the expansion and contraction of mercury or alcohol in a capillary tube and bulb, or by means of a thermocouple, now often with a digital readout. **—ther'mom•e•try,** *n.* **—,ther•mo'met•ric,** *adj.*

ther•mo•nu•cle•ar [,θɜrmou'njukliər] *or* [,θɜrmou'nukliər] *adj.* **1** of or designating the fusion of atoms (as in the hydrogen bomb) through very high temperature: *a thermonuclear reaction.* **2** of, employing, or designating the heat energy released in a nuclear reactor.

ther•mo•phile ['θɜrmə,faɪl] *n.* any organism that thrives in relatively high temperatures. **—,ther•mo'phil•ic** [-'fɪlɪk], *adj.*

ther•mo•pile ['θɜrmə,paɪl] *n.* a device for detecting and measuring very small changes in temperature or for producing a thermo-electric current. It consists of a series of thermocouples.

ther•mo•plas•tic [,θɜrmou'plæstɪk] *adj., n.* *—adj.* becoming soft and malleable when heated.
—n. a thermoplastic material, especially one of certain synthetic resins.

Ther•mos ['θɜrməs] *n. Trademark.* a double-walled bottle or flask made with a vacuum between its inner and outer walls, used to keep a beverage, soup, etc. hot or cold for a long time; vacuum bottle. Also, **Thermos bottle, Thermos flask.** ⟨< Gk. *thermos* hot⟩

ther•mo•set ['θɜrmə,sɛt] *adj., n.* *—adj.* thermosetting.
—n. a thermosetting material, especially a plastic.

ther•mo•set•ting ['θɜrmə,sɛtɪŋ] *adj.* becoming hard and permanently set after being heated: *thermosetting plastics.*

ther•mo•sphere ['θɜrmə,sfir] *n.* the layer of the earth's atmosphere lying above the mesosphere, extending from about 85 km to about 450 km above the earth's surface, where the exosphere begins, and characterized by an increase in temperature with increasing altitude. This is also the region of meteors and aurorae. Air is very thin in the thermosphere, where it is very hot.

ther•mo•stat ['θɜrmə,stæt] *n.* **1** an automatic device for regulating temperature. In most thermostats, the expansion and contraction of a metal, liquid, or gas opens and closes an electric circuit by which an appliance or device, such as an air conditioner or furnace, is made to work or to stop working. **2** a similar device that responds to temperature changes, such as one that will activate a sprinkler system or fire alarm if the temperature increases beyond a certain point. ⟨< *thermo-* + Gk. *-statēs* that stands⟩

ther•mo•stat•ic [ˌθɜrməˈstætɪk] *adj.* of, having to do with, or like a thermostat.

ther•mo•stat•i•cal•ly [ˌθɜrməˈstætɪkli] *adv.* by means of a thermostat.

ther•mo•tax•is [ˌθɜrmouˈtæksɪs] *n.* **1** *Biology.* the movement of an organism toward or away from a source of heat. **2** *Physiology.* the natural regulation of body temperature. **—ˌther•moˈtax•ic** or **ˌther•moˈtac•tic,** *adj.*

ther•mo•trop•ism [θərˈmɒtrəˌpɪzəm] *n. Biology.* the oriented growth of a plant or sessile animal in response to a source of heat, either toward it or away from it. **—ˌther•moˈtrop•ic** [-məˈtrɒpɪk], *adj.*

the•ro•pod [ˈθirəˌpɒd] *n.* any of a suborder (Theropoda) of carnivorous dinosaurs walking primarily on the hind legs and living in Triassic to Cretaceous times. Tyrannosaurs were theropods. ⟨< Gk. *ther* wild beast + *pous, podos* foot⟩

the•sau•rus [θɪˈsɔrəs] *n., pl.* **-ri** [-raɪ] *or* [-ri]. **1** a dictionary or encyclopedia, especially a dictionary in which words are grouped by their semantic relationships; a book of synonyms and antonyms. **2** a computer program serving a similar purpose. **3** *Rare.* a treasury or storehouse. ⟨< L < Gk. *thesauros.* Doublet of TREASURE.⟩

these [ðiz] *adj., pron. —adj.* pl. of the adjective THIS: *These two problems are hard.*
—pron. pl. of the pronoun THIS: *These are my books.* ⟨OE *thǣs,* var. of *thās.* Cf. THOSE.⟩

the•sis [ˈθisɪs] *n., pl.* **-ses** [-siz]. **1** a proposition or statement to be proved or to be maintained against objections. **2** a long essay, especially one based on original research and presented by a candidate for a postgraduate degree or diploma. **3** *Prosody.* the part of a metrical foot that does not bear the stress. In an iambic foot, the first syllable is the thesis. **4** *Philosophy.* in Hegelian dialectic, the first and least satisfactory stage of development, followed by antithesis and synthesis. ⟨< L < Gk. *thesis,* originally, a setting down⟩

Thes•pi•an [ˈθɛspiən] *adj., n. —adj.* **1** having to do with Thespis, a Greek tragic poet who lived about 534 B.C. **2** of or having to do with the drama or tragedy; dramatic; tragic.
—n. an actor. ⟨< *Thespis,* a Greek poet⟩

the•ta [ˈθeitə] *or* [ˈθitə] *n.* the eighth letter (θ) of the Greek alphabet, pronounced as the English 'th' in *thin.*

the•ur•gy [ˈθiərdʒi] *n.* **1** divine or supernatural activity in earthly or human affairs; miracles. **2** the art or practice of trying to influence or cause such activity, as some forms of beneficent magic. ⟨< LL *theurgia* < Gk. *theourgia* < *theos* god + *ergon* work⟩ **—theˈur•gi•cal,** *adj.* **—ˈthe•ur•gist,** *n.*

thews [θjuz] *n.pl.* **1** muscles or sinews. **2** physical strength. ⟨ME *theawes* good quality; strength < OE *thēaw* habit⟩ **—ˈthew•y,** *adj.*

they [ðei] *pron.pl., subj.* **they,** *obj.* **them,** *poss.* **theirs. 1** pl. of HE, SHE, or IT. **2** *Informal.* some unspecified people or people in general: *They say she's really a very serious person. They don't observe Boxing Day in the United States.* ⟨ME < ON *their*⟩

☛ *Usage.* **They** is used in informal speech as an indefinite pronoun but generally it is not so used in writing. Spoken: *They have had no serious accidents at that crossing for over two years.* Written: *There have been no serious accidents…*

they'd [ðeid] **1** they had. **2** they would.

they'll [ðeil] they will.

they're [ðɛr]; *unstressed,* [ðər] they are.
☛ *Hom.* THEIR, THERE.

they've [ðeiv] they have.

THI temperature humidity index.

thi•a•min [ˈθaɪəmɪn] *n.* a white, crystalline organic compound, also known as vitamin B_1, found in cereals, yeast, etc. or prepared synthetically. Also, **thiamine** [-mɪn] *or* [-ˌmin]. *Formula:* $C_{12}H_{17}ClN_4OS$

thi•a•zide [ˈθaɪəˌzaɪd] *n.* any member of a class of diuretics inhibiting the reabsorption of sodium chloride in the kidneys. It is widely used in the treatment of hypertension.

Thi•bet•an [tɪˈbɛtən] *adj. or n.* See TIBETAN.

thick [θɪk] *adj., adv., n. —adj.* **1** of an object or substance, filling much space from one surface to the other; not thin: *The castle has thick stone walls.* **2** large in diameter relative to length: *a thick cable.* **3** measuring between two opposite surfaces of an object or substance: *3 cm thick.* **4** dense, abundant, profuse, or heavy: *thick hair, bullets thick as hail, thick fumes.* **5** filled; covered: *thick with flies.* **6** like glue or syrup, not like water; rather dense of its kind: *Thick liquids pour much more slowly than thin liquids.* **7** of atmospheric conditions, not clear; foggy, muddy, or impenetrable: *thick darkness. The weather was thick and the airports were shut down.* **8** not clear in sound; hoarse, muffled, or husky: *a thick voice.* **9** stupid; dull: *He has a thick head. They are too thick to come in out of the rain.* **10** *Informal.* very friendly; intimate: *She's very thick with the boss these days.* **11** *Informal.* too much to be endured: *They made you work outdoors in this heat? That's a bit thick!*
thick skin, the ability to take criticism, etc. without being affected by it.
—adv. thickly.
lay it on thick, *Informal.* praise or blame too much.
—n. the part that is thickest, most crowded, most active, etc.: *in the thick of the fight.*
through thick and thin, in good times and bad: *A true friend stays loyal through thick and thin.* ⟨OE *thicce*⟩ **—ˈthick•ly,** *adv.*

thick•en [ˈθɪkən] *v.* **1** make or become thick or thicker. **2** of the plot of a play, novel, etc., become more complex or intricate. **—ˈthick•en•er,** *n.*

thick•en•ing [ˈθɪkənɪŋ] *n., v. —n.* **1** a material or ingredient used to thicken something. **2** a thickened part. **3** the act or process of making or becoming thick or thicker.
—v. ppr. of THICKEN.

thick•et [ˈθɪkɪt] *n.* a dense growth of shrubs, bushes, or small trees. ⟨OE *thiccet* < *thicce* thick⟩

thick•head [ˈθɪkˌhɛd] *n.* dolt; stupid person.

thick–head•ed [ˈθɪk ˌhɛdɪd] *adj.* stupid; dull. **—ˈthick-ˌhead•ed•ness,** *n.*

thick•ish [ˈθɪkɪʃ] *adj.* somewhat thick.

thick•ness [ˈθɪknɪs] *n.* **1** the quality or state of being thick. **2** the distance between opposite surfaces; the third measurement of a solid; depth, not length or breadth. **3** the thick part. **4** a layer: *The pad was made up of three thicknesses of blotting paper.*

thick•set [ˈθɪkˌsɛt] *adj., n. —adj.* **1** closely placed, planted, etc.: *a thickset hedge.* **2** thick in form or build: *a thickset man.*
—n. Archaic. thicket.

thick–skinned [ˈθɪk ˈskɪnd] *adj.* **1** having a thick skin. **2** not readily affected by criticism, rebuff, insults, etc.; insensitive.

thick–wit•ted [ˈθɪk ˈwɪtɪd] *adj.* stupid; dull.

thick•wood buffalo [ˈθɪkˌwʊd] *Cdn.* WOOD BUFFALO.

thief [θif] *n., pl.* **thieves.** a person who steals, especially one who steals secretly and without using force. ⟨OE *thēof*⟩

☛ *Syn.* **Thief,** ROBBER = someone who steals. **Thief** applies to someone who takes and, usually, carries away something belonging to another, in a secret or stealthy way: *A thief stole the little girl's bicycle from the yard.* **Robber** applies to one who takes another's property by force or threats of violence: *The robbers bound and gagged the security guard.*

thieve [θiv] *v.* **thieved, thiev•ing.** steal. ⟨OE *thēofian* < *thēof* thief⟩

thiev•er•y [ˈθivəri] *n., pl.* **-er•ies.** the act of stealing; theft.

thieves [θivz] *n.* pl. of THIEF.

thiev•ish [ˈθivɪʃ] *adj.* **1** having the habit of stealing; likely to steal. **2** like a thief; stealthy; sly. **—ˈthiev•ish•ly,** *adv.* **—ˈthiev•ish•ness,** *n.*

thigh [θaɪ] *n.* **1** in humans, the part of the leg between the hip and the knee. See LEG for picture. **2** the femoral region of certain other creatures, especially poultry. ⟨OE *thēoh*⟩

thigh•bone [ˈθaɪˌboun] *n.* the bone of the leg between the hip and the knee; femur. See LEG and PELVIS for pictures.

thig•mot•ro•pism [θɪgˈmɒtrəˌpɪzəm] *n.* the growth of a plant in response to touch, such as when a vine tendril coils around a support. ⟨< Gk. *thigma* touch + E *tropism*⟩ **—ˌthig•moˈtrop•ic** [ˌθɪgməˈtrɒpɪk], *adj.*

thill [θɪl] *n.* either of the shafts between which a single animal drawing a vehicle is placed. ⟨ME *thille*⟩

thim•ble [ˈθɪmbəl] *n.* **1** a small cap of metal, bone, plastic, etc. worn on the finger to protect it when pushing the needle in sewing. **2** a short metal tube. **3** a metal ring having a groove in its outer surface and fitted inside a loop of rope to save wear on the rope. **4** *Computer technology.* a type of printing mechanism in a computer printer. It is like a daisy wheel in which the spokes are bent up so as to look like a thimble. ⟨OE *thȳmel* < *thūma* thumb⟩

thim•ble•ber•ry [ˈθɪmbəlˌbɛri] *n., pl.* **-ries.** any of several plants closely related to and resembling the raspberry, especially a tall, thornless shrub (*Rubus parviflorus*) of central and western North America, having large, very broad, lobed leaves, white flowers, and red, thimble-shaped, edible fruit.

thim•ble•ful ['θɪmbəl,fʊl] *n., pl.* **-fuls.** as much as a thimble will hold; a very small quantity.

thim•ble•rig ['θɪmbəl,rɪg] *n., v.* **-rigged, rig•ging.** *—n.* SHELL GAME.
—v. cheat by or as by the thimblerig. **—'thim•ble,rig•ger,** *n.*

thin [θɪn] *adj.* **thin•ner, thin•nest;** *adv., v.* **thinned, thin•ning.**
—adj. **1** of an object or substance, filling little space from one surface to the other; not thick: *thin paper, thin wire, a thin layer of dust.* **2** having little flesh or fat; slender or lean: *a long, thin face. She is still thin after her illness.* **3** scanty; sparse; not abundant; consisting of few placed far apart: *He has thin hair. The actors played to a thin audience.* **4** not dense: *The air on the top of those high mountains is thin.* **5** not like glue or syrup; like water; of less substance than usual: *thin milk.* **6** not deep or strong: *a thin, shrill voice.* **7** having little depth, fullness, or intensity: *a thin colour.* **8** easily seen through; sheer; transparent or nearly so: *a thin nightie.* **9** of something abstract, insubstantial; not solid; weak or ineffectual: *a thin argument, a thin excuse.*
thin skin, the condition of being easily affected by criticism, etc.
—adv. thinly.
—v. **1** make or become thin: *to thin paint.* **2** make or become less crowded or numerous by the removal or departure of individuals (*often used with* **out**): *to thin a row of beets. The crowds at the festival thinned out as night came on.* ⟨OE *thynne*⟩ **—'thin•ly,** *adv.* **—'thin•ner,** *n.* **—'thin•ness,** *n.*
☛ *Syn. adj.* **2. Thin,** LEAN², GAUNT = having little flesh. **Thin** emphasizes its basic meaning of being not thick through, but sometimes suggests lack of the normal or usual amount of flesh, as from sickness, strain, lack of food, etc.: *She has a thin face.* **Lean** emphasizes lack of fat, and suggests natural thinness with firm, solid flesh: *The forest ranger is lean and brown.* **Gaunt** adds to **thin** the idea of showing the bones, and often suggests a starved or worn look: *Gaunt, bearded men stumbled into camp.*

thine [ðaɪn] *pron., adj. Archaic or poetic. —pron.* the possessive form of THOU: *"For Thine is the kingdom."*
—adj. the form of THY used before a vowel or mute *h*: *thine honour. "Drink to me only with thine eyes."* ⟨OE *thīn*⟩
☛ *Usage.* See note at THOU.

thing [θɪŋ] *n.* **1** any object or substance: *All the things in the house were burned. Put these things away.* **2** whatever is spoken or thought of; any act, deed, fact, event, situation, idea, or concern: *A strange thing happened. It was a good thing to do.* **3 a** a person or creature (referred to with pity, scorn, condescension, etc.): *a silly old thing, a mean thing, a dear little thing, a poor thing.* **b** any object whose name is forgotten or unknown, or which is regarded with contempt: *Don't tell me you're still driving around in that thing.* **4 the thing,** anything considered desirable, suitable, appropriate, important, etc.: *the latest thing in swimsuits, the thing to do. The thing is, how much can you afford?* **5 things,** *pl.* **a** belongings; possessions: *Take your things.* **b** clothes and wearing apparel generally: *Put on your things.* **c** equipment or articles for a given purpose: *I'll need some drafting things for that course.* **d** circumstances: *How are things? Things are easier for her these days.* **6** *Informal.* **a** a person's special interest or strong point: *I decided that gardening was just not my thing.* **b** a complex; an irrational or neurotic aversion to or fondness for someone or something: *He has a thing about driving in the city.*
do (one's) **(own) thing,** *Informal.* express one's personality by doing what one does well or enjoys most.
know a thing or two (about), *Informal.* be experienced (in) or knowledgeable (about).
make a (big) thing (out) of, *Informal.* make an issue of; blow out of proportion, especially so as to cause an argument.
make a good thing of, *Informal.* profit from.
see or **hear things,** have hallucinations; imagine sights or sounds and believe they are real. ⟨OE⟩

thing•a•ma•bob ['θɪŋəmə,bɒb] *n. Informal.* thingamajig. Also, **thingumabub, thingumbob.**

thing•a•ma•jig ['θɪŋəmə,dʒɪg] *n. Informal.* something whose name one forgets or does not bother to mention.

thing•um•my ['θɪŋəmi] *n. Informal.* thingamajig.

think [θɪŋk] *v.* **thought, think•ing;** *n. —v.* **1** use the mind to generate and shape ideas, link concepts, assess ideas of others, etc.: *I can't think very clearly right now.* **2** have in the mind: *He thought that it was wrong. Think pleasant thoughts.* **3** have one's thoughts full of: *She thinks nothing but sports.* **4** have a mental image or concept (*used with* **of**): *He had thought of her as still a child.* **5** have as an opinion; believe: *What do you think about the new federal budget?* **6** reflect; consider: *I must think before answering.* **7** figure out; determine by reasoning or reflection: *She tried to think how she should respond.* **8** imagine: *You can't think how surprised I was.* **9** remember (*often with* **of**): *I can't think of her name. I can't think what I did with that paper.* **10** expect: *I did not think to find you here. He thinks to escape punishment.* **11** consider the needs, rights, or happiness (*of*): *Think of the children. She thinks of no one but herself.* **12** entertain the possibility or prospect of doing something (*usually with a negative*): *I wouldn't think of parking in your spot!*
think aloud, say what one is thinking.
think better of, a change one's mind about; reconsider: *She was going to confront them immediately, but then thought better of it and decided to collect more evidence first.* **b** have a more favourable opinion of (a person, idea, etc.): *She thought better of him for his apology.*
think fit, regard as a suitable course of action: *We thought fit to stay away for a few days.*
think little or **nothing of,** have no scruples about: *They think nothing of taking supplies home from the office.*
think nothing of it, you're welcome (in response to an expression of thanks).
think out, a plan, solve, or understand by thinking: *Bill thought out the reasons for his dad's anger.* **b** think through to the end.
think out loud, say what one is thinking.
think over, consider carefully: *Think it over before you decide.*
think the world (or **much,** etc.) **of,** *Informal.* regard or esteem very highly.
think through, think about until one reaches an understanding or conclusion.
think twice, think again before acting; hesitate: *I'd think twice about jogging after dark if I were you. He didn't think twice about going.*
think up, plan or discover by thinking: *We will have to think up a better strategy.*
—n. Informal. **1** the act or a period of pondering or assessing: *to sit down for a long think on the matter.* **2** (*adjl.*) of, involving, or designed for contemplation or assessment: *a think session.* ⟨OE *thencan* < Gmc.⟩ **—'think•er,** *n.*
☛ *Syn.* **1. Think,** REFLECT, MEDITATE = use the powers of the mind. **Think** is the general word meaning 'to use the mind to form ideas, reach conclusions, understand what is known, etc.': *I must think about your offer before I accept it.* **Reflect** suggests quietly and seriously thinking over a subject, by turning the thoughts (back) upon it: *They need time to reflect on their problems.* **Meditate** suggests focussing one's thoughts on a subject from every point of view, to understand all its sides and relations, often as a spiritual or mentally edifying exercise: *He meditated on the nature of truth.*

think•a•ble ['θɪŋkəbəl] *adj.* capable of being or fit to be thought; conceivable.

think•ing ['θɪŋkɪŋ] *adj., n., v. —adj.* **1** that thinks; reasoning. **2** thoughtful or reflective.
put on (one's) **thinking cap,** take time for thinking over something.
—n. THOUGHT (defs. 2-4).
—v. ppr. of THINK.

think piece *Slang.* a piece of analytic or reflective journalistic writing.

think–tank ['θɪŋk ,tæŋk] *n. Informal.* a centre for technological research, or the people working there, often engaged in government and defence projects: *The Fraser Institute is a well-known Canadian think-tank.*

thin•ner¹ ['θɪnər] *n.* **1** a substance added to another to give it a more fluid consistency, as turpentine or spirits to paint. **2** a person who thins something.

thin•ner² ['θɪnər] *adj.* comparative of THIN.

thin•nish ['θɪnɪʃ] *adj.* somewhat thin.

thin–skinned ['θɪn 'skɪnd] *adj.* **1** having a thin skin. **2** easily affected by criticism, rebuff, etc.; too sensitive; touchy.

thio– *combining form.* sulphur; used to form names of chemical substances in which oxygen atoms have been replaced with sulphur.

thi•o•a•ce•tic acid [,θaɪouə'sitɪk] *or* [-ə'sɛtɪk] a pungent, fuming yellow liquid used as a chemical reagent and tear gas. *Formula*: C_2H_4SO

thi•ol ['θaɪɒl] *n.* any of a class of alcohol-like organic compounds characterized by the substitution of sulphur for oxygen.

thi•o•pen•tal sodium [,θaɪou'pɛntəl] SODIUM PENTOTHAL.

thi•o•u•re•a [,θaɪoujə'riə] *or* [,θaɪou'juriə] *n.* a colourless, crystalline, water-soluble compound derived from urea by replacing the oxygen with sulphur, chiefly used in organic synthesis and in photography. *Formula*: CH_4N_2S

third [θɜrd] *adj., n. —adj.* **1** next after the second; last in a series of three; 3rd. **2** being one of three equal parts.
—n. **1** the next after the second; the last in a series of three. **2** one of three equal parts: *The pizza was divided into thirds.* **3** *Music.* **a** a tone three degrees from another tone. **b** the interval between such tones. **c** the combination of such tones. **4** in automobiles and similar machines, the forward gear or speed next above second; high gear in a three-gear system. **5** *Curling.* the team member next in importance to the skip, and next after the second player in throwing the rock. ⟨OE *thirda,* var. of *thridda* < *thrēo* three⟩

third base *Baseball.* **1** the base across from first base, to the catcher's left and the pitcher's right. **2** the position of the fielder covering this part of the infield.

third class **1** a class after or below the second. **2** the class of mail that includes unsealed greeting cards, printed circulars, books, etc. **3** in some railway, hotel, etc. systems, the least expensive accommodation. **4** by or in third class: *We travelled third class because nothing else was available.* **—'third-'class,** *adj.*

third degree **1** the use of severe treatment by the police to force a person to give information or to make a confession. **2** in Freemasonry, the position or rank of master mason.

third–de•gree ['θɜrd dɪ'gri] *adj.* of a burn, the most severe, damaging the lower layers of tissue.

third estate persons not in the nobility or clergy; common people.

third eye *Hinduism.* an eye in the forehead of an image of a god, especially Siva, representing supernatural insight.

third eyelid NICTITATING MEMBRANE.

third force **1** a political party or bloc in an intermediary position between two established factions representing opposite extremes, especially one exercising a mediating or neutralizing influence. **2** an international coalition formed to take such a position or have such a function.

third•ly ['θɜrdli] *adv.* in the third place.

third party **1 a** a person or group affected by the actions of two major parties in a contract, arrangement, etc. **b** a person or group unaffected by the actions or arrangements of two others, and therefore impartial and objective. **2** in a two-party political system, any party other than the two major ones.

third person **1** the form of a pronoun or verb used to refer to a person who is neither the person speaking nor the one spoken to. The verb *has* is the third person singular of *have.* **2** the category to which such forms belong. *He, she, it,* and *they* are pronouns of the third person. **3** a style of narration that makes use primarily of such forms: *The story is told in the third person.*

third rail a rail parallelling the ordinary rails of a railway. It carries a powerful electric current and is used on some railways instead of an overhead wire.

third–rate ['θɜrd 'reit] *adj.* **1** of the third class. **2** distinctly inferior. **—'third-'rat•er,** *n.*

third stream a musical genre melding jazz and classical music. **—'third-'stream,** *adj.*

Third World the developing countries of the world, especially those emerging in Africa and Asia since World War II. Also, **third world. —'third-'world,** *adj.*

thirst [θɜrst] *n., v. —n.* **1** a dry, uncomfortable feeling in the mouth or throat caused by having had nothing to drink; desire or need for something to drink. **2** a strong desire: *a thirst for adventure.*
—v. **1** feel thirsty; be thirsty. **2** have a strong desire. ⟨OE *thurst* from WGmc.⟩

thirst•y ['θɜrsti] *adj.* **thirst•i•er, thirst•i•est. 1** feeling thirst; having thirst. **2** without water or moisture; dry. **3** *Informal.* arousing thirst: *Mowing the lawn is thirsty work.* **4** having a strong desire; eager. **—'thirst•i•ly,** *adv.* **—'thirst•i•ness,** *n.*

thir•teen ['θɜrt'tin] *n., adj. —n.* **1** three more than ten; 13: *He counted fourteen people, but I counted thirteen.* **2** the numeral 13: *The 13 is very faint.* **3** the thirteenth in a set or series. **4** a set or series of thirteen persons or things.
—adj. **1** being three more than ten; 13. **2** being thirteenth in a set or series (*used after the noun*): *Section thirteen.* ⟨OE *thrēotēne*⟩

Thirteen Colonies See COLONY (def. 7).

thir•teenth ['θɜrt'tinθ] *adj. or n.* **1** next after the 12th; last in a series of thirteen; 13th. **2** one, or being one, of 13 equal parts.

thir•ti•eth ['θɜrtiɪθ] *adj. or n.* **1** next after the 29th; last in a series of thirty; 30th. **2** one, or being one, of 30 equal parts.

thir•ty ['θɜrti] *adj., n., pl.* **-ties.** *—adj.* being three times ten; 30.
—n. **1** three times ten; 30. **2 thirties,** *pl.* the years from thirty through thirty-nine, especially of a century or of a person's life: *His grandfather still vividly remembered the drought of the thirties.* ⟨OE *thrītig*⟩

thir•ty–sec•ond note ['θɜrti 'sɛkənd] *Music.* a note equal to one thirty-second of a whole note. See NOTE for picture.

thir•ty–sec•ond rest ['θɜrti 'sɛkənd] *Music.* a rest lasting as long as a thirty-second note.

this [ðɪs] *adj., pl.* **these;** *pron., pl.* **these;** *adv. —adj.* **1** pointing out, indicating, or emphasizing some person, thing, idea, etc. already mentioned or understood, currently in progress, or just about to be mentioned or presented, especially one present or near in place or time or in the spoken or written context. When used with *that, this* refers to something near and *that* refers to something far or farther away. *Examples*: *I liked this book a lot. This dress is nicer than that one. I'd rather do it this way.* **2** *Informal.* designating a certain unspecified or unidentified person or thing: *I saw this really handsome guy in the coffee shop today.*
—pron. some person, thing, idea, etc. already mentioned or understood or just about to be mentioned or presented, often one that is to be emphasized or contrasted with another farther away in place or time or in the spoken or written context: *This is a better drawing than that. "What's this?" she asked, holding up my torn sweater. After this we'd better go home. I'll read it to you; listen to this.*
—adv. to this extent or degree; so: *You can have this much.* ⟨OE⟩

☛ *Usage. pron.* **This,** like **that,** is regularly used to refer to the idea of a clause or sentence: *He had always had his own way at home, and this made him a poor room-mate.* But usually **this** is preferred for one that is about to be mentioned: *This is my main problem: I just can't concentrate.*

☛ *Usage. adj.* **2.** This use is very informal and is out of place in careful or formal speech or writing. There the indefinite article is always preferred, sometimes followed by 'certain' or something similar: *Once there was a* (not *this*) *girl who…*

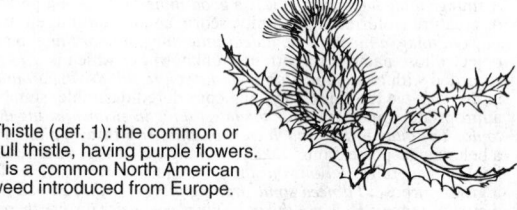

Thistle (def. 1): the common or bull thistle, having purple flowers. It is a common North American weed introduced from Europe.

this•tle ['θɪsəl] *n.* **1** any of numerous plants of the composite family (especially of genus *Cirsium*) having prickly leaves and stem and showy heads of purple, pink, or yellow flowers. Some thistles, such as the common, or bull, thistle (*Cirsium vulgare*) and the Canada thistle (*C. arvense*) are troublesome weeds. **2** any of various other prickly plants. ⟨OE *thistel*⟩

this•tle•down ['θɪsəl,daʊn] *n.* the down or fluff from the ripe flower head of a thistle.

this•tly ['θɪsli] *adj.* **1** like thistles; prickly. **2** having many thistles.

thith•er ['θɪðər] *adv., adj. —adv. Archaic, Poetic, or Formal.* to or toward that place; there.
—adj. located on that side; far or farther: *the thither end of the lane.* ⟨OE *thider*⟩

thith•er•to ['θɪðər'tu] *adv. Archaic, Poetic, or Formal.* up until then; before that time: *Thitherto she had not known love.*

thith•er•ward ['θɪðərwərd] *adv.* thither. Also, **thitherwards.**

thix•ot•ro•py [θɪk'sɒtrəpi] *n.* the property of some gels and emulsions of liquefying when stirred or shaken and congealing again when left standing. ⟨< Gk. *thixis* a touching + *tropos* turn⟩ **—,thix•o'trop•ic** [,θɪksə'trɒpɪk], *adj.*

tho' [ðoʊ] *conj. or adv. Informal.* though.

thole [θoʊl] *n.* a wooden peg or either of a pair of pegs set into the top of the gunwale on each side of a boat to serve as a support for an oar in rowing. Also, **tholepin.** ⟨OE *tholl*⟩

Thom•ism ['toumɪzəm] *n.* the theological and philosophical doctrines of Saint Thomas Aquinas and his followers. **—'Tho•mist,** *n., adj.* **—Tho'mis•tic,** *adj.*

thong [θɒŋ] *n.* **1** a narrow strip of leather, etc., especially one used as a fastening. **2** the lash of a whip. **3** a kind of sandal, especially of rubber, held on the foot by a narrow piece that passes between the first and second toes. ⟨OE *thwang*⟩

Thon•ga ['tɒŋgə] *n.* **1** a Bantu language spoken in Mozambique. **2** a native speaker of this language.

Thor [θɔr] *n. Norse mythology.* the god of thunder, war, and agriculture.

tho•rac•ic [θə'ræsɪk] *adj.* of or having to do with the thorax. The thoracic cavity contains the heart and lungs.

thoracic duct the main duct of the lymphatic system, extending from below the diaphragm up through the thorax to the base of the neck, where it opens into a large vein below the left clavicle.

tho•rax ['θɔræks] *n., pl.* **-rax•es, -ra•ces** [-rə,siz]. **1** the part of the body between the neck and the abdomen. **2** the second division of an insect's body, between the head and the abdomen. ⟨< L < Gk.⟩

tho•ria ['θɔriə] *n.* thorium dioxide, ThO_2, a whitish powder used for incandescent mantles for gas lamps. ⟨< *thorium*⟩

tho•rite ['θɔrəit] *n.* a rare mineral consisting essentially of a silicate of thorium. *Formula*: $ThSiO_4$ ⟨< Swedish *thorit* < ON *Thorr*⟩

tho•ri•um ['θɔriəm] *n.* a radioactive metallic chemical element present in certain rare minerals. *Symbol*: Th; *at.no.* 90; *at.mass* 232.04. ⟨< NL *thorium* < *Thor*⟩ **—'thor•ic,** *adj.*

thorn [θɔrn] *n.* **1** a sharp-pointed, woody growth on a stem or branch of a plant, especially a tree or shrub. **2** a plant having thorns, such as a hawthorn. **3** the wood from any thorn-bearing tree. **4** the third letter of the FUTHORK, the runic alphabet in which early Old English was written, representing the interdental fricatives now spelled *th* in English. It was also borrowed into the roman alphabet, but was replaced by *th* in the Middle Ages.
thorn in the flesh or **side,** a cause of discomfort or irritation. ⟨OE⟩

thorn apple **1** the fruit of a hawthorn; haw. **2** hawthorn. **3** jimsonweed or any other plant of the same genus.

thorn•y ['θɔrni] *adj.* **thorn•i•er, thorn•i•est. 1** full of thorns; having thorns or spines. **2** troublesome; full of difficulties or complexities.

tho•ron ['θɔrɒn] *n.* a radioactive, gaseous isotope of radon, formed in the disintegration of thorium. ⟨< *thor(ium)* + *-on*, as in *neon*⟩

thor•ough ['θɜrou] *or* ['θɜrə] *adj., adv., prep. —adj.* **1** being all that is needed; complete: *a thorough search.* **2** doing all that should be done and neglecting nothing: *The doctor was very thorough in his examination of the patient.* **3** absolute; unqualified; out-and-out: *Now that I've made a thorough fool of myself. . .*
—adv. or prep. Archaic. through. ⟨OE *thuruh*, var. of *thurh* through⟩ **—'thor•ough•ly,** *adv.* **—'thor•ough•ness,** *n.*

thorough bass *Music.* especially in baroque music, a bass part, marked with special figures below it, usually played on a keyboard and accompanied by a stringed bass instrument.

thor•ough•bred ['θɜrə,brɛd] *adj., n. —adj.* **1** of pure breed or stock. **2** of persons, well-bred; thoroughly trained. **3** of or having to do with the Thoroughbreds.
—n. **1 Thoroughbred,** a breed of horse, used especially in racing, originally bred in England from European mares and Arabian stallions. **2** a purebred or pedigreed animal. **3** a well-bred person.

thor•ough•fare ['θɜrə,fɛr] *n.* **1** a passage, road, or street open at both ends. **2** a main road; highway: *The Queen Elizabeth Way is a well-known thoroughfare between Toronto and Niagara Falls.* **3** traffic or passage through: *Mrs. Lee erected a sign prohibiting thoroughfare through her property.*
no thoroughfare, do not go through.

thor•ough•go•ing ['θɜrə,gouɪŋ] *adj.* thorough; complete.

thorp [θɔrp] *n. Archaic.* a village; a small town (*surviving mainly in place names of the form* -thorpe). ⟨OE *thorp, throp* from Gmc.⟩

those [ðouz] *adj., pron. —adj.* pl. of the adjective THAT: *She owns that dog; the boys own those dogs.*
—pron. pl. of the pronoun THAT: *These are her books; those are my books.* ⟨OE *thās* these⟩

Thoth [θouθ] *or* [tout] *n. Egyptian mythology.* the god of wisdom, learning, and magic, represented as a man with the head of a dog or an ibis.

thou¹ [ðaʊ] *pron. Archaic or poetic.* you (sing.); the one spoken to: *"O wild West Wind, thou breath of Autumn's being."* ⟨ME < OE *thū*⟩

☛ *Usage.* **Thou, thee, thine, thy,** and **thyself** are used today only in religious language, as for addressing God, and in poetry. In Middle English they were the general words used for addressing one person.

thou² [θaʊ] *n. Informal.* thousand: *The contract is worth forty thou.*

though [ðou] *conj., adv. —conj.* **1** in spite of the fact that; notwithstanding the fact that: *Though it was pouring, the girls went to school.* **2** yet; still; nevertheless: *He is better, though not yet cured.* **3** even if; granting or supposing that: *Though I fail, I shall try again.*
as though, as if; as it would be if: *You look as though you are tired.*
—adv. however: *I'm sorry about our quarrel; you started it, though.* ⟨ME *thoh* < ON *thó*, with *-h* from OE *thēah*⟩

thought [θɒt] *n., v. —n.* **1** what one thinks; an idea; notion; something conceived or imagined: *The thought of his upcoming visit filled her with excitement.* **2** the power or process of thinking; mental activity: *Plants are incapable of thought.* **3** reasoning; reflection: *lost in thought. He applied thought to the problem.* **4** the intellectual activity or mental product characteristic of the thinkers of a specified group, time, or place: *in modern scientific thought, 16th-century thought.* **5** consideration; attention; care; regard: *Show some thought for others.* **6** intention: *His thought was to avoid controversy.* **7** a little bit; trifle: *Be a thought more polite.*
—v. pt. and pp. of THINK. ⟨OE *thōht*⟩
☛ *Syn. n.* **1.** See note at IDEA.

thought control the strict limiting or regimentation of ideas, reasoning, etc. to make them conform to those of a particular group, government, etc.

thought•ful ['θɒtfəl] *adj.* **1 a** deep in thought; thinking: *He was thoughtful for a while and then replied, "No."* **b** in the habit of thinking critically and seriously: *Thoughtful educators will see at once how poorly-founded this curriculum is.* **2** indicating thought; showing careful thought: *a thoughtful plan. She uttered a thoughtful 'hmmm' and went on reading.* **3** careful of others; considerate: *She is always thoughtful of her mother.*
—'thought•ful•ly, *adv.* **—'thought•ful•ness,** *n.*
☛ *Syn.* **3. Thoughtful,** CONSIDERATE = giving careful attention to the comfort or feelings of others. **Thoughtful** emphasizes concerning oneself with the comfort and welfare of others and doing, without being asked, things that will add to their well-being or happiness: *A thoughtful neighbour, knowing the girl was sick and alone, took her some hot food.* **Considerate** emphasizes concerning oneself with the feelings and rights of others and trying to spare them discomfort, pain, or unhappiness: *He is considerate enough to tell his parents where he is going.*

thought•less ['θɒtlɪs] *adj.* **1** without thought; done, or doing things, without thinking; careless. **2** showing little or no care or regard for others; not considerate. **3** stupid. **—'thought•less•ly,** *adv.* **—'thought•less•ness,** *n.*

thought–out ['θɒt 'ʌut] *adj.* carefully considered; deliberate.

thou•sand ['θaʊzənd] *n. or adj.* **1** ten hundred; 1000.
2 thousands, *pl.* a very large but unstated number: *There were thousands of tourists in town today.* ⟨OE *thūsend*⟩

thou•sand•fold ['θaʊzənd,fould] *adj., adv., or n.* a thousand times as much or as many.

thou•sandth ['θaʊzəndθ] *adj. or n.* **1** the last in a series of a thousand. **2** one, or being one, of a thousand equal parts.

Thra•cian ['θreiʃən] *n., adj. —n.* **1** a native or inhabitant of ancient Thrace, a region in the E part of the Balkan peninsula. **2** the language of ancient Thrace, assumed to be Indo-European and now extinct.
—adj. of or having to do with ancient Thrace or its people.

thral•dom ['θrɒldəm] See THRALLDOM.

thrall [θrɒl] *n.* **1** a person in bondage; slave. **2** thralldom; bondage; slavery. ⟨OE < ON *thræll*⟩

thrall•dom or **thral•dom** ['θrɒldəm] *n.* bondage; slavery.

thrash [θræʃ] *v.* **1** beat severely, often with a SWITCH (def. 4) or cane: *The man thrashed the boy for stealing the apples.* **2** move violently; toss: *Unable to sleep, the patient thrashed about in her bed. He lay on the ground, thrashing his arms and legs in pain.* **3** thresh. **4** defeat thoroughly.
thrash out, settle by thorough discussion: *to thrash out a problem.*
thrash over, go over again and again. ⟨var. of *thresh*⟩

thrash•er ['θræʃər] *n.* **1** any of several North American songbirds (esp. genus *Toxostoma*) belonging to the same family as the mockingbird, having a long tail and long bill. Thrashers are noted for their song. **2** a person or thing that thrashes.

thrash•ing ['θræʃɪŋ] *n., v. —n.* a severe beating; a flogging. *—v.* ppr. of THRASH.

thread [θrɛd] *n., v. —n.* **1 a** cotton, silk, flax, etc. or a synthetic material such as nylon, acrylic, etc., spun out into a fine cord: *Thread is used for sewing.* **b** a similar filament of glass, metal, or plastic. **2** something long and slender like a thread: *Threads of gold could be seen in the ore.* **3** a continuing or connecting element: *She lost the thread of their conversation when she heard the phone ring.* **4** the sloping ridge that winds around a bolt, screw, pipe, joint, etc.: *The thread of a nut interlocks with the thread of a bolt.* **5** a tenuous or slender assurance or support: *a thread of hope.* **6 threads,** *pl. Slang.* clothes, especially an outfit or suit.
hang by or **on a thread,** be in a precarious position.
—v. **1** pass a thread or threads through: *a blue tapestry threaded with silver. He threaded his needle. I threaded a hundred beads.* **2** prepare thread on (a sewing machine or serger) for sewing. **3** form into a thread when poured from a spoon: *Cook the syrup until it threads.* **4** pass like a thread through; pervade. **5** pass (a tape, film, etc.) through (a projector, recorder, etc.) as though threading a needle. **6** make one's way through; make (one's way) carefully; go on a winding course: *She threaded her way through the crowd.* **7** cut threads into (a bolt, screw, pipe, joint, etc.) ⟨OE *thrǣd*⟩ **—'thread,like,** *adj.*

thread•bare ['θrɛd,bɛr] *adj.* **1** having the nap worn off; worn so much that the threads show: *a threadbare coat.* **2** wearing clothes worn to threads; shabby. **3** old and worn; stale.

thread•fin ['θrɛd,fɪn] *n.* any small, tropical, marine percoid fish of the family Polynemidae, having long, threadlike streamers from its pectoral fin.

thread•worm ['θrɛd,wɜrm] *n.* any of various long, thin nematode worms, especially the pinworm.

thread•y ['θrɛdi] *adj.* **1** consisting of or resembling a thread. **2** fibrous; stringy or viscid. **3** of the pulse, thin and feeble. **4** of the voice, etc., lacking in fullness. **—'thread•i•ness,** *n.*

threat [θrɛt] *n.* **1** a statement of what will be done to hurt or punish someone. **2** a sign or cause of possible harm or unpleasantness: *Those black clouds are a threat of rain.* ⟨OE *thrēat* troop, throng; coercion⟩

threat•en ['θrɛtən] *v.* **1** make a threat against (someone); say what will be done to hurt or punish: *to threaten a person with imprisonment. Do you mean to threaten?* **2** declare one's intention to do, inflict, etc.: *Now they have threatened a worse punishment. She threatened to erase all his video games.* **3** be a cause of possible evil or harm to: *A flood threatened the city.* **4** be a sign of (possible evil or harm, etc.): *Black clouds threaten rain.* **5** be a threat; be imminent; be likely (to have some harmful effect): *Darkness threatened; they began to hurry. Her carelessness is threatening to ruin the whole project.* ⟨OE *thrēatnian* urge; coerce⟩ **—'threat•en•er,** *n.* **—'threat•en•ing•ly,** *adv.*

☛ *Syn.* **1. Threaten,** MENACE = promise or warn of harm, injury, or punishment. **Threaten** emphasizes trying to force or influence someone to do (or not to do) something, by stating that some harm or hurt will be inflicted to punish disobedience or to get even: *He threatened to shoot her if she screamed.* **Menace,** which never takes an infinitive complement, emphasizes showing by a look, position, movement, etc. an intention to harm: *He menaced us with a gun.*

threatened species a species that is not yet considered endangered, but whose rarity indicates it may well be so in the near future.

three [θri] *n., adj. —n.* **1** one more than two; 3: *I bought two T-shirts and he bought three.* **2** the numeral 3: *There's a 3 at the bottom of the page.* **3** the third in a set or series; especially, a playing card or side of a die having three spots: *the three of hearts.* **4** a set or series of three persons or things: *The soldiers marched past in threes.*
—adj. **1** being one more than two; 3. **2** being third in a set or series (*used mainly after the noun*): *Have you read Chapter Three?* ⟨OE *thrēo*⟩

three–base hit ['θri 'beis] *Baseball.* a hit which advances the batter to third base.

three–card trick or **monte** ['θri 'kɑrd] a game in which bets are laid on which of three cards, placed face down and, sometimes, moved around, is the queen or some other pre-specified card.

three–col•our process ['θri ,kʌlər] a full colour printing process that reproduces natural colours by combining plates of the three primary colours (red, blue, and yellow).

three–cor•nered ['θri 'kɔrnərd] *adj.* **1** triangular. **2** describing any object having three corners or angles: *a three-cornered hat.* **3** of a contest, game, etc., involving three individual people: *a three-cornered tennis game.*

three–D or **3–D** ['θri 'di] *adj., n. —adj.* being three-dimensional or producing a three-dimensional effect.
—n. **1** a film, etc. having a three-dimensional effect. **2** a system producing this effect.

three–deck•er ['θri 'dɛkər] *n.* **1** any ship having three decks. **2** formerly, a fighting ship having three decks of guns. **3** anything having three storeys, layers, or parts: *a club sandwich is a three-decker.* **4** (*adjl.*) having three storeys, layers, or parts: *We built a three-decker bunkbed at the cottage.*

three–di•men•sion•al ['θri də'mɛnʃənəl] *or* ['θri daɪ'mɛnʃənəl] *adj.* **1** of, having, or having to do with the three dimensions of width, depth, and height. **2** appearing to have depth as well as height and width, especially of flat images which have the illusion of depth. **3** of a film, etc., producing an effect of depth by stereoscopic means. **4** of a character in a novel, play, etc., true to life.

three•fold ['θri,fould] *adj., adv., n. —adj.* **1** three times as much or as many. **2** having three parts.
—adv. or n. three times as much or as many.

three–four ['θri 'fɔr] *adj. Music.* indicating or having three quarter notes in a bar or measure, the first of which is accented, as in a waltz.

three–mile limit ['θri 'mɑɪl] the traditional limit of a nation's territorial waters, according to international law, being three nautical miles (almost 6 km) from shore. This was extended to 12 nautical miles (about 22 km) by international agreement in 1982.

three•pence ['θrʌpəns] *or* ['θrɛpəns] *n. Brit.* the sum of three pence.

three•pen•ny ['θrʌpəni], ['θrɛpəni], *or* ['θri,pɛni] *adj., n. —adj.* **1** of little worth; cheap. **2** *Brit.* formerly, worth or costing three pence.
—n. THREEPENNY BIT.

threepenny bit *Brit.* a former British coin worth three pence.

three–piece ['θri 'pis] *adj.* consisting of three separate but matching pieces, as a man's suit of jacket, vest, and pants, or a living-room suite of chesterfield, chair, and love seat: *a three-piece suit, a three-piece suite.*

three–ply ['θri ,plaɪ] *adj.* having three thicknesses, layers, folds, or strands: *three-ply yarn, three-ply tissue.*

three–point blanket ['θri 'pɔɪnt] *Cdn.* the heaviest grade of POINT BLANKET made by the Hudson's Bay Company.

three–pointer ['θri 'pɔɪntər] *n. Cdn.* THREE-POINT BLANKET.

three–point landing ['θri 'pɔɪnt] of an aircraft, a perfect landing in which the two main wheels and the tail or nose wheel touch down simultaneously.

three–point turn ['θri 'pɔɪnt] a standard method of turning a motor vehicle 180° using forward and reverse gears and involving three steps, each moving the vehicle through an arc.

three–quar•ter ['θri 'kwɔrtər] *adj.* **1** three-four: *three-quarter time.* **2** consisting of three fourths of anything. **3** of a portrait, showing the face at an angle between profile and full face, or going down to the hips: *a three-quarter portrait of the prime minister.* **4** of the binding of a book, using one material, such as leather, for the spine and part of each cover and a different material for the rest.

three R's reading, writing, and arithmetic.

three–ring circus ['θri 'rɪŋ] **1** a circus in which there are simultaneous acts being performed in each of three rings. **2** a situation in which there is a confusing or dazzling array of activities.

three•score ['θri,skɔr] *adj.* three times twenty; 60.

three•some ['θrisəm] *n.* **1** a group of three people. **2** any game played by three people. **3** the players in such a game.

three–wheel•er ['θri ,wilər] *n.* a tricycle or other vehicle with three wheels.

thren•o•dy ['θrɛnədi] *n., pl.* **-dies.** a song of lamentation, especially at a person's death. Also, **threnode** ['θrinoud]. ⟨< Gk. *thrēnōidia* < *thrēnos* lament + *ōidē* song⟩ **—thre'nod•ic** [θrə'nɒdɪk], *adj.* **—'thren•o•dist,** *n.*

thre•o•nine ['θriə,nin] *or* ['θriənɪn] *n.* an essential amino acid, obtained from the hydrolysis of many proteins, and considered essential for growth.

thresh [θrɛʃ] *v.* **1** separate the grain or seeds from (wheat, etc.): *Nowadays most farmers use a machine instead of a flail to thresh their wheat.* **2** toss about; move violently; thrash.
thresh out, settle by thorough discussion.
thresh over, go over again and again. ⟨OE *threscan*⟩

thresh•er ['θrɛʃər] *n.* **1** a person who threshes. **2** a machine used for separating the grain or seeds from the stalks and other parts of wheat, oats, etc. **3** a large shark (*Alopias vulpinus*) having a tail with a very long upper lobe.

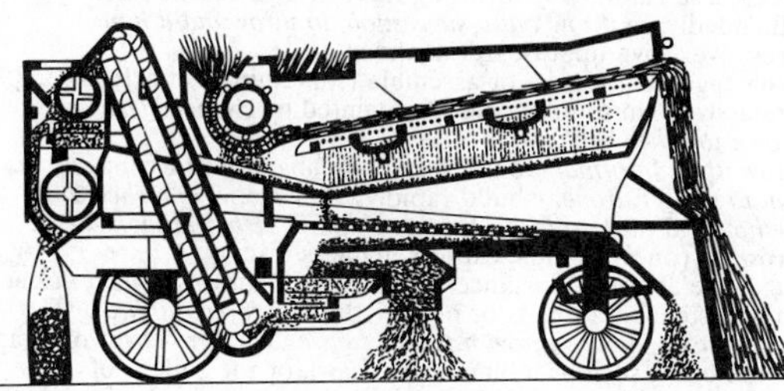

A threshing machine. The whole wheat is put in at the top, and travels along a thresher which separates the grain from the chaff. The chaff is thrown out at the side. The grain travels along conveyor belts, is further threshed and eventually travels up a conveyor belt where it is dropped into a container.

threshing machine a machine for separating the grain, or seeds, from the stalks and other parts of wheat, oats, etc.

thresh•old ['θrɛʃould] *or* ['θrɛʃhould] *n.* **1** a piece of wood or stone under a door. **2** doorway. **3** the point of entering; a beginning point: *The scientist was on the threshold of an important discovery.* **4** *Psychology and physiology.* the limit below which a given stimulus ceases to be perceptible, or the point beyond which two stimuli cannot be differentiated. **5** *Physics.* the limit below which no reaction occurs. ⟨OE *therscold, threscold,* rel. to THRASH tread⟩

threshold trait *Genetics.* a trait with MULTIFACTORIAL INHERITANCE, in which only individuals with genotypes beyond a threshold at the extreme limit of the range are affected. It is characteristic of many common congenital malformations.

threw [θru] *v.* pt. of THROW.

thrice [θrəis] *adv. Archaic or poetic.* **1** three times. **2** three times as many; three times as much. **3** very; extremely. ⟨ME *thries* < OE *thriga* thrice⟩

thrid [θrɪd] *v.* **thrid•ded, thrid•ding.** *Archaic or dialect.* thread.

thrift [θrɪft] *n.* **1** the absence of waste; economical management; the habit of saving: *By thrift she managed to get along on her small salary.* **2** any of several perennial plants (genus *Armeria*) related to the sea lavender, especially *A. maritima*, native to mountainous, marshy, and sandy coastal regions of Eurasia and North America, having clusters of pink or white flowers. ⟨< *thrive*⟩

thrift•less ['θrɪftlɪs] *adj.* without thrift; wasteful. **—'thrift•less•ly,** *adv.* **—'thrift•less•ness,** *n.*

thrift shop a second-hand store, usually managed and staffed by a charitable organization for the benefit of its projects.

thrift•y ['θrɪfti] *adj.* **thrift•i•er, thrift•i•est. 1** careful in spending; economical; saving. **2** thriving or prosperous: *a thrifty plant, a thrifty farm.* **—'thrift•i•ly,** *adv.* **—'thrift•i•ness,** *n.*
☛ *Syn.* **1.** See note at ECONOMICAL.

thrill [θrɪl] *n., v. —n.* **1** a shivering, exciting feeling. **2** a vibrating or quivering; throbbing; tremor. **3** something causing great pleasure, emotion, or excitement: *Being here is a real thrill for me.* **4** thrilling quality: *the thrill of freedom after long imprisonment.*
—v. **1** give a shivering, exciting feeling to: *Stories of adventure thrilled him.* **2** have a shivering, exciting feeling. **3** quiver; tremble: *Her voice thrilled with terror.* ⟨var. of *thirl* < OE *thyrlian* pierce < *thurh* through⟩ **—'thrill•ing•ly,** *adv.*

thrill•er ['θrɪlər] *n.* **1** a person or thing that thrills. **2** *Informal.* a very suspenseful story, play, or film, especially one involving a murder.

thrill•ing ['θrɪlɪŋ] *adj., v. —adj.* exciting.
—v. ppr. of THRILL.

thrips [θrɪps] *n., pl.* **thrips.** any of numerous small or minute insects (order Thysanoptera) having long, narrow wings fringed with hairs, and mouthparts adapted for sucking plant juices. Many thrips are serious plant pests. ⟨< L < Gk. *thrips* woodworm⟩

thrive [θraɪv] *v.* **throve** or **thrived, thrived** or **thriv•en, thriv•ing. 1** grow vigorously and well; flourish: *thriving crops. The garden is thriving under his care.* **2** be successful; prosper: *Her business is thriving.* ⟨ME < ON *thrífa(sk)*⟩ **—'thriv•ing•ly,** *adv.*

thriv•en ['θrɪvən] *v.* a pp. of THRIVE.

throat [θrout] *n.* **1** the front of the neck. **2** the passage from the mouth to the stomach or the lungs. **3** any narrowed opening or passage: *the throat of a mine.*
cut (one's) **own throat,** *Informal.* cause one's own downfall.
jump down (someone's) **throat,** *Informal.* attack or criticize a person with sudden violence.
lump in (one's) **throat, a** a feeling of inability to swallow. **b** a feeling of being about to cry: *The story brought a lump to his throat.*
ram (something) **down** (someone's) **throat,** force (something) on someone's attention; force acceptance of (something).
stick in (one's) **throat, a** be hard or unpleasant to say: *The apology stuck in his throat.* **b** be hard to accept: *Her criticism, though just, stuck in my throat.* ⟨OE *throte*⟩

throat•ed ['θroutɪd] *adj.* having a throat, especially of a specified kind (*usually used in compounds*): *a ruby-throated hummingbird.*

throat•y ['θrouti] *adj.* **throat•i•er, throat•i•est. 1** produced or uttered from far back in the throat; low-pitched and resonant: *a throaty voice.* **2** deep and resonant as if produced far back in the throat. **—'throat•i•ly,** *adv.* **—'throat•i•ness,** *n.*

throb [θrɒb] *v.* **throbbed, throb•bing;** *n. —v.* **1** beat more rapidly or strongly than normally: *Our hearts were still throbbing from the long climb up the hill.* **2** beat or vibrate steadily. **3** quiver; tremble: *They were throbbing with excitement.*
—n. **1** an abnormally rapid or strong beat: *the throb of our hearts.* **2** a steady beat or vibration: *She felt the throb of the little plane's engine.* **3** a quiver; tremble. ⟨ME *throbbe(n)*; ? imitative⟩ **—'throb•bing•ly,** *adv.*

throe [θrou] *n.* Usually, **throes,** *pl.* **1** a violent pang or pangs; great pain: *the throes of death, the throes of childbirth.* **2** a hard or agonizing struggle: *a poet in the throes of creation, the throes of revolution.* ⟨? a fusion of OE *thrōwian* suffer, and *thrāwan* twist; throw⟩
☛ *Hom.* THROW.

throm•bin ['θrɒmbɪn] *n.* the enzyme of the blood, formed from prothrombin, that promotes clotting.

throm•bo•cyte ['θrɒmbə,səit] *n.* a blood cell that initiates clotting; platelet. ⟨< Gk. *thrombos* clot + E *-cyte*⟩ **—,throm•bo'cyt•ic** [-'sɪtɪk], *adj.*

throm•bo•phle•bi•tis [,θrɒmbouflə'bəitis] *n.* inflammation of the lining of a vein due to a blood clot.

throm•bo•sis [θrɒm'bousɪs] *n.* the formation of a blood clot in a blood vessel or in the heart. ⟨< NL < Gk. *thrombōsis*, ult. < *thrombos* clot⟩ **—throm'bot•ic** [-'bɒtɪk], *adj.*

throm•bus ['θrɒmbəs] *n., pl.* **-bi** [-baɪ] *or* [-bi]. a blood clot causing thrombosis.

throne [θroun] *n., v.* **throned, thron•ing;** *—n.* **1** the chair on which a king, queen, bishop, or other person of high rank sits during ceremonies. **2** the power or authority of a king, queen, etc. **3** the person who sits on a throne; sovereign.
—v. enthrone. ⟨ME < OF < L < Gk. *thronos*⟩

throng [θrɒŋ] *n., v. —n.* a crowd; multitude.
—v. **1** crowd; fill with a crowd. **2** come together in a crowd; go or press in large numbers. ⟨OE *(ge)thrang*⟩
☛ *Syn. n.* See note at CROWD.

thros•tle ['θrɒsəl] *n.* **1** a thrush, especially the song thrush. **2** a spinning machine that continuously produces yarn from wool, cotton, etc. ⟨OE⟩

throt•tle ['θrɒtəl] *n., v.* **-tled, -tling.** *—n.* **1** a valve regulating the flow of steam, gasoline vapour, etc. to (an engine); especially, the valve controlling the gasoline vapour entering the cylinders of an internal combustion engine. **2** a lever or pedal working such a valve. The throttle of a car is called an accelerator. **3** throat or windpipe.
—v. **1** lessen the speed of (an engine) or the flow of (fuel, steam, etc.) by closing a throttle (*often used with* **down** *or* **back**): *to*

throttle down a steam engine. **2** stop the breath of by pressure on the throat: choke; strangle: *The thief throttled the dog to keep it from barking.* **3** stop or check the expression or action of; suppress: *Increased tariffs soon throttled trade between the two countries.* ⟨ME; perhaps dim. of *throat*⟩

through [θru] *prep., adv., adj.* —*prep.* **1** from end to end or from side to side of; between the parts of; from beginning to end of; in one side of and out the other: *The soldiers marched through the town. The men cut a tunnel through a mountain.* **2** here and there in or among; over; around: *We travelled through Québec, visiting many old towns. She found weeds coming up all through her tomato plants.* **3** because of; by reason of: *The woman refused help through pride.* **4** by means of; by way of: *He became rich through hard work and ability. We returned from Nova Scotia to Ontario through the States.* **5** at the end of; finished with: *We are through school at three o'clock.* **6** **a** during the whole of; throughout: *to work from dawn through the day and into the night.* **b** during and until the finish of: *to help a person through hard times.* **7** up to and including: *The store is open Monday through Saturday.* **8** past without stopping: *She drove right through a stop sign.*
—*adv.* **1** from end to end; from side to side; between the parts of something; in one side and out the other: *The bullet hit the wall and went through.* **2** completely; thoroughly: *He walked home in the rain and was wet through.* **3** from beginning to end: *She read the book through.* **4** along the whole distance; all the way: *The train goes through to Vancouver.*
through and through, completely; thoroughly. See also idioms with **through** at COME, GET, PULL, PUT, and SEE.
—*adj.* **1** **a** going all the way without change: *a through train from Montréal to Vancouver.* **b** for the whole distance or journey: *a through ticket.* **c** going straight on without stopping: *through traffic.* **2** at the end; done; finished: *I am almost through. I'm through with that good-for-nothing.* **3** passing or extending from one end, side, surface, etc. to or beyond the other. ⟨earlier *thourgh,* OE *thurh*⟩
☛ *Syn. prep.* **3, 4.** See note at BY.

through•out [θru'ʌut] *prep., adv.* —*prep.* all the way through; through all; in every part or during the whole course of: *Canada Day is celebrated throughout Canada. We skied almost every weekend throughout the winter.*
—*adv.* in or to every part or from beginning to end: *The house is well built throughout. He remained stubborn throughout.*

through•put ['θru,pʊt] *n.* **1** the amount of goods or material handled or processed: *The elevator's records show that the throughput of wheat has increased over last year.* **2** the rate of such handling or processing: *The computerized billing system has a throughput of 200 invoices per minute.*

through street a street on which traffic is given the right of way at intersections. Compare STOP STREET.

through•way ['θru,wei] *n.* a thoroughfare, especially an expressway.

throve [θrouv] *v.* a pt. of THRIVE.

throw [θrou] *v.* **threw, thrown, throw•ing;** *n.* —*v.* **1** **a** cast; toss; hurl: *to throw a ball.* **b** propel through the air with the aid of a catapult, gun, hose, etc.: *The fire hose threw water on the fire.* **2** bring to the ground: *His horse threw him.* **3** put carelessly or in haste: *Throw some clothes on and run.* **4** put or move quickly or by force: *to throw oneself onto a bed, to throw a man into prison.* **5** put into a certain condition: *to throw a person into confusion.* **6** turn, direct, or deliver, especially quickly: *to throw a punch. She threw a glance at each car that passed us.* **7** move (a lever, etc.) that connects or disconnects parts of a switch, clutch, or other mechanism. **8** connect or disconnect thus. **9** shed. A snake throws its skin. **10** of some animals, bring forth (young). **11** *Informal.* let an opponent win (a race, game, etc.), often for money. **12** make (a specified cast) with dice: *I threw two sixes.* **13** twist (silk) into threads. **14** shape on a potter's wheel: *to throw a bowl from a ball of clay.* **15** *Informal.* **a** give (a party, etc.). **b** have (a fit, tantrum. etc.) **16** project: *The lamp threw his shadow on the wall.* **17** *Informal.* confuse; disconcert (*often used with* **off**): *Her remark really threw me for a minute.*
throw a monkey wrench into, complicate; make difficult or problematic: *The rail strike threw a monkey wrench into our holiday plans.*
throw away, a get rid of; discard. **b** waste: *to throw away money, to throw away an opportunity.* **c** *Theatre.* speak (a line or speech) in a deliberately casual way.
throw back, revert to an ancestral type.
throw cold water on, discourage by being indifferent or unwilling.
throw in, add as a gift: *Our grocer often throws in an extra apple.*
throw off, a get rid of. **b** cause to lose: *to throw a hound off the scent.* **c** *Informal.* produce (a poem, etc.) in an offhand manner. **d** put out of sync or out of harmony. **e** get free from (a pursuer); shake; evade.
throw (oneself) **at,** try very hard to get the love, friendship, or favour of.
throw (oneself) **into,** engage in wholeheartedly.
throw (oneself) **on** or **upon,** appeal to as one's last or only hope.
throw (one's) **voice,** practise ventriloquism.
throw open, a open suddenly or widely. **b** remove all obstacles or restrictions from.
throw out, a get rid of; discard. **b** reject. **c** expel. **d** *Baseball.* put out (a base runner) by throwing the ball to a base. **e** utter offhandedly: *to throw out a suggestion, to throw out a hint.*
throw over, give up; discard; abandon.
throw together, a make or assemble (something) quickly and carelessly. **b** cause to become acquainted by chance: *They were thrown together by the war.*
throw up, a *Informal.* vomit. **b** give up; abandon: *He threw up his plan to go to Europe.* **c** build rapidly: *They threw up a shed in a few hours.* **d** raise quickly: *He threw up the sash and looked out.*
throw up (one's) **hands,** express helpless dismay.
—*n.* **1** the act or an instance of throwing: *That was a good throw.* **2** the distance a thing is or may be thrown: *a record throw. The river is just a stone's throw from the house.* **3** a light cover or wrap for the body, such as a blanket or shawl, or for a piece of furniture to protect or decorate it. **4** the act or result of casting dice: *a throw of six.* **5** a particular method or technique of throwing. **6** a venture or risk. **7** *Geology.* the vertical displacement of part of a bed of rock, produced by a fault. ⟨OE *thrāwan* twist⟩ —**'throw•er,** *n.*
☛ *Hom.* THROE.
☛ *Syn. v.* **1. Throw,** TOSS, CAST = send something through the air by a sudden twist or quick movement of the arm. **Throw** is the general word: *The children threw pillows at each other.* **Toss** means throw lightly or carelessly: *Please toss me the matches.* **Cast** is literary or archaic in the literal meaning of 'throw with the hand' (except in special uses, as in games, voting, fishing, sailing—*They cast anchor*) but it is often used figuratively: *She cast dignity to the winds and ran.*

throw•a•way ['θrouə,wei] *n.* **1** a free handbill or leaflet carrying advertising or other information; handout. **2** anything designed to be discarded after use. **3** (*adjl.*) meant to be discarded or thrown away after use; disposable: *throwaway bottles.* **4** (*adjl.*) of a remark, a line of dialogue, etc., spoken or delivered in an offhand or casual way: *a throwaway line in a play.* **5** (*adjl.*) accustomed to or inclined toward throwing away or wastefulness: *North America has become a throwaway society; now even cameras are disposable.*

throw•back ['θrou,bæk] *n.* **1** a reversion to an ancestral type or character. **2** an instance of such a reversion: *The boy seemed to be a throwback to his great-grandmother.*

thrown [θroun] *v.* pp. of THROW.

throw rug SCATTER RUG.

thrum[1] [θrʌm] *v.* **thrummed, thrum•ming;** *n.* —*v.* **1** play on (a stringed instrument) by plucking the strings, especially in an idle, mechanical, or unskilful way: *to thrum a guitar.* **2** of a guitar, etc. or its strings, sound when thrummed on. **3** drum or tap idly (on) with the fingers: *to thrum on a table.* **4** **a** recite, speak, or tell in a monotonous or droning way. **b** hum (a melody).
—*n.* **1** the sound made by thrumming. **2** an act of thrumming: *With one thrum on my guitar he broke two strings.* ⟨imitative⟩ —**'thrum•mer,** *n.*

thrum[2] [θrʌm] *n., v.* **thrummed, thrum•ming.** —*n.* **1** the end of the warp thread or threads left unwoven on the loom after the web is cut off. **2** loose thread or yarn. **3** a tuft or fringe.
—*v.* furnish with or make out of thrums. ⟨OE *thrum;* in *tungethrum* tongue ligament⟩

thrush[1] [θrʌʃ] *n.* any of a subfamily (Turdinae, of the family Muscicapidae) of songbirds found throughout the world, especially those species having brownish plumage with a spotted breast. This group includes some of the finest singers among birds, such as the nightingale and the hermit thrush. Some authorities classify thrushes as a separate family (Turdidae). ⟨OE *thrȳsce*⟩

thrush[2] [θrʌʃ] *n.* **1** **a** a contagious disease, especially of very young babies, in which white blisters form in the mouth and throat and on the lips. Thrush is caused by a fungus (*Candida albicans*). **b** a similar vaginal infection. **2** a diseased condition of a horse's foot. ⟨?< ON *thruskr*⟩

thrust [θrʌst] *v.* **thrust, thrust•ing;** *n.* —*v.* **1** push with force: *He thrust his hands into his pockets. She thrust her brother aside and grabbed the plate of cookies.* **2** forcefully push oneself or one's hand; force one's way; lunge: *Drawing a deep breath, she thrust forward into the crowd.* **3** drive (a weapon or instrument)

into something or cause to pierce something by pushing; stab: *He thrust his fork into the potato.* **4** drive a sharp instrument into; pierce; stab: *She thrust her attacker through with her dagger.* **5** put forth; extend; stretch: *The tree thrust its roots deep into the ground. The Sahara thrusts further south every year.*
thrust (something) **on** (someone), force or impose something on someone.
—n. **1** a sudden or forceful push: *With a quick thrust, she hid the book behind the pillow.* **2** a push or lunge with a weapon or instrument, especially a pointed one: *A thrust with the pin broke the balloon.* **3** a sudden attack. **4** *Mechanics.* the continuous sideways force of one part of a structure against another, such as the pressure of an arch against a pillar. **5 a** the endwise push exerted by the rotation of a propeller, producing forward motion. **b** the force exerted by a high-speed jet of gas, etc. ejected to the rear, as in a jet engine, producing forward motion. **6** main purpose or direction: *the thrust of an argument.* **7** *Geology.* a fault that is nearly horizontal, with older strata overlapping more recent ones. ⟨ME < ON *thrýsta*⟩

thrust•er [ˈθrʌstər] *n.* **1** someone or something that thrusts. **2** a small manoeuvring rocket engine that provides extra or correcting thrust on a spacecraft or high-altitude airplane, as on re-entry.

thud [θʌd] *n., v.* **thud•ded, thud•ding.** *—n.* **1** a dull sound caused by a blow or fall: *The book hit the floor with a thud.* **2** a blow or thump.
—v. hit, move, or land with a thud. ⟨? ME *thudden* < OE *thyddan* strike⟩

thug [θʌg] *n.* **1** a ruffian; cutthroat; gangster. **2 Thug,** formerly, in India, a member of a Hindu organization of robbers and murderers in the service of the goddess Kali. ⟨< Hind. < Skt. *sthaga* rogue⟩ **—ˈthug•gish,** *adj.*

thug•gee [θʌˈgi] *or* [ˈθʌgi] *n.* robbery and murder as practised by the Thugs. ⟨< Hind. *thagi*⟩

thug•ger•y [ˈθʌgəri] *n.* violent or brutal acts or behaviour.

thu•ja [ˈθujə] *n.* **1** any coniferous evergreen tree of the genus *Thuja*, having small leaves closely set to the branches or stems. **2** arborvitae.

Thu•le [ˈθuli] *or* (esp. def. 2) [ˈtuli] *n.* **1** the part of the world that the ancient Greeks and Romans regarded as farthest north, that is, some island or region north of Britain. **2** an Inuit culture of N Greenland, lasting from about A.D. 500 to 1400. **3** See ULTIMA THULE. ⟨< L < Gk. *Thoulē*⟩

thu•li•um [ˈθjuliəm] *or* [ˈθuliəm] *n.* a metallic element of the rare-earth group. *Symbol*: Tm; *at.no.* 69; *at.mass* 168.93. ⟨< NL *thulium* < *Thule*⟩

thumb [θʌm] *n., v.* *—n.* **1 a** the short finger of the human hand that is nearest the wrist and can be opposed to the other fingers. **b** the corresponding digital part in some other vertebrates. **2** the part of a glove, mitten, etc. that covers the thumb.
all thumbs, very clumsy, awkward, etc.: *I'm all thumbs when it comes to tying bows.*
thumbs down, a a gesture of disapproval, rejection, or disappointment, made by closing the hand and pointing the thumb downward: *She just gave us a thumbs down when we asked how she liked the slogan.* **b** any expression of disapproval, rejection, or disappointment: *The principal gave them thumbs down on the proposal for another field trip.*
thumbs up, a a gesture of acceptance or satisfaction, made by closing the hand and pointing the thumb up: *He smiled and signalled thumbs up as he came out of the employment office.* **b** an expression of satisfaction: *"Thumbs up!" she called as she came out of the examination room.*
under (someone's) **thumb,** under someone's control or influence: *He's got them all under his thumb and they'll do anything he tells them.*
—v. **1** leaf through or turn (the pages of a book, magazine, etc.) rapidly. **2** soil or wear by or as if by repeated leafing or paging through: *The books were badly thumbed.* **3** *Informal.* ask for or get (a free ride) by signalling with the thumb to passing motorists: *He thumbed a ride into town when his car broke down.* **4** travel by thumbing rides; hitchhike: *She thumbed her way from Calgary to Winnipeg.*
thumb off, *Hockey.* indicate by a jerk of the thumb that (a given player) has been penalized for an infraction of the rules and that he or she is to take his or her place in the penalty box.
thumb (one's) **nose,** express scorn or defiance by or as if by placing one's thumb on the end of one's nose and extending the fingers: *The rude little girl thumbed her nose at a passerby. He thumbed his nose at the promise of success and went on his way.* ⟨OE *thūma*⟩ **—ˈthumb,like,** *adj.* **—ˈthumb•less,** *adj.*

thumb index a series of labelled, usually semi-circular cuts down the side of a reference book, Bible, etc., making it easier to find the desired section.

thumb•nail [ˈθʌm,neil] *n.* **1** the nail of the thumb. **2** something very small or short.

thumbnail sketch **1** a small or quickly drawn picture: *a thumbnail sketch of a child at play.* **2** a short description.

thumb•screw [ˈθʌm,skru] *n.* **1** a screw made so that its head can be easily turned with the thumb and a finger. **2** formerly, an instrument of torture for squeezing the thumbs.

thumb•stall [ˈθʌm,stɒl] *n.* a protective sheath for the thumb.

thumb•tack [ˈθʌm,tæk] *n.* a tack having a broad, flat head, designed to be pressed into a surface with the thumb.

thump [θʌmp] *v., n.* *—v.* **1** strike with something thick and heavy: *He thumped the table with his fist.* **2** strike against (something) heavily and noisily: *The shutters thumped the wall in the wind.* **3** make a dull sound; pound: *The hammer thumped against the wood.* **4** beat violently or heavily: *His heart always thumped as he walked past the cemetery at night.* **5** beat or thrash severely.
—n. **1** a blow with something thick and heavy; a heavy knock. **2** the dull sound made by a blow, knock, or fall. ⟨imitative⟩ **—ˈthump•er,** *n.*

thump•ing [ˈθʌmpɪŋ] *adj., v.* *—adj. Informal.* great; huge; whopping.
—v. ppr. of THUMP. **—ˈthump•ing•ly,** *adv.*

thun•der [ˈθʌndər] *n., v.* *—n.* **1** the loud rumbling or crashing noise that often follows a flash of lightning. It is caused by a disturbance of the air resulting from the discharge of electricity. **2** any noise like thunder: *the thunder of Niagara Falls, a thunder of applause.* **3** threats or denunciations. **4** THUNDERBOLT (def. 1).
in thunder (*intensifier with interrogatives*), ever; on earth: *What in thunder is she doing now?*
steal (someone's) **thunder,** make someone's idea, method, etc. less effective by using it first or doing something better or more startling: *The Liberals stole the Tories' thunder by announcing their election platform first.*
—v. **1** give forth thunder: *We heard it thunder in the distance.* **2** make a noise like thunder. **3** utter very loudly; roar: *to thunder a reply.* **4** utter a threat or denunciation loudly, violently, or impressively: *The newspaper article thundered against the injustices of the political system.* ⟨OE *thunor*⟩ **—ˈthun•der•er,** *n.*

thun•der•bird [ˈθʌndər,bərd] *n.* in the mythology of several First Nations peoples, a huge bird that creates thunder with its beating wings and lightning with its flashing eyes. Carved representations of the thunderbird are often found on totem poles of the Pacific Coast peoples.

thun•der•bolt [ˈθʌndər,boult] *n.* **1** a flash of lightning and the thunder that follows it. **2** a supposed bolt or missile thrown to earth as a destructive force by lightning, especially when indicative of the anger of the gods or of God. **3** something sudden, startling, and terrible: *The news of his death came as a thunderbolt.*

thun•der•clap [ˈθʌndər,klæp] *n.* **1** a loud crash of thunder. **2** something sudden or startling.

thun•der•cloud [ˈθʌndər,klaʊd] *n.* a dark, electrically charged cloud that brings thunder and lightning.

Thun•der•er [ˈθʌndərər] *n.* Jupiter; Zeus.

thun•der•head [ˈθʌndər,hɛd] *n.* one of the round, swelling masses of cumulus clouds often appearing before thunderstorms and frequently developing into thunderclouds.

A thunderhead

thun•der•ing [ˈθʌndərɪŋ] *adj., v.* *—adj.* **1** making thunder; extremely loud. **2** *Informal.* unusual; superlative; extremely big or great.
—v. ppr. of THUNDER. **—ˈthun•der•ing•ly,** *adv.*

thun•der•ous [ˈθʌndərəs] *adj.* **1** producing thunder. **2** making a noise like thunder. **—ˈthun•der•ous•ly,** *adv.*

thun•der•show•er [ˈθʌndər,ʃaʊər] *n.* a rainshower accompanied by thunder and lightning.

thun•der•squall [ˈθʌndər,skwɒl] *n.* a squall accompanied by thunder and lightning.

thun•der•storm [ˈθʌndər,stɔrm] *n.* a storm accompanied by thunder and lightning and, usually, by heavy rain.

thun•der•struck [ˈθʌndər,strʌk] *adj.* overcome, as if hit by a thunderbolt; astonished; amazed.

thun•de•ry [ˈθʌndəri] *adj.* thunderous.

thunk [θʌŋk] *v., n.* —*v.* PLUNK (def. 2).
—*n.* plunk.

thu•ri•ble [ˈθʊrəbəl] *or* [ˈθɜrəbəl] *n.* censer. ⟨ME < L *t(h)uribulum* < *t(h)us, thuris* incense < Gk. *thyos* burnt sacrifice⟩

thu•ri•fer [ˈθʊrəfər] *or* [ˈθɜrəfər] *n. Roman Catholic and Anglican Churches.* the acolyte or server who carries the thurible at High Mass or Sung Eucharist. ⟨< L *thus, thuris* incense + *ferre* carry⟩

Thu•rin•gi•an [θjʊˈrɪndʒiən] *or* [θʊˈrɪndʒiən] *adj., n.* —*adj.* **1** of or having to do with Thuringia, a former state in southern East Germany, or its people. **2** *Geology.* of or having to do with the upper division of the Permian period in Europe.
—*n.* **1** a native or inhabitant of Thuringia. **2** a member of a Germanic tribe living in central Germany till the 6th century.

Thurs. or **Thur.** Thursday.

Thurs•day [ˈθɜrzdei] *or* [ˈθɜrzdi] *n., adv.* —*n.* the fifth day of the week, following Wednesday.
—*adv.* on Thursday: *She's leaving Thursday.* ⟨OE < ON *Thórsdagr*, literally, day of Thor, translation of LL *dies Jovis* day of Jupiter (or Jove)⟩

Thurs•days [ˈθɜrzdeiz] *or* [ˈθɜrzdiz] *adv.* every Thursday: *She works Thursdays.*

thus [ðʌs] *adv.* **1** in this way; in the way just indicated or about to be indicated: *He spoke thus.* **2** accordingly; consequently; therefore: *The evidence was clearly against her claim; thus we decided that she was wrong.* **3** to this extent or degree; so: *thus far.* ⟨OE⟩

thus•ly [ˈðʌsli] *adv. Informal.* THUS (def. 1).

thwack [θwæk] *v., n.* —*v.* strike vigorously with a stick or something flat.
—*n.* a sharp blow with a stick or something flat. ⟨probably imitative⟩

thwart [θwɔrt] *v., n., adj.* —*v.* hinder, defeat, or frustrate; keep from doing something: *The boy's lack of money thwarted his plans for a trip. The enemy's attack was thwarted.*
—*n.* **1** a seat across a boat, on which a rower sits. **2** a brace in a canoe.
—*adj.* lying or situated across something else; transverse or oblique. ⟨ME < ON *thvert*, adv., across, originally neut. of adj. *thverr* transverse⟩
☛ *Syn. v.* See note at FRUSTRATE.

thy [ðaɪ] *adj. Archaic or poetic.* the possessive form of THOU used before a noun beginning with a consonant sound: *"Thy kingdom come, Thy will be done."* Compare THINE. ⟨OE *thīn*⟩
☛ *Usage.* See note at THOU.

thy•la•cine [ˈθaɪlə,saɪn] *or* [ˈθaɪləsɪn] *n.* TASMANIAN WOLF.

thyme [taɪm] *n.* any of several herbs or small shrubs (genus *Thymus*) of the mint family having aromatic leaves, especially a garden herb (*T. vulgaris*) whose dried leaves and flowering tops are used as seasoning. ⟨ME < MF *thym* < L *thymum* < Gk. *thymon*⟩
☛ *Hom.* TIME.

thy•mol [ˈθaɪmoul] *or* [ˈθaɪmɒl] *n.* a crystalline substance obtained from thyme, etc. or made synthetically, used as an antiseptic. *Formula*: $C_{10}H_{13}OH$

thy•mus [ˈθaɪməs] *n.* a ductless, glandlike body situated near the base of the neck, present in the young of most vertebrates but becoming very small or disappearing altogether in adults. The thymus is thought to function in the development of the body's immune system. ⟨< NL < Gk. *thymos*⟩ —**ˈthy•mic,** *adj.*

thy•roid [ˈθaɪrɔɪd] *n.* **1** THYROID GLAND. **2** a medicine made from the thyroid glands of certain animals, used in the treatment of goitre, obesity, etc. **3** THYROID CARTILAGE. **4** (*adjl.*) of or having to do with the thyroid gland or thyroid cartilage. ⟨ult. < Gk. *thyreoeidēs* shieldlike < *thyreos* oblong shield (< *thyra* door) + *eidos* form⟩

thyroid cartilage the principal cartilage of the larynx, which in men forms the Adam's apple.

thyroid gland an important ductless gland in the neck of vertebrates producing a hormone that regulates growth and metabolism.

thy•rox•ine [θaɪˈrɒksin] *or* [θaɪˈrɒksɪn] *n.* an amino acid that is the active hormone produced by the thyroid gland. Thyroxine is also prepared synthetically or obtained from the thyroid glands of animals and is used in the treatment of thyroid disorders. *Formula*: $C_{15}H_{11}I_4NO_4$ Also, **thyroxin.**

thyrse [θɜrs] *n. Botany.* a compound inflorescence (flower cluster), as in the grape and lilac, composed of two simple types of inflorescence: the main axis is a raceme and the secondary axes are cymes. ⟨< F < NL *thyrsus* thyrsus. 17c.⟩

thyr•sus [ˈθɜrsəs] *n., pl.* **-si** [-saɪ] *or* [-si]. **1** *Greek mythology.* a staff or spear tipped with an ornament like a pine cone and sometimes wrapped round with ivy and vine branches, borne by Dionysus (Bacchus) and his followers. **2** thyrse. ⟨< L < Gk. *thyrsos* staff, stem. 18c.⟩

thy•self [ðaɪˈsɛlf] *pron. Archaic or poetic.* the reflexive or intensive form of THOU: *"Thou shalt love thy neighbour as thyself."*
☛ *Usage.* See note at THOU.

ti¹ [ti] *n. Music.* **1** the seventh tone of an eight-tone major scale. **2** the tone B. See DO² for picture. Sometimes, **te.** ⟨See GAMUT⟩
☛ *Hom.* T, TEA, TEE.

ti² [ti] *n.* any Australasian woody plant of the genus *Cordyline* of the agave family, especially *C. terminalis*, having edible roots and leaves used for thatching, fodder, clothing, etc. ⟨various Polynesian langs.⟩
☛ *Hom.* T, TE, TEA, TEE.

Ti titanium.

ti•ar•a [tiˈɛrə] *or* [tiˈɑrə] *n.* **1** a band of gold, jewels, flowers, etc., worn around the head by women as an ornament. **2** *Roman Catholic Church.* **a** the triple crown of the Pope. **b** the position or authority of the Pope. **3** in ancient Persia, a headdress for men. ⟨< L < Gk.⟩

Ti•bet•an [təˈbɛtən] *n., adj.* —*n.* **1** a member of an Asiatic people who are the original inhabitants of Tibet, a region in SW China. **2** a native or inhabitant of Tibet. **3** the language of Tibet, belonging to the Sino-Tibetan language family.
—*adj.* of or having to do with Tibet, its people, or their language.

Ti•bet•o–Bur•man [təˈbɛtou ˈbɜrmən] *n., adj.* —*n.* a branch of the Sino-Tibetan language family. It includes Tibetan and Burmese.
—*adj.* of or relating to this branch or the people who speak these languages.

tib•i•a [ˈtɪbiə] *n., pl.* **-i•ae** [-i,i] *or* [-i,aɪ] or **-i•as. 1** *Anatomy.* the inner and thicker of the two bones of the leg from the knee to the ankle; shinbone. See LEG for picture. **2** in animals or birds, a corresponding bone. **3** the fourth joint of the leg of an insect. **4** in ancient times, a flute originally made from this bone. ⟨< L⟩ —**ˈtib•i•al,** *adj.*

tic [tɪk] *n.* **1** a habitual, involuntary twitching of the muscles, especially those of the face. **2** TIC DOULOUREUX. ⟨< F⟩
☛ *Hom.* TICK.

tic•ca•na•gon [,tɪkəˈnɑgən] *n. Cdn.* See TIKINAGAN.

tic dou•lou•reux [,dulʊˈru]; *French* [duluˈʀœ] trigeminal neuralgia, a disorder characterized by painful spasms in either of the trigeminal nerves. ⟨< F, literally, painful tic⟩

tick¹ [tɪk] *n., v.* —*n.* **1** a sound made by a clock or watch. **2** a sound like it. **3** *Informal.* a moment; instant: *I'll have that ready for you in two ticks.* **4** a small mark used in checking, usually √ or /.
—*v.* **1** make a tick or ticks. **2** mark off by a ticking sound: *The clock ticked away the minutes.* **3** mark an item in a list, etc. with a tick; check (*usually used with* **off**): *I ticked off the groceries I had already bought.* **4** *Informal.* function, work, or go: *What makes that gadget tick?*
tick along, function or proceed smoothly: *The renovations are ticking along just fine.*
ticked off, *Informal.* fed up; annoyed; angry.
tick off, *Informal.* annoy; irritate; anger.
what makes (someone) **tick,** what motivates a person to act or behave in a certain way: *He's very quiet. I wonder what makes him tick.* ⟨probably ult. imitative⟩
☛ *Hom.* TIC.

tick² [tɪk] *n.* **1** any of a large group of small arachnids comprising two families (Ixodidae, the **hard ticks,** and Argasidae, the **soft ticks**), having sucking mouthparts with which they feed on the blood of dogs, cattle, human beings, etc. Some ticks carry infectious diseases. **2** any of various species of usually dipterous insect that live as parasites on cattle, sheep, birds, etc. ⟨OE *ticia*⟩
☛ *Hom.* TIC.

tick³ [tɪk] *n.* **1** the cloth covering of a mattress or pillow. **2** *Informal.* ticking. ⟨probably ult. < L *theca* case < Gk. *thēkē*⟩
☛ *Hom.* TIC.

tick⁴ [tɪk] *n. Informal. Esp. Brit.* credit: *They buy everything on tick.* ⟨< *ticket*⟩

tick•er ['tɪkər] *n.* **1** something that ticks, especially a clock or watch. **2** especially formerly, a telegraphic instrument recording stock market reports or news on a paper tape (**ticker tape**). **3** *Slang.* the heart. ⟨< *tick*¹⟩

tick•et ['tɪkɪt] *n., v.* —*n.* **1** a card or other piece of paper showing that a fee or fare has been paid: *a theatre ticket, an airline ticket, a lottery ticket.* **2** an official notification that a person is charged with a traffic violation: *a parking ticket, a ticket for speeding.* **3** a label or tag attached to an article for sale, showing its size, price, etc. **4** *U.S.* the list of candidates to be voted on that belong to one political party. **5** *Informal.* a certificate: *a chief engineer's ticket.*
that's the ticket, *Informal.* that's the correct or desirable thing.
—*v.* **1** put a ticket on; mark with a ticket: *All articles in the store are ticketed with the price.* **2** describe or mark as if by a ticket; label; designate; characterize. **3** furnish with a ticket, such as a railway or airline ticket. **4** give or attach a ticket to, indicating a traffic violation: *She was ticketed for speeding.* ⟨< F *étiquette* ticket < Gmc.⟩

tick fever ROCKY MOUNTAIN SPOTTED FEVER.

ticking¹ ['tɪkɪŋ] *v.* ppr. of TICK¹.

tick•ing² ['tɪkɪŋ] *n.* a strong cotton or linen cloth, used to cover mattresses and pillows and to make tents and awnings.

tick•le¹ ['tɪkəl] *v.* **-led, -ling;** *n.* —*v.* **1** touch lightly causing little thrills, shivers, or wriggles and, often, laughter. **2** have a feeling like this; cause such a feeling: *My nose tickles.* **3** excite pleasantly; amuse; delight or gratify: *The story tickled her.* **4** play, stir, get, etc. with light touches or strokes. **5** refresh or jog (the memory).
be tickled pink, *Informal.* be very pleased.
tickle (someone's) **fancy,** appeal to someone.
tickle the ivories, *Informal.* play the piano.
—*n.* **1** a tingling or itching feeling. **2** the act or a bout of tickling. ⟨ME *tik(e)le(n)*⟩

tick•le² ['tɪkəl] *n. Cdn., esp. Nfld.* **1** a narrow channel between an island and the mainland or, sometimes, between islands. **2** a narrow entrance to a harbour. ⟨? < Brit. dial. *stickle* rapids, riffle⟩

tick•ler ['tɪklər] *n.* **1** a person or device that tickles. **2** *Informal.* a memorandum book, card index, or other device kept as a reminder. **3** *Informal.* a difficult or puzzling problem.

tick•lish ['tɪklɪʃ] *adj.* **1** sensitive to tickling. **2** requiring careful handling; delicate, precarious, or risky: *a ticklish situation. A canoe is a ticklish craft.* **3** easily annoyed or offended: *a proud man and a ticklish fellow.* —**'tick•lish•ly,** *adv.* —**'tick•lish•ness,** *n.*

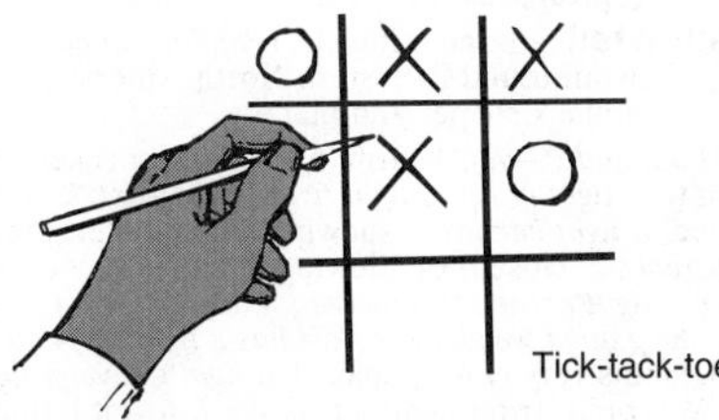
Tick-tack-toe

tick–tack–toe [,tɪk tæk 'tou] *n.* a game in which two players alternately put circles or crosses in a figure of nine squares, each player trying to be the first to fill three spaces in a row with his or her mark. Also, **tic-tac-toe, Xs and Os.**

tick–tock ['tɪk ,tɒk] *n., v.* —*n.* the sound made by a clock having a pendulum.
—*v.* make this sound; tick: *A tall clock tick-tocked on the stair.*

tick•y–tack•y ['tɪki 'tæki] *n., adj. Informal.* —*n.* **1** rubbish; worthless material. **2** anything that reflects poor taste.
—*adj.* worthless; in poor taste.

tic–tac–toe [,tɪk tæk 'tou] *n.* See TICK-TACK-TOE.

t.i.d. of medicine, (take) three times a day (for L *ter in die*).

tid•al ['taɪdəl] *adj.* **1** of, having to do with, caused by, or having tides: *tidal waters, a tidal breeze.* **2** dependent on the state of the tide as to time of arrival and departure: *a tidal steamer.* —**'tid•al•ly,** *adv.*

tidal energy the kinetic energy of large bodies of water, manifested in waves: *Tidal energy can be harnessed to make electricity.*

tidal wave **1** a large wave or sudden increase in the level of water along a shore, caused by unusually strong winds. **2** a destructive ocean wave which is caused by an underwater earthquake. **3** any great movement or manifestation of feeling, opinion, or the like: *a tidal wave of popular indignation.*

tid•bit ['tɪd,bɪt] *n.* a very pleasing bit of food, news, etc. Also, **titbit.** ⟨< *tid* nice + *bit* morsel⟩

tid•dly•winks ['tɪdli,wɪŋks] *n.* a game in which the players try to make small coloured disks jump into a cup by pressing on their edges with a larger disk (*used with a singular verb*). Also, **tiddledywinks** ['tɪdəldi-]. ⟨origin uncertain⟩

tide¹ [taɪd] *n., v.* **tid•ed, tid•ing.** —*n.* **1** the rise and fall of the ocean and connected waterways, usually taking place about every twelve hours, caused by the attraction of the moon and the sun. **2** anything that rises and falls like the tide: *the tide of popular opinion.* **3** a stream; current; flood. **4** *Poetic.* a season; time (*usually used in compounds*): *Eastertide.*
turn the tide, change a condition to the opposite.
—*v.* **1** drift with the tide. **2** get (a ship) into or out of a harbour, etc. with the help of the tide.
tide over, help to overcome a difficulty, etc., with emergency aid in anticipation of a more permanent solution: *He said twenty dollars would tide him over until payday.* ⟨OE *tīd*, originally, time⟩ —**'tide•less,** *adj.*

tide² [taɪd] *v.* **tid•ed, tid•ing.** *Archaic.* betide; happen. ⟨OE *tīdan*⟩

tide•land ['taɪd,lænd] *or* ['taɪdlənd] *n.* land that is under water at high tide and exposed at low tide.

tideland spruce *Cdn.* a tall spruce tree (*Picea sitchensis*) found on the Pacific Slope. Also, **Sitka spruce.**

tide line *Cdn.* a line etched near the top of a glass for use in a beer parlour or pub, intended to show the level to which the glass must legally be filled.

tide•mark ['taɪd,mɑrk] *n.* a mark left by the tide at its highest point, or, sometimes, at its lowest point.

tide•wa•ter ['taɪd,wɒtər] *n.* **1** water affected by tides. **2** an area whose waters are so affected; a low-lying seacoast. **3** water brought by tides; water flooding land at high tide. **4** (*adjl.*) of or being such water or such an area. **5** **Tidewater, a** the eastern part of the state of Virginia in the U.S.; **b** the English dialect of this area.

tide•way ['taɪd,wei] *n.* **1** a channel through which a tide runs. **2** the current or ebb and flow in such a channel. **3** the tidal part of a river.

ti•dings ['taɪdɪŋz] *n.pl.* news; information. ⟨OE *tīdung* < *tīdan* happen, tide²⟩

ti•dy ['taɪdi] *adj.* **-di•er, -di•est;** *v.* **-died, -dy•ing;** *n., pl.* **-dies.** *adj.* **1** neat and in order: *a tidy room.* **2** inclined to keep things neat and in order: *a tidy person.* **3** *Informal.* fairly large; considerable; substantial: *I already have a tidy sum saved up toward a stereo.* **4** *Informal.* fairly good; acceptable; satisfactory: *They've worked out a tidy solution.*
—*v.* put (things) in order; make (a place) tidy (*often used with* **up**): *She quickly tidied the room. We tidied up before we left.*
—*n.* **1** a small decorative cover used to protect the back or arms of a chair, chesterfield, etc.; antimacassar. **2** a small container to hold little miscellaneous items or waste scraps: *a sink tidy.* ⟨ult. < OE *tīd* time⟩ —**'ti•di•ly,** *adv.* —**'ti•di•ness,** *n.*
☛ *Syn. adj.* **1.** See note at NEAT.

tie [taɪ] *v.* **tied, ty•ing;** *n.* —*v.* **1** fasten, attach, or close with cord, ribbon, rope, or the like: *Tie the package securely and tie a label on it. She tied the dog to the fence. Tie your shoes.* **2** arrange to form a bow or knot: *to tie a scarf.* **3** make by tying: *to tie a knot, to tie a fishing fly.* **4** be capable of being tied: *This paper ribbon doesn't tie very well.* **5** be closed or joined by means of cord, ribbon, etc.: *The apron ties at the back.* **6** restrain or limit: *She did not want to be tied to a steady job.* **7** connect or join in any way: *When the river was low, a narrow strip of sand tied the island to the shore.* **8** make the same score (as); be equal (to) in points: *The two teams tied. Halifax tied Charlottetown in the last game of the series.* **9** cause to end in a tie: *The fourth goal tied the game.* **10** *Music.* connect (notes) by a tie.
tie down, a confine or restrict: *She's tied down with a full-time job and night school.* **b** fasten or hold down by tying: *He tied down the tarp to keep it from flapping.*
tie in, a connect: *Where does this line tie in with the main circuit?*

b co-ordinate or relate: *The illustrations tie in very well with the story.*
tie into, *Informal.* start in on vigorously: *She forgot everything else and tied into her food.*
tie off, a close off (a passage) by tying with something. **b** prevent (a seam, etc.) from ravelling by tying thread, yarn, etc., in a knot.
tie one on, *Slang.* get drunk: *He really tied one on last night.*
tie up, a confine in bonds; bind with cord, etc.: *The thieves tied him up and left him.* **b** hinder or stop the progress of: *The stalled truck tied up traffic for half an hour.* **c** engage, occupy, or commit (money, a person, piece of equipment, etc.) so as to make unavailable for other purposes: *Since her money was tied up in real estate, she was unable to buy the bonds. He's tied up and can't make it to the dinner. Don't tie up the phone too long.* **d** complete: bring to completion; conclude: *And that report ties up our program for tonight.* **e** make (a deal, prospect, etc.) certain: *They've nearly got the details tied up.* **f** moor (a boat).
—n. **1** a cord, ribbon, etc. used for fastening parts together, especially one already attached: *An apron has ties. I don't like shoes with ties.* **2** a shaped, folded length of cloth worn under a shirt collar and knotted in front, either to form a bow or, more often, so that the two ends hang straight down: *He always wears a shirt and tie to work.* **3** anything that unites or binds; a bond or obligation: *family ties.* **4** one of the parallel wooden beams placed crosswise at intervals on a railway bed to form a foundation and support for the rails. **5** a connecting beam or rod, as in a framework supporting a roof, etc. **6 a** equality in points, votes, etc.: *The game ended in a tie, 3 to 3.* **b** the game or contest that ends with such an equality: *The election was a tie.* **7** (*adjl.*) being a tie; ending in a tie: *a tie game.* **8** *Music.* a curved line joining two notes of the same pitch to show that they are to be played or sung without a break between them. **9** a shoe fastened by means of a shoelace (*usually used in the plural*). ⟨OE *tīgan* < *tēag* rope⟩ **—'ti•er,** *n.*
☛ *Syn. n.* **3.** See note at BOND.

tie–and–dye ['taɪ ən ˌdaɪ] *n.* TIE-DYE.

tie•back ['taɪˌbæk] *n.* **1** a cord, ribbon, strip of cloth, etc., usually decorative, used to drape a curtain to the side of a window instead of allowing it to hang straight down. **2 tiebacks,** *pl.* curtains having tiebacks.

tie beam a timber or piece serving as a tie; especially, a horizontal beam connecting the lower ends of two opposite principal rafters, thus forming the base of a roof truss.

tie breaker an extra period of play, question period, etc., at the completion of play and often with special rules, held to determine a winner from among contestants with equal scores.

tie clip a long clip, usually having an ornamental face, used to clip a necktie to the front of a shirt. Also, **tie clasp**.

tie–dye ['taɪ ˌdaɪ] *n., v.* **-dyed, -dye•ing.** *—n.* **1** a method of hand-dyeing cloth in patterns by tying parts of the cloth with string so that they will not absorb the dye. **2** a design made in this way. **3** cloth decorated with such a design.
—v. dye (cloth or a garment) in this way: *to tie-dye a scarf.*

tie–in ['taɪ ˌɪn] *n.* a link; association; connection: *There was no tie-in between the murder and the robbery.*

tie line a line connecting points in a system, especially one connecting telephone extensions without going through the main exchange.

tie•pin ['taɪˌpɪn] *n.* a pin, usually having an ornamental head and a protective sheath for the point, used to hold a necktie or cravat in place.

tier [tir] *n., v.* *—n.* one of a series of rows arranged one above another: *tiers of seats in a football stadium.*
—v. arrange in tiers. ⟨< F *tire,* originally, order < *tirer* draw⟩
☛ *Hom.* TEAR[1].

tierce [tirs] *n.* **1 a** a cask of varying sizes, for provisions. **b** the quantity it contains, as a unit of measure. **2** a sequence of three playing cards of the same suit. **3** *Fencing.* the third defensive position. **4** *Music.* a third. **5** the service for the third canonical hour. ⟨ME < OF < L *tertius* third⟩

tier•cel ['tirsəl] *n.* See TERCEL.

tie rod a connecting rod, especially the rod connecting components of the steering system in a motor vehicle.

tie tack a kind of pin to hold a necktie in place, having an ornamental head with a short stud behind it that is passed through the tie and shirt and held in place with a small clasp on the inside.

tie–up ['taɪ ˌʌp] *n.* **1** a stopping of work or action on account of a strike, storm, accident, etc. **2** *Informal.* a connection; relation. **3** a place to moor a boat.

tiff [tɪf] *n., v.* *—n.* **1** a slight quarrel. **2** a slight fit of ill humour or peevishness.
—v. have or be in a tiff. ⟨origin uncertain⟩

tif•fa•ny ['tɪfəni] *n.* very thin, sheer muslin or silk. ⟨< OF *tiphanie* Epiphany; originally a dress worn on Twelfth Night⟩

Tif•fa•ny ['tɪfəni] *adj.* **1** of, being, or having to do with a type of stained glass in an art nouveau style, used for lampshades, windows, etc. **2** of, being, or having to do with a type of setting for a gem in which tiny prongs hold it in place. ⟨< L.C. *Tiffany* and C.L. *Tiffany*, respectively, U.S. designer and his father⟩

tif•fin ['tɪfən] *n. Brit., East Indian.* a light meal, especially at midday; lunch. ⟨Anglo-Indian for *tiffing* < *tiff* drink, of uncertain origin⟩

ti•ger ['taɪgər] *n.* **1** a large, fierce Asiatic feline (*Panthera tigris*) that has dull yellow fur striped with black. **2** a fierce and wild person: *He becomes a tiger if you criticize his work.* **3** a vigorous or energetic person: *a tiger for work.* **4** *Informal.* an extra yell at the end of a cheer.
have a tiger by the tail, be in a difficult situation in which remaining may be preferable to flight. ⟨< L < Gk. *tigris*⟩
—'ti•ger,like, *adj.*

Tigers

tiger beetle any of a large family (Cicindelidae) of beetles found mostly in warm regions, having large, strong jaws and noted for their voracity in going after prey, especially as larvae.

tiger cat 1 any of various medium-sized wild members of the cat family resembling the tiger, such as the ocelot or serval. **2** a striped domestic cat. **3** *Cdn.* formerly, any wild cat, especially the cougar.

ti•ger–eye ['taɪgər ˌaɪ] *n.* tiger's-eye.

ti•ger•ish ['taɪgərɪʃ] *adj.* like a tiger; wild and fierce.

tiger lily 1 a commonly grown garden lily (*Lilium tigrinum*) native to China and Japan, having large, black-spotted orange flowers. 2 any of various lilies with similar flowers, such as the prairie lily.

tiger moth any of a large family (Arctiidae) of nocturnal moths, especially any of the genus *Arctia*, typically having conspicuously spotted or striped wings.

ti•ger's–eye ['taɪgərz ˌaɪ] *n.* a golden-brown semiprecious stone with a changeable lustre, composed chiefly of quartz, coloured with iron oxide.

tiger shark any of various striped or spotted sharks, especially the voracious and omnivorous *Galiocerdo cuvieri*, a requiem shark found in tropical seas.

tiger swallowtail a large butterfly, (*Papilio glaucus*), a species of swallowtail found in eastern North America, having yellow wings with black stripes and margins.

tight [təit] *adj., adv.* *—adj.* **1** firm; held firmly; packed or put together firmly: *a tight grasp, a tight fist, a tight knot.* **2 a** drawn taut; stretched: *a tight canvas.* **b** showing strain or tension: *a tight smile, a tight reply.* **3** close; not allowing much leeway or extra room: *to turn a tight corner, to squeeze something into a tight space. Since she gained weight, her skirt has a tight fit.* **4** dense; having its elements very closely spaced: *a tight weave, a tight schedule.* **5** well-built; trim; neat: *a tight craft.* **6** not letting water, air, or gas in or out (*often in compounds*): *airtight window frames. The caulking on the boat is tight.* **7** not wasteful of words; terse; concise: *tight writing, a tight style.* **8** hard to deal with or manage; difficult: *His lies got him in a tight place.* **9** *Informal.* almost even; close: *It was a tight race.* **10 a** hard to get; scarce: *Money for mortgages is tight just now.* **b** characterized by scarcity or eager demand: *a tight money market.* **11** *Informal.* stingy. **12** *Informal.* drunk. **13** strict; severe: *to rule with a tight hand.* **14** of a group, having such close ties as to be exclusive; not open to outsiders or new people.
(run) a tight ship, (operate or direct) a highly efficient, organized, well-disciplined organization.
—adv. closely; securely; firmly: *The rope was tied too tight.*
sit tight, *Informal.* keep the same position, opinion, etc. and see what develops; refrain from action while waiting alertly.
sleep tight, *Informal.* sleep soundly. ⟨OE *getyht*, pp. of *tyhtan* stretch⟩ **—'tight•ly,** *adv.* **—'tight•ness,** *n.*
☛ *Syn. adj.* **2. Tight,** TAUT = drawn or stretched so as to be not loose or slack. **Tight,** the general word, emphasizes the idea of drawing closely together or of being drawn over or around something so firmly that there

is no looseness: *You need a tight string around that package.* **Taut** emphasizes stretching until the thing described would break, snap, or tear if pulled more tightly, and is used chiefly as a nautical or mechanical term or to describe or suggest strained nerves or muscles: *The covering on a drum must be taut.*

tight•en ['təitən] *v.* make or become tight or tighter. **—'tight•en•er,** *n.*

tight–fist•ed ['təit 'fɪstɪd] *adj.* stingy.

tight•knit ['təit,nɪt] *adj.* **1** of prose, etc., tight. **2** closely united or integrated: *a tightknit family, a tightknit community.*

tight–lipped ['təit 'lɪpt] *adj.* **1** keeping the lips firmly together, as in determination or when controlling strong emotion: *She stood there in tight-lipped fury.* **2** saying little or nothing; reluctant to speak: *He's very tight-lipped; you won't get any information out of him.*

tight•rope ['təit,roup] *n.* a rope or wire stretched tight some distance above the ground, for acrobats to perform on.
on a tightrope, in a dangerous or extremely delicate situation: *She was on a tightrope now; one wrong word and she would lose their confidence.*

tights [təits] *n.pl.* a close-fitting, usually knitted, garment covering the lower body and each leg and foot separately, worn by acrobats, dancers, etc. or as stockings in cold weather.

tight squeeze a difficult situation; narrow escape.

tight•wad ['təit,wɒd] *n. Slang.* a stingy person.

tight•wire ['təit,waɪr] *n.* a wire tightrope.

ti•glon ['taɪglɒn] *or* ['taɪglən] *n.* the progeny of a male tiger and a lioness. Also, **tigon.**

ti•gress ['taɪgrɪs] *n.* **1** an adult female tiger. **2** a woman thought of as being like a tiger in fierceness or wildness.

ti•grish ['taɪgrɪʃ] *adj.* tigerish.

ti•ka ['tikə] *n. Hinduism.* the dot of coloured paste or other type of marking on the forehead. ⟨< Hind.⟩

tike [təik] See TYKE.

ti•ki ['tiki] *n.* **1** in Polynesia, a small sculptured human figure representing an ancestor or god, worn as an amulet. **2** in New Zealand, often a large, wooden human figure. ⟨< Maori⟩

ti•ki•na•gan [,tɪkə'nɑgən] *n. Cdn.* cradle-board. Also, **ticcanagon.**

til [tɪl] *n.* See TILDE (def. 2).

til•ak ['tɪlək] *n.* tika. ⟨< Skt. *tilaka*⟩

til•bu•ry ['tɪlbəri] *n., pl.* **-ries.** a light, two-wheeled, horse-drawn carriage without a top. ⟨< name of a British coach designer⟩

til•de ['tɪldə]; *Spanish,* ['tilde] *n.* **1** a diacritical mark (~) used in Spanish over *n* when it is pronounced [nj], as in *cañón* [ka'njon] **2 a** the same mark, used in Portuguese over certain vowels to indicate that they are nasalized, as in *São* [sɑ̃õ]. The Portuguese name for this mark is **til. b** the same mark used over vowel symbols in the International Phonetic Alphabet, indicating nasalization, as in [bɔ̃] for French *bon.* ⟨< Sp. < L *titulus* title⟩

tile [taɪl] *n., v.* **tiled, til•ing.** *—n.* **1** a thin piece of baked clay, stone, etc. Tiles are used for covering roofs and floors, and for ornamenting. **2** a thin square of plastic, rubber, etc. used for surfacing floors, walls, or ceilings. **3** a short porous pipe or trough, usually earthenware, used for draining land. **4** tiles collectively. **5** (*adjl.*) covered with or made of tile: *a tile floor.* **6** *Informal.* a stiff hat; high silk hat. **7** a thin, flat piece of plastic, polished wood, or ivory used in games such as mah-jongg or Scrabble.
—v. put tiles on or in; cover with tile. ⟨OE *tigele* < L *tegula*⟩

tile•fish ['taɪl,fɪʃ] *n.* a percoid food fish of very deep tropical waters of the Atlantic, *Lopholatilus chamaeleonticeps,* having a bright blue or purple body with yellow spots.

til•er ['taɪlər] *n.* a person who makes or lays tiles.

til•ing ['taɪlɪŋ] *n., v. —n.* **1** tiles collectively. **2** the work of a person who tiles. **3** a surface or structure consisting of tiles.
—v. ppr. of TILE.

till¹ [tɪl] *prep., conj. —prep.* up to the time of; until: *The child played till eight.*
—conj. up to the time when; until: *Walk till you come to a white house.* ⟨OE *til*⟩

☛ *Usage.* **Till, until.** These two words are not distinguishable in meaning, though **until** is usually considered the more formal word and is normally used at the beginning of sentences: *Until she left high school, she had no job. He didn't take any job till (or until) he left high school.* Otherwise, one may choose between the two forms on the basis of stress and rhythm.

till² [tɪl] *v.* cultivate; plough; harrow, etc.: *Farmers till the land.* ⟨OE *tilian*⟩ **—'till•a•ble,** *adj.*

till³ [tɪl] *n.* **1** a drawer or box for money, especially in a store, etc.: *The till is under the counter.* **2** CASH REGISTER. ⟨ult. < OE *-tyllan* draw, as in *betyllan* lure⟩

till⁴ [tɪl] *n.* glacial drift composed of clay, stones, gravel, boulders, etc. mixed together. ⟨origin unknown⟩

till•age ['tɪlɪdʒ] *n.* **1** the cultivation of land. **2** tilled land.

till•er¹ ['tɪlər] *n.* a bar or handle used to turn the rudder in steering a boat. ⟨ME < OF *telier* weaver's beam, ult. < L *tela* web, loom⟩

till•er² ['tɪlər] *n.* **1** a person who tills the land. **2** a machine for tilling; cultivator. ⟨< *till²*⟩

till•er³ ['tɪlər] *n., v. —n.* a shoot springing from the base of the original plant stem; sucker.
—v. send forth tillers. ⟨< OE *telgor* twig⟩

til•li•cum ['tɪləkəm] *n.* **1** on the Pacific coast and in the Northwest, a friend; pal. **2** in First Nations parlance, one's own people. ⟨< Chinook jargon *tillikum* people, person < Chinookan *tilikum* Indian(s)⟩

tilt¹ [tɪlt] *v., n. —v.* **1** slant or cause to slant; incline: *She tilted the board to allow the water to run off. The table is liable to tilt.* **2** bias (a policy, treatment of an issue, etc.) **3** take part in a jousting match, especially one in which the competitors ride toward each other along either side of a barrier to prevent the collision of the horses. Compare JOUST. **4** attack or overthrow (a person) in such a match. **5** thrust or aim: *to tilt a lance.* **6 a** aim or thrust one's lance (at) in a joust: *The black knight tilted him.* **b** attack or charge (*used with* **at**): *tilting at injustice.* **7** forge or work (steel, etc.) with a TILT HAMMER.
tilt at windmills. See WINDMILL.
—n. **1** slope or slant: *the tabletop has a slight tilt.* **2** the act of tilting. **3** a jousting match, especially one in which the competitors ride toward each other along either side of a barrier. **4** the barrier itself. **5** the ground or yard where such contests were held; the lists. **6** a debate or dispute. **7** TILT HAMMER.
(at) full tilt, at full speed or with full force: *The car ran full tilt against the tree.* ⟨ult. < OE *tealt* shaky⟩

tilt² [tɪlt] *n. Cdn.* **1 a** (*esp. Labrador*) a temporary shelter of canvas, sealskins, etc.; tent. **b** (*West*) formerly, the canvas covering of a PRAIRIE SCHOONER. **2** (*esp. Labrador*) **a** a log hut or cabin used by fishers or trappers. **b** any simple dwelling, especially one made of wood. ⟨< ME *telte* < OE *teld;* rel. to G *Zelt* tent⟩

tilth [tɪlθ] *n.* **1** the cultivation of land. **2** tilled land. **3** the condition of tilled soil: *a garden in bad tilth.* ⟨OE *tilth* < *tilian* till²⟩

tilt hammer a drop hammer consisting of a heavy head at the end of a pivot, used in drop-forging.

tilt•me•ter ['tɪlt,mitər] *n.* a device to measure the tilt of the earth.

tim•bal ['tɪmbəl] *n.* kettledrum. ⟨< F *timbale,* ult. < Arabic *at-tabl* the drum⟩

tim•bale [tɪm'bɑl] *or* ['tɪmbəl]; *French,* [tɛ̃'bal] *n.* **1** a food consisting of minced meat, fish, vegetables, etc. prepared with a sauce and cooked in a mould. **2** a cup-shaped pastry mould. ⟨< F *timbale,* originally, *timbal.* See TIMBAL.⟩

tim•ber ['tɪmbər] *n., v., interj. —n.* **1** wood suitable for building and making things. **2** a large squared piece of wood ready to use in building or forming part of a structure. Beams and rafters are timbers. **3** a curved piece forming a rib of a ship. **4** mature growing trees; forest, especially regarded as a source of wood: *Half of their land is covered with timber.* **5** logs, green or cured, cut from such trees. **6** figuratively, calibre or quality: *a woman of her timber.*
—v. cover, support, or furnish with timber or timbers.
—interj. a warning shout that a tree is about to fall. ⟨OE⟩
☛ *Hom.* TIMBRE.

tim•ber•doo•dle ['tɪmbər,dudəl] *n.* woodcock.

tim•bered ['tɪmbərd] *adj., v. —adj.* **1** made or furnished with timber. **2** covered with growing trees.
—v. pt. and pp. of TIMBER.

timber hitch a knot used to fasten a rope around a spar, post, etc. See KNOT¹ for picture.

tim•ber•ing ['tɪmbərɪŋ] *n., v. —n.* **1** building material of wood. **2** timbers collectively. **3** an arrangement or structure of timbers.
—v. ppr. of TIMBER.

tim•ber•land ['tɪmbər,lænd] *n.* land with trees, especially trees that are, or may be, used for timber.

timber licence *Cdn. Lumbering and logging.* a licence permitting the cutting of trees on a TIMBER LIMIT (def. 2), on payment of certain dues to the government.

timber limit *Cdn.* **1** timberline. **2** *Logging.* a tract of land in which a person or company has the right to fell trees and remove timber; concession.

tim•ber•line [ˈtɪmbər,laɪn] *n.* a line on mountains and in high latitudes beyond which trees will not grow because of climatic conditions such as extreme cold and strong winds. In Canada, the country north of the timberline is called the Barrens.

timber raft *Logging.* a collection of logs lashed together for transport in water.

timber wolf *Cdn.* a large grey wolf (*Canis lupus*), especially any of several subspecies found in wooded northern regions of Canada and in Alaska.

A timber wolf

tim•bre [ˈtɪmbər] *or* [ˈtæmbər]; *French,* [tɛ̃bʀ] *n.* the quality in sounds that distinguishes a certain voice, instrument, etc. from other voices, instruments, etc. Notes of the same pitch and loudness may differ in timbre. ⟨< MF *timbre,* ult. < Gk. *tympanon* kettledrum. Doublet of TYMPAN, TYMPANUM.⟩
☛ *Hom.* TIMBER [ˈtɪmbər].

tim•brel [ˈtɪmbrəl] *n. Archaic.* tambourine. ⟨dim. of ME *timbre* < OF *timbre,* a kind of tambourine. See TIMBRE.⟩

time [taɪm] *n., v.* **timed, tim•ing.** *—n.* **1** all the days there have been or ever will be; the past, present, and future: *We measure time in years, months, days, hours, minutes, seconds, etc.* **2** a part of time: *A minute is a short time.* **3 a** a period of history; epoch: *the time of the Stuarts of England.* **b** a particular season; span of the calendar: *haying time, the hot time.* **c** any specified or defined period of time: *Where were you the whole time?* **4** (*adjl.*) of or having to do with time: *time travel.* **5** a term of imprisonment, enlistment, apprenticeship, etc.: *to complete one's time.* **6** a long time: *What a time it took you!* **7** some point in time; a particular point in time: *What time is it?* **8 a** the right, usual, or fixed period or point of time: *It is time to eat.* **b** appointed moment, as of death or childbirth: *I hope I am ready when my time comes.* **c** one's turn (to do something, succeed, etc.): *a leader whose time has come.* **9** (*adjl.*) provided with a clocklike mechanism so that a given action will occur at a given moment: *a time bomb, a time lock.* **10** an occasion: *This time we will succeed.* **11** a way of reckoning time: *daylight-saving time.* **12 times,** *pl.* **a** conditions of life: *War brings hard times.* **b** multiplied by (*prepositional use*): *Four times three is twelve.* **c** multiplied instances: *five times as much.* **d** age; era; period of history: *ancient times, modern times.* **13** amount of time; period used or allotted for some specific activity: *Cooking time, 30 minutes. With every race, she improved her time. I have some time for rest.* **14** (*adjl.*) *Business.* having to do with purchases to be paid for at a future date. **15** an experience during a certain time: *She had a good time at the party.* **16** rate of speed; tempo. **17** *Music.* **a** the length of a note or rest. **b** the grouping of such notes into rhythmic beats, divided into bars or measures of equal length. **c** the tempo of a composition. **d** the rhythm of a composition: *waltz time, march time.* **18** the amount of time that one has worked or should work. **19** the pay for this: *They paid me double time.* **20** leisure: *to have time to read.* **21** *Military.* a rate of stepping; pace: *to march in quick time.* **22** lifetime: *That was before my time. Peace in our time.*
about time, at or near the proper time: *It's about time to go home.*
against time, trying to finish before a certain time.
ahead of time, early; in advance.
at a time, together; in the same period; simultaneously; in one act: *He took the steps two at a time. She reads a lot, often three books at a time.*
at one time, a simultaneously. **b** formerly: *At one time he was the most famous man in the industry.*
at the same time, a simultaneously. **b** however; nevertheless.
at times, now and then; once in a while.
behind the times, old-fashioned; out of date.
do or **serve time,** *Informal.* spend time in prison as a criminal: *a man doing time for bank robbery.*
for the time being, for the present; for now.
from time to time, now and then; once in a while: *From time to time we visited Aunt Leah's fruit farm.*
in good time, a at the right time: *We reached the theatre in good time for the first act.* **b** soon; quickly.
in no time (flat), *Informal.* instantly; instantaneously.
in time, a after a while. **b** soon enough: *We got there just in time, before the bank closed.* **c** *Music.* in the right rate of movement.
it's about time, *Informal.* it's past due: *You're finally cleaning your room? It's about time!*
keep time, a of a watch or clock, go at the correct speed. **b** sound or move at the right rate: *The marchers kept time to the martial music.*
make (good, excellent, etc.**) time,** go with speed.
make time (for), ensure time is available; set aside time (for).
mark time, a beat out the proper time or rhythm. **b** pass time doing nothing; wait.
on (one's) **own time,** outside of one's paid working hours.
on time, a at the right or specified time, or hour; not late: *He's never on time. Be sure you're on time, so we can start promptly at 8.* **b** with time in which to pay; on credit: *She bought a car on time.*
pass the time (away), occupy oneself; stave off boredom; fill empty time: *I passed the time away by knitting.*
tell time, read the clock; tell what time it is by the clock.
time after time or **time and again,** again and again.
time of life, age: *a foolish thing to do at his time of life.*
time out of mind, TIME IMMEMORIAL; time beyond memory or historical record: *People have acted this way since time out of mind.*
—v. **1** measure the duration of: *to time a race.* **2** fix, set, or regulate the length of in time: *to time an exposure correctly.* **3** set, regulate, or adjust (a timepiece): *to time an alarm clock.* **4** do in rhythm with; set the rhythm of: *The dancers timed their steps to the music.* **5** choose the moment or occasion for: *The demonstrators timed their march through the business section so that most shoppers would see them.* ⟨OE *tīma*⟩
☛ *Hom.* THYME.

time–and–a–half [ˈtaɪm ənd ə ˈhæf] *n.* a rate of pay one and a half times the usual, for working overtime or on holidays.

time and motion study a systematic study of the methods and body motions used and the amount of time taken to do the various steps in a certain job, conducted to establish the most effective way of doing it.

time bomb **1** a bomb equipped with a timing device, so that it can be set to explode at a certain moment. **2** *Informal.* a condition or situation leading to inevitable disaster, unless action can be taken to avert it.

time capsule a container with documents and other items representative of the current age, that is buried or sealed into the cornerstone of a building, etc., to be discovered in a future generation.

time•card [ˈtaɪm,kɑrd] *n.* a card used with a time clock for recording the arrival and departure times of an employee.

time clock a clock with a device to stamp an employee's timecard with the time he or she arrives or leaves.

time–con•sum•ing [ˈtaɪm kən,sumɪŋ] *or* [ˈtaɪm kən,sjumɪŋ] *adj.* taking up or requiring a great deal of time: *The calculations weren't hard, but they were time-consuming.*

time draft a draft to be paid at the future time stated in the draft.

time exposure **1** the exposure of a photographic film for a certain time, usually longer than a half second. **2** a photograph taken in this way.

time frame the period of time, usually approximate, projected or allotted for some activity.

time fuse a fuse that will burn for a certain time.

time–hon•oured or **time–hon•ored** [ˈtaɪm ,ɒnərd] *adj.* honoured because old and established: *a time-honoured custom.*

time immemorial **1** a period in time so distant that it is before the beginning of records or known chronology. **2** time so long ago as to be imprecise: *Our family has done it this way from time immemorial.* **3** *Law.* the time before legal records were known. In the United Kingdom, it is fixed by law as the time prior to 1189, the beginning of Richard I's reign.

time•keep•er [ˈtaɪm,kipər] *n.* a measurer of time; a person who or thing that keeps time: *The factory timekeeper keeps account of the hours of work done. My watch is an excellent timekeeper.*

time–lag [ˈtaɪm ,læg] *n.* an interval between the cause of an event or state and its happening or coming on.

time–lapse photography [ˈtaɪm ,læps] motion photography in which separate pictures of a slow-moving object, such as a flower unfolding, are taken at intervals and then projected at normal speed to give the illusion of speeded-up action.

time•less ['taɪmlɪs] *adj.* **1 a** never ending. **b** infinite; eternal. **2** confined to no special time; always applicable or suitable: *timeless classics of literature.* —**'time•less•ly,** *adv.* —**'time•less•ness,** *n.*

time line **a** a usually long line marked with dates and events at approximate intervals, for use in teaching history. It shows which events were concurrent, which important figures were contemporaries, etc. **b** a similar device used to show the sequence or concurrence of events in a detailed plan, such as a Royal Visit, a major project by a team of workers, etc.

time•ly ['taɪmli] *adj.* **-li•er, -li•est.** happening at the right time; suited to the time: *The timely arrival of the police stopped the riot. Your article on Canadian regionalism is very timely.*
—**'time•li•ness,** *n.*

☛ *Syn.* **Timely,** OPPORTUNE = well-timed or especially suited to the time or occasion. **Timely** describes something perfectly suited to the time or circumstance, coming or happening just at a time to be useful or valuable: *Saturday's paper contained a timely article on wise buying and foolish spending.* **Opportune** describes either the moment or occasion most favourable for doing something, or an event or action happening or done at exactly the right and most advantageous moment: *The invitation came at an opportune moment.*

time of day the time as shown by the clock.
give the time of day to, notice or acknowledge; do the least thing for.
know the time of day, know what is going on; know the current state of affairs.
pass the time of day, exchange greetings or brief conversation.

time–out ['taɪm 'ʌut] *n.* **1** *Sports.* an interval during which play is stopped and time not counted, for players to consult about strategy, make substitutions, confer with the umpire about a decision, etc. **2** any interruption for rest or refreshments. **3** a time during which a child is excluded from the company of others, from group activities, etc. as a punishment or as an opportunity to reflect on his or her misbehaviour and plan how to make amends.

time•piece ['taɪm,pis] *n.* a clock or watch.

tim•er ['taɪmər] *n.* **1** a device for indicating or recording intervals of time, such as a stopwatch. **2** a device similar to a clock that can be set to indicate, by means of a buzzer, etc., when a specific period of time has elapsed, or to start or stop another device or mechanism automatically at a predetermined time: *a timer on a stove.* **3** an automatic device in the ignition system of an internal-combustion engine that causes the spark for igniting the charge to occur just at the time required. **4** timekeeper.

time•sav•er ['taɪm,seivər] *n.* a person or thing that saves time.

time•sav•ing ['taɪm,seivɪŋ] *adj.* that saves time: *timesaving household appliances.*

time•serv•er ['taɪm,sɜrvər] *n.* a person who for selfish purposes shapes his or her conduct to conform with the opinions of the time or of the persons in power.

time•serv•ing ['taɪm,sɜrvɪŋ] *n., adj.* —*n.* the practice or behaviour of a timeserver.
—*adj.* having or showing a lack of integrity or independent thinking: *a timeserving little wretch.*

time•shar•ing ['taɪm,ʃɛrɪŋ] *n.* **1** *Computer technology.* a system or technique whereby different users at separate terminals can have access to a single computer at virtually the same time, due to the high speed at which the computer operates. **2** a system whereby several owners occupy a vacation home, condominium, etc., each for a specified period with certain dates. Also, **time-sharing**.

time sheet a sheet on which an employee's hours of work, time off, etc., are recorded.

time signature *Music.* a symbol, usually in the form of a fraction, that is printed or written at the beginning of a composition or where the time changes. The numerator of the fraction indicates the number of beats in a bar or measure; the denominator gives the length of the note that receives one beat. A special symbol, much like a letter C, is sometimes used to indicate 4/4, or common, time.

times table multiplication table.

time study TIME AND MOTION STUDY.

time•ta•ble ['taɪm,teibəl] *n.* any table, list, or schedule showing a planned sequence of events, such as arrival and departure times for public transportation (buses, trains, planes, etc.), times for classes in a school or university, times and places for competitive events, etc.

time–test•ed ['taɪm ,tɛstɪd] *adj.* having a value or effectivensss that has been proven over a long period of time: *a time-tested recipe for bread.*

time warp a theoretical change in the nature of time, according to certain conditions in the universe.

time•worn ['taɪm,wɔrn] *adj.* **1** worn by long existence or use: *They walked up the timeworn steps of the old house.* **2** hackneyed or trite: *a timeworn excuse.* **3** ancient.

The Canadian time zones

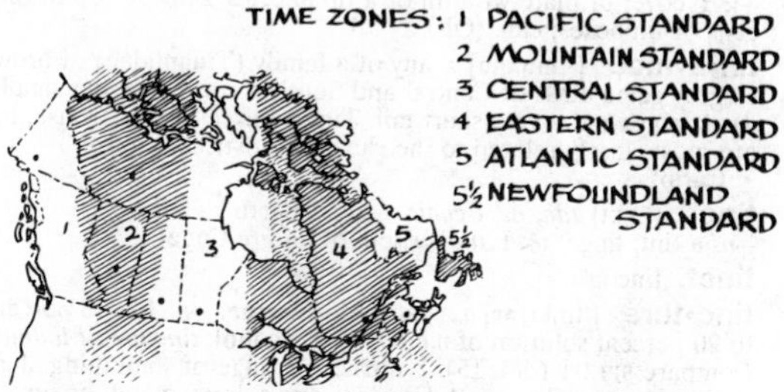

TIME ZONES: 1 PACIFIC STANDARD
2 MOUNTAIN STANDARD
3 CENTRAL STANDARD
4 EASTERN STANDARD
5 ATLANTIC STANDARD
5½ NEWFOUNDLAND STANDARD

time zone a geographical region within which the same standard of time is used. The world is divided into 24 time zones, beginning and ending at the International Date Line, an imaginary line running mostly through the Pacific Ocean at the 180th meridian of longitude.

tim•id ['tɪmɪd] *adj.* **1** lacking courage or self-confidence; easily frightened. **2** showing lack of self-confidence or determination: *a timid voice, a timid excuse.* ⟨< L *timidus* < *timere* to fear⟩
—**'tim•id•ly,** *adv.* —**'tim•id•ness,** *n.*

☛ *Syn.* **Timid,** COWARDLY = lacking courage. **Timid** emphasizes the idea of being always ready to be afraid, especially of anything new, different, uncertain, or unknown: *He does not like his job, but is too timid to try to find another.* **Cowardly** emphasizes the idea of a weak and dishonourable lack of courage in the presence of danger or trouble: *Leaving his wife because she was hopelessly sick was a cowardly thing to do.*

ti•mid•i•ty [tə'mɪdəti] *n.* the quality of being timid: *His timidity prevents him from asking questions.*

tim•ing ['taɪmɪŋ] *n., v.* —*n.* **1** the choice or regulation of the speed, co-ordination, or moment of occurrence of a thing or series of things so as to produce the best possible effect: *The timing of the engine is off. Timing is very important in a golf swing. Her timing couldn't have been worse–she asked for the car just after her mother had discovered the mess in the living room. The comedian's timing was meticulous.* **2** the measurement and recording of the time taken by an action or process: *Timing is often done with a stopwatch.*
—*v.* ppr. of TIME.

Ti•mis•ka•ming [tə'mɪskəmɪŋ] *adj., n. Geology.* —*adj.* of or having to do with the more recent period of the Archaeozoic era.
—*n.* **1** the more recent period of the Archaeozoic era. **2** the rocks or rock formations of this period. ⟨< *Timiskaming,* Ontario⟩

ti•moc•ra•cy [tə'mɒkrəsi] *or* [taɪ'mɒkrəsi] *n., pl.* **-cies. 1** in Plato's political philosophy, a form of government in which the love of honour and power motivates those who rule. **2** in the writings of Aristotle, a form of government in which ownership of property is the requisite for holding office. ⟨< OF *timocracie* < Med.L *timocratia* < Gk. *timokratia* < *time* honour, worth + *kratia* < *kratos* power⟩ —**'ti•mo,crat** ['taɪmə,kræt], *n.*
—**,ti•mo'crat•ic,** *adj.*

Ti•mon ['taɪmən] *n.* a hater of people in general; misanthrope. ⟨after the hero of Shakespeare's play, *Timon of Athens,* noted for his dislike of people⟩

tim•or•ous ['tɪmərəs] *adj.* **1** easily frightened; timid: *a timorous child.* **2** marked or caused by fear or lack of self-confidence: *The puppy's timorous advances were ignored.* ⟨ME < OF < Med.L *timorosus* < L *timor* fear⟩ —**'tim•or•ous•ly,** *adv.*
—**'tim•or•ous•ness,** *n.*

tim•o•thy ['tɪməθi] *n.* a perennial European grass (*Phleum pratense*) having long, cylindrical flower spikes, widely cultivated in temperate regions for hay and as a pasture grass. ⟨< *Timothy* Hanson, an early American cultivator⟩

tim•pa•ni ['tɪmpəni] *n.pl.* a set of kettledrums, each tuned to a different pitch, played by one person in an orchestra or band (*sometimes used with a singular verb*). ⟨< Ital., pl. of *timpano* kettledrum < L *tympanum* drum. See TYMPANUM.⟩

tim•pa•nist ['tɪmpənɪst] *n.* a person who plays the timpani, especially a professional or skilled player.

tin [tɪn] *n., v.* **tinned, tin•ning.** *—n.* **1** a soft, silver-white metallic element used as a coating on other metals and in making alloys. *Symbol*: Sn; *at.no.* 50; *at.mass* 118.69. **2** thin sheets of iron or steel coated with tin. **3** (*adjl.*) made of tin: *tin cans, a tin box.* **4** any box, can, pan, or other container made of tin or tin plate: *a cake tin, a muffin tin. Sardines are packed in tins.* **5** such a container together with its contents: *a tin of peas.*
—v. **1** cover or plate with tin or a tin alloy. **2** *Brit.* put up in tin cans or tin boxes; can. ⟨OE⟩

tin•a•mou ['tɪnə,mu] *n.* any of a family (Tinamidae) of brown or grey game birds of Central and South America having small, weak wings and a very short tail. Tinamous resemble grouse, but are most closely related to the rheas and ostriches. ⟨< F < Carib⟩

tinct [tɪŋkt] *adj., n. Archaic. —adj.* tinged.
—n. a tint; tinge. ⟨< L *tinctus*, pp. of *tingere* tinge⟩

tinct. tincture.

tinc•ture ['tɪŋktʃər] *n., v.* **-tured, -tur•ing.** *—n.* **1** a 10 percent to 20 percent solution of medicine in alcohol: *tincture of iodine.* Compare SPIRIT (def. 15). **2** a trace or tinge of something. **3** a slight colour or flavour. **4** *Heraldry.* any colour, metal, or fur used for the fields, charges, etc. in coats of arms.
—v. **1** give a trace or tinge to (*used with* **with**). **2** affect slightly with a certain quality (*used with* **with**): *Everything he says is tinctured with conceit.* **3** colour or flavour slightly. ⟨< L *tinctura* < *tingere* tinge⟩

tin•der ['tɪndər] *n.* **1** anything that catches fire easily. **2** material used to catch fire from a spark. Before matches were invented people carried a box holding tinder, flint, and steel. ⟨OE *tynder*⟩

tin•der•box ['tɪndər,bɒks] *n.* **1** a box formerly used for holding tinder, flint, and steel for making a fire. **2** an object, structure, etc. that is highly flammable. **3 a** a situation or place likely to burst into conflict or violence of some kind. **b** a very excitable person.

tine [taɪn] *n.* a sharp, projecting point or prong: *the tines of a fork.* ⟨OE *tind*⟩ **-tined,** *adj.*

tin•e•a ['tɪniə] *n.* any of a number of fungal skin diseases such as ringworm. ⟨ME < L, worm⟩

tin ear the inability to perceive the more subtle differences in speech sounds or musical tones. **—'tin-'eared,** *adj.*

tin foil **1** very thin sheeting of tin, aluminum, or an alloy of tin and lead, used for wrapping food products, for insulation, etc. **2** SILVER PAPER.

ting [tɪŋ] *n., v. —n.* a light, clear, ringing sound, as that made by crystal goblets striking each other lightly.
—v. make or cause to make such a sound: *The glass tinged when I touched it with the spoon.* ⟨imitative⟩

tinge [tɪndʒ] *v.* **tinged, tinge•ing** or **ting•ing;** *n. —v.* **1** colour slightly: *A drop of ink will tinge a glass of water.* **2** add a trace of some quality to; change slightly: *Sad memories tinged their present joy.*
—n. **1** a slight colouring or tint. **2** a very small amount; trace. ⟨< L *tingere*⟩

tin•gle ['tɪŋgəl] *v.* **-gled, -gling;** *n. —v.* **1** have a pricking or stinging feeling, especially from excitement, cold, etc.: *He tingled with delight on his first train trip. The cold made his fingers tingle.* **2** cause this feeling (in): *The fine rain tingled her cheeks. Champagne tingles.* **3** be thrilling: *Her account of their misadventures tingled with excitement.* **4** tinkle; jingle.
—n. **1** a pricking, stinging feeling. **2** a tinkle; jingle. ⟨probably var. of *tinkle*⟩ **—'tin•gly,** *adj.*

tin god a person who demands or gets respect out of all proportion to his or her actual merit: *The new CEO, so highly extolled in a recent business journal, was autocratic and distant—a real tin god.*

tink•er[1] ['tɪŋkər] *n., v. —n.* **1** a person who mends pots, pans, etc., usually one who travels from place to place to practise his or her trade. **2** a clumsy or unskilful worker. **3** a person who likes to tinker with mechanical things; a handy person.
—v. **1** mend (things) as a tinker. **2** work on, adjust, or repair in an unskilled or experimental way (*used with* **with**): *Someone has been tinkering with my bicycle. She likes to tinker with old radios and TV sets.* **3** keep busy in an irregular or purposeless way; play; toy (*used with* **with**): *to tinker with a new idea.* ⟨? ult. < *tin*⟩ **—'tink•er•er,** *n.*

tink•er[2] ['tɪŋkər] *n.* **1** *Cdn. Atlantic Provinces.* the razorbill or the common murre. **2** the common mackerel (*Scomber scombrus*) caught off the Atlantic coast. ⟨prob. < *tinkershere*, Brit. name for guillemot, meaning dark or black (tinker's hue)⟩

tinker's damn or **dam** a most worthless or useless thing: *She doesn't give a tinker's damn what I think. His writing is not worth a tinker's damn.* ⟨? from tinkers' reputation for cursing⟩

tin•kle ['tɪŋkəl] *v.* **-kled, -kling;** *n. —v.* **1** make short, light, ringing sounds: *Little bells tinkle.* **2** cause to tinkle. **3** indicate, make known, etc. by tinkling: *The little clock tinkled out the hours.* **4** *Informal.* urinate.
—n. a series of short, light, ringing sounds: *the tinkle of bells.* ⟨ult. imitative⟩ **—'tin•kly,** *adj.*

tin•man ['tɪnmən] *n., pl.* **-men.** tinsmith.

tin•ner ['tɪnər] *n.* **1** a person who works in a tin mine; a tin miner. **2** tinsmith.

tin•ni•tus [tɪ'nəitəs] an abnormal ringing or buzzing in the ears, not caused by any external source of sound. ⟨< L, pp. of *tinnire* ring, tinkle⟩

tin•ny ['tɪni] *adj.* **-ni•er, -ni•est. 1** of or containing tin. **2** shrill or thin in sound; lacking in resonance: *a tinny voice, the tinny music of an old juke box.* **3** thin and cheap; of poor quality: *tinny cutlery, tinny jewellery.* **4** tasting of tin: *The salmon is tinny.* **—'tin•ni•ly,** *adv.* **—'tin•ni•ness,** *n.*

tin–pan alley ['tɪn 'pæn] **1** a district or area of a city serving as a centre for composers and publishers of popular music. **2** the community of people concerned with writing and publishing popular music. ⟨< *Tin Pan Alley*, such a district of New York City⟩

tin pants *Cdn. Slang.* heavy work pants made of canvas or duck, impregnated with a waterproofing solution such as paraffin. ⟨so called because of their stiffness⟩

tin plate thin sheets of iron or steel coated with tin. Ordinary tin cans are made of tin plate.

tin–plate ['tɪn 'pleit] *v.* **-plat•ed, -plat•ing.** coat or plate (metal) with tin.

tin•pot ['tɪn,pɒt] *adj. Informal. Esp. Brit.* inferior; petty; *a tin-pot dictator.* Also, **tin-pot.**

tin•sel ['tɪnsəl] *or* ['tɪnzəl] *n., v.* **-selled** or **-seled, -sel•ling** or **-sel•ing,** *—n.* **1** extremely thin sheets, strips, or threads of a metallic substance, used to add glitter to cloth, yarn, or decorations, ornament Christmas trees, etc. **2** something like tinsel; something showy and attractive, but not worth much. **3** cloth woven with threads of gold, silver, or copper. **4** (*adjl.*) made of or decorated with tinsel. **5** (*adjl.*) showy but cheap; gaudy.
—v. **1** decorate or trim with or as if with tinsel. **2** make artificially glamorous or splendid. ⟨< F *étincelle* spark < L *scintilla.* Doublet of SCINTILLA.⟩ **—'tin•sel-,like,** *adj.* **—'tin•sel•ly,** *adj.*

tin•smith ['tɪn,smɪθ] *n.* a person who works with tin or other light metal; maker of tinware.

tin•stone ['tɪn,stoun] *n.* cassiterite.

tint [tɪnt] *n., v. —n.* **1** a variety of a colour, especially one mixed with white. **2** a suggestion of or tendency toward a different colour: *white with a bluish tint.* **3** a delicate or pale colour. **4** a preparation for colouring hair; dye. **5** *Printing.* a pale coloured background against which to print something. **6** in engraving, a uniform shading achieved by a series of fine parallel lines.
—v. put a tint on or in; colour: *to tint a black-and-white photograph, to tint one's hair.* ⟨earlier *tinct* < L *tinctus* a dyeing < *tingere* dye⟩

tin•tin•nab•u•la•tion [,tɪntə,næbjə'leiʃən] *n.* the ringing of bells. ⟨ult. < L *tintinnabulum* bell⟩

tin•type ['tɪn,təip] *n.* a photograph taken on a sheet of enamelled tin or iron.

tin•ware ['tɪn,wɛr] *n.* articles made of or lined with tin.

ti•ny ['taɪni] *adj.* **-ni•er, -ni•est.** very small; wee. ⟨ME *tine*; origin uncertain⟩ **—'ti•ni•ly,** *adv.* **—'ti•ni•ness,** *n.*

-tion *suffix.* **1** the act or process of ——ing: *addition, opposition.* **2** the condition of being ——ed: *exhaustion.* **3** the result or product of ——ing: *reflection.* ⟨< L *-tio, -onis* < *-t-* of pp. stem + *-io* (cf. *-ion*)⟩

tip[1] [tɪp] *n., v.* **tipped, tip•ping.** *—n.* **1** the end part; end; point: *the tips of the fingers.* **2** a small piece put on the end of something: *a rubber tip for a cane.*
tip of the iceberg, a a problem, issue, etc. that seems small but

has very great hidden ramifications. **b** one or relatively few instances of some problem, of which it is suspected there are many more: *They've caught 200 tax evaders and they say that's just the tip of the iceberg!*
—*v.* **1** put a tip on; furnish with a tip: *spears tipped with steel.* **2** cover or adorn at the tip: *mountains tipped with snow. Sunlight tips the steeple.* **3** be the tip of: *An ornately engraved bronze point tipped the scabbard.*
tip in, insert (an illustration, map, errata slip, etc.) by pasting to the inner margin of a book. ⟨ME *tippe*; ? < MDu. *tip* point⟩

tip² [tɪp] *v.* **tipped, tip•ping;** *n.* —*v.* **1** slope; slant: *She tipped the table toward her. My plants always tip toward the sun.* **2** upset; overturn: *He tipped over the milk jug. We fell in the water when the canoe tipped.* **3** raise (a hat) in greeting: *Men used to tip their hats when meeting a woman.* **4** empty out; dump.
tip the scales at. See SCALE².
—*n.* **1** the act of tipping: *a tip of the hat.* **2** a slope; slant. ⟨ME *tipen*; of certain origin⟩

tip³ [tɪp] *n., v.* **tipped, tip•ping.** —*n.* **1** a small present of money in return for service: *He gave the waiter a tip.* **2** a piece of secret or confidential information: *Alice had a tip that the black horse would win the race.* **3** a useful hint, suggestion, etc.: *a book of tips on caring for your pet.*
—*v.* **1** give a small present of money to: *She tipped the porter.* **2** give a tip or tips: *In Australia they don't tip in restaurants.* **3** give (an amount) as a tip: *I tipped him $5.*
tip off, give secret information or a warning to: *Someone tipped off the criminal and he escaped before the police arrived.*
tip (one's) **hand,** *Informal.* disclose one's secret plans, especially by accident. ⟨origin uncertain⟩ —**'tip•per,** *n.*

tip⁴ [tɪp] *n., v.* **tipped, tip•ping.** —*n.* a slight, sharp blow; tap. —*v.* hit lightly and sharply; tap. ⟨var. of *tap*⟩

tip cart a cart that is easily tipped for emptying, often with its body swivelling on a horizontal axis.

ti•pi ['tipi] See TEEPEE.

tip–off ['tɪp ˌɒf] *n. Informal.* **1** a piece of secret information, especially a warning. **2** the act of giving such information.

tip•pet ['tɪpɪt] *n.* **1** a scarf for the neck and shoulders with ends hanging down in front. **2** a long, narrow strip of cloth hanging from a sleeve, hood, or cape, worn especially in the 16th century. ⟨probably < *tip¹*⟩

tip•ple ['tɪpəl] *v.* **-pled, -pling;** *n.* —*v.* drink (alcoholic liquor) often.
—*n.* alcoholic liquor. ⟨origin uncertain; cf. Norwegian *tipla* drip, tipple⟩

tip•pler ['tɪplər] *n.* a habitual drinker of alcoholic liquor.

tip•py ['tɪpi] *adj.* liable to tip; unsteady or shaky: *Kayaks are tippy craft.*

tip•staff ['tɪpˌstæf] *n., pl.* **-staves** or **-staffs. 1** a staff tipped with metal, formerly carried by constables and other officers of the law. **2** an official who carried such a staff.

tip•ster ['tɪpstər] *n. Informal.* a person who makes a business of furnishing private or secret information for use in betting, speculation, etc. ⟨< *tip* a hint + *-ster*⟩

tip•sy ['tɪpsi] *adj.* **-si•er, -si•est. 1** somewhat intoxicated but not thoroughly drunk. **2** tipping easily; unsteady; tilted. ⟨< *tip²*⟩ —**'tip•si•ly,** *adv.* —**'tip•si•ness,** *n.*

tip•toe ['tɪpˌtou] *n., v.* **-toed, -toe•ing.** —*n.* the tips of the toes.
on tiptoe, a (walking) on the balls and toes of the feet: *I crossed the room on tiptoe to avoid waking her.* **b** eager: *The children were on tiptoe for vacation to begin.* **c** furtively, stealthily, or quietly.
—*v.* walk on the balls and toes of the feet, with the heels raised off the ground: *She tiptoed quietly up the stairs.*

tip•top ['tɪpˌtɒp] *n., adj.* —*n.* the very top; highest point or degree.
—*adj.* **1** situated at the very top or highest point. **2** *Informal.* first-rate; excellent. ⟨< *tip* end + *top*⟩

tip•up ['tɪp ˌʌp] *n. Cdn.* in ice-fishing, a device for supporting a line and indicating when a fish is hooked, as a pole balanced on a fulcrum so that one end (often flagged) tips upward when a fish pulls on the line.

ti•rade ['taɪreid] *or* [taɪ'reid] *n.* a long, vehement, usually scolding, speech. ⟨< F < Ital. *tirata* < *tirare* shoot⟩

ti•rail•leur [tiʀɑ'jœʀ] *n. French.* skirmisher; sharpshooter. ⟨< F *tirailleur* < *tirer* shoot⟩

tire¹ [taɪr] *v.* **tired, tir•ing. 1** lower or use up the energy of; make weary: *The hard work tired him.* **2** become weary: *She tires easily.* **3** wear down the patience, interest, or appreciation of: *Dull filing jobs tired the office boy.* **4** become impatient or bored: *She soon tired of these games.*
tire out, make very weary. ⟨OE *tȳrian*⟩

tire² [taɪr] *n., v.* **tired, tir•ing.** —*n.* **1** a circular rubber tube or ring fitted around the rim of a wheel, as of an automobile, aircraft, or bicycle, to provide a smooth ride and to increase traction. An automobile tire usually consists of an air-filled casing of layered rubberized nylon or steel cord covered with treaded rubber. See WHEEL for picture. **2** a band of rubber or metal around a wheel: *The wagon had iron tires.*
—*v.* furnish with a tire or tires. ⟨< *attire*, in sense of 'covering'⟩

tire³ [taɪr] *n., v.* **tired, tir•ing.** *Archaic.* —*n.* headdress; attire. —*v.* attire or adorn. ⟨short for *attire*⟩

tire chains a set of chains made to be fitted around the tire tread of an automotive vehicle to prevent skidding or slipping on ice or snow.

tired [taɪrd] *adj., v.* —*adj.* **1** weary; wearied; exhausted. **2** trite: *the same tired old arguments.*
—*v.* pt and pp. of TIRE¹.
tired of, no longer interested in; bored with: *I'm tired of hearing about their holidays.* ⟨< *tire¹*⟩ —**'tired•ly,** *adv.* —**'tired•ness,** *n.*
☛ *Syn.* **Tired,** WEARY, EXHAUSTED = having one's physical or mental strength, energy, and power of endurance lowered or drained by hard or long-continued work, strain, etc. **Tired** is the general and least precise word: *I am tired, but I must get back to work.* **Weary** suggests feeling worn out and unable or unwilling to go on: *Weary shoppers waited for buses and streetcars.* **Exhausted** emphasizes being without enough energy or endurance left to be able to go on: *Exhausted by play, the child could not eat.*

-tired *combining form.* having a tire or tires of a specified kind: *a wagon with rubber-tired wheels.* ⟨< *tire²*⟩

tire iron an iron bar about 45 cm long and 1.5 cm thick, slightly curved along its length, for prying a tire off a wheel rim.

tire•less¹ ['taɪrlɪs] *adj.* **1** never becoming tired; requiring little rest: *a tireless worker.* **2** never stopping: *tireless efforts.* —**'tire•less•ly,** *adv.* —**'tire•less•ness,** *n.*

tire•less² ['taɪrlɪs] *adj.* having no tire or tires.

Ti•re•si•as [taɪ'risiəs] *or* [tə'risiəs] *n. Greek legend.* a soothsayer from Thebes who was blinded by Athena because he saw her bathing. In compensation she gave him power to foresee future events, an understanding of birds' language, and a staff to serve as eyes.

tire•some ['taɪrsəm] *adj.* **1** tiring, because boring: *a tiresome speech.* **2** *Informal.* vexing; annoying or irritating. —**'tire•some•ly,** *adv.* —**'tire•some•ness,** *n.*
☛ *Syn.* **Tiresome,** TEDIOUS = tiring or boring, or both. **Tiresome** describes a person or thing that tires or bores one quickly by virtue of being dull and uninteresting: *Our neighbour is good-hearted, but I find her tiresome.* **Tedious** adds the idea of being long or slow or too much the same or, when describing a person, speaking or writing at too great length: *Weeding a garden is tedious work. He is a tedious speaker.*

tire•wom•an ['taɪrˌwʊmən] *n., pl.* **-wom•en.** *Archaic.* a lady's maid. ⟨< *tire* an archaic word for attire (< ME *tiren* shortened from *atiren* attire) + *woman*⟩

tiring room *Archaic.* a dressing room, especially in a theatre. ⟨< *attiring room.* See TIREWOMAN.⟩

ti•ro ['taɪrou] *n., pl.* **-ros.** See TYRO.

Ti•ro•le•an [tə'rouliən] *or* [ˌtirə'liən] *n., adj.* —*n.* a native or inhabitant of Tirol, a region in the Alps, partly in Austria and partly in Italy.
—*adj.* of or having to do with tirol. Also, **Tyrolean.**

Tir•o•lese [ˌtirə'liz] *adj. or n.* Tirolean. Also, **Tyrolese.**

Tir•than•ka•ra [tir'tʌŋkərə] *n.* any of the twenty-four venerated prophets and teachers in Jain belief.

'tis [tɪz] it is.

ti•sane [tɪ'zæn]; *French,* [ti'zan] *n.* an infusion or tea made from dried herbs; herbal tea. ⟨ME < MF < VL *tisana* < L *ptisana* barley groats or a drink made from them < Gk. *ptisane* peeled barley < *ptissein* peel⟩

Tish•ri ['tɪʃri] *n.* in the Hebrew calendar, the seventh month of the ecclesiastical year, and the first month of the civil year, corresponding roughly to October on the Julian calendar.

tis•sue ['tɪʃu] *n.* **1** *Biology.* **a** cells and intercellular material in general that constitute the substance of a plant or animal and distinguish organic structure as opposed to inorganic. **b** a mass of similar cells that together form some specialized part of an animal or a plant: *muscle tissue, skin tissue.* **2** a thin, light cloth. **3** a web; network: *Her whole story was a tissue of lies.* **4** TISSUE PAPER. **5** a thin, soft paper that absorbs moisture easily: *toilet tissue, cleansing tissue.* **6** a piece or a sheet of this paper: *There* *are 450 tissues in each box.* ⟨ME < OF *tissu*, originally pp. of *tistre* weave < L *texere*⟩

tissue culture the establishment and maintenance of living tissue under laboratory conditions allowing proliferation and differentiation. See also CELL CULTURE.

tissue paper a very thin, crisp paper, usually in large sheets and often layered, used mainly for wrapping.

tit[1] [tɪt] *n. Esp. Brit.* **1** any bird of the titmouse family, especially the Old World members of the genus *Parus*, such as the **great tit** (*Parus major*) of Europe, NW Africa, and Asia. **2** any of various similar small birds. ⟨ME; cf. Icelandic *tittr* titmouse⟩

tit[2] [tɪt] *n.* nipple; teat. ⟨OE *titt*⟩

ti•tan ['taitən] *n.* **1 Titan, a** *Greek mythology.* one of a family of giants who ruled the world until they were overthrown by the gods of Olympus. **b** the largest of Saturn's satellites. **2** a person or thing of great size, power, or strength. **3** (*adj.*) having great size, strength, or power; titanic. ⟨< L < Gk.⟩

ti•tan•ate ['taitə,neit] *n.* an ester or salt obtained by reaction of titanium tetrachloride with an alcohol or phenol in the presence of a base. ⟨< *titanium* + *-ate*⟩

ti•tan•ic[1] [tai,tænɪk] *adj.* **1** Usually, **Titanic,** of or like the Titans. **2** having or showing great size, strength, or power; colossal: *titanic energy.* **—ti'tan•i•cal•ly,** *adv.*

ti•tan•ic[2] [tai'tænɪk] containing titanium, especially in tetravalent form.

Ti•tan•ism ['taitə,nɪzəm] *n.* an attitude of rebellion or defiance toward authority, convention, etc.

ti•ta•ni•um [tai'teiniəm] *or* [tə'teiniəm] *n.* a light, strong, silvery or grey metallic element that occurs in ilmenite and rutile, used especially in steel alloys for aircraft parts. *Symbol*: Ti; *at.no.* 22; *at.mass* 47.90. ⟨< *Titan*⟩

titanium dioxide a crystalline, white oxide occurring naturally and used as a white pigment and glaze. Also called **titanium white** or **titanic oxide**. *Formula*: TiO_2

ti•tan•o•saur [tai'tænə,sɔr] *n.* any of a genus (*Titanosaurus*) of plant-eating quadrupedal dinosaurs of the Jurassic and Cretacious periods. ⟨< Gk. *Titan* + *sauros* lizard⟩

ti•tan•o•there [tai'tænə,θir] *n.* any of various extinct, rhinoceroslike mammals (order Perissodactyla) that flourished in North America from the Eocene to the Oligocene epochs, having a large, bulky body, a massive skull often having large horns over the snout, hoofed feet, and a very small, primitive brain. ⟨< Gk. *Titan* Titan + *thērion* beast⟩

ti•tan•ous ['taitənəs] *adj.* containing trivalent titanium.

tit•bit ['tɪt,bɪt] *n.* See TIDBIT.

ti•ter See TITRE.

tit for tat blow for blow; like for like. ⟨? by assimilation < *tip for tap*⟩

tithe [taið] *n., v.* **tithed, tith•ing.** *—n.* **1** one-tenth. **2** Often, **tithes,** *pl.* one-tenth of the yearly produce of land, animals, and personal work, paid as a tax, a donation, or an offering to God, for the support of the church and the clergy and their ministries. **3** a very small part. **4** any small tax, levy, etc.
—v. **1** give one-tenth of (one's income) to the church or to charity. **2** put a tax or a levy of a tenth on. **3** pay such a tax on (one's income, produce, etc.). ⟨OE *teogotha* tenth⟩

tith•ing ['taiðɪŋ] *n.* **1** the practice of giving or imposing a tithe. **2** formerly, in England: **a** a unit of local self-government consisting of ten families or households. **b** the district they occupied.

ti•ti[1] ['titi] *or* ['taitai] *n.* a small evergreen tree (*Cliftonia monophylla*) native to the S United States, having white or pale pink flowers. ⟨origin uncertain⟩

ti•ti[2] [ti'ti] *n.* any monkey of the genus *Callicebus* of South America, having long fur, a long, nonprehensile tail, and a small, round head. ⟨< Sp. *titi* < Aymara, language of an indigenous people of Bolivia and Peru⟩

ti•tian ['tɪʃən] *n. or adj.* auburn; golden red. ⟨< *Titian* (1477-1576), an Italian painter, who used this colour in his paintings⟩

tit•il•late ['tɪtə,leit] *v.* **-lat•ed, -lat•ing. 1** excite pleasantly; stimulate agreeably, often sexually. **2** tickle. ⟨< L *titillare*⟩

tit•il•la•tion [,tɪtə'leiʃən] *n.* **1** pleasant excitement; agreeable stimulation. **2** a tickling.

tit•i•vate or **tit•ti•vate** ['tɪtə,veit] *v.* **-vat•ed, -vat•ing.** *Informal.* dress or spruce up; make smart. ⟨? ult. < *tidy*⟩ **—,tit•i'va•tion** or **,tit•ti'va•tion,** *n.*

tit•lark ['tɪt,lɑrk] *n.* pipit. ⟨< *tit*[1] + *lark*[1]⟩

ti•tle ['taitəl] *n., v.* **-tled, -tling.** *—n.* **1 a** the name of a book, poem, picture, song, etc. **b** TITLE PAGE. **c** a descriptive heading or caption, as of a chapter or section of a book, etc. **2** a book; volume: *There are 5000 titles in our library.* **3** a name showing a person's rank, occupation, or condition in life. *Examples: doctor, professor, Madame, Miss, king, duke, lord, countess, and captain.* **4** a descriptive name or nickname; epithet. *Example*: Robin Hood, *Prince of Thieves.* **5** a first place position; championship: *the tennis title.* **6** *Law.* **a** the legal right to the possession of property. **b** the evidence showing such a right. **7** a recognized right; legitimate claim. **8** a caption, especially one translating dialogue, or a credit, displayed on the screen in a television program or film.
—v. call by a title; name. ⟨ME < OF < L *titulus.* Doublet of TITTLE.⟩
☛ *Syn. n.* **1.** See note at NAME.

ti•tled ['taitəld] *adj., v. —adj.* having a title, such as that of a duke, countess, lord, dame, etc.: *He married a titled diplomat.*
—v. pt. and pp. of TITLE.

title deed a document showing that a person owns certain property.

ti•tle•hold•er ['taitəl,houldər] *n.* the person currently holding the title, or championship, in some sport or competition.

title page the page at the beginning of a book that carries the title, the author's name, etc.

title role or **rôle** the part or character for which a play is named. Hamlet and Othello are title roles.

ti•tlist ['taitəlɪst] *n.* a former or current titleholder.

tit•mouse ['tɪt,mʌus] *n., pl.* **-mice. 1** any of various small, active, insect-eating songbirds (family Paridae), such as the **tufted titmouse** (*Parus bicolor*), which is closely related to the chickadee. **2** (*adj.*) designating the family (Paridae) of songbirds that includes the titmice and chickadees. See also TIT[1]. ⟨ME *titmose* < *tit* a small creature + *mose* titmouse + OE *māse*; influenced by *mouse*⟩

Ti•to•ism ['titou,ɪzəm] *n.* the principles and practices of Marshal Tito (1892-1980), president of the former Yugoslavia, from 1953 until his death, especially a form of Communism that asserted national rather than international interests and did not accept Soviet domination.

ti•trate ['taitreit] *or* ['tɪtreit] *v.* **-trat•ed, -trat•ing. 1** analyse (a solution) by titration. **2** be subjected to titration. ⟨< F *titrer* < *titre* quality⟩

ti•tra•tion [tai'treiʃən] *or* [tɪ'treiʃən] *n.* the process of determining the amount of some substance present in a solution by measuring the amount of a different substance that must be added to cause a chemical change.

ti•tre ['taitər] *or* ['titər] *n. Chemistry.* **1** a standard amount or strength of a solution as established by titration. **2** the minimum quantity of a standard solution needed to produce a given result in titration. Also, **titer.** ⟨< OF *titre* the proportion of gold or silver in an alloy; originally, learned borrowing < L *titulus* inscription⟩
☛ *Hom.* TEETER ['titər].

tit•ter ['tɪtər] *v., n. —v.* **1** laugh or giggle nervously, giddily, or affectedly, especially in a partly checked way: *Some people in the audience tittered nervously when the actor forgot his lines.* **2** say with such a laugh or giggle: *"He's got his sweater on inside out," she tittered.*
—n. a silly or nervous laugh or giggle, usually partly suppressed. **—'tit•ter•er,** *n.*

tit•tle ['tɪtəl] *n.* **1** a very little bit; particle; whit. **2** a small stroke or mark over a letter in writing or printing. The dot over an *i* is a tittle. ⟨ME < Med.L *titulus* diacritical mark < L *titulus* title. Doublet of TITLE.⟩

tit•tle–tat•tle ['tɪtəl ,tætəl] *n. or v.* **-tled, -tling.** gossip. ⟨varied reduplication of *tattle*⟩

tit•u•ba•tion [,tɪtjə'beiʃən] *n. Medicine.* unsteadiness in walking due to a nervous disorder. ⟨< L *titubatio* a staggering, stumbling < *titubare* stagger⟩

tit•u•lar ['tɪtʃələr] *adj., n. —adj.* **1** in title or name only: *He is a titular prince, without any power.* **2** having a title; titled. **3** having to do with a title; referred to in a title: *the titular heroine of Tolstoy's* Anna Karenina.
—n. a person holding a title, usually without actual power or duties of office. ⟨< L *titulus* title⟩ **—'tit•u•lar•ly,** *adv.*

tiz•zy ['tɪzi] *n., pl.* **-zies.** *Slang.* a very excited state; dither. ⟨origin uncertain⟩

TKO, T.K.O., or **t.k.o.** *Boxing.* TECHNICAL KNOCKOUT.

Tl thallium.

TLC *Informal.* tender loving care.

Tlin•git ['tlɪŋgɪt] *n., pl.* (def. 1) **Tlin•git** or **Tlin•gits;** *adj. —n.* **1** a member of a group of First Nations peoples of the northern Pacific coast. **2** the group of languages, thought to be related to Athapascan, spoken by these peoples.
—adj. of or having to do with the Tlingit or their languages.

Tm thulium.

TM trademark.

TM or **T.M.** TRANSCENDENTAL MEDITATION.

tme•sis [tə'misɪs] *or* ['misɪs] *n., pl.* **-ses** [siz]. *Grammar.* the separation of a compound word by an intervening word or words, as in the archaism *to us-ward* for *toward us.* ⟨< LL < Gk. *tmēsis*, originally, a cutting < *temnein* cut⟩

tn. ton(s).

TNT or **T.N.T.** ['ti,ɛn'ti] **1** trinitrotoluene. **2** *Informal.* anything dangerous or explosive.

to¹ [tu]; *unstressed,* [tʊ] *or* [tə] *prep., adv. —prep.* **1 a** in the direction of: *Go to the right.* **b** toward and reaching: *to fall to the floor. We rode to Montréal.* **2** as far as; until: *rotten to the core, faithful to the end, medium to large sizes.* **3** in telling time, before (the hour): *It is ten to four.* **4** for; for the purpose of: *He came to the rescue.* **5** toward or into the position, condition, or state of: *He went to sleep. She tore the letter to pieces.* **6** so as to produce, cause, or result in: *To her horror, the bear kept advancing toward her.* **7** by: *a fact known to few.* **8** along with; with: *We danced to the music.* **9** as a reaction or response stimulated or elicited by: *dogs salivating to the ringing of a bell. Answer to that charge. What did she say to that?* **10** compared with: *Those dogs are as different as black is to white. The score was 9 to 5.* **11** in agreement or accordance with: *It is not to my liking.* **12** as perceived or understood by: *a symptom alarming to the doctor.* **13** belonging with; of: *the key to my room, the lid to this jar.* **14** in honour of: *Drink to the King.* **15** on or onto; against; at: *Fasten it to the wall.* **16** about; concerning: *He did not speak to that issue.* **17** included, contained, or involved in: *seven apples to the kilogram.*
18 *Mathematics.* having; with: *a logarithm to the base ten, X to the exponent 3.* **19** *To* is used to show action directed at or toward: *Give the book to me. Speak to her.*
—adv. (*always stressed*) **1** forward: *He wore his cap wrong side to.* **2** together; touching; closed: *The door slammed to.* **3** to action or work: *We turned to gladly. The hungry girls set to as soon as they were served.* **4** to consciousness: *She came to. The ammonia brought her to.*
to and fro, first one way and then back again; back and forth. ⟨OE *tō*⟩
☛ *Hom.* TOO, TWO.

to² [tu]; *unstressed,* [tʊ] *or* [tə] a grammatical function word marking the infinitive of verbs: *He likes to read. "To err is human; to forgive divine." To* may stand for an understood infinitive and its complements in elliptical constructions: *Stay if you want to. I'll eat your spinach if you're not going to. Ask him? I wouldn't dare to.*

toad [toud] *n.* **1** any of numerous small amphibians (especially family Bufonidae) resembling frogs, but living mostly on land and having a more squat body, weaker hind legs, and rough, dry, often warty skin. Toads return to water to breed. Compare FROG. **2** a contemptible or disgusting person. ⟨OE *tāde*⟩
☛ *Hom.* TOED.

toad•eat•er ['toud,itər] *n.* a servile flatterer; toady. ⟨originally, a quack doctor's attendant who pretended to eat toads, which were thought to be poisonous, to prove the efficacy of his master's 'cure'⟩

toad•fish ['toud,fɪʃ] *n.* any of a family (Batrachoididae) of saltwater fishes having a thick head, a wide mouth, and slimy skin usually without scales.

toad•flax ['toud,flæks] *n.* any of several plants (genus *Linaria*) of the same family as the snapdragon, especially *L. vulgaris,* which has yellow-and-orange flowers.

toad spit or **spittle** CUCKOO SPIT.

toad•stool ['toud,stul] *n.* an umbrella-shaped fungus, especially a poisonous one. Compare MUSHROOM.

toad•y ['toudi] *n., pl.* **toad•ies;** *v.* **toad•ied, toad•y•ing.** *—n.* a fawning flatterer.
—v. **1** act like a toady. **2** fawn upon; flatter. ⟨short for *toadeater*⟩

toad•y•ism ['toudi,ɪzəm] *n.* the action or behaviour of a toady; interested flattery; base servility.

to–and–fro ['tu ən 'frou] *adj.* back-and-forth.

toast¹ [toust] *n., v. —n.* a slice or slices of bread browned by heat.
be toast, *Slang.* be ruined or done for: *Try that once more and you're toast!*
—v. **1** brown or be browned by heat. **2** heat or become heated thoroughly. ⟨ME < OF *toster,* ult. < L *torrere* parch⟩

toast² [toust] *n.* **1** a tribute to a person or thing by a company of people, in which the people raise their drinking glasses, express a wish for the health or success of the person or thing, and take a drink together: *The chairman proposed a toast to the Queen.* **2** a call for or the act of making such a tribute. **3** the person or thing honoured in such a way. **4** a person having many admirers: *She was the toast of the town.*
—v. drink a toast to: *The guests toasted the bride and groom.* ⟨from the custom of putting spiced toast into drinks for flavouring⟩

toast•er ['toustər] *n.* an electrical appliance for toasting bread, etc.

toast•mas•ter ['toust,mæstər] *n.* **1** a person who presides at a dinner and introduces the speakers. **2** a person who proposes toasts. **—'toast,mis•tress** [-,mɪstrɪs], *n.*

toas•ty ['tousti] *adj.* **1** like toast. **2** pleasantly or cosily warm.

to•bac•co [tə'bækou] *n., pl.* **-cos** or **-coes. 1** a plant (*Nicotiana tabacum*) of the nightshade family, widely cultivated in many varieties for its leaves, from which cigarettes, cigars, etc. are made. **2** the prepared leaves of this plant. **3** the products made from such leaves: *Does this store sell tobacco?* **4** the practice of using tobacco for smoking, etc.: *I have sworn off tobacco.* **5** any plant of the genus *Nicotiana,* which includes several species grown for their sweet-smelling flowers. ⟨< Sp. *tabaco* < Carib⟩

tobacco mosaic any of several viral diseases affecting tobacco and related plants, typically manifested in the form of mosaiclike mottling of leaves. The **tobacco mosaic virus** is important in biochemical research.

Tobacco Nation the Petun First Nations people, an Iroquoian people once inhabiting SW Ontario.

to•bac•co•nist [tə'bækənɪst] *n.* a dealer in tobacco.

To•ba•go•ni•an [,toubə'gouniən] *n., adj. —n.* a native or inhabitant of Tobago, an island in the West Indies.
—adj. of or having to do with Tobago.

to•bog•gan [tə'bɒgən] *n., v. Cdn. —n.* a long, light, narrow sleigh with a flat bottom and no runners, having the front end curved up and back.
—v. **1** ride or carry on a toboggan: *We went tobogganing yesterday. The supplies were tobogganed to camp.* **2** decline sharply and rapidly in value: *House prices tobogganed.* ⟨< Cdn.F *tabagane* < Algonquian; cf. Micmac *tobākun*⟩

to•by or **To•by** ['toubi] *n., pl.* **to•bies** or **To•bies.** a small, fat jug or mug in the form of a fat man wearing a long coat and a three-cornered hat. Also, **toby jug** or **Toby jug.** ⟨< *Toby,* proper name, short for *Tobias*⟩

toc•ca•ta [tə'kɑtə] *n. Music.* a composition for the piano, organ, or other keyboard instrument, often intended to exhibit the player's technique. ⟨< Ital. *toccata,* originally pp. of *toccare* touch⟩

To•char•i•an [tə'kæriən], [tə'kɛriən], *or* [tə'kɑriən] *n., adj. —n.* **1 a** an extinct Indo-European language of E Central Asia, current in the first millenium A.D. It is particularly interesting in that it is a centum language in a satem area. **b** either of the written forms of this language, known from texts dating from the 7th and 8th centuries, **Tocharian A** (or Turfanian) in the east and **Tocharian B** (or Kouchean) in the west. **2** a member of the Asian people speaking this language, thought to have had an advanced civilization.
—adj. of or having to do with these people or their language. Also, **Tokharian.**

to•col•o•gy [tə'kɒlədʒi] *n.* obstetrics. ⟨< Gk. *tokos* childbirth + E *-logy*⟩

to•coph•er•ol [tə'kɒfə,rɒl] *n.* any of a number of closely related E vitamins in the form of viscous oils found in wheat germ, cottonseed, egg yolk, and leafy vegetables. ⟨< Gk. *tokos* childbirth, offspring + *pher-* (< *pherein* bear) + E *-ol*⟩

toc•sin ['tɒksən] *n.* **1** an alarm sounded on a bell; a warning signal. **2** a bell used to sound an alarm. ⟨< F < Provençal *tocasenh* < *tocar* strike, touch + *senh* bell⟩
☛ *Hom.* TOXIN.

to•day [tə'dei] *n., adv. —n.* the present day, time, or period: *The photographer of today has many types of film to choose from.*

—*adv.* **1** on or during this day: *I have to go to the dentist today.* **2** at the present time or period; these days: *Most Canadian homes today have a refrigerator.* ⟨OE *tō dœge* on (the) day⟩

tod•dle ['tɒdəl] *v.* **-dled, -dling;** *n.* —*v.* walk with short, unsteady steps, as a baby does.
—*n.* a toddling way of walking. ⟨origin unknown⟩

tod•dler ['tɒdlər] *n.* a young child, especially one between the ages of one and two or three.

tod•dy ['tɒdi] *n., pl.* **-dies. 1** the fresh or fermented sap of various palm trees, especially of the East Indies. **2** a usually hot drink made of an alcoholic liquor such as whisky or brandy mixed with water, sugar, and spices. ⟨< Hind. *tārī* palm sap < *tār* palm⟩

to–do [tə 'du] *n., pl.* **-dos.** *Informal.* a fuss; flurry; excitement: *There was a great to-do when the new puppy arrived.*

toe [tou] *n., v.* **toed, toe•ing.** —*n.* **1** one of the five end parts of the foot. **2** the part of a stocking, shoe, etc. that covers the toes. **3** the forepart of a foot or hoof. **4** anything resembling a toe: *the toe and heel of a golf club.*
on (one's) **toes,** ready for action; alert.
step on (someone's) **toes,** offend someone, especially by infringing on his or her rights or encroaching on his or her domain of responsibility.
—*v.* **1** touch or reach with the toes: *to toe a line.* **2** turn the toes or have toes that turn in walking, standing, dancing, etc.: *to toe in, to toe out.* **3** furnish with a toe or toes. **4** drive (a nail) slantwise. **5** fasten by nails driven slantwise.
toe in, adjust the front wheels of an automobile, etc. so that they point forward and slightly inward.
toe the line, a have one's toes on the starting line of a race. **b** obey rules, conform to a doctrine, etc. strictly. ⟨OE *tā*⟩
—'toe•less, *adj.* **—'toe,like,** *adj.*
☛ *Hom.* TOW.

toea ['touɑ] *n., pl.* **toea** ['touɑ]. a unit of money in Papua New Guinea, equal to ¹⁄₁₀₀ of a kina. See table of money in the Appendix. ⟨< a Papuan language⟩

toe•cap ['tou,kæp] *n.* the outer covering, often reinforced, of the toe of a boot or shoe.

toe clip an attachment on a pedal that fits over the toes of the cyclist, to prevent the foot from slipping off the pedal.

toed [toud] *adj.* **1** having a specified number or kind of toes (*used only in compounds*): *square-toed shoes. The camel is a two-toed animal.* **2** of a nail, driven slantwise. **3** fastened by nails driven slantwise.
☛ *Hom.* TOAD.

toe dance a dance done on tiptoe, as in ballet.
—'toe-,dance, *v.*

toe•hold ['tou,hould] *n.* **1** a small place of support for the toes when climbing: *The climber cut toeholds in the glacier as he went.* **2** any means of support in progressing, especially at the start of a venture, etc.: *She opened a small neighbourhood store to get a toehold in the business.* **3** *Wrestling.* a hold in which an opponent's foot is bent back or twisted.

toe–in ['tou ,ɪn] *n.* the adjustment of the front wheels of a motor vehicle so that they are not perfectly parallel but point slightly inward at the front. This makes for better steering and helps equalize wear on the tires.

toe•nail ['tou,neil] *n., v.* —*n.* **1** the nail growing on a toe. **2** *Carpentry.* a nail driven obliquely.
—*v.* TOE (defs. 4, 5).

toe rubber 1 a very low rubber overshoe, covering only the toe, heel, and sole of the shoe. **2** a similar shoe protector but covering only the toe and having a strap around the heel to secure it.

toe•shoe ['tou,ʃu] *n.* either of a pair of ballet shoes with a flat piece of wood in the toe, on which to balance.

tof•fee ['tɒfi] *n., pl.* **-fees.** taffy. Also, **toffy** (*pl.* **-fies**). ⟨origin uncertain⟩

to•fu ['toufu] *n.* a bland, protein-rich food of a cheeselike consistency, made from soybeans. It is a popular meat substitute. ⟨< Japanese < Chinese *to* bean + *fu* rot⟩

tog [tɒg] *n., v.* **togged, tog•ging.** —*n.* Usually, **togs,** *pl. Informal.* clothes.
—*v.* clothe; dress (*usually with* **out** *or* **up**). ⟨apparently a shortening of obs. *togman;* probably influenced by L *toga*⟩

to•ga ['tougə] *n., pl.* **-gas, -gae** [-dʒi], [-gi], *or* [-gaɪ] **1** in ancient Rome, the loose, flowing outer garment worn by citizens. A toga was made of a single piece of cloth with no sleeves or armholes, covering the whole body except for the right arm. **2** a robe of office. ⟨< L⟩

to•gaed ['tougəd] *adj.* wearing a toga.

to•geth•er [tə'gɛðər] *adv., adj.* —*adv.* **1 a** in company or association; with each other: *They walked down the road together. I like navy and red together. They worked together for many years.* **b** jointly; by a joint or co-operative effort: *Together we can change the world.* **2** in or into one unit, mass, piece, etc.: *She mixed the two colours together.* **3** in or into contact or collision: *Bang the cymbals together.* **4** considered as a whole: *All the dimes and nickles together don't even make up three dollars. All together, there were 25 people at the party.* **5** in or into one gathering, company, or collection: *They get together every Friday to play bridge.* **6** in or into harmony or agreement: *Let's get together on our basic requirements.* **7** at the same time: *Day and night cannot occur together.* **8** without a stop or break; continuously; in succession: *He worked for days together.*
get it (all) together, *Slang.* get affairs under control.
—*adj. Slang.* having a well-adjusted, well-integrated personality: *She is so together, she makes me nervous!*
together with, along with. ⟨OE *tōgædere* < *tō* to + *gædere* together⟩
☛ *Usage.* **Together with.** In writing, a singular subject followed by 'together with—' still takes a singular verb: *My uncle, together with my two cousins, was there to meet me.* Compare this with: *My uncle and my two cousins were there to meet me.*

to•geth•er•ness [tə'gɛðərnɪs] *n.* the condition of being closely associated or united, especially in family or social activities.

tog•ger•y ['tɒgəri] *n. Informal.* **1** garments; clothes. **2** a clothing store.

tog•gle ['tɒgəl] *n., v.* **-gled, -gling.** —*n.* **1** a pin, bolt, or rod put through the eye of a rope or a link of a chain to keep it in place, to hold two ropes together, to serve as a hold for the fingers, etc. **2** an oblong piece that is attached crosswise by its centre and is passed through a loop or hole to act as a fastening for a coat, etc. **3 a** TOGGLE JOINT. **b** TOGGLE SWITCH. **c** a device furnished with either of these. **4** *Computer technology.* a switch or function on a computer that is successively activated and deactivated by the same command, key, or combination of keys.
—*v.* fasten or furnish with a toggle or toggles. ⟨Cf. *tug,* v.⟩

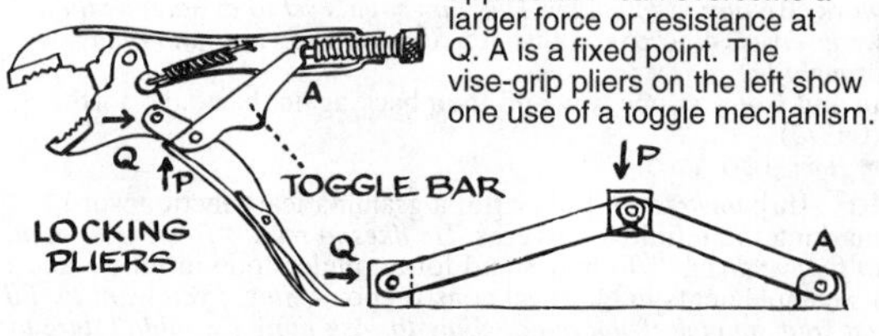

Toggle joint: a small force applied at P can overcome a larger force or resistance at Q. A is a fixed point. The vise-grip pliers on the left show one use of a toggle mechanism.

toggle joint a kneelike joint that transmits pressure at right angles.

toggle switch an electric switch having a projecting lever that is pushed through a small arc to open or close the circuit.

To•go ['tougou] *n.* a republic in W Africa.

To•go•lese [,tougou'liz] *adj., n., pl.* **-lese.** —*adj.* of or having to do with Togo, its people, or their culture.
—*n.* a native or inhabitant of Togo.

togue [toug] *n. Cdn. Maritimes.* LAKE TROUT. ⟨< Cdn.F < Algonquian⟩

toil¹ [tɔɪl] *n., v.* —*n.* hard work or a single piece of hard work; labour: *to succeed finally after years of toil.*
—*v.* **1** work hard: *to toil with one's hands for a living.* **2** move with difficulty, pain or weariness: *They toiled up the hill.* **3** *Archaic.* bring, achieve, or obtain by hard work or effort. ⟨ME < AF *toiler* < OF *toeillier* drag about, make dirty < L *tudiculare* stir up < L *tudicula* olive press < *tundere* pound⟩ **—'toil•er,** *n.*
☛ *Syn. n.* **1.** See note at WORK.

toil² [tɔɪl] *n.* **1** *Archaic.* a net for trapping game. **2 toils,** *pl.* anything that holds one fast; a snare or trap: *caught in the toils of the law.* ⟨< F *toile,* literally, cloth < L *tela* web < *texere* weave⟩

toile [twɑl]; *French,* [twal] *n.* sheer cotton or linen. ⟨< F⟩

toi•let ['tɔɪlɪt] *n.* **1** a fixture, usually a porcelain bowl flushed by water, into which waste from the body is passed. **2** a room or cubicle containing a toilet. **3** (*adjl.*) for a toilet: *a toilet brush.*

4 the act or process of washing, dressing, and grooming oneself: *She took a half-hour to complete her toilet.* **5** (*adjl.*) of or for use in the process of dressing and grooming: *Combs and brushes are toilet articles.* **6** *Archaic.* dressing table. **7** *Archaic.* attire or costume: *Her toilet was elaborate.* **8** *Medicine.* **a** the cleaning and application of dressings to a wound. **b** the cleansing or clearing out of a passage or cavity, as after childbirth.
go to the toilet, *Informal.* urinate or defecate: *The child said he had to go to the toilet.* ⟨< F *toilette*, dim. of *toile*. See TOIL[2].⟩

toi•let•ing ['tɔılətıŋ] *n.* independent use of a toilet (by a small child).

toilet paper thin, soft, absorbent paper for use in a toilet, especially for cleaning the body after passing waste.

toi•let•ry ['tɔılıtri] *n.* Usually, **toiletries,** *pl.* soap, face powder, perfume or cologne, shaving cream, etc. used in washing and grooming oneself.

toilet soap mild soap that is usually perfumed and coloured.

toi•lette [twɑ'lɛt] *n.* **1** the process of washing, dressing, and grooming oneself. **2** fashionable attire or costume. ⟨< F⟩

toilet tissue TOILET PAPER.

toilet training *n.* the process of training a child to control bladder and bowel movements and to use a toilet.
—'toi•let-,train, *v.*

toilet water EAU DE TOILETTE.

toil•some ['tɔılsəm] *adj.* requiring hard work; laborious; wearisome. **—'toil•some•ly,** *adv.* **—'toil•some•ness,** *n.*

toil•worn ['tɔıl,wɔrn] *adj.* worn by toil; showing the effects of toil: *toilworn hands.*

To•kay ['toukei] *n.* **1** a rich, sweet, golden wine made in Hungary. **2** a similar wine made elsewhere. **3** a variety of large, reddish, sweet grape used for making such wine. ⟨< *Tokay*, a town in N Hungary, where this wine was first made⟩

to•ken ['toukən] *n.* **1 a** a mark, symbol, or sign: *Black is a token of mourning.* **b** something that serves to prove; an evidence: *His actions are a token of his sincerity.* **c** a characteristic mark or indication: *the tokens of a good horse, the tokens of a disease.* **2** a sign of friendship; keepsake: *She received many birthday tokens.* **3** a piece of metal, plastic, etc. stamped for a higher value than of the material, often made and sold for use as a single bus or train fare, etc. **4** a piece of metal, plastic, etc. indicating a right or privilege: *This token will admit you to the swimming pool.* **5** something that is a sign of genuineness or authority. **6** (*adjl.*) **a** serving only as a symbol; having no real significance; nominal: *a token payment, token resistance.* **b** included merely as a show of non-discrimination: *the token Asian on the committee.* **7** *Archaic.* a signal.
by the same token, for the same reason; similarly.
in token of, as a token of; to show. ⟨OE *tācen*⟩
☛ *Syn. n.* **1.** See note at MARK.

to•ken•ism ['toukə,nızəm] *n.* the practice or policy of making only a nominal or partial effort, especially in providing equal opportunity to disadvantaged or minority groups: *Putting a few women on boards of directors is just tokenism.*

To•khar•i•an [tə'kæriən], [tə'kɛriən], *or* [tə'kɑriən] *n., adj.* See TOCHARIAN.

to•lar ['toulɑr] *n., pl.* **to•lar•jev** [-,jɛv]. the unit of currency in Slovenia. See table of money in the Appendix.

tol•bu•ta•mide [tɒl'bjutə,maıd] *n.* a crystalline sulphonamide that releases insulin from the pancreas and lowers the blood sugar. It is used orally in the treatment of adult diabetes. *Formula*: $C_{12}H_{18}N_2O_3S$

told [tould] *v.* pt. and pp. of TELL.
all told, including all.

To•le•do [tə'lidou] *n.* a fine sword or sword blade made in Toledo, a city in central Spain.

tol•er•a•ble ['tɒlərəbəl] *adj.* **1** that can be endured: *The pain has not disappeared, but it has become tolerable.* **2** fairly good: *She is in tolerable health.* ⟨ME < OF < L *tolerabilis* < *tolerare* tolerate⟩ **—,tol•er•a'bil•i•ty,** *n.* **—'tol•er•a•bly,** *adv.*
—'tol•er•a•ble•ness, *n.*

tol•er•ance ['tɒlərəns] *n.* **1** a willingness to be tolerant and respectful toward people whose opinions or ways differ from one's own. **2** the power of enduring or resisting the effects of: *a high tolerance for pain, a low tolerance for alcohol.* **3** the act of tolerating. **4** an allowed amount of variation from a standard, as in the mass of coins or the dimensions of a machine or part.
☛ *Syn.* **1.** See note at TOLERATION.

tol•er•ant ['tɒlərənt] *adj.* **1** willing to let other people do as they think best; willing to allow beliefs and actions of which one does not approve: *A more tolerant person would not have walked out in the middle of the meeting.* **2** easy-going; not readily saying no: *The teacher was tolerant toward the high-spirited children.* **3** able to endure or resist the action of a drug, poison, etc.
—'tol•er•ant•ly, *adv.*

tol•er•ate ['tɒlə,reit] *v.* **-at•ed, -at•ing. 1** allow; permit: *He was an informal teacher, but would never tolerate insolence.* **2** bear; endure; put up with: *They tolerated the grouchy old man because he was their employer.* **3** recognize the validity of (the beliefs, practices, etc. of others) although one may not share them. **4** endure or resist the action or effect of. ⟨< L *tolerare*⟩
—'tol•er,a•tor, *n.*

tol•er•a•tion [,tɒlə'reiʃən] *n.* **1** the act or practice of tolerating. **2** the policy or practice of recognizing and guaranteeing people's rights, especially their freedom to worship as they think best without loss of civil rights or social privileges.
☛ *Usage.* **Toleration** (def. 1) and TOLERANCE (def. 1) are associated with the verb **tolerate,** but differ in meaning. **Toleration** = the act of allowing or putting up with actions, beliefs, or people one does not like or approve of, often because of indifference or a desire to avoid conflict: *Toleration of dishonest officials encourages corruption.* **Tolerance** = the state, quality, or attitude of being willing to let others think, live, or worship according to their own beliefs and to refrain from judging harshly or with blind prejudice: *Canadians value tolerance and understanding.*

toll[1] [toul] *v., n.* *—v.* **1** sound (a church bell, etc.) with single strokes slowly and regularly repeated: *Bells were tolled all over the country at the king's death.* **2** of a bell, sound with slow, single strokes: *The bell tolled.* **3** call, announce, etc. by tolling: *The bells tolled the death of the king.*
—n. **1** the stroke or sound of a bell being tolled. **2** the act or fact of tolling. ⟨related to OE *-tyllan* draw. See TILL[3].⟩

toll[2] [toul] *n., v.* *—n.* **1** a tax or fee paid for some right or privilege: *We pay a toll when we use the bridge.* **2** a charge for a certain service. There is a toll on long-distance telephone calls. **3** something paid, lost, suffered, etc.: *Automobile accidents take a heavy toll of human lives.*
—v. Rare. collect as a toll or collect a toll from. ⟨OE *toll*, var. of *toln* < L < Gk. *telōnion* toll house, ult. < *telos* tax⟩

toll[3] [toul] *v., n. Hunting.* *—v.* **1** lure (game) by using a call or other sound. **2** make such a call or sound.
—n. a call or sound thus made. ⟨ME; cf. OE *talu* talk. Akin to TALE.⟩

toll bar a barrier, especially a gate, across a road or bridge where a toll is taken.

toll•booth ['toul,buθ] *n.* a booth, as at the entry to a toll road or toll bridge, where drivers must stop and pay a toll.

toll bridge a bridge at which a toll is charged.

toll call a long-distance telephone call.

toll•er ['toulər] *n. Cdn.* NOVA SCOTIA DUCK TOLLING RETRIEVER.

toll•gate ['toul,geit] *n.* a gate where a toll is collected.

toll•keep•er ['toul,kipər] *n.* a person who collects the toll at a tollgate.

toll road a road on which tolls are charged; turnpike.

Tol•tec ['toultɛk] *or* ['tɒltɛk] *n., adj.* *—n.* a member of a native North American people supposed to have ruled in Mexico before the Aztecs.
—adj. of or having to do with this people or their culture.

to•lu [tou'lu] *n.* a fragrant balsam obtained from a South American tree, used in medicine, perfume, etc. ⟨< Santiago de *Tolú*, a city in Colombia⟩

tol•u•ene ['tɒlju,in] *n.* a colourless liquid hydrocarbon resembling benzene, originally obtained from tolu but now more often from coal tar and coal gas. It is used as a solvent and for making explosives and dyes. *Formula*: $C_6H_5CH_3$ ⟨< *tolu* + *-ene*, as in *benzene*⟩

tol•u•ol ['tɒlju,ɒl] *or* ['tɒlju,oul] *n.* a commercial grade of toluene.

tom [tɒm] *n.* **1** the male of some animals: *This cat is a tom.* **2** (*adjl.*) of some animals, male: *a tom turkey.* ⟨< *Tom*, used as a type name for a common man. Compare TOMCAT.⟩

tom•a•hawk ['tɒmə,hɒk] *n., v.* *—n.* a light axe used by many First Nations peoples as a weapon and as a tool.
bury the tomahawk, stop fighting; make peace.
—v. strike or kill with a tomahawk. ⟨< Algonquian⟩

to•mal•ki [tə'mælki] *n. Cdn. Slang.* an alcoholic drink consisting of tomato juice mixed with any cheap white spirits. Compare REDEYE. ⟨< *tom*(*ato*) + *alki* (< *alcohol*)⟩

tom•al•ley ['tɒmæli] *n.* the cooked liver of a lobster, a Caribbean delicacy. ⟨< Carib *taumali*⟩

to•ma•to [tə'meitou], [tə'mɑtou], *or* [tə'mætou] *n., pl.* **-toes.** **1** a juicy, pulpy, red or yellow fruit commonly eaten as a vegetable, either raw or cooked. **2** the widely cultivated annual plant (*Lycopersicon esculentum*) this fruit grows on, having hairy leaves and stems and small, yellow flowers. ⟨< Sp. < Nahuatl *tomatl*⟩

tomb [tum] *n., v.* *—n.* **1** a vault or chamber for the dead, often built partly or completely above ground. **2** grave. **3** a monument or tombstone to commemorate the dead. **4 the tomb,** death.
—v. Rare. entomb. ⟨ME < AF < LL < Gk. *tymbos* mound⟩
—'tomb•less, *adj.* **—'tomb,like,** *adj.*

tom•bac, tom•back, or **tom•bak** ['tɒmbæk] *n.* any of several alloys consisting of zinc, copper, and sometimes arsenic, used to make cheap jewellery, art objects, etc. Also, **tambac.** ⟨< F *tombac* < Pg. *tambaca* < Malay < Skt. *tamraka*⟩

tom•bo•la [tɒm'boulə] *n.* a kind of lottery in which the prize tickets are drawn from a drum-shaped barrel usually turned by a crank. Tombola is popular at charity balls, community fairs, etc. ⟨< F < Ital. *tombolare* tumble⟩

tom•bo•lo ['tɒmbə,lou] *n.* a ridge of sand, gravel, etc. joining an island to the mainland or to another nearby island. ⟨< Ital. < L *tumulus* mound⟩

tom•boy ['tɒm,bɔi] *n.* a girl who has boyish mannerisms, tries to look like a boy, etc.

tomb•stone ['tum,stoun] *n.* a stone that marks a tomb or grave.

tom•cat ['tɒm,kæt] *n.* a male cat. ⟨< *tom* + *cat*, after *Tom the Cat*, hero of "The Life and Adventures of a Cat" (1760)⟩

tom•cod ['tɒm,kɒd] *n.* TOMMY COD.

Tom, Dick, and Harry people in general; everyone (*usually preceded by* **every** *and often mildly pejorative*).

tome [toum] *n.* a book, especially a large and scholarly book. ⟨< F < L < Gk. *tomos*, originally, piece cut off⟩

to•men•tum [tə'mɛntəm] *n., pl.* **-ta** [-tə]. **1** *Botany.* a downy or woolly growth on stems and leaves. **2** *Anatomy.* a mass of very fine, interconnected blood vessels in the pia matter and cerebral cortex of the human brain. ⟨< NL < L, stuffing for pillows⟩
—to'men•tose or **'to•men,tose** ['toumən,tous], *adj.*

tom•fool ['tɒm,ful] *n., adj.* *—n.* a silly fool; stupid person.
—adj. very stupid or foolish: *That was a tomfool thing to do.*

tom•fool•er•y [,tɒm'fuləri] *n., pl.* **-er•ies.** silly behaviour; nonsense.

Tom•my or **tom•my** ['tɒmi] *n., pl.* **-mies.** a nickname for a British soldier. Also, **Tommy Atkins.** ⟨< *Thomas Atkins*, a fictitious name used since 1815 in British army regulations to represent a private soldier⟩

tommy cod *Cdn.* any of several small saltwater fishes (genus *Microgadus*), especially of the St. Lawrence and adjacent waters, resembling and related to the cod.

tom•my•rot ['tɒmi,rɒt] *n. Slang.* nonsense; rubbish; foolishness. ⟨origin uncertain⟩

to•mo•gram ['toumə,græm] *n.* an X-ray photograph produced by tomography. ⟨< Gk. *tome* a cutting + E *-gram*⟩

to•mog•ra•phy [tə'mɒgrəfi] *n.* an X-ray technique by which only a single plane of the body is displayed. ⟨< Gk. *tome* a cutting off + E *-graphy*⟩

to•mor•row [tə'mɔrou] *n., adv.* *—n.* **1** the day after today. **2** the indefinite future: *the world of tomorrow.*
—adv. **1** on the day after today. **2** at some indefinite time in the future: *Tomorrow these same youth will be leaders of the nation.* ⟨ME *to morowe*⟩

tom•pi•on ['tɒmpiən] *n.* See TAMPION.

Tom Thumb **1** in the children's story, a dwarf no bigger than his father's thumb. **2** any very small thing or person.

tom–tom ['tɒm ,tɒm] *n.* a usually tall or long, narrow drum beaten with the hands; especially, any of various such drums of India or Africa or of the First Nations. ⟨< Hind. *tam-tam*; *of imitative origin*⟩

-to•my *combining form.* a cutting or dividing (used especially in the names of surgical operations): *lobotomy.* ⟨< Gk. *tome* a cutting⟩

ton[1] [tʌn] *n.* **1** either of two formerly standard units for measuring mass: the **short ton,** used in Canada, the United States, etc., equal to 2000 pounds (about 907 kg) and the **long ton,** used in the United Kingdom, equal to 2240 pounds (about 1016 kg). **2** a unit for measuring the internal capacity of a ship, equal to 100 cubic feet (about 2.8 m^3); in full, **register ton. 3** a unit for measuring the cargo or carrying capacity of a ship, equal to 40 cubic feet (about 1.1 m^3); in full, **freight ton** or **measurement ton. 4** a unit for measuring the amount of water a ship will displace, equal to 35 cubic feet (about 1 m^3), which is approximately equal to a long ton mass of sea water; in full, **displacement ton. 5** *Informal.* a very large number or amount: *These books weigh a ton. He's got tons of records.* **6** tonne; METRIC TON. ⟨var. of *tun*⟩
☛ *Hom.* TONNE, TUN.

ton[2] [tɔ̃] *n. French.* style; elegance. ⟨< F⟩

ton•al ['tounəl] *adj.* **1** of or having to do with tones or tone. **2** characterized by TONALITY (def. 1b); based on a scale or mode; having a key: *tonal music.* **—'ton•al•ly,** *adv.*

to•nal•i•ty [tou'næləti] *n., pl.* **-ties. 1** *Music.* **a** the relations existing between the tones that make up a scale or musical system. **b** adherence to a particular arrangement of tones in a scale or musical system; key. **2** in painting, etc., the overall tone or colour scheme of a picture: *The colours in the painting are sombre, but the tonality is good.*

tonal language TONE LANGUAGE.

ton•do ['tɒndou] *n., pl.* **-di** [-di] or **-dos.** a circular painting. ⟨< Ital., plate (originally, round < *rotondo* < L *rotundus*)⟩

tone [toun] *n., v.* **toned, ton•ing.** *—n.* **1** any sound considered with reference to its quality, pitch, strength, source, etc.: *sweet, shrill, or loud tones.* **2** the quality of sound: *a voice silvery in tone.* **3** *Music.* **a** a sound of definite pitch and character. **b** the basic or fundamental frequency of a musical note as opposed to any of its overtones. **c** a difference in pitch of one whole step or degree between two notes: *C and D are one tone apart.* **4** a manner of speaking or writing: *We disliked the haughty tone of her letter.* **5 a** spirit; character; style: *tone of elegance.* **b** mental or emotional state; mood; disposition: *a healthful tone of mind.* **6** condition with regard to health and vigour: *good tone, poor tone.* **7** *Physiology.* normal tension and firmness of healthy muscle at rest. **8** the overall effect of colour and of light and shade in a painting, drawing, etc.: *I like the soft green tone of that painting.* **9 a** a shade of colour: *This room is furnished in tones of brown.* **b** the quality imparted to one colour by another: *That carpet gives the white wall a bluish tone.* **10** *Linguistics.* **a** the pitch of the voice as it is high or low, or as it rises and falls, regarded as a distinctive feature of a language. **b** any of the tonal levels distinctive in a language. **c** the pronunciation characteristic of a particular person, group of people, area, etc.; accent: *plummy British tones.* **11** elegance; good style; distinction.
—v. **1** harmonize (*often used with* **in**): *This rug tones in well with the wallpaper and furniture.* **2** give (a) tone to. **3** change the tone of. **4** *Photography.* chemically alter the colour of (a print, especially a monochrome one).
tone down, soften; make or become less intense.
tone up, give or acquire more sound, colour, or vigour; make or become stronger or more intense. ⟨ME < OF < L *tonus* < Gk. *tonos*, originally, a stretching, taut string⟩

tone arm the part of a record player that carries the pickup and needle. The tone arm moves on a pivot.

tone block one of a set of tuned percussion instruments, consisting of shaped wooden pieces struck with a mallet.

tone control a device, as on an amplifier, to control the relative intensity of high and low frequencies in sound reproduction.

toned [tound] *adj., v.* *—adj.* having (a) tone, especially of a specified kind or number (*used especially in compounds*): *a sweet-toned voice, a high-toned restaurant, a two-toned colour scheme.*
—v. pt. and pp. of TONE.

tone–deaf ['toun ,dɛf] *adj.* not able to distinguish differences in musical pitch accurately. **—tone deafness.**

tone language or **tonal language** a language, such as Yoruba, Swedish, or Mandarin, in which otherwise homophonous words are distinguished in meaning solely by pitch or intonation contour.

tone•less ['tounlɪs] *adj.* **1** lacking in expression or variation of tone: *He spoke in a toneless voice.* **2** having no tone. **—'tone•less•ly,** *adv.* **—'tone•less•ness,** *n.*

tone poem SYMPHONIC POEM.

ton•er ['tounər] *n.* **1** the powdered ink used in xerography, usually in a cartridge. **2** an astringent cleanser for the face.

tone row *Music.* an arrangement of notes, especially the twelve notes of the chromatic scale, in some specific order as the basis of a composition in serial music.

to•nette [tou'nɛt] *n.* a simple flutelike instrument having easy finger guides and range slightly more than an octave, used for basic education in music.

to•ney ['touni] *adj.* See TONY.

tong[1] [tɒŋ] *n.* **1** in China, an association or club. **2** a secret organization or club in North American Chinese communities. ⟨< Chinese *t'ang, t'ong*, originally, meeting hall⟩

tong[2] [tɒŋ] *v.* **1** seize, gather, hold, or handle with tongs. **2** use tongs; work with tongs. ⟨OE *tang*⟩

ton•ga ['tɒŋgə] *n.* on the Indian subcontinent, a two-wheeled vehicle, drawn usually by a horse. ⟨< Hind. *tanga*⟩

Ton•ga ['tɒŋgə] *n.* an island kingdom in the South Pacific.

Ton•gan ['tɒŋgən] *n.* **1** a native or inhabitant of Tonga. **2** the Polynesian language of Tonga.

tongs [tɒŋz] *n.pl.* a tool for seizing, holding, or lifting, usually consisting of two long arms joined like a pair of scissors or by a spring piece. See FIREPLACE for picture.

tongue [tʌŋ] *n., v.* **tongued, tongu•ing.** *—n.* **1 a** the movable fleshy organ in the mouth of human beings and most vertebrates. The tongue is used for tasting and taking and swallowing food and also, in humans, for talking. See WINDPIPE for picture. **b** an analogous part in invertebrates, as the radula of a mollusc or the proboscis of an insect. **2** an animal's tongue used as food. **3** the power of speech: *You are silent—have you lost your tongue?* **4** a way of speaking; speech; talk: *a flattering tongue.* **5** the language of a people: *the English tongue.* **6 tongues,** *pl.* glossolalia; SPEAKING IN TONGUES. **7** *Archaic or Poetic.* a group of people united by one language. **8** the strip of material under the laces of a shoe. **9** a narrow strip of land running out into water. **10** a tapering jet of flame. **11** the pin of a buckle, brooch, etc. **12** the pole by which a team of horses draws a wagon. **13** a projecting strip along the edge of a board for fitting into a groove in another board. **14** the pointer of a dial, balance, etc. **15** the clapper of a bell. **16** in a woodwind, a vibrating reed, etc. **17** the short movable rail of a railway switch. **18** anything shaped or used like a tongue.
find one's tongue, regain the power of speech, as after being surprised or disconcerted.
give tongue, a of hounds, etc., bark or bay. **b** of humans, speak, cry, etc. vociferously (*used facetiously*): *The infant opened her mouth and gave tongue as soon as she was born.*
hold (one's) **tongue,** keep silent.
on the tip of (one's) **tongue, a** almost spoken. **b** ready to be spoken.
speak in tongues, practise glossolalia.
(with one's) **tongue in** (one's) **cheek,** ironically; not seriously; facetiously.
—v. **1** modify tones of (a flute, cornet, etc.) with the tongue. **2** touch or lick with the tongue. **3** articulate with the tongue. **4** furnish (a board) with a tongue. **5** join using a tongue-and-groove joint. ⟨OE *tunge*⟩ **—'tongue•less,** *adj.* **—'tongue,like,** *adj.*

tongue–and–groove joint ['tʌŋ ən 'gruv] *Carpentry.* a joint made by fitting a projecting strip, or tongue, along one edge of a board into a groove in another board.

tongue–in–cheek ['tʌŋ ɪn 'tʃik] *adj.* meant to be ironic or facetious: *a tongue-in-cheek criticism.*

tongue–lash•ing ['tʌŋ ,læʃɪŋ] *n.* a severe scolding: *Her father gave her a tongue-lashing for letting her ice cream drip all over the carpet.* **—'tongue-,lash,** *v.*

tongue–tie ['tʌŋ ,taɪ] *n., v.* **-tied, -ty•ing.** *—n.* a condition in which the motion of the tongue is impeded by an abnormal shortness of the folded membrane below it.
—v. make (someone) unable to speak, because of amazement, fear, shyness, etc.

tongue–tied ['tʌŋ ,taɪd] *adj.* **1** unable to speak because of shyness or embarrassment. **2** having the motion of the tongue hindered or limited because the membrane that connects its lower side to the bottom of the mouth is abnormally short.

tongue twister a phrase or sentence having a sequence of similar sounds or groups of sounds that is difficult to say quickly without getting the sounds mixed up. *Example*: *She sells sea shells on the seashore.*

tongue–twist•ing ['tʌŋ ,twɪstɪŋ] *adj.* of or like a tongue twister; difficult to say quickly without a mistake.

tongu•ing ['tʌŋɪŋ] *n.* use or manipulation of the tongue in playing a wind instrument, in order to interrupt the tone and produce a staccato effect, or to achieve greater accuracy in playing a rapid series of notes.

ton•ic ['tɒnɪk] *n., adj. —n.* **1** anything that gives strength, vigour, or refreshment; a medicine to give strength: *Cod-liver oil is a tonic. Conversation with children was a tonic for the old man.* **2** *Music.* the first note of a scale; keynote. **3** TONIC WATER: *gin and tonic.* **4** *Phonetics.* **a** primary stress. **b** a sound or syllable bearing primary stress.
—adj. **1** restoring to health and vigour; giving strength; bracing: *The mountain air is tonic.* **2 a** having to do with, producing, or restoring normal muscular tension. **b** characterized by continuous contraction of the muscles: *a tonic convulsion.* **3** *Music.* **a** having to do with a tone or tones. **b** of, being, or based on a keynote. **4** *Phonetics.* **a** of stress, primary; having to do with primary stress. **b** of a sound or syllable, bearing primary stress or bearing TONIC ACCENT. ⟨< Gk. *tonikos* < *tonos* tone. See TONE.⟩

tonic accent *Phonetics.* emphasis placed on a syllable by raising its pitch rather than, or sometimes in addition to, increasing its volume or length.

to•nic•i•ty [tə'nɪsəti] *n.* **1** the quality or condition of being tonic. **2** the property of possessing bodily tone; the normal elastic tension of muscles, arteries, etc.

tonic sol–fa a system of teaching music, especially sight-singing and notation, in which the notes of a major scale are sung to sol-fa syllables with *do* as the tonic or keynote of the major keys, and *lah* as the tonic or keynote of the minor keys. See GAMUT, etymology.

tonic water quinine-flavoured carbonated water.

to•night [tə'naɪt] *adv., n. —adv.* on or during the present or the coming night or evening.
—n. the present or the coming night or evening: *I wish tonight would come!* ⟨OE *tō niht*⟩

to•nite ['tounəit] *n.* an explosive used in blasting, consisting of guncotton and barium nitrate. ⟨< *ton-*, abstracted from L *tonare* thunder⟩

ton•ka bean ['tɒŋkə] **1** the black, aromatic seed of a South American leguminous tree (*Dipteryx odorata*), used in making perfumes. **2** the tree bearing these seeds.

Tonkin snub–nosed langur ['tɒŋkə] a species of monkey (*Rhonopithecus avunculus*) found in northern Vietnam. It is an endangered species.

ton•nage ['tʌnɪdʒ] *n.* **1** the internal capacity of a ship expressed in tons of 100 cubic feet, or REGISTER TONS (about 2.8 m³). A ship with a tonnage of 500 has an internal capacity of 50 000 cubic feet. **2** ships in terms of their total carrying capacity or the total amount carried: *the tonnage of Canada's navy.* **3** a duty or tax on ships at so much a ton. **4** total mass in tons.

tonne [tʌn] *n.* a unit used with the SI for measuring mass, equal to one thousand kilograms. A very small car has a mass of about one tonne. Also called **metric ton**. *Symbol*: t
☛ *Hom.* TON, TUN.

ton•neau [tə'nou] *n., pl.* **-neaus** or **-neaux** [-'ouz]. **1** the part of an automobile that contains the back seats, whether enclosed or, as often in small sportcars, open. **2** the cargo compartment of a boat or hatchback. ⟨< F *tonneau*, literally, cask, tun, ult. < Gmc.⟩

to•nom•e•ter [tə'nɒmətər] *n.* **1** an instrument measuring the pitch or frequency of tones. It may be mechanical, as a tuning fork, or electronic. **2** *Medicine.* an instrument measuring the pressure of a bodily fluid. **3** an instrument measuring vapour pressure.

ton•sil ['tɒnsəl] *n.* either of the two oval masses of lymphatic tissue on the inner sides of the throat, at the back of the mouth. ⟨< L *tonsillae*, pl., dim. of *toles*, pl., goiter⟩

ton•sil•lar or **ton•sil•ar** ['tɒnsələr] *adj.* of or having to do with the tonsils.

ton•sil•lec•to•my [,tɒnsə'lɛktəmi] *n., pl.* **-mies.** a removal of the tonsils by surgery. ⟨< L *tonsil* + E *-ectomy*⟩

ton•sil•li•tis [,tɒnsə'ləitɪs] *n.* inflammation of the tonsils. ⟨< NL < L *tonsillae* tonsils + E *-itis*⟩

ton•so•ri•al [tɒn'sɔriəl] *adj. Facetious.* of or having to do with a barber or his or her work. ⟨< L *tonsorius*, ult. < *tondere* shear⟩

ton•sure ['tɒnʃər] *n., v.* **-sured, -sur•ing.** *—n.* **1** the act or the rite of clipping the hair or of shaving a part or the whole of the head of a person entering the priesthood or an order of monks. **2** the shaved part of the head of a priest or monk. **3** the state of

being so shaved.
—*v.* shave the head of. ⟨ME < L *tonsura* < *tondere* shear, shave⟩

ton•tine ['tɒntin] *or* [tɒn'tin] *n.* **1** a form of annuity or insurance in which subscribers share the benefits on such terms that the share of any member who dies or defaults is distributed among the other members until the whole goes to the last surviving member, or until a specified expiration date, when the whole is divided among the remaining members. **2** the total fund accumulated in such a scheme. **3** the share of each member. **4** the members collectively. ⟨< F *tontine* < Lorenzo *Tonti,* an Italian banker, who introduced this system into France in about 1653⟩

to•nus ['tounəs] *n. Physiology.* the normal, slight tension or contraction of a relaxed muscle; tone.

to•ny ['touni] *adj. Informal.* stylish; high-toned; fashionably elegant.

too [tu] *adv.* **1** also; besides: *The dog is hungry, and thirsty too.* **2** beyond what is desirable, proper, or right; more than enough: *My dress is too long for you. He ate too much. The summer passed too quickly.* **3** very; exceedingly: *I am only too glad to help you. I didn't do too well on the exam.* **4** indeed; most definitely (*used to contradict a negative*): *I didn't take it. You did too!* ⟨var. of *to*⟩
☛ *Hom.* TO, TWO.

took [tʊk] *v.* pt. of TAKE.

tool [tul] *n., v.* —*n.* **1** a knife, hammer, saw, shovel, or any instrument used in doing manual work. **2** anything used to achieve some purpose or necessary to one's profession or occupation: *the tools of one's trade. Books are a scholar's tools.* **3** a person used by another like a tool: *He is a tool of the departmental boss.* **4** a part of a machine that cuts, bores, smooths, etc. **5** the whole of such a machine; MACHINE TOOL.
—*v.* **1** work, shape, or cut with a tool: *He tooled beautiful designs in leather with a knife.* **2** ornament by cutting, pressing, etc. with a tool: *to tool leather.* **3** *Slang.* drive or ride, especially fast: *tooling along the highway in a beat-up old car.*
tool up, install equipment (in) for a certain task; prepare for a specific job: *The factory is tooling up for the production of new cars.* ⟨OE *tōl*⟩
☛ *Hom.* TULLE.
☛ *Syn. n.* **1. Tool,** IMPLEMENT = an instrument or other article used in doing work. **Tool** indicates an instrument or simple device especially suited or designed to make a particular kind of work easier, but applies particularly to something held and worked by the hands in doing manual work: *Plumbers, mechanics, carpenters, and shoemakers need tools.* **Implement** is a general word meaning a tool, instrument, utensil, or machine needed to do something: *Hoes and tractors are agricultural implements.*

tool•box ['tul,bɒks] *n.* a box, often open, with variously sized compartments and a handle, for storing and carrying hand tools.

tool chest a toolbox, especially one large enough for big items such as power saws, drills, etc., and having a lid.

tool•ing ['tulɪŋ] *n., v.* —*n.* **1** ornamentation made with a hand tool; especially, lettering or designs made on leather. **2** any work done with a tool. **3** the assembly or installation of machine tools in a factory.
—*v.* ppr. of TOOL.

tool•mak•er ['tul,meikər] *n.* **1** a person who makes tools. **2** a person who makes, repairs, or maintains machine tools.
—'tool,mak•ing, *n.*

tool•push•er ['tul,pʊʃər] *n. Cdn.* a foreman of a drilling operation in the oil industry. Also, **toolpush.**

tool•room ['tul,rum] *or* ['tul,rʊm] *n.* a room, as in a factory, machine shop, railway yard, etc., where tools are stored, repaired, issued, etc.

tool•shed ['tul,ʃɛd] *n.* a small outbuilding housing garden tools, ladders, etc.

toon¹ [tun] *n.* **1** a large Asian tree (*Cedrela toona*) of the mahogany family whose wood is much used for furniture and whose flowers yield a dye. **2** the wood of this tree. ⟨< Hind. *tun*⟩
☛ *Hom.* TUNE.

toon² [tun] *n. Slang.* cartoon; cartoon character. ⟨shortened from *cartoon*⟩
☛ *Hom.* TUNE.

toon•ie or **toon•y** ['tuni] *n., pl.* **-ies.** *Cdn.* the Canadian two-dollar coin. Also, **twoonie, twonie.** ⟨< alteration of *two* + *-nie* on the analogy of *loonie*⟩

toot¹ [tut] *n., v.* —*n.* the short sound of a horn, whistle, etc.
—*v.* **1** give forth a short blast; make a sound like a horn or whistle: *We heard the train toot three times.* **2** sound (a horn, whistle, etc.) in short blasts: *to toot a horn. She tooted as she drove past the house.* **3** sound (a melody, blasts, etc.) on or as if on a horn or whistle. ⟨probably ult. imitative⟩ **—'toot•er,** *n.*

toot² [tut] *n. Slang.* a drinking spree; binge: *go on a toot.* ⟨earlier, a large drink < obs. *toot,* v., drink copiously; origin unknown⟩

tooth [tuθ] *n., pl.* **teeth;** *v.* —*n.* **1** one of the hard, bony, enamel-covered projections in the mouth, used for biting and chewing. See TEETH for picture. **2** something like a tooth. Each one of the projecting parts of a comb, gearwheel, or saw is a tooth. Any of the pointed indentations or lobes in the edge of a leaf is a tooth. **3** a taste; liking: *have no tooth for fruit.*
fight tooth and nail, fight fiercely, with all one's force.
long in the tooth, ageing or old. For idioms with **teeth,** see TEETH.
—*v.* **1** furnish with teeth; put teeth on. **2** cut teeth on the edge of; indent. ⟨OE *tōth*⟩ **—'tooth,like,** *adj.*

tooth•ache ['tuθ,eik] *n.* a pain in a tooth or the teeth.

toothache grass *Cdn.* a species of grass (*Ctenium aromaticum*) having an aromatic flavour and formerly used as a remedy for toothache.

tooth•brush ['tuθ,brʌʃ] *n.* a small, long-handled brush for cleaning the teeth.

toothed [tuθt] *or* [tuðd] *adj., v.* —*adj.* **1** having teeth, especially of a certain kind or number (*often used in compounds*): *yellow-toothed.* **2** notched or indented: *a toothed blade.*
—*v.* pt. and pp. of TOOTH.

toothed whale any of an order (Odontoceta) of whales having teeth as opposed to baleen, and eating fish, molluscs, etc. as opposed to plankton. They include sperm whales, dolphins, and porpoises.

tooth fairy an imaginary character who hides money under a pillow in return for a baby tooth that has fallen out and been placed there by a child.

tooth•less ['tuθlɪs] *adj.* **1** without teeth. **2** without force or effectiveness.

tooth•paste ['tuθ,peist] *n.* an abrasive paste for cleaning the teeth.

tooth•pick ['tuθ,pɪk] *n.* a small, pointed piece of wood, plastic, etc., for removing bits of food from between the teeth.

tooth powder an abrasive powder for cleaning the teeth.

tooth•some ['tuθsəm] *adj.* **1** pleasing to the taste; tasting good. **2** attractive; voluptuous. **—'tooth•some•ly,** *adv.*
—'tooth•some•ness, *n.*

tooth•wort ['tuθ,wɜrt] *n.* any of various plants having rhizomes with toothlike scales on them, especially *Lathraea squamaria* of Europe or any plant of genus *Dentaria* of North America and Eurasia.

too•thy ['tuθi] *adj.* **-thi•er, -thi•est.** having or showing prominent teeth: *a toothy grin.*

too•tle ['tutəl] *v.* **-tled, -tling;** *n.* —*v.* toot softly and continuously, as on a whistle.
—*n.* the act or sound of tootling. ⟨frequentative of TOOT¹.⟩
—'too•tler, *n.*

toot•sie or **toot•sy** ['tʊtsi] *n., pl.* **-sies.** *Slang.* (*a child's term*) foot or toe.

top¹ [tɒp] *n., adj., v.* **topped, top•ping.** —*n.* **1** the highest point or part: *the top of a mountain.* **2** the upper end or surface: *the top of a table.* **3** the highest or leading place, rank, etc.: *He is at the top of his class.* **4** one that occupies the highest or leading position: *She is the top in her profession.* **5** the highest pitch or degree: *The boy was yelling at the top of his voice.* **6** the best or most important part: *the top of the morning.* **7** the part of a plant that grows above ground, especially a plant with edible roots: *carrot tops.* **8** the head. **9** the cover of an automobile, carriage, etc. **10** the upper part of a shoe or boot. **11** a lid or cap: *Put the top back on the bottle.* **12** a piece of clothing for the upper part of the body: *She wore white shorts and a pink top.* **13** on a ship, a platform around the top of a lower mast. See MAST¹ for picture. **14** *Sports.* a stroke above the centre of a ball. **15** a tent used as a covering for a circus or other performance. **16** *Baseball.* the first half of an inning. **17** the first or opening part (of a song, scene, etc. to be performed): *Let's take it from the top.* **18** *Chemistry.* the first part to volatilize of a mixture being distilled. **19 tops,** *pl.* the highest cards in any suit.
blow (one's) **top,** *Slang.* **a** lose one's temper. **b** become insane.
from top to toe, a from head to foot. **b** completely.
off the top, *Informal.* deducted from the gross amount (of income, etc.) before other deductions.
off the top of one's head, without reflection or preparation.
on top, with success; with victory: *to come out on top.*

on top (of), a directly on or upon. b in addition (to); above and beyond. c right after: *The loss of their house came right on top of the death of his mother.* d in control (of): *She is on top of the situation.*
over the top, a over the front of a trench to attack. b over a quantity that is a target or limit: *We aimed for 50 subscriptions to our magazine, but we went over the top and collected 73.* c *Esp. Brit.* excessive; crossing limits prescribed by common sense or convention: *It was a bit over the top to ask her such a personal question in public.*
—adj. 1 having to do with, situated at, or forming the top: *the top shelf.* 2 highest in degree; greatest: *at top speed.* 3 chief; foremost: *top honours.*
—v. 1 put a top on: *to top a box.* 2 be on or at the top of; be the top of: *A church tops the hill.* 3 reach, or reach and go over, the top of: *They topped the mountain.* 4 rise higher than; rise above: *The sun topped the horizon.* 5 be higher than; be greater than. 6 do better than; outdo; excel: *His story topped all the rest.* 7 *Golf.* hit (a ball) above centre. 8 remove the top of (a plant, etc.). 9 in chemical distillation, remove the volatile part from (a liquid); skim.
top off, a finish; end. b complete; put the finishing touches to: *We topped off the evening with an excellent dinner.* c *Slang.* in the West, begin to tame or break (a horse).
top up, replenish or refill (something). ⟨OE *topp*⟩
☛ *Syn. n.* **Top**, SUMMIT, CROWN = the highest point or part of something. **Top** is the general word: *From her first position as office clerk she rose to the top of the corporate structure.* **Summit** is the highest point of a hill, mountain, or pass, but is often used figuratively to mean the highest level that can be reached, or reached toward, by effort: *At last he attained the summit of his ambition.* **Crown,** used figuratively, means the highest degree of perfection or completion or highest state or quality of something: *A Nobel Prize is the crown of success.*

top² [tɒp] *n.* a rounded or cone-shaped toy having a point at one end on which it is made to spin.
sleep like a top, sleep soundly. ⟨OE *topp* of uncertain orig.⟩

to•paz ['toupæz] *or* [tou'pæz] *n.* 1 a mineral that is a silicate of aluminum, occurring usually in transparent or translucent crystals in various colours. Transparent yellow or brownish topaz is used as a gem. *Formula*: $Al_2SiO_4(F, OH)_2$ 2 a gem made from this stone. 3 any of various yellow gemstones, such as a yellow sapphire. ⟨ME < OF < L < Gk. *topazos*⟩

top banana *Slang.* 1 in show business, the star performer, especially the leading comedian in vaudeville, a musical comedy, etc. 2 the leader of any group. ⟨from the banana-shaped club once carried by comedians⟩

top boot a high boot, especially one having the upper part of the top in a different colour or material and made to look as if turned down.

top brass *Slang.* 1 high-ranking officers of the armed forces. 2 high-ranking officials of any organization.

top•coat ['tɒp,kout] *n.* 1 an overcoat, especially a lightweight one. 2 the fur of an animal that covers its back and sides. 3 a finishing coating of paint, etc.

top dog *Informal.* the best, most successful or most important individual or group. ⟨from the position of the winning dog in a dogfight⟩

top dollar a great amount of money (paid or earned for something).

top drawer [drɔr] *Informal.* the highest level of excellence, importance, good breeding, etc.: *a family in the top drawer of society.* **—'top-'draw•er,** *adj.*

top dressing 1 a layer of manure, compost, or rich soil spread on arable land. 2 a top layer of gravel, crushed rock, etc. on a roadway. 3 the application of such dressings. **—'top-,dress,** *v.*

tope¹ [toup] *v.* **toped, top•ing.** drink alcohol excessively or habitually; tipple. ⟨origin uncertain⟩ **—'top•er,** *n.*
☛ *Hom.* TAUPE.

tope² [toup] *n.* a domed Buddhist shrine. ⟨< Hind. *top* < Skt. *stupa*⟩
☛ *Hom.* TAUPE.

tope³ [toup] *n.* any of various small sharks, especially *Galeorhinus galeus*, a small grey requiem shark of Europe.
☛ *Hom.* TAUPE.

top–flight ['tɒp 'fləit] *adj.* superior; of the highest excellence.

top•gal•lant [,tɒp'gælənt] *or* [tə'gælənt] *n., adj. —n.* the mast or sail above the topmast; the third section of a mast above the deck.
—adj. next above the topmast.

top gun the best in its (or his or her) class or field.

top hat a tall, black silk hat worn with formal clothes by men. See HAT for picture.

top–heav•y ['tɒp ,hɛvi] *adj.* 1 too heavy at the top, so as to be likely to fall over. 2 overcapitalized, as a business corporation. 3 having too many officials of high rank: *a school board top-heavy with administrators and consultants.* **—'top-,heav•i•ly,** *adv.* **—'top-,heav•i•ness,** *n.*

To•phet ['toufɪt] *n.* hell. ⟨< Hebrew *Topheth*, the name of a place near Jerusalem used for the worship of idols, and later for burning refuse⟩

to•pi ['toupi] *n.* in the Indian subcontinent: 1 a hat, especially the traditional brimless cap worn by men. 2 PITH HELMET. ⟨< Hind.⟩

to•pi•ar•y ['toupi,ɛri] *adj., n., pl.* **-ar•ies.** *—adj. Gardening.* 1 trimmed or clipped into figures or designs: *topiary shrubs.* 2 of or having to do with such trimming.
—n. 1 the art or practice of such trimming. 2 a topiary garden. ⟨< F *topiare*, ult. < L *topia* fancy gardening < Gk. *topos* place⟩

top•ic ['tɒpɪk] *n.* 1 a subject that people think, write, or talk about: *The main topics at the dinner party were the weather and the election.* 2 a short phrase or sentence used in an outline to give the main point of a part of a speech, writing, etc. 3 *Linguistics.* in a sentence, the known or 'old' information, the part stating the item about which the comment, or new information, is given. In *The peaches are getting ripe, The peaches* is the topic and *are getting ripe* is the comment. In *Car trouble was the excuse he gave, the excuse he gave* is the topic and *car trouble was* is the comment. ⟨sing. of *topics* < L *topica* < Gk. *(ta) topika,* a study of logical and rhetorical commonplaces (by Aristotle) < *topos* place⟩
☛ *Syn.* 1. See note at SUBJECT.

top•i•cal ['tɒpəkəl] *adj.* 1 having to do with topics of the day; of current or local interest. 2 of or using topics; having to do with the topics of a speech, writing, etc.; arranged according to topic: *a topical index.* 3 of or designed for a particular part of the body; local: *a topical medicine.* 4 local; having to do with a particular place. **—,top•i'cal•i•ty,** *n.* **—'top•i•cal•ly,** *adv.*

top•knot ['tɒp,nɒt] *n.* 1 a knot or tuft of hair on the top of the head of a person or animal. 2 a plume or crest of feathers on the head of a bird. 3 a cluster of feathers, a bow, or other decoration worn on the top of the head.

top•less ['tɒplɪs] *adj.* 1 having no top: *a topless table.* 2 wearing no clothes on the upper part of the body: *a topless waitress.* 3 *Informal.* of a restaurant, etc., featuring topless waitresses, dancers, etc. 4 so high or tall that the top cannot be seen.

top–lev•el ['tɒp 'lɛvəl] *adj. Informal.* of the highest importance, authority, etc.: *top-level decisions.*

top•lof•ty ['tɒp,lɒfti] *adj. Informal.* lofty in character or manner; haughty; pompous; pretentious. **—'top,loft•i•ly,** *adv.* **—'top,loft•i•ness,** *n.*

top•mast ['tɒp,mæst] *or* ['tɒpməst] *n.* the second section of a mast above the deck. See MAST¹ for picture.

top•most ['tɒp,moust] *adj.* highest.

top–notch ['tɒp 'nɒtʃ] *adj. Informal.* first-rate; best possible.

top•o•graph•i•cal [,tɒpə'græfəkəl] *adj.* of or having to do with topography. A topographical map shows mountains, rivers, etc. Also, **topographic.** **—,top•o'graph•i•cal•ly,** *adv.*

to•pog•ra•phy [tə'pɒgrəfi] *n., pl.* **-phies.** 1 the art or practice of detailed description or mapping of the natural and artificial features of a region or place. 2 a detailed description of the surface features of a place or region. 3 the features themselves. The topography of a region includes hills, valleys, streams, lakes, bridges, tunnels, roads, etc. 4 topographical surveying. 5 a study or description of an area of the body, of a galaxy, of a field of knowledge, or of any other system, giving the different parts, their features and interrelationships, etc.: *a topography of the human brain, the topography of modern physics.* ⟨< LL < Gk. *topographia* < *topos* place + *graphein* write⟩ **—to'pog•ra•pher,** *n.*

to•pol•o•gy [tə'pɒlədʒi] *n., pl.* **-gies.** 1 a topographical study or analysis. 2 *Mathematics.* the study of the properties of geometric forms and spatial relations that remain unchanged under continuous change of shape or size. ⟨< G *Topologie* < Gk. *topos* place + *-logos* treating of⟩ **—,top•o'log•i•cal,** *adj.* **—,top•o'log•i•cal•ly,** *adv.* **—to'pol•o•gist,** *n.*

top•o•nym ['tɒpə,nɪm] *n.* 1 a place name. 2 a name derived from a place name. ⟨< Gk. *topos* place + *onyma* name⟩

to•pon•y•my [tə'pɒnəmi] *n., pl.* **-mies. 1** the study of the place names of a region, country, etc. **2** a register of such names. **–,top•o'nym•ic,** *adj.* **–to'pon•y•mist,** *n.*

top•per ['tɒpər] *n.* **1** *Slang.* an excellent, first-rate person or thing. **2** *Informal.* TOP HAT. **3** *Informal.* a loose, short topcoat for women. **4** a person or thing that tops something.

top•ping ['tɒpɪŋ] *adj., n., v.* *–adj. Brit. Informal.* excellent; first-rate.
–n. **1** something that forms a top, such as a garnish placed on food to add flavour or for decoration: *pudding with a topping of whipped cream, a cake with a crumb topping.* **2 toppings,** *pl.* branches, stems, etc. cut off in topping trees or plants.
–v. ppr. of TOP.

top•ple ['tɒpəl] *v.* **-pled, -pling. 1** fall forward; tumble down: *The chimney toppled over on the roof.* **2** throw over or down; overturn; cause the fall of: *The wrestler toppled his opponent. The rebel army toppled the government.* **3** hang over in an unsteady way: *beneath toppling crags.* ⟨frequentative of *top*, v. < *top¹*, n.⟩

tops [tɒps] *adj., n. Slang. –adj.* of the highest degree in quality, excellence, popularity, etc. (*never used before a noun*): *She's tops in her field.*
–n.
the tops, an excellent person or thing of its kind.

top•sail ['tɒp,seil] *or* ['tɒpsəl] *n.* the second sail above the deck on a mast.

top–se•cret ['tɒp 'sikrɪt] *adj.* of utmost secrecy; extremely confidential.

top•side ['tɒp,saɪd] *n., adv. –n.* Often, **topsides,** *pl.* **a** the top or upper portion of a ship's sides above the water line. **b** the upper part of a ship, as distinct from the hold, engine room, etc.
–adv. Often, **topsides, 1** to or on the bridge or an upper deck; on deck. **2** *Informal.* on top; up above.

top•soil ['tɒp,sɔɪl] *n.* surface soil suitable for growing plants in: *People buy topsoil for gardens and lawns.*

top•spin ['tɒp,spɪn] *n.* a fast spinning motion applied to a ball, especially in tennis, by hitting it forward and upward, causing it to rotate forward.

top•stitch ['tɒp,stɪtʃ] *v.* decorate or finish with topstitching.

top•stitch•ing ['tɒp,stɪtʃɪŋ] *n.* a decorative line of stitching on the outside of a garment near an edge or seam: *The jacket has topstitching around the collar and down the front.*

top•sy–tur•vy ['tɒpsi 'tɜrvi] *adv., adj., n., pl.* **-vies.** *–adv. or adj.* **1** upside down. **2** in confusion or disorder.
–n. **1** the state of being upside down. **2** confusion; disorder. ⟨probably ult. < *top¹* + *tirve* overturn, related to OE *tearflian* roll over⟩ **–'top•sy-'tur•vi•ly,** *adv.* **–'top•sy-'tur•vi•ness,** *n.*

toque [touk] *n.* **1** a hat with no brim or with very little brim. **2** tuque. **3** in the 16th century, a small hat decorated with a plume, worn in Europe by both men and women. ⟨< F⟩

tor [tɔr] *n.* a high, bare, rocky hill or small mountain. ⟨ME < OE *torr* tower, crag < Celtic⟩
☛ *Hom.* TORE, TORR.

to•rah or **to•ra** ['tɔrə] *n.* in Jewish usage: **1** a doctrine, teaching, or law. **2** Usually, **Torah,** the totality of sacred writings, including actual Scripture, the Talmud, etc. **3 the Torah,** the law of Moses; Pentateuch. **4** a parchment scroll containing any of these. ⟨< Hebrew⟩

torc [tɔrk] *n.* See TORQUE (def. 2).

torch [tɔrtʃ] *n., v. –n.* **1** a makeshift light to be carried around or stuck in a holder on a wall, consisting of a piece of wood or other rigid material, often dipped in pitch, grease, etc., and ignited. A piece of pine wood makes a good torch. **2** a device for producing a very hot flame, used especially to burn off paint, to solder metal, and to melt metal; blowtorch. **3** *Brit.* flashlight. **4** something thought of as a source of enlightenment: *the torch of civilization.*
carry a (or **the**) **torch (for), a** *Slang.* be in love (with); especially, suffer unrequited love (for): *He has been carrying the torch for her for months.* **b** *Informal.* crusade (for); support (a cause).
–v. Slang. set on fire or burn down, especially maliciously. ⟨ME < OF *torche*, probably ult. < L *torquere* twist⟩ **–'torch,like,** *adj.*

torch•bear•er ['tɔrtʃ,bɛrər] *n.* **1** one who carries a torch. **2** one who spreads the light of knowledge, civilization, etc. **3** *Informal.* one who is prominent in support of a crusade, a cause, or an individual.

tor•chiere or **tor•chère** [tɔr'ʃir] *or* [tɔr'ʃɛr] *n.* **1** a floor lamp without a shade but having a concave reflector facing upward for indirect lighting. **2** a tall stand with a small tablelike or slightly concave surface for holding a candlestick or lamp. ⟨< F *torchère* tall candelabrum < OF *torche* torch⟩

torch•light ['tɔrtʃ,ləit] *n.* **1** the light of a torch or torches. **2** (*adj.*) performed or carried out by torchlight: *a torchlight procession.*

tor•chon lace ['tɔrʃən] **1** a handmade linen lace with loosely twisted threads in simple open patterns. **2** a machine-made imitation of this in linen or cotton. ⟨< F *torchon* dishcloth⟩

torch song a popular song having disappointed or unrequited love as its theme.

tore¹ [tɔr] *v.* pt. of TEAR².

tore² [tɔr] *n.* TORUS (defs. 1, 4).
☛ *Hom.* TOR, TORR.

to•re•ro [tə'rɛrou]; *Spanish* [to'rero] *n.* bullfighter. Also called **toreador** ['tɔriə,dɔr]. ⟨< Sp. *torear* to fight bulls, ult. < *toro* bull < L *taurus*⟩

to•reu•tics [tə'rutɪks] *n.pl.* (*used with a singular verb*) the art of embossing or engraving, especially on metal. ⟨< Gk. *toreutikos* < *toreuein* carve, bore⟩ **–to'reu•tic,** *adj.*

to•ri ['tɔraɪ] *or* ['tɔri] *n.* pl. of TORUS.

tor•ic ['tɔrɪk] *adj.* having to do with, or having the form of, a torus.

The torii marking the entrance to the Shinto shrine of Itsukushima on the island of Itsukushima, Japan. It is made of camphor wood.

to•ri•i ['tɔri,i] *n., pl.* **-ri•i.** in Japan, a gateway at the entrance to a Shinto temple, built of two uprights and two crosspieces. ⟨< Japanese⟩

tor•ment *v.* [tɔr'mɛnt]; *n.* ['tɔrmɛnt] *v., n. –v.* **1** cause very great pain or mental anguish to. **2** worry or annoy very much: *He torments everyone with silly questions.*
–n. **1** a cause of very great pain or mental anguish. Instruments of torture were torments. **2** very great pain or mental anguish. **3** a cause of very much worry or annoyance. ⟨ME < OF *tormenter*, ult. < L *tormentum,* originally, twisted sling < *torquere* twist⟩
☛ *Syn. v.* **1. Torment,** TORTURE = cause physical or mental pain or suffering that is hard to bear. **Torment** = hurt or harm again and again and cause sharp, severe pain that continues or is constantly repeated: *She is tormented by a racking cough.* **Torture** = torment so severely that the victim twists and turns in agony. It often suggests a deliberate cruelty out of hatred, an attempt to force a confession, etc.: *We do not believe in torturing prisoners.*

tor•men•tor or **tor•ment•er** [tɔr'mɛntər] *n.* **1** a person or thing that torments. **2** *Theatre.* a framed structure or curtain that projects onto either side of a proscenium stage to hide the wings from the view of the audience, sometimes making it difficult for those seated at the far sides to see the stage.

torn [tɔrn] *v.* pp. of TEAR².

tor•na•do [tɔr'neidou] *n., pl.* **-does** or **-dos. 1** a violent, destructive kind of cyclone a few hundred metres to a few kilometres wide, seen as a slender, funnel-shaped, whirling cloud that moves across the land. **2** any whirlwind or hurricane. **3** a violent outburst. ⟨alteration of Sp. *tronada* < *tronar* thunder⟩ **–tor'nad•ic** [-'nædɪk], *adj.*

to•roid ['tɔrɔid] *n. Geometry.* a surface generated by the rotation of a closed plane curve about a line in the same plane as the curve but not intersecting it. ⟨< *tore²* + *-oid*⟩ **–to'roid•al,** *adj.*

to•rose ['tɔrous] *or* [tɔ'rous] *adj.* **1** *Botany.* cylindrical with knotty bulges at irregular intervals. **2** *Zoology.* knobbly. ⟨< L *torosus* < *torus*. See TORUS.⟩

tor•pe•do [tɔr'pidou] *n., pl.* **-does;** *v.* **-doed, -do•ing.** *–n.* **1** a large, cigar-shaped shell that contains explosives and travels by its own power. Torpedoes are launched under water from a tube on the lower side of a vessel, to blow up enemy ships. **2** a submarine mine, shell, etc. that explodes when hit. **3** an explosive put on a railway track that makes a loud noise for a

signal when a wheel of the engine runs over it. **4** a cartridge of explosives used in an oil well to clear it out. **5** a kind of firework that explodes when it is thrown against something hard. **6** an ELECTRIC RAY, especially any of the genus *Torpedo*.
—*v.* **1** attack or destroy with a torpedo. **2** set off a torpedo in or against. **3** bring completely to an end; destroy: *torpedo a peace conference.* ⟨< L *torpedo* the electric ray (a fish), originally, numbness < *torpere* be numb⟩

torpedo boat a small, fast warship designed for firing torpedoes.

tor•pid ['tɔrpɪd] *adj.* **1** lacking in vigour; dull or sluggish: *a torpid mind.* **2** dormant, as a hibernating animal. **3** numb. ⟨< L *torpidus* < *torpere* be numb⟩ **—'tor•pid•ly,** *adv.* **—'tor•pid•ness,** *n.*

tor•pid•i•ty [tɔr'pɪdəti] *n.* the quality or state of being torpid.

tor•por ['tɔrpər] *n.* **1** a state of being dormant or inactive. **2** sluggishness or dullness. ⟨< L *torpor* < *torpere* be numb⟩

tor•por•if•ic [,tɔrpə'rɪfɪk] *adj.* causing torpor.

torque [tɔrk] *n.* **1 a** a force that produces rotation. The engine of a motor vehicle transmits torque to the axle. **b** a measure of the rotatory tendency of such a force, equalling the force times the perpendicular distance from the line of the force's action to the centre of the rotating body. **2** a necklace of twisted metal, especially such a necklace as worn by the ancient Celts. Also (def. 2), **torc.** ⟨< L *torques* twisted neck chain < *torquere* twist⟩

tor•ques ['tɔrkwiz] *n. Zoology.* a distinctive ring of fur, feathers, skin, etc. around the neck of an animal. ⟨< L. See TORQUE.⟩ **—'tor•quate** [-kwɪt] *or* [-kweit], *adj.*

torque wrench a wrench having a meter or gauge on it indicating the amount of torque being applied to the object being worked on.

torr [tɔr] *n.* a unit of pressure equalling 133.32 pascals, or the amount required to maintain a column of mercury 1 mm high at 0°C and standard gravity.
☛ *Hom.* TOR, TORE.

tor•re•fy ['tɔrə,fai] *v.* **-fied, -fy•ing.** dry or parch with heat: *a torrefied drug, torrefied ores.* ⟨< L *torrefacere* < *torrere* parch + *facere* make⟩ **—,tor•re'fac•tion,** *n.*

tor•rent ['tɔrənt] *n.* **1** a violent, rushing stream of liquid, especially water or lava. **2** any violent, rushing stream or flood: *a torrent of abuse.* **3** a downpour of rain. ⟨< L *torrens, -entis* boiling, parching⟩

tor•ren•tial [tə'rɛnʃəl] *adj.* of, caused by, or like a torrent: *torrential rains, a torrential flow of words.* **—tor'ren•tial•ly,** *adv.*

tor•rid ['tɔrɪd] *adj.* **1** very hot: *a torrid climate.* **2** exposed to great heat; scorched or arid: *the torrid wastes of the Sahara.* **3** passionate; intense: *torrid love letters.* ⟨< L *torridus* < *torrere* parch⟩ **—'tor•rid•ly,** *adv.* **—'tor•rid•ness,** *n.*

tor•rid•i•ty [tə'rɪdəti] *n.* extreme heat.

Torrid Zone the region comprising the low latitudes, between the Tropic of Cancer and the Tropic of Capricorn, forming part of a now obsolete classification system for world climate zones. See also FRIGID ZONE, TEMPERATE ZONE.

tor•sade [tɔr'sɑd] *or* [tɔr'seid] *n.* a twisted cord for decoration, as on a hat, drapery, etc. ⟨< F < Med.L *torsus* twisted⟩

tor•si•bil•i•ty [,tɔrsə'bɪləti] *n.* ability to be twisted or to withstand the effects of twisting.

tor•sion ['tɔrʃən] *n.* **1** the act or process of twisting or wrenching by turning one end of something while the other end is held fast or twisted in the opposite direction. **2** stress, strain, or distortion resulting from such a process. **3** the state of being twisted. **4** the torque exerted by a body being twisted. ⟨ME < OF < LL *torsio, -onis* < L *torquere* twist⟩

tor•sion•al ['tɔrʃənəl] *adj.* of, having to do with, or resulting from torsion. **—'tor•sion•al•ly,** *adv.*

torsion balance an instrument measuring small forces by the torsion they produce in a fine wire.

torsion bar a metal bar forming part of an automobile suspension or of any of various machines, showing resilience under torsion.

torsk [tɔrsk] *n.* any fish of the cod family, especially *Brosmius brosme*, an important food fish of the N Atlantic. ⟨< Norwegian < ON *thorskr* fish for drying⟩

tor•so ['tɔrsou] *n., pl.* **-sos. 1** the trunk or body of a statue without any head, arms, or legs. **2** the trunk of the human body. **3** something left mutilated or unfinished. ⟨< Ital. *torso*, originally, stalk < L < Gk. *thyrsos* wand⟩

tort [tɔrt] *n. Law.* any civil, as opposed to criminal, wrong (except for certain cases involving a breach of contract) for which the law requires damages: *If your automobile breaks a fence, you have committed a tort against the owner.* ⟨ME < OF < Med.L *tortum* injustice < L *torquere* turn awry, twist⟩ **—'tor•tious** ['tɔrʃəs], *adj.* **—'tor•tious•ly,** *adv.*
☛ *Hom.* TORTE.

tor•te ['tɔrtə] *or* [tɔrt] *n., pl.* **tor•tes** or **tor•ten** ['tɔrtən] a rich cake having a filling or topping of cream, fruit, nuts, etc. ⟨< G < Ital. *torta* < LL *torta* (*panis*) round or twisted loaf⟩
☛ *Hom.* TORT [tɔrt].

tor•tel•li•ni [,tɔrtə'lini] *n.* pasta in the form of small, curved, pouchlike pieces filled with meat, etc. in a sauce. ⟨< Ital., dim. of *tortella*, dim. of *torta*. See TORTE.⟩

tort•fea•sor ['tɔrt,fizər] *n. Law.* the committer of a tort. ⟨< F *tortfaiseur* < *tort* wrong + *faiseur* doer < *faire* do⟩

tor•ti•col•lis [,tɔrtə'kɒləs] *n. Medicine.* wryneck.

tor•tile ['tɔrtaɪl] *adj.* twisted; coiled. ⟨< L *tortilus* < *tortus*, pp of *torquere* twist⟩

tor•til•la [tɔr'tijə] *n.* especially in Spanish America, a thin, flat, round corn cake. ⟨< Sp.⟩

tortilla chip a small, crisp, usually triangular and often highly spiced piece of unleavened cornmeal bread, eaten as a snack.

tor•toise ['tɔrtəs] *n., pl.* **-toise** or **-tois•es. 1** a turtle, especially any land-dwelling turtle of the family Testudinidae. **2** a very slow person or thing. ⟨ME < Med.L *tortuca*, ult. < L *torquere* twist⟩

tortoise beetle any of various small, often brilliantly coloured, leaf-eating beetles (family Chrysomelidae) shaped somewhat like turtles.

tortoise shell *n.* **1** the mottled yellow-and-brown shell of some species of turtle, such as the hawksbill turtle, used for ornaments, combs, etc. **2** any synthetic material imitating this. **3** a breed of domestic cat, having a coat of mottled black, tan, and cream. **4** any of various butterflies (genus *Nymphalis*) having orange-and-black wings. **—'tor•toise-,shell,** *adj.*

tor•to•ni [tɔr'touni] *n.* a rich Italian ice cream made with cherries, nuts, sherry, etc. ⟨< *Ital.*⟩

tor•tu•os•i•ty [,tɔrtʃu'ɒsəti] *n., pl.* **-ties. 1** the quality or condition of being tortuous. **2** an instance of being tortuous; a twisted or sharply turning part.

tor•tu•ous ['tɔrtʃuəs] *adj.* **1** full of twists, turns, or bends; twisting; winding; crooked. **2** mentally or morally crooked; not straightforward; devious or indirect: *tortuous reasoning.* ⟨ME < AF < L *tortuosus*, ult. < *torquere* twist⟩ **—'tor•tu•ous•ly,** *adv.* **—'tor•tu•ous•ness,** *n.*
☛ *Usage.* See note at TORTUROUS.

tor•ture ['tɔrtʃər] *n., v.* **-tured, -tur•ing.** *—n.* **1** the act or fact of inflicting extreme pain, especially to make people give evidence about crimes, or to make them confess. **2** extreme pain. **3** something that causes extreme pain. **4** a violent and continuous twisting, pushing, or shaking that taxes a thing to the limit: *the torture of a boat by pounding waves.*
—*v.* **1** cause extreme pain to, especially in order to obtain evidence, a confession, etc. **2** twist the meaning of. **3** twist or force out of its natural or proper form; distort: *Winds tortured the trees. Her essays torture the English language.* **4** puzzle or perplex greatly. ⟨< LL *tortura* < L *torquere* twist⟩ **—'tor•tur•er,** *n.*
☛ *Syn. v.* **1.** See note at TORMENT.

tor•tur•ous ['tɔrtʃərəs] *adj.* full of, involving, or causing torture. **—'tor•tur•ous•ly,** *adv.*
☛ *Usage.* **Torturous** and TORTUOUS are sometimes confused because of their similar sound and form and negative metaphorical meaning. Anything that causes torture or is regarded as if it did by virtue of any of its qualities can be called **torturous. Tortuous** has a much narrower meaning; it means simply 'twisted'.

to•rus ['tɔrəs] *n., pl.* **to•ri** ['tɔraɪ] *or* ['tɔri]. **1** *Architecture.* a large convex moulding, commonly forming the lowest member of the base of a column. **2** *Botany.* the receptacle of a flower. **3** *Anatomy.* a rounded ridge; a protuberant part. **4** *Geometry.* a ring-shaped surface or solid generated by the revolution of a conic about any line that is coplanar with it but not intersecting it. ⟨< L *torus*, originally, cushion, swelling⟩

To•ry ['tɔri] *n., pl.* **-ries;** *adj.* *—n.* **1** in Canada, a member or supporter of the Progressive Conservative Party: *His mother is a Tory.* **2** in the United Kingdom, originally, a member of the political party that favoured royal power and the established church and that opposed change. Strictly speaking, there is no Tory party in the modern United Kingdom, although members of the Conservative Party are often called Tories. **3** *U.S.* during the

American Revolution, a person who supported continued allegiance to Great Britain; Loyalist. **4** Often, **tory,** a person who has extremely conservative political or economic principles.
—adj. of or having to do with the Tories or their policies: *a strong Tory opposition.* ⟨< Irish *tóraí* persecuted person (used of Irishmen dispossessed by the English in the 17c.), outlaw, prob. from *toír* pursuit⟩

To•ry•ism ['tɔri,ɪzəm] *n.* **1** the principles and practices of the Tories. **2** the fact or state of being a Tory.

toss [tɒs] *v.,* **tossed** or *Poetic* **tost, tos•sing.** *n. —v.* **1** throw lightly; cast; fling: *toss a ball.* **2** throw about; agitate; pitch about: *The ship was tossed by the heavy waves.* **3** lift quickly; throw upward: *She tossed her head. He was tossed by the bull.* **4** mix the ingredients of lightly: *to toss a salad.* **5 a** throw (a coin) up in the air to decide something by the side that falls upward. **b** do this with (someone): *I'll toss you for it.* **6** bandy; give or exchange (remarks, ideas, etc.) casually or offhandedly. **7** throw oneself about; roll restlessly. **8** fling oneself: *She tossed out of the room in anger.*
toss off, a do or make quickly and easily. **b** drink all at once: *He tossed off a whole glass of whisky.*
toss up, toss a coin as a way of settling or deciding something: *Let's toss up to see who does the dishes.*
—n. **1** the distance to which something is or can be tossed. **2** a throw; tossing. ⟨? < Scand.; cf. dial. Norwegian *tossa* strew⟩
☛ *Syn. v.* **1.** See note at THROW.

toss–up ['tɒs ˌʌp] *n.* **1** a tossing of a coin to decide something. **2** an even chance: *It was a toss-up whether he or his brother would get the nomination.*

tost [tɒst] *v. Poetic.* a pt. and a pp. of TOSS.

tos•ta•da [tou'stadə] *n.* a crisply fried tortilla. Also, **tostado.** ⟨< Am.Sp., fem of *tostado,* fried < Sp., 'toasted', pp. of *tostar* toast⟩

tot¹ [tɒt] *n.* **1** a little child. **2** *Esp. Brit.* a small portion of alcoholic liquor. ⟨origin uncertain⟩

tot² [tɒt] *v.,* **tot•ted, tot•ting.** *Esp. Brit. Informal.* add (*up*): *Will you tot this bill up for me, please?* ⟨shortened from *total* or from L *totum* all, the whole⟩

to•tal ['toutəl] *adj., n., v.* **-talled** or **-taled, -tal•ling** or **-tal•ing.** *—adj.* **1** whole, especially having all parts or elements included: *The total cost of the furnishings will be $10 000.* **2** complete; absolute: *The lights went out and we were in total darkness.*
—n. the whole amount; sum: *His expenses reached a total of $100.*
—v. **1** find the sum of; add: *Total that column of figures.* **2** reach an amount of; amount (*sometimes used with* **to**): *The money spent yearly on chewing gum totals millions of dollars.* **3** *Slang.* wreck completely: *Her car was totalled in the accident.* ⟨ME < OF < Med.L *totalis* < L *totus* all, the whole⟩

total eclipse an eclipse in which, from some vantage point on the earth, the whole of the eclipsed body is obscured.

to•tal•i•tar•i•an [tou,tælə'tɛriən] *adj., n.—adj.* **1** of, having to do with, or designating a form of government in which a centralized state authority permits no competing political group and exercises strict control over economic, social, and cultural aspects of life. **2** supporting or favouring such a form of government.
—n. a person who supports totalitarianism or is part of such a regime.

to•tal•i•tar•i•an•ism [tou,tælə'tɛriə,nɪzəm] *n.* **1** a totalitarian system of government. **2** the political principle that the individual citizen should be under the complete control of a government or ruler.

to•tal•i•ty [tou'tæləti] *n., pl.* **-ties. 1** a total number or amount; whole; sum. **2** the quality or state of being total; entirety. **3** the total eclipse of the sun or moon, or the period during which this takes place.

to•tal•i•za•tor ['toutələ,zeitər] *or* ['toutəlaɪ,zeitər] *n.* an apparatus for registering and indicating totals of operations, measurements, etc., especially one used for pari-mutuel betting at horse races.

to•tal•ize ['toutə,laɪz] *v.* **-ized, -iz•ing.** make a total; combine into a total.

to•tal•ly ['toutəli] *adv.* wholly; entirely; completely: *The experiment was totally successful.*

total recall the ability to remember clearly every detail about an experience or situation in the past.

total war a war in which all the resources of a nation are used, and in which attack is made not only on the armed forces of the opponent, but also (subject to certain limitations) on all its people and property.

tote¹ [tout] *v.* **tot•ed, tot•ing;** *n. —v. Informal.* carry; haul.
—n. **1** a carrying or hauling. **2** the distance of this; a haul: *a long tote.* **3** TOTE BAG. ⟨origin uncertain⟩

tote² [tout] *n. Slang.* totalizator.

tote bag a large handbag of canvas, straw, vinyl, etc., often open at the top, or other small piece of baggage, used for carrying small packages, clothing, etc.

tote board *Informal.* **1** totalizator. **2** a large, highly visible information board facing the grandstand at a racetrack, on which are displayed the results, odds, etc.

to•tem ['toutəm] *n.* **1** among First Nations peoples of the northern Pacific coast, an animal or plant taken as the emblem of a people, clan, or family. **2** among many peoples throughout the world, a creature or object that is associated with their ancestral traditions and is looked on with awe and reverence by a tribe, clan, etc.: *Many peoples never kill the animals that are their totems.* **3** a representation of a totem, usually carved or painted. **4** anything that is used as an emblem or symbol. ⟨< Algonquian⟩

to•tem•ic [tou'tɛmɪk] *adj.* of or having to do with a totem or totemism.

to•tem•ism ['toutə,mɪzəm] *n.* **1** belief in a mystical relationship or kinship between human beings and animals and plants, usually taking the form of a special reverence felt by a people or a person for particular creatures or objects. **2** the use of totems to distinguish tribes, clans, or families. **—'to•tem•ist,** *n.* **—,to•tem'is•tic,** *adj.*

Haida totem poles in southern British Columbia

totem pole 1 a large upright log carved and painted with representations of totems, traditionally erected by many of the First Nations peoples of the northern Pacific coast. Totem poles serve as a record of the ancestry of a family and sometimes also of historical or mythological happenings. **2** *Informal.* hierarchy; pecking order: *He's low on the totem pole at work.*

tote road an unpaved road or trail for hauling provisions and supplies to a lumber camp.

t'oth•er or **toth•er** ['tʌðər] *adj. or pron. Dialect.* the other. ⟨ME *thet other* the other, pronounced as *the tother*⟩

tot•ter ['tɒtər] *v., n. —v.* **1** walk with shaky, unsteady steps. **2** tremble or rock as if about to fall: *The old wall tottered in the storm and fell.* **3** become unstable; be about to fall or collapse: *The old regime was already tottering before the revolution broke out.*
—n. an unsteady way of walking. ⟨ME; ? < Scand.; cf. dial. Norwegian *totra* quiver⟩ **—'tot•ter•er,** *n.* **—'tot•ter•ing,** *adj.*

tot•ter•y ['tɒtəri] *adj.* tottering; shaky.

tou•can ['tukæn] *or* [tu'kæn] *n.* any of a family (Ramphastidae) of brightly coloured birds of tropical America, having a large but very light beak. ⟨< Carib⟩

A toucan

touch [tʌtʃ] *v., n. —v.* **1** put the hand or some other part of the body on or against: *She touched the pan to see whether it was still hot.* **2** put something against; make contact with: *He touched the post with his umbrella.* **3** be in contact with; come against: *Your sleeve is touching the butter.* **4** be in contact: *Our hands touched.*

5 a border on: *a country that touches the mountains on the north.* **b** in geometry, be tangent (to). **6** strike lightly or gently: *She touched the strings of the harp.* **7** injure slightly: *The flowers were touched by the frost.* **8** affect with some feeling: *The sad story touched us.* **9** affect in some way by contact: *a metal so hard that a file cannot touch it.* **10** *Informal.* make slightly insane. **11** have to do with; concern (*sometimes used with* **on**): *The matter touches your interest.* **12** speak of; deal with; refer to; treat briefly (*used with* **on**): *Our conversation touched on many subjects.* **13** (*used in the negative*) **a** handle; use at all: *She hasn't touched her golf clubs the whole summer. He won't touch liquor or tobacco.* **b** eat or drink the slightest amount of: *You haven't touched your dinner.* **c** be involved in the slightest extent: *I won't touch a bribe. She doesn't touch gossip.* **14** reach; come up to: *His head almost touches the top of the doorway.* **15** stop at; visit in passing: *The ship touched port.* **16** make a brief stop: *Most ships touch at that port.* **17** *Slang.* borrow from: *to touch a man for a fiver.* **18** take, use, or handle without right or so as to disturb, harm, etc.: *Don't you touch my daughter! Who touched this file on my desk?* **19** compare with; rival: *No one in our class can touch her in music.* **20** mark slightly or superficially, as with some colour: *a sky touched with pink.* **21** mark, draw, or delineate, as with strokes of the brush, pencil, etc.

not touch with a bargepole or **ten-foot pole.** See BARGEPOLE.

touch down, a land; alight. **b** *Football.* touch the ground with (the ball) behind the opposing team's goal line.

touch off, a give an exact or clever imitation of; parody. **b** cause to start; provoke (a reaction): *The new tax touched off a rebellion.*

touch on or **upon, a** speak of; treat lightly: *Our conversation touched on many subjects.* **b** come close to.

touch up, a change a little; improve: *He touched up a photograph.* **b** rouse by touching.

–n. **1** a touching or being touched: *A bubble bursts at a touch.* **2** the sense by which a person perceives things by feeling, handling, or coming against them: *People who are blind have keen touch.* **3** the distinctive tactile quality of something that imparts a particular sensation to the toucher; feel: *Silk has a smooth touch.* **4** a coming or being in contact: *the touch of their hands.* **5** communication or connection: *A newspaper keeps one in touch with the world. He has been out of touch with his mother since he left home.* **6** a slight amount; little bit: *It needs a touch more salt.* **7** a stroke with a brush, pencil, pen, etc.: *With a few skilful touches the artist finished my picture.* **8** a detail in any artistic work: *a story with charming poetic touches.* **9** a slight alteration, addition, etc. in a piece of writing, a painting, etc.: *I have to make a few touches to it before handing it in.* **10** a manner of striking, or depressing, keys on a keyboard: *a pianist with an excellent touch. She types with an uneven touch.* **11** of a keyboard instrument or machine, the resistance that the keys offer to the fingers: *A piano should not have too light a touch.* **12** a distinctive manner or quality: *The work showed an expert's touch.* **13** special ability or skill: *The magician seemed to have lost his touch.* **14** a slight attack: *a touch of fever.* **15 a** an official mark put on gold, etc. after testing. **b** a stamp for impressing such a mark. **c** the quality so tested. **16** quality in general. **17** any test. **18** *Slang.* **a** the act of soliciting or getting money as a loan or a gift from a person. **b** money got in this way. **c** a person from whom one has got or expects to get money in this way: *He's a soft touch.* **19** in bell-ringing, any series of permutations numbering less than a full peal. **20** *Football, soccer, etc.* the part of the field, including the sidelines, lying outside of the field of play. ⟨ME < OF *tuchier* < VL *toccare* strike (as a bell); originally imitative⟩
–'touch•a•ble, *adj.* **–'touch•er,** *n.*

touch–and–go ['tʌtʃ ən 'gou] *adj.* uncertain; risky: *So far it's been touch-and-go, but we're still hoping for the best.*

touch•back ['tʌtʃ,bæk] *n. American football.* the act of touching the ball to the ground behind one's own goal line when driven there by the other side.

touch•down ['tʌtʃ,daʊn] *n.* **1** *Football.* **a** the act of scoring by being in possession of the ball on or behind the opponents' goal line. **b** the score made in this way, counting six points. **2** the landing or moment of landing (of an aircraft, spacecraft, etc.).

tou•ché [tu'ʃei] *n., interj. –n.* a touch by an opponent's weapon in fencing.
–interj. **1** an exclamation acknowledging such a touch. **2** an exclamation acknowledging a clever reply or a point well made in discussion. ⟨< F⟩

touched [tʌtʃt] *adj., v. –adj.* **1** stirred emotionally, especially by gratitude or sympathy; moved: *He was touched by their offer to help.* **2** *Informal.* slightly unbalanced mentally.
–v. pt. and pp. of TOUCH.

touch football a variety of football, usually played informally and without protective equipment, in which the person carrying the ball is touched rather than tackled.

touch•hole ['tʌtʃ,houl] *n.* the small opening in early cannon or firearms through which the gunpowder inside was set on fire.

touch•ing ['tʌtʃɪŋ] *adj., prep., v. –adj.* arousing tender feeling.
–prep. concerning; about.
–v. ppr. of TOUCH. **–'touch•ing•ly,** *adv.*

touch•line ['tʌtʃ,laɪn] *n. Rugger and soccer.* a line along one side of the playing field; sideline.

touch–me–not ['tʌtʃ mi 'nɒt] *n.* any of several wild species of impatiens, such as *Impatiens capensis* or *I. pallida*, found in wet places and woods in North America and Europe.

touch•stone ['tʌtʃ,stoun] *n.* **1** a dark stone containing silica, such as jasper or basalt, formerly used to test the purity of gold or silver by the colour of the streak produced on the stone when it was rubbed with the metal. **2** any test or standard for determining the genuineness or value of something: *Her work has for many years been the touchstone of excellence in architecture.*

touch–tone ['tʌtʃ ,toun] *adj.* designating a type of phone having buttons instead of a rotor or dial. The buttons activate fixed electronic tones, giving access to any of a variety of services that operate by responding to these tones.

touch–ty•ping ['tʌtʃ,təipɪŋ] *n.* a method of typing without looking at the keyboard by always using a particular finger to strike a particular key. **–'touch-,type,** *v.*

touch–typ•ist ['tʌtʃ,təipɪst] *n.* a person skilled in touch-typing.

touch•wood ['tʌtʃ,wʊd] *n.* **1** a substance prepared from certain types of fungus (e.g., genus *Formes*) found on tree trunks, used as tinder. **2** PUNK[1].

touch•y ['tʌtʃi] *adj.* **touch•i•er, touch•i•est. 1** apt to take offence at trifles; too sensitive. **2** requiring skill in handling; ticklish; precarious: *It was a touchy situation; we didn't know whether to stay or leave.* **3** of a part of the body, very sensitive to touch: *The skin around the wound is very touchy.* **4** very flammable; easily ignited. **–'touch•i•ly,** *adv.* **–'touch•i•ness,** *n.*

tough [tʌf] *adj., n., v. –adj.* **1** hard to cut, break, tear, or chew: *Leather is tough. The steak was so tough he couldn't eat it.* **2** stiff; sticky: *tough clay.* **3** strong; hardy: *a tough plant. Donkeys are tough little animals and can carry big loads.* **4** showing great mental or moral strength or determination; resolute and stern: *She needs a good dose of tough love.* **5** not easily affected emotionally; not tender-hearted: *He never cries because he thinks he has to be tough.* **6** hard; difficult: *tough work.* **7** hard to bear; bad; unpleasant: *A spell of tough luck discouraged him.* **8** hard to influence; stubborn: *a tough customer.* **9** severe; violent; strenuous: *Football is a tough game.* **10** rough; disorderly: *a tough neighbourhood.*
–n. a rough person; rowdy.
–v.
tough it out, *Slang.* endure a difficulty to the end in a bold or stoic manner. ⟨OE *tōh*⟩ **–'tough•ly,** *adv.* **–'tough•ness,** *n.*

tough•en ['tʌfən] *v.* **1** make tough or tougher. **2** become tough or tougher. **–'tough•en•er,** *n.*

tough•ie ['tʌfi] *n., pl.* **-ies.** *Informal.* something or someone that is tough.

tough–mind•ed ['tʌf ,maɪndɪd] *adj.* practical, realistic, and unemotional.

tou•la•di ['tulə,di] *n., pl.* **-di** or **-dis.** *Cdn.* LAKE TROUT. ⟨< Cdn.F *touladi* < Algonquian (Micmac)⟩

tou•pee [tu'pei] *n.* a wig or patch of false hair worn to cover a bald spot. ⟨< F *toupet* < OF *toupe* tuft < Gmc.⟩

tour [tur] *n., v. –n.* **1** a long journey through a country or countries, often beginning and ending at the same place: *a European tour.* **2** a regular spell or turn of work or duty, or the length of time such a spell lasts: *Her last tour of duty was in France.* **3** a short trip or walk around, as for inspection: *a tour of the boat.*
on tour, of a theatre company, orchestra, entertainer, etc., travelling from place to place, fulfilling engagements: *The choir is on tour for six months of the year.*
–v. **1** travel from place to place: *I'm touring next winter with the Canadian Opera Company.* **2** travel through: *Last year they toured Europe.* **3** *Theatre.* take (a play, etc.) on tour. **4** go through (a building or other structure) to see its different parts, exhibits, etc.: *to tour a museum, to tour a manufacturing plant.* ⟨< F < L *tornus* turner's wheel, lathe < Gk. *tornos.* Related to TURN.⟩

tour de force ['tur də 'fɔrs] *pl.* **tours de force** ['tur də 'fɔrs] **1** a notable feat of strength, skill, or ingenuity. **2** something done that is merely clever or ingenious: *His later work showed* *that his first novel was little more than a tour de force.* ⟨< F, literally, feat of strength⟩

touring car an open automobile, especially of the 1920s and 1930s, usually seating five or six people.

tour•ism ['tʊrɪzəm] *n.* **1** touring or travelling as a pastime or recreation. **2** the business of providing services for tourists. **—tour'is•tic,** *adj.*

tour•ist ['tʊrɪst] *n.* **1** a person travelling for pleasure. **2** TOURIST CLASS. **3** (*adjl.*) of or for tourists.

tourist class the lowest class of accommodation for passengers on a ship, train, etc.; economy class.

tourist court *Esp. U.S.* motel.

tourist trap a place or business establishment that exploits tourists.

tour•ist•y ['tʊrɪsti] *adj. Informal, often pejorative.* **1** like or characteristic of a tourist: *She was wearing a very touristy outfit.* **2** catering to or often visited by tourists: *They tried to avoid the touristy places on their trip.*

tour•ma•line ['tʊrməlɪn] *or* ['tʊrmə,lin] *n.* **1** a complex silicate of aluminum and boron occurring in various colours. The transparent varieties of tourmaline are used for gems. **2** a gem made from this stone. Also, **tourmalin.** ⟨< F < Singhalese *toramalli*⟩

tour•na•ment ['tɜrnəmənt] *or* ['tʊrnəmənt] *n.* **1** a series of contests testing the skill of many persons: *a golf tournament. His aunt won the chess tournament.* **2** in the Middle Ages: **a** a jousting contest between two groups of knights on horseback who fought for a prize. **b** a series of knightly jousts, sports, etc. occurring at one time at a particular place. ⟨ME < OF *torneiement* < *torneier.* See TOURNEY.⟩

tour•ne•dos ['tʊrnə,dou] *or* [,tʊrnə'dou] *n.* a small but thick steak of beef tenderloin. ⟨< F < *tourne* turn + *dos* back⟩

tour•ney ['tɜrni] *or* ['tʊrni] *n., pl.* **-neys;** *v.* **-neyed, -ney•ing.**
—n. tournament.
—v. take part in a tournament. ⟨ME < OF *torneier,* ult. < L *tornus.* See TURN.⟩

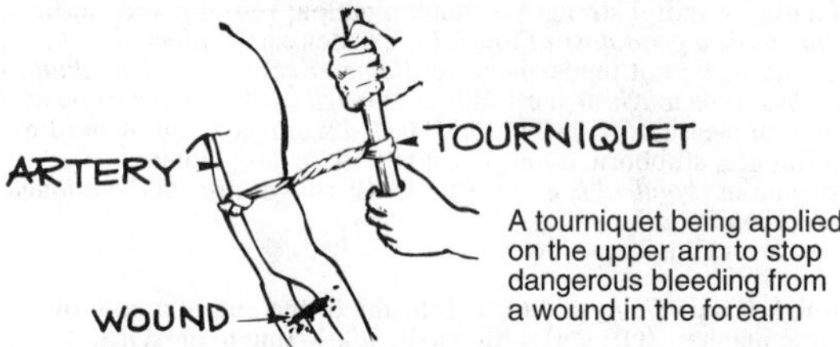

A tourniquet being applied on the upper arm to stop dangerous bleeding from a wound in the forearm

tour•ni•quet ['tʊrnə,ki], ['tʊrnə,kei], ['tɜrnəkɪt] *or* ['tɜrnə,kɛt] *n.* a device for stopping bleeding by compressing a blood vessel. A bandage tightened by twisting with a stick may be used as a tourniquet. ⟨< F *tourniquet* < *tourner* to turn⟩

tour•tière [tʊr'tjɛr]; *French* [tuʀ'tjɛʀ] *n. Cdn.* a pie made with ground pork, often mixed with some veal or chicken, associated especially with French Canada. ⟨< Cdn.F⟩

tou•sle ['taʊzəl] *v.* **-sled, -sling;** *n.* *—v.* put into disorder; make untidy; muss: *She tousled her brother's hair to tease him.*
—n. a disordered or tangled mass of hair, etc. ⟨ME *touse(n)*⟩

tout [tʌut] *v., n. Informal.* *—v.* **1** praise highly and insistently. **2** try to get (customers, jobs, votes, etc.). **3** urge betting on (a racehorse) by claiming to have special information. **4** *Esp. Brit.* spy out (information about racehorses) for use in betting.
—n. a person who touts. ⟨< var. of OE *tȳtan* peep out⟩
—'tout•er, *n.*

tow¹ [tou] *v., n.* *—v.* pull along by a rope, chain, etc.: *The tug is towing three barges.*
—n. **1** the act or an instance of towing: *He charges forty-five dollars for a tow.* **2** the fact or condition of being towed. **3** that which is towed: *Each tug had a tow of three barges.* **4** something used for towing: *a ski tow.*
in tow, a in the state of being towed: *The launch had a sailboat in tow.* **b** under protection or guidance: *He was taken in tow by his aunt as soon as he arrived.* **c** under someone's influence; in the position of follower or dependent: *The movie producer arrived at the reception with several admirers in tow.* ⟨OE *togian* drag⟩
☛ *Hom.* TOE.

tow² [tou] *n.* **1** the coarse, broken fibres of flax, hemp, etc., prepared for spinning. **2** (*adjl.*) made from tow. ⟨OE *tōw-* a spinning⟩
☛ *Hom.* TOE.

tow•age ['touɪdʒ] *n.* **1** towing or being towed. **2** a charge for towing.

to•ward *prep.* [tʊ'wɔrd], [twɔrd], *or* [tɔrd]; *adj.* ['touərd] *or* [tɔrd] *prep., adj.* *—prep.* **1** in the direction of; in a way or course leading to: *I walked toward the north. Let us work toward peace.* **2** with respect to; regarding; about; concerning: *What is your attitude toward war?* **3** just before: *It must be toward four o'clock.* **4** as a help to; for; in order to get: *Will you give something toward our new hospital? They're saving toward a house.*
—adj. **1** *Rare.* about to happen; impending. **2** *Archaic.* promising, hopeful, or apt; docile. ⟨OE *tōweard* < *tō* to + *-weard* -ward⟩

to•wards [tʊ'wɔrdz], [twɔrdz], *or* [tɔrdz] *prep.* toward.

tow bar 1 a bar by which a vehicle is towed. **2** T-BAR.

tow•boat ['tou,bout] *n.* tugboat.

tow•el ['taʊəl] *n., v.* **-elled** or **-eled, -el•ling** or **-el•ing.** *—n.* an absorbent piece of cloth or paper for wiping and drying something wet.
throw or **toss in the towel,** *Informal.* admit defeat.
—v. dry with a towel. ⟨ME < OF *toaille* < Gmc.⟩

tow•el•ette [,taʊə'lɛt] *n.* a small paper towel, usually moistened and perfumed and contained in a small foil package, for wiping the hands after eating, refreshing the face, etc. when travelling or eating out.

tow•el•ling or **tow•el•ing** ['taʊəlɪŋ] *n., v.* *—n.* material used for towels, especially cotton terry or linen.
—v. ppr. of TOWEL.

tow•er¹ ['taʊər] *n., v.* *—n.* **1** a high structure that may be completely walled in or may consist only of a framework of metal or wood, and that may stand alone or form part of a church, castle, etc.: *a lookout tower, a bell tower, a water tower, a fire tower.* **2** a fortress or prison consisting of or including a tower: *the Tower of London.* **3** a very tall building; highrise: *an office tower.* **4** a person or thing that acts as a defence, protection, or support: *She proved to be a tower of strength during the emergency.*
—v. rise or reach to a great height: *He was a giant of a man, towering over all his friends.* ⟨ME < OF < L *turris*⟩ **—'tow•ered,** *adj.*

tow•er² ['touər] *n.* a person, thing, firm, etc. that tows.

tow•er•ing ['taʊərɪŋ] *adj., v.* *—adj.* **1** very high. **2** very tall: *a towering basketball player.* **3** very great: *Making electricity from atomic power is a towering achievement.* **4** very violent: *a towering rage.*
—v. ppr. of TOWER.

tow•er•man ['taʊərmən] *n., pl.* **-men** [-mən]. *Cdn.* a fire-spotter, specifically one who overlooks the forest from a high tower.

tow•er•y ['taʊəri] *adj.* **1** having towers. **2** towering; lofty.

tow•head ['tou,hɛd] *n.* **1** a person having light, pale yellow hair. **2** a head of light-coloured hair.

tow•head•ed ['tou,hɛdɪd] *adj.* having light, pale yellow hair.

tow•hee ['taʊhi] *or* ['touhi] *n.* **1** a long-tailed North American finch (*Pipilo erythrophthalmus*) having a call that sounds somewhat like its name. The male has a black head and back, reddish sides, and a white abdomen. Also called **rufous-sided towhee.** **2** any of various other North American finches (genera *Pipilo* and *Chlorura*). ⟨imitative of its call⟩

tow•line ['tou,laɪn] *n.* a rope, chain, etc. for towing.

town [taʊn] *n.* **1** a large group of houses, stores, schools, churches, etc. that together with the people living there forms a community with fixed boundaries and its own local government. A town is usually smaller than a city but larger than a village. **2** any large place with many people living in it: *Toronto is an exciting town.* **3** the people of a town: *The whole town was having a holiday.* **4** the part of a town or city where the stores and office buildings are: *Let's go into town.* **5** *Cdn.* TOWNSHIP (def. 1). **6** (*adjl.*) of, in, or having to do with town or a town.
go to town, *Informal.* **a** achieve success. **b** do or go through something thoroughly: *The hungry girls really went to town on that pie.*
in town, in a specified town or city: *He is not in town today.*
out of town, happening, located, etc. outside a specified town or city: *The restaurant is a short distance out of town.*
(out) on the town, out for entertainment and pleasure as available in a city or town.
paint the town red, *Slang.* go on a wild spree or party; celebrate in a noisy manner. ⟨OE *tūn*⟩

town clerk an official who keeps the records of a town.

town council *Cdn.* the elected government of a municipality smaller than a city.

town crier formerly, a public crier in a city or town.

town hall the headquarters of a town's government.

town house a house in town, especially in explicit contrast to a house in the country.

town•house ['taʊn,hʌus] *n.* a house that is one of a row of attached houses two or more storeys high, each having its own street entrance and a small yard.

town•ie ['taʊni] *n. Informal.* **1** a permanent resident of a town, especially as contrasted with tourists, students attending the town's university, or residents of the surrounding rural area. **2** *Nfld.* a resident of St. John's as opposed to one who lives in an outport.

town meeting a general meeting of the inhabitants of the town.

town•scape ['taʊn,skeip] *n.* a view of a town or urban area, or a picture portraying it. ⟨< *town* + *(land)scape*⟩

towns•folk ['taʊnz,fouk] *n.pl.* townspeople.

town•ship ['taʊnʃɪp] *n.* **1** in Canada and the United States, a division of a county having certain powers of government; municipality. **2** a land-survey area on which later subdivisions may be based. In the Prairie Provinces, a township is an area of about 93 km², divided into 36 sections. *Abbrev.*: Tp., tp., twp. or Twp. ⟨OE *tunscipe* < *tūn* town + *-scipe* -ship⟩

town•site ['taʊn,səit] *n.* **1** the site of a town. **2** a piece of land being developed or to be developed as a town.

towns•man ['taʊnzmən] *n., pl.* **-men. 1** a man who is a native or resident of a city or town. **2** a man who lives in one's own town.

towns•peo•ple ['taʊnz,pipəl] *n.pl.* the people of a town or city.

towns•wom•an ['taʊnz,wʊmən] *n., pl.* **-wom•en. 1** a woman who is a native or inhabitant of a city or town. **2** a woman who lives in one's own town.

tow•path ['tou,pæθ] *n.* a path along the bank of a canal or river for use in towing boats.

tow•rope ['tou,roup] *n.* a rope used for towing.

tow truck a truck equipped for towing away disabled or illegally parked vehicles.

tox•a•phene ['tɒksə,fin] *n.* a chlorinated, possibly carcinogenic camphene insecticide used for forage crops. *Formula*: $C_{10}H_{10}Cl_8$ ⟨< *toxic* + *(cam)phene*⟩

tox•e•mi•a [tɒk'simiə] *n.* a form of blood poisoning, especially one in which the toxins are produced by the body's own bacteria or cells. Also, **toxaemia.** ⟨< NL *toxaemia* < L *toxicum* poison (See TOXIC) + Gk. *haima* blood⟩

tox•e•mic [tɒk'simɪk] *adj.* **1** of or having to do with toxemia. **2** suffering from toxemia. Also, **toxaemic.**

tox•ic ['tɒksɪk] *adj.* **1** of, having to do with, or caused by a poison or toxin: *a toxic reaction.* **2** poisonous: *Automobile exhaust fumes are toxic.* ⟨< Med.L *toxicus* < L *toxicum* poison < Gk. *toxikon (pharmakon)* (poison) for shooting arrows < *toxon* bow⟩ **—'tox•i•cal•ly,** *adv.*

tox•i•cant ['tɒksəkənt] *adj., n. —adj.* poisonous.
—n. poison; toxic substance.

tox•ic•i•ty [tɒk'sɪsəti] *n., pl.* **-ties.** the quality or state of being toxic.

tox•i•co•gen•ic [,tɒksəkou'dʒɛnɪk] *adj.* that produces toxic substances.

tox•i•co•log•i•cal [,tɒksəkə'lɒdʒəkəl] *adj.* of or having to do with the science of poisons. **—,tox•i•co'log•i•cal•ly,** *adv.*

tox•i•col•o•gist [,tɒksə'kɒlədʒɪst] *n.* a person trained in toxicology, especially one whose work it is.

tox•i•col•o•gy [,tɒksə'kɒlədʒi] *n.* the science that deals with poisons, their effects, antidotes, detection, etc. ⟨< Gk. *toxikon* poison (See TOXIC) + E *-logy*⟩

tox•i•co•sis [,tɒksə'kousɪs] *n.* any disease or diseased condition brought on by poisoning.

toxic shock syndrome an often fatal infection characterized by rapid onset, fever, rash, nausea, vomiting, diarrhea, and symptoms of shock. It is thought to be caused by *Staphylococcus aureus*, a bacterium, and occurs especially in young menstruating women using high-absorbency tampons.

tox•in ['tɒksən] *n.* any poisonous product of animal or vegetable metabolism, especially one of those produced by bacteria. The symptoms of a disease caused by bacteria, such as diphtheria, are due to toxins. ⟨< *toxic*⟩
☛ *Hom.* TOCSIN.

tox•oid ['tɒksɔɪd] *n.* a specially treated form of a toxin used to immunize against a specific disease.

tox•oph•i•lite [tɒk'sɒfə,ləit] *n.* a person devoted to archery. ⟨< *Toxophilus* title of a book by Roger Ascham (1545) < Gk. *toxon* bow + *philos* loving + E *-ite*⟩ **—tox'oph•i•ly,** *n.*

tox•o•plas•mo•sis [,tɒksəplæz'mousɪs] *n.* a mainly tropical disease characterized by jaundice and damage to the internal organs, nervous system, and vision. It is caused by the protozoan *Toxoplasma gondii.*

toy [tɔi] *n., v. —n.* **1** something meant to play with, especially for a child: *Pick up your toys, Carly. Put that carving down; it is not a toy.* **2** (*adjl.*) made for use as a toy; especially, being a small model of a real thing: *a toy truck, a toy soldier.* **3** any thing or person treated as a toy or dallied with: *She was his toy. All his possessions were the toys of the school bully.* **4** something that resembles a child's toy in being small and pleasing or amusing but having little real value, usefulness, or importance, etc.: *That little calculator is nothing but a toy.* **5** (*adjl.*) designating a small variety of certain breeds of dog: *a toy poodle, a toy terrier.* **6** a small breed or variety of dog: *Pekingese, pugs, and chihuahuas are toys.*
—v. handle or deal with in a light, careless, or trifling way (*used with* **with**): *She toyed with her beads as she talked. He has been toying with the idea of writing a book but so far has not done anything about it. Do not toy with my emotions.* ⟨ME *toye* play, n.; cf. Du. *tuig* tools, stuff, and G *Zeug* stuff⟩ **—'toy,like,** *adj.*

to•yon ['toujən] *n.* a shrub (*Photinia arbutifolia*) of the rose family found along the Pacific coast of North America, whose evergreen leaves and scarlet berries look much like holly. ⟨< Am.Sp. *tollon*⟩

toy•shop ['tɔɪ,ʃɒp] *n.* a store whose chief line of merchandise is toys.

t.p. title page.

Tp. or **tp. 1** township. **2** troop.

Tpk. or **Tpke.** turnpike.

tr. 1 transitive. **2** transpose. **3** translation; translator; translated. **4** trace (in lab results). **5** treasurer. **6** train.

tra•be•ate ['treibiɪt] *or* ['treibi,eit] *adj.* **1** constructed with horizontal beams rather than arches. **2** of this method of construction. Also, **trabeated.** ⟨< L *trabs*, pl. *trabes* beam⟩ **—,tra•be'a•tion,** *n.*

trace¹ [treis] *n., v.* **traced, trac•ing.** *—n.* **1** a sign or evidence of the existence, presence, or action of something in the past; vestige: *The explorer found traces of an ancient city.* **2** a footprint or other mark left; track; trail: *We saw traces of rabbits in the snow.* **3** a very small amount; little bit: *There wasn't a trace of grey in her hair.* **4** something marked out or drawn. **5** the record made by the moving pen or stylus of a recording instrument. **6 a** the spot or line shown moving across the screen of a cathode ray tube by the deflection of the electron beam. **b** its path. **7** *Mathematics.* the intersection of a line, curve, or surface with a coordinate plane. **8** *Psychology.* the permanent change in the brain caused by learning something; engram. **9** *Chemistry.* an indication of an amount of some constituent in a compound, usually too small to be measured. **10** *Meteorology.* an amount of precipitation less than 0.127 mm.
—v. **1** follow by means of marks, tracks, or signs: *to trace deer.* **2** follow the course, history, or development of; *He traced the river to its source. He traced his family back through eight generations. Agriculture can be traced back through many millenia.* **3** find by following a trail of evidence; track down: *They have been unable to trace the suspect.* **4** find signs of; observe. **5** mark out; draw: *The spy traced a plan of the fort.* **6** copy by following the lines of: *He put thin paper over the map and traced it.* **7** decorate with tracery. **8** write, especially by forming the letters carefully or laboriously. **9** record in the form of a curving, wavy, or broken line, as a cardiograph, seismograph, etc. ⟨ME < OF *tracier* < VL *tractiare*, ult. < L *trahere* drag⟩
☛ *Syn. n.* **1. Trace,** VESTIGE = a mark or sign of what has existed or happened. **Trace** applies to any noticeable sign or mark left by something that has happened or been present: *The campers removed all traces of their fire.* **Vestige,** sometimes used as a more formal substitute especially when referring to something no longer present or existing, applies particularly to an actual remnant of something that existed in the past: *Some of our common social manners are vestiges of very old customs.*

trace² [treis] *n.* **1** either of the two straps, ropes, or chains by which an animal pulls a wagon, carriage, etc. See HARNESS for

picture. **2** a rod or bar pivoted or hinged at both ends that transmits motion between two parts of a machine.
kick over the traces, throw off control; become unruly. ⟨ME < OF *traiz*, pl. of *trait*, ult. < L *trahere* drag⟩

trace•a•ble ['treisəbəl] *adj.* capable of being traced. **—'trace•a•bly,** *adv.* **—,trace•a'bil•i•ty,** *n.*

trace element any element occurring in very small amounts, especially such an element occurring in an organism and necessary to the physiological and biological processes of the organism.

trac•er ['treisər] *n.* **1** a person whose work is tracing missing persons or property. **2** an inquiry sent from place to place to trace a missing person, letter, parcel, etc. **3** a person whose work is tracing patterns, designs, markings, etc. **4** a device or machine for making tracings of drawings, plans, designs, etc. **5** a bullet or shell containing a substance that marks its course with a trail of smoke or fire. **6** *Chemistry.* an element (**tracer element**) or atom (**tracer atom**), usually radioactive, used in a chemical or biological process to permit the course of the process to be traced, or to find abnormal cells, etc.

trac•er•y ['treisəri] *n., pl.* **-er•ies. 1** ornamental openwork in stone, consisting of branching or interlacing lines, especially such ornament at the top of a window in Gothic architecture. **2** any decorative pattern or natural outline suggesting this: *the tracery in a butterfly's wing. Tracery is sometimes used in embroidery.* **—'trac•er•ied,** *adj.*

tra•che•a ['treikiə] *or* [trə'kiə] *n., pl.* **tra•che•ae** ['treiki,i] *or* ['treiki,aɪ], [trə'kii] *or* [trə'kiaɪ]. **1** the tube extending from the larynx to the bronchi; windpipe. See LUNG and WINDPIPE for pictures. **2** *Zoology.* one of the air-carrying tubes of the respiratory system of insects and other arthropods. **3** *Botany.* a vessel or duct serving to carry water and dissolved minerals. ⟨< LL *trachia*, ult. < Gk. *tracheia (artēria)*, literally, rough (artery)⟩ **—'tra•che•al,** *adj.*

tra•che•id ['treikiɪd] *n. Botany.* any of the nonliving cells occurring in the xylem. They are long and tubular and serve to conduct water.

tra•che•i•tis [,treiki'əitɪs] *n.* inflammation of the trachea.

tra•che•o•phyte ['treikiə,fəit] *n.* any of a division (Tracheophyta) of plants, including club mosses, horsetails, ferns, and flowering plants, all having a vascular system for conducting food and a life cycle showing alternation of generations. ⟨< NL *Tracheophyta* (division name) < *trache-* < Med.L *trachea* trachea + Gk. *phyton* plant⟩

tra•che•ot•o•my [,treiki'ɒtəmi] *n.* a surgical operation that involves cutting an opening into the trachea, especially to relieve an obstruction to breathing. Also, **tracheostomy.** ⟨< Gk. *tracheia* trachea + *tomia* a cutting⟩

tra•cho•ma [trə'koumə] *n.* a contagious disease of the eye caused by a bacterium (*Chlamydia trachomatis*) and characterized by inflamed granulations on the inner surface of the eyelids. ⟨< NL < Gk. *trachōma* roughness < *trachys* rough⟩ **—tra'cho•ma•tous,** *adj.*

tra•chyte ['treikəit] *or* ['trækəit] *n.* a light-coloured igneous rock of fine grain and rough texture, consisting chiefly of alkalic feldspars with other minerals such as mica or hornblende. It is the extrusive form of syenite. ⟨< F < Gk. *trachys* rough⟩ **—tra'chyt•ic** [trə'kɪtɪk], *adj.*

trac•ing ['treisɪŋ] *n., v.* *—n.* **1** a copy of a map, drawing, etc. made by following its lines on a transparent or semi-transparent sheet that has been placed over it. **2** a line made by a recording instrument that registers movement. An electrocardiograph makes tracings of the contractions of the heart, which are used to diagnose heart disease. **3** (*adjl.*) made for the purpose of tracing: *tracing paper.*
—v. ppr. of TRACE.

track [træk] *n., v.* *—n.* **1** Often, **tracks,** *pl.* the pair of parallel steel rails on which a locomotive, etc. runs: *The train disappeared down the track.* **2** a mark or marks left by something that has passed by: *The tires left tracks on the new asphalt. We followed the deer's tracks along the river.* **3** a path or trail: *A track runs through the woods to the farmhouse.* **4** a course for running or racing: *The school has an oval track.* **5** the sport made up of contests in running. See TRACK AND FIELD. **6** (*adjl.*) of or for use in such sports: *track shoes.* **7** a line of motion or travel: *the track of a bullet.* **8** a course of action or way of doing: *going on in the same track year after year.* **9 a** educational stream; program of study geared to a particular level or category of ability and carried on through several grades or levels of schooling: *the academic track, the technical track, the arts track.* **b** a course of career advancement or promotion, not usually officially recognized in a corporation: *the fast track. Few promotions are awarded to those on the 'mommy' track.* **10** a sequence or succession of events, thoughts, etc. **11 a** a path on a magnetic tape, disc, diskette, etc. or along one side of a film, on which sound or information is recorded. **b** *Computer technology.* the part of a storage device (disk, tape, etc.) passing under a particular position of the reading head. **12** a band on a phonograph record. **13** an endless belt of linked steel treads by which a bulldozer, tank, etc. moves over the ground. **14** the transverse distance between the centres of the parallel wheels of a vehicle.
in (one's) **tracks,** *Informal.* right where one is: *He saw the bear and stopped in his tracks.*
keep track of, keep within one's sight, knowledge, or attention: *The noise of the crowd made it difficult to keep track of what was going on.*
lose track of, fail to keep track of.
make tracks, *Informal.* go very fast; run away.
off (the) track, a off the subject. **b** wrong.
on (the) track, a on the subject. **b** right.
the beaten track, the ordinary or usual way.
the wrong (or **other**) **side of the tracks,** the part of town regarded by residents of another part as inferior.
—v. **1** follow by means of footprints, marks, smell, etc.: *The hunter tracked the bear and killed it.* **2** trace in any way until found (*usually with* **down**): *to track down a criminal.* **3** make footprints or other marks on (a floor, etc.) (*usually with* **up**): *Don't track up the floor.* **4** bring (snow, mud, etc.) into a place on one's feet: *to track mud into the house.* **5** follow and plot the course of, as by radar. **6** *Film.* follow (the subject) with a moving camera. **7** *Cdn.* draw or lead (a canoe, boat, scow, etc.) through rapids, shallows, or other difficult stretches of water by means of lines running from the craft to people on the bank or shore. **8** of moving parts (e.g., gears, videotape in a VCR, phonograph stylus, etc.), move or be in proper alignment. **9** of wheels, move so that the rear ones follow exactly in the track left by the front ones. **10** of a vehicle, have a specific distance between parallel wheels. **11** put in or on a track. ⟨ME < OF *trac*, probably < Gmc.⟩ **—'track•er,** *n.*

track•age ['trækɪdʒ] *n.* **1** all the tracks of a railway. **2** the right of one railway to use the tracks of another. **3** the charge for this.

track and field the group of competitive athletic events performed on a running track and a field next to it, including running, jumping, pole-vaulting, and throwing: *Mitch doesn't play hockey but he's good at track and field.* **—'track-and-'field,** *adjl.*

track•ball ['træk,bɒl] *n. Computer technology.* a computer input device that controls the location of an object or a cursor on a screen. The device consists of a rotatable sphere in a special housing. The location of the object on the screen is changed by rotating the ball by hand.

track•ing ['trækɪŋ] *n., v.* *—n.* TRACK SYSTEM.
—v. ppr. of TRACK.

tracking line *Cdn.* trackline.

tracking station any of several telemeter stations built to track the orbit of a satellite and record data from it.

track•lay•er ['træk,leiər] *n.* a person who lays and maintains track for a railway.

track•less ['træklɪs] *adj.* **1** not using or following a track; without tracks: *a trackless streetcar.* **2** not making or leaving any tracks: *the trackless passage of a rabbit over hard, dry ground.* **3** without paths or trails: *the trackless desert.*

track lighting a system of lighting with directional, swivelling lights set in a wired metal rack attached to the wall or ceiling. In some systems, the lights can be moved along the track to different positions.

track•line ['træk,laɪn] *n. Cdn.* a strong line or rope used to TRACK (v. 7) a canoe. Also, **tracking line.**

track meet a series or group of contests in track-and-field events.

track•pad ['træk,pæd] *n. Computer technology.* a pad allowing movement of the cursor or objects on the screen. The user moves his or her fingertip on the pad in a way similar to a mouse or trackball.

track record a record of the past achievements and overall performance of a person or institution, especially in some specific field or with regard to a specific issue: *Their track record in dealing with environmental issues is rather poor.*

track system *Education.* a system whereby students are divided into different TRACKS (def. 9a) following divergent programs of study designed to suit their level and type of ability. Each program spans several years of study and transfer from one to another is sometimes difficult.

tract[1] [trækt] *n.* **1** a stretch of land, water, etc.; extent; area: *A tract of desert land is of little value to farmers.* **2** a system of related parts or organs in the body. The stomach and intestines are part of the digestive tract. **3** a housing development or subdivision. **4** *Archaic.* a period of time. ⟨< L *tractus*, originally, hauling < *trahere* drag. Doublet of TRAIT.⟩

tract[2] [trækt] *n.* a pamphlet on a religious or political subject intended to support or speak out against a particular cause or point of view. ⟨apparently < L *tractatus* a handling, ult. < *trahere* drag⟩

trac•ta•ble ['træktəbəl] *adj.* **1** easily managed or controlled; easy to deal with; docile: *Dogs are more tractable than mules.* **2** easily worked: *Copper and gold are tractable.* ⟨< L *tractabilis* < *tractare.* See TREAT.⟩ **—'trac•ta•ble•ness,** *n.* **—'trac•ta•bly,** *adv.* **—,trac•ta'bil•i•ty,** *n.*

Trac•tar•i•an•ism [træk'tɛriə,nɪzəm] *n.* a movement in the 1830s in the Church of England, also known as the **Oxford Movement**, urging a return to traditional doctrines and forms of worship. ⟨from the 90 'Tracts for the Times' published at Oxford⟩

trac•tate ['trækteit] *n.* a short treatise.

trac•tile ['træktaɪl] *or* ['træktəl] *adj.* capable of being drawn out to a greater length. **—trac'til•i•ty** [-'tɪləti], *n.*

trac•tion ['trækʃən] *n.* **1** the friction between a body and the surface on which it moves enabling the body to move without slipping: *Wheels slip on ice because there is too little traction.* **2** the kind of power used by a locomotive, streetcar, etc.: *Some railways use electric traction.* **3** the act or process of pulling a load or vehicle over a surface, or the state of being pulled. **4** the pulling of neck, leg, or arm muscles by means of a special device, to relieve pressure, bring a fractured bone into place, etc., or the state of tension produced by such a device: *She spent several months in traction as a result of the accident.* ⟨< Med.L *tractio, -onis* < L *trahere* drag⟩ **—'trac•tion•al,** *adj.*

traction engine a steam engine on wheels, used for pulling wagons, ploughs, etc. along roads or over fields.

trac•tive ['træktɪv] *adj.* pulling; used for pulling.

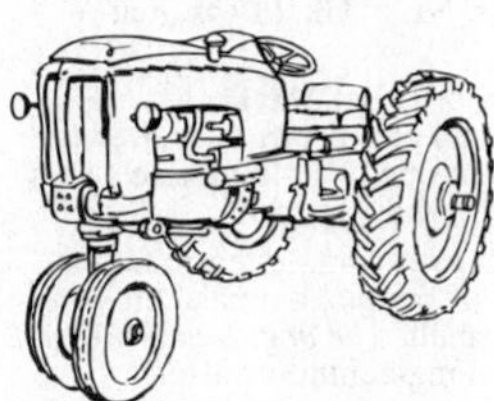

A tractor (def. 1)

A tractor (def. 2) with trailer

trac•tor ['træktər] *n.* **1** a vehicle with a powerful gasoline or diesel engine, having four wheels or running on continuous tracks, used for pulling farm implements, wagons, etc. **2** a powerful truck having a cab for the driver, a short chassis, and no body, used to pull a large trailer or semitrailer along the highway. **3** an aircraft having the propeller in front of the engine. ⟨< Med.L *tractor* < L *trahere* drag⟩

tractor swing *Cdn.* cat-train.

trac•tor–trail•er ['træktər 'treilər] *n.* a very large truck, consisting of a TRACTOR (def. 2) together with a trailer or semitrailer, used for hauling freight.

tractor train *Cdn.* cat-train.

trad [træd] *adj.* TRADITIONAL (def. 2).

trade [treid] *n., v.* **trad•ed, trad•ing.** *—n.* **1** the process of buying and selling; exchange of goods; commerce: *Canada has trade with many foreign countries.* **2** an exchange: *an even trade.* **3** *Informal.* a bargain; business deal: *He made a good trade.* **4** commerce, or the market, related to a specific group of people, commodity, season of the year, etc.: *the book trade, the tourist trade, the Christmas trade.* **5** a kind of work; line of business, especially one requiring skilled mechanical work: *She is learning the carpenter's trade.* **6** people in the same kind of work or business: *The whole building trade is up in arms over the new regulations.* **7** (*adjl.*) of, for, or having to do with trade or a particular trade: *a trade secret, trade journals.* **8** *Informal.* customers: *That store has a lot of trade.* **9 the trades,** *pl.* the TRADE WINDS.

—v. **1** buy and sell; exchange (goods); be in commerce: *Canada trades with many foreign countries.* **2** have dealings; be involved; be an agent of (*used with* **in**): *This organization trades in lies and terror.* **3** swap; exchange: *to trade seats. I traded the book for a compact disc.* **4** make an exchange: *This coat is a better size for you; want to trade?* **5** make an exchange with (someone): *I'll trade you.* **6** bargain; deal. **7** be a customer: *We've been trading at that grocery store for years.*

trade in, give (an automobile, radio, etc.) as part payment for something else, especially for a new item of the same kind: *She traded her old car in for a new one.*

trade off, get rid of by trading.

trade on, take advantage of: *He traded on his father's good name.* ⟨ME < MDu. or MLG *trade* track⟩

☛ *Syn. n.* **1. Trade,** COMMERCE = the buying and selling or exchanging of goods or other commodities. **Trade** applies to the actual buying and selling, or exchange, between countries or within a country: *The government has drawn up new agreements for trade with various countries.* **Commerce** is more general, applying to the whole business of the exchange of commodities, including both trade and transportation, especially as conducted on a large scale between different states or countries.

trade agreement **1** an agreement between nations to promote trade between them. **2** an agreement for a specified time between labour and management concerning job conditions.

trade balance the difference between the value of a country's imports and its exports; BALANCE OF TRADE.

trade barrier anything that restricts or limits international trade: *Tariffs and embargoes are trade barriers.*

trade book a book published for sale to the general public, through retail stores, as opposed to textbooks or other specialized books sold by mail order, etc.

trade discount an amount deducted from the price of a commodity sold by a manufacturer or wholesaler to a retailer or from one establishment to another in the same trade.

trade edition an edition of a book designed for sale to the general public through retail stores, as opposed to a school text edition, etc. Compare TEXT EDITION.

trade gap the difference in value between the total imports and total exports of a country, taking the form of either a **trade surplus** or a **trade deficit.**

trade–in ['treid ,ɪn] *n.* **1** something, such as a used appliance or car, given or accepted as part payment for a new thing of the same kind. **2** the value or price allowed by the seller on a trade-in: *The dealer gave her $600 trade-in on her old car.* **3** a sale or purchase that involves a trade-in. **4** (*adjl.*) of or as a trade-in: *My car has a trade-in value close to zero.*

trade•mark ['treid,mɑrk] *n., v. —n.* a mark, picture, symbol, or name that identifies a product or service as being produced or sold by a particular company, and that is protected by law. A trademark may legally be applied only to goods or services produced or sold by the company that owns it.
—v. **1** distinguish by means of a trademark. **2** register (a name, symbol, etc.) as a trademark.

trade name **1** a distinctive name that identifies a product or service as being produced or sold by a particular company; brand name. **2** the name under which a firm or company conducts its business.

trade–off ['treid,ɒf] *n.* an exchange of one benefit or advantage for another, each entailing some sort of disadvantage, in hopes of a net gain but frequently as a compromise or as an arbitrary selection.

trad•er ['treɪdər] *n.* **1** a person who trades; merchant. **2** a ship used in trading. **3** a person who buys and sells stocks and securities for himself or herself rather than for customers. **4** an item of which a collector has another copy; a duplicate available for trading.

trad•es•can•tia [,trædə'skænʃə] *or* [,trædə'skæntiə] *n.* any of a variety of trailing, hardy perennial houseplants or ground covers such as spiderwort (*T. virginiana*) or wandering Jew (*T. fluminiensis*). ⟨< NL < J. *Tradescant*, an English naturalist (?-1638)⟩

trade school a school where trades are taught.

trades•man ['treidzmən] *n., pl.* **-men. 1** a storekeeper; shopkeeper. **2** one who practises a skilled trade, as, a carpenter, baker, etc. **—'trades,wo•man,** *n.*

trades•peo•ple ['treidz,pipəl] *n.pl.* **1** storekeepers; shopkeepers. **2** people who practise a skilled trade.

trade token *Cdn.* TRADING TOKEN.

trade union an association of workers in any trade or craft or group of allied trades to protect and promote their interests; labour union. Also, *esp. Brit.*, **trades union.**

trade unionism 1 the system of having trade unions. 2 the principles, methods, or practices of trade unions.

trade unionist 1 a member of a trade union. 2 a person who favours trade unionism.

trade winds tropical winds blowing steadily toward the equator from about 30° north latitude to about 30° south latitude. North of the equator, they blow from the northeast; south of the equator, from the southeast.

trading post a store or station of a trader or trading company, especially in a remote place: *The Hudson's Bay Company operates trading posts in the North.*

trading stamp a stamp offered by a merchant to purchasers and redeemable, in certain quantities, for goods to be selected from a special list.

trading token *Cdn.* formerly, one of the coins or tokens constituting beaver currency, a monetary system of the fur trade in which the unit of exchange was the value of one prime beaver pelt. Also, **trade token**.

tra•di•tion [trəˈdɪʃən] *n.* **1** the handing down of beliefs, opinions, customs, stories, etc. from one generation to another. **2** the body of beliefs, opinions, customs, etc. handed down in this way: *a culture strongly steeped in tradition.* **3** an established belief, custom, or practice: *The navy has many old traditions.* **4** *Theology.* **a** in Jewish usage, the unwritten laws and doctrines received from Moses. **b** in Christian usage, the oral teachings of Christ and the apostles, not recorded in the Scriptures. **c** in Muslim usage, the sayings and deeds of Mohammed not recorded in the Koran. **5** *Law.* the formal act of handing something over to someone else; delivery. ⟨< L *traditio, -onis* < *tradere* hand down < *trans-* over + *dare* give. Doublet of TREASON.⟩ **—traˈdi•tion•less,** *adj.* **—traˈdi•tion•ist,** *n.*

tra•di•tion•al [trəˈdɪʃənəl] *adj.* **1** of, based on, or handed down by tradition: *The coronation is a traditional ceremony. They prefer traditional furniture to modern furniture.* **2** of or referring to a style of jazz originating in New Orleans in the early 20th century and revived in the 50s, characterized by improvisation and typically featuring a clarinet, a trombone, and one or two trumpets accompanied by various rhythm instruments, including banjo and tuba. **—traˈdi•tion•al•ly,** *adv.*

tra•di•tion•al•ism [trəˈdɪʃənə,lɪzəm] *n.* **1** strict adherence to tradition. **2** a system of philosophy in which all religious knowledge is held to stem from divine revelation and be transmitted by traditional instruction. **—traˈdi•tion•al•ist,** *n.* **—tra,di•tion•alˈis•tic,** *adj.*

tra•duce [trəˈdjus] *or* [trəˈdus] *v.* **-duced, -duc•ing.** speak evil of (a person) falsely; slander. ⟨< L *traducere* parade in disgrace < *trans-* across + *ducere* lead⟩ **—traˈduc•er,** *n.* **—traˈduce•ment,** *n.*

traf•fic [ˈtræfɪk[*n., v.* **-ficked, -fick•ing.** *—n.* **1** the people, automobiles, wagons, ships, etc. coming and going along a way of travel. **2** buying and selling; commerce or trade in a specific commodity, especially illegal or illicit. **3 a** the business done by a railway line, a steamship line, etc. **b** the number of passengers or the amount of freight carried. **4 a** the volume or rate of movement of vehicles, ships, pedestrians, etc.: *Traffic is slow today. Traffic peaks at 5 p.m.* **b** the total amount of business done by any company or industry within a certain time. **c** the volume of telegrams, calls, etc. transmitted by a communications company in a given period, the amount of electronic mail carried by a computer, etc. **5** (*adjl.*) of, for, or having to do with traffic or its regulation: *traffic signals, traffic duty, traffic court.* **6** intercourse; dealings.
—v. **1** carry on trade; engage in buying, selling, or exchanging: *The men trafficked with the natives for ivory.* **2** have social dealings with; have to do with: *He refuses to traffic with strangers.* ⟨< MF < Ital. *traffico* < *trafficare* < *tras-* across (< L *trans-*) + *ficcare* shove, poke, ult. < L *figere* fix⟩

traffic circle a type of intersection in which traffic to and from different roads moves in a single direction around a circular island, entering and exiting at various points.

traffic island a usually raised area in a road or street designed to direct the flow of traffic into particular lanes, protect pedestrians, etc.

traf•fick•er [ˈtræfɪkər] *n.* a person who buys and sells, especially one who deals illicitly in drugs or other goods.

traffic light an electrically operated device for controlling traffic at intersections, usually consisting of a standard series of coloured lights. A green light means go ahead, an amber light means caution, and a red one means stop. Also, **traffic signal**.

trag•a•canth [ˈtrægə,kænθ] *n.* **1** a gum obtained from certain Asian or eastern European shrubs (genus *Astragalus*) of the pea family used for stiffening cloth, thickening medicines, etc. **2** a plant yielding this gum. ⟨< L < Gk. *tragakantha*, literally, goat's thorn < *tragos* goat + *akantha* thorn⟩

tra•ge•di•an [trəˈdʒidiən] *n.* **1** a writer of tragedies. **2** an actor who specializes in tragic roles.

trag•e•dy [ˈtrædʒədi] *n., pl.* **-dies. 1** a serious play having, usually, a central character and an unhappy or disastrous ending. In many tragedies the hero or heroine experiences great mental suffering and, finally, meets his or her death. *Hamlet* is a tragedy. **2 a** the branch of drama that includes such plays. **b** the writing of such plays. **3** a novel, long poem, etc. similar to a tragic play. **4** a very sad or terrible situation or happening: *The mother's death was a tragedy to her family.* **5** the tragic quality or element of such a happening or piece or writing; tragicalness: *The tragedy of it is that all her talent is going to waste. He was overwhelmed by the tragedy of the situation.* ⟨ME < OF < L < Gk. *tragōidia* < *tragos* goat (connection obscure) + *ōidē* song⟩

trag•ic [ˈtrædʒɪk] *adj.* **1** of or having to do with tragedy: *a tragic actor, a tragic poet, a tragic hero.* **2** very sad or dreadful: *a tragic death, a tragic event.* Also (def. 2), **tragical**. ⟨< L < Gk. *tragikos*⟩ **—ˈtrag•i•cal•ly,** *adv.* **—ˈtrag•i•cal•ness,** *n.*

tragic flaw a flaw in the character of a tragic hero or heroine that brings about his or her downfall.

trag•i•com•e•dy [,trædʒɪˈkɒmədi] *n., pl.* **-dies. 1** a play having both tragic and comic elements. *The Merchant of Venice* is a tragicomedy. **2** a real-life incident or situation in which serious and comic elements are blended. ⟨< F < LL *tragicomoedia* < L *tragicocomoedia* < *tragicus* tragic + *comoedia* comedy⟩

trag•i•com•ic [,trædʒɪˈkɒmɪk] *adj.* having both tragic and comic elements. Also, **tragicomical**. **—,trag•iˈcom•i•cal•ly,** *adv.*

tra•go•pan [ˈtrægə,pæn] *n.* any of a genus of Asiatic pheasants (*Tragopan*) having brightly coloured feathers and two fleshy protuberances on the head. ⟨< NL < Gk. *tragos* goat + *Pan* Pan⟩

tra•gus [ˈtreigəs] *n., pl.* **-gi** [-dʒaɪ] *or* [-dʒi]. the fleshy prominence at the front of the external ear, protruding over the opening. It is the part pushed in when one is 'holding one's ears' ⟨< Gk. *tragos* hairy part of the ear; literally, goat⟩

trail [treil] *n., v. —n.* **1** an unpaved path made intentionally or resulting from the frequent passage of people, animals, etc., often in a wild region. **2** a track or smell: *The dogs found the trail of a rabbit.* **3** anything that follows along behind or after, including a series of conditions, events, etc. arising as a consequence: *The car left a trail of dust behind it. The young man left a trail of misery and broken hearts wherever he went.* **4** the lower end of a gun carriage.
—v. **1** pull or drag or be pulled or dragged along behind: *The child trailed a toy horse after her. Her dress trails on the ground.* **2** hang down or float loosely from something. **3** follow the trail or track of; track: *to trail a bear or thief.* **4** carry or bring by or as if by leaving in a trail behind one; TRACK (def. 4): *to trail snow into a house.* **5** bring or have floating after itself: *a car trailing dust.* **6** follow along behind; follow: *The dog trailed him constantly.* **7** *Sports.* be behind (an opponent) in a game or competition: *trailing by seven points. England was still trailing Sweden in the second half.* **8** move or extend in a long, uneven line: *ivy trailing over an old wall, refugees trailing from their ruined village.* **9** mark out (a trail or track): *to trail a path through the jungle.* **10** go along slowly or wearily; traipse: *children trailing to school.* **11** become gradually less (*used with* **off** *or* **away**): *Her voice trailed off into silence.* ⟨ME < OF *trailler* tow, ult. < L *tragula* dragnet⟩

trail bike a small motorcycle for riding on rough terrain.

trail blaze *Cdn.* See BLAZE[2] (def. 1).

trail•bla•zer [ˈtreil,bleizər] *n.* **1** a person who marks a trail by chipping bark off trees along the way. **2** a person who pioneers or prepares the way to something new.

trail•er [ˈtreilər] *n.* **1** a small or large vehicle having one or more pairs of wheels, designed to be pulled along by a truck, tractor, automobile, etc., and used for transporting goods, animals, a boat or snowmobile, etc. **2** a closed-in vehicle having one or more pairs of wheels, designed to be pulled by an automobile or truck and equipped for use as a dwelling or place of business; a camper, mobile home, etc.: *We have a trailer that we take to the lake every summer. Large trailers are often called mobile homes.* **3** a short film made up of selected scenes from a feature film, shown as an advertisement: *I haven't seen the movie yet, but I saw the trailer on TV.* **4** a short length of blank film at the end of a reel. **5** a trailing plant. **6** a person or animal that follows a trail.

trailer camp or **park** an area equipped to accommodate TRAILERS (def. 2), often having electricity, running water, etc.

trailer hitch a knoblike or hooklike projection for attaching a trailer, fixed to the rear of a vehicle.

trailing arbutus a trailing plant (*Epigaea repens*) of the heath family found in the woodlands of eastern North America, having evergreen leaves and clusters of fragrant, pink or white flowers very early in spring; mayflower. The trailing arbutus is the provincial flower of Nova Scotia.

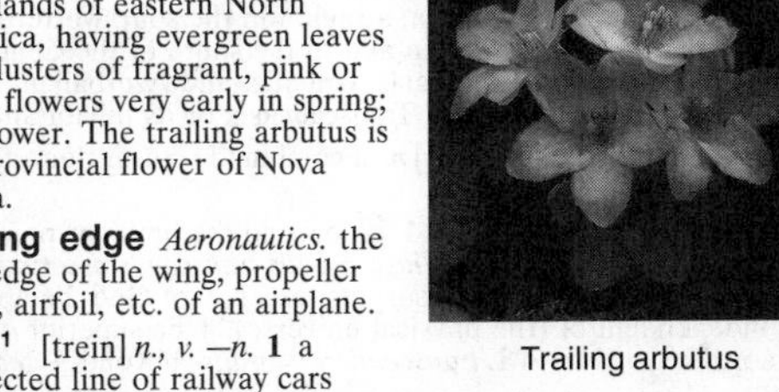
Trailing arbutus

trailing edge *Aeronautics.* the rear edge of the wing, propeller blade, airfoil, etc. of an airplane.

train[1] [trein] *n., v.* —*n.* **1** a connected line of railway cars pulled by an engine. **2** a line of people, animals, wagons, trucks, etc. moving along together. **3** a collection of vehicles, animals, and people accompanying an army to carry supplies, baggage, ammunition, or any equipment or materials. **4** a part of a dress, cloak, or gown that trails behind the wearer: *Two attendants carried the queen's train.* **5** something that is drawn along behind; a trailing part. **6** a tail: *the train of a peacock, the train of a comet.* **7** a group of followers. **8 a** a series; succession: *a long train of misfortunes.* **b** a continuous course: *a train of thought.* **c** a succession of results or conditions following some event: *The flood brought starvation and disease in its train.* **9** a line of gunpowder that acts as a fuse. **10** a series of connected parts, such as wheels and pinions, through which motion is transmitted in a machine.
in train, a in proper order, arrangement, or sequence. **b** in process.
train of thought, a succession of connected thoughts passing through one's mind at a particular time: *From the way the speaker paused, it was obvious that he had lost his train of thought.*
—*v.* **1** bring up; rear; teach: *to train a child.* **2** acquire or impart some skill by teaching and practice: *to train as a nurse. Saint Bernard dogs were trained to hunt for travellers lost in the snow.* **3 a** discipline and instruct (an animal) to be useful, obedient, perform tricks, race, etc.: *to train a horse.* **b** sometimes, specifically, to make (an animal) housebroken. **4** make or become fit for some athletic activity by exercise and diet: *Runners train for races.* **5** point; aim: *to train cannon upon a fort.* **6** bring (plants, etc.) into a particular position so as to direct future growth: *Train the vine around this post.* ⟨ME < OF *trainer* < VL *traginare*, ult. < L *trahere* drag⟩

train[2] [trein] *n. Cdn.* **1** dog-team. **2** a dog-team and dog-sled together. ⟨< Cdn.F *traîne sauvage* toboggan < F *traîneau* sled⟩

train•ee [trei'ni] *n.* one who is receiving training: *She had the trainee observe her for a week before starting duties.*
—train'ee•ship, *n.*

train•er ['treinər] *n.* **1** a person who trains individual athletes or sports teams. **2** a person who trains racehorses, circus beasts, or other animals. **3** a device, machine, etc. used in training: *The pilot was flying a single-engined trainer.*

train•ing ['treinɪŋ] *n., v.* —*n.* **1** practical education in some art, profession, etc.: *training for teachers.* **2** the development of physical or moral strength and endurance.
in training, in the process of being trained or receiving training.
—*v.* ppr. of TRAIN.

training camp a session of intensive training undertaken by a team or an athlete at a place away from home base in preparation for a regular season or for a special contest or event.

training pants thick, absorbent underpants for young children being trained to use the toilet.

training school **1** an institution for the custody and education of juvenile offenders. Training schools in Canada are operated by a provincial government or by a private organization under a provincial charter. **2** *Rare.* TRADE SCHOOL.

training ship a ship, especially a large sailing ship, used for training novices in the art of seamanship, especially for the navy: *HMCS* Oriole *is a Canadian training ship based in Victoria.*

training wheels small wheels attached on either side of the rear wheel of a bicycle to steady the vehicle for a child learning to ride.

train•load ['trein,loud] *n.* as much as a train can hold or carry.

train•man ['treinmən] *n., pl.* **-men.** a man who works on a railway train, especially a brakeman.

train oil oil obtained from a sea animal, especially a whale. ⟨< obs. *train* train oil < MLG *trān* or MDu. *traen* tear, drop; cf. G *Träne*⟩

traipse [treips] *v.* **traipsed, traips•ing;** *n. Informal.* —*v.* walk, wander, or tramp: *I traipsed all over town looking for a gift.*
—*n.* a walk, especially a long or tiring one. ⟨probably < OF *trapasser*, var. of *trespasser.* See TRESPASS.⟩

trait [treit] *n.* a quality of mind, character, etc.; distinguishing feature; characteristic: *Courage, love of justice, and common sense are desirable traits.* ⟨< F *trait* < L *tractus* < *trahere* drag. Doublet of TRACT[1].⟩
☛ *Syn.* See note at FEATURE.

trai•tor ['treitər] *n.* **1** a person who betrays his or her country or ruler; one who commits treason. **2** a person who betrays a trust, duty, friend, etc. ⟨ME < OF *traitor*, ult. < L *traditor*, ult. < *trans-* over + *dare* give⟩

trai•tor•ous ['treitərəs] *adj.* **1** like a traitor; treacherous; faithless. **2** treasonable; that constitutes or involves treason.
—'trai•tor•ous•ly, *adv.* **—'trai•tor•ous•ness,** *n.*

tra•jec•to•ry [trə'dʒɛktəri] *n., pl.* **-ries. 1** the curved path of something moving through space, such as a bullet from a gun or a planet in its orbit. **2** *Geometry.* a curve or surface that intersects all the curves of a family of curves at a given angle. ⟨< Med.L *trajectorius* throwing across, ult. < L *trans-* across + *jacere* throw⟩

tra–la [trɑ'lɑ] *interj.* an expression of glee, nonchalance, etc. ⟨in imitation of the refrain of a song⟩

tram[1] [træm] *n.* **1** a truck or car on which loads are carried in mines. **2** the basket or cage on an overhead conveyor cable. **3** *Esp. Brit.* streetcar. **4** tramway. ⟨< MDu. or MLG *trame* beam⟩

tram[2] [træm] *n.* lightly twisted double silk yarn forming the weft in some velvet or silk weaves. ⟨< F *trame* < L *trama* woof⟩

tram[3] [træm] *n.* TRAMMEL (def. 6).

tram•car ['træm,kar] *n.* **1** *Brit.* streetcar. **2** TRAM[1] (def. 1).

tram•mel ['træməl] *n., v.* **-melled** or **-meled, -mel•ling** or **-mel•ing.** —*n.* **1** Usually, **trammels,** *pl.* anything that hinders or restrains: *A large bequest freed the artist from the trammels of poverty.* **2** a fine net to catch fish, birds, etc. **3** a device in a fireplace having a series of holes by which to hook pots, kettles, etc. at the desired height over the fire. Also, **trammel net. 4** a shackle for controlling the motions of a horse and teaching it to amble. **5** a type of compass for drawing ellipses. **6** a device for making fine adjustments to machine parts.
—*v.* **1** hinder; restrain. **2** entangle. ⟨ME *tramayle* a kind of net < OF < LL *trimaculum* (spelled *tremaculum*) < L *tri-* three + *macula* mesh⟩ **—'tram•mel•ler** or **'tram•mel•er,** *n.*

tra•mon•tane [trə'mɒntein] *or* [,træmən'tein] *adj., n.* —*adj.* **1** having to do with, coming from, or located on the other side of the mountains, especially north of the Alps; transalpine: *a tramontane wind.* **2** foreign.
—*n.* **1** one who lives on the other side of the mountains, especially north of the Alps. **2** foreigner. **3** a cold wind blowing from a mountain range. ⟨< Ital. *tramontana* < L *transmontanus* < *trans* across + *montanus* mountain⟩

tramp [træmp] *v., n.* —*v.* **1** walk heavily: *He tramped across the room in his heavy boots.* **2** step heavily (on); trample; cause to be or go in this way: *He tramped on the flowers. You're tramping my glove into the dirt! She tramped the tin cans flat.* **3** go on foot, especially wearily or for a long way; trudge: *We tramped through the fields.* **4** travel through on foot, especially at length: *to tramp the streets.* **5** walk steadily; march: *We tramped all day.* **6** go or wander as a tramp.
—*n.* **1** the sound of heavy footsteps: *Hear the tramp of the parade.* **2** a long, steady walk; hike. **3** a person who goes about on foot, living by begging, doing odd jobs, etc. **4** a freighter that takes a cargo when and where it can. **5** an iron plate giving extra protection, traction, etc. on the sole of a shoe, as for use when digging with a shovel. **6** *Slang.* a sexually loose woman. ⟨? < LG *trampen*⟩ **—'tramp•er,** *n.*

tram•ple ['træmpəl] *v.* **-pled, -pling;** *n.* —*v.* **1** crush, kill, or destroy by treading heavily (on): *The cattle broke through the* *fence and trampled the farmer's crops.* **2** hurt or violate, as if by treading on (*often used with* **on**): *to trample on someone's rights.* —*n.* the act or sound of trampling: *We heard the trample of many feet.* ⟨< *tramp*⟩ —**'tram•pler,** *n.*

tram•po•line [ˌtræmpə'lin], ['træmpəˌlin], *or* ['træmpəlɪn] *n.* an apparatus for tumbling, acrobatics, etc. consisting of a taut piece of canvas or other sturdy fabric attached by springs to a metal frame. ⟨< Ital. *trampolino* springboard⟩ —**ˌtram•po'lin•ist,** *n.*

tram•way ['træmˌwei] *n.* **1** *Mining.* **a** a track or roadway for carrying ore from mines. **b** a cable or system of cables on which suspended cars carry ore, etc. **2** *Esp. Brit.* a track for streetcars. Also (def. 1a), *esp. U.S.,* **tramroad.**

trance [træns] *n., v.* **tranced, tranc•ing.** —*n.* **1** a state of unconsciousness resembling sleep. A person may be in a trance from illness, from the influence of some other person, or from his or her own will, as a medium during a seance. **2 a** a dreamy, absorbed condition that is like a trance: *The old man sat before the fire in a trance, thinking of his past life.* **b** stupor; daze. **3** a high emotion; rapture; ecstasy, as from extreme religious fervour or a mystical experience.
—*v.* hold in a trance; enchant. ⟨ME < OF *transe,* ult. < L *trans-* across + *ire* go⟩ —**'trance,like,** *adj.*

trank [træŋk] *n., v. Slang.* —*n.* tranquillizer.
—*v.* tranquillize.

tran•quil ['træŋkwəl] *adj.* calm; peaceful; quiet: *a tranquil mood, the tranquil evening air.* ⟨< L *tranquillus*⟩ —**tran'quil•ly,** *adv.*

tran•quil•i•ty [træŋ'kwɪləti] *n.* See TRANQUILLITY.

tran•quil•ize ['trænkwəˌlaɪz] *v.* **-ized, -iz•ing.** See TRANQUILLIZE.

tran•quil•iz•er ['træŋkwəˌlaɪzər] *n.* See TRANQUILLIZER.

tran•quil•li•ty or **tran•quil•i•ty** [træŋ'kwɪləti] *n.* calmness; peacefulness; quiet.

tran•quil•lize or **tran•quil•ize** ['træŋkwəˌlaɪz] *v.* **-lized** or **-ized, -liz•ing** or **-iz•ing. 1** make peaceful or quiet; especially, reduce mental tension and anxiety in (someone) by the use of drugs. **2** become peaceful or quiet. —**ˌtran•quil•li'za•tion,** *n.*

tran•quil•liz•er or **tran•quil•iz•er** ['træŋkwəˌlaɪzər] *n.* a person who or thing that makes someone peaceful or quiet; especially, any of several drugs used to reduce mental tension and anxiety, control certain psychoses, etc.

trans– *prefix.* **1** across, over, or through, as in *transcontinental, transmit.* **2** beyond; on the other side of, as in *Transjordan, transcend.* **3** across, etc., and also beyond, on the other side of, as in *transarctic, transequatorial, transmarine, transoceanic, transpolar,* and many other geographical terms, such as *trans-African.* **4** into a different place, condition, etc., as in *transform, transmute.* **5** *Chemistry.* **a** of an isomer, having a certain atom or group on both sides of a given plane in the molecule: *trans-butene.* **b** of an element, having an atomic number that exceeds that of (another element) in the periodic table: *transuranium.* Also, **tran-** before *s,* and **tra-** before *d, j, l, m, n,* or *v* in words of Latin origin. ⟨< L *trans,* prep.⟩

trans. **1** transitive. **2** transportation. **3** transaction(s). **4** translation; translated; translator. **5** transferred. **6** transpose. **7** transverse.

trans•act [træn'zækt] *v.* manage, negotiate, or carry on (business, etc.): *She transacts business with stores all over the country.* ⟨< L *transactus,* pp. of *transigere* accomplish < *trans-* through + *agere* drive⟩

trans•ac•tion [træn'zækʃən] *n.* **1** the act or an instance of transacting: *Mr. Smith attends to the transaction of important matters himself.* **2** a piece of business: *A record is kept of all the firm's transactions.* **3 transactions,** *pl.* a record of what is done at the meetings of a society, club, etc. ⟨ME < LL *transactio, -onis* < *transigere.* See TRANSACT.⟩ —**trans'ac•tion•al,** *adj.*

transactional analysis *Psychoanalysis.* a form of psychotherapy having as its goal the balance of three postulated states of the individual's ego, namely child, adult, and parent.

trans•ac•tor [træn'zæktər] *n.* a person who transacts business affairs.

trans•al•pine [træn'zælpaɪn] *or* [træn'zælpɪn] *adj., n.* —*adj.* across or beyond the Alps, especially as viewed from Italy.
—*n.* a native or inhabitant of any transalpine country.

trans•am•i•nase [træn'zæməˌneis] *or* [træn'zæməˌneiz] *n.* any of a group of enzymes found in most plant and animal tissues that are agents of transamination.

trans•am•i•na•tion [trænˌzæmə'neiʃən] *n.* the transfer of an amino group from one molecule to another.

trans•at•lan•tic [ˌtrænzət'læntɪk] *adj.* **1** crossing or extending across the Atlantic Ocean. **2** having to do with crossing the Atlantic Ocean: *transatlantic air fares.* **3** on the other side of the Atlantic Ocean.

trans–Can•a•da [ˌtrænz'kænədə] *adj.* **1** extending right across Canada, from the Atlantic to the Pacific Oceans: *the trans-Canada microwave system.* **2** (*noml.*) **Trans-Canada,** the Trans-Canada Highway, a series of paved roads extending across Canada through each province and conforming to agreed standards of construction.

Trans•cau•ca•sian [ˌtrænzkɒ'keiʒən] *n., adj.* —*n.* a native or inhabitant of Transcaucasia, a region in the southwestern part of the former Soviet Union, in and to the south of the Caucasus Mountains, comprising Georgia, Armenia, and Azerbaijan.
—*adj.* of or having to do with Transcaucasia or its inhabitants.

trans•cei•ver [træn'sivər] *n.* a combined transmitter and receiver, as, for radio signals.

tran•scend [træn'sɛnd] *v.* **1** go beyond the limits or powers of; exceed: *The grandeur of Niagara Falls transcends description.* **2** be higher or greater than; surpass; excel. **3** of God, be above and independent of (the physical universe). **4** be superior or extraordinary. ⟨ME < L *transcendere* < *trans-* beyond + *scandere* climb⟩

tran•scend•ence [træn'sɛndəns] *n.* the state or quality of being transcendent.

tran•scend•ent [træn'sɛndənt] *adj.* **1** surpassing ordinary limits; excelling; superior; extraordinary. **2** existing apart from the universe. **3** *Philosophy.* **a** transcending the Aristotelian categories, especially as considered by the medieval scholastics. **b** in Kantian philosophy, not realizable in human experience. —**tran'scend•ent•ly,** *adv.*

tran•scen•den•tal [ˌtrænsɛn'dɛntəl] *adj.* **1** transcendent. **2** supernatural. **3** obscure; incomprehensible; fantastic. **4** abstract or metaphysical. **5** *Philosophy.* implied in and necessary to human experience; transcending sense perception; having to do with those elements of human experience stemming from the mind's inherent organizing processes, necessary to knowledge. **6** *Mathematics.* **a** incapable of being the root of any algebraic equation having coefficients that are rational numbers. **b** of a function, such as a logarithm, incapable of algebraic expression using the variables and constants and the operations multiplication, addition, or involution or their inverses. —**ˌtran•scen'den•tal•ly,** *adv.*

tran•scen•den•tal•ism [ˌtrænsɛn'dɛntəˌlɪzəm] *n.* **1** a transcendental quality, thought, language, or philosophy. **2** any philosophy based upon the doctrine that the principles of reality are to be discovered by a study of the processes of thought, not from experience. **3** obscurity; incomprehensibility; fantasy.

tran•scen•den•tal•ist [ˌtrænsɛn'dɛntəlɪst] *n.* a person who believes in transcendentalism or practises transcendental meditation.

transcendental meditation Sometimes, **Transcendental Meditation,** a technique for detaching oneself from problems, stress, etc. and achieving a state of relaxation through meditation and the recitation of a mantra. It is based on ancient Hindu writings. *Abbrev.:* TM or T.M.

trans•con•ti•nen•tal [ˌtrænzkɒntə'nɛntəl] *adj.* **1** crossing or extending across a continent: *a transcontinental railway.* **2** (*noml.*) a train that crosses a continent. **3** being on the other side of a continent.

tran•scribe [træn'skraɪb] *v.* **-scribed, -scrib•ing. 1** copy in writing or in typewriting: *The account of the trial was transcribed from the stenographer's shorthand notes.* **2** set down in writing or print: *His entire speech was transcribed in the newspapers, word for word.* **3** arrange (a musical composition) for a different instrument or voice. **4** *Radio and television.* make a recording of (a program, commercial, etc.), especially for broadcasting at a later time. **5** broadcast (such a program, commercial, etc.). **6** *Phonetics.* record (speech) in a system of phonetic symbols; represent (a speech sound) by a phonetic symbol. **7** transliterate. ⟨< L *transcribere* < *trans-* over + *scribere* write⟩ —**tran'scrib•er,** *n.*

tran•script ['trænskrɪpt] *n.* **1** a written or typewritten copy: *They were waiting for a transcript of the tapes.* **2** any copy or reproduction: *The university requires a transcript of your high-school grades.* ⟨< L *transcriptum,* pp. neut. of *transcribere.* See TRANSCRIBE.⟩

tran•scrip•tase [træn'skrɪpteis] *n.* an enzyme active in the synthesis of complementary DNA.

tran•scrip•tion [træn'skrɪpʃən] *n.* **1** the act or process of transcribing. **2** a transcript; copy. **3** an arrangement of a musical composition for a different instrument or voice. **4** a recording of a program, commercial, etc. made for broadcasting on radio or television. **5** the act or practice of broadcasting such a recording. **6** *Phonetics.* a written representation of speech in a system of phonetic symbols. **7** a transliterated version of a text. **—tran'scrip•tive,** *adj.*

trans•duce [trænz'djus] *or* [trænz'dus] *v.* **-duced, -duc•ing.** transfer or convert (one form of energy) into another. ⟨< L *transducere* < *trans-* + *ducere* lead⟩

trans•duc•tion [trænz'dʌkʃən] *n.* **1** *Biology.* the transfer of genetic material from one cell to another by means of a bacterial virus. **2** *Physics.* the transfer of one form of energy to another.

trans•du•cer [trænz'djusər] *or* [trænz'dusər] *n.* an electrical device which converts one form of energy into another: *Microphones and loudspeakers are transducers.*

tran•sect [træn'sɛkt] *v.* divide by cutting across. ⟨< *trans-* + L *sectus* pp. of *secare* cut⟩

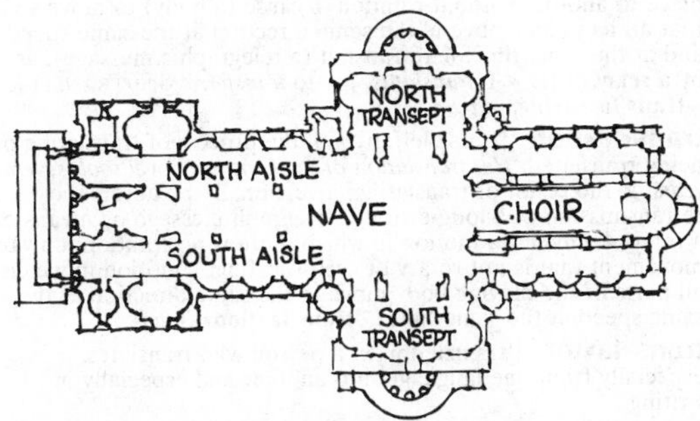

A ground plan of a church showing the north and south transepts

tran•sept ['trænsɛpt] *n.* **1** the part of a cross-shaped church at right angles to the long main part, or nave. **2** either projecting end of this part. ⟨< Med.L *transeptum*, ult. < L *trans-* across + *saeptum* fence⟩

trans•fer *v.* [træns'fɜr], [trænz'fɜr], *or* ['trænsfər]; *n.* ['trænsfər] *v.* **-ferred, -fer•ring;** *n.* *—v.* **1** convey, remove, or cause to go from one person, place, school, department, etc. to another; hand over: *This farm has been transferred from father to son for generations. My trunks were transferred by express. The army transferred her to Kingston.* **2** move or switch, or be moved or switched, to another location, school, course, department, etc.: *She transferred from McGill to Simon Fraser last term.* **3** convey (a drawing, design, pattern) from one surface to another. **4** make over (a title, right, or property) by deed or legal process: *to transfer a bond by endorsement.* **5** change from one streetcar, bus, train, etc. to another without having to pay another fare: *I transferred at Islington station.*
—n. **1** a transferring or being transferred. **2** a drawing, pattern, etc. printed from one surface onto another. **3** a ticket allowing a passenger to continue his or her journey on another streetcar, bus, train, etc. **4** a point or place for transferring. **5** the making over to another of title, right, or property by deed or legal process. **6** a document ordering, authorizing, or effecting a transfer of some sort, such as a transfer of stocks or bonds, a transfer of title, a transfer to another location, etc. **7** a person or thing that is transferred. ⟨ME < L *transferre* < *trans-* across + *ferre* bear⟩ **—trans'fer•rer,** *n.* **—trans'fer•ral,** *n.*

trans•fer•a•bil•i•ty [,trænsfərə'bɪləti] *or* [træns,fɜrə'bɪləti] *n.* the quality of being transferable.

trans•fer•a•ble [træns'fɜrəbəl] *or* ['trænsfərəbəl] *adj.* capable of being transferred.

transferable vote a vote that is transferred to another candidate, indicated by the voter, in the event that the candidate of first choice is eliminated.

trans•fer•ase ['trænsfə,reis] *or* ['trænsfə,reiz] *n.* any of a group of enzymes transferring chemical groups from one molecule to another.

trans•fer•ee [,trænsfə'ri] *n.* **1** a person who has been or is being transferred. **2** a person to whom something, especially property, is transferred.

trans•fer•ence ['trænsfərəns] *or* [træns'fɜrəns] *n.* **1** the act of transferring or the state of being transferred. **2** *Psychoanalysis.* a revival of emotions previously experienced and repressed, as toward a parent, with a new person as the object, often the analyst. **—,trans•fer'en•tial,** *adj.*

trans•fer•or [træns'fɜrər] *n.* *Law.* one from or by whom something is transferred.

trans•fer•rin [træns'fɛrɪn] *n.* a globulin in blood plasma that binds and carries iron. ⟨< *trans-* + L *ferrum* iron + E *-in*⟩

transfer RNA a form of RNA that is involved in transporting amino acids from the cytoplasm to the growing polypeptide chain.

trans•fig•u•ra•tion [træns,fɪgjə'reiʃən] *or* [træns,fɪgə'reiʃən] *n.* **1** a change in form or appearance; transformation. **2 the Transfiguration,** *Christianity.* **a** in the Bible, the change in the appearance of Christ on the mountain. **b** a Christian festival held on August 6 in honour of this.

trans•fig•ure [træns'fɪgjər] *or* [træns'fɪgər] *v.* **-ured, -ur•ing.** **1** change in form or appearance, especially for the better: *New paint had transfigured the old house.* **2** change so as to glorify; exalt. ⟨ME < L *transfigurare* < *trans-* across + *figura* figure⟩

trans•fi•nite [træns'faɪnəɪt] *adj.* **1** that is beyond finitude or the finite. **2** *Mathematics.* of or being a cardinal or ordinal number larger than any positive integer; an infinite cardinal or ordinal number.

trans•fix [træns'fɪks] *v.* **1** pierce through: *The hunter transfixed the wild boar with a spear.* **2** fasten by piercing through with something pointed. **3** make motionless (with amazement, terror, etc.). ⟨< L *transfixus*, pp. of *transfigere* < *trans-* through + *figere* fix⟩ **—trans'fix•ion,** *n.*

trans•form *v.* [træns'fɔrm]; *n.* ['trænsfɔrm] *v., n.* *—v.* **1** change considerably or radically in form, appearance, function, condition, or character: *The blizzard transformed the bushes into glittering mounds of snow. Her face was transformed by a sudden smile. The witch transformed the brothers into pigs.* **2** *Physics.* change (one form of energy) into another. A generator transforms mechanical energy into electricity. **3** change the voltage, etc. of (an electric current) by means of a transformer. **4** *Mathematics.* change (a figure, term, etc.) to another differing in form but having the same value or quantity. **5** *Linguistics.* in TRANSFORMATIONAL GRAMMAR, change (a structure) according to a transformation.
—n. Mathematics, Linguistics. the result of transforming. ⟨ME < L *transformare* < *trans-* across + *forma* form⟩
—trans'form•a•tive, *adj.*

☛ *Syn. v.* **Transform,** TRANSMUTE, CONVERT = change the form, nature, substance, or state of something. **Transform** suggests a thoroughgoing or fundamental change in the appearance, shape, or nature of a thing or person: *Responsibility transformed him from a happy-go-lucky youth into a capable leader.* **Transmute,** formal, implies a complete change in nature or substance, especially a change to a higher level or kind: *She thus transmuted disapproval into admiration.* **Convert** suggests turning from one state or condition to another, especially for a new use or purpose: *convert boxes into furniture.*

trans•for•ma•tion [,trænsfər'meiʃən] *n.* **1** the act or process of transforming or the state of being transformed: *the transformation of a caterpillar into a butterfly.* **2** the result of transforming. **3** *Linguistics.* in TRANSFORMATIONAL GRAMMAR, a rule-governed change by which a surface structure is derived from an underlying structure. An example is the inversion of subject and verb to form an interrogative sentence. **4** *Medicine.* the conversion of a normal cell into a cancer cell.

transformational grammar *Linguistics.* a theory of syntax, especially in generative grammars, positing the existence of underlying structures and surface structures, the former being generated by basic rules and the latter being derived from the underlying structures by means of a series of rule-governed changes or transformations. The theory accounts for every possible grammatical utterance of any language. Also, **transformational generative grammar.**

trans•form•er [træns'fɔrmər] *n.* **1** a device for changing the voltage of an electric current. North American electrical appliances cannot be used in Europe without a transformer because the voltage there is much higher than in North America. **2** a child's toy which, by folding, unfolding, turning, etc. various parts of it, can be converted into a different toy, usually with some space-age motif. **3** any person or thing that transforms another: *Love is a great transformer.*

trans•fuse [træns'fjuz] *v.* **-fused, -fus•ing.** **1** pour from one container into another. **2** transfer (blood) from one person or animal to another intravenously. **3** inject (a solution) into a blood vessel. **4** give a transfusion to (a person or animal). **5** infuse; instil: *The speaker transfused his enthusiasm into the audience.* ⟨ME < L *transfusus*, pp. of *transfundere* < *trans-* across + *fundere* pour⟩

trans•fu•sion [træns'fjuʒən] *n.* **1** the act or process of transfusing; especially, the process of transfusing blood or blood plasma into a blood vessel of a person or animal. **2** an instance of transfusing blood: *She has received three transfusions.*

trans•gene ['trænz,dʒin] *n. Genetics.* a foreign gene carried by an organism as a result of the injection of foreign DNA at the oocyte stage of development. The foreign DNA may be expressed and, if incorporated into the germline, may be transmitted to the progeny. **—trans'gen•ic** [-'dʒɛnɪk], *adj.*

trans•gress [trænz'grɛs] *v.* **1** break a law, command, etc.; sin: *I knew he had transgressed.* **2** go contrary to; sin against: *to transgress the divine law.* **3** go beyond (a boundary or limit): *The interviewer's questions transgressed the bounds of good taste.* ⟨< L *transgressus*, pp. of *transgredi* go beyond < *trans-* across + *gradi* to step⟩ **—trans'gres•sive,** *adj.*

trans•gres•sion [trænz'grɛʃən] *n.* a transgressing; breaking a law, command, etc.; sin. ⟨< L *transgressio, -onis*, originally, a going over < *transgredi.* See TRANSGRESS.⟩

trans•gres•sor [trænz'grɛsər] *n.* a person who transgresses; sinner.

tran•ship [træn'ʃɪp] *v.* **-shipped, -ship•ping.** transship. **—tran'ship•ment,** *n.*

trans•hu•mance [træns'hjuməns] *or* [trænz'hjuməns] *n.* the moving of livestock to more suitable pastures as the seasons change. ⟨< F < Sp., ult. < L *trans-* + *humus* ground⟩ **—trans'hu•mant,** *adj.*

tran•si•ence ['trænziəns] *n.* the quality or state of being transient. Also, **transiency.**

tran•si•ent ['trænziənt] *adj., n.* *—adj.* **1** passing soon; fleeting; not lasting; transitory. **2 a** passing through and not staying long: *a transient guest in a hotel.* **b** serving transient guests, customers, etc.: *a transient hotel.*
—n. **1** a visitor or boarder who stays for a short time. **2** a tramp or hobo. **3** *Electricity.* a sudden surge of voltage or current. ⟨< L *transiens, -entis*, ppr. of *transire* pass through < *trans-* through + *ire* go⟩ **—'tran•si•ent•ly,** *adv.*
☛ *Syn. adj.* **1.** See note at TEMPORARY.

tran•sis•tor [træn'zɪstər] *n.* **1** a small electronic device, similar to an electron tube in use, that amplifies electricity by controlling the flow of electrons. Transistors are used in computers, radios, television sets, etc. **2** a portable radio that has transistors instead of tubes. ⟨< L *trans-* + *sistere* send, convey⟩

tran•sis•tor•ize [træn'zɪstə,raɪz] *v.* **-ized, -iz•ing.** equip with transistors.

trans•it ['trænzɪt] *n., v.* **-it•ed, -it•ing.** *—n.* **1** the act or process or an instance of passing across or through. **2** the process of carrying or being carried across or through: *The goods were damaged in transit.* **3** transportation by trains, buses, etc. **4** transition or change. **5** *Surveying.* in full, **transit theodolite**, an instrument used for measuring angles. It includes a telescope and levels and scales for measuring angles both vertically and horizontally. **6** *Astronomy.* **a** the apparent passage of a heavenly body across the meridian of a place. **b** the passage of a small heavenly body across the disk of a larger one. **7** RAPID TRANSIT.
—v. **1** pass through, over, or across (something or some place). **2** *Surveying.* turn (the telescope of a transit) around its horizontal transverse axis to point in the opposite direction. ⟨< L *transitus* < *transire.* See TRANSIENT.⟩

transit instrument or **telescope** **1** *Astronomy.* a telescope so fixed that it can move only in the plane of the meridian along which it is located, used to determine the time of a heavenly body's transit. **2** a surveyor's transit.

tran•si•tion [træn'zɪʃən] *n.* **1** a change or passing from one condition, place, form, stage, etc. to another: *a transition from poverty to wealth and power, a period of transition in history.* **2** *Music.* **a** a change of key. **b** a passage linking one section, subject, etc. of a composition with another. **3** in writing, a word, phrase, sentence, etc. serving to link ideas or to lead smoothly from one topic to the next. ⟨< L *transitio, -onis* < *transire.* See TRANSIENT.⟩ **—tran'si•tion,ar•y,** *adj.*

tran•si•tion•al [træn'zɪʃənəl] *adj.* of, having to do with, or involving transition: *a transitional stage in his life.* **—tran'si•tion•al•ly,** *adv.*

transition element *Chemistry.* any of several elements having an incomplete electron shell, more than one valence, and a tendency to form complexes. There are three series of such elements in the periodic table.

tran•si•tive ['trænzətɪv] *adj., n.* *—adj.* **1** *Grammar.* of a verb, taking a direct object. *Bring* and *raise* are transitive verbs. Compare INTRANSITIVE. **2** transitional. **3** *Mathematics, Logic.* of or being a relation such that, if A bears this relation to B and B bears it to C, A bears the same relation to C. 'Greater than' is a transitive relation, since if A > B and B > C, then A > C.
—n. Grammar. a transitive verb. **—'tran•si•tive•ly,** *adv.* **—'tran•si•tive•ness** or **,tran•si'tiv•i•ty,** *n.*
☛ *Usage.* See note at VERB.

tran•si•to•ry ['trænzə,tɔri] *adj.* passing soon or quickly; lasting only a short time. **—'tran•si,to•ri•ly,** *adv.* **—'tran•si,to•ri•ness,** *n.*

trans•late ['trænzleit] *or* [trænz'leit] *v.* **-lat•ed, -lat•ing.** **1** change from one language into another: *to translate a book from French into English.* **2** change into other words, especially in order to explain the meaning of: *to translate a scientific treatise for the layman.* **3** change from one place, position, form, or condition to another. **4** *Theology.* take to heaven, especially without death. **5** *Physics.* **a** move (a body) from one point or place to another without rotation. **b** cause (a body) to move so that all its points move in the same direction at the same speed and at the same time. **6** retransmit (a telegraphic message), as by a relay. ⟨ME < L *translatus*, pp. to *transferre.* See TRANSFER.⟩ **—trans'lat•a•ble,** *adj.*

trans•la•tion [trænz'leiʃən] *n.* **1** the process of translating or being translated: *Her translation of the German novel took several years.* **2** the result of translating; a version. **3** the automatic retransmission of a long-distance telegraph message by means of a relay. **4** *Physics.* **a** motion in which there is no rotation; onward movement that is not rotary or reciprocating. **b** motion in which all parts of the moving body move in the same direction at the same speed at the same time. **—trans'la•tion•al,** *adj.*

trans•la•tor ['trænzleitər] *n.* a person who translates, especially from one language into another and especially in writing.

trans•lit•er•ate [trænz'lɪtə,reit] *v.* **-at•ed, -at•ing.** change (letters, words, etc.) into the corresponding characters of another alphabet or language: *We transliterate the Greek* χ *as* ch *and* φ *as* ph. ⟨< *trans-* + L *litera* letter⟩

trans•lit•er•a•tion [trænz,lɪtə'reiʃən] *n.* the act of transliterating; the rendering of a letter or letters of one alphabet by equivalents in another.

trans•lo•cate [,trænzlə'keit] *or* [trænz'loukeit] *v.*, **-cat•ed, -cat•ing.** cause to change location or position; cause to undergo translocation.

trans•lo•ca•tion [,trænzlə'keiʃən] *n.* **1** a change of position or location. **2** *Genetics.* the transfer of a segment of a chromosome to a non-homologous chromosome. **Reciprocal translocation** is the mutual exchange of chromosomal material between two non-homologous chromosomes. **3** *Botany.* the transportation of food material from one part of a plant to another.

trans•lu•cence [trænz'lusəns] *n.* the quality or state of being translucent.

trans•lu•cen•cy [trænz'lusənsi] *n.* **1** translucence. **2** something that is translucent.

trans•lu•cent [trænz'lusənt] *adj.* **1** letting diffused light through; semi-transparent: *Frosted glass is translucent.* **2** transparent; clear. ⟨< L *translucens, -entis*, ppr. of *translucere* < *trans-* through + *lucere* shine⟩ **—trans'lu•cent•ly,** *adv.*

trans•ma•rine [,trænzmə'rin] *adj.* located, originating, or passing across or beyond the sea.

trans•mi•grant [trænz'maɪgrənt] *adj., n.* *—adj.* **1** passing through some place. **2** passing from one state or condition to another.
—n. **1** a person or thing that transmigrates or has transmigrated. **2** a person passing through a place en route to another where he or she plans to settle.

trans•mi•grate [trænz'maɪgreit] *v.* **-grat•ed, -grat•ing.** **1** of the soul, pass at death into another body. **2** move from one place or country to another; migrate. ⟨< L *transmigrare* < *trans-* across + *migrare* move⟩ **—trans'mi•gra,to•ry** [-'maɪgrə,tɔri], *adj.*

trans•mi•gra•tion [,trænzmaɪ'greiʃən] *n.* **1** in certain religions, the passing of the soul at death into another body. **2** the going from one place or country to another; migration.

trans•mis•si•ble [trænz'mɪsəbəl] *adj.* capable of being transmitted: *Scarlet fever is a transmissible disease.* **—trans,mis•si'bil•i•ty,** *n.*

trans•mis•sion [trænz'mɪʃən] *n.* **1** a sending over; passing on or along; letting through: *Mosquitoes are the only means of transmission of malaria.* **2** something transmitted. **3** of a motor vehicle, the part that transmits power from the engine to the driving axle. **4** the passage through space of radio waves from the transmitting station to the receiving station: *When radio transmission is good, distant stations can be received.* ⟨< L *transmissio, -onis* < *transmittere.* See TRANSMIT.⟩ **—trans'mis•sive,** *adj.*

trans•mit [trænz'mɪt] *v.* **-mit•ted, -mit•ting. 1** send over; pass on; pass along; communicate: *I will transmit the news by special messenger. Rats transmit disease. The money was transmitted to the vendor by the bank.* **2** *Physics.* **a** cause (light, heat, sound, etc.) to pass through a medium. **b** convey (force or movement) from one part of a body or mechanism to another. **c** of a medium, allow (light, heat, etc.) to pass through: *Glass transmits light.* **3** send (signals, broadcasts, etc.) through space via radio waves to the receiving station: *The prime minister's message will be transmitted at six o'clock tonight.* ⟨< L *transmittere* < *trans-* across + *mittere* send⟩ **—trans'mit•ta•ble,** *adj.*

trans•mit•tal [trænz'mɪtəl] *n.* the act or process of transmitting.

trans•mit•tance [trænz'mɪtəns] *n.* **1** the ratio of the radiant energy transmitted by a body to the radiant energy received by it. **2** transmittal; transmission.

trans•mit•ter [trænz'mɪtər] *or* ['trænzmɪtər] *n.* **1** the part of a telephone into which one speaks and which contains a device that converts the sound waves of speech into corresponding electric waves. **2** the part of a telegraph by which a message is sent. **3** in radio and television broadcasting, the apparatus that generates and modulates radio-frequency waves and sends them to the station's antenna. **4** any person or thing that transmits.

trans•mog•ri•fy [trænz'mɒgrə,faɪ] *v.* **-fied, -fy•ing.** (*usually jocular*) completely change the appearance or form of, especially in a fantastic or grotesque way: *The handsome prince was transmogrified into a frog.* ⟨origin uncertain; apparently a 16c. or 17c. pseudo-Latinism⟩ **—trans,mog•ri•fi'ca•tion,** *n.*

trans•mon•tane [trænz'mɒntein] *or* [,trænzmɒn'tein] *adj.* beyond a mountain or mountain range; tramontane.

trans•mu•ta•tion [,trænzmju'teiʃən] *n.* **1** a change into another nature, substance, or form. **2** *Physics and chemistry.* the conversion of atoms of one element into atoms of a different element or a different isotope, either naturally, as by radioactive disintegration, or artificially, as by bombardment with neutrons, etc. **3** *Alchemy.* the (attempted) conversion of a baser metal into gold or silver. **—,trans•mu'ta•tion•al,** *adj.* **—trans'mu•ta•tive,** *adj.*

trans•mute [trænz'mjut] *v.* **-mut•ed, -mut•ing. 1** change from one nature, substance, or form into another: *We can transmute water power into electrical power.* **2** *Physics and chemistry.* subject to transmutation. ⟨< L *transmutare* < *trans-* thoroughly + *mutare* change⟩ **—trans'mut•er,** *n.*

☛ *Syn.* See note at TRANSFORM.

trans•na•tion•al [trænz'næʃənəl] *adj.* going beyond the borders, affairs, etc. of a single nation in relevance.

trans•o•ce•an•ic [,trænzouʃi'ænɪk] *adj.* **1** crossing or extending across the ocean: *a transoceanic airline.* **2** on the other side of the ocean.

tran•som ['trænsəm] *n.* **1** a window over a door or other window, usually hinged for opening. **2** a horizontal crossbar in a window, over a door, or between a door and a window above it. **3** any of various other crosspieces, as a beam across a ship's stern, the arm of a gallows, the horizontal piece of a cross, etc. **over the transom,** without being solicited by the publisher. ⟨ME; ult. < L *transtrum*; originally, crossbeam⟩

tran•son•ic [træn'sɒnɪk] *adj.* of, having to do with, or designed for operation at speeds close to the speed of sound in air, which is about 1190 km/h at sea level. Also, **transsonic.**

trans•pa•cif•ic [,trænspə'sɪfɪk] *adj.* **1** crossing or extending across the Pacific Ocean. **2** having to do with crossing the Pacific Ocean: *transpacific air fares.* **3** on the other side of the Pacific Ocean.

trans•par•en•cy [træns'pærənsi] *or* [træns'pɛrənsi] *n., pl.* **-cies. 1** the quality or state of being transparent. **2** something transparent; especially, a photograph, picture, or design on glass or clear plastic made visible by light shining through from below or behind. Also (def. 1), **transparence.**

trans•par•ent [træns'pærənt] *or* [træns'pɛrənt] *adj.* **1** transmitting light so that something behind or beyond can be distinctly seen: *Window glass is transparent.* **2** of fabrics, etc., so fine or open in weave that something on the other side can be seen quite clearly; sheer. **3** easily seen through or detected; obvious: *The excuse he gave was transparent.* **4** free from deceit or guile; frank: *He had led a simple and transparent life.* **5** easily understood; lucid; clear. ⟨< Med.L *transparens, -entis,* ppr. of *transparere* show light through < L *trans-* through + *parere* appear⟩ **—trans'par•ent•ly,** *adv.* **—trans'par•ent•ness,** *n.*

trans•pierce [træns'pirs] *v.* **-pierced, -pierc•ing.** pierce or penetrate completely, to the other side.

tran•spi•ra•tion [,trænspə'reiʃən] *n.* the act or process or an instance of transpiring; especially, the passage of moisture through the pores of the skin or the surface of plant leaves.

tran•spire [træn'spaɪr] *v.* **-spired, -spir•ing. 1** take place; happen. **2** leak out; become known. **3** pass off or send off (moisture) in the form of vapour through a wall or surface, as from the human body or from leaves. **4** of moisture or vapour, be passed off in this way. ⟨< F < L *trans-* through + *spirare* breathe⟩

☛ *Usage.* **Transpire.** The meaning 'happen, take place' was once regarded as not being in good use, but **transpire** in this sense is fairly common in cultivated English today.

trans•plant *v.* [trans'plænt]; *n.* ['trænsplænt] *v., n.* **1** plant again in a different place: *We start the flowers indoors and then transplant them to the garden.* **2** remove from one place to another: *The colony was transplanted to a more healthful location.* **3** transfer (skin, an organ, etc.) from one person or animal to another, or from one part of the body to another: *transplant a kidney.* **4** bear transplanting: *Poppies do not transplant well and should be planted where they are to grow.*
—n. **1** the transfer of an organ, etc. from one person or animal to another, or from one part of the body to another: *a heart transplant.* **2** something transplanted. ⟨ME < LL *transplantare* < L *trans-* across + *plantare* plant⟩ **—trans'plant•a•ble,** *adj.* **—trans'plant•er,** *n.*

trans•plan•ta•tion [,trænsplæn'teiʃən] *n.* **1** a transplanting or being transplanted. **2** something that has been transplanted.

tran•spond•er [træn'spɒndər] *n.* a type of transmitting and receiving system for radio or radar signals that automatically transmits signals when it receives a predetermined signal. ⟨< *trans(mitter)* + *(res)ponder*⟩

trans•pon•tine [træns'pɒntaɪn] *adj.* **1** across or on the other side of a bridge. **2** on the south side of the River Thames in London, England. ⟨< *trans-* + L *pons, pontis* bridge⟩

trans•port *v.* [trans'pɔrt]; *n.* ['trænspɔrt] *v., n.* *—v.* **1** carry from one place to another, especially a relatively distant one: *Wheat is transported from the farm to the mills.* **2** carry away by strong feeling: *She was transported with joy by the good news.* **3** send away to another country as a punishment.
—n. **1** a carrying from one place to another by vehicle: *Trucks are much used for transport.* **2** a system of transportation, especially public. **3** a large truck used to carry freight long distances by road. **4** a ship used to carry passengers and supplies. **5** an airplane that transports passengers, mail, freight, etc. **6** a strong feeling: *a transport of rage.* **7** a transported convict. ⟨ME < L *transportare* < *trans-* across + *portare* carry⟩ **—trans'port•er,** *n.*

☛ *Syn. v.* **1.** See note at CARRY.

trans•port•a•ble [træns'pɔrtəbəl] *adj.* **1** capable of being transported. **2** involving, or liable to, punishment by transportation: *a transportable offence.* **—trans,port•a'bil•i•ty,** *n.*

trans•por•ta•tion [,trænspər'teiʃən] *n.* **1** a transporting or being transported: *The railway allows free transportation for a certain amount of a passenger's baggage.* **2** the business, system, industry, etc. of providing transport. **3** a means of transport. **4** the cost of transport; a ticket for transport. **5** a sending away or being sent to another country as a punishment.

trans•pos•al [træns'pouzəl] *n.* transposition.

trans•pose [træns'pouz] *v.* **-posed, -pos•ing. 1** change the position or order of; interchange. **2** change the usual order of (letters, words, or numbers); invert. *Example*: *Up came the wind, and off went her hat.* **3** *Music.* **a** rewrite in another key. **b** play in another key. **4** *Algebra.* transfer (a term) to the other side of an equation, changing plus to minus or minus to plus. ⟨< F *transposer* < *trans-* across (< L) + *poser* put (See POSE[1])⟩ **—trans'pos•er,** *n.* **—trans'pos•a•ble,** *adj.*

trans•po•si•tion [,trænspə'zɪʃən] *n.* **1** the act of transposing or the state of being transposed. **2** something transposed, such as a piece of music transposed into a different key. **—trans•po'si•tion•al,** *adj.* **—trans'pos•i•tive** [-'pɒzətɪv], *adj.*

trans•pro•vin•cial [ˌtrænsprəˈvɪnʃəl] *adj.* crossing or extending across a province: *transprovincial bus service.*

trans•sex•u•al [trænˈsɛkʃuəl] *n., adj. —n.* **1** a person who identifies so strongly with the opposite sex as to assume its usual roles, clothing, mannerisms, etc. **2** a person of this sort who has undergone surgery and hormone treatment in order to effect a change of sex.
—adj. of, characteristic of, or having to do with a transsexual or transsexuals. **—trans'sex•u•al,ism,** *n.*

trans•ship [trænsˈʃɪp] *or* [trænˈʃɪp] *v.* **-shipped, -ship•ping.** transfer from one ship, train, car, etc. to another. Also, **tranship. —trans'ship•ment,** *n.*

trans•son•ic [trænˈsɒnɪk] *adj.* transonic.

tran•sub•stan•ti•ate [ˌtrænsəbˈstænʃiˌeit] *v.* **-at•ed, -at•ing.** undergo or cause to undergo the change from one substance into another.

tran•sub•stan•ti•a•tion [ˌtrænsəbˌstænʃiˈeiʃən] *n.* **1** a changing of one substance into another. **2** *Theology.* in some Christian belief systems, the miraculous changing of the substance of the bread and wine of the Eucharist into the substance of the body and blood of Christ, only the appearance of the bread and wine remaining. Compare IMPANATION. ⟨< Med.L *transubstantiatio, -onis* < *transubstantiare* transmute < L *trans-* over + *substantia* substance⟩

tran•sude [trænˈsud] *or* [trænˈsjud] *v.* **-sud•ed, -sud•ing.** pass slowly through tiny pores, interstices, etc. of a membrane. ⟨< NL *transudare* < *trans-* across, through + *sudare* sweat⟩ **—,tran•su'da•tion,** *n.*

trans•u•ran•ic [ˌtrænzjəˈrænɪk] *adj.* of or being any of the elements whose atomic number exceeds that of uranium, such as plutonium. Transuranic elements are usually obtained by nuclear bombardment.

trans•ver•sal [trænzˈvɜrsəl] *adj., n. —adj.* transverse.
—n. Geometry. a line intersecting two or more other lines. **—trans'ver•sal•ly,** *adv.*

trans•verse [trænzˈvɜrs] *or* [ˈtrænzvɜrs] *adj., n. —adj.* **1** lying or placed across or crosswise: *The transverse beams in the barn were spruce.* **2** *Geometry.* designating the axis that passes through the foci of a hyperbola.
—n. **1** a transverse part or piece. **2** *Geometry.* the transverse axis. ⟨< L *transversus*, pp. of *transvertere* < *trans-* across + *vertere* turn⟩

trans•verse•ly [trænzˈvɜrsli] *adv.* across; athwart; crosswise; from side to side.

transverse wave *Physics.* a wave whose medium vibrates in a direction perpendicular to the direction in which the wave is propagated.

trans•vest•ism [trænzˈvɛstɪzəm] *n.* the practice of wearing clothing normally associated with the opposite sex. ⟨< G *Transvestismus* < L *trans-* + *vestire* dress⟩

trans•vest•ite [trænzˈvɛstəit] *n.* a person who seeks or derives sexual pleasure from wearing clothing normally associated with the opposite sex.

Tran•syl•va•ni•an [ˌtrænsɪlˈveinjən] *or* [ˌtrænsɪlˈveiniən] *n., adj. —n.* a native or inhabitant of Transylvania, a region in W Romania.
—adj. of or having to do with Transylvania or its people.

trap[1] [træp] *n., v.* **trapped, trap•ping.** *—n.* **1** a device for catching animals, lobsters, birds, etc. **2** a trick or other means for catching someone off guard: *He knew that the question was a trap.* **3** trapdoor. **4** a bend in a pipe for holding a small amount of water to prevent the escape of air, gas, etc. **5** SPEED TRAP. **6** a light two-wheeled carriage. **7** a device to throw clay pigeons, etc. into the air to be shot at. **8** *Golf.* bunker. **9** *Slang.* mouth: *Shut your trap!* **10 traps,** *pl.* drums, cymbals, bells, gongs, etc.
—v. **1** catch in a trap. **2** set traps for animals; especially, engage in trapping animals for their fur. **3** provide with a trap. **4** stop with a trap: *a gutter to trap rainwater.* **5** *Football, Baseball.* catch (a ball) on the first rebound from the ground. ⟨OE *træppe*⟩

☛ *Syn. n.* **1, 2. Trap,** SNARE[1] = something that catches or is contrived to catch an animal or person. **Trap** figuratively suggests a situation deliberately set to catch someone by surprise and destroy him or her or trick him or her into doing or saying something: *Suspecting a trap, the detachment of soldiers withdrew.* **Snare** figuratively applies to a desperate situation someone gets entangled in unawares, or a device to lure him or her into getting caught: *The detectives used marked money as a snare for the thief.*

trap[2] [træp] *v.* **trapped, trap•ping;** *n. —v.* cover with ornamental coverings or dress.
—n. **traps,** *pl. Informal.* belongings; baggage. ⟨ME, alteration of OF *drap* cloth < Med.L *drappus,* of uncertain origin⟩

trap[3] [træp] *n.* any of several dark, fine-grained, igneous rocks of columnar structure, such as basalt. ⟨< Swedish *trapp* < *trappa* stair, from the appearance of the outcroppings⟩

trap•boat [ˈtræpˌbout] *n. Cdn. Nfld.* a boat, 8 m to 12 m long, having low sides and capable of carrying a cod trap.

trap•door [ˈtræpˌdɔr] a hinged or sliding door in a floor, ceiling, or roof, often concealed, to provide access to an attic or cellar or to the space below a stage.

trapdoor spider any of various large North American spiders (family Tenizidae) that make tubular burrowed nests in the ground, covered with a hinged lid of soil and silk.

trapes [treips] See TRAIPSE.

tra•peze [trəˈpiz] *n.* a short horizontal bar hung by ropes like a swing, used in gymnastics and acrobatics. ⟨< F < LL < Gk. *trapezion,* dim. of *trapeza* table < *tra-* (unique for *tetra-*) four + *peza* foot. Doublet of TRAPEZIUM.⟩

tra•pe•zi•um [trəˈpiziəm] *n., pl.* **-zi•ums, -zi•a** [-ziə]. **1** a four-sided plane figure having no sides parallel. See QUADRILATERAL for picture. **2** *Brit.* trapezoid. **3** *Anatomy.* a small bone of the wrist, articulating with the metacarpal bone of the thumb. ⟨< LL < Gk. *trapezion,* originally, little table. Doublet of TRAPEZE.⟩

tra•pe•zi•us [trəˈpiziəs] *n., pl.* **-zi•i** [-ziˌaɪ] *or* [-ziˌi]. *Anatomy.* either of two large, flat, triangular muscles in the back of the neck and upper shoulders, that together resemble a trapezium or similar four-sided figure. ⟨< LL < L < Gk.⟩

trap•e•zoid [ˈtræpəˌzɔɪd] *n., adj. —n.* **1** a four-sided plane figure having two sides parallel and two sides not parallel. See QUADRILATERAL for picture. **2** *Brit.* trapezium. **3** *Anatomy.* a small bone of the wrist, articulating with the metacarpal bone of the index finger.
—adj. of or shaped like a trapezoid. Also (adj.), **trapezoidal.** ⟨< NL < Gk. *trapezoeidēs* < *trapeza* table + *eidos* form⟩

trap•line [ˈtræpˌlaɪn] *n. Cdn.* **1** a series of traps set and maintained by a trapper who periodically goes over the line, removing trapped animals and resetting the traps. **2** the way or route along which such a series of traps is set.

trap•per [ˈtræpər] *n.* a person who traps wild animals for food or for their fur.

trap•pings [ˈtræpɪŋz] *n.pl.* **1** ornamental coverings for a horse. **2** things worn; ornamental dress: *the trappings of a king and his court.* **3** outward appearances: *He had all the trappings of a cowboy, but he couldn't even ride a horse.* ⟨< *trap*[2]⟩

Trap•pist [ˈtræpɪst] *n., adj. —n. Roman Catholic Church.* a monk belonging to an extremely austere branch of the Cistercian order established in 1664.
—adj. of or having to do with the Trappists. ⟨< F *trappiste,* from the monastery of *La Trappe* in N France⟩

trap•shoot•ing [ˈtræpˌʃutɪŋ] *n.* the sport or art of shooting at clay pigeons, etc. thrown into the air. **—'trap,shoot•er,** *n.*

tra•pun•to [trəˈpʊntou] *n.* a type of quilting in which only the areas covered by designs are padded and outlined with stitches. It is used for upholstery or on some clothing. ⟨< Ital. pp.of *trapungere* embroider < *tra-* through + *pungere* prick⟩

trash [træʃ] *n., v. —n.* **1** discarded or worthless stuff; rubbish; garbage. **2** worthless or inferior writing, art, or other work: *That novel is trash; I can't imagine how it ever got published.* **3** a person of worthless character or such persons as a group; riffraff. **4** plant trimmings; leaves, twigs, etc. that have been broken or cut off.
—v. Slang. **1** destroy; vandalize: *Last winter our summer cottage was broken into and trashed by vandals.* **2** put down; criticize severely and harshly: *The reviewer trashed the movie.* **3** reject or discard: *Let's just trash the whole idea.* ⟨< Scand.; cf. dial. Norwegian *trask* lumber, trash and ON *tros* broken twigs⟩

trash•y [ˈtræʃi] *adj.* **trash•i•er, trash•i•est.** like or containing trash; of inferior quality: *a trashy magazine.* **—'trash•i•ly,** *adv.* **—'trash•i•ness,** *n.*

trass [træs] *n.* a type of tuff, powdered and used to make cement. ⟨< G < Du. *tras* < *terras* < MF *terrace*⟩

trat•to•ria [trɑˈtɔriə] *n., pl.* **-ri•e** [-rie] *Italian.* a small, casual Italian restaurant. ⟨< Ital. *trattore* innkeeper⟩

trau•ma [ˈtrɒmə] *or* [ˈtraʊmə] *n., pl.* **-ma•ta** [-mətə] or **-mas. 1** *Medicine.* **a** an injury to living tissue; a wound produced suddenly, as by violence or accident. **b** the resulting physical condition. **2** *Psychiatry.* **a** an emotional shock that has lasting effects on the victim. **b** a state of emotional disturbance resulting from an injury or mental shock. ⟨< Gk. *trauma, -atos* wound⟩

trau•mat•ic [trɒ'mætɪk], [trə'mætɪk], *or* [traʊ'mætɪk] *adj.* **1** of, having to do with, or produced by a trauma. **2** *Informal.* shocking or unpleasant: *It was a traumatic experience to run into her old enemy after all those years.* **—trau'mat•i•cal•ly,** *adv.*

trau•ma•tism ['trɒmə,tɪzəm] *or* ['traʊmə,tɪzəm] *n.* **1** trauma. **2** traumatic quality.

trau•ma•tize ['trɒmə,taɪz] *or* ['traʊmə,taɪz] *v.* **-tized, -tiz•ing.** subject to physical, mental, or emotional trauma.

trav•ail ['træveil] *or (esp. v.)* [trə'veil] *n., v.* *—n.* **1** hard work; toil. **2** trouble or pain. **3** the pains of childbirth; labour pains.
—v. **1** suffer the pains of childbirth. **2** work hard. ⟨ME < OF *travail,* ult. < LL *tripalium* (spelled *trepalium*) torture device, probably ult. < L *tri-* three + *palus* stake⟩

trave [treiv] *n.* **1** a wooden frame to hold a horse being shod. **2** *Architecture.* **a** a crossbeam. **b** a division in a ceiling, etc. bounded by crossbeams. ⟨ME < OF < L *trabs, trabis* beam⟩

trav•el ['trævəl] *v.* **-elled** or **-eled, -el•ling** or **-el•ing;** *n.* *—v.* **1** go on a trip from one place to another; journey: *to travel across the country.* **2** move; proceed; pass; advance: *Light and sound travel in waves.* **3** cover (a given distance): *A deer travels a considerable distance in a day.* **4** go from place to place selling things: *She travels for a large firm.* **5** pass through or over: *to travel a road.* **6** of machine parts, etc., move or have freedom of movement along a fixed course. **7** *Informal.* move rapidly: *That car was really travelling when it hit the abutment!* **8** *Basketball.* commit the fault of moving too far (usually, more than two steps) while holding the ball.
—n. **1 a** the act or practice of going in aircraft, trains, ships, cars, etc. from one place to another; journeying. **b** the industry that facilitates this; the business of helping or serving travellers: *She's training for a career in travel.* **2** movement in general. **3** the length of stroke, speed, way of working, etc. of a part of a machine. **4 travels,** *pl.* **a** journeys. **b** a book about one's experiences, visits, etc. while travelling. ⟨var. of *travail*⟩

travel agency a business that makes arrangements for travellers by booking reservations and securing tickets, drawing up itineraries, etc.

travel agent a trained person who runs, or works in, a travel agency.

travel bureau TRAVEL AGENCY.

trav•elled or **trav•eled** ['trævəld] *adj., v.* *—adj.* **1** that has done much travelling. **2** used by travellers: *It was a well-travelled road.*
—v. pt. and pp. of TRAVEL.

trav•el•ler or **trav•el•er** ['trævələr] *n.* **1** a person who travels or is travelling. **2** sales representative: *He's a traveller for a drug company.* **3** a mechanical part that travels.

traveller's cheque or **traveler's cheque** a cheque issued by a bank or other financial institution, on a special form and in any of various fixed denominations, that is signed by the buyer and must be countersigned by him or her at the time of cashing.

travelling bag or **traveling bag** HANDBAG (def. 2); TOTE BAG.

travelling fellowship or **traveling fellowship** a FELLOWSHIP (def. 4) that enables the holder to travel for purposes of study.

travelling salesman or **traveling salesman** a person whose work is going from place to place, usually in an assigned area, selling things for a company.

trav•e•logue ['trævə,lɒg] *n.* **1** a lecture describing travel, usually accompanied by pictures. **2** a film depicting travel or a place worth travelling to. Also *(esp. U.S.),* **travelog.** ⟨< *travel* + *-logue,* as in *dialogue*⟩

trav•erse *v., adv.* [trə'vɜrs] *or* ['trævərs]; *n., adj.* ['trævərs] *v.* **-ersed, -ers•ing;** *n., adj., adv.* *—v.* **1** pass across, over, or through: *The caravan traversed the desert.* **2** lie, extend, or stretch across; cross; intersect. **3** walk or move in a crosswise or sideways direction; move back and forth or from side to side: *That horse traverses.* **4** go to and fro over or along (a place, etc.). **5** ski diagonally or in a zigzag manner, or climb sideways, across (a slope). **6** read, examine, or consider carefully. **7** *Fencing.* glide the blade along that of the opponent's foil, toward the hilt, while applying pressure. **8** turn (big guns) to right or left. **9** turn on a pivot, or as if on a pivot. **10** oppose; hinder; thwart. **11** *Law.* make a formal denial of (an allegation by the opposing side in a suit).
—n. **1** the act of crossing. **2** something put or lying across. **3** an earth wall protecting a trench or an exposed place in a fortification. **4** in a church, etc., a gallery running from side to side. **5** a distance across. **6 a** a sideways motion of a ship, a part in a machine, mountain climbers, etc. **b** the path of this motion. **7 a** the zigzag line taken by a ship because of contrary winds or currents, or by a skier on a slope. **b** a single leg of such a line or course. **8** a line that crosses other lines. **9** opposition; an obstacle; hindrance. **10 a** the act of changing the direction of a gun to the right or left. **b** the amount of such change. **11** *Law.* a formal denial of something alleged to be a fact by the opposing side. **12** a single survey line across an area or tract.
—adj. **1** lying across; being across. **2** referring to drapes or curtains (or, especially, the rods for them) that hang on hooks and are drawn by a cord hanging down at the side.
—adv. across; crosswise. ⟨ME < OF *traverser* < LL *transversare* < L *transversus.* See TRANSVERSE.⟩ **—tra'vers•a•ble,** *adj.* **—tra'vers•al,** *n.* **—tra'vers•er,** *n.*

trav•er•tine ['trævərtɪn] *or* ['trævər,tin] *n.* a form of limestone deposited by springs, etc., used as building material. Also, **travertin.** ⟨< Ital. *travertino,* var. of *tivertino,* ult. < L *Tibur,* an ancient town in Latium⟩

trav•es•ty ['trævɪsti] *n., pl.* **-ties;** *v.* **-tied, -ty•ing.** *—n.* **1** an imitation of a serious literary work done in such a way as to make it seem ridiculous. **2** any treatment or imitation that makes a serious thing seem ridiculous.
—v. make (a serious subject or matter) ridiculous; imitate in an absurd or grotesque way. ⟨< F *travesti* disguised, ult. < L *trans-* over + *vestire* dress < *vestis* garment⟩

Two kinds of travois

tra•vois [trə'vwɑ] *or* ['trævwɒ], ['trævɔɪ] *or* [trə'vɔɪ]; *French,* [tʀa'vwa] *n., pl.* **-vois** [-vwa]. *Cdn.* formerly: **1** a simple wheelless vehicle used by First Nations peoples of the plains, made of two shafts or poles to which was attached a platform or net for holding the load, and dragged by a dog hitched to the shafts. **2** a larger conveyance of similar design, drawn by a horse or pony, the shafts often doubling as teepee poles. **3** any of a number of similar simple conveyances. **4** a sled used for transporting logs. ⟨< Cdn.F, alteration of F *travail* frame to hold a horse being shod⟩

trawl [trɒl] *n., v.* *—n.* **1** a strong net dragged along the bottom of the sea. Also called **trawl net. 2** a line supported by buoys and having attached to it many short lines with baited hooks. Also called **trawl line.**
—v. **1** fish with a net by dragging it along the bottom of the sea. **2** fish with lines supported by buoys. **3** catch with a trawl: *to trawl fish.* ⟨< MDu. *traghel* < L *tragula* dragnet⟩

trawl•er ['trɒlər] *n.* **1** a boat used in trawling. **2** a person who fishes by trawling.

tray [trei] *n.* **1** a flat, open holder or container with a low rim around it: *We carried the dishes into the dining room on a tray. The sewing basket has an accessory tray that can be lifted out.* **2** a tray together with its contents. ⟨OE *trēg*⟩
☛ *Hom.* TREY.

treach•er•ous ['trɛtʃərəs] *adj.* **1** not to be trusted; not faithful; disloyal: *The treacherous soldier carried reports to the enemy.* **2** having a false appearance of strength, security, etc.; not reliable; deceiving: *Thin ice is treacherous.* **—'treach•er•ous•ly,** *adv.* **—'treach•er•ous•ness,** *n.*

treach•er•y ['trɛtʃəri] *n., pl.* **-er•ies. 1** a breaking of faith; treacherous behaviour; deceit. **2** treason. ⟨ME < OF *trecherie* < *trechier* cheat⟩
☛ *Syn.* **1.** See note at DISLOYALTY.

trea•cle ['trikəl] *n.* **1** *Esp. Brit.* **a** molasses. **b** a syrup produced in the process of refining sugar. **c** this syrup mixed with molasses. **2** anything too sweet or cloyingly sentimental. **3** formerly, a compound much used as an antidote for poison or poisonous bites. ⟨ME *triacle* antidote for bites < OF < L < Gk. *thēriakē*, ult. < *thēr* wild beast⟩ **—'trea•cly,** *adj.*

tread [trɛd] *v.* **trod** or (*archaic*) **trode, trod•den** or **trod, tread•ing;** *n.* *—v.* **1** walk; step; set the foot down: *Don't tread on the flower beds.* **2** set the feet on; walk on or through; step on: *to tread the streets.* **3** press under the feet; trample on; crush: *to tread grapes.* **4** make, form, or do by walking: *Cattle had trodden a path to the pond.* **5** follow; pursue: *to tread the path of virtue.* **6** treat with cruelty; oppress (*used with* **on**). **7** of a male bird, copulate with (a female).
tread on (someone's) **toes,** offend or annoy someone.
tread the boards, be an actor; play a part in a play.
tread water, keep afloat in water, with the body upright and the head above the surface, by slowly moving the legs as if bicycling.
—n. **1** the act or sound of treading: *We heard the tread of marching feet.* **2** a way of walking: *He walks with a heavy tread.* **3** the horizontal part of a step. **4** the width of this, from front to back. **5** the part of something, such as a wheel or shoe, that touches the ground. **6 a** the raised pattern on the surface of a tire or the sole of a shoe or boot: *The tread on the back tires is almost gone.* **b** its thickness or depth. **7** either of the tracks of a caterpillar tractor or similar vehicle. **8** the part of a rail or rails that the wheels touch. **9** the distance between the two front or rear wheels of a motor vehicle: *a car with a wide tread.* **10 a** footprint; shoeprint. **b** tireprint. ⟨OE *tredan*⟩ **—'tread•er,** *n.*

trea•dle ['trɛdəl] *n., v.* **-dled, -dling.** *—n.* a rocking lever or pedal worked by the foot to drive a machine, such as a sewing machine, grindstone, or lathe.
—v. work a treadle. ⟨OE *tredel* < *tredan* tread⟩

tread•mill ['trɛd,mɪl] *n.* **1** an apparatus for producing motion by having a person or animal walk on the moving steps of a wheel or of a sloping, endless belt. **2** any wearisome or monotonous round of work or life that seems to go nowhere.

treas. treasurer; treasury.

trea•son ['trizən] *n.* **1** the act or fact of betraying one's country or ruler. Helping the enemies of one's country is treason. **2** *Rare.* the betrayal of a trust, duty, friend, etc.; treachery. ⟨ME < AF *treson* < L *traditio.* Doublet of TRADITION.⟩
☛ *Syn.* **1.** See note at DISLOYALTY.

trea•son•a•ble ['trizənəbəl] *adj.* having to do with, consisting of, or involving treason. **—'trea•son•a•ble•ness,** *n.* **—'trea•son•a•bly,** *adv.*

trea•son•ous ['trizənəs] *adj.* **1** treasonable. **2** committing treason.

treas•ure ['trɛʒər] *n., v.* **-ured, -ur•ing.** *—n.* **1** wealth or riches stored up; valuable things. **2** any thing or person that is much loved or valued.
—v. **1** value highly. **2** put away for future use; store up. ⟨ME < OF *tresor* < L < Gk. *thēsauros.* Doublet of THESAURUS.⟩

treasure house a place where treasure is kept; a storehouse of anything valuable.

treasure hunt **1** a game in which players are directed from place to place by a series of clues, often hidden ones, ending finally at the spot where some object is concealed. **2** a hunt for buried treasure.

treas•ur•er ['trɛʒərər] *n.* a person in charge of the finances of a club, society, corporation, government body, etc. **—'treas•ur•er,ship,** *n.*

treas•ure–trove ['trɛʒər ,trouv] *n.* **1** money, jewels, or other treasure that a person finds, especially if the owner of it is not known. **2** any valuable discovery. ⟨< AF *tresor trové* treasure found⟩

treas•ur•y ['trɛʒəri] *n., pl.* **-ur•ies. 1** the place where money is kept; especially, one where public revenues are deposited and kept. **2** money belonging to a society, club, etc.; funds: *We paid for the party out of the club treasury.* **3** a government department that has charge of the collection, management, and expenditure of public revenues. **4** a place where treasure or anything valuable is kept. **5** a book, person, etc. thought of as a valued source: *a treasury of adventure stories. He is a treasury of information on rocks.*

Treasury bench or **benches** in the House of Commons or in a legislature, the front benches to the Speaker's right, occupied by the ministers of the government.

treasury bill an obligation issued by the treasury of Canada, bearing no interest but sold at a discount and maturing within less than a year.

Treasury Board *Cdn.* the sole statutory committee of the Cabinet, including the minister of finance, four other ministers appointed by the governor-in-council, and the comptroller general, responsible to oversee the general management of public funds in the administration.

treat [trit] *v., n.* *—v.* **1** act toward; handle: *He treats his dog gently. My father treats our new car with care.* **2** think of; consider; regard: *She treated her mistake as a joke.* **3** deal with to relieve or cure: *The dentist is treating my tooth.* **4** deal with to bring about some special result: *to treat a metal plate with acid in engraving.* **5** deal with; discuss (*sometimes used with* **of**): *Her talk treated of recent political developments in Europe. This magazine treats the progress of medicine.* **6** express in literature, music, or art: *to treat a theme realistically.* **7** discuss terms; arrange terms: *Messengers came to treat for peace.* **8** entertain by giving food, drink, or amusement: *He treated us to lunch.* **9** pay the cost of entertainment: *I'll treat today.*
—n. **1** a gift of food, drink, or amusement: *"This is my treat," she said, as she paid for the tickets.* **2** anything that gives pleasure: *Being in the country is a treat to her.* ⟨ME < OF *traitier* < L *tractare*, originally, drag violently, handle, frequentative of *trahere* drag⟩ **—'treat•er,** *n.*

treat•a•ble ['tritəbəl] *adj.* capable of being treated; that will respond to treatment: *a treatable disease.* **—,treat•a'bil•i•ty,** *n.*

trea•tise ['tritɪs] *n.* a book or writing dealing formally and systematically with some subject. ⟨ME < AF *tretiz*, ult. < L *tractare* treat. See TREAT.⟩

treat•ment ['tritmənt] *n.* **1** the act or process of treating. **2** a way of treating. **3** something done or used to treat something else, especially a disease: *We read about old treatments for colds.*

trea•ty ['triti] *n., pl.* **-ties. 1** an agreement, especially one between nations, signed and approved by each nation. **2** the document embodying such an agreement. **3** *Cdn.* one of a number of official agreements between the federal government and certain bands of First Nations peoples whereby the latter give up their land rights, except for reserves, and accept treaty money and other kinds of government assistance. **4** TREATY MONEY.
take treaty or **take the treaty,** *Cdn.* of a First Nations band or people, accept the terms of treaty with the federal government. ⟨ME < AF *trete*, OF *traitie* < L *tractatus* discussion < *tractare.* See TREAT.⟩

Treaty Day *Cdn.* **1** the day on which treaty was originally taken by a First Nations group. **2** an anniversary of this day, celebrated with festivities. **3 treaty day,** any day on which treaty money is paid.

treaty Indian *Cdn.* a member of a First Nations band or people living on a reserve and receiving treaty money and other treaty rights.

treaty money *Cdn.* an annual payment made by the federal government to treaty Indians.

treaty rights *Cdn.* the rights guaranteed to First Nations people in their treaties with the federal government.

treaty time TREATY DAY (defs. 2, 3).

tre•ble ['trɛbəl] *adj., v.* **-bled, -bling;** *n.* *—adj.* **1** three times as much or as many; threefold; triple. **2** *Music.* having to do with, having the range of, or designed for the treble. **3** of a voice or sound, shrill and high-pitched.
—v. make or become three times as much: *She trebled her income when she changed to a career in advertising.*
—n. **1** *Music.* **a** the highest voice part in choral music, especially for a boys' choir; soprano. **b** a singer who sings such a part. **c** the upper half of the whole musical range of a voice or instrument. Compare BASS[1] (def. 5). **d** an instrument having the highest range in a family of musical instruments. **2** in sound reproduction, the higher portion of the audio-frequency band. **3** a shrill, high-pitched voice or sound. ⟨ME < OF < L *triplus* triple. Doublet of TRIPLE.⟩

treble clef *Music.* **1** a symbol (𝄞) indicating that the pitch of the notes on a staff is above middle C. See CLEF for picture. **2** the range of notes represented on a staff marked with this symbol.

tre•bly ['trɛbli] *adv.* three times.

treb•u•chet ['trɛbjə,ʃɛt] *n.* a large medieval war machine for throwing stones or other missiles, in the form of a sling on a pivoting beam. Also, **trebucket** ['tribʌkɪt]. ⟨ME < OF fr. *trebucher* overthrow; ult. < Frankish⟩

tre•cen•to [trei'tʃɛntou]; *Italian,* [tre'tʃɛnto] *n.* the 14th century, or its characteristic style, etc. in Italian art and literature. ⟨< Ital. *mille trecento* one thousand three hundred⟩

tree [tri] *n., v.* **treed, tree•ing.** *—n.* **1** a large perennial plant having a woody trunk, branches, and leaves. **2** less accurately, any of certain other plants that resemble trees in form or size. **3 a** a part or structure of wood, long and narrow in shape; a beam, bar, pole, handle, etc. **b** a piece or structure of wood, etc. of some other shape, for some special purpose: *a clothes tree, a shoe tree.* **4** anything suggesting a tree and its branches, such as dendrite, or a diagram for syntactic analysis of a sentence. **5** FAMILY TREE. **6** *Archaic.* a gallows. **7** *Archaic.* the cross on which Christ died.
bark up the wrong tree. See BARK.
up a tree, a up in a tree. **b** *Informal.* in a difficult position.
—v. **1** furnish with a tree (beam, bar, wooden handle, etc.). **2** stretch (a shoe) on a shoe tree. **3** assume a treelike or branching form. **4** chase up a tree: *The cat was treed by a dog.* **5** take refuge in a tree. **6** *Informal.* put into a difficult position. ⟨OE *trēo*⟩ **—'tree•less,** *adj.* **—'tree,like,** *adj.*

treed [trid] *adj., v. —adj.* planted or covered with trees: *treed lands.*
—v. pt. and pp. of TREE.

tree farm a privately owned area in which trees are grown under a system of forest management. **—tree farmer. —tree farming.**

tree fern any of numerous tropical ferns (especially of family Cyatheaceae) that grow to the size of a tree, with a trunklike stem and large fronds at the top.

tree frog 1 any of a large family (Hylidae) of frogs found mainly in the New World, most of which live in trees. Tree frogs have suckerlike, sticky disks on the tips of their toes which help them in climbing. **2** any of various other frogs and toads that live in trees.

tree•hop•per ['tri,hɒpər] *n.* any of various homopterous insects of the family Membracidae, having an enlarged prothorax prolonged backward over the abdomen, and feeding on the juices of plants, which may be harmed as a result.

tree house a structure, such as a playhouse, built in the branches of a tree.

tree line a limit on mountains and in high latitudes beyond which trees will not grow because of the cold, etc.; timberline. Also, **treeline.**

treen [trin] *n.* **1** the art and craft of making household utensils carved from wood. Canadian treen ranges from the late 17th century to recent times. **2** treenware. ⟨< OE *trēowen* < *trēow* tree⟩

tree•nail ['trineil], ['trɛnəl], *or* ['trʌnəl] *n.* a round pin of hard wood for fastening timbers together, swelling when moist so as to result in a tight fit. Also, **trenail.**

treen•ware ['trin,wɛr] *n.* household utensils and objects carved from wood, as used by the early settlers.

tree of heaven an Asian ailanthus (*Ailanthus altissima*) that is widely grown as an ornamental and shade tree.

tree ring ANNUAL RING.

tree surgeon one whose work is TREE SURGERY.

tree surgery the cutting and other treatment of diseased trees, and moving of trees for preservation.

tree toad TREE FROG.

tree•top ['tri,tɒp] *n.* the top part of a tree.

tref [treif] *adj. Judaism.* not kosher. ⟨< Yiddish *treif* < Hebrew *terefah* flesh of an animal torn (by other animals)⟩

tre•foil ['trifɔil] *n.* **1** any of various herbs having leaves made up of three leaflets, especially clover. **2** a leaf made up of three leaflets. **3** an ornamental figure shaped like such a leaf. ⟨ME < AF < L *trifolium* < *tri-* three + *folium* leaf⟩

trek [trɛk] *v.* **trekked, trek•king;** *n. —v.* **1** travel, especially slowly and for a long distance or under difficult conditions; migrate. **2** *Informal.* go; proceed; traipse: *to trek down to the office.* **3** especially in South Africa: **a** travel by ox wagon. **b** of an ox, draw (a wagon). **4** go on a long, arduous hike, on foot or horseback and especially through wild country, for recreation or sightseeing: *You need a permit to trek in Nepal.*
—n. **1** a journey, especially a slow or difficult one. **2** especially in South Africa, a journey by ox wagon, specifically, by a group of pioneers into unsettled country. **3** a stage of such a journey, from one stopping place to the next. **4** a long, arduous hike or trip, on foot or horseback, especially through wild country, for recreation or sightseeing: *This travel agent specializes in treks up the Pacific coast.* **5** a traipse. ⟨< Du. *trekken*, originally, draw, pull⟩ **—'trek•ker,** *n.*

trel•lis ['trɛlɪs] *n., v. —n.* **1** a frame of light strips of wood or metal crossing one another with open spaces in between; lattice, especially one supporting growing vines. **2** a summerhouse or other structure with sides of lattice.
—v. **1** furnish with a trellis. **2** support on a trellis. **3** cross or interlace like a trellis; interweave. ⟨ME < OF *trelis*, ult. < L *trilix* triple-twilled < *tri-* three + *licium* thread⟩

trel•lis•work ['trɛlɪs,wɜrk] *n.* trellises; latticework.

trem•a•tode ['trɛmə,toud] *or* ['trimə,toud] *n., adj. —n.* any of a class (Trematoda) of flatworms that live as parasites in or on other animals; fluke.
—adj. of or relating to a trematode. ⟨< NL < Gk. *trēmatōdēs* holed < *trēma, -atos* hole⟩

trem•ble ['trɛmbəl] *v.* **-bled, -bling;** *n. —v.* **1** shake because of fear, excitement, weakness, cold, etc. **2** of a sound, voice, etc., quaver; falter: *His voice trembled noticeably on high notes.* **3** feel fear, anxiety, etc: *She trembled for their safety. He trembled at the thought of having to ask for the money.* **4** move gently.
—n. **1** a trembling or quivering: *There was a tremble in her voice as she began to recite.* **2 trembles,** *pl.* **a** a toxic disease of cattle and sheep characterized by muscular tremors, caused by ingesting a poisonous alcohol contained in white snakeroot. **b** a fit of trembling: *I got the trembles so bad I could hardly write.* ⟨ME < OF *trembler*, ult. < L *tremulus.* See TREMULOUS.⟩ **—trem'bling•ly,** *adv.*
☛ *Syn. v.* **1.** See note at SHAKE.

trembling aspen a North American poplar (*Populus tremuloides*) found throughout the forested regions of Canada, having finely toothed, rounded, hairless leaves that flutter in the slightest breeze. See also ASPEN.

trem•bly ['trɛmbli] *adj.* trembling; tremulous: *His voice was trembly with fear.*

tre•men•dous [trə'mɛndəs] *adj.* **1** dreadful; awful. **2** *Informal.* very great; enormous: *a tremendous house.* **3** *Informal.* especially good: *We saw a tremendous movie yesterday.* ⟨< L *tremendus*, literally, to be trembled at < *tremere* tremble⟩ **—tre'men•dous•ly,** *adv.* **—tre'men•dous•ness,** *n.*

trem•o•lo ['trɛmə,lou] *n., pl.* **-los. 1** *Music.* a trembling or vibrating quality, as produced in singing by a wavering in pitch or on a stringed instrument by a rapid repeating of a tone with fast strokes of the bow. The tremolo is used to express emotion. **2** in an organ, a device used to produce this quality. ⟨< Ital. *tremolo* < L *tremulus.* Doublet of TREMULOUS.⟩

trem•or ['trɛmər] *n.* **1** an involuntary shaking or trembling as from physical weakness, emotional upset, or disease: *a nervous tremor in the voice.* **2** a thrill of emotion or excitement. **3** a shaking movement. An earthquake is called an earth tremor. ⟨< L⟩ **—'trem•or•ous,** *adj.*

trem•u•lous ['trɛmjələs] *adj.* **1** trembling; quivering: *a tremulous voice.* **2** marked by, or showing the effects of, tremors: *tremulous excitement, tremulous handwriting.* **3** timid; fearful. ⟨< L *tremulus* < *tremere* tremble. Doublet of TREMOLO.⟩ **—'trem•u•lous•ly,** *adv.* **—'trem•u•lous•ness,** *n.*

tre•nail ['tri,neil], ['trɛnəl], *or* ['trʌnəl] See TREENAIL.

trench [trɛntʃ] *n., v. —n.* **1** a long, narrow cut in the ground, especially one having the excavated earth thrown up in front, to be used as a defence for soldiers in battle. **2** a long, narrow, deep furrow in the ocean floor.
—v. **1** surround or fortify with a trench or trenches. **2** dig a trench in. **3** dig ditches. **4** make a cut in.
trench on or **upon, a** trespass upon. **b** come close to; border on: *The demagogue's speech trenched closely on treason.* ⟨ME < OF *trenche*, n., *trenchier*, v., to cut, apparently ult. < L *truncare* lop off < *truncus* mutilated⟩

trench•an•cy ['trɛntʃənsi] *n.* the quality or state of being trenchant.

trench•ant ['trɛntʃənt] *adj.* **1** sharp; keen; cutting: *trenchant wit.* **2** vigorous; effective: *a trenchant policy.* **3** clear-cut; distinct: *in trenchant outline against the sky.* ⟨ME < OF *trenchant*, ppr. of *trenchier* cut. See TRENCH.⟩ **—'trench•ant•ly,** *adv.*

trench coat a loose-fitting raincoat worn with a belt, often double-breasted and usually having wide lapels and epaulettes. The classic trench coat is a beige or camel colour.

trench•er ['trɛntʃər] *n.* a wooden platter formerly used for serving food, especially meat. ⟨ME < OF *trencheoir* knife, ult. < *trenchier* cut. See TRENCH.⟩

trench•er•man ['trɛntʃərmən] *n., pl.* **-men. 1** a heavy eater; a person who has a hearty appetite. **2** *Archaic.* a hanger-on; sponger.

trench fever an infectious fever that is transmitted by lice, particularly common among soldiers in the trenches during the First World War.

trench foot injury to the tissues, blood vessels, and nerves of the feet, caused by prolonged exposure to cold and wet, as with soldiers serving in trenches for long periods of time.

trench mouth a contagious disease of the gums and, sometimes, the inside of the lips and cheeks, etc., caused by a bacterium (*Fusobacterium nucleatum*) and characterized by ulceration of the mucous membranes and foul-smelling breath.

trend [trɛnd] *n., v.* —*n.* **1** the general direction; a course or tendency: *a western trend, the trend of modern living.* **2** a current style in fashion, etc.
—*v.* have a general direction; tend; run: *The road trends to the north.* ⟨OE *trendan*⟩
☛ *Syn. n.* See note at DIRECTION.

trend•setter ['trɛnd,sɛtər] *n.* a person, design firm, magazine, etc. that creates or promotes new fashions in clothing or other products, ideas, etc.

trend•y ['trɛndi] *adj.* **trend•i•er, trend•i•est;** *n., pl.* **trend•ies.** *Informal.* —*adj.* following the very latest fashions or trends: *a trendy boutique, trendy styles.*
—*n.* a trendy person. —**'trend•i•ly,** *adv.* —**'trend•i•ness,** *n.*

trente et qua•rante [tʀɑ̃teka'ʀɑ̃t] *French.* ROUGE ET NOIR. ⟨< F, literally, thirty and forty⟩

tre•pan [trɪ'pæn] *n., v.* **-panned, -pan•ning.** —*n.* **1** an early form of the trephine. **2** a boring instrument, used for sinking shafts.
—*v.* **1** operate on with a trepan (trephine). **2** bore through with a trepan; cut a disk out of with a trepan or similar tool. ⟨ME < OF < Med.L < Gk. *trypanon* < *trypaein* bore < *trypē* hole⟩
—**,trep•a'na•tion** [,trɛpə'neiʃən], *n.*

tre•pang [trɪ'pæŋ] *n.* **1** any of various large, edible sea cucumbers found especially on the coral reefs of the SW Pacific Ocean, that are boiled, dried, and smoked for use in soup, especially in E Asia. **2** the body wall of any of these sea cucumbers, prepared for use as food. ⟨< Malay *tripang*⟩

tre•phine [trɪ'faɪn] *or* [trɪ'fin] *n., v.* **-phined, -phin•ing.** —*n.* a cylindrical saw with a removable centre pin, used to cut out circular pieces from the skull.
—*v.* operate on with a trephine. ⟨earlier *trafine*, alteration by inventor Woodall of *trapan* (var. of *trepan*) after L *tres fines* three ends⟩ —**,treph•i'na•tion** [,trɛfə'neiʃən], *n.*

trep•i•da•tion [,trɛpə'deiʃən] *n.* **1** nervous dread; apprehension; fear. **2** a trembling. ⟨< L *trepidatio, -onis,* ult. < *trepidus* alarmed⟩

tres•pass ['trɛspæs] *or* ['trɛspəs] *v., n.* —*v.* **1** go on somebody's property without any right: *The farmer put up 'No Trespassing' signs to keep people off his property.* **2** go beyond the limits of what is right, proper, or polite: *I won't trespass on your time any longer.* **3** do wrong; sin. **4** *Law.* commit a trespass.
—*n.* **1** the act or fact of trespassing. **2** a wrong; a sin. **3** *Law.* **a** an unlawful act done against the person, property, or rights of another. **b** an action to recover damages for such an injury. ⟨ME < OF *trespasser* < *tres-* across (< L *trans-*) + *passer* pass, ult. < L *passus* step⟩ —**'tres•pass•er,** *n.*
☛ *Syn. v.* **1, 2.** See note at INTRUDE.

tress [tres] *n.* **1** a lock, curl, or braid of hair. **2 tresses,** *pl.* a woman's or girl's hair, especially when long: *She had thick, dark brown tresses.* ⟨< ME < OF *tresce*, probably < Gmc.⟩ —**tressed,** *adj.*

tres•sure ['trɛʃər] *n. Heraldry.* a narrow border on a shield, decorated with fleurs-de-lis or other motifs. ⟨ME *tressour* < MF *tresseor* < OF *tresce* tress⟩

tres•tle ['trɛsəl] *n.* **1** a structure, such as a sawhorse, used to support a table top, platform, etc. **2** a framework used as a bridge to support a road, railway tracks, etc. Also (def. 2), **trestle bridge.** ⟨ME < OF *trestel* crossbeam, ult. < L *transtrum*⟩

tres•tle•tree ['trɛsəl,tri] *n.* either of two horizontal, fore-and-aft timbers or bars secured to a ship's masthead, one on each side, in order to support the crosstrees.

tres•tle•work ['trɛsəl,wɜrk] *n.* a system of connected trestles supporting a bridge, etc.

trews [truz] *n.pl. Scottish.* tight-fitting tartan pants. ⟨< Irish *trius* < *triubhas.* Cf. TROUSERS.⟩

trey [trei] *n.* a card, die, or domino, etc. having three spots. ⟨ME < OF *trei* < L *tres* three⟩
☛ *Hom.* TRAY.

tri– *prefix.* **1** three; having three; having three parts, as in *triangle.* **2** three times; triply; into three parts or in three ways, as in *trisect, trilingual.* **3** containing three atoms, etc. of the substance specified, as in *trioxide.* **4** once in three; every third, as in *trimonthly.* ⟨< L or Gk.⟩

tri•a•ble ['traɪəbəl] *adj.* fit for, or subject to, trial in court. —**'tri•a•ble•ness,** *n.*

tri•ac•e•tate [traɪ'æsə,teit] *n.* a cellulose derivative containing three acetate radicals in the molecule. It is used as a base for many synthethic fibres.

tri•ac•id [traɪ'æsɪd] *adj.* **1** of a base, reacting with three molecules of a monobasic acid. **2** of an acid, having three replaceable hydrogen atoms.

tri•ad ['traɪæd] *n.* **1** a group of three, especially of three closely related persons or things. **2** *Music.* a chord of three tones, especially one consisting of the root tone plus the third and fifth tones above it. **3** *Chemistry.* an element, atom, or radical with a valence of three. ⟨< LL *trias, -adis* < Gk. *trias, -ados* < *treis* three⟩ —**tri'ad•ic,** *adj.*

tri•age [tri'ɑʒ] *n.* **1** the sorting of a number of casualties, accident victims, etc. by a system of priorities which ensures that those with the best chance of benefiting from treatment are looked after first. **2** the allocation of a scarce commodity, such as food, by a similar method, giving priority to those who will derive the greatest benefit from it. ⟨< F < *trier* to sort, sift. 18c. See TRY.⟩

tri•al ['traɪəl] *n.* **1** the process of examining and deciding a case in court: *The suspected thief was arrested and brought to trial.* **2** (*adjl.*) of or having to do with a trial in a law court: *trial testimony.* **3** the process of trying or testing: *He gave the machine another trial.* **4** (*adjl.*) being a try or test: *a trial run, a trial model.* **5** experimentation by investigation, tentative action, use, etc.; experiment: *to learn by trial and error.* **6** the condition of being tried or tested; probation: *He is employed on trial.* **7** (*adjl.*) that is on trial: *a trial employee.* **8** a trouble or hardship. **9** a cause of trouble or hardship: *She is a trial to her big sister.* **10** an attempt; effort. **11** a preliminary competition in field or track events at a track meet.
on trial, a being tried in court. **b** experimentally; as a test (of abilities, performance, reception by the market, etc.). **c** being tested or tried out. ⟨< AF *trial* < *trier* try⟩
☛ *Syn. n.* **3. Trial,** TEST, EXPERIMENT = a way of discovering or proving something. **Trial** applies to the process of discovering the qualities of something and establishing its worth, genuineness, strength, effect, etc.: *He gave the new toothpaste a trial.* **Test** applies to a trial to end uncertainty about quality, genuineness, or the presence of some substance or part, as by thorough examination: *The new plane passed all tests.* **Experiment** applies to a process to find out something still unknown or to test conclusions, a hypothesis, etc.: *Experiments indicate the new drug will cure infections.*

trial and error the process of arriving at a solution of a problem by trying several ways and learning from the errors so made. —**'tri•al-and-'er•ror,** *adj.*

trial balance in double-entry bookkeeping, a comparison of debit and credit totals in a ledger. If they are not equal, there is an error.

trial jury a jury selected to hear evidence in a criminal or civil trial and sworn to give a verdict on the basis of facts found from the evidence. In a criminal trial, the jury gives a verdict as to the guilt or innocence in law of the accused. In a civil trial it decides in favour of the plaintiff or the defendant. Also called **petit jury.**

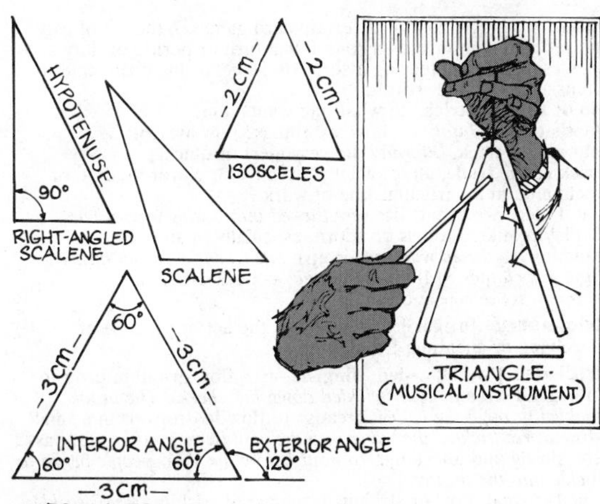

tri•an•gle ['traɪ,æŋgəl] *n.* **1** a plane figure having three sides and three angles. **2** any object, part, or area having three sides or three angles: *Our backyard is a triangle.* **3** a musical instrument consisting of a steel rod bent in a triangle with one corner open, that produces a light ringing sound when struck with a small steel rod. **4** an instrument for drafting, consisting of a flat right-angled triangle of wood, plastic, etc. **5** a situation involving three persons or points of view, especially an emotional relationship involving two men and one woman or two women and one man, with attendant complications: *the eternal triangle.* **6** a group of three. ⟨ME < L *triangulum* < *tri-* three + *angulus* corner⟩

tri•an•gu•lar [traɪ'æŋgjələr] *adj.* **1** of, having to do with, or shaped like a triangle: *a triangular piece of cloth.* **2** having a base or cross-section that is a triangle. **3** concerned with three persons, groups, etc. **—tri,an•gu'lar•i•ty,** *n.* **—tri'an•gu•lar•ly,** *adv.*

tri•an•gu•late *v.* [traɪ'æŋgjə,leit]; *adj.* [traɪ'æŋgjəlɪt] *or* [traɪ'æŋgjə,leit] *v.* **-lat•ed, -lat•ing;** *adj. —v.* **1** divide into triangles. **2** survey or map out (a region) by dividing it into triangles and measuring their angles. **3** find by trigonometry: *to triangulate the height of a mountain.* **4** make triangular.
—adj. **1** composed of or marked with triangles. **2** triangular.

tri•an•gu•la•tion [traɪ,æŋgjə'leiʃən] *n.* **1** a method of survey or measurement done by means of trigonometry, in which an area is divided into a series of connected triangles. **2** a division into triangles.

tri•ar•chy ['traɪɑrki] *n., pl.* **-chies. 1** a system of government in which three persons govern together. **2** a particular instance of this; a specific group of three joint rulers, or a country governed by such a group. **3** a country having three governments. **4** a group of three countries or states in some sort of association, each having its own ruler. ⟨< Gk. *triarchia* < *tri-* three + *archia* < *archein* rule⟩

Tri•as•sic [traɪ'æsɪk] *n., adj. Geology. —n.* **1** the earliest period of the Mesozoic era, beginning approximately 200 million years ago. **2** the rocks formed during this period. See geological time chart in the Appendix.
—adj. of or having to do with the Triassic period or the rocks formed during it. Also (n.), **Trias** ['traɪəs]. ⟨< G *Trias,* the name for a certain series of strata containing three types of deposit < LL *trias.* See TRIAD.⟩

tri•ath•lete [traɪ'æθlit] *n.* one who competes in the triathlon.

tri•ath•lon [traɪ'æθlɒn] *n.* an Olympic sport in which athletes compete in swimming, bicycling, and running. ⟨*tri-* + Gk. *athlon* contest, after *decathlon*⟩

tri•a•tom•ic [,traɪə'tɒmɪk] *adj.* a molecule: **1** made up of three atoms. **2** having three replaceable atoms or groups.

tri•ax•i•al [traɪ'æksiəl] *adj.* having three axes. **—tri'ax•i•al•ly,** *adv.*

trib•al ['traɪbəl] *adj.* of, having to do with, based on, or characteristic of a tribe or tribes: *tribal customs, tribal lore.*

trib•al•ism ['traɪbə,lɪzəm] *n.* **1** social organization according to tribes, the accompanying customs and practices, etc. **2** strong identification with, or loyalty to, a tribe or tribelike group. **—'trib•al•ist,** *n.* **—,trib•al'is•tic,** *adj.*

trib•a•lize ['traɪbə,laɪz] *v.* **-lized, -liz•ing. 1** divide or organize into tribes. **2** confer tribal status on.

trib•al•ly ['traɪbəli] *adv.* according to tribe; by tribe or tribes: *a tribally organized society.*

tri•bas•ic [traɪ'beisɪk] *adj. Chemistry.* **1** of an acid, having three atoms of hydrogen replaceable by basic atoms or radicals. **2** having three atoms or radicals of a univalent metal. **3** having three basic hydroxyl (OH) radicals.

tribe [traɪb] *n.* **1** a group of families, clans, etc. united by ancestry, custom, etc. under one leader or ruling group. The ancient Romans, Greeks, and Hebrews were divided into tribes, as are many non-European peoples today. **2** a group of people, especially a large one, having a common interest, profession, etc.: *a tribe of artists, the whole tribe of gossips.* **3** *Informal.* a large nuclear family. **4** a minor category in the classification of animals and plants ranking between a genus and a subfamily or family. **5** any group, class, or kind of animals, plants, or things. ⟨< L *tribus*⟩

tribes•man ['traɪbzmən] *n., pl.* **-men.** a member of a tribe.

tribo– *combining form.* friction; resulting from or relating to friction: *triboelectricity* = electricity produced by friction; *triboluminescence* = luminescence produced by friction; *tribology* = the systematic study of friction and its effects. ⟨< Gk. *tribein* rub⟩

tri•brach ['traɪbræk] *n. Prosody.* a metrical foot made up of three short syllables. ⟨< Gk. *tri-* three + *brachys* short⟩ **—tri'brach•ic,** *adj.*

trib•u•la•tion [,trɪbjə'leiʃən] *n.* great trouble or affliction, especially as a result of persecution or oppression: *the tribulations of the early Christians.* ⟨ME < OF < LL *tribulatio, -onis,* ult. < L *tribulum* threshing sledge⟩

tri•bu•nal [traɪ'bjunəl] *or* [trɪ'bjunəl] *n.* **1** a court of justice; a place of judgment: *He was brought before the tribunal for trial.* **2** a place where judges sit in a law court. **3** something by or in which judgment is rendered; judicial or deciding authority: *the tribunal of the polls, the tribunal of the press.* ⟨< L *tribunal* < *tribunus.* See TRIBUNE[1].⟩

trib•u•nate ['trɪbjənɪt] *or* ['trɪbjə,neit] *n.* **1** the office, rank, or authority of a tribune. **2** a group of tribunes.

trib•une[1] ['trɪbjun] *n.* **1** in ancient Rome: **a** an official chosen by the plebeians to protect their rights and interests. **b** a military officer, one of six who rotated command of a legion in the course of a year. **2** a defender of the people. ⟨ME < L *tribunus* < *tribus* tribe⟩

trib•une[2] ['trɪbjun] *n.* a raised platform or dais. ⟨< Ital. *tribuna* tribunal⟩

trib•une•ship ['trɪbjun,ʃɪp] *n.* the position, duties, or term of a tribune.

trib•u•tar•y ['trɪbjə,tɛri] *n., pl.* **-tar•ies;** *adj. —n.* **1** a stream that flows into a larger stream or body of water: *The Ottawa River is a tributary of the St. Lawrence.* **2** a person, country, etc. that pays tribute.
—adj. **1** flowing into a larger stream or body of water. **2** paying or required to pay tribute. **3** paid as tribute; of the nature of tribute. **4** contributing; helping.

trib•ute ['trɪbjut] *n.* **1** money paid by one nation to another for peace or protection or because of some agreement. **2** a tax collected to raise this money. **3** a tax paid by a feudal vassal to an overlord, or the duty to pay this tax. **4** any forced payment: *The pirates demanded tribute from passing ships.* **5** an acknowledgment of thanks or respect; compliment: *Remembrance Day is a tribute to our dead servicemen and women.* ⟨ME < L *tributum* < *tribuere* allot < *tribus* tribe⟩

trice[1] [trəis] *v.* **triced, tric•ing.** haul up and fasten with a rope: *to trice up a sail.* ⟨ME < MDu. *trisen* hoist < *trise* pulley⟩

trice[2] [trəis] *n. Archaic* (*except in* **in a trice**). a very short time; moment; instant: *In a trice, he was through the window and in the room.* ⟨abstracted from phrase *at a trice* at a pull. Cf. TRICE[1].⟩

tri•cen•te•nar•y [,traɪsɛn'tɛnəri] *or* [,traɪsɛn'tinəri] *adj. or n., pl.* **-nar•ies.** tricentennial.

tri•cen•ten•ni•al [,traɪsɛn'tɛnjəl] *or* [,traɪsɛn'tɛniəl] *adj., n.*
—adj. **1** of or having to do with a period of 300 years or a 300th anniversary. **2** 300 years old.
—n. **1** a period of 300 years. **2** a 300th anniversary.

tri•ceps ['traɪsɛps] *n., pl.* **-ceps** or **-ceps•es.** *Physiology.* the large muscle at the back of the upper arm. It extends, or straightens, the arm. ⟨< NL < L *triceps* three-headed < *tri-* three + *caput* head⟩

tri•cer•a•tops [trəi'sɛrə,tɒps] *n.* any of various quadripedal, herbivorous dinosaurs of the genus *Triceratops*, order Ornithischia, of the late Cretaceous, having a large bony crest on the back of the neck, a long horn over each eye and a smaller horn on the snout. ⟨< NL < Gk. *tri-* three + *keras, keratos* horn + *ops* face, eye⟩

tri•chi•na [trə'kaɪnə] *n., pl.* **-nae** [-ni] *or* [-naɪ]. a tiny nematode worm (*Trichinella spiralis*) that occurs as a parasite in the intestines and muscles of certain mammals, including humans. Trichinae usually get into the human body from pork that is infected with the larvae and is not cooked long enough to destroy them. ⟨< NL < Gk. *trichinē*, fem. adj., of hair < *thrix, trichos* hair⟩ **—tri'chi•nal,** *adj.*

trich•i•no•sis [,trɪkə'nousɪs] *n.* a disease characterized by fever, muscle fatigue and pain, and diarrhea, caused by the presence of trichinae in the intestines and muscular tissues.

trich•i•nous ['trɪkənəs] *adj.* **1** having trichinosis; infected with trichinae. **2** of, having to do with, or involving trichinae or trichinosis: *a trichinous infection.*

tri•chlo•ride [traɪ'klɔraɪd] *n.* a chloride with three atoms of chlorine per molecule.

tri•chlo•ro•a•ce•tic acid [traɪ,klɔrouə'sitɪk] a toxic, colourless, corrosive, deliquescent crystalline compound $C_2HCl_3O_2$, soluble in water, alcohol, and ether, and used in the synthesis of pharmaceuticals and herbicides. *Abbrev*.: TCA

tri•chlo•ro•eth•yl•ene [traɪ,klɔrou'ɛθə,lin] *n.* a colourless, poisonous, non-flammable liquid, C_2HCl_3, used to degrease metals and as a solvent for fats, oils, and waxes in dry-cleaning. *Abbrev*.: TCE

tricho– *combining form.* hair; resembling hair. ⟨< Gk. *thrix, trichos* hair⟩

trich•oid ['trɪkɔɪd] *adj.* hairlike.

tri•chol•o•gy [trɪ'kɒlədʒi] *n.* the scientific study of hair and diseases of the hair. **—tri'chol•o•gist,** *n.*

tri•chome ['trəikoum] *or* ['trɪkoum] *n.* **1** any of the hairlike growths, such as a prickle, root hair, etc. on the outer surface of a plant. **2** any of the hairlike structures forming the filaments of some algae. **—tri'chom•ic** [-'kɒmɪk] *or* [-'koumɪk], *adj.*

trich•o•mo•nad [,trɪkə'mounæd] *n.* any of a genus (*Trichomonas*) of parasitic flagellate protozoans.

trich•o•mo•ni•a•sis [,trɪkəmə'naɪəsɪs] *n.* an infection caused by infestation with trichomonads, especially in the vaginal, urinary, and digestive tracts.

tri•chop•ter•an [trəi'kɒptərən] *or* [trə'kɒptərən] *n.* CADDIS FLY. ⟨< Gk. *trichos* hair + *pteron* wing + E *-an*⟩ **—tri'chop•ter•ous,** *adj.*

tri•cho•sis [trə'kousɪs] *n.* any hair disease.

tri•chot•o•mize [trəi'kɒtə,maɪz] *v.* **-mized, -mizing.** divide into three mutually exclusive parts or classes; make into or treat as a trichotomy.

tri•chot•o•my [trəi'kɒtəmi] *or* [trə'kɒtəmi] *n., pl.* **-mies.** **1** division into three mutually exclusive groups, classes, parts, etc. **2** an instance of such division; something divided into three. **3** specifically, the division of human nature into body, soul, and spirit. ⟨< NL *trichotomia* < Gk. *trich(a)* in three parts + NL *-tomia* -tomy⟩ **—tri'chot•o•mous,** *adj.* **—tri'chot•o•mous•ly,** *adv.*

tri•chro•ism ['traɪkrou,ɪzəm] *n.* a property of certain crystals whereby they transmit light of a different colour when viewed from each of three different angles. ⟨< Gk. *trichroos* three-coloured < *tri-* three + *chroia* colour⟩ **—tri'chro•ic,** *adj.*

tri•chro•mat•ic [,traɪkrə'mætɪk] *adj.* **1** having, using, or combining three colours, as in colour printing or photography. **2** *Opthalmology*. relating to, or having, normal colour vision fully distinguishing all three primary colours.

trick [trɪk] *n., v.* *—n.* **1** something done to deceive or cheat: *The false message was a trick to get him to leave the house.* **2** something misleading or unreal; illusion: *Those two lines are really the same length, but a trick of vision makes one of them look longer.* **3** a clever act; a feat of skill: *We enjoyed the tricks of the trained animals.* **4** (*adjl.*) using, doing, or involving tricks or illusions; misleading: *trick photography, a trick question.* **5** the best way of dealing with or doing something, especially if not common knowledge: *the trick of making pies.* **6** a piece of mischief; prank: *Stealing Ruth's lunch was a mean trick.* **7** a peculiar habit or way of acting: *He has a trick of pulling at his collar.* **8 a** a single round of certain card games. **b** the set of cards played and won in such a round. **9** a turn or period of duty at a job, especially at steering a ship. **10** *Slang.* a single customer or transaction of a prostitute.

do or **turn the trick,** do what one wants done.

how's tricks? *Informal.* how are things? how are you?

not miss a trick, *Informal.* be very alert or quick.

trick of the trade, an especially effective or clever method or technique in a particular line of work.

—v. **1** deceive; cheat: *We were tricked into buying a poor car.* **2** play pranks. **3** dress or adorn, especially in an ornate or fanciful way (*used with* **out** *or* **up**): *She was tricked out in her mother's clothes.* ⟨ME < OF *trique*⟩ **—'trick•ish,** *adj.*

☛ *Syn. v.* **1.** See note at CHEAT.

trick•er•y ['trɪkəri] *n., pl.* **-er•ies.** the act or practice of deceiving or cheating; fraud.

trick•le ['trɪkəl] *v.* **-led, -ling;** *n.* *—v.* **1** flow or fall in drops or in a small stream: *Tears trickled down her cheeks. The brook trickled through the valley.* **2** cause to flow in drops or in a small stream: *He trickled the water into the container.* **3** come, go, pass, etc. slowly and unevenly: *An hour before the show people began to trickle into the theatre.*

—n. **1** a small flow or stream. **2** the act of trickling. ⟨ME *strikle* < *strike* flow, move, strike < OE *strīcan*⟩

trick•le•down ['trɪkəl,daʊn] *adj.* of or referring to an economic theory that government aid to big business, in the form of loans and tax reduction, will eventually result in benefits to ordinary consumers and to the poor.

trick or treat a call used by children dressed in costumes at Halloween, going from door to door and begging for candy or other gifts under the threat of playing tricks if they are refused.

trick•ster ['trɪkstər] *n.* a cheat; deceiver.

trick•sy ['trɪksi] *adj.* **1** mischievous; playful; frolicsome. **2** tricky. **—'trick•si•ness,** *n.*

trick•y ['trɪki] *adj.* **trick•i•er, trick•i•est. 1** that plays tricks; deceiving; cheating. **2** difficult to do or handle, whether because unreliable, delicate, or requiring skill: *a tricky situation, a tricky piece of work. Our back door has a tricky lock.* **—'trick•i•ly,** *adv.* **—'trick•i•ness,** *n.*

tri•clin•ic [traɪ'klɪnɪk] *adj.* of or referring to a system of crystallization in which there are three unequal axes, none at right angles to any other one. ⟨< *tri-* + Gk. *klinein* incline, lean + E *-ic*⟩

tri•clin•i•um [trəi'klɪniəm] *n., pl.* **-ia.** in ancient Rome: **1** a dining table with couches on three sides, for reclining while eating. **2** a room containing such a table and couches.

tri•col•our or **tri•col•or** ['traɪkʌlər] *adj., n.* *—adj.* having three colours.

—n. a flag having three colours, especially the flag of France, which has three vertical stripes of blue, white, and red. ⟨< F *(drapeau) tricolore* tricoloured (flag)⟩

tri•corne ['traɪkɔrn] *adj., n.* *—adj.* having three 'horns' or corners, as a hat whose brim is folded back up against the crown so as to give it a triangular shape.

—n. a tricorne hat. Also, **tricorn.** ⟨< F *tricorne* < L *tricornis* < *tri-* three + *cornu* horn⟩

tri•cot ['trikou] *n.* **1** a knitted wool, cotton, or synthetic fabric made by hand or machine, having fine vertical ribs on the right side and horizontal ones on the back and used especially for women's garments. **2** a kind of worsted woollen cloth. **3** a close-fitting garment worn by ballet dancers. ⟨< F *tricot*, ult. < Gmc.⟩

tric•o•tine [,trɪkə'tin] *n.* a kind of twilled woollen cloth.

tri•crot•ic [traɪ'krɒtɪk] *adj. Physiology.* of the pulse, having three separate peaks per beat. ⟨< Gk. *trikrotos* with three beats < *tri-* three + *krotein* beat⟩

tri•cus•pid [traɪ'kʌspɪd] *adj., n.* *—adj.* **1** having three points or cusps: *a tricuspid tooth.* **2** having three flaps: *the tricuspid valve of the heart.*

—n. **1** a tricuspid tooth. **2** the tricuspid valve, located between the right auricle and ventricle of the heart. ⟨< L *tricuspis, -idis* three-pointed < *tri-* three + *cuspis* tip⟩

tri•cy•cle ['trəisəkəl] *n.* **1** a three-wheeled vehicle usually worked by pedals attached to the large single wheel in front, now used especially by small children. **2** a three-wheeled motor vehicle designed for use by a disabled person. ⟨< F *tricycle* < *tri-* three (< L or Gk.) + *cycle*, ult. < Gk. *kyklos* ring, circle⟩

tri•cy•clic [traɪ'sɪklɪk] *or* [traɪ'səiklɪk] *adj. Chemistry.* of a compound, having a molecular structure of three fused rings.

tri•dent ['traɪdənt] *n., adj.* *—n.* a three-pronged spear,

especially as the identifying attribute of Poseidon (Neptune), the ancient Greek and Roman god of the sea.
—adj. three-pronged. ⟨< L *tridens, -entis* < *tri-* three + *dens* tooth⟩

tri•den•tate [traɪ'dɛnteit] *adj.* having three teeth or toothlike points; three-pronged.

Tri•den•tine [traɪ'dɛntaɪn] *or* [traɪ'dɛntin] *adj.* of Trent, Italy, or the council held there by the Roman Catholic Church in the mid 16th century as part of the Counter-Reformation. ⟨< NL *Tridentinus* < *Tridentum* Trent⟩

tri•di•men•sion•al [ˌtraɪdə'mɛnʃənəl] *adj.* three-dimensional.

tried [traɪd] *adj., v. —adj.* tested; proved.
tried and true, that has proved effective or successful on many previous occasions.
—v. pt. and pp. of TRY.

tri•en•ni•al [traɪ'ɛniəl] *adj., n. —adj.* **1** lasting three years. **2** occurring every three years.
—n. **1** an event that occurs every three years. **2** the third anniversary of an event. ⟨< L *triennium* three-year period < *tri-* three + *annus* year⟩ **—tri'en•ni•al•ly,** *adv.*

tri•en•ni•um [traɪ'ɛniəm] *n.* a three-year period. ⟨< L⟩

tri•er ['traɪər] *n.* a person who or thing that tries or tests.

tri•er•arch ['traɪəˌrɑrk] *n.* in ancient Greece: **1** the captain or commander of a trireme. **2** a citizen in charge of the building, outfitting, and maintenance of a state trireme. ⟨< L *trierarchus* < Gk. *trierarchos* < *trieres* trireme + *archos* leader, chief⟩ **—'tri•erˌarch•y,** *n.*

tri•eth•yl [traɪ'ɛθəl] *adj.* having three ethyl groups per molecule.

tri•fa•cial [traɪ'feiʃəl] *adj.* trigeminal.

tri•fid ['traɪfɪd] *adj. Botany.* of a leaf, having three parts or lobes. ⟨< L *trifidus* split in three < *tri-* three + *fidus* < *findere* split⟩

tri•fle ['trəifəl] *n., v.* **-fled, -fling.** *—n.* **1** something having little value or importance. **2** a small amount; a little bit. **3** a small amount of money. **4** a rich dessert made of sponge cake, whipped cream, custard, fruit, wine, etc.
—v. **1** talk or act lightly, not seriously: *Don't trifle with serious matters.* **2** play or toy *(with): He trifled with his pencil while he was talking to me.* **3** spend (time, effort, money, etc.) on things having little value: *She had trifled away the whole morning.* ⟨ME < OF *trufle;* origin uncertain⟩
☛ *Syn. v.* **1. Trifle,** DALLY = treat a person or thing without seriousness. **Trifle** means 'talk or act lightly, or playfully', especially about something deserving serious treatment or respect: *She is not one to be trifled with.* **Dally** emphasizes amusing oneself by playing, especially at love or with thoughts, or by flirting with danger or temptation: *I have dallied with the idea of taking a trip.*

tri•fler ['trəiflər] *n.* a frivolous or shallow person.

tri•fling ['trəiflɪŋ] *adj., v. —adj.* **1** having little value; not important; small. **2** frivolous; shallow.
—v. ppr. of TRIFLE. **—'tri•fling,** *adv.*

tri•fo•cal *adj.* [traɪ'foukəl]; *n.* [traɪ'foukəl] *or* ['traɪfoukəl] *adj., n. —adj.* of a lens, etc., adjusted to three focal lengths.
—n. **1** such a lens. **2 trifocals,** *pl.* a pair of glasses with trifocal lenses, the middle section of each being adjusted to an intermediate focal length for objects at a distance of about 76 cm. Also (def. 2), **multifocals.**

tri•fo•li•ate [traɪ'foulirt] *or* [traɪ'fouliˌeit] *adj.* of a plant, having leaves in groups of three. Poison ivy is a trifoliate plant. ⟨< *tri-* + L *foliatus* leaved < *folium* leaf⟩

tri•fo•li•o•late [traɪ'fouliəlɪt] *or* [traɪ'fouliəˌleit] *adj.* of a leaf, divided into three leaflets. A clover leaf is trifoliolate. ⟨< *tri-* + NL *foliolum* dim. of *folium* leaf⟩

tri•fo•ri•um [trəi'fɔriəm] *n., pl.* **-ri•a** [-riə]. a gallery above a side aisle or transept in a church. ⟨< Med.L *triforium,* apparently < L *tri-* three + *foris* door⟩

tri•fur•cate *v.* ['traɪfərˌkeit]; *adj.* [traɪ'fɜrkɪt], [traɪ'fɜrkeɪt], *or* ['traɪfərˌkeit] *v.* **-cat•ed, -cat•ing;** *adj. —v.* separate into three branches.
—adj. having three branches; forked in three ways. ⟨< L *trifurcus* < *tri-* three + *furca* fork + E *-ate*⟩ **—ˌtri•fur'ca•tion,** *n.*

trig [trɪg] *n. Informal.* trigonometry: *We have a test in trig tomorrow.* ⟨shortened < *trigonometry*⟩

tri•gem•i•nal [traɪ'dʒɛmənəl] *adj., n. —adj.* of or referring to either of the fifth pair of cranial nerves, each dividing into an opthalmic, a mandibular, and a maxillary nerve on one side of the head and face.
—n. a trigeminal nerve. ⟨< NL *trigeminus* triplet < *tri-* three + *geminus* twin⟩

trig•ger ['trɪgər] *n., v.* **-gered, -ger•ing.** *—n.* **1** the small lever pulled back by the finger in firing a gun. See FIREARM for picture. **2** any lever that releases a spring, catch, etc. when pulled or pressed. **3** anything that sets off or initiates something else.
quick on the trigger, a quick to shoot. **b** *Informal.* quick to act or speak; mentally alert.
—v. **1** set off or fire; detonate; activate: *The explosion was triggered by a spark.* **2** cause to start; begin: *The fiery speech triggered an outburst of violence.* ⟨ult. < Du. *trekker* < *trekken* pull⟩

trig•ger–hap•py ['trɪgər ˌhæpi] *adj. Informal.* **1** shooting or inclined to shoot or to use armed force at the slightest provocation. **2** too readily inclined to overreact, especially with violent action or adverse criticism.

tri•glyc•er•ide [traɪ'glɪsəˌraɪd] *n.* any ester obtained from glycerol and at least one carboxylic acid, each molecule of glycerol being joined with three molecules of carboxylic acid. Triglycerides occur naturally in animal and vegetable tissues as fats and oils, and are an important source of energy.

tri•glyph ['traɪglɪf] *n. Doric architecture.* the part of a frieze between two metopes, consisting typically of a rectangular block with two vertical grooves and a half groove at each side. ⟨< L < Gk. *triglyphos* < *tri-* three + *glyphē* carving⟩ **—tri'glyph•ic,** *adj.*

trigon. **1** trigonometry; trigonometric.

trig•o•nal ['trɪgənəl] *adj.* **1** of or shaped like a triangle. **2** of or referring to a crystal system having threefold symmetry. ⟨< L *trigonalis* < *trigonum* < Gk. *trigonon* triangle < *tri-* three + *gonia* angle⟩

trig•o•no•met•ric [ˌtrɪgənə'mɛtrɪk] *adj.* of or having to do with trigonometry. Also, **trigonometrical.** **—ˌtrig•o•no'met•ri•cal•ly,** *adv.*

trigonometric function any one of the functions of an angle, such as sine, cosine, tangent, cotangent, secant, or cosecant, that can be expressed as a ratio of two sides of a right triangle. See SINE for picture.

trig•o•nom•e•try [ˌtrɪgə'nɒmətri] *n.* the branch of mathematics that deals with the relations between the sides and angles of triangles and the calculations based on these. The principles of trigonometry are used in surveying, navigation, and engineering. ⟨< NL *trigonometria,* ult. < Gk. *tri-* three + *gōnia* angle + *metron* measure⟩

tri•graph ['traɪgræf] *n.* three letters used to spell a single sound. *Example: the* eau *in* beau.

tri•he•dral [traɪ'hidrəl] *or* [traɪ'hɛdrəl] *adj.* of or having to do with a trihedron; formed by three planes meeting at a point.

tri•he•dron [traɪ'hidrən] *or* [traɪ'hɛdrən] *n., pl.* **-drons, -dra** [-drə]. a figure formed by three planes meeting at a point. ⟨< *tri-* + Gk. *hedra* seat, base⟩

tri•hy•drate [traɪ'haɪdreit] *n.* any chemical compound that contains three water molecules.

tri•hy•drox•y [ˌtraɪhaɪ'drɒksi] *adj.* containing three hydroxyl groups or radicals. Also, **trihydric** [traɪ'haɪdrɪk].

trike [trəik] *n. Informal.* tricycle.

tri•lat•er•al [traɪ'lætərəl] *adj.* having three sides or involving three parties. ⟨< L *trilaterus* < *tri-* three + *latus, lateris* side⟩ **—tri'lat•er•al•ly,** *adv.*

tril•by ['trɪlbi] *n. Esp. Brit.* a man's soft felt hat, floppier than a fedora, with a deeply indented crown. ⟨< *Trilby,* titular heroine of a novel (1893) by George du Maurier⟩

tri•light ['traɪləit] *n.* **1** a lightbulb that can be switched to any of three degrees of brightness. **2** a lamp whose socket is designed to hold such a bulb.

tri•lin•e•ar [traɪ'lɪniər] *adj.* of, relating to, having, or enclosed by three lines.

tri•lin•gual [traɪ'lɪŋgwəl] *or* [traɪ'lɪŋgjəwəl] *adj.* **1** able to speak three languages: *a trilingual person.* **2** using or involving three languages. **—tri'lin•gual•ly,** *adv.*

tri•lit•er•al [traɪ'lɪtərəl] *adj.* **1** consisting of three letters. **2** of or referring to any Semitic language having root forms consisting of three consonants. Derived and inflected forms are produced by interpolating various combinations of vowels between the consonants. **—tri'lit•er•alˌism,** *n.*

trill [trɪl] *v., n. —v.* **1** sing, play, sound, or speak with a quivering, vibrating sound. **2** *Music.* sing or play with a trill. **3** *Phonetics.* pronounce with rapid vibration of the tongue, etc. Many Scots trill the sound of *r.*

—n. **1** the act or sound of trilling. **2** *Music.* a quick alternating of two notes a tone or a half tone apart. **3** *Phonetics.* **a** a rapid vibration of the tongue, etc. **b** a consonant pronounced by such a vibration. The [r] of most Highland Scots is a trill. ⟨< Ital. *trillare* < Gmc.⟩

tril•lion ['trɪljən] *n. or adj.* **1** in Canada and the United States, 1 followed by 12 zeros; 1 000 000 000 000; a million million. **2** in the United Kingdom, France, Germany, etc., 1 followed by 18 zeros; a million million million. ⟨< F *trillion* < *tri-* three, modelled on *million* million⟩

tril•lionth ['trɪljənθ] *adj., n.* **1** last in a series of one trillion. **2** one, or being one, of a trillion equal parts.

tril•li•um ['trɪljəm] *or* ['trɪliəm] *n.* any of a genus (*Trillium*) of small plants of the lily family having a short stem with a whorl of three leaves and a single flower with three narrow green sepals and three white, pink, or reddish petals. The white trillium (*T. grandiflorum*) is the provincial flower of Ontario. ⟨< NL *trillium* < L *tri-* three⟩

Trilliums

tri•lo•bate [traɪ'loubeit] *or* ['traɪlə,beit] *adj.* especially of a leaf, having three lobes. Also, **trilobed** ['traɪloubd].

tri•lo•bite ['traɪlə,bəit] *n.* any of a large group (Trilobata) of extinct marine arthropods that flourished in the Paleozoic era, having a segmented outside skeleton divided by two deep, lengthwise furrows into three lobes. The relationship of trilobites to other arthropods is still unclear. ⟨< NL *trilobita*, < Gk. *tri-* three + *lobos* lobe⟩ **—,tri•lo'bit•ic** [-'bɪtɪk], *adj.*

tril•o•gy ['trɪlədʒi] *n., pl.* **-gies.** three plays, operas, novels, etc. that fit together to make a related series. Any of the three sections of a trilogy is itself a complete work. ⟨< Gk. *trilogia* < *tri-* three + *logos* story⟩

trim [trɪm] *v.* **trimmed, trim•ming;** *adj.* **trim•mer, trim•mest;** *n., adv.* *—v.* **1** put in good order; make neat by cutting away parts: *The lumber has to be trimmed for the carpenter. The gardener trimmed the hedge.* **2** remove (unwanted parts or amounts): *I have to trim 8 kg from my baggage or the airline will charge me extra. He trimmed dead leaves off the plants.* **3** reduce (something) to the required size or shape by cutting out parts: *This year's budget has been trimmed drastically. With rigorous editing she was able to trim her essay down to ten pages.* **4** decorate: *The children trimmed the Christmas tree.* **5** balance (a boat, airplane, etc.) by arranging the load carried, adjusting the stabilizers, etc. **6** be or stay in balance. **7** arrange (the sails) to fit wind and direction. **8** change (opinions, views, etc.) to suit circumstances or to avoid conflict. **9** *Informal.* defeat heavily; beat. **10** *Informal.* scold.
trim (one's) **sails,** alter one's behaviour to suit changing conditions or avoid conflict.
—adj. **1** neat or spruce in appearance: *A trim maid appeared.* **2** that is or appears to be well designed and maintained: *a trim little ketch.*
—n. **1** good condition or order: *to get in trim for a race.* **2** condition; order: *That ship is in poor trim for a voyage.* **3** an act of trimming; a cutting, clipping, etc.: *These hedges are in need of a trim.* **4** a haircut that tidies up the previous cut without changing the style: *They'll give you a shampoo and trim for only $10.* **5** trimming: *the trim on a dress.* **6** woodwork used as a finish or ornament on the inside or outside of a building. **7** the upholstery, handles, and accessories inside an automobile. **8** the chrome, colour scheme, etc. decorating the outside of an automobile. **9** a display in a store window. **10** equipment; outfit. **11 a** the position of a ship or aircraft relative to the horizontal, especially the fore-and-aft axis. **b** properly balanced position relative to this axis: *This vessel is out of trim.* **12** the position or angle of the sails, yards, etc. in relation to the direction of the wind.
—adv. in a trim manner. ⟨OE *trymman* strengthen, make ready⟩ **—'trim•ly,** *adv.* **—'trim•ness,** *n.*
☛ *Syn. adj.* See note at NEAT.

tri•ma•ran ['traɪmə,ræn] *n.* a boat with three hulls side by side. Compare CATAMARAN. ⟨< *tri-* + (*cata*)*maran*⟩

tri•mer ['traɪmər] *n. Chemistry.* **1** a molecule made up of three identical simple molecules. **2** a polymer having such molecules, that is, one derived from three identical molecules. ⟨< *tri-* + Gk. *meros* part⟩ **—tri'mer•ic** [traɪ'mɛrɪk], *adj.*

trim•er•ous ['trɪmərəs] *adj. Botany, Zoology.* having parts divided into three or into groups of three.

tri•mes•ter [traɪ'mɛstər] *or* ['traɪmɛstər] *n.* **1** a third part of a school year. **2** a three-month period; a quarter of a year. ⟨< F *trimestre* < L *trimestris* < *tri-* + *mensis* month⟩

trim•e•ter ['trɪmətər] *n., adj. Prosody.* *—n.* a line of verse having three metrical feet.
—adj. consisting of three feet or measures.

tri•meth•a•di•one [,traɪmɛθə'daɪoun] *n.* a white, crystalline, bitter-tasting compound used in the treatment of epilepsy. *Formula*: $C_6H_9NO_3$ ⟨< *tri-* + *meth*(*yl*) + *di-*[1] + *-one*⟩

tri•met•ric [traɪ'mɛtrɪk] *adj.* **1** being or consisting of a trimeter or trimeters. **2** of or having to do with a crystal system in which three unequal axes intersect one another at right angles. **3** of or referring to a projection, in mechanical drawing, with the three axes at arbitrary angles to one another and, sometimes, using a different linear scale for each. Also, **trimetrical.**

trim line a decorative variation in the interior design of an automobile or aircraft.

trim•mer ['trɪmər] *n.* **1** a person or thing that trims: *a hat trimmer, a window trimmer.* **2** a person who changes his or her opinions, actions, etc. to suit circumstances or avoid conflict, often in an unprincipled manner. **3** a beam or rafter that supports the ends of headers, as around a stairwell, chimney, etc.

trim•ming ['trɪmɪŋ] *n., v.* *—n.* **1** the act or an instance of clipping, cutting, decorating, or making something trim. **2** something added as a decoration or accessory: *I'm putting red and blue trimming on my costume.* **3 trimmings,** *pl.* **a** parts cut away in trimming. **b** *Informal.* garnishes, side dishes, and other accompaniments to a main dish: *We ate turkey with all the trimmings.* **4** the act or practice of adjusting one's views, behaviour, etc. to suit circumstances or avoid conflict, especially in a way that compromises one's integrity. **5** *Informal.* a decisive defeat. **6** *Informal.* a scolding or thrashing.
—v. ppr. of TRIM.

tri•month•ly [traɪ'mʌnθli] *adj.* occurring every three months.

tri•morph ['traɪmɔrf] *n.* a substance, organism, species, etc. that is or contains an instance of trimorphism.

tri•mor•phism [traɪ'mɔrfɪzəm] *n.* **1** *Mineralogy.* the occurrence in the same compound of three different forms of a crystalline substance. **2** *Botany.* the occurrence in the same species or individual plant of three different types of leaf, flower, etc. **3** *Zoology.* the occurrence in one species of three types distinct in size, colour, structure, etc. ⟨< Gk. *trimorphis* < *tri-* + *morphē* form + E *-ism*⟩ **—tri'morph•ic,** *adj.* **—tri'morph•ous,** *adj.*

trim size the finished size of a book or book page, after all extra margins have been trimmed off.

Tri•mur•ti [trɪ'mʊrti] the Hindu trinity, Brahma, Vishnu, and Siva. ⟨< Skt. *tri* three + *murti* form, body⟩

tri•nal ['traɪnəl] *adj.* composed of three parts; threefold.

tri•na•ry ['traɪnəri] *adj.* ternary; triple.

trine [traɪn] *adj., n.* *—adj.* **1** threefold; triple. **2** *Astrology.* of or having to do with the aspect of two planets 120 degrees distant from each other.
—n. **1** any group of three. **2 Trine,** the Trinity. **3** *Astrology.* the aspect, supposed to be favourable, of two planets 120 degrees apart. ⟨< L *trinus* triple⟩

Trin•i•dad and To•ba•go ['trɪnə,dæd ənd tə'beigou] a country of two islands in the West Indies.

Trin•i•dad•ian [,trɪnɪ'dædiən] *or* [,trɪnɪ'deidiən] *n., adj.* *—n.* a native or inhabitant of Trinidad.
—adj. of or having to do with Trinidad or its people.

Trin•i•tar•i•an [,trɪnə'tɛriən] *adj., n.* *—adj.* **1** *Christianity.* **a** believing in the Trinity. **b** having to do with the Trinity. **2 trinitarian,** being or forming a trinity.
—n. Christianity. a person who believes in the Trinity.
—,Trin•i'tar•i•an,ism, *n.*

tri•ni•tro•glyc•er•in [traɪ,nəitrou'glɪsərɪn] *n.* nitroglycerin.

tri•ni•tro•tol•u•ene [traɪ,nəitrou'tɒlju,in] *n.* a powerful explosive formed from toluene, usually known as TNT. Also, **trinitrotoluol.** *Formula*: $CH_3C_6H_2(NO_2)_3$ ⟨< *trinitro-*, a combining form meaning 'of three nitro-groups' (NO_2) + *toluene*⟩

Trin•i•ty ['trɪnəti] *n.* **1** *Christianity.* the union of Father, Son, and Holy Spirit in one divine nature. **2** *Informal.* TRINITY SUNDAY. **3 trinity, a** a group of three closely related persons or things. **b** the state of being threefold. ⟨ME < OF < L *trinitas* < *trinus* triple⟩

Trinity Sunday in the Christian calendar, the first Sunday after Pentecost and the eighth Sunday after Easter, observed as a feast to honour the Trinity.

trin•ket ['trɪŋkɪt] *n.* **1** any small, fancy article, bit of jewellery, etc. **2** a trifle. ⟨ME *trenket* little knife < ONF; ? < OF *trenchier, tranchier* cut⟩

tri•no•mi•al [traɪ'noumiəl] *n., adj.* —*n.* **1** *Mathematics.* an expression consisting of three terms connected by plus or minus signs. *Example*: $a + bx^2 - 2$ **2** *Biology.* the Latin name of an animal or plant consisting of genus, species, and subspecies.
—*adj.* being or having to do with a trinomial or trinomials: *a trinomial expression, trinomial algebra, trinomial nomenclature.* ⟨< *tri-* + *-nomial*, modelled after *binomial*⟩
—tri'no•mi•al•ly, *adv.*

tri•o ['triou] *n., pl.* **-tri•os. 1** a musical composition for three voices or instruments. **2** the second section or theme of a march, scherzo, etc., often quiet and lyrical in character. **3** a group of three singers or players performing together. **4** any group of three persons or things. ⟨< Ital. *trio*, ult. < L *tres* three⟩

tri•ode ['traɪoud] *n. Electronics.* **1** a vacuum tube that has an anode, a cathode, and a controlling grid. **2** any electronic device with three electrodes.

tri•oe•cious [traɪ'iʃəs] *adj. Botany.* having male, female, and bisexual flowers on different individual plants. ⟨< NL *trioecia* < Gk. *tri-* three + *okios* home⟩

tri•o•let ['traɪəlɪt] *n.* a poem having eight lines and only two rhymes. Lines 1, 4, and 7 are identical, as are lines 2 and 8; the rhyme scheme is *abaaabab.* ⟨< F⟩

tri•ox•ide [traɪ'ɒksaɪd] *n.* any oxide having three atoms of oxygen in each molecule.

trip [trɪp] *n., v.* **tripped, trip•ping.** —*n.* **1** a journey; voyage: *We took a trip to Europe.* **2** any act of going and returning: *We bought so much stuff, it took three trips to unload the car.* **3** a stumble; slip. **4** the act of catching a person's foot to throw him or her down. **5** a mistake; blunder. **6** a light, quick tread; stepping lightly. **7 a** a projecting part, catch, etc. on a mechanism or machine for starting or checking some movement. **b** the action of such a part. **8** *Slang.* **a** the mental state or experience induced by hallucinogenic drugs, such as LSD. **b** a period of activity, experience, mode of thinking, etc., that is gratifying, obsessive, intense, or in some other way vaguely analogous to a drug trip: *an ego trip, a guilt trip.*
—*v.* **1** stumble: *to trip on the stairs.* **2** cause to stumble and fall: *The loose board tripped him.* **3** make a mistake; do or say something wrong: *She tripped on that difficult question.* **4** cause to make a mistake or blunder (*sometimes used with* **up**): *The difficult question tripped me.* **5** overthrow by catching in a mistake or blunder; outwit (*usually used with* **up**). **6** detect in an inconsistency or inaccuracy (usually used with **up**): *The examining board tripped him up several times.* **7** take light, quick steps: *She tripped across the floor.* **8** tip; tilt. **9** release the catch of (a wheel, clutch, etc.). **10** activate (a mechanism or machine) by releasing a catch. **11** move past or be released by the pallet, as a cog on an escapement wheel of a watch or clock. **12** *Informal.* make a short tour or journey. **13** *Slang.* experience or have a trip (n. 8) (*often used with* **out**): *ego-tripping, to trip out on LSD.* **14 a** raise (the anchor). **b** turn (a yard) from a horizontal to a vertical position before lowering it. ⟨ME < OF *tripper* < Gmc.⟩

☛ *Syn. n.* **1. Trip,** JOURNEY, VOYAGE = a travelling from one place to another. **Trip** is the general word, usually suggesting return to the starting place, but not suggesting the length, purpose, manner, or means of travel: *How was your trip? He took a trip to Honolulu.* **Journey,** which may have dramatic overtones, applies especially to a long or very tiring trip by land to a place for a definite purpose: *He decided to make the journey to Mexico by car.* **Voyage** applies to a trip, usually long, by water: *The voyage to the Islands will be restful.*

tri•part•ism [traɪ'pɑrtɪzəm] *n. Cdn.* the system of having three main political parties.

tri•par•tite [traɪ'pɑrtəit] *adj.* **1** divided into or composed of three parts. **2** having three corresponding parts or copies. **3** made or shared by three parties: *a tripartite treaty.* ⟨< L *tripartitus* < *tri-* three + *partitus*, pp. of *partiri* divide⟩

tri•par•ti•tion [,traɪpɑr'tɪʃən] *n.* a division into three parts or parties.

tripe [trəip] *n.* **1** the walls of the first and second stomachs of an ox, etc. used as food. **2** *Slang.* something foolish, worthless, or trashy. ⟨ME < OF *tripe* entrails < Arabic *tharb*⟩

trip•ham•mer ['trɪp,hæmər] *n.* a heavy, power-driven hammer, operated by a tripping device by which it is raised and allowed to fall repeatedly.

tri•phen•yl•meth•ane [traɪ,fɛnəl'mɛθein] *n.* a colourless, crystalline solid much used in dyes. *Formula*: $CH(C_6H_5)_3$

tri•phib•i•ous [traɪ'fɪbiəs] *adj.* **1** of warfare, conducted on land, on the sea, and in the air. **2** of an aircraft or other vehicle or piece of equipment, able to take off, land, function, etc. on land, water, and snow or ice, or on land, in water, and in the air. Also, **triphibian.** ⟨< *tri-* + *(am)phibious*⟩

triph•thong ['trɪfθɒŋ] *or* ['trɪpθɒŋ] *n.* **1** a union of three vowel sounds pronounced in one syllable, as in *sour* [saʊə] in some British dialects, or *cow* [kæaʊ] in some American ones. **2** trigraph. ⟨< *diphthong*, with substitution of *tri-* for *di-*⟩
—triph'thong•al, *adj.*

Tri•pit•a•ka [trɪ'pɪtəkə] *n.* the corpus of sacred texts containing the teachings of Buddha, originally written in the Pali language and collected between the 6th and the 1st centuries B.C.

tri•plane ['traiplein] *n.* an airplane having three sets of wings, one above another.

tri•ple ['trɪpəl] *adj., n., v.* **-pled, -pling.** —*adj.* **1** including three; having three parts: *the triple petals of the trillium.* **2** three times as much or as many: *She got triple points for that question.* **3** repeated or occurring three times. **4** *Music.* having three (or a multiple thereof) beats per measure: *triple time.*
—*n.* **1** a number, amount, etc. that is three times as much or as many: *I invested a hundred and got triple back.* **2** *Baseball.* a hit that allows a batter to run three bases. **3** any group of three or threefold thing.
—*v.* **1** make or become three times as much or as many. **2** *Baseball.* **a** hit a triple. **b** advance (another runner) by hitting a triple. ⟨< L *triplus* < *tres* three + *-plus* fold. Doublet of TREBLE.⟩

triple crown 1 *Horse racing.* a championship won by a horse that in a single season wins the three classic races for its category. **2** a similar championship in football, tennis, etc.

triple jump a track-and-field event consisting of three successive jumps preceded by a running start. The contestant must land first on the same foot used for takeoff, then on the other foot, and finally on both feet. The triple jump was formerly called the **hop, step, and jump.**

triple play *Baseball.* a play that puts three players out.

triple point *Physics.* the combination of temperature and pressure at which the solid, liquid, and gaseous phases of a given substance are in equilibrium. The triple point of water is 0.01°C (or 273.16°K) at 4.6 mm of mercury.

tri•plet ['trɪplɪt] *n.* **1** one of three children born at the same time from the same mother. **2** *Music.* a group of three notes to be performed in the time of two notes having the same time value. **3** three successive lines of poetry, usually rhyming and equal in length. **4** *Genetics.* a three-base sequence in DNA or RNA coding for an amino acid or stop signal; codon. **5** any other group of three similar or equal things. ⟨< *triple*⟩

tri•ple•tail ['trɪpəl,teil] *n.* any of a family (Lobotidae) of percoid fishes having trailing, tail-like dorsal and anal fins, especially *Lobster surinamensis,* a food fish off the Atlantic coasts of SE Asia.

triple time *Music.* time or rhythm having three beats to the measure.

triple witching a phenomenon that occurs in the stock market four times a year, with the simultaneous expiry of stock options, stock index futures, and stock index options.

tri•plex ['traɪplɛks] *or* ['trɪplɛks] *adj., n.* —*adj.* triple; threefold. —*n.* **1** *Music.* triple time. **2** *Cdn.* a three-storey building having three apartments. ⟨< L *triplex* < *tri-* three + *plexus* < *plicare* fold⟩

trip•li•cate *v.* ['trɪplə,keit]; *adj., n.* ['trɪpləkɪt] *v.* **-cat•ed, -cat•ing;** *adj., n.* —*v.* **1** make threefold; triple. **2** make three identical copies or repetitions of.
—*adj.* **1** triple; threefold. **2** existing in three identical copies: *As a result of a computer error we received triplicate mailings of that firm's newsletter.*
—*n.* one of three things exactly alike.
in triplicate, in three copies exactly alike. ⟨< L *triplicare* < *triplex* threefold⟩

trip•li•ca•tion [,trɪplə'keiʃən] *n.* **1** a triplicating or being triplicated. **2** the product of triplicating.

tri•plic•i•ty [trɪ'plɪsəti] *n.* **1** the state or condition of being triple. **2** any group of three. **3** *Astrology.* any of the four zodiacal sets of three signs each in which each sign is 120° from the other two. ⟨< LL *triplicitas* < L *triplex* threefold⟩

trip•lo•blas•tic [ˌtrɪplouˈblæstɪk] *adj. Zoology.* of or having to do with the body structure of all multicellular animals except the Cnidarians, developing from three germ layers, the ectoderm, the endoderm, and the mesoderm. ⟨< Gk. *triploos* triple + *blastos* sprout⟩

trip•loid [ˈtrɪplɔid] *adj., n. Genetics. —adj.* having three times the haploid number of chromosomes.
—n. a triploid chromosome set. ⟨< Gk. *triploos* triple + *(hapl)oid*⟩ **—ˈtrip•loi•dy,** *n.*

tri•ply [ˈtrɪpli] *adv.* in a triple manner or to a triple degree; three times.

trip•man [ˈtrɪpˌmæn] *n., pl.* **-men.** *Cdn.* formerly, a temporary hand hired for duty on a canoe or other trip.

tri•pod [ˈtraɪpɒd] *n.* **1** a support or stand having three legs, as for a camera, telescope, etc. **2** a stool or other article having three legs. ⟨< L < Gk. *tripous, -odos* < *tri-* three + *pous* foot⟩ **—ˈtrip•o•dal** [ˈtrɪpədəl], *adj.*

trip•o•li [ˈtrɪpəli] *n.* a very light, porous, mainly siliceous material produced by the weathering of limestone or chert and used as a powder for polishing and filtering. ⟨< *Tripoli,* town in Libya⟩

Tri•pol•i•tan [trɪˈpɒlətən] *n., adj. —n.* a native or inhabitant of Tripoli, a town in Libya.
—adj. of or having to do with Tripoli or its inhabitants.

trip•per [ˈtrɪpər] *n.* **1** a person who or thing that trips; especially, a device in a machine that releases a catch, etc. or one that operates a railway signal. **2** a person who takes a trip or short excursion: *a day tripper.* **3** *Cdn.* **a** a fur trader in charge of a train of dogs. **b** a person who travels the northern bush trails. **c** an experienced wilderness traveller.

trip•pet [ˈtrɪpət] *n.* a mechanical part that regularly strikes or is struck by another. ⟨< *trip*⟩

trip•ping [ˈtrɪpɪŋ] *adj., v. —adj.* light and quick.
—v. ppr. of TRIP. **—ˈtrip•ping•ly,** *adv.*

trip•tane [ˈtrɪptein] *n.* a colourless liquid alkane hydrocarbon used as fuel for aircraft. *Formula*: $(CH_3)_2CHC(CH_3)_3$ ⟨< *trip(en)tane* < *tri-* + *pentane*⟩

trip•tych [ˈtrɪptɪk] *n.* **1** a set of three panels side by side, having pictures, carvings, etc. on them; especially, an altarpiece consisting of a central panel and two smaller, hinged side panels that fold over it. **2** a hinged, three-leaved writing tablet used in ancient Rome. ⟨< Gk. *triptychos* three-layered < *tri-* three + *ptyx* fold⟩

trip•wire [ˈtrɪpˌwaɪr] *n.* a wire stretched across or close to the ground that activates a hidden explosive, camera, trap, etc. when tripped on, stepped on, or driven over.

tri•ra•di•ate [traɪˈreidiɪt] *or* [traɪˈreidiˌeit] *adj.* having three radiating projections or rays.

tri•rat•na [triˈrʌtnə] *n.* in Jainism and Buddhism, the 'three jewels' of belief and practice by which to attain liberation from the world and rebirth, namely: right faith, right knowledge, and right conduct. ⟨< Skt.⟩

tri•reme [ˈtraɪrim] *n.* an ancient Greek or Roman warship having three rows of oars, one above the other, on each side. ⟨< L *triremis* < *tri-* three + *remus* oar⟩

tri•sect [traɪˈsɛkt] *v.* **1** divide into three parts. **2** *Geometry.* divide into three equal parts. ⟨< *tri-* + L *sectus,* pp. of *secare* cut⟩ **—triˈsec•tion,** *n.* **—triˈsect•or,** *n.*

tri•ser•vice or **tri–ser•vice** [traɪˈsɜrvɪs] *adj. Cdn.* of, for, or involving the land, maritime, and air forces or elements of the Canadian Forces.

tris•kai•dek•a•pho•bia [ˌtrɪskaɪˌdɛkəˈfoubiə] *or* [ˌtrɪskəˌdɛkəˈfoubiə] *n.* fear of the number thirteen. ⟨< Gk. *triskaideka* thirteen + E *-phobia*⟩

tris•kel•i•on [trɪˈskɛliˌɒn] *n., pl.* **-i•a.** any of various symbolic designs consisting of three bent or curved lines radiating from a centre. The device of the Isle of Man is a triskelion. Also, **triskele** [ˈtrɪskil]. ⟨< Gk. *triskeles* three-legged (< *tri-* three + *skelos* leg) + *-ion* dim. suffix⟩

tris•mus [ˈtrɪzməs] *n.* a condition symptomatic of tetanus, in which the mouth cannot be opened because the jaw muscles are in a continuous state of contraction; lockjaw. ⟨< NL < Gk. *trismos* grinding⟩ **—ˈtris•mic,** *adj.*

tri•so•my [traɪˈsoumi] *n.* the condition of having three, instead of the usual two, representatives of a given chromosome in all or in a high proportion of body cells. Down syndrome is a form of trisomy, called **trisomy 21.** ⟨< *tri-* + *-some*[3] + *-y*⟩ **—triˈso•mic,** *adj.*

tri•stich [ˈtrɪstɪk] *n. Prosody.* a group, strophe, or stanza consisting of three lines; triplet. **—trisˈtich•ic,** *adj.*

tris•ti•chous [ˈtrɪstɪkəs] *adj. Biology.* arranged, or having elements that are arranged, in three rows, especially the leaves of a plant.

Tris•tram [ˈtrɪstrəm] *n. Arthurian legend.* one of the most famous knights of the Round Table. His love for Iseult, wife of King Mark, is the subject of many stories and poems. Also, **Tristan.**

tri•syl•lab•ic [ˌtraɪsəˈlæbɪk] *adj.* having three syllables. **—ˌtri•sylˈlab•i•cal•ly,** *adv.*

tri•syl•la•ble [traɪˈsɪləbəl] *n.* a word of three syllables. *Educate* is a trisyllable.

trite [trəit] *adj.* **trit•er, trit•est.** ordinary; commonplace; stale or hackneyed; no longer interesting: *The movie turned out to be very trite, so we left early.* ⟨< L *tritus,* pp. of *terere* rub away⟩ **—ˈtrite•ly,** *adv.* **—ˈtrite•ness,** *n.*

tri•the•ism [ˈtraɪθiˌɪzəm] *n.* belief in three gods, especially the belief that the persons of the Christian Trinity (Father, Son, and Holy Spirit) are three separate and undivided gods. **—ˈtri•the•ist,** *n.* **—ˌtri•theˈis•tic,** *adj.*

trit•i•ca•le [ˌtrɪtəˈkeili] *or* [ˌtrɪtəˈkɑli] *n.* a fertile hybrid cereal grain, a cross between wheat and rye that has a high protein content and a high yield. ⟨< NL < *Tritic(um),* genus of wheat + *(Sec)ale,* genus of rye. 20c.⟩

trit•i•um [ˈtrɪtiəm] *or* [ˈtrɪʃiəm] *n.* a radioactive isotope of hydrogen that occurs in minute amounts in natural water, having a mass three times that of ordinary hydrogen. Tritium is used with deuterium in a hydrogen bomb. *Symbol*: T or ^{3}H ⟨< NL < Gk. *tritos* third⟩

tri•ton[1] [ˈtrəitən] *n.* **1 Triton,** *Greek mythology.* a sea god and a son of Poseidon, represented as having the head and body of a man and the tail of a fish, and carrying a conch shell. **2 Triton,** the largest satellite of the planet Neptune. **3 a** any of a family (Cymatiidae) of marine gastropod molluscs found mainly in tropical waters, having an elongated, often brightly coloured, spiral shell. **b** the shell itself.

tri•ton[2] [ˈtraɪtɒn] *n.* the nucleus of a tritium atom. ⟨< *trit(ium)* + *-on,* as in *electron*⟩

tri•tone [ˈtraɪˌtoun] *n. Music.* an interval of three whole tones; an augmented fourth.

trit•u•rate [ˈtrɪtʃəˌreit]; *n.* [ˈtrɪtʃərɪt] *or* [ˈtrɪtʃəˌreit] *v.* **-rat•ed, -rat•ing;** *n. —v.* rub, crush, or grind into a very fine powder.
—n. any substance that is ground into a very fine powder. ⟨< LL *triturare* thresh, ult. < L *terere* rub⟩ **—ˈtrit•u•ra•ble,** *adj.* **—ˈtrit•uˌra•tor,** *n.*

trit•u•ra•tion [ˌtrɪtʃəˈreiʃən] *n.* **1** the act or process of triturating or the state of being triturated. **2** a triturated powder, especially one consisting of a powdered medicinal substance mixed with lactose.

tri•umph [ˈtraɪʌmf] *n., v. —n.* **1** the state of being victorious or successful: *They returned home in triumph.* **2** a great victory, success, or achievement: *a final triumph over the enemy, a triumph of modern science.* **3** joy because of victory or success. **4** in ancient Rome, a procession in honour of a victorious general.
—v. **1** gain victory; win success: *Our team triumphed over theirs.* **2** exult or rejoice because of victory or success: *They triumphed in their success.* ⟨< L *triumphus*⟩
☛ *Syn. n.* **1, 2.** See note at **victory.**

tri•um•phal [traɪˈʌmfəl] *adj.* of, having to do with, or for a triumph; celebrating a victory.

tri•um•phal•ism [traɪˈʌmfəˌlɪzəm] *n.* an arrogant attitude of confidence in the superiority, and eventual dominance, of one's own beliefs or ideas over all others.

tri•um•phant [traɪˈʌmfənt] *adj.* **1** victorious; successful. **2** rejoicing because of victory or success. **—triˈum•phant•ly,** *adv.*

tri•um•vir [traɪˈʌmvər] *or* [traɪˈʊmvir] *n., pl.* **-virs** or **-vi•ri** [-vəˌraɪ] *or* [-vəˌri]. **1** in ancient Rome, one of three men who shared the same public office. **2** one of any three persons sharing power or authority. ⟨< L *triumvir,* abstracted from phrase *trium virorum* 'of three men'⟩ **—triˈum•vi•ral,** *adj.*

tri•um•vi•rate [traɪˈʌmvərɪt] *or* [traɪˈʌmvəˌreit] *n.* **1** the position or term of office of a triumvir. **2** government by three persons together. **3** any association of three in office or authority. **4** any group of three.

tri•une [traɪˈjun] *adj., n. —adj.* that is three in one: *the triune God.*
—n. **Triune,** *Christianity.* Trinity. ⟨< *tri-* + L *unus* one⟩

tri•u•ni•ty [traɪ'junəti] *n.* the state of being triune.

tri•va•lence [traɪ'veiləns] *or* ['trɪvələns] *n.* the state or quality of being trivalent. Also, **trivalency.**

tri•va•lent [traɪ'veilənt] *or* ['trɪvələnt] *adj.* **1** having a valence of three. **2** having three valences. ⟨< *tri-* + L *valens, -entis,* ppr. of *valere* be worth⟩

triv•et ['trɪvɪt] *n.* a stand or support usually having three legs or feet. Trivets are used over fire and under hot platters, etc. ⟨< L *tri-* three + OE *-fēte* footed⟩

triv•i•a ['trɪviə] *n.pl.* **1** trifles; unimportant matters (*sometimes used with a singular verb*). **2** obscure and immaterial bits of information: *He is a storehouse of baseball trivia.* ⟨< L pl. of *trivium,* prob. influenced by trivial⟩

triv•i•al ['trɪviəl] *adj.* **1** minor; not important; trifling; insignificant. **2** *Archaic.* not new or interesting; ordinary. ⟨< L *trivialis* vulgar, originally, of the crossroads, ult. < *tri-* three + *via* road⟩ **—'triv•i•al•ly,** *adv.*

triv•i•al•i•ty [,trɪvi'æləti] *n., pl.* **-ties. 1** the quality or state of being trivial. **2** something trivial; trifle.

triv•i•al•ize ['trɪviə,laɪz] *v.* **-ized, -iz•ing.** downplay; minimize; treat as trivial. **—,triv•i•al•i'za•tion,** *n.*

triv•i•um ['trɪviəm] *n., pl.* **-i•a** [-iə]. in the Middle Ages, grammar, rhetoric, and logic, the first group of the seven liberal arts. Compare QUADRIVIUM. ⟨< Med.L *trivium* a triple way < L *tri-* + *via* way⟩

tri•week•ly [traɪ'wikli] *adv., n., pl.* **-lies;** *adj.* *—adv.* **1** once every three weeks. **2** three times a week.
—n. a newspaper or magazine published triweekly.
—adj. occurring or appearing triweekly.

tro•cha•ic [trou'keiɪk] *adj., n.* *—adj.* of or consisting of trochees.
—n. **1** a line or poem written in trochees. **2** trochee (*usually used in the plural*).

tro•chan•ter [trou'kæntər] *n.* **1** in many vertebrates, any of a characteristic number of processes on the top part of the femur, having muscles attached. **2** the third segment of the leg of an insect. ⟨< F < Gk. *trochanter* < *trechein* run⟩

tro•che ['trouki] *n.* a small, usually round, medicinal lozenge. ⟨< obs. *trochisk* < F < LL *trochiscus* < Gk. *trochiskos,* dim. of *trochos* wheel⟩
☛ *Hom.* TROCHEE.

tro•chee ['trouki] *n. Prosody.* a foot or measure consisting of two syllables, the first accented and the second unaccented or the first long and the second short. *Example*: Síng a | sóng of | síxpence. ⟨< L < Gk. *trochaios,* originally, running < *trochos* a course < *trechein* run⟩
☛ *Hom.* TROCHE.

troch•le•a ['trɒkliə] *n., pl.* **-le•ae** [-li,i] *or* [-li,aɪ]. any part shaped like a pulley, with a groove allowing it to articulate with a bone or tendon sliding over it. ⟨< L < Gk. *trochileia* pulley < *trochos* wheel⟩ **—'troch•le•ar,** *adj.*

trochlear nerve either of the fourth pair of cranial nerves, supplying an upper muscle of the eye.

tro•choid ['troukɔɪd] *n., adj.* *—n.* cycloid.
—adj. rotating or rotatable like a wheel on an axis. Also (adj.), **trochoidal** [trou'kɔɪdəl]. ⟨< Gk. *trochoeides* circular < *trochos* wheel⟩

trod [trɒd] *v.* a pt. and a pp. of TREAD.

trod•den ['trɒdən] *v.* a pp. of TREAD.

trode [troud] *v. Archaic.* a pt. of TREAD.

trof•fer ['trɒfər] *n.* an elongated recess in a ceiling, usually to hold a fluorescent light fixture. ⟨< *trough*⟩

trog•lo•dyte ['trɒglə,dəit] *n.* **1** a member of a prehistoric people who lived in caves. **2** a person who is antisocial or lives in seclusion. **3** an anthropoid ape. ⟨< L < Gk. *trōglodytēs* < *trōglē* cave + *dyein* go in⟩ **—,trog•lo'dyt•ic** [-'dɪtɪk], *adj.*

troi•ka ['trɔɪkə] *n.* **1** a Russian vehicle, especially a sleigh, drawn by three horses abreast. **2** the horses themselves. **3 a** a triumvirate. **b** any group of three. ⟨< Russian < *troie* three together⟩

Tro•jan ['troudʒən] *n., adj.* *—n.* **1** a native or inhabitant of Troy, an ancient city in NW Asia Minor. **2** a person who shows courage or energy: *They all worked like Trojans.*
—adj. of or having to do with Troy or its people. ⟨< L *Trojanus* < *Troja, Troia* Troy < Gk.⟩

Trojan horse 1 *Greek mythology.* a huge wooden horse in which the Greeks concealed soldiers and had them brought into Troy during the Trojan War. **2** any person or group stationed inside a country, institution, etc. to sabotage or otherwise disrupt its activities from within. **3** *Computer technology.* an apparently normal computer program that contains hidden instructions for performing unexpected, and often destructive, processing.

troll[1] [troul] *v., n.* *—v.* **1** fish with a moving line, usually by trailing the line behind the boat near the surface: *He trolled for bass.* **2** draw (a lure or bait) through the water on a line behind a moving boat. **3** fish in (water) in this way: *to troll a lake.* **4** *Archaic.* **a** sing in a full, rolling voice. **b** sing (a song) in a round. **5** revolve or cause to revolve; roll.
—n. **1** a lure or a lure and line used in trolling. **2** *Archaic.* a song whose parts are sung in succession; round. **3** the act or an instance of trolling. ⟨ME *trollen* stroll < OF *troller* wander < Gmc.⟩

troll[2] [troul] *n. Scandinavian folklore.* any of a race of malevolent supernatural beings, thought of as giants or, more recently, as dwarfs. ⟨< ON⟩

troll•er ['troulər] *n.* **1** a person who trolls. **2** a fishing boat equipped with poles for trolling lines behind the boat.

trol•ley ['trɒli] *n., pl.* **-leys. 1** a pulley moving against a wire to carry electricity to a streetcar, electric engine, etc. **2** TROLLEY BUS. **3** streetcar. **4** a basket, carriage, etc., suspended from a pulley running on an overhead track. **5 a** a small cart in the form of a wheeled table or stand with a handle at each end, for serving food. **b** a wheeled contrivance for carrying luggage, etc. **off** (one's) **trolley,** *Slang.* crazy. ⟨probably < *troll*[1] in sense of 'roll'⟩

trolley bus an electrically powered bus having two overhead trolleys and running on tires like a motor bus.

trolley car streetcar.

trol•lop ['trɒləp] *n.* **1** an untidy or slovenly woman. **2** a morally loose woman; slut. **3** prostitute. ⟨probably < *troll*[1]⟩

trom•bi•di•a•sis [,trɒmbə'daɪəsɪs] *n. Veterinary Medicine.* the condition of being infested with mites of the family Trombiculidae. ⟨< NL *trombidium* genus name + E *-iasis* < Gk., condition⟩

A trombone

trom•bone [trɒm'boun] *or* ['trɒmboun] *n.* a musical wind instrument resembling a trumpet and having either a sliding piece or, less often, valves for varying the pitch. ⟨< Ital. *trombone* < *tromba* trumpet < Gmc.⟩

trom•bon•ist [trɒm'bounɪst] *or* ['trɒmbounɪst] *n.* a person who plays the trombone, especially a skilled player.

trom•mel ['trɒməl] *n.* a sieve in the form of a revolving cylinder, used for screening ore. ⟨< G *Trommel* drum⟩

tromp [trɒmp] *v. Informal.* tramp; stamp; stomp. ⟨var. of *tramp*⟩

trompe l'oeil [tRɔ̃p lœj] *French.* **1** a life-size still-life painting, mural, etc. painted so as to create a strong illusion of reality, temporarily deceiving the viewer. **2** an illusion of this kind. ⟨< F, literally, fools the eye⟩

-tron *combining form.* device or instrument, especially an electronic or nuclear one: *magnetron, synchrotron, calutron.* ⟨< Gk. *-tron* suffix of instrument⟩

troop [trup] *n., v.* *—n.* **1** a large group or collection of people or animals: *a troop of deer. A troop of children burst into the kitchen.* **2** a formation of armoured or cavalry forces smaller than a squadron; also, a similar group in other army units. **3 troops,** *pl.* armed forces; soldiers. **4** a group of Scouts or Girl Guides made up of several patrols: *She belongs to the 4th Kingston troop.*
—v. **1** gather or move in a troop or band: *We all trooped into the living room to sing happy birthday.* **2** carry (the colours) before a formation of troops as part of an official ceremony. ⟨< F *troupe,* ult. < LL *troppus* herd < Gmc.⟩
☛ *Hom.* TROUPE.

troop•er ['trupər] *n.* **1** a soldier in a cavalry regiment or an armoured regiment. **2** *Informal.* a hard-working, dependable, persevering or courageous person: *I couldn't have got through this without my wife's support—she's been a real trooper.* **3** a cavalry horse. **4** troopship. **5** a mounted police officer. **6** *U.S.* a state police officer.
☛ *Hom.* TROUPER.

troop leader **1** the person in charge of a military troop. **2** the senior boy or girl of a troop of Scouts or Girl Guides.

Troop Scouter an adult responsible for the operation of a troop of Scouts.

troop•ship ['trup,ʃɪp] *n.* a ship used to carry soldiers; transport.

troost•ite ['trustəit] *n.* a crystalline mineral, reddish or grey in colour, a type of willemite with part of the zinc replaced by manganese. ⟨< Gerard *Troost* (1776-1850), U.S. geologist⟩

tro•pae•o•lum [trə'piələm] *n., pl.* **-lums** or **-la. 1** nasturtium. **2** any of various related garden plants of the genus *Tropaeolum.*

trope *n.* [troup] **1** the use of a word or phrase in a sense different from its ordinary meaning; figurative use of a word or phrase. **2** a word or phrase so used; figure of speech. *Example*:
All in a hot and *copper* sky,
The *bloody* sun at noon. . . . ⟨< L < Gk. *tropos* turn⟩

tro•pe•o•lin [trə'piəlɪn] *n.* any of various complex azo dyes which are a deep orange or orange-yellow in colour. Also, **tropaeolin.** ⟨< *tropaeolum* (because of the colour)⟩

–troph *combining form.* an organism that nourishes itself in a specified way: *autotroph.* ⟨< Gk. *trophe* food⟩

troph•ic ['trɒfɪk] *adj.* of or having to do with nutrition as a process. ⟨< Gk. *trophikos* < *trophe* food⟩

tro•phied ['troufid] *adj.* decorated with trophies: *trophied walls.*

troph•o•blast ['trɒfə,blæst] *n.* in placental mammals, such as humans, a layer of ectoderm enclosing the embryo and attached to the wall of the uterus, from which it absorbs nourishment. ⟨< Gk. *trophe* food + *blastos* sprout, bud⟩ **–,troph•o'blas•tic,** *adj.*

tro•phy ['troufi] *n., pl.* **-phies. 1** something taken or won in war, hunting, etc., especially if displayed as a memorial or souvenir: *The hunter kept the moose's head as a trophy.* **2** a prize, often in the form of a silver cup or statue, awarded in sports or other competitions: *He kept his tennis trophy on the mantelpiece.* **3** in ancient Greece and Rome, captured arms, flags, etc. of a defeated enemy set up on the field of battle or in a public place as a memorial of victory. **4** a representation of such a memorial on a medal or in the form of a monument. **5** anything serving as a remembrance. ⟨< F *trophée* < L *trophaeum,* for *tropaeum* < Gk. *tropaion* < *tropē* rout, originally, turn⟩

trop•ic ['trɒpɪk] *n.* **1** either of two parallels of latitude, one 23°27′ north and the other 23°27′ south of the equator. The northern parallel is the Tropic of Cancer and the southern parallel is the Tropic of Capricorn. **2 the tropics** or **Tropics,** *pl.* the region between these parallels. The equator runs through the middle of the tropics, which include the hottest parts of the earth. **3** (*adjl.*) of or belonging to the tropics. **4** either of two corresponding circles in the celestial sphere, the limits reached by the sun in its apparent journey north and south. ⟨< L *tropicus* < Gk. *tropikos* pertaining to a turn < *tropē* a turn, a change⟩

trop•i•cal ['trɒpəkəl] *adj.* **1** of, characteristic of, or found in the tropics: *tropical fruits, tropical diseases, a tropical climate.* **2** suitable for or used in the tropics: *tropical suiting.* **3** like the tropics; especially, very hot or sultry. **–'trop•i•cal•ly,** *adv.*

tropical year SOLAR YEAR.

tropic bird any of a very small family (Phaethontidae) of web-footed birds of warm seas having white plumage with black markings and having long, streamerlike tail feathers. They belong to the same order as pelicans and cormorants.

Tropic of Cancer the parallel of latitude at 23°27′ north of the equator, that marks the northern limit of the part of the earth where the sun is directly overhead at some time during the year.

Tropic of Capricorn the parallel of latitude at 23°27′ south of the equator, that marks the southern limit of the part of the earth where the sun is directly overhead at some time during the year.

tro•pism ['troupɪzəm] *n. Biology.* the tendency of an animal or plant to turn or move in response to a stimulus. ⟨< Gk. *tropē* a turning⟩ **—tro'pis•tic,** *adj.*

tro•pol•o•gy [trə'pɒlədʒi] *n., pl.* **-gies. 1** the use of figurative language or tropes. **2** a figurative interpretation of a text, especially the Scriptures. **3** the study of, or a treatise on, the use of figurative language. ⟨< *trope* + *-logy*⟩ **–,trop•o'log•i•cal** [,trɒpə'lɒdʒəkəl], *adj.*

trop•o•pause ['trɒpə,pɒz] *n.* the boundary or transition between the troposphere and the stratosphere, distinguished by an increase in temperature and atmospheric stability. ⟨< *tropo*(*sphere*) + *pause*⟩

tro•poph•i•lous [trə'pɒfələs] *adj.* of plants, able to adapt to changing conditions of temperature, moisture, etc. in different seasons. Deciduous trees and perennial flowers are tropophilous. ⟨< Gk. *tropos* a turning or changing + E *-philous* having an affinity for (< Gk. *philos* loving)⟩

trop•o•phyte ['trɒpə,fəit] *n.* a tropophilous plant. ⟨< Gk. *tropos* a turn or change + E *-phyte*⟩ **–,trop•o'phyt•ic** [-'fɪtɪk], *adj.*

trop•o•sphere ['trɒpə,sfir] *n.* the lowest layer of the atmosphere, extending about 10 to 16 km from the earth upward to the stratosphere. The troposphere is characterized by winds, cloud formation, and a rapid decrease in temperature with increase in altitude. ⟨< Gk. *tropē* a turn, a change + E *sphere*⟩ **–,trop•o'spher•ic** [-'sfɛrɪk], *adj.*

trop•po ['trɒpou]; *Italian,* ['trɔppo] *adv. Italian. Music.* too much. *Example*: *allegro ma non troppo,* fast but not too fast.

trot [trɒt] *v.* **trot•ted, trot•ting;** *n.* *—v.* **1** of horses, etc., go at a gait between a walk and a run by lifting the right forefoot and the left hind foot at about the same time and then the other two feet in the same way. **2** ride or drive a horse at such a gait: *We trotted along the path.* **3** cause to trot: *to trot a horse.* **4** of a person, run at a moderate pace: *The child trotted along after her mother.*
trot out, *Informal.* bring out for others to see.
—n. **1** the gait of a trotting animal or person: *We started off at a trot.* **2** the action or exercise of trotting: *to go for a trot.* **3** a brisk, steady movement. **4** the sound of trotting. **5** a single race in a program of harness racing. **6 the trots,** *pl. Slang.* diarrhea. **7** *Fishing.* trotline. ⟨ME < OF *trotter* < Gmc.⟩

troth [trɒθ] *or* [trouθ] *n., v.* *—n.* **1** faithfulness; loyalty. **2** a promise, especially a promise or engagement to marry. **3** truth.
by my troth or **in troth,** truly; upon my word: *By my troth, I'll see you revenged.*
plight (one's) **troth,** pledge one's word, especially in an engagement to marry.
—v. pledge; betroth. ⟨OE *trēowth* < *trēow* faith⟩

trot•line ['trɒt,laɪn] *n. Fishing.* a long line with short lines and baited hooks attached at regular intervals.

Trot•sky•ism ['trɒtski,ɪzəm] *n.* the social, political, and economic principles of Leon Trotsky (1879-1940), a Russian revolutionary leader, especially the principle that worldwide communist revolution must be put before everything else, including the growth and development of existing communist societies. **—'Trot•sky•ist,** *n.*

Trot•sky•ite ['trɒtski,əit] *n.* a follower of Leon Trotsky; a believer in Trotskyism.

trot•ter ['trɒtər] *n.* **1** an animal that trots, especially a horse bred and trained for harness racing. **2** a sheep's or pig's foot used for food.

tro•tyl ['troutɪl] *n.* trinitrotoluene. ⟨< trini*tro*toluene + *-yl*⟩

trou•ba•dour ['trubə,dɔr] *or* ['trubə,dur] *n.* **1** one of a class of medieval lyric poets of southern France, northern Spain, and northern Italy who wrote poems of chivalry and courtly love. The troubadours had great social influence and were often of knightly rank. **2** any minstrel, poet, or singer. ⟨< F < Provençal *trobador,* ult. < LL *tropus* song, mode (in music) < Gk. *tropos* mode, style (in music), originally, a turn⟩

trou•ble ['trʌbəl] *n., v.* **-bled, -bling.** *—n.* **1** distress; worry or difficulty: *That dog has caused them a lot of trouble. We're still having trouble with the furnace.* **2** a distressing or annoying fact, event, or experience: *His life was full of troubles.* **3** an occasion or cause of affliction, distress, vexation, etc.: *Is she a trouble to you?* **4** public disturbance or unrest: *There was some trouble on the picket line.* **5** extra work; bother; effort: *She took the trouble to make extra copies.* **6** illness or disease: *She has stomach trouble.* **7** faulty operation; malfunction: *They were delayed because of engine trouble.* **8 the trouble,** the cause of annoyance, worry, etc.: *The trouble is that he never bothers to let us know. She's just too easygoing, that's the trouble.*
borrow trouble, look on the worst side of a situation; predict problems that may never arise.

in or **into trouble, a** in or into a situation in which one is caught in wrongdoing and is liable to be blamed, punished, etc.: *They're very mischievous and are always getting into trouble. Her boyfriend is in trouble with the police.* **b** *Informal.* pregnant without being married.
make trouble, cause problems or unpleasantness: *Mind your own business and don't make trouble.*
—v. **1** cause distress or worry to: *The lack of business troubled him.* **2** require extra work or effort of: *May I trouble you to do something for me?* **3** cause oneself inconvenience or effort: *Don't trouble to come to the door; I can let myself out.* **4** cause pain or discomfort to; afflict: *His arthritis is troubling him again. The baby has been troubled with colds.* **5** stir; agitate; disturb: *to trouble the silence, to trouble still waters.*
trouble (someone) **for,** ask (someone) to give: *May I trouble you for the salt?* ⟨ME < OF *truble* < *trubler* trouble, ult. < L *turba* turmoil⟩

trou•ble•mak•er ['trʌbəl,meikər] *n.* a person who causes trouble, especially one who deliberately causes disagreement between people.

trou•ble•mak•ing ['trʌbəl,meikɪŋ] *n., adj. —n.* the actions of a troublemaker.
—adj. causing or making trouble.

trou•ble•shoot ['trʌbəl,ʃut] *v.* **-shot, -shoot•ing.** work as a troubleshooter: *She troubleshoots for a large construction firm.*

trou•ble•shoot•er ['trʌbəl,ʃutər] *n.* **1** a person employed to discover and eliminate causes of trouble in equipment, machinery, etc. **2** a person who is skilled in mediating diplomatic or political disputes.

trou•ble•some ['trʌbəlsəm] *adj.* causing trouble; annoying. **—'trou•ble•some•ly,** *adv.* **—trou•ble•some•ness,** *n.*

trou•blous ['trʌbləs] *adj. Archaic or poetic.* **1** disturbed; restless: *troublous times.* **2** troublesome.

trough [trɒf] *n.* **1** a long, narrow container for holding food or water for animals: *a watering trough.* **2** a container shaped like this: *The baker uses a trough for kneading dough.* **3** a channel for carrying water; gutter. **4** a long hollow between two ridges, etc.: *the trough between two waves.* **5** *Meteorology.* a long, narrow area of relatively low barometric pressure. **6** *Geology.* a basin-shaped depression; the lowest part of a synclinal fold. **7** a low point in a cycle. ⟨OE *trōh*⟩ **—'trough,like,** *adj.*

trounce [traʊns] *v.* **trounced, trounc•ing. 1** beat; thrash. **2** *Informal.* defeat severely in a contest, game, etc. ⟨origin uncertain⟩

troupe [trup] *n., v.* **trouped, troup•ing.** *—n.* a troop, band, or company, especially a group of actors, singers, or acrobats.
—v. tour or travel with a troupe. ⟨< F⟩
☛ *Hom.* TROOP.

troup•er ['trupər] *n.* **1** a member of a theatrical troupe. **2** an old, experienced actor.
☛ *Hom.* TROOPER.

trou•pi•al ['trupiəl] *n.* any of several small or medium-sized New World orioles, especially an orange-and-black species (*Icterus icterus*) of Central and South America. ⟨< F *troupiale* < *troupe* troop, because they tend to congregate in large groups⟩

trou•sers ['traʊzərz] *n.pl.* **1** PANTS (defs. 1, 2). **2** (*adjl.*) **trouser,** of, having to do with, or designed for trousers: *trouser cuffs.* ⟨< *trouse* < Irish *triūs*⟩

trous•seau ['trusou] *or* [tru'sou] *n., pl.* **trous•seaux** or **trous•seaus** ['trusouz] *or* [tru'souz]. a bride's outfit of clothes, linen, etc. ⟨< F *trousseau,* originally, bundle⟩

trout [trʌut] *n., pl.* **trout** or **trouts. 1** any of several food and game fishes (genus *Salmo*) of the salmon family found mainly in northern lakes and rivers. Trout belonging to this group, such as the rainbow trout, are often called true trout to distinguish them from char. **2** any of several species of char (genus *Salvelinus*), also of the salmon family, such as the lake trout or brook trout. ⟨OE *trūht* < LL *tructa, tructa,* probably < Gk. *trōktēs,* literally, gnawer < *trōgein* gnaw⟩

trout•perch ['trʌut,pɜrtʃ] *n.* any of a family (Percopsidae) of bony freshwater fishes, especially *Percopsis omiscomaycus,* of central and eastern Canada and the U.S.

trove [trouv] *n.* TREASURE-TROVE.

trow [trou] *or* [traʊ] *v. Archaic.* believe; think. ⟨OE *truwian*⟩

trow•el ['traʊəl] *n., v.* **-elled** or **-eled, -el•ling** or **-el•ing.**
—n. **1** a hand tool with a thin, flat blade, used for smoothing or spreading plaster, mortar, etc. **2** a garden hand tool similar to a scoop, used for taking up plants, loosening dirt, etc.
—v. **1** use a trowel to dig, spread, smooth, etc. **2** apply (plaster) with a trowel. ⟨ME < OF *truele* < LL *truella,* dim. of L *trua* skimmer⟩

troy [trɔi] *adj.* expressed in TROY WEIGHT: *a troy ounce.* ⟨< *Troyes,* a city in France⟩

troy weight a system of units for measuring mass, traditionally used for weighing gems and precious metals. One pound troy weight is equal to about 0.373 kg.

24 grains = 1 pennyweight
20 pennyweight = 1 ounce
12 ounces = 1 pound

Trp. or **trp.** troop.

trs. transpose.

tru•an•cy ['truənsi] *n., pl.* **-cies.** the act or habit of staying away from school without permission; truant behaviour.

tru•ant ['truənt] *n., adj., v. —n.* a person who neglects work, especially a student who stays away from school without permission.
play truant, neglect one's work or duty; especially, stay away from school without permission.
—adj. **1** being a truant; especially, staying away from school without permission. **2** of, like, or characteristic of a truant: *truant habits.* **3** wandering.
—v. be a truant; engage in truancy. ⟨ME < OF *truant,* probably < Celtic⟩

truant officer a school official employed to investigate and deal with cases of truancy.

truce [trus] *n.* **1** a stop in fighting by agreement between opposing armed forces, either temporary or permanent. **2** a rest from quarrelling, turmoil, trouble, etc. ⟨ME *trewes,* pl. of *trewe,* OE *trēow* faith, treaty⟩

truck¹ [trʌk] *n., v. —n.* **1** a motor conveyance designed primarily for carrying heavy things or animals rather than people. **2** any of various strongly built carts, wagons, etc. used, especially formerly, for a similar purpose. **3** a small conveyance, sometimes with a motor, for carrying trunks, boxes, etc.: *Jim uses a truck in the warehouse. The redcap is coming with a truck.* **4** a swivelling frame, with two or more pairs of wheels, supporting each end of a railway car, locomotive, etc. **5** a low, flat railway car. **6** on a ship or boat, a wooden disk at the top of a flagstaff or mast with holes for the ropes. **7** (*adjl.*) of, for, or used on a truck.
—v. **1** carry on a truck. **2** drive a truck. **3** transport goods by truck, especially as a business; make a living as a trucker. ⟨? < L *trochus* iron hoop < Gk. *trochos* wheel⟩

truck² [trʌk] *n., v. —n.* **1** vegetables raised for market. **2** small articles of little value; odds and ends. **3** *Informal.* rubbish. **4** *Informal.* dealings: *He wanted no truck with peddlers.* **5** exchange; barter. **6** the payment of wages in goods, etc. rather than in money; TRUCK SYSTEM.
—v. make an exchange; swap or barter. ⟨ME < OF *troquer* barter, trade⟩

truck•age ['trʌkɪdʒ] *n.* **1** carrying of goods, etc. by trucks. **2** the charge for carrying by truck.

truck•er¹ ['trʌkər] *n.* **1** a person who drives a truck. **2** a person whose business is carrying goods, etc. by trucks.

truck•er² ['trʌkər] *n.* **1** a market gardener; truck farmer. **2** a person who barters or travels as a peddler.

truck farm a farm where vegetables are raised for market; market garden. **—truck farmer. —truck farming.**

truck•ing ['trʌkɪŋ] *n.* **1** the business of driving a truck or transporting goods by truck. **2** the conveyance of goods by truck; TRUCKAGE (def. 1).

truck•le¹ ['trʌkəl] *v.* **-led, -ling.** give up or submit tamely (*usually used with* **to**): *to truckle to one's superiors.* ⟨< obsolete *truckle* to sleep in a truckle bed; with reference to its low position⟩ **—'truck•ler,** *n.* **—'truck•ling•ly,** *adv.*

truck•le² ['trʌkəl] *n., v.* **-led, -ling.** *—n.* **1** a small wheel; caster. **2** TRUNDLE BED.
—v. move or roll on truckles, or casters. Also (n.), **truckle bed.** ⟨< L *trochlea* < Gk. *trochilea* sheaf of a pulley⟩

truck•load ['trʌk,loud] *n.* **1** a load that fills a truck. **2** the minimum weight of specific goods that makes a truckload according to a schedule of rates for shipping by truck.

truck•man ['trʌkmən] *n., pl.* **-men.** TRUCKER¹.

truck stop a restaurant and service station together on a highway, that is frequented by truckers or that caters especially to truckers.

truck system *Cdn. Atlantic Provinces.* a credit system under which a fisher, logger, trapper, etc. gets his or her outfit and supplies for the season as an advance, and is committed to trade only with the merchant extending the credit, all or most dealings being in kind rather than cash.

truc•u•lence ['trʌkjələns] *n.* the quality or state of being truculent. Also, **truculency.**

truc•u•lent ['trʌkjələnt] *adj.* **1** showing a readiness to fight or quarrel; arrogant and hostile: *a truculent attitude.* **2** fierce and cruel: *at the mercy of a truculent ruffian.* **3** of speech or writing, ruthless and scathing; harsh: *truculent satire.* ⟨< L *truculentus* < *trux, trucis* fierce⟩ **—'truc•u•lent•ly,** *adv.*

trudge [trʌdʒ] *v.* **trudged, trudg•ing;** *n.* *—v.* walk, especially wearily or with effort: *The tired hikers trudged home.*
—n. a hard or weary walk: *It was a long trudge up the hill.* ⟨origin uncertain⟩ **—'trudg•er,** *n.*

trudg•en stroke ['trʌdʒən] *Swimming.* a stroke using a double overarm stroke together with a scissors movement of the legs. ⟨after John *Trudgen* (1852-1902), a British swimmer⟩

true [tru] *adj.* **tru•er, tru•est;** *n., v.* **trued, tru•ing;** *adv.* *—adj.* **1** agreeing with fact; not false: *It is true that 6 and 4 are 10.* **2** real; genuine: *true gold, true kindness.* **3** faithful; loyal: *a true patriot.* **4** agreeing with a standard; right; proper; correct; exact; accurate: *a true copy, a true scale, true to type.* **5** representative of the class named: *A sweet potato is not a true potato.* **6** rightful; lawful: *the true heir to the property.* **7** reliable; sure: *a true sign.* **8** accurately formed, fitted, aligned, or placed: *a true angle.* **9** steady in direction, force, etc.; unchanging: *The arrow made a true course through the air.* **10** *Archaic.* truthful. **11** honest.
come true, happen as expected; become real.
true north, etc. north, etc., according to the earth's axis, not the magnetic north.
true to form, behaving according to expectation.
—n. **1** that which is true. **2** exact or accurate formation, position, or alignment: *A slanting door is out of true.*
—v. make true; shape, place, or make in the exact position, form, etc. required (*usually used with* **up**).
—adv. **1** in a true manner; truly; exactly: *Her words ring true.* **2** in agreement with the ancestral type: *breed true.* ⟨OE *trīewe, trēowe*⟩ **—'true•ness,** *n.*
☛ *Syn. adj.* **1.** See note at REAL.

true bill *Esp. U.S. Law.* the endorsement made by a grand jury when satisfied that a bill of indictment is supported by enough evidence to justify the case being brought to trial.

true–blue ['tru 'blu] *adj.* staunch and unchanging; very loyal: *She's a true-blue conservative.*

true–born ['tru 'bɔrn] *adj.* genuine; that is so by birth: *a true-born Ontarian.*

true•bred ['tru,brɛd] *adj.* purebred; of a good or genuine breed.

true–heart•ed ['tru ,hɑrtɪd] *adj.* **1** faithful; loyal. **2** honest, sincere. **—'true-,heart•ed•ly,** *adv.* **—'true-,heart•ed•ness,** *n.*

true–life ['tru 'ləif] *adj.* that corresponds to, or actually occurred in, real life: *a true-life romance.*

true•love ['tru,lʌv] *n.* a faithful lover; sweetheart.

truelove knot a kind of bowknot that is hard to untie, standing for true and lasting love. Also, **true-lover's knot.**

true ribs in vertebrates, ribs joined directly to the sternum or breastbone. In humans, these are the first seven pairs of ribs.

truf•fle ['trʌfəl] *n.* **1** any of several European underground fungi (genus *Tuber*) valued as food. **2** a soft, very rich chocolate candy. ⟨probably ult. < F *truffe*⟩

truffle hound any kind of dog that can be trained to hunt for truffles.

tru•ism ['truɪzəm] *n.* a statement that is obviously true, especially one that is too obvious to mention, such as "You're only young once." **—tru'ist•ic,** *adj.*

trull [trʌl] *n. Archaic.* prostitute; strumpet. ⟨? < G *Trulle* < *trolle.* Related to TROLL¹.⟩

tru•ly ['truli] *adv.* **1** in a true manner; exactly; rightly; faithfully. **2** in fact; really. **3** in the formal closing of a letter, sincerely (often preceded by "Yours (very)").

trump¹ [trʌmp] *n., v.* *—n.* **1** *Card games.* **a** any playing card of a suit that for the duration of a deal or game ranks higher than the other suits. **b** Often, **trumps,** *pl.* the suit itself. **2** any resource or advantage held back until needed. **3** *Informal.* a fine, dependable person.
—v. **1** *Card games.* **a** take (a trick, card, etc.) with a trump: *She trumped my king.* **b** play a trump when another suit was led: *We didn't expect him to trump.* **2** be better than; surpass; beat.
trump up, think up or invent falsely: *He trumped up an excuse for being late.* ⟨alteration of *triumph*⟩

trump² [trʌmp] *n., v. Archaic or poetic.* *—n.* **1** a trumpet. **2** the sound of a trumpet.
—v. trumpet. ⟨ME < OF *trompe* < Gmc.⟩

trump card **1** any playing card of a suit that for a particular hand ranks higher than the other suits. **2** a decisive fact, argument, etc., especially one that is held in reserve until needed; clincher.

trumped–up ['trʌmpt 'ʌp] *adj.* invented in order to deceive; fraudulent: *trumped-up charges.*

trump•er•y ['trʌmpəri] *n., pl.* **-er•ies;** *adj.* *—n.* something showy but without value; worthless ornaments; useless stuff; rubbish; nonsense.
—adj. showy but without value; trifling; worthless; useless; nonsensical. ⟨< F *tromperie* < *tromper* deceive⟩

A trumpet

trump•et ['trʌmpɪt] *n., v.* *—n.* **1** a musical wind instrument having a looped tube that is bell-shaped at one end and has three valves to vary the pitch. The trumpet has a sharp, clear tone and can produce great volume. **2** anything shaped like a trumpet: *Some people used ear trumpets before small hearing aids were invented.* **3** a sound like that of a trumpet. **4** a TRUMPETER (def. 1). **5** an organ stop producing a trumpetlike tone.
blow (one's) **own trumpet,** talk boastfully; praise oneself.
—v. **1** blow a trumpet. **2** make a sound like a trumpet: *The elephant trumpeted in fright.* **3** proclaim loudly or widely: *He'll trumpet that story all over town.* ⟨ME < OF *trompette,* dim. of *trompe.* See TRUMP.⟩

trumpet creeper **1** a climbing woody vine (*Campsis radicans*) native to the warm regions of the western hemisphere, having clusters of large red, trumpet-shaped flowers. **2** any of various other vines of the same family. **3** (*adjl.*) **trumpet-creeper,** designating the family (Bignoniaceae) of mostly trees, shrubs, and vines that includes the trumpet creeper, bignonia, and catalpa.

trum•pet•er ['trʌmpətər] *n.* **1** a person who plays a trumpet, especially a skilled player. **2** any of a genus (*Psophia,* comprising the family Psophidae) of large birds living mainly on the ground in the tropical rain forests of South America, having a long neck and legs, short tail and wings, and mainly black plumage. Trumpeters have a loud, deep call. **3** TRUMPETER SWAN. **4** a breed of domestic pigeon.

trumpeter swan the largest swan (*Olor buccinator,* also classified as *Cygnus buccinator*), found in western Canada and the NW United States, weighing up to 18 kg and with a wingspread of often more than 2.5 m, having a deep, very far-carrying, trumpetlike call.

trumpet flower **1** any of various plants having trumpet-shaped flowers, such as the **trumpet honeysuckle** *(Lonicera sempervirens)* or the TRUMPET CREEPER. **2** the flower of any of these plants.

trumpet vine TRUMPET CREEPER.

trun•cate ['trʌŋkeit] *v.* **-cat•ed, -cat•ing;** *adj.* *—v.* shorten (something) by cutting off the top or end.
—adj. **1** *Botany.* having a blunt or square end: *the truncate leaf of the tulip tree.* See LEAF for picture. **2** *Zoology.* of the shell of some snails, lacking the normal apex. **3** truncated. ⟨< L *truncare* < *truncus* maimed⟩ **—trun'ca•tion,** *n.*

trun•cat•ed ['trʌŋkeitɪd] *adj., v.* *—adj.* **1** *Geometry.* **a** of a cone, pyramid, or other solid figure, having the angles, edges, or apex cut off. **b** of the angles or edges of a solid figure, cut off or replaced by a plane face. **2** that is or has been cut short: *a truncated version of a speech.*
—v. pt. and pp. of TRUNCATE.

trun•cheon ['trʌntʃən] *n., v.* *—n.* **1** *Esp. Brit.* a short stick or club: *a police officer's truncheon.* **2** a staff of office or authority; baton: *a herald's truncheon.*

—*v.* beat with a club. ⟨ME < OF *tronchon,* ult. < *truncus.* See TRUNK.⟩

trun•dle ['trʌndəl] *v.* **-dled, -dling;** *n.* —*v.* **1** roll or push (something) along: *The worker trundled a wheelbarrow full of cement.* **2** roll or revolve: *The empty shopping cart trundled down the ramp.* **3** *Informal.* go on foot: *Just trundle down to the store and pick up some tea, would you?*
—*n.* **1** the motion or sound of rolling. **2** a small wheel; caster. **3** TRUNDLE BED. **4** a low cart or wagon on small wheels. ⟨ME, var. of *trindel* wheel, or of *trendle* < OE *trendel* ring, disk⟩

trundle bed a low bed on small wheels or casters that can be rolled under a higher bed when not in use.

trunk [trʌŋk] *n.* **1** the main stem of a tree, as distinct from the branches and the roots. **2** the main or central part of something, especially the shaft of a column. **3** an enclosed compartment in an automobile for storing luggage, tools, etc. **4** a large, heavy box with a hinged lid, used for transporting or storing clothes and other personal property. **5** the body apart from the head, arms, and legs; torso. **6** the main body of a blood vessel, nerve, or similar structure as distinct from its branches. **7** the long, muscular, flexible snout of an elephant. **8 trunks,** *pl.* very short pants worn by male athletes, swimmers, acrobats, etc. **9** a main channel or passage, such as a shaft carrying cables, air for ventilation, etc. **10** TRUNK LINE. ⟨< L *truncus,* originally adj., mutilated⟩

trunk call *Brit.* a long-distance telephone call.

trunk hose short, full, baggy breeches reaching about halfway down the thigh, worn by men, especially in the 16th and 17th centuries.

trunk line **1** the main line of a railway, canal, etc. **2** a direct link between two central telephone exchanges, for making connections between individual subscribers.

trun•nel ['trʌnəl] *n.* treenail.

trun•nion ['trʌnjən] *n.* **1** either of the two round projections of a cannon, one on each side, which support it on its carriage and allow it to pivot up and down. **2** either of any similar pair of pins or pivots. ⟨< F *trognon* trunk < L *truncus;* influenced by F *moignon* stump of an amputated limb⟩

truss [trʌs] *v., n.* —*v.* **1** tie; fasten; bind (*often used with* **up**): *We trussed the burglar up and called the police.* **2** fasten the wings or legs of (a fowl) with skewers or twine in preparation for cooking. **3** support or strengthen with a truss or trusses. **4** *Archaic.* fasten or tighten (a garment).
—*n.* **1** a framework of beams or other braces for supporting a roof, bridge, etc. **2** a pad or other device worn as a support for a hernia. **3** a bundle or pack; especially in the United Kingdom, a bundle of hay having a specific mass. **4** on a ship or boat, an iron fitting by which a lower yard is fastened to the mast. **5** *Botany.* a flower cluster at the tip of a stem, as on a tomato plant. ⟨ME < OF *trusser,* ult. < L *torquere* twist⟩

truss•ing ['trʌsɪŋ] *n., v.* —*n.* **1** the work of constructing trusses or of putting them in place to make a supporting framework. **2** the materials used to make trusses. **3** trusses collectively.
—*v.* ppr. of TRUSS.

trust [trʌst] *n., v.* —*n.* **1** a firm belief in the honesty, truthfulness, justice, or power of a person or thing; faith: *He put no trust in the strangers or their information.* **2** a person or thing confided or trusted in: *God is our trust.* **3** a confident expectation or hope: *Our trust is that she will soon be well.* **4** either of two similar arrangements which are illegal in Canada if the intent is to frustrate the free market: **a** a group of individuals or companies controlling much of a certain kind of business: *a steel trust.* **b** a group of individuals or firms having a central committee that controls stock of the constituent companies, thus simplifying management and defeating competition. **5** something managed for the benefit of another; something committed to one's care. **6** the obligation or responsibility imposed on a person in whom confidence or authority is placed. **7** the condition of one in whom trust has been placed; being relied on: *A guardian is in a position of trust.* **8** keeping; care: *The will was left in my trust.* **9** *Law.* **a** a confidence reposed in a person by making him or her nominal owner of property, which he or she is to hold, use, or dispose of for the benefit of another. **b** an estate, etc. committed to a trustee or trustees. **c** a trustee or group of trustees. **d** the right of a person to enjoy the use or profits of property held in trust for him or her. **10** (*adjl.*) managing for an owner: *a trust company.* **11** (*adjl.*) of or having to do with a trust or trusts; held in trust: *a trust fund, a trust account for one's children.* **12** confidence in the ability or intention of a person to pay at some future time for goods, etc.; business credit.
in trust, for the benefit of another: *The money was held in trust for her by her guardian.*
on trust, a on business credit; with payment later. **b** without evidence: *We took his assurances on trust.*
—*v.* **1** have faith; rely; be confident: *Trust in God.* **2** believe firmly in the honesty, truth, justice, or power of; have faith in: *He is a man to be trusted.* **3** rely on; depend on: *A forgetful man should not trust his memory.* **4** commit to the care of someone; leave without fear: *Can I trust the keys to her?* **5** confide or entrust something to the care of; invest: *Can I trust her with a large sum of money?* **6** hope; believe: *I trust you will soon feel better.* **7** give business credit to: *The butcher will trust us for the meat.* **8** allow to go somewhere or do something without misgiving or fear of consequences.
trust to, rely on; depend on: *Don't trust to luck.* ⟨ME < ON *traust*⟩ —**'trust•er,** *n.*

trust company a business concern formed primarily to act as a trustee but also often engaged in other financial activities normally performed by banks.

trus•tee [trʌ'sti] *n.* **1** a person responsible for the property or affairs of another person, of a company, or of an institution. **2** a person elected to a board or committee that is responsible for the schools in a district; school trustee. **3** a country made responsible for a trust territory.

trus•tee•ship [trʌ'stiʃɪp] *n.* **1** the position of trustee. **2 a** a commission from the United Nations to administer a TRUST TERRITORY. **b** administration by a country of a trust territory. **c** the status of a trust territory.

trust•ful ['trʌstfəl] *adj.* ready to confide; ready to have faith; believing. —**'trust•ful•ly,** *adv.* —**'trust•ful•ness,** *n.*

trust fund money, property, or other valuables held in trust.

trust•ing ['trʌstɪŋ] *adj., v.* —*adj.* that trusts; trustful: *She has a trusting nature.*
—*v.* ppr. of TRUST. —**'trust•ing•ly,** *adv.* —**trust•ing•ness,** *n.*

trust territory a territory placed under the administrative control of a particular country by the United Nations.

trust•wor•thy ['trʌst,wɜrði] *adj.* that can be trusted; honest: *The class chose a trustworthy boy for treasurer.* —**'trust,wor•thi•ly,** *adv.* —**'trust,wor•thi•ness,** *n.*
☛ *Syn.* See note at RELIABLE.

trust•y ['trʌsti] *adj.* **trust•i•er, trust•i•est;** *n., pl.* **trust•ies.**
—*adj.* that can be depended on; reliable: *a trusty servant.*
—*n.* **1** a prisoner who is given special privileges because of his or her good behaviour. **2** any trusted person. —**'trust•i•ly,** *adv.* —**'trust•i•ness,** *n.*

truth [truθ] *n., pl.* **truths** [truðz] *or* [truθs] **1** the quality or property of being in accord with fact or reality: *She doubted the truth of the story.* **2** something that is in accord with fact or reality: *to tell the whole truth. The truth is that I haven't seen him for over a year.* **3** a fixed or established principle, law, etc.; an accepted or proven doctrine or fact: *a basic scientific truth.* **4** true, exact, honest, sincere, or loyal quality or nature. **5** the true answer(s) to the ultimate questions of existence: *He is studying philosophy in search of truth. Is there a universal truth?*
in truth, truly; really; in fact. ⟨OE *trīewth, trēowth* < *trīewe, trēowe* true⟩

truth•ful ['truθfəl] *adj.* **1** telling the truth: *a truthful child.* **2** conforming to truth: *a truthful report.* —**'truth•ful•ly,** *adv.* —**'truth•ful•ness,** *n.*

truth serum *Informal.* any drug thought to make a person speak freely and openly when questioned.

truth table **1** *Logic.* a list indicating the truth or falsity of all the possible combinations of the variables of a proposition in symbolic logic. **2** *Computer technology.* a similar table for a computer circuit showing the relationships between input and output.

try [traɪ] *v.* **tried, try•ing;** *n., pl.* **tries.** —*v.* **1** make an attempt or effort: *He tried to open the window, but it was stuck. You'll never know till you try. She's going to try for her lifesaving certificate next week.* **2** attempt to do or accomplish: *It seems easy until you try it.* **3** find out the quality or qualities of by experimenting or sampling; test: *Try your skill at trap-shooting. I tried the candy but didn't like it.* **4** find out the effectiveness or usefulness of (an action, process, or thing): *Try opening the window to get the smoke out. Did you try the hardware store to see if they had any?* **5** attempt to open (a door, window, etc.): *Try the doors to see if they are locked.* **6** *Law.* examine (a case) in a court; determine the guilt or innocence of (a person) with respect to a particular accusation: *The woman was tried and found guilty. Judge Marshall tried the case.* **7** put to a severe test; strain: *His constant complaining tried her patience.* **8** subject to trials; afflict: *She was*

greatly tried by so many family tragedies. **9** *Archaic.* settle by test or investigation. **10** melt down or extract by melting (*often used with* **out**): *to try lard, to try out oil from blubber, to try ore.*
try on, put on (clothing, etc.) to test the fit, looks, etc.: *to try on a new suit.*
try one's hand at, attempt.
try out, a test thoroughly by using: *She took the car onto the highway to try it out.* **b** take a test to show fitness for a particular role or place: *to try out for the hockey team, to try out for a part in a play. Are you going to try out?*
—*n.* **1** an attempt; endeavour; effort. **2** a trial; test; experiment. **3** *Rugger.* **a** the act of touching the ball to the ground behind the opponent's goal line. **b** the score (three points) so gained. ⟨ME < OF *trier* cull; sift; origin uncertain⟩

☛ *Syn. v.* **1, 3. Try,** ATTEMPT, ENDEAVOUR= make an effort to or at. **Try** is the general word: *I tried to see him.* **Attempt** is used in more formal style or to suggest making a real effort, trying hard: *I attempted to obtain an interview.* **Endeavour,** fairly formal, suggests both great effort and great obstacles to be overcome: *The United Nations is endeavouring to establish peace.*

☛ *Usage.* **Try and** or **try to.** Although the formal idiom is **try to,** informal English has long used **try and.** Formal: *Let us try to get permission for the bazaar.* Informal: *Let's try and get permission for the bazaar.*

try•ing ['traɪɪŋ] *adj., v.* —*adj.* hard to endure; annoying: *It's been a trying day.*
—*v.* ppr. of TRY. —**'try•ing•ly,** *adj.*

try–on ['traɪ ,ɒn] *n. Informal.* the act or process of trying on an unfinished garment to check the fit, etc.; a fitting: *I have to go to the dressmaker's tomorrow for a try-on.*

try•out ['traɪ,ʌut] *n.* **1** a test made to determine fitness for a particular role or place: *The tryouts are tomorrow.* **2** a preview of a stage play to test the reaction of the audience.

tryp•a•no•some ['trɪpənə,soum] *n.* any of a genus (*Trypanosoma*) of parasitic protozoans that inhabit the blood of vertebrates as a result of a bite from a carrier insect and which cause sleeping sickness, Chagas' disease, and other serious illnesses. ⟨< NL < Gk. *trypanon* borer + *soma* body⟩

tryp•a•no•so•mi•a•sis [,trɪpənousə'maɪəsɪs] *n.* any disease caused by a trypanosome.

tryp•sin ['trɪpsən] *n.* an enzyme in the digestive juice secreted by the pancreas. Trypsin changes proteins into peptones. ⟨irregularly < Gk. *tripsis* rubbing < *tribein* rub⟩ —**tryp•tic,** *adj.*

tryp•sin•o•gen [trɪp'sɪnədʒən] *n.* the precursor of trypsin in the pancreas.

tryp•to•phan ['trɪptə,fæn] *n.* an essential amino acid produced by the action of trypsin on proteins during digestion. Also, **tryptophane.** ⟨< *trypt(ic)* + *-phane* resembling (< Gk. *phainein* appear)⟩

try•sail ['traɪ,seil] *or* ['trəisəl] *n.* a small fore-and-aft sail used in stormy weather on the foremast or mainmast.

try square an instrument for drawing right angles and testing the squareness of anything. See SQUARE for picture.

tryst [trɪst] *n., v.* —*n.* **1** an agreement or appointment to meet at a certain time and place, especially an agreement by lovers for a secret meeting. **2** a meeting held by appointment. **3** a place of meeting.
—*v.* make a tryst. ⟨ME < OF *triste,* in hunting, a place to which game used to be driven, probably < Scand.⟩

trysting place a place where a tryst is to be kept.

try•works ['traɪ,wɜrks] *n.pl.* a place where seal blubber is tried, or melted.

tsar [zar] *or* [tsɑr] See CZAR.

tsar•e•vitch ['zarə,vɪtʃ] *or* ['tsɑrə,vɪtʃ] See CZAREVITCH.

tsa•rev•na [zɑ'rɛvnə] *or* [tsɑ'rɛvnə] *n.* See CZAREVNA.

tsa•ri•na [zɑ'rinə] *or* [tsɑ'rinə] See CZARINA.

tsar•ism ['zɑrɪzəm] *or* ['tsɑrɪzəm] See CZARISM.

tsar•ist ['zɑrɪst] *or* ['tsɑrɪst] See CZARIST.

TSE or **T.S.E.** Toronto Stock Exchange.

tse•tse ['tsitsi] *or* ['tsɛtsi] *n.* TSETSE FLY. Also, **tzetze.**

tsetse disease a disease of cattle in Africa, transmitted by the tsetse fly.

tsetse fly any of several bloodsucking, two-winged flies (genus *Glossina*) of Africa that transmit various diseases, including sleeping sickness in human beings. ⟨*tsetse* < Bantu⟩

TSH thyroid-stimulating hormone.

Tshi•lu•ba [tʃi'lubə] *n.* the Bantu trade language of Zaire.

T–shirt ['ti ,ʃɜrt] *n.* a light, knit sport shirt or undershirt having no collar and, usually, short sleeves.

Tsim•shi•an ['tsɪmʃiən] *or* [tʃɪmʃiən] *n., pl.* **-an** or **-ans. 1** a First Nations people who originally lived in the lower Skeena and Nass Valleys in British Columbia. **2** a member of this people. **3** the language of this people.

tsk [ts]; *often conventionalized as* [tɪsk] *interj.* a sound made by sucking the tongue against the alveolar ridge and releasing it, used to express disapproval, disgust, contempt, or pity, often facetiously.

tsp. teaspoon(s).

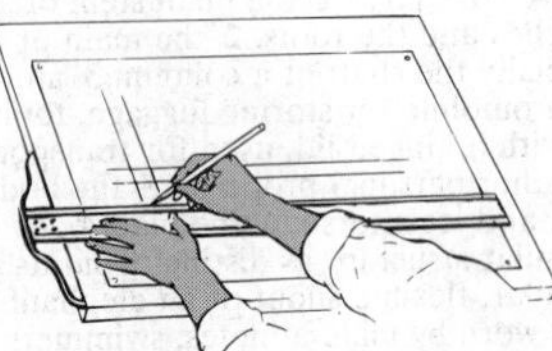
A T-square

T–square ['ti ,skwɛr] a T-shaped ruler used for making parallel lines, etc. The shorter arm of a T-square slides up and down the edge of the drawing board, which serves as a guide.

T–strap ['ti ,stræp] *n.* **1** a T-shaped strap on a shoe or sandal, consisting of a strap along the instep joined to a strap around the ankle. **2** a shoe having such a strap.

tsu•na•mi [tsʊ'nɑmi] *n.* a gigantic sea wave caused by an earthquake on the ocean floor, occurring especially in the Pacific Ocean and often causing great destruction in coastal regions. ⟨< Japanese < *tsu* port + *nami* wave⟩ —**tsu'nam•ic,** *adj.*

Tu. Tuesday.

tu•an or **Tu•an** ['tuɑn] *n.* sir; lord; master; a title of respect originating in SE Asia. ⟨< Malay⟩

Tua•reg ['twɑrɛg] *n.* **1** a member of any of certain Berber or Libyan nomadic peoples of the Sahara. **2** the Afro-Asiatic language of these peoples.

tu•a•ta•ra [,tuə'tɑrə] *n.* a large, amphibious reptile of New Zealand (*Sphenodon punctatus*), the only extant species of a group that flourished in the Mesozoic. It has a row of soft spines along the back and a third eye on the top of the head. ⟨< Maori < *tua* back + *tara* spine⟩

tub [tʌb] *n., v.* **tubbed, tub•bing.** —*n.* **1** bathtub. **2** washtub. **3** *Informal.* bath: *He takes a cold tub every morning.* **4** a usually round, flat-bottomed, open container, especially such a container made of wooden staves bound by hoops, used for holding butter, lard, etc. **5** as much as a tub can hold. **6** *Informal.* a clumsy, slow-moving boat or ship. **7** *Slang.* a fat person. **8** a container, usually wheeled, for carrying ore in a mine.
—*v.* wash or bathe in a tub. ⟨Cf. MDu. or MLG *tubbe*⟩
—**'tub•ba•ble,** *adj.*

A tuba

tu•ba ['tjubə] *or* ['tubə] *n.* **1** a large, brass musical wind instrument resembling a trumpet, having valves to vary the pitch. It has the lowest range of the brasses. **2** an organ stop that produces tubalike tones. ⟨< L *tuba* war trumpet⟩

tub•al ['tjubəl] *or* ['tubəl] *adj.* **1** of or having to do with a tube. **2** of, having to do with, or developing in a Fallopian tube: *a tubal ligation, a tubal pregnancy.*

tub•ate ['tjubeit] *or* ['tubeit] *adj.* forming or possessing a tube or tubes; tubular.

tub•bing ['tʌbɪŋ] *n., v.* —*n.* a bath; washing.
—*v.* ppr. of TUB.

tub•by [ˈtʌbi] *adj.* **-bi•er, -bi•est. 1** like a tub in shape. **2** short and fat or pudgy. **3** of a violin, etc., having a dull, wooden sound; not having proper resonance. **—ˈtub•bi•ness,** *n.*

tub chair a usually upholstered armchair with a rounded back that extends forward on either side to form the arms.

tube [tjub] *or* [tub] *n., v.* **tubed, tub•ing.** *—n.* **1** a long, hollow, rigid or flexible cylinder, especially one used to hold or carry liquids or gases: *The mercury or alcohol of a thermometer is held in a glass tube. A plastic tube runs from the pump to the filter of our fish tank.* **2** a small cylinder of thin, flexible metal or plastic with a cap that screws onto the open end, used for holding paste substances, such as toothpaste or paint, ready for use. **3** a channel in an animal or plant body: *the bronchial tubes.* **4** *Botany.* the lower united portion of a gamopetalous corolla or a gamosepalous calyx. **5** a separate, inflatable casing of rubber that fits inside the outer casing of a tire; inner tube. **6** a pipe or tunnel through which something travels: *The subway runs under the city in a tube.* **7** *Brit. Informal.* subway. **8** ELECTRON TUBE. **9** the picture tube of a television set. **10** *Slang.* television: *What's on the tube tonight?*
(go) **down the tube(s),** *Informal.* (be) destroyed, vanished, failed, or defeated.
—v. **1** furnish or fit with a tube or tubes; insert a tube in. **2** pass through or enclose in a tube. **3** make tubular. ⟨< L *tubus*⟩ **—ˈtube•less,** *adj.* **—ˈtube,like,** *adj.*

tube•less tire [ˈtjublɪs] *or* [ˈtublɪs] a type of tire in which an inner lining is bonded to the outer casing, making a separate inner tube unnecessary.

tube pan a deep, circular cake pan with a vertical hollow tube in the middle.

tu•ber [ˈtjubər] *or* [ˈtubər] *n.* **1** a thick, fleshy underground stem, as of the potato, that is an organ of food storage and from which new plants grow. **2** a thickened root, as of the dahlia, resembling a tuber. **3** a rounded swelling or projection in an animal body. ⟨< L *tuber* lump⟩

tu•ber•cle [ˈtjubərkəl] *or* [ˈtubərkəl] *n.* **1** a small, rounded swelling or knob on an animal or plant. The roots of some plants, such as legumes, have tubercles. In vertebrates, there is a tubercle near the end of each rib where it connects with the backbone. **2** a small, hard, abnormal lump in an organ or the skin, especially such a lump in the lungs that is characteristic of tuberculosis. ⟨< L *tuberculum*, dim. of *tuber* lump⟩

tubercle bacillus the bacterium (*Mycobacterium tuberculosis*) that causes tuberculosis.

tu•ber•cu•lar [tjəˈbɜrkjələr] *or* [təˈbɜrkjələr] *adj., n.* *—adj.* **1** tuberculous. **2** of, having to do with, or having tubercles. Also (def. 2), **tuberculate.**
—n. a person having tuberculosis. **—tuˈber•cu•lar•ly,** *adv.*

tu•ber•cu•la•tion [tjə,bɜrkjəˈleiʃən] *or* [tə,bɜrkjəˈleiʃən] *n.* the formation of tubercles.

tu•ber•cu•lin [tjəˈbɜrkjəlɪn] *or* [təˈbɜrkjəlɪn] *n.* a sterile liquid prepared from a culture of the bacteria that cause tuberculosis, used in the diagnosis of the disease.

tu•ber•cu•loid [tjəˈbɜrkjə,lɔɪd] *or* [təˈbɜrkjə,lɔɪd] *adj.* that resembles a tubercle or tuberculosis.

tu•ber•cu•lo•sis [tjə,bɜrkjəˈlousɪs] *or* [tə,bɜrkjəˈlousɪs] *n.* an infectious disease caused by the tubercle bacillus, affecting human beings and some other mammals, and characterized by the formation of tubercles in various tissues of the body. Tuberculosis in human beings usually affects the lungs. ⟨< NL *tuberculosis* < L *tuberculum.* See TUBERCLE.⟩

tu•ber•cu•lous [tjəˈbɜrkjələs] *or* [təˈbɜrkjələs] *adj.* **1** of, having to do with, or affected with tuberculosis: *a tuberculous patient.* **2** caused by the tubercle bacillus: *tuberculous ulcers in the lungs, a tuberculous infection.*

tube•rose¹ [ˈtjub,rouz] *or* [ˈtub,rouz] *n.* a tropical plant (*Polianthes tuberosa*) of the agave family, having sword-shaped leaves and spikes of very fragrant, white, funnel-shaped flowers. The tuberose grows from a bulb. ⟨< L *tuberosa*, fem. of *tuberosus* tuberous < *tuber* lump; interpreted as if from *tube + rose*⟩

tu•be•rose² [ˈtjubə,rous] *or* [ˈtubə,rous] *adj.* tuberous.

tu•ber•os•i•ty [,tjubəˈrɒsəti] *or* [,tubəˈrɒsəti] *n., pl.* **-ties. 1** the quality or condition of being tuberous. **2** a rounded knob or swelling, especially on a bone where muscles or ligaments are attached.

tu•ber•ous [ˈtjubərəs] *or* [ˈtubərəs] *adj.* **1** of, like, or having a tuber or tubers: *tuberous root.* **2** of, having, or covered with rounded knobs or swellings. ⟨< L *tuberosus* < *tuber* lump⟩

tube sock a sport sock not having a contoured heel but made in the shape of a straight stretchable tube open at one end.

tube top a tight, stretchy top for women consisting of a tube covering only the chest and upper back.

tu•bi•fex [ˈtjubɪ,fɛks] *or* [ˈtubɪ,fɛks] *n.* any of a genus (*Tubifex*) of red annelid worms found in the mud at the bottom of lakes and rivers, used as a food for aquarium fish.

tub•ing [ˈtjubɪŋ] *or* [ˈtubɪŋ] *n., v.* *—n.* **1** material in the form of a tube: *rubber tubing.* **2** a piece of tube. **3** a system of tubes.
—v. ppr. of TUBE.

tub•ist [ˈtjubɪst] *or* [ˈtubɪst] *n.* one who plays the tuba, especially a skilled player.

tub thumper *Informal.* **1** a noisy preacher or speaker who thumps the table, etc.; a loud, emotional orator. **2** a press agent or spokesperson.

tub thumping *Informal.* **1** the actions of a tub thumper. **2** ballyhoo; exaggerated publicity.

tu•bu•lar [ˈtjubjələr] *or* [ˈtubjələr] *adj.* **1** shaped like a tube; cylindrical and hollow: *The tuberose has tubular flowers.* **2** made of or provided with tube-shaped pieces: *tubular furniture.* **3** of or having to do with a tube or tubes. ⟨< L *tubulus*, dim. of *tubus* tube, pipe⟩ **—,tu•buˈlar•i•ty** [-ˈlɛrəti], *n.* **—ˈtu•bu•lar•ly,** *adv.*

tu•bu•late *adj.* [ˈtjubjəlɪt] *or* [ˈtjubjə,leit], [ˈtubjəlɪt] *or* [ˈtubjə,leit]; *v.* [ˈtjubjə,leit] *or* [ˈtubjə,leit] *adj., v.* **-lat•ed, -lat•ing.** *—adj.* tubular.
—v. **1** form into a tube. **2** furnish with a tube. **—,tu•buˈla•tion,** *n.*

tu•bule [ˈtjubjul] *or* [ˈtubjul] *n.* a very small tube, especially a narrow channel in an animal or plant. ⟨< F < L *tubulus*, dim. of *tubus* pipe⟩

tu•bu•li•flo•rous [,tjubjəlɪˈflɔrəs] *or* [,tubjəlɪˈflɔrəs] *adj.* having flowers with tubular corollas. ⟨< LL *tubulus* tubule + *-florus* flowering < *flos, floris* flower⟩

tu•bu•lous [ˈtjubjələs] *or* [ˈtubjələs] *adj.* **1** tubular. **2** having flowers in the shape of small tubes.

tuck [tʌk] *v., n.* *—v.* **1** put (something) into a narrow place or space or a convenient, remote, or unobtrusive spot, where it is held tightly or concealed: *a village tucked away in the mountains. She tucked the newspaper under her arm. He tucked the letter away in an inside pocket.* **2** push the loose edge or end of (something) tightly into place, under or inside something else: *Tuck your shirt in. She tucked a serviette under her chin.* **3** cover snugly by tucking in the bedclothes (*used with* **in**): *He always came up to tuck the children in.* **4** draw close together into a fold or folds; make shorter by gathering or folding together (*used with* **up**): *She tucked up her long skirt and waded into the lake.* **5** sew a tuck or tucks (in) for decoration or to shorten or control fullness: *a dress with a tucked bodice.* **6** fold (the legs) back or up when sitting or lying: *She sat with her legs tucked under her.* **7** eat heartily (*used with* **away**): *He tucked away a big meal.* **8** pull in or back (*used with* **in**): *to tuck in one's stomach.*
tuck in, eat with gusto.
tuck into, eat (something) with gusto.
—n. **1** a narrow, straight fold sewn into a garment, etc. for decoration, to shorten, or to control fullness. **2** *Diving, etc.* a position in which the knees are drawn up to the body. **3** *Informal.* food; eatables, especially candy. **4** the part of the hull of a ship or boat under the stern where the planks or plates meet. ⟨ME *tuke(n)* stretch < OE *tūcian* torment⟩

tuck•a•hoe [ˈtʌkə,hou] *n.* a large, edible fungus (*Poria cocos*) sometimes found on the roots of trees. ⟨< Algonquian⟩

tuck•er¹ [ˈtʌkər] *n.* **1** formerly, a piece of lace, embroidered fabric, etc. worn in or on the bodice of a woman's dress in the 17th and 18th centuries. **2** a person or thing that makes tucks, especially an attachment or device on a sewing machine for making tucks. **3** See BIB AND TUCKER. ⟨< *tuck*⟩

tuck•er² [ˈtʌkər] *v. Informal.* tire; weary; exhaust (*usually used with* **out**): *We were all tuckered out after four hours of wandering around the zoo.* ⟨CF. E dial. *tucked up* worn out, exhausted⟩

tuck–in [ˈtʌk ,ɪn] *n. Informal.* a large, satisfying meal: *After our long hike, we enjoyed a good tuck-in.*

tuck shop a small shop, especially one near or connected with a school, summer camp, etc., in which pastries, drinks, and candies are sold.

–tude *suffix.* the state, quality, or condition of being, as in *aptitude, certitude.* ⟨< F < L *-tudo, -tudinis*⟩

Tu•dor [ˈtjudər] *or* [ˈtudər] *adj., n.* *—adj.* **1** of or having to do with the royal family that ruled England from 1485 to 1603. **2** designating, having to do with, or characteristic of the time of the Tudors, especially of the style of architecture that was

common then. Tudor architecture is characterized by shallow, pointed or slightly rounded arches, half-timbered construction, etc.
—*n.* a member of the Tudor family. Elizabeth I was the last Tudor.

Tues. Tuesday.

Tues•day ['tjuz,dei] *or* ['tuz,dei], ['tjuzdi] *or* ['tuzdi] *n.* the third day of the week, following Monday. ⟨OE *tīwesdæg* day of Tiw (god of war); translation of LL *Martis dies* day of Mars⟩

Tues•days ['tjuz,deiz] *or* ['tuz,deiz], ['tjuzdiz] *or* ['tuzdiz] *adv.* on Tuesday, as a habit; every Tuesday.

tu•fa ['tjufə] *or* ['tufə] *n.* **1** a soft, porous form of limestone produced as a deposit from a spring or stream rich in lime. **2** obsolete form of TUFF. ⟨< Ital. *tufo* < L *tofus.* Doublet of TUFF.⟩ **—tu'fa•ceous** [-'feiʃəs], *adj.*

tuff [tʌf] *n.* a soft, porous rock formed from volcanic ash or dust thrown out by an erupting volcano. Tuff can vary greatly in texture and composition. ⟨< F *tuf* < Ital. *tufo* tufa < L *tofus.* Doublet of TUFA.⟩ **—tuff'a•ceous** [tʌ'feiʃəs], *adj.*

tuf•fet ['tʌfɪt] *n.* **1** a tuft of grass. **2** a low seat or stool.

tuft [tʌft] *n., v.* —*n.* **1** a bunch of feathers, grass, threads, etc. growing from one place or held together at one end: *A goat has a tuft of hair on its chin.* **2** a bunch of short, fluffy, often decorative threads or lengths of yarn held together at one end, especially the ends of thread or yarn sewn through a comforter, mattress, cushion, etc. to keep the padding in place.
—*v.* **1** provide or decorate with a tuft or tufts. **2** secure the padding of (a comforter, etc.) by sewing through it at intervals. **3** grow in or form into tufts. ⟨ME, ? < OF *touffe* < LL *tufa* helmet crest⟩ **—'tuft•y,** *adj.*

tuft•ed ['tʌftɪd] *adj., v.* —*adj.* **1** having or furnished with a tuft or tufts: *a tufted quilt.* **2** of a bird, having a tuft of feathers on the head; crested. **3** formed into a tuft or tufts.
—*v.* pt. and pp. of TUFT.

tug [tʌg] *v.* **tugged, tug•ging;** *n.* —*v.* **1** pull with force or effort; pull hard: *I tugged the rope and it came loose. The child tugged at his mother's hand.* **2** move by pulling hard: *We tugged the boat up onto the sand.* **3** tow by a tugboat.
—*n.* **1** a hard pull. **2** a hard strain, struggle, effort, or contest. **3** tugboat. **4** a rope, chain, or strap used for pulling, especially the harness trace. See HARNESS for picture. ⟨related to *tow*⟩
☛ *Syn. v.* **1.** See note at PULL.

tug•boat ['tʌg,bout] *n.* a small, powerful boat used to tow or push ships or boats.

tug–of–war ['tʌg əv 'wɔr] *n.* **1** a contest between two teams pulling at the ends of a rope, each trying to drag the other over a line marked between them. **2** any hard struggle for power.

tu•grik ['tugrɪk] *n.* the basic unit of money in Mongolia, divided into 100 mongos. See table of money in the Appendix. ⟨< Mongolian⟩

tu•i ['tui] *n.* a bird, a bluish black New Zealand honey-eater (*Prosthemadera novaeseelandia*) having a long bill and a patch of white feathers on the side of the throat. It can mimic human speech and is sometimes tamed as a pet. Also called **parson bird.** ⟨< Maori *tui*⟩

tu•i•tion [tju'ɪʃən] *or* [tu'ɪʃən] *n.* **1** the price of or money paid for instruction: *Her yearly tuition is $5000.* **2** teaching; instruction: *The child made excellent progress under the teacher's capable tuition.* ⟨< L *tuitio, -onis* protection < *tueri* watch over⟩

tu•i•tion•al [tju'ɪʃənəl] *or* [tu'ɪʃənəl] *adj.* of or having to do with tuition.

tuk•tu ['tʌktu] *n. Cdn.* **1** caribou. **2** caribou or reindeer furs. Also, **tuktoo.** ⟨< Inuktitut⟩

tu•la•di ['tulə,di] *Cdn.* See TOULADI. ⟨< Cdn.F *touladi* < Algonquian (Micmac)⟩

tu•la•re•mi•a [,tjulə'rimiə] *or* [,tulə'rimiə] *n.* an acute infectious bacterial disease of rabbits and other rodents, sometimes transmitted to human beings through insect bites or contact with diseased animals. Also, **tularaemia.** ⟨< NL *tularemia* < *(bacterium) tular(ense),* the organism that causes the disease (< *Tulare,* a county in California) + *-emia* < Gk. *haima* blood⟩ **—,tu•la're•mic,** *adj.*

tu•le ['tuli] *n.* either of two large bulrushes (*Scirpus acutus* or *S. lacustris*) having long, round, spiky leaves in clumps and a dark brown, tubular flower head, found in marshy areas of SW Canada and the U.S. The leaves of *S. acutus* are used to make mats and chair seats.
out in the tules, *Cdn., esp. West. Slang.* in the country, away from the urban centres.

tu•lip ['tjulɪp] *or* ['tulɪp] *n.* **1** any of a genus (*Tulipa*) of plants belonging to the lily family that grow from bulbs and have long, pointed leaves and large, cup-shaped, usually single flowers. There are many varieties of cultivated tulips. **2** the flower or bulb of a tulip. ⟨< obs. Du. *tulipa* < F < Turkish *tülbend* < Persian *dulband* turban. Doublet of TURBAN.⟩

tulip tree a large North American hardwood tree (*Liriodendron tulipifera*) of the magnolia family having broad, lobed leaves and large, cup-shaped, greenish yellow flowers that appear after the leaves. In Canada, this tree is native to extreme southern Ontario. Also, **tulip poplar.**

tu•lip•wood ['tjulɪp,wʊd] *or* ['tulɪp,wʊd] *n.* **1** the wood of the tulip tree, used for cabinetwork. **2** any striped or variegated wood of other trees. **3** any of the trees having this type of wood.

tulle [tul] *n.* a fine, stiff, machine-made net, usually of silk or rayon, used especially for bridal veils and ballet costumes. ⟨< *Tulle,* a city in SW France⟩
☛ *Hom.* TOOL.

tul•li•bee ['tulə,bi] *n., pl.* **-bee** or **-bees.** *Cdn.* **1** any of several ciscoes (genus *Coregonus*) found throughout most Canadian lakes from Québec westward, particularly valued as a food fish. **2** a species of whitefish (*Leucicthys tullibee*). ⟨< Cdn.F *toulibi* < Algonquian. Compare Cree *otonabi*⟩

tum•ble ['tʌmbəl] *v.* **-bled, -bling;** *n.* —*v.* **1** fall, especially helplessly, headlong, or end over end: *The child tumbled down the stairs.* **2 a** throw over or down; cause to fall: *The earthquake tumbled several buildings.* **b** collapse; fall in ruins: *Several buildings tumbled during the earthquake.* **3** roll or toss about: *Her apartment had been ransacked and all her things had been tumbled about the room. The clothes were tumbling in the dryer.* **4** move or go in a headlong or awkward way: *He tumbled out of bed to answer the phone. The excited children tumbled through the door.* **5** perform leaps, springs, somersaults, etc.; engage in the sport of tumbling. **6** decline rapidly in amount, power, popularity, etc.: *The stock market tumbled. The Conservatives are tumbling in the polls.* **7** *Informal.* understand; catch on (*used with* **to**): *She tumbled to the trick right away.* **8** mix, cleanse, or polish in a tumbling box, or TUMBLER (def. 8).
—*n.* **1** a fall: *The tumble hurt him badly. He took a tumble on the ice.* **2** a state of confusion or disorder: *Her room was all in a tumble.* **3** a confused or disordered heap: *a tumble of clothes on the floor.* **4** a gymnastic figure, as a somersault, handspring, etc. ⟨ME, ult. < OE *tumbian* dance about⟩

tum•ble•bug ['tʌmbəl,bʌg] *n.* DUNG BEETLE (def. 1), especially any of numerous species that roll dung into balls in which they lay their eggs. The SCARAB (def. 1) is a tumblebug.

tum•ble•down ['tʌmbəl,daʊn] *adj.* ready to fall down; dilapidated.

tum•bler ['tʌmblər] *n.* **1** a person who performs leaps, springs, etc.; acrobat. **2** a glass for drinking out of, made without a handle or a foot or stem, and having a heavy, flat bottom. Tumblers originally had rounded or pointed bottoms so that they could not be set down until empty. **3** the amount a glass will hold: *to drink a tumbler of water.* **4** the part in a lock that must be moved from a certain position in order to release the bolt. **5** the part of a gunlock that forces the hammer forward when the trigger is pulled. **6** a kind of domestic pigeon that does backward somersaults while flying. **7** a toy consisting of a figure with a rounded, weighted bottom that will rock when touched but will always right itself. **8** a revolving device that tumbles things for a particular purpose, such as a box or drum for polishing semiprecious stones or the drum in a clothes dryer. **9** a projecting part on a revolving or rocking shaft that moves another part. **10** a part in an automobile transmission that moves a gear into place.

tum•ble•weed ['tʌmbəl,wid] *n.* any of various plants, such as *Amaranthus graecizans* or *A. albas,* that after drying up in the fall break off from their roots and are blown about by the wind. Russian thistle is a tumbleweed.

tum•bling ['tʌmblɪŋ] *n., v.* —*n.* the sport or practice of performing leaps, somersaults, and other gymnastic feats without the use of any apparatus.
—*v.* ppr. of TUMBLE.

tumbling box or **barrel** TUMBLER (def. 8).

tum•brel or **tum•bril** ['tʌmbrəl] *n.* **1** a farmer's cart that can be tipped for emptying. **2** formerly, **a** an open cart used in the French Revolution to carry prisoners to the guillotine. **b** a two-wheeled covered cart for carrying ammunition and military tools. ⟨probably < OF *tomberel* cart < *tomber* fall < Gmc.⟩

tu•me•fa•cient [ˌtjuməˈfeiʃənt] *or* [ˌtuməˈfeiʃənt] *adj.* causing to swell; that tumefies or causes to swell.

tu•me•fac•tion [ˌtjuməˈfækʃən] *or* [ˌtuməˈfækʃən] *n.* **1** the process of tumefying or swelling, or the condition of being swollen. **2** a swollen part.

tu•me•fy [ˈtjuməˌfaɪ] *or* [ˈtuməˌfaɪ] *v.* **-fied, -fy•ing.** swell or cause to swell. ⟨< L *tumefacere* < *tumere* swell + *facere* make⟩

tu•mes•cence [tjuˈmɛsəns] *or* [tuˈmɛsəns] *n.* **1** the quality or state of being swollen. **2** an instance of swelling; a swollen part.

tu•mes•cent [tjuˈmɛsənt] *or* [tuˈmɛsənt] *adj.* **1** becoming swollen; beginning to swell. **2** somewhat swollen. ⟨< L *tumescens, -entis*, ult. < *tumere* swell⟩

tu•mid [ˈtjumɪd] *or* [ˈtumɪd] *adj.* **1** swollen. **2** of style, swollen with big words; bombastic. ⟨< L *tumidus* < *tumere* swell⟩ **—'tu•mid•ly,** *adv.* **—tu'mid•i•ty** or **'tu•mid•ness,** *n.*

tum•my [ˈtʌmi] *n., pl.* **-mies.** *Informal.* stomach (*a child's word*).

tu•mor•ous [ˈtjumərəs] *or* [ˈtumərəs] *adj.* **1** of or having to do with a tumour or tumours. **2** having a tumour or tumours.

tu•mour or **tu•mor** [ˈtjumər] *or* [ˈtumər] *n.* **1** an abnormal, separate mass of tissue in any part of the body, that develops from existing tissue, but has no physiological function. Tumours can be either benign (doing little or no harm) or malignant (cancerous). **2** any abnormal swelling. ⟨< L *tumour* < *tumere* swell⟩

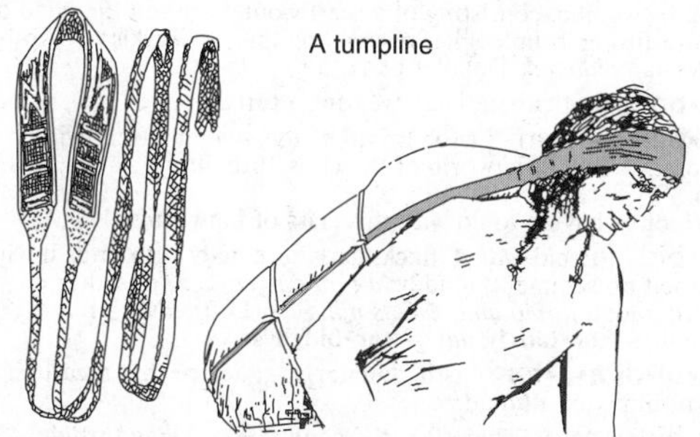
A tumpline

tump•line [ˈtʌmpˌlaɪn] *n.* a kind of harness for carrying or pulling heavy loads, consisting of a long strap with a broad middle part that is placed around the forehead or chest, the two ends being attached to the pack or load. Also, **tump.** ⟨< Algonquian *tump* + E *line.* Cf. METUMP.⟩

tu•mu•lose [ˈtjumjəˌlous] *or* [ˈtumjəˌlous] *adj.* characterized by many tumuli. Also, **tumulous.**

tu•mult [ˈtjumʌlt] *or* [ˈtumʌlt] *n.* **1** a violent disturbance or disorder; uproar: *We heard the tumult of the storm. The shout of "Fire!" caused a tumult in the theatre.* **2** a great disturbance of mind or feeling; confusion and excitement: *His mind was in a tumult.* ⟨< L *tumultus*⟩

tu•mul•tu•ous [tjuˈmʌltʃuəs] *or* [tuˈmʌltʃuəs] *adj.* **1** characterized by tumult; very noisy or disorderly. **2** greatly disturbed. **3** rough; stormy: *Tumultuous waves beat upon the rocks.* **—tu'mul•tu•ous•ly,** *adv.* **—tu'mul•tu•ous•ness,** *n.*

tu•mu•lus [ˈtjumjələs] *or* [ˈtumjələs] *n., pl.* **-lus•es, -li** [-ˌlaɪ] *or* [-ˌli]. a mound of earth, especially over a grave. ⟨< L⟩ **—'tu•mu•lar,** *adj.*

tun [tʌn] *n., v.* **tunned, tun•ning,** *—n.* **1** a large cask for holding liquids, especially wine, beer, or ale. **2** a unit formerly used for measuring the volume of liquids, equal to 252 imperial gallons (about 954 L).
—v. put or keep in a tun. ⟨OE *tunne* from ML *tunna*, probably < Gaulish base⟩
☛ *Hom.* TON, TONNE.

tu•na¹ [ˈtjunə] *or* [ˈtunə] *n.* **1** any of various large, spiny-finned food and game fishes (of genus *Thunnus* and other genera in family Scombridae) found in warm seas throughout the world, having a rounded, tapering body and a crescent-shaped tail. The largest and commercially most important tuna is the **bluefin tuna,** (*Thunnus thunnus*) which may weigh as much as 500 kg. **2** the flesh of a tuna, especially when canned for use as food. ⟨< Am.Sp. *tuna*, ult. < L *thunnus.* See TUNNY.⟩

tu•na² [ˈtjunə] *or* [ˈtunə] *n.* **1** any of various prickly pear cactuses, especially one (*Opuntia tuna*) of tropical America cultivated for its edible fruit. **2** the fruit of a tuna. ⟨< Sp. < Haitian⟩

tun•a•ble or **tune•a•ble** [ˈtjunəbəl] *or* [ˈtunəbəl] *adj.* **1** capable of being tuned. **2** *Archaic.* harmonious; tuneful. **—'tun•a•bly** or **'tune•a•bly,** *adj.*

tuna fish **1** the flesh of a tuna, especially when canned for use as food. **2** (*adjl.*) **tuna-fish,** made with tuna fish: *a tuna-fish casserole.*

tun•dra [ˈtʌndrə] *n.* a vast, level, treeless plain in the arctic regions. The subsoil of the tundra remains frozen all year round. ⟨< Russian⟩

tune [tjun] *or* [tun] *n., v.* **tuned, tun•ing.** *—n.* **1 a** a succession of musical tones in a particular rhythm, forming a unit; melody: *He was humming a tune to himself as he worked.* **b** a particular musical setting of a poem, hymn, psalm, etc., often arranged in four-part harmony and usually having a distinctive name independent of which lyrics are set to it: *Look it up in the alphabetical index of tunes. "Which tune do you sing it to?" "Diadem."* **2** the proper pitch: *She can't sing in tune. The piano is out of tune.* **3** a mood or manner; attitude: *He was very cocky at first, but soon changed his tune.* **4** agreement; harmonious relation: *He's happier now that he's in tune with his surroundings again. She won't be elected because she's out of tune with the times.*
call the tune, have control; be in a position to dictate what will be done: *He talks big to the press, but it is his partner who calls the tune.*
sing a different tune, talk or behave differently: *She's singing a different tune since she lost her job.*
to the tune of, *Informal.* to the amount or sum of, especially when it is considered excessive: *He received a bill to the tune of $800 for car repairs.*
—v. **1** adjust to the proper pitch; put in tune: *to tune a piano or a violin.* **2** of an orchestra, adjust instruments to the proper pitch (*used with* **up**): *The orchestra was already tuning up when we arrived.* **3** adjust; adapt; make sensitive or sympathetic: *You must tune your message to the mood of the audience.* **4** adjust (a motor, etc.) for precise performance (*often used with* **up**). **5 a** adjust (a radio or television set) to receive a particular frequency of signals (*often used with* **in**): *He tuned his radio to the news from Moscow. Tune in tomorrow for another episode.* **b** adjust a radio or television set to receive (a particular frequency of signals) (*used with* **in**): *We tuned in the new FM station.*
tune in, *Informal.* become or make aware: *It took the new executive a while to tune in to the company's innovative philosophy. The experience quickly tuned her in to her family's needs.*
tune out, a adjust a radio or television set to cut out (interference or static). **b** *Slang.* turn one's mind away from; ignore: *Our boss tunes out complaints she doesn't want to hear.* ⟨var. of *tone*⟩

tune•ful [ˈtjunfəl] *or* [ˈtunfəl] *adj.* musical; melodious: *That canary has a tuneful song.* **—'tune•ful•ly,** *adv.* **—'tune•ful•ness,** *n.*

tune•less [ˈtjunlɪs] *or* [ˈtunlɪs] *adj.* **1** not tuneful; not having a pleasing or recognizable tune: *His absent-minded tuneless humming began to get on their nerves.* **2** silent; making no music: *Her guitar, now tuneless, gathered dust in a corner.* **—'tune•less•ly,** *adv.* **—'tune•less•ness,** *n.*

tun•er [ˈtjunər] *or* [ˈtunər] *n.* **1** a person whose work is tuning musical instruments, especially pianos. **2** any person who or thing that tunes. **3** the part of a radio or television receiver that detects broadcast signals and feeds them to other circuits, especially a separate unit of a home entertainment system.

tune•smith [ˈtjunˌsmɪθ] *or* [ˈtunˌsmɪθ] *n. Informal.* songwriter, especially one who composes popular music.

tune–up [ˈtjun ˌʌp] *or* [ˈtun ˌʌp] *n.* adjustment of a motor, etc. to the proper running condition: *He took his car in for an engine tune-up.*

tung oil [tʌŋ] an oil obtained from the seeds of the TUNG TREE, widely used as a drying oil in paints and varnishes, as a waterproofing agent, etc.

tung•sten [ˈtʌŋstən] *n.* a hard, heavy, steel-grey metallic element with a very high melting point, used especially for the filaments of electric light bulbs and in making steel alloys; wolfram. *Symbol*: W; *at.no.* 74; *at.mass* 183.85. ⟨< Swedish *tungsten* < *tung* heavy + *sten* stone⟩

tungsten lamp an incandescent electric lamp of very low wattage, in which the filament is made of tungsten.

tung•stic [ˈtʌŋstɪk] *adj.* of or containing tungsten, especially with a valence of five or six.

tung•stite [ˈtʌŋstait] *n.* a yellowish mineral, tungstic trioxide, occuring naturally with tungsten ores. *Formula*: WO_3

tung tree a tree (*Aleurites fordii*) of the spurge family native to China but now cultivated in other warm regions, having large, heart-shaped leaves and white flowers. The seeds of the tung tree yield oil.

tu•nic ['tjunɪk] *or* ['tunɪk] *n.* **1** a loose garment with or without sleeves, usually reaching to the knees, worn by the ancient Greeks and Romans. **2** a girls' or women's garment somewhat like a dress but shorter, worn over a skirt or long pants: *Sleeveless tunics, sometimes open at the sides, are often worn over blouses and skirts, etc.* **3** a hip-length overblouse. **4** a short, close-fitting coat or jacket worn as part of the uniform by soldiers, police officers, etc. **5** *Anatomy, Zoology, Botany.* a covering or enclosing membrane. ⟨< L *tunica*, ult. < Semitic⟩

tu•ni•ca ['tjunɪkə] *or* ['tunɪkə] *n., pl.* **-cae** [-ˌki], [-ˌkaɪ], *or* [-ˌsi]. TUNIC (def. 5).

tu•ni•cate ['tjunəkɪt] *or* ['tjunəˌkeit], ['tunəkɪt] *or* ['tunəˌkeit] *n., adj.* —*n.* any of a subphylum (Tunicata, also called Urochordata) of marine chordate animals that includes the sea squirts, having in the adult stage a sacklike body with a tough, leathery outer covering (a tunic).
—*adj.* **1** of, having to do with, or being a tunicate. **2** having or made up of concentric layers of tissue, as an onion bulb. ⟨< L *tunicatus*, pp. of *tunicare* clothe with a tunic < *tunica.* See TUNIC.⟩

tuning fork a small, two-pronged steel instrument that sounds a fixed tone when struck, used to determine a standard pitch for singing or for tuning a musical instrument.

Tu•ni•sia [tjʊ'niʒə] *or* [tu'niʒə]; *also,* [-'niʃə], [-'niziə], [-'nisiə], *or* [-'nɪziə] *n.* a country in N Africa.

Tu•ni•sian [tju'niʒən] *or* [tu'niʒən]; *also,* [-'niʃən], [-'niziən], [-'nisiən], *or* [-'nɪziən] *n., adj.* —*n.* a native or inhabitant of Tunisia, or its capital city, Tunis.
—*adj.* of or having to do with Tunisia, Tunis, or the Tunisians.

tun•nel ['tʌnəl] *n., v.* **-nelled** or **-neled, -nel•ling** or **-nel•ing.**
—*n.* **1** an artificial underground passage under a river, road, building, etc. or through a hill or mountain, for a railway, road, or walkway: *The railway passes through several tunnels on its way through the Rockies. There is a tunnel connecting the university residences with the food-services building.* **2** a nearly horizontal passageway in a mine (often used loosely for any drift, level, etc.). **3** any channel or conduit. **4** an animal's burrow.
—*v.* **1** make a tunnel: *The workers are tunnelling under the river.* **2** make a tunnel through or under: *to tunnel a hill or river.* **3** make (one's way or a passage) by tunnelling: *She tunnelled a narrow passage through the snowdrift. They tunnelled their way under the prison wall.* ⟨ME < OF *tonel* cask < *tonne* tun < Celtic⟩ **—'tun•nel•ler** or **'tun•nel•er,** *n.*

tunnel effect *Physics.* a phenomenon in which an elementary particle passes through a potential insurmountable barrier by the operation of certain principles of wave mechanics. Such particles are said to be 'tunnelling'. In a **tunnel diode** electrons tunnel across a narrow and heavily doped positive-negative junction.

tunnel vision **1** a very narrow field of vision; a field of vision that is restricted at the sides. **2** narrow-mindedness.

tun•ny ['tʌni] *n., pl.* **-nies** or **-ny.** TUNA[1]. ⟨< F *thon* < Provençal < L *thunnus, thynnus* < Gk. *thynnos*⟩

tu•pek ['tupək] *Cdn.* See TUPIK.

tu•pe•lo ['tjupəˌlou] *or* ['tupəˌlou] *n.* **1** any of several tall North American trees of the genus *Nyssa,* belonging to the sourgum family, having ovate leaves, clusters of tiny flowers and purple berrylike fruit, found in swampy regions of the eastern, southern, and southwestern U.S. **2** the soft, fine-textured wood of such trees. ⟨< Creek *ito* tree + *opilwa* swamp⟩

Tu•pi [tu'pi] *n., pl.* **-pis** or **-pi.** **1** a member of a group of Indian peoples of Brazil and Paraguay. **2** their language. **3** a language stock that includes seven language families, among them TUPI-GUARANI. **—Tu'pi•an,** *adj.*

Tu•pi–Gua•ra•ni [tu'pi ˌgwɑrɑ'ni] *n.* a language family of central South America consisting principally of the Tupi and Guarani languages and occurring particularly along the lower Amazon.

tu•pik ['tupək] *n. Cdn.* a compact, portable tent of skins, traditionally used by Inuit as a summer dwelling. Also, **tupek.** ⟨< Inuktitut *tupiq*⟩

tup•pence ['tʌpəns] twopence.

tup•pen•ny ['tʌpəni] twopenny.

tuque [tuk] *or* [tjuk] *n. Cdn.* **1** a knitted cap resembling a long stocking, usually knotted at the end: *Tuques are popular at the winter carnival.* **2** a tight-fitting, short knitted cap, often having a round tassel on top. ⟨< Cdn.F var. of F *toque* cap⟩

Tu•ra•ni•an [tjʊ'reiniən] *or* [tʊ'reiniən] *adj. or n.* URAL-ALTAIC. ⟨< Persian *Tūrān*, a district north of the Oxus⟩

A Sikh wearing a turban

tur•ban ['tɜrbən] *n.* **1** a headdress for men worn especially by Muslims and Sikhs, consisting of a scarf wound around the head, sometimes over a cap. **2** any similar headdress, especially one worn by women, consisting of a scarf wound around the head or a close-fitting, brimless hat resembling this. ⟨< Turkish < Arabic < Persian *dulband.* Doublet of TULIP.⟩

tur•baned ['tɜrbənd] *adj.* wearing a turban.

tur•bel•lar•i•an [ˌtɜrbə'lɛriən] *n., adj.* —*n.* any free-living, generally aquatic flatworm of the class Turbellaria, having many cilia.
—*adj.* of or having to do with this class of flatworms.

tur•bid ['tɜrbɪd] *adj.* **1** thick, dark, or cloudy with or as if with churned-up sediment; muddy: *a turbid river.* **2** confused or disordered: *a turbid and restless mind.* ⟨< L *turbidus* < *turba* turmoil⟩ **—'tur•bid•ly,** *adv.* **—'tur•bid•ness,** *n.*

tur•bi•dim•e•ter [ˌtɜrbɪ'dɪmətər] *n.* a device that measures the turbidity of a liquid.

tur•bid•i•ty [tər'bɪdəti] *n.* the condition of being turbid.

tur•bi•nate ['tɜrbənɪt] *or* ['tɜrbəˌneit] *adj., n.* —*adj.* **1** shaped like an upside-down cone. **2** shaped like a spiral or scroll. Many molluscs have turbinate shells. **3** having to do with or designating certain spongy, scroll-shaped bones in the nasal passages.
—*n.* a turbinate shell or bone. Also (adj.), **turbinal.** ⟨< L *turbinatus* < *turbo* whirling object or motion⟩

tur•bine ['tɜrbaɪn] *or* ['tɜrbɪn] *n.* a rotary engine or motor driven by a current of water, steam, or air that pushes against the blades of a wheel or system of wheels attached to a drive shaft, causing the wheel and drive shaft to turn. Turbines are used to turn generators that produce electric power. See JET ENGINE for picture. ⟨< F < L *turbo, -binis* whirling object or motion⟩

tur•bit ['tɜrbɪt] *n.* a breed of domestic pigeon having a crested head and a ruffed neck. ⟨< L *turbo* top[2], because of its stout shape⟩

tur•bo ['tɜrbou] *n.* **1** turbine. **2** turbocharger.

Tur•bo ['tɜrbou] *n. Cdn.* formerly, a train driven by a turbine, running between Toronto and Montréal.

turbo– *combining form.* consisting of or driven by a turbine, as in *turbojet.*

tur•bo•charge ['tɜrbouˌtʃɑrdʒ] *v.* **-charged, -charg•ing.** enhance the action of (an engine) using a turbocharger.

tur•bo•charg•er ['tɜrbouˌtʃɑrdʒər] *n.* a supercharger driven by a turbine that in turn is powered by the engine's exhaust gases.

tur•bo•fan ['tɜrbouˌfæn] *n.* **1** a turbojet engine in which a large fan driven by the turbine draws in additional air which is forced rearward to increase the thrust of the jet. **2** the fan itself, or any fan powered by a turbine.

tur•bo•gen•er•a•tor [ˌtɜrbou'dʒɛnəˌreitər] *n.* a generator attached to a turbine, by which it is driven.

tur•bo•jet ['tɜrbouˌdʒɛt] *n.* **1** TURBOJET ENGINE. **2** an aircraft powered by a turbojet engine or engines.

turbojet engine a jet engine using a turbine to drive an air compressor which supplies compressed air to the combustion chamber. A turbojet engine is started with an auxiliary power source that spins the turbine. Most military aircraft are powered by turbojet engines.

tur•bo•prop ['tɜrbou,prɒp] *n.* **1** TURBOPROP ENGINE. **2** an aircraft powered by a turboprop engine or engines. Also called **propjet**. ⟨*turbo-* (< *turbine*) + *prop*(*eller*)⟩

turboprop engine a jet engine using a propeller and a turbojet engine with two turbines. The turbojet engine is used mainly to turn the propeller, which supplies most of the power for the aircraft. The jet exhaust of a turboprop engine adds only a little to the power provided by the propeller.

tur•bo•su•per•charg•er [,tɜrbou'supər,tʃɑrdʒər] *n.* turbocharger.

tur•bot ['tɜrbət] *n., pl.* **-bot** or **-bots. 1** a large European flatfish (*Scophthalmus maximus*), valued as food, also found in large numbers off the Grand Banks of Newfoundland. **2** any of various similar fishes. ⟨ME < OF < OSwedish *törnbut* (< *törn* thorn, from the fish's prickles)⟩

tur•bu•lence ['tɜrbjələns] *n.* **1** the quality or state of being turbulent; disturbance or commotion: *He was glad to retire from the turbulence of public life.* **2** *Meteorology.* an unstable condition of the atmosphere, characterized by strong, irregular air currents: *The captain is expecting some turbulence and suggests that you fasten your seat belts.* **3** an irregular, tumultuous flow of any gas or fluid.

tur•bu•lent ['tɜrbjələnt] *adj.* **1** greatly disturbed or agitated; characterized by trouble or commotion: *the turbulent sea, a turbulent state of mind.* **2** causing disturbance; unruly; boisterous: *a turbulent mob.* **3** marked by irregular or tumultuous flow or motion. ⟨< L *turbulentus* < *turba* turmoil⟩ **—'tur•bu•lent•ly,** *adv.*

Turco– *combining form.* **1** Turkish or Turkic. **2** Turkey and.

turd [tɜrd] *n.* a piece of excrement. ⟨OE *tord* < Gmc⟩

tu•reen [tjʊ'rin], [tʊ'rin], *or* [tə'rin] *n.* a deep, covered dish for serving soup, etc. ⟨< F *terrine* earthen vessel, ult. < L *terra* earth⟩
☛ *Hom.* TERRENE, TERRINE [tə'rin].

turf [tɜrf] *n., pl.* **turfs** or (*sometimes*) **turves;** *v.* *—n.* **1** grass with its roots and the soil it is growing in, forming a thick layer like a mat. **2** a piece of turf; sod: *We cut turfs from the back lawn to fill in bare spots in the front.* **3** an artificial surface for a playing field, etc., made to resemble grass. **4** Usually, **the turf, a** a track for horse racing. **b** the sport or business of horse racing. **5** *Informal.* a particular territory or area: *She could relax now that she was back on her own turf.* **6** peat, especially a block of peat used for fuel.
—v. **1** cover with turf. **2** *Slang.* dismiss or evict forcefully (*usually used with* **out**): *The restaurant manager had them turfed out when they got rowdy.* ⟨OE⟩

turf•y ['tɜrfi] *adj.* **turf•i•er, turf•i•est. 1** covered with turf; grassy. **2** like turf. **3** full of or like peat. **4** of or having to do with horse racing. **—'turf•i•ness,** *n.*

tur•ges•cent [tər'dʒɛsənt] *adj.* becoming turgid; swelling. ⟨< L *turgescens, -entis,* ppr. of *turgescere* begin to swell < *turgere* swell⟩ **—tur'ges•cence,** *n.*

tur•gid ['tɜrdʒɪd] *adj.* **1** swollen; bloated. **2** using big words and elaborate comparisons; bombastic; inflated; pompous. ⟨< L *turgidus* < *turgere* swell⟩ **—'tur•gid•ly,** *adv.* **—'tur•gid•ness,** *n.*

tur•gid•i•ty [tər'dʒɪdəti] *n.* the quality or state of being turgid.

tur•gor ['tɜrgər] *n.* **1** the state of being swollen or distended; turgescence; turgidity. **2** *Biology.* the normal distension or rigidity of plant or animal cells due to the pressure of the cell contents on the cell walls. ⟨< LL < *turgere* swell⟩

Tu•ring test ['tjʊrɪŋ] *or* ['tʊrɪŋ] a test proposed by Alan Turing in 1950 to determine whether a machine can think. In the test, a person (known as the interrogator) is required to carry on two discussions by typed communication, one with a person and the other with a machine. If the interrogator is unable to distinguish the machine from the person, then the machine is considered able to think.

Turk [tɜrk] *n.* **1** a native or inhabitant of Turkey. **2** a native or inhabitant of the former Ottoman Empire. **3** a member of any of the peoples traditionally speaking Turkic languages and inhabiting the region from the Adriatic Sea to eastern Siberia. **4** a breed of horse closely related to the Arabian. One such horse was one of the three stallions from which all true Thoroughbreds are descended. ⟨ME < Med.L *Turcus* < Persian⟩

tur•key ['tɜrki] *n., pl.* **-keys. 1** a large North American bird (*Meleagris gallopavo*) having a thickset body with metallic green, copper, and bronze plumage and a bare head and neck with wattles. Domestic turkeys are derived from a Mexican subspecies of this bird. **2** a similar bird (*Agriocharis ocellata*) of Central America and northern South America which, together with the North American species, constitutes the gallinaceous family Meleagrididae. **3** the flesh of a domestic turkey, used for food: *Turkey is associated especially with Christmas and Thanksgiving.* **4** *Cdn., esp. Prairie Provinces.* SANDHILL CRANE. **5** *Slang.* a flop or failure, especially a play or motion picture that has failed. **6** *Slang.* an unattractive, stupid, or silly person: *I don't want that turkey as a partner.* **7** *Bowling.* in tenpins, a series of three consecutive strikes.
talk turkey, *Informal.* talk frankly and bluntly: *They decided it was time to get together and talk turkey.* ⟨shortened from *turkey-cock* and *turkey-hen*, names orig. applied to the guinea fowl because it was first imported into England via Turkey, and later applied to the North American bird because it was at first confused with the guinea fowl⟩

Tur•key ['tɜrki] *n.* a country in Asia Minor and SE Europe. See CRETE for picture.
☛ *Hom.* TURKI ['tɜrki].

turkey buzzard TURKEY VULTURE.

turkey•cock ['tɜrki,kɒk] *n.* **1** a male turkey. **2** a strutting, conceited person.

Turkey red 1 bright red. **2** a cotton cloth having this colour.

turkey trot a ragtime one-step of the World War I era.

turkey vulture a vulture (*Cathartes aura*) found in the western hemisphere as far north as southern Canada, having dark plumage and a red upper neck and head that are bare of feathers. The turkey vulture looks somewhat like a turkey.

Tur•ki ['tʊrki] *or* ['tɜrki] *n., adj. —n.* **1** the Turkic languages collectively of central Asia, especially those of the eastern group such as Uzbek or Uighur. **2** (*used with plural verb*) the speakers of these languages.
—adj. noting or pertaining to these languages or their speakers.
☛ *Hom.* TURKEY ['tɜrki].

Turk•ic ['tɜrkɪk] *adj., n. —adj.* **1** of, having to do with, or designating a subfamily of the Altaic family of languages, including Turkish, Turkoman, and Tatar. **2** of or having to do with the peoples speaking Turkic languages.
—n. the Turkic languages collectively.

Turk•ish ['tɜrkɪʃ] *n., adj. —n.* the Turkic language of Turkey.
—adj. of, having to do with, or characteristic of Turkey, its inhabitants, or their language.

Turkish bath 1 a kind of bath in which the bather stays in a hot, usually steam-filled room until he or she sweats freely, and then is washed and massaged. **2** Often, **Turkish baths,** *pl.* a place used for such baths.

Turkish delight a fruit-flavoured candy made of sugar and gelatin, usually cut into cubes and dusted with powdered sugar.

Turkish Empire OTTOMAN EMPIRE.

Turkish towel a thick towel made of cotton terry.

Turk•man ['tɜrkmən] *n., pl.* **-men.** a native or inhabitant of Turkmenistan.

Turk•men ['tɜrkmɛn] *or* ['tɜrkmən] *n., pl.* **-men** or **-mens. 1** a language spoken mainly in Turkmenistan, but also in parts of Russia, Iran, and the Caucasus. **2** TURKOMAN (def. 1).

Turk•men•i•stan [tɜrk'mɛnɪ,stæn] *n.* a country in western Asia, on the Caspian Sea.

Tur•ko•man ['tɜrkəmən] *n., pl.* **-mans;** *adj. —n.* **1** a member of any of several Turkic peoples living mainly in the region around the Aral Sea in the Soviet Union. **2** the Turkic language of the Turkomans.
—adj. of or having to do with the Turkomans or their language.

Turk's–cap lily ['tɜrks ,kæp] any of several varieties of lily whose flowers have recurved petals, making them look like a turban.

Turk's–head ['tɜrks ,hɛd] *n.* a knot resembling a turbaned head, formed by weaving a small cord around a larger one, or a fine line around a rope.

tur•mer•ic ['tɜrmərɪk] *n.* **1** a yellow powder prepared from the underground stem of an East Indian perennial herb (*Curcuma longa*), used as a seasoning, as a yellow dye, and in medicine. **2** the plant itself. **3** the underground stem of this plant. **4** any of a number of similar plants. ⟨earlier *tarmaret* < F < Med.L *terra merita*, literally, worthy earth < L *terra* earth + *merere* deserve⟩

turmeric paper *Chemistry.* a test paper impregnated with turmeric. It turns brown in alkalis and reddish brown in boric acid.

tur•moil ['tɜrmɔil] *n.* a commotion; disturbance; confusion. ⟨origin uncertain⟩

turn [tɜrn] *v., n.* —*v.* **1** move or cause to move around as a wheel does; rotate; spin: *The merry-go-round turned. I turned the crank three times.* **2** move part way around; change in direction or position; change from being on one side, or facing in one way, to the other: *to turn a page. Turn onto your back. She turned the photo sideways.* **3** move or cause to move around in order to open, close, raise, lower, or tighten: *She turned the knob. The key turned in the lock.* **4** perform by revolving, as a somersault. **5** take a new direction: *The road turns to the north here. Their discussion turned to the coming election.* **6** give a new direction to: *He turned his steps to the north. She turned her thoughts toward home.* **7 a** reverse the position of (the turf, soil, etc.) in ploughing or digging so as to bring the under parts to the surface: *to turn the sod before beginning construction.* **b** make by so doing: *to turn a furrow.* **8** empty (something) out of something by inverting or reversing it: *Turn the cake out of the pan after it has cooled. He turned the crumpled bills out of his pockets onto the table.* **9** put the inner side of (a garment, etc.) outward. **10** change or cause to change so as to become (*used with a following adjective or adjectival*): *to turn traitor. She turned pale. All this worry is turning my hair grey.* **11** transform or convert; be transformed or converted (*used with* **to** or **into**): *They turned defeat into victory. The rain turned to snow as the temperature dropped.* **12** change for or to a worse condition; sour; spoil: *Warm weather turns milk. The cream has turned, because you left it out all day.* **13** give form to; make, especially in a skilled way: *He can turn pretty compliments.* **14** change from one language into another; translate: *Turn this text into Latin.* **15** put out of order; unsettle. **16** depend; be contingent: *The success of the picnic turns on the weather.* **17** cause to go; send, etc.: *to turn a person from one's door, to turn someone adrift.* **18** drive back; stop; deflect; repel: *to turn a punch.* **19** direct; aim: *He turned his flashlight on us. They turned their efforts toward making a better plan.* **20** consider in different aspects; revolve in the mind (*often used with* **over**): *to turn a problem in one's mind.* **21** direct one's thought, attention, gaze, etc.: *Let us turn to more global concerns.* **22** put (to use); apply: *to turn money to good use.* **23** move to the other side of; go around or beyond (a corner). **24** shape or be shaped on a lathe. **25** make or become curved, rounded, bent, or twisted. **26** make or become sick or nauseated: *The smell of it turned my stomach.* **27** become dizzy. **28** reach or pass (a particular age, time, or amount): *a man turning sixty. It's just turned six o'clock.* **29** cause (money or commodities) to circulate steadily. **30 a** of leaves, change colour. **b** cause (leaves) to change colour: *They say it's the frost that turns the leaves in the fall, but no one knows for sure.* **31** recoil or cause to recoil or backfire: *His own logic turned against him. Her remarks were turned against her.* **32** change in affections or attitude: *to turn friends against friends. After that, she turned against her mother.* **33** exchange for something else: *to turn stock into cash.* **34** convert: *She has turned to Buddhism. The missionaries tried to turn the people to Christianity, with varying degrees of success.* **35** make; earn (a profit).
turn down, a fold or bend downward. **b** place with face downward. **c** *Informal.* refuse; reject: *to turn down a proposal.* **d** lower; moderate; make less intense. *Would you turn the sound down a bit? Turn down the charm, it's making me sick!*
turn in, a turn and go in. **b** of toes, point inward. **c** *Informal.* go to bed. **d** hand in; deliver. **e** give back. **f** exchange: *to turn an old bike in for a new one.* **g** hand over to the police: *After a long time in hiding, he turned himself in.*
turn loose, free (someone) from restraint and allow to go where, or do as, he or she will: *to turn a prisoner loose.*
turn off, a shut off; stop the flow or operation of; put out (a light, etc.) **b** go aside or branch off from (a main route): *Our street turns off just before the bridge. Where should I turn off Highway 401 to get to your place?* **c** *Slang.* make or become bored, disgusted, etc. (by): *The whole experience turned me off train travel. I just turn off when people start talking like that.*
turn on a start the flow or operation of; put on (a light, etc.) **b** attack; oppose, especially after supporting or having seemed to support. **c** be contingent on; be a function of (something variable). **d** *Slang.* take a narcotic; especially, smoke marijuana. **e** *Slang.* make or become stimulated and elated by, or as if by, the use of a psychedelic drug. **f** *Slang.* make or become enthusiastic (*used with* **to**): *It was Jack who turned me on to jazz. Turn on to the great taste of milk! She turns on whenever they bring up the topic of art.* **g** stimulate or arouse sexually; be so stimulated or aroused.
turn out, a put out; shut off (a light, etc.) **b** let go out: *Turn out the dogs, they're getting restless.* **c** drive out: *They were turned out of their home.* **d** come or go out to some function or event (*used with* **for**): *We all turned out for hockey practice.* **e** make; produce: *That factory turns out 500 chairs a day.* **f** result: *It turned out that we couldn't go after all.* **g** become ultimately; end up: *It turned out all lopsided.* **h** have the hoped-for outcome: *We planned it carefully, but it just didn't turn out.* **i** be found out or known: *It turns out he comes from my grandparents' village in Hungary! They turned out to be a couple of frauds.* **j** equip; fit out or deck out. **k** *Informal.* get out of bed. **l** turn inside out: *He turned out his pockets.*
turn over, a hand over; transfer: *He turned the job over to his assistant.* **b** think carefully about; consider in different ways: *She turned the idea over in her mind.* **c** buy and then sell (stock). **d** invest and get back (capital). **e** convert to different use. **f** do business to the amount of (a given sum). **g** of an engine, start; start (an engine): *It makes a noise but it won't turn over. Turn over the engine and let it warm up on cold mornings.*
turn (someone's) **head,** make someone too proud: *Fame turned his head.*
turn tail, turn one's back to flee.
turn to, a refer to. **b** go to for help. **c** resort to: *They turned to threats and violence.* **d** get busy; set to work: *They rolled up their sleeves and turned to.*
turn up, a fold up or over, especially so as to shorten; give an upward turn to; bring up the underside of. **b** be directed upward: *Her nose turns up at the end.* **c** make brighter, louder, or more intense. **d** turn and go up. **e** appear: *My lost book turned up the other day.* **f** bring to light; unearth: *Her research turned up several interesting facts about medieval dress.*
—*n.* **1** rotating motion like that of a wheel: *The turn of the merry-go-round was making her dizzy.* **2** a single revolution, as of a wheel: *With each turn, the screw goes in further.* **3** a change of direction: *a turn to the left. The conversation took a new turn.* **4** a place where there is such a change: *He stood at the turn in the road.* **5** the act or an instance of winding, twisting, bending, or coiling: *Give that rope a few more turns around the tree.* **6** the condition of being, or the direction in which something is, twisted, bent, or curved: *Her feet have an inward turn.* **7** a change in affairs, conditions, or circumstances: *the turn of a fever, the regular turn of the seasons. The sick man has taken a turn for the better.* **8** the time of a change: *at the turn of the year.* **9** a form; style; cast: *a happy turn of expression, a serious turn of mind, the turn of a vase.* **10** a time or chance to do something, in an ordered series or rotation: *My turn comes after yours.* **11** a time or spell of action: *She took a turn at gardening as a relief from desk work.* **12** a deed; act: *One good turn deserves another.* **13** a stage act or its performers: *The acrobats are the next turn. He did his turn very well.* **14** an inclination; bent: *She has a turn for mathematics.* **15** a short walk, drive, or ride: *a turn in the park.* **16** a spell of dizziness or fainting: *This morning I had one of my turns.* **17** *Informal.* a momentary shock caused by sudden alarm, fright, etc.: *to give someone a bad turn.* **18** a version, application, or interpretation (*used with* **on**): *a new turn on an old idea.* **19** *Music.* an ornamental device of four tones, a principal tone followed usually by one tone above and below it and a return to the principal tone. The order in which the turn is performed is sometimes reversed. **20** a stock market transaction that involves both the purchase and sale of a particular security.
at every turn, a every time; without exception. **b** all the time; constantly.
by turns, one after the other alternately: *She was by turns amused and angered by their prank.*
call the turn, a foretell something correctly. **b** be in control: *He is the nominal head of the company but his secretary really calls the turns.*
in turn, a in proper order. **b** in response or reaction; correspondingly: *He kept overspending; she, in turn, became paranoid about every little expenditure.*
out of turn, a not in proper order. **b** inappropriate(ly) or without right; at the wrong stage, etc.: *He was tactless to speak out of turn like that. Your comments are out of turn.*
take it in turns (to do something), act alternately: *We took it in turns to drive on the long journey.*
take turns, play, act, etc. one after another in proper order.
to a turn, to just the right degree.
turn about or **turn and turn about,** one after another in proper order. ⟨OE *turnian* < L *tornare* turn on a lathe < *tornus* lathe < Gk. *tornos.* Related to TOUR.⟩
➥ *Hom.* TERN.
➥ *Syn. v.* **1. Turn,** REVOLVE, ROTATE = move around in a circle. **Turn** is the general and common word, meaning 'move in a circle or in circle after circle' either on a pivot or axis or around a centre: *That wheel turns freely now.* **Revolve** means especially to go around and around in a circular path around something that serves as a centre. **Rotate** means especially to go around and around on its own axis or around its own centre: *The earth rotates (on its axis) once every 24 hours and revolves around the sun once each year.*

turn•a•bout [ˈtɜrnə,bʌut] *n.* **1** the act of turning so as to face the other way. **2** a changing to an opposite view, policy, etc.; about-face; reversal. **3** a merry-go-round.

turn•a•round [ˈtɜrnə,raʊnd] *n., adj.* —*n.* **1** an about-face or reversal. **2** the time it takes a ship, airplane, etc. to unload, load, and undergo repairs and servicing before being ready to depart. **3** the time taken for any return trip or for any process involving the transfer and return transfer of anything: *The turnaround for your application should be about a week.* **4** a space for vehicles to turn around.
—*adj.* of or having to do with a turnaround: *efforts to reduce turnaround time.*

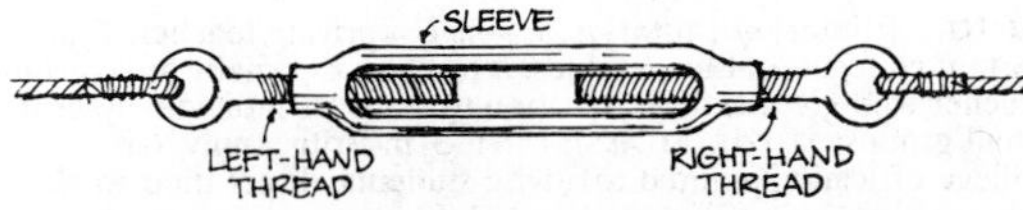

A turnbuckle, used for joining two lengths of wire

turn•buck•le [ˈtɜrn,bʌkəl] *n.* a device for connecting and tightening metal rods, sections of wire, etc., consisting of a hollow metal link with an inside screw thread at either end or a swivel at one end and a screw thread at the other.

turn•coat [ˈtɜrn,kout] *n.* a person who changes his or her political party or principles; a person who goes over to the opposing side.

turn•down [ˈtɜrn,daʊn] *adj., n.* —*adj.* that is or can be turned down; folded or doubled down: *a turndown collar.*
—*n.* **1** a turning down; rejection. **2** a decline; downturn.

turn•er [ˈtɜrnər] *n.* **1** a device or tool that is used for turning: *an egg turner.* **2** a person who forms or shapes things with a lathe.

Turn•er syndrome a syndrome of defective sexual development and other phenotypic features including short stature, typically occurring in individuals with a female phenotype but only 45 chromosomes, only one of which is an X chromosome. Also, **Turner's syndrome.**

turn indicator **1** a flashing light or other device on a motor vehicle for signalling turns. **2** a gyroscopic device that indicates any turning motion around the vertical axis of an airplane.

turn•ing [ˈtɜrnɪŋ] *n., v.* —*n.* **1** the action of a person or object that turns. **2** the point at which something, as a road, turns off or bends. **3** the art or process of forming rounded objects on a lathe.
—*v.* pp. of TURN.

turning circle the minimum circular space needed by a vehicle to turn.

turning point a point in time or space at which a significant change takes place: *That experience was the turning point of his life.*

tur•nip [ˈtɜrnɪp] *n.* **1** a biennial plant (*Brassica rapa*) of the mustard family, having hairy leaves and a thick, round, whitish root. **2** the rutabaga, closely related to this plant. **3** the root of either of these plants, used as a vegetable. ⟨probably ult. < ME *turn* (from its rounded shape) + *nepe* turnip < L *napus*⟩

turn•key [ˈtɜrn,ki] *n., pl.* **-keys;** *adj.* —*n. Archaic.* a person in charge of the keys of a prison; the keeper of a prison.
—*adj.* **1** ready to be put into immediate use; equipped with, or including, everything needed to operate it: *a turnkey computer system with hardware, software, and documentation. The store she purchased was a turnkey operation.* **2** of or referring to a method of construction, production, installation, etc. that ends with everything ready to be put into immediate use by the end user or consumer.

turn•off [ˈtɜrn,ɒf] *n.* **1** the act of turning off. **2** a place where one can leave a highway, especially an exit ramp leading off an expressway: *It's 2 km to the next turnoff.* **3** *Slang.* something or someone that bores or disgusts people, etc.: *This novel is a real turnoff.*

turn-of-the-century [ˈtɜrn əv ðə ˈsɛntʃəri] *adj.* of or having to do with the years around the end of one century and the beginning of the next: *The literary prize is a turn-of-the-century institution.*

turn-on [ˈtɜrn ,ɒn] *n. Slang.* someone or something that makes people interested and enthusiastic, stimulates people, etc.

turn•out [ˈtɜrn,ʌut] *n.* **1 a** a gathering of people for a special purpose or event: *There was a good turnout at the dance.* **b** the number of people gathered: *a turnout of 600.* **2** output. **3** the way in which a person or thing is equipped or dressed; equipment; outfit: *an elegant turnout.* **4** a carriage together with its horse or horses. **5** *Cdn. West.* the time in spring when cattle are turned out to forage for themselves.

turn•o•ver [ˈtɜrn,ouvər] *n.* **1** a small, filled pastry in the shape of a semicircle or triangle made by placing the filling on one half of a piece of rolled-out dough and folding the other half over it. **2 a** the rate at which people leave a job or company and have to be replaced: *The company has had a high turnover in the past year.* **b** the number of workers taken on to replace those leaving during a given time. **3** the amount of business done in a given time: *There was a large turnover on the stock exchange this week.* **4** the paying out and getting back of the money involved in a business transaction: *The store reduced prices to make a quick turnover.* **5** the number of times, or the rate at which, a stock of merchandise is sold out and refilled. **6** *Football, Basketball.* the act or an instance of losing possession of the ball to the opposing team through a fumble, pass interception, etc.: *Two touchdowns were scored as a result of turnovers.* **7** the act or an instance of turning over; upset or reversal. **8** (*adjl.*) that can be or is designed to be turned over: *a turnover collar.*

turn•pike [ˈtɜrn,pəik] *n.* **1** *Esp. U.S.* a road on which a toll is or used to be charged, especially an expressway. **2** tollgate. ⟨< *turn* + *pike* a sharp point; with reference to a spiked barrier across a road, turning on a vertical axis⟩

turn signal TURN INDICATOR (def. 1).

turn•sole [ˈtɜrn,soul] *n.* any of a number of plants having flowers that are said to turn toward the sun. ⟨ME *turnesole* < MF *tournesol* < Ital. *tornasole* < *tornare* turn + *sole* sun⟩

turn•spit [ˈtɜrn,spɪt] *n.* **1** a person or animal formerly employed to operate a device, such as a treadmill, for turning meat on a spit. **2** a spit that turns.

turn•stile [ˈtɜrn,staɪl] *n.* a barrier consisting of bars set into a revolving central post, allowing people to pass through only on foot, one at a time, and only in one direction.

turn•stone [ˈtɜrn,stoun] *n.* any of a small genus (*Arenaria*) of migratory shore birds belonging to the same family as sandpipers, that use their flattened, slightly upturned bill to turn over stones in search of food, especially the **ruddy turnstone** (*A. interpres*) common in Canadian and other arctic areas.

turn•ta•ble [ˈtɜrn,teibəl] *n.* **1** on a record player, **a** the revolving disc on which a record is placed to be played. **b** the entire unit containing the revolving disc and including the tone arm, needle cartridge, etc. **2** any similar disk or platform that revolves, such as a platform with track, used for turning a locomotive around.

tur•pen•tine [ˈtɜrpən,taɪn] *n., v.* **-tined, -tin•ing.** —*n.* **1** a thick, sticky fluid consisting of oil and resin, obtained from pines and various other coniferous trees. **2** a volatile oil distilled from this fluid, used especially as a solvent and thinner for paints, varnishes, etc. **3** any of the oleoresins obtained from conifers, especially from the terebinth.
—*v.* **1** apply turpentine to. **2** extract turpentine from. Also (n. 3), **gum turpentine.** ⟨ME < OF < L *terebinthina* < Gk. *terebinthos* turpentine tree⟩ **—,tur•pen'tin•ic** [,tɜrpənˈtɪnɪk], *adj.* **—,tur•pen'tin•ous** [-ˈtaɪnəs], *adj.*

tur•pi•tude [ˈtɜrpə,tjud] *or* [ˈtɜrpə,tud] *n.* a shameful wickedness; baseness. ⟨< L *turpitudo* < *turpis* vile⟩

turps [tɜrps] *n. Informal.* turpentine ⟨shortened from *turpentine*⟩

tur•quoise [ˈtɜrkɔɪz] *or* [ˈtɜrkwɔɪz] *n., adj.* —*n.* **1** a sky blue or greenish blue precious stone or mineral, consisting of a phosphate of aluminum and copper, which is used as a gem. **2** a gem made from this stone. **3** light greenish blue.
—*adj.* having the colour turquoise. ⟨< F *turquoise,* originally fem. adj., Turkish⟩

turr [tɜr] *n. Cdn.* **1** *Esp. Nfld.* the razorbill (*Alca torda*). **2** *Nfld.* the murre (*Uria aalge* or *U. lomvia*). ⟨probably imitative⟩

tur•ret [ˈtɜrɪt] *n.* **1** a small tower, often on the corner of a building. **2** any of various low, rotating armoured structures in which guns are mounted. **3** an opening in a military aircraft, usually covered by a convex cap of strong, transparent plastic material and containing a machine gun or guns. **4** a kind of tower on wheels, formerly used in attacking walled castles, forts, or towns. **5** a rotating attachment for a lathe, etc. holding a number of tools that can be presented to the work as desired. Also called **turrethead.** ⟨ME < OF *torete,* dim. of *tor* < L *turris* tower⟩

tur•ret•ed ['tɜrətɪd] *adj.* **1** having a turret or turrets. **2** of a shell, having whorls forming a long spiral.

tur•tle¹ ['tɜrtəl] *n.* **1** any of an order (Chelonia) of four-legged, toothless, generally slow-moving reptiles found throughout the world, having the body encased in a protective bony shell with an outside layer of horny plates, or, in some species, tough skin. Most species of turtle can withdraw the head, legs, and tail into the shell for protection. Land turtles are often called tortoises. **2** *Computer technology.* a special cursor that moves about on a computer screen under program control: *The turtle is used to draw lines on a cathode-ray tube.*
turn turtle, turn bottom side up. ⟨< F *tortue* tortoise; influenced by E *turtle* turtledove⟩

tur•tle² ['tɜrtəl] *n. Archaic.* turtledove. ⟨OE *turtle, turtla* < L *turtur*⟩

tur•tle•back ['tɜrtəl,bæk] *n.* an arched projection erected over the deck of a steamship at the bow, and often at the stern also, to guard against damage from heavy seas.

tur•tle•dove ['tɜrtəl,dʌv] *n.* **1** any of a genus (*Streptopelia*) of wild doves, especially a small, grey or brownish European wild dove (*S. turtur*) found in woods and around farms, noted for its sad-sounding cooing and the affection that it appears to have for its mate. **2** MOURNING DOVE. **3** sweetheart; a term of endearment.

turtle•head ['tɜrtəl,hɛd] *n.* any perennial plant of the genus *Chelone* of North America, belonging to the figwort family and having large, tubular white or pink flowers. ⟨< *turtle² + head*⟩

tur•tle•neck ['tɜrtəl,nɛk] *n.* **1** a high, snugly fitting, usually turned-over knit collar, especially on a sweater. See COLLAR for picture. **2** a sweater having such a collar.

Tus•can ['tʌskən] *n., adj.* —*n.* **1** a native or inhabitant of Tuscany, a district in central Italy. **2** the language of Tuscany, regarded as the classical form of Italian and forming the basis of modern standard Italian.
—*adj.* **1** of or having to do with Tuscany or its people.
2 *Architecture.* of, having to do with, or designating an order of architecture developed in ancient Rome, one of the five classical styles of architecture. The characteristic Tuscan column is seven diameters high, with an unfluted shaft and a capital and base having mouldings but no decoration. See ORDER for picture.

Tus•ca•ro•ra [,tʌskə'rɔrə] *n., pl.* **-ra** or **-ras. 1** a member of an American Indian people of Iroquois stock who occupied what is now North Carolina at the time of their first contact with Europeans, but later migrated to New York and Ontario. The Tuscarora were the sixth nation to join the Iroquois Confederacy. **2** the Iroquoian language of the Tuscarora.

tush¹ [tʌʃ] *interj. or n.* an exclamation expressing impatience, contempt, etc.

tush² [tʌʃ] *n.* **1** a canine tooth of a horse. **2** tusk. ⟨OE *tusc.* Related to TOOTH.⟩

tush³ [tʊʃ] *n. Slang.* buttocks. ⟨< Yiddish⟩

tusk [tʌsk] *n., v.* —*n.* **1** a very long, large, pointed tooth, usually one of a pair projecting from the sides of the closed mouth in animals like the elephant, walrus, and wild boar. Animals with tusks use them for digging, as a weapon, etc. **2** any tooth or other object like a tusk.
—*v.* gore, dig up, or tear with the tusks. ⟨ME *tusk*, var. of OE *tux*, var. of *tusc* tush²⟩ **—tusked,** *adj.*

tusk•er ['tʌskər] *n.* an animal with well-developed tusks, such as a mature elephant, walrus, or wild boar.

tus•sah ['tʌsə] *n.* **1 a** a coarse, strong silk from a wild or semi-domesticated silkworm (*Antheraea paphia*) of India or China. Undyed tussah is a brownish colour. **b** cloth made of this silk. **2** the silkworm that produces this silk. The tussah feeds on oak or castor bean leaves and makes a larger cocoon than the domestic silkworm. Also, **tussore.** ⟨< Hind. *tasar* shuttle⟩

tus•sis ['tʌsɪs] *n. Medicine.* a cough. ⟨< L⟩ **—'tus•sive,** *adj.*

tus•sle ['tʌsəl] *n., v.* **-sled, -sling.** —*n.* a scuffle or struggle: *There was a short tussle as everyone tried to get through the door first.*
—*v.* struggle or wrestle: *The two sisters liked to tussle with one another.* ⟨var. of *tousle*⟩

tus•sock ['tʌsək] *n.* a tuft or clump of growing grass, etc. ⟨origin uncertain⟩ **—tus•soc•ky,** *adj.*

tussock moth any of numerous dull-coloured moths (family Lymantriidae) whose larvae have thick tufts of hair.

tus•sore ['tʌsɔr] *n.* See TUSSAH.

tut [tʌt] *interj., n., v.* **tut•ted, tut•ting.** —*interj. or n.* an exclamation of impatience, contempt, or rebuke (*usually reduplicated*); tut-tut.
—*v.* exclaim in this way; utter a tut or tuts.

tu•te•lage ['tjutəlɪdʒ] *or* ['tutəlɪdʒ] *n.* **1** instruction: *They learned very quickly under his expert tutelage.* **2** guardianship; protection. **3** the condition of being in the care of a guardian. ⟨< L *tutela* watching⟩

tu•te•lar•y ['tjutə,lɛri] *or* ['tutə,lɛri] *adj., n., pl.* **-lar•ies.** —*adj.* **1** protecting; guardian: *a tutelary saint.* **2** of or having to do with a guardian.
—*n.* a tutelary saint, spirit, divinity, etc. Also, **tutelar.** ⟨< L *tutelarius* < *tutela* protection < *tueri* watch over⟩

tu•tor ['tjutər] *or* ['tutər] *n., v.* —*n.* **1** a private teacher. **2** in certain colleges and universities, a teacher, especially an assistant teacher who gives extra instruction to students individually or in small groups; TUTORIAL ASSISTANT. **3** in British universities, a college official appointed to advise students, direct their work, etc.
—*v.* **1** teach; instruct, especially individually or privately. **2** act as tutor. **3** *Informal.* be taught by a tutor. ⟨ME < L *tutor* guardian < *tueri* watch over⟩ **—'tu•tor•age,** *n.*

tu•to•ri•al [tju'tɔriəl] *or* [tu'tɔriəl] *adj., n.* —*adj.* **1** of or having to do with a tutor: *tutorial authority.* **2** using tutors for the main work of teaching: *the tutorial system of university instruction.*
—*n.* in some colleges and universities, a class given by a tutor to an individual or a small group of students.

tutorial assistant a graduate student in a university or college who assists a professor by taking some tutorials.
—tutorial assistantship.

tu•tor•ship ['tjutər,ʃɪp] *or* ['tutər,ʃɪp] *n.* the position, rank, or duties of a tutor.

Tut•si ['tʊtsi] *n., pl.* **-si** or **-sis.** a member of a major people group of Rwanda and Burundi. Also, **Watusi.**

tut•ti ['tuti] *Italian,* ['tutti] *adj., n., pl.* **-tis** [-tiz]. *Music.*
—*adj.* for or by all instruments or voices.
—*n.* **1** a passage or section to be performed by all instruments or voices. **2** the tonal effect produced by a tutti performance. ⟨< Ital. *tutti*, pl. of *tutto* all⟩

tut•ti-frut•ti ['tuti 'fruti] *n.* **1** a preserve of mixed fruits. **2** ice cream containing a variety of fruits or fruit flavouring. **3** (*adjl.*) flavoured with mixed fruits. ⟨< Ital. *tutti frutti* all fruits⟩

tut–tut ['tʌt 'tʌt] *interj., n., v.* **-tut•ted, -tut•ting,** —*interj., n.* a clicking noise made with the tongue as a form of mild rebuke, or to express annoyance, sometimes facetiously pronounced as spelled.
—*v.* make such a sound: *He merely tut-tutted when told what his child had done.*

tut•ty ['tʌti] *n.* **1** an impure form of zinc oxide obtained from the flues of smelting furnaces, used as a polishing powder. **2** a similar, naturally occurring substance. ⟨ME *tutie* < MF < ML *tutia* < Arabic *tutiya* oxide of zinc < Persian < Skt. *tuttham* blue vitriol⟩

tu•tu ['tutu]; *French,* [ty'ty] *n.* a ballet dancer's very short, frilly skirt. ⟨< F *tutu*, alteration of *cucu*, child's reduplication of *cul* buttocks < L *culus*⟩

Tu•va•lu ['tuvə,lu] *or* [,tuvə'lu] *n.* a group of islands lying in the Pacific Ocean to the east of the Solomon Islands and north of Fiji, formerly a British colony, now a country.

tu–whit tu–whoo [tu'wɪt tu'wu] *n.* imitation of the vocal sound made by an owl.

tux [tʌks] *n. Informal.* tuxedo.

tux•e•do [tʌk'sidou] *n., pl.* **-dos** or **-does. 1** a man's semiformal jacket for evening wear, usually black with satin or grosgrain lapels and made without tails; dinner jacket. **2** a suit of men's evening clothes including such a jacket. ⟨< *Tuxedo* Park, New York, where it is supposed to have been first worn⟩

tu•yère [twi'jɛr], [tu'jɛr], *or* [twir] *n.* a tube or pipe through which the blast of air enters a blast furnace, forge, etc. ⟨< F *tuyère*, ult. < Gmc.⟩

TV or **tv** terminal velocity.

TV or **T.V.** ['ti 'vi] *n.* **1** television. **2** a television set. **3** (*adjl.*) of or having to do with television or television sets.

TV dinner a frozen, precooked, packaged dinner that is ready to serve after simply being heated in its container.

twad•dle ['twɒdəl] *n., v.* **-dled, -dling.** —*n.* silly, tiresome talk or writing; nonsense; drivel.
—*v.* talk or write in a silly, tiresome way. ⟨alteration of earlier *twattle*, ? < *tattle*⟩ **—'twad•dler,** *n.*

twain [twein] *n. or adj. Archaic or poetic.* two. ⟨OE *twēgen*⟩

twang [twæŋ] *n., v. —n.* **1** a sharp, ringing sound like that made by a bowstring or rubber band when plucked: *We could hear the twang of her bow as she shot the arrow.* **2** a sharp, nasal tone: *Some Nova Scotians speak with a twang.* **3** a dialect having such a characteristic tone: *Some people speak of the "Prairie twang."*
—v. **1** make or cause to make a sharp, ringing sound: *The banjos twanged.* **2** play, pluck, shoot, etc. with a twang: *to twang a guitar. He twanged an arrow into the target.* **3** speak or utter with a sharp, nasal tone. ⟨imitative⟩ **—'twang•y,** *adj.*

'twas [twʌz] *or* [twɒz]; *unstressed,* [twəz] it was.

tway•blade ['twei,bleid] *n.* any of several small, moss-inhabiting orchids of the genera *Listera* and *Liparis,* especially the **heartleaved twayblade** (*Listera cordata*), having two opposing broad leaves and found across Canada, in Alaska, and south to California, New Mexico, and North Carolina. ⟨OE *twegen* twain + *blade*⟩

tweak [twik] *v., n. —v.* pull sharply and twist with the fingers: *She tweaked her little brother's ear and made him cry.*
—n. a sharp pull and twist. ⟨< var. of OE *twiccian* pluck, twitch⟩

tweed [twid] *n.* **1** a woollen cloth with a rough surface, usually woven in a twill weave with yarns of two or more colours, used especially for suits and coats. **2** a garment made of tweed: *He was wearing tweeds.* **3** any of various similar fabrics. ⟨said to be a misreading of *tweel,* var. of *twill*⟩

twee•dle ['twidəl] *v.* **-dled, -dling.** play or produce shrill tones, such as those of a bagpipe or fiddle. ⟨origin uncertain⟩

twee•dle•dum and twee•dle•dee [,twidəl'dʌm ən ,twidəl'di] **1** two persons or things that are practically identical. **2 Tweedledum and Tweedledee,** identical twin brothers in Lewis Carroll's *Through the Looking Glass.* ⟨imitative of the sounds of low-pitched and high-pitched instruments, probably from a rhyme by John Byrom (1692-1763), about a musical battle between Handel and Bononcini, giving them these names⟩

tweed•y ['twidi] *adj.* **tweed•i•er, tweed•i•est. 1** made of tweed; like tweed. **2** in the habit of wearing tweeds or other clothing suggestive of the outdoors; casual and fond of the outdoors or of intellectual or academic pursuits. **3** characteristic of or suited to such people, especially those with a British or liberal arts background: *a tweedy writing style, a tweedy pub.* **—'tweed•i•ness,** *n.*

'tween [twin] *prep. Poetic.* between.

'tween–decks or **'tween–deck** ['twin ,dɛk] *n. Nautical.* an area between the decks of any vessel.

tweet [twit] *n., interj., v. —n. or interj.* the sound made by a small or young bird or an imitation or representation of this sound.
—v. utter a tweet or tweets. ⟨imitative⟩

tweet•er ['twitər] *n.* a small high-fidelity loudspeaker used to reproduce sounds in the higher frequency range. Compare WOOFER.

tweeze [twiz] *v.* pluck or remove with or as if with tweezers.

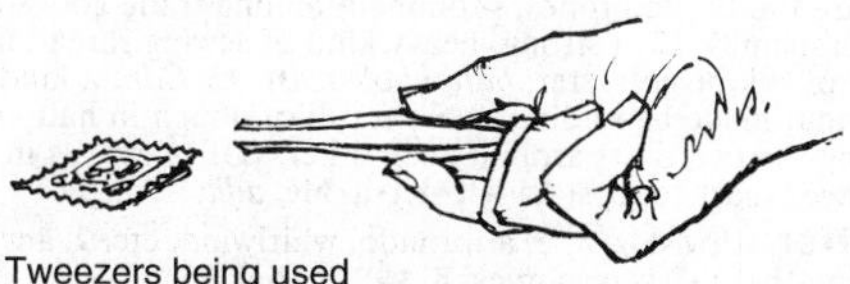

Tweezers being used to pick up a stamp

tweez•ers ['twizərz] *n.pl. or sing.* small pincers or tongs for pulling out hairs or slivers, picking up small objects, etc. ⟨< *tweeze* instrument case, ult. < F *étui* < OF *estuier* keep < VL *studiare* be zealous < L *studium* zeal⟩

twelfth [twɛlfθ] *adj. or n.* **1** next after the 11th; last in a series of twelve; 12th. **2** one, or being one, of 12 equal parts.

Twelfth Day *n.* January 6, the twelfth day after Christmas. On this day the feast of the Epiphany is celebrated. Formerly it marked the end of the Christmas season. **—'Twelfth-'day,** *adj.*

Twelfth Night *n.* the evening or eve of Twelfth Day, often celebrated as the end of Christmas festivities. **—'Twelfth-'night,** *adj.*

twelve [twɛlv] *n., adj. —n.* **1** two more than 10; 12. **2** the numeral 12: *The 12 is too small.* **3** the twelfth in a set or series. **4** a set or series of twelve persons or things. **5 the Twelve,** the twelve Apostles of Jesus.
—adj. **1** being two more than 10. **2** being twelfth in a set or series (*used after the noun*): *Section Twelve.* ⟨OE *twelf*⟩

twelve•fold ['twɛlv,fould] *adj., adv. —adj.* **1** twelve times as much or as many. **2** having twelve parts.
—adv. twelve times as much or as many.

twelve•mo ['twɛlvmou] *n., pl.* **-mos;** *or adj.* duodecimo.

twelve•month ['twɛlv,mʌnθ] *n. Archaic or Brit.* a period of twelve months; a year.

Twelve Tables in ancient Rome, the first written code of laws, produced in 451 and 450 B.C.

twelve–tone ['twɛlv 'toun] *adj.* **1** of or having to do with an atonal musical system developed by Arnold Schönberg (1874-1951), in which all the twelve tones of the chromatic scale are used in an arbitrarily chosen order but without the traditional tone centre or key. **2** using this musical system.

twen•ti•eth ['twɛntiɪθ] *adj. or n.* **1** next after the 19th; last in a series of twenty; 20th. **2** one, or being one, of 20 equal parts.

twen•ty ['twɛnti] *n., pl.* **-ties;** *adj. —n.* **1** two times ten; 20. **2** the numeral 20. **3** the twentieth in a set or series. **4** a 20-dollar bill. **5 twenties,** *pl.* the years from twenty through twenty-nine, especially of a century or of a person's age: *She was in her twenties when her mother died.* **6** a set or series of twenty persons or things.
—adj. **1** being two times ten. **2** being twentieth in a set or series (*used after the noun*): *Lesson Twenty.* ⟨OE *twēntig*⟩

twen•ty•fold ['twɛnti,fould] *adj., adv. —adj.* **1** twenty times as much or as many. **2** having 20 parts.
—adv. twenty times as much or as many.

twenty–one [,twɛnti'wʌn] *n.* blackjack, a card game. ⟨translation of F *vingt-et-un*⟩

twen•ty–twen•ty or **20/20** ['twɛnti 'twɛnti] *adj.* of vision, normally acute: *I'm a bit short-sighted, but my sister has 20/20 vision.* ⟨from a traditional test in which the standard for normal visual acuity is the ability to distinguish at a distance of 20 feet (about 6 m) a character 1/3 inch (about 8 mm) high⟩

'twere [twɜr] *unstressed,* [twər] *Archaic or poetic.* it were.

twerp [twɜrp] *n. Informal.* a person considered insignificant, ridiculous, contemptible. Also, **twirp.**

Twi [twi] *or* [tʃi] *n.* a Kwa language of Ghana, mutually intelligible with Fanti.

twice [twəis] *adv.* **1** two times: *twice a day. Twice two is four.* **2** doubly: *twice as much.* ⟨ME *twies* < OE *twiga* twice⟩

twice–told ['twəis 'tould] *adj.* told many times before; trite or very familiar: *twice-told tales.*

twice–travelled or **–traveled** ['twəis 'trævəld] *adj. Cdn. Nfld.* referring to a very strong variety of port wine that has twice been transported across the Atlantic by ship.

twid•dle ['twɪdəl] *v.* **-dled, -dling;** *n. —v.* **1** twirl: *to twiddle one's pencil.* **2** play with (something) idly.
twiddle (one's) **thumbs, a** keep turning one's thumbs idly about each other. **b** do nothing; be idle.
—n. a twirl. ⟨origin uncertain⟩

twig[1] [twɪg] *n.* a slender shoot or branch of a tree or other woody plant. ⟨OE *twigge*⟩

twig[2] [twɪg] *v.* **twigged, twig•ging.** *Informal.* **1** get the meaning; catch on (*often used with* **to**): *I didn't twig that he wanted a lift. They soon twigged to our plan.* **2** observe; notice. ⟨originally thieves' slang, ult. < Irish *tuigim* I understand⟩

twig•gy ['twɪgi] *adj.* **1** very thin or slender like a twig. **2** full of twigs.

twi•light ['twaɪ,ləit] *n.* **1** the faint light reflected from the sky before the sun rises and after it sets. **2** the period during which this light lasts, especially after sunset. **3** any faint light. **4** a period of gradual decline in fame, vigour, achievement, etc.: *the twilight of a golden age in history, twilight of one's life.* **5** any undefined or intermediate state or condition: *She lived in an uneasy twilight between sickness and health.* **6** (*adjl.*) of, like, or produced by twilight: *the twilight hour, a twilight glow.* ⟨ME *twilight* < *twi-* two, double + *light*[1]⟩

twilight sleep a semiconscious condition produced by the hypodermic injection of scopolamine and morphine, formerly used especially to dull the pain of childbirth. ⟨translation of G *Dämmerschlaf*⟩

twilight zone 1 an area or condition not clearly defined, as that between day and night, good and evil, reality and fantasy, etc. **2** a realm of strange or inexplicable goings-on: *What a* *weirdo! Our conversation was like something out of the twilight zone!*

twi•lit ['twaɪ,lɪt] *adj.* lighted by twilight or as if by twilight; bathed in such diffused light: *We paused to admire the beauty of the twilit forest.*

twill [twɪl] *n., v.* —*n.* **1** a textile weave in which the crosswise threads pass alternately over one and then under two or more lengthwise threads, producing raised diagonal lines. See WEAVE for picture. **2** fabric woven in this way. Denim is a twill.
—*v.* weave (cloth) in the manner of a twill. ⟨OE *twilic* < L *bilix* with a double thread < *bi-* two + *licium* thread, with substitution of *twi-* two for *bi-*⟩
☛ *Hom.* 'TWILL.

'twill [twɪl] *Archaic or poetic.* it will.
☛ *Hom.* TWILL.

twilled [twɪld] *adj.* woven in raised diagonal lines.

twin [twɪn] *n., v.* **twinned, twin•ning.** —*n.* **1** one of two children or animals born at the same time from the same mother. See also FRATERNAL (def. 3) and IDENTICAL (def. 3), MONOZYGOTIC and DIZYGOTIC. **2** (*adjl.*) being two or either one of two born at the same time from the same mother: *twin boys. That's his twin sister.* **3** one of two persons or things very much or exactly alike in structure, appearance, etc.: *This table is the twin of one we have at home.* **4** (*adjl.*) being two or either one of two persons or things very much or exactly alike or closely associated; paired or matching: *twin dresses, twin cities.* **5** (*adjl.*) having or consisting of two identical parts or units; double: *a twin-engined aircraft.* **6** (*adjl.*) of bed linen, designed to fit a TWIN BED. **7** a composite crystal consisting of two crystals, usually equal and similar, united in reversed positions with respect to each other. **8 the Twins,** *Astronomy or astrology.* Gemini.
—*v.* **1** give birth to twins. **2** join or associate closely; pair: *The two swimmers were twinned for the relay competition. Our town is twinned with one in Denmark.* **3** make or be a match of; duplicate. **4** of a crystal, form into a twin. ⟨OE *twinn*⟩

twin bed a single bed about one metre wide. Twin beds are often sold in matching pairs.

twin•ber•ry ['twɪn,bɛri] *n. Cdn.* **1** partridgeberry. **2** a North American honeysuckle (*Lonicera involucrata*) found in moist areas from California to Alaska and eastward, having paired black berries.

twine [twaɪn] *n., v.* **twined, twin•ing.** —*n.* **1** a strong thread or string made of two or more strands twisted together. **2** the act of twisting together, encircling or embracing. **3** something that is twisted together or interlaced; a tangle. **4** a single coil or twist.
—*v.* **1** twist together: *She twined holly into wreaths. According to legend, the two plants twined into a true-lover's knot over the graves of the sweethearts.* **2** make or form by twisting: *to twine a wreath of flowers.* **3** wind or wrap (*around*); cause to encircle something: *We are training the vine to twine around the post. He twined the string around his finger. They twined their arms around each other.* **4** follow a winding course: *The road twined around the lakes and hills.* ⟨OE *twīn*⟩

twin–en•gine ['twɪn 'ɛndʒən] *adj., n.* —*adj.* twin-engined.
—*n.* a twin-engined aircraft.

twin–en•gined ['twɪn 'ɛndʒənd] *adj.* of an aircraft, powered by two engines.

twin•flow•er ['twɪn,flaʊər] *n.* an evergreen trailing shrub (*Linnaea borealis*) of the honeysuckle family having pink or white, fragrant, bell-shaped flowers growing in pairs.

twinge [twɪndʒ] *n., v.* **twinged, twing•ing.** —*n.* **1** a sudden sharp, pinching pain that lasts only a moment: *a twinge of rheumatism.* **2** a sudden, brief mental pain; pang: *a twinge of remorse, a twinge of fear.*
—*v.* feel or cause to feel a twinge: *The theft occasionally twinged his conscience.* ⟨OE *twengan* pinch⟩

twin•kle ['twɪŋkəl] *v.* **-kled, -kling;** *n.* —*v.* **1** shine with quick little gleams: *The stars twinkled.* **2** of a person's eyes, light up or shine with amusement or fun: *Tony's eyes twinkled when he laughed.* **3** of the feet, move quickly: *The dancer's feet twinkled.* **4** wink or blink one's eyes. **5** cause to twinkle.
—*n.* **1** a twinkling; sparkle; gleam. **2** a quick motion, especially of the feet in dancing. **3** a quick motion of the eyelid; a wink; blink. **4** the time required for a wink: *He was gone in a twinkle.* ⟨OE *twinclian*⟩ —**'twin•kler,** *n.*

twin•kling ['twɪŋklɪŋ] *n., v., adj.* —*n.* TWINKLE (defs. 1, 4).
—*v.* ppr. of TWINKLE.
—*adj.* that twinkles: *twinkling stars.*

twin–screw ['twɪn 'skru] *adj., n.* —*adj.* of a steamship, having two screw propellers that revolve in opposite directions.
—*n.* a steamship powered by such propellers.

twin•ship ['twɪn,ʃɪp] *n.* **1** the fact or condition of being a twin or twins. **2** the relation existing between twins.

twin–size ['twɪn ,saɪz] *adj.* **1** designating a TWIN BED. **2** designed for a twin bed: *a twin-size bedspread.* Compare KING-SIZE, QUEEN-SIZE.

twirl [twɜrl] *v., n.* —*v.* **1** revolve rapidly; spin; whirl: *to twirl a top. The skaters twirled over the ice.* **2** turn or twist round and round: *He twirled the ends of his mustache. She twirled her hair with the curling iron.* **3** *Baseball.* throw (a ball); pitch.
—*n.* **1** the act of twirling; spin; whirl: *a twirl in a dance.* **2** a twist, curl, or flourish, as made in writing, etc. ⟨Cf. OE *thwirel* churn staff, and G *zwirlen* twirl⟩ —**'twirl•er,** *n.*

twirp [twɜrp] *n.* See TWERP.

twist [twɪst] *v., n.* —*v.* **1** wind together; twine: *to twist flowers into a wreath.* **2** make by winding together: *to twist a wreath of flowers.* **3** wind (a cord, ribbon, wire, etc.) around something: *She twisted the wire around the post.* **4** wind or coil (around something): *The vine has twisted around the fence post.* **5** give a spiral form to by turning one end while the other remains stationary or is turned in the opposite direction: *to twist a rubber band. The belt is twisted at the back.* **6** take on a spiral form: *This thread twists easily.* **7** move part way around: *He twisted around in his seat to see who had come in. She twisted the steering wheel sharply to the left.* **8** spin or twirl: *leaves twisting along the path in the wind. She twisted the ring on her finger.* **9** pull off or break by turning one end (*used with* **off**): *to twist off the stem of an apple.* **10** pull or force out of the natural shape or position: *I twisted my ankle when I fell. His face was twisted with pain. Your skirt is twisted.* **11** squirm; wriggle; writhe: *The injured worm lay twisting on the pavement. The child was twisting so vigorously in my arms that I had to put her down.* **12** distort the meaning, purpose, or intent of: *Don't twist my words; I didn't mean that at all.* **13** have a winding shape; follow a winding course; have many curves or bends: *The path twists in and out among the rocks.* **14** give an abnormal bias or inclination to; pervert: *Years of bitterness had twisted his mind.* **15** force (something) out of someone's possession; force someone to utter: *She twisted it out of his grasp. They twisted the story out of him.* **16** dance the twist.
twist (someone's) **arm,** force or coerce, either physically or verbally.
—*n.* **1** a wrench or sprain. **2** a twisting or being twisted; a spiral movement. **3** something made by twisting, such as a roll or a loaf of bread made of twisted pieces of dough. **4** a curve or bend, or a place at which something is twisted: *a path full of twists and turns. There's a twist in the rope.* **5** an unexpected change or variation: *an old story with a new twist. The plot had several twists that kept us in suspense right to the end.* **6** a peculiar bias or inclination; quirk: *an action prompted by some mental twist.* **7 a** torsional strain or stress; torque. **b** the degree or angle of this. **8** *Sports.* **a** a lateral spin imparted to a ball in throwing or striking it. **b** a ball thus spun. **9** a dance in which the hips are vigorously turned back and forth while the dancer stands in one place. **10** a small slice of lemon or lime, twisted and added to a drink: *gin and tonic with a twist.* **11** *Cdn.* formerly, tobacco prepared in twisted ropes, prominent among trade goods of the fur companies. **12** a strong, heavy kind of sewing thread usually made of silk or polyester: *buttonhole twist.* **13** *Cdn.* a kind of doughnut made by folding a 15 cm roll of dough in half and twining the two parts around each other. ⟨OE *-twist,* as in *mæsttwist* mast rope, stay⟩ —**'twist•a•ble,** *adj.*

twist•er ['twɪstər] *n.* **1** a tornado, whirlwind, etc. **2** any person or thing that twists or curves. **3** TWIST (def. 13).

twist–tie ['twɪst ,taɪ] *n.* a short length of thin wire between two narrow strips of paper or embedded in a narrow strip of soft plastic, used for closing plastic bags, tying up plants, etc.

twit[1] [twɪt] *v.* **twit•ted, twit•ting;** *n.* —*v.* taunt lightly; make fun of; tease: *His friends twitted him about his schemes to make money.*
—*n.* **1** an act of twitting; a taunt; jibe. **2** *Informal.* an annoyingly silly or stupid person; fool; nitwit. ⟨OE *ætwītan* < *æt* at + *wītan* blame⟩ —**'twit•ter,** *n.*

twit[2] [twɪt] *n.* dither; a state of nervous excitement: *She was all in a twit about the forthcoming interview.* ⟨< *twitter*⟩

twitch [twɪtʃ] *v., n.* —*v.* **1** move with slight, quick jerks: *The child's mouth twitched as if she were about to cry.* **2** pull or move with a sudden tug; jerk: *He twitched the curtain aside.* **3** ache with sudden, sharp pain.
—*n.* **1** a quick, jerky movement of some part of the body. **2** a short, sudden pull or jerk. **3** a sharp pain; twinge. ⟨related to OE *twiccian* pluck⟩

twitch grass COUCH GRASS.

twitch•y ['twɪtʃi] *adj.* **1** nervous or irritable. **2** twitching.

twit•ter ['twɪtər] *v., n.* —*v.* **1** make a series of light, trembling sounds; chirp: *Birds began to twitter just before sunrise.* **2** talk or laugh in a rapid, excited or nervous way; chatter or titter. **3** utter by twittering: *a sparrow twittering its morning song. She nervously twittered a greeting.* **4** tremble with excitement.
—*n.* **1** a series of light, trembling sounds; chirping: *the twitter of birds in the garden.* **2** an excited condition: *My nerves are in a twitter when I have to sing in public.* ⟨imitative⟩ **—'twit•te•ry,** *adj.*

'twixt [twɪkst] *prep. Poetic or dialect.* betwixt; between.

two [tu] *n., pl.* **twos;** *adj.* —*n.* **1** one more than one; 2. **2** the numeral 2: *I can't see it very well, but I think it's a 2.* **3** the second in a set or series; especially, a playing card or side of a die having two spots: *the two of clubs.* **4** *Cdn.* **a** formerly, a two-dollar bill. **b** a two-dollar coin. **5** a set or series of two persons or things: *The audience entered in twos and threes.*
in two, in two parts or pieces: *Break the cookie in two.*
put two and two together, form an obvious conclusion from the facts.
—*adj.* **1** being one more than one. **2** being second in a set or series (*used mainly after the noun*): *Chapter Two tells about his childhood.* ⟨OE *twā*⟩
☛ *Hom.* TO, TOO.

two–bag•ger ['tu 'bægər] *n. Baseball. Informal.* TWO-BASE HIT.

two–base hit ['tu 'beis] *Baseball.* a hit that allows the batter to reach second base.

two–bit ['tu 'bɪt] *adj. Slang.* **1** worth or selling for twenty-five cents. **2** cheap, inferior, or insignificant; small-time: *a two-bit novel, a two-bit gangster.*

two bits *Slang.* twenty-five cents; a quarter.

two–by–four *adj.* ['tu baɪ 'fɔr]; *n.* ['tu baɪ ,fɔr] *adj., n.* —*adj.* **1** especially of lumber, measuring two inches thick by four inches wide, untrimmed (about 5 cm by 10 cm): *They used two-by-four studs for the inside walls.* **2** *Informal.* small; narrow or limited: *a two-by-four apartment.*
—*n.* a piece of lumber two inches thick by four inches wide, untrimmed, equivalent to 1⅝″ × 2⅝″ (4½ cm × 9 cm) when trimmed. Two-by-fours are much used in building.

two–car ['tu 'kɑr] *adj.* owning or having space for two cars: *a two-car family, a two-car garage.*

two cents' worth *Slang.* an individual point of view or opinion on a particular subject: *They said we would all have a chance to put in our two cents' worth.*

two–di•men•sion•al ['tu də'mɛnʃənəl] *adj.* **1** having two dimensions: *Drawing is a two-dimensional art form.* **2** of a character in a novel, play, etc., lacking depth or individuality.

two–edged ['tu 'ɛdʒd] *adj.* **1** of a sword, etc., having two cutting edges; cutting both ways. **2** of a comment, etc., able to be taken in two ways; ambiguous: *a two-edged compliment.* **3** able to be used or to be effective in two ways: *a two-edged policy.*

two–faced ['tu ,feist] *adj.* **1** having two faces. **2** deceitful; hypocritical. **—'two-,fac•ed•ly,** *adv.* **—'two-,fac•ed•ness,** *n.*

two–fist•ed ['tu ,fɪstɪd] *adj. Informal.* vigorous and aggressive: *a two-fisted bully.*

two•fer ['tufər] *n. Informal.* a ticket, coupon, voucher, etc. or special offer allowing the purchaser to buy two items for the approximate price of one: *Our local theatre has a twofer on Tuesdays. Yogurt is on as a twofer this week.* ⟨< *two for* (*one*)⟩

two•fold ['tu,fould] *adj., adv.* —*adj.* **1** two times as much or as many; double. **2** made up of two parts or elements: *Her meaning was twofold: part joking and part serious.*
—*adv.* two times as much or as many; doubly.

two–four ['tu 'fɔr] *adj.* of or designating a musical rhythm with two quarter notes to a bar.

two–hand•ed ['tu 'hændɪd] *adj.* **1** having two hands. **2** using both hands equally well. **3** involving the use of both hands; requiring both hands to wield or manage: *a two-handed sword.* **4** requiring two persons to operate: *a two-handed saw.* **5** engaged in by two persons: *a two-handed game.*

two nations *Cdn.* English and French Canada.

two•nie or **twoo•nie** ['tuni] *n. Cdn.* See TOONIE.

two–part time ['tu ,pɑrt] *Music.* a time or rhythm with two beats to the measure, or a multiple of two beats to the measure.

two–par•ty system ['tu 'pɑrti] a political system in which two political parties predominate over any others, one of the two generally having a majority in the legislature. This system originated in Great Britain in the 17th century, and prevailed until fairly recently in Canada, the United States, and most countries of the English-speaking world.

two•pence ['tʌpəns] *n. Brit.* **1** the sum of two pence. **2** a former British silver coin worth two pence. Also, **tuppence.**

two•pen•ny ['tʌpəni]; *def. 3,* ['tu,pɛni] *adj.* **1** *Brit.* worth or costing two pence. **2** of little worth; cheap. Also, **tuppenny.** **3** referring to a type of nail that is 2.5 cm long and used to sell at two pennies per hundred.

two–phase ['tu ,feiz] *adj. Electricity.* of a circuit, appliance, etc., using or carrying two alternating voltages or currents of equal frequency, their phases differing by 90°.

two–piece *adj.* ['tu 'pis]; *n.* ['tu ,pis] *adj., n.* —*adj.* of a dress, swimsuit, etc., consisting of separate, matching top and bottom parts.
—*n.* a two-piece dress, swimsuit, etc.

two–ply ['tu 'plaɪ] *adj.* having two thicknesses, folds, layers, or strands.

two–seater ['tu 'sitər] *n.* a vehicle with seats to accommodate the driver and one passenger, as a sportscar or a motorcycle.

two–sided ['tu 'saɪdɪd] *adj.* **1** having two sides. **2** having two sides the same or equally usable; reversible: *two-sided fabric* **3** having two aspects: *a two-sided proposition.*

two•some ['tusəm] *n.* **1** a group of two people. **2** a game played by two people. **3** the players in such a game.

two–step ['tu ,stɛp] *n., v.* **-stepped, -step•ping.**
—*n.* **1** a dance in 2/4 time. **2** the music for such a dance.
—*v.* dance the two-step: *They two-stepped across the floor.*

two–stroke ['tu ,strouk] *adj.* of, being, or having to do with an internal-combustion engine in which the piston makes two strokes with every explosion. Compare FOUR-STROKE.

two–time ['tu ,taɪm] *v.* **-timed, -tim•ing.** *Slang.* **1** be unfaithful (to) in love. **2** betray; double cross. **—'two-,tim•er,** *n.* **—'two-,tim•ing,** *adj.*

two–tone ['tu ,toun] *adj.* having two colours or two shades of one colour: *two-tone shoes. His car is two-tone blue.*

'twould [twʊd]; *unstressed,* [twəd] *Archaic or poetic.* it would.

two–way ['tu 'wei] *adj.* **1** of a street, bridge, etc., allowing traffic to move in either direction. **2** of traffic, moving in both directions on the same street, etc. **3** designed for both sending and receiving messages: *a two-way radio.* **4** of or designating a valve, pipe, wire, etc. that connects with two outlets or operates in two directions. **5** involving reciprocal action between two people or groups: *a two-way cultural exchange.* **6** of a fabric or garment, reversible. **7** *Mathematics.* capable of variation in two ways or modes: *a two-way progression.*

two–way street **1** a street allowing traffic in both directions. **2** any activity, relationship, etc. that involves reciprocity: *Communication is a two-way street.*

two–wheel•er ['tu 'wilər] *or* ['tu ,wilər] *n.* a vehicle having two wheels, especially a bicycle or motorcycle.

twp. or Twp. township.

-ty[1] *suffix.* tens, as in *sixty, seventy, eighty.* ⟨OE *-tig*⟩

-ty[2] *noun-forming suffix.* the fact, quality, state, condition, etc. of being——, as in *safety, sovereignty, surety.* See also -ITY. ⟨ME < OF *-te, -tet* < L *-tas, -tatis*⟩

ty•coon [təi'kun] *n.* **1** *Informal.* a person who holds a very important position in business, industry, etc.; magnate. **2** formerly, the title used by foreigners to refer to the Japanese shogun. ⟨< Japanese *taikun* < Chinese *tai* great + *kiun* lord⟩

ty•ee ['taii] *n., pl.* **ty•ee** (def. 2) or **ty•ees.** *Cdn.* **1** a spring salmon, especially one weighing more than about 13 kg. **2** *Esp. British Columbia.* **a** the chief of a First Nations band. **b** any important person; boss. Also (def. 1), **tyee salmon.** ⟨< Chinook Jargon⟩

ty•ing ['taiɪŋ] *v.* ppr. of TIE.

tyke [təik] *n.* **1** *Informal.* a small child. **2** a dog, especially an inferior or worthless one. ⟨ME < ON *tík* bitch⟩

tym•pan ['tɪmpən] *n.* **1** a stretched membrane, or a sheet or plate of some thin material, in an apparatus. **2** *Architecture.* tympanum. **3** *Archaic.* a drum. ⟨< L < Gk. *tympanon.* Doublet of TYMPANUM, TIMBRE.⟩

tym•pa•ni ['tɪmpəni] *n.* See TIMPANI.

tym•pan•ic [tɪm'pænɪk] *adj.* **1** of, having to do with, or being the eardrum or the middle ear. **2** like a drum.

tympanic bone in mammals, the bone in the inner ear that supports the tympanic membrane and encloses part of the middle ear.

tympanic membrane eardrum.

tym•pa•nist ['tɪmpənɪst] *n.* See TIMPANIST.

tym•pa•ni•tes [ˌtɪmpə'nəitiz] *n.* a condition caused by an excessive accumulation of gas in the intestines or peritoneal cavity and characterized by distention of the abdomen. ⟨< LL < Gk. *tympanites* having to do with a drum < *tympanon.* See TYMPANUM.⟩ **—ˌtym•pa'nit•ic** [-'nɪtɪk], *adj.*

tym•pa•ni•tis [ˌtɪmpə'nəitɪs] *n.* inflammation of the middle ear; otitis media.

tym•pa•num ['tɪmpənəm] *n., pl.* **-nums** or **-na** [-nə]. **1** eardrum. **2** the middle ear. **3** a thin membrane covering the organ of hearing of an insect. **4** a drum or drumhead. **5** the diaphragm in a telephone. **6** *Architecture.* **a** the vertical recessed face of a pediment, enclosed by the cornices. **b** a slab or wall between an arch and the horizontal top of a door or window below. ⟨< L *tympanum* drum < Gk. *tympanon.* Doublet of TIMBRE, TYMPAN.⟩

Tyn•dall effect ['tɪndɒl] *Physics.* the scattering of light by particles of matter, as dust, snow, etc. that encounter it, so that the beam of light becomes visible by illuminating the particles. ⟨< John *Tyndall* (1820-1893), Irish physicist⟩

Tyn•wald ['tɪnwɒld] *n.* the parliament of the Isle of Man. ⟨< ON *thing-völlr* place of assembly < *thing* assembly + *völlr* place⟩

type [təip] *n., v.* **typed, typ•ing.** *—n.* **1** a class or group having qualities or characteristics in common: *type O blood, a new type of engine. He doesn't like that type of work.* **2** a person or thing having the qualities or characteristics of a particular class or group; model, representative, or symbol: *She is a perfect type of the conscientious student.* **3** a person or thing that foreshadows, prefigures, evokes, etc. another, especially in literature. **4** the general form, style, character, or combination of qualities that distinguishes some class or group: *They weren't surprised when he got angry, because he was behaving true to type.* **5** *Informal.* an unusual or eccentric person: *She's a real type.* **6** *Printing.* **a** a block, usually of metal, having a raised letter, numeral, or sign in reverse on its upper surface, from which an inked impression can be made. **b** a collection of such pieces: *a box of type.* **c** a collection of letters, numerals, or signs that are reproduced photographically for printing. **d** a particular kind or size of letters, numerals, or signs: *The poem was set in italic type.* **7** printed or typewritten letters, numerals, or signs: *The page looks crowded with so much type on it.* **8** the figure, writing, or design on either side of a coin or medal. **9** *Biology.* **a** sometimes, **type species**, a species, genus, etc. whose characteristics are used as the basis for defining the next highest taxonomic group and for which the group is usually named. **b** sometimes, **type specimen**, the single specimen or series of specimens on which the description of a species for classification is based.
—v. **1** classify according to type: *to type a blood sample. The new boy was immediately typed as a bully.* **2** typecast: *She's been typed as the girl next door ever since her first film.* **3** write with a typewriter. **4** cause (words, letters, etc.) to be displayed on the screen by entering them on a computer keyboard. ⟨< L < Gk. *typos* dent, impression⟩ **—'typ•al,** *adj.*

☛ *Usage.* **Type of.** The idiom should not be shortened by omitting the **of,** as in *this type letter.* Standard usage requires *this type of letter.*

Type A a personality type whose main features are tenseness, aggression, inflexibility, etc. and which is more conducive to heart attacks. ⟨coined by U.S. physicians M. Friedman and R. Rosenman, 1974⟩

Type B a personality type whose main features are a relaxed attitude, adaptability, friendliness, etc. and which is less conducive to heart attacks. ⟨See TYPE A⟩

type•bar ['təip,bɑr] *n.* on a typewriter, one of the metal bars that strike the paper and print a letter, number, etc. when a key is depressed.

type•cast ['təip,kæst] *v.* **-cast, -cast•ing. 1** cast (an actor) in a role to fit his or her personality, appearance, etc. **2** cast (an actor) repeatedly in the same kind of role.

type•cast•er ['təip,kæstər] *n.* a person who casts type.

type•face ['təip,feis] *n.* **1** the face, or printing surface, of type. **2** the design or style of type; face: *an ornate typeface.*

type founder a person who casts metal type in a foundry. **—type founding.**

type genus *Biology.* the genus from which a family name is derived.

type–high ['təip ,hai] *adj.* as high as a standard piece of type, .918 inches (2.33 cm).

type metal metal used for casting type, normally an alloy of tin, lead, and antimony.

type•script ['təip,skrɪpt] *n.* **1** a typewritten manuscript. **2** typewritten matter.

typeset ['təip,sɛt] *v.* **-set, -set•ting.** set (text) in type.

type•set•ter ['təip,sɛtər] *n.* a person, company, or machine that sets type for printing.

type•set•ting ['təip,sɛtɪŋ] *n., adj. —n.* the act or process of setting type for printing.
—adj. of, having to do with, or used for setting type: *typesetting machines, typesetting methods.*

type•write ['təip,rəit] *v.* **-wrote, -writ•ten, -writ•ing.** write with a typewriter; type.

type•writ•er ['təip,rəitər] *n.* **1** a machine for producing letters, numerals, and signs similar to those produced by printer's type, operated by means of a keyboard. When a key is struck, the corresponding type hits an inked ribbon, transferring the imprint of the letter, etc. onto paper behind the ribbon. **2** a style of printer's type, or a computer printer font, meant to resemble the characters produced by a typewriter. **3** *Archaic.* typist.

type•writ•ing ['təip,rəitɪŋ] *n., v. —n.* **1** the act or skill of using a typewriter. **2** work done on a typewriter.
—v. ppr. of TYPEWRITE.

type•writ•ten ['təip,rɪtən] *adj., v. —adj.* written with a typewriter: *a typewritten letter.*
—v. pp. of TYPEWRITE.

ty•phoid ['təifɔɪd] *adj., n. —adj.* **1** of or having to do with TYPHOID FEVER. **2** like typhus.
—n. TYPHOID FEVER. ⟨< *typhus*⟩ **—ty'phoid•al,** *adj.*

typhoid fever a severe infectious disease caused by a bacterium (*Salmonella typhosa*) that enters the body in contaminated food or drink, most often from a polluted public water supply. Typhoid fever is characterized by fever, a rash of small red spots and, often, inflammation of the intestines.

Typhoid Ma•ry 1 a carrier of typhoid. **2** a person who is the source of any noxious influence. ⟨< *Mary* Mallon (d. 1938), a cook in New York who carried typhoid⟩

ty•phoon [təi'fun] *n.* a violent tropical cyclone that forms over the Pacific Ocean. ⟨< Chinese *tai fung* big wind; influenced by Gk. *typhōn* whirlwind⟩ **—ty'phon•ic** [-'fɒnɪk], *adj.*

ty•phus ['təifəs] *n.* any of a group of very serious infectious diseases caused by any of several species of rickettsia which are carried especially by lice or fleas. Epidemic typhus, caused by *Rickettsia prowazekii,* is characterized by chills and fever, dark-red spots on the skin, and extreme weakness; it used to occur in epidemics in which many people died. Also, **typhus fever.** ⟨< NL < Gk. *typhos* stupor, originally, smoke⟩ **—'ty•phous,** *adj.*

typ•i•cal ['tɪpəkəl] *adj.* **1** very much like others of the same type or kind; serving as an example; representative: *a typical Canadian. The typical Thanksgiving dinner has roast turkey as its main course.* **2** of, having to do with, or serving to distinguish a type; characteristic: *the hospitality typical of the pioneer. It was typical of him to sign it without reading it first.* **3** being a type; prefiguring; foreshadowing; symbolic or evocative (*of*). **4** *Biology.* that is the type of the genus, family, etc. Also (defs. 3, 4), **typic.** **—ˌtyp•i'cal•i•ty,** *n.* **—'typ•i•cal•ly,** *adv.* **—'typ•i•cal•ness,** *n.*

typ•i•fy ['tɪpə,fai] *v.* **-fied, -fy•ing. 1** have the common characteristics of; be an example of: *Alexander Mackenzie typifies the adventurous explorer.* **2** be a symbol of; signify or represent: *The dove typifies peace.* **3** prefigure; be a type of; foreshadow. ⟨< L *typus* type + E *-fy*⟩ **—ˌtyp•i•fi'ca•tion,** *n.* **—'typ•i,fi•er,** *n.*

typ•ist ['təipɪst] *n.* a person who types, especially one whose work is typing.

ty•po ['təipou] *n. Informal.* a typographical error; a small mistake made in typing or in setting type.

ty•pog•ra•pher [təi'pɒgrəfər] *n.* printer or typesetter.

ty•po•graph•i•cal [ˌtəipə'græfəkəl] *or* [ˌtɪpə'græfəkəl] *adj.* of or having to do with printing: *typographical errors.* Also, **typographic. —ˌty•po'graph•i•cal•ly,** *adv.*

ty•pog•ra•phy [təi'pɒgrəfi] *n.* **1** the art or process of printing with type; the work of setting and arranging type and of printing from it. **2** the arrangement, appearance, or style of printed matter. ⟨< late Med.L < Gk. *typos* type + *-graphia* writing⟩

ty•po•log•i•cal [ˌtəipəˈlɒdʒəkəl] *adj.* of or having to do with typology.

ty•pol•o•gist [təiˈpɒlədʒɪst] *n.* one who is skilled in typology, especially one whose work it is.

ty•pol•o•gy [təiˈpɒlədʒi] *n.* **1** the classification and study of types, as of remains and specimens in archaeology or grammatical features and word order in languages. **2** the system of types, symbols, etc. used in a body of literature, posited by a school of interpretation, etc.; symbolism. **3** the study of this. ⟨< Gk. *typos* type + E *-logy*⟩

Tyr [tir] *n. Norse mythology.* the god of war, the son of Odin. ⟨< ON⟩

ty•ra•mine [ˈtaɪrɑˌmin] *or* [ˈtirəˌmin] *n.* a colourless crystalline amine occurring in ripe cheese, decayed animal tissue, mistletoe, and ergot fungus, formerly used to treat hypotension. *Formula*: $C_8H_{11}NO$ ⟨< *tyr(osine)* + *amine*⟩

ty•ran•ni•cal [təˈrænəkəl] *or* [taɪˈrænəkəl] *adj.* of or like a tyrant; wielding power in an arbitrary, cruel, or unjust way: *a tyrannical king.* Also, **tyrannic. —ty'ran•ni•cal•ly,** *adv.*

ty•ran•ni•cide [təˈrænəˌsaɪd] *or* [taɪˈrænəˌsaɪd] *n.* **1** the act of killing a tyrant. **2** a person who kills a tyrant. ⟨< L *tyrannicidium* the killing of a tyrant < *tyrannus* tyrant + *-cidium* act of killing (for def. 1); < L *tyrannicida* one who kills a tyrant < *tyrannus* + *-cida* killer (for def. 2)⟩ **—ty,ran•ni'cid•al,** *adj.*

tyr•an•nize [ˈtirəˌnaɪz] *v.* **-nized, -niz•ing.** use power cruelly or unjustly; rule as a tyrant (*sometimes used with* **over**): *Those who are strong should not tyrannize over those who are weaker.* **—'tyr•an,niz•er,** *n.*

ty•ran•no•sau•rus [təˌrænəˈsɔrəs] *n.* a huge carnivorous dinosaur (*Tyrannosaurus rex*) of the late Cretaceous period in North America, noted for its ability to walk upright on its two hind legs. Also, **tyrannosaur** [təˈrænəˌsɔr]. ⟨< NL *Tyrannosaurus*, the genus name < Gk. *tyrannos* tyrant + *sauros* lizard⟩

tyr•an•nous [ˈtirənəs] *adj.* tyrannical; despotic. **—'tyr•an•nous•ly,** *adv.*

tyr•an•ny [ˈtirəni] *n., pl.* **-nies. 1** cruel or unjust use of power. **2** severe or demanding conditions: *the tyranny of public opinion, living all one's life under the tyranny of the clock.* **3** a tyrannical act: *She had suffered many tyrannies.* **4** government by an absolute ruler. **5** any form or system of oppressive or despotic government; totalitarianism. ⟨< LL < Gk. *tyrannia* < *tyrannos.* See TYRANT.⟩

ty•rant [ˈtaɪrənt] *n.* **1** a person who uses his or her power cruelly or unjustly or who exercises complete control over others: *That spoiled child is a regular tyrant in their household.* **2** a cruel or unjust ruler. **3** a ruler with absolute power, especially one who has acquired it illegitimately, regardless of how he or she uses it. Some tyrants in ancient Greece were kind and just rulers. ⟨ME < OF < L < Gk. *tyrannos* (def. 3)⟩

tyrant flycatcher any of a family (Tyrannidae) of passerine New World birds that catch and eat insects in flight; FLYCATCHER (def. 2).

Tyr•i•an [ˈtiriən] *adj., n. —adj.* **1** of or having to do with Tyre, a seaport in ancient Phoenicia. **2** of TYRIAN PURPLE. *—n.* a native of Tyre. ⟨< L < Gk. *Tyrios*⟩

Tyrian purple 1 a crimson or purple dye highly prized by the ancient Greeks and Romans. It was obtained from certain molluscs. **2** a deep purplish red.

ty•ro [ˈtaɪrou] *n., pl.* **-ros.** a beginner in learning anything; novice; greenhorn. Also, **tiro.** ⟨< L *tiro* recruit⟩

Ty•ro•le•an [təˈrouliən] *or* [ˌtirəˈliən] *n., adj.* Tirolean.

Tyr•o•lese [ˌtirəˈliz] Tirolese.

ty•ro•sin•ase [ˈtaɪrousɪˌneis] *or* [taɪˈrɒsɪˌneis] *n.* a plant and animal enzyme involved in the production of the dark pigment melanin, the absence of which results in albinism. ⟨< *tyrosine* + *-ase* enzyme suffix⟩

ty•ro•sine [ˈtaɪrəˌsin] *n.* an amino acid formed by decomposition of proteins and converted by the body into melanin. ⟨< Gk. *tyros* cheese + E *-ine*[2]⟩

tyyn [tin] *n.* a unit of money in Kirghizia and Uzbekistan, equal to 1/100 of a som. See table of money in the Appendix.

tzar [zɑr] *or* [tsɑr] *n.* See CZAR. **—'tsar•ism,** *n.* **—'tsar•ist,** *n., adj.*

tzar•e•vitch [ˈzɑrəˌvɪtʃ] *or* [ˈtsɑrəˌvɪtʃ] *n.* See CZAREVITCH.

tsa•rev•na [zɑˈrɛvnə] *or* [tsɑˈrɛvnə] *n.* See CZAREVNA.

tza•ri•na [zɑˈrinə] *or* [tsɑˈrinə] *n.* See CZARINA.

tze•tze [ˈtsi tsi] *or* [ˈtsɛtsi] *n.* See TSETSE.

tzi•gane [tsiˈgɑn] *n.* often, **Tzigane.** a Gypsy, especially a Hungarian one. ⟨< F < Hungarian *czigány.* 19c.⟩

U u *U u*

u or **U** [ju] *n., pl.* **u's** or **U's. 1** the twenty-first letter of the English alphabet. **2** any speech sound represented by this letter. **3** a person or thing identified as *u,* especially the twenty-first of a series. **4** something shaped like the letter U. **5** (*adjl.*) of or being a U or u. **6** any device, such as a printer's type, a lever, or a key on a keyboard, that produces a U or u.

u unit(s).

u. 1 upper. **2** uncle.

U uranium.

U. 1 University. **2** uncle.

UAE UNITED ARAB EMIRATES.

u•bi•e•ty [ju'baɪəti] *n.* the fact or condition of being in a particular place. ⟨< NL *ubietas* < L *ubi* where⟩

u•biq•ui•tous [ju'bɪkwətəs] *adj.* being or seeming to be everywhere at the same time; found or turning up everywhere: *He wanted a quiet place to read, but found it impossible to escape from his ubiquitous little sister.* ⟨< *ubiquity*⟩ **—u'biq•ui•tous•ly,** *adv.* **—u'biq•ui•tous•ness,** *n.*

u•biq•ui•ty [ju'bɪkwəti] *n.* **1** the fact or condition of being or seeming to be everywhere at the same time. **2** the ability to be everywhere at once. ⟨< NL *ubiquitas* < L *ubique* everywhere⟩

U–boat ['ju ,bout] *n.* a German submarine. ⟨< G *U-boot,* short for *Unterseeboot* undersea boat⟩

U bolt a bolt shaped like the letter U, having both ends threaded to take securing nuts.

u.c. upper case; one or more capital letters.

U.C. 1 Upper Canada. **2** United Church.

ud•der ['ʌdər] *n.* in a cow or female sheep or goat, etc., a large baglike organ containing two or more milk-producing glands, each gland provided with one teat. ⟨OE *ūder*⟩

u•dom•e•ter [ju'dɒmətər] *n.* a rain gauge. ⟨< L *udus* wet + E *-meter*⟩

U.E.L. UNITED EMPIRE LOYALIST.

UFO [,juɛf'ou] *n., pl.* **UFOs** or **UFO's. 1** an unidentified flying object, especially one regarded as possibly being a flying saucer or other spacecraft from another planet. **2** *Cdn.* United Farmers of Ontario.

u•fol•o•gy [ju'fɒlədʒi] *n.* the study of UFOs. **—u'fol•o•gist,** *n.*

U•gan•da [ju'gændə] *or* [ju'gɑndə] *n.* a country in E central Africa. See SUDAN for map.

U•gan•dan [ju'gændən] *n., adj. —n.* a native or inhabitant of Uganda.
—adj. of or having to do with Uganda or its people.

ugh [ʌx], [ʌ], [ʊx], *or* [ʌg] *interj.* an exclamation expressing disgust or horror.

Ug•li ['ʌgli] *n. Trademark.* a large, sweet, citrus fruit of Jamaica, a variety of tangelo having rough, wrinkled skin, hence the name. ⟨< Sp. var. of *ugly*⟩

ug•li•fi•ca•tion [,ʌgləfə'keiʃən] *n.* the act or an instance of uglifying or the state of being uglified.

ug•li•fy ['ʌglə,faɪ] *v.* **-fied, -fy•ing.** make ugly or more ugly: *uglifying the parkway with a lot of billboards.*

ug•ly ['ʌgli] *adj.* **-li•er, -li•est. 1** very unpleasant to look at, hear, smell, etc.: *an ugly house, an ugly sound, ugly fumes.* **2** morally bad; objectionable; vile: *ugly rumours, an ugly deed.* **3** threatening; dangerous: *an ugly wound, ugly clouds.* **4** *Informal.* ill-natured or bad-tempered; quarrelsome: *an ugly dog. He gets ugly when he's drunk.* ⟨ME < ON *uggligr* dreadful⟩ **—'ug•li•ness,** *n.*

☛ *Syn.* **1. Ugly,** UNSIGHTLY, HOMELY = not pleasing in appearance. **Ugly** is the opposite of **beautiful** and means, when restricted to the visual, 'positively unpleasant or offensive in appearance': *There are five ugly lamps in that room.* **Unsightly** emphasizes being unpleasing to the sight, sometimes causing one to turn away to avoid seeing what is described: *Trains approach the city through an unsightly section.* **Homely** emphasizes lack of physical beauty or attractiveness in a person, but does not suggest unpleasant or disagreeable moral qualities: *a homely child.*

ugly duckling a person or thing at first thought to be ugly, unpromising, etc. but that turns out to have unusual beauty, talent, value, etc. ⟨with reference to the cygnet in a story by Hans Christian Andersen (1805-1875), that seems ugly by comparison with its duckling companions, but grows up to be a swan⟩

U•gri•an ['ugriən] *or* ['jugriən] *n., adj. —n.* **1** a member of the branch of the Finno-Ugric peoples that includes the Magyars and certain groups from western Siberia. **2** the languages of these peoples.
—adj. of or designating the Ugrians or their languages.

U•gric ['ugrɪk] *or* ['jugrɪk] *n.* the branch of the Finno-Ugric family of languages that includes Hungarian.

uh [ʌ] *or* [ʌ̃] *interj.* a sound made by a speaker hesitating while he or she thinks of the right word or words to say next.

UHF or **U.H.F.** ULTRAHIGH FREQUENCY.

uh–huh [ʌ̃'hʌ̃] *interj.* an expression of agreement or affirmation; yes.

uh•lan ['ulɑn] *or* [u'lɑn] *n.* formerly: **1** in certain European armies, a lancer and cavalry man of a type first known in Poland. **2** in the German army, a member of the heavy cavalry. ⟨< G < Polish < Turkish *oghlān* boy⟩

uh–uh ['ʌ̃'ʌ̃], ['ʌ̃,ʌ̃], *or* [,ʌ̃'ʌ̃] *interj.* an expression of disagreement, refusal, etc.; no.

UI or **U.I.** UNEMPLOYMENT INSURANCE.

UIC or **U.I.C.** Unemployment Insurance Commission.

u•in•ta•ite or **u•in•ta•hite** [ju'ɪntə,əit] *n.* a very pure, lustrous, black natural form of asphalt, found in parts of Utah and western Colorado, and used in the manufacture of paints and varnishes. ⟨< the *Uinta* Mountains, a range of the Rockies in Utah⟩

uit•land•er ['ɔɪt,lændər] *or* ['əit,lændər] *n.* in South Africa, a foreigner. ⟨< Afrikaans⟩

U–joint ['ju ,dʒɔɪnt] *n.* UNIVERSAL JOINT.

UK or **U.K.** UNITED KINGDOM.

u•kase [ju'keis] *or* ['jukeis] *n.* **1** in czarist Russia, an order or edict of the ruler or government. **2** any official proclamation or order. ⟨< Russian *ukaz*⟩

u•ke•le•le [,jukə'leili] *n.* See UKULELE.

U•kraine [ju'krein] *n.* a large country in SE Europe.

U•krain•i•an [ju'kreinjən] *n., adj. —n.* **1** a native or inhabitant of Ukraine. **2** the Slavic language of the Ukrainians, closely related to Russian. **3** a person of Ukrainian descent: *There are many Ukrainians in Canada, especially in the West.*
—adj. of or having to do with Ukraine, its people, or their language.

Ukrainian Catholic 1 a member of an Eastern rite church within the Catholic Church, originating in E Europe and now active especially in Ukraine, Canada, and the United States. **2** of or having to do with Ukrainian Catholics or their church.

u•ku•le•le [,jukə'leili] *n.* a small, guitar-shaped instrument having four strings. Also, **ukelele.** ⟨< Hawaiian *ukulele,* literally jumping flea < *uku* flea + *lele* jump, leap⟩

A ukulele

u•la•ma [,ulə'mɑ] *or* ['ulə,mɑ] *n.* See ULEMA.

ul•cer ['ʌlsər] *n.* **1** an open sore on the skin or a mucous membrane such as the lining of the stomach or the inside of the mouth. **2** a moral sore spot; corrupting influence. **3** a visual blight: *Those huge open-pit mines are ulcers on the landscape.* ⟨< L *ulcus, ulceris*⟩

ul•cer•ate ['ʌlsə,reit] *v.* **-at•ed, -at•ing. 1** affect or be affected with an ulcer: *An ulcerated tooth may be very painful.* **2** form or be formed into an ulcer; become ulcerous. ⟨< L *ulcerare* < *ulcus* ulcer⟩ **—'ul•cer•a•tive,** *adj.*

ul•cer•a•tion [,ʌlsə'reiʃən] *n.* **1** an ulcerating or being ulcerated. **2** ulcer.

ul•cer•ous ['ʌlsərəs] *adj.* **1** having an ulcer or ulcers. **2** of or having to do with ulcers. **—'ul•cer•ous•ly,** *adv.* **—'ul•cer•ous•ness,** *n.*

-ule *suffix.* small: *globule, module.* ⟨< F < L *-ulus, -ula, -ulum,* diminutive suffix of first, second, and third declension nouns⟩

u•le•ma [,ulə'mɑ] *or* ['ulə,mɑ] *n.pl. Islam.* **1** religious scholars or leaders. **2** (*used with a singular verb*) a group of these; council. ⟨< Turkish < Arabic *ulama*, pl. of *alim* learned < *alima* know⟩

–ulent *suffix.* full of; abounding in: *corpulent, succulent.* ⟨< L *-ulentus*⟩

ul•lage ['ʌlɪdʒ] *n.* **1** the amount by which a container fails to be full. **2** *Rocketry.* the volume of a loaded tank of liquid propellant in excess of the volume of the propellant; the space allowed for thermal expansion of the propellant. ⟨< ME *ulage* < OF *ouillage* filling of a cask < *ouiller* fill a cask < *ouil* eye (fig., bunghole) < L *oculus*⟩

ul•na ['ʌlnə] *n., pl.* **-nae** [-ni] *or* [-naɪ] or **-nas. 1** the bone of the forearm on the side opposite the thumb. See ARM[1] for picture. **2** the corresponding bone in the foreleg of an animal. ⟨< NL < L *ulna* elbow⟩

ul•nar ['ʌlnər] *adj.* **1** of or having to do with the ulna. **2** in or supplying the part of the forearm near the ulna.

–ulous *suffix.* full of; characterized by; tending to: *credulous, pendulous.*

ul•ster ['ʌlstər] *n.* a long, loose, heavy overcoat, often belted at the waist. ⟨< *Ulster*, a province of Ireland⟩

ult. 1 *Archaic.* ultimo. **2** ultimate; ultimately.
☛ *Usage.* See note at INST. (def. 1).

ul•te•ri•or [ʌl'tiriər] *adj.* **1** beyond what is seen or expressed; hidden, especially for a bad purpose: *an ulterior motive.* **2** more distant; on the farther side. **3** further; later. ⟨< L *ulterior*, comparative of root of *ultra, ultro*, adv., beyond⟩ **—ul'te•ri•or•ly,** *adv.*

ul•ti•ma ['ʌltəmə] *n. Linguistics.* the last syllable of a word. ⟨< L *ultima (syllaba)* last (syllable)⟩

ul•ti•mate ['ʌltəmɪt] *adj., n. —adj.* **1** coming at the end; last possible; final: *She never stopped to consider the ultimate result of her actions.* **2** beyond which nothing further may be discovered by investigation or analysis; primary; basic: *the ultimate principle, the ultimate source.* **3** greatest possible.
—n. an ultimate point, result, fact, etc. ⟨< Med.L *ultimatus*, pp. of *ultimare* < Ital. *ultimare* bring to an end < L *ultimare* come to an end < *ultimus* last⟩ **—'ul•ti•ma•cy** or **'ul•ti•mate•ness,** *n.* **—'ul•ti•mate•ly,** *adv.*
☛ *Syn.* **1, 2.** See note at LAST[1].

ultimate strength *Physics.* the maximum stress or tension a substance can bear without tearing or breaking.

ultimate stress *Physics.* the stress or load needed to produce fracture or breakage.

ultima Thu•le ['ʌltəmə 'θuli] *or* ['ʊltɪmɑ 'tuli] **1** the farthest north. **2** any distant unknown place. **3** the farthest limit or point possible. **4** the uttermost degree attainable. ⟨< L *ultima Thule* most remote Thule (a remote Northern region)⟩

ul•ti•ma•tum [,ʌltə'meitəm] *n., pl.* **-tums, -ta** [-tə]. a final proposal, statement of conditions, or demand presented, especially one whose rejection may result in a breaking off of relations between negotiating parties or, sometimes, in international negotiations, a declaration of war. ⟨< NL *ultimatum*, originally neut. of Med.L *ultimatus.* See ULTIMATE.⟩

ul•ti•mo ['ʌltə,mou] *adv. Archaic.* in or of last month. ⟨< Med.L *ultimo (mense)* in the last (month)⟩

ul•ti•mo•gen•i•ture [,ʌltəmou'dʒɛnətʃər] *n.* the right of inheritance or succession through the youngest son. Compare PRIMOGENITURE.

ul•tra ['ʌltrə] *adj., n. —adj.* beyond what is usual; very; excessive; extreme.
—n. a person who holds extreme views or urges extreme measures. ⟨< L *ultra* beyond⟩

ultra– *prefix.* **1** beyond a specified limit, range, or place, as in *ultraviolet, ultramontane.* **2** very; extremely; unusually, as in *ultra-ambitious, ultrafashionable, ultramodest, ultraradical, ultrarefined.* **3** of instruments, machines, etc., useful or operating at an extreme range of speed, size, temperature, etc.: *ultramicrometer, ultracentrifuge.* ⟨< LL *ultra-* < L *ultra*, adv. prep. beyond⟩

ul•tra•cen•tri•fuge [,ʌltrə'sɛntrə,fjudʒ] *n.* a high-speed centrifuge for separating colloids.

ul•tra•dense ['ʌltrə'dɛns] *adj.* of matter, extremely dense, as in a black hole.

ul•tra•high frequency ['ʌltrə'haɪ] the range of radio frequencies between 300 and 3000 megahertz. Ultrahigh frequency is the range next above very high frequency. *Abbrev.:* UHF or U.H.F.

ul•tra•ism ['ʌltrə,ɪzəm] *n.* adherence to an extreme position in politics, religion, etc. **—'ul•tra•ist,** *n.*

ul•tra•light ['ʌltrə,ləit] *or* ['ʌltrə'ləit] *n.* microlight.

ul•tra•ma•rine [,ʌltrəmə'rin] *n., adj. —n.* **1** a deep blue. **2** a blue pigment made from powdered lapis lazuli. **3** a chemically similar pigment made from other substances. Artificial ultramarine is much cheaper than the natural pigment and is also made in reddish and greenish hues.
—adj. **1** having the colour ultramarine. **2** beyond or across the sea. ⟨< Med.L *ultramarinus* < L *ultra* beyond + *mare* sea; used with reference to the source (Asia) of lapis lazuli⟩

ul•tra•mi•cro•scope [,ʌltrə'məikrə,skoup] *n.* a powerful instrument for making visible very tiny particles that are invisible to the common microscope. Light is thrown on the object from one side, over a dark background.

ul•tra•mi•cro•scop•ic [,ʌltrə,məikrə'skɒpɪk] *adj.* **1** too small to be seen with an ordinary microscope. **2** having to do with an ultramicroscope. **—,ul•tra•mi'cros•co•py** [-məi'krɒskəpi], *n.*

ul•tra•mod•ern [,ʌltrə'mɒdərn] *adj.* extremely advanced in design, ideas, or technology.

Ul•tra•mon•tagne [,ʌltrə'mɒntein] *or* [,ʌltrəmɒn'tein] *n., adj. —n. Cdn.* formerly, a member of the extreme right wing of the Conservative Party in Québec.
—adj. of or having to do with this group. ⟨< Cdn.F⟩
☛ *Hom.* ULTRAMONTANE.

ul•tra•mon•tane [,ʌltrə'mɒntein] *or* [,ʌltrəmɒn'tein] *adj., n.*
—adj. **1** beyond the mountains. **2** south of the Alps; Italian. **3** *Roman Catholic Church.* supporting a party or policy advocating extreme centralization of papal power, as opposed to a policy of decentralization.
—n. **1** a person living south of the Alps. **2** a supporter of ultramontane policies. ⟨< Med.L *ultramontanus* < L *ultra* beyond + *mons, montis* mountain⟩
☛ *Hom.* ULTRAMONTAGNE.

ul•tra•mon•tan•ism [,ʌltrə'mɒntə,nɪzəm] *n.* a doctrine or policy favouring extreme centralization of papal power.

ul•tra•mon•ta•nist [,ʌltrə'mɒntənɪst] *n.* a supporter of ultramontanism.

ul•tra•mun•dane [,ʌltrə'mʌndein] *or* [,ʌltrəmʌn'dein] *adj.* **1** beyond the world; beyond the limits of the known universe. **2** beyond this present life. ⟨< LL *ultramundanus* < L *ultra* beyond + *mundus* world⟩

ul•tra•na•tion•al•ism [,ʌltrə'næʃənə,lɪzəm] *n.* extreme or excessive devotion to nationalism. **—,ul•tra'na•tion•al•ist,** *n.* **—,ul•tra,na•tion•al'is•tic,** *adj.*

ul•tra•short [,ʌltrə'ʃɔrt] *adj.* **1** very short. **2** of or having to do with a radio wavelength of less than ten metres in length and above thirty megahertz in frequency.

ul•tra•son•ic [,ʌltrə'sɒnɪk] *adj.* of or designating sound waves having a pitch above the upper limit of human hearing, that is, a frequency above 20 000 hertz. **—,ul•tra'son•ic•al•ly,** *adv.*

ul•tra•son•ics [,ʌltrə'sɒnɪks] *n.* (*used with a singular verb*) the branch of physics that deals with ultrasonic waves.

ul•tra•son•o•gra•phy [,ʌltrəsə'nɒgrəfi] *n. Medicine.* a technique used to visualize deep structures in the body by recording pulses of ultrasonic waves directed into the tissues. It is widely used for medical purposes, including examination of the fetus in prenatal diagnosis, diagnosis of diseases of the liver, gallbladder, etc. **—,ul•tra,son•o'graph•ic** [-,sɒnə'græfɪk], *adj.*

ul•tra•sound ['ʌltrə,saʊnd] *n.* **1** ultrasonography. **2** ultrasonic waves. **3** a single ultrasonographic examination: *I had an ultrasound yesterday.*

ul•tra•struc•ture ['ʌltrə,strʌktʃər] *n. Biology.* structure too small or fine to be seen with an optical microscope. **—,ul•tra'struc•tur•al,** *adj.*

ul•tra•trop•i•cal [,ʌltrə'trɒpəkəl] *adj.* **1** outside of the tropics. **2** warmer than the tropics; very hot.

ul•tra•vi•o•let [,ʌltrə'vaɪəlɪt] *adj., n. —adj.* **1** of, having to do with, or designating the invisible rays, or waves, of the electromagnetic spectrum that are shorter than light rays but longer than X rays. **2** using or producing such radiation.
—n. **1** the part of the electromagnetic spectrum with ultraviolet rays. **2** the rays themselves.

ultraviolet light ultraviolet rays.

ul•tra vi•res ['ʌltrə 'vaɪriz] *Latin.* going beyond the powers granted by authority or by law. ⟨literally, beyond strength⟩

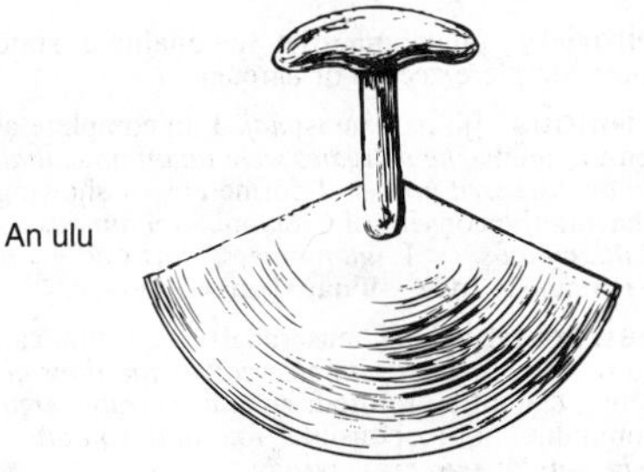

u•lu ['ulu] *n. Cdn.* a knife traditionally used by Inuit women, having a crescent-shaped blade and a handle of bone, ivory, wood, etc. Also, **ooloo.** ⟨< Inuktitut *ulu*⟩

ul•u•lant ['juljələnt] *or* ['ʌljələnt] *adj.* howling or wailing.

ul•u•late ['juljə,leit] *or* ['ʌljə,leit] *v.* **-lat•ed, -lat•ing. 1** of a dog, wolf, etc., howl. **2** lament loudly. ⟨< L *ululare* howl⟩ **—,ul•u'la•tion,** *n.*

U•lys•ses [ju'lɪsiz] *n.* the Latin name for Odysseus, a Greek leader in the Trojan war and the hero of Homer's epic poem the *Odyssey.*

um [ʌm] *interj.* a sound made by a speaker pausing or hesitating.

um•bel ['ʌmbəl] *n.* a type of flower cluster in which stalks nearly equal in length spring from a common centre and form a flat or slightly curved surface, as in parsley. See INFLORESCENCE for picture. ⟨< L *umbella* parasol, dim. of *umbra* shade⟩

um•bel•late ['ʌmbəlɪt] *or* ['ʌmbə,leit] *adj. Botany.* **1** of or like an umbel. **2** having umbels; forming an umbel or umbels. Also, **umbellar. —'um•bel•late•ly,** *adv.*

um•bel•lif•er•ous [,ʌmbə'lɪfərəs] *adj. Botany.* bearing an umbel or umbels. The parsley and carrot are umbelliferous.

um•ber ['ʌmbər] *n., adj. —n.* **1** a heavy, brown earth, consisting mainly of ferric oxide and used in its natural state **(raw umber)** as a brown pigment, or after heating **(burnt umber)** as a reddish brown pigment. **2** a brown or reddish brown.
—adj. brown or reddish brown. ⟨< Ital. *(terra di) ombra* (earth of) shade, but possibly originally < *Umbria,* a district in central Italy⟩

um•bil•i•cal [ʌm'bɪləkəl] *adj.* **1** of or having to do with the navel or umbilical cord. **2** formed, placed, or shaped like a navel or umbilical cord.

umbilical cord 1 in mammals, a cordlike structure through which a fetus in the womb receives food and discharges waste. The cord runs from the navel of the fetus to the placenta. **2** an electric cable, fuel line, or the like, connected to a rocket or spacecraft on its launching site and disconnected just before takeoff. **3** the cable attached to an astronaut to supply him or her with oxygen when working outside the spaceship.

um•bil•i•cate [ʌm'bɪlɪkɪt] *or* [ʌm'bɪlɪ,keit] *adj.* **1** shaped or formed like a navel or umbilicus. **2** having an umbilicus. **—um,bil•i'ca•tion,** *n.*

um•bil•i•cus [ʌm'bɪləkəs] *or* [,ʌmbə'ləikəs] *n., pl.* **-ci** [-saɪ] *or* [-si]. **1** the navel; the depression in the middle of the abdomen, indicating the point where the umbilical cord was attached. **2** a navel-like formation, such as the hilum of a seed. ⟨< L *umbilicus* navel⟩

um•ble pie ['ʌmbəl] HUMBLE PIE.

um•bra ['ʌmbrə] *n., pl.* **-brae** [-bri] *or* [-braɪ]. *Astronomy.* **1** a shadow of the earth or moon that completely hides the sun. See ECLIPSE for picture. **2** of any heavenly body, the region on the side turned away from the sun and receiving none of its light. **3** the dark central part of a sunspot. **4** a shadowy apparition; spectre; ghost. ⟨< L⟩

um•brage ['ʌmbrɪdʒ] *n.* **1** a feeling that one has been slighted or insulted; resentment (*now used mainly in the phrases* **take umbrage** *and* **give umbrage**): *He took umbrage at the slightest criticism. She didn't say anything for fear of giving umbrage to her host.* **2** *Archaic or poetic.* **a** shade. **b** foliage that provides shade. ⟨< F *ombrage,* ult. < L *umbra* shade⟩

um•bra•geous [ʌm'breidʒəs] *adj.* **1 a** giving shade. **b** shaded. **2** likely to take offence. **—um'bra•geous•ly,** *adv.* **—um'bra•geous•ness,** *n.*

um•brel•la [ʌm'brɛlə] *n.* **1** a collapsible device used for protection against rain or sun, especially a small, light one meant to be carried in the hand and consisting of a circular, convex screen of cloth or plastic stretched over a framework of hinged ribs radiating from a central pole. **2** a screen of fighter aircraft or a barrage of gunfire to protect ground forces against enemy aircraft. **3** anything that protects or provides shelter. **4** an official organization, department, etc. uniting, for support or control, a broad range of activities, agencies, or spheres of interest: *The Arts Co-op is an umbrella for all the humanities and fine arts co-op programs. The Community Chest is an umbrella for many local charities.* **5** *(adj.)* **a** pertaining to or being part of an umbrella: *umbrella ribs, umbrella handle.* **b** serving as an umbrella: *an umbrella organization.* **6** the gelatinous body of a jellyfish. ⟨< Ital. *ombrella,* ult. < L *umbra* shade⟩

umbrella plant a common aquatic plant (*Cyperus alternifolius*) of the sedge family, having triangular stems growing upward from a mass of roots and surmounted by an umbrella-shaped cluster of leaves on each stem, cultivated for its ornamental value.

umbrella tree 1 a magnolia (*Magnolia tripetala*) of North America, having umbrellalike clusters of long leaves at the ends of its branches. **2** any of numerous other trees whose leaves or branches grow in an umbrella-shaped formation.

Um•bri•an ['ʌmbriən] *n., adj. —n.* **1** a native or inhabitant of Umbria, a district in central Italy. **2** an extinct Italic language of ancient S Italy.
—adj. of or having to do with Umbria, its people, or their language.

An umiak

u•mi•ak ['umi,æk] *n. Cdn.* a large, flat-bottomed boat made of skins stretched over a wooden frame and propelled by paddles. Umiaks are used by Inuit for carrying freight and are usually worked by women. Also, **oomiak.** ⟨< Inuktitut *umiaq.*⟩

um•laut ['ʊmlʌut] *n., v. Linguistics. —n.* **1** in Germanic languages, the fronting of a vowel sound because of the influence of a front vowel or a palatal glide in the following syllable. In English, plurals such as *feet, mice,* and verbs derived from nouns or adjectives, such as *feed, fill* are the result of umlaut. **2** a vowel that is the result of such a change. **3** the sign (¨) used to indicate such a vowel, as in German *süss* sweet.
—v. modify or be modified by umlaut. ⟨< G *Umlaut* < *um* around + *laut* sound⟩

um•ma ['ʌmə] *n. Islam.* the worldwide community of believers, including Sunnis, Shiites, and other Muslim sects.

ump [ʌmp] *n., v. Informal.* umpire.

um•pire ['ʌmpaɪr] *n., v.* **-pired, -pir•ing.** *—n.* **1** a person who rules on the plays in certain games: *The umpire called the ball a foul.* **2** a person chosen to settle a dispute.
—v. **1** act as umpire. **2** act as umpire in. ⟨earlier *a numpire* (taken as *an umpire*) < OF *nonper* not even, odd < *non* not (< L) + *per* equal < L *par*⟩ **—'um•pir•age,** *n.*

ump•teen ['ʌmp'tin] *adj. Informal.* a great many: *I've heard umpteen different suggestions, but not one of them is practical.*

ump•teenth ['ʌmp'tinθ] *adj. Informal.* the last in an extremely long series: *I've just dialled his number for the umpteenth time, but there's still no answer.*

un–[1] *prefix.* not; the opposite of, as in *unequal, unjust, unobtrusive.* ⟨OE⟩
☛ *Usage.* See note at IN-[1].

un–[2] *prefix.* do the opposite of or do what will reverse the act, as in *undress, unlock, untie.* ⟨OE *un-, on-*⟩

UN or **U.N. 1** UNITED NATIONS. **2** UNION NATIONALE.

un•a•bashed [ˌʌnə'bæʃt] *adj.* not embarrassed, ashamed, or awed. **–ˌun•a'bash•ed•ly,** *adv.*

un•a•ble [ʌn'eibəl] *adj.* **1** not able; lacking ability or power (*to*): *A newborn baby is unable to walk or talk.* **2** incompetent: *He is a most unable leader.*

un•a•bridged [ˌʌnə'brɪdʒd] *adj.* **1** not shortened; complete: *an unabridged book.* **2** of or designating any large dictionary more comprehensive than an ordinary desk dictionary, especially the largest one of a series.

un•ac•com•pa•nied [ˌʌnə'kʌmpənid] *adj.* **1** not accompanied. **2** *Music.* without an accompaniment.

un•ac•com•plished [ˌʌnə'kɒmplɪʃt] *adj.* **1** not completed or finished. **2** lacking in skills or accomplishments.

un•ac•count•a•ble [ˌʌnə'kaʊntəbəl] *adj.* **1** that cannot be accounted for or explained; strange or puzzling: *She suddenly flew into one of her unaccountable rages.* **2** not obliged or bound to account (*for*); not responsible: *The accused was judged insane and therefore unaccountable for his actions.* **–ˌun•ac'count•a•bly,** *adv.* **–ˌun•acˌcount•a'bil•i•ty** or **ˌun•ac'count•a•ble•ness,** *n.*

un•ac•count•ed–for [ˌʌnə'kaʊntɪd ˌfɔr] *adj.* unexplained: *unaccounted-for atmospheric disturbances.*

un•ac•cus•tomed [ˌʌnə'kʌstəmd] *adj.* **1** not used (to); not accustomed. **2** not familiar; unusual; strange: *unaccustomed heat.*

u•na cor•da ['unə 'kɔrdə] *Musical direction.* (in a composition for piano) with the soft pedal down. ⟨< Ital., literally, one string; the soft pedal causes the hammers to strike only one of each set of strings⟩

un•ad•vised [ˌʌnəd'vaɪzd] *adj.* **1** not prudent or discreet; rash. **2** not advised; without advice. **–ˌun•ad'vis•ed•ness,** *n.*

un•ad•vis•ed•ly [ˌʌnəd'vaɪzɪdli] *adv.* in an indiscreet manner; rashly.

un•af•fect•ed[1] [ˌʌnə'fɛktɪd] *adj.* not affected; not influenced: *unaffected by criticism.* ⟨< *un-*[1] + *affected*[1]⟩ **–ˌun•af'fect•ed•ly,** *adv.* **–ˌun•af'fect•ed•ness,** *n.*

un•af•fect•ed[2] [ˌʌnə'fɛktɪd] *adj.* simple and natural; without airs or pretense. ⟨< *un-*[1] + *affected*[2]⟩ **–ˌun•af'fect•ed•ly,** *adv.* **–ˌun•af'fect•ed•ness,** *n.*

un•al•ter•a•ble [ʌn'ɒltərəbəl] *adj.* that cannot be altered; not changeable. **–un'al•ter•a•bly,** *adv.*

un•a•neled [ˌʌnə'nild] *adj. Archaic.* without being anointed by a priest before death; not having received extreme unction. ⟨< *un-*[1] + *anele* give extreme unction to, ME *anelie(n)*, ult. < OE *an-* on + *ele* oil < L *oleum*⟩

u•na•nim•i•ty [ˌjunə'nɪməti] *n.* the quality or state of being unanimous; complete accord or agreement.

u•nan•i•mous [ju'nænəməs] *adj.* **1** in complete accord or agreement; agreed: *The delegates were unanimous that the issue needed to be discussed further.* **2** formed by or showing complete accord; having the consent of everyone: *unanimous consent. The vote was unanimous.* ⟨< L *unanimus* < *unus* one + *animus* mind⟩ **–u'nan•i•mous•ly,** *adv.* **–u'nan•i•mous•ness,** *n.*

un•an•swer•a•ble [ʌn'ænsərəbəl] *adj.* **1** that cannot be answered or has no answer: *unanswerable questions about life and death.* **2** that cannot be refuted: *an unanswerable argument.* **3** unaccountable; not responsible: *You think you are unanswerable to anybody.* **–un'an•swer•a•bly,** *adv.*

un•ap•proach•a•ble [ˌʌnə'proutʃəbəl] *adj.* **1** very hard to approach; aloof; distant. **2** unrivalled; without an equal. **–ˌun•ap'proach•a•ble•ness,** *n.* **–ˌun•ap'proach•a•bly,** *adv.* **–ˌun•apˌproach•a'bil•i•ty,** *n.*

un•apt [ʌn'æpt] *adj.* **1** not suitable; not appropriate. **2** not likely. **3** not skilful; not well qualified. **4** not quick to learn. **–un'apt•ly,** *adv.* **–un'apt•ness,** *n.*

un•arm [ʌn'ɑrm] *v.* **1** take weapons or armour from; disarm. **2** lay down one's weapons. **3** take off one's armour.

un•armed [ʌn'ɑrmd] *adj., v.* *–adj.* **1** without weapons or armour. **2** of plants and animals, without horns, teeth, prickles, spines, thorns, etc.
–v. pt. and pp. of UNARM.

u•na•ry ['junəri] **1** having to do with, consisting of, or involving one; single. **2** *Mathematics.* of or having to do with a function whose domain is a given set and whose range is confined to that set.

un•as•sum•ing [ˌʌnə'sumɪŋ] *or* [ˌʌnə'sjumɪŋ] *adj.* not putting on airs; modest. **–ˌun•as'sum•ing•ly,** *adv.* **–ˌun•as'sum•ing•ness,** *n.*

un•at•tached [ˌʌnə'tætʃt] *adj.* **1** not attached. **2** not connected or associated with a particular body, group, organization, or the like; independent. **3** not married or engaged to be married.

un•at•tend•ed [ˌʌnə'tɛndɪd] *adj.* **1** without attendants or companions; alone. **2** not taken care of; not attended to.

u•nau [u'naʊ] *or* [ju'nɒ] *n.* the two-toed sloth (*Choloepus hoffmanni* or *C. didactylus*) native to South America. ⟨< F < Tupi⟩

un•a•vail•ing [ˌʌnə'veilɪŋ] *adj.* not successful; useless. **–ˌun•a'vail•ing•ly,** *adv.*

un•a•void•a•ble [ˌʌnə'vɔɪdəbəl] *adj.* that cannot be avoided or prevented; inevitable: *an unavoidable delay.* **–ˌun•a'void•a•ble•ness,** *n.* **–ˌun•a'void•a•bly,** *adv.*

In each of the words below **un-** *means* not; *the pronunciation of the main part of each word is not changed.*

ˌun•a'bat•ed
ˌun•ab'bre•viˌat•ed
ˌun•a'bet•ted
ˌun•ab'solved
ˌun•ab'sorbed
ˌun•ac•a'dem•ic
un'ac•cent•ed
ˌun•ac'cen•tuˌat•ed
ˌun•ac'cept•a•ble
ˌun•ac'cept•ed
ˌun•ac'claimed
un'ac•cliˌmat•ed
ˌun•ac'cli•maˌtized
ˌun•ac'com•moˌdat•ing
ˌun•ac'cred•it•ed
ˌun•ac'knowl•edged
ˌun•ac'quaint•ed
ˌun•ac'quit•ted
un'act•ed
un'ac•tion•a•ble
un'ac•tuˌat•ed
ˌun•a'dapt•a•ble
ˌun•a'dapt•ed
ˌun•ad'dressed
ˌun•ad'journed
ˌun•ad'just•a•ble
ˌun•ad'just•ed
ˌun•a'dorned
ˌun•a'dul•terˌat•ed
ˌun•ad•van'ta•geous
ˌun•ad'ven•tur•ous
un'ad•verˌtised
ˌun•ad'vis•a•ble
ˌun•aes'thet•ic
ˌun•af'fil•iˌat•ed
ˌun•a'fraid
ˌun•ag'gres•sive
un'aid•ed
un'aimed
un'aired
ˌun•a'larmed
un'a•li•en•a•ble
ˌun•a'ligned
ˌun•a'like
ˌun•al'layed
ˌun•al'le•viˌat•ed
ˌun•al'lied
ˌun•al'low•a•ble
ˌun•al'loyed
un'al•pha•betˌized
un'al•tered
ˌun•am'big•u•ous
ˌun•am'bi•tious
un'a•mi•a•ble
un'am•i•ca•ble
un'am•pliˌfied
ˌun•a'mused
ˌun•a'mus•ing
un'an•aˌlys•a•ble
un'an•aˌlysed
un'an•iˌmat•ed
ˌun•an'nounced
un'an•swered
ˌun•an'tic•iˌpat•ed
ˌun•aˌpol•o'get•ic
ˌun•ap'par•ent
ˌun•ap'peal•ing
ˌun•ap'peas•a•ble
ˌun•ap'peased
un'ap•peˌtiz•ing
un'ap•pli•ca•ble
ˌun•ap'plied
ˌun•ap'point•ed
ˌun•ap'por•tioned
ˌun•ap'pre•ciˌat•ed
ˌun•ap'pre•ci•a•tive
ˌun•ap•pre'hen•sive
ˌun•ap'proached
ˌun•ap'pro•priˌat•ed
ˌun•ap'proved
un'ar•gu•a•ble
un'ar•moured
ˌun•ar'rest•ed
ˌun•ar'tic•uˌlat•ed
ˌun•ar'tis•tic
ˌun•as•cer'tain•a•ble
ˌun•as•cer'tained
ˌun•a'shamed
un'asked
un'as•piˌrat•ed
ˌun•a'spir•ing
ˌun•as'sail•a•ble
ˌun•as'sailed
ˌun•as'ser•tive
ˌun•as'sessed
ˌun•as'sign•a•ble
ˌun•as'signed
ˌun•as'sim•i•la•ble
ˌun•as'sim•iˌlat•ed
ˌun•as'sist•ed
ˌun•as'sort•ed
ˌun•as'sumed
ˌun•as'sured
ˌun•ath'let•ic
ˌun•a'toned
ˌun•at'tain•a•ble
ˌun•at'tained
ˌun•at'tempt•ed
ˌun•at'test•ed
ˌun•at'tired
ˌun•at'trac•tive
ˌun•aus'pi•cious
ˌun•au'then•tic
ˌun•au'then•tiˌcat•ed
un'au•thorˌized
ˌun•a'vail•a•ble
ˌun•a'venged
ˌun•a'vowed
ˌun•a'wak•ened
ˌun•a'ward•ed

un•a•ware [ˌʌnəˈwɛr] *adj.* **1** not aware; ignorant: *They were unaware of her change in plans. They had gone out in the boat, unaware that there was a storm warning.* **2** (*advl.*) **unawares, a** by surprise: *The police caught the burglar unawares.* **b** without knowing or being aware: *We made the error unawares.*
—ˌun•aˈware•ness, *n.*

un•backed [ʌnˈbækt] *adj.* **1** not backed, helped, or supported; unaided. **2** not bet on. **3** not saddlebroken. **4** having no back or backing.

un•bal•ance [ʌnˈbæləns] *n., v.* **-anced, -anc•ing.** *—n.* lack of balance; imbalance; condition of being out of balance.
—v. throw out of balance; disorder or derange.

un•bal•anced [ʌnˈbælənst] *adj., v. —adj.* **1** not balanced; improperly balanced. **2** mentally disordered; unstable or deranged.
—v. pt. and pp. of UNBALANCE.

un•bar [ʌnˈbɑr] *v.* **-barred, -bar•ring.** remove the bars from; unbolt; open.

un•bear•a•ble [ʌnˈbɛrəbəl] *adj.* that cannot be endured: *unbearable suspense, unbearable pain.* **—unˈbear•a•ble•ness,** *n.* **—unˈbear•ab•ly,** *adv.*

un•beat•en [ʌnˈbitən] *adj.* **1** not defeated or surpassed. **2** not trodden; not travelled: *unbeaten paths.* **3** not beaten or pounded. **4** not mixed by stirring: *Add two unbeaten eggs.*

un•be•com•ing [ˌʌnbɪˈkʌmɪŋ] *adj.* **1** not attractive; not suited to the wearer: *an unbecoming dress.* **2** not fitting or proper: *unbecoming behaviour.* **—ˌun•beˈcom•ing•ly,** *adv.* **—ˌun•beˈcom•ing•ness,** *n.*

un•be•knownst [ˌʌnbɪˈnounst] *adj. Informal.* **1** not known; unbeknown: *Her present whereabouts are unbeknown to me.* **2** without the knowledge of (*used with* **to**): *Unbeknownst to me, they had pulled up all the dahlias.* Also, **unbeknown.**

un•be•lief [ˌʌnbɪˈlif] *n.* a lack of belief, especially in God or in a particular religion or doctrine.
☛ *Syn.* **Unbelief,** DISBELIEF = lack of belief. **Unbelief** suggests only lack of belief in something offered or held as true, with no positive feelings one way or the other: *The Inquisition punished people for their unbelief.* **Disbelief** suggests a positive refusal to believe: *I expressed my disbelief in the value of universal military training.*

un•be•liev•a•ble [ˌʌnbɪˈlivəbəl] *adj.* beyond belief; too unlikely to believe; incredible: *an unbelievable story, a man of almost unbelievable strength.* **—ˌun•beˈliev•a•bly,** *adv.*

un•be•liev•er [ˌʌnbɪˈlivər] *n.* **1** a person who does not believe. **2** a person who does not believe in a particular religion.

un•be•liev•ing [ˌʌnbɪˈlivɪŋ] *adj.* not believing; doubting. **—ˌun•beˈliev•ing•ly,** *adv.*

un•belt•ed [ʌnˈbɛltəd] *adj.* without a belt: *She wore the coat unbelted.*

un•bend [ʌnˈbɛnd] *v.* **-bent, -bend•ing. 1** straighten or become straight. **2** release from strain. **3** relax: *The judge unbent and behaved like a boy.* **4** unfasten (a sail, rope, etc.).

un•bend•ing [ʌnˈbɛndɪŋ] *adj., n., v. —adj.* **1** not bending or curving; rigid: *the unbending boughs of an old oak.* **2** not yielding; firm or inflexible: *an unbending attitude.* **3** of someone's manner, distant; stern.
—n. a relaxing or freeing from constraint: *In a rare moment of unbending, she told us about her childhood.*
—v. ppr. of UNBEND. **—unˈbend•ing•ly,** *adv.* **—unˈbend•ing•ness,** *n.*

un•bent [ʌnˈbɛnt] *v., adj. —v.* pt. and pp. of UNBEND.
—adj. not bent or curved.

un•bi•assed or **un•bi•ased** [ʌnˈbaɪəst] *adj.* not biassed; impartial; fair: *an unbiassed account.*

un•bid•den [ʌnˈbɪdən] *adj.* not bidden; not invited or not commanded.

un•bind [ʌnˈbaɪnd] *v.* **-bound, -bind•ing.** release from bonds or restraint; untie; unfasten; let loose. ⟨OE *unbindan*⟩

un•bit•ted [ʌnˈbɪtɪd] *adj.* **1** not having a bit or bridle. **2** UNBRIDLED (def. 2).

un•bleached [ʌnˈblitʃt] *adj.* not bleached; not made white by bleaching: *unbleached muslin.*

un•blem•ished [ʌnˈblɛmɪʃt] *adj.* without blemishes; flawless: *smooth, unblemished skin, an unblemished reputation.*

un•blessed [ʌnˈblɛst] *adj.* **1** not blessed. **2** wicked, evil, or malignant: *a soul unblessed.* **3** unhappy; miserable; wretched. Also, **unblest.**

un•blood•ed [ʌnˈblʌdɪd] *adj.* **1** not purebred or thoroughbred. **2** uninitiated; inexperienced.

un•blush•ing [ʌnˈblʌʃɪŋ] *adj.* **1** not blushing. **2** shameless or unabashed: *unblushing impudence.* **—unˈblush•ing•ly,** *adv.*

un•bod•ied [ʌnˈbɒdid] *adj.* **1** having no body; incorporeal. **2** disembodied.

un•bolt [ʌnˈboult] *v.* open or unlock (a door, etc.) by drawing back the bolt or bolts.

un•bolt•ed[1] [ʌnˈboultɪd] *adj., v. —adj.* not bolted or fastened: *an unbolted door.*
—v. pt. and pp. of UNBOLT. ⟨< *un-*[1] + *bolt*[1]⟩

un•bolt•ed[2] [ʌnˈboultɪd] *adj.* not sifted: *unbolted flour.* ⟨< *un-*[1] + *bolt*[2]⟩

un•bon•net [ʌnˈbɒnɪt] *v.* **1** remove the headgear from. **2** uncover the head as a mark of respect.

un•bon•net•ed [ʌnˈbɒnətɪd] *adj., v. —adj.* wearing no bonnet or cap; bareheaded.
—v. pt. and pp. of UNBONNET.

un•born [ʌnˈbɔrn] *adj.* **1** within the mother's womb; not yet born: *an unborn child.* **2** not brought into being: *That joke should have stayed unborn.* **3** still to come; future: *unborn generations.*

un•bos•om [ʌnˈbʊzəm] *or* [ʌnˈbuzəm] *v.* **1** relieve (oneself) of feelings, secrets, etc. by revealing them: *I unbosomed myself to my understanding sister.* **2** reveal (thoughts, etc.): *She unbosomed her suspicions to her best friend.* ⟨< *un-*[2] + *bosom,* v.⟩

un•bound [ʌnˈbaʊnd] *adj., v. —adj.* **1** not fastened or bound together; loose; having no binding: *unbound sheets of music, an unbound book.* **2** freed from bonds; released. **3** *Physics.* not in a chemical union with some other substance.
—v. pt. and pp. of UNBIND.

un•bound•ed [ʌnˈbaʊndɪd] *adj.* not bounded or restrained; without bounds or limits; very great: *His unbounded good spirits cheered all of us up.*

un•bowed [ʌnˈbaʊd] *adj.* **1** not bowed or bent. **2** not forced to yield or submit.

un•brace [ʌnˈbreis] *v.* **-braced, -brac•ing. 1** detach or loosen the brace or braces of. **2** make less tense; relax. **3** weaken; make feeble or unsteady.

un•braid [ʌnˈbreid] *v.* separate the strands of.

un•break•a•ble [ʌnˈbreikəbəl] *adj.* not breakable; that cannot be easily broken: *an unbreakable toy.*

un•bri•dle [ʌnˈbraɪdəl] *v.* remove a bridle or restraint from: *to unbridle a horse.*

un•brid•led [ʌnˈbraɪdəld] *adj., v. —adj.* **1** not having a bridle on. **2** not controlled; not restrained.
—v. pt. and pp. of UNBRIDLE.

un•bro•ken [ʌnˈbroukən] *adj.* **1** not broken; whole: *There was only one unbroken cup left in the whole set.* **2** not interrupted; continuous: *He had eight hours of unbroken sleep.* **3** not tamed:

In each of the words below **un-** *means* not; *the pronunciation of the main part of each word is not changed.*

unˈawed
unˈbaked
unˈband•aged
unˈbap•tized
unˈbarbed
unˈbathed
unˈbeat•a•ble
unˈbeau•ti•ful
ˌun•beˈfit•ting
ˌun•beˈfriend•ed
ˌun•beˈgot•ten
ˌun•beˈhold•en
unˈbelt
ˌun•beˈtrothed
ˌun•beˈwailed
unˈblam•a•ble
unˈblamed
unˈbleached
unˈblem•ished
unˈblink•ing
unˈblock
unˈblocked
unˈblurred
unˈboned
unˈbor•rowed
unˈboth•ered
unˈbought
unˈbranched
unˈbrand•ed
unˈbreath•a•ble
unˈbrib•a•ble
unˈbridge•a•ble
unˈbroth•er•ly
unˈbruised
unˈbrushed

an unbroken colt. **4** of a record, not surpassed.
—un'bro•ken•ness, *n.*

un•buck•le [ʌn'bʌkəl] *v.* **-led, -ling.** open the buckle or buckles of: *She unbuckled her belt and took it off.*

un•build [ʌn'bɪld] *v.* **-built, -build•ing.** tear down.

un•built [ʌn'bɪlt] *v., adj. —v.* pt. and pp. of UNBUILD.
—adj. not built.

un•bur•den [ʌn'bɜrdən] *v.* **1** free from a burden. **2** relieve (oneself or one's conscience or mind) by confessing or revealing something: *I decided to unburden myself of the problem. She unburdened her mind to her friend.* **3** confess or reveal (secret thoughts, feelings, etc.) in order to relieve one's mind: *He unburdened his guilt in a long letter.*

un•busi•ness•like [ʌn'bɪznɪs,ləik] *adj.* without system and method; not efficient.

un•but•ton [ʌn'bʌtən] *v.* unfasten the button or buttons of (a garment).

un•but•toned [ʌn'bʌtənd] *adj., v. —adj.* **1** not buttoned: *His coat was unbuttoned.* **2** unrestricted in expression or action; casual; informal: *He was in an unbuttoned mood, talking freely of his past.*
—v. pt. and pp. of UNBUTTON.

un•cage [ʌn'keidʒ] *v.* **-caged, -cag•ing. 1** release from a cage. **2** release.

un•called–for [ʌn'kɒld ,fɔr] *adj.* unnecessary and unjustified; impertinent or rude: *an uncalled-for remark.*

un•can•ny [ʌn'kæni] *adj.* **1** strange and mysterious; eerie: *The trees had uncanny shapes in the dim light.* **2** seeming to have or show powers beyond what is natural or normal: *an uncanny sense of timing, an uncanny knack for solving puzzles.*
—un'can•ni•ly, *adv.* **—un'can•ni•ness,** *n.*
☛ *Syn.* See note at WEIRD.

un•cap [ʌn'kæp] *v.* **-capped, -cap•ping. 1** remove a cap or covering from: *to uncap a bottle.* **2** remove one's hat, especially in deference.

un•cared–for [ʌn'kɛrd ,fɔr] *adj.* not properly looked after; neglected; unkempt.

un•cer•e•mo•ni•ous [,ʌnsɛrə'mouniəs] *adj.* **1** not ceremonious; informal. **2** not as courteous as would be expected; abrupt or rude: *an unceremonious dismissal.*
—,un•cer•e'mo•ni•ous•ly, *adv.* **—,un•cer•e'mo•ni•ous•ness,** *n.*

un•cer•tain [ʌn'sɜrtən] *adj.* **1** not known with certainty; not finally established; indefinite: *The election results are still uncertain. Her arrival time is uncertain.* **2** not assured or secured; problematic: *an uncertain future.* **3** likely to change; unreliable: *a dog of uncertain temper. The weather remains uncertain.* **4** dubious or doubtful; hesitating: *an uncertain smile. He was uncertain about the reception he would get.* **5** indistinct; vague: *an uncertain shape in the mist.* **6** not constant; wavering: *an uncertain flicker of light.* **—un'cer•tain•ly,** *adv.* **—un'cer•tain•ness,** *n.*
☛ *Syn.* **1, 2, 4. Uncertain,** INSECURE = not sure in some way or about something. **Uncertain** emphasizes not knowing definitely or surely about something or not having complete confidence in a thing, a person, or oneself, and thus suggests the presence of doubt: *Their plans for the summer are uncertain.* **Insecure** emphasizes not being protected from or guarded against danger or loss, and suggests the presence of fear or anxiety: *Her position at the bank is insecure.*

un•cer•tain•ty [ʌn'sɜrtənti] *n., pl.* **-ties. 1** the quality or state of being uncertain; doubtfulness. **2** something uncertain: *Our trip is still an uncertainty.*

uncertainty principle *Physics.* the principle of quantum mechanics, properly called the **Heisenberg uncertainty principle**, that two related observable quantities such as the position and the momentum of an electron cannot both be accurately measured at the same time. ⟨after W. *Heisenberg* (1901-1976), G physicist⟩

un•chain [ʌn'tʃein] *v.* release from chains or as if from chains; set free.

un•change•a•ble [ʌn'tʃeindʒəbəl] *adj.* that cannot be changed. **—un'change•a•ble•ness,** *n.* **—un'change•a•bly,** *adv.*

un•changed [ʌn'tʃeindʒd] *adj.* not changed; the same.

un•chang•ing [ʌn'tʃeindʒɪŋ] *adj.* not changing; constant: *listening to the unchanging roar of the sea.*

un•char•i•ta•ble [ʌn'tʃærətəbəl] *or* [ʌn'tʃɛrətəbəl] *adj.* not generous; not charitable or compassionate; severe; harsh.
—un'char•i•ta•ble•ness, *n.* **—un'char•i•ta•bly,** *adv.*

un•chart•ed [ʌn'tʃɑrtɪd] *adj.* not yet mapped; not recorded on a chart: *sailing uncharted seas.*

un•chaste [ʌn'tʃeist] *adj.* not chaste; not virtuous.
—un'chaste•ly, *adv.*

un•chas•ti•ty [ʌn'tʃæstəti] *n.* lack of chastity; unchaste character or behaviour; lewdness.

un•checked [ʌn'tʃɛkt] *adj.* not checked; not restrained.

un•chris•tian [ʌn'krɪstʃən] *adj.* **1** not Christian. **2** unworthy of Christians. **3** *Informal.* such as any civilized person would object to; barbarous; outrageous: *routed out of bed at a most unchristian hour.*

un•church [ʌn'tʃɜrtʃ] *v.* **1** expel from a church; excommunicate. **2** deprive (a congregation) of status and rights as a church.

un•churched [ʌn'tʃɜrtʃt] *adj., v. —adj.* not belonging to or attending any church.
—v. pt. and pp. of UNCHURCH.

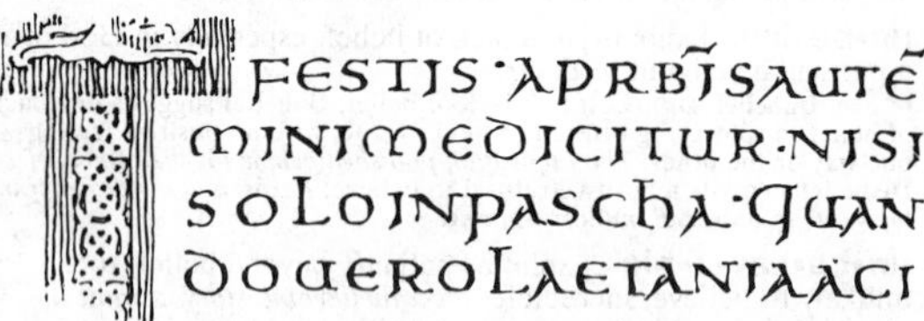

The first section of a page from the 6th-century Latin manuscript "Gregorius Magnus Papa, Liber sacramentorium," written in uncials

un•ci•al ['ʌnʃiəl] *or* ['ʌnʃəl] *n., adj. —n.* **1** a kind of letter or writing having heavy, rounded strokes, used especially in Greek and Latin manuscripts from the 4th to the 8th century.
2 manuscript written in uncial.
—adj. having to do with or written in this style or such letters.
⟨< L *uncialis,* in the sense 'inch-high' < *uncia* inch⟩

un•ci•form ['ʌnsɪ,fɔrm] *adj.* uncinate.

un•ci•nate ['ʌnsənɪt] *or* ['ʌnsə,neit] *adj.* hooked; bent at the end like a hook. ⟨< L *uncinatus,* ult. < *uncus* hook⟩

un•cir•cum•cised [ʌn'sɜrkəm,saɪzd] *adj.* **1** not circumcised. **2** not Jewish; gentile. **3** heathen; spiritually impure; unregenerate.

un•cir•cum•ci•sion [,ʌnsɜrkəm'sɪʒən] *n.* **1** the state of being uncircumcised. **2** people who have not been circumcised; non-Jews; gentiles collectively.

un•civ•il [ʌn'sɪvəl] *adj.* **1** not civil; rude; impolite. **2** not civilized. **—un'civ•il•ly,** *adv.*

un•civ•i•lized [ʌn'sɪvə,laɪzd] *adj.* **1** not civilized; barbarous or unenlightened. **2** *Informal.* badly behaved; rude: *Her friend is an uncivilized lout. It was quite uncivilized of her not to tell us she was leaving.*

In each of the words below **un-** *means* not; *the pronunciation of the main part of each word is not changed.*

un'budg•et•ed
un'bur•ied
un'burn•a•ble
un'burned
un'burnt
un'but•tered
un'can•celled
,un•ca'non•i•cal
un'cap•i•tal,ized
un'car•ing
un'car•pet•ed
un'cashed
un'casked
un'cat•a,logued
,un•cat•e'gor•i•cal
un'caught
un'ceas•ing
un'cel•e,brat•ed
un'cen•sored
un'cen•sured
un'cer•ti,fied
un'chal•lenge•a•ble
un'chal•lenged
un'chap•er,oned
,un•char•ac•ter'is•tic
un'charged
un'char•tered
un'chas•tened
,un•chas'tised
un'cher•ished
un'chewed
un'chilled
un'chiv•al•rous
un'chos•en
un'chris•tened

un•clad [ʌn'klæd] *adj.* not dressed; not clothed; naked.

un•clasp [ʌn'klæsp] *v.* **1** unfasten the clasp or clasps of. **2** release or be released from a clasp or grasp. **3** loosen one's grip.

un•clas•si•fied [ʌn'klæsɪ,faɪd] *adj.* **1** not placed in a category or class. **2** not classified as secret or restricted: *Employees without security clearance have access only to unclassified information.*

un•cle ['ʌŋkəl] *n.* **1** the brother of one's father or mother. **2** the husband of one's aunt. **3** *Informal.* a man considered as friend, adviser, etc. of a younger person or group.
say or **cry uncle,** *Informal.* give in; surrender: *They wouldn't let him up until he said uncle.* ⟨ME < AF < L *avunculus* one's mother's brother⟩

un•clean [ʌn'klin] *adj.* **1** not clean; dirty; filthy. **2** not pure morally; evil. **3** ceremonially unclean; defiled or defiling. ⟨OE *unclǣne*⟩ **—un'clean•ness,** *n.*

un•clean•ly[1] [ʌn'klɛnli] *adj.* not cleanly; unclean. ⟨< *un-[1]* + *cleanly[1]*⟩ **—un'clean•li•ness,** *n.*

un•clean•ly[2] [ʌn'klinli] *adv.* in an unclean manner. ⟨< *unclean*⟩

un•clench [ʌn'klɛntʃ] *v.* open or become opened from a clenched state: *unclench one's fists.*

Uncle Sam [sæm] *Informal.* the government or people of the United States. ⟨< the initials *U.S.*⟩

un•cloak [ʌn'klouk] *v.* **1** remove the coat from. **2** reveal; expose: *to uncloak an impostor.* **3** take off one's cloak or outer garment.

un•clog [ʌn'klɒg] *v.* make free from an obstruction: *to unclog a drain.*

un•close [ʌn'klouz] *v.* **-closed, -clos•ing. 1** open. **2** disclose.

un•clothe [ʌn'klouð] *v.* **-clothed** or **-clad, -cloth•ing. 1** strip (oneself or another) of clothes; undress. **2** lay bare; uncover.

un•coil [ʌn'kɔɪl] *v.* unwind.

un•com•fort•a•ble [ʌn'kʌmfərtəbəl] *adj.* **1** not comfortable: *I am uncomfortable in this chair.* **2** uneasy: *I feel uncomfortable at formal dinners.* **3** disagreeable; causing discomfort: *This is an uncomfortable chair.* **—un'com•fort•a•bly,** *adv.* **—un'com•fort•a•ble•ness,** *n.*

un•com•mer•cial [,ʌnkə'mɜrʃəl] *adv.* **1** not involving or concerned with commerce or business; non-commercial. **2** not following the principles or spirit of business; unbusinesslike. **3** commercially unprofitable.

un•com•mit•ted [,ʌnkə'mɪtɪd] *adj.* **1** not bound or pledged to a certain viewpoint, course of action, association or relationship, etc.: *an uncommitted candidate.* **2** not taking one position or another; neutral or undecided: *uncommitted voters.* **3** lacking in commitment or dedication. **4** not committed to prison or another institution.

un•com•mon [ʌn'kɒmən] *adj.* **1** not commonly encountered; rare; unusual: *The tulip tree is uncommon in most of Canada.* **2** remarkable: *uncommon strength, an uncommon grasp of the subject.* **—un'com•mon•ly,** *adv.* **—un'com•mon•ness,** *n.*

un•com•mu•ni•ca•tive [,ʌnkə'mjunəkətɪv] *or* [,ʌnkə'mjunə,keitɪv] *adj.* not giving out any information, opinions, etc.; silent and reserved; taciturn. **—,un•com'mu•ni•ca•tive•ly,** *adv.* **—,un•com'mu•ni•ca•tive•ness,** *n.*

un•com•pro•mis•ing [ʌn'kɒmprə,maɪzɪŋ] *adj.* unyielding; firm; unwilling to compromise. **—un'com•pro,mis•ing•ly,** *adv.*

un•con•cern [,ʌnkən'sɜrn] *n.* lack of care, interest, or anxiety; indifference: *The children looked with complete unconcern at their strange surroundings.*
☛ *Syn.* See note at INDIFFERENCE.

un•con•cerned [,ʌnkən'sɜrnd] *adj.* **1** free from care, interest, or anxiety; indifferent or nonchalant: *unconcerned about the results of the exam.* **2** not involved: *He was unconcerned with that aspect of the inquiry. They need an unconcerned party to settle the dispute.* **—,un•con'cern•ed•ness** [-'sɜrnɪdnɪs], *n.* **—,un•con'cern•ed•ly** [-'sɜrnɪdli], *adv.*

un•con•di•tion•al [,ʌnkən'dɪʃənəl] *adj.* without conditions; absolute: *unconditional surrender, unconditional love.* **—,un•con'di•tion•al•ly,** *adv.*

un•con•di•tioned [,ʌnkən'dɪʃənd] *adj.* **1** without conditions; unconditional. **2** *Psychology.* not learned; not dependent on conditioning; natural or instinctive: *Withdrawing one's hand on contact with fire is an unconditioned reflex.*

un•con•form•a•ble [,ʌnkən'fɔrməbəl] *adj.* **1** that cannot or does not conform. **2** *Geology.* of strata, showing unconformity in age, direction of stratification, etc. **—,un•con'form•a•bly,** *adv.*

un•con•form•i•ty [,ʌnkən'fɔrməti] *n., pl.* **-ties. 1** lack of conformity. **2** *Geology.* discontinuity in the surface of contact between rock strata of different ages, representing a period of erosion or non-deposition of rock before the upper, younger bed was laid down.

un•con•nect•ed [,ʌnkə'nɛktɪd] *adj.* **1** separated; disconnected. **2** lacking in cohesion or coherence; separate or unrelated: *What she had written was not a paragraph; it was just a series of unconnected sentences.*

un•con•quer•a•ble [ʌn'kɒŋkərəbəl] *adj.* that cannot be conquered. **—un'con•quer•a•bly,** *adv.*

un•con•scion•a•ble [ʌn'kɒnʃənəbəl] *adj.* **1** not sanctioned or guided by conscience; unscrupulous: *unconscionable business practices, an unconscionable liar.* **2** unreasonable; excessive: *to wait an unconscionable time for someone.* **—un'con•scion•a•bly,** *adv.*

un•con•scious [ʌn'kɒnʃəs] *adj., n.* *—adj.* **1** not conscious; not able to feel or think: *to be knocked unconscious. He was unconscious for several days after the accident.* **2** not aware: *The general was unconscious of being followed by a spy.* **3** not deliberate; not intended: *unconscious neglect.* **4** relating to that part of a person's mind or mental activity of which he or she is not normally aware, but which can affect behaviour: *unconscious bigotry.*
—n.
the unconscious, the part of a person's mind of which the person is not normally aware, but which can affect behaviour; a person's unconscious thoughts, desires, fears, etc. **—un'con•scious•ly,** *adv.* **—un'con•scious•ness,** *n.*

un•con•sti•tu•tion•al [,ʌnkɒnstə'tjuʃənəl] *or* [,ʌnkɒnstə'tuʃənəl] *adj.* contrary to the constitution; not

In each of the words below **un-** *means* not; *the pronunciation of the main part of each word is not changed.*

un'claimed
un'clar•i,fied
un'clas•si,fi•a•ble
un'cleaned
un'clear
un'cleared
un'cloud•ed
un'clut•tered
un'coat•ed
un'cocked
,un•co'erced
un'coined
,un•col'lect•a•ble
,un•col'lect•ed
,un•col'lect•i•ble
un'col•on,ized
un'col•oured
un'combed
,un•com'bin•a•ble
,un•com'bined
un'come•ly
un'com•fort•ed
,un•com'mend•a•ble
,un•com'pan•ion•a•ble
un'com•pen,sat•ed
,un•com'pet•i•tive
,un•com'plain•ing
,un•com'plai•sant
,un•com'plet•ed
,un•com'pli•ant
un'com•pli,cat•ed
,un•com•pli'men•ta•ry
,un•com'ply•ing
,un•com'pound•ed
,un•com•pre'hend•ing
,un•com•pre'hen•si•ble
un'com•pro,mised
,un•con'cealed
,un•con'ce•ded
,un•con'cert•ed
,un•con'clud•ed
,un•con'demned
,un•con'densed
,un•con'du•cive
,un•con'fessed
,un•con'fined
,un•con'firmed
,un•con'fused
,un•con'geal•a•ble
,un•con'gealed
,un•con'gen•i•al
,un•con'gest•ed
un'con•quered
,un•con•sci'en•tious
un'con•se,crat•ed
,un•con'sent•ing
,un•con'sid•ered
,un•con'soled
,un•con'sol•i,dat•ed
,un•con'strained
,un•con'strict•ed
,un•con'sumed
un'con•sum,mat•ed
,un•con'tam•i,nat•ed
,un•con'test•ed
,un•con•tra'dict•a•ble
,un•con•tra'dict•ed

constitutional. **—,un•con•sti'tu•tion•al•ly,** *adv.* **—,un•con•sti,tu•tion'al•i•ty,** *n.*

un•con•trol•la•ble [,ʌnkən'troʊləbəl] *adj.* not controllable; that cannot be controlled or held back: *I had to leave quickly because I felt an uncontrollable desire to laugh.* **—,un•con'trol•la•bly,** *adv.*

un•con•ven•tion•al [,ʌkən'vɛnʃənəl] *adj.* not bound by or conforming to convention, rule, or precedent; being out of the ordinary: *an unconventional way of dressing. She is an unconventional person.* **—,un•con'ven•tion•al•ly,** *adv.* **—,un•con,ven•tion'al•i•ty,** *n.*

un•cork [ʌn'kɔrk] *v.* **1** pull the cork from. **2** let go or let out; release: *to uncork a vicious punch, to uncork one's pent-up feelings.*

un•count•ed [ʌn'kaʊntɪd] *adj.* **1** not counted; not reckoned. **2** very many; innumerable.

un•cou•ple [ʌn'kʌpəl] *v.* **-pled, -pling.** disconnect; unfasten; separate.

un•cour•te•ous [ʌn'kɜrtiəs] *adj.* discourteous; impolite; rude. **—un'cour•te•ous•ly,** *adv.*

un•court•li•ness [ʌn'kɔrtlinɪs] *n.* rudeness.

un•couth [ʌn'kuθ] *adj.* **1** awkward or crude in appearance, conduct, etc.: *uncouth manners, an uncouth young man.* **2** *Archaic.* strange; outlandish: *They heard people speaking in an uncouth tongue.* ⟨OE *uncūth* < *un-*[1] + *cūth*, pp. of *cunnan* know⟩ **—un'couth•ly,** *adv.* **—un'couth•ness,** *n.*

un•cov•e•nant•ed [ʌn'kʌvənəntɪd] *adj.* not bound by or promised by a covenant.

un•cov•er [ʌn'kʌvər] *v.* **1** remove the cover from. **2** make known; reveal; expose. **3** remove the hat or cap from (one's head). **4** remove one's hat or cap in respect: *Uncover before the king!*

un•cov•ered [ʌn'kʌvərd] *adj., v.* —*adj.* **1** having no cover or covering: *Don't leave the milk uncovered.* **2** not protected by insurance, etc. **3** not wearing a hat or cap.
—*v.* pt. and pp. of UNCOVER.

un•cross [ʌn'krɒs] *v.* change from a crossed position: *She uncrossed her legs and stretched them out.*

un•crossed [ʌn'krɒst] *v., adj.* —*v.* pt. and pp. of UNCROSS.
—*adj.* not crossed; not marked with a cross-stroke: *You left several t's uncrossed.*

un•crown [ʌn'kraʊn] *v.* take the crown from; depose.

un•crowned [ʌn'kraʊnd] *adj., v.* —*adj.* **1** not crowned; not having yet assumed the crown. **2** having royal power without being king, queen, etc.
—*v.* pt. and pp. of UNCROWN.

unc•tion ['ʌŋkʃən] *n.* **1** the act of anointing with oil, ointment, etc. for medical purposes or as a religious rite: *The priest gave the dying man extreme unction.* **2** the oil, ointment, etc. used for anointing. **3** something soothing or comforting: *the unction of flattery.* **4** a fervent or earnest quality in behaviour or expression. **5** affected fervour or earnestness; unctuousness. ⟨< L *unctio, -onis* < *unguere* anoint⟩

unc•tu•ous ['ʌŋktʃuəs] *adj.* **1** like an oil or ointment; oily or greasy. **2** of or containing oil or grease. **3** of minerals, soapy or greasy to the touch. **4** of a person or a person's manner, very smooth, fervent, or earnest, especially in a false or affected way when trying to please or persuade: *The stranger's unctuous manner made us suspicious.* **5** of ground or soil, soft and clinging, but easily worked; rich in decayed organic matter. **6** of clay, very plastic. ⟨ME < Med.L *unctuosus*, ult. < L *unguere* anoint⟩ **—'unc•tu•ous•ly,** *adv.* **—,unc•tu'os•i•ty** [-'ɒsəti] or **'unc•tu•ous•ness,** *n.*

un•curl [ʌn'kɜrl] *v.* straighten out: *Can you uncurl these pages that have been rolled up for so long? Her carefully set hair uncurled in the dense fog.*

un•cut [ʌn'kʌt] *adj.* **1** not cut into, cut apart, or cut down: *The cake was on the table, still uncut.* **2** of a gem, not shaped: *uncut diamonds.* **3** of a book, having the folded edges of the leaves not cut open, or having untrimmed margins. **4** of a book, film, etc., not shortened; unabridged or unexpurgated: *They saw the uncut version of the film.*

un•daunt•ed [ʌn'dɒntɪd] *adj.* not daunted; not discouraged or dismayed. **—un'daunt•ed•ly,** *adv.* **—un'daunt•ed•ness,** *n.*

un•de•ceive [,ʌndɪ'siv] *v.* **-ceived, -ceiv•ing.** make free from error, illusion, or deception.

un•de•cid•ed [,ʌndɪ'saɪdɪd] *adj.* **1** not decided or settled. **2** not having one's mind made up. **—,un•de'cid•ed•ly,** *adv.* **—,un•de'cid•ed•ness,** *n.*

un•de•fined [,ʌndɪ'faɪnd] *adj.* **1** not defined or explained. **2** indefinite; imprecise or vague.

un•de•ni•a•ble [,ʌndɪ'naɪəbəl] *adj.* **1** that cannot be denied; certain; indisputable: *the undeniable rudeness of his answer, undeniable excellence.* **2** unquestionably genuine or excellent: *Her references were undeniable.* **—,un•de'ni•a•bly,** *adv.*

un•de•nom•i•na•tion•al [,ʌndɪ,nɒmə'neiʃənəl] *adj.* nondenominational; not limited to or belonging to any particular religious group.

un•der ['ʌndər] *prep., adv., adj.* —*prep.* **1** in, at, or to a place or position directly below: *The marble rolled under the table. Write your name under mine.* **2** under and through to the other side of: *The road goes under that bridge.* **3** below the surface of: *under the ground, swimming under water.* **4** on the inside of; covered or hidden by: *She was wearing a heavy sweater under her parka. He has a soft heart under his gruff exterior.* **5** lower than the required or standard degree, amount, etc.: *under par. You cannot sign a contract if you are under legal age.* **6** less than: *It will cost under ten dollars.* **7** subject to the authority, control, influence, or guidance of: *He studied under a famous pianist. The soldiers acted under orders.* **8** during the time of the rule of: *England under Elizabeth I.* **9 a** in the position or state of being affected by: *under the new rules. He doesn't work well under pressure.* **b** undergoing; in the process of: *under renovation, under examination, under discussion.* **10** within a particular group or category: *Books on gymnastics are classified under sports.* **11** represented by: *under a new name.* **12** using as a cover: *Under the guise of friendship, she found out his secret. He entered the house under the pretext of checking the meter.* **13** sowed or planted with: *two hectares under corn.*
under the circumstances, things being as they are (or were, etc.).
—*adv.* **1** in or to a place or position below something: *We saw the swimmer go under.* **2** in or into a condition of subjection, failure,

In each of the words below **un-** *means* not; *the pronunciation of the main part of each word is not changed.*

,un•con'trolled
,un•con•tro'ver•sial
,un•con•tro'vert•i•ble
,un•con'ver•sant
,un•con'vert•ed
,un•con'vinced
,un•con'vinc•ing
un'cooked
un'cooled
,un•co-'op•e•ra•tive
,un•co-'or•di,nat•ed
un'cor•dial
un'corked
,un•cor'rect•ed
,un•cor'rob•o,rat•ed
,un•cor'rupt•ed
un'count•a•ble
un'court•ly
un'crate
,un•cre'at•ed
,un•cre'a•tive
un'cred•it•ed
un'crit•i•cal
un'crit•i,ciz•a•ble
un'cropped
un'crowd•ed
un'crush•a•ble
un'crys•tal,lized
un'cul•ti•va•ble
un'cul•ti,vat•ed
un'cul•tured
un'curbed
un'cured
un'cur•i•ous
un'curled
un'cur•rent
,un•cur'tailed
un'cur•tained
un'cus•tom,a•ry
un'dam•aged
un'damped
un'dat•ed
un'daugh•ter•ly
un'daz•zled
,un•de'bat•a•ble
,un•de'cayed
,un•de'ceiv•a•ble
,un•de'ceived
,un•de'ci•pher•a•ble
,un•de'ci•phered
un'decked
,un•de'clared
,un•de'clin•a•ble
,un•de'clined
un'dec•o,rat•ed
,un•de'faced
,un•de'feat•a•ble
,un•de'feat•ed
,un•de'fend•ed
,un•de'fen•si•ble
,un•de'filed
,un•de'fin•a•ble
,un•de'formed
,un•de'layed
,un•de'lin•e,at•ed
,un•de'liv•er•a•ble
,un•de'liv•ered
,un•de'mand•ing
,un•dem•o'crat•ic
,un•dem•o'crat•i•cal•ly
,un•de'mon•stra•ble
,un•de'mon•stra•tive
,un•de'nied
,un•de'pend•a•ble
,un•de'plet•ed
,un•de'pre•ci,at•ed

unconsciousness, etc.: *His business went under.* **3** less than some quantity or limit: *ten dollars or under.*
—adj. facing or projecting downward: *The under surface was rough.* 〈OE〉

☛ *Syn. prep.* **1, 3, 5. Under,** BELOW, BENEATH express a relation in which one thing is thought of as being lower than another in some way. **Under** suggests being directly lower: *A corporal is under a sergeant.* **Below** suggests being on a lower level, but not necessarily straight below nor without anyone or anything in between: *A corporal is below a major.* **Beneath** can be used in place of either **under** or **below,** but is usually more formal or literary: *She lies buried beneath an ancient oak tree.*

under– *prefix.* **1** that is in, on, or to a lower place or side: *underlip, underparts.* **2** below or beneath: *underground.* **3** that is on or for the inside; covered or concealed: *underwear.* **4** from below; from or in a lower or a concealed position: *undergird, underlie, underdrain.* **5** lower in rank; subordinate: *undersecretary.* **6** not enough; insufficient: *underfed, underripe, underbake, undereducated, underexercise, underemphasize.* **7** less or for less than: *underbid, undersell.* **8** below normal: *undersized, underactive, underconsumption, underdose, underpopulated.*

un•der•a•chieve [ˌʌndərə'tʃiv] *v.* **-chieved, -chiev•ing.** work or perform to a lower standard than expected, especially academically. **—ˌun•der•a'chieve•ment,** *n.*

un•der•a•chiev•er [ˌʌndərə'tʃivər] *n.* a person, especially a student, who fails to work at the level of his or her ability.

un•der•act [ˌʌndər'ækt] *v.* perform (a role in a play) with too little dramatic force; fail to adequately portray (a character).

un•der•age[1] [ˌʌndər'eidʒ] *adj.* **1** of less than full age. **2** of less than the legal age for voting, marrying, drinking liquor in public bars, etc.

un•der•age[2] [ˌʌndərɪdʒ] a shortage; deficiency; the amount by which something is short.

un•der•arm ['ʌndərˌɑrm] *adj., n., adv. —adj.* **1** on or under the inside of the arm where it joins the shoulder; on or under the armpit: *an underarm scar, the underarm seam in a shirt.* **2** of, having to do with, or for the armpit: *underarm deodorant.* **3** underhand: *an underarm throw.*
—n. armpit.
—adv. underhand: *She threw the ball underarm.*

un•der•bel•ly ['ʌndərˌbɛli] *n., pl.* **-lies. 1** the unprotected lower surface or part of the belly. **2** any unprotected or especially vulnerable part.

un•der•bid [ˌʌndər'bɪd] *v.* **-bid, -bid•ding;** *n. —v.* **1** make a lower bid than (another bidder), as in seeking a contract for work, at an auction, etc. **2** bid less than the full value of: *to underbid a hand in bridge.*
—n. the act of underbidding. **—ˌun•der'bid•der,** *n.*

un•der•bo•dy ['ʌndərˌbɒdi] *n.* the underside of an animal or a mechanism.

un•der•bred [ˌʌndər'brɛd] *adj.* **1** marked by lack of good breeding; ill-mannered or vulgar. **2** of a horse, dog, etc., not of pure breed.

un•der•brush ['ʌndərˌbrʌʃ] *n.* bushes and small trees growing under the large trees in a wooded area; undergrowth.

un•der•car•riage ['ʌndərˌkærɪdʒ] *or* ['ʌndərˌkɛrɪdʒ] *n.* **1** the supporting framework of an automobile, carriage, etc. **2** the underpart of an aircraft that receives the impact on landing and supports the aircraft on the ground or water; landing gear.

un•der•charge *v.* [ˌʌndər'tʃɑrdʒ]; *n.* ['ʌndərˌtʃɑrdʒ] *v.* **-charged, -charg•ing;** *n. —v.* **1** put an insufficient charge or load into. **2** charge less than the proper or fair price: *I think the clerk undercharged me. You undercharged me one dollar.*
—n. **1** an insufficient charge or load. **2** a charge or price less than is proper or fair.

un•der•class ['ʌndərˌklæs] *n.* the lowest social class; the poor.

un•der•clothes ['ʌndərˌklouz] *or* ['ʌndərˌklouðz] *n.pl.* underwear.

un•der•cloth•ing ['ʌndərˌklouðɪŋ] *n.* underwear.

un•der•coat ['ʌndərˌkout] *n., v. —n.* **1** a coat or layer of paint, etc. applied before the finishing coat. **2** the soft, thick fur of certain animals that is hidden by the longer, coarser hair of the outer coat. **3** a car undercoating.
—v. apply undercoating or an undercoat to: *to undercoat a car.*

un•der•coat•ing ['ʌndərˌkoutɪŋ] *n., v. —n.* a heavy, tarry coating sprayed on the underside of a motor vehicle to protect it against rust, etc.: *Every new car should have undercoating.*
—v. ppr. of UNDERCOAT.

un•der•cov•er ['ʌndərˌkʌvər] *or* [ˌʌndər'kʌvər] *adj., adv.* *—adj.* **1** working in secret: *The jeweller was an undercover man for*

the police. **2** done in secret: *an undercover attack.*
—adv. secretly: *He was working undercover.*

un•der•croft ['ʌndərˌkrɒft] *n.* crypt.

un•der•cur•rent ['ʌndərˌkɜrənt] *n.* **1** a current flowing below the upper currents or the surface of a body of water, air, etc. **2** an underlying tendency that is often contrary to what is expressed or shown: *There was an undercurrent of sadness beneath her joking manner.*

un•der•cut *v.* [ˌʌndər'kʌt]; *n.* ['ʌndərˌkʌt] *v.* **-cut, -cut•ting;** *n.* *—v.* **1** cut under or beneath; cut away material from so as to leave a portion overhanging. **2** sell or work for less than (a competitor). **3** undermine; weaken: *He is undercutting my authority.* **4** cut a notch in (a tree) below the main cut to ensure falling in the desired direction or to prevent splitting. **5** *Golf, tennis, etc.* hit (a ball) with a downward slant to give it a backward spin.
—n. **1** the act or result of undercutting. **2** a notch cut in a tree below the main cut and on the side toward which the tree is to fall. An undercut prevents the tree from splitting when it falls. **3** *Esp. Brit.* the tenderloin or fillet of beef. **4** *Golf, tennis, etc.* the act or an instance of hitting a ball with a downward slant to give it a backward spin.

un•der•de•vel•oped [ˌʌndərdɪ'vɛləpt] *adj.* **1 a** not developed in a normal way: *an underdeveloped limb.* **b** less fully developed at a certain stage than comparable others. **2** of a region, country, etc., poorly or inadequately developed in industry and commerce and having a relatively low standard of living. **3** of film, a print, etc., showing a less distinct image than it should because too little time or too weak a solution was used in processing it. **—ˌun•der•de'vel•op•ment,** *n.*

un•der•dog ['ʌndərˌdɒg] *n.* **1** a person or group that is expected to lose or is losing a struggle or contest. **2** a person or group that is a victim of persecution or social or political injustice. **3** a dog having the worst of a fight.

un•der•done [ˌʌndər'dʌn] *adj.* not cooked enough; cooked very little.

un•der•drain ['ʌndərˌdrein] *n., v. —n.* an underground drain for cultivated land.
—v. drain (land) using such drains. **—'un•derˌdrain•age,** *n.*

un•der•dress [ˌʌndər'drɛs] *v.* **-dressed, -dres•sing.** dress less formally than the occasion demands. **—ˌun•der'dressed,** *adj.*

un•der•em•ployed [ˌʌndərɛm'plɔɪd] *adj., n. —adj.* of a person in the work force, not adequately or fully employed; employed in a way that does not permit the use of one's true or full abilities and training.
—n. **the underemployed,** all those people not fully employed. **—ˌun•der•em'ploy•ment,** *n.*

un•der•es•ti•mate *v.* [ˌʌndər'ɛstəˌmeit]; *n.* [ˌʌndər'ɛstəmɪt] *v.* **-mat•ed, -mat•ing;** *n.*
—v. estimate at too low a value, amount, rate, etc.
—n. an estimate that is too low. **—ˌun•derˌes•ti'ma•tion,** *n.*

un•der•ex•pose [ˌʌndərɛk'spouz] *v.* **-posed, -pos•ing.** *Photography.* expose to light for too short a time, or to too little light.

un•der•ex•po•sure [ˌʌndərɛk'spouʒər] *n. Photography.* **1** an exposure to the light for too short a time, or to too little light. Underexposure makes a photograph look dim. **2** an underexposed negative or the print or slide made from it: *The film developers did not make me pay for the underexposures. With a lower film speed, most of these would have been underexposures.*

un•der•feed [ˌʌndər'fid] *v.* **-fed, -feed•ing. 1** feed too little. **2** stoke with coal or other solid fuel from the bottom.

un•der•foot [ˌʌndər'fʊt] *adv. or adj.* **1** at, before, or underneath one's feet; down on or against the ground: *enjoying the soft grass underfoot. She crushed the flowers underfoot.* **2** in the way: *That dog is always underfoot. The children were constantly underfoot.*

un•der•fur ['ʌndərˌfɜr] *n.* the soft, thick fur of certain mammals that is hidden by the longer, coarser hair of the outer coat.

un•der•gar•ment ['ʌndərˌgɑrmənt] *n.* any garment worn under outer clothing, especially an article of underwear.

un•der•gird [ˌʌndər'gɜrd] *v.,* **-gird•ed,** or **-girt, -gird•ing. 1** reinforce or brace from beneath. **2** support; strengthen.

un•der•glaze ['ʌndərˌgleiz] *n.* a design, decoration, or colour applied to a ceramic article before the glaze is put on.

un•der•go [ˌʌndər'gou] *v.* **-went, -gone, -go•ing. 1** go through;

be subjected to; experience: *The town has undergone many changes in the past few years.* **2** endure; suffer: *They underwent a great deal of hardship on the long trek.*
☛ *Syn.* See note at EXPERIENCE.

un•der•gone [ˌʌndər'gɒn] *v.* pp. of UNDERGO.

un•der•grad ['ʌndər,græd] *n., adj.* undergraduate.

un•der•grad•u•ate [ˌʌndər'grædʒuɪt] *n., adj. —n.* a university student in a course of study leading to a bachelor's degree.
—adj. **1** for, having to do with, or designating undergraduates: *undergraduate activities.* **2** characteristic of undergraduates.

un•der•ground *adv., adj.* ['ʌndər'graʊnd]; *n.* ['ʌndər,graʊnd] *adv., adj., n. —adv.* **1** beneath the surface of the ground. **2** in or into concealment or secret operation: *The thieves went underground after the robbery.*
—adj. **1** being, working, or used beneath the surface of the ground: *underground telephone cables.* **2** done or operating secretly: *The revolution began as an underground movement in the cities.* **3** of, having to do with, or produced by a group or groups outside the establishment, especially avant-garde or radical groups: *an underground newspaper. Her first plays were produced by an underground theatre.*
—n. **1** *Esp. Brit.* an underground railway system in a city; subway. **2** place or space beneath the surface of the ground. **3** a secret organization of citizens or a grouping of such organizations, working to free a country from foreign domination or an autocratic regime. **4** any avant-garde or revolutionary movement in art, communications, or politics.

Underground Railroad formerly, a secret system set up by opponents of slavery in Canada and the United States before the Civil War to help slaves escape to freedom in the northern states and Canada.

un•der•growth ['ʌndər,grouθ] *n.* **1** underbrush. **2** an animal's underfur.

un•der•hand ['ʌndər,hænd] *adj., adv. —adj.* **1** not open or honest; secret and sly; underhanded. **2** made with an upward movement of the hand from below shoulder level: *an underhand pitch.*
—adv. **1** secretly and slyly; underhandedly. **2** with an upward movement of the hand from below shoulder level: *to throw a ball underhand.*

un•der•hand•ed ['ʌndər'hændɪd] *adj.* **1** not open or honest; secret and sly: *an underhanded trick.* **2** SHORT-HANDED (def. 1).
—ˌun•der'hand•ed•ly, *adv.* **—ˌun•der'hand•ed•ness,** *n.*

un•der•hung ['ʌndər'hʌŋ] *adj.* **1** of the lower jaw, projecting beyond the upper jaw: *A bulldog has an underhung jaw.* **2** having a projecting lower jaw. **3** resting on a track beneath, instead of being hung from above: *underhung sliding doors.* **4** underslung. **5** of meat, not hung long enough to make it tender.

un•der•in•sured [ˌʌndərɪn'ʃʊrd] *adj.* not carrying sufficient insurance.

un•der•jaw ['ʌndər,dʒɒ] *n.* the lower jaw; mandible.

un•der•laid [ˌʌndər'leid] *v.* pt. and pp. of UNDERLAY.

un•der•lain [ˌʌndər'lein] *v.* pp. of UNDERLIE.

un•der•lap [ˌʌndər'læp] *v.* **-lapped, -lap•ping.** be or lie partly covered by (something else).

un•der•lay *v.* [ˌʌndər'lei]; *n.* ['ʌndər,lei]; *v.* **-laid, -lay•ing;** *n.*
—v. **1** lay (something) under something else. **2** raise, support, cushion, etc. with something laid underneath. **3** *Printing.* furnish with an underlay. **4** pt. of UNDERLIE.
—n. **1** something laid beneath to raise, support, cushion, etc.: *The carpet has a foam rubber underlay.* **2** *Printing.* a piece or pieces of paper put under types, etc. to bring them to the proper height for printing. ⟨OE *underlecgan*⟩

un•der•lie [ˌʌndər'laɪ] *v.* **-lay, -lain, -ly•ing.** **1** lie under; be beneath. **2** form the basis of; be a reason or cause for: *Strong resentment underlay his outburst.* **3** *Linguistics.* of something in deep structure, be represented by (another form) in surface structure, according to TRANSFORMATIONAL GRAMMAR. ⟨OE *underlicgan*⟩

un•der•line ['ʌndər,laɪn] *v.* **-lined, -lin•ing;** *n. —v.* **1** draw a line or lines under. **2** emphasize; make emphatic or more emphatic: *Her speech underlined the importance of co-operation.* **3** sew an underlining in (a garment).
—n. a line drawn underneath something: *The underline is too faint.*

un•der•ling ['ʌndərlɪŋ] *n.* a person of lower rank or position; inferior. ⟨OE *underling* < *under* under + *-ling*⟩

un•der•lin•ing ['ʌndər,laɪnɪŋ] *n., v. —n.* a garment lining formed by attaching the individual sections separately to the corresponding garment sections, each garment section with its attached lining being treated as a unit when the garment is sewn together.
—v. ppr. of UNDERLINE.

un•der•lip ['ʌndər,lɪp] *n.* the lower lip.

un•der•ly•ing [ˌʌndər'laɪɪŋ] *adj., v. —adj.* **1** lying under or beneath. **2** fundamental; basic; essential. **3** not clearly evident or expressed; implicit: *His complimentary remarks had an underlying tone of sarcasm.* **4** *Linguistics.* in TRANSFORMATIONAL GRAMMAR, being part of the deep structure and not appearing in the surface structure: *an underlying form.*
—v. ppr. of UNDERLIE.

un•der•manned [ˌʌndər'mænd] *adj.* having not enough crew, staff, etc.; understaffed: *The ship was undermanned, but still carried out its mission.*

un•der•mine [ˌʌndər'maɪn] *v.* **-mined, -min•ing.** **1** wear away the base or foundations of: *The wave had undermined the cliff.* **2** injure or damage by secret or unfair means: *The editorial was obviously intended to undermine her influence in the community.* **3** weaken, wear out, or destroy gradually: *Several months of stress and insufficient sleep had undermined her health.* **4** make a passage or hole under; dig under: *to undermine a wall.*
—ˌun•der'min•er, *n.*

un•der•most ['ʌndər,moust] *adj. or adv.* lowest.

un•der•neath [ˌʌndər'niθ] *prep., adv., adj., n. —prep.* **1** directly below; beneath; under: *a cellar underneath a house. Write the date underneath your name.* **2** on the inside of; covered or hidden by; under: *He wore a T-shirt underneath his shirt.* **3** under the control or authority of: *The clerical staff are underneath the administrative assistants.*
—adv. **1** on the inside of or below something: *He crawled underneath. She was wearing her swimsuit underneath.* **2** on or at the lower part or surface: *The box is wet underneath.*
—adj. lower: *the underneath side.*
—n. the lower part or surface: *Let me see the underneath.* ⟨OE *underneothan* < *under-* under + *neothan* below⟩

un•der•nour•ish [ˌʌndər'nɜrɪʃ] *v.* provide with insufficient food for growth, health, etc.: *The children were badly undernourished.*

un•der•nour•ish•ment [ˌʌndər'nɜrɪʃmənt] *n.* not having enough food; lack of nourishment.

un•der•pants ['ʌndər,pænts] *n.pl.* long or short pants worn as an undergarment.

un•der•part ['ʌndər,pɑrt] *n.* **1** a part that is underneath. **2** a subordinate part, as in a play.

un•der•pass ['ʌndər,pæs] *n.* a way underneath, especially a road under railway tracks or under another road.

un•der•pay [ˌʌndər'pei] *v.* **-paid, -pay•ing.** **1** pay (someone) too little. **2** pay less than (what is due): *We underpaid our rent this month because we didn't know about the increase.*
—ˌun•der'pay•ment, *n.*

un•der•pin [ˌʌndər'pɪn] *v.* **-pinned, -pin•ning.** **1** support or strengthen from below with props, stones, masonry, etc. **2** provide a foundation for; substantiate.

un•der•pin•ning *n.* ['ʌndər,pɪnɪŋ]; *v.* [ˌʌndər'pɪnɪŋ] *n., v. —n.* **1** the material or structure used to support a building or wall from below; a support or prop. **2** Often, **underpinnings,** *pl.* **a** anything used as a foundation or support: *The new evidence provided a good underpinning for the detective's theory.* **b** *Informal.* legs.
—v. ppr. of UNDERPIN.

un•der•play [ˌʌndər'plei] *v.* **1 a** act (a role or scene) in a subdued or restrained manner. **b** play (a role) in too subtle or understated a way. **2** make unimportant or less important; avoid or reduce emphasis on; downplay.

un•der•plot ['ʌndər,plɒt] *n.* subplot.

un•der•priv•i•leged [ˌʌndər'prɪvəlɪdʒd] *adj.* **1** having fewer advantages than most people have, especially because of poor economic or social status. **2** (*noml.*) **the underprivileged,** *pl.* all persons who are underprivileged.

un•der•pro•duce [ˌʌndərprə'djus] *or* [ˌʌndərprə'dus] *v.* **-pro•duced, -pro•duc•ing.** produce less of (something) than is normal or than there is demand for. **—ˌun•der•pro'duc•tion,** *n.*

un•der•proof ['ʌndər'pruf] *adj.* of liquor, containing a lower percentage of alcohol than proof spirit.

un•der•quote [ˌʌndər'kwout] *v.* **-quot•ed, -quot•ing. 1** quote a lower price or rate than (someone else). **2** quote a lower price or rate for (goods or services) than another.

un•der•rate [ˌʌndər'reit] *v.* **-rat•ed, -rat•ing.** rate or estimate too low; put too low a value on.

un•der•re•port [ˌʌndərɪ'pɔrt] *v.* report fewer instances of or less than the true amount of: *Date rape is underreported.*

un•der•ripe [ˌʌndər'rəip] *adj.* not completely ripe or not ripe enough: *The tomatoes were somewhat underripe, but edible.*

un•der•score *v.* [ˌʌndər'skɔr]; *n.* ['ʌndərˌskɔr] *v.* **-scored, -scor•ing;** *n.* —*v.* **1** underline. **2** emphasize.
—*n.* a line underscoring something.

un•der•sea ['ʌndər'si] *adj., adv.* —*adj.* being, carried on, or used beneath the surface of the sea: *an undersea cable, undersea explorations, undersea oil deposits.*
—*adv.* Often, **underseas,** beneath the surface of the seas: *exploring undersea.*

un•der•sec•re•tar•y [ˌʌndər'sɛkrəˌtɛri] *n., pl.* **-tar•ies.** an assistant secretary, especially of a government department.

un•der•sell [ˌʌndər'sɛl] *v.* **-sold, -sell•ing. 1** sell things at a lower price than: *to undersell a competitor.* **2** sell (merchandise, etc.) at less than the actual value; sell at a loss. **3** promote or advertise (merchandise, etc.) in a restrained manner.

un•der•serv•ant ['ʌndərˌsɜrvənt] *n.* a servant who does the simpler or lower tasks, or who is under the authority of another servant.

un•der•set *n.* ['ʌndərˌsɛt]; *v.* [ˌʌndər'sɛt] *n., v.* **-set, -set•ting.**
—*v.* support by setting something under.
—*n.* an undercurrent in the ocean.

un•der•sexed [ˌʌndər'sɛkst] *adj.* having a weaker sexual drive than is considered normal.

un•der•sher•iff ['ʌndərˌʃɛrɪf] *n.* a sheriff's deputy, especially one who acts when the sheriff is not able to act or when there is no sheriff.

un•der•shirt ['ʌndərˌʃɜrt] *n.* a collarless, often sleeveless, knit undergarment for the upper part of the body.

un•der•shoot [ˌʌndər'ʃut] *v.* **-shot, -shoot•ing. 1** of an aircraft, come down short of (the runway or landing field). **2** shoot short of or below (a target, mark, etc.).

un•der•shorts ['ʌndərˌʃɔrts] *n.pl.* short underpants worn by men and boys.

un•der•shot *adj.* ['ʌndərˌʃɒt]; *v.* [ˌʌndər'ʃɒt] *adj., v.* —*adj.* **1** of a water wheel, driven by water passing beneath. See WATER WHEEL for picture. **2** of the lower jaw, projecting beyond the upper; underhung.
—*v.* pt. and pp. of UNDERSHOOT.

un•der•side ['ʌndərˌsaɪd] *n.* the surface lying underneath; the bottom or hidden side.

un•der•signed ['ʌndərˌsaɪnd] *n., adj.* —*n.* **the undersigned,** the person or persons signing a letter or document: *The undersigned accepts the agreement. We, the undersigned, testify that we have read the document.*
—*adj.* signed or having signed at the end of a letter or document: *the undersigned witness.*

un•der•sized ['ʌndər'saɪzd] *adj.* smaller than the usual, desired, or required size: *undersized trout.*

un•der•skirt ['ʌndərˌskɜrt] *n.* a skirt worn under another skirt: *a lace skirt with a satin underskirt.*

un•der•sleeve ['ʌndərˌsliv] *n.* a sleeve worn under an outer sleeve, especially an ornamental inner sleeve extending below the other.

un•der•slung [ˌʌndər'slʌŋ] *adj.* **1** of a vehicle frame, suspended below the axles. **2** having an underslung frame. **3** of a jaw, undershot.

un•der•song ['ʌndərˌsɒŋ] *n.* a song that is sung as an accompaniment to another song.

un•der•staffed [ˌʌndər'stæft] *adj.* having too small a staff; having not enough personnel.

un•der•stand [ˌʌndər'stænd] *v.* **-stood, -stand•ing. 1** get the meaning (of); comprehend: *Now I understand the message.* **2** be in rapport (with); be sympathetic (to): *People listen to him but often do not understand him. Tell your troubles to someone who understands.* **3** learn or hear indirectly; infer from information received: *I understand you've been laid off; I can't imagine why.* **4** know how to deal with; know well; know: *A good teacher should understand children.* **5** comprehend as a fact; grasp clearly; realize: *You understand, don't you, that I will be away for three weeks?* **6** take as a fact; believe implicitly: *It is understood that you will come.* **7** take as the intended meaning; take as meant: *What are we to understand from her words?* **8** supply in the mind. In *He hit the tree harder than I,* the word *did* is understood after *I.*
understand each other, know each other's meaning and wishes; agree. ⟨OE *understandan*⟩
☛ *Syn.* **3.** See note at KNOW.

un•der•stand•a•ble [ˌʌndər'stændəbəl] *adj.* able to be understood. **—ˌun•der'stand•a•bly,** *adv.*

un•der•stand•ing [ˌʌndər'stændɪŋ] *n., adj., v.* —*n.* **1** the mental process or state of one who understands; comprehension; knowledge: *a clear understanding of the problem.* **2** the ability to learn and know; intelligence: *The organist was a woman of understanding.* **3** knowledge of each other's meaning and wishes: *True friendship is based on understanding.* **4** agreement: *You and I must come to an understanding.* **5** an individual's perception or interpretation: *her understanding of the event.*
—*adj.* intelligent and sympathetic: *an understanding reply.*
—*v.* ppr. of UNDERSTAND. **—ˌun•der'stand•ing•ly,** *adv.*

un•der•state [ˌʌndər'steit] *v.* **-stat•ed -stat•ing. 1** state too weakly or in too restrained a manner; say less than the full truth about; minimize. **2** show or express in a subtle or unobtrusive way: *understated elegance, understated humour.*

un•der•state•ment ['ʌndərˌsteitmənt] *or* [ˌʌndər'steitmənt] *n.* **1** a statement that expresses a fact too weakly or in a subtle or restrained way: *To say that he was annoyed is an understatement.* **2** the act or practice of making such a statement or statements: *This humorist makes frequent use of understatement.*

un•der•stood [ˌʌndər'stʊd] *adj., v.* —*adj.* **1** agreed upon; decided in advance. **2** comprehended; known. **3** implied; assumed.
—*v.* pt. and pp. of UNDERSTAND.

un•der•stud•y ['ʌndərˌstʌdi] *n.* **-stud•ies;** *v.* **-stud•ied, -stud•y•ing.** —*n.* a person who is ready to substitute in an emergency for an actor or any other regular performer.
—*v.* **1** learn (a part) in order to replace the regular performer when necessary. **2** act as an understudy to.

un•der•sur•face ['ʌndərˌsɜrfɪs] *n.* underside.

un•der•take [ˌʌndər'teik] *v.* **-took, -tak•en, -tak•ing. 1** set about; try; attempt. **2** agree to do; take upon oneself. **3** promise; guarantee. **4** *Formal.* act on the behalf of (*used with* **for**).

un•der•tak•er ['ʌndərˌteikər] *for 1;* [ˌʌndər'teikər] *for 2. n.* **1** a person whose business is preparing the dead for burial and taking charge of funerals; funeral director. **2** a person who attempts or agrees to do something.

un•der•tak•ing ['ʌndərˌteikɪŋ] *or* [ˌʌndər'teikɪŋ] *for 1 and 2;* ['ʌndərˌteikɪŋ] *for 3. n., v.* —*n.* **1** something undertaken; task; enterprise. **2** a promise; guarantee. **3** the business of preparing the dead for burial and taking charge of funerals.
—*v.* ppr. of UNDERTAKE.

un•der–the–count•er ['ʌndər ðə 'kaʊntər] *adj.* **1** made or sold dishonestly or illegally: *under-the-counter copies.* **2** illegal; clandestine; unauthorized: *an under-the-counter transaction.*

un•der•things ['ʌndərˌθɪŋz] *n.pl.* women's underwear.

un•der•tint ['ʌndərˌtɪnt] *n.* UNDERTONE (def. 2).

un•der•tone ['ʌndərˌtoun] *n.* **1** a low or very quiet tone: *to talk in undertones.* **2** a subdued colour; a colour seen through other colours: *There was an undertone of brown beneath all the gold and crimson of autumn.* **3** a quality or feeling that is beneath the surface: *an undertone of sadness in her gaiety.*

un•der•took [ˌʌndər'tʊk] *v.* pt. of UNDERTAKE.

un•der•tow ['ʌndərˌtou] *n.* **1** any strong current below the surface, moving in a direction different from that of the surface current. **2** the backward flow from waves breaking on a beach.

un•der•val•ue [ˌʌndər'vælju] *v.* **-ued, -u•ing. 1** put too low a value on. **2** esteem too little; appreciate insufficiently. **—ˌun•derˌval•u'a•tion,** *n.*

un•der•vest ['ʌndərˌvɛst] *n. Esp. Brit.* undershirt.

un•der•wa•ter ['ʌndər'wɒtər] *adj., adv.* —*adj.* **1** growing, done, or used below the surface of the water: *underwater plants. A submarine is an underwater ship.* **2** below a ship's waterline.
—*adv.* below the surface of the water: *He stayed underwater for two minutes.*

under way **1** in progress: *Plans are under way for a new city hall.* **2** no longer at rest; travelling: *At last we're under way. The ship got under way at exactly noon.* Also, **underway**.

un•der•wear [ˈʌndər,wɛr] *n.* clothing worn under outer clothing and not meant to be visible when one is fully dressed. Compare OUTERWEAR.

un•der•weight *adj.* [ˈʌndərˈweit]; *n.* [ˈʌndər,weit] *adj., n.* —*adj.* **1** of a person or animal, having a mass that is too small in proportion to height and build. **2** having less mass than is needed, desired, or specified: *He claimed that the roast was underweight.*
—*n.* a mass that is less than needed, desired, or specified.

un•der•went [,ʌndərˈwɛnt] *v.* pt. of UNDERGO.

un•der•whelm [,ʌndərˈwɛlm] *v.* be less than impressive (to); fail to interest or impress: *The new musical is totally underwhelming.* ⟨facetious analogy with *overwhelm*⟩

un•der•wood [ˈʌndər,wʊd] *n.* underbrush; undergrowth.

un•der•world [ˈʌndər,wɜrld] *n.* **1** the criminal part of society. **2** *Greek and Roman mythology.* the world of the dead; Hades. **3** the earth. **4** the opposite side of the earth.

un•der•write [,ʌndərˈrəit] *v.* **-wrote, -writ•ten, -writ•ing.** **1** insure (property) against loss. **2** sign (an insurance policy), thereby accepting the risk of insuring something against loss. **3** write under (other written matter); sign one's name to (a document, etc.). **4** agree to buy (all the stocks or bonds of a certain issue that are not bought by the public): *The bankers underwrote the steel company's bonds.* **5** agree to meet the expenses of; sponsor: *Local businesses underwrote the summer concert series.* **6** agree or subscribe to (a proposal, etc.) as if by signing. **7** be, or work as, an underwriter. ⟨OE *underwrītan*, translation of L *subscribere*⟩

un•der•writ•er [ˈʌndər,rəitər] *n.* **1** a person who underwrites an insurance policy or carries on an insurance business; insurer. **2** an official of an insurance company who determines the risks to be accepted, the premiums to be paid, etc. **3** a person who underwrites (usually with others) issues of bonds, stocks, etc.

un•der•writ•ten [,ʌndərˈrɪtən] *v.* pp. of UNDERWRITE.

un•der•wrote [,ʌndərˈrout] *v.* pt. of UNDERWRITE.

un•de•sir•a•ble [,ʌndɪˈzaɪrəbəl] *adj., n.* —*adj.* objectionable; disagreeable.
—*n.* a person who is not wanted. **—,un•de'sir•a•bly,** *adv.* **—,un•de,sir•a'bil•i•ty,** *n.*

un•de•vel•oped [,ʌndɪˈvɛləpt] *adj.* **1** not fully grown. **2** not put to full use. **3** having resources not yet exploited; having little or no modern technology: *undeveloped countries.*

un•did [ʌnˈdɪd] *v.* pt. of UNDO.

un•dies [ˈʌndiz] *n.pl. Informal.* underthings.

un•dine [ʌnˈdin] *or* [ˈʌndin] *n. European folklore.* a female water sprite who, by marrying a mortal and bearing a child, was supposed to be able to acquire a soul. ⟨< NL *Undina* < L *unda* wave⟩

un•dis•ci•plined [ʌnˈdɪsəplɪnd] *adj.* not disciplined; without proper control; untrained.

un•dis•guised [,ʌndɪsˈgaɪzd] *adj.* **1** not disguised. **2** unconcealed; open; plain; frank. **—,un•dis'guis•ed•ly,** *adv.*

un•dis•posed [,ʌndɪˈspouzd] *adj.* **1** not disposed (of). **2** unwilling; disinclined.

un•dis•put•ed [,ʌndɪˈspjutɪd] *adj.* not disputed; not doubted. **—,un•dis'put•ed•ly,** *adv.*

un•dis•turbed [,ʌndɪˈstɜrbd] *adj.* not disturbed; not troubled; calm.

un•do [ʌnˈdu] *v.* **-did, -done, -do•ing.** **1** unfasten, untie, unwrap, etc.: *We quickly undid the package. I can't undo my shoelace.* **2** do away with; cancel or reverse: *We mended the roof, but a heavy storm undid our work.* **3** bring to ruin; spoil; destroy. **4** *Obsolete.* explain or solve. ⟨OE *undōn*⟩ **—un'do•er,** *n.*
☛ *Hom.* UNDUE.

un•dock [ʌnˈdɒk] *v.* **1** take (a ship) out of a dock. **2** of spacecraft: **a** uncouple one module from another. **b** uncouple a spacecraft from a space station, in space.

un•do•ing [ʌnˈduɪŋ] *n., v.* —*n.* **1** a doing away with; spoiling; destroying. **2** a cause of destruction or ruin: *Drink was his undoing.*
—*v.* ppr. of UNDO.

un•done [ʌnˈdʌn] *adj., v.* —*adj.* **1** not done; not finished: *to leave a job undone.* **2** unfastened or not done up: *The top button was undone.* **3** ruined.
—*v.* pp. of UNDO.

un•doubt•ed [ʌnˈdʌutɪd] *adj.* not doubted; accepted as true. **—un'doubt•ed•ly,** *adv.*

un•dress *v.* [ʌnˈdrɛs]; *n.* [ˈʌn,drɛs] *or* [ʌnˈdrɛs]; *adj.* [ˈʌn,drɛs] *v., n., adj.* —*v.* **1** take the clothes off (someone); strip: *The child undressed the doll and gave it a bath.* **2** to strip of ornament. **3** take dressing from (a wound). **4** take off one's clothes.
—*n.* **1** loose, informal dress or nightclothes. **2** ordinary clothes; civilian clothes; business clothes. **3** lack of clothing; nakedness or partial nakedness.
—*adj.* of or having to do with informal or ordinary clothes.

un•due [ʌnˈdju] *or* [ʌnˈdu] *adj.* **1** not owing or payable. **2** not fitting; not right; improper. **3** too great; too much.
☛ *Hom.* UNDO [ʌnˈdu].

un•du•lant [ˈʌndʒələnt] *or* [ˈʌndjələnt] *adj.* waving; wavy.

undulant fever an infectious disease transmitted to humans by bacteria in the milk of infected cattle, goats, etc. It brings on fever, spleen and bowel disorders, pain in the joints, etc.

un•du•late [ˈʌndʒə,leit] *or* [ˈʌndjə,leit] *v.* **-lat•ed, -lat•ing;** *adj.* —*v.* **1** move in waves: *undulating water.* **2** have a wavy form or surface: *undulating hair.* **3** cause to move in waves. **4** give a wavy form or surface to.
—*adj.* wavy. ⟨< LL *undula* wavelet, L *undulatus* diversified as with waves < *unda* wave⟩

un•du•la•tion [,ʌndʒəˈleiʃən] *or* [,ʌndjəˈleiʃən] *n.* **1** a waving motion. **2** a wavy form. **3** one of a series of wavelike bends, curves, swellings, etc. **4** *Physics.* a wavelike motion in air or some other medium, as in the propagation of sound or light; vibration; wave.

un•du•la•to•ry [ˈʌndʒələ,tɔri] *or* [ˈʌndjələ,tɔri] *adj.* undulating; wavy.

un•du•ly [ʌnˈdjuli] *or* [ʌnˈduli] *adv.* **1** excessively; too much: *unduly harsh, unduly optimistic.* **2** unjustly or improperly.

un•dy•ing [ʌnˈdaɪɪŋ] *adj.* **1** deathless; immortal. **2** enduring: *Her courageous action earned his undying gratitude.* **—un'dy•ing•ly,** *adv.*

In each of the words below **un-** *means* not; *the pronunciation of the main part of each word is not changed.*

,un•de'scend•ed
,un•de'scrib•a•ble
,un•de'served
,un•de'serv•ing
un'des•ig,nat•ed
,un•de'sign•ing
,un•de'sired
,un•de'sir•ous
,un•de'spair•ing
,un•de'stroyed
,un•de'tach•a•ble
,un•de'tached
,un•de'tect•ed
,un•de'ter•mi•na•ble
,un•de'ter•mined
,un•de'terred
un'de•vi,at•ing
,un•de'voured
,un•de'vout
,un•di•ag'nosed
,un•dif•fer'en•ti,at•ed
,un•di'gest•ed
un'dig•ni,fied
,un•di'lut•ed
,un•di'min•ished
,un•di'min•ish•ing
un'dimmed
,un•dip•lo'mat•ic
,un•di'rect•ed
,un•dis'cern•i•ble
,un•dis'cern•ing
,un•dis'charged
,un•dis'closed
,un•dis'cour•aged
,un•dis'cov•er•a•ble
,un•dis'cov•ered
,un•dis'crim•i,nat•ing
,un•dis'heart•ened
,un•dis'hon•oured
,un•dis'mayed
,un•dis'mem•bered
,un•dis'posed
,un•dis'put•a•ble
,un•dis'so•ci,at•ed
,un•dis'solved
,un•dis'tilled
,un•dis'tin•guish•a•ble
,un•dis'tin•guished
,un•dis'tin•guish•ing
,un•dis'tort•ed
,un•dis'tract•ed
,un•dis'tressed
,un•dis'trib•ut•ed
,un•di'ver•si,fied
,un•di'vid•ed
,un•di'vulged
un'doc•u,ment•ed
,un•dog'mat•ic
,un•do'mes•tic
,un•do'mes•ti,cat•ed
un'dou•bled
un'doubt•a•ble
un'doubt•ing
un'drained
,un•dra'mat•ic
un'drape
un'draped
un'dreamed
un'dreamt
un'dressed
un'dried
un'drilled
un'drink•a•ble
un'du•ti•ful
un'dyed

un•earned [ʌn'ɜrnd] *adj.* **1** not earned; not gained by labour or service: *unearned income.* **2** not deserved. **3** *Baseball.* scored because of a defensive error or errors.

unearned income income accruing from rents, investments, etc. and not from wages, royalties, etc.

unearned increment increase in the value of property from natural causes, such as the growth of population, rather than from the labour, improvements, etc. put into it by the owner.

un•earth [ʌn'ɜrθ] *v.* **1** dig up: *to unearth a buried city.* **2** find out; discover: *to unearth a plot.*

un•earth•ly [ʌn'ɜrθli] *adj.* **1** not of this world; supernatural. **2** strange; weird; ghostly. **3** *Informal.* unnatural; extraordinary; preposterous. **—un'earth•li•ness,** *n.*

un•ease [ʌn'iz] *n.* a state of restlessness, perturbation, or anxiety.

un•eas•y [ʌn'izi] *adj.* **-eas•i•er, -eas•i•est. 1** restless; disturbed; anxious. **2** not comfortable. **3** disconcerting; that makes uncomfortable: *an uneasy silence.* **4** not easy in manner; awkward. **—un'eas•i•ly,** *adv.* **—un'eas•i•ness,** *n.*

un•ed•u•cat•ed [ʌn'ɛdʒə,keitɪd] *adj.* not educated; not taught or trained.
☛ *Syn.* See note at IGNORANT.

UNEF ['junɛf] United Nations Emergency Force.

un•em•ploy•a•ble [,ʌnɛm'plɔɪəbəl] *adj., n. —adj.* that cannot be employed.
—n. a person who cannot be given work.

un•em•ployed [,ʌnɛm'plɔɪd] *adj.* **1** not having a job; having no work: *an unemployed person.* **2** (*noml.*) **the unemployed,** people out of work. **3** not employed; not in use: *an unemployed skill.*

un•em•ploy•ment [,ʌnɛm'plɔɪmənt] *n.* **1** a lack of employment; being out of work. **2** the number or percentage of persons unemployed at a particular time: *a period of high unemployment.* **3** UNEMPLOYMENT INSURANCE (def. 2).

unemployment insurance 1 a program providing regular payments of money for a fixed period to persons in the regular labour force who are temporarily unemployed because of layoffs, illness, maternity, etc. Unemployment insurance benefits in Canada are paid for through the contributions of employees, employers, and the federal government. **2** benefits paid through such a program: *She collected unemployment insurance for two months.*

un•e•qual [ʌn'ikwəl] *adj.* **1** not the same in amount, size, number, value, merit, rank, etc. **2** not balanced; not well matched. **3** not fair; one-sided: *an unequal contest.* **4** not enough; not adequate: *Her strength was unequal to the task.* **5** not regular; not even; variable or inconsistent. **—,un'e•qual•ly,** *adv.* **—,un'e•qual•ness,** *n.*

un•e•qualled or **un•e•qualed** [ʌn'ikwəld] *adj.* not equalled; matchless.

un•e•quiv•o•cal [,ʌnɪ'kwɪvəkəl] *adj.* **1** clear; plain. **2** of persons, not inclined to temporize, compromise, or equivocate; speaking frankly and straightforwardly. **—,un•e'quiv•o•cal•ly,** *adv.* **—,un•e'quiv•o•cal•ness,** *n.*

un•err•ing [ʌn'ɛrɪŋ] *or* [ʌn'ɜrɪŋ] *adj.* making no mistakes; exactly right; never missing: *unerring aim.* **—un'err•ing•ly,** *adv.* **—un'err•ing•ness,** *n.*

UNESCO [ju'nɛskou] *n.* the United Nations Educational, Scientific, and Cultural Organization.

un•es•sen•tial [,ʌnə'sɛnʃəl] *adj., n. —adj.* not essential; not of prime importance.
—n. something not essential.

un•e•ven [ʌn'ivən] *adj.* **1** not level: *uneven ground.* **2** not equal; one-sided: *an uneven contest.* **3** of a number, leaving a remainder of 1 when divided by 2; odd. *Examples*: 9, 27, 781. **4** not uniform; irregular or variable: *of uneven thickness. It was an uneven performance, but on the whole very enjoyable.* **5** of lines, crooked; not parallel; not straight. ⟨OE *unefen*⟩ **—un'e•ven•ly,** *adv.* **—un'e•ven•ness,** *n.*

un•e•vent•ful [,ʌnɪ'vɛntfəl] *adj.* without important or striking occurrences. **—,un•e'vent•ful•ly,** *adv.* **—,un•e'vent•ful•ness,** *n.*

un•ex•am•pled [,ʌnɛg'zæmpəld] *adj.* having no equal or like; without precedent or parallel; without anything like it: *This man's run of 100 m in 8 s is unexampled.*

un•ex•cep•tion•a•ble [,ʌnɛk'sɛpʃənəbəl] *adj.* beyond criticism; wholly admirable; sometimes mildly pejorative, as having perfect correctness as its only virtue. **—,un•ex'cep•tion•a•bly,** *adv.*

un•ex•cep•tion•al [,ʌnɛk'sɛpʃənəl] *adj.* **1** ordinary. **2** admitting of no exception. **—,un•ex'cep•tion•al•ly,** *adv.*

un•ex•pect•ed [,ʌnɛk'spɛktɪd] *adj.* not expected. **—,un•ex'pect•ed•ly,** *adv.* **—,un•ex'pect•ed•ness,** *n.*

un•fail•ing [ʌn'feilɪŋ] *adj.* **1** never failing. **2** tireless; dependable. **3** never running short; endless. **4** sure; certain. **—un'fail•ing•ly,** *adv.*

un•fair [ʌn'fɛr] *adj.* not fair; unjust. ⟨OE *unfæger*⟩ **—un'fair•ly,** *adv.* **—un'fair•ness,** *n.*

un•faith•ful [ʌn'feiθfəl] *adj.* **1** not faithful; not true to duty or one's promises; faithless. **2** not accurate; not true to the original or to actual fact: *an unfaithful translation. His revisionist history gives an unfaithful representation of the role of Canada in World War II.* **3** having committed adultery. **—un'faith•ful•ly,** *adv.* **—un'faith•ful•ness,** *n.*

un•fa•mil•iar [,ʌnfə'mɪljər] *adj.* **1** not well-known; unusual; strange: *That face is unfamiliar to me.* **2** not acquainted: *She is unfamiliar with the Greek language.*

un•fa•mil•i•ar•i•ty [,ʌnfəmɪl'jærəti] *or* [,ʌnfəmɪl'jɛrəti], [,ʌnfə,mɪli'ærəti] *or* [,ʌnfə,mɪli'ɛrəti] *n.* lack of familiarity.

un•fas•ten [ʌn'fæsən] *v.* **1** undo; make loose; open. **2** become undone or open: *Your zipper has unfastened.*

un•fath•ered [ʌn'fɒðərd] *adj.* **1** illegitimate; of unknown male parentage; bastard. **2** of unknown authorship.

In each of the words below **un-** *means* not; *the pronunciation of the main part of each word is not changed.*

un'ea•ger
un'eat•a•ble
un'eat•en
,un•e'clipsed
,un•e•co'nom•ic
,un•e•co'nom•i•cal
un'ed•i•ble
un'ed•i,fy•ing
un'ed•it•ed
un'ed•u•ca•ble
,un•ef'faced
,un•e'lim•i,nat•ed
,un•e'man•ci,pat•ed
,un•em'bar•rassed
,un•em'bel•lished
,un•e'mo•tion•al
,un•em'phat•ic
un'emp•tied
,un•en'closed
,un•en'cour•aged
,un•en'cum•bered
,un•en'dan•gered
un'end•ing
,un•en'dorsed
,un•en'dowed
,un•en'dur•a•ble
,un•en'dur•ing
,un•en'force•a•ble
,un•en'forced
,un•en'gaged
,un•en'gag•ing
un-'Eng•lish
,un•en'joy•a•ble
,un•en'larged
,un•en'light•ened
,un•en'riched
,un•en'rolled
,un•en'slaved
,un•en'tan•gled
un'en•tered
un'en•ter,pris•ing
,un•en•ter'tain•ing
,un•en'thralled
,un•en,thu•si'as•tic
,un•en'tit•led
un'en•vi•a•ble
un'en•vied
un'en•vi•ous
,un•e'quipped
,un•e'rased
,un•es'cap•a•ble
,un•es'cort•ed
,un•es'tab•lished
,un•es'thet•ic
un'es•ti,mat•ed
un'eth•i•cal
,un•e'vad•ed
,un•ex'act•ing
,un•ex'ag•ger,at•ed
,un•ex'am•ined
un'ex•ca,vat•ed
,un•ex'ceed•ed
,un•ex'celled
,un•ex'change•a•ble
,un•ex'cit•a•ble
,un•ex'cit•ed
,un•ex'cit•ing
,un•ex'cused
un'ex•e,cut•ed
un'ex•er,cised
,un•ex'haust•ed
,un•ex'pand•ed
,un•ex'pend•ed
,un•ex'pe•ri•enced
un'ex•pert
un'ex•pi,at•ed
,un•ex'pired
,un•ex'plain•a•ble
,un•ex'plained
,un•ex'plic•it
,un•ex'plod•ed
,un•ex'ploit•ed
,un•ex'plored
,un•ex'port•ed
,un•ex'posed
,un•ex'pressed
,un•ex'pres•sive
,un•ex'punged
un'ex•pur,gat•ed
,un•ex'tend•ed
,un•ex'tin•guished
un'fad•a•ble
un'fad•ed
un'fad•ing
un'fal•ter•ing
un'fash•ion•a•ble
un'fas•tened
un'fath•er•ly

un•fath•om•a•ble [ʌn'fæðəməbəl] *adj.* **1** so deep that the bottom cannot be reached. **2** too mysterious or profound to be understood.

un•fath•omed [ʌn'fæðəmd] *adj.* **1** not measured. **2** not understood.

un•fa•vour•a•ble or **un•fa•vor•a•ble** [ʌn'feivərəbəl] *adj.* **1** opposed or adverse: *Most of the reviews were unfavourable.* **2** not propitious or advantageous: *an unfavourable aspect.* **—un'fa•vour•a•ble•ness** or **un'fa•vor•a•ble•ness,** *n.* **—un'fa•vour•a•bly** or **un'fa•vor•a•bly,** *adv.*

un•feel•ing [ʌn'filɪŋ] *adj.* **1** hard-hearted; insensitive: *a cold, unfeeling person.* **2** not able to feel: *numb, unfeeling hands.* **—un'feel•ing•ly,** *adv.* **—un'feel•ing•ness,** *n.*

un•feigned [ʌn'feind] *adj.* sincere; real.

un•feign•ed•ly [ʌn'feinɪdli] *adv.* really; sincerely.

un•fet•ter [ʌn'fɛtər] *v.* remove fetters from; unchain.

un•fin•ished [ʌn'fɪnɪʃt] *adj.* **1** not finished; not complete. **2** without some special finish or final stage of processing; not polished; rough; not painted: *unfinished furniture.*

un•fit [ʌn'fɪt] *adj., v.* **-fit•ted, -fit•ting.** *—adj.* **1** not fit; not suitable. **2** not good enough; unqualified. **3** physically or mentally unsound. **4** not adapted.
—v. make unfit; spoil. **—un'fit•ness,** *n.* **—un'fit•ly,** *adv.*

un•fit•ted [ʌn'fɪtɪd] *adj., v.* *—adj.* **1** inappropriate; not suitable. **2** not tailored or properly fitted: *an unfitted coat.*
—v. pt. and pp. of UNFIT.

un•fix [ʌn'fɪks] *v.* loosen; detach; unfasten.

un•flag•ging [ʌn'flægɪŋ] *adj.* not drooping or failing: *unflagging efforts.* **—un'flag•ging•ly,** *adv.*

un•flap•pa•ble [ʌn'flæpəbəl] *adj. Informal.* having or showing self-control or coolness; imperturbable: *an unflappable teacher.* **—,un•flap•pa'bil•i•ty,** *n.*

un•fledged [ʌn'flɛdʒd] *adj.* **1** of a bird, too young to fly; not having full-grown feathers. **2** undeveloped; immature.

un•flinch•ing [ʌn'flɪntʃɪŋ] *adj.* not drawing back from difficulty, danger, or pain; firm; resolute. **—un'flinch•ing•ly,** *adv.*

un•fold [ʌn'fould] *v.* **1** open the folds of; spread out: *to unfold a serviette.* **2** cause to be no longer bent, coiled, or interlaced; unbend and straighten out: *to unfold your arms.* **3** reveal, show, or explain stage by stage: *to unfold the plot of a story.* **4** open out; develop, literally or figuratively: *Buds unfold into flowers. History is unfolding as it should.* ⟨OE *unfealdan*⟩

un•forced [ʌn'fɔrst] *adj.* **1** not forced; not compelled; willing. **2** natural; spontaneous.

un•fore•seen [,ʌnfɔr'sin] *adj.* not known or thought of beforehand; unexpected.

un•for•get•ta•ble [,ʌnfər'gɛtəbəl] *adj.* that can never be forgotten. **—,un•for'get•ta•bly,** *adv.*

un•formed [ʌn'fɔrmd] *adj.* **1** shapeless. **2** undeveloped. **3** *Biology.* unorganized.

un•for•tu•nate [ʌn'fɔrtʃənɪt] *adj., n.* *—adj.* **1** not lucky; having bad luck. **2** bringing bad luck; inauspicious. **3** not suitable; not fitting: *Dr. Ow is an unfortunate name for a dentist.* **4** unwished-for; undesirable; lamentable or deplorable: *The unfortunate consequence was that most of the original manuscript was lost.*
—n. an unfortunate person. **—un'for•tu•nate•ly,** *adv.* **—un'for•tu•nate•ness,** *n.*

un•found•ed [ʌn'faʊndɪd] *adj.* **1** without foundation; baseless: *an unfounded complaint.* **2** not yet founded or established. **—un'found•ed•ly,** *adv.* **—un'found•ed•ness,** *n.*

un•freeze [ʌn'friz] *v.* **-froze, -fro•zen. 1** cause to melt or thaw. **2** melt or thaw: *That roast you took out this morning hasn't unfrozen yet.* **3** remove financial controls or restrictions from.

un•fre•quent•ed [,ʌnfrɪ'kwɛntɪd] *adj.* not frequented; seldom visited; rarely used.

un•friend•ed [ʌn'frɛndɪd] *adj.* without friends.

un•friend•ly [ʌn'frɛndli] *adj.* **1** not friendly; hostile: *an unfriendly dog.* **2** not favourable: *unfriendly weather.* **—un'friend•li•ness,** *n.*
☛ *Syn.* **1.** See note at HOSTILE.

un•frock [ʌn'frɒk] *v.* deprive (a priest or minister) of his or her rank, position, and privileges; defrock.

un•fruit•ful [ʌn'frutfəl] *adj.* **1** not fruitful; barren; not productive. **2** futile. **—,un'fruit•ful•ly,** *adv.* **—un'fruit•ful•ness,** *n.*

un•furl [ʌn'fɜrl] *v.* spread out; shake out; unfold: *to unfurl a sail.*

un•gain•ly [ʌn'geinli] *adj.* awkward; clumsy. ⟨ME *ungaynly* < *un-* not + *gaynly* agile⟩ **—un'gain•li•ness,** *n.*
☛ *Syn.* See note at AWKWARD.

un•gen•er•ous [ʌn'dʒɛnərəs] *adj.* not generous; mean. **—un'gen•er•ous•ly,** *adv.*

un•glued [ʌn'glud] *adj.* **1** no longer stuck together by glue. **2** with no glue on it.
come unglued, *Informal.* lose one's self-possession; become disquieted.

un•god•li•ness [ʌn'gɒdlinɪs] *n.* **1** lack of godliness. **2** wickedness; sinfulness. **3** *Informal.* the fact or quality of being outrageous, dreadful, extreme, etc.: *Had it not been for the ungodliness of the hour, I would gladly have gone to meet him.*

un•god•ly [ʌn'gɒdli] *adj.* **1** irreligious. **2** wicked; sinful. **3** *Informal.* outrageous; dreadful; shocking: *to pay an ungodly price, to eat an ungodly amount.*

un•gov•ern•a•ble [ʌn'gʌvərnəbəl] *adj.* impossible to control; very hard to control or rule; unruly: *an ungovernable temper.* **—un'gov•ern•a•ble•ness,** *n.* **—un'gov•ern•a•bly,** *adv.*
☛ *Syn.* See note at UNRULY.

un•grace•ful [ʌn'greisfəl] *adj.* not graceful; not elegant or beautiful in motion; clumsy; awkward. **—un'grace•ful•ly,** *adv.* **—un'grace•ful•ness,** *n.*

un•gra•cious [ʌn'greiʃəs] *adj.* **1** not polite; rude. **2** unpleasant; disagreeable. **—un'gra•cious•ly,** *adv.* **—un'gra•cious•ness,** *n.*

un•grate•ful [ʌn'greitfəl] *adj.* **1** characterized by or displaying lack of gratitude: *that ungrateful wretch, an ungrateful silence.* **2** thankless; not appreciated or rewarded: *an ungrateful*

In each of the words below **un-** *means* not; *the pronunciation of the main part of each word is not changed.*

un'fath•om•a•ble	**un'fer•ti,lized**	**un'force•a•ble**	**un'fought**	**un'gen•tle**
un'fath•omed	**un'fet•tered**	**un'ford•a•ble**	**un'found**	**un'gen•tle•man•ly**
,un•fa'tigued	**un'filed**	**,un•fore'see•a•ble**	**un'framed**	**un'gen•u•ine**
un'fa•voured	**un'fil•i•al**	**,un•fore'seen**	**un'free**	**un'gift•ed**
un'fazed	**un'filled**	**un'for•est•ed**	**un'fro•zen**	**un'gird**
un'feared	**un'fil•tered**	**,un•fore'told**	**,un•ful'filled**	**un'glam•or•ous**
un'fea•si•ble	**un'fired**	**un'for•feit•ed**	**un'fund•ed**	**un'glazed**
un'feath•ered	**un'fit•ting**	**,un•for'giv•a•ble**	**un'fun•ny**	**un'glo•ri,fied**
un'fea•tured	**un'flat•ter•ing**	**,un•for'giv•en**	**un'fur•nished**	**un'glossed**
un'fed	**un'fla•voured**	**,un•for'giv•ing**	**un'fur•rowed**	**un'gloved**
un'fed•er,at•ed	**un'flawed**	**,un•for'got•ten**	**un'gained**	**un'gov•erned**
un'felt	**un'flexed**	**un'for•mu,lat•ed**	**un'gal•lant**	**un'gowned**
un'fem•i•nine	**un'fo•cussed**	**,un•for'sak•en**	**un'gar•nished**	**un'grad•ed**
un'fenced	**,un•for'bear•ing**	**,un•forth'com•ing**	**un'gath•ered**	**un'grad•u,at•ed**
,un•fer'ment•ed	**,un•for'bid•den**	**un'for•ti,fied**	**,un•gen'teel**	**,un•gram'mat•i•cal**

task. **3** unpleasant; disagreeable. **—un'grate•ful•ly,** *adv.* **—un'grate•ful•ness,** *n.*

un•grudg•ing [ʌn'grʌdʒɪŋ] *adj.* willing; hearty; liberal. **—un'grudg•ing•ly,** *adv.*

un•gual ['ʌŋgwəl] *adj.* of, having to do with, bearing, or shaped like a nail, claw, or hoof. ⟨< L *unguis* nail, claw, hoof⟩

un•guard•ed [ʌn'gɑrdɪd] *adj.* **1** not protected. **2** careless: *In an unguarded moment, she gave away the secret.* **3** open and free in manner; not hedging, defensive, or sly. **—un'guard•ed•ly,** *adv.* **—un'guard•ed•ness,** *n.*

un•guent ['ʌŋgwənt] *n.* an ointment for sores, burns, etc.; salve. ⟨< L *unguentum* < *unguere* anoint⟩ **—'un•guen,ta•ry,** *adj.*

un•guis ['ʌŋgwɪs] *n., pl.* **-gues** [-gwiz]. **1** *Botany.* the narrow, clawlike part at the base of some petals. **2** *Zoology.* a nail or claw. ⟨< L, a nail⟩

un•gu•la ['ʌŋgjələ] *n., pl.* **-lae** [-,li] *or* [-,laɪ] **1** a hoof. **2** a nail; claw. **3** *Botany.* the claw-shaped base of a petal. **4** *Geometry.* a cylinder, cone, etc., the top part of which has been cut off by a plane oblique to the base. ⟨< L *ungula,* dim. of *unguis* nail, claw, hoof⟩ **—'un•gu•lar,** *adj.*

un•gu•late ['ʌŋgjəlɪt] *or* ['ʌŋgjə,leit] *n., adj.* *—n.* **1** any of a large group of four-footed, plant-eating mammals having hoofed feet. Present-day ungulates comprise four orders: Perissodactyla (horses, rhinoceroses, etc.), Artiodactyla (deer, bovines, camels, etc.), Proboscidae (elephants), and Hyracoidea (hyraxes). This grouping is no longer used in formal classification.
—adj. **1** having hoofs. **2** resembling a hoof. **3** of or having to do with the ungulates. ⟨< L *ungulatus* < *ungula.* See UNGULA.⟩

un•hal•lowed [ʌn'hæloud] *adj.* **1** not made holy; not sacred. **2** wicked.

un•hand [ʌn'hænd] *v. Poetic.* let go of; take the hands from (*often used facetiously*).

un•hand•some [ʌn'hænsəm] *adj.* **1** not good-looking; plain; ugly. **2** ungracious; discourteous; unseemly. **3** not generous; mean. **—un'hand•some•ly,** *adv.*

un•hand•y [ʌn'hændi] *adj.* **1** not easy to handle or manage: *an unhandy tool.* **2** not skilful in using the hands: *an unhandy man.* **—un'hand•i•ly,** *adv.* **—un'hand•i•ness,** *n.*

un•hap•py [ʌn'hæpi] *adj.* **-pi•er, -pi•est. 1** sad; sorrowful. **2** dissatisfied or disappointed; not pleased: *She is unhappy with the recent changes at work.* **3** unlucky. **4** not suitable. **—un'hap•pi•ly,** *adv.* **—un'hap•pi•ness,** *n.*

un•har•ness [ʌn'hɑrnɪs] *v.* **1** remove harness or gear (from): *unharness the horse.* **2** *Archaic.* divest of armour.

un•health•ful [ʌn'hɛlθfəl] *adj.* bad for the health. **—un'health•ful•ly,** *adv.* **—un'health•ful•ness,** *n.*

un•health•y [ʌn'hɛlθi] *adj.* **1** not possessing good health; not well: *an unhealthy child.* **2** characteristic of or resulting from poor health: *an unhealthy paleness.* **3** hurtful to health; unwholesome: *an unhealthy climate.* **4** morally unsound or harmful: *He has an unhealthy preoccupation with gambling.* **5** *Informal.* filled with danger or risk. **—un'health•i•ly,** *adv.* **—un'health•i•ness,** *n.*

un•heard [ʌn'hɜrd] *adj.* **1** not perceived by the ear: *unheard melodies.* **2** not given a hearing: *the unheard minority.* **3** *Archaic.* unheard-of.

un•heard–of [ʌn'hɜrd ,ʌv] *adj.* **1** never heard of; unknown: *The electric light was unheard-of 200 years ago.* **2** unprecedented; outrageous; preposterous: *A price of $6 a dozen for eggs is unheard-of.*

un•hes•i•tat•ing [ʌn'hɛzə,teitɪŋ] *adj.* prompt; ready; immediate: *unhesitating acceptance.* **—un'hes•i,tat•ing•ly,** *adv.*

un•hinge [ʌn'hɪndʒ] *v.* **-hinged, -hing•ing. 1** take (a door, etc.) off its hinges. **2** remove the hinges from. **3** separate from something; detach. **4** unsettle; disorganize; upset: *Trouble has unhinged this poor man's mind.*

un•his•tor•ic [,ʌnhɪ'stɔrɪk] *adj.* **1 a** not famous in history; unimportant: *an unhistoric event.* **b** not having a celebrated heritage: *an unhistoric little town.* **2** unhistorical. **3** *Linguistics.* arising accidentally or arbitrarily rather than by regular development from earlier forms, as the *s* in *island* or the *b* in *thumb.*

un•his•tor•i•cal [,ʌnhɪ'stɔrəkəl] *adj.* **1** not in accordance with the facts of history. **2** not recorded in history; mythological or ahistorical; not amenable to historical analysis. **3** ignorant of the facts of history. **—,un•his'tor•i•cal•ly,** *adv.* **—,un•his'tor•i•cal•ness,** *n.*

un•hitch [ʌn'hɪtʃ] *v.* free from being hitched; unfasten.

un•ho•ly [ʌn'houli] *adj.* **-li•er, -li•est. 1** not hallowed or consecrated. **2** not holy; wicked; sinful. **3** *Informal.* outrageous or dreadful: *They were raising an unholy row.* **—un'ho•li•ness,** *n.*

un•hook [ʌn'hʊk] *v.* **1** remove from a hook or come off a hook. **2** undo or open by unfastening or disengaging a hook or hooks. **3** of something fastened by a hook or hooks, come undone: *My dress has unhooked; will you fasten it for me?*

un•hoped–for [ʌn'houpt ,fɔr] *adj.* unexpected; not hoped for; unanticipated: *an unhoped-for benefit.*

un•horse [ʌn'hɔrs] *v.* **-horsed, -hors•ing. 1** pull or knock from a horse's back; cause to fall from a horse: *The knight was unhorsed by the sharp thrust of his opponent's lance.* **2** dislodge; overthrow: *The prime minister was unhorsed by the rebels in her own party.*

un•hu•man [ʌn'hjumən] *adj.* **1** not human; devoid of human qualities. **2** inhuman. **3** superhuman. **—un'hu•man•ly,** *adv.*

un•hurt [ʌn'hɜrt] *adj.* not hurt; not harmed.

uni– *combining form.* one: *unilateral.* ⟨< L *unus* one⟩

U•ni•at ['juni,æt] *n., adj.* *—n.* a member of any Eastern Christian church that is in communion with the Roman Catholic Church and acknowledges the supremacy of the Pope but keeps its own liturgy and organization.
—adj. of or having to do with such a church or its members. Also, **Uniate** ['juni,ɪt] *or* ['juni,eit]. ⟨< Russian *uniyat* < *uniya* union⟩

u•ni•ax•i•al [,juni'æksiəl] *adj.* having only one axis. **—,u•ni'ax•i•al•ly,** *adv.*

u•ni•cam•er•al [,junə'kæmərəl] *adj.* having only one house in a lawmaking body. All Canadian provinces except Québec have unicameral legislatures. ⟨< *uni-* + L *camera* chamber⟩

UNICEF ['junə,sɛf] *n.* United Nations Children's Fund (originally, United Nations International Children's Emergency Fund).

u•ni•cel•lu•lar [,junə'sɛljələr] *adj.* of an organism, consisting of a single cell. The amoeba is a unicellular animal.

u•ni•corn ['junə,kɔrn] *n.* **1** a legendary animal resembling a horse, and having a single long horn growing from the middle of its forehead, often a symbol of virtue or chastity. **2** a figure, picture, or representation of this animal, often used as a heraldic bearing. **3** in the Bible, a mistranslation of a Hebrew word referring to a two-horned animal, probably the aurochs. ⟨< L *unicornis* < *unus* one + *cornu* horn⟩

u•ni•cy•cle ['junə,səikəl] *n.* a vehicle with a single wheel and a saddle, propelled by pedals: *Unicycles are ridden mostly by acrobats and entertainers.* **—'u•ni,cy•clist,** *n.*

In each of the words below **un-** *means* not; *the pronunciation of the main part of each word is not changed.*

un'grat•i,fied
un'grat•i,fy•ing
un'greased
un'ground•ed
,un•guar•an'teed
un'guess•a•ble
un'guid•ed
un'hack•neyed
un'hailed
un'ham•pered
un'hand•i,capped
un'han•dled
un'hand•some
un'hanged
un'har•assed
un'hard•ened
un'harmed
un'harm•ful
,un•har'mo•ni•ous
un'har•nessed
un'har•rowed
un'har•vest•ed
un'hatched
un'healed
un'heat•ed
un'heed•ed
un'heed•ful
un'heed•ing
un'helped
un'help•ful
un'her•ald•ed
,un•he'ro•ic
un'hes•i•tant
un'hes•i,tat•ing
un'hewn
un'hin•dered
un'hired
un'hon•oured
un'housed
un'hung
un'hur•ried
un'hur•ry•ing
un'hurt•ful
un'husk
,un•hy'gien•ic
un'hy•phen,at•ed
,un•i'de•al

un•i•den•ti•fied flying object [,ʌnaɪ'dɛntə,faɪd] an object in the sky that cannot be identified as a known aircraft from earth or explained as any natural phenomenon. *Abbrev.*: UFO

u•ni•di•men•sion•al [,junədə'mɛnʃənəl] *or* [,junədaɪ'mɛnʃənəl] *adj.* having only one dimension.

u•ni•di•rec•tion•al [,junədə'rɛkʃənəl] *or* [,junədaɪ'rɛkʃənəl] *adj.* functioning or moving in only one direction.

u•ni•fi•ca•tion [,junəfə'keiʃən] *n.* **1** a formation into one unit; union: *the unification of many states into one nation.* **2** a making or being made more alike: *The traffic laws of the different provinces need unification.* **3** the condition or state of being unified. **4** *Cdn.* the policy or action of completely merging the traditional navy, army, and air force into one combined force having a unified command and common uniform and rank structure.

unified field theory *Physics.* any theory purporting to explain or describe, in a single set of equations or propositions, all the different field phenomena, including electromagnetic, gravitational, and nuclear.

u•ni•fo•li•ate [,junə'fouliɪt] *or* [,junə'fouli,eit] *adj. Botany.* **1** bearing only one leaf. **2** unifoliolate.

u•ni•fo•li•o•late [,junə'fouliəlɪt] *or* [,junə'fouliə,leit] *adj. Botany.* **1** having only one leaflet, although compound in structure, as the leaf of an orange tree. **2** bearing such leaves.

u•ni•form ['junə,fɔrm] *adj., n., v. —adj.* **1** always the same; never changing; regular: *The earth turns around at a uniform rate.* **2** all alike; not varying from one to the other in a group: *All the bricks are of a uniform size.* **3** the same throughout a single whole: *lawns of a uniform green.*
—n. the distinctive clothes worn by the members of a group when on duty, by which they may be recognized as belonging to that group: *Soldiers, police officers, and nurses wear uniforms.*
—v. clothe or furnish with a uniform. ⟨< L *uniformis* < *unus* one + *forma* form⟩ **—'u•ni,form•ly,** *adv.* **—'u•ni,form•ness,** *n.*
☛ *Syn.* See note at EVEN.

u•ni•form•i•tar•i•an [,junə,fɔrmɪ'tɛriən] *adj., n. —adj.* **1** relating to, or supporting, the doctrine that all geological formations are explainable in terms of existing physical and chemical processes that have operated continuously and uniformly throughout time. **2** in favour of uniformity in some area of behaviour, dogma, etc.
—n. someone who is uniformitarian.
—,u•ni,form•i'tar•i•an,ism, *n.*

u•ni•form•i•ty [,junə'fɔrməti] *n., pl.* **-ties.** a uniform condition or character; sameness throughout.

u•ni•fy ['junə,faɪ] *v.* **-fied, -fy•ing.** make or form into one; unite. ⟨< LL *unificare* < L *unus* one + *facere* make⟩ **—'u•ni,fi•er,** *n.* **—'u•ni,fi•a•ble,** *adj.*

u•nij•u•gate [ju'nɪdʒəgɪt] *or* [ju'nɪdʒə,geit], [junə'dʒugɪt] *or* [junə'dʒugeit] *adj. Botany.* having a single pair of leaflets.

u•ni•lat•er•al [,junə'lætərəl] *adj.* **1** of, on, or affecting one side only. **2** having all the parts arranged on one side of an axis; turned to one side; one-sided. **3** *Law.* of a contract, etc., done by, affecting, or binding one party or person only: *unilateral disarmament.* **4** concerned with or considering only one side of a matter. **5** unilineal. **—,u•ni'lat•er•al•ly,** *adv.*

u•ni•lat•er•al•ism [,junə'lætərə,lɪzəm] *n.* belief in or advocacy of a unilateral policy, especially in disarmament.

u•ni•lat•er•al•ist [,junə'lætərəlɪst] *adj., n. —adj.* of or having to do with unilateralism or unilateralists.
—n. an advocate or follower of unilateralism.

u•ni•lin•e•al [,junə'lɪniəl] *adj.* showing or tracing descent through only one line of the forebears, either the father's side or the mother's.

u•ni•lin•e•ar [,junə'lɪniər] *adj.* proceeding or developing along a single direct line.

u•ni•lin•gual [,junə'lɪŋgwəl] *adj.* **1** having knowledge or use of only one language. **2** of or having one universal language.

u•ni•lin•gual•ism [,junə'lɪŋgwə,lɪzəm] *n.* **1** the state, condition, or policy of being unilingual. **2** advocacy of or belief in one universal language.

un•im•peach•a•ble [,ʌnɪm'pitʃəbəl] *adj.* free from fault; blameless; above suspicion; impeccable. **—,un•im'peach•a•bly,** *adv.*

un•im•pressed [,ʌnɪm'prɛst] *adj.* **1** not impressed one way or the other; left with no particular impression. **2** negatively or unfavourably impressed.

un•im•proved [,ʌnɪm'pruvd] *adj.* **1** not bettered or developed to the fullest capacity: *unimproved land.* **2** not improved in health, etc. **3** neglected; not enhanced or increased.

un•in•spired [,ʌnɪn'spaɪrd] *adj.* **1** not inspired. **2** dull; tiresome.

un•in•tel•li•gi•ble [,ʌnɪn'tɛlədʒəbəl] *adj.* that cannot be understood. **—,un•in'tel•li•gi•bly,** *adv.*

un•in•ter•est•ed [ʌn'ɪntrɪstɪd] *or* [ʌn'ɪntə,rɛstɪd] *adj.* not interested; showing no interest. **—un'in•ter•est•ed•ly,** *adv.*
☛ *Usage.* See note at DISINTERESTED.

un•in•ter•rupt•ed [,ʌnɪntə'rʌptɪd] *adj.* without interruption; continuous. **—,un•in•ter'rupt•ed•ly,** *adv.*

un•ion ['junjən] *n.* **1** the act of uniting or the state of being united: *The United States was formed by the union of thirteen former British colonies.* **2** something formed by combining two or more members, sets, or parts: *The ten provinces of Canada form a union.* **3** a group of workers joined together to protect and promote their interests; LABOUR UNION; TRADE UNION. **4** marriage. **5** any of various devices for connecting parts of machinery or apparatus, especially a piece to join pipes or tubes together. **6** a device or emblem symbolizing political union on a flag or ensign, as the Union Jack, wherein the crosses of the patron saints of England, Scotland, and Ireland are combined in one device. **7 the Union, a** *Cdn.* formerly, the uniting of Upper and Lower Canada, effected by the Union Act of 1840. **b** *Cdn.* Confederation. **c** the United States or 'North', in the American Civil War, as opposed to the Confederacy of Southern States. ⟨ME < OF < LL *unio, -onis* < *unus* one⟩
☛ *Syn.* **1. Union,** UNITY = a forming or being one. **Union** emphasizes the joining together of two or more things, people, or groups to form a whole, or the state of being joined together as a unit: *A combat team is formed by the union of infantry and other forces.* **Unity** emphasizes a quality and applies to the oneness of the whole that is formed: *The strength of any group is in its unity.*

un•ion•ism ['junjə,nɪzəm] *n.* **1** the principle of union. **2** a

In each of the words below **un-** *means* not; *the pronunciation of the main part of each word is not changed.*

,un•i'den•ti,fi•a•ble
,un•i'den•ti,fied
,un•id•i•o'mat•ic
,un•il'lu•mi,nat•ed
,un•il'lu•min,at•ing
un'il•lus,trat•ed
,un•il'lus•tra•tive
,un•i'mag•i•na•ble
,un•i'mag•i•na•tive
,un•i'mag•ined
,un•im'bued
un'im•i,tat•ed
,un•im'paired
,un•im'pas•sioned
,un•im'ped•ed
un'im•ple,ment•ed
,un•im'por•tance
,un•im'por•tant
,un•im'pos•ing
,un•im'preg•nat•ed
,un•im'pressed
,un•im'pres•si•ble
,un•im'pres•sion•a•ble
,un•im'pres•sive
,un•im'proved
,un•in'cor•po,rat•ed
un'in•cu,bat•ed
,un•in'dem•ni,fied
un'in•dexed
,un•in'dulged
,un•in'dus•tri•al,ized
,un•in'dus•tri•ous
,un•in'fect•ed
,un•in'fest•ed
,un•in'flam•ma•ble
,un•in'flect•ed
un'in•flu•enced
,un•in•flu'en•tial
,un•in'form•a•tive
,un•in'formed
,un•in'hab•it•a•ble
,un•in'hab•it•ed
,un•in'hib•it•ed
,un•i'ni•ti,at•ed
un'in•jured
,un•in'quir•ing
,un•in'quis•i•tive
,un•in'spect•ed
,un•in'spir•ing
,un•in'struct•ed
,un•in'struc•tive
un'in•su,lat•ed
,un•in'sur•a•ble
,un•in'sured
un'in•te,grat•ed
,un•in•tel'lec•tu•al
,un•in'tel•li•gent
,un•in'tend•ed
,un•in'ten•tion•al
un'in•ter•est•ing
,un•in•ter'mit•tent
,un•in•ter'mit•ting
,un•in'ter•pol,at•ed
,un•in'ter•pret•ed
,un•in'tim•i,dat•ed
,un•in'tox•i,cat•ed
,un•in'ven•tive
,un•in'vest•ed
,un•in'ves•ti,gat•ed
,un•in'vit•ed
,un•in'vit•ing
,un•in'voked
,un•in'volved

loyalty to a union. **3** the system, principles, or methods of labour unions.

un•ion•ist ['junjənɪst] *n.* **1** a person who promotes or advocates union or unionism. **2** a member of a labour union. **3 Unionist,** formerly: **a** *Cdn.* a person who was in favour of union among the provinces of British North America, especially of Upper and Lower Canada. **b** a supporter of the federal government of the United States during the Civil War. **c** a person who opposed the political separation of Ireland from Great Britain. **4 Unionist**, since 1920, a person who favours keeping Northern Ireland as part of the United Kingdom.

un•ion•i•za•tion [ˌjunjənə'zeiʃən] *or* [ˌjunjənaɪ'zeiʃən] *n.* the act of unionizing or the state of being unionized.

un•ion•ize ['junjəˌnaɪz] *v.* **-ized, -iz•ing. 1** form into a labour union: *The teaching assistants have decided to unionize themselves.* **2** organize under a labour union: *to unionize an industry. Many professions are not unionized.* **3** join in a labour union: *None of them wants to unionize.* **4** make to conform or subject to the rules and standards of a labour union.

un•i•on•ized [ʌn'aɪənˌaɪzd] *adj.* not ionized.

Union Jack the red, white, and blue flag of the United Kingdom, formed by combining the crosses of St. George, St. Andrew, and St. Patrick, for England, Scotland, and Ireland respectively.

Union Na•tion•ale [ˌnæʃə'næl]; *French,* [ynjɔ̃nasjɔ'nal] a political party in Québec, formed in the early 1930s.

union shop 1 a business establishment that by agreement hires only employees who are, or will become, members of a labour union. **2** the terms and conditions of employment in such an establishment, as agreed upon by the employer and the appropriate labour union or unions.

union station a station used jointly by two or more railways.

union suit long johns and long-sleeved undershirt combined in a one-piece garment for men.

un•i•pa•ren•tal di•so•my [ˌjunəpə'rɛntəl 'dəisəmi] *Genetics.* an abnormal situation in which both members of a pair of homologous chromosomes are inherited from one parent.

u•ni•par•ous [ju'nɪpərəs] *adj.* **1** *Botany.* producing only one axis at each branching. **2** *Zoology.* producing only one ovum or offspring at a time.

u•ni•po•lar [ˌjunə'poulər] *adj.* **1** *Physics.* having or relating to a single electric or magnetic pole. **2** *Biology.* of a nerve cell, having only one pole or process. **3** *Psychiatry.* referring to a type of clinical depression which does not alternate with a manic phase. Compare BIPOLAR AFFECTIVE DISORDER.

u•nique [ju'nik] *adj.* **1** having no like or equal. **2** being the only one; sole. **3** *Informal.* rare; unusual; interestingly original. ⟨< F < L *unicus*⟩ **—u'nique•ly,** *adv.* **—u'nique•ness,** *n.*

☛ *Usage.* In formal English **unique** means 'being one of a kind', and so it cannot be compared or qualified; something is either unique or not. In informal English **unique** has the sense 'unusual and interesting', and so is sometimes used with **more** or **most** or with a qualifier like **quite, rather,** or **really**: *Her clothes are rather unique.* This usage should be avoided in careful speech and writing.

u•ni•sex ['junəˌsɛks] *adj.* of, having to do with, or designating clothing, hairstyles, etc. that are worn by members of both sexes.

u•ni•sex•u•al [ˌjunə'sɛkʃuəl] *adj.* **1** pertaining to or describing one sex only. **2** *Biology.* having only male or female sex organs in one body, as most animals and flowers. **3** unisex. **—ˌu•niˌsex•u'al•i•ty,** *n.* **—ˌu•ni'sex•u•al•ly,** *adv.*

u•ni•son ['junəsən] *or* ['junəzən] *n. Music.* **a** identity of pitch of two or more tones. **b** a performing together by voices, instruments, etc. of the same melody, etc., at the same pitch or an octave apart. **c** the interval between two tones of the same or different quality but identical pitch; PRIME[1].
in unison, together as one, at the same time; united(ly): *They moved and spoke in unison.* ⟨< Med.L *unisonus* sounding the same < LL *unisonus* in immediate sequence in the scale < L *unus* one + *sonus* sound⟩ **—u'nis•on•ant** [ju'nɪsənənt], *adj.* **—u'nis•o•nous** [ju'nɪsənəs], *adj.*

u•nit ['junɪt] *n.* **1** a single thing or person. **2** any group of things or persons considered as one. **3** one of the individual things or discrete parts of which a whole is composed: *the storage unit of a computer. The body consists of units called cells.* **4** a standard quantity or amount, used as a basis for measuring: *A metre is a unit of length; a minute is a unit of time.* **5** the amount of a drug or vaccine needed to produce a certain result in an individual. **6** the smallest whole number; 1. **7** a regiment or other organized body of troops making up a subdivision of a larger group. **8** in schools, a section of a course, usually on one theme or topic. ⟨probably < *unity*⟩

U•ni•tar•i•an [ˌjunə'tɛriən] *n., adj. —n.* a member of a religious denomination rejecting the doctrine of the Trinity, based on the belief that God exists as one, not as the Father, the Son, and the Holy Spirit. Unitarians accept the moral teachings of Jesus and believe in reason, social justice, and tolerance of different religious views.
—adj. of or having to do with Unitarians.

U•ni•tar•i•an•ism [ˌjunə'tɛriəˌnɪzəm] *n.* the doctrines or beliefs of Unitarians.

u•ni•tar•y ['junəˌtɛri] *adj.* **1** of, being, or having to do with a unit or units. **2** having to do with unity. **3** like that of a unit; used as a unit.

u•nite [ju'nəit] *v.* **u•nit•ed, u•nit•ing. 1** join together; make one; combine. **2** adhere or cause to adhere: *to unite bricks with mortar in a wall.* **3** bring together; amalgamate or consolidate into one body; join in action, interest, opinion, feeling, etc.: *Several firms were united to form one company.* **4** join by mutual pledging, covenant, or other formal bond; cause to become a union: *to unite a man and woman in marriage.* **5** have or exhibit in union or combination: *a child uniting his father's temper and his mother's red hair.* **6** become one; join in action, etc. ⟨< L *unitus*, pp. of *unire* < *unus* one⟩ **—u'nit•er,** *n.* **—'u•ni•tive** ['junətɪv], *adj.*

☛ *Syn.* See note at JOIN.

u•nit•ed [ju'nəitɪd] *adj., v. —adj.* **1** fused; combined; joined together to make one. **2** joined together in such a way as to remain distinct. **3 a** having or showing cohesion, harmony, or accord: *a united effort.* **b** acting together or resulting from joint action. **—u'nit•ed•ly,** *adv.*
—v. pt. and pp. of UNITE.

United Arab Em•ir•ates a federation of seven emirates, formerly called the Trucial States, in E Arabia, on the Persian Gulf, and the Gulf of Oman.

United Church of Canada a Christian church formed in 1924-1925 from a union of the Canadian Methodist and Congregationalist churches and two-thirds of the congregations of the Canadian Presbyterian Church. Its doctrines combine selected doctrines of the founding churches.

United Empire Loyalist *Cdn.* any of the Loyalists in the American Revolution who emigrated to what are now Ontario and the Maritimes, or their descendants; especially, any of the people (or their descendants) who are officially recorded as having emigrated before the peace of 1783. Compare LOYALIST.

United Kingdom GREAT BRITAIN and Northern Ireland.

United Nations 1 a worldwide organization devoted to establishing world peace and promoting economic and social welfare. The United Nations charter was put into effect on October 24, 1945. **2** the nations that belong to this organization: *Canada is one of the United Nations.* **3** the ALLIES (def. 2). *Abbrev.*: UN or U.N.

United States of America a large country in North America between Mexico and Canada, including also Alaska and Hawaii.

unit fraction a common fraction in which the numerator is 1. *Examples*: $\frac{1}{8}$, $\frac{1}{100}$.

unit pricing a system of pricing commodities based on a standard unit of measure, such as a millilitre or ounce, rather than on the container such as a box or can.

u•ni•ty ['junəti] *n., pl.* **-ties. 1** oneness; being united: *A circle has unity; a row of dots doesn't. A nation has more unity than a group of tribes.* **2** a union of parts forming a complex whole. **3** a unit; a single, simple, distinct thing. **4 a** harmony: *Brothers and sisters should live together in unity.* **b** constancy or consistency; singleness: *unity of purpose.* **5** the number one (1). **6** an arrangement and choice of material to give a single effect, main idea, etc.: *A pleasing picture has unity; so has a well-written*

In each of the words below **un-** *means* not; *the pronunciation of the main part of each word is not changed.*

un'i•roned **un'is•sued**

composition. **7 the unities,** *pl.* the rules of dramatic structure derived from Aristotle, according to which a play should have one main action occurring on one day in one place. ⟨ME < L *unitas* < *unus* one⟩
☛ *Syn.* **1, 4, 6.** See note at UNION.

Univ. **1** University. **2** Universalist.

u•ni•va•lent [ˌjunə'veilənt] *or* [ju'nɪvələnt] *adj.* **1** *Chemistry.* having a valence of one. **2** *Biology.* of a chromosome, unpaired. ⟨< *uni-* + L *valens, -entis,* ppr. of *valere* be worth⟩
–ˌu•ni'va•lence, *n.*

u•ni•valve ['junəˌvælv] *n., adj. Biology. –n.* **1** a mollusc having a shell consisting of a single piece, called a valve. Gastropods are univalves. **2** the shell of such a mollusc.
–adj. of, having to do with, or designating such molluscs or their shells.

u•ni•ver•sal [ˌjunə'vɜrsəl] *adj., n. –adj.* **1** of, belonging to, concerning, or used or done by all: *Food, fire, and shelter are universal needs.* **2** of or having to do with the universe; existing everywhere: *The law of gravity is universal.* **3** covering a whole class of persons, things, cases, etc.; general. **4** adaptable to different sizes, angles, kinds of work, etc. **5** constituting, existing as, or regarded as a complete whole; complete; entire; whole: *the universal cosmos.* **6** accomplished in or comprising all, or very many, subjects; wide-ranging: *universal knowledge.* **7** allowing or providing for movement in any direction: *a universal joint.*
–n. **1** a proposition that asserts or denies something of every member of a class. *Example*: All people are mortal. **2** something of, belonging to, concerning, or done by all, especially a person or thing that is universally powerful, current, etc. **3** *Philosophy.* **a** an entity that remains unchanged in character through a series of changes or relationships. **b** a general concept or abstraction. ⟨ME < L *universalis* < *universus.* See UNIVERSE.⟩
–ˌu•ni'ver•sal•ly, *adv.*

u•ni•ver•sal•ism [ˌjunə'vɜrsəˌlɪzəm] *n.* **1** universality of interest, application, etc.; comprehensiveness. **2 Universalism,** the doctrines or beliefs of Universalists.

u•ni•ver•sal•ist [ˌjunə'vɜrsəlɪst] *n., adj. –n.* **1** a person whose interests, activities, knowledge, skills, etc. cover a very wide range. **2 Universalist,** a member of a Christian church holding the belief that all people will finally be saved.
–adj. of or having to do with Universalists.

u•ni•ver•sal•i•ty [ˌjunəvər'sæləti] *n., pl.* **-ties. 1** the fact or condition of being universal. **2** something universal.

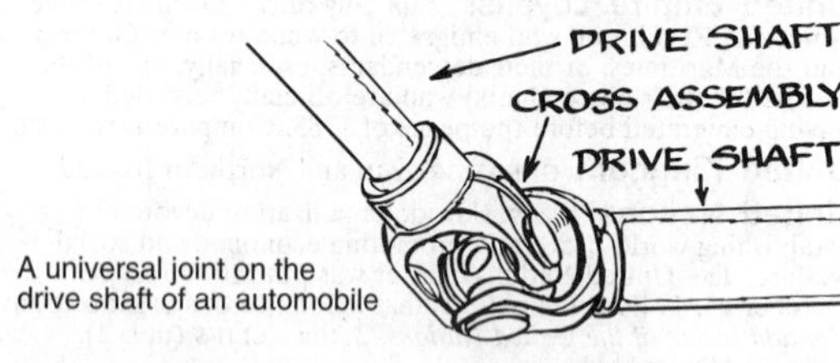

A universal joint on the drive shaft of an automobile

universal joint **1** a joint that moves in any direction. **2** a coupling for transmitting power from one shaft to another when they are not in line.

Universal Product Code *Computer technology.* a barcode printed on consumer products, indicating product classification, price, etc., that can be read by an electronic scanner.

universal time GREENWICH MEAN TIME.

u•ni•verse ['junəˌvɜrs] *n.* **1** all things; everything that exists, including all space and matter. **2** the earth as inhabited by, and often including, all people. **3** a field of thought, area of study, etc. considered as being complete and independent: *the universe of chemistry.* **4** UNIVERSE OF DISCOURSE. **5** *Sociology.* the total population from which a sample population is drawn. ⟨< L *universum,* originally adj., whole, turned into one, neut. of *universus* < *unus* one + *vertere* turn⟩

universe of discourse *Logic and mathematics.* the set of things under discussion or consideration, including the assumptions and presuppositions underlying them and the relations among them.

u•ni•ver•si•ty [ˌjunə'vɜrsəti] *n., pl.* **-ties. 1** an educational institution attended after secondary school for studies leading to a degree. Universities offer advanced courses in general subjects such as literature, history, and science, and also often have schools of law, medicine, business, etc. **2** a building or buildings used by a university. **3** the collective members of a university, including the faculty, the administration, and the students. ⟨ME < OF < Med.L *universitas* corporation < L *universitas* aggregate, whole < *universus.* See UNIVERSE.⟩

u•ni•vo•cal [ju'nɪvəkəl] *or* [ˌjuni'voukəl] *adj.* having only one meaning or nature; unambiguous.

un•joint [ʌn'dʒɔɪnt] *v.* **1** take apart the joints of. **2** dislocate (a joint).

un•just [ʌn'dʒʌst] *adj.* not just; not fair: *It is unjust to punish lawbreakers who are insane.* **–un'just•ly,** *adv.* **–un'just•ness,** *n.*

un•kempt [ʌn'kɛmpt] *adj.* **1** not combed. **2** neglected in appearance; untidy. ⟨< *un-¹* + OE *cembed* combed, pp. of *cemban* < *camb* comb⟩

un•kind [ʌn'kaɪnd] *adj.* harsh; cruel; mean. **–un'kind•ness,** *n.*

un•kind•ly [ʌn'kaɪndli] *adj., adv. –adj.* harsh; unfavourable.
–adv. in an unkind way; harshly. **–un'kind•li•ness,** *n.*

un•knit [ʌn'nɪt] *v.* **-knit•ted** or **-knit, -knit•ting. 1** untie or unfasten (a knot, etc.). **2** ravel out (something knitted). **3** smooth out (something wrinkled).

un•known [ʌn'noun] *adj., n. –adj.* not familiar or known; unidentified, unexplored, etc.: *an unknown country, an unknown number.*
–n. **1** a person who or thing that is unknown: *The diver descended into the unknown. The main actor in this movie is an unknown.* **2** *Mathematics.* a symbol, as in an equation, for a quantity whose value is to be found.

Unknown Soldier an unidentified soldier killed in battle, who is buried in a national monument and honoured as the representative of all unidentified war dead of his or her country.

un•la•boured or **un•la•bored** [ʌn'leibərd] *adj.* **1** effortless; spontaneous; not stiff or stilted: *unlaboured verses.* **2** not produced or cultivated by labour or effort: *unlaboured fields.*

un•lace [ʌn'leis] *v.* **-laced, -lac•ing.** undo the laces of.

un•lade [ʌn'leid] *v.* **-lad•ed, -lad•en** or **-lad•ed, -lad•ing.** unload.

un•lash [ʌn'læʃ] *v.* untie or detach (something fastened by a cord or rope).

un•latch [ʌn'lætʃ] *v.* unfasten or open by lifting a latch.

un•law•ful [ʌn'lɒfəl] *adj.* contrary to law; against a law; forbidden; illegal. **–un'law•ful•ly,** *adv.* **–un'law•ful•ness,** *n.*

un•lead•ed [ʌn'lɛdɪd] *adj., n. –adj.* **1** not containing compounds of lead; lead-free. **2** not having leads separating the lines of type.
–n. lead-free gasoline or other lead-free products.

un•learn [ʌn'lɜrn] *v.* get rid of (learned ideas, habits, or tendencies); forget.

un•learn•ed *adj.* [ʌn'lɜrnɪd] *for 1,* [ʌn'lɜrnd] *for 2; v.* [ʌn'lɜrnd] *adj., v. –adj.* **1** not educated; ignorant; showing lack of education. **2** inherent; innate; instinctive and not learned; known without being learned: *A baby's ability to suck is unlearned.*
–v. pt. and pp. of UNLEARN.

un•leash [ʌn'liʃ] *v.* **1** release from a leash: *to unleash a dog.* **2** let loose: *to unleash one's anger.*

un•leav•ened [ʌn'lɛvənd] *adj.* not leavened. Unleavened bread is made without yeast or any other rising agent such as soda or baking powder.

In each of the words below **un-** *means* not; *the pronunciation of the main part of each word is not changed.*

un'joined
ˌun•ju'di•cial
un'jus•ti,fi•a•ble
un'jus•ti,fied
un'kept
un'kin•dled
un'king•ly
un'kissed
un'knight•ly
un'know•a•ble
un'know•ing
un'la•belled
un'la•dy,like
un'laid
ˌun•la'ment•ed
un'laun•dered
un'leased

un•less [ən'lɛs] *or* [ʌn'lɛs] *conj.* if not (that); in any or every case except if: *We'll go unless it rains. Don't call 911 unless there's a real emergency.* ⟨ME *on lesse (that)* on a less condition (than)⟩

un•let•tered [ʌn'lɛtərd] *adj.* **1** not educated. **2** not able to read or write. **3** not having letters on it.

un•like [ʌn'ləik] *adj., prep.* —*adj.* **1** not similar; different: *The two problems are quite unlike.* **2** different in size or number; unequal: *unlike weights.* **3** *Archaic or dialect.* unlikely.
—*prep.* **1** different from: *act unlike others.* **2** uncharacteristic of: *It's unlike you to be so quiet.*

un•like•li•hood [ʌn'ləikli,hʊd] *n.* improbability; unlikeliness.

un•like•ly [ʌn'ləikli] *adj.* **1** not likely; not probable: *an unlikely story. He is unlikely to win the race.* **2** not likely to succeed: *an unlikely undertaking.* **—un'like•li•ness,** *n.*

un•like•ness [ʌn'ləiknɪs] *n.* the fact of being unlike; difference.

un•lim•ber [ʌn'lɪmbər] *v., adj.* —*v.* **1** detach the limber or forepart of the carriage from (an artillery piece). **2** prepare for action.
—*adj.* inflexible; stiff.

un•lim•it•ed [ʌn'lɪmətɪd] *adj.* **1** without limits; boundless: *The girl seems to have unlimited energy.* **2** not restrained; not restricted, controlled, or checked: *a government of unlimited power.* **3** vast. **—un'lim•it•ed•ness,** *n.*

un•list•ed [ʌn'lɪstɪd] *adj.* not included in a list or reference book: *an unlisted telephone number.*

un•load [ʌn'loud] *v.* **1** remove (a load): *She unloaded the bales of hay.* **2** take the load from: *Help me unload the wagon.* **3** get rid of. **4** remove powder, shot, bullets, or shells from (a gun). **5** be unloaded; be emptied of its cargo: *The ship is unloading.* **6** *Informal.* relieve oneself by expressing (one's bad feelings): *to unload one's frustrations. Can I unload on you for a minute?* **—un'load•er,** *n.*

un•lock [ʌn'lɒk] *v.* **1** open the lock of; open (anything firmly closed). **2** release; let loose. **3** disclose; reveal. **4** become unlocked.

un•looked–for [ʌn'lʊkt ,fɔr] *adj.* unexpected; unforeseen.

un•loose [ʌn'lus] *v.* **-loosed, -loos•ing.** let loose; set free; release.

un•loos•en [ʌn'lusən] *v.* unloose; loosen.

un•love•ly [ʌn'lʌvli] *adj.* without beauty or charm; unpleasing in appearance; unpleasant; objectionable; disagreeable. **—un'love•li•ness,** *n.*

un•luck•y [ʌn'lʌki] *adj.* **1** not lucky; unfortunate. **2** bringing or thought to bring bad luck: *The number 13 is thought to be unlucky by the superstitious.* **—un'luck•i•ly,** *adv.* **—un'luck•i•ness,** *n.*

un•make [ʌn'meik] *v.* **-made, -mak•ing. 1** undo; destroy; ruin. **2** deprive of rank or station; depose. **3** reduce to an original condition or form.

un•man [ʌn'mæn] *v.* **-manned, -man•ning. 1** deprive of the qualities of a man. **2** weaken or break down the spirit of; render abjectly fearful or servile. **3** deprive of virility or manhood; castrate. **4** deprive of men: *to unman a ship.*

un•man•ly [ʌn'mænli] *adj.* **1** not manly; weak; cowardly. **2** not befitting a man; effeminate. **—un'man•li•ness,** *n.*

un•manned [ʌn'mænd] *adj., v.* —*adj.* not operated, attended, occupied, etc. by a crew or other people: *an unmanned spacecraft. You have left all the lookout posts unmanned.*
—*v.* pt. and pp. of UNMAN.

un•man•ner•ly [ʌn'mænərli] *adj., adv.* —*adj.* having bad manners; discourteous.
—*adv.* with bad manners; rudely. **—un'man•ner•li•ness,** *n.*

un•mar•ried [ʌn'mærid] *or* [ʌn'mɛrid] *adj.* not married; single.

un•mask [ʌn'mæsk] *v.* **1** remove a mask or disguise: *The guests unmasked at midnight.* **2** take off a mask or disguise from. **3 a** expose the true character of: *to unmask a hypocrite.* **b** appear in true character; expose one's real self. **4** reveal the presence of (guns, etc.) by firing: *to unmask a battery.*

un•mean•ing [ʌn'minɪŋ] *adj.* **1** without meaning. **2** without sense; without expression: *an unmeaning stare.* **—un'mean•ing•ly,** *adv.*

un•meas•ured [ʌn'mɛʒərd] *adj.* **1** not measured; unlimited; measureless. **2** unrestrained; intemperate.

un•meet [ʌn'mit] *adj. Formal, poetic, or archaic.* not fit; not proper; unsuitable.

un•men•tion•a•ble [ʌn'mɛnʃənəbəl] *adj., n.* —*adj.* that cannot be mentioned; not fit to be spoken about.
—*n.* **unmentionables,** *pl.* **a** things considered improper subjects of conversation; things not to be mentioned or discussed.
b *Informal, humorous.* underclothes.
—un'men•tion•a•ble•ness, *n.* **—un'men•tion•a•bly,** *adv.*

un•mer•ci•ful [ʌn'mɜrsəfəl] *adj.* **1** having or showing no mercy; cruel. **2** excessive: *He kept us waiting an unmerciful length of time.* **—un'mer•ci•ful•ly,** *adv.* **—un'mer•ci•ful•ness,** *n.*

un•mind•ful [ʌn'maɪndfəl] *adj.* regardless; heedless; careless: *They went ahead despite our warning and unmindful of the results.* **—un'mind•ful•ly,** *adv.*

un•mis•tak•a•ble [,ʌnmɪ'steikəbəl] *adj.* that cannot be mistaken or misunderstood; clear; plain; evident.
—,un•mis'tak•a•ble•ness, *n.* **—,un•mis'tak•a•bly,** *adv.*

un•mit•i•gat•ed [ʌn'mɪtə,geitɪd] *adj.* **1** not softened or lessened: *unmitigated harshness.* **2** unqualified or absolute: *an unmitigated fraud.* **—un'mit•i,gat•ed•ly,** *adv.*

un•moor [ʌn'mur] *v. Nautical.* **1** release the moorings of (a vessel). **2** weigh all the anchors of (a vessel) but one. **3** come free of its moorings.

un•mor•al [ʌn'mɔrəl] *adj.* neither moral nor immoral; not perceiving or involving right and wrong; amoral. **—un'mor•al•ly,** *adv.* **—,un•mo'ral•i•ty,** *n.*

un•moved [ʌn'muvd] *adj.* **1** not moved; firm. **2** not disturbed; indifferent; emotionally unaffected.

un•muz•zle [ʌn'mʌzəl] *v.* **-zled, -zling. 1** take off a muzzle from (a dog, etc.). **2** make free from restraint; allow to speak or write freely.

In each of the words below **un-** *means* not; *the pronunciation of the main part of each word is not changed.*

un'les•soned
un'lev•el
un'lev•ied
un'li•censed
un'life•like
un'light•ed
un'lik•a•ble
un'like•a•ble
un'lined
un'link
un'liq•ue,fied
un'liq•ui,dat•ed
un'lit
un'lit•tered
un'liv•a•ble
un'lived
un'live•ly
,un•lo'cat•ed
un'lov•a•ble
un'loved
un'lov•ing
un'lu•bri,cat•ed
un'mag•ni,fied
un'maid•en•ly
un'mail•a•ble
un'mailed
un'mal•le•a•ble
un'man•age•a•ble
,un•ma'nip•u,lat•ed
un'man•nered
,un•man•u'fac•tur•a•ble
,un•man•u'fac•tured
un'mapped
un'marked
un'mar•ket•a•ble
un'marred
un'mar•riage•a•ble
un'mas•tered
un'matched
un'mat•ed
un'mat•ted
,un•ma'tured
un'meant
un'meas•ur•a•ble
,un•me'chan•i•cal
un'med•i,cat•ed
,un•me'lo•di•ous
un'melt•ed
un'mem•or•a•ble
un'mem•o,rized
un'men•ac•ing
un'mend•ed
un'men•tioned
un'mer•cen,a•ry
un'mer•chant•a•ble
un'mer•it•ed
,un•me'thod•i•cal
un'met•ri•cal
un'mil•i,ta•ry
un'milled
un'min•gled
un'mirth•ful
,un•mis'tak•en
,un'mit•i•ga•ble
un'mixed
un'mod•i,fied
un'mod•u,lat•ed
un'mois•tened
,un•mo'lest•ed
un'mol•ten
un'mort•gaged
un'moth•er•ly
un'mo•ti,vat•ed
un'mould•ed
un'mount•ed
un'mourned
un'mov•a•ble
un'mov•ing
un'mown
un'mu•si•cal

un•nat•u•ral [ʌn'nætʃərəl] *adj.* **1** not in accordance with the usual course of nature. **2** totally at variance with natural feeling or normal decency, morality, etc.; depraved; showing perversion: *unnatural cruelty.* **3** artificial or affected: *an unnatural laugh.* **—un'nat•u•ral•ly,** *adv.* **—un'nat•u•ral•ness,** *n.*

un•nec•es•sar•y [ʌn'nɛsə,sɛri] *adj.* not necessary; needless. **—un,nec•es'sar•i•ly,** *adv.* **—un'nec•es,sar•i•ness,** *n.*

un•nerve [ʌn'nɜrv] *v.* **-nerved, -nerv•ing.** deprive of firmness, courage, or composure. **—,un'nerv•ing•ly,** *adv.*

unnil– ['junɪl] *combining form.* one zero. It is the first part of the provisional name for any of a series of elements with atomic numbers from 104 to 109, about which little is known (**unnilquadium**, also called rutherfordium, **unnilpentium**, also called hahnium, **unnilhexium**, and **unnilseptium, unniloctium**, and **unnilennium** respectively). ⟨< L *unlus* one + *nil* nothing, for the first two digits of the atomic numbers⟩

un•num•bered [ʌn'nʌmbərd] *adj.* **1** not numbered; not counted: *The pages of the composition were left unnumbered.* **2** too many to count: *There are unnumbered fish in the ocean.*

un•ob•tru•sive [,ʌnəb'trusɪv] *adj.* not noticeable or intrusive; inconspicuous. **—,un•ob'tru•sive•ly,** *adv.* **—,un•ob'tru•sive•ness,** *n.*

un•oc•cu•pied [ʌn'ɒkjə,paɪd] *adj.* **1** not occupied; vacant: *an unoccupied parking space.* **2** not in action or use; idle: *an unoccupied mind.*

un•or•gan•ized [ʌn'ɔrgə,naɪzd] *adj.* **1** not formed into an organized or systematized whole. **2** not organized into labour unions. **3** not being a living organism. An enzyme is an unorganized ferment. **4** disorganized.

un•pack [ʌn'pæk] *v.* **1** take out (things packed in a box, trunk, etc.): *She unpacked her comb and brush.* **2** take packed things out (of): *I'll come down after I've unpacked. We unpacked our suitcases.* **3** admit of being unpacked: *These deep duffel bags don't unpack easily.*

un•paged [ʌn'peidʒd] *adj.* having unnumbered pages.

un•paid [ʌn'peid] *adj.* **1** not paid: *unpaid bills.* **2** without pay: *Candystripers are unpaid workers.*

un•pal•at•a•ble [ʌn'pælətəbəl] *adj.* not agreeable to the taste; distasteful; unpleasant. **—un'pal•at•a•ble•ness,** *n.* **—un'pal•at•a•bly,** *adv.*

un•par•al•leled [ʌn'pærə,lɛld] *or* [ʌn'pɛrə,lɛld] *adj.* having no parallel; unequalled; matchless.

un•par•lia•men•ta•ry [,ʌnpɑrlə'mɛntəri] *adj.* not in acccordance with parliamentary practice.

un•peg [ʌn'pɛg] *v.* **-pegged, -peg•ging. 1** remove the pegs from. **2** loosen or unfasten by removing pegs. **3** remove controls on the free rise and fall of (wages, prices, etc.).

un•peo•ple [ʌn'pipəl] *v.* **-pled, -pling.** deprive of population.

un•peo•pled [ʌn'pipəld] *adj., v.* *—adj.* **1** not (yet) inhabited. **2** deprived of people. *—v.* pt. and pp. of UNPEOPLE.

un•per•son ['ʌn,pɜrsən] *n.* nonperson.

un•pick [ʌn'pɪk] *v.* remove or take out (stitches) from knitting, sewing, etc.

un•picked [ʌn'pɪkt] *v., adj.* *—v.* pt. and pp. of UNPICK. *—adj.* not chosen or selected.

un•pile [ʌn'paɪl] *v.* **-piled, -pil•ing. 1** take or remove from a pile. **2** take a pile or heap apart.

un•pin [ʌn'pɪn] *v.* **-pinned, -pin•ning.** take out a pin or pins from; unfasten.

un•pleas•ant [ʌn'plɛzənt] *adj.* not pleasant; disagreeable. **—un'pleas•ant•ly,** *adv.*

un•pleas•ant•ness [ʌn'plɛzəntnɪs] *n.* **1** the quality of being unpleasant. **2** something unpleasant. **3** a quarrel.

un•plug [ʌn'plʌg] *v.* **-plugged, -plug•ging. 1** open or set free (something) by removing a plug or stopper. **2** unclog; unblock. **3** disconnect (an electric light, appliance, etc.) by removing the plug from an outlet: *Unplug the kettle before pouring the water.*

un•plumbed [ʌn'plʌmd] *adj.* **1** not fathomed; not measured; of unknown depth. **2** not fully explored or understood: *an unplumbed area of physics.* **3** having no plumbing.

un•pop•u•lar [ʌn'pɒpjələr] *adj.* not generally liked: *an unpopular government policy. He was always unpopular with his colleagues.* **—un'pop•u•lar•ly,** *adv.*

un•pop•u•lar•i•ty [,ʌnpɒpjə'lærəti] *or* [,ʌnpɒpjə'lɛrəti] *n.* lack of popularity; the fact of being unpopular.

un•prac•tised [ʌn'præktɪst] *adj.* **1** not skilled; not expert. **2** not put into practice; not used. **3** unrehearsed. Also, **unpracticed.**

un•prec•e•dent•ed [ʌn'prɛsə,dɛntɪd] *or* [ʌn'prisə,dɛntɪd] *adj.* having no precedent; never done before; never known before.

un•prej•u•diced [ʌn'prɛdʒədɪst] *adj.* **1** without prejudice; impartial. **2** not impaired.

un•pre•pared [,ʌnprɪ'pɛrd] *adj.* **1** not made ready; not worked out ahead: *an unprepared speech.* **2** not ready: *a person unprepared to answer.*

In each of the words below **un-** *means* not; *the pronunciation of the main part of each word is not changed.*

un'mys•ti,fied
un'nam•a•ble
un'name•a•ble
un'named
un'nat•u•ral,ized
un'nav•i•ga•ble
un'nav•i,gat•ed
un'need•ed
un'need•ful
,un•ne'go•tia•ble
,un•ne'go•ti,at•ed
un'neigh•bour•ly
un'notched
un'not•ed
un'note,wor•thy
un'no•tice•a•ble
un'no•ticed
un'nur•tured
,un•o'beyed
,un•ob'jec•tion•a•ble
un'ob•li,gat•ed
,un•o'blig•ing
,un•ob'scured
,un•ob'serv•a•ble
,un•ob'serv•ant
,un•ob'serv•ing
,un•ob'struct•ed
,un•ob'tain•a•ble
,un•ob'tained
,un•ob'trud•ing
,un•ob'tru•sive
,un•ob'tru•sive•ness
,un•oc'ca•sioned
,un•of'fend•ed
,un•of'fend•ing
,un•of'fen•sive
un'of•fered
,un•of'fi•cial
,un•of'fi•cious
un'oiled
un'o•pened
,un•op'posed
,un•op'pressed
,un•op'pres•sive
,un•or'dained
un'or•dered
,un•o'rig•i•nal
,un•or•na'men•tal
un'or•na,ment•ed
un'or•tho,dox
un'or•tho,dox•y
,un•os•ten'ta•tious
un'owned
un'ox•i,dized
un'pac•i,fied
un'paid-,for
un'paint•ed
un'paired
un'pal•at•a•ble
un'par•don•a•ble
un'par•doned
,un•par'ti•tioned
un'pas•teur,ized
un'patched
un'pat•ent•ed
,un•pa•tri'ot•ic
,un•pa•tri'ot•i•cal•ly
un'paved
un'peace•a•ble
un'peace•ful
un'ped•i,greed
un'pen•e,trat•ed
un'pen•sioned
un'pep•pered
,un•per'ceived
,un•per'ceiv•ing
,un•per'cep•tive
,un•per'fect•ed
,un•per'formed
,un•per'plexed
,un•per'suad•a•ble
,un•per'suad•ed
,un•per'sua•sive
,un•per'turb•a•ble
,un•per'turbed
,un•pe'rused
,un•phil•o'soph•ic
,un•phil•o'soph•i•cal
,un•pho'net•ic
un'pierced
un'pit•ied
un'pit•y•ing
un'placed
un'plagued
un'planned
un'plant•ed
un'play•a•ble
un'played
un'pleased
un'pleas•ing
un'pledged
un'pli•ant
un'ploughed
un'plowed
un'plucked
,un•po'et•ic
un'point•ed
un'poised
un'po•lar,ized
,un•po'liced
un'pol•ished
un'pol•i•tic
,un•po'lit•i•cal
un'polled
,un•pol'lut•ed
un'pol•y•mer,ized
un'pop•u,lat•ed
un'posed
un'post•ed
un'prac•ti•ca•ble
un'prac•ti•cal
un'praised
,un•pre'dict•a•ble
,un•pre'dict•ed
,un•pre'med•i,tat•ed

un•pre•tend•ing [ˌʌnprɪ'tɛndɪŋ] *adj.* unassuming; modest. —ˌ**un•pre'tend•ing•ly,** *adv.*

un•pre•ten•tious [ˌʌnprɪ'tɛnʃəs] *adj.* modest; free from self-conscious affectation or airs; simple. —ˌ**un•pre'ten•tious•ly,** *adv.* —ˌ**un•pre'ten•tious•ness,** *n.*

un•prin•ci•pled [ʌn'prɪnsəpəld] *adj.* lacking or resulting from a lack of good moral principles; bad.
☛ *Syn.* See note at UNSCRUPULOUS.

un•print•a•ble [ʌn'prɪntəbəl] *adj.* not fit to be printed.

un•pro•fes•sion•al [ˌʌnprə'fɛʃənəl] *adj.* **1** contrary to professional etiquette; unbecoming in members of a profession. **2** not up to professional standards; amateurish. **3** not having to do with or connected with a profession. **4** not belonging to a profession. —ˌ**un•pro'fes•sion•al•ly,** *adv.*

un•prof•it•a•ble [ʌn'prɒfətəbəl] *adj.* producing no gain or advantage. —**un'prof•it•a•ble•ness,** *n.* —**un'prof•it•a•bly,** *adv.*

un•pro•voked [ˌʌnprə'voukt] *adj.* not provoked: *an unprovoked attack.*

un•qual•i•fied [ʌn'kwɒləˌfaɪd] *adj.* **1** not qualified; not fitted. **2** not modified, limited, or restricted in any way: *unqualified praise.* **3** complete; absolute: *an unqualified failure.* —**un'qual•iˌfied•ly,** *adv.*

un•ques•tion•a•ble [ʌn'kwɛstʃənəbəl] *adj.* **1** beyond dispute or doubt; certain: *an unquestionable advantage.* **2** impeccable in quality or nature; accepted without question or reservation; unexceptionable. —**un'ques•tion•a•ble•ness,** *n.* —**un'ques•tion•a•bly,** *adv.*

un•ques•tioned [ʌn'kwɛstʃənd] *adj.* **1** not questioned; not disputed. **2** not interrogated; not asked any questions.

un•qui•et [ʌn'kwaɪət] *adj., n.* —*adj.* restless; disturbed; uneasy. —*n.* restlessness; disquiet; lack of tranquillity. —**un'qui•et•ly,** *adv.* —**un'qui•et•ness,** *n.*

un•quote [ʌn'kwout] *v.* **-quot•ed, -quot•ing.** mark the end of (a quotation) either in speech or writing, or by a gesture: *He quoted but he didn't unquote, so we couldn't tell where the quotation ended.*

un•rav•el [ʌn'rævəl] *v.* **-elled** or **-eled, -el•ling** or **-el•ing.** **1** separate the threads of; undo: *The kitten unravelled Grandma's knitting.* **2** come apart; ravel: *My knitted gloves are unravelling at the wrist.* **3** bring or come out of a tangled state; clear up: *to unravel a mystery.* **4** make or become confused, distracted, etc.: *I've got to get out of here before my mind completely unravels. Their constant noise is unravelling my thoughts.*

un•read [ʌn'rɛd] *adj.* **1** not read: *an unread book.* **2** **a** not having read much: *an unread person.* **b** not versed or instructed; not familiar with (*used with* **in**): *I'm afraid I'm unread in British politics.*

un•read•y [ʌn'rɛdi] *adj.* **1** not ready; not prepared. **2** not prompt or quick. —**un'read•i•ly,** *adv.* —**un'read•i•ness,** *n.*

un•re•al [ʌn'riəl] *or* [ʌn'ril] *adj.* imaginary; not real; not substantial; fanciful. —**un're•al•ly,** *adv.*
☛ *Hom.* UNREEL [ʌn'ril].

un•re•al•i•ty [ˌʌnri'æləti] *n., pl.* **-ties. 1** lack of reality or substance; an imaginary or fanciful quality. **2** impractical or visionary character or tendency; impracticality. **3** something unreal: *Unrealities, such as elves and goblins, are fun to imagine.*

un•rea•son [ʌn'rizən] *n.* irrationality; action or thought that is not reasonable.

un•rea•son•a•ble [ʌn'rizənəbəl] *adj.* **1** not in accord with reason; not sensible; irrational: *an unreasonable fear of the dark.* **2** not moderate; excessive: *I think $190 is an unreasonable price for those shoes.* —**un'rea•son•a•ble•ness,** *n.* —**un'rea•son•a•bly,** *adv.*

un•rea•son•ing [ʌn'rizənɪŋ] *adj.* not reasoning; not using reason; reasonless; irrational. —**un'rea•son•ing•ly,** *adv.*

un•re•con•struct•ed [ˌʌnrikən'strʌktɪd] *adj.* **1** not reconciled to change; adhering to old and outworn customs, standards, laws, etc. **2** not rebuilt or reconstructed.

un•reel [ʌn'ril] *v.* unwind from a reel.
☛ *Hom.* UNREAL.

un•re•gard•ed [ˌʌnrɪ'gɑrdɪd] *adj.* disregarded; not heeded.

un•re•gen•er•a•cy [ˌʌnrɪ'dʒɛnərəsi] *n.* unregenerate condition; enmity toward God; wickedness.

un•re•gen•er•ate [ˌʌnrɪ'dʒɛnərɪt] *adj.* **1** not born again spiritually; not turned to the love of God. **2** wicked; bad. **3** obstinate; unwilling to change. —ˌ**un•re'gen•er•ate•ly,** *adv.* —ˌ**un•re'gen•er•ate•ness,** *n.*

un•re•lent•ing [ˌʌnrɪ'lɛntɪŋ] *adj.* **1** not yielding to feelings of kindness or compassion; merciless. **2** not slackening or relaxing in force or intensity, effort or determination, speed, etc.; constant. —ˌ**un•re'lent•ing•ly,** *adv.* —ˌ**un•re'lent•ing•ness,** *n.*
☛ *Syn.* **1.** See note at INFLEXIBLE.

un•re•li•gious [ˌʌnrɪ'lɪdʒəs] *adj.* **1** non-religious; not connected with religion. **2** irreligious.

un•re•mit•ting [ˌʌnrɪ'mɪtɪŋ] *adj.* never stopping; not slackening; maintained steadily: *unremitting vigilance.* —ˌ**un•re'mit•ting•ly,** *adv.*

In each of the words below **un-** *means* not; *the pronunciation of the main part of each word is not changed.*

ˌun•pre•pos'sess•ing
ˌun•pre'scribed
ˌun•pre'sent•a•ble
ˌun•pre'served
un'pressed
ˌun•pre'sump•tu•ous
un'pret•ty
ˌun•pre'vail•ing
ˌun•pre'vent•a•ble
un'prince•ly
un'print•ed
un'priv•i•leged
un'prized
un'pro•cessed
ˌun•pro'claimed
ˌun•pro'cur•a•ble
ˌun•pro'duc•tive
ˌun•pro'faned
ˌun•pro'fessed
ˌun•pro'gres•sive
ˌun•pro'hib•it•ed
ˌun•pro'ject•ed
un'prom•is•ing
un'prompt•ed
ˌun•pro'nounce•a•ble
ˌun•pro'nounced
ˌun•pro'pi•tious
ˌun•pro'por•tioned
ˌun•pro'posed
un'pros•per•ous
ˌun•pro'tect•ed
ˌun•pro'test•ed
ˌun•pro'test•ing
un'proved
un'prov•en
ˌun•pro'vid•ed
ˌun•pro'voc•a•tive
un'pruned
un'pub•liˌcized
un'pub•lished
un'punc•tu•al
un'pun•ish•a•ble
un'pun•ished
un'pur•chas•a•ble
un'pu•riˌfied
un'pur•posed
ˌun•pur'su•ing
un'quail•ing
un'qual•iˌfy•ing
un'quelled
un'quench•a•ble
un'quenched
un'quot•a•ble
un'quot•ed
un'raised
un'ran•somed
un'rat•ed
un'rat•iˌfied
un'reach•a•ble
un'read•a•ble
ˌun•re•al'ist•ic
un're•alˌiz•a•ble
un're•alˌized
un'rea•soned
ˌun•re'buked
ˌun•re'ceiv•a•ble
ˌun•re'ceived
ˌun•re'cep•tive
ˌun•re'cip•roˌcat•ed
un'reck•oned
ˌun•re'claimed
un'rec•ogˌniz•a•ble
un'rec•ogˌnized
ˌun•rec•om'mend•ed
un'rec•omˌpensed
ˌun•rec•on'cil•a•ble
un'rec•onˌciled
ˌun•re'cord•ed
ˌun•re'cov•er•a•ble
un'rec•tiˌfied
ˌun•re'deemed
ˌun•re'dressed
ˌun•re'fined
ˌun•re'flect•ing
ˌun•re'formed
ˌun•re'freshed
ˌun•re'gard•ed
un'reg•iˌment•ed
un'reg•is•tered
ˌun•re'gret•ted
un'reg•uˌlat•ed
ˌun•re'hearsed
ˌun•re'lat•ed
ˌun•re'laxed
ˌun•re'lax•ing
ˌun•reˌli•a'bil•i•ty
ˌun•re'li•a•ble
ˌun•re'li•a•bly
ˌun•re'liev•a•ble
ˌun•re'lieved
ˌun•re'mark•a•ble
ˌun•re'marked
un'rem•e•died
ˌun•re'mem•bered
ˌun•re'mit•ted
ˌun•re'morse•ful
ˌun•re'moved
ˌun•re'mu•nerˌat•ed
ˌun•re'mu•ner•a•tive
un'ren•dered
ˌun•re'newed
ˌun•re'nowned
un'rent•ed
ˌun•re'paid
ˌun•re'paired
ˌun•re'pealed
ˌun•re'peat•a•ble
ˌun•re'pent•ant
ˌun•re'pent•ed
ˌun•re'pent•ing
ˌun•re'place•a•ble
ˌun•re'placed
ˌun•re'plen•ished
ˌun•re'port•ed
ˌun•rep•re'sent•a•tive
ˌun•rep•re'sent•ed
ˌun•re'pressed
ˌun•re'prieved
un'rep•riˌmand•ed
ˌun•re'proached
ˌun•re'prov•a•ble
ˌun•re'proved
ˌun•re'quest•ed
ˌun•re'quit•ed
ˌun•re'sent•ful

un•re•serve [ˌʌnrɪ'zɜrv] *n.* frankness; candour; lack of reserve.

un•re•served [ˌʌnrɪ'zɜrvd] *adj.* **1** frank; open: *an unreserved manner.* **2** not restricted or qualified; without reservation: *unreserved praise.* **3** not kept for a special person or purpose: *unreserved seats.*

un•re•serv•ed•ly [ˌʌnrɪ'zɜrvɪdli] *adv.* **1** frankly; openly. **2** without reservation or restriction.

un•rest [ʌn'rɛst] *n.* **1** lack of ease and quiet; restlessness. **2** social or political agitation or disturbance amounting almost to rebellion.

un•re•strained [ˌʌnrɪ'streind] *adj.* **1** not constrained; spontaneous or free: *unrestrained joy.* **2** immoderate or uncontrolled: *unrestrained urban sprawl.*

un•right•eous [ʌn'rəitʃəs] *adj.* **1** wicked; sinful. **2** unjust; unfair. ⟨OE *unrihtwīs*⟩ **—un'right•eous•ly,** *adv.* **—un'right•eous•ness,** *n.*

un•rip [ʌn'rɪp] *v.* **-ripped, -rip•ping.** take apart or undo by ripping.

un•ripe [ʌn'rəip] *adj.* **1** not ripe; green. **2** of persons, plans, etc., not fully developed or grown; immature. **—un'ripe•ness,** *n.*

un•ri•valled or **un•ri•valed** [ʌn'raɪvəld] *adj.* having no rival; without an equal.

un•roll [ʌn'roul] *v.* **1** open or spread out (something rolled). **2** become opened or spread out. **3** unfold; reveal or become revealed, especially gradually: *Our interest increased as the story unrolled.*

un•root [ʌn'rut] *v.* uproot.

un•round [ʌn'raʊnd] *v.* **1** *Phonetics.* pronouce (a usually rounded vowel) without lip-rounding. **2** prevent (the lips) from rounding.

un•ruf•fled [ʌn'rʌfəld] *adj.* **1** not ruffled; smooth. **2** not disturbed; calm.

un•ruled [ʌn'ruld] *adj.* **1** not kept under control; not governed. **2** not marked with lines: *unruled paper.*

un•ru•ly [ʌn'ruli] *adj.* hard to rule or control: *an unruly crowd, an unruly horse.* **—ˌun'ru•li•ness,** *n.*

☛ *Syn.* **Unruly,** UNGOVERNABLE = hard or impossible to control. **Unruly** = not inclined to obey or accept discipline or restraint, and suggests getting out of hand and becoming disorderly, contrary, or obstinately willful, resisting or defying attempts to bring under control: *The angry mob become unruly.* **Ungovernable** = incapable of being controlled or restrained, either because never subjected to rule or direction or because of escape from it: *One of the circus lions became ungovernable.*

UNRWA United Nations Relief and Works Agency.

un•sad•dle [ʌn'sædəl] *v.* **-dled, -dling. 1** take the saddle off (a horse). **2** cause to fall from a horse.

un•safe [ʌn'seif] *adj.* dangerous. **—un'safe•ly,** *adv.* **—un'safe•ness,** *n.*

un•said [ʌn'sɛd] *adj., v.* *—adj.* not said or spoken. *—v.* pt. and pp. of UNSAY.

un•sat•u•rat•ed [ʌn'sætʃəˌreitɪd] *adj.* **1** not saturated; not thoroughly wet. **2** of a solution, able to dissolve or absorb more of a substance. **3** of an organic compound, containing double or triple bonds between carbon atoms, thus able to undergo reactions in which other elements or radicals are taken on. **—ˌun•sat•u'ra•tion,** *n.*

un•sa•vour•y or **un•sa•vor•y** [ʌn'seivəri] *adj.* **1** tasteless. **2** unpleasant in taste or smell. **3** morally unpleasant; offensive: *That man has an unsavoury reputation.* **—un'sa•vour•i•ly** or **un'sa•vor•i•ly,** *adv.* **—un'sa•vour•i•ness** or **un'sa•vor•i•ness,** *n.*

un•say [ʌn'sei] *v.* **-said, -say•ing.** take back or cancel something said: *What is said cannot be unsaid.*

un•scathed [ʌn'skeiðd] *adj.* not harmed; uninjured.

un•schooled [ʌn'skuld] *adj.* **1** not schooled or acquired by schooling; not learned or taught. **2** undisciplined. **3** unstudied; natural.

un•sci•en•tif•ic [ˌʌnsaɪən'tɪfɪk] *adj.* **1** not in accordance with the facts or principles of science: *an unscientific notion.* **2** not acting in accordance with such facts or principles: *an unscientific farmer.* **—ˌun•sci•en'tif•i•cal•ly,** *adv.*

un•scram•ble [ʌn'skræmbəl] *v.* **-bled, -bling. 1** reduce from confusion to order; bring out of a scrambled condition. **2** restore (a transmitted signal, etc.) to the original condition; make intelligible: *unscramble a radio message.* **—un'scram•bler,** *n.*

un•screw [ʌn'skru] *v.* **1** take out the screw or screws from. **2** loosen or take off or out by turning; untwist. **3** unfasten or open by removing a screw or screws. **4** become unscrewed; admit of being unscrewed: *This light bulb doesn't want to unscrew.*

un•scru•pu•lous [ʌn'skrupjələs] *adj.* not careful about right or wrong; showing a lack of principles or conscience: *unscrupulous business practices. The unscrupulous gambler cheated.* **—un'scru•pu•lous•ly,** *adv.* **—un'scru•pu•lous•ness,** *n.*

☛ *Syn.* **Unscrupulous,** UNPRINCIPLED = having or showing no regard for what is morally right. **Unscrupulous,** describing a person's character, acts, or words, means not held back by any scruples of conscience, any doubts about the morality or justice of what one is doing or about to do, or by a sense of honour: *She would stoop to any unscrupulous trick to avoid paying her bills.* **Unprincipled** means being without, or showing an absence of, good moral principles: *Only an unprincipled person would defend that man's conduct.*

un•seal [ʌn'sil] *v.* **1** break or remove the seal of: *unseal a letter.* **2** open: *The threat unsealed her lips.*

un•sealed [ʌn'sild] *adj., v.* *—adj.* not sealed; left open. *—v.* pt. and pp. of UNSEAL.

un•search•a•ble [ʌn'sɜrtʃəbəl] *adj.* not to be searched into; that cannot be understood by searching; mysterious or profound. **—un'search•a•bly,** *adv.*

un•sea•son•a•ble [ʌn'sizənəbəl] *adj.* **1** not suitable to the season. **2** coming at the wrong time. **—un'sea•son•a•ble•ness,** *n.* **—un'sea•son•a•bly,** *adv.*

un•seat [ʌn'sit] *v.* **1** displace from a seat or saddle; unhorse: *The bronco unseated everyone who tried to ride it.* **2** remove from office: *Our previous MP was unseated in the last election.*

un•se•cured [ˌʌnsɪ'kjurd] *adj.* **1** not secure; not held firmly in place: *The boat floated off the beach at high tide because it had been left unsecured.* **2** not insured against loss; not guaranteed by

In each of the words below **un-** *means* not; *the pronunciation of the main part of each word is not changed.*

ˌun•re'signed	**ˌun•reˌturned**	**un'rimed**	**un'sat•ed**	**un'sched•uled**
ˌun•re'sist•ant	**ˌun•re'vealed**	**un'rip•ened**	**un'sa•tiˌat•ed**	**un'schol•ar•ly**
ˌun•re'sist•ed	**ˌun•re'venged**	**un'robe**	**ˌun•sat•is'fac•to•ri•ly**	**un'scorched**
ˌun•re'sist•ing	**ˌun•re'viewed**	**ˌun•ro'man•tic**	**ˌun•sat•is'fac•to•ry**	**un'scoured**
ˌun•re'solved	**ˌun•re'vised**	**un'rum•pled**	**un'sat•isˌfied**	**un'scraped**
ˌun•re'spect•ful	**ˌun•re'voked**	**un'saint•ly**	**un'sat•isˌfy•ing**	**un'scratched**
ˌun•re'spon•sive	**ˌun•re'ward•ed**	**un'sal•a•ble**	**un'saved**	**un'screened**
un'rest•ed	**ˌun•re'ward•ing**	**un'sal•a•ried**	**un'say•a•ble**	**un'scrip•tur•al**
un'rest•ful	**un'rhymed**	**un'sale•a•ble**	**un'scal•a•ble**	**un'sculp•tured**
ˌun•re'strict•ed	**un'rhyth•mic**	**un'salt•ed**	**un'scaled**	**un'sea•son•al**
ˌun•re'ten•tive	**un'rhyth•mi•cal**	**un'sam•pled**	**un'scanned**	**un'sea•soned**
ˌun•re'tract•ed	**un'rid•den**	**un'sanc•tiˌfied**	**un'scared**	**un'seaˌwor•thy**
ˌun•re'trieved	**un'ri•fled**	**un'sanc•tioned**	**un'scarred**	**ˌun•se'clud•ed**
ˌun•re'turn•a•ble	**un'right•ful**	**un'san•iˌta•ry**	**un'scent•ed**	**un'sec•ond•ed**

collateral: *an unsecured loan.* **3** not protected from interference, tampering, intrusion, etc.

un•seem•ly [ʌn'simli] *adj., adv. —adj.* not suitable; improper: *unseemly laughter.*
—adv. improperly; unsuitably. **—un'seem•li•ness,** *n.*

un•seen [ʌn'sin] *adj.* **1** not seen: *an unseen error.* **2** not visible: *an unseen spirit.*

un•self•ish [ʌn'sɛlfɪʃ] *adj.* considerate of others; generous. **—un'self•ish•ly,** *adv.* **—un'self•ish•ness,** *n.*

un•set•tle [ʌn'sɛtəl] *v.* **-tled, -tling.** make or become unstable; disturb or be disturbed; shake; weaken. **—un'set•tle•ment,** *n.*

un•set•tled [ʌn'sɛtəld] *adj.* **1** disordered; not in proper condition or order. **2** not fixed or stable. **3** liable to change; uncertain: *The weather is unsettled.* **4** not adjusted or disposed of: *an unsettled estate, an unsettled bill.* **5** not determined or decided. **6** not inhabited. **7** not having found or chosen a permanent residence. **—un'set•tled•ness,** *n.*

un•sex [ʌn'sɛks] *v.* deprive of sexual capacity or of the attributes of one's sex.

un•shack•le [ʌn'ʃækəl] *v.* **-led, -ling.** remove shackles from; set free.

un•shak•en [ʌn'ʃeikən] *adj.* not shaken; firm: *an unshaken belief in the faithfulness of a friend.*

un•sheathe [ʌn'ʃið] *v.* **-sheathed, -sheath•ing.** draw (a sword, knife, etc.) from a sheath.

un•ship [ʌn'ʃɪp] *v.* **-shipped, -ship•ping. 1** put off or take off from a ship: *to unship a cargo.* **2** remove from the proper place for use: *to unship an oar or tiller.*

un•shod [ʌn'ʃɒd] *adj.* without shoes.

un•sight•ly [ʌn'səitli] *adj.* ugly or unpleasant to look at. **—un'sight•li•ness,** *n.*
☛ *Syn.* See note at UGLY.

un•skil•ful or **un•skill•ful** [ʌn'skɪlfəl] *adj.* awkward; clumsy; inexpert: *This would-be artist's unskilful work needs the tempering of time.* **—un'skil•ful•ly** or **un'skill•ful•ly,** *adv.* **—un'skil•ful•ness** or **un'skill•ful•ness,** *n.*

un•skilled [ʌn'skɪld] *adj.* **1** not skilled or trained: *For a person unskilled in carpentry, you certainly helped a lot with these renovations.* **2** not requiring special skills or training: *unskilled labour.* **3** employed at an unskilled job: *Unskilled workers usually earn less than skilled workers.*

un•snap [ʌn'snæp] *v.* **-snapped, -snap•ping.** unfasten the snap or snaps of.

un•snarl [ʌn'snɑrl] *v.* remove the snarls from; untangle.

un•so•cia•bil•i•ty [ˌʌnsouʃə'bɪləti] *n.* unsociable nature or behaviour; lack of friendliness.

un•so•cia•ble [ʌn'souʃəbəl] *adj.* **1** not sociable; not associating easily with others: *unsociable behaviour, an unsociable hermit.* **2** not conducive to, or preventing, sociability: *an unsociable atmosphere.* **—un'so•cia•ble•ness,** *n.* **—un'so•cia•bly,** *adv.*

un•sol•der [ʌn'sɒdər] *v.* **1** separate (something soldered). **2** break up; divide; dissolve.

un•so•phis•ti•cat•ed [ˌʌnsə'fɪstəˌkeitɪd] *adj.* **1** not sophisticated; simple; natural. **2** not very advanced or highly developed: *unsophisticated methods, unsophisticated technology.* **—ˌun•so'phis•tiˌcat•ed•ly,** *adv.* **—ˌun•soˌphis•ti'ca•tion,** *n.*

un•sound [ʌn'saʊnd] *adj.* **1** not in good condition; not sound: *an unsound business, unsound walls, unsound in body or mind.* **2** not based on truth or fact: *an unsound doctrine, theory, etc.* **3** not restful; disturbed: *an unsound sleep.* **—un'sound•ly,** *adv.* **—un'sound•ness,** *n.*

un•spar•ing [ʌn'spɛrɪŋ] *adj.* **1** very generous; liberal; not sparing. **2** not merciful; severe. **—un'spar•ing•ly,** *adv.* **—un'spar•ing•ness,** *n.*

un•speak•a•ble [ʌn'spikəbəl] *adj.* **1** that cannot be expressed in words: *unspeakable joy, an unspeakable loss.* **2** extremely bad; so bad that it can hardly be spoken of: *That was an unspeakable thing to do!* **3** that may not be uttered: *In some cultures, the name of a dead ancestor is unspeakable.* **—un'speak•a•bly,** *adv.*

un•spot•ted [ʌn'spɒtɪd] *adj.* without spot or stain; pure.

un•sta•ble [ʌn'steibəl] *adj.* **1** not firmly fixed; easily moved, shaken, or overthrown. **2** not constant; variable. **3** *Chemistry.* **a** easily decomposed; readily changing into other compounds. **b** radioactive. **4** unsettled in mind; emotionally unsound. **—un'sta•ble•ness,** *n.* **—un'sta•bly,** *adv.*

unstable element *Chemistry.* a radioactive element that eventually changes into a radioactive isotope.

un•stead•y [ʌn'stɛdi] *adj., v.* **-stead•ied, -stead•y•ing.** *—adj.* **1** not steady; shaky: *an unsteady voice, an unsteady flame.* **2** likely to change; not predictable: *unsteady winds.* **3** not regular in habits.
—v. make unsteady. **—un'stead•i•ly,** *adv.* **—un'stead•i•ness,** *n.*

un•step [ʌn'stɛp] *v.* **-stepped, -step•ping.** remove (a mast, etc.) from its step.

un•stick [ʌn'stɪk] *v.* **-stuck, -stick•ing.** make or become free from being stuck.

un•stop [ʌn'stɒp] *v.* **-stopped, -stop•ping. 1** remove the stopper from (a bottle, etc.). **2** make free from any obstruction; open.

un•strap [ʌn'stræp] *v.* **-strapped, -strap•ping.** loosen the strap of (a trunk, box, etc.).

un•string [ʌn'strɪŋ] *v.* **-strung, -string•ing. 1** take off or loosen the string or strings of. **2** take from a string. **3** weaken the nerves of; make nervous.

un•struc•tured [ʌn'strʌktʃərd] *adj.* having no formal or rigid structure or organization: *unstructured classes.*

un•strung [ʌn'strʌŋ] *adj., v. —adj.* upset; emotionally disturbed.
—v. pt. and pp. of UNSTRING.

un•stuck [ʌn'stʌk] *v., adj. —v.* pt. and pp. of UNSTICK.
—adj. loosened or freed from being stuck.
come unstuck, become disordered or confused; go awry: *The*

In each of the words below **un-** *means* not; *the pronunciation of the main part of each word is not changed.*

ˌun•se'duced
un'seed•ed
un'see•ing
ˌun•seg'ment•ed
un'seg•reˌgat•ed
ˌun•se'lect•ed
ˌun•se'lec•tive
ˌun•self'con•scious
ˌun•sen'sa•tion•al
un'sen•si•tive
ˌun•sen•ti'men•tal
un'sep•aˌrat•ed
un'served
un'serv•ice•a•ble
un'set
un'sewn
un'shad•ed
un'shad•owed
un'shak•a•ble
un'shake•a•ble
un'shaped
un'shape•ly
un'shared
un'sharp•ened
un'shaved
un'shav•en
un'shed
un'shelled
un'shel•tered
un'shield•ed
un'shock•a•ble
un'shorn
un'short•ened
un'shrink•a•ble
un'shrink•ing
un'sift•ed
un'sight•ed
un'signed
un'si•lenced
un'sing•a•ble
un'sink•a•ble
un'sis•ter•ly
un'sized
un'slacked
un'slaked
un'sleep•ing
un'sliced
un'smil•ing
un'snagged
un'so•cial
un'soiled
un'sold
un'sol•dier•ly
ˌun•so'lic•it•ed
ˌun•so'lic•it•ous
un'sol•id
un'solv•a•ble
un'solved
un'soothed
un'sort•ed
un'sought
un'sound•ed
un'soured
un'sowed
un'sown
un'spe•cialˌized
ˌun•spe'cif•ic
un'spe•ciˌfied
ˌun•spec'tac•u•lar
un'spec•u•la•tive
un'spent
un'spiced
un'spir•i•tu•al
un'split
un'spoiled
un'spo•ken
un'sport•ing
un'sports•manˌlike
un'sprung
un'squan•dered
un'stain•a•ble
un'stained
un'stamped
un'stand•ardˌized
un'starched
un'stat•ed
un'states•manˌlike
un'stemmed
un'ster•ile
un'ster•iˌlized
un'stig•maˌtized
un'stint•ed
un'stint•ing
un'stitched
un'stop•pa•ble
un'strained
un'strat•iˌfied
un'stressed
un'stri•at•ed

whole timetable came unstuck when one person wanted to change her time slot.

un•stud•ied [ʌn'stʌdid] *adj.* **1** not contrived; not planned ahead; natural. **2** not skilled, practised or learned (*in* something): *I am quite unstudied in higher math.* **3** that is not a subject of research or study.

un•sub•stan•tial [ˌʌnsəb'stænʃəl] *adj.* **1** not substantial; flimsy; slight; unreal. **2** incorporeal; not of material substance. **—ˌun•sub'stan•tial•ly,** *adv.* **—ˌun•sub,stan•ti'al•i•ty,** *n.*

un•suc•cess•ful [ˌʌnsək'sɛsfəl] *adj.* not successful; without success. **—ˌun•suc'cess•ful•ly,** *adv.*

un•suit•a•bil•i•ty [ˌʌnsutə'bɪləti] *n.* the fact or quality of being unsuitable.

un•suit•a•ble [ʌn'sutəbəl] *adj.* not suitable; unfit. **—un'suit•a•bly,** *adv.*

un•suit•ed [ʌn'sutɪd] *adj.* **1** not suited; unfit. **2** not wearing a suit: *Businesspeople, suited and unsuited, poured into the hall to see the displays.*

un•sung [ʌn'sʌŋ] *adj.* **1** not sung. **2** not honoured in song or poetry; unpraised.

un•sus•pect•ed [ˌʌnsə'spɛktɪd] *adj.* **1** not under suspicion: *He had already committed several burglaries but was still unsuspected.* **2** not thought of or known about: *an unsuspected danger.* **—ˌun•sus'pec•ted•ly,** *adv.*

un•tan•gle [ʌn'tæŋgəl] *v.* **-gled, -gling. 1** take the tangles out of; disentangle. **2** straighten out or clear up (anything confused or perplexing).

un•taught [ʌn'tɒt] *adj.* **1** not instructed; not educated. **2** known without being taught; learned naturally. **3** of a lesson, etc., not delivered or presented: *Owing to time pressures, two units of the course remained untaught.*

un•thank•ful [ʌn'θæŋkfəl] *adj.* ungrateful; thankless.

un•think•able [ʌn'θɪŋkəbəl] *adj.* **1** that cannot be imagined or grasped by the mind; inconceivable: *the unthinkable vastness of the universe.* **2** that cannot be considered; out of the question: *It is unthinkable that she could be a thief.* **—un'think•a•bly,** *adv.*

un•think•ing [ʌn'θɪŋkɪŋ] *adj.* **1** thoughtless; heedless; careless: *An unthinking comment can sometimes cause a lot of trouble. They are not really malicious, just unthinking.* **2** characterized by absence of thought: *blind, unthinking anger.* **3** not having the faculty of thought; unable to think. **—un'think•ing•ly,** *adv.*

un•thought–of [ʌn'θɒt ˌʌv] *adj.* not imagined or considered.

un•thread [ʌn'θrɛd] *v.* **1** take the thread out of. **2** unravel. **3** find one's way through (a maze, etc.).

un•ti•dy [ʌn'taɪdi] *adj.* **1** not in order; not neat. **2** not given to neatness; slovenly: *Unlike her mother, she is a rather untidy person.* **—un'ti•di•ly,** *adv.* **—un'ti•di•ness,** *n.*

un•tie [ʌn'taɪ] *v.* **-tied, -ty•ing. 1** loosen; unfasten; undo: *to untie a knot.* **2** become untied: *A properly tied knot should untie easily.* **3** make free; release: *He untied his horse.* **4** make clear; explain; resolve. ⟨OE *untīgan*⟩

un•til [ən'tɪl] *prep., conj. —prep.* **1** up to the time of: *It was cold from Christmas until April.* **2** before (*used only with a negative*): *She did not leave until morning.*
—conj. **1** up to the time when: *He waited until the sun had set.* **2** before (*used only with a negative*): *He did not come until the meeting was half over.* **3** to the point or stage that: *He worked until he was too tired to do more.* ⟨ME *untill* < ON *und* up to + *till* till[1]⟩
☛ *Usage.* See note at TILL[1].

un•time•ly [ʌn'taɪmli] *adj., adv. —adj.* **1** coming or happening at a wrong time or season: *an untimely snowstorm.* **2** coming or happening too early or too soon: *an untimely death.*
—adv. **1** too early; too soon: *She died untimely.* **2** at a wrong or inopportune time: *They arrived most untimely.*
—un'time•li•ness, *n.*

un•tir•ing [ʌn'taɪrɪŋ] *adj.* tireless; unwearied. **—un'tir•ing•ly,** *adv.*

un•ti•tled [ʌn'təitəld] *adj.* **1** having no title. **2** not distinguished by a title; not of titled rank: *the gentry and other untitled classes.* **3** lacking lawful right; not entitled (to rule).

un•to ['ʌntu]; *before consonants often,* ['ʌntə] *prep. Archaic or poetic.* **1** to. **2** till; until: *The soldier was faithful unto death.* ⟨ME *unto* < *un-* (see UNTIL) + *to*⟩

un•told [ʌn'tould] *adj.* **1** not told; not revealed. **2** too many or much to be counted; countless; immense: *untold wealth. There are untold stars in the sky.* **3** not permitting of being told; untellable or indescribable: *untold grief. He experienced untold horrors in the concentration camp.*

un•touch•a•ble [ʌn'tʌtʃəbəl] *adj., n. —adj.* **1** that cannot be touched; out of reach. **2** that must not be touched. **3** not vulnerable to criticism; beyond suspicion; unimpeachable. **4** too disgusting to touch. **5** of or being an untouchable or untouchables.
—n. **1** in India, a person of the lowest caste whose touch supposedly defiles members of higher castes. It is now illegal in India to discriminate on the basis of caste. **2** any person rejected by his or her social group; social outcast; pariah.
—ˌun•touch•a'bil•i•ty, *n.*

un•touched [ʌn'tʌtʃt] *adj.* **1** not used, consumed, handled, etc.: *The cat left the milk untouched.* **2** not affected or moved: *The miser was untouched by the poor family's story.* **3** not dealt with: *The last topic was left untouched.*

un•tow•ard [ˌʌntə'wɔrd] *or* [ʌn'tɔrd] *adj.* **1** unfavourable; unfortunate: *an untoward wind, an untoward accident.* **2** perverse; stubborn; willful. **3** improper: *untoward behaviour.* ⟨< *un-*[1] + *toward*⟩ **—ˌun•to'ward•ly,** *adv.* **—ˌun•to'ward•ness,** *n.*

un•tram•melled or **un•tram•meled** [ʌn'træməld] *adj.* not hindered; not restrained; free: *untrammelled passions.*

un•tried [ʌn'traɪd] *adj.* **1** not tried; not tested. **2** not tried in a court of law.

un•true [ʌn'tru] *adj.* **1** false; incorrect. **2** not faithful. **3** not true to a standard or rule. ⟨OE *untrēowe*⟩ **—un'tru•ly,** *adv.*

In each of the words below **un-** *means* not; *the pronunciation of the main part of each word is not changed.*

un'stuffed
un'styl•ish
ˌun•sub'dued
ˌun•sub'mis•sive
un'sub•si,dized
ˌun•sub'stan•ti,at•ed
un'sub•tle
ˌun•sug'ges•tive
un'sul•lied
un'sunk
un'sup•er,vised
ˌun•sup'port•a•ble
ˌun•sup'port•ed
ˌun•sup'pressed
un'sure
ˌun•sur'mount•a•ble
ˌun•sur'pass•a•ble
ˌun•sur'passed
ˌun•sur'prised
ˌun•sus'cep•ti•ble
ˌun•sus'pect•ing
ˌun•sus'pi•cious
ˌun•sus'tained
un'swayed
un'sweet•ened
un'swept
un'swerv•ing
un'sworn
ˌun•sym'met•ri•cal
ˌun•sym•pa'thet•ic
ˌun•sym•pa'thet•i•cal•ly
un'sym•pa,thiz•ing
ˌun•sys•tem'at•ic
ˌun•sys•tem'at•i•cal•ly
un'sys•tem•a,tized
un'tab•u,lat•ed
un'tact•ful
un'taint•ed
un'tak•en
un'tal•ent•ed
un'talk•a•tive
un'talked-of
un'tam•a•ble
un'tamed
un'tanned
un'tapped
un'tar•nished
un'tast•ed
un'tax•a•ble
un'taxed
un'teach•a•ble
un'tech•ni•cal
un'tem•pered
un'tempt•ed
un'ten•a•ble
un'ten•ant•ed
un'tend•ed
un'ter•ri,fied
un'test•ed
un'teth•ered
un'thanked
un'thank•ful
un'thatched
un'thawed
ˌun•the'at•ri•cal
un'thought
un'thought•ful
un'thrif•ty
un'til•la•ble
un'tilled
un'tinged
un'tired
un'torn
un'trace•a•ble
un'traced
un'tracked
un'tract•a•ble
ˌun•tra'di•tion•al
un'trained
ˌun•trans'fer•a•ble
ˌun•trans'formed
ˌun•trans'lat•a•ble
un'trans•lat•ed
ˌun•trans'mit•ted
un'trav•elled
ˌun•tra'vers•a•ble
ˌun•tra'versed
un'treat•ed
un'trimmed
un'trod
un'trod•den
un'trou•bled

un•truss [ʌn'trʌs] *v.* unfasten; loose from a truss.

un•truth [ʌn'truθ] *n.* **1** lack of truth; falsity. **2** a lie; falsehood. ⟨OE *untrēowth*⟩

un•truth•ful [ʌn'truθfəl] *adj.* **1** not truthful; contrary to the truth. **2** given to lying. **—un'truth•ful•ly,** *adv.* **—un'truth•ful•ness,** *n.*

un•tu•tored [ʌn'tjutərd] *or* [ʌn'tutərd] *adj.* **1** untaught. **2** simple; natural.

un•twine [ʌn'twaɪn] *v.* **-twined, -twin•ing.** untwist; unwind.

un•twist [ʌn'twɪst] *v.* **1** undo or loosen (something twisted); unravel. **2** become untwisted.

un•used [ʌn'juzd] *adj.* **1** not in use; not being used: *an unused room.* **2** never having been used: *We'll keep the unused paper cups for our next picnic.*
unused [ʌn'just] **to,** unaccustomed to: *The actor's hands were unused to manual labour.*

un•u•su•al [ʌn'juʒuəl] *adj.* not usual; beyond the ordinary; not common; rare. **—un'u•su•al•ly,** *adv.* **—un'u•su•al•ness,** *n.*

un•ut•ter•a•ble [ʌn'ʌtərəbəl] *adj.* that cannot be expressed; unspeakable. **—un'ut•ter•a•bly,** *adv.*

un•var•nished [ʌn'vɑrnɪʃt] *adj.* **1** not varnished. **2** plain; unadorned: *the unvarnished truth.*

un•veil [ʌn'veil] *v.* **1** remove a veil or cover from: *The statue was unveiled in the town square yesterday.* **2** disclose; reveal: *to unveil a secret.* **3** take off one's veil; reveal oneself: *The princess unveiled.*

un•veiled [ʌn'veild] *v., adj.* *—v.* pt. and pp. of UNVEIL. *—adj.* not wearing or covered by a veil: *In former times, Hindi women were not allowed to appear unveiled in public.*

un•voiced [ʌn'vɔɪst] *adj.* **1** not spoken; not expressed in words. **2** *Phonetics.* **a** voiceless. **b** of a normally voiced sound, devoiced as a form of assimilation, as the *r* in *tray.*

un•war•rant•a•ble [ʌn'wɔrəntəbəl] *adj.* not justifiable; indefensible: *an unwarrantable invasion of privacy, unwarrantable rudeness.* **—un'war•rant•a•bly,** *adv.*

un•war•y [ʌn'wɛri] *adj.* not cautious; not careful; unguarded. **—un'war•i•ly,** *adv.* **—un'war•i•ness,** *n.*

un•wea•ried [ʌn'wirid] *adj.* **1** not weary; not tired. **2** never growing weary.

un•weave [ʌn'wiv] *v.* **-wove, -wo•ven, -weav•ing.** take apart (something woven).

un•wel•come [ʌn'wɛlkəm] *adj.* not welcome; not wanted.

un•well [ʌn'wɛl] *adj.* ailing; ill; sick.

un•wept [ʌn'wɛpt] *adj.* **1** not wept for; not mourned. **2** not shed: *unwept tears.*

un•whole•some [ʌn'houlsəm] *adj.* **1** not wholesome; bad for the body or the mind. **2** unhealthy. **—un'whole•some•ly,** *adv.* **—un'whole•some•ness,** *n.*

un•wield•y [ʌn'wildi] *adj.* not easily handled or managed, because of size, shape, or weight; bulky and clumsy: *the unwieldy armour of knights.* **—un'wield•i•ness,** *n.*

un•will•ing [ʌn'wɪlɪŋ] *adj.* **1** not willing; not consenting: *I wanted her to try it, but she was unwilling.* **2** done, said, etc. against one's will: *an unwilling smile, unwilling assistance.* **—un'will•ing•ly,** *adv.* **—un'will•ing•ness,** *n.*

un•wind [ʌn'waɪnd] *v.* **-wound, -wind•ing. 1** wind off; take from a spool, ball, etc. **2 a** uncoil. **b** make (something coiled) less tight: *You should unwind that spring a little or it will snap.* **3** become unwound. **4** disentangle. **5** *Informal.* relax: *I need an hour to unwind when I come home from a meeting.* ⟨OE *unwindan*⟩

un•wise [ʌn'waɪz] *adj.* not wise; not showing good judgment; foolish. ⟨OE *unwīs*⟩ **—un'wise•ly,** *adv.*

un•wit•ting [ʌn'wɪtɪŋ] *adj.* not knowing; unaware; unconscious; unintentional. **—un'wit•ting•ly,** *adv.*

un•won•ted [ʌn'wountɪd] *adj.* **1** not customary; not usual. **2** *Archaic.* not accustomed; not used (*to*). **—un'wont•ed•ly,** *adv.* **—un'wont•ed•ness,** *n.*

un•world•ly [ʌn'wɜrldli] *adj.* **1** not caring much for the things of this world, such as money, pleasure, and power. **2** naïve. **3** not of or concerning this world; spiritual. **—un'world•li•ness,** *n.*

un•wor•thy [ʌn'wɜrði] *adj.* **1** not worthy; not deserving: *Such a silly story is unworthy of belief.* **2** not befitting or becoming; below the proper level or standard: *a gift not unworthy of a king.* **3** base; shameful: *unworthy conduct.* **4** lacking value or merit; worthless. **—un'wor•thi•ness,** *n.* **—un'wor•thi•ly,** *adv.*

un•wound [ʌn'waʊnd] *v.* pt. and pp. of UNWIND.

un•wove [ʌn'wouv] *v.* pt. of UNWEAVE.

un•wo•ven [ʌn'wouvən] *v., adj.* *—v.* pp. of UNWEAVE. *—adj.* not woven: *Felt is an example of unwoven fabric.*

un•wrap [ʌn'ræp] *v.* **-wrapped, -wrap•ping. 1** remove a wrapping from; open. **2** become opened.

un•writ•ten [ʌn'rɪtən] *adj.* **1** not written. **2** understood or customary, but not actually expressed in writing: *unwritten laws, an unwritten contract.* **3** not written on; blank: *an unwritten page.*

unwritten law 1 COMMON LAW. **2** a practice or rule established by general usage. **3** a principle or tradition that a person who commits a crime to avenge personal or family honour is entitled to lenient treatment.

un•yield•ing [ʌn'jildɪŋ] *adj.* **1** hard; resistant to the touch: *an unyielding mattress.* **2** firm; not giving in: *an unyielding determination.*

un•yoke [ʌn'jouk] *v.* **-yoked, -yok•ing. 1** make or become free from a yoke; separate; disconnect. **2** set free from oppression.

un•zip [ʌn'zɪp] *v.* **-zipped, -zip•ping. 1** open the zipper of: *Could you please unzip the back of my dress?* **2** of a zipper, come open: *This zipper unzips at the least strain.*

up [ʌp] *adv., prep., adj., n., v.* **upped, up•ping.** *—adv.* **1** from a lower to a higher place, rank, condition, etc.; to, toward, or near the top: *The bird flew up. She was moved up to a full directorship.* **2** in a higher place or condition; on or at a higher level: *He stayed up in the mountains several days.* **3** from a smaller to a larger amount or degree: *Prices have gone up.* **4** to or at any point, place, or condition that is considered higher: *from childhood up. He lives up north.* **5** above the horizon: *The sun is up.* **6** in or into an erect position: *Stand up.* **7** out of bed: *I usually get up at about seven o'clock.* **8** thoroughly; completely; entirely: *The paper burned up in a few minutes. My eraser is almost used up.* **9** at an end; over: *His time is up now.* **10** in or into being or action: *Don't stir up trouble.* **11** together: *Add these up.* **12** to or in an even position; not behind: *to catch up in a race, to keep up with the times.* **13** in or into view, notice, or

---

In each of the words below **un-** *means* not; *the pronunciation of the main part of each word is not changed.*

un'trust,wor•thy	**un'var•ied**	**un'want•ed**	**un'wea•ry**	**un'wit•nessed**
un'tuft•ed	**un'var•y•ing**	**un'war,like**	**un'wea•ry•ing**	**un'wom•an•ly**
un'tun•a•ble	**un'ven•ti,lat•ed**	**un'warmed**	**un'weath•ered**	**un'won**
un'tuned	**un'ver•i,fi•a•ble**	**un'warned**	**un'wed**	**un'wood•ed**
un'tune•ful	**un'ver•i,fied**	**un'warped**	**un'wed•ded**	**un'wooed**
un'turned	**un'versed**	**un'war•rant•ed**	**un'weed•ed**	**un'work•a•ble**
un'typ•i•cal	**un'vexed**	**un'washed**	**un'weighed**	**un'worked**
un'us•a•ble	**un'vi•a•ble**	**un'wast•ed**	**un'weld•ed**	**un'work•man,like**
un'ut•i,liz•a•ble	**un'vi•o,lat•ed**	**un'watched**	**un'wife•ly**	**un'worn**
un'u•ti,lized	**un'vis•it•ed**	**un'wa•tered**	**un'willed**	**un'wor•ried**
un'ut•tered	**un'vit•ri,fied**	**un'wa•ver•ing**	**un'wink•ing**	**un'wor•shipped**
un'vac•ci,nat•ed	**un'voc•al,ized**	**un'waxed**	**un'wish**	**un'wound•ed**
un'val•ued	**un'wak•ened**	**un'weaned**	**un'wished**	**un'wrin•kle**
un'van•quished	**un'walled**	**un'wear•a•ble**	**un'with•ered**	**un'wrought**

consideration: *to bring up a new topic.* **14** in or into a state of tightness, compactness, etc.: *Shut him up in his cage.* **15** into safekeeping, storage, etc.; aside; by: *to store up supplies.* **16** *Baseball.* to or at bat. **17** of a score in tennis, etc., for each side: *The score is now 30 up.* **18** *Sports.* ahead of a competitor with regard to the number of points, goals, etc.: *At the moment, Price is three up on his nearest opponent.* **19** *Computer technology.* into an operational state: *After the power failure, the computer operator brought the system up again.* **20 up** is also: **a** used with verbs as an intensive: *dress up, tidy up.* **b** added to many verbs as a meaningless element: *light up a cigarette, phone up a friend.*
it's all up with, there's no further hope for.
up against, *Informal.* facing (something) as a thing to be dealt with.
up against it, *Informal.* in difficulties.
up and around or **about,** active as usual, especially after an illness, injury, etc.
up and doing, busy; active.
up and down, here and there; at various points; in many or different places throughout an area, etc.: *She travelled up and down without finding a place to settle.*
up for, a in contention as a candidate or applicant for: *She is up for election to the committee.* **b** before the court on trial for (some charge). **c** in the mood for; expecting to take part in: *Are you up for a game of euchre? Are the Singhs still up for the do on Friday night?*
up on, well informed about: *We are up on the latest methods.*
up to, a occupied with; doing, scheming, planning, etc.: *She is up to some mischief.* **b** equal to; capable of doing: *Do you feel up to going out so soon after being sick?* **c** incumbent on, as a duty or task: *It's up to the judge to decide.* **d** as many as: *You can reuse it up to five times.* **e** as far as: *up to now.* **f** dependent on the free choice or will of: *The format and topic of the oral presentation are up to you.*
up to the ears, eyes, or **neck in,** *Informal.* thoroughly embroiled in (trouble, work, debt, etc.).
what's up? *Informal.* **a** what's going on? **b** what's the matter?
–prep. **1** along or through from the bottom to or toward the top of: *The cat ran up the tree. We walked up the hill. The smoke went up the chimney.* **2** along, especially in a northerly direction: *She walked up the street.* **3** toward the upper end or part of, especially toward the source of (a river): *They sailed up the St. Lawrence from Québec City to Montréal.* **4** at or in a higher part of: *There is soot up the chimney. They live further up the river.*
up and down, everywhere in; from one extremity to the other of: *up and down the country.*
–adj. **1** moving upward; directed upward: *an up trend.* **2** *Computer technology.* operational; in service: *Because the Convict Information System was still up at midnight, the suspect's criminal record could be checked.*
–n. **1** an upward movement, course, or slope. **2** *Informal.* a period of good luck, prosperity, or happiness: *Her life is full of ups and downs.*
on the up and up, a *Informal.* increasing; rising; improving. **b** *Slang.* honest; legitimate.
–v. **1** *Informal.* put, lift, or get up. **2** *Informal.* increase: *They upped the price of eggs.*
up and, suddenly and inexplicably: *He up and left.* ⟨OE *upp(e)*⟩

up– *prefix.* up, as in *upcountry, upgrade, upkeep, uplift, upbringing.* ⟨OE *up-*. Related to UP.⟩

up–and–com•ing ['ʌp ən 'kʌmɪŋ] *adj. Informal.* promising; enterprising; on the way to importance and success: *an up-and-coming actor.*

up–and–down ['ʌp ən 'daʊn] *adj.* **1** characterized by alternate upward and downward motion; rising and falling; fluctuating: *up-and-down sales activity.* **2** vertical; perpendicular. **3** variable: *an up-and-down existence.*

U•pan•i•shad [u'pɑnə,ʃɑd] *or* [u'pænə,ʃæd] *n. Hinduism.* any of a group of philosophical treatises in ancient Sanskrit, including those of the Vedanta. ⟨< Skt.⟩

u•pas ['jupəs] *n.* **1** a tall, SE Asian tree (*Antiaris toxicaria*) of the mulberry family, having whitish bark and a poisonous, milky sap. **2** the sap of this tree, used as poison for arrows. ⟨< Malay *upas* poison⟩

up•beat ['ʌp,bit] *n., adj. –n.* **1** *Music.* an unaccented beat; the beat on which the conductor's hand goes up. **2** revival; upswing.
–adj. **1** *Informal.* rising; hopeful; buoyant: *an upbeat market opening.* **2** *Informal.* cheerful; light; positive: *upbeat music, an upbeat atmosphere.*

up•borne [ʌp'bɔrn] *adj.* borne up; raised aloft; supported.

up•bound ['ʌp,baʊnd] *adj. or adv.* heading in an upward direction.

up•bow ['ʌp,bou] *n.* on the violin, cello, etc., a stroke in which the bow is moved upward, or from tip to frog, across the strings.

up•braid [ʌp'breid] *v.* find fault with; blame; reprove: *The captain upbraided his crew for falling asleep.* ⟨OE *ūpbregdan* < *upp* up + *bregdan* weave, snatch, move suddenly⟩ **–up'braid•er,** *n.*
☛ *Syn.* See note at SCOLD.

up•braid•ing [ʌp'breidɪŋ] *n., v. –n.* a severe reproof; scolding.
–v. ppr. of UPBRAID.

up•bring•ing ['ʌp,brɪŋɪŋ] *n.* the care and training given to a child while growing up; especially, a particular way of training or educating a child: *a very casual upbringing, a Catholic upbringing.*

up•build [ʌp'bɪld] *v.* **-built, -build•ing.** build up; edify; strengthen.

UPC UNIVERSAL PRODUCT CODE.

up•cast ['ʌp,kæst] *n., adj., v.* **-cast, -cast•ing.** *–n.* **1** something thrown or cast up, as when digging earth. **2** the act of casting upward. **3** a ventilating shaft for the upward passage of air, as from a mine. **4** *Geology.* the upwardly displaced portion of strata in a fault.
–adj. thrown or directed upward: *upcast eyes.*
–v. throw upward.

up•chuck ['ʌp,tʃʌk] *v. Informal.* vomit; throw up: *The smell of that rotting garbage is enough to make you upchuck.*

up•com•ing ['ʌp,kʌmɪŋ] *adj.* forthcoming; approaching.

up•coun•try *n.* ['ʌp,kʌntri]; *adv., adj.* ['ʌp'kʌntri]; *n., adv., adj.*
–n. the interior of a country.
–adv. toward or in the interior of a country: *They live upcountry.*
–adj. remote from the coast or border; interior: *an upcountry settlement.*

up•date *v.* [ʌp'deit] *or* ['ʌp,deit]; *n.* ['ʌp,deit] *v.* **-dat•ed, -dat•ing;** *n. –v.* bring up to date: *to update one's wardrobe. The files are updated once a month.*
–n. **1** the act or an instance of updating: *to perform a monthly update.* **2** an updated version, as of accounts, a report, etc.: *a news update.*

up•draft ['ʌp,dræft] *n.* an upward movement of gas, air, etc. Also, **updraught.**

up•end [ʌp'ɛnd] *v.* **1** set on end; stand on end. **2** topple.

up•fold ['ʌp,fould] *n. Geology.* an upward fold; anticline.

up front **1** in or to the front. **2** in or into a prominent position or role. **3** forthright(ly); candid(ly). **4** of payment, on the spot; immediately or in advance, often in anticipation of being reimbursed later on: *My insurance will cover it, but I have to pay the bill up front.* **–'up-'front,** *adj.*

up•grade *n., adv., adj.* ['ʌp,greid]; *v.* [ʌp'greid] *n., adv., adj., v.* **-grad•ed, -grad•ing.** *–n.* **1** an upward slope or incline. **2** something upgraded; a result of upgrading. **3** *Computer technology.* a component which can be installed in a computer system, as an addition or replacement, to upgrade it.
on the upgrade, rising; improving.
–adv. or adj. uphill.
–v. **1** improve the grade, quality, or level of: *to upgrade livestock by selective breeding.* **2** promote to a higher position with a higher salary: *The company has set up a training program to upgrade its secretaries.* **3** *Computer technology.* improve the performance of (a computer) by adding updated or more powerful components; bring to a more advanced state of technology.

up•grad•ing ['ʌp,greidɪŋ] *n., v. –n.* a program for improvement in standing or qualifications: *He took high school upgrading before entering university.*
–v. ppr. of UPGRADE.

up•growth ['ʌp,grouθ] *n.* **1** the process of growing up; rise, increase, or development. **2** something that grows up.

up•heav•al [ʌp'hivəl] *n.* **1** the action or an instance of heaving or lifting up, especially of part of the earth's crust: *Geologists say that the Rocky Mountains were formed by an upheaval of the earth's crust.* **2** a sudden or violent agitation in affairs; social or emotional turmoil: *The sale of the family business caused a great upheaval.*

up•heave [ʌp'hiv] *v.* **-heaved** or **-hove, -heav•ing.** **1** heave up; lift up. **2** rise as a result of force exerted from below.

up•held [ʌp'hɛld] *v.* pt. and pp. of UPHOLD.

up•hill ['ʌp'hɪl] *adj., adv., n. –adj.* **1** sloping or going up: *It is an uphill road all the way.* **2** difficult: *an uphill fight.* **3** situated on higher ground: *Our uphill neighbours have a sea view.*

—adv. up the slope of a hill; upward: *We had to walk uphill for a kilometre.*
—n. a slope: *I could ride my bike OK on the flat, but on the uphills I had to get off and walk.*

up•hold [ʌp'hould] *v.* **-held, -hold•ing. 1** give moral support or encouragement to; affirm: *The children's courage and good spirits upheld their mother through her time of crisis.* **2** hold up; defend; promote; maintain: *We uphold the good name of our school.* **3** approve; confirm; endorse: *The principal upheld the teacher's decision.* **—up'hold•er,** *n.*
☛ *Syn.* See note at SUPPORT.

up•hol•ster [ʌp'houlstər] *v.* provide (furniture) with cushions, springs, padding, etc. and a covering of cloth, leather, vinyl, etc. ⟨back formation < *upholsterer*, ult. < obs. *uphold* keep in repair⟩

up•hol•ster•er [ʌp'houlstərər] *n.* a person whose business is upholstering furniture.

up•hol•ster•y [ʌp'houlstəri] *n., pl.* **-ster•ies. 1** the padding, covering, springs, etc. of an upholstered piece of furniture. **2** the business or craft of upholstering.

up•hove [ʌp'houv] *v.* a pt. and a pp. of UPHEAVE.

UPI United Press International.

up•keep ['ʌp,kip] *n.* **1** the act of maintaining or the state of being maintained in (a given) condition. **2** the cost of maintaining in good condition: *What's the upkeep on your car?*

up•land ['ʌplənd] *or* ['ʌp,lænd] *n.* **1** high land. **2** (*adjl.*) of or found in high land: *an upland meadow, upland flowers.*

upland plover a sandpiper of Canada and the northern U.S. (*Bartramia longicauda*) found in open, grassy uplands, having streaked, buff-coloured plumage, a long neck, and a small head with a straight, somewhat short bill. Also called **upland sandpiper.**

up•lift *v.* [ʌp'lɪft]; *n.* ['ʌp,lɪft] *v., n. —v.* **1** lift up; raise; elevate; especially, cause (a part of the earth's crust) to be raised. **2** improve mentally, spiritually, or morally: *He had been greatly uplifted by his friends' cheerful optimism.*
—n. **1** the act, process, or result of lifting up or of uplifting: *Good music gives her an uplift when she is discouraged.* **2** a special brassiere designed to lift the bosom upward.
—up'lift•er, *n.* **—up'lift•ment,** *n.*

up•link ['ʌp,lɪŋk] *n.* **1** the sending of communication from an earth station to a space station or satellite. **2** the earth station used to send such communication.

up•load ['ʌp,loud] *v., n. Computer technology.* transfer (files, programs, etc.) from a smaller or remote computer to a larger or central computer via a telecommunications link: *The retail outlet's daily sales data were uploaded to the head office's computer in Winnipeg.*
—n. the act or an instance of uploading: *The upload was successful.* Compare DOWNLOAD.

up•most ['ʌpmoust] *adj.* uppermost.

up•on [ə'pɒn] *prep. Formal or poetic.* on. ⟨ME *upon* < *up* + *on*⟩

up•per ['ʌpər] *adj., n. —adj.* **1** higher in position, rank, degree, etc., especially of a set of two similar things: *the upper lip, the upper floor, the upper range of a singer's voice, the upper house of a parliament.* **2 Upper,** *Geology and archaeology.* of or designating a recent or late division or part of a specified period, epoch, system, or formation: *Upper Cambrian.* **3** farther upstream or inland: *the upper St. Lawrence, Upper Canada.* **4** farther north. **5** of clothing, etc., covering the torso above the waist.
—n. **1** the part of a shoe or boot above the sole. **2** an upper berth or bunk: *I had the upper, and my brother had the lower.* **3** an upper tooth or denture: *Her new uppers are much more comfortable than the old ones were.* **4** *Slang.* any drug that acts as a stimulant.
on (one's) **uppers,** in financial difficulty; having very little or no money left: *He was obviously on his uppers but refused to accept charity.*

Upper Canada *Cdn.* **1** *Esp. Maritimes.* the province of Ontario. **2** until 1841, the official name of the region west of the Ottawa River and north of Lakes Ontario and Erie, now included in the province of Ontario. In 1841 Upper and Lower Canada were united in the Province of Canada. Upper Canada was so named because it lay farther up the St. Lawrence than Lower Canada. *Abbrev.*: U.C.

Upper Canadian *Cdn.* of Upper Canada.

upper case capital letters. *Abbrev.*: u.c.

up•per–case ['ʌpər ,keis] *adj., v.* **-cased, -cas•ing,** *—adj.* capital; printed in capital letters.
—v. write or print in, or change to, capital letters.

Upper Chamber or **upper chamber** UPPER HOUSE.

upper class the social class that has the greatest prestige or power in a society, usually because of wealth, birth, or education.

up•per–class ['ʌpər 'klæs] *adj.* **1** of, having to do with, or suitable for the upper class of society: *upper-class tastes.* **2** in universities, schools, etc., of or having to do with the senior classes.

up•per•class•man ['ʌpər'klæsmən] *n., pl.* **-men.** a senior student.

upper crust *Informal.* the upper classes.

up•per•cut ['ʌpər,kʌt] *n., v.* **-cut, -cut•ting.** *—n. Boxing.* a short swinging blow directed upward and toward the chin.
—v. strike with an uppercut.

upper hand a position of control; mastery or advantage: *During the first two periods, the visiting team had the upper hand.*

Upper House or **upper house** in a legislature having two branches, the branch that has the smaller number of members and is less representative. In some countries, the members of the Upper House are elected, as in the United States; in others they are appointed, as in Canada. The Senate is the Upper House of the Canadian Parliament.

Upper Lakes the most northerly of the Great Lakes; Lakes Superior and Huron and, sometimes, Lake Michigan.

up•per•most ['ʌpər,moust] *adj., adv. —adj.* **1** highest; topmost: *the uppermost branches of a tree.* **2** having the most force or influence; most prominent.
—adv. **1** in or into the highest place: *The watch lay with the back turned uppermost.* **2** in or into the first or most prominent position.

up•pish ['ʌpɪʃ] *adj. Esp. Brit. Informal.* uppity. ⟨< *up*, adv.⟩ **—'up•pish•ly,** *adv.* **—'up•pish•ness,** *n.*

up•pi•ty ['ʌpəti] *adj. Informal.* inclined to put on airs; arrogant or conceited. **—'up•pi•ti•ness,** *n.*

up•raise [ʌp'reiz] *v.* **-raised, -rais•ing.** raise or lift up.

up•rate [ʌp'reit] *v.* **up•rat•ed, up•rat•ing.** raise to a higher level of rank, speed, etc.; upgrade.

up•rear [ʌp'rir] *v.* **1** lift up; raise. **2** rear, as a horse.

up•right *adj., adv.* ['ʌprəit] *or* [ʌp'rəit]; *n.* ['ʌp,rəit] *adj., adv., n. —adj.* **1** standing up straight; erect. **2** good; honest; righteous.
—adv. straight up; in or into a vertical position.
—n. **1** something standing erect; a vertical part or piece: *The boards for the fence were nailed across the uprights.* **2** UPRIGHT PIANO.
on the upright, in a vertical or upright position. ⟨OE *upriht*⟩
—'up,right•ly, *adv.* **—'up,right•ness,** *n.*
☛ *Syn. adj.* **1. Upright,** ERECT = straight up. **Upright** literally means 'straight up', standing up straight on a base or in a base or in a position that is straight up and down, not slanting: *After the earthquake not a lamp or chair was upright.* **Erect,** describing the body, a thing, etc. means 'held or set upright', not stooping or bent: *At seventy she still walks erect.*

upright piano a piano with a vertical frame and strings. Compare GRAND PIANO.

up•rise *v.* [ʌp'raɪz]; *n.* [ʌp,raɪz] *v.* **-rose, -ris•en, -ris•ing;** *n. —v.* **1** rise up; be or become upright. **2** slope upward. **3** increase in volume, amount, etc. **4** rise in rebellion.
—n. **1** a rising up. **2** an upward rise.

up•ris•en [ʌp'rɪzən] *v.* pp. of UPRISE.

up•ris•ing ['ʌp,raɪzɪŋ] *or* [ʌp'raɪzɪŋ] *n., v. —n.* **1** a revolt; rebellion: *The revolution began with small uprisings in several towns.* **2** *Archaic.* an upward slope; ascent.
—v. ppr. of UPRISE.

up•riv•er ['ʌp'rɪvər] *adj., adv. —adj.* **1** belonging to or situated farther up, or toward the upper end of, a river. **2** leading or directed toward the source of a river.
—adv. toward or in the direction of the source of a river.

up•roar ['ʌp,rɔr] *n.* **1** a noisy or violent disturbance; tumult; commotion: *We heard an uproar in the hall and went to see what it was. There was a great uproar when the theft was discovered.* **2** a loud or confused noise; din. ⟨< Du. *oproer* insurrection, tumult; influenced by association with *roar*⟩
☛ *Syn.* See note at NOISE.

up•roar•i•ous [ʌp'rɔriəs] *adj.* **1** marked by uproar; noisy and confused: *an uproarious disturbance.* **2** loud and boisterous: *uproarious laughter, in uproarious good spirits.* **3** very funny: *an uproarious comedy, an uproarious scene.* **—up'roar•i•ous•ly,** *adv.* **—up'roar•i•ous•ness,** *n.*

up•root [ʌp'rut] *v.* **1** tear up by the roots: *The storm uprooted two trees. The gardener uprooted the crabgrass.* **2** force away (from a settled position): *Famine uprooted many families from their homes in Ireland during the 1840s.* **3** eradicate or destroy completely: *By these acts, the dictator uprooted the democratic process and the rule of law.* **—up'root•er,** *n.*

up•rose [ʌp'rouz] *v.* pt. of UPRISE.

up•rush ['ʌp,rʌʃ] *n.* **1** an upward rush: *When we drilled for water, there was a sudden uprush when the drill penetrated the rock.* **2** a sudden upturn or increase: *There has been an uprush of registrations lately.*

ups–a–dai•sy ['ʌps ə ,deizi] *interj.* an expression of encouragement used especially to a small child when the child is being lifted or helped up after a fall. Also, **upsy-daisy.**

up•scale *adj.* ['ʌp,skeil]; *v.* [ʌp'skeil] *adj., v.* **-scaled, -scal•ing.** *—adj.* posh; of or for affluent people: *an upscale restaurant, an upscale neighbourhood.*
—v. **1** increase the scale, slope, intensity, etc. of. **2** raise the social status of.

up•set *v., adj.* [ʌp'sɛt]; *n.* ['ʌp,sɛt] *v.* **-set, -set•ting;** *n., adj.* *—v.* **1** tip over; overturning: *to upset a boat.* **2** disturb greatly; disorder physically or emotionally: *Rain upset our plans for a picnic. The shock upset her nerves.* **3** overthrow; defeat: *to upset a will, to upset a regime.*
—n. **1** a tipping over; overturning. **2** a great disturbance; disorder. **3** an overthrowing; an unexpected defeat.
—adj. **1** tipped over; overturned. **2** greatly disturbed; physically or emotionally disordered: *an upset stomach.* **3** conquered; overthrown.
upset price, the lowest price at which a thing offered for sale will be sold.
☛ *Syn. v.* **1. Upset,** OVERTURN = fall, or cause to fall, over or down. **Upset** suggests losing a somewhat precarious balance and tipping over from an upright or proper position as the result of a movement or action by some person or thing: *I accidentally kicked the table and upset the vase of flowers.* **Overturn** suggests turning upside down or, especially, over on one side from an upright position. It also suggests the application of a certain amount of force: *He got up too quickly and overturned his chair.*

up•shot ['ʌp,ʃɒt] *n.* **1** the end result; outcome: *The upshot of all the delays will probably be that we'll have to cancel the program.* **2** the main drift or effect (of a message); significance.

up•side ['ʌp,saɪd] *n.* the upper side.

upside down **1** having or so as to have at the bottom what should be on top. **2** in or into complete disorder: *The room was turned upside down.* ⟨alteration of ME *up so down* up as if down⟩ **—'up,side-'down,** *adj.*

up•side–down cake ['ʌp,saɪd 'daʊn] a cake baked with a layer of fruit on the bottom and served upside down with the fruit on top.

up•si•lon ['ʌpsə,lɒn], ['upsə,lɒn], *or* ['jupsə,lɒn] *n.* the twentieth letter (Υ, υ = English U, u, or Y, y) of the Greek alphabet.

up•stage ['ʌp'steidʒ] *adv., adj., v.* **-staged, -stag•ing.** *—adv.* toward or at the back of the stage of a theatre.
—adj. **1** having to do with the back part of the stage. **2** situated toward or at the back of the stage. **3** haughty; snobbish: *I didn't like his upstage manner.*
upstage of, farther back on the stage than.
—v. **1** force (another actor) to turn away from the audience by moving or staying upstage of him or her. **2** make oneself the centre of attention at the expense of; steal the show from: *She upstaged the hostess by welcoming everyone herself.*

up•stairs ['ʌp'stɛrz] *adv., adj., n.* *—adv.* **1** up the stairs: *I ran upstairs.* **2** on or onto an upper floor: *She lives upstairs. She got upstairs by using a ladder and entering by a second-storey window.*
kick (someone) **upstairs,** get rid of a person by promoting him or her to a higher but ineffectual position.
—adj. on or of an upper floor: *He is waiting in an upstairs hall.*
—n. the upper storey or storeys (*used with a singular verb*): *The upstairs of the house is very small.*

up•stand•ing ['ʌp'stændɪŋ] *adj.* **1** having integrity; honourable: *a fine, upstanding young man.* **2** standing up; erect.

up•start ['ʌp,stɑrt] *n., adj.* *—n.* a person who has suddenly risen from a humble position to wealth, power, or importance, especially one who is unpleasant, conceited, or arrogant.
—adj. suddenly risen from a humble position to wealth, power, or importance, especially when conceited or arrogant. Compare DOWNSTART.

up•stream ['ʌp'strim] *adv. or adj.* in the direction opposite to the current of a stream: *It is hard to swim upstream. They stopped at an upstream camping site.*

up•stretched [ʌp'strɛtʃt] *adj.* especially of the arms, stretched upward.

up•stroke ['ʌp,strouk] *n.* **1** a stroke or movement upward, especially of something that goes up and down repeatedly or rhythmically as a pen, paintbrush, vertical piston, conductor's baton, etc.: *The choir readied themselves on the upstroke.*

up•surge *n.* ['ʌp,sɜrdʒ]; *v.* [ʌp'sɜrdʒ] *n., v.* **-surged, -surg•ing.** *—n.* sudden or rapid rise; a surge of growth, development, emotion, etc.: *an upsurge in prices, an upsurge of feeling.*
—v. surge up; rise rapidly or suddenly.

up•sweep ['ʌp,swip] *n.* **1** a curving or sweeping upward. **2** an upswept hairstyle.

up•swell ['ʌp,swɛl] *n.* an UPWELLING (def. 1) or upsurge.

up•swept ['ʌp,swɛpt] *adj.* **1** curving or sloping upward. **2** of or having to do with a woman's hairstyle in which the hair is brushed upward and piled high on the head.

up•swing *n.* ['ʌp,swɪŋ]; *v.* [ʌp'swɪŋ] *n., v.* **-swung, -swing•ing.** *—n.* **1** a swing or movement upward. **2** a marked improvement; strong advance.
—v. undergo an upswing.

up•sy–dai•sy ['ʌpsi ,deizi] *or* ['ʌpsə ,deizi] *interj.* See UPS-A-DAISY.

up•take ['ʌp,teik] *n.* **1** the act or process of taking or drawing up. **2** a flue or ventilating shaft.
quick (or **slow**) **on the uptake,** quick (or slow) to understand: *He's a very nice fellow, but a little slow on the uptake.*

up–tem•po ['ʌp ,tɛmpou] *adj., adv. Music.* *—adj. or adv.* in or at a fast tempo.

up•throw *n.* ['ʌp,θrou]; *v.* [,ʌp'θrou] *n., v.* **-threw, -thrown, -throw•ing.** *—n.* **1** an upheaval. **2** a casting or throwing upward. **3** *Geology.* upcast; a displacement upward of the rock on one side of a fault.
—v. throw or cast upward.

up•thrust ['ʌp,θrʌst] *n.* **1** an upward push. **2** a movement upward of part of the earth's crust.

up•tight ['ʌp'tɔit] *adj. Informal.* **1** angry and defensive: *Don't get uptight; she didn't mean anything by it.* **2** tense, worried, or anxious: *His mother gets uptight if he's late getting home.* **3** rigid and conformist in attitude; straitlaced: *an uptight approach to new ideas.* **—'up,tight•ness,** *n.*

up•time ['ʌp,taɪm] *n.* the time during which a machine, especially a computer, functions properly and is available for use. Compare DOWNTIME.

up–to–date ['ʌp tə 'deit] *adj.* **1** extending to the present time; including the latest information: *an up-to-date record of sales, an up-to-date map of the city.* **2** keeping up with the times in style, ideas, or methods; modern: *an up-to-date dress shop. He's very up-to-date in his selling methods.* **—'up-to-'date•ness,** *n.*
☛ *Usage.* **Up-to-date** is a compound adjective. Adverbially, the phrase **up to date** is used: *Let me bring you up to date.*

up–to–the–min•ute ['ʌp tə ðə 'mɪnɪt] *adj.* modern; up-to-date; latest.

up•town ['ʌp'taʊn] *adv. or adj., n.* *—adj. or adv.* **1** to or in a main part of a town or city that is away from the main business area, higher, further north, or further from a lake, river, harbour, etc. than other parts: *to go uptown, an uptown store.* **2** in rural areas and small towns, of, to, or in the business district or central area of town.
—n. **1** the better-class neighbourhoods, away from the main business area. **2** the central business area of a small town.

up•turn *v.* [ʌp'tɜrn]; *n.* ['ʌp,tɜrn] *v., n.* *—v.* turn upward or over. *—n.* **1** an upward turn. **2** improvement: *an upturn in business.*

up•turned *adj.* ['ʌp'tɜrnd]; *v.* [ʌp'tɜrnd] *adj., v.* *—adj.* **1** turned upside down; overturned: *He set the upturned chair on its feet.* **2** turned upward: *a mustache with upturned ends. She kissed the child's upturned face.*
—v. pt. and pp. of UPTURN.

UPU Universal Postal Union of the United Nations.

up•ward ['ʌpwərd] *adv., adj.* *—adv.* **1** to or toward a higher place. **2** in the higher or highest position; uppermost: *to store baskets with the bottoms upward.* **3** toward a higher or greater rank, amount, age, etc.: *From public school upward, she studied French.* **4** above; more: *Children of five years and upward must pay bus fare.* **5** to or toward the source (of a river, stream, etc.): *to follow a river upward.*
—adj. directed or moving toward, or situated in, a higher place: *an upward glance.* Also (*adv.*), **upwards.** ⟨OE *upweard*⟩

up•ward•ly ['ʌpwərdli] *adv.* in an upward manner or direction; upward.

upward mobility *Sociology.* movement to a higher socioeconomic status, or opportunity for such movement. **—upwardly mobile.**

up•wards ['ʌpwərdz] *adv.* upward.
upwards of or **upward of,** more than: *Repairs to the car will cost upwards of $800.*

up•well•ing ['ʌp,wɛlɪŋ] *n.* **1** an instance of welling up, as of joy, public opinion, etc. **2** a current of warm water which rises from the depths of the sea to the surface: *An upwelling is rich in nutrients that attract fish.*

up•wind ['ʌp'wɪnd] *adv., adj.* on or toward the side from which the wind is blowing.

ur– or **Ur–** [ʊr-] *prefix.* original or most primitive. ⟨< G⟩

u•ra•cil ['jʊrə,sɪl] *n. Biochemistry.* a pyramidine base, colourless and crystalline, one of the fundamental components of RNA. *Formula*: $C_4H_4N_2O_2$ *Symbol*: U

u•rae•us [jʊ'riəs] *n.* the sacred asp or cobra, symbol of divine power, represented on the royal headdress of the ancient Egyptians. ⟨< NL < LGk. *ouraios* cobra < Egyptian⟩

U•ral–Al•ta•ic ['jʊrəl æl'teiɪk] *or* [ɒl'teiɪk] *adj., n. —adj.* **1** of the region embracing the Ural and Altaic Mountains. **2** of or having to do with a large family of languages spoken in northern Asia and eastern Europe, including the Finno-Ugric, Turkic, Mongolian, and some other languages.
—n. the Ural-Altaic language family.

U•ral•ic [jʊ'rælɪk] *or* [jʊ'reilɪk] *n., adj. —n.* a family of languages comprising the Finno-Ugric and Samoyed sub-families. *—adj.* of or having to do with these languages or their speakers.

U•ra•ni•a [jʊ'reiniə] *n. Greek mythology.* the Muse of astronomy.

u•ran•ic [jʊ'rænɪk] *adj.* of or containing uranium, especially in a high valence.

u•ran•i•nite [jʊ'rænə,nəit] *n.* a blackish green uranium mineral often found in crystal form. When found in veins, it is called **pitchblende.** *Formula*: UO_2

u•ra•ni•um [jʊ'reiniəm] *n.* a heavy, white, radioactive metallic chemical element that occurs in pitchblende and certain other minerals. The uranium isotope, U^{235}, can sustain efficient chain reaction and is for this reason used in nuclear devices. *Symbol*: U; *at.no.* 92; *at.mass* 238.03. ⟨< NL *uranium* < *Uranus*, the planet⟩

u•ran•og•ra•phy [,jʊrə'nɒgrəfi] *n.* celestial cartography. ⟨< Gk. *ouranographia* < *ouranos* heaven + *graphein* to write⟩

u•ran•ous ['jʊrənəs] *adj.* of or containing uranium, especially in a low valence.

U•ra•nus ['jʊrənəs] *or* [ju'reinəs] *n.* **1** *Greek mythology.* the first god of the heavens, original ruler of the world and father of the Titans, the Cyclopes, and the Furies. He was overthrown by his son Cronus. **2** one of the larger planets. It is the seventh in order from the sun.

u•rate ['jʊreit] *n.* a salt of uric acid.

ur•ban ['ɜrbən] *adj.* of, having to do with, or in cities or towns: *an urban district, urban planning, the urban population, urban problems.* ⟨< L *urbanus* < *urbs* city⟩

urban drift the tendency of people to move from rural areas into cities.

ur•bane [ər'bein] *adj.* courteous and refined; smoothly polite; polished. ⟨< L *urbanus*, originally, urban. See URBAN.⟩ **—ur'bane•ly,** *adv.* **—ur'bane•ness,** *n.*

ur•ban•ite ['ɜrbə,nəit] *n.* someone who lives in a city.

ur•ban•i•ty [ər'bænəti] *n., pl.* **-ties. 1** the quality or state of being urbane. **2 urbanities,** *pl.* urbane acts; courteous, polite conduct.

ur•ban•ize ['ɜrbə,naɪz] *v.* **-ized, -iz•ing.** render or become urban: *to urbanize a district or its people.* **—,ur•ban•i'za•tion,** *n.*

urban renewal a program, policy, or the process of rehabilitating or replacing rundown or substandard buildings in a city, as well as upgrading roads, recreation facilities, etc. especially in the downtown core.

urban sprawl the uncontrolled spreading of urban development, in the form of new subdivisions, shopping centres, etc., into rural areas.

ur•ce•o•late ['ɜrsiəlɪt] *or* ['ɜrsiə,leit] *adj. Botany.* shaped like an urn or pitcher. ⟨< NL *urceolatus* < L *urceolus* dim. of *urceus* urn⟩

ur•chin ['ɜrtʃən] *n.* **1** a small child, especially a mischievous one. **2** a poor, ragged child. **3** SEA URCHIN. **4** *Archaic.* hedgehog. **5** *Archaic.* a goblin or elf. ⟨ME < OF *irechon* < L *ericius* an obstacle with spikes < *er* hedgehog⟩

Ur•du ['ʊrdu] *or* ['ɜrdu] *n.* an Indic language closely related to Hindi. Urdu is an official language of Pakistan and is also widely used in India.

–ure *noun-forming suffix.* **1** the act or fact of ——ing: *failure.* **2** the state of being ——ed: *pleasure.* **3** the means or result of ——ing: *enclosure.* **4** the thing that ——s: *legislature.* **5** the thing that is ——ed: *disclosure.* **6** other special meanings: *procedure, sculpture, denture.* ⟨< F *-ure* < L *-ura*⟩

u•re•a [jʊ'riə] *or* ['jʊriə] *n.* a soluble crystalline compound present especially in the urine of mammals. Urea is manufactured synthetically for use in making fertilizers, adhesives, and plastics. *Formula*: $CO(NH_2)_2$ ⟨< NL *urea*, ult. < Gk. *ouron* urine⟩ **—u're•al,** *adj.*

u•re•a–for•mal•de•hyde resin [jʊ'riə fɔr'mældə,haɪd] any of a group of strong, odourless, toxic resins formed by the interaction of urea and formaldehyde in the presence of a catalyst, under conditions including heat and pH control, used in the manufacture of buttons, baking enamel, etc., and as a treatment making fabric resistant to wrinkles. Also, **urea resin.**

u•re•mi•a [jʊ'rimiə] *n. Medicine.* a condition resulting from the accumulation in the blood, due to kidney malfunction, of waste products that should normally be eliminated in the urine. ⟨< NL *uremia* < Gk. *ouron* urine + *haima* blood⟩

u•re•mic [jʊ'rimɪk] *adj.* **1** of or having to do with uremia. **2** suffering from uremia.

u•re•ter [jʊ'ritər] *or* ['jʊrətər] *n.* a duct that carries urine from a kidney to the bladder or the cloaca. See KIDNEY for picture. ⟨< NL < Gk. *ourētēr*, ult. < *ouron* urine⟩ **—u're•ter•al,** *adj.* **—,u•re'ter•ic** [,jʊrə'tɛrɪk], *adj.*

u•re•thane ['jʊrə,θein] *n.* **1** a white, crystalline compound and ethyl derivative used especially in the plastics industry to manufacture polyurethane and in medicine to treat certain forms of leukemia, etc. *Formula*: $C_3H_7NO_2$ **2** polyurethane.

u•re•thra [jʊ'riθrə] *n., pl.* **-thrae** [-θri] *or* [-θraɪ] or **-thras.** in most mammals, the duct by which urine is discharged from the bladder and also, in males, through which semen is discharged. ⟨< LL < Gk. *ourēthra*, ult. < *ouron* urine⟩ **—u're•thral,** *adj.*

u•re•thri•tis [,jʊrə'θraitɪs] *n.* inflammation of the urethra.

u•ret•ic [jʊ'rɛtɪk] *adj.* of, having to do with, or present in the urine.

urge [ɜrdʒ] *v.* **urged, urg•ing;** *n. —v.* **1** push, force, or drive; cause to go faster: *The rider urged his horse on with whip and spurs.* **2** try to persuade with arguments; ask earnestly: *They urged him to stay.* **3** plead or argue earnestly (for); recommend strongly: *Motorists urged better roads.* **4** press upon the attention; refer to often and with emphasis: *to urge a claim, to urge an argument.*
—n. **1** a driving force, impulse, or desire. **2** the act of urging. ⟨< L *urgere*⟩

ur•gen•cy ['ɜrdʒənsi] *n., pl.* **-cies.** the quality or state of being urgent: *They said it was a matter of great urgency. His captors were moved by the urgency of his plea.*

ur•gent ['ɜrdʒənt] *adj.* **1** demanding immediate action or attention; pressing; important: *an urgent need. She said the matter was urgent.* **2** insistent: *an urgent appeal for funds.* ⟨< L *urgens*, *-entis*, ppr. of *urgere* urge⟩ **—'ur•gent•ly,** *adv.*

u•ric ['jʊrɪk] *adj.* of, having to do with, or found in urine.

uric acid a white, odourless, tasteless, crystalline compound only slightly soluble in water, that is found in small quantities in the urine of mammals and in large quantities in the urine of birds and reptiles. *Formula*: $C_5H_4N_4O_3$

u•ri•nal ['jʊrɪnəl] *or* [jʊ'raɪnəl] *n.* **1** an upright plumbing fixture into which to urinate, for use by men and boys. **2** a room or structure containing such fixtures. **3** a container for urine, such as for use by bedridden persons. ⟨< LL *urinal*, ult. < L *urina*⟩

u•ri•nal•y•sis [,jʊrə'næləsɪs] *n., pl.* **-ses** [-,siz]. a chemical analysis of a sample of urine. ⟨alteration of British *uranalysis uro-, ur-* + *analysis*; influenced in spelling by *urine*⟩

u•ri•nar•y ['jʊrə,nɛri] *adj., n., pl.* **-nar•ies.** *—adj.* **1** of, like, or having to do with urine. **2** of or having to do with the organs that secrete and discharge urine: *the urinary tract, a urinary calculus.*
—n. urinal.

urinary bladder *Zoology, Anatomy.* a distendable, membranous sac, used for the temporary storage of urine on its way from the kidneys to the urethra, whence it is discharged from the body.

u•ri•nate ['jʊrə,neit] *v.* **-nat•ed, -nat•ing.** discharge urine from the body. ⟨< Med.L *urinare*⟩ **—,uri'na•tion,** *n.*

u•rine ['jʊrɪn] *n.* waste material that is produced by the kidneys of vertebrates and that forms a clear, usually slightly acid fluid in mammals but is semisolid in birds and reptiles. ⟨< L *urina*⟩ **—'u•ri•nous,** *adj.*

u•ri•no•gen•i•tal [,jʊrənou'dʒɛnətəl] *adj.* See UROGENITAL.

urn [ɜrn] *n.* **1** a vase or similar vessel having a base or pedestal. **2** such a vase used for holding the cremated ashes of the dead. **3** a large coffee percolator or teapot with a tap. **4** *Botany.* the spore-bearing capsule of a moss. Also (def. 2), **funerary urn.** ⟨< L *urna*⟩

☛ *Hom.* EARN, ERNE.

uro– *combining form.* urine; having to do with the urinary tract: *urology = the study of the urinary tract.* Also, before vowels, **ur-.**

u•ro•chord ['jʊrou,kɔrd] *n.* **1** the notochord of a tunicate, especially as confined to the tail region. **2** tunicate. ⟨< Gk. *oura* tail + *chord*[2]⟩ **—,u•ro'chord•al,** *adj.*

u•ro•dele ['jʊrou,dil] *n.* any member of the order Urodela, which includes salamanders and newts. ⟨< Gk. *oura* tail + *delos* visible⟩

u•ro•gen•i•tal [,jʊrou'dʒɛnətəl] *adj.* pertaining to or having to do with the urinary and genital organs. ⟨< Gk. *ouron* urine + E *genital*⟩

u•rog•e•nous [jʊ'rɒdʒənəs] *adj.* **1** producing urine. **2** present in or obtained from urine.

u•ro•lith ['jʊrou,lɪθ] *n.* a calculus occurring in the urinary tract. ⟨< *uro-* + Gk. *lithos* stone⟩

u•rol•o•gist [jʊ'rɒlədʒɪst] *n.* a specialist in urology.

u•rol•o•gy [jʊ'rɒlədʒi] *n.* the branch of medicine concerned with the study of the conditions, diseases, etc. of the urinary tract in the female or of the urogenital tract in the male. ⟨< *uro-* + *-logy*⟩ **—,u•ro'log•i•cal,** *adj.*

u•ro•pyg•i•um [,jʊrou'pɪdʒiəm] *n., pl.* **-i•ums** or **-i•a** [-iə]. the rear portion of a bird's body, bearing the tail feathers and a gland which secretes oil used in preening. ⟨< NL < Gk. *ouropygion*⟩ **—,u•ro'pyg•i•al,** *adj.*

u•ro•sco•py [jʊ'rɒskəpi] *n.* examination of the urine as a way of diagnosing disease. **—,u•ro'scop•ic** [,jʊrə'skɒpɪk], *adj.*

Ur•sa Ma•jor ['ɜrsə 'meidʒər] the most conspicuous northern constellation, situated near the north pole of the heavens and including the stars that form the Big Dipper; the Great Bear. ⟨< L *ursa major* bigger bear⟩

Ur•sa Mi•nor ['ɜrsə 'maɪnər] the northern constellation that includes the north pole of the heavens and the stars that form the Little Dipper; the Little Bear. ⟨< L *ursa minor* smaller bear⟩

ur•si•form ['ɜrsɪ,fɔrm] *adj.* having the appearance of a bear; bear-shaped. ⟨< L *ursus* bear + E *-form*⟩

ur•sine ['ɜrsaɪn] *or* ['ɜrsən] *adj.* of, having to do with, or resembling a bear or the bear family; bearlike. ⟨< L *ursinus* < *ursus* bear⟩

Ur•su•line ['ɜrsəlɪn] *or* ['ɜrsjəlɪn], ['ɜrsə,laɪn] *or* ['ɜrsjə,laɪn] *n., adj. —n.* a member of a Roman Catholic order of nuns founded in 1535 in Brescia, Italy, for the education of girls and for the care of the sick and needy.
—adj. of or having to do with Saint Ursula, a British martyr of the 4th or 5th century, or the Ursulines.

ur•ti•car•i•a [,ɜrtə'kɛriə] *n.* hives. ⟨< NL < L *urtica* nettle⟩ **—,ur•ti'car•i•al,** *adj.*

U•ru•guay ['jʊrə,gwaɪ] *n.* a country in SE South America.

U•ru•guay•an [,jʊrə'gwaɪən] *or* [,jʊrə'gweiən] *n., adj. —n.* a native or inhabitant of Uruguay.
—adj. of or having to do with Uruguay or its people.

u•rus ['jʊrəs] *n.* AUROCHS (def. 1). ⟨< L < Gmc.⟩

us [ʌs]; *unstressed,* [əs] *pron.* **1** the objective form of **we:** *Mom went with us.* **2** *Informal.* we: *It's us against them.* ⟨OE *ūs*⟩

U.S. United States (of America).

USA or **U.S.A.** United States of America.

us•a•bil•i•ty [,juzə'bɪləti] *n.* the quality or state of being usable.

us•a•ble ['juzəbəl] *adj.* that can be used; fit for use. Also, **useable. —'us•a•ble•ness,** *n.* **—'us•a•bly,** *adv.*

us•age ['jusɪdʒ] *or* ['juzɪdʒ] *n.* **1** a way or manner of using; treatment: *The car has had rough usage.* **2** a long-continued practice; customary use; habit; custom: *Travellers should learn many of the usages of the countries they visit.* **3** the customary way of using words: *In Shakespeare's time "most unkindest" was accepted usage.* ⟨ME < OF *usage* < *us,* n., use < L *usus*⟩

us•ance ['juzəns] *n.* **1** *Business.* the time allowed for payment of foreign bills of exchange. **2** the income or benefits of every kind derived from the ownership of wealth; unearned income. ⟨ME < OF *usance* < *user.* See USE.⟩

use *v.* [juz]; *n.* [jus] *v.* **used, us•ing;** *n. —v.* **1** put into action or service; avail oneself of for a particular purpose: *We use our legs in walking. He used a knife to cut the meat. May I use your telephone?* **2** employ or practise actively; exercise, especially habitually or customarily: *to use one's knowledge, authority, or judgment, to use bad language.* **3** partake of, especially habitually: *to use drugs or alcohol. He does not use tobacco.* **4** consume or expend by using: *We have used most of the money. The car uses too much gas.* **5** act toward; treat: *They use their furniture very hard.* **6** act toward (a person or persons) in a particular way for one's own ends; exploit: *She uses people.*
used [just] *or* [jus] **to, a** accustomed to: *She is used to hardships.* **b** had as one's practice, custom, or state in the past: *They used to come by here every day. We used to sit and talk for hours.*
use up, a consume or expend entirely. **b** *Informal.* tire out; weary; exhaust.
—n. **1** the act or an instance of using: *the use of tools, good for up to four uses.* **2** the state of being used: *methods long out of use. Our telephone is in constant use.* **3** employment or usage resulting in or causing wear, damage, etc. **4** usefulness; benefit: *a thing of no practical use. There's no use trying to tell him, he won't do it anyway.* **5** the purpose that a thing is used for; function; service: *to find a new use for something.* **6** a way of using: *a poor use of materials.* **7** the fact or quality of serving the needs or ends (of a person or persons): *a park for the use of all the people.* **8** a need or occasion to use: *She had no further use for it.* **9** the power, right, or privilege of using: *to have the use of a boat for the summer. She has lost the use of her right arm.* **10** a custom; habit; usage: *It was his use to rise early.* **11** *Law.* **a** the act or fact of employing, occupying, possessing, or holding property so as to derive benefit from it. **b** the right of a beneficiary to the benefit or profits of land or tenements held in trust for him or her by another. **c** a trust giving someone title to real property for the benefit of a beneficiary.
have no use for, a not need or want. **b** *Informal.* dislike; be impatient with: *I have no use for people who expect you to guess their thoughts.*
make use of, use; employ: *Can you make use of these old curtains?*
put to use, make use of; utilize; use. ⟨ME < OF *us,* n., *user,* v., < L *usus,* pp. of *uti* to use⟩

☛ *Syn. v.* **1. Use,** EMPLOY, UTILIZE = put into action or service. **Use,** the general and common word, emphasizes putting something or someone into service as a means or help in carrying out a purpose or getting what one wants: *He uses a typewriter for his homework.* **Employ,** more formal, often interchangeable with **use,** emphasizes putting to work for a special purpose or in a profitable way: *That architect frequently employs glass brick.* **Utilize** emphasizes making useful or turning to profitable use: *She utilizes every scrap of food.*

use•a•ble [,juzəbəl] See USABLE.

used [juzd] *adj., v. —adj.* **1** not new; that has belonged to another or others: *a used car.* **2** of a single-use item, spent or soiled by use: *Throw the used paper cups in this bag.*
—v. pt. and pp. of USE.

use•ful ['jusfəl] *adj.* of use; giving service; helpful; effective. **—'use•ful•ly,** *adv.* **—'use•ful•ness,** *n.*

use•less ['juslɪs] *adj.* **1** having no use or being of no use: *She is completely useless in the kitchen. That walkie-talkie is useless for any distance over a kilometre.* **2** futile; ineffective; pointless: *It was useless to complain.* **—'use•less•ly,** *adv.* **—'use•less•ness,** *n.*

us•er ['juzər] *n.* a person or thing that uses: *users of a delivery service, a drug user, a computer user.*

u•ser–friend•ly ['juzər 'frɛndli] *adj. Computer technology.* of a computer or computer program, easy to understand and use; not confusing.

U–shaped ['ju ,ʃeipt] *adj.* having the shape of the letter U: *a U-shaped kitchen counter.*

U•shas ['uʃɑs] the Hindu goddess of the dawn. ⟨< Skt. *Usas* dawn⟩

ush•er ['ʌʃər] *n., v. —n.* **1** a person who shows people to their seats in a church, theatre, etc. **2** a person who has charge of the

door of a court, hall, or chamber. **3** a groom's attendant in a wedding party, especially one who is not the best man. **4** an officer whose duty is to walk before a person of rank: *gentleman usher of the Black Rod.*
—v. **1** act as usher to; conduct; escort: *The patrons were ushered to their seats.* **2** go or come before; introduce or inaugurate (*used with* **in**): *to usher in a new age. Fall was ushered in by a week of cold rains.* ⟨ME < AF *usser*, OF *uissier* < VL *ustiarius* doorkeeper < *ustium*, var. of L *ostium* door⟩

USSR or **U.S.S.R.** Union of Soviet Socialist Republics, the name of the former country which consisted of a union of fifteen E European and N Asian republics, including Russia.

u•su•al ['juʒuəl] *adj.* **1** commonly done, used, occurring, etc.; ordinary or customary: *She didn't take her usual route home last night. It's the usual thing to tip a waiter in a restaurant.* **2** (*noml.*) **the usual,** something that is customarily done, used, etc.: *She sat down at our table and ordered the usual.*
as usual, in the usual manner. ⟨ME < LL *usualis* < L *usus* use, custom < *uti* to use⟩ **—'u•su•al•ly,** *adv.* **—'u•su•al•ness,** *n.*
☛ *Syn.* **1. Usual,** CUSTOMARY = often or commonly seen or found, especially in a certain place or at a given time. **Usual** emphasizes the familiar nature or quality of what is described, and applies to something that is in common use or that commonly or ordinarily happens or occurs: *This is the usual weather at this time of the year.* **Customary** describes something that is according to the usual practices or habits of a particular person or group: *He stayed up long past his customary bedtime.*

u•su•fruct ['juzjə,frʌkt] *or* ['jusjə,frʌkt] *n., adj. —n. Law.* the right of using another's property without injuring or destroying it.
—adj. held in usufruct. ⟨< L *usufructu*, abl. of *ususfructus*, earlier *usus (et) fructus* use and enjoyment⟩

u•su•fruc•tu•a•ry [,juzjə'frʌktʃu,ɛri] *n., adj. —n.* an agent or other person having usufruct property.
—adj. of or of the nature of usufruct property.

u•su•rer ['juʒərər] *n.* **1** a person who lends money at an extremely high or unlawful rate of interest. **2** *Archaic.* any moneylender. ⟨ME < AF *usurer*, var. of OF *usurier* < LL *usurarius* moneylender < L *usurarius* at interest, for use < *usura* use < *uti* use⟩

u•su•ri•ous [ju'ʒʊriəs] *adj.* **1** taking extremely high or unlawful interest for the use of money; practising usury. **2** of, having to do with, or involving usury: *Fifty percent is a usurious rate of interest.* **—u'su•ri•ous•ly,** *adv.* **—u'su•ri•ous•ness,** *n.*

u•surp [ju'sɜrp] *or* [ju'zɜrp] *v.* **1** seize and hold (power, position, authority, etc.) by force or without right: *The king's brother tried to usurp the throne.* **2** infringe or encroach (*on*). ⟨< L *usurpare*, ult. < *usu*, abl., through use + *rapere* seize⟩ **—u'surp•er,** *n.*

u•sur•pa•tion [,jusər'peiʃən] *or* [,juzər'peiʃən] *n.* the act of usurping: *the usurpation of the throne by a pretender.*

u•su•ry ['juʒəri] *n., pl.* **-ries. 1** the lending of money at an extremely high or unlawful rate of interest. **2** an extremely high or unlawful rate or amount of interest. **3** *Archaic.* the lending of money with an interest charge. ⟨ME < Med.L *usuria*, alteration of L *usura.* See USURER.⟩

ut [ut] *or* [ʌt] *n. Music.* formerly, the name of the first note of a scale, and sometimes of the note C, now generally superseded by DO².

UT UNIVERSAL TIME.

U•tah ['jutɑ] *n.* a southwestern state of the United States.

u•tah•rap•tor ['jutɑ,ræptər] *n.* a dinosaur which ran on two legs, each having a large claw, related to birds rather than reptiles.

Ute [jut] *or* ['juti] *n.* **1** a member of a people of the Shoshonean stock of North American Indians, now living mainly in Utah and Colorado. **2** the Uto-Aztecan language of these people.

u•ten•sil [ju'tɛnsəl] *n.* **1** a container or implement used for practical household purposes, especially in the kitchen. Measuring cups, peelers, graters, cutlery, etc. are utensils. **2** an instrument or tool used for some special purpose. Pens and pencils are writing utensils. A mop is a cleaning utensil. ⟨ME < Med.L *utensile* < L *utensilis* that may be used < *uti* use⟩

u•ter•ine ['jutərɪn], ['jutə,raɪn], *or* ['jutə,rin] *adj.* **1** of or having to do with the uterus. **2** having the same mother, but a different father. Uterine brothers are stepbrothers born of the same mother. ⟨ME < LL *uterinus* < L *uterus* uterus⟩

u•ter•us ['jutərəs] *n., pl.* **-ter•i** [-tə,raɪ] *or* [-tə,ri]. in female mammals, a muscular organ lying within the pelvic cavity, that holds and nourishes the young till birth; womb. ⟨< L⟩

U•ther ['uθər] *or* ['juθər] *n.* king of ancient Britain and father of King Arthur. Also, **Uther Pendragon**.

u•tile ['jutaɪl] *or* ['jutəl] *adj.* useful.

u•til•i•dor [ju'tɪlə,dɔr] *n. Cdn. North.* a large insulated tube mounted on short posts above ground and housing water, steam, and sewage pipes that supply services to buildings in a town or settlement built on permafrost. ⟨< *utili(ty)* + *(corri)dor*⟩

u•til•i•tar•i•an [ju,tɪlə'tɛriən] *adj.* **1** of, having to do with, or aimed at utility rather than aesthetic merit: *a utilitarian furniture design.* **2** of, having to do with, or designating utilitarianism: *utilitarian philosophy.*
—n. a person who believes in utilitarianism.

u•til•i•tar•i•an•ism [ju,tɪlə'tɛriə,nɪzəm] *n. Philosophy.* **1** the doctrine or belief, especially as developed in the late 18th and early 19th centuries by Jeremy Bentham and John Stuart Mill, that the greatest good of the greatest number should be the purpose of human conduct. **2** the doctrine or belief that things are good if and only if they are useful. **3** a utilitarian quality or character; attention to utility rather than beauty.

u•til•i•ty [ju'tɪləti] *n., pl.* **-ties. 1** the power to satisfy needs; usefulness: *The cottage was obviously designed more for utility than beauty.* **2** something that is useful. **3** (*adjl.*) designed or serving strictly for usefulness rather than appearance or luxury: *utility furnishings.* **4** (*adjl.*) capable of being used in a number of different ways: *a utility knife.* **5 a** PUBLIC UTILITY. **b utilities,** *pl.* shares in a public utility. **6** the supplying of gas, water, electricity, etc. by a public utility: *They pay a lot more for utilities than we do.* **7** (*adjl.*) designating, of, or having to do with the supplying of such services or the equipment used for this: *The car struck a utility pole.* **8** *Computer technology.* a piece of system software for manipulating different applications, transferring or rearranging stored data, detecting and removing viruses, etc. **9** (*adjl.*) designating the lowest and cheapest government grade of meat: *A utility grade turkey may be an A or B grade that has had the skin broken or has a wing missing, etc.* **10** *Philosophy.* the greatest happiness of the greatest number of people. ⟨ME < OF < L *utilitas*, ult. < *uti* use⟩

utility room a room in a house or apartment where such appliances as the furnace, washing equipment, hot water tank, etc. are located.

u•ti•li•za•tion [,jutələ'zeiʃən] *or* [,jutəlaɪ'zeiʃən] *n.* the act of utilizing or the state of being utilized.

u•ti•lize ['jutə,laɪz] *v.* **-lized, -liz•ing.** make use of; put to some practical use: *to utilize leftovers in cooking.* **—'u•ti,liz•a•ble,** *adj.* **—'u•ti,liz•er,** *n.*
☛ *Syn.* See note at USE.

ut•most ['ʌt,moust] *adj.* **1** of the greatest or highest degree, amount, or quantity: *Sleep is of the utmost importance to health.* **2** farthest or most distant; extreme: *the utmost ends of the earth.*
—n. **1** the most that is possible; extreme limit: *I enjoyed myself to the utmost.* **2** all that one can do; the greatest or highest of one's powers or abilities: *She did her utmost to help him find a good job.* ⟨OE *ūtemest* < *ūte* outside + *-mest* -most⟩

U•to–Az•tec•an ['jutou 'æztɛkən] *n., adj. —n.* an American Indian language family of the western part of North and Central America, including Hopi, Ute, Shoshone, Comanche, etc.
—adj. of or having to do with these languages or their speakers.

u•to•pi•a [ju'toupiə] *n.* **1 Utopia,** an ideal commonwealth where perfect justice and social harmony exist, described in *Utopia* (1516), by Sir Thomas More. **2** an ideal place or state with perfect laws. **3** a visionary, impractical system of political or social perfection. Compare DYSTOPIA. ⟨< NL < Gk. *ou* not + *topos* place⟩

u•to•pi•an [ju'toupiən] *adj., n. —adj.* **1** Usually, **Utopian,** of, having to do with, or characteristic of Utopia. **2** of, having to do with, or like a utopia. **3** visionary; impractical.
—n. **1** an ardent but impractical reformer; idealist. **2 Utopian,** an inhabitant of Utopia.

u•to•pi•an•ism [ju'toupiə,nɪzəm] *n.* **1** the ideas, beliefs, and aims of utopians. **2** ideal schemes for the improvement of life, social conditions, etc.

u•tri•cle ['jutrɪkəl] *n.* **1** *Botany.* **a** a small sac or baglike body, such as an air cell in seaweed. **b** a thin, bladderlike seed vessel. **2** *Anatomy.* the larger of the two sacs of the internal ear. Also, **utriculus** (*pl.* **utriculi**) [ju'trɪkjələs, -,laɪ]. ⟨< L *utriculus*, dim. of *uter* skin bag, skin bottle⟩ **—u'tric•u•lar,** *adj.*

ut•ter¹ ['ʌtər] *adj.* complete; total; absolute: *utter surprise, utter darkness, an utter failure.* ⟨OE *ūtera* outer⟩ **—'ut•ter•ly,** *adv.*

ut•ter² ['ʌtər] *v.* **1** speak; make known; express: *the last words she uttered, to utter one's thoughts.* **2** give out as sound: *He uttered* *a cry of pain.* **3** *Law.* pass off (forged documents, counterfeit money, etc.) as genuine. ⟨ME *uttren*, literally, put forth < OE *ūtor*, comparative of *ūt* out⟩ **—'ut•ter•a•ble,** *adj.* **—'ut•ter•er,** *n.*

ut•ter•ance ['ʌtərəns] *n.* **1** an uttering; expression in words or sounds: *The child gave utterance to her grief.* **2** the power or a way of speaking: *defective utterance.* **3** something uttered; a spoken word or words: *Some of his famous political utterances are included in the book.* **4** *Law.* the passing off of counterfeit money, forged cheques, etc.; uttering: *He was arrested for the utterance of forged cheques worth $75 000.*

ut•ter•most ['ʌtər,moust] *adj. or n.* utmost.

U–turn ['ju ,tɜrn] *n.* **1** a complete reversal of direction on a road, as, from the northbound to the southbound lane: *U-turns are illegal on some roads.* **2** *Informal.* a complete reversal of tactics or policy.

UV ultraviolet.

u•ve•a ['juviə] *n.* the pigmented inner layer of the eye, consisting of the iris, the ciliary body, and the choroid. ⟨< L *uva* grape⟩ **—'u•ve•al,** *adj.*

UV index ultraviolet index, an indication of the strength of ultraviolet radiation on a given date in a given place, intended as a guide to the amount of sunshine one can absorb safely.

u•vu•la ['juvjələ] *n., pl.* **-las** or **-lae** [-,li] *or* [-,laɪ]. the small lobe of flesh hanging down from the soft palate in the back of the mouth. ⟨< LL *uvula*, dim. of L *uva*, originally, grape⟩

u•vu•lar ['juvjələr] *adj., n.* *—adj.* **1** of or having to do with the uvula. **2** of a speech sound, produced or pronounced with the uvula and the back of the tongue. The standard French pronunciation of *r* is uvular.
—n. a uvular speech sound.

ux•o•ri•al [ʌk'sɔriəl] *or* [ʌg'zɔriəl] *adj.* pertaining to or befitting a wife. ⟨< L *uxor* wife⟩ **—ux'o•ri•al•ly,** *adv.*

ux•or•i•cide [ʌk'sɔrə,saɪd] *or* [ʌg'zɔrə,saɪd] *n.* **1** the murder of a wife. **12** a man who murders his wife. ⟨< L *uxor* wife + E *-cide*⟩ **—ux,or•i'ci•dal,** *adj.*

ux•o•ri•ous [ʌk'sɔriəs] *or* [ʌg'zɔriəs] *adj.* excessively or foolishly devoted or subservient to one's wife. ⟨< L *uxorius* < *uxor* wife⟩ **—ux'o•ri•ous•ly,** *adv.* **—ux'o•ri•ous•ness,** *n.*

Uz•bek ['ʊzbɛk] *or* ['ʌzbɛk] *n., adj.* *—n.* **1** a member of a Turkic people of Turkestan, a region in central Asia, especially of Uzbekistan. **2** the Turkic language of the Uzbeks.
—adj. of or having to do with Uzbek, its people, or their language.

Uz•bek•i•stan [ʊz'bɛkə,stɑn] *or* [ʊz'bɛkə,stæn] *n.* a country in central Asia.

V v *V v*

v or **V** [vi] *n., pl.* **v's** or **V's. 1** the twenty-second letter of the English alphabet. **2** any speech sound represented by this letter. **3** a person or thing identified as *v*, especially the twenty-second in a series. **4** something, such as a printer's type, a lever, or a key on a keyboard, that produces a v or V. **5** the Roman numeral for 5. **6** something shaped like the letter V. **7** *(adjl.)* of or being a V or v.

v. 1 verb. **2** verse. **3** versus. **4** see (for L *vide*). **5** voice. **6** vector. **7** volume. **8** von (*used in names*). **9** version. **10** violin. **11** velocity. **12** vocative. **13** very. **14** verso. **15** volt; voltage. **16** ventral.

V 1 vanadium. **2** volt. **3** velocity. **4** victory. **5** vector.

V. 1 Venerable. **2** Viscount. **3** Vice (*used in titles*). **4** Vicar. **5** Victoria. **6** Volunteer.

V.A. VICAR APOSTOLIC.

va•can•cy ['veikənsi] *n., pl.* **-cies. 1** the state of being unoccupied or empty. **2** an unfilled post, office, or position: *The company has a vacancy for a sales representative.* **3** a space, room, apartment, etc. that is unoccupied and available: *There were no vacancies in the parking lot. The hotel had one vacancy.* **4** empty space; void: *He stared into the vacancy of the night.* **5** a gap or opening; a blank; a definite empty space. **6** emptiness of mind; a lack of thought or intelligence. **7** *Archaic.* idleness or an interval of idleness. ⟨< L *vacantia* < *vacans.* See VACANT.⟩

va•cant ['veikənt] *adj.* **1** empty; not occupied or filled: *a vacant post, a vacant chair, vacant space.* **2** having or showing no thought or intelligence: *a vacant smile.* **3** having no expression: *a vacant face.* **4** free from work, business, etc.: *vacant time.* **5** *Law.* having no tenant or claimant, nor any furniture or fixtures. **6** of public lands, unused or ungranted. ⟨ME < L *vacans, -antis,* ppr. of *vacare* be empty⟩ **—'va•cant•ly,** *adv.*

va•cate [vei'keit], [və'keit], *or* ['veikeit] *v.* **-cat•ed, -cat•ing. 1** go away from and leave empty or unoccupied; make vacant: *They will vacate the house next month.* **2** leave (a post or position) empty through resignation, retirement, transfer, or death. **3** leave. **4** make void; annul; cancel. ⟨< L *vacare* be empty⟩

va•ca•tion [vei'keiʃən] *or* [və'keiʃən] *n., v.* *—n.* **1** a scheduled time of rest and freedom from work or activity, especially in schools and courts of law: *The school has a vacation at Christmas.* **2** a period of time spent away from work; holidays: *Is he taking a vacation this year? She spent her vacation at the cottage.* **3** the act or an instance of vacating.
—v. take or spend a vacation: *They are vacationing in the North.* ⟨ME < L *vacatio, -onis* < *vacare* have time (off)⟩
—va'ca•tion•less, *adj.*

va•ca•tion•er [vei'keiʃənər] *or* [və'keiʃənər] *n.* a person who is taking a vacation, especially away from home: *The resort town was crowded with vacationers.*

va•ca•tion•ist [vei'keiʃənɪst] *or* [və'keiʃənɪst] *n.* vacationer.

vac•ci•nate ['væksə,neit] *v.* **-nat•ed, -nat•ing. 1** inoculate with vaccine as a protection against disease. **2** have a policy of performing or practising vaccination.

vac•ci•na•tion [,væksə'neiʃən] *n.* **1** the act or process of vaccinating: *Vaccination has made smallpox a very rare disease.* **2** the sore or the scar left by vaccinating.

vac•cine [væk'sin] *or* ['væksɪn] *n.* **1** a preparation, often made of weakened viruses of a disease, used to inoculate a person in order to protect him or her from that disease by causing the formation of antibodies against it: *Salk vaccine is used against polio.* **2** *Computer technology.* a program whose purpose is to protect a computer from viruses. ⟨< L *vaccinus* pertaining to cows < *vacca* cow, used in the Mod.L phrase *virus vaccinus* virus of cowpox. This virus became the first vaccine when it was found to protect people against smallpox.⟩
—'vac•cin•al, *adj.*

vac•il•lant ['væsələnt] *adj.* vacillating.

vac•il•late ['væsə,leit] *v.* **-lat•ed, -lat•ing. 1** move first one way and then another; alternate; fluctuate; waver. **2** waver in mind or opinion: *She keeps vacillating and finds it hard to make up her mind.* ⟨< L *vacillare*⟩

vac•il•la•tion [,væsə'leiʃən] *n.* **1** the act or an instance of vacillating. **2** a habitual inability to make up one's mind or take a stand.

vac•il•la•to•ry ['væsɪlə,tɔri] *adj.* given to or displaying vacillation.

vac•ua ['vækjuə] *n.pl.* of VACUUM.

va•cu•i•ty [və'kjuəti] *n., pl.* **-ties. 1** the quality or state of being empty or without thought or intelligence. **2** an empty space; vacuum. **3** something, such as an idea, that is foolish or stupid; inanity. **4** absence or lack (*of* something specified). ⟨< L *vacuitas* < *vacuus* vacuous⟩

vac•u•o•la•tion [,vækjuə'leiʃən] *n.* the formation or arrangement of vacuoles.

vac•u•ole ['vækju,oul] *n.* a tiny cavity in the cytoplasm of a living cell, containing fluid. See CELL for picture. ⟨< F *vacuole* < L *vacuus* empty⟩ **—'vac•u•ol•ate** ['vækjuəlɪt] or **,vac•u'ol•ar,** *adj.*

vac•u•ous ['vækjuəs] *adj.* **1** showing no thought or intelligence; foolish; stupid: *a vacuous statement.* **2** empty. ⟨< L *vacuus*⟩ **—'vac•u•ous•ly,** *adv.* **—'vac•u•ous•ness,** *n.*

vac•u•um ['vækjum] *or* ['vækjəm] *n., pl.* **vac•u•ums** or (defs 1-3, 5) **vac•u•a** ['vækjuə]; *v.* *—n.* **1** an empty space utterly devoid of matter, even air. **2** an enclosed space from which almost all air, gas, etc. has been removed. **3 a** a decrease of air pressure below normal atmospheric pressure. **b** the degree to which this pressure has been decreased. **4** *(adjl.)* of, containing, using, or producing a vacuum: *vacuum brakes, a vacuum pump.* **5** an empty space; void; emptiness: *His wife's death left a vacuum in his life.* **6** VACUUM CLEANER.
—v. clean with a vacuum cleaner: *to vacuum a rug. I was vacuuming when I heard the phone ring.* ⟨< L *vacuum,* neut. adj., empty⟩

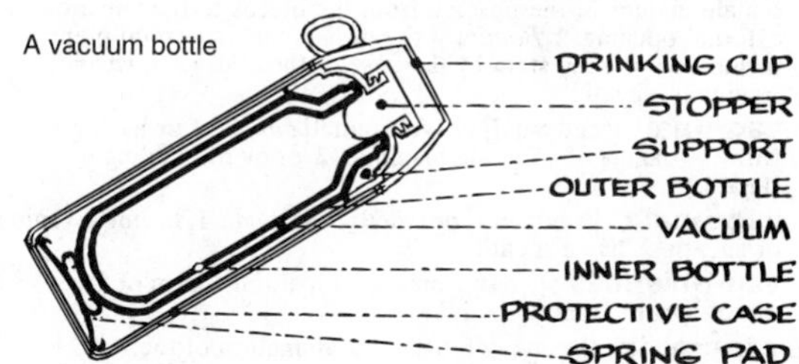

vacuum bottle a bottle or flask made with a vacuum between its inner and outer walls so that its contents will stay hot or cold for a long time. Also, **vacuum flask**.

vacuum cleaner an electrical appliance for cleaning carpets, curtains, floors, etc. by suction.

vacuum flask VACUUM BOTTLE.

vacuum gauge an instrument measuring the pressure in a vacuum or partial vacuum.

vac•u•um–packed ['vækjum ,pækt] *adj.* **1** of a container, having most of the air removed before being sealed in order to preserve the freshness, etc. of the contents: *Coffee, nuts, etc. are often sold in vacuum-packed tins.* **2** packed in such a container: *vacuum-packed tennis balls.*

vacuum pump 1 a pump or device by which a partial vacuum can be produced. **2** a pump in which a partial vacuum is used to raise water.

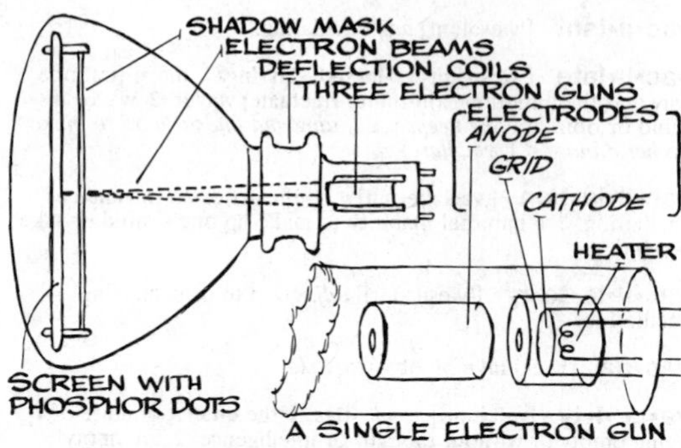

Vacuum tube: a colour television picture tube

vacuum tube an electron tube from which almost all the air has been removed, leaving an almost perfect vacuum through which an electric current can pass freely.

va•de me•cum ['vɑdi 'meikəm] **1** anything a person carries about with him or her because of its usefulness. **2** a book for ready reference; manual; handbook. ⟨< L *vade mecum* go with me⟩

V.Adm. or **VAdm** vice-admiral.

vag•a•bond ['vægə,bɒnd] *n., adj., v.* —*n.* **1** a wanderer, especially a tramp. **2** an idle, shiftless person; rascal.
—*adj.* **1** wandering; drifting; moving from place to place: *The Gypsies are traditionally a vagabond people.* **2** of, having to do with, or characteristic of a wanderer: *a vagabond life.* **3** shiftless and irresponsible.
—*v.* wander as a vagabond. ⟨ME < OF < L *vagabundus*, ult. < *vagus* rambling⟩ —**'vag•a,bond•ish,** *adj.*

vag•a•bond•age ['vægə,bɒndɪdʒ] *n.* **1** the fact or state of being a vagabond; idle wandering. **2** vagabonds as a group. Also (def. 1), **vagabondism.**

va•gal ['veigəl] *adj.* of or pertaining to a vagus nerve.

va•gar•y ['veigəri] *or* [və'gɛri] *n., pl.* **-gar•ies. 1** an odd fancy; extravagant notion: *the vagaries of a dream.* **2** an odd action; caprice: *the vagaries of fashion.* ⟨probably < L *vagari* wander < *vagus* roving⟩ —**va'ga•ri•ous,** *adj.*

va•gi•na [və'dʒaɪnə] *n., pl.* **-nas** or **-nae** [-ni] *or* [-nai]. **1** in female mammals, the passage from the uterus to the vulva or external opening. **2** *Botany.* a sheathlike part in certain plants formed around the stem by the base of the leaf. ⟨< L *vagina*, originally, sheath⟩

vag•i•nal ['vædʒənəl] *or* [və'dʒaɪnəl] *adj.* **1** of or having to do with the vagina of a female mammal. **2** of or resembling a sheath.

vag•i•nate ['vædʒənɪt] *or* ['vædʒə,neit] *adj.* **1** having a vagina or sheath. **2** like a sheath.

vag•i•nis•mus [,vædʒə'nɪzməs] *n.* painful spasm of the muscles of the vagina. ⟨< NL⟩

vag•i•ni•tis [,vædʒə'nəitɪs] *n.* inflammation of the vagina.

va•gran•cy ['veigrənsi] *n., pl.* **-cies. 1** a wandering idly from place to place without proper means or ability to earn a living. **2** *Law.* the criminal offence of being a vagrant: *The tramp was charged with vagrancy.* **3** a wandering or digression of mind or thought.

va•grant ['veigrənt] *n., adj.* —*n.* **1** a wanderer, especially a person who goes from place to place without a regular residence, often living by begging, etc. **2** *Law.* a beggar, prostitute, drunkard, etc. living without lawful or visible means of support.
—*adj.* **1** of, having to do with, or being a vagrant. **2** roving; migrant. **3** moving in no definite direction or course; wandering; random. ⟨? alteration of AF *wacrant* (< Gmc.), influenced by F *vagant* straying (< L *vagari* wander)⟩ —**'va•grant•ly,** *adv.*

vague [veig] *adj.* **va•guer, va•guest. 1** not clearly expressed or defined: *a vague statement, a vague notion, a vague longing.* **2** having no definite meaning or character: *'Nice' is a vague term.* **3** not thinking or expressing oneself clearly: *He was very vague about his plans.* **4** having no definite outline: *a vague shape in the mist.* **5** not established; uncertain; not definitely known: *a vague destination, a vague rumour.* ⟨< MF < L *vagus* wandering. Doublet of VAGUS.⟩ —**'vague•ly,** *adv.* —**'vague•ness,** *n.*
☛ *Syn.* **1, 3.** See note at OBSCURE.

va•gus ['veigəs] *n., pl.* **va•gi** ['veidʒaɪ] *or* ['veidʒi]. either of a pair of nerves extending from the brain to the heart, lungs, stomach, and other organs. Also **vagus nerve.** ⟨< L *vagus* wandering. Doublet of VAGUE.⟩

vail [veil] *n. Archaic.* **1** lower; cause or allow to fall. **2** take off; doff. **3** yield; bow. ⟨< OF *valer*, or < *avale* < OF *avaler*, both ult. < L *ad vallem* to the valley⟩
☛ *Hom.* VALE[1], VEIL.

vain [vein] *adj.* **1** having too much pride in one's looks, ability, etc. **2** of no use; without effect or success; producing no good result: *a vain hope. She made several vain attempts to pull herself out of the icy water.* **3** of no value or importance; worthless; empty: *a vain boast.*
in vain, a without effect or success: *My shout for help was in vain, for no one was near enough to hear me.* **b** in a profane or irreverent way (also used facetiously): *to take the Lord's name in vain. Did I hear somebody taking my name in vain?* ⟨ME < OF < L *vanus*⟩ —**'vain•ly,** *adv.* —**'vain•ness,** *n.*
☛ *Hom.* VANE, VEIN.
☛ *Syn. adj.* **2. Vain,** FUTILE = without effect or success. **Vain** describes thinking, action, effort, etc. that fails to accomplish what is hoped for and aimed at, or to produce any valuable result: *The principal made another vain appeal for better equipment in the high-school laboratories.* **Futile** adds and emphasizes the idea of being inherently incapable of producing the desired, or any, result, and often suggests being useless or unwise to attempt: *Without modern antibiotics, early attempts to treat many diseases were futile.*

vain•glo•ri•ous [,vein'glɔriəs] *adj.* excessively proud or boastful; extremely vain. —**,vain'glo•ri•ous•ly,** *adv.* —**,vain'glo•ri•ous•ness,** *n.*

vain•glo•ry ['vein,glɔri] *or* [,vein'glɔri] *n.* **1** an extreme pride in oneself; boastful vanity. **2** worthless pomp or show. ⟨ME < OF < Med.L *vana gloria*⟩

vair [vɛr] *n.* **1** a grey-and-white squirrel fur used in the Middle Ages for lining and trimming the robes of nobles. **2** *Heraldry.* the representation of this fur by small shield-shaped or bell-shaped figures, usually alternately silver and blue, in alternate or diagonal lines, or alternately upright and inverted. ⟨ME < OF < L *varius* variegated. Doublet of VARIOUS.⟩

Vaish•na•va ['vəiʃnəvə] *n. Hinduism.* a Bakhti sect devoted to Vishnu.

val•ance ['væləns] *n.* **1** a short drapery or a decorative wooden or metal frame around the top of a window, used to hide curtain fixtures, etc. **2** a short curtain hanging around the edge of a bed, dressing table, etc. ⟨probably from *Valence*, a town in SE France⟩

vale[1] [veil] *n. Poetic.* valley. ⟨ME < OF *val* < L *vallis*⟩
☛ *Hom.* VEIL.

va•le[2] ['vɑlei] *or* ['veili] *interj. or n. Latin.* good-bye; farewell.

val•e•dic•tion [,vælə'dɪkʃən] *n.* **1** the act or an instance of bidding farewell. **2** anything said in taking leave. ⟨< L *valedict-*, pp. stem of *valedicere* bid farewell < *vale* be well! + *dicere* say⟩

val•e•dic•to•ri•an [,vælədɪk'tɔriən] *n.* a student who gives the farewell address at the graduation of his or her class.

val•e•dic•to•ry [,vælə'dɪktəri] *n., pl.* **-ries;** *adj.* —*n.* a farewell address, especially at the graduation exercises of a school or college.
—*adj.* of farewell: *a valedictory address.*

va•lence ['veiləns] *n. Chemistry.* the quality of an atom or radical that determines the number of other atoms or radicals with which it can combine, indicated by the number of hydrogen atoms with which it can combine or which it can displace. Elements whose atoms lose electrons, such as hydrogen and the metals, have a positive valence. Elements whose atoms add electrons, such as oxygen and other non-metals, have a negative valence. Oxygen has a negative valence of two; hydrogen has a positive valence of one; one atom of oxygen combines with two of hydrogen to form a molecule of water. ⟨< LL *valentia* strength < *valere* be strong⟩

valence electron *Chemistry.* any of the orbital electrons located in the outermost shell of an atom, that largely determine the characteristics of the atom and can be shared with or transferred to another atom.

Va•len•ci•a or **va•len•ci•a** [və'lɛnʃiə], [və'lɛnʃə], *or* [və'lɛnsiə] *n.* one of the most extensively cultivated varieties of sweet orange, having a thin skin and usually seedless pulp.

Va•len•ci•ennes [və,lɛnsi'ɛn] *or* [,vælənsi'ɛnz]; *French,* [valɑ̃'sjɛn] *n.* **1** a fine, ornate linen lace in which the pattern and background are worked together using the same threads. **2** an imitation of this lace, using cotton thread. ⟨< *Valenciennes*, a city in N France, where this lace was first made⟩

va•len•cy ['veilənsi] *n., pl.* **-cies.** See VALENCE.

-va•lent *combining form.* **1** having a valence of ______. **2** having ______ different valences: *monovalent, trivalent.*

val•en•tine ['vælən,taın] *n.* **1** a greeting card or small gift sent or given on Saint Valentine's Day, February 14. **2** a sweetheart, especially one chosen on this day.

Valentine's Day ['vælən,taınz] in full, **Saint Valentine's Day,** the day on which valentines are exchanged, February 14.

va•le•ri•an [və'lɛriən] *or* [və'liriən] *n.* **1** any of a genus (*Valeriana*) of perennial herbs, especially the common valerian (*V. officinalis*), a tall garden plant having clusters of small, very fragrant, white or reddish flowers and a strong-smelling root. Also called **allheal, vandalroot. 2** a drug made from the dried roots of the common valerian, formerly used in medicine as an antispasmodic and a sedative in nervous diseases. **3** (*adjl.*) designating a family (Valerianaceae) of perennial or annual herbs or shrubs found mainly in the northern hemisphere. The valerian family includes valerian and spikenard. ⟨ME < OF *valeriane* or Med.L *valeriana* < L *Valerius*, a Roman gens name⟩

val•et [væ'lei], ['vælei], *or* ['vælıt] *n., v.* **-et•ed, -et•ing.** *—n.* **1** a male servant who takes care of a man's clothes, helps him dress, etc. **2** an employee of a hotel, etc. who cleans or presses clothes. **3** (*adjl.*) designating any of various services, as in a hotel for cleaning or pressing clothes, or for parking, etc., at some other establishments.
—v. serve as a valet. ⟨< F *valet*, var. of OF *vaslet.* See VARLET.⟩

val•e•tu•di•nar•i•an [,vælə,tjudə'nɛriən] *or* [,vælə,tudə'nɛriən] *n., adj. —n.* a weak or sickly person, especially one who thinks too much about being sick.
—adj. of, having to do with, or characteristic of a valetudinarian. ⟨< L *valetudinarius* sickly < *valetudo* (good or bad) health < *valere* be strong⟩ **—,val•e'tu•di,na•ry,** *adj.* **—,val•e,tu•di'nar•ian,ism,** *n.*

val•gus ['vælgəs] *n., adj. —n.* a deformity in which the foot, hand, knee, or hip is turned or bent outward, as a clubfoot.
—adj. deformed in this way. Compare VARUS. ⟨< NL < L *valgus* bowlegged⟩

Val•hal•la [væl'hælə] *n. Norse mythology.* the hall where the souls of heroes slain in battle feast with the god Odin. ⟨< NL < ON *valhöll* < *valr* those slain in battle + *höll* hall⟩

val•iant ['væljənt] *adj.* **1** courageous; heroic: *a valiant soldier, a valiant deed.* **2** brave; resolute; persevering. ⟨ME < OF *vaillant*, ppr. of *valoir* be strong < L *valere*⟩ **—'val•iance, 'val•ian•cy,** or **'val•iant•ness,** *n.* **—'val•iant•ly,** *adv.*

val•id ['vælıd] *adj.* **1** supported by facts, reason, or authority; sound; true: *a valid argument.* **2** having legal force; legally binding: *A contract made by a minor is not valid.* **3** appropriate in a particular situation or for a particular goal or end; effective: *a valid approach to a problem, a valid excuse.* ⟨< L *validus* strong < *valere* be strong⟩ **—'val•id•ly,** *adv.* **—'val•id•ness,** *n.*

☛ *Syn.* **1. Valid,** SOUND[2], COGENT = strong or convincing with respect to truth, rightness, or reasoning. **Valid,** describing reasons, objections, arguments, evidence, etc., emphasizes being based on truth or fact and supported by correct reasoning: *His objections to women doctors are not valid.* **Sound** emphasizes having a solid foundation of truth or right and being free from defects or errors in reasoning: *The author has sound views on discipline.* **Cogent** means 'so valid or sound as to be convincing': *She gives cogent advice to young people.*

val•i•date ['vælə,deit] *v.* **-dat•ed, -dat•ing. 1** make or declare legally binding; give legal force to: *to validate election results.* **2** support by facts or authority; confirm: *The results of the experiments validated their hypothesis.* **—,val•i'da•tion,** *n.*

va•lid•i•ty [və'lıdəti] *n., pl.* **-ties.** the quality, fact, or condition of being valid: *He questioned the validity of the contract.*

va•line ['vælin] *or* ['vælın], ['veilin] *or* ['veilın] *n.* a white, crystalline, water-soluble essential amino acid, found in small quantities in most plant and animal proteins and essential for growth. *Formula*: $(CH_3)_2CHCH(NH_2)COOH$

va•lise [və'lis] *or* [və'liz] *n.* a travelling bag to hold clothes, etc. ⟨< F < Ital. *valigia*⟩

Val•kyr•ie [væl'kiri] *n. Norse mythology.* one of the handmaidens of Odin who ride through the air and hover over battlefields, choosing the heroes who are to die in battle and afterward leading them to Valhalla. ⟨< ON *valkyrja* < *valr* those slain in battle + *kyrja* chooser⟩ **—Val'ky•ri•an,** *adj.*

val•la•tion [væ'leiʃən] *n.* **1** a trench or rampart. **2** the act, process, or science of building such fortifications. ⟨< LL *vallatio, -onis* < L *vallare* surround with a rampart < *vallum* rampart⟩

val•ley ['væli] *n., pl.* **-leys. 1** an area of low land between hills or mountains, usually having a stream or river flowing through it. **2** a wide region drained by a great river system: *the Ottawa valley.* **3** any hollow or structure like a valley. **4** *Architecture.* a trough formed where two slopes of a roof meet or where a roof meets a wall. ⟨ME < OF *valee* < *val* vale < L *vallis*⟩

va•lo•nia [və'louniə] *n.* the acorn cups, collectively, of a Eurasian oak (*Quercus aegilops*) used for tanning leather and as colouring matter. ⟨< Ital. *vallonia* < Mod.Gk. *balania* oak < Gk. *balanos* acorn⟩

val•or•i•za•tion [,vælərə'zeiʃən] *or* [,vælərai'zeiʃən] *n.* **1** the actual or attempted maintenance of certain prices for a commodity by a government. **2** validation. ⟨< *valour*, in obs. sense of 'value' < LL < L *valere* be worth⟩

val•or•ize ['vælə,raız] *v.* **-ized, -iz•ing. 1** assign a value to. **2** regulate the price of by valorization.

val•or•ous ['vælərəs] *adj.* valiant; displaying valour. **—'val•or•ous•ly,** *adv.* **—'val•or•ous•ness,** *n.*

val•our or **val•or** ['vælər] *n.* great bravery; courage under conditions of extreme danger; heroic or sensational courage, especially in battle: *The Victoria Cross, the highest decoration given for bravery, is inscribed simply 'For Valour'.* ⟨ME < OF < LL *valour* < L *valere* be strong⟩

valse [vɑls] *n. French.* waltz.

val•u•a•ble ['væljəbəl] *or* (*adj. 4*) ['væljuəbəl] *adj., n. —adj.* **1** having value; being worth something. **2** having great value; costly; precious. **3** of great use or benefit; very worthwhile. **4** that can have its value measured.
—n. Usually, **valuables,** *pl.* articles of value: *She keeps her jewellery and other valuables in a safe.* **—'val•u•a•ble•ness,** *n.* **—'val•u•a•bly,** *adv.*

☛ *Syn. adj.* **2. Valuable,** PRECIOUS = worth much. **Valuable** describes something that is worth much money and would bring a high price if sold, or, often, something of great usefulness or benefit to the person (or group) that has it: *He has a valuable stamp collection.* **Precious** describes something that is very valuable because it is rare or unique, or something of great worth which belongs to it by its very nature: *Many precious oriental art treasures are kept in the Royal Ontario Museum.*

val•u•ate ['vælju,eit] *v.* **-at•ed, -at•ing. 1** estimate or determine the objective value of. **2** acknowledge the worth or merit of; treat or regard as valuable or worthy.

val•u•a•tion [,vælju'eiʃən] *n.* **1** value estimated or determined: *The jeweller's valuation of the necklace was $10 000.* **2** an estimating or determining of the value of something. **3** acknowledgment of the worth or merit of anything: *the valuation of Mother Teresa's contribution to society.* **—,val•u'a•tion•al,** *adj.* **—,val•u'a•tion•al•ly,** *adv.*

val•ue ['vælju] *n., v.* **-ued, -u•ing.** *—n.* **1** worth; excellence; usefulness; importance: *the value of education.* **2** the real worth; proper price: *The antique plate was insured for much less than its value.* **3** a proper equivalent in return for money or other payment: *Shop Smith's for value and service.* **4** the current market price: *The value of a house varies greatly over the years.* **5** the power to buy things: *The value of the dollar has varied greatly.* **6** an estimated worth: *He placed a value on his furniture.* **7** the meaning; effect; force: *the value of a symbol.* **8** a number or amount represented by a symbol: *If x is 3, find the value of y.* **9 values,** *pl.* the established ideals of life; principles about what is really important or worthwhile that guide choices and behaviour. **10** *Music.* the relative length of a tone or silence indicated by a note or rest. **11** in speech, the special quality of a sound; the phonological equivalent of a letter or other written symbol. **12** in a painting, etc.: **a** the degree of lightness or darkness. **b** the relative importance or effect of an object, part, spot of colour, etc.
—v. **1** rate at a certain value or price; estimate the value of. **2** think highly of; regard highly: *to value someone's judgment.* **3** ascribe a certain relative worth to (something) in a scale of values: *When it comes to footwear, she values comfort over style.* ⟨ME < OF *valu* < pp. of *valoir* be worth < L *valere*⟩ **—'val•u•er,** *n.*

☛ *Syn. v.* **2. Value,** APPRECIATE, ESTEEM = think highly of a person or thing. **Value** = think highly of people or things because they are considered extremely good, precious, or important: *I value his friendship.* **Appreciate** = think highly of people or things because we can understand them enough to value or enjoy them: *Her classmates appreciate her ready wit.* **Esteem** = value someone or something very highly, respect him or her, and at the same time feel an attachment to him or her: *One esteems a man like Churchill.*

value–added tax in some economies, an excise or sales tax paid on goods or services at each stage of production or distribution and included in the final cost to the consumer. *Abbrev.*: VAT

val•ued ['væljud] *adj., v. –adj.* **1** having its value estimated or determined. **2** highly regarded.
–v. pt. and pp. of VALUE.

value judgment or **judgement** a subjective asessment or judgment of the worth, excellence, desirability, etc. of an action, person, program, etc.

val•ue•less ['væljulɪs] *adj.* without value; worthless.

val•vate ['vælveit] *adj.* **1** furnished with, or opening by, a valve or valves. **2** serving as or resembling a valve. **3** *Botany.* **a** meeting without overlapping, as the parts of certain buds do. **b** composed of, or characterized by, such parts. ⟨< L *valvatus* having folding doors⟩

valve [vælv] *n., v.* **valved, valv•ing.** *–n.* **1** a movable part that controls the flow of a liquid, gas, etc. through a pipe or channel by opening and closing the passage. A tap is one kind of valve. **2** sluicegate. **3** *Anatomy.* a flaplike membrane or structure in a hollow organ or part that works as in def. 1. The valves in the heart permit passage of blood in only one direction. **4** *Zoology.* one of the two halves of the shell of an oyster, clam, etc. **5** *Botany.* **a** one of the sections formed when a seed vessel bursts open. **b** a section of an anther that opens like a lid. **c** either of the halves of the cell wall of a diatom. **6** *Brit.* formerly, a vacuum tube used in a radio. **7** *Music.* a device in certain wind instruments for changing the pitch of the tone by changing the direction and length of the column of air. Cornets, trumpets, and French horns have valves; they are pressed separately or in combination to produce tones between the 'open' tones.
–v. **1** furnish with a valve or valves. **2** control the flow of a liquid, gas, etc. by a valve. **3** discharge gas from a balloon by opening a valve. ⟨< L *valva* one of a pair of folding doors⟩ **–'valve•less,** *adj.* **–'valve,like,** *adj.*

valve trumpet a trumpet played by manipulating valves, as distinct from the old posthorn, which has no valves.

val•vu•lar ['vælvjələr] *adj.* **1** of or having to do with a valve, especially of the heart: *a valvular disorder.* **2** having the form of a valve. **3** furnished with or working by valves.

val•vule ['vælvjul] *n.* a small valve.

val•vu•lit•is [,vælvjə'ləitɪs] *n.* inflammation of a valve, especially in the heart.

va•moose [væ'mus] *v.* **-moosed, -moos•ing.** *Slang.* go away quickly. ⟨< Sp. *vamos* let us go⟩

vamp¹ [væmp] *n., v. –n.* **1** the upper front part of a shoe or boot covering the instep and, sometimes, the toes. **2 a** a piece or patch added to an old thing to make it look new. **b** something so repaired or patched. **3** *Music.* an improvised musical accompaniment, introduction, etc.
–v. **1** furnish or repair with a new vamp. **2** patch up; make (an old thing) look new (*usually used with* **up**). **3** invent, especially in order to deceive (*often used with* **up**): *He vamped up a big story about needing the money to help out a friend.* **4** *Music.* improvise (an accompaniment, introduction, etc.): *'Vamp till ready' is an instruction often given to accompanists.* ⟨ME < AF **vampe*, OF *avanpie* forepart of the foot < *avant* before (< L *ab* from + *ante* before) + *pie* foot < L *pes*⟩ **–'vamp•er,** *n.*

vamp² [væmp] *Slang. n., v. –n.* a woman who seduces and exploits men; unscrupulous flirt.
–v. act as a vamp; use wiles and charm on: *to vamp an unsuspecting man.* ⟨< *vampire*⟩

vam•pire ['væmpaɪr] *n.* **1** an imaginary creature believed to be a corpse that comes back to life at night and sucks the blood of people while they sleep. **2** a person who ruthlessly takes advantage of others. **3** a woman who seduces and ruins men. **4** any of various tropical American bats (genera *Desmodus* and *Diphylla* of the family Desmodontidae) that live by sucking the blood of vertebrates and that can be dangerous to human beings and animals because they transmit diseases such as rabies. **5** any of various other species of bat that are believed to feed on blood but do not actually do so. ⟨< F < Hungarian *vampir*; cf. Turkish *uber* witch⟩

vam•pir•ism ['væmpə,rɪzəm] *or* ['væmpaɪ,rɪzəm] *n.* **1** belief in the existence of VAMPIRES (def. 1). **2** the habits or behaviour of VAMPIRES (def. 1). **3** unscrupulous or ruthless exploitation of, or preying on, others.

van¹ [væn] *n.* the front part or position of an army, fleet, or other advancing group, social or political movement, etc.; vanguard: *The magazine tries to be in the van of current fashion.* ⟨< *vanguard*⟩

van² [væn] *n., v.* **vanned, van•ning.** *–n.* **1** a large, enclosed motor truck or trailer used for moving furniture, etc. **2** a small, buslike vehicle or light motor truck with a completely enclosed body used as a camper, for delivering goods to customers, etc. **3** *Brit.* a railway car for luggage or freight.
–v. Cdn. Alberta. transport (children) to school by bus.
⟨< *caravan*⟩

va•nad•ic acid [və'nædɪk] *or* [və'neidɪk] any of certain acids containing vanadium that apparently do not exist in the free state, especially one with the formula H_3VO_4.

va•na•di•um [və'neidiəm] *n.* a rare, silvery grey, metallic chemical element used in making certain kinds of steel. *Symbol:* V; *at.no.* 23; *at.mass* 50.94. ⟨< NL < ON *Vanadis*, a name for Freya, the Norse goddess of love and beauty⟩ **–'van•a•dous** ['vænədəs], *adj.*

vanadium steel a steel alloy containing vanadium to make it tougher and harder.

Van Al•len belt [vən 'ælən] either of two belts of high-intensity radiation above the earth's atmosphere, produced by a high concentration of charged particles trapped in the magnetic field of the earth. The inner belt is centred at an altitude of 3200 km and the outer at between 14 500 km and 19 000 km. ⟨after J.A. *Van Allen*, U.S. physicist, b. 1914⟩

van•dal ['vændəl] *n.* **1 Vandal, a** a member of a Germanic people originally living in the area south of the Baltic between the Vistula and the Oder, who ravaged Gaul, Spain, and North Africa and in A.D. 455 sacked Rome. Many books and works of art were destroyed by them. **b** (*adjl.*) of or having to do with the Vandals. **2** a person who willfully destroys or damages things, especially beautiful or valuable ones. **3** (*adjl.*) of or like a vandal; willfully or senselessly destructive. ⟨< LL *Vandalus* < Gmc.⟩

van•dal•ism ['vændə,lɪzəm] *n.* willful destruction or defacement of things, especially works of art or other valuable things or property.

van•dal•ize ['vændə,laɪz] *v.* **-ized, -iz•ing.** destroy or damage willfully; subject to vandalism.

van•dal•root ['vændəl,rut] *n.* valerian.

Van de Graaff generator ['væn də, græf] a generator that produces very high electrostatic potentials in the millions of volts. A continuous vertical belt of insulating material gathers an increasing charge from a voltage source and relays it to a hollow, insulated metal dome or sphere. ⟨< R.J. *Van de Graaff* (1901-1967), U.S. physicist⟩

Van der Waals' forces ['væn dər ,wɑlz] weakly attractive electrostatic forces between neutral atoms and molecules, caused by temporary dissymetrics in the arrangement of the electrons.

Van•dyke [vən'dəik] *n.* **1** a short, pointed beard. Also, **vandyke. 2** any of a series of V-shaped points forming a decorative edging on lace, cloth, etc. **3** a large collar, cape, etc. edged with such points. Also, **vandyke. 4** (*adjl.*) in the style of dress characteristic of portraits by the Flemish painter, Sir Anthony Van Dyck (1599-1641). **5** *Printing.* a proof made from a negative or plate, showing white on brown or brown on white.

Vandyke brown 1 a medium to dark, earthy brown colour. **2** a dark brown organic pigment used by the painter Van Dyck; also, any of various other pigments made to imitate this.

vane [vein] *n.* **1** WEATHER VANE. **2** a blade, wing, or similar part attached to an axis, wheel, etc., so as to be turned by a current of air or liquid or to produce a current when turned. The vanes of a windmill are turned by the wind; the vanes of an electric fan produce air currents as they turn. **3** any projecting fixed or movable plane on the outside of a rocket for stability and directional control. **4** *Surveying.* a sight of a quadrant, levelling rod, etc. **5** the flat, soft part of a feather. **6** *Archery.* a stabilizing feather on an arrow. ⟨OE *fana* banner⟩
☛ *Hom.* VAIN, VEIN.

vang [væŋ] *n. Nautical.* either of two ropes steadying the gaff by running from its end to the deck. ⟨< Du., catch⟩

van•guard ['væn,gɑrd] *or* ['væŋ,gɑrd] *n.* **1** a body of soldiers marching ahead of the main part of an army to make sure the way is clear. **2** the foremost or leading position; VAN¹. **3** the leaders of a movement, especially persons who experiment or work with new ideas. ⟨ME < MF *avantgarde* < OF < *avant* before (< L *ab* from + *ante* before) + *garde* guard < Gmc.⟩

va•nil•la [və'nɪlə] *n., adj. –n.* **1** a food flavouring made from vanilla beans. **2** VANILLA BEAN. **3** any of a genus (*Vanilla*) of tropical American orchids, especially *V. planifolia*, which is the chief source of the food flavouring.
–adj. flavoured with or containing vanilla: *vanilla ice cream, vanilla pudding.* ⟨< NL < Sp. *vainilla*, literally, little pod, ult. < L *vagina* sheath⟩

vanilla bean the long, beanlike fruit of a vanilla, especially *V. planifolia*, from which the flavouring vanilla is extracted.

va•nil•lin [və'nɪlɪn] *n.* a white, crystalline, water- and alcohol-soluble solid, the fragrant principle of vanilla, obtained from the vanilla bean or manufactured synthetically, used as a flavouring and in perfumery. *Formula*: $C_8H_8O_3$

van•ish ['vænɪʃ] *v.* **1** pass suddenly out of sight; disappear: *The sun vanished behind a cloud.* **2** pass away; cease to be: *Dinosaurs have vanished from the earth.* **3** *Mathematics.* of a number or function, become zero. ⟨ME < OF *esvaniss-*, a stem of *esvanir*, ult. < L *evanescere* < *ex-* out + *vanus* empty⟩ **—'van•ish•er,** *n.*
☛ *Syn.* **1.** See note at DISAPPEAR.

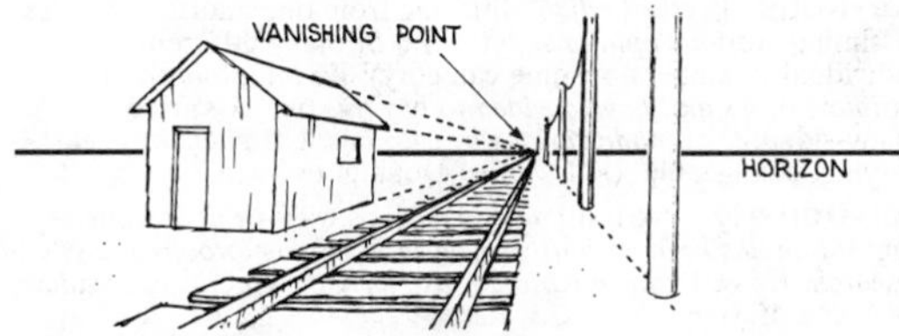

vanishing point **1** the point toward which receding parallel lines seem to converge. **2** a point at which anything disappears.

van•i•ty ['vænəti] *n., pl.* **-ties. 1** too much pride in one's looks, ability, etc. **2** something about which one is vain. **3** a lack of real value; worthlessness: *the vanity of wealth.* **4** a useless or worthless thing or action. **5** worthless pleasure or display. **6** lack of effect or success. **7** VANITY CASE. **8** DRESSING TABLE. **9** a bathroom counter or cabinet with a built-in sink and storage space. ⟨ME < OF < L *vanitas* < *vanus* empty⟩

vanity case a small travelling case used by women, having a mirror fixed on the inside of the lid, and fitted for carrying cosmetics, etc.

Vanity Fair any place or scene, such as the world, a great city, or the world of fashion, regarded as given over to vain pleasure or empty show. ⟨< *Vanity Fair*, a fair described in John Bunyan's *Pilgrim's Progress*, symbolizing the world of vain pleasure or empty show⟩

vanity plate a custom-made licence plate for a motor vehicle, obtainable for a special fee, sometimes bearing the owner's name or other personal code: *I saw a Rover with the licence plate "Ruff."*

vanity press or **publisher** a press or publisher specializing in printing and publishing books at the author's own cost.

van•quish ['væŋkwɪʃ] *v.* conquer; defeat; overcome. ⟨ME < OF *vencus*, pp. of *veintre* or < OF *vainquiss-*, a stem of *vainquir*, both < L *vincere* conquer⟩ **—'van•quish•a•ble,** *adj.* **—'van•quish•er,** *n.*

van•tage ['væntɪdʒ] *n.* a better position or condition; advantage. ⟨ult. < *advantage*⟩

vantage point **1** a superior position from which a person can see to advantage. **2** a favourable condition that gives a person an advantage. Also (*Brit.*), **vantage ground.**

Va•nu•a•tu [,vɑnu'ɑtu] *n.* a country of islands in the South Pacific, east of Australia, formerly called The New Hebrides.

van•ward ['vænwərd] *adj. or adv.* toward the front. ⟨< *van*[1] + *-ward*⟩

vap•id ['væpɪd] *adj.* without much life or flavour; flat; dull. ⟨< L *vapidus*⟩ **—'vap•id•ly,** *adv.* **—'vap•id•ness,** *n.*

va•pid•i•ty [və'pɪdəti] *n., pl.* **-ties. 1** insipidity; flatness of flavour. **2** a vapid thought or remark.

va•por ['veipər] See VAPOUR.

va•por•if•ic [,veipə'rɪfɪk] *adj.* vaporous.

va•por•ize ['veipə,raɪz] *v.* **-ized, -iz•ing.** change or cause to change from a solid or liquid to a vapour: *To distil water, we first have to vaporize it.* **—'va•por,iz•a•ble,** *adj.* **—,va•por•i'za•tion,** *n.*

va•por•iz•er ['veipə,raɪzər] *n.* **1** a device for converting liquid to vapour, as a perfume atomizer. **2** a jet in a carburetor. **3** *Science fiction.* a gunlike weapon that causes the person shot at to disintegrate or vaporize.

va•por•ous [,veipərəs] *adj.* **1** full of vapour; misty. **2** like vapour. **3** exuding, releasing, or forming a vapour. **4** soon passing; ephemeral. **—'va•por•ous•ly,** *adv.* **—'va•por•ous•ness,** *n.*

va•pour•y or **va•por•y** ['veipəri] *adj.* vaporous.

va•pour or **va•por** ['veipər] *n., v.* —*n.* **1** moisture in the air that can be seen; fog; mist. **2** steam from boiling water, as it condenses. **3** *Physics.* **a** a gas formed by heating a substance that is usually a liquid or a solid. **b** a gas below its critical point or below its boiling point. **4 a** a substance, as alcohol, mercury, or benzoin, that has been changed into vapour for use medicinally, industrially, etc. **b** a mixture of a vaporized substance and air, as in an internal-combustion engine. **c** the visible emission or exhalation of such mixtures or of any substance in gaseous form. **5** something without substance; empty fancy. **6 the vapours,** *Archaic.* low spirits.
—*v.* **1** pass off as vapour. **2** send out in vapour. **3** give out vapour. **4** boast; swagger; brag. ⟨< L⟩

va•pour•ish or **va•por•ish** ['veipərɪʃ] *adj.* **1** like vapour. **2** abounding in vapour. **3** *Archaic.* in low spirits. **4** *Archaic.* having to do with or connected with low spirits: *vapourish fears.*

vapour lock or **vapor lock** obstruction of the flow of fuel to an internal-combustion engine because of air bubbles in the liquid fuel, created by overheating.

vapour pressure or **vapor pressure** the pressure of a vapour, especially one in equilibrium with its liquid or solid form.

vapour trail or **vapor trail** a white trail of water droplets or ice crystals that is sometimes seen in the wake of an aircraft flying at high altitudes. A vapour trail is caused by the condensation of moisture in the atmosphere or of exhaust gases from the aircraft.

va•que•ro [vɑ'kɛrou] *n., pl.* **-ros.** a cowboy or herdsman in Spanish America or the SW United States. ⟨< Sp. *vaquero*, ult. < L *vacca* cow. Cf. BUCKAROO.⟩

va•qui•ta [və'kitə] *n.* a dolphin (*Phocoena sinus*) of the Gulf of California. It is an endangered species. ⟨< Sp.⟩

var. **1** variant; variation; variable. **2** variometer. **3** various.

va•rac•tor [və'ræktər] *n.* a semiconductor diode functioning as a capacitor, its capacitance varying with the applied voltage. Compare VARISTOR. ⟨< *var*(*iable*) + (*re*)*act*(*ance*) + *-or*⟩

va•re•ny•ky [və'rɛnəki] *n.pl.* boiled dumplings with any of numerous fillings, such as cottage cheese, fruit, etc. ⟨< Ukrainian⟩

var•i•a•bil•i•ty [,vɛriə'bɪləti] *n.* **1** the fact or quality of being variable. **2** a tendency to vary.

var•i•a•ble ['vɛriəbəl] *adj., n.* —*adj.* **1** apt to change; changeable; uncertain: *variable winds.* **2** likely to shift from one opinion or course of action to another; inconsistent: *a variable frame of mind.* **3** that can be varied; adjustable: *This curtain rod is of variable length.* **4** *Biology.* deviating from the normal species, type, etc. **5** likely to increase or decrease in size, number, amount, degree, etc.; not remaining the same or uniform: *a constant or variable ratio.*
—*n.* **1** a thing, quality, or quantity that varies: *Temperature and rainfall are variables.* **2** *Mathematics, Statistics, Computer technology.* a quantity or function that may assume any value in a set of related values. **3** a shifting wind. **4 the variables,** the region between the northeast and the southeast trade winds. **5** VARIABLE STAR. **—'var•i•a•ble•ness,** *n.* **—'var•i•a•bly,** *adv.*

variable star any of several stars whose brightness varies in more or less regular periods because of influences outside the earth's atmosphere.

var•i•ance ['vɛriəns] *n.* **1** disagreement; dispute; difference of opinion: *She had had a slight variance with her brother over the matter.* **2** *Law.* a difference or discrepancy between two legal statements or documents, as between a writ and a complaint or between evidence and an accusation, sufficient to make them ineffectual. **3 a** a varying or a tendency to vary; variation. **b** the amount or degree of this. **4** *Statistics.* the square of the standard deviation. **5** official permission to do something forbidden by regulations, especially zoning bylaws. **6** *Chemistry.* the number of DEGREES OF FREEDOM of a system.
at variance, a differing; disagreeing; in disagreement: *Her actions are at variance with her promises.* **b** in a state of discord or dissension: *at variance with the neighbours.*

var•i•ant ['vɛriənt] *adj., n.* —*adj.* **1** showing difference, disagreement, or variety: *variant readings of a poem, a variant pronunciation of a word.* **2** *Archaic.* variable; changing.
—*n.* **1** something that is somewhat different from a standard or norm: *She showed us two variants of the original design.* **2** one of two or more slightly different versions of the same thing, especially forms, pronunciations, or spellings of one word: *The*

spellings colour *and* color *are almost equally common variants.* ⟨ME < OF < L *varians, -antis,* ppr. of *variare* change⟩

var•i•ate ['vɛriɪt] *n.* **1** variant. **2** variable. **3** RANDOM VARIABLE.

var•i•a•tion [,vɛri'eiʃən] *n.* **1** a change in condition, degree, etc. **2** the act of changing in condition or degree. **3** the amount of change. **4** a varied or changed form. **5** *Music.* **a** a changing or ornamenting of a tune or theme. **b** one of a series of such modifications upon a theme. **6** *Biology.* **a** a deviation of an animal or plant from type. **b** an animal or plant showing such deviation or divergence. **7** *Astronomy.* the deviation of a heavenly body from its average orbit or motion.

var•i•cel•la [,værə'sɛlə] *or* [,vɛrə'sɛlə] *n.* CHICKEN POX. ⟨< NL, dim. of *variola* pustule⟩

var•i•cel•late [,værɪ'sɛlɪt] *or* [,vɛrɪ'sɛlɪt] *adj. Zoology.* of some shells, having small ridges. ⟨< NL *varicella,* dim. of *varix* dilated vein⟩

var•i•ces ['værəsiz] *or* ['vɛrəsiz] *n.* pl. of VARIX.

var•i•co•cele ['værəkə,sil] *or* ['vɛrəkə,sil] *n.* a varicose condition of the spermatic veins of the scrotum. ⟨< *varico-* (< L *varix* dilated vein) + *-cele* < Gk. *kele* hernia⟩

var•i•col•oured or **var•i•col•ored** ['vɛri,kʌlərd] *adj.* having various colours.

var•i•cose ['værə,kous] *or* ['vɛrə,kous] *adj.* **1** swollen or enlarged: *He has varicose veins in his legs.* **2** of, having to do with, resulting from, or affected with, varicose veins. ⟨< L *varicosus* < *varix, -icis* dilated vein⟩

var•i•co•sis [,værə'kousɪs] *or* [,vɛrə'kousɪs] *n.* a varicose condition of a vein.

var•i•cos•i•ty [,værə'kɒsəti] *or* [,vɛrə'kɒsəti] *n., pl.* **-ties.** **1** the state or condition of being varicose. **2** an abnormally dilated blood or lymph vessel.

var•i•cot•o•my [,værə'kɒtəmi] *or* [,vɛrə'kɒtəmi] *n., pl.* **-mies.** the surgical excision of a varicose vein. ⟨< L *varix, varicis* dilated vein + *-tomia* < Gk. *tome* a cutting⟩

var•ied ['vɛrid] *adj., v. —adj.* **1** of different kinds; having variety: *a varied assortment.* **2** changed; altered. **3** variegated. *—v.* pt. and pp. of VARY. **—'var•ied•ly,** *adj.*

var•i•e•gate ['vɛrɪ,geit] *or* ['vɛriə,geit] *v.* **-gat•ed, -gat•ing.** **1** vary in appearance; mark, spot, or streak with different colours. **2** give variety to. ⟨< L *variegare* < *varius* varied + *agere* drive, make⟩

var•i•e•gat•ed ['vɛrɪ,geitɪd] *or* ['vɛriə,geitɪd] *adj., v. —adj.* **1** varied in appearance; marked with different colours: *variegated pansies.* **2** having variety.
—v. pt. and pp. of VARIEGATE.

var•i•e•ga•tion [,vɛrɪ'geiʃən] *or* [,vɛriə'geiʃən] *n.* a variegating or being variegated; especially, variety of colour.

va•ri•e•tal [və'raɪətəl] *adj., n. —adj.* **1** of, designating, or characteristic of a particular variety. **2** constituting a variety. **3** of wine, made entirely of one variety of grape.
—n. a varietal wine. **—va'ri•e•tal•ly,** *adv.*

va•ri•e•ty [və'raɪəti] *n., pl.* **-ties.** **1** lack of sameness; difference; variation. **2** a number of different kinds: *The store has a great variety of toys.* **3** a kind; sort: *Which variety of cake do you prefer?* **4** *Biology.* **a** a geographical grouping within an animal or plant species, based on inherited biological differences; subspecies. **b** a cultivar of a wild subspecies. **c** an individual or group, fertile within the species, but differing in some characteristics that can be perpetuated. **5** VARIETY SHOW. **6** (*adjl.*) of or in a variety show. ⟨< L *varietas* < *varius* various⟩

☛ *Syn.* **2. Variety,** DIVERSITY = a number of things of different kinds or qualities. **Variety** emphasizes absence of sameness in form or character, and may apply to a number of related things of different kinds or a number of different things of the same general kind: *A teacher has a wide variety of duties.* **Diversity** emphasizes unlikeness, complete difference, in nature, form, or qualities: *A person who has travelled widely has a diversity of interests.*

variety show an entertainment in a theatre or night club, on television, etc., made up of different kinds of acts such as songs, dances, and comic skits.

variety store a store selling a large variety of different things, especially small, inexpensive items such as sewing supplies, small toys, magazines, greeting cards, candy, and tobacco, and now often basic groceries and non-prescription drugs.

var•i•form ['vɛrɪ,fɔrm] *adj.* varied in form; having various forms.

va•ri•o•la [və'raɪələ] *n.* smallpox. ⟨< Med.L *variola* < L *varius* various, spotted⟩ **—va'ri•o•lar** or **va'ri•o•lous,** *adj.*

var•i•om•e•ter [,vɛri'ɒmətər] *n.* **1** an instrument for comparing the intensity of magnetic forces, especially the magnetic force of the earth at different points. **2** *Electricity.* an instrument for varying inductance, consisting of a fixed coil and a movable coil connected in series. **3** *Aeronautics.* a device used to indicate the rate of climb or descent of an airplane. ⟨< L *varius* various + E *-meter*⟩

var•i•o•rum [,vɛri'ɔrəm] *n., adj. —n.* **1** an edition of a book that has the comments and notes of several editors, critics, etc. **2** an edition of a book containing variant versions of the text.
—adj. of or being a variorum. ⟨< L *(cum notis) variorum* (with notes) of various people⟩

var•i•ous ['vɛriəs] *adj.* **1** differing from one another; diverse; dissimilar: *various opinions.* **2** several or many different or individual (members of some category): *We have looked at various houses and have decided to buy this one.* **3** varied; many-sided: *lives made various by learning.* **4** *Archaic or poetic.* varying; changeable. ⟨< L *varius.* Doublet of VAIR.⟩

var•i•ous•ly ['vɛriəsli] *adv.* in various ways or at various times: *She has been variously involved in editing, proofreading, and research. He was known variously as Harry the Hooligan, Deadeye, and Jaws McGee.*

va•ris•tor [və'rɪstər] *n. Electronics.* a semiconductor functioning as resistor in which the resistance varies in proportion to the voltage applied. Compare VARACTOR. ⟨< *var(ious)* + *(res)istor*⟩

var•ix ['værɪks] *or* ['vɛrɪks] *n., pl.* **var•i•ces** [-,siz]. **1** *Medicine.* a varicose vein or other vessel. **2** *Zoology.* any of the ridges crossing the whorls of some univalve shells.

var•let ['vɑrlɪt] *n.* **1** *Archaic.* a low fellow; rascal. **2** formerly, an attendant, specifically the page serving a knight. ⟨ME < OF *varlet,* var. of *vaslet,* originally, young man < Celtic⟩ **—'var•let•ry,** *n.*

var•mint ['vɑrmənt] *n. Informal or dialect.* **1** vermin. **2** an objectionable animal or person.

var•na ['vɑrnə] *n. Hinduism.* caste.

var•nish ['vɑrnɪʃ] *n., v. —n.* **1** a liquid that gives a smooth, glossy appearance to wood, metal, etc., made from resinous substances dissolved in oil or turpentine. **2** any of various other products so used. **3** the smooth, hard surface made by this liquid when dry: *The varnish on the desk has been scratched.* **4** a glossy appearance. **5** a falsely or deceptively attractive appearance; pretence.
—v. **1** put varnish on. **2** give a smooth and glossy appearance to. **3** give a falsely or deceptively attractive appearance to. ⟨ME < OF *vernis,* ult. ? < Gk. *Berenikē,* an ancient city in Libya⟩ **—'var•nish•er,** *n.*

var•si•ty ['vɑrsəti] *n., pl.* **-ties.** **1** *Informal.* university. **2** *Sports.* the principal team representing a school, college, or university. **3** (*adjl.*) of or having to do with a university team or competition: *varsity football.* ⟨clipping from an older pronunciation of *university*⟩

var•us ['vɛrəs] *n., adj. —n.* a deformity in which the foot, knee, etc. is turned inward.
—adj. deformed in this way. Compare VALGUS. ⟨< NL < L *varus* bent, knock-kneed⟩

varve [vɑrv] *n.* one of a pair of stratified bands or layers of alternately light and dark, or fine and coarse, sediment, deposited annually by melting glaciers and useful in determining the age of geological phenomena. The alternating layers represent seasonal deposits, the colour and consistency varying with the seasons. ⟨< Swedish *varv* layer⟩ **—varved,** *adj.*

var•y ['vɛri] *v.* **var•ied, var•y•ing.** **1** make or become different; change: *The driver can vary the speed of an automobile. The weather varies.* **2** be or make different from each other: *The stars vary in brightness. The manufacturers vary the models from year to year.* **3** give variety to: *to vary one's TV viewing.* **4** deviate; diverge; depart (*from*): *The report varies from the first draft only in minor details.* **5** alternate. **6** *Mathematics or physics.* undergo or be subject to a change in value according to some law: *Pressure varies inversely with volume.* **7** *Biology.* exhibit or be subject to variation, as by natural or artificial selection. **8** *Music.* change or ornament (a basic tune or theme). ⟨ME < OF < L *variare* < *varius* various⟩ **—'var•y•ing•ly,** *adv.* **—'var•i•er,** *n.*

☛ *Hom.* VERY.

varying hare *Cdn.* SNOWSHOE HARE.

vas [væs] *n., pl.* **va•sa** ['veisə]. *Anatomy.* a vessel or duct. ⟨< L *vas* vessel⟩ **—'va•sal** ['veisəl], *adj.*

vas•cu•lar ['væskjələr] *adj.* having to do with, made up of, or having vessels that carry blood, sap, etc.: *a vascular plant, vascular tissue.* ⟨< NL *vascularis,* ult. < L *vas* vessel⟩

vascular bundle *Botany.* a unit of the system of specialized, tubelike cells by which food and water are carried through a plant.

vas•cu•lum ['væskjələm] *n., pl.* **-lums** or **-la** [-lə]. a covered, usually metal box used by botanists in the field for holding plant specimens. ⟨< L *vasculum,* dim. of *vas* vase⟩

vas def•er•ens ['dɛfərənz] *or* ['dɛfə,rɛnz] *pl.* **va•sa def•er•en•ti•a** ['veisə ,dɛfə'rɛnʃiə]. especially in higher vertebrates, the duct that carries sperm from the testicles to the penis. ⟨< NL < L *vas* vessel + *deferens,* ppr. of *deferre* to carry away. 16c.⟩

vase [veiz], [vɑz], *or* [vɒz] *n.* an open holder or container, usually taller than it is wide, used for ornament or for holding flowers. ⟨< F < L *vas* vessel⟩ **—'vase,like,** *adj.*

vas•ec•to•my [və'sɛktəmi] *n., pl.* **-mies.** the surgical removal of part or all of the VAS DEFERENS, especially as a method of contraception. ⟨< *vas* + *-ectomy*⟩

Vas•e•line [,væsə'lin] *or* ['væsə,lin] *n. Trademark.* a brand of petroleum jelly. ⟨coined from G *Wasser* water + Gk. *elaion* oil⟩

vas•o•con•strict•or [,væsoukən'strɪktər] *or* [,veizoukən'strɪktər] *adj., n. —adj.* that causes constriction of the blood vessels.
—n. a drug or nerve causing such constriction.
—,vas•o•con'stric•tion, *n.*

vas•o•di•lat•or [,væsou'daɪleitər] *or* [,veizou'daɪleitər] *adj., n. —adj.* that causes dilation of the blood vessels.
—n. a drug or nerve causing such dilation. **—,vas•o•di'la•tion,** *n.*

vas•o•mo•tor [,væsou'moutər] *or* [,veizou'moutər] *adj.* of, designating, or having to do with the nerves that regulate the size of the blood vessels.

vas•o•pres•sin [,væsou'prɛsɪn] *or* [,veizou'presɪn] *n.* a hormone secreted by the pituitary gland, acting to increase blood pressure by causing the contraction of arteries. ⟨< *vas* + *press(ure)* + *-in*⟩

vas•o•spasm ['væsou,spæzəm] *or* ['veizou,spæzəm] *n.* a sudden constriction of a blood vessel, leading to a decrease in the amount of blood it can hold.

vas•sal ['væsəl] *n.* **1** in feudal times, a person who held land from a lord or superior, to whom in return he gave help in war or some other service. A great noble could be a vassal of the king and have many other men as his vassals. **2** (*adjl.*) of, being, or like a vassal. **3** a person in a subordinate position; a servant, slave, etc. ⟨ME < OF < Med.L *vassallus* < LL *vassus* < Celtic⟩

vas•sal•age ['væsəlɪdʒ] *n.* **1** the state of being a vassal. **2** the homage or service due from a vassal to his lord or superior. **3** dependence; servitude. **4** the land held by a vassal. **5** vassals collectively.

vast [væst] *adj.* extremely great; immense: *a vast amount of money, a vast desert. Ontario is a vast province.* ⟨< L *vastus*⟩ **—'vast•ly,** *adv.* **—'vast•ness,** *n.*

vast•y ['væsti] *adj.* **vast•i•er, vast•i•est.** *Poetic.* vast; immense.

vat [væt] *n., v.* **vat•ted, vat•ting.** *—n.* **1** a large container for liquids; tank: *a vat of dye.* **2** a liquid preparation that contains a VAT DYE.
—v. place, store, or treat in a vat. ⟨OE *fæt*⟩

VAT VALUE-ADDED TAX.

vat dye a special type of colourfast dye. It is applied to cloth while in a soluble, colourless state, then coloured and made insoluble by oxidation. **—'vat-,dye,** *v.*

vat•ic ['vætɪk] *adj.* of, pertaining to, or characteristic of a prophet; prophetic. ⟨< L *vates* prophet⟩

Vat•i•can ['vætəkən] *n.* **1** in Vatican City, the buildings of the Roman Catholic Church and the palace of the Pope. **2** the government, office, or authority of the Pope. ⟨< L *Vaticanus (mons)* Vatican (hill), on which the palace of the Pope was built⟩

Vatican City an independent papal state within the city of Rome.

Vatican Council an ecumenical council convoked in 1869-1870 by Pope Pius IX, who promulgated the idea of papal infallibility. Also, **Vatican I.**

Vatican II the twenty-first ecumenical council, convoked in 1962-1965 by Pope John XXIII, which redefined the nature of the Roman Catholic Church.

va•tic•i•nal [və'tɪsɪnəl] *adj.* having the nature of a prophecy.

va•tic•i•nate [və'tɪsə,neit] *v.* **-nat•ed, -nat•ing.** prophesy. ⟨< L *vaticinari* < *vates* seer⟩ **—va,tic•i'na•tion,** *n.*

va•tu ['vɑtu] *n., pl.* **-tu** or **-tus.** the unit of currency of Vanuatu. See table of money in the Appendix.

vaude•ville ['vɒd,vɪl] *or* ['vɒdə,vɪl] *n.* **1** a type of entertainment consisting of a variety of acts, such as singing, dancing, juggling, short plays, and animal acts. **2** a single show of this type. **3** a light, comic stage play with songs interspersed. ⟨< F *vaudeville* < *Vau de Vire,* a valley in Normandy; first applied to the songs composed by Olivier Basselin, a poet of the 15c., who lived in this valley⟩ **—,vaude'vil•li•an** [-'vɪliən], *n.*

Vau•dois [vo'dwa] *n. French.* Waldenses.

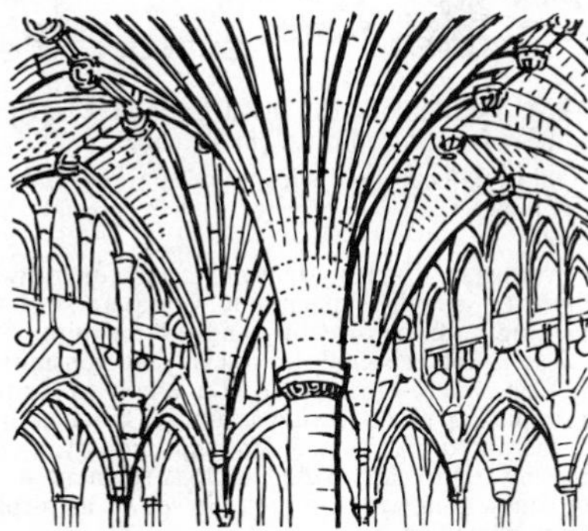

Vault[1]: vaulted ceilings in the Houses of Parliament in Ottawa

vault[1] [vɒlt] *n., v. —n.* **1** an arched roof or ceiling; a series of arches. **2** an arched space or passage. **3** something like an arched roof. The **vault of heaven** means the sky. **4** an underground cellar or storehouse. **5** a place, especially in a bank, for storing valuable things and keeping them safe. Vaults are often made of steel. **6** a place for burial; burial chamber. **7** *Anatomy.* an arched roof of a cavity or other body structure.
—v. **1** make in the form of a vault: *a vaulted roof.* **2** cover with a vault. **3** curve in the shape of a vault: *The ceiling vaults up to a skylight in the roof.* ⟨ME < OF *vaulte,* ult. < L *volvere* roll⟩ **—'vault,like,** *adj.*

vault[2] [vɒlt] *v., n. —v.* **1** jump or leap by resting on one or both hands or by using a pole: *He vaulted the fence. She vaulted from the saddle.* **2** *Gymnastics.* leap or spring over a pommel or vaulting horse, usually using the hands to push off. **3** advance as if by a spring or leap: *She vaulted to the top of her profession before she was 25.*
—n. the act of vaulting. ⟨< OF *volter,* ult. < L *volvere* roll⟩ **—'vault•er,** *n.*

vault•ed ['vɒltɪd] *adj., v. —adj.* **1** in the form of a vault; arched. **2** built or covered with a vault.
—v. pt. and pp. of VAULT.

vault•ing[1] ['vɒltɪŋ] *n., v. —n.* **1** the art, practice, or operation of constructing vaults. **2** a vaulted structure. **3** vaults collectively.
—v. ppr. of VAULT[1].

vault•ing[2] ['vɒltɪŋ] *adj., v. —adj.* **1** reaching or leaping over. **2** too confident; overreaching: *vaulting ambition.* **3** for use in vaulting or gymnastics: *a vaulting horse.*
—v. ppr. of VAULT[2].

vaunt [vɒnt] *v. or n.* boast (about). ⟨< F < LL *vanitare* < *vanus* vain⟩ **—'vaunt•ing•ly,** *adv.*

v. aux. auxiliary verb.

vav [vɒv] *or* [vɑv] *n.* the seventh letter of the Hebrew alphabet. See table of alphabets in the Appendix.

vb. verb; verbal.

V.C. **1** VICTORIA CROSS. **2** a person who has won a Victoria Cross. **3** Vice-Chairman. **4** Vice-Chancellor. **5** Vice-Consul.

VCR VIDEO CASSETTE RECORDER.

v.d. various dates.

VD or **V.D.** VENEREAL DISEASE.

VDT *Computer technology.* video display terminal, another term for VISUAL DISPLAY UNIT.

VDU *Computer technology.* VISUAL DISPLAY UNIT.

've contraction of *have*: *I've got a bad cold. You've nothing to fear from me. They've left at last.*

Ve•a•dar [ˌveiəˈdɑr] *or* [ˈviəˌdɑr] *n.* an intercalary month in the Jewish calendar, coming once every three years, after the month of Adar.

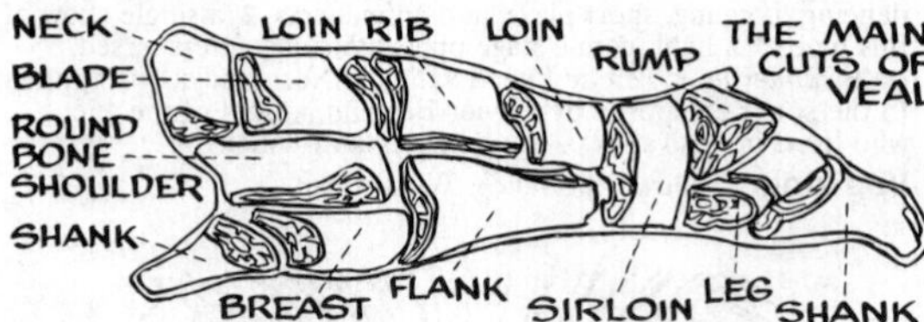

veal [vil] *n.* **1** the flesh of a calf, used for food. **2** vealer. ⟨ME < OF *veel,* ult. < L *vitellus,* dim. of *vitulus* calf⟩

veal•er [ˈvilər] *n.* a calf that is less than 12 weeks old, raised for its tender meat.
☛ *Hom.* VELAR.

vec•tor [ˈvɛktər] *n., v.* —*n.* **1** *Mathematics.* **a** a quantity involving direction as well as magnitude. Compare SCALAR. **b** a line representing both the direction and the magnitude of some force, etc. **2** an agent, especially an insect, that transmits a disease-producing micro-organism from one host to another, either as a simple carrier or serving as a necessary host in the life cycle of the micro-organism. **3** *Molecular biology.* a micro-organism used to carry a cloned DNA segment. **4** a direction or course followed or to be followed by an airplane or missile; compass heading.
—*v.* guide (a pilot, aircraft, or missile) from one point to another within a given time by means of a vector: *He vectored the pilot back to the base.* ⟨< L *vector* carrier < *vehere* carry⟩
—vecˈto•ri•al, *adj.* **—vecˈto•ri•al•ly,** *adv.*

vector analysis the branch of calculus dealing with vectors and the processes involving them.

vector product *Mathematics.* a vector whose magnitude equals the product of the magnitudes of two other vectors and the sine of the angle between them. Its direction is perpendicular to the plane of the first two vectors.

Ve•da [ˈveidə] *or* [ˈvidə] *n.* any or all of the four collections of Hindu sacred writings. ⟨< Skt. *veda* knowledge⟩ **—Ve'da•ic** [vɪˈdeiɪk], *adj.*

Ve•dan•ta [vɪˈdɑntə] *or* [vɪˈdæntə] *n.* one of the leading schools of Hindu religious philosophy based on the Vedas, teaching that everything except Brahma is an illusion. ⟨< Skt. < *veda* sacred knowledge + *-anta* end⟩ **—Ve'dan•tic,** *adj.* **—Ve'dant•ism,** *n.*

V–E Day the day of the Allied victory in Europe in World War II, May 8, 1945.

Ved•da [ˈvɛdə] *n.* a member of an aboriginal people of Sri Lanka. Also, **Veddah. —'Ved•doid,** *adj.*

ve•dette [vəˈdɛt] *n.* **1** a mounted sentry stationed in advance of the outposts of an army. **2** a small naval vessel used for scouting. ⟨< F < Ital. *vedetta,* ult. < L *videre* see⟩

Ve•dic [ˈveidɪk] *or* [ˈvidɪk] *adj., n.* —*adj.* having to do with or found in the Vedas.
—*n.* the form of ancient Sanskrit in which the Vedas are written.

vee [vi] *adj., n.* —*adj.* shaped like the letter V.
—*n.* **1** the letter V. **2** a thing shaped like the letter V.: *"What sort of neckline does your new dress have?" "A vee."*

vee•jay *Informal.* VIDEO JOCKEY. ⟨< the initials *VJ*⟩

veer [vɪr] *v., n.* —*v.* **1** change in direction, especially abruptly; shift; turn: *The wind veered to the south. The talk veered to ghosts.* **2** change the direction of; turn (a vessel) so its stern is toward the wind: *We veered our boat.*
—*n.* a sudden, significant change in direction: *a veer to the left.* ⟨< F *virer*⟩

veer•y [ˈviri] *n., pl.* **veer•ies.** a common North American thrush (*Hylocichla fuscescens*) having a reddish brown back and whitish underparts with very faint spotting on the breast. The veery winters in Central America and N South America. ⟨probably imitative⟩

veg [vɛdʒ] *n., pl.* **vegs** [ˈvɛdʒəz] *v.* **veged, veg•ing.** *Informal.*
—*n.* Usually, **vegs,** *pl.* vegetables.
—*v.* VEGETATE (defs. 2, 3) (*often with* **out**).

Ve•ga [ˈvigə] *or* [ˈveigə] *n. Astronomy.* a bluish white star of the first magnitude, in the constellation Lyra. ⟨< Med.L < Arabic (*al-nasr*) *al-wāqiʻ* the falling (vulture)⟩

ve•gan [ˈvɛdʒən] *or* [ˈvigən] *n.* a vegetarian who eats no flesh foods or animal products, such as eggs or milk.

veg•e•ta•ble [ˈvɛdʒtəbəl] *or* [ˈvɛdʒətəbəl] *n., adj.* —*n.* **1** a part of a plant, such as leaf, seed, root, stem, or fruit, used for food and usually eaten with the main part of the meal. Some common vegetables are potatoes, beans, peas, carrots, cabbage, tomatoes, sweet peppers, and spinach. **2** a usually non-woody plant grown for such parts. **3** *Rare.* any plant. **4** (*adjl.*) of, having to do with, or like plants: *the vegetable kingdom, vegetable life.* **5** (*adjl.*) consisting of, made or derived from vegetables or plants: *vegetable soup, vegetable shortening.* **6** a person apparently lacking in thought or feeling or one who has lost the use of his or her mind and, sometimes, limbs, etc. **7** (*adjl.*) of or designating the life of such a person. ⟨ME (adj.) < OF *vegetable,* or < LL *vegetabilis* vivifying, refreshing < *vegetus* vigorous⟩

vegetable marrow **1** any of several oblong varieties of summer squash having a smooth, whitish or green skin and white flesh. **2** the plant they grow on.

vegetable oil any fatty oil extracted from the seeds or fruit of plants, used in cooking.

vegetable oyster salsify.

veg•e•tal [ˈvɛdʒətəl] *adj.* **1** of, like, or having to do with plants or vegetables. **2** VEGETATIVE (def. 3).

veg•e•tar•i•an [ˌvɛdʒəˈtɛriən] *n., adj.* —*n.* **1** a person who eats no meat or fish and, sometimes, no animal products such as eggs, milk, or cheese, especially one advocating this diet on humanitarian or nutritional grounds.
—*adj.* **1** of or having to do with vegetarians or vegetarianism. **2** containing no meat or fish and, sometimes, no animal products: *a vegetarian meal.* **3** serving only vegetarian foods: *a vegetarian restaurant.*

veg•e•tar•i•an•ism [ˌvɛdʒəˈtɛriəˌnɪzəm] *n.* the practice or principle of living on a diet that contains no meat or fish and, sometimes, no animal products.

veg•e•tate [ˈvɛdʒəˌteit] *v.* **-tat•ed, -tat•ing. 1** grow as plants do. **2** live with very little mental or physical activity; lead a dull, passive existence. **3** be temporarily passive and unstimulated, especially as a respite from too much activity or concentration. ⟨< L *vegetare* enliven < *vegetus* lively⟩

veg•e•ta•tion [ˌvɛdʒəˈteiʃən] *n.* **1** plant life; growing plants: *There is not much vegetation in deserts.* **2** the process of vegetating. **3** a dull, passive existence. **4** any abnormal growth on a part of the body. **—ˌveg•eˈta•tion•al,** *adj.*

veg•e•ta•tive [ˈvɛdʒəˌteitɪv] *adj.* **1** growing as plants do. **2** of plants or plant life. **3** *Botany.* concerned with growth and development rather than reproduction: *vegetative root cells.* **4** causing or promoting growth in plants; productive; fertile: *vegetative mould.* **5** of or having to do with vegetablelike unconscious or involuntary functions of the body: *the vegetative processes of the body, such as growth and repair.* **6** having very little action, thought, or feeling. **7** of or having to do with asexual reproduction, as by budding in plants. **—ˈveg•eˌta•tive•ly,** *adv.* **—ˈveg•eˌta•tive•ness,** *n.*

veg•gie [ˈvɛdʒi] *n. Informal.* a vegetable (*often used in the plural*).

ve•he•mence [ˈviəməns] *n.* the quality or state of being vehement: *The vehemence of her retort surprised us.*

ve•he•ment [ˈviəmənt] *adj.* **1** having, showing, or caused by strong feeling; intense or passionate: *a vehement denial, vehement patriotism. He was vehement about not wanting to go.* **2** forceful; violent: *a vehement onslaught, a vehement wind.* ⟨< L *vehemens, -entis* < *vehere* carry⟩ **—ˈve•he•ment•ly,** *adv.*

ve•hi•cle [ˈviəkəl] *n.* **1** a carriage, cart, wagon, bicycle, automobile, sled, or any other conveyance used on land. **2** any form of conveyance or transportation: *a space vehicle.* **3** a means by which something is communicated, shown, done, etc.: *Language is the vehicle of thought.* **4** **a** a painting medium, such as linseed oil, in which the pigment is suspended. **b** *Pharmacy.* a substance, such as syrup, in which a medicine is mixed and administered. **5** in a metaphor, the term whose meaning is being used figuratively to describe the other term. *Example: tiger* in *Our team captain is a tiger!* Compare TENOR (def. 11) ⟨< L *vehiculum* < *vehere* carry⟩

ve•hic•u•lar [vɪˈhɪkjələr] *adj.* **1** of or having to do with vehicles. **2** serving as a VEHICLE (def. 3): *the vehicular function of language.*

V–8 [ˈvi ˈeit] *adj., n.* —*adj.* of or referring to a type of internal-combustion engine having eight cylinders in two rows of

four which together form a V shape.
—*n.* **1** such an engine. **2** a car with such an engine.

veil [veil] *n., v.* —*n.* **1** a length of cloth worn by women so as to fall over the head and shoulders and, sometimes, the face or part of the face. **2** a piece of very thin cloth or netting attached to a woman's hat or headpiece and falling partway over the head or face as a protection or as an ornament. **3** anything that covers or hides: *A veil of clouds hid the sun.*
take the veil, become a nun.
—*v.* **1** cover with a veil: *In some places, Muslim women still veil their faces before going out in public.* **2** cover, screen, or hide: *Fog veiled the shore. Their plans were veiled in secrecy.* ⟨ME < AF < L *velum* covering. Doublet of VELUM, VOILE.⟩ —**'veil-,like,** *adj.*
☛ *Hom.* VAIL, VALE.

veiled [veild] *adj., v.* —*adj.* **1** wearing a veil. **2** covered with a veil. **3** indirectly expressed: *veiled meaning, veiled threats.* **4** concealed or hidden.
—*v.* pt. and pp. of VEIL.

veil•ing ['veilɪŋ] *n., v.* —*n.* **1** a veil. **2** material for veils.
—*v.* ppr. of VEIL.

vein [vein] *n., v.* —*n.* **1** one of the membranous vessels or tubes that carry blood to the heart from all parts of the body. See HEART and KIDNEY for pictures. **2** a rib of an insect's wing. **3** one of the bundles of vascular tissue forming the principal framework of a leaf. **4** a distinct mass or bed of mineral or ore occurring in a crack in rock or between strata of rock: *a vein of copper.* **5** any streak or marking of a different shade or colour in wood, marble, etc. **6** a strain or streak of some quality in character, conduct, writing, etc.: *There is a vein of fun in these poems. He has a vein of cruelty.* **7** a course of thought, feeling, or action: *If you continue to think in this vein you will just discourage yourself. If this goes over well, we can plan other activities in the same vein.*
—*v.* cover or mark with veins or veinlike lines. ⟨ME < OF < L *vena*⟩ —**'vein•less,** *adj.* —**'vein,like,** *adj.* —**'vein•y,** *adj.*
☛ *Hom.* VAIN, VANE.

veined [veind] *adj., v.* —*adj.* having veins or veinlike markings: *veined marble.*
—*v.* pt. and pp. of VEIN.

vein•ing ['veinɪŋ] *n., v.* —*n.* an arrangement or pattern of veins.
—*v.* ppr. of VEIN.

vein•let ['veinlɪt] *n.* a small vein. Also, **veinule** [-jul].

Ve•la ['vilə] *or* ['veilə] *n. Astronomy.* a constellation in the southern hemisphere, in the Milky Way between Antlia and Carina.

ve•lar ['vilər] *adj., n.* —*adj.* **1** of or having to do with a velum. **2** *Phonetics.* pronounced with the aid of the soft palate. *C* in *coo* represents the velar sound [k].
—*n. Phonetics.* a velar sound. ⟨< L *velaris* < *velum* covering⟩
☛ *Hom.* VEALER.

ve•lar•ize ['vilə,raɪz] *v.* **-ized, -iz•ing.** modify the articulation of (a sound) by raising the back of the tongue toward the velum.

ve•late ['vileit] *adj.* having a velum.

Vel•cro ['vɛlkrou] *n. Trademark.* a type of fastener used for clothing, etc., consisting of two nylon strips or patches, one covered with tiny filaments formed into hooks and the other with loops. The fastener is closed by pressing the two surfaces together so that they engage, and opened by peeling them apart.

veld or **veldt** [vɛlt] *or* [fɛlt] *n.* in South Africa, open country having grass or bushes but few trees. ⟨< Afrikaans *veld* < Du. *veld* field⟩

vel•lum ['vɛləm] *n.* **1** the finest kind of parchment, originally made from calfskin, used especially for writing on or for binding books. **2** a manuscript written on vellum. **3** strong writing paper made to imitate vellum. **4** (*adjl.*) of, resembling, or bound in vellum: *a vellum finish.* ⟨ME < OF *velin* < *veel* calf. See VEAL.⟩

ve•loc•i•pede [və'lɒsə,pid] *n.* **1** tricycle. **2** an early kind of bicycle or tricycle. **3** a railway handcar. ⟨< F *vélocipède* < L *velox, -ocis* swift + *pes, pedis* foot⟩

ve•loc•i•ty [və'lɒsəti] *n., pl.* **-ties. 1** speed; swiftness; quickness of motion: *to fly with the velocity of a bird.* **2** the rate of motion in a particular direction: *The velocity of light is about 300 000 km/s.* **3** the absolute or relative rate of operation or action. ⟨< L *velocitas* < *velox, velocis* swift⟩

ve•lo•drome ['vɛlə,droum] *or* ['vilə,droum] *n.* a building having a track for bicycle racing and, usually, seats and other facilities for spectators.

ve•lour or **ve•lours** [və'lur] *n., pl.* **velours.** any of various fabrics with a nap or pile like velvet, used for upholstery, draperies, clothing, etc. ⟨< F *velours* velvet, earlier *velous* < Provençal *velos,* ult. < L *villus* shaggy hair⟩
☛ *Hom.* VELURE.

ve•lou•té [vəlu'tei] *n.* a rich, creamy white sauce made from stock thickened with flour and, often, egg yolk and butter. ⟨< F, velvety⟩

ve•lum ['viləm] *n., pl.* **-la** [-lə]. a veil-like membrane or membranous part of an animal or plant or of the human body, especially the SOFT PALATE. ⟨< L *velum* covering. Doublet of VEIL, VOILE.⟩

ve•lure [və'lur] *n.* **1** velvet or a fabric like it. **2** a soft pad used for smoothing silk hats. ⟨var. of *velour.* See VELOURS.⟩
☛ *Hom.* VELOUR.

ve•lu•ti•nous [və'lutənəs] *adj. Biology.* covered with short, dense, soft hairs like velvet. ⟨< Ital. *velluto* velvet⟩

vel•vet ['vɛlvət] *n.* **1** cloth, usually of cotton, rayon, or nylon, having a thick, short, cut pile that makes it smooth and soft to the touch. Velvet is made by weaving two layers of fabric together and then shearing the faces apart. **2** (*adjl.*) made of or covered with velvet: *a velvet chesterfield.* **3** (*adjl.*) like velvet; soft, smooth, rich, etc.: *the velvet paws of a kitten, a velvet voice.* **4** something like velvet or suggesting velvet, especially in softness or smoothness. **5** the soft, furry skin that covers and nourishes the growing antlers of a deer. **6** *Slang.* clear profit or gain. **7** *Slang.* money won through gambling.
be on velvet, *Slang.* **a** have previous winnings available for gambling, speculating, etc. **b** be well supplied with money.
play on velvet, *Slang.* gamble or speculate with money won previously. ⟨ME < Med.L *velvetum,* ult. < L *villus* tuft of hair⟩

vel•vet•een [,vɛlvə'tin] *or* ['vɛlvə,tin] *n.* **1** cotton or rayon cloth having a soft, cut pile similar to velvet, but which is woven singly instead of face to face like velvet. **2** (*adjl.*) made of or covered with velveteen. ⟨< *velvet*⟩

vel•vet•y ['vɛlvəti] *adj.* **1** smooth and soft like velvet. **2** of liquor, mellow; smooth in flavour.

Ven. Venerable.

ve•na ca•va ['vinə 'keivə] *pl.* **venae cavae** ['vini 'keivi]. *Anatomy.* either of the two large veins that in air-breathing vertebrates return blood to the right atrium of the heart. See HEART for picture. ⟨< L, literally, hollow vein⟩

ve•nal ['vinəl] *adj.* **1** willing to sell one's services or influence basely; open to bribes; corrupt: *venal judges.* **2** influenced or obtained by bribery: *venal conduct.* ⟨< L *venalis* < *venum* sale⟩ —**'ve•nal•ly,** *adv.*

ve•nal•i•ty [vi'næləti] *or* [və'næləti] *n.* the quality of being venal.

ve•na•tion [vi'neiʃən] *or* [və'neiʃən] *n.* **1** the arrangement of veins in a leaf or in an insect's wing. **2** such veins collectively. ⟨< L *vena* vein⟩

vend [vɛnd] *v.* sell (goods). ⟨< L *vendere* < *venum dare* offer for sale⟩

vend•ee [vɛn'di] *n.* a person to whom a thing is sold; buyer.

vend•er ['vɛndər] *n.* See VENDOR.

ven•det•ta [vɛn'dɛtə] *n.* **1** a feud in which the relatives of a person who has been wronged or murdered try to take vengeance on the wrongdoer or killer or on his or her relatives. **2** any bitter, prolonged quarrel or rivalry: *There has been an ongoing vendetta between the two newspapers for years.* ⟨< Ital. < L *vindicta* revenge, ult. < *vindex, -icis* protector, avenger⟩ —**ven'det•tist,** *n.*

ven•deuse [vɑ̃'dœz] *n. French.* a saleswoman, especially of women's fashions.

vend•i•ble ['vɛndəbəl] *adj., n.* —*adj.* saleable.
—*n.* a saleable thing. —**'vend•i•bly,** *adv.* —**,vend•i'bil•i•ty,** *n.*

vending machine a coin-operated machine from which one may obtain coffee, candy, cigarettes, stamps, etc.

ven•di•tion [vɛn'dɪʃən] *n.* the act of selling.

ven•dor or **ven•der** ['vɛndər] *n.* **1** a person who sells something. **2** VENDING MACHINE. ⟨< AF *vendor* < *vendre* sell < L *vendere.* See VEND.⟩

ven•due ['vɛndju], [vɛn'dju], *or* [vɛn'du] *n.* a public auction. ⟨< Du. < OF *vendue* sale⟩

ve•neer [və'nir] *n., v.* —*n.* **1** a thin layer of fine wood or other material covering a cheaper grade of wood, fibreboard, etc.: *a desk made of pine with a walnut veneer, a wall with a veneer of*

brick. **2** any of the thin layers forming plywood. **3** surface appearance or show: *a veneer of honesty.*
—v. **1** cover with a veneer. **2** glue together (thin layers of wood) to form plywood. **3** conceal (something) under a superficial pleasantness or attractiveness. ⟨earlier *fineer* < G *furnieren* < F *fournir* furnish⟩ **—ve'neer•er,** *n.*

ve•neer•ing [və'nirɪŋ] *n., v. —n.* **1** the act of applying veneer. **2** the surface so achieved. **3** the wood or other material used as a veneer.
—v. ppr. of VENEER.

ven•e•punc•ture ['vɛnə,pʌŋktʃər] *n.* See VENIPUNCTURE.

ven•er•a•ble ['vɛnərəbəl] *adj.* **1** worthy of reverence; deserving respect because of age, character, or associations: *a venerable old matriarch, venerable customs.* **2** *Anglican Church.* **Venerable,** a title of respect for an archdeacon: *The Venerable John Jones.* **3** *Roman Catholic Church.* **Venerable,** designating a person recognized as having attained a degree of virtue but not yet recognized as beatified or canonized: *the Venerable Bede.* ⟨ME < L *venerabilis* < *venerari* venerate⟩ **—'ven•er•a•bly,** *adv.* **—,ven•er•a'bil•i•ty,** *n.* **—'ven•er•a•ble•ness,** *n.*

ven•er•ate ['vɛnə,reit] *v.* **-at•ed, -at•ing.** regard with deep respect; revere: *He venerates his mother's memory.* ⟨< L *venerari* < *Venus, Veneris,* originally, love⟩

ven•er•a•tion [,vɛnə'reiʃən] *n.* **1** deep respect; reverence. **2** the act of venerating or the state of being venerated.

ve•ne•re•al [və'niriəl] *adj.* **1** of or having to do with sexual intercourse. **2** arousing sexual desire. **3** of a disease, transmitted by sexual intercourse. **4** of or having to do with diseases communicated by sexual intercourse. **5** infected with venereal disease. ⟨< L *venereus* < *Venus, Veneris* Venus⟩

venereal disease a contagious disease, such as gonorrhea or syphilis, that is transmitted only or mainly by sexual intercourse.

ve•ne•re•ol•o•gy [və,niri'ɒlədʒi] *n.* the branch of medicine that deals with venereal diseases. **—ve,ne•re•o'log•i•cal,** *adj.* **—ve,ne•re'ol•o•gist,** *n.*

ven•er•y¹ ['vɛnəri] *n. Archaic.* gratification of sexual desire. ⟨< L *Venus, Veneris* Venus⟩

ven•er•y² ['vɛnəri] *n. Archaic.* hunting; the chase. ⟨ME < OF *venerie,* ult. < L *venari* hunt⟩

ven•e•sec•tion ['vɛnə,sɛkʃən] *or* ['vinə,sɛkʃən] *n.* surgical incision into a vein; phlebotomy. ⟨< NL *venae secto* cutting of a vein⟩

Ve•ne•tian [və'niʃən] *n., adj. —n.* **1** a native or inhabitant of Venice, a city on the NE coast of Italy. **2** a dialect of Italian spoken in parts of the province of Veneto.
—adj. of or having to do with Venice or its people.

Venetian blind a window blind consisting of horizontal plastic, metal, or wooden slats that can be set at different angles to vary the amount of light that is let in. Also, **venetian blind.**

Venetian glass a fine, very delicate kind of glassware. ⟨< *Venice,* Italy, where it was first made⟩

Venetian red **1** a red pigment originally prepared from ferric oxides, now made synthetically from a mixture of lime and ferrous sulphate. **2** a rust colour.

Ven•e•zue•la [,vɛnə'zweilə] *n.* a country in N South America.

Ven•e•zue•lan [,vɛnə'zweilən] *n., adj. —n.* a native or inhabitant of Venezuela.
—adj. of or having to do with Venezuela or its people.

venge•ance ['vɛndʒəns] *n.* **1** the inflicting of injury in retaliation for a wrong or injury; revenge: *to swear vengeance for a wrong, to take vengeance on an enemy.* **2** the desire to retaliate in this way: *There was vengeance in his heart.*
with a vengeance, a with great force or intensity: *By six o'clock it was raining with a vengeance. She started in on the job with a vengeance.* **b** to an unusual degree; extremely: *He was getting his own back with a vengeance. That escapade was adventure with a vengeance.* ⟨ME < OF *vengeance,* ult. < L *vindex* avenger⟩

venge•ful ['vɛndʒfəl] *adj.* **1** inflicting vengeance; serving as an instrument of vengeance. **2** seeking vengeance; inclined to avenge oneself; vindictive: *vengeful enemies.* **3** feeling or showing a strong desire for vengeance. **—'venge•ful•ly,** *adv.* **—'venge•ful•ness,** *n.*

ve•ni•al ['viniəl] *or* ['vinjəl] *adj.* of misdeeds or shortcomings, that can be excused or overlooked; not very serious; minor: *venial faults.* ⟨ME < LL *venialis* < *venia* forgiveness⟩ **—'ve•ni•al•ly,** *adv.* **—,ve•ni'al•i•ty,** *n.*

venial sin *Theology.* a minor offence, or any offence that is not committed with full knowledge and consent and so does not deprive the soul of divine grace. Compare MORTAL SIN.

ven•in ['vɛnɪn] *n.* any of several toxic substances found in snake venom. ⟨< *venom* + *-in*⟩

ven•i•punc•ture ['vɛnɪ,pʌŋktʃər] *or* ['vinə,pʌŋktʃər] *n. Medicine.* the puncturing of a vien to take a blood sample or to inject a drug. Also, **venepuncture.**

ve•ni•re [və'naɪri] *or* [və'niri] *n. Law.* a writ authorizing the summoning of persons to serve on a jury. ⟨< L *venire facias,* that you may cause (them) to come⟩

ven•i•son ['vɛnəsən] *or* ['vɛnəzən] *n.* the flesh of a deer, used for food; deer meat. ⟨ME < OF < L *venatio* hunting < *venari* hunt⟩

venison bird *Cdn.* CANADA JAY.

Ve•ni•te [və'nitei] *or* [vɪ'naiti] *n.* the 95th Psalm (94th in the Vulgate), used as a part of certain Christian liturgies. ⟨< L *venite* come (2nd pers. pl. imperative), the first word in the Latin version⟩

ve•ni, vi•di, vi•ci ['veini 'vidi 'vitʃi] *or* ['weini 'widi 'wiki] *Latin.* I came, I saw, I conquered (a report of victory made by Julius Caesar to the Roman Senate).

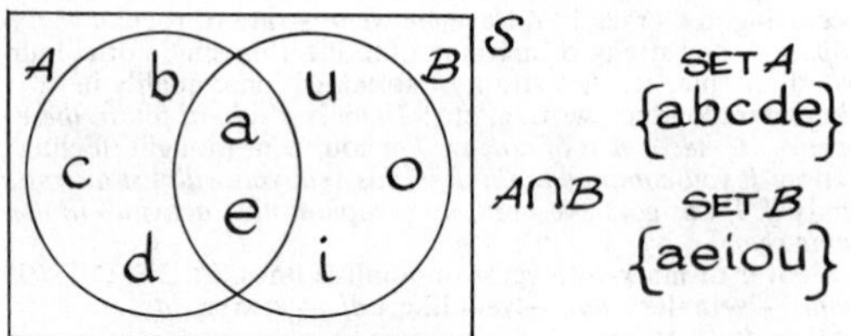

A Venn diagram showing the intersection of two sets having common elements. S is the set of all the letters of the alphabet, A is the set of the first five letters, and B is the set of vowels.

Venn diagram [vɛn] *Mathematics, Logic.* a diagram using circles, rectangles, or ellipses to show the relationships between sets, propositions, etc. ⟨< John *Venn* (1834-1923), an English logician⟩

ven•om ['vɛnəm] *n.* **1** the poison produced by some snakes, spiders, etc. and introduced into the body of prey or an enemy mainly by a bite or sting. **2** spite; malice: *There was venom in her voice.* ⟨ME < OF *venin* < L *venenum* poison⟩ **—'ven•om•less,** *adj.*

ven•om•ous ['vɛnəməs] *adj.* **1** poisonous: *Rattlesnakes are venomous.* **2** spiteful; malicious. **—'ven•om•ous•ly,** *adv.* **—'ven•om•ous•ness,** *n.*

ve•nous ['vinəs] *adj.* **1** of, in, or having to do with veins: *venous blood.* **2** having veins: *the venous wings of insects.* Also, **venose** ['vinous]. ⟨< L *venosus* < *vena* vein⟩ **—ve'nos•i•ty** [vɪ'nɒsəti], *n.* **—'ve•nous•ly,** *adv.*

vent¹ [vɛnt] *n., v. —n.* **1** a hole; opening, especially one serving as an outlet. **2** an outlet; way out: *His great energy found vent in hard work.* **3** expression: *She gave vent to her grief in tears.* **4** the opening of a volcano, through which lava, etc. escapes. **5** the external opening of the intestine, especially in birds, fish, and reptiles. **6** the small opening in the barrel of certain old guns through which the powder was fired; touchhole. **7** in an automobile, etc., a small side window or louvre that can be opened for indirect ventilation.
—v. **1** let out; express freely: *Don't vent your anger on the dog.* **2** make a vent in or for. ⟨partly < MF *vent* wind < L *ventus;* partly < MF *évent* vent, blowhole, ult. < L *ex-* out + *ventus* wind⟩

vent² [vɛnt] *n.* a slit or opening, usually faced or lined, made in a garment for ease of fit, especially in a coat or jacket. ⟨ME *vent,* var. of *fent(e)* < MF *fente* slit, ult. < L *findere* split⟩

vent•age ['vɛntɪdʒ] *n.* a vent; a small hole, especially for the escape or passage of air. The finger holes of a flute are ventages.

ven•ti•fact ['vɛntə,fækt] *n.* a stone shaped and smoothed by the abrasion of wind-driven sand. ⟨< L *ventus* wind + E *(art)ifact*⟩

ven•ti•late ['vɛntə,leit] *v.* **-lat•ed, -lat•ing.** **1** change or freshen the air in: *to ventilate a room by opening windows.* **2** purify by introducing a fresh supply of oxygen: *The lungs ventilate the blood.* **3** make known publicly; discuss openly: *to ventilate a grievance.* **4** furnish with a vent or opening for the escape of air, gas, etc. **5** expose (something) to air or wind for maintenance, freshening, etc.; air. ⟨< L *ventilare* fan < *ventus* wind⟩ **—'ven•ti•la,to•ry** ['vɛntələ,tɔri], *adj.*

ven•ti•la•tion [,vɛntə'leiʃən] *n.* **1** the act or process of ventilating. **2** a means of supplying fresh air: *That small window is the only ventilation in the warehouse.* **3** circulation of air: *The room has good ventilation.* **4** *Physiology.* the circulation and exchange of gases in the lungs in the process of breathing.

ven•ti•la•tor ['vɛntə,leitər] *n.* any apparatus or means for changing or improving the air in an enclosed space.

ven•tral ['vɛntrəl] *adj.* **1** *Anatomy.* of or having to do with the belly; abdominal. **2** *Zoology.* of, having to do with, or located on or near the part or surface opposite the back: *a ventral fin.* **3** *Botany.* of, having to do with, or located on the inner or lower surface of a structure. ⟨< LL *ventralis* < L *venter* belly⟩ **—'ven•tral•ly,** *adv.*

ven•tri•cle ['vɛntrəkəl] *n.* **1** either of the two lower chambers of the heart that receive blood from the upper chambers and force it into the arteries. See HEART for picture. **2** any of the series of four communicating cavities in the brain, which connect with the spinal cord and contain cerebrospinal fluid. See BRAIN for picture. **3** any of various other small cavities in the body. ⟨ME < L *ventriculus*, dim. of *venter* belly⟩

ven•tric•u•lar [vɛn'trɪkjələr] *adj.* **1** of, having to do with, or being a ventricle. **2** having to do with the stomach. **3** swelling out; distended. Also (def. 3), **ventricose**.

ven•tric•u•lus [vɛn'trɪkjələs] *n. Zoology.* **1** the part of the alimentary tract in which digestion takes place, as the lower cavity in an insect. **2** gizzard.

ven•tri•lo•qui•al [,vɛntrə'loukwiəl] *adj.* having to do with ventriloquism.

ven•tril•o•quism [vɛn'trɪlə,kwɪzəm] *n.* the art or practice of speaking or uttering sounds without moving the lips so that the voice may seem to come from some source other than the speaker. Also, **ventriloquy**. ⟨< L *ventriloquus* ventriloquist < *venter* belly + *loqui* speak⟩

ven•tril•o•quist [vɛn'trɪləkwɪst] *n.* a person who is skilled in ventriloquism, especially one who uses it to entertain an audience by appearing to carry on a conversation with a puppet manipulated by hand. **—ven,tril•o'quis•tic,** *adj.*

ven•tril•o•quize [vɛn'trɪlə,kwaɪz] *v.* **-quized, -quiz•ing.** make or utter (sounds) as a ventriloquist.

ven•tril•o•quy [vɛn'trɪləkwi] *n.* ventriloquism.

ven•ture ['vɛntʃər] *n., v.* **-tured, -tur•ing.** *—n.* **1** a risky or daring undertaking: *Her courage was equal to any venture.* **2** a speculation to make money: *A lucky venture in oil stock made his fortune.* **3** the thing risked; stake.
at a venture, at random; by chance.
—v. **1** expose to risk of danger or loss: *People venture their lives in war.* **2** dare (*to*): *No one ventured to interrupt the speaker.* **3** dare to come, go, or proceed: *He ventured out on the thin ice and fell through.* **4** guess (*at*): *to venture at a reason.* **5** brave or face the dangers of (something): *to venture the bitter cold.* **6** utter or offer at the risk of one's hearers' negative reaction: *She ventured a critique of their newly drafted policy.*
nothing ventured, nothing gained, advantage, profit, or other objectives are forfeited by overcautiousness or refusal to risk danger. ⟨< *aventure*, an earlier form of *adventure*⟩
☛ *Syn. v.* **3.** See note at DARE.

venture capital funds invested or available for investment, at risk of loss, in a new or unproven, but potentially highly profitable, business undertaking.

Ven•tur•er ['vɛntʃərər] *n.* a member, aged 14 to 17, of the Scouts.

ven•ture•some ['vɛntʃərsəm] *adj.* **1** inclined to take risks; rash; daring: *a venturesome explorer.* **2** hazardous; risky: *A trip to the moon is a venturesome journey.* **—'ven•ture•some•ly,** *adv.* **—'ven•ture•some•ness,** *n.*

ven•tu•ri (tube) [vɛn'tʃʊri] *or* [vɛn'tʊri] *n.* a short, narrow piece of tubing between wider sections in a pump or pipeline, used to measure or regulate the rate of flow of a liquid or gas. ⟨< G.B. *Venturi* (1746-1822), an Italian physicist⟩

ven•tur•ous ['vɛntʃərəs] *adj.* venturesome. **—'ven•tur•ous•ly,** *adv.* **—'ven•tur•ous•ness,** *n.*

ven•ue ['vɛnju] *n.* **1** *Law.* **a** the place or neighbourhood of a crime or cause of action. **b** the place where the jury is gathered and the case tried. A change of venue is allowed when strong local feeling may prevent a defendant from getting a fair trial. **2** the scene or setting of a real or fictional action or event. **3** the location of a conference, an important sporting event, public entertainment by a performing artist, etc.: *We have done some gigs in nightclubs and are now seeking other venues.* ⟨< OF *venue* coming, ult. < L *venire* come⟩

ven•ule ['vɛnjul] *n.* veinlet; a small vein. **—'ven•u•lar,** *adj.*

Ve•nus ['vinəs] *n.* **1** *Roman mythology.* the goddess of love and beauty, corresponding to the Greek goddess Aphrodite. **2** any very beautiful woman. **3** the most brilliant planet in the solar system, second in distance from the sun and closest to the earth.

Ve•nu•sian [və'nuʒən] *or* [və'nuʃən] *adj., n. —adj.* of or relating to the planet Venus.
—n. in science fiction, an inhabitant of the planet Venus.

Ve•nus's–fly•trap ['vinəsɪz 'flaɪ,træp] *n.* an insect-eating bog plant (*Dionaea muscipula*) of the sundew family native to the E United States, having hairy leaves with two lobes at the end that snap together to trap insects. Also, **Venus'-flytrap.**

ve•ra•cious [və'reiʃəs] *adj.* **1** of a person, truthful; honest. **2** true or accurate in content: *a veracious account.* ⟨< L *verax, -acis* < *verus* true⟩ **—ve'ra•cious•ly,** *adv.* **—ve'ra•cious•ness,** *n.*
☛ *Hom.* VORACIOUS.

ve•rac•i•ty [və'ræsəti] *n., pl.* **-ties. 1** truthfulness. **2** correctness; accuracy: *to check the veracity of a statement.* **3** something that is true. ⟨< Med.L *veracitas* < L *verax, -acis.* See VERACIOUS.⟩
☛ *Hom.* VORACITY.

ve•ran•da or **ve•ran•dah** [və'rændə] *n.* a large covered porch along one or more sides of a house. ⟨< Hind. and other languages of India < Pg. *varanda* railing⟩

verb [vɜrb] *n.* a word that expresses an action, event, or state, and that in many languages has different forms for person, tense, voice, etc. The verb is the main part of the predicate of a sentence. *Examples*: *do, see, impose, introduce, think, be.* ⟨< L *verbum*, originally, word⟩
☛ *Usage.* Verbs are classified on the basis of what complements them as a necessary part of the sentence structure. A verb taking a noun or noun substitute as an object is called **transitive:** She *broke* the mirror. A verb not taking an object is called **intransitive:** They *succeeded.* A verb taking a noun or adjective as a complement referring back to the subject is called a **linking verb:** She *became* a lawyer. He *seems* better. Many verbs in English can be either transitive or intransitive: I *broke* the mirror. The mirror *broke.*

ver•bal ['vɜrbəl] *adj.* **1** in or of words: *A description is a verbal picture.* **2** expressed in spoken words; oral as opposed to written: *a verbal promise, a verbal message.* **3** word for word; literal: *a verbal translation from the French.* **4** *Grammar.* of, having to do with, forming, or derived from a verb: *a verbal noun.* **5** having to do only with words rather than facts, action, thought, or belief: *Her religion is purely verbal. The verbal quality of your paper is excellent, but it lacks original ideas.*
—n. **1** *Grammar.* a verb form that functions as a noun, adjective, or adverb. Participles, gerunds, and infinitives are verbals. **2** *Linguistics.* a word or group of words that functions like a verb. ⟨< LL *verbalis* < L *verbum* word, verb⟩ **—'ver•bal•ly,** *adv.*
☛ *Usage.* See note at ORAL.

ver•bal•ism ['vɜrbə,lɪzəm] *n.* **1** a verbal expression; word, phrase, etc. **2** too much attention to mere words. **3** a stock phrase or statement with little meaning.

ver•bal•ist ['vɜrbəlɪst] *n.* **1** a person who is skilled in the use or choice of words. **2** a person who pays too much attention to mere words. **—,ver•bal'is•tic,** *adj.*

ver•bal•ize ['vɜrbə,laɪz] *v.* **-ized, -iz•ing. 1** use words; use language; speak: *Humans can verbalize.* **2** express in words: *He finds it difficult to verbalize his feelings.* **3** use too many words; be wordy: *The tendency of inexperienced writers is to verbalize.* **4** change (a noun, etc.) into a verb. **—,ver•bal•i'za•tion,** *n.*

verbal noun **1** gerund; the *-ing* form of a verb, used as a noun, as *Swimming* in *Swimming is fun.* **2** in many languages, the infinitive form of a verb similarly used.
☛ *Usage.* See note at GERUND.

ver•ba•tim [vər'beitɪm] *adv. or adj.* word for word; in exactly the same words: *His speech was printed verbatim in the newspaper.* ⟨< Med.L *verbatim* < L *verbum* word⟩

ver•be•na [vər'binə] *n.* **1** any of a genus (*Verbena*) of chiefly New World plants having flowers of various colours growing in clusters or spikes. Some verbenas have long been cultivated as garden plants. **2** (*adjl.*) designating a family (Verbenaceae) of mainly tropical herbs, shrubs, and trees. The verbena family includes the verbenas and also some trees important for timber, such as teak. ⟨< L *verbena* leafy branch. Doublet of VERVAIN.⟩

ver•bi•age ['vɜrbiɪdʒ] *n.* **1** too many words; abundance of useless words: *Cut out the verbiage and make your point.*

2 manner of expression; diction; wording. ⟨< F *verbiage*, ult. < L *verbum* word⟩

ver•bose [vər'bous] *adj.* containing or using too many words; wordy. ⟨< L *verbosus* < *verbum* word⟩ **—ver'bose•ly,** *adv.* **—ver'bose•ness,** *n.*
☛ *Syn.* See note at WORDY.

ver•bos•i•ty [vər'bɒsəti] *n.* the use of too many words; wordiness.

ver•bo•ten [fər'boutən]; *German,* [fɛʀ'botən] *adj.* forbidden, especially by authority.

ver•dant ['vɜrdənt] *adj.* **1** green in colour: *fields covered with verdant grass.* **2** covered with growing green plants: *verdant fields.* **3** inexperienced, unsophisticated, or immature; green. ⟨< *verdure*⟩ **—'ver•dan•cy,** *n.* **—'ver•dant•ly,** *adv.*

verd antique [vɜrd] **1** an ornamental variety of marble, mottled dark green in colour. **2** verdigris. **3** a type of green porphyry.

ver•dict ['vɜrdɪkt] *n.* **1** the decision of a jury: *The jury returned a verdict of not guilty.* **2** any decision or judgment: *the public's verdict, the verdict of history.* ⟨ME < AF *verdit* < *ver* true (< L *verus*) + *dit*, pp. of *dire* speak < L *dicere*⟩

ver•di•gris ['vɜrdə,gris] *or* ['vɜrdəgrɪs] *n.* **1** a green or bluish coating that forms on brass, copper, or bronze when exposed to the air for long periods of time. **2** a green or bluish green poisonous compound of copper and acetic acid, used as a pigment for paints. Also (def. 1), **false verdigris.** ⟨ME < OF *vert de grece*, literally, green of Greece⟩

ver•dure ['vɜrdʒər] *n.* **1** the fresh greenness of growing vegetation. **2** a flourishing growth of vegetation. **3** a condition of freshness and vigour. ⟨ME < OF *verdure*, ult. < L *viridis* green⟩
☛ *Hom.* VERGER.

ver•dur•ous ['vɜrdʒərəs] *adj.* **1** green. **2** healthy, fresh, and vigorous.

verge[1] [vɜrdʒ] *n. or v.* **verged, verg•ing.** *—n.* **1** the point at which something begins or happens; brink: *His business is on the verge of ruin.* **2** a limiting belt, strip, or border of something, as the strip of grass along a sidewalk. **3** a rod, staff, etc. carried as an emblem of authority. **4** *Architecture.* the shaft of a column. **5** the edge of tiling projecting over a gable.
—v. be on the verge; border: *Their silly talk verged on nonsense.* ⟨ME < OF < L *virga* staff⟩

verge[2] [vɜrdʒ] *v.* **verged, verg•ing.** tend or incline (*toward*); pass gradually (*into*): *Her gown was grey, verging into jet black at the bottom. His sadness is verging toward depression.* ⟨< L *vergere* turn, bend⟩

ver•ger ['vɜrdʒər] *n.* **1** in some churches, a sexton or custodian. **2** *Esp. Brit.* an officer or attendant who carries the staff or wand before a bishop, dean, etc. ⟨< MF *verger* < *verge* verge[1] < L *virga* staff⟩
☛ *Hom.* VERDURE.

Ver•gil•i•an [vər'dʒɪliən] See VIRGILIAN.

ver•glas [vɛr'glɑ] *n.* a thin coating of ice or frozen rain on rocks or pavement. ⟨< F < MF *verreglaz* < *verre* glass + *glaz* ice⟩

ve•rid•i•cal [və'rɪdəkəl] *adj.* **1** truthful; veracious. **2** of a dream, vision, etc., corresponding to fact or reality; true or coming true. ⟨< L *veridicus* telling the truth < *verus* truth + *dicere* speak⟩

ver•i•est ['vɛriɪst] *adj.* utmost: *the veriest nonsense.*

ver•i•fi•a•ble ['vɛrə,faɪəbəl] *adj.* capable of being verified; that can be checked for truth or correctness. **—'ver•i,fi•a•bly,** *adv.*

ver•i•fi•ca•tion [,vɛrəfə'keiʃən] *n.* **1** verifying or being verified; proof by evidence or testimony; confirmation. **2** *Law.* an affidavit added to testimony or a statement by the pleading party declaring that his or her allegations are true. **—,ver•i•fi'ca•tion•al,** *adj.*

ver•i•fy ['vɛrə,faɪ] *v.* **-fied, -fy•ing. 1** prove (something) to be true; confirm: *The driver's report of the accident was verified by eyewitnesses.* **2** test the correctness of; check for accuracy: *Verify the spelling of a word by looking in a dictionary.* **3** *Law.* **a** testify or affirm to be true, formally or upon oath. **b** declare that (one's pleading or allegations) are true, by the addition of an affidavit or the adduction of testimony or proof. ⟨ME < OF < Med.L *verificare* < L *verus* true + *facere* make⟩ **—'ver•i,fi•er,** *n.*

ver•i•ly ['vɛrəli] *adv. Archaic or poetic.* in truth; truly; really. ⟨< *very* + *-ly[1]*⟩

ver•i•sim•i•lar [,vɛrə'sɪmələr] *adj.* appearing true or real; probable; plausible or credible.

ver•i•si•mil•i•tude [,vɛrəsə'mɪlə,tjud] *or* [,vɛrəsə'mɪlə,tud] *n.* **1** appearance of truth or reality; probability; plausibility or credibility: *A story must have verisimilitude to interest most people.* **2** something having merely the appearance of truth or reality. ⟨< L *verisimilitudo* < *verus* true + *similis* like⟩

ver•ism ['vɛrɪzəm] *n.* in the arts, realism or naturalism. Also, especially in opera, **verismo** [və'rɪzmou]. ⟨< Ital. *verismo* (< *vero* true) + E *-ism*⟩ **—'ver•ist,** *n.* **—ve'ris•tic,** *adj.*

ver•i•ta•ble ['vɛrətəbəl] *adj.* true; real; actual. ⟨< OF *veritable* < *verité* < L *veritas.* See VERITY.⟩ **—'ver•i•ta•ble•ness,** *n.* **—'ver•i•ta•bly,** *adv.*

ver•i•ty ['vɛrəti] *n., pl.* **-ties. 1** the quality or state of being true or real. **2** something that is true or real, especially a basic principle or belief: *the eternal verities.* ⟨ME < OF < L *veritas* < *verus* true⟩

ver•juice ['vɜr,dʒus] *n.* **1** an acid liquor made from sour juice of crab apples, unripe grapes, etc. Verjuice was formerly used in cooking. **2** sourness, as of temper or expression. ⟨ME < OF *verjus* < *vert* green (< L *viridis*) + *jus* juice < L⟩

ver•juiced ['vɜr,dʒust] *adj.* of or having to do with verjuice; sour.

ver•meil [vər'mei], ['vɜrmeil], *or* ['vɜrməl] *n., adj. —n.* **1** silver, bronze, or copper coated or plated with gold. **2** *Poetic.* vermilion.
—adj. **1** made of vermeil. **2** *Poetic.* vermilion. ⟨ME < OF *vermeil* < L *vermiculus*, dim. of *vermis* worm⟩

ver•mi•cel•li [,vɜrmə'tʃɛli] *or* [,vɜrmə'sɛli]; *Italian,* [,vɛrmi'tʃɛlli] *n.* a kind of pasta similar to spaghetti, but thinner. ⟨< Ital. *vermicelli*, literally, little worms, ult. < L *vermis* worm⟩

ver•mi•cide ['vɜrmə,saɪd] *n.* any agent that kills worms; especially, a drug used to kill parasitic intestinal worms. ⟨< L *vermis* worm + E *-cide[2]*⟩

ver•mic•u•lar [vər'mɪkjələr] *adj.* **1** of, having to do with, or characteristic of a worm or worms. **2** like a worm in nature, form, or method of movement. **3** like the wavy track of a worm; undulating; tortuous. **4** marked with close wavy lines. **5** worm-eaten. **6** formed or caused by worms. ⟨< Med.L *vermicularis*, ult. < L *vermis* worm⟩

ver•mic•u•late *v.* [vər'mɪkjə,leit]; *adj.* [vər'mɪkjəlɪt] *or* [vər'mɪkjə,leit] *v.,* **-late, -lat•ed;** *adj. —v.* ornament with wavy lines (like those left by a worm).
—adj. vermicular. **—ver,mic•u'la•tion,** *n.*

ver•mic•u•lite [vər'mɪkjə,ləit] *n.* any of various silicate minerals in the form of small, lightweight granules or flakes that readily absorb water. Vermiculite is used as a medium for growing seedlings, for insulation, etc. ⟨< L *vermiculus* + E *-ite[1]*. See VERMEIL.⟩

ver•mi•form ['vɜrmə,fɔrm] *adj.* shaped like a worm. ⟨< Med.L *vermiformis* < L *vermis* worm + *forma* form⟩

vermiform appendix a slender tube, closed at one end, growing out of the large intestine in the lower right-hand part of the abdomen. Appendicitis is inflammation of the vermiform appendix.

ver•mi•fuge ['vɜrmə,fjudʒ] *n., adj. —n.* a medicine to expel worms from the intestines.
—adj. serving to expel worms: *to put vermifuge powder in dog food.* ⟨< F < L *vermis* worm + *fugare* cause to flee⟩

ver•mil•ion [vər'mɪljən] *n., adj. —n.* **1** bright, somewhat orangy red. **2** a pigment having this colour, especially one consisting of mercuric sulphide.
—adj. having the colour vermilion. ⟨ME < OF *vermillon* < *vermeil.* See VERMEIL.⟩

ver•min ['vɜrmən] *n.* (*usually functioning as plural*) **1** small animals that are troublesome, objectionable, or destructive, especially insects such as lice, fleas, and bedbugs, or rodents such as rats and mice. **2** a vile, offensive, or dangerous person or persons. ⟨ME < OF *vermin*, ult. < L *vermis* worm⟩

ver•min•ous ['vɜrmənəs] *adj.* **1** infested with vermin. **2** caused by vermin. **3** like vermin; vile; worthless.

Ver•mont [vər'mɒnt] *n.* a northeastern state of the United States.

ver•mouth [vər'muθ] *or* ['vɜrməθ] *n.* a fortified white wine flavoured with herbs and used as a liqueur or in cocktails. Vermouth may be either dry or sweet, and ranges in colour from pale yellow to reddish brown. ⟨< F < G *Wermut(h)* wormwood, with which it was originally flavoured⟩

ver•nac•u•lar [vər'nækjələr] *n., adj. —n.* **1** a native language; language used by the people of a certain country or place.

2 everyday language; informal speech. **3** the language of a profession, trade, etc.: *the vernacular of the lawyers.* **4** a vernacular word or expression, especially the common name of an animal or plant.
—adj. **1** used, practised, etc. by the people of a certain country, place, etc.; native: *vernacular customs. English is our vernacular tongue.* **2** of, using, or in the native or everyday language, rather than a literary or learned language. ⟨< L *vernaculus* domestic, native < *verna* home-born slave⟩

ver•nac•u•lar•ism [vər'nækjələ,rɪzəm] *n.* **1** the use of, or the policy of using, the vernacular language. **2** a vernacular term or usage.

ver•nal ['vɜrnəl] *adj.* **1** of, having to do with, or occurring in spring: *vernal green, vernal flowers, vernal months, the vernal equinox.* **2** like spring; fresh, new, mild, etc. **3** youthful: *Everyone admired the young girl's vernal freshness.* ⟨< L *vernalis* < *ver* spring⟩ **—'ver•nal•ly,** *adv.*

vernal equinox the equinox that occurs on or about March 21.

ver•nal•ize ['vɜrnə,laɪz] *v.* **-ized, -iz•ing.** hasten the flowering of (plants) by cooling the seed before planting.
—,ver•nal•i'za•tion, *n.*

ver•na•tion [vər'neiʃən] *n. Botany.* the arrangement of leaves in a bud. ⟨< NL *vernatio, -onis* < *vernare* bloom, renew itself⟩

Ver•ner's law ['vɜrnərz] *Linguistics.* a statement by K. Verner, a Danish philologist, explaining the regularity of apparent exceptions to GRIMM'S LAW.

ver•ni•er ['vɜrniər] *or* ['vɜrnir] *n., adj. —n.* **1** a small, movable scale for measuring a fractional part of one of the divisions of a fixed scale. **2** any auxiliary device allowing a tool or instrument of measurement to be adjusted to a finer setting.
—adj. of or having a vernier. ⟨after Pierre *Vernier* (1580-1637), a French mathematician⟩

ver•nis•sage [,vɜrnə'sɑʒ]; *French,* [vɛRni'saʒ] *n.* **1** the opening or first showing of an exhibition of artwork. **2** a reception for the artist on this day. ⟨< F, varnishing, because paintings used to be varnished before showing⟩

ve•ron•i•ca [və'rɒnəkə] *n.* **1** speedwell. **2 a** a cloth with an image of Christ's face, especially the cloth said to have been impressed with such an image after being used by St. Veronica to wipe the sweat from Christ's face on the way to Calvary. **b** the image itself. **3** a move in bullfighting where the matador holds the cape away from his body and pivots slowly as the bull charges. ⟨< NL⟩

ver•ru•ca [və'rukə] *n., pl.* **-cas** or **-cae** [-si] *or* [-saɪ]. **1** a wart, especially one on the hand or foot. **2** a wartlike growth or bump on a plant, the skin of an animal, etc. ⟨< L, wart⟩ **—'ver•ru,cose** ['vɛrə,kous], *adj.* **—'ver•ru•cous,** *adj.*

ver•sant ['vɜrsənt] *n.* **1** the side or slope of a mountain or range of mountains. **2** the slope of any region. ⟨< F < L *versare* turn⟩

ver•sa•tile ['vɜrsə,taɪl] *or* ['vɜrsətəl] *adj.* **1** able to do many things well: *He is very versatile; he is an actor, a poet, a singer, and a language teacher.* **2** having many uses: *a versatile dress, suitable for different occasions. A pocketknife is a versatile tool.* **3** *Zoology.* **a** capable of turning forward or backward: *the versatile toe of an owl.* **b** moving freely up and down and from side to side: *versatile antennae.* **4** *Botany.* attached at or near the middle so as to swing or turn freely: *a versatile anther.* **5** *Archaic.* changeable; fickle; inconstant. ⟨< L *versatilis* turning, ult. < *vertere* turn⟩
—'ver•sa,tile•ly, *adv.* **—,ver•sa'til•i•ty** [-'tɪləti], *n.*

verse [vɜrs] *n.* **1** a form of literary expression using lines of words, the lines usually having a regularly repeated stress and often having rhyme; poetry. **2** sometimes, poetry of poor or mediocre quality; doggerel. **3 a** a single line of verse. **b** a single poem. **4** stanza: *Sing the first verse of "O Canada."* **5** a type of verse; METRE (def. 1): *blank verse, iambic verse.* **6** one of the short sections into which the chapters of the books of the Bible are traditionally divided. ⟨late OE *vers* (replacing earlier *fers*) < L *versus,* originally, row, furrow < *vertere* turn around⟩

versed [vɜrst] *adj.* experienced; practised; knowledgeable or informed: *A doctor should be well versed in medical theory.*

ver•si•cle ['vɜrsəkəl] *n.* **1** a little verse. **2** one of a series of short sentences said or sung by the minister or priest during services, to which the people make response. ⟨< L *versiculus,* dim. of *versus.* See VERSE.⟩

ver•si•col•our ['vɜrsə,kʌlər] *adj.* **1** multicoloured; variegated. **2** changing colours in different lights or as seen from different angles; iridescent. Also, **versicoloured.** ⟨< L *versare* change, turn + *color* colour⟩

ver•si•fi•ca•tion [,vɜrsəfə'keiʃən] *n.* **1** the art, theory, or act of writing verses. **2** the form or style of poetry; metrical structure. **3 a** the act or process of putting prose into verse. **b** the resulting piece of writing.

ver•si•fy ['vɜrsə,faɪ] *v.* **-fied, -fy•ing. 1** write verses, especially mediocre ones. **2** tell in verse. **3** turn (prose) into poetry. ⟨< L *versificare* < *versus* verse + *facere* make⟩ **—'ver•si,fi•er,** *n.*

ver•sion ['vɜrʒən] *or* ['vɜrʃən] *n.* **1** a translation from one language to another; especially, a translation of the Bible: *the King James Version.* **2** a statement or description from a particular point of view: *Each of the three boys gave his own version of the quarrel.* **3** a special form or variant of something: *The tent trailer is a modern version of the travois.* **4** *Medicine.* **a** an abnormal, tilted position of the uterus. **b** the turning of a fetus by the midwife or doctor during childbirth for easier delivery. ⟨< L *versio, -onis,* originally, a turning < *vertere* turn⟩
—'ver•sion•al, *adj.*

vers li•bre [vɛr 'librə]; *French,* [vɛR'libR] *French.* free verse; verse that follows no fixed metrical form.

ver•so ['vɜrsou] *n., pl.* **-sos** [-souz]. **1** *Printing.* **a** the back of a sheet of printed paper; the side that is to be read second. **b** the left-hand page of an open book. Compare RECTO. **2** the reverse side of a medal or coin. ⟨< L *verso folio* turned leaf < *versus,* pp. of *vertere* turn⟩

verst [vɛrst] *or* [vɜrst] *n.* formerly, a Russian unit of linear measure, equalling 1.067 km. ⟨< Russian *vyersta* < Old Russian *virsta*⟩

ver•sus ['vɜrsəs] *prep.* **1** against. **2** in contrast to: *the new versus the old, strength versus agility. Abbrev.*: v., vs. ⟨< L *versus* turned toward, pp. of *vertere* turn⟩

vert [vɜrt] *n., adj. Heraldry.* green, represented by diagonal lines upward from left to right. ⟨ME verte < OF < L *viridis* green⟩

vert. vertical.

ver•te•bra ['vɜrtəbrə] *n., pl.* **-brae** [-,brei] *or* [-,bri] or **-bras.** one of the bones of the spinal column. See SPINAL COLUMN for picture. ⟨< L < *vertere* turn⟩

ver•te•bral ['vɜrtəbrəl] *adj.* **1** of, like, or having to do with a vertebra or the vertebrae. **2** composed of vertebrae.

ver•te•brate ['vɜrtəbrɪt] *or* ['vɜrtə,breit] *n., adj. —n.* any animal that has a segmented spinal column, or backbone. Fish, amphibians, reptiles, birds, and mammals are all vertebrates.
—adj. **1** of, having to do with, or designating the vertebrates. **2** vertebral. ⟨< L *vertebratus* jointed < *vertebra.* See VERTEBRA.⟩

ver•te•bra•tion [,vɜrtə'breiʃən] *n.* division into segments like those of the spinal column; vertebrate formation.

ver•tex ['vɜrtɛks] *n., pl.* **-tex•es** or **-ti•ces** [-tə,siz]. **1** the highest point; top; summit. **2** *Mathematics.* **a** the point opposite to and farthest away from the base of a triangle, pyramid, etc. **b** the point of meeting of lines that form an angle. **c** a point where the axis of a hyperbola, parabola, or ellipse intersects it. **d** any point of a triangle or polygon. **3** *Astronomy.* a point in the heavens directly overhead. **4** *Anatomy, Zoology.* the top of the head. ⟨< L *vertex,* originally, whirl, n. < *vertere* turn⟩

ver•ti•cal ['vɜrtəkəl] *adj., n. —adj.* **1** straight up and down; perpendicular to a horizontal surface. A person standing up straight is in a vertical position. See HORIZONTAL for picture. **2** of or at the highest point; of the vertex. **3** directly overhead; at the zenith. **4** *Industry.* of or including many or all stages in production, strata of organization, etc.: *a vertical union, vertical trusts, vertical mobility.*
—n. a vertical line, plane, circle, position, part, etc. ⟨< LL *verticalis* < *vertex* highest point. See VERTEX.⟩ **—'ver•ti•cal•ly,** *adv.* **—,ver•ti'cal•i•ty** [-'kæləti], *n.*

vertical circle *Astronomy.* any great circle of the celestial sphere perpendicular to the horizon and passing through the zenith.

vertical file a file, as in a library, cataloguing or bringing together various different media, such as photographs, articles, drawings, recordings, etc., organized by subject.

vertical union a labour union to which all workers in a given industry may belong, regardless of their particular trade or craft.

ver•ti•ces ['vɜrtə,siz] *n.* a pl. of VERTEX.

ver•ti•cil ['vɜrtə,sɪl] *n. Biology.* a whorl or circle of parts, such as leaves, hairs, etc., growing around a stem or central point. ⟨< L *verticillus,* dim. of *vertex.* See VERTEX.⟩ **—ver'tic•il•late** [vər'tɪsəlɪt], *adj.*

ver•tig•i•nous [vər'tɪdʒənəs] *adj.* **1** whirling; rotary. **2** affected with vertigo; dizzy. **3** of the nature of or having to do with vertigo; likely to cause vertigo. **4** fickle; unstable. ⟨< L *vertiginosus* suffering from dizziness < *vertigo.* See VERTIGO.⟩ **—ver'tig•i•nous•ly,** *adv.* **—ver'tig•i•nous•ness,** *n.*

ver•ti•go ['vɜrtə,gou] *n., pl.* **ver•ti•goes** or **ver•tig•i•nes** [vər'tɪdʒə,niz]. a sensation of dizziness or of giddiness. ⟨< L *vertigo* < *vertere* turn⟩

ver•tu [vər'tu] *or* ['vɜrtu] See VIRTU.

ver•vain ['vɜrvein] *n.* verbena; especially, any of several wild North American herbs or a European species (*Verbena officinalis*) formerly used in medicine. ⟨ME < OF < L *verbena* leafy bough. Doublet of VERBENA.⟩

verve [vɜrv] *n.* enthusiasm; energy; vigour; spirit; liveliness. ⟨< F⟩

ver•vet ['vɜrvɪt] *n.* a small guenon monkey (*Circopethecus pygerythrus*) of Africa, related to the grivet and to the green monkey but having a rust-coloured patch at the base of the tail. ⟨< F, prob. < *ver(t)* green + *(gri)vet*⟩

ver•y ['vɛri] *adv. or adj.* **ver•i•er, ver•i•est.** *—adv.* **1** much; greatly; extremely: *The sun is very hot.* **2** absolutely; exactly: *in the very same place.*
—adj. **1** same; identical: *The very people who used to love her hate her now.* **2** mere; sheer: *The very thought of blood makes him sick. They wept for very joy.* **3** utter; absolute; complete: *He did the very opposite. She is the very slave of her mother.* **4** actual: *He was caught in the very act of stealing.* **5** exactly right or suitable: *That picture is the very thing for our living room wall.* **6** *Archaic.* real; true; genuine: *She seemed a very queen.* ⟨ME < OF *verai*, ult. < L *verus* true⟩
☛ *Hom.* VARY.

very high frequency the band of radio frequencies between 30 and 300 kilohertz. Very high frequency is the range next above high frequency. *Abbrev.*: VHF, V.H.F.

Ver•y light ['vɛri] *or* ['viri] a coloured light fired from a pistol as a signal or for temporary illumination. ⟨< Edward W. *Very* (1847-1910), a U.S. naval officer who invented it⟩

very low frequency the band of radio frequencies between 3 and 30 kilohertz. Very low frequency is the range next above voice frequency. *Abbrev.*: VLF, V.L.F.

Very pistol ['vɛri] *or* ['viri] a pistol for firing a VERY LIGHT.

Very Reverend a title of respect for any of various Christian ecclesiastical officials, such as a dean or canon or a rector of a college or seminary.

ves•i•ca ['vɛsəkə] *n., pl.* **-cas** or **-cae** [-,si] *or* [-,saɪ]. bladder, especially the urinary bladder. ⟨< L⟩ **—'ves•i•cal,** *adj.*

ves•i•cant ['vɛsəkənt] *adj., n. —adj.* that causes blistering.
—n. **1** an agent or substance that causes blistering. **2** in chemical warfare, an agent, such as mustard gas, that burns and destroys tissue, both internally and externally.

ves•i•cate ['vɛsə,keit] *v.* **-cat•ed, -cat•ing.** cause blisters on; blister. **—,ves•i'ca•tion,** *n.*

ves•i•cle ['vɛsəkəl] *n.* **1** a small bladder, pouch, sac, or cyst in a plant or animal. **2** a small, abnormal, raised part in the outer layer of skin, containing a watery fluid; blister. **3** *Geology.* a small cavity, the result of trapped gas, in a rock or mineral, especially in volcanic rock. ⟨< L *vesicula*, dim. of *vesica* bladder, blister⟩

ve•sic•u•lar [və'sɪkjələr] *adj.* **1** of, having to do with, or having vesicles. **2** like a vesicle; having the form or structure of a vesicle.

ve•sic•u•late *v.* [və'sɪkjə,leit]; *adj.* [və'sɪkjəlɪt] *or* [və'sɪkjə,leit] *v.* **-lat•ed, -lat•ing;** *adj. —v.* make or become vesicular.
—adj. vesicular.

ves•per ['vɛspər] *n.* **1** *Archaic or poetic.* evening. **2 vespers** or **Vespers,** *pl.* **a** a Christian church service held in the late afternoon or in the evening. **b** the sixth of the canonical hours. **3** a bell calling people to vespers. **4 Vesper,** the evening star. **5** (*adj.*) of or having to do with evening or vespers. ⟨< Med.L < L *vespera* evening⟩

vesper sparrow a grey-brown sparrow, *Pooecetes gramineus*, ranging from Canada to the south central U.S., having white outer tail feathers, a whitish eye-ring, and chestnut wing bend. Its song is heard in the evening.

ves•per•tine ['vɛspər,taɪn] *or* ['vɛspərtɪn] *adj.* **1** of or occurring in the evening. **2** *Biology.* **a** of animals or birds, active in the evening. **b** of flowers, opening in the evening. **3** of stars, setting near the time of sunset. ⟨< L *vespertinus* < *vesper* evening⟩

ves•pi•ar•y ['vɛspi,ɛri] *n., pl.* **-ies.** a nest or colony of wasps. ⟨< L *vespa* wasp + E *(ap)iary*⟩

ves•pine ['vɛspaɪn] *or* ['vɛspɪn] *adj.* of or having to do with wasps or resembling a wasp. ⟨< L *vespa* wasp⟩

ves•sel ['vɛsəl] *n.* **1** a ship or large boat. **2** an airship. **3** a hollow holder or container. Cups, bowls, pitchers, bottles, barrels, tubs, etc. are vessels. **4 a** a tube carrying blood or other body fluid. Veins and arteries are blood vessels. **b** a tube or duct in the xylem of plants, carrying fluids and made up of a row of cells whose end walls have broken down. **5** a person regarded as a container of some quality or as made for some purpose (used chiefly in or after Biblical expressions): *a vessel of purity.* ⟨ME < OF < L *vascellum*, double dim. of *vas* vessel⟩

vest [vɛst] *n., adj. —n.* **1** a usually close-fitting, sleeveless, waist-length garment, either with a front closure or pulled on and off over the head. **2** a garment or piece of equipment of this general form, serving a specific purpose: *a life vest, an ammunition vest.* **3** an undershirt, especially for women or children. **4** *Archaic.* clothing; a garment.
—v. **1 a** clothe; robe; dress in vestments: *The vested priest stood before the altar.* **b** put on garments or vestments. **2** furnish with powers, authority, rights, etc.: *Parliament is vested with power to declare war.* **3** put in the possession or control of a person or persons: *The management of the hospital is vested in a board of trustees.* **4** of property, a right, etc. pass into the possession of (a person); become vested (*in*). ⟨ME < OF *veste*, ult. < L *vestis* garment⟩ **—'vest•less,** *adj.*

Ves•ta ['vɛstə] *n.* **1** *Roman mythology.* the goddess of the hearth, corresponding to the Greek goddess Hestia. A sacred fire was always kept burning in the temple of Vesta. **2** the brightest of the four largest asteroids. **3 vesta,** a kind of short, usually wooden, friction match.

ves•tal ['vɛstəl] *adj., n. —adj.* **1** of or having to do with the Roman goddess Vesta. **2** of or having to do with the VESTAL VIRGINS. **3** chaste; pure; virginal.
—n. **1** a chaste woman, especially a nun or a virgin. **2** VESTAL VIRGIN.

vestal virgin a virgin consecrated to the service of the Roman goddess Vesta. Six vestal virgins tended an undying fire in honour of Vesta at her temple in Rome.

vest•ed ['vɛstɪd] *adj., v. —adj.* **1** *Law.* placed in the permanent possession or control of a person or persons; fixed; absolute: *vested rights.* **2** clothed or robed, especially in church garments: *a vested choir.*
—v. pt. and pp. of VEST.

vested interest **1** a legally established right to the possession of real or personal property. **2** a self-interested concern for something; favourable involvement in or leaning toward something which is to one's own advantage (*used with* **in**): *Manufacturers have a vested interest in low freight rates.* **3** a person, group, or institution having such a concern.

vest•ee [vɛs'ti] *n.* a fabric insert, with or without a collar, in the front of a dress, jacket, or blouse. ⟨< *vest* + *-ee*, dim. suffix⟩

ves•ti•a•ry ['vɛsti,ɛri] *n., adj. —n.* **1** VESTRY (def. 1). **2** a robing room, as for clergy or choir.
—adj. relating to clothing or vestments.

ves•tib•u•lar [vɛ'stɪbjələr] *adj.* of or having to do with a vestibule.

ves•ti•bule ['vɛstə,bjul] *n.* **1** a passage or hall between the outer door and the inside of a building, or between an anteroom and a larger room. **2** the enclosed space at the end of a railway passenger car, for entering and exiting, especially when moving between cars. **3** *Anatomy, Zoology.* a cavity of the body that leads to another cavity. The vestibule of the ear is the central cavity of the internal ear. See EAR[1] for picture. ⟨< L *vestibulum*⟩

ves•tige ['vɛstɪdʒ] *n.* **1** a slight remnant; trace: *Ghost stories are vestiges of a former widespread belief in ghosts.* **2** *Biology.* a part, organ, etc. that is no longer fully developed or useful. **3** *Rare.* footprint. Also (def. 2), **vestigium.** ⟨< F < L *vestigium* footprint⟩
☛ *Syn.* **1.** See note at TRACE.

ves•tig•i•al [vɛ'stɪdʒiəl] *adj.* **1** remaining as a vestige of something that has disappeared. **2** *Biology.* no longer fully developed or useful. **—ves'tig•i•al•ly,** *adv.*

vest•ment ['vɛstmənt] *n.* **1** an outer garment, especially for ceremonial or official wear. **2** any of the official garments worn by some members of the Christian clergy and assistants during church services. **3 vestments,** *pl.* clothing. **4** *Poetic.* something that covers like a garment: *rooftops with a vestment of snow.* ⟨ME < OF *vestement*, ult. < L *vestis* garment⟩

vest–pock•et ['vɛst ˌpɒkɪt] *adj.* **1** able to fit into a vest pocket. **2** very small.

ves•try ['vɛstri] *n., pl.* **-tries. 1** a room in a Christian church, where vestments, etc. are kept; sacristy. **2** a room in a church or an attached building, used for Sunday school, prayer meetings, etc. **3** *Anglican Church.* **a** a committee that helps manage church business. **b** a meeting of parishioners on church business. **c** the place where either of these groups meets. ⟨ME *vestry* < *vest* vest + *-(e)ry* -ery⟩

ves•try•man ['vɛstrimən] *n., pl.* **-men.** a member of a committee that helps manage the business of a Christian church.

ves•ture ['vɛstʃər] *n., v.* **-tured, -tur•ing.** *—n.* **1** *Poetic.* **a** clothing; garments. **b** a covering. **2** *Law.* everything growing on or covering land, excluding trees.
—v. clothe; cover. ⟨ME < OF *vesture*, ult. < L *vestis* garment⟩

Ve•su•vi•an [və'suviən] *adj., n. —adj.* of, having to do with, or resembling Mount Vesuvius, an active volcano near Naples, Italy; volcanic.
—n. **vesuvian**, formerly, a type of match used especially for lighting cigars.

ve•su•vi•an•ite [və'suviəˌnəit] *n.* a glassy, brown or green mineral, a hydrated silicate of calcium, magnesium, iron, and aluminum, sometimes used as a gemstone.

vet[1] [vɛt] *n., v.* **vet•ted, vet•ting.** *Informal. —n.* veterinarian.
—v. **1** examine and care for as a veterinarian or, sometimes, as a doctor. **2** examine carefully; check: *to vet a report.* **3** practise veterinary medicine.

vet[2] [vɛt] *n. Informal.* VETERAN (def. 1).

vet[3] [vɛt] *n.* the third letter of the Hebrew alphabet. See table of alphabets in the Appendix.

vet. 1 veteran. **2** veterinarian; veterinary.

vetch [vɛtʃ] *n.* any of a genus (*Vicia*) of trailing or climbing plants of the pea family, including several species that are valuable fodder and soil-enriching plants. ⟨< dial. OF < L *vicia*⟩

vet•er•an ['vɛtərən] *n., adj. —n.* **1** a person who has served in the armed forces, especially during wartime. **2** a person who has had (much) experience in war; an old soldier, sailor, airman, etc. **3** (*adjl.*) having had (much) experience in war: *Veteran troops fought side by side with new recruits.* **4** a person who has had much experience in some position, occupation, etc.: *veterans on a teaching staff.* **5** (*adjl.*) grown old in service; having had much experience: *a veteran farmer.* ⟨< L *veteranus* < *vetus, -teris* old⟩

Veterans Affairs Canada *Cdn.* a branch of the federal government dealing with the needs and rights of former service personnel.

vet•er•i•nar•i•an [ˌvɛtərə'nɛriən] *n.* a person trained in veterinary medicine, especially one whose work it is.

vet•er•i•nar•y ['vɛtrəˌnɛri] *or* ['vɛtərəˌnɛri] *adj., n., pl.* **-nar•ies.** *—adj.* having to do with the medical or surgical treatment of animals.
—n. veterinarian. ⟨< L *veterinarius* < *veterinus* pertaining to beasts of burden and draft, probably < *vetus, veteris* old (i.e., good for nothing else)⟩

veterinary surgeon *Esp. Brit.* veterinarian.

vet•i•ver ['vɛtəvər] *n.* **1** a grass (*Vetiveria zizanioides*) of India from whose roots a fragrant oil is obtained, used in perfumes. **2** the roots themselves. ⟨< F *vétiver* < Tamil *vettiveru* root that is dug up < *ver* root⟩

ve•to ['vitou] *n., pl.* **-toes;** *v.* **-toed, -to•ing.** *—n.* **1** the right or power to forbid or reject: *The Senate has the power of veto over most bills passed in the House of Commons.* **2** the use of this right; a refusal of consent: *The school's veto on baseball caps in the classroom may be hard to enforce.* **3** a statement of the reasons for disapproval of a bill passed by a legislature. **4** (*adjl.*) having to do with a veto: *veto power.* Also (def. 3), **veto message.**
—v. **1** reject formally by a veto. **2** refuse to consent to: *Her parents vetoed her plan to buy a motorcycle.* ⟨< L *veto* I forbid⟩ **—'ve•to•er,** *n.*

vex [vɛks] *v.* **1** anger by trifles; annoy; provoke. **2** disturb; trouble. ⟨< L *vexare*⟩

vex•a•tion [vɛk'seiʃən] *n.* **1** the quality or state of being vexed: *His vexation at the delay was obvious.* **2** the act of vexing. **3** something that vexes.

vex•a•tious [vɛk'seiʃəs] *adj.* **1** vexing; annoying. **2** *Law.* of legal action, brought with insufficient grounds and merely in order to annoy the defendant. **—vex'a•tious•ly,** *adv.* **—vex'a•tious•ness,** *n.*

vex•ed•ly ['vɛksɪdli] *adv.* with vexation; with a sense of annoyance or vexation.

vexed question a question causing much difficulty and debate.

vex•il•lol•o•gist [ˌvɛksə'lɒlədʒɪst] *n.* a person who studies flags.

vex•il•lol•o•gy [ˌvɛksə'lɒlədʒi] *n.* the study of flags. ⟨< L *vexillum* flag + *-logy*⟩ **—ˌvex•il•lo'log•i•cal,** *adj.*

vex•il•lum [vɛk'sɪləm] *n., pl.* **-il•la** [-ɪlə]. **1** *Zoology.* the vane of a feather. **2** *Botany.* the large, erect petal of certain butterfly-shaped flowers, as those of the pea family. The other, somewhat smaller petal hangs downward. **3** a processional or military banner or standard; flag. ⟨< L *vexillum* flag⟩ **—'vex•il,la•ry** ['vɛksəˌlɛri], *adj.* **—'vex•il•late** ['vɛksəˌlɪt], *adj.*

VHF or **V.H.F.** VERY HIGH FREQUENCY.

VHS *Trademark.* an electronic audio and video recording system. ⟨< *v*ideo *h*ome *s*ystem⟩

v.i. intransitive verb (for L *verbum intransitivum*).

vi•a ['vaɪə] *or* ['viə] *prep.* **1** by way of; by a route that passes through or along: *They travelled from Winnipeg to Saskatoon via Regina.* **2** by means or through the medium of: *We sent the package via airmail.* ⟨< L *via*, abl. of *via* way⟩

vi•a•ble ['vaɪəbəl] *adj.* **1** able to stay alive or to survive the passage of time. **2** able to keep operating or functioning: *a viable economy.* **3** workable; practicable; serviceable: *That is not a viable solution to our problem.* **4** of a fetus or newborn infant, sufficiently developed to maintain life outside the uterus. **5** *Botany.* capable of living and growing, as a spore or seed. ⟨< F < *vie* life < L *vita*⟩ **—'vi•a•bly,** *adv.* **—ˌvi•a'bil•i•ty,** *n.*

Vi•a Dol•o•ro•sa ['viə ˌdɒlə'rousə] *or* [ˌdoulə'rousə] *Latin.* **1** the road in Jerusalem travelled by Jesus from the judgment hall to Calvary. **2 via dolorosa,** a path of suffering or torment. ⟨literally, sorrowful way⟩

vi•a•duct ['vaɪəˌdʌkt] *n.* a bridge, especially one consisting of a series of arches or short spans resting on high piers or towers, for carrying a road or railway over a valley, a part of a city, etc. ⟨< L *via* road + *ductus* a leading; patterned on *aqueduct*⟩

vi•al ['vaɪəl] *n.* a small bottle, especially a glass bottle, for holding medicines, perfumes, etc. ⟨var. of *phial*⟩
☛ *Hom.* VIOL.

vi•a me•di•a ['vaɪə 'midiə] *or* ['viə 'midiə] *Latin.* a middle way; a course of moderation between two extremes.

vi•and ['vaɪənd] *or* ['viənd] *n.* Usually, **viands,** *pl.* articles of food, especially choice food. ⟨ME < OF *viande* < LL *vivenda* things for living < L *vivenda*, pl., to be lived⟩

vi•at•i•cum [vaɪ'ætəkəm] *or* [vi'ætəkəm] *n., pl.* **-ca** [-kə] or **-cums. 1** Holy Communion given to a person dying or in danger of death. **2** supplies or money for a journey. ⟨< L *viaticum*, ult. < *via* road. Doublet of VOYAGE.⟩

vibes [vaɪbz] *n.pl. Informal.* **1** vibraphone. **2** a distinctive emotional atmosphere or reaction; VIBRATIONS (def. 3): *He left the party early because the vibes were bad.*

vib•ist ['vaɪbɪst] *n. Informal.* vibraphonist.

vi•brac•u•lum [vaɪ'brækjələm] *n., pl.* **-la.** *Zoology.* any of the specialized whiplike structures of bryozoans which serve to bring food within reach and to prevent the settling of parasites. ⟨< NL < L *vibrare* vibrate⟩

vi•brant ['vaɪbrənt] *adj.* **1** vibrating. **2** throbbing with vitality, enthusiasm, etc.; full of life and vigour: *a vibrant personality.* **3 a** of sounds, resounding or resonant: *a vibrant voice.* **b** of colours, bright and rich: *vibrant reds and greens.* ⟨< L *vibrans, -antis*, ppr. of *vibrare* vibrate⟩ **—'vi•brant•ly,** *adv.* **—'vi•bran•cy,** *n.*

vi•bra•phone ['vaɪbrəˌfoun] *n.* a musical instrument similar to a xylophone but having motor-driven resonators and metal tubes that produce a vibrato.

vi•bra•phon•ist ['vaɪbrəˌfounɪst] *n.* a person who plays the vibraphone, especially a skilled player.

vi•brate ['vaɪbreit] *v.* **-brat•ed, -brat•ing. 1** move or cause to move rapidly to and fro: *A piano string vibrates and makes a sound when a key is struck.* **2** swing or cause to swing to and fro; set in motion. **3** measure by moving to and fro: *A pendulum vibrates seconds.* **4** respond with feeling; thrill: *Their hearts vibrated to the appeal.* **5** resound: *The clanging vibrated in our ears.* **6** vascillate; waver back and forth between options. ⟨< L *vibrare* shake⟩

vi•bra•tile ['vaɪbrəˌtaɪl] *or* ['vaɪbrətɪl] *adj.* **1** capable of vibrating or of being vibrated. **2** having a vibratory motion. **3** having to do with vibration. **—,vi•bra'til•i•ty,** *n.*

vi•bra•tion [vaɪ'breiʃən] *n.* **1** a rapid movement to and fro; quivering motion; the act of vibrating: *The buses shake the house so much that we feel the vibration.* **2** motion back and forth across a position of equilibrium. **3** an emotional stimulus or reaction. **4** a wavering between two options; vacillation. **—vi'bra•tion•al,** *adj.* **—vi'bra•tion•less,** *adj.*

vi•bra•to [vɪ'brɑtou] *or* [vaɪ'brɑtou] *n., pl.* **-tos.** *Music.* a vibrating or tremulous effect, produced by slight variations of pitch. ⟨< Ital. < L *vibrare* to shake⟩

vi•bra•tor ['vaɪbreitər] *n.* **1** an electrical appliance or device that vibrates, used in massage. **2** a vibrating device in an electric bell or buzzer. **3** *Electricity.* **a** an apparatus for setting a given component in vibration by means of continual impulses. **b** a device for causing oscillations.

vi•bra•to•ry ['vaɪbrə,tɔri] *adj.* **1** vibrating or capable of vibration. **2** having to do with or causing vibration: *a vibratory force.* **3** consisting of vibration: *a vibratory movement.*

vi•bris•sa [vaɪ'brɪsə] *n., pl.* **-sae** [-si] *or* [-saɪ]. **1** any of the bristly, sensitive hairs growing near the mouth or nostrils of most mammals, such as a cat's whiskers. **2** a long, slender, bristlelike feather that grows near the mouth of certain birds, especially insect-eaters. ⟨< NL < L, ult. < *vibrare* vibrate⟩

vi•bur•num [vaɪ'bɜrnəm] *n.* **1** any of a genus (*Viburnum*) of shrubs and small trees of the honeysuckle family. The snowball is a viburnum. **2** the bark of certain of these shrubs, used for medicinal purposes. ⟨< L⟩

vic•ar ['vɪkər] *n.* **1** *Anglican Church.* a member of the clergy who carries out the duties of a parish but is not officially the rector. A rector may be responsible for several parishes, with a different vicar representing him or her in each one. **2** *Roman Catholic Church.* **a** a deputy or representative of the pope or a bishop. The cardinal vicar of Rome is appointed to represent the pope. **b Vicar of Christ**, the pope thought of as Christ's representative on earth. **3** any person who takes the place of another; a substitute or representative. ⟨ME < OF < L *vicarius,* originally, adj., substitute < *vicis* (gen. of **vix* change)⟩

vic•ar•age ['vɪkərɪdʒ] *n.* **1** the residence of a vicar. **2** the position or duties of a vicar. **3** the benefice or salary of a vicar.

vicar apostolic *Roman Catholic Church.* a missionary or titular bishop stationed either in a country where no episcopal see has yet been established, or in one where the succession of bishops has been interrupted.

vic•ar–gen•er•al ['vɪkər 'dʒɛnərəl] *n., pl.* **vic•ars-gen•er•al.** **1** *Roman Catholic Church.* a deputy of a bishop or an archbishop, assisting him or her in the government of the diocese. **2** *Anglican Church.* a church officer, usually a lay person, who assists a bishop or an archbishop.

vi•car•i•al [vəi'kɛriəl] *or* [vɪ'kɛriəl] *adj.* **1** of or having to do with a vicar. **2** delegated; VICARIOUS (def. 4).

vi•car•i•ate [vəi'kɛriɪt] *or* [vɪ'kɛriɪt] *n.* the office, authority, or administrative jurisdiction of a vicar.

vi•car•i•ous [vəi'kɛriəs] *or* [vɪ'kɛriəs] *adj.* **1** felt or realized by sharing in one's imagination the actual experience of another person: *She obtains a vicarious delight in foreign countries from reading travel books.* **2** done or suffered for others: *vicarious work, a vicarious sacrifice.* **3** taking the place of or doing the work of another: *As a ghost writer, he is a vicarious autobiographer.* **4** delegated: *vicarious authority.* **5** especially of menstrual bleeding, occurring in an unexpected or abnormal part of the body. ⟨< L *vicarius.* See VICAR.⟩ **—vi'car•i•ous•ly,** *adv.* **—vi'car•i•ous•ness,** *n.*

vic•ar•ship ['vɪkər,ʃɪp] *n.* the office or position of a vicar.

vice[1] [vəis] *n.* **1** moral corruption; evil; wickedness. **2** an evil or immoral habit, character trait, practice, etc.: *the vice of gluttony.* **3** a fault; a bad habit: *You said that this horse had no vices.* **4** prostitution. ⟨ME < OF < L *vitium*⟩
☛ *Hom.* VISE.

vice[2] [vəis] See VISE.

vice[3] [vəis] *n. Informal.* a vice-principal, vice-president, vice-chairman, etc. ⟨See VICE[4]⟩

vi•ce[4] ['vəisi] *prep.* instead of; in the place of. ⟨< L *vice* (abl. of **vix, vicis* turn, change⟩

vice– *prefix.* substitute; deputy; subordinate, as in *vice-president, vice-chairman, vice-chancellor.* ⟨See VICE[4]⟩

vice–ad•mi•ral ['vəis 'ædmərəl] *n.* **1** *Canadian Forces.* in Maritime Command, the equivalent of a lieutenant-general. See chart of ranks in the Appendix. **2** a naval officer of similar rank in other countries. *Abbrev.*: V.Adm. or VAdm **—'vice-'ad•mi•ral•ty,** *n.*

vice–chan•cel•lor ['vəis 'tʃænsələr] *n.* a person who substitutes for or acts as assistant to a chancellor. **—'vice-'chan•cel•lor•ship,** *n.*

vice–con•sul ['vəis 'kɒnsəl] *n.* a person next in rank below a consul. **—'vice-'con•su•lar,** *adj.*

vice•ge•ren•cy [,vəis'dʒirənsi] *n., pl.* **-cies.** the rank, office, or jurisdiction of a vicegerent.

vice•ge•rent [,vəis'dʒirənt] *n., adj.* *—n.* a person exercising the powers or authority of another; a deputy, especially of a ruler.
—adj. acting as vicegerent. ⟨< Med.L *vicegerens* < L *vice* instead (of) + *gerere* manage⟩

vic•e•nar•y ['vɪsə,nɛri] *adj.* **1** of, relating to or consisting of 20. **2** *Mathematics.* using a base of 20. ⟨< L *vicenarius* < *viceni* twenty each < *viginti* twenty⟩

vi•cen•ni•al [vəi'sɛniəl] *adj.* **1** of or for twenty years. **2** occurring once every twenty years. ⟨< L *vicennium* twenty-year period < stem of *vicies* twenty times + *annus* year⟩

vice–pres•i•den•cy ['vəis 'prɛzədənsi] *n.* the office or position of vice-president.

vice–pres•i•dent ['vəis 'prɛzədənt] *n.* **1** the officer next in rank to the president, who takes the president's place when necessary. *Abbrev.*: VP, V.P. or V.Pres. **2** one of several officers next in rank to a president, each of whom oversees a particular department or has a special function: *the vice-president, academic. She is vice-president, Human Resource Systems.*

vice–pres•i•den•tial ['vəis ,prɛzə'dɛnʃəl] *adj.* of or having to do with the vice-president.

vice•re•gal [,vəis'rigəl] *adj.* of or having to do with a viceroy. **—,vice-'re•gal•ly,** *adv.*

vice–re•gent ['vəis 'ridʒənt] *n.* a deputy of a regent.

vice•reine ['vəis,rein] *n.* **1** the wife of a viceroy. **2** a woman holding the rank or office of viceroy. ⟨< F *vice-* vice- + *reine* queen⟩

vice•roy ['vəis,rɔɪ] *n.* **1** a person governing a province or colony as the representative of the sovereign. **2** a North American butterfly (*Limenitis archipus*) similar to the monarch in coloration, but smaller. ⟨< F *vice-roi* < *vice* vice[2] (< L) + *roi* king < L *rex*⟩ **—'vice•roy,ship,** *n.*

vice•roy•al•ty [,vəɪs'rɔɪəlti] *n.* the position, term of office, or district of a viceroy.

vice squad a division of a police force, concerned especially with the enforcement of prostitution and gambling laws.

vice ver•sa ['vəis 'vɜrsə] *or* ['vəisə 'vɜrsə] the other way round; conversely: *Jake blamed Hilary, and vice versa (Hilary blamed Jake).* ⟨< L⟩

Vich•y ['vɪʃi] *n.* VICHY WATER.

vi•chys•soise [,vɪʃi'swɑz] *n.* a cream soup made chiefly of potatoes and leeks and sprinkled with chopped chives, usually served cold. ⟨< F < *Vichy,* a city in France, where it originated⟩

Vichy water **1** a natural mineral water from springs at Vichy, France, containing sodium bicarbonate and other salts, used in the treatment of digestive disturbances, gout, etc. **2** a natural or artificial water of similar composition.

vic•i•nage ['vɪsənɪdʒ] *n.* neighbourhood; vicinity or surrounding district or its residents. ⟨ME < OF < L *vicinus.* See VICINITY.⟩

vic•i•nal ['vɪsənəl] *adj.* **1** neighbouring. **2** local; having to do with a neighbourhood. ⟨< L *vicinalis* < *vicinus.* See VICINITY.⟩

vi•cin•i•ty [və'sɪnəti] *n., pl.* **-ties.** **1** a region near or about a place; neighbourhood; surrounding district: *He knew many people in Toronto and its vicinity.* **2** a nearness in place; closeness: *The vicinity of the school to the house was an advantage on rainy days.* **in the vicinity of, a** near: *a farm in the vicinity of Cloverdale.* **b** approximately: *Costs were in the vicinity of $2000.* ⟨< L *vicinitas* < *vicinus* neighbouring < *vicus* quarter, village⟩

vi•cious ['vɪʃəs] *adj.* **1** depraved or wicked; full of vice: *He had led a vicious life.* **2** dangerously aggressive or unruly: *a vicious dog, a vicious horse.* **3** fierce or violent: *a vicious brawl.* **4** spiteful; malicious: *a vicious rumour, a vicious retort.* **5** *Informal.* severe: *a vicious headache.* **6** morally unwholesome; having a bad effect; leading to vice: *a vicious influence, vicious amusements.* **7** of arguments, reasoning, etc., unsound or invalid;

fallacious. ⟨ME < OF *vicieux* < L *vitiosus*⟩ **—'vi•cious•ly,** *adv.* **—'vi•cious•ness,** *n.*

vicious circle or **cycle** **1** two or more undesirable things, each of which keeps causing the other. **2** a situation where the resolution of one problem creates another whose resolution in turn leads back to the first, often in a still worse form than before. **3** in logic, false reasoning that uses one statement to prove a second statement when the first statement really depends upon the second for proof.

vi•cis•si•tude [və'sɪsə,tjud] *or* [və'sɪsə,tud] *n.* **1** a change in circumstances, fortune, etc. that occurs by chance: *The vicissitudes of life may suddenly make a rich man poor or a poor man rich.* **2** constant change or variation; mutability. **3** a regular alternation or succession: *the vicissitude of day and night.* ⟨< L *vicissitudo* < *vicis* (gen.) change. Cf. VICE[3].⟩
—vi,cis•si'tu•di•nous, *adj.*

vi•comte [vi'kɔ̃t] *n. French.* viscount. **—vi•com'tesse,** *n.fem.*

vic•tim ['vɪktəm] *n.* **1** a person or animal injured, killed, or mistreated: *victims of war, a victim of heart disease, victims of an unjust economic system. She has been the victim of several harsh attacks in the press.* **2** a person tricked by another; dupe: *the victim of a swindler.* **3** a person or animal sacrificed as part of a religious rite. ⟨< L *victima*⟩ **—'vic•tim•less,** *adj.*

vic•tim•i•za•tion [,vɪktəmə'zeiʃən] *or* [,vɪktəmaɪ'zeiʃən] *n.* the act of victimizing or the state of being victimized.

vic•tim•ize ['vɪktə,maɪz] *v.* **-ized, -iz•ing. 1** make a victim of; cause to suffer. **2** cheat; swindle. **—'vic•tim,iz•er,** *n.*

vic•tor ['vɪktər] *n.* **1** a winner; conqueror. **2** (*adjl.*) victorious. ⟨< L *victor* < *vincere* conquer⟩

vic•to•ri•a [vɪk'tɔriə] *n.* **1** a low, four-wheeled carriage with a folding top and a seat for two passengers: *A victoria is a type of phaeton.* **2** an early touring car having a folding top covering the back seat. **3** any of a genus (*Victoria*) of South American water lilies having huge, rose-white, night-blooming flowers and gigantic leaves measuring up to 2.5 m across. ⟨after Queen *Victoria* (1819-1901), Queen of Great Britain and Ireland from 1837 to 1901⟩

Victoria Cross a bronze medal in the shape of a Maltese cross, the highest award given in the Commonwealth to members of the armed forces for conspicuous bravery in the presence of the enemy. See MEDAL for picture. ⟨Queen *Victoria*, who instituted the award in 1856⟩

Victoria Day in Canada, a national holiday established in 1845 to celebrate the birthday of Queen Victoria (May 24); since 1952, celebrated on the Monday immediately preceding May 25.

Vic•to•ri•an [vɪk'tɔriən] *adj., n.* *—adj.* **1** of or having to do with the reign of Victoria (1819-1901), Queen of Great Britain and Ireland and Empress of India from 1837 to 1901. **2** possessing characteristics attributed to Victorians, such as prudishness, smugness, bigotry, etc. **3** of or having to do with the style of architecture, decor, furniture, etc., usually ornate and massive, of the latter half of Queen Victoria's reign. **4** of or having to do with the city of Victoria, British Columbia, or any other place called Victoria.
—n. **1** a person, especially an author, who lived during the reign of Queen Victoria. **2** a native or inhabitant of any place called Victoria, such as Victoria, B.C. or the state of Victoria, Australia.

Vic•to•ri•an•a [vɪk,tɔri'ænə] *n.* Victorian phenomena collectively; objects, writings, attitudes, etc. of the Victorian age.

Vic•to•ri•an•ism [vɪk'tɔriə,nɪzəm] *n.* **1** the quality or state of being Victorian, especially in attitudes or tastes. **2** an idea, belief, etc. common during the Victorian age.

vic•to•ri•ous [vɪk'tɔriəs] *adj.* **1** having won a victory; conquering: *a victorious army.* **2** of or having to do with victory: *a victorious procession through the streets.* **—vic'to•ri•ous•ly,** *adv.* **—vic'to•ri•ous•ness,** *n.*

vic•to•ry ['vɪktəri] *n., pl.* **-ries. 1** the defeat of an enemy, antagonist, or opponent. **2** the achievement of success in a struggle against a difficulty or problem. ⟨< L *victoria*, ult. < *vincere* conquer⟩

☛ *Syn.* **Victory,** CONQUEST, TRIUMPH = success in a contest or struggle. **Victory** emphasizes winning a contest or fight of any kind, and implies defeating the opponent or enemy: *We celebrated our victory.* **Conquest** adds and emphasizes bringing the defeated thing or country under complete or absolute control and reducing defeated people to subjects or slaves: *Some day we may complete the conquest of disease.* **Triumph** applies to a glorious victory or conquest: *The granting of the vote to women was a triumph for the suffragettes.*

vict•ual ['vɪtəl] *n., v.* **-ualled** or **-ualed, -ual•ling** or **-ual•ing.** *—n.* **victuals,** *pl.* food or provisions, especially when prepared for use.
—v. **1** supply with food or provisions: *The captain victualled his ship for the voyage.* **2** take on a supply of food or provisions: *The ship will victual before sailing.* ⟨ME < OF *vitaille* < LL *victualia*, pl., ult. < *vivere* live⟩

vict•ual•ler or **vict•ual•er** ['vɪtələr] *n.* **1** a person who supplies food or provisions to a ship, an army, etc. **2** *Brit.* the keeper of an inn, tavern, saloon, etc. **3** a ship that carries provisions for other ships or for troops.

vi•cu•ña [vɪ'kjunjə] *or* [vɪ'kunjə], [vɪ'kjunə] *or* [vɪ'kunə] *n.* **1** a wild animal (*Lama vicugna*) of South America closely related to the llama and alpaca, highly valued for its soft, fine wool. **2** the wool of a vicuña. **3** a cloth made from this wool, or from some substitute. ⟨< Sp. < Quechua⟩

vi•de ['videi] *v. Latin.* see.
vide infra, see below.
vide supra, see above.

vi•de•li•cet [və'dɛləsɪt] *adv. Latin.* to wit; namely (*usually abbreviated to* **viz.**). ⟨< *videre licet* it is permissible to see⟩
☛ *Usage.* See note at VIZ.

vid•e•o ['vɪdi,ou] *adj., n.* *—adj.* **1** of or used in the transmission or reception of television images. **2** making use of, or shown on, a computer screen.
—n. **1** television. **2** the visual part, as opposed to the sound, of a film or television program. **3** a presentation, performance, etc., videotaped or designed to be videotaped and shown on a TV or VCR: *My job is to prepare videos for training employees on different systems. The rock group is working on a video to accompany their new hit.* **4 a** a videotape or video cassette, especially one on which a movie or other entertainment or performance has been recorded. *This cabinet will store up to 30 videos.* **b** what is recorded on it: *Let's watch a video.* ⟨< L *video* I see⟩

video camera a camera for recording sounds and moving images simultaneously. It may be connected to a VCR containing a cassette, or it may be completely self-contained with its own cassette.

video cassette a videotape mounted in a cassette, for recording and playing back video programs.

video cassette recorder a device for recording and playing back video cassettes. It may be connected to a television or to a video camera. *Abbrev.*: VCR

vid•e•o•con•fer•ence ['vɪdiou,kɒnfərəns] *n.* a teleconference using any electronic link involving both voice and image, such as videophones. **—,vid•e•o 'con•fer•enc•ing,** *n.*

vid•e•o•disk ['vɪdiou,dɪsk] *n.* a disk on which video and, usually, audio signals have been recorded for playback on a television or computer screen by means of a special player using laser.

video game an electronic game in which the player manipulates the action on a screen.

vid•e•og•ra•phy [,vɪdi'ɒgrəfi] *n.* **1** videos collectively and the making of videos. **2** the study of this. **—,vid•e'og•ra•pher,** *n.* **—,vid•e•o'graph•i•cal,** *adj.*

video jockey a person who chooses, introduces, and plays videos, especially music videos, for a TV program.

vid•e•o•phone ['vɪdiou,foun] *n.* a telephone equipped to send and receive both audio and video signals so that the users can see as well as hear each other.

video recorder VIDEO CASSETTE RECORDER.

vid•e•o•tape ['vɪdiou,teip] *n., v.* **-taped, -tap•ing.** *—n.* **1** a magnetic tape for recording video and audio signals. **2** a recording made on such a tape.
—v. record on videotape.

vid•e•o•tex ['vɪdiou,tɛks] *n.* any interactive system for the electronic retrieval and distribution of textual information, used with display terminals connected to telephone or television. Also, **videotext.** ⟨< *video* + *tex(t)*⟩

vi•dette [vɪ'dɛt] See VEDETTE.

vie [vaɪ] *v.* **vied, vy•ing.** strive for superiority; contend in rivalry; compete. ⟨< F *envier* challenge < L *invitare* invite⟩

Vi•en•na sausage [vi'ɛnə] a miniature frankfurter for use as an hors d'oeuvre.

Vi•en•nese [,viə'niz] *n., pl.* **-nese;** *adj.* *—n.* a native or inhabitant of Vienna, the capital of Austria.
—adj. of or having to do with Vienna or its people.

Vi•et•nam [ˌviət'nɑm] *or* [ˌvjɛt'nɑm] *n.* a country in SE Asia, properly called the Socialist Republic of Vietnam.

Vi•et•nam•ese [ˌviətnə'miz] *or* [ˌvjɛtnə'miz] *n., adj.* —*n.* **1** a native or inhabitant of Vietnam. **2** the official language of Vietnam, belonging to the Austroasiatic family.
—*adj.* of or having to do with Vietnam, its people, or their language.

view [vju] *n., v.* —*n.* **1** an act of seeing; sight: *It was our first view of the ocean.* **2** the power or opportunity of seeing; the range of the eye: *A ship came into view.* **3** something seen; a scene: *The view from our house is beautiful.* **4** a picture of some scene: *Various views of the mountains hung on the walls.* **5** a mental picture; idea: *This book will give you a general view of the way the pioneers lived.* **6** a way of looking at or considering a matter; opinion: *A child's view of school is different from a teacher's.* **7** aim or purpose. **8** a prospect; expectation: *with no view of success.*
in view, a in sight; within range of the eye: *As long as the cliffs were in view, she could find her way.* **b** under consideration: *Keep the teacher's advice in view as you try to improve your work.* **c** as a purpose or intention: *He works hard and has a definite aim in view.* **d** as a hope; as an expectation.
in view of, considering; because of.
on view, to be seen; open for people to see: *The exhibit is on view from 9 a.m. to 5 p.m.*
take a dim view of, look upon or regard with disapproval, doubt, pessimism, etc.
with a view to, a with the purpose or intention of: *He worked hard after school with a view to earning money for a new bicycle.* **b** with a hope of; expecting to.
—*v.* **1** see; look at; survey: *They viewed the scene with pleasure.* **2** consider; regard mentally: *The plan was viewed favourably.* **3** watch (especially something televised or filmed). ⟨ME < AF *vewe* < OF *veoir* see < L *videre*⟩
☛ *Syn. n.* **3. View,** SCENE = something seen. **View** emphasizes the idea of something actually seen through the eyes, and applies to what is presented to the sight, or within the range of vision, of someone looking from a certain point or position: *That new building spoils the view from our windows.* **Scene** emphasizes the idea of something that can be seen, and applies to a landscape or setting that is spread out before the eyes: *We stopped to gaze at the mountain scene. n.* **6.** See note at OPINION.

view•er ['vjuər] *n.* **1** a person who views: *a television viewer.* **2** a device for viewing, especially a small instrument for viewing photographic transparencies. **3** *Law.* a person appointed by a court to inspect and report on property.

view•find•er ['vju,faɪndər] *n. Photography.* a device on a camera that shows the scene or area within view of the lens. Also, **view finder.**

view•ing ['vjuɪŋ] *n.* **1** an occasion for looking at or inspecting, as of articles to be sold at auction, etc. **2** a time for people to see a dead person's remains laid out at a funeral parlour for the paying of last respects, etc.: *I would like to go to the viewing as I won't be able to make it to the funeral.* **3** an act of watching, especially television.

view•less ['vjulɪs] *adj.* **1** without views or opinions. **2** without a view or any hopeful prospect: *a viewless room, a viewless future.*

view•point ['vju,pɔɪnt] *n.* **1** the place from which one looks at something. **2** mental perspective; point of view: *A heavy rain that is good from the viewpoint of farmers may be bad from the viewpoint of tourists.*

vi•ges•i•mal [vaɪ'dʒɛsəməl] *adj.* **1** twentieth. **2** done or progressing, etc. in or by twenties; based on the number twenty. ⟨< L *vigesimus* twentieth⟩

vig•il ['vɪdʒəl] *n.* **1** a staying awake for some purpose; a watching; watch: *All night the mother kept vigil over the sick child.* **2** a night spent in prayer. **3** the day and night before a solemn church festival. **4** Often, **vigils,** *pl.* devotions, prayers, services, etc. on the night before a religious festival. ⟨ME < OF < L *vigilia* < *vigil* watchful⟩

vig•i•lance ['vɪdʒələns] *n.* the quality or state of being vigilant; watchfulness or alertness.

vigilance committee a self-appointed committee of citizens organized for protection or to maintain order and punish criminals in places or situations where official law enforcement appears inadequate.

vig•i•lant ['vɪdʒələnt] *adj.* watchful; alert: *a vigilant guard.* ⟨< L *vigilans, -antis* watching < *vigil* watchful⟩ —**'vig•i•lant•ly,** *adv.*
☛ *Syn.* See note at WATCHFUL.

vig•i•lan•te [ˌvɪdʒə'læntɪ] *n.* a member of a VIGILANCE COMMITTEE. ⟨< Sp. *vigilante* vigilant⟩ —**ˌvig•i'lan•tism,** *n.* —**ˌvig•i'lan•tist,** *adj.*

vi•gnette [vɪn'jɛt] *n., v.* **-gnet•ted, -gnet•ting.** —*n.* **1** a decorative design on a page of a book, especially on the title page. **2** a literary sketch; a short verbal description. **3** a short and memorable or striking incident or scene, as in a movie or play. **4** an engraving, drawing, photograph, or the like, that shades off gradually at the edge.
—*v.* **1** make a vignette of. **2** finish (a photograph or portrait) in the manner of a vignette. ⟨< F *vignette,* dim. of *vigne* vine⟩ —**vi'gnet•tist,** *n.*

vig•or ['vɪgər] See VIGOUR.

vi•go•ro•so [ˌvigou'rousou] *adj., adv. Music.* —*adj.* vigorous; energetic.
—*adv.* vigorously. ⟨< Ital.⟩

vig•or•ous ['vɪgərəs] *adj.* **1** full of vigour; strong and active: *The old man is still vigorous and lively.* **2** requiring or carried out with vigour; done energetically: *a vigorous denial, vigorous exercises, a vigorous election campaign.* **3** of plants, growing strongly. —**'vig•or•ous•ly,** *adv.*

vig•our or **vig•or** ['vɪgər] *n.* **1** active physical strength or force; flourishing physical condition. **2** mental energy or power. **3** strong or energetic action; intensity of action: *They opposed all such military measures with great vigour. The vigour of her refusal surprised me.* **4** legal or binding force; validity: *a law in full vigour.* ⟨ME < OF < L < *vigere* thrive⟩

Vi•king or **vi•king** ['vaɪkɪŋ] *n., adj.* —*n.* **1** one of the bands of Norsemen who raided the coasts of Europe during the 8th, 9th, and 10th centuries A.D. Some of them reached as far as North America. **2** any sea rover.
—*adj.* of or being a Viking or Vikings. ⟨< ON *vikingr;* cf. OE *wicing* < *wic* camp < L *vicus* village⟩

vil•a•yet [vɪ'lajɛt] *or* [ˌvɪla'jɛt] *n.* in Turkey, a province or main governmental division. ⟨< Turkish < Arabic *welāyet*⟩

vile [vaɪl] *adj.* **vil•er, vil•est. 1** despicable or evil: *a vile attempt to defraud an old man of his savings.* **2** physically repulsive: *the vile smell of rotting garbage.* **3** very bad or unpleasant: *vile language. The weather has turned really vile. She has a vile temper.* **4** degrading or degraded; mean and low: *vile servitude.* **5** *Archaic.* of little worth or account. ⟨ME < OF < L *vilis* cheap⟩ —**'vile•ly,** *adv.* —**'vile•ness,** *n.*
☛ *Syn.* See note at BASE[2].

vil•i•fi•ca•tion [ˌvɪləfə'keiʃən] *n.* a vilifying or being vilified.

vil•i•fy ['vɪlə,faɪ] *v.* **-fied, -fy•ing.** speak evil of; revile; slander. ⟨ME < LL *vilificare* < L *vilis* vile + *facere* make⟩ —**'vil•i,fi•er,** *n.*

vil•la ['vɪlə] *n.* a house in the country or suburbs, sometimes at the seashore; a country house as opposed to a town house. A villa is usually a large or elegant dwelling, used as a summer or holiday residence. ⟨< Ital. < L⟩

vil•lage ['vɪlɪdʒ] *n.* **1** a group of houses, stores, schools, churches, etc. that together with the people living there form a community with fixed boundaries and some local powers of government. In Canada, a village is the smallest community that can have its own local government. **2** the people of a village: *The whole village was out to see the fire.* **3** an informal or non-political section of a large urban centre, regarded as a relatively cohesive community or neighbourhood having its own distinctive character: *We do all our shopping in Cook Street village. Bloor West Village is her favourite part of Toronto.* ⟨ME < OF *village,* ult. < L *villa* country house⟩

vil•lag•er ['vɪlɪdʒər] *n.* a person who lives in a village.

vil•lain ['vɪlən] *n.* **1** a scoundrel; wicked person. **2** an unsympathetic character, the main antagonist in a play, novel, etc. whose evil motives or actions form an important element in the plot. **3** a person or thing blamed for a particular problem: *City health experts studying the epidemic decided the chief villain was overcrowding.* **4** See VILLEIN. **5** *Informal.* rascal or rogue. **6** *Archaic.* a rude or clumsy person; boor. ⟨ME < OF < Med.L *villanus* farmhand < L *villa* country house⟩
☛ *Hom.* VILLEIN.

vil•lain•ous ['vɪlənəs] *adj.* **1** very wicked. **2** extremely bad; vile. —**'vil•lain•ous•ly,** *adv.* —**'vil•lain•ous•ness,** *n.*

vil•lain•y ['vɪləni] *n., pl.* **-lain•ies. 1** great wickedness. **2** a very wicked act; crime.

vil•la•nel•la [ˌvɪlə'nɛlə] *n.* **1** an unaccompanied rustic Italian part song. **2** a dance performed to such a song. ⟨< Ital. See VILLANELLE.⟩

vil•la•nelle [ˌvɪlə'nɛl] *n.* a form of poem having nineteen lines with two rhymes, written in five tercets with a final quatrain. ⟨< F < Ital. *villanella* < *villa* villa⟩

-ville *combining form.* **1** town; city (*in place names*): *Oakville, Maillardville.* **2** place, event, situation, etc. full of or characterized by (in slang nonce compounds): *thrillsville, dullsville.*

vil•lein ['vɪlən] *n.* in the Middle Ages, one of a class of half-free peasants. A villein was under the control of the local lord, but in relations with other people had the rights of a freeman. ⟨var. of *villain*⟩
☛ *Hom.* VILLAIN.

vil•lein•age ['vɪlənɪdʒ] *n.* **1** the fact or state of being a villein. **2** the conditions under which a villein held land.

vil•li ['vɪlaɪ] *or* ['vɪli] *n.* pl. of VILLUS. **1** tiny hairlike parts growing out of the mucous membrane of the small intestine. The villi absorb certain substances. **2** soft, hairlike outgrowths on some plants, as on the stems of certain mosses. ⟨< L *villi,* pl. of *villus* tuft of hair⟩ **—'vil•li,form** ['vɪlə,fɔrm], *adj.*

vil•lous ['vɪləs] *adj.* having villi; covered with villi. Also, **villose. —vil'los•i•ty** [-'lɒsəti], *n.*

vil•lus ['vɪləs] *n.* sing. of VILLI.

vim [vɪm] *n.* vitality and enthusiasm; energy: *full of vim after a good night's sleep.* ⟨< L *vim,* accus. of *vis* force⟩

vi•men ['vaɪmɛn] *n., pl.* **vi•mi•na** ['vɪmənə]. *Botany.* a long shoot or slender, flexible branch. ⟨< L *vimen* twig, osier⟩ **—vi'min•e•ous** [vɪ'mɪniəs], *adj.*

vi•na ['vinə] *n.* a traditional seven-stringed instrument of India. It has two sets of strings, one for the melody and the other for accompaniment, with gourds attached to each end for resonance. ⟨< Skt.⟩

vi•na•ceous [vɪ'neiʃəs] *or* [vaɪ'neiʃəs] *adj.* **1** resembling wine or grapes. **2** wine red in colour. ⟨< L *vinaceus* < *vinum* wine⟩

vin•ai•grette [,vɪnə'grɛt] *n.* **1** a salad dressing made of seasoned oil and vinegar, and, often, chopped chives or green onions, etc. Also, **vinaigrette sauce** or **dressing. 2** (*adjl.*) served with vinaigrette (*used only after the noun*): *artichokes vinaigrette.* **3** an ornamental bottle or box for smelling salts, etc. ⟨< F *vinaigrette* < *vinaigre.* See VINEGAR.⟩

vin•ci•ble ['vɪnsəbəl] *adj.* conquerable. ⟨< L *vincibilis* < *vincere* conquer⟩ **—,vin•ci'bil•i•ty,** *n.*

vin•cu•lum ['vɪŋkjələm] *n., pl.* **-la** [-lə]. **1** *Mathematics.* a line drawn over two or more terms in an expression to show that they are to be considered together. A vinculum is equivalent to parentheses. *Example:* $\overline{a+b} \times c = (a+b) \times c$. **2** *Anatomy.* a band or bandlike structure connecting parts. **3** *Rare.* a bond or tie. ⟨< L *vinculum* bond < *vincire* bind⟩

vin•di•cate ['vɪndə,keit] *v.* **-cat•ed, -cat•ing. 1** clear from suspicion, dishonour, hint or charge of wrongdoing, etc.: *The verdict of "Not guilty" vindicated the accused.* **2** defend successfully against opposition: *He vindicated his claim to his uncle's fortune.* **3** confirm or justify: *Their faith in her has been vindicated.* ⟨< L *vindicare* < *vindex, vindicis* defender⟩ **—'vin•di•ca•ble,** *adj.* **—'vin•di,ca•tor,** *n.* **—'vin•di,ca•to•ry,** *adj.*

vin•di•ca•tion [,vɪndə'keiʃən] *n.* **1** the act or process of clearing from any charge of wrongdoing. **2** something which justifies or vindicates: *The successful invention was a vindication of his new idea.*

vin•dic•a•tive [vɪn'dɪkətɪv] *or* ['vɪndə,keitɪv] *adj.* tending to vindicate; justifying.

vin•dic•tive [vɪn'dɪktɪv] *adj.* **1** feeling a strong tendency toward revenge; bearing a grudge: *He is so vindictive that he never forgives anybody.* **2** intended for revenge; involving revenge: *vindictive punishment.* **3** spiteful; malicious: *He has a vindictive nature. She writes a vindictive column in the local paper.* ⟨< L *vindicta* revenge⟩ **—vin'dic•tive•ly,** *adv.* **—vin'dic•tive•ness,** *n.*

vine [vaɪn] *n.* **1** any plant having a long, slender stem that does not stand up by itself, but creeps along the ground or climbs on a support by twining or by putting out tendrils: *Melons and pumpkins grow on vines. Ivy is a vine.* **2** the main stem of such a plant. **3** grapevine: *the fruit of the vine.* ⟨ME < OF < L *vinea* < *vinum* wine⟩ **—'vine,like,** *adj.*

vine•dress•er ['vaɪn,drɛsər] *n.* a person who tends grapevines.

vin•e•gar ['vɪnəgər] *n.* **1** a sour liquid produced by the fermentation of cider, wine, etc. and consisting largely of dilute, impure acetic acid. Vinegar is used in flavouring and preserving food. **2** speech or temper of a sour or acid character. ⟨ME < MF *vinaigre* < *vin* wine (< L *vinum*) + *aigre* sour < L *acer*⟩

vin•e•gar•y ['vɪnəgəri] *adj.* of or like vinegar; sour. Also, **vinegarish.**

vi•ne•ry ['vaɪnəri] *n.* **1** an area or building in which vines, especially grapevines, are grown. **2** the vines collectively.

vine•yard ['vɪnjərd] *n.* **1** a place planted with grapevines. **2** a field or sphere of activity, especially religious work. ⟨< *vine* + *yard*[1]⟩

vingt–et–un [vɛ̃te'œ̃] *n.* twenty-one; BLACKJACK (def. 5). ⟨< F⟩

vi•ni– *combining form.* wine. Also, before vowels, **vin-.** ⟨< L *vinum* wine⟩

vin•i•cul•ture ['vɪnɪ,kʌltʃər] *or* ['vaɪnɪ,kʌltʃər] *n.* **1** the cultivation of grapes for wine. **2** the art or science of making wines.

vi•ni•fer•ous [vɪ'nɪfərəs] *or* [vaɪ'nɪfərəs] *adj.* suitable for making wine; yielding wine: *viniferous grapes.*

vin•i•fy ['vɪnə,faɪ] *v.* **-fied, -fy•ing.** ferment (juice); make (grapes) into wine. **—,vin•i•fi'ca•tion,** *n.*

Vin•land ['vɪnlənd] *n.* a coastal area of eastern North America, thought to be somewhere from Newfoundland to Virginia, visited and described by Norsemen led by Leif Erikson c. A.D. 1000. ⟨< ON, wine-land, because of the wild berries and grapes found there⟩

vi•no ['vinou] *n. Informal.* any inexpensive red wine, especially Italian. ⟨< Ital.⟩

vin or•di•naire [vɛ̃ɔRdi'nɛR] *French.* any inexpensive table wine of unspecified origin. ⟨literally, ordinary wine⟩

vi•nous ['vaɪnəs] *adj.* **1** of, like, or having to do with wine. **2** caused by drinking wine. ⟨< L *vinosus* < *vinum* wine⟩ **—vi'nos•i•ty** [-'nɒsəti], *n.*

vin•tage ['vɪntɪdʒ] *n., adj.* —*n.* **1** the wine or grapes of one season or from a particular vineyard or region: *Wines of Niagara vintage are making a hit nowadays.* **2** the year of the harvest from which a particular wine was produced: *The vintage of this wine is 1978.* **3** the gathering of grapes for making wine. **4** the season of gathering grapes and making wine. **5** a character or kind typical of a particular period or year of origin: *songs of prewar vintage.* —*adj.* **1** of a good vintage; of superior quality: *a cellar full of vintage wines.* **2** being or representing the best example or model; classic: Sunshine Sketches of a Little Town *is vintage Stephen Leacock.* **3** of or belonging to an earlier time; old or old-fashioned: *shelves full of vintage comic books. She rattled around town in her vintage Ford.* ⟨ME < AF *vintage,* alteration of OF *vendange* < L *vindemia* < *vinum* wine + *demere* take off; influenced by *vintner*⟩

vin•tag•er ['vɪntədʒər] *n.* a person who harvests grapes to be made into wine.

vintage year **1** a year in which a vintage wine is produced: *The year 1972 was a vintage year.* **2** an outstandingly successful year: *a vintage year in the history of sports.*

vint•ner ['vɪntnər] *n.* **1** a person who buys and sells wine; a dealer in wine. **2** a person who makes wine. ⟨earlier *vinter* < AF *vinetier,* ult. < L *vinum* wine⟩

vi•ny ['vaɪni] *adj.* **1** of or having to do with the nature of vines. **2 a** filled or covered with vines. **b** producing vines, especially in quantity.

vi•nyl ['vaɪnəl] *n.* **1** (*adjl.*) of, designating, or containing a univalent group of atoms (CH_2CH-) derived from ethylene: *a vinyl polymer, vinyl acetate.* **2** a polymer of any of several organic compounds containing this group of atoms, used for the manufacture of floor and furniture coverings, toys, phonograph records, etc. **3** (*adjl.*) made of such a polymer: *The car has a vinyl roof.* ⟨< *vini-* + *-yl*⟩

vinyl chloride a colourless, flammable gas made by chlorinating ethylene. It is used as a refrigerant and in the manufacture of polyvinyl chloride or PVC. *Formula:* CH_2:CHCl

vi•ol ['vaɪəl] *n.* one of a family of usually six-stringed musical instruments similar to the violin family, used mainly in the 16th and 17th centuries. Viols are played with a curved bow and have a softer, less rich and varied tone than the violin. ⟨ME *viel* < OF *viole, vielle* < Med.L *vitula* fiddle < *Vituala* goddess of joy⟩
☛ *Hom.* VIAL.

vi•o•la[1] [vi'oulə] *n.* a musical instrument of the violin family that is slightly larger and tuned a fifth lower than the violin. ⟨< Ital.⟩

vi•o•la[2] [vaɪ'oulə] *or* ['vaɪələ] *n.* any of a genus (*Viola*) of plants that includes the violets and pansies; especially, any of numerous garden varieties that are hybrids, having yellow, purple, or white flowers somewhat smaller than pansies.

vi•o•la•ble ['vaɪələbəl] *adj.* that can be violated. ⟨< L *violabilis* < *violare.* See VIOLATE.⟩ **—ˌvi•o•la'bil•i•ty,** *n.* **—'vi•o•la•bly,** *adv.*

vi•o•la•ceous [ˌvaɪə'leiʃəs] *adj.* **1** belonging to the violet family (Violaceae) of plants. **2** violet coloured; purplish blue.

viola da brac•cio [də 'brɑtʃiou] an early member of the viol family, more or less equivalent to the modern viola, held on the shoulder. ⟨< Ital., literally, violin for the arm⟩

viola da gam•ba [də 'gɑmbɑ] *or* ['gæmbə] a bass member of the viol family, resembling a modern cello. It was the most important solo instrument of the family. Also called **bass viol.** ⟨< Ital., literally, violin for the leg⟩

viola d'a•mo•re [dɑ'mɔrei] a tenor member of the viol family whose extra set of strings gives it a very sweet, clear tone. It is held under the chin. ⟨< Ital., literally, viol of love⟩

vi•o•late ['vaɪəˌleit] *v.* **-lat•ed, -lat•ing. 1** break (a law, rule, agreement, promise, etc.); act contrary to; fail to perform: *Speeding violates the traffic regulations.* **2** treat with disrespect or contempt: *The soldiers violated the church by using it as a stable.* **3** offend; be an outrage to; be utterly incompatible with: *Such treatment violates all sense of decency. To call that society 'free' violates the meaning of the word.* **4** break in upon; disturb: *The sound of the explosion violated the usual calm of Sunday morning.* **5** trespass on; infringe on: *to violate the right of free speech.* **6** commit rape on. ⟨ME < L *violare* < *vis* violence⟩ **—'vi•oˌla•tor,** *n.* **—'vi•o•la•tive,** *adj.*

vi•o•la•tion [ˌvaɪə'leiʃən] *n.* **1** a violating or being violated; infringement of a law, rule, agreement, promise, etc. **2** an interruption or disturbance. **3** the treatment of a holy thing with disrespect or contempt. **4** use of force; violence. **5** rape.

vi•o•lence ['vaɪələns] *n.* **1** rough force in action: *He slammed the door with violence.* **2** rough or harmful action or treatment. **3** the illegal or unjust use of physical force to injure or damage persons or property. **4** strength of feeling: *We were shocked by the violence of her hate.* **5** rape.
do violence to, violate: *It would do violence to her principles to work on Sunday.* ⟨ME < OF < L *violentia*⟩

vi•o•lent ['vaɪələnt] *adj.* **1** acting or done with, or characterized by the use of, strong, rough, harmful force: *a violent blow, a violent person, a violent relationship.* **2** caused by strong, rough force: *a violent death.* **3** showing or caused by very strong feeling, action, etc.: *violent language, a violent disagreement.* **4** depicting, promoting, exploiting or based on violence: *violent films, violent toys, violent video games.* **5** severe; extreme; very great: *a violent pain.* **6** that tends to distort meaning: *a violent use of a word.* ⟨ME < OF < L *violentus* < *vis* force⟩ **—'vi•o•lent•ly,** *adv.*

vi•o•let ['vaɪəlɪt] *n.* **1** any of numerous plants (genus *Viola*) having small, solid-coloured, usually yellow, white, or purple flowers. The purple violet (*V. papilionacea*) is the provincial flower of New Brunswick. **2** any plant of the genus *Viola*; VIOLA². **3** the flower of a violet. **4** (*adjl.*) designating a worldwide family (Violaceae) of herbs, shrubs, and small trees to which the violets belong. The violet family is made up of 800 species. **5** any of various unrelated plants having violetlike flowers: *dogtooth violet, African violet.* **6** a medium bluish purple. *—adj.* having the colour violet. ⟨ME < OF *violette,* ult. < L *viola*⟩

violet rays the shortest rays of the visible spectrum, with wavelengths whose range is just above that of the invisible ultraviolet rays.

vi•o•lin [ˌvaɪə'lɪn] *n.* **1** a musical instrument with four strings tuned at intervals of a fifth, played by drawing a bow across the strings: *The violin can produce tones of great variety and richness.* **2** (*adjl.*) designating a family of stringed musical instruments of which the violin is the smallest. The other members of the violin family are the viola, cello, and double bass. ⟨< Ital. *violino,* dim. of *viola* viol⟩

A violin

vi•o•lin•ist [ˌvaɪə'lɪnɪst] *n.* a person who plays the violin, especially a skilled player.

vi•ol•ist ['vaɪəlɪst] *for def. 1,* [vi'oulɪst] *for def. 2. n.* **1** a person who plays the viol, especially a skilled player. **2** a person who plays the viola, especially a skilled player.

vi•o•lon•cel•list [ˌvaɪələn'tʃɛlɪst] *or* [ˌviələn'tʃɛlɪst] *n.* a cellist.

vi•o•lon•cel•lo [ˌvaɪələn'tʃɛlou] *or* [ˌviələn'tʃɛlou] *n., pl.* **-los.** a cello. ⟨< Ital. *violoncello,* ult. < *viola* viol⟩

vi•o•lo•ne [vjou'lounei] *n.* a double-bass viol; the member of the viol family having the lowest tone and the largest size. Its range is an octave below that of the viola da gamba.

vi•os•ter•ol [vaɪ'ɒstəˌrɒl] *or* [vaɪ'ɒstəˌroul] *n.* an oil containing a form of vitamin D, used as a medicine to prevent or cure rickets. ⟨< (*ultra*)*vio*(*let*) + (*ergo*)*sterol*⟩

VIP *Informal.* very important person.

vi•per [ˌvəipər] *n.* **1** any of a family (Viperidae) of Old World poisonous snakes having hollow fangs in the upper jaw, through which poison is injected. The fangs are attached to movable bones and folded back when the mouth is closed. **2** PIT VIPER. **3** any of various other snakes that are poisonous or thought to be poisonous. **4** an extremely spiteful or treacherous person. ⟨< L *vipera* < *vivus* alive + *parere* bring forth⟩

vi•per•ine ['vəipəˌraɪn] *or* ['vəipərɪn] *n.* of, having to do with, or resembling a viper.

vi•per•ous ['vəipərəs] *adj.* like a viper; treacherous and malicious. Also, **viperish. —'vi•per•ous•ly,** *adv.* **—'vi•per•ous•ness,** *n.*

vi•ra•go [və'rɑgou] *or* [və'reigou] *n., pl.* **-goes** or **-gos.** a violent, bad-tempered, or scolding woman. ⟨< L *virago* < *vir* man⟩

vi•ral ['vaɪrəl] *adj.* of, having to do with, or caused by a virus: *viral pneumonia.*

vir•e•lay ['vɪrəˌlei] *n.* an old French form of short poem with two rhymes to a stanza. Also, **virelai.** ⟨ME < OF *virelai* < *vireli* a refrain⟩

vir•e•o ['vɪriˌou] *n., pl.* **-e•os.** any of a family (Vireonidae) of small, typically green-and-white, insect-eating, New World songbirds, resembling warblers, but less active and having a stouter bill that is hooked and notched at the tip. ⟨< L *vireo* a small bird, possibly the greenfinch⟩ **—'vir•e•oˌnine** [-ˌnaɪn], *adj.*

vi•res•cence [vaɪ'rɛsəns] *or* [vɪ'rɛsəns] *n.* **1** greenness; a turning green. **2** *Botany.* the unusual greening, due to the abnormal presence of chlorophyll, of parts normally having bright colour, such as petals.

vi•res•cent [vaɪ'rɛsənt] *or* [vɪ'rɛsənt] *adj.* turning green; tending to a green colour; greenish. ⟨< L *virescens, -entis,* ppr. of *virescere* turn green⟩

vir•ga ['vɜrgə] *n. Meteorology.* long wisps or streamers of rain or snow trailing from clouds and evaporating before they reach the earth. ⟨< L, streak⟩

vir•gate ['vɜrgɪt] *adj. Botany.* slender, tall, erect, and unbranching. ⟨< L *virgatus* of twigs < *virga* twig⟩

Vir•gil•i•an [vər'dʒɪliən] *adj.* of, having to do with, or in the style of the Roman poet Virgil (70-19 B.C.).

vir•gin ['vɜrdʒən] *n., adj. —n.* **1** a person, especially a woman, who has never had sexual intercourse. **2** an unmarried girl or young woman. **3** a member of any religious order of women who have vowed to remain virgins. **4 the Virgin,** the VIRGIN MARY. **5 Virgin,** a picture or statue of the Virgin Mary. **6 the Virgin,** *Astronomy or Astrology.* Virgo. **7** *Zoology.* **a** a female animal that has not mated. **b** a female insect that lays eggs without impregnation by a male.
—adj. **1** having to do with or suitable for a virgin: *virgin modesty.* **2** being a virgin. **3** pure or spotless; untouched: *virgin snow.* **4** not yet used or altered by human beings: *virgin forest.* **5** of wool, spun or woven only once or not yet spun at all. **6** initial; first: *a virgin effort.* **7** of oil, obtained from the first pressing, without the use of heat: *virgin olive oil.* **8** of metal, obtained directly from an ore, rather than being made out of scrap. ⟨ME < OF < L *virgo, -inis*⟩

vir•gin•al¹ ['vɜrdʒənəl] *adj.* **1** of or suitable for a virgin; maidenly. **2** fresh; pure; unsullied; untouched. **3** remaining in a state of virginity. ⟨ME < L *virginalis* < *virgo, -inis* maiden⟩ **—'vir•gin•al•ly,** *adv.*

vir•gin•al² ['vɜrdʒənəl] *n.* a musical instrument like a small harpsichord, but set in a box without legs. It was much used, especially in England, in the 16th and 17th centuries. Also, **(pair of) virginals.** ⟨apparently < *virginal¹*⟩

virgin birth *Biology.* parthenogenesis.

Virgin Birth the doctrine that Jesus had no human father, but was miraculously conceived by the Virgin Mary through the power of the Holy Spirit.

Vir•gin•ia [vər'dʒɪnjə] *n.* an eastern state of the United States.

Virginia creeper a woody North American vine

(*Parthenocissus quinquefolia*) of the grape family having compound leaves, bluish black berries, and tendrils by means of which it climbs.

Virginia deer WHITE-TAILED DEER.

Virginia reel 1 a North American country dance in which the partners perform in parallel lines. **2** the music for such a dance.

vir•gin•i•ty [vər'dʒɪnəti] *n.* the quality or state of being virgin; maidenhood.

Virgin Mary the mother of Jesus Christ.

vir•gin's–bow•er ['vɜrdʒənz 'baʊər] *n.* any of several North American species of clematis having clusters of small white flowers, such as *Clematis virginiana.*

Vir•go ['vɜrgou] *n.* **1** *Astronomy.* a constellation on the celestial equator thought of as having the form of a woman. **2** *Astrology.* **a** the sixth sign of the zodiac. The sun enters Virgo about August 22. See ZODIAC for picture. **b** a person born under this sign. ⟨< L *virgo* maiden⟩

vir•gule ['vɜrgjul] *n.* a slanting stroke (/) between two words, indicating that either word applies, as in *and/or,* also used sometimes in fractions (1/2), in dates to separate day, month, and year (26/04/96), and to express 'per' as in *ft/sec* (feet per second). ⟨< L *virgula* little rod⟩

vi•ri•cide ['vaɪrə,saɪd] *n.* a substance that can destroy viruses. **—,vi•ri'ci•dal,** *adj.*

vir•i•des•cence [,virə'dɛsəns] *n.* the condition of being viridescent.

vir•i•des•cent [,virə'dɛsənt] *adj.* **1** greenish. **2** turning green. ⟨< LL *viridescens, -entis,* ppr. of *viridescere* turn green < L *viridis* green⟩

vir•i•di•an [və'rɪdiən] *n., adj. —n.* **1** a bluish green pigment, a hydrated oxide of chromium. *Formula*: Cr_2O_3 **2** a bluish green. *—adj.* bluish green.

vi•rid•i•ty [və'rɪdəti] *n.* **1** greenness; verdancy. **2** youthful freshness or vigour. ⟨< L *viridis* green⟩

vir•ile ['viraɪl] *or* ['virəl] *adj.* **1** belonging to or characteristic of a man; masculine; manly. **2** having masculine vigour or forcefulness: *a virile writing style.* **3** of a male, capable of copulation; sexually potent. ⟨< L *virilis* < *vir* man⟩

vi•ril•ism ['virə,lɪzəm] *n.* the development in women of secondary male sex characteristics, as hirsutism and a lowered voice, caused by conditions affecting hormonal regulation.

vi•ril•i•ty [və'rɪləti] *n., pl.* **-ties.** the quality or state of being virile.

vi•roid ['vaɪrɔɪd] *n.* a source of infection in plants, resembling a virus but smaller, being only a strand of RNA with no protein coating.

vi•rol•o•gist [vaɪ'rɒlədʒɪst] *n.* a person who is trained in virology, especially one whose work it is.

vi•rol•o•gy [vaɪ'rɒlədʒi] *n.* the study of viruses and virus diseases. **—,vi•ro'log•i•cal,** *adj.*

vir•tu [vər'tu] *or* ['vɜrtu] *n.* **1** excellence or merit in an object of art because of its quality, rarity, antiquity, etc. **2** objects of art collectively; choice curios. **3** a taste for objects of art; knowledge of objects of art. Also, **vertu.** ⟨< Ital. *virtù* excellence < L *virtus* virtue. Doublet of VIRTUE.⟩

vir•tu•al ['vɜrtʃuəl] *adj.* **1** being something in effect, though not so in name or according to strict definition: *a virtual promise. The battle was won with so great a loss of soldiers that it was a virtual defeat. He is the virtual president, though his title is secretary.* **2** *Computer technology.* **a** of a kind of data storage or memory that is temporary, consisting only in the use of disk space to store information while a large program, occupying all or most of the regular memory, is being run. **b** of, having to do with, or making use of VIRTUAL REALITY. **3** *Physics.* **a** of a particle, too short-lived to be detectable, exchanged by other interacting particles. **b** of or having to do with a VIRTUAL IMAGE. **—,vir•tu'al•i•ty** [,vɜrtʃu'æləti], *n.*

virtual image *Physics.* an optical image which is the apparent point of divergence of light rays, even though the rays do not actually pass through it.

vir•tu•al•ly ['vɜrtʃuəli] *adv.* almost entirely or for all practical purposes: *The house was virtually destroyed in the fire. The two houses are virtually identical.*

virtual office any place, such as one's home or car, or a hotel room, that is computerized and equipped to handle office business.

virtual reality *Computer technology.* a highly effective simulation of reality achieved through video and audio programming, in which the user or viewer actually experiences the physical sensations associated with the scenes, events, environment, etc. represented on the computer system, and can interact with them as though they were real.

vir•tue ['vɜrtʃu] *n.* **1** moral excellence; goodness. **2** a particular kind of moral goodness: *Justice and kindness are virtues.* **3 a** the quality of being worthwhile; merit or value: *There is virtue in making a detailed plan.* **b** a specific feature that has merit or value: *He praised the virtues of his car.* **4** chastity, especially in a woman. **5** the power to produce effects: *There is little virtue in that medicine.*

by or **in virtue of,** relying on; because of; on account of: *By virtue of getting to the theatre early, they got the best seats. She was able to get a copy of the letter by virtue of her position in the company.*

make a virtue (out) of necessity, do willingly or graciously what must be done anyway. ⟨ME < L *virtus* manliness < *vir* man. Doublet of VIRTU.⟩

☛ *Syn.* **1.** See note at GOODNESS.

vir•tu•os•i•ty [,vɜrtʃu'ɒsəti] *n., pl.* **-ties. 1** the character or skill of a virtuoso. **2** interest or taste in the fine arts.

vir•tu•o•so [,vɜrtʃu'ousou] *n., pl.* **-sos, -si** [-si]; *adj. —n.* **1** a person highly skilled in the methods of an art, especially in playing a musical instrument. **2** a person who has a cultivated appreciation of artistic excellence. **3** a student or collector of objects of art, curios, antiquities, etc.
—adj. showing the artistic qualities and skills of a virtuoso: *a virtuoso performance.* ⟨< Ital. *virtuoso* learned⟩ **—,vir•tu'o•sa,** *n. fem., pl.* **-se.**

vir•tu•ous ['vɜrtʃuəs] *adj.* **1** good; moral; righteous. **2** chaste. **—'vir•tu•ous•ly,** *adv.* **—'vir•tu•ous•ness,** *n.*

vir•u•lence ['virələns] *or* [,virjələns] *n.* **1** the quality of being very poisonous or harmful; deadliness. **2** intense bitterness or spite; violent hostility. **3** the degree of infectiousness of any desease-causing entity. Also, **virulency.**

vir•u•lent ['virələnt] *or* ['virjələnt] *adj.* **1** very poisonous or harmful; deadly: *a virulent poison.* **2** of disease, characterized by a rapid and severe malignant or infectious condition. **3** of a micro-organism, able to cause a disease by breaking down the protective mechanisms of the host. **4** intensely bitter or spiteful; violently hostile. ⟨< L *virulentus* < *virus* poison⟩ **—'vir•u•lent•ly,** *adv.*

vi•rus ['vaɪrəs] *n.* **1** any of a large group of submicroscopic entities typically consisting of a core of RNA or DNA material surrounded by a coat of protein, that are capable of reproduction and growth only in living cells. Viruses are regarded either as the simplest micro-organisms or as very complex molecules. Many of them are agents of disease. **2** a disease caused by a virus: *She's been off work for two weeks with a bad virus.* **3** a corrupting influence: *the virus of prejudice.* **4** *Computer technology.* a piece of code inserted in a computer program so as to be very hard to detect, having a destructive or corrupting effect on the system and any data stored in it. It originates as a piece of sabotage but may be passed accidentally from system to system through the exchange of software by unsuspecting users. ⟨< L *virus* poison⟩

vis [vɪs] *n., pl.* **vi•res** ['vaɪriz] *or* ['vireis]. *Latin.* force.
vis major, act of God.

vi•sa ['vizə] *n., v.* **-saed, -sa•ing.** *—n.* an official document or endorsement on a passport allowing the person or persons identified in the passport to visit a particular country or region. Some countries will not allow a foreign traveller to enter without a visa.
—v. **1** give a visa to. **2** put a visa on or in (a passport): *Has your passport been visaed for Thailand?* ⟨< F *visa,* ult. < L *videre* see⟩

vis•age ['vɪzɪdʒ] *n.* **1** the face, especially with reference to its form or expression: *a grim visage, a visage of despair.* **2** appearance; aspect: *the sad visage of late autumn.* ⟨ME < OF *visage* < *vis* face < L *visus* a look < *videre* see⟩

☛ *Syn.* **1.** See note at FACE.

vis–à–vis [,vi zə 'vi] *adv., adj., prep., n. —adv. or adj.* face to face; opposite: *We sat vis-à-vis. They found themselves in a vis-à-vis position.*
—prep. **1** face to face with; opposite: *She sat vis-à-vis the guest of honour. The hotel is situated vis-à-vis the plaza.* **2** in comparison with or in relation to: *Vis-à-vis their competitors, they were doing very well.*
—n. **1** a person or thing that is face to face with or opposite another. **2** a person who corresponds to one in another group, etc.; counterpart. **3** any of various things in or on which people assume a position facing each other. ⟨< F⟩

Vi•sa•yan [vɪ'saɪən] *n., adj. —n.* **1** a member of the largest of the Philippines' indigenous peoples. **2** the Austronesian language of this group.
—adj. of, being, or having to do with this people group, its language, or its culture.

vis•ca•cha [vɪ'skɑtʃə] *n.* any burrowing rodent of the South American genera *Logostomus* and *Lagidium*, valued for their fur. ⟨< Am.Sp. *vizcacha* < Quechua *uiscacha*⟩

vis•cer•a ['vɪsərə] *n.* pl. of **vis•cus** ['vɪskəs]. the internal organs of the body, especially those in the cavity of the trunk, such as the stomach, intestines, kidneys, and liver. ⟨< L *viscera*, pl. of *viscus* internal body part⟩

vis•cer•al ['vɪsərəl] *adj.* **1** of, having to do with, or affecting the viscera. **2** of or springing from instinct or emotion, rather than reason: *a visceral reaction.* **—'vis•cer•al•ly,** *adv.*

vis•cid ['vɪsɪd] *adj.* **1** thick and sticky like heavy syrup or glue. **2** *Botany.* covered with a sticky substance. ⟨< LL *viscidus* < L *viscum* bird lime⟩ **—vis'cid•i•ty,** *n.* **—'vis•cid•ly,** *adv.*

vis•co•me•ter [vɪ'skɒmətər] *n.* a device for measuring viscosity.

vis•cose ['vɪskous] *n., adj. —n.* **1** a viscous solution made from cellulose and used especially in making rayon. **2** rayon fibres, yarn, or fabric. **3** (*adjl.*) of, having to do with, or made of viscose: *viscose rayon.*
—adj. viscous. ⟨< L *viscosus.* See VISCOUS.⟩

vis•cos•i•ty [vɪ'skɒsəti] *n., pl.* **-ties. 1** the quality or property of being viscous. **2** *Physics.* the property of a fluid that tends to prevent it from flowing; the frictional resistance of a fluid to the motion of its molecules.

vis•count ['vaɪ,kaʊnt] *n.* **1** a nobleman ranking next below an earl or count and next above a baron. **2** formerly, in England, a sheriff, or deputy of an earl. ⟨ME < AF < OF *visconte* < *vis-* vice- + *comte* count[2]⟩

vis•count•cy ['vaɪ,kaʊntsi] *n.* the title, rank, or dignity of a viscount. Also, **viscountship, viscounty.**

vis•count•ess ['vaɪ,kaʊntɪs] *n.* **1** the wife or widow of a viscount. **2** a woman who holds in her own right a rank equivalent to that of a viscount.

vis•cous ['vɪskəs] *adj.* **1** of a liquid, sticky; thick like syrup or glue; viscid. **2** *Physics.* having the property of viscosity. ⟨ME < LL *viscosus* < *viscum* birdlime⟩ **—'vis•cous•ly,** *adj.* **—'vis•cous•ness,** *n.*
☛ *Hom.* VISCUS.

vis•cus ['vɪskəs] *n.* sg. of VISCERA.
☛ *Hom.* VISCOUS.

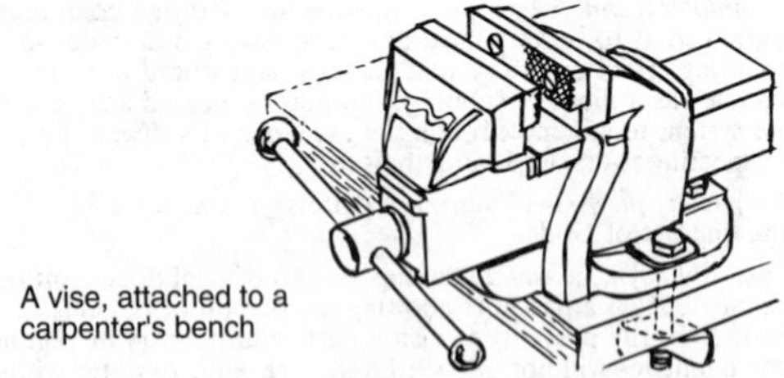
A vise, attached to a carpenter's bench

vise or **vice** [vəis] *n., v.* **vised, vis•ing.** *—n.* a tool having two jaws moved by a screw or lever, etc., used to hold an object firmly while work is being done on it.
—v. hold, press, or squeeze with a vise, or as if with a vise. ⟨ME < OF *vis* screw < VL *vitium* < L *vitis* vine⟩
☛ *Hom.* VICE.

vise–grip pliers ['vəis ,grɪp] pliers with a grip like that of a vise.

Vish•nu ['vɪʃnu] *n. Hinduism.* one of the three great divinities of classical Hinduism, regarded as the highest god, and usually worshipped in one of his human forms, especially Krishna or Rama. ⟨< Skt.⟩ **—'vish•nu,ism,** *n.*

vis•i•bil•i•ty [,vɪzə'bɪləti] *n., pl.* **-ties. 1 a** the quality or state of being visible. **b** the relative probability of being seen or noticed under specific conditions of light, atmosphere, etc.: *White clothing gives pedestrians higher visibility at night.* **2 a** the condition of light, atmosphere, etc. with reference to the distance at which things can be clearly seen: *Poor visibility was the main reason for the accident.* **b** this distance: *Fog and rain decreased visibility to about 50 m.* **3** the structural ability to provide a wide range of unobstructed vision: *Because of the angle of the dash, the windshield in this car has good visibility.*

vis•i•ble ['vɪzəbəl] *adj.* **1** that can be seen: *The shore was barely visible through the fog. Bacteria are visible only with the aid of a microscope.* **2** that can be observed; apparent; obvious: *There was no visible improvement in the patient's condition. The tramp had no visible means of support.* **3** available; already existing: *visible assets.* **4** visually represented; made so as to bring parts not normally seen into view. ⟨ME < L *visibilis* < *videre* see⟩ **—'vis•i•bly,** *adv.*

Vis•i•goth ['vɪzə,gɒθ] *n.* a member of the western division of the Goths. The Goths plundered Rome in A.D. 410, and formed a monarchy in France and N Spain about A.D. 418. ⟨< LL *Visigothi* < Gmc.; taken as 'the western Goths'⟩ **—,Vis•i'goth•ic,** *adj.*

vi•sion ['vɪʒən] *n., v. —n.* **1** the power of seeing; sense of sight: *He wears glasses because of poor vision.* **2** the act or fact of seeing; sight. **3** the power of perceiving by the imagination, by supernatural revelation, or by clear thinking: *a prophet of great vision.* **4 a** something seen in the imagination, in a dream, in a supernatural revelation, in one's thoughts, etc.: *visions of doom, visions of great wealth.* **b** such an image adopted as a goal or objective: *As the new president, what is your vision for the company?* **5** a phantom. **6** a very beautiful person, scene, etc.
—v. imagine or envision. ⟨ME < L *visio, -onis* < *videre* see⟩ **—'vi•sion•al,** *adj.*

vi•sion•ar•y ['vɪʒə,nɛri] *adj., n., pl.* **-ar•ies.** *—adj.* **1** having a tendency to indulge in fanciful and impractical schemes or theories: *a visionary thinker.* **2** not practical; fanciful or utopian: *a visionary scheme for a just society.* **3** having or characterized by ideas that are far more advanced than others of the current time. **4 a** of, having to do with, or seen in a vision: *The visionary scene faded and she awoke.* **b** imaginary; only in the mind. **5** able or likely to see visions.
—n. **1** a person whose schemes or theories are fanciful and impractical. **2** a person who sees visions. **3** a person whose ideas are far more advanced than others of the current time.

vis•it ['vɪzɪt] *v., n. —v.* **1** make a call on or stay with for social reasons: *I'm going to visit my aunt tomorrow. They're visiting friends in Halifax this month.* **2** go or come to see or stay at (a place), especially for sightseeing, etc.: *Last year we visited Newfoundland.* **3** go or come to see officially for inspection or examination: *The inspector visits the factory once a month. I must visit my doctor.* **4** make a call or stay as a guest or for the purpose of inspection, etc.: *They are visiting in the country. The teachers were nervous whenever the chairman of the school board was visiting.* **5** *Informal.* converse; chat amicably: *We sat visiting for an hour after the gifts were opened.* **6 a** come upon; afflict: *The poor old man was visited by many troubles.* **b** occur to; come to: *She was visited by a strange premonition.* **7** send; inflict: *He visited his anger upon them.* **8** punish or avenge (a sin, etc.): *to visit the sins of the fathers upon the children.*
—n. **1** a call or stay as a guest or for the purpose of inspection, etc.: *They had to cut their visit short because she got sick.* **2** *Informal.* a friendly talk or chat: *We had a nice visit while we were waiting.* **3** *Maritime Law.* an inspection of a ship by an officer of a warring nation to search it, determine nationality, etc. ⟨< L *visitare*, ult. < *videre* see⟩

vis•it•ant ['vɪzətənt] *n., adj. —n.* **1** a visitor, especially one from a strange or distant place, or one thought to be supernatural. **2** *Zoology.* a migrating bird in any of the places it stays temporarily.
—adj. Archaic or poetic. paying a visit; visiting.

vis•it•a•tion [,vɪzə'teiʃən] *n.* **1** the act or an instance of visiting; especially, a visit involving some degree of protocol, as one customarily made to a family in mourning, to a parishioner by a spiritual leader, or for the purpose of inspection or examination: *the visitation of a foreign ship.* **2 a** the rights accorded a divorced parent to visit his or her child. **b** such a visit. **3** a punishment, reward, vision, etc. sent by a deity. **4** any severe affliction, blow, or trial. **5 Visitation, a** the visit of the Virgin Mary to Elizabeth, her cousin. **b** a festival of the Roman Catholic Church, held July 2, in honour of this visit.

vis•i•ta•to•ri•al [,vɪzətə'tɔriəl] *adj.* **1** having the right or power of official visitation. **2** of or having to do with official visitation or inspection, or with an official visitor or inspector.

visiting card CALLING CARD.

visiting fireman *Informal.* **1** an important or influential person accorded special privileges or treatment while visiting a city or institution: *There were a lot of visiting firemen in Victoria* *during the Commonwealth Games.* **2** a tourist, vacationer, or conventioneer, etc., presumed to be a big spender.

vis•i•tor ['vɪzətər] *n.* a person who visits or is visiting: *I don't live here; I'm just a visitor. The zoo had more visitors than ever last summer.*

☛ *Syn.* **Visitor,** GUEST = someone who comes to see or stay with another or in a place. **Visitor** is the general word, applying to anyone who comes to see a person or place or makes a call or stay, long or short, for any reason: *Our visitors from the East arrived last night.* **Guest** emphasizes the idea of being entertained, and applies especially to someone invited to come or stay: *He usually entertains his guests at the club.*

vi•sor ['vaɪzər] *n., v.* —*n.* **1** formerly, the movable front part of a knight's or warrior's helmet, covering the face. See ARMOUR for picture. **2** a movable section made of safety glass or acrylic, attached to a safety helmet to protect the eyes of welders, motorcyclists, etc. **3** a projecting part, such as the peak of a cap, intended to protect the eyes from the sun or other strong light. See CAP for picture. **4** a type of peaked cap having no crown: *a golf visor.* **5** a small movable shade attached inside an automobile at the top of the windshield. **6** a mask or disguise.
—*v.* cover or protect with a visor. ⟨ME < AF *viser* < *vis* face, ult. < L *videre* see⟩

vi•sored ['vaɪzərd] *adj.* furnished or equipped with a visor.

vis•ta ['vɪstə] *n.* **1** a view seen through a narrow opening or passage: *The opening between two rows of trees afforded a vista of the lake.* **2** such an opening or passage itself: *a shady vista of elms.* **3** a mental view, especially over a period of time or series of events in the past or future: *The book had opened up a new vista for her future.* ⟨< Ital. *vista,* ult. < L *videre* see⟩

vis•u•al ['vɪʒuəl] *adj., n.* —*adj.* **1** of, having to do with, received through, or used in sight or vision: *Near-sightedness is a visual defect.* **2** that can be seen; visible: *the visual arts.* **3** done by sight only: *visual navigation.* **4** of the nature of a mental vision; produced or occurring as a picture in the mind: *to form a visual image from an author's description.* **5** *Optics.* optical.
—*n.* **1** VISUAL AID. **2** Usually, **visuals,** *pl.* the picture or graphic elements of a movie, TV show, etc. as distinct from the sound, etc.: *The screenplay is mediocre, but the visuals are great.* ⟨< LL *visualis* < L *visus* sight < *videre* see⟩ —**'vis•u•al•ly,** *adv.*

visual aid a device or means such as a chart, diagram, motion picture, etc. for aiding communication through the sense of sight.

visual binary a binary star close enough that it can actually be seen, with a telescope or the naked eye (i.e., without recourse to spectrum analysis), to have two distinct components.

visual display unit *Computer technology.* a device displaying computer data on a screen; a monitor, often incorporating a keyboard for user interaction.

vis•u•al•i•za•tion [,vɪʒuələ'zeiʃən] *or* [,vɪʒuəlaɪ'zeiʃən] *n.* **1** the act or process of visualizing or the state of being visualized. **2** the thing visualized.

vis•u•al•ize ['vɪʒuə,laɪz] *v.* **-ized, -iz•ing. 1** form a mental picture of: *I can visualize his reaction when he hears the news.* **2** make visible; especially, make (an internal organ) visible by surgical means or X ray. **3** form mental pictures, especially of oneself realizing some objective, as a form of positive thinking.

vi•ta ['vitə] *n., pl.* **-tae** [-taɪ] *or* [-ti]. an autobiographical sketch or summary; CURRICULUM VITAE. ⟨< L *vita* life⟩

vi•tal ['vəitəl] *adj., n.* —*adj.* **1** of, having to do with, or necessary to life: *vital forces. Eating is a vital function. The heart is one of the vital organs of the body.* **2** of the greatest importance; essential: *vital national interests. Perfect timing was vital to the success of her plan.* **3** causing death, failure, or ruin: *a vital wound, a vital blow to an industry.* **4** full of life and spirit; lively.
—*n.* **vitals,** *pl.* **a** the vital organs, such as the heart, brain, lungs, etc. **b** the essential parts or elements of anything. ⟨ME < L *vitalis* < *vita* life⟩ —**'vi•tal•ly,** *adv.*

vital capacity *Physiology.* the volume of air that can be exhaled from the lungs after the greatest possible amount has been inhaled.

vital force a hypothetical force held to be the source and organizing or driving principle of all living things; ÉLAN VITAL.

vi•tal•ism ['vəitə,lɪzəm] *n.* a doctrine that the behaviour of a living organism is, at least in part, due to a VITAL FORCE that cannot possibly be explained by physics and chemistry. —**'vi•tal•ist,** *n.* —**,vi•tal'is•tic,** *adj.*

vi•tal•i•ty [vəi'tæləti] *n., pl.* **-ties. 1** mental or physical vigour; liveliness: *She has great vitality.* **2** the power to endure or remain active: *the vitality of a tradition.* **3** vital force; the power to live; that which distinguishes the living from the non-living.

vi•tal•ize ['vəitə,laɪz] *v.* **-ized, -iz•ing. 1** put vitality into. **2** give life to. —**,vi•tal•i'za•tion,** *n.* —**'vi•tal,iz•er,** *n.*

vital signs physical signs of life, such as pulse, breathing, and temperature.

vital statistics 1 facts or data about births, deaths, marriages, etc. **2** *Slang.* a woman's bust, waist, and hip measurements. **3** *Informal.* any of various other kinds of numerical data, such as the achievements of an athlete, considered important.

vi•ta•min ['vəitəmɪn] *n.* **1** any of certain complex organic substances required for the normal growth and nourishment of the body, found especially in milk, butter, raw fruits and vegetables, brewers' yeast, wheat, and cod-liver oil. Lack of vitamins in food causes such diseases as rickets and scurvy as well as general poor health. **2** (*adjl.*) of, having to do with, or containing vitamins: *a vitamin deficiency, vitamin pills.* ⟨< L *vita* life + E *amine (< ammonia)*⟩ —**,vi•ta'min•ic,** *adj.*

vitamin A a fat-soluble vitamin occurring in two known forms, A_1 and A_2, and found especially in animal products such as milk, butter, cod-liver oil, egg yolk, and liver, and in leafy green vegetables. Vitamin A helps the body resist infection and prevents night blindness. *Formula for A_1*: $C_{20}H_{30}O$; *for A_2*: $C_{20}H_{28}O$

vitamin B_1 thiamine.

vitamin B_2 riboflavin. Also, **vitamin G.**

vitamin B_6 pyridoxine.

vitamin B_{12} a complex crystalline compound found especially in liver, that is necessary for blood formation and proper neurological functioning and is used particularly in treating pernicious anemia. *Formula*: $C_{63}H_{90}N_{14}O_{14}PCo$

vitamin B complex a group of different water-soluble vitamins found especially in yeast, liver, eggs, and seed germs. They include thiamine, riboflavin, pyridoxine, vitamin B_{12}, biotin, choline, nicotinic acid, folic acid, and pantothenic acid.

vitamin C a water-soluble compound found especially in citrus fruits and also made synthetically; ASCORBIC ACID. It is used especially for the prevention and treatment of scurvy and the common cold. *Formula*: $C_6H_8O_6$

vitamin D any of several fat-soluble compounds that are necessary for normal growth of bones and teeth and found especially in fish-liver oils, egg yolk, and milk. The most abundant form of this vitamin is D_3, which is found in fish-liver oils and is also formed in the skin by the action of sunlight. *Formula for D_3*: $C_{27}H_{43}OH$

vitamin E any of several fat-soluble vitamins found especially in leaves and seed germ oils, whole grain cereals, butter, and eggs. It is important as an antioxidant for inhibiting the destruction of cell tissues. *Formula*: $C_{29}H_{50}O_2$

vitamin G vitamin B_2; riboflavin.

vitamin H biotin.

vi•ta•min•ize ['vəitəmɪ,naɪz] *v.* **-ized, -iz•ing.** provide with vitamins; add vitamins to: *This breakfast cereal has been vitaminized.*

vitamin K 1 either of two fat-soluble compounds necessary to the normal clotting of blood, found especially in leafy vegetables, alfalfa, etc. and formed in the intestines of mammals by the action of bacteria. *Formula for K_1*: $C_{31}H_{46}O_2$ *Formula for K_2*: $C_{41}H_{56}O_2$ **2** any of several synthetically produced compounds closely related to vitamins K_1 and K_2 and having a similar function.

vitamin L a vitamin found in beef liver (vitamin L_1) and yeast (vitamin L_2) that promotes normal lactation.

vitamin P bioflavonoid.

vi•tel•lin [vɪ'tɛlən] *or* [vəi'tɛlən] *n.* a protein contained in the yolk of eggs. ⟨< L *vitellus* egg yolk⟩

vi•tel•line [vɪ'tɛlɪn] *or* [vɪ'tɛlaɪn], [vəi'tɛlɪn] *or* [vəi'tɛlaɪn] *adj.* **1** of or having to do with the yolk of an egg. **2** having the colour of an egg yolk.

vi•tel•lus [vɪ'tɛləs] *or* [vəi'tɛləs] *n.* egg yolk. ⟨< L⟩

vi•ti•ate ['vɪʃi,eit] *v.* **-at•ed, -at•ing. 1** impair the quality of; spoil: *His illness vitiated his chances of success.* **2** destroy the legal force or authority of: *The contract was vitiated because one person signed under compulsion.* **3** corrupt; debase. ⟨< L *vitiare* < *vitium* fault⟩ —**,vi•ti'a•tion,** *n.* —**'vi•ti•a•ble,** *adj.*

vit•i•cul•ture ['vɪtə,kʌltʃər] *or* ['vəitə,kʌltʃər] *n.* the cultivation of grapes. ⟨< L *vitis* vine + E *culture*⟩
—**,vi•ti'cul•tur•al,** *adj.* —**,vi•ti'cul•tur•ist,** *n.*

vit•re•ous ['vɪtriəs] *adj.* **1** of, having to do with, derived from, or consisting of glass. **2** like glass in texture, brittleness, etc.; glassy: *vitreous rocks.* **3** of or having to do with the VITREOUS HUMOUR. ⟨< L *vitreus* < *vitrum* glass⟩ **—'vit•re•ous•ness** or **ˌvit•re'os•i•ty** [ˌvɪtri'ɒsəti], *n.*

vitreous humour or **humor** the transparent, jellylike substance that fills the interior of the eyeball behind the lens. See EYE for picture.

vi•tres•cent [vɪ'trɛsənt] *adj.* **1** becoming or tending to become glass. **2** capable of being made into glass. **—vi'tres•cence,** *n.*

vit•ric ['vɪtrɪk] *adj., n.* —*adj.* of or having to do with glass; like glass.
—*n.* **1 vitrics** (*used with a singular verb*), the study of glass and glassmaking. **2 vitrics,** *pl.,* glassware; glass articles.

vit•ri•fac•tion [ˌvɪtrə'fækʃən] *n.* vitrification.

vit•ri•fi•ca•tion [ˌvɪtrəfə'keiʃən] *n.* **1** the process of vitrifying. **2** a product of vitrifying.

vit•ri•form ['vɪtrəˌfɔrm] *adj.* having the structure or appearance of glass. ⟨< F < L *vitrum* glass + *facere* make⟩

vit•ri•fy ['vɪtrəˌfaɪ] *v.* **-fied, -fy•ing.** change into glass or a glasslike substance by heat and fusion. **—'vit•riˌfi•a•ble,** *adj.*

vi•trine [vɪ'trin] *n.* a glass display case or cabinet. ⟨< F < *vitre* glass pane < L *vitrum* glass⟩

vit•ri•ol ['vɪtriˌɒl] *or* ['vɪtriəl] *n.* **1** any of certain sulphates, as of copper **(blue vitriol),** iron **(green vitriol),** or zinc **(white vitriol). 2** SULPHURIC ACID. Vitriol burns deeply and leaves very bad scars. **3** very sharp speech or severe criticism. ⟨ME < Med.L *vitriolum,* ult. < L *vitrum* glass⟩

vit•ri•ol•ic [ˌvɪtri'ɒlɪk] *adj.* **1** of or containing vitriol. **2** like vitriol. **3** bitterly severe; extremely harsh: *vitriolic criticism.*

vit•ri•ol•ize ['vɪtriəˌlaɪz] *v.* **-ized, iz•ing. 1** convert into vitriol. **2** treat or injure with vitriol.

vit•ta ['vɪtə] *n., pl.* **-tae** [-ti] *or* [-taɪ]. **1** *Botany.* a tube containing oil in a fruit, especially the fruit of an umbelliferous plant. **2** *Zoology.* a stripe of colour. ⟨< NL < L *vitta* headband⟩ **—'vit•tate** [-eit], *adj.*

vit•u•line ['vɪtʃəˌlaɪn] *or* ['vɪtʃəlɪn] *adj.* of or resembling a calf or veal. ⟨< L *vitulinus* < *vitulus* calf⟩

vi•tu•per•ate [vɪ'tjupəˌreit] *or* [vɪ'tupəˌreit] *v.* **-at•ed, -at•ing.** find fault with in abusive words; revile. ⟨< L *vituperare* < *vitium* fault + *parare* prepare⟩

vi•tu•per•a•tion [vɪˌtjupə'reiʃən] *or* [vɪˌtupə'reiʃən] *n.* bitter abuse in words; very severe scolding.

vi•tu•per•a•tive [vɪ'tjupərətɪv] *or* [vɪ'tupərətɪv] *adj.* abusive; reviling. **—vi'tu•per•a•tive•ly,** *adv.* **—vi'tu•per•a•tive•ness,** *n.*

vi•va ['vivə] *interj., n.* —*interj.* an exclamation used as a salute or expression of approval: *Viva Italia!*
—*n.* a shout of applause or good will: *The crowd greeted her with a loud viva.* ⟨< Ital.⟩

vi•va•ce [vi'vɑtʃei] *adj., adv., n. Music.* —*adj.* quick; lively.
—*adv.* in a lively manner.
—*n.* a lively movement or passage; composition to be played or sung in this manner. ⟨< Ital. < L *vivax, -acis*⟩

vi•va•cious [vɪ'veiʃəs] *or* [vaɪ'veiʃəs] *adj.* lively; sprightly; animated: *a vivacious personality, a vivacious smile.* ⟨< L *vivax, -acis*⟩ **—vi'va•cious•ly,** *adv.* **—vi'va•cious•ness,** *n.*

vi•vac•i•ty [vɪ'væsəti] *or* [vaɪ'væsəti] *n., pl.* **-ties.** liveliness; sprightliness; animation; gaiety. ⟨< L *vivacitas* < *vivax, -acis* lively⟩

vi•var•i•um [vɪ'vɛriəm] *n., pl.* **-i•ums** or **-i•a** [-iə]. an enclosed place for keeping animals in an environment as close as possible to their natural one. ⟨< L⟩

vi•va vo•ce ['vivə 'voutʃei] *or* ['vaɪvə 'vousi] **1** spoken; oral: *a viva voce examination.* **2** orally: *We voted viva voce instead of by ballot.* ⟨< L *viva voce,* literally, by living voice⟩

vive [viv] *French. interj.* a word used in exclamation of praise or as a salute. *Vive la France!* means *Long live France!*

vi•ver•rine [vɪ'vɛraɪn], [vɪ'vɛrɪn], *or* [vaɪ'vɛraɪn] *adj., n.* —*adj.* of, having to do with, or belonging to the family Viverridae, of small, slender, carnivorous mammals such as civets, mongooses, genets, etc.
—*n.* such an animal. ⟨< L *viverra* ferret + *-ine*⟩

viv•id ['vɪvɪd] *adj.* **1** brilliant; strikingly bright; brightly coloured: *vivid fabric. Dandelions are a vivid yellow.* **2** full of life; lively: *a vivid personality.* **3 a** clearly and strikingly perceived or felt: *a vivid impression, a vivid sensation.* **b** very evocative: *a vivid description, vivid imagery.* **4** very strong and active: *a vivid imagination.* ⟨< L *vividus* < *vivus* alive⟩ **—'viv•id•ly,** *adv.* **—'viv•id•ness,** *n.*

viv•i•fy ['vɪvəˌfaɪ] *v.* **-fied, -fy•ing.** give life or vigour to; animate; enliven; make vivid. ⟨< L *vivificare* < *vivus* alive + *facere* make⟩ **—ˌviv•i•fi'ca•tion,** *n.*

vi•vip•a•rous [vɪ'vɪpərəs] *or* [vaɪ'vɪpərəs] *adj.* **1** *Zoology.* bringing forth living young rather than eggs, as most mammals, and some reptiles and fishes. Compare OVIPAROUS. **2** *Botany.* having seeds or bulbs that germinate while still on the parent plant. ⟨< L *viviparus* < *vivus* alive + *parere* bring forth⟩ **—ˌviv•i'par•i•ty** [ˌvɪvə'pærəti], *n.* **—vi'vip•a•rous•ly,** *adv.*

viv•i•sect ['vɪvəˌsɛkt] *or* [ˌvɪvə'sɛkt] *v.* **1** perform vivisection on: *to vivisect an animal.* **2** practise vivisection.

viv•i•sec•tion [ˌvɪvə'sɛkʃən] *n.* the act or practice of cutting into or experimenting on living animals for scientific study. ⟨< L *vivus* alive + E *section*⟩ **—ˌviv•i'sec•tion•al,** *adj.*

viv•i•sec•tion•ist [ˌvɪvə'sɛkʃənɪst] *n.* **1** vivisector. **2** a person who favours or defends vivisection.

viv•i•sec•tor ['vɪvəˌsɛktər] *n.* a person who practises vivisection.

vix•en ['vɪksən] *n.* **1** a female fox. **2** a bad-tempered or quarrelsome woman. ⟨OE **fyxen* < *fox* fox⟩ **—'vix•en•ish,** *adj.*

Vi•yel•la [vaɪ'ɛlə] *n. Trademark.* a soft, lightweight, washable fabric, a blend of wool and cotton.

viz. to wit; namely (abbreviation of L *videlicet*): *Two members have been asked to attend the conference, viz., Ms. Sanchez and Mr. Faber.* ⟨< L *videlicet* as *vi* + *z,* the Med.L symbol of the abbreviation of *-et*⟩

☛ *Usage.* **Viz.** is used mainly in rather formal documents or reference works. It is a written form that is not pronounced [vɪz], except humorously, but is usually spoken or read as 'namely'.

viz•ard ['vɪzərd] *n. Archaic.* a mask; VISOR (def. 3). ⟨alteration of *visor*⟩

vi•zier [vɪ'zir] *or* ['vɪzjər] *n.* in Muslim countries, especially in the former Turkish Empire, a high official or minister of state. ⟨< Turkish < Arabic *wazīr,* originally, porter⟩ **—vi'zier•al,** *adj.* **—vi'zier•ate** or **vi'zier•ship,** *n.*

vi•zir [vɪ'zir] See VIZIER.

viz•sla or **Viz•sla** ['vizlə], ['vɪʒlɒ], *or* ['vislə] *n.* a medium-sized Hungarian hunting dog, 53-57 cm at the shoulder, having a short, smooth, rusty gold or sandy yellow coat, and usually a docked tail. ⟨< *Vizla,* a town in Hungary⟩

VJ ['vi ˌdʒei] VIDEO JOCKEY.

V–J Day the date of the Allied victory over Japan in World War II, either August 15, 1945 (when the fighting officially ended) or September 2, 1945 (the signing of the formal surrender).

VL or **V.L.** VULGAR LATIN.

VLCT very large commercial transport, a plane carrying 550-800 passengers.

VLF or **V.L.F.** VERY LOW FREQUENCY.

VLSI an electronic circuit on a small semiconductor chip, having an extremely high number of microcircuits. ⟨*v*ery *l*arge *s*cale *i*ntegration⟩

V neck a garment neckline that is V-shaped at the front. Also, **V-neck. —'V-ˌneck** or **'V-ˌnecked,** *adjl.*

vo•ca•ble ['voukəbəl] *n.* a word, especially as heard or seen without consideration of its meaning. ⟨< L *vocabulum* < *vocare* call⟩

vo•cab•u•lar•y [və'kæbjəˌlɛri] *or* [vou'kæbjəˌlɛri] *n., pl.* **-lar•ies. 1** the stock of words known to or used by a person, class of people, profession, etc.: *Reading will increase your vocabulary.* **2** a collection or list of words, usually in alphabetical order, with their translations or meanings: *There is a vocabulary in the back of our French book.* **3** all the words of a language; LEXICON (def. 2). **4** the characteristic expressions of a quality, feeling, art, etc.: *the vocabulary of prejudice, the vocabulary of music.* ⟨< Med.L *vocabularius* < L *vocabulum.* See VOCABLE.⟩

vo•cal ['voukəl] *adj., n.* —*adj.* **1** of, by, for, made or done with, or otherwise having to do with the voice: *vocal organs, vocal power, a vocal message, vocal music.* **2** having a voice; giving forth sound: *We are vocal beings. The gorge was vocal with the roar of the cataract.* **3** aroused to speech; inclined to talk freely: *He became vocal with indignation. One of the twins is very reserved; the other is quite vocal.* **4** *Phonetics.* of a vowel or vowels.
—*n.* **1** a vocal sound. **2** *Music.* **a** a composition for the voice. **b** the part of a composition that is sung: *She did the background*

vocals for this song. ⟨< L *vocalis* < *vox* voice. Doublet of VOWEL.⟩ **—'vo•cal•ly,** *adv.*

vocal cords either of two pairs of folds of membrane in the larynx. Voice is produced when the edges of the lower pair of folds vibrate as air from the lungs passes between them. See WINDPIPE for picture. Also, VOCAL BANDS.

vo•cal•ic [vou'kælɪk] *adj. Phonetics.* **1** of, having to do with, or consisting of a vowel or vowels: *a vocalic sound.* I *is a vocalic word.* **2** being or functioning as a vowel: *The word* pyre *has a vocalic* y. **—vo'cal•i•cal•ly,** *adv.*

vo•cal•ise [,voukə'liz] *n. Music.* a piece of music sung on one vowel sound or on sol fa syllables as a voice exercise. ⟨< F *vocaliser* vocalize⟩

vo•cal•ist ['voukəlɪst] *n.* singer.

vo•cal•ize ['voukə,laɪz] *v.* **-ized, -iz•ing. 1** speak, sing, shout, etc.; use the voice. **2** make vocal; utter; articulate; express with the voice: *The dog vocalized its pain in a series of long howls.* **3** *Phonetics.* **a** change into or pronounce as a vowel. **b** voice. **4** add vowel points to (text in Hebrew or other purely consonantal script). **—,vo•cal•i'za•tion,** *n.*

vo•ca•tion [vou'keiʃən] *n.* **1** an occupation, business, profession, or trade: *He chose teaching as his vocation.* **2 a** an inclination or summons to a particular activity, especially to religious work: *Since childhood she felt a vocation for nursing.* **b** the work to which one is so called. ⟨ME < L *vocatio, -onis,* literally, a calling < *vocare* call⟩

☛ *Usage.* **Vocation,** AVOCATION are often confused. **Vocation** applies to a person's regular occupation, the way he or she earns his or her living. **Avocation** applies to a kind of work a person does in his or her spare time, a hobby: *Bookkeeping is her vocation, and photography is her avocation.*

vo•ca•tion•al [vou'keiʃənəl] *adj.* of or having to do with some occupation, trade, etc. Trades and skills such as carpentry, stenography, hairdressing, and printing are taught in vocational schools. **—vo'ca•tion•al•ly,** *adv.*

voc•a•tive ['vɒkətɪv] *adj., n.* —*adj.* **1** *Grammar.* of, having to do with, or being the grammatical case, found in Latin and some other languages, that shows that a noun, pronoun, or adjective refers to a person or thing being addressed or invoked. **2** of, having to do with, or characterized by calling.
—*n. Grammar.* **1** the vocative case. **2** a word or construction in the vocative case. ⟨< L *vocativus* < *vocare* call⟩ **—'voc•a•tive•ly,** *adv.*

vo•cif•er•ant [və'sɪfərənt] *or* [vou'sɪfərənt] *adj., n.* —*adj.* vociferating.
—*n.* a person who vociferates.

vo•cif•er•ate [və'sɪfə,reit] *or* [vou'sɪfə,reit] *v.* **-at•ed, -at•ing.** cry out loudly or noisily; shout. ⟨< L *vociferari* < *vox, vocis* voice + *ferre* bear⟩

vo•cif•er•a•tion [və,sɪfə'reiʃən] *or* [vou,sɪfə'reiʃən] *n.* a vociferating; noisy oratory or clamour.

vo•cif•er•ous [və'sɪfərəs] *or* [vou'sɪfərəs] *adj.* loud and noisy; shouting; clamouring: *a vociferous person, vociferous cheers.* ⟨< L *vociferari.* See VOCIFERATE.⟩ **—vo'cif•er•ous•ly,** *adv.* **—vo'cif•er•ous•ness,** *n.*

vod•ka ['vɒdkə] *n.* a colourless alcoholic liquor distilled from a mash of rye, wheat, etc. ⟨< Russian *vodka,* dim. of *voda* water⟩

vogue [voug] *n.* **1** something that is in fashion at a particular time; the popular style: *Hoopskirts were the vogue many years ago.* **2** general favour; popularity: *the colours that are in vogue this spring. This song had a great vogue at one time.* **3** a period of popularity: *a short vogue.* **4** (*adjl.*) popular or fashionable: *vogue colours, a vogue word.* ⟨< F *vogue* a rowing, course, success < *voguer* float < Ital. *vogare*⟩ **—'vogu•ish,** *adj.*

voice [vɔɪs] *n., v.* **voiced, voic•ing.** —*n.* **1** the sound produced by the organs in the throat and uttered through the mouth and nose, especially the sounds human beings make in speaking, singing, shouting, etc.: *The voices of the children could be heard coming from the playground.* **2** such sound regarded as having a particular quality that distinguishes one person from another, expresses emotion, etc.: *to recognize someone's voice, a low voice, a gentle voice, an angry voice.* **3** the ability to make such sounds: *His voice was gone because of a sore throat.* **4** anything thought of as being like speech or song: *the voice of the wind, the voice of one's conscience.* **5** *Music.* **a** a musical sound made by the vocal cords and resonated by several head and throat cavities; the tones made in singing. **b** ability as a singer: *She has a very good voice.* **c** singer: *The chorus consists of 70 voices.* **d** a part of a composition for one kind of singer or instrument. **6** expression: *They gave voice to their joy.* **7** an expressed opinion, choice, wish, etc.: *His voice was for compromise.* **8** a means or instrument of expression: *That newspaper claims to be the voice of the people.* **9** the right to express an opinion or choice: *We have no voice in the matter.* **10** *Grammar.* **a** a form of a verb showing the relation of the subject of the verb to the action expressed by the verb. The active voice, as *sees* in *he sees,* shows that the subject is performing the action. The passive voice, as *is seen* in *he is seen,* shows that the subject is receiving the action. **b** the category to which such forms belong. **11** *Phonetics.* the characteristic feature of a sound uttered with vibration of the vocal cords, not with mere breath. **12** the art or science of the proper use of the voice, as in acting or singing: *She is studying voice.*
in voice, in condition to sing or speak well.
lift up (one's) **voice, a** shout; yell. **b** protest; complain.
with one voice, unanimously.
—*v.* **1** express; utter: *They voiced their approval of the plan.* **2** *Phonetics.* utter with vibration of the vocal cords, not with breath alone. The consonants *z, v,* and *d* are voiced; *s, f,* and *t* are not. **3** *Music.* **a** regulate the tone of (an organ, etc.). **b** write the parts of (a piece of music) for one kind of singer or instrument. ⟨ME < OF *vois, voiz* < L *vox*⟩

voice box larynx.

voiced [vɔɪst] *adj., v.* —*adj.* **1** having a voice, especially of a particular kind (*usually used in compounds*): *deep-voiced.* **2** *Phonetics.* produced or uttered with vibration of the vocal cords. All vowel sounds are voiced; many consonants, such as *b, d,* and *g* are also voiced. Compare VOICELESS.
—*v.* pt. and pp. of VOICE.

voice frequency the range of sound frequencies between 300 and 3000 hertz. Voice frequency is the second lowest range in the radio spectrum, above extremely low frequency.

voice•less ['vɔɪslɪs] *adj.* **1** having no voice; mute; speechless. **2** unspoken; not expressed. **3** not accorded the right or opportunity to express one's views or desires. **4** *Phonetics.* produced or uttered without vibration of the vocal cords; not voiced. The consonants *p, t,* and *k* are voiceless. Compare VOICED. **—'voice•less•ly,** *adv.* **—'voice•less•ness,** *n.*

voice mail 1 an automated answering system for telephone networks having touch tone, using a series of prerecorded prompts to which callers may respond by pressing the appropriate button to transfer them quickly and efficiently to the line they need. On completion of such a transfer, callers may listen to a recorded message dealing with the subject of their inquiry, speak to a real person, or leave their own recorded message. **2** a message or messages recorded on such a system. **3** a message recorded on any telephone answering machine.

voice–o•ver ['vɔɪs ,ouvər] *n.* **1 a** the voice of an unseen narrator or commentator in a film or on television. **b** the narration or comment itself: *The film itself came out well, but the voice-over was a disaster.* **2** a film, television ad, etc. with such narration. **3** (*adjl.*) made with an unseen narrator: *She does voice-over commercials for television.*

voice•print ['vɔɪs,prɪnt] *n.* a graphic representation of an individual's voice. It is an electronic record of the duration, amplitude, and frequency of the sound or sounds uttered, and is unique to the individual. **—'voice,print•ing,** *n.*

void [vɔɪd] *adj., v., n.* —*adj.* **1** *Law.* without legal force or effect; not binding: *A contract made by a person under legal age is void.* **2** empty; vacant: *a void space.* **3** without effect; useless. **4** *Card games.* holding no cards (*in* a given suit).
void of, devoid of; without; lacking.
—*v.* **1** make invalid; nullify; cancel: *to void a contract, to void a transaction on a cash register.* **2** excrete (urine or feces): *The nurse asked if I had voided this morning.* **3** empty. **4** *Card games.* play cards so as to make (oneself) void (*in a given suit*). **5** *Archaic.* leave.
—*n.* **1** an empty space. **2** a feeling of loss or emptiness: *The death of his wife left an aching void in Bob's heart.* **3** *Card games.* complete lack of cards (*in* a given suit) in one's hand as dealt: *a void in hearts.* ⟨ME < OF *voide* < VL *vocitus,* ult. < var. of L *vacuus* empty⟩ **—'void•er,** *n.*

void•a•ble ['vɔɪdəbəl] *adj.* capable of being voided or given up: *The contract was voidable by either party after twelve months.*

void•ance ['vɔɪdəns] *n.* **1** an act of voiding. **2** annulment, as of a contract. **3** vacancy of a benefice.

voi•là [vwɑ'lɑ] *interj. French.* there it is; behold.

voile [vɔɪl]; *French,* [vwal] *n.* a thin, sheer, somewhat crisp cloth in a plain weave, used for blouses, light dresses, curtains, etc. Voile is usually made of cotton or a cotton blend. ⟨< F *voile,* originally, veil < L *vela,* pl. of *velum* covering. Doublet of VEIL, VELUM.⟩

voir dire ['vwɑr 'dir] *Law.* **1** a preliminary examination by a judge to determine the competence, interest, etc. of a trial witness or the voluntary nature of an accused person's confession to a police officer. **2** the oath administered to such a person. ⟨< OF < *voire* truly + *dire* to speak. 17c.⟩

vol. **1** volume. **2** volunteer. **3** volcano.

vo•lant ['voulənt] *adj.* **1** flying; able to fly. **2** *Heraldry.* represented as flying. **3** nimble; quick. ⟨< L *volans, -antis,* ppr. of *volare* fly⟩

Vo•la•puk or **Vo•la•pük** [,voulɑ'pyk] *or* ['vɒlə,pʊk] *n.* an artificial language based on major European languages, invented c. 1879 by Johann Schleyer. ⟨< *vol* world + *a-* connective + *pük* speak⟩

vo•lar ['voulər] *adj.* of or having to do with the palm of the hand or the sole of the foot. ⟨< L *vol(a)* hollow of hand, sole of foot + *-ar*⟩

vol•a•tile ['vɒlə,taɪl] *or* ['vɒlətəl] *adj., n.* —*adj.* **1** evaporating rapidly; changing into vapour easily at a relatively low temperature: *Gasoline is volatile.* **2** changing rapidly from one mood or interest to another; fickle; frivolous: *of a volatile disposition.* **3** of an unstable social or political situation, likely to break into open revolt; unpredictable. **4** transient; short-lived. **5** *Computer technology.* of memory, not retaining data when the power is cut off.
—*n.* a volatile substance. ⟨< L *volatilis* flying < *volare* fly⟩ **—'vol•a,tile•ness,** *n.*

volatile oil ESSENTIAL OIL.

vol•a•til•i•ty [,vɒlə'tɪləti] *n.* the quality or state of being volatile.

vol•a•til•ize ['vɒlətə,laɪz] *v.* **-ized, -iz•ing.** change or be changed into vapour; evaporate or cause to evaporate. **—,vol•a•til•i'za•tion,** *n.*

vol–au–vent [vɔlo'vɑ̃] *n.* a shell of puff pastry, to be filled with a meat, vegetable, or fish mixture, with a sauce: *Chicken vol-au-vent is a favourite entrée at formal luncheons.* ⟨< F, literally, flight on the wind⟩

vol•can•ic [vɒl'kænɪk] *adj.* **1** of, having to do with, or caused by a volcano: *a volcanic eruption.* **2** characterized by the presence of volcanoes. **3** made of materials from volcanoes: *volcanic rock.* **4** like a volcano in breaking forth violently: *a volcanic temper.* **—vol'can•i•cal•ly,** *adv.* **—,vol•ca'nic•i•ty** [,vɒlkə'nɪsəti], *n.*

volcanic glass a natural glass formed by the quick cooling of lava; obsidian.

vol•can•ism ['vɒlkə,nɪzəm] *n.* phenomena connected with volcanoes and volcanic activity.

vol•can•ize ['vɒlkə,naɪz] *v.* **-ized, -iz•ing.** subject to volcanic heat.

vol•ca•no [vɒl'keinou] *n., pl.* **-noes** or **-nos. 1** an opening in the earth's crust through which steam, ashes, and lava are expelled. **2** a hill or mountain around this opening, built up of the material that has been forced out. ⟨< Ital. < L *Vulcanus* Vulcan⟩

vol•ca•nol•o•gy [,vɒlkə'nɒlədʒi] *n.* the scientific study of volcanoes and volcanic phenomena. **—,vol•ca'nol•o•gist** or **'vol•can•ist,** *n.* **—,vol•ca•no'log•i•cal,** *adj.*

vole [voul] *n.* any of numerous rodents (family Cricetidae, especially in genus *Microtus*) resembling mice, but having a plumper body, a blunt nose, very short ears, and a short tail. The common field mouse is a vole. ⟨< *volemouse* < *voll* field (< Scand.; cf. ON *völlr*) + *mouse*⟩

vo•li•tion [və'lɪʃən] *n.* **1** the act or an instance of using one's will to make a choice or decision: *He gave himself up to the police of his own volition.* **2** the power of making a choice or decision; will: *By a tremendous exercise of volition, she made one last effort.* ⟨< Med.L *volitio, -onis* < L *volo* I wish⟩ **—vo'li•tion•al,** *adj.* **—vo'li•tion•al•ly,** *adv.*

vol•i•tive ['vɒlətɪv] *adj.* **1** of or having to do with the will. **2** *Grammar.* desiderative.

Volks•lied ['fɔlks,lit] *n., pl.* **-lied•er** [-,lidəʀ]. folk song. ⟨< G⟩

vol•ley ['vɒli] *n., pl.* **-leys;** *v.* **-leyed, -ley•ing.** —*n.* **1** the discharge of a number of guns or other weapons at once. **2** a shower of stones, bullets, arrows, etc. **3** a burst or outpouring of words, oaths, shouts, cheers, etc.: *A volley of questions met the prime minister as he stepped from the car.* **4** *Tennis, volleyball, etc.* **a** the hitting or return of the ball before it touches the ground. **b** an uninterrupted series of such returns, in a game or as a warmup exercise.
—*v.* **1** discharge or be discharged in a volley: *Cannon volleyed on all sides.* **2** *Tennis, volleyball, etc.* **a** hit or return (the ball) before it touches the ground. **b** engage in an uninterrupted series of such returns, in a game or as a warmup exercise. ⟨< F *volée* flight < *voler* fly < L *volare*⟩

vol•ley•ball ['vɒli,bɒl] *n.* **1** a game played with a large ball and a high net. Two teams of players hit the ball with their hands back and forth across the net without letting it touch the ground. **2** the ball used in this game.

vol•plane ['vɒl,plein] *v.* **-planed, -plan•ing;** *n.* —*v.* glide toward the earth in an airplane without using motor power.
—*n.* the act of gliding in this way. ⟨< F *vol plané* gliding flight⟩

Vol•sun•ga Saga ['vɒlsʊŋgə] an Icelandic version of the NIBELUNGENLIED, dating from about the 13th century.

volt [voult] *n.* an SI unit for measuring the pressure, or push, of an electric current. One volt of pressure is needed to drive a current of one ampere through a conductor with a resistance of one ohm. *Symbol:* V ⟨after Count Alessandro *Volta* (1745-1827), an Italian physicist⟩

volt•age ['voultɪdʒ] *n.* the strength of electric pressure measured in volts. A current of high voltage is used in transmitting electric power over long distances.

vol•ta•ic [vɒl'teiɪk] *adj.* of, having to do with, or producing direct electric current by chemical action; galvanic: *a voltaic cell.*

voltaic battery *Electricity.* **1** a battery composed of VOLTAIC CELLS. **2** VOLTAIC CELL.

voltaic cell *Electricity.* ELECTROCHEMICAL CELL.

voltaic pile *Electricity.* a device that produces an electric current from an electrolyte in which are placed two plates of different metals.

vol•tam•e•ter [vɒl'tæmətər] *n.* a device for measuring the quantity of electricity passing through a conductor by indicating the amount of gas produced or of metal deposited on an electrode. ⟨< *volta(ic)* + *meter*[2]⟩ **—,vol•ta'met•ric,** *adj.*

volt•am•me•ter ['voult,æm,mitər] *n.* a device for measuring voltage or amperage.

volt–am•pere ['voult 'æmpɛr] *n.* the product of one volt and one ampere, i.e., one watt.

volte face [,vɒlt 'fɑs]; *French,* [vɔlt 'fas] *n.* an about-face; reversal in attitude. ⟨< F < Ital. *voltafaccia* < *volta* a turning + *faccia* face < L *facies*⟩

volt•me•ter ['voult,mitər] *n.* an instrument for measuring electromotive force.

vol•u•ble ['vɒljəbəl] *adj.* **1** ready to talk much; talkative. **2** characterized by a rapid or ready flow of words: *a voluble protest. She was voluble in her account of the accident.* **3** *Botany.* of vines, twining around a support. ⟨< L *volubilis,* originally, rolling < *volvere* roll⟩ **—'vol•u•bly,** *adv.* **—,vol•u'bil•i•ty** or **'vol•u•ble•ness,** *n.*
☛ *Syn.* **1, 2.** See note at FLUENT.

vol•ume ['vɒljəm] *or* ['vɒljum] *n.* **1** a collection of printed or written sheets bound together to form a book; book: *We own a library of five hundred volumes.* **2** a book forming part of a set or series: *His memoirs were published in three volumes.* **3** a series of a periodical, usually all the issues published in one year. **4** space occupied or contained, measured in cubic units: *The storeroom has a volume of 20 m³.* **5** an amount or quantity, especially a large quantity: *Volumes of smoke poured from the chimneys of the factory.* **6** degree of loudness or fullness of tone: *A pipe organ gives much more volume than a violin or flute.* **7** a roll of parchment, papyrus, etc. containing written matter (the ancient form of a book); scroll.
speak volumes, express much; be full of meaning: *His loving glance spoke volumes.* ⟨ME < OF < L *volumen* book roll, scroll < *volvere* roll⟩
☛ *Syn.* **4.** See note at SIZE[1].

vo•lu•me•ter [və'lumətər] *n.* an instrument for measuring the volume of a liquid, solid, or gas. ⟨< *volu(me)* + *meter*⟩

vol•u•met•ric [,vɒljə'mɛtrɪk] *adj.* of or having to do with measurement by volume. **—,vol•u'met•ri•cal•ly,** *adv.*

volumetric analysis *Chemistry.* quantitative analysis of a solution by finding what volumes of it react with known volumes of known reagents.

vo•lu•mi•nous [və'lumənəs] *adj.* **1** of great size or volume; very bulky or full: *A voluminous cloak covered her from head to foot.* **2** forming or filling a large book or several books: *a voluminous report.* **3** writing or speaking much: *a voluminous author.* ⟨< LL *voluminosus* with many coils < L *volumen, -minis.*

See VOLUME.⟩ **—vo'lu•mi•nous•ly,** *adv.* **—vo,lu•mi'nos•i•ty** [-'nɒsəti] or **vo'lu•mi•nous•ness,** *n.*

vol•un•tar•ism ['vɒləntə,rɪzəm] *n.* **1** *Philosophy.* any theory stating that will is the fundamental or dominant principle or factor in history or in the individual's experience. **2** the principle of relying on voluntary contributions rather than on government support, as in churches, schools, hospitals, etc. **3** voluntary participation in organizations, causes, etc.: *The current rise in voluntarism has benefited many social agencies.*

vol•un•tar•y ['vɒlən,tɛri] *adj., n., pl.* **-tar•ies.** *—adj.* **1** done, made, given, etc. of one's own free will; not forced or compelled: *Churches are supported by voluntary contributions.* **2** supported entirely by voluntary gifts: *She works for several voluntary organizations.* **3** acting of one's own free will or choice: *Voluntary workers built a road to the boys' camp.* **4** able to act of one's own free will: *a voluntary agent.* **5** *Physiology.* controlled by the will: *Talking is voluntary; breathing is only partly so.* **6** VOLUNTEER (def. 4). **7** *Law.* **a** done, given, or proceeding from the free or unconstrained will of a person: *a voluntary affidavit.* **b** acting or done without obligation or without receiving a valuable consideration: *a voluntary partition of land.* **c** deliberately intended; done on purpose: *voluntary manslaughter.*
—n. **1** anything done, made, given, etc. of one's own free will. **2** *Music.* **a** a composition, often extemporized, that is used as a prelude. **b** an organ solo played before, during, or after a church service. **3** volunteer. ⟨ME < L *voluntarius* < *voluntas* will < *volo* I wish⟩ **—,vol•un'tar•i•ly,** *adv.*

☛ *Syn. adj.* **1. Voluntary,** SPONTANEOUS = done, made, given, etc. without being forced or compelled. **Voluntary** emphasizes the idea of something done of one's own free will or choice, not in obedience to the will of another: *The state is supported by taxes, the church by voluntary contributions.* **Spontaneous** emphasizes the idea of something neither compelled by another nor directed by one's own will, but done from natural impulse, without thought or intention: *The laughter at her jokes is never forced, but always spontaneous.*

vol•un•teer [,vɒlən'tir] *n., v.* *—n.* **1** a person who offers or performs a voluntary service, especially a public service. **2** a person who enters military service of his or her own free will. **3** a person who serves without pay: *In some towns, the firefighters are volunteers.* **4** (*adjl.*) being, made up of, or done by a volunteer or volunteers: *a volunteer firefighter, a volunteer organization.* **5** a plant that grows from seed dropped by a previous crop or generation of plants, rather than from seed deliberately sown. **6** (*adjl.*) designating such a plant or crop.
—v. **1** offer one's services as a volunteer: *As soon as war was declared, many citizens volunteered.* **2** offer of one's own free will: *He volunteered to do the job.* **3** tell or say voluntarily: *She volunteered the information.* ⟨< F *volontaire*, originally adj. < L *voluntarius.* See VOLUNTARY.⟩

vol•un•teer•ism [,vɒlən'tirɪzəm] *n.* VOLUNTARISM (defs. 2, 3).

vo•lup•tu•ar•y [və'lʌptʃu,ɛri] *n., pl.* **-ar•ies;** *adj.* *—n.* a person who cares much for luxury and sensual pleasures.
—adj. of, concerned with, or promoting luxury and sensual pleasures. ⟨< L *voluptuarius* < *voluptas* pleasure. See VOLUPTUOUS.⟩

vo•lup•tu•ous [və'lʌptʃuəs] *adj.* **1** full of or giving pleasure to the senses: *voluptuous music, a voluptuous dance.* **2** occupied with, directed toward, or derived from luxury and the pleasures of the senses. **3** of a woman, shapely; having a sexually attractive figure. ⟨ME < L *voluptuosus* < *voluptas* pleasure < *volup(e)*, neut., agreeable⟩ **—vo'lup•tu•ous•ly,** *adv.* **—vo'lup•tu•ous•ness,** *n.*

vo•lute [və'lut] *n., adj.* *—n.* **1** a spiral or scroll-shaped thing or form. **2** *Architecture.* a spiral or scroll-like ornament, especially as an Ionic capital. See ORDER for picture. **3** *Zoology.* **a** any of a family (Volutidae) of tropical marine gastropod molluscs typically having a short spiral shell. **b** the shell or one of the whorls of the shell of such a gastropod.
—adj. **1** rolled up or spiral: *a volute spring.* **2** *Zoology.* of or being a volute. ⟨< F *volute* < Ital. < L *voluta*, fem. pp. of *volvere* roll⟩ **—vo'lu•tion,** *n.*

vol•va ['vɒlvə] *n. Botany.* the small cuplike structure around the base of the stalk in certain mushrooms. In the early stages of growth it encloses the whole mushroom. ⟨< NL < L *vulva* womb, wrapper⟩ **—'vol•vate,** *adj.*

vol•vox ['vɒlvɒks] *n.* any of genus *Volvox* of flagellate freshwater algae, living as a colony in the form of a green multicellular globe that rolls around in the water. ⟨< NL < L *volvere* roll⟩

vo•mer ['voumər] *n. Anatomy.* the thin, flat bone in the septum separating the nasal passages. ⟨< NL < L *vomer* plowshare⟩

vom•it ['vɒmɪt] *v., n.* *—v.* **1** expel the contents of the stomach through the mouth; throw up (something eaten). **2** throw up or out with force: *The chimneys vomited forth smoke.* **3** come out with force or violence: *smoke vomiting from the chimneys.*
—n. **1** the substance thrown up from the stomach in vomiting. **2** the act or an instance of vomiting. **3** *Archaic.* emetic. ⟨ME < L *vomitus*, pp. of *vomere* spew forth⟩ **—'vom•i•tive,** *adj.* **—'vom•i•tous,** *adj.*

vom•i•to•ry ['vɒmə,tɔri] *n.* any of a series of large openings, as in a stadium or theatre, through which large numbers of people are able to enter or leave. Also, **vomitorium.** ⟨< L *vomere* vomit + *-torius*; in a Roman amphitheatre the spectators were discharged through these areas⟩

vom•i•tu•ri•tion [,vɒmɪtʃə'rɪʃən] *n.* repeated but ineffectual or unproductive vomiting; retching.

vom•i•tus ['vɒmɪtəs] *n.* **1** vomited matter. **2** the act of vomiting.

voo•doo ['vudu] *n., pl.* **-doos;** *adj., v.* **-doo•ed, -doo•ing.**
—n. **1** a polytheistic religion that originated in Africa and is still practised among some peoples. Voodoo involves belief in the existence of spirits which act as guides or protectors of individuals or families, and belief in the magical power of charms and spells. **2** a person who practises this religion. **3** a charm, curse, or fetish of voodoo origin.
—adj. of or having to do with voodoo.
—v. affect by voodoo sorcery, magic, or conjuration. ⟨of African origin⟩

voo•doo•ism ['vudu,ɪzəm] *n.* **1** the belief in or practice of voodoo. **2** voodoo rites or practices.

voo•doo•ist ['vuduɪst] *n.* a person who believes in or practises voodoo.

voo•doo•is•tic [,vudu'ɪstɪk] *adj.* of or having to do with voodooism.

vo•ra•cious [vɔ'reiʃəs] *or* [və'reiʃəs] *adj.* **1** eating much; having an enormous appetite; ravenous: *voracious sharks.* **2** very eager; unable to be satisfied: *She is a voracious reader.* ⟨< L *vorax, -acis* greedy⟩ **—vo'ra•cious•ly,** *adv.* **—vo'ra•cious•ness,** *n.*

☛ *Hom.* VERACIOUS [və'reiʃəs].

vo•rac•i•ty [vɔ'ræsəti] *or* [və'ræsəti] *n.* the quality or state of being voracious.

☛ *Hom.* VERACITY [və'ræsəti].

-vorous *suffix.* eating; feeding on: *carnivorous, omnivorous.* ⟨< L *-vorus* < *vorare* devour⟩

vor•tex ['vɔrtɛks] *n., pl.* **-tex•es** or **-ti•ces. 1** a whirling mass of water, air, etc. that sucks everything near it into its centre. A whirlpool is a kind of vortex. **2** a whirl of activity or other situation of rapidly increasing involvement, from which it is hard to escape: *The two nations were unwillingly drawn into the vortex of war.* ⟨< L var. of *vertex.* See VERTEX.⟩

vor•ti•cal ['vɔrtəkəl] *adj., n.* *—adj.* of or causing motion like that of a vortex; spinning; eddying.
—n. a vortical motion. **—'vor•ti•cal•ly,** *adv.*

vor•ti•cel•la [,vɔrtə'sɛlə] *n., pl.* **-cel•lae** [-'sɛli] *or* [-'sɛlaɪ]. any of a genus (*Vorticella*) of protozoans having a bell-shaped body with cilia at the oral end and a slender, contractile stalk at the other end, often found attached to a plant or other object under water. ⟨< NL *vorticella*, dim. of L *vortex.* See VORTEX.⟩

vor•ti•ces ['vɔrtə,siz] *n.* a pl. of VORTEX.

vor•ti•cose ['vɔrtə,kous] *adj.* vortical; vortiginous.

vor•tig•i•nous [vɔr'tɪdʒənəs] *adj.* moving in a vortex; vortical. ⟨< L *vortigo, -inis*, var. of *vertigo* a whirling⟩

vot•a•ble ['voutəbəl] *adj.* capable of being submitted to a vote; that can be voted on. Also, **voteable.**

vo•ta•ress ['voutərɪs] *n.* a female votary.

vo•ta•rist ['voutərɪst] *n.* votary.

vo•ta•ry ['voutəri] *n., pl.* **-ries;** *adj.* *—n.* **1** an adherent or ardent devotee of a particular religion, cause, ideal, etc. **2** a person, such as a monk or nun, bound by vows to a religious life. **3** a person very interested in or attracted to something; fan: *He was a votary of oriental music.*
—adj. of, like, or consecrated by a vow. ⟨< L *votum* vow⟩

vote [vout] *n., v.* **vot•ed, vot•ing.** *—n.* **1** a formal expression of a person's opinion or decision in response to a specific question, a choice between candidates, etc.: *She won the election by twenty votes.* **2** the formal decision or expression of opinion by a group resulting from the majority of the individual choices of its members: *The vote may go against the government.* **3** the right to

contribute to such a formal decision: *In our club, only those who have paid their fees have a vote.* **4** the written or printed slip, token, etc. used to indicate one's decision; ballot: *The votes were placed in a sealed box.* **5** what is expressed or decided by a majority of voters: *a vote of confidence, a vote of $200 000 for a new gymnasium.* **6** the total number of votes cast; votes collectively: *The vote was higher than in the last election.* **7** a particular group of voters or their votes: *the labour vote, the under-25 vote.* **8** the act or process of voting: *The matter was decided by vote.* **9** a choice or preference of an individual or group, not necessarily formally expressed: *My vote is for peace.*
put to a vote, decide (a matter) by voting.
take a vote, vote.
—v. **1** give or cast a vote: *He voted for the Liberals. She has gone to vote.* **2** support by one's vote: *Vote Lynn McGregor for president.* **3** declare oneself to be by casting a vote: *to vote Conservative.* **4** pass, determine, put, or grant by a vote: *The committee voted $30 000 for renovating the building. He was voted into the presidency.* **5** declare by general consent: *The trip was voted a success.* **6** *Informal.* suggest: *I vote that we go.* **7** make a choice or preference known: *Consumers vote with their dollars.*
vote down, defeat (especially a motion or proposal) by voting against.
vote in, elect.
vote out, defeat (an incumbent) by voting against. ⟨ME < L *votum* vow. Doublet of VOW.⟩ **—'vote•less,** *adj.*

vote of confidence **1** in parliament, a majority vote of support for the government, especially in a crisis and when defeat of the government would have forced it to resign. **2** any show of support or approval.

vot•er ['voutər] *n.* **1** a person who votes. **2** a person who has the right to vote.

voters' list at an election, a list giving the names, addresses, and occupations of all those entitled to vote in a given riding, ward, etc.

voting machine a mechanical device for registering and counting votes.

vo•tive ['voutɪv] *adj.* **1** done, given, etc. to express or fulfill a vow or promise. **2** *Roman Catholic Church.* voluntarily done or given, especially for a special intention or occasion: *a votive mass, a votive offering, a votive candle.* ⟨< L *votivus* < *votum* vow⟩

vouch [vʌutʃ] *v.* **1** be responsible; give a guarantee; answer *(for): I can vouch for the truth of the story. The principal vouched for Sarah's honesty.* **2** confirm; guarantee: *The union rep vouched that all workers would return to their jobs.* **3** give evidence or assurance *(for): The success of the attack vouches for the general's ability.* **4** *Law.* call into court to give warranty of title. **5** sponsor or recommend (a person or thing); support; back (*used with* **for**). ⟨ME < AF *voucher* < L *vocare* call⟩

vouch•er ['vʌutʃər] *n.* **1** a person or thing that vouches for something. **2** a written evidence of payment in advance, as a bonus coupon, gift certificate, meal chit, etc., entitling the holder to get something. **3** receipt. Cancelled cheques returned from one's bank are a type of voucher.

vouch•safe [,vʌutʃ'seif] *v.* **-safed, -saf•ing.** be willing to grant or give; condescend to do or give: *The proud man vouchsafed no reply when we spoke to him.* ⟨original meaning 'guarantee', to *vouch* for as *safe*⟩

vous•soir [vu'swɑr] *n. Architecture.* any of the wedge-shaped pieces forming an arch or vault. See ARCH for picture. ⟨< F < VL *volsorium* < *volvere* roll⟩

vow [vaʊ] *n., v.* *—n.* **1** a solemn promise: *a vow of secrecy.* **2** a promise made to God: *a nun's vows, marriage vows.* **3** any solemn declaration, personal pledge, etc.: *a vow of revenge, a vow of eternal friendship.*
take vows, become a member of a religious order.
—v. **1** make a vow. **2** make a vow to do, give, get, etc.: *to vow revenge.* **3** declare earnestly or emphatically: *She vowed she would never shop there again.* ⟨ME < OF *vou* < L *votum* < *vovere* vow. Doublet of VOTE.⟩

vow•el ['vaʊəl] *n.* **1** a speech sound in which the vocal cords are vibrating and the breath is not blocked at any point in the mouth by the tongue, teeth, or lips. When you say *awe*, you are uttering a vowel. The vowel is the most prominent sound in a syllable. **2** a letter or symbol representing such a sound. The vowels used in writing English are *a, e, i, o, u,* and sometimes *y.* **3** (*adjl.*) of or having to do with a vowel: Voluntary *has four vowel sounds*; strength *has only one.* ⟨ME < OF < L *(littera) vocalis* sounding (letter) < *vox* voice. Doublet of VOCAL.⟩

vow•el•ize ['vaʊə,laɪz] *v.* **-ized, -iz•ing.** VOCALIZE (def. 4).

vowel point any one of a set of dots or other symbols used to indicate vowels in a consonant-root based writing system such as Hebrew.

vox [vɒks] *n., pl.* **vo•ces** ['vousiz]. *Latin.* voice; sound; word; expression.

vox hu•ma•na [hju'mɑnə] *or* [hju'mænə] *n.* an organ reed stop, intended to be an imitation of the human voice. ⟨< L *vox humana* the human voice⟩

vox po•pu•li ['pɒpjə,laɪ] *or* ['pɒpjə,li] *Latin.* the voice or opinion of the people.

voy•age ['vɔɪɪdʒ] *n., v.* **-aged, -ag•ing.** *—n.* **1** a journey by water, especially a long journey: *a voyage to Japan.* **2** a journey through the air or through space: *an airplane voyage, the earth's voyage around the sun.* **3** a written account of a voyage, especially by sea.
—v. **1** make or take a voyage; travel by water or air: *Columbus voyaged on unknown seas.* **2** traverse; travel over or through. ⟨< F *voyage* < L *viaticum.* Doublet of VIATICUM.⟩
☛ *Syn. n.* **1.** See note at TRIP.

voy•ag•er ['vɔɪɪdʒər] *n.* **1** a person who makes a voyage; traveller. **2** *Cdn.* voyageur.

vo•ya•geur [,vɔɪə'ʒɜr]; *French,* [vwaja'ʒœʀ] *n., pl.* **-geurs** [-'ʒɜrz]; *French,* [-'ʒœʀ] *Cdn.* **1** formerly, a canoeman or boatman, especially a French Canadian, in the service of the early fur-trading companies. **2** a person who travels the northern wilderness, especially by canoe. ⟨< F *voyageur,* ult. < *voyage* voyage⟩

voy•eur [vwɑ'jɜr] *or* [vɔɪ'jɜr] *n.* a person who finds sexual gratification in observing the nude bodies or sexual acts of others. ⟨< F *voyeur* < *voir* to see < L *videre*⟩

voy•eur•ism [vwɑ'jɜrɪzəm] *or* [vɔɪ'jɜrɪzəm] *n.* the habits and practices of a voyeur. **—,voy•eur'ist•ic,** *adj.*

VP, V.P., or **V.Pres.** vice-president.

V.R. Queen Victoria (for L *Victoria Regina*).

V.Rev. Very Reverend.

vroom [vrum] *interj.* an exclamation imitating the sound of a motor vehicle revving or accelerating. ⟨imitative⟩

vs. **1** versus. **2** verse.

v.s. vide supra (see above).

V–shaped ['vi ,ʃeipt] *adj.* shaped like the letter V.

V sign **1** a victory sign made by raising the index and middle fingers, first used during World War II. **2** a sign of approval.

V–6 ['vee 'sɪks] *n., adj.* *–n.* **1** a six-cylinder automobile engine laid out in a V. **2** a car with such an engine.
—adj. of or having to do with such an engine.

V/STOL vertical or short take-off and landing (aircraft).

v.t. transitive verb (for L *verbum transitivum*). Also, **vt.**

VTOL ['vi,tɒl] vertical takeoff and landing.

VTR videotape recorder.

vug or **vugg** [vʌg] *n. Mining.* a cavity in a rock or vein, especially one lined with crystals. ⟨< Cornish *vooga* cave⟩

Vul•can ['vʌlkən] *n. Roman mythology.* the god of fire and metalworking, corresponding to the Greek god Hephaestus.

vul•ca•ni•an [vʌl'keiniən] *adj.* **1 Vulcanian,** *Roman mythology.* of or relating to the god Vulcan. **2** *Geology.* **a** volcanic. **b** of or relating to a volcanic eruption in which large quantities of gas and fine ash are ejected along with viscous lava that hardens in the air while still in the crater.

vul•can•ite ['vʌlkə,nəit] *n.* a hard black rubber made by treating crude rubber with sulphur and heating it to high temperatures; ebonite.

vul•can•ize ['vʌlkə,naɪz] *v.* **-ized, -iz•ing.** treat (crude rubber or a similar synthetic material) chemically, especially with sulphur and intense heat, to make it stronger and more elastic. ⟨< *Vulcan*⟩ **—,vul•can•i'za•tion,** *n.* **—'vul•can,iz•er,** *n.*

vul•gar ['vʌlgər] *adj.* **1** utterly lacking in good manners, taste, sensitivity, etc.; coarse; boorish: *vulgar ambition, such a vulgar show of wealth.* **2** indecent; lewd; obscene: *vulgar language.* **3** in common use; ordinary. **4** of the common people: *Modern French, Italian, Portuguese, and Spanish developed from vulgar varieties of Latin.* **5** (*noml.*) **the vulgar,** *Archaic.* the common people. ⟨ME < L *vulgaris* < *vulgus* common people⟩ **—'vul•gar•ly,** *adv.* **—'vul•gar•ness,** *n.*
☛ *Syn. adj.* **1.** See note at COARSE.

vulgar fraction COMMON FRACTION.

vul•gar•i•an [vʌl'gɛriən] *n.* a vulgar person, especially a rich person who lacks good manners, taste, etc.

vul•gar•ism ['vʌlgə,rɪzəm] *n.* **1** a word, phrase, or expression that is regarded as substandard, coarse, or obscene. **2** vulgarity.

vul•gar•i•ty [vʌl'gɛrəti] *n., pl.* **-ties. 1** the quality or state of being vulgar. **2** an action, habit, remark, etc. that is vulgar.

vul•gar•ize ['vʌlgə,raɪz] *n.* **-ized, -iz•ing. 1** make vulgar; make cheap, coarse, or indecent. **2** make widely known; popularize. **—'vul•gar,iz•er,** *n.* **—,vul•gar•i'za•tion,** *n.*

Vulgar Latin the nonclassical, spoken form of ancient Latin, established as the main source of the modern Romance languages.

Vul•gate ['vʌlgeit] *n., adj. —n.* **1** the Latin translation of the Bible made by Saint Jerome in the 4th century A.D., used in subsequently revised form by the Roman Catholic Church as the authoritative text. **2 vulgate,** *Rare.* **a** the traditionally accepted text or reading of any author. **b** common speech; vernacular.
—adj. **1** of, in, or having to do with the Vulgate. **2 vulgate,** commonly accepted or used; popular. ⟨< L *vulgata (editio)* popular (edition)⟩

vul•ner•a•bil•i•ty [,vʌlnərə'bɪləti] *n., pl.* **-ties. 1** the quality or state of the fact of being vulnerable; the fact of being open to attack or injury. **2** a specific respect in which one is vulnerable; weak point.

vul•ner•a•ble ['vʌlnərəbəl] *adj.* **1** capable of being wounded or injured; open to attack: *The head is a vulnerable part of the body. The fort was vulnerable while the walls were being repaired.* **2** open to criticism, moral attack, or temptation. **3** sensitive to or affected by certain influences (*used with* **to**): *Most people are vulnerable to ridicule.* **4** *Contract bridge.* in the position where penalties and premiums are increased. ⟨< LL *vulnerabilis* wounding, ult. < *vulnus, -neris* wound⟩ **—'vul•ner•a•bly,** *adv.* **—'vul•ner•a•ble•ness,** *n.*

vul•ner•a•ry ['vʌlnə,rɛri] *adj., n. —adj.* that can be or is used to heal wounds.
—n. a drug, herb, etc. that can be so used. ⟨< L *vulnerarius* < *vulnus* wound⟩

vul•pine ['vʌlpaɪn] *or* ['vʌlpɪn] *adj.* **1** of, having to do with, or like a fox. **2** clever; crafty; cunning. ⟨< L *vulpinus* < *vulpes* fox⟩

vul•ture ['vʌltʃər] *n.* **1** any of a family (Cathartidae) of large, carrion-eating, New World birds having a naked head and neck and relatively weak feet and claws, including the condors and the turkey vulture. **2** any of a subfamily (Aegypiinae) of similar carrion-eating, Old World birds of the same family as hawks and eagles, also typically having a bare head. **3** a greedy, ruthless person who preys on others. ⟨< L < *vultur*⟩

vul•tur•ine ['vʌltʃə,raɪn] *or* ['vʌltʃərɪn] *adj.* **1** of, having to do with, or characteristic of a vulture. **2** resembling a vulture in voracious or predatory qualities. Also, **vulturous.**

vul•va ['vʌlvə] *n., pl.* **-vae** [-vi] *or* [-vaɪ] or **-vas.** the external parts of the genital organs of female mammals. ⟨< L *vulva* womb⟩ **—'vul•vi,form,** *adj.* **—'vul•var,** *adj.* **—'vul•vate,** *adj.*

vul•vi•tis [vʌl'vəitɪs] *n.* inflammation of the vulva.

vv 1 verses. **2** violins. **3** volumes.

v.v. VICE VERSA.

vy•ing ['vaɪɪŋ] *adj., v. —adj.* competing.
—v. ppr. of VIE.

W w *W w*

w or **W** ['dʌbəl,ju] *n., pl.* **w's** or **W's. 1** the twenty-third letter of the English alphabet. **2** any speech sound represented by this letter. **3** a person or thing identified as *w*, especially the twenty-third in a series. **4** something shaped like the letter W. **5** (*adj.*) of or being a W or w. **6** something, such as a printer's type, a lever, or a key on a keyboard, that produces a w or W.

w. 1 week(s). **2** wide; width. **3** weight. **4** wife. **5** with. **6** west; western. **7** wins; won.

W 1 watt. **2** west; western. **3** *Chemistry.* tungsten (for *wolfram*). **4** *Physics.* work; energy or force.

W. 1 Wednesday. **2** west; western. **3** Wales; Welsh.

W.A. Women's Auxiliary.

wab•ble ['wɒbəl] *n.* WARBLE[2].

wack•y ['wæki] *adj.* **-i•er, -i•est.** *Slang.* unconventional in behaviour; eccentric; crazy. Also, **whacky.**

wad [wɒd] *n., v.* **wad•ded, wad•ding.** *—n.* **1** a small, soft, or loose mass of material, such as cotton batting or crumpled paper: *He plugged his ears with wads of cotton to keep out the noise. She threw a wad of paper into the wastebasket.* **2** a small compact lump of something: *a wad of chewing gum.* **3** *Informal.* a roll of paper money: *He took a wad out of his pocket and counted off five tens.* **4** *Slang.* a large amount of money; wealth: *She made her wad in real estate.* **5** a round plug of felt, cardboard, etc. used in a gun or cartridge to hold powder and shot in place.
—v. **1** crush, press, or roll into a wad: *He wadded up the paper and threw it into the wastebasket.* **2** stuff with a wad: *to wad a gun.* **3** hold in place by a wad: *to wad a charge in a gun.* **4** pad or line with wadding. ⟨origin uncertain⟩

wad•ding ['wɒdɪŋ] *n., v.* *—n.* **1** a soft material for padding, stuffing, packing, etc.; especially, carded cotton in sheets. **2** material for making wads for guns or cartridges. **3** a wad or wads.
—v. ppr. of WAD.

wad•dle ['wɒdəl] *v.* **-dled, -dling;** *n.* *—v.* walk with short steps and an awkward, swaying motion, like a duck.
—n. an awkward, swaying gait. ⟨< *wade*⟩ **—'wad•dler,** *n.*

wade [weid] *v.* **wad•ed, wad•ing;** *n.* *—v.* **1** walk through water, snow, sand, mud, or anything that hinders free motion. **2** walk about in shallow water for amusement: *We loved to go wading in the spring.* **3** cross or pass through by wading. **4** make one's way with difficulty (*used with* **through**): *to wade through an uninteresting book.* **5** *Informal.* attack or go to work vigorously (*used with* **in** *or* **into**): *He waded right in and got the job done in half an hour.*
—n. the act or an instance of wading. ⟨OE *wadan* proceed⟩

wad•er ['weidər] *n.* **1** Usually, **waders,** *pl.* high waterproof boots or pants with feet in them used for wading, especially by fishers, etc. **2** WADING BIRD. **3** any person who or thing that wades.

wa•di ['wɑdi] *n., pl.* **-dis. 1** in parts of the Arabian peninsula, N Africa, etc., a valley or ravine through which a stream flows during the rainy season. **2** a stream or torrent running through such a ravine. **3** an oasis. Also, **wady.** ⟨< Arabic⟩

wading bird any long-legged bird that wades in water to look for food, as herons, cranes, sandpipers, and flamingos.

wading pool 1 a shallow, round pool with a cement bottom, inclined from the edges to the centre, provided, as in a public park, for small children to play in. **2** a small, shallow, portable pool of plastic, fibreglass, etc. for small children to play in.

wa•dy ['wɑdi] *n., pl.* **-dies.** See WADI.

wa•fer ['weifər] *n., v.* *—n.* **1** a very thin, crisp biscuit or cookie. **2** a very thin piece of candy: *a chocolate wafer.* **3** in some Christian churches, a thin, round piece of unleavened bread used in the Eucharist. **4** *Electronics.* a thin piece of semiconductor used as a base material with integrated circuits or single transistors on it; part of a chip. **5** a small disk of paper or, formerly, dried paste, used as a seal on letters, documents, etc.
—v. fasten or seal with a wafer or wafers. ⟨ME < AF *wafre* < Gmc.⟩ **—'wa•fer,like,** *adj.*

wa•fer–thin ['weifər 'θɪn] *adj.* exceedingly thin: *wafer-thin cucumber slices.*

wa•fer•y ['weifəri] *adj.* like a wafer.

waf•fle[1] ['wɒfəl] *n.* a light, thin, crisp, moulded cake made from a batter and baked in a WAFFLE IRON. ⟨< Du. *wafel*⟩

waf•fle[2] ['wɒfəl] *v.* **-fled, -fling;** *n.* *—v.* **1** avoid making a decision or commitment by speaking ambiguously or evasively: *The ratepayers' association accused their MP of waffling on the airport issue.* **2** talk nonsense; prattle; talk on and on.
—n. **1** vague, evasive talk. **2** nonsense; foolish talk. ⟨< Brit. dial. *waff* to yelp + *-le*⟩

waffle iron a device for cooking waffles, consisting of two hinged metal plates with a gridlike pattern of surface projections; the two plates close together and cook the waffles between them.

waft [wɒft] *or* [wæft] *v., n.* *—v.* **1** carry over water or through air: *The waves wafted the boat to shore. The night wind wafted the sound of singing across the lake.* **2** transport or transfer very quickly or as if by magic: *to be wafted by plane from Toronto to London.* **3** float: *A single feather wafted down to the ground.* **4** of a breeze, blow gently; stir.
—n. **1** the act of wafting. **2** a breath or puff of air, wind, etc. **3** something, such as a scent, wafted through the air. **4** a waving movement. **5** *Nautical.* a distress signal made by flying a rolled or knotted flag or pennant, or a garment, sometimes in the rigging rather than on the mast. ⟨< earlier *wafter* convoy ship < Du. and LG *wachter* guard⟩

wag [wæg] *v.* **wagged, wag•ging;** *n.* *—v.* **1** move or cause to move from side to side or up and down, especially rapidly and repeatedly: *He wagged his finger at me in disapproval. The dog's tail started wagging even before the car turned into the driveway. She wagged her head in agreement.* **2** of a person's tongue, move in speaking, especially to chatter or gossip: *Tongues began to wag almost immediately after the police left.* **3** move (the tongue) in chatter or gossip: *They don't really know anything about it; they're just wagging their tongues.*
—n. **1** the act of wagging. **2** a person who is fond of making jokes. ⟨ME; cf. OE *wagian*⟩

wage [weidʒ] *n., v.* **waged, wag•ing.** *—n.* **1** Often, **wages,** *pl.* an amount paid for work, especially work on an hourly, daily, or piecework basis: *That company pays good wages. He is paid the minimum wage.* **2** Usually, **wages,** something given in return (*used with a singular or plural verb*): *Her illness taught her the wages of poor eating.* **3 wages,** *pl. Economics.* the part of the total monetary product of industry that goes to labour as opposed to that part going to capital.
—v. carry on: *to wage war, to wage a campaign.* ⟨ME < AF. Doublet of *wage*, GAGE[1].⟩ **—'wage•less,** *adj.*
☛ *Syn.* See note at SALARY.

wage earner a person who works for wages or a salary.

wa•ger ['weidʒər] *n., v.* *—n.* **1** an agreement between two persons that the one who is proved wrong about the outcome of an event will give a particular thing or sum of money to the person who is proved right; bet: *They made a wager on the result of the election.* **2** the thing or sum risked in a wager; stake: *What's your wager? He paid the wager promptly.*
—v. **1** make a wager; bet; gamble: *She wagered two dollars on the first race.* **2** be fairly certain; say with some certainty: *I wager he'll come if you stop coaxing him.* ⟨ME < AF *wageure* < OF *wage* pledge. See WAGE.⟩ **—'wa•ger•er,** *n.*

wage scale a schedule of wages paid to workers, taking into account the degree of skill and responsibility, seniority or experience, and other factors.

wage•work•er ['weidʒ,wɜrkər] *n.* WAGE EARNER.

wag•ger•y ['wægəri] *n., pl.* **-ger•ies. 1** joking or merriment. **2** a joke, especially a practical joke. ⟨*wag* + *-ery*⟩

wag•gish ['wægɪʃ] *adj.* **1** fond of making jokes. **2** done or made in fun; playful or funny; characteristic of a wag: *a waggish look.* ⟨*wag* + *-ish*⟩ **—'wag•gish•ly,** *adv.* **—'wag•gish•ness,** *n.*

wag•gle ['wægəl] *v.* **-gled, -gling;** *n.* *—v.* **1** move quickly and repeatedly from side to side; wag. **2** wobble or waver while moving along: *The ball waggled into the hole.*
—n. a waggling motion. ⟨frequentative of *wag*⟩ **—'wag•gly,** *adj.*

wag•on ['wægən] *n.* **1** a four-wheeled vehicle, usually drawn by a horse or tractor; especially, such a vehicle used for carrying loads: *a milk wagon, a hay wagon.* **2** a child's four-wheeled cart, usually low, shallow, and steered by a pole handle. **3** STATION WAGON. **4** PATROL WAGON.
fix (someone's) **wagon,** *Informal.* hurt someone to avenge real or imagined wrong.
hitch (one's) **wagon to a star,** have high hopes and ambitions; aim high.

off the wagon, *Slang.* drinking alcoholic liquors again after a period of abstaining from them.
on the wagon, *Slang.* no longer drinking alcoholic liquors. ⟨< Du. *wagen.* Akin to WAIN.⟩

wag•on•er ['wægənər] *n.* **1** a person who drives a wagon. **2 Wagoner,** *Astronomy.* the northern constellation Auriga, between Camelopardalis and Orion.

wag•on•ette [,wægə'nɛt] *n.* a four-wheeled, horse-drawn carriage with a seat in front running crosswise and two lengthwise seats facing each other in the back.

wa•gon–lit [vagɔ̃'li] *n., pl.* **wa•gons-lits** [vagɔ̃'li]. *French.* in Europe, a railway sleeping car. ⟨< F *wagon* railway coach + *lit* bed⟩

wag•on•load ['wægən,loud] *n.* the load carried by a wagon.

wagon train **1** a group of wagons moving along in a line one after another; especially, such a group carrying a company of settlers travelling together for protection. **2** *Esp. U.S.* a convoy of wagons carrying military supplies.

wag•tail ['wæg,teil] *n.* any of various small, chiefly Old World songbirds (family Motacillidae) having a very long tail that wags up and down as the bird walks or stands.

Wah•ha•bi or **Wa•ha•bi** [wɑ'hɑbi] *n.* a member of a very strict, conservative Muslim sect founded in the 18th century and existing mainly among Saudi Arabians. Also, **Wahhabite** or **Wahabite.** ⟨< Arabic⟩ **—Wah'ha•bism** or **Wa'ha•bism,** *n.*

wa•hi•ne [wɑ'hinei] *or* [wɑ'hini] *n.* **1** a Polynesian woman. **2** an attractive young woman, especially one who surfs or frequents beaches. ⟨< Hawaiian or Maori *wahine* woman⟩

wa•hoo[1] ['wɑhu] *or* [wɑ'hu] *n.* **1** an elm of the southeastern parts of North America (*Ulmus alata*) having corky ridges. **2** any of certain other North American trees, including the cascara. ⟨< Creek *uhawhu*⟩

wa•hoo[2] ['wɑhu] *or* [wɑ'hu] *n.* a large food and game fish (*Acanthocybium solanderi*) of the same family (Scombridae) as the mackerels, found in tropical seas. ⟨origin unknown⟩

wah–wah ['wɑ ,wɑ] *n. Music.* **1** a wailing effect, much used in jazz, created by muting and unmuting a brass instrument in quick succession, or by intermittently applying a foot pedal on an amplifier attached to any other instrument. **2** the device used to produce this effect. ⟨imitative⟩

waif [weif] *n.* **1** a person without home or friends, especially a homeless or neglected child. **2** anything without an owner; a stray thing, animal, etc. found and not claimed. ⟨ME < AF *waif,* probably < Scand.⟩

wail [weil] *v., n.* —*v.* **1** cry loud and long because of grief or pain; lament; mourn. **2** make a mournful sound: *The wind wailed around the old house.*
—*n.* **1** a long cry of grief or pain. **2** a sound like such a cry: *the wail of a hungry coyote.* ⟨ME; ? < ON *vǽla* < *vǽ, vei,* interj., woe⟩ **—'wail•er,** *n.*
☛ *Hom.* WALE, WHALE.

Wailing Wall a high wall in Jerusalem, Israel, at which Jews have traditionally gathered for prayer, believed to have been part of the western section of the wall protecting Herod's Temple. Also called **Western Wall.**

wain [wein] *n. Archaic or poetic.* wagon. ⟨OE *wægn*⟩
☛ *Hom.* WANE.

wain•scot ['wein,skɒt] *or* ['weinskət] *n., v.* **-scot•ted** or **-scot•ed, -scot•ting** or **-scot•ing.** —*n.* **1** a facing of wood, usually in panels, on the walls of a room. **2** such panelling, or other finish such as tile, applied only to the lower part of a wall. **3** the lower part of the wall of a room when it is decorated differently from the upper part.
—*v.* line with wainscotting: *a room wainscotted in oak.* ⟨ME < MLG *wagenschot* < *wagen* wagon + *schot* partition⟩

wain•scot•ting or **wain•scot•ing** ['wein,skɒtɪŋ] *n., v.* —*n.* **1** material used for wainscots. **2** wainscots collectively.
—*v.* ppr. of WAINSCOT.

wain•wright ['wein,rɔit] *n.* one who makes and repairs wagons.

waist [weist] *n.* **1** the part of the human body between the ribs and the hips. **2** waistline. **3** a garment or part of a garment covering the body from the neck or shoulders to the waistline. **4** a narrow middle part: *the waist of a violin, the waist of a wasp or ant.* **5** *Nautical.* the part of a ship amidships, as that between the forecastle and the quarterdeck of a sailing vessel, or between the forward and stern superstructure of an oil tanker. **6** the middle section of the fuselage of an aircraft, especially that of a bomber. ⟨ME *wast,* probably < OE *wæst, weahst.* Related to WAX[2].⟩
☛ *Hom.* WASTE.

waist•band ['weist,bænd] *n.* a band of cloth attached to the top of a skirt or pants to fit around the waist: *a wide waistband. The waistband on these shorts is too loose.*

waist•cloth ['weist,klɒθ] *n.* loincloth.

waist•coat ['weist,kout] *or* ['wɛskət] *n.* **1** *Brit.* a man's vest. **2** the garment from which this is derived, a hip-length, ornate sleeveless jacket worn under a doublet by British and European men in the 16th century.

waist•line ['weist,laɪn] *n.* **1** an imaginary line around the body at the smallest part of the waist. **2** the measurement around the body at this part: *Her waistline is 84 cm.* **3** the part of a garment that fits around the waist: *The dress has an elasticized waistline.* **4** the line where the bodice and skirt of a dress are joined together: *a loose-fitting dress without a waistline.*

wait [weit] *v., n.* —*v.* **1** stay or be inactive until someone comes or something happens: *Let's wait in the shade. We waited for him for two hours.* **2** *Informal.* put off serving (a meal): *Can you wait dinner for her?* **3** look forward expectantly: *They were waiting impatiently for the holidays.* **4** await; wait for: *to wait one's chance. Wait your turn.* **5** be ready and available: *The car was waiting for us when we got there.* **6** be left undone; be put off: *That matter can wait till tomorrow.* **7** be in store; be about to be encountered or experienced: *We do not know what waits for us around the next bend. A surprise is waiting for you at home.* **8** be a waiter or waitress (*usually used in the phrase* **wait (on** *or* **at) table**): *He waits tables in a hotel dining room.*
wait on, supply the wants of, as a clerk in a store, a waiter in a restaurant, etc.; serve: *A polite elderly man waited on us.*
wait on or **upon,** *Formal.* **a** be a servant to: *He waits on the prince.* **b** pay a respectful visit to (a superior): *Tomorrow the prime minister will wait on the Queen.*
wait out, a do nothing until (something) has passed or is finished: *There was nothing to do but wait out the storm.* **b** *Baseball.* refrain from swinging at the pitches of (a pitcher), in the hope of being walked.
wait up, a delay going to bed until someone comes or something happens: *I'll probably be late, so don't wait up for me.* **b** *Informal.* stop and wait for someone to catch up: *Wait up! He's fallen behind again.*
—*n.* **1** the act or an instance of waiting: *I had a long wait at the doctor's office.* **2** *Theatre.* the time of an audience's waiting between acts or of an actor's waiting between appearances on stage. **3 waits,** *pl.* formerly, in England: **a** a group of singers and musicians who went about the streets singing and playing at Christmastime. **b** any of the tunes sung or played by such a group, especially a Christmas carol.
lie in wait, stay hidden ready to surprise or attack: *Two assassins were lying in wait for the dictator.* ⟨ME < ONF *waitier,* originally, watch < Gmc.⟩
☛ *Hom.* WEIGHT.
☛ *Usage.* **Wait,** AWAIT. Wait chiefly means 'stay inactive or in a place until something expected happens or comes', and only in a few phrases is followed directly by a grammatical object: *We can wait here until he comes.* **Await** almost always is followed by the grammatical object, and means 'wait *for* someone or something', to look forward to or be ready for a coming or expected event or person: *We are eagerly awaiting your arrival.*

wait–a–bit ['weit ə ,bɪt] *n.* any of numerous plants having hooked thorns or other sharp or prickly appendages that easily catch in clothing, such as the greenbrier. ⟨< Afrikaans *wag-'n-bietjie* < Du. *wacht een beetje*⟩

wait•er ['weitər] *n.* **1** a person who waits on table in a hotel, restaurant, etc. **2** a person who waits. **3** a tray for carrying dishes.

wait•ing ['weitɪŋ] *n., adj., v.* —*n.* the act of a person who waits.
in waiting, in attendance on royalty: *in waiting to the queen.*
—*adj.* **1** that waits: *a waiting crowd.* **2** used to wait in: *a waiting room.* **3** that is employed to wait on or serve someone: *a waiting maid, a waiting man.*
—*v.* ppr. of WAIT.

waiting game a strategy whereby a person or group temporarily avoids action or a decision in the hope of gaining some advantage or of being able to act or decide more effectively at a later date.

waiting list a list of people who have applied for something that may become available in the future, and who will be accommodated in order of application when it becomes available: *There is already a long waiting list so you probably won't get on that flight.*

wait–list ['weit ˌlɪst] *v.* enter on a list of persons waiting, especially for a seat on an airliner: *She is booked to fly tomorrow morning, but she is wait-listed for tonight's flight.*

wait•ress ['weitrɪs] *n., v.* —*n.* a woman who waits on table in a hotel, restaurant, etc.
—*v.* work as a waitress.

waive [weiv] *v.* **waived, waiv•ing. 1** refrain from claiming, requiring, or insisting on; give up or forgo: *The defendant's lawyer waived her right to cross-examine the witness. The professor waived the prerequisite course in view of all the independent reading the student had done.* **2** put off; postpone; delay. ⟨ME < AF *weyver* abandon, probably < Scand. Related to WAIF.⟩
☛ *Hom.* WAVE.

waiv•er ['weivər] *n.* **1** *Law.* **a** a giving up of a right, claim, etc. **b** a written statement of this: *For $5000 the man signed a waiver of all claims against the railway.* **2** *Professional sports.* (*usually in the phrase* **on waivers**) provisions which a club must follow to dispose of the services of any player in which it has a proprietary interest. The player's contract is offered to other clubs in the league at a fixed price. If they decline, the contract may be taken up by a team from another league. ⟨< AF *weyver,* infin. used as n. See WAIVE.⟩
☛ *Hom.* WAVER.

Wa•kan•da [wɑ'kɑndɑ] *n. Cdn.* among certain Plains peoples of the First Nations, such as the Assiniboines, a supernatural power found in living things and inanimate objects; GREAT SPIRIT. ⟨< Siouan *wakanda* regard as sacred < *wakan* sacred spirit⟩

Wa•kash•an [wɑ'kæʃən] *or* ['wɒkəˌʃæn] *n., pl.* **-an** or **-ans.** a family of First Nations languages of British Columbia and Washington, including Nootka, Kwakwala, Bella Bella, and Makah.

wake[1] [weik] *v.* **woke** or **waked, wo•ken** or **waked, wak•ing** (defs. 1-5); **waked, wak•ing** (def. 6); *n.* —*v.* **1** stop sleeping (*often used with* **up**): *to wake up early in the morning.* **2** rouse from sleep; cause to stop sleeping (*often used with* **up**): *The noise will wake the baby. Wake me up early.* **3** be or stay awake: *Waking or sleeping, he could not seem to get the accusation out of his mind.* **4** become alive or active (*often used with* **up**): *Her conscience woke. The flowers wake in the spring.* **5** make alive or active; rouse to action, alertness, or liveliness (*often used with* **up**): *He needs some interest to wake him up.* **6** *Dialect.* **a** keep a watch or vigil, especially over a corpse. **b** keep watch over (a corpse) until burial.
wake (up) to, become conscious or aware of: *She finally woke up to the fact that her money was almost gone.*
—*n.* a watch held around the body of a dead person before burial, sometimes accompanied by festivities. ⟨OE *wacian*⟩

wake[2] [weik] *n.* **1** the track left behind a moving ship. **2** the track left by anything.
in the wake of, a close behind; very soon after: *Floods came in the wake of the hurricane.* **b** as a consequence or result of. ⟨< MDu.⟩

wake•ful ['weikfəl] *adj.* **1** not able to sleep: *She was still wakeful long after midnight.* **2** without sleep; sleepless: *They spent a wakeful night.* **3** watchful; alert. **—'wake•ful•ly,** *adv.* **—'wake•ful•ness,** *n.*

wak•en ['weikən] *v.* WAKE[1]. ⟨OE *wæcnan*⟩ **—'wak•en•er,** *n.*

wake–rob•in ['weik ˌrɒbən] *n.* **1** trillium. **2** *Brit.* any of various plants of the arum family.

waking ['weikɪŋ] *adj., v.* —*adj.* **1** that is awake or becoming awake. **2** spent awake: *60 percent of our waking hours.*
—*v.* ppr. of WAKE.

Wal•den•ses [wɒl'dɛnsiz] *n.pl.* a Christian sect formed by Pierre Waldo in Lyons, France about 1170 and initially condemned by the popes and subjected to much persecution. Their present headquarters is in Italy.

Wal•den•si•an [wɒl'dɛnsiən] *or* [wɒl'dɛnʃən] *adj., n.* —*adj.* of or having to do with the Waldenses.
—*n.* a member of the Waldenses.

wald•grave ['wɒld,greiv] *n.* in medieval Germany, an officer having jurisdiction over a royal forest. ⟨< G *Waldgraf* < *Wald* woods < *Graf* count⟩

Wal•dorf salad ['wɒl,dɔrf] a salad of diced apples, celery, and walnuts, with a mayonnaise dressing. ⟨< *Waldorf*-Astoria Hotel in New York City⟩

wale [weil] *n., v.* **waled, wal•ing.** —*n.* **1** a streak or ridge made on the skin by a stick or whip; welt. **2** a long, narrow, raised surface, especially one of a series of parallel ribs or ridges in cloth such as corduroy. **3** the texture of weave of such cloth: *corduroy of fine wale.* **4** Usually, **wales,** *pl.* a continuous line of thick, outside planking on the sides of a wooden ship. **5** a strong band around the outside of a woven basket to reinforce it.
—*v.* **1** raise welts on. **2** weave with ridges. ⟨OE *walu*⟩
☛ *Hom.* WAIL, WHALE.

walk [wɒk] *v., n.* —*v.* **1** go on foot. **2** stroll for pleasure, exercise, fresh air, etc.; take a walk or walks. **3** take for such a walk: *to walk one's dog every morning. He walked the baby in her stroller till she fell asleep.* **4** go over, on, or through on foot: *The captain walked the deck.* **5** make, put, drive, etc. by walking: *to walk off a headache.* **6** go on foot in such a way that one foot (or three, for quadrupeds) is always touching the ground: *Walk, do not run.* **7** cause to walk: *The rider walked his horse.* **8** accompany or escort in walking; conduct on foot: *to walk a guest to the door.* **9** push (a bicycle, etc.) while walking beside it: *Walk your bike across the street.* **10** traverse on foot in order to measure, examine, etc.; pace off or over: *to walk the back line of a piece of property.* **11** roam: *The ghost will walk tonight.* **12** of things, move or shake in a manner suggestive of walking. **13** *Baseball.* **a** of a batter, go to first base after the pitcher has thrown four balls. See BALL[1] (def. 5). **b** of a pitcher, allow (a batter) to do this. **c** cause (a run) to be scored in this way. (*used with* **in**). **14** *Basketball.* commit a foul by taking two or more steps while holding the ball. **15** conduct oneself in a particular manner; follow a particular course in life: *to walk justly.* **16** take part in a formal walking event for some cause, such as a walkathon or a demonstration: *Walk for peace on June 13! I'm walking for cancer; will you sponsor me?* **17** leave or cause to leave negotiations, a position, opportunity, etc. in dissatisfaction: *The sales representative was fired for walking too many customers. If you don't pay your people enough, they'll walk.* **18** be released or acquitted or fined instead of sentenced to prison after committing an offence: *If they don't present better evidence than this, he'll walk.*
walk (all) over, a defeat easily and by a wide margin. **b** *Informal.* treat contemptuously: *Don't let them walk all over you.*
walk away from, a progress much faster than. **b** reject, refuse, or renounce flatly. **c** survive (an accident or other ordeal) unhurt.
walk off, a walk away (from), especially in an abrupt manner: *to walk off the job. She walked off without saying anything.* **b** get rid of by walking: *to walk off extra weight. He walked off his anger.*
walk off or **away with, a** take; get; win. **b** steal.
walk out, a *Informal.* go on strike. **b** leave suddenly.
walk out on, *Informal.* desert.
walk tall, have self-respect.
walk through, do a walk-through of (a play, scene, etc.)
—*n.* **1** the act of walking, especially walking for pleasure or exercise: *a walk in the country.* **2** a distance to walk: *It is a long walk from here.* **3** a manner or way of walking; gait: *We knew the man was a sailor from his rolling walk.* **4** the relatively slow pace of a person who or animal that walks: *As she neared the house, she slowed to a walk.* **5** a sidewalk or path for walking: *We always preferred the walk down by the river. I shovelled the snow off the walk.* **6** the regular route covered by a letter carrier, patroller, etc. **7** occupation or social position: *An electrician and a farmer are in different walks of life.* **8** a manner of living or conducting oneself. **9** *Baseball.* the advance of a batter to first base by walking. **10** an enclosed place for animals; tract: *a poultry walk.*
take a walk, *Informal.* get out of here. ⟨OE *wealcan* roll⟩
☛ *Syn. v.* **1. Walk,** STRIDE, PLOD = go on foot at a pace slower than a run. **Walk** is the general word: *He walked downstairs.* **Stride** means 'walk with long, regular steps', especially in haste, annoyance, or self-importance, or with healthy energy: *When we walk for exercise, we should stride briskly.* **Plod** means 'walk heavily, slowly, and with effort': *The old horse plodded up the road.*
☛ *Hom.* WOK.

walk•a•bout ['wɒkə,bʌut] *n.* **1** a relatively informal stroll taken by royalty or a politician to greet the public. **2** *Australian.* a temporary return to the outback by an Aborigine to wander the bush and renew traditional skills and practices.

walk•a•thon ['wɒkə,θɒn] *n.* a long-distance walk: **a** for competition in speed and endurance. **b** to raise money for a cause, with sponsors pledging a certain amount for every kilometre walked.

walk•a•way ['wɒkə,wei] *n. Informal.* an easy victory.

walk•er ['wɒkər] *n.* **1** a person who walks, especially one who walks in a particular way: *She's a fast walker.* **2 a** a framework on wheels designed to support a child learning to walk. **b** a framework designed to help a disabled or elderly person walk.

walk•ie–talk•ie ['wɒki 'tɒki] *n., pl.* **-talk•ies.** a small, portable two-way radio set for communication over short distances, originally developed for military use during World War II. Also, **walky-talky**.

walk–in ['wɒk ,ɪn] *adj., n.* *—adj.* **1** large enough to be walked into: *a walk-in closet.* **2** of any residence, business establishment, professional office, etc., having an entrance directly off the street rather than by way of a hall or lobby. **3 a** of a clinic or other professional or service agency, taking clients without an appointment. **b** referring to such a client.
—n. **1** a sure or easy victory. **2** a walk-in closet, office, apartment, etc. **3** a client who comes to a clinic or other service agency without an appointment.

walk•ing ['wɒkɪŋ] *n., adj., v.* *—n.* **1** the action of a person who or thing that walks: *Walking is good exercise.* **2** the quality or condition of a road, sidewalk, etc. for walking: *The walking was treacherous after the ice storm.*
—adj. **1** for use in walking: *Bring your walking shoes.* **2** including or consisting of the action of walking: *We went on a walking tour of the city centre.* **3** in human form; personified: *She's a walking encyclopedia.*
—v. ppr. of WALK.

walking fern a North American fern (*Camptosorus rhizophyllus*) having long, tapering, evergreen fronds whose tips take root wherever they touch the ground, producing a new plant.

walking papers *Informal.* dismissal from a position, etc.

walking pneumonia a case of pneumonia that does not prevent the patient from getting around.

walking shorts shorts ending just above the knee and cut very full for ease of movement.

walking stick **1** a stick used for support in walking; cane. **2** STICK INSECT; especially, any of several North American species, such as *Diapheromera femorata.*

walking wounded **1** those whose battle wounds do not force them to be bedridden. **2** those suffering emotional or mental problems.

Walk•man ['wɒkmən] *n. Trademark.* a pocket-sized stereo cassette or CD player with headphones, often including a radio.

walk–on ['wɒk ,ɒn] *n.* **1** a small part in a dramatic production in which an actor appears on stage but usually has no lines to speak. **2** an actor having such a part.

walk•out ['wɒk,ʌut] *n.* **1** a work stoppage; strike. **2** the departure of a group of people from a meeting, etc. as a protest.

walk•o•ver ['wɒk,ouvər] *n.* **1** *Informal.* an easy victory. **2** a race in which only one horse is entered, winnable by simply walking over the course.

walk–through ['wɒk ,θru] *n.* a rehearsal of a play in an early phase, when the lines are read, accompanied only by rough stage action.

walk–up ['wɒk ,ʌp] *n.* **1** an apartment house or office building of more than two storeys having no elevator. **2** a room, apartment, or office above the ground floor in such a building. **3** (*adjl.*) located above the ground floor in such a building: *a walk-up apartment.* **4** (*adjl.*) having several storeys and no elevator: *There is a walk-up annex.*

walk•way ['wɒk,wei] *n.* **1** a pathway, passage, or walk specially constructed for the use of pedestrians, for their safety or to prevent walking on the adjacent surface. **2** a raised framework or structure on which to walk, often sheltered, as between buildings over a street, around the wall above a room full of machines, etc.

walk•y–talk•y ['wɒki 'tɒki] *n., pl.* **-talk•ies.** See WALKIE-TALKIE.

wall [wɒl] *n., v.* *—n.* **1** the side of a building or room joining the floor or foundation and the ceiling or roof. **2** a solid structure of stone, brick, or other material built up to enclose, divide, support, or protect. **3** something like a wall in looks or function: *a wall of water 4 m high. I can't seem to get past his wall of indifference.* **4** the side of any hollow thing: *the wall of a cylinder, the wall of the heart.*
come, be, etc. **up against a blank wall,** be completely unsuccessful, as when seeking information; be stymied: *She tried several angles, but always came up against a blank wall.*
drive or **push to the wall,** make desperate or helpless: *driven to the wall by debts.*
go to the wall, a give way; be defeated. **b** fail in business.
off the wall, *Slang.* eccentric; bizarre; crazy; unreasonable.
up the wall, *Informal.* frantic with frustration or anger: *His constant whining drives me up the wall!*
with (one's) **back to** or **against the wall,** in an extreme or desperate situation.
—v. **1** enclose, divide, or protect with a wall, or as if with a wall: *The garden is walled.* **2** close or fill with a wall (*often used with* **up**): *Workers walled up the doorway.* ⟨OE *weall* < L *vallum*⟩
—'wall-less, *adj.* **—'wall-,like,** *adj.*

wal•la ['wʌlə] *n.* See WALLAH.

wal•la•by ['wɒləbi] *n., pl.* **-bies** or (*esp. collectively*) **-by.** any of various small or medium-sized marsupials of the same family (Macropodidae) as the kangaroo, many of them no larger than a rabbit. ⟨< native Australian *wolabā*⟩

wal•lah ['wʌlə] *n.* **1** *Informal.* a chap; fellow. **2** *Anglo-Indian.* one who is connected with some special work or area: *a kitchen wallah.* Also, **walla.** ⟨originally < Hind. *-wala*, adj. suffix, perhaps < Skt. *bala* boy⟩

wal•la•roo [,wɒlə'ru] *n.* a large kangaroo (*Macropus robustus*) found in rocky regions of Australia, having thick, coarse, dark grey or reddish brown fur, a stocky body, and thickly padded feet. ⟨< native Australian *wolarū*⟩

wall•board ['wɒl,bɔrd] *n.* any of various types of board, such as plasterboard, particleboard, or hardboard, used in place of plaster or wooden panelling to finish interior walls and ceilings.

walled [wɒld] *adj., v.* *—adj.* surrounded by walls: *a walled garden.*
—v. pt. and pp. of WALL.

wal•let ['wɒlɪt] *n.* **1** a small, flat, folding case, usually made of leather, vinyl, fabric, or other supple material, having compartments for carrying paper money, credit cards, driver's licence, etc. and, often, coins. **2** *Archaic.* a bag for carrying food and small articles for personal use on a journey. ⟨ME *walet*; origin uncertain⟩

wall•eye ['wɒl,aɪ] *n.* **1** especially in a horse, an eye with a light-coloured or white iris. **2** an eye having an opaque, white cornea. **3** opacity of the cornea. **4** a condition of the eyes in which one or both eyes are turned outward because of an imbalance of the muscles; strabismus. **5** an eye that turns outward. **6** a large, staring eye, as in some fish. **7 a** *Cdn.* a common North American freshwater fish (*Stizostedion vitreum*) of the perch family that is one of the most important food and game fishes of Canada's inland waters, ranging in colour from mainly olive brown to yellow, and occasionally greyish, speckled with gold or yellow, and having smoky, silvery eyes thought to resemble those of walleyed domestic animals. A bluish subspecies (the **blue walleye,** or **blue pike**) was formerly found in Lakes Erie and Ontario. Also called **yellow walleye, pickerel, yellow pickerel, pikeperch, walleyed pike, doré,** and **dory. b** any of various other similar fishes with prominent, glossy eyes. ⟨back formation from *walleyed*⟩

wall•eyed ['wɒl,aɪd] *adj.* having a walleye or walleyes. ⟨ME, by folk etymology < ON *vagl-eygr* < *vagl*, probably, speck in the eye + *auga* eye⟩

walleyed pike or **walleye pike** *Cdn.* WALLEYE (def. 7a).

wall fern a small, hardy fern (*Polypodium vulgare* or *P. virginianum*) found on cliffs and walls, and often grown in gardens.

wall•flow•er ['wɒl,flaʊər] *n.* **1** *Informal.* a person, especially a girl or woman, who remains on the sidelines at a dance, either from shyness or because of not being asked to dance. **2** any of numerous perennial plants (genera *Cheiranthus* and *Erysimum*) of the mustard family that often grow from chinks in walls. Several wallflowers having fragrant yellow, orange, or red flowers are widely cultivated as perennials.

wall hanging a large woven, knotted, appliquéd, etc. decoration hung on a wall.

Wal•loon [wɒ'lun] *n., adj.* *—n.* **1** a member of a Celtic people inhabiting chiefly the southern parts of Belgium and adjacent regions in France. **2** their language, the French dialect of Belgium.
—adj. of or having to do with the Walloons or their language. ⟨< F *Wallon* < Med.L *Wallo* < Gmc.⟩

wal•lop ['wɒləp] *v., n. Informal.* *—v.* **1** beat soundly; thrash. **2** hit very hard; strike with a vigorous blow. **3** defeat thoroughly, as in a game. **4** move along rapidly and awkwardly: *The St. Bernard puppy walloped across the lawn to meet us.*
—n. **1** a very hard blow. **2** the power to deal very hard blows: *He's got a real wallop!* **3** a very forceful effect or impression: *When you've recovered from the wallop delivered by this film, you may want to see some of the director's other works.*
pack a wallop, *Informal.* deliver, or be capable of delivering, a very forceful effect or impression: *That punch she made for the*

party certainly packed a wallop! ⟨ME < ONF *waloper* gallop < Gmc.⟩

wal•lop•ing ['wɒləpɪŋ] *n., adj., adv., v. Informal. —n.* **1** a sound beating or thrashing. **2** a thorough defeat.
—adj. very big or impressive; whopping: *That's a walloping serving of ice cream!*
—adv. extraordinarily; extremely: *a walloping big baby.*
—v. ppr. of WALLOP.

wal•low ['wɒlou] *v., n. —v.* **1** roll about lazily or pleasurably, as animals in dust or mud: *The pigs wallowed in the cool mud.* **2** roll about clumsily or out of control: *The boat wallowed helplessly in the stormy sea.* **3** indulge oneself excessively in some pleasure, state of mind, way of living, etc.: *to wallow in luxury, to wallow in self-pity.*
—n. **1** the act of wallowing. **2** a place where an animal wallows. ⟨OE *wealwian* roll⟩

wall•pa•per ['wɒl,peipər] *n., v. —n.* paper, usually having a printed or embossed design, used for covering the walls and, occasionally, the ceiling of rooms, hallways, etc.
—v. paste wallpaper (on a wall, ceiling, etc.): *We decided to wallpaper the room instead of painting it. They spent all weekend wallpapering.*

wall plate a horizontal timber on the top edge of a wall, distributing the weight of the rafters or joists whose ends rest upon it.

wall rue a fern resembling rue (*Asplenium rutamuraria*) and growing on walls or rockfaces in Europe and North America.

Wall Street the money market or the financiers of the United States. ⟨< *Wall Street*, a street in downtown New York City, the chief financial centre of the United States⟩

wall–to–wall ['wɒl tə 'wɒl] *adj.* **1** covering a floor from one wall to the other in both dimensions. **2** so abundant as to seem to be everywhere in a place: *In the den of the tennis star's home there were wall-to-wall trophies.*

wal•nut ['wɒl,nʌt] *or* ['wɒlnət] *n., adj. —n.* **1** any of a genus (*Juglans*) of hardwood trees found in many parts of the world, having compound leaves with from five to twenty-three toothed leaflets and fruit that is a large woody nut enclosed in a thick husk. Two species of walnut, the **butternut** and **black walnut**, are native to eastern Canada. **2** the roundish, edible nut of any of these trees. **3** the hard, dark wood of any of these trees, valued for making furniture, etc. **4** (*adjl.*) designating a family (Juglandaceae) of trees, including the walnuts and hickories. **5** medium reddish brown.
—adj. having the colour walnut. ⟨OE *wealhhnutu* < *wealh* foreign + *hnutu* nut⟩

Wal•pur•gis Night [vɑl'purgɪs] the night of April 30th, the eve of May Day, when witches formerly held what were believed to be revels with the devil. Also, **Walpurgisnacht** [-,naxt]. ⟨< St. *Walpurga*, English abbess and missionary to Germany (710-780), whose feast day is May 1⟩

wal•rus ['wɒlrəs] *n., pl.* **-rus•es** or **-rus.** a large sea mammal (*Odobenus rosmarus*) of the Arctic regions, resembling a seal but larger and having long tusks. Walruses have long been hunted, especially for their thick hide, their ivory tusks, and the oil obtained from their blubber. ⟨< Du. *walrus, walros* < *wal(vis)* whale + *ros* horse⟩

Walruses

walrus mustache a thick, heavy mustache, hanging down over the upper lip and drooping at both ends, like the hairs on the face of a walrus.

waltz [wɒlts] *n., v. —n.* **1** a smooth, even, gliding ballroom dance in 3/4 time. **2** the music for such a dance. **3** any musical composition or part of a composition written in 3/4 time. **4** *Informal.* something achieved effortlessly, such as an easy victory: *We won in a waltz, 15 to 0.* **5** (*adjl.*) of or having to do with the waltz: *waltz time.*
—v. **1** dance a waltz. **2** dance with or lead (someone) in a waltz: *He waltzed her across the ballroom floor.* **3** move nimbly, quickly, or showily: *She waltzed through the room, cheerfully greeting all the guests.* **4** *Informal.* advance or proceed easily and successfully: *She waltzed through the exam in half the time it took me.* **5** *Informal.* move or lead briskly: *His mother waltzed him into the living room to apologize to his brother.*
waltz up to, *Informal.* approach boldly or abruptly; accost: *He just waltzed up to the supervisor and said he was quitting.* ⟨< G *Walzer* < *walzen* roll⟩ **—'waltz•er,** *n.*

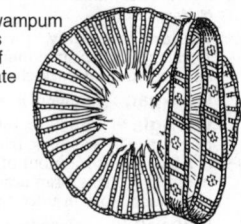

Wampum. The circular piece is the wampum record of the founding of the Iroquois League of Five Nations. It consists of an outer ring of shells with 50 separate strings representing the 50 chiefs of the League. The other piece is a standard Iroquois wampum sash.

wam•pum ['wɒmpəm] *n.* **1** beads made from polished shells (*Venus mercenaria*) strung in belts and sashes, formerly used by eastern First Nations peoples as money, as a reminder of a treaty, and as ornament. The white form was more common, but the black or dark purple was of greater value. **2** *Slang.* money. ⟨< Algonquian: Narraganset *wampompeag* strings of white (things) < *wampan* white + *api* string + *-ag* pl. suffix⟩

wan [wɒn] *adj.* **wan•ner, wan•nest. 1** pale and sickly; lacking natural colour: *Her face looked wan after her long illness.* **2** looking worn or tired; faint or weak: *The sick boy gave the doctor a wan smile.* ⟨OE *wann* dark⟩ **—'wan•ly,** *adv.* **—'wan•ness,** *n.*
☛ *Syn.* **1.** See note at PALE.

wand [wɒnd] *n.* **1** a slender stick or rod that has, or is used as if it had, power to release magic: *The magician waved his wand.* **2** a rod or staff symbolizing authority. **3** *Informal.* the baton of a conductor. **4** a long, slender hand-held electronic device that reads bar codes by being passed over them. **5** any slender stick or rod, including a stem or shoot of a young tree. ⟨ME < ON *vöndr*⟩ **—'wand,like,** *adj.*

wan•der ['wɒndər] *v.* **1** move about without any special purpose: *I was too early for my appointment, so I wandered through the stores for a while.* **2** go aimlessly over or through: *to wander the streets.* **3** depart from the right way; stray: *The dog wandered off and got lost. The student driver wandered into the wrong lane. Your account wanders from the truth in places.* **4** proceed in a leisurely, casual, or indirect way: *I think I'll just wander over to the buffet table; my plate's empty.* **5** talk or think in a rambling or incoherent way: *The fever made his mind wander. As she talked, she kept wandering away from her subject and glancing at the door.* **6** of a river, path, etc., follow a winding, irregular course; meander. **7** of the hands, gaze, etc., move as if idly from one thing to another. ⟨OE *wandrian*⟩ **—'wan•der•er,** *n.*
☛ *Syn.* **1. Wander,** STRAY= go from place to place more or less aimlessly or without a settled course. **Wander** emphasizes moving about from place to place without a definite course or destination: *We wandered through the stores, hoping to get ideas for Christmas presents.* **Stray** emphasizes going aimlessly beyond the usual or proper limits or away from the regular path or course, and often suggests getting lost: *Two of the children strayed from the picnic grounds.*

wan•der•ing ['wɒndərɪŋ] *adj., n., v. —adj.* **1** that wanders: *a wandering stream.* **2** of peoples, nomadic.
—n. **1** an aimless roving about; a travelling from place to place in an aimless or leisurely manner. **2** Usually, **wanderings,** *pl.* **a** travels, especially long or casual ones. **b** thought or discourse that is incoherent; raving; delirium.
—v. ppr. of WANDER.

wandering Jew 1 any of several trailing or creeping plants of the spiderwort family (especially *Tradescantia fluminensis* or *Zebrina pendula*) having showy leaves that are striped with white or cream on the upper side and are reddish purple beneath. Wandering Jews are commonly grown as house plants.
2 Wandering Jew, in medieval legend, a Jew who insulted Christ on the way to the Crucifixion and was condemned to wander on earth till Christ's second coming.

wan•der•lust ['wɒndər,lʌst] *n.* a strong desire to travel: *His wanderlust led him all over the world.* ⟨< G *Wanderlust* < *wandern* wander + *lust* desire⟩

wane [wein] *v.* **waned, wan•ing;** *n. —v.* **1** of the moon, go through the regular decrease in the size of its visible portion: *The moon wanes after it has become full.* **2** become less brilliant or intense: *The light of day wanes in the evening.* **3** lose strength, power, or importance: *Her influence in the club has waned.* **4** of a period of time, draw to a close: *Summer wanes as autumn nears.*

—*n.* **1** the process or period of waning. **2** the defective, unsquared or bark-covered edge or corner of a piece of lumber. **on the wane,** growing less; waning: *His popularity was on the wane.* ⟨OE *wanian*⟩
☛ *Hom.* WAIN.

wane•y or **wan•y** ['weini] *adj.* **wan•i•er, wan•i•est.** **1** waning; decreasing; diminished. **2** of a piece of lumber, having an unsquared or bark-covered edge or corner.

wan•gan ['wɒŋgən] *n. Cdn.* WANIGAN (def. 3).

wan•gle ['wæŋgəl] *v.* **-gled, -gling.** *Informal.* **1** manage to get or arrange by schemes, tricks, manipulation, persuasion, etc. **2** make (one's way) out of difficulties or obligations in this manner. **3** change (an account, report, etc.) dishonestly for one's advantage. ⟨origin uncertain⟩

wan•i•gan ['wɒnəgən] *n. Cdn.* **1** a logger's chest or trunk. **2** a large sled equipped as living quarters and pulled by tracked vehicles as part of a train for carrying troops and supplies in the North. **3** a kind of boat used by loggers for carrying supplies, tools, etc. and as a houseboat. ⟨< Algonquian *waniigan* trap, place for stray objects⟩

Wan•kel engine ['wæŋkəl] *or* ['vɑŋkəl] a rotary, or non-reciprocating, internal-combustion engine having an elliptical chamber in which a more or less triangular shaft or piston rotates continuously. It is not as powerful, efficient, or complex as a reciprocating engine. ⟨< Felix *Wankel* (1902-1988), a German inventor and engineer⟩

wan•nish ['wɒnɪʃ] *adj.* somewhat wan. **—'wan•nish•ly,** *adv.* **—'wan•nish•ness,** *n.*

want [wɒnt] *v., n.* —*v.* **1** wish (for); desire: *He wants to become a singer. She wants a new car.* **2** be without (what is desired or needed); lack: *a reply that wants courtesy. The building fund still wants several thousand dollars.* **3** need; require; ought to have: *Plants want water. You want more exercise.* **4** *Informal.* ought (*to*): *You want to eat a balanced diet.* **5** *Informal.* wish to come or go: *The dog wants in. He was very enthusiastic at first, but now he wants out of the project.* **6** wish to see, speak to, or use the help of (a person): *Call me if you want me. You're wanted on the phone.* **7** seek or go after in order to question or arrest: *The police want him for questioning. She is wanted for theft.* **8** suffer from a lack, especially of the necessities of life: *In spite of the new aid program, many people are still wanting.* **9** be short or lacking by (a given amount): *It wants an hour until train time.* **want for,** have or feel a lack or shortage of: *She is very popular and has never wanted for friends.*
—*n.* **1** a desire or need: *The new park supplied a long-felt want. He is a man of few wants.* **2** the quality or state of lacking something desired or needed; shortage or lack: *The plant died for want of water.* **3** extreme poverty: *Many families were in want this past winter.* ⟨ME < ON *vant* < *vanr* lacking⟩
☛ *Syn. v.* **2.** See note at LACK. *n.* **3.** See note at POVERTY.
☛ *Hom.* WONT [wɒnt].

want ad *Informal.* a notice in a newspaper that an employee, job or position, apartment, car, etc. is wanted or that an apartment, car, etc. is for sale or rent.

want•ing ['wɒntɪŋ] *adj., prep., v.* —*adj.* **1** not coming up to a standard or need; not satisfactory: *The stranger was wanting in courtesy.* **2** lacking; missing: *One volume of the set is wanting.*
—*prep.* **1** without: *an old chair wanting a back.* **2** minus; less: *a month, wanting three days.*
—*v.* ppr. of WANT.

wan•ton ['wɒntən] *adj., n., v.* —*adj.* **1** without excuse or reason; senseless, reckless, or heartless: *a wanton attack, a wanton disregard of others' rights. His mistreatment of animals is wanton cruelty.* **2** sexually immoral; not chaste. **3** *Archaic or poetic.* **a** playful and unrestrained; frolicsome or frisky: *a wanton mood, a wanton child, a wanton breeze.* **b** of vegetation, profuse in growth, luxuriant; rank. **4** extravagant; lavish: *a wanton display of wealth.*
—*n.* an immoral or unchaste person.
—*v.* **1** act in a wanton manner: *The wind wantoned with the leaves.* **2** squander (*often used with* **away**). ⟨ME *wantowen* < OE *wan-* deficient + *togen* brought up, pp. of *tēon* bring⟩ **—'wan•ton•ly,** *adv.* **—'wan•ton•ness,** *n.*

wap•i•ti ['wɒpɪti] *n., pl.* **-ti** or **-tis.** *Cdn.* the North American elk. See ELK (def. 1). ⟨< Algonquian⟩

war [wɔr] *n., v.* **warred, war•ring.** —*n.* **1** open fighting carried on by armed forces between nations or groups. **2** any active struggle, rivalry, or conflict: *the war against disease, a price war.* **3** the art or science of fighting against an opposing armed force; military science: *Soldiers are trained in war.* **4** (*adjl.*) of, having to do with, or used in war: *war materials, war crimes.*
at war, taking part in a war; warring: *France was at war with Great Britain. Her emotions were at war with one another.*
go to war, a start or enter a war. **b** go as a soldier.
—*v.* fight or contend; make war: *warring against poverty. Germany warred against France.* ⟨ME *werre* < AF var. of OF *guerre* < Gmc.⟩ **—'war•less,** *adj.*

war•ble[1] ['wɔrbəl] *v.* **-bled, -bling;** *n.* —*v.* **1** sing in a lilting, melodious way, with trills, quavers, etc.: *Birds warbled in the trees.* **2** make a sound like that of a bird warbling: *The brook warbled over its rocky bed.* **3** express by warbling: *to warble a greeting.*
—*n.* **1** the act of warbling. **2** a bird's song or a sound like it. ⟨ME < ONF *werbler* < Gmc.⟩

war•ble[2] ['wɔrbəl] *n.* **1** a small abscess under the hide, especially of cattle or horses, caused by a larva of the WARBLE FLY or botfly. **2** the larva of a warble fly. **3** a hard lump on a horse's back, caused by prolonged rubbing of a saddle. Also, **wabble.** ⟨< Swedish *varbulde* < *var* pus + *bulde* swelling⟩

war•bled ['wɔrbəld] *adj.* attacked or infected by warbles.

warble fly any of various two-winged flies (family Oestridae) whose larvae burrow under the hide of cattle, horses, and other mammals, causing warbles.

war•bler ['wɔrblər] *n.* **1** any of a subfamily (Sylviinae, of the family Muscicapidae) of small, active, chiefly Old World songbirds typically having brown, dull olive green, or greyish plumage, and including some species noted for their song. Some authorities classify warblers as a separate family (Sylviidae). **2** WOOD WARBLER. **3** any person who or thing that warbles.

war bonnet a ceremonial headdress traditionally worn as a mark of honour among First Nations peoples of the North American plains, consisting of a row or rows of feathers attached to a headband and trailing down the back.

war bride **1** a woman who marries a soldier during wartime, especially a soldier about to go overseas. **2** a woman who marries a soldier met during wartime, especially a foreign soldier, and then returns with him to his country: *After World War II many war brides came to Canada from Great Britain and the Netherlands.*

war club a heavy club used as a weapon.

war correspondent a journalist assigned to send back reports and commentary directly from a war zone.

war crime any violation of the rules of warfare, especially atrocities against civilians, political prisoners, etc.

war criminal one who is convicted of committing a war crime.

war cry **1** a word or phrase shouted in fighting; battle cry. **2** a slogan in any contest.

ward [wɔrd] *n., v.* —*n.* **1** a division of a hospital, especially a section for a particular class or group of patients, consisting of one large room or a group of rooms: *a maternity ward, the children's ward.* **2** a division of a prison, such as a block of cells. **3** a political subdivision of a city, especially one represented by a municipal councillor. **4** a person under the care of a guardian or of a court: *a ward of the Children's Aid Society.* **5** the act of keeping guard or watch: *The soldiers kept ward over the castle.* **6** the state of being kept under guard or in custody. **7** *Fencing, etc.* a movement or position of defence. **8** a notch or groove in a key. **9** the corresponding ridge in a lock. **10** the large open space within the walls of a castle or fortress; bailey.
—*v.* turn aside or keep away; avert (*usually used with* **off**): *He warded off the blow with his arm. She raised her collar to ward off the icy wind.* ⟨OE *weardian* guard < Gmc. Doublet of GUARD.⟩

-ward *suffix.* in or to a particular direction or point in time: *backward, seaward, upward.* See also -WARDS. ⟨OE *-weard*⟩
☛ *Usage.* **-ward, -wards.** Of variants such as **downward—downwards** and **forward—forwards,** only the **-ward** form is used as adjective or noun: *a forward movement, looking to the westward.* Either variant may be used as adverb or preposition: *He fell forward* (or *forwards*). *She came toward* (or *towards*) *me.*

war dance a tribal dance performed before going to war or to celebrate a victory.

ward•en ['wɔrdən] *n.* **1** an official who enforces certain laws or rules: *a fire warden. A game warden enforces hunting restrictions.* **2** a person in charge of the operation of a prison. **3** in certain colleges, churches, or other institutions, an official with administrative, academic, or supervisory duties. **4** *Cdn.* in provinces having county governments, the head of the county council, generally chosen by the members from among themselves. ⟨ME < ONF *wardein*, var. of *g(u)arden*, ult. < Gmc. Doublet of GUARDIAN.⟩ **—'ward•en,ship,** *n.*

ward•er ['wɔrdər] *n.* **1** a guard or watchman. **2** a jailer. **—'ward•er,ship,** *n.*

ward•robe ['wɔr,droub] *n.* **1** a stock of clothes: *She is shopping for her spring wardrobe.* **2** a closet, built-in or free-standing, for holding clothes. **3** a room in which clothes are kept. **4** all the costumes of a theatrical show or film. **5** the department in charge of clothing and regalia for the members of a royal or noble household. ⟨ME < ONF *warderobe*, var. of OF *garderobe* < *garder* keep (< Gmc.) + *robe* gown (< Gmc.)⟩

wardrobe trunk a large trunk or chest used as a portable wardrobe. It is placed on end and contains drawers, rails, or compartments for storing clothes.

ward•room ['wɔrd,rum] *or* ['wɔrd,rʊm] *n.* **1** on a warship, the living and eating quarters for all the commissioned officers except the commanding officer. **2** these officers collectively.

–wards *suffix.* in or to a particular direction or point in time: *afterwards, backwards, towards.* See also -WARD.

☛ *Usage.* **-wards.** Used originally and chiefly in adverbs. See note at -WARD.

ward•ship ['wɔrdʃɪp] *n.* **1** guardianship or custody, especially over a minor or other ward. **2** the condition of being a ward, or under a legal or feudal guardian.

ware[1] [wɛr] *n.* **1** Usually, **wares,** *pl.* manufactured articles or goods for sale (as by merchants, peddlers, etc.); merchandise: *He peddled his wares from door to door.* **2** articles or goods of a particular kind or used for a particular purpose (*now used mainly in compounds*): *tinware, hardware, kitchenware. The silverware needs polishing.* **3** articles of fired clay; pottery: *blue-and-white ware from Delft. Biscuit ware is unglazed porcelain.* ⟨OE *waru*⟩

☛ *Hom.* WEAR, WHERE.

ware[2] [wɛr] *adj., v.* **wared, war•ing.** *Archaic or poetic.* *—adj.* aware.

—v. look out for; beware of. ⟨OE *wær*⟩

☛ *Hom.* WEAR, WHERE.

ware•house *n.* ['wɛr,hʌus]; *v.* ['wɛr,haʊz] *or* ['wɛr,hʌus] *n., pl.* **-hous•es** [-,haʊzɪz]; *v.* **-housed, -hous•ing.** *—n.* **1** a building or large room where goods are stored. **2** a wholesale or large, reasonably-priced retail outlet.

—v. put or keep in a warehouse.

ware•house•man ['wɛr,hʌusmən] *n.* **-men.** a man who owns or works in a warehouse.

war•fare ['wɔr,fɛr] *n.* **1** war; fighting. **2** any struggle or contest. ⟨ME *warfare* < *war* + *fare* a going, OE *faru* journey⟩

war•fa•rin ['wɔrfərɪn] *n.* **1** *Chemistry.* a colourless, odourless, tasteless crystalline anticoagulant, $C_{19}H_{16}O_4$, chiefly used as a rodenticide. It causes internal bleeding. **2** *Pharmacy.* a preparation of this, neutralized with sodium hydroxide, used to treat blood clotting disorders. ⟨< *W*isconsin *A*lumni *R*esearch *F*oundation (holders of the patent) + (*coum*)*arin*⟩

war game a training exercise that simulates war. It may be an exercise on a map or a computer, or it may be manoeuvres with actual troops, weapons, and equipment.

war•head ['wɔr,hɛd] *n.* the forward part of a rocket, missile, torpedo, etc.: *The warhead contains the explosive charge.*

war•horse **1** a horse used in war. **2** *Informal.* a person, especially a veteran soldier or a person in public life, who has survived many battles or struggles. **3** *Informal.* a piece of music, a play, etc. so often performed as to become overly familiar and uninteresting: *The last symphony concert was full of old warhorses, but it was fun anyway.* Also (esp. def. 1), **war horse.**

war•like ['wɔr,ləik] *adj.* **1** fond of and ready for war: *a warlike nature, warlike peoples.* **2** threatening war; belligerent: *a warlike speech.* **3** of, for, or having to do with war: *warlike preparations.*

☛ *Syn.* See note at MILITARY.

war•lock ['wɔr,lɒk] *n.* a man who practises black magic; sorcerer. Compare WITCH. ⟨OE *wǣrloga* traitor, oath-breaker < *wǣr* covenant + *-loga* one who denies⟩

war•lord ['wɔr,lɔrd] *n.* **1** a military commander, especially one who has supreme civil authority in a particular region, often in defiance of a weak central government. **2** any tyrant or dictator who is quick to resort to arms or who has overthrown a government in a military coup.

warm [wɔrm] *adj., v.* *—adj.* **1** more hot than cold; having or giving forth some heat: *Whoever had built the fire could not have been gone long—the ashes were still warm. Don't leave the apple juice out or it'll get warm.* **2 a** having the natural body heat of living beings. **b** having a feeling of greater than usual body heat: *She was warm from running.* **3** that makes or keeps warm: *a warm coat, warm work.* **4** having or showing affection, enthusiasm, etc.: *a warm welcome, a warm friend, a warm heart.* **5** quick to show irritation or anger: *a warm temper.* **6** showing irritation or anger: *a warm dispute.* **7** of a trail, scent, etc., recent and strong. **8** *Informal.* in games, treasure hunts, etc., near what one is searching for. **9** of a colour, suggesting warmth; mainly red or yellow in tone. **10** uncomfortable; unpleasant: *to make things warm for a person.*

—v. **1** make or become warm: *to warm a room.* **2** make or become cheered, interested, friendly, or sympathetic: *Their kindness warmed our hearts.* **3** bask; luxuriate; feel pleasure.

warm over, reheat (leftover food, etc.). **b** rehash; rework with tiresome effect.

warm to, become more and more enthusiastic about or sympathetic toward: *The speaker warmed to his subject. She quickly warmed to them after a few more encounters.*

warm up, a heat or cook again. **b** make or become more interested, friendly, etc. **c** practise or exercise for a few minutes before entering a game, contest, etc. **d** of an engine, etc., run or operate in order to reach a proper working temperature: *It takes the car a long time to warm up on cold mornings.* **e** run or operate (an engine, etc.) until it reaches a proper working temperature. ⟨OE *wearm*⟩ **—'warm•er,** *n.* **—'warm•ly,** *adv.* **—'warm•ness,** *n.*

warm–blood•ed ['wɔrm 'blʌdɪd] *adj.* **1** having warm blood that stays about the same temperature regardless of the surrounding air or water. Warm-blooded animals have body temperatures between 36°C and 44°C. **2** having or showing a passionate or ardent spirit.

warmed–o•ver ['wɔrmd 'ouvər] *adj.* **1** of food, warmed again; reheated: *warmed-over chili.* **2** of ideas, etc., not new or fresh or interesting; stale and trite.

warm front *Meteorology.* the front edge of a warm air mass advancing into and replacing a colder one.

warm–heart•ed ['wɔrm 'hɑrtɪd] *adj.* having or showing a kind, sympathetic, affectionate, or friendly nature: *a warm-hearted person, a warm-hearted response.*

warming pan a covered pan having a long handle and designed to hold hot coals, formerly used to warm beds.

warm•ish ['wɔrmɪʃ] *adj.* somewhat warm. **—'warm•ish•ly,** *adv.* **—'warm•ish•ness,** *n.*

war•mon•ger ['wɔr,mʌŋgər] *or* ['wɔr,mɒŋgər] *n.* a person who is in favour of war or attempts to bring about war.

warmth [wɔrmθ] *n.* **1** the quality or state of being more hot than cold; being warm: *the warmth of an open fire.* **2** liveliness, excitement, fervour, etc.: *He spoke with warmth of the natural beauty of the countryside.* **3** a friendly, affectionate, or kind feeling or nature: *the warmth of family life.* **4** in painting, interior decorating, etc., a glowing effect produced by the use of reds and yellows.

warm–up ['wɔrm ,ʌp] *n.* **1** the act or an instance of warming up: *a quick warm-up before the game.* **2** exercises or a routine used for warming up, as before a game, contest, etc.

warn [wɔrn] *v.* **1** give notice (to) in advance about a possible or approaching unpleasantness or danger; put (someone) on guard: *The clouds warned of the coming storm. They had been warned against using the old bridge.* **2** give notice of something that requires attention or action; inform: *His mother warned us that we would have to leave by 8 o'clock.* **3** give notice to stay away, go away, keep out, etc. (*used with* **off** or **away**): *There was a sign warning off trespassers.* **4** caution or admonish (*with an infinitive*): *They warned us not to smoke in the auditorium. She warned us to keep away from the dog.* ⟨OE *warnian*⟩ **—'warn•er,** *n.*

☛ *Hom.* WORN.

☛ *Syn.* **Warn,** CAUTION = give someone notice of possible or coming danger, harm, risk, unpleasantness, consequences of an action or practice, etc. **Warn** emphasizes giving information or a hint that lets a person avoid or prepare for what is coming or likely to come: *Her mother warned her not to speak to strangers.* **Caution** emphasizes giving advice to be on one's guard against something (or someone) or suggesting steps that can be taken: *Drivers are cautioned against driving too long without a break.*

warn•ing ['wɔrnɪŋ] *n., adj., v.* *—n.* something that warns; notice given in advance.

—adj. that warns.

—v. ppr. of WARN. **—'warn•ing•ly,** *adv.*

War of 1812 a war between the United States and Great Britain, 1812-1815, fought on the Atlantic Ocean and in North America. This war confirmed Canada's independence of the United States.

War of Independence *U.S.* See REVOLUTIONARY WAR.

war of nerves a conflict or struggle characterized by the use of propaganda, bluffing, threats, etc. in order to break the morale of an opponent or enemy.

warp [wɔrp] *v., n.* —*v.* **1** bend or twist out of shape: *The heat from the radiator has warped the table. If you use green wood to build something, it is liable to warp.* **2** make or become perverted or distorted: *Prejudice warps our judgment. He has a warped sense of humour. This columnist gives a warped account of the events at Concordia.* **3** *Nautical.* move (a ship, etc.) by pulling on a rope fastened at one end to a fixed object. **4** arrange (threads or yarn) on a loom so as to form a warp.
—*n.* **1** the condition of being bent or twisted out of shape, especially as a result of heat or dampness. **2** a bend or twist in something that should be straight: *This board has a warp.* **3** a distortion of the mind, judgment, etc.; a bias or quirk.
4 *Nautical.* a rope used for warping a ship or boat. **5** the threads stretched lengthwise in a loom, through which the crosswise threads are woven. See WEAVE for picture. **6** the basis or foundation of something (often in **warp and woof**): *the warp of our society.* **7** See TIME WARP. ⟨OE *weorpan* throw⟩

warp•age ['wɔrpɪdʒ] *n.* **1** a warping or being warped. **2** the amount or degree of warping. **3** a charge for warping a ship into a harbour.

war paint **1** paint put on the face or body by certain peoples, such as, formerly, some First Nations peoples, before going to war. **2** *Informal.* make-up; cosmetics for the face. **3** *Informal.* ceremonial costume; full dress.

war•path ['wɔr,pæθ] *n. Cdn.* the way or route taken by a fighting expedition of First Nations peoples.
on the warpath, a on a warlike expedition or at war. **b** looking for a fight; very angry.

warp beam a roller at the back of a loom, on which the top ends of the warp threads are wound.

war•plane ['wɔr,plein] *n.* an aircraft used in war.

war•rant ['wɔrənt] *n., v.* —*n.* **1** a written order giving legal authority for something, especially one authorizing a search, arrest etc.: *The police have a warrant for his arrest.* **2** something that gives a right; authorization or sanction: *Their vote of confidence was his warrant to continue his investigation.* **3** a good and sufficient reason for an action, belief, etc.; justification or grounds: *She had no warrant for her suspicions.* **4** a promise; guarantee. **5** a document certifying something, especially to a purchaser. **6** *Military.* formerly, the official certificate of appointment of a WARRANT OFFICER.
—*v.* **1** justify: *It was a crisis that warranted immediate action.* **2** guarantee (something) to (someone): *to warrant the genuineness of goods purchased.* **3** *Informal.* declare positively or confidently: *I warrant I'll get there before you.* **4** authorize: *The law warrants his arrest. The judge warranted the police to search the drug dealer's apartment.* ⟨ME < ONF *warant* < Gmc.⟩

war•rant•a•ble ['wɔrəntəbəl] *adj.* capable of being warranted; justifiable. —**'war•rant•a•ble•ness,** *n.* —**'war•rant•a•bly,** *adv.*

war•ran•tee [,wɔrən'ti] *n.* a person to whom a warranty is made.

war•rant•er ['wɔrəntər] See WARRANTOR.

warrant officer **1** *Canadian Forces.* a non-commissioned officer ranking next above a sergeant and below a master warrant officer. **2** a non-commissioned officer of similar rank in the armed forces of other countries. *Abbrev.:* WO or W.O.

war•ran•tor ['wɔrəntər] *or* ['wɔrən,tɔr] *n.* a person who makes a warranty; guarantor.

war•ran•ty ['wɔrənti] *n., pl.* **-ties. 1** a usually written promise or pledge that a product is what it is claimed to be and that the manufacturer will take the responsibility for repairing or replacing it if it proves to be defective. **2** a pledge or affirmation by an insured person that a statement is true or that certain conditions will be met. **3** authorization or justification; warrant. ⟨< OF *warantie* (var. of *guarantie*) < *warantir* warrant < *warant* a warrant < Gmc. Doublet of GUARANTY.⟩

war•ren ['wɔrən] *n.* **1** an area of ground having many interconnected burrows where rabbits live. **2** the rabbits living in a warren. **3** a crowded district or building. **4** *Esp. Brit.* an enclosed area where small game, such as rabbits or pheasants, are kept and bred. ⟨ME < AF *warenne* < Celtic⟩

war•ri•or ['wɔriər] *n.* a person who engages in armed combat; an experienced soldier. ⟨ME < OF *werreieor* < *werreier* wage war < *werre* war. See WAR.⟩ —**'war•ri•or,like,** *adj.*

War•saw Pact ['wɔrsɒ] a collective defence alliance of Albania, Bulgaria, the former Czechoslovakia, the former German Democratic Republic, Hungary, Poland, Romania, and the former Soviet Union, signed in Warsaw on May 14, 1955.

war•ship ['wɔr,ʃɪp] *n.* a ship used in war.

wart [wɔrt] *n.* **1** a small, usually hard growth on the skin, caused by a virus. **2** anything resembling a wart, such as a hard lump on a plant. **3** a defect or imperfection. ⟨OE *wearte*⟩

wart hog a wild pig (*Phacochoerus aethiopicus*) of Africa having large tusks and large wartlike growths on its face. Also, **warthog.**

war•time ['wɔr,taɪm] *n., adj.* —*n.* a time of active hostilities or open fighting.
—*adj.* of such a time; that happens or exists during time of war: *wartime rationing.*

wart•y ['wɔrti] *adj.* **wart•i•er, wart•i•est. 1** having warts, or lumps or defects that are like warts. **2** of or like a wart.

war whoop a war cry, especially of First Nations people.

war•y ['wɛri] *adj.* **war•i•er, war•i•est. 1** on one's guard against danger, deception, etc.; cautious and watchful (**of**): *a wary fox. Be wary of gossip. They were wary of the stranger.* **2** showing or done with caution: *She gave wary answers to all of the stranger's questions.* ⟨< *ware*[2]⟩ —**'war•i•ly,** *adv.*
—**'war•i•ness,** *n.*
☛ *Syn.* See note at CAREFUL.
☛ *Hom.* WHERRY.

was [wʌz]; *unstressed,* [wəz] *v.* the 1st and 3rd pers. sing., past indicative, of BE: *I was late. Was he late, too?* ⟨OE *wæs*⟩

wash[1] [wɒʃ] *v., n.* —*v.* **1** clean (anything) with water or other liquid: *to wash clothes, to wash one's face, to wash dishes.* **2** agitate in soapy or sudsy water, as a phase of the cleansing process distinct from, and opposed to, rinsing. **3** make clean; purify; purge: *This one act of heroism washed him of all his guilty past.* **4** remove (dirt, stains, paint, etc.) by or as if by the action of water: *to wash a spot out.* **5** wash oneself: *He washed before eating dinner.* **6** wash clothes: *She washes for a living.* **7** undergo washing without damage: *That cloth washes well.* **8** of a stain, etc., be removed by washing (*used with* **out**): *That ink won't wash out.* **9** wear away, erode, carry, or be carried by the action of water or other liquid (*often used with* **away, out,** *etc.*): *The bridge was washed out during the storm. Wood is often washed ashore by the waves. The rain washed deep channels in the laneway.* **10** flow (over) or beat (against) with a lapping sound: *The waves washed upon the shore. The river washed the rocks along its edge.* **11** make wet: *The flowers are washed with dew.* **12** cover with a thin coating of colour or of metal: *to wash walls with blue, to wash silver with gold.* **13** *Mining.* **a** sift (earth, ore, etc.) by action of water to separate valuable material. **b** extract (valuable material) in this way: *You won't wash any gold out of this heap of gravel!* **14** *Informal.* of an excuse, account, etc., stand up under scrutiny or careful evaluation: *Sorry, that story just won't wash; what's the truth?*
wash down, a wash from top to bottom or from end to end. **b** swallow liquid along with or after (solid food) to help in swallowing or digestion.
wash out, a *Slang.* fail or cause to fail an examination, course, etc. **b** cause to lose colour, body, or vigour. **c** *Informal.* cancel: *The whole program was washed out.*
wash up, a wash the hands and face, as before meals. **b** wash the dishes after meals: *We washed up right after supper.*
—*n.* **1** a washing or being washed. **2** a quantity of clothes washed or to be washed. **3** (*adjl.*) that can be washed without damage: *a wash dress.* **4** the process or period of being agitated in soapy water as distinct from and opposed to the process or period of rinsing. **5** *Geology.* the material carried along by moving water and then deposited as sediment: *A delta is formed by the wash of a river.* **6** the motion, rush, or sound of water: *We listened to the wash of the waves against the boat.* **7** wear or erosion by moving water. **8** a tract of land sometimes overflowed with water and sometimes left dry; a tract of shallow water; fen, marsh, or bog. **9** a liquid for a special use: *a hair wash, a mouthwash.* **10** waste liquid matter; liquid garbage. **11** watery or weak liquid food. **12** a thin coating of colour, as in water painting, or metal. **13** *Mining.* earth, etc. from which gold or the like can be washed. **14 a** the rough or broken water left behind a moving ship. **b** the disturbed air left behind a moving plane or propeller. **15** the fermented liquid before distillation in making whisky or other spirits.
come out in the wash, *Informal.* resolve itself, be revealed, or be clarified with the passage of time. ⟨OE *wascan*⟩

wash² [wɒʃ] *n. Cdn.* **1** any of the underwater exits from a beaver lodge. **2** a bear's den. ⟨< Algonquian (Ojibway)⟩

wash•a•ble ['wɒʃəbəl] *adj.* **1** that can be washed without damage: *washable silk.* **2** that can be removed by washing: *washable paint or ink.*

wash–and–wear ['wɒʃ ən 'wɛr] *adj.* of a fabric or garment, easily washed and dried and needing little or no ironing.

wash•ba•sin ['wɒʃ,beisən] *n.* a basin for holding water to wash one's face and hands, do laundry by hand, etc.; sometimes also used of the porcelain, metal, or plastic fixture in a bathroom, with attached water taps and a drain.

wash•board ['wɒʃ,bɔrd] *n.* **1** a rectangular sheet of heavy glass, metal, etc. with a surface of rounded crosswise ridges, set in a wooden frame and used for rubbing the dirt out of clothes, etc. **2** a road having a surface with many crosswise ridges.

wash•bowl ['wɒʃ,boul] *n.* a bowl for holding water to wash one's face and hands.

wash•cloth ['wɒʃ,klɒθ] *n.* **1** a small cloth for washing oneself; facecloth. **2** dishcloth.

wash•day ['wɒʃ,dei] *n.* a day when clothes and household linens are washed: *Monday is their traditional washday.*

washed–out ['wɒʃt 'ʌut] *adj.* **1** lacking colour; pale or faded, as if from much washing: *a washed-out green, washed-out photos, an old, washed-out shirt.* **2** *Informal.* tired; lacking vigour or spirit; exhausted: *She was feeling washed-out after a day of meetings.*

washed–up ['wɒʃt 'ʌp] *adj. Informal.* **1** no longer able to function; failed; finished: *After three unsuccessful films, he is probably washed-up as a director.* **2** fatigued; washed-out.

wash•er ['wɒʃər] *n.* **1** a person who or thing that washes, especially an automatic washing machine. **2** a flat ring of metal, rubber, leather, etc. used to protect surfaces held by bolts or nuts, to seal joints, to reduce friction, etc.

wash•er•wom•an ['wɒʃər,wʊmən] *n., pl.* **-wom•en** [,wɪmən]. a woman whose work is washing clothes and linens; laundress.

wash•ing ['wɒʃɪŋ] *n., v.* —*n.* **1** clothes or linens that have been washed or are to be washed; laundry; WASH¹ (def. 2).
2 Sometimes, **washings,** *pl.* material obtained in washing something: *washings of gold obtained from earth.* **3** the act of a person who or thing that cleans with water.
—*v.* ppr. of WASH¹.

washing machine a machine for washing clothes, etc.

washing soda a crystalline form of sodium carbonate, used dissolved in water for washing clothes, etc.

Wash•ing•ton ['wɒʃɪŋtən] *n.* **1** a northwestern state of the United States. **2** the capital of the United States, situated in the District of Columbia.

Washington pie a Boston cream pie having jam instead of custard between the layers.

Washington treaty OREGON TREATY.

wash•out ['wɒʃ,ʌut] *n.* **1** a washing away of earth, a road, etc. by rainfall, a flood, or other sudden rush of water. **2** the hole or break made by such action. **3** *Slang.* an utter failure: *The party was a complete washout. He turned out to be a washout as a sales rep.*

wash•rag ['wɒʃ,ræg] *n.* a washcloth.

wash•room ['wɒʃ,rum] *or* ['wɒʃ,rʊm] *n.* **1** a room equipped with a toilet and sink, especially such a room in a public building: *Most restaurants and gas stations have washrooms for their customers.* **2** especially in industry, a room for washing fabrics or other materials that are being processed.

wash sale *Esp. U.S.* the illegal practice of buying and selling the same stocks in order to create a false impression of market activity.

wash•stand ['wɒʃ,stænd] *n.* **1** a stand for holding a washbowl, pitcher, etc. for washing. **2** a small basin or sink with pipes and taps for running water to wash one's hands and face.

wash•tub ['wɒʃ,tʌb] *n.* a tub or large, deep, usually square sink, used to wash or soak laundry in.

wash•wom•an ['wɒʃ,wʊmən] *n., pl.* **-wom•en** [,wɪmən]. See WASHERWOMAN.

wash•y ['wɒʃi] *adj.* **wash•i•er, wash•i•est. 1** too watery or thin: *washy tea.* **2** too weak; not having enough colour, substance, or force; insipid: *washy colours, washy poetry.*

was•n't ['wʌzənt] was not.

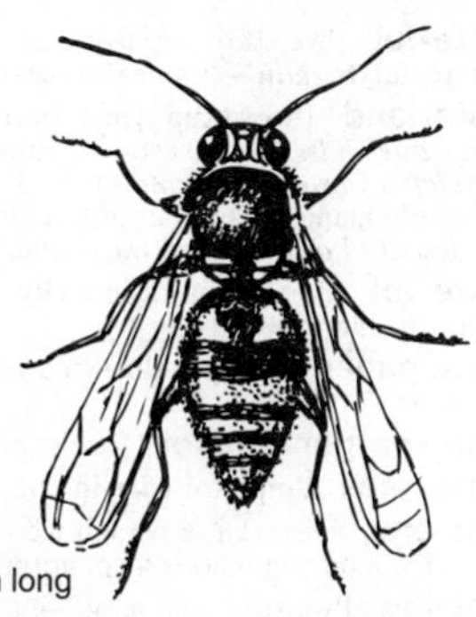

A wasp, about 18 mm long

wasp [wɒsp] *n.* **1** any of numerous winged insects (order Hymenoptera, especially family Vespidae) having biting mouthparts, a slender body with the abdomen attached to the thorax by a thin stalk, and, in the females and workers, a powerful sting. Some species of wasps live in colonies, but most do not. Wasps belong to the same order as bees, ants, and sawflies. A hornet is a type of wasp. **2** a person who is irritable or petulant for no apparent reason. ⟨OE *wæsp*⟩ —**'wasp,like,** *adj.*

wasp•ish ['wɒspɪʃ] *adj.* **1** of or like a wasp. **2** having a wasplike slim waist. **3** irritable or snappish: *a waspish temper.* —**'wasp•ish•ly,** *adv.* —**'wasp•ish•ness,** *n.*

wasp waist a very slender waist. —**'wasp-,waist•ed,** *adj.*

wasp•y ['wɒspi] *adj.* **-i•er, -i•est. 1** like a wasp. **2** waspish.

was•sail ['wɒsəl], ['wɒseil], [wɒ'seil], *or* ['wæsəl] *n., v., interj.* —*n.* **1** a drinking party; revel with drinking of healths, especially during the Christmas season. **2** spiced ale or other liquor drunk at a wassail. **3** an old English toast meaning "Your health!"
—*v.* **1** take part in a wassail; revel. **2** drink to the health of.
—*interj.* "Your health!" ⟨ME *wassayl* < ON *ves heill* be healthy! Cf. OE *wes hāl*⟩ —**'was•sail•er,** *n.*

Wassermann test a test for syphilis, made on a sample of a person's blood or spinal fluid. ⟨< August von *Wassermann* (1866-1925), a German physician who invented this test⟩

wast [wʌst]; *unstressed,* [wəst] *v. Archaic or poetic.* 2nd pers. sing., past indicative of BE. *Thou wast* means *you* (sing.) *were.*

wast•age ['weistɪdʒ] *n.* **1** loss by use, wear, decay, leakage, etc.; especially, preventable loss of something useful or valuable; waste. **2** the material or amount wasted.

waste [weist] *v.* **wast•ed, wast•ing;** *n., adj.* —*v.* **1** make poor use of; spend uselessly; fail to get value from: *Don't waste time or money.* **2** wear or be worn down little by little; destroy or be destroyed or lose gradually: *The sick man was wasted by disease. She was wasting before our very eyes.* **3** damage greatly; destroy: *The soldiers wasted the enemy's fields.*
—*n.* **1** poor use; useless spending; failure to get the most out of something. **2** useless or worthless material; stuff to be thrown away: *Garbage or sewage is waste.* **3** bare or wild land; desert; wilderness. **4** a wearing down little by little; gradual destruction or loss. **5** that which is excreted from the body. **6** destruction or devastation caused by war, floods, fires, etc. **7** a vast, dreary, desolate, or empty expanse or tract, as of water or snow-covered land. **8** material left over or rejected during the manufacture of textiles, used to wipe off oil, dirt, etc.
go to waste, be wasted.
—*adj.* **1** thrown away as useless or worthless. **2** left over; not used. **3** not cultivated; that is a desert or wilderness; bare; wild. **4** in a state of desolation or ruin. **5** carrying off or holding refuse: *a waste drain.* **6** unused by or unusable to, and therefore excreted by, an animal or human body.
lay waste, damage greatly; destroy; ravage: *The invading army laid waste the countryside.* ⟨ME < ONF *waster,* var. of OF *guaster* < L *vastare* lay waste < *vastus* vast, waste; influenced in OF by cognate Gmc. word⟩
☛ *Hom.* WAIST.

waste•bas•ket ['weist,bæskɪt] *n.* a basket or other open container for waste paper, etc.

waste•ful ['weistfəl] *adj.* using or spending too much. **—'waste•ful•ly,** *adv.* **—'waste•ful•ness,** *n.*

waste•land ['weist,lænd] *n.* **1** barren, uncultivated land: *desert wastelands.* **2** a devastated, ruined region: *The advancing troops left a wasteland behind them.* **3** anything that has been improperly managed or is unproductive or barren: *Television has been described as a cultural wasteland.*

waste lot *n.* a vacant lot in a city, especially one neglected and left to run to weeds.

waste paper *n.* paper thrown away or to be thrown away as useless or worthless.

waste•pa•per basket ['weist,peipər] See WASTEBASKET.

waste pipe a pipe for carrying off waste water, etc.

wast•er ['weistər] *n.* a person who or thing that wastes; especially, a person who is a spendthrift.

wast•ing ['weistɪŋ] *adj., n., v.* *—adj.* **1** gradually destructive to the body: *Tuberculosis is a wasting disease.* **2** laying waste; devastating.
—n. the act of a person who or thing that wastes.
—v. ppr. of WASTE.

wast•rel ['weistrəl] *n.* **1** a waster. **2** a good-for-nothing.

wa•tap [wɑ'tɑp] *n. Cdn.* fibrous roots, especially of the spruce, once much used by First Nations people for sewing birchbark canoes, for weaving watertight bowls and dishes, and for other purposes. Also, **watape, wattape, wattap.** ⟨< Algonquian; cf. Ojibway *watapi*⟩

watch [wɒtʃ] *v., n.* *—v.* **1** look attentively or carefully; observe closely: *The medical students watched while the doctor performed the operation.* **2** look at; observe; view: *to watch a play.* **3** look or wait with care and attention; be on the alert (for): *The boy watched for a chance to cross the busy street.* **4** keep guard: *She watched throughout the night.* **5** keep guard over; guard: *The dog watched the child.* **6** stay awake for some purpose: *The nurse watched with the patient.* **7** maintain an interest in; regard mentally; follow or keep track of: *to watch one's children growing up, to watch the stock markets.*
watch oneself, be careful, discreet, and restrained.
watch out, be careful; be on guard.
watch over, guard or supervise; protect or preserve from danger, harm, error, etc.
—n. **1** a careful looking; attitude of attention: *Be on the watch for cars when you cross the street.* **2** a protecting; a guarding: *A security guard keeps watch over the bank at night.* **3** formerly, a person or persons kept as a guard: *The man's cry aroused the town watch, who came running to his aid.* **4** a period of time for guarding: *a watch in the night.* **5** a staying awake for some purpose. **6** a spring-driven or electronic device for indicating time, small enough to be carried in a pocket or worn on the wrist. **7** *Nautical.* **a** the time of duty of one part of a ship's crew. A watch usually lasts four hours. **b** the part of a crew on duty at one time.
watch and ward, a the act of guarding. **b** continuous watch; vigil. ⟨OE *wæccan*⟩ **—'watch•er,** *n.*

watch•band ['wɒtʃ,bænd] *n.* a band or strap of leather, metal, etc. for holding a wristwatch on the wrist.

watch•case ['wɒtʃ,keis] *n.* the outer covering for the works of a watch.

watch chain a chain attached to a watch and fastened to one's clothing or worn around one's neck.

watch•dog ['wɒtʃ,dɒg] *n.* **1** a dog kept to guard property. **2** a watchful guardian; a person or organization whose mandate is to keep guard against immoral or unethical behaviour, practices, etc.: *a consumer watchdog.*

watch fire a fire kept burning at night in camps, etc.

watch•ful ['wɒtʃfəl] *adj.* watching carefully; on the lookout; alert and vigilant: *a watchful guard. He is watchful of his health.* **—'watch•ful•ly,** *adv.* **—'watch•ful•ness,** *n.*

☛ *Syn.* **Watchful,** VIGILANT, ALERT = wide-awake and attentive or on the lookout for something good or harmful. **Watchful** is the general word, particularly suggesting paying close attention and observing carefully or keeping careful guard: *She is watchful of her children.* **Vigilant** suggests being constantly and keenly watchful for a definite reason or purpose, especially to see and avoid danger: *The new mayor is vigilant against attempts to take advantage of her lack of experience.* **Alert** emphasizes being wide-awake and ready to meet what comes: *The alert driver avoided an accident.*

watching brief **1** a brief directing a lawyer to observe proceedings on a client's behalf. **2** any position or task involving similar watchfulness.

watch•ma•ker ['wɒtʃ,meikər] *n.* a person who makes and repairs watches and clocks. **—'watch,making,** *n.*

watch•man ['wɒtʃmən] *n., pl.* **-men.** a person who keeps watch; guard: *A watchman guards the grounds at night.*

watch night New Year's Eve, observed in some Christian churches with social gatherings and religious services which last until the arrival of the new year.

watch pocket a small pocket for holding a watch.

watch•tow•er ['wɒtʃ,taʊər] *n.* a tower from which watch is kept for enemies, fires, ships, etc.

watch•word ['wɒtʃ,wɜrd] *n.* **1** a secret word that allows a person to pass a guard; password: *We gave the watchword, and the sentinel let us pass.* **2** a motto; slogan: *"Truth" is our watchword.*

wa•ter ['wɑtər] *n., v.* *—n.* **1** the liquid that falls as rain and makes up the seas, lakes, and rivers, and that is also the main constituent of all living matter. Pure water is a transparent, colourless, odourless, tasteless compound of hydrogen and oxygen (H_2O) that can be converted into steam by heating it to 100°C and into ice by cooling it to 0°C. **2** a body of water; a sea, river, lake, etc.: *He lived across the water from them.* **3** (*adjl.*) found or living in or near water: *water rodents, water lilies, waterfowl.* **4** (*adjl.*) in, on, using, or operated by means of water: *water sports, water power, water transport, water colour.* **5 waters,** *pl.* **a** a particular part of the ocean, a lake, etc.: *fishing in Canadian waters, the upper waters of the St. Lawrence, warm Pacific waters.* **b** mineral or spring water, as at a spa: *to take the waters.* **6** the water of a river, etc. with reference to the tide: *high or low water.* **7** the surface of a body of water: *to swim under water.* **8 a** a liquid containing water: *rose water, soda water.* **b** a liquid resembling water: *When you cry, water runs from your eyes.* **9** *Jewellery.* the degree of clearness and brilliance of a precious stone. A diamond of the first water is a very clear and brilliant one. **10** *Business.* additional shares or securities issued without a corresponding increase of capital or assets, so that the book value of the company's capital is inflated. **11** the amnion, the fluid-filled sac enclosing a fetus, or the fluid itself: *When her water broke, she called her midwife.*
back water, a make a boat go backward. **b** reverse one's course; withdraw from a position, claim, etc.
by water, by means of a ship or boat: *She would rather travel by water than by air.*
hold water, pass the test; be shown to be consistent, logical, effective, etc.: *That argument won't hold water.*
keep (one's) **head above water,** keep out of trouble or difficulty, especially financial difficulty: *Business is so bad that he is finding it hard to keep his head above water.*
like water, very freely or recklessly: *to spend money like water. Blood flowed like water.*
make or **pass water,** urinate.
make water, of a boat, ship, etc., take in water through leaks or over the side.
of the first or **purest water,** of the highest quality or most extreme degree: *a musical composition of the first water. He is a bungler of the first water.*
throw or **pour cold water on,** actively discourage or belittle: *She didn't tell her friends her scheme because she knew they'd throw cold water on it.*
tread water, a keep afloat in the water, with the body upright and the head above the surface, by slowly moving the legs as if bicycling. **b** maintain one's position in the face of adversity.
water under the bridge or **over the dam,** something done and finished with.
—v. **1** sprinkle or wet with water: *to water the grass.* **2** provide with water to drink: *to water the horses.* **3** supply water to (a region, etc.): *British Columbia is well watered by rivers and streams.* **4** fill with or discharge water: *Her mouth watered when she saw the cake. Strong sunlight can make your eyes water.* **5** weaken by adding water; adulterate with water. **6** get or take in a supply of water: *A ship waters before sailing.* **7** of animals, drink water: *The cattle usually watered at the creek.* **8** make a wavy pattern on: *to water silk.* **9** *Business.* increase (stock, etc.) by issuing additional shares or securities without a corresponding increase in capital or assets.
make (someone's) **mouth water,** arouse an appetite or desire (for something): *a sports car to make your mouth water.*
water down, a reduce in strength by diluting with water: *We watered down the punch because it was too strong.* **b** reduce the effectiveness or force of by altering; weaken: *The original bill had been watered down before being presented to Parliament.* ⟨OE *wæter*⟩ **—'wa•ter•er,** *n.*

water arum CALLA (def. 1).

Water Bearer *Astronomy. Astrology.* Aquarius.

water bed a bed having a mattress that is a padded,

water-filled plastic bag supported at the bottom and on all four sides by a wooden frame.

water beetle any of numerous beetles belonging to several different families, all having broad, fringed hind legs well adapted for swimming. Water beetles are found in freshwater streams and lakes.

water bird a bird that swims or wades in water.

water biscuit a thin, crisp, crackerlike biscuit, made from flour and water, often served with cheese.

water blister a blister containing a clear, watery fluid rather than blood.

water boatman any of various bugs (family Corixidae) that live in water and have paddlelike legs used in swimming.

water bomber an aircraft equipped with special tanks filled with water, used for fighting forest fires. **—water bombing.**

wa•ter–borne ['wɒtər ˌbɔrn] *adj.* **1** supported, carried, or transmitted by water; floating. **2** conveyed by a boat or the like.

water bottle a bottle, rubberized bag, etc. for holding water.

water brash [bræʃ] *n.* heartburn.

wa•ter•buck ['wɒtər,bʌk] *n.* any of several large African antelopes (genus *Kobus*) found near rivers and in marshy areas. ⟨< Du. *waterbok*⟩

water buffalo the common buffalo (*Bubalus bubalis*) of S Asia and the Philippines, having large, spreading horns. The water buffalo is used as a draft animal.

water bug **1** CROTON BUG. **2** WATER BOATMAN.

Water Carrier *Astronomy. Astrology.* Aquarius.

water chestnut **1** a Chinese sedge (*Eleocharis tuberosa*) having a button-shaped, edible tuber. **2** the tuber of this plant, used especially in Chinese cooking. **3** a floating, aquatic, Old World plant (*Trapa natans*) of the evening-primrose family having an edible, nutlike fruit.

water clock an instrument for measuring time by the flow of water.

water closet **1** a room or compartment having a toilet with a bowl that can be flushed with water. **2** the toilet itself. *Abbrev.*: W.C. or w.c.

water colour or **color** **1** paint mixed with water instead of oil. **2** the art or skill of painting with water colours: *He is good at water colour.* **3** a picture painted with water colours. Also, **watercolour.**

wa•ter–col•our or **wa•ter–col•or** ['wɒtər ˌkʌlər] *adj.* made with paint mixed with water instead of oil: *a water-colour painting.* Also, **watercolour.**

water cooler a device for cooling and, usually, dispensing drinking water.

wa•ter•course ['wɒtər,kɔrs] *n.* **1** a stream of water; a river or brook. **2** a natural or artificial channel for water; a stream bed, canal, etc.

wa•ter•craft ['wɒtər,kræft] *n.* **1** skill in handling boats or in water sports. **2** any ship or boat. **3** boats and ships collectively.

wa•ter•cress ['wɒtər,krɛs] *n.* a perennial plant (*Nasturtium officinale*) of the mustard family that grows in running water and has crisp leaves often used in salads, sandwiches, etc.

water cure the treatment of disease by the use of water; hydropathy; hydrotherapy.

water dog **1** a dog that swims well, especially one that retrieves game from water. **2** *Informal.* a person at home on or in the water, such as a sailor or a good swimmer. **3** MUD PUPPY.

wa•ter•fall ['wɒtər,fɒl] *n.* a stream or river falling over a cliff or down a very steep hill; cataract.

water flea any of numerous tiny aquatic crustaceans (order Cladocera) that swim with a skipping motion, by means of branched antennae.

wa•ter•fowl ['wɒtər,faʊl] *n.* **-fowl** (*esp. collectively*) or **-fowls.** **1** a water bird, especially one that swims. **2** swimming game birds as a group, as opposed to shore birds, etc.

wa•ter•front ['wɒtər,frʌnt] *n.* **1** the part of a city, town, etc. beside a river, lake, or harbour. **2** land at the water's edge. **3** (*adjl.*) of, having to do with, or on the waterfront: *a waterfront hotel.*

water gap a gap in a mountain ridge through which a stream flows.

water gas a poisonous gas used for fuel or lighting, consisting of carbon monoxide and hydrogen with small amounts of methane, carbon dioxide, and nitrogen. It is produced by passing steam over very hot coal or coke.

water gate **1** a gate that controls the flow of water; floodgate. **2** a gate giving access to a river, etc., as at a landing.

wa•ter•glass ['wɒtər,glæs] *n.* sodium or potassium silicate, a substance used especially to coat eggs in order to preserve them. Also, **water glass.**

water glass a glass to hold water; tumbler.

water gun WATER PISTOL.

water hemlock any of a number of poisonous plants of the genus *Cicuta*, especially *C. maculata*, having lacy leaves and umbelliferous clusters of small white flowers, and growing in wet or swampy ground.

water hen **1** MOORHEN (def. 2). **2** the American coot (*Frulica americana*). See COOT.

water hole **1** a hole in the ground where water collects; small pond or pool. **2** a hole in the frozen surface of a body of water. **3** a source of drinking water, as a spring in the desert. **4** WATERING PLACE.

water ice **1** a confection or dessert consisting of a frozen mixture of water, sugar, and flavouring. **2** solid ice formed by the direct freezing of water, as distinct from the compacting of snow.

watering can a container with a handle and a spout, often ending in a flared perforated cap, for sprinkling or pouring water on plants, etc.

watering hole **1** *Informal.* a bar, nightclub, etc., where alcoholic beverages are served. **2** WATER HOLE (def. 3) or WATERING PLACE (def. 1).

watering place **1** a place where water may be obtained, especially a pool, a part of a stream, etc. where animals go to drink. **2** *Informal.* WATERING HOLE (def. 1). **3** a spa or health resort, usually near a lake, the sea, or mineral springs.

watering pot WATERING CAN.

water jacket a casing with water or other liquid in it, surrounding something to keep it at a certain temperature; especially, in an internal-combustion engine, the part of the cylinder block that contains the coolant.

water jump a water-filled ditch, a stream, or a channel that a horse must clear in a steeplechase or Grand Prix event.

wa•ter•less ['wɒtərlɪs] *adj.* **1** not having water; dry. **2** not needing or using water: *waterless cookware.*

water level **1** the surface level of a body of water. **2** WATER TABLE. **3** waterline; WATERMARK (def. 1).

water lily **1** any of a family (Nymphaeaceae) of water plants found in temperate and tropical parts of the world, having floating leaves and showy, fragrant flowers. The stems of a water lily grow from thick, creeping underground stems buried in the mud at the bottom of a pond, etc. **2** the flower of any of these plants.

Water lilies

wa•ter•line ['wɒtər,laɪn] *n.* **1** the line where the surface of the water touches the side of a ship or boat. **2** any of several lines marked on a ship's hull to show the depth to which it sinks when unloaded, partly loaded, or fully loaded. **3** a line or mark showing how high water has risen or may rise; WATERMARK (def. 1).

wa•ter–logged ['wɒtər ˌlɒgd] *adj.* **1** of a boat, etc., so full of water that it will barely float. **2** completely soaked with water. Also, **waterlogged.**

Wa•ter•loo [ˌwɒtər'lu] *n.* any decisive or crushing defeat: *She has met her Waterloo and will not run for election again. His first international tennis competition turned out to be his Waterloo.* ⟨< *Waterloo*, a town in central Belgium, where Napoleon was finally defeated in 1815 by the allied armies under Wellington and Blücher⟩

water main a main conduit in a system of water pipes.

wa•ter•man ['wɒtərmən] *n., pl.* **-men.** **1** a boatman, especially one who rents out boats. **2** an oarsman.

wa•ter•mark ['wɒtər,mɑrk] *n., v.* *—n.* **1** a mark showing how high water has risen or may rise. **2** **a** a faint mark produced on some paper by pressure of a projecting design during manufacture, indicating the maker, etc. The watermark may be seen by holding the paper up to the light. **b** the design. *—v.* put a watermark on: *Fine writing paper is often watermarked.*

wa•ter•mel•on ['wɒtər,mɛlən] *n.* **1** a large, oblong or roundish edible fruit having sweet, juicy, red, pink, or yellowish pulp with seeds scattered through it and a hard, thick green rind. **2** the trailing vine (*Citrullus vulgaris*) it grows on. The watermelon, which is native to Africa, is a member of the gourd family.

water meter a device that registers the quantity of water supplied to a house, etc. through a water supply system.

water milfoil any of a genus (*Myriophyllum*) of submerged or floating aquatic plants having whorls of finely divided leaves and tiny flowers. Some species are cultivated in ponds and aquariums.

water mill a mill whose machinery is run by water power.

water moccasin 1 a large, dark-coloured, poisonous snake (*Agkistrodon piscivorus*), a kind of pit viper most often found in the swamps and rivers of the S United States. **2** any of various similar but harmless snakes, especially a **water snake.**

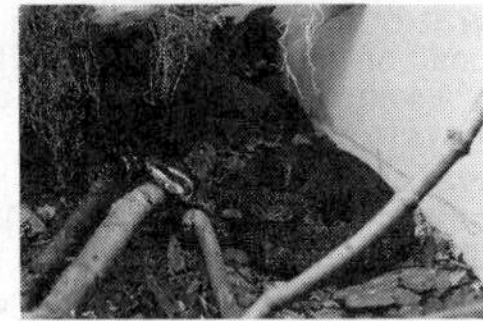

A water moccasin

water nymph 1 a nymph or goddess associated with some body of water. **2** a nymph supposed to live in water.

water of crystallization *Chemistry.* water that is a constituent of certain crystalline substances and that usually is necessary to maintain a particular crystalline structure. When water of crystallization is removed by heating, the crystals usually break up into a powder.

water ouzel DIPPER (def. 2).

water parsnip any of a genus (*Sium*) of marsh plants of the parsley family having primately compound leaves.

water pipe 1 a pipe for conveying water. **2** hookah.

water pistol a toy gun designed to shoot a jet of water.

water polo a game played in a swimming pool by two teams of seven players each who try to throw or push a round inflated ball into the opponents' goal.

water power 1 the power from flowing or falling water, used to drive machinery and make electricity. **2** a fall in a stream that can supply power.

wa•ter•proof ['wɒtər,pruf] *adj., n., v.* —*adj.* that will not let water through; sealed, or treated or coated with something so as to keep water out: *a waterproof tarpaulin, a waterproof watch.*
—*n.* **1** a waterproof material. **2** *Esp. Brit.* a raincoat.
—*v.* make waterproof.

wa•ter•proof•ing ['wɒtər,prufɪŋ] *n., v.* **1** any substance used to make something waterproof: *The waterproofing is wearing off my raincoat, and I got quite wet.* **2** the act or process of making something waterproof.
—*v.* ppr. of WATERPROOF.

water rat 1 a large vole (*Arvicola terrestris*) found along the banks of streams and lakes in Europe and Asia. **2** *Cdn.* a muskrat. **3** any of various semi-aquatic rodents (subfamily Hydromyinae of family Muridae) of Australia, New Guinea, and the Philippines. **4** *Slang.* a waterfront petty thief or ruffian.

wa•ter–re•pel•lent ['wɒtər rɪ,pɛlənt] *adj.* resistant to water; that repels water but is not waterproof: *Most raincoats are water-repellent but those treated or coated with rubber or plastic are waterproof.*

wa•ter–re•sis•tant ['wɒtər rɪ,zɪstənt] *adj.* water-repellant: *a water-resistant watch.*

water right the right to use the water of a given stream, lake, or other body of water.

wa•ter•shed ['wɒtər,ʃɛd] *n.* **1** a high ridge of land that divides two areas drained by different river systems; a divide. On one side of a watershed, rivers and streams flow in one direction; on the other side, they flow in a different direction. **2** the region drained by one river system. **3** an important point of division or decision; turning point: *Hitler's decision to invade Poland was one of the watersheds of 20th century history.* ⟨< *water* + *shed*[2]⟩

wa•ter•side ['wɒtər,saɪd] *n.* **1** land along the sea, a lake, a river, etc. **2** (*adjl.*) of, at, or on the waterside: *a waterside park.*

water ski a broad ski, usually one of a pair, for skimming over the water while being towed by a boat.

wa•ter–ski ['wɒtər ,ski] *v.* **-skied, -ski•ing.** skim over the water on water skis. —**'wa•ter-,ski•er,** *n.* —**'wa•ter-,ski•ing,** *n.*

water snake any of various snakes (family Colubridae) that live in or near water, especially any of numerous harmless snakes of the genus *Natrix.*

wa•ter–soak ['wɒtər ,souk] *v.* soak thoroughly with water.

water softener 1 a chemical added to hard water to give it more sudsing capability by dissolving and removing minerals. **2** a device using such a chemical and attached to a water supply.

wa•ter–sol•u•ble ['wɒtər ,sɒljəbəl] *adj.* capable of being dissolved in water.

water spaniel either of two breeds of spaniel, the **Irish water spaniel** or the **American water spaniel**, both having thick, curly, reddish brown hair and often trained to retrieve game birds from water.

wa•ter•spout ['wɒtər,spʌut] *n.* **1** a pipe that spouts water, or that carries it away, as from an eavestrough, and empties it somewhere else; downspout. **2** a rotating funnel-shaped or tube-shaped column of spray and water between a cloud and the surface of the ocean or of a large lake, produced by the action of a whirlwind.

water sprite a sprite supposed to live in water.

water table the level below which the ground is saturated with water.

water taxi a motorboat that transports people from place to place for a fare.

wa•ter•tight ['wɒtər,təit] *adj.* **1** so tight that no water can get in or out. Large ships are often divided into watertight compartments by watertight partitions. **2** leaving no opening for misunderstanding, criticism, etc.; perfect: *a watertight argument.*
—**'wa•ter,tight•ness,** *n.*

water torture a form of torture in which water is let fall in a steady, slow drip on the victim's forehead.

water tower 1 an elevated tank or reservoir for storing water and maintaining a steady pressure in a water supply system. **2** any of several types of firefighting equipment designed to deliver water under pressure to a nozzle at a great height for fighting fires in the upper parts of tall buildings. The original water tower was a large, vertical, telescoping steel pipe with a nozzle at the top.

water vapour or **vapor** water in a gaseous state, especially when below the boiling point and fairly diffused, as in the atmosphere. Compare STEAM.

wa•ter•way ['wɒtər,wei] *n.* **1** a river, canal, or other body of water that ships can go on. **2** a channel for water.

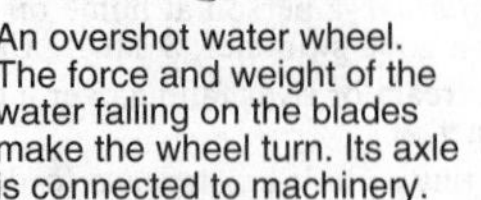

An overshot water wheel. The force and weight of the water falling on the blades make the wheel turn. Its axle is connected to machinery.

An undershot water wheel. The force of the water pushing against the blades makes the wheel turn. Its axle is connected to machinery.

water wheel 1 a wheel turned by running or falling water, used to supply power. **2** a wheel having buckets around the rim, for drawing water. **3** the paddle wheel of a steamboat.

water wings a device consisting of two air-filled floats joined together, designed to give support to a swimmer or a person learning to swim. Water wings are worn around the upper arms or under the arms, extending out behind the shoulders.

water witch a person who uses a divining rod to locate underground water sources; dowser. —**'wa•ter-,witch,** *v.* —**water witching,** *n.*

wa•ter•works ['wɒtər,wɜrks] *n.pl. or sing.* **1** a system of pipes, reservoirs, water towers, pumps, etc. for supplying a city or town with water. **2** a building containing engines and pumps for

pumping water; pumping station. **3** *Slang.* a flow of tears, especially a sudden or violent flow.
turn on the waterworks, *Slang.* begin to shed tears, weep, especially deliberately.

wa•ter•worn ['wɒtər,wɔrn] *adj.* worn or smoothed by the action of water.

wa•ter•y ['wɒtəri] *adj.* **1** too wet; soaked; sodden; soggy: *watery soil. The potatoes were overcooked and watery.* **2** of eyes, full of tears; tending to water: *The old man's eyes were watery.* **3** of a liquid, too thin; containing too much water: *watery soup, watery tea.* **4** like water in consistency or appearance: *A blister is filled with a watery fluid.* **5** weak or pale: *a watery blue, watery winter sunlight.* **6** indicating rain: *a watery sky.* **7** consisting of water: *a watery grave.* **8** uninteresting; insipid; lacking force.

watt [wɒt] *n.* an SI unit used to measure the electric power, or energy available per second, needed to send one ampere of electric current across one volt. One watt is equal to one joule of energy per second. *Symbol:* W ⟨after James *Watt* (1736-1819), a Scottish engineer and inventor⟩
☛ *Hom.* WOT.

watt•age ['wɒtɪdʒ] *n.* electric power expressed in watts: *Our new heater has a higher wattage than our old one.*

wat•tap or **wat•tape** [wɑ'tɑp] *n. Cdn.* See WATAP.

watt hour a unit of electrical energy, equal to the power of one watt maintained for one hour. A watt hour is equal to 3.6 kilojoules. *Symbol:* W•h

wat•tle ['wɒtəl] *n., v.* **-tled, -tling.** *—n.* **1** a construction of sticks interwoven with slender branches, twigs, or reeds to form a wall, fence, etc.: *a hut built of wattle.* **2** Often, **wattles,** *pl.* poles used to support a roof of thatch. **3** (*adjl.*) made or built of wattle: *a wattle roof.* **4** *Australian.* any of various acacia trees whose long, pliant branches were used by early settlers for making wattle. **5** the fleshy, wrinkled skin hanging down from the throat of certain birds. The wattle of a turkey is bright red. **6** the barbel of a fish.
—v. **1** build or form of wattle: *to wattle a fence.* **2** twist or weave together into wattle: *to wattle twigs and branches.* ⟨OE *watul*⟩

wat•tled ['wɒtəld] *adj., v. —adj.* **1** having wattles. **2** formed by interwoven twigs; interlaced.
—v. pt. and pp. of WATTLE.

watt•me•ter ['wɒt,mitər] *n.* an instrument for measuring in watts the power developed in an electric circuit.

wave [weiv] *v.* **waved, wav•ing;** *n. —v.* **1** move or cause to move back and forth or up and down from a fixed base, with a slow, sweeping or undulating motion, as in a current of air or water: *A flag waved in the breeze.* **2** make a signal or greeting with an up-and-down or back-and-forth movement of the hand or arm: *We waved until the train was out of sight.* **3** make a signal or greeting by such a movement of (something held in the hand): *She waved her handkerchief.* **4** signal or direct by waving: *He waved us away. She waved goodbye.* **5** shake in the air; brandish: *He waved the stick at them.* **6** have a wavelike form or follow a curving line: *Her hair waves naturally.* **7** give a wavelike form or pattern to: *to wave hair.*
—n. **1** the action of waving, especially as a signal or greeting: *a wave of the hand.* **2** a moving ridge or swell of water, as on the sea: *The boat rose and fell on the waves.* **3** a group or one of a series of groups advancing, swaying, etc. in a surging or swelling movement, like ocean waves: *waves of grain. A wave of new settlers followed the completion of the railway.* **4** an emotion, activity, etc. passing from one person to the next in a group: *A wave of hysteria passed through the crowd.* **5** a swell or sudden temporary increase of emotion, influence, activity, hot or cold weather, etc.; upsurge or rush: *We're having a heat wave. A wave of fear swept over him.* **6** a curve or series of curves or gentle curls: *hair set in waves.* **7** PERMANENT WAVE. **8** *Physics.* a periodic disturbance propagated through a medium or through space, in which energy is carried forward through local displacement of particles in a medium (as in a wave of water or sound) or through a change in temperature, strength of electromagnetic field, etc. (as in electromagnetic waves). **9** Often, **waves,** *pl. Poetic.* a body of water, especially the sea.
make waves, cause a stir; disturb a peaceful situation or attract attention. ⟨OE *wafian*⟩ **—'wave,like,** *adj.* **—'wav•er,** *n.*
☛ *Hom.* WAIVE.
☛ *Syn. n.* **1. Wave,** BREAKER[1], RIPPLE = a moving ridge on the surface of water. **Wave** is the general word: *The raft rose and fell on the waves.* **Breaker** applies to a heavy wave of the ocean, that breaks into foam as it nears the shore or strikes rocks: *Our favourite sport is riding the breakers in.* **Ripple** applies to a tiny wave, such as one caused by the ruffling of a smooth surface by a breeze: *There is scarcely a ripple on the lake tonight.*

wave band *Radio. Television.* a range of frequencies between certain limits.

wave front *Physics.* a surface, at right angles to a disturbance, containing adjacent points affected by the wave oscillation at the same time.

wave•length ['weiv,lɛŋθ] *n. Physics.* the distance between any point in a wave and the next point that is in the same phase, as from one peak to the next. Radio wavelengths are measured in metres.
on someone's (or **the same**) **wavelength,** *Informal.* sharing a line of thought: *He and I were just never on the same wavelength.*

wave•less ['weivlɪs] *adj.* having no waves; still.

wave•let ['weivlɪt] *n.* a little wave.

wa•ver ['weivər] *v., n. —v.* **1** move unsteadily to and fro; wobble or totter. **2** vary in intensity; flicker: *a wavering light.* **3** hesitate between choices; be undecided in opinion, direction, etc.: *She wavered, not knowing which road to take.* **4** grow fainter, then louder, or change pitch, speed, etc. up and down fairly quickly; quaver, tremble, or pulsate. **5** become unsteady; be about to give way; falter: *The battle line wavered and then broke.* **6** of things that are quantities, fluctuate; vary: *Real estate prices have wavered considerably over the last few years.*
—n. the act of wavering. ⟨ult. < *wave*⟩ **—'wa•ver•er,** *n.* **—'wa•ver•ing•ly,** *adv.*
☛ *Hom.* WAIVER.
☛ *Syn. v.* **3.** See note at HESITATE.

wa•vey ['weivi] *n. Cdn.* a wild goose, especially the snow goose. ⟨< Cdn.F < Cree⟩
☛ *Hom.* WAVY.

wav•y ['weivi] *adj.* **wav•i•er, wav•i•est. 1** having or marked by undulations or curves: *wavy hair, a wavy line.* **2** moving or proceeding in waves, or undulating curves. **—'wav•i•ness,** *n.* **—'wav•i•ly,** *adv.*
☛ *Hom.* WAVEY.

wa•wa ['wɑwɑ] *or* ['wɑwə] *n. Cdn.* See WAVEY.

wax[1] [wæks] *n., v. —n.* **1** a yellowish, pleasant-smelling substance akin to fats and oils, secreted by bees for constructing their honeycomb cells; beeswax. Wax is hard when cold, but can be easily shaped when warm; it is used for candles, modelling, etc. **2** any of various substances resembling this. Paraffin, commonly used for candles, etc., is often called wax. Sealing wax is a mixture of resin and turpentine. Scale insects secrete a kind of wax. **3** cerumen. **4** (*adjl.*) made of wax: *a wax model for a sculpture.*
be wax in (someone's) **hands,** be totally under the influence of (someone).
—v. rub or treat with wax or something like wax to polish, stiffen, condition, etc.: *We wax that floor once a month.* ⟨OE *weax*⟩ **—'wax,like,** *adj.*

wax[2] [wæks] *v.* **waxed, waxed** or (*archaic*) **wax•en, wax•ing. 1** of the moon, go through the regular increase in the size of its visible portion. The moon waxes till it becomes full and then it wanes. **2** grow bigger or greater; increase in size, strength, prosperity, numbers, etc.: *During this period her wealth waxed steadily.* **3** grow or become: *to wax indignant. The party waxed merry.* ⟨OE *weaxan*⟩

wax bean 1 a variety of garden bean having yellow pods which are used as a vegetable while still young and tender. **2** the immature pod of this bean.

wax•ber•ry ['wæks,bɛri] *n.* **1** snowberry. **2** BAYBERRY (defs. 1, 2).

wax•en[1] ['wæksən] *adj.* **1** *Archaic.* made of or covered with wax. **2** like wax in being smooth, pale, and lustrous: *a waxen skin.*

wax•en[2] ['wæksən] *v. Archaic or poetic.* a pp. of WAX[2].

wax museum a museum containing effigies in wax of famous persons, historical tableaux, etc.

wax myrtle 1 BAYBERRY (def. 1). **2** (*adjl.*) **wax-myrtle,** designating a small family (Myricaceae) of aromatic trees and shrubs found in many parts of the world. The wax-myrtle family includes the **bayberry** and **sweet gale.**

wax paper or **waxed paper** paper made water-repellent by being coated with a waxy substance such as paraffin, used mostly for wrapping food.

wax•wing ['wæks,wɪŋ] *n.* any of a small genus (*Bombycilla,* constituting the family Bombycillidae) of small, crested songbirds of the northern hemisphere, having sleek, greyish or brownish plumage, a narrow black stripe over the eye and, often, red, waxlike tips on the secondary wing feathers. See also BOHEMIAN WAXWING, CEDAR WAXWING.

wax•work ['wæks,wɜrk] *n.* **1** a figure or figures made of wax. **2 waxworks,** *pl.* an exhibition of such figures, especially one showing figures of famous or notorious people; WAX MUSEUM.

wax•y ['wæksi] *adj.* **wax•i•er, wax•i•est. 1** made of, containing, or covered with wax: *The candles left a waxy mess on the tablecloth.* **2** like wax; smooth, glossy, pale, etc.: *waxy skin. Bayberries are waxy.* **—'wax•i•ness,** *n.*

way [wei] *n., adv. —n.* **1** a manner or style: *a queer way of talking.* **2** a method or means: *Doctors are using new ways of preventing disease.* **3** a point or feature; respect; detail: *This plan is bad in several ways.* **4** a direction; a specified route: *Look this way. This is not the way to the store.* **5** movement or progress along a course: *The guide led the way.* **6** a distance: *The sun is a long way off.* **7** a road; path; street; course: *a way through the forest.* **8** a space for passing or going ahead: *Clear a way for the movers, they're bringing the furniture in.* **9** Often, **ways,** *pl.* habit; custom: *Don't mind his teasing; it's just his way.* **10** one's wish; will: *Spoiled children want their own way all the time.* **11** *Informal.* a condition; state: *That patient is in a bad way.* **12** movement; forward motion: *The ship slowly gathered way.* **13** the range of experience or notice: *The best idea that ever landed in my way.* **14** a course of life, action, or experience: *Let us choose the way of non-violence and co-operation.* **15** *Informal.* district; area; region: *She lives out our way.* **16 ways,** *pl.* the timbers on which a ship is built and launched. **17** RIGHT OF WAY (def. 2).
by the way, a along the side of the road, path, etc. **b** in that connection; incidentally.
by way of, a by the route of; through. **b** as; for: *By way of an answer he just nodded.* **c** making a profession of or having a reputation for (being or doing something): *She is by way of being a clever cartoonist.*
come (one's) **way,** meet or happen to one.
give way, a make way; retreat; yield. **b** break down or fall: *Several people were hurt when the platform gave way.* **c** abandon oneself (to emotion): *to give way to tears.*
go (one's) **way, a** depart. **b** turn out as desired.
go out of (one's or **the**) **way,** make a special effort.
have a way with (one), be persuasive: *When it comes to getting what she wants, she has a real way with her.*
in a way, to some extent; from one point of view.
in the (or one's) **way,** being an obstacle, hindrance, etc.
in the way of, a in a favourable position for doing or getting: *He put me in the way of a good investment.* **b** in the category of: *Would you have anything in the way of hedge clippers?*
in the worst way, *Informal.* to an extraordinary degree: *I need a new skirt in the worst way.*
lead the way, take the initiative; act as a guide or example.
lose (one's) **way,** not know any longer where one is or how to get to where one is going.
make (one's) **way, a** go: *They made their way through the bushes to the road.* **b** get ahead; succeed: *He's sure to make his way in the world.*
make way, a give space for passing or going ahead; make room. **b** move forward; progress.
no way, *Informal.* absolutely not.
on the (or one's) **way,** in the process of going.
once in a way, occasionally.
out of the way, a so as not to be an obstacle, hindrance, etc.: *If we take the chair out of the way, we can move the couch to that wall.* **b** far from where most people live or go; awkward to reach. **c** unusual; strange. **d** finished; taken care of: *I'd like to get this job out of the way first.* **e** out of reach; not in danger. **f** improper or wrong. **g** mislaid, hidden, or lost.
pay (one's) **way, a** pay one's fare. **b** contribute one's share.
put out of the way, put to death; kill or murder.
see (one's) **way (clear),** be willing or able: *Can you see your way clear to help with the party?*
take (one's) **way,** go.
—adv. Informal. at or to a great distance; far: *The cloud of smoke stretched way out to the pier.* ⟨OE *weg*⟩
☛ *Hom.* WEIGH, WHEY.
☛ *Syn. n.* **1, 2. Way,** METHOD, MANNER = a mode or means of doing or happening. **Way** is the common and general word, sometimes general in meaning, sometimes suggesting a very personal or special manner or method: *The way in which she spoke hurt me.* **Method** applies to an orderly way of doing something, and suggests a definite arrangement of steps or a special system: *Follow her method of cooking.* **Manner** applies to a characteristic or individual method or particular way of acting or happening: *He rides in the western manner.*
☛ *Usage.* **Way, ways.** Way, meaning distance (def. 6), is standard; **ways** is non-standard: *a long way* (not *ways*) *off.*

way•bill ['wei,bɪl] *n.* a paper listing the goods in a shipment and stating where the goods are to be shipped, by what route, and the cost involved. The waybill is sent with the shipment.

way•far•er ['wei,fɛrər] *n.* a traveller, especially one who travels on foot.

way•far•ing ['wei,fɛrɪŋ] *adj.* travelling, especially on foot.

way•laid [,wei'leid] *or* ['wei,leid] *v.* pt. and pp. of WAYLAY.

Way•land (the) Smith ['weilənd] in Germanic and English legend, a marvellously skilled elvish smith who was normally invisible.

way•lay [wei'lei] *or* ['wei,lei] *v.* **-laid, -lay•ing. 1** lie in wait for and attack; ambush: *Robin Hood waylaid and robbed rich travellers.* **2** stop (a person) on his or her way. ⟨< *way* + *lay, v.*, after MLG or MDu. *wegelagen*⟩ **—way'lay•er,** *n.*

way–out ['wei 'ʌut] *adj. Slang.* far away from the ordinary; very unconventional or experimental: *His clothes are way-out.*

–ways *suffix.* in a particular direction, position, or manner: *edgeways, sideways.* ⟨< *way*⟩

ways and means 1 the resources, methods, etc. available or used to accomplish a particular purpose, especially of some administrative body: *The plan seemed attractive but the committee still had to consider ways and means.* **2** methods, including legislation, used by a government to generate revenue.

way•side ['wei,saɪd] *n., adj. —n.* **1** the edge of a road or path. **2** *Cdn.* a railway station intermediate between major stations.
fall or **go by the wayside,** fail to continue or to be completed: *The rally weekend fell by the wayside for lack of interest.*
—adj. along the edge of a road or path.

way station 1 a station between main stations on a railway, etc. **2** any stopping place along a route.

way train a railway train that stops at all or most of the stations on its way.

way•ward ['weiwərd] *adj.* **1** tending to go against the advice, wishes, or orders of others; wrong-headed; willful. **2** irregular; unpredictable. ⟨ME *weiward,* for *aweiward* turned away⟩ **—'way•ward•ly,** *adv.* **—'way•ward•ness,** *n.*

way•worn ['wei,wɔrn] *adj.* wearied by travelling.

W.B. or **w.b.** waybill.

W.C. or **w.c.** *Brit. Informal.* WATER CLOSET.

W.C. or **W/C** WING COMMANDER.

WCC World Council of Churches.

we [wi] *pron.pl., subj.* **we,** *obj.* **us,** *poss.* **ours. 1** the speaker or writer plus the person or persons spoken or written to or about: *Bring your swimsuit so we can go to the pool. We've been invited but you haven't.* **2** the speaker or writer, thinking of himself or herself as in a formal or official role. Authors, sovereigns, judges, and newspaper editors sometimes use *we* when others would say *I.* **3** people in general, including the speaker; ONE (def. 2); YOU (def. 2): *We need some fibre in our diet.* **4** you (slightly patronizing, as to a child or invalid): *Shall we take our bath now?* ⟨OE *we*⟩
☛ *Hom.* WEE, WHEE.

weak [wik] *adj.* **1** lacking physical strength or health: *She is still weak from her illness. He realized he was too weak to move the rock.* **2** resulting from or showing lack of normal strength or health: *weak eyes. He spoke in a weak voice. She gave the door a weak push.* **3** that can too easily be broken, crushed, torn, overcome, etc.; inadequate, defective, etc.: *weak defences, a weak link in a chain, weak faith. The building collapsed because the foundation was weak.* **4** lacking authority, force, or power: *a weak government, a weak argument.* **5** lacking mental power: *a weak mind.* **6** lacking moral strength or firmness; not able to resist persuasion or temptation: *a weak character.* **7** suggesting a lack of strength: *a weak chin.* **8** containing less of the active ingredient or ingredients than is usual or desired: *a weak solution of boric acid. The tea is too weak.* **9** less strong or potent than is usual or normal: *a weak strain of a virus.* **10** lacking loudness: *a weak radio signal.* **11** lacking skill or aptitude: *The weaker students were given extra help in the subject.* **12** designating an aspect, field, etc. in which a person lacks skill or aptitude: *My weakest subject is history.* **13** lacking or poor in a particular thing: *The composition was weak in spelling, but otherwise quite good. This novel is a little weak on character development, but it has an exciting plot.* **14** *Business.* of prices on an exchange, etc.: **a** having a downward tendency; not firm. **b** characterized by a fluctuating or downward tendency: *a weak market.* **15** *Grammar.* **a** of verbs, inflected by the addition of an inflectional suffix to the stem, not by an internal vowel change, as in the Germanic languages. English weak verbs form the past tense and past participle by adding *-ed, -d,* or *-t.* **b** in Germanic languages, referring to nouns and adjectives, or their endings, following the

most regular pattern. For adjectives, this depends on the determiner used. **16** *Phonetics.* **a** of a syllable, not stressed. **b** of a stress, light; not strong. ⟨ME < ON *veikr*⟩
☛ *Hom.* WEEK.

weak•en ['wikən] *v.* **1** make weak or weaker: *You can weaken tea by adding water. The new evidence weakened the case against her.* **2** become weak or weaker: *The patient was gradually weakening. He weakened when the child began to cry.*
—'weak•en•er, *n.*

weak•fish ['wik,fɪʃ] *n., pl.* **-fish** or **-fish•es.** any of various spiny-finned marine fishes (family Sciaenidae) named for their weak mouths with easily torn flesh, especially a food and game fish (*Cynoscion regalis*) of the Atlantic coast of the United States. See also SEA TROUT.

weak force or **interaction** *Physics.* the interaction between elementary particles that causes BETA DECAY. Compare STRONG FORCE.

weak–kneed ['wik ,nid] *adj.* lacking determination or resolution; giving in easily to opposition, intimidation, etc.

weak•ling ['wiklɪŋ] *n.* a weak person or animal. ⟨< *weak* + *-ling*⟩

weak•ly ['wikli] *adv., adj.* **-li•er, -li•est.** *—adv.* in a weak manner.
—adj. weak; feeble; sickly. **—'weak•li•ness,** *n.*
☛ *Hom.* WEEKLY.

weak–mind•ed ['wik 'maɪndɪd] *adj.* **1** having or showing little intelligence; feeble-minded. **2** lacking firmness of mind.
—'weak-'mind•ed•ness, *n.*

weak•ness ['wiknɪs] *n.* **1** the condition of being weak; lack of power, force, or vigour. **2** a weak point; fault. **3** fondness: *She has a weakness for chocolate.* **4** something very difficult to resist or of which one is extraordinarily fond: *Chocolate is my weakness.*

weal[1] [wil] *n. Archaic.* well-being; prosperity; happiness: *Good citizens act for the public weal.* ⟨OE *wela*⟩
☛ *Hom.* WE'LL, WHEAL, WHEEL.

weal[2] [wil] *n.* a streak or ridge on the skin made by a stick or whip; welt. ⟨var. of *wale*⟩
☛ *Hom.* WE'LL, WHEAL, WHEEL.

weald [wild] *n.* **1** *Archaic or poetic.* country or wilderness, either open or forested. **2 the Weald,** a district in SE England including parts of Kent, Surrey, and Sussex, formerly forested. ⟨OE *weald* woods⟩
☛ *Hom.* WHEELED, WIELD.

wealth [wɛlθ] *n.* **1** much money or property; riches. **2** *Economics.* all things that have money value or that add to the capacity for production. **3** a large quantity; abundance: *a wealth of hair, a wealth of words.* ⟨< *well*[1] or *weal*[1]⟩

wealth•y ['wɛlθi] *adj.* **wealth•i•er, wealth•i•est.** having much money or property; rich. **—'wealth•i•ly,** *adv.* **—'wealth•i•ness,** *n.*
☛ *Syn.* See note at RICH.

Wealth•y ['wɛlθi] *n.* a red fall apple.

wean [win] *n.* **1** accustom (a child or young animal) to food other than its mother's milk or milk from a bottle with a nipple. **2** accustom (a person) to do without something; cause to turn away (*from*): *The young delinquent was sent away to wean him from his bad companions.* ⟨OE *wenian*⟩
☛ *Hom.* WEEN.

wean•ling ['winlɪŋ] *n., adj.* *—n.* a child or animal recently weaned.
—adj. recently weaned.

weap•on ['wɛpən] *n.* **1** any instrument or device designed or used to injure or kill, such as a sword, gun, bomb, club, or knife: *weapons of war. The murder weapon was a rock.* **2** an organ or part of an animal or plant used for fighting or protection, such as claws, horns, teeth, or stings. **3** a procedure or means used to get the better of an opponent: *Drugs are used as weapons against disease.* ⟨OE *wǣpen*⟩ **—'weap•on•less,** *adj.* **—'weap•oned,** *adj.*

weap•on•ry ['wɛpənri] *n.* **1** weapons collectively. **2** the design and production of weapons.

wear[1] [wɛr] *v.* **wore, worn, wear•ing;** *n.* *—v.* **1** have or carry on the body as clothing, adornment, etc.: *He always wears a suit to work. She was wearing pearls. He wore a sword.* **2** have habitually as part of one's person: *He wears a beard. I used to wear my hair long.* **3** carry on the body to assist or replace a natural part or organ: *She wears a hearing aid. She wore a brace on her leg.* **4** show as part of one's appearance: *wearing a grin. The old house wore an air of sadness.* **5** have as a quality or attribute; bear: *to wear one's honours modestly.* **6** of a ship, fly (a flag or colours).

7 change, make less, or damage by constant handling, using, rubbing, etc.: *These shoes are badly worn. Water had worn the stones smooth. The mountains were worn down by glacial action.* **8** suffer damage or deterioration from constant handling, using, rubbing, etc. (*often used with* **away** *or* **down**): *The cuffs of the shirt are starting to wear at the edges.* **9** produce gradually by rubbing, scraping, washing away, etc.: *I wore a hole in my shoe.* **10** tire; exhaust (*often used with* **out**): *The job was extremely wearing. A visit with him always wears me out.* **11** endure being used; last under use: *This coat has worn well. The shoes are beautiful but they won't wear.* **12** stand the test of experience, familiarity, criticism, etc.: *a friendship that did not wear.* **13** of time, pass or go gradually: *It grew hotter as the day wore on.* **14** pass (time) gradually (*used with* **away** *or* **out**): *to wear one's life away in regrets.* **15** hold the rank or office symbolized by (an ornament or article of dress): *"Uneasy lies the head that wears a crown."*
wear down, a overcome by persistent effort: *She tried to wear her parents down by asking again and again why she couldn't go.* **b** make less, smaller, lower, etc. by wearing: *The shoes were worn down at the heel.* **c** tire out or weary (someone): *She was worn down by the constant struggle of surviving poor crops and low prices.*
wear off, a gradually disappear or become less: *As the freezing wore off, my tooth started to ache.* **b** take or come off through much scraping, washing, using, etc.: *You won't be able to get that dye off your hands right away; you'll have to let it wear off.*
wear out, a wear until no longer fit for use; make useless by long or hard wear: *She wore the shoes out in six months.* **b** become useless from long or hard wear: *I don't think this coat will ever wear out.* **c** make very tired or weary.
wear thin, a become weak from being used too much: *My patience was wearing thin.* **b** become tiresome and unconvincing because of repetition: *That excuse of his is wearing thin.*
—n. **1** the act of wearing or the state of being worn: *clothing for summer wear.* **2** things worn or to be worn; clothing: *children's wear. Casual wear is sold on the second floor.* **3** damage or deterioration due to use: *The rug showed signs of wear.* **4** capacity for resisting deterioration and damage through use; lasting quality: *The shoes still have lots of wear in them.* ⟨OE *werian*⟩
—'wear•a•ble, *adj.* **—'wear•er,** *n.*
☛ *Hom.* WARE, WHERE.

wear[2] [wɛr] *v.* **wore, worn, wear•ing.** of a ship, turn or be turned so that the bow is pointing away from the wind.
☛ *Hom.* WARE, WHERE.

wear and tear damage or deterioration as a result of ordinary use over a period of time.

wea•ri•some ['wirisəm] *adj.* wearying; tiring; tiresome.
—'wea•ri•some•ly, *adv.* **—'wea•ri•some•ness,** *n.*

wea•ry ['wiri] *adj.* **-ri•er, -ri•est;** *v.* **-ried, -ry•ing.**
—adj. **1** tired: *weary feet. We were all weary after the long ride.* **2** causing tiredness; tiring: *a weary wait.* **3** having one's patience, liking, or tolerance exhausted (*used with* **of**): *She was weary of his stupid jokes.* **4** showing weariness: *a weary smile.* **5** causing impatience or dissatisfaction; tedious: *I know Dickens is a great author but I can't stand his long, weary descriptions.*
—v. make or become weary. ⟨OE *wērig*⟩ **—wea'ri•ly,** *adv.*
—'wea•ri•ness, *n.*
☛ *Syn. adj.* **1.** See note at TIRED.

wea•sand ['wizənd] *n. Archaic or dialect.* **1** windpipe. **2** throat. ⟨OE *wǣsend*⟩

A weasel

wea•sel ['wizəl] *n., v.* **-selled** or **-seled, -sel•ling** or **-sel•ing.** *—n.* **1** any of several small, carnivorous mammals (genus *Mustela*) having a long, slender body, a long, flexible neck, short legs, and short, thick fur that is mainly reddish brown above and creamy below. Northern weasels turn white in winter. **2** (*adjl.*) designating a family (Mustelidae) of carnivorous mammals that includes the weasels, minks, and otters. The weasel family is found throughout the world. **3** a sly and sneaky person.
—v. **1** use misleading or ambiguous words to avoid committing oneself or making a direct statement: *Stop weaselling and give me a straight answer.* **2** escape from or evade some responsibility in a crafty way; get out of a situation or obligation (*used with* **out**): *She had promised to help but weaselled out at the last minute.* ⟨OE *weosule*⟩ **—'wea•sel•ly,** *adj.*

weasel word Often, **weasel words,** *pl.* a word intended to soften what one says, making the message vague or confusing. ⟨prob. from the weasel's habit of sucking eggs so as to remove the yolk and white while leaving the shell intact⟩

weath•er ['wɛðər] *n., v.* *—n.* **1** the condition of the atmosphere at a particular time and place with respect to temperature, moisture, cloudiness, or windiness: *windy weather. The weather was beautiful for the entire trip.* **2** disagreeable conditions of the atmosphere, such as wind, rain, storm, or cold; bad weather: *a shelter for protection against the weather.* **3** (*adjl.*) of or designating the side of a ship toward the wind; windward.
under the weather, *Informal.* **a** somewhat sick; ailing: *He's been feeling under the weather for several days.* **b** slightly drunk.
—v. **1** expose to the weather; subject to the action of sun, rain, frost, etc.: *Wood turns grey if weathered for a long time. Many plants started indoors need to be weathered in stages before being planted outdoors.* **2** become discoloured or worn by air, rain, sun, frost, etc. **3** pass safely through (bad weather or a difficult time): *The ship weathered the storm.* **4** *Nautical.* sail to the windward of: *The ship weathered the cape.* **5** make (boards, tiles, etc.) overlap and slope downward so as to shed water. **6** resist the effects of the weather: *This paint weathers well.* ⟨OE *weder*⟩
☛ *Hom.* WETHER, WHETHER.

weather beam the side of a ship toward the wind.

weath•er–beat•en ['wɛðər ˌbitən] *adj.* worn or hardened by the wind, rain, sun, and other forces of the weather.

weath•er•board ['wɛðərˌbɔrd] *n., v.* *—n.* **1** clapboard; siding. **2** a piece of clapboard or siding. **3** the side of a ship toward the wind; weather beam.
—v. cover with weatherboard.

weath•er–bound ['wɛðər ˌbaʊnd] *adj.* delayed or immobilized by bad weather: *a weather-bound ship.*

weather breeder a fine, clear day, popularly supposed to be a sign of a coming storm.

weath•er•cock ['wɛðərˌkɒk] *n.* **1** a weather vane, especially one in the shape of a rooster. **2** someone who easily changes opinions or loyalties: *As far as his politics are concerned, he's a real weathercock.*

weather eye **1** the vision or watchful look of a person alert to signs of change in the weather. **2** a close watch for expected change of any kind: *The news media were keeping a weather eye on the labour situation.*

weath•er•glass ['wɛðərˌglæs] *n.* any of various instruments that measure atmospheric changes, especially a barometer.

weath•er•ing ['wɛðərɪŋ] *n., v.* *—n.* the destructive or discolouring action of air, water, frost, etc., especially on rocks.
—v. ppr. of WEATHER.

weath•er•man ['wɛðərˌmæn] *n., pl.* **-men.** *Informal.* **1** a person who forecasts the weather, especially a meteorologist. **2** a person who reports weather conditions and forecasts on radio or television.

weath•er•proof ['wɛðərˌpruf] *adj., v.* *—adj.* protected against rain, snow, or wind; able to stand exposure to all kinds of weather.
—v. make weatherproof.

weath•er•proof•ing ['wɛðərˌprufɪŋ] *n., v.* *—n.* a material for making something weatherproof.
—v. ppr. of WEATHERPROOF.

weather strip a narrow strip, usually of metal or thick felt, to fill or cover the space between a door or window and the casing, so as to keep out rain, snow, and wind. Also, **weatherstrip.**

weath•er–strip ['wɛðər ˌstrɪp] *v.* **-stripped, -strip•ping.** fit with weather strips.

weather stripping **1** a WEATHER STRIP or weather strips collectively. **2** material for weather strips.

weather vane a device for showing the direction of the wind, consisting of a blade or a flat cutout figure mounted on a vertical axis in an exposed place, such as the peak of a roof or spire, so that it will turn with the wind.

weath•er–wise ['wɛðər ˌwaɪz] *adj.* skilful in forecasting the changes of the weather.

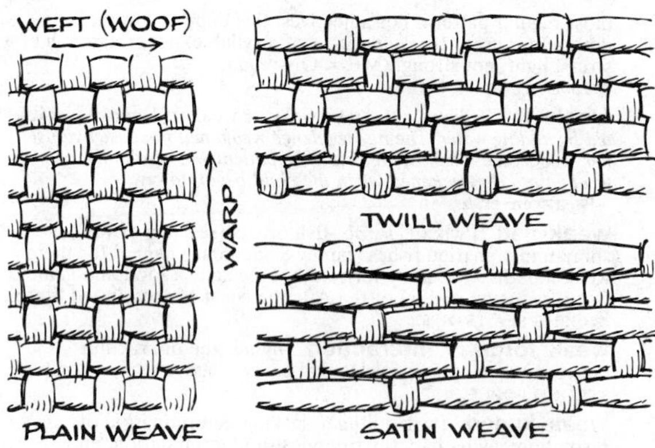

The three basic weaves for cloth

weave [wiv] *v.* **wove** or (rare) **weaved, wo•ven** or **wove, weav•ing;** *n.* *—v.* **1** form (threads or strips) into a texture or fabric; interlace. People weave thread into cloth, straw into hats, reeds into baskets. **2** make by interlacing threads or strips in this way: *She is weaving a rug.* **3** make fabric by this method; do weaving, especially on a loom. **4** combine into a whole: *The author wove three plots together into one story.* **5** make by combining parts: *The author wove a story from three plots.*
6 include or introduce deftly, so as to make seem a natural or integral part: *The author wove regionalisms into the dialogue.*
7 construct mentally by skilfully combining various elements and details: *to weave a tale. P.D. James weaves her plots with great skill and complexity, challenging the reader to follow the intricacies.*
8 proceed or cause to proceed by twisting and turning.
weave (one's) **way,** make one's way by twisting and turning.
—n. a method or pattern of weaving: *Homespun is a cloth of coarse weave.* ⟨OE *wefan*⟩
☛ *Hom.* WE'VE.
☛ *Usage.* **Woven, wove. Woven** is the usual past participle. **Wove** is now chiefly used in certain technical terms, such as *wire-wove* and *wove paper.*

weav•er ['wivər] *n.* **1** a person who weaves, especially one whose work it is. **2** weaverbird.

weav•er•bird ['wivərˌbɜrd] *n.* any of a family (Ploceidae) of Old World, seed-eating birds resembling finches, named for the elaborate woven nests made by many species.

web [wɛb] *n., v.* **web•bed, web•bing.** *—n.* **1** a woven length of fabric, especially while on the loom or as it comes off the loom. **2** a cobweb or something similar produced by any of various insects. **3** any complicated network, especially one that entangles like a cobweb: *a web of lies.* **4** the skin joining the toes of swimming birds and animals. **5** the vane of a feather. **6** a thin metal sheet or plate joining the rims of a girder, etc.
7 CONNECTIVE TISSUE. **8** **a** a continuous sheet of paper as it is being manufactured or as it emerges from the paper machine. After the water is pressed out of the web, it enters the drying section. **b** an uncut roll of paper, especially newsprint, for use in rotary presses. **9** *Cdn.* a snowshoe. **10** *Computer technology.* **the Web,** *Informal.* WORLD WIDE WEB.
—v. **1** provide or cover with a web. **2** trap or entwine in a web. ⟨OE *webb*⟩ **—'web,like,** *adj.*

webbed [wɛbd] *adj., v.* *—adj.* **1** formed like a web or with a web. **2** of feet, having the digits joined by a web. Ducks have webbed feet. **3** of digits, joined by a web: *webbed toes.*
—v. pt. and pp. of WEB.

web•bing ['wɛbɪŋ] *n., v.* *—n.* **1** cloth woven into strong strips, used in upholstery and for belts. **2** the plain foundation fabric left for protection at the edge of some rugs, etc. **3** skin joining the digits, as in a duck's feet. **4** something resembling this, as the leather connecting the thumb and forefinger of a baseball mitt.
5 any netlike structure of interlaced cords, thongs, etc. having a latticelike appearance, as the face of snowshoes, tennis rackets, etc.
—v. ppr. of WEB.

web•er ['wɛbər] *or* ['veibər] *n.* an SI unit of magnetic flux, equal to 10^8 maxwells. ⟨after Wilhelm E. *Weber* (1804-1891), German physicist⟩

web•foot ['wɛbˌfʊt] *n., pl.* **-feet. 1** a foot in which the toes are joined by a web. **2** a bird or animal having webfeet.

web–foot•ed ['wɛb ˌfʊtɪd] *adj.* having the toes joined by a web.

web–toed ['wɛb ˌtoud] *adj.* web-footed.

wed [wɛd] *v.* **wed•ded, wed•ded** or **wed, wed•ding. 1 a** marry (someone else) in a formal ceremony: *Debbie wedded her best friend Jan last Saturday.* **b** join or unite (a couple) in matrimony: *The minister who wedded them was an old family friend.* **2** unite; bind by close ties. ⟨OE *weddian*⟩

we'd [wid]; *unstressed,* [wɪd] **1** we had. **2** we would.
☛ *Hom.* WEED.

Wed. Wednesday.

wed•ded ['wɛdɪd] *adj., v. –adj.* **1 a** married. **b** of marriage or married persons: *wedded bliss.* **2** united. **3** devoted; obstinately attached (to an opinion, habit, etc.): *She was wedded to the notion that all people are equal.*
–v. pt. and a pp. of WED.

wed•ding ['wɛdɪŋ] *n., v. –n.* **1** a marriage ceremony and the subsequent celebration. **2** an anniversary of the day of marriage, especially any of several specific anniversaries, such as the 25th (silver wedding) or the 50th (golden wedding). **3** a joining or uniting: *His writing shows a remarkable wedding of thought and language.*
–v. ppr. of WED. ⟨OE *weddung*⟩
☛ *Syn.* **1.** See note at MARRIAGE.

wedge [wɛdʒ] *n., v.* **wedged, wedg•ing.** *–n.* **1** a piece of wood or metal with a tapering thin edge, used in splitting, separating, etc. **2** something tapered from a wide edge to a point: *He cut the big pie into ten wedges.* **3** a character or part of a character in cuneiform writing. **4** something used like a wedge to make an opening or opportunity: *Her constant namedropping was a wedge to get onto the Advisory Council.* **5** *Golf.* a club used for high, short shots, lofting the ball out of traps, heavy grass, etc., so called because of the shape of the club head. **6** anything that divides in some way: *Their disagreement about politics drove a wedge between the friends.*
–v. **1** split or separate with or as with a wedge. **2** brace or tighten with a wedge or something squeezed in. **3** thrust or pack in tightly; squeeze: *She wedged herself through the narrow window.* **4** force (a way): *She wedged her way through the crowd.* ⟨OE *wecg*⟩

wed•gie ['wɛdʒi] *n.* a shoe with a wedge-shaped heel and sole all in one piece.

Wedg•wood ['wɛdʒwʊd] *n.* **1** *Trademark.* a kind of fine, unglazed pottery having a raised, decorative design of white Greek and Roman figures against a tinted ground. **2** a kind of fine china. **3** something made of either the pottery or the china. ⟨after Josiah *Wedgwood* (1730-1795), the British potter who originated it⟩

wed•lock ['wɛd,lɒk] *n.* married life; marriage. ⟨OE *wedlāc* pledge < *wedd* pledge + *-lāc,* noun suffix denoting activity⟩

Wednes•day ['wɛnzdei] *or* ['wɛnzdi] *n.* the fourth day of the week, following Tuesday. ⟨OE *Wōdnes dæg* Woden's day; translation of LL *Mercurii dies* day of Mercury⟩

Wednes•days ['wɛnzdeiz] *or* ['wɛnzdiz] *adv.* every Wednesday: *They do the grocery shopping Wednesdays.*

wee [wi] *adj.* **we•er, we•est.** very small; tiny. ⟨from the phrase *a little wee* a little bit, OE *wǣg* weight⟩
☛ *Hom.* WE, WHEE.

weed[1] [wid] *n., v. –n.* **1** a wild plant growing where it is not wanted, as in grainfields, gardens, lawns, pastures, etc., especially one that grows fast and is hard to get rid of. Russian thistle, milkweed, ragweed, and wild mustard are common weeds. **2** something useless or troublesome, especially a horse unfit for racing or breeding. **3** *Informal.* a cigarette or cigar. **4** *Informal.* a marijuana cigarette. **5 the weed,** *Informal.* tobacco or marijuana.
–v. **1** take weeds out of: *to weed a garden.* **2** take out weeds: *I spent all morning weeding.* **3** remove elements seen as superfluous from: *You'll have to weed this composition thoroughly before handing it in.* **4** remove or discard as not wanted (*usually used with* **out**): *The weak players were weeded out before the regular season began.* ⟨OE *wēod*⟩ **–'weed,like,** *adj.*
☛ *Hom.* WE'D.

weed[2] [wid] *n.* **1 weeds,** *pl.* mourning garments: *a widow's weeds.* **2** *Archaic.* a garment. ⟨OE *wǣd*⟩
☛ *Hom.* WE'D.

weed•er ['widər] *n.* **1** a person who weeds. **2** a tool or machine for digging up weeds.

weed•y ['widi] *adj.* **weed•i•er, weed•i•est. 1** full of weeds: *a weedy garden.* **2** of or like a weed or weeds, especially in fast and vigorous growth. **3** thin and lanky: *a tall and weedy youth.* **–'weed•i•ly,** *adv.* **–'weed•i•ness,** *n.*

wee hours the hours after midnight; the early morning hours.

week [wik] *n.* **1** seven days, one after another. **2** the time from one Sunday through the following Saturday. **3** seven successive days specified as set aside for some particular purpose: *Christmas week.* **4** the seven days following a specified day: *the week of June 4th.* **5** the working days or hours of a seven-day period: *A school week is five days. The typical full-time work week is 40 hours.*
a week Monday (or **Tuesday**, etc.), the Monday one week from this Monday (or Tuesday, etc.).
a week today, one week from today.
week in, week out, week after week. ⟨OE *wice*⟩
☛ *Hom.* WEAK.

week•day ['wik,dei] *n.* **1** any day except Sunday or other weekly holy day in various religions. **2** any day except Saturday or Sunday. **3** (*adjl.*) of or on a weekday.

week•end ['wik,ɛnd] *n., v. –n.* **1** Saturday and Sunday and occasionally Monday or Friday in case of a holiday, as a time for recreation, visiting, etc.; the time between the end of one week of work or school and the beginning of the next: *a weekend in the country, the Monday of Thanksgiving weekend.* **2** (*adjl.*) of or on a weekend.
–v. spend a weekend: *They are weekending at their cottage.*

week•end•er ['wik,ɛndər] *n.* **1** one who spends a weekend at a holiday resort or friend's house. **2** a small suitcase capable of holding enough clothes, etc. for a weekend.

week•ly ['wikli] *adj., adv., n., pl.* **-lies.** *–adj.* **1** of a week; for a week; lasting a week: *His weekly wage is $360.* **2** done or happening once a week: *a weekly letter home.*
–adv. once each week; every week.
–n. a newspaper or magazine published once a week.
☛ *Hom.* WEAKLY.

ween [win] *v. Archaic.* think; suppose; believe; expect. ⟨OE *wēnan*⟩
☛ *Hom.* WEAN.

weep [wip] *v.* **wept, weep•ing;** *n. –v.* **1** shed tears; cry. **2** shed tears (*for*); mourn; grieve: *She wept for her dead husband.* **3** spend in crying: *to weep one's life away.* **4** let fall in drops; shed: *They wept bitter tears.* **5** put into a specified condition by shedding tears: *to weep one's eyes dry.* **6** give off (moisture) in drops; ooze or drip: *That basement wall sometimes weeps. The infected sore on his leg wept a serous fluid.*
–n. Often, **the weeps,** *pl.* a period or fit of weeping: *She has the weeps.* ⟨OE *wēpan*⟩

weep•er ['wipər] *n.* **1** a person who weeps. **2** a person hired to weep at funerals; professional mourner.

weep•ing ['wipɪŋ] *adj., v. –adj.* **1** shedding tears for; crying; mourning. **2** giving off moisture; oozing; dripping. **3** having thin, drooping branches: *a weeping fig tree.*
–v. ppr. of WEEP.

weeping birch SILVER BIRCH (def. 1).

weeping willow a large willow (*Salix babylonica*) native to E Asia, having long, feathery, drooping branches. Weeping willows are often planted as ornamental trees in Europe and North America.

weep•y ['wipi] *adj.* **-i•er, -i•est. 1** inclined to shed tears on slight provocation; tearful; lachrymose. **2** *Informal.* sad or sentimental: *a weepy book.* **3** exuding moisture.

wee•vil ['wivəl] *n.* **1** any of a family (Curculionidae) of beetles having an elongated, usually downward-curving snout called a rostrum. Many weevils are serious agricultural pests, feeding on fruit, nuts, and grains, as well as on living plants. **2** any of various other similar beetles, as of the family Bruchidae. ⟨OE *wifel*⟩

wee•vil•ly or **wee•vil•y** ['wivəli] *adj.* infested with weevils.

weft [wɛft] *n.* the threads running from side to side across a woven fabric; woof. See WEAVE for picture. ⟨OE *weft* < *wefan* weave⟩

Wehr•macht ['vɛr,mɑxt] *n. German.* the armed forces of Germany before and during World War II. ⟨< G, *defence force*⟩

weigh [wei] *v.* **1** determine the mass of by means of scales or a balance: *I weighed myself this morning.* **2** have as a measure of mass: *I weigh 50 kg. Things weigh much less on the moon than on earth.* **3** measure (a quantity of something) by mass (*usually used with* **out**): *The grocer weighed out 2 kg of potatoes.* **4** hold or balance (something) in one's hand(s) to estimate its mass. **5** balance in the mind; consider carefully so as to choose: *She weighed her words before speaking.* **6** have importance or

influence: *The amount of his salary does not weigh with Mr. Black at all, because he is very rich.* **7** have an oppressive effect: *The mistake weighed heavily upon her mind.* **8** *Nautical.* **a** lift up (an anchor). **b** lift anchor.
weigh down, a bend by weight: *The boughs of the apple tree are weighed down with fruit.* **b** burden: *She is weighed down with many troubles.*
weigh in, find out one's weight before a contest.
weigh in at, weigh (a given amount).
weigh on, be a burden to. ⟨OE *wegan*⟩ **—'weigh•er,** *n.*
☛ *Hom.* WAY, WHEY.
☛ *Syn.* **5.** See note at CONSIDER.

weigh•mas•ter ['wei,mæstər] *n.* **1** an official in charge of public weighing scales. **2** a worker in charge of registering by weight the amount of a commodity produced, mined, etc.

weigh scales scales built into a pull-off area of a highway, where loaded trucks must be weighed to determine that their loaded weight is within the legal limit for that load.

weight [weit] *n., v. —n.* **1** MASS (def. 6): *The dog's weight is 20 kg.* **2** a piece of metal having a particular mass, used to weigh something on a balance: *a 50 g weight.* **3** how heavy a thing is; the quality of anything that makes it tend toward the centre of the earth: *Gas has hardly any weight at all. Your weight is a little less on a mountain than at sea level.* **4** a system of units for expressing mass: *avoirdupois weight, troy weight.* **5** a unit of such a system. **6** a quantity that has a certain mass: *a weight of gold dust.* **7** something heavy used to hold down light things or maintain balance; something useful because of its heaviness: *A weight keeps the papers in place.* **8** a load or burden: *a weight of care. Pillars support the weight of the roof.* **9** influence or importance: *What he says carries a lot of weight around here.* **10** preponderant portion: *The weight of public opinion was against it.* **11** the relative heaviness of an article of clothing appropriate to the season's weather: *summer weight.* **12** *Statistics.* **a** a number assigned to an item in a statistical compilation, as in a cost-of-living index, to make its effect on the compilation reflect its importance. **b** the frequency of an item in a statistical compilation. **13** *Sports.* a metal ball, barbell, etc. thrown, pushed, or lifted in contests of strength. **14** a class in which contestants are placed according to their mass, especially in boxing, wrestling, weight-lifting, etc. **15** the total mass of the saddle, leads, and jockey that a horse must carry in a given race: *Secretariat was given a weight of 57.3 kg.*
by weight, as measured by weighing.
pull (one's) **weight,** do one's part or share.
throw (one's) **weight around,** *Informal.* make too much use of one's rank or position; assert one's importance improperly or excessively.
—v. **1** load down; burden. **2** add weight to; put weight on: *The scales are weighted too heavily. The drapes were weighted to prevent them from blowing apart.* **3** attach importance or value to. **4** treat (cloth or thread) with mineral to make it seem of better quality: *to weight silk.* **5** *Statistics.* give a weight to: *to weight an average.* **6** *Skiing.* direct all or most of the downward thrust onto: *to weight the left ski.* ⟨OE *wiht* < *wegan* weigh⟩
☛ *Hom.* WAIT.

weight–arm ['weit ,ɑrm] *n.* in a lever, the distance from the weight to the fulcrum.

weight•less ['weitlɪs] *adj.* **1** appearing to have no weight: *The snow was weightless on my shoulders.* **2** being free from the pull of gravity: *In outer space, all things are weightless.*
—'weight•less•ly, *adv.* **—'weight•less•ness,** *n.*

weight•y ['weiti] *adj.* **weight•i•er, weight•i•est. 1** heavy. **2** oppressively heavy; burdensome: *weighty cares of state.* **3** important; influential: *a weighty speaker.* **4** convincing: *weighty arguments.* **—'weight•i•ly,** *adv.* **—'weight•i•ness,** *n.*
☛ *Syn.* See note at HEAVY.

Wei•ma•ra•ner ['vaɪmə,rɑnər] *or* ['waɪmə,rɑnər] *n.* a breed of medium-sized hunting dog having a short, grey coat. ⟨< *Weimar,* a city in Germany, where the breed was developed⟩

wei•ner ['winər] *n.* See WIENER.

weir [wir] *n.* **1** a dam in a river to raise the level of the water or to divert its flow. **2** a fence of stakes or broken branches put in a stream or channel to catch fish. Compare POUND NET. **3** an obstruction erected across a channel or stream to divert the water through a special opening in order to measure the rate of flow. ⟨OE *wer*⟩
☛ *Hom.* WE'RE.

weird [wird] *adj.* **1** unearthly; mysterious: *They were awakened by a weird shriek. The shadows made weird figures on the wall.* **2** *Informal.* odd; eccentric; queer: *She's been pretty weird lately, ever since her marriage broke up.* **3** *Archaic or Scottish.* having to do with fate or destiny. ⟨OE *wyrd* fate⟩ **—'weird•ly,** *adv.* **—'weird•ness,** *n.*
☛ *Syn.* **1. Weird,** EERIE, UNCANNY = mysteriously or frighteningly strange. **Weird** describes something that seems not of this world or that is caused by something above or beyond nature: *All night weird cries came from the jungle.* **Eerie** suggests the frightening effect of something weird or ghostly or vaguely mysterious: *The light from the single candle made eerie shadows in the cave.* **Uncanny** suggests a strangeness that is disturbing because it seems unnatural: *I had an uncanny feeling that eyes were peering from the darkness.*

weird•o ['wir,dou] *n. Slang.* a very odd or eccentric person; a person who is very strange or unconventional in appearance or behaviour. Also called **weirdie.**

Weird Sisters 1 the Fates. **2** the witches in Shakespeare's *Macbeth.*

Weis•mann•ism ['vəismə,nɪzəm] *n. Genetics.* a theory of heredity, holding that the germ plasm carries the inheritable characteristics and that acquired characteristics cannot be passed on to the next generation. ⟨after August *Weismann* (1834-1914), German biologist⟩

welch [wɛltʃ] *or* [wɛlʃ] *v.* See WELSH.

wel•come ['wɛlkəm] *v.* **-comed, -com•ing;** *n., adj., interj. —v.* **1** greet in a friendly and kindly way: *to welcome a guest.* **2** receive gladly: *We welcome new ideas and suggestions.* **3** greet or receive in a specified way, usually unfriendly: *He was welcomed rather coldly. She welcomed us with a volley of questions.*
—n. **1** a friendly and kindly reception. *You will always have a welcome here.* **2** an expression of greeting or reception.
wear out (one's) **welcome,** visit a person too often or too long.
—adj. **1** gladly received; pleasing: *a welcome visitor, a welcome letter, a welcome rest.* **2** gladly or freely permitted: *You are welcome to pick the flowers.* **3** free to have or do something, to enjoy some favour, etc. without a feeling of indebtedness or obligation: *You are quite welcome.*
you're welcome, a reply to thanks.
—interj. an exclamation of friendly greeting: *Welcome!* ⟨original meaning 'agreeable guest', OE *wilcuma* < *wil-* (related to *will* pleasure) + *cuma* comer, contaminated by translation of *bien* well from F *bien venue* welcome⟩ **—'wel•com•er,** *n.*

welcome mat doormat.
put out the welcome mat, *Informal.* offer any enthusiastic reception or welcome.

weld [wɛld] *v., n. —v.* **1** join together (metal) by hammering or pressing while hot and soft: *She welded the broken metal rod.* **2** unite closely: *Working together for a month welded them into a strong team.* **3** be welded or be capable of being welded: *Some metals weld better than others.*
—n. **1** a welded joint. **2** an act of welding. ⟨< *well*[2], v.⟩
—'weld•er, *n.*

wel•fare ['wɛl,fɛr] *n.* **1** health, happiness, and prosperity; a condition of being or doing well: *Uncle Charles asked about the welfare of everyone in our family.* **2** WELFARE WORK.
on welfare, receiving benefits from the government or from some organization to provide a basic standard of living: *There was no harvest and many families were on welfare.* ⟨ME *wel fare* < *wel* well < *fare* go⟩

welfare state a state whose government provides for the welfare of its citizens through old-age pensions, unemployment insurance, medical treatment, etc.

welfare work work done to improve the lives and living conditions of people who need help because of poverty, sickness, family problems, etc. Welfare work is carried on by governments, private organizations, and sometimes individuals.

welfare worker a person who does WELFARE WORK.

wel•kin ['wɛlkən] *n. Archaic.* the sky: *The welkin rang with the people's shouts.* ⟨OE *wolcen* cloud⟩

well[1] [wɛl] *adv., adj.* **bet•ter, best;** *interj. —adv.* **1** in a satisfactory, favourable, or advantageous manner; all right: *You would do well to start an RRSP now. Is everything going well at school?* **2** thoroughly; fully: *Shake well before using.* **3** to a considerable degree; much: *The fair brought in well over a hundred dollars.* **4** easily or reasonably: *I couldn't very well refuse. You might well ask what he was doing there. They could well be here before dark.* **5** in a friendly or kind manner: *to treat them well.* **6** in an excellent manner: *Julia draws well.* **7** without doubt: *You know very well what I meant.*
as well, a also; besides. **b** equally.
as well as, a in addition to; besides. **b** and also: *Igor is witty as well as handsome.*
—adj. **1** satisfactory; good; right. *All is not well with their*

marriage. **2** in good health: *I am very well.* **3** desirable; advisable: *It is always well to start a bit early.*
all very well, an expression used concessively: *It's all very well for you to criticize, but can you do better?*
well and good, I am content (though not particularly excited) about that.
–interj. an expression used to show mild surprise, agreement, etc. or merely to fill in: *Well! Well! Here's Jack. Well, I'm not sure.* ⟨OE *wel*⟩
☛ *Usage.* See note at GOOD.
☛ *Spelling.* Hyphenated compounds consisting of *well* plus a participle are spelled as two separate words after a linking verb: *a well-founded faith. Your suspicions are well founded.*

well² [wɛl] *n., v. –n.* **1** a hole dug or bored in the ground to find or obtain water, oil, gas, etc. **2** a spring or other natural source of water from the earth. **3** fountain or source: *Our class president is a well of ideas.* **4** something like a well in shape or use: *the well of a fountain pen.* **5** a shaft for light, or for stairs or an elevator, extending vertically through the floors of a building. **6** a compartment around the pumps on a ship. **7** a storage compartment for fish in the hold of a fishing boat, kept filled with water to keep the catch alive.
–v. spring; rise; gush: *Tears welled in his eyes. A deep joy welled up inside her at the sight of her baby.* ⟨OE *wella,* n., *wiellan,* v.⟩

we'll [wil]; *unstressed,* [wɪl] we shall; we will.
☛ *Hom.* WEAL, WHEAL, WHEEL.

well•a•day [ˌwɛlə'dei] *interj. Archaic.* See WELLAWAY.

well–ad•just•ed ['wɛl ə'dʒʌstɪd] *adj.* of persons, emotionally balanced and mature; able to cope with stress and change.

well–ad•vised ['wɛl əd'vaɪzd] *adj.* **1** proceeding with wisdom, care, or deliberation. **2** based on wise counsel or prudence.

well–ap•point•ed ['wɛl ə'pɔɪntɪd] *adj.* having good furnishings or equipment.

well•a•way [ˌwɛlə'wei] *interj. Archaic.* alas!

well–bal•anced ['wɛl 'bælənst] *adj.* **1** rightly balanced, adjusted, or regulated. **2** sensible; sane.

well–be•haved ['wɛl bɪ'heivd] *adj.* showing good manners or conduct.

well–be•ing ['wɛl 'biɪŋ] *n.* health and happiness; welfare.

well•born ['wɛl'bɔrn] *adj.* belonging to a socially respected family.

well–bred ['wɛl 'brɛd] *adj.* **1** well brought up; having or showing good manners. **2** of animals, of good stock or pedigree.

well–con•nect•ed ['wɛl kə'nɛktɪd] *adj.* **1** of a well-known family; related to important or distinguished people. **2** put together well; carefully planned: *well-connected paragraphs.*

well–con•tent ['wɛl kən'tɛnt] *adj.* highly pleased or satisfied. Also, **well-contented.**

well–de•fined ['wɛl dɪ'faɪnd] *adj.* clearly defined or indicated; distinct.

well–dis•posed ['wɛl dɪs'pouzd] *adj.* favourably or kindly disposed; having sympathetic or friendly feelings.

well–do•ing ['wɛl 'duɪŋ] *n.* the act of doing right; good conduct.

well–done ['wɛl 'dʌn] *adj.* **1** performed or executed with skill and efficiency. **2** of meat, thoroughly cooked.

well–fa•voured or **well–fa•vored** ['wɛl 'feivərd] *adj.* of pleasing appearance; good-looking.

well–fed ['wɛl 'fɛd] *adj.* showing the result of good feeding; fat; plump.

well–fixed ['wɛl 'fɪkst] *adj. Informal.* WELL-TO-DO.

well–found ['wɛl 'faʊnd] *adj.* supplied or equipped with what is needed.

well–found•ed ['wɛl 'faʊndɪd] *adj.* rightly or justly founded: *a well-founded faith in discipline.*

well–groomed ['wɛl 'grumd] *adj.* well cared for; neat and trim: *She always presents a well-groomed appearance, even though the house is a mess.*

well–ground•ed ['wɛl 'graʊndɪd] *adj.* **1** based on good reasons. **2** thoroughly instructed in the fundamental principles of a subject.

well•head ['wɛlˌhɛd] *n.* **1** the source of a spring or stream; fountainhead. **2** the top of a well or a structure built around it.

well–heeled ['wɛl 'hild] *adj. Slang.* prosperous; well-to-do.

wel•lies ['wɛliz] *n.pl. Brit. Informal.* WELLINGTON BOOTS (def. 2).

well–in•formed ['wɛl ɪn'fɔrmd] *adj.* **1** having reliable or full information on a subject. **2** having information on a wide variety of subjects.

Wellington boot or **Wel•ling•ton** ['wɛlɪŋtən] *n.* **1** a very high leather boot that comes above the knee in front and is cut away behind. **2** a rubber boot coming nearly up to the knees. Also, **wellington.** ⟨worn by the first Duke of *Wellington* (1769-1852), a British general⟩

well–kept ['wɛl 'kɛpt] *adj.* well cared for; carefully tended.

well–knit ['wɛl 'nɪt] *adj.* **1** firmly constructed or joined together; closely connected or linked. **2** of a person's body, of strong, supple build; well-built.

well–known ['wɛl 'noun] *adj.* fully or widely known.

well–man•nered ['wɛl 'mænərd] *adj.* having or showing good manners; polite; courteous.

well–marked ['wɛl 'mɑrkt] *adj.* clearly marked or distinguished; distinct.

well–mean•ing ['wɛl 'minɪŋ] *adj.* **1** having good intentions. **2** proceeding from good intentions. Also, **well-meant.**

well•ness ['wɛlnɪs] *n.* the state or condition of being maximally healthy, physically or mentally.

well–nigh ['wɛl 'naɪ] *adv.* very nearly; almost.

well–off ['wɛl 'ɒf] *adj.* **1** in a good condition or position: *Your whole family is healthy, so you should consider yourself well-off.* **2** fairly rich; prosperous.

well–or•dered ['wɛl 'ɔrdərd] *adj.* ordered or arranged well; well-regulated.

well–placed ['wɛl 'pleist] *adj.* **1** well aimed. **2** conveniently placed; accessible. **3** having a good official or social position.

well–pre•served ['wɛl prɪ'zɜrvd] *adj.* showing few signs of age or use.

well–pro•por•tioned ['wɛl prə'pɔrʃənd] *adj.* having good or correct proportions; having a pleasing shape.

well–read ['wɛl 'rɛd] *adj.* having read much; knowing a great deal about books and literature.

well–round•ed ['wɛl 'raʊndɪd] *adj.* **1** properly balanced, as a program or education. **2** having a variety of interests or attainments. **3** fully developed.

well–spo•ken ['wɛl 'spoukən] *adj.* **1** speaking well, fluently, or pleasingly; polite in speech. **2** spoken well, fittingly or justly.

well•spring ['wɛlˌsprɪŋ] *n.* **1** fountainhead. **2** a source, especially of a supply that never fails.

well–suit•ed ['wɛl 'sutɪd] *adj.* suitable; appropriate.

well sweep a device used to draw water from a well, consisting of a pole on a pivot, with a bucket at one end.

well–thought–of ['wɛl 'θɒt ʌv] *adj.* esteemed; of good repute or reputation.

well–timed ['wɛl 'taɪmd] *adj.* timely.

well–to–do ['wɛl tə 'du] *adj.* having enough money to live well; prosperous.

well–turned ['wɛl 'tɜrnd] *adj.* **1** well-shaped; rounded expertly. **2** gracefully or elegantly expressed: *a well-turned phrase.*

well–turned–out ['wɛl 'tɜrnd 'ʌut] *adj.* elegantly or fashionably dressed.

well–wish•er ['wɛl ˌwɪʃər] *n.* a person who wishes well to a person, cause, etc. **–'well-ˌwish•ing,** *adj., n.*

well–worn ['wɛl 'wɔrn] *adj.* **1** much worn by use. **2** used too much; trite; stale.

welsh [wɛlʃ] *v. Slang.* **1** cheat by failing to pay a bet. **2** evade the fulfilment of an obligation.
welsh on, fail to keep an agreement with. Also, **welch.** ⟨origin uncertain⟩ **–'welsh•er,** *n.*

Welsh [wɛlʃ] *n., adj. –n.* **1 the Welsh,** *pl.* the people of Wales, a division of the United Kingdom. **2** the Celtic language of Wales.
–adj. of or having to do with Wales, its people, or their Celtic language. ⟨OE *Welisc* < *wealh* stranger (a non-Saxon)⟩

Welsh corgi one of either of two breeds of dog having short legs, erect ears, and a foxy head, originally bred for herding cattle. The Pembroke Welsh corgi has no tail; the Cardigan has a full tail and larger ears.

Welsh•man ['wɛlʃmən] *n., pl.* **-men. 1** a man who is a native or inhabitant of Wales. **2** a man of Welsh descent.

Welsh rabbit a mixture containing cheese, cooked and served on toast. Also, **Welsh rarebit**.

Welsh springer spaniel a medium-sized spaniel similar to but lighter in build than the English springer, and having a rich dark red-and-white coat.

Welsh•wom•an ['wɛlʃ,wʊmən] *n., pl.* **-wom•en. 1** a woman who is a native or inhabitant of Wales. **2** a woman of Welsh descent.

welt [wɛlt] *n., v.* —*n.* **1** a strip of leather between the upper part and the sole of a shoe. **2** the narrow border, trimming, etc. on the edge of a garment or upholstery. **3** a seam similar to a flat fell seam, used in tailoring. **4** a streak or ridge made on the skin by a blow, especially from a stick or whip. **5** a heavy blow.
—*v.* **1** put a welt on. **2** *Informal.* beat severely. ⟨ME *welte, walte*⟩

Welt•an•schau•ung ['vɛlt,anʃaʊʊŋ] *n. German.* a mental scheme or conception of life, history, reality, etc.; one's way of looking at the world; literally, worldview.

Welt•an•sicht ['vɛlt,anzɪxt] *n. German.* a special interpretation of reality; literally, worldview.

wel•ter ['wɛltər] *v., n.* —*v.* **1** roll or toss about; wallow. **2** lie soaked in some liquid; be drenched.
—*n.* **1** a surging or confused mass: *The fighting children were a welter of arms and legs.* **2** confusion; commotion. ⟨< MDu. and MLG *welteren*⟩

wel•ter•weight ['wɛltər,weit] *n.* a boxer weighing between 63.5 kg and 67 kg. ⟨earlier *welter*, literally, beater (ult. < *welt*) + *weight*⟩

Welt•schmerz ['vɛlt,ʃmɛRts] *n. German.* sadness or melancholy arising from life in an imperfect world; world-weariness. ⟨< G, literally 'world pain'⟩

wen [wɛn] *n. Pathology.* a benign tumour of the skin. ⟨OE *wenn*⟩
☛ *Hom.* WHEN.

wench [wɛntʃ] *n., v.* —*n.* **1** *Facetious*. a girl or young woman. **2** *Archaic.* a female servant.
—*v.* seek out and consort with wenches. ⟨< *wenchel* child, OE *wencel*⟩

wend [wɛnd] *v.* **wend•ed** or (*archaic*) **went, wend•ing. 1** direct (one's way): *We wended our way home.* **2** *Archaic.* go. ⟨OE *wendan*⟩

Wend [wɛnd] *n.* a member of a Slavic people living in central Germany. See SORB. ⟨< G *Wende*⟩ —**'Wend•ish,** *adj.*

wen•di•go ['wɛndɪ,gou] *n., pl.* **-gos** *for 1;* **-go** or **-gos** *for 2. Cdn.* **1** *Algonquian mythology.* an evil spirit of a cannibalistic nature. Also, **windigo. 2** a hybrid trout; splake. ⟨< Algonquian (Ojibway) *weendigo* cannibal⟩

went [wɛnt] *v.* **1** pt. of GO. **2** *Archaic.* a pt. of WEND.

wen•tle•trap ['wɛntəl,træp] *n.* one of a number of marine gastropods of the family Epitorii (Scalariidae) having a spiral, whitish shell. ⟨< Du. *wenteltrap* < *wendeltrap* spiral staircase⟩

wept [wɛpt] *v.* pt. and pp. of WEEP.

were [wɜr]; *unstressed,* [wər] *v.* **1** pl. and 2nd pers. sing., past indicative, of BE: *The officers were obeyed by the soldiers.* **2** past subjunctive of BE: *If I were rich, I would travel.*
as it were, as if it were; so to speak. ⟨OE *wǣron*⟩
☛ *Hom.* WHIR.
☛ *Usage.* **Were.** For subjunctive uses, in expressing wishes not yet realized, conditions that are merely hypothetical, etc., **were** is used with all persons irrespective of number: *I wish it were warmer. She looked as though she were ill.*

we're [wir] we are.
☛ *Hom.* WEIR.

weren't [wɜrnt] *or* [wɛrnt] were not.

were•wolf ['wɛr,wʊlf], ['wɜr,wʊlf], *or* ['wir,wʊlf] *n., pl.* **-wolves** [-,wʊlvz]. *Folklore.* a person, especially a man or boy, who has been changed into a wolf or who can change himself into a wolf, while retaining human intelligence. ⟨OE *werwulf* < *wer* man + *wulf* wolf⟩

wer•geld ['wɜr,gɛld] *or* ['wɛr,gɛld] *n.* **1** in early Anglo-Saxon and Germanic law, money paid to the family of a murdered person by the murderer in order to prevent reprisal or a blood feud. **2** a price fixed as compensation for the killing or disablement of another person, according to the victim's rank. Also, **weregild, wergild.** ⟨ME *weregylt* < OE *wergild* < *wer* man + *gild* payment⟩

wert [wɜrt] *or* [wɛrt]; *unstressed,* [wərt] *v. Archaic.* 2nd pers. sing. past tense of BE. *Thou wert* means *you* (sing.) *were.*

wer•wolf ['wɛr,wʊlf], ['wɜr,wʊlf], *or* ['wir,wʊlf] *n., pl.* **-wolves** [-wʊlvz]. See WEREWOLF.

Wes•ak ['wɛsæk] *n. Buddhism*. the New Year festival, celebrated at the full moon in the month of May and commemorating the birth, enlightenment, and death of Buddha.

Wes•ley•an ['wɛsliən] *or* ['wɛzliən] *n., adj.* —*n.* a member of the church founded by John Wesley (1703-1791), an English clergyman; Methodist.
—*adj.* of or having to do with John Wesley or the Methodist Church. —**'Wes•ley•an,ism,** *n.*

Wes•sex ['wɛsɪks] *n.* **1** an Anglo-Saxon kingdom comprising parts of what are now Hampshire, Wiltshire, and Dorsetshire, with its capital at Winchester. **2** in modern England, the unofficial name of the same area, mainly in Dorset, especially as the scene of the novels of Thomas Hardy.

west [wɛst] *n., adv., adj.* —*n.* **1** the direction of the sunset; the point of the compass to the left as one faces north. **2** Also, **West,** the part of the world, or of a given country or continent, toward the west. **3 the West, a** *Cdn.* the western part of Canada or the United States. **b** the countries in Europe and the Americas as distinguished from those in Asia, especially SW Asia. **c** the United States, the United Kingdom, and their allies as distinguished from Russia and its allies. **d** formerly, the Western Roman Empire.
out West, *Cdn.* **a** any point to the west of about Winnipeg. **b** in or toward any place west of about Winnipeg. **4** the point on a compass directly opposite east.
—*adv.* toward the west: *They travelled west for two days.*
—*adj.* **1** toward or farther toward the west. **2** from the west: *a west wind.* **3** situated or found in the west or the western part: *the west wing of a house.* **4** designating that part of a church opposite the altar.
west of, farther west than: *Alberta is west of Saskatchewan.* ⟨OE⟩

west•bound ['wɛst,baʊnd] *adj.* going toward the west.

West Coast *Cdn.* the western coast of Canada, especially southwestern British Columbia, including Vancouver Island, the Gulf Islands, and the Queen Charlotte Islands.

west•er ['wɛstər] *v., n.* —*v.* turn or move westward; shift to the west.
—*n.* a wind or storm from the west.

west•er•ly ['wɛstərli] *adj., adv., n., pl.* **west•er•lies** [-liz]. —*adj. or adv.* **1** in or toward the west: *walking in a westerly direction.* **2** from the west: *a westerly wind.*
—*n.* a wind that blows from the west.

west•ern ['wɛstərn] *adj., n.* —*adj.* **1** toward the west. **2** from the west. **3** of or in the western part of the world or a given country or continent: *Vancouver is a western Canadian port.* **4** of, in, or having to do with the West. Also, **Western.**
—*n. Informal.* **1** a story or film dealing with life in the western part of North America, especially cowboy life in the United States in the late 19th century. **2** WESTERN SANDWICH; WESTERN OMELETTE.

western anemone CHALICE FLOWER.

Western Church **1** the part of the Catholic Church that acknowledges the Pope as its spiritual leader and follows the Latin Rite; Roman Catholic Church. **2** all the Christian churches of Western Europe and the Americas, especially the Roman Catholic and Anglican Churches.

Western civilization the civilization of Europe and the Americas as contrasted with Oriental civilization.

Western Empire See WESTERN ROMAN EMPIRE.

West•ern•er ['wɛstərnər] *n., Cdn.* a native or inhabitant of western Canada. Also, **westerner.**

western flowering dogwood a tree of the dogwood family, having blossoms with white petal-like bracts, red berries, and hard wood. The blossom of the western flowering dogwood is the floral emblem of British Columbia.

western hemisphere the half of the terrestrial globe that includes North and South America with their neighbouring islands and surrounding waters.

western hemlock **1** a tall hemlock (*Tsuga heterophylla*) found in the forest regions of British Columbia and the NW United States, an important timber-producing tree having flat needles and small, egg-shaped cones. **2** the moderately light, hard, and strong wood of this tree.

west•ern•ize ['wɛstər,naɪz] *v.* **-ized, -iz•ing.** introduce or adopt, or cause to introduce or adopt western ideas, customs, culture, etc. —**'west•ern,iz•er,** *n.* —**'west•ern•i'za•tion,** *n.*

western juniper ROCKY MOUNTAIN JUNIPER.

western larch a very tall larch (*Larix occidentalis*) found mainly in the forests of southern British Columbia, often growing to heights of 30 m to 50 m, having oval cones and heavy, hard, strong wood. The western larch is one of the most important timber-producing trees in western Canada.

west•ern•most ['wɛstərn,moust] *adj.* farthest west.

western omelette or **omelet** an omelette made with the addition of chopped green peppers, chopped onions, and ham.

western red cedar a very large arborvitae (*Thuja plicata*) found along the Pacific coast and in interior British Columbia, a very long-lived tree often reaching a height of 45 m to 60 m and a diameter of 2.5 m or more. The western red cedar is used by the people of the First Nations of the Pacific northwest for carving totem poles and building canoes and lodges.

Western Roman Empire the western part of the Roman Empire after the division in A.D. 395. The Western Roman Empire came to an end in A.D. 476; the Eastern Empire continued as the Byzantine Empire until A.D. 1453.

Western saddle a saddle with a high pommel and cantle, and a horn on the pommel, originally intended to tie a rope to when lassoing cattle. See SADDLE for picture.

Western Sa•ha•ra [sə'hærə], [sə'hɛrə], *or* [sə'hɑrə] a country in NW Africa.

Western Samoa a country comprising the western part of Samoa.

western sandwich a sandwich with a filling of scrambled eggs, minced ham, peppers, and onions.

Western Wall See WAILING WALL.

western yew a yew (*Taxus brevifolia*) occurring as a small tree or shrub in the forests of British Columbia. The hard, strong wood of the western yew is valued for archery bows, canoe paddles, and carving, and the bark is used in the production of a cancer-treating medication.

West Germanic a subgroup of the Germanic languages including Afrikaans, Dutch, English, Flemish, Frisian, German, Yiddish, and their various dialects and earlier forms.

West Highland white terrier one of a breed of small (4.5 cm at the shoulder), sturdy Scottish terriers, having a pure white coat, erect tail, and short ears. Originally bred to hunt small game, they are very successful as companion dogs.

West Indian *n., adj. —n.* **1** a native or inhabitant of the WEST INDIES. **2** a person whose recent ancestors came from the West Indies.
—adj. of or having to do with the West Indies or the peoples of these islands.

West In•dies ['ɪndiz] a large group of islands and island countries between Florida and South America.

west•ing ['wɛstɪŋ] *n.* the distance travelled in a westerly direction.

West•min•ster [,wɛst'mɪnstər] *or* ['wɛst,mɪnstər] *n. Brit. Informal.* Parliament, or the British government. ⟨< *Westminster*, the part of London that contains the Houses of Parliament⟩

west–north•west ['wɛst ,nɔrθ'wɛst] *n., adj., adv. —n.* a direction or compass point midway between west and northwest.
—adj. or adv. in, toward, or from this direction.

West Saxon **1** an inhabitant or native of the kingdom of Wessex. **2** **a** a dialect of Old English used by the West Saxons. **b** the major literary dialect of Old English before the Norman Conquest in A.D. 1066.

west–south•west ['wɛst ,sʌuθ'wɛst] *n., adj., adv. —n.* a direction or compass point midway between west and southwest.
—adj. or adv. in, toward, or from this direction.

West Virginia an eastern state of the United States, west of Virginia.

west•ward ['wɛstwərd] *adj., adv., n. —adj. or adv.* toward the west; west: *He walked westward. We live on the westward slope of the hill.* Also (*adv.*), **westwards**.
—n. a westward part, direction, or point.

west•ward•ly ['wɛstwərdli] *adj. or adv.* **1** toward the west. **2** of winds, from the west.

west•wards ['wɛstwərdz] *adv.* westward.

wet [wɛt] *adj.* **wet•ter, wet•test;** *v.* **wet** or **wet•ted, wet•ting;** *n.*
—adj. **1** covered, moistened, or soaked with water or other liquid: *wet hands, a wet sponge.* **2** not yet dry: *Don't touch wet paint.* **3** rainy: *wet weather.* **4** watery: *Her eyes were wet with tears.* **5** having or serving alcoholic drinks: *a wet bar.* **6** having or favouring laws that permit the making and selling of alcoholic drinks: *a wet town*. **7** using water; performed under water, as some mining and manufacturing processes.
all wet, *Informal.* completely wrong; completely mistaken.
wet behind the ears, *Informal.* too young to know very much; immature; inexperienced.
—v. **1** make or become wet. **2** pass urine; make wet by passing urine.
—n. **1** water or other liquid: *I dropped my scarf in the wet.* **2** wet weather; rain: *We enjoy walking in the wet.* **3** wetness; moisture. **4** a person who favours laws that permit the making and selling of alcoholic drinks. ⟨ME *wett*, pp. of *wete(n)*, OE *wǣtan*⟩
—'wet•ly, *adv.* **—'wet•ness,** *n.* **—'wet•ter,** *n.*
☛ *Hom.* WHET.
☛ *Syn. v.* **Wet,** DRENCH, SOAK = make or become covered or spread through with liquid. **Wet** is the general word: *Wet the material well before applying soap.* **Drench** means 'wet thoroughly' by pouring liquid: *Drench the ashes and ground before leaving a campfire.* **Soak** means 'wet thoroughly' by putting and keeping, or lying, in or under liquid, especially until the liquid has spread through the fibres or substance of the thing: *Soak the stained spot in soda water.*

wet blanket *Informal.* a person who has a discouraging or depressing effect.

wet cell *Electricity.* an electrochemical cell having a liquid electrolyte.

wet dream an erotic dream with ejaculation of semen.

wet fly an artificial fishing fly designed to imitate an underwater insect. Compare DRY FLY.

weth•er ['wɛðər] *n.* a castrated male sheep. ⟨OE⟩
☛ *Hom.* WEATHER, WHETHER.

wet•land ['wɛt,lænd] *or* ['wɛtlənd] *n.* **1** a marsh or swamp. **2** Usually, **wetlands,** *pl.* a swampy or marshy area set aside for the preservation of wildlife.

wet nurse a woman employed to suckle the infant of another.

wet–nurse ['wɛt ,nɜrs] *v.* **-nursed, -nurs•ing. 1** act as a wet nurse to. **2** treat with special care; coddle; pamper.

wet strength a quality of some paper, enabling it to hold together and not tear or disintegrate even when wet.

wet suit a skin-tight suit of sponge rubber or a similar material that is not watertight but that will retain body heat, worn especially by skindivers in cold water.

wetting agent *Chemistry*. any admixture to a liquid which will increase the liquid's spreadability or power of penetration.

wet•tish ['wɛtɪʃ] *adj.* somewhat wet.

we've [wiv]; *unstressed*, [wɪv] we have.
☛ *Hom.* WEAVE.

wf or **w.f.** *Printing.* wrong font.

WFTU or **W.F.T.U.** World Federation of Trade Unions.

W•h WATT HOUR(s).

whack [wæk] *n., v. —n.* **1** *Informal.* a sharp, resounding blow or the sound of such a blow. **2** *Slang.* portion; share: *Each of the thieves took his whack and left town.*
have or **take a whack at,** *Slang.* make an attempt at; try: *I'd like to take a whack at flying a glider.*
out of whack, *Slang.* not in proper condition; out of order: *The timing of the engine is out of whack.*
—v. **1** *Informal.* strike with a sharp, resounding blow: *The batter whacked the ball out of the park.* **2** *Informal.* beat or win in a contest. **3** *Slang.* chop or take (*off*): *She whacked off a couple of branches with her axe.*
whack up, *Slang.* share; divide. ⟨? imitative⟩

whacked [wækt] *adj., v. —adj. Slang.* **1** exhausted; worn out. **2** heavily intoxicated.
—v. pt. and pp. of WHACK.

whack•ing ['wækɪŋ] *adj., adv., v. —adj. Informal.* large or tremendous: *a whacking success.*
—adv. Informal. very: *a whacking good story.*
—v. ppr. of WHACK.

whack•y ['wæki] *adj.* See WACKY.

A whale

whale[1] [weil] *n., pl.* **whales** or **whale;** *v.* **whaled, whal•ing.**
–n. any of an order (Cetacea) of aquatic mammals that are shaped like fish; especially, any of the larger members of this order as distinguished from the porpoises and dolphins. Whales breathe air and bear live young.
a whale of a, *Informal.* a big or impressive example or type of: *a whale of a car, a whale of a good time.*
–v. hunt and catch whales. ⟨OE *hwæl*⟩
☛ *Hom.* WAIL, WALE.

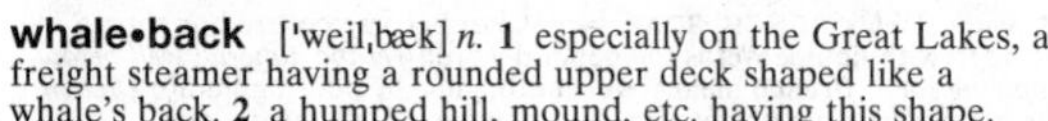

whale[2] [weil] *v.* **whaled, whal•ing.** *Informal.* **1** beat; whip severely. **2** hit hard. ⟨apparently var. of *wale*⟩
☛ *Hom.* WAIL, WALE.

whale•back ['weil,bæk] *n.* **1** especially on the Great Lakes, a freight steamer having a rounded upper deck shaped like a whale's back. **2** a humped hill, mound, etc. having this shape.

whale•boat ['weil,bout] *n.* a long, narrow rowboat, sharp at both ends, formerly much used in whaling, now used mainly as a lifeboat or utility boat.

whale•bone ['weil,boun] *n.* **1** the horny substance growing in the mouth of baleen whales; baleen. **2** a thin strip of this, especially as formerly used for stays in corsets, dresses, etc.

whalebone whale BALEEN WHALE.

whal•er ['weilər] *n.* **1** a person who hunts whales. **2** a ship used for hunting and catching whales.

whal•ing[1] ['weilɪŋ] *n., v.* *–n.* **1** the hunting and killing of whales. **2** the industry concerned with the hunting, killing, and processing of whales.
–v. ppr. of WHALE[1].

whal•ing[2] ['weilɪŋ] *n., v.* *–n.* a beating or thrashing.
–v. ppr. of WHALE[2].

wham [wæm] *n., interj., v.* **whammed, wham•ming.** *Informal.*
–n. a loud bang; the sound of a hard impact.
–interj. an exclamation representing the sound of a hard impact. Also, **whammo.**
–v. hit with a bang; smash; beat. ⟨imitative⟩

wham•my ['wæmi] *n., pl.* **-mies.** *Slang.* **1** a magical power or spell bringing bad luck; jinx: *The magician put the whammy on him.* **2** a catastrophe; devastating blow: *The over-fishing and the increase in the seal population were a double whammy for the fishing industry.*

whang [wæŋ] *n., v. Informal.* *–n.* a resounding blow or bang.
–v. strike with a blow or bang. ⟨imitative⟩

whang•ee ['wæŋi] *n.* **1** a type of bamboo (genus *Phyllostachys*) found in China and Japan. **2** a cane or walking stick made from this. ⟨< Chinese *huang-i* < *huang* a hard bamboo + *-i* ? to lean on⟩

whap [wæp] *v.* **whapped, whap•ping;** *n.* whop.

wharf [wɔrf] *n., pl.* **wharves** or **wharfs;** *v.* *–n.* a platform built on the shore or out from the shore, beside which ships can load and unload.
–v. **1** provide or furnish with a wharf or wharves. **2** unload or store on a wharf. ⟨OE *hwearf*⟩

wharf•age ['wɔrfɪdʒ] *n.* **1** the use of a wharf for mooring a ship, storing and handling goods, etc. **2** the charge made for this. **3** wharves: *There are miles of wharfage in Montréal.*

wharf•in•ger ['wɔrfɪndʒər] *n.* a person who owns or has charge of a wharf. ⟨for *wharfager* < *wharfage* with *n* added as in *passenger*⟩

wharves [wɔrvz] *n.* a pl. of WHARF.

what [wʌt]; *unstressed,* [wət] *pron., adj., adv., interj., conj.*
–pron. **1** as an interrogative pronoun, a word used in asking the identity of a thing: *What is your name? What is the matter? She asked the sobbing child what was wrong.* **2** as a relative pronoun: **a** that which: *I know what you mean.* **b** whatever; anything that: *Do what you please.* **3** what it is; what to do, etc.: *I'll tell you what: you can go see and I'll save your spot.*
and what not, and all kinds of other things.
give (someone) **what for,** *Informal.* give one something to cry, suffer, or be miserable for; punish; castigate.
what for, why; for what purpose.
what have you, *Informal.* anything else like this; and so on.
what if, a what would happen if. **b** what difference does it make if: *And what if he did tell her? I don't care!*
what's what, *Informal.* the true state of affairs: *I'm still trying to find out what's what.*
what with, on account of (an accumulation of things): *What with our long walk and all the excitement, we were exhausted.*
–adj. **1** as an interrogative adjective, a word used in asking the identity of persons or things: *What time is it? She asked me what I was doing.* **2** as a relative adjective: **a** that —— which; which: *Put back what money is left.* **b** whatever; any —— that: *Take what supplies you will need.* **3** as a generalized exclamatory adjective, how great, wonderful, bad, etc.: *What a cad!*
–adv. **1** how much; how: *What does it matter?* **2** a word used to intensify an adjective in an exclamation: *What a good time we had!*
–interj. a word used to show surprise, doubt, anger, liking, etc. or to add emphasis: *What? Are you late again?*
–conj.
but what, *Informal.* but that. ⟨OE *hwæt*⟩

what•ev•er [wət'ɛvər] *pron., adj.* *–pron.* **1** anything or everything that: *Do whatever you like.* **2** no matter what: *Whatever happens, he is safe.* **3** *Informal.* a word used for emphasis instead of *what* (emphatic): *Whatever do you mean?* **4** any of a number of specified or unspecified things that will qualify (*also used dismissively or concessively as a sentence substitute*): *Cake and jelly and whatever. "It's a spade, not a shovel." "Whatever."*
–adj. **1** any that: *Ask whatever girls you like to the party.* **2** no matter what: *Whatever excuse he makes, it will not be believed.* **3** (*after the noun*) at all: *Any person whatever can tell you.*

what•not ['wʌt,nɒt] *n.* **1** a stand with several shelves for books, ornaments, etc. **2** a thing that or person who may be variously named or described; nondescript.

what's [wʌts] **1** what is: *What's the latest news?* **2** what has: *What's been going on here lately?* **3** *Informal.* what does: *What's she want now?*

what•so•ev•er [,wʌtsou'ɛvər] *pron. or adj.* whatever.

wheal [wil] *n.* **1** a small burning or itching swelling on the skin. **2** Also, **weal.** a ridge on the skin made by a whip; welt. ⟨Cf. OE *hwelian* suppurate⟩
☛ *Hom.* WEAL, WE'LL, WHEEL.

wheat [wit] *n.* any of a genus (*Triticum*) of cereal grasses bearing grain in dense spikes. There are thousands of varieties of wheat cultivated throughout the world. **2** the grain yielded by any of these plants, one of the world's most important sources of flour for bread, pasta, etc. ⟨OE *hwǣte*⟩

Wheat Belt *Cdn.* the large tract on the Prairies mainly given over to the growing of wheat.

wheat•ear ['wit,ir] *n.* any of a genus (*Oenanthe*) of small northern thrushes, especially *O. oenanthe,* having grey-and-black upper parts and light brown underparts with a white rump.

wheat•en ['witən] *adj.* **1** made of wheat or wheat flour. **2** of or having to do with wheat. **3** being the colour of wheat, a pale yellow or yellow brown.

wheat germ the tiny, golden embryo of the wheat kernel, used as a cereal and as a vitamin supplement.

wheat pool *Cdn.* **1** a co-operative founded by western farmers to handle the wheat they produce. **2** the total annual amount of wheat handled by such a co-operative.

Wheat•stone bridge ['wit,stoun] *Electricity.* **1** a divided bridge circuit for measuring an unknown electrical resistance by comparing it with a known resistance. **2** a device that contains a circuit of this kind. ⟨after Sir Charles *Wheatstone* (1802-1875), English physicist⟩

whee [wi] *interj.* whoopee!; an exclamation of joy, delight, etc.
☛ *Hom.* WE, WEE.

whee•dle ['widəl] *v.* **-dled, -dling. 1** persuade by flattery, smooth words, caresses, etc.; coax: *The children wheedled their mother into letting them go out.* **2** get by wheedling: *They finally wheedled the secret out of him.* ⟨OE *wǣdlian* beg⟩ **–'whee•dler,** *n.* **–'whee•dling•ly,** *adv.*

A wheel

wheel [wil] *n., v.* *—n.* **1** a round frame or disk that can turn on a pin or shaft in its centre. **2** any instrument, machine, apparatus, etc. shaped or moving like a wheel. A **ship's wheel** is used in steering. Clay is shaped into pots, etc. on a **potter's wheel.**
3 *Informal.* **a** a bicycle. **b** a bicycle ride. **4** any force thought of as moving or propelling: *the wheels of government.* **5** a circling or circular motion or movement; rotation (not necessarily completed around); revolution: *The skaters made a wheel in the middle of the arena.* **6** a pivoting movement by which dancers, troops, or ships in line change direction while maintaining a straight line. **7** *Informal.* BIG WHEEL. **8 wheels,** *pl. Informal.* a motor vehicle, especially an automobile: *Do you have wheels?*
at or **behind the wheel, a** at the steering wheel. **b** in control: *The variety night is bound to be a success with Mari at the wheel.*
wheels within wheels, complicated circumstances, motives, influences, etc.
—v. **1** *Informal.* go by bicycle: *She wheeled along happily till she hit a bump and fell off.* **2** turn: *She wheeled around suddenly.*
3 cause to turn: *The rider wheeled her horse about.* **4** move or perform in a curved or circular direction: *The flight of geese wheeled across the sunset sky.* **5** move on wheels; push a wheeled object: *The worker was wheeling a load of bricks on a wheelbarrow.*
6 travel along smoothly. **7** provide with wheels.
wheel and deal, *Slang.* do business or trade freely and rapidly, especially in an aggressive or somewhat unscrupulous way. ⟨OE *hwēol*⟩
☛ *Hom.* WEAL, WE'LL, WHEAL.

wheel•bar•row ['wil,bærou] *or* ['wil,bɛrou] *n.* a small vehicle for carrying loads, having one wheel at the front and two legs at the back, and handles for tilting and pushing it.

wheel•base ['wil,beis] *n.* in motor vehicles, the distance from the centre of the front axle to the centre of the rear axle, measured in millimetres.

wheelchair ['wil,tʃɛr] *n.* a chair mounted on wheels so that it can be pushed from behind or moved by the person sitting in it. Wheelchairs are used by invalids and people who are paralysed or have injuries to their feet or legs.

wheel dog *Cdn.* of a dog team, the dog nearest the sled in a tandem hitch, or either of the two dogs nearest the sled in a fan hitch.

wheeled [wild] *adj., v.* *—adj.* **1** having a wheel or wheels.
2 having wheels of a specified number: *a three-wheeled bicycle.*
3 moving or mounted on wheels: *a wheeled table.*
—v. pt. and pp. of WHEEL.
☛ *Hom.* WEALD, WIELD.

wheel•er ['wilər] *n.* **1** a person who or thing that wheels. **2** a thing that has a wheel or wheels of a specified kind or number: *a two-wheeler.* **3** WHEEL HORSE (def. 1). **4** WHEEL DOG.

wheel•er–deal•er ['wilər 'dilər] *n. Informal.* a person who wheels and deals.

wheel horse **1** a horse nearest to the front wheels of the vehicle being pulled. **2** *Informal.* a person who works hard, long, and effectively.

wheel•house ['wil,hʌus] *n.* a small, enclosed place on a ship to shelter the steering wheel and those who steer the ship; pilot house.

wheel•wright ['wil,rəit] *n.* a person whose work is making or repairing wheels, carriages, and wagons.

wheeze [wiz] *v.* **wheezed, wheez•ing;** *n.* *—v.* **1** breathe with difficulty and with a whistling sound. **2** make a sound like this: *The old engine wheezed, but it didn't stop.* **3** say with a wheeze.
—n. **1** a whistling sound caused by difficult breathing. **2** a breath taken with difficulty and with a whistling sound. **3** *Slang.* a funny saying or story, especially one that has been told many times; an old or familiar joke. ⟨probably < ON *hvæsa* hiss⟩

wheez•y ['wizi] *adj.* **-i•er, -i•est.** habitually wheezing: *a fat, wheezy old dog.* **—'wheez•i•ly,** *adv.* **—'wheez•i•ness,** *n.*

The shell of a whelk—about 7 cm long

whelk[1] [wɛlk] *n.* any of a family (Buccinidae) of carnivorous marine gastropod molluscs typically having a thick, strong, spiral shell. ⟨OE *weoloc*⟩

whelk[2] [wɛlk] *n.* a pimple; pustule. ⟨OE *hwylca*⟩

whelm [wɛlm] *v.* **1** overwhelm. **2** submerge or engulf. ⟨related to OE *-hwelfan,* as in *āhwelfan* cover over; influenced by *helmian* cover⟩

whelp [wɛlp] *n., v.* *—n.* **1** a young animal, especially a puppy or wolf cub. **2** a good-for-nothing boy or young man. **3** *Machinery.* **a** a tooth on a sprocket wheel. **b** any of the longitudinal projections or ridges on the barrel of a capstan, windlass, etc.
—v. give birth to one or more puppies or cubs. ⟨OE *hwelp*⟩

when [wɛn]; *unstressed,* [wən] *adv., conj., pron., n.* *—adv.* at what time or stage: *When does school close? When do you want to change sides?*
—conj. **1** at the time that: *Rise when your name is called.* **2** at any time that: *He is impatient when he is kept waiting.* **3** at which time; and then: *The dog growled till its owner spoke, when it gave a joyful bark.* **4** whereas: *We have only three books when we need five.* **5** considering that; inasmuch as; since: *How can I help you when I don't know how to do the problems myself?*
—pron. **1** what time; which time: *Since when have they had a car?*
2 at which: *That was a time when every penny counted.*
—n. the time or occasion: *the when and where of an act.* ⟨OE *hwænne*⟩
☛ *Hom.* WEN.

when•as [wɛn'æz] *conj. Archaic.* when; while; whereas.

whence [wɛns] *adv., pron. Archaic or formal.* *—adv.* from what place, source, or cause: *Whence do you come? They wondered whence he had learned so much about their affairs.*
—pron. from which or from where: *Let them return to the country whence they came.* ⟨ME *whennes* < OE *whannon(e)*⟩

whence•so•ev•er [,wɛnssou'ɛvər] *conj. Archaic or formal.* from whatever place, source, or cause.

when•ev•er [wɛn'ɛvər] *conj. or adv.* at whatever time; when (*emphatic*); at any time that.

when•so•ev•er [,wɛnsou'ɛvər] *conj. or adv. Archaic.* whenever; at whatever time.

where [wɛr] *adv., pron., n., conj.* *—adv.* **1** in what place; at what place: *Where is she?* **2** to what place: *Where are you going? I don't know where she is.* **3** from what place or source: *Where did you get that story?* **4** in which; at which: *the house where he was born.*
5 to which: *the place where he is going.* **6** in what way; in what respect: *Where is the harm in trying?* **7** in what position or state: *Where would I be without her?*
—pron. what place: *Where does he come from?*
—n. the place or scene: *the when and the where of it.*
—conj. **1** to the place to or at which: *I will go where you go. She goes where she likes.* **2** in the place in which; at the place at which: *The book is where you left it.* **3** in any place in which; at any place at which: *Use the salve where the pain is felt.* **4** in or at which place: *They came to the town, where they stayed for the night.* **5** in the case, circumstances, respect, etc. in which: *Some people worry where it does no good.* **6** *Informal.* that: *Did you read where Munro is suing the Liberal Party?* ⟨OE *hwǣr*⟩
☛ *Hom.* WARE, WEAR.

where•a•bout ['wɛrə,bʌut] *adv., n. Rare.* whereabouts.

where•a•bouts ['wɛrə,bʌuts] *adv., n.* *—adv.* where; near what place: *Whereabouts can I find a doctor? We did not know whereabouts we were.*
—n.pl. or sing. the place where a person or thing is: *Do you know the whereabouts of the cottage?*

where•as ['wɛrəz] *or* [wɛr'æz] *conj.* **1** on the contrary; but; while: *Some people like opera whereas others do not.*
2 considering that; since, often used at the beginning of a formal proclamation, resolution, etc.: *Whereas all people are human, so all people should show humanity.*

where•at [wɛr'æt] *adv. or conj. Archaic.* at what; at which.

where•by [wɛr'baɪ] *adv. or conj.* by what; by which: *There is no other way whereby she can be saved.*

where•fore ['wɛrfɔr] *adv., conj., n.* *—adv. Archaic.* for what reason; why: *Wherefore do you weep? I think I know wherefore she is angry.*
—conj. Archaic or formal. for which reason; therefore; so: *He has been found guilty, wherefore he must be banished.*
—n. Usually, **wherefores,** *pl.* an explanation or reason: *I don't want to hear all the whys and wherefores.* ⟨< *where* + *fore,* prep.⟩

where•from [wɛr'frʌm] *adv. Archaic.* whence.

where•in [wɛr'ɪn] *adv., conj. Archaic or formal.* *–adv.* in what place or respect: *Wherein had he erred?*
–conj. in which place or respect: *the place wherein they lived.*

where•of [wɛr'ʌv] *adv. or conj. Archaic or formal.* of what, which, or whom: *I know whereof I speak.*

where•on [wɛr'ɒn] *adv. or conj. Archaic or formal.* on which or what.

where•so•ev•er [,wɛrsou'ɛvər] *conj. or adv. Archaic.* wherever.

where•to [wɛr'tu] *adv. or conj. Archaic or formal.* **1** to what; to which; where: *He went to that place whereto he had been sent.* **2** for what purpose; why: *Whereto do you lay up riches?*

where•up•on [,wɛrə'pɒn] *adv., conj. –adv.* upon what; upon which: *Whereupon do you propose to base these accusations? The foundation whereupon we build our children's future must be a secure one.*
–conj. at which point; after which event: *She read him the letter, whereupon he flew into a rage.*

wher•ev•er [wɛr'ɛvər] *conj. or adv.* **1** where; to whatever place; in whatever place: *Wherever are you going? Sit wherever you like.* **2** no matter where: *Wherever I go, her face appears before me.*

where•with•al *n.* ['wɛrwɪð,ɒl] *or* ['wɛrwɪθ,ɒl]; *adv. and pron.* [,wɛrwɪð'ɒl] *or* [,wɛrwɪθ'ɒl] *n., adv. –n.* means, supplies, or money needed: *Does she have the wherewithal to pay for the trip?*
–adv. Archaic. with what; with which: *the garments wherewithal ye are clothed. Wherewithal shall we be fed?*

wher•ry ['wɛri] *n., pl.* **-ries. 1** a light, shallow rowboat for carrying passengers and goods on rivers. **2** a light rowboat for one person, used for racing. ⟨origin unknown⟩
☛ *Hom.* WARY.

whet [wɛt] *v.* **whet•ted, whet•ting;** *n. –v.* **1** sharpen by rubbing on a stone: *to whet a knife.* **2** stir up; awaken: *The smell of food whetted my appetite. An exciting story whets your interest.*
–n. **1** the act of whetting. **2** something that whets. **3** appetizer. ⟨OE *hwettan*⟩
☛ *Hom.* WET.

wheth•er ['wɛðər] *conj., pron. –conj.* **1** *Whether* is a conjunction expressing a choice or an alternative: *It matters little whether we go or stay. He does not know whether to work or play. Whether sick or well, she is always cheerful. Whether she works out of the house or buys a car, she will have the same opportunities.* **2** if (*in indirect questions*): *He asked whether he should finish the work.*
whether or no, in any case; no matter what happens.
–pron. Archaic. which of two. ⟨OE *hwether*⟩
☛ *Hom.* WEATHER, WETHER.

whet•stone ['wɛt,stoun] *n.* a stone for sharpening knives or tools.

whew [hwju] *interj. or n.* an exclamation of surprise, relief, dismay, exhaustion, etc.: *Whew! it's hot!*

whey [wei] *n.* the watery part of milk that separates from the curd when milk sours and becomes coagulated or when cheese is made. ⟨OE *hwǣg*⟩
☛ *Hom.* WAY, WEIGH.

which [wɪtʃ] *pron., adj. –pron.* **1** an interrogative pronoun used to introduce direct or indirect questions that single out one or more members of a group: *Which seems the best plan? Tell me which you like best.* **2** as a relative pronoun, a word used, sometimes with a preposition before it, to introduce a clause telling about a place or thing just mentioned: *Take the book which is on the desk. The boat in which you are sitting leaks.* **3** a thing or fact that: *And, which was worse, he was late.*
which is which, which is one and which is the other: *They look so much alike, it's hard to tell which is which.*
–adj. **1** an interrogative adjective used to introduce direct or indirect questions that single out one or more members of a group: *Which boy won the prize? Which books are yours? I don't know which dress to wear.* **2** a word used to raise the possibility of alternatives between or among members of a group: *Be careful which way you turn. No matter which camera he uses, his pictures never turn out.* ⟨OE *hwilc*⟩
☛ *Hom.* WITCH.
☛ *Usage.* **Which.** As a relative pronoun **which** refers to things and to groups of people regarded impersonally: *They returned for his axe, which they had forgotten. The legislature, which passed the act this afternoon, deserves much credit.* See also the note at THAT.
☛ *Usage.* **Of which, whose.** See note at WHO.

which•ev•er [wɪtʃ'ɛvər] *pron. or adj.* **1** any one that; any that: *Take whichever you want. Buy whichever hat you like.* **2** no matter which: *Whichever side wins, I shall be satisfied.*

which•so•ev•er [,wɪtʃsou'ɛvər] *pron. or adj. Archaic.* whichever.

whick•er ['wɪkər] *n., v. –n.* a soft whinny. ⟨imitative⟩
–v. whinny softly.
☛ *Hom.* WICKER.

whiff [wɪf] *n., v. –n.* **1** a slight gust; puff; breath; blow; puff: *A whiff of fresh air cleared his head.* **2** a slight smell; puff of air having an odour: *Take a whiff of this perfume.* **3** a puff of tobacco smoke. **4** a slight outburst. **5** *Informal.* **a** *Baseball, golf, etc.* a swing at a ball without hitting it. **b** *Baseball.* a strikeout.
–v. **1** breathe in or out gently. **2** puff tobacco smoke from (a pipe, etc.); smoke. **3** *Informal. Baseball.* strike out or be struck out. ⟨probably imitative; partly < ME *weffe* vapour, whiff⟩

whif•fet ['wɪfɪt] *n.* **1** *Informal.* an insignificant person or thing. **2** a small dog. ⟨? < *whiff*⟩

whif•fle ['wɪfəl] *v.* **-fled, -fling. 1** blow in puffs or gusts. **2** veer; shift; vacillate; waffle: *Stop whiffling and say what you really think.* **3** blow lightly; scatter. ⟨< *whiff*⟩ **—'whif•fler,** *n.*

whif•fle•tree ['wɪfəl,tri] *n.* whippletree.

Whig [wɪg] *n.* formerly: **1** a member or supporter of a British political party of the 18th and 19th centuries that favoured sweeping social and political reforms. The Whig Party became the Liberal Party. **2** in the United States, a person living in any one of the Thirteen Colonies who supported the rebellion against Great Britain. **3** a member of a U.S. political party in the 19th century, opposed to the Democratic Party. **4** *Cdn.* in colonial times, a person in favour of self-government.
5 (*adjl.*) being, composed of, having to do with, or characteristic of a Whig or Whigs.
☛ *Hom.* WIG.

Whig•ger•y ['wɪgəri] *n.* the principles or practices of Whigs.

Whig•gish ['wɪgɪʃ] *adj.* **1** of or having to do with Whigs. **2** like Whigs.

while [waɪl] *n., conj., v.* **whiled, whil•ing.** *–n.* **1** a time; space of time: *He kept us waiting a long while. The mail came a while ago.* **2** *Archaic.* a particular time.
(all) the while, at or during the same time.
between whiles, at times; at intervals.
worth (one's) **while,** worth time, attention, or effort: *The business trip to Montréal was hardly worth their while, as all their contacts were out celebrating St. Jean Baptiste Day.*
–conj. **1** during the time that; in the time that; in the same time that: *While I was speaking, she said nothing. Summer is pleasant while it lasts.* **2** in contrast with the fact that; although: *While I like the colour of the hat, I don't like the style.*
–v. pass or spend in an easy, pleasant manner (*usually used with* **away**): *We whiled away the day playing at the beach.* ⟨OE *hwīl*⟩
☛ *Hom.* WILE.
☛ *Usage.* **While** is used principally as a subordinating conjunction introducing adverbial clauses of time: *They waited on the bank while she swam to the raft.* **While** is also used, rather weakly, in the sense of **although, whereas,** or **but:** *While the doctor did all she could, she couldn't save the child. Walnut is a hard wood, while pine is soft.* **While** is sometimes used for **and,** but not often: *The second number was an acrobatic exhibition, while the third was a trapeze artist.*

whiles [waɪlz] *adv., conj. Archaic or dialect.*
–adv. **1** sometimes. **2** in the meantime.
–conj. while.

whi•lom ['waɪləm] *adj., adv. Archaic. –adj.* former: *a whilom friend.*
–adv. formerly; once. ⟨OE *hwīlum* at times, dat. pl. of *hwīl* while⟩

whilst [waɪlst] *conj. Brit.* while.

whim [wɪm] *n.* **1** a sudden fancy or notion; freakish or capricious idea or desire: *Her whim for gardening won't last long.* **2** *Mining.* a kind of capstan used in hoisting.
on a whim, without planning or purpose: *She went to Alberta on a whim.* ⟨probably < Scand.; cf. Icelandic *hvim* unsteady look⟩

whim•brel ['wɪmbrəl] *n.* a large grey-brown shorebird (*Numenius phaeopus*) of the curlew family, having a curved bill and a striped crown. It is found in both the Old and New Worlds; it breeds in Arctic regions and winters in South America and southern Africa.

whim•per ['wɪmpər] *v., n. –v.* **1** cry with soft, broken sounds: *The sick child whimpered.* **2** say with a whimper. **3** complain in a weak way; whine.
–n. a whimpering cry or sound. ⟨probably imitative; cf. G *wimmern*⟩ **—'whim•per•er,** *n.* **—'whim•per•ing•ly,** *adv.*

whim•sey ['wɪmzi] *n., pl.* **-seys.** See WHIMSY.

whim•si•cal ['wɪmzɪkəl] *adj.* **1** having many playfully odd notions or fancies; full of whimsy. **2** full of caprice or whims. **—'whim•si•cal•ly,** *adv.*

whim•si•cal•i•ty [,wɪmzɪ'kæləti] *n., pl.* **-ties. 1** a whimsical character or quality. **2** a whimsical notion, speech, act, etc.

whim•sy ['wɪmzi] *n., pl.* **-sies. 1** an odd or fanciful idea; whim: *It was just one of her whimsies; don't take it seriously.* **2** odd or fanciful humour; quaintness: *The story* Alice's Adventures in Wonderland *is full of whimsy.* **3** an object or creation showing whimsy. Also, **whimsey.** ⟨< *whim*⟩

whin [wɪn] *n.* furze. ⟨Cf. Icel. *hvingras* bent grass⟩
☛ *Hom.* WIN.

whine [waɪn] *v.* **whined, whin•ing;** *n.* *—v.* **1** make a high-pitched, drawn-out, complaining cry or sound: *The dog whined to go out with us. The electric saw whined.* **2** complain in a peevish, childish way: *Some people are always whining about trifles.* **3** say with a whine.
—n. **1** a high-pitched, drawn-out, complaining cry or sound. **2** a peevish, childish complaint. ⟨OE *hwīnan*⟩ **—'whin•er,** *n.* **—'whin•ing•ly,** *adv.*
☛ *Hom.* WINE.

whin•ny ['wɪni] *n., pl.* **-nies;** *v.* **-nied, -ny•ing.** *—n.* a soft neighing sound.
—v. of a horse, utter such a sound. ⟨related to WHINE⟩

whin•stone ['wɪn,stoun] *n.* basalt or some similar hard rock. ⟨< *whin* whinstone (of uncertain origin) + *stone*⟩

whin•y ['waɪni] *adj.* **-i•er, -i•est.** habitually whining.

whip [wɪp] *n., v.* **whipped** or **whipt, whip•ping.** *—n.* **1** a flexible thing to strike or beat with, usually a stick with a cord or thong at the end. **2** a whipping motion. **3** a dessert made by beating cream, eggs, fruit, etc. into a froth: *Prune whip is my favourite dessert.* **4** WHISK (def. 3). **5 a** a member of a political party who controls and directs the other members in a lawmaking body, as by seeing that they attend meetings in which important votes will be taken. **b** a call made on members of a political party in a legislature to attend a given session or remain in attendance for it. **6** a person who manages the hounds of a hunting pack. **7** a driver; coachman. **8** a rope and pulley.
—v. **1** strike or beat with or as with a whip; lash: *He whipped the horse to make it go faster.* **2** move, put, or pull quickly and suddenly: *He whipped off his coat and whipped out his knife. The chipmunk whipped behind a tree and escaped.* **3** flap about in a whiplike manner, as flags or clothing in a high wind. **4** bring, get, make, or produce by or as if by whipping: *to whip the nonsense out of someone.* **5** incite; rouse; revive: *The speaker whipped her audience into a fervour.* **6** criticize or reprove with cutting severity. **7** *Informal.* defeat: *The mayor whipped her opponent in the election.* **8** summon (*in, up*) to attend, as the members of a political party in a legislative body, for united action. **9** beat (cream, eggs, etc.) to a froth. **10** whipstitch. **11** wind (a rope, stick, etc.) closely with thread or string; wind (cord, twine, or thread) around something. **12** cast a fishing line with a motion like that of using a whip. **13** fish, using this type of cast: *to whip a stream.*
whip up, a prepare or make quickly: *She whipped up some masks for us to wear on Halloween.* **b** stir up: *We are trying to whip up some interest in speed skating.* ⟨Cf. MDu. and MLG *wippe* swing⟩ **—'whip,like,** *adj.* **—'whip•per,** *n.*

whip•cord ['wɪp,kɔrd] *n.* **1** a strong, twisted cord, sometimes used for the lashes of whips. **2** a strong worsted cloth with diagonal ridges on it.

whip hand 1 the hand that holds the whip while driving a horse-drawn vehicle. **2** a position of control; advantage: *A clever person often gets the whip hand over others.*

whip•lash ['wɪp,læʃ] *n.* **1** the lash of a whip. **2** anything considered as similar to this: *the whiplash of fear.* **3** an injury to the neck caused by a sudden jolt that snaps the head backward and then forward, or forward and then backward. A person in a vehicle that is struck from behind by another vehicle can suffer whiplash.

whip•per–snap•per ['wɪpər ,snæpər] *n.* an insignificant person, especially a young one who thinks he or she is important.

whip•pet ['wɪpɪt] *n.* a breed of swift, lean racing and hunting dog that looks like a small greyhound. The whippet was developed from a cross between the greyhound and a terrier. ⟨< *whip* in the sense of 'move quickly'⟩

whip•ping ['wɪpɪŋ] *n., v.* *—n.* **1** a beating; flogging. **2** an arrangement of cord, twine, or the like, wound around a thing: *We fastened the broken rod with a whipping of wire.*
—v. ppr. of WHIP.

whipping boy 1 formerly, a boy who was educated with a young prince and made to take punishment due to the prince. **2** any person who takes the blame for the wrongdoings of others; a scapegoat.

whipping cream heavy fresh cream with a sufficiently high butterfat content that it can be beaten until stiff.

whipping post formerly, a post to which lawbreakers were tied to be whipped.

whip•ple•tree ['wɪpəl,tri] *n.* the swinging bar of a carriage or wagon, to which the traces of a harness are fastened. Also, **singletree, swingletree, whiffletree.** ⟨? < *whip*⟩

whip•poor•will ['wɪpər,wɪl] *n.* a goatsucker (*Caprimulgus vociferus*) of central and E North America having soft, mottled brown-and-black plumage, a small bill, and an enormous mouth. Also, **whip-poor-will.** ⟨imitative of the bird's cry⟩

whip•saw ['wɪp,sɒ] *n., v.* *—n.* a long, narrow, two-handed saw with each end held in a frame.
—v. **1** cut with a whipsaw. **2** *Informal.* get the better of (a person) no matter what he or she does, or in more than one way at once.

whip•stitch ['wɪp,stɪtʃ] *v., n.* *—v.* sew with stitches passing over and over an edge; overcast (the edge of a garment, fabric, etc.).
—n. a stitch made in whipstitching.

whip•stock ['wɪp,stɒk] *n.* the handle of a whip.

whipt [wɪpt] *v.* a pt. and pp. of WHIP.

whip•worm ['wɪp,wɜrm] *n.* any of various nematodes of the genus *Trichuris* having a slender, whiplike front part. Whipworms are parasitic in the intestines of mammals.

whir or **whirr** [wɜr] *n., v.* **whirred, whir•ring.** *—n.* a soft buzzing noise as of something turning at high speed: *the whir of a small machine, the whir of a hummingbird's wings.*
—v. operate or move with such a noise: *The motor whirred.* ⟨Cf. Danish *hvirre* whirl⟩
☛ *Hom.* WERE.

whirl [wɜrl] *v., n.* *—v.* **1** cause to turn or swing round and round; spin: *He whirled the club.* **2** move round and round: *The dancers whirled about the room. The leaves whirled in the wind.* **3** move or carry quickly: *We were whirled away in an airplane.* **4** become or be dizzy or giddy; reel: *Her mind was whirling.*
—n. **1** a whirling movement. **2** something that whirls. **3** a dizzy or confused condition: *His thoughts were in a whirl.* **4** great activity; a rapid round of happenings, parties, etc.: *We had a rest after the whirl of Christmas holidays.* **5** *Informal.* an attempt; try: *She had never been in a canoe before, but decided to give it a whirl.* ⟨ME, probably < ON *hvirfla* < *hverfla* turn⟩ **—'whirl•er,** *n.*
☛ *Hom.* WHORL [wɜrl].

whirl•i•gig ['wɜrli,gɪg] *n.* **1** a toy that whirls. **2** a merry-go-round. **3** something that whirls or seems to whirl round and round. **4** a whirling movement. ⟨< *whirly-* (obs. var. of *whirl*) + *gig* something that whirls (of uncertain origin)⟩

whirligig beetle any of a family (Gyrinidae) of beetles commonly seen circling and spinning around on the surface of ponds or lakes.

whirl•pool ['wɜrl,pul] *n.* **1** water whirling round and round rapidly and violently, creating a current that sucks things downward. **2** anything like a whirlpool.

whirl•wind ['wɜrl,wɪnd] *n., adj.* *—n.* **1** a current of air whirling violently round and round; a whirling windstorm. **2** anything like a whirlwind, as an overwhelming, inexorable or rapid series of events.
—adj. like a whirlwind; fast: *a whirlwind romance.* ⟨< *whirl* + *wind*, after ON *hvirfilvindr*⟩

whirl•y•bird ['wɜrli,bɜrd] *n.* *Informal.* a helicopter.

whirr [wɜr] *n., v.* See WHIR.

whish [wɪʃ] *n., v.* *—n.* a soft rushing sound; whizz; swish.
—v. make a soft rushing sound. ⟨imitative⟩
☛ *Hom.* WISH.

whisht [wɪʃt] *interj.* *Dialect.* Hush! be quiet! ⟨ME; probably imitative⟩

whisk [wɪsk] *v., n.* *—v.* **1** remove, wipe, brush, etc. with a quick sweeping motion: *He whisked the crumbs from the table. She whisked the letter out of sight. The waiter whisked my plate away.* **2** move or carry quickly or nimbly: *They whisked the children off to bed. The mouse whisked into its hole. The prime minister was whisked away in her limousine.* **3** beat or whip (eggs, etc.) to a froth.
—n. **1** a quick sweeping or whipping movement: *with a whisk of the broom, a whisk of the horse's tail.* **2** WHISK BROOM. **3** a small

wire kitchen utensil for beating eggs, cream, etc. by hand. ⟨ME *visk*, prob. < Scand.; cf. ON *visk* wisp⟩

whisk broom a small, short-handled broom for brushing away crumbs, dirt, etc.

whisk•er [ˈwɪskər] *n.* **1** Usually, **whiskers,** *pl.* the hair growing on a man's face, especially that on his cheeks and chin. **2** one of the hairs growing on a man's face. **3** any of the long, stiff sensory hairs growing near the mouth of a cat, rat, etc. **4** *Crystallography.* a thin single-crystal filament of high tensile strength, several millimetres long and one or two microns in diameter, that grows on certain metals and reinforces them. **5** a very small amount: *Could you move over just a whisker, please?* ⟨< *whisk*⟩

whisk•ered [ˈwɪskərd] *adj.* having whiskers.

whisk•er•y [ˈwɪskəri] *adj.* **1** whiskered. **2** resembling whiskers.

whisk•y or **whiskey** [ˈwɪski] *n., pl.* **-kies. 1** a strong alcoholic drink made from grain. **2** a drink of whisky: *She often has a whisky before dinner.* ⟨short for *whiskybae* < Gaelic *uisge beatha*, literally, water of life⟩

whis•ky–jack [ˈwɪski ˌdʒæk] *n. Cdn.* CANADA JAY. Also, **whiskey-jack.** ⟨< obs. *whisky-john*, alteration of Cree *weskuchanis*⟩

whisky sour a cocktail consisting of whisky, lemon juice, and sugar, usually served with an orange slice and a cherry. Also, **whiskey sour.**

whis•per [ˈwɪspər] *v., n.* —*v.* **1** speak or utter very softly, with little or no vibration of the vocal cords: *We could hear them whispering behind us.* **2** talk or tell secretly or privately: *It is whispered that his health is failing.* **3** make a soft, rustling sound: *The wind whispered in the pines.*
—*n.* **1** the act or an instance of whispering; speech without vibration of the vocal cords: *She spoke in a whisper. They were speaking in whispers.* **2** something told secretly or privately. **3** a soft, rustling sound. ⟨OE *hwisprian*⟩ —**ˈwhis•per•er,** *n.*

whispering campaign a campaign of discreditation, defamation, etc., using gossip.

whis•pe•ry [ˈwɪspəri] *adj.* having the characteristics of a WHISPER (defs. 1, 3).

whist[1] [wɪst] *n.* a card game, resembling bridge, for two pairs of players. Auction and contract bridge developed from whist. ⟨alteration of *whisk*, influenced by *whist*[2]⟩

whist[2] [wɪst] *interj., adj.* —*interj.* hush! silence!
—*adj. Archaic.* hushed; silent. ⟨imitative⟩

whis•tle [ˈwɪsəl] *v.* **-tled, -tling;** *n.* —*v.* **1** make a clear, shrill, often musical sound by forcing breath through one's teeth or pursed lips: *We heard him whistling as he walked along.* **2** make or utter a shrill sound resembling this: *The old steam engine whistled. The widgeons whistled as they flew over.* **3** produce or utter by whistling: *to whistle a tune.* **4** blow a whistle. **5** call, signal, or direct by a whistle: *The police officer whistled the motorist to stop.* **6** move with a shrill sound: *The wind whistled around the house.*
whistle for, *Informal.* go without; fail to get.
whistle in the dark, try or pretend to be courageous or hopeful in a fearful or trying situation.
—*n.* **1** the sound made by whistling. **2** a device for making shrill sounds by means of forced air or steam.
blow the whistle (on), inform (on).
wet (one's) **whistle,** *Informal.* take a drink. ⟨OE *hwistlian*⟩

whis•tler [ˈwɪslər] *n.* **1** a person who or thing that whistles. **2** any of various birds having a whistling call (such as the **whistling swan**) or making a whistling sound in flight (such as the **goldeneye**). **3** *Cdn.* **a** HOARY MARMOT. **b** pika.

whist•le–stop [ˈwɪsəl ˌstɒp] *n., v.* **-stopped, -stop•ping.** *Informal.* —*n.* **1** a small, little-known town along a railway line at which a train stops only when signalled. **2** a stop at such a town or station for a brief appearance or speech, as in a political campaign tour. **3** (*adjl.*) of, having to do with, or characterized by whistle-stops: *a whistle-stop campaign.*
—*v.* make a series of electioneering appearances or speeches at various small towns along a route.

whistling swan a North American swan (*Olor columbianus*, also classified as *Cygnus columbianus*) that nests in the Arctic, having white plumage and a black bill, named for its whistling call.

whit [wɪt] *n.* a very small bit: *The sick woman is not a whit better.* ⟨var. of OE *wiht* thing, wight⟩
☛ *Hom.* WIT.

white [wəit] *n., adj.* **whit•er, whit•est;** *v.* **whit•ed, whit•ing.**
—*n.* **1** the colour of fresh snow or salt; the opposite of black. **2** the quality of being white; white coloration or appearance; whiteness. **3** a white colouring matter. **4** often, **whites,** *pl.* white cloth or clothing. **5** something white; a white or colourless part: *the white of an egg, the whites of the eyes.* **6** a member of a light-skinned race. **7** *Archery.* the outermost ring of a butt (formerly painted white). **8** *Printing.* a blank space. **9** an ultraconservative; reactionary; royalist. **10** *Chess, checkers, or backgammon.* **a** the light-coloured squares or other shapes on the board. **b** the white or light-coloured pieces. **c** the player holding these pieces.
—*adj.* **1** having the colour of snow or salt; reflecting light without absorbing any of the rays composing it. **2** having a colour that approaches this. **3** pale: *She turned white with fear.* **4** light-coloured: *white wines, white meat.* **5** having a light-coloured skin; of or having to do with the Caucasian race. **6** silvery or grey: *white hair.* **7** snowy: *a white winter.* **8** *Printing.* blank: *white space.* **9** spotless; pure; innocent. **10** wearing white clothing. **11** Often, **White,** ultraconservative; reactionary; royalist. **12** good; beneficent: *white magic.* **13** being at white heat.
bleed (someone) **white,** gradually use up or take away all of (someone's) money, strength, etc.
—*v.* **1** make or become white. **2** remove (an error) by covering it with white (*usually with* **out**). ⟨OE *hwīt*⟩ —**ˈwhite•ness,** *n.*
☛ *Hom.* WIGHT.

white admiral a butterfly (*Limenitis arthemis*) having prominent white bands on its wings, common to Canada and the eastern U.S.

white ant a termite.

white•bait [ˈwəit,beit] *n., pl.* **-bait. 1** a young herring or sprat about 3 cm to 5 cm long. **2** any of various very small fish used for food.

white•bark pine [ˈwəit,bɑrk] **1** a small, often shrubby, mountain pine (*Pinus albicaulis*) of W North America, having bluish green needles, egg-shaped or almost round cones, and smooth, chalky white bark on young stems. **2** the light, medium-soft wood of this tree.

white bear *Cdn.* POLAR BEAR.

white birch 1 a large North American birch (*Betula papyrifera*), common throughout most of Canada and noted especially for its papery white bark, which can be readily peeled off in layers and which was traditionally used by North American First Nations peoples of the eastern woodlands for making canoes, etc. **2** any of various other birches with white bark, such as the European silver birch. **3** the wood of any of these trees.

white blood cell any of the white or colourless blood cells found in the blood and lymph of vertebrates; leucocyte. White blood cells help the body to fight infection.

white•cap [ˈwəit,kæp] *n.* a wave with a foaming white crest.

white cedar 1 an arborvitae (*Thuja occidentalis*) of E North America, found in Canada from Nova Scotia to Manitoba. **2** a coniferous evergreen tree (*Chamaecyparis thyoides*) of the cypress family, found in wetlands of the eastern U.S. **3** the wood of any of these trees.

A white cedar

white clover a low-growing, creeping, Eurasian clover (*Trifolium repens*) having white flower heads, widely cultivated as a forage crop and also used in mixtures for lawn grass.

white coal *Cdn.* **1** water used as a source of power. **2** the power so generated.

white•coat [ˈwəit,kout] *n.* **1** a young harp seal. It has a coat of white hair. **2** the skin of a whitecoat.

white–col•lar [ˈwəit ˈkɒlər] *adj.* of or having to do with clerical, professional, or business work or workers.

white corpuscle WHITE BLOOD CELL.

whit•ed sepulchre [wəitɪd] a hypocrite. ⟨a term used in the Christian Bible⟩

white dwarf *Astronomy.* a small star, about the size of the earth and of little brightness, that is in the final stage of evolution for low-mass stars, having undergone gravitational collapse. Compare RED GIANT.

white elephant 1 something rare or valuable that is expensive and troublesome to keep and take care of. 2 something very costly or elaborate that turns out to be useless or not worthwhile: *The new airport is just a white elephant.* 3 a possession that may have some intrinsic or potential value but is unwanted by its owner: *Several neighbours decided to have a garage sale to get rid of white elephants.* ⟨with reference to a rare albino or pale grey variety of Indian elephant held sacred in parts of S Asia⟩

white–faced ['wəit ˌfeist] *adj.* 1 wan; pallid; pale. 2 of an animal, having large white patches of hair on the head: *a white-faced horse.* 3 having a white front or surface.

white feather a symbol of cowardice.
show the white feather, act like a coward.

white•fish ['wəitˌfɪʃ] *n., pl.* **-fish** or **-fish•es.** any of a subfamily (Coregoninae, of the family Salmonidae) of silvery, large-scaled, freshwater fishes of northern regions that are important food fishes. Some authorities classify the whitefishes in a separate family (Coregonidae).

white flag a plain white flag or piece of cloth, used as a sign of truce or surrender.

white•fly ['wəitˌflaɪ] *n.* any of a variety of plant-sucking insects of the family Aleyrodidae, having scalelike larvae. The winged adults are covered with a white, powdery wax and are a considerable garden and greenhouse pest in some areas of Canada and the U.S.

white–foot•ed mouse ['wəit ˌfʊtɪd] DEER MOUSE.

white fox 1 the winter colour phase of the Arctic fox. 2 the valuable fur of this animal.

white friar a Carmelite monk. ⟨from the distinctive white cloak worn by members of the order⟩

white garden lily MADONNA LILY.

white gold an alloy of gold, nickel or platinum, and some zinc and copper, that looks much like platinum and is used for jewellery.

white–haired ['wəit ˌhɛrd] *adj.* 1 having white or very fair hair. 2 favourite; darling: *the white-haired boy of the Liberal party.*

White•hall ['wəitˌhɒl] *n.* 1 a former palace in London. 2 a street in London where many government offices are located. 3 the British government or its policies.

white heat 1 an intense heat at which things give off a dazzling, white light. 2 a state of intense activity, excitement, or feeling.

white heather *Cdn.* a small, evergreen shrub (*Cassiope tetragona*) of the heath family, found in Arctic regions and having scalelike leaves and nodding, bell-shaped flowers.

white–hot ['wəit 'hɒt] *adj.* 1 white with heat; extremely hot. 2 very enthusiastic; excited; intense.

White House 1 the official residence of the President of the United States, in Washington, D.C. 2 *Informal.* the office, authority, opinion, etc. of the President of the United States: *What is the opinion of the White House on this matter?*

white lead [lɛd] 1 a heavy, white, poisonous compound of lead, used in making paint; basic carbonate of lead. *Formula*: $2PbCO_3Pb(OH)_2$ 2 lead sulphate or various other white pigments that contain lead.

white lie a lie about some small matter, especially one told to avoid being rude or hurting someone's feelings.

white light *Physics.* light that is a mixture of wavelengths ranging from red to violet, but is perceived by the eye as having the quality of noontime sunlight.

white–liv•ered ['wəit ˌlɪvərd] *adj.* 1 cowardly. 2 pale; unhealthy looking.

white magic good magic. Compare BLACK MAGIC.

white matter *Anatomy.* tissue of the brain, spinal cord, etc. that consists chiefly of nerve fibres. Compare GREY MATTER (def. 1).

white meat any light-coloured meat or poultry such as veal, pork, breast of poultry or game birds, etc.

whit•en ['wəitən] *v.* 1 make or become white: *to whiten sheets with bleach.* 2 make or become pale or paler: *He whitened when he heard the bad news.* **—'whit•en•er,** *n.* **—'whit•en•ing,** *n.*

☛ *Syn.* **1. Whiten,** BLEACH = make white or nearly white. **Whiten,** the general word, often suggests applying a substance on the outside of something: *toothpaste that whitens one's teeth.* **Bleach** means to make white, lighter, or colourless by exposing to sunlight and air or by using chemicals: *Cotton can be bleached in the sun.*

white noise the sound produced by using the whole range of audible frequencies at once. Also, **white sound.** ⟨by analogy with *white light*, which contains all the wavelengths of the visible spectrum⟩

white oak 1 a tall oak (*Quercus alba*) of E North America having shiny, bright green, very deeply lobed leaves, light grey or whitish bark, and a hard, durable wood. 2 any of various similar oaks. 3 the wood of any of these trees, highly valued for lumber.

white•out ['wəitˌʌut] *n. Cdn.* 1 an arctic weather condition in which the snow-covered ground, the cloudy sky, and the horizon become a continuous, shadowless mass of dazzling white. 2 the inability to distinguish objects, or sky from land, resulting from this condition. 3 a winter weather condition in which blowing snow completely fills the range of vision: *Many highway traffic accidents are caused by whiteouts.* 4 an opaque liquid used to erase errors in typing or writing. ⟨modelled on *blackout*⟩

white paper a government report concerning matters of lesser importance than those appearing in BLUE BOOKS.

white pepper a hot-tasting seasoning made by grinding the dried, husked berries of the black pepper vine. Compare BLACK PEPPER.

white pine 1 any of various pines having soft, light wood; especially, the **eastern white pine** (*Pinus strobus*) of the Great Lakes and St. Lawrence forest regions and the **western white pine** (*P. monticola*) of southern British Columbia and the NW United States. 2 the wood of any of these trees, much used for building.

white plague tuberculosis.

white poplar 1 a large Eurasian poplar (*Populus alba*) having a dense covering of white, woolly hairs on the underside of the lobed leaves and on the twigs and buds. It is widely cultivated as an ornamental tree. 2 TREMBLING ASPEN.

white potato the common potato.

White Russian 1 a Russian living in Belarus north of Ukraine. 2 a Russian who recognizes the former czarist government of Russia as the legal government of that country.

white sale a sale of household linens such as sheets, pillowcases, towels, etc. ⟨from the fact of all these articles having been at one time made from white fabrics⟩

white sauce a sauce made of milk, butter, flour, and seasonings cooked together.

white shark a large, ferocious shark (*Carcharodon carcharias*), widely distributed in temperate and tropical seas, having a greyish back and white underside. The white shark is a man-eater.

white slave 1 a girl or woman who is forced to be a prostitute. 2 a white person held as a slave. **—'white-'slave,** *adj.*

white slaver a person who keeps, controls, or deals in WHITE SLAVES.

white slavery 1 the condition of white slaves. 2 traffic in WHITE SLAVES.

white sound WHITE NOISE.

white spruce a common spruce (*Picea glauca*) of the northern forest, also found throughout the rest of Canada, larger and taller than the black spruce, having long, slender cones, and bluish green needles often covered with a whitish, powdery coating called a bloom.

white supremacist a person who believes or supports the belief that the white race is superior to other races.

white supremacy the belief that the white race is superior to other races, especially the black and oriental races, and should therefore occupy the highest social, economic, and governmental positions, achieving these goals through deportation, oppression, and, in extreme cases, extermination of those believed to be inferior.

white–tail ['wəit ˌteil] *n.* WHITE-TAILED DEER.

white–tailed deer ['wəit ˌteild] a North American deer (*Odocoileus virginianus*) closely resembling the mule deer, but having a broad, relatively long tail with a wide, white fringe and underside, and antlers that arch forward.

White-tailed deer

white•thorn ['wəit,θɔrn] *n.* hawthorn.

white•throat ['wəit,θrout] *n.* **1** an Old World warbler (*Sylvia communis*) having mainly brownish plumage with a white throat. **2** WHITE-THROATED SPARROW.

white–throat•ed sparrow ['wəit ˌθroutɪd] a common, grey-and-brown, North American sparrow (*Zonotrichia albicollis*) having broad stripes across the top of the head, from front to back, and a white throat patch.

white tie 1 a white bow tie for men, worn with formal evening dress and some university regalia. **2** men's formal evening dress with tailcoat and white tie. Compare BLACK TIE.

white•wash ['wəit,wɒʃ] *n., v. —n.* **1** a liquid for whitening walls, woodwork, etc., usually made of lime and water. **2** a covering up of faults or mistakes. **3** anything that covers up faults or mistakes. **4** *Informal. Sports.* a defeat in which the loser fails to score. **5** a cosmetic used for making the skin fairer.
—v. **1** whiten with whitewash. **2** cover up the faults or mistakes of. **3** *Informal. Sports.* defeat in a shutout.

white water rapids.

white–wa•ter ['wəit ˌwɒtər] *adj.* of or having to do with movement through or across rapids, especially as recreation: *white-water rafting.*

white whale BELUGA (def. 1).

white•wood ['wəit,wʊd] *n.* **1** a tree with light-coloured wood, such as a tulip tree, linden, etc. **2** its wood. **3** cottonwood.

whith•er ['wɪðər] *adv. or conj. Archaic or poetic.* to what or which place, situation, condition, etc.; where. ⟨OE *hwider*⟩
☛ *Hom.* WITHER.

whith•er•so•ev•er [ˌwɪðərsou'ɛvər] *adv. or conj. Archaic.* wherever; to whatever place.

whit•ing[1] ['wəitɪŋ] *n., pl.* **-ing** or **-ings. 1** an important European marine food fish (*Merlangius merlangus*, also classified as *Gadus merlangus*) of the cod family. **2** any of various related or similar marine fishes. ⟨ME < MDu. *wijting* < *wit* white; cf. OE *hwītling*⟩

whit•ing[2] ['wəitɪŋ] *n., v. —n.* a powdered white chalk, used in making putty, whitewash, and silver polish. ⟨< *white* + *ing*⟩
—v. ppr. of WHITE.

whit•ish ['wəitɪʃ] *adj.* almost white. **—'whit•ish•ness,** *n.*

whit•low ['wɪtlou] *n.* a usually pus-filled inflammation of a finger or toe, especially near the nail; FELON[2]. ⟨earlier *whitflaw*, probably < *white* + *flaw*⟩

Whit•mon•day ['wɪt'mʌndei] *or* ['wɪt'mʌndi] *n.* the Monday after Whitsunday.

Whit•sun ['wɪtsən] *adj.* of or having to do with Whitsunday or Whitsuntide.

Whit•sun•day ['wɪt'sʌndei] *or* ['wɪt'sʌndi] *n. Christianity.* the seventh Sunday after Easter; Pentecost. ⟨< *white* + *Sunday*⟩

Whit•sun•tide ['wɪtsən,taid] *n.* the week beginning with Whitsunday, especially the first three days.

whit•tle ['wɪtəl] *v.* **-tled, -tling. 1** cut (shavings or chips) from (wood, etc.) with a knife. **2** shape or make by whittling: *to whittle a boat.*
whittle down or **away,** cut down little by little: *We tried to whittle down our expenses.* ⟨earlier *thwittle*, ult. < OE *thwītan* cut⟩
—'whit•tler, *n.*

whiz[1] [wɪz] *n. Informal.* a person who is very good in a particular field or activity: *a computer whiz.* ⟨alteration of *wiz* < *wizard*⟩

whiz[2] or **whizz** [wɪz] *n., pl.* **whiz•zes;** *v.* **whizzed, whiz•zing.** *—n.* **1** a humming or hissing sound, especially such a sound made by very rapid movement. **2** *Slang.* something very excellent, snazzy, etc.: *That's a whiz of a bike you've got there!*
—v. make a humming or hissing sound; move or rush or cause to rush with such a sound: *An arrow whizzed past his head.* ⟨imitative⟩

whiz–kid or **whiz kid** ['wɪz ˌkɪd] *n.* a young person who is unusually talented, expert, or influential for his or her age in a given field.

who [hu] *pron. poss.* **whose** [huz], *obj.* **whom** [hum]. **1** what person(s) or which person(s); an interrogative pronoun used in direct or indirect questions about the identity of a person or persons: *Who is she? Who told you? I don't know who did it.* **2** a relative pronoun used to introduce a clause giving extra information about someone just mentioned: *The girl who spoke has left. We saw the men who were hired.*
as who should say, *Archaic.* in a manner of speaking.
who's who, a which is one person and which is another. **b** which people are important. ⟨OE *hwā*⟩
☛ *Usage.* **Who** refers to people, to personified objects (such as a ship, a country, etc.), and occasionally to animals. See also the note at THAT.
☛ *Usage.* In informal English **who** is commonly used in both subject and object positions, though **whom** is obligatory immediately after a preposition: *Who did you speak to?* but *I saw the man to whom you spoke yesterday.* Formal and written English require **whom** in object position.
☛ *Usage.* The use of **whose** as a relative referring to a non-personal antecedent (e.g., *generators whose combined capacity*. . .) is acceptable in both formal and informal situations when the construction **of which** would make the sentence seem clumsy.

WHO WORLD HEALTH ORGANIZATION.

whoa [wou] *interj.* (*used especially to horses*) stop!
☛ *Hom.* WO, WOE.

who'd [hud] **1** who would: *Who'd like to go along?* **2** who had: *The girl who'd been to the party was tired.*

who•dun•it [hu'dʌnɪt] *n. Slang.* a story, film, or play dealing with crime, especially murder, and its detection. ⟨< *who* + *done* + *it*⟩

who•ev•er [hu'ɛvər] *pron.* **1** who; any person that: *Whoever wants the book may have it.* **2** no matter who: *Whoever else goes hungry, he won't.* **3** an emphatic version of the interrogative *who*: *Whoever thought that up?*

whole [houl] *adj., n. —adj.* **1** having all its parts or elements; complete: *He gave her a whole set of dishes.* **2** comprising the full quantity, amount, extent, number, etc.; entire: *a whole page. He worked the whole day.* **3** not injured, broken, or defective: *to get out of a fight with a whole skin.* **4** in one piece; undivided: *to swallow a piece of meat whole.* **5** *Mathematics.* not fractional; integral: *a whole number.* **6** well; healthy. **7** having the same father and mother: *They are whole brothers.*
made out of whole cloth, *Informal.* entirely false or made-up.
—n. **1** all of a thing; the total: *Four quarters make a whole. She will regret that for the whole of her life.* **2** any thing or group of things having unity and completeness; a system.
as a whole, as one complete thing; altogether.
on the whole, a considering everything. **b** for the most part. ⟨dial. var. of ME *hole*, OE *hāl*⟩ **—'whole•ness,** *n.*
☛ *Hom.* HOLE.

whole blood 1 blood used for transfusions that is exactly as taken from the donor, having had none of the elements removed. **2** a relationship to someone through both parents.

whole gale wind having a speed of 89-102 km/h. See chart of Beaufort scale in the Appendix.

whole–heart•ed ['houl 'hɑrtɪd] *adj.* earnest; sincere; hearty. **—'whole-'heart•ed•ly,** *adv.* **—'whole-'heart•ed•ness,** *n.*

whole–hog ['houl 'hɒg] *adv. Slang.* completely; unreservedly: *She gives herself whole-hog to any project she takes up.*

whole language *Education.* the teaching of reading and writing in context, i.e., by its use in learning other things, rather than artificially and in isolation.

whole milk milk with none of the butterfat or trace elements removed.

whole note *Music.* a note having the longest time value in standard notation, used as the basis for determining the time value of all other notes. It is equal to two half notes, four quarter notes, etc. See NOTE for picture.

whole number a number denoting zero or one or more whole things or units; a number that does not contain a fraction; integer. *Examples*: 0, 1, 3, –47, 2052

whole rest *Music.* a rest lasting as long as a WHOLE NOTE. See REST[1] for picture.

whole•sale ['houl,seil] *n., adj., adv., v.* **-saled, -sal•ing.** *—n.* the sale of goods in large quantities at a time, usually to retailers rather than to consumers directly: *He buys at wholesale and sells at retail.* Compare RETAIL.
—adj. of or having to do with sale in large quantities: *a wholesale fruit business. The wholesale price of this coat is $100; the retail*

price is $150. **3** broad and general; extensive and indiscriminate: *Avoid wholesale condemnation.*
–adv. **1** in large lots or quantities. **2** at a wholesale price: *I can get it for you wholesale.* **3** indiscriminately or on a large scale.
–v. sell or be sold in large quantities: *They wholesale these jackets at $10 each. Such jackets usually wholesale for much more.*

whole•sal•er ['houl,seilər] *n.* a merchant who sells goods wholesale.

whole•some ['houlsəm] *adj.* **1** good for the health; healthful: *wholesome food.* **2** healthy-looking; suggesting health: *a wholesome face.* **3** good for the mind or morals; beneficial: *wholesome books.* ⟨ME *holsum* < *hol* whole + *-sum* -some[1]⟩ **–'whole•some•ly,** *adv.* **–'whole•some•ness,** *n.*
☛ *Syn.* See note at HEALTHY.

whole step *Music.* an interval consisting of two adjoining semitones and equal to one-sixth of an octave, such as D to E, or E to F♯.

whole tone WHOLE STEP.

whole–wheat ['houl 'wit] *adj.* made of the entire wheat kernel or from the flour derived from this.

whol•ism ['houlɪzəm] *n.* See HOLISM.

whol•is•tic [hou'lɪstɪk] *adj.* See HOLISTIC.

who'll [hul] who will; who shall.

whol•ly ['houlli] *or* ['houli] *adv.* to the whole amount or extent; completely; entirely; totally.
☛ *Hom.* HOLEY, HOLI, HOLY ['houli].

whom [hum] *pron.* the objective form of WHO: *No one knows for whom that house is being built. Whom do you wish to see?* ⟨OE *hwām*, dat. of *hwā* who⟩
☛ *Usage.* See note at WHO.

whom•ev•er [hum'ɛvər] *pron.* **1** whom; any person whom. **2** no matter whom. **3** used interrogatively, whom (*emphatic*): *Whomever could he have meant?*

whom•so•ev•er [,humsou'ɛvər] *pron. Archaic.* any person whom; whomever.

whoop [hup] *or* [wup] *n., v.* *–n.* **1** a loud cry or shout: *When land was sighted, the sailor let out a whoop of joy.* **2** the cry of an owl, crane, etc.; hoot. **3** the loud, gasping noise a person with whooping cough makes after a fit of coughing.
–v. **1** shout loudly. **2** call, urge, drive, etc. with shouts: *to whoop the dogs on.* **3** hoot. **4** make a loud gasping noise, as in whooping cough.
whoop it up, *Slang.* make a noisy disturbance, as in celebrating. ⟨imitative⟩
☛ *Hom.* HOOP [hup].

whoop–de–do ['hup] *or* ['wup di du] *n. Informal.* **1** loud commotion or display; uproar. **2** *Ironic.* big deal; so what. Also, **whoop-de-doo.**

whoop•ee ['wʊpi] *or* [wʊpi]; *also, for n. 1,* ['wʊ'pi] *interj., n.* *–interj.* an exclamation of hilarious, unrestrained joy or pleasure.
–n. **1** a shout of "whoopee!" **2** loud excitement; hilarity.
make whoopee, a have a noisy, hilarious good time. **b** make love. ⟨< *whoop*⟩

whoop•er ['hupər] *or* ['wupər] *n.* **1** WHOOPING CRANE. **2** WHOOPER SWAN. **3** a person who or animal that whoops.

whooper swan a large, white, Old World swan (*Cygnus cygnus*) having a black bill with a yellow base, named for its whooping call.

whoop•ing cough ['hupɪŋ] *or* ['wupɪŋ] *Pathology.* an infectious disease of children, characterized by fits of coughing ending with a loud, gasping sound. In Canada, whooping cough, also called pertussis, is now largely prevented by vaccination.

Whooping cranes—about 135 cm long including the tail; height about 120 cm

whooping crane ['wupɪŋ] *or* ['hupɪŋ] a very large white North American crane (*Grus americana*) having a long neck and legs, with black wing tips and a red patch on the face. The whooping crane, which is the tallest of Canadian birds, is almost extinct.

whoop•la ['hupla] *n.* See HOOPLA.

whoops [wʊps] *interj.* oops.

whoop–up ['hup ,ʌp] *or* ['wup ,ʌp] *n. Cdn., esp. West. Slang.* a noisy party or other celebration. ⟨< *v. whoop it up*, enjoy oneself in a boisterous way⟩

whoosh [wuʃ] *or* [wʊʃ] *n., v.* *–n.* **1** a loud, fast rushing noise, as of air or water. **2** a movement causing this sound.
–v. move or cause to move with such a sound.

whop [wɒp] *v.* **whopped, whop•ping;** *n.* *–v.* **1** *Informal.* strike hard or beat. **2** defeat soundly.
–n. a heavy blow or bump. Also, **whap.**

whop•per ['wɒpər] *n. Informal.* **1** something very large. **2** a big lie.

whop•ping ['wɒpɪŋ] *adj., v.* *–adj. Informal.* very large of its kind; huge.
–v. ppr. of WHOP.

whore [hɔr] *or* [hur] *n., v.* **whored, whor•ing.** *–n.* a promiscuous woman or one who is a prostitute.
–v. **1** have intercourse with whores. **2** of a woman, be or act as a whore. **3** pursue (something unworthy) (*used with* **after**). ⟨OE *hōre*⟩
☛ *Hom.* HOAR [hɔr].

who're ['huər] *v.* who are: *Who're the new people in the house?*

whore•house ['hɔr,hʌus] *or* ['hur,hʌus] *n.* brothel.

whorl [wɔrl] *or* [wɜrl] *n.* **1** a circle of leaves or flowers around the stem of a plant. **2** one of the turns of a spiral shell. **3** any coil or curl, especially of something that is whirling or that suggests a whirling movement. **4** a type of fingerprint in which the ridges in the centre turn through at least one complete circle. ⟨probably var. of *whirl*⟩
☛ *Hom.* WHIRL [wɜrl].

whorled [wɔrld] *or* [wɜrld] *adj.* **1** having a whorl or whorls. **2** arranged in a whorl.
☛ *Hom.* WORLD [wɜrld].

whor•tle•ber•ry ['wɜrtəl,bɛri] *n., pl.* **-ries. 1** a low-growing Eurasian shrub (*Vaccinium myrtillus*) closely related to the blueberry, having sweet, blackish, edible berries. **2** the berry of this shrub. Also called **bilberry.** ⟨< *whortle* (ult. < OE *horte* whortleberry) + *berry*⟩

who's [huz] **1** who is. **2** who has: *Who's been eating my porridge?*
☛ *Hom.* WHOSE.

whose [huz] *pron., adj.* the possessive form of WHO and of WHICH; of or relating to whom or which: *I found this pen, but I don't know whose it is. Whose car is that?* ⟨OE *hwæs*, gen. of *hwā* who; influenced in ME by nominative *who*⟩
☛ *Hom.* WHO'S.
☛ *Usage.* **Whose** is always used when referring to people, but it can also be used for things, in order to make a long written or spoken sentence smoother. For instance, it is easier to read the second of the following sentences than the first: **1.** *The plant has three new generators, the combined capacity of which is greater than that of the five we had before.* **2.** *The plant has three new generators whose combined capacity is greater than that of the five we had before.*

whose•so•ev•er [,huzsou'ɛvər] *pron. Archaic or formal.* whose; of any person whatsoever; no matter whose: *I will accept whosesoever help is offered.*

who•sis ['huzɪs] *n. Informal.* a person or thing whose name has been forgotten: *Could you get me the whosis on the shelf over the sink? Have you ever met little Whosis over there?*

who•so ['husou] *pron. Archaic.* whoever.

who•so•ev•er [,husou'ɛvər] *pron. Archaic or formal.* whoever; anybody who.

why [waɪ] *adv. or conj., n., pl.* **whys;** *interj.* *–adv. or conj.* **1** for what cause, reason, or purpose: *Why did you do it? I don't know why I did it. That is why he raised the question.* **2** for which; because of which: *That is the reason why he failed.*
why not, *Informal.* OK; let's try it.
–n. the cause; reason: *I can't understand the whys and wherefores of her behaviour.*
–interj. an expression used to show surprise, doubt, etc. or just to fill in: *Why! The cage is empty. Why, yes, I will if you wish.* ⟨OE *hwȳ*, instrumental case of *hwā* who and *hwæt* what⟩
☛ *Hom.* WYE, Y.

WI or **W.I.** WOMEN'S INSTITUTE.

Wic•ca ['wɪkə] *n.* the belief in the power of the old pagan religion of northern Europe, whose followers are organized in groups called covens. ⟨OE *wicca* wizard⟩

Wic•can ['wɪkən] *n., adj.* —*n.* a devotee of Wicca. —*adj.* of or having to do with Wicca.

wick[1] [wɪk] *n.* the part of an oil lamp or candle that is lighted, usually a loosely-twisted cord through which oil or melted wax is drawn up and burned. ⟨OE *wēoce*⟩

wick[2] [wɪk] *v., n. Curling.* —*v.* curl (a stone) so that it glances off another already played.
—*n.* a shot played in this way.

wick•ed ['wɪkɪd] *adj.* **1** bad; evil; sinful: *a wicked person, wicked deeds.* **2** mischievous; playfully sly: *a wicked smile.* **3** *Informal.* unpleasant; severe: *a wicked task, a wicked storm.* **4** *Slang.* skilful; masterful: *a wicked golfer, to play a wicked game of tennis.* ⟨< *wick* wicked, probably ult. < OE *wicca* wizard⟩ **—'wick•ed•ly,** *adv.*

wick•ed•ness ['wɪkɪdnɪs] *n.* **1** sinfulness; the state of being wicked. **2** a wicked thing or act; sin; something evil.

wick•er ['wɪkər] *n.* **1** slender, easily bent branches or twigs that can be woven together. Wicker is used in making baskets and furniture. **2** (*adjl.*) made of wicker. **3** (*adjl.*) covered with wicker. **4** a slender, flexible branch or twig; a withe. **5** wickerwork. ⟨ME < Scand.; cf. dial. Swedish *vikker* willow⟩
☛ *Hom.* WHICKER.

wick•er•work ['wɪkər,wɜrk] *n.* **1** twigs or branches woven together; wicker. **2** anything made of wicker. **3** the art or business of making things out of wicker.

wick•et ['wɪkɪt] *n.* **1** a small door or gate: *The big door has a wicket in it.* **2** a small window or opening at a counter, till, etc., often protected by a screen or grating: *Buy your tickets at this wicket.* **3** a small gate or valve for emptying the chamber of a canal lock, or in the chute of a water wheel for regulating the passage of water. **4** *Croquet.* a wire arch stuck in the ground to knock the ball through. **5** *Cricket.* **a** either of the two sets of sticks that one side tries to hit with the ball. **b** the level space between these. **c** one batsman's turn. **d** the period during which two players bat together. ⟨ME < AF *wiket,* ult. < Gmc., cf. MDu. *wicket*⟩

wick•et•keep•er ['wɪkɪt,kipər] *n. Cricket.* the player who stands behind the wicket.

wick•ing ['wɪkɪŋ] *n., v.* —*n.* material for lamp or candle wicks. —*v.* ppr. of WICK[2].

wick•i•up ['wɪki,ʌp] *n. Cdn.* **1** a brush- or mat-covered shelter among certain Algonquian First Nations people. **2** a crude shelter, such as a lean-to. ⟨< Algonquian; cf. Fox *wikiyap* dwelling⟩

wid•der•shins ['wɪdər,ʃɪnz] *adv. Scottish.* **1** in the opposite or contrary direction. **2** in a direction contrary to the apparent course of the sun, considered to be unlucky. Also, **withershins.** ⟨< MLG < MHG *widersinnes* < *wider* against, opposed + *-sinn* way, direction + *-es*⟩

wide [waɪd] *adj.* **wid•er, wid•est;** *adv., n.* —*adj.* **1** filling much space from side to side; not narrow; broad: *a wide street, the wide ocean.* **2** extending a certain distance from side to side, measured at right angles to length: *The door is 90 cm wide.* **3** full; ample; roomy: *a wide room.* **4** of great range: *wide reading.* **5** far or fully open; distended: *to stare with wide eyes.* **6** far from a named point, object, target, etc.: *a wide shot. His guess was wide of the truth.*
—*adv.* **1** to a great or relatively great extent from side to side: *wide apart.* **2** over an extensive space or region: *They travel far and wide.* **3** to the full extent; fully: *Open your mouth wide.* **4** aside; astray: *Her shot went wide.*
—*n.* **1** a wide space or expanse. **2** *Cricket.* a ball bowled wide of the wicket, counting as a run for the batsman's side. ⟨OE *wīd*⟩ **—'wide•ness,** *n.*
☛ *Syn. adj.* **1, 2. Wide,** BROAD = far or large across, especially when it is larger than average. Although they are often used interchangeably, **wide** emphasizes the distance from one side to the other; **broad** emphasizes size or expanse of what is between the two sides: *A wide ocean separates Canada from Europe. Ships sail on the broad ocean.*

wide–a•wake ['waɪd ə'weik] *adj.* **1** with the eyes wide open; fully awake. **2** alert; keen; knowing.

wide–eyed ['waɪd ,aɪd] *adj.* with or as if with the eyes wide open, as with innocence, sleeplessness, or surprise.

wide•ly ['waɪdli] *adv.* **1** to a great extent; throughout a large area; to a great many people; over a wide range: *a widely distributed plant, a man who is widely known, to be widely read, eyes opened widely.* **2** very; extremely: *The boys gave two widely different accounts of the quarrel.*

wid•en ['waɪdən] *v.* make or become wide or wider: *She widened the path through the forest. The river widens as it flows.*

wide–o•pen ['waɪd 'oupən] *adj.* (*only before the noun; two words elsewhere*) **1** opened as much as possible. **2** lax in the enforcement of laws, especially those having to do with the sale of liquor, gambling, and prostitution. **3** quite unsettled or undecided: *a wide-open question.* ⟨late ME⟩

wide•spread ['waɪd,sprɛd] *adj.* **1** spread widely or fully: *widespread wings.* **2** spread over a wide space: *a widespread flood.* **3** occurring in many places or among many persons far apart: *a widespread belief.*

widg•eon ['wɪdʒən] *n., pl.* **-eons** or **-eon.** any of several freshwater ducks (genus *Anas,* also classified as *Mareca*), such as the North American baldpate; also, a Eurasian species (*A. penelope*), the male of which has mainly grey-and-white plumage with a reddish brown head and breast. See also BALDPATE (def. 2). ⟨Cf. MF *vigeon* wild duck⟩

wid•get ['wɪdʒɪt] *n.* a small, unspecified tool or gadget, especially a hypothetical one.

wid•ow ['wɪdou] *n., v.* —*n.* **1** a woman whose husband is dead and who has not married again. **2** *Card games.* **a** a person holding a hand, or group of cards, not dealt to any player but capable of being used by a player who bids for it. **b** a hand dealt to the table. **3** *Printing.* a word or group of words constituting less than a full line at the head of a column or page. **4** a woman whose husband is often away or preoccupied because of some overindulged pastime: *a computer game widow.*
—*v.* make a widow or widower of: *She was widowed when she was only thirty years old.* ⟨OE *widewe*⟩

wid•ow•er ['wɪdouər] *n.* a man whose wife is dead and who has not married again. ⟨ME, alteration of OE *widewa,* masculine of *widewe*⟩

wid•ow•hood ['wɪdou,hʊd] *n.* the condition or time of being a widow.

widow's mite a small amount of money given cheerfully by a poor person. ⟨with reference to the biblical story of a poor widow's gift to the temple⟩

widow's peak a V-shaped point formed by the hairline in the middle of the forehead. ⟨from a belief that it was a sign of early widowhood⟩

widow's walk a railing-enclosed platform on the roof of some coastal houses, formerly for watching for ships returning from sea.

width [wɪdθ] *or* [wɪtθ] *n.* **1** how wide a thing is; distance across; breadth: *The width of the room is 4 m.* **2** a piece of a certain width: *curtains taking two widths of cloth.* **3** extension or breadth in general; quality of wideness: *great width of mind, vision, etc.*

wield [wild] *v.* hold and use; manage; exercise: *The soldier wielded his sword well. The people wield the power in a democracy.* ⟨OE *wieldan*⟩ **—'wield•er,** *n.*
☛ *Hom.* WEALD, WHEELED.

wie•ner ['winər] *n.* a bland, reddish sausage usually made of finely ground beef and pork or chicken; frankfurter. ⟨shortened form of G *Wienerwurst* Vienna sausage⟩

wiener roast an outdoor social function at which wieners are roasted or boiled over an open fire.

wife [wəif] *n., pl.* **wives. 1** a married woman, especially when considered with reference to her husband. **2** *Archaic.* a woman, as in *fishwife.*
take (someone) **to wife,** marry (someone). ⟨OE *wīf*⟩ **—'wife•less,** *adj.*

wife•hood ['wəif,hʊd] *n.* the condition of being a wife.

wife•ly ['wəifli] *adj.* **-li•er, -li•est.** of a wife; like a wife; suitable for a wife.

wig [wɪg] *n., v.* **wigged, wig•ging.** —*n.* an artificial covering of hair for the head: *The bald man wore a wig.*
—*v.* supply with, or cover with, a wig or wigs. ⟨< *periwig*⟩
☛ *Hom.* WHIG.

wig•gle ['wɪgəl] *v.* **-gled, -gling;** *n.* —*v.* move or shake with short, quick or twisting movements from side to side; wriggle: *The restless children wiggled in their chairs. This key doesn't work unless you wiggle it in the lock.*
—*n.* a wiggling movement. ⟨ME *wigle(n),* frequentative of dial. *wig* wag; cf. Du., LG *wiggelen*⟩

wig•gler ['wɪglər] *n.* **1** a person or thing that wiggles. **2** WRIGGLER (def. 2).

wig•gly ['wɪgli] *adj.* **-gli•er, -gli•est. 1** wiggling: *a wiggly little caterpillar.* **2** wavy: *He drew a wiggly line under the heading.*

wight [wəit] *n. Archaic or dialect.* a human being; person. ⟨OE *wiht*⟩
☛ *Hom.* WHITE.

wig•wag ['wɪg,wæg] *v.* **-wagged, -wag•ging;** *n.* *—v.* **1** move to and fro. **2** signal (a message) by movements of arms, flags, lights, etc. according to a code.
—n. **1** signalling by movements of arms, flags, lights, etc. **2** the message signalled. ⟨< *wig*, v. (related to WIGGLE) + *wag*, v.; modelled on *zigzag*⟩ **—'wig,wag•ger,** *n.*

wig•wam ['wɪg,wɒm] *n.* **1** a kind of dwelling traditionally used by First Nations peoples from Manitoba to the Atlantic Provinces, consisting of an arched or cone-shaped framework of poles covered with hide, bark, mats made from rushes, etc. Compare TEEPEE. **2** teepee. ⟨< Algonquian (Ojibway)⟩

wil•co ['wɪlkou] *interj. Radiotelephony.* will comply.

wild [waɪld] *adj., n., adv. —adj.* **1** living or growing in the forests or fields; not tamed or cultivated: *The tiger is a wild animal. The daisy is a wild flower.* **2** with no people living in it; uncultivated: *wild land.* **3** not civilized; savage or primitive. **4** not controlled; not restrained: *a wild rush for the ball.* **5** resisting control or restraint; unruly or insubordinate: *Nobody appreciates a wild child.* **6** dissolute; dissipated; licentious: *to live a wild life.* **7** not in proper control or order: *wild hair.* **8** violently excited; frantic or distracted: *a wild rage.* **9** violent: *a wild storm.* **10** rash; crazy: *wild schemes.* **11** *Informal.* very eager. **12** unconventional, bizarre, or fanciful: *a wild tune or song.* **13** going, landing, or hitting far from the mark; WIDE (def. 6). **14** *Card games.* of a card, able to be used to represent any number or suit.
run wild, live or grow without restraint.
wild about, extremely fond of or impressed by: *I'm not wild about Harry's affair with my niece.*
wild and woolly, a rough and uncivilized like the American West during frontier times; rough-and-tumble. **b** very unconventional: *She's got a lot of wild and woolly ideas about parenting.*
—n. **1** Often, **wilds,** *pl.* an uncultivated or desolate region or tract; waste; desert. **2** wild country. **3** a wild state.
—adv. in a wild manner or to a wild degree. ⟨OE *wilde*⟩ **—'wild•ly,** *adv.* **—'wild•ness,** *n.*

wild boar a wild pig (*Sus scrofa*) of Europe, N Africa, and Asia, from which most domestic breeds of pig have been derived.

wild card 1 *Cards.* a card declared wild and therefore substitutable for any other card at the whim of the player. **2** *Sports.* a team or player who, although not qualifying, is admitted to a tournament at the discretion of the organizing committee: *In tennis, wild cards sometimes get to the final rounds.* **3** a completely unpredictable or uncontrollable variable.

wild carrot QUEEN ANNE'S LACE.

wild•cat ['waɪld,kæt] *n., v.* **-cat•ted, -cat•ting.** *—n.* **1** any of various small- or medium-sized wild members of the cat family, such as the lynx, bobcat, or ocelot. **2** a wild animal (*Felis sylvestris*) of Europe, resembling the domestic cat but somewhat larger and heavier and having a bushy tail. The wildcat is generally thought to be one of the ancestors of the domestic cat. **3** *Cdn.* **a** one of several varieties of lynx, especially the Canada lynx. **b** the flesh of the lynx used as food. **4** a person who has a wild temper or is a fierce fighter. **5** a well drilled for oil or gas in a region where none has been found before; a test well. **6** a risky or unsafe commercial enterprise. **7** a railway locomotive in operation without cars. **8** (*adjl.*) of a strike, etc., begun or taking place illegally or without proper union approval. **9** (*adjl.*) of, having to do with, or resulting from an unsound or risky business enterprise.
—v. **1** drill wells in regions not known to contain oil. **2** engage in wildcat striking or business activity. **—'wild,cat•ter,** *n.*

wild celery TAPE GRASS.

wild dog any of various wild members of the dog family, such as the dingo of Australia.

wil•de•beest ['wɪldə,bist] *n.* the gnu, an African antelope. ⟨< Afrikaans < Du. *wildebeest* wild beast⟩

wil•der ['wɪldər] *v. Poetic or archaic.* **1** bewilder or be bewildered. **2** lose or cause to lose one's way. ⟨apparently < *wilderness*⟩ **—'wil•der•ment,** *n.*

wil•der•ness ['wɪldərnɪs] *n.* **1** a wild or desolate region with few or no people living in it. **2** a bewildering mass or collection: *a wilderness of streets.* **3** any empty or open expanse, as an ocean.
voice (crying) in the wilderness, someone whose calls for reform go unheeded. ⟨ME *wilderne* wild, OE *wildēorn*, ult. < *wilde* wild + *dēor* animal⟩
☛ *Syn.* **1.** See note at DESERT[1].

wilderness area an area of crown land set aside as an ecological preserve in its wild state, with no roads or trails, tourist facilities, etc.

wild–eyed ['waɪld ,aɪd] *adj.* **1** having wild eyes. **2** staring wildly or angrily. **3** irrational; impractical; radical: *a wild-eyed scheme.*

wild•fire ['waɪld,faɪr] *n.* **1** a substance that burns fiercely and is hard to put out, formerly used in warfare. **2** any large, destructive fire that spreads rapidly and is hard to put out. **3** will-o'-the-wisp; IGNIS FATUUS. **4** any of various inflammatory, eruptive diseases, especially of sheep.
like wildfire, very rapidly: *The news spread like wildfire.*

wild•flower ['waɪld,flaʊər] *n.* **1** any flowering plant that grows in the woods, fields, etc.; an uncultivated plant. **2** a flower of such a plant. Also, **wild flower.**

wild•fowl ['waɪld,faʊl] *n.* birds ordinarily hunted, such as wild ducks or geese, partridges, grouse, quail, and pheasants.

wild–goose chase ['waɪld 'gus] a useless search or pursuit.

wild•ing ['waɪldɪŋ] *n.* **1** a wild plant or its fruit. **2** any plant that grows wild, especially one once domesticated. **3** a wild animal. **4** the act of a mob of uncontrolled young people surging through an area and causing destruction and injury.

wild•life ['waɪld,ləif] *n.* wild animals and birds as a group, especially those native to a particular area: *the northern wildlife.*

wild•ling [ˌwaɪldlɪŋ] *n.* WILDING (defs. 1, 2, 3).

wild mustard one of the commonest Canadian weeds, an annual plant (*Sinapsis arvensis*, sometimes classified as *Brassica kaber*) growing up to 1 m high, having somewhat hairy leaves and clusters of small, bright yellow flowers. Wild mustard was introduced to North America from Europe and Asia.

wild oats 1 a an Old World annual grass (*Avena fatua*) closely related to and resembling cultivated oats, that has been introduced to North America, where it has become a troublesome weed, especially in prairie grainfields. **b** any of several other wild grasses of the same genus. **2** *Cdn.* formerly, WILD RICE.
sow (one's) **wild oats,** indulge in youthful dissipation before settling down in life. ⟨translation of < F *folle avoine*⟩

wild pansy a common European wildflower, a violet (*Viola tricolour*) having small, usually purple flowers. The pansy commonly found in gardens is derived mainly from the wild pansy.

wild parsnip *Cdn.* the poisonous WATER HEMLOCK.

wild rice *Cdn.* **1** a tall North American grass (*Zizania aquatica*) that grows in wet places, as along the edges of lakes. **2** its edible, ricelike grain, which resembles rice, especially when grown as a commercial crop.

wild rose *Cdn.* any uncultivated rose, especially the prickly rose (*Rosa spina*). The wild rose (*R. acicularis*) is the floral emblem of Alberta.

wild turkey the North American bird (*Meleagris gallopavo*) considered to be the ancestor of the domesticated turkey.

wild type *Genetics.* the standard or normal type of a species, that has not been bred or selected for some special quality.

wild West or **Wild West** the western United States during pioneer days, when it was uncultivated and unpoliced.

wild•wood ['waɪld,wʊd] *n. Poetic.* trees growing in their natural state; forest.

wile [waɪl] *n., v.* **wiled, wil•ing.** *—n.* **1** a trick to deceive; a cunning way. **2** subtle trickery; slyness; craftiness.
—v. coax; lure; entice: *The sunshine wiled me from my work.*
wile away, while away; spend (time, a vacation, etc.) easily or pleasantly. ⟨OE *wīgle* magic, probably < confusion with *while*⟩
☛ *Hom.* WHILE.

wil•ful ['wɪlfəl] *adj.* See WILLFUL. **—'wil•ful•ness,** *n.* **—'wil•ful•ly,** *adv.*

will[1] [wɪl]; *unstressed,* [wəl] *v.* pt. **would,** pres. sing. or pl. **will.** a modal auxiliary verb used: **1** to refer to future happenings: *The train will be late. If they leave now, they will arrive in time for dinner.* **2** to express a promise: *I will come at 4 o'clock.* **3** to introduce a polite request or offer: *Will you please hand me that book? Will you have another slice?* **4** to express a capacity or power that something has: *This pail will hold 8 L.* **5** to express inevitability, probability, inclination, or habit: *She will read for hours at a time.* **6** as an imperative with the subject *you*: *Don't argue with me; you will do it at once!* ⟨OE *willan*⟩
☛ *Usage.* **Will,** SHALL. **Will** is the usual auxiliary for forming the future

tense: *I will be there. Tomorrow will come.* In formal English, however, some people still prefer to use **shall** when the subject is **I** or **we**: *We shall arrive before lunch.* For an emphatic future, the auxiliary (**will** or **shall**) is stressed in speech, but in writing **shall** is used with all subjects: *You will* (or *shall*) *be home by midnight. I shall not fail. This shall be done.*

will² [wɪl] *n., v.* **willed, will•ing.** —*n.* **1** the power of the mind to decide and do; deliberate control over thought and action: *A good leader must have a strong will.* **2** the act of choosing to do something, sometimes including also all deliberation that precedes making the choice; volition: *Nobody forced him; he did it of his own will.* **3** purpose; determination: *the will to live.* **4** an order, command, or decree. **5** what is chosen to be done; (one's or its) pleasure; wish; desire. **6** *Law.* **a** a legal statement of a person's wishes about what is to be done with his or her property after he or she is dead. **b** a document containing such a statement. **7** feeling toward another: *good will, ill will.*
at will, whenever one wishes.
do the will of, obey.
with a will, with energy and determination.
—*v.* **1** decide by using the power of the mind to choose and do; use the will: *She willed herself to keep awake.* **2** influence or try to influence by deliberate control over thought and action: *She willed the person in front of her to turn around.* **3** determine: *Fate has willed it otherwise.* **4** give by a will: *to will a house to someone.* **5** wish; desire: *All right, dear, as you will; but next time I get to pick the movie.* ⟨OE⟩

willed [wɪld] *adj., v.* —*adj.* having —— will: *strong-willed.*
—*v.* pt. and pp. of WILL².

wil•lem•ite ['wɪlə,məit] *n.* a white or colourless mineral consisting of silicate of zinc. *Formula:* Zn_2SiO_4 ⟨after *Willem* I, king of the Netherlands (1772-1834)⟩

wil•let ['wɪlɪt] *n.* a large shore bird (*Catoptrophorus semipalmatus*) of the western hemisphere, belonging to the same family as the sandpipers and having a long bill and grey, black, and white plumage. ⟨< *pilly-will-willet*, imitative of its call⟩

will•ful or **wil•ful** ['wɪlfəl] *adj.* **1** wanting or taking one's own way; stubborn. **2** done on purpose; intended: *willful murder, willful waste.* ⟨< *will*² + *-ful*⟩ —**'will•ful•ness** or **'wil•ful•ness,** *n.* —**'will•ful•ly** or **'wil•ful•ly,** *adv.*

wil•lies ['wɪliz] *n.* **the willies,** *Informal.* a feeling of nervousness and uneasiness; jitters. ⟨origin unknown⟩

will•ing ['wɪlɪŋ] *adj., v.* —*adj.* **1** ready; consenting: *He is willing to wait.* **2** cheerfully ready: *a willing worker.* **3** cheerfully and readily done or given: *willing obedience.*
—*v.* ppr. of WILL². —**'will•ing•ly,** *adv.* —**'will•ing•ness,** *n.*

wil•li•waw ['wɪlə,wɒ] *n.* **1** a sudden, violent gust of wind moving down to the sea from mountains along the coast. **2** any commotion or agitation. ⟨origin unknown⟩

will–o'–the–wisp ['wɪl ə ðə 'wɪsp] *n.* **1** a moving light appearing at night over marshy places, caused by the combustion of marsh gas. **2** something that deceives or misleads by luring on.

wil•low ['wɪlou] *n., v.* —*n.* **1** any of a genus (*Salix*) of trees and shrubs found mainly in the northern hemisphere, usually having long, narrow, pointed leaves arranged alternately on the twigs, and flowers that appear in early spring before or at the same time as the leaves. Many willows have tough, slender branches that bend easily. **2** the wood of any of these trees or shrubs. **3** (*adjl.*) made of willow. **4** (*adjl.*) designating a family (Salicaceae) of trees and shrubs that consists of the willows and poplars. **5** a cylindrical machine having internal revolving spikes, used for cleaning raw wool, cotton, or other natural fibres. **6** *Informal.* a baseball or cricket bat.
—*v.* clean (fibres) with a willow. Also (*n.* 5 and *v.*), **willy.** ⟨ult. < OE *welig*⟩

willow grouse *Cdn.* **1** WILLOW PTARMIGAN. **2** *Esp. B.C.* RUFFED GROUSE. **3** *Esp. Yukon.* SHARP-TAILED GROUSE.

willow herb **1** any of several plants (genus *Epilobium*) of the evening-primrose family, found in temperate and arctic regions and typically having narrow, willowlike leaves. See also FIREWEED. **2** the golden loosestrife.

willow ptarmigan *Cdn.* a ptarmigan (*Lagopus lagopus*) found throughout the arctic regions of the world, having all-white winter plumage except for the black outer tail feathers, the male being distinguished in summer by its reddish brown head, neck, and breast.

wil•low•y ['wɪloui] *adj.* **1** like a willow; slender; supple; graceful. **2** having many willows.

will•pow•er ['wɪl,paʊər] *n.* power exercised by the will; self-control or determination: *He hasn't got enough willpower to keep to a diet.*

wil•ly–nil•ly ['wɪli 'nɪli] *adv., adj.* —*adv.* willingly or not; whether one wishes it or not: *He found himself involved willy-nilly in the promotion campaign.*
—*adj.* that is or happens whether one wishes it or not: *a willy-nilly candidate.* ⟨< *will I* (*he, ye*), *nill I* (*he, ye*); *nill* not will, OE *nyllan* < *ne* not + *willan* will⟩

Wilson's thrush veery.

Wilson's warbler a small, olive green and yellow North American warbler (*Wilsonia persilla*) with a round black cap in the male. Also called **pileated warbler.**

wilt¹ [wɪlt] *v., n.* —*v.* **1** become limp and drooping; wither. **2** lose strength, vigour, assurance, etc. **3** cause to wilt.
—*n.* a disease of plants characterized by drying, drooping, and withering of the leaves, resulting from various causes, especially an inadequate water supply. ⟨var. of *welt* wither, alteration of *welk*; cf. MDu. and MLG *welken*⟩

wilt² [wɪlt] *v. Archaic.* 2nd pers. sing. present tense of WILL¹. *Thou wilt* means *you* (sing.) *will.*

Wil•ton ['wɪltən] *n.* a kind of velvety carpet. ⟨< *Wilton*, a town in Wiltshire, England, famous for such carpets⟩

Wilt•shire ['wɪltʃər] *n.* **1** a breed of British sheep having white faces and long, backward-spiralled horns. **2** a British cheese similar to cheddar but moister. ⟨a county of S England⟩

wil•y ['waili] *adj.* **wil•i•er, wil•i•est.** using subtle tricks to deceive; crafty; cunning; sly. —**'wil•i•ly,** *adv.* —**'wil•i•ness,** *n.*

wim•ble ['wɪmbəl] *n.* a tool for boring. ⟨ME < AF < MLG *wemel*⟩

wimp [wɪmp] *n. Slang.* a timid and weak-willed individual who is filled with pity for himself or herself. ⟨probably from *whimper*⟩

wim•ple ['wɪmpəl] *n., v.* **-pled, -pling.** —*n.* a cloth draped closely about the face and covering the head and neck, worn by women in the Middle Ages and still forming part of the habit of some nuns.
—*v.* **1** cover or muffle with a wimple. **2** ripple or cause to ripple. **3** *Archaic.* lie or lay in folds, as a veil. ⟨OE *wimpel*⟩

win [wɪn] *v.* **won, win•ning;** *n.* —*v.* **1** finish first in (a race or competition): *to win a race. Her horse won by a length.* Compare PLACE (def. 8b) and SHOW (def. 16b). **2** gain (a prize, first place, etc.) in a race or competition: *Our display won first prize. They won the pennant.* **3** get victory or success (in); overcome an adversary: *You'll never win if the chairperson is against the idea. The English eventually won the Hundred Years' War.* **4** gain (something) by effort, as if in a competition: *to win recognition for a new refining process.* **5** gain the favour or support of (often used with **over**): *The speaker soon won the audience. We won most of the undecided voters over to our side.* **6** gain the love, sympathy, etc. of; attract. **7** persuade to marry. **8** get to; reach, often by effort: *to win the summit of a mountain.*
win out, *Informal.* get victory or success; prevail: *Reason won out over stubbornness in the end.*
—*n.* **1** *Informal.* the act or fact of winning; success; victory: *We had five wins and no defeats.* **2** the position of the horse and rider or driver that come first in a race. ⟨OE *winnan*⟩
—**'win•na•ble,** *adj.*
☛ *Hom.* WHIN.

wince [wɪns] *v.* **winced, winc•ing;** *n.* —*v.* draw back suddenly; flinch slightly, often with a grimace: *The boy winced at the sight of the dentist's drill.*
—*n.* the act of wincing. ⟨ME < AF *wencir*, var. of OF *guencir* < Gmc.⟩

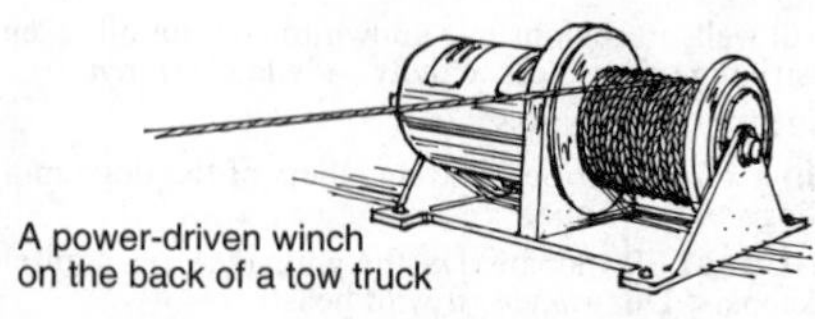
A power-driven winch on the back of a tow truck

winch [wɪntʃ] *n., v.* —*n.* **1** a machine for lifting or pulling, having a roller around which a rope or cable is wound. The crank of a winch is turned by hand or by an engine. **2** any crank or handle used for transmitting motion, as in hoisting. See RATCHET WHEEL for another picture.
—*v.* move by a winch. ⟨OE *wince*⟩

wind¹ *n.* [wɪnd] *or, archaic or poetic,* [waind]; *v.* [wɪnd] *n., v.* **wind•ed, wind•ing.** —*n.* **1** air in motion. The wind may vary in force from a slight breeze to a strong gale, and may arise naturally or be created by a fan, etc. **2** a strong wind; gale. **3** gas

in the stomach or bowels. **4** *Music.* **a** a wind instrument. **b winds,** *pl.* the section of an orchestra or band composed of wind instruments. **5** the power of breathing freely; breath: *A runner needs good wind.* **6** empty, useless talk. **7** vanity; conceit.
before the wind, in the direction toward which the wind is blowing.
between wind and water, a near the water line of a ship. **b** in a dangerous place.
break wind, pass gass.
get or **have the wind up,** become nervous, alarmed, or worried: *Ever since they announced the reorganization of the company, he's really had the wind up.*
get wind of, a find out about; get a hint of: *Don't let them get wind of our plans.* **b** smell: *The deer soon got wind of the hunter.*
in the eye or **teeth of the wind,** directly against the wind.
in the wind, happening; about to happen; impending: *There's an election in the wind.*
into the wind, pointing toward the direction from which the wind is blowing.
off the wind, with the wind blowing from behind.
on the wind, a as nearly as possible in the direction from which the wind is blowing. **b** carried by the wind: *She caught the aroma of woodsmoke on the wind.*
sail close to the wind, a manage with close calculation or the utmost economy. **b** come very near to imprudence, dishonesty, indecency, etc.
take the wind out of (someone's) **sails,** take away someone's advantage, argument, pride, excitement, etc. suddenly or unexpectedly, showing that it has been done, thought of, or said before.
to or **from the four winds,** in or from all directions of the compass.
to the wind, to the point from which the wind blows.
—v. **1** expose to wind or air. **2** follow by scent; smell. **3** put out of breath; cause difficulty in breathing: *The fat man was winded by walking up the steep hill.* **4** let recover breath: *They stopped in order to wind their horses.* ⟨OE⟩

☛ *Syn. n.* **1. Wind,** BREEZE = air in motion. **Wind** is the general word: *The wind is from the north.* **Breeze,** except as a technical term (in meteorology), means a light, gentle wind, especially one that is cool or refreshing: *We nearly always have a breeze at night.*

wind[2] [waɪnd] *v.* **wound** or (rare) **wind•ed, wind•ing;** *n.*
—v. **1** move or cause to move this way and that; move in a crooked way; change direction; turn: *A brook winds through the woods. We wound our way through the narrow streets.* **2 a** proceed in a roundabout or indirect manner: *His speech wound slowly toward its conclusion.* **b** introduce in an indirect or unobtrusive manner; weave: *Her political bias is wound into every story.* **3** fold, wrap, or entwine about something: *The mother wound her arms about the child. He wound the string around the package several times to secure it.* **4** cover with something twined, wrapped, or folded around: *The man's arm is wound with bandages.* **5** roll into a ball or on a spool: *The old woman was winding yarn. Thread comes wound on spools. The thread winds around the bobbin when you press the control.* **6** twist or turn around something several times: *The vine winds around a pole.* **7** become warped or twisted: *That board will wind.* **8** make (a machine) go by turning some part of it: *to wind a clock.* **9** be wound: *This clock winds easily.* **10** haul or hoist by means of a winch, windlass, or the like. **11** of a musical instrument, tighten the strings, pegs, etc.; tune.
wind back, double on one's track to throw off pursuers.
wind down, a bring or come gradually to a conclusion. **b** relax.
wind off, unwind; take off by unwinding.
wind up, a end; settle; conclude: *We expect to wind up the project tomorrow.* **b** *Baseball.* make swinging and twisting movements of the arm and body just before pitching the ball. **c** roll, coil, or wind completely. **d** put into a state of tension, great strain, intensity of feeling, etc.; excite. **e** entangle; involve: *I don't want to get wound up in that business.* **f** end up: *If you keep spending like that, you'll wind up destitute.*
—n. a bend; turn; twist. ⟨OE *windan*⟩ **—'wind•er,** *n.*

wind[3] [waɪnd] *or* [wɪnd] *v.* **wind•ed** or **wound, wind•ing.** blow; sound (a signal or note) on (a horn): *The hunter winds his horn.* ⟨special use of *wind[1]*⟩

wind•age ['wɪndɪdʒ] *n.* **1** the power of the wind to turn a missile from its course. **2** the distance that a missile is turned from its course by the wind. **3** a change in aim to compensate for windage. **4** atmospheric disturbance produced by the passage of a bullet, shell, or other missile. **5** the part of a ship's surface exposed to or affected by the action of wind. **6** the slight difference between the diameter of a bullet, shell, etc. and of the bore of a gun of the same calibre.

wind•bag ['wɪnd,bæg] *n. Slang.* a person who talks a great deal but does not say much that is significant.

wind–blown ['wɪnd ,bloun] *adj.* **1** blown by the wind. **2** of a hairstyle, etc., appearing as if blown by the wind.

wind–borne ['wɪnd ,bɔrn] *adj.* of pollen, seed, etc., carried by the wind.

wind•break ['wɪnd,breik] *n. Cdn.* **1** a row or clump of trees or bushes planted to provide protection from the wind and, often, to prevent soil erosion. **2** any temporary shelter from the wind.

wind•break•er ['wɪnd,breikər] *n. Cdn.* a short outdoor jacket of wool, leather, nylon, etc. that closes to the neck and has close-fitting cuffs and waist.

wind–bro•ken ['wɪnd ,broukən] *adj.* of horses, etc., having the breathing restricted or impaired; having the heaves.

wind–charg•er ['wɪnd ,tʃardʒər] *n. Cdn.* **1** a windmill driving a generator, the electricity generated being used to charge storage batteries. Wind-chargers were formerly much used on the Prairies to supply electricity for individual homes. **2** the generator of a wind-charger.

wind chill *Cdn.* the chilling effect of wind in combination with low temperature.

wind chill factor *Cdn.* a measure of the combined chilling effect of wind and low temperature on living things or inanimate objects, expressed in watts per square metre. See Appendix for chart.

wind•ed ['wɪndɪd] *adj., v. —adj.* **1** out of breath. **2** having breath, or wind, of a specified kind or strength (*used only in compounds*): *short-winded.*
—v. pt. and pp. of WIND[1].

wind•fall ['wɪnd,fɒl] *n.* **1** fruit blown down by the wind: *These apples are windfalls.* **2** a tree blown down by the wind. **3** an unexpected piece of good luck.

wind•flow•er ['wɪnd,flaʊər] *n. Cdn.* in the West, any of several anemones, especially the prairie crocus or chalice flower.

wind gauge **1** anemometer. **2** a graduated scale on the rear sight of a rifle, that can be adjusted to allow for WINDAGE (def. 3).

win•di•go ['wɪndɪ,gou] *n., pl.* **-gos.** WENDIGO (def. 1).

wind•ing ['waɪndɪŋ] *n., adj., v. —n.* **1** the act of one who or that which winds. **2** a bend; turn. **3** something that is wound or coiled. **4** *Electricity.* **a** a continuous coil of wire forming a conductor in a generator, motor, etc. **b** the manner in which the wire is coiled: *a series winding.*
—adj. bending; turning.
—v. ppr. of WIND[2]. **—'wind•ing•ly,** *adv.*

winding sheet a cloth in which a dead person is wrapped for burial.

wind instrument a musical instrument sounded by blowing air into it by mouth. Trumpets, flutes, clarinets, harmonicas, and oboes are wind instruments.

wind•jam•mer ['wɪnd,dʒæmər] *n. Informal.* **1** formerly, in the merchant navy, a sailing ship as opposed to a steamship. **2** a member of its crew.

wind•lass ['wɪndləs] *n.* a machine for pulling or lifting things; winch. See WINCH for picture. ⟨ME *windelass,* an alteration (influenced by ME *windel* wheel, winder) of ME *windass* < ON *vindáss* < *vinde* wind + *áss* beam, pole⟩

wind•mill ['wɪnd,mɪl] *n.* **1** a mill or machine operated by the action of the wind upon a wheel of vanes or sails mounted on a tower. The motion thus produced is transmitted to a millstone, water pump, etc. **2** something that acts like or suggests a windmill, such as a pinwheel or helicopter.
tilt at (or **fight**) **windmills,** expend one's energy in futile attacks on what cannot be overcome or in a chase after imaginary foes (in allusion to the story of Don Quixote tilting at windmills under the illusion that they were giants).

A windmill

win•dow ['wɪndou] *n., v. —n.* **1** an opening in the wall or roof of a building, boat, car, etc. to let in light or air. **2** such an opening with the frame, panes of glass, etc. that fill it. **3** the sashes and panes

that fit such an opening: *to open the window.* **4** a windowpane: *to break a window.* **5 a** an opening like a window in shape or function, such as the transparent part of some envelopes through which the address is seen. **b** anything suggesting a window in giving access or view: *This play opens a new window on human nature.* **6** *Computer technology.* **a** means of interrupting a computer program to perform some other function without disturbing the existing file. **b** the boxlike screen compartment displaying activity in such a function. **7** a period of time favourable for launching a spacecraft, or for any other undertaking.
–v. furnish with windows. ⟨ME < ON *vindauga* < *vindr* wind + *auga* eye⟩ **–'win•dow•less,** *adj.*

window blind BLIND (*n.* def. 1).

window box **1** a long, narrow box placed outside a window, or inside on a window sill, and used for growing plants and flowers. **2** a groove on the side of a window frame to hold the weights that counterbalance a vertically sliding sash.

window dresser a person who is responsible for displaying merchandise in a shop window.

window dressing **1** the art of attractively displaying merchandise in shop windows. **2** any display or statement made, often misleadingly, to create a favourable impression: *Much of the president's report was window dressing.*

window envelope an envelope with a transparent space where the address on the enclosure can show through.

win•dow•pane ['wɪndou,pein] *n.* a piece of glass in a window.

window sash the frame for the glass in a window.

window seat a bench built into the wall of a room, under a window.

win•dow–shop ['wɪndou ʃɒp] *v.* **-shopped, -shop•ping.** look at articles in store windows without going in to buy anything. **–'win•dow-,shop•per,** *n.*

window sill a piece of wood, stone, etc. across the bottom of a window.

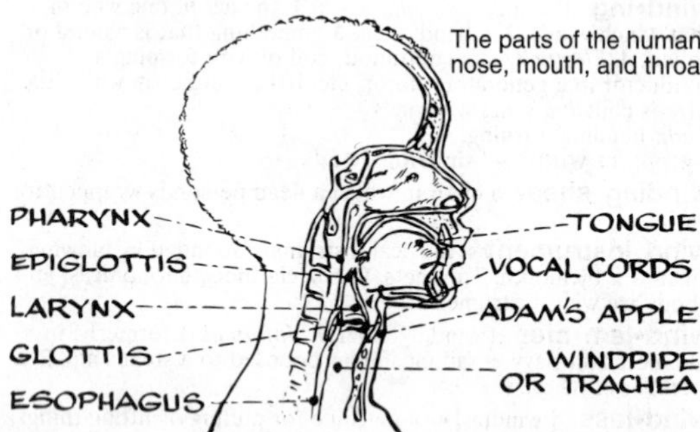

wind•pipe ['wɪnd,pəip] *n.* the passage by which air is carried from the throat to the lungs; trachea. See LUNG for another picture.

wind•row ['wɪnd,rou] *n., v.* *–n.* **1** a row of hay raked together to dry before being made into cocks or heaps. **2** any similar row, as of sheaves of grain, made for the purpose of drying. **3** a row of dry leaves, dust, etc. swept together by wind or the like.
–v. arrange in a windrow or windrows. ⟨< *wind*[1] + *row*[1]⟩

wind•screen ['wɪnd,skrin] *n. Brit.* windshield.

wind shear a sudden, violent change in the direction or speed of the wind: *Wind shear can cause aircraft to crash.*

wind–shell ['wɪnd ,ʃɛl] *n. Cdn.* a light, unlined outer garment serving as protection from the wind.

wind•shield ['wɪnd,ʃild] *n.* **1** the sheet of glass or plastic, usually curved, that forms the front window of a motor vehicle. **2** a sheet of glass or plastic forming a screen from the wind at the front of a motorcycle, motorboat, etc.

wind sleeve windsock.

wind•sock ['wɪnd,sɒk] *n.* a long, cone-shaped canvas bag open at both ends, mounted on a pole with the narrower opening outward, so that the wind filling it will cause it to billow out, indicating the direction of the wind.

Wind•sor ['wɪnzər] *n.* the family name of the royal house of the United Kingdom since 1917. ⟨< *Windsor* Castle, a residence of the British sovereigns⟩

Windsor chair a kind of wooden chair, with or without arms, having a rounded and arched spindle back, slanting legs, and a flat or slightly hollowed seat, especially popular in England and North America during the 18th century. ⟨< *Windsor,* a town in Berkshire, England, where such chairs were first made⟩

Windsor knot a double slipknot used in tying a four-in-hand tie, resulting in a wide, triangular knot.

Windsor tie a wide necktie of soft silk, tied in a loose bow.

wind speed the velocity of the wind blowing from a specific direction, as measured at a particular point on an anemometer, or wind gauge: *The wind speed today at the airport is from the SE at 25 knots.*

wind•storm ['wɪnd,stɔrm] *n.* a storm with much wind but little or no rain.

wind•surf•ing ['wɪnd,sɜrfɪŋ] *n.* the sport of gliding over water on a board (sailboard) that is like a surfboard equipped with a sail. The operator, standing, controls the craft by leaning in a particular direction as he or she grasps one of the curved horizontal bars on either side of the sail. **–'wind,surf•er,** *n.*

wind tunnel a tunnel-like chamber in which the effect of air pressures on aircraft, missiles, etc. can be calculated by means of artificially made winds.

wind–up ['waɪnd ,ʌp] *n.* **1** a winding up; ending; close; conclusion. **2** *Baseball.* a series of movements made by a pitcher just before throwing the ball. Also, **windup.**

wind•ward ['wɪndwərd]; *Nautical* ['wɪndərd] *adv., adj., n.*
–adv. **1** in the direction from which the wind is blowing. **2** toward the wind.
–adj. **1** situated on the side toward the wind. **2** proceeding in the direction from which the wind is blowing.
–n.
to windward, in the direction from which the wind is blowing: *They saw a ship to windward.*

wind•y ['wɪndi] *adj.* **wind•i•er, wind•i•est. 1** having much wind: *a windy street, windy weather.* **2** made of wind; empty: *windy talk.* **3** talking a great deal; voluble. **4** causing or having gas in the stomach or intestines. ⟨OE *windig*⟩ **–'wind•i•ly,** *adv.* **–'wind•i•ness,** *n.*

wine [waɪn] *n., adj., v.* **wined, win•ing.** *–n.* **1** the juice of grapes that has been fermented and contains alcohol. **2** the fermented juice of other fruits of plants: *currant wine, dandelion wine.* **3** the colour of red wine; a dark purplish red. **4** something that exhilarates or intoxicates like wine.
new wine in old bottles, something new imposed on an old form or system, or without a necessary change of structure or attitude.
–adj. having the colour wine.
–v. **1** entertain with wine. **2** drink wine: *After a day of seminars they spent the whole evening wining and dining.* ⟨OE *wīn,* ult. < L *vinum*⟩
☛ *Hom.* WHINE.

wine•bib•ber ['waɪn,bɪbər] *n.* a person who drinks much wine. ⟨(translation of G *Weinsäufer*) < *wine* + *bibber* < ME *bibbe(n)* drink, ? < L *bibere*⟩

wine cellar **1** a cellar where wine is stored. **2** the collection of wines stored there.

wine gallon an old British gallon equal to 231 cubic inches (about 3.8 L), now the standard United States gallon.

wine•glass ['waɪn,glæs] *n.* a stemmed drinking glass for wine.

wine•grow•er ['waɪn,grouər] *n.* a person who cultivates grapes and makes wine.

wine•grow•ing ['waɪn,grouɪŋ] *n., adj.* *–n.* the business of a winegrower.
–adj. engaged in, or having to do with, the business of growing grapes and making wine.

wine•mak•er ['waɪn,meikər] *n.* **1** one who is expert in the production of wines. **2** winegrower.

wine press **1** a machine for pressing the juice from grapes. **2** a vat in which grapes are trodden in the process of making wine.

win•er•y ['waɪnəri] *n., pl.* **-er•ies.** a place where wine is made.

Wine•sap or **wine•sap** ['waɪn,sæp] *n.* a variety of red winter apple.

wine•skin ['waɪn,skɪn] *n.* a container made of the nearly complete skin of a goat, hog, etc. and used, especially in some Eastern countries, for holding wine.

wing [wɪŋ] *n., v.* *–n.* **1 a** the part of a bird, insect, or bat used

in flying. **b** a corresponding part in flightless birds or insects. **2** in art, myth, etc., a similar structure attributed to angels, dragons, demons, etc. or symbolizing speed, flight, etc. **3** anything like a wing in shape or use, such as one of the major lifting and supporting surfaces of an airplane, a vane of a windmill, or the feather of an arrow. **4** a part that sticks out from the main part or body, such as an extension at the side of a building, etc. often reserved for a specialized use: *the maternity wing.* **5** a part of an organization; faction, especially one whose view, activities, etc. contrast with those of the mainstream: *Wilson has joined the left wing.* **6** the condition of flying; winged flight. **7** *Hockey, lacrosse, etc.* **a** a player whose position is on either side of the centre. **b** the position played by this player. **8** *Theatre.* **a** any of the pieces of side scenery on the stage. **b wings,** *pl.* the area at either side of the stage, out of sight of the audience. **9** either of the parts that project forward from the sides of the back of a wing chair. **10** an air-force unit made up of several squadrons. **11 wings,** *pl.* the insignia, or badge, of an aircraft pilot. **12** that part of a military force to the right or left of the main body. **13** *Facetious.* a foreleg or arm, especially the pitching or throwing arm of a baseball player.
clip (someone's) **wings,** restrict or confine someone.
get (one's) **wings, a** be awarded one's pilot's licence. **b** earn recognition and status as a full-fledged, competent performer in some field by passing some test of ability.
lend or **give wings to,** cause to fly or to seem to fly.
on a wing and a prayer, with slim chances of success.
on the wing, a flying. **b** moving; active; busy. **c** going away. **d** while flying, moving, etc.
take wing, a fly away. **b** depart in haste.
under (someone's) **wing,** under someone's protection or sponsorship.
(waiting) in the wings, ready to intervene or be used if necessary.
—v. **1** fly or fly through: *The birds are winging south.* **2** supply with wings. **3** make able to fly; give speed to: *Terror winged his steps as the bear drew nearer.* **4** wound in the wing or arm: *The bullet winged the bird but did not kill it.*
wing it, *Informal.* speak, perform, or execute an action with little preparation or planning; ad lib; improvise. ⟨ME < ON *vængr*⟩ **—'wing•less,** *adj.* **—'wing,like,** *adj.*

wing case either of the hardened front wings of certain insects.

wing chair a completely upholstered, high-backed armchair having WINGS (def. 9) on the sides of the back.

wing commander formerly, an air-force officer ranking next above a squadron leader and below a group captain. *Abbrev.:* W.C. or W/C

wing•ding or **wing–ding** ['wɪŋ,dɪŋ] *n. Slang.* **1** a lively, lavish party or celebration. **2** something remarkable or memorable of its kind: *a wingding of a fight.*

winged [wɪŋd]; *esp. poetic,* ['wɪŋɪd] *adj., v. —adj.* **1** having wings. **2** swift; rapid. **3** of words, elevated; sublime.
—v. pt. and pp. of WING.

wing•er ['wɪŋər] *n. Cdn. Hockey, lacrosse, etc.* WING (def. 7).

wing nut 1 a NUT (def. 3) having a flat, projecting piece on either side of the top so that it can be turned with the thumb and forefinger. **2** *Slang.* NUT (def. 6).

wing shot *Hunting.* **1** a shot at a bird in flight or a clay pigeon. **2** an expert at making such shots.

wing•span ['wɪŋ,spæn] *n.* the distance between the tips of the wings of a bird or insect when they are spread out, or between the tips of the wings of an airplane.

wing•spread ['wɪŋ,sprɛd] *n.* wingspan.

wing tip 1 the outer end of the wing of a bird or airplane. **2** a special decoration on the toe of a shoe. **3** a shoe with such a decorated toe. Also (esp. defs. 2 & 3) **wingtip.**

wink [wɪŋk] *v., n. —v.* **1** close the eyes and open them again quickly. **2** close one eye and open it again as a hint or signal. **3** move by winking: *to wink back tears.* **4** twinkle: *The stars winked.* **5** give a signal or express (a message) by a winking of the eye, a flashlight, etc.
wink at, pretend not to see.
—n. **1** the act or an instance of winking. **2** a hint or signal given by winking. **3** a twinkle. **4** a very short time: *I'll be back in a wink.* **5** the very shortest bit of sleep: *I didn't sleep a wink.*
forty winks, a short sleep; nap. ⟨OE *wincian*⟩

wink•er ['wɪŋkər] *n.* **1** a person who or thing that winks. **2** *Informal.* an eyelash. **3** a blinder or blinker for a horse's eye.

win•kle ['wɪŋkəl] *n., v.* **wink•led, wink•ling.** *—n.* any of various gastropod molluscs; PERIWINKLE[2].
—v. extract with difficulty; pry or root out from cover (*used with* **out**): *The pen was stuck down the side of the chair, but I managed to winkle it out.* ⟨OE *-wincle,* as in *pinewincle* periwinkle[2]⟩

win•ner ['wɪnər] *n.* **1** a person who or thing that wins. **2** someone or something that seems sure to succeed.

winners' circle 1 *Horse racing.* a small, usually circular enclosure at a racetrack where winning horses and their jockeys, owners, trainers, etc. receive their prizes. **2** any chosen group of high achievers: *Several B.C. wines have made it into the winners' circle recently.*

win•ning ['wɪnɪŋ] *adj., n., v. —adj.* **1** that wins: *a winning team.* **2** charming; attractive: *a winning smile.*
—n. **1 winnings,** *pl.* what is won; money won: *She pocketed her winnings.* **2** a shaft or bed in a coal mine ready for mining.
—v. ppr. of WIN. **—'win•ning•ly,** *adv.*

winning post a post on a racecourse marking the end of the race.

Win•ni•peg couch ['wɪnə,pɛg] *Cdn.* a kind of couch having no arms or back and opening out into a double bed.

Winnipeg goldeye *Cdn.* goldeye.

win•now ['wɪnou] *v., n. —v.* **1** blow off the chaff from (grain). **2** drive or blow away (chaff). **3** sort out; separate; sift: *to winnow truth from falsehood. I suggest you go through your poetry collection a few times and winnow it before sending it to a publisher.* **4** *Archaic or poetic.* beat (the air) with or as if with wings.
—n. **1** a contrivance for winnowing grain. **2** the act of winnowing or a motion resembling it. ⟨OE *windwian* < *wind* wind[1]⟩ **—'win•now•er,** *n.*

wi•no ['waɪnou] *n., pl.* **-nos.** *Slang.* an alcoholic who is addicted to cheap wine.

win•some ['wɪnsəm] *adj.* charming; attractive; pleasing: *a winsome child.* ⟨OE *wynsum* < *wynn* joy⟩ **—'win•some•ly,** *adv.* **—'win•some•ness,** *n.*

win•ter ['wɪntər] *n., v. —n.* **1** the coldest of the four seasons; the time of the year between fall and spring. **2** a year as denoted by this season: *a man of eighty winters.* **3** (*adjl.*) of, having to do with, or characteristic of winter: *winter clothes, winter weather.* **4** (*adjl.*) of the kind that may be kept for use during the winter: *winter apples.* **5** the last period of life. **6** a period of decline, dreariness, or adversity.
—v. **1** pass the winter: *Many Canadians winter in Florida or Hawaii.* **2** keep, feed, or manage during winter: *We wintered our cattle in the warm valley.* ⟨OE⟩

winter•ber•ry ['wɪntər,bɛri] *n.* any of several North American hollies (genus *Ilex*), especially the black alder, or Canada holly, having red, black, or purple berries that last over the winter.

winter carnival a carnival featuring winter sports and crafts.

winter dance *Cdn. Pacific coast.* formerly, a ceremonial performance given by one of the Dancing Societies of the Kwakiutl and other coastal peoples during the winter months.

win•ter•er ['wɪntərər] *n. Cdn.* formerly: **1** a seasoned fur trader or voyageur who spent his winters in the fur country. **2** WINTERING PARTNER.

win•ter•green ['wɪntər,grin] *n.* **1** any of several evergreen shrubs (genus *Gaultheria*) of the heath family, especially a low-growing species (*G. procumbens*) of E North America having shiny, aromatic leaves and edible red berries. **2 oil of wintergreen, a** an aromatic oil used for flavouring and in medicine, originally made from the leaves of the wintergreen, but now usually synthesized. **b** the flavour of this oil or of anything flavoured with it. **3** any of a genus (*Pyrola*) of perennial herbs of temperate and arctic regions having shiny, rounded leaves and fragrant, typically cup-shaped flowers. **4** any of various plants of related genera, such as the **one-flowered wintergreen** (*Moneses uniflora*). **5** (*adjl.*) designating the family (Pyrolaceae) of low-growing perennial herbs that includes the wintergreens (genera *Pyrola, Moneses,* etc.) and pipsissewas.

winter ice sea ice that is more than about 20 cm thick and has formed and developed in one winter.

wintering partner *Cdn.* formerly, **1** a stock-holding partner in the Montréal fur companies, especially the North West Company, who represented the company the year round at trading posts in the fur country. **2** in the Hudson's Bay Company, a commissioned officer in charge of business at a trading post. He held no stock but received a share of the profits.

win•ter•ize ['wɪntə,raɪz] *v.* **-ized, -iz•ing. 1** make (an automobile, etc.) ready for operation or use during the winter. **2** prepare (a building, such as a cottage) for use in winter. **3** safeguard (an unoccupied building) against damage in winter by draining taps, boarding windows, etc.

win•ter•kill ['wɪntər,kɪl] *v., n. —v.* kill by or die from exposure to cold weather: *The rosebushes were winterkilled.*
—n. the death of plants and animals resulting from winter conditions.

winter range *Cdn. West.* a region suitable for the grazing of cattle, sheep, or horses in winter.

winter solstice *Astronomy.* for the northern hemisphere, the time when the sun is farthest south from the equator, and the daylight hours are fewest, December 21 or 22.

winter squash 1 the large, edible fruit of a trailing vine (*Cucurbita maxima*) of the gourd family, greatly variable in size, shape, and colour. The numerous varieties of winter squash are harvested in fall and can be stored many months. **2** a plant that produces such fruits.

win•ter•tide ['wɪntər,taɪd] *n. Archaic.* wintertime.

win•ter•time ['wɪntər,taɪm] *n.* the season of winter.

winter wheat wheat planted in the fall to ripen in the following spring or summer.

win•ter•y ['wɪntəri] *adj.* **-ter•i•er, -ter•i•est.** See WINTRY.

win•try ['wɪntri] *adj.* **-tri•er, -tri•est. 1** of or having to do with winter; like winter: *a wintry sky.* **2** devoid of fervour or affection; cold; chilling: *a wintry smile.* **3** destitute of warmth or brightness; dismal; dreary; cheerless: *a wintry gathering.* **—'win•tri•ness,** *n.* **—'win•tri•ly,** *adv.*

win•y ['waɪni] *adj.* **-i•er, -i•est.** tasting, smelling, or looking like wine.

winze [wɪnz] *n. Mining.* a small inclined shaft or passage connecting one level with another. ⟨< earlier *winds,* perhaps < *wind²*⟩

wipe [wəip] *v.* **wiped, wip•ing;** *n. —v.* **1** rub with paper, cloth, etc. in order to clean or dry: *to wipe the table.* **2** take (away, off, or out) by rubbing: *Wipe away your tears. She wiped off the dust.* **3** remove. **4** rub or draw (something) over a surface. **5** apply (a soft substance) by rubbing it on with a cloth, pad, etc.: *to wipe wax on a table.* **6** form (a joint in lead pipe) by spreading solder with a leather pad.
wipe out, a destroy completely: *The pollution in the river has wiped out all the fish.* **b** cancel: *The generous man wiped out all the debts owed him.* **c** erase: *The rain wiped out all the footprints.* **d** *Slang.* slip and fall; skid; lose control; capsize: *When the wind caught her sails, she wiped out.* **e** *Slang.* fail miserably: *I really wiped out on that exam!*
—n. **1** the act of wiping: *She gave his face a hasty wipe.* **2** a piece of moistened, absorbent material, usually disposable, for wiping any of various surfaces: *Using alcohol-free, fragrance-free baby wipes reduces the risk of diaper rash.* ⟨OE *wīpian*⟩

wipe•out ['wəip,ʌut] *n. Slang.* an act or instance of wiping out.

wip•er ['wəipər] *n.* **1** a person who wipes. **2** anything used for wiping. **3** an automatic device consisting of a rubber blade set in a metal or plastic arm that moves back and forth across the windshield of a vehicle to clear it of rain or snow.

wire [waɪr] *n., v.* **wired, wir•ing.** *—n.* **1** metal drawn out into a thin, flexible rod or thread: *copper wire.* **2** (*adjl.*) made of or consisting of wire: *a wire fence.* **3** netting, etc. made of wire. **4** a piece of such metal: *She used a wire to connect the two batteries.* **5** something made of wire, such as a barbed-wire fence or a snare. **6** *Informal.* **a** telegraph: *He sent a message by wire.* **b** a telegram. **7** a metal string of a guitar, piano, etc. **8** a wire above the finish line of a racecourse, that is broken as the winner runs through it.
down to the wire, *Informal.* up to or at the very end or the very last moment.
get (in) under the wire, *Informal.* arrive or finish just before it is too late.
pull wires, *Informal.* use one's influence to gain an advantage for oneself or others.
—v. **1** furnish with wire or wiring: *to wire a house for electricity.* **2** fasten with wire: *He wired the two pieces together.* **3** fence (*in*) with wire. **4** stiffen with wire. **5** place on a wire. **6** catch by a wire or wires. **7** *Informal.* telegraph: *to wire a birthday greeting. I'll wire you if my plans change.* **8** *Informal.* attach concealed electronic recording equipment in (a place) or on (a person): *The police often wire an informant in order to get accurate information.* ⟨OE *wīr*⟩ **—'wire,like,** *adj.* **—'wir•er,** *n.*

wire birch *Cdn.* a small species of birch tree (*Betula populifolia*), native to the Maritimes, southern Québec, and eastern Ontario.

wire brush a small brush with bristles made of wire, used for scraping metal before repainting, etc.

wire cutter a scissorlike tool for cutting wire.

wired [waɪrd] *adj., v. —adj. Slang.* extremely excited, tense, edgy, disoriented, etc.
—v. pt. and pp. of WIRE.

wire•drawn ['waɪr,drɒn] *adj.* **1** drawn out into a wire. **2** of ideas, comparisons, descriptions, etc., given in great detail; intricate. **3** too fine or subtle.

wire gauge a device, usually a disk with different-sized notches in it, for measuring the diameter of wire, the thickness of metal sheets, etc.

wire gauze a very fine netting of woven wire.

wire–haired ['waɪr ,hɛrd] *adj.* having coarse, stiff hair: *a wire-haired fox terrier.*

wire•less ['waɪrlɪs] *adj., n., v. —adj.* **1** using no wires; transmitting by radio waves instead of by electric wires: *wireless telegraphy.* **2** *Esp. Brit.* radio.
—n. **1** *Esp. Brit.* **a** a radio. **b** a message sent by radio. **2 a** wireless telegraphy. **b** wireless telephony.
—v. Esp. Brit. send or transmit by radio; communicate with by radio.
☛ *Usage.* The British usage is no longer common.

wire nail a small, thin nail made from iron or steel wire, with a small head produced by the compression of one end.

Wire•pho•to ['waɪr,foutou] *n. Trademark.* **1** a method for transmitting photographs by reproducing a facsimile through electric signals. **2** a photograph transmitted in this fashion.

wire pulling *Informal.* the use of personal influence to accomplish a purpose. **—wire puller.**

wire recorder an early type of magnetic audio recorder that used wire instead of tape.

wire service a business organization that collects news stories, photos, stock market prices, etc. and distributes them to newspapers and radio and television stations that subscribe to their service; news service.

wire•tap ['waɪr,tæp] *n., v.* **-tapped, -tap•ping.** *—n.* **1** an instance of wiretapping. **2** the information obtained by wiretapping.
—v. **1** engage in wiretapping, legally or illegally. **2** record (something) by wiretapping. ⟨back formation < *wiretapping*⟩ **—'wire,tap•per,** *n.*

wire•tap•ping ['waɪr,tæpɪŋ] *n., v. —n.* the act or practice of making a secret connection with telephone or telegraph wires to find out the messages sent over them.
—v. ppr. of WIRETAP.

wire•worm ['waɪr,wɜrm] *n.* **1** the slender, hard-bodied larva of any of various click beetles. Wireworms feed on the roots of plants and do much damage to crops. **2** a millipede (*Julus diplopoda*). **3** a parasitic roundworm (*Haemonchus contortus*) that infests the stomach and small intestine of cattle and sheep.

wire–wove ['waɪr ,wouv] *n.* a grade of very smooth paper made in a frame of fine wire.

wir•ing ['waɪrɪŋ] *n., v. —n. Electricity.* a system of wires to carry an electric current.
—v. ppr. of WIRE.

wir•y ['waɪri] *adj.* **wir•i•er, wir•i•est. 1** made of wire. **2** like wire. **3** lean, strong, and tough. **—'wir•i•ly,** *adv.* **—'wir•i•ness,** *n.*

wis [wɪs] *v. Archaic.* know (used only in *I wis,* parenthetically). ⟨ME *iwis* certainly (taken as *I wis*) < OE *gewiss*⟩

Wis•con•sin [wɪ'skɒnsɪn] *n.* a north central state of the United States.

wis•dom ['wɪzdəm] *n.* **1** knowledge and good judgment based on experience; the quality of being wise. **2** wise conduct; wise words. **3** scholarly knowledge. ⟨OE *wīsdōm* < *wīs* wise⟩

wisdom tooth the back tooth, or third molar, on either side of the upper and lower jaw, ordinarily appearing between the ages of 17 and 25.

wise¹ [waɪz] *adj.* **wis•er, wis•est;** *v.* **wised, wis•ing.**
—adj. **1** having knowledge and good judgment: *a wise counsellor.* **2** showing wisdom: *wise advice.* **3** having knowledge or information; informed: *We are none the wiser for her explanations.* **4** learned; erudite. **5** *Slang.* annoyingly know-it-all. **6** *Archaic.* having knowledge of occult or supernatural things.

get wise, *Slang.* **a** find out; understand; realize (*often with* **to**). **b** get saucy.
put (someone) **wise to,** *Slang.* enlighten (someone) about.
wise to, *Slang.* aware of; informed about.
—v.
wise up, *Slang.* **a** inform or enlighten (a person). **b** become enlightened; gain awareness or understanding. ⟨OE *wīs*⟩
—'wise•ly, *adv.* **—'wise•ness,** *n.*

☛ *Syn.* **1, 2. Wise,** SAGE[1] = having or showing knowledge and good judgment in using and applying that knowledge. **Wise** emphasizes knowledge and understanding of people and of what is true and right in life and conduct, together with sound judgment in deciding and acting: *His wise mother knows how to handle him.* **Sage** suggests deep wisdom based on wide knowledge and experience and profound thought and understanding: *The old professor gave us sage advice that we have never forgotten.*

wise² [waiz] *n. Formal.* way; manner: *John is in no wise a student; he prefers sports and machinery.* ⟨OE *wīse.* Akin to GUISE.⟩

-wise *suffix.* **1** in —— manner: *anywise* and *likewise.* **2** in a ——ing manner: *slantwise.* **3** in the characteristic way of a ——: *clockwise.* **4** in the —— respect or case: *leastwise, otherwise.* **5** in the direction of ——: *lengthwise.* **6** with regard to ——: *businesswise.* **7** special meanings: *sidewise.* ⟨< *wise*²⟩

☛ *Usage.* **6.** In Old and Middle English **-wise** was freely added to nouns to form adverbs of manner. This usage has recently been revived and is popularly used to form words as needed: *He is doing well salarywise.* However, many people regard the usage as a fad appropriate only to informal speech and professional jargon. It should, therefore, be used with discretion, especially in writing.

wise•a•cre ['waiz,eikər] *n.* a person who thinks that he or she knows everything. ⟨< MDu. *wijssegger* soothsayer < G *Weissager*⟩

wise•crack ['waiz,kræk] *n., v. Slang.* *—n.* a smart remark; a quick, witty reply.
—v. make wisecracks. **—'wise,crack•er,** *n.*

wise guy *Slang.* **1** someone who is conceited, impudent, cocky; a know-it-all. **2** someone who works undercover for a government department or agency. **—'wise-,guy,** *adj.*

wi•sent ['vizənt] *n.* the European bison (*Bison bonasus*), somewhat smaller than the North American bison, or buffalo, and having a much smaller hump over the shoulder. The wisent is now nearly extinct as a wild animal, but survives in parks.

wish [wɪʃ] *v., n.* *—v.* **1** have a need or longing (for); desire; want: *Do you wish to go home?* **2** have or express a desire or hope (for): *He wished for a new house. I wish that I had enough money to buy that model boat. We wish peace for all humankind.* **3** express a desire or hope with respect to (a person or thing): *I wish you a Happy New Year. She wished him dead.* **4** request or command (a thing or action, or a person to do something): *Do you wish me to send her in now?* **5** pass or impose (something undesirable or unwanted); foist (*used with* **on**): *They wished the hardest job on him.* **6** cause to be, etc., by sheer force of wishing: *We can't just wish this war away.*
—n. **1** the act or an instance of wishing: *She had no wish to be president of the company. Turn your wishes into action.* **2** Usually, **wishes,** *pl.* the expressed desire for someone's happiness, fortune, etc.: *She sends you best wishes for a Happy New Year.* **3** the thing wished for: *They got their wishes.*
make a wish, have or express a wish. ⟨OE *wȳscan*⟩ **—'wish•er,** *n.*

☛ *Syn. v.* **1. Wish,** DESIRE = want or long for something. **Wish** is the less emphatic word, sometimes suggesting only that one would like to have, do, or get a certain thing, sometimes suggesting a longing that can never be satisfied: *I wish I could travel round the world.* **Desire,** sometimes used as a formal substitute for **wish** or, especially, **want,** particularly suggests wishing strongly and often a willingness or determination to work or struggle to get it: *She finally received the position she desired.*
☛ *Hom.* WHISH.

wish•bone ['wɪʃ,boun] *n.* in poultry and other birds, the forked bone in the front of the breast. ⟨from the custom of two people wishing on this bone, which they then pull apart; the wish of the person holding the longer end will supposedly be granted⟩

wish•ful ['wɪʃfəl] *adj.* having or expressing a wish; desiring; desirous; longing. **—'wish•ful•ly,** *adv.* **—'wish•ful•ness,** *n.*

wish fulfilment *Psychology.* the satisfaction of a subconscious desire through fantasy.

wishful thinking a believing something to be true that one wishes or wants to be true.

wish list a hypothetical list of things wished for, and usually unlikely to be received.

wish•y–wash•y ['wɪʃi ,wɒʃi] *adj.* **1** thin and weak; watery; insipid. **2** lacking in substantial qualities; indecisive; vacillating. **—'wish•y-,wash•i•ly,** *adv.* **—'wish•y-,wash•i•ness,** *n.*

wisp [wɪsp] *n.* **1** a small bundle or bunch: *a wisp of hay.* **2** a slender, fine bit of something insubstantial: *a wisp of smoke.* **3** a small and delicate or slight person or thing: *a wisp of a girl.* ⟨ME *wisp, wips;* cf. W Frisian *wisp.* Akin to WIPE.⟩

wisp•y ['wɪspi] *adj.* **wisp•i•er, wisp•i•est. 1** like a wisp; thin; slight. **2** of women's hair, trimmed to irregular thicknesses or lengths so as to appear finer or lighter, as on the back of the neck or on the forehead.

wist [wɪst] *v. Archaic.* pt. and pp. of WIT².

wis•tar•i•a [wɪ'stɛriə] *n.* See WISTERIA.

wis•te•ri•a [wɪ'stiriə] *or* [wɪ'stɛriə] *n.* any of a genus (*Wisteria*) of twining, mostly woody, vines of the pea family having compound leaves and large, drooping clusters of blue, purple, white, or rose flowers. Some wisterias are widely cultivated as ornamentals. ⟨after Caspar *Wistar* (1761-1818), U.S. scientist⟩

wist•ful ['wɪstfəl] *adj.* **1** longing; yearning: *A child stood looking with wistful eyes at the toys in the window.* **2** pensive; melancholy. ⟨< obs. *wist* attentive (< *wistly* intently, of uncertain origin) + *-ful*⟩ **—'wist•ful•ly,** *adv.* **—'wist•ful•ness,** *n.*

wit¹ [wɪt] *n.* **1** the power to perceive quickly and express cleverly or incisively ideas that are unusual, striking, and amusing. **2** a person with such power. **3** Often, **wits,** *pl.* the power of understanding; mind; good sense: *People with quick wits learn easily. The children were out of their wits with fright. That poor man hasn't wit enough to earn a living.*
at (one's) **wits' end,** not knowing what to do or say.
have or **keep** (one's) **wits about** (one), be alert; have presence of mind; remain calm and in control of one's thoughts: *You have to keep your wits about you to understand her lectures.*
live by (one's) **wits,** make one's living by clever or crafty devices rather than by any settled occupation. ⟨OE *witt*⟩
☛ *Hom.* WHIT.
☛ *Syn.* **1. Wit,** HUMOUR = power to see and express what is amusing or causes laughter. **Wit** = a mental sharpness and quickness in perceiving what is striking, unusual, inconsistent, or out of keeping and in expressing it in cleverly surprising and amusing sayings: *Bernard Shaw was famous for his wit.* **Humour** = a power to see and show with warm sympathy and kindness the things in life and human nature that are funny or absurdly out of the ordinary: *Her sense of humour makes her popular.*

wit² [wɪt] *v. pres. 1st pers. sing.* **wot,** *2nd pers. sing.* **wost,** *3rd pers. sing.* **wot,** *pl.* **wit;** *pt. and pp.* **wist;** *ppr.* **wit•ting.** *Archaic.* know or learn.
to wit, that is to say; namely: *To my son I leave all I own–to wit, my house, what is in it, and the land on which it stands.* ⟨OE *witan*⟩
☛ *Hom.* WHIT.

witch [wɪtʃ] *n., v.* *—n.* **1** a person, especially a woman, who practises usually black magic. Compare WARLOCK. **2 a** a Wiccan priest or priestess. **b** a devotee of Wicca. **3** *Informal.* a charming or fascinating girl or woman. **4** *Informal.* a woman of any age who is malicious or scheming.
—v. **1** use the power of a witch on (a person or thing). **2** charm; fascinate; bewitch. **3** use a divining rod. ⟨OE *wicce*⟩ **—'witch•y,** *adv.* **—'witch,like,** *adj.*
☛ *Hom.* WHICH.

witch•craft ['wɪtʃ,kræft] *n.* **1** the practices and the cult of witches; the power or art of evoking supernatural forces or spirits to control or change the natural course of events, especially in order to work evil. **2** an influence or fascination suggesting such power or art.

witch doctor a professional practitioner of magic among certain preliterate peoples, who uses his or her power especially in healing the sick.

witch•er•y ['wɪtʃəri] *n., pl.* **-er•ies. 1** witchcraft; magic. **2** charm; fascination.

witches' Sabbath Sabbat.

witch hazel 1 any of a genus (*Hamamelis*) of shrubs and small trees native to E Asia and E North America, having small clusters of yellow flowers; especially, a North American species (*H. virginiana*) which is the source of a medicinal lotion. **2** the lotion prepared from the bark and leaves of the common North American witch hazel, used for cooling and soothing the skin.

witch hunt *Slang.* a campaign to seek out and harrass, malign, or purge all those who disagree with a given platform, or who may be accused of disloyalty, subversion, etc., often on slight or unsubstantiated evidence. **—witch hunter.**

witch•ing ['wɪtʃɪŋ] *n., adj., v.* *—n.* the practice of a person who claims to be or is suspected of being a witch.
—adj. bewitching; magical; enchanting.
—v. ppr. of WITCH. **—'witch•ing•ly,** *adv.*

witching hour, the midnight.

wit•e•na•ge•mot ['wɪtənəgə,mout] *n.* the royal council of the Anglo-Saxons. ⟨OE *witenagemōt* < *witena*, gen. pl. of *wita* councillor + *gemōt* meeting⟩

with [wɪθ] *or* [wɪð] *prep.* **1** in the company of: *Come with me.* **2** into or among: *They will mix with the crowd. Mix the butter with the sugar.* **3** having, wearing, carrying, etc.: *a man with brains, a telegram with bad news.* **4** by means of; by using: *to cut meat with a knife.* **5** using; showing: *Work with care.* **6** as an addition to; added to: *Do you want sugar with your tea?* **7** including; and: *tea with sugar and lemon.* **8** in relation to; in co-operation with: *They are friendly with us.* **9** in regard to: *We are pleased with the house.* **10** in proportion to: *An army's power increases with its size.* **11** because of: *to shake with cold.* **12** in the keeping or care of: *Leave the dog with me.* **13** in the region, sphere, experience, opinion, or view of: *It is day with us while it is night with the Chinese. High taxes are unpopular with many people.* **14** at the same time as: *Go to bed with the sun.* **15** following upon; after: *With this stern warning, she wheeled and left the room.* **16** in the same direction as: *The boat floated along with the current.* **17** on the side of; for; of the same view or opinion as: *They are with us in our plan.* **18** from: *I hate to part with my favourite things.* **19** against: *We fought with that gang.* **20** receiving; having; being given; endorsed; backed by: *I went with his permission. She comes to us with Shelagh's recommendation.* **21** in spite of: *With all his size he was not a strong man.* **22** on, in, attached to, etc. and therefore in the same rhythm, direction, etc. as: *The duck rose and fell with the waves.*
with it, *Slang.* **a** up to date; in the know; hip. **b** alert; following and understanding what is being said or done: *For her age, Anne's grandmother is really with it.*
with that, when that occurred; whereupon: *The train reached the station, and, with that, our long trip ended.* ⟨OE *with* against⟩
☛ *Hom.* WITHE [wɪθ] *or* [wɪð].
☛ *Syn.* **4.** See note at BY.

with– *prefix.* **1** against: *withstand.* **2** back; away: *withdraw, withhold.* **3** along with; alongside; toward: *without, within.* ⟨OE⟩

with•al [wɪ'ðɒl] *or* [wɪ'θɒl] *adv., prep. Archaic. —adv.* with it all; as well; besides; also: *The lady is rich and fair and wise withal.*
—prep. with: *He had not even a blanket to cover himself withal.* ⟨< *with* + *all*⟩

with•draw [wɪθ'drɒ] *or* [wɪð'drɒ] *v.* **-drew, -drawn, -draw•ing.** **1** draw back; draw away: *He quickly withdrew his hand from the hot stove. She tried to kiss him, but he withdrew from her touch.* **2** take back; remove: *to withdraw money from an account. Worn-out paper money is withdrawn from use by the government.* **3** go away: *She withdrew from the room.* **4** take back or retract (a statement, motion, proposal, etc.). **5** cease one's involvement with some activity, commitment, etc.: *to withdraw from active service.* **6** *Psychology.* retreat from reality. ⟨< *with-* away + *draw*⟩
☛ *Syn.* **3.** See note at DEPART.

with•draw•al [wɪθ'drɒəl] *or* [wɪð'drɒəl] *n.* **1** the act or an instance of drawing back or taking back, taking away or going away: *The chairperson noticed her withdrawal from the meeting. You cannot make withdrawals on this account.* **2** the amount or thing withdrawn: *The Jupiter 600 is the second withdrawal from the car market this spring due to manufacturing defects.* **3** *Psychology.* a mental condition during which a person ceases to communicate with others and draws back into himself or herself. **4** the complex of effects experienced by a person trying to overcome an addiction.

with•drawn [wɪθ'drɒn] *or* [wɪð'drɒn] *v., adj. —v.* pp. of WITHDRAW.
—adj. unsociable or unresponsive; introverted.

with•drew [wɪθ'dru] *or* [wɪð'dru] *v.* pt. of WITHDRAW.

withe [waɪð], [wɪθ], *or* [wɪð] *n., v.* **withed, with•ing.** *—n.* **1** a willow twig. **2** any tough, easily bent twig suitable for binding things together.
—v. bind with withes. ⟨OE *withthe*⟩
☛ *Hom.* WITH [wɪθ] *or* [wɪð].

with•er ['wɪðər] *v.* **1** lose or cause to lose freshness, vigour, etc.; dry up or fade: *a face withered with age. Flowers wither after they are cut.* **2** cause to feel ashamed or confused: *She blushed under her aunt's withering look.* ⟨ME *wideren*, var. of *wederen* weather⟩ **—'with•er•ing•ly,** *adv.*
☛ *Hom.* WHITHER.

with•ers ['wɪðərz] *n.pl.* the highest part of a horse's or other animal's back, behind the neck. See HORSE for picture. ⟨OE *withre* resistance < *wither* to; from the fact that a horse opposes this part to the load it is pulling⟩

with•er•shins ['wɪðər,ʃɪnz] *adv. Scottish.* See WIDDERSHINS.

with•held [wɪθ'hɛld] *or* [wɪð'hɛld] *v.* pt. and pp. of WITHHOLD.

with•hold [wɪθ'hould] *or* [wɪð'hould] *v.* **-held, -hold•ing.** **1** refrain from giving or granting: *The play cannot be put on if the principal withholds her consent.* **2** forbear; hold back; keep back: *The captain withheld his men from attack.* ⟨< *with-* + *hold*⟩
☛ *Syn.* **1.** See note at KEEP.

with•in [wɪ'ðɪn] *or* [wɪ'θɪn] *prep., adv. —prep.* **1** inside the limits of; not beyond: *The task was within the man's powers. He guessed my weight within 2 kg.* **2** in or into the inner part of; inside of: *to see within the body by means of X rays.* **3** in the inner being, soul, or mind of.
—adv. **1** in or into the inner part; inside: *The house has been painted within and without. We saw a figure approach the tower and disappear within.* **2** in the inner being; in the being, soul, or mind; inwardly: *to keep one's grief within.* ⟨OE *withinnan*⟩

with•out [wɪ'ðʌut] *or* [wɪ'θʌut] *prep., adv., conj. —prep.* **1** with no; not having; free from; lacking: *A cat walks without noise. I drink tea without sugar.* **2** so as to omit, avoid, or neglect: *She walked past without looking at us.* **3** *Archaic.* outside of; beyond: *Soldiers are camped within and without the city walls.*
—adv. Archaic or poetic. on or at the outside; externally: *The house is clean within and without.*
do or **go without,** remain in want of something; manage in spite of not having a certain thing: *Either cook your own supper or go without.*
—conj. Dialect. unless. ⟨OE *withūtan*⟩

with•stand [wɪθ'stænd] *or* [wɪð'stænd] *v.* **-stood, -stand•ing.** stand against; hold out against; endure; oppose, especially successfully: *The pioneers withstood many hardships. These shoes will withstand hard wear.* ⟨OE *withstandan* < *with-* against + *standan* stand⟩
☛ *Syn.* See note at OPPOSE.

with•stood [wɪθ'stʊd] *or* [wɪð'stʊd] *v.* pt. and pp. of WITHSTAND.

with•y ['wɪði] *or* ['wɪθi] *n., pl.* **with•ies.** **1** willow or osier; withe. **2** a band or halter made of withes. ⟨OE *wīthig*⟩

wit•less ['wɪtlɪs] *adj.* lacking intelligence; stupid; foolish. **—'wit•less•ly,** *adv.* **—'wit•less•ness,** *n.*

wit•ness ['wɪtnɪs] *n., v. —n.* **1** a person who is present when something happens; one who has direct or first-hand knowledge of an event. **2** a person who gives evidence or testifies under oath before a judge, coroner, etc. **3** evidence; testimony. **4** a person who signs a document to show that another person's signature on it is genuine.
bear witness, be evidence; give evidence; testify: *A wife need not bear witness against her husband. The man's fingerprints bore witness to his guilt.*
—v. **1** see; perceive: *He witnessed the accident.* **2** testify to; give evidence of: *Her whole manner witnessed her surprise.* **3** give evidence; testify. **4** sign (a document) as a witness: *to witness a will.* ⟨OE *witnes* knowledge < *wit* wit[1]⟩

witness box the place where a witness stands or sits to give evidence in a court of law.

witness post a post driven into the ground, to mark the area where a mining claim has been staked.

witness stand WITNESS BOX.

wit•ti•cism ['wɪtə,sɪzəm] *n.* a witty remark. ⟨< *witty*, on the model of *criticism*⟩

wit•ting ['wɪtɪŋ] *adj., v. —adj.* knowing; conscious; deliberate or intentional: *His witting false claim will get him into trouble.*
—v. Archaic. ppr. of WIT[2]. **—'wit•ting•ly,** *adv.*

wit•ty ['wɪti] *adj.* **-ti•er, -ti•est.** full of wit; clever and amusing: *a witty person, a witty remark.* ⟨OE *wittig*⟩ **—'wit•ti•ly,** *adv.* **—'wit•ti•ness,** *n.*

wive [waɪv] *v.* **wived, wiv•ing.** *Archaic.* **1** marry (a woman). **2** supply with a wife. ⟨OE *wīfian*⟩

wi•vern ['waɪvərn] *n.* See WYVERN.

wives [waɪvz] *n.* pl. of WIFE.

wiz [wɪz] *n.* WHIZ[1].

wiz•ard ['wɪzərd] *n., adj. —n.* **1** a man supposed to have magic power. **2** *Informal.* a person of amazing skill or accomplishment.
—adj. **1** magic. **2** of or having to do with wizards or wizardry. ⟨ult. < *wise*[1]⟩ **—'wiz•ard•ly,** *adj.*

wiz•ar•dry ['wɪzərdri] *n.* **1** magic; magic skill. **2** exceptional skill or expertness: *The chef at the new restaurant displays absolute wizardry in the kitchen.*

wiz•en ['wɪzən] *v.* dry up. ⟨ME *wisenen* < OE *wisnian* become dry⟩

wiz•ened ['wɪzənd] *adj., v. —adj.* dried up; withered; shrivelled: *a wizened apple, a wizened face.*
—v. pt. and pp. of WIZEN. ⟨pp. of dial. *wizen,* OF *wisnian* shrivel⟩

wk. 1 week. 2 work.

wkly. weekly.

w.l. or **WL** 1 WATER LINE. 2 wavelength.

w.long. west longitude.

WMO World Meteorological Organization.

WNW or **W.N.W.** west-northwest.

wo [wou] *Archaic.* See WOE.
☛ *Hom.* WHOA.

WO or **W.O.** WARRANT OFFICER.

w/o without.

woad [woud] *n.* 1 a European herb (*Isatis tinctoria*) of the mustard family formerly cultivated for its leaves, from which a blue dye was made. 2 the dye itself. ⟨OE *wād*⟩

wob•ble ['wɒbəl] *v.* **-bled, -bling;** *n. —v.* 1 move unsteadily from side to side; shake; tremble. 2 incline or move from side to side when rotating, as a top or an unevenly balanced wheel. 3 cause to wobble. 4 be uncertain, unsteady, or inconstant; waver.
—n. a wobbling motion. ⟨Cf. LG *wabbeln*⟩ **—'wob•bler,** *n.* **—'wob•bly,** *adj.* **—'wob•bli•ness,** *n.*

Wo•den ['woudən] *n.* the most important Anglo-Saxon god, corresponding to Odin in Norse mythology. Also, **Wodan.** ⟨OE⟩

woe [wou] *n., interj. —n.* 1 great grief, trouble, or distress: *Sickness and poverty are common woes.* 2 a cause of this.
—interj. Archaic. an exclamation of grief, trouble, or distress (*now usually jocular*): *Woe is me!* Also, **wo.** ⟨OE *wā,* interj.⟩
☛ *Hom.* WHOA.

woe•be•gone ['woubɪ,gɒn] *adj.* looking sad, sorrowful, or wretched. ⟨ME *wo begon* surrounded with woe < wot *begon,* pp. of *begon* < OE *began* surround, besiege⟩

woe•ful ['woufəl] *adj.* 1 full of woe; sad; sorrowful; wretched: *a woeful expression.* 2 pitiful: *a woeful sight.* 3 of very poor quality. **—'woe•ful•ly,** *adv.* **—'woe•ful•ness,** *n.*

wok [wɒk] *n.* a wide, somewhat shallow metal cooking utensil used especially in Chinese cooking, having sides that curve in to a small, flat bottom. ⟨< Guangdong dial. *wohk* pan⟩
☛ *Hom.* WALK.

woke [wouk] *v.* a pt. of WAKE[1].

wo•ken ['woukən] *v.* a pp. of WAKE[1].

wold [would] *n. Poetic.* an area of high, rolling country, bare of woods. ⟨OE *wald, weald* a wood⟩

wolf [wʊlf] *n., pl.* **wolves;** *v. —n.* 1 either of two wild members (genus *Canis*) of the dog family formerly widespread throughout the northern hemisphere but now greatly reduced in range and numbers, having a large, broad head, a deep, narrow chest, long legs, a long, bushy tail, and a coat that may be white, greyish, black, or reddish brown. The relatively small **red wolf** (*Canis rufus*) of south central United States is considered by many authorities to be of the same species as the timber wolf (grey wolf). See also TIMBER WOLF. 2 any of several similar wild members of the dog family. 3 a cruel, savage, or greedy person. 4 *Slang.* a man who makes a habit of aggressively flirting with or trying to seduce women. 5 *Music.* **a** a discordant sound heard in chords produced on a keyboard instrument when tuned in a system of unequal temperament. **b** the chord in which it appears. **c** in stringed instruments played with a bow, a dissonance or breaking of tone caused by a defect in structure or adjustment.
cry wolf, give a false alarm.
keep the wolf from the door, keep safe from hunger or poverty.
wolf in sheep's clothing, a person who pretends to be friendly or harmless, but intends to do harm.
—v. Informal. eat greedily (*often used with* **down**): *to wolf down one's dinner.* ⟨OE *wulf*⟩ **—'wolf,like,** *adj.*

wolf•ber•ry ['wʊlf,bɛri] *n.* snowberry.

wolf call *Slang.* a characteristic whistle or shout made by a male expressing appreciation of an attractive female.

Wolf Cub a member, aged eight to ten, of the Scouts.

wolf dog 1 any of various dogs used in hunting wolves. 2 a dog, especially a sled dog, having some wolf ancestry. 3 *Cdn.* in the North, an Eskimo dog or husky.

wolf eel any of a family (Anarhichadidae) of large fishes of the N Atlantic and Pacific Oceans belonging to the same suborder as the blennies, having long, pointed front teeth, especially a N Atlantic species (*Anarhichas lupus*) valued as a food fish.

wolf•er ['wʊlfər] *n. Cdn.* a wolf hunter. Formerly, **wolver.**

Wolff•i•an body ['wʊlfiən] *Embryology.* the excretory organ in the embryonic form of higher vertebrates, which is later replaced by the kidney. ⟨after K.F. *Wolff* (1733-1794), the German anatomist who first described it⟩

wolf•fish or **wolf fish** ['wʊlf,fɪʃ] *n., pl.* **-fish** or **-fish•es.** a large spiny-finned fish of the genus *Anarhichas,* especially *A. lupus* of the northern Atlantic, noted for its ferocious appearance and habits.

wolf•hound ['wʊlf,haʊnd] *n.* any of several breeds of very large dog, such as the **borzoi** or the **Irish wolfhound,** formerly used in hunting wolves.

wolf•ish ['wʊlfɪʃ] *adj.* 1 of or having to do with wolves. 2 resembling a wolf: *a wolfish dog.* 3 cruel, savage, or greedy: *He ate with wolfish impatience.* **—'wolf•ish•ly,** *adv.* **—'wolf•ish•ness,** *n.*

wolf•ram ['wʊlfrəm] *n.* 1 *Chemistry.* tungsten. 2 wolframite. ⟨< G⟩

wolf•ram•ite ['wʊlfrə,məit] *n.* an ore consisting of compounds of tungsten with iron and manganese.

wolfs•bane or **wolf's–bane** ['wʊlfs,bein] *n.* aconite, especially a poisonous species (*Aconitum lycoctonum*) having dull yellow flowers, found in the mountainous regions of Europe.

wolf spider any of a family (Lycosidae) of ground spiders ranging in size from a body length of about 6 mm to about 45 mm, that do not spin webs but leap on their prey. Some wolf spiders, such as the European tarantula, live in silk-lined burrows in the ground; others live in the open.

wolf willow or **wolf–wil•low** ['wʊlf ,wɪlou] *n. Cdn.* a North American shrub (*Elaeagnus commutata*) of the oleaster family found especially in the Prairies, having oblong, silvery leaves, small, fragrant flowers that are silver outside and yellow inside, and silvery fruit that is edible, but dry and mealy.

wol•las•ton•ite ['wʊləstə,nəit] *n.* a whitish mineral, silicate of calcium, occurring in metamorphic rocks and having a variety of industrial uses. ⟨after W. *Wollaston,* English physicist (1766-1828)⟩

wol•ver•ine ['wʊlvə,rin] *or* [,wʊlvə'rin] *n.* 1 a very powerful, heavily built, carnivorous mammal (*Gulo gulo*) of the weasel family found in the northern forests of North America and Eurasia, having a long, thick, coarse coat that is blackish brown with a light brown stripe along each side of the body. 2 the fur of this animal. ⟨earlier *wolvering* < *wolf*⟩

A wolverine

wolves [wʊlvz] *n.* pl. of WOLF.

wom•an ['wʊmən] *n., pl.* **wom•en** ['wɪmən] 1 an adult female human being. 2 women as a group; the average woman: *a magazine designed for the modern woman.* 3 (*adjl.*) female: *a woman cab driver. One of her women friends was asking about her.* 4 feminine nature or emotions; womanliness. 5 a female servant or attendant. 6 *Informal or dialect.* a wife. 7 a mistress; paramour. 8 a man considered as being womanish: *He's a fussy old woman.* 9 (*adjl.*) of or characteristic of a woman or women; womanly: *woman talk.*
be one's own woman. See MAN. ⟨OE *wīfman* < *wīf* woman + *man* human being⟩ **—'wom•an•less,** *adj.*
☛ *Usage.* See note at LADY.

wom•an•hood ['wʊmən,hʊd] *n.* 1 the condition or time of being a woman. 2 the character or qualities of a woman. 3 women as a group: *Marie Curie was an honour to womanhood.*

wom•an•ish ['wʊmənɪʃ] *adj.* 1 not suitable to a man of strong character. 2 effeminate: *He had a womanish way about him.* **—'wom•an•ish•ly,** *adv.* **—'wom•an•ish•ness,** *n.*

wom•an•ize ['wʊmə,naɪz] *v.* **-ized, -iz•ing.** 1 of a man, indulge frequently in casual sexual relationships with women. 2 make effeminate. **—'wom•an,iz•er,** *n.*

wom•an•kind ['wʊmən,kaɪnd] *n.* women collectively.

wom•an•like ['wʊmən,ləik] *adj.* **1** like a woman; womanly. **2** suitable for a woman.

wom•an•ly ['wʊmənli] *adj.* **1** having or showing the best qualities of a woman: *a womanly nature. She is very womanly.* **2** proper or suitable for a woman: *Hockey, sewing, and business are all equally womanly pursuits.* **—'wom•an•li•ness,** *n.*

woman of God **1** a holy woman; saint. **2** a female member of the clergy.

woman of letters **1** a woman writer. **2** a woman who has a wide knowledge of literature.

woman of the world a woman who has wide experience of different kinds of people and customs; a sophisticated and worldly-wise or practical woman.

woman suffrage the political right of women to vote.

wom•an–suf•fra•gist ['wʊmən 'sʌfrədʒɪst] *n.* a person who favours the right of women to vote.

womb [wum] *n.* **1** the uterus of the human female and of the female of certain higher mammals. **2** a place where something is conceived or generated and developed. ⟨OE *wamb*⟩

wom•bat ['wɒmbæt] *n.* either of two burrowing Australian marsupials (*Vombatus ursinus* and *Lasiorhinus latifrons*, constituting the family Vombatidae, also called Phascolomidae) that resemble small bears. ⟨< a native Australian language⟩

wom•en ['wɪmən] *n.* pl. of WOMAN.

wom•en•folk ['wɪmən,fouk] *n.pl. Informal.* **1** women collectively. **2** a particular group of women, such as the female members of a family.

Women's Institute a society for women (originally, rural women) that promotes interest in agriculture and industry, home management, citizenship, and cultural activities. The first Women's Institute was formed in Stoney Creek, Ontario, in 1897. The movement spread to England in 1915. *Abbrev.*: WI or W.I.

women's lib *Informal.* WOMEN'S LIBERATION.

Women's Liberation a movement beginning in the late 1960s, committed to combatting sexual discrimination and to obtaining full legal, economic, and social rights equal to those granted to men.

women's rights social, political, and legal rights for women, equal to those of men.

won[1] [wʌn] *v.* pt. and pp. of WIN.

won[2] [wɒn] *n., pl.* **won. 1** the basic unit of money in Korea, divided into 100 chon. See table of money in the Appendix. **2** a coin or note worth one won. ⟨< Korean⟩

won•der ['wʌndər] *n., v.* *—n.* **1** a strange and surprising, awesome, beautiful thing or event; awe; intense admiration and curiosity mixed: *He saw the wonders of the city. It is a wonder she turned down the offer.* **2** the feeling caused by what is strange and surprising, awesome, beautiful, etc.: *The baby looked with wonder at the Christmas tree.* **3** (*adjl.*) amazingly effective, brilliant, etc.: *a wonder drug.*
do or **work wonders,** do wonderful things; achieve or produce extraordinary results.
for a wonder, as a strange and surprising thing; for once.
no (or **small** or **little**) **wonder, a** it is nothing surprising; not surprising: *No wonder he resigned.* **b** now I know why; that explains it.
wonders (will) never cease, what a (pleasant) surprise.
—v. **1** feel wonder: *We wonder at the splendour of the stars.* **2** feel some doubt or curiosity; wish to know or learn; speculate: *to wonder about his sudden departure. I wonder what happened.* **3** be surprised or astonished: *I shouldn't wonder if she wins the prize.* **4** ask oneself; ask inwardly or in one's thoughts: "Where could she have gone?" he wondered. ⟨OE *wundor*⟩ **—'won•der•er,** *n.* **—'won•der•ing•ly,** *adv.*

won•der•ful ['wʌndərfəl] *adj.* **1** causing wonder; marvellous; remarkable: *The explorer had wonderful adventures.* **2** *Informal.* excellent; splendid; fine: *We had a wonderful time at the party.* ⟨OE *wunderfull*⟩ **—'won•der•ful•ly,** *adv.* **—'won•der•ful•ness,** *n.*
☛ *Syn.* **1. Wonderful,** MARVELLOUS = causing wonder. **Wonderful** describes something so new and unfamiliar, out of the ordinary, beyond expectation, or imperfectly understood that it excites a feeling of surprise, admiration, puzzled interest, or, sometimes, astonishment: *The boys from India saw some wonderful sights on their first trip across Canada.* **Marvellous** describes something so extraordinary, surprising, or astonishing that it seems hardly believable: *The machine that can translate from a foreign language is a marvellous scientific invention.*

won•der•land ['wʌndər,lænd] *n.* a land, realm, etc. full of wonders.

won•der•ment ['wʌndərmənt] *n.* **1** wonder; surprise. **2** something that causes wonder; a marvel.

won•drous ['wʌndrəs] *adj., adv.* *—adj.* wonderful. *—adv. Poetic.* wonderfully: *wondrous strange.* ⟨alteration of *wonders* (gen. of *wonder*) wondrous, with the suffix *-ous,* as in *marvellous*⟩ **—'won•drous•ly,** *adv.* **—'won•drous•ness,** *n.*

won•ky ['wɒŋki] *adj. Slang.* shaky; out of kilter; out of whack; not functioning, or appearing not to function normally: *You must have a fever; your eyes look wonky.* ⟨? alteration of dial. *wankle,* ult. < OE *wancol* shaky⟩

wont [wount] *or* [wɒnt] *adj., n.* *—adj.* accustomed: *She was wont to read the paper at breakfast.*
—n. a custom or habit: *He rose early, as was his wont.* ⟨originally pp., ult. < OE *wunian* be accustomed⟩
☛ *Hom.* WON'T [wount], WANT [wɒnt].

won't ['wount] will not.
☛ *Hom.* WONT [wount].

wont•ed ['wountɪd] *or* ['wɒntɪd] *adj.* accustomed; customary; usual: *My wonted route to work was blocked off, so I had to go the long way around.* **—'wont•ed•ness,** *n.*

won ton ['wɒn ,tɒn] a Chinese dumpling consisting of chopped meat, etc. in a very thin casing of dough, served either fried or in broth. ⟨< Cantonese *wan t'an* dumpling⟩

woo [wu] *v.* **1** seek to marry; court. **2** seek to win; try to get: *Some people woo fame; some woo riches.* ⟨OE *wōgian*⟩

wood [wʊd] *n., v.* *—n.* **1** the hard substance beneath the bark of trees and shrubs. **2** trees cut up for use: *The carpenter brought wood to build a garage.* **3** (*adjl.*) made of wood; wooden: *a wood house.* **4** a thing or things made of wood. **5** a cask; barrel; keg: *wine drawn from the wood.* **6** (*adjl.*) used for or on wood: *We have a wood basket for the fireplace.* **7** *Printing.* **a** a woodcut. **b** woodcuts collectively. **8** *Music.* **a** a wooden wind instrument; woodwind. **b woods,** *pl.* the woodwinds of a band or orchestra. **9** Usually, **woods,** *pl.* a large number of growing trees; forest: *looking for wildflowers in the woods.* **10** (*adjl.*) dwelling or growing in the woods: *wood moss.* **11** a golf club, usually a driver, originally with a wooden head. **12 woods,** (*adjl.*) having to do with a forest: *a woods camp.*
out of the woods, out of danger or difficulty.
saw wood, *Informal.* **a** work steadily at one's task, without attention to anything else. **b** sleep heavily; snore.
—v. **1** supply with wood; get wood for. **2** get supplies of wood. **3** plant with trees. ⟨OE *wudu*⟩
☛ *Hom.* WOULD.
☛ *Usage.* **Woods** is treated as singular and as plural. We speak of *a woods* but ordinarily use it with a plural verb: *The woods are pretty in the fall.* In proper names, **woods** is frequently used with a singular verb. When used to qualify another noun, **woods** often refers particularly to forest areas as the site of logging operations: *a woods camp, a woods superintendent.*

wood alcohol methanol; METHYL ALCOHOL.

wood anemone any of several woodland anemones, especially *Anemone quinquefolia* of E North America and *A. nemorosa* of Europe.

wood•bine ['wʊd,baɪn] *n.* **1** honeysuckle, especially a common Eurasian species (*Lonicera periclymenum*) having fragrant yellow flowers. **2** VIRGINIA CREEPER. ⟨OE *wudubind(e)* < *wudu* wood + *binde* wreath⟩

wood block **1** a block of wood. **2** WOODCUT (def. 1).

wood buffalo *Cdn.* a variety of bison (*Bison bison athabascae*) found in lightly wooded regions of northern Alberta and the Mackenzie District. Also, **woods buffalo.**

wood•carv•ing ['wʊd,kɑrvɪŋ] *n.* **1** the art or craft of carving wood. **2** an object or work of art carved out of wood. **—'wood,carv•er,** *n.*

wood•chuck ['wʊd,tʃʌk] *n. Cdn.* a groundhog. ⟨< Algonquian (Ojibway) *wejack*; influenced by *wood*⟩

wood•cock ['wʊd,kɒk] *n., pl.* **-cock** or **-cocks. 1** an Old World game bird (*Scolopax rusticola*) belonging to the sandpiper family, having reddish plumage, a long bill, and short legs. **2** a smaller shore bird (*Philohela minor*) of the same family, found in E North America. ⟨OE *wuducoc*⟩

wood•craft ['wʊd,kræft] *n.* **1** knowledge about how to get food and shelter in the woods; skill in hunting, trapping, finding one's way, etc. **2** skill in making things out of wood.

wood•cut ['wʊd,kʌt] *n.* **1** a block of wood with a pattern, design, or illustration cut into the surface, from which prints are made. **2** a print from such a block.

wood•cut•ter ['wʊd,kʌtər] *n.* a person who fells trees or chops wood. **—'wood,cut•ting,** *n.*

wood duck a highly coloured, surface-feeding North American duck (*Aix sponsa*) having a white belly and a long, dark, square tail. It nests in tree cavities near wooded swamps, rivers, and ponds in NW Canada and U.S.

wood•ed ['wʊdɪd] *adj., v. —adj.* filled with trees: *The park is well wooded.*
—v. pt. and pp. of WOOD.

wood•en ['wʊdən] *adj.* **1** made of wood. **2** stiff; awkward: *The boy gave a wooden bow and left the stage.* **3** dull; stupid; insensitive. **4** lifeless; hollow; lacking in animation, resonance, or reality. **—'wood•en•ly,** *adv.* **—'wood•en•ness,** *n.*

wood engraving **1** the art or process of engraving designs in relief on a wood block. **2** a woodcut. The distinction is often made that a **wood engraving** is cut on the end grain of the wood, while a **woodcut** is made with the grain.

wood•en–head•ed ['wʊdən ˌhɛdɪd] *adj. Informal.* dull; stupid.

wooden horse TROJAN HORSE.

wood•en•ware ['wʊdən,wɛr] *n.* containers, utensils, etc. made of wood, as wooden salad bowls, trays, spice racks, etc.

wood•land ['wʊdlənd] *n.* **1** land covered with trees. **2** (*adjl.*) of, in, or having to do with woods.

woodland caribou *Cdn.* a species of caribou (*Rangifer tarandus*) of the forested areas of northern Canada.

Woodland Cree SWAMPY CREE.

wood•land•er ['wʊdləndər] *n.* one who lives in the woods.

wood•lark ['wʊd,lɑrk] *n.* a European lark (*Lullula arborea*), resembling the skylark, but somewhat smaller.

wood lily PRAIRIE LILY.

wood•lot ['wʊd,lɒt] *n.* a piece of land on which trees are grown and cut; a bush lot.

wood louse *pl.* **wood lice. 1** any of various small, terrestrial crustaceans (order Isopoda, especially genera *Oniscus*, *Porcellio*, etc.) found in dark, damp places, such as underneath stones, having a flattened, oval, segmented body covered with protective plates. Many species can roll into a ball if disturbed. **2** any of various small, wingless insects (order Corrodentia) that live under bark, in the woodwork of houses, etc.

wood•man ['wʊdmən] *n., pl.* **-men. 1** a woodcutter. **2** See WOODSMAN.

wood note a musical sound made by a bird or animal of the forest.

wood nymph **1** a nymph supposed to live in the woods; dryad. **2** a moth (*Minois alope*) that destroys grapevines.

A downy woodpecker—about 17 cm long including the tail

wood•peck•er ['wʊd,pɛkər] *n.* any of a family (Picidae) of climbing birds found almost worldwide, typically having showy, multicoloured plumage, a long, straight, strong bill adapted for chiselling through the bark or wood of trees in search of insects, a long, extensile tongue with a horny spear at the tip for removing insects from deep cavities, and stiff tail feathers used in climbing.

wood pigeon a large Eurasian pigeon (*Columba palumbus*) having whitish patches on the neck and wings.

wood•pile ['wʊd,paɪl] *n.* a pile of wood, especially wood cut for fuel.

wood pulp wood made into pulp for making paper.

wood rat any of a genus (*Neotoma*) of rats of W North America having large ears, a furry tail, and thick grey fur. Wood rats are the only rats native to Canada.

wood•ruff ['wʊdrəf] *or* ['wʊdrʌf] *n.* any of several plants (genus *Asperula*) of the madder family having small, fragrant flowers and narrow, pointed, fragrant leaves; especially, a Eurasian species (*Galium odorata*). ⟨OE *wudurōfe*⟩

woods buffalo See WOOD BUFFALO.

wood screw a sharp-pointed screw with a slotted head, used in woodworking.

wood•shed ['wʊd,ʃɛd] *n.* a shed for storing wood.

woods•man ['wʊdzmən] *n., pl.* **-men.** a man who lives, works, or frequently engages in recreation in the woods, especially one who is skilled in making his way in the woods and in hunting, fishing, trapping, etc.

wood sorrel any of a genus (*Oxalis*) of herbs found in temperate and tropical regions, having sour stem juice and compound leaves. The **white wood sorrel** (*O. acetosella*), which has leaves composed of three heart-shaped leaflets, is one of the plants considered to be the true shamrock.

woods•y ['wʊdzi] *adj.* **-i•er, -i•est. 1** of or like the woods. **2** of people, at home in or enjoying the woods. **—'woods•i•ness,** *n.*

wood tar a dark brown, sticky substance obtained from the distillation of wood and containing turpentine, resins, etc.

wood thrush *Cdn.* a large thrush (*Hylocichla mustelina*) common in the thickets and woods of eastern North America, noted for its beautiful, clear song.

wood tick *n.* a kind of tick (*Dermacentor andersoni*), a carrier of ROCKY MOUNTAIN SPOTTED FEVER.

wood turning the making of pieces of wood into various shapes by turning on a lathe. **—'wood-,turn•er,** *n.*

wood warbler any of a New World family (Parulidae) of small, active, often brightly coloured songbirds similar to the Old World warblers but generally not having a musical song.

wood•wind ['wʊd,wɪnd] *n.* **1 woodwinds,** *pl.* certain wind instruments of an orchestra, including clarinets, oboes, etc. Woodwinds were formerly made of wood, but many are now made of metal. **2** any of this group of instruments. **3** (*adjl.*) of or having to do with woodwinds.

wood•work ['wʊd,wɜrk] *n.* **1** things made of wood, especially the doors, stairs, mouldings, etc. inside a house. **2** the work involved in producing such articles. **3** the craft of making things out of wood.
come out of the woodwork, *Informal.* make an unexpected and often unwanted appearance.

wood•work•er ['wʊd,wɜrkər] *n.* a person who makes things out of wood.

wood•work•ing ['wʊd,wɜrkɪŋ] *n., adj. —n.* the act, process, or craft of making or shaping things of wood.
—adj. pertaining to this craft: *woodworking tools.*

wood•worm ['wʊd,wɜrm] *n.* any of various insect larvae that bore in wood, especially the larva of a beetle (*Anobium punctatum*) that is destructive to furniture and buildings.

wood•y ['wʊdi] *adj.* **wood•i•er, wood•i•est. 1** having many trees; covered with trees: *a woody hillside.* **2** of a plant, having stems containing lignin, the main element of wood. Trees, shrubs, and some vines are woody plants. **3** consisting of wood: *the woody parts of a shrub.* **4** like wood; tough and stringy; no longer succulent: *Turnips become woody when they are left in the ground too long.* **—'wood•i•ness,** *n.*

woo•er ['wuər] *n.* a person who woos; suitor.

woof [wuf] *n.* **1** the crosswise threads of a fabric; weft. **2** woven fabric or its texture. See WEAVE for picture. ⟨ME *oof* < OE *ōwef* < *on* on + *wefan* weave⟩

wool [wʊl] *n.* **1** the soft, curly hair or fur of sheep and some other animals. **2** short, thick, curly hair. **3** something like wool, such as a fibrous mass of inorganic material, or the downy or hairy substance found on plants or insect larvae. Glass wool, used for insulation, is made from fibres of glass. **4** yarn, cloth, or garments made of wool. **5** (*adjl.*) made of wool: *a wool sweater.*
pull the wool over (someone's) **eyes,** *Informal.* deceive someone. ⟨OE *wull*⟩

wool•en ['wʊlən] *adj., n.* See WOOLLEN.

wool fat lanolin.

wool•gath•er•ing ['wʊl,gæðərɪŋ] *n., adj. —n.* absorption in thinking or daydreaming; absent-mindedness.
—adj. inattentive; absent-minded; dreamy. **—'wool,gath•er•er,** *n.*

wool•grow•er ['wʊl,grouər] *n.* a person who raises sheep for their wool.

wool•len or **wool•en** ['wʊlən] *adj., n. —adj.* **1** made of wool: *a woollen suit.* **2** of or having to do with wool or cloth made of wool: *a woollen mill.*
—n. Usually, **woollens** or **woolens,** *pl.* cloth or clothing made of wool.

wool•ly ['wʊli] *adj.* **-li•er, -li•est;** *n., pl.* **-lies.**
—adj. **1** consisting of wool. **2** like wool. **3** covered with wool or

something like it. **4** not definite; confused; muddled: *woolly thinking.*
—n. Informal. an article of clothing made from wool, as winter underwear. Also, **wooly. —'wool•li•ness,** *n.*

woolly bear a hairy brown or black caterpillar, especially of the tiger moth.

woolly dog *Cdn. Pacific coast.* an extinct breed of dog somewhat resembling a Pomeranian, whose wool was used by the Coast Salish First Nations people to weave their blankets.

wool•ly–mind•ed ['wʊli ˌmaɪndəd] *adj.* confused; muddled; not thinking clearly. Also, **woolly-headed.**

wool•pack ['wʊl,pæk] *n.* **1** a large cloth bag for packing wool. **2** formerly, a bundle or bale of wool weighing 240 pounds. **3** a round, fleecy cloud.

wool•sack ['wʊl,sæk] *n.* **1** a bag for wool. **2** in the British House of Lords, the cushion, originally stuffed with wool, on which the Lord Chancellor sits. **3** the office of Lord Chancellor.

wool•shed ['wʊl,ʃɛd] *n.* a building in which sheep are sheared and the fleeces prepared for marketing.

wool•y ['wʊli] *adj., n.* See WOOLLY.

wooz•y ['wuzi] *adj. Slang.* **1** somewhat dizzy or weak; slightly nauseated: *to feel woozy.* **2** muddled; confused. **3** slightly drunk; tipsy. **—'wooz•i•ly,** *adv.* **—'wooz•i•ness,** *n.*

Worces•ter•shire sauce ['wʊstərʃər] *n.* a highly seasoned sauce made of soya sauce, vinegar, spices, etc. ⟨< *Worcester,* a city in W England, where it was made originally⟩

word [wɜrd] *n., v. —n.* **1** a sound or a group of sounds that has meaning and is an independent unit of speech. **2** the writing or printing that stands for a word. *Bat, bet, bit,* and *but* are words. **3** a short talk: *May I have a word with you?* **4** speech: *honest in word and deed.* **5** a brief expression or comment: *The teacher gave us a word of advice.* **6** a command; order: *We have to wait till she gives the word.* **7** a verbal signal, as a password or watchword: *The word for tonight is "change."* **8** a promise: *The boy kept his word.* **9** news: *No word has come from the battlefront.* **10 words,** *pl.* **a** angry talk; a quarrel or dispute: *They had words about whose fault it was.* **b** the text of a song as distinguished from the music. **11 the Word,** *Christianity.* **a** the Bible. **b** the message of the gospel. **c** the second person of the Trinity. **12** *Computer technology.* a unit that can be processed by a computer.
a good word, a favourable comment; commendation: *Put in a good word for me, will you?*
a man or **woman of his** or **her word,** a man or woman who keeps his or her promise.
be as good as (one's) **word,** keep one's promise.
by word of mouth, by spoken words; orally.
eat (one's) **words,** take back what one has said; retract.
hang on (someone's) **words,** listen attentively and admiringly to someone.
have the last word, in an argument, have the final, decisive say.
in a word, briefly.
in so many words, exactly; precisely; explicitly.
mince words, avoid coming to the point, telling the truth, or taking a stand by using ambiguous or evasive words.
my word! an expression of surprise.
of few words, not talkative.
take (someone) **at his** or **her word,** take (someone's) words seriously and act accordingly.
take (someone's) **word for it,** believe because someone has said so.
take the words out of (someone's) **mouth,** say exactly what someone was just going to say.
the last word, a the last or latest thing or example in a class or field. **b** the final thing or example, beyond which no advance or improvement is possible.
upon my word, a I promise. **b** *Brit.* an expression of surprise.
word for word, in the exact words.
words fail me, I can't believe it; I'm left speechless.
—v. put into words: *Word your ideas clearly.* ⟨OE⟩

word blindness loss of the ability to read; inability to distinguish words in print or writing because of a brain defect; alexia. **—'word-ˌblind,** *adj.*

word•book ['wɜrd,bʊk] *n.* a list of words, usually with explanations, etc.; dictionary; vocabulary.

word class 1 PART OF SPEECH. **2** a group of words all belonging to the same part of speech.

word deafness inability to distinguish the meanings of spoken words, caused by a defect in the auditory centre of the brain; auditory aphasia. **—'word-ˌdeaf,** *adj.*

word element a COMBINING FORM, such as a base or root, affix, etc.

word–for–word ['wɜrd fər 'wɜrd] *adj.* **1** of a translation, done one word at a time, according to the individual meanings and with no regard to the sense of the whole. **2** reproduced verbatim; in exactly the same words.

word•ing ['wɜrdɪŋ] *n., v. —n.* the way of saying a thing; the choice and use of words: *Careful wording made the meaning clear.*
—v. ppr. of WORD.
☛ *Syn. n.* See note at DICTION.

word•less ['wɜrdlɪs] *adj.* **1** without words; speechless. **2** not put into words; unexpressed or inexpressible. **—'word•less•ly,** *adv.*

word of honour or **honor** a solemn promise.

word–of–mouth ['wɜrd əv 'mʌuθ] *adj.* communicated orally, usually in an informal way.

word order the arrangement of words in a sentence, phrase, etc.
☛ *Usage.* In English the usual word order for statements is subject + verb + complement, as in *John hit the ball. The ball hit John.* Some other patterns of word order (*Away ran John. Him I can't stand! Sweet are the uses of adversity.*) are chiefly rhetorical and poetic. In English, with its relatively few inflections, word order is the chief grammatical device for indicating the function of words and their relation to each other.

word•play ['wɜrd,pleɪ] *n.* **1** verbal wit; the manipulation of words and meanings for the purpose of entertaining, making a point, or showing off. **2** a play on words; pun.

word processing *Computer technology.* the input, editing, organization, storage, and retrieval of information in the form of words, using electronic means. **—'word-ˌpro•ces•sing,** *adj.*

word processor *Computer technology.* **1** a type of computer specifically designed for use in word processing, including a keyboard, printer, storage, memory, and, usually, a display screen. **2** a person who operates a word processing system.

word•y ['wɜrdi] *adj.* **word•i•er, word•i•est. 1** using too many words. **2** consisting of or expressed in words; verbal: *a wordy war.* **—'word•i•ly,** *adv.* **—'word•i•ness,** *n.*
☛ *Syn.* **1. Wordy,** VERBOSE = using more words than are necessary. **Wordy** emphasizes the use of many words to say something that could be expressed more clearly and effectively in a few. Example: *There are many reasons that he has for going,* instead of *He has many reasons for going.* **Verbose,** a more formal word used especially to describe public speakers, writers, speeches, and writings, adds the idea of using too many long, high-sounding words and long, roundabout sentences that do not express meaning clearly or interestingly: *Our quadruped companions* is a verbose way of saying *our pets.*

wore [wɔr] *v.* pt. of WEAR.

work [wɜrk] *n., v.* **worked** or (*archaic*) **wrought, work•ing.** *—n.* **1** the effort of doing or making something: *Moving the piano was hard work.* **2** something to do; occupation; employment: *He is out of work.* **3** something made or done, especially something creative; the result of effort: *The artist considers that picture to be her greatest work.* **4** a particular task, job, or undertaking: *to plan one's work for the day.* **5** one's place of employment: *She sometimes took her baby to work with her. I left my umbrella at work.* **6** material or a piece of material on which effort is expended: *The dressmaker took her work out on the porch.* **7 works,** *pl.* **a** a factory or other place for doing some kind of work: *Her first job was in the boiler works.* **b** the moving parts of a machine or device: *the works of a watch.* **c** buildings, bridges, docks, etc. **d** actions; deeds: *good works.* **8** a fortification. **9** *Physics.* **a** the transference of energy from one body or system to another. **b** that which is accomplished by a force when it acts through a distance; force multiplied by distance. **10** the action, activity, or operation (of a person or thing), especially of a particular kind and with reference to result: *The medicine and suggestion have done their work.* **11** handwork embroidery; needlework. **12 works,** *pl.* the business of erecting and maintaining public buildings: *the department of public works.* **13 the (whole) works,** *Slang.* everything involved; the complete set or treatment: *He invested $50 000 and lost the works.*
at work, working or operating.
give (someone) **the works,** *Slang.* **a** abuse; treat harshly or cruelly. **b** give someone everything.
in the works, *Informal.* in the planning stage; upcoming.
make short or **quick work of,** do or get rid of quickly.
out of work, having no job; unemployed.
—v. **1** do work; labour: *Most people must work for a living.* **2** work for pay; be employed: *He works in a bank.* **3** carry on operations in (districts, etc.): *The sales rep worked the Toronto area. He worked his farm with success. The police officer was working her beat.* **4** function; operate, especially effectively: *This pump will not work. The plan worked.* **5** produce an effect or exert an influence: *He decided to memorize the whole of his part at once*

and let it work in his mind and soul. **6** put into operation; use; manage: *to work a scheme.* **7** cause to do work: *He works his men long hours.* **8** treat or handle in making; knead; mix; be treated, kneaded, mixed, etc.: *Dough is worked to mix it thoroughly. This clay does not work easily.* **9** make, get, do, or bring about by effort: *She worked her way through college.* **10** move as if with effort: *His face worked as he tried to keep back the tears.* **11** bring about; cause; do: *The plan worked harm.* **12** go or do slowly or with effort: *The ship worked to windward. Work the cork loose.* **13** gradually become: *The window catch has worked loose.* **14** form; shape: *She worked a silver dollar into a bracelet.* **15** influence; persuade: *to work people to one's will.* **16** move; stir; excite: *Don't work yourself into a temper.* **17** solve: *Work all the problems on the page.* **18** *Informal.* use tricks on to get something: *to work a friend for a loan.* **19** ferment: *Yeast makes the brew work.*

work a room or **crowd,** move through a room or crowd greeting people, shaking hands, etc.

work in, put in, especially with effort.

work off, a get rid of by working. **b** pay (a debt, etc.) with work rather than money.

work on, a try to persuade or influence. **b** try to make or accomplish: *I'm working on getting this spot out of the rug.*

work out, a plan; develop fully. **b** solve; find out. **c** use up by working. **d** give exercise to; practise. **e** accomplish by work. **f** result; turn out. **g** pay (a debt, etc.) by working. **h** add up to a specified total (*used with* **at** *or* **to**). **i** engage in a program for physical fitness; exercise: *I work out at Trim That Body every Wednesday.* **j** succeed; prove to be satisfactory: *We hired a nanny but she didn't work out and we fired her the following week.* **k** devise. **l** get or take out with effort.

work to rule, of employees, work only as much as is demanded by terms of employment (without overtime, extraordinary effort, etc.), as a form of protest.

work up, a plan; develop. **b** excite; stir up. **c** manipulate, mix, etc. into a specified object: *She took the leftover fabric and trim and worked it up into a costume for Halloween.* **d** bring about (a sweat or appetite) by vigorous activity. ⟨OE *weorc,* n., *wyrcean,* v.⟩

☛ *Syn. n.* **1. Work,** LABOUR, TOIL[1] = effort or exertion turned to making or doing something. **Work** is the general word, applying to physical or mental effort or to the activity of a force or machine: *Keeping house is not easy work.* **Labour** applies to hard physical or mental work: *That student's understanding of her subjects shows the amount of labour she puts into her homework.* **Toil,** a word with some literary flavour, applies to long and wearying labour: *The farmer's toil was rewarded with good crops.*

work•a•ble ['wɜrkəbəl] *adj.* that can work or be worked.

work•a•day ['wɜrkəˌdei] *adj.* of or for working days; practical; commonplace; ordinary.

work•a•hol•ic [ˌwɜrkə'hɒlɪk] *n. Informal.* someone addicted to his or her work, often to the detriment of social and familial relations.

work•bag ['wɜrkˌbæg] *n.* a bag to hold the things that a person works with, especially a bag for sewing materials.

work•bench ['wɜrkˌbɛntʃ] *n.* a table at which a mechanic, carpenter, artisan, etc. works.

work•book ['wɜrkˌbʊk] *n.* **1** a book containing outlines for the study of some subject, questions to be answered, etc.; a book in which a student does parts of his or her written work. **2** a book containing rules for doing certain work. **3** a book for notes of work planned or work done.

work•box ['wɜrkˌbɒks] *n.* a box to hold the materials and tools that a person works with.

work•day ['wɜrkˌdei] *n., adj.* —*n.* **1** a day for work; a day that is not one's regular day off or a holiday. **2** the part of a day during which work is done. **3** the number of hours required to complete a day's work.
—*adj.* workaday.

worked [wɜrkt] *adj., v.* —*adj.* wrought; crafted.
—*v.* pt. and pp. of WORK.

work•er ['wɜrkər] *n.* **1** a person who or thing that works, especially a person who does a specified kind of work or works in a specified way: *a research worker, a volunteer worker. He's not a very good worker.* **2** a person who works hard: *She's really a worker.* **3** a manual labourer or one who works with industrial machines; a member of the working class. **4** in a colony of bees, ants, wasps, or termites, one of a class of usually sterile individuals that care for the larvae, find food for the colony, etc.

workers' compensation compensation for personal injuries suffered at work or diseases arising from work, that are not due to the employee's willful misconduct or gross negligence.

work force 1 the total number of people employed by a particular company or working on a particular project, etc. **2** the total number of people potentially available for employment.

work•horse ['wɜrkˌhɔrs] *n.* **1** a horse used mostly for work, not for racing, hunting, or showing. **2** a person who is an exceptionally hard worker. **3** a machine that is especially powerful, productive, etc. Also, **work horse.**

work•house ['wɜrkˌhʌus] *n. Esp. Brit.* formerly, a house where very poor people were lodged and were expected to perform some work in return.

work•ing ['wɜrkɪŋ] *n., adj., v.* —*n.* **1** the action, method, or performance of one who or that which works. **2** Often, **workings.** operations; action: *the workings of one's mind. Do you understand the workings of this machine?* **3** Usually, **workings,** *pl.* the parts of a mine, quarry, tunnel, etc. where work is being done.
—*adj.* **1** that works. **2** used in working. **3** used to operate with or by: *a working majority.* **4 a** performing its function; that goes: *a working model of a train.* **b** that can be arranged or accomplished; workable: *a working agreement, a working arrangement.* **5** providing a basis for further work: *a working hypothesis.* **6** moving convulsively, as the features from emotion. **7** of liquor, etc., fermenting.
—*v.* ppr. of WORK.

working capital 1 the amount of capital needed to operate a business. **2** *Accounting.* the amount left when current liabilities are subtracted from current assets. **3** *Business.* the liquid, or immediately usable, capital of a business, as distinguished from frozen assets, such as property, machinery, etc.

working class a group thought of as including all those people who work for wages, especially manual and industrial workers.

working day workday.

work•ing–day ['wɜrkɪŋ ˌdei] *adj.* workaday; everyday.

working hypothesis a theory accepted only to guide investigations.

work•ing•man ['wɜrkɪŋˌmæn] *n., pl.* **-men.** a man who works for wages, especially one who works with his hands or with machines.

working stiff *Slang.* a workingman.

work•ing•wom•an ['wɜrkɪŋˌwʊmən] *n., pl.* **-wom•en** [-ˌwɪmən]. a woman who works for wages, especially one who works with her hands or with machines.

work•load ['wɜrkˌloud] *n.* the amount of work assigned to a person, position, department, etc.

work•man ['wɜrkmən] *n., pl.* **-men. 1** a workingman. **2** a man who is skilled in a trade or craft; craftsman.

work•man•like ['wɜrkmənˌləik] *adj.* worthy of a careful worker; skilful: *The job was done quickly and in a workmanlike manner.* Also, **workmanly.**

work•man•ship ['wɜrkmənˌʃɪp] *n.* **1** the art or skill of a skilled worker; craftsmanship: *His workmanship is not always good.* **2** the quality of something that has been made: *jewellery of fine workmanship.* **3** the work done.

work of art 1 a product of any of the arts, especially a painting, statue, or literary or musical work. **2** anything done or made with great artistry or skill: *He makes lunch a work of art.*

work•out ['wɜrkˌʌut] *n. Informal.* **1** a session of vigorous physical or mental exercise, practice, or training: *Doing these problems will give your math skills a real workout.* **2** a trial; test.

work•place ['wɜrkˌpleis] *n.* **1** the specific location, as on an assembly line, at a desk, etc., where one does one's job: *Plant employees are not allowed to smoke at their workplace.* **2** the environment in which one works at one's job.

work•room ['wɜrkˌrum] *or* ['wɜrkˌrʊm] *n.* a room set aside for working in: *We have a workroom in the basement.*

work•sheet ['wɜrkˌʃit] *n.* **1** a sheet of paper on which a record of work, including times, productivity, etc. is kept. **2** a sheet of paper printed with practice drills, exercises, problems, etc. on which students work and record their answers. **3** a paper containing preliminary notes, sketches, etc.

work•shop ['wɜrkˌʃɒp] *n.* **1** a room or building where work, especially manual work, is done. **2** a meeting of people for discussion, study, etc. of a particular subject: *The social studies teachers had a workshop in September.* **3** the group of people so meeting.

work•shy ['wɜrkˌʃaɪ] *adj.* lazy.

work station a desk and other equipment where a computer system is set up for work by one person. Also, **workstation.**

work–stu•dy ['wɜrk ˌstʌdi] *adj.* of or having to do with a program, sometimes government-supported, at secondary or post-secondary educational institutions, that enables students to do part-time work that is related to their fields of study.

work•ta•ble ['wɜrk,teibəl] *n.* a table to work at.

work•week ['wɜrk,wik] *n.* the standard number of hours or days constituting a week of work.

work•wom•an ['wɜrk,wʊmən] *n., pl.* **-wom•en** [-,wɪmən]. a workingwoman.

world [wɜrld] *n.* **1** the earth: *Ships can sail around the world.* **2** all of certain parts, people, or things of the earth: *the insect world, the Third World. The New World is North America and South America. The Old World is Europe, Asia, Australia, and Africa.* **3** a sphere of interest, activity, thought, etc.: *the world of music, the world of fashion.* **4** human affairs; the activities and circumstances of social, business, and public life: *a man of the world. The young graduate was ready to go out into the world.* **5** the things of this life and the people devoted to them: *Monks and nuns live apart from the world.* **6** the human race. **7** people in general; the public: *The whole world knows it.* **8** a star or planet, especially when considered as inhabited. **9** any time, condition, or place of life: *the medieval world.* **10** all things; everything; the universe. **11** a great deal; very much; large amount: *The rest did her a world of good.* **12** individual experience or outlook: *He lives in a small world. Taking a job like this for a year or two will broaden your world.*
bring into the world, a give birth to. **b** help deliver (a baby).
come into the world, be born.
for all the world, in every respect; exactly.
in the world, a anywhere. **b** at all; ever: *Why in the world not?*
not for worlds or **not for (all) the world,** in no way; not for any reason.
on top of the world, in high spirits: *I was on top of the world when I found out I had won.*
out of this world, *Informal.* **a** great; wonderful; distinctive: *Our plans for the decorations are out of this world.* **b** unearthly.
think the world of, regard (someone or something) highly.
world without end, forever. ⟨OE *weorold*⟩
☛ *Hom.* WHORLED [wɜrld].
☛ *Syn.* See note at EARTH.

World Bank the International Bank for Reconstruction and Development, an agency of the United Nations established in 1945 for the purpose of making loans to member nations.

world–class ['wɜrld 'klæs] *adj.* **1** capable of competing at the highest levels, as in the Commonwealth Games or the Olympics: *a world-class athlete.* **2** of a very high standard: *Toronto is now a world-class city.*

World Court a court made up of representatives of various nations, established as the Permanent Court of International Justice in 1920 under the covenant of the League of Nations to settle disputes between nations, and continued as the International Court of Justice under the United Nations.

World Health Organization a United Nations organization, established in 1945 with a mandate to improve health conditions worldwide and to prevent and control communicable diseases by means of various scientific projects and programs.

world island *Geopolitics.* the land mass that constitutes Asia, Africa, and Europe.

world•ling ['wɜrldlɪŋ] *n.* a person who cares much for the interests and pleasures of this world. ⟨< *world* + *-ling*⟩

world•ly ['wɜrldli] *adj.* **-li•er, -li•est. 1** of this world; not of heaven: *worldly wealth.* **2** absorbed in or caring much for the interests and pleasures of this world. **3** worldly-wise.
—'world•li•ness, *n.*
☛ *Syn.* **1.** See note at EARTHLY.

world•ly–mind•ed ['wɜrldli 'maɪndɪd] *adj.* having or showing a worldly mind; caring much for the interests and pleasures of this world.

world•ly–wise ['wɜrldli ,waɪz] *adj.* wise about the ways and affairs of this world; sophisticated.

world power an institution, organization, or nation powerful enough to influence worldwide events.

World Series *Baseball.* the series of games played each fall between the winners of the two major league championships to decide the professional championship of the United States and Canada. ⟨after the Chicago *World*, the newspaper that first sponsored it⟩

world•view ['wɜrld,vju] *n.* a comprehensive concept or philosophy of life as it relates to the world or the universe.

World War I the war fought in Europe, Asia, Africa, and at sea, from July 28, 1914 to November 11, 1918. The United Kingdom, France, Russia, Canada, the United States (1917-1918), and their allies were on one side; Germany, Austria-Hungary, and their allies were on the other side.

World War II the war fought mainly in Europe, Asia, Africa, and at sea, from September 1, 1939 to August 14, 1945, beginning as a war between the United Kingdom, France, Poland, Canada, and their allies on one side and Germany and Italy on the other, and ultimately involving most of the world's nations, notably the United States, Japan, and the Soviet Union.

world–wea•ry ['wɜrld ,wiri] *adj.* weary of this world; tired of living. **—'world-,wea•ri•ness,** *n.*

world•wide ['wɜrld'waɪd] *adj. or adv.* throughout the world.

World Wide Web *Computer technology.* a logical network of text files, linked solely by hypertext and accessible through the Internet using any of various specialized pieces of software. The files, or pages, originate with a wide variety of international private and public users. Also called **the Web.** ⟨coined by Tim Burners-Lee⟩

worm [wɜrm] *n., v.* *—n.* **1** any of numerous small, slender, elongated, often segmented invertebrates, usually soft-bodied and legless, as the anclids (earthworms, etc.), flatworms (tapeworms, etc.), and nematodes (roundworms). **2** the wormlike larva of any of various insects. **3** *Archaic.* a serpent, snake, or dragon. **4** something like a worm in shape or movement, as the thread of a screw. **5** a short, continuously threaded shaft or screw, the thread of which gears with the teeth of a toothed wheel. **6** a force or agent that torments or slowly eats away from within. **7** a person who is the object of contempt or pity; wretch. **8 worms,** *pl. Pathology.* a disease caused by parasitic worms in the body.
can of worms, *Informal.* an unlooked-for and complicated, usually unpleasant, problem.
—v. **1** move like a worm; crawl or creep like a worm: *The soldier wormed his way toward the enemy's lines.* **2** insinuate; work insidiously (into): *She wormed herself into their confidence.* **3** wriggle (out of trouble, etc.). **4** work or get by persistent and devious means: *They tried to worm the secret out of me.* **5** look for or catch worms. **6** purge worms from (plants or animals): *Puppies should be wormed before going to their new owners.* ⟨OE *wyrm*⟩ **—'worm•er,** *n.* **—'worm,like,** *adj.*

worm–eat•en ['wɜrm ,itən] *adj.* **1** eaten into by worms: *worm-eaten timbers.* **2** worn-out; worthless; out-of-date.

worm gear 1 WORM WHEEL. **2** a worm wheel and an endless screw together. A worm gear can transmit the rotary motion of one shaft to another shaft at right angles to it. See GEAR for picture.

worm•hole ['wɜrm,houl] *n.* a hole made by a worm.

worm•seed ['wɜrm,sid] *n.* **1** any of a number of plants of the goosefoot family, especially *Chenopodium ambrosioides,* or **American wormseed,** formerly regarded as a remedy for parasitic worms, but now realized to have harmful side effects. **2** the seed of any of these plants.

worm wheel a wheel with teeth that mesh with the thread of a revolving screw called a worm. See GEAR for picture.

worm•wood ['wɜrm,wʊd] *n.* **1** any of various bitter herbs and shrubs (genus *Artemesia*) of the composite family, especially a European species (*A. absinthium*) that yields a bitter oil used in making absinthe. **2** something bitter or extremely unpleasant, such as a painful or mortifying experience. ⟨OE *wermōd,* influenced by *worm, wood*⟩

worm•y ['wɜrmi] *adj.* **worm•i•er, worm•i•est. 1** having worms; containing many worms. **2** resembling a worm. **3** damaged by worms. **4** contemptible; pitiable: *a wormy creature.*
—'worm•i•ness, *n.*

worn [wɔrn] *v., adj.* *—v.* pp. of WEAR.
—adj. **1** damaged by use: *worn rugs.* **2** tired; wearied: *a worn face.*
☛ *Hom.* WARN.

worn–out ['wɔrn 'ʌut] *adj.* **1** used until no longer fit for use. **2** exhausted; fatigued.

wor•ri•ment ['wɜrimənt] *n. Informal.* **1** the act of worrying. **2 a** worry; anxiety. **b** a cause of worry.

wor•ri•some ['wɜrisəm] *adj.* **1** causing worry. **2** inclined to worry. **—'wor•ri•some•ly,** *adv.* **—'wor•ri•some•ness,** *n.*

wor•ry ['wɜri] *v.* **-ried, -ry•ing;** *n., pl.* **-ries.** *—v.* **1** feel anxious or uneasy: *She will worry if we are late.* **2** cause to feel anxious or troubled: *The problem worried him.* **3** annoy; bother: *Don't worry*

me with so many questions. **4** seize and shake with the teeth; bite at; snap at: *A dog will worry a rat.* **5** harass, as if by repeated biting, etc.; harry by rough treatment or repeated attacks.
not to worry! don't worry!
worry along or **through,** manage somehow.
worry at, keep picking at: *Stop worrying at that scab; you'll make it bleed!*
—n. **1** anxiety; uneasiness; trouble; care; the act of worrying: *Worry kept her awake.* **2** a cause of trouble or care: *A mother of sick children has many worries.* ⟨OE *wyrgan* strangle⟩
—'wor•ri•er, *n.*

☛ *Syn. v.* **Worry,** ANNOY, HARASS = disturb or distress a person with constant troubles, interference, etc. **Worry** emphasizes causing great uneasiness, care, or anxiety: worried by doubts, worried by a recurring sense of guilt. **Annoy** particularly suggests constant interference, inconvenience, or irritation: *The new employee annoys her fellow workers by interrupting their work to ask foolish questions.* **Harass** emphasizes persistent or repeated demands or burdens: *He is harassed by business troubles and a nagging boss.*

wor•ry•wart ['wɜri,wɔrt] *n.* someone who constantly worries, especially over insignificant matters; a fusspot.

worse [wɜrs] *adj. comparative of* BAD; *adv.,* comparative of BADLY and ILL; *n. —adj.* **1** more harmful, painful, regrettable, unpleasant, unfavourable, etc.: *It could be worse.* **2** more unattractive, unsuitable, faulty, incorrect, ill-advised, etc.: *His pen was poor and his writing even worse.* **3** more bad or evil: *She is dishonest enough, but her sister is much worse.* **4** of even lower quality or value; inferior: *The soil is worse in the valley.* **5** more ill: *The patient is worse today.* **6** less fortunate or well off.
worse off, a in a worse condition. **b** having less money.
—adv. in a worse manner or to a worse extent or degree: *It is raining worse than ever.*
—n. that which is worse: *She thought the loss of her property bad enough, but worse followed.*
for the worse, to a worse state: *The change was for the worse.*
go from bad to worse, worsen.
none (or **a little, somewhat**, etc.) **the worse for,** not (or a little, etc.) suffering or damaged because of: *Pearl was rescued from the water, and was none the worse for her adventure.* ⟨OE *wyrsa*⟩

wor•sen ['wɜrsən] *v.* make or become worse: *You will only worsen the situation if you talk about it. She was taken to hospital, but her condition worsened through the night.*

wor•ship ['wɜrʃɪp] *n., v.* **-shipped** or **-shiped, -ship•ping** or **-ship•ing.** *—n.* **1** great honour and respect paid to a deity: *the worship of God, idol worship.* **2** religious ceremonies or services in which one pays such respect: *Prayers and hymns are part of worship.* **3** great love and admiration: *hero worship.* **4 Worship,** a title used in addressing or referring to a mayor or, especially in the United Kingdom, to certain magistrates: *a letter addressed to Her Worship the mayor. "Thank you, Your Worship," he said.*
—v. **1** honour, adore, or venerate as a deity: *Muslims worship Allah.* **2** take part in a religious act, rite, or service. **3** consider extremely precious; love and admire very much; idolize: *He worships his big brother. A miser worships money.* ⟨OE *weorthscipe* < *weorth* worth + *-scipe* -ship⟩ **—'wor•ship•per** or **'wor•ship•er,** *n.*

wor•ship•ful ['wɜrʃɪpfəl] *adj.* **1** having or showing reverence: *worshipful silence.* **2** Often, **Worshipful,** *Esp. Brit.* a title of respect for mayors and certain other people of distinguished rank. **3** *Archaic or formal.* worthy of respect and honour.
—'wor•ship•ful•ly, *adv.*

worst [wɜrst] *adj. superlative of* BAD; *adv.,* superlative of BADLY and ILL; *n., v. —adj.* **1** most harmful, painful, regrettable, unpleasant, unfavourable, etc.: *the worst diet imaginable, the worst sheep of the herd, the worst room in the hotel.* **2** most unattractive, unsuitable, faulty, incorrect, ill-advised, etc.: *That's the worst writing I've ever seen.* **3** most bad or evil: *It was the worst murder of the century.* **4** of the poorest quality or value: *This district has some of the worst soil in the province.*
—adv. in the worst manner or to the worst extent or degree: *He acts worst when he's tired.*
—n. that which is worst: *That was bad, but the worst is yet to come.*
at worst, under the least favourable circumstances.
give (someone) **the worst of it,** defeat someone.
if (the) worst comes to (the) worst, if the very worst thing happens.
—v. beat, defeat: *The hero worsted his enemies.* ⟨OE *wyrresta*⟩

wor•sted ['wɜrstɪd] *or* ['wʊstid] *n.* **1** smooth, firm yarn or thread made from long wool fibres that have been combed. Worsted is used especially for firm, smooth-finished fabrics, carpets, and in knitting. **2** fabric made from worsted. **3** (*adjl.*) made of worsted. ⟨< *Worsted* (now Worstead), a town in E England, where it was made originally⟩

wort[1] [wɜrt] *n.* the liquid made from malt that, after fermentation, becomes beer, ale, or other liquor. ⟨OE *wyrt*⟩

wort[2] [wɜrt] *n.* a plant, especially any of various herbaceous plants formerly used in medicine (*now used chiefly in compounds*): *liverwort, figwort.* ⟨OE *wyrt*⟩

worth [wɜrθ] *adj., n. —adj. (functioning prepositionally)* **1** good or important enough for; deserving of: *Vancouver is a city worth visiting.* **2** equal in value to: *That stamp is worth at least twenty dollars.* **3** having property that amounts to: *That woman is worth millions.*
for all (one) **is worth,** to the full extent of one's power or ability: *She ran for all she was worth.*
—n. **1** merit; usefulness; importance; excellent quality: *We should read books of real worth.* **2** value in money: *He needed money and had to sell his car for less than its worth.* **3** a quantity of something of specified value: *a dollar's worth of sugar.* **4** *Archaic.* property; wealth. ⟨OE *weorth*⟩
☛ *Syn. n.* **1.** See note at MERIT.

worth•less ['wɜrθlɪs] *adj.* without worth; good-for-nothing; useless. **—'worth•less•ly,** *adv.* **—'worth•less•ness,** *n.*

worth•while ['wɜrθ'waɪl] *adj.* worth time, attention, or effort; having real merit: *He ought to do some worthwhile reading.*

wor•thy ['wɜrði] *adj.* **-thi•er, -thi•est;** *n., pl.* **-thies.**
—adj. **1** having worth or merit: *She presents a very worthy analysis of a complicated situation.* **2** deserving; meriting.
worthy of, a deserving. **b** having enough worth for.
—n. a person of great merit; an admirable person. **—'wor•thi•ly,** *adv.* **—'wor•thi•ness,** *n.*

-wor•thy *suffix.* **1** worthy of: *noteworthy, praiseworthy.* **2** capable of being used in or on a ——: *roadworthy, seaworthy.*

wost [wɒst] *v. Archaic.* 2nd pers. sing., present tense of WIT[2].

wot [wɒt] *v. Archaic.* 1st and 3rd pers. sing., present tense, of WIT[2]. *I wot* means *I know.* ⟨OE *wāt*⟩
☛ *Hom.* WATT.

would [wʊd]; *unstressed,* [wəd] *v.* **1** an auxiliary verb used: **a** to introduce a request or command in a polite manner: *Would you please close the window?* **b** to soften a statement or express uncertainty: *I don't know whose that would be.* **c** to express the hypothetical consequence of an unlikely or an impossible condition or, sometimes, to express the condition itself: *If I asked him, he would say no. If I knew the way, I would tell you. If you would ask her just once, she might surprise you.* **d** to express repeated, or habitual, action in the past: *When we were small, we would spend hours playing in the sand.* **e** to express desire: *Nutritionists would have us all eat whole grains.* **2** pt. of WILL[1]. ⟨OE *wolde*⟩
☛ *Hom.* WOOD.
☛ *Usage.* **Would** as the past tense of WILL is used most often in reported speech. Compare *He said, "I will come."* with *He said that he would come.* **Would rather** is used to express a strong preference: *She would rather stay home than have to dance with him.*

would–be ['wʊd ,bi] *adj.* **1** wishing or pretending to be. **2** intended to be.

would•n't ['wʊdənt] would not.

wouldst [wʊdst] *v. Archaic or poetic.* 2nd pers. sing., form of WOULD. *Thou wouldst* means *you* (sing.) *would.*

wound[1] [wund] *n., v. —n.* **1** a hurt or injury caused by cutting, stabbing, shooting, etc. **2** in a tree or plant, a similar injury due to external violence. **3** any hurt or injury to feelings, reputation, etc.: *The loss of her job was a wound to her pride.*
—v. **1** injure by cutting, stabbing, shooting, etc.; hurt. **2** injure in feelings, reputation, etc.: *His words wounded her.* ⟨OE *wund*⟩

wound[2] [waʊnd] *v.* a pt. and a pp. of WIND[2].

wound[3] [waʊnd] *v.* a pt. and a pp. of WIND[3].

wove [woʊv] *v.* a pt. and a pp. of WEAVE.

wo•ven ['woʊvən] *v.* a pp. of WEAVE.

wow[1] [waʊ] *n.* **1** a wail. **2** a short explosive noise like a bark. **3** a variation in the sound pitch of a phonograph or tape recorder, caused by a slight irregularity in the speed of the driving mechanism. ⟨imitative⟩

wow[2] [waʊ] *n., v., interj. Slang. —n.* a complete success; a hit: *The clown's act was a wow!*
—v. dazzle or impress: *My father really wowed everyone with his new suit.*
—interj. an exclamation of delight, admiration, etc.

wpm words per minute.

wrack[1] [ræk] *n., v.* —*n.* **1** wreckage; especially, a wrecked ship. **2** ruin; destruction. **3** seaweed cast ashore.
—*v.* wreck; ruin. ⟨< MDu. and MLG *wrak* wreck⟩
☛ *Hom.* RACK.

wrack[2] [ræk] *v.* **1** hurt very much; torture: *wracked by convulsions.* **2** stretch; strain. **3** torture on the rack. ⟨var. of *rack*[1]⟩
☛ *Hom.* RACK.

wraith [reiθ] *n.* **1** the ghost of a person seen before or soon after his or her death. **2** a ghost; spectre. **3** something pale, thin, or insubstantial: *wraiths of fog lingering over the fields. She looks like a wraith of her former self.* ⟨< Scottish, ? < ON *vörthr* guardian spirit⟩ **—'wraith•like,** *adj.*

wran•gle[1] ['ræŋgəl] *v.* **-gled, -gling;** *n.* —*v.* argue or dispute in a noisy or angry way; quarrel: *The children wrangled about who should sit in front.*
—*n.* a noisy dispute or quarrel. ⟨? < LG *wrangeln*⟩
—'wran•gler, *n.*

wran•gle[2] ['ræŋgəl] *n.* **-gled, -gling.** *Cdn. West.* in the western parts of Canada and the United States, herd or tend (horses, etc.) on the range. ⟨< Sp. *caverango,* hostler, prob. influenced by E *wrangle* quarrel, struggle⟩ **—'wran•gler,** *n.*

wrap [ræp] *v.* **wrapped** or **wrapt, wrap•ping;** *n.* —*v.* **1** cover by winding or folding something around: *She wrapped herself in a shawl.* **2** wind or fold as a covering: *Wrap a shawl around you.* **3** cover with paper, etc. and tie up or fasten: *to wrap a gift.* **4** cover; envelop; hide: *The mountain peak is wrapped in clouds. She sat wrapped in thought.*
wrapped up in, a devoted to; thinking mainly of: *He is wrapped up in his children.* **b** involved in; associated with.
wrap up, a put on warm outer clothes. **b** *Informal.* bring to a successful conclusion; clinch: *They wrapped up the game with three runs in the ninth.* **c** *Informal.* settle or finish: *to wrap up a meeting.* **d** come to the end (of a presentation, discussion, etc.): *I'll just make one more point and then I'll wrap up.* **e** wrap.
—*n.* **1 a** a loose outer garment, especially one worn draped or wrapped about the shoulders, such as a shawl or cape. **b wraps,** *pl.* overcoat, scarf, etc.: *Just throw your wraps on the bed in the guest room.* **2** wrapping paper: *gift wrap.*
under wraps, secret or concealed. ⟨ME *wrappen*⟩
☛ *Hom.* RAP.

wrap•per ['ræpər] *n.* **1** a person who or thing that wraps. **2** anything in which something is wrapped; covering; cover. **3** a woman's long, loose-fitting garment for wearing in the house. **4** the leaf or leaves rolled around smaller leaves or pieces to form the outside layer of tobacco in a cigar.

wrap•ping ['ræpɪŋ] *n., v.* —*n.* Often, **wrappings,** *pl.* the paper, or other material, in which something is wrapped.
—*v.* ppr. of WRAP.

wrapt [ræpt] *v.* a pt. and a pp. of WRAP.

wrap–up ['ræp ˌʌp] *adj., n. Informal.* —*adj.* concluding; bringing to an end; summarizing: *She will give the wrap-up presentation at the seminar.*
—*n.* **1** a concluding or summarizing statement or report. **2** the act of concluding or summarizing.

wrasse [ræs] *n.* any of a family (Labridae) of usually brightly coloured fishes of warm and temperate seas, having thick, fleshy lips, powerful teeth, and spiny fins. ⟨< Cornish *wrach*⟩

wrath [ræθ], [rɑθ], *or* [rɒθ] *n.* **1** very great anger; rage. **2** righteous anger. ⟨OE *wrǣththu*⟩
☛ *Syn.* See note at ANGER.

wrath•ful ['ræθfəl], ['rɑθfəl], *or* ['rɒθfəl] *adj.* feeling or showing wrath; very angry. **—'wrath•ful•ly,** *adv.*
—'wrath•ful•ness, *n.*

wrath•y ['ræθi], ['rɑθi], *or* ['rɒθi] *adj.* **wrath•i•er, wrath•i•est.** wrathful.

wreak [rik] *v.* **1** give expression to; work off (negative feelings, desires, etc.): *The bully wreaked his bad temper on his dog.* **2** inflict: *The hurricane wreaked havoc on the city.* **3** *Archaic.* avenge. ⟨OE *wrecan*⟩
☛ *Hom.* REEK.

wreath [riθ] *n., pl.* **wreaths** [riðz] *or* [rɪθs]. **1** a ring of flowers, leaves, or twigs twisted together. Wreaths are used as decorations, symbols of victory, tokens of remembrance, bridesmaids' headdresses, etc. **2** something suggesting a wreath: *a wreath of smoke.* **3 Wreath,** *Astrology.* Corona Australis (the Southern Crown), a southern constellation. ⟨OE *wrǣth*⟩

wreathe [rið] *v.* **wreathed, wreath•ing. 1** make into a wreath; twist or twine together in a circle. **2** decorate or adorn with wreaths. **3** make a ring around; encircle: *Mist wreathed the hills.* **4** move in rings: *The smoke wreathed upward.*
wreathed in smiles, smiling broadly. ⟨partly < ME *wrethen,* pp. of *writhen* writhe, partly < *wreath*⟩

wreck [rɛk] *n., v.* —*n.* **1** the destruction, either accidental or deliberate, of a ship, building, train, automobile, or aircraft: *The hurricane caused many wrecks.* **2** any destruction or serious physical or mental injury: *Heavy rains caused the wreck of many crops.* **3** what is left of anything that has been destroyed or severely damaged: *The wreck of a ship was cast upon the shore.* **4** a person or animal that has lost physical or mental health. **5** goods cast up by the sea, especially after a shipwreck.
—*v.* **1** cause the wreck of; destroy or ruin: *Their house was wrecked in the hurricane. The many years as a miner had wrecked his health.* **2** suffer wreck. **3** work as a wrecker. ⟨ME < AF < ON *wrek* < Gmc. *wrecan* to drive⟩
☛ *Hom.* RECK.

wreck•age ['rɛkɪdʒ] *n.* **1** what is left by wreck or wrecks: *The shore was covered with the wreckage of ships.* **2** a wrecking or being wrecked: *the wreckage of one's hopes.*

wreck•er ['rɛkər] *n.* **1** a person who or machine that tears down buildings: *Mario operates the wrecker that is demolishing the vacant building.* **2** a person, car, train, or machine that removes wrecks and salvages and sells parts that are still usable. **3** a person or ship that recovers wrecked or disabled ships or their cargoes. **4** a person who causes shipwrecks by false lights on shore so as to plunder the wrecks.

wren [rɛn] *n.* **1** any of a family (Troglodytidae) of small, energetic, insect-eating songbirds having mostly brownish plumage and a short, cocked tail. The North American **house wren** (*Troglodytes acdon*) is a common summer resident throughout much of Canada, often nesting near houses. The **winter wren** (*T. troglodytes*), the common wren of the United Kingdom, is a tiny wren found throughout the northern hemisphere. **2** any of several other passerine birds. ⟨OE *wrenna*⟩

wrench [rɛntʃ] *n., v.* —*n.* **1** a violent twist or twisting pull: *She broke the branch off the tree with a sudden wrench. He gave his ankle a wrench when he jumped off the bus.* **2** an injury caused by twisting. **3** a pang or surge of grief or pain: *She felt a sudden wrench as she saw him wave from the train and disappear.* **4** a cause of grief or pain: *It was a wrench to leave our old home.* **5** a tool for holding, turning, or twisting something, such as a nut, bolt, or pipe. **6** distortion of the proper or original meaning, interpretation, etc.
—*v.* **1** twist or pull violently: *The police officer wrenched the gun out of the man's hand.* **2** injure by twisting: *He wrenched his back in falling from the horse.* **3** give pain or anguish to. **4** twist or distort the meaning of. ⟨OE *wrencan* twist⟩

wrest [rɛst] *v., n.* —*v.* **1** twist, pull, or tear away with force; wrench away: *He wrested the knife from his assailant.* **2** take by force, persistence, or persuasion: *The usurper wrested the power from the king.* **3** twist, pervert, or turn from the proper meaning, use, etc.
—*n.* **1** the act of wresting; a forcible twist, pull, or tear. **2** *Archaic.* a small, wrenchlike key used for turning the WREST PINS on a harp or piano. ⟨OE *wrǣstan*⟩ **—'wrest•er,** *n.*
☛ *Hom.* REST.

wres•tle ['rɛsəl] *v.* **-tled, -tling;** *n.* —*v.* **1** fight or grapple with (an opponent) by holding, throwing, tripping, etc., but without striking with the fist. **2** struggle or contend (*with*): *wrestling with a problem, wrestling with inflation.* **3** move (something) laboriously, with or as if with wrestling movements: *He managed to wrestle the couch down the stairs.*
—*n.* the act or an instance of wrestling; especially, a wrestling match. ⟨ult. < *wrest*⟩ **—'wres•tler,** *n.*

wres•tling ['rɛslɪŋ] *n., v.* —*n.* a sport or contest in which each of two opponents tries to throw or force the other to the ground. The rules for wrestling do not allow using the fists or certain holds on the body.
—*v.* ppr. of WRESTLE.

wrest pin one of the pins on a piano, harpsichord, or harp around which one end of each string is coiled. The tension, and therefore pitch, of the strings may be changed by turning the wrest pins.

wretch [rɛtʃ] *n.* **1** a very unfortunate or unhappy person. **2** a scoundrel. ⟨OE *wrecca* exile⟩
☛ *Hom.* RETCH.

wretch•ed ['rɛtʃɪd] *adj.* **1** very unfortunate or unhappy. **2** very unsatisfactory; miserable: *a wretched hut.* **3** characterized by misfortune, misery, or distress. **4** vicious; wicked; degenerate;

contemptible: *a wretched traitor.* **—'wretch•ed•ly,** *adv.* **—'wretch•ed•ness,** *n.*

☛ *Syn.* **1. Wretched,** MISERABLE = very unhappy or deeply disturbed. **Wretched** suggests a state of unhappinesss and extreme lowness of spirits marked by discouragement and hopelessness, caused by sorrow, sickness, worry, etc.: *He felt wretched when he failed the examination again.* **Miserable** suggests a state of severe suffering or distress of mind, caused especially by conditions or circumstances such as poverty, humiliation, or misfortune: *After the loss of their savings and their home, they felt too miserable to see their old friends.*

wrig•gle ['rɪgəl] *v.* **-gled, -gling;** *n.* *—v.* **1** twist and turn; squirm: *Children wriggle when they are restless.* **2** move by twisting and turning: *A snake wriggled across the road. She managed to wriggle her suitcase out of the closely-packed closet.* **3** make one's way by tricks, excuses, etc.: *Some people can wriggle out of any difficulty.*
—n. the act of wriggling: *With one wriggle, he was under the bed.* ⟨Cf. Du. *wriggelen*⟩

wrig•gler ['rɪglər] *n.* **1** a person who or thing that wriggles. **2** the larva of a mosquito.

wrig•gly ['rɪgli] *adj.* **wrig•gli•er, wrig•gli•est,** twisting and turning.

wright [rəit] *n.* a person who makes, creates, or fixes something (*usually used in compounds*): *wheelwright, shipwright, playwright.* ⟨OE *wryhta,* var. of *wyrhta* < *weorc* work⟩
☛ *Hom.* RIGHT, RITE, WRITE.

wring [rɪŋ] *v.* **wrung, wring•ing;** *n.* *—v.* **1** twist and squeeze hard, especially so as to extract moisture (*often used with* **out**): *to wring clothes.* **2** force by twisting and squeezing: *The hikers wrung water from their soaking clothes.* **3** twist violently; wrench: *to wring a chicken's neck.* **4** get by force, effort, or persuasion: *The old beggar could wring money from anyone by his sad story.* **5** clasp; press: *They wrung their old friend's hand. She wrung her hands in distress.* **6** cause pain or pity in: *Their poverty wrung my heart.*
—n. the act of twisting and squeezing: *She gave her swimsuit a good wring.* ⟨OE *wringan*⟩
☛ *Hom.* RING.

wring•er ['rɪŋər] *n.* a person who or thing that wrings; especially, a device or machine for squeezing water from clothes.
put (someone) **through the wringer,** *Slang.* subject (someone) to an ordeal.
☛ *Hom.* RINGER.

wrin•kle¹ ['rɪŋkəl] *n., v.* **-kled, -kling.** *—n.* **1** an irregular ridge or fold; crease: *An old person's face has wrinkles. When she unpacked the dress she found it was full of wrinkles.* **2** a small problem to be overcome; hitch: *The plan has a few wrinkles, but I think we can make it work.*
—v. **1** make a wrinkle or wrinkles in: *He wrinkled his forehead.* **2** have or acquire wrinkles: *The label says the shirt won't wrinkle.* ⟨Cf. OE *gewrinclod,* pp., twisted, winding⟩

wrin•kle² ['rɪŋkəl] *n. Informal.* a useful hint or idea; clever trick. ⟨? special use of *wrinkle¹*⟩

wrin•kly ['rɪŋkli] *adj.* **-kli•er, -kli•est.** wrinkled or prone to wrinkling: *The problem with rayon is it's so wrinkly.*

wrist [rɪst] *n.* **1** the part of the human arm between the hand and the forearm. See ARM for picture. **2** a corresponding part of the forelimb of an animal. **3** the joint formed by the end of the larger bone of the forearm and the carpus, connecting the arm with the hand. **4** one or more of the bones of this joint. **5** the part of a sleeve, glove, or mitten covering the wrist.
slap on the wrist, *Informal.* a punishment that is much lighter than deserved. ⟨OE⟩

wrist•band ['rɪst,bænd] *n.* **1** the band of a sleeve or mitten, etc. fitting around the wrist. **2** a strap worn around the wrist, as of a wristwatch.

wrist•let ['rɪstlɪt] *n.* **1** a band worn around the wrist to keep it warm. **2** a bracelet.

wrist pin *Machinery.* a stud or pin projecting from the side of a crank, wheel, or the like, and forming a means of attachment to a connecting rod.

wrist shot *Sports.* a shot or stroke in which the power is provided by a flick of the wrist, rather than the arm.

wrist•watch ['rɪst,wɒtʃ] *n., pl.* **wrist•watch•es.** a watch worn on a strap around the wrist.

writ¹ [rɪt] *n.* **1** *Law.* a formal written order directing a person to do or not to do something: *A writ from the judge ordered the prisoner's release from jail.* **2** something written; a piece of writing. ⟨OE *writ* < *wrītan* write⟩

writ² [rɪt] *v. Archaic.* a pt. and a pp. of WRITE.

write [rəit] *v.* **wrote** or (*archaic*) **writ, writ•ten** or (*archaic*) **writ, writ•ing. 1** make (letters or words), especially in cursive style, with pen, pencil, chalk, etc.: *He learned to write.* **2** mark with the required letters or words: *to write a cheque.* **3** put down or form the letters, words, etc. of: *Write your name and address.* **4** give in writing; record: *She writes all that happens.* **5** make up (books, stories, articles, poems, letters, etc.); compose: *He writes reviews for the magazines.* **6** be a writer: *Her ambition was to write.* **7** write a letter: *He writes to her every week.* **8** write a letter to: *I wrote him yesterday.* **9** show plainly: *Honesty is written on her face.* **10** *Computer technology.* record (data) in memory, on a tape or a disk, for use by a computer. **11** of an instrument, produce writing of a certain kind: *A sharp pencil writes more clearly.*
write down, a put into writing: *Many early folk songs were never written down.* **b** put a lower value on.
write home about. See HOME.
write in, a insert (a fact, statement, etc.) in a piece of writing. **b** *U.S.* cast a vote for (an unlisted candidate) by writing his or her name on a ballot.
write off, a cancel (an entry in an account) as uncollectable: *My father agreed to write off my debt to him.* **b** note the deduction of for depreciation. **c** give up on; dismiss or treat as if nonexistent. **d** amortize.
write out, a put into writing. **b** write in full: *She made quick notes during the interview and wrote out her report later.* **c** exhaust (oneself) by prolific writing: *The poet Nelligan wrote himself out in a few years.* **d** eliminate (a character) from a television or radio script by means of story events: *When her contract ended, they wrote her out in a murder episode.*
write up, a write a description or account of. **b** write in detail. **c** bring up to date in writing. **d** put a higher value on. ⟨OE *wrītan,* originally, scratch⟩
☛ *Hom.* RIGHT, RITE, WRIGHT.

write–in ['rəit ,ɪn] *adj., n. U.S.* *—adj.* in an election, of or having to do with a person who is not officially listed as a candidate but who is voted for by his or her name being written in on a ballot.
—n. a write-in candidate or vote.

write–off ['rəit ,ɒf] *n.* **1** something cancelled or recognized as a loss: *We treated the money we had lent him as a write-off.* **2** *Informal.* a total wreck, such as might be written off as a loss: *They weren't hurt badly in the accident, but their car was a write-off.*

writ•er ['rəitər] *n.* a person who writes, especially one whose profession or business is writing; an author or journalist.

write–up ['rəit ,ʌp] *n. Informal.* a written description or account.

writhe [raɪð] *v.* **writhed, writhed** or (*archaic or poetic*) **writh•en** ['rɪðən], **writh•ing;** *n.* *—v.* **1** twist and turn; squirm: *to writhe in pain.* **2** suffer intense embarrassment, revulsion, annoyance, etc.: *He writhed when he thought of the blunder he had made.*
—n. a writhing movement; a twist of the body: *She gave a final writhe of pain and then lay still.* ⟨OE *wrīthan*⟩

writ•ing ['rəitɪŋ] *n., v.* *—n.* **1** written form: *Put your ideas in writing.* **2** handwriting. **3** something written; a letter, paper, document, etc. **4** the act of writing. **5** a literary work; a book or other literary production: *the writings of Judge Haliburton.* **6** the profession or business of a person who writes. **7** (*adjl.*) used in writing: *writing paper.*
—v. ppr. of WRITE.

writ•ten ['rɪtən] *adj., v.* *—adj.* put down in a form intended to be read; not spoken: *the written word.*
—v. a pp. of WRITE.

wrong [rɒŋ] *adj., adv., n., v.* *—adj.* **1** not right; immoral; unjust; unlawful: *It is wrong to tell lies.* **2** incorrect; in error: *She gave the wrong answer.* **3** unsuitable; improper; inappropriate: *the wrong clothes for the occasion.* **4** in a bad state or condition; out of order; amiss: *Something is wrong with the car.* **5** not meant to be seen or shown: *the wrong side of the cloth.*
go wrong, a turn out badly. **b** stop being good and become bad.
—adv. in a wrong way, direction, etc.; so as to be wrong: *to guess wrong. You put the pieces together wrong.*
get (someone or something) **wrong,** misinterpret; misunderstand (someone or something).
—n. **1** what is wrong; wrong thing or things: *Two wrongs do not make a right.* **2** an injustice; injury: *to do someone a wrong.*
in the wrong, at fault; guilty; in error: *He argues all the more vehemently when he suspects he's in the wrong.*
—v. **1** do wrong to; treat unjustly; injure: *She forgave those who had wronged her.* **2** discredit or dishonour unjustly by statement, opinion, etc.; impute evil to undeservedly. **3** cheat or defraud (a

person of something). ⟨OE *wrang* < ON *wrangr, rangr* crooked⟩ **—'wrong•ly,** *adv.* **—'wrong•ness,** *n.*

wrong•do•er ['rɒŋ,duər] *n.* a person who does wrong.

wrong•do•ing ['rɒŋ,duɪŋ] *n.* the doing of wrong; bad acts: *The thief was guilty of wrongdoing.*

wrong•ful ['rɒŋfəl] *adj.* **1** wrong; unjust. **2** unlawful. **—'wrong•ful•ly,** *adv.* **—'wrong•ful•ness,** *n.*

wrong–head•ed ['rɒŋ 'hɛdɪd] *adj.* **1** wrong in judgment or opinion. **2** stubborn even when wrong. **—'wrong-'head•ed•ly,** *adv.* **—'wrong-'head•ed•ness,** *n.*

wrote [rout] *v.* a pt. of WRITE.

wroth [rɒθ] *or* [rouθ] *adj. Archaic or poetic.* angry; wrathful. ⟨OE *wrāth*⟩

wrought [rɒt] *adj., v.* *—adj.* **1** shaped or formed with skill and care; fashioned: *wrought vases.* **2** of metals, **a** shaped by hammering, etc.: *a plate of wrought silver.* **b** made with elaborate decoration.
—v. Archaic. a pt. and a pp. of WORK.
☛ *Hom.* ROT.

wrought iron a tough, durable form of iron that is soft enough to be easily forged and welded, but that will not break as easily as cast iron. Wrought iron is often used for decorative furniture, gates, or railings. **—'wrought-'i•ron,** *adj.*

wrought–up ['rɒt 'ʌp] *adj.* stirred up; excited.

wrung [rʌŋ] *v.* pt. and pp. of WRING.

wry [raɪ] *adj.* **wri•er** or **wry•er, wri•est** or **wry•est. 1** made by distorting the mouth or other features to show disgust, bitterness, doubt, or irony: *a wry face, a wry grin.* **2** marked by grim or bitter irony: *wry humour, wry remarks.* **3** turned to one side in an abnormal way: *a wry nose.* **4** perversely wrong or inappropriate: *wry behaviour.* ⟨ult. < OE *wrīgian* turn⟩ **—'wry•ly,** *adv.*
☛ *Hom.* RYE.

wry•neck ['raɪ,nɛk] *n.* **1** either of two Old World woodpeckers (constituting the genus *Jynx* and the subfamily Jynginae) having mottled greyish brown plumage and differing from typical woodpeckers in having soft tail feathers, a small bill not adapted for drumming on trees, and the habit of twisting their necks about when disturbed. **2** a spasmodic or congenital contraction of the neck muscles, causing the head to be pulled or twisted to the side; torticollis.

WSW or **W.S.W.** west-southwest.

wt. weight.

Wun•der•kind or **wun•der•kind** ['vʊndəʀ,kɪnt] *n. German.* a child prodigy.

WWI WORLD WAR I.

WWII WORLD WAR II.

Wy•an•dot ['waɪən'dɒt] *n., pl.* **-dots** or **-dot. 1** a member of a First Nations group originating among Huron-speaking peoples of Ontario and formerly living in Ontario and adjacent states of the U.S. Their current home is in Oklahoma. **2** their Iroquoian language.

Wy•an•dotte ['waɪən,dɒt] *n.* an American breed of medium-sized, hardy chickens. ⟨< *Wyandot*⟩

wye [waɪ] *n.* **1** the letter Y. **2** anything made or arranged in the shape of the letter Y.
☛ *Hom.* WHY.

Wy•o•ming [waɪ'oumɪŋ] *n.* a northwestern state of the United States.

wy•vern ['waɪvərn] *n. Heraldry.* a two-legged, winged dragon with a barbed tail. Also, **wivern.** ⟨ME *wyvre* < AF *wivre* (OF *guivre*), ult. < OHG *wipera* < L *vipera* viper⟩

X x *X x*

x or **X** [ɛks] *n., pl.* **x's** or **X's. 1** the twenty-fourth letter of the English alphabet. **2** any speech sound represented by this letter. **3** a person or thing identified as *x,* especially the twenty-fourth of a series or the first of a pair or a series consisting of x, y, and, sometimes, z. **4 X,** the Roman numeral for 10. **5** *x, Algebra.* an unknown quantity, as in $x + y = 5$. **6** *Geometry.* an abscissa. **7 X,** an unidentified person or thing: *Ms. X.* **8** something shaped like the letter X. **9** *(adjl.)* of or being an X or x. **10 x** or **X** is also used: **a** to indicate a certain place on a map, etc.: *X marks the spot.* **b** to symbolize a kiss. **c** to represent the signature of a person who cannot write. **d** to indicate fineness of sugar or flour. **11** something, such as a printer's type, a lever, or a key on a keyboard, that produces an x or X. **12 x** is also used to indicate multiplication or dimensions: $3 x 2 = 6$; a 2 × 4 (two by four) is a piece of wood measuring 4 inches wide and 2 inches thick, of any desired length. **13 X,** extra or oversize: *XL, XXL;* or children's sizes: *2X, 4X.* **14** out of; foaled by: *a filly by Supercharger X Ballet Dancer.* **15** used to make one's choice or answer on a ballot, questionnaire, survey, etc. **16 X,** Christ, especially in abbreviations: *Xmas.*

x [ɛks] *v.* **x•ed** or **x'd, x•ing** or **x'ing. 1** mark with an x. **2** cancel or cross out with an x or a series of x's (*often used with* **out**): *to x out a mistake.*

xanth– *combining form.* yellow. ⟨< NL < Gk. *xanthos* yellow⟩

xan•thate ['zænθeit] *n. Chemistry.* a salt or ester of xanthic acid.

xan•thic ['zænθɪk] *adj.* **1** yellow or yellowish in colour. **2** *Chemistry.* of or from xanthine or xanthic acid.

xanthic acid 1 *Chemistry.* an unstable colourless acid that decomposes into ethyl alcohol and carbon disulphide at 24°C. Its methyl and ethyl esters are colourless, oily liquids having a penetrating odour. *Formula*: $C_3H_6OS_2$ **2** any of a series of acids containing the group OCS_2H.

xan•thine ['zænθin] *or* ['zænθɪn] *n. Biochemistry.* a crystalline, nitrogenous compound related to uric acid and present in blood, urine, and certain plant tissues. *Formula*: $C_5H_4N_4O_2$

Xan•thip•pe [zæn'tɪpi] *n.* a scolding woman; shrew. ⟨< *Xanthippe,* the wife of Socrates, notorious as a scold⟩

xan•thous ['zænθəs] *adj.* **1** of or having to do with peoples having yellowish, reddish, or light brown hair. **2** of or having to do with peoples having a yellowish skin, as the Mongolians. **3** yellow. ⟨< Gk. *xanthos* yellow⟩

x–ax•is ['ɛks ,æksɪs] *n., pl.* **x-ax•es** ['ɛks ,æksiz] *Geometry.* **1** in a plane Cartesian coordinate system, the horizontal axis along which the abscissa is measured and from which the ordinate is measured. **2** in a three-dimensional Cartesian coordinate system, the axis along which values of *x* are measured and at which *y* and *z* each equal zero. Compare Y-AXIS, Z-AXIS.

X chromosome *Biology.* one of the two chromosomes bearing the genes that determine sex in human beings and many animals. Each female body cell normally contains two X chromosomes and each egg cell contains one X chromosome. Compare Y CHROMOSOME.

Xe xenon.

xe•bec ['zibɛk] *n.* a small, three-masted vessel of the Mediterranean. Also, **zebec, zebeck.** ⟨< F *xebec* < earlier *chebec,* influenced by Sp. *xabeque,* ult. < Arabic *shabbāk*⟩

xe•ni•a ['ziniə] *n. Botany.* the effects or changes in a seed resulting directly from cross-pollination. ⟨< NL < Gk. *xenia* hospitality < Gk. *xenos* guest, stranger⟩

xeno– *combining form.* **1** stranger; foreigner: *xenophobia.* **2** strange; foreign: *xenomorphic.* ⟨< Gk. *xenos* guest, stranger⟩

xen•o•lith ['zɛnə,lɪθ] *n.* a rock fragment different from the igneous rock which surrounds it. **–,xen•o'lith•ic,** *adj.*

xen•o•mor•phic [,zɛnə'mɔrfɪk] *adj.* of rock, having a form distorted from the normal form as a result of pressure. **–,xen•o'mor•phi•cal•ly,** *adv.*

xe•non ['zinɒn] *or* ['zɛnɒn] *n. Chemistry.* a rare, heavy, colourless, gaseous element that is chemically inactive. It occurs in the air in minute quantities. *Symbol*: Xe; *at.no.* 54; *at.mass* 131.30. ⟨< Gk. *xenon,* neut. of *xenos* strange⟩

xen•o•phi•lia [,zɛnə'fɪliə] *n.* an attraction to strange or foreign peoples, cultures, or customs.

xen•o•phobe ['zɛnə,foub] *n.* one who has a morbid fear or dislike of foreign persons or things.

xen•o•pho•bi•a [,zɛnə'foubiə] *n.* a hatred or fear of foreigners or foreign things. **–,xen•o'pho•bic,** *adj.*

xe•ric ['zirɪk] *adj.* pertaining to or adapted to a dry or desertlike environment. ⟨< Gk. *xeros* dry⟩

xero– *combining form.* dry; dryness: *xerophyte.* ⟨< Gk. *xēros* dry⟩

xe•ro•graph•ic [,zirə'græfɪk] *adj.* of or having to do with xerography.

xe•rog•ra•phy [zɪ'rɒgrəfi] *n.* a process for making copies of written or printed material, pictures, etc., by the action of magnetic attraction rather than ink and pressure. Tiny, negatively-charged particles are spread on positively-charged paper in an arrangement that exactly copies the printing, etc. on the original paper. ⟨< *xero-* + *-graph* + *-y*⟩

xe•roph•i•lous [zɪ'rɒfələs] *adj. Botany. Zoology.* of certain plants and animals, capable of living and flourishing in, or adapting to, a hot, dry environment.

xe•ro•phyte ['zirə,fəit] *n.* a plant that needs very little water and can grow in deserts or very dry ground. Cactuses, sagebrush, etc. are xerophytes. **–,xe•ro'phyt•ic** [,zirə'fɪtɪk], *adj.*

xe•ro•sis [zi'rousɪs] *n. Medicine.* abnormal dryness of the skin, eyes, or mucous membranes.

Xer•ox ['zirɒks] *n. Trademark.* a copying process or machine using xerography.

Xho•sa ['kousə] *or* ['kouzə] *n., pl.* **-sa** or **-sas;** *adj.* *–n.* **1** a member of a group of Bantu-speaking peoples of southern Africa. **2** the Bantu language of the Xhosa, closely related to Zulu and characterized by the use of clicks.
–adj. of or having to do with the Xhosa or their culture or language.

Xho•san ['kousən] *or* ['kouzən] *adj.* of or having to do with Xhosa.

xi [saɪ], [zaɪ], *or* [ksi] *n.* the fourteenth letter (Ξ, ξ = English X, x) of the Greek alphabet.

xiph•i•ster•num [,zɪfɪ'stɜrnəm] *n. Anatomy. Zoology.* the lowest of the three sections of the sternum. ⟨< NL < Gk. *xiphos* sword + NL *sternum* sternum⟩

xiph•oid ['zɪfɔɪd] *adj., n.* *–adj. Anatomy. Zoology.* **1** sword-shaped. **2** of or relating to the xiphisternum.
–n. the xiphisternum. Also called **xiphoid process.**

X–linkage ['ɛks ,lɪŋkədʒ] *n. Genetics.* the pattern of inheritance of genes located on the X chromosome.

X–linked ['ɛks ,lɪŋkt] *adj. Genetics.* **1** of a gene, located on the X chromosome. **2** involving traits determined by such genes: *X-linked inheritance.* See DOMINANT INHERITANCE, RECESSIVE INHERITANCE.

Xmas ['ɛksməs] *or* ['krɪsməs] *n. Informal.* Christmas.

X ray or **X–ray** ['ɛks ,rei] *n.* **1** radiation of the same type as visible radiation (i.e., light) but having an extremely short wavelength, 0.1–10 nanometres. It can go through substances that ordinary light rays cannot penetrate, but will act in the same way as light does on a photographic film or plate to produce a picture. X rays are used to locate breaks in bones, a bullet lodged in the body, etc., and in treating certain diseases. **2** a picture obtained by means of X rays. **3** *(adjl.)* **X-ray** or **x-ray,** made by or using X rays. ⟨translation of G *X-Strahlen,* pl., < *X,* in sense of 'unknown', + *Strahl* ray, beam⟩

X–ray or **x–ray** ['ɛks ,rei] *v.* examine, photograph, or treat with X rays.

X–ray tube an electronic, cathode-ray tube in which a metal target is bombarded by high energy electrons and emits X rays as a result.

Xs and Os TICK-TACK-TOE.

xylo– *combining form.* wood. Also, before vowels, **xyl-.** ⟨< Gk. *xylon*⟩

xy•lem ['zaɪləm] *n. Botany.* the more rigid tissue in the vascular system of plants and trees that conducts water and mineral salts up from the roots and supports the softer tissue. Compare PHLOEM.

xy•lene ['zaɪlin] *n. Chemistry.* any of three colourless, oily, toxic isomeric hydrocarbons of the benzene series, obtained chiefly from coal tar but also from wood tar and petroleum, and used in the manufacture of antiseptics, dyes, and solvents. *Formula*: C_8H_{10}

xy•li•tol ['zaɪlɪ,tɒl] *or* ['zaɪlɪ,toul] *n.* a naturally occurring crystalline alcohol used especially by diabetics as a substitute for sucrose. *Formula*: $C_5H_{12}O_5$

xy•lo•graph ['zaɪlə,græf] *n.* an engraving on wood; a woodcut or wood carving, especially an early one.

xy•log•ra•phy [zaɪ'lɒgrəfi] *n.* the practice, especially early or primitive, of making engravings on wood, or woodcuts, and of printing from these.

xy•loph•a•gous [zaɪ'lɒfəgəs] *adj.* eating or living in wood, as certain insect larvae, etc. Termites are xylophagous.

xy•lo•phone ['zaɪlə,foun] *n.* a musical percussion instrument consisting of two rows of wooden bars that are graduated in length to produce the tones of two octaves of the chromatic scale. It is played by striking the bars with wooden hammers.
—'xy•lo,phon•ist, *n.*

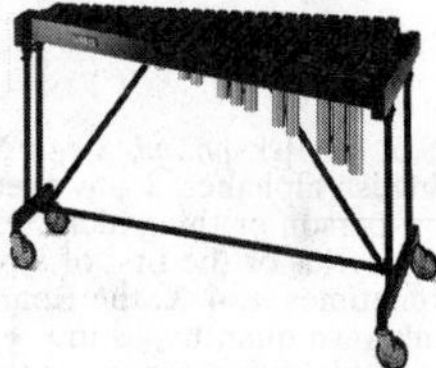
A xylophone

xy•ster ['zɪstər] *n.* a surgical instrument for scraping bones.
⟨< NL < Gk., scraping tool < *xyein* scrape⟩

Y y *Y y*

y or **Y** [waɪ] *n.* **y's** or **Y's. 1** the twenty-fifth letter of the English alphabet. **2** any speech sound represented by this letter. **3** a person or thing identified as *y*, especially the twenty-fifth of a series or the second of a pair or a series consisting of x, y, and, sometimes, z. **4** *y, Algebra.* an unknown quantity, as in $2x + 3y = 7$. **5** *Geometry.* an ordinate. **6** something shaped like the letter Y. **7** *(adjl.)* of or being a Y or y. **8** something, such as a printer's type, a lever, or a key on a keyboard, that produces a y or Y. **9 the Y,** *Informal.* YMCA; YWCA; YMHA; YWHA.
☛ *Hom.* WHY.

–y[1] *suffix.* **1** full of, composed of, containing, having, or characterized by ——: *airy, cloudy, dewy, icy, juicy, watery.* **2** somewhat ——: *chilly, salty.* **3** inclined to ——: *chatty, fidgety.* **4** resembling or suggesting ——: *sloppy, sugary, willowy.* **5** *Archaic or poetic.* very ——: *stilly, vasty.* ⟨OE *-ig*⟩

–y[2] *suffix.* used to indicate that someone or something is considered as small and attractive, thought of with affection, etc.: *doggy, dolly, Mommy, softy.* ⟨ME⟩

–y[3] *suffix.* **1** a —— state or quality: *jealousy, victory.* **2** an activity: *delivery, entreaty.* **3** a collective group of people or things: *soldiery, confectionery.* ⟨< F *-ie* < L *-ia,* Gk. *-ia*⟩

y. 1 yard(s). **2** year(s).

Y 1 yttrium. **2** YEN[1].

yacht [jɒt] *n., v.* —*n.* **1** a light sailing vessel having graceful lines, designed for racing. **2** a similar, often luxuriously equipped vessel having sails and/or motor power, used for private pleasure cruising.
—*v.* sail, race, or cruise on a yacht. ⟨< Early Mod.Du. *jaghte* (now *jacht*) < *jaghtschip* chasing ship⟩

yacht•ing [ˈjɒtɪŋ] *n., adj., v.* —*n.* **1** the art of sailing a yacht. **2** the pastime of sailing on a yacht.
—*adj.* of or having to do with yachting or yachts.
—*v.* ppr. of YACHT.

yachts•man [ˈjɒtsmən] *n., pl.* **-men.** a man who owns or sails a yacht.

yachts•man•ship [ˈjɒtsmən,ʃɪp] *n.* skill or ability in handling a yacht.

yack [jæk] *v. Slang.* See YAK[2].

yah [jɑ] *interj.* an exclamation used to express derision, disgust, or impatience.

Ya•hoo *n.* [ˈjæhu] *or* [ˈjɑhu]; *interj.* [jæˈhu] *n., pl.* **-hoos;** *interj.* —*n.* **1** in Swift's *Gulliver's Travels,* a type of brute in human shape who works for a race of intelligent horses. **2 yahoo,** any rough, coarse, or uncouth person.
—*interj.* **yahoo,** a cry of delight: *School's out! Yahoo!*

Yah•weh or **Yah•we** [ˈjɑwei] *or* [ˈjɑwɛ] *n.* the name of God in the Hebrew Bible (the Old Testament). Also, **Yahveh, Yahve, Jahve, Jahveh.** ⟨< Hebrew. See JEHOVAH.⟩ **—ˈYah•wism,** *n.* **—ˈYah•wist,** *n.*

yak[1] [jæk] *n.* a large, long-haired animal (*Bos grunniens*) of central Asia, related to the North American buffalo and to cattle. Yaks are often domesticated and used for food and as beasts of burden. ⟨< Tibetan *gyag*⟩

A yak

yak[2] [jæk] *v.* **yakked, yak•king;** *n. Slang.* —*v.* chatter; talk idly and constantly.
—*n.* persistent, idle chatter. Also, **yack, yak-yak, yakety-yak.** ⟨imitative⟩

Ya•kut [jəˈkut] *n.* **1** a Turkic-speaking people of the Lena River valley of eastern Siberia. **2** the Turkic language spoken by these people.

yam [jæm] *n.* **1** the edible, starchy tuber of any of several tropical and subtropical climbing vines (genus *Dioscorea,* of the family Dioscoreaceae), used as a staple food in tropical regions. **2** any of the vines that produce these tubers. **3** any of several varieties of sweet potato. ⟨< Sp. *iñame,* ult. < Senegalese *nyami* eat⟩

yam•mer [ˈjæmər] *v., n.* —*v.* **1** whine or whimper in a complaining way. **2** utter (complaints, etc.) persistently. **3** howl, yell, or clamour: *dogs yammering for their food.* **4** talk loudly and persistently.
—*n.* a yammering sound or utterance. ⟨ME *yameren* < OE *geomerian* complain, lament; possibly influenced by MDu. *jam(m)eren*⟩

yang [jæŋ] *n.* **1** *Taoism.* the positive force in the cosmos; the counterpart to the yin. **2** *Chinese philosophy.* the male principle, active and positive, the source of heat and light, complementary to and contrasting with the yin. Compare YIN.

yank [jæŋk] *v., n. Informal.* —*v.* pull with a sudden motion; jerk: *You almost yanked my arm off! She yanked the sweater out of the drawer.*
—*n.* a sudden pull; jerk: *He gave the door a yank.* ⟨origin uncertain⟩

Yank [jæŋk] *n. or adj. Slang.* Yankee.

Yan•kee [ˈjæŋki] *n., adj.* —*n.* **1** a native or inhabitant of the United States; an American. **2** a native or inhabitant of one of the six New England states of the northeastern part of the United States. **3** a native or inhabitant of any of the northern states of the United States. **4** a Union, or northern, soldier in the American Civil War.
—*adj.* of, having to do with, or characteristic of Yankees: *Yankee shrewdness.* ⟨probably ult. < Du. *Jan Kees* John Cheese (nickname), the *-s* being taken for pl. ending⟩

yap [jæp] *n., v.* **yapped, yap•ping.** —*n.* **1** a snappish bark; yelp. **2** *Slang.* snappish, noisy, or foolish talk. **3** *Slang.* a peevish or noisy person. **4** *Slang.* the mouth.
—*v.* **1** bark snappishly; yelp. **2** *Slang.* talk snappishly, noisily, or foolishly; chatter or talk idly. ⟨imitative⟩ **—ˈyap•py,** *adj.*

Ya•qui [ˈjɑki] *n., pl.* **-qui** or **-quis.** a member of a Native American people of S Arizona and NW Mexico.

yar•bor•ough [ˈjɑrbərə] *n. Bridge. Whist.* a hand of thirteen cards with no card higher than a nine. ⟨after the second Earl of *Yarborough* (died 1897), who is said to have bet a thousand to one against the occurrence of such a hand. 19c.⟩

yard[1] [jɑrd] *n., v.* —*n.* **1** the piece of ground adjacent to or around a house, barn, school, etc. **2** a piece of ground surrounded by a building or buildings: *a courtyard, a farmyard.* **3** a piece of enclosed ground for some special purpose or business: *a chicken yard.* **4** *Railroads.* a space with tracks where railway cars are stored, switched, etc. **5** *Cdn.* **a** a clearing where a group of moose or deer feed in winter. **b** the moose or deer so grouped. **6** a place where musk-oxen huddle together for warmth and protection. **7** *Cdn. Logging.* an assembly point for logs. **8 the Yard,** *Brit.* SCOTLAND YARD.
—*v.* **1** put into or enclose in a yard. **2** *Cdn.* of moose or deer, be in, settle, or come together in a yard (*often used with* **up**). ⟨OE *geard*⟩

yard[2] [jɑrd] *n.* **1** a unit for measuring length, equal to 3 feet or 36 inches (about 91.4 cm). *Abbrev.:* y. or yd. **2** a cubic yard: *It took two yards of gravel to surface the driveway.* **3** *Nautical.* **a** a long, slender beam, or spar, with tapered ends, fastened across a mast and used to support a sail. **b** a similar member of a mast on a non-sailing vessel, used for holding signal flags, lights, etc. **make yards, a** *Football.* advance the ball from the line of scrimmage. **b** *Informal.* advance; make headway: *She has already made yards in her new business.* ⟨OE *gierd* rod⟩

yard•age[1] [ˈjɑrdɪdʒ] *n.* **1** length in yards. **2** a quantity of something, such as cloth, that is measured in yards: *a large yardage of silk.* **3** YARD GOODS. **4** *Football.* the number of yards by which a team or player advances the ball from the line of scrimmage. **5** *Informal.* advance; gain; benefit.

yard•age[2] [ˈjɑrdɪdʒ] *n.* **1** the use of a yard or enclosure, as in loading or unloading cattle, etc. at a railway station. **2** the charge made for such use.

yard•arm [ˈjɑrd,ɑrm] *n. Nautical.* either end of a yard supporting a sail on a square-rigged ship.

yard•er [ˈjɑrdər] *n. Cdn. Logging.* **1** a DONKEY (def. 4) or other engine rigged to haul logs from the woods to the track, skid road, or landing. **2** a vehicle used for hauling logs to a YARD[1] (def. 7).

yard goods cloth, etc. sold by the yard.

yard•ing ['jɑrdɪŋ] *n., v.* *—n. Cdn. Logging.* the assembly and stacking of logs in a YARD[1] (def. 7).
—v. ppr. of YARD[1].

yard•mas•ter ['jɑrd,mæstər] *n.* the manager of a railway yard.

yard of ale **1** the amount of ale or beer (between about 1 and 1.7 L) contained in a very narrow, horn-shaped glass about one yard (91.4 cm) tall. **2** the glass itself.

yard sale an informal sale of personal possessions, used furniture, etc., usually held in a private yard and patronized mostly by neighbours and passers-by. See also GARAGE SALE.

yard•stick ['jɑrd,stɪk] *n.* **1** a stick one yard long, used for measuring. **2** any standard of judgment or comparison.

yare [jɛr] *or* [jɑr] *adj.* **yar•er, yar•est. 1** *Nautical.* responding easily to the helm. **2** agile; quick; lively. **3** *Archaic.* ready; prepared.

yar•mul•ke ['jɑrməlkə] *n.* a skullcap worn especially by Orthodox and Conservative Jewish men and boys for prayer and ceremonial occasions or, by strongly religious Jews, at all times. Also, **yarmulka.** ⟨< Yiddish < Ukrainian, Polish *yarmulka* cap⟩

yarn [jɑrn] *n., v.* *—n.* **1** any spun thread, especially that prepared for weaving or knitting. **2** the spun fibre used for making rope. **2** *Informal.* an exaggerated, often humorous, tale or story: *Who told you that yarn?*
spin a yarn, *Informal.* tell such a story.
—v. Informal. tell stories. ⟨OE *gearn*⟩

yar•row ['jærou] *or* ['jɛrou] *n.* any of several plants (genus *Achillea*) of the composite family, especially the common yarrow (*A. millefolium*) having finely divided leaves and flat clusters of white or pink flowers. ⟨OE *gearwe*⟩

yash•mak or **yash•mac** [jɑʃ'mɑk] *or* ['jæʃmæk] *n.* a veil worn in public by Muslim women. ⟨< Turkish *yasmak*⟩

yat•a•ghan ['jætə,gæn] *or* [ˌjɑtɑ'gɑn] *n.* a doubly curved sword used by Muslims, having no guard for the hand and no crosspiece, but usually a large pommel. ⟨< Turkish⟩

yaw [jɒ] *v., n.* *—v.* **1** turn from a straight course; go unsteadily. **2** of a ship, swing from side to side across a horizontal course. **3** of an aircraft, turn from a straight course by a motion about its vertical axis. **4** of a rocket or guided missile, wobble or swing on the longitudinal axis in the horizontal plane.
—n. a movement from a straight course. ⟨possibly < ON *jaga* sway, move back and forth⟩

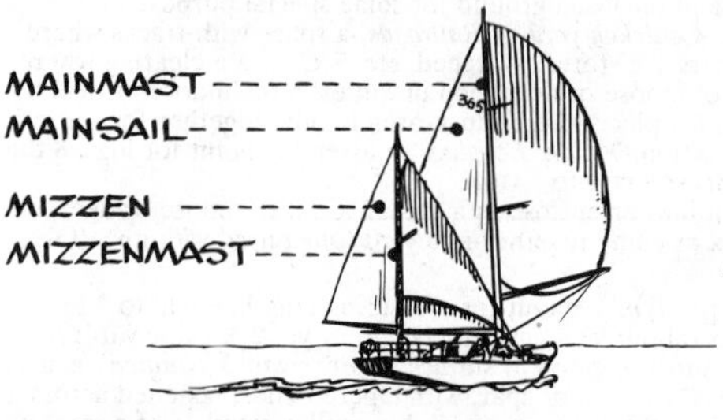

MAINMAST
MAINSAIL
MIZZEN
MIZZENMAST

A yawl

yawl [jɒl] *n.* **1** a boat similar to a ketch, having a large mast near the bow and a short mast near the stern. A yawl has its sails rigged fore-and-aft. **2** a ship's boat rowed by four or six oars. ⟨< Du. *jol*⟩

yawn [jɒn] *v., n.* *—v.* **1** open the mouth widely and inhale deeply as an involuntary effect of sleepiness, boredom, etc. **2** express with a yawn. **3** be wide open, like a yawning mouth; gape: *A wide gorge yawned beneath our feet.*
—n. **1** the act or an instance of yawning. **2** a person or thing sufficiently tiresome or boring to cause a yawn. ⟨OE *geonian*⟩
—'yawn•er, *n.*

yawp [jɒp] *v., n. Dialect or informal.* *—v.* utter a loud, harsh cry.
—n. a loud, harsh cry. ⟨imitative⟩ **—'yawp•er,** *n.*

yaws [jɒz] *n.pl. Pathology.* a contagious disease of the tropics, characterized by sores on the skin. ⟨< Carib⟩

y–axis ['waɪ ,æksɪs] *n. Geometry.* **1** in a plane Cartesian coordinate system, the vertical axis along which the ordinate is measured and from which the abscissa is measured. **2** in a three-dimensional Cartesian coordinate system, the axis along which the values of *y* are measured and at which *x* and *z* each equal zero. Compare X-AXIS, Z-AXIS.

Yb ytterbium.

Y chromosome *Biology.* one of the two chromosomes bearing the genes that determine sex in human beings and many animals. Each male body cell normally contains one Y and one X chromosome and each sperm contains either a Y or an X chromosome. If an egg cell is fertilized by a sperm with an X chromosome, the resulting embryo will be a female; if the sperm is one with a Y chromosome, the embryo will be a male. Compare X CHROMOSOME.

y•clept [ɪ'klɛpt] *adj. Archaic.* called; named; styled. Also, **ycleped.** ⟨OE *gecleopod* named⟩

yd. yard(s).

ye[1] [ji]; *unstressed,* [jɪ] *pron. Archaic, poetic, or dialect.* you (plural); the ones spoken to: *ye brooks and hills.* ⟨OE *gē*⟩

ye[2] [ði] *definite article. Archaic spelling of* THE[1].
☛ *Usage.* **Ye.** In Old and Middle English **the** was commonly written as þe. The early printers, who ordinarily did not have this consonant symbol (called 'thorn') in their fonts, substituted y for it, but this was never intended to be read with the value of *y.*

yea [jei] *adv., n., interj.* *—adv.* **1** aye; yes (*used for affirmation or assent, as in voting*). **2** *Archaic.* indeed; truly (*used to introduce a clause*). **3** *Archaic.* not only that, but even: *willing, yea eager.* **4** *Informal.* so; this: *a piece about yea big.*
—n. an affirmative vote or voter.
—interj. Informal. an exclamation used in cheering someone on: *Yea, team!* ⟨OE *gēa*⟩

yeah [jæ] *adv. Informal.* yes.

yean [jin] *v.* give birth to (a lamb or kid). ⟨OE *geēanian*; cf. *ēanian* yean, *geēan,* adj., pregnant⟩

yean•ling ['jinlɪŋ] *n.* a lamb or kid; the young of a sheep or a goat.

year [jir] *n.* **1** in the Gregorian calendar, a period of 365 or, in a leapyear, 366 days; January 1 to December 31. **2** a period of approximately the same length in other calendars. **3** 12 months reckoned from any point. A **fiscal year** is a period of 12 months at the end of which the accounts of a government, business, etc. are balanced: *We moved here five years ago this week. They came with their six-year-old daughter.* **4** the part of a year spent in a certain activity: *The school year goes from September to June.* **5** *Astronomy.* **a** the exact period of the earth's revolution around the sun. The **solar** or **astronomical year** is 365 days, 5 hours, 48 minutes, 46 seconds. **b** the time it takes for the apparent travelling of the sun from a given fixed star back to it again. The **sidereal year** is 20 minutes, 23 seconds longer than the solar year. **c** the time in which any planet completes its revolution around the sun. **d** LUNAR YEAR. **6 years,** *pl.* **a** age: *a child of tender years.* **b** a very long time: *I hadn't seen them for years.*
a year and a day, *Law.* a period constituting a term for certain purposes, in order to ensure that a full year is completed.
year by year, with each succeeding year; as years go by.
year in, year out, always; continuously: *She has always worked hard, year in, year out.* ⟨OE *gēar*⟩

year•book ['jir,bʊk] *n.* **1** a book or report published every year. **2** an annual school publication containing pictures of students and information about school activities.

year–end ['jir 'ɛnd] *n., adj.* *—n.* the end of a calendar or fiscal year.
adj. done, occurring, etc. at the end of a year.

year•ling ['jirlɪŋ] *n.* **1** an animal one year old: *The rancher decided to sell his yearlings.* **2** *Horse racing.* a horse reckoned to be one year old on January 1st of the year after foaling. A horse born on December 31st becomes a yearling the next day. **3** (*adjl.*) being a yearling: *a yearling colt.* ⟨< *year* + *-ling*⟩

year•long ['jir'lɒŋ] *adj., adv.* *—adj.* **1** lasting for a year. **2** lasting for years.
—adv. all year long: *She works yearlong.*

year•ly ['jirli] *adj., adv.* *—adj.* **1** happening, done, etc. once a year; in every year: *She takes a yearly trip to Toronto.* **2** lasting a year: *The earth makes a yearly revolution around the sun.* **3** for a year: *a yearly salary of $44 000.*
—adv. **1** once a year; annually: *A new volume comes out yearly.* **2** for a year: *She gets $34 000 yearly.*

yearn [jɜrn] *v.* **1** feel a deep longing or desire; desire earnestly: *He yearns for home.* **2** feel pity; have strong, tender feelings: *Her heart yearned for the homeless children.* ⟨OE *giernan*⟩

yearn•ing ['jɜrnɪŋ] *n., v.* *—n.* an earnest or strong desire; longing.
—v. ppr. of YEARN.

year–round ['jir 'raʊnd] *adj. or adv.* (staying, used, happening, etc.) throughout the year: *year-round residents.*

yeast [jist] *n.* **1** a yellowish, frothy substance consisting mainly of cells of very small fungi (genus *Saccharomyces* and related genera) which grow especially on the surface of liquids containing sugar, producing fermentation. Yeast is used as a leavening agent for bread, in the making of beer and other alcoholic liquors, etc. **2 a** a particular yeast (*Saccheromyces cerevisiae*) used in brewing beer. **b** yeast as a by-product of brewing, often used as a dietary supplement. **3** a single yeast cell. **4** a product containing yeast, often in the form of dried granules or a small pressed block or cake. **5** something that acts like yeast in causing activity or ferment: *the yeast of rebellion.* **6** foam; froth. **7** any fungus of genus *Saccharomyces* that may infest moist, protected areas of the human body. ⟨OE *gist*⟩

yeast•y ['jisti] *adj.* **-i•er, -i•est. 1** of, containing, or resembling yeast. **2** frothy or foamy: *yeasty waves.* **3** light or trifling; frivolous. **4** restless; agitated.

yech [jɛx], [jʌk], *or* [jʌx] *interj. Slang.* an exclamation used to express disgust, extreme distaste, etc.

yegg [jɛg] *n. Slang.* **1** a burglar who robs safes. **2** any burglar. ⟨origin uncertain⟩

yell [jɛl] *v., n.* *—v.* **1** cry out with a strong, loud sound. **2** say in a loud, strong voice: *He yelled out his instructions to the crew.*
—n. **1** a strong, loud cry. **2** a special shout or cheer, especially one used by a school or college to encourage its sports team. ⟨OE *giellan*⟩

yel•low ['jɛlou] *n., adj., v.* *—n.* **1** the colour of gold, butter, or ripe lemons. **2** a yellow pigment or dye. **3** something yellow, especially the yolk of an egg: *We used the whites of six eggs for cake and the yellows for custards.*
—adj. **1** having the colour yellow, including through age: *a yellow ball. The map was brittle and yellow.* **2** having a yellowish brown skin. **3** *Informal.* cowardly. **4** cheaply sensational: *a yellow journal.*
—v. **1** become yellow: *Paper yellows with age.* **2** make yellow: *Buttercups yellowed the field.* ⟨OE *geolu*⟩ **—'yel•lo•wy,** *adj.* **—'yel•low•ness,** *n.*

yel•low–bel•lied sapsucker ['jɛlou ,bɛlid] a sapsucker (*Sphyrapicus varius*) of Canada and the western U.S. having a red forehead patch, yellowish underparts, and a long, white wing patch. The male also has a red throat.

yel•low–bel•ly ['jɛlou ,bɛli] *n., pl.* **-lies.** someone with no courage or nerve; coward.

yel•low•bird ['jɛlou,bɜrd] *n.* any of various birds having yellow plumage, such as a North American goldfinch or the yellow warbler.

yellow cake *Cdn.* semirefined uranium ore; uranium oxide concentrate used to produce fuel elements for nuclear reactors. *Formula*: U_3O_8

yellow cypress or **cedar** a medium-large evergreen tree (*Chamaecyparis nootkatensis*) of the cypress family found along the Pacific coast of North America, usually about 25 m tall, having small, sharply pointed, scalelike leaves and small, round, reddish brown cones. The hard wood of the yellow cypress is much used for boat building.

yellow fever a dangerous, infectious disease of warm climates, caused by a virus transmitted by the bite of a mosquito and characterized by high fever, jaundice, vomiting, etc.

yel•low•ham•mer ['jɛlou,hæmər] *n.* **1** a common Eurasian bunting (*Emberiza citrinella*) having mainly yellowish plumage. **2** the yellow-shafted flicker. See FLICKER[2]. ⟨earlier *yelambre* < OE *geolu* yellow + *amore*, a kind of bird; the *h* may have resulted from the influence of obs. *yellowham* of the same meaning < OE *geolu* yellow + *hama* covering, feathers⟩

yel•low•ish ['jɛlouɪʃ] *adj.* somewhat yellow.

yellow jack 1 YELLOW FEVER. **2** a yellow flag used as a signal of quarantine.

yellow jacket any of a genus (*Vespa*) of wasps having bright yellow markings, that nest in colonies, usually in the ground.

Yel•low•knife ['jɛlou,naif] *n., pl.* **-knife** or **-knives. 1** a group of First Nations people, closely allied to the Chipewyan, originally living in the region between Great Bear Lake and Great Slave Lake to the east. **2** a member of this group. **3** the Athapascan language of these people. **4** the capital of the Northwest Territories.

yel•low•legs ['jɛlou,lɛgz] *n.* either of two North American shore birds, the **greater yellowlegs** (*Tringa melanoleuca*) and the **lesser yellowlegs** (*T. flavipes*), belonging to the sandpiper family, having yellow legs, a brownish back streaked with white, and a white breast with brown markings.

yellow metal 1 gold. **2** a yellowish alloy containing copper and zinc.

yellow no. 5 *U.S.* tartrazine.

yellow pages a telephone directory, or a part of one, printed on yellow paper, that lists and advertises firms and professionals classified by the nature of their business.

yellow perch a small freshwater food fish (*Perca flavescens*) of North America. Also called **raccoon perch, ringed perch.**

yellow pickerel WALLEYE (def. 7).

yellow pine 1 any of several species of pine having relatively hard wood, especially the **ponderosa pine. 2** the wood of any of these pines.

yellow walleye WALLEYE (def. 7).

yellow warbler a New World warbler (*Dendroica petechia*) that is common throughout much of Canada, often found nesting in shrubbery around dwellings, having mainly yellowish green plumage with bright yellow patches on the tail.

yelp [jɛlp] *n., v.* *—n.* a quick, sharp bark or cry.
—v. **1** make a quick, sharp bark or cry. **2** utter with a yelp. ⟨OE *gielpan* boast⟩

Ye•men ['jɛmən] *or* ['jeimən] *n.* a country in the S Arabian peninsula, formed from the union of the Yemen Arab Republic with the People's Democratic Republic of Yemen.

Yem•e•ni ['jɛməni] *n., adj.* *—n.* a native or inhabitant of Yemen.
—adj. of or having to do with Yemen or its inhabitants. Also, **Yemenite.**

yen¹ [jɛn] *n., pl.* **yen. 1** the basic unit of money in Japan. See table of money in the Appendix. **2** a coin worth one yen. ⟨< Japanese⟩

yen² [jɛn] *n., v.* **yenned, yen•ning.** *Informal.* *—n.* **1** a deep or fanciful desire or longing: *a yen to see the world.* **2** a desire: a *yen for Chinese food.*
—v. have a desire. ⟨< Chinese (Pekinese) *yen* opium (lit. smoke)⟩

yeo•man ['joumən] *n., pl.* **-men. 1** a naval petty officer, especially the chief signals officer on a ship. **2** *Brit.* formerly, a member of a class of people who owned a small amount of land. **3** *Archaic.* a servant or attendant of a lord or king. **4** YEOMAN OF THE GUARD.
yeoman service or **yeoman's service,** extremely valuable service or assistance. ⟨ME *yoman*; origin uncertain⟩

yeo•man•ly ['joumənli] *adj., adv.* *—adj.* having to do with or suitable for a yeoman; sturdy; honest.
—adv. like a yeoman; bravely.

yeoman of the guard in England, a member of a force once forming the sovereign's bodyguard, now having ceremonial duties and providing warders for the Tower of London; BEEFEATER (def. 2).

yeo•man•ry ['joumənri] *n.* yeomen collectively.

yer•ba bue•na ['jɛrbə 'bweinə] *or* ['jɜrbə] a creeping perennial plant (*Satureja douglasii*) of the mint family, native to the Pacific coast of North America from Los Angeles county to British Columbia. The dried leaves can be used to make a pleasant tea. ⟨< Sp., good herb⟩

yes [jɛs] *adv., n., pl.* **yes•es;** *v.* **yessed, yes•sing.** *—adv.* **1** a word used to indicate that one can or will, or that something is so; a word used to affirm, accept, or agree: *"Yes, five and two are seven," said Bob. Will you go? Yes.* **2** and what is more; in addition to that: *The soldier found that he could endure hardships, yes, even enjoy them.* **3** as an inquiry in response to being called or addressed, to mean "What is it? What would you like me to do?", etc. or as an expression of interest meaning "Oh, is it so?" or "Go on talking; I'm listening."
—n. agreement; acceptance; consent: *You have my yes to that.*
—v. say yes (to): *She yessed my request for more funds.* ⟨OE *gēse* < *gēa* yea + *sī* let it be⟩
☛ *Usage.* **Yes** and NO¹, when used as adverbs, may modify a sentence (*Yes, you're right*) or may have the value of a co-ordinate clause (*No; but you should have told me*) or may stand as complete sentences (*Do you really intend to go with him? Yes.*).

ye•shi•va [jə'ʃivə] *or* [jəʃi'vɑ] *n., pl.* **ye•shi•vas** or **ye•shi•voth** [jəʃi'vout]. **1** a Jewish school for higher studies, often a seminary for the rabbinate. **2** a Jewish day school. ⟨< Hebrew *yeshibah* sitting⟩

yes man *Slang.* a man who always agrees with his employer, superior officer, etc., in order to curry favour.

yes•ter•day ['jɛstər,dei] *or* ['jɛstərdi] *n., adv., adj.* *—n.* **1** the

day before today. **2** the recent past: *We are often amused by the fashions of yesterday.*
—adv. **1** on the day before today: *Yesterday we went to the beach.* **2** recently.
—adj. of yesterday: *yesterday afternoon.* ⟨OE *geostrandæg* < *geostran* yesterday + *dæg* day⟩

yes•ter•eve [ˌjɛstərˈiv] *n. or adv. Archaic or poetic.* yesterday evening. Also, **yesterevening.**

yes•ter•morn [ˌjɛstərˈmɔrn] *n. or adv. Archaic or poetic.* yesterday morning.

yes•ter•night [ˌjɛstərˈnəit] *n. or adv. Archaic or poetic.* last night; the night before today.

yes•ter•year [ˈjɛstərˌjir] *n. or adv. Poetic.* **1** last year; the year before this. **2** (in) recent years. ⟨coined by the poet Dante Gabriel Rossetti (1828–1882) to render the French *antan*⟩

yes•treen [jɛˈstrin] *n. or adv. Scottish.* yesterday evening.

yet [jɛt] *adv., conj. —adv.* **1** (*used with a negative or interrogative*) up to this or that time; thus far: *Are you finished yet? It was not yet dark.* **2** (*used with a negative*) at this or that time, as opposed to later on: *Don't go yet. He decided he couldn't tell her just yet.* **3** still; even: *speaking yet more loudly. Yet once more she urged them to reconsider.* **4** besides; to boot: *a huge dinner, with two desserts yet! Kind, strong, and handsome—and a doctor yet!* **5** sometime: *The thief will be caught yet.* **6** even now; in the time still remaining: *The new legislation may yet be introduced before summer recess.* **7** still at this or that time; continuing from an earlier time: *I can see it in my mind's eye yet.*
as yet, up to now.
nor yet, not even: *She hasn't bought him a gift, nor yet a card.*
—conj. but; nevertheless; however: *The work is good, yet it could be better.* ⟨OE *gīet(a)*⟩

ye•ti [ˈjɛti] *n.* ABOMINABLE SNOWMAN. ⟨< Tibetan. 20c.⟩

yew [ju] *n.* **1** any of a genus (*Taxus*) of evergreen trees and shrubs of the northern hemisphere, having broad, flat needles that are dark green above and light green below and small, red, berrylike cones. **2** the wood of the yew, especially the hard, fine-grained wood of the English yew (*T. baccata*), used in cabinetmaking and for archery bows. **3** (*adjl.*) designating the family (Taxaceae) of evergreen trees and shrubs that includes the yews. ⟨OE *īw*⟩
☛ *Hom.* EWE, YOU.

Ygg•dra•sil [ˈɪgdrəˌsɪl] *n. Norse mythology.* the ash tree that binds together earth, heaven, and hell. Also, **Ygdrasil.**

Yid•dish [ˈjɪdɪʃ] *n., adj. —n.* a language that developed from a dialect of Middle High German, written in Hebrew characters. Yiddish, which today contains many Hebrew and Slavic words, is spoken by Jews in eastern and central Europe and is much used in Jewish communities elsewhere.
—adj. having to do with this language. ⟨< G *jüdisch* Jewish⟩

yield [jild] *v., n. —v.* **1** produce; bear: *This land yields good crops. Mines yield ore.* **2** give; grant: *to yield one's consent.* **3** give up or in; submit; surrender: *The enemy yielded their fort up to our soldiers. I yielded to temptation and ate all the candy.* **4 a** give way: *The door yielded to her touch.* **b** let the other motorist(s) have the right of way. **5** give up one's place or right; defer. **6** *Archaic.* pay; reward.
—n. the amount yielded; product: *This year's yield from the silver mine was very large.* ⟨OE *gieldan* pay⟩
☛ *Syn. v.* **3. Yield,** SUBMIT = give in to someone or something. **Yield** particularly suggests giving way before, or giving up to, a stronger force and, usually, ceasing to fight against it: *The obstinate man will not yield in an argument even when he is proved wrong.* **Submit** suggests giving up all resistance and giving in to the power, will, or authority of another: *Finally she submitted to the unjust treatment. —n.* See note at CROP.

yield•ing [ˈjildɪŋ] *adj., v. —adj.* **1** not resisting; submissive: *a yielding nature.* **2** soft; giving way under weight or force: *We lay back in the yielding grass.*
—v. ppr. of YIELD.

yikes [jəiks] *interj.* an exclamation of alarm. Also, **yipe** [jəip] or **yipes.**

yin [jɪn] *n.* **1** *Taoism.* the negative cosmic force; the counterpart to the yang. **2** *Chinese philosophy.* the female principle, passive and negative, the source of dark, complementary to and contrasting with the yang. Compare YANG.

yip [jɪp] *v.* **yipped, yip•ping;** *n. Informal. —v.* especially of dogs, bark or yelp briskly.
—n. a sharp barking sound. ⟨imitative⟩

-yl *suffix. Chemistry.* denoting a radical such as *ethyl* or *hydroxyl.* ⟨< Gk. *hylē* wood, material⟩

y•lang–y•lang [ˈilæŋ ˈilæŋ] *n.* See ILANG-ILANG.

YMCA or **Y.M.C.A.** Young Men's Christian Association.

YMHA or **Y.M.H.A.** Young Men's Hebrew Association.

Y•mir [ˈimir] *n. Norse mythology.* a giant from whose body the gods made the universe.

yod [jɒd] *n.* the eleventh letter of the Hebrew alphabet. See table of alphabets in the Appendix.

yo•del [ˈjoudəl] *v.* **-delled** or **-deled, -del•ling** or **-del•ing;** *n. —v.* sing or call with frequent, sudden changes from the ordinary voice pitch to a much higher pitch or to a falsetto in the manner of mountaineers of Switzerland and Tyrol.
—n. the act or sound of yodelling. Also, **yodle.** ⟨< G *jodeln*⟩ **—'yo•del•ler** or **'yo•de•ler,** *n.*

yo•dle [ˈjoudəl] *v.* **-dled, -dling;** *n.* See YODEL. **—'yo•dler,** *n.*

yo•ga or **Yo•ga** [ˈjougə] *n.* a system to improve the condition of the body under the control of the mind and spirit through the practice of slow, rhythmic body movements, controlled breathing exercises, and complete relaxation of the body and the mind. Yoga originated in India about 6000 years ago as one of the six systems of Hindu philosophy. ⟨< Hind. < Skt. *yoga* union⟩ **—'yo•gic,** *adj.*

yo•gi [ˈjougi] *n., pl.* **-gis.** one who practises or follows yoga.

yo•gurt [ˈjougərt] *n.* a semisolid food made from milk fermented by a bacterial culture and often sweetened and flavoured with honey, fruit, etc. Also, **yoghurt, yoghourt.** ⟨< Turkish *yōghurt*⟩

yo–heave–ho [ˈjou ˈhiv ˈhou] *interj.* an exclamation formerly used by sailors in pulling or lifting together.

yoke [jouk] *n., v.* **yoked, yok•ing.** *—n.* **1** a wooden frame which fits around the neck of two work animals to fasten them together for pulling a plough or vehicle. **2** a pair fastened together by a yoke: *The plough was drawn by a yoke of oxen.* **3** any frame connecting two other parts: *The man carried two buckets on a yoke, one at each end.* **4** *Electronics.* a collection of coils and magnetic material placed around the neck of a cathode-ray tube and producing and controlling the scanning motion of the electron beam. **5** a separate upper section of a shirt, blouse, etc. that fits closely over the shoulder area and to which the main part of the bodice is attached. **6** a separate upper section of a skirt, fitting closely about the hips and to which the main part of the skirt is pleated or gathered. **7** a modified crosshead used instead of a connecting rod between the piston and crankshaft in certain small engines. **8** a crossbar at the top of a rudder of a boat, and having two lines or ropes attached for steering. **9** a crossbar connecting the tongue of a wagon, carriage, etc. to the collars of two horses, mules, etc. **10** *Electricity.* a magnetic bar connecting the poles of an electromagnet and not having a coil winding. **11** among the ancient Romans and others: **a** a contrivance similar to a yoke for oxen, etc. placed on the neck of a captive. **b** a symbol of this consisting of two upright spears with a third placed across them, under which captives were forced to walk. **12** something that binds together: *the yoke of marriage.* **13** something that holds people in slavery or submission: *Throw off your yoke and be free.* **14** rule; dominion: *Slaves are under their master's yoke.*
—v. **1** put a yoke on; fasten with a yoke. **2** harness or fasten a work animal or animals to: *The farmer yoked her plough.* **3** join; unite: *to be yoked in marriage.* ⟨OE *geoc*⟩
☛ *Hom.* YOLK.

yoke•fel•low [ˈjoukˌfɛlou] *n. Archaic or poetic.* a close companion, partner, or mate.

yo•kel [ˈjoukəl] *n.* a person who lives in or comes from a rural area and is perceived as being simple, backward, etc. ⟨origin uncertain⟩

yolk[1] [jouk] *n.* **1** the yellow and principal substance of an egg, as distinguished from the white. **2** the corresponding part in any animal ovum, which serves for the nutrition of the embryo. ⟨OE *geolca* < *geolu* yellow⟩
☛ *Hom.* YOKE.

yolk[2] [jouk] *n.* the fat or grease in sheep's wool. ⟨? < earlier *yoak* < OE **ēowoca*, from Gmc. root of OE *ēowu* ewe; influenced by *yolk*[1]⟩
☛ *Hom.* YOKE.

yolk sac **1** in birds, reptiles, and fish, a membranous sac containing yolk, growing from the ventral surface of the embryo. **2** a corresponding organ in the embryo of a mammal, but containing no yolk and becoming vestigial early in the embryo's development.

Yom Kip•pur [jɒm ˈkɪpər] *or* [jɒm kɪˈpʊr] *Judaism.* the Day of Atonement, an annual day of fasting and atoning for sin, observed on the tenth day of the month of Tishri, which is the first month of the Jewish civil year. ⟨< Hebrew *yōm kippūr*⟩

yon [jɒn] *adj., adv., pron. —adj. or adv. Archaic or dialect* (*except in* **hither and yon**). yonder.
hither and yon. See HITHER.
—pron. Esp. Brit. the one yonder: *Yon's the best man for the job.* ⟨OE *geon*⟩

yond [jɒnd] *adj. or adv. Archaic or dialect.* yonder. ⟨OE *geond*⟩

yon•der ['jɒndər] *adv., adj. —adv.* within sight, but not near; over there: *Look yonder.*
—adj. **1** situated over there; being within sight, but not near: *She lives in yonder cottage.* **2** farther; more distant; other: *There is snow on the yonder side of the mountains.* ⟨ME, extension of *yond*; cf. Gothic *jaindrē*⟩

yore [jɔr] *n. Archaic or poetic.*
of yore, of long ago; of time long past: *in days of yore.* ⟨OE *geāra*, gen. pl. of *gēar* year⟩
☛ *Hom.* YOUR.

York [jɔrk] *n.* **1** the royal house of England from 1461 to 1485. Its emblem was a white rose. **2** the name of Toronto from 1793 to 1834.

A York boat

York boat *Cdn.* formerly, a type of heavy freight vessel developed by the Hudson's Bay Company at York Factory on Hudson Bay, used especially on inland waterways from about 1820 to 1930, when the last one was retired from service.

York•ist ['jɔrkɪst] *n., adj. —n.* an adherent or member of the English royal family of York, especially at the time of the Wars of the Roses (1455-1485).
—adj. of or having to do with the English royal family of York.

York rite one of the two advanced divisions of Masonic membership, leading to the Knights Templar degree. Compare SCOTTISH RITE.

York•shire pudding ['jɔrkʃər] in traditional British cuisine, a light, puffy, baked dish made from a batter of flour, milk, and eggs, and usually served with roast beef. ⟨< *Yorkshire*, a county in N England⟩

Yorkshire terrier a breed of small dog having long, silky, greyish blue hair.

Yo•ru•ba ['jɔrʊbə] *n.* **1** a people of western Nigeria and neighbouring areas. **2** their Niger-Congo language.

you [ju]; *unstressed,* [jə] *pron. sing. or pl., subj. or obj.* **you,** *poss.* **yours. 1** the person or persons spoken to: *Are you ready? I'll bring you the book tomorrow.* **2** one; anybody: *You press this button to turn it on. You never can tell. His lectures put you to sleep.* ⟨OE *ēow*, dat. and accus. of *gē* ye[1]⟩
☛ *Usage.* The use of **you** and **your** to refer to people in general is common in speech: *The pay is good if you can stand the long hours.* In formal writing, however, most people prefer **one** or some other impersonal construction: *This work develops one's powers of concentration.* The important thing is to be consistent; avoid using **you** and **one** for the same purpose in the same piece of writing.
☛ *Hom.* EWE, YEW.

you'd [jud], *unstressed,* [jəd] **1** you had: *You'd better go quickly.* **2** you would: *You'd like this story.*

you'll [jul]; *unstressed,* [jəl] you will.
☛ *Hom.* YULE.

young [jʌŋ] *adj.* **young•er** ['jʌŋgər], **young•est** ['jʌŋgɪst]; *n.*
—adj. **1** in the early part of life or growth; not old: *A puppy is a young dog.* **2** having the looks or qualities of youth or a young person; youthful; lively: *She looks and acts young for her age.* **3** of youth; early: *one's young days.* **4** not so old as another of the same name: *Young Mr. Jones worked for his mother.* **5** in an early stage; not far advanced: *The night was still young when we left the party.* **6** without much experience or practice: *He was too young in the business to be successful.* **7** representing or advocating recent or progressive tendencies.
—n. **1** young offspring: *An animal will fight to protect its young.* **2 the young,** *pl.* young people.
with young, pregnant. ⟨OE *geong*⟩
☛ *Syn. adj.* **1-3. Young,** YOUTHFUL, JUVENILE = of or pertaining to persons in the early part of life. **Young** emphasizes age, being in the early part of life: *too young to marry.* **Youthful** emphasizes having the qualities of a young person, especially freshness and vitality: *youthful vigour and enthusiasm.* **Juvenile** stresses immaturity, and describes things having to do with young people: *juvenile behaviour, a juvenile novel.*

young blood 1 young people. **2** youthful vigour, energy, enthusiasm, etc.

young•ish ['jʌŋɪʃ] *adj.* rather young.

young•ling ['jʌŋlɪŋ] *n., adj. Poetic. —n.* **1** a young person, animal, or plant. **2** a novice; beginner.
—adj. young; youthful. ⟨OE *geongling*⟩

young•ster ['jʌŋstər] *or* ['jʌŋkstər] *n.* **1** a child: *She is a lively youngster.* **2** a young person: *They have hired several youngsters for the summer.*

young turk [tɜrk] **1** one of a group wishing or seeking to reform or take control of a political party, organization, country, etc. **2** someone who aggressively supports progressive or reformist tactics.

youn•ker ['jʌŋkər] *n. Archaic.* a young fellow. ⟨< MDu. *jonckher, jonchere* < *jonc* young + *here* lord, master⟩

your [jɔr] *or* [jʊr]; *unstressed,* [jər] *adj.* **1** a possessive form of YOU: of, belonging to, or made or done by you or yourself: *Give me your hand. Is this your pen? We enjoyed your visit.* **2** of, having to do with, or belonging to anybody or to people in general: *The government guarantees your basic freedoms.* **3** *Informal.* that you know or speak of: *your real lover of music, your modern girl.* **4 Your,** a word used as part of certain formal titles when using the title to address the person holding it: *Your Highness, Your Ladyship, Your Worship.* ⟨OE *ēower*, gen. of *gē* ye[1]⟩
☛ *Hom.* YORE [jɔr], YOU'RE [jʊr].

you're [jʊr]; *unstressed,* [jər] you are.
☛ *Hom.* YOUR.

yours [jɔrz] *or* [jʊrz] *pron. sing and pl.* **1** a possessive form of YOU: that which belongs to you: *I think this scarf is yours. I don't like our set as well as yours.* **2** at your service: *yours sincerely. I am yours to command.*
of yours, belonging to or having to do with you: *Is she a friend of yours?*

your•self [jər'sɛlf] *pron., pl.* **-selves. 1** a reflexive pronoun, the form of YOU used as an object when it refers to the same person as the subject: *You will hurt yourself if you aren't careful.* **2** a form of YOU added for emphasis: *You yourself know the story is not true.* **3** your usual self: *Come see us when you feel better and are yourself again.*

yours truly 1 a phrase often used at the end of a letter, before the signature. **2** *Informal.* I; me.

youth [juθ] *n., pl.* **youths** [juðz] *or* [juθs] or (*collectively*) **youth. 1** the fact or quality of being young: *He has the vigour of youth.* **2** the appearance, freshness, vigour, or some other quality characteristic of the young: *She keeps her youth well.* **3** the time between childhood and adulthood. **4** a young man. **5** young people collectively (*used with a singular or plural verb*). **6** the first or early stage of anything; the early period of growth or development: *during the youth of this country.* ⟨OE *geoguth*⟩

youth•ful ['juθfəl] *adj.* **1** young. **2** of youth; suitable for young people: *Everyone admired her youthful enthusiasm.* **3** having the looks or qualities of youth; fresh and lively: *The old man had a happy and youthful spirit.* **4** early; new. **—'youth•ful•ly,** *adv.* **—'youth•ful•ness,** *n.*
☛ *Syn.* **2.** See note at YOUNG.

youth hostel a supervised, inexpensive lodging place for travelling young people, usually one of a system of such places.

you've [juv]; *unstressed,* [jəv] you have: *You've gone too far.*

yowl [jaʊl] *n., v. —n.* a long, distressful, or dismal cry; howl.
—v. howl. ⟨imitative⟩

yo–yo ['joujou] *n., pl.* **-yos;** *adj. —n.* **1** a small wheel-shaped toy made of two disks, usually wooden, joined by a central peg around which a string is wound. The toy is spun out and reeled in on the string, one end of which is looped around the player's finger. **2** *Slang.* a dull, stupid person, especially one who is silly, gullible, or easily manipulated.
—adj. Informal. fluctuating between extremes: *yo-yo dieting.* ⟨< *Yoyo*, a trademark; origin uncertain⟩

yr. 1 year(s). **2** your; yours.

yrs. 1 years. **2** yours.

YT YUKON TERRITORY (*used esp. in computerized address systems*).

Y.T. YUKON TERRITORY.

yt•ter•bi•a [ɪ'tɜrbiə] *n. Chemistry.* a heavy, white substance that forms colourless salts. Also called **ytterbium oxide.** *Formula*: Yb_2O_3

yt•ter•bi•um [ɪ'tɜrbiəm] *n. Chemistry.* a rare metallic chemical element belonging to the YTTRIUM GROUP. *Symbol*: Yb; *at.no.* 70; *at.mass* 173.04. ⟨< NL *yttrium*, ult. < *Ytterby*, a town in Sweden⟩

yt•tri•a ['ɪtriə] *n. Chemistry.* a heavy, insoluble white powder, used in electronics. Also called **yttrium oxide.** *Formula*: Y_2O_3

yt•tri•um ['ɪtriəm] *n. Chemistry.* a rare metallic chemical element. Compounds of yttrium are used for incandescent gas mantles. *Symbol*: Y; *at.no.* 39; *at.mass* 88.91. ⟨< NL *yttrium*, ult. < *Ytterby*, a town in Sweden⟩

yttrium group a series of related metallic elements including yttrium, holmium, erbium, thulium, ytterbium, lutetium, terbium, gadolinium, and dysprosium.

yu•an [ju'ɑn] *n., pl.* **yu•an. 1** the basic unit of money in the People's Republic of China, divided into 10 chiao and 100 fen. See table of money in the Appendix. **2** the basic unit of money in Taiwan, divided into 10 chiao and 100 cents. **3** a coin or note worth one yuan. ⟨< Chinese *yüan* round, a circle⟩

Yu•ca•tec ['jukə,tɛk] *n.* **1** a member of an Indian people of the Yucatán Peninsula in Mexico. **2** the Mayan language of these people. **–,Yu•ca'tec•an,** *adj.*

yuc•ca ['jʌkə] *n.* any of a tropical and subtropical American genus (*Yucca*) of plants of the lily family having long, stiff, sword-shaped leaves and a single erect cluster of large, white, lilylike flowers. ⟨< NL < Sp. *yuca*⟩

yuck [jʌk] *interj., n. Slang. –interj.* an expression of disgust or distaste.
–n. something unpleasant, disgusting, or distasteful: *That pizza was a real yuck.* **–'yuck•y,** *adj.*
☛ *Hom.* YUK.

yuk [yʌk] *n., v.* **yukked, yuk•king.** *Slang. –n.* **1** a loud and hearty laugh. **2** something evoking such a laugh.
–v. laugh loudly and heartily.
☛ *Hom.* YUCK.

Yu•kon•er ['jukɒnər] *n.* a native or long-term resident of the Yukon Territory.

Yu•kon Territory ['jukɒn] a territory of Canada, north of British Columbia.

Yule or **yule** [jul] *n. Archaic or poetic.* Christmas; Christmastime. ⟨ME < OE *geol, iul* a festival held at the time of the winter solstice⟩
☛ *Hom.* YOU'LL.

Yule log 1 a large log burned at Christmas, originally one that burned as the base of a fire throughout the Christmas season. **2** a Christmas confection made of ice cream, cake, and icing, decorated to resemble a Yule log.

Yule•tide or **yule•tide** ['jul,taɪd] *n., adj. Archaic or poetic.*
–n. Christmastime; the Christmas season.
–adj. of Christmastime: *Yuletide cheer.*

yum•my ['jʌmi] *adj., n., pl.* **-mies;** *interj. Slang. –adj.* delighting the senses, especially the taste; delicious.
–n. something very tasty or delicious.
–interj. an exclamation expressing pleasure or delight at the taste of something. ⟨< *yum* exclamation of pleasure + *-y*[1]⟩

Yup•pie or **yup•pie** ['jʌpi] *n.* a young urban professional, regarded as a member of a social class characterized by similar tastes, values, etc.

yurt [jʊrt] *n.* a portable, domed tent made of felt stretched over a framework of branches, used by the Mongolian nomads of Siberia. ⟨< Russian *yurta* < Turkic⟩

YWCA or **Y.W.C.A.** Young Women's Christian Association.

YWHA or **Y.W.H.A.** Young Women's Hebrew Association.

y•wis [ɪ'wɪs] *adv. Archaic.* certainly; indeed; iwis. ⟨OE *gewis*, ult. < Gmc. *wid- know⟩

Z z Z z

z or **Z** [zɛd] *n., pl.* **z's** or **Z's. 1** the twenty-sixth and last letter of the English alphabet. **2** any speech sound represented by this letter. **3** a person or thing identified as *z*, especially the twenty-sixth of a series or the last in a series consisting of x, y, and z. **4** *z, Algebra.* an unknown quantity. **5** something shaped like the letter Z. **6** (*adjl.*) of or being a Z or z. **7** **Z**, the Roman numeral for 2000. **8** something, such as a printer's type, a lever, or a key on a keyboard, that produces a z or Z.

z. or **Z.** zone.

Z ATOMIC NUMBER.

zad•dick ['tsɑdɪk] *n., pl.* **zad•dik•im** [tsɑ'dikɪm]. **1** an outstandingly just and virtuous person. **2** the leader of a Hasidic group or community. ⟨< Hebrew *tsadike* to be right⟩

zaf•fre or **zaf•fer** ['zæfər] *n.* an artificial mixture of impure oxides of cobalt and, usually, silica, resembling smalt and used to produce a blue colour in ceramic glazes and glass. ⟨< F *zafre*; ult. origin uncertain⟩

zag [zæg] *n., v.* **zagged, zag•ging.** *—n.* one of the two directions involved in a zigzag pattern, course, etc.
—v. move in one of these directions: *We zigged and zagged to avoid the potholes in the road.* Compare ZIG.

zai•bat•su ['zaɪbɑt'su] *n.pl. or sing.* the leading families of Japan, who direct its industries. ⟨< Japanese *zai* property + *batsu* family⟩

za•ire or **za•ïre** [zɑ'ir] *n., pl.* **zaire** or **zaïre. 1** the basic unit of money in Zaire, divided into 100 makuta (*singular* likuta). See table of money in the Appendix. **2** a note worth one zaire.

Za•ire [zɑ'ir] *n.* an independent country in central Africa, formerly the Democratic Republic of the Congo. See SUDAN for map. **—Za'ir•i•an,** *adj.*

Zam•bia ['zæmbiə] *n.* an independent country in east central Africa, formerly called Northern Rhodesia. **—'Zam•bi•an,** *adj.*

Zam•bo•ni [zæm'bouni] *n. Trademark.* an apparatus for scraping off the surface of an ice rink and laying down a new surface in a single operation.

za•ny ['zeini] *adj.* **-i•er, -i•est;** *n., pl.* **-nies.** *—adj.* comically foolish or absurd.
—n. **1** a zany person. **2** formerly, in old comedies, an assistant clown or buffoon who tried to mimic the principal clown. ⟨< F < dial. Ital. *zanni*, originally var. of *Giovanni* John⟩ **—'za•ni•ly,** *adv.* **—'za•ni•ness,** *n.*

zap [zæp] *interj., n., v.* **zapped, zap•ping.** *Slang. —interj.* a word used to express or indicate a sudden, swift happening: *I was just standing there when—zap—something hit me on the head.*
—n. the sound of a sudden slap, blow, blast, etc.
—v. **1** hit with a hard blow. **2** kill. **3** beat; defeat. **4** move very fast; zip; zoom. **5** delete (commercials) while videotaping a television program. **6** heat quickly in a microwave oven.

Zap•o•tec ['zæpə,tɛk] *n., adj., —n.* **1** a member of an Indian people of Oaxaca state in southern Mexico. **2** the Oto-Manguean language of these people.
—adj. **1** of or having to do with these people, their culture, or their language. **2** *Archaeology.* of or having to do with a Mesoamerican Indian civilization.

Zar•a•thus•tra [,zɑrə'θustrə] *n.* ZOROASTER. **—,Zar•a'thus•tri•an,** *adj.*

zar•zue•la [zɑr'zweilə] *n.* a type of Spanish opera having spoken dialogue and often a topical theme treated satirically or comically. ⟨< Sp., after *La Zarzuela,* palace in Madrid where originally performed⟩

za•stru•gi [zə'strugi] *n.pl.* See SASTRUGI.

z-axis ['zɛd ,æksɪs] *n. Geometry.* in a three-dimensional Cartesian coordinate system, the axis along which values of *z* are measured, and at which *x* and *y* each equal zero. Compare X-AXIS, Y-AXIS.

za•yin ['zɑjin] *n.* the eighth letter of the Hebrew alphabet. See table of alphabets in the Appendix.

zeal [zil] *n.* intense or fervent devotion to or enthusiasm for something or someone, as displayed in action. ⟨ME < LL < Gk. *zēlos* < *zēein* to boil⟩

zeal•ot ['zɛlət] *n.* **1** a person who shows too much zeal; a fanatic. **2** **Zealot,** a member of a radical, intensely patriotic Jewish political sect which advocated the overthrow of the Roman domination of Palestine until c. A.D. 70. ⟨< L *zelotes* < Gk. *zēlōtēs* < *zēlos* zeal⟩

zeal•ot•ry ['zɛlətri] *n.* too great zeal; fanaticism.

zeal•ous ['zɛləs] *adj.* full of zeal; eager; earnest; enthusiastic: *The children made zealous efforts to clean up the house for the party.* ⟨< Med.L *zelosus* < L *zelus* < Gk.⟩ **—'zeal•ous•ly,** *adv.* **—'zeal•ous•ness,** *n.*

ze•bec or **ze•beck** ['zibɛk] *n.* See XEBEC.

A zebra

ze•bra ['zibrə] *or* ['zɛbrə] *n.* any of several wild mammals (genus *Equus*) of Africa, closely related to and resembling the horse and donkey but marked with conspicuous black or brown stripes on a white or light tan background. ⟨< Portuguese < Bantu⟩ **—'zeb•rine** ['zibraɪn] *or* ['zibrɪn], *adj.*

ze•bu ['zibju] *or* ['zibu] *n.* any of numerous breeds of domestic cattle originally developed in India from an Asiatic wild ox (*Bos indicus*) closely related to the aurochs (the ancestor of European cattle), all breeds being characterized by a hump over the shoulders, a long head, and loose folds of skin hanging from the throat and chest. Zebus are widely used in tropical Africa, Asia, and South America as draft animals and for milk and meat. ⟨< F⟩

zech•in ['zɛkɪn] *n.* SEQUIN (def. 2).

zed [zɛd] *n.* the name of the letter Z. ⟨< F *zède* < LL < Gk. *zēta*⟩

Zee•man effect ['zeimɑn] *Physics. Optics.* the division of a spectral line or lines as a result of the placement of a radiation source in a magnetic field. A split into two or three equally spaced lines is a **normal Zeeman effect,** while a split into three or more unequally spaced lines is an **anomalous Zeeman effect.** ⟨after Pieter *Zeeman* (1865-1943), a Dutch physicist⟩

Zeit•geist ['tsaɪt,gaɪst] *n. German.* a pattern of thought or feeling characteristic of a particular period of time. ⟨< G *Zeit* time + *Geist* spirit⟩

zem•stvo ['zɛmstvou] *n., pl.* **-vos.** in Imperial Russia, a local assembly managing the affairs of a district. ⟨< Russian *zemstvo* < *zemlya* country⟩

ze•na•na [zɛ'nɑnə] *n.* in India and Persia, the part of a house set aside for the women. ⟨< Hind. < Persian *zanāna* < *zan* woman⟩

Zen (Buddhism) [zɛn] *n.* **1** a mystical Japanese form of Buddhism that emphasizes contemplation and solitary study to achieve self-discipline and intuitive spiritual enlightenment. **2** (*adjl.*) of, having to do with, or designating this religion. ⟨< Japanese *zen* contemplation⟩

Zen Buddhist a believer in or follower of Zen.

Zend [zɛnd] *n.* **1** *Zoroastrianism.* the translation of the Avesta into Pahlavi or Middle Persian. **2** the old name for the Avestan language, closely related to Old Persian.

Zend-A•ves•ta ['zɛnd ə'vɛstə] *n.* the sacred writings of the Zoroastrian religion.

ze•nith ['zinɪθ] *or* ['zɛnɪθ] *n.* **1** the point in the heavens directly overhead. See NADIR for picture. **2** the highest or greatest point: *At the zenith of its power Rome ruled the whole of civilized Europe.* ⟨ME < OF or Med.L *senit* < Arabic *samt* (*ar-rās*) the way (over the head)⟩

ze•o•lite ['ziə,laɪt] *n.* any of various minerals consisting of hydrous silicates of aluminum, lime, and sodium, usually found in veins or cavities of basaltic rock. ⟨< Swedish *zeolit* < Gk. *zēein* to boil + *-lite*, because it swells or boils under a blowpipe⟩

zeph•yr ['zɛfər] *n.* **1** the west wind. **2** any soft, gentle wind; mild breeze. **3** a fine, soft yarn or worsted fabric. ⟨< L < Gk. *zephyros*⟩

Zeph•y•rus ['zɛfərəs] *n. Greek mythology.* the personification of the west wind, thought of as the most gentle of gods.

Zep•pe•lin or **zep•pe•lin** ['zɛpələn] *n.* an early type of airship shaped like a cigar with pointed ends, having compartments for gas, engines, passengers, etc. ⟨after Count Ferdinand von *Zeppelin* (1838-1917), a German airship builder⟩

ze•ro ['zirou] *n., pl.* **-ros** or **-roes;** *adj., v.* **-roed, -ro•ing.** —*n.* **1** nought; the figure 0: *There are three zeros in 40 006.* **2** the point marked as 0 on the scale of a thermometer, etc. A Celsius thermometer reads up and down from zero. **3** the temperature that corresponds to zero on the scale of a thermometer: *The forecast is zero. Water freezes at zero.* **4** the complete absence of quantity; nothing. **5** the lowest point: *The team's spirit sank to zero after its third defeat.* **6** a sight setting on a gun that takes into account wind and elevation.
—*adj.* **1** of or at zero: *a zero score.* **2** not any; none at all: *a zero chance of survival, zero gravity.* **3** *Meteorology. Aeronautics.* **a** designating a cloud ceiling limiting visibility to 15 m or less. **b** designating a horizontal visibility of 50 m or less. **4** *Linguistics.* designating a hypothetical morphological form having no realization as a sequence of phonemes. The plural of *sheep* requires the zero allomorph.
—*v.* adjust (an instrument or device) to a zero point or line or to any given point from which readings will then be measured.
zero in, adjust the sights of (a rifle) for a given range so a bullet will strike the centre of the target.
zero in on, a locate as a target; get the range of by adjusting the sights of a firearm, etc. **b** direct attention or focus with precision toward. ⟨< Ital. < Arabic *sifr* empty. Doublet of CIPHER.⟩

zero gravity a condition in which gravity appears not to operate, as with objects in outer space; weightlessness.

zero hour 1 the time for beginning an attack, etc. **2** any point in time viewed as similar to this; crucial moment.

zero magnitude *Astronomy.* a degree of brilliance indicating a brightness 2½ times greater than that of first magnitude stars.

ze•ro–ze•ro ['zirou 'zirou] *adj. Aeronautics. Meteorology.* of or having to do with atmospheric conditions in which visibility is reduced to zero in both vertical and horizontal directions.

zest [zɛst] *n., v.* —*n.* **1** keen enjoyment; relish: *The hungry child ate with zest. She has a great zest for life.* **2** a pleasant or exciting quality, flavour, etc.: *Wit gives zest to conversation.* **3** the thin, outer peel of a citrus fruit, used as flavouring.
—*v.* give an exciting flavour or quality to (*usually used with* **up**). ⟨< F *zeste* orange or lemon peel⟩ **—'zest•y,** *adj.*

zest•ful ['zɛstfəl] *adj.* characterized by zest. **—'zest•ful•ly,** *adv.* **—'zest•ful•ness,** *n.*

ze•ta ['zeitə] *or* ['zitə] *n.* the sixth letter (Z, ζ = English Z, z) of the Greek alphabet.

zeug•ma ['zugmə] *n.* a figure of speech in which one word governs or modifies two or more others that are normally related to the first in different ways. *Example*: *She put out the cat and the light.*

Zeus [zus] *n. Greek mythology.* the king of the gods and of humankind and husband of Hera. Zeus corresponds to the Roman god Jupiter.

zig [zɪg] *n., v.* **zigged, zig•ging.** —*n.* one of the two directions involved in a zigzag pattern, course, etc.
—*v.* move in this direction: *We zigged and zagged to avoid the potholes in the road.* Compare ZAG.

zig•gu•rat ['zɪgə,ræt] *n.* an ancient Assyrian or Babylonian temple in the form of a pyramid of terraced towers. Also, **zikkurat.** ⟨< Akkadian *ziqqurata* pinnacle, tower⟩

A zigzag design

zig•zag ['zɪg,zæg] *adj., adv., v.* **-zagged, -zag•ging;** *n.*
—*adj.* with short, sharp turns, from one side to the other: *to go in a zigzag course.*
—*adv.* turning sharply from one side to the other: *The path ran zigzag up the hill.*
—*v.* move in a zigzag way: *Lightning zigzagged across the sky.*
—*n.* **1** a zigzag line or course. **2** a sequence of two or more sharp turns first to one side and then the other. ⟨< F⟩

zigzag fence *Cdn.* a SNAKE FENCE, usually one made of split rails.

zik•ku•rat ['zɪkə,ræt] *n.* See ZIGGURAT.

zilch [zɪltʃ] *n. Slang.* nothing; zero. ⟨originally a character in the magazine *Ballyhoo,* in the 1930s⟩

zil•li•on ['zɪlijən] *n. Informal.* an extremely large but indefinite number. ⟨formed by analogy with *million, billion,* etc.⟩

Zim•bab•we [zɪm'bɒbwei] *n.* a country in east central Africa, formerly called Southern Rhodesia. **—Zim'bab•we•an,** *adj.*

zinc [zɪŋk] *n., v.* **zincked** or **zinced** [zɪŋkt], **zinck•ing** or **zinc•ing** ['zɪŋkɪŋ]. —*n. Chemistry.* a bluish white metallic chemical element that, at ordinary temperatures, is little affected by air and moisture. Zinc is used as a roofing material, in battery electrodes, in paint, in medicine, and for coating some metals. *Symbol*: Zn; *at.no.* 30; *at.mass* 65.38.
—*v.* coat or cover with zinc. ⟨< G *Zink*⟩

zinc chloride *Chemistry.* a white, crystalline, water-soluble poisonous solid used as a wood preservative, antiseptic and disinfectant, and in the manufacture of adhesives, embalming fluids, etc. *Formula*: $ZnCl_2$

zinc ointment *Pharmacy.* a salve containing zinc oxide, used especially in treating skin disorders.

zinc oxide *Chemistry. Pharmacy.* an insoluble white powder used in making paint, rubber, glass, cosmetics, ointments, etc. Also called **zinc white, Chinese white**. *Formula*: ZnO

zinc sulphate *Chemistry.* a colourless, water-soluble powder used in medicine as an astringent, emetic, and styptic, and otherwise in wood and skin preservation, in the bleaching of paper, and as a mordant in dyeing, etc. *Formula*: $ZnSO_4 \cdot 7H_2O$

zinc sulphide *Chemistry.* a yellowish white to yellow crystalline powder, soluble in acids but not in water, used chiefly as a phosphor on X-ray or television screens. *Formula*: ZnS

zing [zɪŋ] *n., v.* —*n.* **1** a sharp humming sound. **2** spirit; vitality; liveliness; zest.
—*v.* make a sharp humming sound, especially in going fast: *A bullet zinged by her ear.* ⟨imitative⟩

zin•ga•ro ['tsiŋgaro] *n., pl.* **-ri** [-ri]. *Italian.* a gypsy.

zing•er ['zɪŋər] *n.* a person, remark, etc. showing spirit or zest.

zin•ni•a ['zɪniə] *or* ['zɪnjə] *n.* any of a genus (*Zinnia*) of tropical and subtropical American plants of the composite family, cultivated in many varieties for their showy flower heads. ⟨< NL; after Johann G. *Zinn* (1727-1759), a German botanist⟩

Zi•on ['zaɪən] *n.* **1** the hill in Jerusalem on which the royal palace and the temple were built, used as a symbol of the city itself. **2** the land of Israel; the people of Israel. **3** heaven; the heavenly city. **4** the church or Kingdom of God. Also, **Sion.** ⟨OE *Sion* < LL < Gk. *Seōn* < Hebrew *tsīyōn* hill⟩

Zi•on•ism ['zaɪə,nɪzəm] *n.* a movement, begun in the late 19th century, to make modern Palestine (now Israel) a Jewish national state; now, a movement supporting this state.

Zi•on•ist ['zaɪənɪst] *n.* an advocate of Zionism.

Zi•on•is•tic [,zaɪə'nɪstɪk] *adj.* of, having to do with, or resembling Zionism.

zip [zɪp] *n., v.* **zipped, zip•ping.** —*n.* **1** a sudden, brief hissing sound, as of a flying bullet. **2** *Informal.* energy or vim. **3** *Esp. Brit.* a zipper. **4** *Informal.* nothing; zero; a score of nil: *I did all that work and got zip for it. The score was 4-zip.*
—*v.* **1** make a sudden, brief hissing sound. **2** *Informal.* act, go, etc. with speed and energy. **3** fasten or close the zipper of (*often with* **up**): *She zipped up her jacket.* **4** be fastened or unfastened by means of a zipper: *This jumpsuit zips up the back.* ⟨imitative⟩

Zi•pan•gu [zɪ'pæŋgu] *n.* Marco Polo's name for Japan.

zip code 1 a system for addressing and sorting mail in the United States, in which a five-digit identifying number is assigned to each postal delivery area in the country. **2** an identifying number in this system. Some zip codes have more than five digits. ⟨< *Z*one *I*mprovement *P*lan⟩

zip gun *n.* a homemade toy pistol or gun consisting of a piece of tubing, a wooden handle, and a rubber band or spring to fire the bullet.

zip•per ['zɪpər] *n., v.* —*n.* a flexible fastening device for clothing, boots, cushion covers, etc., consisting of two parallel rows of plastic or metal coils or teeth on either side of an opening, and a sliding tab that either interlocks or opens them when pulled.
—*v.* ZIP (def. 3, 4). ⟨< *Zipper*, a trademark⟩

zip•pered ['zɪpərd] *adj., v. —adj.* equipped with a zipper: *a zippered jacket.*
—v. pt. and pp. of ZIPPER.

zip•py ['zɪpi] *adj.* **-pi•er, -pi•est.** *Informal.* full of energy; lively; quick.

zir•con ['zɜrkɒn] *n.* **1** a crystalline mineral consisting of zirconium silicate, that occurs in various forms and colours. *Formula*: $ZrSiO_4$ **2** a gem made from this mineral. ⟨probably < F < Arabic *zarqūn*⟩

zir•co•nia [zər'kouniə] *n. Chemistry.* ZIRCONIUM OXIDE.

zir•co•ni•um [zər'kouniəm] *n. Chemistry.* a rare, ductile, metallic chemical element used in alloys for wires, filaments, and for cladding for nuclear fuel, etc. *Symbol*: Zr; *at.no.* 40; *at.mass* 91.22. ⟨< NL⟩

zirconium oxide *Chemistry.* a heavy, white, infusible, water-soluble powder used in the manufacture of paints, refractory crucibles, furnace linings, etc. *Formula*: ZrO_2

zith•er ['zɪðər] *n.* a musical instrument having 30 to 40 strings over a flat sounding board, played with a plectrum and the fingers. ⟨< G *Zither* < L *cithara* < Gk. *kithara.* Doublet of CITHARA and GUITAR.⟩

A zither

zith•ern ['zɪθərn] *n.* **1** cittern. **2** zither. Also, **zittern** ['zɪtərn].

zlo•ty ['zlouti] *n., pl.* **-tys** or **-ty. 1** the basic unit of money in Poland, divided into 100 groszy. See table of money in the Appendix. **2** a coin worth one zloty. ⟨< Polish⟩

Zn zinc.

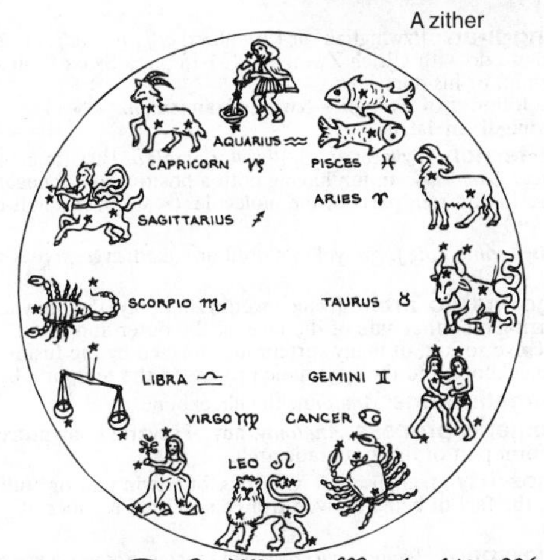

The zodiac

zo•di•ac ['zoudi,æk] *n.* **1** an imaginary belt of the heavens extending on both sides of the apparent yearly path of the sun. The zodiac is divided into 12 equal parts, called signs, named after 12 groups of stars. **2** a diagram representing the zodiac, used in astrology. ⟨ME < OF < L < Gk. *zōdiakos (kyklos)*, literally, (circle) of the animals, ult. < *zōion* animal⟩

zo•di•a•cal [zou'daɪəkəl] *adj.* **1** of or having to do with the zodiac. **2** situated in the zodiac.

zodiacal light a faint luminosity in the sky, seen in the west after sunset or in the east before sunrise.

Zoll•ver•ein ['tsɔlfə,raɪn] *n. German.* **1** a union of German states from 1819 to 1871 to promote uniform conditions of trade among themselves and between themselves and other nations. **2** any similar union of states or countries. ⟨< G *Zollverein* toll union⟩

zom•bi ['zɒmbi] *n., pl.* **-bis.** See ZOMBIE.

zom•bie ['zɒmbi] *n., pl.* **-bies. 1** a corpse supposedly brought back to life by a supernatural power. **2** in certain West African voodoo cults, the python god. **3** the snake god of voodoo, derived from this. **4 a** a supernatural power or force by which the dead may be endowed with a capacity for mute trancelike action somewhat resembling life, alleged to be possessed by certain practitioners of West Indian voodoo. **b** a corpse animated by this force. **5** *Cdn. Slang.* in World War II, a person conscripted for service in the army but refusing to serve overseas. **6** *Slang.* a dazed, apathetic, or lethargic person. **7** a drink of several kinds of rum, fruit juice, sugar, and brandy. ⟨< Haitian Creole *zõbi* < West African (Congo) *zumbi* good-luck fetish⟩

zon•al ['zounəl] *adj.* **1** of a zone; having to do with zones. **2** divided into zones. **—'zon•al•ly,** *adv.*

zo•na•tion [zou'neiʃən] *n.* **1** the state or condition of being arranged in zones; the state of being zonal. **2** an arrangement or distribution in zones.

zone [zoun] *n., v.* **zoned, zon•ing.** *—n.* **1** an area, region, district, etc. set off as distinct from surrounding or neighbouring areas, etc.: *a hospital zone, a parking zone on a street, an industrial zone in a city. A combat zone is a region where fighting is going on.* **2** a region or area having a particular environment or climate and characterized by certain forms of plant and animal life. **3** a district or area within which certain rates are charged for such services as public transit, parcel post, etc., the rates changing at the borders of the area. **4** *Mathematics.* a part of the surface of a sphere contained between two parallel planes. **5** *Archaic or poetic.* a belt; girdle. **6** an encircling or enclosing line, band, or ring, sometimes differing in colour, texture, etc. from the surrounding medium. **7** *Sports.* a designated area of a game surface, as a football field, hockey rink, etc.
—v. **1** set (an area or areas) apart for a special purpose, especially in a city or town: *This area is zoned for apartment buildings.* **2** divide into or mark with zones. **3** surround with or as if with a zone; encircle. ⟨< L *zona* < Gk. *zōnē*, originally, girdle⟩

zoned ['zound] *adj., v. —adj.* **1** marked with or having zones. **2** divided into zones.
—v. pt. and pp. of ZONE.

zon•ing ['zounɪŋ] *n., v., adj. —n.* building restrictions in an area of a city or town.
—v. ppr. of ZONE.
—adj. of or having to do with building restrictions: *zoning bylaws.*

zonked [zɒŋkt] *adj. Slang.* **1** totally exhausted or tired out: *I was really zonked after climbing those hills all day.* **2** high on drugs; intoxicated; drunk. ⟨imitative⟩

zoo [zu] *n.* **1** a place where animals, especially wild animals, are kept and shown. **2** any very busy, overwhelming, chaotic place or situation: *Town was a real zoo today, with all the Christmas shoppers.* ⟨short for *zoological garden*⟩

zoo– *combining form.* living being; animal: *zoology.* ⟨< Gk. *zōion* animal⟩

zo•o•gen•ic [,zouə'dʒɛnɪk] *adj.* **1** caused by or originating in animals, as some diseases. **2** pertaining to development or evolution in animals.

zo•o•ge•og•ra•phy [,zouədʒi'ɒgrəfi] *n.* the study of the distribution of animals over the surface of the earth.
—,zo•o•ge'og•ra•pher, *n.* **—,zo•o,ge•o'graph•ic** [,zouə,dʒiə'græfɪk], *adj.* **—,zo•o,ge•o'graph•i•cal•ly,** *adv.*

zo•og•ra•phy [zou'ɒgrəfi] *n.* the branch of zoology that describes animals and their habits; descriptive zoology.
—,zo•o'graph•ic [,zouə'græfɪk], *adj.*

zo•oid ['zouɔɪd] *n. Zoology.* **1** any animal organism capable of separate existence and reproduced by methods other than sexual reproduction, such as fission, gemmation, etc. **2** any distinct member of a colonial or compound animal organism, whether detached or detachable or not.

zool. zoology; zoologist; zoological.

zo•ol•at•ry [zou'ɒlətri] *n.* animal worship; excessive attention to animals.

zo•o•lite ['zouə,ləit] *n.* a fossil animal. ⟨< *zoo-* + *-lite*⟩

zo•o•log•i•cal [,zouə'lɒdʒɪkəl] *or* [,zuə'lɒdʒɪkəl] *adj.* **1** of animals and animal life. **2** having to do with zoology: *zoological science.* **—,zo•o'log•i•cal•ly,** *adv.*

zoological garden a zoo.

zo•ol•o•gist [zou'ɒlədʒɪst] *or* [zu'ɒlədʒɪst] *n.* a person trained in zoology, especially one whose work it is.

zo•ol•o•gy [zou'ɒlədʒi] *or* [zu'ɒlədʒi] *n.* **1** the science that deals with animals and animal life. Zoology deals with the form, structure, physiology, development, and classification of animals, including the study of special groups such as birds, insects, snakes, mammals, etc. **2** a textbook or handbook dealing with this subject.

zoom [zum] *v., n.* —*v.* **1** move or travel rapidly. **2** of an aircraft, fly suddenly upward in a nearly vertical ascent at great speed: *The airplane zoomed.* **3** increase sharply or rapidly: *Prices zoomed.* **4** make a loud, continuous, low-pitched humming or buzzing sound. **5** travel or move with a loud humming or buzzing sound. **6** move rapidly from one focal length to another, as with a ZOOM LENS.
zoom in on, photograph by means of a zoom lens.
—*n.* **1** a sudden upward flight or increase. **2** a humming or buzzing sound, especially of something moving.

zoom lens *Photography.* a type of lens that can be adjusted between telephoto close-ups and wide-angle shots without loss of focus.

zo•o•mor•phism [,zouə'mɔrfɪzəm] *n.* **1** *Art.* the depiction of animals or animal forms. **2** the representation of a god or other superhuman in the form or with the characteristics of an animal. ⟨< E *zoo-* + Gk. *morphē* form + E *-ism*⟩ **—,zo•o'morph•ic,** *adj.*

zo•on•o•sis [zou'ɒnəsɪs] *or* [,zouə'nousɪs] *n., pl.* **-ses** [-siz]. *Pathology.* any infection or infestation that can be transmitted to humans from lower vertebrates under natural conditions. ⟨< NL < *zoo-* + Gk. *nosos* disease⟩

zo•oph•a•gous [zou'ɒfəgəs] *adj.* carnivorous.

zo•o•pho•bia [,zouə'foubiə] *n.* an abnormal fear of animals. **—,zo•o'phob•ic,** *adj.* **—'zo•o,phobe,** *n.*

zo•o•phyte ['zouə,fəit] *n.* any of various invertebrate animals that resemble plants in form, such as corals, sponges, or sea anemones. **—,zo•o'phyt•ic** [,zouə'fɪtɪk] or **,zo•o'phyt•ical,** *adj.*

zo•o•plank•ton [,zouə'plæŋktən] *n.* a plankton made up of animal organisms, such as protozoans, rotifers, etc.

zo•o•plast•y ['zouə,plæsti] *n., pl.* **-ties.** *Surgery.* plastic surgery in which living tissue from a lower animal is grafted onto a human body. ⟨< *zoo-* + Gk. *plastikos,* ult. < *plassein* to form, shape⟩ **—,zo•o'plas•tic,** *adj.*

zo•o•spore ['zouə,spɔr] *n. Botany.* a spore that has cilia, flagella, etc. and can move about. Some algae and fungi produce zoospores. **—,zo•o'spor•ic,** *adj.* **—,zo•o'spor•ous,** *adj.*

zoot suit [zut] *Slang.* a man's flashy suit with large shoulders, a long coat, and tight trouser cuffs, popular in the early 1940s. ⟨< *suit* by reduplication⟩

Zo•ro•as•ter [,zɔrou'æstər] *or* ['zɔrou,æstər] *n.* the prophet and founder of Zoroastrianism, born in Persia about 600 B.C. His birthday is celebrated each year by Zoroastrians on the 26th of March. Also called **Zarathustra**.

Zo•ro•as•tri•an [,zɔrou'æstriən] *adj., n.* —*adj.* of or having to do with Zoroastrianism or Zoroaster.
—*n.* a follower of Zoroaster or believer in Zoroastrianism.

Zo•ro•as•tri•an•ism [,zɔrou'æstriə,nɪzəm] *n.* a religion founded by the Persian prophet Zoroaster in the 6th century B.C. It is expounded in the Zend-Avesta and teaches that the supreme god Ormazd (or Ahura Mazda) is struggling continuously with Ahriman, the spirit of evil, and needs the good deeds of people to help him ultimately to overcome evil.

Zou•ave [zu'ɑv] *or* [zwɑv] *n.* **1** formerly, a member of a French infantry unit originally composed of Algerian recruits who were noted for their fighting ability, precision drilling, and colourful uniforms. **2** a member of any of various military units patterned after the French Zouaves, such as a body of volunteers called Papal Zouaves, originally organized at the call of the Pope for the protection of the Papal States in the 1860s. Zouaves were recruited in several cities of Québec. ⟨< F < *Zwāwa,* name of Algerian Berber tribe from which first Zouaves came⟩

zounds [zaʊndz] *or* [zundz] *interj. Archaic.* an oath expressing surprise or anger. ⟨< God*'s wounds!*⟩

Zr zirconium.

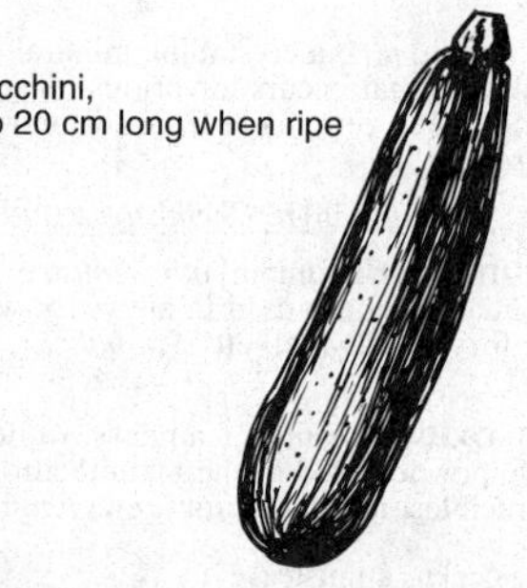

A zucchini,
15 to 20 cm long when ripe

zuc•chi•ni [zu'kini] *or* [zə'kini] *n., pl.* **-ni** or **-nis. 1** a small, oblong variety of summer squash having a smooth, dark green or bright yellow skin and white flesh with small seeds. **2** the plant it grows on. ⟨< Ital. *zucchino,* dim. of *zuccho* gourd, squash⟩

Zu•lu ['zulu] *n., pl.* **-lus** or **-lu;** *adj.* —*n.* **1** a member of a Bantu-speaking people of Natal in South Africa. **2** a Bantu language spoken by the Zulus. Zulu is an important literary language of southern Africa.
—*adj.* of or having to do with the Zulus or their language.

Zu•ñi or **Zu•ni** ['zunji] *or* ['zuni] *n., pl.* **-ñi** or **-ñis, -ni** or **-nis. 1** a member of an Indian people of W New Mexico. **2** the language of the Zuñi, of no known relationship to other languages. ⟨< Am.Sp.⟩

zwie•back ['zwi,bɑk], ['zwi,bæk], ['swi,bɑk], *or* ['swi,bæk]; *German,* ['tsvibɑk] *n.* a kind of bread cut into slices and toasted dry in an oven. ⟨< G *Zwieback* biscuit < *zwie-* two + *backen* bake⟩

Zwing•li•an ['zwɪŋgliən] *or* ['tsvɪŋliən] *adj., n.* —*adj.* of or having to do with Ulrich Zwingli (1484-1531), a Swiss Protestant reformer, or his doctrines.
—*n.* a follower of Zwingli. **—'zwing•li•an,ism,** *n.* **—'Zwing•li•an•ist,** *n.*

zwit•ter•ion ['zwɪtər,aɪən], ['tswɪtər,aɪən], *or* ['tsvɪtər,aɪən] *n. Physical Chemistry.* an ion having both a positive and a negative charge in different parts of the molecule. ⟨< G *Zwitter* half-breed + E *ion*⟩

zygo– *combining form.* yoke; paired or yoked: *zygospore.* ⟨< Gk. *zygon* yoke⟩

zy•go•mat•ic arch [,zaɪgə'mætɪk] *Anatomy.* the bony arch occurring on either side of the face, at the outer and lower edge of the eye socket, of many vertebrates, formed by the fusion of the cheekbone and the zygomatic process of the temporal bone.

zygomatic bone *Anatomy.* the cheekbone.

zygomatic process *Anatomy.* any of several bony processes that form part of the zygomatic arch.

zy•gos•i•ty [zaɪ'gɒsəti] *n. Genetics.* of a twin pair or multiple birth, the fact of being derived from a specified number of zygotes.

zy•go•spore ['zaɪgə,spɔr] *or* ['zɪgə,spɔr] *n. Botany.* a spore formed by the union of two similar gametes. **—,zy•go'spor•ic,** *adj.*

zy•gote ['zaɪgout] *or* ['zɪgout] *n. Biology.* any cell formed by the union of two gametes (i.e., reproductive cells). A fertilized egg is a zygote. ⟨< Gk. *zygotos* yoked < *zygon* yoke⟩ **—zy'got•ic** [zaɪ'gɒtɪk] *or* [zɪ'gɒtɪk], *adj.* **—zy'got•i•cal•ly,** *adv.*

zy•mase ['zaɪmeis] *n. Biochemistry.* an enzyme in yeast that changes sugar into alcohol and carbon dioxide. ⟨< F < Gk. *zymē* leaven⟩

zyme [zaɪm] *n.* **1** any ferment, enzyme, virus, etc. that causes an infectious or contagious disease. **2** any ferment or enzyme. ⟨< Gk. *zymē* leaven⟩

zymo– *combining form.* fermentation: *zymology.*

zy•mol•o•gy [zaɪ'mɒlədʒi] *n.* the science that deals with fermentation. **—,zy•mo'log•i•cal,** *adj.*

zy•mo•sis [zaɪ'mousɪs] *n.* **1** fermentation. **2** *Medicine.* **a** an internal process akin to fermentation, formerly supposed to cause an infectious disease. **b** any zymotic disease. **c** the development and spread of a zymotic disease. ⟨< NL *zymōsis* < Gk. *zymosis,* ult. < *zymē* leaven⟩

zy•mot•ic [zaɪ'mɒtɪk] *adj., n.* *—adj.* **1** having to do with, causing, or caused by fermentation. **2** having to do with or denoting any infectious disease caused by a ferment or virus, originally thought to be caused by an internal process akin to fermentation.
—n. a zymotic disease. ⟨< Gk. *zymōtikos* causing fermentation⟩
—zy'mot•i•cal•ly, *adv.*

zy•mur•gy ['zaɪmərdʒi] *n.* the branch of chemistry dealing with the processes of fermentation, as in brewing, etc. ⟨ult. < Gk. *zymē* leaven + *ergon* work⟩

Appendix

AIR QUALITY INDEX

The Air quality index measures levels of the six most common air pollutants: Carbon Monoxide (CO); Nitrogen Dioxide (NO_2); Ozone (O_3); Sulphur Dioxide (SO_2); Suspended Particles[2] (SP); Total Reduced Sulphur (TRS).

An unusually high concentration of these pollutants in the air can affect health, decrease visibility, corrode metal, and destroy vegetation.

Here is a chart which describes the harmful effects of air pollution.

	0-15 Very Good	16-31 Good	32-49 Moderate	50-99 Poor	100+ Very Poor
CO	no effects	no effects	some changes in blood chemistry but no discomfort	smokers experience cardiovascular difficulties	non-smokers experience cardiovascular difficulties
NO_2	no effects	slight odour	rather noticeable odour	asthma sufferers experience mild discomfort, very bad odour	bronchitis and asthma sufferers feel short of breath, foul odour
O_3	no effects	harmful to many plants	harmful to most vegetation	athletes will not perform up to potential	light exercise is painful for those with lung disease
SO_2	no effects	harmful to some plants	harmful to some plants	very harmful to vegetation, unpleasant odour	bronchitis and asthma sufferers feel short of breath, foul odour
SP	no effects	no effects	slightly decreased visibility	greatly decreased visibility, people with breathing disorders experience discomfort	bronchitis and asthma sufferers feel short of breath
TRS	no effects	slight odour	unpleasant odour	very unpleasant odour	possible headache and nausea due to severe odour

THE BIOLOGICAL CLASSIFICATION OF ANIMALS AND PLANTS

The chart below gives the main categories, or groupings, used in the classification of animals and plants. The examples (the *coyote* and the *rose*) are given to show how particular animals and plants fit into the system. As one goes from the most specific to the most general, more and more animals or plants are included, and the relationships between the more general groups become more distant. For instance, coyotes are more closely related to dogs and wolves than to foxes; and coyotes, dogs, wolves, and foxes are more closely related to each other than they are to cats or bears.

Animals	Plants
SPECIES: *Canis latrans* The coyote.	SPECIES: *Rosa acicularis* The prickly rose, a wild rose.
GENUS: *Canis* Dogs and their close relatives; 8 species. (The coyote, domestic dog, dingo, wolves, and jackals.)	GENUS: *Rosa* Wild roses and garden roses.
FAMILY: *Canidae* Dog family, made up of 14 genera. (Includes also foxes, the African hunting dog, etc.)	FAMILY: *Rosaceae* Rose family, made up of about 100 genera. (Roses; also spireas, apples, pears, plums, strawberries, etc.)
ORDER: *Carnivora* Carnivorous, or meat-eating, animals, made up of 7 families. (Includes also cats, bears, weasels, skunks, etc.)	ORDER: *Rosales* Rose order, made up of about 3 families. (Includes also sycamore, mock orange, hydrangeas, clovers, etc.)
CLASS: *Mammalia* Mammals, made up of 18 orders. (Includes also humans, apes, whales, camels, rodents, bats, etc.)	CLASS: *Magnoliopsida* (or *Dicotyledones*) Dicotyledons, made up of 74 orders. (Includes also willows, maples, cactuses, peppers, violets, daisies, etc.)
PHYLUM: *Chordata* Chordates, animals with some form of spinal cord, made up of 9 classes. (Includes also birds, reptiles, amphibians, fishes, etc.)	DIVISION: *Magnoliophyta* (or *Anthophyta*) The flowering plants, or angiosperms, made up of 2 classes. (Includes also grasses, palms, bulrushes, lilies, orchids, etc.)
KINGDOM: *Animalia* All animals.	KINGDOM: *Plantae* All plants.

COMPARATIVE TABLE OF ALPHABETS

The sounds are represented by symbols of the International Phonetic Alphabet.

GREEK			ARABIC			HEBREW			CYRILLIC		
Form	**Name**	**Sound**	**Form**	**Name**	**Sound**	**Form**	**Name**	**Sound**	**Form**	**Name**	**Sound**
Α α	alpha	[a]	ا	alif	[ʔ]	א	alef	[ʔ]	А а	ah	[ɑ]
Β β	beta	[b]	ب	bā	[b]	בּ	bet	[b]	Б б	beh	[b]
Γ γ	gamma	[g], [ŋ]	ت	tā	[t̪]	ב	vet	[v]	В в	veh	[v]
Δ δ	delta	[d]	ث	thā	[θ]	ג	gimel	[g]	Г г	geh	[g]
Ε ε	epsilon	[ɛ]	ج	jīm	[dʒ]	ד	dalet	[d]	Д д	deh	[d]
Ζ ζ	zeta	[z]	ح	hā	[ħ]	ה	he	[h]	Е е	yeh	[jɛ]
Η η	eta	[e]	خ	khā	[x]	ו	vav	[v]	Ё ё	yo	[jɔ]
Θ θ	theta	[θ]	د	dāl	[d̪]	ז	zayin	[z]	Ж ж	zheh	[ʒ]
Ι ι	iota	[i]	ذ	dhāl	[ð]	ח	ḥet	[x]	З з	zeh	[z]
Κ κ	kappa	[k]	ر	rā	[r]	ט	ṭet	[t]	И и	ee	[i]
Λ λ	lambda	[l]	ز	zāy	[z]	י	yod	[j]	Й й	ee krátkoye	[ɪ]
Μ μ	mu	[m]	س	sīn	[s]	כ ך	kaf	[k]	К к	kah	[k]
Ν ν	nu	[n]	ش	shīn	[ʃ]	ל	lamed	[l]	Л л	el	[l]
Ξ ξ	xi	[ks]	ص	şād	[ʂ]	מ ם	mem	[m]	М м	em	[m]
Ο ο	omicron	[ɔ]	ض	d̦ad	[đ]	נ ן	nun	[n]	Н н	en	[n]
Π π	pi	[p]	ط	ţā	[ŧ]	ס	samekh	[s]	О о	o	[ɒ]
Ρ ρ	rho	[r]	ظ	z̧ā	[ð]	ע	ayin	[ʕ]	П п	peh	[p]
Σ σ ς	sigma	[s]	ع	ʻayn	[ʕ]	פּ ף	pe	[p]	Р р	err	[r]
Τ τ	tau	[t]	غ	ghayn	[ʁ]	פ	fe	[f]	С с	ess	[s]
Υ υ	upsilon	[y], [u]	ف	fā	[f]	צ ץ	sade	[ts]	Т т	teh	[t]
Φ φ	phi	[f]	ق	qāf	[q]	ק	qof	[k]	У у	oo	[u]
Χ χ	chi	[x]	ك	kāf	[k]	ר	resh	[r]	Ф ф	eff	[f]
Ψ ψ	psi	[ps]	ل	lām	[l]	שׁ	shin	[ʃ]	Х х	kha	[x]
Ω ω	omega	[o]	م	mīm	[m]	שׂ	sin	[s]	Ц ц	tseh	[ts]
			ن	nūn	[n]	ת	tav	[t]	Ч ч	cheh	[tʃ]
			ه	hā	[h]				Ш ш	shah	[ʃ]
			و	wāw	[w]				Щ щ	shehah	[ʃtʃ]
			ى	yā	[j]				Ъ ъ	tvyórdy znak	hard sign
									Ы ы	yerrý	[ɪ]
									Ь ь	myáhki znak	soft sign
									Э э	e	[ɛ]
									Ю ю	yoo	[ju]
									Я я	yah	[jɑ]
When *gamma* precedes *kappa, xi, chi,* or another *gamma*, it is transliterated *n*; the letter *upsilon* is transliterated *u* as the final element in diphthongs. The second lowercase form of *sigma* is used only in the final position.			The forms shown are those used when the letters are used in conjunction with other letters. These forms may change when used in isolation. The letter *alif* represents no sound in itself.			Where two forms are shown, the second is used at the end of a word. Hebrew letters are primarily consonants; vowels are shown by the addition of subscript and superscript dots. *Alef* is a glottal stop.			The above table shows the sounds as used in Russian. Other languages using the Cyrillic alphabet, such as Bulgarian, Ukrainian, etc., assign different sound values to some letters.		

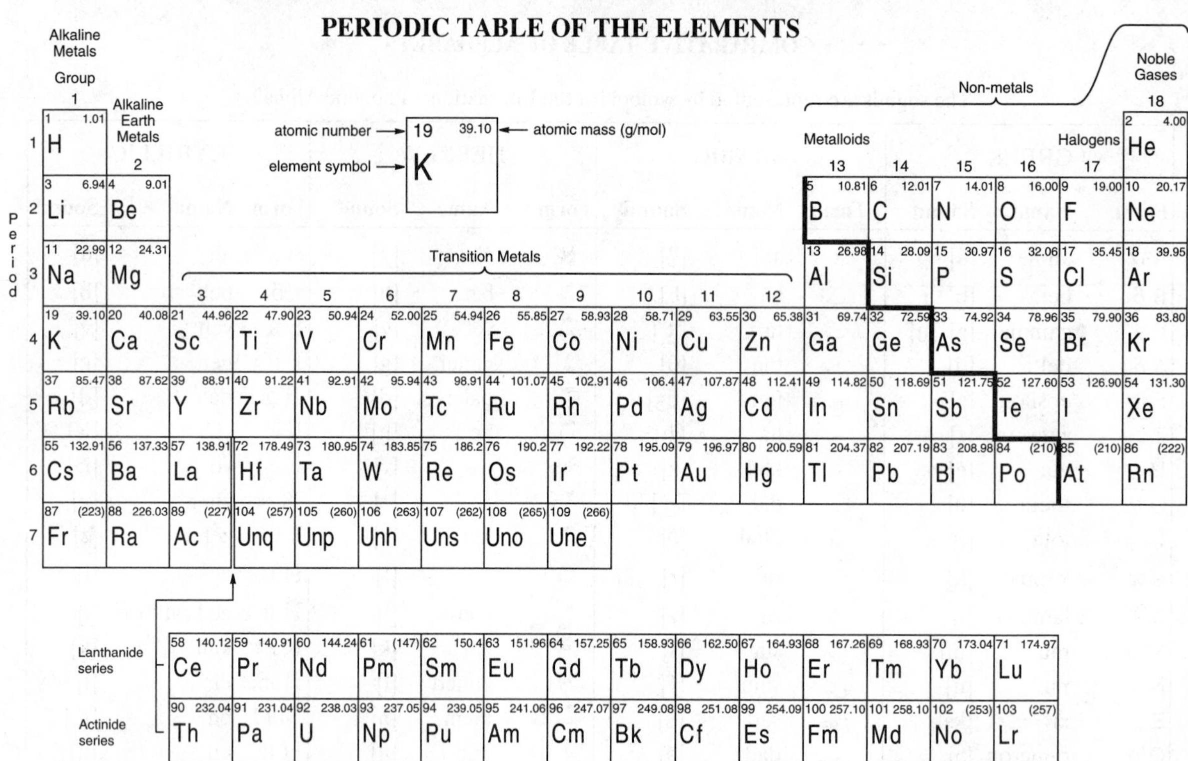

ALPHABETICAL LIST OF THE ELEMENTS, WITH THEIR SYMBOLS AND ATOMIC NUMBERS

Symbol	Name	Atomic Number	Symbol	Name	Atomic Number	Symbol	Name	Atomic Number	Symbol	Name	Atomic Number
Ac	actinium	89	Fm	fermium	100	Np	neptunium	93	Sr	strontium	38
Al	aluminum	13	F	fluorine	9	Ni	nickel	28	S	sulphur	16
Am	americium	95	Fr	francium	87	Nb	niobium	41	Ta	tantalum	73
Sb	antimony	51	Gd	gadolinium	64	N	nitrogen	7	Tc	technetium	43
Ar	argon	18	Ga	gallium	31	No	nobelium	102	Te	tellurium	52
As	arsenic	33	Ge	germanium	32	Os	osmium	76	Tb	terbium	65
At	astatine	85	Au	gold	79	O	oxygen	8	Tl	thallium	81
Ba	barium	56	Hf	hafnium	72	Pd	palladium	46	Th	thorium	90
Bk	berkelium	97	He	helium	2	P	phosphorus	15	Tm	thulium	69
Be	beryllium	4	Ho	holmium	67	Pt	platinum	78	Sn	tin	50
Bi	bismuth	83	H	hydrogen	1	Pu	plutonium	94	Ti	titanium	22
B	boron	5	In	indium	49	Po	polonium	84	Unh	unnilhexium	106
Br	bromine	35	I	iodine	53	K	potassium	19	Une	unnilennium	109
Cd	cadmium	48	Ir	iridium	77	Pr	praseodymium	59	Uno	unniloctium	108
Ca	calcium	20	Fe	iron	26	Pm	promethium	61	Unp	unnilpentium	105
Cf	californium	98	Kr	krypton	36	Pa	protactinium	91	Uns	unnilseptium	107
C	carbon	6	La	lanthanum	57	Ra	radium	88	Unq	unnilquadium	104
Ce	cerium	58	Lr	lawrencium	103	Rn	radon	86	U	uranium	92
Cs	cesium	55	Pb	lead	82	Re	rhenium	75	V	vanadium	23
Cl	chlorine	17	Li	lithium	3	Rh	rhodium	45	W	tungsten	74
Cr	chromium	24	Lu	lutetium	71	Rb	rubidium	37	Xe	xenon	54
Co	cobalt	27	Mg	magnesium	12	Ru	ruthenium	44	Yb	ytterbium	70
Cu	copper	29	Mn	manganese	25	Sm	samarium	62	Y	yttrium	39
Cm	curium	96	Md	mendelevium	101	Sc	scandium	21	Zn	zinc	30
Dy	dysprosium	66	Hg	mercury	80	Se	selenium	34	Zr	zirconium	40
Es	einsteinium	99	Mo	molybdenum	42	Si	silicon	14			
Er	erbium	68	Nd	neodymium	60	Ag	silver	47			
Eu	europium	63	Ne	neon	10	Na	sodium	11			

GEOLOGICAL TIME CHART

Eras	Periods, Epochs, and Their Beginnings (years ago)	Changes and Characteristics
CENOZOIC ERA	Quaternary Period: Recent or Holocene Epoch (11 thousand)	Glaciers melt and Great Lakes are formed. Climate warm. Humans live in most parts of the earth, develop agriculture, use metals, domesticate animals.
	Quaternary Period: Pleistocene Epoch (2 million)	Great ice sheets cover northern hemisphere. Climate cool. Mountains continue to rise in western North America. Early humans reach Europe and North America. Massive extinctions of plants and animals.
	Tertiary Period: Pliocene Epoch (11 million)	Climate cooling. Grasslands replace forests. Many volcanoes. Birds and mammals spread around the world. Humans appear near end of epoch.
	Tertiary Period: Miocene Epoch (24 million)	Climate mild. Sierra Nevadas forming. Flowering plants and trees resemble modern kinds. Apes first appear.
	Tertiary Period: Oligocene Epoch (37 million)	Climate mild. Hawaiian Islands start to form. Red Sea opens up.
	Tertiary Period: Eocene Epoch (57 million)	Climate mild. Seas flood shores of continents. Primitive apes, early horses, and elephants appear.
	Tertiary Period: Paleocene Epoch (66 million)	Dinosaurs are extinct. First placental mammals appear.
MESOZOICERA	Cretaceous Period (144 million)	Seas spread over the land. Flowering plants appear. Dinosaurs die out. Rockies, Himalayas, Alps, and Andes begin to form.
	Jurassic Period (208 million)	Shallow seas invade continents. Dinosaurs reach their largest size. First birds and simple mammals appear.
	Triassic Period (245 million)	Dinosaurs first appear. Continents rise and deserts form.
PALEOZOIC ERA	Permian Period (280 million)	Ural Mountains are formed. Major glaciation occurs. Major extinction of plants and animals.
	Carboniferous Period (360 million)	Warm, moist climate produces great forests that later become coal beds. Large insects and reptiles appear. Appalachian and central European mountains are formed.
	Devonian Period (405 million)	Many kinds of fish in seas and fresh water. Immense trees. Climate warm and humid.
	Ordovician Period (505 million)	Coral reefs are formed. First amphibians and forests of fernlike trees appear. Land starts to emerge from sea and dry out.
	Cambrian Period (570 million)	Seas spread across North America. First fishes appear. Greatest development of invertebrates.
PRECAMBRIAN TIME (4.5 billion?)		Cooling and melting of the earth's crust. Evidence of bacteria, the first known living things, about 3.5 billion years ago.

MONEY: MAJOR CURRENCIES OF THE WORLD

Country	Currency Unit	Lesser Unit
Afghanistan	afghani	100 puls
Albania	lek	100 qindarka
Algeria	dinar	100 centimes
Angola	kwanza	100 lwei
Argentina	peso	100 centavos
Armenia	dram	100 lumma
Australia	dollar	100 cents
Austria	schilling	100 groschen
Azerbaijan	manat	100 qepiq
Bahamas	dollar	100 cents
Bahrain	dinar	1000 fils
Bangladesh	taka	100 poisha
Barbados	dollar	100 cents
Belarus	ruble	100 kapeik
Belgium	franc	100 centimes
Belize	dollar	100 cents
Benin	franc CFA	100 centimes
Bermuda	dollar	100 cents
Bhutan	ngultrum	100 chetrums
Bolivia	Boliviano	100 centavos
Bosnia-Hercegovina	new dinar	
Botswana	pula	100 thebe
Brazil	real	100 centavos
Brunei	ringgit	100 cents
Bulgaria	lev	100 stotinki
Burkina Faso	franc CFA	100 centimes
Burundi	franc	100 centimes
Cameroon	franc CFA	100 centimes
Canada	dollar	100 cents
Cape Verde	escudo	100 centavos
Cayman Islands	dollar	100 cents
Central African Republic	franc CFA	100 centimes
Chad	franc CFA	100 centimes
Chile	peso	100 centavos
People's Republic of China	yuan	100 fen
Colombia	peso	100 centavos
Congo	franc CFA	100 centimes
Costa Rica	colon	100 centimos
Croatia	kuna	100 lipa
Cuba	peso	100 centavos
Cyprus	pound	100 cents
Czech Republic	koruna	100 haléru
Denmark	krone	100 öre
Djibouti	franc	100 centimes
Dominican Republic	peso oro	100 centavos
Ecuador	sucre	100 centavos
Egypt	pound	100 piastres
El Salvador	colón	100 centavos
Equatorial Guinea	franc CFA	100 centimes
Eritrea	birr	100 cents
Estonia	kroon	100 senti
Ethiopia	birr	100 cents
Fiji Islands	dollar	100 cents
Finland	markka	100 pennia
France	franc	100 centimes
Gabon	franc CFA	100 centimes
Gambia	dalasi	100 bututs
Georgia	kupon	
Germany	Deutsche mark	100 pfennige
Ghana	cedi	100 pesewas
Greece	drachma	100 lepta
Grenada	dollar EC	100 cents
Guatemala	quetzal	100 centavos
Guinea	franc	100 centimes
Guinea-Bissau	peso	100 centavos
Guyana	dollar	100 cents
Haïti	gourde	100 centimes
Honduras	lempira	100 centavos
Hong Kong	dollar	100 cents
Hungary	forint	100 fillér
Iceland	króna	100 aurar
India	rupee	100 paise
Indonesia	rupiah	100 sen

Country	Currency Unit	Lesser Unit
Iran	rial	100 dinars
Iraq	dinar	1000 fils
Ireland	pound	100 pence
Israel	shequel	100 agorot
Italy	lira	100 centesimi
Ivory Coast	franc CFA	100 centimes
Jamaica	dollar	100 cents
Japan	yen	100 sen
Jordan	dinar	1000 fils
Kampuchea	riel	100 su
Kazakhstan	tenge	100 cents
Kenya	shilling	100 cents
Kirghizia	som	100 tyyn
Korea	won	100 chon
Kuwait	dinar	1000 fils
Laos	kip	100 att
Latvia	lat	100 santimi
Lebanon	livre	100 piastres
Lesotho	loti	100 lisente
Liberia	dollar	100 cents
Libya	dinar	1000 dirhams
Liechtenstein	Swiss franc	100 centimes
Lithuania	lita	100 centas
Luxembourg	franc	100 centimes
Macao	pataca	100 avos
Macedonia	denar	100 deni
Madagascar	franc	100 centimes
Malaŵi	kwacha	100 tambala
Malaysia	ringgit	100 sen
Maldives	rufiyaa	100 lari
Mali	franc CFA	100 centimes
Malta	lira	100 cents
Mauritania	ougiya	5 khoum
Mauritius	rupee	100 cents
Mexico	peso	100 centavos
Moldova	leu	100 bani
Monaco	French franc	100 centimes
Mongolia	tugrik	100 mongo
Morocco	dirham	100 centimes
Mozambique	metical	100 centavos
Myanmar	kyat	100 pyas
Namibia	dollar	100 cents
Nepal	rupee	100 paisa
The Netherlands	gulden	100 cents
New Zealand	dollar	100 cents
Nicaragua	córdoba	100 centavos
Niger	franc CFA	100 centimes
Nigeria	naira	100 kobo
Norway	krone	100 öre
Oman	rial	1000 baisa
Pakistan	rupee	100 paisas
Panama	balboa	100 centésimos
Papua New Guinea	kina	100 toea
Paraguay	guaraní	100 céntimos
Peru	nuevo sol	100 centimos
Philippines	piso	100 sentimos
Poland	zloty	100 groszy
Portugal	escudo	100 centavos
Qatar	riyal	100 dirhems
Romania	leu	100 bani
Russia	ruble	100 kopeks
Rwanda	franc	100 centimes
São Tomé e Principe	dobra	100 centimos
Saudi Arabia	riyal	100 halalas
Senegal	franc CFA	100 centimes
Serbia	dinar	100 paras
Seychelles	rupee	100 cents
Sierra Leone	leone	100 cents
Singapore	dollar	100 cents
Slovak Republic	koruna	100 halier
Slovenia	tolar	
Solomon Islands	dollar	100 cents
Somalia	shilin	100 senti
South Africa	rand	100 cents
Spain	peseta	100 céntimos

Country	Currency Unit	Lesser Unit
Sri Lanka	rupee	100 cents
Sudan	dinar	10 pounds
Surinam	gulden	100 cents
Swaziland	lilangeni	100 cents
Sweden	krona	100 öre
Switzerland	franc	100 centimes
Syria	pound	100 piastres
Tajikistan	ruble	
Taiwan	yuan	100 cents
Tanzania	shilingi	100 senti
Thailand	baht	100 satang
Togo	franc CFA	100 centimes
Tonga	pa'anga	100 seniti
Trinidad and Tobago	dollar	100 cents
Tunisia	dinar	1000 millim
Turkey	lira	100 kurus
Turkmenistan	manat	100 tenesi
Uganda	shilling	100 cents
Ukraine	karbovanets	
United Arab Emirates	dirham	100 fils
United Kingdom	pound sterling	100 pence
United States	dollar	100 cents
Uruguay	peso Uruguayo	100 centésimos
Uzbekistan	som	100 tyyn
Vanuatu	vatu	
Venezuela	bolívar	100 céntimos
Vietnam	dong	10 hao
Western Samoa	tala	100 sene
Yemen	rial	100 fils
Zaïre	nouveau zaïre	100 makuta
Zambia	kwacha	100 ngwee
Zimbabwe	dollar	100 cents

CANADIAN MILITARY RANKS

Land and Air Command

COMMISSIONED RANKS

General
Lieutenant-General
Major-General
Brigadier-General
Colonel
Lieutenant-Colonel
Major
Captain
Lieutenant
2nd Lieutenant
Officer Cadet

NON-COMMISSIONED RANKS

Chief Warrant Officer
Master Warrant Officer
Warrant Officer
Sergeant
Master Corporal
Corporal
Private

Maritime Command

COMMISSIONED RANKS

Admiral
Vice Admiral
Rear-Admiral
Commodore
Captain (N)
Commander
Lieutenant Commander
Lieutenant (N)
Sub Lieutenant
Acting Sub Lieutenant
Officer Cadet or Midshipman

NON-COMMISSIONED RANKS

Chief Petty Officer 1st Class
Chief Petty Officer 2nd Class
Petty Officer 1st Class
Petty Officer 2nd Class
Master Seaman
Leading Seaman
{ Able Seaman
{ Ordinary Seaman

EXAMPLES OF WIND CHILL FACTOR

Wind Chill Factor	*Description*
700	**Conditions considered comfortable when dressed for skiing.**
1200	**Conditions no longer pleasant for outdoor activities on overcast days.**
1400	**Conditions no longer pleasant for outdoor activities on sunny days.**
1600	**Freezing of exposed skin begins for most people, depending on the degree of activity and the amount of sunshine.**
2300	**Conditions for outdoor travel such as walking become dangerous. Exposed areas of the face freeze in less than 1 minute for the average person.**
2700	**Exposed flesh will freeze within half a minute for the average person.**

Atmospheric Environmental Service. Government of Canada

BEAUFORT SCALE OF WIND SPEEDS

Beaufort Number	*International Description*	*Wind Speed km/h*
0	**Calm**	**0-1**
1	**Light air**	**1-5**
2	**Light breeze**	**6-11**
3	**Gentle breeze**	**12-19**
4	**Moderate breeze**	**20-28**
5	**Fresh breeze**	**29-38**
6	**Strong breeze**	**39-49**
7	**Moderate gale**	**50-61**
8	**Fresh gale**	**62-74**
9	**Strong gale**	**75-88**
10	**Whole gale**	**89-102**
11	**Storm**	**103-117**
12-17	**Hurricane**	**above 117**

TABLE OF MEASURES

The International System (SI) as Used in Canada

SI base units

name	symbol	quantity
metre	m	length
kilogram	kg	mass
second	s	time
ampere	A	electric current
kelvin	K	thermodynamic temperature
mole	mol	amount of substance
candela	cd	luminous intensity

SI prefixes

name	symbol	multiplying factor*
exa-	E	$\times 10^{18}$
peta-	P	$\times 10^{15}$
tera-	T	$\times 10^{12}$
giga-	G	$\times 10^{9}$
mega-	M	$\times 10^{6}$
kilo-	k	$\times 10^{3}$
hecto-	h	$\times 10^{2}$
deca-	da	$\times 10$
deci-	d	$\times 10^{-1}$
centi-	c	$\times 10^{-2}$
milli-	m	$\times 10^{-3}$
micro-	µ	$\times 10^{-6}$
nano-	n	$\times 10^{-9}$
pico-	p	$\times 10^{-12}$
femto-	f	$\times 10^{-15}$
atto-	a	$\times 10^{-18}$

*$10^2 = 100$; $10^3 = 1000$
$10^{-1} = 0.1$; $10^{-2} = 0.01$
Thus, $2 \text{ km} = 2 \times 1000 = 2000 \text{ m}$
$3 \text{ cm} = 3 \times 0.01 = 0.03 \text{ m}$

Common SI derived units with special names

name	symbol	quantity
hertz	Hz	frequency
pascal	Pa	pressure, stress
watt	W	power, radiant flux
volt	V	electric potential, electromotive force
newton	N	force
joule	J	energy, work
coulomb	C	electric charge
ohm	Ω	electric resistance
farad	F	electric capacitance

Common units used with the SI

name	symbol	quantity
litre	L	volume or capacity (= 1 dm^3)
degree Celsius	°C	temperature (= 1 K; 0°C = 273.2 K)
hectare	ha	area (= 10 000 m^2)
tonne	t	mass (= 1000 kg)
electronvolt	eV	energy (= 0.160 aJ)
nautical mile	M	distance (navigation)(= 1852 m)
knot	kn	speed (navigation)(= 1 M/h)

SI supplementary units

name	symbol	quantity
radian	rad	plane angle
steradian	sr	solid angle

Common Conversion Factors

1 centimetre	=	0.39 in.
1 metre	=	39.4 in.
1 kilometre	=	0.62 mi.
1 gram	=	0.04 oz.
1 kilogram	=	2.20 lb.
1 tonne	=	1.10 short tons
1 square centimetre	=	0.16 sq.in.
1 square metre	=	1.20 sq.yd.
1 litre	=	0.88 qt.
1 cubic centimetre	=	0.06 cu.in.
1 cubic metre	=	1.31 cu.yd.

Conversion factors for common U.S. liquid measures

U.S.	Cdn.	metric
1 fl.oz.	= 1.041 fl.oz.	(29.57 cm^3)
1 pt.	= 0.833 pt.	(0.473 dm^3)
1 qt.	= 0.833 qt.	(0.946 dm^3)
1 gal.	= 0.833 gal.	(3.785 dm^3)

Traditional Canadian Measures

name	abbrev. or symbol	equivalent in related units	metric equivalent
LENGTH			
inch	in. *or* ″	—	2.54 cm
foot	ft. *or* ′	12 in.	30.48 cm
yard	yd.	3 ft.; 36 in.	0.91 m
mile	mi.	1760 yd.; 5280 ft.	1.609 km
MASS (WEIGHT)			
grain	gr.	—	0.06 g
dram	dr.	27.343 gr.	1.77 g
ounce	oz.	16 dr.	28.35 g
pound	lb.	16 oz.	0.453 kg
hundredweight			
(short)	cwt.	100 lb.	45.36 kg
(long)	cwt.	112 lb.	50.80 kg
ton (short)	—	2000 lb.	0.907 t
ton (long)	—	2240 lb.	1.016 t
VOLUME AND CAPACITY			
fluid dram	fl.dr.	0.22 cu.in.	3.55 cm^3
fluid ounce	fl.oz.	8 fl.dr.; 1.7 cu.in.	28.41 cm^3
pint	pt.	20 fl.oz.; 34.7 cu.in.	568.3 cm^3
quart	qt.	2 pt.; 69.4 cu.in.	1.14 dm^3
gallon	gal.	4 qt.; 277 cu.in.	4.55 dm^3
peck	pk.	2 gal.; 555 cu.in.	9.09 dm^3
bushel	bu.	4 pk.; 2219 cu.in.	36.37 dm^3
barrel (oil)	—	35 gal.	159 dm^3
AREA			
acre	—	4840 sq.yd.	4047 m^2
square mile	sq.mi.	640 acres	2.590 km^2